THE OFFICIAL® 2007 PRICE GUIDE TO FOOTBALL CARDS

DR. JAMES BECKETT

TWENTY-SIXTH EDITION

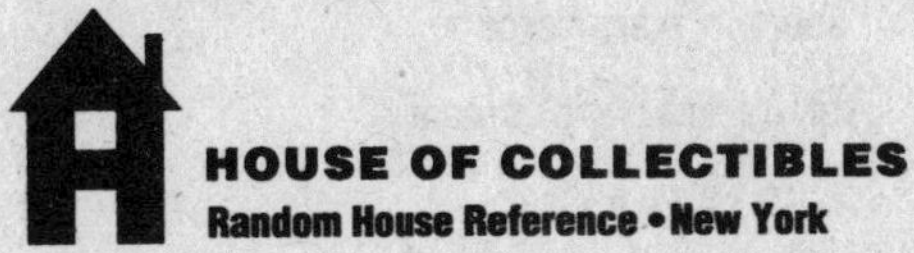

Important Notice: All of the information, including valuations, in this book has been compiled from the most reliable sources, and every effort has been made to eliminate errors and questionable data. Nevertheless, the possibility of error, in a work of such immense scope, always exists. The publisher will not be held responsible for losses that may occur in the purchase, sale, or other transaction of items because of information contained herein. Readers who feel they have discovered errors are invited to *write* and inform us, so they may be corrected in subsequent editions. Those seeking further information on the topics covered in this book are advised to refer to the complete line of *Official Price Guides* published by the House of Collectibles.

House of Collectibles and colophon
are trademarks of Random House, Inc.

www.houseofcollectibles.com

Published by:
House of Collectibles
Random House Reference
New York, New York

Distributed by The Random House Information Group,
a division of Random House, Inc.,
New York, and simultaneously in Canada by
Random House of Canada Limited, Toronto.
Random House is a registered trademark of Random House, Inc.

www.randomhouse.com

Manufactured in the United States of America

ISSN: 0748-1365

ISBN-10: 0-375-72103-7

ISBN-13: 978-0-375-72103-8

10 9 8 7 6 5 4 3 2 1

Twenty-Sixth Edition: August 2006

Table of Contents

About the Author xi
How to Use This Book xi
Prices in This Guide xii
Acknowledgments xii
Introduction xii
How to Collect 1
Obtaining Cards 1
Preserving Your Cards 2
Collecting vs. Investing 2
Terminology 3
Glossary/Legend 3
Understanding Card Values 7
Determining Value 7
Regional Variation 8
Set Prices 8
Scarce Series 9
Grading Your Cards 9
Centering 9
Corner Wear 10
Creases 10
Alterations 10
Categorization of Defects 11
Condition Guide 11
Selling Your Cards 12
Interesting Notes 14
History of Football Cards 14
Additional Reading 18

1995 Absolute 19
1996 Absolute 19
1997 Absolute 20
1998 Absolute Hobby 21
1999 Absolute EXP 22
1999 Absolute SSD 23
2000 Absolute 24
2001 Absolute Memorabilia 25
2002 Absolute Memorabilia 26
2003 Absolute Memorabilia 27
2004 Absolute Memorabilia 28
2005 Absolute Memorabilia 29
2005 Absolute Memorabilia Retail 30
1995 Action Packed ....
Rookies/Stars 30
2002 Atomic 31
1998 Aurora 31
1999 Aurora 32
2000 Aurora 33
2004 Bazooka 34
2005 Bazooka 35
1948 Bowman 36
1950 Bowman 36
1951 Bowman 37
1952 Bowman Large 38
1952 Bowman Small 38
1953 Bowman 39
1954 Bowman 39
1955 Bowman 40
1991 Bowman 41
1992 Bowman 43
1993 Bowman 46
1994 Bowman 48
1995 Bowman 49
1998 Bowman 51
1999 Bowman 52
2000 Bowman 53
2001 Bowman 54
2002 Bowman 55
2003 Bowman 56
2004 Bowman 58
2005 Bowman 59
1998 Bowman Chrome 60
1999 Bowman Chrome 61
2000 Bowman Chrome 62
2001 Bowman Chrome 63
2002 Bowman Chrome 64
2003 Bowman Chrome 66
2004 Bowman Chrome 67
2004 Bowman Chrome Super ....
Bowl XXXIX Unsigned ....
Draft Picks 68

Table of Contents

2005 Bowman Chrome 68
2000 Bowman Reserve 69
1995 Bowman's Best 70
1996 Bowman's Best 71
1997 Bowman's Best 71
1998 Bowman's Best 72
1999 Bowman's Best 73
2000 Bowman's Best 73
2001 Bowman's Best 74
2002 Bowman's Best 75
2003 Bowman's Best 76
2004 Bowman's Best 76
2005 Bowman's Best 77
1994 Classic NFL Experience ..78
1994 Collector's Choice 79
1995 Collector's Choice 80
1995 Collector's Choice Update ..82
1996 Collector's Choice 83
1996 Collector's Choice Update ..85
1997 Collector's Choice 85
1996 Donruss 88
1997 Donruss 89
1999 Donruss 90
2000 Donruss 91
2002 Donruss 92
2001 Donruss Classics 93
2002 Donruss Classics 94
2003 Donruss Classics 95
2004 Donruss Classics 96
2005 Donruss Classics 97
1999 Donruss Elite 99
2000 Donruss Elite 100
2001 Donruss Elite 100
2002 Donruss Elite 101
2003 Donruss Elite 102
2004 Donruss Elite 103
2005 Donruss Elite 104
2005 Donruss Gridiron Gear 105
1997 Donruss Preferred 106
1999 Donruss Preferred QBC 106
2000 Donruss Preferred 107
2005 Exquisite Collection 108
1992 Finest 108
1994 Finest 108
1995 Finest 109
1996 Finest 111
1997 Finest 112
1998 Finest 114
1999 Finest 115
2000 Finest 116
2001 Finest 117
2002 Finest 118
2003 Finest 118
2004 Finest 119
2005 Finest 120
1995 Flair 120
2002 Flair 121
2003 Flair 122
2004 Flair 123
1997 Flair Showcase Row 2 123
1998 Flair Showcase Row 3 124
1999 Flair Showcase 124
1960 Fleer 125
1961 Fleer 126
1962 Fleer 127
1963 Fleer 127
1990 Fleer 128
1990 Fleer Update 129
1991 Fleer 130
1992 Fleer 132
1993 Fleer 134
1994 Fleer 136
1995 Fleer 138
1996 Fleer 140

Table of Contents

1997 Fleer 141
2001 Fleer Hot Prospects 143
2002 Fleer Hot Prospects 143
2003 Fleer Hot Prospects 144
2004 Fleer Hot Prospects 144
2004 Fleer Inscribed 145
2001 Fleer Premium 146
2002 Fleer Premium 147
2000 Fleer Showcase 148
2001 Fleer Showcase 148
2002 Fleer Showcase 149
2003 Fleer Showcase 150
2004 Fleer Showcase 150
2004 Fleer Sweet Sigs 151
1998 Fleer Tradition 152
1999 Fleer Tradition 153
2000 Fleer Tradition 154
2001 Fleer Tradition 156
2001 Fleer Tradition Glossy ..158
2002 Fleer Tradition 160
2003 Fleer Tradition 161
2004 Fleer Tradition 163
2000 Greats of the Game 164
2004 Greats of the Game 165
2002 Gridiron Kings 165
2003 Gridiron Kings 166
1948 Leaf 167
1949 Leaf 167
1996 Leaf 168
1997 Leaf 169
1999 Leaf Certified 169
2000 Leaf Certified 170
2001 Leaf Certified Materials 172
2002 Leaf Certified 172
2003 Leaf Certified Materials 173
2004 Leaf Certified Materials 174
2005 Leaf Certified Materials 175
2000 Leaf Limited 176
2003 Leaf Limited 178
2004 Leaf Limited 178
2005 Leaf Limited 180
1998 Leaf Rookies and Stars 181
1999 Leaf Rookies and Stars 182
2000 Leaf Rookies and Stars 183
2001 Leaf Rookies and Stars 185
2002 Leaf Rookies and Stars 186
2003 Leaf Rookies and Stars 187
2004 Leaf Rookies and Stars 189
2005 Leaf Rookies and Stars 190
1991 Pacific 191
1992 Pacific 194
1993 Pacific 197
1994 Pacific 199
1995 Pacific 201
1996 Pacific 203
1997 Pacific 205
1998 Pacific 207
1999 Pacific 209
2000 Pacific 211
2001 Pacific 213
2002 Pacific 215
1996 Pacific Dynagon 218
1997 Pacific Dynagon 218
2001 Pacific Dynagon 219
1998 Pacific Omega 220
1999 Pacific Omega 221
2000 Pacific Omega 222
1997 Pacific Philadelphia 223
1964 Philadelphia 225
1965 Philadelphia 226
1966 Philadelphia 227
1967 Philadelphia 228
1991 Pinnacle 229
1992 Pinnacle 230

Table of Contents

1993 Pinnacle 232
1994 Pinnacle 234
1995 Pinnacle 235
1996 Pinnacle 236
1997 Pinnacle 237
1997 Pinnacle Certified 238
1997 Pinnacle Inscriptions ..239
1997 Pinnacle Inside 239
1997 Pinnacle Totally Certified Platinum Red 240
1992 Playoff 240
1993 Playoff 241
1994 Playoff 243
1993 Playoff Contenders 244
1994 Playoff Contenders 245
1995 Playoff Contenders 245
1997 Playoff Contenders 246
1998 Playoff Contenders Ticket ..247
1999 Playoff Contenders SSD 247
2000 Playoff Contenders 248
2001 Playoff Contenders 249
2002 Playoff Contenders 250
2003 Playoff Contenders 251
2004 Playoff Contenders 252
2005 Playoff Contenders 253
2003 Playoff Hogg Heaven ..254
2004 Playoff Hogg Heaven ..255
2001 Playoff Honors 256
2002 Playoff Honors 257
2003 Playoff Honors 258
2004 Playoff Honors 259
2005 Playoff Honors 260
1998 Playoff Momentum Hobby ..261
1999 Playoff Momentum SSD ..262
2000 Playoff Momentum 263
1998 Playoff Prestige Hobby 264
1999 Playoff Prestige EXP 265
1999 Playoff Prestige SSD ..266
2000 Playoff Prestige 267
2002 Playoff Prestige 269
2003 Playoff Prestige 270
2004 Playoff Prestige 271
2005 Playoff Prestige 272
1996 Playoff Prime 273
2002 Playoff Prime Signatures ..274
2004 Playoff Prime Signatures ..274
1995 Pro Line 275
1995 Pro Line Series 2 277
1996 Pro Line 277
1997 Pro Line 279
1989 Pro Set 280
1990 Pro Set 283
1991 Pro Set 287
1991 Pro Set Platinum 290
1992 Pro Set 292
1993 Pro Set 295
2000 Quantum Leaf 297
2001 Quantum Leaf 299
2004 Reflections 300
2005 Reflections 301
1997 Revolution 303
1998 Revolution 304
1999 Revolution 304
2000 Revolution 305
1989 Score 306
1989 Score Supplemental 307
1990 Score 308
1990 Score Supplemental 311
1991 Score 311
1991 Score Supplemental 315
1992 Score 315
1993 Score 318
1994 Score 319
1995 Score 321

Table of Contents

1996 Score 322
1997 Score 324
1998 Score 325
1999 Score 326
1999 Score Supplemental 328
2000 Score 328
2001 Score 330
2002 Score 331
2003 Score 333
2004 Score 334
2005 Score 336
2002 Score QBC Materials 338
2001 Score Select 338
1993 Select 339
1994 Select 340
1996 Select 341
1995 Select Certified 342
1996 Select Certified 343
2000 SkyBox 344
1992 SkyBox Impact 345
1993 SkyBox Impact 347
1994 SkyBox Impact 348
1995 SkyBox Impact 350
1996 SkyBox Impact 351
1996 SkyBox Impact Rookies 352
1997 SkyBox Impact 352
2003 SkyBox LE 354
2004 SkyBox LE 354
1993 SkyBox Premium 355
1994 SkyBox Premium 356
1995 SkyBox Premium 357
1996 SkyBox Premium 358
1997 SkyBox Premium 359
1998 SkyBox Premium 361
1999 SkyBox Premium 362
1993 SP 363
1994 SP 364
1995 SP 365
1995 SP Championship 366
1996 SP 367
1997 SP Authentic 368
1998 SP Authentic 369
1999 SP Authentic 370
2000 SP Authentic 370
2001 SP Authentic 371
2002 SP Authentic 372
2003 SP Authentic 373
2004 SP Authentic 375
2005 SP Authentic 376
2001 SP Game Used Edition 377
2003 SP Game Used Edition 378
2004 SP Game Used Edition 378
2002 SP Legendary Cuts 379
1999 SP Signature 380
2003 SP Signature 381
1999 Sports Illustrated 382
1996 SPx 383
1997 SPx 383
1998 SPx 383
1998 SPx Finite 384
1999 SPx 385
2000 SPx 386
2001 SPx 387
2002 SPx 388
2003 SPx 389
2004 SPx 390
2005 SPx 391
1991 Stadium Club 392
1992 Stadium Club 394
1993 Stadium Club 397
1994 Stadium Club 400
1995 Stadium Club 402
1996 Stadium Club 404
1997 Stadium Club 405

Table of Contents

1998 Stadium Club 407
1999 Stadium Club 408
2000 Stadium Club 409
2001 Stadium Club 409
2002 Stadium Club 410
1999 Stadium Club Chrome 411
2002 Sweet Spot 412
2003 Sweet Spot 412
2004 Sweet Spot 413
2005 Sweet Spot 414
2005 Throwback Threads 416
1950 Topps Felt Backs 417
1951 Topps Magic 417
1955 Topps All-American 418
1956 Topps 418
1957 Topps 419
1958 Topps 419
1959 Topps 420
1960 Topps 421
1961 Topps 421
1962 Topps 422
1963 Topps 423
1964 Topps 424
1965 Topps 425
1966 Topps 425
1967 Topps 426
1968 Topps 426
1969 Topps 427
1970 Topps 428
1971 Topps 430
1972 Topps 431
1973 Topps 432
1974 Topps 434
1975 Topps 436
1976 Topps 438
1977 Topps 440
1978 Topps 443
1979 Topps 445
1980 Topps 447
1981 Topps 449
1982 Topps 451
1983 Topps 453
1984 Topps 455
1984 Topps USFL 456
1985 Topps 457
1985 Topps USFL 458
1986 Topps 459
1987 Topps 461
1988 Topps 462
1989 Topps 464
1989 Topps Traded 465
1990 Topps 466
1990 Topps Traded 468
1991 Topps 469
1992 Topps 471
1993 Topps 474
1994 Topps 477
1995 Topps 480
1996 Topps 482
1997 Topps 483
1998 Topps 485
1999 Topps 486
2000 Topps 488
2001 Topps 490
2002 Topps 491
2003 Topps 493
2004 Topps 494
2005 Topps 496
2003 Topps All American 498
2005 Topps All American 498
1996 Topps Chrome 499
1997 Topps Chrome 499
1998 Topps Chrome 500
1999 Topps Chrome 501

Table of Contents

2000 Topps Chrome 502
2001 Topps Chrome 503
2002 Topps Chrome 504
2003 Topps Chrome 505
2004 Topps Chrome 506
2005 Topps Chrome 507
2001 Topps Debut 509
2002 Topps Debut 509
2003 Topps Draft Picks and Prospects 510
2004 Topps Draft Picks and Prospects 511
2005 Topps Draft Picks and Prospects 512
2004 Topps Fan Favorites 512
1997 Topps Gallery 513
2000 Topps Gallery 513
2001 Topps Gallery 514
2002 Topps Gallery 515
2001 Topps Heritage 516
2002 Topps Heritage 516
2005 Topps Heritage 517
2002 Topps Pristine 519
2003 Topps Pristine 519
2004 Topps Pristine 520
2005 Topps Pristine 521
2004 Topps Signature 522
2003 Topps Total 522
2004 Topps Total 524
2005 Topps Total 526
2005 Topps Turkey Red 528
2004 UD Diamond All-Star ..529
2004 UD Diamond Pro Sigs 530
2005 UD Mini Jersey Collection ..531
2005 UD Portraits 531
2003 Ultimate Collection 532
2004 Ultimate Collection 532
2005 Ultimate Collection 533
1991 Ultra 534
1991 Ultra Update 536
1992 Ultra 536
1993 Ultra 538
1994 Ultra 540
1995 Ultra 542
1996 Ultra 544
1997 Ultra 545
1998 Ultra 546
1999 Ultra 548
2000 Ultra 549
2001 Ultra 550
2002 Ultra 552
2003 Ultra 553
2004 Ultra 554
2005 Ultra 555
1991 Upper Deck 556
1992 Upper Deck 558
1992 Upper Deck Gold 561
1993 Upper Deck 561
1994 Upper Deck 563
1995 Upper Deck 565
1996 Upper Deck 566
1997 Upper Deck 567
1998 Upper Deck 568
1999 Upper Deck 569
2000 Upper Deck 571
2001 Upper Deck 572
2002 Upper Deck 573
2003 Upper Deck 574
2004 Upper Deck 575
2005 Upper Deck 576
2005 Upper Deck AFL 578
2006 Upper Deck AFL 578
2005 Upper Deck ESPN 579
2004 Upper Deck Foundations 579

Table of Contents

2005 Upper Deck Foundations ..581
2005 Upper Deck Kickoff 582
1997 Upper Deck Legends ..582
2000 Upper Deck Legends ..583
2001 Upper Deck Legends ..584
2004 Upper Deck Legends ..585
2005 Upper Deck Legends ..585
2000 Upper Deck Pros and Prospects 586
2001 Upper Deck Pros and Prospects 587
2003 Upper Deck Pros and Prospects 587
2005 Upper Deck Rookie Debut 588
2005 Upper Deck Rookie Materials 589
2004 Upper Deck Rookie Premiere 590
2005 Upper Deck Rookie Premiere 590
1995 Zenith 590
1996 Zenith 591
1997 Zenith 592
2005 Zenith 592
1996 Press Pass 593
1996 Press Pass Paydirt 593
1997 Press Pass 594
1998 Press Pass 594
1999 Press Pass 594
2000 Press Pass 595
2001 Press Pass 595
2002 Press Pass 595
2003 Press Pass 595
2004 Press Pass 596
2005 Press Pass 596
2006 Press Pass 596
2002 Press Pass JE 597
2003 Press Pass JE 597
2001 Press Pass SE 597
2004 Press Pass SE 597
2005 Press Pass SE 598
2006 Press Pass SE 598
1999 SAGE 598
2000 SAGE 598
2001 SAGE 599
2002 SAGE 599
2003 SAGE 599
2004 SAGE 599
2005 SAGE 600
2000 SAGE HIT 600
2001 SAGE HIT 600
2002 SAGE HIT 601
2003 SAGE HIT 601
2004 SAGE HIT 601
2005 SAGE HIT 602
2006 SAGE HIT 602
2004 SAGE Jersey Update 602
2005 SAGE Premium Action Autographs Gold 602
1991 Wild Card Draft 603
Acknowledgments 604

About the Author

Jim Beckett, the leading authority on sports card values in the United States, maintains a wide range of activities in the world of sports. He possesses one of the finest collections of sportscards and autographs in the world, has made numerous appearances on radio and television, and has been frequently cited in many national publications. He was awarded the first "Special Achievement Award for Contributions to the Hobby" by the National Sports Collectors Convention in 1980, the "Jock-Jaspersen Award for Hobby Dedication" in 1983, and the "Buck Barker, Spirit of the Hobby Award" in 1991.

Dr. Beckett is the author of *Beckett Baseball Card Price Guide, The Official Price Guide to Baseball Cards, The Sport Americana Price Guide to Baseball Collectibles, Beckett Almanac of Baseball Cards and Collectibles, The Sport Americana Baseball Memorabilia and Autograph Price Guide, Beckett Football Card Price Guide, The Official Price Guide to Football Cards, Beckett Hockey Card Price Guide and Alphabetical Checklist, Beckett Basketball Card Price Guide, The Official Price Guide to Basketball Cards,* and *Beckett Baseball Card Alphabetical Checklist.* In addition, he is the founder, and publisher, of sports collectible magazines: *Beckett Baseball, Beckett Basketball, Beckett Football, Beckett Hockey,* and *Beckett.*

Jim Beckett received his Ph.D. in Statistics from Southern Methodist University in 1975. Prior to starting Beckett Publications in 1984, Dr. Beckett served as an Associate Professor of Statistics at Bowling Green State University and as a Vice President of a consulting firm in Dallas, Texas. He currently resides in Dallas.

How to Use This Book

Isn't it great? Every year this book gets better with all the new sets coming out. But even more exciting is that every year there are more attractive choices and, subsequently, more interest in the cards we love so much. This edition has been enhanced and expanded from the previous edition. The cards you collect—who appears on them, what they look like, where they are from, and (most important to most of you) what their current values are—are enumerated within. Many of the features contained in the other *Beckett Price Guides* have been incorporated into this volume since condition-grading, terminology, and many other aspects of collecting are common to the card hobby in general. We hope you find the book both interesting and useful in your collecting pursuits.

The Beckett Guide has been successful where other attempts have failed because it is complete, current, and valid. This price guide contains not just one, but two prices by condition for all the football cards listed. These account for most of the football cards in existence. The prices were added to the card lists just prior to printing and reflect not the author's opinions or desires but the going retail prices for each card, based on the marketplace (sports memorabilia conventions and shows, sportscard shops, hobby papers, current mail-order catalogs, Internet sales, auction results, and other firsthand reporting of actually realized prices).

What is the best price guide available on the market today? Of course card sellers will prefer the price guide with the highest prices, while card buyers will naturally prefer the one with the lowest prices. Accuracy, however, is the true test. Use the price guide used by more collectors and dealers than all the others combined. Look for the Beckett name. I won't put my name on anything I won't stake my reputation on. Not the lowest and not the highest—but the most accurate, with integrity.

To facilitate your use of this book, read the complete introductory section on the following pages before going to the pricing pages. Every collectible field has its own terminology; we've tried to capture most of these terms and definitions in our glossary. Please read carefully the section on grading and the condition of your cards, as you will not be able to determine which price column is appropriate for a given card without first knowing its condition.

Prices in This Guide

Prices found in this guide reflect current retail rates just prior to the printing of this book. They do not reflect the for-sale prices of the author, the publisher, the distributors, the advertisers, or any card dealers associated with this guide. No one is obligated in any way to buy, sell, or trade his or her cards based on these prices. The price listings were compiled by the author from actual buy/sell transactions at sports conventions, sportscard shops, buy/sell advertisements in the hobby papers, for-sale prices from dealer catalogs and price lists, and discussions with leading hobbyists in the U.S. and Canada. All prices are in U.S. dollars.

Acknowledgments

A great deal of diligence, hard work, and dedicated effort went into this year's volume. The high standards to which we hold ourselves, however, could not have been met without the expert input and generous amount of time contributed by many people. Our sincere thanks are extended to each and every one of you.

A complete list of these invaluable contributors appears after the Price Guide section.

Introduction

Welcome to the exciting world of sportscard collecting, one of America's most popular avocations. You have made a good choice in buying this book, since it will open up to you the entire panorama of this field in the simplest, most concise way.

The growth of *Beckett Baseball, Beckett Basketball, Beckett Football, Beckett Hockey,* and *Beckett Racing* is an indication of the unprecedented popularity of sportscards. Founded in 1984 by Dr. James Beckett, *Beckett Baseball* contains the most extensive and accepted monthly price guide, collectible glossy superstar covers, colorful feature articles, "Hot List," Convention Calendar, tips for beginners, "Readers Write" letters to and responses from the editor, information on errors and varieties, autograph collecting tips, and profiles of the sport's hottest stars. Published every month, *Beckett Baseball* is the hobby's largest paid circulation periodical. The other five magazines were built on the success of Baseball.

So collecting sportscards—while still pursued as a hobby with youthful exuberance by kids in the neighborhood—has also taken on the trappings of an industry, with thousands of full- and part-time card dealers, as well as vendors of supplies, clubs, and conventions. In fact, each year since 1980 thousands of hobbyists have assembled for a National Sports Collectors Convention, at which hundreds of dealers have displayed their wares, seminars have been conducted, autographs penned by sports notables, and millions of cards changed hands. The Beckett Guide is the best annual guide available to the exciting world of football cards. Read it and use it. May your enjoyment and your card collection increase in the coming months and years.

How to Collect

Each collection is personal and reflects the individuality of its owner. There are no set rules on how to collect cards. Since card collecting is a hobby or leisure pastime, what you collect, how much you collect, and how much time and money you spend collecting are entirely up to you. The funds you have available for collecting and your own personal taste should determine how you collect. The information and ideas presented here are intended to help you get the most enjoyment from this hobby.

It is impossible to collect every card ever produced. Therefore, beginners as well as intermediate and advanced collectors usually specialize in some way. One of the reasons this hobby is popular is that individual collectors can define and tailor their collecting methods to match their own tastes. To give you some ideas of the various approaches to collecting, we will list some of the more popular areas of specialization.

Many collectors select complete sets from particular years. For example, they may concentrate on assembling complete sets from all the years since their birth or since they became avid sports fans. They may try to collect a card for every player during that specified period of time. Many others wish to acquire only certain players. Usually such players are the superstars of the sport, but occasionally collectors will specialize in all the cards of players who attended a particular college or came from a certain town. Some collectors are only interested in the first cards or Rookie Cards of certain players.

Another fun way to collect cards is by team. Most fans have a favorite team, and it is natural for that loyalty to be translated into a desire for cards of the players on that favorite team. For most of the recent years, team sets (all the cards from a given team for that year) are readily available at a reasonable price. See Beckett.com for searchable player checklists.

Obtaining Cards

Several avenues are open to card collectors. Cards still can be purchased in the traditional way: by the pack at the local discount, grocery, or convenience stores. But there are also thousands of card shops across the country that specialize in selling cards individually or by the pack, box, or set. Another alternative is the thousands of card shows held each month around the country, which feature anywhere from five to 800 tables of sports cards and memorabilia for sale.

For many years, it has been possible to purchase complete sets of cards through mail-order advertisers found in traditional sports media publications, such as *The Sporting News, Football Digest, Street & Smith* yearbooks, and others. These sets also are advertised in the card collecting periodicals. Many collectors will begin by subscribing to at least one of the hobby periodicals, all with good up-to-date information. Another way of obtaining cards and information is through Beckett's Web site, www.beckett.com.

Most serious card collectors obtain old (and new) cards from one or more of several main sources: (1) trading or buying from other collectors or dealers; (2) responding to sale or auction ads in the hobby publications; (3) buying at a local hobby store; (4) attending sports collectibles shows or conventions; and/or (5) purchasing cards over the Internet.

We advise that you try all four methods since each has its own distinct advantages: (1) trading is a great way to make new friends; (2) hobby periodicals help you keep up with what's going on in the hobby (including when and where the conventions are happening); (3) stores provide the opportunity to enjoy personalized service and consider a great diversity of material in a relaxed sports-oriented atmosphere; (4) shows allow you to choose from multiple dealers and thousands of cards under one roof in a competitive situation; and (5) the Internet allows you to purchase cards in a convenient manner from almost anywhere in the world.

Preserving Your Cards

Cards are fragile. They must be handled properly in order to retain their value. Careless handling can easily result in creased or bent cards. It is, however, not recommended that tweezers or tongs be used to pick up your cards since such utensils might mar or indent card surfaces and thus reduce those cards' conditions and values. In general, your cards should be handled directly as little as possible. This is sometimes easier to say than to do.

Although there are still many who use custom boxes, storage trays, or even shoe boxes, plastic sheets are the preferred method of many collectors for storing cards. A collection stored in plastic pages in a three-ring album allows you to view your collection at any time without the need to touch the card itself. Cards can also be kept in single holders (of various types and thicknesses) designed for the enjoyment of each card individually. For a large collection, some collectors may use a combination of the above methods. When purchasing plastic sheets for your cards, be sure that you find the pocket size that fits the cards snugly. Don't put your 1951 Bowman in a sheet designed to fit 1981 Topps.

Most hobby and collectibles shops and virtually all collectors' conventions will have these plastic pages available in quantity for the various sizes offered, or you can purchase them directly from the advertisers in this book. Also, remember that pocket size isn't the only factor to consider when looking for plastic sheets. Other factors such as safety, economy, appearance, availability, or personal preference also may indicate which types of sheets a collector may want to buy.

Damp, sunny, and/or hot conditions. No, this is not a weather forecast, but rather three elements to avoid in extremes if you are interested in preserving your collection. Too much (or too little) humidity can cause gradual deterioration of a card. Direct, bright sun (or fluorescent light) over time will bleach out the color of a card. Extreme heat accelerates the decomposition of the card. On the other hand, many cards have lasted more than 50 years without much scientific intervention. So be cautious, even if the above factors typically present a problem only when present in the extreme. It never hurts to be prudent.

Collecting vs. Investing

Collecting individual players and collecting complete sets are both popular vehicles for investment and speculation. Most investors and speculators stock up on complete sets or on quantities of players they think have good investment potential.

There is obviously no guarantee in this book, or anywhere else for that matter, that cards will outperform the stock market or other investment alternatives in the future. After all, football cards do not pay quarterly dividends and cards cannot be sold at their "current values" as easily as stocks or bonds.

Nevertheless, investors have noticed a favorable long-term trend in the past performance of sports collectibles, and certain cards and sets have outperformed just about any other investment in some years. Many hobbyists maintain that the best investment is and always will be the building of a collection, which traditionally has held up better than outright speculation.

Some of the obvious questions are Which cards? When to buy? When to sell? The best investment you can make is in your own education. The more you know about your collection and the hobby, the more informed decisions you will be able to make. We're not selling investment tips. We're selling information about the current value of football cards. It's up to you to use that information to your best advantage.

Terminology

Each hobby has its own language to describe its area of interest. The terminology traditionally used for trading cards is derived from the American Card Catalog, published in 1960 by Nostalgia Press. That catalog, written by Jefferson Burdick (who is called the "Father of Card Collecting" for his pioneering work), uses letter and number designations for each separate set of cards. The letter used in the ACC designation refers to the generic type of card. While both sport and non-sport issues are classified in the ACC, we shall confine ourselves to the sport issues. The following list defines the letters and their meanings as used by the American Card Catalog, as applied to football cards:

(none) or **N** - 19th Century U.S. Tobacco
F - Food Inserts
H - Advertising
M - Periodicals
N - 19th Century U.S. Tobacco
PC - Postcards
R - Recent Candy and Gum Cards, 1930 to Present
UO - Gas and Oil Inserts
V - Canadian Candy
W - Exhibits, Strip Cards, Team Cards

Following the letter prefix and an optional hyphen are one-, two-, or three-digit numbers, R(-)999. These typically represent the company or entity issuing the cards. In several cases, the ACC number is extended by an additional hyphen and another one- or two-digit numerical suffix. For example, the 1957 Topps regular-series football card issue carries an ACC designation of R415-5. The "R" indicates a Candy or Gum card produced since 1930. The "415" is the ACC designation for the 1957 regular issue (Topps fifth football set).

Like other traditional methods of identification, this system provides order to the process of cataloging cards; however, most serious collectors learn the ACC designation of the popular sets by repetition and familiarity, rather than by attempting to "figure out" what they might or should be. From 1948 forward, collectors and dealers commonly refer to all sets by their year, maker, type of issue, and any other distinguishing characteristic. For example, such a characteristic could be an unusual issue or one of several regular issues put out by a specific maker in a single year. Regional issues are usually referred to by year, maker, and sometimes by title or theme of the set.

Glossary/Legend

Our glossary defines terms frequently used in the card collecting hobby. Many of these terms are also common to other types of sports memorabilia collecting. Some terms may have several meanings depending on use and context.

ACC - Acronym for American Card Catalog.

ACETATE - A transparent plastic.

AFC - American Football Conference.

AFL - American Football League.

AS - All-Star.

ATG - All Time Great card.

AU(TO) - An autographed card.

BRICK - A group or "lot" or cards, usually 50 or more having common characteristics, that is intended to be bought, sold, or traded as a unit.

C - Center.

CB - Cornerback.

CFL - Canadian Football League.

CL - Checklist card. A card that lists in order the cards and players in the set or series. Older checklist cards in mint condition that have not been checked off are very desirable and command large premiums.

CO - Coach card.

COLLECTOR ISSUE - A set produced for the sake of the card itself, with no product or service sponsor. It derives its name from the fact that most of these sets are produced for sale directly to the hobby market.

COMBINATION CARD - A single card depicting two or more players (not including team cards).

COMMON CARD - The typical card of any set; it has no premium value accruing from subject matter, numerical scarcity, popular demand, or anomaly.

CONVENTION - A large gathering of dealers and collectors at a single location for the purpose of buying, selling, and sometimes trading sports memorabilia items. Conventions are open to the public and sometimes also feature autograph guests, door prizes, films, contests, etc. More commonly called "shows."

COR - Corrected card. A version of an error card that was fixed by the manufacturer.

DB - Defensive back.

DIE-CUT - A card with its stock partially cut. In some cases, after removal or appropriate folding, the remaining part of the card can be made to stand up.

DISC - A circular-shaped card.

DISPLAY SHEET - A clear, plastic page that is punched for insertion into a binder (with standard three-ring spacing) containing pockets for displaying cards. Many different styles of sheets exist with pockets of varying sizes to hold the many differing card formats. The vast majority of current cards measure 2-1/2 by 3-1/2 inches and fit in nine-pocket sheets.

DP - Double Print. A card that was printed in approximately double the quantity compared to other cards in the same series, or draft pick card.

DT - Defensive tackle or Dream Team.

DUFEX - A method of card manufacturing technology patented by Pinnacle Brands, Inc. It involves a refractive quality to a card with a foil coating.

EMBOSSED - A raised surface; features of a card that are projected from a flat background.

ERR - Error card. A card with erroneous information, spelling, or depiction on either side of the card. Most errors are never corrected by the producing card company.

ETCHED - Impressions within the surface of a card.

EXHIBIT - The generic name given to thick-stock, postcard-size cards with single-color, obverse pictures. The name is derived from the Exhibit Supply Co. of Chicago, the principal manufacturer of this type of card. These are also known as Arcade cards since they were found in many arcades.

FB - Fullback.

FDP - First (round) draft pick.

FG - Field goal.

FOIL - A special type of sticker with a metallic-looking surface.

FULL-BLEED - A borderless card; a card containing a photo that encompasses the entire card.

FULL SHEET - A complete sheet of cards that has not been cut into individual cards by the manufacturer. Also called an uncut sheet.

G - Guard.

GLOSS - A card with luster; a shiny finish as in a card with UV coating.

HIGH NUMBER - The cards in the last series of number, in a year in which such higher-numbered cards were printed or distributed in significantly lesser amount than the lower-numbered cards. The high-number designation refers to a scarcity of the high-numbered cards.

HL - Highlight card, for example from the 1978 Topps subset.

HOF - Hall of Fame, or Hall of Famer (also abbreviated HOFer).

HOLOGRAM - A three-dimensional photographic image.

HOR - Horizontal pose on a card as opposed to the standard vertical orientation found on most cards.

IA - In Action card. A special type of card depicting a player in an action photo, such as the 1982 Topps cards.

IL - Inside linebacker.

INSERT - A card of a different type, e.g., a poster, or any other sports collectible contained and sold in the same package along with a card or cards of a major set.

INTERACTIVE - A concept that involves collector participation.

K - Kicker.

KARAT - A unit of measure for the fineness of gold; i.e., 24K.

KP - Kid Picture card.

LAYERING - The separation or peeling of one or more layers of the card stock, usually at the corner of the card. Also see the Condition Guide.

LB - Linebacker.

LID - A circular-shaped card (possibly with tab) that forms the top of the container for the product being promoted.

LL - League leader card. A card depicting the leader or leaders in a specific statistical category from the previous season. Not to be confused with team leader (TL).

LOGO - NFLPA logo on card.

MAJOR SET - A set produced by a national manufacturer of cards, containing a large number of cards. Usually 100 or more different cards comprise a major set.

MEM - Memorial.

METALLIC - A glossy design that enhances card features.

MINI - A small card or stamp (specifically the 1969 Topps Four-in-One football inserts or the 1987 Topps mini football set issued for the United Kingdom).

MVP - Most Valuable Player.

NFLPA - National Football League Players Association.

NO LOGO - No NFLPA logo on card.

NO TR - No trade reference on card.

NPO - No position.

NT - Nose tackle.

OFF - Officials cards.

O-ROY - Offensive Rookie of the Year.

OT - Offensive tackle.

P - Punter.

P1 - First Printing.

P2 - Second Printing.

PACKS - A means with which cards are issued in terms of pack type (wax, cello, foil, rack, etc.) and channels of distribution (hobby, retail, etc.).

PANEL - An extended card that is composed of multiple individual cards.

PARALLEL - A card that is similar in design to its counterpart from a basic set, but offers a distinguishing quality.

PB - Pro Bowl.

PLATINUM - A metallic element used in the process of creating a glossy card.

POY - Player of the Year.

PREMIUM - A card, sometimes on photographic stock, that is purchased or obtained in conjunction with (or redeemed for) another card or product. This term applies mainly to older products, as newer cards distributed in this manner are generally lumped together as peripheral sets.

PREMIUM CARDS - A class of products introduced recently, intended to have higher quality card stock and photography than regular cards, but more limited production and higher cost. Defining what is and isn't a premium card is somewhat subjective.

PRISMATIC/PRISM - A glossy or bright design that refracts or disperses light.

PROMOTIONAL SET - A set, usually containing a small number of cards, issued by a national card producer and distributed in limited quantities or to a select group of people, such as major show attendees or dealers with wholesale accounts. Presumably, the purpose of a promo set is to stir up demand for an upcoming set. Also called a preview, prototype, or test set.

QB - Quarterback.

RARE - A card or series of cards of very limited availability. Unfortunately, "rare" is a subjective term sometimes used indiscriminately. Using the strict definitions, rare cards are harder to obtain than scarce cards.

RB - Record Breaker card or running back.

RC - Rookie Card. A player's first appearance on a regular issue card from one of the major card companies. With a few exceptions, each player has only one RC in any given set. A Rookie Card typically cannot be an All-Star, Highlight, In Action, league leader, Super Action, or team leader card. It can, however, be a coach card or draft pick card.

REDEMPTION - A program established by manufacturers that allows collectors to mail in a special card (usually a random insert) in return for special cards, sets, or other prizes not available through conventional channels.

REFRACTORS - A card that features a design element which enhances (distorts) its color/appearance through deflecting light.

REGIONAL - A card issued and distributed only in a limited geographical area of the country. The producer may or may not be a major, national producer of trading cards. The key is whether the set was distributed nationally in any form or not.

REPLICA - An identical copy or reproduction.

RET - Retired.

REV NEG - Reversed or flopped photo side of the card. This is a major type of error card, but only some are corrected.

ROY - Rookie of the Year.

S - Safety.

SB - Super Bowl.

SCARCE - A card or series of cards of limited availability. This subjective term is sometimes used indiscriminately to promote or hype value. Using strict definitions, scarce cards are easier to obtain than rare cards.

SEMI-HIGH - A card from the next-to-last series of a sequentially issued set. It has more value than an average card and generally less value than a high number. A card is not called a semi-high unless its next-to-last series has an additional premium attached to it.

SERIES - The entire set of cards issued by a particular producer in a particular year, e.g., the 1978 Topps series. Also, within a particular set, series can refer to a group of (consecutively numbered) cards printed at the same time, e.g., the first series of the 1948 Leaf set (#1 through #49).

SET - One each of an entire run of cards of the same type, produced by a particular manufacturer during a single season. In other words, if you have a complete set of 1975 Topps football cards, then you have every card from #1 up to and including #528; i.e., all the different cards that were produced.

SHEEN - Brightness or luster emitted by a card.

SKIP-NUMBERED - A set that has many unissued card numbers between the lowest number in the set and the highest number in the set, e.g., the 1949 Leaf football set contains 49 cards skip-numbered from number 1 to number 144. A major set in which a few numbers were not printed is not considered to be skip-numbered.

SP - Single or Short Print. A card which was printed in lesser quantity compared to the other cards in the same series (also see DP). This term can only be used in a relative sense and in reference to one particular set. For instance, the 1989 Pro Set Pete Rozelle SP is less common than the other cards in that set, but it isn't necessarily scarcer than regular cards of any other set.

SPECIAL CARD - A card that portrays something other than a single player or team; for example, the 1990 Fleer Joe Montana/Jerry Rice Super Bowl

MVPs card #397.

SR - Super Rookie.

STAMP - Adhesive-backed papers depicting a player. The stamp may be individual or in a sheet of many stamps. Moisture must be applied to the adhesive in order for the stamp to be attached to another surface.

STAR CARD - A card that portrays a player of some repute, usually determined by his ability, but sometimes referring to sheer popularity.

STICKER - A card-like item with a removable layer that can be affixed to another surface. Example: 1983 Topps inserts.

STOCK - The cardboard or paper on which the card is printed.

SUPERIMPOSED - To be affixed on top of something, i.e., a player photo over a solid background.

SUPERSTAR CARD - A card that portrays a superstar, e.g., a Hall of Fame member or a player whose current performance may eventually warrant serious Hall of Fame consideration.

TAB - A card portion set off from the rest of the card, usually with perforations, that may be removed without damaging the central character or event depicted by the card.

TC - Team card or team checklist card.

TEAM CARD - A card that depicts an entire team.

THREE-DIMENSIONAL (3D) - A visual image that provides an illusion of depth and perspective.

TL - Team leader card or Top Leader.

TOPICAL - A subset or group of cards that have a common theme, i.e., MVP award winners.

TR - Trade reference on card.

TRANSPARENT - Clear, see-through.

TRIMMED - A card cut down from its original size. Trimmed cards are undesirable to most collectors, and are therefore less valuable than otherwise identical, untrimmed cards. Also see the Condition Guide.

UER - Uncorrected error card.

USFL - United States Football League.

UV - Ultraviolet, a glossy coating used in producing cards.

VAR - Variation card. One of two or more cards from the same series, with the same card number (or player with identical pose, if the series is unnumbered) differing from one another in some aspect, from the printing, stock, or other feature of the card. This is often caused when the manufacturer of the cards notices an error, in a particular card, corrects the error and then resumes the print run. In this case there will be two versions or variations of the same card. Sometimes one of the variations is relatively scarce. Variations also can result from accidental or deliberate design changes, information updates, photo substitutions, etc.

VERT - Vertical pose on a card.

WFL - World Football League.

WLAF - World League of American Football.

WR - Wide receiver.

XRC - Extended Rookie Card. A player's first appearance on a card, but issued in a set that was not distributed nationally or in packs. In football sets, this term generally refers to the 1984 and 1985 Topps USFL sets.

Understanding Card Values

Determining Value

Why are some cards more valuable than others? Obviously, the economic laws of supply and demand are applicable to card collecting just as they are to any other field where a commodity is bought, sold, or traded in a free, unregulated market.

Supply (the number of cards available on the market) is less than the total number of cards originally produced since attrition diminishes that original quantity. Each year a percentage of cards is typically thrown away, destroyed, or otherwise lost to collectors. This percentage is much, much smaller today than it was in the past because more and more people have become increasingly aware of the value of their cards.

For those who collect only mint condition cards, the supply of older cards can be quite small indeed. Until recently, collectors were not so conscious of the need to preserve the condition of their cards. For this reason, it is difficult to know exactly how many 1962 Topps are currently available, mint or otherwise. It is generally accepted that there are fewer 1962 Topps available than 1972, 1982, or 1992 Topps cards. If demand were equal for each of these sets, the law of supply and demand would increase the price for the least available sets.

Demand, however, is never equal for all sets, so price correlations can be complicated. The demand for a card is influenced by many factors. These include: (1) the age of the card; (2) the number of cards printed; (3) the player(s) portrayed on the card; (4) the attractiveness and popularity of the set; and (5) the physical condition of the card.

In general, (1) the older the card, (2) the fewer the number of the cards printed, (3) the more famous, popular, and talented the player, (4) the more attractive and popular the set, and (5) the better the condition of the card, the higher the value of the card will be. There are exceptions to all but one of these factors: the condition of the card. Given two cards similar in all respects except condition, the one in the better condition will always be valued higher.

While those guidelines help to establish the value of a card, the countless exceptions and peculiarities make any simple, direct mathematical formula to determine card values impossible.

Regional Variation

Since the market varies from region to region, card prices of local players may be higher. This is known as a regional premium. How significant the premium is—and if there is any premium at all—depends on the local popularity of the team and the player.

The largest regional premiums usually do not apply to superstars, who often are so well known nationwide that the prices of their key cards are too high for local dealers to realize a premium.

Lesser stars often command the strongest premiums. Their popularity is concentrated in their home region, creating local demand that greatly exceeds overall demand.

Regional premiums can apply to popular retired players and sometimes can be found in the areas where the players grew up or starred in college.

A regional discount is the converse of a regional premium. Regional discounts occur when a player has been so popular in his region for so long that local collectors and dealers have accumulated quantities of his cards. The abundant supply may make the cards available in that area at the lowest prices anywhere.

Set Prices

A somewhat paradoxical situation exists in the price of a complete set vs. the combined cost of the individual cards in the set. In nearly every case, the sum of the prices for the individual cards is higher than the cost for the complete set. This is prevalent especially in the cards of the past few years. The reasons for this apparent anomaly stem from the habits of collectors and from the carrying costs to dealers. Today, each card in a set normally is produced in the same quantity as all others in its set.

Many collectors pick up only stars, superstars, and particular teams. As a result, the dealer is left with a shortage of certain player cards and an abundance of others. He therefore incurs an expense in simply "carrying" these less desirable cards in stock. On the other hand, if he sells a complete set, he gets rid of large numbers of cards at one time. For this reason, he generally is willing to receive less money for a complete set. By doing this, he recovers all of his costs and also makes a profit.

Set prices do not include rare card varieties, unless specifically stated. Of course, the prices for sets do include one example of each type for the given set, but this is the least expensive variety.

Scarce Series

Scarce series occur because cards issued before 1973 were made available to the public each year in several series of finite numbers of cards, rather than all cards of the set being available for purchase at one time. At some point during the season, interest in current year cards waned. Consequently, the manufacturers produced smaller numbers of these later-series cards. Nearly all nationwide issues from post World War II manufacturers (1948 to 1972) exhibit these series variations.

In the past, Topps, for example, may have issued series consisting of many different numbers of cards, including 55, 66, 80, 88, 110, and others. However, after 1968, the sheet size generally has been 132. Despite Topps' standardization of the sheet size, the company double-printed one sheet in 1983 and possibly in 1984 and 1985, too. This was apparently an effort to induce collectors to buy more packs.

We are always looking for information or photographs of printing sheets of cards for research. Each year, we try to update the hobby's knowledge of distribution anomalies. Please let us know at the address in this book if you have firsthand knowledge that would be helpful in this pursuit.

Grading Your Cards

Each hobby has its own grading terminology—stamps, coins, comic books, record collecting, etc. Collectors of sports cards are no exception. The one invariable criterion for determining the value of a card is its condition: the better the condition of the card, the more valuable it is. Condition grading, however, is subjective. Individual card dealers and collectors differ in the strictness of their grading, but the stated condition of a card should be determined without regard to whether it is being bought or sold.

No allowance is made for age. A 1952 card is judged by the same standards as a 1992 card. But there are specific sets and cards that are condition-sensitive because of their border color, consistently poor centering, etc. Such cards and sets sometimes command premiums above the listed percentages in mint condition.

Centering

Current centering terminology uses numbers representing the percentage of border on either side of the main design. Obviously, centering is diminished in importance for borderless cards such as Stadium Club.

Slightly Off-Center (60/40) - A slightly off-center card is one that upon close inspection is found to have one border bigger than the opposite border.

This degree once was offensive only to purists, but now some hobbyists try to avoid cards that are anything other than perfectly centered.

Off-Center (70/30) - An off-center card has one border that is noticeably more than twice as wide as the opposite border.

Badly Off-Center (80/20 or worse) - A badly off-center card has virtually no border on one side of the card.

Miscut - A miscut card actually shows part of the adjacent card in its larger border and consequently a corresponding amount of its card is cut off.

Corner Wear

Corner wear is the most scrutinized grading criteria in the hobby. These are the major categories of corner wear:

Corner with a slight touch of wear - The corner still is sharp, but there is a slight touch of wear showing. On a dark-bordered card, this shows as a dot of white.

Fuzzy corner - The corner still comes to a point, but the point has just begun to fray. A slightly "dinged" corner is considered the same as a fuzzy corner.

Slightly rounded corner - The fraying of the corner has increased to where there is only a hint of a point. Mild layering may be evident. A "dinged" corner is considered the same as a slightly rounded corner.

Rounded corner - The point is completely gone. Some layering is noticeable.

Badly rounded corner - The corner is completely round and rough. Severe layering is evident.

Creases

A third common defect is the crease. The degree of creasing in a card is difficult to show in a drawing or picture. On giving the specific condition of an expensive card for sale, the seller should note any creases additionally. Creases can be categorized as to severity according to the following scale.

Light Crease - A light crease is a crease that is barely noticeable upon close inspection. In fact, when cards are in plastic sheets or holders, a light crease may not be seen (until the card is taken out of the holder). A light crease on the front is much more serious than a light crease on the card back only.

Medium Crease - A medium crease is noticeable when held and studied at arm's length by the naked eye, but does not overly detract from the appearance of the card. It is an obvious crease, but not one that breaks the picture surface of the card.

Heavy Crease - A heavy crease is one that has torn or broken through the card's picture surface, e.g., puts a tear in the photo surface.

Alterations

Deceptive Trimming - This occurs when someone alters the card in order (1) to shave off edge wear, (2) to improve the sharpness of the corners, or (3) to improve centering. Obviously their objective is to falsely increase the perceived value of the card to an unsuspecting buyer. The shrinkage usually is evident only if the trimmed card is compared to an adjacent full-sized card or if the trimmed card is itself measured.

Obvious Trimming - Obvious trimming is noticeable and unfortunate. It is usually performed by non-collectors who give no thought to the present or future value of their cards.

Deceptively Retouched Borders - This occurs when the borders (especially on those cards with dark borders) are touched up on the edges and corners with magic marker or crayons of appropriate color in order to make the card appear to be mint.

Categorization of Defects

Miscellaneous Flaws

The following are common minor flaws that, depending on severity, lower a card's condition by one to four grades and often render it no better than excellent-mint: bubbles (lumps in surface), gum and wax stains, diamond cutting (slanted borders), notching, off-centered backs, paper wrinkles, scratched-off cartoons or puzzles on back, rubber band marks, scratches, surface impressions, and warping.

The following are common serious flaws that, depending on severity, lower a card's condition at least four grades and often render it no better than good: chemical or sun fading, erasure marks, mildew, miscutting (severe off-centering), holes, bleached or retouched borders, tape marks, tears, trimming, water or coffee stains, and writing.

Condition Guide

Grades

Mint (Mt) - A card with no flaws or wear. The card has four perfect corners, 55/45 or better centering from top to bottom and from left to right, original gloss, smooth edges, and original color borders. A mint card does not have print spots, color, or focus imperfections.

Near Mint-Mint (NrMt-Mt) - A card with one minor flaw. Any one of the following would lower a mint card to near mint-mint: one corner with a slight touch of wear, barely noticeable print spots, color or focus imperfections. The card must have 60/40 or better centering in both directions, original gloss, smooth edges, and original color borders.

Near Mint (NrMt) - A card with one minor flaw. Any one of the following would lower a mint card to near mint: one fuzzy corner or two to four corners with slight touches of wear, 70/30 to 60/40 centering, slightly rough edges, minor print spots, color or focus imperfections. The card must have original gloss and original color borders.

Excellent-Mint (ExMt) - A card with two or three fuzzy, but not rounded, corners and centering no worse than 80/20. The card may have no more than two of the following: slightly rough edges, very slightly discolored borders, minor print spots, color or focus imperfections. The card must have original gloss.

Excellent (Ex) - A card with four fuzzy but definitely not rounded corners and centering no worse than 80/20. The card may have a small amount of original gloss lost, rough edges, slightly discolored borders and minor print spots, color or focus imperfections.

Very Good (Vg) - A card that has been handled but not abused: slightly rounded corners with slight layering, slight notching on edges, a significant amount of gloss lost from the surface but no scuffing and moderate discoloration of borders. The card may have a few light creases.

Good (G), Fair (F), Poor (P) - A well-worn, mishandled, or abused card: badly rounded and layered corners, scuffing, most or all original gloss missing, seriously discolored borders, moderate or heavy creases, and one or more serious flaws. The grade of good, fair, or poor depends on the severity of wear and flaws. Good, fair, and poor cards generally are used only as fillers.

The most widely used grades are defined above. Obviously, many cards will not perfectly fit one of the definitions.

Therefore, categories between the major grades known as in-between grades are used, such as good to very good (G-Vg), very good to excellent (VgEx), and excellent-mint to near nint (ExMt-NrMt). Such grades indicate a card with all qualities of the lower category but with at least a few qualities of the higher category.

The Beckett Guide lists each card and set in three grades, with the middle grade valued at about 40%–45% of the top grade, and the bottom grade valued at about 10%–15% of the top grade.

The value of cards that fall between the listed columns can also be calculated using a percentage of the top grade. For example, a card that falls between the top and middle grades (Ex, ExMt, or NrMt in most cases) will generally be valued at anywhere from 50% to 90% of the top grade.

Similarly, a card that falls between the middle and bottom grades (G-Vg, Vg, or VgEx in most cases) will generally be valued at anywhere from 20% to 40% of the top grade.

There are also cases where cards are in better condition than the top grade or worse than the bottom grade. Cards that grade worse than the lowest grade are generally valued at 5%–10% of the top grade.

When a card exceeds the top grade by one—such as NrMt-Mt when the top grade is NrMt, or Mint when the top grade is NrMt-Mt—a premium of up to 50% is possible, with 10%–20% the usual norm.

When a card exceeds the top grade by two—such as Mint when the top grade is NrMt, or NrMt-Mt when the top grade is ExMt—a premium of 25%–50% is the usual norm. But certain condition-sensitive cards or sets, particularly those from the pre-war era, can bring premiums of up to 100% or even more.

Unopened packs, boxes, and factory-collated sets are considered mint in their unknown (and presumed perfect) state. Once opened, however, each card can be graded (and valued) in its own right by taking into account any defects that may be present in spite of the fact that the card has never been handled.

Selling Your Cards

Just about every collector sells cards or will sell cards eventually. Someday you may be interested in selling your duplicates or maybe even your whole collection. You may sell to other collectors, friends, or dealers. You may even sell cards you purchased from a certain dealer back to that same dealer. In any event, it helps to know some of the mechanics of the typical transaction between buyer and seller.

Dealers will buy cards in order to resell them to other collectors who are interested in the cards. Dealers will always pay a higher percentage for items that (in their opinion) can be resold quickly, and a much lower percentage for those items that are perceived as having low demand and hence are slow moving. In either case, dealers must buy at a price that allows for the expense of doing business and a margin for profit.

If you have cards for sale, the best advice we can give is that you get several offers for your cards—either from card shops or at a card show—and take the best offer, all things considered. Note, the "best" offer may not be the one for the highest amount. And remember, if a dealer really wants your cards, he won't let you get away without making his best competitive offer. Another alternative is to place your cards in an auction as one or several lots.

Many people think nothing of going into a department store and paying $15 for an item of clothing for which the store paid $5. But if you were selling your $15 card to a dealer and he offered you $5 for it, you might think his markup unreasonable. To complete the analogy, most department stores (and card dealers) that consistently pay $10 for $15 items eventually go out of business.

Centering

Well-Centered

Slightly Off-Centered

Off-Centered

Badly Off-Centered

Miscut

An exception is when the dealer has lined up a willing buyer for the item(s) you are attempting to sell, or if the cards are so hot that it's likely he'll have to hold the cards for only a short period of time.

In those cases, an offer of up to 75% of book value still will allow the dealer to make a reasonable profit considering the short time he will need to hold the merchandise. In general, however, most cards and collections will bring offers in the range of 25% to 50% of retail price. Also consider that most material from the past five to 20 years is plentiful. If that's what you're selling, don't be surprised if your best offer is well below that range.

Interesting Notes

The first card numerically of an issue is the single card most likely to obtain excessive wear. Consequently, you typically will find the price on the #1 card (in NrMt or mint condition) somewhat higher than might otherwise be the case. Similarly, but to a lesser extent (because normally the less important, reverse side of the card is the one exposed), the last card numerically in an issue also is prone to abnormal wear. This extra wear and tear occurs because the first and last cards are exposed to the elements (human element included) more than any other cards. They are generally end cards in any brick formations, rubber bandings, stackings on wet surfaces, and like activities.

Sports cards have no intrinsic value. The value of a card, like the value of other collectibles, can be determined only by you and your enjoyment in viewing and possessing these cardboard treasures.

Remember, the buyer ultimately determines the price of each card. You are the determining price factor because you have the ability to say "No" to the price of any card by not exchanging your hard-earned money for a given card. When the cost of a trading card exceeds the enjoyment you will receive from it, your answer should be "No." We assess and report the prices. You set them!

We are always interested in receiving the price input of collectors and dealers from around the country. We happily credit major contributors. We welcome your opinions, since your contributions assist us in ensuring a better guide each year. If you would like to join our survey list for the next editions of this book and others authored by Dr. Beckett, please send your name and address to Dr. James Beckett, 15850 Dallas Parkway, Dallas, TX 75248.

History of Football Cards

Until the 1930s, the only set devoted exclusively to football players was the Mayo N302 set. The first bubblegum issue dedicated entirely to football players did not appear until the National Chicle issue of 1935. Before this, athletes from several sports were pictured in the multi-sport Goudey Sport Kings issue of 1933. In that set, football was represented by three legends whose fame has not diminished through the years: Red Grange, Knute Rockne, and Jim Thorpe.

But it was not until 1948, and the post-war bubblegum boom, that the next football issues appeared. Bowman and Leaf Gum companies both issued football card sets in that year. From this point on, football cards have been issued annually by one company or another up to the present time, with Topps being the only major card producer until 1989, when Pro Set and Score debuted and sparked a football card boom.

Football cards depicting players from the Canadian Football League (CFL) did not appear until Parkhurst issued a 100-card set in 1952. Four years later, Parkhurst issued another CFL set with 50 small cards this time. Topps began issuing CFL sets in 1958 and continued annually until 1965, although from 1961 to 1965 these cards were printed in Canada by O-Pee-Chee. Post

Corner Wear

The partial cards here have been photographed at 300%. This was done in order to magnify each card's corner wear to such a degree that differences could be shown on a printed page.

This 1985 Topps Fred Quillan card has a fuzzy corner. Notice the extremely slight fraying on the corner.

This 1985 Topps Fred Smerlas card has a slightly rounded corner. Notice that there is no longer a sharp corner but heavy wear.

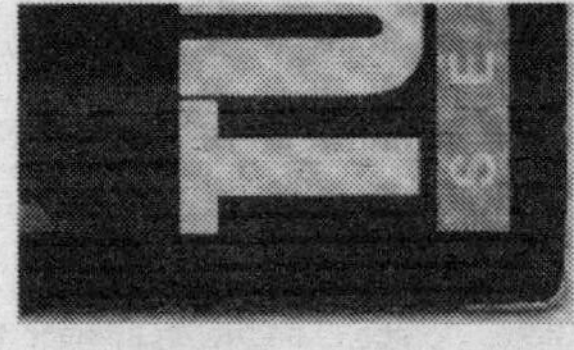

This 1985 Topps Daryl Turner card has a rounded corner evident by the lack of a sharp point and heavy wear on both edges.

This 1985 Topps Kim Bokamper card displays a badly rounded corner. Notice a large portion of missing cardboard accompanied by heavy wear and excessive fraying.

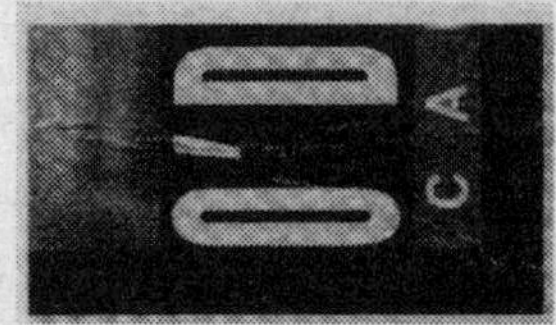

This 1985 Topps Neil O'Donaghue card displays creases of varying degrees. Light creases (left side of the card) may not break the card's surface, while heavy creases (right side) will.

Cereal issued two CFL sets in 1962 and 1963; these cards formed the backs of boxes of Post Cereals distributed in Canada. The O-Pee-Chee company, which has maintained a working relationship with the Topps Gum Company, issued four CFL sets in the years 1968, 1970, 1971, and 1972. Since 1981, the JOGO Novelties Company has been producing a number of CFL sets depicting past and present players.

Returning to American football issues, Bowman resumed its football cards (by then with full-color fronts) from 1950 to 1955. The company twice increased the size of its card during that period. Bowman was unopposed during most of the early 1950s as the sole producer of cards featuring pro football players.

Topps issued its first football card set in 1950 with a group of very small, felt-back cards. In 1951 Topps issued what is referred to as the "Magic Football Card" set. This set of 75 has a scratch-off section on the back which answers a football quiz. Topps did not issue another football set until 1955 when its All-American Football set paid tribute to past college football greats. In January 1956, Topps Gum Company (of Brooklyn) purchased the Bowman Company (of Philadelphia).

After the purchase, Topps issued sets of National Football League (NFL) players up until 1963. The 1961 Topps football set also included American Football League (AFL) players in the high-number series (133–198). Topps sets from 1964 to 1967 contained AFL players only. From 1968 to the present, Topps has issued a major set of football cards each year.

When the AFL was founded in 1960, Fleer produced a 132-card set of AFL players and coaches. In 1961, Fleer issued a 220-card set (even larger than the Topps issue of that year) featuring players from both the NFL and AFL. Apparently, for that one year, Topps and Fleer tested a reciprocal arrangement, trading the card printing rights to each other's contracted players. The 1962 and 1963 Fleer sets feature only AFL players. Both sets are relatively small at 88 cards each.

Post Cereal issued a 200-card set of National League football players in 1962 which contains numerous scarcities, namely those players appearing on unpopular varieties of Post Cereal. From 1964 to 1967, the Philadelphia Gum company issued four 198-card NFL player sets.

In 1984 and 1985, Topps produced a set for the now defunct United States Football League, in addition to its annual NFL set. The 1984 set in particular is quite scarce, due to both low distribution and the high demand for the extended Rookie Cards of current NFL superstars Jim Kelly and Reggie White, among others.

In 1986, McDonald's Restaurants generated the most excitement in football cards in many years. McDonald's created a nationwide football card promotion in which customers could receive a card or two per food purchase, upon request. However, the cards distributed were only of the local team, or of the "McDonald's All-Stars" for areas not near NFL cities. Also, each set was produced with four possible color tabs: blue, black, gold, and green. The tab color distributed depended on the week of the promotion. In general, cards with blue tabs are the scarcest, although for some teams the cards with black tabs are the hardest to find. The tabs were intended to be scratched off and removed by customers to be redeemed for food and other prizes, but among collectors, cards with scratched or removed tabs are categorized as having a major defect, and therefore are valued considerably less.

The entire set, including four color tabs for all 29 subsets, totals over 2,800 different cards. The hoopla over the McDonald's cards fell off precipitously after 1988 as collector interest shifted to the new 1989 Score and Pro

Set issues.

The popularity of football cards has continued to grow since 1986. Topps introduced "Super Rookie" cards in 1987. Card companies other than Topps noticed the burgeoning interest in football cards, resulting in the two landmark 1989 football sets: a 330-card Score issue, and a 440-card Pro Set release. Score later produced a self-contained 110-card supplemental set, while Pro Set printed 100 Series II cards and a 21-card "Final Update" set. Topps, Pro Set, and Score all improved card quality and increased the size of their sets for 1990. That season also marked Fleer's return to football cards and Action Packed's first major set.

In 1991, Pacific, Pro Line, Upper Deck, and Wild Card joined a market that is now at least as competitive as the baseball card market. And the premium card trend that began in baseball cards spilled over to the gridiron in the form of Fleer Ultra, Pro Set Platinum, Score Pinnacle, and Topps Stadium Club sets.

The year 1992 brought even more growth with the debuts of All World, Collectors Edge, GameDay, Playoff, Pro Set Power, SkyBox Impact, and SkyBox Primetime.

The football card market stabilized somewhat in 1993 thanks to an agreement between the long-feuding NFL licensing bodies, NFL Properties and the NFL Players Association. Also helping the stabilization was the emergence of several promising rookies, including Drew Bledsoe, Jerome Bettis, and Rick Mirer. Limited production became the industry buzzword in sports cards, and football was no exception. The result was the success of three new product lines: 1993 Playoff Contenders, 1993 Select, and 1993 SP.

The year 1994 brought further stabilization and limited production. Pro Set and Wild Card dropped out, while no new card companies joined the ranks. However, several new NFL sets were added to the mix by existing manufacturers: Classic NFL Experience, Collector's Choice, Excalibur, Finest, and Sportflics. The new trend centered around multi-level parallel sets and interactive game inserts with parallel prizes. Another strong rookie crop and reported production cutbacks contributed to strong football card sales throughout 1994.

The football card market continued to grow between 1995 and 1998. Many new sets were released by the major manufacturers and a few new players entered the hobby. Companies continued to push the limits of printing technology with issues printed on plastic, leather, cloth, and various metals. Rookie Cards once more came into vogue and the "1-of-1" insert card was born. There are more choices than ever before for the football card collector; most like it that way. In the last couple of years, more changes have occurred in the football card market. The Rookie Card popularity continued but with a twist. Since 1998, many Rookie Cards have been sequentially numbered and/or printed to a shorter supply than other cards in the set they are in.

Also, many companies have begun to issue "game-worn jerseys" or certified autographed cards of leading players, both active and retired.

In addition, graded cards, old and new, have revitalized the card market. Many collectors and dealers have been able to trade over Internet services such as eBay or the many different ways cards are available on beckett.com.

The trend towards short printed Rookie Cards as well as a growing use of memorablia on card continued through the 2001 seasons.

Many of the key Rookie Cards are now issued with some combination of either an autograph, uniform swatch or even both. In addition, the print run of many of these is smaller each and every year.

In addition, a significant amount of the autographs are no longer actually signed on the cards but are signed on stickers which are then affixed to a card.

One after-effect of all this emphasis on Rookie and Memorabilia cards is that many supposed "second-tier" players just do not have many cards issued. The most notable example for 2001 card season was that Tom Brady (who quarterbacked the Patriots to a Super Bowl championship) had less than five cards issued in more than 50 sets.

The 2002 football card season saw an increase in the number of memorabilia cards being issued, and a slight decrease in the number of certified autograph cards being released. Michael Vick was at the forefront of a strong collecting season, as he and several other young players look to establish themselves in the market, as many of the NFL's superstars grow older and near retirement.

While some collectors are frustrated by the changing hobby, others are thrilled because there are more choices than ever for the football card collector—and many of the collectors like it that way.

Additional Reading

Each year Beckett Publications produces comprehensive annual price guides for each of the four major sports: *Beckett Baseball Card Price Guide, Beckett Football Card Price Guide, Beckett Basketball Card Price Guide*, and *Beckett Hockey Card Price Guide*. The aim of these annual guides is to provide information and accurate pricing on a wide array of sports cards, ranging from main issues by the major card manufacturers to various regional, promotional, and food issues. Also other alphabetical checklists, such as *The Beckett Baseball Card Alphabetical, The Beckett Football Card Alphabetical, The Beckett Basketball Card Alphabetical*, and *The Beckett Hockey Card Price Guide and Alphabetical*, are published to assist the collector in identifying all the cards of any particular player. Our Web site Beckett.com was created to allow our readers with Internet access an avenue for buying and selling cards as well as participating in online auctions and interactive price guides. The seasoned collector will find these tools valuable sources of information that will enable him to pursue his hobby interests.

In addition, abridged editions of the Beckett Price Guides have been published for each of the three major sports as part of the House of Collectibles series: *The Official Price Guide to Baseball Cards, The Official Price Guide to Football Cards*, and *The Official Price Guide to Basketball Cards*. Published in a convenient mass-market paperback format, these price guides provide information and accurate pricing on all the important issues by the major card manufacturers.

1995 Absolute

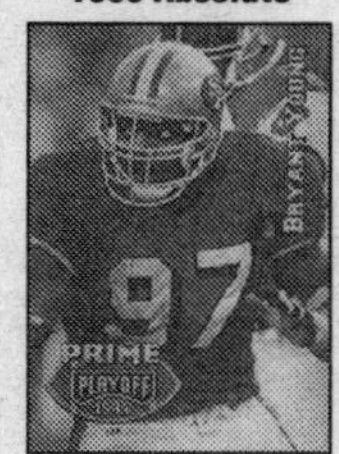

❑ COMPLETE SET (200)	20.00	7.50
❑ 1 John Elway	2.00	.75
❑ 2 Reggie White	.40	.15
❑ 3 Errict Rhett	.20	.07
❑ 4 Deion Sanders	.50	.20
❑ 5 Rocket Ismail	.20	.07
❑ 6 Jerome Bettis	.40	.15
❑ 7 Randall Cunningham	.40	.15
❑ 8 Mario Bates	.20	.07
❑ 9 Dave Brown	.20	.07
❑ 10 Stan Humphries	.20	.07
❑ 11 Drew Bledsoe	.60	.25
❑ 12 Neil O'Donnell	.20	.07
❑ 13 Dan Marino	2.00	.75
❑ 14 Larry Centers	.20	.07
❑ 15 Craig Heyward	.20	.07
❑ 16 Bruce Smith	.40	.15
❑ 17 Erik Kramer	.10	.02
❑ 18 Jeff Blake RC	1.00	.40
❑ 19 Vinny Testaverde	.20	.07
❑ 20 Barry Sanders	1.50	.60
❑ 21 Boomer Esiason	.20	.07
❑ 22 Emmitt Smith	1.50	.60
❑ 23 Warren Moon	.20	.07
❑ 24 Junior Seau	.40	.15
❑ 25 Heath Shuler	.20	.07
❑ 26 Jackie Harris	.10	.02
❑ 27 Terance Mathis	.20	.07
❑ 28 Raymont Harris	.10	.02
❑ 29 Jim Kelly	.40	.15
❑ 30 Dan Wilkinson	.20	.07
❑ 31 Herman Moore	.40	.15
❑ 32 Shannon Sharpe	.20	.07
❑ 33 Antonio Langham	.10	.02
❑ 34 Charles Haley	.20	.07
❑ 35 Brett Favre	2.00	.75
❑ 36 Marshall Faulk	1.25	.50
❑ 37 Neil Smith	.20	.07
❑ 38 Harvey Williams	.10	.02
❑ 39 Johnny Bailey	.10	.02
❑ 40 O.J. McDuffie	.40	.15
❑ 41 David Palmer	.20	.07
❑ 42 Willie McGinest	.20	.07
❑ 43 Quinn Early	.20	.07
❑ 44 Johnny Johnson	.10	.02
❑ 45 Derek Brown TE	.10	.02
❑ 46 Charlie Garner	.40	.15
❑ 47 Byron Bam Morris	.10	.02
❑ 48 Natrone Means	.20	.07
❑ 49 Ken Norton Jr.	.20	.07
❑ 50 Troy Aikman	1.00	.40
❑ 51 Reggie Brooks	.20	.07
❑ 52 Trent Dilfer	.40	.15
❑ 53 Cortez Kennedy	.20	.07
❑ 54 Chuck Levy	.10	.02
❑ 55 Jeff George	.20	.07
❑ 56 Steve Young	.75	.30
❑ 57 Lewis Tillman	.10	.02
❑ 58 Carl Pickens	.20	.07
❑ 59 Jake Reed	.20	.07
❑ 60 Jay Novacek	.20	.07
❑ 61 Greg Hill	.20	.07
❑ 62 James Jett	.20	.07
❑ 63 Terry Kirby	.20	.07
❑ 64 Qadry Ismail	.20	.07
❑ 65 Ben Coates	.20	.07
❑ 66 Kevin Greene	.20	.07
❑ 67 Bryant Young	.20	.07
❑ 68 Brian Mitchell	.10	.02
❑ 69 Steve Walsh	.10	.02
❑ 70 Darnay Scott	.20	.07
❑ 71 Daryl Johnston	.20	.07
❑ 72 Glyn Milburn	.10	.02
❑ 73 Tim Brown	.40	.15
❑ 74 Isaac Bruce	.75	.30
❑ 75 Bernie Parmalee	.20	.07
❑ 76 Terry Allen	.20	.07
❑ 77 Jim Everett	.10	.02
❑ 78 Thomas Lewis	.20	.07
❑ 79 Vaughn Hebron	.10	.02
❑ 80 Rod Woodson	.20	.07
❑ 81 Rick Mirer	.20	.07
❑ 82 Dana Stubblefield	.20	.07
❑ 83 Bert Emanuel	.40	.15
❑ 84 Andre Reed	.20	.07
❑ 85 Jeff Graham	.10	.02
❑ 86 Johnnie Morton	.20	.07
❑ 87 LeShon Johnson	.20	.07
❑ 88 Michael Irvin	.40	.15
❑ 89 Derrick Alexander WR	.40	.15
❑ 90 Lake Dawson	.20	.07
❑ 91 Cody Carlson	.10	.02
❑ 92 Chris Warren	.20	.07
❑ 93 William Floyd	.20	.07
❑ 94 Charles Johnson	.20	.07
❑ 95 Roosevelt Potts	.10	.02
❑ 96 Cris Carter	.40	.15
❑ 97 Aaron Glenn	.10	.02
❑ 98 Curtis Conway	.40	.15
❑ 99 Kevin Williams WR	.20	.07
❑ 100 Jerry Rice	1.00	.40
❑ 101 Frank Reich	.10	.02
❑ 102 Harold Green	.10	.02
❑ 103 Russell Copeland	.10	.02
❑ 104 Rob Moore	.20	.07
❑ 105 Edgar Bennett	.20	.07
❑ 106 Darren Carrington	.10	.02
❑ 107 Tommy Maddox	.40	.15
❑ 108 Dave Meggett	.10	.02
❑ 109 Fred Barnett	.20	.07
❑ 110 Mark Seay	.20	.07
❑ 111 Gus Frerotte	.20	.07
❑ 112 Brent Jones	.10	.02
❑ 113 Chris Miller	.10	.02
❑ 114 Cedric Tillman	.10	.02
❑ 115 Mark Ingram	.10	.02
❑ 116 Eric Turner	.10	.02
❑ 117 Mark Carrier WR	.20	.07
❑ 118 Garrison Hearst	.40	.15
❑ 119 Craig Erickson	.10	.02
❑ 120 Derek Russell	.10	.02
❑ 121 Mike Sherrard	.10	.02
❑ 122 Horace Copeland	.10	.02
❑ 123 Jack Trudeau	.10	.02
❑ 124 Leroy Hoard	.10	.02
❑ 125 Gary Brown	.10	.02
❑ 126 Mel Gray	.10	.02
❑ 127 Steve Beuerlein	.20	.07
❑ 128 Marcus Allen	.40	.15
❑ 129 Irving Fryar	.20	.07
❑ 130 Marion Butts	.10	.02
❑ 131 Ricky Watters	.20	.07
❑ 132 Tony Martin	.20	.07
❑ 133 Lawrence Dawsey	.10	.02
❑ 134 Ronnie Harmon	.10	.02
❑ 135 Herschel Walker	.20	.07
❑ 136 Michael Haynes	.20	.07
❑ 137 Eric Green	.10	.02
❑ 138 Steve Bono	.20	.07
❑ 139 Jamir Miller	.10	.02
❑ 140 Rod Smith DB	.20	.07
❑ 141 Andre Rison	.20	.07
❑ 142 Eric Metcalf	.20	.07
❑ 143 Michael Timpson	.10	.02
❑ 144 Cornelius Bennett	.20	.07
❑ 145 Sean Dawkins	.20	.07
❑ 146 Scott Mitchell	.20	.07
❑ 147 Ray Childress	.10	.02
❑ 148 Jim Harbaugh	.20	.07
❑ 149 Reggie Cobb	.10	.02
❑ 150 Willie Roaf	.10	.02
❑ 151 Stevie Anderson	.10	.02
❑ 152 Barry Foster	.20	.07
❑ 153 Joe Montana	2.00	.75
❑ 154 David Klingler	.20	.07
❑ 155 Chris Chandler	.20	.07
❑ 156 Carnell Lake	.10	.02
❑ 157 Calvin Williams	.20	.07
❑ 158 Kenneth Davis	.10	.02
❑ 159 Tydus Winans	.10	.02
❑ 160 Sam Adams	.10	.02
❑ 161 Ronald Moore	.10	.02
❑ 162 Vincent Brisby	.10	.02
❑ 163 Alvin Harper	.10	.02
❑ 164 Jake Reed	.20	.07
❑ 165 Jeff Hostetler	.20	.07
❑ 166 Mark Brunell	.60	.25
❑ 167 Leonard Russell	.10	.02
❑ 168 Greg Truitt	.10	.02
❑ 169 Pete Metzelaars	.10	.02
❑ 170 Dave Krieg	.10	.02
❑ 171 Lorenzo White	.10	.02
❑ 172 Robert Brooks	.40	.15
❑ 173 Willie Davis	.20	.07
❑ 174 Irving Spikes	.20	.07
❑ 175 Rodney Hampton	.20	.07
❑ 176 Erric Pegram	.20	.07
❑ 177 Brian Blades	.20	.07
❑ 178 Shawn Jefferson	.10	.02
❑ 179 Tyrone Poole RC	.40	.15
❑ 180 Rob Johnson RC	1.50	.60
❑ 181 Ki-Jana Carter RC	.40	.15
❑ 182 Steve McNair RC	5.00	2.00
❑ 183 Michael Westbrook RC	.40	.15
❑ 184 Kerry Collins RC	2.50	1.00
❑ 185 Kevin Carter RC	.40	.15
❑ 186 Tony Boselli RC	.40	.15
❑ 187 Joey Galloway RC	2.50	1.00
❑ 188 Kyle Brady RC	.40	.15
❑ 189 J.J. Stokes RC	.40	.15
❑ 190 Warren Sapp RC	2.50	1.00
❑ 191 Tyrone Wheatley RC	1.50	.60
❑ 192 Napoleon Kaufman RC	2.00	.75
❑ 193 James O. Stewart RC	1.50	.60
❑ 194 Rashaan Salaam RC	.20	.07
❑ 195 Ray Zellars RC	.20	.07
❑ 196 Todd Collins RC	.20	.07
❑ 197 Sherman Williams RC	.10	.02
❑ 198 Frank Sanders RC	.40	.15
❑ 199 Terrell Fletcher RC	.10	.02
❑ 200 Chad May RC	.10	.02
❑ DP1G Tony Boselli Draft Gold	3.00	1.50
❑ DP1S Tony Boselli Draft Silver	2.00	.75
❑ DP2G Kerry Collins Draft Gold	5.00	2.00
❑ DP2S Kerry Collins Draft Silver	5.00	2.00

1996 Absolute

❑ COMPLETE SET (200)	60.00	25.00
❑ COMP.RED SET (100)	15.00	6.00
❑ 1 Jim Kelly	.60	.25
❑ 2 Michael Irvin	.60	.25
❑ 3 Jim Harbaugh	.30	.10
❑ 4 Warren Moon	.30	.10
❑ 5 Rick Mirer	.30	.10
❑ 6 Drew Bledsoe	1.00	.40
❑ 7 Steve Young	1.25	.50
❑ 8 Junior Seau	.60	.25
❑ 9 Sherman Williams	.15	.05
❑ 10 Jay Novacek	.15	.05
❑ 11 Bill Brooks	.15	.05
❑ 12 Steve Bono	.15	.05
❑ 13 Leroy Hoard	.15	.05

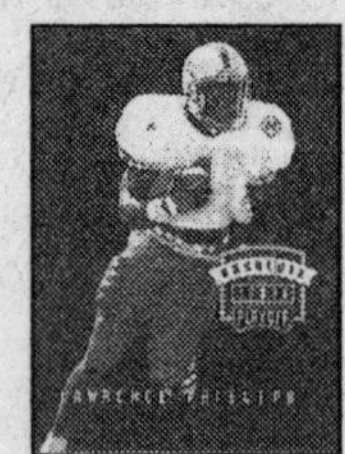

❑ 14	Willie Jackson	.30	.10
❑ 15	Irving Fryar	.30	.10
❑ 16	Tony McGee	.15	.05
❑ 17	Neil O'Donnell	.30	.10
❑ 18	Fred Barnett	.15	.05
❑ 19	Erric Pegram	.15	.05
❑ 20	Derrick Moore	.15	.05
❑ 21	Johnnie Morton	.30	.10
❑ 22	James Jett	.30	.10
❑ 23	Tim Brown	.60	.25
❑ 24	Kevin Miniefield	.15	.05
❑ 25	Jim McMahon	.30	.10
❑ 26	Brian Blades	.15	.05
❑ 27	Henry Ellard	.15	.05
❑ 28	Calvin Williams	.15	.05
❑ 29	Chris Chandler	.30	.10
❑ 30	Rod Woodson	.30	.10
❑ 31	Ronnie Harmon	.15	.05
❑ 32	Brent Jones	.15	.05
❑ 33	Qadry Ismail	.30	.10
❑ 34	Steve Tasker	.15	.05
❑ 35	Eric Green	.15	.05
❑ 36	Brian Mitchell	.15	.05
❑ 37	Herschel Walker	.30	.10
❑ 38	Sean Dawkins	.15	.05
❑ 39	Bryce Paup	.15	.05
❑ 40	Dorsey Levens	.60	.25
❑ 41	Andre Rison	.30	.10
❑ 42	Lamont Warren	.15	.05
❑ 43	Earnest Byner	.15	.05
❑ 44	Bobby Engram RC	.60	.25
❑ 45	Simeon Rice RC	1.50	.60
❑ 46	Michael Jackson	.30	.10
❑ 47	Marvin Harrison RC	4.00	1.50
❑ 48	Thurman Thomas	.60	.25
❑ 49	Charles Haley	.30	.10
❑ 50	Rob Moore	.30	.10
❑ 51	Bryan Cox	.15	.05
❑ 52	Horace Copeland	.15	.05
❑ 53	Rodney Peete	.15	.05
❑ 54	Jeff Graham	.15	.05
❑ 55	Charles Johnson	.15	.05
❑ 56	Natrone Means	.30	.10
❑ 57	Terrell Fletcher	.15	.05
❑ 58	Eric Bieniemy	.15	.05
❑ 59	Karim Abdul-Jabbar RC	.60	.25
❑ 60	Quinn Early	.15	.05
❑ 61	Mark Bruener	.15	.05
❑ 62	Shawn Jefferson	.15	.05
❑ 63	Vinny Testaverde	.30	.10
❑ 64	Derrick Mayes RC	.60	.25
❑ 65	Mario Bates	.30	.10
❑ 66	J.J. Birden	.15	.05
❑ 67	Eddie Kennison RC	.60	.25
❑ 68	Steve Walsh	.15	.05
❑ 69	Mark Chmura	.30	.10
❑ 70	Mike Sherrard	.15	.05
❑ 71	Boomer Esiason	.30	.10
❑ 72	Alex Van Dyke RC	.30	.10
❑ 73	Jake Reed	.30	.10
❑ 74	Jackie Harris	.15	.05
❑ 75	Mark Rypien	.15	.05
❑ 76	Chris Calloway	.15	.05
❑ 77	Amani Toomer RC	1.50	.60
❑ 78	Terrell Davis	3.00	1.25
❑ 79	Rocket Ismail	.15	.05
❑ 80	Derek Loville	.15	.05
❑ 81	Ben Coates	.30	.10
❑ 82	Kyle Brady	.15	.05
❑ 83	Willie Green	.15	.05
❑ 84	Randall Cunningham	.60	.25
❑ 85	Amp Lee	.15	.05
❑ 86	Bert Emanuel	.30	.10
❑ 87	Jason Dunn RC	.30	.10
❑ 88	Michael Haynes	.15	.05
❑ 89	Robert Green	.15	.05
❑ 90	Willie Davis	.15	.05
❑ 91	O.J. McDuffie	.30	.10
❑ 92	Harold Green	.15	.05
❑ 93	Ken Dilger	.30	.10
❑ 94	Brett Perriman	.15	.05
❑ 95	Eric Zeier	.15	.05
❑ 96	Jerome Bettis	.60	.25
❑ 97	Rickey Dudley RC	.60	.25
❑ 98	Darnay Scott	.30	.10
❑ 99	Mark Brunell	1.00	.40
❑ 100	Christian Fauria	.15	.05
❑ 101	Jeff Blake	1.50	.60
❑ 102	Troy Aikman	4.00	1.50
❑ 103	John Elway	8.00	3.00
❑ 104	Barry Sanders	6.00	2.50
❑ 105	Curtis Conway	1.50	.60
❑ 106	Wayne Chrebet	2.00	.75
❑ 107	Lake Dawson	.75	.30
❑ 108	Jerry Rice	4.00	1.50
❑ 109	Kevin Williams	.25	.08
❑ 110	Zack Crockett	.25	.08
❑ 111	Vincent Brisby	.25	.08
❑ 112	Rodney Thomas	.25	.08
❑ 113	Rodney Hampton	.75	.30
❑ 114	Adrian Murrell	.30	.10
❑ 115	Bruce Smith	1.50	.60
❑ 116	Napoleon Kaufman	1.50	.60
❑ 117	Byron Bam Morris	.25	.08
❑ 118	Anthony Miller	.75	.30
❑ 119	Aaron Hayden RC	.75	.30
❑ 120	Joey Galloway	.60	.25
❑ 121	Trent Dilfer	.75	.30
❑ 122	Stoney Case	.25	.08
❑ 123	Tamarick Vanover	.30	.10
❑ 124	Eric Metcalf	.75	.30
❑ 125	Marcus Allen	1.50	.60
❑ 126	James O. Stewart	.75	.30
❑ 127	Charlie Garner	.75	.30
❑ 128	Yancey Thigpen	.75	.30
❑ 129	William Floyd	.75	.30
❑ 130	Terry Allen	.75	.30
❑ 131	Robert Smith	.75	.30
❑ 132	Todd Kinchen	.25	.08
❑ 133	Gus Frerotte	.75	.30
❑ 134	Frank Sanders	.75	.30
❑ 135	Scott Mitchell	.75	.30
❑ 136	Greg Hill	.75	.30
❑ 137	Edgar Bennett	.75	.30
❑ 138	Alvin Harper	.25	.08
❑ 139	Reggie White	1.50	.60
❑ 140	Craig Heyward	.25	.08
❑ 141	Todd Collins	.75	.30
❑ 142	Ernie Mills	.25	.08
❑ 143	Keyshawn Johnson RC	2.50	1.00
❑ 144	Mark Carrier WR	.25	.08
❑ 145	Robert Brooks	1.50	.60
❑ 146	Bernie Parmalee	.25	.08
❑ 147	Carl Pickens	.75	.30
❑ 148	Kevin Hardy RC	1.50	.60
❑ 149	Jonathan Ogden RC	1.50	.60
❑ 150	Lawrence Phillips RC	1.50	.60
❑ 151	Emmitt Smith	10.00	4.00
❑ 152	Brett Favre	12.00	5.00
❑ 153	Dan Marino	12.00	5.00
❑ 154	Jim Everett	.60	.25
❑ 155	Dave Brown	1.25	.50
❑ 156	Jeff Hostetler	1.25	.50
❑ 157	Heath Shuler	1.25	.50
❑ 158	Daryl Johnston	1.25	.50
❑ 159	Terance Mathis	1.25	.50
❑ 160	Curtis Martin	5.00	2.00
❑ 161	Ray Zellars	.60	.25
❑ 162	Ricky Watters	1.25	.50
❑ 163	Chris Warren	1.25	.50
❑ 164	Larry Centers	1.25	.50
❑ 165	Steve McNair	5.00	2.00
❑ 166	Terry Kirby	1.25	.50
❑ 167	Rob Johnson	2.50	1.00
❑ 168	Dave Meggett	.60	.25
❑ 169	Antonio Freeman	.60	.25
❑ 170	Marshall Faulk	4.00	1.50
❑ 171	Andre Hastings	.15	.05
❑ 172	Stan Humphries	1.25	.50
❑ 173	Errict Rhett	1.25	.50
❑ 174	Michael Westbrook	2.50	1.00
❑ 175	Deion Sanders	4.00	1.50
❑ 176	Jeff George	1.25	.50
❑ 177	Cris Carter	2.50	1.00
❑ 178	Chris Sanders	1.25	.50
❑ 179	Ki-Jana Carter	1.25	.50
❑ 180	Kordell Stewart	2.50	1.00
❑ 181	Isaac Bruce	2.50	1.00
❑ 182	Terry Glenn RC	5.00	2.00
❑ 183	Garrison Hearst	1.25	.50
❑ 184	Erik Kramer	.60	.25
❑ 185	Leeland McElroy RC	1.25	.50
❑ 186	Rashaan Salaam	1.25	.50
❑ 187	Kimble Anders	.60	.25
❑ 188	Chad May	.60	.25
❑ 189	Tony Martin	1.25	.50
❑ 190	J.J. Stokes	2.50	1.00
❑ 191	Darick Holmes	.60	.25
❑ 192	Eric Moulds RC	6.00	2.50
❑ 193	Shannon Sharpe	1.25	.50
❑ 194	Tim Biakabutuka RC	2.50	1.00
❑ 195	Eddie George RC	6.00	2.50
❑ 196	Mike Alstott RC	5.00	2.00
❑ 197	Kerry Collins	2.50	1.00
❑ 198	Harvey Williams	.60	.25
❑ 199	Herman Moore	1.25	.50
❑ 200	Tyrone Wheatley	1.25	.50

1997 Absolute

❑	COMPLETE SET (200)	80.00	30.00
❑	COMP.GREEN SET (100)	25.00	10.00
❑ 1	Marcus Allen	.50	.20
❑ 2	Eric Bieniemy	.20	.07
❑ 3	Jason Dunn	.20	.07
❑ 4	Jim Harbaugh	.30	.10
❑ 5	Michael Westbrook	.30	.10
❑ 6	Tiki Barber RC	4.00	1.50
❑ 7	Frank Reich	.20	.07
❑ 8	Irving Fryar	.30	.10
❑ 9	Courtney Hawkins	.20	.07
❑ 10	Eric Zeier	.30	.10
❑ 11	Kent Graham	.20	.07
❑ 12	Trent Dilfer	.50	.20
❑ 13	Neil O'Donnell	.30	.10
❑ 14	Reidel Anthony RC	.50	.20
❑ 15	Jeff Hostetler	.20	.07
❑ 16	Lawrence Phillips	.20	.07
❑ 17	Dave Brown	.20	.07

❑ 18 Mike Tomczak .20 .07
❑ 19 Jake Reed .30 .10
❑ 20 Anthony Miller .20 .07
❑ 21 Eric Metcalf .30 .10
❑ 22 Sedrick Shaw RC .30 .10
❑ 23 Anthony Johnson .20 .07
❑ 24 Mario Bates .20 .07
❑ 25 Dorsey Levens .50 .20
❑ 26 Stan Humphries .30 .10
❑ 27 Ben Coates .30 .10
❑ 28 Tyrone Wheatley .30 .10
❑ 29 Adrian Murrell .30 .10
❑ 30 William Henderson .30 .10
❑ 31 Warrick Dunn RC 1.50 .60
❑ 32 LeShon Johnson .20 .07
❑ 33 James O.Stewart .30 .10
❑ 34 Edgar Bennett .30 .10
❑ 35 Raymont Harris .20 .07
❑ 36 LeRoy Butler .20 .07
❑ 37 Darren Woodson .20 .07
❑ 38 Darnell Autry RC .30 .10
❑ 39 Johnnie Morton .30 .10
❑ 40 William Floyd .30 .10
❑ 41 Terrell Fletcher .20 .07
❑ 42 Leonard Russell .20 .07
❑ 43 Henry Ellard .20 .07
❑ 44 Terrell Owens .50 .20
❑ 45 John Friesz .20 .07
❑ 46 Antowain Smith RC 1.50 .60
❑ 47 Charles Johnson .30 .10
❑ 48 Rickey Dudley .30 .10
❑ 49 Lake Dawson .20 .07
❑ 50 Bert Emanuel .30 .10
❑ 51 Zach Thomas .50 .20
❑ 52 Earnest Byner .20 .07
❑ 53 Yatil Green RC .30 .10
❑ 54 Chris Spielman .20 .07
❑ 55 Muhsin Muhammad .30 .10
❑ 56 Bobby Engram .30 .10
❑ 57 Eric Bjornson .20 .07
❑ 58 Willie Green .20 .07
❑ 59 Derrick Mayes .30 .10
❑ 60 Chris Sanders .20 .07
❑ 61 Jimmy Smith .30 .10
❑ 62 Tony Gonzalez RC 2.00 .75
❑ 63 Rich Gannon .50 .20
❑ 64 Stanley Pritchett .20 .07
❑ 65 Brad Johnson .50 .20
❑ 66 Rodney Peete .20 .07
❑ 67 Sam Gash .20 .07
❑ 68 Chris Calloway .20 .07
❑ 69 Chris T. Jones .20 .07
❑ 70 Will Blackwell RC .30 .10
❑ 71 Mark Bruener .20 .07
❑ 72 Terry Kirby .30 .10
❑ 73 Brian Blades .20 .07
❑ 74 Craig Heyward .20 .07
❑ 75 Jamie Asher .20 .07
❑ 76 Terance Mathis .30 .10
❑ 77 Troy Davis RC .30 .10
❑ 78 Bruce Smith .30 .10
❑ 79 Simeon Rice .30 .10
❑ 80 Fred Barnett .20 .07
❑ 81 Tim Brown .50 .20
❑ 82 James Jett .30 .10
❑ 83 Mark Carrier WR .20 .07
❑ 84 Shawn Jefferson .20 .07
❑ 85 Ken Dilger .20 .07
❑ 86 Rae Carruth RC .20 .07
❑ 87 Keenan McCardell .30 .10
❑ 88 Michael Irvin .50 .20
❑ 89 Mark Chmura .30 .10
❑ 90 Derrick Alexander WR .30 .10
❑ 91 Andre Reed .30 .10
❑ 92 Ed McCaffrey .30 .10
❑ 93 Erik Kramer .20 .07
❑ 94 Albert Connell RC .50 .20
❑ 95 Frank Wycheck .20 .07
❑ 96 Zack Crockett .20 .07
❑ 97 Jim Everett .20 .07
❑ 98 Michael Haynes .20 .07
❑ 99 Jeff Graham .20 .07
❑ 100 Brent Jones .30 .10
❑ 101 Troy Aikman 3.00 1.25
❑ 102 Byron Hanspard RC .30 .10
❑ 103 Robert Brooks 1.25 .50
❑ 104 Karim Abdul-Jabbar 1.25 .50
❑ 105 Drew Bledsoe 1.50 .60
❑ 106 Napoleon Kaufman 1.25 .50
❑ 107 Steve Young 2.00 .75
❑ 108 Leeland McElroy .20 .07
❑ 109 Jamal Anderson .50 .20
❑ 110 David LaFleur RC .50 .20
❑ 111 Vinny Testaverde .75 .30
❑ 112 Eric Moulds 1.25 .50
❑ 113 Tim Biakabutuka 1.25 .50
❑ 114 Rick Mirer .50 .20
❑ 115 Jeff Blake 1.25 .50
❑ 116 Jim Schwantz RC .50 .20
❑ 117 Herman Moore .75 .30
❑ 118 Ike Hilliard RC 2.50 1.00
❑ 119 Reggie White 1.25 .50
❑ 120 Steve McNair 2.00 .75
❑ 121 Marshall Faulk 2.00 .75
❑ 122 Natrone Means .75 .30
❑ 123 Greg Hill .75 .30
❑ 124 O.J. McDuffie .75 .30
❑ 125 Robert Smith .75 .30
❑ 126 Bryant Westbrook RC 1.25 .50
❑ 127 Ray Zellars .50 .20
❑ 128 Rodney Hampton .75 .30
❑ 129 Wayne Chrebet .50 .20
❑ 130 Desmond Howard .75 .30
❑ 131 Ty Detmer .75 .30
❑ 132 Erric Pegram .50 .20
❑ 133 Yancey Thigpen .75 .30
❑ 134 Danny Wuerffel RC .50 .20
❑ 135 Charlie Jones .50 .20
❑ 136 Chris Warren .75 .30
❑ 137 Isaac Bruce 1.25 .50
❑ 138 Errict Rhett .75 .30
❑ 139 Gus Frerotte 1.25 .50
❑ 140 Frank Sanders .75 .30
❑ 141 Todd Collins .75 .30
❑ 142 Jake Plummer RC 12.00 5.00
❑ 143 Darnay Scott .75 .30
❑ 144 Rashaan Salaam 1.25 .50
❑ 145 Terrell Davis 2.00 .75
❑ 146 Scott Mitchell .75 .30
❑ 147 Junior Seau 1.25 .50
❑ 148 Warren Moon .75 .30
❑ 149 Wesley Walls .50 .20
❑ 150 Daryl Johnston .75 .30
❑ 151 Brett Favre 12.00 5.00
❑ 152 Emmitt Smith 10.00 4.00
❑ 153 Dan Marino 12.00 5.00
❑ 154 Larry Centers 1.25 .50
❑ 155 Michael Jackson 1.25 .50
❑ 156 Kerry Collins .50 .20
❑ 157 Curtis Conway 1.25 .50
❑ 158 Peter Boulware RC 2.00 .75
❑ 159 Carl Pickens 1.25 .50
❑ 160 Shannon Sharpe 1.25 .50
❑ 161 Brett Perriman .75 .30
❑ 162 Eddie George 2.00 .75
❑ 163 Mark Brunell 4.00 1.50
❑ 164 Tamarick Vanover 1.25 .50
❑ 165 Cris Carter 2.00 .75
❑ 166 Corey Dillon RC 15.00 6.00
❑ 167 Curtis Martin 4.00 1.50
❑ 168 Amani Toomer 1.25 .50
❑ 169 Jeff George 1.25 .50
❑ 170 Kordell Stewart 2.00 .75
❑ 171 Garrison Hearst 1.25 .50
❑ 172 Tony Banks 1.25 .50
❑ 173 Mike Alstott 2.00 .75
❑ 174 Jim Druckenmiller RC .30 .10
❑ 175 Chris Chandler 1.25 .50
❑ 176 Byron Bam Morris .75 .30
❑ 177 Billy Joe Hobert 1.25 .50
❑ 178 Ernie Mills .75 .30
❑ 179 Ki-Jana Carter .75 .30
❑ 180 Deion Sanders 2.00 .75
❑ 181 Ricky Watters 1.25 .50
❑ 182 Shawn Springs RC 2.00 .75
❑ 183 Barry Sanders 10.00 4.00
❑ 184 Antonio Freeman 2.00 .75
❑ 185 Marvin Harrison 2.00 .75
❑ 186 Elvis Grbac 1.25 .50
❑ 187 Terry Glenn 2.00 .75
❑ 188 Willie Roaf .75 .30
❑ 189 Keyshawn Johnson 2.00 .75
❑ 190 Orlando Pace RC 2.00 .75
❑ 191 Jerome Bettis 2.00 .75
❑ 192 Tony Martin 1.25 .50
❑ 193 Jerry Rice 6.00 2.50
❑ 194 Joey Galloway 1.25 .50
❑ 195 Terry Allen 2.00 .75
❑ 196 Eddie Kennison 1.25 .50
❑ 197 Thurman Thomas 2.00 .75
❑ 198 Darrell Russell RC .75 .30
❑ 199 Rob Moore 1.25 .50
❑ 200 John Elway 12.00 5.00

1998 Absolute Hobby

❑ COMPLETE SET (200) 100.00 40.00
❑ 1 John Elway 10.00 4.00
❑ 2 Marcus Nash RC 1.50 .60
❑ 3 Brian Griese RC 6.00 2.50
❑ 4 Terrell Davis 2.50 1.00
❑ 5 Rod Smith WR 1.50 .60
❑ 6 Shannon Sharpe 1.50 .60
❑ 7 Ed McCaffrey 1.50 .60
❑ 8 Brett Favre 10.00 4.00
❑ 9 Dorsey Levens 2.50 1.00
❑ 10 Derrick Mayes 1.50 .60
❑ 11 Antonio Freeman 2.50 1.00
❑ 12 Robert Brooks 1.50 .60
❑ 13 Mark Chmura 1.50 .60
❑ 14 Reggie White 2.50 1.00
❑ 15 Kordell Stewart 2.50 1.00
❑ 16 Hines Ward RC 12.00 6.00
❑ 17 Jerome Bettis 2.50 1.00
❑ 18 Charles Johnson 1.00 .40
❑ 19 Courtney Hawkins 1.00 .40
❑ 20 Will Blackwell 1.00 .40
❑ 21 Mark Bruener 1.00 .40
❑ 22 Steve Young 4.00 1.50
❑ 23 Jim Druckenmiller 1.00 .40
❑ 24 Garrison Hearst 2.50 1.00
❑ 25 R.W. McQuarters RC 2.50 1.00
❑ 26 Marc Edwards 1.00 .40
❑ 27 Irv Smith 1.00 .40
❑ 28 Jerry Rice 5.00 2.00
❑ 29 Terrell Owens 2.50 1.00
❑ 30 J.J. Stokes 1.50 .60
❑ 31 Elvis Grbac 1.50 .60
❑ 32 Rashaan Shehee RC 2.50 1.00
❑ 33 Donnell Bennett 1.00 .40
❑ 34 Kimble Anders 1.50 .60
❑ 35 Ted Popson 1.00 .40
❑ 36 Derrick Alexander WR 1.50 .60
❑ 37 Tony Gonzalez 2.50 1.00
❑ 38 Andre Rison 1.50 .60

❑ 39 Brad Johnson	2.50	1.00
❑ 40 Randy Moss RC	20.00	7.50
❑ 41 Robert Smith	2.50	1.00
❑ 42 Leroy Hoard	1.00	.40
❑ 43 Cris Carter	2.50	1.00
❑ 44 Jake Reed	1.50	.60
❑ 45 Drew Bledsoe	4.00	1.50
❑ 46 Tony Simmons RC	2.50	1.00
❑ 47 Chris Floyd RC	1.50	.60
❑ 48 Robert Edwards RC	2.50	1.00
❑ 49 Shawn Jefferson	1.00	.40
❑ 50 Ben Coates	1.50	.60
❑ 51 Terry Glenn	2.50	1.00
❑ 52 Trent Dilfer	2.50	1.00
❑ 53 Jacquez Green RC	2.50	1.00
❑ 54 Warrick Dunn	2.50	1.00
❑ 55 Mike Alstott	2.50	1.00
❑ 56 Reidel Anthony	1.50	.60
❑ 57 Bert Emanuel	1.50	.60
❑ 58 Warren Sapp	1.50	.60
❑ 59 Charlie Batch RC	3.00	1.25
❑ 60 Germane Crowell RC	2.50	1.00
❑ 61 Scott Mitchell	1.50	.60
❑ 62 Barry Sanders	8.00	3.00
❑ 63 Tommy Vardell	1.00	.40
❑ 64 Herman Moore	1.50	.60
❑ 65 Johnnie Morton	1.50	.60
❑ 66 Mark Brunell	2.50	1.00
❑ 67 Jonathan Quinn RC	3.00	1.25
❑ 68 Fred Taylor RC	5.00	2.00
❑ 69 James Stewart	1.50	.60
❑ 70 Jimmy Smith	1.50	.60
❑ 71 Damon Jones	1.00	.40
❑ 72 Keenan McCardell	1.50	.60
❑ 73 Dan Marino	10.00	4.00
❑ 74 Larry Shannon RC	1.50	.60
❑ 75 John Avery RC	2.50	1.00
❑ 76 Troy Drayton	1.00	.40
❑ 77 Stanley Pritchett	1.00	.40
❑ 78 Karim Abdul-Jabbar	2.50	1.00
❑ 79 O.J. McDuffie	1.50	.60
❑ 80 Yatil Green	1.00	.40
❑ 81 Danny Kanell	1.50	.60
❑ 82 Tiki Barber	2.50	1.00
❑ 83 Tyrone Wheatley	1.50	.60
❑ 84 Charles Way	1.00	.40
❑ 85 Gary Brown	1.00	.40
❑ 86 Brian Alford RC	1.50	.60
❑ 87 Joe Jurevicius RC	3.00	1.25
❑ 88 Ike Hilliard	1.50	.60
❑ 89 Troy Aikman	5.00	2.00
❑ 90 Deion Sanders	2.50	1.00
❑ 91 Emmitt Smith	8.00	3.00
❑ 92 Chris Warren	1.50	.60
❑ 93 Daryl Johnston	1.50	.60
❑ 94 Michael Irvin	2.50	1.00
❑ 95 David LaFleur	1.00	.40
❑ 96 Kevin Dyson RC	3.00	1.25
❑ 97 Steve McNair	2.50	1.00
❑ 98 Eddie George	2.50	1.00
❑ 99 Yancey Thigpen	1.00	.40
❑ 100 Frank Wycheck	1.00	.40
❑ 101 Glenn Foley	1.50	.60
❑ 102 Vinny Testaverde	1.50	.60
❑ 103 Keyshawn Johnson	2.50	1.00
❑ 104 Curtis Martin	2.50	1.00
❑ 105 Keith Byars	1.00	.40
❑ 106 Scott Frost RC	1.50	.60
❑ 107 Wayne Chrebet	2.50	1.00
❑ 108 Warren Moon	2.50	1.00
❑ 109 Ahman Green RC	15.00	6.00
❑ 110 Steve Broussard	1.00	.40
❑ 111 Ricky Watters	1.50	.60
❑ 112 Joey Galloway	1.50	.60
❑ 113 Mike Pritchard	1.00	.40
❑ 114 Brian Blades	1.00	.40
❑ 115 Gus Frerotte	1.00	.40
❑ 116 Skip Hicks RC	2.50	1.00
❑ 117 Terry Allen	2.50	1.00
❑ 118 Michael Westbrook	1.50	.60

❑ 119 Jamie Asher	1.00	.40
❑ 120 Leslie Shepherd	1.00	.40
❑ 121 Jeff Blake	1.50	.60
❑ 122 Corey Dillon	2.50	1.00
❑ 123 Carl Pickens	1.50	.60
❑ 124 Tony McGee	1.00	.40
❑ 125 Darnay Scott	1.50	.60
❑ 126 Kerry Collins	1.50	.60
❑ 127 Fred Lane	1.00	.40
❑ 128 William Floyd	1.00	.40
❑ 129 Rae Carruth	1.00	.40
❑ 130 Wesley Walls	1.50	.60
❑ 131 Muhsin Muhammad	1.50	.60
❑ 132 Jake Plummer	2.50	1.00
❑ 133 Adrian Murrell	1.50	.60
❑ 134 Michael Pittman RC	4.00	2.00
❑ 135 Larry Centers	1.00	.40
❑ 136 Frank Sanders	1.50	.60
❑ 137 Rob Moore	1.50	.60
❑ 138 Andre Wadsworth RC	2.50	1.00
❑ 139 Mario Bates	1.50	.60
❑ 140 Chris Chandler	1.50	.60
❑ 141 Byron Hanspard	1.00	.40
❑ 142 Jamal Anderson	2.50	1.00
❑ 143 Terance Mathis	1.50	.60
❑ 144 O.J. Santiago	1.00	.40
❑ 145 Tony Martin	1.50	.60
❑ 146 Jammi German RC	1.50	.60
❑ 147 Jim Harbaugh	1.50	.60
❑ 148 Errict Rhett	1.50	.60
❑ 149 Michael Jackson	1.00	.40
❑ 150 Pat Johnson RC	2.50	1.00
❑ 151 Eric Green	1.00	.40
❑ 152 Doug Flutie	2.50	1.00
❑ 153 Rob Johnson	1.50	.60
❑ 154 Antowain Smith	2.50	1.00
❑ 155 Bruce Smith	1.50	.60
❑ 156 Eric Moulds	2.50	1.00
❑ 157 Andre Reed	1.50	.60
❑ 158 Erik Kramer	1.00	.40
❑ 159 Darnell Autry	1.00	.40
❑ 160 Edgar Bennett	1.00	.40
❑ 161 Curtis Enis RC	1.50	.60
❑ 162 Curtis Conway	1.50	.60
❑ 163 E.G. Green RC	2.50	1.00
❑ 164 Jerome Pathon RC	3.00	1.25
❑ 165 Peyton Manning RC	30.00	12.50
❑ 166 Marshall Faulk	3.00	1.25
❑ 167 Zack Crockett	1.00	.40
❑ 168 Ken Dilger	1.00	.40
❑ 169 Marvin Harrison	2.50	1.00
❑ 170 Danny Wuerffel	1.50	.60
❑ 171 Lamar Smith	1.50	.60
❑ 172 Ray Zellars	1.00	.40
❑ 173 Qadry Ismail	1.50	.60
❑ 174 Sean Dawkins	1.00	.40
❑ 175 Andre Hastings	1.00	.40
❑ 176 Jeff George	1.50	.60
❑ 177 Charles Woodson RC	4.00	1.50
❑ 178 Napoleon Kaufman	2.50	1.00
❑ 179 Jon Ritchie RC	2.50	1.00
❑ 180 Desmond Howard	1.50	.60
❑ 181 Tim Brown	2.50	1.00
❑ 182 James Jett	1.50	.60
❑ 183 Rickey Dudley	1.00	.40
❑ 184 Bobby Hoying	1.50	.60
❑ 185 Rodney Peete	1.00	.40
❑ 186 Charlie Garner	1.50	.60
❑ 187 Irving Fryar	1.50	.60
❑ 188 Chris T. Jones	1.00	.40
❑ 189 Jason Dunn	1.00	.40
❑ 190 Tony Banks	1.50	.60
❑ 191 Robert Holcombe RC	2.50	1.00
❑ 192 Craig Heyward	1.00	.40
❑ 193 Isaac Bruce	2.50	1.00
❑ 194 Az-Zahir Hakim RC	3.00	1.25
❑ 195 Eddie Kennison	1.50	.60
❑ 196 Mikhael Ricks RC	2.50	1.00
❑ 197 Ryan Leaf RC	3.00	1.25
❑ 198 Natrone Means	1.50	.60
❑ 199 Junior Seau	2.50	1.00
❑ 200 Freddie Jones	1.00	.40

1999 Absolute EXP

❑ COMPLETE SET (200)	50.00	25.00
❑ 1 Tim Couch RC	1.25	.50
❑ 2 Donovan McNabb RC	6.00	2.50
❑ 3 Akili Smith RC	.75	.30
❑ 4 Edgerrin James RC	5.00	2.00
❑ 5 Ricky Williams RC	2.50	1.00
❑ 6 Torry Holt RC	3.00	1.25
❑ 7 Champ Bailey RC	1.50	.60
❑ 8 David Boston RC	1.25	.50
❑ 9 Chris Claiborne RC	.50	.20
❑ 10 Chris McAlister RC	.75	.30
❑ 11 Daunte Culpepper RC	5.00	2.00
❑ 12 Cade McNown RC	.75	.30
❑ 13 Troy Edwards RC	.75	.30
❑ 14 Kevin Johnson RC	1.25	.50
❑ 15 James Johnson RC	.75	.30
❑ 16 Rob Konrad RC	1.25	.50
❑ 17 Jim Kleinsasser RC	1.25	.50
❑ 18 Kevin Faulk RC	1.25	.50
❑ 19 Joe Montgomery RC	.75	.30
❑ 20 Shaun King RC	.75	.30
❑ 21 Peerless Price RC	1.25	.50
❑ 22 Mike Cloud RC	.75	.30
❑ 23 Jermaine Fazande RC	.75	.30
❑ 24 D'Wayne Bates RC	.75	.30
❑ 25 Brock Huard RC	1.25	.50
❑ 26 Marty Booker RC	1.25	.50
❑ 27 Karsten Bailey RC	.75	.30
❑ 28 Shawn Bryson RC	1.25	.50
❑ 29 Jeff Paulk RC	.50	.20
❑ 30 Sedrick Irvin RC	.50	.20
❑ 31 Craig Yeast RC	.75	.30
❑ 32 Joe Germaine RC	.75	.30
❑ 33 Dameane Douglas RC	1.25	.50
❑ 34 Brandon Stokley RC	1.50	.60
❑ 35 Larry Parker RC	1.25	.50
❑ 36 Wane McGarity RC	.50	.20
❑ 37 Na Brown RC	.75	.30
❑ 38 Cecil Collins RC	.50	.20
❑ 39 Darrin Chiaverini RC	.75	.30
❑ 40 Madre Hill RC	.50	.20
❑ 41 Adrian Murrell	.50	.20
❑ 42 Jake Plummer	.50	.20
❑ 43 Frank Sanders	.50	.20
❑ 44 Rob Moore	.50	.20
❑ 45 Andre Wadsworth	.30	.10
❑ 46 Simeon Rice	.50	.20
❑ 47 Eric Swann	.30	.10
❑ 48 Terance Mathis	.50	.20
❑ 49 Tim Dwight	.75	.30
❑ 50 Jamal Anderson	.75	.30
❑ 51 Chris Chandler	.50	.20
❑ 52 Chris Calloway	.30	.10
❑ 53 O.J. Santiago	.30	.10
❑ 54 Jermaine Lewis	.50	.20
❑ 55 Priest Holmes	1.25	.50
❑ 56 Scott Mitchell	.30	.10
❑ 57 Tony Banks	.50	.20
❑ 58 Rod Woodson	.50	.20
❑ 59 Andre Reed	.50	.20

❑ 60 Thurman Thomas .50 .20
❑ 61 Bruce Smith .50 .20
❑ 62 Rob Johnson .50 .20
❑ 63 Eric Moulds .75 .30
❑ 64 Doug Flutie .75 .30
❑ 65 Antowain Smith .75 .30
❑ 66 Tim Biakabutuka .50 .20
❑ 67 Muhsin Muhammad .50 .20
❑ 68 Steve Beuerlein .30 .10
❑ 69 Bobby Engram .50 .20
❑ 70 Curtis Conway .50 .20
❑ 71 Curtis Enis .30 .10
❑ 72 Edgar Bennett .30 .10
❑ 73 Jeff Blake .50 .20
❑ 74 Darnay Scott .30 .10
❑ 75 Carl Pickens .50 .20
❑ 76 Corey Dillon .75 .30
❑ 77 Ty Detmer .50 .20
❑ 78 Leslie Shepherd .30 .10
❑ 79 Sedrick Shaw .30 .10
❑ 80 Rocket Ismail .50 .20
❑ 81 Emmitt Smith 1.50 .60
❑ 82 Michael Irvin .50 .20
❑ 83 Troy Aikman 1.50 .60
❑ 84 Deion Sanders .75 .30
❑ 85 Darren Woodson .30 .10
❑ 86 Chris Warren .30 .10
❑ 87 John Elway 2.50 1.00
❑ 88 Brian Griese .75 .30
❑ 89 Shannon Sharpe .50 .20
❑ 90 Terrell Davis .75 .30
❑ 91 Bubby Brister .30 .10
❑ 92 Ed McCaffrey .50 .20
❑ 93 Rod Smith .50 .20
❑ 94 Germane Crowell .30 .10
❑ 95 Johnnie Morton .50 .20
❑ 96 Barry Sanders 2.50 1.00
❑ 97 Herman Moore .50 .20
❑ 98 Charlie Batch .75 .30
❑ 99 Mark Chmura .30 .10
❑ 100 Derrick Mayes .30 .10
❑ 101 Dorsey Levens .75 .30
❑ 102 Brett Favre 2.50 1.00
❑ 103 Antonio Freeman .75 .30
❑ 104 Robert Brooks .50 .20
❑ 105 Desmond Howard .50 .20
❑ 106 Jerome Pathon .30 .10
❑ 107 Marvin Harrison .75 .30
❑ 108 Peyton Manning 2.50 1.00
❑ 109 E.G. Green .30 .10
❑ 110 Tavian Banks .30 .10
❑ 111 Keenan McCardell .50 .20
❑ 112 Jimmy Smith .50 .20
❑ 113 Mark Brunell .75 .30
❑ 114 Fred Taylor .75 .30
❑ 115 Byron Bam Morris .30 .10
❑ 116 Andre Rison .50 .20
❑ 117 Elvis Grbac .50 .20
❑ 118 Warren Moon .75 .30
❑ 119 Tony Gonzalez .75 .30
❑ 120 Derrick Alexander WR .50 .20
❑ 121 Rashaan Shehee .30 .10
❑ 122 Zach Thomas .75 .30
❑ 123 Oronde Gadsden .50 .20
❑ 124 Dan Marino 2.50 1.00
❑ 125 Karim Abdul-Jabbar .50 .20
❑ 126 O.J. McDuffie .50 .20
❑ 127 Jake Reed .50 .20
❑ 128 John Randle .50 .20
❑ 129 Randy Moss 2.00 .75
❑ 130 Cris Carter .75 .30
❑ 131 Randall Cunningham .75 .30
❑ 132 Robert Smith .75 .30
❑ 133 Terry Glenn .75 .30
❑ 134 Ben Coates .50 .20
❑ 135 Drew Bledsoe 1.00 .40
❑ 136 Ty Law .50 .20
❑ 137 Tony Simmons .30 .10
❑ 138 Eddie Kennison .50 .20
❑ 139 Cam Cleeland .30 .10
❑ 140 Ike Hilliard .30 .10
❑ 141 Joe Jurevicius .50 .20
❑ 142 Gary Brown .30 .10
❑ 143 Kerry Collins .50 .20
❑ 144 Tiki Barber .75 .30
❑ 145 Jason Sehorn .30 .10
❑ 146 Dedric Ward .30 .10
❑ 147 Vinny Testaverde .50 .20
❑ 148 Wayne Chrebet .50 .20
❑ 149 Curtis Martin .75 .30
❑ 150 Keyshawn Johnson .75 .30
❑ 151 James Jett .50 .20
❑ 152 Napoleon Kaufman .75 .30
❑ 153 Tim Brown .75 .30
❑ 154 Charles Woodson .75 .30
❑ 155 Rickey Dudley .30 .10
❑ 156 Charles Johnson .30 .10
❑ 157 Duce Staley .75 .30
❑ 158 Chris Fuamatu-Ma'afala .30 .10
❑ 159 Jerome Bettis .75 .30
❑ 160 Kordell Stewart .50 .20
❑ 161 Levon Kirkland .30 .10
❑ 162 Hines Ward .75 .30
❑ 163 Mikhael Ricks .30 .10
❑ 164 Natrone Means .50 .20
❑ 165 Ryan Leaf .75 .30
❑ 166 Jim Harbaugh .50 .20
❑ 167 Junior Seau .75 .30
❑ 168 Steve Young 1.00 .40
❑ 169 J.J. Stokes .50 .20
❑ 170 Terrell Owens .75 .30
❑ 171 Jerry Rice 1.50 .60
❑ 172 Garrison Hearst .50 .20
❑ 173 Ricky Watters .50 .20
❑ 174 Jon Kitna .75 .30
❑ 175 Joey Galloway .50 .20
❑ 176 Ahman Green .75 .30
❑ 177 Isaac Bruce .75 .30
❑ 178 Marshall Faulk 1.00 .40
❑ 179 Trent Green .75 .30
❑ 180 Amp Lee .30 .10
❑ 181 Greg Hill .30 .10
❑ 182 Warren Sapp .30 .10
❑ 183 Hardy Nickerson .30 .10
❑ 184 Trent Dilfer .50 .20
❑ 185 Reidel Anthony .50 .20
❑ 186 Jacquez Green .30 .10
❑ 187 Warrick Dunn .75 .30
❑ 188 Mike Alstott .75 .30
❑ 189 Kevin Dyson .50 .20
❑ 190 Eddie George .75 .30
❑ 191 Yancey Thigpen .30 .10
❑ 192 Steve McNair .75 .30
❑ 193 Chris Sanders .30 .10
❑ 194 Frank Wycheck .30 .10
❑ 195 Darrell Green .30 .10
❑ 196 Stephen Alexander .30 .10
❑ 197 Albert Connell .30 .10
❑ 198 Michael Westbrook .50 .20
❑ 199 Brad Johnson .75 .30
❑ 200 Skip Hicks .30 .10

1999 Absolute SSD

❑ COMPLETE SET (200) 250.00 125.00
❑ 1 Rob Moore 1.25 .50
❑ 2 Frank Sanders 1.25 .50
❑ 3 Jake Plummer 1.25 .50
❑ 4 Adrian Murrell 1.25 .50
❑ 5 Chris Chandler 1.25 .50
❑ 6 Jamal Anderson 2.00 .75
❑ 7 Tim Dwight 2.00 .75
❑ 8 Terance Mathis 1.25 .50
❑ 9 Priest Holmes 3.00 1.25
❑ 10 Jermaine Lewis 1.25 .50
❑ 11 Antowain Smith 2.00 .75
❑ 12 Doug Flutie 2.00 .75
❑ 13 Eric Moulds 2.00 .75
❑ 14 Muhsin Muhammad 1.25 .50
❑ 15 Tim Biakabutuka 1.25 .50
❑ 16 Curtis Enis .75 .30
❑ 17 Curtis Conway 1.25 .50
❑ 18 Bobby Engram 1.25 .50
❑ 19 Corey Dillon 2.00 .75
❑ 20 Carl Pickens 1.25 .50
❑ 21 Darnay Scott .75 .30
❑ 22 Sedrick Shaw .75 .30
❑ 23 Leslie Shepherd .75 .30
❑ 24 Ty Detmer 1.25 .50
❑ 25 Deion Sanders 2.00 .75
❑ 26 Troy Aikman 4.00 1.50
❑ 27 Michael Irvin 1.25 .50
❑ 28 Emmitt Smith 4.00 1.50
❑ 29 Rocket Ismail 1.25 .50
❑ 30 Rod Smith WR 1.25 .50
❑ 31 Ed McCaffrey 1.25 .50
❑ 32 Bubby Brister .75 .30
❑ 33 Terrell Davis 2.00 .75
❑ 34 Shannon Sharpe 1.25 .50
❑ 35 Brian Griese 2.00 .75
❑ 36 John Elway 6.00 2.50
❑ 37 Charlie Batch 2.00 .75
❑ 38 Herman Moore 1.25 .50
❑ 39 Barry Sanders 6.00 2.50
❑ 40 Johnnie Morton 1.25 .50
❑ 41 Antonio Freeman 2.00 .75
❑ 42 Brett Favre 6.00 2.50
❑ 43 Dorsey Levens 2.00 .75
❑ 44 Derrick Mayes 1.25 .50
❑ 45 Mark Chmura .75 .30
❑ 46 Peyton Manning 6.00 2.50
❑ 47 Marvin Harrison 2.00 .75
❑ 48 Jerome Pathon .75 .30
❑ 49 Fred Taylor 2.00 .75
❑ 50 Mark Brunell 2.00 .75
❑ 51 Jimmy Smith 1.25 .50
❑ 52 Keenan McCardell 1.25 .50
❑ 53 Elvis Grbac 1.25 .50
❑ 54 Andre Rison 1.25 .50
❑ 55 Byron Bam Morris .75 .30
❑ 56 O.J. McDuffie 1.25 .50
❑ 57 Karim Abdul-Jabbar 1.25 .50
❑ 58 Dan Marino 6.00 2.50
❑ 59 Oronde Gadsden 1.25 .50
❑ 60 Robert Smith 2.00 .75
❑ 61 Randall Cunningham 2.00 .75
❑ 62 Cris Carter 2.00 .75
❑ 63 Randy Moss 5.00 2.00
❑ 64 Drew Bledsoe 2.50 1.00
❑ 65 Ben Coates 1.25 .50
❑ 66 Terry Glenn 2.00 .75
❑ 67 Cam Cleeland .75 .30
❑ 68 Eddie Kennison 1.25 .50
❑ 69 Kerry Collins 1.25 .50
❑ 70 Gary Brown .75 .30
❑ 71 Joe Jurevicius 1.25 .50
❑ 72 Ike Hilliard .75 .30
❑ 73 Keyshawn Johnson 2.00 .75
❑ 74 Curtis Martin 2.00 .75
❑ 75 Wayne Chrebet 1.25 .50
❑ 76 Tim Brown 2.00 .75
❑ 77 Napoleon Kaufman 2.00 .75
❑ 78 James Jett 1.25 .50
❑ 79 Duce Staley 2.00 .75

❑	80	Charles Johnson	.75	.30
❑	81	Kordell Stewart	1.25	.50
❑	82	Jerome Bettis	2.00	.75
❑	83	Chris Fuamatu-Ma'afala	.75	.30
❑	84	Jim Harbaugh	1.25	.50
❑	85	Ryan Leaf	2.00	.75
❑	86	Natrone Means	1.25	.50
❑	87	Mikhael Ricks	.75	.30
❑	88	Garrison Hearst	1.25	.50
❑	89	Jerry Rice	4.00	1.50
❑	90	Terrell Owens	2.00	.75
❑	91	J.J. Stokes	1.25	.50
❑	92	Steve Young	2.50	1.00
❑	93	Joey Galloway	1.25	.50
❑	94	Jon Kitna	2.00	.75
❑	95	Ricky Watters	1.25	.50
❑	96	Trent Green	2.00	.75
❑	97	Marshall Faulk	2.50	1.00
❑	98	Isaac Bruce	2.00	.75
❑	99	Mike Alstott	2.00	.75
❑	100	Warrick Dunn	2.00	.75
❑	101	Jacquez Green	.75	.30
❑	102	Reidel Anthony	1.25	.50
❑	103	Trent Dilfer	1.25	.50
❑	104	Steve McNair	2.00	.75
❑	105	Yancey Thigpen	.75	.30
❑	106	Eddie George	2.00	.75
❑	107	Kevin Dyson	1.25	.50
❑	108	Skip Hicks	.75	.30
❑	109	Brad Johnson	2.00	.75
❑	110	Michael Westbrook	1.25	.50
❑	111	Thurman Thomas CA	4.00	1.50
❑	112	Andre Reed CA	4.00	1.50
❑	113	Emmitt Smith CA	10.00	4.00
❑	114	Troy Aikman CA	10.00	4.00
❑	115	Deion Sanders CA	5.00	2.00
❑	116	John Elway CA	15.00	6.00
❑	117	Terrell Davis CA	5.00	2.00
❑	118	Barry Sanders CA	15.00	6.00
❑	119	Brett Favre CA	15.00	6.00
❑	120	Warren Moon CA	5.00	2.00
❑	121	Dan Marino CA	15.00	6.00
❑	122	Cris Carter CA	5.00	2.00
❑	124	Tim Brown CA	5.00	2.00
❑	125	Jerome Bettis CA	4.00	1.50
❑	126	Junior Seau CA	5.00	2.00
❑	127	Jerry Rice CA	10.00	4.00
❑	127	Vinny Testaverde CA	4.00	1.50
❑	128	Steve Young CA	6.00	2.50
❑	129	Eddie George CA	5.00	2.00
❑	130	Cardinals CL	3.00	1.25
❑	131	Falcons CL	3.00	1.25
❑	132	Ravens CL	8.00	3.00
❑	133	Bills CL	6.00	2.50
❑	134	Panthers CL	3.00	1.25
❑	135	Bears CL	4.00	1.50
❑	136	Bengals CL	3.00	1.25
❑	137	Browns CL	8.00	3.00
❑	138	Cowboys CL	8.00	3.00
❑	139	Broncos CL	8.00	3.00
❑	140	Lions CL	8.00	3.00
❑	141	Packers CL	8.00	3.00
❑	142	Colts CL	8.00	3.00
❑	143	Jaguars CL	4.00	1.50
❑	144	Chiefs CL	3.00	1.25
❑	145	Dolphins CL	3.00	1.25
❑	146	Vikings CL	8.00	3.00
❑	147	Patriots CL	3.00	1.25
❑	148	Saints CL	8.00	3.00
❑	149	Giants CL	3.00	1.25
❑	150	Jets CL	4.00	1.50
❑	151	Raiders CL	4.00	1.50
❑	152	Eagles CL	4.00	1.50
❑	153	Steelers CL	3.00	1.25
❑	154	Chargers CL	8.00	3.00
❑	155	49ers CL	8.00	3.00
❑	156	Seahawks CL	3.00	1.25
❑	157	Rams CL	4.00	1.50
❑	158	Buccaneers CL	3.00	1.25
❑	159	Titans CL	4.00	1.50
❑	160	Redskins CL	3.00	1.25
❑	161	Tim Couch RC	2.50	1.00
❑	162	Donovan McNabb RC	12.00	5.00
❑	163	Akili Smith RC	4.00	1.50
❑	164	Edgerrin James RC	10.00	4.00
❑	165	Ricky Williams RC	5.00	2.00
❑	166	Torry Holt RC	6.00	2.50
❑	167	Champ Bailey RC	3.00	1.25
❑	168	David Boston RC	5.00	2.00
❑	169	Chris Claiborne RC	1.00	.40
❑	170	Chris McAlister RC	1.50	.60
❑	171	Daunte Culpepper RC	10.00	4.00
❑	172	Cade McNown RC	1.50	.60
❑	173	Troy Edwards RC	1.50	.60
❑	174	Kevin Johnson RC	2.50	1.00
❑	175	James Johnson RC	1.50	.60
❑	176	Rob Konrad RC	2.50	1.00
❑	177	Jim Kleinsasser RC	2.50	1.00
❑	178	Kevin Faulk RC	2.50	1.00
❑	179	Joe Montgomery RC	1.50	.60
❑	180	Shaun King RC	1.50	.60
❑	181	Peerless Price RC	2.50	1.00
❑	182	Mike Cloud RC	1.50	.60
❑	183	Jermaine Fazande RC	1.50	.60
❑	184	D'Wayne Bates RC	1.50	.60
❑	185	Brock Huard RC	2.50	1.00
❑	186	Marty Booker RC	2.50	1.00
❑	187	Karsten Bailey RC	1.50	.60
❑	188	Shawn Bryson RC	2.50	1.00
❑	189	Jeff Paulk RC	1.00	.40
❑	190	Sedrick Irvin RC	1.00	.40
❑	191	Craig Yeast RC	1.50	.60
❑	192	Joe Germaine RC	1.50	.60
❑	193	Dameane Douglas RC	2.50	1.00
❑	194	Brandon Stokley RC	3.00	1.25
❑	195	Larry Parker RC	2.50	1.00
❑	196	Wane McGarity RC	1.00	.40
❑	197	Na Brown RC	1.50	.60
❑	198	Cecil Collins RC	1.00	.40
❑	199	Darrin Chiaverini RC	1.50	.60
❑	200	Madre Hill RC	1.00	.40

2000 Absolute

❑		COMPLETE SET (250)	250.00	125.00
❑		COMP.SET w/o SP's (150)	20.00	7.50
❑	1	Frank Sanders	.50	.20
❑	2	Rob Moore	.50	.20
❑	3	Jake Plummer	.50	.20
❑	4	David Boston	.75	.30
❑	5	Chris Chandler	.50	.20
❑	6	Tim Dwight	.75	.30
❑	7	Terance Mathis	.50	.20
❑	8	Jamal Anderson	.75	.30
❑	9	Priest Holmes	1.00	.40
❑	10	Tony Banks	.50	.20
❑	11	Jermaine Lewis	.30	.10
❑	12	Qadry Ismail	.50	.20
❑	13	Brandon Stokley	.50	.20
❑	14	Shannon Sharpe	.50	.20
❑	15	Trent Dilfer	.50	.20
❑	16	Eric Moulds	.75	.30
❑	17	Doug Flutie	.75	.30
❑	18	Antowain Smith	.50	.20
❑	19	Jonathan Linton	.30	.10
❑	20	Peerless Price	.50	.20
❑	21	Rob Johnson	.50	.20
❑	22	Muhsin Muhammad	.50	.20
❑	23	Wesley Walls	.30	.10
❑	24	Tim Biakabutuka	.50	.20
❑	25	Steve Beuerlein	.50	.20
❑	26	Patrick Jeffers	.75	.30
❑	27	Natrone Means	.30	.10
❑	28	Curtis Enis	.30	.10
❑	29	Bobby Engram	.50	.20
❑	30	Marcus Robinson	.75	.30
❑	31	Marty Booker	.50	.20
❑	32	Cade McNown	.30	.10
❑	33	Darnay Scott	.50	.20
❑	34	Carl Pickens	.50	.20
❑	35	Corey Dillon	.75	.30
❑	36	Akili Smith	.30	.10
❑	37	Michael Basnight	.30	.10
❑	38	Karim Abdul-Jabbar	.50	.20
❑	39	Tim Couch	.50	.20
❑	40	Kevin Johnson	.75	.30
❑	41	Darrin Chiaverini	.30	.10
❑	42	Errict Rhett	.50	.20
❑	43	Emmitt Smith	1.50	.60
❑	44	Michael Irvin	.50	.20
❑	45	Rocket Ismail	.50	.20
❑	46	Troy Aikman	1.50	.60
❑	47	Jason Tucker	.30	.10
❑	48	Randall Cunningham	.75	.30
❑	49	Joey Galloway	.50	.20
❑	50	Ed McCaffrey	.75	.30
❑	51	Rod Smith	.50	.20
❑	52	Brian Griese	.75	.30
❑	53	John Elway	2.50	1.00
❑	54	Terrell Davis	.75	.30
❑	55	Olandis Gary	.75	.30
❑	56	Johnnie Morton	.50	.20
❑	57	Charlie Batch	.75	.30
❑	58	Barry Sanders	2.00	.75
❑	59	Germane Crowell	.30	.10
❑	60	Herman Moore	.50	.20
❑	61	James Stewart	.50	.20
❑	62	Corey Bradford	.30	.10
❑	63	Dorsey Levens	.50	.20
❑	64	Antonio Freeman	.75	.30
❑	65	Brett Favre	2.50	1.00
❑	66	Bill Schroeder	.50	.20
❑	67	Marvin Harrison	.75	.30
❑	68	Peyton Manning	1.50	.60
❑	69	Terrence Wilkins	.30	.10
❑	70	Edgerrin James	1.25	.50
❑	71	Keenan McCardell	.50	.20
❑	72	Mark Brunell	.75	.30
❑	73	Fred Taylor	.75	.30
❑	74	Jimmy Smith	.50	.20
❑	75	Elvis Grbac	.50	.20
❑	76	Tony Gonzalez	.50	.20
❑	77	Donnell Bennett	.30	.10
❑	78	Warren Moon	.75	.30
❑	79	Kimble Anders	.30	.10
❑	80	Dan Marino	2.50	1.00
❑	81	O.J. McDuffie	.50	.20
❑	82	Tony Martin	.50	.20
❑	83	James Johnson	.30	.10
❑	84	Thurman Thomas	.50	.20
❑	85	Randy Moss	1.25	.50
❑	86	Cris Carter	.75	.30
❑	87	Robert Smith	.75	.30
❑	88	Daunte Culpepper	1.00	.40
❑	89	Terry Glenn	.50	.20
❑	90	Drew Bledsoe	1.00	.40
❑	91	Kevin Faulk	.50	.20
❑	92	Ricky Williams	.75	.30
❑	93	Jeff Blake	.50	.20
❑	94	Jake Reed	.50	.20
❑	95	Amani Toomer	.50	.20
❑	96	Kerry Collins	.50	.20
❑	97	Tiki Barber	.75	.30
❑	98	Ike Hilliard	.50	.20
❑	99	Curtis Martin	.75	.30

❑ 100	Vinny Testaverde	.50	.20
❑ 101	Wayne Chrebet	.50	.20
❑ 102	Ray Lucas	.50	.20
❑ 103	Tyrone Wheatley	.50	.20
❑ 104	Napoleon Kaufman	.50	.20
❑ 105	Tim Brown	.75	.30
❑ 106	Rich Gannon	.75	.30
❑ 107	Duce Staley	.75	.30
❑ 108	Donovan McNabb	1.25	.50
❑ 109	Kordell Stewart	.50	.20
❑ 110	Jerome Bettis	.75	.30
❑ 111	Troy Edwards	.30	.10
❑ 112	Junior Seau	.75	.30
❑ 113	Jim Harbaugh	.50	.20
❑ 114	Ryan Leaf	.50	.20
❑ 115	Jermaine Fazande	.30	.10
❑ 116	Curtis Conway	.50	.20
❑ 117	Terrell Owens	.75	.30
❑ 118	Charlie Garner	.50	.20
❑ 119	Jerry Rice	1.50	.60
❑ 120	Steve Young	1.00	.40
❑ 121	Jeff Garcia	.75	.30
❑ 122	Derrick Mayes	.50	.20
❑ 123	Ricky Watters	.50	.20
❑ 124	Jon Kitna	.75	.30
❑ 125	Sean Dawkins	.30	.10
❑ 126	Az-Zahir Hakim	.50	.20
❑ 127	Isaac Bruce	.75	.30
❑ 128	Marshall Faulk	1.00	.40
❑ 129	Trent Green	.75	.30
❑ 130	Kurt Warner	1.50	.60
❑ 131	Torry Holt	.75	.30
❑ 132	Jacquez Green	.30	.10
❑ 133	Warren Sapp	.50	.20
❑ 134	Mike Alstott	.75	.30
❑ 135	Warrick Dunn	.75	.30
❑ 136	Shaun King	.30	.10
❑ 137	Keyshawn Johnson	.75	.30
❑ 138	Eddie George	.75	.30
❑ 139	Yancey Thigpen	.30	.10
❑ 140	Steve McNair	.75	.30
❑ 141	Kevin Dyson	.50	.20
❑ 142	Frank Wycheck	.30	.10
❑ 143	Jevon Kearse	.75	.30
❑ 144	Stephen Davis	.75	.30
❑ 145	Brad Johnson	.75	.30
❑ 146	Michael Westbrook	.50	.20
❑ 147	Albert Connell	.30	.10
❑ 148	Bruce Smith	.50	.20
❑ 149	Jeff George	.50	.20
❑ 150	Deion Sanders	.75	.30
❑ 151	Peter Warrick RC	4.00	1.50
❑ 152	Courtney Brown RC	4.00	1.50
❑ 153	Plaxico Burress RC	8.00	3.00
❑ 154	Corey Simon RC	4.00	1.50
❑ 155	Thomas Jones RC	6.00	2.50
❑ 156	Travis Taylor RC	4.00	1.50
❑ 157	Shaun Alexander RC	15.00	6.00
❑ 158	Chris Redman RC	3.00	1.25
❑ 159	Chad Pennington RC	10.00	4.00
❑ 160	Jamal Lewis RC	10.00	4.00
❑ 161	Brian Urlacher RC	20.00	7.50
❑ 162	Bubba Franks RC	4.00	1.50
❑ 163	Dez White RC	4.00	1.50
❑ 164	Ahmed Plummer RC	4.00	1.50
❑ 165	Ron Dayne RC	4.00	1.50
❑ 166	Shaun Ellis RC	4.00	1.50
❑ 167	Sylvester Morris RC	.50	.20
❑ 168	Deltha O'Neal RC	4.00	1.50
❑ 169	R.Jay Soward RC	3.00	1.25
❑ 170	Sherrod Gideon RC	2.00	.75
❑ 171	John Abraham RC	4.00	1.50
❑ 172	Travis Prentice RC	3.00	1.25
❑ 173	Darrell Jackson RC	8.00	3.00
❑ 174	Giovanni Carmazzi RC	2.00	.75
❑ 175	Anthony Lucas RC	2.00	.75
❑ 176	Danny Farmer RC	3.00	1.25
❑ 177	Dennis Northcutt RC	4.00	1.50
❑ 178	Troy Walters RC	4.00	1.50
❑ 179	Laveranues Coles RC	5.00	2.00
❑ 180	Kwame Cavil RC	2.00	.75
❑ 181	Tee Martin RC	4.00	1.50
❑ 182	J.R. Redmond RC	3.00	1.25
❑ 183	Tim Rattay RC	4.00	1.50
❑ 184	Jerry Porter RC	5.00	2.00
❑ 185	Sebastian Janikowski RC	4.00	1.50
❑ 186	Michael Wiley RC	3.00	1.25
❑ 187	Reuben Droughns RC	5.00	2.00
❑ 188	Trung Canidate RC	3.00	1.25
❑ 189	Shyrone Stith RC	3.00	1.25
❑ 190	Ian Gold RC	3.00	1.25
❑ 191	Hank Poteat RC	3.00	1.25
❑ 192	Darren Howard RC	3.00	1.25
❑ 193	Rob Morris RC	3.00	1.25
❑ 194	Marc Bulger RC	8.00	3.00
❑ 195	Tom Brady RC	40.00	20.00
❑ 196	Doug Johnson RC	4.00	1.50
❑ 197	Todd Husak RC	4.00	1.50
❑ 198	Gari Scott RC	2.00	.75
❑ 199	Erron Kinney RC	4.00	1.50
❑ 200	Nate Webster RC	2.00	.75
❑ 201	Anthony Becht RC	4.00	1.50
❑ 202	Sammy Morris RC	3.00	1.25
❑ 203	Rondell Mealey RC	2.00	.75
❑ 204	Doug Chapman RC	3.00	1.25
❑ 205	Rogers Beckett RC	3.00	1.25
❑ 206	Ron Dugans RC	2.00	.75
❑ 207	Deon Dyer RC	3.00	1.25
❑ 208	Marcus Knight RC	3.00	1.25
❑ 209	Thomas Hamner RC	2.00	.75
❑ 210	Joe Hamilton RC	3.00	1.25
❑ 211	Todd Pinkston RC	4.00	1.50
❑ 212	Chris Cole RC	3.00	1.25
❑ 213	Ron Dixon RC	3.00	1.25
❑ 214	JaJuan Dawson RC	2.00	.75
❑ 215	Terrelle Smith RC	3.00	1.25
❑ 216	Curtis Keaton RC	3.00	1.25
❑ 217	Keith Bulluck RC	4.00	1.50
❑ 218	John Engelberger RC	3.00	1.25
❑ 219	Raynoch Thompson RC	3.00	1.25
❑ 220	Cornelius Griffin RC	3.00	1.25
❑ 221	William Bartee RC	3.00	1.25
❑ 222	Fred Robbins RC	2.00	.75
❑ 223	Dwayne Goodrich RC	2.00	.75
❑ 224	Deon Grant RC	3.00	1.25
❑ 225	Jacoby Shepherd RC	3.00	1.25
❑ 226	Ben Kelly RC	2.00	.75
❑ 227	Corey Moore RC	2.00	.75
❑ 228	Aaron Shea RC	3.00	1.25
❑ 229	Trevor Gaylor RC	3.00	1.25
❑ 230	Frank Moreau RC	3.00	1.25
❑ 231	Avion Black RC	3.00	1.25
❑ 232	Paul Smith RC	3.00	1.25
❑ 233	Dante Hall RC	8.00	3.00
❑ 234	Muneer Moore RC	2.00	.75
❑ 235	James Whalen RC	2.00	.75
❑ 236	Chad Morton RC	4.00	1.50
❑ 237	Frank Murphy RC	2.00	.75
❑ 238	Mareno Philyaw RC	2.00	.75
❑ 239	James Williams RC	3.00	1.25
❑ 240	Mike Anderson RC	5.00	2.00
❑ 241	Jarious Jackson RC	3.00	1.25
❑ 242	Demario Brown RC	2.00	.75
❑ 243	Chris Coleman RC	4.00	1.50
❑ 244	Rashard Anderson RC	3.00	1.25
❑ 245	John Jones RC	3.00	1.25
❑ 246	Erik Flowers RC	3.00	1.25
❑ 247	JaJuan Seider RC	2.00	.75
❑ 248	Leon Murray RC	2.00	.75
❑ 249	Bashir Yamini RC	2.00	.75
❑ 250	Na'il Diggs RC	3.00	1.25

2001 Absolute Memorabilia

❑	COMP.SET w/o SP's (100)	30.00	12.50
❑ 1	David Boston	1.25	.50
❑ 2	Jake Plummer	.75	.30
❑ 3	Thomas Jones	.75	.30
❑ 4	Jamal Anderson	1.25	.50
❑ 5	Chris Redman	.50	.20
❑ 6	Jamal Lewis	2.00	.75
❑ 7	Qadry Ismail	.75	.30
❑ 8	Ray Lewis	1.25	.50
❑ 9	Shannon Sharpe	.75	.30
❑ 10	Travis Taylor	.75	.30
❑ 11	Trent Dilfer	.75	.30
❑ 12	Elvis Grbac	.75	.30
❑ 13	Eric Moulds	.75	.30
❑ 14	Rob Johnson	.75	.30
❑ 15	Muhsin Muhammad	.75	.30
❑ 16	Brian Urlacher	2.00	.75
❑ 17	Cade McNown	.50	.20
❑ 18	Marcus Robinson	1.25	.50
❑ 19	Akili Smith	.50	.20
❑ 20	Corey Dillon	1.25	.50
❑ 21	Peter Warrick	1.25	.50
❑ 22	Courtney Brown	.75	.30
❑ 23	Tim Couch	.75	.30
❑ 24	Emmitt Smith	2.50	1.00
❑ 25	Troy Aikman	2.00	.75
❑ 26	Brian Griese	1.25	.50
❑ 27	Ed McCaffrey	1.25	.50
❑ 28	John Elway	4.00	1.50
❑ 29	Mike Anderson	1.25	.50
❑ 30	Rod Smith	.75	.30
❑ 31	Terrell Davis	1.25	.50
❑ 32	Barry Sanders	2.50	1.00
❑ 33	James Stewart	.75	.30
❑ 34	Ahman Green	1.25	.50
❑ 35	Antonio Freeman	1.25	.50
❑ 36	Brett Favre	4.00	1.50
❑ 37	Edgerrin James	1.50	.60
❑ 38	Marvin Harrison	1.25	.50
❑ 39	Peyton Manning	3.00	1.25
❑ 40	Fred Taylor	1.25	.50
❑ 41	Jimmy Smith	.75	.30
❑ 42	Keenan McCardell	.50	.20
❑ 43	Mark Brunell	1.25	.50
❑ 44	Sylvester Morris	.50	.20
❑ 45	Tony Gonzalez	.75	.30
❑ 46	Dan Marino	4.00	1.50
❑ 47	Jay Fiedler	1.25	.50
❑ 48	Lamar Smith	.75	.30
❑ 49	Cris Carter	1.25	.50
❑ 50	Daunte Culpepper	1.25	.50
❑ 51	Randy Moss	2.50	1.00
❑ 52	Drew Bledsoe	1.50	.60
❑ 53	Terry Glenn	.75	.30
❑ 54	Aaron Brooks	1.25	.50
❑ 55	Joe Horn	.75	.30
❑ 56	Ricky Williams	1.25	.50
❑ 57	Amani Toomer	.75	.30
❑ 58	Ike Hilliard	.75	.30
❑ 59	Kerry Collins	.75	.30
❑ 60	Ron Dayne	1.25	.50
❑ 61	Tiki Barber	1.25	.50
❑ 62	Chad Pennington	2.00	.75
❑ 63	Curtis Martin	1.25	.50
❑ 64	Laveranues Coles	1.25	.50
❑ 65	Vinny Testaverde	.75	.30
❑ 66	Wayne Chrebet	.75	.30
❑ 67	Charles Woodson	.75	.30
❑ 68	Rich Gannon	1.25	.50

❑ 69 Tim Brown 1.25 .50
❑ 70 Tyrone Wheatley .75 .30
❑ 71 Corey Simon .75 .30
❑ 72 Donovan McNabb 1.50 .60
❑ 73 Duce Staley 1.25 .50
❑ 74 Jerome Bettis 1.25 .50
❑ 75 Plaxico Burress 1.25 .50
❑ 76 Doug Flutie 1.25 .50
❑ 77 Junior Seau 1.25 .50
❑ 78 Charlie Garner .75 .30
❑ 79 Jeff Garcia 1.25 .50
❑ 80 Jerry Rice 2.50 1.00
❑ 81 Steve Young 1.25 .50
❑ 82 Terrell Owens 1.25 .50
❑ 83 Darrell Jackson 1.25 .50
❑ 84 Ricky Watters .50 .20
❑ 85 Shaun Alexander 1.50 .60
❑ 86 Isaac Bruce 1.25 .50
❑ 87 Kurt Warner 2.50 1.00
❑ 88 Marshall Faulk 1.50 .60
❑ 89 Torry Holt 1.25 .50
❑ 90 Brad Johnson 1.25 .50
❑ 91 Keyshawn Johnson 1.25 .50
❑ 92 Mike Alstott 1.25 .50
❑ 93 Shaun King .50 .20
❑ 94 Warren Sapp .75 .30
❑ 95 Warrick Dunn 1.25 .50
❑ 96 Eddie George 1.25 .50
❑ 97 Jevon Kearse .75 .30
❑ 98 Steve McNair 1.25 .50
❑ 99 Jeff George .75 .30
❑ 100 Stephen Davis 1.25 .50
❑ 101 Jason McKinley RC 4.00 1.50
❑ 102 Bobby Newcombe RC 4.00 1.50
❑ 103 Cedrick Wilson RC 6.00 2.50
❑ 104 Ken-Yon Rambo RC 4.00 1.50
❑ 105 Kevin Kasper RC 6.00 2.50
❑ 106 Jamal Reynolds RC 6.00 2.50
❑ 107 Scotty Anderson RC 4.00 1.50
❑ 108 T.J. Houshmandzadeh RC 6.00 2.50
❑ 109 Chris Taylor RC 4.00 1.50
❑ 110 Vinny Sutherland RC 4.00 1.50
❑ 111 Jabari Holloway RC 4.00 1.50
❑ 112 Shad Meier RC 4.00 1.50
❑ 113 Correll Buckhalter RC 8.00 3.00
❑ 114 Dan Alexander RC 6.00 2.50
❑ 115 David Allen RC 4.00 1.50
❑ 116 LaMont Jordan RC 12.00 5.00
❑ 117 Nate Clements RC 6.00 2.50
❑ 118 Reggie White RC 4.00 1.50
❑ 119 Javon Green RC 4.00 1.50
❑ 120 Shaun Rogers RC 6.00 2.50
❑ 121 Heath Evans RC 4.00 1.50
❑ 122 Moran Norris RC 2.50 1.00
❑ 123 Ben Leard RC 4.00 1.50
❑ 124 David Rivers RC 4.00 1.50
❑ 125 A.J. Feeley RC 6.00 2.50
❑ 126 Boo Williams RC 4.00 1.50
❑ 127 Ronney Daniels RC 2.50 1.00
❑ 128 Alge Crumpler RC 8.00 4.00
❑ 129 Todd Heap RC 6.00 2.50
❑ 130 Tim Hasselbeck RC 6.00 2.50
❑ 131 Josh Booty RC 6.00 2.50
❑ 132 Jamie Winborn RC 4.00 1.50
❑ 133 Brian Allen RC 2.50 1.00
❑ 134 Sedrick Hodge RC 2.50 1.00
❑ 135 Tommy Polley RC 6.00 2.50
❑ 136 Torrance Marshall RC 6.00 2.50
❑ 137 Damione Lewis RC 4.00 1.50
❑ 138 Marcus Stroud RC 6.00 2.50
❑ 139 Aaron Schobel RC 6.00 2.50
❑ 140 DeLawrence Grant RC 2.50 1.00
❑ 141 Fred Smoot RC 6.00 2.50
❑ 142 Jamar Fletcher RC 4.00 1.50
❑ 143 Ken Lucas RC 4.00 1.50
❑ 144 Will Allen RC 4.00 1.50
❑ 145 Adam Archuleta RC 6.00 2.50
❑ 146 Derrick Gibson RC 4.00 1.50
❑ 147 Jarrod Cooper RC 6.00 2.50
❑ 148 Eddie Berlin RC 4.00 1.50
❑ 149 Steve Smith RC 15.00 7.50
❑ 150 Willie Middlebrooks RC 4.00 1.50
❑ 151 Michael Vick RPM RC 80.00 30.00
❑ 152 Drew Brees RPM RC 40.00 15.00
❑ 153 Chris Weinke RPM RC 15.00 6.00
❑ 154 Mar Tuiasosopo RPM RC 15.00 6.00
❑ 155 Mike McMahon RPM RC 15.00 6.00
❑ 156 Deuce McAllister RPM RC 30.00 12.50
❑ 157 Leonard Davis RPM RC 10.00 4.00
❑ 158 LaD Tomlinson RPM RC 60.00 30.00
❑ 159 Anthony Thomas RPM RC 15.00 6.00
❑ 160 Travis Henry RPM RC 15.00 6.00
❑ 161 James Jackson RPM RC 15.00 6.00
❑ 162 Michael Bennett RPM RC 25.00 10.00
❑ 163 Kevan Barlow RPM RC 15.00 6.00
❑ 164 Travis Minor RPM RC 10.00 4.00
❑ 165 David Terrell RPM RC 15.00 6.00
❑ 166 Santana Moss RPM RC 25.00 10.00
❑ 167 Rod Gardner RPM RC 15.00 6.00
❑ 168 Quincy Morgan RPM RC 15.00 6.00
❑ 169 Freddie Mitchell RPM RC 15.00 6.00
❑ 170 Reggie Wayne RPM RC 30.00 12.50
❑ 171 Koren Robinson RPM RC 15.00 6.00
❑ 172 Chad Johnson RPM RC 40.00 15.00
❑ 173 Chris Chambers RPM RC 25.00 10.00
❑ 174 Josh Heupel RPM RC 15.00 6.00
❑ 175 Andre Carter RPM RC 15.00 6.00
❑ 176 Justin Smith RPM RC 15.00 6.00
❑ 177 Richard Seymour RPM RC 15.00 6.00
❑ 178 Dan Morgan RPM RC 15.00 6.00
❑ 179 Gerard Warren RPM RC 15.00 6.00
❑ 180 Robert Ferguson RPM RC 15.00 6.00
❑ 181 Sage Rosenfels RPM RC 15.00 6.00
❑ 182 Rudi Johnson RPM RC 30.00 12.50
❑ 183 Snoop Minnis RPM RC 10.00 4.00
❑ 184 Jesse Palmer RPM RC 15.00 6.00
❑ 185 Quincy Carter RPM RC 15.00 6.00

2002 Absolute Memorabilia

❑ COMP.SET w/o SP's (150) 30.00 12.50
❑ 1 Aaron Brooks 1.25 .50
❑ 2 Ahman Green 1.25 .50
❑ 3 Alge Crumpler .75 .30
❑ 4 Amani Toomer .75 .30
❑ 5 Andre Carter .50 .20
❑ 6 Anthony Thomas .75 .30
❑ 7 Antonio Freeman 1.25 .50
❑ 8 Antowain Smith .75 .30
❑ 9 Az-Zahir Hakim .50 .20
❑ 10 Bill Schroeder .75 .30
❑ 11 Brad Johnson .75 .30
❑ 12 Brett Favre 3.00 1.25
❑ 13 Brian Griese 1.25 .50
❑ 14 Brian Urlacher 2.00 .75
❑ 15 Chad Johnson 1.25 .50
❑ 16 Chad Pennington 1.50 .60
❑ 17 Champ Bailey .75 .30
❑ 18 Charles Woodson .75 .30
❑ 19 Charlie Batch .75 .30
❑ 20 Charlie Garner .75 .30
❑ 21 Chris Chambers 1.25 .50
❑ 22 Chris Redman .50 .20
❑ 23 Chris Weinke .75 .30
❑ 24 Corey Dillon .75 .30
❑ 25 Correll Buckhalter .75 .30
❑ 26 Cris Carter 1.25 .50
❑ 27 Curtis Martin 1.25 .50
❑ 28 Darnay Scott .75 .30
❑ 29 Darrell Jackson .75 .30
❑ 30 Daunte Culpepper 1.25 .50
❑ 31 David Boston 1.25 .50
❑ 32 David Terrell 1.25 .50
❑ 33 Derrick Alexander .75 .30
❑ 34 Derrick Mason .75 .30
❑ 35 Deuce McAllister 1.50 .60
❑ 36 Dominic Rhodes .75 .30
❑ 37 Donald Hayes .50 .20
❑ 38 Donovan McNabb 1.50 .60
❑ 39 Doug Flutie 1.25 .50
❑ 40 Drew Bledsoe 1.50 .60
❑ 41 Drew Brees 1.25 .50
❑ 42 Duce Staley 1.25 .50
❑ 43 Ed McCaffrey 1.25 .50
❑ 44 Eddie George 1.25 .50
❑ 45 Edgerrin James 1.50 .60
❑ 46 Elvis Joseph .50 .20
❑ 47 Emmitt Smith 3.00 1.25
❑ 48 Eric Moulds .75 .30
❑ 49 Frank Sanders .50 .20
❑ 50 Fred Taylor 1.25 .50
❑ 51 Freddie Mitchell .75 .30
❑ 52 Garrison Hearst .75 .30
❑ 53 Gerard Warren .50 .20
❑ 54 Germane Crowell .50 .20
❑ 55 Isaac Bruce 1.25 .50
❑ 56 Jake Plummer .75 .30
❑ 57 Jamal Anderson .75 .30
❑ 58 Jamal Lewis 1.25 .50
❑ 59 James Allen .75 .30
❑ 60 James Jackson .50 .20
❑ 61 James Stewart .75 .30
❑ 62 Jason Brookins .50 .20
❑ 63 Jay Fiedler .75 .30
❑ 64 Jeff Garcia 1.25 .50
❑ 65 Jerome Bettis 1.25 .50
❑ 66 Jerry Rice 2.50 1.00
❑ 67 Jevon Kearse .75 .30
❑ 68 Jim Miller .50 .20
❑ 69 Jimmy Smith .75 .30
❑ 70 Joe Horn .75 .30
❑ 71 Joey Galloway .75 .30
❑ 72 Jon Kitna .75 .30
❑ 73 Junior Seau 1.25 .50
❑ 74 Keenan McCardell .50 .20
❑ 75 Kendrell Bell 1.25 .50
❑ 76 Kerry Collins .75 .30
❑ 77 Kevan Barlow .75 .30
❑ 78 Kevin Dyson .75 .30
❑ 79 Kevin Johnson .75 .30
❑ 80 Kevin Kasper .50 .20
❑ 81 Keyshawn Johnson 1.25 .50
❑ 82 Kordell Stewart .75 .30
❑ 83 Koren Robinson .75 .30
❑ 84 Kurt Warner 1.25 .50
❑ 85 LaDainian Tomlinson 2.50 1.00
❑ 86 Lamar Smith .75 .30
❑ 87 Laveranues Coles .75 .30
❑ 88 MarTay Jenkins .50 .20
❑ 89 Mark Brunell 1.25 .50
❑ 90 Marshall Faulk 1.25 .50
❑ 91 Marty Booker .75 .30
❑ 92 Marvin Harrison 1.25 .50
❑ 93 Snoop Minnis .50 .20
❑ 94 Michael Bennett .75 .30
❑ 95 Michael Strahan .75 .30
❑ 96 Michael Vick 4.00 1.50
❑ 97 Mike Alstott 1.25 .50
❑ 98 Mike Anderson 1.25 .50
❑ 99 Mike McMahon 1.25 .50
❑ 100 Muhsin Muhammad .75 .30
❑ 101 Nate Clements .50 .20
❑ 102 Oronde Gadsden .75 .30
❑ 103 Peter Warrick .75 .30

❑ 104 Peyton Manning 2.50 1.00
❑ 105 Plaxico Burress .75 .30
❑ 106 Priest Holmes 1.50 .60
❑ 107 Quincy Carter .75 .30
❑ 108 Quincy Morgan .75 .30
❑ 109 Rocket Ismail .75 .30
❑ 110 Randy Moss 2.50 1.00
❑ 111 Ray Lewis 1.25 .50
❑ 112 Reggie Wayne 1.25 .50
❑ 113 Rich Gannon 1.25 .50
❑ 114 Rickey Dudley .50 .20
❑ 115 Ricky Watters .75 .30
❑ 116 Ricky Williams 1.25 .50
❑ 117 Rod Gardner .75 .30
❑ 118 Rod Smith .75 .30
❑ 119 Robert Ferguson .50 .20
❑ 120 Santana Moss 1.25 .50
❑ 121 Shaun Alexander 1.50 .60
❑ 122 Stephen Davis .75 .30
❑ 123 Steve McNair 1.25 .50
❑ 124 Steve Smith 1.25 .50
❑ 125 Terrell Davis 1.25 .50
❑ 126 Terrell Owens 1.25 .50
❑ 127 Terry Glenn .75 .30
❑ 128 Thomas Jones .75 .30
❑ 129 Tiki Barber 1.25 .50
❑ 130 Tim Brown 1.25 .50
❑ 131 Tim Couch .75 .30
❑ 132 Todd Heap .75 .30
❑ 133 Todd Pinkston .75 .30
❑ 134 Tom Brady 3.00 1.25
❑ 135 Tony Boselli .50 .20
❑ 136 Tony Gonzalez .75 .30
❑ 137 Torry Holt 1.25 .50
❑ 138 Travis Henry 1.25 .50
❑ 139 Travis Taylor .75 .30
❑ 140 Trent Dilfer .75 .30
❑ 141 Trent Green .75 .30
❑ 142 Troy Brown .75 .30
❑ 143 Troy Hambrick .50 .20
❑ 144 Trung Canidate .75 .30
❑ 145 Vinny Testaverde .75 .30
❑ 146 Warren Sapp .75 .30
❑ 147 Warrick Dunn 1.25 .50
❑ 148 Wayne Chrebet .75 .30
❑ 149 Wesley Walls .50 .20
❑ 150 Zach Thomas 1.25 .50
❑ 151 Quentin Jammer RC 6.00 2.50
❑ 152 Randy Fasani RC 5.00 2.00
❑ 153 Kurt Kittner RC 5.00 2.00
❑ 154 Chad Hutchinson RC 5.00 2.00
❑ 155 Major Applewhite RC 6.00 2.50
❑ 156 Wes Pate RC 3.00 1.25
❑ 157 J.T. O'Sullivan RC 5.00 2.00
❑ 158 Ryan Denney RC 5.00 2.00
❑ 159 Ronald Curry RC 6.00 2.50
❑ 160 Lamar Gordon RC 6.00 2.50
❑ 161 Brian Westbrook RC 10.00 4.00
❑ 162 Jonathan Wells RC 6.00 2.50
❑ 163 Ricky Williams RC 5.00 2.00
❑ 164 Verron Haynes RC 6.00 2.50
❑ 165 Josh Scobey RC 6.00 2.50
❑ 166 Larry Ned RC 5.00 2.00
❑ 167 Adrian Peterson RC 6.00 2.50
❑ 168 Chester Taylor RC 6.00 2.50
❑ 169 Luke Staley RC 5.00 2.00
❑ 170 Damien Anderson RC 5.00 2.00
❑ 171 Lee Mays RC 5.00 2.00
❑ 172 Deion Branch RC 12.00 5.00
❑ 173 Terry Charles RC 5.00 2.00
❑ 174 Woody Dantzler RC 5.00 2.00
❑ 175 Jason McAddley RC 5.00 2.00
❑ 176 Kelly Campbell RC 5.00 2.00
❑ 177 Freddie Milons RC 5.00 2.00
❑ 178 Kahlil Hill RC 5.00 2.00
❑ 179 Brian Poli-Dixon RC 5.00 2.00
❑ 180 Mike Echols RC 3.00 1.25
❑ 181 Pete Rebstock RC 3.00 1.25
❑ 182 Dwight Freeney RC 8.00 3.00
❑ 183 Bryan Thomas RC 5.00 2.00
❑ 184 Charles Grant RC 6.00 2.50
❑ 185 Kalimba Edwards RC 6.00 2.50
❑ 186 Ryan Sims RC 6.00 2.50
❑ 187 John Henderson RC 6.00 2.50
❑ 188 Wendell Bryant RC 3.00 1.25
❑ 189 Albert Haynesworth RC 5.00 2.00
❑ 190 Larry Tripplett RC 3.00 1.25
❑ 191 Phillip Buchanon RC 6.00 2.50
❑ 192 Lito Sheppard RC 6.00 2.50
❑ 193 Mike Rumph RC 6.00 2.50
❑ 194 Levar Fisher RC 3.00 1.25
❑ 195 Ed Reed RC 10.00 4.00
❑ 196 Rocky Calmus RC 6.00 2.50
❑ 197 Michael Lewis RC 6.00 2.50
❑ 198 Napoleon Harris RC 6.00 2.50
❑ 199 Robert Thomas RC 6.00 2.50
❑ 200 Anthony Weaver RC 5.00 2.00
❑ 201 Ladell Betts RPM RC 12.00 6.00
❑ 202 Antonio Bryant RPM RC 12.00 6.00
❑ 203 Reche Caldwell RPM RC 12.00 6.00
❑ 204 David Carr RPM RC 25.00 10.00
❑ 205 Tim Carter RPM RC 6.00 3.00
❑ 206 Eric Crouch RPM RC 12.00 6.00
❑ 207 Rohan Davey RPM RC 12.00 6.00
❑ 208 Andre Davis RPM RC 6.00 3.00
❑ 209 T.J. Duckett RPM RC 20.00 7.50
❑ 210 DeShaun Foster RPM RC 12.00 6.00
❑ 211 Jabar Gaffney RPM RC 12.00 6.00
❑ 212 Daniel Graham RPM RC 12.00 6.00
❑ 213 William Green RPM RC 12.00 6.00
❑ 214 Joey Harrington RPM RC 25.00 10.00
❑ 215 David Garrard RPM RC 8.00 3.00
❑ 216 Ron Johnson RPM RC 6.00 3.00
❑ 217 Ashley Lelie RPM RC 25.00 10.00
❑ 218 Josh McCown RPM RC 15.00 6.00
❑ 219 Maurice Morris RPM RC 12.00 6.00
❑ 220 Julius Peppers RPM RC 25.00 12.50
❑ 221 Clinton Portis RPM RC 30.00 12.50
❑ 222 Patrick Ramsey RPM RC 15.00 6.00
❑ 223 Antwaan Randle El RPM RC 20.00 7.50
❑ 224 Josh Reed RPM RC 12.00 6.00
❑ 225 Cliff Russell RPM RC 6.00 3.00
❑ 226 Jeremy Shockey RPM RC 30.00 12.50
❑ 227 Donte Stallworth RPM RC 25.00 10.00
❑ 228 Travis Stephens RPM RC 6.00 3.00
❑ 229 Javon Walker RPM RC 25.00 12.50
❑ 230 Marquise Walker RPM RC 6.00 3.00
❑ 231 Roy Williams RPM RC 30.00 12.50
❑ 232 Mike Williams RPM RC 6.00 3.00

2003 Absolute Memorabilia

❑ COMP.SET w/o SP's (100) 25.00 10.00
❑ 1 Jamal Lewis 1.25 .50
❑ 2 Ray Lewis 1.25 .50
❑ 3 Todd Heap .75 .30
❑ 4 Drew Bledsoe 1.25 .50
❑ 5 Travis Henry .75 .30
❑ 6 Peerless Price .75 .30
❑ 7 Corey Dillon .75 .30
❑ 8 Chad Johnson 1.25 .50
❑ 9 Tim Couch .50 .20
❑ 10 William Green .75 .30
❑ 11 Andre Davis .50 .20
❑ 12 Brian Griese 1.25 .50
❑ 13 Ashley Lelie 1.25 .50
❑ 14 Clinton Portis 2.00 .75
❑ 15 Rod Smith .75 .30
❑ 16 David Carr 2.00 .75
❑ 17 Corey Bradford .50 .20
❑ 18 Jonathan Wells .50 .20
❑ 19 Peyton Manning 2.00 .75
❑ 20 Edgerrin James 1.25 .50
❑ 21 Marvin Harrison 1.25 .50
❑ 22 Mark Brunell .75 .30
❑ 23 Fred Taylor 1.25 .50
❑ 24 Jimmy Smith .75 .30
❑ 25 Trent Green .75 .30
❑ 26 Priest Holmes 1.50 .60
❑ 27 Tony Gonzalez .75 .30
❑ 28 Jay Fiedler .75 .30
❑ 29 Ricky Williams 1.25 .50
❑ 30 Chris Chambers 1.25 .50
❑ 31 Zach Thomas 1.25 .50
❑ 32 Tom Brady 3.00 1.25
❑ 33 Troy Brown .75 .30
❑ 34 Antowain Smith .75 .30
❑ 35 Chad Pennington 1.50 .60
❑ 36 Curtis Martin 1.25 .50
❑ 37 Laveranues Coles .75 .30
❑ 38 Rich Gannon .75 .30
❑ 39 Charlie Garner .50 .20
❑ 40 Jerry Rice 2.50 1.00
❑ 41 Tim Brown 1.25 .50
❑ 42 Tommy Maddox 1.25 .50
❑ 43 Jerome Bettis 1.25 .50
❑ 44 Plaxico Burress .75 .30
❑ 45 Hines Ward 1.25 .50
❑ 46 Drew Brees 1.25 .50
❑ 47 LaDainian Tomlinson 1.25 .50
❑ 48 Junior Seau 1.25 .50
❑ 49 Steve McNair 1.25 .50
❑ 50 Eddie George .75 .30
❑ 51 Jevon Kearse .75 .30
❑ 52 Jake Plummer .75 .30
❑ 53 David Boston .75 .30
❑ 54 Marcel Shipp .75 .30
❑ 55 Michael Vick 3.00 1.25
❑ 56 T.J. Duckett .75 .30
❑ 57 Warrick Dunn .75 .30
❑ 58 Muhsin Muhammad .75 .30
❑ 59 Julius Peppers 1.25 .50
❑ 60 Steve Smith 1.25 .50
❑ 61 Anthony Thomas .75 .30
❑ 62 Brian Urlacher 2.00 .75
❑ 63 Marty Booker .75 .30
❑ 64 Antonio Bryant .75 .30
❑ 65 Chad Hutchinson .50 .20
❑ 66 Roy Williams 1.25 .50
❑ 67 Emmitt Smith 3.00 1.25
❑ 68 Joey Harrington 2.00 .75
❑ 69 James Stewart .75 .30
❑ 70 Az-Zahir Hakim .50 .20
❑ 71 Brett Favre 3.00 1.25
❑ 72 Ahman Green 1.25 .50
❑ 73 Donald Driver .75 .30
❑ 74 Daunte Culpepper 1.25 .50
❑ 75 Randy Moss 2.00 .75
❑ 76 Michael Bennett .75 .30
❑ 77 Aaron Brooks 1.25 .50
❑ 78 Deuce McAllister 1.25 .50
❑ 79 Donte Stallworth 1.25 .50
❑ 80 Tiki Barber 1.25 .50
❑ 81 Kerry Collins .75 .30
❑ 82 Jeremy Shockey 2.00 .75
❑ 83 Donovan McNabb 1.50 .60
❑ 84 Duce Staley .75 .30
❑ 85 Antonio Freeman .75 .30
❑ 86 Jeff Garcia 1.25 .50
❑ 87 Terrell Owens 1.25 .50
❑ 88 Garrison Hearst .75 .30
❑ 89 Matt Hasselbeck .75 .30
❑ 90 Koren Robinson .75 .30
❑ 91 Shaun Alexander 1.25 .50

❑ 92 Kurt Warner 1.25 .50
❑ 93 Marshall Faulk 1.25 .50
❑ 94 Isaac Bruce 1.25 .50
❑ 95 Brad Johnson .75 .30
❑ 96 Keyshawn Johnson 1.25 .50
❑ 97 Warren Sapp .75 .30
❑ 98 Patrick Ramsey 1.25 .50
❑ 99 Rod Gardner .75 .30
❑ 100 Stephen Davis .75 .30
❑ 101 Jason Gesser RC 6.00 2.50
❑ 102 Brandon Lloyd RC 8.00 3.00
❑ 103 Ken Dorsey RC 6.00 2.50
❑ 104 Avon Cobourne RC 3.00 1.25
❑ 105 Cecil Sapp RC 5.00 2.00
❑ 106 Derek Watson RC 5.00 2.00
❑ 107 Dwone Hicks RC 3.00 1.25
❑ 108 Earnest Graham RC 5.00 2.00
❑ 109 LaBrandon Toefield RC 6.00 2.50
❑ 110 Quentin Griffin RC 6.00 2.50
❑ 111 Sultan McCullough RC 5.00 2.00
❑ 112 Lee Suggs RC 12.00 5.00
❑ 113 Talman Gardner RC 6.00 2.50
❑ 114 Arnaz Battle RC 6.00 2.50
❑ 115 Billy McMullen RC 5.00 2.00
❑ 116 Doug Gabriel RC 6.00 2.50
❑ 117 Justin Gage RC 6.00 2.50
❑ 118 Kareem Kelly RC 5.00 2.00
❑ 119 Paul Arnold RC 5.00 2.00
❑ 120 Sam Aiken RC 5.00 2.00
❑ 121 Shaun McDonald RC 6.00 2.50
❑ 122 Terrence Edwards 5.00 2.00
❑ 123 Walter Young RC 3.00 1.25
❑ 124 Ryan Hoag RC 3.00 1.25
❑ 125 Jason Witten RC 12.00 5.00
❑ 126 Bennie Joppru RC 6.00 2.50
❑ 127 George Wrighster RC 5.00 2.00
❑ 128 L.J. Smith RC 6.00 2.50
❑ 129 Robert Johnson RC 3.00 1.25
❑ 130 Chris Kelsay RC 6.00 2.50
❑ 131 Cory Redding RC 5.00 2.00
❑ 132 DeWayne White RC 5.00 2.00
❑ 133 Kenny Peterson RC 5.00 2.00
❑ 134 Jerome McDougle RC 6.00 2.50
❑ 135 Michael Haynes RC 6.00 2.50
❑ 136 Jimmy Kennedy RC 6.00 2.50
❑ 137 Kevin Williams RC 6.00 2.50
❑ 138 Johnathan Sullivan RC 5.00 2.00
❑ 139 Rien Long RC 3.00 1.25
❑ 140 Ty Warren RC 6.00 2.50
❑ 141 William Joseph RC 6.00 2.50
❑ 142 E.J. Henderson RC 6.00 2.50
❑ 143 Boss Bailey RC 6.00 2.50
❑ 144 Dennis Weathersby RC 3.00 1.25
❑ 145 Chris Simms RC 10.00 4.00
❑ 146 Rashean Mathis RC 5.00 2.00
❑ 147 Charles Rogers RC 6.00 2.50
❑ 148 Andre Woolfolk RC 6.00 2.50
❑ 149 Troy Polamalu RC 25.00 12.50
❑ 150 Mike Doss RC 6.00 2.50
❑ 151 Carson Palmer RPM RC 40.00 20.00
❑ 152 Byron Leftwich RPM RC 30.00 12.50
❑ 153 Kyle Boller RPM RC 20.00 7.50
❑ 154 Rex Grossman RPM RC 15.00 6.00
❑ 155 Dave Ragone RPM RC 12.00 5.00
❑ 156 Kliff Kingsbury RPM RC 10.00 4.00
❑ 157 Seneca Wallace RPM RC 12.00 5.00
❑ 158 Larry Johnson RPM RC 40.00 20.00
❑ 159 Willis McGahee RPM RC 25.00 12.50
❑ 160 Justin Fargas RPM RC 12.00 5.00
❑ 161 Onterrio Smith RPM RC 12.00 5.00
❑ 162 Chris Brown RPM RC 15.00 6.00
❑ 163 Musa Smith RPM RC 12.00 5.00
❑ 164 Artose Pinner RPM RC 12.00 5.00
❑ 165 Andre Johnson RPM RC 20.00 7.50
❑ 166 Kelley Washington RPM RC 12.00 5.00
❑ 167 Taylor Jacobs RPM RC 10.00 4.00
❑ 168 Bryant Johnson RPM RC 12.00 5.00
❑ 169 Tyrone Calico RPM RC 15.00 6.00
❑ 170 Anquan Boldin RPM RC 25.00 10.00
❑ 171 Bethel Johnson RPM RC 12.00 5.00
❑ 172 Nate Burleson RPM RC 15.00 6.00
❑ 173 Kevin Curtis RPM RC 12.00 5.00
❑ 174 Dallas Clark RPM RC 12.00 5.00
❑ 175 Teyo Johnson RPM RC 12.00 5.00
❑ 176 Terrell Suggs RPM RC 20.00 7.50
❑ 177 DeWayne Robertson RPM RC 12.00 5.00
❑ 178 Brian St.Pierre RPM RC 12.00 5.00
❑ 179 Terence Newman RPM RC 20.00 7.50
❑ 180 Marcus Trufant RPM RC 12.00 5.00

2004 Absolute Memorabilia

❑ COMP.SET w/o SP's (150) 80.00 40.00
❑ 1-150 PRINT RUN 1150 SER.#'d SETS
❑ 151-233 PRINT RUN 750 SER.#'d SETS
❑ UNPRICED SPECTRUM PLATINUM #'d TO 1
❑ 1 Anquan Boldin 3.00 1.25
❑ 2 Emmitt Smith 6.00 2.50
❑ 3 Josh McCown 2.00 .75
❑ 4 Marcel Shipp 2.00 .75
❑ 5 Michael Vick 6.00 2.50
❑ 6 Peerless Price 2.00 .75
❑ 7 T.J. Duckett 2.00 .75
❑ 8 Warrick Dunn 2.00 .75
❑ 9 Jamal Lewis 3.00 1.25
❑ 10 Kyle Boller 3.00 1.25
❑ 11 Ray Lewis 3.00 1.25
❑ 12 Terrell Suggs 2.00 .75
❑ 13 Drew Bledsoe 3.00 1.25
❑ 14 Eric Moulds 2.00 .75
❑ 15 Josh Reed 1.25 .50
❑ 16 Travis Henry 2.00 .75
❑ 17 DeShaun Foster 2.00 .75
❑ 18 Jake Delhomme 3.00 1.25
❑ 19 Julius Peppers 3.00 1.25
❑ 20 Muhsin Muhammad 2.00 .75
❑ 21 Stephen Davis 2.00 .75
❑ 22 Steve Smith 3.00 1.25
❑ 23 Anthony Thomas 2.00 .75
❑ 24 Brian Urlacher 4.00 1.50
❑ 25 Marty Booker 2.00 .75
❑ 26 Rex Grossman 3.00 1.25
❑ 27 Carson Palmer 4.00 1.50
❑ 28 Chad Johnson 3.00 1.25
❑ 29 Corey Dillon 2.00 .75
❑ 30 Peter Warrick 2.00 .75
❑ 31 Rudi Johnson 2.00 .75
❑ 32 Andre Davis 1.25 .50
❑ 33 Dennis Northcutt 1.25 .50
❑ 34 Lee Suggs 3.00 1.25
❑ 35 Tim Couch 1.25 .50
❑ 36 Jeff Garcia 3.00 1.25
❑ 37 William Green 2.00 .75
❑ 38 Antonio Bryant 2.00 .75
❑ 39 Quincy Carter 2.00 .75
❑ 40 Roy Williams S 2.00 .75
❑ 41 Terence Newman 2.00 .75
❑ 42 Keyshawn Johnson 2.00 .75
❑ 43 Garrison Hearst 2.00 .75
❑ 44 Champ Bailey 2.00 .75
❑ 45 Ashley Lelie 2.00 .75
❑ 46 Jake Plummer 2.00 .75
❑ 47 Rod Smith 2.00 .75
❑ 48 Shannon Sharpe 2.00 .75
❑ 49 Charles Rogers 2.00 .75
❑ 50 Joey Harrington 3.00 1.25
❑ 51 Ahman Green 3.00 1.25
❑ 52 Brett Favre 8.00 3.00
❑ 53 Donald Driver 2.00 .75
❑ 54 Javon Walker 2.00 .75
❑ 55 Robert Ferguson 1.25 .50
❑ 56 Andre Johnson 3.00 1.25
❑ 57 David Carr 3.00 1.25
❑ 58 Domanick Davis 3.00 1.25
❑ 59 Edgerrin James 3.00 1.25
❑ 60 Marvin Harrison 3.00 1.25
❑ 61 Peyton Manning 5.00 2.00
❑ 62 Reggie Wayne 2.00 .75
❑ 63 Byron Leftwich 4.00 1.50
❑ 64 Fred Taylor 2.00 .75
❑ 65 Jimmy Smith 2.00 .75
❑ 66 Dante Hall 3.00 1.25
❑ 67 Priest Holmes 4.00 1.50
❑ 68 Tony Gonzalez 2.00 .75
❑ 69 Trent Green 2.00 .75
❑ 70 Chris Chambers 2.00 .75
❑ 71 Jay Fiedler 1.25 .50
❑ 72 David Boston 2.00 .75
❑ 73 Ricky Williams 3.00 1.25
❑ 74 Zach Thomas 3.00 1.25
❑ 75 Daunte Culpepper 3.00 1.25
❑ 76 Michael Bennett 2.00 .75
❑ 77 Moe Williams 1.25 .50
❑ 78 Randy Moss 4.00 1.50
❑ 79 David Givens 2.00 .75
❑ 80 Deion Branch 3.00 1.25
❑ 81 Kevin Faulk 1.25 .50
❑ 82 Richard Seymour 1.25 .50
❑ 83 Tom Brady 8.00 3.00
❑ 84 Troy Brown 2.00 .75
❑ 85 Ty Law 2.00 .75
❑ 86 Aaron Brooks 2.00 .75
❑ 87 Deuce McAllister 3.00 1.25
❑ 88 Donte Stallworth 2.00 .75
❑ 89 Joe Horn 2.00 .75
❑ 90 Amani Toomer 2.00 .75
❑ 91 Jeremy Shockey 3.00 1.25
❑ 92 Kerry Collins 2.00 .75
❑ 93 Michael Strahan 2.00 .75
❑ 94 Tiki Barber 3.00 1.25
❑ 95 Chad Pennington 3.00 1.25
❑ 96 Curtis Martin 3.00 1.25
❑ 97 Santana Moss 2.00 .75
❑ 98 Wayne Chrebet 2.00 .75
❑ 99 Justin McCareins 1.25 .50
❑ 100 Charles Woodson 2.00 .75
❑ 101 Jerry Porter 2.00 .75
❑ 102 Jerry Rice 6.00 2.50
❑ 103 Rich Gannon 2.00 .75
❑ 104 Tim Brown 3.00 1.25
❑ 105 Warren Sapp 2.00 .75
❑ 106 A.J. Feeley 3.00 1.25
❑ 107 Brian Westbrook 2.00 .75
❑ 108 Correll Buckhalter 2.00 .75
❑ 109 Donovan McNabb 4.00 1.50
❑ 110 Freddie Mitchell 2.00 .75
❑ 111 Terrell Owens 3.00 1.25
❑ 112 Jevon Kearse 2.00 .75
❑ 113 Todd Pinkston 1.25 .50
❑ 114 Antwaan Randle El 3.00 1.25
❑ 115 Hines Ward 3.00 1.25
❑ 116 Jerome Bettis 3.00 1.25
❑ 117 Kendrell Bell 2.00 .75
❑ 118 Plaxico Burress 2.00 .75
❑ 119 Tommy Maddox 2.00 .75
❑ 120 Duce Staley 2.00 .75
❑ 121 Drew Brees 3.00 1.25
❑ 122 LaDainian Tomlinson 4.00 1.50
❑ 123 Kevan Barlow 2.00 .75
❑ 124 Tai Streets 1.25 .50
❑ 125 Tim Rattay 1.25 .50
❑ 126 Darrell Jackson 2.00 .75
❑ 127 Koren Robinson 2.00 .75
❑ 128 Matt Hasselbeck 2.00 .75

❑ 129 Shaun Alexander 3.00 1.25
❑ 130 Isaac Bruce 2.00 .75
❑ 131 Kurt Warner 3.00 1.25
❑ 132 Marc Bulger 3.00 1.25
❑ 133 Marshall Faulk 3.00 1.25
❑ 134 Torry Holt 3.00 1.25
❑ 135 Derrick Brooks 2.00 .75
❑ 136 Keenan McCardell 1.25 .50
❑ 137 Mike Alstott 2.00 .75
❑ 138 Thomas Jones 2.00 .75
❑ 139 Charlie Garner 2.00 .75
❑ 140 Derrick Mason 2.00 .75
❑ 141 Drew Bennett 2.00 .75
❑ 142 Eddie George 2.00 .75
❑ 143 Keith Bulluck 1.25 .50
❑ 144 Steve McNair 3.00 1.25
❑ 145 LaVar Arrington 6.00 2.50
❑ 146 Laveranues Coles 2.00 .75
❑ 147 Patrick Ramsey 2.00 .75
❑ 148 Rod Gardner 2.00 .75
❑ 149 Clinton Portis 3.00 1.25
❑ 150 Mark Brunell 2.00 .75
❑ 151 Craig Krenzel AU RC EXCH 15.00 7.50
❑ 152 Andy Hall AU RC EXCH 12.00 6.00
❑ 153 Josh Harris RC 6.00 2.50
❑ 154 Jim Sorgi AU RC 15.00 7.50
❑ 155 Jeff Smoker AU RC 15.00 7.50
❑ 156 John Navarre AU RC EXCH 15.00 7.50
❑ 157 Jared Lorenzen AU RC 12.00 6.00
❑ 158 Cody Pickett AU RC 15.00 7.50
❑ 159 Casey Bramlet RC 5.00 2.00
❑ 160 Matt Mauck AU RC 15.00 7.50
❑ 161 B.J. Symons AU RC 15.00 7.50
❑ 162 Bradlee Van Pelt RC 10.00 4.00
❑ 163 Ryan Dinwiddie RC 5.00 2.00
❑ 164 Michael Turner RC 6.00 2.50
❑ 165 Drew Henson RC 6.00 2.50
❑ 166 Troy Fleming RC 5.00 2.00
❑ 167 Adimchinobe Echemandu RC 5.00 2.00
❑ 168 Quincy Wilson RC 5.00 2.00
❑ 169 Derrick Ward RC 3.00 1.25
❑ 170 Bruce Perry RC 6.00 2.50
❑ 171 Brandon Miree RC 5.00 2.00
❑ 172 Jarrett Payton AU RC 25.00 10.00
❑ 173 Ran Carthon RC 5.00 2.00
❑ 174 Carlos Francis AU RC EXCH 12.00 6.00
❑ 175 Samie Parker RC 6.00 2.50
❑ 176 Jerricho Cotchery RC 6.00 2.50
❑ 177 Ernest Wilford RC 6.00 2.50
❑ 178 Johnnie Morant RC 6.00 2.50
❑ 179 Maurice Mann AU RC 15.00 7.50
❑ 180 D.J. Hackett RC 5.00 2.00
❑ 181 Drew Carter RC 6.00 2.50
❑ 182 P.K. Sam RC 5.00 2.00
❑ 183 Jamaar Taylor RC 6.00 2.50
❑ 184 Ryan Krause RC 5.00 2.00
❑ 185 Triandos Luke RC 6.00 2.50
❑ 186 Jeris McIntyre RC 5.00 2.00
❑ 187 Clarence Moore AU RC 15.00 7.50
❑ 188 Mark Jones RC 5.00 2.00
❑ 189 Sloan Thomas AU RC 12.00 6.00
❑ 190 Sean Taylor RC 8.00 3.00
❑ 191 Derek Abney RC 6.00 2.50
❑ 192 Jonathan Vilma RC 6.00 2.50
❑ 193 Tommie Harris RC 6.00 2.50
❑ 194 D.J. Williams RC 8.00 3.00
❑ 195 Will Smith RC 6.00 2.50
❑ 196 Kenechi Udeze RC 6.00 2.50
❑ 197 Vince Wilfork RC 8.00 3.00
❑ 198 Ahmad Carroll RC 8.00 3.00
❑ 199 Jason Babin RC 6.00 2.50
❑ 200 Chris Gamble RC 8.00 3.00
❑ 201 Larry Fitzgerald RPM RC 25.00 10.00
❑ 202 DeAngelo Hall RPM RC 10.00 4.00
❑ 203 Matt Schaub RPM RC 12.00 5.00
❑ 204 Michael Jenkins RPM AU RC 25.00 12.50
❑ 205 Devard Darling RPM AU RC 25.00 10.00
❑ 206 J.P. Losman RPM RC 15.00 6.00
❑ 207 Lee Evans RPM RC 10.00 4.00
❑ 208 Keary Colbert RPM AU RC 30.00 15.00
❑ 209 Bernard Berrian RPM AU RC 25.00 10.00
❑ 210 Chris Perry RPM RC 12.00 5.00
❑ 211 Kellen Winslow RPM RC 15.00 6.00
❑ 212 Luke McCown RPM RC 8.00 3.00
❑ 213 Julius Jones RPM RC 30.00 12.50
❑ 214 Darius Watts RPM RC 8.00 3.00
❑ 215 Tatum Bell RPM AU RC 40.00 15.00
❑ 216 Kevin Jones RPM RC 25.00 10.00
❑ 217 Roy Williams RPM RC 20.00 7.50
❑ 218 Dunta Robinson RPM RC 8.00 3.00
❑ 219 Greg Jones RPM AU RC 25.00 12.50
❑ 220 Reggie Williams RPM RC 10.00 4.00
❑ 221 Mewelde Moore RPM RC 10.00 4.00
❑ 222 Ben Watson RPM RC 8.00 3.00
❑ 223 Cedric Cobbs RPM RC 15.00 7.50
❑ 224 Dev Henderson RPM AU RC 25.00 10.00
❑ 225 Eli Manning RPM RC 50.00 20.00
❑ 226 Robert Gallery RPM RC 12.00 5.00
❑ 227 Roethlisberger RPM RC 60.00 35.00
❑ 228 Philip Rivers RPM RC 25.00 12.50
❑ 229 Derrick Hamilton RPM RC 6.00 2.50
❑ 230 Rashaun Woods RPM RC 8.00 3.00
❑ 231 Steven Jackson RPM RC 25.00 10.00
❑ 232 Michael Clayton RPM RC 15.00 6.00
❑ 233 Ben Troupe RPM RC 8.00 3.00

2005 Absolute Memorabilia

❑ 151-205 PRINT RUN 999 SER.#'d SETS
❑ 206-234 PRINT RUN 750 SER.#'d SETS
❑ UNPRICED PLATINUM PRINT RUN 1 SET
❑ HOBBY PRINTED ON HOLOFOIL STOCK
❑ 1 Anquan Boldin 2.00 .75
❑ 2 Kurt Warner 2.00 .75
❑ 3 Josh McCown 2.00 .75
❑ 4 Larry Fitzgerald 3.00 1.25
❑ 5 Alge Crumpler 2.00 .75
❑ 6 Michael Vick 5.00 2.00
❑ 7 Peerless Price 1.50 .60
❑ 8 T.J. Duckett 2.00 .75
❑ 9 Warrick Dunn 2.00 .75
❑ 10 Deion Sanders 3.00 1.25
❑ 11 Derrick Mason 2.00 .75
❑ 12 Ed Reed 2.00 .75
❑ 13 Jamal Lewis 3.00 1.25
❑ 14 Kyle Boller 2.00 .75
❑ 15 Ray Lewis 3.00 1.25
❑ 16 Todd Heap 2.00 .75
❑ 17 Eric Moulds 2.00 .75
❑ 18 J.P. Losman 3.00 1.25
❑ 19 Lee Evans 2.00 .75
❑ 20 Travis Henry 2.00 .75
❑ 21 Willis McGahee 3.00 1.25
❑ 22 DeShaun Foster 2.00 .75
❑ 23 Jake Delhomme 3.00 1.25
❑ 24 Julius Peppers 2.00 .75
❑ 25 Keary Colbert 2.00 .75
❑ 26 Stephen Davis 2.00 .75
❑ 27 Steve Smith 2.00 .75
❑ 28 Brian Urlacher 3.00 1.25
❑ 29 Muhsin Muhammad 2.00 .75
❑ 30 Thomas Jones 2.00 .75
❑ 31 Rex Grossman 2.00 .75
❑ 32 Carson Palmer 3.00 1.25
❑ 33 Chad Johnson 3.00 1.25
❑ 34 Peter Warrick 1.50 .60
❑ 35 Rudi Johnson 2.00 .75
❑ 36 T.J. Houshmandzadeh 1.50 .60
❑ 37 Antonio Bryant 1.50 .60
❑ 38 Dennis Northcutt 1.50 .60
❑ 39 Trent Dilfer 2.00 .75
❑ 40 Kellen Winslow 3.00 1.25
❑ 41 Lee Suggs 2.00 .75
❑ 42 Reuben Droughns 2.00 .75
❑ 43 Drew Bledsoe 3.00 1.25
❑ 44 Jason Witten 2.00 .75
❑ 45 Julius Jones 4.00 1.50
❑ 46 Keyshawn Johnson 2.00 .75
❑ 47 Terence Newman 1.50 .60
❑ 48 Roy Williams S 2.00 .75
❑ 49 Jake Plummer 2.00 .75
❑ 50 Rod Smith 2.00 .75
❑ 51 Ashley Lelie 2.00 .75
❑ 52 Tatum Bell 2.00 .75
❑ 53 Charles Rogers 2.00 .75
❑ 54 Joey Harrington 3.00 1.25
❑ 55 Kevin Jones 3.00 1.25
❑ 56 Roy Williams WR 3.00 1.25
❑ 57 Ahman Green 3.00 1.25
❑ 58 Brett Favre 8.00 3.00
❑ 59 Donald Driver 2.00 .75
❑ 60 Javon Walker 2.00 .75
❑ 61 Andre Johnson 2.00 .75
❑ 62 David Carr 3.00 1.25
❑ 63 Domanick Davis 2.00 .75
❑ 64 Brandon Stokley 2.00 .75
❑ 65 Dallas Clark 1.50 .60
❑ 66 Edgerrin James 3.00 1.25
❑ 67 Marvin Harrison 3.00 1.25
❑ 68 Peyton Manning 5.00 2.00
❑ 69 Reggie Wayne 2.00 .75
❑ 70 Reggie Williams 2.00 .75
❑ 71 Byron Leftwich 3.00 1.25
❑ 72 Fred Taylor 2.00 .75
❑ 73 Jimmy Smith 2.00 .75
❑ 74 Priest Holmes 3.00 1.25
❑ 75 Tony Gonzalez 2.00 .75
❑ 76 Dante Hall 2.00 .75
❑ 77 Trent Green 2.00 .75
❑ 78 Eddie Kennison 1.50 .60
❑ 79 A.J. Feeley 2.00 .75
❑ 80 Chris Chambers 2.00 .75
❑ 81 Zach Thomas 3.00 1.25
❑ 82 Junior Seau 2.00 .75
❑ 83 Marty Booker 2.00 .75
❑ 84 Daunte Culpepper 3.00 1.25
❑ 85 Nate Burleson 2.00 .75
❑ 86 Michael Bennett 2.00 .75
❑ 87 Onterrio Smith 2.00 .75
❑ 88 Corey Dillon 2.00 .75
❑ 89 Deion Branch 2.00 .75
❑ 90 Tom Brady 8.00 3.00
❑ 91 Troy Brown 2.00 .75
❑ 92 Tedy Bruschi 2.00 .75
❑ 93 Aaron Brooks 2.00 .75
❑ 94 Donte Stallworth 2.00 .75
❑ 95 Joe Horn 2.00 .75
❑ 96 Deuce McAllister 3.00 1.25
❑ 97 Amani Toomer 2.00 .75
❑ 98 Plaxico Burress 2.00 .75
❑ 99 Jeremy Shockey 3.00 1.25
❑ 100 Eli Manning 6.00 2.50
❑ 101 Tiki Barber 3.00 1.25
❑ 102 Chad Pennington 3.00 1.25
❑ 103 Laveranues Coles 2.00 .75
❑ 104 Curtis Martin 3.00 1.25
❑ 105 Justin McCareins 1.50 .60
❑ 106 Wayne Chrebet 2.00 .75
❑ 107 Jerry Porter 2.00 .75
❑ 108 LaMont Jordan 3.00 1.25
❑ 109 Randy Moss 3.00 1.25
❑ 110 Kerry Collins 2.00 .75
❑ 111 Charles Woodson 2.00 .75
❑ 112 Brian Westbrook 2.00 .75

❑ 113	Donovan McNabb	4.00	1.50
❑ 114	Jevon Kearse	2.00	.75
❑ 115	Terrell Owens	3.00	1.25
❑ 116	Ben Roethlisberger	8.00	3.00
❑ 117	Hines Ward	3.00	1.25
❑ 118	Duce Staley	2.00	.75
❑ 119	Jerome Bettis	3.00	1.25
❑ 120	Antonio Gates	3.00	1.25
❑ 121	Eric Parker	1.50	.60
❑ 122	Keenan McCardell	1.50	.60
❑ 123	Drew Brees	3.00	1.25
❑ 124	LaDainian Tomlinson	4.00	1.50
❑ 125	Brandon Lloyd	1.50	.60
❑ 126	Kevan Barlow	2.00	.75
❑ 127	Tim Rattay	1.50	.60
❑ 128	Koren Robinson	2.00	.75
❑ 129	Darrell Jackson	2.00	.75
❑ 130	Jerry Rice	6.00	2.50
❑ 131	Matt Hasselbeck	2.00	.75
❑ 132	Shaun Alexander	4.00	1.25
❑ 133	Isaac Bruce	2.00	.75
❑ 134	Marc Bulger	3.00	1.25
❑ 135	Marshall Faulk	3.00	1.25
❑ 136	Steven Jackson	4.00	1.50
❑ 137	Torry Holt	3.00	1.25
❑ 138	Brian Griese	2.00	.75
❑ 139	Michael Clayton	3.00	1.25
❑ 140	Michael Pittman	1.50	.60
❑ 141	Mike Alstott	2.00	.75
❑ 142	Chris Brown	2.00	.75
❑ 143	Drew Bennett	2.00	.75
❑ 144	Steve McNair	3.00	1.25
❑ 145	Clinton Portis	3.00	1.25
❑ 146	LaVar Arrington	3.00	1.25
❑ 147	Santana Moss	2.00	.75
❑ 148	Patrick Ramsey	2.00	.75
❑ 149	Rod Gardner	2.00	.75
❑ 150	Sean Taylor	2.00	.75
❑ 151	DeMarcus Ware RC	10.00	4.00
❑ 152	Shawne Merriman RC	10.00	4.00
❑ 153	Thomas Davis RC	6.00	2.50
❑ 154	Derrick Johnson RC	10.00	4.00
❑ 155	Travis Johnson RC	5.00	2.00
❑ 156	David Pollack RC	6.00	2.50
❑ 157	Erasmus James RC	6.00	2.50
❑ 158	Marcus Spears RC	6.00	2.50
❑ 159	Fabian Washington RC	6.00	2.50
❑ 160	Marlin Jackson RC	6.00	2.50
❑ 161	Cedric Benson RC	12.00	5.00
❑ 162	Matt Roth RC	6.00	2.50
❑ 163	Dan Cody RC	6.00	2.50
❑ 164	Bryant McFadden RC	6.00	2.50
❑ 165	Chris Henry RC	6.00	2.50
❑ 166	Brandon Jones RC	6.00	2.50
❑ 167	Marion Barber RC	10.00	4.00
❑ 168	Brandon Jacobs RC	8.00	3.00
❑ 169	Jerome Mathis RC	6.00	2.50
❑ 170	Craphonso Thorpe RC	5.00	2.00
❑ 171	Alvin Pearman RC	6.00	2.50
❑ 172	Darren Sproles RC	6.00	2.50
❑ 173	Fred Gibson RC	5.00	2.00
❑ 174	Roydell Williams RC	6.00	2.50
❑ 175	Airese Currie RC	6.00	2.50
❑ 176	Damien Nash RC	5.00	2.00
❑ 177	Dan Orlovsky RC	8.00	3.00
❑ 178	Adrian McPherson RC	6.00	2.50
❑ 179	Larry Brackins RC	3.00	1.25
❑ 180	Aaron Rodgers RC	20.00	8.00
❑ 181	Cedric Houston RC	6.00	2.50
❑ 182	Mike Williams	12.00	5.00
❑ 183	Heath Miller RC	15.00	6.00
❑ 184	Dante Ridgeway RC	5.00	2.00
❑ 185	Craig Bragg RC	5.00	2.00
❑ 186	Deandra Cobb RC	5.00	2.00
❑ 187	Derek Anderson RC	6.00	2.50
❑ 188	Paris Warren RC	5.00	2.00
❑ 189	David Greene RC	6.00	2.50
❑ 190	Lionel Gates RC	5.00	2.00
❑ 191	Anthony Davis RC	5.00	2.00
❑ 192	Noah Herron RC	6.00	2.50
❑ 193	Ryan Fitzpatrick RC	10.00	4.00
❑ 194	J.R. Russell RC	5.00	2.00
❑ 195	Jason White RC	6.00	2.50
❑ 196	Kay-Jay Harris RC	5.00	2.00
❑ 197	Steve Savoy RC	3.00	1.25
❑ 198	T.A. McLendon RC	3.00	1.25
❑ 199	Taylor Stubblefield RC	3.00	1.25
❑ 200	Josh Davis RC	5.00	2.00
❑ 201	Shaun Cody RC	6.00	2.50
❑ 202	Rasheed Marshall RC	6.00	2.50
❑ 203	Chad Owens RC	6.00	2.50
❑ 204	Tab Perry RC	6.00	2.50
❑ 205	James Kilian RC	6.00	2.50
❑ 206	Adam Jones RPM RC	10.00	4.00
❑ 207	Alex Smith QB RPM RC	30.00	12.50
❑ 208	Antrel Rolle RPM RC	10.00	4.00
❑ 209	Andrew Walter RPM RC	15.00	6.00
❑ 210	Braylon Edwards RPM RC	30.00	12.50
❑ 211	Carnell Williams RPM RC	40.00	15.00
❑ 212	Carlos Rogers RPM RC	12.00	5.00
❑ 213	Charlie Frye RPM RC	20.00	10.00
❑ 214	Ciatrick Fason RPM RC	10.00	4.00
❑ 215	Courtney Roby RPM RC	10.00	4.00
❑ 216	Eric Shelton RPM RC	10.00	4.00
❑ 217	Frank Gore RPM RC	15.00	6.00
❑ 218	J.J. Arrington RPM RC	15.00	6.00
❑ 219	Kyle Orton RPM RC	15.00	6.00
❑ 220	Jason Campbell RPM RC	15.00	6.00
❑ 221	Mark Bradley RPM RC	10.00	4.00
❑ 222	Mark Clayton RPM RC	12.00	5.00
❑ 223	Matt Jones RPM RC	25.00	10.00
❑ 224	Maurice Clarett RPM	10.00	4.00
❑ 225	Reggie Brown RPM RC	10.00	4.00
❑ 226	Ronnie Brown RPM RC	30.00	12.50
❑ 227	Roddy White RPM RC	10.00	4.00
❑ 228	Ryan Moats RPM RC	10.00	4.00
❑ 229	Roscoe Parrish RPM RC	10.00	4.00
❑ 230	Stefan LeFors RPM RC	10.00	4.00
❑ 231	Terrence Murphy RPM RC	10.00	4.00
❑ 232	Troy Williamson RPM RC	20.00	8.00
❑ 233	Vernand Morency RPM RC	10.00	4.00
❑ 234	Vincent Jackson RPM RC	10.00	4.00

2005 Absolute Memorabilia Retail

❑ COMPLETE SET (150) 30.00 15.00

❑ *VETERANS: .1X TO .25X BASIC CARDS

❑ *ROOKIES 151-205: .2X TO .5X BASIC CARDS

❑ RETAIL PRINTED ON WHITE STOCK

1995 Action Packed Rookies/Stars

❑ COMPLETE SET (105) 20.00 7.50

❑ 1	Steve Young	1.25	.50
❑ 2	Steve Bono	.25	.08
❑ 3	Natrone Means	.25	.08
❑ 4	Steve Beuerlein	.25	.08
❑ 5	Neil O'Donnell	.25	.08
❑ 6	Marshall Faulk	2.00	.75
❑ 7	Ricky Watters	.25	.08
❑ 8	Gary Brown	.10	.02
❑ 9	Jeff Hostetler	.25	.08
❑ 10	Robert Brooks	.50	.20
❑ 11	Johnny Mitchell	.10	.02
❑ 12	Barry Sanders	2.50	1.00
❑ 13	Dave Brown	.25	.08
❑ 14	John Elway	3.00	1.25
❑ 15	Garrison Hearst	.50	.20
❑ 16	Jim Everett	.10	.02
❑ 17	Michael Irvin	.50	.20
❑ 18	Dan Marino	3.00	1.25
❑ 19	Jeff George	.25	.08
❑ 20	Ben Coates	.25	.08
❑ 21	Charles Johnson	.25	.08
❑ 22	Carl Pickens	.25	.08
❑ 23	Deion Sanders	1.00	.40
❑ 24	Errict Rhett	.25	.08
❑ 25	Steve Walsh	.10	.02
❑ 26	Bruce Smith	.50	.20
❑ 27	Andre Rison	.25	.08
❑ 28	Warren Moon	.25	.08
❑ 29	Terry Allen	.25	.08
❑ 30	Desmond Howard	.25	.08
❑ 31	Shannon Sharpe	.25	.08
❑ 32	Dave Krieg	.10	.02
❑ 33	Byron Bam Morris	.10	.02
❑ 34	Rodney Hampton	.25	.08
❑ 35	Scott Mitchell	.25	.08
❑ 36	Alvin Harper	.10	.02
❑ 37	Robert Smith	.50	.20
❑ 38	Troy Aikman	1.50	.60
❑ 39	William Floyd	.25	.08
❑ 40	Randall Cunningham	.50	.20
❑ 41	Mario Bates	.25	.08
❑ 42	Reggie White	.50	.20
❑ 43	Chris Chandler	.25	.08
❑ 44	Erik Kramer	.10	.02
❑ 45	Emmitt Smith	2.50	1.00
❑ 46	Irving Fryar	.25	.08
❑ 47	Jeff Blake RC	.75	.30
❑ 48	Drew Bledsoe	1.00	.40
❑ 49	Anthony Miller	.25	.08
❑ 50	Marcus Allen	.50	.20
❑ 51	Leroy Hoard	.10	.02
❑ 52	Stan Humphries	.25	.08
❑ 53	Eric Green	.10	.02
❑ 54	Herschel Walker	.25	.08
❑ 55	Junior Seau	.50	.20
❑ 56	Terance Mathis	.25	.08
❑ 57	Boomer Esiason	.25	.08
❑ 58	Lorenzo White	.10	.02
❑ 59	Tim Brown	.50	.20
❑ 60	Brett Favre	3.00	1.25
❑ 61	Craig Erickson	.10	.02
❑ 62	Rod Woodson	.25	.08
❑ 63	Frank Reich	.10	.02
❑ 64	Cris Carter	.50	.20
❑ 65	Jerry Rice	1.50	.60
❑ 66	Greg Hill	.25	.08
❑ 67	Andre Reed	.25	.08
❑ 68	Trent Dilfer	.50	.20
❑ 69	Eric Metcalf	.25	.08
❑ 70	Jim Kelly	.50	.20
❑ 71	Herman Moore	.50	.20
❑ 72	Vinny Testaverde	.25	.08
❑ 73	Jeff Graham	.10	.02
❑ 74	Edgar Bennett	.25	.08
❑ 75	Jerome Bettis	.50	.20
❑ 76	Heath Shuler	.25	.08
❑ 77	Chris Warren	.25	.08
❑ 78	Reggie Brooks	.25	.08
❑ 79	Rick Mirer	.25	.08
❑ 80	Chris Miller	.10	.02
❑ 81	Napoleon Kaufman RC	1.25	.50
❑ 82	Christian Fauria RC	.25	.08
❑ 83	Todd Collins RC	.25	.08
❑ 84	J.J. Stokes RC	.50	.20
❑ 85	Mark Bruener RC	.25	.08
❑ 86	Frank Sanders RC	.50	.20
❑ 87	Chad May RC	.10	.02
❑ 88	Kordell Stewart RC	1.50	.60
❑ 89	Ki-Jana Carter RC	.50	.20

❑	90 Curtis Martin RC	3.00	1.25
❑	91 Sherman Williams RC	.10	.02
❑	92 Terrell Davis RC	2.50	1.00
❑	93 Chris Sanders RC	.25	.08
❑	94 Kyle Brady RC	.50	.20
❑	95 Tyrone Wheatley RC	1.25	.50
❑	96 Rodney Thomas RC	.25	.08
❑	97 James O. Stewart RC	1.25	.50
❑	98 Kerry Collins RC	1.50	.60
❑	99 Rashaan Salaam RC	.25	.08
❑	100 Stoney Case RC	.10	.02
❑	101 Steve McNair RC	3.00	1.25
❑	102 Joey Galloway RC	1.50	.60
❑	103 Michael Westbrook RC	.50	.20
❑	104 Eric Zeier RC	.50	.20
❑	105 Ray Zellars RC	.25	.08

2002 Atomic

❑	COMP.SET w/o SP's (100)	50.00	20.00
❑	1 David Boston	2.00	.75
❑	2 Thomas Jones	1.25	.50
❑	3 Jake Plummer	1.25	.50
❑	4 Jamal Anderson	1.25	.50
❑	5 Warrick Dunn	2.00	.75
❑	6 Michael Vick	6.00	2.50
❑	7 Jamal Lewis	2.00	.75
❑	8 Chris Redman	.75	.30
❑	9 Travis Taylor	1.25	.50
❑	10 Travis Henry	2.00	.75
❑	11 Eric Moulds	1.25	.50
❑	12 Peerless Price	1.25	.50
❑	13 Muhsin Muhammad	1.25	.50
❑	14 Lamar Smith	1.25	.50
❑	15 Chris Weinke	1.25	.50
❑	16 Marty Booker	.75	.30
❑	17 Jim Miller	.75	.30
❑	18 Anthony Thomas	1.25	.50
❑	19 Corey Dillon	1.25	.50
❑	20 Jon Kitna	1.25	.50
❑	21 Peter Warrick	1.25	.50
❑	22 Tim Couch	1.25	.50
❑	23 Kevin Johnson	1.25	.50
❑	24 Quincy Morgan	.75	.30
❑	25 Quincy Carter	1.25	.50
❑	26 Joey Galloway	1.25	.50
❑	27 Emmitt Smith	5.00	2.00
❑	28 Terrell Davis	2.00	.75
❑	29 Brian Griese	2.00	.75
❑	30 Ed McCaffrey	2.00	.75
❑	31 Rod Smith	1.25	.50
❑	32 Scotty Anderson	.75	.30
❑	33 Az-Zahir Hakim	.75	.30
❑	34 Mike McMahon	2.00	.75
❑	35 Brett Favre	5.00	2.00
❑	36 Terry Glenn	1.25	.50
❑	37 Ahman Green	2.00	.75
❑	38 James Allen	1.25	.50
❑	39 Corey Bradford	.75	.30
❑	40 Jermaine Lewis	.75	.30
❑	41 Marvin Harrison	2.00	.75
❑	42 Edgerrin James	2.50	1.00
❑	43 Peyton Manning	4.00	1.50
❑	44 Mark Brunell	2.00	.75
❑	45 Jimmy Smith	1.25	.50
❑	46 Fred Taylor	2.00	.75
❑	47 Tony Gonzalez	1.25	.50
❑	48 Trent Green	1.25	.50
❑	49 Priest Holmes	2.50	1.00
❑	50 Chris Chambers	2.00	.75
❑	51 Jay Fiedler	1.25	.50
❑	52 Ricky Williams	2.00	.75
❑	53 Michael Bennett	1.25	.50
❑	54 Daunte Culpepper	2.00	.75
❑	55 Randy Moss	4.00	1.50
❑	56 Tom Brady	5.00	2.00
❑	57 Troy Brown	1.25	.50
❑	58 Antowain Smith	1.25	.50
❑	59 Aaron Brooks	2.00	.75
❑	60 Joe Horn	1.25	.50
❑	61 Deuce McAllister	2.50	1.00
❑	62 Tiki Barber	2.00	.75
❑	63 Kerry Collins	1.25	.50
❑	64 Ron Dayne	1.25	.50
❑	65 Wayne Chrebet	1.25	.50
❑	66 Curtis Martin	2.00	.75
❑	67 Vinny Testaverde	1.25	.50
❑	68 Tim Brown	2.00	.75
❑	69 Rich Gannon	2.00	.75
❑	70 Charlie Garner	1.25	.50
❑	71 Jerry Rice	4.00	1.50
❑	72 Correll Buckhalter	1.25	.50
❑	73 Donovan McNabb	2.50	1.00
❑	74 Duce Staley	2.00	.75
❑	75 Jerome Bettis	2.00	.75
❑	76 Kordell Stewart	1.25	.50
❑	77 Hines Ward	2.00	.75
❑	78 Isaac Bruce	2.00	.75
❑	79 Marshall Faulk	2.00	.75
❑	80 Torry Holt	2.00	.75
❑	81 Kurt Warner	2.00	.75
❑	82 Drew Brees	2.00	.75
❑	83 Tim Dwight	1.25	.50
❑	84 Doug Flutie	2.00	.75
❑	85 LaDainian Tomlinson	3.00	1.25
❑	86 Jeff Garcia	2.00	.75
❑	87 Garrison Hearst	1.25	.50
❑	88 Terrell Owens	2.00	.75
❑	89 Shaun Alexander	2.50	1.00
❑	90 Trent Dilfer	1.25	.50
❑	91 Darrell Jackson	1.25	.50
❑	92 Mike Alstott	2.00	.75
❑	93 Brad Johnson	1.25	.50
❑	94 Keyshawn Johnson	2.00	.75
❑	95 Eddie George	2.00	.75
❑	96 Derrick Mason	1.25	.50
❑	97 Steve McNair	2.00	.75
❑	98 Stephen Davis	1.25	.50
❑	99 Rod Gardner	1.25	.50
❑	100 Jacquez Green	.75	.30
❑	101 Damien Anderson RC	6.00	2.50
❑	102 Ladell Betts RC	8.00	3.00
❑	103 Antonio Bryant RC	8.00	3.00
❑	104 Reche Caldwell RC	8.00	3.00
❑	105 Kelly Campbell RC	6.00	2.50
❑	106 David Carr RC	20.00	7.50
❑	107 Rohan Davey RC	8.00	3.00
❑	108 Andre Davis RC	6.00	2.50
❑	109 T.J. Duckett RC	12.00	5.00
❑	110 DeShaun Foster RC	8.00	3.00
❑	111 David Garrard RC	8.00	3.00
❑	112 Lamar Gordon RC	8.00	3.00
❑	113 William Green RC	8.00	3.00
❑	114 Joey Harrington RC	20.00	7.50
❑	115 Kurt Kittner RC	6.00	2.50
❑	116 Ashley Lelie RC	15.00	6.00
❑	117 Josh McCown RC	10.00	4.00
❑	118 Clinton Portis RC	25.00	10.00
❑	119 Patrick Ramsey RC	10.00	4.00
❑	120 Antwaan Randle El RC	12.00	5.00
❑	121 Josh Reed RC	8.00	3.00
❑	122 Luke Staley RC	6.00	2.50
❑	123 Donte Stallworth RC	15.00	6.00
❑	124 Marquise Walker RC	6.00	2.50
❑	125 Brian Westbrook RC	12.00	5.00
❑	126 Jason McAddley RC	6.00	2.50
❑	127 Josh Scobey RC	8.00	3.00
❑	128 Kahlil Hill RC	6.00	2.50
❑	129 Ron Johnson RC	6.00	2.50
❑	130 Julius Peppers RC	15.00	6.00
❑	131 Adrian Peterson RC	8.00	3.00
❑	132 Woody Dantzler RC	6.00	2.50
❑	133 Roy Williams RC	20.00	10.00
❑	134 Najeh Davenport RC	8.00	3.00
❑	135 Javon Walker RC	15.00	6.00
❑	136 Jabar Gaffney RC	8.00	3.00
❑	137 John Henderson RC	8.00	3.00
❑	138 Leonard Henry RC	6.00	2.50
❑	139 Daniel Graham RC	8.00	3.00
❑	140 Jeremy Shockey RC	25.00	10.00
❑	141 Ronald Curry RC	8.00	3.00
❑	142 Napoleon Harris RC	8.00	3.00
❑	143 Freddie Milons RC	6.00	2.50
❑	144 Lito Sheppard RC	8.00	3.00
❑	145 Eric Crouch RC	8.00	3.00
❑	146 Robert Thomas RC	8.00	3.00
❑	147 Quentin Jammer RC	8.00	3.00
❑	148 Maurice Morris RC	8.00	3.00
❑	149 Travis Stephens RC	6.00	2.50
❑	150 Cliff Russell RC	6.00	2.50
❑	151 Dameon Hunter RC	4.00	1.50
❑	152 Javin Hunter RC	4.00	1.50
❑	153 Tellis Redmon RC	6.00	2.50
❑	154 Chester Taylor RC	8.00	3.00
❑	155 Randy Fasani RC	6.00	2.50
❑	156 Jamin Elliott RC	4.00	1.50
❑	157 Chad Hutchinson RC	6.00	2.50
❑	158 Eddie Drummond RC	6.00	2.50
❑	159 Craig Nall RC	8.00	3.00
❑	160 Jarrod Baxter RC	6.00	2.50
❑	161 Jonathan Wells RC	8.00	3.00
❑	162 Shaun Hill RC	8.00	3.00
❑	163 Deion Branch RC	15.00	6.00
❑	164 J.T. O'Sullivan RC	6.00	2.50
❑	165 Tim Carter RC	6.00	2.50
❑	166 Daryl Jones RC	6.00	2.50
❑	167 Lee Mays RC	10.00	4.00
❑	168 Seth Burford RC	6.00	2.50
❑	169 Brandon Doman RC	6.00	2.50
❑	170 Jerramy Stevens RC	8.00	3.00

1998 Aurora

❑	COMPLETE SET (200)	60.00	30.00
❑	1 Rob Moore	.60	.25
❑	2 Jake Plummer	1.00	.40
❑	3 Frank Sanders	.60	.25
❑	4 Eric Swann	.40	.15
❑	5 Jamal Anderson	1.00	.40
❑	6 Chris Chandler	.60	.25
❑	7 Byron Hanspard	.40	.15
❑	8 Terance Mathis	.60	.25
❑	9 O.J. Santiago	.40	.15
❑	10 Chuck Smith	.40	.15
❑	11 Jessie Tuggle	.40	.15
❑	12 Jay Graham	.40	.15
❑	13 Jim Harbaugh	.60	.25
❑	14 Michael Jackson	.40	.15
❑	15 Pat Johnson RC	1.50	.60
❑	16 Jermaine Lewis	.60	.25

❑ 17 Errict Rhett	.60	.25
❑ 18 Rod Woodson	.60	.25
❑ 19 Quinn Early	.40	.15
❑ 20 Andre Reed	.60	.25
❑ 21 Antowain Smith	1.00	.40
❑ 22 Bruce Smith	.60	.25
❑ 23 Thurman Thomas	1.00	.40
❑ 24 Ted Washington	.40	.15
❑ 25 Michael Bates	.40	.15
❑ 26 Rae Carruth	.40	.15
❑ 27 Kerry Collins	.60	.25
❑ 28 Fred Lane	.40	.15
❑ 29 Wesley Walls	.60	.25
❑ 30 Edgar Bennett	.40	.15
❑ 31 Curtis Conway	.60	.25
❑ 32 Curtis Enis RC	1.00	.40
❑ 33 Walt Harris	.40	.15
❑ 34 Erik Kramer	.40	.15
❑ 35 Barry Minter	.40	.15
❑ 36 Jeff Blake	.60	.25
❑ 37 Corey Dillon	1.00	.40
❑ 38 Carl Pickens	.60	.25
❑ 39 Darnay Scott	.60	.25
❑ 40 Troy Aikman	2.00	.75
❑ 41 Michael Irvin	1.00	.40
❑ 42 Deion Sanders	1.00	.40
❑ 43 Emmitt Smith	3.00	1.50
❑ 44 Chris Warren	.60	.25
❑ 45 Terrell Davis	1.00	.40
❑ 46 John Elway	4.00	1.50
❑ 47 Brian Griese RC	4.00	1.50
❑ 48 Ed McCaffrey	.60	.25
❑ 49 John Mobley	.40	.15
❑ 50 Shannon Sharpe	.60	.25
❑ 51 Neil Smith	.60	.25
❑ 52 Rod Smith WR	.60	.25
❑ 53 Stephen Boyd	.40	.15
❑ 54 Scott Mitchell	.60	.25
❑ 55 Herman Moore	.60	.25
❑ 56 Johnnie Morton	.60	.25
❑ 57 Robert Porcher	.40	.15
❑ 58 Barry Sanders	3.00	1.25
❑ 59 Robert Brooks	.60	.25
❑ 60 Mark Chmura	.60	.25
❑ 61 Brett Favre	4.00	2.00
❑ 62 Antonio Freeman	1.00	.40
❑ 63 Vonnie Holliday RC	1.50	.60
❑ 64 Dorsey Levens	1.00	.40
❑ 65 Ross Verba	.40	.15
❑ 66 Reggie White	1.00	.40
❑ 67 Elijah Alexander	.40	.15
❑ 68 Ken Dilger	.40	.15
❑ 69 Marshall Faulk	1.25	.50
❑ 70 Marvin Harrison	1.00	.40
❑ 71 Peyton Manning RC	20.00	7.50
❑ 72 Bryan Barker	.40	.15
❑ 73 Mark Brunell	1.00	.40
❑ 74 Keenan McCardell	.60	.25
❑ 75 Jimmy Smith	.60	.25
❑ 76 James Stewart	.60	.25
❑ 77 Derrick Alexander WR	.60	.25
❑ 78 Kimble Anders	.60	.25
❑ 79 Donnell Bennett	.40	.15
❑ 80 Elvis Grbac	.60	.25
❑ 81 Andre Rison	.60	.25
❑ 82 Rashaan Shehee RC	1.50	.60
❑ 83 Derrick Thomas	1.00	.40
❑ 84 Karim Abdul-Jabbar	1.00	.40
❑ 85 Trace Armstrong	.40	.15
❑ 86 Charles Jordan	.40	.15
❑ 87 Dan Marino	4.00	1.50
❑ 88 O.J. McDuffie	.60	.25
❑ 89 Zach Thomas	1.00	.40
❑ 90 Cris Carter	1.00	.40
❑ 91 Charles Evans	.40	.15
❑ 92 Andrew Glover	.40	.15
❑ 93 Brad Johnson	1.00	.40
❑ 94 Randy Moss RC	12.00	5.00
❑ 95 John Randle	.60	.25
❑ 96 Jake Reed	.60	.25
❑ 97 Robert Smith	1.00	.40
❑ 98 Bruce Armstrong	.40	.15
❑ 99 Drew Bledsoe	1.50	.60
❑ 100 Ben Coates	.60	.25
❑ 101 Robert Edwards RC	1.50	.60
❑ 102 Terry Glenn	1.00	.40
❑ 103 Willie McGinest	.40	.15
❑ 104 Sedrick Shaw	.40	.15
❑ 105 Tony Simmons RC	1.50	.60
❑ 106 Chris Slade	.40	.15
❑ 107 Billy Joe Hobert	.40	.15
❑ 108 Qadry Ismail	.60	.25
❑ 109 Heath Shuler	.40	.15
❑ 110 Lamar Smith	.60	.25
❑ 111 Ray Zellars	.40	.15
❑ 112 Tiki Barber	1.00	.40
❑ 113 Chris Calloway	.40	.15
❑ 114 Ike Hilliard	.60	.25
❑ 115 Joe Jurevicius RC	2.00	.75
❑ 116 Danny Kanell	.60	.25
❑ 117 Amani Toomer	.60	.25
❑ 118 Charles Way	.40	.15
❑ 119 Tyrone Wheatley	.60	.25
❑ 120 Wayne Chrebet	1.00	.40
❑ 121 John Elliott	.40	.15
❑ 122 Glenn Foley	.60	.25
❑ 123 Scott Frost RC	.40	.15
❑ 124 Aaron Glenn	.40	.15
❑ 125 Keyshawn Johnson	1.00	.40
❑ 126 Curtis Martin	1.00	.40
❑ 127 Vinny Testaverde	.60	.25
❑ 128 Tim Brown	1.00	.40
❑ 129 Rickey Dudley	.40	.15
❑ 130 Jeff George	.60	.25
❑ 131 James Jett	.60	.25
❑ 132 Napoleon Kaufman	1.00	.40
❑ 133 Darrell Russell	.40	.15
❑ 134 Charles Woodson RC	2.50	1.00
❑ 135 James Darling RC	.40	.15
❑ 136 Koy Detmer	1.00	.40
❑ 137 Irving Fryar	.60	.25
❑ 138 Charlie Garner	.60	.25
❑ 139 Bobby Hoying	.60	.25
❑ 140 Chad Lewis	.60	.25
❑ 141 Duce Staley	1.25	.50
❑ 142 Kevin Turner	.40	.15
❑ 143 Jerome Bettis	1.00	.40
❑ 144 Will Blackwell	.40	.15
❑ 145 Mark Bruener	.40	.15
❑ 146 Dermontti Dawson	.40	.15
❑ 147 Charles Johnson	.40	.15
❑ 148 Levon Kirkland	.40	.15
❑ 149 Tim Lester	.40	.15
❑ 150 Kordell Stewart	1.00	.40
❑ 151 Tony Banks	.60	.25
❑ 152 Isaac Bruce	1.00	.40
❑ 153 Robert Holcombe RC	1.50	.60
❑ 154 Eddie Kennison	.60	.25
❑ 155 Amp Lee	.40	.15
❑ 156 Jerald Moore	.40	.15
❑ 157 Charlie Jones	.40	.15
❑ 158 Freddie Jones	.40	.15
❑ 159 Ryan Leaf RC	2.00	.75
❑ 160 Natrone Means	.60	.25
❑ 161 Junior Seau	1.00	.40
❑ 162 Bryan Still	.40	.15
❑ 163 Marc Edwards	.40	.15
❑ 164 Merton Hanks	.40	.15
❑ 165 Garrison Hearst	1.00	.40
❑ 166 Terrell Owens	1.00	.40
❑ 167 Jerry Rice	2.00	.75
❑ 168 J.J. Stokes	.60	.25
❑ 169 Bryant Young	.40	.15
❑ 170 Steve Young	1.25	.50
❑ 171 Chad Brown	.40	.15
❑ 172 Joey Galloway	.60	.25
❑ 173 Walter Jones	.40	.15
❑ 174 Cortez Kennedy	.40	.15
❑ 175 Jon Kitna	1.00	.40
❑ 176 James McKnight	1.00	.40
❑ 177 Warren Moon	1.00	.40
❑ 178 Michael Sinclair	.40	.15
❑ 179 Mike Alstott	1.00	.40
❑ 180 Reidel Anthony	.60	.25
❑ 181 Derrick Brooks	1.00	.40
❑ 182 Trent Dilfer	1.00	.40
❑ 183 Warrick Dunn	1.00	.40
❑ 184 Hardy Nickerson	.40	.15
❑ 185 Warren Sapp	.60	.25
❑ 186 Willie Davis	.40	.15
❑ 187 Eddie George	1.00	.40
❑ 188 Steve McNair	1.00	.40
❑ 189 Jon Runyan	.40	.15
❑ 190 Chris Sanders	.40	.15
❑ 191 Frank Wycheck	.40	.15
❑ 192 Stephen Alexander RC	1.50	.60
❑ 193 Terry Allen	1.00	.40
❑ 194 Stephen Davis	.40	.15
❑ 195 Cris Dishman	.40	.15
❑ 196 Gus Frerotte	.40	.15
❑ 197 Darrell Green	.60	.25
❑ 198 Skip Hicks RC	1.50	.60
❑ 199 Dana Stubblefield	.40	.15
❑ 200 Michael Westbrook	.60	.25
❑ S1 Warrick Dunn Sample	1.00	.40

1999 Aurora

❑ COMPLETE SET (150)	40.00	15.00
❑ 1 David Boston RC	1.50	.60
❑ 2 Larry Centers	.25	.08
❑ 3 Rob Moore	.40	.15
❑ 4 Adrian Murrell	.40	.15
❑ 5 Jake Plummer	.40	.15
❑ 6 Jamal Anderson	.60	.25
❑ 7 Chris Chandler	.40	.15
❑ 8 Tim Dwight	.60	.25
❑ 9 Terance Mathis	.40	.15
❑ 10 O.J. Santiago	.25	.08
❑ 11 Priest Holmes	1.00	.40
❑ 12 Michael Jackson	.25	.08
❑ 13 Jermaine Lewis	.40	.15
❑ 14 Ray Lewis	.60	.25
❑ 15 Michael McCrary	.25	.08
❑ 16 Doug Flutie	.60	.25
❑ 17 Eric Moulds	.60	.25
❑ 18 Peerless Price RC	1.50	.60
❑ 19 Antowain Smith	.60	.25
❑ 20 Bruce Smith	.40	.15
❑ 21 Steve Beuerlein	.40	.15
❑ 22 Tim Biakabutuka	.40	.15
❑ 23 Kevin Greene	.25	.08
❑ 24 Muhsin Muhammad	.40	.15
❑ 25 Wesley Walls	.40	.15
❑ 26 Curtis Conway	.40	.15
❑ 27 Bobby Engram	.40	.15
❑ 28 Curtis Enis	.25	.08
❑ 29 Erik Kramer	.25	.08
❑ 30 Cade McNown RC	1.25	.50
❑ 31 Jeff Blake	.40	.15
❑ 32 Corey Dillon	.60	.25
❑ 33 Carl Pickens	.40	.15
❑ 34 Darnay Scott	.25	.08
❑ 35 Akili Smith RC	1.25	.50
❑ 36 Tim Couch RC	1.50	.60

❑ 37 Ty Detmer .40 .15
❑ 38 Kevin Johnson RC 1.50 .60
❑ 39 Terry Kirby .25 .08
❑ 40 Troy Aikman 1.25 .50
❑ 41 Michael Irvin .40 .15
❑ 42 Rocket Ismail .40 .15
❑ 43 Deion Sanders .60 .25
❑ 44 Emmitt Smith 1.25 .50
❑ 45 Bubby Brister .25 .08
❑ 46 Terrell Davis .60 .25
❑ 47 Brian Griese .60 .25
❑ 48 Ed McCaffrey .40 .15
❑ 49 Shannon Sharpe .40 .15
❑ 50 Rod Smith .40 .15
❑ 51 Charlie Batch .60 .25
❑ 52 Sedrick Irvin RC .25 .08
❑ 53 Herman Moore .40 .15
❑ 54 Johnnie Morton .40 .15
❑ 55 Barry Sanders 2.00 .75
❑ 56 Robert Brooks .40 .15
❑ 57 Brett Favre 2.00 .75
❑ 58 Antonio Freeman .60 .25
❑ 59 Dorsey Levens .60 .25
❑ 60 Derrick Mayes .25 .08
❑ 61 Marvin Harrison .60 .25
❑ 62 Edgerrin James RC 6.00 2.50
❑ 63 Peyton Manning 2.00 .75
❑ 64 Jerome Pathon .25 .08
❑ 65 Tavian Banks .25 .08
❑ 66 Mark Brunell .60 .25
❑ 67 Keenan McCardell .40 .15
❑ 68 Jimmy Smith .40 .15
❑ 69 Fred Taylor .60 .25
❑ 70 Derrick Alexander .40 .15
❑ 71 Kimble Anders .40 .15
❑ 72 Mike Cloud RC 1.25 .50
❑ 73 Elvis Grbac .40 .15
❑ 74 Andre Rison .40 .15
❑ 75 Karim Abdul-Jabbar .40 .15
❑ 76 James Johnson RC 1.25 .50
❑ 77 Dan Marino 2.00 .75
❑ 78 O.J. McDuffie .40 .15
❑ 79 Lamar Thomas .25 .08
❑ 80 Cris Carter .60 .25
❑ 81 Daunte Culpepper RC 6.00 2.50
❑ 82 Randall Cunningham .60 .25
❑ 83 Randy Moss 1.50 .60
❑ 84 John Randle .40 .15
❑ 85 Robert Smith .60 .25
❑ 86 Drew Bledsoe .75 .30
❑ 87 Ben Coates .40 .15
❑ 88 Kevin Faulk RC 1.50 .60
❑ 89 Terry Glenn .60 .25
❑ 90 Ty Law .40 .15
❑ 91 Cam Cleeland .25 .08
❑ 92 Andre Hastings .25 .08
❑ 93 Billy Joe Hobert .25 .08
❑ 94 Ricky Williams RC 3.00 1.25
❑ 95 Tiki Barber .60 .25
❑ 96 Kent Graham .25 .08
❑ 97 Ike Hilliard .25 .08
❑ 98 Charles Way .25 .08
❑ 99 Wayne Chrebet .40 .15
❑ 100 Keyshawn Johnson .60 .25
❑ 101 Curtis Martin .60 .25
❑ 102 Vinny Testaverde .40 .15
❑ 103 Dedric Ward .25 .08
❑ 104 Tim Brown .60 .25
❑ 105 Rickey Dudley .25 .08
❑ 106 James Jett .40 .15
❑ 107 Napoleon Kaufman .60 .25
❑ 108 Charles Woodson .60 .25
❑ 109 Jeff Graham .25 .08
❑ 110 Charles Johnson .25 .08
❑ 111 Donovan McNabb RC 8.00 3.00
❑ 112 Duce Staley .60 .25
❑ 113 Jerome Bettis .60 .25
❑ 114 Troy Edwards RC 1.25 .50
❑ 115 Courtney Hawkins .25 .08
❑ 116 Kordell Stewart .40 .15
❑ 117 Amos Zereoue RC 1.50 .60
❑ 118 Isaac Bruce .60 .25
❑ 119 Marshall Faulk .75 .30
❑ 120 Joe Germaine RC 1.25 .50
❑ 121 Torry Holt RC 4.00 1.50
❑ 122 Amp Lee .25 .08
❑ 123 Charlie Jones .25 .08
❑ 124 Ryan Leaf .60 .25
❑ 125 Natrone Means .40 .15
❑ 126 Junior Seau .60 .25
❑ 127 Garrison Hearst .40 .15
❑ 128 Terrell Owens .60 .25
❑ 129 Jerry Rice 1.25 .50
❑ 130 J.J. Stokes .40 .15
❑ 131 Steve Young .75 .30
❑ 132 Chad Brown .25 .08
❑ 133 Joey Galloway .40 .15
❑ 134 Brock Huard RC 1.50 .60
❑ 135 Jon Kitna .60 .25
❑ 136 Ricky Watters .40 .15
❑ 137 Mike Alstott .60 .25
❑ 138 Reidel Anthony .40 .15
❑ 139 Trent Dilfer .40 .15
❑ 140 Warrick Dunn .60 .25
❑ 141 Jacquez Green .25 .08
❑ 142 Shaun King RC 1.25 .50
❑ 143 Eddie George .60 .25
❑ 144 Steve McNair .60 .25
❑ 145 Yancey Thigpen .25 .08
❑ 146 Frank Wycheck .25 .08
❑ 147 Champ Bailey RC 2.00 .75
❑ 148 Skip Hicks .25 .08
❑ 149 Brad Johnson .60 .25
❑ 150 Michael Westbrook .40 .15
❑ AU1 T.Owens AUTO/197 40.00 20.00

2000 Aurora

❑ COMPLETE SET (150) 30.00 12.50
❑ 1 David Boston .60 .25
❑ 2 Thomas Jones RC 1.50 .60
❑ 3 Rob Moore .40 .15
❑ 4 Jake Plummer .40 .15
❑ 5 Frank Sanders .40 .15
❑ 6 Jamal Anderson .60 .25
❑ 7 Chris Chandler .40 .15
❑ 8 Tim Dwight .60 .25
❑ 9 Doug Johnson RC 1.00 .40
❑ 10 Tony Banks .40 .15
❑ 11 Qadry Ismail .40 .15
❑ 12 Jamal Lewis RC 2.50 1.00
❑ 13 Chris Redman RC .75 .30
❑ 14 Travis Taylor RC 1.00 .40
❑ 15 Doug Flutie .60 .25
❑ 16 Rob Johnson .40 .15
❑ 17 Eric Moulds .60 .25
❑ 18 Peerless Price .40 .15
❑ 19 Antowain Smith .40 .15
❑ 20 Steve Beuerlein .40 .15
❑ 21 Tim Biakabutuka .40 .15
❑ 22 Patrick Jeffers .60 .25
❑ 23 Muhsin Muhammad .40 .15
❑ 24 Curtis Enis .25 .08
❑ 25 Cade McNown .25 .08
❑ 26 Marcus Robinson .60 .25
❑ 27 Dez White RC 1.00 .40
❑ 28 Corey Dillon .60 .25
❑ 29 Ron Dugans RC .75 .30
❑ 30 Darnay Scott .40 .15
❑ 31 Akili Smith .25 .08
❑ 32 Peter Warrick RC 1.00 .40
❑ 33 Tim Couch .40 .15
❑ 34 JaJuan Dawson RC .75 .30
❑ 35 Kevin Johnson .60 .25
❑ 36 Dennis Northcutt RC 1.00 .40
❑ 37 Travis Prentice RC 1.00 .40
❑ 38 Troy Aikman 1.25 .50
❑ 39 Rocket Ismail .40 .15
❑ 40 Emmitt Smith 1.25 .50
❑ 41 Jason Tucker .25 .08
❑ 42 Terrell Davis .60 .25
❑ 43 Olandis Gary .60 .25
❑ 44 Brian Griese .60 .25
❑ 45 Ed McCaffrey .60 .25
❑ 46 Rod Smith .40 .15
❑ 47 Charlie Batch .60 .25
❑ 48 Germane Crowell .25 .08
❑ 49 Reuben Droughns RC 1.25 .50
❑ 50 Herman Moore .40 .15
❑ 51 Barry Sanders 1.50 .60
❑ 52 Brett Favre 2.00 .75
❑ 53 Bubba Franks RC 1.00 .40
❑ 54 Antonio Freeman .60 .25
❑ 55 Dorsey Levens .40 .15
❑ 56 Bill Schroeder .40 .15
❑ 57 Marvin Harrison .60 .25
❑ 58 Edgerrin James 1.00 .40
❑ 59 Peyton Manning 1.50 .60
❑ 60 Terrence Wilkins .25 .08
❑ 61 Mark Brunell .60 .25
❑ 62 Keenan McCardell .40 .15
❑ 63 Jimmy Smith .40 .15
❑ 64 R.Jay Soward RC .75 .30
❑ 65 Shyrone Stith RC 1.00 .40
❑ 66 Fred Taylor .60 .25
❑ 67 Derrick Alexander .40 .15
❑ 68 Donnell Bennett .25 .08
❑ 69 Tony Gonzalez .40 .15
❑ 70 Elvis Grbac .40 .15
❑ 71 Sylvester Morris RC .75 .30
❑ 72 Damon Huard .60 .25
❑ 73 James Johnson .25 .08
❑ 74 Dan Marino 2.00 .75
❑ 75 Tony Martin .40 .15
❑ 76 O.J. McDuffie .40 .15
❑ 77 Quinton Spotwood RC .75 .30
❑ 78 Cris Carter .60 .25
❑ 79 Daunte Culpepper .75 .30
❑ 80 Randy Moss 1.25 .50
❑ 81 Robert Smith .60 .25
❑ 82 Troy Walters RC 1.00 .40
❑ 83 Drew Bledsoe .75 .30
❑ 84 Tom Brady RC 15.00 7.50
❑ 85 Kevin Faulk .40 .15
❑ 86 Terry Glenn .40 .15
❑ 87 J.R. Redmond RC .75 .30
❑ 88 Marc Bulger RC 2.00 .75
❑ 89 Sherrod Gideon RC .75 .30
❑ 90 Keith Poole .25 .08
❑ 91 Ricky Williams .60 .25
❑ 92 Kerry Collins .40 .15
❑ 93 Ron Dayne RC 1.00 .40
❑ 94 Ike Hilliard .40 .15
❑ 95 Amani Toomer .25 .08
❑ 96 Wayne Chrebet .40 .15
❑ 97 Laveranues Coles RC 1.25 .50
❑ 98 Curtis Martin .60 .25
❑ 99 Chad Pennington RC 2.50 1.00
❑ 100 Vinny Testaverde .40 .15
❑ 101 Tim Brown .60 .25
❑ 102 Rich Gannon .60 .25
❑ 103 Napoleon Kaufman .40 .15
❑ 104 Jerry Porter RC 1.25 .50
❑ 105 Tyrone Wheatley .40 .15
❑ 106 Charles Johnson .40 .15

❑	107	Donovan McNabb	1.00	.40
❑	108	Todd Pinkston RC	1.00	.40
❑	109	Duce Staley	.60	.25
❑	110	Jerome Bettis	.60	.25
❑	111	Plaxico Burress RC	2.00	.75
❑	112	Troy Edwards	.25	.08
❑	113	Richard Huntley	.25	.08
❑	114	Tee Martin RC	1.00	.40
❑	115	Kordell Stewart	.40	.15
❑	116	Isaac Bruce	.60	.25
❑	117	Trung Canidate RC	.75	.30
❑	118	Marshall Faulk	.75	.30
❑	119	Torry Holt	.60	.25
❑	120	Kurt Warner	1.25	.50
❑	121	Jermaine Fazande	.25	.08
❑	122	Trevor Gaylor RC	.75	.30
❑	123	Jim Harbaugh	.40	.15
❑	124	Junior Seau	.60	.25
❑	125	Giovanni Carmazzi RC	.75	.30
❑	126	Charlie Garner	.40	.15
❑	127	Terrell Owens	.60	.25
❑	128	Jerry Rice	1.25	.50
❑	129	J.J. Stokes	.40	.15
❑	130	Steve Young	.75	.30
❑	131	Shaun Alexander RC	5.00	2.00
❑	132	Christian Fauria	.25	.08
❑	133	Jon Kitna	.60	.25
❑	134	Derrick Mayes	.40	.15
❑	135	Ricky Watters	.40	.15
❑	136	Mike Alstott	.60	.25
❑	137	Warrick Dunn	.60	.25
❑	138	Jacquez Green	.25	.08
❑	139	Joe Hamilton RC	.75	.30
❑	140	Shaun King	.25	.08
❑	141	Eddie George	.60	.25
❑	142	Jevon Kearse	.60	.25
❑	143	Steve McNair	.60	.25
❑	144	Yancey Thigpen	.25	.08
❑	145	Frank Wycheck	.25	.08
❑	146	Albert Connell	.25	.08
❑	147	Stephen Davis	.60	.25
❑	148	Todd Husak RC	1.00	.40
❑	149	Brad Johnson	.60	.25
❑	150	Michael Westbrook	.40	.15
❑	S1	Jon Kitna Sample	1.00	.40

2004 Bazooka

❑		COMPLETE SET (220)	50.00	20.00
❑	1	Peyton Manning	1.25	.50
❑	2	Rod Gardner	.50	.20
❑	3	Marc Bulger	.75	.30
❑	4	Champ Bailey	.50	.20
❑	5	Moe Williams	.40	.15
❑	6	Andre' Davis	.40	.15
❑	7	Corey Dillon	.50	.20
❑	8	Trent Green	.50	.20
❑	9	Daunte Culpepper	.75	.30
❑	10	Chad Pennington	.75	.30
❑	11	Hines Ward	.75	.30
❑	12	Tim Brown	.75	.30
❑	13	Jerome Pathon	.40	.15
❑	14	Drew Brees	.75	.30
❑	15	Eddie George	.50	.20
❑	16	Duce Staley	.50	.20
❑	17	Marques Tuiasosopo	.50	.20
❑	18	Willis McGahee	.75	.30
❑	19	T.J. Duckett	.50	.20
❑	20	Brian Urlacher	1.00	.40
❑	21	Ashley Lelie	.50	.20
❑	22	Robert Ferguson	.40	.15
❑	23	Tai Streets	.40	.15
❑	24	Junior Seau	.75	.30
❑	25	Priest Holmes	1.00	.40
❑	26	Ty Law	.50	.20
❑	27	Correll Buckhalter	.50	.20
❑	28	Plaxico Burress	.50	.20
❑	29	Brad Johnson	.50	.20
❑	30	Shaun Alexander	.75	.30
❑	31	Mark Brunell	.50	.20
❑	32	Julian Peterson	.40	.15
❑	33	Marcel Shipp	.50	.20
❑	34	Kyle Boller	.75	.30
❑	35	Rudi Johnson	.50	.20
❑	36	Quincy Carter	.50	.20
❑	37	Jabar Gaffney	.50	.20
❑	38	Reggie Wayne	.50	.20
❑	39	Deion Branch	.75	.30
❑	40	Terrell Owens	.75	.30
❑	41	Chris Brown	.75	.30
❑	42	Bobby Engram	.40	.15
❑	43	Josh Reed	.40	.15
❑	44	Thomas Jones	.50	.20
❑	45	Stephen Davis	.50	.20
❑	46	Mike Anderson	.50	.20
❑	47	Javon Walker	.50	.20
❑	48	Edgerrin James	.75	.30
❑	49	Randy McMichael	.40	.15
❑	50	Deuce McAllister	.75	.30
❑	51	Nate Burleson	.75	.30
❑	52	Jevon Kearse	.50	.20
❑	53	Jay Fiedler	.40	.15
❑	54	Patrick Ramsey	.50	.20
❑	55	Brian Westbrook	.50	.20
❑	56	Tyrone Calico	.50	.20
❑	57	Alge Crumpler	.50	.20
❑	58	Josh McCown	.50	.20
❑	59	Quincy Morgan	.50	.20
❑	60	Jeff Garcia	.75	.30
❑	61	Garrison Hearst	.50	.20
❑	62	Chad Johnson	.75	.30
❑	63	Byron Leftwich	1.00	.40
❑	64	Donald Driver	.50	.20
❑	65	Ricky Williams	.75	.30
❑	66	Todd Pinkston	.40	.15
❑	67	Amani Toomer	.50	.20
❑	68	David Givens	.50	.20
❑	69	Jerome Bettis	.75	.30
❑	70	Derrick Mason	.50	.20
❑	71	Darrell Jackson	.50	.20
❑	72	Kassim Osgood	.40	.15
❑	73	Todd Heap	.50	.20
❑	74	Warrick Dunn	.50	.20
❑	75	Brett Favre	2.00	.75
❑	76	Chris Chambers	.50	.20
❑	77	Fred Taylor	.50	.20
❑	78	Charles Rogers	.50	.20
❑	79	Onterrio Smith	.50	.20
❑	80	Joe Horn	.50	.20
❑	81	Justin McCareins	.40	.15
❑	82	Ike Hilliard	.40	.15
❑	83	Kevan Barlow	.50	.20
❑	84	Charlie Garner	.50	.20
❑	85	Anquan Boldin	.75	.30
❑	86	Anthony Thomas	.50	.20
❑	87	Julius Peppers	.75	.30
❑	88	Dat Nguyen	.40	.15
❑	89	Peerless Price	.50	.20
❑	90	Randy Moss	1.00	.40
❑	91	Jamie Sharper	.40	.15
❑	92	Travis Henry	.50	.20
❑	93	Terrell Suggs	.50	.20
❑	94	Joey Galloway	.50	.20
❑	95	Torry Holt	.75	.30
❑	96	Freddie Mitchell	.50	.20
❑	97	Jerry Porter	.50	.20
❑	98	Dwight Freeney	.50	.20
❑	99	Joey Harrington	.75	.30
❑	100	Michael Vick	1.50	.60
❑	101	Kelley Washington	.40	.15
❑	102	Marty Booker	.50	.20
❑	103	Tim Rattay	.40	.15
❑	104	Derrick Brooks	.50	.20
❑	105	Laveranues Coles	.50	.20
❑	106	Ray Lewis	.75	.30
❑	107	Jon Kitna	.50	.20
❑	108	Terry Glenn	.40	.15
❑	109	Steve Smith	.75	.30
❑	110	Ahman Green	.75	.30
❑	111	Andre Johnson	.75	.30
❑	112	Dallas Clark	.50	.20
❑	113	Kevin Faulk	.40	.15
❑	114	Michael Bennett	.50	.20
❑	115	Tony Gonzalez	.50	.20
❑	116	Michael Strahan	.50	.20
❑	117	Tommy Maddox	.50	.20
❑	118	Isaac Bruce	.50	.20
❑	119	Brandon Lloyd	.50	.20
❑	120	Steve McNair	.75	.30
❑	121	Keith Brooking	.40	.15
❑	122	Drew Bledsoe	.75	.30
❑	123	Peter Warrick	.50	.20
❑	124	Antonio Bryant	.50	.20
❑	125	Clinton Portis	.75	.30
❑	126	Kelly Holcomb	.50	.20
❑	127	Jake Delhomme	.75	.30
❑	128	Rod Smith	.50	.20
❑	129	Lee Suggs	.75	.30
❑	130	Domanick Davis	.75	.30
❑	131	Carson Palmer	1.00	.40
❑	132	Kerry Collins	.50	.20
❑	133	Teyo Johnson	.40	.15
❑	134	Curtis Martin	.75	.30
❑	135	Matt Hasselbeck	.50	.20
❑	136	Cedrick Wilson	.40	.15
❑	137	Eric Moulds	.50	.20
❑	138	Keyshawn Johnson	.50	.20
❑	139	Dante Hall	.75	.30
❑	140	Jamal Lewis	.75	.30
❑	141	Kelly Campbell	.40	.15
❑	142	Jeremy Shockey	.75	.30
❑	143	Jerry Rice	1.50	.60
❑	144	Kurt Warner	.75	.30
❑	145	Jake Plummer	.50	.20
❑	146	Keenan McCardell	.40	.15
❑	147	Jimmy Smith	.50	.20
❑	148	Zach Thomas	.75	.30
❑	149	Eddie Kennison	.40	.15
❑	150	Tom Brady	2.00	.75
❑	151	Donte' Stallworth	.50	.20
❑	152	John Abraham	.40	.15
❑	153	Koren Robinson	.50	.20
❑	154	Rex Grossman	.75	.30
❑	155	Donovan McNabb	1.00	.40
❑	156	David Carr	.75	.30
❑	157	David Boston	.50	.20
❑	158	Tiki Barber	.75	.30
❑	159	Santana Moss	.50	.20
❑	160	LaDainian Tomlinson	1.25	.50
❑	161	Justin Fargas	.50	.20
❑	162	Troy Brown	.50	.20
❑	163	Marshall Faulk	.75	.30
❑	164	Aaron Brooks	.50	.20
❑	165	Marvin Harrison	.75	.30
❑	166	Kevin Jones RC	5.00	2.00
❑	167	Michael Clayton RC	3.00	1.25
❑	168	Bernard Berrian RC	1.50	.60
❑	169	Ben Watson RC	1.50	.60
❑	170	Philip Rivers RC	5.00	2.00
❑	171	Vince Wilfork RC	2.00	.75
❑	172	Jason Babin RC	1.50	.60
❑	173	Marcus Tubbs RC	1.50	.60
❑	174	Sean Taylor RC	2.00	.75
❑	175	Larry Fitzgerald RC	5.00	2.00
❑	176	Craig Krenzel RC	1.50	.60

❑ 177 Cedric Cobbs RC 1.50 .60
❑ 178 Lee Evans RC 2.00 .75
❑ 179 Johnnie Morant RC 1.50 .60
❑ 180 Kellen Winslow RC 3.00 1.25
❑ 181 Mewelde Moore RC 2.00 .75
❑ 182 Carlos Francis RC 1.25 .50
❑ 183 Josh Harris RC 1.50 .60
❑ 184 Julius Jones RC 6.00 2.50
❑ 185 Reggie Williams RC 2.00 .75
❑ 186 DeAngelo Hall RC 2.00 .75
❑ 187 D.J. Williams RC 2.00 .75
❑ 188 Cody Pickett RC 1.50 .60
❑ 189 Dunta Robinson RC 1.50 .60
❑ 190 J.P. Losman RC 3.00 1.25
❑ 191 Jonathan Vilma RC 1.50 .60
❑ 192 Jerricho Cotchery RC 1.50 .60
❑ 193 Keary Colbert RC 2.00 .75
❑ 194 Ben Troupe RC 1.50 .60
❑ 195 Drew Henson RC 1.50 .60
❑ 196 Chris Gamble RC 2.00 .75
❑ 197 Samie Parker RC 1.50 .60
❑ 198 Tatum Bell RC 3.00 1.25
❑ 199 Robert Gallery RC 2.50 1.00
❑ 200 Eli Manning RC 12.00 5.00
❑ 201 Ahmad Carroll RC 2.00 .75
❑ 202 Devery Henderson RC 1.25 .50
❑ 203 Matt Schaub RC 2.50 1.00
❑ 204 Greg Jones RC 1.50 .60
❑ 205 Roy Williams RC 4.00 1.50
❑ 206 Tommie Harris RC 1.50 .60
❑ 207 Jeff Smoker RC 1.50 .60
❑ 208 Kenechi Udeze RC 1.50 .60
❑ 209 Derrick Hamilton RC 1.25 .50
❑ 210 Ben Roethlisberger RC 20.00 10.00
❑ 211 Darius Watts RC 1.50 .60
❑ 212 John Navarre RC 1.50 .60
❑ 213 Ernest Wilford RC 1.50 .60
❑ 214 Rashaun Woods RC 1.50 .60
❑ 215 Steven Jackson RC 5.00 2.00
❑ 216 Michael Jenkins RC 1.50 .60
❑ 217 Will Smith RC 1.50 .60
❑ 218 Devard Darling RC 1.50 .60
❑ 219 Chris Perry RC 2.50 1.00
❑ 220 Luke McCown RC 1.50 .60

2005 Bazooka

❑ COMPLETE SET (220) 50.00 20.00
❑ COMP.SET w/o RC's (165) 25.00 10.00
❑ 1 Willis McGahee .75 .30
❑ 2 Aaron Brooks .50 .20
❑ 3 Allen Rossum .40 .15
❑ 4 Brett Favre 2.00 .75
❑ 5 Donovan McNabb 1.00 .40
❑ 6 Torry Holt .75 .30
❑ 7 Michael Vick 1.25 .50
❑ 8 David Carr .75 .30
❑ 9 Eric Moulds .50 .20
❑ 10 Chad Pennington .75 .30
❑ 11 Larry Fitzgerald .75 .30
❑ 12 Tom Brady 2.00 .75
❑ 13 Derrick Brooks .50 .20
❑ 14 Brandon Stokley .50 .20
❑ 15 Justin McCareins .40 .15
❑ 16 Champ Bailey .50 .20
❑ 17 Jake Delhomme .75 .30
❑ 18 Peyton Manning 1.25 .50
❑ 19 Keyshawn Johnson .50 .20
❑ 20 Daunte Culpepper .75 .30
❑ 21 Chester Taylor .50 .20
❑ 22 Kurt Warner .50 .20
❑ 23 Cedrick Wilson .40 .15
❑ 24 Brian Westbrook .50 .20
❑ 25 Rodney Harrison .50 .20
❑ 26 Clinton Portis .75 .30
❑ 27 A.J. Feeley .50 .20
❑ 28 Curtis Martin .75 .30
❑ 29 Chris Perry .50 .20
❑ 30 Randy Moss .75 .30
❑ 31 Darrell Jackson .50 .20
❑ 32 Edgerrin James .75 .30
❑ 33 Ben Roethlisberger 2.00 .75
❑ 34 Kevin Jones .75 .30
❑ 35 LaMont Jordan .75 .30
❑ 36 Jerome Bettis .75 .30
❑ 37 Ahman Green .75 .30
❑ 38 Tyrone Calico .50 .20
❑ 39 Anquan Boldin .50 .20
❑ 40 Dante Hall .50 .20
❑ 41 Todd Heap .50 .20
❑ 42 Corey Dillon .50 .20
❑ 43 Julius Peppers .50 .20
❑ 44 Antonio Bryant .40 .15
❑ 45 Dunta Robinson .50 .20
❑ 46 Michael Pittman .40 .15
❑ 47 Billy Volek .50 .20
❑ 48 Jimmy Smith .50 .20
❑ 49 Carson Palmer .75 .30
❑ 50 Derrick Blaylock .40 .15
❑ 51 Deuce McAllister .75 .30
❑ 52 Ray Lewis .75 .30
❑ 53 Chad Johnson .75 .30
❑ 54 Zach Thomas .75 .30
❑ 55 Julius Jones 1.00 .40
❑ 56 D.J. Williams .40 .15
❑ 57 Stephen Davis .50 .20
❑ 58 Greg Jones .40 .15
❑ 59 J.P. Losman .75 .30
❑ 60 Trent Green .50 .20
❑ 61 Drew Bennett .50 .20
❑ 62 Joe Horn .50 .20
❑ 63 Mewelde Moore .50 .20
❑ 64 Alge Crumpler .50 .20
❑ 65 Javon Walker .50 .20
❑ 66 Jake Plummer .50 .20
❑ 67 Aaron Stecker .40 .15
❑ 68 Keary Colbert .50 .20
❑ 69 Joey Harrington .75 .30
❑ 70 Brian Urlacher .75 .30
❑ 71 Jeremy Shockey .75 .30
❑ 72 Duce Staley .50 .20
❑ 73 Tim Rattay .40 .15
❑ 74 Jerry Porter .50 .20
❑ 75 Steven Jackson 1.00 .40
❑ 76 David Givens .50 .20
❑ 77 Byron Leftwich .75 .30
❑ 78 T.J. Duckett .50 .20
❑ 79 Jason Witten .50 .20
❑ 80 Andre Johnson .50 .20
❑ 81 Amani Toomer .50 .20
❑ 82 Kellen Winslow .75 .30
❑ 83 Kyle Boller .50 .20
❑ 84 Santana Moss .50 .20
❑ 85 Antonio Gates .75 .30
❑ 86 Lee Evans .50 .20
❑ 87 Larry Johnson .75 .30
❑ 88 Plaxico Burress .50 .20
❑ 89 Reuben Droughns .50 .20
❑ 90 Eli Manning 1.50 .60
❑ 91 Lito Sheppard .40 .15
❑ 92 DeAngelo Hall .50 .20
❑ 93 Josh McCown .50 .20
❑ 94 Eric Parker .40 .15
❑ 95 Drew Brees .75 .30
❑ 96 Fred Taylor .50 .20
❑ 97 Jonathan Vilma .50 .20
❑ 98 Michael Strahan .50 .20
❑ 99 Dwight Freeney .50 .20
❑ 100 Kerry Collins .50 .20
❑ 101 Hines Ward .75 .30
❑ 102 Lee Suggs .50 .20
❑ 103 Luke McCown .40 .15
❑ 104 Laveranues Coles .50 .20
❑ 105 LaDainian Tomlinson 1.00 .40
❑ 106 Jeff Garcia .50 .20
❑ 107 Michael Clayton .75 .30
❑ 108 DeShaun Foster .50 .20
❑ 109 Rex Grossman .50 .20
❑ 110 Priest Holmes .75 .30
❑ 111 Roy Williams WR .75 .30
❑ 112 Drew Henson .50 .20
❑ 113 Derrick Mason .50 .20
❑ 114 Michael Bennett .50 .20
❑ 115 Chris Simms .50 .20
❑ 116 Isaac Bruce .50 .20
❑ 117 Deion Branch .50 .20
❑ 118 Rudi Johnson .50 .20
❑ 119 Nate Burleson .50 .20
❑ 120 Warrick Dunn .50 .20
❑ 121 Brian Griese .50 .20
❑ 122 T.J. Houshmandzadeh .40 .15
❑ 123 Jamaar Taylor .40 .15
❑ 124 Drew Bledsoe .75 .30
❑ 125 Najeh Davenport .40 .15
❑ 126 Charles Rogers .50 .20
❑ 127 Ronald Curry .50 .20
❑ 128 Chris Brown .50 .20
❑ 129 Doug Gabriel .40 .15
❑ 130 Todd Pinkston .40 .15
❑ 131 Marc Bulger .75 .30
❑ 132 Marshall Faulk .75 .30
❑ 133 Marvin Harrison .75 .30
❑ 134 Matt Hasselbeck .50 .20
❑ 135 Tiki Barber .75 .30
❑ 136 Muhsin Muhammad .50 .20
❑ 137 Kevan Barlow .50 .20
❑ 138 Chris Chambers .50 .20
❑ 139 Donald Driver .50 .20
❑ 140 Jamal Lewis .75 .30
❑ 141 Rashaun Woods .50 .20
❑ 142 Steve McNair .75 .30
❑ 143 Reggie Wayne .50 .20
❑ 144 Jevon Kearse .50 .20
❑ 145 Domanick Davis .50 .20
❑ 146 Donte Stallworth .50 .20
❑ 147 Chris Gamble .50 .20
❑ 148 Philip Rivers .75 .30
❑ 149 Sean Taylor .50 .20
❑ 150 Antwaan Randle El .50 .20
❑ 151 Koren Robinson .50 .20
❑ 152 Tatum Bell .50 .20
❑ 153 Tony Gonzalez .50 .20
❑ 154 Reggie Williams .50 .20
❑ 155 Onterrio Smith .50 .20
❑ 156 Patrick Ramsey .50 .20
❑ 157 Thomas Jones .50 .20
❑ 158 Michael Jenkins .50 .20
❑ 159 Rod Smith .50 .20
❑ 160 Trent Dilfer .50 .20
❑ 161 Randy McMichael .40 .15
❑ 162 Terrell Owens .75 .30
❑ 163 Travis Henry .50 .20
❑ 164 Travis Taylor .40 .15
❑ 165 Shaun Alexander 1.00 .40
❑ 166 J.J. Arrington RC 2.00 .75
❑ 167 Cedric Benson RC 3.00 1.25
❑ 168 Carlos Rogers RC 2.00 .75
❑ 169 Troy Williamson RC 3.00 1.25
❑ 170 Ronnie Brown RC 5.00 2.00
❑ 171 Jason Campbell RC 2.50 1.00
❑ 172 Alvin Pearman RC 1.50 .60
❑ 173 Reggie Brown RC 1.50 .60
❑ 174 Lionel Gates RC 1.25 .50
❑ 175 Derek Anderson RC 1.50 .60
❑ 176 Craphonso Thorpe RC 1.25 .50

❑ 177 Frank Gore RC	2.50	1.00
❑ 178 David Greene RC	1.50	.60
❑ 179 Vincent Jackson RC	1.50	.60
❑ 180 Adam Jones RC	1.50	.60
❑ 181 Derrick Johnson RC	2.50	1.00
❑ 182 Stefan LeFors RC	1.50	.60
❑ 183 Heath Miller RC	4.00	1.50
❑ 184 Ryan Moats RC	1.50	.60
❑ 185 Vernand Morency RC	1.50	.60
❑ 186 Brandon Jacobs RC	2.00	.75
❑ 187 Kyle Orton RC	2.50	1.00
❑ 188 Roscoe Parrish RC	1.50	.60
❑ 189 Courtney Roby RC	1.50	.60
❑ 190 Aaron Rodgers RC	6.00	2.50
❑ 191 Marion Barber RC	2.50	1.00
❑ 192 Antrel Rolle RC	1.50	.60
❑ 193 Airese Currie RC	1.50	.60
❑ 194 Alex Smith QB RC	6.00	2.50
❑ 195 Andrew Walter RC	2.50	1.00
❑ 196 Roddy White RC	1.50	.60
❑ 197 Carnell Williams RC	5.00	2.00
❑ 198 Mike Williams	3.00	1.25
❑ 199 Rasheed Marshall RC	1.50	.60
❑ 200 Charlie Frye RC	3.00	1.25
❑ 201 Justin Miller RC	1.25	.50
❑ 202 Fabian Washington RC	1.50	.60
❑ 203 Mark Bradley RC	1.50	.60
❑ 204 Adrian McPherson RC	1.50	.60
❑ 205 Marcus Spears RC	1.50	.60
❑ 206 Matt Jones RC	4.00	1.50
❑ 207 Darren Sproles RC	1.50	.60
❑ 208 Eric Shelton RC	1.50	.60
❑ 209 Fred Gibson RC	1.25	.50
❑ 210 Anthony Davis RC	1.25	.50
❑ 211 Mark Clayton RC	2.00	.75
❑ 212 Braylon Edwards RC	5.00	2.00
❑ 213 Ciatrick Fason RC	1.50	.60
❑ 214 DeMarcus Ware RC	2.50	1.00
❑ 215 Dan Orlovsky RC	2.00	.75
❑ 216 Maurice Clarett	1.50	.60
❑ 217 Erasmus James RC	1.50	.60
❑ 218 Chris Henry RC	1.50	.60
❑ 219 Jerome Mathis RC	1.50	.60
❑ 220 Terrence Murphy RC	1.50	.60

1948 Bowman

❑ COMPLETE SET (108)	6000.00	4500.00
❑ COMMON 1/4/7/-/-/-	20.00	12.00
❑ COMMON 2/5/8/-/-/-	25.00	15.00
❑ COMMON SP 3/6/9 /-/-/-	100.00	65.00
❑ WRAPPER (1-CENT)	250.00	150.00
❑ 1 Joe Tereshinski RC !	150.00	80.00
❑ 2 Larry Olsonoski	25.00	15.00
❑ 3 Johnny Lujack RC SP	350.00	250.00
❑ 4 Ray Poole	20.00	12.00
❑ 5 Bill DeCorrevont RC	25.00	15.00
❑ 6 Paul Briggs SP	100.00	65.00
❑ 7 Steve Van Buren RC	200.00	125.00
❑ 8 Kenny Washington RC	60.00	40.00
❑ 9 Nolan Luhn SP	100.00	65.00
❑ 10 Chris Iversen	20.00	12.00
❑ 11 Jack Wiley	25.00	15.00
❑ 12 Charley Conerly RC SP	350.00	250.00
❑ 13 Hugh Taylor RC	25.00	15.00
❑ 14 Frank Seno	25.00	15.00
❑ 15 Gil Bouley SP	100.00	65.00
❑ 16 Tommy Thompson RC	35.00	20.00
❑ 17 Charley Trippi RC	100.00	60.00
❑ 18 Vince Banonis SP	100.00	65.00
❑ 19 Art Faircloth	20.00	12.00
❑ 20 Clyde Goodnight	25.00	15.00
❑ 21 Bill Chipley SP	100.00	65.00
❑ 22 Sammy Baugh RC	500.00	350.00
❑ 23 Don Kindt	25.00	15.00
❑ 24 John Koniszewski SP	100.00	65.00
❑ 25 Pat McHugh	20.00	12.00
❑ 26 Bob Waterfield RC	200.00	125.00
❑ 27 Tony Compagno SP	100.00	65.00
❑ 28 Paul Governali RC	25.00	15.00
❑ 29 Pat Harder RC	60.00	40.00
❑ 30 Vic Lindskog SP	100.00	65.00
❑ 31 Salvatore Rosato	20.00	12.00
❑ 32 John Mastrangelo	25.00	15.00
❑ 33 Fred Gehrke SP	100.00	65.00
❑ 34 Bosh Pritchard	20.00	12.00
❑ 35 Mike Micka	25.00	15.00
❑ 36 Bulldog Turner RC SP	250.00	160.00
❑ 37 Len Younce	20.00	12.00
❑ 38 Pat West	25.00	15.00
❑ 39 Russ Thomas SP	100.00	65.00
❑ 40 James Peebles	20.00	12.00
❑ 41 Bob Skoglund	25.00	15.00
❑ 42 Walt Stickle SP	100.00	65.00
❑ 43 Whitey Wistert RC	25.00	15.00
❑ 44 Paul Christman RC	60.00	40.00
❑ 45 Jay Rhodemyre SP	100.00	65.00
❑ 46 Tony Minisi	20.00	12.00
❑ 47 Bob Mann	25.00	15.00
❑ 48 Mal Kutner RC SP	110.00	70.00
❑ 49 Dick Poillon	20.00	12.00
❑ 50 Charles Cherundolo	25.00	15.00
❑ 51 Gerald Cowhig SP	100.00	65.00
❑ 52 Neill Armstrong RC	25.00	15.00
❑ 53 Frank Maznicki	25.00	15.00
❑ 54 John Sanchez SP	100.00	65.00
❑ 55 Frank Reagan	20.00	12.00
❑ 56 Jim Hardy	25.00	15.00
❑ 57 John Badaczewski SP	100.00	65.00
❑ 58 Robert Nussbaumer	20.00	12.00
❑ 59 Marvin Pregulman	25.00	15.00
❑ 60 Elbie Nickel RC SP	125.00	75.00
❑ 61 Alex Wojciechowicz RC	150.00	90.00
❑ 62 Walt Schlinkman	25.00	15.00
❑ 63 Pete Pihos RC SP	225.00	150.00
❑ 64 Joseph Sulaitis	20.00	12.00
❑ 65 Mike Holovak RC	50.00	30.00
❑ 66 Cy Souders SP RC	100.00	65.00
❑ 67 Paul McKee	20.00	12.00
❑ 68 Bill Moore	25.00	15.00
❑ 69 Frank Minini SP	100.00	65.00
❑ 70 Jack Ferrante	20.00	12.00
❑ 71 Les Horvath RC	50.00	35.00
❑ 72 Ted Fritsch Sr. RC SP	110.00	70.00
❑ 73 Tex Coulter RC	25.00	15.00
❑ 74 Boley Dancewicz	25.00	15.00
❑ 75 Dante Mangani SP	100.00	65.00
❑ 76 James Hefti	20.00	12.00
❑ 77 Paul Sarringhaus	25.00	15.00
❑ 78 Joe Scott SP	100.00	65.00
❑ 79 Bucko Kilroy RC	25.00	15.00
❑ 80 Bill Dudley RC	125.00	75.00
❑ 81 Mar.Goldberg RC SP	110.00	70.00
❑ 82 John Cannady	20.00	12.00
❑ 83 Perry Moss	25.00	15.00
❑ 84 Harold Crisler RC SP	110.00	70.00
❑ 85 Bill Gray	20.00	12.00
❑ 86 John Clement	25.00	15.00
❑ 87 Dan Sandifer SP	100.00	65.00
❑ 88 Ben Kish	20.00	12.00
❑ 89 Herbert Banta	25.00	15.00
❑ 90 Bill Garnaas SP	100.00	65.00
❑ 91 Jim White RC	20.00	12.00
❑ 92 Frank Barzilauskas	25.00	15.00
❑ 93 Vic Sears SP	100.00	65.00
❑ 94 John Adams	20.00	12.00
❑ 95 George McAfee RC	150.00	90.00
❑ 96 Ralph Heywood SP	100.00	65.00
❑ 97 Joe Muha	20.00	12.00
❑ 98 Fred Enke	25.00	15.00
❑ 99 Harry Gilmer RC SP	175.00	100.00
❑ 100 Bill Miklich	20.00	12.00
❑ 101 Joe Gottlieb	25.00	15.00
❑ 102 Bud Angsman RC SP	110.00	70.00
❑ 103 Tom Farmer	20.00	12.00
❑ 104 Bruce Smith RC	75.00	40.00
❑ 105 Bob Cifers SP	100.00	65.00
❑ 106 Ernie Steele	20.00	12.00
❑ 107 Sid Luckman RC	300.00	175.00
❑ 108 Buford Ray RC SP !	400.00	250.00

1950 Bowman

❑ COMPLETE SET (144)	4000.00	3000.00
❑ WRAPPER (5-CENT)	175.00	100.00
❑ 1 Doak Walker !	250.00	150.00
❑ 2 John Greene	25.00	18.00
❑ 3 Bob Nowasky	25.00	18.00
❑ 4 Jonathan Jenkins	25.00	18.00
❑ 5 Y.A.Tittle RC	250.00	175.00
❑ 6 Lou Groza RC	175.00	100.00
❑ 7 Alex Agase RC	30.00	20.00
❑ 8 Mac Speedie RC	50.00	30.00
❑ 9 Tony Canadeo RC	90.00	50.00
❑ 10 Larry Craig	30.00	20.00
❑ 11 Ted Fritsch Sr.	30.00	20.00
❑ 12 Joe Golding	25.00	18.00
❑ 13 Martin Ruby	25.00	18.00
❑ 14 George Taliaferro	30.00	20.00
❑ 15 Tank Younger RC	50.00	30.00
❑ 16 Glenn Davis RC	125.00	75.00
❑ 17 Bob Waterfield	125.00	75.00
❑ 18 Val Jansante	25.00	18.00
❑ 19 Joe Geri	25.00	18.00
❑ 20 Jerry Nuzum	25.00	18.00
❑ 21 Elmer Bud Angsman	25.00	18.00
❑ 22 Billy Dewell	25.00	18.00
❑ 23 Steve Van Buren	90.00	50.00
❑ 24 Cliff Patton	25.00	18.00
❑ 25 Bosh Pritchard	25.00	18.00
❑ 26 Johnny Lujack	80.00	50.00
❑ 27 Sid Luckman	125.00	75.00
❑ 28 Bulldog Turner	60.00	35.00
❑ 29 Bill Dudley	60.00	35.00
❑ 30 Hugh Taylor	30.00	20.00
❑ 31 George Thomas	25.00	18.00
❑ 32 Ray Poole	25.00	18.00
❑ 33 Travis Tidwell	25.00	18.00
❑ 34 Gail Bruce	25.00	18.00
❑ 35 Joe Perry RC	200.00	125.00
❑ 36 Frankie Albert RC	40.00	25.00
❑ 37 Bobby Layne	200.00	125.00
❑ 38 Leon Hart	40.00	25.00
❑ 39 B.Hoernschemeyer RC	30.00	20.00
❑ 40 Dick Barwegan RC	25.00	18.00
❑ 41 Adrian Burk RC	30.00	20.00
❑ 42 Barry French	25.00	18.00
❑ 43 Marion Motley RC	250.00	150.00
❑ 44 Jim Martin	30.00	20.00
❑ 45 Otto Graham RC	450.00	300.00
❑ 46 Al Baldwin	25.00	18.00
❑ 47 Larry Coutre	30.00	20.00
❑ 48 John Rauch	25.00	18.00
❑ 49 Sam Tamburo	25.00	18.00

❑ 50 Mike Swistowicz	25.00	18.00
❑ 51 Tom Fears RC	150.00	90.00
❑ 52 Elroy Hirsch RC	225.00	125.00
❑ 53 Dick Huffman	25.00	18.00
❑ 54 Bob Gage	25.00	18.00
❑ 55 Buddy Tinsley	25.00	18.00
❑ 56 Bill Blackburn	25.00	18.00
❑ 57 John Cochran	25.00	18.00
❑ 58 Bill Fischer	25.00	18.00
❑ 59 Whitey Wistert	30.00	20.00
❑ 60 Clyde Scott	25.00	18.00
❑ 61 Walter Barnes	25.00	18.00
❑ 62 Bob Perina	25.00	18.00
❑ 63 Bill Wightkin	25.00	18.00
❑ 64 Bob Goode	25.00	18.00
❑ 65 Al Demao	25.00	18.00
❑ 66 Harry Gilmer	30.00	20.00
❑ 67 Bill Austin	25.00	18.00
❑ 68 Joe Scott	25.00	18.00
❑ 69 Tex Coulter	30.00	20.00
❑ 70 Paul Salata	25.00	18.00
❑ 71 Emil Sitko RC	30.00	20.00
❑ 72 Bill Johnson C	25.00	18.00
❑ 73 Don Doll RC	25.00	18.00
❑ 74 Dan Sandifer	25.00	18.00
❑ 75 John Panelli	25.00	18.00
❑ 76 Bill Leonard	25.00	18.00
❑ 77 Bob Kelly	25.00	18.00
❑ 78 Dante Lavelli RC	150.00	90.00
❑ 79 Tony Adamle	30.00	20.00
❑ 80 Dick Wildung	25.00	18.00
❑ 81 Tobin Rote RC	50.00	30.00
❑ 82 Paul Burris	25.00	18.00
❑ 83 Lowell Tew	25.00	18.00
❑ 84 Barney Poole	25.00	18.00
❑ 85 Fred Naumetz	25.00	18.00
❑ 86 Dick Hoerner	25.00	18.00
❑ 87 Bob Reinhard	25.00	18.00
❑ 88 Howard Hartley RC	25.00	18.00
❑ 89 Darrell Hogan RC	25.00	18.00
❑ 90 Jerry Shipkey	25.00	18.00
❑ 91 Frank Tripucka	30.00	20.00
❑ 92 Buster Ramsey RC	25.00	18.00
❑ 93 Pat Harder	30.00	20.00
❑ 94 Vic Sears	25.00	18.00
❑ 95 Tommy Thompson QB	30.00	20.00
❑ 96 Bucko Kilroy	30.00	20.00
❑ 97 George Connor	50.00	30.00
❑ 98 Fred Morrison	25.00	18.00
❑ 99 Rookie	25.00	18.00
❑ 100 Sammy Baugh	250.00	150.00
❑ 101 Harry Ulinski	25.00	18.00
❑ 102 Frank Spaniel	25.00	18.00
❑ 103 Charley Conerly	90.00	50.00
❑ 104 Dick Hensley	25.00	18.00
❑ 105 Eddie Price	25.00	18.00
❑ 106 Ed Carr	25.00	18.00
❑ 107 Leo Nomellini	75.00	45.00
❑ 108 Verl Lillywhite	25.00	18.00
❑ 109 Wallace Triplett	25.00	18.00
❑ 110 Joe Watson	25.00	18.00
❑ 111 Cloyce Box RC	30.00	20.00
❑ 112 Billy Stone	25.00	18.00
❑ 113 Earl Murray	25.00	18.00
❑ 114 Chet Mutryn RC	30.00	20.00
❑ 115 Ken Carpenter	30.00	20.00
❑ 116 Lou Rymkus RC	30.00	20.00
❑ 117 Dub Jones RC	30.00	20.00
❑ 118 Clayton Tonnemaker	25.00	18.00
❑ 119 Walt Schlinkman	25.00	18.00
❑ 120 Billy Grimes	25.00	18.00
❑ 121 George Ratterman RC	30.00	20.00
❑ 122 Bob Mann	25.00	18.00
❑ 123 Buddy Young RC	40.00	25.00
❑ 124 Jack Zilly	25.00	18.00
❑ 125 Tom Kalmanir	25.00	18.00
❑ 126 Frank Sinkovitz	25.00	18.00
❑ 127 Elbert Nickel	30.00	20.00
❑ 128 Jim Finks RC	75.00	40.00
❑ 129 Charley Trippi	60.00	35.00
❑ 130 Tom Wham	25.00	18.00
❑ 131 Ventan Yablonski	25.00	18.00
❑ 132 Chuck Bednarik	125.00	75.00
❑ 133 Joe Muha	25.00	18.00
❑ 134 Pete Pihos	80.00	45.00
❑ 135 Washington Serini	25.00	18.00
❑ 136 George Gulyanics	25.00	18.00
❑ 137 Ken Kavanaugh	30.00	20.00
❑ 138 Howie Livingston	25.00	18.00
❑ 139 Joe Tereshinski	25.00	18.00
❑ 140 Jim White	25.00	18.00
❑ 141 Gene Roberts	25.00	18.00
❑ 142 Bill Swiacki	30.00	20.00
❑ 143 Norm Standlee	25.00	18.00
❑ 144 Knox Ramsey RC !	100.00	50.00

1951 Bowman

❑ COMPLETE SET (144)	3500.00	2500.00
❑ WRAPPER (1-CENT)	250.00	150.00
❑ WRAPPER (5-CENT)	300.00	175.00
❑ 1 Weldon Humble RC !	80.00	50.00
❑ 2 Otto Graham	200.00	125.00
❑ 3 Mac Speedie	35.00	20.00
❑ 4 Norm Van Brocklin RC	300.00	200.00
❑ 5 Woodley Lewis RC	25.00	15.00
❑ 6 Tom Fears	50.00	30.00
❑ 7 George Musacco	20.00	12.00
❑ 8 George Taliaferro	25.00	15.00
❑ 9 Barney Poole	20.00	12.00
❑ 10 Steve Van Buren	60.00	35.00
❑ 11 Whitey Wistert	25.00	15.00
❑ 12 Chuck Bednarik	80.00	50.00
❑ 13 Bulldog Turner	50.00	30.00
❑ 14 Bob Williams	20.00	12.00
❑ 15 Johnny Lujack	60.00	35.00
❑ 16 Roy Rebel Steiner	20.00	12.00
❑ 17 Jug Girard	25.00	15.00
❑ 18 Bill Neal	20.00	12.00
❑ 19 Travis Tidwell	20.00	12.00
❑ 20 Tom Landry RC	500.00	350.00
❑ 21 Arnie Weinmeister RC	60.00	35.00
❑ 22 Joe Geri	20.00	12.00
❑ 23 Bill Walsh C RC	25.00	15.00
❑ 24 Fran Rogel	20.00	12.00
❑ 25 Doak Walker	60.00	35.00
❑ 26 Leon Hart	35.00	20.00
❑ 27 Thurman McGraw	20.00	12.00
❑ 28 Buster Ramsey	20.00	12.00
❑ 29 Frank Tripucka	35.00	20.00
❑ 30 Don Paul DB	20.00	12.00
❑ 31 Alex Loyd	20.00	12.00
❑ 32 Y.A.Tittle	135.00	75.00
❑ 33 Verl Lillywhite	20.00	12.00
❑ 34 Sammy Baugh	175.00	110.00
❑ 35 Chuck Drazenovich	20.00	12.00
❑ 36 Bob Goode	20.00	12.00
❑ 37 Horace Gillom RC	25.00	15.00
❑ 38 Lou Rymkus	25.00	15.00
❑ 39 Ken Carpenter	20.00	12.00
❑ 40 Bob Waterfield	75.00	45.00
❑ 41 Vitamin Smith RC	25.00	15.00
❑ 42 Glenn Davis	60.00	35.00
❑ 43 Dan Edwards	20.00	12.00
❑ 44 John Rauch	20.00	12.00
❑ 45 Zollie Toth	20.00	12.00
❑ 46 Pete Pihos	60.00	35.00
❑ 47 Russ Craft	20.00	12.00
❑ 48 Walter Barnes	20.00	12.00
❑ 49 Fred Morrison	20.00	12.00
❑ 50 Ray Bray	20.00	12.00
❑ 51 Ed Sprinkle RC	25.00	15.00
❑ 52 Floyd Reid	20.00	12.00
❑ 53 Billy Grimes	20.00	12.00
❑ 54 Ted Fritsch Sr.	25.00	15.00
❑ 55 Al DeRogatis	25.00	15.00
❑ 56 Charley Conerly	75.00	45.00
❑ 57 Jon Baker	20.00	12.00
❑ 58 Tom McWilliams	20.00	12.00
❑ 59 Jerry Shipkey	20.00	12.00
❑ 60 Lynn Chandnois RC	25.00	15.00
❑ 61 Don Doll	20.00	12.00
❑ 62 Lou Creekmur	50.00	30.00
❑ 63 Bob Hoernschemeyer	25.00	15.00
❑ 64 Tom Wham	20.00	12.00
❑ 65 Bill Fischer	20.00	12.00
❑ 66 Robert Nussbaumer	20.00	12.00
❑ 67 Gordy Soltau RC	20.00	12.00
❑ 68 Visco Grgich	20.00	12.00
❑ 69 John Strzykalski RC	20.00	12.00
❑ 70 Pete Stout	20.00	12.00
❑ 71 Paul Lipscomb	20.00	12.00
❑ 72 Harry Gilmer	35.00	20.00
❑ 73 Dante Lavelli	50.00	30.00
❑ 74 Dub Jones	25.00	15.00
❑ 75 Lou Groza	75.00	45.00
❑ 76 Elroy Hirsch	75.00	45.00
❑ 77 Tom Kalmanir	20.00	12.00
❑ 78 Jack Zilly	20.00	12.00
❑ 79 Bruce Alford	20.00	12.00
❑ 80 Art Weiner	20.00	12.00
❑ 81 Brad Ecklund	20.00	12.00
❑ 82 Bosh Pritchard	20.00	12.00
❑ 83 John Green	20.00	12.00
❑ 84 Ebert Van Buren	20.00	12.00
❑ 85 Julie Rykovich	20.00	12.00
❑ 86 Fred Davis	20.00	12.00
❑ 87 John Hoffman RC	20.00	12.00
❑ 88 Tobin Rote	25.00	15.00
❑ 89 Paul Burris	20.00	12.00
❑ 90 Tony Canadeo	50.00	30.00
❑ 91 Emlen Tunnell RC	100.00	60.00
❑ 92 Otto Schnellbacher RC	20.00	12.00
❑ 93 Ray Poole	20.00	12.00
❑ 94 Darrell Hogan	20.00	12.00
❑ 95 Frank Sinkovitz	20.00	12.00
❑ 96 Ernie Stautner	75.00	45.00
❑ 97 Elmer Bud Angsman	20.00	12.00
❑ 98 Jack Jennings	20.00	12.00
❑ 99 Jerry Groom	20.00	12.00
❑ 100 John Prchlik	20.00	12.00
❑ 101 J. Robert Smith	20.00	12.00
❑ 102 Bobby Layne	135.00	75.00
❑ 103 Frankie Albert	35.00	20.00
❑ 104 Gail Bruce	20.00	12.00
❑ 105 Joe Perry	75.00	45.00
❑ 106 Leon Heath	20.00	12.00
❑ 107 Ed Quirk	20.00	12.00
❑ 108 Hugh Taylor	25.00	15.00
❑ 109 Marion Motley	100.00	60.00
❑ 110 Tony Adamle	20.00	12.00
❑ 111 Alex Agase	25.00	15.00
❑ 112 Tank Younger	35.00	20.00
❑ 113 Bob Boyd	20.00	12.00
❑ 114 Jerry Williams	20.00	12.00
❑ 115 Joe Golding	20.00	12.00
❑ 116 Sherman Howard	20.00	12.00
❑ 117 John Wozniak	20.00	12.00
❑ 118 Frank Reagan	20.00	12.00
❑ 119 Vic Sears	20.00	12.00
❑ 120 Clyde Scott	20.00	12.00
❑ 121 George Gulyanics	20.00	12.00
❑ 122 Bill Wightkin	20.00	12.00
❑ 123 Chuck Hunsinger	20.00	12.00
❑ 124 Jack Cloud	20.00	12.00

❑ 125 Abner Wimberly	20.00	12.00
❑ 126 Dick Wildung	20.00	12.00
❑ 127 Eddie Price	20.00	12.00
❑ 128 Joe Scott	20.00	12.00
❑ 129 Jerry Nuzum	20.00	12.00
❑ 130 Jim Finks	35.00	20.00
❑ 131 Bob Gage	20.00	12.00
❑ 132 Bill Swiacki	25.00	15.00
❑ 133 Joe Watson	20.00	12.00
❑ 134 Ollie Cline	20.00	12.00
❑ 135 Jack Lininger	20.00	12.00
❑ 136 Fran Polsfoot	20.00	12.00
❑ 137 Charley Trippi	50.00	30.00
❑ 138 Ventan Yablonski	20.00	12.00
❑ 139 Emil Sitko	20.00	12.00
❑ 140 Leo Nomellini	60.00	30.00
❑ 141 Norm Standlee	20.00	12.00
❑ 142 Eddie Saenz	20.00	12.00
❑ 143 Al Demao	20.00	12.00
❑ 144 Bill Dudley !	150.00	75.00
❑ NNO Johnny Lujack Proof	300.00	175.00
❑ NNO Bob Gage Proof	125.00	75.00
❑ NNO Darrell Hogan Proof	125.00	75.00

1952 Bowman Large

❑ COMPLETE SET (144)	12500.00	9500.00
❑ COMMON CARD (1-72)	35.00	20.00
❑ COMMON CARD (73-144)	40.00	25.00
❑ WRAPPER (5-CENT)	60.00	30.00
❑ 1 Norm Van Brocklin SP !	500.00	350.00
❑ 2 Otto Graham	300.00	200.00
❑ 3 Doak Walker	100.00	60.00
❑ 4 Steve Owen RC CO	75.00	40.00
❑ 5 Frankie Albert	50.00	30.00
❑ 6 Laurie Niemi	35.00	20.00
❑ 7 Chuck Hunsinger	35.00	20.00
❑ 8 Ed Modzelewski	50.00	30.00
❑ 9 Joe Spencer SP	75.00	40.00
❑ 10 Chuck Bednarik SP	300.00	200.00
❑ 11 Barney Poole	35.00	20.00
❑ 12 Charley Trippi	75.00	40.00
❑ 13 Tom Fears	75.00	40.00
❑ 14 Paul Brown RC CO	250.00	150.00
❑ 15 Leon Hart	50.00	30.00
❑ 16 Frank Gifford RC	500.00	350.00
❑ 17 Y.A.Tittle	300.00	200.00
❑ 18 Charlie Justice SP	175.00	100.00
❑ 19 George Connor SP	175.00	100.00
❑ 20 Lynn Chandnois	35.00	20.00
❑ 21 Billy Howton RC	50.00	30.00
❑ 22 Kenneth Snyder	35.00	20.00
❑ 23 Gino Marchetti RC	250.00	150.00
❑ 24 John Karras	35.00	20.00
❑ 25 Tank Younger	50.00	30.00
❑ 26 Tommy Thompson LB	35.00	20.00
❑ 27 Bob Miller SP RC!	300.00	200.00
❑ 28 Kyle Rote RC SP	175.00	100.00
❑ 29 Hugh McElhenny RC	250.00	150.00
❑ 30 Sammy Baugh	350.00	225.00
❑ 31 Jim Dooley RC	45.00	25.00
❑ 32 Ray Mathews	35.00	20.00
❑ 33 Fred Cone	35.00	20.00
❑ 34 Al Pollard	35.00	20.00
❑ 35 Brad Ecklund	35.00	20.00
❑ 36 John Hancock RC SP!	350.00	225.00
❑ 37 Elroy Hirsch SP	200.00	125.00
❑ 38 Keever Jankovich	35.00	20.00
❑ 39 Emlen Tunnell	125.00	75.00
❑ 40 Steve Dowden	35.00	20.00
❑ 41 Claude Hipps	35.00	20.00
❑ 42 Norm Standlee	35.00	20.00
❑ 43 Dick Todd CO	35.00	20.00
❑ 44 Babe Parilli	50.00	30.00
❑ 45 Steve Van Buren SP	300.00	200.00
❑ 46 Art Donovan RC SP	350.00	250.00
❑ 47 Bill Fischer	35.00	20.00
❑ 48 George Halas RC CO	275.00	160.00
❑ 49 Jerrell Price	35.00	20.00
❑ 50 John Sandusky RC	35.00	20.00
❑ 51 Ray Beck	35.00	20.00
❑ 52 Jim Martin	45.00	25.00
❑ 53 Joe Bach CO UER	35.00	20.00
❑ 54 Glen Christian SP	75.00	40.00
❑ 55 Andy Davis SP	75.00	40.00
❑ 56 Tobin Rote	45.00	25.00
❑ 57 Wayne Millner RC CO	90.00	50.00
❑ 58 Zollie Toth	35.00	20.00
❑ 59 Jack Jennings	35.00	20.00
❑ 60 Bill McColl	35.00	20.00
❑ 61 Les Richter RC	45.00	25.00
❑ 62 Walt Michaels RC	45.00	25.00
❑ 63 Charley Conerly SP	700.00	400.00
❑ 64 Howard Hartley SP	75.00	40.00
❑ 65 Jerome Smith	35.00	20.00
❑ 66 James Clark	35.00	20.00
❑ 67 Dick Logan	35.00	20.00
❑ 68 Wayne Robinson	35.00	20.00
❑ 69 James Hammond	35.00	20.00
❑ 70 Gene Schroeder	35.00	20.00
❑ 71 Tex Coulter	45.00	25.00
❑ 72 John Schweder RC SP!	600.00	400.00
❑ 73 Vitamin Smith SP	150.00	90.00
❑ 74 Joe Campanella RC	40.00	25.00
❑ 75 Joe Kuharich RC CO	50.00	30.00
❑ 76 Herman Clark	40.00	25.00
❑ 77 Dan Edwards	40.00	25.00
❑ 78 Bobby Layne	300.00	175.00
❑ 79 Bob Hoernschemeyer	50.00	30.00
❑ 80 John Carr Blount	40.00	25.00
❑ 81 John Kastan RC SP	150.00	90.00
❑ 82 Harry Minarik RC SP	150.00	90.00
❑ 83 Joe Perry	100.00	60.00
❑ 84 Buddy Parker RC CO	50.00	30.00
❑ 85 Andy Robustelli RC	200.00	125.00
❑ 86 Dub Jones	50.00	30.00
❑ 87 Mal Cook	40.00	25.00
❑ 88 Billy Stone	40.00	25.00
❑ 89 George Taliaferro	50.00	30.00
❑ 90 Thomas Johnson RC SP	150.00	90.00
❑ 91 Leon Heath SP	100.00	60.00
❑ 92 Pete Pihos	100.00	60.00
❑ 93 Fred Benners	40.00	25.00
❑ 94 George Tarasovic	40.00	25.00
❑ 95 Buck Shaw RC CO	40.00	25.00
❑ 96 Bill Wightkin	40.00	25.00
❑ 97 John Wozniak	40.00	25.00
❑ 98 Bobby Dillon RC	50.00	30.00
❑ 99 Joe Stydahar RC SP CO!	650.00	450.00
❑ 100 Dick Alban RC SP	150.00	90.00
❑ 101 Arnie Weinmeister	60.00	35.00
❑ 102 Bobby Cross	40.00	25.00
❑ 103 Don Paul DB	40.00	25.00
❑ 104 Buddy Young	60.00	35.00
❑ 105 Lou Groza	125.00	75.00
❑ 106 Ray Pelfrey	40.00	25.00
❑ 107 Maurice Nipp	40.00	25.00
❑ 108 Hubert Johnston RC SP!	650.00	450.00
❑ 109 Vol.Quinlan RC SP	100.00	60.00
❑ 110 Jack Simmons	40.00	25.00
❑ 111 George Ratterman	50.00	30.00
❑ 112 John Badaczewski	40.00	25.00
❑ 113 Bill Reichardt	40.00	25.00
❑ 114 Art Weiner	40.00	25.00
❑ 115 Keith Flowers	40.00	25.00
❑ 116 Russ Craft	40.00	25.00
❑ 117 J.O'Donahue RC SP	150.00	90.00
❑ 118 Darrell Hogan SP	100.00	60.00
❑ 119 Frank Ziegler	40.00	25.00
❑ 120 Dan Towler	60.00	35.00
❑ 121 Fred Williams	40.00	25.00
❑ 122 Jimmy Phelan CO	40.00	25.00
❑ 123 Eddie Price	40.00	25.00
❑ 124 Chet Ostrowski	40.00	25.00
❑ 125 Leo Nomellini	100.00	60.00
❑ 126 S.Romanik RC SP!	300.00	200.00
❑ 127 Ollie Matson RC SP	300.00	200.00
❑ 128 Dante Lavelli	90.00	50.00
❑ 129 Jack Christiansen RC	175.00	100.00
❑ 130 Dom Moselle	40.00	25.00
❑ 131 John Rapacz	40.00	25.00
❑ 132 Chuck Ortmann UER	40.00	25.00
❑ 133 Bob Williams	40.00	25.00
❑ 134 Chuck Ulrich	40.00	25.00
❑ 135 Gene Ronzani CO SP RC!	650.00	450.00
❑ 136 Bert Rechichar SP	100.00	60.00
❑ 137 Bob Waterfield	125.00	75.00
❑ 138 Bobby Walston RC	50.00	30.00
❑ 139 Jerry Shipkey	40.00	25.00
❑ 140 Yale Lary RC	175.00	100.00
❑ 141 Gordy Soltau	40.00	25.00
❑ 142 Tom Landry	600.00	450.00
❑ 143 John Papit	40.00	25.00
❑ 144 Jim Lansford RC SP!	3000.00	1800.00

1952 Bowman Small

❑ COMPLETE SET (144)	5000.00	3500.00
❑ COMMON CARD (1-72)	25.00	15.00
❑ COMMON CARD (73-144)	30.00	18.00
❑ WRAPPER (1-CENT)	60.00	40.00
❑ 1 Norm Van Brocklin !	350.00	200.00
❑ 2 Otto Graham	200.00	125.00
❑ 3 Doak Walker	60.00	35.00
❑ 4 Steve Owen RC CO	60.00	35.00
❑ 5 Frankie Albert	35.00	20.00
❑ 6 Laurie Niemi	25.00	15.00
❑ 7 Chuck Hunsinger	25.00	15.00
❑ 8 Ed Modzelewski	35.00	20.00
❑ 9 Joe Spencer	25.00	15.00
❑ 10 Chuck Bednarik	75.00	45.00
❑ 11 Barney Poole	25.00	15.00
❑ 12 Charley Trippi	60.00	35.00
❑ 13 Tom Fears	60.00	35.00
❑ 14 Paul Brown RC CO	150.00	90.00
❑ 15 Leon Hart	35.00	20.00
❑ 16 Frank Gifford RC	400.00	200.00
❑ 17 Y.A.Tittle	125.00	75.00
❑ 18 Charlie Justice	45.00	30.00
❑ 19 George Connor	35.00	20.00
❑ 20 Lynn Chandnois	25.00	15.00
❑ 21 Billy Howton RC	40.00	25.00
❑ 22 Kenneth Snyder	25.00	15.00
❑ 23 Gino Marchetti RC	125.00	75.00
❑ 24 John Karras	25.00	15.00
❑ 25 Tank Younger	35.00	20.00
❑ 26 Tommy Thompson LB	25.00	15.00
❑ 27 Bob Miller RC	25.00	15.00
❑ 28 Kyle Rote RC	50.00	30.00
❑ 29 Hugh McElhenny RC	175.00	100.00

❑ 30 Sammy Baugh	250.00	150.00
❑ 31 Jim Dooley RC	30.00	18.00
❑ 32 Ray Mathews	25.00	15.00
❑ 33 Fred Cone	25.00	15.00
❑ 34 Al Pollard	25.00	15.00
❑ 35 Brad Ecklund	25.00	15.00
❑ 36 John Lee Hancock	25.00	15.00
❑ 37 Elroy Hirsch	60.00	35.00
❑ 38 Keever Jankovich	25.00	15.00
❑ 39 Emlen Tunnell	50.00	30.00
❑ 40 Steve Dowden	25.00	15.00
❑ 41 Claude Hipps	25.00	15.00
❑ 42 Norm Standlee	25.00	15.00
❑ 43 Dick Todd CO	25.00	15.00
❑ 44 Babe Parilli	35.00	20.00
❑ 45 Steve Van Buren	75.00	40.00
❑ 46 Art Donovan RC	200.00	125.00
❑ 47 Bill Fischer	25.00	15.00
❑ 48 George Halas RC CO	250.00	150.00
❑ 49 Jerrell Price	25.00	15.00
❑ 50 John Sandusky RC	25.00	15.00
❑ 51 Ray Beck	25.00	15.00
❑ 52 Jim Martin	30.00	18.00
❑ 53 Joe Bach CO UER	25.00	15.00
❑ 54 Glen Christian	25.00	15.00
❑ 55 Andy Davis	25.00	15.00
❑ 56 Tobin Rote	30.00	18.00
❑ 57 Wayne Millner RC CO	50.00	30.00
❑ 58 Zollie Toth	25.00	15.00
❑ 59 Jack Jennings	25.00	15.00
❑ 60 Bill McColl	25.00	15.00
❑ 61 Les Richter RC	30.00	18.00
❑ 62 Walt Michaels RC	30.00	18.00
❑ 63 Charley Conerly	75.00	40.00
❑ 64 Howard Hartley	25.00	15.00
❑ 65 Jerome Smith	25.00	15.00
❑ 66 James Clark	25.00	15.00
❑ 67 Dick Logan	25.00	15.00
❑ 68 Wayne Robinson	25.00	15.00
❑ 69 James Hammond	25.00	15.00
❑ 70 Gene Schroeder	25.00	15.00
❑ 71 Tex Coulter	30.00	18.00
❑ 72 John Schweder	25.00	15.00
❑ 73 Vitamin Smith	35.00	20.00
❑ 74 Joe Campanella RC	30.00	18.00
❑ 75 Joe Kuharich RC CO	35.00	20.00
❑ 76 Herman Clark	30.00	18.00
❑ 77 Dan Edwards	30.00	18.00
❑ 78 Bobby Layne	150.00	90.00
❑ 79 Bob Hoernschemeyer	35.00	20.00
❑ 80 John Carr Blount	30.00	18.00
❑ 81 John Kastan RC	30.00	18.00
❑ 82 Harry Minarik	30.00	18.00
❑ 83 Joe Perry	75.00	40.00
❑ 84 Buddy Parker RC CO	35.00	20.00
❑ 85 Andy Robustelli RC	125.00	75.00
❑ 86 Dub Jones	35.00	20.00
❑ 87 Mal Cook	30.00	18.00
❑ 88 Billy Stone	30.00	18.00
❑ 89 George Taliaferro	35.00	20.00
❑ 90 Thomas Johnson RC	30.00	18.00
❑ 91 Leon Heath	30.00	18.00
❑ 92 Pete Pihos	50.00	35.00
❑ 93 Fred Benners	30.00	18.00
❑ 94 George Tarasovic	30.00	18.00
❑ 95 Buck Shaw RC CO	30.00	18.00
❑ 96 Bill Wightkin	30.00	18.00
❑ 97 John Wozniak	30.00	18.00
❑ 98 Bobby Dillon RC	35.00	20.00
❑ 99 Joe Stydahar RC CO	45.00	30.00
❑ 100 Dick Alban RC	30.00	18.00
❑ 101 Arnie Weinmeister	40.00	25.00
❑ 102 Bobby Cross	30.00	18.00
❑ 103 Don Paul DB	30.00	18.00
❑ 104 Buddy Young	40.00	25.00
❑ 105 Lou Groza	75.00	45.00
❑ 106 Ray Pelfrey	30.00	18.00
❑ 107 Maurice Nipp	30.00	18.00
❑ 108 Hubert Johnston	30.00	18.00
❑ 109 Volney Quinlan RC	30.00	18.00
❑ 110 Jack Simmons	30.00	18.00
❑ 111 George Ratterman	35.00	20.00
❑ 112 John Badaczewski	30.00	18.00
❑ 113 Bill Reichardt	30.00	18.00
❑ 114 Art Weiner	30.00	18.00
❑ 115 Keith Flowers	30.00	18.00
❑ 116 Russ Craft	30.00	18.00
❑ 117 Jim O'Donahue RC	30.00	18.00
❑ 118 Darrell Hogan	30.00	18.00
❑ 119 Frank Ziegler	30.00	18.00
❑ 120 Dan Towler	40.00	25.00
❑ 121 Fred Williams	30.00	18.00
❑ 122 Jimmy Phelan CO	30.00	18.00
❑ 123 Eddie Price	30.00	18.00
❑ 124 Chet Ostrowski	30.00	18.00
❑ 125 Leo Nomellini	75.00	40.00
❑ 126 Steve Romanik	30.00	18.00
❑ 127 Ollie Matson RC	125.00	75.00
❑ 128 Dante Lavelli	60.00	35.00
❑ 129 Jack Christiansen RC	80.00	50.00
❑ 130 Dom Moselle	30.00	18.00
❑ 131 John Rapacz	30.00	18.00
❑ 132 Chuck Ortmann UER	30.00	18.00
❑ 133 Bob Williams	30.00	18.00
❑ 134 Chuck Ulrich	30.00	18.00
❑ 135 Gene Ronzani RC CO	30.00	18.00
❑ 136 Bert Rechichar	35.00	20.00
❑ 137 Bob Waterfield	75.00	45.00
❑ 138 Bobby Walston RC	35.00	20.00
❑ 139 Jerry Shipkey	30.00	18.00
❑ 140 Yale Lary RC	80.00	50.00
❑ 141 Gordy Soltau	30.00	18.00
❑ 142 Tom Landry	400.00	250.00
❑ 143 John Papit	30.00	18.00
❑ 144 Jim Lansford RC !	175.00	100.00

1953 Bowman

❑ COMPLETE SET (96)	3400.00	2200.00
❑ WRAPPER (5-CENT)	150.00	90.00
❑ 1 Eddie LeBaron RC !	125.00	75.00
❑ 2 John Dottley	30.00	18.00
❑ 3 Babe Parilli	35.00	20.00
❑ 4 Bucko Kilroy	35.00	20.00
❑ 5 Joe Tereshinski	30.00	18.00
❑ 6 Doak Walker	75.00	45.00
❑ 7 Fran Polsfoot	30.00	18.00
❑ 8 Sisto Averno	30.00	18.00
❑ 9 Marion Motley	75.00	45.00
❑ 10 Pat Brady	30.00	18.00
❑ 11 Norm Van Brocklin	125.00	75.00
❑ 12 Bill McColl	30.00	18.00
❑ 13 Jerry Groom	30.00	18.00
❑ 14 Al Pollard	30.00	18.00
❑ 15 Dante Lavelli	50.00	30.00
❑ 16 Eddie Price	30.00	18.00
❑ 17 Charley Trippi	50.00	30.00
❑ 18 Elbert Nickel	35.00	20.00
❑ 19 George Taliaferro	35.00	20.00
❑ 20 Charley Conerly	80.00	50.00
❑ 21 Bobby Layne	125.00	75.00
❑ 22 Elroy Hirsch	100.00	60.00
❑ 23 Jim Finks	40.00	25.00
❑ 24 Chuck Bednarik	75.00	45.00
❑ 25 Kyle Rote	40.00	25.00
❑ 26 Otto Graham	175.00	100.00
❑ 27 Harry Gilmer	35.00	20.00
❑ 28 Tobin Rote	35.00	20.00
❑ 29 Billy Stone	30.00	18.00
❑ 30 Buddy Young	40.00	25.00
❑ 31 Leon Hart	40.00	25.00
❑ 32 Hugh McElhenny	75.00	45.00
❑ 33 Dale Samuels	30.00	18.00
❑ 34 Lou Creekmur	50.00	30.00
❑ 35 Tom Catlin	30.00	18.00
❑ 36 Tom Fears	60.00	35.00
❑ 37 George Connor	40.00	25.00
❑ 38 Bill Walsh C	30.00	18.00
❑ 39 Leo Sanford SP	45.00	30.00
❑ 40 Horace Gillom	35.00	20.00
❑ 41 John Schweder SP	45.00	30.00
❑ 42 Tom O'Connell	30.00	18.00
❑ 43 Frank Gifford SP	300.00	175.00
❑ 44 Frank Continetti SP	45.00	30.00
❑ 45 John Olszewski SP	45.00	30.00
❑ 46 Dub Jones	35.00	20.00
❑ 47 Don Paul LB SP	45.00	30.00
❑ 48 Gerald Weatherly	30.00	18.00
❑ 49 Fred Bruney SP	45.00	30.00
❑ 50 Jack Scarbath	30.00	18.00
❑ 51 John Karras	30.00	18.00
❑ 52 Al Conway	30.00	18.00
❑ 53 Emlen Tunnell SP	125.00	75.00
❑ 54 Gern Nagler SP	45.00	30.00
❑ 55 Kenneth Snyder SP	45.00	30.00
❑ 56 Y.A.Tittle	150.00	90.00
❑ 57 John Rapacz SP	45.00	30.00
❑ 58 Harley Sewell SP	45.00	30.00
❑ 59 Don Bingham	30.00	18.00
❑ 60 Darrell Hogan	30.00	18.00
❑ 61 Tony Curcillo	30.00	18.00
❑ 62 Ray Renfro RC SP	50.00	30.00
❑ 63 Leon Heath	30.00	18.00
❑ 64 Tex Coulter SP	45.00	30.00
❑ 65 Dewayne Douglas	30.00	18.00
❑ 66 J. Robert Smith SP	45.00	30.00
❑ 67 Bob McChesney SP	45.00	30.00
❑ 68 Dick Alban SP	45.00	30.00
❑ 69 Andy Kozar	30.00	18.00
❑ 70 Merwin Hodel SP	45.00	30.00
❑ 71 Thurman McGraw	30.00	18.00
❑ 72 Cliff Anderson	30.00	18.00
❑ 73 Pete Pihos	60.00	35.00
❑ 74 Julie Rykovich	30.00	18.00
❑ 75 John Kreamcheck SP	45.00	30.00
❑ 76 Lynn Chandnois	30.00	18.00
❑ 77 Cloyce Box SP	45.00	30.00
❑ 78 Ray Mathews	30.00	18.00
❑ 79 Bobby Walston	35.00	20.00
❑ 80 Jim Dooley	30.00	18.00
❑ 81 Pat Harder SP	45.00	30.00
❑ 82 Jerry Shipkey	30.00	18.00
❑ 83 Bobby Thomason RC	30.00	18.00
❑ 84 Hugh Taylor	35.00	20.00
❑ 85 George Ratterman	35.00	20.00
❑ 86 Don Stonesifer	30.00	18.00
❑ 87 John Williams SP RC	45.00	30.00
❑ 88 Leo Nomellini	50.00	30.00
❑ 89 Frank Ziegler	30.00	18.00
❑ 90 Don Paul DB UER	30.00	18.00
❑ 91 Tom Dublinski	30.00	18.00
❑ 92 Ken Carpenter	30.00	18.00
❑ 93 Ted Marchibroda RC	40.00	25.00
❑ 94 Chuck Drazenovich	30.00	18.00
❑ 95 Lou Groza SP	125.00	75.00
❑ 96 William Cross RC SP !	100.00	50.00

1954 Bowman

❑ COMPLETE SET (128)	1800.00	1200.00
❑ COMMON CARD (1-64)	5.00	3.00
❑ COMMON SP (65-96)	25.00	15.00
❑ COMMON CARD (97-128)	5.00	3.00
❑ WRAPPER (1-CENT)	15.00	10.00
❑ WRAPPER (5-CENT)	30.00	25.00
❑ 1 Ray Mathews !	30.00	15.00

2 John Huzvar	5.00	3.00
3 Jack Scarbath	5.00	3.00
4 Doug Atkins RC	50.00	30.00
5 Bill Stits	5.00	3.00
6 Joe Perry	30.00	18.00
7 Kyle Rote	15.00	7.50
8 Norm Van Brocklin	50.00	25.00
9 Pete Pihos	20.00	12.00
10 Babe Parilli	8.00	4.00
11 Zeke Bratkowski RC	25.00	15.00
12 Ollie Matson	25.00	15.00
13 Pat Brady	5.00	3.00
14 Fred Enke	5.00	3.00
15 Harry Ulinski	5.00	3.00
16 Bob Garrett	5.00	3.00
17 Bill Bowman	5.00	3.00
18 Leo Rucka	5.00	3.00
19 John Cannady	5.00	3.00
20 Tom Fears	25.00	15.00
21 Norm Willey	5.00	3.00
22 Floyd Reid	5.00	3.00
23 George Blanda RC	175.00	100.00
24 Don Doheney	5.00	3.00
25 John Schweder	5.00	3.00
26 Bert Rechichar	5.00	3.00
27 Harry Dowda	5.00	3.00
28 John Sandusky	5.00	3.00
29 Les Bingaman RC	15.00	7.50
30 Joe Arenas	5.00	3.00
31 Ray Wietecha RC	5.00	3.00
32 Elroy Hirsch	30.00	18.00
33 Harold Giancanelli	5.00	3.00
34 Billy Howton	8.00	4.00
35 Fred Morrison	5.00	3.00
36 Bobby Cavazos	5.00	3.00
37 Darrell Hogan	5.00	3.00
38 Buddy Young	8.00	4.00
39 Charlie Justice	20.00	12.00
40 Otto Graham	80.00	50.00
41 Doak Walker	35.00	20.00
42 Y.A.Tittle	60.00	35.00
43 Buford Long	5.00	3.00
44 Volney Quinlan	5.00	3.00
45 Bobby Thomason	5.00	3.00
46 Fred Cone	5.00	3.00
47 Gerald Weatherly	5.00	3.00
48 Don Stonesifer	5.00	3.00
49A Lynn Chandnois ERR	5.00	3.00
49B Lynn Chandnois COR	5.00	3.00
50 George Taliaferro	5.00	3.00
51 Dick Alban	5.00	3.00
52 Lou Groza	35.00	20.00
53 Bobby Layne	60.00	35.00
54 Hugh McElhenny	40.00	20.00
55 Frank Gifford	100.00	60.00
56 Leon McLaughlin	5.00	3.00
57 Chuck Bednarik	40.00	20.00
58 Art Hunter	5.00	3.00
59 Bill McColl	5.00	3.00
60 Charley Trippi	25.00	15.00
61 Jim Finks	15.00	7.50
62 Bill Lange G	5.00	3.00
63 Laurie Niemi	5.00	3.00
64 Ray Renfro	8.00	4.00
65 Dick Chapman	25.00	15.00
66 Bob Hantla	25.00	15.00
67 Ralph Starkey	25.00	15.00
68 Don Paul LB	25.00	15.00
69 Kenneth Snyder	25.00	15.00
70 Tobin Rote SP	30.00	18.00
71 Art DeCarlo	25.00	15.00
72 Rookie	25.00	15.00
73 Hugh Taylor SP	30.00	18.00
74 Warren Lahr RC SP	25.00	15.00
75 Jim Neal	25.00	15.00
76 Leo Nomellini SP	60.00	35.00
77 Dick Yelvington	25.00	15.00
78 Les Richter SP	30.00	18.00
79 Bucko Kilroy SP	30.00	18.00
80 John Martinkovic	25.00	15.00
81 Dale Dodrill RC SP	25.00	15.00
82 Ken Jackson	25.00	15.00
83 Paul Lipscomb	25.00	15.00
84 John Bauer	25.00	15.00
85 Lou Creekmur SP	50.00	30.00
86 Eddie Price	25.00	15.00
87 Kenneth Farragut	25.00	15.00
88 Dave Hanner RC SP	30.00	18.00
89 Don Boll	25.00	15.00
90 Chet Hanulak	25.00	15.00
91 Thurman McGraw	25.00	15.00
92 Don Heinrich RC SP	30.00	18.00
93 Dan McKown	25.00	15.00
94 Bob Fleck	25.00	15.00
95 Jerry Hilgenberg	25.00	15.00
96 Bill Walsh C	25.00	15.00
97A Tom Finnin ERR	60.00	35.00
97B Tom Finnan COR	8.00	4.00
98 Paul Barry	5.00	3.00
99 Chick Jagade	5.00	3.00
100 Jack Christiansen	20.00	12.00
101 Gordy Soltau	5.00	3.00
102A Emlen Tunnel ERR	20.00	12.00
102B Emlen Tunnell COR	20.00	12.00
102C Emlen Tunnell COR	20.00	12.00
103 Stan West	5.00	3.00
104 Jerry Williams	5.00	3.00
105 Veryl Switzer	5.00	3.00
106 Billy Stone	5.00	3.00
107 Jerry Watford	5.00	3.00
108 Elbert Nickel	8.00	4.00
109 Ed Sharkey	5.00	3.00
110 Steve Meilinger	5.00	3.00
111 Dante Lavelli	20.00	12.00
112 Leon Hart	15.00	7.50
113 Charley Conerly	30.00	18.00
114 Richard Lemmon	5.00	3.00
115 Al Carmichael	5.00	3.00
116 George Connor	20.00	12.00
117 John Olszewski	5.00	3.00
118 Ernie Stautner	25.00	15.00
119 Ray Smith	5.00	3.00
120 Neil Worden	5.00	3.00
121 Jim Dooley	5.00	3.00
122 Arnold Galiffa	5.00	3.00
123 Kline Gilbert	5.00	3.00
124 Bob Hoernschemeyer	8.00	4.00
125 Wilford White RC	15.00	7.50
126 Art Spinney	5.00	3.00
127 Joe Koch	5.00	3.00
128 John Lattner RC !	80.00	40.00

1955 Bowman

COMPLETE SET (160)	1600.00	1000.00
COMMON CARD (1-64)	5.00	3.00
COMMON CARD (65-160)	8.00	5.00
WRAPPER (1-CENT)	225.00	150.00
WRAPPER (5-CENT)	100.00	60.00
1 Doak Walker !	75.00	40.00
2 Mike McCormack RC	30.00	18.00
3 John Olszewski	5.00	3.00
4 Dorne Dibble	5.00	3.00
5 Lindon Crow	5.00	3.00
6 Hugh Taylor UER	8.00	4.00

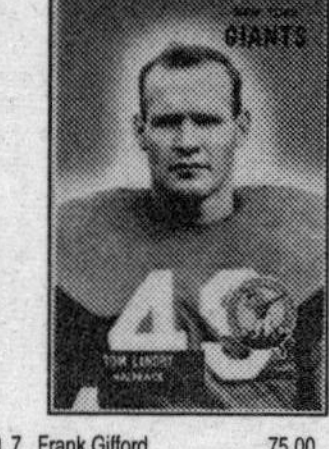

7 Frank Gifford	75.00	45.00
8 Alan Ameche RC	40.00	25.00
9 Don Stonesifer	5.00	3.00
10 Pete Pihos	15.00	7.50
11 Bill Austin	5.00	3.00
12 Dick Alban	5.00	3.00
13 Bobby Walston	8.00	4.00
14 Len Ford RC	40.00	25.00
15 Jug Girard	5.00	3.00
16 Charley Conerly	25.00	15.00
17 Volney Peters	5.00	3.00
18 Max Boydston	5.00	3.00
19 Leon Hart	12.00	6.00
20 Bert Rechichar	5.00	3.00
21 Lee Riley	5.00	3.00
22 Johnny Carson	5.00	3.00
23 Harry Thompson	5.00	3.00
24 Ray Wietecha	5.00	3.00
25 Ollie Matson	25.00	15.00
26 Eddie LeBaron	15.00	7.50
27 Jack Simmons	5.00	3.00
28 Jack Christiansen	15.00	7.50
29 Bucko Kilroy	8.00	4.00
30 Tom Keane	5.00	3.00
31 Dave Leggett	5.00	3.00
32 Norm Van Brocklin	40.00	25.00
33 Harlon Hill RC	8.00	4.00
34 Robert Haner	5.00	3.00
35 Veryl Switzer	5.00	3.00
36 Dick Stanfel RC	12.00	6.00
37 Lou Groza	25.00	15.00
38 Tank Younger	12.00	6.00
39 Dick Flanagan	5.00	3.00
40 Jim Dooley	5.00	3.00
41 Ray Collins	5.00	3.00
42 John Henry Johnson RC	40.00	25.00
43 Tom Fears	15.00	7.50
44 Joe Perry	30.00	18.00
45 Gene Brito RC	5.00	3.00
46 Bill Johnson C	5.00	3.00
47 Dan Towler	12.00	6.00
48 Dick Moegle	8.00	4.00
49 Kline Gilbert	5.00	3.00
50 Les Gobel	5.00	3.00
51 Ray Krouse RC	5.00	3.00
52 Pat Summerall RC	70.00	35.00
53 Ed Brown RC	12.00	6.00
54 Lynn Chandnois	5.00	3.00
55 Joe Heap	5.00	3.00
56 John Hoffman	5.00	3.00
57 Howard Ferguson	5.00	3.00
58 Bobby Watkins	5.00	3.00
59 Charlie Ane RC	5.00	3.00
60 Ken MacAfee E RC	8.00	4.00
61 Ralph Guglielmi RC	8.00	4.00
62 George Blanda	60.00	35.00
63 Kenneth Snyder	5.00	3.00
64 Chet Ostrowski	5.00	3.00
65 Buddy Young	15.00	7.50
66 Gordy Soltau	8.00	5.00
67 Eddie Bell	8.00	5.00
68 Ben Agajanian RC	12.00	6.00
69 Tom Dahms	8.00	5.00
70 Jim Ringo RC	50.00	30.00

❑ 71 Bobby Layne	75.00	45.00
❑ 72 Y.A.Tittle	75.00	45.00
❑ 73 Bob Gaona	8.00	5.00
❑ 74 Tobin Rote	12.00	6.00
❑ 75 Hugh McElhenny	30.00	18.00
❑ 76 John Kreamcheck	8.00	5.00
❑ 77 Al Dorow	12.00	6.00
❑ 78 Bill Wade	15.00	7.50
❑ 79 Dale Dodrill	8.00	5.00
❑ 80 Chuck Drazenovich	8.00	5.00
❑ 81 Billy Wilson RC	12.00	6.00
❑ 82 Les Richter	12.00	6.00
❑ 83 Pat Brady	8.00	5.00
❑ 84 Bob Hoernschemeyer	12.00	6.00
❑ 85 Joe Arenas	8.00	5.00
❑ 86 Len Szafaryn UER	8.00	5.00
❑ 87 Rick Casares RC	20.00	12.00
❑ 88 Leon McLaughlin	8.00	5.00
❑ 89 Charley Toogood	8.00	5.00
❑ 90 Tom Bettis	8.00	5.00
❑ 91 John Sandusky	8.00	5.00
❑ 92 Bill Wightkin	8.00	5.00
❑ 93 Darrel Brewster	8.00	5.00
❑ 94 Marion Campbell	15.00	7.50
❑ 95 Floyd Reid	8.00	5.00
❑ 96 Chick Jagade	8.00	5.00
❑ 97 George Taliaferro	8.00	5.00
❑ 98 Carlton Massey	8.00	5.00
❑ 99 Fran Rogel	8.00	5.00
❑ 100 Alex Sandusky	8.00	5.00
❑ 101 Bob St.Clair RC	35.00	20.00
❑ 102 Al Carmichael	8.00	5.00
❑ 103 Carl Taseff RC	8.00	5.00
❑ 104 Leo Nomellini	25.00	15.00
❑ 105 Tom Scott	8.00	5.00
❑ 106 Ted Marchibroda	15.00	7.50
❑ 107 Art Spinney	8.00	5.00
❑ 108 Wayne Robinson	8.00	5.00
❑ 109 Jim Ricca	8.00	5.00
❑ 110 Lou Ferry	8.00	5.00
❑ 111 Roger Zatkoff	8.00	5.00
❑ 112 Lou Creekmur	15.00	7.50
❑ 113 Kenny Konz	8.00	5.00
❑ 114 Doug Eggers	8.00	5.00
❑ 115 Bobby Thomason	8.00	5.00
❑ 116 Bill McPeak	8.00	5.00
❑ 117 William Brown	8.00	5.00
❑ 118 Royce Womble	8.00	5.00
❑ 119 Frank Gatski RC	35.00	20.00
❑ 120 Jim Finks	15.00	7.50
❑ 121 Andy Robustelli	25.00	15.00
❑ 122 Bobby Dillon	8.00	5.00
❑ 123 Leo Sanford	8.00	5.00
❑ 124 Elbert Nickel	12.00	6.00
❑ 125 Wayne Hansen	8.00	5.00
❑ 126 Buck Lansford RC	8.00	5.00
❑ 127 Gern Nagler	8.00	5.00
❑ 128 Jim Salsbury	8.00	5.00
❑ 129 Dale Atkeson RC	8.00	5.00
❑ 130 John Schweder	8.00	5.00
❑ 131 Dave Hanner	12.00	6.00
❑ 132 Eddie Price	8.00	5.00
❑ 133 Vic Janowicz	30.00	15.00
❑ 134 Ernie Stautner	25.00	15.00
❑ 135 James Parmer	8.00	5.00
❑ 136 Emlen Tunnell UER	20.00	12.00
❑ 137 Kyle Rote	15.00	7.50
❑ 138 Norm Willey	8.00	5.00
❑ 139 Charley Trippi	20.00	12.00
❑ 140 Billy Howton	12.00	6.00
❑ 141 Bobby Clatterbuck	8.00	5.00
❑ 142 Bob Boyd	8.00	5.00
❑ 143 Bob Toneff RC	12.00	6.00
❑ 144 Jerry Helluin	8.00	5.00
❑ 145 Adrian Burk	8.00	5.00
❑ 146 Walt Michaels	12.00	6.00
❑ 147 Zollie Toth	8.00	5.00
❑ 148 Frank Varrichione RC	8.00	5.00
❑ 149 Dick Bielski RC	8.00	5.00
❑ 150 George Ratterman	12.00	6.00
❑ 151 Mike Jarmoluk	8.00	5.00
❑ 152 Tom Landry	200.00	125.00
❑ 153 Ray Renfro	12.00	6.00
❑ 154 Zeke Bratkowski	12.00	6.00
❑ 155 Jerry Norton	8.00	5.00
❑ 156 Maurice Bassett	8.00	5.00
❑ 157 Volney Quinlan	8.00	5.00
❑ 158 Chuck Bednarik	30.00	18.00
❑ 159 Don Colo	8.00	5.00
❑ 160 L.G. Dupre RC !	40.00	20.00

1991 Bowman

❑ COMPLETE SET (561)	12.00	5.00
❑ COMP.FACT.SET (561)	12.00	5.00
❑ 1 Jeff George RS	.25	.08
❑ 2 Richmond Webb RS	.04	.01
❑ 3 Emmitt Smith RS	1.25	.50
❑ 4 Mark Carrier DB RS UER	.04	.01
❑ 5 Steve Christie RS	.04	.01
❑ 6 Keith Sims RS	.04	.01
❑ 7 Rob Moore RS UER	.25	.08
❑ 8 Johnny Johnson RS	.04	.01
❑ 9 Eric Green RS	.04	.01
❑ 10 Ben Smith RS	.04	.01
❑ 11 Tory Epps RS	.04	.01
❑ 12 Andre Rison	.10	.02
❑ 13 Shawn Collins	.04	.01
❑ 14 Chris Hinton	.04	.01
❑ 15 Deion Sanders	.40	.15
❑ 16 Darion Conner	.04	.01
❑ 17 Michael Haynes	.25	.08
❑ 18 Chris Miller	.10	.02
❑ 19 Jessie Tuggle	.04	.01
❑ 20 Scott Fulhage	.04	.01
❑ 21 Bill Fralic	.04	.01
❑ 22 Floyd Dixon	.04	.01
❑ 23 Oliver Barnett	.04	.01
❑ 24 Mike Rozier	.04	.01
❑ 25 Tory Epps	.04	.01
❑ 26 Tim Green	.04	.01
❑ 27 Steve Broussard	.04	.01
❑ 28 Bruce Pickens RC	.04	.01
❑ 29 Mike Pritchard RC	.25	.08
❑ 30 Andre Reed	.10	.02
❑ 31 Darryl Talley	.04	.01
❑ 32 Nate Odomes	.04	.01
❑ 33 Jamie Mueller	.04	.01
❑ 34 Leon Seals	.04	.01
❑ 35 Keith McKeller	.04	.01
❑ 36 Al Edwards	.04	.01
❑ 37 Butch Rolle	.04	.01
❑ 38 Jeff Wright RC	.04	.01
❑ 39 Will Wolford	.04	.01
❑ 40 James Williams	.04	.01
❑ 41 Kent Hull	.04	.01
❑ 42 James Lofton	.10	.02
❑ 43 Frank Reich	.10	.02
❑ 44 Bruce Smith	.25	.08
❑ 45 Thurman Thomas	.25	.08
❑ 46 Leonard Smith	.04	.01
❑ 47 Shane Conlan	.04	.01
❑ 48 Steve Tasker	.10	.02
❑ 49 Ray Bentley	.04	.01
❑ 50 Cornelius Bennett	.10	.02
❑ 51 Stan Thomas	.04	.01
❑ 52 Shaun Gayle	.04	.01
❑ 53 Wendell Davis	.04	.01
❑ 54 James Thornton	.04	.01
❑ 55 Mark Carrier DB	.10	.02
❑ 56 Richard Dent	.10	.02
❑ 57 Ron Morris	.04	.01
❑ 58 Mike Singletary	.10	.02
❑ 59 Jay Hilgenberg	.04	.01
❑ 60 Donnell Woolford	.04	.01
❑ 61 Jim Covert	.04	.01
❑ 62 Jim Harbaugh	.25	.08
❑ 63 Neal Anderson	.10	.02
❑ 64 Brad Muster	.04	.01
❑ 65 Kevin Butler	.04	.01
❑ 66 Trace Armstrong UER	.04	.01
❑ 67 Ron Cox	.04	.01
❑ 68 Peter Tom Willis	.04	.01
❑ 69 Johnny Bailey	.04	.01
❑ 70 Mark Bortz UER	.04	.01
❑ 71 Chris Zorich RC	.25	.08
❑ 72 Lamar Rogers RC	.04	.01
❑ 73 David Grant UER	.04	.01
❑ 74 Lewis Billups	.04	.01
❑ 75 Harold Green	.10	.02
❑ 76 Ickey Woods	.04	.01
❑ 77 Eddie Brown	.04	.01
❑ 78 David Fulcher	.04	.01
❑ 79 Anthony Munoz	.10	.02
❑ 80 Carl Zander	.04	.01
❑ 81 Rodney Holman	.04	.01
❑ 82 James Brooks	.10	.02
❑ 83 Tim McGee	.04	.01
❑ 84 Boomer Esiason	.10	.02
❑ 85 Leon White	.04	.01
❑ 86 James Francis UER	.04	.01
❑ 87 Mitchell Price RC	.04	.01
❑ 88 Ed King RC	.04	.01
❑ 89 Eric Turner RC	.10	.02
❑ 90 Rob Burnett RC	.10	.02
❑ 91 Leroy Hoard	.10	.02
❑ 92 Kevin Mack UER	.04	.01
❑ 93 Thane Gash UER	.04	.01
❑ 94 Gregg Rakoczy	.04	.01
❑ 95 Clay Matthews	.10	.02
❑ 96 Eric Metcalf	.10	.02
❑ 97 Stephen Braggs	.04	.01
❑ 98 Frank Minnifield	.04	.01
❑ 99 Reggie Langhorne	.04	.01
❑ 100 Mike Johnson	.04	.01
❑ 101 Brian Brennan	.04	.01
❑ 102 Anthony Pleasant	.04	.01
❑ 103 Godfrey Myles RC UER	.04	.01
❑ 104 Russell Maryland RC	.25	.08
❑ 105 James Washington RC	.04	.01
❑ 106 Nate Newton	.10	.02
❑ 107 Jimmie Jones	.04	.01
❑ 108 Jay Novacek	.25	.08
❑ 109 Alexander Wright	.04	.01
❑ 110 Jack Del Rio	.10	.02
❑ 111 Jim Jeffcoat	.04	.01
❑ 112 Mike Saxon	.04	.01
❑ 113 Troy Aikman	.75	.30
❑ 114 Issiac Holt	.04	.01
❑ 115 Ken Norton	.10	.02
❑ 116 Kelvin Martin	.04	.01
❑ 117 Emmitt Smith	2.50	1.00
❑ 118 Ken Willis	.04	.01
❑ 119 Daniel Stubbs	.04	.01
❑ 120 Michael Irvin	.25	.08
❑ 121 Danny Noonan	.04	.01
❑ 122 Alvin Harper RC	.25	.08
❑ 123 Reggie Johnson RC	.04	.01
❑ 124 Vance Johnson	.04	.01
❑ 125 Steve Atwater	.04	.01
❑ 126 Greg Kragen	.04	.01
❑ 127 John Elway	1.25	.50
❑ 128 Simon Fletcher	.04	.01
❑ 129 Wymon Henderson	.04	.01
❑ 130 Ricky Nattiel	.04	.01

❑	131	Shannon Sharpe	.50	.20
❑	132	Ron Holmes	.04	.01
❑	133	Karl Mecklenburg	.04	.01
❑	134	Bobby Humphrey	.04	.01
❑	135	Clarence Kay	.04	.01
❑	136	Dennis Smith	.04	.01
❑	137	Jim Juriga	.04	.01
❑	138	Melvin Bratton	.04	.01
❑	139	Mark Jackson UER	.04	.01
❑	140	Michael Brooks	.04	.01
❑	141	Alton Montgomery	.04	.01
❑	142	Mike Croel RC	.04	.01
❑	143	Mel Gray	.10	.02
❑	144	Michael Cofer	.04	.01
❑	145	Jeff Campbell	.04	.01
❑	146	Dan Owens	.04	.01
❑	147	Robert Clark UER	.04	.01
❑	148	Jim Arnold	.04	.01
❑	149	William White	.04	.01
❑	150	Rodney Peete	.10	.02
❑	151	Jerry Ball	.04	.01
❑	152	Bennie Blades	.04	.01
❑	153	Barry Sanders UER	1.25	.50
❑	154	Andre Ware	.10	.02
❑	155	Lomas Brown	.04	.01
❑	156	Chris Spielman	.10	.02
❑	157	Kelvin Pritchett RC	.10	.02
❑	158	Herman Moore RC	.25	.08
❑	159	Chris Jacke	.04	.01
❑	160	Tony Mandarich	.04	.01
❑	161	Perry Kemp	.04	.01
❑	162	Johnny Holland	.04	.01
❑	163	Mark Lee	.04	.01
❑	164	Anthony Dilweg	.04	.01
❑	165	Scott Stephen RC	.04	.01
❑	166	Ed West	.04	.01
❑	167	Mark Murphy	.04	.01
❑	168	Darrell Thompson	.04	.01
❑	169	James Campen RC	.04	.01
❑	170	Jeff Query	.04	.01
❑	171	Brian Noble	.04	.01
❑	172	Sterling Sharpe UER	.25	.08
❑	173	Robert Brown	.04	.01
❑	174	Tim Harris	.04	.01
❑	175	LeRoy Butler	.10	.02
❑	176	Don Majkowski	.04	.01
❑	177	Vinnie Clark RC	.04	.01
❑	178	Esera Tuaolo RC	.04	.01
❑	179	Lorenzo White UER	.04	.01
❑	180	Warren Moon	.25	.08
❑	181	Sean Jones	.10	.02
❑	182	Curtis Duncan	.04	.01
❑	183	Al Smith	.04	.01
❑	184	Richard Johnson CB RC	.04	.01
❑	185	Tony Jones WR	.04	.01
❑	186	Bubba McDowell	.04	.01
❑	187	Bruce Matthews	.10	.02
❑	188	Ray Childress	.04	.01
❑	189	Haywood Jeffires	.10	.02
❑	190	Ernest Givins	.10	.02
❑	191	Mike Munchak	.10	.02
❑	192	Greg Montgomery	.04	.01
❑	193	Cody Carlson RC	.04	.01
❑	194	Johnny Meads	.04	.01
❑	195	Drew Hill UER	.04	.01
❑	196	Mike Dumas RC	.04	.01
❑	197	Darryll Lewis RC	.10	.02
❑	198	Rohn Stark	.04	.01
❑	199	Clarence Verdin UER	.04	.01
❑	200	Mike Prior	.04	.01
❑	201	Eugene Daniel	.04	.01
❑	202	Dean Biasucci	.04	.01
❑	203	Jeff Herrod	.04	.01
❑	204	Keith Taylor	.04	.01
❑	205	Jon Hand	.04	.01
❑	206	Pat Beach	.04	.01
❑	207	Duane Bickett	.04	.01
❑	208	Jessie Hester UER	.04	.01
❑	209	Chip Banks	.04	.01
❑	210	Ray Donaldson	.04	.01
❑	211	Bill Brooks	.04	.01
❑	212	Jeff George	.25	.08
❑	213	Tony Siragusa RC	.10	.02
❑	214	Albert Bentley	.04	.01
❑	215	Joe Valerio	.04	.01
❑	216	Chris Martin	.04	.01
❑	217	Christian Okoye	.04	.01
❑	218	Stephone Paige	.04	.01
❑	219	Percy Snow	.04	.01
❑	220	David Szott	.04	.01
❑	221	Derrick Thomas	.25	.08
❑	222	Todd McNair	.04	.01
❑	223	Albert Lewis	.04	.01
❑	224	Neil Smith	.25	.08
❑	225	Barry Word	.04	.01
❑	226	Robb Thomas	.04	.01
❑	227	John Alt	.04	.01
❑	228	Jonathan Hayes	.04	.01
❑	229	Kevin Ross	.04	.01
❑	230	Nick Lowery	.04	.01
❑	231	Tim Grunhard	.04	.01
❑	232	Dan Saleaumua	.04	.01
❑	233	Steve DeBerg	.04	.01
❑	234	Harvey Williams RC	.25	.08
❑	235	Nick Bell RC UER	.04	.01
❑	236	Mervyn Fernandez UER	.04	.01
❑	237	Howie Long	.25	.08
❑	238	Marcus Allen	.25	.08
❑	239	Eddie Anderson	.04	.01
❑	240	Ethan Horton	.04	.01
❑	241	Lionel Washington	.04	.01
❑	242	Steve Wisniewski UER	.04	.01
❑	243	Bo Jackson UER	.30	.10
❑	244	Greg Townsend	.04	.01
❑	245	Jeff Jaeger	.04	.01
❑	246	Aaron Wallace	.04	.01
❑	247	Garry Lewis	.04	.01
❑	248	Steve Smith	.04	.01
❑	249	Willie Gault UER	.04	.01
❑	250	Scott Davis	.04	.01
❑	251	Jay Schroeder	.04	.01
❑	252	Don Mosebar	.04	.01
❑	253	Todd Marinovich RC	.04	.01
❑	254	Irv Pankey	.04	.01
❑	255	Flipper Anderson	.04	.01
❑	256	Tom Newberry	.04	.01
❑	257	Kevin Greene	.10	.02
❑	258	Mike Wilcher	.04	.01
❑	259	Bern Brostek	.04	.01
❑	260	Buford McGee	.04	.01
❑	261	Cleveland Gary	.04	.01
❑	262	Jackie Slater	.04	.01
❑	263	Henry Ellard	.10	.02
❑	264	Alvin Wright	.04	.01
❑	265	Darryl Henley RC	.04	.01
❑	266	Damone Johnson RC	.04	.01
❑	267	Frank Stams	.04	.01
❑	268	Jerry Gray	.04	.01
❑	269	Jim Everett	.10	.02
❑	270	Pat Terrell	.04	.01
❑	271	Todd Lyght RC	.04	.01
❑	272	Aaron Cox	.04	.01
❑	273	Barry Sanders LL	.50	.20
❑	274	Jerry Rice LL	.40	.15
❑	275	Derrick Thomas LL	.25	.08
❑	276	Mark Carrier DB LL	.10	.02
❑	277	Warren Moon LL	.25	.08
❑	278	Randall Cunningham LL	.10	.02
❑	279	Nick Lowery LL	.04	.01
❑	280	Clarence Verdin LL	.04	.01
❑	281	Thurman Thomas LL	.25	.08
❑	282	Mike Horan LL	.04	.01
❑	283	Flipper Anderson LL	.04	.01
❑	284	John Offerdahl	.04	.01
❑	285	Dan Marino UER	1.25	.50
❑	286	Mark Clayton	.10	.02
❑	287	Tony Paige	.04	.01
❑	288	Keith Sims	.04	.01
❑	289	Jeff Cross	.04	.01
❑	290	Pete Stoyanovich	.04	.01
❑	291	Ferrell Edmunds	.04	.01
❑	292	Reggie Roby	.04	.01
❑	293	Louis Oliver	.04	.01
❑	294	Jarvis Williams	.04	.01
❑	295	Sammie Smith	.04	.01
❑	296	Richmond Webb	.04	.01
❑	297	J.B. Brown	.04	.01
❑	298	Jim C.Jensen	.04	.01
❑	299	Mark Duper	.10	.02
❑	300	David Griggs	.04	.01
❑	301	Randal Hill RC	.10	.02
❑	302	Aaron Craver RC	.04	.01
❑	303	Keith Millard	.04	.01
❑	304	Steve Jordan	.04	.01
❑	305	Anthony Carter	.10	.02
❑	306	Mike Merriweather	.04	.01
❑	307	Audray McMillian RC UER	.04	.01
❑	308	Randall McDaniel	.04	.01
❑	309	Gary Zimmerman	.04	.01
❑	310	Carl Lee	.04	.01
❑	311	Reggie Rutland	.04	.01
❑	312	Hassan Jones	.04	.01
❑	313	Kirk Lowdermilk UER	.04	.01
❑	314	Herschel Walker	.10	.02
❑	315	Chris Doleman	.04	.01
❑	316	Joey Browner	.04	.01
❑	317	Wade Wilson	.10	.02
❑	318	Henry Thomas	.04	.01
❑	319	Rich Gannon	.25	.08
❑	320	Al Noga UER	.04	.01
❑	321	Pat Harlow RC	.04	.01
❑	322	Bruce Armstrong	.04	.01
❑	323	Maurice Hurst	.04	.01
❑	324	Brent Williams	.04	.01
❑	325	Chris Singleton	.04	.01
❑	326	Jason Staurovsky	.04	.01
❑	327	Marvin Allen	.04	.01
❑	328	Hart Lee Dykes	.04	.01
❑	329	Johnny Rembert	.04	.01
❑	330	Andre Tippett	.04	.01
❑	331	Greg McMurtry	.04	.01
❑	332	John Stephens	.04	.01
❑	333	Ray Agnew	.04	.01
❑	334	Tommy Hodson	.04	.01
❑	335	Ronnie Lippett	.04	.01
❑	336	Marv Cook	.04	.01
❑	337	Tommy Barnhardt RC	.04	.01
❑	338	Dalton Hilliard	.04	.01
❑	339	Sam Mills	.04	.01
❑	340	Morten Andersen	.04	.01
❑	341	Stan Brock	.04	.01
❑	342	Brett Maxie	.04	.01
❑	343	Steve Walsh	.04	.01
❑	344	Vaughan Johnson	.04	.01
❑	345	Rickey Jackson	.04	.01
❑	346	Renaldo Turnbull	.04	.01
❑	347	Joel Hilgenberg	.04	.01
❑	348	Toi Cook RC	.04	.01
❑	349	Robert Massey	.04	.01
❑	350	Pat Swilling	.10	.02
❑	351	Eric Martin	.04	.01
❑	352	Rueben Mayes UER	.04	.01
❑	353	Vince Buck	.04	.01
❑	354	Brett Perriman	.25	.08
❑	355	Wesley Carroll RC	.04	.01
❑	356	Jarrod Bunch RC	.04	.01
❑	357	Pepper Johnson	.04	.01
❑	358	Dave Meggett	.10	.02
❑	359	Mark Collins	.04	.01
❑	360	Sean Landeta	.04	.01
❑	361	Maurice Carthon	.04	.01
❑	362	Mike Fox UER	.04	.01
❑	363	Jeff Hostetler	.10	.02
❑	364	Phil Simms	.10	.02
❑	365	Leonard Marshall	.04	.01
❑	366	Gary Reasons	.04	.01
❑	367	Rodney Hampton	.25	.08
❑	368	Greg Jackson RC	.04	.01
❑	369	Jumbo Elliott	.04	.01
❑	370	Bob Kratch RC	.04	.01

❑ 371 Lawrence Taylor .25 .08
❑ 372 Erik Howard .04 .01
❑ 373 Carl Banks .04 .01
❑ 374 Stephen Baker .04 .01
❑ 375 Mark Ingram .10 .02
❑ 376 Browning Nagle RC .04 .01
❑ 377 Jeff Lageman .04 .01
❑ 378 Ken O'Brien .04 .01
❑ 379 Al Toon .10 .02
❑ 380 Joe Prokop .04 .01
❑ 381 Tony Stargell .04 .01
❑ 382 Blair Thomas .04 .01
❑ 383 Erik McMillan .04 .01
❑ 384 Dennis Byrd .04 .01
❑ 385 Freeman McNeil .04 .01
❑ 386 Brad Baxter .04 .01
❑ 387 Mark Boyer .04 .01
❑ 388 Terance Mathis .10 .02
❑ 389 Jim Sweeney .04 .01
❑ 390 Kyle Clifton .04 .01
❑ 391 Pat Leahy .04 .01
❑ 392 Rob Moore .25 .08
❑ 393 James Hasty .04 .01
❑ 394 Blaise Bryant .04 .01
❑ 395A Jesse Campbell RC ERR 1.00 .40
❑ 395B Jesse Campbell RC COR .04 .01
❑ 396 Keith Jackson .10 .02
❑ 397 Jerome Brown .04 .01
❑ 398 Keith Byars .04 .01
❑ 399 Seth Joyner .10 .02
❑ 400 Mike Bellamy .04 .01
❑ 401 Fred Barnett .25 .08
❑ 402 Reggie Singletary RC .04 .01
❑ 403 Reggie White .25 .08
❑ 404 Randall Cunningham .25 .08
❑ 405 Byron Evans .04 .01
❑ 406 Wes Hopkins .04 .01
❑ 407 Ben Smith .04 .01
❑ 408 Roger Ruzek .04 .01
❑ 409 Eric Allen UER .04 .01
❑ 410 Anthony Toney UER .04 .01
❑ 411 Clyde Simmons .04 .01
❑ 412 Andre Waters .04 .01
❑ 413 Calvin Williams .10 .02
❑ 414 Eric Swann RC .25 .08
❑ 415 Eric Hill .04 .01
❑ 416 Tim McDonald .04 .01
❑ 417 Luis Sharpe .04 .01
❑ 418 Ernie Jones UER .04 .01
❑ 419 Ken Harvey .10 .02
❑ 420 Ricky Proehl .04 .01
❑ 421 Johnny Johnson .04 .01
❑ 422 Anthony Bell .04 .01
❑ 423 Timm Rosenbach .04 .01
❑ 424 Rich Camarillo .04 .01
❑ 425 Walter Reeves .04 .01
❑ 426 Freddie Joe Nunn .04 .01
❑ 427 Anthony Thompson UER .04 .01
❑ 428 Bill Lewis .04 .01
❑ 429 Jim Wahler RC .04 .01
❑ 430 Cedric Mack .04 .01
❑ 431 Mike Jones DE RC .04 .01
❑ 432 Ernie Mills RC .10 .02
❑ 433 Tim Worley .04 .01
❑ 434 Greg Lloyd .25 .08
❑ 435 Dermontti Dawson .04 .01
❑ 436 Louis Lipps .04 .01
❑ 437 Eric Green .04 .01
❑ 438 Donald Evans .04 .01
❑ 439 D.J. Johnson .04 .01
❑ 440 Tunch Ilkin .04 .01
❑ 441 Bubby Brister .04 .01
❑ 442 Chris Calloway .04 .01
❑ 443 David Little .04 .01
❑ 444 Thomas Everett .04 .01
❑ 445 Carnell Lake .04 .01
❑ 446 Rod Woodson .25 .08
❑ 447 Gary Anderson K .04 .01
❑ 448 Merril Hoge .04 .01
❑ 449 Gerald Williams .04 .01
❑ 450 Eric Moten RC .04 .01
❑ 451 Marion Butts .10 .02
❑ 452 Leslie O'Neal .10 .02
❑ 453 Ronnie Harmon .04 .01
❑ 454 Gill Byrd .04 .01
❑ 455 Junior Seau .25 .08
❑ 456 Nate Lewis RC .04 .01
❑ 457 Leo Goeas .04 .01
❑ 458 Burt Grossman .04 .01
❑ 459 Courtney Hall .04 .01
❑ 460 Anthony Miller .10 .02
❑ 461 Gary Plummer .04 .01
❑ 462 Billy Joe Tolliver .04 .01
❑ 463 Lee Williams .04 .01
❑ 464 Arthur Cox .04 .01
❑ 465 John Kidd UER .04 .01
❑ 466 Frank Cornish .04 .01
❑ 467 John Carney .04 .01
❑ 468 Eric Bieniemy RC .04 .01
❑ 469 Don Griffin .04 .01
❑ 470 Jerry Rice .75 .30
❑ 471 Keith DeLong .04 .01
❑ 472 John Taylor .10 .02
❑ 473 Brent Jones .25 .08
❑ 474 Pierce Holt .04 .01
❑ 475 Kevin Fagan .04 .01
❑ 476 Bill Romanowski .04 .01
❑ 477 Dexter Carter .04 .01
❑ 478 Guy McIntyre .04 .01
❑ 479 Joe Montana 1.25 .50
❑ 480 Charles Haley .10 .02
❑ 481 Mike Cofer .04 .01
❑ 482 Jesse Sapolu .04 .01
❑ 483 Eric Davis .04 .01
❑ 484 Mike Sherrard .04 .01
❑ 485 Steve Young .75 .30
❑ 486 Darryl Pollard .04 .01
❑ 487 Tom Rathman .04 .01
❑ 488 Michael Carter .04 .01
❑ 489 Ricky Watters RC 1.50 .60
❑ 490 John Johnson RC .04 .01
❑ 491 Eugene Robinson .04 .01
❑ 492 Andy Heck .04 .01
❑ 493 John L. Williams .04 .01
❑ 494 Norm Johnson .04 .01
❑ 495 David Wyman .04 .01
❑ 496 Derrick Fenner UER .04 .01
❑ 497 Rick Donnelly .04 .01
❑ 498 Tony Woods .04 .01
❑ 499 Derrick Loville RC .04 .01
❑ 500 Dave Krieg .10 .02
❑ 501 Joe Nash .04 .01
❑ 502 Brian Blades .10 .02
❑ 503 Cortez Kennedy .25 .08
❑ 504 Jeff Bryant .04 .01
❑ 505 Tommy Kane .04 .01
❑ 506 Travis McNeal .04 .01
❑ 507 Terry Wooden .04 .01
❑ 508 Chris Warren .25 .08
❑ 509A Dan McGwire RC ERR .04 .01
❑ 509B Dan McGwire RC COR .04 .01
❑ 510 Mark Robinson .04 .01
❑ 511 Ron Hall .04 .01
❑ 512 Paul Gruber .04 .01
❑ 513 Harry Hamilton .04 .01
❑ 514 Keith McCants .04 .01
❑ 515 Reggie Cobb .04 .01
❑ 516 Steve Christie UER .04 .01
❑ 517 Broderick Thomas .04 .01
❑ 518 Mark Carrier WR .25 .08
❑ 519 Vinny Testaverde .10 .02
❑ 520 Ricky Reynolds .04 .01
❑ 521 Jesse Anderson .04 .01
❑ 522 Reuben Davis .04 .01
❑ 523 Wayne Haddix .04 .01
❑ 524 Gary Anderson RB UER .04 .01
❑ 525 Bruce Hill .04 .01
❑ 526 Kevin Murphy .04 .01
❑ 527 Lawrence Dawsey RC .10 .02
❑ 528 Ricky Ervins RC .10 .02
❑ 529 Charles Mann .04 .01
❑ 530 Jim Lachey .04 .01
❑ 531 Mark Rypien UER .10 .02
❑ 532 Darrell Green .04 .01
❑ 533 Stan Humphries .25 .08
❑ 534 Jeff Bostic UER .04 .01
❑ 535 Earnest Byner .04 .01
❑ 536 Art Monk UER .10 .02
❑ 537 Don Warren .04 .01
❑ 538 Darryl Grant .04 .01
❑ 539 Wilber Marshall .04 .01
❑ 540 Kurt Gouveia RC .04 .01
❑ 541 Markus Koch .04 .01
❑ 542 Andre Collins .04 .01
❑ 543 Chip Lohmiller .04 .01
❑ 544 Alvin Walton .04 .01
❑ 545 Gary Clark .25 .08
❑ 546 Ricky Sanders .04 .01
❑ 547 Redskins vs. Eagles .04 .01
❑ 548 Bengals vs. Oilers .04 .01
❑ 549 Dolphins vs. Chiefs .04 .01
❑ 550 Bears vs. Saints UER .04 .01
❑ 551 Playoffs/Thurman Thomas .10 .02
❑ 552 49ers vs. Redskins .04 .01
❑ 553 Giants vs. Bears .04 .01
❑ 554 Playoffs/Bo Jackson .10 .02
❑ 555 AFC Championship .04 .01
❑ 556 NFC Championship .04 .01
❑ 557 Super Bowl XXV .04 .01
❑ 558 Checklist 1-140 .04 .01
❑ 559 Checklist 141-280 .04 .01
❑ 560 Checklist 281-420 UER .04 .01
❑ 561 Checklist 421-561 UER .04 .01

1992 Bowman

❑ COMPLETE SET (573) 50.00 25.00
❑ 1 Reggie White 1.00 .40
❑ 2 Johnny Meads .25 .08
❑ 3 Chip Lohmiller .25 .08
❑ 4 James Lofton .50 .20
❑ 5 Ray Horton .25 .08
❑ 6 Rich Moran .25 .08
❑ 7 Howard Cross .25 .08
❑ 8 Mike Horan .25 .08
❑ 9 Erik Kramer .50 .20
❑ 10 Steve Wisniewski .25 .08
❑ 11 Michael Haynes .50 .20
❑ 12 Donald Evans .25 .08
❑ 13 Michael Irvin FOIL 1.00 .40
❑ 14 Gary Zimmerman .25 .08
❑ 15 John Friesz .50 .20
❑ 16 Mark Carrier WR 1.00 .40
❑ 17 Mark Duper .25 .08
❑ 18 James Thornton .25 .08
❑ 19 Jon Hand .25 .08
❑ 20 Sterling Sharpe 1.00 .40
❑ 21 Jacob Green .25 .08
❑ 22 Wesley Carroll .25 .08
❑ 23 Clay Matthews .50 .20
❑ 24 Kevin Greene .50 .20
❑ 25 Brad Baxter .25 .08
❑ 26 Don Griffin .25 .08
❑ 27 Robert Delpino 1.50 .60
❑ 28 Lee Johnson .25 .08

❑ 29 Jim Wahler .25 .08
❑ 30 Leonard Russell .50 .20
❑ 31 Eric Moore .25 .08
❑ 32 Dino Hackett .25 .08
❑ 33 Simon Fletcher .25 .08
❑ 34 Al Edwards .25 .08
❑ 35 Brad Edwards .25 .08
❑ 36 James Joseph .25 .08
❑ 37 Rodney Peete .50 .20
❑ 38 Ricky Reynolds .25 .08
❑ 39 Eddie Anderson .25 .08
❑ 40 Ken Clarke .25 .08
❑ 41 Tony Bennett .50 .20
❑ 42 Larry Brown DB .25 .08
❑ 43 Ray Childress .25 .08
❑ 44 Mike Kenn .25 .08
❑ 45 Vestee Jackson .25 .08
❑ 46 Neil O'Donnell .50 .20
❑ 47 Bill Brooks .25 .08
❑ 48 Kevin Butler .25 .08
❑ 49 Joe Phillips .25 .08
❑ 50 Cortez Kennedy .50 .20
❑ 51 Rickey Jackson .25 .08
❑ 52 Vinnie Clark .25 .08
❑ 53 Michael Jackson .50 .20
❑ 54 Ernie Jones .25 .08
❑ 55 Tom Newberry .25 .08
❑ 56 Pat Harlow .25 .08
❑ 57 Craig Taylor .25 .08
❑ 58 Joe Prokop .25 .08
❑ 59 Warren Moon FOIL SP 2.00 .75
❑ 60 Jeff Lageman .25 .08
❑ 61 Neil Smith 1.00 .40
❑ 62 Jim Jeffcoat .25 .08
❑ 63 Bill Fralic .25 .08
❑ 64 Mark Schlereth RC .25 .08
❑ 65 Keith Byars .25 .08
❑ 66 Jeff Hostetler .50 .20
❑ 67 Joey Browner .25 .08
❑ 68 Bobby Hebert FOIL SP 1.50 .60
❑ 69 Keith Sims .25 .08
❑ 70 Warren Moon 1.00 .40
❑ 71 Pio Sagapolutele RC .25 .08
❑ 72 Cornelius Bennett .50 .20
❑ 73 Greg Davis .25 .08
❑ 74 Ronnie Harmon .25 .08
❑ 75 Ron Hall .25 .08
❑ 76 Howie Long 1.00 .40
❑ 77 Greg Lewis .25 .08
❑ 78 Carnell Lake .25 .08
❑ 79 Ray Crockett .25 .08
❑ 80 Tom Waddle .25 .08
❑ 81 Vincent Brown .25 .08
❑ 82 Bill Brooks .50 .20
❑ 83 John L. Williams .25 .08
❑ 84 Floyd Turner .25 .08
❑ 85 Scott Radecic .25 .08
❑ 86 Anthony Munoz .50 .20
❑ 87 Lonnie Young .25 .08
❑ 88 Dexter Carter .25 .08
❑ 89 Tony Zendejas .25 .08
❑ 90 Tim Jorden .25 .08
❑ 91 LeRoy Butler .25 .08
❑ 92 Richard Brown RC .25 .08
❑ 93 Erric Pegram .50 .20
❑ 94 Sean Landeta .25 .08
❑ 95 Clyde Simmons .25 .08
❑ 96 Martin Mayhew .25 .08
❑ 97 Jarvis Williams .25 .08
❑ 98 Barry Word .25 .08
❑ 99 John Taylor FOIL .50 .20
❑ 100 Emmitt Smith 8.00 3.00
❑ 101 Leon Seals .25 .08
❑ 102 Marion Butts .25 .08
❑ 103 Mike Merriweather .25 .08
❑ 104 Ernest Givins .50 .20
❑ 105 Wymon Henderson .25 .08
❑ 106 Robert Wilson .25 .08
❑ 107 Bobby Hebert .25 .08
❑ 108 Terry McDaniel .25 .08
❑ 109 Jerry Ball .25 .08
❑ 110 John Taylor .50 .20
❑ 111 Rob Moore .50 .20
❑ 112 Thurman Thomas FOIL 1.00 .40
❑ 113 Checklist 1-115 .25 .08
❑ 114 Brian Blades .50 .20
❑ 115 Larry Kelm .25 .08
❑ 116 James Francis .25 .08
❑ 117 Rod Woodson 1.00 .40
❑ 118 Trace Armstrong .25 .08
❑ 119 Eugene Daniel .25 .08
❑ 120 Andre Tippett .25 .08
❑ 121 Chris Jacke .25 .08
❑ 122 Jessie Tuggle .25 .08
❑ 123 Chris Chandler 1.00 .40
❑ 124 Tim Johnson .25 .08
❑ 125 Mark Collins .25 .08
❑ 126 Aeneas Williams SP 1.50 .60
❑ 127 James Jones DT .25 .08
❑ 128 George Jamison .25 .08
❑ 129 Deron Cherry .25 .08
❑ 130 Mark Clayton .50 .20
❑ 131 Keith DeLong .25 .08
❑ 132 Marcus Allen 1.00 .40
❑ 133 Joe Walter RC .25 .08
❑ 134 Reggie Rutland .25 .08
❑ 135 Kent Hull .25 .08
❑ 136 Jeff Feagles .25 .08
❑ 137 Ronnie Lott FOIL SP 2.00 .75
❑ 138 Henry Rolling .25 .08
❑ 139 Gary Anderson RB .25 .08
❑ 140 Morten Andersen .25 .08
❑ 141 Cris Dishman .25 .08
❑ 142 David Treadwell .25 .08
❑ 143 Kevin Gogan .25 .08
❑ 144 James Hasty .25 .08
❑ 145 Robert Delpino .25 .08
❑ 146 Patrick Hunter .25 .08
❑ 147 Gary Anderson K .25 .08
❑ 148 Chip Banks .25 .08
❑ 149 Dan Fike .25 .08
❑ 150 Chris Miller .50 .20
❑ 151 Hugh Millen .25 .08
❑ 152 Courtney Hall .25 .08
❑ 153 Gary Clark .50 .20
❑ 154 Michael Brooks .25 .08
❑ 155 Jay Hilgenberg .25 .08
❑ 156 Tim McDonald .25 .08
❑ 157 Andre Tippett .50 .20
❑ 158 Doug Riesenberg .25 .08
❑ 159 Bill Maas .25 .08
❑ 160 Fred Barnett .50 .20
❑ 161 Pierce Holt .25 .08
❑ 162 Brian Noble .25 .08
❑ 163 Harold Green .25 .08
❑ 164 Joel Hilgenberg .25 .08
❑ 165 Mervyn Fernandez .25 .08
❑ 166 John Offerdahl .25 .08
❑ 167 Shane Conlan .25 .08
❑ 168 Mark Higgs FOIL SP 1.50 .60
❑ 169 Bubba McDowell .25 .08
❑ 170 Barry Sanders 6.00 2.50
❑ 171 Larry Roberts .25 .08
❑ 172 Herschel Walker .50 .20
❑ 173 Steve McMichael .50 .20
❑ 174 Kelly Stouffer .25 .08
❑ 175 Louis Lipps .25 .08
❑ 176 Jim Everett .50 .20
❑ 177 Tony Tolbert .25 .08
❑ 178 Mike Baab .25 .08
❑ 179 Eric Swann .50 .20
❑ 180 Emmitt Smith FOIL SP 12.00 5.00
❑ 181 Tim Brown 1.00 .40
❑ 182 Dennis Smith .25 .08
❑ 183 Moe Gardner .25 .08
❑ 184 Derrick Walker .25 .08
❑ 185 Reyna Thompson .25 .08
❑ 186 Esera Tuaolo .25 .08
❑ 187 Jeff Wright .25 .08
❑ 188 Mark Rypien .25 .08
❑ 189 Quinn Early .50 .20
❑ 190 Christian Okoye .25 .08
❑ 191 Keith Jackson .50 .20
❑ 192 Doug Smith .25 .08
❑ 193 John Elway FOIL 10.00 4.00
❑ 194 Reggie Cobb .25 .08
❑ 195 Reggie Roby .25 .08
❑ 196 Clarence Verdin .25 .08
❑ 197 Jim Breech .25 .08
❑ 198 Jim Sweeney .25 .08
❑ 199 Marv Cook .25 .08
❑ 200 Ronnie Lott .50 .20
❑ 201 Mel Gray .50 .20
❑ 202 Maury Buford .25 .08
❑ 203 Lorenzo Lynch .25 .08
❑ 204 Jesse Sapolu .25 .08
❑ 205 Steve Jordan .25 .08
❑ 206 Don Majkowski .25 .08
❑ 207 Flipper Anderson .25 .08
❑ 208 Ed King .25 .08
❑ 209 Tony Woods .25 .08
❑ 210 Ron Heller .25 .08
❑ 211 Greg Kragen .25 .08
❑ 212 Scott Case .25 .08
❑ 213 Tommy Barnhardt .25 .08
❑ 214 Charles Mann .25 .08
❑ 215 David Griggs .25 .08
❑ 216 Kenneth Davis FOIL SP 1.50 .60
❑ 217 Lamar Lathon .25 .08
❑ 218 Nate Odomes .25 .08
❑ 219 Vinny Testaverde .50 .20
❑ 220 Rod Bernstine .25 .08
❑ 221 Barry Sanders FOIL 10.00 4.00
❑ 222 Carlton Haselrig RC .25 .08
❑ 223 Steve Beuerlein .50 .20
❑ 224 John Alt .25 .08
❑ 225 Pepper Johnson .25 .08
❑ 226 Checklist 116-230 .25 .08
❑ 227 Irv Eatman .25 .08
❑ 228 Greg Townsend .25 .08
❑ 229 Mark Jackson .25 .08
❑ 230 Robert Blackmon .25 .08
❑ 231 Terry Allen 1.00 .40
❑ 232 Bennie Blades .25 .08
❑ 233 Sam Mills 1.00 .40
❑ 234 Richmond Webb .25 .08
❑ 235 Richard Dent .50 .20
❑ 236 Alonzo Mitz RC .25 .08
❑ 237 Steve Young 5.00 2.00
❑ 238 Pat Swilling .25 .08
❑ 239 James Campen .25 .08
❑ 240 Earnest Byner .25 .08
❑ 241 Pat Terrell .25 .08
❑ 242 Carwell Gardner .25 .08
❑ 243 Charles McRae .25 .08
❑ 244 Vince Newsome .25 .08
❑ 245 Eric Hill .25 .08
❑ 246 Steve Young FOIL 5.00 2.00
❑ 247 Nate Lewis .25 .08
❑ 248 William Fuller .25 .08
❑ 249 Andre Waters .25 .08
❑ 250 Dean Biasucci .25 .08
❑ 251 Andre Rison .50 .20
❑ 252 Brent Williams .25 .08
❑ 253 Todd McNair .25 .08
❑ 254 Jeff Davidson RC .25 .08
❑ 255 Art Monk .50 .20
❑ 256 Kirk Lowdermilk .25 .08
❑ 257 Bob Golic .25 .08
❑ 258 Michael Irvin 1.00 .40
❑ 259 Eric Green .25 .08
❑ 260 David Fulcher .50 .20
❑ 261 Damone Johnson .25 .08
❑ 262 Marc Spindler .25 .08
❑ 263 Alfred Williams .25 .08
❑ 264 Donnie Elder .25 .08
❑ 265 Keith McKeller .25 .08
❑ 266 Steve Bono RC 1.00 .40
❑ 267 Jumbo Elliott .25 .08
❑ 268 Randy Hilliard RC .25 .08

❑ 269 Rufus Porter	.25	.08
❑ 270 Neal Anderson	.25	.08
❑ 271 Dalton Hilliard	.25	.08
❑ 272 Michael Zordich RC	.25	.08
❑ 273 Cornelius Bennett FOIL	.50	.20
❑ 274 Louie Aguiar RC	.25	.08
❑ 275 Aaron Craver	.25	.08
❑ 276 Tony Bennett	.25	.08
❑ 277 Terry Wooden	.25	.08
❑ 278 Mike Munchak	.50	.20
❑ 279 Chris Hinton	.25	.08
❑ 280 John Elway	6.00	2.50
❑ 281 Randall McDaniel	.25	.08
❑ 282 Brad Baxter	.50	.20
❑ 283 Wes Hopkins	.25	.08
❑ 284 Scott Davis	.25	.08
❑ 285 Mark Tuinei	.25	.08
❑ 286 Broderick Thompson	.25	.08
❑ 287 Henry Ellard	.50	.20
❑ 288 Adrian Cooper	.25	.08
❑ 289 Don Warren	.25	.08
❑ 290 Rodney Hampton	.50	.20
❑ 291 Kevin Ross	.25	.08
❑ 292 Mark Carrier DB	.25	.08
❑ 293 Ian Beckles	.25	.08
❑ 294 Gene Atkins	.25	.08
❑ 295 Mark Rypien FOIL	.50	.20
❑ 296 Eric Metcalf	.50	.20
❑ 297 Howard Ballard	.25	.08
❑ 298 Nate Newton	.25	.08
❑ 299 Dan Owens	.25	.08
❑ 300 Tim McGee	.25	.08
❑ 301 Greg McMurtry	.25	.08
❑ 302 Walter Reeves	.25	.08
❑ 303 Jeff Herrod	.25	.08
❑ 304 Darren Comeaux	.25	.08
❑ 305 Pete Stoyanovich	.25	.08
❑ 306 Johnny Holland	.25	.08
❑ 307 Jay Novacek	.50	.20
❑ 308 Steve Broussard	.25	.08
❑ 309 Darrell Green	.25	.08
❑ 310 Sam Mills	.25	.08
❑ 311 Tim Barnett	.25	.08
❑ 312 Steve Atwater	.25	.08
❑ 313 Tom Waddle FOIL	.50	.20
❑ 314 Felix Wright	.25	.08
❑ 315 Sean Jones	.25	.08
❑ 316 Jim Harbaugh	1.00	.40
❑ 317 Eric Allen	.25	.08
❑ 318 Don Mosebar	.25	.08
❑ 319 Rob Taylor	.25	.08
❑ 320 Terance Mathis	.50	.20
❑ 321 Leroy Hoard	.50	.20
❑ 322 Kenneth Davis	.25	.08
❑ 323 Guy McIntyre	.25	.08
❑ 324 Deron Cherry	.50	.20
❑ 325 Tunch Ilkin	.25	.08
❑ 326 Willie Green	.25	.08
❑ 327 Darryl Henley	.25	.08
❑ 328 Shawn Jefferson	.25	.08
❑ 329 Greg Jackson	.25	.08
❑ 330 John Roper	.25	.08
❑ 331 Bill Lewis	.25	.08
❑ 332 Rodney Holman	.25	.08
❑ 333 Bruce Armstrong	.25	.08
❑ 334 Robb Thomas	.25	.08
❑ 335 Alvin Harper	.50	.20
❑ 336 Brian Jordan	.50	.20
❑ 337 Morten Andersen	.50	.20
❑ 338 Dermontti Dawson	.25	.08
❑ 339 Checklist 231-345	.25	.08
❑ 340 Louis Oliver	.25	.08
❑ 341 Paul McJulien RC	.25	.08
❑ 342 Karl Mecklenburg	.25	.08
❑ 343 Lawrence Dawsey	.50	.20
❑ 344 Kyle Clifton	.25	.08
❑ 345 Jeff Bostic	.25	.08
❑ 346 Cris Carter	1.50	.60
❑ 347 Al Smith	.25	.08
❑ 348 Mark Kelso	.25	.08
❑ 349 Art Monk FOIL	1.00	.40
❑ 350 Michael Carter	.25	.08
❑ 351 Ethan Horton	.25	.08
❑ 352 Andy Heck	.25	.08
❑ 353 Gill Fenerty	.25	.08
❑ 354 David Brandon RC	.25	.08
❑ 355 Anthony Johnson	1.00	.40
❑ 356 Mike Golic	.25	.08
❑ 357 Ferrell Edmunds	.25	.08
❑ 358 Dennis Gibson	.25	.08
❑ 359 Gill Byrd	.25	.08
❑ 360 Todd Lyght	.25	.08
❑ 361 Jayice Pearson RC	.25	.08
❑ 362 John Rade	.25	.08
❑ 363 Keith Van Horne	.25	.08
❑ 364 John Kasay	.25	.08
❑ 365 Broderick Thomas	1.50	.60
❑ 366 Ken Harvey	.25	.08
❑ 367 Rich Gannon	1.00	.40
❑ 368 Darrell Thompson	.25	.08
❑ 369 Jon Vaughn	.25	.08
❑ 370 Jesse Solomon	.25	.08
❑ 371 Erik McMillan	.25	.08
❑ 372 Bruce Matthews	.25	.08
❑ 373 Wilber Marshall	.25	.08
❑ 374 Brian Blades	1.50	.60
❑ 375 Vance Johnson	.25	.08
❑ 376 Eddie Brown	.25	.08
❑ 377 Don Beebe	.25	.08
❑ 378 Brent Jones	.50	.20
❑ 379 Matt Bahr	.25	.08
❑ 380 Dwight Stone	.25	.08
❑ 381 Tony Casillas	.25	.08
❑ 382 Jay Schroeder	.25	.08
❑ 383 Byron Evans	.25	.08
❑ 384 Dan Saleaumua	.25	.08
❑ 385 Wendell Davis	.25	.08
❑ 386 Ron Holmes	.25	.08
❑ 387 George Thomas RC	.25	.08
❑ 388 Ray Berry	.25	.08
❑ 389 Eric Martin	.25	.08
❑ 390 Kevin Mack	.25	.08
❑ 391 Natu Tuatagaloa RC	.25	.08
❑ 392 Bill Romanowski	.25	.08
❑ 393 Nick Bell FOIL SP	1.50	.60
❑ 394 Grant Feasel	.25	.08
❑ 395 Eugene Lockhart	.25	.08
❑ 396 Lorenzo White	.25	.08
❑ 397 Mike Farr	.25	.08
❑ 398 Eric Bieniemy	.25	.08
❑ 399 Kevin Murphy	.25	.08
❑ 400 Luis Sharpe	.25	.08
❑ 401 Jessie Tuggle	1.50	.60
❑ 402 Cleveland Gary	.25	.08
❑ 403 Tony Mandarich	.25	.08
❑ 404 Bryan Cox	.50	.20
❑ 405 Marvin Washington	.25	.08
❑ 406 Fred Stokes	.25	.08
❑ 407 Duane Bickett	.25	.08
❑ 408 Leonard Marshall	.25	.08
❑ 409 Barry Foster	.50	.20
❑ 410 Thurman Thomas	1.00	.40
❑ 411 Willie Gault	.50	.20
❑ 412 Vinson Smith RC	.25	.08
❑ 413 Mark Bortz	.25	.08
❑ 414 Johnny Johnson	.25	.08
❑ 415 Rodney Hampton FOIL	1.00	.40
❑ 416 Steve Wallace	.25	.08
❑ 417 Fuad Reveiz	.25	.08
❑ 418 Derrick Thomas	.50	.20
❑ 419 Jackie Harris RC	1.00	.40
❑ 420 Derek Russell	.25	.08
❑ 421 David Grant	.25	.08
❑ 422 Tommy Kane	.25	.08
❑ 423 Stan Brock	.25	.08
❑ 424 Haywood Jeffires	.50	.20
❑ 425 Broderick Thomas	.25	.08
❑ 426 John Kidd	.25	.08
❑ 427 Shawn McCarthy RC FOIL	.50	.20
❑ 428 Jim Arnold	.25	.08
❑ 429 Scott Fulhage	.25	.08
❑ 430 Jackie Slater	.25	.08
❑ 431 Scott Galbraith RC	.25	.08
❑ 432 Roger Ruzek	.25	.08
❑ 433 Irving Fryar	.50	.20
❑ 434A D.Thomas FOIL ERR 494	1.00	.40
❑ 434B D.Thomas FOIL COR	1.00	.40
❑ 435 D.J. Johnson	.25	.08
❑ 436 Jim C.Jensen	.25	.08
❑ 437 James Washington	.25	.08
❑ 438 Phil Hansen	.25	.08
❑ 439 Rohn Stark	.25	.08
❑ 440 Jarrod Bunch	.25	.08
❑ 441 Todd Marinovich	.25	.08
❑ 442 Brett Perriman	1.00	.40
❑ 443 Eugene Robinson	.25	.08
❑ 444 Robert Massey	.25	.08
❑ 445 Nick Lowery	.25	.08
❑ 446 Rickey Dixon	.25	.08
❑ 447 Jim Lachey	.25	.08
❑ 448 Johnny Hector	.50	.20
❑ 449 Gary Plummer	.25	.08
❑ 450 Robert Brown	.25	.08
❑ 451 Gaston Green	.25	.08
❑ 452 Checklist 346-459	.25	.08
❑ 453 Darion Conner	.25	.08
❑ 454 Mike Cofer	.25	.08
❑ 455 Craig Heyward	.50	.20
❑ 456 Anthony Carter	.50	.20
❑ 457 Pat Coleman RC	.25	.08
❑ 458 Jeff Bryant	.25	.08
❑ 459 Mark Gunn RC	.25	.08
❑ 460 Stan Thomas	.25	.08
❑ 461 Simon Fletcher	1.50	.60
❑ 462 Ray Agnew	.25	.08
❑ 463 Jessie Hester	.25	.08
❑ 464 Rob Burnett	.25	.08
❑ 465 Mike Croel	.25	.08
❑ 466 Mike Pitts	.25	.08
❑ 467 Darryl Talley	.25	.08
❑ 468 Rich Camarillo	.25	.08
❑ 469 Reggie White FOIL	1.00	.40
❑ 470 Nick Bell	.25	.08
❑ 471 Tracy Hayworth RC	.25	.08
❑ 472 Eric Thomas	.25	.08
❑ 473 Paul Gruber	.25	.08
❑ 474 David Richards	.25	.08
❑ 475 T.J. Turner	.25	.08
❑ 476 Mark Ingram	.25	.08
❑ 477 Tim Grunhard	.25	.08
❑ 478 Marion Butts FOIL	.50	.20
❑ 479 Tom Rathman	.25	.08
❑ 480 Brian Mitchell	.50	.20
❑ 481 Bryce Paup	1.00	.40
❑ 482 Mike Pritchard	.50	.20
❑ 483 Ken Norton Jr.	.50	.20
❑ 484 Roman Phifer	.25	.08
❑ 485 Greg Lloyd	.50	.20
❑ 486 Brett Maxie	.25	.08
❑ 487 Richard Dent FOIL SP	1.50	.60
❑ 488 Curtis Duncan	.25	.08
❑ 489 Chris Burkett	.25	.08
❑ 490 Travis McNeal	.25	.08
❑ 491 Carl Lee	.25	.08
❑ 492 Clarence Kay	.25	.08
❑ 493 Tom Thayer	.25	.08
❑ 494 Erik Kramer FOIL SP	2.00	.75
❑ 495 Perry Kemp	.25	.08
❑ 496 Jeff Jaeger	.25	.08
❑ 497 Eric Sanders	.25	.08
❑ 498 Burt Grossman	.25	.08
❑ 499 Ben Smith	.25	.08
❑ 500 Keith McCants	.25	.08
❑ 501 John Stephens	.25	.08
❑ 502 John Rienstra	.25	.08
❑ 503 Jim Ritcher	.25	.08
❑ 504 Harris Barton	.25	.08
❑ 505 Andre Rison FOIL SP	2.00	.75
❑ 506 Chris Martin	.25	.08
❑ 507 Freddie Joe Nunn	.25	.08

Card	Price 1	Price 2
❑ 508 Mark Higgs	.25	.08
❑ 509 Norm Johnson	.25	.08
❑ 510 Stephen Baker	.25	.08
❑ 511 Ricky Sanders	.25	.08
❑ 512 Ray Donaldson	.25	.08
❑ 513 David Fulcher	.25	.08
❑ 514 Gerald Williams	.25	.08
❑ 515 Toi Cook	.25	.08
❑ 516 Chris Warren	1.00	.40
❑ 517 Jeff Gossett	.25	.08
❑ 518 Ken Lanier	.25	.08
❑ 519 Haywood Jeffires FOIL SP	2.00	.75
❑ 520 Kevin Glover	.25	.08
❑ 521 Mo Lewis	.25	.08
❑ 522 Bern Brostek	.25	.08
❑ 523 Bo Orlando RC	.25	.08
❑ 524 Mike Saxon	.25	.08
❑ 525 Seth Joyner	.25	.08
❑ 526 John Carney	.25	.08
❑ 527 Jeff Cross	.25	.08
❑ 528 Gary Anderson K FOIL SP	1.50	.60
❑ 529 Chuck Cecil	.25	.08
❑ 530 Tim Green	.25	.08
❑ 531 Kevin Porter	.25	.08
❑ 532 Chris Spielman	.50	.20
❑ 533 Willie Drewrey	.25	.08
❑ 534 Chris Singleton UER	.25	.08
❑ 535 Matt Stover	.25	.08
❑ 536 Andre Collins	.25	.08
❑ 537 Erik Howard	.25	.08
❑ 538 Steve Tasker	.50	.20
❑ 539 Anthony Thompson	.25	.08
❑ 540 Charles Haley	.50	.20
❑ 541 Mike Merriweather	.50	.20
❑ 542 Henry Thomas	.25	.08
❑ 543 Scott Stephen	.25	.08
❑ 544 Bruce Kozerski	.25	.08
❑ 545 Tim McKyer	.25	.08
❑ 546 Chris Doleman	.25	.08
❑ 547 Riki Ellison	.25	.08
❑ 548 Mike Prior	.25	.08
❑ 549 Dwayne Harper	.25	.08
❑ 550 Bubby Brister	.25	.08
❑ 551 Dave Meggett	.50	.20
❑ 552 Greg Montgomery	.25	.08
❑ 553 Kevin Mack	.50	.20
❑ 554 Mark Stepnoski	.50	.20
❑ 555 Kenny Walker	.25	.08
❑ 556 Eric Moten	.25	.08
❑ 557 Michael Stewart	.25	.08
❑ 558 Calvin Williams	.50	.20
❑ 559 Johnny Hector	.25	.08
❑ 560 Tony Paige	.25	.08
❑ 561 Tim Newton	.25	.08
❑ 562 Brad Muster	.25	.08
❑ 563 Aeneas Williams	.50	.20
❑ 564 Herman Moore	1.00	.40
❑ 565 Checklist 460-573	.25	.08
❑ 566 Jerome Henderson	.25	.08
❑ 567 Danny Copeland	.25	.08
❑ 568 Alexander Wright	.50	.20
❑ 569 Tim Harris	.25	.08
❑ 570 Jonathan Hayes	.25	.08
❑ 571 Tony Jones T	.25	.08
❑ 572 Carlton Bailey RC	.25	.08
❑ 573 Vaughan Johnson	.25	.08

1993 Bowman

Card	Price 1	Price 2
❑ COMPLETE SET (423)	25.00	10.00
❑ 1 Troy Aikman FOIL	3.00	1.50
❑ 2 John Parrella RC	.20	.07
❑ 3 Dana Stubblefield RC	.75	.30
❑ 4 Mark Higgs	.20	.07
❑ 5 Tom Carter RC	.40	.15
❑ 6 Nate Lewis	.20	.07
❑ 7 Vaughn Hebron RC	.20	.07
❑ 8 Ernest Givins	.40	.15
❑ 9 Vince Buck	.20	.07
❑ 10 Levon Kirkland	.20	.07
❑ 11 J.J. Birden	.20	.07
❑ 12 Steve Jordan	.20	.07
❑ 13 Simon Fletcher	.20	.07
❑ 14 Willie Green	.20	.07
❑ 15 Pepper Johnson	.20	.07
❑ 16 Roger Harper RC	.20	.07
❑ 17 Rob Moore	.40	.15
❑ 18 David Lang	.20	.07
❑ 19 David Klingler	.20	.07
❑ 20 Garrison Hearst RC FOIL	2.00	.75
❑ 21 Anthony Johnson	.40	.15
❑ 22 Eric Curry RC FOIL	.40	.15
❑ 23 Nolan Harrison	.20	.07
❑ 24 Earl Dotson RC	.20	.07
❑ 25 Leonard Russell	.40	.15
❑ 26 Doug Riesenberg	.20	.07
❑ 27 Dwayne Harper	.20	.07
❑ 28 Richard Dent	.40	.15
❑ 29 Victor Bailey RC	.20	.07
❑ 30 Junior Seau	.75	.30
❑ 31 Steve Tasker	.40	.15
❑ 32 Kurt Gouveia	.20	.07
❑ 33 Renaldo Turnbull UER	.20	.07
❑ 34 Dale Carter	.20	.07
❑ 35 Russell Maryland	.20	.07
❑ 36 Dana Hall	.20	.07
❑ 37 Marco Coleman	.20	.07
❑ 38 Greg Montgomery	.20	.07
❑ 39 Deon Figures RC	.20	.07
❑ 40 Troy Drayton RC	.40	.15
❑ 41 Eric Metcalf	.40	.15
❑ 42 Michael Husted RC	.20	.07
❑ 43 Harry Newsome	.20	.07
❑ 44 Kelvin Pritchett	.20	.07
❑ 45 Andre Rison FOIL	.75	.40
❑ 46 John Copeland RC	.40	.15
❑ 47 Greg Biekert RC	.20	.07
❑ 48 Johnny Johnson	.20	.07
❑ 49 Chuck Cecil	.20	.07
❑ 50 Rick Mirer RC FOIL	1.50	.60
❑ 51 Rod Bernstine	.20	.07
❑ 52 Steve McMichael	.40	.15
❑ 53 Roosevelt Potts RC	.20	.07
❑ 54 Mike Sherrard	.20	.07
❑ 55 Terrell Buckley	.20	.07
❑ 56 Eugene Chung	.20	.07
❑ 57 Kimble Anders RC	.75	.30
❑ 58 Daryl Johnston	.75	.30
❑ 59 Harris Barton	.20	.07
❑ 60 Thurman Thomas FOIL	1.50	.60
❑ 61 Eric Martin	.20	.07
❑ 62 Reggie Brooks RC FOIL	.40	.15
❑ 63 Eric Bieniemy	.20	.07
❑ 64 John Offerdahl	.20	.07
❑ 65 Wilber Marshall	.20	.07
❑ 66 Mark Carrier WR	.40	.15
❑ 67 Merril Hoge	.20	.07
❑ 68 Cris Carter	.75	.30
❑ 69 Marty Thompson RC	.20	.07
❑ 70 Randall Cunningham FOIL	1.50	.60
❑ 71 Winston Moss	.20	.07
❑ 72 Doug Pelfrey RC	.20	.07
❑ 73 Jackie Slater	.20	.07
❑ 74 Pierce Holt	.20	.07
❑ 75 Hardy Nickerson	.40	.15
❑ 76 Chris Burkett	.20	.07
❑ 77 Michael Brandon	.20	.07
❑ 78 Tom Waddle	.20	.07
❑ 79 Walter Reeves	.20	.07
❑ 80 Lawrence Taylor FOIL	.75	.40
❑ 81 Wayne Simmons RC	.20	.07
❑ 82 Brent Williams	.20	.07
❑ 83 Shannon Sharpe	.75	.30
❑ 84 Robert Blackmon	.20	.07
❑ 85 Keith Jackson	.40	.15
❑ 86 A.J. Johnson	.20	.07
❑ 87 Ryan McNeil RC	.75	.30
❑ 88 Michael Dean Perry	.40	.15
❑ 89 Russell Copeland RC	.40	.15
❑ 90 Sam Mills	.20	.07
❑ 91 Courtney Hall	.20	.07
❑ 92 Gino Torretta RC	.40	.15
❑ 93 Artie Smith RC	.20	.07
❑ 94 David Whitmore	.20	.07
❑ 95 Charles Haley	.40	.15
❑ 96 Rod Woodson	.75	.30
❑ 97 Lorenzo White	.20	.07
❑ 98 Tom Scott OL RC	.20	.07
❑ 99 Tyji Armstrong	.20	.07
❑ 100 Boomer Esiason	.40	.15
❑ 101 Rocket Ismail FOIL	.75	.40
❑ 102 Mark Carrier DB	.20	.07
❑ 103 Broderick Thompson	.20	.07
❑ 104 Bob Whitfield	.20	.07
❑ 105 Ben Coleman RC	.20	.07
❑ 106 Jon Vaughn	.20	.07
❑ 107 Marcus Buckley RC	.20	.07
❑ 108 Cleveland Gary	.20	.07
❑ 109 Ashley Ambrose	.20	.07
❑ 110 Reggie White FOIL	1.50	.60
❑ 111 Arthur Marshall RC	.20	.07
❑ 112 Greg McMurtry	.20	.07
❑ 113 Mike Johnson	.20	.07
❑ 114 Tim McGee	.20	.07
❑ 115 John Carney	.20	.07
❑ 116 Neil Smith	.75	.30
❑ 117 Mark Stepnoski	.20	.07
❑ 118 Don Beebe	.20	.07
❑ 119 Scott Mitchell	.75	.30
❑ 120 Randall McDaniel	.20	.07
❑ 121 Chidi Ahanotu RC	.20	.07
❑ 122 Ray Childress	.20	.07
❑ 123 Tony McGee RC	.40	.15
❑ 124 Marc Boutte	.20	.07
❑ 125 Ronnie Lott	.40	.15
❑ 126 Jason Elam RC	.75	.30
❑ 127 Martin Harrison RC	.20	.07
❑ 128 Leonard Renfro RC	.20	.07
❑ 129 Jessie Armstead RC	.40	.15
❑ 130 Quentin Coryatt	.40	.15
❑ 131 Luis Sharpe	.20	.07
❑ 132 Bill Maas	.20	.07
❑ 133 Jesse Solomon	.20	.07
❑ 134 Kevin Greene	.40	.15
❑ 135 Derek Brown RC RBK	.40	.15
❑ 136 Greg Townsend	.20	.07
❑ 137 Neal Anderson	.20	.07
❑ 138 John L. Williams	.20	.07
❑ 139 Vincent Brisby RC	.75	.30
❑ 140 Barry Sanders FOIL	5.00	2.00
❑ 141 Charles Mann	.20	.07
❑ 142 Ken Norton	.40	.15
❑ 143 Eric Moten	.20	.07
❑ 144 John Alt	.20	.07
❑ 145 Dan Footman RC	.20	.07
❑ 146 Bill Brooks	.20	.07
❑ 147 James Thornton	.20	.07
❑ 148 Martin Mayhew	.20	.07
❑ 149 Andy Harmon	.40	.15
❑ 150 Dan Marino FOIL	6.00	2.50
❑ 151 Micheal Barrow RC	.75	.30
❑ 152 Flipper Anderson	.20	.07
❑ 153 Jackie Harris	.20	.07
❑ 154 Todd Kelly RC	.20	.07
❑ 155 Dan Williams RC	.20	.07

❑ 156 Harold Green .20 .07
❑ 157 David Treadwell .20 .07
❑ 158 Chris Doleman .20 .07
❑ 159 Eric Hill .20 .07
❑ 160 Lincoln Kennedy RC .20 .07
❑ 161 Devon McDonald RC .20 .07
❑ 162 Natrone Means RC .75 .30
❑ 163 Rick Hamilton RC .20 .07
❑ 164 Kelvin Martin .20 .07
❑ 165 Jeff Hostetler .40 .15
❑ 166 Mark Brunell RC 4.00 1.50
❑ 167 Tim Barnett .20 .07
❑ 168 Ray Crockett .20 .07
❑ 169 William Perry .40 .15
❑ 170 Michael Irvin .75 .30
❑ 171 Marvin Washington .20 .07
❑ 172 Irving Fryar .40 .15
❑ 173 Scott Sisson RC .20 .07
❑ 174 Gary Anderson K .20 .07
❑ 175 Bruce Smith .75 .30
❑ 176 Clyde Simmons .20 .07
❑ 177 Russell White RC .40 .15
❑ 178 Irv Smith RC .20 .07
❑ 179 Mark Wheeler .20 .07
❑ 180 Warren Moon .75 .30
❑ 181 Del Speer RC .20 .07
❑ 182 Henry Thomas .20 .07
❑ 183 Keith Kartz .20 .07
❑ 184 Ricky Ervins .20 .07
❑ 185 Phil Simms .40 .15
❑ 186 Tim Brown .75 .30
❑ 187 Willis Peguese .20 .07
❑ 188 Rich Moran .20 .07
❑ 189 Robert Jones .20 .07
❑ 190 Craig Heyward .40 .15
❑ 191 Ricky Watters .75 .30
❑ 192 Stan Humphries .40 .15
❑ 193 Larry Webster .20 .07
❑ 194 Brad Baxter .20 .07
❑ 195 Randal Hill .20 .07
❑ 196 Robert Porcher .20 .07
❑ 197 Patrick Robinson RC .20 .07
❑ 198 Ferrell Edmunds .20 .07
❑ 199 Melvin Jenkins .20 .07
❑ 200 Joe Montana FOIL 6.00 2.50
❑ 201 Marv Cook .20 .07
❑ 202 Henry Ellard .40 .15
❑ 203 Calvin Williams .40 .15
❑ 204 Craig Erickson .40 .15
❑ 205 Steve Atwater .20 .07
❑ 206 Najee Mustafaa .20 .07
❑ 207 Darryl Talley .20 .07
❑ 208 Jarrod Bunch .20 .07
❑ 209 Tim McDonald .20 .07
❑ 210 Patrick Bates RC .20 .07
❑ 211 Sean Jones .20 .07
❑ 212 Leslie O'Neal .40 .15
❑ 213 Mike Golic .20 .07
❑ 214 Mark Clayton .20 .07
❑ 215 Leonard Marshall .20 .07
❑ 216 Curtis Conway RC 1.50 .60
❑ 217 Andre Hastings RC .40 .15
❑ 218 Barry Word .20 .07
❑ 219 Will Wolford .20 .07
❑ 220 Desmond Howard .40 .15
❑ 221 Rickey Jackson .20 .07
❑ 222 Alvin Harper .40 .15
❑ 223 William White .20 .07
❑ 224 Steve Broussard .20 .07
❑ 225 Aeneas Williams .20 .07
❑ 226 Michael Brooks .20 .07
❑ 227 Reggie Cobb .20 .07
❑ 228 Derrick Walker .20 .07
❑ 229 Marcus Allen .75 .30
❑ 230 Jerry Ball .20 .07
❑ 231 J.B. Brown .20 .07
❑ 232 Terry McDaniel .20 .07
❑ 233 LeRoy Butler .20 .07
❑ 234 Kyle Clifton .20 .07
❑ 235 Henry Jones .20 .07
❑ 236 Shane Conlan .20 .07
❑ 237 Michael Bates RC .20 .07
❑ 238 Vincent Brown .20 .07
❑ 239 William Fuller .20 .07
❑ 240 Ricardo McDonald .20 .07
❑ 241 Gary Zimmerman .20 .07
❑ 242 Fred Barnett .40 .15
❑ 243 Elvis Grbac RC 4.00 1.50
❑ 244 Myron Baker RC .20 .07
❑ 245 Steve Emtman .20 .07
❑ 246 Mike Compton RC .75 .30
❑ 247 Mark Jackson .20 .07
❑ 248 Santo Stephens RC .20 .07
❑ 249 Tommie Agee .20 .07
❑ 250 Broderick Thomas .20 .07
❑ 251 Fred Baxter RC .20 .07
❑ 252 Andre Collins .20 .07
❑ 253 Ernest Dye RC .20 .07
❑ 254 Raylee Johnson RC .40 .15
❑ 255 Rickey Dixon .20 .07
❑ 256 Ron Heller .20 .07
❑ 257 Joel Steed .20 .07
❑ 258 Everett Lindsay RC .20 .07
❑ 259 Tony Smith RB .20 .07
❑ 260 Sterling Sharpe UER .75 .30
❑ 261 Tommy Vardell .20 .07
❑ 262 Morten Andersen .20 .07
❑ 263 Eddie Robinson .20 .07
❑ 264 Jerome Bettis RC 8.00 4.00
❑ 265 Alonzo Spellman .20 .07
❑ 266 Harvey Williams .40 .15
❑ 267 Jason Belser RC .20 .07
❑ 268 Derek Russell .20 .07
❑ 269 Derrick Lassic RC .20 .07
❑ 270 Steve Young FOIL 3.00 1.50
❑ 271 Adrian Murrell RC .75 .30
❑ 272 Lewis Tillman .20 .07
❑ 273 O.J.McDuffie RC .75 .30
❑ 274 Marty Carter .20 .07
❑ 275 Ray Seals .20 .07
❑ 276 Earnest Byner .20 .07
❑ 277 Marion Butts .20 .07
❑ 278 Chris Spielman .40 .15
❑ 279 Carl Pickens .40 .15
❑ 280 Drew Bledsoe RC FOIL 6.00 2.50
❑ 281 Mark Kelso .20 .07
❑ 282 Eugene Robinson .20 .07
❑ 283 Eric Allen .20 .07
❑ 284 Ethan Horton .20 .07
❑ 285 Greg Lloyd .40 .15
❑ 286 Anthony Carter .40 .15
❑ 287 Edgar Bennett .75 .30
❑ 288 Bobby Hebert .20 .07
❑ 289 Haywood Jeffires .40 .15
❑ 290 Glyn Milburn RC .75 .30
❑ 291 Bernie Kosar .40 .15
❑ 292 Jumbo Elliott .20 .07
❑ 293 Jessie Hester .20 .07
❑ 294 Brent Jones .40 .15
❑ 295 Carl Banks .20 .07
❑ 296 Brian Washington .20 .07
❑ 297 Steve Beuerlein .40 .15
❑ 298 John Lynch RC 2.00 .75
❑ 299 Troy Vincent .20 .07
❑ 300 Emmitt Smith FOIL 5.00 2.50
❑ 301 Chris Zorich .20 .07
❑ 302 Wade Wilson .20 .07
❑ 303 Darrien Gordon RC .20 .07
❑ 304 Fred Stokes .20 .07
❑ 305 Nick Lowery .20 .07
❑ 306 Rodney Peete .20 .07
❑ 307 Chris Warren .40 .15
❑ 308 Herschel Walker .40 .15
❑ 309 Aundray Bruce .20 .07
❑ 310 Barry Foster FOIL .40 .15
❑ 311 George Teague RC .40 .15
❑ 312 Darryl Williams .20 .07
❑ 313 Thomas Smith RC .40 .15
❑ 314 Dennis Brown .20 .07
❑ 315 Marvin Jones RC FOIL .40 .15
❑ 316 Andre Tippett .20 .07
❑ 317 Demetrius DuBose RC .20 .07
❑ 318 Kirk Lowdermilk .20 .07
❑ 319 Shane Dronett .20 .07
❑ 320 Terry Kirby RC .75 .30
❑ 321 Qadry Ismail RC .75 .30
❑ 322 Lorenzo Lynch .20 .07
❑ 323 Willie Drewrey .20 .07
❑ 324 Jessie Tuggle .20 .07
❑ 325 Leroy Hoard .40 .15
❑ 326 Mark Collins .20 .07
❑ 327 Darrell Green .20 .07
❑ 328 Anthony Miller .40 .15
❑ 329 Brad Muster .20 .07
❑ 330 Jim Kelly FOIL 1.50 .60
❑ 331 Sean Gilbert .40 .15
❑ 332 Tim McKyer .20 .07
❑ 333 Scott Mersereau .20 .07
❑ 334 Willie Davis .75 .30
❑ 335 Brett Favre FOIL 6.00 3.00
❑ 336 Kevin Gogan .20 .07
❑ 337 Jim Harbaugh .75 .30
❑ 338 James Trapp RC .20 .07
❑ 339 Pete Stoyanovich .20 .07
❑ 340 Jerry Rice FOIL 3.00 1.50
❑ 341 Gary Anderson RB .20 .07
❑ 342 Carlton Gray RC .20 .07
❑ 343 Dermontti Dawson .20 .07
❑ 344 Ray Buchanan RC .75 .30
❑ 345 Derrick Fenner .20 .07
❑ 346 Dennis Smith .20 .07
❑ 347 Todd Rucci RC .20 .07
❑ 348 Seth Joyner .20 .07
❑ 349 Jim McMahon .40 .15
❑ 350 Rodney Hampton .40 .15
❑ 351 Al Smith .20 .07
❑ 352 Steve Everitt RC .20 .07
❑ 353 Vinnie Clark .20 .07
❑ 354 Eric Swann .40 .15
❑ 355 Brian Mitchell .40 .15
❑ 356 Will Shields RC .75 .30
❑ 357 Cornelius Bennett .40 .15
❑ 358 Darrin Smith RC .40 .15
❑ 359 Chris Mims .20 .07
❑ 360 Blair Thomas .20 .07
❑ 361 Dennis Gibson .20 .07
❑ 362 Santana Dotson .40 .15
❑ 363 Mark Ingram .20 .07
❑ 364 Don Mosebar .20 .07
❑ 365 Ty Detmer .75 .30
❑ 366 Bob Christian RC .20 .07
❑ 367 Adrian Hardy .20 .07
❑ 368 Vaughan Johnson .20 .07
❑ 369 Jim Everett .40 .15
❑ 370 Ricky Sanders .20 .07
❑ 371 Jonathan Hayes .20 .07
❑ 372 Bruce Matthews .20 .07
❑ 373 Darren Drozdov RC .75 .30
❑ 374 Scott Brumfield RC .20 .07
❑ 375 Cortez Kennedy .40 .15
❑ 376 Tim Harris .20 .07
❑ 377 Neil O'Donnell .75 .30
❑ 378 Robert Smith RC 3.00 1.25
❑ 379 Mike Caldwell RC .20 .07
❑ 380 Burt Grossman .20 .07
❑ 381 Corey Miller .20 .07
❑ 382 Kev.Williams WR FOIL RC .40 .15
❑ 383 Ken Harvey .20 .07
❑ 384 Greg Robinson RC .20 .07
❑ 385 Harold Alexander RC .20 .07
❑ 386 Andre Reed .40 .15
❑ 387 Reggie Langhorne .20 .07
❑ 388 Courtney Hawkins .20 .07
❑ 389 James Hasty .20 .07
❑ 390 Pat Swilling .20 .07
❑ 391 Chris Slade RC .40 .15
❑ 392 Keith Byars .20 .07
❑ 393 Dalton Hilliard .20 .07
❑ 394 David Williams .20 .07
❑ 395 Terry Obee RC .20 .07

396	Heath Sherman	.20	.07
397	John Taylor	.40	.15
398	Irv Eatman	.20	.07
399	Johnny Holland	.20	.07
400	John Elway FOIL	6.00	2.50
401	Clay Matthews	.40	.15
402	Dave Meggett	.20	.07
403	Eric Green	.20	.07
404	Bryan Cox	.20	.07
405	Jay Novacek	.40	.15
406	Kenneth Davis	.20	.07
407	Lamar Thomas RC	.20	.07
408	Lance Gunn RC	.20	.07
409	Audray McMillian	.20	.07
410	Derrick Thomas FOIL	1.50	.60
411	Rufus Porter	.20	.07
412	Coleman Rudolph RC	.20	.07
413	Mark Rypien	.20	.07
414	Duane Bickett	.20	.07
415	Chris Singleton	.20	.07
416	Mitch Lyons RC	.20	.07
417	Bill Fralic	.20	.07
418	Gary Plummer	.20	.07
419	Ricky Proehl	.20	.07
420	Howie Long	.75	.30
421	Willie Roaf RC FOIL	.75	.40
422	Checklist 1-212	.20	.07
423	Checklist 213-423	.20	.07

1994 Bowman

	COMPLETE SET (390)	50.00	20.00
1	Dan Wilkinson RC	.40	.15
2	Marshall Faulk RC	15.00	6.00
3	Heath Shuler RC	.75	.30
4	Willie McGinest RC	.75	.30
5	Trent Dilfer RC	3.00	1.25
6	Brent Jones	.40	.15
7	Sam Adams RC	.40	.15
8	Randy Baldwin	.20	.07
9	Jamir Miller RC	.40	.15
10	John Thierry RC	.20	.07
11	Aaron Glenn RC	.75	.30
12	Joe Johnson RC	.20	.07
13	Bernard Williams RC	.20	.07
14	Wayne Gandy RC	.20	.07
15	Aaron Taylor RC	.20	.07
16	Charles Johnson RC	.75	.30
17	Dew.Washington RC UER 309	.40	.15
18	Bernie Kosar	.40	.15
19	Johnnie Morton RC	2.50	1.00
20	Rob Fredrickson RC	.40	.15
21	Shante Carver RC	.20	.07
22	Thomas Lewis RC	.40	.15
23	Greg Hill RC	.75	.30
24	Cris Dishman	.20	.07
25	Jeff Burris RC	.40	.15
26	Isaac Davis RC	.20	.07
27	Bert Emanuel RC	.75	.30
28	Allen Aldridge RC	.20	.07
29	Kevin Lee RC	.20	.07
30	Chris Brantley RC	.20	.07
31	Rich Braham RC	.20	.07
32	Ricky Watters	.40	.15
33	Quentin Coryatt	.20	.07
34	Hardy Nickerson	.40	.15
35	Johnny Johnson	.20	.07
36	Ken Harvey	.20	.07
37	Chris Zorich	.20	.07
38	Chris Warren	.40	.15
39	David Palmer RC	.75	.30
40	Chris Miller	.20	.07
41	Ken Ruettgers	.20	.07
42	Joe Panos RC	.20	.07
43	Mario Bates RC	.75	.30
44	Harry Colon	.20	.07
45	Barry Foster	.20	.07
46	Steve Tasker	.40	.15
47	Richmond Webb	.20	.07
48	James Folston RC	.20	.07
49	Erik Williams	.20	.07
50	Rodney Hampton	.40	.15
51	Derek Russell	.20	.07
52	Greg Montgomery	.20	.07
53	Anthony Phillips	.20	.07
54	Andre Coleman RC	.20	.07
55	Gary Brown	.20	.07
56	Neil Smith	.40	.15
57	Myron Baker	.20	.07
58	Sean Dawkins RC	.75	.30
59	Marvin Washington	.20	.07
60	Steve Beuerlein	.40	.15
61	Brentson Buckner RC	.20	.07
62	William Gaines RC	.20	.07
63	LeShon Johnson RC	.40	.15
64	Errict Rhett RC	.75	.30
65	Jim Everett	.40	.15
66	Desmond Howard	.40	.15
67	Jack Del Rio	.20	.07
68	Isaac Bruce RC	12.00	6.00
69	Van Malone RC	.20	.07
70	Jim Kelly	.75	.30
71	Leon Lett	.20	.07
72	Greg Robinson	.20	.07
73	Ryan Yarborough RC	.20	.07
74	Terry Wooden	.20	.07
75	Eric Allen	.20	.07
76	Ernest Givins	.40	.15
77	Marcus Spears RC	.20	.07
78	Thomas Randolph RC	.20	.07
79	Willie Clark RC	.20	.07
80	John Elway	4.00	1.50
81	Aubrey Beavers RC	.20	.07
82	Jeff Cothran RC	.20	.07
83	Norm Johnson	.20	.07
84	Donnell Bennett RC	.75	.30
85	Phillippi Sparks	.20	.07
86	Scott Mitchell	.40	.15
87	Bucky Brooks RC	.20	.07
88	Courtney Hawkins	.20	.07
89	Kevin Greene	.40	.15
90	Doug Nussmeier RC	.20	.07
91	Floyd Turner	.20	.07
92	Anthony Newman	.20	.07
93	Vinny Testaverde	.40	.15
94	Ronnie Lott	.40	.15
95	Troy Aikman	2.00	.75
96	John Taylor	.40	.15
97	Henry Ellard	.40	.15
98	Carl Lee	.20	.07
99	Terry McDaniel	.20	.07
100	Joe Montana	4.00	1.50
101	David Klingler	.20	.07
102	Bruce Walker RC	.20	.07
103	Rick Cunningham RC	.20	.07
104	Robert Delpino	.20	.07
105	Mark Ingram	.20	.07
106	Leslie O'Neal	.20	.07
107	Darrell Thompson	.20	.07
108	Dave Meggett	.20	.07
109	Chris Gardocki	.20	.07
110	Andre Rison	.40	.15
111	Kelvin Martin	.20	.07
112	Marcus Robertson	.20	.07
113	Jason Gildon RC	3.00	1.25
114	Mel Gray	.20	.07
115	Tommy Vardell	.20	.07
116	Dexter Carter	.20	.07
117	Scottie Graham RC	.40	.15
118	Horace Copeland	.20	.07
119	Cornelius Bennett	.40	.15
120	Chris Maumalanga RC	.20	.07
121	Mo Lewis	.20	.07
122	Toby Wright RC	.20	.07
123	George Hegamin RC	.20	.07
124	Chip Lohmiller	.20	.07
125	Calvin Jones RC	.20	.07
126	Steve Shine	.20	.07
127	Chuck Levy RC	.20	.07
128	Sam Mills	.20	.07
129	Terance Mathis	.40	.15
130	Randall Cunningham	.75	.30
131	John Fina	.20	.07
132	Reggie White	.75	.30
133	Tom Waddle	.20	.07
134	Chris Calloway	.20	.07
135	Kevin Mawae RC	.75	.30
136	Lake Dawson RC	.40	.15
137	Alai Kalaniubalu	.20	.07
138	Tom Nalen RC	.75	.30
139	Cody Carlson	.20	.07
140	Dan Marino	4.00	1.50
141	Harris Barton	.20	.07
142	Don Mosebar	.20	.07
143	Romeo Bandison	.20	.07
144	Bruce Smith	.75	.30
145	Warren Moon	.75	.30
146	David Lutz	.20	.07
147	Dermontti Dawson	.20	.07
148	Ricky Proehl	.20	.07
149	Lou Benfatti RC	.20	.07
150	Craig Erickson	.20	.07
151	Sean Gilbert	.20	.07
152	Zefross Moss	.20	.07
153	Darnay Scott RC	1.25	.50
154	Courtney Hall	.20	.07
155	Brian Mitchell	.20	.07
156	Joe Burch RC UER 333	.20	.07
157	Terry Mickens	.20	.07
158	Jay Novacek	.40	.15
159	Chris Gedney	.20	.07
160	Bruce Matthews	.20	.07
161	Mario Perry RC	.20	.07
162	Vince Buck	.20	.07
163	Michael Bates	.20	.07
164	Willie Davis	.40	.15
165	Mike Pritchard	.20	.07
166	Doug Riesenberg	.20	.07
167	Herschel Walker	.40	.15
168	Tim Ruddy RC	.20	.07
169	William Floyd RC	.75	.30
170	John Randle	.40	.15
171	Winston Moss	.20	.07
172	Thurman Thomas	.75	.30
173	Eric England RC	.20	.07
174	Vincent Brisby	.40	.15
175	Greg Lloyd	.40	.15
176	Paul Gruber	.20	.07
177	Brad Ottis RC	.20	.07
178	George Teague	.20	.07
179	Willie Jackson RC	.75	.30
180	Barry Sanders	3.00	1.25
181	Brian Washington	.20	.07
182	Michael Jackson	.40	.15
183	Jason Mathews RC	.20	.07
184	Chester McGlockton	.20	.07
185	Tydus Winans RC	.20	.07
186	Michael Haynes	.40	.15
187	Erik Kramer	.40	.15
188	Chris Doleman	.20	.07
189	Haywood Jeffires	.40	.15
190	Larry Whigham RC	.20	.07
191	Shawn Jefferson	.20	.07
192	Pete Stoyanovich	.20	.07
193	Rod Bernstine	.20	.07

❑ 194 William Thomas .20 .07
❑ 195 Marcus Allen .75 .30
❑ 196 Dave Brown .40 .15
❑ 197 Harold Bishop RC .20 .07
❑ 198 Lorenzo Lynch .20 .07
❑ 199 Dwight Stone .20 .07
❑ 200 Jerry Rice 2.00 .75
❑ 201 Rocket Ismail .40 .15
❑ 202 LeRoy Butler .20 .07
❑ 203 Glenn Parker .20 .07
❑ 204 Bruce Armstrong .20 .07
❑ 205 Shane Conlan .20 .07
❑ 206 Russell Maryland .20 .07
❑ 207 Herman Moore .75 .30
❑ 208 Eric Martin .20 .07
❑ 209 John Friesz .40 .15
❑ 210 Boomer Esiason .40 .15
❑ 211 Jim Harbaugh .75 .30
❑ 212 Harold Green .20 .07
❑ 213 Perry Klein RC .20 .07
❑ 214 Eric Metcalf .40 .15
❑ 215 Steve Everitt .20 .07
❑ 216 Victor Bailey .20 .07
❑ 217 Lincoln Kennedy .20 .07
❑ 218 Glyn Milburn .40 .15
❑ 219 John Copeland .20 .07
❑ 220 Drew Bledsoe 2.00 .75
❑ 221 Kevin Williams WR .40 .15
❑ 222 Roosevelt Potts .20 .07
❑ 223 Troy Drayton .20 .07
❑ 224 Terry Kirby .75 .30
❑ 225 Ronald Moore .20 .07
❑ 226 Tyrone Hughes .40 .15
❑ 227 Wayne Simmons .20 .07
❑ 228 Tony McGee .20 .07
❑ 229 Derek Brown RBK .20 .07
❑ 230 Jason Elam .40 .15
❑ 231 Qadry Ismail .75 .30
❑ 232 O.J.McDuffie .75 .30
❑ 233 Mike Caldwell .20 .07
❑ 234 Reggie Brooks .40 .15
❑ 235 Rick Mirer .75 .30
❑ 236 Steve Tovar .20 .07
❑ 237 Patrick Robinson .20 .07
❑ 238 Tom Carter .20 .07
❑ 239 Ben Coates .40 .15
❑ 240 Jerome Bettis 1.25 .50
❑ 241 Garrison Hearst .75 .30
❑ 242 Natrone Means .75 .30
❑ 243 Dana Stubblefield .40 .15
❑ 244 Willie Roaf .20 .07
❑ 245 Cortez Kennedy .40 .15
❑ 246 Todd Steussie RC .40 .15
❑ 247 Pat Coleman .20 .07
❑ 248 David Wyman .20 .07
❑ 249 Jeremy Lincoln .20 .07
❑ 250 Carlester Crumpler .20 .07
❑ 251 Dale Carter .20 .07
❑ 252 Corey Raymond RC .20 .07
❑ 253 Bryan Cox .20 .07
❑ 254 Charlie Garner RC 3.00 1.25
❑ 255 Jeff Hostetler .40 .15
❑ 256 Shane Bonham RC .20 .07
❑ 257 Thomas Everett .20 .07
❑ 258 John Jackson T .20 .07
❑ 259 Terry Irving RC .20 .07
❑ 260 Corey Sawyer .40 .15
❑ 261 Rob Waldrop .20 .07
❑ 262 Curtis Conway .75 .30
❑ 263 Winfred Tubbs RC .40 .15
❑ 264 Sean Jones .20 .07
❑ 265 James Washington .20 .07
❑ 266 Lonnie Johnson RC .20 .07
❑ 267 Rob Moore .40 .15
❑ 268 Flipper Anderson .20 .07
❑ 269 Jon Hand .20 .07
❑ 270 Joe Patton RC .20 .07
❑ 271 Howard Ballard .20 .07
❑ 272 Fernando Smith RC .20 .07
❑ 273 Jessie Tuggle .20 .07
❑ 274 John Alt .20 .07
❑ 275 Corey Miller .20 .07
❑ 276 Gus Frerotte RC .75 .30
❑ 277 Jeff Cross .20 .07
❑ 278 Kevin Smith .20 .07
❑ 279 Corey Louchiey RC .20 .07
❑ 280 Micheal Barrow .20 .07
❑ 281 Jim Flanigan RC .40 .15
❑ 282 Calvin Williams .40 .15
❑ 283 Jeff Jaeger .20 .07
❑ 284 John Reece RC .20 .07
❑ 285 Jason Hanson .20 .07
❑ 286 Kurt Haws RC .20 .07
❑ 287 Eric Davis .20 .07
❑ 288 Maurice Hurst .20 .07
❑ 289 Kirk Lowdermilk .20 .07
❑ 290 Rod Woodson .40 .15
❑ 291 Andre Reed .40 .15
❑ 292 Vince Workman .20 .07
❑ 293 Wayne Martin .20 .07
❑ 294 Keith Lyle RC .20 .07
❑ 295 Brett Favre 4.00 1.50
❑ 296 Doug Brien RC .20 .07
❑ 297 Junior Seau .75 .30
❑ 298 Randall McDaniel .20 .07
❑ 299 Johnny Mitchell .20 .07
❑ 300 Emmitt Smith 3.00 1.25
❑ 301 Michael Brooks .20 .07
❑ 302 Steve Jackson .20 .07
❑ 303 Jeff George .75 .30
❑ 304 Irving Fryar .40 .15
❑ 305 Derrick Thomas .75 .30
❑ 306 Dante Jones .20 .07
❑ 307 Darrell Green .20 .07
❑ 308 Mark Bavaro .20 .07
❑ 309 Eugene Robinson .20 .07
❑ 310 Shannon Sharpe .40 .15
❑ 311 Michael Timpson .20 .07
❑ 312 Kevin Mitchell RC .20 .07
❑ 313 Stevon Moore .20 .07
❑ 314 Eric Swann .40 .15
❑ 315 James Bostic RC .75 .30
❑ 316 Robert Brooks .75 .30
❑ 317 Pete Pierson RC .20 .07
❑ 318 Jim Sweeney .20 .07
❑ 319 Anthony Smith .20 .07
❑ 320 Rohn Stark .20 .07
❑ 321 Gary Anderson K .20 .07
❑ 322 Robert Porcher .20 .07
❑ 323 Darryl Talley .20 .07
❑ 324 Stan Humphries .40 .15
❑ 325 Shelly Hammonds RC .20 .07
❑ 326 Jim McMahon .40 .15
❑ 327 Lamont Warren RC .20 .07
❑ 328 Chris Penn RC .20 .07
❑ 329 Tony Woods .20 .07
❑ 330 Raymont Harris RC .75 .30
❑ 331 Mitch Davis RC .20 .07
❑ 332 Michael Irvin .75 .30
❑ 333 Kent Graham .40 .15
❑ 334 Brian Blades .40 .15
❑ 335 Lomas Brown .20 .07
❑ 336 Willie Drewrey .20 .07
❑ 337 Russell Freeman .20 .07
❑ 338 Eric Zomalt RC .20 .07
❑ 339 Santana Dotson .40 .15
❑ 340 Sterling Sharpe .40 .15
❑ 341 Ray Crittenden RC .20 .07
❑ 342 Perry Carter RC .20 .07
❑ 343 Austin Robbins .20 .07
❑ 344 Mike Wells DT RC .20 .07
❑ 345 Toddrick McIntosh RC .20 .07
❑ 346 Mark Carrier WR .40 .15
❑ 347 Eugene Daniel .20 .07
❑ 348 Tre Johnson RC .20 .07
❑ 349 D.J. Johnson .20 .07
❑ 350 Steve Young 1.50 .60
❑ 351 Jim Pyne RC .20 .07
❑ 352 Jocelyn Borgella RC .20 .07
❑ 353 Pat Carter .20 .07
❑ 354 Sam Rogers RC .20 .07
❑ 355 Jason Sehorn RC 1.25 .50
❑ 356 Darren Carrington .20 .07
❑ 357 Lamar Smith RC 4.00 1.50
❑ 358 James Burton RC .20 .07
❑ 359 Darrin Smith .20 .07
❑ 360 Marco Coleman .20 .07
❑ 361 Webster Slaughter .20 .07
❑ 362 Lewis Tillman .20 .07
❑ 363 David Alexander .20 .07
❑ 364 Bradford Banta RC .20 .07
❑ 365 Erric Pegram .20 .07
❑ 366 Mike Fox .20 .07
❑ 367 Jeff Lageman .20 .07
❑ 368 Kurt Gouveia .20 .07
❑ 369 Tim Brown .75 .30
❑ 370 Seth Joyner .20 .07
❑ 371 Irv Eatman .20 .07
❑ 372 Dorsey Levens RC 4.00 1.50
❑ 373 Anthony Pleasant .20 .07
❑ 374 Henry Jones .20 .07
❑ 375 Cris Carter 1.00 .40
❑ 376 Morten Andersen .20 .07
❑ 377 Neil O'Donnell .75 .30
❑ 378 Tyronne Drakeford RC .20 .07
❑ 379 John Carney .20 .07
❑ 380 Vincent Brown .20 .07
❑ 381 J.J. Birden .20 .07
❑ 382 Chris Spielman .40 .15
❑ 383 Mark Bortz .20 .07
❑ 384 Ray Childress .20 .07
❑ 385 Carlton Bailey .20 .07
❑ 386 Charles Haley .40 .15
❑ 387 Shane Dronett .20 .07
❑ 388 Jon Vaughn .20 .07
❑ 389 Checklist 1-195 .20 .07
❑ 390 Checklist 196-390 .20 .07

1995 Bowman

❑ COMPLETE SET (357) 60.00 25.00
❑ 1 Ki-Jana Carter RC .75 .30
❑ 2 Tony Boselli RC .75 .30
❑ 3 Steve McNair RC 8.00 3.00
❑ 4 Michael Westbrook RC .60 .25
❑ 5 Kerry Collins RC 4.00 1.50
❑ 6 Kevin Carter RC .75 .30
❑ 7 Mike Mamula RC .20 .05
❑ 8 Joey Galloway RC 4.00 1.50
❑ 9 Kyle Brady RC .75 .30
❑ 10 J.J. Stokes RC .75 .30
❑ 11 Derrick Alexander DE RC .20 .05
❑ 12 Warren Sapp RC 4.00 1.50
❑ 13 Mark Fields RC .75 .30
❑ 14 Ruben Brown RC .75 .30
❑ 15 Ellis Johnson RC .20 .05
❑ 16 Hugh Douglas RC .75 .30
❑ 17 Mike Pelton RC .20 .05
❑ 18 Napoleon Kaufman RC 3.00 1.25
❑ 19 James O. Stewart RC 2.50 1.00
❑ 20 Luther Elliss RC .20 .05
❑ 21 Rashaan Salaam RC .40 .15
❑ 22 Tyrone Poole RC .75 .30
❑ 23 Ty Law RC 3.00 1.25
❑ 24 Korey Stringer RC .40 .15

❑ 25 Billy Milner RC .20 .05
❑ 26 Devin Bush RC .20 .05
❑ 27 Mark Bruener RC .40 .15
❑ 28 Derrick Brooks RC 4.00 1.50
❑ 29 Blake Brockermeyer RC .20 .05
❑ 30 Alundis Brice RC .20 .05
❑ 31 Trezelle Jenkins RC .20 .05
❑ 32 Craig Newsome RC .20 .05
❑ 33 Fred Barnett .30 .10
❑ 34 Ray Childress .15 .05
❑ 35 Chris Miller .15 .05
❑ 36 Charles Haley .30 .10
❑ 37 Ray Crittenden .15 .05
❑ 38 Gus Frerotte .30 .10
❑ 39 Jeff George .30 .10
❑ 40 Dan Marino 3.00 1.25
❑ 41 Shawn Lee .15 .05
❑ 42 Herman Moore .60 .25
❑ 43 Chris Calloway .15 .05
❑ 44 Jeff Graham .15 .05
❑ 45 Ray Buchanan .15 .05
❑ 46 Doug Pelfrey .15 .05
❑ 47 Lake Dawson .30 .10
❑ 48 Glenn Parker .15 .05
❑ 49 Terry McDaniel .15 .05
❑ 50 Rod Woodson .30 .10
❑ 51 Santana Dotson .15 .05
❑ 52 Anthony Miller .30 .10
❑ 53 Bo Orlando .15 .05
❑ 54 David Palmer .30 .10
❑ 55 William Floyd .30 .10
❑ 56 Edgar Bennett .30 .10
❑ 57 Jeff Blake RC 2.50 1.00
❑ 58 Anthony Pleasant .15 .05
❑ 59 Quinn Early .30 .10
❑ 60 Bobby Houston .15 .05
❑ 61 Terrell Fletcher RC .20 .05
❑ 62 Gary Brown .15 .05
❑ 63 Dwayne Sabb .15 .05
❑ 64 Roman Phifer .15 .05
❑ 65 Sherman Williams RC .20 .05
❑ 66 Roosevelt Potts .15 .05
❑ 67 Darnay Scott .30 .10
❑ 68 Charlie Garner .60 .25
❑ 69 Bert Emanuel .60 .25
❑ 70 Herschel Walker .30 .10
❑ 71 Lorenzo Styles RC .20 .05
❑ 72 Andre Coleman .15 .05
❑ 73 Tyronne Drakeford .15 .05
❑ 74 Jay Novacek .30 .10
❑ 75 Raymont Harris .15 .05
❑ 76 Tamarick Vanover RC .75 .30
❑ 77 Tom Carter .15 .05
❑ 78 Eric Green .15 .05
❑ 79 Patrick Hunter .15 .05
❑ 80 Jeff Hostetler .30 .10
❑ 81 Robert Blackmon .15 .05
❑ 82 Anthony Cook RC .20 .05
❑ 83 Craig Erickson .15 .05
❑ 84 Glyn Milburn .15 .05
❑ 85 Greg Lloyd .30 .10
❑ 86 Brent Jones .15 .05
❑ 87 Barrett Brooks RC .20 .05
❑ 88 Alvin Harper .15 .05
❑ 89 Sean Jones .15 .05
❑ 90 Cris Carter .60 .25
❑ 91 Russell Copeland .15 .05
❑ 92 Frank Sanders RC .75 .30
❑ 93 Mo Lewis .15 .05
❑ 94 Michael Haynes .30 .10
❑ 95 Andre Rison .30 .10
❑ 96 Jesse James RC .20 .05
❑ 97 Stan Humphries .30 .10
❑ 98 James Hasty .15 .05
❑ 99 Ricardo McDonald .15 .05
❑ 100 Jerry Rice 1.50 .60
❑ 101 Chris Hudson RC .20 .05
❑ 102 Dave Meggett .15 .05
❑ 103 Brian Mitchell .15 .05
❑ 104 Mike Johnson .15 .05
❑ 105 Kordell Stewart RC 4.00 1.50
❑ 106 Michael Brooks .15 .05
❑ 107 Steve Walsh .15 .05
❑ 108 Eric Metcalf .30 .10
❑ 109 Ricky Watters .30 .10
❑ 110 Brett Favre 3.00 1.25
❑ 111 Aubrey Beavers .15 .05
❑ 112 Brian Williams LB RC .20 .05
❑ 113 Eugene Robinson .15 .05
❑ 114 Matt O'Dwyer RC .20 .05
❑ 115 Micheal Barrow .15 .05
❑ 116 Rocket Ismail .30 .10
❑ 117 Scott Gragg RC .20 .05
❑ 118 Leon Lett .15 .05
❑ 119 Reggie Roby .15 .05
❑ 120 Marshall Faulk 2.00 .75
❑ 121 Jack Jackson RC .20 .05
❑ 122 Keith Byars .15 .05
❑ 123 Eric Hill .15 .05
❑ 124 Todd Sauerbrun RC .20 .05
❑ 125 Dexter Carter .15 .05
❑ 126 Vinny Testaverde .30 .10
❑ 127 Shane Conlan .15 .05
❑ 128 Terrance Shaw RC .20 .05
❑ 129 Willie Roaf .15 .05
❑ 130 Jim Kelly .60 .25
❑ 131 Neil O'Donnell .30 .10
❑ 132 Ray McElroy RC .20 .05
❑ 133 Ed McDaniel .15 .05
❑ 134 Brian Gelzheiser RC .20 .05
❑ 135 Marcus Allen .60 .25
❑ 136 Carl Pickens .30 .10
❑ 137 Mike Verstegan RC .20 .05
❑ 138 Chris Mims .15 .05
❑ 139 Darryl Pounds RC .20 .05
❑ 140 Emmitt Smith 2.50 1.25
❑ 141 Mike Frederick RC .20 .05
❑ 142 Henry Ellard .30 .10
❑ 143 Willie McGinest .30 .10
❑ 144 Michael Roan RC .20 .05
❑ 145 Chris Spielman .30 .10
❑ 146 Darryl Talley .15 .05
❑ 147 Randall Cunningham .60 .25
❑ 148 Andrew Greene RC .20 .05
❑ 149 George Teague .15 .05
❑ 150 Tyrone Hughes .30 .10
❑ 151 Ron Davis RC .20 .05
❑ 152 Stevon Moore .15 .05
❑ 153 Merton Hanks .15 .05
❑ 154 Darren Perry .15 .05
❑ 155 Dave Brown .30 .10
❑ 156 Mike Morton RC .20 .05
❑ 157 Seth Joyner .15 .05
❑ 158 Bryan Cox .15 .05
❑ 159 Corey Fuller RC .20 .05
❑ 160 John Elway 3.00 1.25
❑ 161 Dewayne Washington .30 .10
❑ 162 Chris Warren .30 .10
❑ 163 Jeff Kopp RC .20 .05
❑ 164 Sean Dawkins .30 .10
❑ 165 Mark Carrier DB .15 .05
❑ 166 Andre Hastings .30 .10
❑ 167 Derek West RC .20 .05
❑ 168 Glenn Montgomery .15 .05
❑ 169 Trent Dilfer .60 .25
❑ 170 Rob Johnson RC 2.50 1.00
❑ 171 Todd Scott .15 .05
❑ 172 Charles Johnson .30 .10
❑ 173 Kez McCorvey RC .20 .05
❑ 174 Rob Fredrickson .15 .05
❑ 175 Corey Sawyer .15 .05
❑ 176 Brett Perriman .30 .10
❑ 177 Ken Dilger RC .75 .30
❑ 178 Dana Stubblefield .30 .10
❑ 179 Eric Allen .15 .05
❑ 180 Drew Bledsoe 1.00 .40
❑ 181 Tyrone Davis RC .20 .05
❑ 182 Reggie Brooks .30 .10
❑ 183 Dale Carter .30 .10
❑ 184 William Henderson RC 3.00 1.25
❑ 185 Reggie White .60 .25
❑ 186 Lorenzo White .15 .05
❑ 187 Leslie O'Neal .30 .10
❑ 188 Stoney Case RC .20 .05
❑ 189 Jeff Burris .15 .05
❑ 190 Leroy Hoard .15 .05
❑ 191 Thomas Randolph .15 .05
❑ 192 Rodney Thomas RC .40 .15
❑ 193 Quentin Coryatt .30 .10
❑ 194 Terry Wooden .15 .05
❑ 195 David Sloan RC .20 .05
❑ 196 Bernie Parmalee .30 .10
❑ 197 Zack Crockett RC .40 .15
❑ 198 Troy Aikman 1.50 .60
❑ 199 Bruce Smith .60 .25
❑ 200 Eric Zeier RC .75 .30
❑ 201 Anthony Smith .15 .05
❑ 202 Jake Reed .30 .10
❑ 203 Hardy Nickerson .15 .05
❑ 204 Patrick Riley RC .20 .05
❑ 205 Bruce Matthews .15 .05
❑ 206 Larry Centers .30 .10
❑ 207 Troy Drayton .15 .05
❑ 208 John Burrough RC .20 .05
❑ 209 Jason Elam .30 .10
❑ 210 Donnell Woolford .15 .05
❑ 211 Sam Shade RC .20 .05
❑ 212 Kevin Greene .30 .10
❑ 213 Ronald Moore .15 .05
❑ 214 Shane Hannah RC .20 .05
❑ 215 Jim Everett .15 .05
❑ 216 Scott Mitchell .30 .10
❑ 217 Antonio Freeman RC 3.00 1.25
❑ 218 Tony McGee .15 .05
❑ 219 Clay Matthews .30 .10
❑ 220 Neil Smith .30 .10
❑ 221 Mark Williams FOIL .40 .15
❑ 222 Derrick Graham FOIL .40 .15
❑ 223 Mike Hollis FOIL .40 .15
❑ 224 Darion Conner FOIL .40 .15
❑ 225 Steve Beuerlein FOIL .40 .15
❑ 226 Rod Smith DB FOIL .40 .15
❑ 227 James Williams LB FOIL .40 .15
❑ 228 Bob Christian FOIL .40 .15
❑ 229 Jeff Lageman FOIL .40 .15
❑ 230 Frank Reich FOIL .40 .15
❑ 231 Harry Colon FOIL .40 .15
❑ 232 Carlton Bailey FOIL .40 .15
❑ 233 Mickey Washington FOIL .40 .15
❑ 234 Shawn Bouwens FOIL .40 .15
❑ 235 Don Beebe FOIL .40 .15
❑ 236 Kelvin Pritchett FOIL .40 .15
❑ 237 Tommy Barnhardt FOIL .40 .15
❑ 238 Mike Dumas FOIL .40 .15
❑ 239 Brett Maxie FOIL .40 .15
❑ 240 Desmond Howard FOIL .40 .15
❑ 241 Sam Mills FOIL .40 .15
❑ 242 Keith Goganious FOIL .40 .15
❑ 243 Bubba McDowell FOIL .40 .15
❑ 244 Vinnie Clark FOIL .40 .15
❑ 245 Lamar Lathon FOIL .40 .15
❑ 246 Bryan Barker FOIL .40 .15
❑ 247 Darren Carrington FOIL .40 .15
❑ 248 Jay Barker RC .20 .05
❑ 249 Eric Davis .15 .05
❑ 250 Heath Shuler .30 .10
❑ 251 Donta Jones RC .20 .05
❑ 252 LeRoy Butler .15 .05
❑ 253 Michael Zordich .15 .05
❑ 254 Cortez Kennedy .30 .10
❑ 255 Brian DeMarco RC .20 .05
❑ 256 Randal Hill .15 .05
❑ 257 Michael Irvin .60 .25
❑ 258 Natrone Means .30 .10
❑ 259 Linc Harden RC .20 .05
❑ 260 Jerome Bettis .60 .25
❑ 261 Tony Bennett .15 .05
❑ 262 Dameian Jeffries RC .20 .05
❑ 263 Cornelius Bennett .30 .10
❑ 264 Chris Zorich .15 .05

❑ 265 Bobby Taylor RC .75 .30
❑ 266 Terrell Buckley .15 .05
❑ 267 Troy Dumas RC .20 .05
❑ 268 Rodney Hampton .30 .10
❑ 269 Steve Everitt .15 .05
❑ 270 Mel Gray .15 .05
❑ 271 Antonio Armstrong RC .20 .05
❑ 272 Jim Harbaugh .30 .10
❑ 273 Gary Clark .15 .05
❑ 274 Tau Pupua RC .20 .05
❑ 275 Warren Moon .30 .10
❑ 276 Corey Croom .15 .05
❑ 277 Tony Berti RC .20 .05
❑ 278 Shannon Sharpe .30 .10
❑ 279 Boomer Esiason .30 .10
❑ 280 Aeneas Williams .15 .05
❑ 281 Lethon Flowers RC .20 .05
❑ 282 Derek Brown TE .15 .05
❑ 283 Charlie Williams RC .20 .05
❑ 284 Dan Wilkinson .30 .10
❑ 285 Mike Sherrard .15 .05
❑ 286 Evan Pilgrim RC .20 .05
❑ 287 Kimble Anders .30 .10
❑ 288 Greg Jefferson RC .20 .05
❑ 289 Ken Norton .30 .10
❑ 290 Terance Mathis .30 .10
❑ 291 Torey Hunter RC .20 .05
❑ 292 Ken Harvey .15 .05
❑ 293 Irving Fryar .30 .10
❑ 294 Michael Reed RC .20 .05
❑ 295 Andre Reed .30 .10
❑ 296 Vencie Glenn .15 .05
❑ 297 Corey Swinson .15 .05
❑ 298 Harvey Williams .15 .05
❑ 299 Willie Davis .30 .10
❑ 300 Barry Sanders 2.50 1.00
❑ 301 Curtis Martin RC 8.00 3.00
❑ 302 Johnny Mitchell .15 .05
❑ 303 Daryl Johnston .30 .10
❑ 304 Lorenzo Lynch .15 .05
❑ 305 Christian Fauria RC .40 .15
❑ 306 Sean Gilbert .30 .10
❑ 307 Ray Zellars RC .40 .15
❑ 308 William Strong RC .20 .05
❑ 309 Jack Del Rio .15 .05
❑ 310 Junior Seau .60 .25
❑ 311 Justin Armour RC .20 .05
❑ 312 Eric Bjornson RC .20 .05
❑ 313 Vincent Brown .15 .05
❑ 314 Darius Holland RC .20 .05
❑ 315 Chad May RC .20 .05
❑ 316 Simon Fletcher .15 .05
❑ 317 Roell Preston RC .30 .10
❑ 318 John Thierry .15 .05
❑ 319 Orlando Thomas RC .20 .05
❑ 320 Zach Wiegert RC .20 .05
❑ 321 Derrick Alexander WR .60 .25
❑ 322 Chris Cowart RC .20 .05
❑ 323 Chris Sanders RC .40 .15
❑ 324 Robert Brooks .60 .25
❑ 325 Todd Collins RC .40 .15
❑ 326 Ken Irvin RC .20 .05
❑ 327 Erric Pegram .30 .10
❑ 328 Damien Covington RC .20 .05
❑ 329 Brendan Stai RC .20 .05
❑ 330 James A.Stewart RC .20 .05
❑ 331 Jessie Tuggle .15 .05
❑ 332 Marco Coleman .15 .05
❑ 333 Steve Young 1.25 .50
❑ 334 Greg Hill .30 .10
❑ 335 Darryl Williams .15 .05
❑ 336 Calvin Williams .30 .10
❑ 337 Cris Dishman .15 .05
❑ 338 Anthony Morgan .15 .05
❑ 339 Renaldo Turnbull .15 .05
❑ 340 Rick Mirer .30 .10
❑ 341 Tim Brown .60 .25
❑ 342 Dennis Gibson .15 .05
❑ 343 Brad Baxter .15 .05
❑ 344 Henry Jones .15 .05
❑ 345 Johnny Bailey .15 .05
❑ 346 Rocket Ismail .30 .10
❑ 347 Richmond Webb .15 .05
❑ 348 Robert Jones .15 .05
❑ 349 Garrison Hearst .60 .25
❑ 350 Errict Rhett .30 .10
❑ 351 Steve Atwater .15 .05
❑ 352 Joe Cain .15 .05
❑ 353 Ben Coates .30 .10
❑ 354 Aaron Glenn .15 .05
❑ 355 Antonio Langham .15 .05
❑ 356 Eugene Daniel .15 .05
❑ 357 Tim Bowens .15 .05

1998 Bowman

❑ COMPLETE SET (220) 50.00 20.00
❑ 1 Peyton Manning RC 20.00 7.50
❑ 2 Keith Brooking RC 1.50 .60
❑ 3 Duane Starks RC .75 .30
❑ 4 Takeo Spikes RC 1.50 .60
❑ 5 Andre Wadsworth RC 1.25 .50
❑ 6 Greg Ellis RC .75 .30
❑ 7 Brian Griese RC 3.00 1.25
❑ 8 Germane Crowell RC 1.25 .50
❑ 9 Jerome Pathon RC 1.50 .60
❑ 10 Ryan Leaf RC 1.50 .60
❑ 11 Fred Taylor RC 2.50 1.00
❑ 12 Robert Edwards RC 1.25 .50
❑ 13 Grant Wistrom RC 1.25 .50
❑ 14 Robert Holcombe RC 1.25 .50
❑ 15 Tim Dwight RC 1.50 .60
❑ 16 Jacquez Green RC 1.25 .50
❑ 17 Marcus Nash RC .75 .30
❑ 18 Jason Peter RC .75 .30
❑ 19 Anthony Simmons RC 1.25 .50
❑ 20 Curtis Enis RC .75 .30
❑ 21 John Avery RC 1.25 .50
❑ 22 Pat Johnson RC 1.25 .50
❑ 23 Joe Jurevicius RC 1.50 .60
❑ 24 Brian Simmons RC 1.25 .50
❑ 25 Kevin Dyson RC 1.50 .60
❑ 26 Skip Hicks RC 1.25 .50
❑ 27 Hines Ward RC 8.00 3.00
❑ 28 Tavian Banks RC 1.25 .50
❑ 29 Ahman Green RC 8.00 3.00
❑ 30 Tony Simmons RC 1.25 .50
❑ 31 Charles Johnson .30 .10
❑ 32 Freddie Jones .30 .10
❑ 33 Joey Galloway .50 .20
❑ 34 Tony Banks .50 .20
❑ 35 Jake Plummer .75 .30
❑ 36 Reidel Anthony .50 .20
❑ 37 Steve McNair .75 .30
❑ 38 Michael Westbrook .50 .20
❑ 39 Chris Sanders .30 .10
❑ 40 Isaac Bruce .75 .30
❑ 41 Charlie Garner .50 .20
❑ 42 Wayne Chrebet .75 .30
❑ 43 Michael Strahan .50 .20
❑ 44 Brad Johnson .75 .30
❑ 45 Mike Alstott .75 .30
❑ 46 Tony Gonzalez .75 .30
❑ 47 Johnnie Morton .50 .20
❑ 48 Darnay Scott .50 .20
❑ 49 Rae Carruth .30 .10
❑ 50 Terrell Davis .75 .30
❑ 51 Jermaine Lewis .50 .20
❑ 52 Frank Sanders .50 .20
❑ 53 Byron Hanspard .30 .10
❑ 54 Gus Frerotte .30 .10
❑ 55 Terry Glenn .75 .30
❑ 56 J.J. Stokes .50 .20
❑ 57 Will Blackwell .30 .10
❑ 58 Keyshawn Johnson .75 .30
❑ 59 Tiki Barber .75 .30
❑ 60 Dorsey Levens .75 .30
❑ 61 Zach Thomas .75 .30
❑ 62 Corey Dillon .75 .30
❑ 63 Antowain Smith .75 .30
❑ 64 Michael Sinclair .30 .10
❑ 65 Rod Smith .50 .20
❑ 66 Trent Dilfer .75 .30
❑ 67 Warren Sapp .50 .20
❑ 68 Charles Way .30 .10
❑ 69 Tamarick Vanover .30 .10
❑ 70 Drew Bledsoe 1.25 .50
❑ 71 John Mobley .30 .10
❑ 72 Kerry Collins .50 .20
❑ 73 Peter Boulware .30 .10
❑ 74 Simeon Rice .50 .20
❑ 75 Eddie George .75 .30
❑ 76 Fred Lane .30 .10
❑ 77 Jamal Anderson .75 .30
❑ 78 Antonio Freeman .75 .30
❑ 79 Jason Sehorn .50 .20
❑ 80 Curtis Martin .75 .30
❑ 81 Bobby Hoying .50 .20
❑ 82 Garrison Hearst .75 .30
❑ 83 Glenn Foley .50 .20
❑ 84 Danny Kanell .50 .20
❑ 85 Kordell Stewart .75 .30
❑ 86 O.J. McDuffie .50 .20
❑ 87 Marvin Harrison .75 .30
❑ 88 Bobby Engram .50 .20
❑ 89 Chris Slade .30 .10
❑ 90 Warrick Dunn .75 .30
❑ 91 Ricky Watters .50 .20
❑ 92 Rickey Dudley .30 .10
❑ 93 Terrell Owens .75 .30
❑ 94 Karim Abdul-Jabbar .75 .30
❑ 95 Napoleon Kaufman .75 .30
❑ 96 Darrell Green .50 .20
❑ 97 Levon Kirkland .30 .10
❑ 98 Jeff George .50 .20
❑ 99 Andre Hastings .30 .10
❑ 100 John Elway 3.00 1.25
❑ 101 John Randle .50 .20
❑ 102 Andre Rison .50 .20
❑ 103 Keenan McCardell .50 .20
❑ 104 Marshall Faulk 1.00 .40
❑ 105 Emmitt Smith 2.50 1.00
❑ 106 Robert Brooks .50 .20
❑ 107 Scott Mitchell .50 .20
❑ 108 Shannon Sharpe .50 .20
❑ 109 Deion Sanders .75 .30
❑ 110 Jerry Rice 1.50 .60
❑ 111 Erik Kramer .30 .10
❑ 112 Michael Jackson .30 .10
❑ 113 Aeneas Williams .30 .10
❑ 114 Terry Allen .75 .30
❑ 115 Steve Young 1.00 .40
❑ 116 Warren Moon .75 .30
❑ 117 Junior Seau .75 .30
❑ 118 Jerome Bettis .75 .30
❑ 119 Irving Fryar .50 .20
❑ 120 Barry Sanders 2.50 1.00
❑ 121 Tim Brown .75 .30
❑ 122 Chad Brown .30 .10
❑ 123 Ben Coates .50 .20
❑ 124 Robert Smith .75 .30
❑ 125 Brett Favre 3.00 1.25
❑ 126 Derrick Thomas .75 .30
❑ 127 Reggie White .75 .30
❑ 128 Troy Aikman 1.50 .60

❑ 129	Jeff Blake	.50	.20
❑ 130	Mark Brunell	.75	.30
❑ 131	Curtis Conway	.50	.20
❑ 132	Wesley Walls	.50	.20
❑ 133	Thurman Thomas	.75	.30
❑ 134	Chris Chandler	.50	.20
❑ 135	Dan Marino	3.00	1.25
❑ 136	Larry Centers	.30	.10
❑ 137	Shawn Jefferson	.30	.10
❑ 138	Andre Reed	.50	.20
❑ 139	Jake Reed	.50	.20
❑ 140	Cris Carter	.75	.30
❑ 141	Elvis Grbac	.50	.20
❑ 142	Mark Chmura	.50	.20
❑ 143	Michael Irvin	.75	.30
❑ 144	Carl Pickens	.50	.20
❑ 145	Herman Moore	.50	.20
❑ 146	Marvin Jones	.30	.10
❑ 147	Terance Mathis	.50	.20
❑ 148	Rob Moore	.50	.20
❑ 149	Bruce Smith	.50	.20
❑ 150	Rob Johnson CL	.30	.10
❑ 151	Leslie Shepherd	.30	.10
❑ 152	Chris Spielman	.30	.10
❑ 153	Tony McGee	.30	.10
❑ 154	Kevin Smith	.30	.10
❑ 155	Bill Romanowski	.30	.10
❑ 156	Stephen Boyd	.30	.10
❑ 157	James Stewart	.50	.20
❑ 158	Jason Taylor	.50	.20
❑ 159	Troy Drayton	.30	.10
❑ 160	Mark Fields	.30	.10
❑ 161	Jessie Armstead	.30	.10
❑ 162	James Jett	.50	.20
❑ 163	Bobby Taylor	.30	.10
❑ 164	Kimble Anders	.50	.20
❑ 165	Jimmy Smith	.50	.20
❑ 166	Quentin Coryatt	.30	.10
❑ 167	Bryant Westbrook	.30	.10
❑ 168	Neil Smith	.50	.20
❑ 169	Darren Woodson	.30	.10
❑ 170	Ray Buchanan	.30	.10
❑ 171	Earl Holmes	.30	.10
❑ 172	Ray Lewis	.75	.30
❑ 173	Steve Broussard	.30	.10
❑ 174	Derrick Brooks	.75	.30
❑ 175	Ken Harvey	.30	.10
❑ 176	Darryll Lewis	.30	.10
❑ 177	Derrick Rodgers	.30	.10
❑ 178	James McKnight	.75	.30
❑ 179	Cris Dishman	.30	.10
❑ 180	Hardy Nickerson	.30	.10
❑ 181	Charles Woodson RC	2.00	.75
❑ 182	Randy Moss RC	10.00	4.00
❑ 183	Stephen Alexander RC	1.25	.50
❑ 184	Samari Rolle RC	.75	.30
❑ 185	Jamie Duncan RC	.75	.30
❑ 186	Lance Schulters RC	.75	.30
❑ 187	Tony Parrish RC	1.50	.60
❑ 188	Corey Chavous RC	1.50	.60
❑ 189	Jammi German RC	.75	.30
❑ 190	Sam Cowart RC	1.25	.50
❑ 191	Donald Hayes RC	1.25	.50
❑ 192	R.W. McQuarters RC	1.25	.50
❑ 193	Az-Zahir Hakim RC	1.50	.60
❑ 194	Chris Fuamatu-Ma'afala RC	1.25	.50
❑ 195	Allen Rossum RC	1.25	.50
❑ 196	Jon Ritchie RC	1.25	.50
❑ 197	Blake Spence RC	.75	.30
❑ 198	Brian Alford RC	.75	.30
❑ 199	Fred Weary RC	.75	.30
❑ 200	Rod Rutledge RC	.75	.30
❑ 201	Michael Myers RC	.75	.30
❑ 202	Rashaan Shehee RC	1.25	.50
❑ 203	Donovin Darius RC	1.25	.50
❑ 204	E.G. Green RC	1.25	.50
❑ 205	Vonnie Holliday RC	1.25	.50
❑ 206	Charlie Batch RC	1.50	.60
❑ 207	Michael Pittman RC	2.00	.75
❑ 208	Artrell Hawkins RC	.75	.30
❑ 209	Jonathan Quinn RC	1.50	.60
❑ 210	Kailee Wong RC	.75	.30
❑ 211	DeShea Townsend RC	.75	.30
❑ 212	Patrick Surtain RC	1.50	.60
❑ 213	Brian Kelly RC	1.25	.50
❑ 214	Tebucky Jones RC	.75	.30
❑ 215	Pete Gonzalez RC	.75	.30
❑ 216	Shaun Williams RC	1.25	.50
❑ 217	Scott Frost RC	.75	.30
❑ 218	Leonard Little RC	1.50	.60
❑ 219	Alonzo Mayes RC	.75	.30
❑ 220	Cordell Taylor RC	.75	.30

1999 Bowman

❑	COMPLETE SET (220)	40.00	15.00
❑ 1	Dan Marino	2.50	1.00
❑ 2	Michael Westbrook	.50	.20
❑ 3	Yancey Thigpen	.30	.10
❑ 4	Tony Martin	.50	.20
❑ 5	Michael Strahan	.50	.20
❑ 6	Dedric Ward	.30	.10
❑ 7	Joey Galloway	.50	.20
❑ 8	Bobby Engram	.50	.20
❑ 9	Frank Sanders	.50	.20
❑ 10	Jake Plummer	.50	.20
❑ 11	Eddie Kennison	.50	.20
❑ 12	Curtis Martin	.75	.30
❑ 13	Chris Spielman	.30	.10
❑ 14	Trent Dilfer	.50	.20
❑ 15	Tim Biakabutuka	.50	.20
❑ 16	Elvis Grbac	.50	.20
❑ 17	Charlie Batch	.75	.30
❑ 18	Takeo Spikes	.30	.10
❑ 19	Tony Banks	.50	.20
❑ 20	Doug Flutie	.75	.30
❑ 21	Ty Law	.50	.20
❑ 22	Isaac Bruce	.75	.30
❑ 23	James Jett	.50	.20
❑ 24	Kent Graham	.30	.10
❑ 25	Derrick Mayes	.30	.10
❑ 26	Amani Toomer	.30	.10
❑ 27	Ray Lewis	.75	.30
❑ 28	Shawn Springs	.30	.10
❑ 29	Warren Sapp	.30	.10
❑ 30	Jamal Anderson	.75	.30
❑ 31	Byron Bam Morris	.30	.10
❑ 32	Johnnie Morton	.30	.10
❑ 33	Terance Mathis	.30	.10
❑ 34	Terrell Davis	.75	.30
❑ 35	John Randle	.50	.20
❑ 36	Vinny Testaverde	.30	.10
❑ 37	Junior Seau	.75	.30
❑ 38	Reidel Anthony	.50	.20
❑ 39	Brad Johnson	.30	.10
❑ 40	Emmitt Smith	1.50	.60
❑ 41	Mo Lewis	.30	.10
❑ 42	Terry Glenn	.75	.30
❑ 43	Dorsey Levens	.75	.30
❑ 44	Thurman Thomas	.50	.20
❑ 45	Rob Moore	.50	.20
❑ 46	Corey Dillon	.75	.30
❑ 47	Jessie Armstead	.30	.10
❑ 48	Marshall Faulk	1.00	.40
❑ 49	Charles Woodson	.30	.10
❑ 50	John Elway	2.50	1.00
❑ 51	Kevin Dyson	.50	.20
❑ 52	Tony Simmons	.30	.10
❑ 53	Keenan McCardell	.50	.20
❑ 54	O.J. Santiago	.30	.10
❑ 55	Jermaine Lewis	.50	.20
❑ 56	Herman Moore	.50	.20
❑ 57	Gary Brown	.30	.10
❑ 58	Jim Harbaugh	.50	.20
❑ 59	Mike Alstott	.75	.30
❑ 60	Brett Favre	2.50	1.00
❑ 61	Tim Brown	.75	.30
❑ 62	Steve McNair	.75	.30
❑ 63	Ben Coates	.50	.20
❑ 64	Jerome Pathon	.30	.10
❑ 65	Ray Buchanan	.30	.10
❑ 66	Troy Aikman	1.50	.60
❑ 67	Andre Reed	.50	.20
❑ 68	Bubby Brister	.30	.10
❑ 69	Karim Abdul-Jabbar	.50	.20
❑ 70	Peyton Manning	2.50	1.00
❑ 71	Charles Johnson	.30	.10
❑ 72	Natrone Means	.50	.20
❑ 73	Michael Sinclair	.30	.10
❑ 74	Skip Hicks	.30	.10
❑ 75	Derrick Alexander	.50	.20
❑ 76	Wayne Chrebet	.50	.20
❑ 77	Rod Smith	.50	.20
❑ 78	Carl Pickens	.50	.20
❑ 79	Adrian Murrell	.50	.20
❑ 80	Fred Taylor	.75	.30
❑ 81	Eric Moulds	.75	.30
❑ 82	Lawrence Phillips	.50	.20
❑ 83	Marvin Harrison	.75	.30
❑ 84	Cris Carter	.75	.30
❑ 85	Ike Hilliard	.30	.10
❑ 86	Hines Ward	.75	.30
❑ 87	Terrell Owens	.75	.30
❑ 88	Ricky Proehl	.30	.10
❑ 89	Bert Emanuel	.50	.20
❑ 90	Randy Moss	2.00	.75
❑ 91	Aaron Glenn	.30	.10
❑ 92	Robert Smith	.75	.30
❑ 93	Andre Hastings	.30	.10
❑ 94	Jake Reed	.50	.20
❑ 95	Curtis Enis	.30	.10
❑ 96	Andre Wadsworth	.30	.10
❑ 97	Ed McCaffrey	.50	.20
❑ 98	Zach Thomas	.75	.30
❑ 99	Kerry Collins	.50	.20
❑ 100	Drew Bledsoe	1.00	.40
❑ 101	Germane Crowell	.30	.10
❑ 102	Bryan Still	.30	.10
❑ 103	Chad Brown	.30	.10
❑ 104	Jacquez Green	.30	.10
❑ 105	Garrison Hearst	.50	.20
❑ 106	Napoleon Kaufman	.75	.30
❑ 107	Ricky Watters	.50	.20
❑ 108	O.J. McDuffie	.50	.20
❑ 109	Keyshawn Johnson	.75	.30
❑ 110	Jerome Bettis	.75	.30
❑ 111	Duce Staley	.75	.30
❑ 112	Curtis Conway	.50	.20
❑ 113	Chris Chandler	.50	.20
❑ 114	Marcus Nash	.30	.10
❑ 115	Stephen Alexander	.30	.10
❑ 116	Darnay Scott	.30	.10
❑ 117	Bruce Smith	.50	.20
❑ 118	Priest Holmes	1.25	.50
❑ 119	Mark Brunell	.75	.30
❑ 120	Jerry Rice	1.50	.60
❑ 121	Randall Cunningham	.75	.30
❑ 122	Scott Mitchell	.30	.10
❑ 123	Antonio Freeman	.75	.30
❑ 124	Kordell Stewart	.50	.20
❑ 125	Jon Kitna	.75	.30
❑ 126	Ahman Green	.75	.30
❑ 127	Warrick Dunn	.75	.30
❑ 128	Robert Brooks	.50	.20
❑ 129	Derrick Thomas	.75	.30

❑	130	Steve Young	1.00	.40
❑	131	Peter Boulware	.30	.10
❑	132	Michael Irvin	.50	.20
❑	133	Shannon Sharpe	.30	.10
❑	134	Jimmy Smith	.50	.20
❑	135	John Avery	.30	.10
❑	136	Fred Lane	.30	.10
❑	137	Trent Green	.75	.30
❑	138	Andre Rison	.50	.20
❑	139	Antowain Smith	.30	.10
❑	140	Eddie George	.75	.30
❑	141	Jeff Blake	.50	.20
❑	142	Rocket Ismail	.50	.20
❑	143	Rickey Dudley	.30	.10
❑	144	Courtney Hawkins	.30	.10
❑	145	Mikhael Ricks	.30	.10
❑	146	J.J. Stokes	.50	.20
❑	147	Levon Kirkland	.30	.10
❑	148	Deion Sanders	.75	.30
❑	149	Barry Sanders	2.50	1.00
❑	150	Tiki Barber	.75	.30
❑	151	David Boston RC	2.00	.75
❑	152	Chris McAlister RC	1.50	.60
❑	153	Peerless Price RC	2.00	.75
❑	154	D'Wayne Bates RC	1.50	.60
❑	155	Cade McNown RC	1.50	.60
❑	156	Akili Smith RC	1.50	.60
❑	157	Kevin Johnson RC	2.00	.75
❑	158	Tim Couch RC	2.00	.75
❑	159	Sedrick Irvin RC	.75	.30
❑	160	Chris Claiborne RC	.75	.30
❑	161	Edgerrin James RC	8.00	3.00
❑	162	Mike Cloud RC	1.50	.60
❑	163	Cecil Collins RC	.75	.30
❑	164	James Johnson RC	1.50	.60
❑	165	Rob Konrad RC	2.00	.75
❑	166	Daunte Culpepper RC	8.00	3.00
❑	167	Kevin Faulk RC	2.00	.75
❑	168	Donovan McNabb RC	10.00	4.00
❑	169	Troy Edwards RC	1.50	.60
❑	170	Amos Zereoue RC	2.00	.75
❑	171	Karsten Bailey RC	1.50	.60
❑	172	Brock Huard RC	2.00	.75
❑	173	Joe Germaine RC	1.50	.60
❑	174	Torry Holt RC	5.00	2.00
❑	175	Shaun King RC	1.50	.60
❑	176	Jevon Kearse RC	3.00	1.25
❑	177	Champ Bailey RC	2.50	1.00
❑	178	Ebenezer Ekuban RC	1.50	.60
❑	179	Andy Katzenmoyer	1.50	.60
❑	180	Antoine Winfield RC	1.50	.60
❑	181	Jermaine Fazande RC	1.50	.60
❑	182	Ricky Williams RC	4.00	1.50
❑	183	Joel Makovicka RC	2.00	.75
❑	184	Reginald Kelly RC	.75	.30
❑	185	Brandon Stokley RC	2.50	1.00
❑	186	L.C. Stevens RC	.75	.30
❑	187	Marty Booker RC	2.00	.75
❑	188	Jerry Azumah	2.00	.75
❑	189	Ted White RC	.75	.30
❑	190	Scott Covington RC	2.00	.75
❑	191	Tim Alexander RC	.75	.30
❑	192	Darrin Chiaverini RC	1.50	.60
❑	193	Dat Nguyen RC	2.00	.75
❑	194	Wane McGarity RC	.75	.30
❑	195	Al Wilson RC	2.00	.75
❑	196	Travis McGriff RC	.75	.30
❑	197	Stacey Mack RC	2.00	.75
❑	198	Antuan Edwards RC	.75	.30
❑	199	Aaron Brooks RC	4.00	1.50
❑	200	De'Mond Parker RC	.75	.30
❑	201	Jed Weaver RC	.75	.30
❑	202	Madre Hill RC	.75	.30
❑	203	Jim Kleinsasser RC	2.00	.75
❑	204	Michael Bishop RC	2.00	.75
❑	205	Michael Basnight RC	.75	.30
❑	206	Sean Bennett RC	.75	.30
❑	207	Dameane Douglas RC	1.50	.60
❑	208	Na Brown RC	1.50	.60
❑	209	Patrick Kerney RC	2.00	.75
❑	210	Malcolm Johnson RC	.75	.30
❑	211	Dre Bly RC	2.00	.75
❑	212	Terry Jackson RC	1.50	.60
❑	213	Eugene Baker RC	.75	.30
❑	214	Autry Denson RC	1.50	.60
❑	215	Darnell McDonald RC	1.50	.60
❑	216	Charlie Rogers RC	1.50	.60
❑	217	Joe Montgomery RC	1.50	.60
❑	218	Cecil Martin RC	1.50	.60
❑	219	Larry Parker RC	2.00	.75
❑	220	Mike Peterson RC	2.00	.75

2000 Bowman

❑		COMPLETE SET (240)	40.00	15.00
❑	1	Eddie George	.60	.25
❑	2	Ike Hilliard	.40	.15
❑	3	Terrell Owens	.60	.25
❑	4	James Stewart	.40	.15
❑	5	Joey Galloway	.40	.15
❑	6	Jake Reed	.40	.15
❑	7	Derrick Alexander	.40	.15
❑	8	Jeff George	.40	.15
❑	9	Kerry Collins	.40	.15
❑	10	Tony Gonzalez	.40	.15
❑	11	Marcus Robinson	.60	.25
❑	12	Charles Woodson	.40	.15
❑	13	Germane Crowell	.25	.08
❑	14	Yancey Thigpen	.25	.08
❑	15	Tony Martin	.40	.15
❑	16	Frank Sanders	.40	.15
❑	17	Napoleon Kaufman	.40	.15
❑	18	Jay Fiedler	.60	.25
❑	19	Patrick Jeffers	.60	.25
❑	20	Steve McNair	.60	.25
❑	21	Herman Moore	.40	.15
❑	22	Tim Brown	.60	.25
❑	23	Olandis Gary	.60	.25
❑	24	Corey Dillon	.60	.25
❑	25	Warren Sapp	.40	.15
❑	26	Curtis Enis	.25	.08
❑	27	Vinny Testaverde	.40	.15
❑	28	Tim Biakabutuka	.40	.15
❑	29	Kevin Johnson	.60	.25
❑	30	Charlie Batch	.60	.25
❑	31	Jermaine Fazande	.25	.08
❑	32	Shaun King	.25	.08
❑	33	Errict Rhett	.40	.15
❑	34	O.J. McDuffie	.40	.15
❑	35	Bruce Smith	.40	.15
❑	36	Antonio Freeman	.60	.25
❑	37	Tim Couch	.40	.15
❑	38	Duce Staley	.60	.25
❑	39	Jeff Blake	.40	.15
❑	40	Jim Harbaugh	.40	.15
❑	41	Jeff Graham	.25	.08
❑	42	Drew Bledsoe	.75	.30
❑	43	Mike Alstott	.60	.25
❑	44	Terance Mathis	.40	.15
❑	45	Antowain Smith	.40	.15
❑	46	Johnnie Morton	.40	.15
❑	47	Chris Chandler	.40	.15
❑	48	Keith Poole	.40	.15
❑	49	Ricky Watters	.40	.15
❑	50	Darnay Scott	.40	.15
❑	51	Damon Huard	.60	.25
❑	52	Peerless Price	.40	.15
❑	53	Brian Griese	.60	.25
❑	54	Frank Wycheck	.25	.08
❑	55	Kevin Dyson	.40	.15
❑	56	Junior Seau	.60	.25
❑	57	Curtis Conway	.40	.15
❑	58	Jamal Anderson	.60	.25
❑	59	Jim Miller	.25	.08
❑	60	Rob Johnson	.25	.08
❑	61	Mark Brunell	.60	.25
❑	62	Wayne Chrebet	.40	.15
❑	63	James Johnson	.25	.08
❑	64	Sean Dawkins	.25	.08
❑	65	Stephen Davis	.60	.25
❑	66	Daunte Culpepper	.75	.30
❑	67	Doug Flutie	.60	.25
❑	68	Pete Mitchell	.25	.08
❑	69	Bill Schroeder	.40	.15
❑	70	Terrence Wilkins	.25	.08
❑	71	Cade McNown	.25	.08
❑	72	Muhsin Muhammad	.40	.15
❑	73	E.G. Green	.25	.08
❑	74	Edgerrin James	1.00	.40
❑	75	Troy Edwards	.25	.08
❑	76	Terry Glenn	.40	.15
❑	77	Tony Banks	.40	.15
❑	78	Derrick Mayes	.40	.15
❑	79	Curtis Martin	.60	.25
❑	80	Kordell Stewart	.40	.15
❑	81	Amani Toomer	.40	.15
❑	82	Dorsey Levens	.40	.15
❑	83	Brad Johnson	.60	.25
❑	84	Ed McCaffrey	.60	.25
❑	85	Charlie Garner	.40	.15
❑	86	Brett Favre	2.00	.75
❑	87	J.J. Stokes	.40	.15
❑	88	Steve Young	.75	.30
❑	89	Jonathan Linton	.25	.08
❑	90	Isaac Bruce	.60	.25
❑	91	Shawn Jefferson	.25	.08
❑	92	Rod Smith	.40	.15
❑	93	Champ Bailey	.40	.15
❑	94	Ricky Williams	.60	.25
❑	95	Priest Holmes	.75	.30
❑	96	Corey Bradford	.40	.15
❑	97	Eric Moulds	.60	.25
❑	98	Warrick Dunn	.60	.25
❑	99	Jevon Kearse	.60	.25
❑	100	Albert Connell	.25	.08
❑	101	Az-Zahir Hakim	.25	.08
❑	102	Marvin Harrison	.60	.25
❑	103	Qadry Ismail	.40	.15
❑	104	Oronde Gadsden	.40	.15
❑	105	Rob Moore	.40	.15
❑	106	Marshall Faulk	.75	.30
❑	107	Steve Beuerlein	.25	.08
❑	108	Torry Holt	.60	.25
❑	109	Donovan McNabb	1.00	.40
❑	110	Rich Gannon	.60	.25
❑	111	Jerome Bettis	.60	.25
❑	112	Peyton Manning	1.50	.60
❑	113	Cris Carter	.60	.25
❑	114	Jake Plummer	.40	.15
❑	115	Kent Graham	.25	.08
❑	116	Keenan McCardell	.40	.15
❑	117	Tim Dwight	.60	.25
❑	118	Fred Taylor	.60	.25
❑	119	Jerry Rice	1.25	.50
❑	120	Michael Westbrook	.40	.15
❑	121	Kurt Warner	1.25	.50
❑	122	Jimmy Smith	.40	.15
❑	123	Emmitt Smith	1.25	.50
❑	124	Terrell Davis	.60	.25
❑	125	Randy Moss	1.25	.50
❑	126	Akili Smith	.25	.08
❑	127	Rocket Ismail	.40	.15
❑	128	Jon Kitna	.60	.25
❑	129	Elvis Grbac	.40	.15
❑	130	Wesley Walls	.25	.08

❑ 131 Torrance Small .25 .08
❑ 132 Tyrone Wheatley .40 .15
❑ 133 Carl Pickens .40 .15
❑ 134 Zach Thomas .60 .25
❑ 135 Jacquez Green .25 .08
❑ 136 Robert Smith .60 .25
❑ 137 Keyshawn Johnson .60 .25
❑ 138 Matthew Hatchette .25 .08
❑ 139 Troy Aikman 1.25 .50
❑ 140 Charles Johnson .40 .15
❑ 141 Terry Battle EP .30 .12
❑ 142 Pepe Pearson EP RC .75 .30
❑ 143 Cory Sauter EP .30 .12
❑ 144 Brian Shay EP .30 .12
❑ 145 Marcus Crandell EP RC .50 .20
❑ 146 Danny Wuerffel EP .50 .20
❑ 147 L.C. Stevens EP .30 .12
❑ 148 Ted White EP .30 .12
❑ 149 Matt Lytle EP RC .50 .20
❑ 150 Vershan Jackson EP RC .30 .12
❑ 151 Mario Bailey EP .30 .12
❑ 152 Darryl Daniel EP RC .50 .20
❑ 153 Sean Morey EP RC .50 .20
❑ 154 Jim Kubiak EP RC .50 .20
❑ 155 Aaron Stecker EP RC .75 .30
❑ 156 Damon Dunn EP RC .50 .20
❑ 157 Kevin Daft EP .30 .12
❑ 158 Corey Thomas EP .30 .12
❑ 159 Deon Mitchell EP RC .50 .20
❑ 160 Todd Floyd EP RC .30 .12
❑ 161 Norman Miller EP RC .30 .12
❑ 162 Jeremaine Copeland EP .30 .12
❑ 163 Michael Blair EP .30 .12
❑ 164 Ron Powlus EP RC .75 .30
❑ 165 Pat Barnes EP .50 .20
❑ 166 Dez White RC 1.00 .40
❑ 167 Trung Canidate RC .75 .30
❑ 168 Thomas Jones RC 1.50 .60
❑ 169 Courtney Brown RC 1.00 .40
❑ 170 Jamal Lewis RC 2.50 1.00
❑ 171 Chris Redman RC .75 .30
❑ 172 Ron Dayne RC 1.00 .40
❑ 173 Chad Pennington RC 2.50 1.00
❑ 174 Plaxico Burress RC 2.00 .75
❑ 175 R.Jay Soward RC .75 .30
❑ 176 Travis Taylor RC 1.00 .40
❑ 177 Shaun Alexander RC 5.00 2.00
❑ 178 Brian Urlacher RC 4.00 1.50
❑ 179 Danny Farmer RC .75 .30
❑ 180 Tee Martin RC 1.00 .40
❑ 181 Sylvester Morris RC .75 .30
❑ 182 Curtis Keaton RC .75 .30
❑ 183 Peter Warrick RC 1.00 .40
❑ 184 Anthony Becht RC 1.00 .40
❑ 185 Travis Prentice RC 1.00 .40
❑ 186 J.R. Redmond RC .75 .30
❑ 187 Bubba Franks RC 1.00 .40
❑ 188 Ron Dugans RC .50 .20
❑ 189 Reuben Droughns RC 1.25 .50
❑ 190 Corey Simon RC 1.00 .40
❑ 191 Joe Hamilton RC .75 .30
❑ 192 Laveranues Coles RC 1.25 .50
❑ 193 Todd Pinkston RC 1.00 .40
❑ 194 Jerry Porter RC 1.25 .50
❑ 195 Dennis Northcutt RC 1.00 .40
❑ 196 Tim Rattay RC 1.00 .40
❑ 197 Giovanni Carmazzi RC .50 .20
❑ 198 Mareno Philyaw RC .50 .20
❑ 199 Avion Black RC .75 .30
❑ 200 Chafie Fields RC .50 .20
❑ 201 Rondell Mealey RC .50 .20
❑ 202 Troy Walters RC 1.00 .40
❑ 203 Frank Moreau RC .75 .30
❑ 204 Vaughn Sanders RC .50 .20
❑ 205 Sherrod Gideon RC .50 .20
❑ 206 Doug Chapman RC .75 .30
❑ 207 Marcus Knight RC .75 .30
❑ 208 Jamel White RC .75 .30
❑ 209 Windrell Hayes RC .75 .30
❑ 210 Reggie Jones RC 1.00 .40
❑ 211 Jarious Jackson RC .75 .30
❑ 212 Ronney Jenkins RC .75 .30
❑ 213 Quinton Spotwood RC .50 .20
❑ 214 Rob Morris RC .75 .30
❑ 215 Gari Scott RC .50 .20
❑ 216 Kevin Thompson RC .50 .20
❑ 217 Trevor Insley RC .50 .20
❑ 218 Frank Murphy RC .50 .20
❑ 219 Patrick Pass RC .75 .30
❑ 220 Mike Anderson RC 1.25 .50
❑ 221 Derrius Thompson RC 1.00 .40
❑ 222 John Abraham RC 1.00 .40
❑ 223 Dante Hall RC 2.00 .75
❑ 224 Chad Morton RC 1.00 .40
❑ 225 Ahmed Plummer RC 1.00 .40
❑ 226 Julian Peterson RC 1.00 .40
❑ 227 Mike Green RC .75 .30
❑ 228 Michael Wiley RC .75 .30
❑ 229 Spergon Wynn RC .75 .30
❑ 230 Trevor Gaylor RC .75 .30
❑ 231 Doug Johnson RC 1.00 .40
❑ 232 Marc Bulger RC 2.00 .75
❑ 233 Ron Dixon RC .75 .30
❑ 234 Aaron Shea RC .75 .30
❑ 235 Thomas Hamner RC .50 .20
❑ 236 Tom Brady RC 25.00 12.50
❑ 237 Deltha O'Neal RC 1.00 .40
❑ 238 Todd Husak RC 1.00 .40
❑ 239 Erron Kinney RC 1.00 .40
❑ 240 JaJuan Dawson RC .50 .20

2001 Bowman

❑ COMPLETE SET (275) 60.00 25.00
❑ 1 Emmitt Smith 1.25 .50
❑ 2 James Stewart .40 .15
❑ 3 Jeff Graham .25 .08
❑ 4 Keyshawn Johnson .60 .25
❑ 5 Stephen Davis .60 .25
❑ 6 Chad Lewis .25 .08
❑ 7 Drew Bledsoe .75 .30
❑ 8 Fred Taylor .60 .25
❑ 9 Mike Anderson .60 .25
❑ 10 Tony Gonzalez .40 .15
❑ 11 Aaron Brooks .60 .25
❑ 12 Vinny Testaverde .40 .15
❑ 13 Jerome Bettis .60 .25
❑ 14 Marshall Faulk .75 .30
❑ 15 Jeff Garcia .60 .25
❑ 16 Terry Glenn .40 .15
❑ 17 Jay Fiedler .60 .25
❑ 18 Ahman Green .60 .25
❑ 19 Cade McNown .25 .08
❑ 20 Rob Johnson .40 .15
❑ 21 Jamal Anderson .60 .25
❑ 22 Corey Dillon .60 .25
❑ 23 Jake Plummer .40 .15
❑ 24 Rod Smith .40 .15
❑ 25 Trent Green .60 .25
❑ 26 Ricky Williams .60 .25
❑ 27 Charlie Garner .40 .15
❑ 28 Shaun Alexander .75 .30
❑ 29 Jeff George .40 .15
❑ 30 Torry Holt .60 .25
❑ 31 James Thrash .40 .15
❑ 32 Rich Gannon .60 .25
❑ 33 Ron Dayne .60 .25
❑ 34 Dedric Ward .25 .08
❑ 35 Edgerrin James .75 .30
❑ 36 Cris Carter .60 .25
❑ 37 Derrick Mason .40 .15
❑ 38 Brad Johnson .60 .25
❑ 39 Charlie Batch .60 .25
❑ 40 Joey Galloway .40 .15
❑ 41 James Allen .40 .15
❑ 42 Tim Biakabutuka .40 .15
❑ 43 Ray Lewis .60 .25
❑ 44 David Boston .60 .25
❑ 45 Kevin Johnson .40 .15
❑ 46 Jimmy Smith .40 .15
❑ 47 Joe Horn .40 .15
❑ 48 Terrell Owens .60 .25
❑ 49 Eddie George .60 .25
❑ 50 Brett Favre 2.00 .75
❑ 51 Wayne Chrebet .40 .15
❑ 52 Hines Ward .60 .25
❑ 53 Warrick Dunn .60 .25
❑ 54 Matt Hasselbeck .40 .15
❑ 55 Tiki Barber .60 .25
❑ 56 Lamar Smith .40 .15
❑ 57 Tim Couch .40 .15
❑ 58 Eric Moulds .40 .15
❑ 59 Shawn Jefferson .25 .08
❑ 60 Donald Hayes .25 .08
❑ 61 Brian Urlacher 1.00 .40
❑ 62 Steve McNair .60 .25
❑ 63 Kurt Warner 1.25 .50
❑ 64 Tim Brown .60 .25
❑ 65 Troy Brown .40 .15
❑ 66 Albert Connell .25 .08
❑ 67 Peyton Manning 1.50 .60
❑ 68 Peter Warrick .60 .25
❑ 69 Elvis Grbac .40 .15
❑ 70 Chris Chandler .40 .15
❑ 71 Akili Smith .25 .08
❑ 72 Keenan McCardell .25 .08
❑ 73 Kerry Collins .40 .15
❑ 74 Junior Seau .60 .25
❑ 75 Donovan McNabb .75 .30
❑ 76 Tony Banks .40 .15
❑ 77 Steve Beuerlein .25 .08
❑ 78 Daunte Culpepper .60 .25
❑ 79 Darrell Jackson .60 .25
❑ 80 Isaac Bruce .60 .25
❑ 81 Tyrone Wheatley .40 .15
❑ 82 Derrick Alexander .40 .15
❑ 83 Germane Crowell .25 .08
❑ 84 Jon Kitna .40 .15
❑ 85 Jamal Lewis 1.00 .40
❑ 86 Ed McCaffrey .60 .25
❑ 87 Mark Brunell .60 .25
❑ 88 Jeff Blake .40 .15
❑ 89 Duce Staley .60 .25
❑ 90 Doug Flutie .60 .25
❑ 91 Kordell Stewart .40 .15
❑ 92 Randy Moss 1.25 .50
❑ 93 Marvin Harrison .60 .25
❑ 94 Muhsin Muhammad .40 .15
❑ 95 Brian Griese .60 .25
❑ 96 Antonio Freeman .60 .25
❑ 97 Amani Toomer .40 .15
❑ 98 Oronde Gadsden .40 .15
❑ 99 Curtis Martin .60 .25
❑ 100 Jerry Rice 1.25 .50
❑ 101 Michael Pittman .25 .08
❑ 102 Shannon Sharpe .40 .15
❑ 103 Peerless Price .40 .15
❑ 104 Bill Schroeder .40 .15
❑ 105 Ike Hilliard .40 .15
❑ 106 Freddie Jones .25 .08
❑ 107 Tai Streets .25 .08
❑ 108 Ricky Watters .40 .15
❑ 109 Az-Zahir Hakim .25 .08
❑ 110 Jacquez Green .25 .08
❑ 111 Bobby Shaw .25 .08

❑ 112	Johnnie Morton	.40	.15
❑ 113	Laveranues Coles	.60	.25
❑ 114	Chad Pennington	1.00	.40
❑ 115	Champ Bailey	.40	.15
❑ 116	Charles Woodson	.40	.15
❑ 117	Curtis Conway	.40	.15
❑ 118	Marcus Robinson	.60	.25
❑ 119	Michael Westbrook	.40	.15
❑ 120	Mike Alstott	.60	.25
❑ 121	Priest Holmes	.75	.30
❑ 122	Qadry Ismail	.40	.15
❑ 123	Rocket Ismail	.40	.15
❑ 124	Shawn Bryson	.25	.08
❑ 125	Jeff Lewis	.25	.08
❑ 126	Jeremy Mcdaniel	.25	.08
❑ 127	Terance Mathis	.25	.08
❑ 128	Travis Prentice	.25	.08
❑ 129	Warren Sapp	.40	.15
❑ 130	Jevon Kearse	.40	.15
❑ 131	George Layne RC	.75	.30
❑ 132	Correll Buckhalter RC	1.50	.60
❑ 133	Tony Stewart RC	1.25	.50
❑ 134	Chris Barnes RC	.75	.30
❑ 135	A.J. Feeley RC	1.25	.50
❑ 136	Margin Hooks RC	.50	.20
❑ 137	Anthony Henry RC	1.25	.50
❑ 138	Dwight Smith RC	.50	.20
❑ 139	Torrance Marshall RC	1.25	.50
❑ 140	Gary Baxter RC	.75	.30
❑ 141	Derek Combs RC	.75	.30
❑ 142	Marcus Bell DT RC	.75	.30
❑ 143	Delawrence Grant RC	.50	.20
❑ 144	Jameel Cook RC	.75	.30
❑ 145	Eric Downing RC	.50	.20
❑ 146	Marlon McCree RC	.75	.30
❑ 147	Tay Cody RC	.50	.20
❑ 148	Mario Monds RC	.50	.20
❑ 149	Kenny Smith RC	.75	.30
❑ 150	Sedrick Hodge RC	.50	.20
❑ 151	Marcus Stroud RC	1.25	.50
❑ 152	Steve Smith RC	3.00	1.25
❑ 153	Tyrone Robertson RC	.50	.20
❑ 154	James Reed RC	.50	.20
❑ 155	Kris Kocurek RC	.50	.20
❑ 156	Dan O'Leary RC	.75	.30
❑ 157	Harold Blackmon RC	.50	.20
❑ 158	Fred Smoot RC	1.25	.50
❑ 159	Billy Baber RC	.50	.20
❑ 160	Jarrod Cooper RC	1.25	.50
❑ 161	Travis Henry RC	1.25	.50
❑ 162	David Terrell RC	1.25	.50
❑ 163	Josh Heupel RC	1.25	.50
❑ 164	Drew Brees RC	3.00	1.25
❑ 165	T.J. Houshmandzadeh RC	1.25	.50
❑ 166	Rod Gardner RC	1.25	.50
❑ 167	Richard Seymour RC	1.25	.50
❑ 168	Koren Robinson RC	1.25	.50
❑ 169	Scotty Anderson RC	.75	.30
❑ 170	Marques Tuiasosopo RC	1.25	.50
❑ 171	John Capel RC	.75	.30
❑ 172	LaMont Jordan RC	2.50	1.00
❑ 173	James Jackson RC	1.25	.50
❑ 174	Bobby Newcombe RC	1.25	.50
❑ 175	Anthony Thomas RC	1.25	.50
❑ 176	Dan Alexander RC	1.25	.50
❑ 177	Quincy Carter RC	1.25	.50
❑ 178	Morlon Greenwood RC	.75	.30
❑ 179	Robert Ferguson RC	1.25	.50
❑ 180	Sage Rosenfels RC	1.25	.50
❑ 181	Michael Stone RC	.50	.20
❑ 182	Chris Weinke RC	1.25	.50
❑ 183	Travis Minor RC	.75	.30
❑ 184	Gerard Warren RC	1.25	.50
❑ 185	Jamar Fletcher RC	.75	.30
❑ 186	Andre Carter RC	1.25	.50
❑ 187	Deuce McAllister RC	2.50	1.00
❑ 188	Dan Morgan RC	1.25	.50
❑ 189	Todd Heap RC	1.25	.50
❑ 190	Snoop Minnis RC	.75	.30
❑ 191	Will Allen RC	.75	.30
❑ 192	Freddie Mitchell RC	1.25	.50
❑ 193	Rudi Johnson RC	2.50	1.00
❑ 194	Kevan Barlow RC	1.25	.50
❑ 195	Jamie Winborn RC	.75	.30
❑ 196	Onomo Ojo RC	.75	.30
❑ 197	Leonard Davis RC	.75	.30
❑ 198	Santana Moss RC	2.00	.75
❑ 199	Chris Chambers RC	2.00	.75
❑ 200	Michael Vick RC	8.00	4.00
❑ 201	Michael Bennett RC	2.00	.75
❑ 202	Mike McMahon RC	1.25	.50
❑ 203	Jonathan Carter RC	.75	.30
❑ 204	Jamal Reynolds RC	1.25	.50
❑ 205	Justin Smith RC	1.25	.50
❑ 206	Quincy Morgan RC	1.25	.50
❑ 207	Chad Johnson RC	3.00	1.25
❑ 208	Jesse Palmer RC	1.25	.50
❑ 209	Reggie Wayne RC	2.50	1.00
❑ 210	LaDainian Tomlinson RC	6.00	3.00
❑ 211	Andre King RC	.75	.30
❑ 212	Richmond Flowers RC	.75	.30
❑ 213	Derrick Blaylock RC	1.25	.50
❑ 214	Cedrick Wilson RC	1.25	.50
❑ 215	Zeke Moreno RC	1.25	.50
❑ 216	Tommy Polley RC	1.25	.50
❑ 217	Damione Lewis RC	.75	.30
❑ 218	Aaron Schobel RC	1.25	.50
❑ 219	Alge Crumpler RC	1.50	.60
❑ 220	Nate Clements RC	1.25	.50
❑ 221	Quentin McCord RC	.75	.30
❑ 222	Ken-Yon Rambo RC	.75	.30
❑ 223	Milton Wynn RC	.75	.30
❑ 224	Derrick Gibson RC	.75	.30
❑ 225	Chris Taylor RC	.75	.30
❑ 226	Corey Hall RC	.50	.20
❑ 227	Vinny Sutherland RC	.75	.30
❑ 228	Kendrell Bell RC	2.00	.75
❑ 229	Casey Hampton RC	1.25	.50
❑ 230	Demetric Evans RC	.50	.20
❑ 231	Brian Allen RC	.50	.20
❑ 232	Rodney Bailey RC	.50	.20
❑ 233	Otis Leverette RC	.50	.20
❑ 234	Ron Edwards RC	.50	.20
❑ 235	Michael Jameson RC	.50	.20
❑ 236	Markus Steele RC	.75	.30
❑ 237	Jimmy Williams RC	.50	.20
❑ 238	Roger Knight RC	.50	.20
❑ 239	Randy Garner RC	.50	.20
❑ 240	Raymond Perryman RC	.50	.20
❑ 241	Karon Riley RC	.50	.20
❑ 242	Adam Archuleta RC	1.25	.50
❑ 243	Arnold Jackson RC	.75	.30
❑ 244	Ryan Pickett RC	.50	.20
❑ 245	Shad Meier RC	.75	.30
❑ 246	Reggie Germany RC	.75	.30
❑ 247	Justin McCareins RC	1.25	.50
❑ 248	Idrees Bashir RC	.50	.20
❑ 249	Josh Booty RC	1.25	.50
❑ 250	Eddie Berlin RC	.75	.30
❑ 251	Heath Evans RC	.75	.30
❑ 252	Alex Bannister RC	.75	.30
❑ 253	Corey Alston RC	.50	.20
❑ 254	Reggie White RC	.75	.30
❑ 255	Orlando Huff RC	.50	.20
❑ 256	Ken Lucas RC	.75	.30
❑ 257	Matt Stewart RC	.50	.20
❑ 258	Cedric Scott RC	.75	.30
❑ 259	Ronney Daniels RC	.50	.20
❑ 260	Kevin Kasper RC	1.25	.50
❑ 261	Tony Driver RC	.75	.30
❑ 262	Kyle Vanden Bosch RC	1.25	.50
❑ 263	T.J. Turner RC	.50	.20
❑ 264	Eric Westmoreland RC	.75	.30
❑ 265	Ronald Flemons RC	.50	.20
❑ 266	Eric Kelly RC	.50	.20
❑ 267	Moran Norris RC	.50	.20
❑ 268	Damerien McCants RC	.75	.30
❑ 269	James Boyd RC	.50	.20
❑ 270	Keith Adams RC	.50	.20
❑ 271	Brandon Manumaleuna RC	.75	.30
❑ 272	Dee Brown RC	1.25	.50
❑ 273	Ross Kolodziej RC	.50	.20
❑ 274	Boo Williams RC	.75	.30
❑ 275	Patrick Chukwurah RC	.50	.20

2002 Bowman

❑	COMPLETE SET (275)	50.00	20.00
❑ 1	Emmitt Smith	1.50	.60
❑ 2	Drew Brees	.60	.25
❑ 3	Duce Staley	.60	.25
❑ 4	Curtis Martin	.60	.25
❑ 5	Isaac Bruce	.60	.25
❑ 6	Stephen Davis	.40	.15
❑ 7	Darrell Jackson	.40	.15
❑ 8	James Stewart	.40	.15
❑ 9	Tim Couch	.40	.15
❑ 10	Travis Henry	.60	.25
❑ 11	Thomas Jones	.40	.15
❑ 12	Jamal Lewis	.60	.25
❑ 13	Chris Chambers	.60	.25
❑ 14	Jeff Blake	.40	.15
❑ 15	Plaxico Burress	.60	.25
❑ 16	Michael Pittman	.25	.08
❑ 17	Jeff Garcia	.60	.25
❑ 18	Tim Brown	.60	.25
❑ 19	Kent Graham	.25	.08
❑ 20	Shannon Sharpe	.40	.15
❑ 21	Corey Dillon	.40	.15
❑ 22	Muhsin Muhammad	.40	.15
❑ 23	Tony Gonzalez	.40	.15
❑ 24	Qadry Ismail	.40	.15
❑ 25	Mike McMahon	.60	.25
❑ 26	Edgerrin James	.75	.30
❑ 27	Daunte Culpepper	.60	.25
❑ 28	Deuce McAllister	.75	.30
❑ 29	Kerry Collins	.40	.15
❑ 30	Eddie George	.60	.25
❑ 31	Torry Holt	.60	.25
❑ 32	Todd Pinkston	.40	.15
❑ 33	Quincy Carter	.40	.15
❑ 34	Rod Smith	.40	.15
❑ 35	Michael Vick	2.00	.75
❑ 36	Jim Miller	.25	.08
❑ 37	Troy Brown	.40	.15
❑ 38	Wayne Chrebet	.40	.15
❑ 39	Curtis Conway	.25	.08
❑ 40	Reidel Anthony	.25	.08
❑ 41	Mark Brunell	.60	.25
❑ 42	Chris Weinke	.40	.15
❑ 43	Eric Moulds	.40	.15
❑ 44	Ike Hilliard	.25	.08
❑ 45	Jay Fiedler	.40	.15
❑ 46	Keyshawn Johnson	.60	.25
❑ 47	Rod Gardner	.40	.15
❑ 48	Chris Redman	.25	.08
❑ 49	James Allen	.40	.15
❑ 50	Kordell Stewart	.40	.15
❑ 51	Priest Holmes	.75	.30
❑ 52	Anthony Thomas	.40	.15
❑ 53	Peter Warrick	.40	.15
❑ 54	Jake Plummer	.40	.15
❑ 55	Jerry Rice	1.25	.50
❑ 56	Joe Horn	.40	.15
❑ 57	Derrick Mason	.40	.15

No.	Player	Hi	Lo
❑ 58	Kurt Warner	.60	.25
❑ 59	Antowain Smith	.40	.15
❑ 60	Randy Moss	1.25	.50
❑ 61	Warrick Dunn	.60	.25
❑ 62	Laveranues Coles	.40	.15
❑ 63	LaDainian Tomlinson	1.00	.40
❑ 64	Michael Westbrook	.25	.08
❑ 65	Travis Taylor	.25	.08
❑ 66	Brian Griese	.60	.25
❑ 67	Bill Schroeder	.40	.15
❑ 68	Ahman Green	.60	.25
❑ 69	Jimmy Smith	.40	.15
❑ 70	Charlie Garner	.40	.15
❑ 71	Terrell Owens	.60	.25
❑ 72	Brad Johnson	.40	.15
❑ 73	James Thrash	.40	.15
❑ 74	Marvin Harrison	.60	.25
❑ 75	Brett Favre	1.50	.60
❑ 76	Rocket Ismail	.40	.15
❑ 77	David Boston	.60	.25
❑ 78	Jermaine Lewis	.25	.08
❑ 79	Aaron Brooks	.60	.25
❑ 80	Shaun Alexander	.75	.30
❑ 81	Steve McNair	.60	.25
❑ 82	Marshall Faulk	.60	.25
❑ 83	Terrell Davis	.60	.25
❑ 84	Corey Bradford	.25	.08
❑ 85	David Terrell	.60	.25
❑ 86	Kevin Johnson	.40	.15
❑ 87	Jon Kitna	.40	.15
❑ 88	Az-Zahir Hakim	.25	.08
❑ 89	Drew Bledsoe	.75	.30
❑ 90	Garrison Hearst	.40	.15
❑ 91	Doug Flutie	.60	.25
❑ 92	Jerome Bettis	.60	.25
❑ 93	Vinny Testaverde	.40	.15
❑ 94	Tiki Barber	.60	.25
❑ 95	Johnnie Morton	.40	.15
❑ 96	Lamar Smith	.40	.15
❑ 97	Marcus Robinson	.40	.15
❑ 98	Fred Taylor	.60	.25
❑ 99	Tom Brady	1.50	.60
❑ 100	Peyton Manning	1.25	.50
❑ 101	Donovan McNabb	.75	.30
❑ 102	Rich Gannon	.60	.25
❑ 103	Hines Ward	.60	.25
❑ 104	Michael Bennett	.60	.25
❑ 105	Ricky Williams	.60	.25
❑ 106	Germane Crowell	.25	.08
❑ 107	Joey Galloway	.40	.15
❑ 108	Amani Toomer	.40	.15
❑ 109	Trent Green	.40	.15
❑ 110	Terry Glenn	.40	.15
❑ 111	Donte Stallworth RC	3.00	1.25
❑ 112	Mike Williams RC	1.25	.50
❑ 113	Kurt Kittner RC	1.25	.50
❑ 114	Josh Reed RC	1.50	.60
❑ 115	Raonall Smith RC	1.25	.50
❑ 116	David Garrard RC	1.50	.60
❑ 117	Eric Crouch RC	1.50	.60
❑ 118	Bryan Thomas RC	1.25	.50
❑ 119	Levi Jones RC	1.25	.50
❑ 120	Andre Davis RC	1.25	.50
❑ 121	Herb Haygood RC	.75	.30
❑ 122	Josh McCown RC	2.00	.75
❑ 123	Quentin Jammer RC	1.50	.60
❑ 124	Cliff Russell RC	1.25	.50
❑ 125	Jeremy Shockey RC	5.00	2.00
❑ 126	Jamin Elliott RC	.75	.30
❑ 127	Roy Williams RC	4.00	1.50
❑ 128	Marquise Walker RC	1.25	.50
❑ 129	Kalimba Edwards RC	1.50	.60
❑ 130	Daniel Graham RC	1.50	.60
❑ 131	Freddie Milons RC	1.25	.50
❑ 132	Anthony Weaver RC	1.25	.50
❑ 133	Jake Schifino RC	1.25	.50
❑ 134	Antonio Bryant RC	1.50	.60
❑ 135	DeShaun Foster RC	1.50	.60
❑ 136	Antwaan Randle El RC	2.50	1.00
❑ 137	William Green RC	1.50	.60
❑ 138	Ed Reed RC	2.50	1.00
❑ 139	Maurice Morris RC	1.50	.60
❑ 140	Joey Harrington RC	4.00	1.50
❑ 141	T.J. Duckett RC	2.50	1.00
❑ 142	Javon Walker RC	3.00	1.25
❑ 143	Albert Haynesworth RC	1.25	.50
❑ 144	Julius Peppers RC	3.00	1.25
❑ 145	Clinton Portis RC	5.00	2.00
❑ 146	Craig Nall RC	1.50	.60
❑ 147	Ashley Lelie RC	3.00	1.25
❑ 148	Reche Caldwell RC	1.50	.60
❑ 149	Rohan Davey RC	1.50	.60
❑ 150	Patrick Ramsey RC	2.00	.75
❑ 151	Jabar Gaffney RC	1.50	.60
❑ 152	Tank Williams RC	1.25	.50
❑ 153	Ron Johnson RC	1.25	.50
❑ 154	Ladell Betts RC	1.50	.60
❑ 155	Brian Westbrook RC	2.50	1.00
❑ 156	Jamar Martin RC	1.25	.50
❑ 157	Travis Stephens RC	1.25	.50
❑ 158	Tim Carter RC	1.25	.50
❑ 159	Darrell Hill RC	1.50	.60
❑ 160	Luke Staley RC	1.25	.50
❑ 161	Randy Fasani RC	1.25	.50
❑ 162	Matt Schobel RC	1.25	.50
❑ 163	Jon McGraw RC	.75	.30
❑ 164	Dwight Freeney RC	2.00	.75
❑ 165	Chad Hutchinson RC	1.25	.50
❑ 166	Adrian Peterson RC	1.50	.60
❑ 167	Josh Scobey RC	1.50	.60
❑ 168	Jonathan Wells RC	1.50	.60
❑ 169	Sam Simmons RC	.75	.30
❑ 170	Jerramy Stevens RC	1.50	.60
❑ 171	Jason McAddley RC	1.25	.50
❑ 172	Ken Simonton RC	.75	.30
❑ 173	Chester Taylor RC	1.50	.60
❑ 174	Brandon Doman RC	1.25	.50
❑ 175	Javin Hunter RC	.75	.30
❑ 176	Eddie Drummond RC	1.25	.50
❑ 177	Andre Lott RC	1.50	.60
❑ 178	Travis Fisher RC	1.50	.60
❑ 179	Jarvis Green RC	1.25	.50
❑ 180	Ross Tucker RC	.75	.30
❑ 181	Lamont Brightful RC	.75	.30
❑ 182	Rocky Calmus RC	1.50	.60
❑ 183	Wes Pate RC	.75	.30
❑ 184	Lamar Gordon RC	1.50	.60
❑ 185	Terry Jones RC	1.25	.50
❑ 186	Kyle Johnson RC	.75	.30
❑ 187	Daryl Jones RC	1.25	.50
❑ 188	Tellis Redmon RC	1.25	.50
❑ 189	Howard Green RC	.75	.30
❑ 190	Jarrod Baxter RC	1.25	.50
❑ 191	Delvon Flowers RC	1.25	.50
❑ 192	Kevin Curtis RC	.75	.30
❑ 193	Kelly Campbell RC	1.25	.50
❑ 194	Eddie Freeman RC	.75	.30
❑ 195	Atrews Bell RC	.75	.30
❑ 196	Omar Easy RC	1.50	.60
❑ 197	Jeremy Allen RC	.75	.30
❑ 198	Andra Davis RC	1.25	.50
❑ 199	Jack Brewer RC	1.25	.50
❑ 200	Mike Rumph RC	1.50	.60
❑ 201	Seth Burford RC	1.25	.50
❑ 202	Marquand Manuel RC	.75	.30
❑ 203	Marques Anderson RC	1.50	.60
❑ 204	Ben Leber RC	1.50	.60
❑ 205	Ryan Denney RC	1.25	.50
❑ 206	Justin Peelle RC	.75	.30
❑ 207	Lito Sheppard RC	1.50	.60
❑ 208	Damien Anderson RC	1.25	.50
❑ 209	Lamont Thompson RC	1.25	.50
❑ 210	David Priestley RC	1.25	.50
❑ 211	Michael Lewis RC	1.50	.60
❑ 212	Lee Mays RC	1.25	.50
❑ 213	Alan Harper RC	.75	.30
❑ 214	Verron Haynes RC	1.50	.60
❑ 215	Chris Hope RC	1.50	.60
❑ 216	David Thornton RC	.75	.30
❑ 217	Derek Ross RC	1.25	.50
❑ 218	Brett Keisel RC	4.00	1.50
❑ 219	Joseph Jefferson RC	1.25	.50
❑ 220	Andre Goodman RC	1.50	.60
❑ 221	Robert Royal RC	1.50	.60
❑ 222	Sheldon Brown RC	1.50	.60
❑ 223	DeVeren Johnson RC	1.25	.50
❑ 224	Rock Cartwright RC	2.00	.75
❑ 225	Quincy Monk RC	.75	.30
❑ 226	Nick Rogers RC	1.25	.50
❑ 227	Kendall Simmons RC	1.25	.50
❑ 228	Joe Burns RC	1.25	.50
❑ 229	Wesly Mallard RC	1.25	.50
❑ 230	Chris Cash RC	1.25	.50
❑ 231	David Givens RC	5.00	2.00
❑ 232	John Owens RC	1.25	.50
❑ 233	Jarrett Ferguson RC	1.25	.50
❑ 234	Randy McMichael RC	2.50	1.00
❑ 235	Chris Baker RC	1.25	.50
❑ 236	Rashad Bauman RC	1.25	.50
❑ 237	Matt Murphy RC	1.25	.50
❑ 238	LaVar Glover RC	.75	.30
❑ 239	Steve Bellisari RC	1.25	.50
❑ 240	Chad Williams RC	1.25	.50
❑ 241	Kevin Thomas RC	1.25	.50
❑ 242	Carlos Hall RC	1.50	.60
❑ 243	Nick Greisen RC	.75	.30
❑ 244	Justin Bannan RC	1.25	.50
❑ 245	Charles Hill RC	.75	.30
❑ 246	Mark Anelli RC	.75	.30
❑ 247	Coy Wire RC	1.50	.60
❑ 248	Darnell Sanders RC	1.25	.50
❑ 249	Larry Foote RC	4.00	1.50
❑ 250	David Carr RC	4.00	1.50
❑ 251	Ricky Williams RC	1.25	.50
❑ 252	Napoleon Harris RC	1.50	.60
❑ 253	Ennis Haywood RC	1.25	.50
❑ 254	Keyuo Craver RC	1.25	.50
❑ 255	Kahlil Hill RC	1.25	.50
❑ 256	J.T. O'Sullivan RC	1.25	.50
❑ 257	Woody Dantzler RC	1.25	.50
❑ 258	Phillip Buchanon RC	1.50	.60
❑ 259	Charles Grant RC	1.50	.60
❑ 260	Dusty Bonner RC	.75	.30
❑ 261	James Allen RC	.75	.30
❑ 262	Ronald Curry RC	1.50	.60
❑ 263	Deion Branch RC	3.00	1.25
❑ 264	Larry Ned RC	1.25	.50
❑ 265	Mel Mitchell RC	1.25	.50
❑ 266	Kendall Newson RC	.75	.30
❑ 267	Shaun Hill RC	1.50	.60
❑ 268	David Pugh RC	.75	.30
❑ 269	Dante Wesley RC	.75	.30
❑ 270	Josh Mallard RC	.75	.30
❑ 271	Akin Ayodele RC	.75	.30
❑ 272	Pete Hunter RC	1.25	.50
❑ 273	Kevin McCadam RC	1.25	.50
❑ 274	Jeff Kelly RC	1.25	.50
❑ 275	John Henderson RC	1.50	.60

2003 Bowman

No.	Player	Hi	Lo
❑	COMPLETE SET (273)	60.00	30.00
❑ 1	Brett Favre	2.00	.75
❑ 2	Jeremy Shockey	1.25	.50
❑ 3	Fred Taylor	.75	.30

❑	4	Rich Gannon	.50	.20
❑	5	Joey Galloway	.50	.20
❑	6	Ray Lewis	.75	.30
❑	7	Jeff Blake	.30	.10
❑	8	Stacey Mack	.30	.10
❑	9	Matt Hasselbeck	.50	.20
❑	10	Laveranues Coles	.50	.20
❑	11	Brad Johnson	.50	.20
❑	12	Tommy Maddox	.75	.30
❑	13	Curtis Martin	.75	.30
❑	14	Tom Brady	2.00	.75
❑	15	Ricky Williams	.75	.30
❑	16	Stephen Davis	.50	.20
❑	17	Chad Johnson	.75	.30
❑	18	Joey Harrington	1.25	.50
❑	19	Tony Gonzalez	.50	.20
❑	20	Peerless Price	.50	.20
❑	21	LaDainian Tomlinson	.75	.30
❑	22	James Thrash	.30	.10
❑	23	Charlie Garner	.50	.20
❑	24	Eddie George	.50	.20
❑	25	Terrell Owens	.75	.30
❑	26	Brian Urlacher	1.25	.50
❑	27	Eric Moulds	.50	.20
❑	28	Emmitt Smith	2.00	.75
❑	29	Tim Couch	.30	.10
❑	30	Jake Plummer	.50	.20
❑	31	Marvin Harrison	.75	.30
❑	32	Chris Chambers	.75	.30
❑	33	Tiki Barber	.75	.30
❑	34	Kurt Warner	.75	.30
❑	35	Michael Pittman	.30	.10
❑	36	Kevin Dyson	.50	.20
❑	37	Clinton Portis	1.25	.50
❑	38	Peyton Manning	1.25	.50
❑	39	Travis Taylor	.50	.20
❑	40	Jeff Garcia	.75	.30
❑	41	Patrick Ramsey	.75	.30
❑	42	Shaun Alexander	.75	.30
❑	43	Joe Horn	.50	.20
❑	44	Daunte Culpepper	.75	.30
❑	45	Travis Henry	.50	.20
❑	46	Brian Finneran	.30	.10
❑	47	William Green	.50	.20
❑	48	Kordell Stewart	.50	.20
❑	49	Reggie Wayne	.50	.20
❑	50	Priest Holmes	1.00	.40
❑	51	Jay Fiedler	.50	.20
❑	52	Corey Dillon	.50	.20
❑	53	Jamal Lewis	.75	.30
❑	54	Mark Brunell	.50	.20
❑	55	Santana Moss	.50	.20
❑	56	Duce Staley	.50	.20
❑	57	Torry Holt	.75	.30
❑	58	Rod Gardner	.50	.20
❑	59	Kerry Collins	.50	.20
❑	60	Randy Moss	1.25	.50
❑	61	Jerry Porter	.50	.20
❑	62	Plaxico Burress	.50	.20
❑	63	Steve McNair	.75	.30
❑	64	Muhsin Muhammad	.50	.20
❑	65	Drew Bledsoe	.75	.30
❑	66	T.J. Duckett	.50	.20
❑	67	Ahman Green	.75	.30
❑	68	Rod Smith	.50	.20
❑	69	Jimmy Smith	.50	.20
❑	70	Trent Green	.50	.20
❑	71	Tim Brown	.75	.30
❑	72	Jerome Bettis	.75	.30
❑	73	Isaac Bruce	.75	.30
❑	74	Derrick Mason	.50	.20
❑	75	Donovan McNabb	1.00	.40
❑	76	Deuce McAllister	.75	.30
❑	77	Zach Thomas	.75	.30
❑	78	Garrison Hearst	.50	.20
❑	79	Koren Robinson	.50	.20
❑	80	Marshall Faulk	.75	.30
❑	81	Keyshawn Johnson	.75	.30
❑	82	Jake Delhomme	.75	.30
❑	83	Marty Booker	.50	.20
❑	84	James Stewart	.50	.20
❑	85	Corey Bradford	.30	.10
❑	86	Dernius Thompson	.30	.10
❑	87	Edgerrin James	.75	.30
❑	88	Darrell Jackson	.50	.20
❑	89	Hines Ward	.75	.30
❑	90	David Boston	.50	.20
❑	91	Curtis Conway	.50	.20
❑	92	David Patten	.30	.10
❑	93	Michael Bennett	.50	.20
❑	94	Todd Pinkston	.50	.20
❑	95	Jerry Rice	1.50	.60
❑	96	Jon Kitna	.50	.20
❑	97	Ed McCaffrey	.75	.30
❑	98	Donald Driver	.50	.20
❑	99	Anthony Thomas	.50	.20
❑	100	Michael Vick	2.00	.75
❑	101	Terry Glenn	.30	.10
❑	102	Quincy Morgan	.50	.20
❑	103	David Carr	1.25	.50
❑	104	Troy Brown	.50	.20
❑	105	Aaron Brooks	.75	.30
❑	106	Amani Toomer	.50	.20
❑	107	Drew Brees	.75	.30
❑	108	Chad Hutchinson	.30	.10
❑	109	Warrick Dunn	.50	.20
❑	110	Chad Pennington	1.00	.40
❑	111	Carson Palmer RC	6.00	2.50
❑	112	Brian St.Pierre RC	1.50	.60
❑	113	Keenan Howry RC	1.50	.60
❑	114	Sultan McCullough RC	1.25	.50
❑	115	Terence Newman RC	3.00	1.25
❑	116	Kelley Washington RC	1.50	.60
❑	117	Musa Smith RC	1.50	.60
❑	118	Kevin Williams RC	1.50	.60
❑	119	Jordan Gross RC	1.25	.50
❑	120	Lance Briggs RC	2.00	.75
❑	121	Victor Hobson RC	1.50	.60
❑	122	Bryant Johnson RC	1.50	.60
❑	123	Travis Anglin RC	.75	.30
❑	124	Artose Pinner RC	1.50	.60
❑	125	Willis McGahee RC	4.00	1.50
❑	126	Rashean Mathis RC	1.25	.50
❑	127	B.J. Askew RC	1.50	.60
❑	128	DeWayne White RC	1.25	.50
❑	129	Kevin Curtis RC	1.50	.60
❑	130	Tyrone Calico RC	2.00	.75
❑	131	Julian Battle RC	1.25	.50
❑	132	Ricky Manning RC	1.50	.60
❑	133	Cory Redding RC	1.25	.50
❑	134	Michael Haynes RC	1.50	.60
❑	135	Dallas Clark RC	1.50	.60
❑	136	Shaun McDonald RC	1.50	.60
❑	137	Marcus Trufant RC	1.50	.60
❑	138	Kareem Kelly RC	1.25	.50
❑	139	Sam Aiken RC	1.25	.50
❑	140	Terrell Suggs RC	2.50	1.00
❑	141	Gibran Hamdan RC	.75	.30
❑	142	Bobby Wade RC	1.50	.60
❑	143	Aaron Walker RC	1.25	.50
❑	144	Calvin Pace RC	1.25	.50
❑	145	Quentin Griffin RC	1.50	.60
❑	146	Ken Dorsey RC	1.50	.60
❑	147	Jerome McDougle RC	1.50	.60
❑	148	Earnest Graham RC	1.25	.50
❑	149	Rashad Moore RC	1.25	.50
❑	150	Charles Rogers RC	1.50	.60
❑	151	Cecil Sapp RC	1.25	.50
❑	152	Cato June RC	1.50	.60
❑	153	Ahmaad Galloway RC	1.25	.50
❑	154	William Joseph RC	1.50	.60
❑	155	Anquan Boldin RC	4.00	1.50
❑	156	L.J. Smith RC	1.50	.60
❑	157	Antwoine Sanders RC	.75	.30
❑	158	Justin Griffith RC	1.25	.50
❑	159	Kevin Garrett RC	.75	.30
❑	160	Teyo Johnson RC	1.50	.60
❑	161	Chris Crocker RC	1.50	.60
❑	162	Brad Banks RC	1.25	.50
❑	163	Justin Gage RC	1.50	.60
❑	164	Doug Gabriel RC	1.50	.60
❑	165	Terry Pierce RC	1.25	.50
❑	166	Bradie James RC	1.50	.60
❑	167	Bennie Joppru RC	1.50	.60
❑	168	Malaefou Mackenzie RC	.75	.30
❑	169	Terrence Edwards RC	1.25	.50
❑	170	E.J. Henderson RC	1.50	.60
❑	171	Tony Romo RC	1.50	.60
❑	172	DeWayne Robertson RC	1.50	.60
❑	173	Dwone Hicks RC	.75	.30
❑	174	Carl Ford RC	.75	.30
❑	175	Byron Leftwich RC	5.00	2.00
❑	176	Ken Hamlin RC	1.50	.60
❑	177	Domanick Davis RC	2.50	1.00
❑	178	Adrian Madise RC	1.25	.50
❑	179	Siddeeq Shabazz RC	.75	.30
❑	180	Dave Ragone RC	1.50	.60
❑	181	Mike Seidman RC	.75	.30
❑	182	Brooks Bollinger RC	1.50	.60
❑	183	DeAndrew Rubin RC	.75	.30
❑	184	Mike Pinkard RC	.75	.30
❑	185	Nate Burleson RC	2.00	.75
❑	186	LaBrandon Toefield RC	1.50	.60
❑	187	Angelo Crowell RC	1.25	.50
❑	188	J.R. Tolver RC	1.25	.50
❑	189	Osi Umenyiora RC	2.50	1.00
❑	190	Larry Johnson RC	6.00	3.00
❑	191	Nick Barnett RC	2.50	1.00
❑	192	Brandon Drumm RC	.75	.30
❑	193	Rien Long RC	.75	.30
❑	194	Zuriel Smith RC	.75	.30
❑	195	Onterrio Smith RC	1.50	.60
❑	196	Ronald Bellamy RC	1.25	.50
❑	197	Kenny Peterson RC	1.25	.50
❑	198	Charles Tillman RC	2.00	.75
❑	199	Chaun Thompson RC	.75	.30
❑	200	Andre Johnson RC	3.00	1.25
❑	201	Gerald Hayes RC	.75	.30
❑	202	Terrence Holt RC	1.25	.50
❑	203	Ovie Mughelli RC	.75	.30
❑	204	Talman Gardner RC	1.50	.60
❑	205	Bethel Johnson RC	1.50	.60
❑	206	Avon Cobourne RC	.75	.30
❑	207	Brandon Lloyd RC	2.00	.75
❑	208	Andre Woolfolk RC	1.50	.60
❑	209	George Wrighster RC	1.25	.50
❑	210	Justin Fargas RC	1.50	.60
❑	211	Jimmy Kennedy RC	1.50	.60
❑	212	Arnaz Battle RC	1.50	.60
❑	213	Marquel Blackwell RC	.75	.30
❑	214	Walter Young RC	.75	.30
❑	215	Kliff Kingsbury RC	1.25	.50
❑	216	Kawika Mitchell RC	1.50	.60
❑	217	Drayton Florence RC	.75	.30
❑	218	Jeremi Johnson RC	1.25	.50
❑	219	Billy McMullen RC	1.25	.50
❑	220	Lee Suggs RC	3.00	1.25
❑	221	David Kircus RC	1.25	.50
❑	222	Rod Babers RC	1.25	.50
❑	223	Jon Olinger RC	.75	.30
❑	224	Ty Warren RC	1.50	.60
❑	225	Kyle Boller RC	3.00	1.25
❑	226	Danny Curley RC	.75	.30
❑	227	Andrew Pinnock RC	1.25	.50
❑	228	Kirk Farmer RC	.75	.30
❑	229	Tully Banta-Cain RC	1.25	.50
❑	230	Alonzo Jackson RC	1.25	.50
❑	231	Anthony Adams RC	1.25	.50
❑	232	Trent Smith RC	1.50	.60
❑	233	Seneca Wallace RC	1.50	.60
❑	234	Shane Walton RC	.75	.30
❑	235	Chris Brown RC	2.00	.75
❑	236	Dahrran Diedrick RC	1.50	.60
❑	237	Juston Wood RC	.75	.30
❑	238	Mike Doss RC	1.50	.60
❑	239	Visanthe Shiancoe RC	1.25	.50
❑	240	Rex Grossman RC	2.50	1.00
❑	241	David Young RC	.75	.30
❑	242	Jimmy Wilkerson RC	1.25	.50
❑	243	Jason Witten RC	2.50	1.00

❑	244	Dennis Weathersby RC	.75	.30
❑	245	Taylor Jacobs RC	1.25	.50
❑	246	Chris Davis RC	1.25	.50
❑	247	LaTarence Dunbar RC	1.25	.50
❑	248	Eugene Wilson RC	1.50	.60
❑	249	Ryan Hoag RC	.75	.30
❑	250	Chris Simms RC	2.50	1.00
❑	251	Ike Taylor RC	2.50	1.00
❑	252	Brock Forsey RC	1.50	.60
❑	253	Curt Anes RC	.75	.30
❑	254	Taco Wallace RC	1.25	.50
❑	255	Johnathan Sullivan RC	1.25	.50
❑	256	David Tyree RC	1.25	.50
❑	257	Troy Polamalu RC	15.00	7.50
❑	258	Nate Hybl RC	1.50	.60
❑	259	Spencer Nead RC	1.25	.50
❑	260	Boss Bailey RC	1.50	.60
❑	261	LaMarcus McDonald RC	.75	.30
❑	262	Casey Moore RC	1.25	.50
❑	263	Pisa Tinoisamoa RC	1.50	.60
❑	264	Willie Ponder RC	.75	.30
❑	265	Donald Lee RC	1.25	.50
❑	266	Nnamdi Asomugha RC	1.25	.50
❑	267	Sammy Davis RC	1.50	.60
❑	268	Joffrey Reynolds RC	.75	.30
❑	269	Eddie Moore RC	1.25	.50
❑	270	Tony Hollings RC	1.50	.60
❑	271	Nick Maddox RC	.75	.30
❑	272	Kevin Walter RC	1.25	.50
❑	273	Dan Klecko RC	1.50	.60
❑	274	Antwan Peek RC	1.25	.50
❑	275	Tyler Brayton RC	1.50	.60

2004 Bowman

❑		COMPLETE SET (275)	60.00	30.00
❑	1	Brett Favre	2.00	.75
❑	2	Jay Fiedler	.30	.10
❑	3	Andre Davis	.30	.10
❑	4	Travis Henry	.50	.20
❑	5	Jimmy Smith	.50	.20
❑	6	Santana Moss	.50	.20
❑	7	Correll Buckhalter	.50	.20
❑	8	Randy Moss	1.00	.40
❑	9	Edgerrin James	.75	.30
❑	10	Marc Bulger	.75	.30
❑	11	Derrick Mason	.50	.20
❑	12	Mark Brunell	.50	.20
❑	13	Donte' Stallworth	.50	.20
❑	14	Deion Branch	.75	.30
❑	15	Jake Plummer	.50	.20
❑	16	Steve Smith	.75	.30
❑	17	Jon Kitna	.50	.20
❑	18	Andre Johnson	.75	.30
❑	19	A.J. Feeley	.75	.30
❑	20	Drew Bledsoe	.75	.30
❑	21	Antonio Bryant	.50	.20
❑	22	Reggie Wayne	.50	.20
❑	23	Thomas Jones	.50	.20
❑	24	Alge Crumpler	.50	.20
❑	25	Anquan Boldin	.75	.30
❑	26	Tim Rattay	.30	.10
❑	27	Charlie Garner	.50	.20
❑	28	James Thrash	.30	.10
❑	29	Koren Robinson	.50	.20
❑	30	Terrell Owens	.75	.30
❑	31	Amani Toomer	.50	.20
❑	32	Kelly Campbell	.30	.10
❑	33	Patrick Ramsey	.50	.20
❑	34	Plaxico Burress	.50	.20
❑	35	Chad Pennington	.75	.30
❑	36	Fred Taylor	.50	.20
❑	37	Domanick Davis	.75	.30
❑	38	DeShaun Foster	.50	.20
❑	39	T.J. Duckett	.50	.20
❑	40	Ahman Green	.75	.30
❑	41	Lee Suggs	.75	.30
❑	42	Tony Gonzalez	.50	.20
❑	43	Rich Gannon	.50	.20
❑	44	Kevan Barlow	.50	.20
❑	45	Torry Holt	.75	.30
❑	46	Aaron Brooks	.50	.20
❑	47	Tyrone Calico	.50	.20
❑	48	Keenan McCardell	.30	.10
❑	49	Hines Ward	.75	.30
❑	50	LaDainian Tomlinson	1.00	.40
❑	51	Dante Hall	.75	.30
❑	52	Marcus Pollard	.30	.10
❑	53	Corey Dillon	.50	.20
❑	54	Justin McCareins	.30	.10
❑	55	Stephen Davis	.50	.20
❑	56	Jeff Garcia	.75	.30
❑	57	Ashley Lelie	.50	.20
❑	58	Javon Walker	.50	.20
❑	59	Kyle Boller	.75	.30
❑	60	Chad Johnson	.75	.30
❑	61	Anthony Thomas	.50	.20
❑	62	Byron Leftwich	1.00	.40
❑	63	David Boston	.50	.20
❑	64	Onterrio Smith	.50	.20
❑	65	Deuce McAllister	.75	.30
❑	66	Antwaan Randle El	.75	.30
❑	67	Justin Fargas	.50	.20
❑	68	Laveranues Coles	.50	.20
❑	69	Quincy Morgan	.50	.20
❑	70	Priest Holmes	1.00	.40
❑	71	Robert Ferguson	.30	.10
❑	72	Charles Rogers	.50	.20
❑	73	Drew Brees	.75	.30
❑	74	Matt Hasselbeck	.50	.20
❑	75	Peyton Manning	1.25	.50
❑	76	Rudi Johnson	.50	.20
❑	77	Jake Delhomme	.75	.30
❑	78	Tiki Barber	.75	.30
❑	79	Brad Johnson	.50	.20
❑	80	Steve McNair	.75	.30
❑	81	Willis McGahee	.75	.30
❑	82	Josh McCown	.50	.20
❑	83	Garrison Hearst	.50	.20
❑	84	Quincy Carter	.50	.20
❑	85	Ricky Williams	.75	.30
❑	86	Trent Green	.50	.20
❑	87	Curtis Martin	.75	.30
❑	88	Jerry Porter	.50	.20
❑	89	Brian Westbrook	.50	.20
❑	90	Clinton Portis	.75	.30
❑	91	Eric Moulds	.50	.20
❑	92	Marcel Shipp	.50	.20
❑	93	Joey Harrington	.75	.30
❑	94	David Carr	.75	.30
❑	95	Marvin Harrison	.75	.30
❑	96	Joe Horn	.50	.20
❑	97	Chris Chambers	.50	.20
❑	98	Darrell Jackson	.50	.20
❑	99	Eddie George	.50	.20
❑	100	Donovan McNabb	1.00	.40
❑	101	Marshall Faulk	.75	.30
❑	102	Rex Grossman	.75	.30
❑	103	Tai Streets	.30	.10
❑	104	Jeremy Shockey	.75	.30
❑	105	Jamal Lewis	.75	.30
❑	106	Tom Brady	2.00	.75
❑	107	Shaun Alexander	.75	.30
❑	108	Carson Palmer	1.00	.40
❑	109	Daunte Culpepper	.75	.30
❑	110	Michael Vick	1.50	.60
❑	111	Eli Manning RC	12.00	5.00
❑	112	Kevin Jones RC	5.00	2.00
❑	113	Philip Rivers RC	5.00	2.00
❑	114	Ben Roethlisberger RC	20.00	10.00
❑	115	Roy Williams RC	4.00	1.50
❑	116	Tommie Harris RC	1.50	.60
❑	117	Vontez Duff RC	1.25	.50
❑	118	Karlos Dansby RC	1.50	.60
❑	119	Thomas Tapeh RC	1.25	.50
❑	120	Matt Schaub RC	2.50	1.00
❑	121	Dexter Reid RC	.75	.30
❑	122	Jonathan Smith RC	1.25	.50
❑	123	Ricardo Colclough RC	1.50	.60
❑	124	Jeff Dugan RC	.75	.30
❑	125	Larry Fitzgerald RC	5.00	2.00
❑	126	Gibril Wilson RC	1.50	.60
❑	127	Sean Taylor RC	2.00	.75
❑	128	Marquise Hill RC	1.25	.50
❑	129	Ernest Wilford RC	1.50	.60
❑	130	Cedric Cobbs RC	1.50	.60
❑	131	Rich Gardner RC	1.25	.50
❑	132	Chris Cooley RC	1.50	.60
❑	133	Kenechi Udeze RC	1.50	.60
❑	134	John Navarre RC	1.50	.60
❑	135	Ben Troupe RC	1.50	.60
❑	136	Dave Ball RC	.75	.30
❑	137	Antwan Odom RC	1.50	.60
❑	138	Stuart Schweigert RC	1.50	.60
❑	139	Derek Abney RC	1.50	.60
❑	140	Keary Colbert RC	2.00	.75
❑	141	Jeris McIntyre RC	1.25	.50
❑	142	Matt Kranchick RC	1.50	.60
❑	143	Rodney Leisle RC	.75	.30
❑	144	Vince Wilfork RC	2.00	.75
❑	145	Lee Evans RC	2.00	.75
❑	146	Darnell Dockett RC	1.25	.50
❑	147	Jeremy LeSueur RC	1.25	.50
❑	148	Gilbert Gardner RC	1.25	.50
❑	149	Amon Gordon RC	.75	.30
❑	150	Darius Watts RC	1.50	.60
❑	151	Junior Siavii RC	1.50	.60
❑	152	Igor Olshansky RC	1.50	.60
❑	153	Courtney Watson RC	1.50	.60
❑	154	D.J. Williams RC	2.00	.75
❑	155	Mewelde Moore RC	2.00	.75
❑	156	Teddy Lehman RC	1.50	.60
❑	157	Nathan Vasher RC	2.00	.75
❑	158	Randy Starks RC	1.25	.50
❑	159	Isaac Sopoaga RC	.75	.30
❑	160	Drew Henson RC	1.50	.60
❑	161	Erik Coleman RC	1.50	.60
❑	162	Robert Kent RC	.75	.30
❑	163	Jammal Lord RC	1.50	.60
❑	164	Richard Seigler RC	1.25	.50
❑	165	Jeff Smoker RC	1.50	.60
❑	166	Niko Koutouvides RC	1.25	.50
❑	167	Adimchinobe Echemandu RC	1.25	.50
❑	168	Matt Mauck RC	1.50	.60
❑	169	Brandon Miree RC	1.25	.50
❑	170	Dunta Robinson RC	1.50	.60
❑	171	B.J. Symons RC	1.50	.60
❑	172	Courtney Anderson RC	1.25	.50
❑	173	Bruce Perry RC	1.50	.60
❑	174	Shaun Phillips RC	1.25	.50
❑	175	Greg Jones RC	1.50	.60
❑	176	Ryan Krause RC	1.25	.50
❑	177	Charlie Anderson RC	.75	.30
❑	178	Tank Johnson RC	1.25	.50
❑	179	Dwan Edwards RC	.75	.30
❑	180	Julius Jones RC	6.00	2.50
❑	181	Chad Lavalais RC	1.25	.50
❑	182	Tim Anderson RC	1.50	.60
❑	183	Jarrett Payton RC	2.00	.75
❑	184	Matt Ware RC	1.50	.60
❑	185	DeAngelo Hall RC	2.00	.75
❑	186	Ben Hartsock RC	1.50	.60
❑	187	Bradlee Van Pelt RC	2.50	1.00
❑	188	Michael Boulware RC	1.50	.60
❑	189	Keith Smith RC	1.25	.50

❑	190	Michael Jenkins RC	1.50	.60
❑	191	Quincy Wilson RC	1.25	.50
❑	192	Dontarrious Thomas RC	1.50	.60
❑	193	Sloan Thomas RC	1.25	.50
❑	194	Tony Hargrove RC	1.25	.50
❑	195	Ben Watson RC	1.50	.60
❑	196	Craig Krenzel RC	1.50	.60
❑	197	Jason Babin RC	1.50	.60
❑	198	Jim Sorgi RC	1.50	.60
❑	199	Triandos Luke RC	1.50	.60
❑	200	Kellen Winslow RC	3.00	1.25
❑	201	Patrick Crayton RC	1.50	.60
❑	202	Michael Waddell RC	.75	.30
❑	203	Chris Gamble RC	2.00	.75
❑	204	Josh Harris RC	1.50	.60
❑	205	Devard Darling RC	1.50	.60
❑	206	Shawntae Spencer RC	1.50	.60
❑	207	Will Smith RC	1.50	.60
❑	208	Samie Parker RC	1.50	.60
❑	209	Darrion Scott RC	1.50	.60
❑	210	Chris Perry RC	2.50	1.00
❑	211	P.K. Sam RC	1.25	.50
❑	212	Wes Welker RC	1.50	.60
❑	213	Ryan Dinwiddie RC	1.25	.50
❑	214	Rod Davis RC	.75	.30
❑	215	Casey Clausen RC	1.50	.60
❑	216	Clarence Moore RC	1.50	.60
❑	217	D.J. Hackett RC	1.25	.50
❑	218	Casey Bramlet RC	1.25	.50
❑	219	Jared Lorenzen RC	1.25	.50
❑	220	Devery Henderson RC	1.25	.50
❑	221	Sean Jones RC	1.25	.50
❑	222	Maurice Mann RC	1.25	.50
❑	223	Jared Allen RC	2.00	.75
❑	224	Bruce Thornton RC	.75	.30
❑	225	Tatum Bell RC	3.00	1.25
❑	226	Leon Joe RC	.75	.30
❑	227	Tim Euhus RC	1.50	.60
❑	228	John Standeford RC	1.25	.50
❑	229	Reggie Torbor RC	1.25	.50
❑	230	Rashaun Woods RC	1.50	.60
❑	231	Jason Shivers RC	.75	.30
❑	232	Jason Peters RC	1.50	.60
❑	233	Ahmad Carroll RC	2.00	.75
❑	234	Jason David RC	1.50	.60
❑	235	Keyaron Fox RC	1.25	.50
❑	236	Corey Williams RC	.75	.30
❑	237	Raheem Orr RC	.75	.30
❑	238	Carlos Francis RC	1.25	.50
❑	239	Von Hutchins RC	1.25	.50
❑	240	Marcus Tubbs RC	1.50	.60
❑	241	Daryl Smith RC	1.50	.60
❑	242	Robert Gallery RC	2.50	1.00
❑	243	Sean Tufts RC	1.25	.50
❑	244	Marquis Cooper RC	1.25	.50
❑	245	Bernard Berrian RC	1.50	.60
❑	246	Derrick Strait RC	1.50	.60
❑	247	Travis LaBoy RC	1.50	.60
❑	248	Johnnie Morant RC	1.50	.60
❑	249	Caleb Miller RC	1.25	.50
❑	250	Michael Clayton RC	3.00	1.25
❑	251	Will Poole RC	1.50	.60
❑	252	Andy Hall RC	1.25	.50
❑	253	Demorrio Williams RC	1.50	.60
❑	254	Chris Thompson RC	.75	.30
❑	255	Derrick Hamilton RC	1.25	.50
❑	256	Glenn Earl RC	1.25	.50
❑	257	Jonathan Vilma RC	1.50	.60
❑	258	Donnell Washington RC	1.50	.60
❑	259	Drew Carter RC	1.50	.60
❑	260	Steven Jackson RC	5.00	2.00
❑	261	Jamaar Taylor RC	1.50	.60
❑	262	Nate Lawrie RC	1.25	.50
❑	263	Cody Pickett RC	1.50	.60
❑	264	Keiwan Ratliff RC	1.25	.50
❑	265	Luke McCown RC	1.50	.60
❑	266	Jerricho Cotchery RC	1.50	.60
❑	267	Joey Thomas RC	1.50	.60
❑	268	Shawn Andrews RC	1.50	.60
❑	269	Derrick Ward RC	.75	.30
❑	270	Reggie Williams RC	2.00	.75
❑	271	Rod Rutherford RC	1.25	.50
❑	272	Michael Turner RC	1.50	.60
❑	273	Michael Gaines RC	1.25	.50
❑	274	Will Allen RC	1.50	.60
❑	275	J.P. Losman RC	3.00	1.25

2005 Bowman

❑ COMP.SET w/o AU's (270) 60.00 25.00

❑ UNPRICED PRINT PLATES SER.#'d TO 1

❑	1	Peyton Manning	1.25	.50
❑	2	Antonio Gates	.75	.30
❑	3	Priest Holmes	.75	.30
❑	4	Anquan Boldin	.50	.20
❑	5	Donovan McNabb	1.00	.40
❑	6	Drew Bennett	.50	.20
❑	7	Michael Vick	1.25	.50
❑	8	David Carr	.75	.30
❑	9	Drew Brees	.75	.30
❑	10	Trent Green	.50	.20
❑	11	Drew Bledsoe	.75	.30
❑	12	Randy Moss	.75	.30
❑	13	Terrell Owens	.75	.30
❑	14	Donte Stallworth	.50	.20
❑	15	Alge Crumpler	.50	.20
❑	16	Jake Plummer	.50	.20
❑	17	Curtis Martin	.75	.30
❑	18	Jason Witten	.50	.20
❑	19	Tom Brady	2.00	.75
❑	20	Thomas Jones	.50	.20
❑	21	Tiki Barber	.75	.30
❑	22	Maurice Carthon CO	.50	.20
❑	23	Rex Grossman	.50	.20
❑	24	Brett Favre	2.00	.75
❑	25	Marshall Faulk	.75	.30
❑	26	LaMont Jordan	.75	.30
❑	27	Kurt Warner	.50	.20
❑	28	Corey Dillon	.50	.20
❑	29	Julius Jones	1.00	.40
❑	30	Ahman Green	.75	.30
❑	31	Jamal Lewis	.75	.30
❑	32	Ben Roethlisberger	2.00	.75
❑	33	Keary Colbert	.50	.20
❑	34	Mike Nolan CO RC	.75	.30
❑	35	Joey Harrington	.75	.30
❑	36	Brian Westbrook	.50	.20
❑	37	Domanick Davis	.50	.20
❑	38	Carson Palmer	.75	.30
❑	39	Stephen Davis	.50	.20
❑	40	Eli Manning	1.50	.60
❑	41	Edgerrin James	.75	.30
❑	42	Jonathan Vilma	.50	.20
❑	43	Brad Childress CO RC	.50	.20
❑	44	Willis McGahee	.75	.30
❑	45	Steve McNair	.75	.30
❑	46	Plaxico Burress	.50	.20
❑	47	Rudi Johnson	.50	.20
❑	48	Jerry Porter	.50	.20
❑	49	Chad Pennington	.75	.30
❑	50	Charles Rogers	.50	.20
❑	51	Patrick Ramsey	.50	.20
❑	52	Dwight Freeney	.50	.20
❑	53	Brian Griese	.50	.20
❑	54	Jerome Bettis	.75	.30
❑	55	Tim Lewis CO	.40	.15
❑	56	Aaron Brooks	.50	.20
❑	57	Matt Hasselbeck	.50	.20
❑	58	Chris Chambers	.50	.20
❑	59	Kyle Boller	.50	.20
❑	60	Brandon Lloyd	.40	.15
❑	61	Marc Bulger	.75	.30
❑	62	Isaac Bruce	.50	.20
❑	63	Jake Delhomme	.75	.30
❑	64	Chad Johnson	.75	.30
❑	65	Shaun Alexander	1.00	.40
❑	66	Kevin Jones	.75	.30
❑	67	Eric Moulds	.50	.20
❑	68	Laveranues Coles	.50	.20
❑	69	A.J. Feeley	.50	.20
❑	70	Sean Taylor	.50	.20
❑	71	Romeo Crennel CO RC	.75	.30
❑	72	Ashley Lelie	.50	.20
❑	73	Nick Saban CO RC	.75	.30
❑	74	Deuce McAllister	.75	.30
❑	75	Kerry Collins	.50	.20
❑	76	Chris Brown	.50	.20
❑	77	Steven Jackson	1.00	.40
❑	78	Nate Burleson	.50	.20
❑	79	LaDainian Tomlinson	1.00	.40
❑	80	Darrell Jackson	.50	.20
❑	81	Torry Holt	.75	.30
❑	82	Lee Suggs	.50	.20
❑	83	Lee Evans	.50	.20
❑	84	Santana Moss	.50	.20
❑	85	Jeremy Shockey	.75	.30
❑	86	Hines Ward	.75	.30
❑	87	Muhsin Muhammad	.50	.20
❑	88	Daunte Culpepper	.75	.30
❑	89	Deion Branch	.50	.20
❑	90	DeShaun Foster	.50	.20
❑	91	Travis Henry	.50	.20
❑	92	Jerry Rice	1.50	.60
❑	93	Reggie Wayne	.50	.20
❑	94	Roy Williams WR	.75	.30
❑	95	Michael Jenkins	.50	.20
❑	96	Tatum Bell	.50	.20
❑	97	Andre Johnson	.50	.20
❑	98	Dante Hall	.50	.20
❑	99	Javon Walker	.50	.20
❑	100	Larry Fitzgerald	.75	.30
❑	101	Joe Horn	.50	.20
❑	102	Marvin Harrison	.75	.30
❑	103	Fred Taylor	.50	.20
❑	104	Byron Leftwich	.75	.30
❑	105	Tony Gonzalez	.50	.20
❑	106	T.J. Houshmandzadeh	.40	.15
❑	107	J.P. Losman	.75	.30
❑	108	Michael Clayton	.75	.30
❑	109	Clinton Portis	.75	.30
❑	110	Ted Cottrell CO RC	.40	.15
❑	111	Braylon Edwards RC	5.00	2.00
❑	112	Aaron Rodgers RC	5.00	2.00
❑	113	Ronnie Brown RC	5.00	2.00
❑	114	Alex Smith QB RC	6.00	2.50
❑	115	Carnell Williams RC	8.00	3.00
❑	116	Ciatrick Fason RC	1.50	.60
❑	117	Derrick Johnson RC	2.50	1.00
❑	118	Carlos Rogers RC	2.00	.75
❑	119	Ryan Moats RC	1.50	.60
❑	120	Alvin Pearman RC	1.50	.60
❑	121	Stefan LeFors RC	1.50	.60
❑	122	Brandon Jacobs RC	2.00	.75
❑	123	Kyle Orton RC	2.50	1.00
❑	124	Marion Barber RC	2.50	1.00
❑	125	Mark Bradley RC	1.50	.60
❑	126	Travis Johnson RC	1.25	.50
❑	127	Antrel Rolle RC	1.50	.60
❑	128	Jason Campbell RC	2.50	1.00
❑	129	DeMarcus Ware RC	2.50	1.00
❑	130	Frank Gore RC	2.50	1.00
❑	131	Justin Miller RC	1.25	.50
❑	132	J.J. Arrington RC	2.00	.75
❑	133	Marcus Spears RC	1.50	.60

❑ 134 Roddy White RC 1.50 .60
❑ 135 Fabian Washington RC 1.50 .60
❑ 136 Vincent Jackson RC 1.50 .60
❑ 137 Erasmus James RC 1.50 .60
❑ 138 Roscoe Parrish RC 1.50 .60
❑ 139 Airese Currie RC 1.50 .60
❑ 140 Heath Miller RC 4.00 1.50
❑ 141 Mike Patterson RC 1.50 .60
❑ 142 Troy Williamson RC 3.00 1.25
❑ 143 Terrence Murphy RC 1.50 .60
❑ 144 Dan Orlovsky RC 2.00 .75
❑ 145 Eric Shelton RC 1.50 .60
❑ 146 Thomas Davis RC 1.50 .60
❑ 147 Cedric Benson RC 3.00 1.25
❑ 148 Noah Herron RC 1.50 .60
❑ 149 Vernand Morency RC 1.50 .60
❑ 150 Darren Sproles RC 1.50 .60
❑ 151 Alex Smith TE RC 1.50 .60
❑ 152 Mark Clayton RC 2.00 .75
❑ 153 Craphonso Thorpe RC 1.25 .50
❑ 154 Mike Williams 3.00 1.25
❑ 155 Anthony Davis RC 1.25 .50
❑ 156 Charlie Frye RC 3.00 1.25
❑ 157 Fred Gibson RC 1.25 .50
❑ 158 Reggie Brown RC 1.50 .60
❑ 159 Andrew Walter RC 2.50 1.00
❑ 160 Adam Jones RC 1.50 .60
❑ 161 David Greene RC 1.50 .60
❑ 162 Maurice Clarett 1.50 .60
❑ 163 Courtney Roby RC 1.50 .60
❑ 164 Derek Anderson RC 1.50 .60
❑ 165 Matt Jones RC 4.00 1.50
❑ 166 Chris Henry RC 1.50 .60
❑ 167 Shaun Cody RC 1.50 .60
❑ 168 Khalif Barnes RC 1.25 .50
❑ 169 Matt Roth RC 1.50 .60
❑ 170 Lionel Gates RC 1.25 .50
❑ 171 Kevin Burnett RC 1.50 .60
❑ 172 Taylor Stubblefield RC .75 .30
❑ 173 Zach Tuiasosopo RC .75 .30
❑ 174 Alex Barron RC .75 .30
❑ 175 Mike Nugent RC 1.50 .60
❑ 176 Barrett Ruud RC 1.50 .60
❑ 177 Brock Berlin RC 1.25 .50
❑ 178 Kirk Morrison RC 1.50 .60
❑ 179 David Pollack RC 1.50 .60
❑ 180 Ryan Fitzpatrick RC 2.50 1.00
❑ 181 Kay-Jay Harris RC 1.25 .50
❑ 182 Dan Cody RC 1.50 .60
❑ 183 Chad Owens RC 1.50 .60
❑ 184 Stanley Wilson RC 1.25 .50
❑ 185 Rasheed Marshall RC 1.50 .60
❑ 186 Bryant McFadden RC 1.50 .60
❑ 187 Joel Dreessen RC 1.25 .50
❑ 188 Donte Nicholson RC 1.50 .60
❑ 189 Scott Starks RC 1.25 .50
❑ 190 Walter Reyes RC 1.25 .50
❑ 191 Stanford Routt RC 1.25 .50
❑ 192 Lance Mitchell RC 1.25 .50
❑ 193 Rian Wallace RC 1.25 .50
❑ 194 Timmy Chang RC 1.25 .50
❑ 195 Oshiomogho Atogwe RC 1.25 .50
❑ 196 Larry Brackins RC 1.25 .50
❑ 197 Jovan Witherspoon RC .75 .30
❑ 198 Boomer Grigsby RC 2.00 .75
❑ 199 Darryl Blackstock RC 1.25 .50
❑ 200 Jerome Mathis RC 1.50 .60
❑ 201 Ellis Hobbs RC 1.50 .60
❑ 202 Dante Ridgeway RC 1.25 .50
❑ 203 James Kilian RC 1.50 .60
❑ 204 Patrick Estes RC 1.25 .50
❑ 205 Justin Tuck RC 1.50 .60
❑ 206 Channing Crowder RC 1.50 .60
❑ 207 Dustin Fox RC 1.50 .60
❑ 208 Marlin Jackson RC 1.50 .60
❑ 209 Luis Castillo RC 1.50 .60
❑ 210 Paris Warren RC 1.25 .50
❑ 211 J.R. Russell RC 1.25 .50
❑ 212 Cedric Houston RC 1.50 .60
❑ 213 Corey Webster RC 1.50 .60
❑ 214 Craig Bragg RC 1.25 .50
❑ 215 Tab Perry RC 1.50 .60
❑ 216 Ryan Riddle RC .75 .30
❑ 217 Gino Guidugli RC .75 .30
❑ 218 Deandra Cobb RC 1.25 .50
❑ 219 Travis Daniels RC 1.25 .50
❑ 220 Marcus Maxwell RC 1.25 .50
❑ 221 Eric King RC 1.25 .50
❑ 222 Matt Cassel RC 2.50 1.00
❑ 223 Justin Green RC 1.50 .60
❑ 224 Steve Savoy RC .75 .30
❑ 225 Shawne Merriman RC 2.50 1.00
❑ 226 Damien Nash RC 1.25 .50
❑ 227 T.A. McLendon RC .75 .30
❑ 228 Vincent Fuller RC 1.25 .50
❑ 229 Jordan Beck RC 1.25 .50
❑ 230 Lofa Tatupu RC 2.00 .75
❑ 231 Will Peoples RC 1.25 .50
❑ 232 Chad Friehauf RC 1.25 .50
❑ 233 Brady Poppinga RC 1.50 .60
❑ 234 Anttaj Hawthorne RC 1.25 .50
❑ 235 Adrian McPherson RC 1.50 .60
❑ 236 Nick Collins RC 1.50 .60
❑ 237 Roydell Williams RC 1.50 .60
❑ 238 Craig Ochs RC 1.25 .50
❑ 239 Billy Bajema RC 1.25 .50
❑ 240 Jon Goldsberry RC 1.50 .60
❑ 241 Jared Newberry RC 1.25 .50
❑ 242 Odell Thurman RC 1.50 .60
❑ 243 Kelvin Hayden RC 1.25 .50
❑ 244 Jamaal Brimmer RC .75 .30
❑ 245 Jonathan Babineaux RC 1.25 .50
❑ 246 Bo Scaife RC 1.25 .50
❑ 247 Chris Spencer RC 1.50 .60
❑ 248 Manuel White RC 1.25 .50
❑ 249 Josh Davis RC 1.25 .50
❑ 250 Bryan Randall RC 1.25 .50
❑ 251 James Butler RC 1.25 .50
❑ 252 Harry Williams RC 1.25 .50
❑ 253 Leroy Hill RC 1.50 .60
❑ 254 Josh Bullocks RC 1.50 .60
❑ 255 Alfred Fincher RC 1.25 .50
❑ 256 Antonio Perkins RC 1.25 .50
❑ 257 Bobby Purify RC 1.25 .50
❑ 258 Rick Razzano RC 1.50 .60
❑ 259 Darrent Williams RC 1.50 .60
❑ 260 Darian Durant RC 1.50 .60
❑ 261 Fred Amey RC 1.25 .50
❑ 262 Ronald Bartell RC 1.25 .50
❑ 263 Kerry Rhodes RC 1.50 .60
❑ 264 Jerome Carter RC 1.25 .50
❑ 265 Marcus Randall RC 1.25 .50
❑ 266 Nehemiah Broughton RC 1.25 .50
❑ 267 Keron Henry RC .75 .30
❑ 268 Jerome Collins RC 1.25 .50
❑ 269 Trent Cole RC 1.50 .60
❑ 270 Alphonso Hodge RC .75 .30
❑ 271 Brandon Jones RC 1.50 .60
❑ 272 Chase Lyman RC 1.25 .50
❑ 273 Marviel Underwood RC 1.25 .50
❑ 274 Maurice Washington RC 1.25 .50
❑ 275 Madison Hedgecock RC 1.50 .60

1998 Bowman Chrome

❑ COMPLETE SET (220) 100.00 50.00
❑ 1 Peyton Manning RC 40.00 15.00
❑ 2 Keith Brooking RC 4.00 1.50
❑ 3 Duane Starks RC 2.00 .75
❑ 4 Takeo Spikes RC 4.00 1.50
❑ 5 Andre Wadsworth RC 3.00 1.25
❑ 6 Greg Ellis RC 2.00 .75
❑ 7 Brian Griese RC 8.00 3.00
❑ 8 Germane Crowell RC 3.00 1.25
❑ 9 Jerome Pathon RC 4.00 1.50
❑ 10 Ryan Leaf RC 4.00 1.50
❑ 11 Fred Taylor RC 6.00 2.50
❑ 12 Robert Edwards RC 3.00 1.25
❑ 13 Grant Wistrom RC 3.00 1.25
❑ 14 Robert Holcombe RC 3.00 1.25
❑ 15 Tim Dwight RC 4.00 1.50
❑ 16 Jacquez Green RC 3.00 1.25
❑ 17 Marcus Nash RC 2.00 .75
❑ 18 Jason Peter RC 2.00 .75
❑ 19 Anthony Simmons RC 3.00 1.25
❑ 20 Curtis Enis RC 2.00 .75
❑ 21 John Avery RC 3.00 1.25
❑ 22 Pat Johnson RC 3.00 1.25
❑ 23 Joe Jurevicius RC 4.00 1.50
❑ 24 Brian Simmons RC 3.00 1.25
❑ 25 Kevin Dyson RC 4.00 1.50
❑ 26 Skip Hicks RC 3.00 1.25
❑ 27 Hines Ward RC 15.00 7.50
❑ 28 Tavian Banks RC 3.00 1.25
❑ 29 Ahman Green RC 20.00 10.00
❑ 30 Tony Simmons RC 3.00 1.25
❑ 31 Charles Johnson .50 .20
❑ 32 Freddie Jones .50 .20
❑ 33 Joey Galloway .75 .30
❑ 34 Tony Banks .75 .30
❑ 35 Jake Plummer 1.25 .50
❑ 36 Reidel Anthony .75 .30
❑ 37 Steve McNair 1.25 .50
❑ 38 Michael Westbrook .75 .30
❑ 39 Chris Sanders .50 .20
❑ 40 Isaac Bruce .50 .20
❑ 41 Charlie Garner .75 .30
❑ 42 Wayne Chrebet 1.25 .50
❑ 43 Michael Strahan .75 .30
❑ 44 Brad Johnson 1.25 .50
❑ 45 Mike Alstott .50 .20
❑ 46 Tony Gonzalez 1.25 .50
❑ 47 Johnnie Morton .75 .30
❑ 48 Darnay Scott .75 .30
❑ 49 Rae Carruth .50 .20
❑ 50 Terrell Davis 1.25 .50
❑ 51 Jermaine Lewis .75 .30
❑ 52 Frank Sanders .75 .30
❑ 53 Byron Hanspard .50 .20
❑ 54 Gus Frerotte .50 .20
❑ 55 Terry Glenn 1.25 .50
❑ 56 J.J. Stokes .75 .30
❑ 57 Will Blackwell .50 .20
❑ 58 Keyshawn Johnson 1.25 .50
❑ 59 Tiki Barber 1.25 .50
❑ 60 Dorsey Levens 1.25 .50
❑ 61 Zach Thomas 1.25 .50
❑ 62 Corey Dillon 1.25 .50
❑ 63 Antowain Smith 1.25 .50
❑ 64 Michael Sinclair .50 .20
❑ 65 Rod Smith .75 .30
❑ 66 Trent Dilfer 1.25 .50
❑ 67 Warren Sapp .75 .30
❑ 68 Charles Way .50 .20
❑ 69 Tamarick Vanover .50 .20
❑ 70 Drew Bledsoe 2.00 .75
❑ 71 John Mobley .50 .20
❑ 72 Kerry Collins .75 .30
❑ 73 Peter Boulware .50 .20
❑ 74 Simeon Rice .75 .30
❑ 75 Eddie George 1.25 .50
❑ 76 Fred Lane .50 .20
❑ 77 Jamal Anderson 1.25 .50
❑ 78 Antonio Freeman 1.25 .50
❑ 79 Jason Sehorn .75 .30

❑	80 Curtis Martin	1.25	.50
❑	81 Bobby Hoying	.75	.30
❑	82 Garrison Hearst	1.25	.50
❑	83 Glenn Foley	.75	.30
❑	84 Danny Kanell	.75	.30
❑	85 Kordell Stewart	1.25	.50
❑	86 O.J. McDuffie	.75	.30
❑	87 Marvin Harrison	1.25	.50
❑	88 Bobby Engram	.75	.30
❑	89 Chris Slade	.50	.20
❑	90 Warrick Dunn	1.25	.50
❑	91 Ricky Watters	.75	.30
❑	92 Rickey Dudley	.50	.20
❑	93 Terrell Owens	1.25	.50
❑	94 Karim Abdul-Jabbar	1.25	.50
❑	95 Napoleon Kaufman	1.25	.50
❑	96 Darrell Green	.75	.30
❑	97 Levon Kirkland	.50	.20
❑	98 Jeff George	.75	.30
❑	99 Andre Hastings	.50	.20
❑	100 John Elway	5.00	2.00
❑	101 John Randle	.75	.30
❑	102 Andre Rison	.75	.30
❑	103 Keenan McCardell	.75	.30
❑	104 Marshall Faulk	1.50	.60
❑	105 Emmitt Smith	4.00	1.50
❑	106 Robert Brooks	.75	.30
❑	107 Scott Mitchell	.75	.30
❑	108 Shannon Sharpe	.75	.30
❑	109 Deion Sanders	1.25	.50
❑	110 Jerry Rice	2.50	1.00
❑	111 Erik Kramer	.50	.20
❑	112 Michael Jackson	.50	.20
❑	113 Aeneas Williams	.50	.20
❑	114 Terry Allen	1.25	.50
❑	115 Steve Young	1.50	.60
❑	116 Warren Moon	1.25	.50
❑	117 Junior Seau	1.25	.50
❑	118 Jerome Bettis	1.25	.50
❑	119 Irving Fryar	.75	.30
❑	120 Barry Sanders	4.00	1.50
❑	121 Tim Brown	.50	.20
❑	122 Chad Brown	.50	.20
❑	123 Ben Coates	.75	.30
❑	124 Robert Smith	1.25	.50
❑	125 Brett Favre	5.00	2.00
❑	126 Derrick Thomas	1.25	.50
❑	127 Reggie White	1.25	.50
❑	128 Troy Aikman	2.50	1.00
❑	129 Jeff Blake	.75	.30
❑	130 Mark Brunell	1.25	.50
❑	131 Curtis Conway	.75	.30
❑	132 Wesley Walls	.75	.30
❑	133 Thurman Thomas	1.25	.50
❑	134 Chris Chandler	.75	.30
❑	135 Dan Marino	5.00	2.00
❑	136 Larry Centers	.50	.20
❑	137 Shawn Jefferson	.50	.20
❑	138 Andre Reed	.75	.30
❑	139 Jake Reed	.75	.30
❑	140 Cris Carter	1.25	.50
❑	141 Elvis Grbac	.75	.30
❑	142 Mark Chmura	.75	.30
❑	143 Michael Irvin	1.25	.50
❑	144 Carl Pickens	.75	.30
❑	145 Herman Moore	.75	.30
❑	146 Marvin Jones	.50	.20
❑	147 Terance Mathis	.75	.30
❑	148 Rob Moore	.75	.30
❑	149 Bruce Smith	.75	.30
❑	150 Rob Johnson CL	.50	.20
❑	151 Leslie Shepherd	.50	.20
❑	152 Chris Spielman	.50	.20
❑	153 Tony McGee	.50	.20
❑	154 Kevin Smith	.50	.20
❑	155 Bill Romanowski	.50	.20
❑	156 Stephen Boyd	.50	.20
❑	157 James Stewart	.75	.30
❑	158 Jason Taylor	.75	.30
❑	159 Troy Drayton	.50	.20
❑	160 Mark Fields	.50	.20
❑	161 Jessie Armstead	.50	.20
❑	162 James Jett	.75	.30
❑	163 Bobby Taylor	.50	.20
❑	164 Kimble Anders	.75	.30
❑	165 Jimmy Smith	.75	.30
❑	166 Quentin Coryatt	.50	.20
❑	167 Bryant Westbrook	.50	.20
❑	168 Neil Smith	.75	.30
❑	169 Darren Woodson	.50	.20
❑	170 Ray Buchanan	.50	.20
❑	171 Earl Holmes	.50	.20
❑	172 Ray Lewis	1.25	.50
❑	173 Steve Broussard	.50	.20
❑	174 Derrick Brooks	1.25	.50
❑	175 Ken Harvey	.50	.20
❑	176 Darryll Lewis	.50	.20
❑	177 Derrick Rodgers	.50	.20
❑	178 James McKnight	1.25	.50
❑	179 Cris Dishman	.50	.20
❑	180 Hardy Nickerson	.50	.20
❑	181 Charles Woodson RC	5.00	2.00
❑	182 Randy Moss RC	20.00	7.50
❑	183 Stephen Alexander RC	3.00	1.25
❑	184 Samari Rolle RC	2.00	.75
❑	185 Jamie Duncan RC	2.00	.75
❑	186 Lance Schulters RC	2.00	.75
❑	187 Tony Parrish RC	4.00	1.50
❑	188 Corey Chavous RC	4.00	1.50
❑	189 Jammi German RC	2.00	.75
❑	190 Sam Cowart RC	3.00	1.25
❑	191 Donald Hayes RC	3.00	1.25
❑	192 R.W. McQuarters RC	3.00	1.25
❑	193 Az-Zahir Hakim RC	4.00	1.50
❑	194 Chris Fuamatu-Ma'afala RC	3.00	1.25
❑	195 Allen Rossum RC	2.00	.75
❑	196 Jon Ritchie RC	3.00	1.25
❑	197 Blake Spence RC	2.00	.75
❑	198 Brian Alford RC	2.00	.75
❑	199 Fred Weary RC	2.00	.75
❑	200 Rod Rutledge RC	2.00	.75
❑	201 Michael Myers RC	2.00	.75
❑	202 Rashaan Shehee RC	3.00	1.25
❑	203 Donovin Darius RC	3.00	1.25
❑	204 E.G. Green RC	3.00	1.25
❑	205 Vonnie Holliday RC	3.00	1.25
❑	206 Charlie Batch RC	4.00	1.50
❑	207 Michael Pittman RC	4.00	1.50
❑	208 Artrell Hawkins RC	2.00	.75
❑	209 Jonathan Quinn RC	4.00	1.50
❑	210 Kailee Wong RC	2.00	.75
❑	211 Deshea Townsend RC	2.00	.75
❑	212 Patrick Surtain RC	4.00	1.50
❑	213 Brian Kelly RC	3.00	1.25
❑	214 Tebucky Jones RC	2.00	.75
❑	215 Pete Gonzalez RC	2.00	.75
❑	216 Shaun Williams RC	3.00	1.25
❑	217 Scott Frost RC	2.00	.75
❑	218 Leonard Little RC	4.00	1.50
❑	219 Alonzo Mayes RC	2.00	.75
❑	220 Cordell Taylor RC	2.00	.75

1999 Bowman Chrome

❑	COMPLETE SET (220)	80.00	40.00
❑	1 Dan Marino	4.00	1.50
❑	2 Michael Westbrook	.75	.30
❑	3 Yancey Thigpen	.50	.20
❑	4 Tony Martin	.75	.30
❑	5 Michael Strahan	.75	.30
❑	6 Dedric Ward	.50	.20
❑	7 Joey Galloway	.75	.30
❑	8 Bobby Engram	.75	.30
❑	9 Frank Sanders	.75	.30
❑	10 Jake Plummer	.75	.30
❑	11 Eddie Kennison	.75	.30
❑	12 Curtis Martin	1.25	.50
❑	13 Chris Spielman	.50	.20
❑	14 Trent Dilfer	.75	.30
❑	15 Tim Biakabutuka	.75	.30
❑	16 Elvis Grbac	.75	.30
❑	17 Charlie Batch	1.25	.50
❑	18 Takeo Spikes	.50	.20
❑	19 Tony Banks	.75	.30
❑	20 Doug Flutie	1.25	.50
❑	21 Ty Law	.75	.30
❑	22 Isaac Bruce	1.25	.50
❑	23 James Jett	.75	.30
❑	24 Kent Graham	.50	.20
❑	25 Derrick Mayes	.50	.20
❑	26 Amani Toomer	.50	.20
❑	27 Ray Lewis	1.25	.50
❑	28 Shawn Springs	.50	.20
❑	29 Warren Sapp	.50	.20
❑	30 Jamal Anderson	1.25	.50
❑	31 Byron Bam Morris	.50	.20
❑	32 Johnnie Morton	.50	.20
❑	33 Terance Mathis	.50	.20
❑	34 Terrell Davis	1.25	.50
❑	35 John Randle	.75	.30
❑	36 Vinny Testaverde	.50	.20
❑	37 Junior Seau	1.25	.50
❑	38 Reidel Anthony	.75	.30
❑	39 Brad Johnson	.50	.20
❑	40 Emmitt Smith	2.50	1.00
❑	41 Mo Lewis	.50	.20
❑	42 Terry Glenn	1.25	.50
❑	43 Dorsey Levens	1.25	.50
❑	44 Thurman Thomas	.75	.30
❑	45 Rob Moore	.75	.30
❑	46 Corey Dillon	1.25	.50
❑	47 Jessie Armstead	.50	.20
❑	48 Marshall Faulk	1.50	.60
❑	49 Charles Woodson	.50	.20
❑	50 John Elway	4.00	1.50
❑	51 Kevin Dyson	.75	.30
❑	52 Tony Simmons	.50	.20
❑	53 Keenan McCardell	.75	.30
❑	54 O.J. Santiago	.50	.20
❑	55 Jermaine Lewis	.75	.30
❑	56 Herman Moore	.75	.30
❑	57 Gary Brown	.50	.20
❑	58 Jim Harbaugh	.75	.30
❑	59 Mike Alstott	1.25	.50
❑	60 Brett Favre	4.00	1.50
❑	61 Tim Brown	1.25	.50
❑	62 Steve McNair	.50	.20
❑	63 Ben Coates	.75	.30
❑	64 Jerome Pathon	.50	.20
❑	65 Ray Buchanan	.50	.20
❑	66 Troy Aikman	2.50	1.00
❑	67 Andre Reed	.75	.30
❑	68 Bubby Brister	.50	.20
❑	69 Karim Abdul-Jabbar	.75	.30
❑	70 Peyton Manning	4.00	1.50
❑	71 Charles Johnson	.50	.20
❑	72 Natrone Means	.75	.30
❑	73 Michael Sinclair	.50	.20
❑	74 Skip Hicks	.50	.20
❑	75 Derrick Alexander	.50	.20
❑	76 Wayne Chrebet	.75	.30
❑	77 Rod Smith	.75	.30
❑	78 Carl Pickens	.75	.30
❑	79 Adrian Murrell	.75	.30
❑	80 Fred Taylor	1.25	.50
❑	81 Eric Moulds	1.25	.50

❑ 82 Lawrence Phillips .75 .30
❑ 83 Marvin Harrison 1.25 .50
❑ 84 Cris Carter 1.25 .50
❑ 85 Ike Hilliard .50 .20
❑ 86 Hines Ward 1.25 .50
❑ 87 Terrell Owens 1.25 .50
❑ 88 Ricky Proehl .50 .20
❑ 89 Bert Emanuel .75 .30
❑ 90 Randy Moss 3.00 1.25
❑ 91 Aaron Glenn .50 .20
❑ 92 Robert Smith 1.25 .50
❑ 93 Andre Hastings .50 .20
❑ 94 Jake Reed .75 .30
❑ 95 Curtis Enis .50 .20
❑ 96 Andre Wadsworth .50 .20
❑ 97 Ed McCaffrey .75 .30
❑ 98 Zach Thomas 1.25 .50
❑ 99 Kerry Collins .75 .30
❑ 100 Drew Bledsoe 1.50 .60
❑ 101 Germane Crowell .50 .20
❑ 102 Bryan Still .50 .20
❑ 103 Chad Brown .50 .20
❑ 104 Jacquez Green .50 .20
❑ 105 Garrison Hearst .75 .30
❑ 106 Napoleon Kaufman 1.25 .50
❑ 107 Ricky Watters .75 .30
❑ 108 O.J. McDuffie .75 .30
❑ 109 Keyshawn Johnson 1.25 .50
❑ 110 Jerome Bettis 1.25 .50
❑ 111 Duce Staley 1.25 .50
❑ 112 Curtis Conway .75 .30
❑ 113 Chris Chandler .75 .30
❑ 114 Marcus Nash .50 .20
❑ 115 Stephen Alexander .50 .20
❑ 116 Darnay Scott .75 .30
❑ 117 Bruce Smith .75 .30
❑ 118 Priest Holmes 2.00 .75
❑ 119 Mark Brunell 1.25 .50
❑ 120 Jerry Rice 2.50 1.00
❑ 121 Randall Cunningham 1.25 .50
❑ 122 Scott Mitchell .50 .20
❑ 123 Antonio Freeman 1.25 .50
❑ 124 Kordell Stewart .75 .30
❑ 125 Jon Kitna 1.25 .50
❑ 126 Ahman Green 1.25 .50
❑ 127 Warrick Dunn 1.25 .50
❑ 128 Robert Brooks .75 .30
❑ 129 Derrick Thomas 1.25 .50
❑ 130 Steve Young 1.50 .60
❑ 131 Peter Boulware .50 .20
❑ 132 Michael Irvin .75 .30
❑ 133 Shannon Sharpe .75 .30
❑ 134 Jimmy Smith .75 .30
❑ 135 John Avery .50 .20
❑ 136 Fred Lane .50 .20
❑ 137 Trent Green 1.25 .50
❑ 138 Andre Rison .75 .30
❑ 139 Antowain Smith 1.25 .50
❑ 140 Eddie George 1.25 .50
❑ 141 Jeff Blake .75 .30
❑ 142 Rocket Ismail .75 .30
❑ 143 Rickey Dudley .50 .20
❑ 144 Courtney Hawkins .50 .20
❑ 145 Mikhael Ricks .50 .20
❑ 146 J.J. Stokes .75 .30
❑ 147 Levon Kirkland .50 .20
❑ 148 Deion Sanders 1.25 .50
❑ 149 Barry Sanders 4.00 1.50
❑ 150 Tiki Barber 1.25 .50
❑ 151 David Boston RC 2.00 .75
❑ 152 Chris McAlister RC 1.25 .50
❑ 153 Peerless Price RC 2.00 .75
❑ 154 D'Wayne Bates RC 1.25 .50
❑ 155 Cade McNown RC 1.25 .50
❑ 156 Akili Smith RC 1.25 .50
❑ 157 Kevin Johnson RC 2.00 .75
❑ 158 Tim Couch RC 2.00 .75
❑ 159 Sedrick Irvin RC 1.00 .40
❑ 160 Chris Claiborne RC 1.00 .40
❑ 161 Edgerrin James RC 10.00 4.00
❑ 162 Mike Cloud RC 1.25 .50
❑ 163 Cecil Collins RC 1.00 .40
❑ 164 James Johnson RC 1.25 .50
❑ 165 Rob Konrad RC 2.00 .75
❑ 166 Daunte Culpepper RC 10.00 4.00
❑ 167 Kevin Faulk RC 2.00 .75
❑ 168 Donovan McNabb RC 12.00 5.00
❑ 169 Troy Edwards RC 1.25 .50
❑ 170 Amos Zereoue RC 2.00 .75
❑ 171 Karsten Bailey RC 1.25 .50
❑ 172 Brock Huard RC 2.00 .75
❑ 173 Joe Germaine RC 1.25 .50
❑ 174 Torry Holt RC 6.00 2.50
❑ 175 Shaun King RC 1.25 .50
❑ 176 Jevon Kearse RC 4.00 1.50
❑ 177 Champ Bailey RC 3.00 1.25
❑ 178 Ebenezer Ekuban RC 1.25 .50
❑ 179 Andy Katzenmoyer RC 1.25 .50
❑ 180 Antoine Winfield RC 1.25 .50
❑ 181 Jermaine Fazande RC 1.25 .50
❑ 182 Ricky Williams RC 5.00 2.00
❑ 183 Joel Makovicka RC 2.00 .75
❑ 184 Reginald Kelly RC 1.25 .50
❑ 185 Brandon Stokley RC 2.50 1.00
❑ 186 L.C. Stevens RC 1.00 .40
❑ 187 Marty Booker RC 2.00 .75
❑ 188 Jerry Azumah RC 1.25 .50
❑ 189 Ted White RC 1.00 .40
❑ 190 Scott Covington RC 2.00 .75
❑ 191 Tim Alexander RC 1.00 .40
❑ 192 Darrin Chiaverini RC 1.25 .50
❑ 193 Dat Nguyen RC 2.00 .75
❑ 194 Wane McGarity RC 1.00 .40
❑ 195 Al Wilson RC 2.00 .75
❑ 196 Travis McGriff RC 1.00 .40
❑ 197 Stacey Mack RC 2.00 .75
❑ 198 Antuan Edwards RC 1.00 .40
❑ 199 Aaron Brooks RC 5.00 2.00
❑ 200 De'Mond Parker RC 1.00 .40
❑ 201 Jed Weaver RC 1.00 .40
❑ 202 Madre Hill RC 1.00 .40
❑ 203 Jim Kleinsasser RC 2.00 .75
❑ 204 Michael Bishop RC 2.00 .75
❑ 205 Michael Basnight RC 1.00 .40
❑ 206 Sean Bennett RC 1.00 .40
❑ 207 Dameane Douglas RC 1.25 .50
❑ 208 Na Brown RC 1.25 .50
❑ 209 Patrick Kerney RC 2.00 .75
❑ 210 Malcolm Johnson RC 1.00 .40
❑ 211 Dre Bly RC 2.00 .75
❑ 212 Terry Jackson RC 1.25 .50
❑ 213 Eugene Baker RC 1.00 .40
❑ 214 Autry Denson RC 1.25 .50
❑ 215 Darnell McDonald RC 1.25 .50
❑ 216 Charlie Rogers RC 1.25 .50
❑ 217 Joe Montgomery RC 1.25 .50
❑ 218 Cecil Martin RC 1.25 .50
❑ 219 Larry Parker RC 2.00 .75
❑ 220 Mike Peterson RC 1.25 .50

2000 Bowman Chrome

❑ 1 Eddie George 1.00 .40
❑ 2 Ike Hilliard .60 .25
❑ 3 Terrell Owens 1.00 .40
❑ 4 James Stewart .60 .25
❑ 5 Joey Galloway .60 .25
❑ 6 Jake Reed .40 .15
❑ 7 Derrick Alexander .60 .25
❑ 8 Jeff George .60 .25
❑ 9 Kerry Collins .60 .25
❑ 10 Tony Gonzalez .60 .25
❑ 11 Marcus Robinson 1.00 .40
❑ 12 Charles Woodson .60 .25
❑ 13 Germane Crowell .40 .15
❑ 14 Yancey Thigpen .40 .15
❑ 15 Tony Martin .40 .15
❑ 16 Frank Sanders .60 .25
❑ 17 Napoleon Kaufman .60 .25
❑ 18 Jay Fiedler 1.00 .40
❑ 19 Patrick Jeffers 1.00 .40
❑ 20 Steve McNair 1.00 .40
❑ 21 Herman Moore .60 .25
❑ 22 Tim Brown 1.00 .40
❑ 23 Olandis Gary 1.00 .40
❑ 24 Corey Dillon 1.00 .40
❑ 25 Warren Sapp .60 .25
❑ 26 Curtis Enis .40 .15
❑ 27 Vinny Testaverde .60 .25
❑ 28 Tim Biakabutuka .60 .25
❑ 29 Kevin Johnson 1.00 .40
❑ 30 Charlie Batch 1.00 .40
❑ 31 Jermaine Fazande .60 .25
❑ 32 Shaun King .40 .15
❑ 33 Errict Rhett .60 .25
❑ 34 O.J. McDuffie .60 .25
❑ 35 Bruce Smith .60 .25
❑ 36 Antonio Freeman 1.00 .40
❑ 37 Tim Couch .60 .25
❑ 38 Duce Staley 1.00 .40
❑ 39 Jeff Blake .60 .25
❑ 40 Jim Harbaugh .60 .25
❑ 41 Jeff Graham .40 .15
❑ 42 Drew Bledsoe 1.25 .50
❑ 43 Mike Alstott 1.00 .40
❑ 44 Terance Mathis .60 .25
❑ 45 Antowain Smith .60 .25
❑ 46 Johnnie Morton .60 .25
❑ 47 Chris Chandler .60 .25
❑ 48 Keith Poole .40 .15
❑ 49 Ricky Watters .60 .25
❑ 50 Darnay Scott .40 .15
❑ 51 Damon Huard .60 .25
❑ 52 Peerless Price .60 .25
❑ 53 Brian Griese 1.00 .40
❑ 54 Frank Wycheck .60 .25
❑ 55 Kevin Dyson .60 .25
❑ 56 Junior Seau 1.00 .40
❑ 57 Curtis Conway .60 .25
❑ 58 Jamal Anderson 1.00 .40
❑ 59 Jim Miller .40 .15
❑ 60 Rob Johnson .60 .25
❑ 61 Mark Brunell 1.00 .40
❑ 62 Wayne Chrebet .60 .25
❑ 63 James Johnson .40 .15
❑ 64 Sean Dawkins .40 .15
❑ 65 Stephen Davis 1.00 .40
❑ 66 Daunte Culpepper 1.25 .50
❑ 67 Doug Flutie 1.00 .40
❑ 68 Pete Mitchell .40 .15
❑ 69 Bill Schroeder .40 .15
❑ 70 Terrence Wilkins .40 .15
❑ 71 Cade McNown .40 .15
❑ 72 Muhsin Muhammad .60 .25
❑ 73 E.G. Green .40 .15
❑ 74 Edgerrin James 1.50 .60
❑ 75 Troy Edwards .40 .15
❑ 76 Terry Glenn .60 .25
❑ 77 Tony Banks .60 .25
❑ 78 Derrick Mayes .60 .25
❑ 79 Curtis Martin 1.00 .40
❑ 80 Kordell Stewart .60 .25
❑ 81 Amani Toomer .60 .25
❑ 82 Dorsey Levens .60 .25
❑ 83 Brad Johnson 1.00 .40

❑ 84	Ed McCaffrey	1.00	.40
❑ 85	Charlie Garner	.60	.25
❑ 86	Brett Favre	3.00	1.25
❑ 87	J.J. Stokes	.60	.25
❑ 88	Steve Young	1.25	.50
❑ 89	Jonathan Linton	.40	.15
❑ 90	Isaac Bruce	1.00	.40
❑ 91	Shawn Jefferson	.40	.15
❑ 92	Rod Smith	.60	.25
❑ 93	Champ Bailey	.60	.25
❑ 94	Ricky Williams	1.00	.40
❑ 95	Priest Holmes	1.25	.50
❑ 96	Corey Bradford	.60	.25
❑ 97	Eric Moulds	1.00	.40
❑ 98	Warrick Dunn	1.00	.40
❑ 99	Jevon Kearse	1.00	.40
❑ 100	Albert Connell	.40	.15
❑ 101	Az-Zahir Hakim	.40	.15
❑ 102	Marvin Harrison	1.00	.40
❑ 103	Qadry Ismail	.60	.25
❑ 104	Oronde Gadsden	.60	.25
❑ 105	Rob Moore	.60	.25
❑ 106	Marshall Faulk	1.50	.60
❑ 107	Steve Beuerlein	.60	.25
❑ 108	Torry Holt	1.00	.40
❑ 109	Donovan McNabb	1.50	.60
❑ 110	Rich Gannon	1.00	.40
❑ 111	Jerome Bettis	1.00	.40
❑ 112	Peyton Manning	2.50	1.00
❑ 113	Cris Carter	1.00	.40
❑ 114	Jake Plummer	.60	.25
❑ 115	Kent Graham	.40	.15
❑ 116	Keenan McCardell	.60	.25
❑ 117	Tim Dwight	1.00	.40
❑ 118	Fred Taylor	1.00	.40
❑ 119	Jerry Rice	2.00	.75
❑ 120	Michael Westbrook	.60	.25
❑ 121	Kurt Warner	2.00	.75
❑ 122	Jimmy Smith	.60	.25
❑ 123	Emmitt Smith	2.00	.75
❑ 124	Terrell Davis	1.00	.40
❑ 125	Randy Moss	2.00	.75
❑ 126	Akili Smith	.40	.15
❑ 127	Rocket Ismail	.60	.25
❑ 128	Jon Kitna	1.00	.40
❑ 129	Elvis Grbac	.60	.25
❑ 130	Wesley Walls	.40	.15
❑ 131	Torrance Small	.40	.15
❑ 132	Tyrone Wheatley	.60	.25
❑ 133	Carl Pickens	.40	.15
❑ 134	Zach Thomas	1.00	.40
❑ 135	Jacquez Green	.40	.15
❑ 136	Robert Smith	1.00	.40
❑ 137	Keyshawn Johnson	1.00	.40
❑ 138	Matthew Hatchette	.40	.15
❑ 139	Troy Aikman	2.00	.75
❑ 140	Charles Johnson	.60	.25
❑ 141	Terry Battle EP	1.00	.40
❑ 142	Pepe Pearson EP RC	2.00	.75
❑ 143	Cory Sauter EP	1.00	.40
❑ 144	Brian Shay EP	1.00	.40
❑ 145	Marcus Crandell EP RC	1.50	.60
❑ 146	Danny Wuerffel EP	1.50	.60
❑ 147	L.C. Stevens EP	1.00	.40
❑ 148	Ted White EP	1.00	.40
❑ 149	Matt Lytle EP RC	1.50	.60
❑ 150	Vershan Jackson EP RC	1.00	.40
❑ 151	Mario Bailey EP	1.00	.40
❑ 152	Darryl Daniel EP RC	1.50	.60
❑ 153	Sean Morey EP RC	1.50	.60
❑ 154	Jim Kubiak EP RC	1.50	.60
❑ 155	Aaron Stecker EP RC	2.00	.75
❑ 156	Damon Dunn EP RC	1.50	.60
❑ 157	Kevin Daft EP	1.00	.40
❑ 158	Corey Thomas EP	1.00	.40
❑ 159	Deon Mitchell EP RC	1.50	.60
❑ 160	Todd Floyd EP RC	1.00	.40
❑ 161	Norman Miller EP RC	1.00	.40
❑ 162	Jeremaine Copeland EP	1.00	.40
❑ 163	Michael Blair EP	1.00	.40
❑ 164	Ron Powlus EP RC	2.00	.75
❑ 165	Pat Barnes EP	1.50	.60
❑ 166	Dez White RC	4.00	1.50
❑ 167	Trung Canidate SP RC	25.00	10.00
❑ 168	Thomas Jones SP RC	40.00	20.00
❑ 169	Courtney Brown SP RC	30.00	12.50
❑ 170	Jamal Lewis SP RC	50.00	20.00
❑ 171	Chris Redman SP RC	25.00	10.00
❑ 172	Ron Dayne SP RC	30.00	12.50
❑ 173	Chad Pennington SP RC	50.00	25.00
❑ 174	Plaxico Burress SP RC	60.00	25.00
❑ 175	R.Jay Soward SP RC	25.00	10.00
❑ 176	Travis Taylor SP RC	30.00	12.50
❑ 177	Shaun Alexander SP RC	80.00	40.00
❑ 178	Brian Urlacher RC	20.00	7.50
❑ 179	Danny Farmer RC	3.00	1.25
❑ 180	Tee Martin SP RC	30.00	12.50
❑ 181	Sylvester Morris SP RC	25.00	10.00
❑ 182	Curtis Keaton RC	3.00	1.25
❑ 183	Peter Warrick SP RC	30.00	12.50
❑ 184	Anthony Becht RC	4.00	1.50
❑ 185	Travis Prentice SP RC	30.00	12.50
❑ 186	J.R. Redmond SP RC	25.00	10.00
❑ 187	Bubba Franks SP RC	30.00	12.50
❑ 188	Ron Dugans SP RC	20.00	7.50
❑ 189	Reuben Droughns RC	5.00	2.00
❑ 190	Corey Simon RC	2.00	.75
❑ 191	Joe Hamilton RC	3.00	1.25
❑ 192	Laveranues Coles RC	5.00	2.00
❑ 193	Todd Pinkston SP RC	30.00	12.50
❑ 194	Jerry Porter SP RC	50.00	20.00
❑ 195	Dennis Northcutt RC	4.00	1.50
❑ 196	Tim Rattay RC	4.00	1.50
❑ 197	Giovanni Carmazzi RC	2.00	.75
❑ 198	Mareno Philyaw RC	2.00	.75
❑ 199	Avion Black RC	3.00	1.25
❑ 200	Chafie Fields RC	2.00	.75
❑ 201	Rondell Mealey RC	2.00	.75
❑ 202	Troy Walters RC	4.00	1.50
❑ 203	Frank Moreau RC	3.00	1.25
❑ 204	Vaughn Sanders RC	2.00	.75
❑ 205	Sherrod Gideon RC	2.00	.75
❑ 206	Doug Chapman RC	3.00	1.25
❑ 207	Marcus Knight RC	3.00	1.25
❑ 208	Jamel White RC	3.00	1.25
❑ 209	Windrell Hayes RC	3.00	1.25
❑ 210	Reggie Jones RC	2.00	.75
❑ 211	Jarious Jackson RC	3.00	1.25
❑ 212	Ronney Jenkins RC	3.00	1.25
❑ 213	Quinton Spotwood RC	2.00	.75
❑ 214	Rob Morris RC	3.00	1.25
❑ 215	Gari Scott RC	2.00	.75
❑ 216	Kevin Thompson RC	2.00	.75
❑ 217	Trevor Insley RC	2.00	.75
❑ 218	Frank Murphy RC	2.00	.75
❑ 219	Patrick Pass RC	3.00	1.25
❑ 220	Mike Anderson RC	2.50	1.00
❑ 221	Derrius Thompson RC	4.00	1.50
❑ 222	John Abraham RC	6.00	2.50
❑ 223	Dante Hall RC	8.00	3.00
❑ 224	Chad Morton RC	4.00	1.50
❑ 225	Ahmed Plummer RC	4.00	1.50
❑ 226	Julian Peterson RC	4.00	1.50
❑ 227	Mike Green RC	3.00	1.25
❑ 228	Michael Wiley RC	3.00	1.25
❑ 229	Spergon Wynn RC	3.00	1.25
❑ 230	Trevor Gaylor RC	3.00	1.25
❑ 231	Doug Johnson RC	4.00	1.50
❑ 232	Marc Bulger RC	8.00	3.00
❑ 233	Ron Dixon RC	3.00	1.25
❑ 234	Aaron Shea RC	1.50	.60
❑ 235	Thomas Hamner RC	2.00	.75
❑ 236	Tom Brady RC	60.00	30.00
❑ 237	Deltha O'Neal RC	4.00	1.50
❑ 238	Todd Husak RC	4.00	1.50
❑ 239	Erron Kinney RC	4.00	1.50
❑ 240	JaJuan Dawson RC	2.00	.75
❑ 241	Nick Williams	1.00	.40
❑ 242	Deon Grant RC	3.00	1.25
❑ 243	Brad Hoover RC	3.00	1.25
❑ 244	Kamil Loud	.40	.15
❑ 245	Rashard Anderson RC	3.00	1.25
❑ 246	Clint Stoerner RC	1.50	.60
❑ 247	Antwan Harris RC	2.00	.75
❑ 248	Jason Webster RC	2.00	.75
❑ 249	Kevin McDougal RC	3.00	1.25
❑ 250	Tony Scott RC	2.00	.75
❑ 251	Thabiti Davis RC	2.00	.75
❑ 252	Ian Gold RC	3.00	1.25
❑ 253	Sammy Morris RC	3.00	1.25
❑ 254	Raynoch Thompson RC	3.00	1.25
❑ 255	Jeremy McDaniel	1.00	.40
❑ 256	Terrelle Smith RC	3.00	1.25
❑ 257	Deon Dyer RC	3.00	1.25
❑ 258	Na'il Diggs RC	3.00	1.25
❑ 259	Brandon Short RC	3.00	1.25
❑ 260	Mike Brown RC	8.00	3.00
❑ 261	John Engelberger RC	3.00	1.25
❑ 262	Rogers Beckett RC	3.00	1.25
❑ 263	JaJuan Seider RC	2.00	.75
❑ 264	Desmond Kitchings RC	3.00	1.25
❑ 265	Reggie Davis RC	3.00	1.25
❑ 266	Corey Moore RC	2.00	.75
❑ 267	Cornelius Griffin RC	3.00	1.25
❑ 268	Stockar McDougle RC	2.00	.75
❑ 269	James Williams RC	3.00	1.25
❑ 270	Darrell Jackson RC	6.00	2.50

2001 Bowman Chrome

❑	COMP.SET w/o SP's (110)	25.00	10.00
❑ 1	Emmitt Smith	2.00	.75
❑ 2	James Stewart	.60	.25
❑ 3	Jeff Graham	.40	.15
❑ 4	Keyshawn Johnson	1.00	.40
❑ 5	Stephen Davis	1.00	.40
❑ 6	Chad Lewis	.40	.15
❑ 7	Drew Bledsoe	1.25	.50
❑ 8	Fred Taylor	1.00	.40
❑ 9	Mike Anderson	1.00	.40
❑ 10	Tony Gonzalez	.60	.25
❑ 11	Aaron Brooks	1.00	.40
❑ 12	Vinny Testaverde	.60	.25
❑ 13	Jerome Bettis	1.00	.40
❑ 14	Marshall Faulk	1.25	.50
❑ 15	Jeff Garcia	1.00	.40
❑ 16	Terry Glenn	.60	.25
❑ 17	Jay Fiedler	1.00	.40
❑ 18	Ahman Green	1.00	.40
❑ 19	Cade McNown	.40	.15
❑ 20	Rob Johnson	.60	.25
❑ 21	Jamal Anderson	1.00	.40
❑ 22	Corey Dillon	1.00	.40
❑ 23	Jake Plummer	.60	.25
❑ 24	Rod Smith	.60	.25
❑ 25	Trent Green	1.00	.40
❑ 26	Ricky Williams	1.00	.40
❑ 27	Charlie Garner	.60	.25
❑ 28	Shaun Alexander	1.25	.50
❑ 29	Jeff George	.60	.25
❑ 30	Torry Holt	1.00	.40
❑ 31	James Thrash	.60	.25
❑ 32	Rich Gannon	1.00	.40
❑ 33	Ron Dayne	1.00	.40
❑ 34	Dedric Ward	.40	.15

❑ 35 Edgerrin James 1.25 .50
❑ 36 Cris Carter 1.00 .40
❑ 37 Derrick Mason .60 .25
❑ 38 Brad Johnson 1.00 .40
❑ 39 Charlie Batch 1.00 .40
❑ 40 Joey Galloway .60 .25
❑ 41 James Allen .60 .25
❑ 42 Tim Biakabutuka .60 .25
❑ 43 Ray Lewis 1.00 .40
❑ 44 David Boston 1.00 .40
❑ 45 Kevin Johnson .60 .25
❑ 46 Jimmy Smith .60 .25
❑ 47 Joe Horn .60 .25
❑ 48 Terrell Owens 1.00 .40
❑ 49 Eddie George 1.00 .40
❑ 50 Brett Favre 3.00 1.25
❑ 51 Wayne Chrebet .60 .25
❑ 52 Hines Ward 1.00 .40
❑ 53 Warrick Dunn 1.00 .40
❑ 54 Matt Hasselbeck .60 .25
❑ 55 Tiki Barber 1.00 .40
❑ 56 Lamar Smith .60 .25
❑ 57 Tim Couch .60 .25
❑ 58 Eric Moulds .60 .25
❑ 59 Shawn Jefferson .40 .15
❑ 60 Donald Hayes .40 .15
❑ 61 Brian Urlacher 1.50 .60
❑ 62 Steve McNair 1.00 .40
❑ 63 Kurt Warner 2.00 .75
❑ 64 Tim Brown 1.00 .40
❑ 65 Troy Brown .60 .25
❑ 66 Albert Connell .40 .15
❑ 67 Peyton Manning 2.50 1.00
❑ 68 Peter Warrick 1.00 .40
❑ 69 Elvis Grbac .60 .25
❑ 70 Chris Chandler .60 .25
❑ 71 Akili Smith .40 .15
❑ 72 Keenan McCardell .40 .15
❑ 73 Kerry Collins .60 .25
❑ 74 Junior Seau 1.00 .40
❑ 75 Donovan McNabb 1.25 .50
❑ 76 Tony Banks .60 .25
❑ 77 Steve Beuerlein .60 .25
❑ 78 Daunte Culpepper 1.00 .40
❑ 79 Darrell Jackson 1.00 .40
❑ 80 Isaac Bruce 1.00 .40
❑ 81 Tyrone Wheatley .60 .25
❑ 82 Derrick Alexander .60 .25
❑ 83 Germane Crowell .40 .15
❑ 84 Jon Kitna .60 .25
❑ 85 Jamal Lewis 1.50 .60
❑ 86 Ed McCaffrey 1.00 .40
❑ 87 Mark Brunell 1.00 .40
❑ 88 Jeff Blake .60 .25
❑ 89 Duce Staley 1.00 .40
❑ 90 Doug Flutie 1.00 .40
❑ 91 Kordell Stewart .60 .25
❑ 92 Randy Moss 2.00 .75
❑ 93 Marvin Harrison 1.00 .40
❑ 94 Muhsin Muhammad .60 .25
❑ 95 Brian Griese 1.00 .40
❑ 96 Antonio Freeman 1.00 .40
❑ 97 Amani Toomer .60 .25
❑ 98 Oronde Gadsden .60 .25
❑ 99 Curtis Martin 1.00 .40
❑ 100 Jerry Rice 2.00 .75
❑ 101 Michael Pittman .40 .15
❑ 102 Shannon Sharpe .60 .25
❑ 103 Peerless Price .60 .25
❑ 104 Bill Schroeder .60 .25
❑ 105 Ike Hilliard .60 .25
❑ 106 Freddie Jones .40 .15
❑ 107 Tai Streets .40 .15
❑ 108 Ricky Watters .60 .25
❑ 109 Az-Zahir Hakim .40 .15
❑ 110 Jacquez Green .40 .15
❑ 111 George Layne RC 5.00 2.00
❑ 112 Correll Buckhalter RC 10.00 4.00
❑ 113 Tony Stewart RC 8.00 3.00
❑ 114 Chris Barnes RC 5.00 2.00
❑ 115 A.J. Feeley RC 8.00 3.00
❑ 116 Margin Hooks RC 3.00 1.25
❑ 117 Anthony Henry RC 8.00 3.00
❑ 118 Dwight Smith RC 3.00 1.25
❑ 119 Torrance Marshall RC 8.00 3.00
❑ 120 Gary Baxter RC 5.00 2.00
❑ 121 Derek Combs RC 5.00 2.00
❑ 122 Marcus Bell RC 5.00 2.00
❑ 123 DeLawrence Grant RC 3.00 1.25
❑ 124 Jameel Cook RC 5.00 2.00
❑ 125 Eric Downing RC 3.00 1.25
❑ 126 Marlon McCree RC 5.00 2.00
❑ 127 Tay Cody RC 3.00 1.25
❑ 128 Mario Monds RC 3.00 1.25
❑ 129 Kenny Smith RC 5.00 2.00
❑ 130 Sedrick Hodge RC 3.00 1.25
❑ 131 Marcus Stroud RC 8.00 3.00
❑ 132 Steve Smith RC 30.00 15.00
❑ 133 Tyrone Robertson RC 3.00 1.25
❑ 134 James Reed RC 3.00 1.25
❑ 135 Kris Kocurek RC 3.00 1.25
❑ 136 Dan O'Leary RC 5.00 2.00
❑ 137 Harold Blackmon RC 3.00 1.25
❑ 138 Fred Smoot RC 8.00 3.00
❑ 139 Billy Baber RC 3.00 1.25
❑ 140 Jarrod Cooper RC 8.00 3.00
❑ 141 Travis Henry RC 8.00 3.00
❑ 142 David Terrell RC 8.00 3.00
❑ 143 Josh Heupel RC 8.00 3.00
❑ 144 Drew Brees RC 25.00 10.00
❑ 145 T.J. Houshmandzadeh RC 8.00 3.00
❑ 146 Rod Gardner RC 8.00 3.00
❑ 147 Richard Seymour RC 8.00 3.00
❑ 148 Koren Robinson RC 8.00 3.00
❑ 149 Scotty Anderson RC 5.00 2.00
❑ 150 Marques Tuiasosopo RC 8.00 3.00
❑ 151 John Capel RC 5.00 2.00
❑ 152 LaMont Jordan RC 15.00 6.00
❑ 153 James Jackson RC 8.00 3.00
❑ 154 Bobby Newcombe RC 5.00 2.00
❑ 155 Anthony Thomas RC 8.00 3.00
❑ 156 Dan Alexander RC 8.00 3.00
❑ 157 Quincy Carter RC 8.00 3.00
❑ 158 Morlon Greenwood RC 5.00 2.00
❑ 159 Robert Ferguson RC 8.00 3.00
❑ 160 Sage Rosenfels RC 8.00 3.00
❑ 161 Michael Stone RC 3.00 1.25
❑ 162 Chris Weinke RC 8.00 3.00
❑ 163 Travis Minor RC 5.00 2.00
❑ 164 Gerard Warren RC 8.00 3.00
❑ 165 Jamar Fletcher RC 5.00 2.00
❑ 166 Andre Carter RC 8.00 3.00
❑ 167 Deuce McAllister RC 15.00 6.00
❑ 168 Dan Morgan RC 8.00 3.00
❑ 169 Todd Heap RC 8.00 3.00
❑ 170 Snoop Minnis RC 5.00 2.00
❑ 171 Will Allen RC 5.00 2.00
❑ 172 Freddie Mitchell RC 8.00 3.00
❑ 173 Rudi Johnson RC 15.00 6.00
❑ 174 Kevan Barlow RC 8.00 3.00
❑ 175 Jamie Winborn RC 5.00 2.00
❑ 176 Onome Ojo RC 5.00 2.00
❑ 177 Leonard Davis RC 5.00 2.00
❑ 178 Santana Moss RC 12.00 5.00
❑ 179 Chris Chambers RC 12.00 5.00
❑ 180 Michael Vick RC 80.00 40.00
❑ 181 Michael Bennett RC 12.00 5.00
❑ 182 Mike McMahon RC 8.00 3.00
❑ 183 Jonathan Carter RC 5.00 2.00
❑ 184 Jamal Reynolds RC 8.00 3.00
❑ 185 Justin Smith RC 8.00 3.00
❑ 186 Quincy Morgan RC 8.00 3.00
❑ 187 Chad Johnson RC 25.00 10.00
❑ 188 Jesse Palmer RC 8.00 3.00
❑ 189 Reggie Wayne RC 15.00 6.00
❑ 190 LaDainian Tomlinson RC 60.00 35.00
❑ 191 Andre King RC 5.00 2.00
❑ 192 Richmond Flowers RC 5.00 2.00
❑ 193 Derrick Blaylock RC 8.00 3.00
❑ 194 Cedrick Wilson RC 8.00 3.00
❑ 195 Zeke Moreno RC 8.00 3.00
❑ 196 Tommy Polley RC 8.00 3.00
❑ 197 Damione Lewis RC 5.00 2.00
❑ 198 Aaron Schobel RC 8.00 3.00
❑ 199 Alge Crumpler RC 10.00 5.00
❑ 200 Nate Clements RC 8.00 3.00
❑ 201 Quentin McCord RC 5.00 2.00
❑ 202 Ken-Yon Rambo RC 5.00 2.00
❑ 203 Milton Wynn RC 5.00 2.00
❑ 204 Derrick Gibson RC 5.00 2.00
❑ 205 Chris Taylor RC 5.00 2.00
❑ 206 Corey Hall RC 3.00 1.25
❑ 207 Vinny Sutherland RC 5.00 2.00
❑ 208 Kendrell Bell RC 12.00 5.00
❑ 209 Casey Hampton RC 8.00 3.00
❑ 210 Demetric Evans RC 3.00 1.25
❑ 211 Brian Allen RC 3.00 1.25
❑ 212 Rodney Bailey RC 3.00 1.25
❑ 213 Otis Leverette RC 3.00 1.25
❑ 214 Ron Edwards RC 3.00 1.25
❑ 215 Michael Jameson RC 3.00 1.25
❑ 216 Markus Steele RC 5.00 2.00
❑ 217 Jimmy Williams RC 3.00 1.25
❑ 218 Roger Knight RC 3.00 1.25
❑ 219 Randy Garner RC 3.00 1.25
❑ 220 Raymond Perryman RC 3.00 1.25
❑ 221 Karon Riley RC 3.00 1.25
❑ 222 Adam Archuleta RC 8.00 3.00
❑ 223 Arnold Jackson RC 5.00 2.00
❑ 224 Ryan Pickett RC 3.00 1.25
❑ 225 Shad Meier RC 5.00 2.00
❑ 226 Reggie Germany RC 5.00 2.00
❑ 227 Justin McCareins RC 8.00 3.00
❑ 228 Idrees Bashir RC 3.00 1.25
❑ 229 Josh Booty RC 8.00 3.00
❑ 230 Eddie Berlin RC 5.00 2.00
❑ 231 Heath Evans RC 5.00 2.00
❑ 232 Alex Bannister RC 5.00 2.00
❑ 233 Corey Alston RC 3.00 1.25
❑ 234 Reggie White RC 5.00 2.00
❑ 235 Orlando Huff RC 3.00 1.25
❑ 236 Ken Lucas RC 5.00 2.00
❑ 237 Matt Stewart RC 3.00 1.25
❑ 238 Cedric Scott RC 5.00 2.00
❑ 239 Ronney Daniels RC 3.00 1.25
❑ 240 Kevin Kasper RC 8.00 3.00
❑ 241 Tony Driver RC 5.00 2.00
❑ 242 Kyle Vanden Bosch RC 8.00 3.00
❑ 243 T.J. Turner RC 3.00 1.25
❑ 244 Eric Westmoreland RC 5.00 2.00
❑ 245 Ronald Flemons RC 3.00 1.25
❑ 246 Eric Kelly RC 3.00 1.25
❑ 247 Moran Norris RC 3.00 1.25
❑ 248 Damerien McCants RC 5.00 2.00
❑ 249 James Boyd RC 3.00 1.25
❑ 250 Keith Adams RC 3.00 1.25
❑ 251 Brandon Manumaleuna RC 5.00 2.00
❑ 252 Dee Brown RC 8.00 3.00
❑ 253 Ross Kolodziej RC 3.00 1.25
❑ 254 Boo Williams RC 5.00 2.00
❑ 255 Patrick Chukwurah RC 3.00 1.25

2002 Bowman Chrome

	COMP.SET w/o SP's (110)	25.00	10.00
1	Emmitt Smith	2.50	1.00
2	Drew Brees	1.00	.40
3	Duce Staley	1.00	.40
4	Curtis Martin	1.00	.40
5	Isaac Bruce	1.00	.40
6	Stephen Davis	.60	.25
7	Darrell Jackson	.60	.25
8	James Stewart	.60	.25
9	Tim Couch	.60	.25
10	Travis Henry	1.00	.40
11	Thomas Jones	.60	.25
12	Jamal Lewis	1.00	.40
13	Chris Chambers	1.00	.40
14	Jeff Blake	.60	.25
15	Plaxico Burress	.60	.25
16	Michael Pittman	.40	.15
17	Jeff Garcia	1.00	.40
18	Tim Brown	1.00	.40
19	Kent Graham	.40	.15
20	Shannon Sharpe	.60	.25
21	Corey Dillon	.60	.25
22	Muhsin Muhammad	.60	.25
23	Tony Gonzalez	.60	.25
24	Qadry Ismail	.60	.25
25	Mike McMahon	1.00	.40
26	Edgerrin James	1.25	.50
27	Daunte Culpepper	1.00	.40
28	Deuce McAllister	1.25	.50
29	Kerry Collins	.60	.25
30	Eddie George	1.00	.40
31	Torry Holt	1.00	.40
32	Todd Pinkston	.60	.25
33	Quincy Carter	.60	.25
34	Rod Smith	.60	.25
35	Michael Vick	3.00	1.25
36	Jim Miller	.60	.25
37	Troy Brown	.60	.25
38	Wayne Chrebet	.60	.25
39	Curtis Conway	.40	.15
40	Reidel Anthony	.40	.15
41	Mark Brunell	1.00	.40
42	Chris Weinke	.60	.25
43	Eric Moulds	.60	.25
44	Ike Hilliard	.60	.25
45	Jay Fiedler	.60	.25
46	Keyshawn Johnson	1.00	.40
47	Rod Gardner	.60	.25
48	Chris Redman	.40	.15
49	James Allen	.60	.25
50	Kordell Stewart	.60	.25
51	Priest Holmes	1.25	.50
52	Anthony Thomas	.60	.25
53	Peter Warrick	.60	.25
54	Jake Plummer	.60	.25
55	Jerry Rice	2.00	.75
56	Joe Horn	.60	.25
57	Derrick Mason	.60	.25
58	Kurt Warner	1.00	.40
59	Antowain Smith	.60	.25
60	Randy Moss	2.00	.75
61	Warrick Dunn	1.00	.40
62	Laveranues Coles	.60	.25
63	LaDainian Tomlinson	1.50	.60
64	Michael Westbrook	.60	.25
65	Travis Taylor	.60	.25
66	Brian Griese	1.00	.40
67	Bill Schroeder	.60	.25
68	Ahman Green	1.00	.40
69	Jimmy Smith	.60	.25
70	Charlie Garner	.60	.25
71	Terrell Owens	1.00	.40
72	Brad Johnson	.60	.25
73	James Thrash	.60	.25
74	Marvin Harrison	1.00	.40
75	Brett Favre	2.50	1.00
76	Rocket Ismail	.60	.25
77	David Boston	1.00	.40
78	Jermaine Lewis	.40	.15
79	Aaron Brooks	1.00	.40
80	Shaun Alexander	1.25	.50
81	Steve McNair	1.00	.40
82	Marshall Faulk	1.00	.40
83	Terrell Davis	1.00	.40
84	Corey Bradford	.40	.15
85	David Terrell	1.00	.40
86	Kevin Johnson	.60	.25
87	Jon Kitna	.60	.25
88	Az-Zahir Hakim	.40	.15
89	Drew Bledsoe	1.25	.50
90	Garrison Hearst	.60	.25
91	Doug Flutie	1.00	.40
92	Jerome Bettis	1.00	.40
93	Vinny Testaverde	.60	.25
94	Tiki Barber	1.00	.40
95	Johnnie Morton	.60	.25
96	Lamar Smith	.60	.25
97	Marcus Robinson	.60	.25
98	Fred Taylor	1.00	.40
99	Tom Brady	2.50	1.00
100	Peyton Manning	2.00	.75
101	Donovan McNabb	1.25	.50
102	Rich Gannon	1.00	.40
103	Hines Ward	1.00	.40
104	Michael Bennett	.60	.25
105	Ricky Williams	1.00	.40
106	Germane Crowell	.40	.15
107	Joey Galloway	.60	.25
108	Amani Toomer	.60	.25
109	Trent Green	.60	.25
110	Terry Glenn	.60	.25
111	Donte Stallworth RC	10.00	4.00
112	Mike Williams RC	4.00	1.50
113	Kurt Kittner RC	4.00	1.50
114	Josh Reed RC	5.00	2.00
115	Raonall Smith RC	4.00	1.50
116	David Garrard RC	5.00	2.00
117	Eric Crouch RC	5.00	2.00
118	Levi Jones RC	4.00	1.50
119	Quentin Jammer RC	5.00	2.00
120	Cliff Russell RC	4.00	1.50
121	Jamin Elliott RC	2.50	1.00
122	Roy Williams RC	12.00	5.00
123	Marquise Walker RC	4.00	1.50
124	Kalimba Edwards RC	5.00	2.00
125	Daniel Graham RC	5.00	2.00
126	Anthony Weaver RC	4.00	1.50
127	Antonio Bryant RC	5.00	2.00
128	DeShaun Foster RC	5.00	2.00
129	Antwaan Randle El RC	8.00	3.00
130	William Green RC	5.00	2.00
131	Joey Harrington RC	12.00	5.00
132	T.J. Duckett RC	8.00	3.00
133	Javon Walker RC	10.00	4.00
134	Albert Haynesworth RC	4.00	1.50
135	Julius Peppers RC	10.00	4.00
136	Clinton Portis RC	15.00	6.00
137	Ashley Lelie RC	10.00	4.00
138	Reche Caldwell RC	5.00	2.00
139	Rohan Davey RC	5.00	2.00
140	Patrick Ramsey RC	6.00	2.50
141	Ron Johnson RC	4.00	1.50
142	Jamar Martin RC	4.00	1.50
143	Travis Stephens RC	4.00	1.50
143AU	Travis Stephens AU	12.00	5.00
144	Darrell Hill RC	4.00	1.50
145	Jon McGraw RC	2.50	1.00
146	Javin Hunter RC	2.50	1.00
146AU	Javin Hunter AU	10.00	4.00
147	Eddie Drummond RC	4.00	1.50
148	Andre Lott RC	5.00	2.00
149	Travis Fisher RC	5.00	2.00
150	Lamont Brightful RC	2.50	1.00
151	Rocky Calmus RC	5.00	2.00
152	Wes Pate RC	2.50	1.00
152AU	Wes Pate AU	10.00	4.00
153	Lamar Gordon RC	5.00	2.00
154	Terry Jones RC	4.00	1.50
155	Kyle Johnson RC	2.50	1.00
155AU	Kyle Johnson AU	10.00	4.00
156	Daryl Jones RC	4.00	1.50
157	Tellis Redmon RC	4.00	1.50
158	Jarrod Baxter RC	4.00	1.50
159	Delvon Flowers RC	4.00	1.50
160	Kelly Campbell RC	4.00	1.50
161	Eddie Freeman RC	2.50	1.00
162	Atrews Bell RC	2.50	1.00
163	Omar Easy RC	5.00	2.00
164	Jeremy Allen RC	2.50	1.00
165	Andra Davis RC	4.00	1.50
166	Mike Rumph RC	5.00	2.00
167	Seth Burford RC	4.00	1.50
168	Marquand Manuel RC	2.50	1.00
169	Marques Anderson RC	5.00	2.00
170	Ben Leber RC	5.00	2.00
171	Ryan Denney RC	4.00	1.50
172	Justin Peelle RC	2.50	1.00
173	Lito Sheppard RC	5.00	2.00
174	Damien Anderson RC	4.00	1.50
175	Lamont Thompson RC	4.00	1.50
176	David Priestley RC	4.00	1.50
177	Michael Lewis RC	5.00	2.00
178	Lee Mays RC	4.00	1.50
179	Alan Harper RC	2.50	1.00
180	Verron Haynes RC	5.00	2.00
181	Chris Hope RC	5.00	2.00
182	Derek Ross RC	4.00	1.50
183	Joseph Jefferson RC	4.00	1.50
184	Carlos Hall RC	5.00	2.00
185	Robert Royal RC	5.00	2.00
186	Sheldon Brown RC	5.00	2.00
187	DeVeren Johnson RC	4.00	1.50
188	Rock Cartwright RC	6.00	2.50
189	Kendall Simmons RC	4.00	1.50
190	Joe Burns RC	4.00	1.50
191	David Givens RC	15.00	6.00
192	John Owens RC	4.00	1.50
193	Jarrett Ferguson RC	4.00	1.50
194	Randy McMichael RC	8.00	3.00
195	Chris Baker RC	4.00	1.50
196	Rashad Bauman RC	4.00	1.50
197	Matt Murphy RC	4.00	1.50
198	Steve Bellisari RC	4.00	1.50
199	Jeff Kelly RC	4.00	1.50
200	Mark Anelli RC	2.50	1.00
201	Darnell Sanders RC	4.00	1.50
202	Coy Wire RC	5.00	2.00
203	Ricky Williams RC	4.00	1.50
204	Napoleon Harris RC	5.00	2.00
205	Ennis Haywood RC	4.00	1.50
206	Keyuo Craver RC	4.00	1.50
207	Kahlil Hill RC	4.00	1.50
208	J.T. O'Sullivan RC	4.00	1.50
209	Woody Dantzler RC	4.00	1.50
210	Phillip Buchanon RC	5.00	2.00
211	Charles Grant RC	5.00	2.00
212	Dusty Bonner RC	2.50	1.00
213	James Allen RC	2.50	1.00
214	Ronald Curry RC	5.00	2.00
215	Deion Branch RC	10.00	4.00
216	Larry Ned RC	4.00	1.50
217	Kendall Newson RC	2.50	1.00
218	Shaun Hill RC	5.00	2.00
219	Akin Ayodele RC	2.50	1.00
220	John Henderson RC	5.00	2.00
221	Andre Davis AU A RC	12.00	5.00
222	Bryan Thomas AU A RC	20.00	7.50
223	Brian Westbrook AU C RC	60.00	25.00
224	Chad Hutchinson AU C RC	12.00	5.00
225	Craig Nall AU D RC	25.00	10.00
226	David Carr AU A RC	60.00	30.00
227	Dwight Freeney AU D RC	30.00	15.00
228	Adrian Peterson AU A RC	20.00	7.50
229	Randy Fasani AU E RC	12.00	5.00
230	Ed Reed AU A RC	30.00	15.00
231	Freddie Milons AU B RC	12.00	5.00
232	Herb Haygood AU E RC	10.00	4.00
233	Jabar Gaffney AU A RC	20.00	7.50
234	Josh McCown AU A RC	30.00	15.00
235	Jeremy Shockey AU A RC	80.00	40.00

- ❑ 236 Jake Schifino AU F RC 12.00 5.00
- ❑ 237 Josh Scobey AU E RC 20.00 7.50
- ❑ 238 Jonathan Wells AU D RC 20.00 7.50
- ❑ 239 Ladell Betts AU A RC 25.00 10.00
- ❑ 240 Luke Staley AU E RC 12.00 5.00
- ❑ 241 Maurice Morris AU B RC 20.00 7.50
- ❑ 242 Matt Schobel AU D RC 12.00 5.00
- ❑ 243 Sam Simmons AU C RC 10.00 4.00
- ❑ 244 Tim Carter AU A RC 12.00 5.00
- ❑ 245 Tank Williams AU E RC 12.00 5.00
- ❑ 246 Jerramy Stevens AU A RC 20.00 7.50
- ❑ 247 Jason McAddley AU C RC 12.00 5.00
- ❑ 248 Ken Simonton AU D RC 10.00 4.00
- ❑ 249 Chester Taylor AU F RC 30.00 15.00
- ❑ 250 Brandon Doman AU C RC 12.00 5.00

2003 Bowman Chrome

- ❑ COMP.SET w/o SP's (110) 25.00 10.00
- ❑ 1 Brett Favre 2.50 1.00
- ❑ 2 Jeremy Shockey 1.50 .60
- ❑ 3 Fred Taylor 1.00 .40
- ❑ 4 Rich Gannon .60 .25
- ❑ 5 Joey Galloway .60 .25
- ❑ 6 Ray Lewis 1.00 .40
- ❑ 7 Jeff Blake .40 .15
- ❑ 8 Stacey Mack .40 .15
- ❑ 9 Matt Hasselbeck .60 .25
- ❑ 10 Laveranues Coles .60 .25
- ❑ 11 Brad Johnson .60 .25
- ❑ 12 Tommy Maddox 1.00 .40
- ❑ 13 Curtis Martin 1.00 .40
- ❑ 14 Tom Brady 2.50 1.00
- ❑ 15 Ricky Williams 1.00 .40
- ❑ 16 Stephen Davis .60 .25
- ❑ 17 Chad Johnson 1.00 .40
- ❑ 18 Joey Harrington 1.50 .60
- ❑ 19 Tony Gonzalez .60 .25
- ❑ 20 Peerless Price .60 .25
- ❑ 21 LaDainian Tomlinson 1.00 .40
- ❑ 22 James Thrash .60 .25
- ❑ 23 Charlie Garner .60 .25
- ❑ 24 Eddie George .60 .25
- ❑ 25 Terrell Owens 1.00 .40
- ❑ 26 Brian Urlacher 1.50 .60
- ❑ 27 Eric Moulds .60 .25
- ❑ 28 Emmitt Smith 2.50 1.00
- ❑ 29 Tim Couch .40 .15
- ❑ 30 Jake Plummer .60 .25
- ❑ 31 Marvin Harrison 1.00 .40
- ❑ 32 Chris Chambers 1.00 .40
- ❑ 33 Tiki Barber 1.00 .40
- ❑ 34 Kurt Warner 1.00 .40
- ❑ 35 Michael Pittman .40 .15
- ❑ 36 Kevin Dyson .60 .25
- ❑ 37 Clinton Portis 1.50 .60
- ❑ 38 Peyton Manning 1.50 .60
- ❑ 39 Travis Taylor .60 .25
- ❑ 40 Jeff Garcia 1.00 .40
- ❑ 41 Patrick Ramsey 1.00 .40
- ❑ 42 Shaun Alexander 1.00 .40
- ❑ 43 Joe Horn .60 .25
- ❑ 44 Daunte Culpepper 1.00 .40
- ❑ 45 Travis Henry .60 .25
- ❑ 46 Brian Finneran .40 .15
- ❑ 47 William Green .60 .25
- ❑ 48 Kordell Stewart .60 .25
- ❑ 49 Reggie Wayne .60 .25
- ❑ 50 Priest Holmes 1.25 .50
- ❑ 51 Jay Fiedler .60 .25
- ❑ 52 Corey Dillon .60 .25
- ❑ 53 Jamal Lewis 1.00 .40
- ❑ 54 Mark Brunell .60 .25
- ❑ 55 Santana Moss .60 .25
- ❑ 56 Duce Staley .60 .25
- ❑ 57 Torry Holt 1.00 .40
- ❑ 58 Rod Gardner .60 .25
- ❑ 59 Kerry Collins .60 .25
- ❑ 60 Randy Moss 1.50 .60
- ❑ 61 Jerry Porter .60 .25
- ❑ 62 Plaxico Burress .60 .25
- ❑ 63 Steve McNair 1.00 .40
- ❑ 64 Muhsin Muhammad .60 .25
- ❑ 65 Drew Bledsoe 1.00 .40
- ❑ 66 T.J. Duckett .60 .25
- ❑ 67 Ahman Green 1.00 .40
- ❑ 68 Rod Smith .60 .25
- ❑ 69 Jimmy Smith .60 .25
- ❑ 70 Trent Green .60 .25
- ❑ 71 Tim Brown 1.00 .40
- ❑ 72 Jerome Bettis 1.00 .40
- ❑ 73 Isaac Bruce 1.00 .40
- ❑ 74 Derrick Mason .60 .25
- ❑ 75 Donovan McNabb 1.25 .50
- ❑ 76 Deuce McAllister 1.00 .40
- ❑ 77 Zach Thomas 1.00 .40
- ❑ 78 Garrison Hearst .60 .25
- ❑ 79 Koren Robinson .60 .25
- ❑ 80 Marshall Faulk 1.00 .40
- ❑ 81 Keyshawn Johnson 1.00 .40
- ❑ 82 Jake Delhomme 1.00 .40
- ❑ 83 Marty Booker .60 .25
- ❑ 84 James Stewart .60 .25
- ❑ 85 Corey Bradford .40 .15
- ❑ 86 Derrius Thompson .40 .15
- ❑ 87 Edgerrin James 1.00 .40
- ❑ 88 Darrell Jackson .60 .25
- ❑ 89 Hines Ward 1.00 .40
- ❑ 90 David Boston .60 .25
- ❑ 91 Curtis Conway .40 .15
- ❑ 92 David Patten .40 .15
- ❑ 93 Michael Bennett .60 .25
- ❑ 94 Todd Pinkston .60 .25
- ❑ 95 Jerry Rice 2.00 .75
- ❑ 96 Jon Kitna .60 .25
- ❑ 97 Ed McCaffrey 1.00 .40
- ❑ 98 Donald Driver .60 .25
- ❑ 99 Anthony Thomas .60 .25
- ❑ 100 Michael Vick 2.50 1.00
- ❑ 101 Terry Glenn .40 .15
- ❑ 102 Quincy Morgan .60 .25
- ❑ 103 David Carr 1.50 .60
- ❑ 104 Troy Brown .60 .25
- ❑ 105 Aaron Brooks 1.00 .40
- ❑ 106 Amani Toomer .60 .25
- ❑ 107 Drew Brees 1.00 .40
- ❑ 108 Chad Hutchinson .40 .15
- ❑ 109 Warrick Dunn .60 .25
- ❑ 110 Chad Pennington 1.25 .50
- ❑ 111 Brian St.Pierre RC 5.00 2.00
- ❑ 112 Keenan Howry RC 5.00 2.00
- ❑ 113 Sultan McCullough RC 4.00 1.50
- ❑ 114 Terence Newman RC 10.00 4.00
- ❑ 115 Kelley Washington RC 5.00 2.00
- ❑ 116 Musa Smith RC 5.00 2.00
- ❑ 117 Victor Hobson RC 5.00 2.00
- ❑ 118 Travis Anglin RC 2.50 1.00
- ❑ 119 Artose Pinner RC 5.00 2.00
- ❑ 120 Rashean Mathis RC 4.00 1.50
- ❑ 121 DeWayne White RC 4.00 1.50
- ❑ 122 Kevin Curtis RC 5.00 2.00
- ❑ 123 Tyrone Calico RC 6.00 2.50
- ❑ 124 Ricky Manning RC 5.00 2.00
- ❑ 125 Cory Redding RC 4.00 1.50
- ❑ 126 Dallas Clark RC 5.00 2.00
- ❑ 127 Marcus Trufant RC 5.00 2.00
- ❑ 128 Terrell Suggs RC 8.00 3.00
- ❑ 129 Aaron Walker RC 4.00 1.50
- ❑ 130 Calvin Pace RC 4.00 1.50
- ❑ 131 Ken Dorsey RC 5.00 2.00
- ❑ 132 Earnest Graham RC 4.00 1.50
- ❑ 133 Cecil Sapp RC 4.00 1.50
- ❑ 134 William Joseph RC 5.00 2.00
- ❑ 135 Anquan Boldin RC 15.00 6.00
- ❑ 136 Justin Griffith RC 4.00 1.50
- ❑ 137 Teyo Johnson RC 5.00 2.00
- ❑ 138 Chris Crocker RC 2.50 1.00
- ❑ 139 Doug Gabriel RC 6.00 2.50
- ❑ 140 Terry Pierce RC 4.00 1.50
- ❑ 141 Bradie James RC 5.00 2.00
- ❑ 142 Terrence Edwards RC 4.00 1.50
- ❑ 143 E.J. Henderson RC 5.00 2.00
- ❑ 144 Tony Romo RC 5.00 2.00
- ❑ 145 DeWayne Robertson RC 5.00 2.00
- ❑ 146 Dwone Hicks RC 2.50 1.00
- ❑ 147 Carl Ford RC 2.50 1.00
- ❑ 148 Ken Hamlin RC 5.00 2.00
- ❑ 149 Adrian Madise RC 4.00 1.50
- ❑ 150 Siddeeq Shabazz RC 2.50 1.00
- ❑ 151 Dave Ragone RC 5.00 2.00
- ❑ 152 Mike Seidman RC 2.50 1.00
- ❑ 153 DeAndrew Rubin RC 2.50 1.00
- ❑ 154 Mike Pinkard RC 2.50 1.00
- ❑ 155 Nate Burleson RC 6.00 2.50
- ❑ 156 Angelo Crowell RC 4.00 1.50
- ❑ 157 J.R. Tolver RC 4.00 1.50
- ❑ 158 Osi Umenyiora RC 8.00 3.00
- ❑ 159 Nick Barnett RC 8.00 3.00
- ❑ 160 Brandon Drumm RC 2.50 1.00
- ❑ 161 Rien Long RC 2.50 1.00
- ❑ 162 Zuriel Smith RC 2.50 1.00
- ❑ 163 Onterrio Smith RC 5.00 2.00
- ❑ 164 Kenny Peterson RC 4.00 1.50
- ❑ 165 Chaun Thompson RC 2.50 1.00
- ❑ 166 Terrence Holt RC 4.00 1.50
- ❑ 167 Ovie Mughelli RC 2.50 1.00
- ❑ 168 Bethel Johnson RC 5.00 2.00
- ❑ 169 Avon Cobourne RC 2.50 1.00
- ❑ 170 Andre Woolfolk RC 5.00 2.00
- ❑ 171 George Wrighster RC 4.00 1.50
- ❑ 172 Justin Fargas RC 5.00 2.00
- ❑ 173 Marquel Blackwell RC 2.50 1.00
- ❑ 174 Walter Young RC 2.50 1.00
- ❑ 175 Kawika Mitchell RC 5.00 2.00
- ❑ 176 Drayton Florence RC 2.50 1.00
- ❑ 177 Jeremi Johnson RC 4.00 1.50
- ❑ 178 Lee Suggs RC 10.00 4.00
- ❑ 179 David Kircus RC 4.00 1.50
- ❑ 180 Rex Grossman RC 8.00 3.00
- ❑ 180AU Rex Grossman AU B 40.00 15.00
- ❑ 181 Jon Olinger RC 2.50 1.00
- ❑ 182 Dan Curley RC 2.50 1.00
- ❑ 183 Andrew Pinnock RC 4.00 1.50
- ❑ 184 Kirk Farmer RC 2.50 1.00
- ❑ 185 Charles Rogers RC 5.00 2.00
- ❑ 186 Alonzo Jackson RC 4.00 1.50
- ❑ 187 Trent Smith RC 4.00 1.50
- ❑ 188 Seneca Wallace RC 5.00 2.00
- ❑ 189 Shane Walton RC 2.50 1.00
- ❑ 190 Chris Brown RC 6.00 2.50
- ❑ 191 Dahrran Diedrick RC 5.00 2.00
- ❑ 192 Juston Wood RC 2.50 1.00
- ❑ 193 Mike Doss RC 5.00 2.00
- ❑ 194 Visanthe Shiancoe RC 4.00 1.50
- ❑ 195 Andre Johnson RC 10.00 4.00
- ❑ 196 Dennis Weathersby RC 2.50 1.00
- ❑ 197 Chris Davis RC 4.00 1.50
- ❑ 198 LaTarence Dunbar RC 4.00 1.50
- ❑ 199 Eugene Wilson RC 5.00 2.00
- ❑ 200 Ryan Hoag RC 2.50 1.00
- ❑ 201 Chris Simms RC 8.00 3.00
- ❑ 202 Curt Anes RC 2.50 1.00
- ❑ 203 Taco Wallace RC 4.00 1.50
- ❑ 204 David Tyree RC 4.00 1.50
- ❑ 205 Nate Hybl RC 5.00 2.00

❑ 206 Willis McGahee RC 15.00 6.00
❑ 207 Casey Moore RC 4.00 1.50
❑ 208 Pisa Tinoisamoa RC 5.00 2.00
❑ 209 Willie Ponder RC 2.50 1.00
❑ 210 Donald Lee RC 4.00 1.50
❑ 211 Nnamdi Asomugha RC 4.00 1.50
❑ 212 Sammy Davis RC 5.00 2.00
❑ 213 Joffrey Reynolds RC 2.50 1.00
❑ 214 Eddie Moore RC 4.00 1.50
❑ 215 Tony Hollings RC 5.00 2.00
❑ 216 Nick Maddox RC 2.50 1.00
❑ 217 Kevin Walter RC 4.00 1.50
❑ 218 Dan Klecko RC 5.00 2.00
❑ 219 Antwan Peek RC 4.00 1.50
❑ 220 Tyler Brayton RC 5.00 2.00
❑ 221 Byron Leftwich AU B RC 100.00 40.00
❑ 222 Bobby Wade AU D RC 15.00 6.00
❑ 223 Jerome McDougle AU C RC 12.00 5.00
❑ 224 Michael Haynes AU D RC 12.00 5.00
❑ 225 Taylor Jacobs AU C RC 20.00 7.50
❑ 226 Shaun McDonald AU D RC 12.00 5.00
❑ 227 Bry.Johnson AU B RC EXCH 15.00 6.00
❑ 228 Talman Gardner AU D RC 12.00 5.00
❑ 229 Domanick Davis AU D RC 40.00 15.00
❑ 230 Jason Witten AU D RC 25.00 12.50
❑ 231 Kyle Boller AU B RC 50.00 25.00
❑ 232 L.J. Smith AU C RC 20.00 7.50
❑ 233 Boss Bailey AU C RC 15.00 6.00
❑ 234 Billy McMullen AU D RC 10.00 4.00
❑ 235 Larry Johnson AU B RC 250.00 150.00
❑ 236 Kareem Kelly AU E RC 10.00 4.00
❑ 237 Carson Palmer AU A RC 250.00 150.00
❑ 238 Quentin Griffin AU D RC 20.00 7.50
❑ 239 Kevin Garrett AU E RC 10.00 4.00
❑ 240 Charles Tillman AU E RC 20.00 7.50
❑ 241 Arnaz Battle AU D RC 15.00 6.00
❑ 242 Brooks Bollinger AU E RC 12.00 5.00
❑ 243 LaBrandon Toefield AU D RC 12.00 5.00
❑ 244 Sam Aiken AU D RC 10.00 4.00
❑ 245 Justin Gage AU D RC 12.00 5.00
❑ 246 Gibran Hamdan AU D RC 10.00 4.00

2004 Bowman Chrome

❑ COMP.SET w/o SP's (220) 175.00 100.00
❑ COMP.SET w/o RC's (110) 30.00 12.50
❑ ONE ROOKIE CARD PER PACK
❑ ROOKIE AU/199 GROUP A ODDS 1:603
❑ ROOKIE AU GROUP B ODDS 1:1293
❑ ROOKIE AU GROUP C ODDS 1:359
❑ ROOKIE AU GROUP D ODDS 1:21
❑ 1 Brett Favre 2.50 1.00
❑ 2 Jay Fiedler .40 .15
❑ 3 Andre Davis .40 .15
❑ 4 Travis Henry .60 .25
❑ 5 Jimmy Smith .60 .25
❑ 6 Santana Moss .60 .25
❑ 7 Correll Buckhalter .60 .25
❑ 8 Randy Moss 1.25 .50
❑ 9 Edgerrin James 1.00 .40
❑ 10 Marc Bulger 1.00 .40
❑ 11 Derrick Mason .60 .25
❑ 12 Mark Brunell .60 .25
❑ 13 Donte Stallworth .60 .25
❑ 14 Deion Branch 1.00 .40
❑ 15 Jake Plummer .60 .25
❑ 16 Steve Smith 1.00 .40
❑ 17 Jon Kitna .60 .25
❑ 18 Andre Johnson 1.00 .40
❑ 19 A.J. Feeley 1.00 .40
❑ 20 Drew Bledsoe 1.00 .40
❑ 21 Antonio Bryant .60 .25
❑ 22 Reggie Wayne .60 .25
❑ 23 Thomas Jones .60 .25
❑ 24 Alge Crumpler .60 .25
❑ 25 Anquan Boldin 1.00 .40
❑ 26 Tim Rattay .40 .15
❑ 27 Charlie Garner .60 .25
❑ 28 James Thrash .40 .15
❑ 29 Koren Robinson .60 .25
❑ 30 Terrell Owens 1.00 .40
❑ 31 Amani Toomer .60 .25
❑ 32 Kelly Campbell .40 .15
❑ 33 Patrick Ramsey .60 .25
❑ 34 Plaxico Burress .60 .25
❑ 35 Chad Pennington 1.00 .40
❑ 36 Fred Taylor .60 .25
❑ 37 Domanick Davis 1.00 .40
❑ 38 DeShaun Foster .60 .25
❑ 39 T.J. Duckett .60 .25
❑ 40 Ahman Green 1.00 .40
❑ 41 Lee Suggs 1.00 .40
❑ 42 Tony Gonzalez .60 .25
❑ 43 Rich Gannon .60 .25
❑ 44 Kevan Barlow .60 .25
❑ 45 Torry Holt 1.00 .40
❑ 46 Aaron Brooks .60 .25
❑ 47 Tyrone Calico .60 .25
❑ 48 Keenan McCardell .40 .15
❑ 49 Hines Ward 1.00 .40
❑ 50 LaDainian Tomlinson 1.25 .50
❑ 51 Dante Hall 1.00 .40
❑ 52 Marcus Pollard .40 .15
❑ 53 Corey Dillon .60 .25
❑ 54 Justin McCareins .40 .15
❑ 55 Stephen Davis .60 .25
❑ 56 Jeff Garcia 1.00 .40
❑ 57 Ashley Lelie .60 .25
❑ 58 Javon Walker .60 .25
❑ 59 Kyle Boller 1.00 .40
❑ 60 Chad Johnson 1.00 .40
❑ 61 Anthony Thomas .60 .25
❑ 62 Byron Leftwich 1.25 .50
❑ 63 David Boston .60 .25
❑ 64 Onterrio Smith .60 .25
❑ 65 Deuce McAllister 1.00 .40
❑ 66 Antwaan Randle El 1.00 .40
❑ 67 Justin Fargas .60 .25
❑ 68 Laveranues Coles .60 .25
❑ 69 Quincy Morgan .60 .25
❑ 70 Priest Holmes 1.25 .50
❑ 71 Robert Ferguson .40 .15
❑ 72 Charles Rogers .60 .25
❑ 73 Drew Brees 1.00 .40
❑ 74 Matt Hasselbeck .60 .25
❑ 75 Peyton Manning 1.50 .60
❑ 76 Rudi Johnson .60 .25
❑ 77 Jake Delhomme 1.00 .40
❑ 78 Tiki Barber 1.00 .40
❑ 79 Brad Johnson .60 .25
❑ 80 Steve McNair 1.00 .40
❑ 81 Willis McGahee 1.00 .40
❑ 82 Josh McCown .60 .25
❑ 83 Garrison Hearst .60 .25
❑ 84 Quincy Carter .60 .25
❑ 85 Ricky Williams 1.00 .40
❑ 86 Trent Green .60 .25
❑ 87 Curtis Martin 1.00 .40
❑ 88 Jerry Porter .60 .25
❑ 89 Brian Westbrook .60 .25
❑ 90 Clinton Portis 1.00 .40
❑ 91 Eric Moulds .60 .25
❑ 92 Marcel Shipp .60 .25
❑ 93 Joey Harrington 1.00 .40
❑ 94 David Carr 1.00 .40
❑ 95 Marvin Harrison 1.00 .40
❑ 96 Joe Horn .60 .25
❑ 97 Chris Chambers .60 .25
❑ 98 Darrell Jackson .60 .25
❑ 99 Eddie George .60 .25
❑ 100 Donovan McNabb 1.25 .50
❑ 101 Marshall Faulk 1.00 .40
❑ 102 Rex Grossman 1.00 .40
❑ 103 Tai Streets .40 .15
❑ 104 Jeremy Shockey 1.00 .40
❑ 105 Jamal Lewis 1.00 .40
❑ 106 Tom Brady 2.50 1.00
❑ 107 Shaun Alexander 1.00 .40
❑ 108 Carson Palmer 1.25 .50
❑ 109 Daunte Culpepper 1.00 .40
❑ 110 Michael Vick 2.00 .75
❑ 111 Roethlis AU/199 RC 450.00 300.00
❑ 112 Tommie Harris RC 4.00 1.50
❑ 113 Thomas Tapeh RC 3.00 1.25
❑ 114 Matt Schaub RC 6.00 2.50
❑ 115 Jonathan Smith RC 3.00 1.25
❑ 116 Ricardo Colclough RC 4.00 1.50
❑ 117 Jeff Dugan RC 2.00 .75
❑ 118 Larry Fitzgerald RC 12.00 5.00
❑ 119 Gibril Wilson RC 4.00 1.50
❑ 120 Sean Taylor RC 5.00 2.00
❑ 121 Marquise Hill RC 3.00 1.25
❑ 122 Cedric Cobbs RC 4.00 1.50
❑ 123 Rich Gardner RC 3.00 1.25
❑ 124 Chris Cooley RC 4.00 1.50
❑ 125 Ben Troupe RC 4.00 1.50
❑ 126 Antwan Odom RC 4.00 1.50
❑ 127 Stuart Schweigert RC 4.00 1.50
❑ 128 Derek Abney RC 4.00 1.50
❑ 129 Keary Colbert RC 5.00 2.00
❑ 130 Jeris McIntyre RC 3.00 1.25
❑ 131 Matt Kranchick RC 4.00 1.50
❑ 132 Rodney Leisle RC 2.00 .75
❑ 133 Vince Wilfork RC 5.00 2.00
❑ 134 Darnell Dockett RC 3.00 1.25
❑ 135 Jeremy LeSueur RC 3.00 1.25
❑ 136 Gilbert Gardner RC 3.00 1.25
❑ 137 Amon Gordon RC 2.00 .75
❑ 138 Darius Watts RC 4.00 1.50
❑ 139 Junior Siavii RC 4.00 1.50
❑ 140 Igor Olshansky RC 4.00 1.50
❑ 141 Mewelde Moore RC 5.00 2.00
❑ 142 Nathan Vasher RC 5.00 2.00
❑ 143 Randy Starks RC 3.00 1.25
❑ 144 Isaac Sopoaga RC 2.00 .75
❑ 145 Drew Henson RC 4.00 1.50
❑ 146 Erik Coleman RC 4.00 1.50
❑ 147 Robert Kent RC 2.00 .75
❑ 148 Jammal Lord RC 4.00 1.50
❑ 149 Richard Seigler RC 3.00 1.25
❑ 150 Niko Koutouvides RC 3.00 1.25
❑ 151 Brandon Miree RC 3.00 1.25
❑ 152 Dunta Robinson RC 4.00 1.50
❑ 153 Courtney Anderson RC 3.00 1.25
❑ 154 Bruce Perry RC 4.00 1.50
❑ 155 Shaun Phillips RC 3.00 1.25
❑ 156 Greg Jones RC 4.00 1.50
❑ 157 Tank Johnson RC 3.00 1.25
❑ 158 Dwan Edwards RC 2.00 .75
❑ 159 Julius Jones RC 15.00 6.00
❑ 160 Chad Lavalais RC 3.00 1.25
❑ 161 Tim Anderson RC 4.00 1.50
❑ 162 Jarrett Payton RC 5.00 2.00
❑ 163 Matt Ware RC 4.00 1.50
❑ 164 DeAngelo Hall RC 5.00 2.00
❑ 165 Ben Hartsock RC 4.00 1.50
❑ 166 Keith Smith RC 3.00 1.25
❑ 167 Michael Jenkins RC 4.00 1.50
❑ 168 Quincy Wilson RC 3.00 1.25
❑ 169 Dontarrious Thomas RC 4.00 1.50
❑ 170 Tony Hargrove RC 3.00 1.25
❑ 171 Ben Watson RC 4.00 1.50
❑ 172 Triandos Luke RC 4.00 1.50
❑ 173 Kellen Winslow RC 8.00 3.00
❑ 174 Patrick Crayton RC 4.00 1.50

❑ 175 Devard Darling RC 4.00 1.50
❑ 176 Shawntae Spencer RC 4.00 1.50
❑ 177 Will Smith RC 4.00 1.50
❑ 178 Darrion Scott RC 4.00 1.50
❑ 179 Wes Welker RC 4.00 1.50
❑ 180 Ryan Dinwiddie RC 3.00 1.25
❑ 181 Rod Davis RC 2.00 .75
❑ 182 Casey Clausen RC 4.00 1.50
❑ 183 Clarence Moore RC 4.00 1.50
❑ 184 D.J. Hackett RC 3.00 1.25
❑ 185 Devery Henderson RC 3.00 1.25
❑ 186 Sean Jones RC 3.00 1.25
❑ 187 Bruce Thornton RC 2.00 .75
❑ 188 Tatum Bell RC 8.00 3.00
❑ 189 Tim Euhus RC 4.00 1.50
❑ 190 John Standeford RC 3.00 1.25
❑ 191 Reggie Torbor RC 3.00 1.25
❑ 192 Rashaun Woods RC 4.00 1.50
❑ 193 Jason Shivers RC 2.00 .75
❑ 194 Ahmad Carroll RC 5.00 2.00
❑ 195 Keyaron Fox RC 3.00 1.25
❑ 196 Von Hutchins RC 3.00 1.25
❑ 197 Marcus Tubbs RC 4.00 1.50
❑ 198 Daryl Smith RC 4.00 1.50
❑ 199 Robert Gallery RC 6.00 2.50
❑ 200 Marquis Cooper RC 3.00 1.25
❑ 201 Bernard Berrian RC 4.00 1.50
❑ 202 Derrick Strait RC 4.00 1.50
❑ 203 Travis LaBoy RC 4.00 1.50
❑ 204 Caleb Miller RC 3.00 1.25
❑ 205 Michael Clayton RC 8.00 3.00
❑ 206 Will Poole RC 4.00 1.50
❑ 207 Derrick Hamilton RC 3.00 1.25
❑ 208 Glenn Earl RC 3.00 1.25
❑ 209 Donnell Washington RC 4.00 1.50
❑ 210 Nate Lawrie RC 3.00 1.25
❑ 211 Keiwan Ratliff RC 3.00 1.25
❑ 212 Luke McCown RC 4.00 1.50
❑ 213 Joey Thomas RC 4.00 1.50
❑ 214 Shawn Andrews RC 4.00 1.50
❑ 215 Derrick Ward RC 2.00 .75
❑ 216 Reggie Williams RC 5.00 2.00
❑ 217 Rod Rutherford RC 3.00 1.25
❑ 218 Michael Gaines RC 3.00 1.25
❑ 219 Will Allen RC 4.00 1.50
❑ 220 J.P. Losman RC 8.00 3.00
❑ 221 Roy Williams AU/199 RC 120.0060.00
❑ 222 Kevin Jones AU/199 RC 175.00 90.00
❑ 223 Philip Rivers AU/199 RC 225.00150.00
❑ 224 Steven Jackson AU/199 RC 200.00 100.00
❑ 225 Eli Manning AU/199 RC 300.00 175.00
❑ 226 Cody Pickett AU D RC 20.00 7.50
❑ 227 P.K. Sam AU D RC 15.00 6.00
❑ 228 Maurice Mann AU D RC 15.00 6.00
❑ 229 Andy Hall AU D RC 15.00 6.00
❑ 230 Chris Perry AU D RC 25.00 10.00
❑ 231 Ernest Wilford AU C RC 20.00 7.50
❑ 232 Kenechi Udeze AU D RC 20.00 7.50
❑ 233 Michael Boulware AU D RC 20.007.50
❑ 234 B.J. Symons AU D RC 20.00 7.50
❑ 235 Jared Lorenzen AU D RC 15.00 6.00
❑ 236 Matt Mauck AU D RC 20.00 7.50
❑ 237 Carlos Francis AU D RC 15.00 6.00
❑ 238 Michael Turner AU D RC 25.00 12.50
❑ 239 Lee Evans AU B RC 40.00 20.00
❑ 240 Jerricho Cotchery AU D RC 20.007.50
❑ 241 John Navarre AU D RC 20.00 7.50
❑ 242 Jonathan Vilma AU D RC 25.00 10.00
❑ 243 Josh Harris AU D RC 20.00 7.50
❑ 244 Jeff Smoker AU C RC 20.00 7.50
❑ 245 Jamaar Taylor AU D RC 20.00 7.50

2004 Bowman Chrome Super Bowl XXXIX Unsigned Draft Picks

❑ COMPLETE SET (26) 200.00 75.00
❑ 111 Ben Roethlisberger 80.00 40.00
❑ 221 Roy Williams WR 25.00 10.00
❑ 222 Kevin Jones 30.00 12.50

❑ 223 Philip Rivers 30.00 12.50
❑ 224 Steven Jackson 30.00 12.50
❑ 225 Eli Manning 50.00 20.00
❑ 226 Cody Pickett 10.00 4.00
❑ 227 P.K. Sam 8.00 3.00
❑ 228 Maurice Mann 8.00 3.00
❑ 229 Andy Hall 8.00 3.00
❑ 230 Chris Perry 15.00 6.00
❑ 231 Ernest Wilford 10.00 4.00
❑ 232 Kenechi Udeze 10.00 4.00
❑ 233 Michael Boulware 10.00 4.00
❑ 234 B.J. Symons 10.00 4.00
❑ 235 Jared Lorenzen 8.00 3.00
❑ 236 Matt Mauck 10.00 4.00
❑ 237 Carlos Francis 8.00 3.00
❑ 238 Michael Turner 10.00 4.00
❑ 239 Lee Evans 12.00 5.00
❑ 240 Jerricho Cotchery 10.00 4.00
❑ 241 John Navarre 10.00 4.00
❑ 242 Jonathan Vilma 10.00 4.00
❑ 243 Josh Harris 10.00 4.00
❑ 244 Jeff Smoker 10.00 4.00
❑ 245 Jamaar Taylor 10.00 4.00

2005 Bowman Chrome

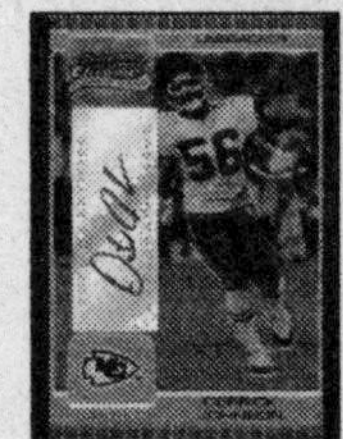

❑ COMP.SET w/o AU's (220) 100.00 40.00
❑ COMP.SET w/o RC's (110) 30.00 12.50
❑ ROOK.AU GROUP A ODDS 1:381 H, 1:1011 R
❑ ROOK.AU GROUP B ODDS 1:156 H, 1:449 R
❑ ROOK.AU GROUP C ODDS 1:318 H, 1:899 R
❑ ROOK.AU GROUP D ODDS 1:296 H, 1:899 R
❑ ROOK.AU GROUP E ODDS 1:281 H, 1:809 R
❑ ROOK.AU GROUP F ODDS 1:132 H, 404 R
❑ ROOK.AU GROUP G ODDS 1:39 H, 1:108 R
❑ ROOKIE AU/199 ODDS 1:685 H, 1:1348 R
❑ UNPRICED PRINT.PLATE 1/1 ODDS 1:975 H
❑ 1 Peyton Manning 1.50 .60
❑ 2 Priest Holmes 1.00 .40
❑ 3 Anquan Boldin .60 .25
❑ 4 Michael Vick 1.50 .60
❑ 5 Drew Brees 1.00 .40
❑ 6 Terrell Owens 1.00 .40
❑ 7 Curtis Martin 1.00 .40
❑ 8 Tom Brady 2.50 1.00
❑ 9 Maurice Carthon CO .60 .25
❑ 10 Brett Favre 2.50 1.00
❑ 11 Marshall Faulk 1.00 .40
❑ 12 Corey Dillon .60 .25
❑ 13 Julius Jones 1.25 .50
❑ 14 Jamal Lewis 1.00 .40
❑ 15 Keary Colbert .60 .25
❑ 16 Joey Harrington 1.00 .40
❑ 17 Domanick Davis .60 .25
❑ 18 Eli Manning 2.00 .75
❑ 19 Brad Childress CO .60 .25
❑ 20 Steve McNair 1.00 .40
❑ 21 Plaxico Burress .60 .25
❑ 22 Chad Pennington 1.00 .40
❑ 23 Patrick Ramsey .60 .25
❑ 24 Brian Griese .60 .25
❑ 25 Matt Hasselbeck .60 .25
❑ 26 Chris Chambers .60 .25
❑ 27 Marc Bulger 1.00 .40
❑ 28 Jake Delhomme 1.00 .40
❑ 29 Shaun Alexander 1.25 .50
❑ 30 Laveranues Coles .60 .25
❑ 31 A.J. Feeley .60 .25
❑ 32 Ashley Lelie .60 .25
❑ 33 Deuce McAllister 1.00 .40
❑ 34 Chris Brown .60 .25
❑ 35 Nate Burleson .60 .25
❑ 36 Darrell Jackson .60 .25
❑ 37 Lee Evans .60 .25
❑ 38 Jeremy Shockey 1.00 .40
❑ 39 Muhsin Muhammad .60 .25
❑ 40 Deion Branch .60 .25
❑ 41 DeShaun Foster .60 .25
❑ 42 Reggie Wayne .60 .25
❑ 43 Michael Jenkins .60 .25
❑ 44 Andre Johnson .60 .25
❑ 45 Javon Walker .60 .25
❑ 46 Joe Horn .60 .25
❑ 47 Fred Taylor .60 .25
❑ 48 Tony Gonzalez .60 .25
❑ 49 J.P. Losman 1.00 .40
❑ 50 Clinton Portis 1.00 .40
❑ 51 Randy Moss 1.00 .40
❑ 52 Jake Plummer .60 .25
❑ 53 Tiki Barber 1.00 .40
❑ 54 Edgerrin James 1.00 .40
❑ 55 Jerome Bettis 1.00 .40
❑ 56 Brandon Lloyd .50 .20
❑ 57 Romeo Crennel CO 1.00 .40
❑ 58 Antonio Gates 1.00 .40
❑ 59 Donovan McNabb 1.25 .50
❑ 60 Drew Bennett .60 .25
❑ 61 David Carr 1.00 .40
❑ 62 Trent Green .60 .25
❑ 63 Drew Bledsoe 1.00 .40
❑ 64 Donte Stallworth .60 .25
❑ 65 Alge Crumpler .60 .25
❑ 66 Jason Witten .60 .25
❑ 67 Thomas Jones .60 .25
❑ 68 Rex Grossman .60 .25
❑ 69 LaMont Jordan 1.00 .40
❑ 70 Kurt Warner .60 .25
❑ 71 Ahman Green 1.00 .40
❑ 72 Ben Roethlisberger 2.50 1.00
❑ 73 Mike Nolan CO 1.00 .40
❑ 74 Brian Westbrook .60 .25
❑ 75 Carson Palmer 1.00 .40
❑ 76 Stephen Davis .60 .25
❑ 77 Jonathan Vilma .60 .25
❑ 78 Willis McGahee 1.00 .40
❑ 79 Rudi Johnson .60 .25
❑ 80 Jerry Porter .60 .25
❑ 81 Charles Rogers .60 .25
❑ 82 Dwight Freeney .60 .25
❑ 83 Tim Lewis CO .50 .20
❑ 84 Aaron Brooks .60 .25
❑ 85 Kyle Boller .60 .25
❑ 86 Isaac Bruce .60 .25
❑ 87 Chad Johnson 1.00 .40
❑ 88 Kevin Jones 1.00 .40
❑ 89 Eric Moulds .60 .25
❑ 90 Sean Taylor .60 .25
❑ 91 Chris Perry .60 .25
❑ 92 Kerry Collins .60 .25
❑ 93 Steven Jackson 1.25 .50

❑ 94 LaDainian Tomlinson 1.25 .50
❑ 95 Torry Holt 1.00 .40
❑ 96 Lee Suggs .60 .25
❑ 97 Santana Moss .60 .25
❑ 98 Hines Ward 1.00 .40
❑ 99 Daunte Culpepper 1.00 .40
❑ 100 Travis Henry .60 .25
❑ 101 Ricky Williams .60 .25
❑ 102 Roy Williams WR 1.00 .40
❑ 103 Tatum Bell .60 .25
❑ 104 Dante Hall .60 .25
❑ 105 Larry Fitzgerald 1.00 .40
❑ 106 Marvin Harrison 1.00 .40
❑ 107 Byron Leftwich 1.00 .40
❑ 108 T.J. Houshmandzadeh .50 .20
❑ 109 Michael Clayton 1.00 .40
❑ 110 Ted Cottrell CO .50 .20
❑ 111 Carlos Rogers RC 5.00 2.00
❑ 112 Kyle Orton RC 6.00 2.50
❑ 113 Marion Barber RC 6.00 2.50
❑ 114 Mark Bradley RC 4.00 1.50
❑ 115 Travis Johnson RC 3.00 1.25
❑ 116 Antrel Rolle RC 4.00 1.50
❑ 117 Jason Campbell RC 6.00 2.50
❑ 118 Justin Miller RC 3.00 1.25
❑ 119 J.J. Arrington RC 5.00 2.00
❑ 120 Marcus Spears RC 4.00 1.50
❑ 121 Vincent Jackson RC 4.00 1.50
❑ 122 Erasmus James RC 4.00 1.50
❑ 123 Heath Miller RC 10.00 4.00
❑ 124 Eric Shelton RC 4.00 1.50
❑ 125 Cedric Benson RC 8.00 3.00
❑ 126 Mark Clayton RC 5.00 2.00
❑ 127 Anthony Davis RC 3.00 1.25
❑ 128 Charlie Frye RC 8.00 3.00
❑ 129 Fred Gibson RC 3.00 1.25
❑ 130 Reggie Brown RC 4.00 1.50
❑ 131 Andrew Walter RC 6.00 2.50
❑ 132 Adam Jones RC 4.00 1.50
❑ 133 David Greene RC 4.00 1.50
❑ 134 Maurice Clarett 4.00 1.50
❑ 135 Roscoe Parrish RC 4.00 1.50
❑ 136 Chris Henry RC 4.00 1.50
❑ 137 Mike Nugent RC 4.00 1.50
❑ 138 Kevin Burnett RC 4.00 1.50
❑ 139 Matt Roth RC 4.00 1.50
❑ 140 Barrett Ruud RC 4.00 1.50
❑ 141 Kirk Morrison RC 4.00 1.50
❑ 142 Brock Berlin RC 3.00 1.25
❑ 143 Bryant McFadden RC 4.00 1.50
❑ 144 Scott Starks RC 3.00 1.25
❑ 145 Stanford Routt RC 3.00 1.25
❑ 146 Oshiomogho Atogwe RC 3.00 1.25
❑ 147 Jovan Witherspoon RC 2.00 .75
❑ 148 Boomer Grigsby RC 5.00 2.00
❑ 149 Lance Mitchell RC 3.00 1.25
❑ 150 Darryl Blackstock RC 3.00 1.25
❑ 151 Ellis Hobbs RC 4.00 1.50
❑ 152 James Kilian RC 4.00 1.50
❑ 153 Willie Parker 10.00 4.00
❑ 154 Justin Tuck RC 4.00 1.50
❑ 155 Luis Castillo RC 4.00 1.50
❑ 156 Paris Warren RC 3.00 1.25
❑ 157 Corey Webster RC 4.00 1.50
❑ 158 Tab Perry RC 4.00 1.50
❑ 159 Rian Wallace RC 3.00 1.25
❑ 160 Joel Dreessen RC 3.00 1.25
❑ 161 Khalif Barnes RC 3.00 1.25
❑ 162 David Pollack RC 4.00 1.50
❑ 163 Zach Tuiasosopo RC 2.00 .75
❑ 164 Ryan Riddle RC 2.00 .75
❑ 165 Travis Daniels RC 3.00 1.25
❑ 166 Eric King RC 3.00 1.25
❑ 167 Justin Green RC 4.00 1.50
❑ 168 Manuel White RC 3.00 1.25
❑ 169 Jordan Beck RC 3.00 1.25
❑ 170 Lofa Tatupu RC 5.00 2.00
❑ 171 Will Peoples RC 3.00 1.25
❑ 172 Chad Friehauf RC 3.00 1.25
❑ 173 Brady Poppinga RC 4.00 1.50
❑ 174 Anttaj Hawthorne RC 3.00 1.25
❑ 175 Nick Collins RC 4.00 1.50
❑ 176 Craig Ochs RC 3.00 1.25
❑ 177 Billy Bajema RC 3.00 1.25
❑ 178 Jon Goldsberry RC 4.00 1.50
❑ 179 Jared Newberry RC 3.00 1.25
❑ 180 Odell Thurman RC 4.00 1.50
❑ 181 Kelvin Hayden RC 3.00 1.25
❑ 182 Jamaal Brimmer RC 2.00 .75
❑ 183 Jonathan Babineaux RC 3.00 1.25
❑ 184 Bo Scaife RC 3.00 1.25
❑ 185 Bryan Randall RC 3.00 1.25
❑ 186 James Butler RC 3.00 1.25
❑ 187 Harry Williams RC 3.00 1.25
❑ 188 Leroy Hill RC 4.00 1.50
❑ 189 Josh Bullocks RC 4.00 1.50
❑ 190 Alfred Fincher RC 3.00 1.25
❑ 191 Antonio Perkins RC 3.00 1.25
❑ 192 Bobby Purify RC 3.00 1.25
❑ 193 Darrent Williams RC 4.00 1.50
❑ 194 Darian Durant RC 4.00 1.50
❑ 195 Fred Amey RC 3.00 1.25
❑ 196 Ronald Bartell RC 3.00 1.25
❑ 197 Kerry Rhodes RC 4.00 1.50
❑ 198 Jerome Carter RC 3.00 1.25
❑ 199 Roddy White RC 4.00 1.50
❑ 200 Nehemiah Broughton RC 3.00 1.25
❑ 201 Keron Henry RC 2.00 .75
❑ 202 Jerome Collins RC 3.00 1.25
❑ 203 Trent Cole RC 4.00 1.50
❑ 204 Alphonso Hodge RC 2.00 .75
❑ 205 Marviel Underwood RC 3.00 1.25
❑ 206 Marlin Jackson RC 4.00 1.50
❑ 207 Madison Hedgecock RC 4.00 1.50
❑ 208 Chris Spencer RC 4.00 1.50
❑ 209 Vincent Fuller RC 3.00 1.25
❑ 210 Marcus Maxwell RC 3.00 1.25
❑ 211 Dustin Fox RC 4.00 1.50
❑ 212 Timmy Chang RC 3.00 1.25
❑ 213 Walter Reyes RC 3.00 1.25
❑ 214 Donte Nicholson RC 4.00 1.50
❑ 215 Stanley Wilson RC 3.00 1.25
❑ 216 Dan Cody RC 4.00 1.50
❑ 217 Alex Barron RC 2.00 .75
❑ 218 Taylor Stubblefield RC 2.00 .75
❑ 219 Shaun Cody RC 4.00 1.50
❑ 220 Steve Savoy RC 2.00 .75
❑ 221 Aaron Rodgers AU/199 RC 200.00 125.00
❑ 222 Alex Smith QB AU/199 RC 200.00 125.00
❑ 223 Braylon Edwards AU/199 RC 175.00 100.00
❑ 224 Carnell Williams AU/199 RC 250.00 150.00
❑ 225 Mike Williams AU/199 150.00 75.00
❑ 226 Ronnie Brown AU/199 RC 200.00 125.00
❑ 227 Troy Williamson AU/199 RC 100.00 60.00
❑ 228 Dante Ridgeway AU B RC 12.00 5.00
❑ 229 Channing Crowder AU G RC 15.00 6.00
❑ 230 Chase Lyman AU E RC 12.00 5.00
❑ 231 Courtney Roby AU F RC 15.00 6.00
❑ 232 Damien Nash AU G RC 12.00 5.00
❑ 233 Dan Orlovsky AU C RC 20.00 10.00
❑ 234 Fabian Washington AU B RC 20.00 7.50
❑ 235 Shawne Merriman AU B RC 30.00 15.00
❑ 236 Cedric Houston AU G RC 15.00 7.50
❑ 237 Alex Smith TE AU D RC 15.00 6.00
❑ 238 Brandon Jones AU B RC 15.00 6.00
❑ 239 Alvin Pearman AU G RC 15.00 6.00
❑ 240 Derek Anderson AU C RC 15.00 6.00
❑ 241 J.R. Russell AU G RC 12.00 5.00
❑ 242 Jerome Mathis AU F RC 12.00 5.00
❑ 243 Josh Davis AU A RC 15.00 6.00
❑ 244 Kay-Jay Harris AU G RC 12.00 5.00
❑ 245 Rasheed Marshall AU F RC 12.005.00
❑ 246 Matt Jones AU/199 RC 135.00 75.00
❑ 247 Chad Owens AU G RC 15.00 6.00
❑ 248 Larry Brackins AU A RC 15.00 6.00
❑ 249 Matt Cassel AU G RC 25.00 10.00
❑ 250 Noah Herron AU G RC 15.00 6.00
❑ 251 Roydell Williams AU G RC 15.00 6.00
❑ 252 Ryan Fitzpatrick AU F RC 25.00 10.00
❑ 253 Derrick Johnson AU E RC 25.00 10.00
❑ 254 DeMarcus Ware AU D RC 25.00 10.00
❑ 255 Brandon Jacobs AU A RC 30.00 15.00
❑ 256 Craig Bragg AU G RC 12.00 5.00
❑ 257 Ryan Moats AU G RC 25.00 12.50
❑ 258 Stefan LeFors AU G RC 15.00 6.00
❑ 259 Frank Gore AU B RC 30.00 15.00
❑ DSB Bogut/A.Smith QB AU/100 200.00 150.00

2000 Bowman Reserve

❑ COMP.SET w/o SP's (100) 40.00 15.00
❑ 1 Chad Pennington RC 40.00 15.00
❑ 2 Shaun Alexander RC 50.00 25.00
❑ 3 Thomas Jones RC 25.00 10.00
❑ 4 Courtney Brown RC 15.00 6.00
❑ 5 Curtis Keaton RC 12.00 5.00
❑ 6 Jerry Porter RC 20.00 7.50
❑ 7 Jamal Lewis RC 40.00 15.00
❑ 8 Ron Dayne RC 15.00 6.00
❑ 9 R.Jay Soward RC 12.00 5.00
❑ 10 Tee Martin RC 15.00 6.00
❑ 11 Travis Taylor RC 15.00 6.00
❑ 12 Plaxico Burress RC 30.00 12.50
❑ 13 Giovanni Carmazzi RC 12.00 5.00
❑ 14 Sylvester Morris RC 12.00 5.00
❑ 15 Chris Redman RC 12.00 5.00
❑ 16 Trung Canidate RC 12.00 5.00
❑ 17 J.R. Redmond RC 12.00 5.00
❑ 18 Bubba Franks RC 15.00 6.00
❑ 19 Travis Prentice RC 12.00 5.00
❑ 20 Peter Warrick RC 15.00 6.00
❑ 21 Frank Sanders .75 .30
❑ 22 Edgerrin James 2.00 .75
❑ 23 Marcus Robinson 1.25 .50
❑ 24 Mike Alstott 1.25 .50
❑ 25 Jerry Rice 2.50 1.00
❑ 26 Marshall Faulk 1.50 .60
❑ 27 Brad Johnson 1.25 .50
❑ 28 Elvis Grbac .75 .30
❑ 29 Wayne Chrebet .75 .30
❑ 30 Akili Smith .50 .20
❑ 31 Rob Johnson .75 .30
❑ 32 Brett Favre 4.00 1.50
❑ 33 Ricky Williams 1.25 .50
❑ 34 Donovan McNabb 2.00 .75
❑ 35 Cris Carter 1.25 .50
❑ 36 Ricky Watters .75 .30
❑ 37 Steve McNair 2.00 .75
❑ 38 Stephen Davis 1.25 .50
❑ 39 Fred Taylor 1.25 .50
❑ 40 Rocket Ismail .75 .30
❑ 41 Terry Glenn .75 .30
❑ 42 Ed McCaffrey 1.25 .50
❑ 43 Patrick Jeffers 1.25 .50
❑ 44 Jake Plummer .75 .30
❑ 45 Doug Flutie 1.25 .50
❑ 46 Terrell Davis 1.25 .50
❑ 47 Marvin Harrison 1.25 .50
❑ 48 Amani Toomer .75 .30
❑ 49 Tyrone Wheatley .75 .30
❑ 50 Charlie Garner .75 .30
❑ 51 Jevon Kearse 1.25 .50
❑ 52 Michael Westbrook .75 .30
❑ 53 Eddie George 1.25 .50

❑ 54 Robert Smith 1.25 .50
❑ 55 Keyshawn Johnson 1.25 .50
❑ 56 Torry Holt 1.25 .50
❑ 57 Jon Kitna 1.25 .50
❑ 58 Curtis Conway .75 .30
❑ 59 Jeff Garcia 1.25 .50
❑ 60 Randy Moss 2.50 1.00
❑ 61 Jimmy Smith .75 .30
❑ 62 James Stewart .75 .30
❑ 63 Troy Aikman 2.50 1.00
❑ 64 Cade McNown .50 .20
❑ 65 Natrone Means .75 .30
❑ 66 Jamal Anderson 1.25 .50
❑ 67 Warrick Dunn 1.25 .50
❑ 68 Kordell Stewart .75 .30
❑ 69 Duce Staley 1.25 .50
❑ 70 Rich Gannon 1.25 .50
❑ 71 Curtis Martin 1.25 .50
❑ 72 Kerry Collins .75 .30
❑ 73 Jeff Blake .75 .30
❑ 74 Drew Bledsoe 1.50 .60
❑ 75 Kevin Dyson .75 .30
❑ 76 Tony Gonzalez .75 .30
❑ 77 Mark Brunell 1.25 .50
❑ 78 Peyton Manning 3.00 1.25
❑ 79 Dorsey Levens .75 .30
❑ 80 Germane Crowell .50 .20
❑ 81 Brian Griese 1.25 .50
❑ 82 Steve Beuerlein .75 .30
❑ 83 Eric Moulds 1.25 .50
❑ 84 Tony Banks .75 .30
❑ 85 Chris Chandler .75 .30
❑ 86 Isaac Bruce 1.25 .50
❑ 87 Terrell Owens 1.25 .50
❑ 88 Jerome Bettis 1.25 .50
❑ 89 Daunte Culpepper 1.50 .60
❑ 90 Emmitt Smith 2.50 1.00
❑ 91 Curtis Enis .50 .20
❑ 92 Shaun King .50 .20
❑ 93 Tim Brown 1.25 .50
❑ 94 Antonio Freeman 1.25 .50
❑ 95 Charlie Batch 1.25 .50
❑ 96 Tim Couch .75 .30
❑ 97 Corey Dillon 1.25 .50
❑ 98 Muhsin Muhammad .75 .30
❑ 99 Joey Galloway .75 .30
❑ 100 Kurt Warner 2.50 1.00
❑ 101 David Boston 1.25 .50
❑ 102 Rod Smith .50 .20
❑ 103 Derrick Mayes .75 .30
❑ 104 Tony Martin .75 .30
❑ 105 Darnay Scott .75 .30
❑ 106 Joe Horn .75 .30
❑ 107 Troy Edwards .50 .20
❑ 108 James Johnson .50 .20
❑ 109 Vinny Testaverde .75 .30
❑ 110 Qadry Ismail .75 .30
❑ 111 Andre Reed .75 .30
❑ 112 Zach Thomas 1.25 .50
❑ 113 Ike Hilliard .75 .30
❑ 114 Herman Moore .75 .30
❑ 115 Kevin Johnson 1.25 .50
❑ 116 Shawn Jefferson .50 .20
❑ 117 Terance Mathis .75 .30
❑ 118 Peerless Price .75 .30
❑ 119 Bert Emanuel .50 .20
❑ 120 Terrence Wilkins .50 .20
❑ 121 Mike Anderson RC 20.00 7.50
❑ 122 Dez White RC 15.00 6.00
❑ 123 Todd Pinkston RC 15.00 6.00
❑ 124 Reuben Droughns RC 20.00 7.50
❑ 125 Danny Farmer RC 12.00 5.00

1995 Bowman's Best

❑ COMPLETE SET (180) 100.00 40.00
❑ R1 Ki-Jana Carter RC 1.50 .60
❑ R2 Tony Boselli RC 1.50 .60
❑ R3 Steve McNair RC 15.00 6.00
❑ R4 Michael Westbrook RC 1.50 .60
❑ R5 Kerry Collins RC 6.00 2.50
❑ R6 Kevin Carter RC 1.50 .60
❑ R7 Mike Mamula RC .40 .15
❑ R8 Joey Galloway RC 6.00 2.50
❑ R9 Kyle Brady RC 1.50 .60
❑ R10 Ray McElroy RC .40 .15
❑ R11 Derrick Alexander DE RC .40 .15
❑ R12 Warren Sapp RC 6.00 2.50
❑ R13 Mark Fields RC 1.50 .60
❑ R14 Ruben Brown RC 1.50 .60
❑ R15 Ellis Johnson RC .40 .15
❑ R16 Hugh Douglas RC 1.50 .60
❑ R17 Alundis Brice RC .40 .15
❑ R18 Napoleon Kaufman RC 5.00 2.00
❑ R19 James O. Stewart RC 3.00 1.25
❑ R20 Luther Elliss RC .40 .15
❑ R21 Rashaan Salaam RC .75 .30
❑ R22 Tyrone Poole RC 1.50 .60
❑ R23 Ty Law RC 4.00 1.50
❑ R24 Korey Stringer RC .75 .30
❑ R25 Billy Milner RC .40 .15
❑ R26 Roell Preston RC .75 .30
❑ R27 Mark Bruener RC .75 .30
❑ R28 Derrick Brooks RC 6.00 2.50
❑ R29 Blake Brockermeyer RC .40 .15
❑ R30 Mike Frederick RC .40 .15
❑ R31 Trezelle Jenkins RC .40 .15
❑ R32 Craig Newsome RC .40 .15
❑ R33 Matt O'Dwyer RC .40 .15
❑ R34 Terrance Shaw RC .40 .15
❑ R35 Anthony Cook RC .40 .15
❑ R36 Darick Holmes RC .75 .30
❑ R37 Cory Raymer RC .40 .15
❑ R38 Zach Wiegert RC .40 .15
❑ R39 Sam Shade RC .40 .15
❑ R40 Brian DeMarco RC .40 .15
❑ R41 Ron Davis RC .40 .15
❑ R42 Orlando Thomas RC .40 .15
❑ R43 Derek West RC .40 .15
❑ R44 Ray Zellars RC .75 .30
❑ R45 Todd Collins RC .75 .30
❑ R46 Linc Harden RC .40 .15
❑ R47 Frank Sanders RC 1.50 .60
❑ R48 Ken Dilger RC 1.50 .60
❑ R49 Barrett Robbins RC .40 .15
❑ R50 Bobby Taylor RC 2.50 1.00
❑ R51 Terrell Fletcher RC .40 .15
❑ R52 Jack Jackson RC .40 .15
❑ R53 Jeff Kopp RC .40 .15
❑ R54 Brendan Stai RC .40 .15
❑ R55 Corey Fuller RC .40 .15
❑ R56 Todd Sauerbrun RC .40 .15
❑ R57 Dameian Jeffries RC .40 .15
❑ R58 Troy Dumas RC .40 .15
❑ R59 Charlie Williams RC .40 .15
❑ R60 Kordell Stewart RC 6.00 2.50
❑ R61 Jay Barker RC .40 .15
❑ R62 Jesse James RC .40 .15
❑ R63 Shane Hannah RC .40 .15
❑ R64 Rob Johnson RC 4.00 1.50
❑ R65 Darius Holland RC .40 .15
❑ R66 William Henderson RC 5.00 2.00
❑ R67 Chris Sanders RC .75 .30
❑ R68 Darryl Pounds RC .40 .15
❑ R69 Melvin Tuten RC .40 .15
❑ R70 David Sloan RC .40 .15
❑ R71 Chris Hudson RC .40 .15
❑ R72 William Strong RC .40 .15
❑ R73 Brian Williams LB RC .40 .15
❑ R74 Curtis Martin RC 15.00 6.00
❑ R75 Mike Verstegen RC .40 .15
❑ R76 Justin Armour RC .40 .15
❑ R77 Lorenzo Styles RC .40 .15
❑ R78 Oliver Gibson RC .40 .15
❑ R79 Zack Crockett RC .75 .30
❑ R80 Tau Pupua RC .40 .15
❑ R81 Tamarick Vanover RC 1.50 .60
❑ R82 Steve McLaughlin RC .40 .15
❑ R83 Sean Harris RC .40 .15
❑ R84 Eric Zeier RC 1.50 .60
❑ R85 Rodney Young RC .40 .15
❑ R86 Chad May RC .40 .15
❑ R87 Evan Pilgrim RC .40 .15
❑ R88 James A.Stewart RC .40 .15
❑ R89 Torey Hunter RC .40 .15
❑ R90 Antonio Freeman RC 4.00 1.50
❑ V1 Rob Moore .60 .25
❑ V2 Craig Heyward .60 .25
❑ V3 Jim Kelly 1.25 .50
❑ V4 John Kasay .30 .10
❑ V5 Jeff Graham .30 .10
❑ V6 Jeff Blake RC 2.50 1.00
❑ V7 Antonio Langham .30 .10
❑ V8 Troy Aikman 3.00 1.25
❑ V9 Simon Fletcher .30 .10
❑ V10 Barry Sanders 5.00 2.00
❑ V11 Edgar Bennett .60 .25
❑ V12 Ray Childress .30 .10
❑ V13 Ray Buchanan .30 .10
❑ V14 Desmond Howard .60 .25
❑ V15 Dale Carter .60 .25
❑ V16 Troy Vincent .30 .10
❑ V17 David Palmer .60 .25
❑ V18 Ben Coates .60 .25
❑ V19 Derek Brown TE .30 .10
❑ V20 Dave Brown .60 .25
❑ V21 Mo Lewis .30 .10
❑ V22 Harvey Williams .30 .10
❑ V23 Randall Cunningham 1.25 .50
❑ V24 Kevin Greene .60 .25
❑ V25 Junior Seau 1.25 .50
❑ V26 Merton Hanks .30 .10
❑ V27 Cortez Kennedy .60 .25
❑ V28 Troy Drayton .30 .10
❑ V29 Hardy Nickerson .30 .10
❑ V30 Brian Mitchell .30 .10
❑ V31 Raymont Harris .30 .10
❑ V32 Keith Goganious .30 .10
❑ V33 Andre Reed .60 .25
❑ V34 Terance Mathis .60 .25
❑ V35 Garrison Hearst 1.25 .50
❑ V36 Glyn Milburn .30 .10
❑ V37 Emmitt Smith 5.00 2.00
❑ V38 Vinny Testaverde .60 .25
❑ V39 Darnay Scott .60 .25
❑ V40 Mickey Washington .30 .10
❑ V41 Craig Erickson .30 .10
❑ V42 Chris Chandler 1.25 .50
❑ V43 Brett Favre 6.00 2.50
❑ V44 Scott Mitchell .60 .25
❑ V45 Chris Slade .30 .10
❑ V46 Warren Moon .60 .25
❑ V47 Dan Marino 6.00 2.50
❑ V48 Greg Hill .60 .25
❑ V49 Rocket Ismail .60 .25
❑ V50 Bobby Houston .30 .10
❑ V51 Rodney Hampton .60 .25
❑ V52 Jim Everett .30 .10
❑ V53 Rick Mirer .60 .25
❑ V54 Steve Young 2.50 1.00
❑ V55 Dennis Gibson .30 .10
❑ V56 Rod Woodson .60 .25
❑ V57 Calvin Williams .60 .25
❑ V58 Tom Carter .30 .10
❑ V59 Trent Dilfer 1.25 .50

❑ V60 Shane Conlan .30 .10
❑ V61 Cornelius Bennett .60 .25
❑ V62 Eric Metcalf .60 .25
❑ V63 Frank Reich .30 .10
❑ V64 Eric Hill .30 .10
❑ V65 Erik Kramer .30 .10
❑ V66 Michael Irvin 1.25 .50
❑ V67 Tony McGee .30 .10
❑ V68 Andre Rison .60 .25
❑ V69 Shannon Sharpe .60 .25
❑ V70 Quentin Coryatt .60 .25
❑ V71 Robert Brooks 1.25 .50
❑ V72 Steve Beuerlein .60 .25
❑ V73 Herman Moore 1.25 .50
❑ V74 Jack Del Rio .30 .10
❑ V75 Dave Meggett .30 .10
❑ V76 Pete Stoyanovich .30 .10
❑ V77 Neil Smith .60 .25
❑ V78 Corey Miller .30 .10
❑ V79 Tim Brown 1.25 .50
❑ V80 Tyrone Hughes .60 .25
❑ V81 Boomer Esiason .60 .25
❑ V82 Natrone Means .60 .25
❑ V83 Chris Warren .60 .25
❑ V84 Byron Bam Morris .30 .10
❑ V85 Jerry Rice 3.00 1.25
❑ V86 Michael Zordich .30 .10
❑ V87 Errict Rhett .60 .25
❑ V88 Henry Ellard .60 .25
❑ V89 Chris Miller .30 .10
❑ V90 John Elway 6.00 2.50

1996 Bowman's Best

❑ COMPLETE SET (180) 80.00 40.00
❑ 1 Emmitt Smith 3.00 1.25
❑ 2 Kordell Stewart .75 .30
❑ 3 Mark Chmura .40 .15
❑ 4 Sean Dawkins .20 .07
❑ 5 Steve Young 1.50 .60
❑ 6 Tamarick Vanover .40 .15
❑ 7 Scott Mitchell .40 .15
❑ 8 Aaron Hayden .20 .07
❑ 9 William Thomas .20 .07
❑ 10 Dan Marino 4.00 1.50
❑ 11 Curtis Conway .75 .30
❑ 12 Steve Atwater .20 .07
❑ 13 Derrick Brooks .75 .30
❑ 14 Rick Mirer .40 .15
❑ 15 Mark Brunell 1.00 .40
❑ 16 Garrison Hearst .40 .15
❑ 17 Eric Turner .20 .07
❑ 18 Mark Carrier WR .20 .07
❑ 19 Darnay Scott .40 .15
❑ 20 Steve McNair 1.50 .60
❑ 21 Jim Everett .20 .07
❑ 22 Wayne Chrebet 1.00 .40
❑ 23 Ben Coates .40 .15
❑ 24 Harvey Williams .20 .07
❑ 25 Michael Westbrook .75 .30
❑ 26 Kevin Carter .20 .07
❑ 27 Dave Brown .20 .07
❑ 28 Jake Reed .40 .15
❑ 29 Thurman Thomas .75 .30
❑ 30 Jeff George .40 .15
❑ 31 Carnell Lake .20 .07
❑ 32 J.J. Stokes .75 .30
❑ 33 Jay Novacek .20 .07
❑ 34 Brett Perriman .20 .07
❑ 35 Robert Brooks .75 .30
❑ 36 Neil Smith .40 .15
❑ 37 Chris Zorich .20 .07
❑ 38 Micheal Barrow .20 .07
❑ 39 Quentin Coryatt .20 .07
❑ 40 Kerry Collins .75 .30
❑ 41 Aeneas Williams .20 .07
❑ 42 James O.Stewart .40 .15
❑ 43 Warren Moon .40 .15
❑ 44 Willie McGinest .20 .07
❑ 45 Rodney Hampton .40 .15
❑ 46 Jeff Hostetler .20 .07
❑ 47 Darrell Green .20 .07
❑ 48 Warren Sapp .20 .07
❑ 49 Troy Drayton .20 .07
❑ 50 Junior Seau .75 .30
❑ 51 Mike Mamula .20 .07
❑ 52 Antonio Langham .20 .07
❑ 53 Eric Metcalf .20 .07
❑ 54 Adrian Murrell .40 .15
❑ 55 Joey Galloway .75 .30
❑ 56 Anthony Miller .40 .15
❑ 57 Carl Pickens .40 .15
❑ 58 Bruce Smith .40 .15
❑ 59 Merton Hanks .20 .07
❑ 60 Troy Aikman 2.00 .75
❑ 61 Erik Kramer .20 .07
❑ 62 Tyrone Poole .20 .07
❑ 63 Michael Jackson .40 .15
❑ 64 Rob Moore .40 .15
❑ 65 Marcus Allen .75 .30
❑ 66 Orlando Thomas .20 .07
❑ 67 Dave Meggett .20 .07
❑ 68 Trent Dilfer .75 .30
❑ 69 Herman Moore .40 .15
❑ 70 Brett Favre 4.00 1.50
❑ 71 Blaine Bishop .20 .07
❑ 72 Eric Allen .20 .07
❑ 73 Bernie Parmalee .20 .07
❑ 74 Kyle Brady .20 .07
❑ 75 Terry McDaniel .20 .07
❑ 76 Rodney Peete .20 .07
❑ 77 Yancey Thigpen .40 .15
❑ 78 Stan Humphries .40 .15
❑ 79 Craig Heyward .20 .07
❑ 80 Rashaan Salaam .40 .15
❑ 81 Shannon Sharpe .40 .15
❑ 82 Jim Harbaugh .40 .15
❑ 83 Vinnie Clark .20 .07
❑ 84 Steve Bono .20 .07
❑ 85 Drew Bledsoe 1.00 .40
❑ 86 Ken Norton .20 .07
❑ 87 Brian Mitchell .20 .07
❑ 88 Hardy Nickerson .20 .07
❑ 89 Todd Lyght .20 .07
❑ 90 Barry Sanders 3.00 1.25
❑ 91 Robert Blackmon .20 .07
❑ 92 Larry Centers .40 .15
❑ 93 Jim Kelly .75 .30
❑ 94 Lamar Lathon .20 .07
❑ 95 Cris Carter .75 .30
❑ 96 Hugh Douglas .40 .15
❑ 97 Michael Strahan .40 .15
❑ 98 Lee Woodall .20 .07
❑ 99 Michael Irvin .75 .30
❑ 100 Marshall Faulk 1.00 .40
❑ 101 Terance Mathis .20 .07
❑ 102 Eric Zeier .20 .07
❑ 103 Marty Carter .20 .07
❑ 104 Steve Tovar .20 .07
❑ 105 Isaac Bruce .75 .30
❑ 106 Tony Martin .40 .15
❑ 107 Dale Carter .20 .07
❑ 108 Terry Kirby .40 .15
❑ 109 Tyrone Hughes .20 .07
❑ 110 Bryce Paup .20 .07
❑ 111 Errict Rhett .40 .15
❑ 112 Ricky Watters .40 .15
❑ 113 Chris Chandler .40 .15
❑ 114 Edgar Bennett .40 .15
❑ 115 John Elway 4.00 1.50
❑ 116 Sam Mills .20 .07
❑ 117 Seth Joyner .20 .07
❑ 118 Jeff Lageman .20 .07
❑ 119 Chris Calloway .20 .07
❑ 120 Curtis Martin 1.50 .60
❑ 121 Ken Harvey .20 .07
❑ 122 Eugene Daniel .20 .07
❑ 123 Tim Brown .75 .30
❑ 124 Mo Lewis .20 .07
❑ 125 Jeff Blake .75 .30
❑ 126 Jessie Tuggle .20 .07
❑ 127 Vinny Testaverde .40 .15
❑ 128 Chris Warren .40 .15
❑ 129 Terrell Davis 1.50 .60
❑ 130 Greg Lloyd .40 .15
❑ 131 Deion Sanders 1.00 .40
❑ 132 Derrick Thomas .75 .30
❑ 133 Darryll Lewis .20 .07
❑ 134 Reggie White .75 .30
❑ 135 Jerry Rice 2.00 .75
❑ 136 Tony Banks RC 1.00 .40
❑ 137 Derrick Mayes RC 1.00 .40
❑ 138 Leeland McElroy RC .50 .20
❑ 139 Bryan Still RC .50 .20
❑ 140 Tim Biakabutuka RC 1.00 .40
❑ 141 Rickey Dudley RC 1.00 .40
❑ 142 Tory James RC .50 .20
❑ 143 Lawyer Milloy RC 1.25 .50
❑ 144 Mike Ulufale RC .25 .08
❑ 145 Bobby Engram RC 1.00 .40
❑ 146 Willie Anderson RC .25 .08
❑ 147 Terrell Owens RC 15.00 7.50
❑ 148 Jonathan Ogden RC 1.00 .40
❑ 149 Darrius Johnson RC .25 .08
❑ 150 Kevin Hardy RC 1.00 .40
❑ 151 Simeon Rice RC 2.50 1.00
❑ 152 Alex Molden RC .25 .08
❑ 153 Cedric Jones RC .25 .08
❑ 154 Duane Clemons RC .25 .08
❑ 155 Karim Abdul-Jabbar RC 1.00 .40
❑ 156 Dedric Mathis RC .25 .08
❑ 157 John Michels RC .25 .08
❑ 158 Winslow Oliver RC .25 .08
❑ 159 Stepfret Williams RC .25 .08
❑ 160 Eddie Kennison RC 1.00 .40
❑ 161 Marcus Coleman RC .25 .08
❑ 162 Tedy Bruschi RC 25.00 10.00
❑ 163 Detron Smith RC .25 .08
❑ 164 Ray Lewis RC 25.00 12.50
❑ 165 Marvin Harrison RC 15.00 7.50
❑ 166 Je'rod Cherry RC .25 .08
❑ 167 Jerris McPhail RC .25 .08
❑ 168 Eric Moulds RC 8.00 3.00
❑ 169 Walt Harris RC .25 .08
❑ 170 Eddie George RC 8.00 3.00
❑ 171 Jermaine Lewis RC 1.00 .40
❑ 172 Jeff Lewis RC .50 .20
❑ 173 Ray Mickens RC .25 .08
❑ 174 Amani Toomer RC 5.00 2.00
❑ 175 Zach Thomas RC 3.00 1.25
❑ 176 Lawrence Phillips RC .50 .20
❑ 177 John Mobley RC .25 .08
❑ 178 Anthony Dorsett RC .25 .08
❑ 179 DeRon Jenkins .20 .07
❑ 180 Keyshawn Johnson RC 6.00 2.50

1997 Bowman's Best

❑ COMPLETE SET (125) 30.00 12.50
❑ 1 Brett Favre 4.00 1.50
❑ 2 Larry Centers .60 .25
❑ 3 Trent Dilfer 1.00 .40
❑ 4 Rodney Hampton .60 .25
❑ 5 Wesley Walls .60 .25
❑ 6 Jerome Bettis 1.00 .40
❑ 7 Keyshawn Johnson 1.00 .40

❑ 8 Keenan McCardell .60 .25
❑ 9 Terry Allen 1.00 .40
❑ 10 Troy Aikman 2.00 .75
❑ 11 Tony Banks .60 .25
❑ 12 Ty Detmer .60 .25
❑ 13 Chris Chandler .60 .25
❑ 14 Marshall Faulk 1.25 .50
❑ 15 Heath Shuler .40 .15
❑ 16 Stan Humphries .60 .25
❑ 17 Bryan Cox .40 .15
❑ 18 Chris Spielman .40 .15
❑ 19 Derrick Thomas 1.00 .40
❑ 20 Steve Young 1.25 .50
❑ 21 Desmond Howard .60 .25
❑ 22 Jeff Blake .60 .25
❑ 23 Michael Jackson .60 .25
❑ 24 Cris Carter 1.00 .40
❑ 25 Joey Galloway .60 .25
❑ 26 Simeon Rice .60 .25
❑ 27 Reggie White 1.00 .40
❑ 28 Dave Brown .40 .15
❑ 29 Mike Alstott 1.00 .40
❑ 30 Emmitt Smith 3.00 1.25
❑ 31 Anthony Johnson .40 .15
❑ 32 Mark Brunell 1.25 .50
❑ 33 Ricky Watters .60 .25
❑ 34 Terrell Davis 1.25 .50
❑ 35 Ben Coates .60 .25
❑ 36 Gus Frerotte .40 .15
❑ 37 Andre Reed .60 .25
❑ 38 Isaac Bruce 1.00 .40
❑ 39 Junior Seau 1.00 .40
❑ 40 Eddie George 1.00 .40
❑ 41 Adrian Murrell .60 .25
❑ 42 Jake Reed .60 .25
❑ 43 Karim Abdul-Jabbar .60 .25
❑ 44 Scott Mitchell .60 .25
❑ 45 Ki-Jana Carter .40 .15
❑ 46 Curtis Conway .60 .25
❑ 47 Jim Harbaugh .60 .25
❑ 48 Tim Brown 1.00 .40
❑ 49 Mario Bates .40 .15
❑ 50 Jerry Rice 2.00 .75
❑ 51 Byron Bam Morris .40 .15
❑ 52 Marcus Allen 1.00 .40
❑ 53 Errict Rhett .40 .15
❑ 54 Steve McNair 1.25 .50
❑ 55 Kerry Collins 1.00 .40
❑ 56 Bert Emanuel .60 .25
❑ 57 Curtis Martin 1.25 .50
❑ 58 Bryce Paup .40 .15
❑ 59 Brad Johnson 1.00 .40
❑ 60 John Elway 4.00 1.50
❑ 61 Natrone Means .60 .25
❑ 62 Deion Sanders 1.00 .40
❑ 63 Tony Martin .60 .25
❑ 64 Michael Westbrook .60 .25
❑ 65 Chris Calloway .40 .15
❑ 66 Antonio Freeman 1.00 .40
❑ 67 Rob Johnson 1.00 .40
❑ 68 Kent Graham .40 .15
❑ 69 O.J. McDuffie .60 .25
❑ 70 Barry Sanders 3.00 1.25
❑ 71 Chris Warren .60 .25
❑ 72 Kordell Stewart 1.00 .40
❑ 73 Thurman Thomas 1.00 .40
❑ 74 Marvin Harrison 1.00 .40
❑ 75 Carl Pickens .60 .25
❑ 76 Brent Jones .40 .15
❑ 77 Irving Fryar .60 .25
❑ 78 Neil O'Donnell .60 .25
❑ 79 Elvis Grbac .60 .25
❑ 80 Drew Bledsoe 1.25 .50
❑ 81 Shannon Sharpe .60 .25
❑ 82 Vinny Testaverde .60 .25
❑ 83 Chris Sanders .40 .15
❑ 84 Herman Moore .60 .25
❑ 85 Jeff George .60 .25
❑ 86 Bruce Smith .60 .25
❑ 87 Robert Smith .60 .25
❑ 88 Kevin Hardy .40 .15
❑ 89 Kevin Greene .60 .25
❑ 90 Dan Marino 4.00 1.50
❑ 91 Michael Irvin 1.00 .40
❑ 92 Garrison Hearst .60 .25
❑ 93 Lake Dawson .40 .15
❑ 94 Lawrence Phillips .40 .15
❑ 95 Terry Glenn 1.00 .40
❑ 96 Jake Plummer RC 6.00 2.50
❑ 97 Byron Hanspard RC .60 .25
❑ 98 Bryant Westbrook RC .40 .15
❑ 99 Troy Davis RC .60 .25
❑ 100 Danny Wuerffel RC 1.00 .40
❑ 101 Tony Gonzalez RC 4.00 1.50
❑ 102 Jim Druckenmiller RC .60 .25
❑ 103 Kevin Lockett RC .60 .25
❑ 104 Renaldo Wynn RC .40 .15
❑ 105 James Farrior RC 1.00 .40
❑ 106 Rae Carruth RC .40 .15
❑ 107 Tom Knight RC .40 .15
❑ 108 Corey Dillon RC 8.00 3.00
❑ 109 Kenny Holmes RC 1.00 .40
❑ 110 Orlando Pace RC 1.00 .40
❑ 111 Reidel Anthony RC 1.00 .40
❑ 112 Chad Scott RC .60 .25
❑ 113 Antowain Smith RC 3.00 1.25
❑ 114 David LaFleur RC .40 .15
❑ 115 Yatil Green RC .60 .25
❑ 116 Darrell Russell RC .40 .15
❑ 117 Joey Kent RC 1.00 .40
❑ 118 Darnell Autry RC .60 .25
❑ 119 Peter Boulware RC 1.00 .40
❑ 120 Shawn Springs RC .60 .25
❑ 121 Ike Hilliard RC 1.50 .60
❑ 122 Dwayne Rudd RC 1.00 .40
❑ 123 Reinard Wilson RC .60 .25
❑ 124 Michael Booker RC .40 .15
❑ 125 Warrick Dunn RC 3.00 1.25

1998 Bowman's Best

❑ COMPLETE SET (125) 80.00 30.00
❑ 1 Emmitt Smith 3.00 1.25
❑ 2 Reggie White 1.00 .40
❑ 3 Jake Plummer 1.00 .40
❑ 4 Ike Hilliard .40 .15
❑ 5 Isaac Bruce .40 .15
❑ 6 Trent Dilfer 1.00 .40
❑ 7 Ricky Watters .60 .25
❑ 8 Jeff George .60 .25
❑ 9 Wayne Chrebet 1.00 .40
❑ 10 Brett Favre 4.00 1.50
❑ 11 Terry Allen 1.00 .40
❑ 12 Bert Emanuel .40 .15
❑ 13 Andre Reed .60 .25
❑ 14 Andre Rison .60 .25
❑ 15 Jeff Blake .60 .25
❑ 16 Steve McNair 1.00 .40
❑ 17 Joey Galloway .60 .25
❑ 18 Irving Fryar .60 .25
❑ 19 Dorsey Levens 1.00 .40
❑ 20 Jerry Rice 2.00 .75
❑ 21 Kerry Collins .60 .25
❑ 22 Michael Jackson .40 .15
❑ 23 Kordell Stewart 1.00 .40
❑ 24 Junior Seau 1.00 .40
❑ 25 Jimmy Smith .60 .25
❑ 26 Michael Westbrook .60 .25
❑ 27 Eddie George 1.00 .40
❑ 28 Cris Carter 1.00 .40
❑ 29 Jason Sehorn .60 .25
❑ 30 Warrick Dunn 1.00 .40
❑ 31 Garrison Hearst 1.00 .40
❑ 32 Erik Kramer .40 .15
❑ 33 Chris Chandler .60 .25
❑ 34 Michael Irvin 1.00 .40
❑ 35 Marshall Faulk 1.25 .50
❑ 36 Warren Moon 1.00 .40
❑ 37 Rickey Dudley .40 .15
❑ 38 Drew Bledsoe 1.50 .60
❑ 39 Antowain Smith 1.00 .40
❑ 40 Terrell Davis 1.00 .40
❑ 41 Gus Frerotte .40 .15
❑ 42 Robert Brooks .60 .25
❑ 43 Tony Banks .60 .25
❑ 44 Terrell Owens 1.00 .40
❑ 45 Edgar Bennett .40 .15
❑ 46 Rob Moore .60 .25
❑ 47 J.J. Stokes .60 .25
❑ 48 Yancey Thigpen .40 .15
❑ 49 Elvis Grbac .60 .25
❑ 50 John Elway 4.00 1.50
❑ 51 Charles Johnson .40 .15
❑ 52 Karim Abdul-Jabbar 1.00 .40
❑ 53 Carl Pickens .60 .25
❑ 54 Peter Boulware .40 .15
❑ 55 Chris Warren .40 .15
❑ 56 Terance Mathis .60 .25
❑ 57 Andre Hastings .40 .15
❑ 58 Jake Reed .60 .25
❑ 59 Mike Alstott .40 .15
❑ 60 Mark Brunell 1.00 .40
❑ 61 Herman Moore .60 .25
❑ 62 Troy Aikman 2.00 .75
❑ 63 Fred Lane .40 .15
❑ 64 Rod Smith .60 .25
❑ 65 Terry Glenn 1.00 .40
❑ 66 Jerome Bettis 1.00 .40
❑ 67 Derrick Thomas 1.00 .40
❑ 68 Marvin Harrison 1.00 .40
❑ 69 Adrian Murrell .40 .15
❑ 70 Curtis Martin 1.00 .40
❑ 71 Bobby Hoying .60 .25
❑ 72 Darrell Green .60 .25
❑ 73 Sean Dawkins .40 .15
❑ 74 Robert Smith 1.00 .40
❑ 75 Antonio Freeman 1.00 .40
❑ 76 Scott Mitchell .60 .25
❑ 77 Curtis Conway .60 .25
❑ 78 Rae Carruth .40 .15
❑ 79 Jamal Anderson 1.00 .40
❑ 80 Dan Marino 4.00 1.50
❑ 81 Brad Johnson 1.00 .40
❑ 82 Danny Kanell .60 .25
❑ 83 Charlie Garner .60 .25
❑ 84 Rob Johnson .60 .25
❑ 85 Natrone Means .60 .25
❑ 86 Tim Brown 1.00 .40
❑ 87 Keyshawn Johnson 1.00 .40

❑ 88	Ben Coates	.60	.25
❑ 89	Derrick Alexander	.60	.25
❑ 90	Steve Young	1.25	.50
❑ 91	Shannon Sharpe	.60	.25
❑ 92	Corey Dillon	1.00	.40
❑ 93	Bruce Smith	.60	.25
❑ 94	Errict Rhett	.60	.25
❑ 95	Jim Harbaugh	.40	.15
❑ 96	Napoleon Kaufman	1.00	.40
❑ 97	Glenn Foley	.60	.25
❑ 98	Tony Gonzalez	1.00	.40
❑ 99	Keenan McCardell	.60	.25
❑ 100	Barry Sanders	3.00	1.25
❑ 101	Charles Woodson RC	3.00	1.25
❑ 102	Tim Dwight RC	2.50	1.00
❑ 103	Marcus Nash RC	1.25	.50
❑ 104	Joe Jurevicius RC	2.50	1.00
❑ 105	Jacquez Green RC	2.00	.75
❑ 106	Kevin Dyson RC	2.50	1.00
❑ 107	Keith Brooking RC	2.50	1.00
❑ 108	Andre Wadsworth RC	2.00	.75
❑ 109	Randy Moss RC	15.00	6.00
❑ 110	Robert Edwards RC	2.00	.75
❑ 111	Pat Johnson RC	2.00	.75
❑ 112	Peyton Manning RC	25.00	10.00
❑ 113	Duane Starks RC	1.25	.50
❑ 114	Grant Wistrom RC	2.00	.75
❑ 115	Anthony Simmons RC	2.00	.75
❑ 116	Takeo Spikes RC	2.50	1.00
❑ 117	Tony Simmons RC	2.00	.75
❑ 118	Jerome Pathon RC	2.50	1.00
❑ 119	Ryan Leaf RC	2.50	1.00
❑ 120	Skip Hicks RC	2.00	.75
❑ 121	Curtis Enis RC	1.25	.50
❑ 122	Germane Crowell RC	2.00	.75
❑ 123	John Avery RC	2.00	.75
❑ 124	Hines Ward RC	10.00	5.00
❑ 125	Fred Taylor RC	4.00	1.50

1999 Bowman's Best

❑	COMPLETE SET (133)	80.00	30.00
❑ 1	Randy Moss	2.50	1.00
❑ 2	Skip Hicks	.40	.15
❑ 3	Robert Smith	1.00	.40
❑ 4	Drew Bledsoe	1.25	.50
❑ 5	Tim Brown	1.00	.40
❑ 6	Marshall Faulk	1.25	.50
❑ 7	Terance Mathis	.60	.25
❑ 8	Sean Dawkins	.40	.15
❑ 9	Ed McCaffrey	.60	.25
❑ 10	Jamal Anderson	1.00	.40
❑ 11	Antonio Freeman	1.00	.40
❑ 12	Terry Kirby	.60	.25
❑ 13	Vinny Testaverde	.60	.25
❑ 14	Eddie George	1.00	.40
❑ 15	Ricky Watters	.60	.25
❑ 16	Johnnie Morton	.60	.25
❑ 17	Natrone Means	.60	.25
❑ 18	Terry Glenn	1.00	.40
❑ 19	Michael Westbrook	.60	.25
❑ 20	Doug Flutie	1.00	.40
❑ 21	Jake Plummer	.60	.25
❑ 22	Darnay Scott	.60	.25
❑ 23	Andre Rison	.60	.25
❑ 24	Jon Kitna	1.00	.40
❑ 25	Dan Marino	3.00	1.25
❑ 26	Ike Hilliard	.60	.25
❑ 27	Warrick Dunn	1.00	.40
❑ 28	Jerome Bettis	1.00	.40
❑ 29	Curtis Conway	.60	.25
❑ 30	Emmitt Smith	2.00	.75
❑ 31	Jimmy Smith	.60	.25
❑ 32	Isaac Bruce	1.00	.40
❑ 33	Jerry Rice	2.00	.75
❑ 34	Curtis Martin	1.00	.40
❑ 35	Steve McNair	1.00	.40
❑ 36	Jeff Blake	.60	.25
❑ 37	Rob Moore	.60	.25
❑ 38	Dorsey Levens	1.00	.40
❑ 39	Terrell Davis	1.00	.40
❑ 40	John Elway	3.00	1.25
❑ 41	Trent Dilfer	.60	.25
❑ 42	Joey Galloway	.60	.25
❑ 43	Keyshawn Johnson	1.00	.40
❑ 44	O.J. McDuffie	.60	.25
❑ 45	Fred Taylor	1.00	.40
❑ 46	Andre Reed	.60	.25
❑ 47	Frank Sanders	.60	.25
❑ 48	Keenan McCardell	.60	.25
❑ 49	Elvis Grbac	.60	.25
❑ 50	Barry Sanders	3.00	1.25
❑ 51	Terrell Owens	1.00	.40
❑ 52	Trent Green	1.00	.40
❑ 53	Brad Johnson	1.00	.40
❑ 54	Rich Gannon	1.00	.40
❑ 55	Randall Cunningham	1.00	.40
❑ 56	Tony Martin	.60	.25
❑ 57	Rod Smith	.60	.25
❑ 58	Eric Moulds	1.00	.40
❑ 59	Yancey Thigpen	.40	.15
❑ 60	Brett Favre	3.00	1.25
❑ 61	Cris Carter	1.00	.40
❑ 62	Marvin Harrison	1.00	.40
❑ 63	Chris Chandler	.60	.25
❑ 64	Antowain Smith	1.00	.40
❑ 65	Carl Pickens	.60	.25
❑ 66	Shannon Sharpe	.60	.25
❑ 67	Mike Alstott	1.00	.40
❑ 68	J.J. Stokes	.60	.25
❑ 69	Ben Coates	.60	.25
❑ 70	Peyton Manning	3.00	1.25
❑ 71	Duce Staley	1.00	.40
❑ 72	Michael Irvin	.60	.25
❑ 73	Tim Biakabutuka	.60	.25
❑ 74	Priest Holmes	1.50	.60
❑ 75	Steve Young	1.25	.50
❑ 76	Jerome Pathon	.60	.25
❑ 77	Wayne Chrebet	1.00	.40
❑ 78	Bert Emanuel	.40	.15
❑ 79	Curtis Enis	.40	.15
❑ 80	Mark Brunell	1.00	.40
❑ 81	Herman Moore	.60	.25
❑ 82	Corey Dillon	1.00	.40
❑ 83	Jim Harbaugh	.60	.25
❑ 84	Gary Brown	.40	.15
❑ 85	Kordell Stewart	.60	.25
❑ 86	Garrison Hearst	.60	.25
❑ 87	Rocket Ismail	.60	.25
❑ 88	Charlie Batch	1.00	.40
❑ 89	Napoleon Kaufman	1.00	.40
❑ 90	Troy Aikman	2.00	.75
❑ 91	Brett Favre BP	1.50	.60
❑ 92	Randy Moss BP	1.25	.50
❑ 93	Terrell Davis BP	1.00	.40
❑ 94	Barry Sanders BP	1.50	.60
❑ 95	Peyton Manning BP	1.50	.60
❑ 96	Troy Edwards BP	.60	.25
❑ 97	Cade McNown BP	.60	.25
❑ 98	Edgerrin James BP	2.50	1.00
❑ 99	Torry Holt BP	1.00	.40
❑ 100	Tim Couch BP	1.00	.40
❑ 101	Chris Claiborne RC	1.00	.40
❑ 102	Brock Huard RC	2.00	.75
❑ 103	Amos Zereoue RC	2.00	.75
❑ 104	Sedrick Irvin RC	1.00	.40
❑ 105	Kevin Faulk RC	2.00	.75
❑ 106	Ebenezer Ekuban RC	1.00	.40
❑ 107	Daunte Culpepper RC	8.00	3.00
❑ 108	Rob Konrad RC	1.50	.60
❑ 109	James Johnson RC	1.50	.60
❑ 110	Kurt Warner RC	10.00	4.00
❑ 111	Mike Cloud RC	1.50	.60
❑ 112	Andy Katzenmoyer RC	1.50	.60
❑ 113	Jevon Kearse RC	3.00	1.25
❑ 114	Akili Smith RC	1.50	.60
❑ 115	Edgerrin James RC	8.00	3.00
❑ 116	Cecil Collins RC	1.00	.40
❑ 117	Chris McAlister RC	1.50	.60
❑ 118	Donovan McNabb RC	10.00	4.00
❑ 119	Kevin Johnson RC	2.00	.75
❑ 120	Torry Holt RC	5.00	2.00
❑ 121	Antoine Winfield RC	1.50	.60
❑ 122	Michael Bishop RC	2.00	.75
❑ 123	Joe Germaine RC	1.50	.60
❑ 124	David Boston RC	2.00	.75
❑ 125	D'Wayne Bates RC	1.50	.60
❑ 126	Champ Bailey RC	2.50	1.00
❑ 127	Cade McNown RC	1.50	.60
❑ 128	Shaun King RC	1.50	.60
❑ 129	Peerless Price RC	2.00	.75
❑ 130	Troy Edwards RC	1.50	.60
❑ 131	Karsten Bailey RC	1.50	.60
❑ 132	Tim Couch RC	2.00	.75
❑ 133	Ricky Williams RC	4.00	1.50
❑ C1	Rookie Class Photo	8.00	3.00

2000 Bowman's Best

❑	COMPLETE SET (150)	500.00	250.00
❑ 1	Troy Edwards	.30	.10
❑ 2	Kurt Warner	1.50	.60
❑ 3	Steve McNair	.75	.30
❑ 4	Terry Glenn	.50	.20
❑ 5	Charlie Batch	.75	.30
❑ 6	Patrick Jeffers	.75	.30
❑ 7	Jake Plummer	.50	.20
❑ 8	Derrick Alexander	.50	.20
❑ 9	Joey Galloway	.50	.20
❑ 10	Tony Banks	.50	.20
❑ 11	Robert Smith	.75	.30
❑ 12	Jerry Rice	1.50	.60
❑ 13	Jeff Garcia	.75	.30
❑ 14	Michael Westbrook	.50	.20
❑ 15	Curtis Conway	.50	.20
❑ 16	Brian Griese	.75	.30
❑ 17	Peyton Manning	2.00	.75
❑ 18	Daunte Culpepper	1.00	.40
❑ 19	Frank Sanders	.50	.20
❑ 20	Muhsin Muhammad	.50	.20
❑ 21	Corey Dillon	.75	.30
❑ 22	Brett Favre	2.50	1.00
❑ 23	Warrick Dunn	.75	.30
❑ 24	Tim Brown	.75	.30
❑ 25	Kerry Collins	.50	.20
❑ 26	Brad Johnson	.75	.30
❑ 27	Rocket Ismail	.50	.20
❑ 28	Jamal Anderson	.75	.30
❑ 29	Jimmy Smith	.50	.20
❑ 30	Torry Holt	.75	.30

❑ 31	Duce Staley	.75	.30
❑ 32	Drew Bledsoe	1.00	.40
❑ 33	Jerome Bettis	.75	.30
❑ 34	Keyshawn Johnson	.75	.30
❑ 35	Fred Taylor	.75	.30
❑ 36	Akili Smith	.30	.10
❑ 37	Rob Johnson	.50	.20
❑ 38	Elvis Grbac	.50	.20
❑ 39	Antonio Freeman	.75	.30
❑ 40	Curtis Enis	.30	.10
❑ 41	Terance Mathis	.50	.20
❑ 42	Terrell Davis	.75	.30
❑ 43	Randy Moss	1.50	.60
❑ 44	Jon Kitna	.75	.30
❑ 45	Curtis Martin	.75	.30
❑ 46	Terrell Owens	.75	.30
❑ 47	Robert Smith	.75	.30
❑ 48	Albert Connell	.30	.10
❑ 49	Edgerrin James	1.25	.50
❑ 50	Tony Gonzalez	.50	.20
❑ 51	Eric Moulds	.75	.30
❑ 52	Natrone Means	.50	.20
❑ 53	Carl Pickens	.50	.20
❑ 54	Mark Brunell	.75	.30
❑ 55	Rob Moore	.50	.20
❑ 56	Marshall Faulk	1.00	.40
❑ 57	Stephen Davis	.75	.30
❑ 58	Rich Gannon	.75	.30
❑ 59	Ricky Williams	.75	.30
❑ 60	Emmitt Smith	1.50	.60
❑ 61	Germane Crowell	.30	.10
❑ 62	Doug Flutie	.75	.30
❑ 63	O.J. McDuffie	.50	.20
❑ 64	Chris Chandler	.50	.20
❑ 65	Qadry Ismail	.50	.20
❑ 66	Tim Couch	.50	.20
❑ 67	James Stewart	.50	.20
❑ 68	Marvin Harrison	.75	.30
❑ 69	Cris Carter	.75	.30
❑ 70	Cade McNown	.30	.10
❑ 71	Marcus Robinson	.75	.30
❑ 72	Steve Beuerlein	.50	.20
❑ 73	Jevon Kearse	.75	.30
❑ 74	Eddie George	.75	.30
❑ 75	Donovan McNabb	1.25	.50
❑ 76	Jeff Blake	.50	.20
❑ 77	Wayne Chrebet	.50	.20
❑ 78	Kordell Stewart	.50	.20
❑ 79	Steve Young	1.00	.40
❑ 80	Mike Alstott	.75	.30
❑ 81	Ricky Watters	.50	.20
❑ 82	Charlie Garner	.50	.20
❑ 83	Troy Aikman	1.50	.60
❑ 84	Dorsey Levens	.50	.20
❑ 85	Ike Hilliard	.50	.20
❑ 86	Shaun King	.30	.10
❑ 87	Isaac Bruce	.75	.30
❑ 88	Tyrone Wheatley	.50	.20
❑ 89	Amani Toomer	.50	.20
❑ 90	Ed McCaffrey	.75	.30
❑ 91	E.James/M.Faulk BP	.75	.30
❑ 92	D.Bledsoe/B.Johnson BP	.75	.30
❑ 93	J.Smith/R.Moss BP	1.00	.40
❑ 94	E.George/S.Davis BP	.50	.20
❑ 95	M.Brunell/T.Aikman BP	1.00	.40
❑ 96	M.Harrison/C.Carter BP	.75	.30
❑ 97	C.Martin/E.Smith BP	1.00	.40
❑ 98	T.Brown/I.Bruce BP	.50	.20
❑ 99	F.Taylor/R.Williams BP	.75	.30
❑ 100	K.Warner/P.Manning BP	1.00	.40
❑ 101	Shaun Alexander RC	30.00	15.00
❑ 102	Thomas Jones RC	12.00	5.00
❑ 103	Courtney Brown RC	8.00	3.00
❑ 104	Curtis Keaton RC	6.00	2.50
❑ 105	Jerry Porter RC	10.00	4.00
❑ 106	Corey Simon RC	8.00	3.00
❑ 107	Dez White RC	8.00	3.00
❑ 108	Jamal Lewis RC	15.00	6.00
❑ 109	Ron Dayne RC	8.00	3.00
❑ 110	R.Jay Soward RC	6.00	2.50
❑ 111	Tee Martin RC	8.00	3.00
❑ 112	Brian Urlacher RC	25.00	10.00
❑ 113	Reuben Droughns RC	10.00	4.00
❑ 114	Travis Taylor RC	8.00	3.00
❑ 115	Plaxico Burress RC	15.00	6.00
❑ 116	Chad Pennington RC	15.00	6.00
❑ 117	Sylvester Morris RC	6.00	2.50
❑ 118	Ron Dugans RC	4.00	1.50
❑ 119	Joe Hamilton RC	6.00	2.50
❑ 120	Chris Redman RC	6.00	2.50
❑ 121	Trung Canidate RC	6.00	2.50
❑ 122	J.R. Redmond RC	6.00	2.50
❑ 123	Danny Farmer RC	6.00	2.50
❑ 124	Todd Pinkston RC	8.00	3.00
❑ 125	Dennis Northcutt RC	8.00	3.00
❑ 126	Laveranues Coles RC	10.00	4.00
❑ 127	Bubba Franks RC	8.00	3.00
❑ 128	Travis Prentice RC	6.00	2.50
❑ 129	Peter Warrick RC	8.00	3.00
❑ 130	Anthony Becht RC	8.00	3.00
❑ 131	Ike Charlton RC	4.00	1.50
❑ 132	Shaun Ellis RC	8.00	3.00
❑ 133	Sean Morey RC	6.00	2.50
❑ 134	Sebastian Janikowski RC	8.00	3.00
❑ 135	Aaron Stecker RC	8.00	3.00
❑ 136	Ronney Jenkins RC	6.00	2.50
❑ 137	Jamel White RC	6.00	2.50
❑ 138	Nick Williams	4.00	1.50
❑ 139	Andy McCullough	4.00	1.50
❑ 140	Kevin Daft	4.00	1.50
❑ 141	Thomas Hamner RC	4.00	1.50
❑ 142	Tim Rattay RC	8.00	3.00
❑ 143	Spergon Wynn RC	6.00	2.50
❑ 144	Brandon Short RC	6.00	2.50
❑ 145	Chad Morton RC	8.00	3.00
❑ 146	Gari Scott RC	4.00	1.50
❑ 147	Frank Murphy RC	4.00	1.50
❑ 148	James Williams RC	6.00	2.50
❑ 149	Windrell Hayes RC	6.00	2.50
❑ 150	Doug Johnson RC	8.00	3.00

2001 Bowman's Best

❑	COMP.SET w/o SP's (100)	20.00	7.50
❑ 1	Jerry Rice	1.50	.60
❑ 2	Doug Flutie	.75	.30
❑ 3	Drew Bledsoe	1.00	.40
❑ 4	Edgerrin James	1.00	.40
❑ 5	Muhsin Muhammad	.50	.20
❑ 6	Charlie Batch	.75	.30
❑ 7	Marshall Faulk	1.00	.40
❑ 8	Trent Green	.75	.30
❑ 9	Rich Gannon	.75	.30
❑ 10	Emmitt Smith	1.50	.60
❑ 11	Steve McNair	.75	.30
❑ 12	Darrell Jackson	.75	.30
❑ 13	Amani Toomer	.50	.20
❑ 14	Jimmy Smith	.50	.20
❑ 15	Kevin Johnson	.50	.20
❑ 16	Ray Lewis	.75	.30
❑ 17	Peter Warrick	.75	.30
❑ 18	Cris Carter	.75	.30
❑ 19	Jerome Bettis	.75	.30
❑ 20	Keyshawn Johnson	.75	.30
❑ 21	Joey Galloway	.50	.20
❑ 22	Chris Chandler	.50	.20
❑ 23	Brett Favre	2.50	1.00
❑ 24	Aaron Brooks	.75	.30
❑ 25	Kurt Warner	1.50	.60
❑ 26	Jeff Graham	.30	.10
❑ 27	Curtis Martin	.75	.30
❑ 28	Mike Anderson	.75	.30
❑ 29	Eric Moulds	.50	.20
❑ 30	David Boston	.75	.30
❑ 31	Elvis Grbac	.50	.20
❑ 32	James Stewart	.50	.20
❑ 33	Randy Moss	1.50	.60
❑ 34	Donovan McNabb	1.00	.40
❑ 35	Matt Hasselbeck	.50	.20
❑ 36	Stephen Davis	.75	.30
❑ 37	Brad Johnson	.75	.30
❑ 38	Jamal Anderson	.75	.30
❑ 39	Tim Biakabutuka	.50	.20
❑ 40	Antonio Freeman	.75	.30
❑ 41	Mark Brunell	.75	.30
❑ 42	Tiki Barber	.75	.30
❑ 43	Charlie Garner	.50	.20
❑ 44	Eddie George	.75	.30
❑ 45	Ricky Williams	.75	.30
❑ 46	Rob Johnson	.50	.20
❑ 47	Jake Plummer	.50	.20
❑ 48	Peyton Manning	2.00	.75
❑ 49	Lamar Smith	.50	.20
❑ 50	Corey Dillon	.75	.30
❑ 51	Derrick Alexander	.50	.20
❑ 52	Troy Brown	.50	.20
❑ 53	Wayne Chrebet	.50	.20
❑ 54	Shaun Alexander	1.00	.40
❑ 55	Jeff George	.50	.20
❑ 56	Tim Brown	.75	.30
❑ 57	Brian Griese	.75	.30
❑ 58	Cade McNown	.30	.10
❑ 59	Jamal Lewis	1.25	.50
❑ 60	Germane Crowell	.30	.10
❑ 61	Junior Seau	.75	.30
❑ 62	Warrick Dunn	.75	.30
❑ 63	Isaac Bruce	.75	.30
❑ 64	Terry Glenn	.50	.20
❑ 65	Fred Taylor	.75	.30
❑ 66	Tim Couch	.50	.20
❑ 67	Akili Smith	.30	.10
❑ 68	Tony Gonzalez	.50	.20
❑ 69	Kerry Collins	.50	.20
❑ 70	James Thrash	.50	.20
❑ 71	Terrell Owens	.75	.30
❑ 72	Derrick Mason	.50	.20
❑ 73	Tyrone Wheatley	.50	.20
❑ 74	Oronde Gadsden	.50	.20
❑ 75	Ahman Green	.75	.30
❑ 76	Jon Kitna	.50	.20
❑ 77	Tony Banks	.50	.20
❑ 78	Marvin Harrison	.75	.30
❑ 79	Daunte Culpepper	.75	.30
❑ 80	Vinny Testaverde	.50	.20
❑ 81	Chad Lewis	.30	.10
❑ 82	Torry Holt	.75	.30
❑ 83	Jeff Garcia	.75	.30
❑ 84	Rod Smith	.50	.20
❑ 85	Marcus Robinson	.75	.30
❑ 86	Keenan McCardell	.30	.10
❑ 87	Joe Horn	.50	.20
❑ 88	Kordell Stewart	.50	.20
❑ 89	Jay Fiedler	.75	.30
❑ 90	Ed McCaffrey	.75	.30
❑ 91	E.George/S.Davis	.50	.20
❑ 92	P.Manning/J.Garcia	1.50	.60
❑ 93	R.Smith/T.Holt	.75	.30
❑ 94	E.James/M.Faulk	1.50	.60
❑ 95	E.Grbac/D.Culpepper	.75	.30
❑ 96	M.Harrison/R.Moss	1.25	.50
❑ 97	M.Anderson/E.Smith	.75	.30
❑ 98	B.Griese/K.Warner	1.00	.40
❑ 99	M.Muhammad/E.McCaffrey	.75	.30
❑ 100	E.Moulds/T.Owens	.75	.30
❑ 101	David Terrell JSY RC	8.00	3.00

❑ 102	Kevan Barlow JSY RC	8.00	3.00
❑ 103	Quincy Morgan JSY RC	8.00	3.00
❑ 104	Chris Weinke JSY RC	8.00	3.00
❑ 105	Josh Heupel JSY RC	8.00	3.00
❑ 106	Chris Chambers JSY RC	15.00	6.00
❑ 107	Reggie Wayne JSY RC	20.00	7.50
❑ 108	Gerard Warren JSY RC	8.00	3.00
❑ 109	Freddie Mitchell JSY RC	8.00	3.00
❑ 110	Anthony Thomas JSY RC	8.00	3.00
❑ 111	Robert Ferguson JSY RC	8.00	3.00
❑ 112	Deuce McAllister JSY RC	20.00	7.50
❑ 113	Travis Henry JSY RC	8.00	3.00
❑ 114	Rod Gardner JSY RC	8.00	3.00
❑ 115	Michael Bennett JSY RC	15.00	6.00
❑ 116	Santana Moss JSY RC	15.00	6.00
❑ 117	Chad Johnson JSY RC	25.00	10.00
❑ 118	Jesse Palmer JSY RC	8.00	3.00
❑ 119	James Jackson JSY RC	8.00	3.00
❑ 120	Dan Morgan JSY RC	8.00	3.00
❑ 121	Drew Brees RC	15.00	6.00
❑ 122	Travis Minor RC	4.00	1.50
❑ 123	Quincy Carter RC	6.00	2.50
❑ 124	LaDainian Tomlinson RC	30.00	15.00
❑ 125	Michael Vick RC	40.00	20.00
❑ 126	Ryan Pickett RC	2.50	1.00
❑ 127	Mike McMahon RC	6.00	2.50
❑ 128	Alex Bannister RC	4.00	1.50
❑ 129	A.J. Feeley RC	6.00	2.50
❑ 130	Shad Meier RC	4.00	1.50
❑ 131	Jamie Winborn RC	4.00	1.50
❑ 132	Fred Smoot RC	6.00	2.50
❑ 133	Milton Wynn RC	4.00	1.50
❑ 134	Onome Ojo RC	4.00	1.50
❑ 135	Jonathan Carter RC	4.00	1.50
❑ 136	Todd Heap RC	6.00	2.50
❑ 137	Bobby Newcombe RC	4.00	1.50
❑ 138	Tony Stewart RC	6.00	2.50
❑ 139	Torrance Marshall RC	6.00	2.50
❑ 140	Jamal Reynolds RC	6.00	2.50
❑ 141	Jamar Fletcher RC	4.00	1.50
❑ 142	Richard Seymour RC	6.00	2.50
❑ 143	Tay Cody RC	2.50	1.00
❑ 144	Koren Robinson RC	6.00	2.50
❑ 145	Eddie Berlin RC	4.00	1.50
❑ 146	Damione Lewis RC	4.00	1.50
❑ 147	Marques Tuiasosopo RC	8.00	3.00
❑ 148	Snoop Minnis RC	4.00	1.50
❑ 149	Chris Barnes RC	4.00	1.50
❑ 150	Leonard Davis RC	4.00	1.50
❑ 151	Vinny Sutherland RC	4.00	1.50
❑ 152	Rudi Johnson RC	12.00	5.00
❑ 153	Derrick Gibson RC	4.00	1.50
❑ 154	Dan Alexander RC	6.00	2.50
❑ 155	Damerien McCants RC	4.00	1.50
❑ 156	Adam Archuleta RC	6.00	2.50
❑ 157	Correll Buckhalter RC	8.00	3.00
❑ 158	LaMont Jordan RC	12.00	5.00
❑ 159	Quentin McCord RC	4.00	1.50
❑ 160	Justin Smith RC	6.00	2.50
❑ 161	Nate Clements RC	6.00	2.50
❑ 162	Alge Crumpler RC	8.00	4.00
❑ 163	Dan O'Leary RC	4.00	1.50
❑ 164	Sage Rosenfels RC	8.00	3.00
❑ 165	Andre Carter RC	6.00	2.50
❑ 166	Marcus Stroud RC	6.00	2.50
❑ 167	Will Allen RC	4.00	1.50
❑ 168	Tommy Polley RC	6.00	2.50
❑ 169	Justin McCareins RC	6.00	2.50
❑ 170	Josh Booty RC	6.00	2.50

2002 Bowman's Best

❑	COMP.SET w/o SP's (90)	40.00	15.00
❑ 1	Peyton Manning	3.00	1.25
❑ 2	Chris Weinke	1.00	.40
❑ 3	Daunte Culpepper	1.50	.60
❑ 4	Deuce McAllister	2.00	.75
❑ 5	Duce Staley	1.50	.60
❑ 6	Koren Robinson	1.00	.40
❑ 7	Emmitt Smith	4.00	1.50
❑ 8	Jamal Lewis	1.50	.60

❑ 9	Jake Plummer	1.00	.40
❑ 10	Tim Brown	1.50	.60
❑ 11	LaDainian Tomlinson	2.50	1.00
❑ 12	Derrick Mason	1.00	.40
❑ 13	Keyshawn Johnson	1.50	.60
❑ 14	Priest Holmes	2.00	.75
❑ 15	Marcus Robinson	1.00	.40
❑ 16	Drew Bledsoe	2.00	.75
❑ 17	Troy Brown	1.00	.40
❑ 18	Ahman Green	1.50	.60
❑ 19	Edgerrin James	2.00	.75
❑ 20	Hines Ward	1.50	.60
❑ 21	Marshall Faulk	1.50	.60
❑ 22	Rod Gardner	1.00	.40
❑ 23	Amani Toomer	1.00	.40
❑ 24	Ricky Williams	1.50	.60
❑ 25	Peter Warrick	1.00	.40
❑ 26	Ray Lewis	1.50	.60
❑ 27	Warrick Dunn	1.50	.60
❑ 28	Jermaine Lewis	1.00	.40
❑ 29	Mark Brunell	1.50	.60
❑ 30	Randy Moss	3.00	1.25
❑ 31	Laveranues Coles	1.00	.40
❑ 32	Kordell Stewart	1.00	.40
❑ 33	Darrell Jackson	1.00	.40
❑ 34	Jeff Garcia	1.50	.60
❑ 35	Eddie George	1.50	.60
❑ 36	Tim Dwight	1.00	.40
❑ 37	Trent Green	1.00	.40
❑ 38	Quincy Carter	1.00	.40
❑ 39	Mike McMahon	1.50	.60
❑ 40	Corey Dillon	1.00	.40
❑ 41	Corey Bradford	.60	.25
❑ 42	Aaron Brooks	1.50	.60
❑ 43	Todd Pinkston	1.00	.40
❑ 44	Isaac Bruce	1.50	.60
❑ 45	Shane Matthews	1.00	.40
❑ 46	Eric Moulds	1.00	.40
❑ 47	Anthony Thomas	1.00	.40
❑ 48	David Boston	1.50	.60
❑ 49	Kevin Johnson	1.00	.40
❑ 50	Brett Favre	4.00	1.50
❑ 51	Ron Dayne	1.00	.40
❑ 52	Donovan McNabb	2.00	.75
❑ 53	Brad Johnson	1.00	.40
❑ 54	Garrison Hearst	1.00	.40
❑ 55	Jimmy Smith	1.00	.40
❑ 56	Muhsin Muhammad	1.00	.40
❑ 57	Michael Vick	5.00	2.00
❑ 58	Kerry Collins	1.00	.40
❑ 59	Jerome Bettis	1.50	.60
❑ 60	Trent Dilfer	1.00	.40
❑ 61	Torry Holt	1.50	.60
❑ 62	Stephen Davis	1.00	.40
❑ 63	Steve McNair	1.50	.60
❑ 64	Marvin Harrison	1.50	.60
❑ 65	Zach Thomas	1.50	.60
❑ 66	Antowain Smith	1.00	.40
❑ 67	Joe Horn	1.00	.40
❑ 68	Jim Miller	1.00	.40
❑ 69	Travis Taylor	1.00	.40
❑ 70	James Allen	1.00	.40
❑ 71	Tom Brady	4.00	1.50
❑ 72	Tiki Barber	1.50	.60
❑ 73	Doug Flutie	1.50	.60
❑ 74	Rich Gannon	1.50	.60
❑ 75	Kurt Warner	1.50	.60
❑ 76	Michael Pittman	.60	.25
❑ 77	Curtis Martin	1.50	.60
❑ 78	Plaxico Burress	1.50	.60
❑ 79	Terrell Owens	1.50	.60
❑ 80	Tony Gonzalez	1.00	.40
❑ 81	Michael Bennett	1.50	.60
❑ 82	Brian Griese	1.50	.60
❑ 83	Tim Couch	1.00	.40
❑ 84	Shaun Alexander	2.00	.75
❑ 85	Drew Brees	1.50	.60
❑ 86	Vinny Testaverde	1.00	.40
❑ 87	Chris Chambers	1.50	.60
❑ 88	David Terrell	1.50	.60
❑ 89	Rod Smith	1.00	.40
❑ 90	Jerry Rice	3.00	1.25
❑ 91	David Carr JSY RC	20.00	7.50
❑ 92	Joey Harrington JSY RC	20.00	7.50
❑ 93	Marquise Walker JSY RC	6.00	2.50
❑ 94	Ladell Betts JSY RC	8.00	3.00
❑ 95	David Garrard JSY RC	10.00	4.00
❑ 96	Antwaan Randle El JSY RC	15.00	6.00
❑ 97	Antonio Bryant JSY RC	8.00	3.00
❑ 98	Eric Crouch JSY RC	8.00	3.00
❑ 99	Tim Carter JSY RC	6.00	2.50
❑ 100	William Green JSY RC	8.00	3.00
❑ 101	Rohan Davey JSY RC	8.00	3.00
❑ 102	Julius Peppers JSY RC	15.00	6.00
❑ 103	Donte Stallworth JSY RC	15.00	6.00
❑ 104	Ashley Lelie JSY RC	15.00	6.00
❑ 105	Jeremy Shockey JSY RC	25.00	10.00
❑ 106	Javon Walker JSY RC	15.00	7.50
❑ 107	Patrick Ramsey JSY RC	12.00	5.00
❑ 108	Roy Williams JSY RC	20.00	7.50
❑ 109	T.J. Duckett JSY RC	12.00	5.00
❑ 110	Jabar Gaffney JSY RC	8.00	3.00
❑ 111	Andre Davis JSY RC	6.00	2.50
❑ 112	Reche Caldwell JSY RC	8.00	3.00
❑ 113	Josh McCown JSY RC	10.00	4.00
❑ 114	Maurice Morris JSY RC	8.00	3.00
❑ 115	Ron Johnson JSY RC	6.00	2.50
❑ 116	DeShaun Foster JSY RC	8.00	3.00
❑ 117	Clinton Portis JSY RC	25.00	10.00
❑ 118	Aaron Lockett AU RC	6.00	2.50
❑ 119	Robert Thomas AU RC	12.00	5.00
❑ 121	Atrews Bell AU RC	6.00	2.50
❑ 122	Brandon Doman AU RC	10.00	4.00
❑ 124	Bryan Thomas AU RC	10.00	4.00
❑ 125	Bryant McKinnie AU RC	10.00	4.00
❑ 126	Chad Hutchinson AU RC	10.00	4.00
❑ 127	Charles Grant AU RC	12.00	5.00
❑ 128	Chester Taylor AU RC	25.00	10.00
❑ 129	Craig Nall AU RC	25.00	10.00
❑ 130	Deion Branch AU RC	40.00	15.00
❑ 131	Doug Jolley AU RC	12.00	5.00
❑ 132	Dwight Freeney AU RC	30.00	15.00
❑ 133	Ed Reed AU RC	40.00	15.00
❑ 134	Freddie Milons AU RC	10.00	4.00
❑ 135	Herb Haygood AU RC	6.00	2.50
❑ 136	J.T. O'Sullivan AU RC	10.00	4.00
❑ 137	Jake Schifino AU RC	10.00	4.00
❑ 138	Jason McAddley AU RC	10.00	4.00
❑ 139	Jeff Kelly AU RC	10.00	4.00
❑ 140	Jerramy Stevens AU RC	12.00	5.00
❑ 141	John Henderson AU RC	12.00	5.00
❑ 142	Jonathan Wells AU RC	12.00	5.00
❑ 143	Josh Scobey AU RC	12.00	5.00
❑ 144	Kelly Campbell AU RC	10.00	4.00
❑ 145	Kahlil Hill AU RC	10.00	4.00
❑ 146	Kalimba Edwards AU RC	12.00	5.00
❑ 147	Ken Simonton AU RC	6.00	2.50
❑ 148	Kurt Kittner AU RC	10.00	4.00
❑ 149	Lamar Gordon AU RC	12.00	5.00
❑ 150	Leonard Henry AU RC	10.00	4.00
❑ 151	Lito Sheppard AU RC	12.00	5.00
❑ 152	Luke Staley AU RC	10.00	4.00
❑ 153	Matt Schobel AU RC	10.00	4.00
❑ 154	Mike Rumph AU RC	12.00	5.00

❑ 155 Najeh Davenport AU RC 12.00 5.00
❑ 156 Napoleon Harris AU RC 12.00 5.00
❑ 158 Quentin Jammer AU RC 12.00 5.00
❑ 159 Randy Fasani AU RC 10.00 4.00
❑ 160 Ronald Curry AU RC 12.00 5.00
❑ 161 Ryan Sims AU RC 12.00 5.00
❑ 162 Sam Simmons AU RC 6.00 2.50
❑ 163 Seth Burford AU RC 10.00 4.00
❑ 164 Tellis Redmon AU RC 10.00 4.00
❑ 165 Terry Charles AU RC 10.00 4.00
❑ 166 Tracey Wistrom AU RC 10.00 4.00
❑ 167 Verron Haynes AU RC 20.00 7.50
❑ 168 Wes Pate AU RC 6.00 2.50
❑ 169 Wendell Bryant AU RC 6.00 2.50
❑ 170 Damien Anderson AU RC 10.00 4.00

2003 Bowman's Best

❑ COMP.SET w/o SP's (80) 30.00 12.50
❑ ROOKIE AU STATED ODDS 1:136
❑ CARDS 170, 175 NOT RELEASED
❑ 1 Terrell Owens 1.50 .60
❑ 2 Peerless Price 1.00 .40
❑ 3 Joey Harrington 2.50 1.00
❑ 4 Ricky Williams 1.50 .60
❑ 5 David Boston 1.00 .40
❑ 6 Troy Brown 1.00 .40
❑ 7 Deuce McAllister 1.50 .60
❑ 8 Marvin Harrison 1.50 .60
❑ 9 Ahman Green 1.50 .60
❑ 10 Emmitt Smith 4.00 1.50
❑ 11 Brian Urlacher 2.50 1.00
❑ 12 Jamal Lewis 1.50 .60
❑ 13 Keyshawn Johnson 1.50 .60
❑ 14 Kurt Warner 1.50 .60
❑ 15 Rod Gardner 1.00 .40
❑ 16 Plaxico Burress 1.00 .40
❑ 17 Chad Pennington 2.00 .75
❑ 18 Jeremy Shockey 2.50 1.00
❑ 19 Donovan McNabb 2.00 .75
❑ 20 T.J. Duckett 1.00 .40
❑ 21 Fred Taylor 1.50 .60
❑ 22 Daunte Culpepper 1.50 .60
❑ 23 Tiki Barber 1.50 .60
❑ 24 Brian Griese 1.50 .60
❑ 25 Chad Johnson 1.50 .60
❑ 26 Julius Peppers 1.50 .60
❑ 27 Chad Hutchinson .60 .25
❑ 28 Eddie George 1.00 .40
❑ 29 Torry Holt 1.50 .60
❑ 30 Drew Brees 1.50 .60
❑ 31 Rich Gannon 1.00 .40
❑ 32 Trent Green 1.00 .40
❑ 33 Clinton Portis 2.50 1.00
❑ 34 Tom Brady 4.00 1.50
❑ 35 Aaron Brooks 1.50 .60
❑ 36 Ray Lewis 1.50 .60
❑ 37 David Carr 2.50 1.00
❑ 38 Chris Chambers 1.50 .60
❑ 39 Brad Johnson 1.00 .40
❑ 40 Tommy Maddox 1.50 .60
❑ 41 Curtis Martin 1.50 .60
❑ 42 Travis Henry 1.00 .40
❑ 43 Brett Favre 4.00 1.50
❑ 44 Randy Moss 2.50 1.00
❑ 45 Jimmy Smith 1.00 .40
❑ 46 Joey Galloway 1.00 .40
❑ 47 Derrick Mason 1.00 .40
❑ 48 Darrell Jackson 1.00 .40
❑ 49 Curtis Conway .60 .25
❑ 50 Michael Vick 4.00 1.50
❑ 51 Rod Smith 1.00 .40
❑ 52 Muhsin Muhammad 1.00 .40
❑ 53 Drew Bledsoe 1.50 .60
❑ 54 Michael Bennett 1.00 .40
❑ 55 Joe Horn 1.00 .40
❑ 56 Stephen Davis 1.00 .40
❑ 57 Isaac Bruce 1.50 .60
❑ 58 Shaun Alexander 1.50 .60
❑ 59 Jerry Rice 3.00 1.25
❑ 60 Peyton Manning 2.50 1.00
❑ 61 Tony Gonzalez 1.00 .40
❑ 62 Jake Plummer 1.00 .40
❑ 63 Tim Couch .60 .25
❑ 64 Marty Booker 1.00 .40
❑ 65 Corey Dillon 1.00 .40
❑ 66 Steve McNair 1.50 .60
❑ 67 Jeff Garcia 1.50 .60
❑ 68 Hines Ward 1.50 .60
❑ 69 Laveranues Coles 1.00 .40
❑ 70 Amani Toomer 1.00 .40
❑ 71 Eric Moulds 1.00 .40
❑ 72 Donald Driver 1.00 .40
❑ 73 Jay Fiedler 1.00 .40
❑ 74 Charlie Garner 1.00 .40
❑ 75 Priest Holmes 2.00 .75
❑ 76 Edgerrin James 1.50 .60
❑ 77 Kerry Collins 1.00 .40
❑ 78 LaDainian Tomlinson 1.50 .60
❑ 79 Mark Brunell 1.00 .40
❑ 80 Marshall Faulk 1.50 .60
❑ 81 Lee Suggs RC 8.00 3.00
❑ 82 William Joseph RC 4.00 1.50
❑ 83 Brandon Lloyd RC 5.00 2.00
❑ 84 Nick Barnett RC 6.00 2.50
❑ 85 Andre Woolfolk RC 4.00 1.50
❑ 86 Jimmy Kennedy RC 4.00 1.50
❑ 87 Kliff Kingsbury RC 4.00 1.50
❑ 88 Andrew Williams RC 4.00 1.50
❑ 89 Mike Doss RC 4.00 1.50
❑ 90 Troy Polamalu RC 20.00 10.00
❑ 91 Bryant Johnson JSY RC 6.00 2.50
❑ 92 Justin Fargas JSY RC 6.00 2.50
❑ 93 Terence Newman JSY RC 12.00 6.00
❑ 94 Brian St.Pierre JSY RC 6.00 2.50
❑ 95 DeWayne Robertson JSY RC 6.00 2.50
❑ 96 Dave Ragone JSY RC 6.00 2.50
❑ 97 Teyo Johnson JSY RC 6.00 2.50
❑ 98 Bethel Johnson JSY RC 6.00 2.50
❑ 99 Tyrone Calico JSY RC 8.00 3.00
❑ 100 Carson Palmer JSY RC 25.00 12.50
❑ 101 Marcus Trufant JSY RC 6.00 2.50
❑ 102 Nate Burleson JSY RC 8.00 3.00
❑ 103 Musa Smith JSY RC 6.00 2.50
❑ 104 Anquan Boldin JSY RC 15.00 6.00
❑ 105 Chris Simms JSY RC 10.00 4.00
❑ 106 Taylor Jacobs JSY RC 6.00 2.50
❑ 107 Dallas Clark JSY RC 6.00 2.50
❑ 108 Seneca Wallace JSY RC 6.00 2.50
❑ 109 Ken Dorsey JSY RC 6.00 2.50
❑ 110 Willis McGahee JSY RC 15.00 6.00
❑ 111 Chris Brown JSY RC 8.00 3.00
❑ 112 Terrell Suggs JSY RC 10.00 4.00
❑ 113 Kelley Washington JSY RC 6.00 2.50
❑ 114 Onterrio Smith JSY RC 6.00 2.50
❑ 115 Rex Grossman JSY RC 10.00 4.00
❑ 116 LaBrandon Toefield AU RC 12.00 5.00
❑ 117 Sam Aiken AU RC 10.00 4.00
❑ 118 Malaefou Mackenzie AU RC 8.00 3.00
❑ 119 David Tyree AU RC 10.00 4.00
❑ 120 Jerome McDougle AU RC 12.00 5.00
❑ 121 DeWayne White AU RC 10.00 4.00
❑ 122 Zuriel Smith AU RC 8.00 3.00
❑ 123 Shaun McDonald AU RC 12.00 5.00
❑ 124 Andre Johnson AU/199 RC 60.0030.00
❑ 125 Ahmaad Galloway AU RC 10.00 4.00
❑ 126 Keenan Howry AU RC 12.00 5.00
❑ 127 Kareem Kelly AU RC 10.00 4.00
❑ 128 Brooks Bollinger AU RC 12.00 5.00
❑ 129 Arnaz Battle AU RC 15.00 6.00
❑ 130 Adrian Madise AU RC 10.00 4.00
❑ 131 LaTarence Dunbar AU RC 10.00 4.00
❑ 132 L.J. Smith AU RC 12.00 5.00
❑ 133 B.J. Askew AU RC 12.00 5.00
❑ 134 Michael Haynes AU RC 12.00 5.00
❑ 135 David Kircus AU RC 10.00 4.00
❑ 136 Kyle Boller AU/199 RC 50.00 20.00
❑ 137 Domanick Davis AU RC 40.00 15.00
❑ 138 Osi Umenyiora AU RC 30.00 15.00
❑ 139 Bobby Wade AU RC 12.00 5.00
❑ 140 Boss Bailey AU RC 15.00 6.00
❑ 141 Billy McMullen AU RC 10.00 4.00
❑ 142 Doug Gabriel AU RC 12.00 5.00
❑ 143 J.R. Tolver AU RC 10.00 4.00
❑ 144 Gibran Hamdan AU RC 8.00 3.00
❑ 145 Walter Young AU RC 8.00 3.00
❑ 146 Carl Ford AU RC 8.00 3.00
❑ 147 Andrew Pinnock AU RC 10.00 4.00
❑ 148 Byron Leftwich AU/199 RC 100.00 50.00
❑ 149 Ty Warren AU RC 12.00 5.00
❑ 150 Visanthe Shiancoe AU RC 10.00 4.00
❑ 151 Justin Gage AU RC 12.00 5.00
❑ 152 Brock Forsey AU RC 12.00 5.00
❑ 153 Casey Moore AU RC 10.00 4.00
❑ 154 Juston Wood AU RC 8.00 3.00
❑ 155 Aaron Walker AU RC 10.00 4.00
❑ 156 Trent Smith AU RC 12.00 5.00
❑ 157 Travis Anglin AU RC 8.00 3.00
❑ 158 Jeremi Johnson AU RC 10.00 4.00
❑ 159 Justin Griffith AU RC 10.00 4.00
❑ 160 Chris Davis AU RC 10.00 4.00
❑ 161 J.T. Wall AU RC 8.00 3.00
❑ 162 Larry Johnson AU/199 RC 135.0075.00
❑ 163 Jon Olinger AU RC 10.00 4.00
❑ 164 Donald Lee AU RC 10.00 4.00
❑ 165 Taco Wallace AU RC 10.00 4.00
❑ 166 DeAndrew Rubin AU RC 8.00 3.00
❑ 167 Ryan Hoag AU RC 8.00 3.00
❑ 168 Kevin Williams AU RC 12.00 5.00
❑ 169 Ovie Mughelli AU RC 8.00 3.00
❑ 171 Brandon Drumm AU RC 10.00 4.00
❑ 172 Brad Banks AU RC 10.00 4.00
❑ 173 Talman Gardner AU RC 12.00 5.00
❑ 174 Jason Witten AU RC 25.00 12.50

2004 Bowman's Best

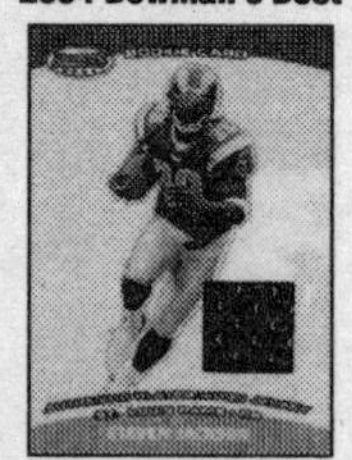

❑ COMP.SET w/o SP's (100) 50.00 25.00
❑ RC JSY GROUP A ODDS 1:130
❑ RC JSY GROUP B ODDS 1:236
❑ RC JSY GROUP C ODDS 1:86
❑ RC JSY GROUP D ODDS 1:38
❑ RC JSY GROUP E ODDS 1:31
❑ RC JSY GROUP F ODDS 1:27
❑ RC JSY GROUP G ODDS 1:50
❑ RC JSY GROUP H ODDS 1:89
❑ RC JSY GROUP I ODDS 1:29
❑ RC AU/199 STATED ODDS 1:311
❑ RC AU STATED ODDS 1:3
❑ 1 Brett Favre 4.00 1.50

❑ 2 Chris Chambers 1.00 .40
❑ 3 Kyle Boller 1.50 .60
❑ 4 Brian Urlacher 2.00 .75
❑ 5 Marvin Harrison 1.50 .60
❑ 6 Matt Hasselbeck 1.00 .40
❑ 7 Aaron Brooks 1.00 .40
❑ 8 Curtis Martin 1.50 .60
❑ 9 Keenan McCardell .60 .25
❑ 10 Terrell Owens 1.50 .60
❑ 11 Jimmy Smith 1.00 .40
❑ 12 Garrison Hearst 1.00 .40
❑ 13 Joe Horn 1.00 .40
❑ 14 David Carr 1.50 .60
❑ 15 Tom Brady 4.00 1.50
❑ 16 Shaun Alexander 1.50 .60
❑ 17 Tommy Maddox 1.00 .40
❑ 18 Tiki Barber 1.50 .60
❑ 19 Trent Green 1.00 .40
❑ 20 Anquan Boldin 1.50 .60
❑ 21 Peerless Price 1.00 .40
❑ 22 Jake Delhomme 1.50 .60
❑ 23 Eric Moulds 1.00 .40
❑ 24 Quincy Carter 1.00 .40
❑ 25 Steve McNair 1.50 .60
❑ 26 Tim Rattay .60 .25
❑ 27 Laveranues Coles 1.00 .40
❑ 28 Corey Dillon 1.00 .40
❑ 29 Byron Leftwich 2.00 .75
❑ 30 Chad Pennington 1.50 .60
❑ 31 Koren Robinson 1.00 .40
❑ 32 Plaxico Burress 1.00 .40
❑ 33 Steve Smith 1.50 .60
❑ 34 Warrick Dunn 1.00 .40
❑ 35 Jamal Lewis 1.50 .60
❑ 36 Charles Rogers 1.00 .40
❑ 37 Tony Gonzalez 1.00 .40
❑ 38 Jake Plummer 1.00 .40
❑ 39 Chad Johnson 1.50 .60
❑ 40 Peyton Manning 2.50 1.00
❑ 41 Daunte Culpepper 1.50 .60
❑ 42 Fred Taylor 1.00 .40
❑ 43 Amani Toomer 1.00 .40
❑ 44 Santana Moss 1.00 .40
❑ 45 Deuce McAllister 1.50 .60
❑ 46 Rex Grossman 1.50 .60
❑ 47 Ray Lewis 1.50 .60
❑ 48 Hines Ward 1.50 .60
❑ 49 Darrell Jackson 1.00 .40
❑ 50 Randy Moss 2.00 .75
❑ 51 Carson Palmer 2.00 .75
❑ 52 Rod Smith 1.00 .40
❑ 53 Drew Bledsoe 1.50 .60
❑ 54 Brad Johnson 1.00 .40
❑ 55 Travis Henry 1.00 .40
❑ 56 Joey Harrington 1.50 .60
❑ 57 Edgerrin James 1.50 .60
❑ 58 Kurt Warner 1.50 .60
❑ 59 Josh McCown 1.00 .40
❑ 60 Clinton Portis 1.50 .60
❑ 61 Brian Westbrook 1.00 .40
❑ 62 Marc Bulger 1.50 .60
❑ 63 Charlie Garner 1.00 .40
❑ 64 Torry Holt 1.50 .60
❑ 65 LaDainian Tomlinson 2.00 .75
❑ 66 Mark Brunell 1.00 .40
❑ 67 Derrick Mason 1.00 .40
❑ 68 Andre Johnson 1.50 .60
❑ 69 Keyshawn Johnson 1.00 .40
❑ 70 Ahman Green 1.50 .60
❑ 71 Rudi Johnson 1.00 .40
❑ 72 Stephen Davis 1.00 .40
❑ 73 Jeff Garcia 1.50 .60
❑ 74 Michael Strahan 1.00 .40
❑ 75 Michael Vick 3.00 1.25
❑ 76 Ricky Williams 1.50 .60
❑ 77 Domanick Davis 1.50 .60
❑ 78 Priest Holmes 2.00 .75
❑ 79 Marshall Faulk 1.50 .60
❑ 80 Donovan McNabb 2.00 .75
❑ 81 Dunta Robinson RC 4.00 1.50
❑ 82 Robert Gallery RC 6.00 2.50
❑ 83 Ben Troupe RC 4.00 1.50
❑ 84 Antwan Odom RC 4.00 1.50
❑ 85 Brandon Miree RC 3.00 1.25
❑ 86 Darnell Dockett RC 3.00 1.25
❑ 87 Vince Wilfork RC 5.00 2.00
❑ 88 Randy Starks RC 3.00 1.25
❑ 89 Chris Cooley RC 4.00 1.50
❑ 90 Dwan Edwards RC 2.00 .75
❑ 91 Patrick Crayton RC 4.00 1.50
❑ 92 Sean Jones RC 3.00 1.25
❑ 93 Sean Ryan RC 3.00 1.25
❑ 94 Chris Gamble RC 5.00 2.00
❑ 95 Will Smith RC 4.00 1.50
❑ 96 Sloan Thomas RC 3.00 1.25
❑ 97 Tim Euhus RC 4.00 1.50
❑ 98 Tommie Harris RC 4.00 1.50
❑ 99 Will Poole RC 4.00 1.50
❑ 100 Karlos Dansby RC 4.00 1.50
❑ 101 Bernard Berrian JSY RC D 6.00 2.50
❑ 102 DeAngelo Hall JSY RC A 8.00 3.00
❑ 103 Mewelde Moore JSY RC G 8.00 3.00
❑ 104 Rashaun Woods JSY RC G 6.00 2.50
❑ 105 Reggie Williams JSY RC 8.00 3.00
❑ 106 Derrick Hamilton JSY RC F 5.00 2.00
❑ 107 Kellen Winslow JSY RC C 12.00 5.00
❑ 108 Devard Darling JSY RC D 6.00 2.50
❑ 109 Michael Clayton JSY RC B 12.00 5.00
❑ 110 Larry Fitzgerald JSY RC E 20.00 7.50
❑ 111 Greg Jones JSY RC E 6.00 2.50
❑ 112 Chris Perry JSY RC H 12.00 5.00
❑ 113 Lee Evans JSY RC F 8.00 3.00
❑ 114 Tatum Bell JSY RC E 12.00 5.00
❑ 115 Steven Jackson JSY RC I 20.00 7.50
❑ 116 Matt Schaub JSY RC A 10.00 4.00
❑ 117 Ben Troupe JSY 6.00 2.50
❑ 118 Devery Henderson JSY RC F 5.002.00
❑ 119 Ben Watson JSY RC E 6.00 2.50
❑ 120 J.P. Losman JSY RC I 12.00 5.00
❑ 121 Keary Colbert JSY RC F 8.00 3.00
❑ 122 Darius Watts JSY RC C 6.00 2.50
❑ 123 Cedric Cobbs JSY RC D 6.00 2.50
❑ 124 Luke McCown JSY RC A 6.00 2.50
❑ 125 Michael Jenkins JSY RC A 6.00 2.50
❑ 126 Eli Manning AU/199 RC 150.00 90.00
❑ 127 Roy Williams AU/199 RC 80.00 30.00
❑ 128 Kevin Jones AU/199 RC 120.00 50.00
❑ 129 Philip Rivers AU/199 RC 80.00 60.00
❑ 130 Roethlis AU/199 RC 350.00 200.00
❑ 131 Carlos Francis AU RC 12.00 5.00
❑ 132 Bradlee Van Pelt AU RC 25.00 12.50
❑ 133 Michael Turner AU RC 20.00 7.50
❑ 134 Kenechi Udeze AU RC 15.00 6.00
❑ 135 Jeff Smoker AU RC 15.00 6.00
❑ 136 Josh Harris AU RC 12.00 5.00
❑ 137 Derrick Strait AU RC 12.00 5.00
❑ 138 Jonathan Vilma AU RC 20.00 7.50
❑ 139 Triandos Luke AU RC 12.00 5.00
❑ 140 Jim Sorgi AU RC 15.00 6.00
❑ 141 Ryan Krause AU RC 12.00 5.00
❑ 142 Julius Jones AU RC 80.00 40.00
❑ 143 Mark Jones AU RC 12.00 5.00
❑ 144 P.K. Sam AU RC 12.00 5.00
❑ 145 B.J. Symons AU RC 15.00 6.00
❑ 146 Adimchinobe Echemandu AU RC 12.00 5.00
❑ 147 Casey Bramlet AU RC 12.00 5.00
❑ 148 Clarence Moore AU RC 15.00 6.00
❑ 149 D.J. Williams AU RC 15.00 6.00
❑ 150 Jeris McIntyre AU RC 12.00 5.00
❑ 151 Jerricho Cotchery AU RC 15.00 6.00
❑ 152 Andy Hall AU RC 12.00 5.00
❑ 153 Samie Parker AU RC 15.00 6.00
❑ 154 Maurice Mann AU RC 12.00 5.00
❑ 155 Jonathan Smith AU RC 12.00 5.00
❑ 156 Derrick Ward AU RC 10.00 4.00
❑ 157 D.J. Hackett AU RC 12.00 5.00
❑ 158 Craig Krenzel AU RC 15.00 6.00
❑ 159 Jared Lorenzen AU RC 12.00 5.00
❑ 160 Cody Pickett AU RC 15.00 6.00
❑ 161 Jamaar Taylor AU RC 15.00 6.00
❑ 162 Michael Boulware AU RC 15.00 6.00
❑ 163 Matt Mauck AU RC 12.00 5.00
❑ 164 John Navarre AU RC 15.00 6.00
❑ 165 Ahmad Carroll AU RC 15.00 6.00
❑ 166 Bruce Perry AU RC 15.00 6.00
❑ 167 Erik Jensen AU RC 12.00 5.00
❑ 168 Matt Kranchick AU RC 15.00 6.00
❑ 169 Courtney Anderson AU RC 12.00 5.00
❑ 170 Nate Lawrie AU RC 12.00 5.00
❑ 171 Thomas Tapeh AU RC 12.00 5.00
❑ 172 Courtney Watson AU RC 15.00 6.00
❑ 173 Drew Carter AU RC 15.00 6.00
❑ 174 Ricardo Colclough AU RC 15.00 6.00
❑ 175 Dontarrious Thomas AU RC 15.006.00
❑ 176 Ernest Wilford AU RC 15.00 6.00
❑ 177 Quincy Wilson AU RC 12.00 5.00
❑ 178 Derek Abney AU RC 15.00 6.00
❑ 179 Jeff Dugan AU RC 10.00 4.00
❑ 180 Ben Hartsock AU RC 15.00 6.00
❑ 181 Matt Kegel AU RC 15.00 6.00
❑ 182 Derrick Knight AU RC 12.00 5.00
❑ 183 Teddy Lehman AU RC 15.00 6.00
❑ 184 Johnnie Morant AU RC 15.00 6.00
❑ 185A B.Sanders AU RC Long AU 150.00 90.00
❑ 185B B.Sanders AU RC Short AU 100.00 50.00
❑ 186 Michael Gaines AU RC 12.00 5.00
❑ 187 Daryl Smith AU RC 15.00 6.00
❑ 188 Jason Babin AU RC 15.00 6.00

2005 Bowman's Best

❑ COMP.SET w/o SPs (100) 40.00 15.00
❑ ROOKIE JSY STATED ODDS 1:14
❑ ROOKIE JSY PRINT RUN 799 SER.#'d SETS
❑ COMMON ROOKIE AU 8.00 3.00
❑ ROOKIE AU SEMISTARS 10.00 4.00
❑ ROOKIE AU UNL.STARS 12.00 5.00
❑ ROOKIE AU/999 STATED ODDS 1:8
❑ ROOKIE AU/199 STATED ODDS 1:296
❑ ROOKIE AU PRINT RUN 999 SER.#'d SETS
❑ AU EXCH EXPIRATION: 10/31/2007
❑ UNPRICED GOLD PRINT RUN 1 SET
❑ UNPRICED PRINT.PLATE PRINT RUN 1 SET
❑ 1 Tiki Barber 1.00 .40
❑ 2 Peyton Manning 2.50 1.00
❑ 3 Tony Gonzalez .60 .25
❑ 4 Terrell Owens 1.00 .40
❑ 5 Brett Favre 2.50 1.00
❑ 6 Rudi Johnson .60 .25
❑ 7 Hines Ward 1.00 .40
❑ 8 Andre Johnson .60 .25
❑ 9 Tom Brady 2.50 1.00
❑ 10 LaDainian Tomlinson 1.25 .50
❑ 11 Daunte Culpepper 1.00 .40
❑ 12 Muhsin Muhammad .60 .25
❑ 13 Dwight Freeney .60 .25
❑ 14 Curtis Martin 1.00 .40
❑ 15 Eli Manning 1.50 .60
❑ 16 Willis McGahee 1.00 .40
❑ 17 Steve McNair 1.00 .40
❑ 18 Jamal Lewis 1.00 .40
❑ 19 Reggie Wayne .60 .25
❑ 20 Trent Green .60 .25
❑ 21 Isaac Bruce .60 .25
❑ 22 Edgerrin James 1.00 .40

❑ 23	Marc Bulger	1.00	.40
❑ 24	Torry Holt	1.00	.40
❑ 25	Deuce McAllister	1.00	.40
❑ 26	Jake Plummer	.60	.25
❑ 27	Randy Moss	1.00	.40
❑ 28	Drew Brees	1.00	.40
❑ 29	Ahman Green	1.00	.40
❑ 30	Marvin Harrison	1.00	.40
❑ 31	Michael Vick	1.50	.60
❑ 32	Julius Jones	1.25	.50
❑ 33	Matt Hasselbeck	.60	.25
❑ 34	Priest Holmes	1.00	.40
❑ 35	Drew Bennett	.60	.25
❑ 36	Donovan McNabb	1.25	.50
❑ 37	Chad Johnson	1.00	.40
❑ 38	Fred Taylor	.60	.25
❑ 39	Chris Brown	.60	.25
❑ 40	Jake Delhomme	1.00	.40
❑ 41	Joe Horn	.60	.25
❑ 42	Chad Pennington	1.00	.40
❑ 43	Corey Dillon	.60	.25
❑ 44	Byron Leftwich	1.00	.40
❑ 45	Javon Walker	.60	.25
❑ 46	Ben Roethlisberger	2.50	1.00
❑ 47	Eric Moulds	.60	.25
❑ 48	Domanick Davis	.60	.25
❑ 49	Steven Jackson	1.25	.50
❑ 50	Shaun Alexander	1.25	.50
❑ 51	Stanford Routt RC	4.00	1.50
❑ 52	Marion Barber RC	8.00	3.00
❑ 53	Matt Roth RC	5.00	2.00
❑ 54	James Kilian RC	5.00	2.00
❑ 55	Alex Barron RC	2.50	1.00
❑ 56	Madison Hedgecock RC	5.00	2.00
❑ 57	Patrick Estes RC	4.00	1.50
❑ 58	Bryant McFadden RC	5.00	2.00
❑ 59	Dan Cody RC	5.00	2.00
❑ 60	Justin Miller RC	4.00	1.50
❑ 61	Paris Warren RC	4.00	1.50
❑ 62	Marcus Spears RC	5.00	2.00
❑ 63	Odell Thurman RC	5.00	2.00
❑ 64	Craphonso Thorpe RC	4.00	1.50
❑ 65	Dustin Fox RC	5.00	2.00
❑ 66	David Pollack RC	5.00	2.00
❑ 67	Anthony Davis RC	4.00	1.50
❑ 68	Mike Nugent RC	5.00	2.00
❑ 69	David Greene RC	5.00	2.00
❑ 70	Rick Razzano RC	5.00	2.00
❑ 70AU	Rick Razzano AU	12.00	5.00
❑ 71	Mike Patterson RC	5.00	2.00
❑ 72	Derek Anderson RC	5.00	2.00
❑ 72AU	Derek Anderson AU	12.00	5.00
❑ 73	Marlin Jackson RC	5.00	2.00
❑ 73AU	Marlin Jackson AU	12.00	5.00
❑ 74	Boomer Grigsby RC	6.00	2.50
❑ 75	Kevin Burnett RC	5.00	2.00
❑ 76	Ryan Riddle RC	2.50	1.00
❑ 77	Brock Berlin RC	4.00	1.50
❑ 78	Khalif Barnes RC	4.00	1.50
❑ 79	Marcus Maxwell RC	4.00	1.50
❑ 80	Fred Gibson RC	4.00	1.50
❑ 81	T.A. McLendon RC	2.50	1.00
❑ 82	Kirk Morrison RC	5.00	2.00
❑ 83	Sean Considine RC	5.00	2.00
❑ 84	Luis Castillo RC	5.00	2.00
❑ 85	Darryl Blackstock RC	4.00	1.50
❑ 86	Airese Currie RC	5.00	2.00
❑ 87	Corey Webster RC	5.00	2.00
❑ 88	Kurt Campbell RC	4.00	1.50
❑ 89	Ellis Hobbs RC	5.00	2.00
❑ 90	Timmy Chang RC	4.00	1.50
❑ 91	Travis Johnson RC	4.00	1.50
❑ 92	Eric Moore RC	4.00	1.50
❑ 93	Barrett Ruud RC	5.00	2.00
❑ 94	Erasmus James RC	5.00	2.00
❑ 95	Anttaj Hawthorne RC	4.00	1.50
❑ 96	Manuel White RC	4.00	1.50
❑ 97	Rian Wallace RC	4.00	1.50
❑ 98	Justin Tuck RC	5.00	2.00
❑ 99	Travis Daniels RC	4.00	1.50
❑ 100	Donte Nicholson RC	5.00	2.00
❑ 101	Matt Jones JSY RC	15.00	6.00
❑ 102	J.J. Arrington JSY RC	10.00	4.00
❑ 103	Mark Bradley JSY RC	10.00	4.00
❑ 104	Reggie Brown JSY RC	8.00	3.00
❑ 105	Jason Campbell JSY RC	10.00	4.00
❑ 106	Maurice Clarett JSY	8.00	3.00
❑ 107	Mark Clayton JSY RC	10.00	4.00
❑ 108	Braylon Edwards JSY RC	15.00	6.00
❑ 109	Ciatrick Fason JSY RC	8.00	3.00
❑ 110	Charlie Frye JSY RC	12.00	5.00
❑ 111	Frank Gore JSY RC	10.00	4.00
❑ 112	Vincent Jackson JSY RC	8.00	3.00
❑ 113	Adam Jones JSY RC	8.00	3.00
❑ 114	Stefan LeFors JSY	8.00	3.00
❑ 114AU	Stefan LeFors AU RC	12.00	5.00
❑ 115	Ryan Moats JSY	8.00	3.00
❑ 115AU	Ryan Moats AU RC	20.00	7.50
❑ 116	Vernand Morency JSY RC	8.00	3.00
❑ 117	Terrence Murphy JSY RC	8.00	3.00
❑ 118	Kyle Orton JSY RC	10.00	4.00
❑ 119	Roscoe Parrish JSY RC	8.00	3.00
❑ 120	Courtney Roby JSY RC	8.00	3.00
❑ 121	Carlos Rogers JSY RC	10.00	4.00
❑ 122	Antrel Rolle JSY RC	8.00	3.00
❑ 123	Eric Shelton JSY RC	8.00	3.00
❑ 124	Andrew Walter JSY RC	10.00	4.00
❑ 125	Roddy White JSY RC	8.00	3.00
❑ 126	Carnell Williams JSY RC	25.00	10.00
❑ 127	Troy Williamson JSY RC	12.00	5.00
❑ 128	Cedric Benson AU/199 RC	60.00	30.00
❑ 129	Aaron Rodgers AU/199 RC	100.00	50.00
❑ 130	Alex Smith QB AU/199 RC	120.00	60.00
❑ 131	Mike Williams AU/199	60.00	30.00
❑ 132	Ronnie Brown AU/199 RC	120.00	60.00
❑ 133	Adrian McPherson AU RC	15.00	6.00
❑ 134	Brandon Jacobs AU RC	15.00	6.00
❑ 135	Chad Owens AU RC	12.00	5.00
❑ 136	Chase Lyman AU RC	10.00	4.00
❑ 137	Chris Henry AU RC EXCH	12.00	5.00
❑ 138	Craig Bragg AU RC	10.00	4.00
❑ 139	Damien Nash AU RC	10.00	4.00
❑ 140	Dante Ridgeway AU RC	10.00	4.00
❑ 141	Darren Sproles AU RC	12.00	5.00
❑ 142	Deandra Cobb AU RC	10.00	4.00
❑ 143	Gino Guidugli AU RC	8.00	3.00
❑ 144	J.R. Russell AU RC	10.00	4.00
❑ 145	Jerome Mathis AU RC EXCH	12.00	5.00
❑ 146	Josh Davis AU RC	10.00	4.00
❑ 147	Kay-Jay Harris AU RC	10.00	4.00
❑ 148	Larry Brackins AU RC	10.00	4.00
❑ 149	Matt Cassel AU RC	15.00	6.00
❑ 150	Noah Herron AU RC	12.00	5.00
❑ 151	Rasheed Marshall AU RC	12.00	5.00
❑ 152	Roydell Williams AU RC	12.00	5.00
❑ 153	Ryan Fitzpatrick AU RC	25.00	10.00
❑ 154	Steve Savoy AU RC	8.00	3.00
❑ 155	Tab Perry AU RC	12.00	5.00
❑ 156	Shawne Merriman AU RC	30.00	12.50
❑ 157	Charles Frederick AU RC	10.00	4.00
❑ 158	Alvin Pearman AU RC	12.00	5.00
❑ 159	Channing Crowder AU RC	12.00	5.00
❑ 160	Fabian Washington AU RC	12.00	5.00
❑ 161	Dan Orlovsky AU RC	15.00	6.00
❑ 162	Derrick Johnson AU RC	20.00	7.50
❑ 163	Alex Smith TE AU RC	12.00	5.00
❑ 164	Cedric Houston AU RC EXCH	12.00	5.00
❑ 165	Brandon Jones AU RC	12.00	5.00
❑ 166	DeMarcus Ware AU RC	20.00	7.50
❑ 167	Lionel Gates AU RC	10.00	4.00

1994 Classic NFL Experience

❑	COMPLETE SET (100)	10.00	4.00
❑ 1	Checklist 1	.05	.01
❑ 2	Checklist 2	.05	.01
❑ 3	Bobby Hebert	.05	.01
❑ 4	Erric Pegram	.05	.01
❑ 5	Andre Rison	.10	.02
❑ 6	Deion Sanders	.40	.15
❑ 7	Cornelius Bennett	.10	.02
❑ 8	Jim Kelly	.20	.07
❑ 9	Andre Reed	.10	.02
❑ 10	Bruce Smith	.20	.07
❑ 11	Thurman Thomas	.20	.07
❑ 12	Curtis Conway	.20	.07
❑ 13	Jim Harbaugh	.20	.07
❑ 14	John Copeland	.05	.01
❑ 15	David Klingler	.05	.01
❑ 16	Carl Pickens	.10	.02
❑ 17	Eric Metcalf	.10	.02
❑ 18	Vinny Testaverde	.10	.02
❑ 19	Eric Turner	.05	.01
❑ 20	Tommy Vardell	.05	.01
❑ 21	Troy Aikman	.75	.30
❑ 22	Michael Irvin	.20	.07
❑ 23	Emmitt Smith	1.25	.50
❑ 24	Kevin Williams WR	.10	.02
❑ 25	John Elway	1.50	.60
❑ 26	Glyn Milburn	.10	.02
❑ 27	Shannon Sharpe	.10	.02
❑ 28	Herman Moore	.20	.07
❑ 29	Rodney Peete	.05	.01
❑ 30	Barry Sanders	1.25	.50
❑ 31	Pat Swilling	.05	.01
❑ 32	Brett Favre	1.50	.60
❑ 33	Sterling Sharpe	.10	.02
❑ 34	Reggie White	.20	.07
❑ 35	Haywood Jeffires	.10	.02
❑ 36	Warren Moon	.20	.07
❑ 37	Webster Slaughter	.05	.01
❑ 38	Lorenzo White	.05	.01
❑ 39	Quentin Coryatt	.05	.01
❑ 40	Jeff George	.20	.07
❑ 41	Roosevelt Potts	.05	.01
❑ 42	Marcus Allen	.20	.07
❑ 43	Joe Montana	1.50	.60
❑ 44	Neil Smith	.10	.02
❑ 45	Derrick Thomas	.20	.07
❑ 46	Tim Brown	.20	.07
❑ 47	Jeff Hostetler	.10	.02
❑ 48	Rocket Ismail	.10	.02
❑ 49	Anthony Smith	.05	.01
❑ 50	Jerome Bettis	.40	.15
❑ 51	Jim Everett	.10	.02
❑ 52	T.J.Rubley RC	.05	.01
❑ 53	Keith Jackson	.05	.01
❑ 54	Terry Kirby	.20	.07
❑ 55	Dan Marino	1.50	.60
❑ 56	O.J.McDuffie	.20	.07
❑ 57	Scott Mitchell	.10	.02
❑ 58	Cris Carter	.40	.15
❑ 59	Chris Doleman	.05	.01
❑ 60	Robert Smith	.20	.07
❑ 61	Drew Bledsoe	.60	.25
❑ 62	Vincent Brisby	.10	.02
❑ 63	Derek Brown RBK	.05	.01
❑ 64	Willie Roaf	.05	.01
❑ 65	Irv Smith	.05	.01
❑ 66	Renaldo Turnbull	.05	.01
❑ 67	Rodney Hampton	.10	.02
❑ 68	Phil Simms	.10	.02
❑ 69	Lawrence Taylor	.20	.07
❑ 70	Boomer Esiason	.10	.02

❑ 71 Marvin Jones	.05	.01
❑ 72 Ronnie Lott	.10	.02
❑ 73 Johnny Mitchell	.05	.01
❑ 74 Rob Moore	.10	.02
❑ 75 Victor Bailey	.05	.01
❑ 76 Randall Cunningham	.20	.07
❑ 77 Ken O'Brien	.05	.01
❑ 78 Steve Beuerlein	.10	.02
❑ 79 Garrison Hearst	.20	.07
❑ 80 Ronald Moore	.05	.01
❑ 81 Ricky Proehl	.05	.01
❑ 82 Deon Figures	.05	.01
❑ 83 Barry Foster	.05	.01
❑ 84 Neil O'Donnell	.20	.07
❑ 85 Rod Woodson	.10	.02
❑ 86 Natrone Means	.20	.07
❑ 87 Anthony Miller	.10	.02
❑ 88 Junior Seau	.20	.07
❑ 89 Jerry Rice	.75	.30
❑ 90 Ricky Watters	.10	.02
❑ 91 Steve Young	.75	.30
❑ 92 Brian Blades	.10	.02
❑ 93 Cortez Kennedy	.10	.02
❑ 94 Rick Mirer	.20	.07
❑ 95 Stan Humphries	.10	.02
❑ 96 Eric Curry	.05	.01
❑ 97 Craig Erickson	.05	.01
❑ 98 Reggie Brooks	.10	.02
❑ 99 Desmond Howard	.10	.02
❑ 100 Mark Rypien	.05	.01
❑ SP1 Troy Aikman/1994	40.00	15.00

1994 Collector's Choice

❑ COMPLETE SET (384)	20.00	7.50
❑ 1 Antonio Langham RC	.10	.02
❑ 2 Aaron Glenn RC	.25	.08
❑ 3 Sam Adams RC	.10	.02
❑ 4 Dewayne Washington RC	.10	.02
❑ 5 Dan Wilkinson RC	.10	.02
❑ 6 Bryant Young RC	.25	.08
❑ 7 Aaron Taylor RC	.05	.01
❑ 8 Willie McGinest RC	.25	.08
❑ 9 Trev Alberts RC	.10	.02
❑ 10 Jamir Miller RC	.10	.02
❑ 11 John Thierry RC	.05	.01
❑ 12 Heath Shuler RC	.25	.08
❑ 13 Trent Dilfer RC	1.25	.50
❑ 14 Marshall Faulk RC	5.00	2.00
❑ 15 Greg Hill RC	.25	.08
❑ 16 William Floyd RC	.25	.08
❑ 17 Chuck Levy RC	.05	.01
❑ 18 Charlie Garner RC	1.25	.50
❑ 19 Mario Bates RC	.25	.08
❑ 20 Donnell Bennett RC	.25	.08
❑ 21 LeShon Johnson RC	.10	.02
❑ 22 Calvin Jones RC	.05	.01
❑ 23 Darnay Scott RC	.50	.20
❑ 24 Charles Johnson RC	.25	.08
❑ 25 Johnnie Morton RC	.50	.20
❑ 26 Shante Carver RC	.05	.01
❑ 27 Derrick Alexander WR RC	.25	.08
❑ 28 David Palmer RC	.25	.08
❑ 29 Ryan Yarborough RC	.05	.01
❑ 30 Errict Rhett RC	.25	.08
❑ 31 James Washington I93	.05	.01
❑ 32 Sterling Sharpe I93	.05	.01
❑ 33 Drew Bledsoe I93	.25	.08
❑ 34 Eric Allen I93	.05	.01
❑ 35 Jerome Bettis I93	.25	.08
❑ 36 Joe Montana I93	.60	.25
❑ 37 John Carney I93	.05	.01
❑ 38 Emmitt Smith I93	.50	.20
❑ 39 Chris Warren I93	.25	.08
❑ 40 Reggie Brooks I93	.05	.01
❑ 41 Gary Brown I93	.05	.01
❑ 42 Tim Brown I93	.10	.02
❑ 43 Erric Pegram I93	.05	.01
❑ 44 Ronald Moore I93	.05	.01
❑ 45 Jerry Rice I93	.40	.15
❑ 46 Ricky Watters TE	.10	.02
❑ 47 Joe Montana TE	.60	.25
❑ 48 Reggie Brooks TE	.05	.01
❑ 49 Rick Mirer TE	.25	.08
❑ 50 Rocket Ismail TE	.10	.02
❑ 51 Curtis Conway TE	.10	.02
❑ 52 Junior Seau TE	.25	.08
❑ 53 Mark Carrier DB TE	.05	.01
❑ 54 Ronnie Lott TE	.10	.02
❑ 55 Marcus Allen TE	.25	.08
❑ 56 Michael Irvin TE	.25	.08
❑ 57 Bennie Blades	.05	.01
❑ 58 Randal Hill	.05	.01
❑ 59 Brian Blades	.10	.02
❑ 60 Russell Maryland	.05	.01
❑ 61 Jim Kelly	.25	.08
❑ 62 Arthur Marshall	.05	.01
❑ 63 Webster Slaughter	.05	.01
❑ 64 Dave Krieg	.10	.02
❑ 65 Steve Jordan	.05	.01
❑ 66 Neil O'Donnell	.25	.08
❑ 67 Andre Reed	.10	.02
❑ 68 Mike Croel	.05	.01
❑ 69 Al Smith	.05	.01
❑ 70 Joe Montana	1.50	.60
❑ 71 Randall McDaniel	.05	.01
❑ 72 Greg Lloyd	.10	.02
❑ 73 Thomas Smith	.05	.01
❑ 74 Glyn Milburn	.10	.02
❑ 75 Lorenzo White	.05	.01
❑ 76 Neil Smith	.10	.02
❑ 77 John Randle	.10	.02
❑ 78 Rod Woodson	.10	.02
❑ 79 Russell Maryland	.05	.01
❑ 80 Rodney Peete	.05	.01
❑ 81 Jackie Harris	.05	.01
❑ 82 James Jett	.05	.01
❑ 83 Rodney Hampton	.10	.02
❑ 84 Bill Romanowski	.05	.01
❑ 85 Ken Norton Jr.	.10	.02
❑ 86 Barry Sanders	1.25	.50
❑ 87 Johnny Holland	.05	.01
❑ 88 Terry McDaniel	.05	.01
❑ 89 Greg Jackson	.05	.01
❑ 90 Dana Stubblefield	.10	.02
❑ 91 Jay Novacek	.10	.02
❑ 92 Chris Spielman	.10	.02
❑ 93 Ken Ruettgers	.05	.01
❑ 94 Greg Robinson	.05	.01
❑ 95 Mark Jackson	.05	.01
❑ 96 John Taylor	.10	.02
❑ 97 Roger Harper	.05	.01
❑ 98 Jerry Ball	.05	.01
❑ 99 Keith Byars	.05	.01
❑ 100 Morten Andersen	.05	.01
❑ 101 Eric Allen	.05	.01
❑ 102 Marion Butts	.05	.01
❑ 103 Michael Haynes	.10	.02
❑ 104 Rob Burnett	.05	.01
❑ 105 Marco Coleman	.05	.01
❑ 106 Derek Brown RBK	.05	.01
❑ 107 Andy Harmon	.05	.01
❑ 108 Darren Carrington	.05	.01
❑ 109 Bobby Hebert	.05	.01
❑ 110 Mark Carrier WR	.10	.02
❑ 111 Bryan Cox	.05	.01
❑ 112 Toi Cook	.05	.01
❑ 113 Tim Harris	.05	.01
❑ 114 John Friesz	.10	.02
❑ 115 Neal Anderson	.05	.01
❑ 116 Jerome Bettis	.40	.15
❑ 117 Bruce Armstrong	.05	.01
❑ 118 Brad Baxter	.05	.01
❑ 119 Johnny Bailey	.05	.01
❑ 120 Brian Blades	.10	.02
❑ 121 Mark Carrier DB	.05	.01
❑ 122 Shane Conlan	.05	.01
❑ 123 Drew Bledsoe	.60	.25
❑ 124 Chris Burkett	.05	.01
❑ 125 Steve Beuerlein	.10	.02
❑ 126 Ferrell Edmunds	.05	.01
❑ 127 Curtis Conway	.25	.08
❑ 128 Troy Drayton	.05	.01
❑ 129 Vincent Brown	.05	.01
❑ 130 Boomer Esiason	.10	.02
❑ 131 Larry Centers	.25	.08
❑ 132 Carlton Gray	.05	.01
❑ 133 Chris Miller	.05	.01
❑ 134 Eric Metcalf	.10	.02
❑ 135 Mark Higgs	.05	.01
❑ 136 Tyrone Hughes	.10	.02
❑ 137 Randall Cunningham	.25	.08
❑ 138 Ronnie Harmon	.05	.01
❑ 139 Andre Rison	.10	.02
❑ 140 Eric Turner	.05	.01
❑ 141 Terry Kirby	.25	.08
❑ 142 Eric Martin	.05	.01
❑ 143 Seth Joyner	.05	.01
❑ 144 Stan Humphries	.10	.02
❑ 145 Deion Sanders	.40	.15
❑ 146 Vinny Testaverde	.10	.02
❑ 147 Dan Marino	1.50	.60
❑ 148 Renaldo Turnbull	.05	.01
❑ 149 Herschel Walker	.10	.02
❑ 150 Anthony Miller	.10	.02
❑ 151 Richard Dent	.10	.02
❑ 152 Jim Everett	.10	.02
❑ 153 Ben Coates	.10	.02
❑ 154 Jeff Lageman	.05	.01
❑ 155 Garrison Hearst	.25	.08
❑ 156 Kelvin Martin	.05	.01
❑ 157 Dante Jones	.05	.01
❑ 158 Sean Gilbert	.05	.01
❑ 159 Leonard Russell	.05	.01
❑ 160 Ronnie Lott	.10	.02
❑ 161 Randal Hill	.05	.01
❑ 162 Rick Mirer	.25	.08
❑ 163 Alonzo Spellman	.05	.01
❑ 164 Todd Lyght	.05	.01
❑ 165 Chris Slade	.05	.01
❑ 166 Johnny Mitchell	.05	.01
❑ 167 Ronald Moore	.05	.01
❑ 168 Eugene Robinson	.05	.01
❑ 169 Chris Hinton	.05	.01
❑ 170 Dan Footman	.05	.01
❑ 171 Keith Jackson	.05	.01
❑ 172 Rickey Jackson	.05	.01
❑ 173 Heath Sherman	.05	.01
❑ 174 Chris Mims	.05	.01
❑ 175 Erric Pegram	.05	.01
❑ 176 Leroy Hoard	.05	.01
❑ 177 O.J.McDuffie	.25	.08
❑ 178 Wayne Martin	.05	.01
❑ 179 Clyde Simmons	.05	.01
❑ 180 Leslie O'Neal	.05	.01
❑ 181 Mike Pritchard	.05	.01
❑ 182 Michael Jackson	.10	.02
❑ 183 Scott Mitchell	.10	.02
❑ 184 Lorenzo Neal	.05	.01
❑ 185 William Thomas	.05	.01
❑ 186 Junior Seau	.25	.08
❑ 187 Chris Gedney	.05	.01
❑ 188 Tim Lester	.05	.01
❑ 189 Sam Gash	.05	.01
❑ 190 Johnny Johnson	.05	.01

❑	191	Chuck Cecil	.05	.01
❑	192	Cortez Kennedy	.10	.02
❑	193	Jim Harbaugh	.25	.08
❑	194	Roman Phifer	.05	.01
❑	195	Pat Harlow	.05	.01
❑	196	Rob Moore	.10	.02
❑	197	Gary Clark	.10	.02
❑	198	Jon Vaughn	.05	.01
❑	199	Craig Heyward	.10	.02
❑	200	Michael Stewart	.05	.01
❑	201	Greg McMurtry	.05	.01
❑	202	Brian Washington	.05	.01
❑	203	Ken Harvey	.05	.01
❑	204	Chris Warren	.10	.02
❑	205	Bruce Smith	.25	.08
❑	206	Tom Rouen	.05	.01
❑	207	Cris Dishman	.05	.01
❑	208	Keith Cash	.05	.01
❑	209	Carlos Jenkins	.05	.01
❑	210	Levon Kirkland	.05	.01
❑	211	Pete Metzelaars	.05	.01
❑	212	Shannon Sharpe	.10	.02
❑	213	Cody Carlson	.05	.01
❑	214	Derrick Thomas	.25	.08
❑	215	Emmitt Smith	1.25	.50
❑	216	Robert Porcher	.05	.01
❑	217	Sterling Sharpe	.10	.02
❑	218	Anthony Smith	.05	.01
❑	219	Mike Sherrard	.05	.01
❑	220	Tom Rathman	.05	.01
❑	221	Nate Newton	.05	.01
❑	222	Pat Swilling	.05	.01
❑	223	George Teague	.05	.01
❑	224	Greg Townsend	.05	.01
❑	225	Eric Guliford RC	.10	.02
❑	226	Leroy Thompson	.05	.01
❑	227	Thurman Thomas	.25	.08
❑	228	Dan Williams	.05	.01
❑	229	Bubba McDowell	.05	.01
❑	230	Tracy Simien	.05	.01
❑	231	Scottie Graham RC	.10	.02
❑	232	Eric Green	.05	.01
❑	233	Phil Simms	.10	.02
❑	234	Ricky Watters	.10	.02
❑	235	Kevin Williams WR	.10	.02
❑	236	Brett Perriman	.10	.02
❑	237	Reggie White	.25	.08
❑	238	Steve Wisniewski	.05	.01
❑	239	Mark Collins	.05	.01
❑	240	Steve Young	.75	.30
❑	241	Steve Tovar	.05	.01
❑	242	Jason Belser	.05	.01
❑	243	Ray Seals	.05	.01
❑	244	Earnest Byner	.05	.01
❑	245	Ricky Proehl	.05	.01
❑	246	Rich Miano	.05	.01
❑	247	Alfred Williams	.05	.01
❑	248	Ray Buchanan UER	.05	.01
❑	249	Hardy Nickerson	.10	.02
❑	250	Brad Edwards	.05	.01
❑	251	Jerrol Williams	.05	.01
❑	252	Marvin Washington	.05	.01
❑	253	Tony McGee	.05	.01
❑	254	Jeff George	.25	.08
❑	255	Ron Hall	.05	.01
❑	256	Tim Johnson	.05	.01
❑	257	Willie Roaf	.05	.01
❑	258	Corwin Brown RC	.05	.01
❑	259	Ricardo McDonald	.05	.01
❑	260	Jeff Herrod	.05	.01
❑	261	Demetrius DuBose	.05	.01
❑	262	Ricky Sanders	.05	.01
❑	263	John L. Williams	.05	.01
❑	264	John Lynch	.25	.08
❑	265	Lance Gunn	.05	.01
❑	266	Jessie Hester	.05	.01
❑	267	Mark Wheeler	.05	.01
❑	268	Chip Lohmiller	.05	.01
❑	269	Eric Swann	.10	.02
❑	270	Byron Evans	.05	.01
❑	271	Gary Plummer	.05	.01
❑	272	Roger Duffy RC	.05	.01
❑	273	Irv Smith	.05	.01
❑	274	Todd Collins	.05	.01
❑	275	Robert Blackmon	.05	.01
❑	276	Reggie Roby	.05	.01
❑	277	Russell Copeland	.05	.01
❑	278	Simon Fletcher	.05	.01
❑	279	Ernest Givins	.10	.02
❑	280	Tim Barnett	.05	.01
❑	281	Chris Doleman	.05	.01
❑	282	Jeff Graham	.05	.01
❑	283	Kenneth Davis	.05	.01
❑	284	Vance Johnson	.05	.01
❑	285	Haywood Jeffires	.10	.02
❑	286	Todd McNair	.05	.01
❑	287	Daryl Johnston	.10	.02
❑	288	Ryan McNeil	.05	.01
❑	289	Terrell Buckley	.05	.01
❑	290	Ethan Horton	.05	.01
❑	291	Corey Miller	.05	.01
❑	292	Marc Logan	.05	.01
❑	293	Lincoln Coleman RC	.05	.01
❑	294	Derrick Moore	.05	.01
❑	295	LeRoy Butler	.05	.01
❑	296	Jeff Hostetler	.10	.02
❑	297	Qadry Ismail	.25	.08
❑	298	Andre Hastings	.10	.02
❑	299	Henry Jones	.05	.01
❑	300	John Elway	1.50	.60
❑	301	Warren Moon	.25	.08
❑	302	Willie Davis	.10	.02
❑	303	Vencie Glenn	.05	.01
❑	304	Kevin Greene	.10	.02
❑	305	Marcus Buckley	.05	.01
❑	306	Tim McDonald	.05	.01
❑	307	Michael Irvin	.25	.08
❑	308	Herman Moore	.25	.08
❑	309	Brett Favre	1.50	.60
❑	310	Rocket Ismail	.10	.02
❑	311	Jarrod Bunch	.05	.01
❑	312	Don Beebe	.05	.01
❑	313	Steve Atwater	.05	.01
❑	314	Gary Brown	.05	.01
❑	315	Marcus Allen	.25	.08
❑	316	Terry Allen	.10	.02
❑	317	Chad Brown	.05	.01
❑	318	Cornelius Bennett	.10	.02
❑	319	Rod Bernstine	.05	.01
❑	320	Greg Montgomery	.05	.01
❑	321	Kimble Anders	.10	.02
❑	322	Charles Haley	.10	.02
❑	323	Mel Gray	.05	.01
❑	324	Edgar Bennett	.25	.08
❑	325	Eddie Anderson	.05	.01
❑	326	Derek Brown TE	.05	.01
❑	327	Steve Bono	.10	.02
❑	328	Alvin Harper	.10	.02
❑	329	Willie Green	.05	.01
❑	330	Robert Brooks	.25	.08
❑	331	Patrick Bates	.05	.01
❑	332	Anthony Carter	.10	.02
❑	333	Barry Foster	.05	.01
❑	334	Bill Brooks	.05	.01
❑	335	Jason Elam	.10	.02
❑	336	Ray Childress	.05	.01
❑	337	J.J. Birden	.05	.01
❑	338	Cris Carter	.40	.15
❑	339	Deon Figures	.05	.01
❑	340	Carlton Bailey	.05	.01
❑	341	Brent Jones	.10	.02
❑	342	Troy Aikman UER	.75	.30
❑	343	Rodney Holman	.05	.01
❑	344	Tony Bennett	.05	.01
❑	345	Tim Brown	.25	.08
❑	346	Michael Brooks	.05	.01
❑	347	Martin Harrison	.05	.01
❑	348	Jerry Rice	.75	.30
❑	349	John Copeland	.05	.01
❑	350	Kerry Cash	.05	.01
❑	351	Reggie Cobb	.05	.01
❑	352	Brian Mitchell	.05	.01
❑	353	Derrick Fenner	.05	.01
❑	354	Roosevelt Potts	.05	.01
❑	355	Courtney Hawkins	.05	.01
❑	356	Carl Banks	.05	.01
❑	357	Harold Green	.05	.01
❑	358	Steve Emtman	.05	.01
❑	359	Santana Dotson	.10	.02
❑	360	Reggie Brooks	.10	.02
❑	361	Terry Obee	.05	.01
❑	362	David Klingler	.05	.01
❑	363	Quentin Coryatt	.05	.01
❑	364	Craig Erickson	.05	.01
❑	365	Desmond Howard	.10	.02
❑	366	Carl Pickens	.10	.02
❑	367	Lawrence Dawsey	.05	.01
❑	368	Henry Ellard	.10	.02
❑	369	Shaun Gayle	.05	.01
❑	370	David Lang	.05	.01
❑	371	Anthony Johnson	.10	.02
❑	372	Darnell Walker RC	.05	.01
❑	373	Pepper Johnson	.05	.01
❑	374	Kurt Gouveia	.05	.01
❑	375	Louis Oliver	.05	.01
❑	376	Lincoln Kennedy	.05	.01
❑	377	Anthony Pleasant	.05	.01
❑	378	Irving Fryar	.10	.02
❑	379	Carolina Panthers Logo	.25	.08
❑	380	Jacksonville Jaguars Logo	.05	.01
❑	381	Sterling Sharpe CL UER	.10	.02
❑	382	Dan Marino ART CL	.25	.08
❑	383	Jerry Rice ART CL	.25	.08
❑	384	Joe Montana ART CL	.25	.08
❑	P19	Joe Montana Promo	2.00	.75

1995 Collector's Choice

❑		COMPLETE SET (348)	20.00	10.00
❑	1	Ki-Jana Carter RC	.25	.08
❑	2	Tony Boselli RC	.25	.08
❑	3	Steve McNair RC	2.50	1.00
❑	4	Michael Westbrook RC	.25	.08
❑	5	Kerry Collins RC	1.25	.50
❑	6	Kevin Carter RC	.25	.08
❑	7	Mike Mamula RC	.05	.01
❑	8	Joey Galloway RC	1.25	.50
❑	9	Kyle Brady RC	.25	.08
❑	10	J.J. Stokes RC	.25	.08
❑	11	Derrick Alexander DE RC	.05	.01
❑	12	Warren Sapp RC	1.25	.50
❑	13	Mark Fields RC	.25	.08
❑	14	Tyrone Wheatley RC	1.00	.40
❑	15	Napoleon Kaufman RC	1.00	.40
❑	16	James O. Stewart RC	1.00	.40
❑	17	Luther Elliss RC	.05	.01
❑	18	Rashaan Salaam RC	.10	.02
❑	19	Ty Law RC	1.25	.50
❑	20	Mark Bruener RC	.10	.02
❑	21	Derrick Brooks RC	1.25	.50
❑	22	Christian Fauria RC	.10	.02
❑	23	Ray Zellars RC	.10	.02
❑	24	Todd Collins RC	.10	.02
❑	25	Sherman Williams RC	.05	.01
❑	26	Frank Sanders RC	.25	.08

❑	27	Rodney Thomas RC	.10	.02
❑	28	Rob Johnson RC	.75	.30
❑	29	Steve Stenstrom RC	.05	.01
❑	30	James A.Stewart RC	.05	.01
❑	31	Barry Sanders DYK	.60	.25
❑	32	Marshall Faulk DYK	.40	.15
❑	33	Darnay Scott DYK	.10	.02
❑	34	Joe Montana DYK	.60	.25
❑	35	Michael Irvin DYK	.10	.02
❑	36	Jerry Rice DYK	.40	.15
❑	37	Errict Rhett DYK	.10	.02
❑	38	Drew Bledsoe DYK	.25	.08
❑	39	Dan Marino DYK	.60	.25
❑	40	Terance Mathis DYK	.05	.01
❑	41	Natrone Means DYK	.10	.02
❑	42	Tim Brown DYK	.10	.02
❑	43	Steve Young DYK	.30	.10
❑	44	Mel Gray DYK	.05	.01
❑	45	Jerome Bettis DYK	.25	.08
❑	46	Aeneas Williams DYK	.05	.01
❑	47	Charlie Garner DYK	.10	.02
❑	48	Deion Sanders DYK	.25	.08
❑	49	Ken Harvey DYK	.05	.01
❑	50	Emmitt Smith DYK	.50	.20
❑	51	Andre Reed	.10	.02
❑	52	Sean Dawkins	.10	.02
❑	53	Irving Fryar	.10	.02
❑	54	Vincent Brisby	.05	.01
❑	55	Rob Moore	.10	.02
❑	56	Carl Pickens	.10	.02
❑	57	Vinny Testaverde	.10	.02
❑	58	Webster Slaughter	.05	.01
❑	59	Eric Green	.05	.01
❑	60	Anthony Miller	.10	.02
❑	61	Lake Dawson	.10	.02
❑	62	Tim Brown	.25	.08
❑	63	Stan Humphries	.10	.02
❑	64	Rick Mirer	.10	.02
❑	65	Gary Clark	.05	.01
❑	66	Troy Aikman	.75	.30
❑	67	Mike Sherrard	.05	.01
❑	68	Fred Barnett	.10	.02
❑	69	Henry Ellard	.10	.02
❑	70	Terry Allen	.10	.02
❑	71	Jeff Graham	.05	.01
❑	72	Herman Moore	.25	.08
❑	73	Brett Favre	1.50	.60
❑	74	Trent Dilfer	.25	.08
❑	75	Derek Brown RBK	.05	.01
❑	76	Andre Rison	.10	.02
❑	77	Flipper Anderson	.05	.01
❑	78	Jerry Rice	.75	.30
❑	79	Thurman Thomas	.25	.08
❑	80	Marshall Faulk	1.00	.40
❑	81	O.J. McDuffie	.25	.08
❑	82	Ben Coates	.10	.02
❑	83	Johnny Mitchell	.05	.01
❑	84	Darnay Scott	.10	.02
❑	85	Derrick Alexander WR	.25	.08
❑	86	Micheal Barrow	.05	.01
❑	87	Charles Johnson	.10	.02
❑	88	John Elway	1.50	.60
❑	89	Willie Davis	.10	.02
❑	90	James Jett	.10	.02
❑	91	Mark Seay	.10	.02
❑	92	Brian Blades	.10	.02
❑	93	Ricky Proehl	.05	.01
❑	94	Charles Haley	.10	.02
❑	95	Chris Calloway	.05	.01
❑	96	Calvin Williams	.10	.02
❑	97	Ethan Horton	.05	.01
❑	98	Cris Carter	.25	.08
❑	99	Curtis Conway	.25	.08
❑	100	Lomas Brown	.05	.01
❑	101	Edgar Bennett	.10	.02
❑	102	Craig Erickson	.05	.01
❑	103	Jim Everett	.05	.01
❑	104	Terance Mathis	.10	.02
❑	105	Wayne Gandy	.05	.01
❑	106	Brent Jones	.05	.01
❑	107	Bruce Smith	.25	.08
❑	108	Roosevelt Potts	.05	.01
❑	109	Dan Marino	1.50	.60
❑	110	Michael Timpson	.05	.01
❑	111	Boomer Esiason	.10	.02
❑	112	David Klingler	.10	.02
❑	113	Eric Metcalf	.10	.02
❑	114	Lorenzo White	.05	.01
❑	115	Neil O'Donnell	.10	.02
❑	116	Shannon Sharpe	.10	.02
❑	117	Joe Montana	1.50	.60
❑	118	Jeff Hostetler	.10	.02
❑	119	Ronnie Harmon	.05	.01
❑	120	Chris Warren	.10	.02
❑	121	Randal Hill	.05	.01
❑	122	Alvin Harper	.05	.01
❑	123	Dave Brown	.10	.02
❑	124	Randall Cunningham	.25	.08
❑	125	Heath Shuler	.10	.02
❑	126	Jake Reed	.10	.02
❑	127	Donnell Woolford	.05	.01
❑	128	Scott Mitchell	.10	.02
❑	129	Reggie White	.25	.08
❑	130	Lawrence Dawsey	.05	.01
❑	131	Michael Haynes	.10	.02
❑	132	Bert Emanuel	.25	.08
❑	133	Troy Drayton	.05	.01
❑	134	Merton Hanks	.05	.01
❑	135	Jim Kelly	.25	.08
❑	136	Tony Bennett	.05	.01
❑	137	Terry Kirby	.10	.02
❑	138	Drew Bledsoe	.50	.20
❑	139	Johnny Johnson	.05	.01
❑	140	Dan Wilkinson	.10	.02
❑	141	Leroy Hoard	.05	.01
❑	142	Gary Brown	.05	.01
❑	143	Barry Foster	.10	.02
❑	144	Shane Dronett	.05	.01
❑	145	Marcus Allen	.25	.08
❑	146	Harvey Williams	.05	.01
❑	147	Tony Martin	.10	.02
❑	148	Rod Stephens	.05	.01
❑	149	Ronald Moore	.05	.01
❑	150	Michael Irvin	.25	.08
❑	151	Rodney Hampton	.10	.02
❑	152	Herschel Walker	.10	.02
❑	153	Reggie Brooks	.10	.02
❑	154	Qadry Ismail	.10	.02
❑	155	Chris Zorich	.05	.01
❑	156	Barry Sanders	1.25	.50
❑	157	Sean Jones	.05	.01
❑	158	Errict Rhett	.10	.02
❑	159	Tyrone Hughes	.10	.02
❑	160	Jeff George	.10	.02
❑	161	Chris Miller	.05	.01
❑	162	Steve Young	.60	.25
❑	163	Cornelius Bennett	.10	.02
❑	164	Trev Alberts	.05	.01
❑	165	J.B. Brown	.05	.01
❑	166	Marion Butts	.05	.01
❑	167	Aaron Glenn	.05	.01
❑	168	James Francis	.05	.01
❑	169	Eric Turner	.05	.01
❑	170	Darryll Lewis	.05	.01
❑	171	John L. Williams	.05	.01
❑	172	Simon Fletcher	.05	.01
❑	173	Neil Smith	.10	.02
❑	174	Chester McGlockton	.10	.02
❑	175	Natrone Means	.10	.02
❑	176	Michael Sinclair	.05	.01
❑	177	Larry Centers	.10	.02
❑	178	Daryl Johnston	.10	.02
❑	179	Dave Meggett	.05	.01
❑	180	Greg Jackson	.05	.01
❑	181	Ken Harvey	.05	.01
❑	182	Warren Moon	.10	.02
❑	183	Steve Walsh	.05	.01
❑	184	Chris Spielman	.10	.02
❑	185	Bryce Paup	.10	.02
❑	186	Courtney Hawkins	.05	.01
❑	187	Willie Roaf	.05	.01
❑	188	Chris Doleman	.05	.01
❑	189	Jerome Bettis	.25	.08
❑	190	Ricky Watters	.10	.02
❑	191	Henry Jones	.05	.01
❑	192	Quentin Coryatt	.10	.02
❑	193	Bryan Cox	.05	.01
❑	194	Kevin Turner	.05	.01
❑	195	Siupeli Malamala	.05	.01
❑	196	Louis Oliver	.05	.01
❑	197	Rob Burnett	.05	.01
❑	198	Cris Dishman	.05	.01
❑	199	Byron Bam Morris	.05	.01
❑	200	Ray Crockett	.05	.01
❑	201	Jon Vaughn	.05	.01
❑	202	Nolan Harrison	.05	.01
❑	203	Leslie O'Neal	.10	.02
❑	204	Sam Adams	.05	.01
❑	205	Eric Swann	.10	.02
❑	206	Jay Novacek	.10	.02
❑	207	Keith Hamilton	.05	.01
❑	208	Charlie Garner	.25	.08
❑	209	Tom Carter	.05	.01
❑	210	Henry Thomas	.05	.01
❑	211	Lewis Tillman	.05	.01
❑	212	Pat Swilling	.05	.01
❑	213	Terrell Buckley	.05	.01
❑	214	Hardy Nickerson	.05	.01
❑	215	Mario Bates	.10	.02
❑	216	D.J. Johnson	.05	.01
❑	217	Robert Young	.05	.01
❑	218	Dana Stubblefield	.10	.02
❑	219	Jeff Burris	.05	.01
❑	220	Floyd Turner	.05	.01
❑	221	Troy Vincent	.05	.01
❑	222	Willie McGinest	.10	.02
❑	223	James Hasty	.05	.01
❑	224	Jeff Blake RC	.60	.25
❑	225	Stevon Moore	.05	.01
❑	226	Ernest Givins	.05	.01
❑	227	Greg Lloyd	.10	.02
❑	228	Steve Atwater	.05	.01
❑	229	Dale Carter	.10	.02
❑	230	Terry McDaniel	.05	.01
❑	231	John Carney	.05	.01
❑	232	Cortez Kennedy	.10	.02
❑	233	Clyde Simmons	.05	.01
❑	234	Emmitt Smith	1.25	.50
❑	235	Thomas Lewis	.10	.02
❑	236	William Fuller	.05	.01
❑	237	Ricky Ervins	.05	.01
❑	238	John Randle	.10	.02
❑	239	John Thierry	.05	.01
❑	240	Mel Gray	.05	.01
❑	241	George Teague	.05	.01
❑	242	Charles Wilson Bucs	.05	.01
❑	243	Joe Johnson	.05	.01
❑	244	Chuck Smith	.05	.01
❑	245	Sean Gilbert	.10	.02
❑	246	Bryant Young	.10	.02
❑	247	Bucky Brooks	.05	.01
❑	248	Ray Buchanan	.05	.01
❑	249	Tim Bowens	.05	.01
❑	250	Vincent Brown	.05	.01
❑	251	Marcus Turner	.05	.01
❑	252	Derrick Fenner	.05	.01
❑	253	Antonio Langham	.05	.01
❑	254	Cody Carlson	.05	.01
❑	255	Kevin Greene	.10	.02
❑	256	Leonard Russell	.05	.01
❑	257	Donnell Bennett	.10	.02
❑	258	Rocket Ismail	.10	.02
❑	259	Alfred Pupunu RC	.05	.01
❑	260	Eugene Robinson	.05	.01
❑	261	Seth Joyner	.05	.01
❑	262	Darren Woodson	.10	.02
❑	263	Phillippi Sparks	.05	.01
❑	264	Andy Harmon	.05	.01
❑	265	Brian Mitchell	.05	.01
❑	266	Fuad Reveiz	.05	.01

❑ 267 Mark Carrier DB .05 .01
❑ 268 Johnnie Morton .10 .02
❑ 269 LeShon Johnson .10 .02
❑ 270 Eric Curry .05 .01
❑ 271 Quinn Early .10 .02
❑ 272 Elbert Shelley .05 .01
❑ 273 Roman Phifer .05 .01
❑ 274 Ken Norton Jr. .10 .02
❑ 275 Steve Tasker .10 .02
❑ 276 Jim Harbaugh .10 .02
❑ 277 Aubrey Beavers .05 .01
❑ 278 Chris Slade .05 .01
❑ 279 Mo Lewis .05 .01
❑ 280 Alfred Williams .05 .01
❑ 281 Michael Dean Perry UER .05 .01
❑ 282 Marcus Robertson .05 .01
❑ 283 Rod Woodson .10 .02
❑ 284 Glyn Milburn .05 .01
❑ 285 Greg Hill .10 .02
❑ 286 Rob Fredrickson .05 .01
❑ 287 Junior Seau .25 .08
❑ 288 Rick Tuten .05 .01
❑ 289 Aeneas Williams .05 .01
❑ 290 Darrin Smith .05 .01
❑ 291 John Booty .05 .01
❑ 292 Eric Allen .05 .01
❑ 293 Reggie Roby .05 .01
❑ 294 David Palmer .10 .02
❑ 295 Trace Armstrong .05 .01
❑ 296 Dave Krieg .05 .01
❑ 297 Robert Brooks .25 .08
❑ 298 Brad Culpepper .05 .01
❑ 299 Wayne Martin .05 .01
❑ 300 Craig Heyward .10 .02
❑ 301 Isaac Bruce .40 .15
❑ 302 Deion Sanders .40 .15
❑ 303 Matt Darby .05 .01
❑ 304 Kirk Lowdermilk .05 .01
❑ 305 Bernie Parmalee .10 .02
❑ 306 Leroy Thompson .05 .01
❑ 307 Ronnie Lott .10 .02
❑ 308 Steve Tovar .05 .01
❑ 309 Michael Jackson .10 .02
❑ 310 Al Smith .05 .01
❑ 311 Chad Brown .10 .02
❑ 312 Elijah Alexander .05 .01
❑ 313 Kimble Anders .10 .02
❑ 314 Anthony Smith .05 .01
❑ 315 Andre Coleman .05 .01
❑ 316 Terry Wooden .05 .01
❑ 317 Garrison Hearst .25 .08
❑ 318 Russell Maryland .05 .01
❑ 319 Michael Brooks .05 .01
❑ 320 Bernard Williams .05 .01
❑ 321 Andre Collins .05 .01
❑ 322 Dewayne Washington .10 .02
❑ 323 Raymont Harris .05 .01
❑ 324 Brett Perriman .10 .02
❑ 325 LeRoy Butler .05 .01
❑ 326 Santana Dotson .05 .01
❑ 327 Irv Smith .05 .01
❑ 328 Ron George .05 .01
❑ 329 Marquez Pope .05 .01
❑ 330 William Floyd .10 .02
❑ 331 Mickey Washington .05 .01
❑ 332 Keith Goganious .05 .01
❑ 333 Derek Brown TE .05 .01
❑ 334 Steve Beuerlein .10 .02
❑ 335 Reggie Cobb .05 .01
❑ 336 Jeff Lageman .05 .01
❑ 337 Kelvin Martin .05 .01
❑ 338 Darren Carrington .05 .01
❑ 339 Mark Carrier WR .10 .02
❑ 340 Willie Green .05 .01
❑ 341 Frank Reich .05 .01
❑ 342 Don Beebe .05 .01
❑ 343 Lamar Lathon .05 .01
❑ 344 Tim McKyer .05 .01
❑ 345 Pete Metzelaars .05 .01
❑ 346 Vernon Turner .05 .01
❑ 347 Dan Marino CL .25 .08
❑ 348 Joe Montana CL .25 .08
❑ PC1 Joe Montana Promo 1.00 .40
❑ P1 Joe Montana Promo 1.00 .40

1995 Collector's Choice Update

❑ COMPLETE SET (225) 15.00 7.50
❑ U1 Roell Preston RC .10 .02
❑ U2 Lorenzo Styles RC .05 .01
❑ U3 Todd Collins .25 .08
❑ U4 Darick Holmes RC .10 .02
❑ U5 Justin Armour RC .05 .01
❑ U6 Tony Cline RC .05 .01
❑ U7 Tyrone Poole .10 .02
❑ U8 Kerry Collins .25 .08
❑ U9 Sean Harris .05 .01
❑ U10 Steve Stenstrom .05 .01
❑ U11 Rashaan Salaam .10 .02
❑ U12 Ki-Jana Carter .25 .08
❑ U13 Craig Powell RC .05 .01
❑ U14 Eric Zeier RC .25 .08
❑ U15 Ernest Hunter .05 .01
❑ U16 Sherman Williams .05 .01
❑ U17 Terrell Davis RC 2.00 .75
❑ U18 Luther Elliss .05 .01
❑ U19 Craig Newsome .05 .01
❑ U20 Steve McNair 1.25 .50
❑ U21 Chris Sanders RC .10 .02
❑ U22 Rodney Thomas .10 .02
❑ U23 Ellis Johnson RC .05 .01
❑ U24 Ken Dilger RC .25 .08
❑ U25 Zack Crockett RC .10 .02
❑ U26 Tony Boselli .25 .08
❑ U27 Rob Johnson .40 .15
❑ U28 James O. Stewart .50 .20
❑ U29 Tamarick Vanover RC .25 .08
❑ U30 Napoleon Kaufman .50 .20
❑ U31 Kevin Carter .10 .02
❑ U32 Steve McLaughlin .05 .01
❑ U33 Lovell Pinkney .05 .01
❑ U34 Pete Mitchell RC .10 .02
❑ U35 James A.Stewart .05 .01
❑ U36 Chad May RC .05 .01
❑ U37 Derrick Alexander DE .05 .01
❑ U38 Curtis Martin RC 2.50 1.00
❑ U39 Will Moore RC .05 .01
❑ U40 Ty Law .50 .20
❑ U41 Ray Zellars .10 .02
❑ U42 Mark Fields .10 .02
❑ U43 Tyrone Wheatley .50 .20
❑ U44 Kyle Brady .25 .08
❑ U45 Mike Mamula .05 .01
❑ U46 Bobby Taylor RC .25 .08
❑ U47 Chris T.Jones RC .05 .01
❑ U48 Frank Sanders .10 .02
❑ U49 Stoney Case RC .05 .01
❑ U50 Mark Bruener .10 .02
❑ U51 Kordell Stewart RC 1.25 .50
❑ U52 Jimmy Oliver RC .05 .01
❑ U53 Terrance Shaw RC .05 .01
❑ U54 Terrell Fletcher RC .05 .01
❑ U55 J.J. Stokes .25 .08
❑ U56 Christian Fauria .05 .01
❑ U57 Joey Galloway .25 .08
❑ U58 Warren Sapp .25 .08
❑ U59 Derrick Brooks .60 .25
❑ U60 Michael Westbrook .25 .08
❑ U61 Emmitt Smith K .75 .30
❑ U62 Barry Sanders K .75 .30
❑ U63 Marshall Faulk K .60 .25
❑ U64 Troy Aikman K .50 .20
❑ U65 Steve Young K .40 .15
❑ U66 Junior Seau K .25 .08
❑ U67 John Elway K 1.00 .40
❑ U68 Dan Marino K 1.00 .40
❑ U69 Drew Bledsoe K .25 .08
❑ U70 Errict Rhett K .10 .02
❑ U71 Natrone Means K .10 .02
❑ U72 Deion Sanders K .30 .10
❑ U73 Brett Favre K 1.00 .40
❑ U74 Cris Carter K .25 .08
❑ U75 Ben Coates K .10 .02
❑ U76 Jerome Bettis K .25 .08
❑ U77 Reggie White K .25 .08
❑ U78 Stan Humphries K .05 .01
❑ U79 Michael Westbrook K .25 .08
❑ U80 Steve McNair K .50 .20
❑ U81 Kevin Greene K .10 .02
❑ U82 Joey Galloway K .25 .08
❑ U83 Napoleon Kaufman K .25 .08
❑ U84 Jerry Rice K .50 .20
❑ U85 Andre Rison K .10 .02
❑ U86 Eric Metcalf K .10 .02
❑ U87 Kerry Collins K .10 .02
❑ U88 Chris Warren K .10 .02
❑ U89 Irving Fryar K .10 .02
❑ U90 Michael Irvin K .25 .08
❑ U91 Don Beebe .05 .01
❑ U92 Pete Metzelaars .05 .01
❑ U93 Mark Carrier .05 .01
❑ U94 Frank Reich .05 .01
❑ U95 Randy Baldwin .05 .01
❑ U96 Bob Christian .05 .01
❑ U97 John Kasay .05 .01
❑ U98 Lamar Lathon .05 .01
❑ U99 Sam Mills .10 .02
❑ U100 Carlton Bailey .05 .01
❑ U101 Darion Conner .05 .01
❑ U102 Blake Brockermeyer .05 .01
❑ U103 Gerald Williams .05 .01
❑ U104 Willie Green .05 .01
❑ U105 Derrick Moore .05 .01
❑ U106 Desmond Howard .10 .02
❑ U107 Harry Colon .05 .01
❑ U108 Steve Beuerlein .10 .02
❑ U109 Reggie Cobb .05 .01
❑ U110 Jeff Lageman .05 .01
❑ U111 Mark Brunell 1.00 .40
❑ U112 Darren Carrington .05 .01
❑ U113 Brian DeMarco .10 .02
❑ U114 Ernest Givins .05 .01
❑ U115 Le'shai Maston .05 .01
❑ U116 Willie Jackson .10 .02
❑ U117 Keith Goganious .05 .01
❑ U118 Kelvin Pritchett .05 .01
❑ U119 Ryan Christopherson .05 .01
❑ U120 Bryan Schwartz .05 .01
❑ U121 Dave Kreig .05 .01
❑ U122 Darryl Talley .05 .01
❑ U123 Bryce Paup .10 .02
❑ U124 Anthony Johnson .10 .02
❑ U125 Eric Bieniemy .05 .01
❑ U126 Andre Rison .10 .02
❑ U127 Rodney Peete .05 .01
❑ U128 Aaron Craver .05 .01
❑ U129 Henry Thomas .05 .01
❑ U130 Antonio Freeman RC 1.00 .40
❑ U131 Chris Chandler .10 .02
❑ U132 Craig Erickson .05 .01
❑ U133 Roell Preston .10 .02
❑ U134 Brian Washington .05 .01
❑ U135 Eric Green .05 .01
❑ U136 Broderick Thomas .05 .01

❑ U137 Dave Meggett .05 .01
❑ U138 Eric Allen .05 .01
❑ U139 Herschel Walker .10 .02
❑ U140 Dexter Carter .05 .01
❑ U141 Kerry Cash .05 .01
❑ U142 Kelvin Martin .05 .01
❑ U143 Erric Pegram .10 .02
❑ U144 Bo Orlando .05 .01
❑ U145 Ricky Ervins .05 .01
❑ U146 John Friesz .10 .02
❑ U147 Alexander Wright .05 .01
❑ U148 Alvin Harper .05 .01
❑ U149 Gus Frerotte .10 .02
❑ U150 Duval Love .05 .01
❑ U151 Eric Metcalf .10 .02
❑ U152 Ruben Brown RC .25 .08
❑ U153 Marty Carter .05 .01
❑ U154 James Joseph .05 .01
❑ U155 Hugh Douglas RC .25 .08
❑ U156 Wade Wilson .05 .01
❑ U157 Britt Hager .05 .01
❑ U158 Mark Schlereth .05 .01
❑ U159 Cory Schlesinger RC UER .10 .02
❑ U160 Mark Ingram .05 .01
❑ U161 Mark Stepnoski .05 .01
❑ U162 Flipper Anderson .05 .01
❑ U163 Donta Jones .05 .01
❑ U164 James Hasty .05 .01
❑ U165 Gary Clark .05 .01
❑ U166 David Sloan RC .05 .01
❑ U167 Jeff Dellenbach .05 .01
❑ U168 Rufus Porter .05 .01
❑ U169 Mike Croel .05 .01
❑ U170 Charles Wilson Jets UER 242 .05 .01
❑ U171 Pat Swilling .05 .01
❑ U172 Kurt Gouveia .05 .01
❑ U173 Norm Johnson .05 .01
❑ U174 Shaun Gayle .05 .01
❑ U175 Marquez Pope .05 .01
❑ U176 Tyronne Stowe .05 .01
❑ U177 Anthony Parker .05 .01
❑ U178 Kenneth Gant .05 .01
❑ U179 James Washington .05 .01
❑ U180 Rob Moore .10 .02
❑ U181 Alundis Brice RC .05 .01
❑ U182 Lamont Warren .05 .01
❑ U183 Michael Timpson .05 .01
❑ U184 Lorenzo White .05 .01
❑ U185 Charlie Williams RC .05 .01
❑ U186 Ed McCaffrey .25 .08
❑ U187 James Jones .05 .01
❑ U188 Derrick Fenner .05 .01
❑ U189 Mel Gray .05 .01
❑ U190 James Williams LB .05 .01
❑ U191 Jeff Criswell .05 .01
❑ U192 Randal Hill .05 .01
❑ U193 Terry Allen .10 .02
❑ U194 Joel Smeenge .05 .01
❑ U195 Ricky Watters .10 .02
❑ U196 Don Sasa .05 .01
❑ U197 Steve Bono .10 .02
❑ U198 Steve Broussard .05 .01
❑ U199 Carlos Jenkins .05 .01
❑ U200 Reggie Roby .05 .01
❑ U201 Stanley Richard .05 .01
❑ U202 Vince Workman .05 .01
❑ U203 Eric Guliford .05 .01
❑ U204 Lionel Washington .05 .01
❑ U205 Brian Williams LB .05 .01
❑ U206 Ronnie Lott .10 .02
❑ U207 Corey Harris .05 .01
❑ U208 Harlon Barnett .05 .01
❑ U209 Bubby Brister .05 .01
❑ U210 Darren Bennett RC .05 .01
❑ U211 Winston Moss .05 .01
❑ U212 Leonard Russell .05 .01
❑ U213 Ron Davis .05 .01
❑ U214 Curtis Whitley .05 .01
❑ U215 Webster Slaughter .05 .01
❑ U216 Korey Stringer RC .10 .02
❑ U217 Don Davey .05 .01
❑ U218 Mark Rypien .05 .01
❑ U219 Chad Cota .05 .01
❑ U220 Tim Ruddy .05 .01
❑ U221 Corey Fuller .05 .01
❑ U222 Mike Dumas .05 .01
❑ U223 Eddie Murray .05 .01
❑ U224 Dan Marino CL .50 .20
❑ U225 Dan Marino CL .50 .20
❑ P1 M.Westbrook Promo .50 .20
❑ P2 Dan Marino Promo 1.00 .40
❑ P3 Marino/West./Brown Promo .75 .30

1996 Collector's Choice

❑ COMPLETE SET (375) 25.00 10.00
❑ COMP.FACT.SET (395) 30.00 20.00
❑ 1 Keyshawn Johnson RC 1.00 .40
❑ 2 Kevin Hardy RC .40 .15
❑ 3 Simeon Rice RC .75 .30
❑ 4 Jonathan Ogden RC .40 .15
❑ 5 Cedric Jones RC .10 .02
❑ 6 Lawrence Phillips RC .40 .15
❑ 7 Tim Biakabutuka RC .40 .15
❑ 8 Terry Glenn RC 1.00 .40
❑ 9 Rickey Dudley RC .40 .15
❑ 10 Regan Upshaw RC .10 .02
❑ 11 Walt Harris RC .10 .02
❑ 12 Eddie George RC 1.25 .50
❑ 13 John Mobley RC .10 .02
❑ 14 Duane Clemons RC .10 .02
❑ 15 Marvin Harrison RC 2.50 1.00
❑ 16 Daryl Gardener RC .10 .02
❑ 17 Pete Kendall RC .10 .02
❑ 18 Marcus Jones RC .10 .02
❑ 19 Eric Moulds RC 1.25 .50
❑ 20 Ray Lewis RC 2.50 1.00
❑ 21 Alex Van Dyke RC .20 .07
❑ 22 Leeland McElroy RC .20 .07
❑ 23 Mike Alstott RC 1.00 .40
❑ 24 Lawyer Milloy RC .40 .15
❑ 25 Marco Battaglia RC .10 .02
❑ 26 Je'rod Cherry RC .10 .02
❑ 27 Israel Ifeanyi RC .10 .02
❑ 28 Bobby Engram RC .40 .15
❑ 29 Jason Dunn RC .20 .07
❑ 30 Derrick Mayes RC .40 .15
❑ 31 Stepfret Williams RC .20 .07
❑ 32 Bobby Hoying RC .40 .15
❑ 33 Karim Abdul-Jabbar RC .40 .15
❑ 34 Danny Kanell RC .40 .15
❑ 35 Chris Darkins RC .10 .02
❑ 36 Charlie Jones RC .40 .15
❑ 37 Tedy Bruschi RC 4.00 1.50
❑ 38 Stanley Pritchett RC .20 .07
❑ 39 Donnie Edwards RC .40 .15
❑ 40 Jeff Lewis RC .20 .07
❑ 41 Stephen Davis RC 1.50 .60
❑ 42 Winslow Oliver RC .10 .02
❑ 43 Mercury Hayes RC .10 .02
❑ 44 Jon Runyan RC .10 .02
❑ 45 Steve Taneyhill RC .10 .02
❑ 46 Eric Metcalf SR .10 .02
❑ 47 Bryce Paup SR .10 .02
❑ 48 Kerry Collins SR .20 .07
❑ 49 Rashaan Salaam SR .20 .07
❑ 50 Carl Pickens SR .20 .07
❑ 51 Emmitt Smith SR .50 .20
❑ 52 Michael Irvin SR .20 .07
❑ 53 Troy Aikman SR .40 .15
❑ 54 Terrell Davis SR .20 .07
❑ 55 John Elway SR .75 .30
❑ 56 Herman Moore SR .20 .07
❑ 57 Brett Favre SR .75 .30
❑ 58 Rodney Thomas SR .10 .02
❑ 59 Jim Harbaugh SR .20 .07
❑ 60 Mark Brunell SR .20 .07
❑ 61 Marcus Allen SR .20 .07
❑ 62 Tamarick Vanover SR .20 .07
❑ 63 Steve Bono SR .10 .02
❑ 64 Dan Marino SR .75 .30
❑ 65 Warren Moon SR .10 .02
❑ 66 Curtis Martin SR .20 .07
❑ 67 Tyrone Hughes SR .10 .02
❑ 68 Rodney Hampton SR .10 .02
❑ 69 Hugh Douglas SR .10 .02
❑ 70 Tim Brown SR .20 .07
❑ 71 Ricky Watters SR .20 .07
❑ 72 Kordell Stewart SR .40 .15
❑ 73 Andre Coleman SR .10 .02
❑ 74 Jerry Rice SR .40 .15
❑ 75 Joey Galloway SR .20 .07
❑ 76 Isaac Bruce SR .20 .07
❑ 77 Errict Rhett SR .20 .07
❑ 78 Michael Westbrook SR .10 .02
❑ 79 Brian Mitchell SR .10 .02
❑ 80 Aeneas Williams .10 .02
❑ 81 Andre Reed .20 .07
❑ 82 Brett Maxie .10 .02
❑ 83 Jim Flanigan .10 .02
❑ 84 Jeff Blake .40 .15
❑ 85 Mike Frederick .10 .02
❑ 86 Michael Irvin .40 .15
❑ 87 Aaron Craver .10 .02
❑ 88 Barry Sanders 1.25 .50
❑ 89 Travis Jervey RC .40 .15
❑ 90 Chris Sanders .20 .07
❑ 91 Marshall Faulk .40 .15
❑ 92 Bryan Schwartz .10 .02
❑ 93 Tamarick Vanover .20 .07
❑ 94 Troy Vincent .10 .02
❑ 95 Robert Smith .20 .07
❑ 96 Drew Bledsoe .50 .20
❑ 97 Quinn Early .10 .02
❑ 98 Wayne Chrebet .40 .15
❑ 99 Tim Brown .40 .15
❑ 100 Charlie Garner .20 .07
❑ 101 Yancey Thigpen .20 .07
❑ 102 Isaac Bruce .40 .15
❑ 103 Natrone Means .20 .07
❑ 104 Jerry Rice .75 .30
❑ 105 Chris Warren .20 .07
❑ 106 Errict Rhett .20 .07
❑ 107 Heath Shuler .20 .07
❑ 108 Eric Swann .10 .02
❑ 109 Jeff George .20 .07
❑ 110 Steve Tasker .10 .02
❑ 111 Sam Mills .10 .02
❑ 112 Jeff Graham .10 .02
❑ 113 Carl Pickens .20 .07
❑ 114 Vinny Testaverde .20 .07
❑ 115 Emmitt Smith 1.25 .50
❑ 116 John Elway 1.50 .60
❑ 117 Henry Thomas .10 .02
❑ 118 LeRoy Butler .10 .02
❑ 119 Blaine Bishop .10 .02
❑ 120 Floyd Turner .10 .02
❑ 121 Jeff Lageman .10 .02
❑ 122 Kimble Anders .20 .07
❑ 123 Bryan Cox .10 .02
❑ 124 Qadry Ismail .20 .07
❑ 125 Ted Johnson RC .40 .15
❑ 126 Wesley Walls .20 .07
❑ 127 Rodney Hampton .20 .07
❑ 128 Adrian Murrell .20 .07

❑	129	Daryl Hobbs RC	.10	.02
❑	130	Ricky Watters	.20	.07
❑	131	Carnell Lake	.10	.02
❑	132	Toby Wright	.10	.02
❑	133	Darren Bennett	.10	.02
❑	134	J.J. Stokes	.40	.15
❑	135	Eugene Robinson	.10	.02
❑	136	Eric Curry	.10	.02
❑	137	Tom Carter	.10	.02
❑	138	Dave Krieg	.10	.02
❑	139	Eric Metcalf	.10	.02
❑	140	Bill Brooks	.10	.02
❑	141	Pete Metzelaars	.10	.02
❑	142	Kevin Butler	.10	.02
❑	143	John Copeland	.10	.02
❑	144	Keenan McCardell	.40	.15
❑	145	Larry Brown	.10	.02
❑	146	Jason Elam	.20	.07
❑	147	Willie Clay	.10	.02
❑	148	Robert Brooks	.40	.15
❑	149	Chris Chandler	.20	.07
❑	150	Quentin Coryatt	.10	.02
❑	151	Pete Mitchell	.20	.07
❑	152	Martin Bayless	.10	.02
❑	153	Pete Stoyanovich	.10	.02
❑	154	Cris Carter	.40	.15
❑	155	Jimmy Hitchcock RC	.10	.02
❑	156	Mario Bates	.20	.07
❑	157	Mike Sherrard	.10	.02
❑	158	Boomer Esiason	.20	.07
❑	159	Chester McGlockton	.10	.02
❑	160	Bobby Taylor	.10	.02
❑	161	Kordell Stewart	.40	.15
❑	162	Kevin Carter	.10	.02
❑	163	Junior Seau	.40	.15
❑	164	Derek Loville	.10	.02
❑	165	Brian Blades	.10	.02
❑	166	Jackie Harris	.10	.02
❑	167	Michael Westbrook	.40	.15
❑	168	Rob Moore	.20	.07
❑	169	Jessie Tuggle	.10	.02
❑	170	Darick Holmes	.10	.02
❑	171	Tim McKyer	.10	.02
❑	172	Erik Kramer	.10	.02
❑	173	Harold Green	.10	.02
❑	174	Stevon Moore	.10	.02
❑	175	Deion Sanders	.40	.15
❑	176	Anthony Miller	.20	.07
❑	177	Herman Moore	.20	.07
❑	178	Brett Favre	1.50	.60
❑	179	Rodney Thomas	.10	.02
❑	180	Ken Dilger	.20	.07
❑	181	Mark Brunell	.50	.20
❑	182	Marcus Allen	.40	.15
❑	183	Dan Marino	1.50	.60
❑	184	John Randle	.20	.07
❑	185	Ben Coates	.20	.07
❑	186	Tyrone Hughes	.10	.02
❑	187	Dave Brown	.10	.02
❑	188	Johnny Mitchell	.10	.02
❑	189	Harvey Williams	.10	.02
❑	190	Andy Harmon	.10	.02
❑	191	Kevin Greene	.20	.07
❑	192	D'Marco Farr	.10	.02
❑	193	Andre Coleman	.10	.02
❑	194	Bryant Young	.20	.07
❑	195	Rick Mirer	.20	.07
❑	196	Horace Copeland	.10	.02
❑	197	Leslie Shepherd	.10	.02
❑	198	Jamir Miller	.10	.02
❑	199	Bert Emanuel	.20	.07
❑	200	Steve Christie	.10	.02
❑	201	Kerry Collins	.40	.15
❑	202	Rashaan Salaam	.20	.07
❑	203	Steve Tovar	.10	.02
❑	204	Michael Jackson	.20	.07
❑	205	Kevin Williams	.10	.02
❑	206	Glyn Milburn	.10	.02
❑	207	Johnnie Morton	.20	.07
❑	208	Antonio Freeman	.40	.15
❑	209	Cris Dishman	.10	.02
❑	210	Ellis Johnson	.10	.02
❑	211	Cedric Tillman	.10	.02
❑	212	Steve Bono	.10	.02
❑	213	Eric Green	.10	.02
❑	214	David Palmer	.10	.02
❑	215	Vincent Brisby	.10	.02
❑	216	Michael Haynes	.10	.02
❑	217	Chris Calloway	.10	.02
❑	218	Kyle Brady	.10	.02
❑	219	Terry McDaniel	.10	.02
❑	220	Calvin Williams	.10	.02
❑	221	Greg Lloyd	.20	.07
❑	222	Jerome Bettis	.40	.15
❑	223	Stan Humphries	.20	.07
❑	224	Lee Woodall	.10	.02
❑	225	Robert Blackmon	.10	.02
❑	226	Warren Sapp	.10	.02
❑	227	Brian Mitchell	.10	.02
❑	228	Garrison Hearst	.20	.07
❑	229	Terance Mathis	.10	.02
❑	230	Bryce Paup	.10	.02
❑	231	Derrick Moore	.10	.02
❑	232	Curtis Conway	.40	.15
❑	233	Darnay Scott	.20	.07
❑	234	Andre Rison	.20	.07
❑	235	Jay Novacek	.10	.02
❑	236	Terrell Davis	.50	.20
❑	237	David Sloan	.10	.02
❑	238	Reggie White	.40	.15
❑	239	Todd McNair	.10	.02
❑	240	Ray Buchanan	.10	.02
❑	241	Steve Beuerlein	.20	.07
❑	242	Dan Saleaumua	.10	.02
❑	243	Bernie Parmalee	.10	.02
❑	244	Warren Moon	.20	.07
❑	245	Ty Law	.40	.15
❑	246	Torrance Small	.10	.02
❑	247	Phillippi Sparks	.10	.02
❑	248	Mo Lewis	.10	.02
❑	249	Jeff Hostetler	.10	.02
❑	250	Rodney Peete	.10	.02
❑	251	Byron Bam Morris	.10	.02
❑	252	Chris Miller	.10	.02
❑	253	Tony Martin	.20	.07
❑	254	Eric Davis	.10	.02
❑	255	Joey Galloway	.40	.15
❑	256	Derrick Brooks	.40	.15
❑	257	Ken Harvey	.10	.02
❑	258	Frank Sanders	.20	.07
❑	259	Morten Andersen	.10	.02
❑	260	Marlon Kerner	.10	.02
❑	261	Mark Carrier WR	.10	.02
❑	262	Mark Carrier DB	.10	.02
❑	263	Tony McGee	.10	.02
❑	264	Eric Zeier	.10	.02
❑	265	Darren Woodson	.20	.07
❑	266	Shannon Sharpe	.20	.07
❑	267	Brett Perriman	.10	.02
❑	268	Edgar Bennett	.20	.07
❑	269	Darryll Lewis	.10	.02
❑	270	Jim Harbaugh	.20	.07
❑	271	Desmond Howard	.20	.07
❑	272	Derrick Thomas	.40	.15
❑	273	Irving Fryar	.20	.07
❑	274	Jake Reed	.20	.07
❑	275	Curtis Martin	.50	.20
❑	276	Eric Allen	.10	.02
❑	277	Thomas Lewis	.10	.02
❑	278	Hugh Douglas	.20	.07
❑	279	Pat Swilling	.10	.02
❑	280	William Thomas	.10	.02
❑	281	Norm Johnson	.10	.02
❑	282	Roman Phifer	.10	.02
❑	283	Chris Mims	.10	.02
❑	284	Steve Young	.60	.25
❑	285	Cortez Kennedy	.10	.02
❑	286	Trent Dilfer	.40	.15
❑	287	Terry Allen	.20	.07
❑	288	Clyde Simmons	.10	.02
❑	289	Craig Heyward	.10	.02
❑	290	Jim Kelly	.40	.15
❑	291	Tyrone Poole	.10	.02
❑	292	Chris Zorich	.10	.02
❑	293	Dan Wilkinson	.10	.02
❑	294	Antonio Langham	.10	.02
❑	295	Troy Aikman	.75	.30
❑	296	Steve Atwater	.10	.02
❑	297	Scott Mitchell	.20	.07
❑	298	Mark Chmura	.20	.07
❑	299	Steve McNair	.50	.20
❑	300	Tony Bennett	.10	.02
❑	301	Willie Jackson	.20	.07
❑	302	Neil Smith	.20	.07
❑	303	Terry Kirby	.20	.07
❑	304	Orlando Thomas	.10	.02
❑	305	Willie McGinest	.10	.02
❑	306	Wayne Martin	.10	.02
❑	307	Michael Brooks	.10	.02
❑	308	Marvin Washington	.10	.02
❑	309	Nolan Harrison	.10	.02
❑	310	William Fuller	.10	.02
❑	311	Willie Williams	.10	.02
❑	312	Troy Drayton	.10	.02
❑	313	Shawn Lee	.10	.02
❑	314	Ken Norton	.10	.02
❑	315	Terry Wooden	.10	.02
❑	316	Hardy Nickerson	.10	.02
❑	317	Gus Frerotte	.20	.07
❑	318	Oscar McBride	.10	.02
❑	319	Merton Hanks	.10	.02
❑	320	Justin Armour	.10	.02
❑	321	Willie Green	.10	.02
❑	322	Roger Jones RC	.10	.02
❑	323	Leroy Hoard	.10	.02
❑	324	Chris Boniol	.10	.02
❑	325	Jason Hanson	.10	.02
❑	326	Sean Jones	.10	.02
❑	327	Roosevelt Potts	.10	.02
❑	328	Greg Hill	.20	.07
❑	329	O.J. McDuffie	.20	.07
❑	330	Amp Lee	.10	.02
❑	331	Chris Slade	.10	.02
❑	332	Jim Everett	.10	.02
❑	333	Tyrone Wheatley	.20	.07
❑	334	Charles Wilson	.10	.02
❑	335	Napoleon Kaufman	.40	.15
❑	336	Fred Barnett	.10	.02
❑	337	Neil O'Donnell	.20	.07
❑	338	Sean Gilbert	.10	.02
❑	339	Aaron Hayden RC	.10	.02
❑	340	Brent Jones	.10	.02
❑	341	Christian Fauria	.10	.02
❑	342	Alvin Harper	.10	.02
❑	343	Henry Ellard	.10	.02
❑	344	Willie Davis	.10	.02
❑	345	Charles Haley	.20	.07
❑	346	Chris Jacke	.10	.02
❑	347	Allen Aldridge	.10	.02
❑	348	Jeff Herrod	.10	.02
❑	349	Rocket Ismail	.20	.07
❑	350	Leslie O'Neal	.10	.02
❑	351	Marquez Pope	.10	.02
❑	352	Brock Marion	.10	.02
❑	353	Ernie Mills	.10	.02
❑	354	Larry Centers	.20	.07
❑	355	Chris Doleman	.10	.02
❑	356	Bruce Smith	.20	.07
❑	357	John Kasay	.10	.02
❑	358	Donnell Woolford	.10	.02
❑	359	David Dunn	.10	.02
❑	360	Eric Turner	.10	.02
❑	361	Sherman Williams	.10	.02
❑	362	Chris Spielman	.10	.02
❑	363	Craig Newsome	.10	.02
❑	364	Sean Dawkins	.10	.02
❑	365	James O. Stewart	.20	.07
❑	366	Dale Carter	.10	.02
❑	367	Marco Coleman	.10	.02
❑	368	Dave Meggett	.10	.02

❑ 369 Irv Smith .10 .02
❑ 370 Mike Mamula .10 .02
❑ 371 Erric Pegram .10 .02
❑ 372 Dana Stubblefield .20 .07
❑ 373 Terrance Shaw .10 .02
❑ 374 Jerry Rice CL .40 .15
❑ 375 Dan Marino CL .40 .15
❑ P1 Jerry Rice Promo 1.00 .40
❑ P2 Dan Marino Promo 1.00 .40

1996 Collector's Choice Update

❑ COMPLETE SET (200) 15.00 7.50
❑ U1 Zach Thomas RC .60 .25
❑ U2 Simeon Rice .50 .20
❑ U3 Jonathan Ogden .30 .10
❑ U4 Eric Moulds .30 .10
❑ U5 Tim Biakabutuka .30 .10
❑ U6 Walt Harris .10 .02
❑ U7 Willie Anderson .10 .02
❑ U8 Ricky Whittle .10 .02
❑ U9 John Mobley .10 .02
❑ U10 Reggie Brown RC .10 .02
❑ U11 John Michels .10 .02
❑ U12 Eddie George .60 .25
❑ U13 Marvin Harrison 1.25 .50
❑ U14 Kevin Hardy .20 .07
❑ U15 Kavika Pittman RC .10 .02
❑ U16 Daryl Gardener .10 .02
❑ U17 Duane Clemons .10 .02
❑ U18 Terry Glenn .30 .10
❑ U19 Alex Molden RC .10 .02
❑ U20 Cedric Jones .10 .02
❑ U21 Keyshawn Johnson .50 .20
❑ U22 Rickey Dudley .30 .10
❑ U23 Jason Dunn .10 .02
❑ U24 Jamain Stephens .10 .02
❑ U25 Lawrence Phillips .30 .10
❑ U26 Bryan Still RC .20 .07
❑ U27 Israel Ifeanyi .10 .02
❑ U28 Pete Kendall .10 .02
❑ U29 Regan Upshaw .10 .02
❑ U30 Andre Johnson RC .10 .02
❑ U31 Leeland McElroy .10 .02
❑ U32 Ray Lewis 1.25 .50
❑ U33 Sean Moran RC .10 .02
❑ U34 Muhsin Muhammad RC .75 .30
❑ U35 Bobby Engram .30 .10
❑ U36 Marco Battaglia .10 .02
❑ U37 Stepfret Williams .10 .02
❑ U38 Jeff Lewis .20 .07
❑ U39 Derrick Mayes .20 .07
❑ U40 Reggie Tongue RC .10 .02
❑ U41 Tory James RC .20 .07
❑ U42 Tony Banks RC .30 .10
❑ U43 Tedy Bruschi 3.00 1.25
❑ U44 Mike Alstott .50 .20
❑ U45 Anthony Dorsett .10 .02
❑ U46 Tony Brackens RC .30 .10
❑ U47 Bryant Mix .10 .02
❑ U48 Karim Abdul-Jabbar .30 .10
❑ U49 Moe Williams RB RC .75 .30
❑ U50 Lawyer Milloy .20 .07
❑ U51 Je'rod Cherry .10 .02
❑ U52 Amani Toomer RC 1.00 .40
❑ U53 Alex Van Dyke .20 .07
❑ U54 Lance Johnstone RC .20 .07
❑ U55 Bobby Hoying .30 .10
❑ U56 Jon Witman RC .20 .07
❑ U57 Eddie Kennison RC .30 .10
❑ U58 Brian Roche RC .10 .02
❑ U59 Terrell Owens RC 2.50 1.00
❑ U60 Stephen Davis .75 .30
❑ U61 Jeff George FP .20 .07
❑ U62 Darick Holmes FP .10 .02
❑ U63 Kerry Collins FP .30 .10
❑ U64 Rashaan Salaam FP .20 .07
❑ U65 Jeff Blake FP .20 .07
❑ U66 Emmitt Smith FP .75 .30
❑ U67 Troy Aikman FP .50 .20
❑ U68 John Elway FP 1.00 .40
❑ U69 Terrell Davis FP .40 .15
❑ U70 Barry Sanders FP .75 .30
❑ U71 Herman Moore FP .20 .07
❑ U72 Brett Favre FP 1.00 .40
❑ U73 Robert Brooks FP .20 .07
❑ U74 Steve McNair FP .40 .15
❑ U75 Marshall Faulk FP .30 .10
❑ U76 Marcus Allen FP .30 .10
❑ U77 Dan Marino FP 1.00 .40
❑ U78 Warren Moon FP .10 .02
❑ U79 Drew Bledsoe FP .30 .10
❑ U80 Curtis Martin FP .40 .15
❑ U81 Mario Bates FP .20 .07
❑ U82 Tim Brown FP .30 .10
❑ U83 Charlie Garner FP .20 .07
❑ U84 Kordell Stewart FP .30 .10
❑ U85 Isaac Bruce FP .30 .10
❑ U86 Tony Martin FP .10 .02
❑ U87 Jerry Rice FP .50 .20
❑ U88 J.J. Stokes FP .30 .10
❑ U89 Joey Galloway FP .30 .10
❑ U90 Errict Rhett FP .20 .07
❑ U91 Mike Pritchard .10 .02
❑ U92 Jerome Bettis .30 .10
❑ U93 Winslow Oliver .10 .02
❑ U94 David Klingler .10 .02
❑ U95 Lawrence Dawsey .10 .02
❑ U96 Charlie Jones .20 .07
❑ U97 Dave Krieg .10 .02
❑ U98 Chris Spielman .10 .02
❑ U99 Stanley Pritchett .10 .02
❑ U100 Sean Gilbert .10 .02
❑ U101 Tommy Vardell .10 .02
❑ U102 DeRon Jenkins .10 .02
❑ U103 Larry Bowie .10 .02
❑ U104 Kyle Wachholtz .10 .02
❑ U105 Brady Smith RC .10 .02
❑ U106 Steve Walsh .10 .02
❑ U107 Wesley Walls .20 .07
❑ U108 Kevin Ross .10 .02
❑ U109 Willie Clay .10 .02
❑ U110 Olanda Truitt .10 .02
❑ U111 Calvin Williams .10 .02
❑ U112 Chris Doleman .10 .02
❑ U113 Irving Fryar .20 .07
❑ U114 Jimmy Spencer .10 .02
❑ U115 Reggie Barlow RC .10 .02
❑ U116 Reggie Brown RBK RC .10 .02
❑ U117 Dixon Edwards .10 .02
❑ U118 Haywood Jeffires .10 .02
❑ U119 Santana Dotson .10 .02
❑ U120 Herschel Walker .20 .07
❑ U121 Darryl Williams .10 .02
❑ U122 Bryan Cox .10 .02
❑ U123 Lamar Thomas .10 .02
❑ U124 Hendrick Lusk .10 .02
❑ U125 Jahine Arnold RC .10 .02
❑ U126 Boomer Esiason .20 .07
❑ U127 Willie Davis .10 .02
❑ U128 Pete Stoyanovich .10 .02
❑ U129 Bill Romanowski .10 .02
❑ U130 Tim McKyer .10 .02
❑ U131 Patrick Sapp .10 .02
❑ U132 Natrone Means .20 .07
❑ U133 Quinn Early .10 .02
❑ U134 Leslie O'Neal .10 .02
❑ U135 Mark Seay .10 .02
❑ U136 Pete Metzelaars .10 .02
❑ U137 Jay Leeuwenburg UER .10 .02
❑ U138 Buster Owens .10 .02
❑ U139 Todd McNair .10 .02
❑ U140 Eugene Robinson .10 .02
❑ U141 Sean Salisbury .10 .02
❑ U142 Eddie Robinson .10 .02
❑ U143 Jerris McPhail .10 .02
❑ U144 Ray Farmer RC .10 .02
❑ U145 Garrison Hearst .20 .07
❑ U146 Leonard Russell .10 .02
❑ U147 Roy Barker .10 .02
❑ U148 Larry Brown .10 .02
❑ U149 Webster Slaughter .10 .02
❑ U150 Roman Oben RC .10 .02
❑ U151 LeShon Johnson .10 .02
❑ U152 Patrick Bates .10 .02
❑ U153 Iheanyi Uwaezuoke RC .30 .10
❑ U154 Scott Slutzker .10 .02
❑ U155 John Jurkovic .10 .02
❑ U156 Brian Milne .10 .02
❑ U157 Mike Sherrard .10 .02
❑ U158 Neil O'Donnell .20 .07
❑ U159 Roger Harper .10 .02
❑ U160 Desmond Howard .20 .07
❑ U161 Alfred Williams .10 .02
❑ U162 Ronnie Harmon .10 .02
❑ U163 Sammie Burroughs RC .10 .02
❑ U164 Keenan McCardell .30 .10
❑ U165 Shane Dronett .10 .02
❑ U166 Jeff Graham .10 .02
❑ U167 Bill Brooks .10 .02
❑ U168 Shawn Jefferson .10 .02
❑ U169 Detron Smith .10 .02
❑ U170 Danny Kanell .30 .10
❑ U171 Jevon Langford .10 .02
❑ U172 Russell Maryland .10 .02
❑ U173 Scott Milanovich RC .30 .10
❑ U174 Eric Davis .10 .02
❑ U175 Ernie Conwell .10 .02
❑ U176 Kurt Gouveia .10 .02
❑ U177 Andre Rison .20 .07
❑ U178 Harold Green .10 .02
❑ U179 Frank Reich .10 .02
❑ U180 Glyn Milburn .10 .02
❑ U181 Nilo Silvan .10 .02
❑ U182 Cornelius Bennett .10 .02
❑ U183 Freddie Solomon RC .10 .02
❑ U184 Pat Terrell .10 .02
❑ U185 Miles Macik .10 .02
❑ U186 Bo Orlando .10 .02
❑ U187 Kelvin Martin .10 .02
❑ U188 Todd Kinchen .10 .02
❑ U189 Reggie Brooks .10 .02
❑ U190 Steve Beuerlein .20 .07
❑ U191 Marco Coleman .10 .02
❑ U192 Johnny Johnson .10 .02
❑ U193 Dedric Mathis .10 .02
❑ U194 Leon Searcy .10 .02
❑ U195 Kevin Greene .20 .07
❑ U196 Daniel Stubbs .10 .02
❑ U197 Ray Mickens .10 .02
❑ U198 Devin Wyman .10 .02
❑ U199 Lorenzo Lynch .10 .02
❑ U200 Rice/Marino CL .30 .10

1997 Collector's Choice

❑ COMPLETE SET (565) 30.00 12.50
❑ COMP.SERIES 1 (310) 20.00 7.50
❑ COMP.FACT.SER.1(330) 25.00 10.00
❑ COMP.SERIES 2 (255) 12.00 5.00
❑ 1 Orlando Pace RC .50 .20
❑ 2 Darrell Russell RC .20 .07
❑ 3 Shawn Springs RC .30 .10
❑ 4 Peter Boulware RC .50 .20
❑ 5 Bryant Westbrook RC .20 .07

❑ 6 Tom Knight RC .20 .07
❑ 7 Ike Hilliard RC .75 .30
❑ 8 James Farrior RC .50 .20
❑ 9 Chris Naeole RC .20 .07
❑ 10 Michael Booker RC .20 .07
❑ 11 Warrick Dunn RC 1.25 .50
❑ 12 Tony Gonzalez RC 1.50 .60
❑ 13 Reinard Wilson RC .30 .10
❑ 14 Yatil Green RC .30 .10
❑ 15 Reidel Anthony RC .50 .20
❑ 16 Kenard Lang RC .30 .10
❑ 17 Kenny Holmes RC .50 .20
❑ 18 Tarik Glenn RC .20 .07
❑ 19 Dwayne Rudd RC .50 .20
❑ 20 Renaldo Wynn RC .20 .07
❑ 21 David LaFleur RC .20 .07
❑ 22 Antowain Smith RC 1.25 .50
❑ 23 Jim Druckenmiller RC .30 .10
❑ 24 Rae Carruth RC .20 .07
❑ 25 Jared Tomich RC .20 .07
❑ 26 Chris Canty RC .20 .07
❑ 27 Jake Plummer RC 2.50 1.00
❑ 28 Troy Davis RC .30 .10
❑ 29 Sedrick Shaw RC .30 .10
❑ 30 Jamie Sharper RC .30 .10
❑ 31 Tiki Barber RC 3.00 1.25
❑ 32 Byron Hanspard RC .30 .10
❑ 33 Darnell Autry RC .30 .10
❑ 34 Corey Dillon RC 3.00 1.25
❑ 35 Joey Kent RC .50 .20
❑ 36 Nathan Davis RC .20 .07
❑ 37 Will Blackwell RC .30 .10
❑ 38 Kim Herring RC .20 .07
❑ 39 Pat Barnes RC .50 .20
❑ 40 Kevin Lockett RC .30 .10
❑ 41 Trevor Pryce RC .50 .20
❑ 42 Matt Russell RC .20 .07
❑ 43 Greg Jones RC .20 .07
❑ 44 Antonio Anderson RC .20 .07
❑ 45 George Jones RC .30 .10
❑ 46 Steve Young NG .50 .20
❑ 47 Jerry Rice NG .50 .20
❑ 48 Curtis Conway NG .20 .07
❑ 49 Jeff Blake NG .30 .10
❑ 50 Carl Pickens NG .30 .10
❑ 51 Bruce Smith NG .20 .07
❑ 52 John Elway NG 1.00 .40
❑ 53 Terrell Davis NG .50 .20
❑ 54 Shannon Sharpe NG .20 .07
❑ 55 Junior Seau NG .20 .07
❑ 56 Darren Bennett NG .20 .07
❑ 57 Jim Harbaugh NG .30 .10
❑ 58 Marshall Faulk NG .50 .20
❑ 59 Emmitt Smith NG .75 .30
❑ 60 Troy Aikman NG .50 .20
❑ 61 Deion Sanders NG .50 .20
❑ 62 Dan Marino NG 1.00 .40
❑ 63 Ricky Watters NG .20 .07
❑ 64 Mark Brunell NG .50 .20
❑ 65 Keenan McCardell NG .20 .07
❑ 66 Keyshawn Johnson NG .50 .20
❑ 67 Barry Sanders NG .75 .30
❑ 68 Herman Moore NG .30 .10
❑ 69 Eddie George NG .50 .20
❑ 70 Steve McNair NG .50 .20
❑ 71 Brett Favre NG 1.00 .40
❑ 72 Reggie White NG .30 .10
❑ 73 Edgar Bennett NG .20 .07
❑ 74 Kerry Collins NG .30 .10
❑ 75 Kevin Greene NG .20 .07
❑ 76 Drew Bledsoe NG .30 .10
❑ 77 Terry Glenn NG .30 .10
❑ 78 Curtis Martin NG .50 .20
❑ 79 Jeff Hostetler NG .20 .07
❑ 80 Napoleon Kaufman NG .50 .20
❑ 81 Isaac Bruce NG .50 .20
❑ 82 Terry Allen NG .30 .10
❑ 83 Joey Galloway NG .30 .10
❑ 84 Kordell Stewart NG .50 .20
❑ 85 Jerome Bettis NG .50 .20
❑ 86 Dana Stubblefield .20 .07
❑ 87 Merton Hanks .20 .07
❑ 88 Terrell Owens .60 .25
❑ 89 Brent Jones .20 .07
❑ 90 Ken Norton Jr. .20 .07
❑ 91 Jerry Rice 1.00 .40
❑ 92 Terry Kirby .30 .10
❑ 93 Bryant Young .20 .07
❑ 94 Raymont Harris .20 .07
❑ 95 Jeff Jaeger .20 .07
❑ 96 Curtis Conway .30 .10
❑ 97 Walt Harris .20 .07
❑ 98 Bobby Engram .30 .10
❑ 99 Donnell Woolford .20 .07
❑ 100 Rashaan Salaam .20 .07
❑ 101 Jeff Blake .30 .10
❑ 102 Tony McGee .20 .07
❑ 103 Ashley Ambrose .20 .07
❑ 104 Dan Wilkinson .20 .07
❑ 105 Jevon Langford .20 .07
❑ 106 Darnay Scott .30 .10
❑ 107 David Dunn .20 .07
❑ 108 Eric Moulds .50 .20
❑ 109 Darick Holmes .20 .07
❑ 110 Thurman Thomas .50 .20
❑ 111 Quinn Early .20 .07
❑ 112 Jim Kelly .50 .20
❑ 113 Bryce Paup .20 .07
❑ 114 Bruce Smith .30 .10
❑ 115 Todd Collins .20 .07
❑ 116 Tory James .20 .07
❑ 117 Anthony Miller .20 .07
❑ 118 Terrell Davis .60 .25
❑ 119 Tyrone Braxton .20 .07
❑ 120 John Mobley .20 .07
❑ 121 Bill Romanowski .20 .07
❑ 122 Vaughn Hebron .20 .07
❑ 123 Mike Alstott .50 .20
❑ 124 Errict Rhett .20 .07
❑ 125 Trent Dilfer .50 .20
❑ 126 Courtney Hawkins .20 .07
❑ 127 Hardy Nickerson .20 .07
❑ 128 Donnie Abraham RC .50 .20
❑ 129 Regan Upshaw .20 .07
❑ 130 Kent Graham .20 .07
❑ 131 Rob Moore .30 .10
❑ 132 Simeon Rice .30 .10
❑ 133 LeShon Johnson .20 .07
❑ 134 Frank Sanders .30 .10
❑ 135 Leeland McElroy .20 .07
❑ 136 Seth Joyner .20 .07
❑ 137 Andre Coleman .20 .07
❑ 138 Stan Humphries .30 .10
❑ 139 Charlie Jones .20 .07
❑ 140 Junior Seau .50 .20
❑ 141 Rodney Harrison RC 1.00 .40
❑ 142 Darrien Gordon .20 .07
❑ 143 Terrell Fletcher .20 .07
❑ 144 Tamarick Vanover .30 .10
❑ 145 Greg Hill .20 .07
❑ 146 Marcus Allen .50 .20
❑ 147 Lake Dawson .20 .07
❑ 148 Dale Carter .20 .07
❑ 149 Kimble Anders .30 .10
❑ 150 Chris Penn .20 .07
❑ 151 Sean Dawkins .20 .07
❑ 152 Ken Dilger .20 .07
❑ 153 Marvin Harrison .50 .20
❑ 154 Jeff Herrod .20 .07
❑ 155 Jim Harbaugh .30 .10
❑ 156 Cary Blanchard .20 .07
❑ 157 Aaron Bailey .20 .07
❑ 158 Deion Sanders .50 .20
❑ 159 Jim Schwantz RC .20 .07
❑ 160 Michael Irvin .50 .20
❑ 161 Herschel Walker .30 .10
❑ 162 Emmitt Smith 1.50 .60
❑ 163 Chris Boniol .20 .07
❑ 164 Eric Bjornson .20 .07
❑ 165 Karim Abdul-Jabbar .30 .10
❑ 166 O.J. McDuffie .30 .10
❑ 167 Troy Drayton .20 .07
❑ 168 Zach Thomas .50 .20
❑ 169 Irving Spikes .20 .07
❑ 170 Shane Burton RC .30 .10
❑ 171 Stanley Pritchett .20 .07
❑ 172 Ty Detmer .30 .10
❑ 173 Chris T. Jones .20 .07
❑ 174 Troy Vincent .20 .07
❑ 175 Brian Dawkins .50 .20
❑ 176 Irving Fryar .30 .10
❑ 177 Charlie Garner .30 .10
❑ 178 Bobby Taylor .20 .07
❑ 179 Jamal Anderson .50 .20
❑ 180 Terance Mathis .30 .10
❑ 181 Craig Heyward .20 .07
❑ 182 Cornelius Bennett .20 .07
❑ 183 Jessie Tuggle .20 .07
❑ 184 Devin Bush .20 .07
❑ 185 Dave Brown .20 .07
❑ 186 Danny Kanell .20 .07
❑ 187 Rodney Hampton .30 .10
❑ 188 Tyrone Wheatley .30 .10
❑ 189 Amani Toomer .30 .10
❑ 190 Phillippi Sparks .20 .07
❑ 191 Thomas Lewis .20 .07
❑ 192 Jimmy Smith .30 .10
❑ 193 Pete Mitchell .20 .07
❑ 194 Natrone Means .30 .10
❑ 195 Mark Brunell .60 .25
❑ 196 Kevin Hardy .20 .07
❑ 197 Tony Brackens .20 .07
❑ 198 Aaron Beasley RC .20 .07
❑ 199 Chris Hudson .20 .07
❑ 200 Wayne Chrebet .50 .20
❑ 201 Keyshawn Johnson .50 .20
❑ 202 Adrian Murrell .30 .10
❑ 203 Neil O'Donnell .30 .10
❑ 204 Hugh Douglas .20 .07
❑ 205 Mo Lewis .20 .07
❑ 206 Glenn Foley .20 .07
❑ 207 Aaron Glenn .20 .07
❑ 208 Johnnie Morton .30 .10
❑ 209 Reggie Brown LB .30 .10
❑ 210 Barry Sanders 1.50 .60
❑ 211 Glyn Milburn .20 .07
❑ 212 Bennie Blades .20 .07
❑ 213 Steve McNair .60 .25
❑ 214 Frank Wycheck .20 .07
❑ 215 Chris Sanders .20 .07
❑ 216 Blaine Bishop .20 .07
❑ 217 Willie Davis .20 .07
❑ 218 Darryll Lewis .20 .07
❑ 219 Marcus Robertson .20 .07
❑ 220 Robert Brooks .30 .10
❑ 221 Antonio Freeman .50 .20
❑ 222 Keith Jackson .20 .07
❑ 223 Mark Chmura .30 .10
❑ 224 Brett Favre 2.00 .75
❑ 225 Sean Jones .20 .07
❑ 226 Reggie White .50 .20
❑ 227 LeRoy Butler .20 .07
❑ 228 Craig Newsome .20 .07
❑ 229 Wesley Walls .30 .10

❑ 230 Mark Carrier WR .20 .07
❑ 231 Muhsin Muhammad .30 .10
❑ 232 John Kasay .20 .07
❑ 233 Anthony Johnson .20 .07
❑ 234 Kerry Collins .50 .20
❑ 235 Kevin Greene .30 .10
❑ 236 Sam Mills .20 .07
❑ 237 Ben Coates .30 .10
❑ 238 Terry Glenn .50 .20
❑ 239 Willie McGinest .20 .07
❑ 240 Ted Johnson .20 .07
❑ 241 Lawyer Milloy .30 .10
❑ 242 Drew Bledsoe .60 .25
❑ 243 Willie Clay .20 .07
❑ 244 Chris Slade .20 .07
❑ 245 Tim Brown .50 .20
❑ 246 Daryl Hobbs .20 .07
❑ 247 Rickey Dudley .30 .10
❑ 248 Joe Aska .20 .07
❑ 249 Chester McGlockton .20 .07
❑ 250 Rob Fredrickson .20 .07
❑ 251 Terry McDaniel .20 .07
❑ 252 Tony Banks .30 .10
❑ 253 Lawrence Phillips .20 .07
❑ 254 Isaac Bruce .50 .20
❑ 255 Eddie Kennison .30 .10
❑ 256 Kevin Carter .20 .07
❑ 257 Roman Phifer .20 .07
❑ 258 Keith Lyle .20 .07
❑ 259 Vinny Testaverde .30 .10
❑ 260 Derrick Alexander WR .30 .10
❑ 261 Ray Lewis .75 .30
❑ 262 Jermaine Lewis .50 .20
❑ 263 Byron Bam Morris .20 .07
❑ 264 Stevon Moore .20 .07
❑ 265 Antonio Langham .20 .07
❑ 266 Brian Mitchell .20 .07
❑ 267 Henry Ellard .20 .07
❑ 268 Leslie Shepherd .20 .07
❑ 269 Michael Westbrook .30 .10
❑ 270 Jamie Asher .20 .07
❑ 271 Ken Harvey .20 .07
❑ 272 Gus Frerotte .20 .07
❑ 273 Michael Haynes .20 .07
❑ 274 Ray Zellars .20 .07
❑ 275 Jim Everett .20 .07
❑ 276 Tyrone Hughes .20 .07
❑ 277 Joe Johnson .20 .07
❑ 278 Eric Allen .20 .07
❑ 279 Brady Smith .20 .07
❑ 280 Mario Bates .20 .07
❑ 281 Torrance Small .20 .07
❑ 282 John Friesz .20 .07
❑ 283 Brian Blades .20 .07
❑ 284 Chris Warren .30 .10
❑ 285 Joey Galloway .30 .10
❑ 286 Michael Sinclair .20 .07
❑ 287 Lamar Smith .50 .20
❑ 288 Mike Pritchard .20 .07
❑ 289 Jerome Bettis .50 .20
❑ 290 Charles Johnson .30 .10
❑ 291 Mike Tomczak .20 .07
❑ 292 Levon Kirkland .20 .07
❑ 293 Carnell Lake .20 .07
❑ 294 Erric Pegram .20 .07
❑ 295 Kordell Stewart .50 .20
❑ 296 Greg Lloyd .20 .07
❑ 297 Dixon Edwards .20 .07
❑ 298 Cris Carter .50 .20
❑ 299 Brad Johnson .50 .20
❑ 300 Qadry Ismail .30 .10
❑ 301 John Randle .30 .10
❑ 302 Orlanda Thomas .20 .07
❑ 303 Dewayne Washington .20 .07
❑ 304 Jake Reed .30 .10
❑ 305 Derrick Alexander DE .20 .07
❑ 306 Eddie George CL .50 .20
❑ 307 Dan Marino CL .40 .15
❑ 308 Curtis Martin CL .30 .10
❑ 309 Troy Aikman CL .50 .20
❑ 310 Marcus Allen CL .50 .20
❑ 311 Jim Druckenmiller .20 .07
❑ 312 Greg Clark RC .20 .07
❑ 313 Darnell Autry .30 .10
❑ 314 Reinard Wilson .20 .07
❑ 315 Corey Dillon 1.25 .50
❑ 316 Antowain Smith .50 .20
❑ 317 Trevor Pryce .30 .10
❑ 318 Warrick Dunn .50 .20
❑ 319 Reidel Anthony .30 .10
❑ 320 Jake Plummer 1.00 .40
❑ 321 Tom Knight .20 .07
❑ 322 Freddie Jones RC .30 .10
❑ 323 Tony Gonzalez .60 .25
❑ 324 Pat Barnes .30 .10
❑ 325 Kevin Lockett .30 .10
❑ 326 Tarik Glenn .20 .07
❑ 327 David LaFleur .20 .07
❑ 328 Antonio Anderson .20 .07
❑ 329 Yatil Green .30 .10
❑ 330 Jason Taylor RC 1.00 .40
❑ 331 Brian Manning RC .20 .07
❑ 332 Michael Booker .20 .07
❑ 333 Byron Hanspard .30 .10
❑ 334 Ike Hilliard .50 .20
❑ 335 Tiki Barber 1.25 .50
❑ 336 Renaldo Wynn .20 .07
❑ 337 Damon Jones RC .20 .07
❑ 338 James Farrior .30 .10
❑ 339 Dedric Ward RC .30 .10
❑ 340 Bryant Westbrook .20 .07
❑ 341 Joey Kent .50 .20
❑ 342 Kenny Holmes .20 .07
❑ 343 Darren Sharper RC .50 .20
❑ 344 Rae Carruth .20 .07
❑ 345 Chris Canty .20 .07
❑ 346 Darrell Russell .20 .07
❑ 347 Orlando Pace .50 .20
❑ 348 Peter Boulware .30 .10
❑ 349 Kenard Lang .20 .07
❑ 350 Danny Wuerffel RC .50 .20
❑ 351 Troy Davis .20 .07
❑ 352 Shawn Springs .30 .10
❑ 353 Walter Jones RC .50 .20
❑ 354 Will Blackwell .20 .07
❑ 355 Dwayne Rudd .20 .07
❑ 356 49ers BB .20 .07
❑ 357 Bears BB .20 .07
❑ 358 Bengals BB .20 .07
❑ 359 Bills BB .20 .07
❑ 360 Broncos BB .30 .10
❑ 361 Buccaneers BB .20 .07
❑ 362 Cardinals BB .30 .10
❑ 363 Chargers BB .20 .07
❑ 364 Chiefs BB .30 .10
❑ 365 Colts BB .30 .10
❑ 366 Cowboys BB .20 .07
❑ 367 Dolphins BB .20 .07
❑ 368 Eagles BB .20 .07
❑ 369 Falcons BB .20 .07
❑ 370 Giants BB .20 .07
❑ 371 Jaguars BB .20 .07
❑ 372 Jets BB .20 .07
❑ 373 Lions BB .20 .07
❑ 374 Oilers BB .20 .07
❑ 375 Packers BB .50 .20
❑ 376 Panthers BB .20 .07
❑ 377 Patriots BB .20 .07
❑ 378 Raiders BB .20 .07
❑ 379 Rams BB .20 .07
❑ 380 Ravens BB .20 .07
❑ 381 Redskins BB .20 .07
❑ 382 Saints BB .20 .07
❑ 383 Seahawks BB .20 .07
❑ 384 Steelers BB .30 .10
❑ 385 Vikings BB .30 .10
❑ 386 William Floyd .30 .10
❑ 387 Steve Young .60 .25
❑ 388 Lee Woodall .20 .07
❑ 389 J.J. Stokes .30 .10
❑ 390 Marc Edwards .20 .07
❑ 391 Rod Woodson .30 .10
❑ 392 Jim Schwantz .20 .07
❑ 393 Garrison Hearst .30 .10
❑ 394 Rick Mirer .20 .07
❑ 395 Alonzo Spellman .20 .07
❑ 396 Tom Carter .20 .07
❑ 397 Bryan Cox .20 .07
❑ 398 John Allred RC .20 .07
❑ 399 Ricky Proehl .20 .07
❑ 400 Tyrone Hughes .20 .07
❑ 401 Carl Pickens .30 .10
❑ 402 Tremain Mack RC .20 .07
❑ 403 Boomer Esiason .30 .10
❑ 404 Ki-Jana Carter .20 .07
❑ 405 Steve Tovar .20 .07
❑ 406 Billy Joe Hobert .30 .10
❑ 407 Andre Reed .30 .10
❑ 408 Marcellus Wiley RC .30 .10
❑ 409 Steve Tasker .20 .07
❑ 410 Chris Spielman .20 .07
❑ 411 Alfred Williams .20 .07
❑ 412 John Elway 2.00 .75
❑ 413 Shannon Sharpe .30 .10
❑ 414 Steve Atwater .20 .07
❑ 415 Neil Smith .30 .10
❑ 416 Darrien Gordon .20 .07
❑ 417 Jeff Lewis .20 .07
❑ 418 Flipper Anderson .20 .07
❑ 419 Willie Green .20 .07
❑ 420 Jackie Harris .20 .07
❑ 421 Steve Walsh .20 .07
❑ 422 Anthony Parker .20 .07
❑ 423 Ronde Barber RC 1.00 .40
❑ 424 Warren Sapp .30 .10
❑ 425 Aeneas Williams .20 .07
❑ 426 Larry Centers .30 .10
❑ 427 Eric Swann .20 .07
❑ 428 Kevin Williams .20 .07
❑ 429 Darren Bennett .20 .07
❑ 430 Tony Martin .30 .10
❑ 431 John Carney .20 .07
❑ 432 Jim Everett .20 .07
❑ 433 William Fuller .20 .07
❑ 434 Latario Rachal RC .20 .07
❑ 435 Erric Pegram .20 .07
❑ 436 Eric Metcalf .30 .10
❑ 437 Jerome Woods .20 .07
❑ 438 Derrick Thomas .50 .20
❑ 439 Elvis Grbac .30 .10
❑ 440 Terry Wooden .20 .07
❑ 441 Andre Rison .30 .10
❑ 442 Brett Perriman .20 .07
❑ 443 Paul Justin .20 .07
❑ 444 Robert Blackmon .20 .07
❑ 445 Carlton Gray .20 .07
❑ 446 Chris Gardocki .20 .07
❑ 447 Marshall Faulk .60 .25
❑ 448 Sammie Burroughs .20 .07
❑ 449 Quentin Coryatt .20 .07
❑ 450 Troy Aikman 1.00 .40
❑ 451 Daryl Johnston .30 .10
❑ 452 Tony Tolbert .20 .07
❑ 453 Brock Marion .20 .07
❑ 454 Billy Davis RC .20 .07
❑ 455 Stepfret Williams .20 .07
❑ 456 Anthony Miller .20 .07
❑ 457 Dan Marino 2.00 .75
❑ 458 Jerris McPhail .20 .07
❑ 459 Terrell Buckley .20 .07
❑ 460 Daryl Gardener .20 .07
❑ 461 George Teague .20 .07
❑ 462 Derrick Rodgers RC .20 .07
❑ 463 Fred Barnett .20 .07
❑ 464 Darrin Smith .20 .07
❑ 465 Michael Timpson .20 .07
❑ 466 Jon Harris .20 .07
❑ 467 Jason Dunn .20 .07
❑ 468 Bobby Hoying .30 .10
❑ 469 Ricky Watters .30 .10

❑ 470	Derrick Witherspoon	.20	.07
❑ 471	Chris Chandler	.30	.10
❑ 472	Ray Buchanan	.20	.07
❑ 473	Michael Haynes	.20	.07
❑ 474	O.J. Santiago RC	.30	.10
❑ 475	Morten Andersen	.20	.07
❑ 476	Bert Emanuel	.30	.10
❑ 477	Chris Calloway	.20	.07
❑ 478	Jason Sehorn	.30	.10
❑ 479	John Jurkovic	.20	.07
❑ 480	Keenan McCardell	.30	.10
❑ 481	James O. Stewart	.30	.10
❑ 482	Rob Johnson	.50	.20
❑ 483	Mike Logan RC	.20	.07
❑ 484	Deon Figures	.20	.07
❑ 485	Kyle Brady	.20	.07
❑ 486	Alex Van Dyke	.20	.07
❑ 487	Jeff Graham	.20	.07
❑ 488	Jason Hanson	.20	.07
❑ 489	Herman Moore	.30	.10
❑ 490	Scott Mitchell	.30	.10
❑ 491	Tommy Vardell	.20	.07
❑ 492	Derrick Mason RC	1.00	.40
❑ 493	Rodney Thomas	.20	.07
❑ 494	Ronnie Harmon	.20	.07
❑ 495	Eddie George	.50	.20
❑ 496	Edgar Bennett	.30	.10
❑ 497	William Henderson	.30	.10
❑ 498	Dorsey Levens	.50	.20
❑ 499	Gilbert Brown	.30	.10
❑ 500	Steve Bono	.30	.10
❑ 501	Derrick Mayes	.30	.10
❑ 502	Fred Lane RC	.30	.10
❑ 503	Ernie Mills	.20	.07
❑ 504	Tim Biakabutuka	.30	.10
❑ 505	Michael Bates	.20	.07
❑ 506	Winslow Oliver	.20	.07
❑ 507	Ty Law	.30	.10
❑ 508	Shawn Jefferson	.20	.07
❑ 509	Vincent Brisby	.20	.07
❑ 510	Henry Thomas	.20	.07
❑ 511	Tedy Bruschi	1.00	.40
❑ 512	Curtis Martin	.60	.25
❑ 513	Jeff George	.30	.10
❑ 514	Desmond Howard	.30	.10
❑ 515	Napoleon Kaufman	.50	.20
❑ 516	Kenny Shedd RC	.20	.07
❑ 517	Russell Maryland	.20	.07
❑ 518	Lance Johnstone	.20	.07
❑ 519	Eric Turner	.20	.07
❑ 520	Dexter McCleon RC	.20	.07
❑ 521	Craig Heyward	.20	.07
❑ 522	Ryan McNeil	.20	.07
❑ 523	Mark Rypien	.20	.07
❑ 524	Mike Jones LB	.20	.07
❑ 525	Jamie Sharper	.20	.07
❑ 526	Tony Siragusa	.20	.07
❑ 527	Michael Jackson	.30	.10
❑ 528	Floyd Turner	.20	.07
❑ 529	Eric Green	.20	.07
❑ 530	Michael McCrary	.20	.07
❑ 531	Jay Graham RC	.30	.10
❑ 532	Terry Allen	.50	.20
❑ 533	Sean Gilbert	.20	.07
❑ 534	Scott Turner	.20	.07
❑ 535	Cris Dishman	.20	.07
❑ 536	Darrell Green	.30	.10
❑ 537	Stephen Davis	.50	.20
❑ 538	Alvin Harper	.20	.07
❑ 539	Daryl Hobbs	.20	.07
❑ 540	Wayne Martin	.20	.07
❑ 541	Heath Shuler	.20	.07
❑ 542	Andre Hastings	.20	.07
❑ 543	Jared Tomich	.20	.07
❑ 544	Nicky Savoie RC	.20	.07
❑ 545	Cortez Kennedy	.20	.07
❑ 546	Warren Moon	.50	.20
❑ 547	Chad Brown	.20	.07
❑ 548	Willie Williams	.20	.07
❑ 549	Bennie Blades	.20	.07
❑ 550	Darren Perry	.20	.07
❑ 551	Mark Bruener	.20	.07
❑ 552	Yancey Thigpen	.30	.10
❑ 553	Courtney Hawkins	.20	.07
❑ 554	Chad Scott RC	.30	.10
❑ 555	George Jones	.30	.10
❑ 556	Robert Tate RC	.20	.07
❑ 557	Torrian Gray RC	.20	.07
❑ 558	Robert Griffith RC	.20	.07
❑ 559	Leroy Hoard	.20	.07
❑ 560	Robert Smith	.30	.10
❑ 561	Randall Cunningham	.50	.20
❑ 562	Darrell Russell CL	.20	.07
❑ 563	Troy Aikman CL	.50	.20
❑ 564	Dan Marino CL	.40	.15
❑ 565	Jim Druckenmiller CL	.20	.07

1996 Donruss

❑	COMPLETE SET (240)	20.00	7.50
❑ 1	Barry Sanders	1.50	.60
❑ 2	Flipper Anderson	.10	.02
❑ 3	Ben Coates	.20	.07
❑ 4	Rob Johnson	.40	.15
❑ 5	Rodney Hampton	.20	.07
❑ 6	Desmond Howard	.20	.07
❑ 7	Craig Heyward	.10	.02
❑ 8	Alvin Harper	.10	.02
❑ 9	Todd Collins	.20	.07
❑ 10	Ken Norton Jr.	.10	.02
❑ 11	Stan Humphries	.20	.07
❑ 12	Aeneas Williams	.10	.02
❑ 13	Jeff Hostetler	.10	.02
❑ 14	Frank Sanders	.20	.07
❑ 15	J.J. Birden	.10	.02
❑ 16	Bryce Paup	.10	.02
❑ 17	Bill Brooks	.10	.02
❑ 18	Kevin Williams	.10	.02
❑ 19	Boomer Esiason	.20	.07
❑ 20	O.J. McDuffie	.20	.07
❑ 21	Eric Swann	.10	.02
❑ 22	Neil Smith	.20	.07
❑ 23	Charlie Garner	.20	.07
❑ 24	Greg Lloyd	.20	.07
❑ 25	Willie Jackson	.20	.07
❑ 26	Shawn Jefferson	.10	.02
❑ 27	Rodney Peete	.10	.02
❑ 28	Michael Westbrook	.40	.15
❑ 29	J.J. Stokes	.40	.15
❑ 30	Troy Aikman	1.00	.40
❑ 31	Sean Dawkins	.10	.02
❑ 32	Larry Centers	.20	.07
❑ 33	Herschel Walker	.20	.07
❑ 34	Stoney Case	.10	.02
❑ 35	Kevin Greene	.20	.07
❑ 36	Quinn Early	.10	.02
❑ 37	Fred Barnett	.10	.02
❑ 38	Andre Coleman	.10	.02
❑ 39	Mark Chmura	.20	.07
❑ 40	Adrian Murrell	.20	.07
❑ 41	Roosevelt Potts	.10	.02
❑ 42	Jay Novacek	.10	.02
❑ 43	Derrick Alexander	.20	.07
❑ 44	Ken Dilger	.20	.07
❑ 45	Rob Moore	.20	.07
❑ 46	Cris Carter	.40	.15
❑ 47	Jeff Blake	.40	.15
❑ 48	Derek Loville	.10	.02
❑ 49	Tyrone Wheatley	.20	.07
❑ 50	Terrell Fletcher	.10	.02
❑ 51	Sherman Williams	.10	.02
❑ 52	Justin Armour	.10	.02
❑ 53	Kordell Stewart	.40	.15
❑ 54	Tim Brown	.40	.15
❑ 55	Kevin Carter	.10	.02
❑ 56	Andre Rison	.20	.07
❑ 57	James O.Stewart	.20	.07
❑ 58	Brent Jones	.10	.02
❑ 59	Erik Kramer	.10	.02
❑ 60	Floyd Turner	.10	.02
❑ 61	Ricky Watters	.20	.07
❑ 62	Hardy Nickerson	.10	.02
❑ 63	Aaron Craver	.10	.02
❑ 64	Dave Krieg	.10	.02
❑ 65	Warren Moon	.20	.07
❑ 66	Wayne Chrebet	.50	.20
❑ 67	Napoleon Kaufman	.40	.15
❑ 68	Terance Mathis	.10	.02
❑ 69	Chad May	.10	.02
❑ 70	Andre Reed	.20	.07
❑ 71	Reggie White	.40	.15
❑ 72	Brett Favre	2.00	.75
❑ 73	Chris Zorich	.10	.02
❑ 74	Kerry Collins	.40	.15
❑ 75	Herman Moore	.20	.07
❑ 76	Yancey Thigpen	.20	.07
❑ 77	Glenn Foley	.20	.07
❑ 78	Quentin Coryatt	.10	.02
❑ 79	Terry Kirby	.20	.07
❑ 80	Edgar Bennett	.20	.07
❑ 81	Mark Brunell	.60	.25
❑ 82	Heath Shuler	.20	.07
❑ 83	Gus Frerotte	.20	.07
❑ 84	Deion Sanders	.60	.25
❑ 85	Calvin Williams	.10	.02
❑ 86	Junior Seau	.40	.15
❑ 87	Jim Kelly	.40	.15
❑ 88	Daryl Johnston	.20	.07
❑ 89	Irving Fryar	.20	.07
❑ 90	Brian Blades	.10	.02
❑ 91	Willie Davis	.10	.02
❑ 92	Jerome Bettis	.40	.15
❑ 93	Marcus Allen	.40	.15
❑ 94	Jeff Graham	.10	.02
❑ 95	Rick Mirer	.20	.07
❑ 96	Harvey Williams	.10	.02
❑ 97	Steve Atwater	.10	.02
❑ 98	Carl Pickens	.20	.07
❑ 99	Darick Holmes	.10	.02
❑ 100	Bruce Smith	.20	.07
❑ 101	Vinny Testaverde	.20	.07
❑ 102	Thurman Thomas	.40	.15
❑ 103	Drew Bledsoe	.60	.25
❑ 104	Bernie Parmalee	.10	.02
❑ 105	Greg Hill	.20	.07
❑ 106	Steve McNair	.75	.30
❑ 107	Andre Hastings	.10	.02
❑ 108	Eric Metcalf	.10	.02
❑ 109	Kimble Anders	.20	.07
❑ 110	Steve Tasker	.10	.02
❑ 111	Mark Carrier WR	.10	.02
❑ 112	Jerry Rice	1.00	.40
❑ 113	Joey Galloway	.40	.15
❑ 114	Robert Smith	.20	.07
❑ 115	Hugh Douglas	.20	.07
❑ 116	Willie McGinest	.10	.02
❑ 117	Terrell Davis	.75	.30
❑ 118	Cortez Kennedy	.10	.02
❑ 119	Marshall Faulk	.50	.20
❑ 120	Michael Haynes	.10	.02
❑ 121	Isaac Bruce	.40	.15
❑ 122	Brian Mitchell	.10	.02
❑ 123	Bryan Cox	.10	.02
❑ 124	Tamarick Vanover	.20	.07
❑ 125	William Floyd	.20	.07

❑ 126	Chris Chandler	.20	.07
❑ 127	Carnell Lake	.10	.02
❑ 128	Aaron Bailey	.10	.02
❑ 129	Darnay Scott	.20	.07
❑ 130	Darren Woodson	.20	.07
❑ 131	Ernie Mills	.10	.02
❑ 132	Charles Haley	.20	.07
❑ 133	Rocket Ismail	.10	.02
❑ 134	Bert Emanuel	.20	.07
❑ 135	Lake Dawson	.10	.02
❑ 136	Jake Reed	.20	.07
❑ 137	Dave Brown	.10	.02
❑ 138	Steve Bono	.10	.02
❑ 139	Terry Allen	.20	.07
❑ 140	Errict Rhett	.20	.07
❑ 141	Rod Woodson	.20	.07
❑ 142	Charles Johnson	.10	.02
❑ 143	Emmitt Smith	1.50	.60
❑ 144	Ki-Jana Carter	.20	.07
❑ 145	Garrison Hearst	.20	.07
❑ 146	Rashaan Salaam	.20	.07
❑ 147	Tony Boselli	.10	.02
❑ 148	Derrick Thomas	.40	.15
❑ 149	Mark Seay	.10	.02
❑ 150	Derrick Alexander	.10	.02
❑ 151	Christian Fauria	.10	.02
❑ 152	Aaron Hayden	.10	.02
❑ 153	Chris Warren	.20	.07
❑ 154	Dave Meggett	.10	.02
❑ 155	Jeff George	.20	.07
❑ 156	Jackie Harris	.10	.02
❑ 157	Michael Irvin	.40	.15
❑ 158	Scott Mitchell	.20	.07
❑ 159	Trent Dilfer	.40	.15
❑ 160	Kyle Brady	.10	.02
❑ 161	Dan Marino	2.00	.75
❑ 162	Curtis Martin	.75	.30
❑ 163	Mario Bates	.20	.07
❑ 164	Erric Pegram	.10	.02
❑ 165	Eric Zeier	.10	.02
❑ 166	Rodney Thomas	.10	.02
❑ 167	Neil O'Donnell	.20	.07
❑ 168	Warren Sapp	.10	.02
❑ 169	Jim Harbaugh	.20	.07
❑ 170	Henry Ellard	.10	.02
❑ 171	Anthony Miller	.20	.07
❑ 172	Derrick Moore	.10	.02
❑ 173	John Elway	2.00	.75
❑ 174	Vincent Brisby	.10	.02
❑ 175	Antonio Freeman	.40	.15
❑ 176	Chris Sanders	.20	.07
❑ 177	Steve Young	.75	.30
❑ 178	Shannon Sharpe	.20	.07
❑ 179	Brett Perriman	.10	.02
❑ 180	Orlando Thomas	.10	.02
❑ 181	Eric Bjornson	.10	.02
❑ 182	Natrone Means	.20	.07
❑ 183	Jim Everett	.10	.02
❑ 184	Curtis Conway	.40	.15
❑ 185	Robert Brooks	.40	.15
❑ 186	Tony Martin	.20	.07
❑ 187	Mark Carrier DB	.10	.02
❑ 188	LeShon Johnson	.10	.02
❑ 189	Bernie Kosar	.10	.02
❑ 190	Ray Zellars	.10	.02
❑ 191	Steve Walsh	.10	.02
❑ 192	Craig Erickson	.10	.02
❑ 193	Tommy Maddox	.40	.15
❑ 194	Leslie O'Neal	.10	.02
❑ 195	Harold Green	.10	.02
❑ 196	Steve Beuerlein	.20	.07
❑ 197	Ronald Moore	.10	.02
❑ 198	Leslie Shepherd	.10	.02
❑ 199	Leroy Hoard	.10	.02
❑ 200	Michael Jackson	.20	.07
❑ 201	Will Moore	.10	.02
❑ 202	Ricky Ervins	.10	.02
❑ 203	Keith Jennings	.10	.02
❑ 204	Eric Green	.10	.02
❑ 205	Mark Rypien	.10	.02
❑ 206	Torrance Small	.10	.02
❑ 207	Sean Gilbert	.10	.02
❑ 208	Mike Alstott RC	1.00	.40
❑ 209	Willie Anderson RC	.10	.02
❑ 210	Alex Molden RC	.10	.02
❑ 211	Jonathan Ogden RC	.40	.15
❑ 212	Stepfret Williams RC	.20	.07
❑ 213	Jeff Lewis RC	.20	.07
❑ 214	Regan Upshaw RC	.10	.02
❑ 215	Daryl Gardener RC	.10	.02
❑ 216	Danny Kanell RC	.40	.15
❑ 217	John Mobley RC	.10	.02
❑ 218	Reggie Brown LB RC	.10	.02
❑ 219	Muhsin Muhammad RC	.75	.30
❑ 220	Kevin Hardy RC	.40	.15
❑ 221	Stanley Pritchett RC	.20	.07
❑ 222	Cedric Jones RC	.10	.02
❑ 223	Marco Battaglia RC	.10	.02
❑ 224	Duane Clemons RC	.10	.02
❑ 225	Jerald Moore RC	.20	.07
❑ 226	Simeon Rice RC	1.00	.40
❑ 227	Chris Darkins RC	.10	.02
❑ 228	Bobby Hoying RC	.40	.15
❑ 229	Stephen Davis RC	1.50	.60
❑ 230	Walt Harris RC	.10	.02
❑ 231	Jermane Mayberry RC	.10	.02
❑ 232	Tony Brackens RC	.40	.15
❑ 233	Eric Moulds RC	1.25	.50
❑ 234	Alex Van Dyke RC	.20	.07
❑ 235	Marvin Harrison RC	2.50	1.00
❑ 236	Rickey Dudley RC	.40	.15
❑ 237	Terrell Owens RC	2.50	1.00
❑ 238	Jerry Rice CL	.40	.15
❑ 239	Dan Marino CL	.40	.15
❑ 240	Emmitt Smith CL	.40	.15

1997 Donruss

❑	COMPLETE SET (230)	20.00	7.50
❑ 1	Dan Marino	2.00	.75
❑ 2	Brett Favre	2.00	.75
❑ 3	Emmitt Smith	1.50	.60
❑ 4	Eddie George	.50	.20
❑ 5	Karim Abdul-Jabbar	.30	.10
❑ 6	Terrell Davis	.60	.25
❑ 7	Curtis Martin	.60	.25
❑ 8	Drew Bledsoe	.60	.25
❑ 9	Jerry Rice	1.00	.40
❑ 10	Troy Aikman	1.00	.40
❑ 11	Barry Sanders	1.50	.60
❑ 12	Mark Brunell	.60	.25
❑ 13	Kerry Collins	.50	.20
❑ 14	Steve Young	.60	.25
❑ 15	Kordell Stewart	.50	.20
❑ 16	Eddie Kennison	.30	.10
❑ 17	Terry Glenn	.50	.20
❑ 18	John Elway	2.00	.75
❑ 19	Joey Galloway	.30	.10
❑ 20	Deion Sanders	.50	.20
❑ 21	Keyshawn Johnson	.50	.20
❑ 22	Lawrence Phillips	.20	.07
❑ 23	Ricky Watters	.30	.10
❑ 24	Marvin Harrison	.50	.20
❑ 25	Bobby Engram	.30	.10
❑ 26	Marshall Faulk	.60	.25
❑ 27	Carl Pickens	.30	.10
❑ 28	Isaac Bruce	.50	.20
❑ 29	Herman Moore	.30	.10
❑ 30	Jerome Bettis	.50	.20
❑ 31	Rashaan Salaam	.20	.07
❑ 32	Errict Rhett	.20	.07
❑ 33	Tim Biakabutuka	.30	.10
❑ 34	Robert Brooks	.30	.10
❑ 35	Antonio Freeman	.50	.20
❑ 36	Steve McNair	.60	.25
❑ 37	Jeff Blake	.30	.10
❑ 38	Tony Banks	.30	.10
❑ 39	Terrell Owens	.60	.25
❑ 40	Eric Moulds	.50	.20
❑ 41	Leeland McElroy	.20	.07
❑ 42	Chris Sanders	.20	.07
❑ 43	Thurman Thomas	.50	.20
❑ 44	Bruce Smith	.30	.10
❑ 45	Reggie White	.50	.20
❑ 46	Chris Warren	.30	.10
❑ 47	J.J. Stokes	.30	.10
❑ 48	Ben Coates	.30	.10
❑ 49	Tim Brown	.50	.20
❑ 50	Marcus Allen	.50	.20
❑ 51	Michael Irvin	.50	.20
❑ 52	William Floyd	.30	.10
❑ 53	Ken Dilger	.20	.07
❑ 54	Bobby Taylor	.20	.07
❑ 55	Keenan McCardell	.30	.10
❑ 56	Raymont Harris	.20	.07
❑ 57	Keith Byars	.20	.07
❑ 58	O.J. McDuffie	.30	.10
❑ 59	Robert Smith	.30	.10
❑ 60	Bert Emanuel	.30	.10
❑ 61	Rick Mirer	.20	.07
❑ 62	Vinny Testaverde	.30	.10
❑ 63	Kyle Brady	.20	.07
❑ 64	Mark Bruener	.20	.07
❑ 65	Neil O'Donnell	.30	.10
❑ 66	Anthony Johnson	.20	.07
❑ 67	Ken Norton	.20	.07
❑ 68	Warren Sapp	.30	.10
❑ 69	Amani Toomer	.30	.10
❑ 70	Simeon Rice	.30	.10
❑ 71	Kevin Hardy	.20	.07
❑ 72	Junior Seau	.50	.20
❑ 73	Neil Smith	.30	.10
❑ 74	LeShon Johnson	.20	.07
❑ 75	Quinn Early	.20	.07
❑ 76	Andre Reed	.30	.10
❑ 77	Jake Reed	.30	.10
❑ 78	Elvis Grbac	.30	.10
❑ 79	Tyrone Wheatley	.30	.10
❑ 80	Adrian Murrell	.30	.10
❑ 81	Fred Barnett	.20	.07
❑ 82	Darrell Green	.30	.10
❑ 83	Stan Humphries	.30	.10
❑ 84	Troy Drayton	.20	.07
❑ 85	Steve Atwater	.20	.07
❑ 86	Quentin Coryatt	.20	.07
❑ 87	Dan Wilkinson	.20	.07
❑ 88	Scott Mitchell	.30	.10
❑ 89	Willie McGinest	.20	.07
❑ 90	Kevin Smith	.20	.07
❑ 91	Gus Frerotte	.20	.07
❑ 92	Byron Bam Morris	.20	.07
❑ 93	Darick Holmes	.20	.07
❑ 94	Zach Thomas	.50	.20
❑ 95	Tom Carter	.20	.07
❑ 96	Cortez Kennedy	.20	.07
❑ 97	Kevin Williams	.20	.07
❑ 98	Michael Haynes	.20	.07
❑ 99	Lamont Warren	.20	.07
❑ 100	Jeff Graham	.20	.07
❑ 101	Alex Van Dyke	.20	.07
❑ 102	Jim Everett	.20	.07
❑ 103	Chris Chandler	.30	.10
❑ 104	Qadry Ismail	.30	.10
❑ 105	Ray Zellars	.20	.07
❑ 106	Chris T. Jones	.20	.07

	Card	Player	Mint	NrMt
❑	107	Charlie Garner	.30	.10
❑	108	Bobby Hoying	.30	.10
❑	109	Mark Chmura	.30	.10
❑	110	Cris Carter	.50	.20
❑	111	Darnay Scott	.30	.10
❑	112	Anthony Miller	.20	.07
❑	113	Desmond Howard	.30	.10
❑	114	Terance Mathis	.30	.10
❑	115	Rodney Hampton	.30	.10
❑	116	Napoleon Kaufman	.50	.20
❑	117	Jim Harbaugh	.30	.10
❑	118	Shannon Sharpe	.30	.10
❑	119	Irving Fryar	.30	.10
❑	120	Garrison Hearst	.30	.10
❑	121	Terry Allen	.50	.20
❑	122	Larry Centers	.30	.10
❑	123	Sean Dawkins	.20	.07
❑	124	Jeff George	.30	.10
❑	125	Tony Martin	.30	.10
❑	126	Mike Alstott	.50	.20
❑	127	Rickey Dudley	.30	.10
❑	128	Kevin Carter	.20	.07
❑	129	Derrick Alexander WR	.30	.10
❑	130	Greg Lloyd	.20	.07
❑	131	Bryce Paup	.20	.07
❑	132	Derrick Thomas	.50	.20
❑	133	Greg Hill	.20	.07
❑	134	Jamal Anderson	.50	.20
❑	135	Curtis Conway	.30	.10
❑	136	Frank Sanders	.30	.10
❑	137	Brett Perriman	.20	.07
❑	138	Edgar Bennett	.30	.10
❑	139	Wayne Chrebet	.50	.20
❑	140	Natrone Means	.30	.10
❑	141	Eric Metcalf	.30	.10
❑	142	Trent Dilfer	.50	.20
❑	143	Terry Kirby	.30	.10
❑	144	Johnnie Morton	.30	.10
❑	145	Dale Carter	.20	.07
❑	146	Michael Westbrook	.30	.10
❑	147	Stanley Pritchett	.20	.07
❑	148	Todd Collins	.20	.07
❑	149	Tamarick Vanover	.30	.10
❑	150	Kevin Greene	.30	.10
❑	151	Lamar Lathon	.20	.07
❑	152	Muhsin Muhammad	.30	.10
❑	153	Dorsey Levens	.50	.20
❑	154	Rod Woodson	.30	.10
❑	155	Brent Jones	.20	.07
❑	156	Michael Jackson	.30	.10
❑	157	Shawn Jefferson	.20	.07
❑	158	Kimble Anders	.30	.10
❑	159	Sean Gilbert	.20	.07
❑	160	Carnell Lake	.20	.07
❑	161	Darren Woodson	.20	.07
❑	162	Dave Meggett	.20	.07
❑	163	Henry Ellard	.20	.07
❑	164	Eric Swann	.20	.07
❑	165	Tony Boselli	.20	.07
❑	166	Daryl Johnston	.30	.10
❑	167	Willie Jackson	.20	.07
❑	168	Wesley Walls	.30	.10
❑	169	Mario Bates	.20	.07
❑	170	Lake Dawson	.20	.07
❑	171	Mike Mamula	.20	.07
❑	172	Ed McCaffrey	.30	.10
❑	173	Tony Brackens	.20	.07
❑	174	Craig Heyward	.20	.07
❑	175	Harvey Williams	.20	.07
❑	176	Dave Brown	.20	.07
❑	177	Aaron Glenn	.20	.07
❑	178	Jeff Hostetler	.20	.07
❑	179	Alvin Harper	.20	.07
❑	180	Ty Detmer	.30	.10
❑	181	James Jett	.30	.10
❑	182	James O.Stewart	.30	.10
❑	183	Warren Moon	.50	.20
❑	184	Herschel Walker	.30	.10
❑	185	Ki-Jana Carter	.20	.07
❑	186	Leslie O'Neal	.20	.07
❑	187	Danny Kanell	.20	.07
❑	188	Eric Bjornson	.20	.07
❑	189	Alex Molden	.20	.07
❑	190	Bryant Young	.20	.07
❑	191	Merton Hanks	.20	.07
❑	192	Heath Shuler	.20	.07
❑	193	Brian Blades	.20	.07
❑	194	Steve Bono	.30	.10
❑	195	Wayne Simmons	.20	.07
❑	196	Warrick Dunn RC	1.25	.50
❑	197	Peter Boulware RC	.50	.20
❑	198	David LaFleur RC	.20	.07
❑	199	Shawn Springs RC	.30	.10
❑	200	Reidel Anthony RC	.50	.20
❑	201	Jim Druckenmiller RC	.30	.10
❑	202	Orlando Pace RC	.50	.20
❑	203	Yatil Green RC	.30	.10
❑	204	Bryant Westbrook RC	.20	.07
❑	205	Tiki Barber RC	3.00	1.25
❑	206	James Farrior RC	.50	.20
❑	207	Rae Carruth RC	.20	.07
❑	208	Danny Wuerffel RC	.50	.20
❑	209	Corey Dillon RC	3.00	1.25
❑	210	Ike Hilliard RC	.75	.30
❑	211	Tony Gonzalez RC	1.50	.60
❑	212	Antowain Smith RC	1.25	.50
❑	213	Pat Barnes RC	.50	.20
❑	214	Troy Davis RC	.30	.10
❑	215	Byron Hanspard RC	.30	.10
❑	216	Joey Kent RC	.50	.20
❑	217	Jake Plummer RC	2.50	1.00
❑	218	Kenny Holmes RC	.50	.20
❑	219	Darnell Autry RC	.30	.10
❑	220	Darrell Russell RC	.20	.07
❑	221	Walter Jones RC	.50	.20
❑	222	Dwayne Rudd RC	.50	.20
❑	223	Tom Knight RC	.20	.07
❑	224	Kevin Lockett RC	.30	.10
❑	225	Will Blackwell RC	.30	.10
❑	226	Dan Marino CL	.40	.15
❑	227	Brett Favre CL	.40	.15
❑	228	Emmitt Smith CL	.50	.20
❑	229	Barry Sanders CL	.50	.20
❑	230	Jerry Rice CL	.25	.08
❑	P1	Drew Bledsoe Promo	1.00	.40
❑	P2	Mark Brunell Promo	1.00	.40
❑	P3	Barry Sanders Promo	1.50	.60

1999 Donruss

	Card	Player	Mint	NrMt
❑		COMPLETE SET (200)	100.00	40.00
❑		COMP.SET w/o SP's (150)	20.00	10.00
❑	1	Jake Plummer	.40	.15
❑	2	Rob Moore	.40	.15
❑	3	Adrian Murrell	.40	.15
❑	4	Frank Sanders	.40	.15
❑	5	Jamal Anderson	.60	.25
❑	6	Tim Dwight	.40	.15
❑	7	Terance Mathis	.40	.15
❑	8	Chris Chandler	.40	.15
❑	9	Byron Hanspard	.25	.08
❑	10	Priest Holmes	1.00	.40
❑	11	Jermaine Lewis	.40	.15
❑	12	Errict Rhett	.40	.15
❑	13	Doug Flutie	.60	.25
❑	14	Eric Moulds	.60	.25
❑	15	Antowain Smith	.60	.25
❑	16	Thurman Thomas	.40	.15
❑	17	Andre Reed	.40	.15
❑	18	Bruce Smith	.40	.15
❑	19	Tim Biakabutuka	.40	.15
❑	20	Rae Carruth	.25	.08
❑	21	Muhsin Muhammad	.40	.15
❑	22	Curtis Enis	.25	.08
❑	23	Curtis Conway	.40	.15
❑	24	Bobby Engram	.40	.15
❑	25	Corey Dillon	.60	.25
❑	26	Carl Pickens	.40	.15
❑	27	Jeff Blake	.40	.15
❑	28	Darnay Scott	.40	.15
❑	29	Ty Detmer	.40	.15
❑	30	Leslie Shepherd	.25	.08
❑	31	Emmitt Smith	1.25	.50
❑	32	Troy Aikman	1.25	.50
❑	33	Michael Irvin	.40	.15
❑	34	Deion Sanders	.60	.25
❑	35	Rocket Ismail	.40	.15
❑	36	John Elway	2.00	.75
❑	37	Terrell Davis	.60	.25
❑	38	Ed McCaffrey	.40	.15
❑	39	Shannon Sharpe	.40	.15
❑	40	Rod Smith	.40	.15
❑	41	Bubby Brister	.25	.08
❑	42	Brian Griese	.60	.25
❑	43	Barry Sanders	2.00	.75
❑	44	Charlie Batch	.60	.25
❑	45	Herman Moore	.40	.15
❑	46	Germane Crowell	.25	.08
❑	47	Johnnie Morton	.40	.15
❑	48	Ron Rivers	.25	.08
❑	49	Brett Favre	2.00	.75
❑	50	Antonio Freeman	.60	.25
❑	51	Dorsey Levens	.60	.25
❑	52	Mark Chmura	.25	.08
❑	53	Corey Bradford	.60	.25
❑	54	Bill Schroeder	.60	.25
❑	55	Peyton Manning	2.00	.75
❑	56	Marvin Harrison	.60	.25
❑	57	E.G. Green	.25	.08
❑	58	Fred Taylor	.60	.25
❑	59	Mark Brunell	.60	.25
❑	60	Tavian Banks	.25	.08
❑	61	Jimmy Smith	.40	.15
❑	62	Keenan McCardell	.40	.15
❑	63	Warren Moon	.60	.25
❑	64	Derrick Alexander WR	.40	.15
❑	65	Byron Bam Morris	.25	.08
❑	66	Elvis Grbac	.40	.15
❑	67	Andre Rison	.40	.15
❑	68	Dan Marino	2.00	.75
❑	69	Karim Abdul-Jabbar	.40	.15
❑	70	O.J. McDuffie	.40	.15
❑	71	Tony Martin	.25	.08
❑	72	Randy Moss	1.50	.60
❑	73	Cris Carter	.60	.25
❑	74	Randall Cunningham	.60	.25
❑	75	Robert Smith	.60	.25
❑	76	Jeff George	.40	.15
❑	77	Jake Reed	.40	.15
❑	78	Terry Allen	.40	.15
❑	79	Drew Bledsoe	.75	.30
❑	80	Terry Glenn	.60	.25
❑	81	Ben Coates	.40	.15
❑	82	Tony Simmons	.25	.08
❑	83	Cam Cleeland	.25	.08
❑	84	Eddie Kennison	.40	.15
❑	85	Kerry Collins	.25	.08
❑	86	Ike Hilliard	.25	.08
❑	87	Gary Brown	.25	.08
❑	88	Joe Jurevicius	.40	.15
❑	89	Kent Graham	.25	.08
❑	90	Wayne Chrebet	.40	.15
❑	91	Keyshawn Johnson	.60	.25
❑	92	Curtis Martin	.60	.25
❑	93	Vinny Testaverde	.40	.15

❑ 94 Tim Brown .60 .25
❑ 95 Napoleon Kaufman .60 .25
❑ 96 Charles Woodson .60 .25
❑ 97 Tyrone Wheatley .40 .15
❑ 98 Rich Gannon .60 .25
❑ 99 Charles Johnson .25 .08
❑ 100 Duce Staley .60 .25
❑ 101 Kordell Stewart .40 .15
❑ 102 Jerome Bettis .60 .25
❑ 103 Hines Ward .60 .25
❑ 104 Ryan Leaf .60 .25
❑ 105 Natrone Means .40 .15
❑ 106 Jim Harbaugh .40 .15
❑ 107 Junior Seau .60 .25
❑ 108 Mikhael Ricks .25 .08
❑ 109 Jerry Rice 1.25 .50
❑ 110 Steve Young .75 .30
❑ 111 Garrison Hearst .40 .15
❑ 112 Terrell Owens .60 .25
❑ 113 Lawrence Phillips .40 .15
❑ 114 J.J. Stokes .40 .15
❑ 115 Sean Dawkins .25 .08
❑ 116 Derrick Mayes .25 .08
❑ 117 Joey Galloway .40 .15
❑ 118 Jon Kitna .60 .25
❑ 119 Ahman Green .60 .25
❑ 120 Ricky Watters .40 .15
❑ 121 Isaac Bruce .60 .25
❑ 122 Marshall Faulk .75 .30
❑ 123 Az-Zahir Hakim .25 .08
❑ 124 Warrick Dunn .60 .25
❑ 125 Mike Alstott .60 .25
❑ 126 Trent Dilfer .40 .15
❑ 127 Reidel Anthony .40 .15
❑ 128 Jacquez Green .25 .08
❑ 129 Warren Sapp .40 .15
❑ 130 Eddie George .60 .25
❑ 131 Steve McNair .60 .25
❑ 132 Kevin Dyson .40 .15
❑ 133 Yancey Thigpen .25 .08
❑ 134 Frank Wycheck .25 .08
❑ 135 Stephen Davis .60 .25
❑ 136 Brad Johnson .60 .25
❑ 137 Skip Hicks .25 .08
❑ 138 Michael Westbrook .40 .15
❑ 139 Darrell Green .25 .08
❑ 140 Albert Connell .25 .08
❑ 141 Tim Couch RC 2.00 .75
❑ 142 Donovan McNabb RC 8.00 3.00
❑ 143 Akili Smith RC 1.50 .60
❑ 144 Edgerrin James RC 6.00 2.50
❑ 145 Ricky Williams RC 3.00 1.25
❑ 146 Torry Holt RC 4.00 1.50
❑ 147 Champ Bailey RC 2.50 1.00
❑ 148 David Boston RC 2.00 .75
❑ 149 Andy Katzenmoyer RC 1.50 .60
❑ 150 Chris McAlister RC 1.50 .60
❑ 151 Daunte Culpepper RC 6.00 2.50
❑ 152 Cade McNown RC 1.50 .60
❑ 153 Troy Edwards RC 1.50 .60
❑ 154 Kevin Johnson RC 2.00 .75
❑ 155 James Johnson RC 1.50 .60
❑ 156 Rob Konrad RC 1.50 .60
❑ 157 Jim Kleinsasser RC 2.00 .75
❑ 158 Kevin Faulk RC 2.00 .75
❑ 159 Joe Montgomery RC 1.50 .60
❑ 160 Shaun King RC 1.50 .60
❑ 161 Peerless Price RC 2.00 .75
❑ 162 Mike Cloud RC 1.50 .60
❑ 163 Jermaine Fazande RC 1.50 .60
❑ 164 D'Wayne Bates RC 1.50 .60
❑ 165 Brock Huard RC 2.00 .75
❑ 166 Marty Booker RC 2.00 .75
❑ 167 Karsten Bailey RC 1.50 .60
❑ 168 Shawn Bryson RC 2.00 .75
❑ 169 Jeff Paulk RC 1.00 .40
❑ 170 Travis McGriff RC 1.00 .40
❑ 171 Amos Zereoue RC 2.00 .75
❑ 172 Craig Yeast RC 1.50 .60
❑ 173 Joe Germaine RC 1.50 .60
❑ 174 Dameane Douglas RC 1.50 .60
❑ 175 Brandon Stokley RC 2.50 1.00
❑ 176 Larry Parker RC 2.00 .75
❑ 177 Joel Makovicka RC 2.00 .75
❑ 178 Wane McGarity RC 1.00 .40
❑ 179 Na Brown RC 1.50 .60
❑ 180 Cecil Collins RC 1.00 .40
❑ 181 Nick Williams RC 1.50 .60
❑ 182 Charlie Rogers RC 1.50 .60
❑ 183 Darrin Chiaverini RC 1.50 .60
❑ 184 Terry Jackson RC 1.50 .60
❑ 185 De'Mond Parker RC 1.00 .40
❑ 186 Sedrick Irvin RC 1.00 .40
❑ 187 MarTay Jenkins RC 2.00 .75
❑ 188 Kurt Warner RC 12.00 5.00
❑ 189 Michael Bishop RC 2.00 .75
❑ 190 Sean Bennett RC 1.00 .40
❑ 191 Jamal Anderson CL .25 .08
❑ 192 Eric Moulds CL .25 .08
❑ 193 Terrell Davis CL .60 .25
❑ 194 John Elway CL .75 .30
❑ 195 Barry Sanders CL .75 .30
❑ 196 Peyton Manning CL .75 .30
❑ 197 Fred Taylor CL .60 .25
❑ 198 Dan Marino CL .75 .30
❑ 199 Randy Moss CL .60 .25
❑ 200 Terrell Owens CL .40 .15

2000 Donruss

❑ COMPLETE SET (250) 400.00 150.00
❑ 1 Jake Plummer .30 .10
❑ 2 Frank Sanders .30 .10
❑ 3 Rob Moore .30 .10
❑ 4 David Boston .50 .20
❑ 5 Tim Dwight .50 .20
❑ 6 Jamal Anderson .50 .20
❑ 7 Chris Chandler .30 .10
❑ 8 Terance Mathis .30 .10
❑ 9 Tony Banks .30 .10
❑ 10 Jermaine Lewis .30 .10
❑ 11 Shannon Sharpe .30 .10
❑ 12 Trent Dilfer .30 .10
❑ 13 Qadry Ismail .30 .10
❑ 14 Eric Moulds .50 .20
❑ 15 Doug Flutie .50 .20
❑ 16 Antowain Smith .30 .10
❑ 17 Jonathan Linton .20 .07
❑ 18 Peerless Price .30 .10
❑ 19 Rob Johnson .30 .10
❑ 20 Natrone Means .30 .10
❑ 21 Muhsin Muhammad .30 .10
❑ 22 Wesley Walls .30 .10
❑ 23 Tim Biakabutuka .30 .10
❑ 24 Steve Beuerlein .30 .10
❑ 25 Patrick Jeffers .50 .20
❑ 26 Curtis Enis .20 .07
❑ 27 Cade McNown .20 .07
❑ 28 Bobby Engram .30 .10
❑ 29 Marcus Robinson .50 .20
❑ 30 Marty Booker .30 .10
❑ 31 Corey Dillon .50 .20
❑ 32 Darnay Scott .30 .10
❑ 33 Carl Pickens .30 .10
❑ 34 Akili Smith .20 .07
❑ 35 Michael Basnight .20 .07
❑ 36 Tim Couch .30 .10
❑ 37 Kevin Johnson .50 .20
❑ 38 Karim Abdul-Jabbar .30 .10
❑ 39 Errict Rhett .30 .10
❑ 40 Darrin Chiaverini .20 .07
❑ 41 Emmitt Smith 1.00 .40
❑ 42 Troy Aikman 1.00 .40
❑ 43 Joey Galloway .30 .10
❑ 44 Randall Cunningham .50 .20
❑ 45 Michael Irvin .30 .10
❑ 46 Rocket Ismail .30 .10
❑ 47 Jason Tucker .20 .07
❑ 48 Terrell Davis .50 .20
❑ 49 John Elway 1.50 .60
❑ 50 Olandis Gary .30 .10
❑ 51 Ed McCaffrey .50 .20
❑ 52 Rod Smith .30 .10
❑ 53 Brian Griese .50 .20
❑ 54 Charlie Batch .50 .20
❑ 55 Barry Sanders 1.25 .50
❑ 56 Herman Moore .30 .10
❑ 57 Johnnie Morton .30 .10
❑ 58 Germane Crowell .20 .07
❑ 59 James Stewart .30 .10
❑ 60 Brett Favre 1.50 .60
❑ 61 Dorsey Levens .30 .10
❑ 62 Antonio Freeman .50 .20
❑ 63 Corey Bradford .30 .10
❑ 64 Bill Schroeder .30 .10
❑ 65 E.G. Green .20 .07
❑ 66 Peyton Manning 1.25 .50
❑ 67 Edgerrin James .75 .30
❑ 68 Marvin Harrison .50 .20
❑ 69 Terrence Wilkins .20 .07
❑ 70 Mark Brunell .50 .20
❑ 71 Fred Taylor .50 .20
❑ 72 Keenan McCardell .30 .10
❑ 73 Jimmy Smith .30 .10
❑ 74 Warren Moon .50 .20
❑ 75 Elvis Grbac .30 .10
❑ 76 Tony Gonzalez .30 .10
❑ 77 Dan Marino 1.50 .60
❑ 78 O.J. McDuffie .30 .10
❑ 79 Tony Martin .30 .10
❑ 80 James Johnson .20 .07
❑ 81 Thurman Thomas .30 .10
❑ 82 Randy Moss 1.00 .40
❑ 83 Daunte Culpepper .60 .25
❑ 84 Cris Carter .50 .20
❑ 85 Robert Smith .50 .20
❑ 86 John Randle .30 .10
❑ 87 Drew Bledsoe .60 .25
❑ 88 Terry Glenn .30 .10
❑ 89 Kevin Faulk .30 .10
❑ 90 Ricky Williams .50 .20
❑ 91 Jeff Blake .30 .10
❑ 92 Jake Reed .30 .10
❑ 93 Amani Toomer .30 .10
❑ 94 Kerry Collins .30 .10
❑ 95 Tiki Barber .50 .20
❑ 96 Ike Hilliard .30 .10
❑ 97 Curtis Martin .50 .20
❑ 98 Vinny Testaverde .30 .10
❑ 99 Wayne Chrebet .30 .10
❑ 100 Ray Lucas .30 .10
❑ 101 Charles Woodson .30 .10
❑ 102 Napoleon Kaufman .30 .10
❑ 103 Tim Brown .50 .20
❑ 104 Tyrone Wheatley .30 .10
❑ 105 Rich Gannon .50 .20
❑ 106 Duce Staley .50 .20
❑ 107 Donovan McNabb .75 .30
❑ 108 Amos Zereoue .50 .20
❑ 109 Kordell Stewart .30 .10
❑ 110 Jerome Bettis .50 .20
❑ 111 Troy Edwards .20 .07
❑ 112 Ryan Leaf .30 .10
❑ 113 Junior Seau .50 .20
❑ 114 Jim Harbaugh .30 .10

❑	115	Jermaine Fazande	.20	.07
❑	116	Curtis Conway	.30	.10
❑	117	Steve Young	.60	.25
❑	118	Jerry Rice	1.00	.40
❑	119	Terrell Owens	.50	.20
❑	120	Charlie Garner	.30	.10
❑	121	Jeff Garcia	.50	.20
❑	122	Jon Kitna	.50	.20
❑	123	Derrick Mayes	.30	.10
❑	124	Ricky Watters	.30	.10
❑	125	Kurt Warner	1.00	.40
❑	126	Marshall Faulk	.60	.25
❑	127	Torry Holt	.50	.20
❑	128	Az-Zahir Hakim	.30	.10
❑	129	Isaac Bruce	.50	.20
❑	130	Mike Alstott	.50	.20
❑	131	Warrick Dunn	.50	.20
❑	132	Shaun King	.20	.07
❑	133	Keyshawn Johnson	.50	.20
❑	134	Jacquez Green	.20	.07
❑	135	Reidel Anthony	.30	.10
❑	136	Warren Sapp	.30	.10
❑	137	Eddie George	.50	.20
❑	138	Steve McNair	.50	.20
❑	139	Yancey Thigpen	.20	.07
❑	140	Kevin Dyson	.30	.10
❑	141	Frank Wycheck	.30	.10
❑	142	Jevon Kearse	.50	.20
❑	143	Stephen Davis	.50	.20
❑	144	Skip Hicks	.20	.07
❑	145	Brad Johnson	.50	.20
❑	146	Bruce Smith	.30	.10
❑	147	Michael Westbrook	.30	.10
❑	148	Albert Connell	.20	.07
❑	149	Jeff George	.30	.10
❑	150	Deion Sanders	.50	.20
❑	151	Courtney Brown RC	6.00	2.50
❑	152	Corey Simon RC	6.00	2.50
❑	153	Brian Urlacher RC	25.00	10.00
❑	154	Shaun Ellis RC	6.00	2.50
❑	155	John Abraham RC	6.00	2.50
❑	156	Deltha O'Neal RC	6.00	2.50
❑	157	Ahmed Plummer RC	6.00	2.50
❑	158	Chris Hovan RC	5.00	2.00
❑	159	Rob Morris RC	5.00	2.00
❑	160	Keith Bulluck RC	6.00	2.50
❑	161	Darren Howard RC	5.00	2.00
❑	162	John Engelberger RC	5.00	2.00
❑	163	Raynoch Thompson RC	5.00	2.00
❑	164	Cornelius Griffin RC	5.00	2.00
❑	165	William Bartee RC	5.00	2.00
❑	166	Fred Robbins RC	3.00	1.25
❑	167	Micheal Boireau RC	3.00	1.25
❑	168	Brandon Short RC	5.00	2.00
❑	169	Jacoby Shepherd RC	3.00	1.25
❑	170	Peter Warrick RC	6.00	2.50
❑	171	Jamal Lewis RC	15.00	6.00
❑	172	Thomas Jones RC	10.00	4.00
❑	173	Plaxico Burress RC	12.00	5.00
❑	174	Travis Taylor RC	6.00	2.50
❑	175	Ron Dayne RC	6.00	2.50
❑	176	Bubba Franks RC	6.00	2.50
❑	177	Sebastian Janikowski RC	6.00	2.50
❑	178	Chad Pennington RC	15.00	6.00
❑	179	Shaun Alexander RC	30.00	15.00
❑	180	Sylvester Morris RC	5.00	2.00
❑	181	Anthony Becht RC	6.00	2.50
❑	182	R.Jay Soward RC	5.00	2.00
❑	183	Trung Canidate RC	5.00	2.00
❑	184	Dennis Northcutt RC	6.00	2.50
❑	185	Todd Pinkston RC	6.00	2.50
❑	186	Jerry Porter RC	8.00	3.00
❑	187	Travis Prentice RC	5.00	2.00
❑	188	Giovanni Carmazzi RC	3.00	1.25
❑	189	Ron Dugans RC	3.00	1.25
❑	190	Erron Kinney RC	6.00	2.50
❑	191	Dez White RC	6.00	2.50
❑	192	Chris Cole RC	5.00	2.00
❑	193	Ron Dixon RC	5.00	2.00
❑	194	Chris Redman RC	5.00	2.00
❑	195	J.R. Redmond RC	5.00	2.00
❑	196	Laveranues Coles RC	8.00	3.00
❑	197	JaJuan Dawson RC	3.00	1.25
❑	198	Darrell Jackson RC	12.00	5.00
❑	199	Reuben Droughns RC	8.00	3.00
❑	200	Doug Chapman RC	5.00	2.00
❑	201	Terrelle Smith RC	5.00	2.00
❑	202	Curtis Keaton RC	5.00	2.00
❑	203	Gari Scott RC	3.00	1.25
❑	204	Danny Farmer RC	5.00	2.00
❑	205	Hank Poteat RC	5.00	2.00
❑	206	Ben Kelly RC	3.00	1.25
❑	207	Corey Moore RC	3.00	1.25
❑	208	Na'il Diggs RC	5.00	2.00
❑	209	Aaron Shea RC	5.00	2.00
❑	210	Trevor Gaylor RC	5.00	2.00
❑	211	Julian Peterson RC	6.00	2.50
❑	212	Frank Moreau RC	5.00	2.00
❑	213	Deon Dyer RC	5.00	2.00
❑	214	Avion Black RC	5.00	2.00
❑	215	Paul Smith RC	5.00	2.00
❑	216	Michael Wiley RC	5.00	2.00
❑	217	Dante Hall RC	12.00	5.00
❑	218	Mike Brown RC	10.00	4.00
❑	219	Sammy Morris RC	5.00	2.00
❑	220	Billy Volek RC	10.00	4.00
❑	221	Tee Martin RC	6.00	2.50
❑	222	Troy Walters RC	6.00	2.50
❑	223	Chad Morton RC	6.00	2.50
❑	224	Erik Flowers RC	5.00	2.00
❑	225	Ronney Jenkins RC	5.00	2.00
❑	226	Thomas Hamner RC	3.00	1.25
❑	227	Mareno Philyaw RC	3.00	1.25
❑	228	James Williams RC	5.00	2.00
❑	229	Mike Anderson RC	8.00	3.00
❑	230	Tom Brady RC	80.00	40.00
❑	231	Mike Green RC	5.00	2.00
❑	232	Todd Husak RC	6.00	2.50
❑	233	Tim Rattay RC	6.00	2.50
❑	234	Jarious Jackson RC	5.00	2.00
❑	235	Joe Hamilton RC	5.00	2.00
❑	236	Shyrone Stith RC	5.00	2.00
❑	237	Rondell Mealey RC	3.00	1.25
❑	238	Demario Brown RC	3.00	1.25
❑	239	Chris Coleman RC	6.00	2.50
❑	240	Dwayne Goodrich RC	3.00	1.25
❑	241	Drew Haddad RC	3.00	1.25
❑	242	Doug Johnson RC	6.00	2.50
❑	243	Windrell Hayes RC	5.00	2.00
❑	244	Charles Lee RC	3.00	1.25
❑	245	Kevin McDougal RC	5.00	2.00
❑	246	Spergon Wynn RC	5.00	2.00
❑	247	Shockmain Davis RC	3.00	1.25
❑	248	Jamel White RC	5.00	2.00
❑	249	Bashir Yamini RC	3.00	1.25
❑	250	Kwame Cavil RC	3.00	1.25

2002 Donruss

❑		COMPLETE SET (300)	150.00	75.00
❑		COMP.SET w/o SP's (100)	20.00	7.50
❑	1	Jake Plummer	.30	.10
❑	2	David Boston	.50	.20
❑	3	MarTay Jenkins	.20	.07
❑	4	Thomas Jones	.30	.10
❑	5	Frank Sanders	.20	.07
❑	6	Shawn Jefferson	.20	.07
❑	7	Alge Crumpler	.30	.10
❑	8	Michael Vick	1.50	.60
❑	9	Jamal Anderson	.30	.10
❑	10	Warrick Dunn	.50	.20
❑	11	Peter Boulware	.20	.07
❑	12	Jamal Lewis	.50	.20
❑	13	Jeff Blake	.20	.07
❑	14	Travis Taylor	.30	.10
❑	15	Ray Lewis	.50	.20
❑	16	Todd Heap	.20	.07
❑	17	Nate Clements	.20	.07
❑	18	Alex Van Pelt	.20	.07
❑	19	Reggie Germany	.20	.07
❑	20	Larry Centers	.20	.07
❑	21	Eric Moulds	.30	.10
❑	22	Travis Henry	.50	.20
❑	23	Wesley Walls	.20	.07
❑	24	Steve Smith	.50	.20
❑	25	Lamar Smith	.30	.10
❑	26	Patrick Jeffers	.20	.07
❑	27	Chris Weinke	.30	.10
❑	28	Muhsin Muhammad	.30	.10
❑	29	Marcus Robinson	.30	.10
❑	30	Jim Miller	.20	.07
❑	31	Anthony Thomas	.30	.10
❑	32	David Terrell	.50	.20
❑	33	Brian Urlacher	.75	.30
❑	34	Marty Booker	.20	.07
❑	35	Darnay Scott	.20	.07
❑	36	Jon Kitna	.30	.10
❑	37	Chad Johnson	.50	.20
❑	38	T.J. Houshmandzadeh	.30	.10
❑	39	Corey Dillon	.30	.10
❑	40	Peter Warrick	.30	.10
❑	41	Gerard Warren	.20	.07
❑	42	Anthony Henry	.20	.07
❑	43	Quincy Morgan	.20	.07
❑	44	JaJuan Dawson	.20	.07
❑	45	Tim Couch	.30	.10
❑	46	Kevin Johnson	.30	.10
❑	47	James Jackson	.20	.07
❑	48	La'Roi Glover	.20	.07
❑	49	Anthony Wright	.20	.07
❑	50	Rocket Ismail	.30	.10
❑	51	Troy Hambrick	.20	.07
❑	52	Emmitt Smith	1.25	.50
❑	53	Quincy Carter	.30	.10
❑	54	Joey Galloway	.30	.10
❑	55	Shannon Sharpe	.30	.10
❑	56	Kevin Kasper	.20	.07
❑	57	Olandis Gary	.30	.10
❑	58	Brian Griese	.50	.20
❑	59	Rod Smith	.30	.10
❑	60	Terrell Davis	.50	.20
❑	61	Ed McCaffrey	.50	.20
❑	62	Mike Anderson	.50	.20
❑	63	Bill Schroeder	.30	.10
❑	64	Scotty Anderson	.20	.07
❑	65	Mike McMahon	.50	.20
❑	66	James Stewart	.30	.10
❑	67	Az-Zahir Hakim	.20	.07
❑	68	Germane Crowell	.20	.07
❑	69	Kabeer Gbaja-Biamila	.30	.10
❑	70	LeRoy Butler	.20	.07
❑	71	Antonio Freeman	.50	.20
❑	72	Bubba Franks	.30	.10
❑	73	Brett Favre	1.25	.50
❑	74	Ahman Green	.50	.20
❑	75	Terry Glenn	.30	.10
❑	76	Jamie Sharper	.20	.07
❑	77	Tony Simmons	.20	.07
❑	78	James Allen	.30	.10
❑	79	Terrence Wilkins	.20	.07
❑	80	Dominic Rhodes	.30	.10
❑	81	Qadry Ismail	.30	.10
❑	82	Peyton Manning	1.00	.40
❑	83	Edgerrin James	.60	.25
❑	84	Marvin Harrison	.50	.20

❑ 85 Reggie Wayne .50 .20
❑ 86 Fred Taylor .50 .20
❑ 87 Elvis Joseph .20 .07
❑ 88 Mark Brunell .50 .20
❑ 89 Keenan McCardell .20 .07
❑ 90 Jimmy Smith .30 .10
❑ 91 Kyle Brady .20 .07
❑ 92 Derrick Alexander .30 .10
❑ 93 Johnnie Morton .30 .10
❑ 94 Trent Green .30 .10
❑ 95 Priest Holmes .60 .25
❑ 96 Tony Gonzalez .30 .10
❑ 97 Snoop Minnis .20 .07
❑ 98 Travis Minor .20 .07
❑ 99 Oronde Gadsden .30 .10
❑ 100 Jay Fiedler .30 .10
❑ 101 Chris Chambers .50 .20
❑ 102 Ricky Williams .50 .20
❑ 103 Zach Thomas .50 .20
❑ 104 Byron Chamberlain .20 .07
❑ 105 Todd Bouman .20 .07
❑ 106 Daunte Culpepper .50 .20
❑ 107 Michael Bennett .30 .10
❑ 108 Randy Moss 1.00 .40
❑ 109 Cris Carter .50 .20
❑ 110 David Patten .20 .07
❑ 111 Donald Hayes .20 .07
❑ 112 Tom Brady 1.25 .50
❑ 113 Antowain Smith .30 .10
❑ 114 Troy Brown .30 .10
❑ 115 Drew Bledsoe .60 .25
❑ 116 Bryan Cox .20 .07
❑ 117 Boo Williams .20 .07
❑ 118 Aaron Brooks .50 .20
❑ 119 Deuce McAllister .60 .25
❑ 120 Joe Horn .30 .10
❑ 121 Amani Toomer .30 .10
❑ 122 Ron Dayne .30 .10
❑ 123 Kerry Collins .30 .10
❑ 124 Ike Hilliard .30 .10
❑ 125 Tiki Barber .50 .20
❑ 126 Michael Strahan .30 .10
❑ 127 Chad Pennington .60 .25
❑ 128 Santana Moss .50 .20
❑ 129 LaMont Jordan .50 .20
❑ 130 Curtis Martin .50 .20
❑ 131 Wayne Chrebet .30 .10
❑ 132 Laveranues Coles .30 .10
❑ 133 Vinny Testaverde .30 .10
❑ 134 Charles Woodson .30 .10
❑ 135 Tyrone Wheatley .30 .10
❑ 136 Jerry Porter .20 .07
❑ 137 Rich Gannon .50 .20
❑ 138 Charlie Garner .30 .10
❑ 139 Tim Brown .50 .20
❑ 140 Jerry Rice 1.00 .40
❑ 141 James Thrash .30 .10
❑ 142 Todd Pinkston .30 .10
❑ 143 A.J. Feeley .50 .20
❑ 144 Donovan McNabb .60 .25
❑ 145 Duce Staley .50 .20
❑ 146 Freddie Mitchell .30 .10
❑ 147 Correll Buckhalter .30 .10
❑ 148 Casey Hampton .20 .07
❑ 149 Hines Ward .50 .20
❑ 150 Chris Fuamatu-Ma'afala .20 .07
❑ 151 Jerome Bettis .50 .20
❑ 152 Kordell Stewart .30 .10
❑ 153 Plaxico Burress .30 .10
❑ 154 Kendrell Bell .50 .20
❑ 155 Trevor Gaylor .20 .07
❑ 156 Curtis Conway .20 .07
❑ 157 Doug Flutie .50 .20
❑ 158 Drew Brees .50 .20
❑ 159 LaDainian Tomlinson .75 .30
❑ 160 Junior Seau .50 .20
❑ 161 Bryant Young .20 .07
❑ 162 Andre Carter .20 .07
❑ 163 Eric Johnson .20 .07
❑ 164 Jeff Garcia .50 .20
❑ 165 Garrison Hearst .30 .10
❑ 166 Terrell Owens .50 .20
❑ 167 Kevan Barlow .30 .10
❑ 168 Levon Kirkland .20 .07
❑ 169 Ricky Watters .20 .07
❑ 170 Trent Dilfer .30 .10
❑ 171 Shaun Alexander .60 .25
❑ 172 Koren Robinson .30 .10
❑ 173 Darrell Jackson .30 .10
❑ 174 Adam Archuleta .20 .07
❑ 175 Aeneas Williams .20 .07
❑ 176 Trung Canidate .30 .10
❑ 177 Kurt Warner .50 .20
❑ 178 Marshall Faulk .50 .20
❑ 179 Torry Holt .50 .20
❑ 180 Isaac Bruce .50 .20
❑ 181 John Lynch .30 .10
❑ 182 Joe Jurevicius .20 .07
❑ 183 Brad Johnson .30 .10
❑ 184 Rob Johnson .30 .10
❑ 185 Keyshawn Johnson .50 .20
❑ 186 Mike Alstott .50 .20
❑ 187 Warren Sapp .30 .10
❑ 188 Drew Bennett .50 .20
❑ 189 Frank Wycheck .20 .07
❑ 190 Kevin Dyson .30 .10
❑ 191 Steve McNair .50 .20
❑ 192 Eddie George .50 .20
❑ 193 Jevon Kearse .30 .10
❑ 194 Derrick Mason .30 .10
❑ 195 Champ Bailey .30 .10
❑ 196 Darrell Green .20 .07
❑ 197 Bruce Smith .20 .07
❑ 198 Jacquez Green .20 .07
❑ 199 Stephen Davis .30 .10
❑ 200 Rod Gardner .30 .10
❑ 201 David Carr RC 8.00 3.00
❑ 202 Joey Harrington RC 8.00 3.00
❑ 203 Patrick Ramsey RC 4.00 1.50
❑ 204 Kurt Kittner RC 2.50 1.00
❑ 205 Rohan Davey RC 3.00 1.25
❑ 206 Josh McCown RC 4.00 1.50
❑ 207 David Garrard RC 3.00 1.25
❑ 208 Randy Fasani RC 2.50 1.00
❑ 209 Atrews Bell RC 1.50 .60
❑ 210 Brandon Doman RC 2.50 1.00
❑ 211 Eric Crouch RC 3.00 1.25
❑ 212 Woody Dantzler RC 2.50 1.00
❑ 213 Chad Hutchinson RC 2.50 1.00
❑ 214 Zak Kustok RC 3.00 1.25
❑ 215 Ronald Curry RC 3.00 1.25
❑ 216 William Green RC 3.00 1.25
❑ 217 T.J. Duckett RC 5.00 2.00
❑ 218 Clinton Portis RC 10.00 4.00
❑ 219 DeShaun Foster RC 3.00 1.25
❑ 220 Lamar Gordon RC 3.00 1.25
❑ 221 Jonathan Wells RC 3.00 1.25
❑ 222 Adrian Peterson RC 3.00 1.25
❑ 223 Ladell Betts RC 3.00 1.25
❑ 224 Maurice Morris RC 3.00 1.25
❑ 225 Brian Westbrook RC 5.00 2.00
❑ 226 Luke Staley RC 2.50 1.00
❑ 227 Travis Stephens RC 2.50 1.00
❑ 228 Craig Nall RC 3.00 1.25
❑ 229 Chester Taylor RC 3.00 1.25
❑ 230 Ken Simonton RC 1.50 .60
❑ 231 Verron Haynes RC 3.00 1.25
❑ 232 Tellis Redmon RC 2.50 1.00
❑ 233 J.T. O'Sullivan RC 2.50 1.00
❑ 234 Major Applewhite RC 3.00 1.25
❑ 235 Ricky Williams RC 2.50 1.00
❑ 236 James Mungro RC 3.00 1.25
❑ 237 Josh Scobey RC 3.00 1.25
❑ 238 Najeh Davenport RC 3.00 1.25
❑ 239 Dicenzo Miller RC 1.50 .60
❑ 240 Ennis Haywood RC 2.50 1.00
❑ 241 Jabar Gaffney RC 3.00 1.25
❑ 242 Antonio Bryant RC 3.00 1.25
❑ 243 Donte Stallworth RC 6.00 2.50
❑ 244 Josh Reed RC 3.00 1.25
❑ 245 Ashley Lelie RC 6.00 2.50
❑ 246 Reche Caldwell RC 3.00 1.25
❑ 247 Marquise Walker RC 2.50 1.00
❑ 248 Javon Walker RC 6.00 2.50
❑ 249 Andre Davis RC 2.50 1.00
❑ 250 Antwaan Randle El RC 5.00 2.00
❑ 251 Kelly Campbell RC 2.50 1.00
❑ 252 Cliff Russell RC 2.50 1.00
❑ 253 Kahlil Hill RC 2.50 1.00
❑ 254 Ron Johnson RC 2.50 1.00
❑ 255 Deion Branch RC 6.00 2.50
❑ 256 Brian Poli-Dixon RC 2.50 1.00
❑ 257 Freddie Milons RC 2.50 1.00
❑ 258 Lee Mays RC 2.50 1.00
❑ 259 Tim Carter RC 2.50 1.00
❑ 260 Terry Charles RC 2.50 1.00
❑ 261 Jamar Martin RC 2.50 1.00
❑ 262 Jason McAddley RC 2.50 1.00
❑ 263 Chris Hope RC 3.00 1.25
❑ 264 Howard Green RC 1.50 .60
❑ 265 Jeremy Shockey RC 10.00 4.00
❑ 266 Daniel Graham RC 3.00 1.25
❑ 267 Eddie Freeman RC 1.50 .60
❑ 268 Julius Peppers RC 6.00 2.50
❑ 269 Kalimba Edwards RC 3.00 1.25
❑ 270 Dwight Freeney RC 4.00 1.50
❑ 271 Dennis Johnson RC 1.50 .60
❑ 272 Alex Brown RC 3.00 1.25
❑ 273 Bryan Thomas RC 2.50 1.00
❑ 274 Bryan Fletcher RC 1.50 .60
❑ 275 Will Overstreet RC 1.50 .60
❑ 276 Ryan Denney RC 2.50 1.00
❑ 277 Charles Grant RC 3.00 1.25
❑ 278 John Henderson RC 3.00 1.25
❑ 279 Albert Haynesworth RC 2.50 1.00
❑ 280 Wendell Bryant RC 1.50 .60
❑ 281 Ryan Sims RC 3.00 1.25
❑ 282 Anthony Weaver RC 2.50 1.00
❑ 283 Larry Tripplett RC 1.50 .60
❑ 284 Alan Harper RC 1.50 .60
❑ 285 Napoleon Harris RC 3.00 1.25
❑ 286 Robert Thomas RC 3.00 1.25
❑ 287 Levar Fisher RC 1.50 .60
❑ 288 Andra Davis RC 2.50 1.00
❑ 289 Quentin Jammer RC 3.00 1.25
❑ 290 Phillip Buchanon RC 3.00 1.25
❑ 291 Keyuo Craver RC 2.50 1.00
❑ 292 Lito Sheppard RC 3.00 1.25
❑ 293 Rocky Calmus RC 3.00 1.25
❑ 294 Mike Rumph RC 3.00 1.25
❑ 295 Mike Echols RC 1.50 .60
❑ 296 Joseph Jefferson RC 2.50 1.00
❑ 297 Roy Williams RC 8.00 3.00
❑ 298 Ed Reed RC 5.00 2.00
❑ 299 Michael Lewis RC 3.00 1.25
❑ 300 Eddie Drummond RC 2.50 1.00

2001 Donruss Classics

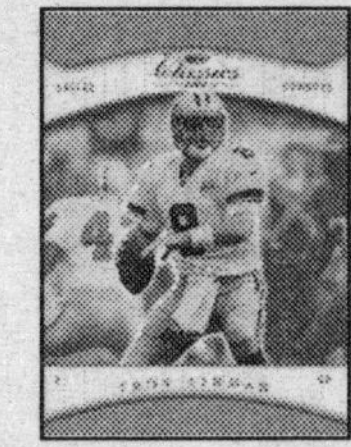

❑ COMP.SET w/o SPs (100) 20.00 7.50
❑ 1 David Boston .75 .30
❑ 2 Jake Plummer .50 .20
❑ 3 Thomas Jones .50 .20
❑ 4 Jamal Anderson .75 .30
❑ 5 Chris Redman .30 .10

❑ 6 Elvis Grbac .50 .20
❑ 7 Jamal Lewis 1.25 .50
❑ 8 Qadry Ismail .50 .20
❑ 9 Ray Lewis .75 .30
❑ 10 Shannon Sharpe .50 .20
❑ 11 Travis Taylor .50 .20
❑ 12 Eric Moulds .50 .20
❑ 13 Rob Johnson .50 .20
❑ 14 Muhsin Muhammad .50 .20
❑ 15 Brian Urlacher 1.25 .50
❑ 16 Cade McNown .30 .10
❑ 17 Marcus Robinson .75 .30
❑ 18 Akili Smith .30 .10
❑ 19 Corey Dillon .75 .30
❑ 20 Peter Warrick .75 .30
❑ 21 Courtney Brown .50 .20
❑ 22 Tim Couch .50 .20
❑ 23 Emmitt Smith 1.50 .60
❑ 24 Brian Griese .75 .30
❑ 25 Ed McCaffery .75 .30
❑ 26 Olandis Gary .50 .20
❑ 27 Mike Anderson .75 .30
❑ 28 Rod Smith .50 .20
❑ 29 Terrell Davis .75 .30
❑ 30 Charlie Batch .75 .30
❑ 31 James Stewart .50 .20
❑ 32 Ahman Green .75 .30
❑ 33 Antonio Freeman .75 .30
❑ 34 Brett Favre 2.50 1.00
❑ 35 Edgerrin James 1.00 .40
❑ 36 Marvin Harrison .75 .30
❑ 37 Peyton Manning 2.00 .75
❑ 38 Fred Taylor .75 .30
❑ 39 Jimmy Smith .50 .20
❑ 40 Keenan McCardell .30 .10
❑ 41 Mark Brunell .75 .30
❑ 42 Sylvester Morris .30 .10
❑ 43 Tony Gonzalez .50 .20
❑ 44 Zach Thomas .75 .30
❑ 45 Jay Fiedler .75 .30
❑ 46 Lamar Smith .50 .20
❑ 47 Cris Carter .75 .30
❑ 48 Daunte Culpepper .75 .30
❑ 49 Randy Moss 1.50 .60
❑ 50 Drew Bledsoe 1.00 .40
❑ 51 Terry Glenn .50 .20
❑ 52 Aaron Brooks .75 .30
❑ 53 Joe Horn .50 .20
❑ 54 Ricky Williams .75 .30
❑ 55 Amani Toomer .50 .20
❑ 56 Ike Hilliard .50 .20
❑ 57 Kerry Collins .50 .20
❑ 58 Ron Dayne .75 .30
❑ 59 Tiki Barber .75 .30
❑ 60 Chad Pennington 1.25 .50
❑ 61 Curtis Martin .75 .30
❑ 62 Laveranues Coles .75 .30
❑ 63 Vinny Testaverde .50 .20
❑ 64 Wayne Chrebet .50 .20
❑ 65 Charles Woodson .50 .20
❑ 66 Rich Gannon .75 .30
❑ 67 Tim Brown .75 .30
❑ 68 Tyrone Wheatley .50 .20
❑ 69 Corey Simon .50 .20
❑ 70 Donovan McNabb 1.00 .40
❑ 71 Duce Staley .75 .30
❑ 72 Jerome Bettis .75 .30
❑ 73 Plaxico Burress .75 .30
❑ 74 Doug Flutie .75 .30
❑ 75 Junior Seau .75 .30
❑ 76 Jeff Garcia .75 .30
❑ 77 Jerry Rice 1.50 .60
❑ 78 Giovanni Carmazzi .30 .10
❑ 79 Terrell Owens .75 .30
❑ 80 Darrell Jackson .75 .30
❑ 81 Ricky Watters .50 .20
❑ 82 Shaun Alexander 1.00 .40
❑ 83 Isaac Bruce .75 .30
❑ 84 Kurt Warner 2.50 1.00
❑ 85 Marshall Faulk 1.00 .40
❑ 86 Torry Holt .75 .30
❑ 87 Brad Johnson .75 .30
❑ 88 Keyshawn Johnson .75 .30
❑ 89 Mike Alstott .75 .30
❑ 90 Shaun King .30 .10
❑ 91 Warren Sapp .50 .20
❑ 92 Warrick Dunn .75 .30
❑ 93 Eddie George .75 .30
❑ 94 Jevon Kearse .50 .20
❑ 95 Steve McNair .75 .30
❑ 96 Jeff George .50 .20
❑ 97 Stephen Davis .75 .30
❑ 98 Charlie Garner .50 .20
❑ 99 Trent Dilfer .50 .20
❑ 100 Troy Aikman 1.25 .50
❑ 101 Michael Vick RC 60.00 25.00
❑ 102 Drew Brees RC 25.00 10.00
❑ 103 Chris Weinke RC 10.00 4.00
❑ 104 Mike McMahon RC 10.00 4.00
❑ 105 Jesse Palmer RC 10.00 4.00
❑ 106 Quincy Carter RC 10.00 4.00
❑ 107 Josh Heupel RC 10.00 4.00
❑ 108 Tim Hasselbeck RC 10.00 4.00
❑ 109 LaDainian Tomlinson RC 50.00 25.00
❑ 110 Deuce McAllister RC 20.00 7.50
❑ 111 Michael Bennett RC 15.00 6.00
❑ 112 Anthony Thomas RC 10.00 4.00
❑ 113 LaMont Jordan RC 20.00 7.50
❑ 114 Travis Henry RC 10.00 4.00
❑ 115 Kevan Barlow RC 10.00 4.00
❑ 116 Travis Minor RC 6.00 2.50
❑ 117 Rudi Johnson RC 20.00 7.50
❑ 118 David Allen RC 6.00 2.50
❑ 119 Heath Evans RC 6.00 2.50
❑ 120 Moran Norris RC 4.00 1.50
❑ 121 David Terrell RC 10.00 4.00
❑ 122 Koren Robinson RC 10.00 4.00
❑ 123 Rod Gardner RC 10.00 4.00
❑ 124 Santana Moss RC 15.00 6.00
❑ 125 Freddie Mitchell RC 10.00 4.00
❑ 126 Reggie Wayne RC 20.00 7.50
❑ 127 Quincy Morgan RC 10.00 4.00
❑ 128 Chad Johnson RC 25.00 10.00
❑ 129 Robert Ferguson RC 10.00 4.00
❑ 130 Chris Chambers RC 15.00 6.00
❑ 131 Snoop Minnis RC 6.00 2.50
❑ 132 Eddie Berlin RC 6.00 2.50
❑ 133 Alex Bannister RC 6.00 2.50
❑ 134 Todd Heap RC 10.00 4.00
❑ 135 Alge Crumpler RC 12.00 6.00
❑ 136 Justin Smith RC 10.00 4.00
❑ 137 Andre Carter RC 10.00 4.00
❑ 138 Jamal Reynolds RC 10.00 4.00
❑ 139 Richard Seymour RC 10.00 4.00
❑ 140 Marcus Stroud RC 10.00 4.00
❑ 141 Casey Hampton RC 10.00 4.00
❑ 142 Gerard Warren RC 10.00 4.00
❑ 143 Torrance Marshall RC 10.00 4.00
❑ 144 Brian Allen RC 4.00 1.50
❑ 145 Morlon Greenwood RC 6.00 2.50
❑ 146 Keith Adams RC 4.00 1.50
❑ 147 Will Allen RC 6.00 2.50
❑ 148 Nate Clements RC 10.00 4.00
❑ 149 Adam Archuleta RC 10.00 4.00
❑ 150 Hakim Akbar RC 4.00 1.50
❑ 151 James Lofton 1.00 .40
❑ 152 Jim Kelly 2.50 1.00
❑ 153 Gale Sayers 2.50 1.00
❑ 154 Mike Singletary 2.00 .75
❑ 155 Boomer Esiason 1.50 .60
❑ 156 Charlie Joiner 1.00 .40
❑ 157 Ken Anderson 1.50 .60
❑ 158 Y.A. Tittle 2.00 .75
❑ 159 Jim Brown 3.00 1.25
❑ 160 Otto Graham 1.50 .60
❑ 161 Ozzie Newsome 1.00 .40
❑ 162 Drew Pearson 1.50 .60
❑ 163 Lance Alworth 1.50 .60
❑ 164 Roger Staubach 4.00 1.50
❑ 165 Tony Dorsett 2.00 .75
❑ 166 John Elway 5.00 2.00
❑ 167 Barry Sanders 3.00 1.25
❑ 168 Bart Starr 4.00 1.50
❑ 169 Paul Hornung 2.00 .75
❑ 170 Earl Campbell 2.00 .75
❑ 171 Warren Moon 2.00 .75
❑ 172 Johnny Unitas 3.00 1.25
❑ 173 Deacon Jones 1.50 .60
❑ 174 Eric Dickerson 1.50 .60
❑ 175 Bob Griese 2.00 .75
❑ 176 Dan Marino 5.00 2.00
❑ 177 Larry Csonka 2.00 .75
❑ 178 Paul Warfield 2.00 .75
❑ 179 Fran Tarkenton 2.50 1.00
❑ 180 Archie Manning 1.50 .60
❑ 181 Frank Gifford 2.00 .75
❑ 182 Lawrence Taylor 2.00 .75
❑ 183 Dan Fouts 2.00 .75
❑ 184 Don Maynard 1.50 .60
❑ 185 Joe Namath 4.00 1.50
❑ 186 Fred Biletnikoff 2.00 .75
❑ 187 Marcus Allen 2.50 1.00
❑ 188 Jim Plunkett 1.50 .60
❑ 189 Franco Harris 2.50 1.00
❑ 190 Terry Bradshaw 4.00 1.50
❑ 191 Joe Montana 10.00 4.00
❑ 192 Roger Craig 1.50 .60
❑ 193 Steve Young 2.50 1.00
❑ 194 Dwight Clark 1.50 .60
❑ 195 Steve Largent 2.00 .75
❑ 196 Art Monk 1.50 .60
❑ 197 Charley Taylor 1.50 .60
❑ 198 Joe Theismann 2.00 .75
❑ 199 Sammy Baugh 2.00 .75
❑ 200 Sonny Jurgensen 2.00 .75

2002 Donruss Classics

❑ COMP.SET w/o SP's (100) 20.00 7.50
❑ 1 David Boston .75 .30
❑ 2 Jake Plummer .50 .20
❑ 3 Jamal Anderson .50 .20
❑ 4 Michael Vick 2.50 1.00
❑ 5 Chris Weinke .50 .20
❑ 6 Muhsin Muhammad .50 .20
❑ 7 Steve Smith .75 .30
❑ 8 Anthony Thomas .50 .20
❑ 9 David Terrell .75 .30
❑ 10 Brian Urlacher 1.25 .50
❑ 11 Marty Booker .50 .20
❑ 12 Quincy Carter .50 .20
❑ 13 Emmitt Smith 2.00 .75
❑ 14 Mike McMahon .75 .30
❑ 15 James Stewart .50 .20
❑ 16 Brett Favre 2.00 .75
❑ 17 Ahman Green .75 .30
❑ 18 Antonio Freeman .75 .30
❑ 19 Michael Bennett .50 .20
❑ 20 Randy Moss 1.50 .60
❑ 21 Cris Carter .75 .30
❑ 22 Daunte Culpepper .75 .30
❑ 23 Aaron Brooks .75 .30
❑ 24 Ricky Williams .75 .30
❑ 25 Deuce McAllister 1.00 .40
❑ 26 Kerry Collins .50 .20

❑ 27	Michael Strahan	.50	.20
❑ 28	Donovan McNabb	1.00	.40
❑ 29	Duce Staley	.75	.30
❑ 30	Freddie Mitchell	.50	.20
❑ 31	Correll Buckhalter	.50	.20
❑ 32	Jeff Garcia	.75	.30
❑ 33	Terrell Owens	.75	.30
❑ 34	Garrison Hearst	.50	.20
❑ 35	Marshall Faulk	.75	.30
❑ 36	Isaac Bruce	.75	.30
❑ 37	Kurt Warner	.75	.30
❑ 38	Torry Holt	.75	.30
❑ 39	Brad Johnson	.50	.20
❑ 40	Keyshawn Johnson	.75	.30
❑ 41	Mike Alstott	.75	.30
❑ 42	Warrick Dunn	.75	.30
❑ 43	Stephen Davis	.50	.20
❑ 44	Rod Gardner	.50	.20
❑ 45	Bruce Smith	.30	.10
❑ 46	Elvis Grbac	.50	.20
❑ 47	Ray Lewis	.75	.30
❑ 48	Jamal Lewis	.75	.30
❑ 49	Rob Johnson	.50	.20
❑ 50	Eric Moulds	.50	.20
❑ 51	Travis Henry	.75	.30
❑ 52	Corey Dillon	.50	.20
❑ 53	Peter Warrick	.50	.20
❑ 54	Tim Couch	.50	.20
❑ 55	James Jackson	.30	.10
❑ 56	Kevin Johnson	.50	.20
❑ 57	Brian Griese	.75	.30
❑ 58	Terrell Davis	.75	.30
❑ 59	Rod Smith	.50	.20
❑ 60	Mike Anderson	.75	.30
❑ 61	Peyton Manning	1.50	.60
❑ 62	Marvin Harrison	.75	.30
❑ 63	Edgerrin James	1.00	.40
❑ 64	Dominic Rhodes	.50	.20
❑ 65	Mark Brunell	.75	.30
❑ 66	Fred Taylor	.75	.30
❑ 67	Jimmy Smith	.50	.20
❑ 68	Tony Gonzalez	.50	.20
❑ 69	Trent Green	.50	.20
❑ 70	Priest Holmes	1.00	.40
❑ 71	Snoop Minnis	.30	.10
❑ 72	Jay Fiedler	.50	.20
❑ 73	Lamar Smith	.50	.20
❑ 74	Chris Chambers	.75	.30
❑ 75	Tom Brady	2.00	.75
❑ 76	Drew Bledsoe	1.00	.40
❑ 77	Antowain Smith	.50	.20
❑ 78	Troy Brown	.50	.20
❑ 79	Vinny Testaverde	.50	.20
❑ 80	Curtis Martin	.75	.30
❑ 81	Wayne Chrebet	.50	.20
❑ 82	Laveranues Coles	.50	.20
❑ 83	Tim Brown	.75	.30
❑ 84	Jerry Rice	1.50	.60
❑ 85	Rich Gannon	.75	.30
❑ 86	Charlie Garner	.50	.20
❑ 87	Kordell Stewart	.50	.20
❑ 88	Jerome Bettis	.75	.30
❑ 89	Kendrell Bell	.75	.30
❑ 90	Plaxico Burress	.50	.20
❑ 91	Drew Brees	.75	.30
❑ 92	LaDainian Tomlinson	1.25	.50
❑ 93	Doug Flutie	.75	.30
❑ 94	Shaun Alexander	1.00	.40
❑ 95	Matt Hasselbeck	.50	.20
❑ 96	Koren Robinson	.50	.20
❑ 97	Steve McNair	.75	.30
❑ 98	Eddie George	.75	.30
❑ 99	Derrick Mason	.50	.20
❑ 100	Jevon Kearse	.50	.20
❑ 101	Joe Montana	12.00	5.00
❑ 102	Joe Namath	5.00	2.00
❑ 103	Warren Moon	3.00	1.25
❑ 104	Dan Marino	10.00	4.00
❑ 105	Steve Bartkowski	2.50	1.00
❑ 106	John Elway	10.00	4.00
❑ 107	Troy Aikman	5.00	2.00
❑ 108	Steve Young	3.00	1.25
❑ 109	Terry Bradshaw	5.00	2.00
❑ 110	Bart Starr	6.00	2.50
❑ 111	Bert Jones	1.50	.60
❑ 112	Craig Morton	2.50	1.00
❑ 113	Bob Griese	3.00	1.25
❑ 114	Dan Fouts	3.00	1.25
❑ 115	Phil Simms	2.50	1.00
❑ 116	Jim McMahon	4.00	1.50
❑ 117	Joe Theismann	3.00	1.25
❑ 118	Ken Stabler	5.00	2.00
❑ 119	Johnny Unitas	5.00	2.00
❑ 120	Roger Staubach	5.00	2.00
❑ 121	Len Dawson	3.00	1.25
❑ 122	Tony Dorsett	4.00	1.50
❑ 123	Gale Sayers	5.00	2.00
❑ 124	Jim Kelly	4.00	1.50
❑ 125	Herschel Walker	2.50	1.00
❑ 126	John Riggins	4.00	1.50
❑ 127	Eric Dickerson	2.50	1.00
❑ 128	Franco Harris	4.00	1.50
❑ 129	Earl Campbell	3.00	1.25
❑ 130	Thurman Thomas	2.50	1.00
❑ 131	Barry Sanders	5.00	2.00
❑ 132	Marcus Allen	4.00	1.50
❑ 134	Natrone Means	1.50	.60
❑ 135	Steve Largent	3.00	1.25
❑ 136	Don Maynard	2.50	1.00
❑ 137	Henry Ellard	2.50	1.00
❑ 138	Sterling Sharpe	3.00	1.25
❑ 139	Art Monk	2.50	1.00
❑ 140	Andre Reed	2.50	1.00
❑ 141	Raymond Berry	2.50	1.00
❑ 142	Ozzie Newsome	2.50	1.00
❑ 143	William Perry	2.50	1.00
❑ 144	Deacon Jones	2.50	1.00
❑ 145	Howie Long	4.00	1.50
❑ 146	L.C. Greenwood	2.50	1.00
❑ 147	Ronnie Lott	2.50	1.00
❑ 148	Dick Butkus	5.00	2.00
❑ 149	Fran Tarkenton	4.00	1.50
❑ 150	Mike Singletary	3.00	1.25
❑ 151	David Carr RC	15.00	6.00
❑ 152	Joey Harrington RC	15.00	6.00
❑ 153	Patrick Ramsey RC	8.00	3.00
❑ 154	Kurt Kittner RC	5.00	2.00
❑ 155	DeShaun Foster RC	6.00	2.50
❑ 156	William Green RC	6.00	2.50
❑ 157	Clinton Portis RC	20.00	7.50
❑ 158	T.J. Duckett RC	10.00	4.00
❑ 159	Cliff Russell RC	5.00	2.00
❑ 160	Antonio Bryant RC	6.00	2.50
❑ 161	Donte Stallworth RC	12.00	5.00
❑ 162	Reche Caldwell RC	6.00	2.50
❑ 163	Jabar Gaffney RC	6.00	2.50
❑ 164	Ashley Lelie RC	12.00	5.00
❑ 165	Andre Davis RC	5.00	2.00
❑ 166	Josh Reed RC	6.00	2.50
❑ 167	Ron Johnson RC	5.00	2.00
❑ 168	Kelly Campbell RC	5.00	2.00
❑ 169	Javon Walker RC	12.00	5.00
❑ 170	Antwaan Randle El RC	10.00	4.00
❑ 171	Marquise Walker RC	5.00	2.00
❑ 172	Jeremy Shockey RC	20.00	7.50
❑ 173	Jerramy Stevens RC	6.00	2.50
❑ 174	Daniel Graham RC	6.00	2.50
❑ 175	Julius Peppers RC	12.00	5.00
❑ 176	Kalimba Edwards RC	6.00	2.50
❑ 177	Alex Brown RC	6.00	2.50
❑ 178	Will Overstreet RC	5.00	2.00
❑ 179	Dwight Freeney RC	8.00	3.00
❑ 180	John Henderson RC	6.00	2.50
❑ 181	Ryan Sims RC	6.00	2.50
❑ 182	Albert Haynesworth RC	5.00	2.00
❑ 183	Wendell Bryant RC	3.00	1.25
❑ 184	Anthony Weaver RC	5.00	2.00
❑ 185	Napoleon Harris RC	6.00	2.50
❑ 186	Robert Thomas RC	6.00	2.50
❑ 187	Quentin Jammer RC	6.00	2.50
❑ 188	Ed Reed RC	10.00	4.00
❑ 189	Roy Williams RC	15.00	6.00
❑ 190	Phillip Buchanon RC	6.00	2.50
❑ 191	Lito Sheppard RC	6.00	2.50
❑ 192	Mike Rumph RC	6.00	2.50
❑ 193	Keyuo Craver RC	5.00	2.00
❑ 194	Randy Fasani RC	5.00	2.00
❑ 195	Rohan Davey RC	6.00	2.50
❑ 196	Chad Hutchinson RC	5.00	2.00
❑ 197	Eric Crouch RC	6.00	2.50
❑ 198	Lamar Gordon RC	6.00	2.50
❑ 199	Brian Westbrook RC	10.00	4.00
❑ 200	Adrian Peterson RC	6.00	2.50

2003 Donruss Classics

❑	COMP.SET w/o SP's (100)	20.00	7.50
❑ 1	Jake Plummer	.50	.20
❑ 2	Marcel Shipp	.50	.20
❑ 3	David Boston	.50	.20
❑ 4	Michael Vick	2.00	.75
❑ 5	T.J. Duckett	.50	.20
❑ 6	Warrick Dunn	.50	.20
❑ 7	Ray Lewis	.75	.30
❑ 8	Jamal Lewis	.75	.30
❑ 9	Todd Heap	.50	.20
❑ 10	Drew Bledsoe	.75	.30
❑ 11	Travis Henry	.50	.20
❑ 12	Peerless Price	.50	.20
❑ 13	Eric Moulds	.50	.20
❑ 14	Julius Peppers	.75	.30
❑ 15	Steve Smith	.75	.30
❑ 16	Lamar Smith	.30	.10
❑ 17	Anthony Thomas	.50	.20
❑ 18	Marty Booker	.50	.20
❑ 19	Brian Urlacher	1.25	.50
❑ 20	Corey Dillon	.50	.20
❑ 21	Chad Johnson	.75	.30
❑ 22	Tim Couch	.30	.10
❑ 23	William Green	.50	.20
❑ 24	Quincy Morgan	.50	.20
❑ 25	Chad Hutchinson	.30	.10
❑ 26	Emmitt Smith	2.00	.75
❑ 27	Antonio Bryant	.50	.20
❑ 28	Roy Williams	.75	.30
❑ 29	Brian Griese	.75	.30
❑ 30	Clinton Portis	1.25	.50
❑ 31	Rod Smith	.50	.20
❑ 32	Ashley Lelie	.75	.30
❑ 33	Joey Harrington	1.25	.50
❑ 34	James Stewart	.50	.20
❑ 35	Bill Schroeder	.50	.20
❑ 36	Brett Favre	2.00	.75
❑ 37	Ahman Green	.75	.30
❑ 38	Donald Driver	.50	.20
❑ 39	David Carr	1.25	.50
❑ 40	Jonathan Wells	.30	.10
❑ 41	Corey Bradford	.30	.10
❑ 42	Peyton Manning	1.25	.50
❑ 43	Edgerrin James	.75	.30
❑ 44	Marvin Harrison	.75	.30
❑ 45	Mark Brunell	.50	.20
❑ 46	Fred Taylor	.75	.30
❑ 47	Jimmy Smith	.50	.20
❑ 48	Trent Green	.50	.20

❑ 49	Priest Holmes	1.00	.40
❑ 50	Tony Gonzalez	.50	.20
❑ 51	Ricky Williams	.75	.30
❑ 52	Chris Chambers	.75	.30
❑ 53	Zach Thomas	.75	.30
❑ 54	Daunte Culpepper	.75	.30
❑ 55	Michael Bennett	.50	.20
❑ 56	Randy Moss	1.25	.50
❑ 57	Tom Brady	2.00	.75
❑ 58	Antowain Smith	.50	.20
❑ 59	Troy Brown	.50	.20
❑ 60	Aaron Brooks	.75	.30
❑ 61	Deuce McAllister	.75	.30
❑ 62	Donte Stallworth	.75	.30
❑ 63	Kerry Collins	.50	.20
❑ 64	Jeremy Shockey	1.25	.50
❑ 65	Amani Toomer	.50	.20
❑ 66	Chad Pennington	1.00	.40
❑ 67	Curtis Martin	.75	.30
❑ 68	Laveranues Coles	.50	.20
❑ 69	Rich Gannon	.50	.20
❑ 70	Charlie Garner	.50	.20
❑ 71	Jerry Rice	1.50	.60
❑ 72	Tim Brown	.75	.30
❑ 73	Donovan McNabb	1.00	.40
❑ 74	Duce Staley	.50	.20
❑ 75	Todd Pinkston	.50	.20
❑ 76	Tommy Maddox	.75	.30
❑ 77	Jerome Bettis	.75	.30
❑ 78	Plaxico Burress	.50	.20
❑ 79	Hines Ward	.75	.30
❑ 80	Drew Brees	.75	.30
❑ 81	LaDainian Tomlinson	.75	.30
❑ 82	Junior Seau	.75	.30
❑ 83	Jeff Garcia	.75	.30
❑ 84	Garrison Hearst	.50	.20
❑ 85	Terrell Owens	.75	.30
❑ 86	Matt Hasselbeck	.50	.20
❑ 87	Shaun Alexander	.75	.30
❑ 88	Koren Robinson	.50	.20
❑ 89	Kurt Warner	.75	.30
❑ 90	Marshall Faulk	.75	.30
❑ 91	Isaac Bruce	.75	.30
❑ 92	Brad Johnson	.50	.20
❑ 93	Mike Alstott	.75	.30
❑ 94	Keyshawn Johnson	.75	.30
❑ 95	Steve McNair	.75	.30
❑ 96	Eddie George	.50	.20
❑ 97	Derrick Mason	.50	.20
❑ 98	Patrick Ramsey	.75	.30
❑ 99	Stephen Davis	.50	.20
❑ 100	Rod Gardner	.50	.20
❑ 101	Archie Manning	3.00	1.25
❑ 102	Bo Jackson	6.00	2.50
❑ 103	Bob Griese	3.00	1.25
❑ 104	Bob Lilly	2.50	1.00
❑ 105	Craig James	2.50	1.00
❑ 106	Cliff Branch	2.50	1.00
❑ 107	Dan Fouts	3.00	1.25
❑ 108	Daryl Johnston	3.00	1.25
❑ 109	Daryle Lamonica	1.50	.60
❑ 110	Dick Butkus	5.00	2.00
❑ 111	Don Maynard	2.50	1.00
❑ 112	Ed Too Tall Jones	2.50	1.00
❑ 113	Franco Harris	4.00	1.50
❑ 114	Frank Gifford	3.00	1.25
❑ 115	Fred Biletnikoff	3.00	1.25
❑ 116	Gale Sayers	5.00	2.00
❑ 117	George Blanda	3.00	1.25
❑ 118	Herman Edwards	2.50	1.00
❑ 119	Herschel Walker	2.50	1.00
❑ 120	Jack Ham	2.50	1.00
❑ 121	Jack Tatum	1.50	.60
❑ 122	Jack Youngblood	1.50	.60
❑ 123	James Lofton	1.50	.60
❑ 124	Jay Novacek	1.50	.60
❑ 125	Jim Brown	6.00	2.50
❑ 126	Jim McMahon/100	40.00	20.00
❑ 127	Jim Plunkett	2.50	1.00
❑ 128	Jimmy Johnson/100 EXCH		

❑ 129	Joe Greene	3.00	1.25
❑ 130	Joe Montana	12.00	5.00
❑ 131	John Riggins	4.00	1.50
❑ 132	John Stallworth	2.50	1.00
❑ 133	John Taylor/100	3.00	1.25
❑ 134	Ken Stabler	5.00	2.00
❑ 135	L.C. Greenwood	2.50	1.00
❑ 136	Lance Alworth	2.50	1.00
❑ 137	Mel Blount	2.50	1.00
❑ 138	Mike Ditka/100	5.00	2.00
❑ 139	Paul Hornung	3.00	1.25
❑ 140	Randy White	2.50	1.00
❑ 141	Raymond Berry	2.50	1.00
❑ 142	Roger Craig	2.50	1.00
❑ 143	Roger Staubach	5.00	2.00
❑ 144	Ron Jaworski	1.50	.60
❑ 145	Sammy Baugh	3.00	1.25
❑ 146	Sonny Jurgenson	2.50	1.00
❑ 147	Steve Young	3.00	1.25
❑ 148	Ted Hendricks	1.50	.60
❑ 149	Thurman Thomas	2.50	1.00
❑ 150	Tom Jackson/100	3.00	1.25
❑ 151	Brian St.Pierre RC	6.00	2.50
❑ 152	Byron Leftwich RC	20.00	7.50
❑ 153	Carson Palmer RC	25.00	10.00
❑ 154	Chris Simms RC	10.00	4.00
❑ 155	Dave Ragone RC	6.00	2.50
❑ 156	Ken Dorsey RC	6.00	2.50
❑ 157	Kliff Kingsbury RC	5.00	2.00
❑ 158	Kyle Boller RC	12.00	5.00
❑ 159	Rex Grossman RC	10.00	4.00
❑ 160	Seneca Wallace RC	6.00	2.50
❑ 161	Jason Gesser RC	6.00	2.50
❑ 162	Artose Pinner RC	6.00	2.50
❑ 163	Avon Cobourne RC	3.00	1.25
❑ 164	Cecil Sapp RC	5.00	2.00
❑ 165	Chris Brown RC	8.00	3.00
❑ 166	Derek Watson RC	5.00	2.00
❑ 167	Domanick Davis RC	10.00	4.00
❑ 168	Dwone Hicks RC	3.00	1.25
❑ 169	Earnest Graham RC	5.00	2.00
❑ 170	Justin Fargas RC	6.00	2.50
❑ 171	Larry Johnson RC	25.00	12.50
❑ 172	Lee Suggs RC	12.00	5.00
❑ 173	Musa Smith RC	6.00	2.50
❑ 174	Onterrio Smith RC	6.00	2.50
❑ 175	Quentin Griffin RC	6.00	2.50
❑ 176	Willis McGahee RC	15.00	6.00
❑ 177	Sultan McCullough RC	5.00	2.00
❑ 178	LaBrandon Toefield RC	6.00	2.50
❑ 179	B.J. Askew RC	6.00	2.50
❑ 180	Andre Johnson RC	12.00	5.00
❑ 181	Anquan Boldin RC	15.00	6.00
❑ 182	Arnaz Battle RC	6.00	2.50
❑ 183	Bethel Johnson RC	6.00	2.50
❑ 184	Billy McMullen RC	5.00	2.00
❑ 185	Bobby Wade RC	6.00	2.50
❑ 186	Brandon Lloyd RC	8.00	3.00
❑ 187	Bryant Johnson RC	6.00	2.50
❑ 188	Charles Rogers RC	6.00	2.50
❑ 189	Doug Gabriel RC	6.00	2.50
❑ 190	Justin Gage RC	6.00	2.50
❑ 191	Kareem Kelly RC	5.00	2.00
❑ 192	Kelley Washington RC	6.00	2.50
❑ 193	Kevin Curtis RC	6.00	2.50
❑ 194	Nate Burleson RC	8.00	3.00
❑ 195	Sam Aiken RC	5.00	2.00
❑ 196	Shaun McDonald RC	6.00	2.50
❑ 197	Talman Gardner RC	6.00	2.50
❑ 198	Taylor Jacobs RC	5.00	2.00
❑ 199	Terrence Edwards RC	5.00	2.00
❑ 200	Tyrone Calico RC	8.00	3.00
❑ 201	Walter Young RC	3.00	1.25
❑ 202	Ryan Hoag/100 RC	12.00	5.00
❑ 203	Paul Arnold RC	5.00	2.00
❑ 204	Bennie Joppru RC	6.00	2.50
❑ 205	Dallas Clark RC	6.00	2.50
❑ 206	George Wrighster RC	5.00	2.00
❑ 207	Jason Witten RC	10.00	4.00
❑ 208	Mike Pinkard RC	3.00	1.25

❑ 209	Robert Johnson RC	3.00	1.25
❑ 210	Teyo Johnson RC	6.00	2.50
❑ 211	Calvin Pace RC	5.00	2.00
❑ 212	Chris Kelsay RC	6.00	2.50
❑ 213	Cory Redding RC	5.00	2.00
❑ 214	DeWayne Robertson RC	6.00	2.50
❑ 215	DeWayne White RC	5.00	2.00
❑ 216	Jerome McDougle RC	6.00	2.50
❑ 217	Kenny Peterson RC	5.00	2.00
❑ 218	Kindal Moorehead RC	5.00	2.00
❑ 219	Michael Haynes RC	6.00	2.50
❑ 220	Terrell Suggs RC	10.00	4.00
❑ 221	Tully Banta-Cain RC	5.00	2.00
❑ 222	Jimmy Kennedy RC	6.00	2.50
❑ 223	Johnathan Sullivan RC	5.00	2.00
❑ 224	Kevin Williams RC	6.00	2.50
❑ 225	Nick Eason/100 RC	12.00	5.00
❑ 226	Rien Long RC	3.00	1.25
❑ 227	Ty Warren RC	6.00	2.50
❑ 228	William Joseph RC	6.00	2.50
❑ 229	Boss Bailey RC	6.00	2.50
❑ 230	Bradie James RC	6.00	2.50
❑ 231	Victor Hobson RC	6.00	2.50
❑ 232	Clifton Smith RC	3.00	1.25
❑ 233	E.J. Henderson/100 RC	12.00	5.00
❑ 234	Gerald Hayes/100 RC	12.00	5.00
❑ 235	LaMarcus McDonald RC	3.00	1.25
❑ 236	Nick Barnett RC	10.00	4.00
❑ 237	Terry Pierce RC	5.00	2.00
❑ 238	Andre Woolfolk RC	6.00	2.50
❑ 239	Dennis Weathersby RC	3.00	1.25
❑ 240	Drayton Florence RC	3.00	1.25
❑ 241	Eugene Wilson RC	6.00	2.50
❑ 242	Marcus Trufant RC	6.00	2.50
❑ 243	Rashean Mathis RC	5.00	2.00
❑ 244	Ricky Manning RC	6.00	2.50
❑ 245	Sammy Davis/100 RC	12.00	5.00
❑ 246	Terence Newman RC	12.00	5.00
❑ 247	Julian Battle RC	5.00	2.00
❑ 248	Ken Hamlin RC	6.00	2.50
❑ 249	Mike Doss RC	6.00	2.50
❑ 250	Troy Polamalu RC	25.00	12.50

2004 Donruss Classics

❑ COMP.SET w/o SP's (100) 20.00 7.50

❑ 101-150 LEG PRINT RUN 2000 SER.#'d SETS

❑ 151-175 RC PRINT RUN 1850 SER.#'d SETS

❑ 176-200 RC PRINT RUN 1250 SER.#'d SETS

❑ 201-225 RC PRINT RUN 925 SER.#'d SETS

❑ 226-250 RC PRINT RUN 500 SER.#'d SETS

❑ 1	Anquan Boldin	.75	.30
❑ 2	Emmitt Smith	1.50	.60
❑ 3	Michael Vick	1.50	.60
❑ 4	Peerless Price	.50	.20
❑ 5	Warrick Dunn	.50	.20
❑ 6	Jamal Lewis	.75	.30
❑ 7	Kyle Boller	.75	.30
❑ 8	Terrell Suggs	.50	.20
❑ 9	Todd Heap	.50	.20
❑ 10	Drew Bledsoe	.75	.30
❑ 11	Travis Henry	.50	.20
❑ 12	DeShaun Foster	.50	.20
❑ 13	Jake Delhomme	.75	.30
❑ 14	Stephen Davis	.50	.20

❑ 15 Steve Smith .75 .30
❑ 16 Anthony Thomas .50 .20
❑ 17 Brian Urlacher 1.00 .40
❑ 18 Rex Grossman .75 .30
❑ 19 Chad Johnson .75 .30
❑ 20 Carson Palmer 1.00 .40
❑ 21 Rudi Johnson .50 .20
❑ 22 Andre Davis .30 .10
❑ 23 Lee Suggs .75 .30
❑ 24 Quincy Carter .50 .20
❑ 25 Roy Williams S .50 .20
❑ 26 Clinton Portis .75 .30
❑ 27 Jake Plummer .50 .20
❑ 28 Rod Smith .50 .20
❑ 29 Charles Rogers .50 .20
❑ 30 Joey Harrington .75 .30
❑ 31 Ahman Green .75 .30
❑ 32 Brett Favre 2.00 .75
❑ 33 Javon Walker .50 .20
❑ 34 Andre Johnson .75 .30
❑ 35 David Carr .75 .30
❑ 36 Domanick Davis .75 .30
❑ 37 Edgerrin James .75 .30
❑ 38 Marvin Harrison .75 .30
❑ 39 Peyton Manning 1.25 .50
❑ 40 Reggie Wayne .50 .20
❑ 41 Byron Leftwich 1.00 .40
❑ 42 Fred Taylor .50 .20
❑ 43 Jimmy Smith .50 .20
❑ 44 Priest Holmes 1.00 .40
❑ 45 Dante Hall .75 .30
❑ 46 Tony Gonzalez .50 .20
❑ 47 Trent Green .50 .20
❑ 48 Chris Chambers .50 .20
❑ 49 Ricky Williams .75 .30
❑ 50 Zach Thomas .75 .30
❑ 51 Daunte Culpepper .75 .30
❑ 52 Michael Bennett .50 .20
❑ 53 Randy Moss 1.00 .40
❑ 54 Deion Branch .75 .30
❑ 55 Adam Vinatieri .75 .30
❑ 56 Tedy Bruschi .50 .20
❑ 57 Tom Brady 2.00 .75
❑ 58 Aaron Brooks .50 .20
❑ 59 Deuce McAllister .75 .30
❑ 60 Donte' Stallworth .50 .20
❑ 61 Joe Horn .50 .20
❑ 62 Jeremy Shockey .75 .30
❑ 63 Kerry Collins .50 .20
❑ 64 Michael Strahan .50 .20
❑ 65 Tiki Barber .75 .30
❑ 66 Chad Pennington .75 .30
❑ 67 Curtis Martin .75 .30
❑ 68 Santana Moss .50 .20
❑ 69 Jerry Rice 1.50 .60
❑ 70 Charles Woodson .50 .20
❑ 71 Rod Woodson .50 .20
❑ 72 Tim Brown .75 .30
❑ 73 Brian Westbrook .50 .20
❑ 74 Correll Buckhalter .50 .20
❑ 75 Donovan McNabb 1.00 .40
❑ 76 Antwaan Randle El .75 .30
❑ 77 Hines Ward .75 .30
❑ 78 Kendrell Bell .50 .20
❑ 79 David Boston .50 .20
❑ 80 Drew Brees .75 .30
❑ 81 LaDainian Tomlinson 1.00 .40
❑ 82 Jeff Garcia .75 .30
❑ 83 Kevan Barlow .50 .20
❑ 84 Terrell Owens .75 .30
❑ 85 Koren Robinson .50 .20
❑ 86 Matt Hasselbeck .50 .20
❑ 87 Shaun Alexander .75 .30
❑ 88 Isaac Bruce .50 .20
❑ 89 Marc Bulger .75 .30
❑ 90 Marshall Faulk .75 .30
❑ 91 Torry Holt .75 .30
❑ 92 Brad Johnson .50 .20
❑ 93 Keenan McCardell .30 .10
❑ 94 Keyshawn Johnson .50 .20
❑ 95 Derrick Mason .50 .20
❑ 96 Eddie George .50 .20
❑ 97 Steve McNair .75 .30
❑ 98 LaVar Arrington 1.50 .60
❑ 99 Laveranues Coles .50 .20
❑ 100 Patrick Ramsey .50 .20
❑ 101 Archie Manning 2.00 .75
❑ 102 Bart Starr 5.00 2.00
❑ 103 Bo Jackson 4.00 1.50
❑ 104 Bob Griese 2.00 .75
❑ 105 Christian Okoye 1.00 .40
❑ 106 Daryl Johnston 2.00 .75
❑ 107 Deacon Jones 1.50 .60
❑ 108 Deion Sanders 3.00 1.25
❑ 109 Dick Butkus 3.00 1.25
❑ 110 Lynn Swann 2.50 1.00
❑ 111 Don Maynard 1.50 .60
❑ 112 Don Shula 2.00 .75
❑ 113 Franco Harris 2.50 1.00
❑ 114 Fred Biletnikoff 2.00 .75
❑ 115 Gale Sayers 2.50 1.00
❑ 116 George Blanda 2.00 .75
❑ 117 Herman Edwards 1.50 .60
❑ 118 Herschel Walker 1.50 .60
❑ 119 Jack Lambert 3.00 1.25
❑ 120 James Lofton 1.00 .40
❑ 121 Jim Plunkett 1.50 .60
❑ 122 Jim Thorpe 2.00 .75
❑ 123 Joe Greene 2.00 .75
❑ 124 John Riggins 2.50 1.00
❑ 125 L.C. Greenwood 1.50 .60
❑ 126 Larry Csonka 2.00 .75
❑ 127 Leroy Kelly 1.50 .60
❑ 128 Walter Payton 8.00 3.00
❑ 129 Marcus Allen 2.00 .75
❑ 130 Mark Bavaro 1.00 .40
❑ 131 Mel Blount 1.50 .60
❑ 132 Michael Irvin 2.00 .75
❑ 133 Mike Ditka 2.00 .75
❑ 134 Mike Singletary 2.00 .75
❑ 135 Ozzie Newsome 1.50 .60
❑ 136 Paul Hornung 2.00 .75
❑ 137 Paul Warfield 1.50 .60
❑ 138 Randall Cunningham 1.50 .60
❑ 139 Ray Nitschke 2.00 .75
❑ 140 Reggie White 2.00 .75
❑ 141 Richard Dent 1.00 .40
❑ 142 Sammy Baugh 2.00 .75
❑ 143 Sonny Jurgensen 1.50 .60
❑ 144 Sterling Sharpe 1.50 .60
❑ 145 Steve Largent 2.00 .75
❑ 146 Terrell Davis 2.00 .75
❑ 147 Terry Bradshaw 4.00 1.50
❑ 148 Thurman Thomas 1.50 .60
❑ 149 Tony Dorsett 2.00 .75
❑ 150 Warren Moon 1.50 .60
❑ 151 John Navarre RC 5.00 2.00
❑ 152 Derek Abney RC 5.00 2.00
❑ 153 Ryan Dinwiddie RC 4.00 1.50
❑ 154 Bruce Perry/100 RC 20.00 7.50
❑ 155 Adimchinobe Echemandu RC 4.001.50
❑ 156 Troy Fleming RC 4.00 1.50
❑ 157 Brandon Miree RC 4.00 1.50
❑ 158 Jarrett Payton RC 6.00 2.50
❑ 159 Ben Hartsock RC 5.00 2.00
❑ 160 Chris Cooley RC 5.00 2.00
❑ 161 Derrick Ward RC 2.50 1.00
❑ 162 Triandos Luke RC 5.00 2.00
❑ 163 Clarence Moore RC 5.00 2.00
❑ 164 D.J. Hackett RC 4.00 1.50
❑ 165 Mark Jones RC 4.00 1.50
❑ 166 Sloan Thomas RC 4.00 1.50
❑ 167 Jamaar Taylor RC 5.00 2.00
❑ 168 Casey Bramlet RC 4.00 1.50
❑ 169 Drew Carter RC 5.00 2.00
❑ 170 Antwan Odom RC 5.00 2.00
❑ 171 Marquise Hill RC 4.00 1.50
❑ 172 Ricardo Colclough RC 5.00 2.00
❑ 173 Keith Smith RC 4.00 1.50
❑ 174 Joey Thomas RC 5.00 2.00
❑ 175 Stuart Schweigert RC 5.00 2.00
❑ 176 Cody Pickett RC 6.00 2.50
❑ 177 B.J. Symons RC 6.00 2.50
❑ 178 Matt Mauck RC 6.00 2.50
❑ 179 Bradlee Van Pelt RC 10.00 4.00
❑ 180 Jim Sorgi RC 6.00 2.50
❑ 181 Ernest Wilford RC 6.00 2.50
❑ 182 Bernard Berrian RC 6.00 2.50
❑ 183 Darius Watts RC 6.00 2.50
❑ 184 Derrick Hamilton RC 5.00 2.00
❑ 185 Jerricho Cotchery RC 6.00 2.50
❑ 186 Jeris McIntyre RC 5.00 2.00
❑ 187 Carlos Francis RC 5.00 2.00
❑ 188 Maurice Mann RC 5.00 2.00
❑ 189 Randy Starks RC 5.00 2.00
❑ 190 Darnell Dockett RC 5.00 2.00
❑ 191 Marcus Tubbs RC 6.00 2.50
❑ 192 Daryl Smith RC 6.00 2.50
❑ 193 Karlos Dansby RC 6.00 2.50
❑ 194 Michael Boulware RC 6.00 2.50
❑ 195 Teddy Lehman RC 6.00 2.50
❑ 196 Will Poole RC 6.00 2.50
❑ 197 Derrick Strait RC 8.00 3.00
❑ 198 Ahmad Carroll RC 8.00 3.00
❑ 199 Jeremy LeSueur RC 5.00 2.00
❑ 200 Bob Sanders RC 12.00 5.00
❑ 201 J.P. Losman RC 15.00 6.00
❑ 202 Matt Schaub RC 10.00 4.00
❑ 203 Josh Harris RC 6.00 2.50
❑ 204 Luke McCown RC 6.00 2.50
❑ 205 Quincy Wilson RC 5.00 2.00
❑ 206 Michael Turner RC 6.00 2.50
❑ 207 Mewelde Moore RC 8.00 3.00
❑ 208 Cedric Cobbs RC 6.00 2.50
❑ 209 Ben Watson RC 6.00 2.50
❑ 210 Michael Jenkins RC 6.00 2.50
❑ 211 Devery Henderson RC 5.00 2.00
❑ 212 Johnnie Morant RC 6.00 2.50
❑ 213 Keary Colbert RC 8.00 3.00
❑ 214 Devard Darling RC 6.00 2.50
❑ 215 P.K. Sam RC 5.00 2.00
❑ 216 Samie Parker RC 6.00 2.50
❑ 217 Jason Babin RC 6.00 2.50
❑ 218 Tommie Harris RC 6.00 2.50
❑ 219 Vince Wilfork RC 8.00 3.00
❑ 220 Jonathan Vilma RC 6.00 2.50
❑ 221 D.J. Williams RC 8.00 3.00
❑ 222 Chris Gamble RC 8.00 3.00
❑ 223 Matt Ware RC 6.00 2.50
❑ 224 Shawntae Spencer RC 6.00 2.50
❑ 225 Sean Jones RC 5.00 2.00
❑ 226 Drew Henson RC 8.00 3.00
❑ 227 Ben Roethlisberger RC 60.00 35.00
❑ 228 Eli Manning RC 40.00 20.00
❑ 229 Philip Rivers RC 25.00 12.50
❑ 230 Steven Jackson RC 25.00 10.00
❑ 231 Kevin Jones RC 25.00 10.00
❑ 232 Chris Perry RC 12.00 5.00
❑ 233 Greg Jones RC 8.00 3.00
❑ 234 Tatum Bell RC 15.00 6.00
❑ 235 Jeff Smoker RC 8.00 3.00
❑ 236 Julius Jones RC 30.00 12.50
❑ 237 Kellen Winslow RC 15.00 6.00
❑ 238 Ben Troupe RC 8.00 3.00
❑ 239 Larry Fitzgerald RC 25.00 10.00
❑ 240 Craig Krenzel RC 8.00 3.00
❑ 241 Roy Williams RC 20.00 7.50
❑ 242 Reggie Williams RC 10.00 4.00
❑ 243 Michael Clayton RC 15.00 6.00
❑ 244 Lee Evans RC 8.00 3.00
❑ 245 Rashaun Woods RC 8.00 3.00
❑ 246 Kenechi Udeze RC 8.00 3.00
❑ 247 Will Smith RC 8.00 3.00
❑ 248 DeAngelo Hall RC 10.00 4.00
❑ 249 Dunta Robinson RC 8.00 3.00
❑ 250 Sean Taylor RC 10.00 4.00

2005 Donruss Classics

❑ COMP.SET w/o SP's (100) 20.00 7.50
❑ 101-150 LEG PRINT RUN 1000 SER.#'d SETS

- ❑ 151-175 PRINT RUN 1999 SER.#'d SETS
- ❑ 176-200 PRINT RUN 1499 SER.#'d SETS
- ❑ 201-225 PRINT RUN 999 SER.#'d SETS
- ❑ 226-250 AU PRINT RUN 499 SER.#'d SETS

❑	1	Kurt Warner	.50	.20
❑	2	Josh McCown	.50	.20
❑	3	Larry Fitzgerald	.75	.30
❑	4	Alge Crumpler	.50	.20
❑	5	Michael Vick	1.25	.50
❑	6	Warrick Dunn	.50	.20
❑	7	Todd Heap	.50	.20
❑	8	Jamal Lewis	.75	.30
❑	9	Kyle Boller	.50	.20
❑	10	Drew Bledsoe	.75	.30
❑	11	Lee Evans	.50	.20
❑	12	Willis McGahee	.75	.30
❑	13	Steve Smith	.50	.20
❑	14	Jake Delhomme	.75	.30
❑	15	Muhsin Muhammad	.50	.20
❑	16	Brian Urlacher	.75	.30
❑	17	Rex Grossman	.50	.20
❑	18	Thomas Jones	.50	.20
❑	19	Carson Palmer	.75	.30
❑	20	Chad Johnson	.75	.30
❑	21	Rudi Johnson	.50	.20
❑	22	Antonio Bryant	.40	.15
❑	23	Kellen Winslow Jr.	.75	.30
❑	24	Lee Suggs	.50	.20
❑	25	Julius Jones	1.00	.40
❑	26	Keyshawn Johnson	.50	.20
❑	27	Roy Williams S	.50	.20
❑	28	Jake Plummer	.50	.20
❑	29	Rod Smith	.50	.20
❑	30	Tatum Bell	.50	.20
❑	31	Joey Harrington	.75	.30
❑	32	Kevin Jones	.75	.30
❑	33	Roy Williams WR	.75	.30
❑	34	Ahman Green	.75	.30
❑	35	Brett Favre	2.00	.75
❑	36	Javon Walker	.50	.20
❑	37	Andre Johnson	.50	.20
❑	38	David Carr	.75	.30
❑	39	Domanick Davis	.50	.20
❑	40	Edgerrin James	.75	.30
❑	41	Marvin Harrison	.75	.30
❑	42	Peyton Manning	1.25	.50
❑	43	Reggie Wayne	.50	.20
❑	44	Byron Leftwich	.75	.30
❑	45	Fred Taylor	.50	.20
❑	46	Jimmy Smith	.50	.20
❑	47	Priest Holmes	.75	.30
❑	48	Tony Gonzalez	.50	.20
❑	49	Trent Green	.50	.20
❑	50	A.J. Feeley	.50	.20
❑	51	Chris Chambers	.50	.20
❑	52	Zach Thomas	.75	.30
❑	53	Daunte Culpepper	.75	.30
❑	54	Michael Bennett	.50	.20
❑	55	Randy Moss	.75	.30
❑	56	Corey Dillon	.50	.20
❑	57	David Givens	.50	.20
❑	58	Tom Brady	2.00	.75
❑	59	Aaron Brooks	.50	.20
❑	60	Deuce McAllister	.75	.30
❑	61	Joe Horn	.50	.20
❑	62	Eli Manning	1.50	.60
❑	63	Jeremy Shockey	.75	.30
❑	64	Tiki Barber	.75	.30
❑	65	Chad Pennington	.75	.30
❑	66	Curtis Martin	.75	.30
❑	67	Santana Moss	.50	.20
❑	68	Jerry Porter	.50	.20
❑	69	Kerry Collins	.50	.20
❑	70	J.P. Losman	.75	.30
❑	71	Brian Westbrook	.50	.20
❑	72	Donovan McNabb	1.00	.40
❑	73	Terrell Owens	.75	.30
❑	74	Ben Roethlisberger	2.00	.75
❑	75	Duce Staley	.50	.20
❑	76	Hines Ward	.75	.30
❑	77	Jerome Bettis	.75	.30
❑	78	Antonio Gates	.75	.30
❑	79	Drew Brees	.75	.30
❑	80	LaDainian Tomlinson	1.00	.40
❑	81	Brandon Lloyd	.40	.15
❑	82	Kevan Barlow	.50	.20
❑	83	Laveranues Coles	.50	.20
❑	84	Darrell Jackson	.50	.20
❑	85	Jerry Rice	1.50	.60
❑	86	Matt Hasselbeck	.50	.20
❑	87	Shaun Alexander	1.00	.40
❑	88	Isaac Bruce	.50	.20
❑	89	Marc Bulger	.75	.30
❑	90	Steven Jackson	1.00	.40
❑	91	Torry Holt	.75	.30
❑	92	Brian Griese	.50	.20
❑	93	Michael Clayton	.75	.30
❑	94	Mike Alstott	.50	.20
❑	95	Chris Brown	.50	.20
❑	96	Drew Bennett	.50	.20
❑	97	Steve McNair	.75	.30
❑	98	Clinton Portis	.75	.30
❑	99	LaVar Arrington	.75	.30
❑	100	Patrick Ramsey	.50	.20
❑	101	Don Shula	3.00	1.25
❑	102	James Lofton	2.50	1.00
❑	103	Thurman Thomas	3.00	1.25
❑	104	Gale Sayers	5.00	2.00
❑	105	Mike Singletary	4.00	1.50
❑	106	Boomer Esiason	3.00	1.25
❑	107	Cris Collinsworth	3.00	1.25
❑	108	Ickey Woods	2.50	1.00
❑	109	Jim Brown	6.00	2.50
❑	110	Leroy Kelly	3.00	1.25
❑	111	Ozzie Newsome	3.00	1.25
❑	112	Paul Warfield	3.00	1.25
❑	113	Deion Sanders	4.00	1.50
❑	114	Herschel Walker	3.00	1.25
❑	115	Mike Ditka	4.00	1.50
❑	116	Michael Irvin	4.00	1.50
❑	117	Roger Staubach	6.00	2.50
❑	118	Tony Dorsett	4.00	1.50
❑	119	Troy Aikman	5.00	2.00
❑	120	John Elway	6.00	2.50
❑	121	Barry Sanders	6.00	2.50
❑	122	Bart Starr	6.00	2.50
❑	123	Paul Hornung	4.00	1.50
❑	124	Sterling Sharpe	3.00	1.25
❑	125	Warren Moon	4.00	1.50
❑	126	Christian Okoye	3.00	1.25
❑	127	Marcus Allen	4.00	1.50
❑	128	Deacon Jones	3.00	1.25
❑	129	Bob Griese	4.00	1.50
❑	130	Dan Marino	8.00	3.00
❑	131	Fran Tarkenton	5.00	2.00
❑	132	Y.A. Tittle	4.00	1.50
❑	133	Don Maynard	3.00	1.25
❑	134	Joe Namath	5.00	2.00
❑	135	Jim Plunkett	3.00	1.25
❑	136	Bo Jackson	5.00	2.00
❑	137	Herman Edwards	3.00	1.25
❑	138	Randall Cunningham	3.00	1.25
❑	139	Franco Harris	5.00	2.00
❑	140	Jack Lambert	5.00	2.00
❑	141	Joe Greene	4.00	1.50
❑	142	L.C. Greenwood	3.00	1.25
❑	143	Terry Bradshaw	6.00	2.50
❑	144	Dan Fouts	4.00	1.50
❑	145	Joe Montana	10.00	4.00
❑	146	John Taylor	3.00	1.25
❑	147	Roger Craig	4.00	1.50
❑	148	Steve Young	5.00	2.00
❑	149	Steve Largent	4.00	1.50
❑	150	Sonny Jurgensen	3.00	1.25
❑	151	Adam Jones RC	5.00	2.00
❑	152	Antrel Rolle RC	5.00	2.00
❑	153	Carlos Rogers RC	6.00	2.50
❑	154	DeMarcus Ware RC	8.00	3.00
❑	155	Shawne Merriman RC	8.00	3.00
❑	156	Thomas Davis RC	5.00	2.00
❑	157	Derrick Johnson RC	8.00	3.00
❑	158	Travis Johnson RC	4.00	1.50
❑	159	David Pollack RC	6.00	2.50
❑	160	Erasmus James RC	6.00	2.50
❑	161	Marcus Spears RC	6.00	2.50
❑	162	Fabian Washington RC	5.00	2.00
❑	163	Luis Castillo RC	5.00	2.00
❑	164	Marlin Jackson RC	5.00	2.00
❑	165	Mike Patterson RC	5.00	2.00
❑	166	Brodney Pool RC	5.00	2.00
❑	167	Barrett Ruud RC	5.00	2.00
❑	168	Shaun Cody RC	5.00	2.00
❑	169	Stanford Routt RC	4.00	1.50
❑	170	Josh Bullocks RC	5.00	2.00
❑	171	Kevin Burnett RC	5.00	2.00
❑	172	Corey Webster RC	5.00	2.00
❑	173	Lofa Tatupu RC	6.00	2.50
❑	174	Justin Miller RC	4.00	1.50
❑	175	Odell Thurman RC	4.00	1.50
❑	176	Heath Miller RC	15.00	6.00
❑	177	Vernand Morency RC	6.00	2.50
❑	178	Ryan Moats RC	6.00	2.50
❑	179	Courtney Roby RC	6.00	2.50
❑	180	Alex Smith TE RC	6.00	2.50
❑	181	Kevin Everett RC	6.00	2.50
❑	182	Brandon Jones RC	6.00	2.50
❑	183	Maurice Clarett	6.00	2.50
❑	184	Marion Barber RC	10.00	4.00
❑	185	Brandon Jacobs RC	8.00	3.00
❑	186	Matt Cassel RC	15.00	6.00
❑	187	Stefan LeFors RC	6.00	2.50
❑	188	Alvin Pearman RC	6.00	2.50
❑	189	James Kilian RC	6.00	2.50
❑	190	Airese Currie RC	6.00	2.50
❑	191	Damien Nash RC	5.00	2.00
❑	192	Dan Orlovsky RC	8.00	3.00
❑	193	Larry Brackins RC	3.00	1.25
❑	194	Rasheed Marshall RC	6.00	2.50
❑	195	Marcus Maxwell RC	5.00	2.00
❑	196	LeRon McCoy RC	5.00	2.00
❑	197	Harry Williams RC	5.00	2.00
❑	198	Noah Herron RC	6.00	2.50
❑	199	Tab Perry RC	6.00	2.50
❑	200	Chad Owens RC	6.00	2.50
❑	201	Alex Smith QB RC	25.00	10.00
❑	202	Ronnie Brown RC	20.00	7.50
❑	203	Braylon Edwards RC	20.00	7.50
❑	204	Cedric Benson RC	12.00	5.00
❑	205	Carnell Williams RC	30.00	12.50
❑	206	Troy Williamson RC	12.00	5.00
❑	207	Mike Williams	12.00	5.00
❑	208	Matt Jones RC	15.00	6.00
❑	209	Mark Clayton RC	6.00	2.50
❑	210	Aaron Rodgers RC	20.00	7.50
❑	211	Jason Campbell RC	10.00	4.00
❑	212	Roddy White RC	6.00	2.50
❑	213	Reggie Brown RC	6.00	2.50
❑	214	Mark Bradley RC	6.00	2.50
❑	215	J.J. Arrington RC	8.00	3.00
❑	216	Eric Shelton RC	6.00	2.50
❑	217	Roscoe Parrish RC	6.00	2.50
❑	218	Terrence Murphy RC	6.00	2.50
❑	219	Vincent Jackson RC	6.00	2.50

❑ 220 Frank Gore RC 10.00 4.00
❑ 221 Charlie Frye RC 12.00 5.00
❑ 222 Andrew Walter RC 10.00 4.00
❑ 223 David Greene RC 6.00 2.50
❑ 224 Kyle Orton RC 10.00 4.00
❑ 225 Ciatrick Fason RC 5.00 2.00
❑ 226 Cedric Houston AU RC EXCH 15.00 6.00
❑ 227 Dante Ridgeway AU RC 12.00 5.00
❑ 228 Craig Bragg AU RC 12.00 5.00
❑ 229 Deandra Cobb AU RC 10.00 4.00
❑ 230 Derek Anderson AU RC 15.00 6.00
❑ 231 Paris Warren AU RC 12.00 5.00
❑ 232 Lionel Gates AU RC 12.00 5.00
❑ 233 Anthony Davis AU RC 12.00 5.00
❑ 234 Ryan Fitzpatrick AU RC 25.00 12.50
❑ 235 J.R. Russell AU RC 12.00 5.00
❑ 236 Dan Cody AU RC 15.00 6.00
❑ 237 Bryant McFadden AU RC 20.00 7.50
❑ 238 Adrian McPherson AU RC 20.00 7.50
❑ 239 Chris Henry AU RC 15.00 6.00
❑ 240 Craphonso Thorpe AU RC 12.00 5.00
❑ 241 Darren Sproles AU RC EXCH 15.00 6.00
❑ 242 Fred Gibson AU RC EXCH 12.00 5.00
❑ 243 Jerome Mathis AU RC 15.00 6.00
❑ 244 Josh Davis AU RC 12.00 5.00
❑ 245 Kay-Jay Harris AU RC 12.00 5.00
❑ 246 Matt Roth AU RC 20.00 7.50
❑ 247 Roydell Williams AU RC 15.00 6.00
❑ 248 Steve Savoy AU RC 10.00 4.00
❑ 249 T.A. McLendon AU RC 10.00 4.00
❑ 250 Taylor Stubblefield AU RC 10.00 4.00

1999 Donruss Elite

❑ COMPLETE SET (200) 100.00 40.00
❑ COMP.SET w/o SP's (160) 30.00 15.00
❑ 1 Warren Moon 1.25 .50
❑ 2 Terry Allen .75 .30
❑ 3 Jeff George .75 .30
❑ 4 Brett Favre 4.00 1.50
❑ 5 Rob Moore .75 .30
❑ 6 Bubby Brister .50 .20
❑ 7 John Elway 4.00 1.50
❑ 8 Troy Aikman 2.50 1.00
❑ 9 Steve McNair 1.25 .50
❑ 10 Charlie Batch 1.25 .50
❑ 11 Elvis Grbac .75 .30
❑ 12 Trent Dilfer .75 .30
❑ 13 Kerry Collins .75 .30
❑ 14 Neil O'Donnell .50 .20
❑ 15 Tony Simmons .50 .20
❑ 16 Ryan Leaf 1.25 .50
❑ 17 Bobby Hoying .75 .30
❑ 18 Marvin Harrison 1.25 .50
❑ 19 Keyshawn Johnson 1.25 .50
❑ 20 Cris Carter 1.25 .50
❑ 21 Deion Sanders 1.25 .50
❑ 22 Emmitt Smith 2.50 1.00
❑ 23 Antowain Smith 1.25 .50
❑ 24 Terry Fair .50 .20
❑ 25 Robert Holcombe .50 .20
❑ 26 Napoleon Kaufman 1.25 .50
❑ 27 Eddie George 1.25 .50
❑ 28 Corey Dillon 1.25 .50
❑ 29 Adrian Murrell .75 .30
❑ 30 Charles Way .50 .20
❑ 31 Amp Lee .50 .20
❑ 32 Ricky Watters .75 .30
❑ 33 Gary Brown .50 .20
❑ 34 Thurman Thomas .75 .30
❑ 35 Pat Johnson .50 .20
❑ 36 Jerome Bettis 1.25 .50
❑ 37 Muhsin Muhammad .75 .30
❑ 38 Kimble Anders .75 .30
❑ 39 Curtis Enis .50 .20
❑ 40 Mike Alstott 1.25 .50
❑ 41 Charles Johnson .50 .20
❑ 42 Chris Warren .50 .20
❑ 43 Tony Banks .75 .30
❑ 44 Leroy Hoard .50 .20
❑ 45 Chris Fuamatu-Ma'afala .50 .20
❑ 46 Michael Irvin 1.25 .50
❑ 47 Robert Edwards .50 .20
❑ 48 Hines Ward 1.25 .50
❑ 49 Trent Green 1.25 .50
❑ 50 Eric Zeier .50 .20
❑ 51 Sean Dawkins .50 .20
❑ 52 Yancey Thigpen .50 .20
❑ 53 Jacquez Green .50 .20
❑ 54 Zach Thomas 1.25 .50
❑ 55 Junior Seau 1.25 .50
❑ 56 Darnay Scott .50 .20
❑ 57 Kent Graham .50 .20
❑ 58 O.J. Santiago .50 .20
❑ 59 Tony Gonzalez 1.25 .50
❑ 60 Ty Detmer .50 .20
❑ 61 Albert Connell .50 .20
❑ 62 James Jett .75 .30
❑ 63 Bert Emanuel .75 .30
❑ 64 Derrick Alexander WR .75 .30
❑ 65 Wesley Walls .75 .30
❑ 66 Jake Reed .75 .30
❑ 67 Randall Cunningham 1.25 .50
❑ 68 Leslie Shepherd .50 .20
❑ 69 Mark Chmura .50 .20
❑ 70 Bobby Engram .75 .30
❑ 71 Rickey Dudley .50 .20
❑ 72 Darick Holmes .50 .20
❑ 73 Andre Reed .75 .30
❑ 74 Az-Zahir Hakim .50 .20
❑ 75 Cameron Cleeland .50 .20
❑ 76 Lamar Thomas .50 .20
❑ 77 Oronde Gadsden .75 .30
❑ 78 Ben Coates .75 .30
❑ 79 Bruce Smith .75 .30
❑ 80 Jerry Rice 2.50 1.00
❑ 81 Tim Brown 1.25 .50
❑ 82 Michael Westbrook .75 .30
❑ 83 J.J. Stokes .75 .30
❑ 84 Shannon Sharpe .75 .30
❑ 85 Reidel Anthony .75 .30
❑ 86 Antonio Freeman 1.25 .50
❑ 87 Keenan McCardell .75 .30
❑ 88 Terry Glenn 1.25 .50
❑ 89 Andre Rison .75 .30
❑ 90 Neil Smith .75 .30
❑ 91 Terrance Mathis .75 .30
❑ 92 Rocket Ismail .75 .30
❑ 93 Byron Bam Morris .50 .20
❑ 94 Ike Hilliard .50 .20
❑ 95 Eddie Kennison .75 .30
❑ 96 Tavian Banks .50 .20
❑ 97 Yatil Green .50 .20
❑ 98 Frank Wycheck .50 .20
❑ 99 Warren Sapp .50 .20
❑ 100 Germane Crowell .50 .20
❑ 101 Curtis Martin 2.50 1.00
❑ 102 John Avery 1.00 .40
❑ 103 Eric Moulds 2.50 1.00
❑ 104 Randy Moss 8.00 3.00
❑ 105 Terrell Owens 2.50 1.00
❑ 106 Vinny Testaverde 1.50 .60
❑ 107 Doug Flutie 1.25 .50
❑ 108 Mark Brunell 1.25 .50
❑ 109 Isaac Bruce 2.50 1.00
❑ 110 Kordell Stewart 1.50 .60
❑ 111 Drew Bledsoe 3.00 1.25
❑ 112 Chris Chandler 1.50 .60
❑ 113 Dan Marino 8.00 3.00
❑ 114 Brian Griese 2.50 1.00
❑ 115 Carl Pickens 1.50 .60
❑ 116 Jake Plummer 1.50 .60
❑ 117 Natrone Means 1.50 .60
❑ 118 Peyton Manning 10.00 4.00
❑ 119 Garrison Hearst 2.50 1.00
❑ 120 Barry Sanders 8.00 3.00
❑ 121 Steve Young 3.00 1.25
❑ 122 Rashaan Shehee 1.00 .40
❑ 123 Ed McCaffrey 1.50 .60
❑ 124 Charles Woodson 2.50 1.00
❑ 125 Dorsey Levens 2.50 1.00
❑ 126 Robert Smith 2.50 1.00
❑ 127 Greg Hill 1.00 .40
❑ 128 Fred Taylor 2.50 1.00
❑ 129 Marcus Nash 1.00 .40
❑ 130 Terrell Davis 2.50 1.00
❑ 131 Ahman Green 2.50 1.00
❑ 132 Jamal Anderson 2.50 1.00
❑ 133 Karim Abdul-Jabbar 1.50 .60
❑ 134 Jermaine Lewis 1.50 .60
❑ 135 Jerome Pathon 1.50 .60
❑ 136 Brad Johnson 2.50 1.00
❑ 137 Herman Moore 1.50 .60
❑ 138 Tim Dwight 2.50 1.00
❑ 139 Johnnie Morton 1.00 .40
❑ 140 Marshall Faulk 3.00 1.25
❑ 141 Frank Sanders 1.50 .60
❑ 142 Kevin Dyson 1.50 .60
❑ 143 Curtis Conway 1.50 .60
❑ 144 Derrick Mayes 1.00 .40
❑ 145 O.J. McDuffie 1.50 .60
❑ 146 Joe Jurevicius 1.50 .60
❑ 147 Jon Kitna 2.50 1.00
❑ 148 Joey Galloway 1.50 .60
❑ 149 Jimmy Smith 1.50 .60
❑ 150 Skip Hicks 1.00 .40
❑ 151 Rod Smith 1.50 .60
❑ 152 Duce Staley 2.50 1.00
❑ 153 James Stewart 1.00 .40
❑ 154 Rob Johnson 1.50 .60
❑ 155 Mikhael Ricks 1.00 .40
❑ 156 Wayne Chrebet 1.50 .60
❑ 157 Robert Brooks 1.50 .60
❑ 158 Tim Biakabutuka 1.50 .60
❑ 159 Priest Holmes 4.00 1.25
❑ 160 Warrick Dunn 2.50 1.00
❑ 161 Champ Bailey RC 5.00 2.00
❑ 162 D'Wayne Bates RC 2.50 1.00
❑ 163 Michael Bishop RC 3.00 1.25
❑ 164 David Boston RC 3.00 1.25
❑ 165 Na Brown RC 2.50 1.00
❑ 166 Chris Claiborne RC 1.50 .60
❑ 167 Joe Montgomery RC 2.50 1.00
❑ 168 Mike Cloud RC 2.50 1.00
❑ 169 Travis McGriff RC 1.50 .60
❑ 170 Tim Couch RC 3.00 1.25
❑ 171 Daunte Culpepper RC 12.00 5.00
❑ 172 Autry Denson RC 2.50 1.00
❑ 173 Jermaine Fazande RC 2.50 1.00
❑ 174 Troy Edwards RC 2.50 1.00
❑ 175 Kevin Faulk RC 3.00 1.25
❑ 176 Dee Miller RC 1.50 .60
❑ 177 Brock Huard RC 3.00 1.25
❑ 178 Torry Holt RC 8.00 3.00
❑ 179 Sedrick Irvin RC 1.50 .60
❑ 180 Edgerrin James RC 12.00 5.00
❑ 181 Joe Germaine RC 2.50 1.00
❑ 182 James Johnson RC 2.50 1.00
❑ 183 Kevin Johnson RC 2.50 1.00
❑ 184 Andy Katzenmoyer RC 2.50 1.00
❑ 185 Jevon Kearse RC 6.00 2.50
❑ 186 Shaun King RC 2.50 1.00
❑ 187 Rob Konrad RC 3.00 1.25
❑ 188 Jim Kleinsasser RC 3.00 1.25
❑ 189 Chris McAlister RC 2.50 1.00

- ❑ 190 Donovan McNabb RC 15.00 6.00
- ❑ 191 Cade McNown RC 2.50 1.00
- ❑ 192 De'Mond Parker RC 1.00 .40
- ❑ 193 Craig Yeast RC 2.50 1.00
- ❑ 194 Shawn Bryson RC 3.00 1.25
- ❑ 195 Peerless Price RC 3.00 1.25
- ❑ 196 Darnell McDonald RC 2.50 1.00
- ❑ 197 Akili Smith RC 1.50 .60
- ❑ 198 Tai Streets RC 3.00 1.25
- ❑ 199 Ricky Williams RC 6.00 2.50
- ❑ 200 Amos Zereoue RC 2.50 1.00

2000 Donruss Elite

- ❑ COMPLETE SET (200) 500.00 300.00
- ❑ 1 Jake Plummer .50 .20
- ❑ 2 David Boston .75 .30
- ❑ 3 Rob Moore .50 .20
- ❑ 4 Chris Chandler .50 .20
- ❑ 5 Tim Dwight .75 .30
- ❑ 6 Terance Mathis .50 .20
- ❑ 7 Jamal Anderson .75 .30
- ❑ 8 Priest Holmes 1.00 .40
- ❑ 9 Tony Banks .50 .20
- ❑ 10 Shannon Sharpe .50 .20
- ❑ 11 Qadry Ismail .50 .20
- ❑ 12 Eric Moulds .75 .30
- ❑ 13 Doug Flutie .75 .30
- ❑ 14 Antowain Smith .50 .20
- ❑ 15 Peerless Price .50 .20
- ❑ 16 Muhsin Muhammad .50 .20
- ❑ 17 Tim Biakabutuka .50 .20
- ❑ 18 Patrick Jeffers .75 .30
- ❑ 19 Steve Beuerlein .50 .20
- ❑ 20 Wesley Walls .30 .10
- ❑ 21 Curtis Enis .30 .10
- ❑ 22 Marcus Robinson .75 .30
- ❑ 23 Carl Pickens .50 .20
- ❑ 24 Corey Dillon .75 .30
- ❑ 25 Akili Smith .30 .10
- ❑ 26 Darnay Scott .50 .20
- ❑ 27 Kevin Johnson .75 .30
- ❑ 28 Errict Rhett .50 .20
- ❑ 29 Emmitt Smith 1.50 .60
- ❑ 30 Deion Sanders .75 .30
- ❑ 31 Troy Aikman 1.50 .60
- ❑ 32 Joey Galloway .50 .20
- ❑ 33 Michael Irvin .50 .20
- ❑ 34 Rocket Ismail .50 .20
- ❑ 35 Jason Tucker .30 .10
- ❑ 36 Ed McCaffrey .75 .30
- ❑ 37 Rod Smith .50 .20
- ❑ 38 Brian Griese .75 .30
- ❑ 39 Terrell Davis .75 .30
- ❑ 40 Olandis Gary .75 .30
- ❑ 41 Charlie Batch .75 .30
- ❑ 42 Johnnie Morton .50 .20
- ❑ 43 Herman Moore .50 .20
- ❑ 44 James Stewart .50 .20
- ❑ 45 Dorsey Levens .50 .20
- ❑ 46 Antonio Freeman .75 .30
- ❑ 47 Brett Favre 2.50 1.00
- ❑ 48 Bill Schroeder .50 .20
- ❑ 49 Peyton Manning 2.00 .75
- ❑ 50 Keenan McCardell .50 .20
- ❑ 51 Fred Taylor .75 .30
- ❑ 52 Jimmy Smith .50 .20
- ❑ 53 Elvis Grbac .50 .20
- ❑ 54 Tony Gonzalez .50 .20
- ❑ 55 Derrick Alexander .50 .20
- ❑ 56 Dan Marino 2.50 1.00
- ❑ 57 Tony Martin .50 .20
- ❑ 58 James Johnson .30 .10
- ❑ 59 Damon Huard .75 .30
- ❑ 60 Thurman Thomas .50 .20
- ❑ 61 Robert Smith .75 .30
- ❑ 62 Randall Cunningham .75 .30
- ❑ 63 Jeff George .50 .20
- ❑ 64 Terry Glenn .50 .20
- ❑ 65 Drew Bledsoe 1.00 .40
- ❑ 66 Jeff Blake .50 .20
- ❑ 67 Amani Toomer .50 .20
- ❑ 68 Kerry Collins .50 .20
- ❑ 69 Joe Montgomery .30 .10
- ❑ 70 Vinny Testaverde .50 .20
- ❑ 71 Ray Lucas .50 .20
- ❑ 72 Keyshawn Johnson .75 .30
- ❑ 73 Wayne Chrebet .50 .20
- ❑ 74 Napoleon Kaufman .50 .20
- ❑ 75 Tim Brown .75 .30
- ❑ 76 Rich Gannon .75 .30
- ❑ 77 Duce Staley .75 .30
- ❑ 78 Kordell Stewart .50 .20
- ❑ 79 Jerome Bettis .75 .30
- ❑ 80 Troy Edwards .30 .10
- ❑ 81 Natrone Means .30 .10
- ❑ 82 Curtis Conway .50 .20
- ❑ 83 Jim Harbaugh .50 .20
- ❑ 84 Junior Seau .75 .30
- ❑ 85 Jermaine Fazande .30 .10
- ❑ 86 Terrell Owens .75 .30
- ❑ 87 Charlie Garner .50 .20
- ❑ 88 Steve Young 1.00 .40
- ❑ 89 Jeff Garcia .75 .30
- ❑ 90 Derrick Mayes .50 .20
- ❑ 91 Ricky Watters .50 .20
- ❑ 92 Az-Zahir Hakim .50 .20
- ❑ 93 Torry Holt .75 .30
- ❑ 94 Warren Sapp .50 .20
- ❑ 95 Mike Alstott .75 .30
- ❑ 96 Warrick Dunn .75 .30
- ❑ 97 Kevin Dyson .50 .20
- ❑ 98 Bruce Smith .50 .20
- ❑ 99 Albert Connell .30 .10
- ❑ 100 Michael Westbrook .50 .20
- ❑ 101 Cade McNown .30 .10
- ❑ 102 Tim Couch 2.00 .75
- ❑ 103 John Elway 6.00 2.50
- ❑ 104 Barry Sanders 5.00 2.00
- ❑ 105 Germane Crowell 1.25 .50
- ❑ 106 Marvin Harrison 2.00 .75
- ❑ 107 Edgerrin James 3.00 1.25
- ❑ 108 Mark Brunell 2.00 .75
- ❑ 109 Randy Moss 4.00 1.50
- ❑ 110 Cris Carter 2.00 .75
- ❑ 111 Daunte Culpepper 2.50 1.00
- ❑ 112 Ricky Williams .75 .30
- ❑ 113 Curtis Martin 2.00 .75
- ❑ 114 Donovan McNabb 3.00 1.25
- ❑ 115 Jerry Rice 4.00 1.50
- ❑ 116 Jon Kitna 2.00 .75
- ❑ 117 Isaac Bruce 2.00 .75
- ❑ 118 Marshall Faulk 2.50 1.00
- ❑ 119 Kurt Warner 4.00 1.50
- ❑ 120 Shaun King .30 .10
- ❑ 121 Eddie George 2.00 .75
- ❑ 122 Steve McNair 2.00 .75
- ❑ 123 Jevon Kearse 2.00 .75
- ❑ 124 Stephen Davis 2.00 .75
- ❑ 125 Brad Johnson 2.00 .75
- ❑ 126 Mike Anderson RC 2.50 1.00
- ❑ 127 Peter Warrick RC 5.00 2.00
- ❑ 128 Courtney Brown RC 2.00 .75
- ❑ 129 Plaxico Burress RC 10.00 4.00
- ❑ 130 Corey Simon RC 5.00 2.00
- ❑ 131 Thomas Jones RC 8.00 3.00
- ❑ 132 Travis Taylor RC 2.00 .75
- ❑ 133 Shaun Alexander RC 25.00 10.00
- ❑ 134 Deon Grant RC 4.00 1.50
- ❑ 135 Chris Redman RC 4.00 1.50
- ❑ 136 Chad Pennington RC 12.00 5.00
- ❑ 137 Jamal Lewis RC 12.00 5.00
- ❑ 138 Brian Urlacher RC 20.00 7.50
- ❑ 139 Keith Bulluck RC 5.00 2.00
- ❑ 140 Bubba Franks RC 5.00 2.00
- ❑ 141 Dez White RC 5.00 2.00
- ❑ 142 Na'il Diggs RC 4.00 1.50
- ❑ 143 Ahmed Plummer RC 5.00 2.00
- ❑ 144 Ron Dayne RC 5.00 2.00
- ❑ 145 Shaun Ellis RC 5.00 2.00
- ❑ 146 Sylvester Morris RC 4.00 1.50
- ❑ 147 Deltha O'Neal RC 5.00 2.00
- ❑ 148 Raynoch Thompson RC 4.00 1.50
- ❑ 149 R.Jay Soward RC 4.00 1.50
- ❑ 150 Mario Edwards RC 4.00 1.50
- ❑ 151 John Engelberger RC 4.00 1.50
- ❑ 152 Dwayne Goodrich RC 5.00 2.00
- ❑ 153 Sherrod Gideon RC 2.50 1.00
- ❑ 154 John Abraham RC 5.00 2.00
- ❑ 155 Ben Kelly RC 5.00 2.00
- ❑ 156 Travis Prentice RC 4.00 1.50
- ❑ 157 Darrell Jackson RC 10.00 4.00
- ❑ 158 Giovanni Carmazzi RC 2.50 1.00
- ❑ 159 Anthony Lucas RC 2.50 1.00
- ❑ 160 Danny Farmer RC 4.00 1.50
- ❑ 161 Dennis Northcutt RC 5.00 2.00
- ❑ 162 Troy Walters RC 5.00 2.00
- ❑ 163 Laveranues Coles RC 6.00 2.50
- ❑ 164 Tee Martin RC 5.00 2.00
- ❑ 165 J.R. Redmond RC 4.00 1.50
- ❑ 166 Tim Rattay RC 5.00 2.00
- ❑ 167 Jerry Porter RC 6.00 2.50
- ❑ 168 Sebastian Janikowski RC 5.00 2.00
- ❑ 169 Michael Wiley RC 4.00 1.50
- ❑ 170 Reuben Droughns RC 6.00 2.50
- ❑ 171 Trung Canidate RC 4.00 1.50
- ❑ 172 Shyrone Stith RC 5.00 2.00
- ❑ 173 Chris Hovan RC 4.00 1.50
- ❑ 174 Brandon Short RC 5.00 2.00
- ❑ 175 Mark Roman RC 4.00 1.50
- ❑ 176 Trevor Gaylor RC 4.00 1.50
- ❑ 177 Chris Cole RC 4.00 1.50
- ❑ 178 Hank Poteat RC 4.00 1.50
- ❑ 179 Darren Howard RC 4.00 1.50
- ❑ 180 Rob Morris RC 5.00 2.00
- ❑ 181 Spergon Wynn RC 4.00 1.50
- ❑ 182 Marc Bulger RC 10.00 5.00
- ❑ 183 Tom Brady RC 60.00 35.00
- ❑ 184 Todd Husak RC 5.00 2.00
- ❑ 185 Gari Scott RC 2.50 1.00
- ❑ 186 Erron Kinney RC 4.00 1.50
- ❑ 187 Julian Peterson RC 5.00 2.00
- ❑ 188 Sammy Morris RC 4.00 1.50
- ❑ 189 Rondell Mealey RC 2.50 1.00
- ❑ 190 Doug Chapman RC 4.00 1.50
- ❑ 191 Ron Dugans RC 2.50 1.00
- ❑ 192 Deon Dyer RC 4.00 1.50
- ❑ 193 Fred Robbins RC 2.50 1.00
- ❑ 194 Ike Charlton RC 5.00 2.00
- ❑ 195 Mareno Philyaw RC 2.50 1.00
- ❑ 196 Thomas Hamner RC 2.50 1.00
- ❑ 197 Jarious Jackson RC 4.00 1.50
- ❑ 198 Anthony Becht RC 5.00 2.00
- ❑ 199 Joe Hamilton RC 4.00 1.50
- ❑ 200 Todd Pinkston RC 5.00 2.00

2001 Donruss Elite

- ❑ COMP.SET w/o SP's (100) 20.00 7.50
- ❑ 1 David Boston .60 .25
- ❑ 2 Jake Plummer .40 .15
- ❑ 3 Thomas Jones .40 .15
- ❑ 4 Jamal Anderson .60 .25
- ❑ 5 Chris Redman .25 .08
- ❑ 6 Jamal Lewis 1.00 .40
- ❑ 7 Shannon Sharpe .40 .15

❑	8 Travis Taylor	.40	.15
❑	9 Trent Dilfer	.40	.15
❑	10 Doug Flutie	.60	.25
❑	11 Eric Moulds	.40	.15
❑	12 Rob Johnson	.40	.15
❑	13 Muhsin Muhammad	.40	.15
❑	14 Steve Beuerlein	.25	.08
❑	15 Brian Urlacher	1.00	.40
❑	16 Cade McNown	.25	.08
❑	17 Marcus Robinson	.60	.25
❑	18 Akili Smith	.25	.08
❑	19 Corey Dillon	.60	.25
❑	20 Peter Warrick	.60	.25
❑	21 Kevin Johnson	.40	.15
❑	22 Tim Couch	.40	.15
❑	23 Emmitt Smith	1.25	.50
❑	24 Troy Aikman	1.00	.40
❑	25 Brian Griese	.60	.25
❑	26 John Elway	2.00	.75
❑	27 Mike Anderson	.60	.25
❑	28 Rod Smith	.40	.15
❑	29 Terrell Davis	.60	.25
❑	30 Barry Sanders	1.25	.50
❑	31 Charlie Batch	.60	.25
❑	32 James Stewart	.40	.15
❑	33 Ahman Green	.60	.25
❑	34 Antonio Freeman	.60	.25
❑	35 Brett Favre	2.00	.75
❑	36 Edgerrin James	.75	.30
❑	37 Marvin Harrison	.60	.25
❑	38 Peyton Manning	1.50	.60
❑	39 Fred Taylor	.60	.25
❑	40 Jimmy Smith	.40	.15
❑	41 Keenan McCardell	.25	.08
❑	42 Mark Brunell	.60	.25
❑	43 Derrick Alexander	.40	.15
❑	44 Elvis Grbac	.40	.15
❑	45 Sylvester Morris	.25	.08
❑	46 Tony Gonzalez	.40	.15
❑	47 Dan Marino	2.00	.75
❑	48 Jay Fiedler	.60	.25
❑	49 Lamar Smith	.40	.15
❑	50 Oronde Gadsden	.40	.15
❑	51 Cris Carter	.60	.25
❑	52 Daunte Culpepper	.60	.25
❑	53 Randy Moss	1.25	.50
❑	54 Robert Smith	.40	.15
❑	55 Drew Bledsoe	.75	.30
❑	56 Terry Glenn	.25	.08
❑	57 Aaron Brooks	.60	.25
❑	58 Joe Horn	.40	.15
❑	59 Ricky Williams	.60	.25
❑	60 Amani Toomer	.25	.08
❑	61 Ike Hilliard	.40	.15
❑	62 Kerry Collins	.40	.15
❑	63 Ron Dayne	.60	.25
❑	64 Tiki Barber	.60	.25
❑	65 Chad Pennington	1.00	.40
❑	66 Curtis Martin	.60	.25
❑	67 Vinny Testaverde	.40	.15
❑	68 Wayne Chrebet	.40	.15
❑	69 Rich Gannon	.60	.25
❑	70 Tim Brown	.60	.25
❑	71 Tyrone Wheatley	.40	.15
❑	72 Donovan McNabb	.75	.30
❑	73 Jerome Bettis	.60	.25
❑	74 Plaxico Burress	.60	.25
❑	75 Junior Seau	.60	.25
❑	76 Charlie Garner	.40	.15
❑	77 Jeff Garcia	.60	.25
❑	78 Jerry Rice	1.25	.50
❑	79 Terrell Owens	.60	.25
❑	80 Darrell Jackson	.60	.25
❑	81 Ricky Watters	.40	.15
❑	82 Shaun Alexander	.75	.30
❑	83 Isaac Bruce	.60	.25
❑	84 Kurt Warner	1.25	.50
❑	85 Marshall Faulk	.75	.30
❑	86 Torry Holt	.60	.25
❑	87 Trent Green	.60	.25
❑	88 Keyshawn Johnson	.60	.25
❑	89 Shaun King	.25	.08
❑	90 Warren Sapp	.40	.15
❑	91 Warrick Dunn	.60	.25
❑	92 Eddie George	.60	.25
❑	93 Jevon Kearse	.40	.15
❑	94 Steve McNair	.60	.25
❑	95 Albert Connell	.25	.08
❑	96 Jeff George	.40	.15
❑	97 Brad Johnson	.60	.25
❑	98 Bruce Smith	.25	.08
❑	99 Michael Westbrook	.40	.15
❑	100 Stephen Davis	.60	.25
❑	101 Michael Vick RC	80.00	40.00
❑	102 Drew Brees RC	30.00	12.50
❑	103 Chris Weinke RC	10.00	4.00
❑	104 Quincy Carter RC	10.00	4.00
❑	105 Sage Rosenfels RC	10.00	4.00
❑	106 Josh Heupel RC	10.00	4.00
❑	107 Tony Driver RC	6.00	2.50
❑	108 Ben Leard RC	6.00	2.50
❑	109 Marques Tuiasosopo RC	10.00	4.00
❑	110 Tim Hasselbeck RC	10.00	4.00
❑	111 Mike McMahon RC	10.00	4.00
❑	112 Deuce McAllister RC	25.00	10.00
❑	113 LaMont Jordan RC	25.00	10.00
❑	114 LaDainian Tomlinson RC	60.00	30.00
❑	115 James Jackson RC	10.00	4.00
❑	116 Anthony Thomas RC	10.00	4.00
❑	117 Travis Henry RC	10.00	4.00
❑	118 DeAngelo Evans RC	6.00	2.50
❑	119 Travis Minor RC	6.00	2.50
❑	120 Rudi Johnson RC	25.00	12.50
❑	121 Michael Bennett RC	15.00	6.00
❑	122 Kevan Barlow RC	10.00	4.00
❑	123 Dan Alexander RC	10.00	4.00
❑	124 David Allen RC	6.00	2.50
❑	125 Correll Buckhalter RC	12.00	5.00
❑	126 David Rivers RC	6.00	2.50
❑	127 Reggie White RC	6.00	2.50
❑	128 Moran Norris RC	4.00	1.50
❑	129 Ja'Mar Toombs RC	6.00	2.50
❑	130 Jason McKinley RC	6.00	2.50
❑	131 Scotty Anderson RC	6.00	2.50
❑	132 Dustin McClintock RC	10.00	4.00
❑	133 Heath Evans RC	6.00	2.50
❑	134 David Terrell RC	10.00	4.00
❑	135 Santana Moss RC	25.00	10.00
❑	136 Rod Gardner RC	10.00	4.00
❑	137 Quincy Morgan RC	10.00	4.00
❑	138 Freddie Mitchell RC	10.00	4.00
❑	139 Boo Williams RC	6.00	2.50
❑	140 Reggie Wayne RC	25.00	10.00
❑	141 Ronney Daniels RC	4.00	1.50
❑	142 Bobby Newcombe RC	6.00	2.50
❑	143 Reggie Germany/250 RC	12.00	5.00
❑	144 Jesse Palmer RC	10.00	4.00
❑	145 Robert Ferguson RC	10.00	4.00
❑	146 Ken-Yon Rambo RC	6.00	2.50
❑	147 Alex Bannister RC	6.00	2.50
❑	148 Koren Robinson RC	10.00	4.00
❑	149 Chad Johnson RC	30.00	12.50
❑	150 Chris Chambers RC	15.00	6.00
❑	151 Javon Green RC	6.00	2.50
❑	152 Snoop Minnis RC	6.00	2.50
❑	153 Vinny Sutherland RC	6.00	2.50
❑	154 Cedrick Wilson RC	10.00	4.00
❑	155 John Capel/250 RC	12.00	5.00
❑	156 T.J. Houshmandzadeh RC	10.00	4.00
❑	157 Todd Heap RC	10.00	4.00
❑	158 Alge Crumpler RC	15.00	6.00
❑	159 Jabari Holloway RC	6.00	2.50
❑	160 Marcellus Rivers RC	6.00	2.50
❑	161 Rashon Burns RC	4.00	1.50
❑	162 Tony Stewart RC	10.00	4.00
❑	163 Jevaris Johnson RC	4.00	1.50
❑	164 Jamal Reynolds RC	10.00	4.00
❑	165 Andre Carter RC	10.00	4.00
❑	166 David Warren RC	4.00	1.50
❑	167 Justin Smith RC	10.00	4.00
❑	168 Josh Booty RC	10.00	4.00
❑	169 Karon Riley RC	4.00	1.50
❑	170 Cedric Scott RC	4.00	1.50
❑	171 Kenny Smith RC	6.00	2.50
❑	172 Richard Seymour RC	10.00	4.00
❑	173 Willie Howard RC	6.00	2.50
❑	174 Markus Steele RC	6.00	2.50
❑	175 Marcus Stroud RC	10.00	4.00
❑	176 Damione Lewis RC	6.00	2.50
❑	177 Casey Hampton RC	10.00	4.00
❑	178 Ennis Davis RC	4.00	1.50
❑	179 Gerard Warren RC	.60	.25
❑	180 Tommy Polley RC	10.00	4.00
❑	181 Kendrell Bell/250 RC	50.00	25.00
❑	182 Dan Morgan RC	10.00	4.00
❑	183 Morlon Greenwood RC	6.00	2.50
❑	184 Quinton Caver/250	10.00	4.00
❑	185 Keith Adams RC	4.00	1.50
❑	186 Brian Allen RC	4.00	1.50
❑	187 Carlos Polk RC	4.00	1.50
❑	188 Torrance Marshall RC	10.00	4.00
❑	189 Jamie Winborn RC	6.00	2.50
❑	190 Jamar Fletcher RC	6.00	2.50
❑	191 Ken Lucas RC	6.00	2.50
❑	192 Fred Smoot RC	10.00	4.00
❑	193 Nate Clements RC	10.00	4.00
❑	194 Will Allen RC	6.00	2.50
❑	195 Willie Middlebrooks/250 RC	10.00	4.00
❑	196 Gary Baxter RC	6.00	2.50
❑	197 Derrick Gibson RC	6.00	2.50
❑	198 Robert Carswell/250 RC	10.00	4.00
❑	199 Hakim Akbar RC	4.00	1.50
❑	200 Adam Archuleta RC	10.00	4.00

2002 Donruss Elite

❑	COMP.SET w/o SP's (100)	20.00	7.50
❑	1 Elvis Grbac	.30	.10
❑	2 Jamal Lewis	.50	.20
❑	3 Ray Lewis	.50	.20
❑	4 Travis Henry	.50	.20
❑	5 Eric Moulds	.30	.10
❑	6 Corey Dillon	.30	.10
❑	7 Peter Warrick	.30	.10
❑	8 Tim Couch	.30	.10
❑	9 James Jackson	.20	.07
❑	10 Kevin Johnson	.30	.10
❑	11 Mike Anderson	.50	.20
❑	12 Terrell Davis	.50	.20

	No.	Player	Hi	Lo
❑	13	Brian Griese	.50	.20
❑	14	Rod Smith	.30	.10
❑	15	Marvin Harrison	.50	.20
❑	16	Reggie Wayne	.50	.20
❑	17	Dominic Rhodes	.30	.10
❑	18	Edgerrin James	.60	.25
❑	19	Mark Brunell	.50	.20
❑	20	Keenan McCardell	.20	.07
❑	21	Jimmy Smith	.30	.10
❑	22	Tony Gonzalez	.30	.10
❑	23	Trent Green	.30	.10
❑	24	Priest Holmes	.60	.25
❑	25	Snoop Minnis	.20	.07
❑	26	Chris Chambers	.50	.20
❑	27	Jay Fiedler	.30	.10
❑	28	Travis Minor	.20	.07
❑	29	Lamar Smith	.30	.10
❑	30	Tom Brady	1.25	.50
❑	31	Troy Brown	.30	.10
❑	32	Antowain Smith	.30	.10
❑	33	Laveranues Coles	.30	.10
❑	34	Curtis Martin	.50	.20
❑	35	Vinny Testaverde	.30	.10
❑	36	Wayne Chrebet	.30	.10
❑	37	Tim Brown	.50	.20
❑	38	Rich Gannon	.50	.20
❑	39	Jerry Rice	1.00	.40
❑	40	Charlie Garner	.30	.10
❑	41	Jerome Bettis	.50	.20
❑	42	Plaxico Burress	.30	.10
❑	43	Kordell Stewart	.30	.10
❑	44	Kendrell Bell	.50	.20
❑	45	Doug Flutie	.50	.20
❑	46	LaDainian Tomlinson	.75	.30
❑	47	Junior Seau	.50	.20
❑	48	Drew Brees	.50	.20
❑	49	Shaun Alexander	.60	.25
❑	50	Koren Robinson	.30	.10
❑	51	Ricky Watters	.30	.10
❑	52	Eddie George	.50	.20
❑	53	Derrick Mason	.30	.10
❑	54	Steve McNair	.50	.20
❑	55	David Boston	.50	.20
❑	56	Jake Plummer	.30	.10
❑	57	Chris Chandler	.30	.10
❑	58	Jamal Anderson	.30	.10
❑	59	Michael Vick	1.50	.60
❑	60	Wesley Walls	.20	.07
❑	61	Chris Weinke	.30	.10
❑	62	David Terrell	.50	.20
❑	63	Anthony Thomas	.30	.10
❑	64	Brian Urlacher	.75	.30
❑	65	Quincy Carter	.30	.10
❑	66	Rocket Ismail	.30	.10
❑	67	Emmitt Smith	1.25	.50
❑	68	James Stewart	.30	.10
❑	69	Germane Crowell	.20	.07
❑	70	Mike McMahon	.50	.20
❑	71	Brett Favre	1.25	.50
❑	72	Ahman Green	.50	.20
❑	73	Antonio Freeman	.50	.20
❑	74	Michael Bennett	.30	.10
❑	75	Cris Carter	.50	.20
❑	76	Daunte Culpepper	.50	.20
❑	77	Randy Moss	1.00	.40
❑	78	Aaron Brooks	.50	.20
❑	79	Deuce McAllister	.60	.25
❑	80	Ricky Williams	.50	.20
❑	81	Kerry Collins	.30	.10
❑	82	Ron Dayne	.30	.10
❑	83	Amani Toomer	.30	.10
❑	84	Correll Buckhalter	.30	.10
❑	85	James Thrash	.30	.10
❑	86	Freddie Mitchell	.30	.10
❑	87	Duce Staley	.50	.20
❑	88	Jeff Garcia	.50	.20
❑	89	Garrison Hearst	.30	.10
❑	90	Terrell Owens	.50	.20
❑	91	Isaac Bruce	.50	.20
❑	92	Marshall Faulk	.50	.20
❑	93	Torry Holt	.50	.20
❑	94	Kurt Warner	.50	.20
❑	95	Mike Alstott	.50	.20
❑	96	Brad Johnson	.30	.10
❑	97	Keyshawn Johnson	.50	.20
❑	98	Stephen Davis	.30	.10
❑	99	Rod Gardner	.30	.10
❑	100	Tony Banks	.20	.07
❑	101	David Carr RC	50.00	20.00
❑	102	Joey Harrington RC	40.00	15.00
❑	103	Rohan Davey RC	15.00	6.00
❑	104	Chad Hutchinson RC	12.00	5.00
❑	105	Patrick Ramsey RC	20.00	7.50
❑	106	Kurt Kittner RC	12.00	5.00
❑	107	Eric Crouch RC	15.00	6.00
❑	108	David Garrard RC	15.00	6.00
❑	109	Ronald Curry RC	15.00	6.00
❑	110	Zak Kustok RC	15.00	6.00
❑	111	Woody Dantzler RC	12.00	5.00
❑	112	Wes Pate RC	6.00	2.50
❑	113	Brian Westbrook RC	25.00	10.00
❑	114	Josh McCown RC	20.00	7.50
❑	115	Travis Stephens RC	12.00	5.00
❑	116	Luke Staley RC	12.00	5.00
❑	117	William Green RC	15.00	6.00
❑	118	Clinton Portis RC	50.00	20.00
❑	119	DeShaun Foster RC	15.00	6.00
❑	120	Verron Haynes RC	15.00	6.00
❑	121	T.J. Duckett RC	25.00	10.00
❑	122	Antwoine Womack RC	12.00	5.00
❑	123	Leonard Henry RC	12.00	5.00
❑	124	Lamar Gordon RC	15.00	6.00
❑	125	Adrian Peterson RC	15.00	6.00
❑	126	Chester Taylor RC	15.00	6.00
❑	127	Damien Anderson RC	12.00	5.00
❑	128	Maurice Morris RC	15.00	6.00
❑	129	Ricky Williams RC	12.00	5.00
❑	130	Terry Charles RC	12.00	5.00
❑	131	Demontray Carter RC	6.00	2.50
❑	132	Jason McAddley RC	12.00	5.00
❑	133	Ladell Betts RC	15.00	6.00
❑	134	Cortlen Johnson RC	6.00	2.50
❑	135	James Mungro RC	15.00	6.00
❑	136	Atrews Bell RC	6.00	2.50
❑	137	Josh Scobey RC	15.00	6.00
❑	138	Justin Peelle RC	6.00	2.50
❑	139	Najeh Davenport RC	15.00	6.00
❑	140	Josh Reed RC	15.00	6.00
❑	141	Marquise Walker RC	12.00	5.00
❑	142	Jabar Gaffney RC	15.00	6.00
❑	143	Antwaan Randle El RC	25.00	10.00
❑	144	Ashley Lelie RC	30.00	12.50
❑	145	Tavon Mason RC	6.00	2.50
❑	146	Antonio Bryant RC	15.00	6.00
❑	147	Javon Walker RC	30.00	12.50
❑	148	Kelly Campbell RC	12.00	5.00
❑	149	Ron Johnson RC	12.00	5.00
❑	150	Andre Davis RC	12.00	5.00
❑	151	Cliff Russell RC	12.00	5.00
❑	152	Reche Caldwell RC	15.00	6.00
❑	153	Kyle Johnson RC	6.00	2.50
❑	154	Freddie Milons RC	12.00	5.00
❑	155	Brian Poli-Dixon RC	12.00	5.00
❑	156	David Thornton RC	6.00	2.50
❑	157	Bryan Thomas RC	12.00	5.00
❑	158	Kahlil Hill RC	12.00	5.00
❑	159	Deion Branch RC	25.00	12.50
❑	160	Akin Ayodele RC	6.00	2.50
❑	161	Donte Stallworth RC	30.00	12.50
❑	162	Tim Carter RC	12.00	5.00
❑	163	Kenyon Coleman RC	6.00	2.50
❑	164	Jeremy Shockey RC	40.00	15.00
❑	165	Eddie Freeman RC	6.00	2.50
❑	166	Tracey Wistrom RC	12.00	5.00
❑	167	Daniel Graham RC	15.00	6.00
❑	168	Julius Peppers RC	30.00	12.50
❑	169	Alex Brown RC	15.00	6.00
❑	170	Dwight Freeney RC	20.00	7.50
❑	171	Kalimba Edwards RC	15.00	6.00
❑	172	Dennis Johnson RC	6.00	2.50
❑	173	Travis Fisher RC	15.00	6.00
❑	174	John Henderson RC	15.00	6.00
❑	175	Anthony Weaver RC	12.00	5.00
❑	176	Ryan Sims RC	15.00	6.00
❑	177	Alan Harper RC	6.00	2.50
❑	178	Larry Tripplett RC	6.00	2.50
❑	179	Wendell Bryant RC	6.00	2.50
❑	180	Albert Haynesworth RC	12.00	5.00
❑	181	Levar Fisher RC	6.00	2.50
❑	182	Andra Davis RC	12.00	5.00
❑	183	Joseph Jefferson RC	12.00	5.00
❑	184	Lamont Thompson RC	12.00	5.00
❑	185	Robert Thomas RC	15.00	6.00
❑	186	Michael Lewis RC	15.00	6.00
❑	187	Rocky Calmus RC	15.00	6.00
❑	188	Napoleon Harris RC	15.00	6.00
❑	189	Lito Sheppard RC	15.00	6.00
❑	190	Quentin Jammer RC	15.00	6.00
❑	191	Roy Williams RC	40.00	20.00
❑	192	Marques Anderson RC	15.00	6.00
❑	193	Chris Hope RC	15.00	6.00
❑	194	Raonall Smith RC	12.00	5.00
❑	195	Mike Rumph RC	15.00	6.00
❑	196	James Allen RC	6.00	2.50
❑	197	Ed Reed RC	25.00	12.50
❑	198	Mike Williams RC	12.00	5.00
❑	199	Phillip Buchanon RC	15.00	6.00
❑	200	Bryant McKinnie RC	12.00	5.00

2003 Donruss Elite

	No.	Player	Hi	Lo
❑		COMP.SET w/o SP's (100)	20.00	7.50
❑	1	Jamal Lewis	.50	.20
❑	2	Ray Lewis	.50	.20
❑	3	Todd Heap	.30	.10
❑	4	Drew Bledsoe	.50	.20
❑	5	Travis Henry	.30	.10
❑	6	Eric Moulds	.30	.10
❑	7	Peerless Price	.30	.10
❑	8	Jon Kitna	.30	.10
❑	9	Corey Dillon	.30	.10
❑	10	Chad Johnson	.50	.20
❑	11	Tim Couch	.20	.08
❑	12	William Green	.30	.10
❑	13	Andre Davis	.20	.08
❑	14	Brian Griese	.50	.20
❑	15	Ashley Lelie	.50	.20
❑	16	Clinton Portis	.75	.30
❑	17	Rod Smith	.30	.10
❑	18	David Carr	.75	.30
❑	19	Jonathan Wells	.20	.08
❑	20	Jabar Gaffney	.30	.10
❑	21	Peyton Manning	.75	.30
❑	22	Edgerrin James	.50	.20
❑	23	Marvin Harrison	.50	.20
❑	24	Mark Brunell	.30	.10
❑	25	Jimmy Smith	.30	.10
❑	26	Fred Taylor	.50	.20
❑	27	Priest Holmes	.60	.25
❑	28	Trent Green	.30	.10
❑	29	Tony Gonzalez	.30	.10
❑	30	Chris Chambers	.50	.20
❑	31	Zach Thomas	.30	.10
❑	32	Ricky Williams	.50	.20
❑	33	Tom Brady	1.25	.50

❑ 34	Antowain Smith	.30	.10
❑ 35	Troy Brown	.30	.10
❑ 36	Chad Pennington	.60	.25
❑ 37	Curtis Martin	.50	.20
❑ 38	Laveranues Coles	.30	.10
❑ 39	Tim Brown	.50	.20
❑ 40	Rich Gannon	.30	.10
❑ 41	Jerry Rice	1.00	.40
❑ 42	Charlie Garner	.30	.10
❑ 43	Antwaan Randle El	.50	.20
❑ 44	Plaxico Burress	.30	.10
❑ 45	Tommy Maddox	.50	.20
❑ 46	Jerome Bettis	.50	.20
❑ 47	Drew Brees	.50	.20
❑ 48	LaDainian Tomlinson	.50	.20
❑ 49	Junior Seau	.50	.20
❑ 50	Eddie George	.30	.10
❑ 51	Steve McNair	.50	.20
❑ 52	Derrick Mason	.30	.10
❑ 53	David Boston	.30	.10
❑ 54	Jake Plummer	.30	.10
❑ 55	Marcel Shipp	.30	.10
❑ 56	Michael Vick	1.25	.50
❑ 57	T.J. Duckett	.30	.10
❑ 58	Warrick Dunn	.30	.10
❑ 59	Julius Peppers	.50	.20
❑ 60	Steve Smith	.50	.20
❑ 61	Muhsin Muhammad	.30	.10
❑ 62	Anthony Thomas	.30	.10
❑ 63	Brian Urlacher	.75	.30
❑ 64	Marty Booker	.30	.10
❑ 65	Chad Hutchinson	.20	.08
❑ 66	Antonio Bryant	.30	.10
❑ 67	Emmitt Smith	1.25	.50
❑ 68	Joey Harrington	.75	.30
❑ 69	Germane Crowell	.20	.08
❑ 70	James Stewart	.30	.10
❑ 71	Brett Favre	1.25	.50
❑ 72	Donald Driver	.30	.10
❑ 73	Ahman Green	.50	.20
❑ 74	Randy Moss	.75	.30
❑ 75	Michael Bennett	.30	.10
❑ 76	Daunte Culpepper	.50	.20
❑ 77	Aaron Brooks	.50	.20
❑ 78	Deuce McAllister	.50	.20
❑ 79	Donte Stallworth	.50	.20
❑ 80	Tiki Barber	.50	.20
❑ 81	Jeremy Shockey	.75	.30
❑ 82	Kerry Collins	.30	.10
❑ 83	Donovan McNabb	.60	.25
❑ 84	James Thrash	.20	.08
❑ 85	Duce Staley	.30	.10
❑ 86	Jeff Garcia	.50	.20
❑ 87	Terrell Owens	.50	.20
❑ 88	Garrison Hearst	.30	.10
❑ 89	Shaun Alexander	.50	.20
❑ 90	Darrell Jackson	.30	.10
❑ 91	Koren Robinson	.20	.08
❑ 92	Marshall Faulk	.50	.20
❑ 93	Kurt Warner	.50	.20
❑ 94	Isaac Bruce	.50	.20
❑ 95	Keyshawn Johnson	.50	.20
❑ 96	Brad Johnson	.30	.10
❑ 97	Warren Sapp	.30	.10
❑ 98	Patrick Ramsey	.50	.20
❑ 99	Rod Gardner	.30	.10
❑ 100	Stephen Davis	.30	.10
❑ 101	Brian St.Pierre RC	12.00	5.00
❑ 102	Byron Leftwich RC	40.00	15.00
❑ 103	Carson Palmer RC	50.00	20.00
❑ 104	Chris Simms RC	20.00	7.50
❑ 105	Dave Ragone RC	12.00	5.00
❑ 106	Ken Dorsey RC	12.00	5.00
❑ 107	Kliff Kingsbury RC	10.00	4.00
❑ 108	Kyle Boller RC	25.00	10.00
❑ 109	Rex Grossman RC	20.00	7.50
❑ 110	Seneca Wallace RC	12.00	5.00
❑ 111	Jason Gesser RC	12.00	5.00
❑ 112	Artose Pinner RC	12.00	5.00
❑ 113	Avon Cobourne RC	6.00	2.50

❑ 114	Cecil Sapp RC	10.00	4.00
❑ 115	Chris Brown RC	15.00	6.00
❑ 116	Derek Watson RC	10.00	4.00
❑ 117	Domanick Davis RC	20.00	7.50
❑ 118	Dwone Hicks/100 RC	30.00	15.00
❑ 119	Earnest Graham RC	10.00	4.00
❑ 120	Justin Fargas RC	12.00	5.00
❑ 121	Larry Johnson RC	50.00	25.00
❑ 122	Lee Suggs RC	25.00	10.00
❑ 123	Musa Smith RC	12.00	5.00
❑ 124	Onterrio Smith RC	12.00	5.00
❑ 125	Quentin Griffin RC	12.00	5.00
❑ 126	Willis McGahee RC	30.00	15.00
❑ 127	Sultan McCullough RC	10.00	4.00
❑ 128	LaBrandon Toefield RC	12.00	5.00
❑ 129	B.J. Askew RC	12.00	5.00
❑ 130	Andre Johnson RC	25.00	10.00
❑ 131	Anquan Boldin RC	30.00	12.50
❑ 132	Arnaz Battle RC	12.00	5.00
❑ 133	Bethel Johnson RC	12.00	5.00
❑ 134	Billy McMullen RC	10.00	4.00
❑ 135	Bobby Wade RC	12.00	5.00
❑ 136	Brandon Lloyd RC	15.00	6.00
❑ 137	Bryant Johnson RC	12.00	5.00
❑ 138	Charles Rogers RC	12.00	5.00
❑ 139	Doug Gabriel RC	12.00	5.00
❑ 140	Justin Gage RC	12.00	5.00
❑ 141	Kareem Kelly RC	10.00	4.00
❑ 142	Kelley Washington RC	12.00	5.00
❑ 143	Kevin Curtis RC	12.00	5.00
❑ 144	Nate Burleson RC	15.00	6.00
❑ 145	Sam Aiken RC	10.00	4.00
❑ 146	Shaun McDonald RC	12.00	5.00
❑ 147	Talman Gardner RC	12.00	5.00
❑ 148	Taylor Jacobs RC	10.00	4.00
❑ 149	Terrence Edwards RC	10.00	4.00
❑ 150	Tyrone Calico RC	15.00	6.00
❑ 151	Walter Young RC	6.00	2.50
❑ 152	Ryan Hoag/100 RC	30.00	15.00
❑ 153	Paul Arnold/100 RC	30.00	15.00
❑ 154	Bennie Joppru RC	12.00	5.00
❑ 155	Dallas Clark RC	12.00	5.00
❑ 156	George Wrighster RC	10.00	4.00
❑ 157	Jason Witten RC	20.00	7.50
❑ 158	Mike Pinkard RC	6.00	2.50
❑ 159	Robert Johnson/100 RC	30.00	15.00
❑ 160	Teyo Johnson RC	12.00	5.00
❑ 161	Andrew Williams RC	10.00	4.00
❑ 162	Chris Kelsay RC	12.00	5.00
❑ 163	Cory Redding RC	10.00	4.00
❑ 164	DeWayne Robertson RC	12.00	5.00
❑ 165	DeWayne White RC	10.00	4.00
❑ 166	Jerome McDougle RC	12.00	5.00
❑ 167	Kenny Peterson RC	10.00	4.00
❑ 168	Kindal Moorehead RC	10.00	4.00
❑ 169	Michael Haynes RC	12.00	5.00
❑ 170	Terrell Suggs RC	20.00	7.50
❑ 171	Tully Banta-Cain RC	10.00	4.00
❑ 172	Jimmy Kennedy RC	12.00	5.00
❑ 173	Johnathan Sullivan RC	6.00	2.50
❑ 174	Kevin Williams RC	12.00	5.00
❑ 175	Nick Eason/100 RC	30.00	15.00
❑ 176	Rien Long RC	6.00	2.50
❑ 177	Ty Warren RC	12.00	5.00
❑ 178	William Joseph RC	12.00	5.00
❑ 179	Boss Bailey RC	12.00	5.00
❑ 180	Bradie James RC	12.00	5.00
❑ 181	Victor Hobson RC	12.00	5.00
❑ 182	Clifton Smith/100 RC	30.00	15.00
❑ 183	E.J. Henderson/100 RC	30.00	15.00
❑ 184	Gerald Hayes/100 RC	30.00	15.00
❑ 185	LaM McDonald/100 RC	30.00	15.00
❑ 186	Nick Barnett RC	20.00	7.50
❑ 187	Terry Pierce RC	10.00	4.00
❑ 188	Andre Woolfolk RC	12.00	5.00
❑ 189	Dennis Weathersby RC	6.00	2.50
❑ 190	Drayton Florence/100 RC	30.00	15.00
❑ 191	Eugene Wilson RC	12.00	5.00
❑ 192	Marcus Trufant RC	12.00	5.00
❑ 193	Rashean Mathis RC	10.00	4.00

❑ 194	Ricky Manning RC	12.00	5.00
❑ 195	Sammy Davis/100 RC	30.00	15.00
❑ 196	Terence Newman RC	25.00	10.00
❑ 197	Julian Battle RC	10.00	4.00
❑ 198	Ken Hamlin RC	12.00	5.00
❑ 199	Mike Doss RC	12.00	5.00
❑ 200	Troy Polamalu/100 RC	100.00	60.00

2004 Donruss Elite

❑ COMP.SET w/o SP's (100) 20.00 7.50

❑ ROOKIE PRINT RUN 500 SER.#'d SETS

❑ 1	Emmitt Smith	2.00	.75
❑ 2	Anquan Boldin	1.00	.40
❑ 3	Michael Vick	2.00	.75
❑ 4	Peerless Price	.60	.25
❑ 5	T.J. Duckett	.60	.25
❑ 6	Warrick Dunn	.60	.25
❑ 7	Jamal Lewis	1.00	.40
❑ 8	Kyle Boller	1.00	.40
❑ 9	Todd Heap	.60	.25
❑ 10	Ray Lewis	1.00	.40
❑ 11	Drew Bledsoe	1.00	.40
❑ 12	Eric Moulds	.60	.25
❑ 13	Travis Henry	.60	.25
❑ 14	Jake Delhomme	1.00	.40
❑ 15	Stephen Davis	.60	.25
❑ 16	Steve Smith	1.00	.40
❑ 17	Anthony Thomas	.60	.25
❑ 18	Brian Urlacher	1.25	.50
❑ 19	Rex Grossman	1.00	.40
❑ 20	Chad Johnson	1.00	.40
❑ 21	Carson Palmer	1.25	.50
❑ 22	Rudi Johnson	.60	.25
❑ 23	Peter Warrick	.60	.25
❑ 24	Andre Davis	.40	.15
❑ 25	Tim Couch	.40	.15
❑ 26	Quincy Carter	.60	.25
❑ 27	Roy Williams S	.60	.25
❑ 28	Terence Newman	.60	.25
❑ 29	Clinton Portis	1.00	.40
❑ 30	Jake Plummer	.60	.25
❑ 31	Rod Smith	.60	.25
❑ 32	Charles Rogers	.60	.25
❑ 33	Joey Harrington	1.00	.40
❑ 34	Ahman Green	1.00	.40
❑ 35	Brett Favre	2.50	1.00
❑ 36	Javon Walker	.60	.25
❑ 37	Andre Johnson	1.00	.40
❑ 38	David Carr	1.00	.40
❑ 39	Domanick Davis	1.00	.40
❑ 40	Edgerrin James	1.00	.40
❑ 41	Marvin Harrison	1.00	.40
❑ 42	Peyton Manning	1.50	.60
❑ 43	Reggie Wayne	.60	.25
❑ 44	Byron Leftwich	1.25	.50
❑ 45	Fred Taylor	.60	.25
❑ 46	Jimmy Smith	.60	.25
❑ 47	Priest Holmes	1.25	.50
❑ 48	Tony Gonzalez	.60	.25
❑ 49	Trent Green	.60	.25
❑ 50	Chris Chambers	.60	.25
❑ 51	Ricky Williams	1.00	.40
❑ 52	Zach Thomas	1.00	.40

❑ 53 Daunte Culpepper 1.00 .40
❑ 54 Michael Bennett .60 .25
❑ 55 Moe Williams .40 .15
❑ 56 Randy Moss 1.25 .50
❑ 57 Deion Branch 1.00 .40
❑ 58 Tom Brady 2.50 1.00
❑ 59 Tedy Bruschi .60 .25
❑ 60 Aaron Brooks .60 .25
❑ 61 Deuce McAllister 1.00 .40
❑ 62 Joe Horn .60 .25
❑ 63 Jeremy Shockey 1.00 .40
❑ 64 Kerry Collins .60 .25
❑ 65 Michael Strahan .60 .25
❑ 66 Tiki Barber 1.00 .40
❑ 67 Chad Pennington 1.00 .40
❑ 68 Curtis Martin 1.00 .40
❑ 69 Santana Moss .60 .25
❑ 70 Jerry Porter .60 .25
❑ 71 Jerry Rice 2.00 .75
❑ 72 Tim Brown 1.00 .40
❑ 73 Brian Westbrook .60 .25
❑ 74 Correll Buckhalter .60 .25
❑ 75 Donovan McNabb 1.25 .50
❑ 76 Hines Ward 1.00 .40
❑ 77 Kendrell Bell .60 .25
❑ 78 Plaxico Burress .60 .25
❑ 79 David Boston .60 .25
❑ 80 Drew Brees 1.00 .40
❑ 81 LaDainian Tomlinson 1.25 .50
❑ 82 Jeff Garcia 1.00 .40
❑ 83 Kevan Barlow .60 .25
❑ 84 Terrell Owens 1.00 .40
❑ 85 Koren Robinson .60 .25
❑ 86 Matt Hasselbeck .60 .25
❑ 87 Shaun Alexander 1.00 .40
❑ 88 Isaac Bruce .60 .25
❑ 89 Marc Bulger 1.00 .40
❑ 90 Marshall Faulk 1.00 .40
❑ 91 Torry Holt 1.00 .40
❑ 92 Brad Johnson .60 .25
❑ 93 Derrick Brooks .60 .25
❑ 94 Keenan McCardell .40 .15
❑ 95 Derrick Mason .60 .25
❑ 96 Eddie George .60 .25
❑ 97 Steve McNair 1.00 .40
❑ 98 Jevon Kearse .60 .25
❑ 99 Laveranues Coles .60 .25
❑ 100 Patrick Ramsey .60 .25
❑ 101 Adimchinobe Echemandu RC 6.002.50
❑ 102 Ahmad Carroll RC 10.00 4.00
❑ 103 Antwan Odom RC 8.00 3.00
❑ 104 B.J. Johnson RC 6.00 2.50
❑ 105 Ben Roethlisberger RC 80.00 50.00
❑ 106 Ben Troupe RC 8.00 3.00
❑ 107 Ben Watson RC 8.00 3.00
❑ 108 Bernard Berrian RC 8.00 3.00
❑ 109 Bob Sanders RC 15.00 6.00
❑ 110 Brandon Everage RC 6.00 2.50
❑ 111 Brandon Miree RC 6.00 2.50
❑ 112 Carlos Francis RC 6.00 2.50
❑ 113 Cedric Cobbs RC 10.00 4.00
❑ 114 Chad Lavalais RC 6.00 2.50
❑ 115 Chris Collins RC 6.00 2.50
❑ 116 Chris Gamble RC 10.00 4.00
❑ 117 Chris Perry RC 12.00 5.00
❑ 118 Cody Pickett RC 8.00 3.00
❑ 119 Craig Krenzel RC 8.00 3.00
❑ 120 D.J. Hackett RC 6.00 2.50
❑ 121 D.J. Williams RC 10.00 4.00
❑ 122 Darius Watts RC 8.00 3.00
❑ 123 Darnell Dockett RC 6.00 2.50
❑ 124 DeAngelo Hall RC 10.00 4.00
❑ 125 Derek Abney RC 8.00 3.00
❑ 126 Derrick Hamilton RC 6.00 2.50
❑ 127 Derrick Strait RC 8.00 3.00
❑ 128 Devard Darling RC 8.00 3.00
❑ 129 Devery Henderson RC 6.00 2.50
❑ 130 Dontarrious Thomas RC 8.00 3.00
❑ 131 Drew Henson RC 8.00 3.00
❑ 132 Dunta Robinson RC 8.00 3.00
❑ 133 Dwan Edwards RC 4.00 1.50
❑ 134 Eli Manning RC 50.00 25.00
❑ 135 Ernest Wilford RC 8.00 3.00
❑ 136 Fred Russell RC 8.00 3.00
❑ 137 Greg Jones RC 8.00 3.00
❑ 138 Igor Olshansky RC 8.00 3.00
❑ 139 J.P. Losman RC 15.00 6.00
❑ 140 Jared Lorenzen RC 6.00 2.50
❑ 141 Jarrett Payton RC 10.00 4.00
❑ 142 Jason Babin RC 8.00 3.00
❑ 143 Jason Fife RC 6.00 2.50
❑ 144 Jeff Smoker RC 8.00 3.00
❑ 145 Jeremy LeSueur RC 6.00 2.50
❑ 146 Jerricho Cotchery RC 8.00 3.00
❑ 147 John Navarre RC 8.00 3.00
❑ 148 John Standeford RC 6.00 2.50
❑ 149 Johnnie Morant RC 8.00 3.00
❑ 150 Jonathan Vilma RC 8.00 3.00
❑ 151 Josh Davis RC 6.00 2.50
❑ 152 Josh Harris RC 8.00 3.00
❑ 153 Julius Jones RC 30.00 12.50
❑ 154 Justin Jenkins RC 6.00 2.50
❑ 155 Karlos Dansby RC 8.00 3.00
❑ 156 Keary Colbert RC 10.00 4.00
❑ 157 Keith Smith RC 6.00 2.50
❑ 158 Keiwan Ratliff RC 6.00 2.50
❑ 159 Kellen Winslow RC 15.00 6.00
❑ 160 Kendrick Starling RC 4.00 1.50
❑ 161 Kenechi Udeze RC 8.00 3.00
❑ 162 Kevin Jones RC 25.00 10.00
❑ 163 Larry Fitzgerald RC 30.00 12.50
❑ 164 Lee Evans RC 10.00 4.00
❑ 165 Luke McCown RC 8.00 3.00
❑ 166 Marquise Hill RC 6.00 2.50
❑ 167 Matt Schaub RC 12.00 5.00
❑ 168 Matt Ware RC 8.00 3.00
❑ 169 Matt Mauck RC 8.00 3.00
❑ 170 Maurice Mann RC 6.00 2.50
❑ 171 Mewelde Moore RC 10.00 4.00
❑ 172 Michael Boulware RC 8.00 3.00
❑ 173 Michael Clayton RC 15.00 6.00
❑ 174 Michael Jenkins RC 8.00 3.00
❑ 175 Michael Turner RC 8.00 3.00
❑ 176 B.J. Symons RC 8.00 3.00
❑ 177 Nathan Vasher RC 10.00 4.00
❑ 178 P.K. Sam RC 6.00 2.50
❑ 179 Philip Rivers RC 25.00 12.50
❑ 180 Quincy Wilson RC 6.00 2.50
❑ 181 Ran Carthon RC 6.00 2.50
❑ 182 Randy Starks RC 6.00 2.50
❑ 183 Rashaun Woods RC 8.00 3.00
❑ 184 Reggie Williams RC 10.00 4.00
❑ 185 Ricardo Colclough RC 8.00 3.00
❑ 186 Robert Kent RC 4.00 1.50
❑ 187 Roy Williams RC 25.00 10.00
❑ 188 Samie Parker RC 8.00 3.00
❑ 189 Scott Rislov RC 8.00 3.00
❑ 190 Sean Jones RC 6.00 2.50
❑ 191 Sean Taylor RC 10.00 4.00
❑ 192 Steven Jackson RC 25.00 10.00
❑ 193 Stuart Schweigert RC 8.00 3.00
❑ 194 Tatum Bell RC 15.00 6.00
❑ 195 Teddy Lehman RC 8.00 3.00
❑ 196 Tommie Harris RC 8.00 3.00
❑ 197 Troy Fleming RC 6.00 2.50
❑ 198 Vince Wilfork RC 10.00 4.00
❑ 199 Will Poole RC 8.00 3.00
❑ 200 Will Smith RC 8.00 3.00

2005 Donruss Elite

❑ COMP.SET w/o SP's (100) 20.00 7.50
❑ 101-200 PRINT RUN 499 SER.#'d SETS

❑ 1 Kurt Warner .60 .25
❑ 2 Larry Fitzgerald 1.00 .40
❑ 3 Anquan Boldin .60 .25
❑ 4 Emmitt Smith 2.00 .75
❑ 5 Michael Vick 1.50 .60
❑ 6 Warrick Dunn .60 .25
❑ 7 Alge Crumpler .60 .25
❑ 8 Jamal Lewis 1.00 .40
❑ 9 Kyle Boller .60 .25
❑ 10 Ray Lewis 1.00 .40
❑ 11 Drew Bledsoe 1.00 .40
❑ 12 Willis McGahee 1.00 .40
❑ 13 Travis Henry .60 .25
❑ 14 Eric Moulds .60 .25
❑ 15 Rex Grossman .60 .25
❑ 16 Brian Urlacher 1.00 .40
❑ 17 Thomas Jones .60 .25
❑ 18 Carson Palmer 1.00 .40
❑ 19 Rudi Johnson .60 .25
❑ 20 Chad Johnson 1.00 .40
❑ 21 J.P. Losman 1.00 .40
❑ 22 Lee Suggs .60 .25
❑ 23 Antonio Bryant .50 .20
❑ 24 Julius Jones 1.25 .50
❑ 25 Roy Williams S .60 .25
❑ 26 Keyshawn Johnson .60 .25
❑ 27 Jake Plummer .60 .25
❑ 28 Tatum Bell .60 .25
❑ 29 Rod Smith .60 .25
❑ 30 Joey Harrington 1.00 .40
❑ 31 Kevin Jones 1.00 .40
❑ 32 Roy Williams WR 1.00 .40
❑ 33 Brett Favre 2.50 1.00
❑ 34 Ahman Green 1.00 .40
❑ 35 Javon Walker .60 .25
❑ 36 David Carr 1.00 .40
❑ 37 Andre Johnson .60 .25
❑ 38 Domanick Davis .60 .25
❑ 39 Peyton Manning 1.50 .60
❑ 40 Edgerrin James 1.00 .40
❑ 41 Brandon Stokley .60 .25
❑ 42 Reggie Wayne .60 .25
❑ 43 Marvin Harrison 1.00 .40
❑ 44 Byron Leftwich 1.00 .40
❑ 45 Jimmy Smith .60 .25
❑ 46 Fred Taylor .60 .25
❑ 47 Trent Green .60 .25
❑ 48 Priest Holmes 1.00 .40
❑ 49 Tony Gonzalez .60 .25
❑ 50 A.J. Feeley .60 .25
❑ 51 Chris Chambers .60 .25
❑ 52 Daunte Culpepper 1.00 .40
❑ 53 Randy Moss 1.00 .40
❑ 54 Onterrio Smith .60 .25
❑ 55 Corey Dillon .60 .25
❑ 56 Tom Brady 2.50 1.00
❑ 57 David Givens .60 .25
❑ 58 Aaron Brooks .60 .25
❑ 59 Deuce McAllister 1.00 .40
❑ 60 Joe Horn .60 .25
❑ 61 Eli Manning 2.00 .75
❑ 62 Tiki Barber 1.00 .40
❑ 63 Jeremy Shockey 1.00 .40
❑ 64 Chad Pennington 1.00 .40
❑ 65 Curtis Martin 1.00 .40
❑ 66 Santana Moss .60 .25
❑ 67 Kerry Collins .60 .25
❑ 68 Jerry Porter .60 .25
❑ 69 Donovan McNabb 1.25 .50
❑ 70 Terrell Owens 1.00 .40
❑ 71 Brian Westbrook .60 .25

- ❑ 72 Ben Roethlisberger 2.50 1.00
- ❑ 73 Plaxico Burress .60 .25
- ❑ 74 Hines Ward 1.00 .40
- ❑ 75 Jerome Bettis 1.00 .40
- ❑ 76 Duce Staley .60 .25
- ❑ 77 Antonio Gates 1.00 .40
- ❑ 78 Drew Brees 1.00 .40
- ❑ 79 LaDainian Tomlinson 1.25 .50
- ❑ 80 Brandon Lloyd .50 .20
- ❑ 81 Kevan Barlow .60 .25
- ❑ 82 Matt Hasselbeck .60 .25
- ❑ 83 Shaun Alexander 1.25 .50
- ❑ 84 Darrell Jackson .60 .25
- ❑ 85 Jerry Rice 2.00 .75
- ❑ 86 Marc Bulger 1.00 .40
- ❑ 87 Marshall Faulk 1.00 .40
- ❑ 88 Steven Jackson 1.25 .50
- ❑ 89 Isaac Bruce .60 .25
- ❑ 90 Torry Holt 1.00 .40
- ❑ 91 Michael Clayton 1.00 .40
- ❑ 92 Brian Griese .60 .25
- ❑ 93 Mike Alstott .60 .25
- ❑ 94 Steve McNair 1.00 .40
- ❑ 95 Derrick Mason .60 .25
- ❑ 96 Chris Brown .60 .25
- ❑ 97 Drew Bennett .60 .25
- ❑ 98 Patrick Ramsey .60 .25
- ❑ 99 Clinton Portis 1.00 .40
- ❑ 100 LaVar Arrington 1.00 .40
- ❑ 101 Aaron Rodgers RC 40.00 15.00
- ❑ 102 Adam Jones RC 10.00 4.00
- ❑ 103 Adrian McPherson RC 10.00 4.00
- ❑ 104 Alex Smith TE ERR RC 20.00 7.50
- ❑ 105 Alex Smith QB ERR RC 50.00 25.00
- ❑ 106 Alvin Pearman RC 10.00 4.00
- ❑ 107 Andrew Walter RC 15.00 6.00
- ❑ 108 Anthony Davis RC 8.00 3.00
- ❑ 109 Antrel Rolle RC 10.00 4.00
- ❑ 110 Anttaj Hawthorne RC 8.00 3.00
- ❑ 111 Brandon Browner RC 8.00 3.00
- ❑ 112 Brandon Jacobs RC 12.00 5.00
- ❑ 113 Braylon Edwards RC 40.00 15.00
- ❑ 114 Brock Berlin RC 8.00 3.00
- ❑ 115 Brandon Jones RC 10.00 4.00
- ❑ 116 Bryant McFadden RC 10.00 4.00
- ❑ 117 Carlos Rogers RC 12.00 5.00
- ❑ 118 Carnell Williams RC 50.00 20.00
- ❑ 119 Cedric Benson RC 25.00 10.00
- ❑ 120 Cedric Houston RC 10.00 4.00
- ❑ 121 Channing Crowder RC 10.00 4.00
- ❑ 122 Charles Frederick RC 8.00 3.00
- ❑ 123 Charlie Frye RC 20.00 7.50
- ❑ 124 Chase Lyman RC 8.00 3.00
- ❑ 125 Chris Henry RC 10.00 4.00
- ❑ 126 Chris Rix RC 8.00 3.00
- ❑ 127 Ciatrick Fason RC 10.00 4.00
- ❑ 128 Corey Webster RC 10.00 4.00
- ❑ 129 Courtney Roby RC 10.00 4.00
- ❑ 130 Craig Bragg RC 8.00 3.00
- ❑ 131 Craphonso Thorpe RC 8.00 3.00
- ❑ 132 Damien Nash RC 8.00 3.00
- ❑ 133 Dan Cody RC 10.00 4.00
- ❑ 134 Dan Orlovsky RC 12.00 5.00
- ❑ 135 Dante Ridgeway RC 8.00 3.00
- ❑ 136 Darian Durant RC 10.00 4.00
- ❑ 137 Darren Sproles RC 10.00 4.00
- ❑ 138 Darryl Blackstock RC 8.00 3.00
- ❑ 139 David Greene RC 10.00 4.00
- ❑ 140 David Pollack RC 10.00 4.00
- ❑ 141 DeMarcus Ware RC 15.00 6.00
- ❑ 142 Derek Anderson RC 10.00 4.00
- ❑ 143 Derrick Johnson RC 15.00 6.00
- ❑ 144 Erasmus James RC 10.00 4.00
- ❑ 145 Eric Shelton RC 10.00 4.00
- ❑ 146 Ernest Shazor RC 10.00 4.00
- ❑ 147 Fabian Washington RC 10.00 4.00
- ❑ 148 Frank Gore UER RC 15.00 6.00
- ❑ 149 Fred Amey RC 8.00 3.00
- ❑ 150 Fred Gibson RC 8.00 3.00
- ❑ 151 Maurice Clarett 10.00 4.00
- ❑ 152 Gino Guidugli RC 5.00 2.00
- ❑ 153 Heath Miller RC 30.00 12.50
- ❑ 154 J.J. Arrington RC 12.00 5.00
- ❑ 155 J.R. Russell RC 8.00 3.00
- ❑ 156 Jason Campbell RC 15.00 6.00
- ❑ 157 Jason White RC 10.00 4.00
- ❑ 158 Jerome Mathis RC 10.00 4.00
- ❑ 159 Josh Bullocks RC 10.00 4.00
- ❑ 160 Josh Davis RC 8.00 3.00
- ❑ 161 Justin Miller RC 8.00 3.00
- ❑ 162 Justin Tuck RC 10.00 4.00
- ❑ 163 Kay-Jay Harris RC 8.00 3.00
- ❑ 164 Kevin Burnett RC 10.00 4.00
- ❑ 165 Kyle Orton RC 15.00 6.00
- ❑ 166 Larry Brackins RC 5.00 2.00
- ❑ 167 Marcus Spears RC 10.00 4.00
- ❑ 168 Marion Barber RC 15.00 6.00
- ❑ 169 Mark Bradley RC 10.00 4.00
- ❑ 170 Mark Clayton RC 12.00 5.00
- ❑ 171 Marlin Jackson RC 10.00 4.00
- ❑ 172 Matt Jones RC 30.00 12.50
- ❑ 173 Matt Roth RC 10.00 4.00
- ❑ 174 Mike Patterson RC 10.00 4.00
- ❑ 175 Mike Williams 30.00 12.50
- ❑ 176 Airese Currie RC 10.00 4.00
- ❑ 177 Reggie Brown RC 10.00 4.00
- ❑ 178 Roddy White RC 10.00 4.00
- ❑ 179 Ronnie Brown RC 40.00 20.00
- ❑ 180 Roscoe Parrish RC 10.00 4.00
- ❑ 181 Roydell Williams RC 10.00 4.00
- ❑ 182 Ryan Fitzpatrick RC 15.00 6.00
- ❑ 183 Rasheed Marshall RC 10.00 4.00
- ❑ 184 Ryan Moats RC 10.00 4.00
- ❑ 185 Shaun Cody RC 10.00 4.00
- ❑ 186 Shawne Merriman RC 15.00 6.00
- ❑ 187 Chad Owens RC 10.00 4.00
- ❑ 188 Stefan LeFors RC 10.00 4.00
- ❑ 189 Steve Savoy RC 5.00 2.00
- ❑ 190 T.A. McLendon RC 5.00 2.00
- ❑ 191 Tab Perry RC 10.00 4.00
- ❑ 192 Taylor Stubblefield RC 5.00 2.00
- ❑ 193 Terrence Murphy RC 10.00 4.00
- ❑ 194 Thomas Davis RC 10.00 4.00
- ❑ 195 Timmy Chang RC 8.00 3.00
- ❑ 196 Travis Johnson RC 8.00 3.00
- ❑ 197 Troy Williamson RC 25.00 10.00
- ❑ 198 Vernand Morency RC 10.00 4.00
- ❑ 199 Vincent Jackson RC 10.00 4.00
- ❑ 200 Walter Reyes RC 8.00 3.00

2005 Donruss Gridiron Gear

- ❑ COMP.SET w/o RC's (100) 25.00 10.00
- ❑ 101-150 PRINT RUN 399 SER.#'d SETS

- ❑ 1 Aaron Brooks .60 .25
- ❑ 2 Ahman Green 1.00 .40
- ❑ 3 Alge Crumpler .60 .25
- ❑ 4 Amani Toomer .60 .25
- ❑ 5 Andre Johnson .60 .25
- ❑ 6 Anquan Boldin .60 .25
- ❑ 7 Antonio Gates 1.00 .40
- ❑ 8 Antwaan Randle El .60 .25
- ❑ 9 Ashley Lelie .60 .25
- ❑ 10 Barry Sanders 4.00 1.50
- ❑ 11 Ben Roethlisberger 2.50 1.00
- ❑ 12 Bob Griese 2.50 1.00
- ❑ 13 Brandon Lloyd .60 .25
- ❑ 14 Brett Favre 2.50 1.00
- ❑ 15 Brian Urlacher 1.00 .40
- ❑ 16 Brian Westbrook .60 .25
- ❑ 17 Byron Leftwich 1.00 .40
- ❑ 18 Carson Palmer 1.00 .40
- ❑ 19 Chad Johnson .60 .25
- ❑ 20 Chad Pennington 1.00 .40
- ❑ 21 Champ Bailey .60 .25
- ❑ 22 Chris Brown .60 .25
- ❑ 23 Chris Chambers .60 .25
- ❑ 24 Clinton Portis 1.00 .40
- ❑ 25 Corey Dillon .60 .25
- ❑ 26 Curtis Martin 1.00 .40
- ❑ 27 Daunte Culpepper 1.00 .40
- ❑ 28 David Carr 1.00 .40
- ❑ 29 Deion Sanders 1.25 .50
- ❑ 30 Derrick Brooks .60 .25
- ❑ 31 Deuce McAllister 1.00 .40
- ❑ 32 Domanick Davis .60 .25
- ❑ 33 Don Maynard .75 .30
- ❑ 34 Donovan McNabb 1.25 .50
- ❑ 35 Drew Bledsoe 1.00 .40
- ❑ 36 Drew Brees .60 .25
- ❑ 37 Edgerrin James 1.00 .40
- ❑ 38 Eli Manning 2.00 .75
- ❑ 39 Eric Moulds .60 .25
- ❑ 40 Fred Taylor .60 .25
- ❑ 41 Hines Ward 1.00 .40
- ❑ 42 Ickey Woods .60 .25
- ❑ 43 Isaac Bruce .60 .25
- ❑ 44 J.P. Losman 1.00 .40
- ❑ 45 Jake Delhomme 1.00 .40
- ❑ 46 Jake Plummer .60 .25
- ❑ 47 Jamal Lewis .60 .25
- ❑ 48 Javon Walker .60 .25
- ❑ 49 Jeremy Shockey 1.00 .40
- ❑ 50 Jerome Bettis 1.00 .40
- ❑ 51 Jerry Porter .60 .25
- ❑ 52 Jevon Kearse .60 .25
- ❑ 53 Jimmy Smith .60 .25
- ❑ 54 Joe Namath 1.25 .50
- ❑ 55 Joey Harrington 1.00 .40
- ❑ 56 Josh McCown .60 .25
- ❑ 57 Josh Reed .50 .20
- ❑ 58 Julius Jones 1.25 .50
- ❑ 59 Julius Peppers .60 .25
- ❑ 60 Keary Colbert .60 .25
- ❑ 61 Kerry Collins .60 .25
- ❑ 62 Kevin Jones 1.25 .50
- ❑ 63 Kyle Boller .60 .25
- ❑ 64 LaDainian Tomlinson 1.25 .50
- ❑ 65 LaMont Jordan .60 .25
- ❑ 66 Larry Fitzgerald 1.00 .40
- ❑ 67 Lee Evans .60 .25
- ❑ 68 Marc Bulger 1.00 .40
- ❑ 69 Marvin Harrison 1.00 .40
- ❑ 70 Matt Hasselbeck .60 .25
- ❑ 71 Michael Clayton 1.00 .40
- ❑ 72 Michael Vick 1.50 .60
- ❑ 73 Mike Alstott .60 .25
- ❑ 74 Muhsin Muhammad .60 .25
- ❑ 75 Nate Burleson .60 .25
- ❑ 76 Peyton Manning 1.50 .60
- ❑ 77 Plaxico Burress .60 .25
- ❑ 78 Priest Holmes 1.00 .40
- ❑ 79 Randy Moss 1.00 .40
- ❑ 80 Ray Lewis 1.00 .40
- ❑ 81 Reggie Wayne .60 .25
- ❑ 82 Rex Grossman .60 .25
- ❑ 83 Rod Smith .60 .25
- ❑ 84 Roy Williams S .60 .25
- ❑ 85 Roy Williams WR 1.00 .40
- ❑ 86 Rudi Johnson .60 .25
- ❑ 87 Shaun Alexander 1.00 .40
- ❑ 88 Sonny Jurgensen .75 .30
- ❑ 89 Stephen Davis .60 .25

❑ 90 Steve McNair	1.00	.40
❑ 91 Steve Smith	.50	.20
❑ 92 Steven Jackson	1.25	.50
❑ 93 Terrell Owens	1.00	.40
❑ 94 Tiki Barber	1.00	.40
❑ 95 Todd Heap	.60	.25
❑ 96 Tom Brady	2.00	.75
❑ 97 Tony Gonzalez	.60	.25
❑ 98 Torry Holt	.60	.25
❑ 99 Trent Green	.60	.25
❑ 100 Willis McGahee	1.00	.40
❑ 101 Alex Smith QB RC	15.00	6.00
❑ 102 Ronnie Brown RC	12.00	5.00
❑ 103 Braylon Edwards RC	12.00	5.00
❑ 104 Cedric Benson RC	8.00	3.00
❑ 105 Carnell Williams RC	20.00	8.00
❑ 106 Adam Jones RC	4.00	1.50
❑ 107 Troy Williamson RC	8.00	3.00
❑ 108 Mike Williams	8.00	3.00
❑ 109 Derrick Johnson RC	4.00	1.50
❑ 110 Demarcus Ware RC	6.00	2.50
❑ 111 Matt Jones RC	10.00	4.00
❑ 112 Mark Clayton RC	5.00	2.00
❑ 113 Aaron Rodgers RC	12.00	5.00
❑ 114 Jason Campbell RC	6.00	2.50
❑ 115 Roddy White RC	4.00	1.50
❑ 116 Heath Miller RC	10.00	4.00
❑ 117 Reggie Brown RC	4.00	1.50
❑ 118 Mark Bradley RC	4.00	1.50
❑ 119 J.J. Arrington RC	5.00	2.00
❑ 120 Odell Thurman RC	4.00	1.50
❑ 121 Roscoe Parrish RC	4.00	1.50
❑ 122 Terrence Murphy RC	4.00	1.50
❑ 123 Vincent Jackson RC	4.00	1.50
❑ 124 Frank Gore RC	6.00	2.50
❑ 125 Charlie Frye RC	8.00	3.00
❑ 126 Courtney Roby RC	4.00	1.50
❑ 127 Andrew Walter RC	6.00	2.50
❑ 128 Vernand Morency RC	4.00	1.50
❑ 129 Ryan Moats RC	4.00	1.50
❑ 130 Chris Henry RC	4.00	1.50
❑ 131 David Greene RC	4.00	1.50
❑ 132 Brandon Jones RC	4.00	1.50
❑ 133 Kyle Orton RC	8.00	3.00
❑ 134 Marion Barber RC	6.00	2.50
❑ 135 Brandon Jacobs RC	5.00	2.00
❑ 136 Ciatrick Fason RC	4.00	1.50
❑ 137 Lofa Tatupu RC	8.00	3.00
❑ 138 Stefan LeFors RC	4.00	1.50
❑ 139 Alvin Pearman RC	4.00	1.50
❑ 140 Darren Sproles RC	4.00	1.50
❑ 141 Samkon Gado RC	40.00	20.00
❑ 142 Antrel Rolle RC	4.00	1.50
❑ 143 Maurice Clarett	4.00	1.50
❑ 144 Adrian McPherson RC	4.00	1.50
❑ 145 Eric Shelton RC	4.00	1.50
❑ 146 Bo Scaife RC	3.00	1.25
❑ 147 Carlos Rogers RC	5.00	2.00
❑ 148 Otis Amey RC	3.00	1.25
❑ 149 Alex Smith TE RC	4.00	1.50
❑ 150 Jerome Mathis RC	4.00	1.50

1997 Donruss Preferred

❑ COMPLETE SET (150)	300.00	150.00
❑ COMP.BRONZE SET (80)	25.00	10.00
❑ 1 Emmitt Smith P	20.00	7.50
❑ 2 Steve Young G	8.00	3.00
❑ 3 Cris Carter S	6.00	2.50
❑ 4 Tim Biakabutuka B	.60	.25
❑ 5 Brett Favre P	25.00	10.00
❑ 6 Troy Aikman G	12.00	5.00
❑ 7 Eddie Kennison S	4.00	1.50
❑ 8 Ben Coates B	.60	.25
❑ 9 Dan Marino P	25.00	10.00
❑ 10 Deion Sanders G	6.00	2.50
❑ 11 Curtis Conway S	4.00	1.50
❑ 12 Jeff George B	.60	.25
❑ 13 Barry Sanders P	20.00	7.50
❑ 14 Kerry Collins G	6.00	2.50
❑ 15 Marvin Harrison S	6.00	2.50
❑ 16 Bobby Engram B	.60	.25
❑ 17 Jerry Rice P	12.00	5.00
❑ 18 Kordell Stewart G	6.00	2.50
❑ 19 Tony Banks S	6.00	2.50
❑ 20 Jim Harbaugh B	.60	.25
❑ 21 Mark Brunell P	8.00	3.00
❑ 22 Steve McNair G	8.00	3.00
❑ 23 Terrell Owens S	8.00	3.00
❑ 24 Raymont Harris B	.40	.15
❑ 25 Curtis Martin P	8.00	3.00
❑ 26 Karim Abdul-Jabbar G	6.00	2.50
❑ 27 Joey Galloway S	4.00	1.50
❑ 28 Bobby Hoying B	.60	.25
❑ 29 Terrell Davis P	8.00	3.00
❑ 30 Terry Glenn G	4.00	1.50
❑ 31 Antonio Freeman S	6.00	2.50
❑ 32 Brad Johnson B	1.00	.40
❑ 33 Drew Bledsoe P	8.00	3.00
❑ 34 John Elway G	25.00	10.00
❑ 35 Herman Moore G	4.00	1.50
❑ 36 Robert Brooks S	4.00	1.50
❑ 37 Rod Smith B	1.00	.40
❑ 38 Eddie George P	6.00	2.50
❑ 39 Keyshawn Johnson G	6.00	2.50
❑ 40 Greg Hill S	2.50	1.00
❑ 41 Scott Mitchell B	.60	.25
❑ 42 Muhsin Muhammad B	.60	.25
❑ 43 Isaac Bruce G	6.00	2.50
❑ 44 Jeff Blake S	4.00	1.50
❑ 45 Neil O'Donnell B	.60	.25
❑ 46 Jimmy Smith B	.60	.25
❑ 47 Jerome Bettis G	6.00	2.50
❑ 48 Terry Allen S	4.00	1.50
❑ 49 Andre Reed B	.60	.25
❑ 50 Frank Sanders B	.60	.25
❑ 51 Tim Brown G	6.00	2.50
❑ 52 Thurman Thomas S	4.00	1.50
❑ 53 Heath Shuler B	.40	.15
❑ 54 Vinny Testaverde B	.60	.25
❑ 55 Marcus Allen S	6.00	2.50
❑ 56 Napoleon Kaufman B	1.00	.40
❑ 57 Derrick Alexander WR B	.60	.25
❑ 58 Carl Pickens G	4.00	1.50
❑ 59 Marshall Faulk S	8.00	3.00
❑ 60 Mike Alstott B	1.00	.40
❑ 61 Jamal Anderson B	1.00	.40
❑ 62 Ricky Watters G	4.00	1.50
❑ 63 Dorsey Levens S	6.00	2.50
❑ 64 Todd Collins B	.40	.15
❑ 65 Trent Dilfer B	1.00	.40
❑ 66 Natrone Means S	4.00	1.50
❑ 67 Gus Frerotte B	.40	.15
❑ 68 Irving Fryar B	.60	.25
❑ 69 Adrian Murrell S	4.00	1.50
❑ 70 Rodney Hampton B	.60	.25
❑ 71 Garrison Hearst B	.60	.25
❑ 72 Reggie White S	6.00	2.50
❑ 73 Anthony Johnson B	.40	.15
❑ 74 Tony Martin B	.60	.25
❑ 75 Chris Sanders S	2.50	1.00
❑ 76 O.J. McDuffie B	.60	.25
❑ 77 Leeland McElroy B	.40	.15
❑ 78 Ki-Jana Carter S	4.00	1.50
❑ 79 Anthony Miller B	.40	.15
❑ 80 Johnnie Morton B	.60	.25
❑ 81 Robert Smith S	.60	.25
❑ 82 Brett Perriman B	.40	.15
❑ 83 Errict Rhett B	.40	.15
❑ 84 Michael Irvin S	4.00	1.50
❑ 85 Darnay Scott B	.60	.25
❑ 86 Shannon Sharpe B	.60	.25
❑ 87 Lawrence Phillips S	4.00	1.50
❑ 88 Bruce Smith B	.60	.25
❑ 89 James O.Stewart B	.60	.25
❑ 90 J.J. Stokes B	.60	.25
❑ 91 Chris Warren B	.60	.25
❑ 92 Daryl Johnston B	.60	.25
❑ 93 Andre Rison B	.60	.25
❑ 94 Rashaan Salaam B	.40	.15
❑ 95 Amani Toomer B	.60	.25
❑ 96 Warrick Dunn RC G	20.00	7.50
❑ 97 Tiki Barber RC S	15.00	6.00
❑ 98 Peter Boulware RC B	1.00	.40
❑ 99 Ike Hilliard RC G	12.00	5.00
❑ 100 Antowain Smith RC S	10.00	4.00
❑ 101 Yatil Green RC S	4.00	1.50
❑ 102 Tony Gonzalez RC B	6.00	2.50
❑ 103 Reidel Anthony RC G	6.00	2.50
❑ 104 Troy Davis RC S	4.00	1.50
❑ 105 Rae Carruth RC S	2.50	1.00
❑ 106 David LaFleur RC B	.40	.15
❑ 107 Jim Druckenmiller RC G	4.00	1.50
❑ 108 Joey Kent RC S	6.00	2.50
❑ 109 Byron Hanspard RC S	4.00	1.50
❑ 110 Darrell Russell RC B	.40	.15
❑ 111 Danny Wuerffel RC S	6.00	2.50
❑ 112 Jake Plummer RC S	12.00	5.00
❑ 113 Jay Graham RC B	.60	.25
❑ 114 Corey Dillon RC S	15.00	6.00
❑ 115 Orlando Pace RC B	1.00	.40
❑ 116 Pat Barnes RC S	4.00	1.50
❑ 117 Shawn Springs RC B	.60	.25
❑ 118 Troy Aikman NT B	2.00	.75
❑ 119 Drew Bledsoe NT B	1.25	.50
❑ 120 Mark Brunell NT B	1.25	.50
❑ 121 Kerry Collins NT B	1.00	.40
❑ 122 Terrell Davis NT B	1.25	.50
❑ 123 Jerome Bettis NT B	1.00	.40
❑ 124 Brett Favre NT B	4.00	2.00
❑ 125 Eddie George NT B	1.00	.40
❑ 126 Terry Glenn NT B	1.00	.40
❑ 127 Karim Abdul-Jabbar NT B	.60	.25
❑ 128 Keyshawn Johnson NT B	1.00	.40
❑ 129 Dan Marino NT B	4.00	2.00
❑ 130 Curtis Martin NT B	1.25	.50
❑ 131 Natrone Means NT B	.60	.25
❑ 132 Herman Moore NT S	4.00	1.50
❑ 133 Jerry Rice NT B	2.00	.75
❑ 134 Barry Sanders NT B	3.00	1.25
❑ 135 Deion Sanders NT B	1.00	.40
❑ 136 Emmitt Smith NT B	3.00	1.50
❑ 137 Kordell Stewart NT B	1.00	.40
❑ 138 Steve Young NT B	1.25	.50
❑ 139 Carl Pickens NT S	4.00	1.50
❑ 140 Isaac Bruce NT S	6.00	2.50
❑ 141 Steve McNair NT S	5.00	2.00
❑ 142 John Elway NT S	10.00	5.00
❑ 143 Cris Carter NT B	.60	.25
❑ 144 Tim Brown NT B	.60	.25
❑ 145 Ricky Watters NT B	.40	.15
❑ 146 Robert Brooks NT B	.60	.25
❑ 147 Jeff Blake NT B	.60	.25
❑ 148 Tiki Barber CL B	1.50	.60
❑ 149 Jim Druckenmiller CL B	.40	.15
❑ 150 Warrick Dunn CL B	1.00	.40

1999 Donruss Preferred QBC

❑ COMPLETE SET (120)	150.00	75.00
❑ COMP.BRONZE SET (45)	25.00	12.50
❑ 1 Troy Aikman B	1.50	.60
❑ 2 Tony Banks B	.50	.20

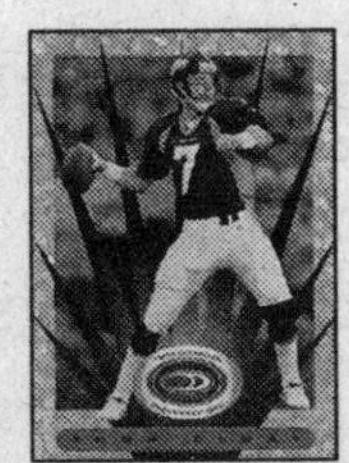

❑ 3	Jeff Blake B	.50	.20
❑ 4	Drew Bledsoe B	1.00	.40
❑ 5	Bubby Brister B	.30	.10
❑ 6	Chris Chandler B	.50	.20
❑ 7	Kerry Collins B	.50	.20
❑ 8	Randall Cunningham B	.75	.30
❑ 9	Terrell Davis B	.75	.30
❑ 10	Trent Dilfer B	.50	.20
❑ 11	John Elway B	2.50	1.00
❑ 12	Boomer Esiason B	.30	.10
❑ 13	Jim Everett B	.30	.10
❑ 14	Brett Favre B	2.50	1.00
❑ 15	Doug Flutie B	.75	.30
❑ 16	Gus Frerotte B	.30	.10
❑ 17	Jeff George B	.50	.20
❑ 18	Elvis Grbac B	.50	.20
❑ 19	Jim Harbaugh B	.50	.20
❑ 20	Michael Irvin B	.50	.20
❑ 21	Brad Johnson B	.75	.30
❑ 22	Keyshawn Johnson B	.75	.30
❑ 23	Danny Kanell B	.30	.10
❑ 24	Jim Kelly B	.30	.10
❑ 25	Bernie Kosar B	.30	.10
❑ 26	Erik Kramer B	.30	.10
❑ 27	Ryan Leaf B	.75	.30
❑ 28	Peyton Manning B	2.50	1.00
❑ 29	Dan Marino B	2.50	1.00
❑ 30	Donovan McNabb RC B	6.00	2.50
❑ 31	Steve McNair B	.75	.30
❑ 32	Cade McNown RC B	1.00	.40
❑ 33	Scott Mitchell B	.30	.10
❑ 34	Warren Moon B	.75	.30
❑ 35	Neil O'Donnell B	.50	.20
❑ 36	Jake Plummer B	.50	.20
❑ 37	Jerry Rice B	1.50	.60
❑ 38	Barry Sanders B	2.50	1.00
❑ 39	Junior Seau B	.75	.30
❑ 40	Phil Simms B	.30	.10
❑ 41	Kordell Stewart B	.50	.20
❑ 42	Vinny Testaverde B	.50	.20
❑ 43	Ricky Williams RC B	2.50	1.00
❑ 44	Steve Young B	1.00	.40
❑ 45	Marino/Favre/Elway B	3.00	1.25
❑ 46	Troy Aikman S	2.50	1.00
❑ 47	Tony Banks S	.75	.30
❑ 48	Drew Bledsoe S	1.50	.60
❑ 49	Bubby Brister S	.50	.20
❑ 50	Chris Chandler S	.75	.30
❑ 51	Kerry Collins S	1.25	.50
❑ 52	Randall Cunningham S	1.25	.50
❑ 53	Terrell Davis S	1.25	.50
❑ 54	Trent Dilfer S	.75	.30
❑ 55	John Elway S	4.00	1.50
❑ 56	Boomer Esiason S	.75	.30
❑ 57	Brett Favre S	4.00	1.50
❑ 58	Doug Flutie S	1.25	.50
❑ 59	Elvis Grbac S	.75	.30
❑ 60	Jim Harbaugh S	.75	.30
❑ 61	Michael Irvin S	1.25	.50
❑ 62	Brad Johnson S	.75	.30
❑ 63	Keyshawn Johnson S	1.25	.50
❑ 64	Jim Kelly S	1.25	.50
❑ 65	Ryan Leaf S	.50	.20
❑ 66	Peyton Manning S	4.00	1.50
❑ 67	Dan Marino S	4.00	1.50
❑ 68	Donovan McNabb S	8.00	3.00
❑ 69	Steve McNair S	1.25	.50
❑ 70	Cade McNown S	2.00	.75
❑ 71	Warren Moon S	1.25	.50
❑ 72	Jake Plummer S	.75	.30
❑ 73	Jerry Rice S	2.50	1.00
❑ 74	Barry Sanders S	4.00	1.50
❑ 75	Junior Seau S	1.25	.50
❑ 76	Phil Simms S	.75	.30
❑ 77	Kordell Stewart S	.75	.30
❑ 78	Vinny Testaverde S	.75	.30
❑ 79	Ricky Williams S	3.00	1.25
❑ 80	Steve Young S	1.50	.60
❑ 81	Troy Aikman G	5.00	2.00
❑ 82	Drew Bledsoe G	3.00	1.25
❑ 83	Bubby Brister G	1.00	.40
❑ 84	Chris Chandler G	1.50	.60
❑ 85	Randall Cunningham G	1.50	.60
❑ 86	Terrell Davis G	2.50	1.00
❑ 87	John Elway G	8.00	3.00
❑ 88	Brett Favre G	8.00	3.00
❑ 89	Doug Flutie G	2.50	1.00
❑ 90	Brad Johnson G	1.50	.60
❑ 91	Keyshawn Johnson G	2.50	1.00
❑ 92	Ryan Leaf G	1.00	.40
❑ 93	Peyton Manning G	8.00	3.00
❑ 94	Dan Marino G	8.00	3.00
❑ 95	Donovan McNabb G	15.00	6.00
❑ 96	Steve McNair G	2.50	1.00
❑ 97	Cade McNown G	4.00	1.50
❑ 98	Warren Moon G	2.50	1.00
❑ 99	Jake Plummer G	1.50	.60
❑ 100	Jerry Rice G	5.00	2.00
❑ 101	Barry Sanders G	8.00	3.00
❑ 102	Kordell Stewart G	1.50	.60
❑ 103	Vinny Testaverde G	1.50	.60
❑ 104	Ricky Williams G	6.00	2.50
❑ 105	Steve Young G	3.00	1.25
❑ 106	Troy Aikman P	8.00	3.00
❑ 107	Drew Bledsoe P	5.00	2.00
❑ 108	Terrell Davis P	4.00	1.50
❑ 109	John Elway P	12.00	5.00
❑ 110	Brett Favre P	12.00	5.00
❑ 111	Keyshawn Johnson P	4.00	1.50
❑ 112	Peyton Manning P	12.00	5.00
❑ 113	Dan Marino P	12.00	5.00
❑ 114	Donovan McNabb P	20.00	7.50
❑ 115	Cade McNown P	5.00	2.00
❑ 116	Jake Plummer P	2.50	1.00
❑ 117	Jerry Rice P	8.00	3.00
❑ 118	Barry Sanders P	12.00	5.00
❑ 119	Kordell Stewart P	2.50	1.00
❑ 120	Ricky Williams P	8.00	3.00

2000 Donruss Preferred

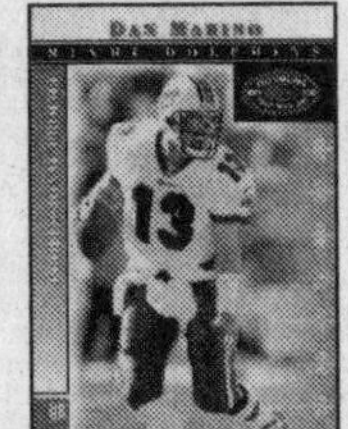

❑	COMPLETE SET (103)	25.00	10.00
❑ 1	Jake Plummer	.30	.10
❑ 2	Chris Chandler	.30	.10
❑ 3	Trent Dilfer	.30	.10
❑ 4	Doug Flutie	.50	.20
❑ 5	Cade McNown	.20	.07
❑ 6	Michael Irvin	.30	.10
❑ 7	Troy Aikman	1.00	.40
❑ 8	Terrell Davis	.50	.20
❑ 9	John Elway	1.50	.60
❑ 10	Brett Favre	1.50	.60
❑ 11	Peyton Manning	1.25	.50
❑ 12	Warren Moon	.50	.20
❑ 13	Randall Cunningham	.50	.20
❑ 14	Drew Bledsoe	.60	.25
❑ 15	Ricky Williams	.50	.20
❑ 16	Kerry Collins	.30	.10
❑ 17	Vinny Testaverde	.30	.10
❑ 18	Donovan McNabb	.75	.30
❑ 19	Jim Harbaugh	.30	.10
❑ 20	Jerry Rice	1.00	.40
❑ 21	Steve Young	.60	.25
❑ 22	Keyshawn Johnson	.50	.20
❑ 23	Neil O'Donnell	.30	.10
❑ 24	Steve McNair	.50	.20
❑ 25	Brad Johnson	.50	.20
❑ 26	Jeff George	.30	.10
❑ 27	Dan Marino	1.50	.60
❑ 28	Jim Kelly	.50	.20
❑ 29	Barry Sanders	1.25	.50
❑ 30	Phil Simms	.30	.10
❑ 31	Gus Frerotte	.20	.07
❑ 32	Elvis Grbac	.30	.10
❑ 33	Jeff Blake	.20	.07
❑ 34	Kordell Stewart	.30	.10
❑ 35	Tony Banks	.30	.10
❑ 36	Doug Flutie C	.50	.20
❑ 37	Cade McNown C	.20	.07
❑ 38	Troy Aikman C	1.00	.40
❑ 39	Terrell Davis C	.50	.20
❑ 40	John Elway C	1.50	.60
❑ 41	Brett Favre C	1.50	.60
❑ 42	Peyton Manning C	1.00	.40
❑ 43	Drew Bledsoe C	.60	.25
❑ 44	Ricky Williams C	.50	.20
❑ 45	Kerry Collins C	.30	.10
❑ 46	Vinny Testaverde C	.30	.10
❑ 47	Donovan McNabb C	.60	.25
❑ 48	Kordell Stewart C	.30	.10
❑ 49	Ryan Leaf C	.30	.10
❑ 50	Jerry Rice C	1.00	.40
❑ 51	Steve Young C	.60	.25
❑ 52	Keyshawn Johnson C	.50	.20
❑ 53	Steve McNair C	.50	.20
❑ 54	Jeff George C	.30	.10
❑ 55	Dan Marino C	1.50	.60
❑ 56	Jim Kelly C	.50	.20
❑ 57	Barry Sanders C	1.25	.50
❑ 58	Bernie Kosar C	.20	.07
❑ 59	Chris Chandler C	.30	.10
❑ 60	Jim Everett C	.20	.07
❑ 61	Jake Plummer HS	.30	.10
❑ 62	Cade McNown HS	.50	.20
❑ 63	Troy Aikman HS	1.00	.40
❑ 64	Ricky Williams HS	.50	.20
❑ 65	Donovan McNabb HS	.60	.25
❑ 66	Steve Young HS	.60	.25
❑ 67	Brad Johnson HS	.50	.20
❑ 68	Kerry Collins HS	.30	.10
❑ 69	Ryan Leaf HS	.30	.10
❑ 70	Drew Bledsoe HS	.60	.25
❑ 71	Jake Plummer PS	.30	.10
❑ 72	Chris Chandler PS	.20	.07
❑ 73	Michael Irvin PS	.30	.10
❑ 74	Troy Aikman PS	1.00	.40
❑ 75	Terrell Davis PS	.50	.20
❑ 76	John Elway PS	1.50	.60
❑ 77	Brett Favre PS	1.50	.60
❑ 78	Peyton Manning PS	1.00	.40
❑ 79	Drew Bledsoe PS	.60	.25
❑ 80	Junior Seau PS	.50	.20
❑ 81	Jerry Rice PS	1.00	.40
❑ 82	Steve Young PS	.60	.25
❑ 83	Keyshawn Johnson PS	.50	.20
❑ 84	Steve McNair PS	.50	.20
❑ 85	Brad Johnson PS	.50	.20
❑ 86	Dan Marino PS	1.50	.60
❑ 87	Jim Kelly PS	.50	.20

❑ 88 Barry Sanders PS 1.25 .50
❑ 89 Phil Simms PS .30 .10
❑ 90 Boomer Esiason PS .30 .10
❑ 91 Jake Plummer OF .30 .10
❑ 92 Chris Chandler OF .30 .10
❑ 93 Bubby Brister OF .20 .07
❑ 94 Cade McNown OF .50 .20
❑ 95 Jim Harbaugh OF .30 .10
❑ 96 Peyton Manning OF 1.00 .40
❑ 97 Donovan McNabb OF .60 .25
❑ 98 Jim Kelly OF .50 .20
❑ 99 Brad Johnson OF .50 .20
❑ 100 Kordell Stewart OF .30 .10
❑ 101 Rob Johnson SP 1.00 .40
❑ 102 Jevon Kearse SP 1.00 .40
❑ 103 Rich Gannon SP 1.00 .40

2005 Exquisite Collection

❑ COMPLETE SET (127)
❑ COMP.SET w/o SP's (42)
❑ COMMON CARD (1-42) 12.00 5.00
❑ SEMISTARS 12.00 5.00
❑ UNLISTED STARS 20.00 8.00
❑ PRINT RUN 150 SER.#'d SETS
❑ ROOKIE AU PRINT RUN 150 SER.#'d SETS
❑ ROOKIE JSY AU PRINT RUN 199 SER.#'d SETS
❑ 1 Larry Fitzgerald 20.00 8.00
❑ 2 Michael Vick 30.00 12.00
❑ 3 Jamal Lewis 12.00 5.00
❑ 4 Ray Lewis 20.00 8.00
❑ 5 Willis McGahee 20.00 8.00
❑ 6 Jake Delhomme 20.00 8.00
❑ 7 Brian Urlacher 20.00 8.00
❑ 8 Carson Palmer 20.00 8.00
❑ 9 Julius Jones 25.00 10.00
❑ 10 Drew Bledsoe 20.00 8.00
❑ 11 Jake Plummer 12.00 5.00
❑ 12 Kevin Jones 25.00 10.00
❑ 13 Roy Williams WR 20.00 8.00
❑ 14 Ahman Green 20.00 8.00
❑ 15 Brett Favre 50.00 20.00
❑ 16 David Carr 20.00 8.00
❑ 17 Edgerrin James 20.00 8.00
❑ 18 Marvin Harrison 20.00 8.00
❑ 19 Peyton Manning 30.00 12.00
❑ 20 Byron Leftwich 20.00 8.00
❑ 21 Priest Holmes 20.00 8.00
❑ 22 Daunte Culpepper 20.00 8.00
❑ 23 Tom Brady 40.00 15.00
❑ 24 Deuce McAllister 20.00 8.00
❑ 25 Eli Manning 40.00 15.00
❑ 26 Jeremy Shockey 20.00 8.00
❑ 27 Chad Pennington 20.00 8.00
❑ 28 Curtis Martin 20.00 8.00
❑ 29 Randy Moss 20.00 8.00
❑ 30 Donovan McNabb 25.00 10.00
❑ 31 Terrell Owens 20.00 8.00
❑ 32 Jerome Bettis 20.00 8.00
❑ 33 Ben Roethlisberger 50.00 20.00
❑ 34 Drew Brees 12.00 5.00
❑ 35 LaDainian Tomlinson 25.00 10.00
❑ 36 Antonio Gates 20.00 8.00
❑ 37 Shaun Alexander 20.00 8.00
❑ 38 Marc Bulger 20.00 8.00
❑ 39 Torry Holt 12.00 5.00
❑ 40 Steven Jackson 25.00 10.00
❑ 41 Steve McNair 20.00 8.00
❑ 42 Clinton Portis 20.00 8.00
❑ 43 Dan Orlovsky AU RC 60.00 25.00
❑ 44 Darren Sproles AU RC 50.00 20.00
❑ 45 Marion Barber AU RC 80.00 30.00
❑ 46 Chris Henry AU RC 50.00 20.00
❑ 47 Derek Anderson AU RC 50.00 20.00
❑ 48 Erasmus James AU RC 40.00 15.00
❑ 49 Thomas Davis AU RC 40.00 15.00
❑ 50 David Pollack AU RC 60.00 25.00
❑ 51 Fred Gibson AU RC 40.00 15.00
❑ 52 Craphonso Thorpe AU RC 40.00 15.00
❑ 53 Derrick Johnson AU RC 80.00 30.00
❑ 54 Brandon Jacobs AU RC 60.00 25.00
❑ 55 Adrian McPherson AU RC 50.00 20.00
❑ 56 Matt Cassel AU RC 100.00 50.00
❑ 57 Anthony Davis AU RC 40.00 15.00
❑ 58 Alvin Pearman AU RC 50.00 20.00
❑ 59 Brandon Jones AU RC 50.00 20.00
❑ 60 Jerome Mathis AU RC 50.00 20.00
❑ 61 Chase Lyman AU RC 25.00 10.00
❑ 62 Roydell Williams AU RC 40.00 15.00
❑ 63 DeMarcus Ware AU RC 80.00 30.00
❑ 64 Mike Patterson AU RC 50.00 20.00
❑ 65 Mike Nugent AU RC 50.00 20.00
❑ 66 Ryan Fitzpatrick AU RC 80.00 30.00
❑ 67 Barrett Ruud AU RC 50.00 20.00
❑ 68 Kevin Burnett AU RC 50.00 20.00
❑ 69 J.R. Russell AU RC 40.00 15.00
❑ 70 C.Houston AU RC EXCH 50.00 20.00
❑ 71 Marlin Jackson AU RC 50.00 20.00
❑ 72 Shawne Merriman AU RC 120.00 60.00
❑ 73 Alex Smith TE AU RC 50.00 20.00
❑ 74 Fabian Washington AU RC 50.00 20.00
❑ 75 Corey Webster AU RC 40.00 15.00
❑ 76 Larry Brackins AU RC 40.00 15.00
❑ 77 Kay-Jay Harris AU RC 40.00 15.00
❑ 78 Airese Currie AU RC 40.00 15.00
❑ 79 Taylor Stubblefield AU RC 25.00 10.00
❑ 80 James Kilian AU RC 40.00 15.00
❑ 81 Travis Johnson AU RC 25.00 10.00
❑ 82 Walter Reyes AU RC 25.00 10.00
❑ 83 Anttaj Hawthorne AU RC 40.00 15.00
❑ 84 Chad Owens AU RC 50.00 20.00
❑ 85 J.J. Arrington JSY AU RC 80.00 40.00
❑ 86 Mark Bradley JSY AU RC 100.00 50.00
❑ 87 Reggie Brown JSY AU RC 120.0050.00
❑ 88 Jason Campbell JSY AU RC 200.00125.00
❑ 89 Maurice Clarett JSY AU 60.00 25.00
❑ 90 Mark Clayton JSY AU RC 150.00 60.00
❑ 91 Ciatrick Fason JSY AU RC 100.0040.00
❑ 92 Charlie Frye JSY AU RC 300.00 175.00
❑ 93 Frank Gore JSY AU RC 175.00 100.00
❑ 94 David Greene JSY AU RC 100.0040.00
❑ 95 Vincent Jackson JSY AU RC 100.00 40.00
❑ 96 Adam Jones JSY AU RC 80.00 30.00
❑ 97 Matt Jones JSY AU RC 200.00 100.00
❑ 98 Stefan LeFors JSY AU RC 80.00 30.00
❑ 99 Heath Miller JSY AU RC 250.00 125.00
❑ 100 Ryan Moats JSY AU RC 120.00 60.00
❑ 101 Vernand Morency JSY AU RC 60.00 25.00
❑ 102 Terrence Murphy JSY AU RC 80.00 30.00
❑ 103 Kyle Orton JSY AU RC 120.00 60.00
❑ 104 Roscoe Parrish JSY AU RC 80.00 30.00
❑ 105 Courtney Roby JSY AU RC 80.0030.00
❑ 106 Aaron Rodgers JSY AU RC 600.00 300.00
❑ 107 Carlos Rogers JSY AU RC 80.0030.00
❑ 108 Antrel Rolle JSY AU RC 80.00 30.00
❑ 109 Eric Shelton JSY AU RC 80.00 30.00
❑ 110 Andrew Walter JSY AU RC 120.00 60.00
❑ 111 Roddy White JSY AU RC 100.0040.00
❑ 112 Troy Williamson JSY AU/99 RC 250.00 150.00
❑ 113 Mike Williams JSY AU 175.00 90.00
❑ 114 Ronnie Brown JSY AU/99 RC 700.00 400.00
❑ 115 Braylon Edwards JSY AU/99 RC 350.00 200.00
❑ 116 Cedric Benson JSY AU/99 RC 550.00 350.00
❑ 117 Carnell Williams JSY AU/99 RC 1250.00 750.00
❑ 118 Alex Smith QB JSY AU/99 RC 800.00 500.00
❑ 120 Tyson Thompson AU RC 60.00 25.00
❑ 121 Chris Carr AU RC 40.00 15.00
❑ 122 Fred Amey AU RC 40.00 15.00
❑ 123 Brodney Pool AU RC 40.00 15.00
❑ 124 Stanford Routt AU RC 40.00 15.00
❑ 125 Justin Tuck AU RC 50.00 20.00
❑ 126 Luis Castillo AU RC 50.00 20.00
❑ 127 Kirk Morrison AU RC 50.00 20.00
❑ 128 DeAndra Cobb AU RC 40.00 15.00

1992 Finest

❑ COMPLETE SET (45) 20.00 7.50
❑ 1 Neal Anderson .50 .20
❑ 2 Cornelius Bennett .50 .20
❑ 3 Marion Butts .30 .10
❑ 4 Anthony Carter .50 .20
❑ 5 Mike Croel .30 .10
❑ 6 John Elway 5.00 2.00
❑ 7 Jim Everett .50 .20
❑ 8 Ernest Givins .30 .10
❑ 9 Rodney Hampton .50 .20
❑ 10 Alvin Harper .30 .10
❑ 11 Michael Irvin 1.00 .40
❑ 12 Rickey Jackson .30 .10
❑ 13 Seth Joyner .30 .10
❑ 14 James Lofton .50 .20
❑ 15 Ronnie Lott .50 .20
❑ 16 Eric Metcalf .50 .20
❑ 17 Chris Miller .50 .20
❑ 18 Art Monk .50 .20
❑ 19 Warren Moon 1.00 .40
❑ 20 Rob Moore .50 .20
❑ 21 Anthony Munoz .50 .20
❑ 22 Christian Okoye .30 .10
❑ 23 Andre Rison .50 .20
❑ 24 Leonard Russell .30 .10
❑ 25 Mark Rypien .50 .20
❑ 26 Barry Sanders 5.00 2.00
❑ 27 Emmitt Smith 6.00 2.50
❑ 28 Pat Swilling .30 .10
❑ 29 John Taylor .50 .20
❑ 30 Derrick Thomas 1.00 .40
❑ 31 Thurman Thomas 1.00 .40
❑ 32 Reggie White 1.00 .40
❑ 33 Rod Woodson 1.00 .40
❑ 34 Edgar Bennett .50 .20
❑ 35 Terrell Buckley .30 .10
❑ 36 Keith Hamilton .50 .20
❑ 37 Amp Lee .30 .10
❑ 38 Ricardo McDonald .30 .10
❑ 39 Chris Mims .30 .10
❑ 40 Robert Porcher 1.00 .40
❑ 41 Leon Searcy .30 .10
❑ 42 Siran Stacy .30 .10
❑ 43 Tommy Vardell .30 .10
❑ 44 Bob Whitfield .30 .10
❑ NNO Checklist .30 .10

1994 Finest

❑ COMPLETE SET (220) 40.00 15.00
❑ 1 Emmitt Smith 6.00 2.50
❑ 2 Calvin Williams .60 .25
❑ 3 Mark Collins .30 .10

❑ 4 Steve McMichael .60 .25
❑ 5 Jim Kelly 1.25 .50
❑ 6 Michael Dean Perry .60 .25
❑ 7 Wayne Simmons .30 .10
❑ 8 Rocket Ismail .60 .25
❑ 9 Mark Rypien .30 .10
❑ 10 Brian Blades .60 .25
❑ 11 Barry Word .30 .10
❑ 12 Jerry Rice 4.00 1.50
❑ 13 Derrick Fenner .30 .10
❑ 14 Karl Mecklenburg .30 .10
❑ 15 Reggie Cobb .30 .10
❑ 16 Eric Swann .60 .25
❑ 17 Neil Smith .60 .25
❑ 18 Barry Foster .30 .10
❑ 19 Willie Roaf .30 .10
❑ 20 Troy Drayton .30 .10
❑ 21 Warren Moon 1.25 .50
❑ 22 Richmond Webb .30 .10
❑ 23 Anthony Miller .60 .25
❑ 24 Chris Slade .30 .10
❑ 25 Mel Gray .30 .10
❑ 26 Ronnie Lott .60 .25
❑ 27 Andre Rison .60 .25
❑ 28 Jeff George 1.25 .50
❑ 29 John Copeland .30 .10
❑ 30 Derrick Thomas 1.25 .50
❑ 31 Sterling Sharpe .60 .25
❑ 32 Chris Doleman .30 .10
❑ 33 Monte Coleman .30 .10
❑ 34 Mark Bavaro .30 .10
❑ 35 Kevin Williams WR .60 .25
❑ 36 Eric Metcalf .60 .25
❑ 37 Brent Jones .60 .25
❑ 38 Steve Tasker .60 .25
❑ 39 Dave Meggett .30 .10
❑ 40 Howie Long 1.25 .50
❑ 41 Rick Mirer 1.25 .50
❑ 42 Jerome Bettis 4.00 1.50
❑ 43 Marion Butts .30 .10
❑ 44 Barry Sanders 6.00 2.50
❑ 45 Jason Elam .60 .25
❑ 46 Broderick Thomas .30 .10
❑ 47 Derek Brown RBK .30 .10
❑ 48 Lorenzo White .30 .10
❑ 49 Neil O'Donnell 1.25 .50
❑ 50 Chris Burkett .30 .10
❑ 51 John Offerdahl .30 .10
❑ 52 Rohn Stark .30 .10
❑ 53 Neal Anderson .30 .10
❑ 54 Steve Beuerlein .60 .25
❑ 55 Bruce Armstrong .30 .10
❑ 56 Lincoln Kennedy .30 .10
❑ 57 Darrell Green .30 .10
❑ 58 Ricardo McDonald .30 .10
❑ 59 Chris Warren .60 .25
❑ 60 Mark Jackson .30 .10
❑ 61 Pepper Johnson .30 .10
❑ 62 Chris Spielman .60 .25
❑ 63 Marcus Allen 1.25 .50
❑ 64 Jim Everett .60 .25
❑ 65 Greg Townsend .30 .10
❑ 66 Cris Carter 1.50 .60
❑ 67 Don Beebe .30 .10
❑ 68 Reggie Langhorne .30 .10
❑ 69 Randall Cunningham 1.25 .50
❑ 70 Johnny Holland .30 .10
❑ 71 Morten Andersen .30 .10
❑ 72 Leonard Marshall .30 .10
❑ 73 Keith Jackson .30 .10
❑ 74 Leslie O'Neal .30 .10
❑ 75 Hardy Nickerson .60 .25
❑ 76 Dan Williams .30 .10
❑ 77 Steve Young 3.00 1.25
❑ 78 Deon Figures .30 .10
❑ 79 Michael Irvin 1.25 .50
❑ 80 Luis Sharpe .30 .10
❑ 81 Andre Tippett .30 .10
❑ 82 Ricky Sanders .30 .10
❑ 83 Erric Pegram .30 .10
❑ 84 Albert Lewis .30 .10
❑ 85 Anthony Blaylock .30 .10
❑ 86 Pat Swilling .30 .10
❑ 87 Duane Bickett .30 .10
❑ 88 Myron Guyton .30 .10
❑ 89 Clay Matthews .30 .10
❑ 90 Jim McMahon .60 .25
❑ 91 Bruce Smith 1.25 .50
❑ 92 Reggie White 1.25 .50
❑ 93 Shannon Sharpe .60 .25
❑ 94 Rickey Jackson .30 .10
❑ 95 Ronnie Harmon .30 .10
❑ 96 Terry McDaniel .30 .10
❑ 97 Bryan Cox .30 .10
❑ 98 Webster Slaughter .30 .10
❑ 99 Boomer Esiason .60 .25
❑ 100 Tim Krumrie .30 .10
❑ 101 Cortez Kennedy .60 .25
❑ 102 Henry Ellard .60 .25
❑ 103 Clyde Simmons .30 .10
❑ 104 Craig Erickson .30 .10
❑ 105 Eric Green .30 .10
❑ 106 Gary Clark .60 .25
❑ 107 Jay Novacek .60 .25
❑ 108 Dana Stubblefield .60 .25
❑ 109 Mike Johnson .30 .10
❑ 110 Ray Crockett .30 .10
❑ 111 Leonard Russell .30 .10
❑ 112 Robert Smith 1.25 .50
❑ 113 Art Monk .60 .25
❑ 114 Ray Childress .30 .10
❑ 115 O.J.McDuffie 1.25 .50
❑ 116 Tim Brown 1.25 .50
❑ 117 Kevin Ross .30 .10
❑ 118 Richard Dent .60 .25
❑ 119 John Elway 8.00 3.00
❑ 120 James Hasty .30 .10
❑ 121 Gary Plummer .30 .10
❑ 122 Pierce Holt .30 .10
❑ 123 Eric Martin .30 .10
❑ 124 Brett Favre 8.00 3.00
❑ 125 Cornelius Bennett .60 .25
❑ 126 Jessie Hester .30 .10
❑ 127 Lewis Tillman .30 .10
❑ 128 Qadry Ismail 1.25 .50
❑ 129 Jay Schroeder .30 .10
❑ 130 Curtis Conway 1.25 .50
❑ 131 Santana Dotson .60 .25
❑ 132 Nick Lowery .30 .10
❑ 133 Lomas Brown .30 .10
❑ 134 Reggie Roby .30 .10
❑ 135 John L. Williams .30 .10
❑ 136 Vinny Testaverde .60 .25
❑ 137 Seth Joyner .30 .10
❑ 138 Ethan Horton .30 .10
❑ 139 Jackie Slater .30 .10
❑ 140 Rod Bernstine .30 .10
❑ 141 Rob Moore .60 .25
❑ 142 Dan Marino 8.00 3.00
❑ 143 Ken Harvey .30 .10
❑ 144 Ernest Givins .60 .25
❑ 145 Russell Maryland .30 .10
❑ 146 Drew Bledsoe 3.00 1.25
❑ 147 Kevin Greene .60 .25
❑ 148 Bobby Hebert .30 .10
❑ 149 Junior Seau 1.25 .50
❑ 150 Tim McDonald .30 .10
❑ 151 Thurman Thomas 1.25 .50
❑ 152 Phil Simms .60 .25
❑ 153 Terrell Buckley .30 .10
❑ 154 Sam Mills .30 .10
❑ 155 Anthony Carter .60 .25
❑ 156 Kelvin Martin .30 .10
❑ 157 Shane Conlan .30 .10
❑ 158 Irving Fryar .60 .25
❑ 159 Demetrius DuBose .30 .10
❑ 160 David Klingler .30 .10
❑ 161 Herman Moore 1.25 .50
❑ 162 Jeff Hostetler .60 .25
❑ 163 Tommy Vardell .30 .10
❑ 164 Craig Heyward .60 .25
❑ 165 Wilber Marshall .30 .10
❑ 166 Quentin Coryatt .30 .10
❑ 167 Glyn Milburn .60 .25
❑ 168 Fred Barnett .60 .25
❑ 169 Charles Haley .60 .25
❑ 170 Carl Banks .30 .10
❑ 171 Ricky Proehl .30 .10
❑ 172 Joe Montana 8.00 3.00
❑ 173 Johnny Mitchell .30 .10
❑ 174 Andre Reed .60 .25
❑ 175 Marco Coleman .30 .10
❑ 176 Vaughan Johnson .30 .10
❑ 177 Carl Pickens .60 .25
❑ 178 Dwight Stone .30 .10
❑ 179 Ricky Watters .60 .25
❑ 180 Michael Haynes .60 .25
❑ 181 Roger Craig .60 .25
❑ 182 Cleveland Gary .30 .10
❑ 183 Steve Emtman .30 .10
❑ 184 Patrick Bates .30 .10
❑ 185 Mark Carrier WR .60 .25
❑ 186 Brad Hopkins .30 .10
❑ 187 Dennis Smith .30 .10
❑ 188 Natrone Means 1.25 .50
❑ 189 Michael Jackson .60 .25
❑ 190 Ken Norton Jr. .60 .25
❑ 191 Carlton Gray .30 .10
❑ 192 Edgar Bennett 1.25 .50
❑ 193 Lawrence Taylor 1.25 .50
❑ 194 Marv Cook .30 .10
❑ 195 Eric Curry .30 .10
❑ 196 Victor Bailey .30 .10
❑ 197 Ryan McNeil .30 .10
❑ 198 Rod Woodson .60 .25
❑ 199 Earnest Byner .30 .10
❑ 200 Marvin Jones .30 .10
❑ 201 Thomas Smith .30 .10
❑ 202 Troy Aikman 4.00 1.50
❑ 203 Audray McMillian .30 .10
❑ 204 Wade Wilson .30 .10
❑ 205 George Teague .30 .10
❑ 206 Deion Sanders 2.00 .75
❑ 207 Will Shields .60 .25
❑ 208 John Taylor .60 .25
❑ 209 Jim Harbaugh 1.25 .50
❑ 210 Micheal Barrow .30 .10
❑ 211 Harold Green .30 .10
❑ 212 Steve Everitt .30 .10
❑ 213 Flipper Anderson .30 .10
❑ 214 Rodney Hampton .60 .25
❑ 215 Steve Atwater .30 .10
❑ 216 James Trapp .30 .10
❑ 217 Terry Kirby 1.25 .50
❑ 218 Garrison Hearst 1.25 .50
❑ 219 Jeff Bryant .30 .10
❑ 220 Roosevelt Potts .30 .10

1995 Finest

❑ COMPLETE SET (275) 80.00 30.00
❑ COMP.SERIES 1 (165) 20.00 10.00
❑ COMP.SERIES 2 (110) 60.00 25.00
❑ 1 Natrone Means .60 .25
❑ 2 Dave Meggett .25 .08

❑ 3 Tim Bowens	.25	.08
❑ 4 Jay Novacek	.60	.25
❑ 5 Michael Jackson	.60	.25
❑ 6 Calvin Williams	.60	.25
❑ 7 Neil Smith	.60	.25
❑ 8 Chris Gardocki	.25	.08
❑ 9 Jeff Burris	.25	.08
❑ 10 Warren Moon	.60	.25
❑ 11 Gary Anderson K	.25	.08
❑ 12 Bert Emanuel	1.25	.50
❑ 13 Rick Tuten	.25	.08
❑ 14 Steve Wallace	.25	.08
❑ 15 Marion Butts	.25	.08
❑ 16 Johnnie Morton	.60	.25
❑ 17 Rob Moore	.60	.25
❑ 18 Wayne Gandy	.25	.08
❑ 19 Quentin Coryatt	.60	.25
❑ 20 Richmond Webb	.25	.08
❑ 21 Errict Rhett	.60	.25
❑ 22 Joe Johnson	.25	.08
❑ 23 Gary Brown	.25	.08
❑ 24 Jeff Hostetler	.60	.25
❑ 25 Larry Centers	.60	.25
❑ 26 Tom Carter	.25	.08
❑ 27 Steve Atwater	.25	.08
❑ 28 Doug Pelfrey	.25	.08
❑ 29 Bryce Paup	.60	.25
❑ 30 Erik Williams	.25	.08
❑ 31 Henry Jones	.25	.08
❑ 32 Stanley Richard	.25	.08
❑ 33 Marcus Allen	1.25	.50
❑ 34 Antonio Langham	.25	.08
❑ 35 Lewis Tillman	.25	.08
❑ 36 Thomas Randolph	.25	.08
❑ 37 Byron Bam Morris	.25	.08
❑ 38 David Palmer	.60	.25
❑ 39 Ricky Watters	.60	.25
❑ 40 Brett Perriman	.60	.25
❑ 41 Will Wolford	.25	.08
❑ 42 Burt Grossman	.25	.08
❑ 43 Vincent Brisby	.25	.08
❑ 44 Ronnie Lott	.60	.25
❑ 45 Brian Blades	.60	.25
❑ 46 Brent Jones	.25	.08
❑ 47 Anthony Newman	.25	.08
❑ 48 Willie Roaf	.25	.08
❑ 49 Paul Gruber	.25	.08
❑ 50 Jeff George	.60	.25
❑ 51 Jamir Miller	.25	.08
❑ 52 Anthony Miller	.60	.25
❑ 53 Darrell Green	.25	.08
❑ 54 Steve Wisniewski	.25	.08
❑ 55 Dan Wilkinson	.60	.25
❑ 56 Brett Favre	5.00	2.00
❑ 57 Leslie O'Neal	.60	.25
❑ 58 Keith Byars	.25	.08
❑ 59 James Washington	.25	.08
❑ 60 Andre Reed	.60	.25
❑ 61 Ken Norton Jr.	.60	.25
❑ 62 John Randle	.60	.25
❑ 63 Lake Dawson	.60	.25
❑ 64 Greg Montgomery	.25	.08
❑ 65 Erric Pegram	.60	.25
❑ 66 Steve Everitt	.25	.08
❑ 67 Chris Brantley	.25	.08
❑ 68 Rod Woodson	.60	.25
❑ 69 Eugene Robinson	.25	.08
❑ 70 Dave Brown	.60	.25
❑ 71 Ricky Reynolds	.25	.08
❑ 72 Rohn Stark	.25	.08
❑ 73 Randal Hill	.25	.08
❑ 74 Brian Washington	.25	.08
❑ 75 Heath Shuler	.60	.25
❑ 76 Darion Conner	.25	.08
❑ 77 Terry McDaniel	.25	.08
❑ 78 Al Del Greco	.25	.08
❑ 79 Allen Aldridge	.25	.08
❑ 80 Trace Armstrong	.25	.08
❑ 81 Darnay Scott	.60	.25
❑ 82 Charlie Garner	1.25	.50
❑ 83 Harold Bishop	.25	.08
❑ 84 Reggie White	1.25	.50
❑ 85 Shawn Jefferson	.25	.08
❑ 86 Irving Spikes	.60	.25
❑ 87 Mel Gray	.25	.08
❑ 88 D.J. Johnson	.25	.08
❑ 89 Daryl Johnston	.60	.25
❑ 90 Joe Montana	5.00	2.00
❑ 91 Michael Strahan	1.25	.50
❑ 92 Robert Blackmon	.25	.08
❑ 93 Ryan Yarborough	.60	.25
❑ 94 Terry Allen	.60	.25
❑ 95 Michael Haynes	.60	.25
❑ 96 Jim Harbaugh	.60	.25
❑ 97 Micheal Barrow	.25	.08
❑ 98 John Thierry	.25	.08
❑ 99 Seth Joyner	.25	.08
❑ 100 Deion Sanders	2.00	.75
❑ 101 Eric Turner	.25	.08
❑ 102 LeShon Johnson	.60	.25
❑ 103 John Copeland	.25	.08
❑ 104 Cornelius Bennett	.60	.25
❑ 105 Sean Gilbert	.60	.25
❑ 106 Herschel Walker	.60	.25
❑ 107 Henry Ellard	.60	.25
❑ 108 Neil O'Donnell	.60	.25
❑ 109 Charles Wilson	.25	.08
❑ 110 Willie McGinest	.60	.25
❑ 111 Tim Brown	1.25	.50
❑ 112 Simon Fletcher	.25	.08
❑ 113 Broderick Thomas	.25	.08
❑ 114 Tom Waddle	.25	.08
❑ 115 Jessie Tuggle	.25	.08
❑ 116 Maurice Hurst	.25	.08
❑ 117 Aubrey Beavers	.25	.08
❑ 118 Donnell Bennett	.60	.25
❑ 119 Shante Carver	.25	.08
❑ 120 Eric Metcalf	.60	.25
❑ 121 John Carney	.25	.08
❑ 122 Thomas Lewis	.60	.25
❑ 123 Johnny Mitchell	.25	.08
❑ 124 Trent Dilfer	1.25	.50
❑ 125 Marshall Faulk	3.00	1.25
❑ 126 Ernest Givins	.25	.08
❑ 127 Aeneas Williams	.25	.08
❑ 128 Bucky Brooks	.25	.08
❑ 129 Todd Steussie	.25	.08
❑ 130 Randall Cunningham	1.25	.50
❑ 131 Reggie Brooks	.60	.25
❑ 132 Morten Andersen	.25	.08
❑ 133 James Jett	.60	.25
❑ 134 George Teague	.25	.08
❑ 135 John Taylor	.25	.08
❑ 136 Charles Johnson	.60	.25
❑ 137 Isaac Bruce	2.50	1.00
❑ 138 Jason Elam	.60	.25
❑ 139 Carl Pickens	.60	.25
❑ 140 Chris Warren	.60	.25
❑ 141 Bruce Armstrong	.25	.08
❑ 142 Mark Carrier DB	.25	.08
❑ 143 Irving Fryar	.60	.25
❑ 144 Van Malone	.25	.08
❑ 145 Charles Haley	.60	.25
❑ 146 Chris Calloway	.25	.08
❑ 147 J.J. Birden	.25	.08
❑ 148 Tony Bennett	.25	.08
❑ 149 Lincoln Kennedy	.25	.08
❑ 150 Stan Humphries	.60	.25
❑ 151 Hardy Nickerson	.25	.08
❑ 152 Randall McDaniel	.25	.08
❑ 153 Marcus Robertson	.25	.08
❑ 154 Ronald Moore	.25	.08
❑ 155 Thurman Thomas	1.25	.50
❑ 156 Tommy Vardell	.25	.08
❑ 157 Ken Ruettgers	.25	.08
❑ 158 Rob Fredrickson	.25	.08
❑ 159 Johnny Bailey	.25	.08
❑ 160 Greg Lloyd	.60	.25
❑ 161 David Alexander	.25	.08
❑ 162 Kevin Mawae	.25	.08
❑ 163 Derek Brown RBK	.25	.08
❑ 164 William Floyd	.60	.25
❑ 165 Aaron Glenn	.25	.08
❑ 166 Joey Galloway RC	8.00	3.00
❑ 167 Troy Drayton	.25	.08
❑ 168 Dermontti Dawson	.60	.25
❑ 169 Ronald Moore	.25	.08
❑ 170 Dan Marino	5.00	2.00
❑ 171 Dennis Gibson	.25	.08
❑ 172 Raymont Harris	.25	.08
❑ 173 Shannon Sharpe	.60	.25
❑ 174 Kevin Williams	.60	.25
❑ 175 Jim Everett	.25	.08
❑ 176 Rocket Ismail	.60	.25
❑ 177 Mark Fields RC	1.25	.50
❑ 178 George Koonce	.25	.08
❑ 179 Chris Hudson	.25	.08
❑ 180 Jerry Rice	2.50	1.00
❑ 181 Dewayne Washington	.60	.25
❑ 182 Dale Carter	.60	.25
❑ 183 Pete Stoyanovich	.25	.08
❑ 184 Blake Brockermeyer	.25	.08
❑ 185 Troy Aikman	2.50	1.00
❑ 186 Jeff Blake RC	2.50	1.00
❑ 187 Troy Vincent	.25	.08
❑ 188 Lamar Lathon	.25	.08
❑ 189 Tony Boselli	1.25	.50
❑ 190 Emmitt Smith	4.00	1.50
❑ 191 Bobby Houston	.25	.08
❑ 192 Edgar Bennett	.60	.25
❑ 193 Derrick Brooks RC	8.00	3.00
❑ 194 Ricky Proehl	.25	.08
❑ 195 Rodney Hampton	.60	.25
❑ 196 Dave Krieg	.25	.08
❑ 197 Vinny Testaverde	.60	.25
❑ 198 Erik Kramer	.25	.08
❑ 199 Ben Coates	.60	.25
❑ 200 Steve Young	2.00	.75
❑ 201 Glyn Milburn	.25	.08
❑ 202 Bryan Cox	.25	.08
❑ 203 Luther Elliss	.25	.08
❑ 204 Mark McMillian	.25	.08
❑ 205 Jerome Bettis	1.25	.50
❑ 206 Craig Heyward	.60	.25
❑ 207 Ray Buchanan	.25	.08
❑ 208 Kimble Anders	.60	.25
❑ 209 Kevin Greene	.60	.25
❑ 210 Eric Allen	.25	.08
❑ 211 Ricardo McDonald	.25	.08
❑ 212 Ruben Brown RC	1.50	.60
❑ 213 Harvey Williams	.25	.08
❑ 214 Broderick Thomas	.25	.08
❑ 215 Frank Reich	.25	.08
❑ 216 Frank Sanders RC	1.50	.60
❑ 217 Craig Newsome	.25	.08
❑ 218 Merton Hanks	.25	.08
❑ 219 Chris Miller	.25	.08
❑ 220 John Elway	5.00	2.00
❑ 221 Ernest Givins	.25	.08
❑ 222 Boomer Esiason	.60	.25
❑ 223 Reggie Roby	.25	.08
❑ 224 Qadry Ismail	.60	.25
❑ 225 Ki-Jana Carter RC	1.50	.60
❑ 226 Leon Lett	.25	.08

❑ 227	Eric Hill	.25	.08
❑ 228	Scott Mitchell	.60	.25
❑ 229	Craig Erickson	.25	.08
❑ 230	Drew Bledsoe	2.00	.75
❑ 231	Sean Landeta	.25	.08
❑ 232	Barrett Brooks	.25	.08
❑ 233	Brian Mitchell	.25	.08
❑ 234	Tyrone Poole	1.25	.50
❑ 235	Desmond Howard	.60	.25
❑ 236	Wayne Simmons	.25	.08
❑ 237	Michael Westbrook RC	1.50	.60
❑ 238	Quinn Early	.60	.25
❑ 239	Willie Davis	.60	.25
❑ 240	Rashaan Salaam RC	.75	.30
❑ 241	Devin Bush	.25	.08
❑ 242	Dana Stubblefield	.60	.25
❑ 243	Dexter Carter	.25	.08
❑ 244	Shane Conlan	.25	.08
❑ 245	Keith Elias RC	.25	.08
❑ 246	Robert Brooks	1.25	.50
❑ 247	Garrison Hearst	1.25	.50
❑ 248	Eric Zeier RC	1.50	.60
❑ 249	Nate Newton	.60	.25
❑ 250	Barry Sanders	4.00	1.50
❑ 251	Dave Meggett	.25	.08
❑ 252	Courtney Hawkins	.25	.08
❑ 253	Cortez Kennedy	.60	.25
❑ 254	Mario Bates	.60	.25
❑ 255	Junior Seau	1.25	.50
❑ 256	Brian Washington	.25	.08
❑ 257	Darius Holland	.25	.08
❑ 258	Jeff Graham	.25	.08
❑ 259	Rob Moore	.60	.25
❑ 260	Andre Rison	.60	.25
❑ 261	Kerry Collins RC	8.00	3.00
❑ 262	Roosevelt Potts	.25	.08
❑ 263	Cris Carter	1.25	.50
❑ 264	Curtis Martin RC	15.00	6.00
❑ 265	Rick Mirer	.60	.25
❑ 266	Mo Lewis	.25	.08
❑ 267	Mike Sherrard	.25	.08
❑ 268	Herman Moore	1.25	.50
❑ 269	Eric Metcalf	.60	.25
❑ 270	Ray Childress	.25	.08
❑ 271	Chris Slade	.25	.08
❑ 272	Michael Irvin	1.25	.50
❑ 273	Jim Kelly	1.25	.50
❑ 274	Terance Mathis	.60	.25
❑ 275	LeRoy Butler	.25	.08

1996 Finest

❑	COMPLETE SET (359)	400.00	150.00
❑	COMP.SERIES 1 (191)	250.00	100.00
❑	COMP.SERIES 2 (168)	150.00	60.00
❑	COMP.BRONZE SER.1 (110)	40.00	15.00
❑	COMP.BRONZE SER.2 (110)	40.00	15.00
❑ B2	Jay Novacek B	.60	.25
❑ B3	Ray Buchanan B	.30	.10
❑ B5	Phil Hansen B	.30	.10
❑ B6	Mike Mamula B	.30	.10
❑ B9	Bernie Parmalee B	.30	.10
❑ B10	Herman Moore B	.60	.25
❑ B11	Shawn Jefferson B	.30	.10
❑ B12	Chris Doleman B	.30	.10
❑ B13	Erik Kramer B	.60	.25
❑ B15	Orlando Thomas B	.30	.10
❑ B16	Terrell Davis B	4.00	1.50
❑ B18	Roman Phifer B	.30	.10
❑ B19	Trent Dilfer B	.60	.25
❑ B21	Darnay Scott B	.60	.25
❑ B22	Steve McNair B	4.00	1.50
❑ B23	Lamar Lathon B	.30	.10
❑ B26	Thomas Randolph B	.30	.10
❑ B27	Michael Jackson B	.60	.25
❑ B28	Seth Joyner B	.30	.10
❑ B29	Jeff Lageman B	.30	.10
❑ B30	Darryl Williams B	.30	.10
❑ B32	Erric Pegram B	.60	.25
❑ B34	Sean Dawkins B	.60	.25
❑ B38	Dan Saleaumua B UER 28	.30	.10
❑ B39	Henry Thomas B	.30	.10
❑ B43	Pat Swilling B	.30	.10
❑ B44	Marty Carter B	.30	.10
❑ B45	Anthony Miller B	.60	.25
❑ B48	Chris Warren B	.60	.25
❑ B49	Derek Brown RBK B	.30	.10
❑ B51	Blaine Bishop B	.30	.10
❑ B52	Jake Reed B	.60	.25
❑ B55	Vencie Glenn B	.30	.10
❑ B58	Derrick Alexander WR B	.60	.25
❑ B64	Jessie Tuggle B	.30	.10
❑ B65	Terrance Shaw B	.30	.10
❑ B66	David Sloan B	.60	.25
❑ B68	Brent Jones B	.30	.10
❑ B70	William Thomas B	.30	.10
❑ B71	Robert Smith B	.60	.25
❑ B72	Wayne Simmons B	.30	.10
❑ B73	Jim Harbaugh B	.60	.25
❑ B76	Wayne Chrebet B	2.00	.75
❑ B77	Chris Hudson B	.30	.10
❑ B79	Stevon Moore B	.30	.10
❑ B80	Chris Calloway B	.30	.10
❑ B81	Tom Carter B	.30	.10
❑ B82	Dave Meggett B	.30	.10
❑ B83	Sam Mills B	.60	.25
❑ B86	Renaldo Turnbull B	.30	.10
❑ B87	Derrick Brooks B	1.00	.40
❑ B89	Eugene Robinson B	.30	.10
❑ B91	Rodney Thomas B	.30	.10
❑ B92	Dan Wilkinson B	.30	.10
❑ B93	Mark Fields B	.30	.10
❑ B94	Warren Sapp B	.30	.10
❑ B95	Curtis Martin B	4.00	1.50
❑ B97	Ray Crockett B	.30	.10
❑ B98	Ed McDaniel B	.30	.10
❑ B101	Craig Heyward B	.30	.10
❑ B102	Ellis Johnson B	.30	.10
❑ B104	O.J. McDuffie B	.60	.25
❑ B105	J.J. Stokes B	1.00	.40
❑ B106	Mo Lewis B	.30	.10
❑ B108	Rob Moore B	.60	.25
❑ B110	Tyrone Wheatley B	.60	.25
❑ B111	Ken Harvey B	.30	.10
❑ B113	Willie Green B	.30	.10
❑ B114	Willie Davis B	.60	.25
❑ B115	Andy Harmon B	.30	.10
❑ B117	Bryan Cox B	.30	.10
❑ B119	Bert Emanuel B	.60	.25
❑ B120	Greg Lloyd B	.60	.25
❑ B122	Willie Jackson B	.60	.25
❑ B123	Lorenzo Lynch B	.30	.10
❑ B124	Pepper Johnson B	.30	.10
❑ B128	Tyrone Poole B	.30	.10
❑ B129	Neil Smith B	.60	.25
❑ B130	Eddie Robinson B	.30	.10
❑ B131	Bryce Paup B	.60	.25
❑ B134	Troy Aikman B	5.00	2.00
❑ B136	Chris Sanders B	.60	.25
❑ B138	Jim Everett B	.30	.10
❑ B139	Frank Sanders B	.60	.25
❑ B141	Cortez Kennedy B	.60	.25
❑ B143	Derrick Alexander DE B	.30	.10
❑ B144	Rob Fredrickson B	.30	.10
❑ B145	Chris Zorich B	.30	.10

❑ B146	Devin Bush B	.30	.10
❑ B149	Troy Vincent B	.30	.10
❑ B151	Deion Sanders B	2.50	1.00
❑ B152	James O. Stewart B	.60	.25
❑ B156	Lawrence Dawsey B	.30	.10
❑ B157	Robert Brooks B	1.00	.40
❑ B158	Rashaan Salaam B	.60	.25
❑ B161	Tim Brown B	.60	.25
❑ B162	Brendan Stai B	.30	.10
❑ B163	Sean Gilbert B	.30	.10
❑ B169	Calvin Williams B	.60	.25
❑ B171	Ruben Brown B	.30	.10
❑ B172	Eric Green B	.30	.10
❑ B175	Jerry Rice B	5.00	2.00
❑ B176	Bruce Smith B	1.00	.40
❑ B177	Mark Bruener B	.30	.10
❑ B179	Lamont Warren B	.30	.10
❑ B180	Tamarick Vanover B	1.00	.40
❑ B182	Scott Mitchell B	.60	.25
❑ B186	Terry Wooden B	.30	.10
❑ B187	Ken Norton B	.60	.25
❑ B188	Jeff Herrod B	.30	.10
❑ B192	Gus Frerotte B	.60	.25
❑ B194	Brett Maxie B	.30	.10
❑ B198	Eddie Kennison B RC	1.25	.50
❑ B201	Marcus Jones B RC	.30	.10
❑ B202	Terry Allen B	.60	.25
❑ B203	Leroy Hoard B	.30	.10
❑ B205	Reggie White B	1.00	.40
❑ B206	Larry Centers B	.60	.25
❑ B208	Vincent Brisby B	.30	.10
❑ B209	Michael Timpson B	.30	.10
❑ B211	John Mobley B RC	.30	.10
❑ B212	Clay Matthews B	.60	.25
❑ B213	Shannon Sharpe B	.60	.25
❑ B214	Tony Bennett B	.30	.10
❑ B216	Mickey Washington B	.30	.10
❑ B217	Fred Barnett B	.60	.25
❑ B218	Michael Haynes B	.60	.25
❑ B219	Stan Humphries B	.60	.25
❑ B221	Winston Moss B	.30	.10
❑ B222	Tim Biakabutuka B RC	1.25	.50
❑ B223	Leeland McElroy B RC	.60	.25
❑ B224	Vinnie Clark B	.30	.10
❑ B225	Keyshawn Johnson B RC	5.00	2.00
❑ B228	Tony Woods B	.30	.10
❑ B231	Anthony Pleasant B	.30	.10
❑ B232	Jeff George B	.60	.25
❑ B233	Curtis Conway B	1.00	.40
❑ B235	Jeff Lewis B RC	.60	.25
❑ B236	Edgar Bennett B	.60	.25
❑ B237	Regan Upshaw B RC	.30	.10
❑ B238	William Fuller B	.30	.10
❑ B241	Willie Anderson B RC	.30	.10
❑ B242	Derrick Thomas B	1.00	.40
❑ B243	Marvin Harrison B RC	15.00	6.00
❑ B244	Darion Conner B	.30	.10
❑ B245	Antonio Langham B	.30	.10
❑ B246	Rodney Peete B	.30	.10
❑ B247	Tim McDonald B	.30	.10
❑ B248	Robert Jones B	.30	.10
❑ B251	Mark Carrier DB B	.30	.10
❑ B252	Stephen Grant B	.30	.10
❑ B254	Jeff Hostetler B	.60	.25
❑ B255	Darrell Green B	.30	.10
❑ B261	Eric Swann B	.60	.25
❑ B263	Irv Smith B	.30	.10
❑ B264	Tim McKyer B	.30	.10
❑ B266	Sean Jones B	.30	.10
❑ B271	Yancey Thigpen B	.60	.25
❑ B273	Quentin Coryatt B	.30	.10
❑ B274	Hardy Nickerson B	.30	.10
❑ B275	Ricardo McDonald B	.30	.10
❑ B277	Robert Blackmon B	.30	.10
❑ B279	Alonzo Spellman B	.30	.10
❑ B281	Rickey Dudley B RC	1.25	.50
❑ B282	Joe Cain B	.30	.10
❑ B284	John Randle B	.60	.25
❑ B286	Vinny Testaverde B	.60	.25
❑ B289	Henry Jones B	.30	.10

❑ B290	Simeon Rice B RC	3.00	1.25
❑ B295	Leslie O'Neal B	.30	.10
❑ B297	Greg Hill B	.60	.25
❑ B301	Eric Metcalf B	.60	.25
❑ B303	Jerome Woods B RC	.30	.10
❑ B306	Anthony Smith B	.30	.10
❑ B307	Darren Perry B	.30	.10
❑ B311	James Hasty B	.30	.10
❑ B312	Cris Carter B	1.00	.40
❑ B314	Lawrence Phillips B RC	.60	.25
❑ B317	Aeneas Williams B	.30	.10
❑ B318	Eric Hill B	.30	.10
❑ B319	Kevin Hardy B RC	1.25	.50
❑ B321	Chris Chandler B	.60	.25
❑ B322	Rocket Ismail B	.60	.25
❑ B323	Anthony Parker B	.30	.10
❑ B324	John Thierry B	.30	.10
❑ B325	Micheal Barrow B	.30	.10
❑ B326	Henry Ford B	.30	.10
❑ B327	Aaron Hayden B RC	.30	.10
❑ B328	Terance Mathis B	.30	.10
❑ B329	Kirk Pointer B RC	.30	.10
❑ B330	Ray Mickens B RC	.30	.10
❑ B331	Jermane Mayberry B RC	.30	.10
❑ B332	Mario Bates B	.60	.25
❑ B333	Carlton Gray B	.30	.10
❑ B334	Derek Loville B	.30	.10
❑ B335	Mike Alstott B RC	5.00	2.00
❑ B336	Eric Guliford B	.30	.10
❑ B337	Marvcus Patton B	.30	.10
❑ B338	Terrell Owens B RC	15.00	6.00
❑ B339	Lance Johnstone B RC	.60	.25
❑ B340	Lake Dawson B	.60	.25
❑ B341	Winslow Oliver B RC	.30	.10
❑ B342	Adrian Murrell B	.60	.25
❑ B343	Jason Belser B	.30	.10
❑ B344	Brian Dawkins B RC	6.00	2.50
❑ B345	Reggie Brown B RC	.30	.10
❑ B346	Shaun Gayle B	.30	.10
❑ B347	Tony Brackens B RC	1.25	.50
❑ B348	Thomas Lewis B	.30	.10
❑ B349	Kelvin Pritchett B	.30	.10
❑ B350	Bobby Engram B RC	1.25	.50
❑ B351	Moe Williams B RC	3.00	1.25
❑ B352	Thomas Smith B	.30	.10
❑ B353	Dexter Carter B	.30	.10
❑ B354	Qadry Ismail B	.60	.25
❑ B355	Marco Battaglia B RC	.30	.10
❑ B356	Levon Kirkland B	.30	.10
❑ B357	Eric Allen B	.30	.10
❑ B358	Bobby Hoying B RC	1.25	.50
❑ B359	Checklist B	.30	.10
❑ G1	Kordell Stewart G	5.00	2.00
❑ G7	Kimble Anders G	1.50	.60
❑ G8	Merton Hanks G	1.50	.60
❑ G17	Rick Mirer G	3.00	1.25
❑ G33	Craig Newsome G	1.50	.60
❑ G36	Bryce Paup G	3.00	1.25
❑ G40	Dan Marino G	20.00	7.50
❑ G42	Andre Coleman G	1.50	.60
❑ G47	Kevin Carter G	1.50	.60
❑ G60	Mark Brunell G	8.00	3.00
❑ G61	David Palmer G	3.00	1.25
❑ G75	Carnell Lake G	1.50	.60
❑ G96	Joey Galloway G	5.00	2.00
❑ G112	Melvin Tuten G	1.50	.60
❑ G121	Aaron Glenn G	1.50	.60
❑ G132	Brett Favre G	20.00	7.50
❑ G133	Ken Dilger G	3.00	1.25
❑ G140	Barry Sanders G	20.00	7.50
❑ G142	Glyn Milburn G	1.50	.60
❑ G148	Brett Perriman G	3.00	1.25
❑ G160	Kerry Collins G	5.00	2.00
❑ G164	Lee Woodall G	1.50	.60
❑ G173	Marshall Faulk G	6.00	2.50
❑ G178	Troy Aikman G	12.00	5.00
❑ G190	Drew Bledsoe G	8.00	3.00
❑ G191	Checklist G	1.50	.60
❑ G193	Michael Irvin G	5.00	2.00
❑ G196	Warren Moon G	3.00	1.25
❑ G200	Steve Young G	10.00	4.00
❑ G207	Alex Van Dyke G RC	3.00	1.25
❑ G220	Cris Carter G	5.00	2.00
❑ G230	John Elway G	20.00	7.50
❑ G234	Charles Haley G	3.00	1.25
❑ G240	Jim Kelly G	5.00	2.00
❑ G250	Rodney Hampton G	3.00	1.25
❑ G256	Errict Rhett G	3.00	1.25
❑ G257	Alex Molden G	1.50	.60
❑ G260	Kevin Hardy G	3.00	1.25
❑ G267	Bryant Young G	3.00	1.25
❑ G268	Jeff Blake G	5.00	2.00
❑ G270	Keyshawn Johnson G	5.00	2.00
❑ G278	Junior Seau G	5.00	2.00
❑ G285	Terry Kirby G	3.00	1.25
❑ G293	Hugh Douglas G	3.00	1.25
❑ G296	Reggie White G	5.00	2.00
❑ G298	Elvis Grbac G	5.00	2.00
❑ G300	Emmitt Smith G	15.00	6.00
❑ G309	Ricky Watters G	3.00	1.25
❑ S4	Brett Favre S	15.00	6.00
❑ S14	Chester McGlockton S	.75	.30
❑ S20	Tyrone Hughes S	.75	.30
❑ S24	Ty Law S	3.00	1.25
❑ S25	Brian Mitchell S	.75	.30
❑ S31	Darren Woodson S	1.50	.60
❑ S35	Brian Mitchell S	.75	.30
❑ S37	Dana Stubblefield S	1.50	.60
❑ S41	Kerry Collins S	3.00	1.25
❑ S46	Orlando Thomas S	.75	.30
❑ S50	Jerry Rice S	8.00	3.00
❑ S53	Willie McGinest S	.75	.30
❑ S54	Blake Brockermeyer S	.75	.30
❑ S56	Michael Westbrook S	3.00	1.25
❑ S57	Garrison Hearst S	3.00	1.25
❑ S59	Kyle Brady S	1.50	.60
❑ S62	Tim Brown S	1.50	.60
❑ S63	Jeff Graham S	.75	.30
❑ S67	Dan Marino S	15.00	6.00
❑ S69	Tamarick Vanover S	3.00	1.25
❑ S74	Daryl Johnston S	1.50	.60
❑ S78	Frank Sanders S	1.50	.60
❑ S84	Darryll Lewis S	.75	.30
❑ S85	Carl Pickens S	1.50	.60
❑ S88	Jerome Bettis S	3.00	1.25
❑ S90	Terrell Davis S	6.00	2.50
❑ S99	Napoleon Kaufman S	3.00	1.25
❑ S100	Rashaan Salaam S	1.50	.60
❑ S103	Barry Sanders S	15.00	6.00
❑ S107	Tony Boselli S	1.50	.60
❑ S109	Eric Zeier S	1.50	.60
❑ S116	Bruce Smith S	3.00	1.25
❑ S118	Zack Crockett S	.75	.30
❑ S125	Joey Galloway S	3.00	1.25
❑ S126	Heath Shuler S	1.50	.60
❑ S127	Curtis Martin S	6.00	2.50
❑ S135	Greg Lloyd S	1.50	.60
❑ S137	Marshall Faulk S	4.00	1.50
❑ S147	Tyrone Poole S	.75	.30
❑ S150	J.J. Stokes S	3.00	1.25
❑ S153	Drew Bledsoe S	5.00	2.00
❑ S154	Terry McDaniel S	.75	.30
❑ S155	Terrell Fletcher S	.75	.30
❑ S159	Dave Brown S	.75	.30
❑ S165	Jim Harbaugh S	1.50	.60
❑ S166	Larry Brown S	.75	.30
❑ S167	Neil Smith S	1.50	.60
❑ S168	Herman Moore S	1.50	.60
❑ S170	Deion Sanders S	5.00	2.00
❑ S174	Mark Chmura S	1.50	.60
❑ S181	Chris Warren S	1.50	.60
❑ S183	Robert Brooks S	3.00	1.25
❑ S184	Steve McNair S	6.00	2.50
❑ S185	Kordell Stewart S	3.00	1.25
❑ S189	Charlie Garner S	1.50	.60
❑ S195	Harvey Williams S	.75	.30
❑ S197	Jeff George S	1.50	.60
❑ S199	Ricky Watters S	1.50	.60
❑ S204	Steve Bono S	1.50	.60
❑ S210	Jeff Blake S	3.00	1.25
❑ S215	Phillippi Sparks S	.75	.30
❑ S226	William Floyd S	1.50	.60
❑ S227	Troy Drayton S	.75	.30
❑ S229	Rodney Hampton S	1.50	.60
❑ S239	Duane Clemons S RC	.75	.30
❑ S249	Curtis Conway S	3.00	1.25
❑ S253	John Mobley S	.75	.30
❑ S258	Chris Slade S	.75	.30
❑ S259	Derrick Thomas S	3.00	1.25
❑ S262	Eric Metcalf S	1.50	.60
❑ S265	Emmitt Smith S	12.00	5.00
❑ S269	Jeff Hostetler S	1.50	.60
❑ S272	Thurman Thomas S	3.00	1.25
❑ S276	Steve Atwater S	.75	.30
❑ S280	Isaac Bruce S	3.00	1.25
❑ S283	Neil O'Donnell S	1.50	.60
❑ S287	Jim Kelly S	3.00	1.25
❑ S288	Lawrence Phillips S	3.00	1.25
❑ S291	Terance Mathis S	.75	.30
❑ S292	Errict Rhett S	1.50	.60
❑ S294	Santo Stephens S	.75	.30
❑ S299	Walt Harris S RC	.75	.30
❑ S302	Jamir Miller S	.75	.30
❑ S304	Ben Coates S	1.50	.60
❑ S305	Marcus Allen S	3.00	1.25
❑ S308	Jonathan Ogden S RC	3.00	1.25
❑ S310	John Elway S	15.00	6.00
❑ S313	Irving Fryar S	1.50	.60
❑ S315	Junior Seau S	3.00	1.25
❑ S316	Alex Molden S RC	.75	.30
❑ S320	Steve Young S	6.00	2.50

1997 Finest

❑	COMPLETE SET (350)	500.00	250.00
❑	COMP.SERIES 1 SET (175)	250.00	125.00
❑	COMP.SERIES 2 SET (175)	250.00	125.00
❑	COMP.BRONZE SER.1 (100)	25.00	10.00
❑	COMP.BRONZE SER.2 (100)	40.00	15.00
❑ 1	Mark Brunell B	2.00	.75
❑ 2	Chris Slade B	.60	.25
❑ 3	Chris Doleman B	.60	.25
❑ 4	Chris Hudson B	.60	.25
❑ 5	Karim Abdul-Jabbar B	1.00	.40
❑ 6	Darren Perry B	.60	.25
❑ 7	Daryl Johnston B	1.00	.40
❑ 8	Rob Moore B UER	1.00	.40
❑ 9	Robert Smith B	1.00	.40
❑ 10	Terry Allen B	1.50	.60
❑ 11	Jason Dunn B	.60	.25
❑ 12	Henry Thomas B	.60	.25
❑ 13	Rod Stephens B	.60	.25
❑ 14	Ray Mickens B	.60	.25
❑ 15	Ty Detmer B	1.00	.40
❑ 16	Fred Barnett B	.60	.25
❑ 17	Derrick Alexander WR B	1.00	.40
❑ 18	Marcus Robertson B	.60	.25
❑ 19	Robert Blackmon B	.60	.25
❑ 20	Isaac Bruce B	1.50	.60
❑ 21	Chester McGlockton B	.60	.25
❑ 22	Stan Humphries B	1.00	.40
❑ 23	Lonnie Marts B	.60	.25
❑ 24	Jason Sehorn B	1.00	.40
❑ 25	Bobby Engram B UER	1.00	.40
❑ 26	Brett Perriman B UER	.60	.25

❑ 27 Stevon Moore B .60 .25
❑ 28 Jamal Anderson B 1.50 .60
❑ 29 Wayne Martin B .60 .25
❑ 30 Michael Irvin B UER 1.50 .60
❑ 31 Thomas Smith B .60 .25
❑ 32 Tony Brackens B .60 .25
❑ 33 Eric Davis B .60 .25
❑ 34 James O.Stewart B 1.00 .40
❑ 35 Ki-Jana Carter B .60 .25
❑ 36 Ken Norton B .60 .25
❑ 37 William Thomas B .60 .25
❑ 38 Tim Brown B 1.50 .60
❑ 39 Lawrence Phillips B .60 .25
❑ 40 Ricky Watters B 1.00 .40
❑ 41 Tony Bennett B .60 .25
❑ 42 Jessie Armstead B .60 .25
❑ 43 Trent Dilfer B 1.50 .60
❑ 44 Rodney Hampton B 1.00 .40
❑ 45 Sam Mills B .60 .25
❑ 46 Rodney Harrison B RC 3.00 1.25
❑ 47 Rob Fredrickson B .60 .25
❑ 48 Eric Hill B .60 .25
❑ 49 Bennie Blades B .60 .25
❑ 50 Eddie George B 1.50 .60
❑ 51 Dave Brown B .60 .25
❑ 52 Raymont Harris B .60 .25
❑ 53 Steve Tovar B .60 .25
❑ 54 Thurman Thomas B 1.50 .60
❑ 55 Leeland McElroy B .60 .25
❑ 56 Brian Mitchell B UER .60 .25
❑ 57 Eric Allen B .60 .25
❑ 58 Vinny Testaverde B 1.00 .40
❑ 59 Marvin Washington B .60 .25
❑ 60 Junior Seau B 1.50 .60
❑ 61 Bert Emanuel B 1.00 .40
❑ 62 Kevin Carter B .60 .25
❑ 63 Mark Carrier DB B .60 .25
❑ 64 Andre Coleman B .60 .25
❑ 65 Chris Warren B 1.00 .40
❑ 66 Aeneas Williams B .60 .25
❑ 67 Eugene Robinson B .60 .25
❑ 68 Darren Woodson B .60 .25
❑ 69 Anthony Johnson B .60 .25
❑ 70 Terry Glenn B 1.50 .60
❑ 71 Troy Vincent B .60 .25
❑ 72 John Copeland B .60 .25
❑ 73 Warren Sapp B 1.00 .40
❑ 74 Bobby Hebert B .60 .25
❑ 75 Jeff Hostetler B .60 .25
❑ 76 Willie Davis B .60 .25
❑ 77 Mickey Washington B .60 .25
❑ 78 Cortez Kennedy B .60 .25
❑ 79 Michael Strahan B 1.00 .40
❑ 80 Jerome Bettis B 1.50 .60
❑ 81 Andre Hastings B UER .60 .25
❑ 82 Simeon Rice B 1.00 .40
❑ 83 Cornelius Bennett B .60 .25
❑ 84 Napoleon Kaufman B 1.50 .60
❑ 85 Jim Harbaugh B 1.00 .40
❑ 86 Aaron Hayden B .60 .25
❑ 87 Gus Frerotte B .60 .25
❑ 88 Jeff Blake B 1.00 .40
❑ 89 Anthony Miller B UER .60 .25
❑ 90 Deion Sanders B 1.50 .60
❑ 91 Curtis Conway B 1.00 .40
❑ 92 William Floyd B 1.00 .40
❑ 93 Eric Moulds B UER 1.50 .60
❑ 94 Mel Gray B .60 .25
❑ 95 Andre Rison B UER 1.00 .40
❑ 96 Eugene Daniel B .60 .25
❑ 97 Jason Belser B .60 .25
❑ 98 Mike Mamula B .60 .25
❑ 99 Jim Everett B .60 .25
❑ 100 Checklist B .60 .25
❑ 101 Drew Bledsoe S 4.00 1.50
❑ 102 Shannon Sharpe S 2.00 .75
❑ 103 Ken Harvey S 1.25 .50
❑ 104 Isaac Bruce S 3.00 1.25
❑ 105 Terry Allen S 3.00 1.25
❑ 106 Lawyer Milloy S 2.00 .75
❑ 107 Ashley Ambrose S 1.25 .50
❑ 108 Alfred Williams S 1.25 .50
❑ 109 Hugh Douglas S 1.25 .50
❑ 110 Junior Seau S 3.00 1.25
❑ 111 Kordell Stewart S 3.00 1.25
❑ 112 Adrian Murrell S 2.00 .75
❑ 113 Byron Bam Morris S 1.25 .50
❑ 114 Terrell Buckley S 1.25 .50
❑ 115 Dan Marino S 12.00 5.00
❑ 116 Willie Clay S 1.25 .50
❑ 117 Neil Smith S 2.00 .75
❑ 118 Blaine Bishop S 1.25 .50
❑ 119 John Mobley S 1.25 .50
❑ 120 Herman Moore S 2.00 .75
❑ 121 Keyshawn Johnson S 3.00 1.25
❑ 122 Boomer Esiason S 2.00 .75
❑ 123 Marshall Faulk S 4.00 1.50
❑ 124 Keith Jackson S 1.25 .50
❑ 125 Ricky Watters S 2.00 .75
❑ 126 Carl Pickens S 2.00 .75
❑ 127 Cris Carter S 3.00 1.25
❑ 128 Mike Alstott S 3.00 1.25
❑ 129 Simeon Rice S 2.00 .75
❑ 130 Troy Aikman S 6.00 2.50
❑ 131 Tamarick Vanover S 2.00 .75
❑ 132 Marquez Pope S 1.25 .50
❑ 133 Winslow Oliver S 1.25 .50
❑ 134 Edgar Bennett S 2.00 .75
❑ 135 Dave Meggett S 1.25 .50
❑ 136 Marcus Allen S 3.00 1.25
❑ 137 Jerry Rice S 6.00 2.50
❑ 138 Steve Atwater S 1.25 .50
❑ 139 Tim McDonald S 1.25 .50
❑ 140 Barry Sanders S 10.00 4.00
❑ 141 Eddie George S 3.00 1.25
❑ 142 Wesley Walls S 1.25 .50
❑ 143 Jerome Bettis S 3.00 1.25
❑ 144 Kevin Greene S 2.00 .75
❑ 145 Terrell Davis S 4.00 1.50
❑ 146 Gus Frerotte S 2.00 .75
❑ 147 Joey Galloway S 2.00 .75
❑ 148 Vinny Testaverde S 2.00 .75
❑ 149 Hardy Nickerson S 1.25 .50
❑ 150 Brett Favre S 12.00 5.00
❑ 151 Desmond Howard G 1.50 .60
❑ 152 Keyshawn Johnson G 5.00 2.00
❑ 153 Tony Banks G 5.00 2.00
❑ 154 Chris Spielman G 1.50 .60
❑ 155 Reggie White G 5.00 2.00
❑ 156 Zach Thomas G 5.00 2.00
❑ 157 Carl Pickens G 3.00 1.25
❑ 158 Karim Abdul-Jabbar G 5.00 2.00
❑ 159 Chad Brown G 1.50 .60
❑ 160 Kerry Collins G 5.00 2.00
❑ 161 Marvin Harrison G 5.00 2.00
❑ 162 Steve Young G 6.00 2.50
❑ 163 Deion Sanders G 5.00 2.00
❑ 164 Trent Dilfer G 5.00 2.00
❑ 165 Barry Sanders G 15.00 6.00
❑ 166 Cris Carter G 5.00 2.00
❑ 167 Keenan McCardell G 3.00 1.25
❑ 168 Terry Glenn G 5.00 2.00
❑ 169 Emmitt Smith G 15.00 6.00
❑ 170 John Elway G 20.00 7.50
❑ 171 Jerry Rice G 10.00 4.00
❑ 172 Troy Aikman G 10.00 4.00
❑ 173 Curtis Martin G 6.00 2.50
❑ 174 Darrell Green G 1.50 .60
❑ 175 Mark Brunell G 6.00 2.50
❑ 176 Corey Dillon B RC 12.00 5.00
❑ 177 Tyrone Poole B .60 .25
❑ 178 Anthony Pleasant B .60 .25
❑ 179 Frank Sanders B 1.00 .40
❑ 180 Troy Aikman B 3.00 1.50
❑ 181 Bill Romanowski B .60 .25
❑ 182 Ty Law B 1.00 .40
❑ 183 Orlando Thomas B .60 .25
❑ 184 Quentin Coryatt B .60 .25
❑ 185 Kenny Holmes RC B 1.25 .50
❑ 186 Bryant Young B .60 .25
❑ 187 Michael Sinclair B .60 .25
❑ 188 Mike Tomczak B .60 .25
❑ 189 Bobby Taylor B .60 .25
❑ 190 Brett Favre B 6.00 3.00
❑ 191 Kent Graham B .60 .25
❑ 192 Jessie Tuggle B .60 .25
❑ 193 Jimmy Smith B 1.00 .40
❑ 194 Greg Hill B .60 .25
❑ 195 Yatil Green B RC .75 .30
❑ 196 Mark Fields B .60 .25
❑ 197 Phillippi Sparks B .60 .25
❑ 198 Aaron Glenn B .60 .25
❑ 199 Pat Swilling B .60 .25
❑ 200 Barry Sanders B 5.00 2.00
❑ 201 Mark Chmura B 1.00 .40
❑ 202 Marco Coleman B .60 .25
❑ 203 Merton Hanks B .60 .25
❑ 204 Brian Blades B .60 .25
❑ 205 Errict Rhett B .60 .25
❑ 206 Henry Ellard B .60 .25
❑ 207 Andre Reed B 1.00 .40
❑ 208 Bryan Cox B .60 .25
❑ 209 Darnay Scott B 1.00 .40
❑ 210 John Elway B 6.00 3.00
❑ 211 Glyn Milburn B .60 .25
❑ 212 Don Beebe B .60 .25
❑ 213 Kevin Lockett B RC .75 .30
❑ 214 Dorsey Levens B 1.50 .60
❑ 215 Kordell Stewart B 1.50 .60
❑ 216 Larry Centers B 1.00 .40
❑ 217 Cris Carter B 1.50 .60
❑ 218 Willie McGinest B .60 .25
❑ 219 Renaldo Wynn RC B .30 .10
❑ 220 Jerry Rice B 3.00 1.50
❑ 221 Reidel Anthony B RC .75 .30
❑ 222 Mark Carrier WR B .60 .25
❑ 223 Quinn Early B .60 .25
❑ 224 Chris Sanders B .60 .25
❑ 225 Shawn Springs B RC .75 .30
❑ 226 Kevin Smith B .60 .25
❑ 227 Ben Coates B 1.00 .40
❑ 228 Tyrone Wheatley B 1.00 .40
❑ 229 Antonio Freeman B 1.50 .60
❑ 230 Dan Marino B 6.00 3.00
❑ 231 Dwayne Rudd RC B 1.25 .50
❑ 232 Leslie O'Neal B .60 .25
❑ 233 Brent Jones B .60 .25
❑ 234 Jake Plummer B RC 10.00 4.00
❑ 235 Kerry Collins B 1.50 .60
❑ 236 Rashaan Salaam B .60 .25
❑ 237 Tyrone Braxton B .60 .25
❑ 238 Herman Moore B 1.00 .40
❑ 239 Keyshawn Johnson B 1.50 .60
❑ 240 Drew Bledsoe B 2.00 .75
❑ 241 Rickey Dudley B 1.00 .40
❑ 242 Antowain Smith B RC 5.00 2.00
❑ 243 Jeff Lageman B .60 .25
❑ 244 Chris T. Jones B .60 .25
❑ 245 Steve Young B 2.00 .75
❑ 246 Eddie Robinson B .60 .25
❑ 247 Chad Cota B .60 .25
❑ 248 Michael Jackson B 1.00 .40
❑ 249 Robert Porcher B .60 .25
❑ 250 Reggie White B 1.50 .60
❑ 251 Carnell Lake B .60 .25
❑ 252 Chris Calloway B .60 .25
❑ 253 Terance Mathis B 1.00 .40
❑ 254 Carl Pickens B 1.00 .40
❑ 255 Curtis Martin B 2.00 .75
❑ 256 Jeff Graham B .60 .25
❑ 257 Regan Upshaw RC B .30 .10
❑ 258 Sean Gilbert B .60 .25
❑ 259 Will Blackwell B RC .75 .30
❑ 260 Emmitt Smith B 5.00 2.50
❑ 261 Reinard Wilson RC B .75 .30
❑ 262 Darrell Russell RC B .30 .10
❑ 263 Wayne Chrebet B 1.00 .40
❑ 264 Kevin Hardy B .60 .25
❑ 265 Shannon Sharpe B 1.00 .40
❑ 266 Harvey Williams B .60 .25

❑ 267 John Randle B 1.00 .40
❑ 268 Tim Bowens B .60 .25
❑ 269 Tony Gonzalez B RC 6.00 2.50
❑ 270 Warrick Dunn B RC 5.00 2.00
❑ 271 Sean Dawkins B .60 .25
❑ 272 Darryll Lewis B .60 .25
❑ 273 Alonzo Spellman B .60 .25
❑ 274 Mark Collins B .60 .25
❑ 275 Checklist Card B .60 .25
❑ 276 Pat Barnes S RC 2.00 .75
❑ 277 Dana Stubblefield S 2.00 .75
❑ 278 Dan Wilkinson S 1.25 .50
❑ 279 Bryce Paup S 1.25 .50
❑ 280 Kerry Collins S 3.00 1.25
❑ 281 Derrick Brooks S 3.00 1.25
❑ 282 Walter Jones S RC 3.00 1.25
❑ 283 Terry McDaniel S 1.25 .50
❑ 284 James Farrior RC S 3.00 1.25
❑ 285 Curtis Martin S 4.00 1.50
❑ 286 O.J. McDuffie S 2.00 .75
❑ 287 Natrone Means S 2.00 .75
❑ 288 Bryant Westbrook RC S 2.00 .75
❑ 289 Peter Boulware RC S 3.00 1.25
❑ 290 Emmitt Smith S 10.00 4.00
❑ 291 Joey Kent S RC 3.00 1.25
❑ 292 Eddie Kennison S 2.00 .75
❑ 293 LeRoy Butler S 1.25 .50
❑ 294 Dale Carter S 1.25 .50
❑ 295 Jim Druckenmiller S RC 2.00 .75
❑ 296 Byron Hanspard S RC 2.00 .75
❑ 297 Jeff Blake S 2.00 .75
❑ 298 Levon Kirkland S 1.25 .50
❑ 299 Michael Westbrook S 2.00 .75
❑ 300 John Elway S 12.00 5.00
❑ 301 Lamar Lathon S 1.25 .50
❑ 302 Ray Lewis S 5.00 2.00
❑ 303 Steve McNair S 4.00 1.50
❑ 304 Shawn Springs S 2.00 .75
❑ 305 Karim Abdul-Jabbar S 2.00 .75
❑ 306 Orlando Pace S RC 3.00 1.25
❑ 307 Scott Mitchell S 1.25 .50
❑ 308 Walt Harris S 1.25 .50
❑ 309 Bruce Smith S 2.00 .75
❑ 310 Reggie White S 3.00 1.25
❑ 311 Eric Swann S 1.25 .50
❑ 312 Derrick Thomas S 3.00 1.25
❑ 313 Tony Martin S 2.00 .75
❑ 314 Darrell Russell RC S 2.00 .75
❑ 315 Mark Brunell S 4.00 1.50
❑ 316 Trent Dilfer S 3.00 1.25
❑ 317 Irving Fryar S 1.25 .50
❑ 318 Amani Toomer S 2.00 .75
❑ 319 Jake Reed S 2.00 .75
❑ 320 Steve Young S 4.00 1.50
❑ 321 Troy Davis S RC 2.00 .75
❑ 322 Jim Harbaugh S 2.00 .75
❑ 323 Neil O'Donnell S 1.25 .50
❑ 324 Terry Glenn S 3.00 1.25
❑ 325 Deion Sanders S 3.00 1.25
❑ 326 Gus Frerotte G 3.00 1.25
❑ 327 Tom Knight RC G 3.00 1.25
❑ 328 Peter Boulware G 3.00 1.25
❑ 329 Jerome Bettis G 5.00 2.00
❑ 330 Orlando Pace G 5.00 2.00
❑ 331 Darnell Autry G RC 3.00 1.25
❑ 332 Ike Hilliard G RC 12.00 5.00
❑ 333 David LaFleur G RC 1.50 .60
❑ 334 Jim Harbaugh G 3.00 1.25
❑ 335 Eddie George G 5.00 2.00
❑ 336 Vinny Testaverde G 3.00 1.25
❑ 337 Terry Allen G 3.00 1.25
❑ 338 Jim Druckenmiller G 3.00 1.25
❑ 339 Ricky Watters G 3.00 1.25
❑ 340 Brett Favre G 20.00 7.50
❑ 341 Simeon Rice G 3.00 1.25
❑ 342 Shannon Sharpe G 3.00 1.25
❑ 343 Kordell Stewart G 5.00 2.00
❑ 344 Isaac Bruce G 5.00 2.00
❑ 345 Drew Bledsoe G 6.00 2.50
❑ 346 Jeff Blake G 3.00 1.25
❑ 347 Herman Moore G 3.00 1.25
❑ 348 Junior Seau G 5.00 2.00
❑ 349 Rae Carruth G RC 1.50 .60
❑ 350 Dan Marino G 20.00 7.50
❑ P5 K.Abdul-Jabbar Promo 1.50 .60
❑ P32 Tony Brackens Promo 1.50 .60
❑ P45 Sam Mills Promo 1.50 .60
❑ P70 Terry Glenn Promo 1.50 .60
❑ P87 Gus Frerotte Promo 1.50 .60

1998 Finest

❑ COMPLETE SET (270) 80.00 30.00
❑ COMP.SERIES 1 (150) 50.00 20.00
❑ COMP.SERIES 2 (120) 30.00 12.50
❑ 1 John Elway 4.00 1.50
❑ 2 Terance Mathis .60 .25
❑ 3 Jermaine Lewis .60 .25
❑ 4 Fred Lane .40 .15
❑ 5 Simeon Rice .60 .25
❑ 6 David Dunn .40 .15
❑ 7 Dexter Coakley .40 .15
❑ 8 Carl Pickens .60 .25
❑ 9 Antonio Freeman 1.00 .40
❑ 10 Herman Moore .60 .25
❑ 11 Kevin Hardy .40 .15
❑ 12 Tony Gonzalez 1.00 .40
❑ 13 O.J. McDuffie .60 .25
❑ 14 David Palmer .40 .15
❑ 15 Lawyer Milloy .60 .25
❑ 16 Danny Kanell .60 .25
❑ 17 Randal Hill .40 .15
❑ 18 Chris Slade .40 .15
❑ 19 Charlie Garner .60 .25
❑ 20 Mark Brunell 1.00 .40
❑ 21 Donnell Woolford .40 .15
❑ 22 Freddie Jones .40 .15
❑ 23 Ken Norton .40 .15
❑ 24 Tony Banks .60 .25
❑ 25 Isaac Bruce 1.00 .40
❑ 26 Willie Davis .40 .15
❑ 27 Cris Dishman .40 .15
❑ 28 Aeneas Williams .40 .15
❑ 29 Michael Booker .40 .15
❑ 30 Cris Carter 1.00 .40
❑ 31 Michael McCrary .40 .15
❑ 32 Eric Moulds 1.00 .40
❑ 33 Rae Carruth .40 .15
❑ 34 Bobby Engram .60 .25
❑ 35 Jeff Blake .60 .25
❑ 36 Deion Sanders 1.00 .40
❑ 37 Rod Smith .60 .25
❑ 38 Bryant Westbrook .40 .15
❑ 39 Mark Chmura .60 .25
❑ 40 Tim Brown 1.00 .40
❑ 41 Bobby Taylor .40 .15
❑ 42 James Stewart .60 .25
❑ 43 Kimble Anders .60 .25
❑ 44 Karim Abdul-Jabbar 1.00 .40
❑ 45 Willie McGinest .40 .15
❑ 46 Jessie Armstead .40 .15
❑ 47 Brad Johnson 1.00 .40
❑ 48 Greg Lloyd .40 .15
❑ 49 Stephen Davis .40 .15
❑ 50 Jerome Bettis 1.00 .40
❑ 51 Warren Sapp .60 .25
❑ 52 Horace Copeland .40 .15
❑ 53 Chad Brown .40 .15
❑ 54 Chris Canty .40 .15
❑ 55 Robert Smith 1.00 .40
❑ 56 Pete Mitchell .40 .15
❑ 57 Aaron Bailey .40 .15
❑ 58 Robert Porcher .40 .15
❑ 59 John Mobley .40 .15
❑ 60 Tony Martin .60 .25
❑ 61 Michael Irvin 1.00 .40
❑ 62 Charles Way .40 .15
❑ 63 Raymont Harris .40 .15
❑ 64 Chuck Smith .40 .15
❑ 65 Larry Centers .40 .15
❑ 66 Greg Hill .40 .15
❑ 67 Kenny Holmes .40 .15
❑ 68 John Lynch .60 .25
❑ 69 Michael Sinclair .40 .15
❑ 70 Steve Young 1.25 .50
❑ 71 Michael Strahan .60 .25
❑ 72 Levon Kirkland .40 .15
❑ 73 Rickey Dudley .40 .15
❑ 74 Marcus Allen 1.00 .40
❑ 75 John Randle .60 .25
❑ 76 Erik Kramer .40 .15
❑ 77 Neil Smith .60 .25
❑ 78 Byron Hanspard .40 .15
❑ 79 Quinn Early .40 .15
❑ 80 Warren Moon 1.00 .40
❑ 81 William Thomas .40 .15
❑ 82 Ben Coates .60 .25
❑ 83 Lake Dawson .40 .15
❑ 84 Steve McNair 1.00 .40
❑ 85 Gus Frerotte .40 .15
❑ 86 Rodney Harrison .60 .25
❑ 87 Reggie White 1.00 .40
❑ 88 Derrick Thomas 1.00 .40
❑ 89 Dale Carter .40 .15
❑ 90 Warrick Dunn 1.00 .40
❑ 91 Will Blackwell .40 .15
❑ 92 Troy Vincent .40 .15
❑ 93 Johnnie Morton .60 .25
❑ 94 David LaFleur .40 .15
❑ 95 Tony McGee .40 .15
❑ 96 Lonnie Johnson .40 .15
❑ 97 Thurman Thomas 1.00 .40
❑ 98 Chris Chandler .60 .25
❑ 99 Jamal Anderson 1.00 .40
❑ 100 Checklist .40 .15
❑ 101 Marshall Faulk 1.50 .60
❑ 102 Chris Calloway .40 .15
❑ 103 Chris Spielman .40 .15
❑ 104 Zach Thomas 1.00 .40
❑ 105 Jeff George .60 .25
❑ 106 Darrell Russell .40 .15
❑ 107 Darryll Lewis .40 .15
❑ 108 Reidel Anthony .60 .25
❑ 109 Terrell Owens 1.00 .40
❑ 110 Rob Moore .60 .25
❑ 111 Darrell Green .60 .25
❑ 112 Merton Hanks .40 .15
❑ 113 Shawn Jefferson .40 .15
❑ 114 Chris Sanders .40 .15
❑ 115 Scott Mitchell .60 .25
❑ 116 Vaughn Hebron .40 .15
❑ 117 Ed McCaffrey .60 .25
❑ 118 Bruce Smith .60 .25
❑ 119 Peter Boulware .40 .15
❑ 120 Brett Favre 4.00 1.50
❑ 121 Peyton Manning RC 30.00 12.50
❑ 122 Brian Griese RC 5.00 2.00
❑ 123 Tavian Banks RC 1.50 .60
❑ 124 Duane Starks RC 1.00 .40
❑ 125 Robert Holcombe RC 1.50 .60
❑ 126 Brian Simmons RC 1.50 .60
❑ 127 Skip Hicks RC 1.50 .60
❑ 128 Keith Brooking RC 2.50 1.00
❑ 129 Ahman Green RC 12.00 5.00
❑ 130 Jerome Pathon RC 2.50 1.00

❑ 131 Curtis Enis RC 1.00 .40
❑ 132 Grant Wistrom RC 1.50 .60
❑ 133 Germane Crowell RC 1.50 .60
❑ 134 Jacquez Green RC 1.50 .60
❑ 135 Randy Moss RC 15.00 6.00
❑ 136 Jason Peter RC 1.00 .40
❑ 137 John Avery RC 1.50 .60
❑ 138 Takeo Spikes RC 2.50 1.00
❑ 139 Pat Johnson RC 1.50 .60
❑ 140 Andre Wadsworth RC 1.50 .60
❑ 141 Fred Taylor RC 4.00 1.50
❑ 142 Charles Woodson RC 3.00 1.25
❑ 143 Marcus Nash RC 1.00 .40
❑ 144 Robert Edwards RC 1.50 .60
❑ 145 Kevin Dyson RC 2.50 1.00
❑ 146 Joe Jurevicius RC 2.50 1.00
❑ 147 Anthony Simmons RC 1.50 .60
❑ 148 Hines Ward RC 10.00 5.00
❑ 149 Greg Ellis RC 1.00 .40
❑ 150 Ryan Leaf RC 2.50 1.00
❑ 151 Jerry Rice 2.00 .75
❑ 152 Tony Martin .60 .25
❑ 153 Checklist .40 .15
❑ 154 Rob Johnson .60 .25
❑ 155 Shannon Sharpe .60 .25
❑ 156 Bert Emanuel .60 .25
❑ 157 Eric Metcalf .40 .15
❑ 158 Natrone Means .60 .25
❑ 159 Derrick Alexander .60 .25
❑ 160 Emmitt Smith 3.00 1.25
❑ 161 Jeff Burris .40 .15
❑ 162 Chris Warren .60 .25
❑ 163 Corey Fuller .40 .15
❑ 164 Courtney Hawkins .40 .15
❑ 165 James McKnight 1.00 .40
❑ 166 Shawn Springs .40 .15
❑ 167 Wayne Martin .40 .15
❑ 168 Michael Westbrook .60 .25
❑ 169 Michael Jackson .40 .15
❑ 170 Dan Marino 4.00 1.50
❑ 171 Amp Lee .40 .15
❑ 172 James Jett .60 .25
❑ 173 Ty Law .60 .25
❑ 174 Kerry Collins .60 .25
❑ 175 Robert Brooks .60 .25
❑ 176 Blaine Bishop .40 .15
❑ 177 Stephen Boyd .40 .15
❑ 178 Keyshawn Johnson 1.00 .40
❑ 179 Deon Figures .40 .15
❑ 180 Allen Aldridge .40 .15
❑ 181 Corey Miller .40 .15
❑ 182 Chad Lewis .60 .25
❑ 183 Derrick Rodgers .40 .15
❑ 184 Troy Drayton .40 .15
❑ 185 Darren Woodson .40 .15
❑ 186 Ken Dilger .40 .15
❑ 187 Elvis Grbac .60 .25
❑ 188 Terrell Fletcher .40 .15
❑ 189 Frank Sanders .60 .25
❑ 190 Curtis Martin 1.00 .40
❑ 191 Derrick Brooks 1.00 .40
❑ 192 Darrien Gordon .40 .15
❑ 193 Andre Reed .60 .25
❑ 194 Damay Scott .60 .25
❑ 195 Curtis Conway .60 .25
❑ 196 Tim McDonald .40 .15
❑ 197 Sean Dawkins .40 .15
❑ 198 Napoleon Kaufman 1.00 .40
❑ 199 Willie Clay .40 .15
❑ 200 Terrell Davis 1.00 .40
❑ 201 Wesley Walls .60 .25
❑ 202 Santana Dotson .40 .15
❑ 203 Frank Wycheck .40 .15
❑ 204 Wayne Chrebet 1.00 .40
❑ 205 Andre Rison .60 .25
❑ 206 Jason Sehorn .60 .25
❑ 207 Jessie Tuggle .40 .15
❑ 208 Kevin Turner .40 .15
❑ 209 Jason Taylor .60 .25
❑ 210 Yancey Thigpen .40 .15
❑ 211 Jake Reed .60 .25
❑ 212 Carnell Lake .40 .15
❑ 213 Joey Galloway .60 .25
❑ 214 Andre Hastings .40 .15
❑ 215 Terry Allen 1.00 .40
❑ 216 Jim Harbaugh .60 .25
❑ 217 Tony Banks .60 .25
❑ 218 Greg Clark .40 .15
❑ 219 Corey Dillon 1.00 .40
❑ 220 Troy Aikman 2.00 .75
❑ 221 Antowain Smith 1.00 .40
❑ 222 Steve Atwater .40 .15
❑ 223 Trent Dilfer 1.00 .40
❑ 224 Junior Seau 1.00 .40
❑ 225 Garrison Hearst 1.00 .40
❑ 226 Eric Allen .40 .15
❑ 227 Chad Cota .40 .15
❑ 228 Vinny Testaverde .60 .25
❑ 229 Duce Staley 1.25 .50
❑ 230 Drew Bledsoe 1.50 .60
❑ 231 Charles Johnson .40 .15
❑ 232 Jake Plummer 1.00 .40
❑ 233 Errict Rhett .60 .25
❑ 234 Doug Evans .40 .15
❑ 235 Phillippi Sparks .40 .15
❑ 236 Ashley Ambrose .40 .15
❑ 237 Bryan Cox .40 .15
❑ 238 Kevin Smith .40 .15
❑ 239 Hardy Nickerson .40 .15
❑ 240 Terry Glenn 1.00 .40
❑ 241 Lee Woodall .40 .15
❑ 242 Andre Coleman .40 .15
❑ 243 Michael Bates .40 .15
❑ 244 Mark Fields .40 .15
❑ 245 Eddie Kennison .60 .25
❑ 246 Dana Stubblefield .40 .15
❑ 247 Bobby Hoying .60 .25
❑ 248 Mo Lewis .40 .15
❑ 249 Derrick Mayes .60 .25
❑ 250 Eddie George 1.00 .40
❑ 251 Mike Alstott 1.00 .40
❑ 252 J.J. Stokes .60 .25
❑ 253 Adrian Murrell .60 .25
❑ 254 Kevin Greene .60 .25
❑ 255 LeRoy Butler .40 .15
❑ 256 Glenn Foley .60 .25
❑ 257 Jimmy Smith .60 .25
❑ 258 Tiki Barber 1.00 .40
❑ 259 Irving Fryar .60 .25
❑ 260 Ricky Watters .60 .25
❑ 261 Jeff Graham .40 .15
❑ 262 Kordell Stewart 1.00 .40
❑ 263 Rod Woodson .60 .25
❑ 264 Leslie Shepherd .40 .15
❑ 265 Ryan McNeil .40 .15
❑ 266 Ike Hilliard .60 .25
❑ 267 Keenan McCardell .60 .25
❑ 268 Marvin Harrison 1.00 .40
❑ 269 Dorsey Levens 1.00 .40
❑ 270 Barry Sanders 3.00 1.25

1999 Finest

❑ COMPLETE SET (175) 80.00 30.00
❑ COMP.SET w/o SPs (124) 30.00 15.00
❑ 1 Peyton Manning 3.00 1.25
❑ 2 Priest Holmes 1.50 .60
❑ 3 Kordell Stewart .60 .25
❑ 4 Shannon Sharpe .60 .25
❑ 5 Andre Rison .60 .25
❑ 6 Rickey Dudley .40 .15
❑ 7 Duce Staley 1.00 .40
❑ 8 Randall Cunningham 1.00 .40
❑ 9 Warrick Dunn 1.00 .40
❑ 10 Dan Marino 3.00 1.25
❑ 11 Kevin Greene .40 .15
❑ 12 Garrison Hearst .60 .25
❑ 13 Eric Moulds 1.00 .40
❑ 14 Marvin Harrison 1.00 .40
❑ 15 Eddie George 1.00 .40
❑ 16 Vinny Testaverde .60 .25
❑ 17 Brad Johnson 1.00 .40
❑ 18 Derrick Thomas 1.00 .40
❑ 19 Chris Chandler .60 .25
❑ 20 Troy Aikman 2.00 .75
❑ 21 Terance Mathis .60 .25
❑ 22 Terrell Owens 1.00 .40
❑ 23 Junior Seau 1.00 .40
❑ 24 Cris Carter 1.00 .40
❑ 25 Fred Taylor 1.00 .40
❑ 26 Adrian Murrell .60 .25
❑ 27 Terry Glenn 1.00 .40
❑ 28 Rod Smith .60 .25
❑ 29 Damay Scott .60 .25
❑ 30 Brett Favre 3.00 1.25
❑ 31 Cam Cleeland .40 .15
❑ 32 Ricky Watters .60 .25
❑ 33 Derrick Alexander .60 .25
❑ 34 Bruce Smith .60 .25
❑ 35 Steve McNair 1.00 .40
❑ 36 Wayne Chrebet .60 .25
❑ 37 Herman Moore .60 .25
❑ 38 Bert Emanuel .60 .25
❑ 39 Michael Irvin .60 .25
❑ 40 Steve Young 1.25 .50
❑ 41 Napoleon Kaufman 1.00 .40
❑ 42 Tim Biakabutuka .60 .25
❑ 43 Isaac Bruce 1.00 .40
❑ 44 J.J. Stokes .60 .25
❑ 45 Antonio Freeman 1.00 .40
❑ 46 John Randle .60 .25
❑ 47 Frank Sanders .60 .25
❑ 48 O.J. McDuffie .60 .25
❑ 49 Keenan McCardell .60 .25
❑ 50 Randy Moss 2.50 1.00
❑ 51 Ed McCaffrey .60 .25
❑ 52 Yancey Thigpen .40 .15
❑ 53 Curtis Conway .60 .25
❑ 54 Mike Alstott 1.00 .40
❑ 55 Deion Sanders 1.00 .40
❑ 56 Dorsey Levens 1.00 .40
❑ 57 Joey Galloway .60 .25
❑ 58 Natrone Means .60 .25
❑ 59 Tim Brown 1.00 .40
❑ 60 Jerry Rice 2.00 .75
❑ 61 Robert Smith 1.00 .40
❑ 62 Carl Pickens .60 .25
❑ 63 Ben Coates .60 .25
❑ 64 Jerome Bettis 1.00 .40
❑ 65 Corey Dillon 1.00 .40
❑ 66 Curtis Martin 1.00 .40
❑ 67 Jimmy Smith .60 .25
❑ 68 Keyshawn Johnson 1.00 .40
❑ 69 Charlie Batch 1.00 .40
❑ 70 Jamal Anderson 1.00 .40
❑ 71 Mark Brunell 1.00 .40
❑ 72 Antowain Smith 1.00 .40
❑ 73 Aeneas Williams .40 .15
❑ 74 Wesley Walls .60 .25
❑ 75 Jake Plummer .60 .25
❑ 76 Oronde Gadsden .60 .25
❑ 77 Gary Brown .40 .15
❑ 78 Peter Boulware .40 .15
❑ 79 Stephen Alexander .40 .15
❑ 80 Barry Sanders 3.00 1.25

❑ 81 Warren Sapp .60 .25
❑ 82 Michael Sinclair .40 .15
❑ 83 Freddie Jones .40 .15
❑ 84 Ike Hilliard .40 .15
❑ 85 Jake Reed .60 .25
❑ 86 Tim Dwight 1.00 .40
❑ 87 Johnnie Morton .60 .25
❑ 88 Robert Brooks .60 .25
❑ 89 Rocket Ismail .60 .25
❑ 90 Emmitt Smith 2.00 .75
❑ 91 Ricky Proehl .40 .15
❑ 92 James Jett .60 .25
❑ 93 Karim Abdul-Jabbar .60 .25
❑ 94 Mark Chmura .40 .15
❑ 95 Andre Reed .60 .25
❑ 96 Michael Westbrook .60 .25
❑ 97 Michael Strahan .60 .25
❑ 98 Chad Brown .40 .15
❑ 99 Trent Dilfer .60 .25
❑ 100 Terrell Davis 1.00 .40
❑ 101 Aaron Glenn .40 .15
❑ 102 Skip Hicks .40 .15
❑ 103 Tony Gonzalez 1.00 .40
❑ 104 Ty Law .60 .25
❑ 105 Jermaine Lewis .60 .25
❑ 106 Ray Lewis 1.00 .40
❑ 107 Zach Thomas 1.00 .40
❑ 108 Reidel Anthony .60 .25
❑ 109 Levon Kirkland .40 .15
❑ 110 Drew Bledsoe 1.25 .50
❑ 111 Bobby Engram .60 .25
❑ 112 Jerome Pathon .40 .15
❑ 113 Muhsin Muhammad .60 .25
❑ 114 Vonnie Holliday .40 .15
❑ 115 Bill Romanowski .40 .15
❑ 116 Marshall Faulk 1.25 .50
❑ 117 Ty Detmer .60 .25
❑ 118 Mo Lewis .40 .15
❑ 119 Charles Woodson 1.00 .40
❑ 120 Doug Flutie 1.00 .40
❑ 121 Jon Kitna 1.00 .40
❑ 122 Courtney Hawkins .40 .15
❑ 123 Trent Green 1.00 .40
❑ 124 John Elway 3.00 1.25
❑ 125 Barry Sanders GM 5.00 2.00
❑ 126 Brett Favre GM 5.00 2.00
❑ 127 Curtis Martin GM 1.50 .60
❑ 128 Dan Marino GM 5.00 2.00
❑ 129 Eddie George GM 1.00 .40
❑ 130 Emmitt Smith GM 5.00 2.00
❑ 131 Jamal Anderson GM 1.50 .60
❑ 132 Jerry Rice GM 3.00 1.25
❑ 133 John Elway GM 5.00 2.00
❑ 134 Terrell Davis GM 2.50 1.00
❑ 135 Troy Aikman GM 3.00 1.25
❑ 136 Skip Hicks SN .40 .15
❑ 137 Charles Woodson SN 1.00 .40
❑ 138 Charlie Batch SN 2.50 1.00
❑ 139 Curtis Enis SN 1.50 .60
❑ 140 Fred Taylor SN 2.50 1.00
❑ 141 Jake Plummer SN 1.50 .60
❑ 142 Peyton Manning SN 5.00 2.00
❑ 143 Randy Moss SN 4.00 1.50
❑ 144 Corey Dillon SN 1.50 .60
❑ 145 Priest Holmes SN 1.50 .60
❑ 146 Warrick Dunn SN 1.50 .60
❑ 147 Jevon Kearse RC 4.00 1.50
❑ 148 Chris Claiborne RC 1.50 .60
❑ 149 Akili Smith RC 1.50 .60
❑ 150 Brock Huard RC 3.00 1.25
❑ 151 Daunte Culpepper RC 10.00 4.00
❑ 152 Edgerrin James RC 10.00 4.00
❑ 153 Cecil Collins RC 1.50 .60
❑ 154 Kevin Faulk RC 3.00 1.25
❑ 155 Amos Zereoue RC 3.00 1.25
❑ 156 James Johnson RC 2.50 1.00
❑ 157 Sedrick Irvin RC 1.50 .60
❑ 158 Ricky Williams RC 5.00 2.00
❑ 159 Mike Cloud RC 2.50 1.00
❑ 160 Chris McAlister 1.50 .60
❑ 161 Rob Konrad RC 2.50 1.00
❑ 162 Champ Bailey RC 3.00 1.25
❑ 163 Ebenezer Ekuban RC 2.50 1.00
❑ 164 Tim Couch RC 3.00 1.25
❑ 165 Cade McNown RC 2.50 1.00
❑ 166 Donovan McNabb RC 12.00 5.00
❑ 167 Joe Germaine RC 2.50 1.00
❑ 168 Shaun King RC 2.50 1.00
❑ 169 Peerless Price RC 3.00 1.25
❑ 170 Kevin Johnson RC 2.50 1.00
❑ 171 Troy Edwards RC 2.50 1.00
❑ 172 Karsten Bailey RC 2.50 1.00
❑ 173 David Boston RC 3.00 1.25
❑ 174 D'Wayne Bates RC 2.50 1.00
❑ 175 Torry Holt RC 6.00 2.50

2000 Finest

❑ COMPLETE SET (205) 400.00 150.00
❑ 1 Tim Dwight .75 .30
❑ 2 Cade McNown .30 .10
❑ 3 Drew Bledsoe 1.00 .40
❑ 4 Torry Holt .75 .30
❑ 5 Derrick Mayes .50 .20
❑ 6 Vinny Testaverde .50 .20
❑ 7 Patrick Jeffers .75 .30
❑ 8 Dorsey Levens .50 .20
❑ 9 James Johnson .30 .10
❑ 10 Champ Bailey .50 .20
❑ 11 Jeff George .50 .20
❑ 12 Shawn Jefferson .30 .10
❑ 13 Terrence Wilkins .30 .10
❑ 14 J.J. Stokes .50 .20
❑ 15 Doug Flutie .75 .30
❑ 16 Corey Dillon .75 .30
❑ 17 Rod Smith .50 .20
❑ 18 Jimmy Smith .50 .20
❑ 19 Amani Toomer .50 .20
❑ 20 Curtis Conway .50 .20
❑ 21 Brad Johnson .75 .30
❑ 22 Edgerrin James 1.25 .50
❑ 23 Derrick Alexander .50 .20
❑ 24 Terrell Owens .75 .30
❑ 25 Kurt Warner 1.50 .60
❑ 26 Frank Sanders .50 .20
❑ 27 Tony Banks .50 .20
❑ 28 Troy Aikman 1.50 .60
❑ 29 Curtis Enis .30 .10
❑ 30 Eddie George .75 .30
❑ 31 Bill Schroeder .50 .20
❑ 32 Kent Graham .30 .10
❑ 33 Mike Alstott .75 .30
❑ 34 Steve Young 1.00 .40
❑ 35 Jacquez Green .30 .10
❑ 36 Frank Wycheck .30 .10
❑ 37 Kerry Collins .50 .20
❑ 38 Stephen Davis .75 .30
❑ 39 Tony Gonzalez .50 .20
❑ 40 Tyrone Wheatley .50 .20
❑ 41 Brett Favre 2.50 1.00
❑ 42 Joey Galloway .50 .20
❑ 43 Terrell Davis .75 .30
❑ 44 Marvin Harrison .75 .30
❑ 45 Zach Thomas .75 .30
❑ 46 Jerry Rice 1.50 .60
❑ 47 Keyshawn Johnson .75 .30
❑ 48 Rob Johnson .50 .20
❑ 49 Rocket Ismail .50 .20
❑ 50 Elvis Grbac .50 .20
❑ 51 Warrick Dunn .75 .30
❑ 52 Jevon Kearse .75 .30
❑ 53 Albert Connell .30 .10
❑ 54 Muhsin Muhammad .50 .20
❑ 55 Carl Pickens .50 .20
❑ 56 Peyton Manning 2.00 .75
❑ 57 Daunte Culpepper 1.00 .40
❑ 58 Ike Hilliard .50 .20
❑ 59 Steve McNair .75 .30
❑ 60 Sean Dawkins .30 .10
❑ 61 Steve Beuerlein .50 .20
❑ 62 Priest Holmes 1.00 .40
❑ 63 Jim Harbaugh .50 .20
❑ 64 Germane Crowell .30 .10
❑ 65 Cris Carter .75 .30
❑ 66 Jamal Anderson .75 .30
❑ 67 Kevin Johnson .75 .30
❑ 68 Herman Moore .50 .20
❑ 69 Ricky Williams .75 .30
❑ 70 Rich Gannon .75 .30
❑ 71 Isaac Bruce .75 .30
❑ 72 Peerless Price .50 .20
❑ 73 Az-Zahir Hakim .50 .20
❑ 74 Mark Brunell .75 .30
❑ 75 Rob Moore .50 .20
❑ 76 Antowain Smith .50 .20
❑ 77 Tim Biakabutuka .50 .20
❑ 78 Ed McCaffrey .75 .30
❑ 79 Tony Martin .50 .20
❑ 80 Marcus Robinson .75 .30
❑ 81 Kevin Dyson .50 .20
❑ 82 Wesley Walls .30 .10
❑ 83 Chris Chandler .50 .20
❑ 84 Keenan McCardell .50 .20
❑ 85 Napoleon Kaufman .50 .20
❑ 86 Emmitt Smith 1.50 .60
❑ 87 James Stewart .50 .20
❑ 88 Tim Brown .75 .30
❑ 89 Ricky Watters .50 .20
❑ 90 Johnnie Morton .50 .20
❑ 91 Jake Plummer .50 .20
❑ 92 Olandis Gary .75 .30
❑ 93 Jerome Bettis .75 .30
❑ 94 Terry Glenn .50 .20
❑ 95 Kordell Stewart .50 .20
❑ 96 Charlie Garner .50 .20
❑ 97 Yancey Thigpen .30 .10
❑ 98 Michael Westbrook .50 .20
❑ 99 Bobby Engram .50 .20
❑ 100 Eric Moulds .75 .30
❑ 101 Darnay Scott .50 .20
❑ 102 Antonio Freeman .75 .30
❑ 103 Wayne Chrebet .50 .20
❑ 104 Akili Smith .30 .10
❑ 105 Jeff Blake .50 .20
❑ 106 Curtis Martin .75 .30
❑ 107 Errict Rhett .50 .20
❑ 108 Damon Huard .75 .30
❑ 109 Jeff Graham .30 .10
❑ 110 Terance Mathis .50 .20
❑ 111 Jon Kitna .75 .30
❑ 112 Tim Couch .50 .20
❑ 113 Fred Taylor .75 .30
❑ 114 Qadry Ismail .50 .20
❑ 115 Donovan McNabb 1.25 .50
❑ 116 Charles Johnson .50 .20
❑ 117 Troy Edwards .30 .10
❑ 118 Shaun King .30 .10
❑ 119 Charlie Batch .75 .30
❑ 120 Robert Smith .75 .30
❑ 121 Marshall Faulk 1.00 .40
❑ 122 Brian Griese .75 .30
❑ 123 O.J. McDuffie .50 .20
❑ 124 Randy Moss 1.50 .60
❑ 125 Duce Staley .75 .30
❑ 126 Peter Warrick RC 8.00 3.00

❑ 127	Dez White RC	8.00	3.00
❑ 128	Ron Dayne RC	8.00	3.00
❑ 129	J.R. Redmond RC	6.00	2.50
❑ 130	Thomas Jones RC	12.00	5.00
❑ 131	Plaxico Burress RC	15.00	6.00
❑ 132	Reuben Droughns RC	10.00	4.00
❑ 133	Shaun Alexander RC	40.00	20.00
❑ 134	Ron Dugans RC	6.00	2.50
❑ 135	Travis Prentice RC	6.00	2.50
❑ 136	Joe Hamilton RC	6.00	2.50
❑ 137	Curtis Keaton RC	6.00	2.50
❑ 138	Chris Redman RC	6.00	2.50
❑ 139	Chad Pennington RC	20.00	7.50
❑ 140	Travis Taylor RC	8.00	3.00
❑ 141	Bubba Franks RC	8.00	3.00
❑ 142	Dennis Northcutt RC	8.00	3.00
❑ 143	Jerry Porter RC	10.00	4.00
❑ 144	Sylvester Morris RC	6.00	2.50
❑ 145	Anthony Becht RC	8.00	3.00
❑ 146	Trung Canidate RC	6.00	2.50
❑ 147	Jamal Lewis RC	20.00	7.50
❑ 148	R.Jay Soward RC	6.00	2.50
❑ 149	Tee Martin RC	8.00	3.00
❑ 150	Courtney Brown RC	8.00	3.00
❑ 151	Brian Urlacher RC	30.00	12.50
❑ 152	Danny Farmer RC	6.00	2.50
❑ 153	Laveranues Coles RC	10.00	4.00
❑ 154	Todd Pinkston RC	8.00	3.00
❑ 155	Corey Simon RC	8.00	3.00
❑ 156	Spergon Wynn RC	6.00	2.50
❑ 157	Tim Rattay RC	8.00	3.00
❑ 158	Todd Husak RC	8.00	3.00
❑ 159	Aaron Shea RC	6.00	2.50
❑ 160	Giovanni Carmazzi RC	6.00	2.50
❑ 161	Trevor Gaylor RC	6.00	2.50
❑ 162	JaJuan Dawson RC	6.00	2.50
❑ 163	Jarious Jackson RC	6.00	2.50
❑ 164	Chris Samuels RC	6.00	2.50
❑ 165	Rob Morris RC	6.00	2.50
❑ 166	P.Warrick/R.Moss IF	2.00	.75
❑ 167	R.Moss/P.Warrick IF	2.00	.75
❑ 168	T.Prentice/S.Davis IF	1.50	.60
❑ 169	S.Davis/T.Prentice IF	1.50	.60
❑ 170	C.Redman/K.Warner IF	1.50	.60
❑ 171	K.Warner/C.Redman IF	1.50	.60
❑ 172	Syl.Morris/J.Smith IF	1.50	.60
❑ 173	J.Smith/Syl.Morris IF	1.50	.60
❑ 174	C.Pennington/P.Manning IF	4.00	1.50
❑ 175	P.Manning/C.Pennington IF	4.00	1.50
❑ 176	R.Soward/M.Harrison IF	1.50	.60
❑ 177	M.Harrison/R.Soward IF	1.50	.60
❑ 178	R.Dayne/J.Anderson IF	1.50	.60
❑ 179	J.Anderson/R.Dayne IF	1.50	.60
❑ 180	S.Alexander/E.George IF	4.00	1.50
❑ 181	E.George/S.Alexander IF	3.00	1.25
❑ 182	C.Brown/B.Smith IF	1.50	.60
❑ 183	B.Smith/C.Brown IF	1.50	.60
❑ 184	J.Lewis/E.James IF	3.00	1.25
❑ 185	E.James/J.Lewis IF	3.00	1.25
❑ 186	T.Canidate/E.Smith IF	3.00	1.25
❑ 187	E.Smith/T.Canidate IF	3.00	1.25
❑ 188	T.Taylor/C.Carter IF	2.00	.75
❑ 189	C.Carter/T.Taylor IF	2.00	.75
❑ 190	C.Keaton/M.Faulk IF	2.00	.75
❑ 191	M.Faulk/C.Keaton IF	2.00	.75
❑ 192	P.Burress/J.Rice IF	3.00	1.25
❑ 193	J.Rice/P.Burress IF	3.00	1.25
❑ 194	T.Jones/T.Davis IF	2.00	.75
❑ 195	T.Davis/T.Jones IF	2.00	.75
❑ 196	Peyton Manning GM	5.00	2.00
❑ 197	Randy Moss GM	4.00	1.50
❑ 198	Terrell Davis GM	1.50	.60
❑ 199	Marshall Faulk GM	2.50	1.00
❑ 200	Edgerrin James GM	4.00	1.50
❑ 201	Emmitt Smith GM	4.00	1.50
❑ 202	Ricky Williams GM	1.50	.60
❑ 203	Kurt Warner GM	3.00	1.25
❑ 204	Eddie George GM	1.50	.60
❑ 205	Brett Favre GM	6.00	2.50

2001 Finest

❑	COMP.SET w/o SP's (100)	40.00	20.00
❑ 1	Eddie George	1.25	.50
❑ 2	Jay Fiedler	1.25	.50
❑ 3	Peter Warrick	1.25	.50
❑ 4	Vinny Testaverde	.75	.30
❑ 5	Charles Johnson	.50	.20
❑ 6	Ahman Green	1.25	.50
❑ 7	Isaac Bruce	1.25	.50
❑ 8	Junior Seau	1.25	.50
❑ 9	Daunte Culpepper	1.25	.50
❑ 10	Ike Hilliard	.75	.30
❑ 11	Tony Banks	.75	.30
❑ 12	Steve Beuerlein	.75	.30
❑ 13	Jamal Anderson	1.25	.50
❑ 14	Tyrone Wheatley	.75	.30
❑ 15	Sylvester Morris	.50	.20
❑ 16	Edgerrin James	1.50	.60
❑ 17	Shaun King	.50	.20
❑ 18	Terrell Owens	1.25	.50
❑ 19	Donovan Mcnabb	1.50	.60
❑ 20	Cade Mcnown	.50	.20
❑ 21	Elvis Grbac	.75	.30
❑ 22	James Stewart	.75	.30
❑ 23	Joe Horn	.75	.30
❑ 24	Randy Moss	2.50	1.00
❑ 25	Matt Hasselbeck	.75	.30
❑ 26	Jerome Bettis	1.25	.50
❑ 27	Bill Schroeder	.75	.30
❑ 28	Jake Plummer	.75	.30
❑ 29	Rod Smith	.75	.30
❑ 30	Akili Smith	.50	.20
❑ 31	Jimmy Smith	.75	.30
❑ 32	Oronde Gadsden	.75	.30
❑ 33	Kerry Collins	.75	.30
❑ 34	Warrick Dunn	1.25	.50
❑ 35	Jeff Graham	.50	.20
❑ 36	Ray Lewis	1.25	.50
❑ 37	Joey Galloway	.75	.30
❑ 38	Tim Brown	1.25	.50
❑ 39	Derrick Alexander	.75	.30
❑ 40	Jerry Rice	2.50	1.00
❑ 41	Muhsin Muhammad	.75	.30
❑ 42	Shawn Jefferson	.50	.20
❑ 43	Curtis Martin	1.25	.50
❑ 44	Terry Glenn	.75	.30
❑ 45	Marvin Harrison	1.25	.50
❑ 46	Mike Anderson	1.25	.50
❑ 47	Stephen Davis	1.25	.50
❑ 48	Chad Lewis	.50	.20
❑ 49	Fred Taylor	1.25	.50
❑ 50	Corey Dillon	1.25	.50
❑ 51	Charlie Batch	1.25	.50
❑ 52	Kevin Johnson	.75	.30
❑ 53	Brett Favre	4.00	1.50
❑ 54	Marshall Faulk	1.50	.60
❑ 55	Kordell Stewart	.75	.30
❑ 56	Steve McNair	1.25	.50
❑ 57	Jeff Blake	.75	.30
❑ 58	Eric Moulds	.75	.30
❑ 59	Emmitt Smith	2.50	1.00
❑ 60	David Boston	1.25	.50
❑ 61	Cris Carter	1.25	.50
❑ 62	Peyton Manning	3.00	1.25
❑ 63	Keyshawn Johnson	1.25	.50
❑ 64	Doug Flutie	1.25	.50
❑ 65	Drew Bledsoe	1.50	.60
❑ 66	Ricky Williams	1.25	.50
❑ 67	Keenan Mccardell	.50	.20
❑ 68	Brian Urlacher	2.00	.75
❑ 69	Jamal Lewis	2.00	.75
❑ 70	Ed McCaffrey	1.25	.50
❑ 71	Antonio Freeman	1.25	.50
❑ 72	Darrell Jackson	1.25	.50
❑ 73	Jeff George	.75	.30
❑ 74	Chris Chandler	.75	.30
❑ 75	Germane Crowell	.50	.20
❑ 76	Tim Biakabutuka	.75	.30
❑ 77	Jon Kitna	.75	.30
❑ 78	Troy Brown	.75	.30
❑ 79	Lamar Smith	.75	.30
❑ 80	Derrick Mason	.75	.30
❑ 81	Hines Ward	1.25	.50
❑ 82	Mark Brunell	1.25	.50
❑ 83	Trent Dilfer	.75	.30
❑ 84	Tim Couch	.75	.30
❑ 85	Donald Hayes	.50	.20
❑ 86	Amani Toomer	.75	.30
❑ 87	Tony Gonzalez	.75	.30
❑ 88	Rich Gannon	1.25	.50
❑ 89	Rob Johnson	.75	.30
❑ 90	Torry Holt	1.25	.50
❑ 91	Jeff Garcia	1.25	.50
❑ 92	Kurt Warner	2.50	1.00
❑ 93	Aaron Brooks	1.25	.50
❑ 94	Brian Griese	1.25	.50
❑ 95	James Allen	.75	.30
❑ 96	Wayne Chrebet	.75	.30
❑ 97	Tiki Barber	1.25	.50
❑ 98	Brad Johnson	1.25	.50
❑ 99	Ricky Watters	.75	.30
❑ 100	Charlie Garner	.75	.30
❑ 101	Andre Carter RC	10.00	4.00
❑ 102	Dan Morgan RC	10.00	4.00
❑ 103	Gerard Warren RC	10.00	4.00
❑ 104	Jesse Palmer RC	10.00	4.00
❑ 105	Josh Heupel RC	10.00	4.00
❑ 106	Justin Smith RC	10.00	4.00
❑ 107	LaMont Jordan RC	20.00	10.00
❑ 108	Leonard Davis RC	6.00	2.50
❑ 109	Marques Tuiasosopo RC	10.00	4.00
❑ 110	Snoop Minnis RC	6.00	2.50
❑ 111	Quincy Carter RC	10.00	4.00
❑ 112	Quincy Morgan RC	10.00	4.00
❑ 113	Richard Seymour RC	10.00	4.00
❑ 114	Rudi Johnson RC	20.00	7.50
❑ 115	Sage Rosenfels RC	10.00	4.00
❑ 116	Todd Heap RC	10.00	4.00
❑ 117	Travis Minor RC	6.00	2.50
❑ 118	Will Allen RC	6.00	2.50
❑ 119	Jamal Reynolds RC	10.00	4.00
❑ 120	Scotty Anderson RC	6.00	2.50
❑ 121	Anthony Thomas RC	10.00	4.00
❑ 122	Chad Johnson RC	25.00	10.00
❑ 123	Chris Chambers RC	15.00	6.00
❑ 124	Chris Weinke RC	10.00	4.00
❑ 125	David Terrell RC	10.00	4.00
❑ 126	Deuce McAllister RC	20.00	7.50
❑ 127	Drew Brees RC	25.00	10.00
❑ 128	Freddie Mitchell RC	10.00	4.00
❑ 129	James Jackson RC	10.00	4.00
❑ 130	Kevan Barlow RC	10.00	4.00
❑ 131	Koren Robinson RC	10.00	4.00
❑ 132	LaDainian Tomlinson RC	50.00	30.00
❑ 133	Michael Bennett RC	15.00	6.00
❑ 134	Michael Vick RC	60.00	30.00
❑ 135	Mike McMahon RC	10.00	4.00
❑ 136	Reggie Wayne RC	20.00	7.50
❑ 137	Robert Ferguson RC	10.00	4.00
❑ 138	Rod Gardner RC	10.00	4.00
❑ 139	Santana Moss RC	15.00	6.00
❑ 140	Travis Henry RC	10.00	4.00

2002 Finest

❑ COMP.SET w/o SP's (62)	40.00	15.00
❑ 1 Peyton Manning	2.50	1.00
❑ 2 Troy Brown	.75	.30
❑ 3 Curtis Martin	1.25	.50
❑ 4 Kordell Stewart	.75	.30
❑ 5 Michael Pittman	.50	.20
❑ 6 Rod Gardner	.75	.30
❑ 7 Germane Crowell	.50	.20
❑ 8 Terrell Davis	1.25	.50
❑ 9 Eric Moulds	.75	.30
❑ 10 Jake Plummer	.75	.30
❑ 11 Tony Gonzalez	.75	.30
❑ 12 Ricky Williams	1.25	.50
❑ 13 Deuce McAllister	1.50	.60
❑ 14 Jerry Rice	2.50	1.00
❑ 15 Torry Holt	1.25	.50
❑ 16 Michael Vick	4.00	1.50
❑ 17 David Terrell	1.25	.50
❑ 18 Terry Glenn	.75	.30
❑ 19 Mark Brunell	1.25	.50
❑ 20 Vinny Testaverde	.75	.30
❑ 21 Jerome Bettis	1.25	.50
❑ 22 Randy Moss	2.50	1.00
❑ 23 Marvin Harrison	1.25	.50
❑ 24 Chris Weinke	.75	.30
❑ 25 Tiki Barber	1.25	.50
❑ 26 Corey Bradford	.50	.20
❑ 27 David Boston	1.25	.50
❑ 28 Emmitt Smith	3.00	1.25
❑ 29 Santana Moss	1.25	.50
❑ 30 Brian Griese	1.25	.50
❑ 31 Priest Holmes	1.50	.60
❑ 32 Rich Gannon	1.25	.50
❑ 33 Antowain Smith	.75	.30
❑ 34 Marcus Robinson	.75	.30
❑ 35 Warrick Dunn	1.25	.50
❑ 36 Daunte Culpepper	1.25	.50
❑ 37 Shaun Alexander	1.50	.60
❑ 38 Kurt Warner	1.25	.50
❑ 39 Quincy Carter	.75	.30
❑ 40 Ray Lewis	1.25	.50
❑ 41 Aaron Brooks	1.25	.50
❑ 42 Plaxico Burress	.75	.30
❑ 43 Jamal Lewis	1.25	.50
❑ 44 Ahman Green	1.25	.50
❑ 45 Rod Smith	.75	.30
❑ 46 Tim Couch	.75	.30
❑ 47 Muhsin Muhammad	.75	.30
❑ 48 Drew Bledsoe	1.50	.60
❑ 49 Anthony Thomas	.75	.30
❑ 50 Tom Brady	3.00	1.25
❑ 51 Trent Green	.75	.30
❑ 52 Charlie Garner	.75	.30
❑ 53 Darrell Jackson	.75	.30
❑ 54 Mike McMahon	1.25	.50
❑ 55 Donovan McNabb	1.50	.60
❑ 56 Fred Taylor	1.25	.50
❑ 57 Corey Dillon	.75	.30
❑ 58 Keyshawn Johnson	1.25	.50
❑ 59 Drew Brees	1.25	.50
❑ 60 Steve McNair	1.25	.50
❑ 61 Jimmy Smith	.75	.30
❑ 62 Terrell Owens	1.25	.50
❑ 63 Eddie George JSY/499	20.00	7.50
❑ 64 Jeff Garcia JSY/999	15.00	6.00
❑ 65 LaDain Tomlinson JSY/999	25.00	10.00
❑ 66 Cris Carter JSY/499	20.00	7.50
❑ 67 Chris Chambers JSY/499	20.00	7.50
❑ 68 Brian Urlacher JSY/999	25.00	10.00
❑ 69 Tim Brown JSY/999	15.00	6.00
❑ 70 Marshall Faulk JSY/999	20.00	7.50
❑ 71 Stephen Davis JSY/999	12.00	5.00
❑ 72 Jevon Kearse JSY/999	12.00	5.00
❑ 73 Edgerrin James JSY/999	15.00	6.00
❑ 74 Mike Anderson JSY/999	15.00	6.00
❑ 75 Warren Sapp JSY/499	20.00	7.50
❑ 76 Brett Favre JSY/499	30.00	15.00
❑ 77 Julius Peppers RC	6.00	2.50
❑ 78 Tim Carter RC	3.00	1.25
❑ 79 Travis Stephens RC	3.00	1.25
❑ 80 Jabar Gaffney RC	4.00	1.50
❑ 81 Cliff Russell RC	3.00	1.25
❑ 82 Reche Caldwell RC	4.00	1.50
❑ 83 Maurice Morris RC	4.00	1.50
❑ 84 Antwaan Randle El RC	6.00	2.50
❑ 85 Ladell Betts RC	4.00	1.50
❑ 86 Daniel Graham RC	4.00	1.50
❑ 87 Jeremy Shockey RC	12.00	5.00
❑ 88 Mike Williams RC	3.00	1.25
❑ 89 Josh McCown RC	5.00	2.00
❑ 90 Rohan Davey RC	4.00	1.50
❑ 91 David Garrard RC	4.00	1.50
❑ 92 Dwight Freeney RC	5.00	2.00
❑ 93 Leonard Henry RC	3.00	1.25
❑ 94 Albert Haynesworth RC	3.00	1.25
❑ 95 Herb Haygood RC	2.00	.75
❑ 96 Kurt Kittner RC	3.00	1.25
❑ 97 Jason McAddley RC	3.00	1.25
❑ 98 Bryan Thomas RC	3.00	1.25
❑ 99 Wendell Bryant RC	2.00	.75
❑ 100 Mike Rumph RC	4.00	1.50
❑ 101 Chad Hutchinson RC	3.00	1.25
❑ 102 Brian Westbrook RC	6.00	2.50
❑ 103 Deion Branch RC	8.00	4.00
❑ 104 John Henderson RC	4.00	1.50
❑ 105 Jerramy Stevens RC	4.00	1.50
❑ 106 Tracey Wistrom RC	3.00	1.25
❑ 107 Phillip Buchanon RC	4.00	1.50
❑ 108 Matt Schobel RC	3.00	1.25
❑ 109 Ed Reed RC	6.00	2.50
❑ 110 Randy Fasani RC	3.00	1.25
❑ 111 Josh Scobey RC	4.00	1.50
❑ 112 Luke Staley RC	3.00	1.25
❑ 113 Anthony Weaver RC	3.00	1.25
❑ 114 Kyle Johnson RC	2.00	.75
❑ 115 David Carr AU RC	50.00	20.00
❑ 116 Joey Harrington AU RC	50.00	20.00
❑ 117 Donte Stallworth AU RC	30.00	12.50
❑ 118 Ashley Lelie AU RC	40.00	15.00
❑ 119 Patrick Ramsey AU RC	30.00	12.50
❑ 120 William Green AU RC	20.00	7.50
❑ 121 Josh Reed AU RC	20.00	7.50
❑ 122 Clinton Portis AU RC	60.00	25.00
❑ 123 Antonio Bryant AU RC	20.00	7.50
❑ 124 Javon Walker AU RC	40.00	20.00
❑ 125 Roy Williams AU RC	40.00	20.00
❑ 126 Marquise Walker AU RC	20.00	7.50
❑ 127 Quentin Jammer AU RC	20.00	7.50
❑ 128 DeShaun Foster AU RC	30.00	15.00
❑ 129 Andre Davis AU RC	20.00	7.50
❑ 130 Ron Johnson AU RC	20.00	7.50
❑ 131 Lamar Gordon AU RC	20.00	7.50
❑ 132 T.J. Duckett AU/300 RC	50.00	20.00
❑ 133 Freddie Milons AU RC	20.00	7.50
❑ 134 Eric Crouch AU RC	20.00	7.50
❑ 135 Adrian Peterson AU RC	20.00	7.50
❑ 136 Damien Anderson AU RC	20.00	7.50

2003 Finest

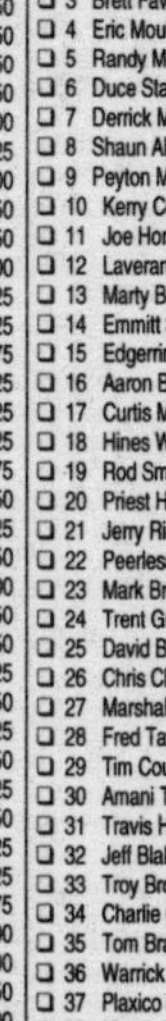

❑ COMP.SET w/o SP's (100)	50.00	20.00
❑ 101-118 GROUP A ODDS 1:171 MINI-BOXES		
❑ 101-118 GROUP B ODDS 1:38 MINI-BOXES		
❑ 101-118 GROUP C ODDS 1:4 MINI-BOXES		
❑ ROOKIE AU/399 ODDS 1:30 MINI-BOXES		
❑ ROOKIE AU/999 ODDS 1:3 MINI-BOXES		
❑ 1 Chad Pennington	1.50	.60
❑ 2 Tommy Maddox	1.25	.50
❑ 3 Brett Favre	3.00	1.25
❑ 4 Eric Moulds	.75	.30
❑ 5 Randy Moss	2.00	.75
❑ 6 Duce Staley	.75	.30
❑ 7 Derrick Mason	.75	.30
❑ 8 Shaun Alexander	1.25	.50
❑ 9 Peyton Manning	2.00	.75
❑ 10 Kerry Collins	.75	.30
❑ 11 Joe Horn	.75	.30
❑ 12 Laveranues Coles	.75	.30
❑ 13 Marty Booker	.75	.30
❑ 14 Emmitt Smith	3.00	1.25
❑ 15 Edgerrin James	1.25	.50
❑ 16 Aaron Brooks	1.25	.50
❑ 17 Curtis Martin	1.25	.50
❑ 18 Hines Ward	1.25	.50
❑ 19 Rod Smith	.75	.30
❑ 20 Priest Holmes	1.50	.60
❑ 21 Jerry Rice	2.50	1.00
❑ 22 Peerless Price	.75	.30
❑ 23 Mark Brunell	.75	.30
❑ 24 Trent Green	.75	.30
❑ 25 David Boston	.75	.30
❑ 26 Chris Chambers	1.25	.50
❑ 27 Marshall Faulk	1.25	.50
❑ 28 Fred Taylor	1.25	.50
❑ 29 Tim Couch	.50	.20
❑ 30 Amani Toomer	.75	.30
❑ 31 Travis Henry	.75	.30
❑ 32 Jeff Blake	.50	.20
❑ 33 Troy Brown	.75	.30
❑ 34 Charlie Garner	.75	.30
❑ 35 Tom Brady	3.00	1.25
❑ 36 Warrick Dunn	.75	.30
❑ 37 Plaxico Burress	.75	.30
❑ 38 Marvin Harrison	1.25	.50
❑ 39 Clinton Portis	2.00	.75
❑ 40 Deuce McAllister	1.25	.50
❑ 41 Matt Hasselbeck	.75	.30
❑ 42 Jeff Garcia	1.25	.50
❑ 43 David Carr	2.00	.75
❑ 44 Ahman Green	1.25	.50
❑ 45 Eddie George	.75	.30
❑ 46 Drew Brees	1.25	.50
❑ 47 Tiki Barber	1.25	.50
❑ 48 Jay Fiedler	.75	.30
❑ 49 Curtis Conway	.75	.30
❑ 50 Steve McNair	1.25	.50
❑ 51 Donald Driver	.75	.30
❑ 52 Jake Plummer	.75	.30
❑ 53 Jamal Lewis	1.25	.50
❑ 54 Corey Dillon	.75	.30
❑ 55 Stephen Davis	.75	.30
❑ 56 Terrell Owens	1.25	.50
❑ 57 Torry Holt	1.25	.50
❑ 58 Chad Johnson	1.25	.50
❑ 59 Chad Hutchinson	.50	.20
❑ 60 Kurt Warner	1.25	.50

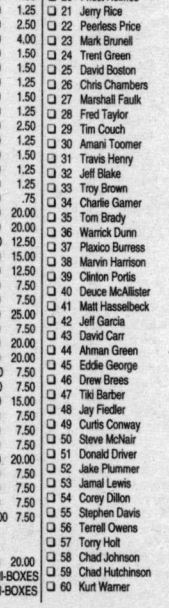

No.	Player	Hi	Lo
61	Troy Polamalu RC	20.00	10.00
62	Eugene Wilson RC	3.00	1.25
63	Juston Wood RC	1.50	.60
64	Anquan Boldin RC	8.00	3.00
65	Doug Gabriel RC	3.00	1.25
66	Domanick Davis RC	5.00	2.00
67	J.R. Tolver RC	2.50	1.00
68	Jerome McDougle RC	3.00	1.25
69	Keenan Howry RC	3.00	1.25
70	Teyo Johnson RC	3.00	1.25
71	Bethel Johnson RC	3.00	1.25
72	Ken Hamlin RC	3.00	1.25
73	L.J. Smith RC	3.00	1.25
74	Rashean Mathis RC	1.50	.60
75	Arnaz Battle RC	3.00	1.25
76	B.J. Askew RC	3.00	1.25
77	Mike Doss RC	3.00	1.25
78	Kevin Curtis RC	3.00	1.25
79	Terence Newman RC	6.00	2.50
80	Shaun McDonald RC	3.00	1.25
81	Kevin Williams RC	3.00	1.25
82	Nate Burleson RC	4.00	1.50
83	Tyrone Calico RC	4.00	1.50
84	DeWayne White RC	2.50	1.00
85	Marcus Trufant RC	3.00	1.25
86	Nick Barnett RC	5.00	2.00
87	Bennie Joppru RC	3.00	1.25
88	Andre Woolfolk RC	3.00	1.25
89	Billy McMullen RC	2.50	1.00
90	Boss Bailey RC	3.00	1.25
91	William Joseph RC	3.00	1.25
92	Michael Haynes RC	3.00	1.25
93	DeWayne Robertson RC	3.00	1.25
94	LaTarence Dunbar RC	2.50	1.00
95	David Tyree RC	2.50	1.00
96	Walter Young RC	1.50	.60
97	E.J. Henderson RC	3.00	1.25
98	Ty Warren RC	3.00	1.25
99	Zuriel Smith RC	1.50	.60
100	Brock Forsey RC	3.00	1.25
101	Ricky Williams JSY C	12.00	5.00
102	Drew Bledsoe JSY C	12.00	5.00
103	Joey Harrington JSY C	15.00	6.00
104	Tim Brown JSY C	15.00	6.00
105	Brian Urlacher JSY C	20.00	7.50
106	Zach Thomas JSY C	12.00	5.00
107	Jeremy Shockey JSY C	15.00	6.00
108	Michael Strahan JSY A	12.00	5.00
109	Jason Taylor JSY C	12.00	5.00
110	Donovan McNabb JSY C	20.00	7.50
111	LaDainian Tomlinson JSY B	15.00	6.00
112	Rich Gannon JSY C	12.00	5.00
113	Brad Johnson JSY C	12.00	5.00
114	Daunte Culpepper JSY C	12.00	5.00
115	Michael Vick JSY C	25.00	10.00
116	Jimmy Smith JSY B	10.00	4.00
117	Keyshawn Johnson JSY C	12.00	5.00
118	Keith Brooking JSY C	10.00	4.00
119	Carson Palmer AU/399 RC	150.00	75.00
120	Byron Leftwich AU/399 RC	100.00	40.00
121	Chris Simms AU/399 RC	40.00	25.00
122	Kyle Boller AU/399 RC	50.00	20.00
123	Justin Fargas AU RC	15.00	6.00
124	Seneca Wallace AU RC	15.00	6.00
125	Larry Johnson AU RC	120.00	60.00
126	Kareem Kelly AU RC	15.00	6.00
127	Willis McGahee AU/399 RC	80.00	40.00
128	Kelley Washington AU RC	15.00	6.00
129	Brian St.Pierre AU RC	15.00	6.00
130	Kliff Kingsbury AU RC	15.00	6.00
131	Ken Dorsey AU RC	15.00	6.00
132	Bryant Johnson AU RC	15.00	6.00
133	Dallas Clark AU RC	15.00	6.00
134	Chris Brown AU RC	25.00	10.00
135	Taylor Jacobs AU RC	15.00	6.00
136	Artose Pinner AU RC	15.00	6.00
137	Lee Suggs AU RC	30.00	12.50
138	LaBrandon Toefield AU RC	15.00	6.00
139	Jason Witten AU RC	30.00	15.00
140	Brad Banks AU RC	15.00	6.00
141	Earnest Graham AU RC	15.00	6.00
142	Bobby Wade AU RC	15.00	6.00
143	Talman Gardner AU RC	15.00	6.00
144	Justin Gage AU RC	15.00	6.00
145	Sam Aiken AU RC	15.00	6.00
146	Musa Smith AU RC	15.00	6.00
147	Terrell Suggs AU RC	20.00	7.50
148	Brandon Lloyd AU RC	25.00	12.50
150	Rex Grossman AU RC	30.00	12.50

2004 Finest

No.	Player	Hi	Lo
	COMP.SET w/o SP's (100)	40.00	15.00
	COMP.SET w/o RC's (60)	12.00	5.00
	VETERAN JERSEY STATED ODDS 1:36		
	108-134 AU/399 RC STATED ODDS 1:120		
	108-134 AU/999 RC STATED ODDS 1:12		
	UNPRICED PRINT PLATES #'d TO 1		
1	Steve McNair	.75	.30
2	Corey Dillon	.50	.20
3	Joey Harrington	.75	.30
4	Travis Henry	.50	.20
5	Donovan McNabb	1.00	.40
6	Jamal Lewis	.75	.30
7	Jeff Garcia	.75	.30
8	Fred Taylor	.50	.20
9	Aaron Brooks	.50	.20
10	Marc Bulger	.75	.30
11	Keenan McCardell	.30	.10
12	David Carr	.75	.30
13	Charles Rogers	.50	.20
14	Ray Lewis	.75	.30
15	Priest Holmes	1.00	.40
16	Curtis Martin	.75	.30
17	Plaxico Burress	.50	.20
18	Shaun Alexander	.75	.30
19	Brad Johnson	.50	.20
20	Marvin Harrison	.75	.30
21	Rod Smith	.50	.20
22	Jake Delhomme	.75	.30
23	Santana Moss	.50	.20
24	Trent Green	.50	.20
25	Michael Vick	1.50	.60
26	Tim Rattay	.30	.10
27	Chris Chambers	.50	.20
28	Robert Ferguson	.30	.10
29	Tiki Barber	.75	.30
30	Terrell Owens	.75	.30
31	Marshall Faulk	.75	.30
32	Quincy Carter	.50	.20
33	Stephen Davis	.50	.20
34	Josh McCown	.50	.20
35	Jeremy Shockey	.75	.30
36	Tommy Maddox	.50	.20
37	Derrick Mason	.50	.20
38	Kerry Collins	.50	.20
39	Jimmy Smith	.50	.20
40	Chad Pennington	.75	.30
41	Domanick Davis	.75	.30
42	Darrell Jackson	.50	.20
43	Steve Smith	.75	.30
44	Drew Bledsoe	.75	.30
45	Deuce McAllister	.75	.30
46	Jerry Porter	.50	.20
47	Peerless Price	.50	.20
48	Eric Moulds	.50	.20
49	Garrison Hearst	.50	.20
50	Brett Favre	3.00	1.25
51	Amani Toomer	.50	.20
52	Andre Johnson	.75	.30
53	Edgerrin James	.75	.30
54	Rex Grossman	.75	.30
55	Daunte Culpepper	.75	.30
56	Tony Gonzalez	.50	.20
57	Byron Leftwich	1.00	.40
58	Mark Brunell	.50	.20
59	Laveranues Coles	.50	.20
60	Matt Hasselbeck	.50	.20
61	Chris Gamble RC	2.50	1.00
62	Michael Turner RC	2.00	.75
63	Julius Jones RC	12.00	5.00
64	Dunta Robinson RC	2.00	.75
65	Sean Taylor RC	2.50	1.00
66	Ahmad Carroll RC	2.50	1.00
67	Derrick Strait RC	2.00	.75
68	Dontarrious Thomas RC	2.00	.75
69	Jason Babin RC	2.00	.75
70	Reggie Williams RC	2.50	1.00
71	Dwan Edwards RC	1.00	.40
72	Rashaun Woods RC	2.00	.75
73	Ricardo Colclough RC	2.00	.75
74	Will Smith RC	2.00	.75
75	Kellen Winslow RC	4.00	1.50
76	Roy Williams RC	5.00	2.00
77	B.J. Symons RC	2.00	.75
78	Carlos Francis RC	1.50	.60
79	Triandos Luke RC	2.00	.75
80	Drew Henson RC	2.00	.75
81	Keiwan Ratliff RC	1.50	.60
82	Will Poole RC	2.00	.75
83	Tommie Harris RC	2.00	.75
84	Steven Jackson RC	6.00	2.50
85	Greg Jones RC	2.00	.75
86	Vince Wilfork RC	2.50	1.00
87	DeAngelo Hall RC	2.50	1.00
88	Daryl Smith RC	2.00	.75
89	Teddy Lehman RC	2.00	.75
90	Casey Bramlet RC	1.50	.60
91	Marcus Tubbs RC	2.00	.75
92	Andy Hall RC	1.50	.60
93	Jim Sorgi RC	2.00	.75
94	Kenechi Udeze RC	2.00	.75
95	Darius Watts RC	2.00	.75
96	Tank Johnson RC	1.50	.60
97	Matt Mauck RC	2.00	.75
98	Bradlee Van Pelt RC	3.00	1.25
99	D.J. Williams RC	2.50	1.00
100	Larry Fitzgerald RC	6.00	2.50
101	Peyton Manning JSY	15.00	6.00
102	Clinton Portis JSY	8.00	3.00
103	Chad Johnson JSY	8.00	3.00
104	Randy Moss JSY	10.00	4.00
105	Tom Brady JSY	20.00	7.50
106	LaDainian Tomlinson JSY	10.00	4.00
107	Ahman Green JSY	8.00	3.00
108	Roethlisberger AU/399 RC	300.00	175.00
109	Philip Rivers AU/399 RC	100.00	50.00
110	Eli Manning AU/399 RC	200.00	125.00
111	Kevin Jones AU/399 RC	80.00	30.00
112	Bernard Berrian AU RC	15.00	6.00
113	Jeff Smoker AU RC	15.00	6.00
114	Mewelde Moore AU RC	20.00	7.50
115	Michael Clayton AU RC	30.00	12.50
116	Jonathan Vilma AU RC	20.00	7.50
117	J Morant AU RC EXCH	15.00	6.00
118	Devard Darling AU RC	15.00	6.00
119	Cedric Cobbs AU RC	15.00	6.00
120	Chris Perry AU/399 RC	30.00	12.50
121	Ernest Wilford AU RC	15.00	6.00
122	Michael Jenkins AU RC	20.00	7.50
123	Jerricho Cotchery AU RC	15.00	6.00
124	P.K. Sam AU RC	12.00	5.00
125	Tatum Bell AU RC	30.00	12.50
126	Derrick Hamilton AU RC	12.00	5.00

- ❑ 127 Luke McCown AU RC 15.00 6.00
- ❑ 128 Devery Henderson AU RC 12.00 5.00
- ❑ 129 Craig Krenzel AU RC 15.00 6.00
- ❑ 130 J.P. Losman AU RC 30.00 12.50
- ❑ 131 Lee Evans AU RC 20.00 10.00
- ❑ 132 Matt Schaub AU RC 25.00 12.50
- ❑ 133 Robert Gallery AU RC 20.00 7.50
- ❑ 134 Keary Colbert AU RC 20.00 7.50

2005 Finest

- ❑ COMPLETE SET (183)
- ❑ UNPRICED FRAMED REF. PRINT RUN 1 SET
- ❑ UNPRICED FRAM.XFRAC. PRINT RUN 1 SET
- ❑ UNPRICED GOLD XFRAC.PRINT RUN 10 SETS
- ❑ UNPRICED PRINT.PLATE PRINT RUN 1 SET
- ❑ UNPRICED SUPERFRACTORS #'d TO 1
- ❑ 1 Muhsin Muhammad .50 .20
- ❑ 2 Kevin Jones .75 .30
- ❑ 3 Eli Manning 1.50 .60
- ❑ 4 Kevan Barlow .50 .20
- ❑ 5 Randy Moss .75 .30
- ❑ 6 Brian Griese .50 .20
- ❑ 7 Dante Hall .50 .20
- ❑ 8 Chris Brown .50 .20
- ❑ 9 Antonio Gates .75 .30
- ❑ 10 Champ Bailey .50 .20
- ❑ 11 Eric Moulds .50 .20
- ❑ 12 Ray Lewis .75 .30
- ❑ 13 Larry Fitzgerald .75 .30
- ❑ 14 Byron Leftwich .75 .30
- ❑ 15 Marvin Harrison .75 .30
- ❑ 16 Stephen Davis .50 .20
- ❑ 17 Laveranues Coles .50 .20
- ❑ 18 Shaun Alexander 1.00 .40
- ❑ 19 Drew Bledsoe .75 .30
- ❑ 20 Sean Taylor .50 .20
- ❑ 21 Deuce McAllister .75 .30
- ❑ 22 Nate Burleson .50 .20
- ❑ 23 A.J. Feeley .50 .20
- ❑ 24 Jerome Bettis .75 .30
- ❑ 25 Torry Holt .75 .30
- ❑ 26 LaDainian Tomlinson 1.00 .40
- ❑ 27 Travis Henry .50 .20
- ❑ 28 T.J. Houshmandzadeh .40 .15
- ❑ 29 Fred Taylor .50 .20
- ❑ 30 Michael Jenkins .50 .20
- ❑ 31 Edgerrin James .75 .30
- ❑ 32 Terrell Owens .75 .30
- ❑ 33 Jason Witten .50 .20
- ❑ 34 Clinton Portis .75 .30
- ❑ 35 Deion Branch .50 .20
- ❑ 36 Priest Holmes .75 .30
- ❑ 37 Javon Walker .50 .20
- ❑ 38 Rex Grossman .50 .20
- ❑ 39 Domanick Davis .50 .20
- ❑ 40 Allen Rossum .40 .15
- ❑ 41 Dwight Freeney .50 .20
- ❑ 42 Jimmy Smith .50 .20
- ❑ 43 Tiki Barber .75 .30
- ❑ 44 Steve McNair .75 .30
- ❑ 45 Steven Jackson 1.00 .40
- ❑ 46 Joe Horn .50 .20
- ❑ 47 Randy McMichael .40 .15
- ❑ 48 J.P. Losman .75 .30
- ❑ 49 Warrick Dunn .50 .20
- ❑ 50 Tatum Bell .50 .20
- ❑ 51 Roy Williams WR .75 .30
- ❑ 52 Curtis Martin .75 .30
- ❑ 53 Donovan McNabb 1.00 .40
- ❑ 54 LaMont Jordan .75 .30
- ❑ 55 Marc Bulger .75 .30
- ❑ 56 Drew Bennett .50 .20
- ❑ 57 Julius Jones 1.00 .40
- ❑ 58 Santana Moss .50 .20
- ❑ 59 Michael Bennett .50 .20
- ❑ 60 Tony Gonzalez .50 .20
- ❑ 61 Jamal Lewis .75 .30
- ❑ 62 Keary Colbert .50 .20
- ❑ 63 Carson Palmer .75 .30
- ❑ 64 Dunta Robinson .50 .20
- ❑ 65 Brandon Stokley .50 .20
- ❑ 66 Brett Favre 2.00 .75
- ❑ 67 Jonathan Vilma .50 .20
- ❑ 68 Darrell Jackson .50 .20
- ❑ 69 Michael Pittman .40 .15
- ❑ 70 Drew Brees .75 .30
- ❑ 71 Amani Toomer .50 .20
- ❑ 72 Corey Dillon .50 .20
- ❑ 73 Willis McGahee .75 .30
- ❑ 74 Michael Vick 1.25 .50
- ❑ 75 Chad Johnson .75 .30
- ❑ 76 Anquan Boldin .50 .20
- ❑ 77 Kerry Collins .50 .20
- ❑ 78 Marshall Faulk .75 .30
- ❑ 79 Roy Williams S .50 .20
- ❑ 80 Trent Green .50 .20
- ❑ 81 Chris Gamble .50 .20
- ❑ 82 Ahman Green .75 .30
- ❑ 83 Todd Heap .50 .20
- ❑ 84 Brandon Lloyd .40 .15
- ❑ 85 Andre Johnson .50 .20
- ❑ 86 Lee Suggs .50 .20
- ❑ 87 Plaxico Burress .50 .20
- ❑ 88 Hines Ward .75 .30
- ❑ 89 Rod Smith .50 .20
- ❑ 90 Joey Harrington .75 .30
- ❑ 91 Derrick Mason .50 .20
- ❑ 92 Rudi Johnson .50 .20
- ❑ 93 Isaac Bruce .50 .20
- ❑ 94 Chris Chambers .50 .20
- ❑ 95 Matt Hasselbeck .50 .20
- ❑ 96 Donte Stallworth .50 .20
- ❑ 97 Philip Rivers .75 .30
- ❑ 98 Michael Clayton .75 .30
- ❑ 99 Alge Crumpler .50 .20
- ❑ 100 Chad Pennington .75 .30
- ❑ 101 Brian Westbrook .50 .20
- ❑ 102 Daunte Culpepper .75 .30
- ❑ 103 Jeremy Shockey .75 .30
- ❑ 104 Jerry Porter .50 .20
- ❑ 105 Tom Brady 2.00 .75
- ❑ 106 Lee Evans .50 .20
- ❑ 107 Jake Delhomme .75 .30
- ❑ 108 Ben Roethlisberger 2.00 .75
- ❑ 109 Jake Plummer .50 .20
- ❑ 110 Charles Rogers .50 .20
- ❑ 111 Patrick Ramsey .50 .20
- ❑ 112 Reggie Wayne .50 .20
- ❑ 113 Reuben Droughns .50 .20
- ❑ 114 Aaron Brooks .50 .20
- ❑ 115 David Carr .75 .30
- ❑ 116 Thomas Jones .50 .20
- ❑ 117 Ashley Lelie .50 .20
- ❑ 118 Donald Driver .50 .20
- ❑ 119 Billy Volek .50 .20
- ❑ 120 Peyton Manning 1.25 .50
- ❑ 121 Frank Gore RC 4.00 1.50
- ❑ 122 Adam Jones RC 2.50 1.00
- ❑ 123 Antrel Rolle RC 2.50 1.00
- ❑ 124 Roddy White RC 2.50 1.00
- ❑ 125 Derrick Johnson RC 4.00 1.50
- ❑ 126 Troy Williamson RC 5.00 2.00
- ❑ 127 Maurice Clarett 2.50 1.00
- ❑ 128 Dan Orlovsky RC 3.00 1.25
- ❑ 129 Andrew Walter RC 4.00 1.50
- ❑ 130 Reggie Brown RC 2.50 1.00
- ❑ 131 Matt Jones RC 6.00 2.50
- ❑ 132 David Greene RC 2.50 1.00
- ❑ 133 Jerome Mathis RC 2.50 1.00
- ❑ 134 Thomas Davis RC 2.50 1.00
- ❑ 135 Roscoe Parrish RC 2.50 1.00
- ❑ 136 Ciatrick Fason RC 2.50 1.00
- ❑ 137 David Pollack RC 2.50 1.00
- ❑ 138 Kyle Orton RC 4.00 1.50
- ❑ 139 Heath Miller RC 6.00 2.50
- ❑ 140 Courtney Roby RC 2.50 1.00
- ❑ 141 Terrence Murphy RC 2.50 1.00
- ❑ 142 DeMarcus Ware RC 4.00 1.50
- ❑ 143 Fabian Washington RC 2.50 1.00
- ❑ 144 J.J. Arrington RC 3.00 1.25
- ❑ 145 Fred Gibson RC 2.00 .75
- ❑ 146 Carlos Rogers RC 3.00 1.25
- ❑ 147 Eric Shelton RC 2.50 1.00
- ❑ 148 Craphonso Thorpe RC 2.00 .75
- ❑ 149 Anthony Davis RC 2.00 .75
- ❑ 150 Marion Barber RC 4.00 1.50
- ❑ 151 Aaron Rodgers AU/299 RC 100.00 50.00
- ❑ 152 Alex Smith QB AU/299 RC 120.00 50.00
- ❑ 153 Braylon Edwards AU/299 RC 80.00 30.00
- ❑ 154 Carnell Williams AU/299 RC 150.00 75.00
- ❑ 155 Cedric Benson AU/299 RC 80.0030.00
- ❑ 156 Charlie Frye AU/299 RC 60.00 30.00
- ❑ 157 Jason Campbell AU/299 RC 60.00 30.00
- ❑ 158 Mark Clayton AU/299 RC 40.00 20.00
- ❑ 159 Mike Williams AU/299 50.00 20.00
- ❑ 160 Ronnie Brown AU/299 RC 100.0050.00
- ❑ 161 Alex Smith TE AU RC 12.00 5.00
- ❑ 162 Alvin Pearman AU RC 12.00 5.00
- ❑ 163 Brandon Jacobs AU RC 20.00 7.50
- ❑ 164 Channing Crowder AU RC 12.00 5.00
- ❑ 165 Chris Henry AU RC 15.00 6.00
- ❑ 166 Courtney Roby AU RC 12.00 5.00
- ❑ 167 Derek Anderson AU RC 12.00 5.00
- ❑ 168 Mark Bradley AU RC 15.00 6.00
- ❑ 169 Ryan Fitzpatrick AU RC 20.00 7.50
- ❑ 170 Ryan Moats AU RC 20.00 7.50
- ❑ 171 Stefan LeFors AU RC 12.00 5.00
- ❑ 172 Steve Savoy AU RC 10.00 4.00
- ❑ 173 Tab Perry AU RC 12.00 5.00
- ❑ 174 Timmy Chang AU RC 15.00 6.00
- ❑ 175 Vincent Jackson AU RC 12.00 5.00
- ❑ 176 Charles Frederick AU RC 12.00 5.00
- ❑ 177 Kay-Jay Harris AU RC 10.00 4.00
- ❑ 178 Darren Sproles AU RC 12.00 5.00
- ❑ 179 Adrian McPherson AU RC 15.00 6.00
- ❑ 180 Craig Bragg AU RC 10.00 4.00
- ❑ 181 J.R. Russell AU RC 10.00 4.00
- ❑ 182 Gino Guidugli AU RC 10.00 4.00
- ❑ 183 Vernand Morency AU RC 12.00 5.00

1995 Flair

- ❑ COMPLETE SET (220) 30.00 12.50
- ❑ 1 Larry Centers .40 .15
- ❑ 2 Garrison Hearst .75 .30
- ❑ 3 Seth Joyner .20 .07
- ❑ 4 Dave Krieg .20 .07
- ❑ 5 Rob Moore .40 .15

❑ 6 Frank Sanders RC .75 .30
❑ 7 Eric Swann .40 .15
❑ 8 Devin Bush .20 .07
❑ 9 Chris Doleman .20 .07
❑ 10 Bert Emanuel .75 .30
❑ 11 Jeff George .40 .15
❑ 12 Craig Heyward .40 .15
❑ 13 Terance Mathis .40 .15
❑ 14 Eric Metcalf .40 .15
❑ 15 Cornelius Bennett .40 .15
❑ 16 Jeff Burris .20 .07
❑ 17 Todd Collins RC .40 .15
❑ 18 Russell Copeland .20 .07
❑ 19 Jim Kelly .75 .30
❑ 20 Andre Reed .40 .15
❑ 21 Bruce Smith .75 .30
❑ 22 Don Beebe .20 .07
❑ 23 Mark Carrier WR .40 .15
❑ 24 Kerry Collins RC 2.00 .75
❑ 25 Barry Foster .40 .15
❑ 26 Pete Metzelaars .20 .07
❑ 27 Tyrone Poole .75 .30
❑ 28 Frank Reich .20 .07
❑ 29 Curtis Conway .75 .30
❑ 30 Chris Gedney .20 .07
❑ 31 Jeff Graham .20 .07
❑ 32 Raymont Harris .20 .07
❑ 33 Erik Kramer .20 .07
❑ 34 Rashaan Salaam RC .40 .15
❑ 35 Lewis Tillman .20 .07
❑ 36 Michael Timpson .20 .07
❑ 37 Jeff Blake RC 1.00 .40
❑ 38 Ki-Jana Carter RC .75 .30
❑ 39 Tony McGee .20 .07
❑ 40 Carl Pickens .40 .15
❑ 41 Corey Sawyer .20 .07
❑ 42 Darnay Scott .40 .15
❑ 43 Dan Wilkinson .40 .15
❑ 44 Derrick Alexander WR .75 .30
❑ 45 Leroy Hoard .20 .07
❑ 46 Michael Jackson .40 .15
❑ 47 Antonio Langham .20 .07
❑ 48 Andre Rison .40 .15
❑ 49 Vinny Testaverde .40 .15
❑ 50 Eric Turner .20 .07
❑ 51 Troy Aikman 2.00 .75
❑ 52 Charles Haley .40 .15
❑ 53 Michael Irvin .75 .30
❑ 54 Daryl Johnston .40 .15
❑ 55 Leon Lett .20 .07
❑ 56 Jay Novacek .40 .15
❑ 57 Emmitt Smith 3.00 1.25
❑ 58 Kevin Williams WR .40 .15
❑ 59 Steve Atwater .20 .07
❑ 60 Rod Bernstine .20 .07
❑ 61 John Elway 4.00 1.50
❑ 62 Glyn Milburn .20 .07
❑ 63 Anthony Miller .40 .15
❑ 64 Mike Pritchard .20 .07
❑ 65 Shannon Sharpe .40 .15
❑ 66 Scott Mitchell .40 .15
❑ 67 Herman Moore .75 .30
❑ 68 Johnnie Morton .40 .15
❑ 69 Brett Perriman .40 .15
❑ 70 Barry Sanders 3.00 1.25
❑ 71 Chris Spielman .40 .15
❑ 72 Edgar Bennett .40 .15
❑ 73 Robert Brooks .75 .30
❑ 74 Brett Favre 4.00 1.50
❑ 75 LeShon Johnson .40 .15
❑ 76 Sean Jones .20 .07
❑ 77 George Teague .20 .07
❑ 78 Reggie White .75 .30
❑ 79 Micheal Barrow .20 .07
❑ 80 Gary Brown .20 .07
❑ 81 Mel Gray .20 .07
❑ 82 Haywood Jeffires .20 .07
❑ 83 Steve McNair RC 4.00 1.50
❑ 84 Rodney Thomas RC .40 .15
❑ 85 Trev Alberts .20 .07
❑ 86 Flipper Anderson .20 .07
❑ 87 Tony Bennett .20 .07
❑ 88 Quentin Coryatt .40 .15
❑ 89 Sean Dawkins .40 .15
❑ 90 Craig Erickson .20 .07
❑ 91 Marshall Faulk 2.50 1.00
❑ 92 Steve Beuerlein .40 .15
❑ 93 Tony Boselli RC .75 .30
❑ 94 Reggie Cobb .20 .07
❑ 95 Ernest Givins .20 .07
❑ 96 Desmond Howard .40 .15
❑ 97 Jeff Lageman .20 .07
❑ 98 James O. Stewart RC 1.50 .60
❑ 99 Marcus Allen .75 .30
❑ 100 Steve Bono .40 .15
❑ 101 Dale Carter .40 .15
❑ 102 Willie Davis .40 .15
❑ 103 Lake Dawson .40 .15
❑ 104 Greg Hill .40 .15
❑ 105 Neil Smith .40 .15
❑ 106 Tim Bowens .20 .07
❑ 107 Bryan Cox .20 .07
❑ 108 Irving Fryar .40 .15
❑ 109 Eric Green .20 .07
❑ 110 Terry Kirby .40 .15
❑ 111 Dan Marino 4.00 1.50
❑ 112 O.J. McDuffie .75 .30
❑ 113 Bernie Parmalee .40 .15
❑ 114 Derrick Alexander DE RC .20 .07
❑ 115 Cris Carter .75 .30
❑ 116 Qadry Ismail .40 .15
❑ 117 Warren Moon .40 .15
❑ 118 Jake Reed .40 .15
❑ 119 Robert Smith .75 .30
❑ 120 Dewayne Washington .40 .15
❑ 121 Drew Bledsoe 1.25 .50
❑ 122 Vincent Brisby .20 .07
❑ 123 Ben Coates .40 .15
❑ 124 Curtis Martin RC 4.00 1.50
❑ 125 Willie McGinest .40 .15
❑ 126 Dave Meggett .20 .07
❑ 127 Chris Slade UER 126 .20 .07
❑ 128 Eric Allen .20 .07
❑ 129 Mario Bates .40 .15
❑ 130 Jim Everett .20 .07
❑ 131 Michael Haynes .40 .15
❑ 132 Tyrone Hughes .40 .15
❑ 133 Renaldo Turnbull .20 .07
❑ 134 Ray Zellars RC .40 .15
❑ 135 Michael Brooks .20 .07
❑ 136 Dave Brown .40 .15
❑ 137 Rodney Hampton .40 .15
❑ 138 Thomas Lewis .40 .15
❑ 139 Mike Sherrard .20 .07
❑ 140 Herschel Walker .40 .15
❑ 141 Tyrone Wheatley RC 1.50 .60
❑ 142 Kyle Brady RC .75 .30
❑ 143 Boomer Esiason .40 .15
❑ 144 Aaron Glenn .20 .07
❑ 145 Mo Lewis .20 .07
❑ 146 Johnny Mitchell .20 .07
❑ 147 Ronald Moore .20 .07
❑ 148 Joe Aska .40 .15
❑ 149 Tim Brown .75 .30
❑ 150 Jeff Hostetler .40 .15
❑ 151 Rocket Ismail .40 .15
❑ 152 Napoleon Kaufman RC 1.50 .60
❑ 153 Chester McGlockton .40 .15
❑ 154 Harvey Williams .20 .07
❑ 155 Fred Barnett .40 .15
❑ 156 Randall Cunningham .75 .30
❑ 157 Charlie Garner .75 .30
❑ 158 Mike Mamula RC .20 .07
❑ 159 Kevin Turner .20 .07
❑ 160 Ricky Watters .40 .15
❑ 161 Calvin Williams .40 .15
❑ 162 Mark Bruener RC .40 .15
❑ 163 Kevin Greene .40 .15
❑ 164 Charles Johnson .40 .15
❑ 165 Greg Lloyd .40 .15
❑ 166 Byron Bam Morris .20 .07
❑ 167 Neil O'Donnell .40 .15
❑ 168 Kordell Stewart RC 2.00 .75
❑ 169 John L. Williams .20 .07
❑ 170 Rod Woodson .40 .15
❑ 171 Jerome Bettis .75 .30
❑ 172 Isaac Bruce 1.25 .50
❑ 173 Kevin Carter RC .75 .30
❑ 174 Troy Drayton .20 .07
❑ 175 Sean Gilbert .40 .15
❑ 176 Carlos Jenkins .20 .07
❑ 177 Todd Lyght .20 .07
❑ 178 Chris Miller .20 .07
❑ 179 Andre Coleman .20 .07
❑ 180 Stan Humphries .40 .15
❑ 181 Shawn Jefferson .20 .07
❑ 182 Natrone Means .40 .15
❑ 183 Leslie O'Neal .40 .15
❑ 184 Junior Seau .75 .30
❑ 185 Mark Seay .40 .15
❑ 186 William Floyd .40 .15
❑ 187 Merton Hanks .20 .07
❑ 188 Brent Jones .20 .07
❑ 189 Ken Norton .40 .15
❑ 190 Jerry Rice 2.00 .75
❑ 191 Deion Sanders 1.00 .40
❑ 192 J.J. Stokes RC .75 .30
❑ 193 Dana Stubblefield .40 .15
❑ 194 Steve Young 1.50 .60
❑ 195 Sam Adams .20 .07
❑ 196 Brian Blades .40 .15
❑ 197 Joey Galloway RC 2.00 .75
❑ 198 Cortez Kennedy .40 .15
❑ 199 Rick Mirer .40 .15
❑ 200 Chris Warren .40 .15
❑ 201 Derrick Brooks RC 2.00 .75
❑ 202 Lawrence Dawsey .20 .07
❑ 203 Trent Dilfer .75 .30
❑ 204 Alvin Harper .20 .07
❑ 205 Jackie Harris .20 .07
❑ 206 Courtney Hawkins .20 .07
❑ 207 Hardy Nickerson .20 .07
❑ 208 Errict Rhett .40 .15
❑ 209 Warren Sapp RC 2.00 .75
❑ 210 Terry Allen .40 .15
❑ 211 Tom Carter .20 .07
❑ 212 Henry Ellard .40 .15
❑ 213 Darrell Green .20 .07
❑ 214 Brian Mitchell .20 .07
❑ 215 Heath Shuler .40 .15
❑ 216 Michael Westbrook RC .75 .30
❑ 217 Tydus Winans .20 .07
❑ 218 Checklist .20 .07
❑ 219 Checklist .20 .07
❑ 220 Checklist .40 .15
❑ S1 Michael Irvin Sample 1.25 .50

2002 Flair

❑ COMP.SET w/o SP's (90) 25.00 10.00
❑ 1 Jeff Garcia 1.25 .50
❑ 2 Jevon Kearse .75 .30
❑ 3 Chris Weinke .75 .30
❑ 4 Ray Lewis 1.25 .50
❑ 5 Donovan McNabb 1.50 .60

❑	6 Tiki Barber	1.25	.50
❑	7 Rich Gannon	1.25	.50
❑	8 Jamal Anderson	.75	.30
❑	9 Curtis Martin	1.25	.50
❑	10 Darrell Jackson	.75	.30
❑	11 Ricky Williams	1.25	.50
❑	12 Drew Brees	1.25	.50
❑	13 Mark Brunell	1.25	.50
❑	14 Johnnie Morton	.75	.30
❑	15 Quincy Carter	.75	.30
❑	16 Brian Urlacher	2.00	.75
❑	17 Peerless Price	.75	.30
❑	18 Drew Bledsoe	1.50	.60
❑	19 Aaron Brooks	1.25	.50
❑	20 Derrick Mason	.75	.30
❑	21 Charlie Garner	.75	.30
❑	22 Mike Alstott	1.25	.50
❑	23 Freddie Mitchell	.75	.30
❑	24 Isaac Bruce	1.25	.50
❑	25 Hines Ward	1.25	.50
❑	26 Doug Flutie	1.25	.50
❑	27 Terrell Owens	1.25	.50
❑	28 Peyton Manning	2.50	1.00
❑	29 Ron Dayne	.75	.30
❑	30 Peter Warrick	.75	.30
❑	31 Randy Moss	2.50	1.00
❑	32 Priest Holmes	1.50	.60
❑	33 Joey Galloway	.75	.30
❑	34 Jimmy Smith	.75	.30
❑	35 Marvin Harrison	1.25	.50
❑	36 Junior Seau	1.25	.50
❑	37 Zach Thomas	1.25	.50
❑	38 Antowain Smith	.75	.30
❑	39 Marty Booker	.75	.30
❑	40 Deuce McAllister	1.50	.60
❑	41 Rod Smith	.75	.30
❑	42 Michael Westbrook	.50	.20
❑	43 Antonio Freeman	1.25	.50
❑	44 Kerry Collins	.75	.30
❑	45 Koren Robinson	.75	.30
❑	46 Jamal Lewis	1.25	.50
❑	47 Duce Staley	1.25	.50
❑	48 Jerome Bettis	1.25	.50
❑	49 David Terrell	1.25	.50
❑	50 Daunte Culpepper	1.25	.50
❑	51 Tim Couch	.75	.30
❑	52 Brian Griese	1.25	.50
❑	53 Marshall Faulk	1.25	.50
❑	54 Brad Johnson	.75	.30
❑	55 Eddie George	1.25	.50
❑	56 Kurt Warner	1.25	.50
❑	57 Steve McNair	1.25	.50
❑	58 Stephen Davis	.75	.30
❑	59 Corey Dillon	.75	.30
❑	60 Troy Brown	.75	.30
❑	61 Warrick Dunn	1.25	.50
❑	62 Ed McCaffrey	1.25	.50
❑	63 Amani Toomer	.75	.30
❑	64 Rod Gardner	.75	.30
❑	65 Mike McMahon	1.25	.50
❑	66 Wayne Chrebet	.75	.30
❑	67 Jake Plummer	.75	.30
❑	68 Edgerrin James	1.50	.60
❑	69 Eric Moulds	.75	.30
❑	70 Tony Gonzalez	.75	.30
❑	71 Marcus Robinson	.75	.30
❑	72 Muhsin Muhammad	.75	.30
❑	73 Trent Dilfer	.75	.30
❑	74 Kevin Johnson	.75	.30
❑	75 Fred Taylor	1.25	.50
❑	76 Terrell Davis	1.25	.50
❑	77 Emmitt Smith	3.00	1.25
❑	78 Az-Zahir Hakim	.50	.20
❑	79 Tim Brown	1.25	.50
❑	80 Jerry Rice	2.50	1.00
❑	81 Warren Sapp	.75	.30
❑	82 Michael Strahan	.75	.30
❑	83 Garrison Hearst	.75	.30
❑	84 David Boston	1.25	.50
❑	85 Michael Vick	4.00	1.50
❑	86 Anthony Thomas	.75	.30
❑	87 Ahman Green	1.25	.50
❑	88 Chris Chambers	1.25	.50
❑	89 Tom Brady	3.00	1.25
❑	90 Plaxico Burress	.75	.30
❑	91 LaDainian Tomlinson	2.00	.75
❑	92 Shaun Alexander	1.50	.60
❑	93 Torry Holt	1.25	.50
❑	94 Kordell Stewart	.75	.30
❑	95 Chad Pennington	1.50	.60
❑	96 Chris Redman	.50	.20
❑	97 Kendrell Bell	1.25	.50
❑	98 Michael Bennett	.75	.30
❑	99 Joe Horn	.75	.30
❑	100 Brett Favre	3.00	1.25
❑	101 David Carr RC	15.00	6.00
❑	102 Joey Harrington RC	15.00	6.00
❑	103 Ashley Lelie RC	12.00	5.00
❑	104 Javon Walker RC	12.00	5.00
❑	105 Reche Caldwell RC	6.00	2.50
❑	106 Andre Davis RC	5.00	2.00
❑	107 William Green RC	6.00	2.50
❑	108 Antonio Bryant RC	6.00	2.50
❑	109 Clinton Portis RC	20.00	7.50
❑	110 Luke Staley RC	5.00	2.00
❑	111 Josh Reed RC	6.00	2.50
❑	112 Ron Johnson RC	5.00	2.00
❑	113 Lamar Gordon RC	6.00	2.50
❑	114 Cliff Russell RC	5.00	2.00
❑	115 Eric Crouch RC	6.00	2.50
❑	116 Ladell Betts RC	6.00	2.50
❑	117 Patrick Ramsey RC	8.00	3.00
❑	118 Adrian Peterson RC	6.00	2.50
❑	119 DeShaun Foster RC	6.00	2.50
❑	120 Tim Carter RC	5.00	2.00
❑	121 Jabar Gaffney RC	6.00	2.50
❑	122 T.J. Duckett RC	10.00	4.00
❑	123 Julius Peppers RC	12.00	5.00
❑	124 Rohan Davey RC	6.00	2.50
❑	125 Antwaan Randle El RC	10.00	4.00
❑	126 Jeremy Shockey RC	20.00	7.50
❑	127 Donte Stallworth RC	12.00	5.00
❑	128 Marquise Walker RC	5.00	2.00
❑	129 Brian Westbrook RC	10.00	4.00
❑	130 Randy Fasani RC	5.00	2.00
❑	131 Jonathan Wells RC	6.00	2.50
❑	132 Travis Stephens RC	5.00	2.00
❑	133 Daniel Graham RC	6.00	2.50
❑	134 Maurice Morris RC	6.00	2.50
❑	135 David Garrard RC	6.00	2.50

2003 Flair

❑	COMP.SET w/o SP's (90)	25.00	10.00
❑	1 Jamal Lewis	1.25	.50
❑	2 Aaron Brooks	1.25	.50
❑	3 Joey Harrington	2.00	.75
❑	4 Brett Favre	3.00	1.25
❑	5 Donovan McNabb	1.50	.60
❑	6 Marcel Shipp	.75	.30
❑	7 Michael Vick	3.00	1.25
❑	8 David Carr	2.00	.75
❑	9 Tommy Maddox	1.25	.50
❑	10 Drew Brees	1.25	.50
❑	11 Chad Pennington	1.50	.60
❑	12 Drew Bledsoe	1.25	.50
❑	13 Rich Gannon	.75	.30
❑	14 Kurt Warner	1.25	.50
❑	15 Brian Griese	1.25	.50
❑	16 William Green	.75	.30
❑	17 Jake Plummer	.75	.30
❑	18 Eric Moulds	.75	.30
❑	19 Peyton Manning	2.00	.75
❑	20 Keyshawn Johnson	1.25	.50
❑	21 Travis Henry	.75	.30
❑	22 Tiki Barber	1.25	.50
❑	23 Emmitt Smith	3.00	1.25
❑	24 Michael Bennett	.75	.30
❑	25 Curtis Martin	1.25	.50
❑	26 Donald Driver	.75	.30
❑	27 Clinton Portis	2.00	.75
❑	28 Eddie George	.75	.30
❑	29 Marshall Faulk	1.25	.50
❑	30 Jeremy Shockey	2.00	.75
❑	31 Ahman Green	1.25	.50
❑	32 Priest Holmes	1.50	.60
❑	33 Edgerrin James	1.25	.50
❑	34 Plaxico Burress	.75	.30
❑	35 Ricky Williams	1.25	.50
❑	36 Anthony Thomas	.75	.30
❑	37 Jerome Bettis	1.25	.50
❑	38 Shaun Alexander	1.25	.50
❑	39 Fred Taylor	1.25	.50
❑	40 Isaac Bruce	1.25	.50
❑	41 Mike Alstott	1.25	.50
❑	42 Peerless Price	.75	.30
❑	43 Corey Dillon	.75	.30
❑	44 Amani Toomer	.75	.30
❑	45 Warrick Dunn	.75	.30
❑	46 Tim Brown	1.25	.50
❑	47 Deuce McAllister	1.25	.50
❑	48 Terrell Owens	1.25	.50
❑	49 Stephen Davis	.75	.30
❑	50 Torry Holt	1.25	.50
❑	51 Duce Staley	.75	.30
❑	52 Jimmy Smith	.75	.30
❑	53 Ray Lewis	1.25	.50
❑	54 Brian Urlacher	2.00	.75
❑	55 Zach Thomas	1.25	.50
❑	56 Joey Galloway	.75	.30
❑	57 LaDainian Tomlinson	1.25	.50
❑	58 Chris Chambers	1.25	.50
❑	59 Ronde Barber	.50	.20
❑	60 Randy Moss	2.00	.75
❑	61 Tom Brady	3.00	1.25
❑	62 Jerry Porter	.75	.30
❑	63 Patrick Ramsey	1.25	.50
❑	64 Derrick Mason	.75	.30
❑	65 Daunte Culpepper	1.25	.50
❑	66 Marty Booker	.75	.30
❑	67 Steve McNair	1.25	.50
❑	68 Hines Ward	1.25	.50
❑	69 Matt Hasselbeck	.75	.30
❑	70 Joe Horn	.75	.30
❑	71 Mark Brunell	.75	.30
❑	72 Laveranues Coles	.75	.30
❑	73 Chad Hutchinson	.50	.20
❑	74 Tony Gonzalez	.75	.30
❑	75 Jeff Garcia	1.25	.50
❑	76 Kendrell Bell	.75	.30
❑	77 Kerry Collins	.75	.30
❑	78 Warren Sapp	.75	.30
❑	79 Tim Couch	.50	.20
❑	80 Jerry Rice	2.50	1.00
❑	81 Koren Robinson	.75	.30
❑	82 Antwaan Randle El	1.25	.50
❑	83 Donte Stallworth	1.25	.50
❑	84 Shannon Sharpe	.75	.30
❑	85 Chad Johnson	1.25	.50
❑	86 Todd Heap	.75	.30
❑	87 Rod Gardner	.75	.30
❑	88 Marvin Harrison	1.25	.50
❑	89 David Boston	.75	.30
❑	90 Julius Peppers	1.25	.50
❑	91 Byron Leftwich RC	40.00	15.00

❑ 92 Terrell Suggs RC	20.00	7.50
❑ 93 Kelley Washington RC	12.00	5.00
❑ 94 Brandon Lloyd RC	15.00	6.00
❑ 95 Kliff Kingsbury RC	10.00	4.00
❑ 96 Willis McGahee RC	30.00	12.50
❑ 97 Terence Newman RC	25.00	10.00
❑ 98 Bryant Johnson RC	12.00	5.00
❑ 99 Musa Smith RC	12.00	5.00
❑ 100 Ken Dorsey RC	12.00	5.00
❑ 101 Larry Johnson RC	50.00	25.00
❑ 102 DeWayne Robertson RC	12.00	5.00
❑ 103 Onterrio Smith RC	12.00	5.00
❑ 104 Tyrone Calico RC	15.00	6.00
❑ 105 Kareem Kelly RC	10.00	4.00
❑ 106 Chris Brown RC	15.00	6.00
❑ 107 Andrew Pinnock RC	10.00	4.00
❑ 108 Taylor Jacobs RC	10.00	4.00
❑ 109 Dallas Clark RC	12.00	5.00
❑ 110 Marcus Trufant RC	12.00	5.00
❑ 111 Charles Rogers RC	12.00	5.00
❑ 112 Lee Suggs RC	25.00	10.00
❑ 113 Rex Grossman RC	20.00	7.50
❑ 114 Doug Gabriel RC	12.00	5.00
❑ 115 Arnaz Battle RC	12.00	5.00
❑ 116 William Joseph RC	12.00	5.00
❑ 117 Justin Fargas RC	12.00	5.00
❑ 118 Anquan Boldin RC	30.00	12.50
❑ 119 Teyo Johnson RC	12.00	5.00
❑ 120 Bobby Wade RC	12.00	5.00
❑ 121 Brian St.Pierre RC	12.00	5.00
❑ 122 Carson Palmer RC	50.00	25.00
❑ 123 Kyle Boller RC	25.00	10.00
❑ 124 Andre Johnson RC	25.00	10.00
❑ 125 Dave Ragone RC	12.00	5.00
❑ 126 Chris Simms RC	20.00	7.50
❑ 127 Seneca Wallace RC	12.00	5.00
❑ 128 Justin Gage RC	12.00	5.00
❑ 129 LaBrandon Toefield RC	12.00	5.00
❑ 130 Talman Gardner RC	12.00	5.00

2004 Flair

❑ COMP.SET w/o SP's (60) 40.00 20.00
❑ ROOKIE STATED ODDS 1:100 RETAIL
❑ ROOKIE PRINT RUN 799 SER.#'d SETS

❑ 1 Clinton Portis	2.00	.75
❑ 2 Deuce McAllister	2.00	.75
❑ 3 Marshall Faulk	2.00	.75
❑ 4 Tom Brady	5.00	2.00
❑ 5 Ahman Green	2.00	.75
❑ 6 LaDainian Tomlinson	2.50	1.00
❑ 7 Lee Suggs	2.00	.75
❑ 8 Amani Toomer	1.25	.50
❑ 9 Priest Holmes	2.50	1.00
❑ 10 Peerless Price	1.25	.50
❑ 11 Warren Sapp	1.25	.50
❑ 12 Andre Davis	.75	.30
❑ 13 Chad Pennington	2.00	.75
❑ 14 Quincy Carter	1.25	.50
❑ 15 Santana Moss	1.25	.50
❑ 16 Antonio Bryant	1.25	.50
❑ 17 Jerry Porter	1.25	.50
❑ 18 Laveranues Coles	1.25	.50
❑ 19 Daunte Culpepper	2.00	.75
❑ 20 Stephen Davis	1.25	.50
❑ 21 Rich Gannon	1.25	.50
❑ 22 Chad Johnson	2.00	.75
❑ 23 Ashley Lelie	1.25	.50
❑ 24 Ray Lewis	2.00	.75
❑ 25 Joey Harrington	2.00	.75
❑ 26 Brian Westbrook	1.25	.50
❑ 27 Marvin Harrison	2.00	.75
❑ 28 Torry Holt	2.00	.75
❑ 29 Kevan Barlow	1.25	.50
❑ 30 Peyton Manning	3.00	1.25
❑ 31 Andre Johnson	2.00	.75
❑ 32 Steve Smith	2.00	.75
❑ 33 Troy Brown	1.25	.50
❑ 34 Brian Urlacher	2.50	1.00
❑ 35 Anquan Boldin	2.00	.75
❑ 36 Matt Hasselbeck	1.25	.50
❑ 37 Edgerrin James	2.00	.75
❑ 38 Dante Hall	2.00	.75
❑ 39 Brad Johnson	1.25	.50
❑ 40 Jamal Lewis	2.00	.75
❑ 41 Rudi Johnson	1.25	.50
❑ 42 Michael Strahan	1.25	.50
❑ 43 Donovan McNabb	2.50	1.00
❑ 44 Steve McNair	2.00	.75
❑ 45 Ricky Williams	2.00	.75
❑ 46 Jake Delhomme	2.00	.75
❑ 47 Patrick Ramsey	1.25	.50
❑ 48 Randy Moss	2.50	1.00
❑ 49 David Carr	2.00	.75
❑ 50 Jeff Garcia	2.00	.75
❑ 51 Shaun Alexander	2.00	.75
❑ 52 Byron Leftwich	2.50	1.00
❑ 53 Michael Vick	4.00	1.50
❑ 54 Brett Favre	5.00	2.00
❑ 55 Hines Ward	2.00	.75
❑ 56 Chris Chambers	1.25	.50
❑ 57 Eddie George	1.25	.50
❑ 58 Eric Moulds	1.25	.50
❑ 59 Plaxico Burress	1.25	.50
❑ 60 Charles Rogers	1.25	.50
❑ 61 Eli Manning RC	25.00	10.00
❑ 62 Larry Fitzgerald RC	15.00	6.00
❑ 63 Chris Perry RC	8.00	3.00
❑ 64 Ben Roethlisberger RC	40.00	20.00
❑ 65 Roy Williams RC	12.00	5.00
❑ 66 Kellen Winslow RC	10.00	4.00
❑ 67 Steven Jackson RC	15.00	6.00
❑ 68 Kevin Jones RC	15.00	6.00
❑ 69 Reggie Williams RC	6.00	2.50
❑ 70 Michael Clayton RC	10.00	4.00
❑ 71 Rashaun Woods RC	5.00	2.00
❑ 72 Ben Troupe RC	5.00	2.00
❑ 73 Greg Jones RC	5.00	2.00
❑ 74 J.P. Losman RC	10.00	4.00
❑ 75 Philip Rivers RC	15.00	7.50
❑ 76 Michael Jenkins RC	5.00	2.00
❑ 77 Darius Watts RC	5.00	2.00
❑ 78 Michael Turner RC	5.00	2.00
❑ 79 Lee Evans RC	6.00	2.50
❑ 80 Drew Henson RC	5.00	2.00
❑ 81 Luke McCown RC	5.00	2.00
❑ 82 Julius Jones RC	20.00	7.50
❑ 83 Bernard Berrian RC	5.00	2.00
❑ 84 Keary Colbert RC	6.00	2.50
❑ 85 Tatum Bell RC	10.00	4.00

1997 Flair Showcase Row 2

❑ COMPLETE SET (120) 40.00 15.00

❑ 1 Jerry Rice	2.00	.75
❑ 2 Mark Brunell	1.25	.50
❑ 3 Eddie Kennison	.60	.25
❑ 4 Brett Favre	4.00	1.50
❑ 5 Karim Abdul-Jabbar	.60	.25
❑ 6 David LaFleur RC	.40	.15
❑ 7 John Elway	4.00	1.50
❑ 8 Troy Aikman	2.00	.75
❑ 9 Steve McNair	1.25	.50
❑ 10 Kordell Stewart	1.00	.40

❑ 11 Drew Bledsoe	1.25	.50
❑ 12 Kerry Collins	1.00	.40
❑ 13 Dan Marino	4.00	1.50
❑ 14 Steve Young	1.25	.50
❑ 15 Marvin Harrison	1.00	.40
❑ 16 Lawrence Phillips	.40	.15
❑ 17 Jeff Blake	.60	.25
❑ 18 Yatil Green RC	.60	.25
❑ 19 Jake Plummer RC	8.00	3.00
❑ 20 Barry Sanders	3.00	1.25
❑ 21 Deion Sanders	1.00	.40
❑ 22 Emmitt Smith	3.00	1.25
❑ 23 Rae Carruth RC	.40	.15
❑ 24 Chris Warren	.60	.25
❑ 25 Terry Glenn	1.00	.40
❑ 26 Jim Druckenmiller RC	.60	.25
❑ 27 Eddie George	1.00	.40
❑ 28 Curtis Martin	1.25	.50
❑ 29 Warrick Dunn RC	4.00	1.50
❑ 30 Terrell Davis	1.25	.50
❑ 31 Rashaan Salaam	.40	.15
❑ 32 Marcus Allen	1.00	.40
❑ 33 Jeff George	.60	.25
❑ 34 Thurman Thomas	1.00	.40
❑ 35 Keyshawn Johnson	1.00	.40
❑ 36 Jerome Bettis	1.00	.40
❑ 37 Larry Centers	.60	.25
❑ 38 Tony Banks	.60	.25
❑ 39 Marshall Faulk	1.25	.50
❑ 40 Mike Alstott	1.00	.40
❑ 41 Elvis Grbac	.60	.25
❑ 42 Errict Rhett	.40	.15
❑ 43 Edgar Bennett	.60	.25
❑ 44 Jim Harbaugh	.60	.25
❑ 45 Antonio Freeman	1.25	.50
❑ 46 Tiki Barber RC	10.00	4.00
❑ 47 Tim Biakabutuka	.60	.25
❑ 48 Joey Galloway	.75	.30
❑ 49 Tony Gonzalez RC	5.00	2.00
❑ 50 Keenan McCardell	.60	.25
❑ 51 Darnay Scott	.60	.25
❑ 52 Brad Johnson	1.25	.50
❑ 53 Herman Moore	.60	.25
❑ 54 Reidel Anthony RC	1.25	.50
❑ 55 Junior Seau	1.00	.40
❑ 56 Ricky Watters	.60	.25
❑ 57 Amani Toomer	.60	.25
❑ 58 Andre Reed	.60	.25
❑ 59 Antowain Smith RC	4.00	2.00
❑ 60 Ike Hilliard RC	2.50	1.00
❑ 61 Byron Hanspard RC	.75	.30
❑ 62 Robert Smith	.60	.25
❑ 63 Gus Frerotte	.40	.15
❑ 64 Charles Way	.40	.15
❑ 65 Trent Dilfer	1.00	.40
❑ 66 Adrian Murrell	.60	.25
❑ 67 Stan Humphries	.60	.25
❑ 68 Robert Brooks	.60	.25
❑ 69 Jamal Anderson	1.00	.40
❑ 70 Natrone Means	.60	.25
❑ 71 John Friesz	.40	.15
❑ 72 Ki-Jana Carter	.40	.15
❑ 73 Marc Edwards RC	.40	.15
❑ 74 Michael Westbrook	.60	.25

❑ 75 Neil O'Donnell .60 .25
❑ 76 Scott Mitchell .60 .25
❑ 77 Wesley Walls .60 .25
❑ 78 Bruce Smith .60 .25
❑ 79 Corey Dillon RC 10.00 4.00
❑ 80 Wayne Chrebet 1.00 .40
❑ 81 Tony Martin .60 .25
❑ 82 Jimmy Smith .60 .25
❑ 83 Terry Allen 1.00 .40
❑ 84 Shannon Sharpe .60 .25
❑ 85 Derrick Alexander WR .60 .25
❑ 86 Garrison Hearst .60 .25
❑ 87 Tamarick Vanover .60 .25
❑ 88 Michael Irvin 1.00 .40
❑ 89 Mark Chmura .60 .25
❑ 90 Bert Emanuel .60 .25
❑ 91 Eric Metcalf .60 .25
❑ 92 Reggie White 1.00 .40
❑ 93 Carl Pickens .60 .25
❑ 94 Chris Sanders .40 .15
❑ 95 Frank Sanders .60 .25
❑ 96 Desmond Howard .60 .25
❑ 97 Michael Jackson .60 .25
❑ 98 Tim Brown 1.00 .40
❑ 99 O.J. McDuffie .60 .25
❑ 100 Mario Bates .40 .15
❑ 101 Warren Moon 1.00 .40
❑ 102 Curtis Conway .60 .25
❑ 103 Irving Fryar .60 .25
❑ 104 Isaac Bruce 1.00 .40
❑ 105 Cris Carter 1.00 .40
❑ 106 Chris Chandler .60 .25
❑ 107 Charles Johnson .60 .25
❑ 108 Kevin Lockett RC .60 .25
❑ 109 Rob Moore .60 .25
❑ 110 Napoleon Kaufman 1.00 .40
❑ 111 Henry Ellard .40 .15
❑ 112 Vinny Testaverde .60 .25
❑ 113 Rick Mirer .40 .15
❑ 114 Ty Detmer .60 .25
❑ 115 Todd Collins .40 .15
❑ 116 Jake Reed .60 .25
❑ 117 Dave Brown .40 .15
❑ 118 Dedric Ward RC .60 .25
❑ 119 Heath Shuler .40 .15
❑ 120 Ben Coates .60 .25
❑ S1 Rae Carruth Sample .25 .10

1998 Flair Showcase Row 3

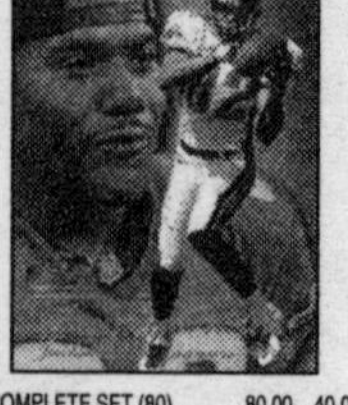

❑ COMPLETE SET (80) 80.00 40.00
❑ 1 Brett Favre 3.00 1.25
❑ 2 Emmitt Smith 2.50 1.00
❑ 3 Peyton Manning RC 15.00 6.00
❑ 4 Mark Brunell 1.00 .40
❑ 5 Randy Moss RC 10.00 4.00
❑ 6 Jerry Rice 1.50 .60
❑ 7 John Elway 3.00 1.25
❑ 8 Troy Aikman 1.50 .60
❑ 9 Warrick Dunn 1.00 .40
❑ 10 Kordell Stewart 1.00 .40
❑ 11 Drew Bledsoe 1.25 .50
❑ 12 Eddie George 1.00 .40
❑ 13 Dan Marino 3.00 1.25
❑ 14 Antowain Smith 1.00 .40
❑ 15 Curtis Enis RC .75 .30
❑ 16 Jake Plummer 1.00 .40
❑ 17 Steve Young 1.00 .40
❑ 18 Ryan Leaf RC 1.50 .60
❑ 19 Terrell Davis 1.00 .40
❑ 20 Barry Sanders 2.50 1.00
❑ 21 Corey Dillon 1.00 .40
❑ 22 Fred Taylor RC 2.50 1.00
❑ 23 Herman Moore .60 .25
❑ 24 Marshall Faulk 1.25 .50
❑ 25 John Avery RC .60 .25
❑ 26 Terry Glenn 1.00 .40
❑ 27 Keyshawn Johnson 1.00 .40
❑ 28 Charles Woodson RC 2.00 .75
❑ 29 Garrison Hearst 1.00 .40
❑ 30 Steve McNair 1.00 .40
❑ 31 Deion Sanders 1.00 .40
❑ 32 Robert Holcombe RC .60 .25
❑ 33 Jerome Bettis 1.00 .40
❑ 34 Robert Edwards RC 1.25 .50
❑ 35 Skip Hicks RC 1.25 .50
❑ 36 Marcus Nash RC .75 .30
❑ 37 Fred Lane .40 .15
❑ 38 Kevin Dyson RC 1.50 .60
❑ 39 Dorsey Levens 1.00 .40
❑ 40 Jacquez Green RC 1.25 .50
❑ 41 Shannon Sharpe .75 .30
❑ 42 Michael Irvin 1.25 .50
❑ 43 Jim Harbaugh .75 .30
❑ 44 Curtis Martin 1.25 .50
❑ 45 Bobby Hoying .75 .30
❑ 46 Trent Dilfer 1.25 .50
❑ 47 Yancey Thigpen .50 .20
❑ 48 Warren Moon 1.25 .50
❑ 49 Danny Kanell .75 .30
❑ 50 Rob Johnson .75 .30
❑ 51 Carl Pickens .75 .30
❑ 52 Scott Mitchell .75 .30
❑ 53 Tim Brown 1.25 .50
❑ 54 Tony Banks 1.25 .50
❑ 55 Jamal Anderson 1.25 .50
❑ 56 Kerry Collins .75 .30
❑ 57 Elvis Grbac .75 .30
❑ 58 Mike Alstott 1.25 .50
❑ 59 Glenn Foley .75 .30
❑ 60 Brad Johnson 1.25 .50
❑ 61 Robert Brooks 1.25 .50
❑ 62 Irving Fryar 1.25 .50
❑ 63 Natrone Means 1.25 .50
❑ 64 Rae Carruth .75 .30
❑ 65 Isaac Bruce 2.00 .75
❑ 66 Andre Rison 1.25 .50
❑ 67 Jeff George 1.25 .50
❑ 68 Charles Way .75 .30
❑ 69 Derrick Alexander 1.25 .50
❑ 70 Michael Jackson .75 .30
❑ 71 Rob Moore 1.25 .50
❑ 72 Ricky Watters 1.25 .50
❑ 73 Curtis Conway 1.25 .50
❑ 74 Antonio Freeman 2.00 .75
❑ 75 Jimmy Smith 1.25 .50
❑ 76 Troy Davis .75 .30
❑ 77 Robert Smith 2.00 .75
❑ 78 Terry Allen 2.00 .75
❑ 79 Joey Galloway 1.25 .50
❑ 80 Charles Johnson .75 .30
❑ NNO Checklist Card .40 .15

1999 Flair Showcase

❑ COMPLETE SET (192) 600.00 300.00
❑ COMP.SET w/o SPs (160) 50.00 20.00
❑ 1 Troy Aikman PW 2.00 .75
❑ 2 Jamal Anderson PW .40 .15
❑ 3 Charlie Batch PW 1.00 .40
❑ 4 Jerome Bettis PW .40 .15
❑ 5 Drew Bledsoe PW 1.25 .50
❑ 6 Mark Brunell PW 1.00 .40
❑ 7 Randall Cunningham PW 1.00 .40
❑ 8 Terrell Davis PW 1.00 .40

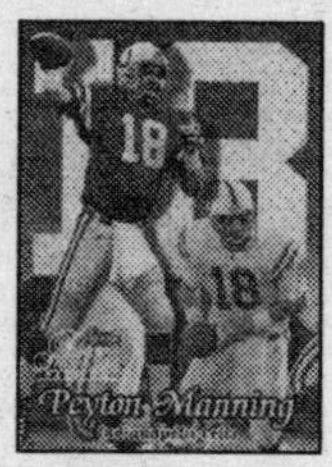

❑ 9 Corey Dillon PW 1.00 .40
❑ 10 Warrick Dunn PW 1.00 .40
❑ 11 Curtis Enis PW .40 .15
❑ 12 Marshall Faulk PW 1.25 .50
❑ 13 Brett Favre PW 3.00 1.25
❑ 14 Doug Flutie PW 1.00 .40
❑ 15 Eddie George PW 1.00 .40
❑ 16 Brian Griese PW 1.00 .40
❑ 17 Keyshawn Johnson PW 1.00 .40
❑ 18 Peyton Manning PW 3.00 1.25
❑ 19 Dan Marino PW 3.00 1.25
❑ 20 Curtis Martin PW 1.00 .40
❑ 21 Steve McNair PW 1.00 .40
❑ 22 Randy Moss PW 2.50 1.00
❑ 23 Terrell Owens PW 1.00 .40
❑ 24 Jake Plummer PW .60 .25
❑ 25 Jerry Rice PW 2.00 .75
❑ 26 Barry Sanders PW 3.00 1.25
❑ 27 Antowain Smith PW 1.00 .40
❑ 28 Emmitt Smith PW 2.00 .75
❑ 29 Kordell Stewart PW .60 .25
❑ 30 J.J. Stokes PW .60 .25
❑ 31 Fred Taylor PW 1.00 .40
❑ 32 Steve Young PW 1.25 .50
❑ 33 Troy Aikman PN 2.00 .75
❑ 34 Mike Alstott PN 1.00 .40
❑ 35 Jamal Anderson PN 1.00 .40
❑ 36 Charlie Batch PN 1.00 .40
❑ 37 Jerome Bettis PN 1.00 .40
❑ 38 Drew Bledsoe PN 1.25 .50
❑ 39 Mark Brunell PN 1.00 .40
❑ 40 Cris Carter PN 1.00 .40
❑ 41 Mark Chmura PN .40 .15
❑ 42 Wayne Chrebet PN .60 .25
❑ 43 Kerry Collins PN .40 .15
❑ 44 Randall Cunningham PN 1.00 .40
❑ 45 Terrell Davis PN 1.00 .40
❑ 46 Trent Dilfer PN .60 .25
❑ 47 Corey Dillon PN 1.00 .40
❑ 48 Warrick Dunn PN 1.00 .40
❑ 49 Kevin Dyson PN .60 .25
❑ 50 Curtis Enis PN .40 .15
❑ 51 Marshall Faulk PN 1.25 .50
❑ 52 Brett Favre PN 3.00 1.25
❑ 53 Doug Flutie PN 1.00 .40
❑ 54 Antonio Freeman PN 1.00 .40
❑ 55 Eddie George PN 1.00 .40
❑ 56 Terry Glenn PN 1.00 .40
❑ 57 Tony Gonzalez PN 1.00 .40
❑ 58 Elvis Grbac PN .60 .25
❑ 59 Jacquez Green PN .40 .15
❑ 60 Brian Griese PN 1.00 .40
❑ 61 Marvin Harrison PN 1.00 .40
❑ 62 Garrison Hearst PN .60 .25
❑ 63 Skip Hicks PN .40 .15
❑ 64 Priest Holmes PN 1.50 .60
❑ 65 Michael Irvin PN .60 .25
❑ 66 Brad Johnson PN .60 .25
❑ 67 Keyshawn Johnson PN 1.00 .40
❑ 68 Napoleon Kaufman PN 1.00 .40
❑ 69 Dorsey Levens PN 1.00 .40
❑ 70 Peyton Manning PN 3.00 1.25
❑ 71 Dan Marino PN 3.00 1.25
❑ 72 Curtis Martin PN 1.00 .40

❑ 73 Ed McCaffrey PN .60 .25
❑ 74 Keenan McCardell PN .60 .25
❑ 75 O.J. McDuffie PN .60 .25
❑ 76 Steve McNair PN 1.00 .40
❑ 77 Scott Mitchell PN .40 .15
❑ 78 Randy Moss PN 2.50 1.00
❑ 79 Eric Moulds PN 1.00 .40
❑ 80 Terrell Owens PN 1.00 .40
❑ 81 Lawrence Phillips PN .60 .25
❑ 82 Jake Plummer PN .60 .25
❑ 83 Jerry Rice PN 2.00 .75
❑ 84 Andre Rison PN .60 .25
❑ 85 Barry Sanders PN 3.00 1.25
❑ 86 Shannon Sharpe PN .60 .25
❑ 87 Antowain Smith PN 1.00 .40
❑ 88 Emmitt Smith PN 2.00 .75
❑ 89 Rod Smith PN .60 .25
❑ 90 Duce Staley PN 1.00 .40
❑ 91 Kordell Stewart PN .60 .25
❑ 92 J.J. Stokes PN .60 .25
❑ 93 Fred Taylor PN 1.00 .40
❑ 94 Vinny Testaverde PN .60 .25
❑ 95 Ricky Watters PN .60 .25
❑ 96 Steve Young PN 1.25 .50
❑ 97 Mike Alstott 1.00 .40
❑ 98 Jamal Anderson 1.00 .40
❑ 99 Charlie Batch 1.00 .40
❑ 100 Jerome Bettis 1.00 .40
❑ 101 Tim Biakabutuka .60 .25
❑ 102 Drew Bledsoe 1.25 .50
❑ 103 Tim Brown 1.00 .40
❑ 104 Mark Brunell 1.00 .40
❑ 105 Cris Carter 1.00 .40
❑ 106 Chris Chandler .60 .25
❑ 107 Mark Chmura .40 .15
❑ 108 Wayne Chrebet .60 .25
❑ 109 Ben Coates .60 .25
❑ 110 Kerry Collins .60 .25
❑ 111 Randall Cunningham 1.00 .40
❑ 112 Trent Dilfer .60 .25
❑ 113 Corey Dillon 1.00 .40
❑ 114 Warrick Dunn 1.00 .40
❑ 115 Kevin Dyson .60 .25
❑ 116 Curtis Enis .40 .15
❑ 117 Marshall Faulk 1.25 .50
❑ 118 Doug Flutie 1.00 .40
❑ 119 Antonio Freeman 1.00 .40
❑ 120 Joey Galloway .60 .25
❑ 121 Rich Gannon 1.00 .40
❑ 122 Eddie George 1.00 .40
❑ 123 Terry Glenn 1.00 .40
❑ 124 Tony Gonzalez 1.00 .40
❑ 125 Elvis Groac .60 .25
❑ 126 Jacquez Green .40 .15
❑ 127 Brian Griese 1.00 .40
❑ 128 Marvin Harrison 1.00 .40
❑ 129 Garrison Hearst .60 .25
❑ 130 Skip Hicks .40 .15
❑ 131 Priest Holmes 1.50 .60
❑ 132 Michael Irvin .60 .25
❑ 133 Brad Johnson .60 .25
❑ 134 Napoleon Kaufman 1.00 .40
❑ 135 Terry Kirby .40 .15
❑ 136 Dorsey Levens 1.00 .40
❑ 137 Curtis Martin 1.00 .40
❑ 138 Ed McCaffrey .60 .25
❑ 139 Keenan McCardell .60 .25
❑ 140 O.J. McDuffie .60 .25
❑ 141 Steve McNair 1.00 .40
❑ 142 Natrone Means .60 .25
❑ 143 Scott Mitchell .40 .15
❑ 144 Herman Moore .60 .25
❑ 145 Eric Moulds 1.00 .40
❑ 146 Terrell Owens 1.00 .40
❑ 147 Lawrence Phillips .60 .25
❑ 148 Jerry Rice 2.00 .75
❑ 149 Andre Rison .60 .25
❑ 150 Deion Sanders 1.00 .40
❑ 151 Shannon Sharpe .60 .25
❑ 152 Antowain Smith 1.00 .40
❑ 153 Rod Smith .60 .25
❑ 154 Duce Staley 1.00 .40
❑ 155 Kordell Stewart .60 .25
❑ 156 J.J. Stokes .60 .25
❑ 157 Vinny Testaverde .60 .25
❑ 158 Yancey Thigpen .40 .15
❑ 159 Ricky Watters .60 .25
❑ 160 Steve Young 1.25 .50
❑ 161 Troy Aikman SP 12.00 6.00
❑ 162 Champ Bailey RC 12.00 5.00
❑ 163 Karsten Bailey RC 8.00 3.00
❑ 164 D'Wayne Bates RC 8.00 3.00
❑ 165 David Boston RC 10.00 4.00
❑ 166 Mike Cloud RC 8.00 3.00
❑ 167 Cecil Collins RC 5.00 2.00
❑ 168 Tim Couch RC 10.00 4.00
❑ 169 Daunte Culpepper RC 40.00 15.00
❑ 170 Terrell Davis SP 6.00 2.50
❑ 171 Troy Edwards RC 8.00 3.00
❑ 172 Kevin Faulk RC 10.00 4.00
❑ 173 Brett Favre SP 20.00 10.00
❑ 174 Torry Holt RC 25.00 10.00
❑ 175 Sedrick Irvin RC 5.00 2.00
❑ 176 Edgerrin James RC 40.00 15.00
❑ 177 James Johnson RC 8.00 3.00
❑ 178 Kevin Johnson RC 10.00 4.00
❑ 179 Keyshawn Johnson SP 5.00 2.00
❑ 180 Peyton Manning SP 20.00 10.00
❑ 181 Dan Marino SP 20.00 10.00
❑ 182 Donovan McNabb RC 50.00 20.00
❑ 183 Cade McNown RC 8.00 3.00
❑ 184 Joe Montgomery RC 8.00 3.00
❑ 185 Randy Moss SP 15.00 6.00
❑ 186 Jake Plummer SP 6.00 2.50
❑ 187 Peerless Price RC 10.00 4.00
❑ 188 Barry Sanders SP 20.00 10.00
❑ 189 Akili Smith RC 8.00 3.00
❑ 190 Emmitt Smith SP 12.00 6.00
❑ 191 Fred Taylor SP 8.00 3.00
❑ 192 Ricky Williams RC 20.00 7.50
❑ P24 Jake Plummer PW Promo 1.00 .40
❑ P82 Jake Plummer PN Promo 1.00 .40
❑ P147 Jake Plummer Promo 1.00 .40

1960 Fleer

❑ COMPLETE SET (132) 750.00 500.00
❑ WRAPPER (5-CENT) 25.00 20.00
❑ 1 Harvey White RC ! 20.00 12.00
❑ 2 Tom Corky Tharp 3.50 2.00
❑ 3 Dan McGrew 3.50 2.00
❑ 4 Bob White 3.50 2.00
❑ 5 Dick Jamieson 3.50 2.00
❑ 6 Sam Salerno 3.50 2.00
❑ 7 Sid Gillman RC CO ! 20.00 12.00
❑ 8 Ben Preston 3.50 2.00
❑ 9 George Blanch 3.50 2.00
❑ 10 Bob Stransky 3.50 2.00
❑ 11 Fran Curci 3.50 2.00
❑ 12 George Shirkey 3.50 2.00
❑ 13 Paul Larson 3.50 2.00
❑ 14 John Stolte 3.50 2.00
❑ 15 Serafino Fazio RC 5.00 2.50
❑ 16 Tom Dimitroff 3.50 2.00
❑ 17 Elbert Dubenion RC 12.00 6.00
❑ 18 Hogan Wharton 3.50 2.00
❑ 19 Tom O'Connell 3.50 2.00
❑ 20 Sammy Baugh CO 50.00 30.00
❑ 21 Tony Sardisco 3.50 2.00
❑ 22 Alan Cann 3.50 2.00
❑ 23 Mike Hudock 3.50 2.00
❑ 24 Bill Atkins 3.50 2.00
❑ 25 Charlie Jackson 3.50 2.00
❑ 26 Frank Tripucka 6.00 3.00
❑ 27 Tony Teresa 3.50 2.00
❑ 28 Joe Amstutz 3.50 2.00
❑ 29 Bob Fee RC 3.50 2.00
❑ 30 Jim Baldwin 3.50 2.00
❑ 31 Jim Yates 3.50 2.00
❑ 32 Don Flynn 3.50 2.00
❑ 33 Ken Adamson 3.50 2.00
❑ 34 Ron Drzewiecki 3.50 2.00
❑ 35 J.W. Slack 3.50 2.00
❑ 36 Bob Yates 3.50 2.00
❑ 37 Gary Cobb 3.50 2.00
❑ 38 Jacky Lee RC 5.00 2.50
❑ 39 Jack Spikes RC 5.00 2.50
❑ 40 Jim Padgett 3.50 2.00
❑ 41 Jack Larscheid UER RC 3.50 2.00
❑ 42 Bob Reifsnyder RC 3.50 2.00
❑ 43 Fran Rogel 3.50 2.00
❑ 44 Ray Moss 3.50 2.00
❑ 45 Tony Banfield RC 5.00 2.50
❑ 46 George Herring 3.50 2.00
❑ 47 Willie Smith RC 3.50 2.00
❑ 48 Buddy Allen 3.50 2.00
❑ 49 Bill Brown LB 3.50 2.00
❑ 50 Ken Ford RC 3.50 2.00
❑ 51 Billy Kinard 3.50 2.00
❑ 52 Buddy Mayfield 3.50 2.00
❑ 53 Bill Krisher 3.50 2.00
❑ 54 Frank Bernardi 3.50 2.00
❑ 55 Lou Saban RC CO 5.00 2.50
❑ 56 Gene Cockrell 3.50 2.00
❑ 57 Sam Sanders 3.50 2.00
❑ 58 George Blanda 50.00 30.00
❑ 59 Sherrill Headrick RC 5.00 2.50
❑ 60 Carl Larpenter 3.50 2.00
❑ 61 Gene Prebola 3.50 2.00
❑ 62 Dick Chorovich 3.50 2.00
❑ 63 Bob McNamara 3.50 2.00
❑ 64 Tom Saidock 3.50 2.00
❑ 65 Willie Evans 3.50 2.00
❑ 66 Billy Cannon RC UER 18.00 10.00
❑ 67 Sam McCord 3.50 2.00
❑ 68 Mike Simmons 3.50 2.00
❑ 69 Jim Swink RC 5.00 2.50
❑ 70 Don Hitt 3.50 2.00
❑ 71 Gerhard Schwedes 3.50 2.00
❑ 72 Thurlow Cooper 3.50 2.00
❑ 73 Abner Haynes RC 18.00 10.00
❑ 74 Billy Shoemake 3.50 2.00
❑ 75 Marv Lasater 3.50 2.00
❑ 76 Paul Lowe RC 15.00 7.50
❑ 77 Bruce Hartman 3.50 2.00
❑ 78 Blanche Martin 3.50 2.00
❑ 79 Gene Grabosky 3.50 2.00
❑ 80 Lou Rymkus CO 5.00 2.50
❑ 81 Chris Burford RC 8.00 4.00
❑ 82 Don Allen 3.50 2.00
❑ 83 Bob Nelson C 3.50 2.00
❑ 84 Jim Woodard 3.50 2.00
❑ 85 Tom Rychlec 3.50 2.00
❑ 86 Bob Cox 3.50 2.00
❑ 87 Jerry Cornelison 3.50 2.00
❑ 88 Jack Work 3.50 2.00
❑ 89 Sam DeLuca 3.50 2.00
❑ 90 Rommie Loudd 3.50 2.00
❑ 91 Teddy Edmondson 3.50 2.00
❑ 92 Buster Ramsey CO 3.50 2.00
❑ 93 Doug Asad 3.50 2.00
❑ 94 Jimmy Harris 3.50 2.00
❑ 95 Larry Cundiff 3.50 2.00
❑ 96 Richie Lucas RC 6.00 3.00
❑ 97 Don Norwood 3.50 2.00

❑ 98 Larry Grantham RC 5.00 2.50
❑ 99 Bill Mathis RC 6.00 3.00
❑ 100 Mel Branch RC 5.00 2.50
❑ 101 Marvin Terrell 3.50 2.00
❑ 102 Charlie Flowers 3.50 2.00
❑ 103 John McMullan 3.50 2.00
❑ 104 Charlie Kaaihue 3.50 2.00
❑ 105 Joe Schaffer 3.50 2.00
❑ 106 Al Day 3.50 2.00
❑ 107 Johnny Carson 3.50 2.00
❑ 108 Alan Goldstein 3.50 2.00
❑ 109 Doug Cline 3.50 2.00
❑ 110 Al Carmichael 3.50 2.00
❑ 111 Bob Dee 3.50 2.00
❑ 112 John Bredice 3.50 2.00
❑ 113 Don Floyd 3.50 2.00
❑ 114 Ronnie Cain 3.50 2.00
❑ 115 Stan Flowers 3.50 2.00
❑ 116 Hank Stram RC CO 40.00 25.00
❑ 117 Bob Dougherty 3.50 2.00
❑ 118 Ron Mix RC 40.00 25.00
❑ 119 Roger Ellis 3.50 2.00
❑ 120 Elvin Caldwell 3.50 2.00
❑ 121 Bill Kimber 3.50 2.00
❑ 122 Jim Matheny 3.50 2.00
❑ 123 Curley Johnson RC 3.50 2.00
❑ 124 Jack Kemp RC 175.00 90.00
❑ 125 Ed Denk 3.50 2.00
❑ 126 Jerry McFarland 3.50 2.00
❑ 127 Dan Lanphear 3.50 2.00
❑ 128 Paul Maguire RC 18.00 10.00
❑ 129 Ray Collins 3.50 2.00
❑ 130 Ron Burton RC 6.00 3.00
❑ 131 Eddie Erdelatz CO 3.50 2.00
❑ 132 Ron Beagle RC ! 15.00 7.50

1961 Fleer

❑ COMPLETE SET (220) 1600.00 1000.00
❑ COMMON CARD (1-132) 4.00 2.50
❑ COMMON CARD (133-220) 6.00 3.50
❑ WRAPPER (5-CENT, SER.1) 25.00 20.00
❑ WRAPPER (5-CENT, SER.2) 30.00 25.00
❑ 1 Ed Brown ! 15.00 7.50
❑ 2 Rick Casares 6.00 3.00
❑ 3 Willie Galimore 6.00 3.00
❑ 4 Jim Dooley 4.00 2.50
❑ 5 Harlon Hill 4.00 2.50
❑ 6 Stan Jones 7.00 3.50
❑ 7 J.C. Caroline 4.00 2.50
❑ 8 Joe Fortunato 4.00 2.50
❑ 9 Doug Atkins 8.00 4.00
❑ 10 Milt Plum 6.00 3.00
❑ 11 Jim Brown 150.00 90.00
❑ 12 Bobby Mitchell 10.00 5.00
❑ 13 Ray Renfro 6.00 3.00
❑ 14 Gern Nagler 4.00 2.50
❑ 15 Jim Shofner 4.00 2.50
❑ 16 Vince Costello 4.00 2.50
❑ 17 Galen Fiss 4.00 2.50
❑ 18 Walt Michaels 6.00 3.00
❑ 19 Bob Gain 4.00 2.50
❑ 20 Mal Hammack 4.00 2.50
❑ 21 Frank Mestnik RC 4.00 2.50
❑ 22 Bobby Joe Conrad 6.00 3.00
❑ 23 John David Crow 6.00 3.00
❑ 24 Sonny Randle RC 6.00 3.00
❑ 25 Don Gillis 4.00 2.50
❑ 26 Jerry Norton 4.00 2.50
❑ 27 Bill Stacy 4.00 2.50
❑ 28 Leo Sugar 4.00 2.50
❑ 29 Frank Fuller 4.00 2.50
❑ 30 Johnny Unitas 60.00 35.00
❑ 31 Alan Ameche 7.00 3.50
❑ 32 Lenny Moore 15.00 7.50
❑ 33 Raymond Berry 15.00 7.50
❑ 34 Jim Mutscheller 4.00 2.50
❑ 35 Jim Parker 7.00 3.50
❑ 36 Bill Pellington 4.00 2.50
❑ 37 Gino Marchetti 10.00 5.00
❑ 38 Gene Lipscomb 7.00 3.50
❑ 39 Art Donovan 15.00 7.50
❑ 40 Eddie LeBaron 6.00 3.00
❑ 41 Don Meredith RC 150.00 90.00
❑ 42 Don McIlhenny 4.00 2.50
❑ 43 L.G. Dupre 4.00 2.50
❑ 44 Fred Dugan 4.00 2.50
❑ 45 Billy Howton 6.00 3.00
❑ 46 Duane Putnam 4.00 2.50
❑ 47 Gene Cronin 4.00 2.50
❑ 48 Jerry Tubbs 4.00 2.50
❑ 49 Clarence Peaks 4.00 2.50
❑ 50 Ted Dean RC 4.00 2.50
❑ 51 Tommy McDonald 8.00 4.00
❑ 52 Bill Barnes 4.00 2.50
❑ 53 Pete Retzlaff 6.00 3.00
❑ 54 Bobby Walston 4.00 2.50
❑ 55 Chuck Bednarik 12.00 6.00
❑ 56 Maxie Baughan RC 6.00 3.00
❑ 57 Bob Pellegrini 4.00 2.50
❑ 58 Jesse Richardson 4.00 2.50
❑ 59 John Brodie RC 50.00 30.00
❑ 60 J.D. Smith RB 6.00 3.00
❑ 61 Ray Norton RC 4.00 2.50
❑ 62 Monty Stickles RC 4.00 2.50
❑ 63 Bob St.Clair 7.00 3.50
❑ 64 Dave Baker 4.00 2.50
❑ 65 Abe Woodson 4.00 2.50
❑ 66 Matt Hazeltine 4.00 2.50
❑ 67 Leo Nomellini 10.00 5.00
❑ 68 Charley Conerly 10.00 5.00
❑ 69 Kyle Rote 7.00 3.50
❑ 70 Jack Stroud 4.00 2.50
❑ 71 Roosevelt Brown 7.00 3.50
❑ 72 Jim Patton 4.00 2.50
❑ 73 Erich Barnes 4.00 2.50
❑ 74 Sam Huff 15.00 7.50
❑ 75 Andy Robustelli 10.00 5.00
❑ 76 Dick Modzelewski 4.00 2.50
❑ 77 Roosevelt Grier 7.00 3.50
❑ 78 Earl Morrall 7.00 3.50
❑ 79 Jim Ninowski 4.00 2.50
❑ 80 Nick Pietrosante RC 6.00 3.00
❑ 81 Howard Cassady 6.00 3.00
❑ 82 Jim Gibbons 4.00 2.50
❑ 83 Gail Cogdill RC 6.00 3.00
❑ 84 Dick Lane 7.00 3.50
❑ 85 Yale Lary 7.00 3.50
❑ 86 Joe Schmidt 8.00 4.00
❑ 87 Darris McCord 4.00 2.50
❑ 88 Bart Starr 60.00 35.00
❑ 89 Jim Taylor 50.00 30.00
❑ 90 Paul Hornung 55.00 30.00
❑ 91 Tom Moore RC 8.00 4.00
❑ 92 Boyd Dowler RC 15.00 7.50
❑ 93 Max McGee 7.00 3.50
❑ 94 Forrest Gregg 8.00 4.00
❑ 95 Jerry Kramer 10.00 5.00
❑ 96 Jim Ringo 8.00 4.00
❑ 97 Bill Forester 6.00 3.00
❑ 98 Frank Ryan 6.00 3.00
❑ 99 Ollie Matson 12.00 6.00
❑ 100 Jon Arnett 6.00 3.00
❑ 101 Dick Bass RC 6.00 3.00
❑ 102 Jim Phillips 4.00 2.50
❑ 103 Del Shofner 6.00 3.00
❑ 104 Art Hunter 4.00 2.50
❑ 105 Lindon Crow 4.00 2.50
❑ 106 Les Richter 6.00 3.00
❑ 107 Lou Michaels 4.00 2.50
❑ 108 Ralph Guglielmi 4.00 2.50
❑ 109 Don Bosseler 4.00 2.50
❑ 110 John Olszewski 4.00 2.50
❑ 111 Bill Anderson 4.00 2.50
❑ 112 Joe Walton 4.00 2.50
❑ 113 Jim Schrader 4.00 2.50
❑ 114 Gary Glick 4.00 2.50
❑ 115 Ralph Felton 4.00 2.50
❑ 116 Bob Toneff 4.00 2.50
❑ 117 Bobby Layne 40.00 25.00
❑ 118 John Henry Johnson 7.00 3.50
❑ 119 Tom Tracy 6.00 3.00
❑ 120 Jimmy Orr RC 7.00 3.50
❑ 121 John Nisby 4.00 2.50
❑ 122 Dean Derby 4.00 2.50
❑ 123 John Reger 4.00 2.50
❑ 124 George Tarasovic 4.00 2.50
❑ 125 Ernie Stautner 10.00 5.00
❑ 126 George Shaw 4.00 2.50
❑ 127 Hugh McElhenny 12.00 6.00
❑ 128 Dick Haley 4.00 2.50
❑ 129 Dave Middleton 4.00 2.50
❑ 130 Perry Richards 4.00 2.50
❑ 131 Gene Johnson DB 4.00 2.50
❑ 132 Don Joyce ! 4.00 2.50
❑ 133 Johnny Green ! 8.00 4.00
❑ 134 Wray Carlton RC 8.00 4.00
❑ 135 Richie Lucas 8.00 4.00
❑ 136 Elbert Dubenion ! 8.00 4.00
❑ 137 Tom Rychlec 6.00 3.50
❑ 138 Mack Yoho 6.00 3.50
❑ 139 Phil Blazer 6.00 3.50
❑ 140 Dan McGrew 6.00 3.50
❑ 141 Bill Atkins 6.00 3.50
❑ 142 Archie Matsos RC 6.00 3.50
❑ 143 Gene Grabosky 6.00 3.50
❑ 144 Frank Tripucka 10.00 5.00
❑ 145 Al Carmichael 6.00 3.50
❑ 146 Bob McNamara 6.00 3.50
❑ 147 Lionel Taylor RC 15.00 7.50
❑ 148 Eldon Danenhauer 6.00 3.50
❑ 149 Willie Smith 6.00 3.50
❑ 150 Carl Larpenter 6.00 3.50
❑ 151 Ken Adamson 6.00 3.50
❑ 152 Goose Gonsoulin RC UER 10.00 5.00
❑ 153 Joe Young 6.00 3.50
❑ 154 Gordy Holz RC 6.00 3.50
❑ 155 Jack Kemp 120.00 60.00
❑ 156 Charlie Flowers 6.00 3.50
❑ 157 Paul Lowe 10.00 5.00
❑ 158 Don Norton 6.00 3.50
❑ 159 Howard Clark 6.00 3.50
❑ 160 Paul Maguire 15.00 7.50
❑ 161 Ernie Wright RC 8.00 4.00
❑ 162 Ron Mix 15.00 7.50
❑ 163 Fred Cole 6.00 3.50
❑ 164 Jim Sears 6.00 3.50
❑ 165 Volney Peters 6.00 3.50
❑ 166 George Blanda 45.00 25.00
❑ 167 Jacky Lee 8.00 4.00
❑ 168 Bob White 6.00 3.50
❑ 169 Doug Cline 6.00 3.50
❑ 170 Dave Smith RB 6.00 3.50
❑ 171 Billy Cannon 15.00 7.50
❑ 172 Bill Groman 6.00 3.50
❑ 173 Al Jamison 6.00 3.50
❑ 174 Jim Norton 6.00 3.50
❑ 175 Dennit Morris 6.00 3.50
❑ 176 Don Floyd 6.00 3.50
❑ 177 Butch Songin 6.00 3.50
❑ 178 Billy Lott 6.00 3.50
❑ 179 Ron Burton 10.00 5.00
❑ 180 Jim Colclough 6.00 3.50
❑ 181 Charley Leo 6.00 3.50
❑ 182 Walt Cudzik 6.00 3.50

❑ 183 Fred Bruney	6.00	3.50
❑ 184 Ross O'Hanley	6.00	3.50
❑ 185 Tony Sardisco	6.00	3.50
❑ 186 Harry Jacobs	6.00	3.50
❑ 187 Bob Dee	6.00	3.50
❑ 188 Tom Flores RC	30.00	15.00
❑ 189 Jack Larscheid	6.00	3.50
❑ 190 Dick Christy	6.00	3.50
❑ 191 Alan Miller RC	6.00	3.50
❑ 192 James Smith	6.00	3.50
❑ 193 Gerald Burch	6.00	3.50
❑ 194 Gene Prebola	6.00	3.50
❑ 195 Alan Goldstein	6.00	3.50
❑ 196 Don Manoukian	6.00	3.50
❑ 197 Jim Otto RC	75.00	40.00
❑ 198 Wayne Crow	6.00	3.50
❑ 199 Cotton Davidson RC	8.00	4.00
❑ 200 Randy Duncan RC	8.00	4.00
❑ 201 Jack Spikes	8.00	4.00
❑ 202 Johnny Robinson RC	15.00	7.50
❑ 203 Abner Haynes	15.00	7.50
❑ 204 Chris Burford	8.00	4.00
❑ 205 Bill Krisher	6.00	3.50
❑ 206 Marvin Terrell	6.00	3.50
❑ 207 Jimmy Harris	6.00	3.50
❑ 208 Mel Branch	8.00	4.00
❑ 209 Paul Miller	6.00	3.50
❑ 210 Al Dorow	6.00	3.50
❑ 211 Dick Jamieson	6.00	3.50
❑ 212 Pete Hart	6.00	3.50
❑ 213 Bill Shockley	6.00	3.50
❑ 214 Dewey Bohling	6.00	3.50
❑ 215 Don Maynard RC	80.00	40.00
❑ 216 Bob Mischak	6.00	3.50
❑ 217 Mike Hudock	6.00	3.50
❑ 218 Bob Reifsnyder	6.00	3.50
❑ 219 Tom Saidock	6.00	3.50
❑ 220 Sid Youngelman !	20.00	12.00

1962 Fleer

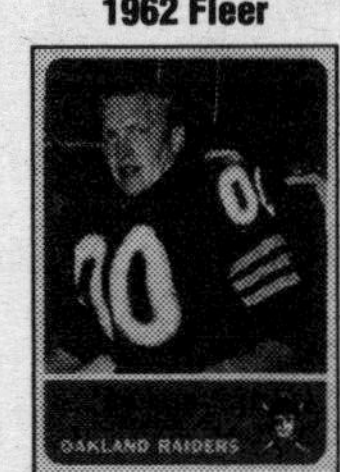

❑ COMPLETE SET (88)	900.00	500.00
❑ WRAPPER (5-CENT)	200.00	100.00
❑ 1 Billy Lott !	16.00	8.00
❑ 2 Ron Burton	10.00	5.00
❑ 3 Gino Cappelletti RC	15.00	7.50
❑ 4 Babe Parilli	10.00	5.00
❑ 5 Jim Colclough	7.00	3.50
❑ 6 Tony Sardisco	7.00	3.50
❑ 7 Walt Cudzik	7.00	3.50
❑ 8 Bob Dee	7.00	3.50
❑ 9 Tommy Addison RC	8.00	4.00
❑ 10 Harry Jacobs	7.00	3.50
❑ 11 Ross O'Hanley	7.00	3.50
❑ 12 Art Baker	7.00	3.50
❑ 13 Johnny Green	7.00	3.50
❑ 14 Elbert Dubenion	10.00	5.00
❑ 15 Tom Rychlec	7.00	3.50
❑ 16 Billy Shaw RC	30.00	18.00
❑ 17 Ken Rice	7.00	3.50
❑ 18 Bill Atkins	7.00	3.50
❑ 19 Richie Lucas	8.00	4.00
❑ 20 Archie Matsos	7.00	3.50
❑ 21 Laverne Torczon	7.00	3.50
❑ 22 Warren Rabb	7.00	3.50
❑ 23 Jack Spikes	8.00	4.00
❑ 24 Cotton Davidson	8.00	4.00
❑ 25 Abner Haynes	15.00	7.50
❑ 26 Jimmy Saxton	7.00	3.50
❑ 27 Chris Burford	8.00	4.00
❑ 28 Bill Miller	7.00	3.50
❑ 29 Sherrill Headrick	8.00	4.00
❑ 30 E.J.Holub RC	8.00	4.00
❑ 31 Jerry Mays RC	10.00	5.00
❑ 32 Mel Branch	8.00	4.00
❑ 33 Paul Rochester RC	7.00	3.50
❑ 34 Frank Tripucka	10.00	5.00
❑ 35 Gene Mingo	7.00	3.50
❑ 36 Lionel Taylor	12.00	6.00
❑ 37 Ken Adamson	7.00	3.50
❑ 38 Eldon Danenhauer	7.00	3.50
❑ 39 Goose Gonsoulin	10.00	5.00
❑ 40 Gordy Holz	7.00	3.50
❑ 41 Bud McFadin	8.00	4.00
❑ 42 Jim Stinnette	7.00	3.50
❑ 43 Bob Hudson RC	7.00	3.50
❑ 44 George Herring	7.00	3.50
❑ 45 Charley Tolar RC	7.00	3.50
❑ 46 George Blanda	50.00	30.00
❑ 47 Billy Cannon	15.00	7.50
❑ 48 Charlie Hennigan RC	15.00	7.50
❑ 49 Bill Groman	7.00	3.50
❑ 50 Al Jamison	7.00	3.50
❑ 51 Tony Banfield	7.00	3.50
❑ 52 Jim Norton	7.00	3.50
❑ 53 Dennit Morris	7.00	3.50
❑ 54 Don Floyd	7.00	3.50
❑ 55 Ed Husmann UER	7.00	3.50
❑ 56 Robert Brooks	7.00	3.50
❑ 57 Al Dorow	7.00	3.50
❑ 58 Dick Christy	7.00	3.50
❑ 59 Don Maynard	50.00	30.00
❑ 60 Art Powell	10.00	5.00
❑ 61 Mike Hudock	7.00	3.50
❑ 62 Bill Mathis	8.00	4.00
❑ 63 Butch Songin	7.00	3.50
❑ 64 Larry Grantham	7.00	3.50
❑ 65 Nick Mumley	7.00	3.50
❑ 66 Tom Saidock	7.00	3.50
❑ 67 Alan Miller	7.00	3.50
❑ 68 Tom Flores	15.00	7.50
❑ 69 Bob Coolbaugh	7.00	3.50
❑ 70 George Fleming	7.00	3.50
❑ 71 Wayne Hawkins RC	8.00	4.00
❑ 72 Jim Otto	40.00	25.00
❑ 73 Wayne Crow	7.00	3.50
❑ 74 Fred Williamson RC	30.00	18.00
❑ 75 Tom Louderback	7.00	3.50
❑ 76 Volney Peters	7.00	3.50
❑ 77 Charley Powell	7.00	3.50
❑ 78 Don Norton	7.00	3.50
❑ 79 Jack Kemp	200.00	125.00
❑ 80 Paul Lowe	10.00	5.00
❑ 81 Dave Kocourek	7.00	3.50
❑ 82 Ron Mix	15.00	7.50
❑ 83 Ernie Wright	10.00	5.00
❑ 84 Dick Harris	7.00	3.50
❑ 85 Bill Hudson	7.00	3.50
❑ 86 Ernie Ladd RC	25.00	15.00
❑ 87 Earl Faison RC	8.00	4.00
❑ 88 Ron Nery !	18.00	9.00

1963 Fleer

❑ COMPLETE SET (88)	1800.00	1200.00
❑ WRAPPER (5-CENT)	120.00	60.00
❑ 1 Larry Garron RC !	20.00	10.00
❑ 2 Babe Parilli	10.00	5.00
❑ 3 Ron Burton	12.00	6.00
❑ 4 Jim Colclough	8.00	4.00
❑ 5 Gino Cappelletti	12.00	6.00
❑ 6 Charles Long RC SP	150.00	75.00
❑ 7 Billy Neighbors RC	8.00	4.00
❑ 8 Dick Felt	8.00	4.00
❑ 9 Tommy Addison	8.00	4.00
❑ 10 Nick Buoniconti RC	80.00	45.00

❑ 11 Larry Eisenhauer RC	8.00	4.00
❑ 12 Bill Mathis	8.00	4.00
❑ 13 Lee Grosscup RC	10.00	5.00
❑ 14 Dick Christy	8.00	4.00
❑ 15 Don Maynard	50.00	30.00
❑ 16 Alex Kroll RC	8.00	4.00
❑ 17 Bob Mischak	8.00	4.00
❑ 18 Dainard Paulson	8.00	4.00
❑ 19 Lee Riley	8.00	4.00
❑ 20 Larry Grantham	10.00	5.00
❑ 21 Hubert Bobo	8.00	4.00
❑ 22 Nick Mumley	8.00	4.00
❑ 23 Cookie Gilchrist RC	50.00	30.00
❑ 24 Jack Kemp	150.00	75.00
❑ 25 Wray Carlton	8.00	4.00
❑ 26 Elbert Dubenion	10.00	5.00
❑ 27 Ernie Warlick RC	10.00	5.00
❑ 28 Billy Shaw	15.00	7.50
❑ 29 Ken Rice	8.00	4.00
❑ 30 Booker Edgerson	8.00	4.00
❑ 31 Ray Abruzzese	8.00	4.00
❑ 32 Mike Stratton RC	15.00	7.50
❑ 33 Tom Sestak RC	10.00	5.00
❑ 34 Charley Tolar	8.00	4.00
❑ 35 Dave Smith RB	8.00	4.00
❑ 36 George Blanda	55.00	30.00
❑ 37 Billy Cannon	15.00	7.50
❑ 38 Charlie Hennigan	10.00	5.00
❑ 39 Bob Talamini RC	8.00	4.00
❑ 40 Jim Norton	8.00	4.00
❑ 41 Tony Banfield	8.00	4.00
❑ 42 Doug Cline	8.00	4.00
❑ 43 Don Floyd	8.00	4.00
❑ 44 Ed Husmann	8.00	4.00
❑ 45 Curtis McClinton RC	15.00	7.50
❑ 46 Jack Spikes	10.00	5.00
❑ 47 Len Dawson RC	200.00	125.00
❑ 48 Abner Haynes	15.00	7.50
❑ 49 Chris Burford	10.00	5.00
❑ 50 Fred Arbanas RC	12.00	6.00
❑ 51 Johnny Robinson	10.00	5.00
❑ 52 E.J. Holub	10.00	5.00
❑ 53 Sherrill Headrick	10.00	5.00
❑ 54 Mel Branch	10.00	5.00
❑ 55 Jerry Mays	10.00	5.00
❑ 56 Cotton Davidson	10.00	5.00
❑ 57 Clem Daniels RC	15.00	7.50
❑ 58 Bo Roberson RC	10.00	5.00
❑ 59 Art Powell	12.00	6.00
❑ 60 Bob Coolbaugh	8.00	4.00
❑ 61 Wayne Hawkins	8.00	4.00
❑ 62 Jim Otto	30.00	18.00
❑ 63 Fred Williamson	20.00	10.00
❑ 64 Bob Dougherty SP	120.00	60.00
❑ 65 Dalva Allen	8.00	4.00
❑ 66 Chuck McMurtry	8.00	4.00
❑ 67 Gerry McDougall RC	8.00	4.00
❑ 68 Tobin Rote	10.00	5.00
❑ 69 Paul Lowe	12.00	6.00
❑ 70 Keith Lincoln RC	40.00	25.00
❑ 71 Dave Kocourek	8.00	4.00
❑ 72 Lance Alworth RC	250.00	125.00
❑ 73 Ron Mix	25.00	15.00
❑ 74 Charley McNeil RC	8.00	4.00

❑ 75 Emil Karas	8.00	4.00
❑ 76 Ernie Ladd	20.00	10.00
❑ 77 Earl Faison	8.00	4.00
❑ 78 Jim Stinnette	8.00	4.00
❑ 79 Frank Tripucka	12.00	6.00
❑ 80 Don Stone	8.00	4.00
❑ 81 Bob Scarpitto	8.00	4.00
❑ 82 Lionel Taylor	12.00	6.00
❑ 83 Jerry Tarr	8.00	4.00
❑ 84 Eldon Danenhauer	8.00	4.00
❑ 85 Goose Gonsoulin	10.00	5.00
❑ 86 Jim Fraser	8.00	4.00
❑ 87 Chuck Gavin	8.00	4.00
❑ 88 Bud McFadin !	20.00	10.00
❑ NNO Checklist SP !	350.00	250.00

1990 Fleer

❑ COMPLETE SET (400)	10.00	4.00
❑ 1 Harris Barton	.04	.01
❑ 2 Chet Brooks	.04	.01
❑ 3 Michael Carter	.04	.01
❑ 4 Mike Cofer UER	.04	.01
❑ 5 Roger Craig	.10	.02
❑ 6 Kevin Fagan RC	.04	.01
❑ 7 Charles Haley UER	.10	.02
❑ 8 Pierce Holt RC	.04	.01
❑ 9 Ronnie Lott	.10	.02
❑ 10A Joe Montana ERR	1.25	.50
❑ 10B Joe Montana COR	1.25	.50
❑ 11 Bubba Paris	.04	.01
❑ 12 Tom Rathman	.04	.01
❑ 13 Jerry Rice	.75	.30
❑ 14 John Taylor	.25	.08
❑ 15 Keena Turner	.04	.01
❑ 16 Michael Walter	.04	.01
❑ 17 Steve Young	.50	.20
❑ 18 Steve Atwater	.04	.01
❑ 19 Tyrone Braxton	.04	.01
❑ 20 Michael Brooks RC	.04	.01
❑ 21 John Elway	1.25	.50
❑ 22 Simon Fletcher	.04	.01
❑ 23 Bobby Humphrey	.04	.01
❑ 24 Mark Jackson	.04	.01
❑ 25 Vance Johnson	.04	.01
❑ 26 Greg Kragen	.04	.01
❑ 27 Ken Lanier RC	.04	.01
❑ 28 Karl Mecklenburg	.04	.01
❑ 29 Orson Mobley RC	.04	.01
❑ 30 Steve Sewell	.04	.01
❑ 31 Dennis Smith	.04	.01
❑ 32 David Treadwell	.04	.01
❑ 33 Flipper Anderson	.04	.01
❑ 34 Greg Bell	.04	.01
❑ 35 Henry Ellard	.10	.02
❑ 36 Jim Everett	.10	.02
❑ 37 Jerry Gray	.04	.01
❑ 38 Kevin Greene	.10	.02
❑ 39 Pete Holohan	.04	.01
❑ 40 LeRoy Irvin	.04	.01
❑ 41 Mike Lansford	.04	.01
❑ 42 Buford McGee RC	.04	.01
❑ 43 Tom Newberry	.04	.01
❑ 44 Vince Newsome RC	.04	.01
❑ 45 Jackie Slater	.04	.01
❑ 46 Mike Wilcher	.04	.01
❑ 47 Matt Bahr	.04	.01
❑ 48 Brian Brennan	.04	.01
❑ 49 Thane Gash RC	.04	.01
❑ 50 Mike Johnson	.04	.01
❑ 51 Bernie Kosar	.10	.02
❑ 52 Reggie Langhorne	.04	.01
❑ 53 Tim Manoa	.04	.01
❑ 54 Clay Matthews	.10	.02
❑ 55 Eric Metcalf	.25	.08
❑ 56 Frank Minnifield	.04	.01
❑ 57 Gregg Rakoczy RC UER	.04	.01
❑ 58 Webster Slaughter	.10	.02
❑ 59 Bryan Wagner	.04	.01
❑ 60 Felix Wright	.04	.01
❑ 61 Raul Allegre	.04	.01
❑ 62 Ottis Anderson UER	.10	.02
❑ 63 Carl Banks	.04	.01
❑ 64 Mark Bavaro	.04	.01
❑ 65 Maurice Carthon	.04	.01
❑ 66 Mark Collins UER	.04	.01
❑ 67 Jeff Hostetler RC	.25	.08
❑ 68 Erik Howard	.04	.01
❑ 69 Pepper Johnson	.04	.01
❑ 70 Sean Landeta	.04	.01
❑ 71 Lionel Manuel	.04	.01
❑ 72 Leonard Marshall	.04	.01
❑ 73 Dave Meggett	.10	.02
❑ 74 Bart Oates	.04	.01
❑ 75 Doug Riesenberg RC	.04	.01
❑ 76 Phil Simms	.10	.02
❑ 77 Lawrence Taylor	.25	.08
❑ 78 Eric Allen	.04	.01
❑ 79 Jerome Brown	.04	.01
❑ 80 Keith Byars	.04	.01
❑ 81 Cris Carter	.50	.20
❑ 82A Byron Evans RC ERR	.15	.05
❑ 82B Randall Cunningham	.15	.05
❑ 83A Ron Heller RC OT ERR	.15	.05
❑ 83B Byron Evans RC COR	.15	.05
❑ 84 Ron Heller RC OT COR	.04	.01
❑ 85 Terry Hoage RC	.04	.01
❑ 86 Keith Jackson	.10	.02
❑ 87 Seth Joyner	.10	.02
❑ 88 Mike Quick	.04	.01
❑ 89 Mike Schad	.04	.01
❑ 90 Clyde Simmons	.04	.01
❑ 91 John Teltschik	.04	.01
❑ 92 Anthony Toney	.04	.01
❑ 93 Reggie White	.25	.08
❑ 94 Ray Berry	.04	.01
❑ 95 Joey Browner	.04	.01
❑ 96 Anthony Carter	.10	.02
❑ 97 Chris Doleman	.04	.01
❑ 98 Rick Fenney	.04	.01
❑ 99 Rich Gannon RC	1.50	.60
❑ 100 Hassan Jones	.04	.01
❑ 101 Steve Jordan	.04	.01
❑ 102 Rich Karlis	.04	.01
❑ 103 Andre Ware RC	.25	.08
❑ 104 Kirk Lowdermilk	.04	.01
❑ 105 Keith Millard	.04	.01
❑ 106 Scott Studwell	.04	.01
❑ 107 Herschel Walker	.10	.02
❑ 108 Wade Wilson	.10	.02
❑ 109 Gary Zimmerman	.04	.01
❑ 110 Don Beebe	.10	.02
❑ 111 Cornelius Bennett	.10	.02
❑ 112 Shane Conlan	.04	.01
❑ 113 Jim Kelly	.25	.08
❑ 114 Scott Norwood UER	.04	.01
❑ 115 Mark Kelso UER	.04	.01
❑ 116 Larry Kinnebrew	.04	.01
❑ 117 Pete Metzelaars	.04	.01
❑ 118 Scott Radecic	.04	.01
❑ 119 Andre Reed	.25	.08
❑ 120 Jim Ritcher RC	.04	.01
❑ 121 Bruce Smith	.25	.08
❑ 122 Leonard Smith	.04	.01
❑ 123 Art Still	.04	.01
❑ 124 Thurman Thomas	.25	.08
❑ 125 Steve Brown	.04	.01
❑ 126 Ray Childress	.04	.01
❑ 127 Ernest Givins	.10	.02
❑ 128 John Grimsley	.04	.01
❑ 129 Alonzo Highsmith	.04	.01
❑ 130 Drew Hill	.04	.01
❑ 131 Bruce Matthews	.10	.02
❑ 132 Johnny Meads	.04	.01
❑ 133 Warren Moon UER	.25	.08
❑ 134 Mike Munchak	.10	.02
❑ 135 Mike Rozier	.04	.01
❑ 136 Dean Steinkuhler	.04	.01
❑ 137 Lorenzo White	.04	.01
❑ 138 Tony Zendejas	.04	.01
❑ 139 Gary Anderson K	.04	.01
❑ 140 Bubby Brister	.04	.01
❑ 141 Thomas Everett	.04	.01
❑ 142 Derek Hill	.04	.01
❑ 143 Merril Hoge	.04	.01
❑ 144 Tim Johnson	.04	.01
❑ 145 Louis Lipps	.10	.02
❑ 146 David Little	.04	.01
❑ 147 Greg Lloyd	.25	.08
❑ 148 Mike Mularkey	.04	.01
❑ 149 John Rienstra RC	.04	.01
❑ 150 Gerald Williams RC UER	.04	.01
❑ 151 Keith Willis UER	.04	.01
❑ 152 Rod Woodson	.25	.08
❑ 153 Tim Worley	.04	.01
❑ 154 Gary Clark	.25	.08
❑ 155 Darryl Grant	.04	.01
❑ 156 Darrell Green	.10	.02
❑ 157 Joe Jacoby	.04	.01
❑ 158 Jim Lachey	.04	.01
❑ 159 Chip Lohmiller	.04	.01
❑ 160 Charles Mann	.04	.01
❑ 161 Wilber Marshall	.04	.01
❑ 162 Mark May	.04	.01
❑ 163 Ralf Mojsiejenko	.04	.01
❑ 164 Art Monk UER	.10	.02
❑ 165 Gerald Riggs	.10	.02
❑ 166 Mark Rypien	.10	.02
❑ 167 Ricky Sanders	.04	.01
❑ 168 Don Warren	.04	.01
❑ 169 Robert Brown RC	.04	.01
❑ 170 Blair Bush	.04	.01
❑ 171 Brent Fullwood	.04	.01
❑ 172 Tim Harris	.04	.01
❑ 173 Chris Jacke	.04	.01
❑ 174 Perry Kemp	.04	.01
❑ 175 Don Majkowski	.04	.01
❑ 176 Tony Mandarich	.04	.01
❑ 177 Mark Murphy	.04	.01
❑ 178 Brian Noble	.04	.01
❑ 179 Ken Ruettgers	.04	.01
❑ 180 Sterling Sharpe	.25	.08
❑ 181 Ed West RC	.04	.01
❑ 182 Keith Woodside	.04	.01
❑ 183 Morten Andersen	.04	.01
❑ 184 Stan Brock	.04	.01
❑ 185 Jim Dombrowski RC	.04	.01
❑ 186 John Fourcade	.04	.01
❑ 187 Bobby Hebert	.04	.01
❑ 188 Craig Heyward	.10	.02
❑ 189 Dalton Hilliard	.04	.01
❑ 190 Rickey Jackson	.10	.02
❑ 191 Buford Jordan	.04	.01
❑ 192 Eric Martin	.04	.01
❑ 193 Robert Massey	.04	.01
❑ 194 Sam Mills	.10	.02
❑ 195 Pat Swilling	.10	.02
❑ 196 Jim Wilks	.04	.01
❑ 197 John Alt RC	.04	.01
❑ 198 Walker Lee Ashley	.04	.01
❑ 199 Steve DeBerg	.04	.01
❑ 200 Leonard Griffin	.04	.01
❑ 201 Albert Lewis	.04	.01
❑ 202 Nick Lowery	.04	.01
❑ 203 Bill Maas	.04	.01

❑ 204 Pete Mandley .04 .01
❑ 205 Chris Martin RC .04 .01
❑ 206 Christian Okoye .04 .01
❑ 207 Stephone Paige .04 .01
❑ 208 Kevin Porter RC .04 .01
❑ 209 Derrick Thomas .25 .08
❑ 210 Lewis Billups .04 .01
❑ 211 James Brooks .10 .02
❑ 212 Jason Buck .04 .01
❑ 213 Rickey Dixon RC .04 .01
❑ 214 Boomer Esiason .10 .02
❑ 215 David Fulcher .04 .01
❑ 216 Rodney Holman .04 .01
❑ 217 Lee Johnson .04 .01
❑ 218 Tim Krumrie .04 .01
❑ 219 Tim McGee .04 .01
❑ 220 Anthony Munoz .10 .02
❑ 221 Bruce Reimers RC .04 .01
❑ 222 Leon White .04 .01
❑ 223 Ickey Woods .04 .01
❑ 224 Harvey Armstrong RC .04 .01
❑ 225 Michael Ball RC .04 .01
❑ 226 Chip Banks .04 .01
❑ 227 Pat Beach .04 .01
❑ 228 Duane Bickett .04 .01
❑ 229 Bill Brooks .04 .01
❑ 230 Jon Hand .04 .01
❑ 231 Andre Rison .25 .08
❑ 232 Rohn Stark .04 .01
❑ 233 Donnell Thompson .04 .01
❑ 234 Jack Trudeau .04 .01
❑ 235 Clarence Verdin .04 .01
❑ 236 Mark Clayton .10 .02
❑ 237 Jeff Cross .04 .01
❑ 238 Jeff Dellenbach RC .04 .01
❑ 239 Mark Duper .10 .02
❑ 240 Ferrell Edmunds .04 .01
❑ 241 Hugh Green UER .04 .01
❑ 242 E.J. Junior .04 .01
❑ 243 Marc Logan .04 .01
❑ 244 Dan Marino 1.25 .50
❑ 245 John Offerdahl .04 .01
❑ 246 Reggie Roby .04 .01
❑ 247 Sammie Smith .04 .01
❑ 248 Pete Stoyanovich .04 .01
❑ 249 Marcus Allen .25 .08
❑ 250 Eddie Anderson RC .04 .01
❑ 251 Steve Beuerlein .10 .02
❑ 252 Mike Dyal .04 .01
❑ 253 Mervyn Fernandez .04 .01
❑ 254 Bob Golic .04 .01
❑ 255 Mike Harden .04 .01
❑ 256 Bo Jackson .30 .10
❑ 257 Howie Long UER .25 .08
❑ 258 Don Mosebar .04 .01
❑ 259 Jay Schroeder .04 .01
❑ 260 Steve Smith .04 .01
❑ 261 Greg Townsend .04 .01
❑ 262 Lionel Washington .04 .01
❑ 263 Brian Blades .10 .02
❑ 264 Jeff Bryant .04 .01
❑ 265 Grant Feasel RC .04 .01
❑ 266 Jacob Green .04 .01
❑ 267 James Jefferson .04 .01
❑ 268 Norm Johnson .04 .01
❑ 269 Dave Krieg UER .10 .02
❑ 270 Travis McNeal .04 .01
❑ 271 Joe Nash .04 .01
❑ 272 Rufus Porter .04 .01
❑ 273 Kelly Stouffer .04 .01
❑ 274 John L. Williams .04 .01
❑ 275 Jim Arnold .04 .01
❑ 276 Jerry Ball .04 .01
❑ 277 Bennie Blades .04 .01
❑ 278 Lomas Brown .04 .01
❑ 279 Michael Cofer .04 .01
❑ 280 Bob Gagliano .04 .01
❑ 281 Richard Johnson .04 .01
❑ 282 Eddie Murray .04 .01
❑ 283 Rodney Peete .10 .02
❑ 284 Barry Sanders 1.25 .50
❑ 285 Eric Sanders .04 .01
❑ 286 Chris Spielman .25 .08
❑ 287 Eric Williams RC .04 .01
❑ 288 Neal Anderson .10 .02
❑ 289A Kevin Butler P/P .25 .08
❑ 289B Kevin Butler K/P .25 .08
❑ 289C Kevin Butler P/K .25 .08
❑ 289D Kevin Butler K/K .04 .01
❑ 290 Jim Covert .04 .01
❑ 291 Richard Dent .10 .02
❑ 292 Dennis Gentry .04 .01
❑ 293 Jim Harbaugh .25 .08
❑ 294 Jay Hilgenberg .04 .01
❑ 295 Vestee Jackson .04 .01
❑ 296 Steve McMichael .10 .02
❑ 297 Ron Morris .04 .01
❑ 298 Brad Muster .04 .01
❑ 299 Mike Singletary .10 .02
❑ 300 James Thornton UER .04 .01
❑ 301 Mike Tomczak .10 .02
❑ 302 Keith Van Horne .04 .01
❑ 303 Chris Bahr UER .04 .01
❑ 304 Martin Bayless RC .04 .01
❑ 305 Marion Butts .10 .02
❑ 306 Gill Byrd .04 .01
❑ 307 Arthur Cox .04 .01
❑ 308 Burt Grossman .04 .01
❑ 309 Jamie Holland .04 .01
❑ 310 Jim McMahon .10 .02
❑ 311 Anthony Miller .25 .08
❑ 312 Leslie O'Neal .10 .02
❑ 313 Billy Ray Smith .04 .01
❑ 314 Tim Spencer .04 .01
❑ 315 Broderick Thompson RC .04 .01
❑ 316 Lee Williams .04 .01
❑ 317 Bruce Armstrong .04 .01
❑ 318 Tim Goad RC .04 .01
❑ 319 Steve Grogan .10 .02
❑ 320 Roland James .04 .01
❑ 321 Cedric Jones .04 .01
❑ 322 Fred Marion .04 .01
❑ 323 Stanley Morgan .04 .01
❑ 324 Robert Perryman .04 .01
❑ 325 Johnny Rembert .04 .01
❑ 326 Ed Reynolds .04 .01
❑ 327 Kenneth Sims .04 .01
❑ 328 John Stephens .04 .01
❑ 329 Danny Villa RC .04 .01
❑ 330 Robert Awalt .04 .01
❑ 331 Anthony Bell .04 .01
❑ 332 Rich Camarillo .04 .01
❑ 333 Earl Ferrell .04 .01
❑ 334 Roy Green .10 .02
❑ 335 Gary Hogeboom .04 .01
❑ 336 Cedric Mack .04 .01
❑ 337 Freddie Joe Nunn .04 .01
❑ 338 Luis Sharpe .04 .01
❑ 339 Vai Sikahema .04 .01
❑ 340 J.T. Smith .04 .01
❑ 341 Tom Tupa RC .04 .01
❑ 342 Percy Snow RC .04 .01
❑ 343 Mark Carrier WR .25 .08
❑ 344 Randy Grimes .04 .01
❑ 345 Paul Gruber .04 .01
❑ 346 Ron Hall .04 .01
❑ 347 Jeff George RC .50 .20
❑ 348 Bruce Hill UER .04 .01
❑ 349 William Howard UER .04 .01
❑ 350 Donald Igwebuike .04 .01
❑ 351 Chris Mohr RC .04 .01
❑ 352 Winston Moss RC .04 .01
❑ 353 Ricky Reynolds .04 .01
❑ 354 Mark Robinson .04 .01
❑ 355 Lars Tate .04 .01
❑ 356 Vinny Testaverde .10 .02
❑ 357 Broderick Thomas .04 .01
❑ 358 Troy Benson .04 .01
❑ 359 Jeff Criswell RC .04 .01
❑ 360 Tony Eason .04 .01
❑ 361 James Hasty .04 .01
❑ 362 Johnny Hector .04 .01
❑ 363 Bobby Humphery UER .04 .01
❑ 364 Pat Leahy .04 .01
❑ 365 Erik McMillan .04 .01
❑ 366 Freeman McNeil .04 .01
❑ 367 Ken O'Brien .04 .01
❑ 368 Ron Stallworth .04 .01
❑ 369 Al Toon .10 .02
❑ 370 Blair Thomas RC .04 .01
❑ 371 Aundray Bruce .04 .01
❑ 372 Tony Casillas .04 .01
❑ 373 Shawn Collins .04 .01
❑ 374 Evan Cooper .04 .01
❑ 375 Bill Fralic .04 .01
❑ 376 Scott Funhage .04 .01
❑ 377 Mike Gann .04 .01
❑ 378 Ron Heller TE .04 .01
❑ 379 Keith Jones .04 .01
❑ 380 Mike Kenn .04 .01
❑ 381 Chris Miller .25 .08
❑ 382 Deion Sanders UER .50 .20
❑ 383 John Settle .04 .01
❑ 384 Troy Aikman .75 .30
❑ 385 Bill Bates .10 .02
❑ 386 Willie Broughton .04 .01
❑ 387 Steve Folsom .04 .01
❑ 388 Ray Horton UER .04 .01
❑ 389 Michael Irvin .25 .08
❑ 390 Jim Jeffcoat .04 .01
❑ 391 Eugene Lockhart .04 .01
❑ 392 Kelvin Martin RC .04 .01
❑ 393 Nate Newton .10 .02
❑ 394 Mike Saxon UER .04 .01
❑ 395 Derrick Shepard .04 .01
❑ 396 Steve Walsh .10 .02
❑ 397 Joe Montana/Rice MVP's .75 .30
❑ 398 Checklist Card UER .04 .01
❑ 399 Checklist Card UER .04 .01
❑ 400 Checklist Card .04 .01

1990 Fleer Update

❑ COMP.FACT.SET (120) 25.00 12.50
❑ U1 Albert Bentley .08 .02
❑ U2 Dean Biasucci .08 .02
❑ U3 Ray Donaldson .08 .02
❑ U4 Jeff George 1.25 .50
❑ U5 Ray Agnew RC .08 .02
❑ U6 Greg McMurtry RC .08 .02
❑ U7 Chris Singleton RC .08 .02
❑ U8 James Francis RC .08 .02
❑ U9 Harold Green RC .30 .10
❑ U10 John Elliott .08 .02
❑ U11 Rodney Hampton RC .30 .10
❑ U12 Gary Reasons .08 .02
❑ U13 Lewis Tillman .08 .02
❑ U14 Everson Walls .08 .02
❑ U15 David Alexander RC .08 .02
❑ U16 Jim McMahon .15 .05
❑ U17 Ben Smith RC .08 .02
❑ U18 Andre Waters .08 .02
❑ U19 Calvin Williams RC .15 .05
❑ U20 Earnest Byner .08 .02
❑ U21 Andre Collins RC .08 .02

❑ U22 Russ Grimm	.08	.02
❑ U23 Stan Humphries RC	.30	.10
❑ U24 Martin Mayhew RC	.08	.02
❑ U25 Barry Foster RC	.30	.10
❑ U26 Eric Green RC	.15	.05
❑ U27 Tunch Ilkin	.08	.02
❑ U28 Hardy Nickerson	.15	.05
❑ U29 Jerrol Williams	.08	.02
❑ U30 Mike Baab	.08	.02
❑ U31 Leroy Hoard RC	.50	.20
❑ U32 Eddie Johnson RC	.08	.02
❑ U33 William Fuller	.15	.05
❑ U34 Haywood Jeffires RC	.30	.10
❑ U35 Don Maggs RC	.08	.02
❑ U36 Allen Pinkett	.08	.02
❑ U37 Robert Awalt	.08	.02
❑ U38 Dennis McKinnon	.08	.02
❑ U39 Ken Norton Jr. RC	.30	.10
❑ U40 Emmitt Smith RC	20.00	7.50
❑ U41 Alexander Wright RC	.08	.02
❑ U42 Eric Hill	.08	.02
❑ U43 Johnny Johnson RC	.15	.05
❑ U44 Timm Rosenbach	.08	.02
❑ U45 Anthony Thompson RC	.08	.02
❑ U46 Dexter Carter RC	.08	.02
❑ U47 Eric Davis RC UER	.15	.05
❑ U48 Keith DeLong	.08	.02
❑ U49 Brent Jones RC	.30	.10
❑ U50 Darryl Pollard RC	.08	.02
❑ U51 Steve Wallace RC	.30	.10
❑ U52 Bern Brostek RC	.08	.02
❑ U53 Aaron Cox	.08	.02
❑ U54 Cleveland Gary	.08	.02
❑ U55 Fred Strickland RC	.08	.02
❑ U56 Pat Terrell RC	.08	.02
❑ U57 Steve Broussard RC	.08	.02
❑ U58 Scott Case	.08	.02
❑ U59 Brian Jordan RC	.15	.05
❑ U60 Andre Rison	.30	.10
❑ U61 Kevin Haverdink	.08	.02
❑ U62 Rueben Mayes	.08	.02
❑ U63 Steve Walsh	.15	.05
❑ U64 Greg Bell	.08	.02
❑ U65 Tim Brown	.30	.10
❑ U66 Willie Gault	.15	.05
❑ U67 Vance Mueller RC	.08	.02
❑ U68 Bill Pickel	.08	.02
❑ U69 Aaron Wallace RC	.08	.02
❑ U70 Glenn Parker RC	.08	.02
❑ U71 Frank Reich	.30	.10
❑ U72 Leon Seals RC	.08	.02
❑ U73 Darryl Talley	.08	.02
❑ U74 Brad Baxter RC	.08	.02
❑ U75 Jeff Criswell	.08	.02
❑ U76 Jeff Lageman	.08	.02
❑ U77 Rob Moore RC	1.50	.60
❑ U78 Blair Thomas	.15	.05
❑ U79 Louis Oliver	.08	.02
❑ U80 Tony Paige	.08	.02
❑ U81 Richmond Webb RC	.08	.02
❑ U82 Robert Blackmon RC	.08	.02
❑ U83 Derrick Fenner RC	.08	.02
❑ U84 Andy Heck	.08	.02
❑ U85 Cortez Kennedy RC	.30	.10
❑ U86 Terry Wooden RC	.08	.02
❑ U87 Jeff Donaldson	.08	.02
❑ U88 Tim Grunhard RC	.08	.02
❑ U89 Emile Harry RC	.08	.02
❑ U90 Dan Saleaumua	.08	.02
❑ U91 Percy Snow	.08	.02
❑ U92 Andre Ware	.30	.10
❑ U93 Darrell Fullington RC	.08	.02
❑ U94 Mike Merriweather	.08	.02
❑ U95 Henry Thomas	.08	.02
❑ U96 Robert Brown	.08	.02
❑ U97 LeRoy Butler RC	.30	.10
❑ U98 Anthony Dilweg	.08	.02
❑ U99 Darrell Thompson RC	.08	.02
❑ U100 Keith Woodside	.08	.02
❑ U101 Gary Plummer	.08	.02
❑ U102 Junior Seau RC	5.00	2.00
❑ U103 Billy Joe Tolliver	.08	.02
❑ U104 Mark Vlasic	.08	.02
❑ U105 Gary Anderson RB	.08	.02
❑ U106 Ian Beckles RC	.08	.02
❑ U107 Reggie Cobb RC	.08	.02
❑ U108 Keith McCants RC	.08	.02
❑ U109 Mark Bortz RC	.08	.02
❑ U110 Maury Buford	.08	.02
❑ U111 Mark Carrier RC DB	.30	.10
❑ U112 Dan Hampton	.15	.05
❑ U113 William Perry	.15	.05
❑ U114 Ron Rivera	.08	.02
❑ U115 Lemuel Stinson	.08	.02
❑ U116 Melvin Bratton RC	.08	.02
❑ U117 Gary Kubiak RC	.30	.10
❑ U118 Alton Montgomery RC	.08	.02
❑ U119 Ricky Nattiel	.08	.02
❑ U120 Checklist 1-132	.08	.02

1991 Fleer

❑ COMPLETE SET (432)	8.00	4.00
❑ 1 Shane Conlan	.04	.01
❑ 2 John Davis RC	.04	.01
❑ 3 Kent Hull	.04	.01
❑ 4 James Lofton	.10	.02
❑ 5 Keith McKeller	.04	.01
❑ 6 Scott Norwood	.04	.01
❑ 7 Nate Odomes	.04	.01
❑ 8 Andre Reed	.10	.02
❑ 9 Jim Ritcher	.04	.01
❑ 10 Leon Seals	.04	.01
❑ 11 Bruce Smith	.25	.08
❑ 12 Leonard Smith	.04	.01
❑ 13 Steve Tasker	.10	.02
❑ 14 Thurman Thomas	.25	.08
❑ 15 Lewis Billups	.04	.01
❑ 16 James Brooks	.10	.02
❑ 17 Eddie Brown	.04	.01
❑ 18 Carl Carter	.04	.01
❑ 19 Boomer Esiason	.10	.02
❑ 20 James Francis	.04	.01
❑ 21 David Fulcher	.04	.01
❑ 22 Harold Green	.10	.02
❑ 23 Rodney Holman	.04	.01
❑ 24 Bruce Kozerski	.04	.01
❑ 25 Tim McGee	.04	.01
❑ 26 Anthony Munoz	.10	.02
❑ 27 Bruce Reimers	.04	.01
❑ 28 Ickey Woods	.04	.01
❑ 29 Carl Zander	.04	.01
❑ 30 Mike Baab	.04	.01
❑ 31 Brian Brennan	.04	.01
❑ 32 Rob Burnett RC	.10	.02
❑ 33 Paul Farren	.04	.01
❑ 34 Thane Gash	.04	.01
❑ 35 David Grayson	.04	.01
❑ 36 Mike Johnson	.04	.01
❑ 37 Reggie Langhorne	.04	.01
❑ 38 Kevin Mack	.04	.01
❑ 39 Eric Metcalf	.10	.02
❑ 40 Frank Minnifield	.04	.01
❑ 41 Gregg Rakoczy	.04	.01
❑ 42 Felix Wright	.04	.01
❑ 43 Steve Atwater	.04	.01
❑ 44 Michael Brooks	.04	.01
❑ 45 John Elway	1.25	.50
❑ 46 Simon Fletcher	.04	.01
❑ 47 Bobby Humphrey	.04	.01
❑ 48 Mark Jackson	.04	.01
❑ 49 Keith Kartz	.04	.01
❑ 50 Clarence Kay	.04	.01
❑ 51 Greg Kragen	.04	.01
❑ 52 Karl Mecklenburg	.04	.01
❑ 53 Warren Powers	.04	.01
❑ 54 Dennis Smith	.04	.01
❑ 55 Jim Szymanski	.04	.01
❑ 56 David Treadwell	.04	.01
❑ 57 Michael Young	.04	.01
❑ 58 Ray Childress	.04	.01
❑ 59 Curtis Duncan	.04	.01
❑ 60 William Fuller	.10	.02
❑ 61 Ernest Givins	.10	.02
❑ 62 Drew Hill	.04	.01
❑ 63 Haywood Jeffires	.10	.02
❑ 64 Richard Johnson DB	.04	.01
❑ 65 Sean Jones	.10	.02
❑ 66 Don Maggs	.04	.01
❑ 67 Bruce Matthews	.10	.02
❑ 68 Johnny Meads	.04	.01
❑ 69 Greg Montgomery	.04	.01
❑ 70 Warren Moon	.25	.08
❑ 71 Mike Munchak	.10	.02
❑ 72 Allen Pinkett	.04	.01
❑ 73 Lorenzo White	.04	.01
❑ 74 Pat Beach	.04	.01
❑ 75 Albert Bentley	.04	.01
❑ 76 Dean Biasucci	.04	.01
❑ 77 Duane Bickett	.04	.01
❑ 78 Bill Brooks	.04	.01
❑ 79 Sam Clancy	.04	.01
❑ 80 Ray Donaldson	.04	.01
❑ 81 Jeff George	.25	.08
❑ 82 Alan Grant	.04	.01
❑ 83 Jessie Hester	.04	.01
❑ 84 Jeff Herrod	.04	.01
❑ 85 Rohn Stark	.04	.01
❑ 86 Jack Trudeau	.04	.01
❑ 87 Clarence Verdin	.04	.01
❑ 88 John Alt	.04	.01
❑ 89 Steve DeBerg	.04	.01
❑ 90 Tim Grunhard	.04	.01
❑ 91 Dino Hackett	.04	.01
❑ 92 Jonathan Hayes	.04	.01
❑ 93 Albert Lewis	.04	.01
❑ 94 Nick Lowery	.04	.01
❑ 95 Bill Maas UER	.04	.01
❑ 96 Christian Okoye	.04	.01
❑ 97 Stephone Paige	.04	.01
❑ 98 Kevin Porter	.04	.01
❑ 99 David Szott	.04	.01
❑ 100 Derrick Thomas	.25	.08
❑ 101 Barry Word FFC	.04	.01
❑ 102 Marcus Allen	.25	.08
❑ 103 Thomas Benson	.04	.01
❑ 104 Tim Brown	.25	.08
❑ 105 Riki Ellison	.04	.01
❑ 106 Mervyn Fernandez	.04	.01
❑ 107 Willie Gault	.10	.02
❑ 108 Bob Golic	.04	.01
❑ 109 Ethan Horton FFC	.04	.01
❑ 110 Bo Jackson	.30	.10
❑ 111 Howie Long	.25	.08
❑ 112 Don Mosebar	.04	.01
❑ 113 Jerry Robinson	.04	.01
❑ 114 Jay Schroeder	.04	.01
❑ 115 Steve Smith	.04	.01
❑ 116 Greg Townsend	.04	.01
❑ 117 Steve Wisniewski	.04	.01
❑ 118 Mark Clayton	.10	.02
❑ 119 Mark Duper	.10	.02
❑ 120 Ferrell Edmunds	.04	.01
❑ 121 Hugh Green	.04	.01
❑ 122 David Griggs	.04	.01

❑ 123 Jim C. Jensen .04 .01
❑ 124 Dan Marino 1.25 .50
❑ 125 Tim McKyer .04 .01
❑ 126 John Offerdahl .04 .01
❑ 127 Louis Oliver .04 .01
❑ 128 Tony Paige .04 .01
❑ 129 Reggie Roby .04 .01
❑ 130 Keith Sims .04 .01
❑ 131 Sammie Smith .04 .01
❑ 132 Pete Stoyanovich .04 .01
❑ 133 Richmond Webb .04 .01
❑ 134 Bruce Armstrong .04 .01
❑ 135 Vincent Brown .04 .01
❑ 136 Hart Lee Dykes .04 .01
❑ 137 Irving Fryar .10 .02
❑ 138 Tim Goad .04 .01
❑ 139 Tommy Hodson .04 .01
❑ 140 Maurice Hurst .04 .01
❑ 141 Ronnie Lippett .04 .01
❑ 142 Greg McMurtry .04 .01
❑ 143 Ed Reynolds .04 .01
❑ 144 John Stephens .04 .01
❑ 145 Andre Tippett .04 .01
❑ 146 Danny Villa .04 .01
❑ 147 Brad Baxter .04 .01
❑ 148 Kyle Clifton .04 .01
❑ 149 Jeff Criswell .04 .01
❑ 150 James Hasty .04 .01
❑ 151 Jeff Lageman .04 .01
❑ 152 Pat Leahy .04 .01
❑ 153 Rob Moore .25 .08
❑ 154 Al Toon .10 .02
❑ 155 Gary Anderson K .04 .01
❑ 156 Bubby Brister .04 .01
❑ 157 Chris Calloway .04 .01
❑ 158 Donald Evans .04 .01
❑ 159 Eric Green .04 .01
❑ 160 Bryan Hinkle .04 .01
❑ 161 Merril Hoge .04 .01
❑ 162 Tunch Ilkin .04 .01
❑ 163 Louis Lipps .04 .01
❑ 164 David Little .04 .01
❑ 165 Mike Mularkey .04 .01
❑ 166 Gerald Williams .04 .01
❑ 167 Warren Williams .04 .01
❑ 168 Rod Woodson .25 .08
❑ 169 Tim Worley .04 .01
❑ 170 Martin Bayless .04 .01
❑ 171 Marion Butts .10 .02
❑ 172 Gill Byrd .04 .01
❑ 173 Frank Cornish .04 .01
❑ 174 Arthur Cox .04 .01
❑ 175 Burt Grossman .04 .01
❑ 176 Anthony Miller .10 .02
❑ 177 Leslie O'Neal .10 .02
❑ 178 Gary Plummer .04 .01
❑ 179 Junior Seau .25 .08
❑ 180 Billy Joe Tolliver .04 .01
❑ 181 Derrick Walker RC .04 .01
❑ 182 Lee Williams .04 .01
❑ 183 Robert Blackmon .04 .01
❑ 184 Brian Blades .10 .02
❑ 185 Grant Feasel .04 .01
❑ 186 Derrick Fenner .04 .01
❑ 187 Andy Heck .04 .01
❑ 188 Norm Johnson .04 .01
❑ 189 Tommy Kane .04 .01
❑ 190 Cortez Kennedy .25 .08
❑ 191 Dave Krieg .10 .02
❑ 192 Travis McNeal .04 .01
❑ 193 Eugene Robinson .04 .01
❑ 194 Chris Warren FFC .25 .08
❑ 195 John L. Williams .04 .01
❑ 196 Steve Broussard .04 .01
❑ 197 Scott Case .04 .01
❑ 198 Shawn Collins .04 .01
❑ 199 Darion Conner UER .04 .01
❑ 200 Tory Epps .04 .01
❑ 201 Bill Fralic .04 .01
❑ 202 Michael Haynes FFC .25 .08
❑ 203 Chris Hinton .04 .01
❑ 204 Keith Jones .04 .01
❑ 205 Brian Jordan .10 .02
❑ 206 Mike Kenn .04 .01
❑ 207 Chris Miller .10 .02
❑ 208 Andre Rison .10 .02
❑ 209 Mike Rozier .04 .01
❑ 210 Deion Sanders .40 .15
❑ 211 Gary Wilkins .04 .01
❑ 212 Neal Anderson .10 .02
❑ 213 Trace Armstrong .04 .01
❑ 214 Mark Bortz .04 .01
❑ 215 Kevin Butler .04 .01
❑ 216 Mark Carrier DB .10 .02
❑ 217 Wendell Davis FFC .04 .01
❑ 218 Richard Dent .10 .02
❑ 219 Dennis Gentry .04 .01
❑ 220 Jim Harbaugh .25 .08
❑ 221 Jay Hilgenberg .04 .01
❑ 222 Steve McMichael .10 .02
❑ 223 Ron Morris .04 .01
❑ 224 Brad Muster .04 .01
❑ 225 Mike Singletary .10 .02
❑ 226 James Thornton .04 .01
❑ 227 Tommie Agee .04 .01
❑ 228 Troy Aikman .75 .30
❑ 229 Jack Del Rio .10 .02
❑ 230 Issiac Holt .04 .01
❑ 231 Ray Horton .04 .01
❑ 232 Jim Jeffcoat .04 .01
❑ 233 Eugene Lockhart .04 .01
❑ 234 Kelvin Martin .04 .01
❑ 235 Nate Newton .10 .02
❑ 236 Mike Saxon .04 .01
❑ 237 Emmitt Smith 2.50 1.00
❑ 238A Daniel Stubbs .10 .02
❑ 238B Daniel Stubbs .10 .02
❑ 239 Jim Arnold .04 .01
❑ 240 Jerry Ball .04 .01
❑ 241 Bennie Blades .04 .01
❑ 242 Lomas Brown .04 .01
❑ 243 Robert Clark .04 .01
❑ 244 Mike Cofer .04 .01
❑ 245 Mel Gray .10 .02
❑ 246 Rodney Peete .10 .02
❑ 247 Barry Sanders 1.25 .50
❑ 248 Andre Ware .10 .02
❑ 249 Matt Brock RC .04 .01
❑ 250 Robert Brown .04 .01
❑ 251 Anthony Dilweg .04 .01
❑ 252 Johnny Holland .04 .01
❑ 253 Tim Harris .04 .01
❑ 254 Chris Jacke .04 .01
❑ 255 Perry Kemp .04 .01
❑ 256 Don Majkowski UER .04 .01
❑ 257 Tony Mandarich .04 .01
❑ 258 Mark Murphy .04 .01
❑ 259 Brian Noble .04 .01
❑ 260 Jeff Query .04 .01
❑ 261 Sterling Sharpe .25 .08
❑ 262 Ed West .04 .01
❑ 263 Keith Woodside .04 .01
❑ 264 Flipper Anderson .04 .01
❑ 265 Aaron Cox .04 .01
❑ 266 Henry Ellard .10 .02
❑ 267 Jim Everett .10 .02
❑ 268 Cleveland Gary .04 .01
❑ 269 Kevin Greene .10 .02
❑ 270 Pete Holohan .04 .01
❑ 271 Mike Lansford .04 .01
❑ 272 Duval Love RC .04 .01
❑ 273 Buford McGee .04 .01
❑ 274 Tom Newberry .04 .01
❑ 275 Jackie Slater .04 .01
❑ 276 Frank Stams .04 .01
❑ 277 Alfred Anderson .04 .01
❑ 278 Joey Browner .04 .01
❑ 279 Anthony Carter .10 .02
❑ 280 Chris Doleman .04 .01
❑ 281 Rick Fenney .04 .01
❑ 282 Rich Gannon .25 .08
❑ 283 Hassan Jones .04 .01
❑ 284 Steve Jordan .04 .01
❑ 285 Carl Lee .04 .01
❑ 286 Randall McDaniel .04 .01
❑ 287 Keith Millard .04 .01
❑ 288 Herschel Walker .10 .02
❑ 289 Wade Wilson .10 .02
❑ 290 Gary Zimmerman .04 .01
❑ 291 Morten Andersen .04 .01
❑ 292 Jim Dombrowski .04 .01
❑ 293 Gill Fenerty .04 .01
❑ 294 Craig Heyward .10 .02
❑ 295 Dalton Hilliard .04 .01
❑ 296 Rickey Jackson .04 .01
❑ 297 Vaughan Johnson .04 .01
❑ 298 Eric Martin .04 .01
❑ 299 Robert Massey .04 .01
❑ 300 Rueben Mayes .04 .01
❑ 301 Sam Mills .04 .01
❑ 302 Brett Perriman .25 .08
❑ 303 Pat Swilling .10 .02
❑ 304 Steve Walsh .04 .01
❑ 305 Ottis Anderson .10 .02
❑ 306 Matt Bahr .04 .01
❑ 307 Mark Bavaro .04 .01
❑ 308 Maurice Carthon .04 .01
❑ 309 Mark Collins .04 .01
❑ 310 John Elliott .04 .01
❑ 311 Rodney Hampton .25 .08
❑ 312 Jeff Hostetler .10 .02
❑ 313 Erik Howard .04 .01
❑ 314 Pepper Johnson .04 .01
❑ 315 Sean Landeta .04 .01
❑ 316 Dave Meggett .10 .02
❑ 317 Bart Oates .04 .01
❑ 318 Phil Simms .10 .02
❑ 319 Lawrence Taylor .25 .08
❑ 320 Reyna Thompson .04 .01
❑ 321 Everson Walls .04 .01
❑ 322 Eric Allen .04 .01
❑ 323 Fred Barnett FFC .25 .08
❑ 324 Jerome Brown .04 .01
❑ 325 Keith Byars .04 .01
❑ 326 Randall Cunningham .25 .08
❑ 327 Byron Evans .04 .01
❑ 328 Ron Heller .04 .01
❑ 329 Keith Jackson .10 .02
❑ 330 Seth Joyner .10 .02
❑ 331 Heath Sherman .04 .01
❑ 332 Clyde Simmons .04 .01
❑ 333 Ben Smith .04 .01
❑ 334 Anthony Toney .04 .01
❑ 335 Andre Waters .04 .01
❑ 336 Reggie White .25 .08
❑ 337 Calvin Williams .10 .02
❑ 338 Anthony Bell .04 .01
❑ 339 Rich Camarillo .04 .01
❑ 340 Roy Green .04 .01
❑ 341 Tim Jorden RC .04 .01
❑ 342 Cedric Mack .04 .01
❑ 343 Dexter Manley .04 .01
❑ 344 Freddie Joe Nunn .04 .01
❑ 345 Ricky Proehl .04 .01
❑ 346 Tootie Robbins .04 .01
❑ 347 Timm Rosenbach .04 .01
❑ 348 Luis Sharpe .04 .01
❑ 349 Vai Sikahema .04 .01
❑ 350 Anthony Thompson .04 .01
❑ 351 Lonnie Young .04 .01
❑ 352 Dexter Carter .04 .01
❑ 353 Mike Cofer .04 .01
❑ 354 Kevin Fagan .04 .01
❑ 355 Don Griffin .04 .01
❑ 356 Charles Haley UER .10 .02
❑ 357 Pierce Holt .04 .01
❑ 358 Brent Jones .25 .08
❑ 359 Guy McIntyre .04 .01
❑ 360 Joe Montana 1.25 .50
❑ 361 Darryl Pollard .04 .01

❑ 362 Tom Rathman .04 .01
❑ 363 Jerry Rice .75 .30
❑ 364 Bill Romanowski .04 .01
❑ 365 John Taylor .10 .02
❑ 366 Steve Wallace .10 .02
❑ 367 Steve Young .75 .30
❑ 368 Gary Anderson RB .04 .01
❑ 369 Ian Beckles .04 .01
❑ 370 Mark Carrier WR .25 .08
❑ 371 Reggie Cobb .04 .01
❑ 372 Reuben Davis .04 .01
❑ 373 Randy Grimes .04 .01
❑ 374 Wayne Haddix .04 .01
❑ 375 Ron Hall .04 .01
❑ 376 Harry Hamilton .04 .01
❑ 377 Bruce Hill .04 .01
❑ 378 Keith McCants .04 .01
❑ 379 Bruce Perkins .04 .01
❑ 380 Vinny Testaverde UER .10 .02
❑ 381 Broderick Thomas .04 .01
❑ 382 Jeff Bostic .04 .01
❑ 383 Earnest Byner .04 .01
❑ 384 Gary Clark .25 .08
❑ 385 Darryl Grant .04 .01
❑ 386 Darrell Green .04 .01
❑ 387 Stan Humphries .25 .08
❑ 388 Jim Lachey .04 .01
❑ 389 Charles Mann .04 .01
❑ 390 Wilber Marshall .04 .01
❑ 391 Art Monk .10 .02
❑ 392 Gerald Riggs .04 .01
❑ 393 Mark Rypien .10 .02
❑ 394 Ricky Sanders .04 .01
❑ 395 Don Warren .04 .01
❑ 396 Bruce Smith HIT .10 .02
❑ 397 Reggie White HIT .10 .02
❑ 398 Lawrence Taylor HIT .10 .02
❑ 399 David Fulcher HIT .04 .01
❑ 400 Derrick Thomas HIT .10 .02
❑ 401 Mark Carrier DB HIT .04 .01
❑ 402 Mike Singletary HIT .10 .02
❑ 403 Charles Haley HIT .04 .01
❑ 404 Jeff Cross HIT .04 .01
❑ 405 Leslie O'Neal HIT .10 .02
❑ 406 Tim Harris HIT .04 .01
❑ 407 Steve Atwater HIT .04 .01
❑ 408 Joe Montana LL UER .50 .20
❑ 409 Randall Cunningham LL .10 .02
❑ 410 Warren Moon LL .10 .02
❑ 411 Andre Rison LL UER 412 .10 .02
❑ 412 Haywood Jeffires LL .10 .02
❑ 413 Stephone Paige LL .04 .01
❑ 414 Phil Simms LL .10 .02
❑ 415 Barry Sanders LL .50 .20
❑ 416 Bo Jackson LL .10 .02
❑ 417 Thurman Thomas LL .10 .02
❑ 418 Emmitt Smith LL 1.25 .50
❑ 419 John L. Williams LL .04 .01
❑ 420 Nick Bell RC .04 .01
❑ 421 Eric Bieniemy RC .04 .01
❑ 422 Mike Dumas RC UER .04 .01
❑ 423 Russell Maryland RC .25 .08
❑ 424 Derek Russell RC .04 .01
❑ 425 Chris Smith RC .04 .01
❑ 426 Mike Stonebreaker RP .04 .01
❑ 427 Pat Tyrance RP .04 .01
❑ 428 Kenny Walker RC .04 .01
❑ 429 Checklist 1-108 UER .04 .01
❑ 430 Checklist 109-216 .04 .01
❑ 431 Checklist 217-324 .04 .01
❑ 432 Checklist 325-432 .04 .01

1992 Fleer

❑ COMPLETE SET (480) 10.00 5.00
❑ 1 Steve Broussard .04 .01
❑ 2 Rick Bryan .04 .01
❑ 3 Scott Case .04 .01
❑ 4 Tory Epps .04 .01
❑ 5 Bill Fralic .04 .01
❑ 6 Moe Gardner .04 .01
❑ 7 Michael Haynes .10 .02
❑ 8 Chris Hinton .04 .01
❑ 9 Brian Jordan .10 .02
❑ 10 Mike Kenn .04 .01
❑ 11 Tim McKyer .04 .01
❑ 12 Chris Miller .10 .02
❑ 13 Erric Pegram .10 .02
❑ 14 Mike Pritchard .10 .02
❑ 15 Andre Rison .10 .02
❑ 16 Jessie Tuggle .04 .01
❑ 17 Carlton Bailey RC .10 .02
❑ 18 Howard Ballard .04 .01
❑ 19 Don Beebe .04 .01
❑ 20 Cornelius Bennett .10 .02
❑ 21 Shane Conlan .04 .01
❑ 22 Kent Hull .04 .01
❑ 23 Mark Kelso .04 .01
❑ 24 James Lofton .10 .02
❑ 25 Keith McKeller .04 .01
❑ 26 Scott Norwood .04 .01
❑ 27 Nate Odomes .04 .01
❑ 28 Frank Reich .10 .02
❑ 29 Jim Ritcher .04 .01
❑ 30 Leon Seals .04 .01
❑ 31 Darryl Talley .04 .01
❑ 32 Steve Tasker .10 .02
❑ 33 Thurman Thomas .25 .08
❑ 34 Will Wolford .04 .01
❑ 35 Neal Anderson .04 .01
❑ 36 Trace Armstrong .04 .01
❑ 37 Mark Carrier DB .04 .01
❑ 38 Richard Dent .10 .02
❑ 39 Shaun Gayle .04 .01
❑ 40 Jim Harbaugh .25 .08
❑ 41 Jay Hilgenberg .04 .01
❑ 42 Darren Lewis .04 .01
❑ 43 Steve McMichael .10 .02
❑ 44 Brad Muster .04 .01
❑ 45 William Perry .10 .02
❑ 46 John Roper .04 .01
❑ 47 Lemuel Stinson .04 .01
❑ 48 Stan Thomas .04 .01
❑ 49 Keith Van Horne .04 .01
❑ 50 Tom Waddle .04 .01
❑ 51 Donnell Woolford .04 .01
❑ 52 Chris Zorich .10 .02
❑ 53 Eddie Brown .04 .01
❑ 54 James Francis .04 .01
❑ 55 David Fulcher .04 .01
❑ 56 David Grant .04 .01
❑ 57 Harold Green .04 .01
❑ 58 Rodney Holman .04 .01
❑ 59 Lee Johnson .04 .01
❑ 60 Tim Krumrie .04 .01
❑ 61 Anthony Munoz .10 .02
❑ 62 Joe Walter RC .04 .01
❑ 63 Mike Baab .04 .01
❑ 64 Stephen Braggs .04 .01
❑ 65 Richard Brown RC .04 .01
❑ 66 Dan Fike .04 .01
❑ 67 Scott Galbraith RC .04 .01
❑ 68 Randy Hilliard RC .04 .01
❑ 69 Michael Jackson .10 .02
❑ 70 Tony Jones T .04 .01
❑ 71 Ed King .04 .01
❑ 72 Kevin Mack .04 .01
❑ 73 Clay Matthews .10 .02
❑ 74 Eric Metcalf .10 .02
❑ 75 Vince Newsome .04 .01
❑ 76 John Rienstra .04 .01
❑ 77 Steve Beuerlein .10 .02
❑ 78 Larry Brown DB .04 .01
❑ 79 Tony Casillas .04 .01
❑ 80 Alvin Harper .10 .02
❑ 81 Issiac Holt .04 .01
❑ 82 Ray Horton .04 .01
❑ 83 Michael Irvin .25 .08
❑ 84 Daryl Johnston .25 .08
❑ 85 Kelvin Martin .04 .01
❑ 86 Nate Newton .10 .02
❑ 87 Ken Norton .10 .02
❑ 88 Jay Novacek .10 .02
❑ 89 Emmitt Smith 1.50 .60
❑ 90 Vinson Smith RC .04 .01
❑ 91 Mark Stepnoski .10 .02
❑ 92 Steve Atwater .04 .01
❑ 93 Mike Croel .04 .01
❑ 94 John Elway 1.25 .50
❑ 95 Simon Fletcher .04 .01
❑ 96 Gaston Green .04 .01
❑ 97 Mark Jackson .04 .01
❑ 98 Keith Kartz .04 .01
❑ 99 Greg Kragen .04 .01
❑ 100 Greg Lewis .04 .01
❑ 101 Karl Mecklenburg .04 .01
❑ 102 Derek Russell .04 .01
❑ 103 Steve Sewell .04 .01
❑ 104 Dennis Smith .04 .01
❑ 105 David Treadwell .04 .01
❑ 106 Kenny Walker .04 .01
❑ 107 Doug Widell .04 .01
❑ 108 Michael Young .04 .01
❑ 109 Jerry Ball .04 .01
❑ 110 Bennie Blades .04 .01
❑ 111 Lomas Brown .04 .01
❑ 112 Scott Conover RC .04 .01
❑ 113 Ray Crockett .04 .01
❑ 114 Mike Farr .04 .01
❑ 115 Mel Gray .10 .02
❑ 116 Willie Green .04 .01
❑ 117 Tracy Hayworth RC .04 .01
❑ 118 Erik Kramer .10 .02
❑ 119 Herman Moore .25 .08
❑ 120 Dan Owens .04 .01
❑ 121 Rodney Peete .10 .02
❑ 122 Brett Perriman .25 .08
❑ 123 Barry Sanders 1.25 .50
❑ 124 Chris Spielman .10 .02
❑ 125 Marc Spindler .04 .01
❑ 126 Tony Bennett .04 .01
❑ 127 Matt Brock .04 .01
❑ 128 LeRoy Butler .04 .01
❑ 129 Johnny Holland .04 .01
❑ 130 Perry Kemp .04 .01
❑ 131 Don Majkowski .04 .01
❑ 132 Mark Murphy .04 .01
❑ 133 Brian Noble .04 .01
❑ 134 Bryce Paup .25 .08
❑ 135 Sterling Sharpe .25 .08
❑ 136 Scott Stephen .04 .01
❑ 137 Darrell Thompson .04 .01
❑ 138 Mike Tomczak .04 .01
❑ 139 Esera Tuaolo .04 .01
❑ 140 Keith Woodside .04 .01
❑ 141 Ray Childress .04 .01
❑ 142 Cris Dishman .04 .01
❑ 143 Curtis Duncan .04 .01
❑ 144 John Flannery .04 .01
❑ 145 William Fuller .10 .02
❑ 146 Ernest Givins .10 .02
❑ 147 Haywood Jeffires .10 .02
❑ 148 Sean Jones .10 .02
❑ 149 Lamar Lathon .04 .01
❑ 150 Bruce Matthews .04 .01

❑ 151 Bubba McDowell	.04	.01
❑ 152 Johnny Meads	.04	.01
❑ 153 Warren Moon	.25	.08
❑ 154 Mike Munchak	.10	.02
❑ 155 Al Smith	.04	.01
❑ 156 Doug Smith	.04	.01
❑ 157 Lorenzo White	.04	.01
❑ 158 Michael Ball	.04	.01
❑ 159 Chip Banks	.04	.01
❑ 160 Duane Bickett	.04	.01
❑ 161 Bill Brooks	.04	.01
❑ 162 Ken Clark	.04	.01
❑ 163 Jon Hand	.04	.01
❑ 164 Jeff Herrod	.04	.01
❑ 165 Jessie Hester	.04	.01
❑ 166 Scott Radecic	.04	.01
❑ 167 Rohn Stark	.04	.01
❑ 168 Clarence Verdin	.04	.01
❑ 169 John Alt	.04	.01
❑ 170 Tim Barnett	.04	.01
❑ 171 Tim Grunhard	.04	.01
❑ 172 Dino Hackett	.04	.01
❑ 173 Jonathan Hayes	.04	.01
❑ 174 Bill Maas	.04	.01
❑ 175 Chris Martin	.04	.01
❑ 176 Christian Okoye	.04	.01
❑ 177 Stephone Paige	.04	.01
❑ 178 Jayice Pearson RC	.04	.01
❑ 179 Kevin Porter	.04	.01
❑ 180 Kevin Ross	.04	.01
❑ 181 Dan Saleaumua	.04	.01
❑ 182 Tracy Simien RC	.04	.01
❑ 183 Neil Smith	.25	.08
❑ 184 Derrick Thomas	.25	.08
❑ 185 Robb Thomas	.04	.01
❑ 186 Mark Vlasic	.04	.01
❑ 187 Barry Word	.04	.01
❑ 188 Marcus Allen	.25	.08
❑ 189 Eddie Anderson	.04	.01
❑ 190 Nick Bell	.04	.01
❑ 191 Tim Brown	.25	.08
❑ 192 Scott Davis	.04	.01
❑ 193 Riki Ellison	.04	.01
❑ 194 Mervyn Fernandez	.04	.01
❑ 195 Willie Gault	.10	.02
❑ 196 Jeff Gossett	.04	.01
❑ 197 Ethan Horton	.04	.01
❑ 198 Jeff Jaeger	.04	.01
❑ 199 Howie Long	.25	.08
❑ 200 Ronnie Lott	.10	.02
❑ 201 Todd Marinovich	.04	.01
❑ 202 Don Mosebar	.04	.01
❑ 203 Jay Schroeder	.04	.01
❑ 204 Greg Townsend	.04	.01
❑ 205 Lionel Washington	.04	.01
❑ 206 Steve Wisniewski	.04	.01
❑ 207 Flipper Anderson	.04	.01
❑ 208 Bern Brostek	.04	.01
❑ 209 Robert Delpino	.04	.01
❑ 210 Henry Ellard	.10	.02
❑ 211 Jim Everett	.10	.02
❑ 212 Cleveland Gary	.04	.01
❑ 213 Kevin Greene	.10	.02
❑ 214 Darryl Henley	.04	.01
❑ 215 Damone Johnson	.04	.01
❑ 216 Larry Kelm	.04	.01
❑ 217 Todd Lyght	.04	.01
❑ 218 Jackie Slater	.04	.01
❑ 219 Michael Stewart	.04	.01
❑ 220 Pat Terrell UER	.04	.01
❑ 221 Robert Young	.04	.01
❑ 222 Mark Clayton	.10	.02
❑ 223 Bryan Cox	.10	.02
❑ 224 Aaron Craver	.04	.01
❑ 225 Jeff Cross	.04	.01
❑ 226 Mark Duper	.04	.01
❑ 227 Harry Galbreath	.04	.01
❑ 228 David Griggs	.04	.01
❑ 229 Mark Higgs	.04	.01
❑ 230 Vestee Jackson	.04	.01
❑ 231 John Offerdahl	.04	.01
❑ 232 Louis Oliver	.04	.01
❑ 233 Tony Paige	.04	.01
❑ 234 Reggie Roby	.04	.01
❑ 235 Sammie Smith	.04	.01
❑ 236 Pete Stoyanovich	.04	.01
❑ 237 Richmond Webb	.04	.01
❑ 238 Terry Allen	.25	.08
❑ 239 Ray Berry	.04	.01
❑ 240 Joey Browner	.04	.01
❑ 241 Anthony Carter	.10	.02
❑ 242 Cris Carter	.50	.20
❑ 243 Chris Doleman	.04	.01
❑ 244 Rich Gannon	.25	.08
❑ 245 Tim Irwin	.04	.01
❑ 246 Steve Jordan	.04	.01
❑ 247 Carl Lee	.04	.01
❑ 248 Randall McDaniel	.04	.01
❑ 249 Mike Merriweather	.04	.01
❑ 250 Harry Newsome	.04	.01
❑ 251 John Randle	.10	.02
❑ 252 Henry Thomas	.04	.01
❑ 253 Herschel Walker	.10	.02
❑ 254 Ray Agnew	.04	.01
❑ 255 Bruce Armstrong	.04	.01
❑ 256 Vincent Brown	.04	.01
❑ 257 Marv Cook	.04	.01
❑ 258 Irving Fryar	.10	.02
❑ 259 Pat Harlow	.04	.01
❑ 260 Tommy Hodson	.04	.01
❑ 261 Maurice Hurst	.04	.01
❑ 262 Ronnie Lippett	.04	.01
❑ 263 Eugene Lockhart	.04	.01
❑ 264 Greg McMurtry	.04	.01
❑ 265 Hugh Millen	.04	.01
❑ 266 Leonard Russell	.10	.02
❑ 267 Andre Tippett	.04	.01
❑ 268 Brent Williams	.04	.01
❑ 269 Morten Andersen	.04	.01
❑ 270 Gene Atkins	.04	.01
❑ 271 Wesley Carroll	.04	.01
❑ 272 Jim Dombrowski	.04	.01
❑ 273 Quinn Early	.10	.02
❑ 274 Gill Fenerty	.04	.01
❑ 275 Bobby Hebert	.04	.01
❑ 276 Joel Hilgenberg	.04	.01
❑ 277 Rickey Jackson	.04	.01
❑ 278 Vaughan Johnson	.04	.01
❑ 279 Eric Martin	.04	.01
❑ 280 Brett Maxie	.04	.01
❑ 281 Fred McAfee RC	.04	.01
❑ 282 Sam Mills	.04	.01
❑ 283 Pat Swilling	.10	.02
❑ 284 Floyd Turner	.04	.01
❑ 285 Steve Walsh	.04	.01
❑ 286 Frank Warren	.04	.01
❑ 287 Stephen Baker	.04	.01
❑ 288 Maurice Carthon	.04	.01
❑ 289 Mark Collins	.04	.01
❑ 290 John Elliott	.04	.01
❑ 291 Myron Guyton	.04	.01
❑ 292 Rodney Hampton	.10	.02
❑ 293 Jeff Hostetler	.10	.02
❑ 294 Mark Ingram	.04	.01
❑ 295 Pepper Johnson	.04	.01
❑ 296 Sean Landeta	.04	.01
❑ 297 Leonard Marshall	.04	.01
❑ 298 Dave Meggett	.10	.02
❑ 299 Bart Oates	.04	.01
❑ 300 Phil Simms	.10	.02
❑ 301 Reyna Thompson	.04	.01
❑ 302 Lewis Tillman	.04	.01
❑ 303 Brad Baxter	.04	.01
❑ 304 Kyle Clifton	.04	.01
❑ 305 James Hasty	.04	.01
❑ 306 Joe Kelly	.04	.01
❑ 307 Jeff Lageman	.04	.01
❑ 308 Mo Lewis	.04	.01
❑ 309 Erik McMillan	.04	.01
❑ 310 Rob Moore	.10	.02
❑ 311 Tony Stargell	.04	.01
❑ 312 Jim Sweeney	.04	.01
❑ 313 Marvin Washington	.04	.01
❑ 314 Lonnie Young	.04	.01
❑ 315 Eric Allen	.04	.01
❑ 316 Fred Barnett	.25	.08
❑ 317 Jerome Brown	.04	.01
❑ 318 Keith Byars	.04	.01
❑ 319 Wes Hopkins	.04	.01
❑ 320 Keith Jackson	.10	.02
❑ 321 James Joseph	.04	.01
❑ 322 Seth Joyner	.10	.02
❑ 323 Jeff Kemp	.04	.01
❑ 324 Roger Ruzek	.04	.01
❑ 325 Clyde Simmons	.04	.01
❑ 326 William Thomas	.04	.01
❑ 327 Reggie White	.25	.08
❑ 328 Calvin Williams	.10	.02
❑ 329 Rich Camarillo	.04	.01
❑ 330 Ken Harvey	.04	.01
❑ 331 Eric Hill	.04	.01
❑ 332 Johnny Johnson	.04	.01
❑ 333 Ernie Jones	.04	.01
❑ 334 Tim Jorden	.04	.01
❑ 335 Tim McDonald	.04	.01
❑ 336 Freddie Joe Nunn	.04	.01
❑ 337 Luis Sharpe	.04	.01
❑ 338 Eric Swann	.10	.02
❑ 339 Aeneas Williams	.10	.02
❑ 340 Gary Anderson K	.04	.01
❑ 341 Bubby Brister	.04	.01
❑ 342 Adrian Cooper	.04	.01
❑ 343 Barry Foster	.10	.02
❑ 344 Eric Green	.04	.01
❑ 345 Bryan Hinkle	.04	.01
❑ 346 Tunch Ilkin	.04	.01
❑ 347 Carnell Lake	.04	.01
❑ 348 Louis Lipps	.04	.01
❑ 349 David Little	.04	.01
❑ 350 Greg Lloyd	.10	.02
❑ 351 Neil O'Donnell	.25	.08
❑ 352 Dwight Stone	.04	.01
❑ 353 Rod Woodson	.25	.08
❑ 354 Rod Bernstine	.04	.01
❑ 355 Eric Bieniemy	.04	.01
❑ 356 Marion Butts	.04	.01
❑ 357 Gill Byrd	.04	.01
❑ 358 John Friesz	.10	.02
❑ 359 Burt Grossman	.04	.01
❑ 360 Courtney Hall	.04	.01
❑ 361 Ronnie Harmon	.04	.01
❑ 362 Shawn Jefferson	.04	.01
❑ 363 Nate Lewis	.04	.01
❑ 364 Craig McEwen RC	.04	.01
❑ 365 Eric Moten	.04	.01
❑ 366 Joe Phillips	.04	.01
❑ 367 Gary Plummer	.04	.01
❑ 368 Henry Rolling	.04	.01
❑ 369 Broderick Thompson	.04	.01
❑ 370 Harris Barton	.04	.01
❑ 371 Steve Bono RC	.25	.08
❑ 372 Todd Bowles	.04	.01
❑ 373 Dexter Carter	.04	.01
❑ 374 Michael Carter	.04	.01
❑ 375 Mike Cofer	.04	.01
❑ 376 Keith DeLong	.04	.01
❑ 377 Charles Haley	.10	.02
❑ 378 Merton Hanks	.10	.02
❑ 379 Tim Harris	.04	.01
❑ 380 Brent Jones	.10	.02
❑ 381 Guy McIntyre	.04	.01
❑ 382 Tom Rathman	.04	.01
❑ 383 Bill Romanowski	.04	.01
❑ 384 Jesse Sapolu	.04	.01
❑ 385 John Taylor	.10	.02
❑ 386 Steve Young	.60	.25
❑ 387 Robert Blackmon	.04	.01
❑ 388 Brian Blades	.10	.02
❑ 389 Jacob Green	.04	.01
❑ 390 Dwayne Harper	.04	.01

❑ 391	Andy Heck	.04	.01
❑ 392	Tommy Kane	.04	.01
❑ 393	John Kasay	.04	.01
❑ 394	Cortez Kennedy	.10	.02
❑ 395	Bryan Millard	.04	.01
❑ 396	Rufus Porter	.04	.01
❑ 397	Eugene Robinson	.04	.01
❑ 398	John L. Williams	.04	.01
❑ 399	Terry Wooden	.04	.01
❑ 400	Gary Anderson RB	.04	.01
❑ 401	Ian Beckles	.04	.01
❑ 402	Mark Carrier WR	.10	.02
❑ 403	Reggie Cobb	.04	.01
❑ 404	Lawrence Dawsey	.10	.02
❑ 405	Ron Hall	.04	.01
❑ 406	Keith McCants	.04	.01
❑ 407	Charles McRae	.04	.01
❑ 408	Tim Newton	.04	.01
❑ 409	Jesse Solomon	.04	.01
❑ 410	Vinny Testaverde	.10	.02
❑ 411	Broderick Thomas	.04	.01
❑ 412	Robert Wilson	.04	.01
❑ 413	Jeff Bostic	.04	.01
❑ 414	Earnest Byner	.04	.01
❑ 415	Gary Clark	.25	.08
❑ 416	Andre Collins	.04	.01
❑ 417	Brad Edwards	.04	.01
❑ 418	Kurt Gouveia	.04	.01
❑ 419	Darrell Green	.04	.01
❑ 420	Joe Jacoby	.04	.01
❑ 421	Jim Lachey	.04	.01
❑ 422	Chip Lohmiller	.04	.01
❑ 423	Charles Mann	.04	.01
❑ 424	Wilber Marshall	.04	.01
❑ 425	Ron Middleton RC	.04	.01
❑ 426	Brian Mitchell	.10	.02
❑ 427	Art Monk	.10	.02
❑ 428	Mark Rypien	.04	.01
❑ 429	Ricky Sanders	.04	.01
❑ 430	Mark Schlereth RC	.04	.01
❑ 431	Fred Stokes	.04	.01
❑ 432	Edgar Bennett RC	.25	.08
❑ 433	Brian Bollinger RC	.04	.01
❑ 434	Joe Bowden RC	.04	.01
❑ 435	Terrell Buckley RC	.04	.01
❑ 436	Willie Clay RC	.04	.01
❑ 437	Steve Gordon RC	.04	.01
❑ 438	Keith Hamilton RC	.10	.02
❑ 439	Carlos Huerta	.04	.01
❑ 440	Matt LaBounty RC	.04	.01
❑ 441	Amp Lee RC	.04	.01
❑ 442	Ricardo McDonald RC	.04	.01
❑ 443	Chris Mims RC	.10	.02
❑ 444	Michael Moody RC	.04	.01
❑ 445	Patrick Rowe RC	.04	.01
❑ 446	Leon Searcy RC	.10	.02
❑ 447	Siran Stacy RC	.04	.01
❑ 448	Kevin Turner RC	.04	.01
❑ 449	Tommy Vardell RC	.10	.02
❑ 450	Bob Whitfield RC	.04	.01
❑ 451	Darryl Williams RC	.04	.01
❑ 452	Thurman Thomas LL	.10	.02
❑ 453	Emmitt Smith LL	.75	.30
❑ 454	Haywood Jeffires LL	.04	.01
❑ 455	Michael Irvin LL	.10	.02
❑ 456	Mark Clayton LL	.04	.01
❑ 457	Barry Sanders LL	.60	.25
❑ 458	Pete Stoyanovich LL	.04	.01
❑ 459	Chip Lohmiller LL	.04	.01
❑ 460	William Fuller LL	.04	.01
❑ 461	Pat Swilling LL	.04	.01
❑ 462	Ronnie Lott LL	.04	.01
❑ 463	Ray Crockett LL	.04	.01
❑ 464	Tim McKyer LL	.04	.01
❑ 465	Aeneas Williams LL	.04	.01
❑ 466	Rod Woodson LL	.10	.02
❑ 467	Mel Gray LL	.04	.01
❑ 468	Nate Lewis LL	.04	.01
❑ 469	Steve Young LL	.30	.10
❑ 470	Reggie Roby LL	.04	.01
❑ 471	John Elway PV	.60	.25
❑ 472	Ronnie Lott PV	.04	.01
❑ 473	Art Monk PV UER	.04	.01
❑ 474	Warren Moon PV	.10	.02
❑ 475	Emmitt Smith PV	.75	.30
❑ 476	Thurman Thomas PV	.10	.02
❑ 477	Checklist 1-120	.04	.01
❑ 478	Checklist 121-240	.04	.01
❑ 479	Checklist 241-360	.04	.01
❑ 480	Checklist 361-480	.04	.01

1993 Fleer

❑	COMPLETE SET (500)	20.00	10.00
❑ 1	Dan Saleaumua	.05	.01
❑ 2	Bryan Cox	.05	.01
❑ 3	Dermontti Dawson	.05	.01
❑ 4	Michael Jackson	.10	.02
❑ 5	Calvin Williams	.10	.02
❑ 6	Terry McDaniel	.05	.01
❑ 7	Jack Del Rio	.05	.01
❑ 8	Steve Atwater	.05	.01
❑ 9	Ernie Jones	.05	.01
❑ 10	Brad Muster	.05	.01
❑ 11	Harold Green	.05	.01
❑ 12	Eric Bieniemy	.05	.01
❑ 13	Eric Dorsey	.05	.01
❑ 14	Fred Barnett	.10	.02
❑ 15	Cleveland Gary	.05	.01
❑ 16	Darion Conner	.05	.01
❑ 17	Jerry Ball	.05	.01
❑ 18	Tony Casillas	.05	.01
❑ 19	Brian Blades	.10	.02
❑ 20	Tony Bennett	.05	.01
❑ 21	Reggie Cobb	.05	.01
❑ 22	Kurt Gouveia	.05	.01
❑ 23	Greg McMurtry	.05	.01
❑ 24	Kyle Clifton	.05	.01
❑ 25	Trace Armstrong	.05	.01
❑ 26	Terry Allen	.25	.08
❑ 27	Steve Bono	.10	.02
❑ 28	Barry Word	.05	.01
❑ 29	Mark Duper	.05	.01
❑ 30	Nate Newton	.10	.02
❑ 31	Will Wolford	.05	.01
❑ 32	Curtis Duncan	.05	.01
❑ 33	Nick Bell	.05	.01
❑ 34	Don Beebe	.05	.01
❑ 35	Mike Croel	.05	.01
❑ 36	Rich Camarillo	.05	.01
❑ 37	Wade Wilson	.05	.01
❑ 38	John Taylor	.10	.02
❑ 39	Marion Butts	.05	.01
❑ 40	Rodney Hampton	.10	.02
❑ 41	Seth Joyner	.05	.01
❑ 42	Wilber Marshall	.05	.01
❑ 43	Bobby Hebert	.05	.01
❑ 44	Bennie Blades	.05	.01
❑ 45	Thomas Everett	.05	.01
❑ 46	Ricky Sanders	.05	.01
❑ 47	Matt Brock	.05	.01
❑ 48	Lawrence Dawsey	.05	.01
❑ 49	Brad Edwards	.05	.01
❑ 50	Vincent Brown	.05	.01
❑ 51	Jeff Lageman	.05	.01
❑ 52	Mark Carrier DB	.05	.01
❑ 53	Cris Carter	.25	.08
❑ 54	Brent Jones	.10	.02
❑ 55	Barry Foster	.10	.02
❑ 56	Derrick Thomas	.25	.08
❑ 57	Scott Zolak	.05	.01
❑ 58	Mark Stepnoski	.05	.01
❑ 59	Eric Metcalf	.10	.02
❑ 60	Al Smith	.05	.01
❑ 61	Ronnie Harmon	.05	.01
❑ 62	Cornelius Bennett	.10	.02
❑ 63	Karl Mecklenburg	.05	.01
❑ 64	Chris Chandler	.10	.02
❑ 65	Toi Cook	.05	.01
❑ 66	Tim Krumrie	.05	.01
❑ 67	Gill Byrd	.05	.01
❑ 68	Mark Jackson	.05	.01
❑ 69	Tim Harris	.05	.01
❑ 70	Shane Conlan	.05	.01
❑ 71	Moe Gardner	.05	.01
❑ 72	Lomas Brown	.05	.01
❑ 73	Charles Haley	.10	.02
❑ 74	Mark Rypien	.05	.01
❑ 75	LeRoy Butler	.05	.01
❑ 76	Steve DeBerg	.05	.01
❑ 77	Darrell Green	.05	.01
❑ 78	Marv Cook	.05	.01
❑ 79	Chris Burkett	.05	.01
❑ 80	Richard Dent	.10	.02
❑ 81	Roger Craig	.10	.02
❑ 82	Amp Lee	.05	.01
❑ 83	Eric Green	.05	.01
❑ 84	Willie Davis	.25	.08
❑ 85	Mark Higgs	.05	.01
❑ 86	Carlton Haselrig	.05	.01
❑ 87	Tommy Vardell	.05	.01
❑ 88	Haywood Jeffires	.10	.02
❑ 89	Tim Brown	.25	.08
❑ 90	Randall McDaniel	.05	.01
❑ 91	John Elway	1.50	.60
❑ 92	Ken Harvey	.05	.01
❑ 93	Joel Hilgenberg	.05	.01
❑ 94	Steve Wallace	.05	.01
❑ 95	Stan Humphries	.10	.02
❑ 96	Greg Jackson	.05	.01
❑ 97	Clyde Simmons	.05	.01
❑ 98	Jim Everett	.10	.02
❑ 99	Michael Haynes	.10	.02
❑ 100	Mel Gray	.10	.02
❑ 101	Alvin Harper	.10	.02
❑ 102	Art Monk	.10	.02
❑ 103	Brett Favre	2.00	.75
❑ 104	Keith McCants	.05	.01
❑ 105	Charles Mann	.05	.01
❑ 106	Leonard Russell	.10	.02
❑ 107	Mo Lewis	.05	.01
❑ 108	Shaun Gayle	.05	.01
❑ 109	Chris Doleman	.05	.01
❑ 110	Tim McDonald	.05	.01
❑ 111	Louis Oliver	.05	.01
❑ 112	Greg Lloyd	.10	.02
❑ 113	Chip Banks	.05	.01
❑ 114	Sean Jones	.05	.01
❑ 115	Ethan Horton	.05	.01
❑ 116	Kenneth Davis	.05	.01
❑ 117	Simon Fletcher	.05	.01
❑ 118	Johnny Johnson	.05	.01
❑ 119	Vaughan Johnson	.05	.01
❑ 120	Derrick Fenner	.05	.01
❑ 121	Nate Lewis	.05	.01
❑ 122	Pepper Johnson	.05	.01
❑ 123	Heath Sherman	.05	.01
❑ 124	Darryl Henley	.05	.01
❑ 125	Pierce Holt	.05	.01
❑ 126	Herman Moore	.25	.08
❑ 127	Michael Irvin	.25	.08
❑ 128	Tommy Kane	.05	.01
❑ 129	Jackie Harris	.05	.01
❑ 130	Hardy Nickerson	.10	.02
❑ 131	Chip Lohmiller	.05	.01

❑ 132 Andre Tippett .05 .01
❑ 133 Leonard Marshall .05 .01
❑ 134 Craig Heyward .10 .02
❑ 135 Anthony Carter .10 .02
❑ 136 Tom Rathman .05 .01
❑ 137 Lorenzo White .05 .01
❑ 138 Nick Lowery .05 .01
❑ 139 John Offerdahl .05 .01
❑ 140 Neil O'Donnell .25 .08
❑ 141 Clarence Verdin .05 .01
❑ 142 Ernest Givins .10 .02
❑ 143 Todd Marinovich .05 .01
❑ 144 Jeff Wright .05 .01
❑ 145 Michael Brooks .05 .01
❑ 146 Freddie Joe Nunn .05 .01
❑ 147 William Perry .10 .02
❑ 148 Daniel Stubbs .05 .01
❑ 149 Morten Andersen .05 .01
❑ 150 Dave Meggett .05 .01
❑ 151 Andre Waters .05 .01
❑ 152 Todd Lyght .05 .01
❑ 153 Chris Miller .10 .02
❑ 154 Rodney Peete .05 .01
❑ 155 Jim Jeffcoat .05 .01
❑ 156 Cortez Kennedy .10 .02
❑ 157 Johnny Holland .05 .01
❑ 158 Ricky Reynolds .05 .01
❑ 159 Kevin Greene .10 .02
❑ 160 Jeff Herrod .05 .01
❑ 161 Bruce Matthews .05 .01
❑ 162 Anthony Smith .05 .01
❑ 163 Henry Jones .05 .01
❑ 164 Rob Burnett .05 .01
❑ 165 Eric Swann .10 .02
❑ 166 Tom Waddle .05 .01
❑ 167 Alfred Williams .05 .01
❑ 168 Darren Carrington RC .05 .01
❑ 169 Mike Sherrard .05 .01
❑ 170 Frank Reich .10 .02
❑ 171 Anthony Newman RC .05 .01
❑ 172 Mike Pritchard .10 .02
❑ 173 Andre Ware .05 .01
❑ 174 Daryl Johnston .25 .08
❑ 175 Rufus Porter .05 .01
❑ 176 Reggie White .25 .08
❑ 177 Charles Mincy RC .05 .01
❑ 178 Pete Stoyanovich .05 .01
❑ 179 Rod Woodson .25 .08
❑ 180 Anthony Johnson .10 .02
❑ 181 Cody Carlson .05 .01
❑ 182 Gaston Green .05 .01
❑ 183 Audray McMillian .05 .01
❑ 184 Mike Johnson .05 .01
❑ 185 Aeneas Williams .05 .01
❑ 186 Jarrod Bunch .05 .01
❑ 187 Dennis Smith .05 .01
❑ 188 Quinn Early .10 .02
❑ 189 James Hasty .05 .01
❑ 190 Darryl Talley .05 .01
❑ 191 Jon Vaughn .05 .01
❑ 192 Andre Rison .10 .02
❑ 193 Kelvin Pritchett .05 .01
❑ 194 Ken Norton Jr. .10 .02
❑ 195 Chris Warren .10 .02
❑ 196 Sterling Sharpe .25 .08
❑ 197 Christian Okoye .05 .01
❑ 198 Richmond Webb .05 .01
❑ 199 James Francis .05 .01
❑ 200 Reggie Langhorne .05 .01
❑ 201 J.J. Birden .05 .01
❑ 202 Aaron Wallace .05 .01
❑ 203 Henry Thomas .05 .01
❑ 204 Clay Matthews .10 .02
❑ 205 Robert Massey .05 .01
❑ 206 Donnell Woolford .05 .01
❑ 207 Ricky Watters .25 .08
❑ 208 Wayne Martin .05 .01
❑ 209 Rob Moore .10 .02
❑ 210 Steve Tasker .10 .02
❑ 211 Jackie Slater .05 .01
❑ 212 Steve Young .75 .30
❑ 213 Barry Sanders 1.25 .50
❑ 214 Jay Novacek .10 .02
❑ 215 Eugene Robinson .05 .01
❑ 216 Duane Bickett .05 .01
❑ 217 Broderick Thomas .05 .01
❑ 218 David Fulcher .05 .01
❑ 219 Rohn Stark .05 .01
❑ 220 Warren Moon .25 .08
❑ 221 Steve Wisniewski .05 .01
❑ 222 Nate Odomes .05 .01
❑ 223 Shannon Sharpe .25 .08
❑ 224 Byron Evans .05 .01
❑ 225 Mark Collins .05 .01
❑ 226 Rod Bernstine .05 .01
❑ 227 Sam Mills .05 .01
❑ 228 Marvin Washington .05 .01
❑ 229 Thurman Thomas .25 .08
❑ 230 Brent Williams .05 .01
❑ 231 Jessie Tuggle .05 .01
❑ 232 Chris Spielman .10 .02
❑ 233 Emmitt Smith 1.50 .60
❑ 234 John L. Williams .05 .01
❑ 235 Jeff Cross .05 .01
❑ 236 Chris Doleman AW .05 .01
❑ 237 John Elway AW .75 .30
❑ 238 Barry Foster AW .05 .01
❑ 239 Cortez Kennedy AW .05 .01
❑ 240 Steve Young AW .40 .15
❑ 241 Barry Foster LL .05 .01
❑ 242 Warren Moon LL .05 .01
❑ 243 Sterling Sharpe LL .05 .01
❑ 244 Emmitt Smith LL .75 .30
❑ 245 Thurman Thomas LL .10 .02
❑ 246 Michael Irvin PV .10 .02
❑ 247 Steve Young PV .40 .15
❑ 248 Barry Foster PV .05 .01
❑ 249 Checklist .05 .01
❑ 250 Checklist .05 .01
❑ 251 Checklist .05 .01
❑ 252 Checklist .05 .01
❑ 253 Troy Aikman AW .40 .15
❑ 254 Jason Hanson AW .05 .01
❑ 255 Carl Pickens AW .10 .02
❑ 256 Santana Dotson AW .05 .01
❑ 257 Dale Carter AW .05 .01
❑ 258 Clyde Simmons LL .05 .01
❑ 259 Audray McMillian LL .05 .01
❑ 260 Henry Jones LL .05 .01
❑ 261 Deion Sanders LL .25 .08
❑ 262 Haywood Jeffires LL .05 .01
❑ 263 Deion Sanders PV .25 .08
❑ 264 Andre Reed PV .10 .02
❑ 265 Vince Workman .05 .01
❑ 266 Robert Brown .05 .01
❑ 267 Ray Agnew .05 .01
❑ 268 Ronnie Lott .10 .02
❑ 269 Wesley Carroll .05 .01
❑ 270 John Randle .10 .02
❑ 271 Rodney Culver .05 .01
❑ 272 David Alexander .05 .01
❑ 273 Troy Aikman .75 .30
❑ 274 Bernie Kosar .10 .02
❑ 275 Scott Case .05 .01
❑ 276 Dan McGwire .05 .01
❑ 277 John Alt .05 .01
❑ 278 Dan Marino 1.50 .60
❑ 279 Santana Dotson .10 .02
❑ 280 Johnny Mitchell .05 .01
❑ 281 Alonzo Spellman .05 .01
❑ 282 Adrian Cooper .05 .01
❑ 283 Gary Clark .10 .02
❑ 284 Vance Johnson .05 .01
❑ 285 Eric Martin .05 .01
❑ 286 Jesse Solomon .05 .01
❑ 287 Carl Banks .05 .01
❑ 288 Harris Barton .05 .01
❑ 289 Jim Harbaugh .25 .08
❑ 290 Bubba McDowell .05 .01
❑ 291 Anthony McDowell RC .05 .01
❑ 292 Terrell Buckley .05 .01
❑ 293 Bruce Armstrong .05 .01
❑ 294 Kurt Barber .05 .01
❑ 295 Reginald Jones .05 .01
❑ 296 Steve Jordan .05 .01
❑ 297 Kerry Cash .05 .01
❑ 298 Ray Crockett .05 .01
❑ 299 Keith Byars .05 .01
❑ 300 Russell Maryland .05 .01
❑ 301 Johnny Bailey .05 .01
❑ 302 Vinnie Clark .05 .01
❑ 303 Terry Wooden .05 .01
❑ 304 Harvey Williams .10 .02
❑ 305 Marco Coleman .05 .01
❑ 306 Mark Wheeler .05 .01
❑ 307 Greg Townsend .05 .01
❑ 308 Tim McGee .05 .01
❑ 309 Donald Evans .05 .01
❑ 310 Randal Hill .05 .01
❑ 311 Kenny Walker .05 .01
❑ 312 Dalton Hilliard .05 .01
❑ 313 Howard Ballard .05 .01
❑ 314 Phil Simms .10 .02
❑ 315 Jerry Rice 1.00 .40
❑ 316 Courtney Hall .05 .01
❑ 317 Darren Lewis .05 .01
❑ 318 Greg Montgomery .05 .01
❑ 319 Paul Gruber .05 .01
❑ 320 George Koonce RC .05 .01
❑ 321 Eugene Chung .05 .01
❑ 322 Mike Brim .05 .01
❑ 323 Patrick Hunter .05 .01
❑ 324 Todd Scott .05 .01
❑ 325 Steve Emtman .05 .01
❑ 326 Andy Harmon RC .10 .02
❑ 327 Larry Brown DB .05 .01
❑ 328 Chuck Cecil .05 .01
❑ 329 Tim McKyer .05 .01
❑ 330 Jeff Bryant .05 .01
❑ 331 Tim Barnett .05 .01
❑ 332 Irving Fryar .10 .02
❑ 333 Tyji Armstrong .05 .01
❑ 334 Brad Baxter .05 .01
❑ 335 Shane Collins .05 .01
❑ 336 Jeff Graham .10 .02
❑ 337 Ricky Proehl .05 .01
❑ 338 Tommy Maddox .25 .08
❑ 339 Jim Dombrowski .05 .01
❑ 340 Bill Brooks .05 .01
❑ 341 Dave Brown RC .25 .08
❑ 342 Eric Davis .05 .01
❑ 343 Leslie O'Neal .10 .02
❑ 344 Jim Morrissey .05 .01
❑ 345 Mike Munchak .10 .02
❑ 346 Ron Hall .05 .01
❑ 347 Brian Noble .05 .01
❑ 348 Chris Singleton .05 .01
❑ 349 Boomer Esiason .10 .02
❑ 350 Ray Roberts .05 .01
❑ 351 Gary Zimmerman .05 .01
❑ 352 Quentin Coryatt .10 .02
❑ 353 Willie Green .05 .01
❑ 354 Randall Cunningham .25 .08
❑ 355 Kevin Smith .10 .02
❑ 356 Michael Dean Perry .10 .02
❑ 357 Tim Green .05 .01
❑ 358 Dwayne Harper .05 .01
❑ 359 Dale Carter .05 .01
❑ 360 Keith Jackson .10 .02
❑ 361 Martin Mayhew .05 .01
❑ 362 Brian Washington .05 .01
❑ 363 Earnest Byner .05 .01
❑ 364 D.J. Johnson .05 .01
❑ 365 Timm Rosenbach .05 .01
❑ 366 Doug Widell .05 .01
❑ 367 Vaughn Dunbar .05 .01
❑ 368 Phil Hansen .05 .01
❑ 369 Mike Fox .05 .01
❑ 370 Dana Hall .05 .01
❑ 371 Junior Seau .25 .08

❑ 372	Steve McMichael	.10	.02
❑ 373	Eddie Robinson	.05	.01
❑ 374	Milton Mack RC	.05	.01
❑ 375	Mike Prior	.05	.01
❑ 376	Jerome Henderson	.05	.01
❑ 377	Scott Mersereau	.05	.01
❑ 378	Neal Anderson	.05	.01
❑ 379	Harry Newsome	.05	.01
❑ 380	John Baylor	.05	.01
❑ 381	Bill Fralic	.05	.01
❑ 382	Mark Bavaro	.05	.01
❑ 383	Robert Jones	.05	.01
❑ 384	Tyronne Stowe	.05	.01
❑ 385	Deion Sanders	.50	.20
❑ 386	Robert Blackmon	.05	.01
❑ 387	Neil Smith	.25	.08
❑ 388	Mark Ingram	.05	.01
❑ 389	Mark Carrier WR	.10	.02
❑ 390	Browning Nagle	.05	.01
❑ 391	Ricky Ervins	.05	.01
❑ 392	Carnell Lake	.05	.01
❑ 393	Luis Sharpe	.05	.01
❑ 394	Greg Kragen	.05	.01
❑ 395	Tommy Barnhardt	.05	.01
❑ 396	Mark Kelso	.05	.01
❑ 397	Kent Graham RC	.25	.08
❑ 398	Bill Romanowski	.05	.01
❑ 399	Anthony Miller	.10	.02
❑ 400	John Roper	.05	.01
❑ 401	Lamar Rogers	.05	.01
❑ 402	Troy Auzenne	.05	.01
❑ 403	Webster Slaughter	.05	.01
❑ 404	David Brandon	.05	.01
❑ 405	Chris Hinton	.05	.01
❑ 406	Andy Heck	.05	.01
❑ 407	Tracy Simien	.05	.01
❑ 408	Troy Vincent	.05	.01
❑ 409	Jason Hanson	.05	.01
❑ 410	Rod Jones CB RC	.05	.01
❑ 411	Al Noga	.05	.01
❑ 412	Ernie Mills	.05	.01
❑ 413	Willie Gault	.05	.01
❑ 414	Henry Ellard	.10	.02
❑ 415	Rickey Jackson	.05	.01
❑ 416	Bruce Smith	.25	.08
❑ 417	Derek Brown TE	.05	.01
❑ 418	Kevin Fagan	.05	.01
❑ 419	Gary Plummer	.05	.01
❑ 420	Wendell Davis	.05	.01
❑ 421	Craig Thompson	.05	.01
❑ 422	Wes Hopkins	.05	.01
❑ 423	Ray Childress	.05	.01
❑ 424	Pat Harlow	.05	.01
❑ 425	Howie Long	.25	.08
❑ 426	Shane Dronett	.05	.01
❑ 427	Sean Salisbury	.05	.01
❑ 428	Dwight Hollier RC	.05	.01
❑ 429	Brett Perriman	.25	.08
❑ 430	Donald Hollas RC	.05	.01
❑ 431	Jim Lachey	.05	.01
❑ 432	Darren Perry	.05	.01
❑ 433	Lionel Washington	.05	.01
❑ 434	Sean Gilbert	.10	.02
❑ 435	Gene Atkins	.05	.01
❑ 436	Jim Kelly	.25	.08
❑ 437	Ed McCaffrey	.25	.08
❑ 438	Don Griffin	.05	.01
❑ 439	Jerrol Williams	.05	.01
❑ 440	Bryce Paup	.10	.02
❑ 441	Darryl Williams	.05	.01
❑ 442	Vai Sikahema	.05	.01
❑ 443	Cris Dishman	.05	.01
❑ 444	Kevin Mack	.05	.01
❑ 445	Winston Moss	.05	.01
❑ 446	Tyrone Braxton	.05	.01
❑ 447	Mike Merriweather	.05	.01
❑ 448	Tony Paige	.05	.01
❑ 449	Robert Porcher	.05	.01
❑ 450	Ricardo McDonald	.05	.01
❑ 451	Danny Copeland	.05	.01
❑ 452	Tony Tolbert	.05	.01
❑ 453	Eric Dickerson	.10	.02
❑ 454	Flipper Anderson	.05	.01
❑ 455	Dave Krieg	.10	.02
❑ 456	Brad Lamb RC	.05	.01
❑ 457	Bart Oates	.05	.01
❑ 458	Guy McIntyre	.05	.01
❑ 459	Stanley Richard	.05	.01
❑ 460	Edgar Bennett	.25	.08
❑ 461	Pat Carter	.05	.01
❑ 462	Eric Allen	.05	.01
❑ 463	William Fuller	.05	.01
❑ 464	James Jones DT	.05	.01
❑ 465	Chester McGlockton	.10	.02
❑ 466	Charles Dimry	.05	.01
❑ 467	Tim Grunhard	.05	.01
❑ 468	Jarvis Williams	.05	.01
❑ 469	Tracy Scroggins	.05	.01
❑ 470	David Klingler	.05	.01
❑ 471	Andre Collins	.05	.01
❑ 472	Erik Williams	.05	.01
❑ 473	Eddie Anderson	.05	.01
❑ 474	Marc Boutte	.05	.01
❑ 475	Joe Montana	1.50	.60
❑ 476	Andre Reed	.10	.02
❑ 477	Lawrence Taylor	.25	.08
❑ 478	Jeff George	.25	.08
❑ 479	Chris Mims	.05	.01
❑ 480	Ken Ruettgers	.05	.01
❑ 481	Roman Phifer	.05	.01
❑ 482	William Thomas	.05	.01
❑ 483	Lamar Lathon	.05	.01
❑ 484	Vinny Testaverde	.10	.02
❑ 485	Mike Kenn	.05	.01
❑ 486	Greg Lewis	.05	.01
❑ 487	Chris Martin	.05	.01
❑ 488	Maurice Hurst	.05	.01
❑ 489	Pat Swilling	.05	.01
❑ 490	Carl Pickens	.10	.02
❑ 491	Tony Smith RB	.05	.01
❑ 492	James Washington	.05	.01
❑ 493	Jeff Hostetler	.10	.02
❑ 494	Jeff Chadwick	.05	.01
❑ 495	Kevin Ross	.05	.01
❑ 496	Jim Ritcher	.05	.01
❑ 497	Jessie Hester	.05	.01
❑ 498	Burt Grossman	.05	.01
❑ 499	Keith Van Horne	.05	.01
❑ 500	Gerald Robinson	.05	.01
❑ P1	Promo Panel	5.00	2.00

1994 Fleer

❑	COMPLETE SET (480)	20.00	10.00
❑ 1	Michael Bankston	.05	.01
❑ 2	Steve Beuerlein	.10	.02
❑ 3	John Booty	.05	.01
❑ 4	Rich Camarillo	.05	.01
❑ 5	Chuck Cecil	.05	.01
❑ 6	Larry Centers	.25	.08
❑ 7	Gary Clark	.10	.02
❑ 8	Garrison Hearst	.25	.08
❑ 9	Eric Hill	.05	.01
❑ 10	Randal Hill	.05	.01
❑ 11	Ronald Moore	.05	.01
❑ 12	Ricky Proehl	.05	.01
❑ 13	Luis Sharpe	.05	.01
❑ 14	Clyde Simmons	.05	.01
❑ 15	Tyronne Stowe	.05	.01
❑ 16	Eric Swann	.10	.02
❑ 17	Aeneas Williams	.05	.01
❑ 18	Darion Conner	.05	.01
❑ 19	Moe Gardner	.05	.01
❑ 20	Jumpy Geathers	.05	.01
❑ 21	Jeff George	.25	.08
❑ 22	Roger Harper	.05	.01
❑ 23	Bobby Hebert	.05	.01
❑ 24	Pierce Holt	.05	.01
❑ 25	D.J. Johnson	.05	.01
❑ 26	Mike Kenn	.05	.01
❑ 27	Lincoln Kennedy	.05	.01
❑ 28	Erric Pegram	.05	.01
❑ 29	Mike Pritchard	.05	.01
❑ 30	Andre Rison	.10	.02
❑ 31	Deion Sanders	.50	.20
❑ 32	Tony Smith RB	.05	.01
❑ 33	Jesse Solomon	.05	.01
❑ 34	Jessie Tuggle	.05	.01
❑ 35	Don Beebe	.05	.01
❑ 36	Cornelius Bennett	.10	.02
❑ 37	Bill Brooks	.05	.01
❑ 38	Kenneth Davis	.05	.01
❑ 39	John Fina	.05	.01
❑ 40	Phil Hansen	.05	.01
❑ 41	Kent Hull	.05	.01
❑ 42	Henry Jones	.05	.01
❑ 43	Jim Kelly	.25	.08
❑ 44	Pete Metzelaars	.05	.01
❑ 45	Marvcus Patton	.05	.01
❑ 46	Andre Reed	.10	.02
❑ 47	Frank Reich	.10	.02
❑ 48	Bruce Smith	.25	.08
❑ 49	Thomas Smith	.05	.01
❑ 50	Darryl Talley	.05	.01
❑ 51	Steve Tasker	.10	.02
❑ 52	Thurman Thomas	.25	.08
❑ 53	Jeff Wright	.05	.01
❑ 54	Neal Anderson	.05	.01
❑ 55	Trace Armstrong	.05	.01
❑ 56	Troy Auzenne	.05	.01
❑ 57	Joe Cain RC	.05	.01
❑ 58	Mark Carrier DB	.05	.01
❑ 59	Curtis Conway	.25	.08
❑ 60	Richard Dent	.10	.02
❑ 61	Shaun Gayle	.05	.01
❑ 62	Andy Heck	.05	.01
❑ 63	Dante Jones	.05	.01
❑ 64	Erik Kramer	.10	.02
❑ 65	Steve McMichael	.10	.02
❑ 66	Terry Obee	.05	.01
❑ 67	Vinson Smith	.05	.01
❑ 68	Alonzo Spellman	.05	.01
❑ 69	Tom Waddle	.05	.01
❑ 70	Donnell Woolford	.05	.01
❑ 71	Tim Worley	.05	.01
❑ 72	Chris Zorich	.05	.01
❑ 73	Mike Brim	.05	.01
❑ 74	John Copeland	.05	.01
❑ 75	Derrick Fenner	.05	.01
❑ 76	James Francis	.05	.01
❑ 77	Harold Green	.05	.01
❑ 78	Rod Jones CB	.05	.01
❑ 79	David Klingler	.05	.01
❑ 80	Bruce Kozerski	.05	.01
❑ 81	Tim Krumrie	.05	.01
❑ 82	Ricardo McDonald	.05	.01
❑ 83	Tim McGee	.05	.01
❑ 84	Tony McGee	.05	.01
❑ 85	Louis Oliver	.05	.01
❑ 86	Carl Pickens	.10	.02
❑ 87	Jeff Query	.05	.01
❑ 88	Daniel Stubbs	.05	.01
❑ 89	Steve Tovar	.05	.01
❑ 90	Alfred Williams	.05	.01
❑ 91	Darryl Williams	.05	.01

❑	92 Rob Burnett	.05	.01
❑	93 Mark Carrier WR	.10	.02
❑	94 Leroy Hoard	.05	.01
❑	95 Michael Jackson	.10	.02
❑	96 Mike Johnson	.05	.01
❑	97 Pepper Johnson	.05	.01
❑	98 Tony Jones T	.05	.01
❑	99 Clay Matthews	.05	.01
❑	100 Eric Metcalf	.10	.02
❑	101 Stevon Moore	.05	.01
❑	102 Michael Dean Perry	.10	.02
❑	103 Anthony Pleasant	.05	.01
❑	104 Vinny Testaverde	.10	.02
❑	105 Eric Turner	.05	.01
❑	106 Tommy Vardell	.05	.01
❑	107 Troy Aikman	1.00	.40
❑	108 Larry Brown DB	.05	.01
❑	109 Dixon Edwards	.05	.01
❑	110 Charles Haley	.10	.02
❑	111 Alvin Harper	.10	.02
❑	112 Michael Irvin	.25	.08
❑	113 Jim Jeffcoat	.05	.01
❑	114 Daryl Johnston	.10	.02
❑	115 Leon Lett	.05	.01
❑	116 Russell Maryland	.05	.01
❑	117 Nate Newton	.05	.01
❑	118 Ken Norton Jr.	.10	.02
❑	119 Jay Novacek	.10	.02
❑	120 Darrin Smith	.05	.01
❑	121 Emmitt Smith	1.50	.60
❑	122 Kevin Smith	.05	.01
❑	123 Mark Stepnoski	.05	.01
❑	124 Tony Tolbert	.05	.01
❑	125 Erik Williams	.05	.01
❑	126 Kevin Williams WR	.10	.02
❑	127 Darren Woodson	.10	.02
❑	128 Steve Atwater	.05	.01
❑	129 Rod Bernstine	.05	.01
❑	130 Ray Crockett	.05	.01
❑	131 Mike Croel	.05	.01
❑	132 Robert Delpino	.05	.01
❑	133 Shane Dronett	.05	.01
❑	134 Jason Elam	.10	.02
❑	135 John Elway	2.00	.75
❑	136 Simon Fletcher	.05	.01
❑	137 Greg Kragen	.05	.01
❑	138 Karl Mecklenburg	.05	.01
❑	139 Glyn Milburn	.10	.02
❑	140 Anthony Miller	.10	.02
❑	141 Derek Russell	.05	.01
❑	142 Shannon Sharpe	.10	.02
❑	143 Dennis Smith	.05	.01
❑	144 Dan Williams	.05	.01
❑	145 Gary Zimmerman	.05	.01
❑	146 Bennie Blades	.05	.01
❑	147 Lomas Brown	.05	.01
❑	148 Bill Fralic	.05	.01
❑	149 Mel Gray	.05	.01
❑	150 Willie Green	.05	.01
❑	151 Jason Hanson	.05	.01
❑	152 Robert Massey	.05	.01
❑	153 Ryan McNeil	.05	.01
❑	154 Scott Mitchell	.10	.02
❑	155 Derrick Moore	.05	.01
❑	156 Herman Moore	.25	.08
❑	157 Brett Perriman	.10	.02
❑	158 Robert Porcher	.05	.01
❑	159 Kelvin Pritchett	.05	.01
❑	160 Barry Sanders	1.50	.60
❑	161 Tracy Scroggins	.05	.01
❑	162 Chris Spielman	.10	.02
❑	163 Pat Swilling	.05	.01
❑	164 Edgar Bennett	.25	.08
❑	165 Robert Brooks	.25	.08
❑	166 Terrell Buckley	.05	.01
❑	167 LeRoy Butler	.05	.01
❑	168 Brett Favre	2.00	.75
❑	169 Harry Galbreath	.05	.01
❑	170 Jackie Harris	.05	.01
❑	171 Johnny Holland	.05	.01
❑	172 Chris Jacke	.05	.01
❑	173 George Koonce	.05	.01
❑	174 Bryce Paup	.10	.02
❑	175 Ken Ruettgers	.05	.01
❑	176 Sterling Sharpe	.10	.02
❑	177 Wayne Simmons	.05	.01
❑	178 George Teague	.05	.01
❑	179 Darrell Thompson	.05	.01
❑	180 Reggie White	.25	.08
❑	181 Gary Brown	.05	.01
❑	182 Cody Carlson	.05	.01
❑	183 Ray Childress	.05	.01
❑	184 Cris Dishman	.05	.01
❑	185 Ernest Givins	.10	.02
❑	186 Haywood Jeffires	.10	.02
❑	187 Sean Jones	.05	.01
❑	188 Lamar Lathon	.05	.01
❑	189 Bruce Matthews	.05	.01
❑	190 Bubba McDowell	.05	.01
❑	191 Glenn Montgomery	.05	.01
❑	192 Greg Montgomery	.05	.01
❑	193 Warren Moon	.25	.08
❑	194 Bo Orlando	.05	.01
❑	195 Marcus Robertson	.05	.01
❑	196 Eddie Robinson	.05	.01
❑	197 Webster Slaughter	.05	.01
❑	198 Lorenzo White	.05	.01
❑	199 John Baylor	.05	.01
❑	200 Jason Belser	.05	.01
❑	201 Tony Bennett	.05	.01
❑	202 Dean Biasucci	.05	.01
❑	203 Ray Buchanan	.05	.01
❑	204 Kerry Cash	.05	.01
❑	205 Quentin Coryatt	.05	.01
❑	206 Eugene Daniel	.05	.01
❑	207 Steve Emtman	.05	.01
❑	208 Jon Hand	.05	.01
❑	209 Jim Harbaugh	.25	.08
❑	210 Jeff Herrod	.05	.01
❑	211 Anthony Johnson	.10	.02
❑	212 Roosevelt Potts	.05	.01
❑	213 Rohn Stark	.05	.01
❑	214 Will Wolford	.05	.01
❑	215 Marcus Allen	.25	.08
❑	216 John Alt	.05	.01
❑	217 Kimble Anders	.10	.02
❑	218 J.J. Birden	.05	.01
❑	219 Dale Carter	.05	.01
❑	220 Keith Cash	.05	.01
❑	221 Tony Casillas	.05	.01
❑	222 Willie Davis	.10	.02
❑	223 Tim Grunhard	.05	.01
❑	224 Nick Lowery	.05	.01
❑	225 Charles Mincy	.05	.01
❑	226 Joe Montana	2.00	.75
❑	227 Dan Saleaumua	.05	.01
❑	228 Tracy Simien	.05	.01
❑	229 Neil Smith	.10	.02
❑	230 Derrick Thomas	.25	.08
❑	231 Eddie Anderson	.05	.01
❑	232 Tim Brown	.25	.08
❑	233 Nolan Harrison	.05	.01
❑	234 Jeff Hostetler	.10	.02
❑	235 Rocket Ismail	.10	.02
❑	236 Jeff Jaeger	.05	.01
❑	237 James Jett	.05	.01
❑	238 Joe Kelly	.05	.01
❑	239 Albert Lewis	.05	.01
❑	240 Terry McDaniel	.05	.01
❑	241 Chester McGlockton	.05	.01
❑	242 Winston Moss	.05	.01
❑	243 Gerald Perry	.05	.01
❑	244 Greg Robinson	.05	.01
❑	245 Anthony Smith	.05	.01
❑	246 Steve Smith	.05	.01
❑	247 Greg Townsend	.05	.01
❑	248 Lionel Washington	.05	.01
❑	249 Steve Wisniewski	.05	.01
❑	250 Alexander Wright	.05	.01
❑	251 Flipper Anderson	.05	.01
❑	252 Jerome Bettis	.50	.20
❑	253 Marc Boutte	.05	.01
❑	254 Shane Conlan	.05	.01
❑	255 Troy Drayton	.05	.01
❑	256 Henry Ellard	.10	.02
❑	257 Sean Gilbert	.05	.01
❑	258 Nate Lewis	.05	.01
❑	259 Todd Lyght	.05	.01
❑	260 Chris Miller	.05	.01
❑	261 Anthony Newman	.05	.01
❑	262 Roman Phifer	.05	.01
❑	263 Henry Rolling	.05	.01
❑	264 T.J.Rubley RC	.05	.01
❑	265 Jackie Slater	.05	.01
❑	266 Fred Stokes	.05	.01
❑	267 Robert Young	.05	.01
❑	268 Gene Atkins	.05	.01
❑	269 J.B. Brown	.05	.01
❑	270 Keith Byars	.05	.01
❑	271 Marco Coleman	.05	.01
❑	272 Bryan Cox	.05	.01
❑	273 Jeff Cross	.05	.01
❑	274 Irving Fryar	.10	.02
❑	275 Mark Higgs	.05	.01
❑	276 Dwight Hollier	.05	.01
❑	277 Mark Ingram	.05	.01
❑	278 Keith Jackson	.05	.01
❑	279 Terry Kirby	.25	.08
❑	280 Bernie Kosar	.10	.02
❑	281 Dan Marino	2.00	.75
❑	282 O.J.McDuffie	.25	.08
❑	283 Keith Sims	.05	.01
❑	284 Pete Stoyanovich	.05	.01
❑	285 Troy Vincent	.05	.01
❑	286 Richmond Webb	.05	.01
❑	287 Terry Allen	.10	.02
❑	288 Anthony Carter	.10	.02
❑	289 Cris Carter	.50	.20
❑	290 Jack Del Rio	.05	.01
❑	291 Chris Doleman	.05	.01
❑	292 Vencie Glenn	.05	.01
❑	293 Scottie Graham RC	.10	.02
❑	294 Chris Hinton	.05	.01
❑	295 Qadry Ismail	.25	.08
❑	296 Carlos Jenkins	.05	.01
❑	297 Steve Jordan	.05	.01
❑	298 Carl Lee	.05	.01
❑	299 Randall McDaniel	.05	.01
❑	300 John Randle	.10	.02
❑	301 Todd Scott	.05	.01
❑	302 Robert Smith	.25	.08
❑	303 Fred Strickland	.05	.01
❑	304 Henry Thomas	.05	.01
❑	305 Bruce Armstrong	.05	.01
❑	306 Harlon Barnett	.05	.01
❑	307 Drew Bledsoe	.75	.30
❑	308 Vincent Brown	.05	.01
❑	309 Ben Coates	.10	.02
❑	310 Todd Collins	.05	.01
❑	311 Myron Guyton	.05	.01
❑	312 Pat Harlow	.05	.01
❑	313 Maurice Hurst	.05	.01
❑	314 Leonard Russell	.05	.01
❑	315 Chris Slade	.05	.01
❑	316 Michael Timpson	.05	.01
❑	317 Andre Tippett	.05	.01
❑	318 Morten Andersen	.05	.01
❑	319 Derek Brown RBK	.05	.01
❑	320 Vince Buck	.05	.01
❑	321 Toi Cook	.05	.01
❑	322 Quinn Early	.10	.02
❑	323 Jim Everett	.10	.02
❑	324 Michael Haynes	.10	.02
❑	325 Tyrone Hughes	.10	.02
❑	326 Rickey Jackson	.05	.01
❑	327 Vaughan Johnson	.05	.01
❑	328 Eric Martin	.05	.01
❑	329 Wayne Martin	.05	.01
❑	330 Sam Mills	.05	.01
❑	331 Willie Roaf	.05	.01

❑ 332 Irv Smith .05 .01
❑ 333 Keith Taylor .05 .01
❑ 334 Renaldo Turnbull .05 .01
❑ 335 Carlton Bailey .05 .01
❑ 336 Michael Brooks .05 .01
❑ 337 Jarrod Bunch .05 .01
❑ 338 Chris Calloway .05 .01
❑ 339 Mark Collins .05 .01
❑ 340 Howard Cross .05 .01
❑ 341 Stacey Dillard RC .05 .01
❑ 342 John Elliott .05 .01
❑ 343 Rodney Hampton .10 .02
❑ 344 Greg Jackson .05 .01
❑ 345 Mark Jackson .05 .01
❑ 346 Dave Meggett .05 .01
❑ 347 Corey Miller .05 .01
❑ 348 Mike Sherrard .05 .01
❑ 349 Phil Simms .10 .02
❑ 350 Lewis Tillman .05 .01
❑ 351 Brad Baxter .05 .01
❑ 352 Kyle Clifton .05 .01
❑ 353 Boomer Esiason .10 .02
❑ 354 James Hasty .05 .01
❑ 355 Bobby Houston .05 .01
❑ 356 Johnny Johnson .05 .01
❑ 357 Jeff Lageman .05 .01
❑ 358 Mo Lewis .05 .01
❑ 359 Ronnie Lott .10 .02
❑ 360 Leonard Marshall .05 .01
❑ 361 Johnny Mitchell .05 .01
❑ 362 Rob Moore .10 .02
❑ 363 Eric Thomas .05 .01
❑ 364 Brian Washington .05 .01
❑ 365 Marvin Washington .05 .01
❑ 366 Eric Allen .05 .01
❑ 367 Fred Barnett .10 .02
❑ 368 Bubby Brister .05 .01
❑ 369 Randall Cunningham .25 .08
❑ 370 Byron Evans .05 .01
❑ 371 William Fuller .05 .01
❑ 372 Andy Harmon .05 .01
❑ 373 Seth Joyner .05 .01
❑ 374 William Perry .10 .02
❑ 375 Leonard Renfro .05 .01
❑ 376 Heath Sherman .05 .01
❑ 377 Ben Smith .05 .01
❑ 378 William Thomas .05 .01
❑ 379 Herschel Walker .10 .02
❑ 380 Calvin Williams .10 .02
❑ 381 Chad Brown .05 .01
❑ 382 Dermontti Dawson .05 .01
❑ 383 Deon Figures .05 .01
❑ 384 Barry Foster .05 .01
❑ 385 Jeff Graham .05 .01
❑ 386 Eric Green .05 .01
❑ 387 Kevin Greene .10 .02
❑ 388 Carlton Haselrig .05 .01
❑ 389 Levon Kirkland .05 .01
❑ 390 Carnell Lake .05 .01
❑ 391 Greg Lloyd .10 .02
❑ 392 Neil O'Donnell .25 .08
❑ 393 Darren Perry .05 .01
❑ 394 Dwight Stone .05 .01
❑ 395 Leroy Thompson .05 .01
❑ 396 Rod Woodson .10 .02
❑ 397 Marion Butts .05 .01
❑ 398 John Carney .05 .01
❑ 399 Darren Carrington .05 .01
❑ 400 Burt Grossman .05 .01
❑ 401 Courtney Hall .05 .01
❑ 402 Ronnie Harmon .05 .01
❑ 403 Stan Humphries .10 .02
❑ 404 Shawn Jefferson .05 .01
❑ 405 Vance Johnson .05 .01
❑ 406 Chris Mims .05 .01
❑ 407 Leslie O'Neal .05 .01
❑ 408 Stanley Richard .05 .01
❑ 409 Junior Seau .25 .08
❑ 410 Harris Barton .05 .01
❑ 411 Dennis Brown .05 .01
❑ 412 Eric Davis .05 .01
❑ 413 Merton Hanks .10 .02
❑ 414 John Johnson .05 .01
❑ 415 Brent Jones .10 .02
❑ 416 Marc Logan .05 .01
❑ 417 Tim McDonald .05 .01
❑ 418 Gary Plummer .05 .01
❑ 419 Tom Rathman .05 .01
❑ 420 Jerry Rice 1.00 .40
❑ 421 Bill Romanowski .05 .01
❑ 422 Jesse Sapolu .05 .01
❑ 423 Dana Stubblefield .10 .02
❑ 424 John Taylor .10 .02
❑ 425 Steve Wallace .05 .01
❑ 426 Ted Washington .05 .01
❑ 427 Ricky Watters .10 .02
❑ 428 Troy Wilson RC .05 .01
❑ 429 Steve Young .75 .30
❑ 430 Howard Ballard .05 .01
❑ 431 Michael Bates .05 .01
❑ 432 Robert Blackmon .05 .01
❑ 433 Brian Blades .10 .02
❑ 434 Ferrell Edmunds .05 .01
❑ 435 Carlton Gray .05 .01
❑ 436 Patrick Hunter .05 .01
❑ 437 Cortez Kennedy .10 .02
❑ 438 Kelvin Martin .05 .01
❑ 439 Rick Mirer .25 .08
❑ 440 Nate Odomes .05 .01
❑ 441 Ray Roberts .05 .01
❑ 442 Eugene Robinson .05 .01
❑ 443 Rod Stephens .05 .01
❑ 444 Chris Warren .10 .02
❑ 445 John L. Williams .05 .01
❑ 446 Terry Wooden .05 .01
❑ 447 Marty Carter .05 .01
❑ 448 Reggie Cobb .05 .01
❑ 449 Lawrence Dawsey .05 .01
❑ 450 Santana Dotson .10 .02
❑ 451 Craig Erickson .05 .01
❑ 452 Thomas Everett .05 .01
❑ 453 Paul Gruber .05 .01
❑ 454 Courtney Hawkins .05 .01
❑ 455 Martin Mayhew .05 .01
❑ 456 Hardy Nickerson .10 .02
❑ 457 Ricky Reynolds .05 .01
❑ 458 Vince Workman .05 .01
❑ 459 Reggie Brooks .10 .02
❑ 460 Earnest Byner .05 .01
❑ 461 Andre Collins .05 .01
❑ 462 Brad Edwards .05 .01
❑ 463 Kurt Gouveia .05 .01
❑ 464 Darrell Green .05 .01
❑ 465 Ken Harvey .05 .01
❑ 466 Ethan Horton .05 .01
❑ 467 A.J. Johnson .05 .01
❑ 468 Tim Johnson .05 .01
❑ 469 Jim Lachey .05 .01
❑ 470 Chip Lohmiller .05 .01
❑ 471 Art Monk .10 .02
❑ 472 Sterling Palmer RC .05 .01
❑ 473 Mark Rypien .05 .01
❑ 474 Ricky Sanders .05 .01
❑ 475 Checklist 1-106 .05 .01
❑ 476 Checklist 107-214 .05 .01
❑ 477 Checklist 215-317 .05 .01
❑ 478 Checklist 318-409 .05 .01
❑ 479 Checklist 410-480/Inserts .05 .01
❑ 480 Inserts Checklist .05 .01
❑ P244 Jerome Bettis Promo 1.00 .40

1995 Fleer

❑ COMPLETE SET (400) 25.00 10.00
❑ 1 Michael Bankston .10 .02
❑ 2 Larry Centers .20 .07
❑ 3 Gary Clark .10 .02
❑ 4 Eric Hill .10 .02
❑ 5 Seth Joyner .10 .02
❑ 6 Dave Krieg .10 .02
❑ 7 Lorenzo Lynch .10 .02 
❑ 8 Jamir Miller .10 .02
❑ 9 Ronald Moore .10 .02
❑ 10 Ricky Proehl .10 .02
❑ 11 Clyde Simmons .10 .02
❑ 12 Eric Swann .20 .07
❑ 13 Aeneas Williams .10 .02
❑ 14 J.J. Birden .10 .02
❑ 15 Chris Doleman .10 .02
❑ 16 Bert Emanuel .30 .10
❑ 17 Jumpy Geathers .10 .02
❑ 18 Jeff George .20 .07
❑ 19 Roger Harper .10 .02
❑ 20 Craig Heyward .20 .07
❑ 21 Pierce Holt .10 .02
❑ 22 D.J. Johnson .10 .02
❑ 23 Terance Mathis .20 .07
❑ 24 Clay Matthews .20 .07
❑ 25 Andre Rison .20 .07
❑ 26 Chuck Smith .10 .02
❑ 27 Jessie Tuggle .10 .02
❑ 28 Cornelius Bennett .20 .07
❑ 29 Bucky Brooks .10 .02
❑ 30 Jeff Burris .10 .02
❑ 31 Russell Copeland .10 .02
❑ 32 Matt Darby .10 .02
❑ 33 Phil Hansen .10 .02
❑ 34 Henry Jones .10 .02
❑ 35 Jim Kelly .30 .10
❑ 36 Mark Maddox RC .10 .02
❑ 37 Bryce Paup .20 .07
❑ 38 Andre Reed .20 .07
❑ 39 Bruce Smith .30 .10
❑ 40 Darryl Talley .10 .02
❑ 41 Dewell Brewer RC .10 .02
❑ 42 Mike Fox .10 .02
❑ 43 Eric Guliford .10 .02
❑ 44 Lamar Lathon .10 .02
❑ 45 Pete Metzelaars .10 .02
❑ 46 Sam Mills .20 .07
❑ 47 Frank Reich .10 .02
❑ 48 Rod Smith DB .20 .07
❑ 49 Jack Trudeau .10 .02
❑ 50 Trace Armstrong .10 .02
❑ 51 Joe Cain .10 .02
❑ 52 Mark Carrier DB .10 .02
❑ 53 Curtis Conway .30 .10
❑ 54 Shaun Gayle .10 .02
❑ 55 Jeff Graham .10 .02
❑ 56 Raymont Harris .10 .02
❑ 57 Erik Kramer .10 .02
❑ 58 Lewis Tillman .10 .02
❑ 59 Tom Waddle .10 .02
❑ 60 Steve Walsh .10 .02
❑ 61 Donnell Woolford .10 .02
❑ 62 Chris Zorich .10 .02
❑ 63 Jeff Blake RC .60 .25
❑ 64 Mike Brim .10 .02
❑ 65 Steve Broussard .10 .02
❑ 66 James Francis .10 .02
❑ 67 Ricardo McDonald .10 .02
❑ 68 Tony McGee .10 .02
❑ 70 Darnay Scott .20 .07
❑ 71 Steve Tovar .10 .02
❑ 72 Dan Wilkinson .20 .07

	Card	Player	Price 1	Price 2
❑	73	Alfred Williams	.10	.02
❑	74	Darryl Williams	.10	.02
❑	75	Derrick Alexander WR	.30	.10
❑	76	Randy Baldwin	.10	.02
❑	77	Carl Banks	.10	.02
❑	78	Rob Burnett	.10	.02
❑	79	Steve Everitt	.10	.02
❑	80	Leroy Hoard	.10	.02
❑	81	Michael Jackson	.20	.07
❑	82	Pepper Johnson	.10	.02
❑	83	Tony Jones T	.10	.02
❑	84	Antonio Langham	.10	.02
❑	85	Eric Metcalf	.20	.07
❑	86	Stevon Moore	.10	.02
❑	87	Anthony Pleasant	.10	.02
❑	88	Vinny Testaverde	.20	.07
❑	89	Eric Turner	.10	.02
❑	90	Troy Aikman	1.00	.40
❑	91	Charles Haley	.20	.07
❑	92	Michael Irvin	.30	.10
❑	93	Daryl Johnston	.20	.07
❑	94	Robert Jones	.10	.02
❑	95	Leon Lett	.10	.02
❑	96	Russell Maryland	.10	.02
❑	97	Nate Newton	.20	.07
❑	98	Jay Novacek	.20	.07
❑	99	Darrin Smith	.10	.02
❑	100	Emmitt Smith	1.50	.60
❑	101	Kevin Smith	.10	.02
❑	102	Erik Williams	.10	.02
❑	103	Kevin Williams WR	.20	.07
❑	104	Darren Woodson	.20	.07
❑	105	Elijah Alexander	.10	.02
❑	106	Steve Atwater	.10	.02
❑	107	Ray Crockett	.10	.02
❑	108	Shane Dronett	.10	.02
❑	109	Jason Elam	.20	.07
❑	110	John Elway	2.00	.75
❑	111	Simon Fletcher	.10	.02
❑	112	Glyn Milburn	.10	.02
❑	113	Anthony Miller	.20	.07
❑	114	Michael Dean Perry	.10	.02
❑	115	Mike Pritchard	.10	.02
❑	116	Derek Russell	.10	.02
❑	117	Leonard Russell	.10	.02
❑	118	Shannon Sharpe	.20	.07
❑	119	Gary Zimmerman	.10	.02
❑	120	Bennie Blades	.10	.02
❑	121	Lomas Brown	.10	.02
❑	122	Willie Clay	.10	.02
❑	123	Mike Johnson	.10	.02
❑	124	Robert Massey	.10	.02
❑	125	Scott Mitchell	.20	.07
❑	126	Herman Moore	.30	.10
❑	127	Brett Perriman	.20	.07
❑	128	Robert Porcher	.10	.02
❑	129	Barry Sanders	1.50	.60
❑	130	Chris Spielman	.20	.07
❑	131	Henry Thomas	.10	.02
❑	132	Edgar Bennett	.20	.07
❑	134	LeRoy Butler	.10	.02
❑	135	Brett Favre	2.00	.75
❑	136	Sean Jones	.10	.02
❑	137	John Jurkovic	.10	.02
❑	138	George Koonce	.10	.02
❑	139	Wayne Simmons	.10	.02
❑	140	George Teague	.10	.02
❑	141	Reggie White	.30	.10
❑	142	Micheal Barrow	.10	.02
❑	143	Gary Brown	.10	.02
❑	144	Cody Carlson	.10	.02
❑	145	Ray Childress	.10	.02
❑	146	Cris Dishman	.10	.02
❑	147	Ernest Givins	.10	.02
❑	148	Mel Gray	.10	.02
❑	149	Darryll Lewis	.10	.02
❑	150	Bruce Matthews	.10	.02
❑	151	Marcus Robertson	.10	.02
❑	152	Webster Slaughter	.10	.02
❑	153	Al Smith	.10	.02
❑	154	Mark Stepnoski	.10	.02
❑	155	Trev Alberts	.10	.02
❑	156	Flipper Anderson	.10	.02
❑	157	Jason Belser	.10	.02
❑	158	Tony Bennett	.10	.02
❑	159	Ray Buchanan	.10	.02
❑	160	Quentin Coryatt	.20	.07
❑	161	Sean Dawkins	.20	.07
❑	162	Steve Emtman	.10	.02
❑	163	Marshall Faulk	1.25	.50
❑	164	Stephen Grant RC	.10	.02
❑	165	Jim Harbaugh	.20	.07
❑	166	Jeff Herrod	.10	.02
❑	167	Tony Siragusa	.10	.02
❑	168	Steve Beuerlein	.20	.07
❑	169	Darren Carrington	.10	.02
❑	170	Reggie Cobb	.10	.02
❑	171	Kelvin Martin	.10	.02
❑	172	Kelvin Pritchett	.10	.02
❑	173	Joel Smeenge	.10	.02
❑	174	James Williams LB	.10	.02
❑	175	Marcus Allen	.30	.10
❑	176	Kimble Anders	.20	.07
❑	177	Dale Carter	.20	.07
❑	178	Mark Collins	.10	.02
❑	179	Willie Davis	.20	.07
❑	180	Lake Dawson	.20	.07
❑	181	Greg Hill	.20	.07
❑	182	Darren Mickell	.10	.02
❑	183	Joe Montana	2.00	.75
❑	184	Tracy Simien	.10	.02
❑	185	Neil Smith	.20	.07
❑	186	William White	.10	.02
❑	187	Greg Biekert	.10	.02
❑	188	Tim Brown	.30	.10
❑	189	Rob Fredrickson	.10	.02
❑	190	Andrew Glover RC	.10	.02
❑	191	Nolan Harrison	.10	.02
❑	192	Jeff Hostetler	.20	.07
❑	193	Rocket Ismail	.20	.07
❑	194	Terry McDaniel	.10	.02
❑	195	Chester McGlockton	.20	.07
❑	196	Winston Moss	.10	.02
❑	197	Anthony Smith	.10	.02
❑	198	Harvey Williams	.10	.02
❑	199	Steve Wisniewski	.10	.02
❑	200	Johnny Bailey	.10	.02
❑	201	Jerome Bettis	.30	.10
❑	202	Isaac Bruce	.50	.20
❑	203	Shane Conlan	.10	.02
❑	204	Troy Drayton	.10	.02
❑	205	Sean Gilbert	.20	.07
❑	206	Jessie Hester	.10	.02
❑	207	Jimmie Jones	.10	.02
❑	208	Todd Lyght	.10	.02
❑	209	Chris Miller	.10	.02
❑	210	Roman Phifer	.10	.02
❑	211	Marquez Pope	.10	.02
❑	212	Robert Young	.10	.02
❑	213	Gene Atkins	.10	.02
❑	214	Aubrey Beavers	.10	.02
❑	215	Tim Bowens	.10	.02
❑	216	Bryan Cox	.10	.02
❑	217	Jeff Cross	.10	.02
❑	218	Irving Fryar	.20	.07
❑	219	Eric Green	.10	.02
❑	220	Mark Ingram	.10	.02
❑	221	Terry Kirby	.20	.07
❑	222	Dan Marino	2.00	.75
❑	223	O.J. McDuffie	.30	.10
❑	224	Bernie Parmalee	.20	.07
❑	225	Keith Sims	.10	.02
❑	226	Irving Spikes	.20	.07
❑	227	Michael Stewart	.10	.02
❑	228	Troy Vincent	.10	.02
❑	229	Richmond Webb	.10	.02
❑	230	Terry Allen	.20	.07
❑	231	Cris Carter	.30	.10
❑	232	Jack Del Rio	.10	.02
❑	233	Vencie Glenn	.10	.02
❑	234	Qadry Ismail	.20	.07
❑	235	Carlos Jenkins	.10	.02
❑	236	Ed McDaniel	.10	.02
❑	237	Randall McDaniel	.10	.02
❑	238	Warren Moon	.20	.07
❑	239	Anthony Parker	.10	.02
❑	240	John Randle	.20	.07
❑	241	Jake Reed	.20	.07
❑	242	Fuad Reveiz	.10	.02
❑	243	Broderick Thomas	.10	.02
❑	244	Dewayne Washington	.20	.07
❑	245	Bruce Armstrong	.10	.02
❑	246	Drew Bledsoe	.60	.25
❑	247	Vincent Brisby	.10	.02
❑	248	Vincent Brown	.10	.02
❑	249	Marion Butts	.10	.02
❑	250	Ben Coates	.20	.07
❑	251	Tim Goad	.10	.02
❑	252	Myron Guyton	.10	.02
❑	253	Maurice Hurst	.10	.02
❑	254	Mike Jones	.10	.02
❑	255	Willie McGinest	.20	.07
❑	256	Dave Meggett	.10	.02
❑	257	Ricky Reynolds	.10	.02
❑	258	Chris Slade	.20	.07
❑	259	Michael Timpson	.10	.02
❑	260	Mario Bates	.20	.07
❑	261	Derek Brown RBK	.10	.02
❑	262	Darion Conner	.10	.02
❑	263	Quinn Early	.20	.07
❑	264	Jim Everett	.10	.02
❑	265	Michael Haynes	.20	.07
❑	266	Tyrone Hughes	.20	.07
❑	267	Joe Johnson	.10	.02
❑	268	Wayne Martin	.10	.02
❑	269	Willie Roaf	.10	.02
❑	270	Irv Smith	.10	.02
❑	271	Jimmy Spencer	.10	.02
❑	272	Winfred Tubbs	.10	.02
❑	273	Renaldo Turnbull	.10	.02
❑	274	Michael Brooks	.10	.02
❑	275	Dave Brown	.20	.07
❑	276	Chris Calloway	.10	.02
❑	277	Jesse Campbell	.10	.02
❑	278	Howard Cross	.10	.02
❑	279	John Elliott	.10	.02
❑	280	Keith Hamilton	.10	.02
❑	281	Rodney Hampton	.20	.07
❑	282	Thomas Lewis	.20	.07
❑	283	Thomas Randolph	.10	.02
❑	284	Mike Sherrard	.10	.02
❑	285	Michael Strahan	.30	.10
❑	286	Brad Baxter	.10	.02
❑	287	Tony Casillas	.10	.02
❑	288	Kyle Clifton	.10	.02
❑	289	Boomer Esiason	.20	.07
❑	290	Aaron Glenn	.10	.02
❑	291	Bobby Houston	.10	.02
❑	292	Johnny Johnson	.10	.02
❑	293	Jeff Lageman	.10	.02
❑	294	Mo Lewis	.10	.02
❑	295	Johnny Mitchell	.10	.02
❑	296	Rob Moore	.20	.07
❑	297	Marcus Turner	.10	.02
❑	298	Marvin Washington	.10	.02
❑	299	Eric Allen	.10	.02
❑	300	Fred Barnett	.20	.07
❑	301	Randall Cunningham	.30	.10
❑	302	Byron Evans	.10	.02
❑	303	William Fuller	.10	.02
❑	304	Charlie Garner	.30	.10
❑	305	Andy Harmon	.10	.02
❑	306	Greg Jackson	.10	.02
❑	307	Bill Romanowski	.10	.02
❑	308	William Thomas	.10	.02
❑	309	Herschel Walker	.20	.07
❑	310	Calvin Williams	.20	.07
❑	311	Michael Zordich	.10	.02
❑	312	Chad Brown	.20	.07
❑	313	Dermontti Dawson	.20	.07

❑ 314 Barry Foster .20 .07
❑ 315 Kevin Greene .20 .07
❑ 316 Charles Johnson .20 .07
❑ 317 Levon Kirkland .10 .02
❑ 318 Carnell Lake .10 .02
❑ 319 Greg Lloyd .20 .07
❑ 320 Byron Bam Morris .10 .02
❑ 321 Neil O'Donnell .20 .07
❑ 322 Darren Perry .10 .02
❑ 323 Ray Seals .10 .02
❑ 324 John L. Williams .10 .02
❑ 325 Rod Woodson .20 .07
❑ 326 John Carney .10 .02
❑ 327 Andre Coleman .10 .02
❑ 328 Courtney Hall .10 .02
❑ 329 Ronnie Harmon .10 .02
❑ 330 Dwayne Harper .10 .02
❑ 331 Stan Humphries .20 .07
❑ 332 Shawn Jefferson .10 .02
❑ 333 Tony Martin .20 .07
❑ 334 Natrone Means .20 .07
❑ 335 Chris Mims .10 .02
❑ 336 Leslie O'Neal .20 .07
❑ 337 Alfred Pupunu RC .10 .02
❑ 338 Junior Seau .30 .10
❑ 339 Mark Seay .20 .07
❑ 340 Eric Davis .10 .02
❑ 341 William Floyd .20 .07
❑ 342 Merton Hanks .10 .02
❑ 343 Rickey Jackson .10 .02
❑ 344 Brent Jones .10 .02
❑ 345 Tim McDonald .10 .02
❑ 346 Ken Norton Jr. .20 .07
❑ 347 Gary Plummer .10 .02
❑ 348 Jerry Rice 1.00 .40
❑ 349 Deion Sanders .40 .15
❑ 350 Jesse Sapolu .10 .02
❑ 351 Dana Stubblefield .20 .07
❑ 352 John Taylor .10 .02
❑ 353 Steve Wallace .10 .02
❑ 354 Ricky Watters .20 .07
❑ 355 Lee Woodall .10 .02
❑ 356 Bryant Young .20 .07
❑ 357 Steve Young .75 .30
❑ 358 Sam Adams .10 .02
❑ 359 Howard Ballard .10 .02
❑ 360 Robert Blackmon .10 .02
❑ 361 Brian Blades .20 .07
❑ 362 Carlton Gray .10 .02
❑ 363 Cortez Kennedy .20 .07
❑ 364 Rick Mirer .20 .07
❑ 365 Eugene Robinson .10 .02
❑ 366 Chris Warren .20 .07
❑ 367 Terry Wooden .10 .02
❑ 368 Brad Culpepper .10 .02
❑ 369 Lawrence Dawsey .10 .02
❑ 370 Trent Dilfer .30 .10
❑ 371 Santana Dotson .10 .02
❑ 372 Craig Erickson .10 .02
❑ 373 Thomas Everett .10 .02
❑ 374 Paul Gruber .10 .02
❑ 375 Alvin Harper .10 .02
❑ 376 Jackie Harris .10 .02
❑ 377 Courtney Hawkins .10 .02
❑ 378 Martin Mayhew .10 .02
❑ 379 Hardy Nickerson .10 .02
❑ 380 Errict Rhett .20 .07
❑ 381 Charles Wilson .10 .02
❑ 382 Reggie Brooks .20 .07
❑ 383 Tom Carter .10 .02
❑ 384 Andre Collins .10 .02
❑ 385 Henry Ellard .20 .07
❑ 386 Ricky Ervins .10 .02
❑ 387 Darrell Green .10 .02
❑ 388 Ken Harvey .10 .02
❑ 389 Brian Mitchell .10 .02
❑ 390 Stanley Richard .10 .02
❑ 391 Heath Shuler .20 .07
❑ 392 Rod Stephens .10 .02
❑ 393 Tyronne Stowe .10 .02
❑ 394 Tydus Winans .10 .02
❑ 395 Tony Woods .10 .02
❑ 396 Checklist .10 .02
❑ 397 Checklist .10 .02
❑ 398 Checklist .10 .02
❑ 399 Checklist .10 .02
❑ 400 Checklist .10 .02
❑ P1 Promo Panel/Bettis/Mirer/R.Brooks 2.50 1.00

1996 Fleer

❑ COMPLETE SET (200) 20.00 7.50
❑ 1 Garrison Hearst .20 .07
❑ 2 Rob Moore .20 .07
❑ 3 Frank Sanders .20 .07
❑ 4 Eric Swann .10 .02
❑ 5 Aeneas Williams .10 .02
❑ 6 Jeff George .20 .07
❑ 7 Craig Heyward .10 .02
❑ 8 Terance Mathis .10 .02
❑ 9 Eric Metcalf .10 .02
❑ 10 Michael Jackson .20 .07
❑ 11 Andre Rison .20 .07
❑ 12 Vinny Testaverde .20 .07
❑ 13 Eric Turner .10 .02
❑ 14 Darick Holmes .10 .02
❑ 15 Jim Kelly .30 .10
❑ 16 Bryce Paup .10 .02
❑ 17 Bruce Smith .20 .07
❑ 18 Thurman Thomas .30 .10
❑ 19 Kerry Collins .30 .10
❑ 20 Lamar Lathon .10 .02
❑ 21 Derrick Moore .10 .02
❑ 22 Tyrone Poole .10 .02
❑ 23 Curtis Conway .30 .10
❑ 24 Bryan Cox .10 .02
❑ 25 Erik Kramer .10 .02
❑ 26 Rashaan Salaam .20 .07
❑ 27 Jeff Blake .30 .10
❑ 28 Ki-Jana Carter .20 .07
❑ 29 Carl Pickens .20 .07
❑ 30 Darnay Scott .20 .07
❑ 31 Troy Aikman .75 .30
❑ 32 Charles Haley .20 .07
❑ 33 Michael Irvin .30 .10
❑ 34 Daryl Johnston .20 .07
❑ 35 Jay Novacek .10 .02
❑ 36 Deion Sanders .40 .15
❑ 37 Emmitt Smith 1.25 .50
❑ 38 Steve Atwater .10 .02
❑ 39 Terrell Davis .60 .25
❑ 40 John Elway 1.50 .60
❑ 41 Anthony Miller .20 .07
❑ 42 Shannon Sharpe .20 .07
❑ 43 Scott Mitchell .20 .07
❑ 44 Herman Moore .20 .07
❑ 45 Johnnie Morton .20 .07
❑ 46 Brett Perriman .10 .02
❑ 47 Barry Sanders 1.25 .50
❑ 48 Edgar Bennett .20 .07
❑ 49 Robert Brooks .30 .10
❑ 50 Mark Chmura .20 .07
❑ 51 Brett Favre 1.50 .60
❑ 52 Reggie White .30 .10
❑ 53 Mel Gray .10 .02
❑ 54 Steve McNair .60 .25
❑ 55 Chris Sanders .20 .07
❑ 56 Rodney Thomas .10 .02
❑ 57 Quentin Coryatt .10 .02
❑ 58 Sean Dawkins .10 .02
❑ 59 Ken Dilger .20 .07
❑ 60 Marshall Faulk .40 .15
❑ 61 Jim Harbaugh .20 .07
❑ 62 Tony Boselli .10 .02
❑ 63 Mark Brunell .50 .20
❑ 64 Natrone Means .20 .07
❑ 65 James O.Stewart .20 .07
❑ 66 Marcus Allen .30 .10
❑ 67 Steve Bono .10 .02
❑ 68 Neil Smith .20 .07
❑ 69 Derrick Thomas .30 .10
❑ 70 Tamarick Vanover .20 .07
❑ 71 Fred Barnett .10 .02
❑ 72 Eric Green .10 .02
❑ 73 Dan Marino 1.50 .60
❑ 74 O.J. McDuffie .20 .07
❑ 75 Bernie Parmalee .10 .02
❑ 76 Cris Carter .30 .10
❑ 77 Qadry Ismail .20 .07
❑ 78 Warren Moon .20 .07
❑ 79 Jake Reed .20 .07
❑ 80 Robert Smith .20 .07
❑ 81 Drew Bledsoe .50 .20
❑ 82 Vincent Brisby .10 .02
❑ 83 Ben Coates .20 .07
❑ 84 Curtis Martin .60 .25
❑ 85 Dave Meggett .10 .02
❑ 86 Mario Bates .20 .07
❑ 87 Jim Everett .10 .02
❑ 88 Michael Haynes .10 .02
❑ 89 Renaldo Turnbull .10 .02
❑ 90 Dave Brown .10 .02
❑ 91 Rodney Hampton .20 .07
❑ 92 Thomas Lewis .10 .02
❑ 93 Tyrone Wheatley .20 .07
❑ 94 Kyle Brady .10 .02
❑ 95 Hugh Douglas .20 .07
❑ 96 Aaron Glenn .10 .02
❑ 97 Jeff Graham .10 .02
❑ 98 Adrian Murrell .20 .07
❑ 99 Neil O'Donnell .20 .07
❑ 100 Tim Brown .30 .10
❑ 101 Jeff Hostetler .10 .02
❑ 102 Napoleon Kaufman .30 .10
❑ 103 Chester McGlockton .10 .02
❑ 104 Harvey Williams .10 .02
❑ 105 William Fuller .10 .02
❑ 106 Charlie Garner .20 .07
❑ 107 Ricky Watters .20 .07
❑ 108 Calvin Williams .10 .02
❑ 109 Jerome Bettis .30 .10
❑ 110 Greg Lloyd .20 .07
❑ 111 Byron Bam Morris .10 .02
❑ 112 Kordell Stewart .30 .10
❑ 113 Yancey Thigpen .20 .07
❑ 114 Rod Woodson .20 .07
❑ 115 Isaac Bruce .30 .10
❑ 116 Troy Drayton .10 .02
❑ 117 Leslie O'Neal .10 .02
❑ 118 Steve Walsh .10 .02
❑ 119 Marco Coleman .10 .02
❑ 120 Aaron Hayden .10 .02
❑ 121 Stan Humphries .20 .07
❑ 122 Junior Seau .30 .10
❑ 123 William Floyd .20 .07
❑ 124 Brent Jones .10 .02
❑ 125 Ken Norton .10 .02
❑ 126 Jerry Rice .75 .30
❑ 127 J.J. Stokes .30 .10
❑ 128 Steve Young .60 .25
❑ 129 Brian Blades .10 .02
❑ 130 Joey Galloway .30 .10
❑ 131 Rick Mirer .20 .07
❑ 132 Chris Warren .20 .07
❑ 133 Trent Dilfer .30 .10

❑	134	Alvin Harper	.10	.02
❑	135	Hardy Nickerson	.10	.02
❑	136	Errict Rhett	.20	.07
❑	137	Terry Allen	.20	.07
❑	138	Henry Ellard	.10	.02
❑	139	Heath Shuler	.20	.07
❑	140	Michael Westbrook	.30	.10
❑	141	Karim Abdul-Jabbar RC	.30	.10
❑	142	Mike Alstott RC	1.00	.40
❑	143	Marco Battaglia RC	.10	.02
❑	144	Tim Biakabutuka RC	.30	.10
❑	145	Tony Brackens RC	.30	.10
❑	146	Duane Clemons RC	.10	.02
❑	147	Ernie Conwell RC	.10	.02
❑	148	Chris Darkins RC	.10	.02
❑	149	Stephen Davis RC	1.50	.60
❑	150	Brian Dawkins RC	1.25	.50
❑	151	Rickey Dudley RC	.30	.10
❑	152	Jason Dunn RC	.20	.07
❑	153	Bobby Engram RC	.30	.10
❑	154	Daryl Gardener RC	.10	.02
❑	155	Eddie George RC	1.25	.50
❑	156	Terry Glenn RC	1.00	.40
❑	157	Kevin Hardy RC	.30	.10
❑	158	Walt Harris RC	.10	.02
❑	159	Marvin Harrison RC	2.50	1.00
❑	160	Bobby Hoying RC	.30	.10
❑	161	Keyshawn Johnson RC	1.00	.40
❑	162	Cedric Jones RC	.10	.02
❑	163	Marcus Jones RC	.10	.02
❑	164	Eddie Kennison RC	.30	.10
❑	165	Ray Lewis RC	2.50	1.00
❑	166	Derrick Mayes RC	.30	.10
❑	167	Leeland McElroy RC	.20	.07
❑	168	Johnny McWilliams RC	.20	.07
❑	169	John Mobley RC	.10	.02
❑	170	Alex Molden RC	.10	.02
❑	171	Eric Moulds RC	1.25	.50
❑	172	Muhsin Muhammad RC	.75	.30
❑	173	Jonathan Ogden RC	.30	.10
❑	174	Lawrence Phillips RC	.30	.10
❑	175	Stanley Pritchett RC	.20	.07
❑	176	Simeon Rice RC	.75	.30
❑	177	Bryan Still RC	.20	.07
❑	178	Amani Toomer RC	1.00	.40
❑	179	Regan Upshaw RC	.10	.02
❑	180	Alex Van Dyke RC	.20	.07
❑	181	Barry Sanders PFW	.60	.25
❑	182	Marcus Allen PFW	.30	.10
❑	183	Bryce Paup PFW	.10	.02
❑	184	Jerry Rice PFW	.40	.15
❑	185	D.Howard/B.Christian PFW	.20	.07
❑	186	Leon Lett PFW	.10	.02
❑	187	Brett Favre PFW	.75	.30
❑	188	G.Lloyd/D.Thomas PFW	.10	.02
❑	189	Jeff Blake PFW	.20	.07
❑	190	Emmitt Smith PFW	.60	.25
❑	191	J.Elway/J.Hostetler PFW	.40	.15
❑	192	Chiefs PFW	.10	.02
❑	193	Marshall Faulk PFW	.30	.10
❑	194	T.Aikman/S.Young PFW	.40	.15
❑	195	Dan Marino PFW	.75	.30
❑	196	Donta Jones PFW	.10	.02
❑	197	Jim Kelly PFW	.30	.10
❑	198	Checklist	.10	.02
❑	199	Checklist	.10	.02
❑	200	Checklist	.10	.02
❑	P1	Promo Sheet/WFloyd/TDil/Favre	4.00	1.50

1997 Fleer

❑		COMPLETE SET (450)	40.00	15.00
❑	1	Mark Brunell	1.00	.40
❑	2	Andre Reed	.50	.20
❑	3	Darrell Green	.50	.20
❑	4	Mario Bates	.30	.10
❑	5	Eddie George	.75	.30
❑	6	Cris Carter	.75	.30
❑	7	Terrell Owens	1.00	.40
❑	8	Bill Romanowski	.30	.10
❑	9	Isaac Bruce	.75	.30

❑	10	Eric Curry	.30	.10
❑	11	Danny Kanell	.30	.10
❑	12	Ki-Jana Carter	.30	.10
❑	13	Antonio Freeman	.75	.30
❑	14	Ricky Watters	.50	.20
❑	15	Ty Law	.50	.20
❑	16	Alonzo Spellman	.30	.10
❑	17	Kordell Stewart	.75	.30
❑	18	Jerry Rice	1.50	.60
❑	19	Derrick Alexander WR	.50	.20
❑	20	Barry Sanders	2.50	1.00
❑	21	Keyshawn Johnson	.75	.30
❑	22	Emmitt Smith	2.50	1.00
❑	23	Ricky Proehl	.30	.10
❑	24	Daryl Gardener	.30	.10
❑	25	Dan Saleaumua	.30	.10
❑	26	Kevin Greene	.50	.20
❑	27	Junior Seau	.75	.30
❑	28	Randall McDaniel	.30	.10
❑	29	Marshall Faulk	1.00	.40
❑	30	Lorenzo Lynch	.30	.10
❑	31	Terance Mathis	.50	.20
❑	32	Warren Sapp	.50	.20
❑	33	Chris Sanders	.30	.10
❑	34	Tom Carter	.30	.10
❑	35	Aeneas Williams	.30	.10
❑	36	Lawrence Phillips	.30	.10
❑	37	John Elway	3.00	1.25
❑	38	Stanley Richard	.30	.10
❑	39	Darryl Williams	.30	.10
❑	40	Phillippi Sparks	.30	.10
❑	41	Tedy Bruschi	1.50	.60
❑	42	Merton Hanks	.30	.10
❑	43	Ray Lewis	1.25	.50
❑	44	Erik Williams	.30	.10
❑	45	Jason Gildon	.30	.10
❑	46	George Koonce	.30	.10
❑	47	Louis Oliver	.30	.10
❑	48	Muhsin Muhammad	.50	.20
❑	49	Daryl Hobbs	.30	.10
❑	50	Terry Glenn	.75	.30
❑	51	Marvin Harrison	.75	.30
❑	52	Brian Dawkins	.75	.30
❑	53	Dale Carter	.30	.10
❑	54	Alex Molden	.30	.10
❑	55	Raymont Harris	.30	.10
❑	56	Jeff Burris	.30	.10
❑	57	Don Beebe	.30	.10
❑	58	Jamir Miller	.30	.10
❑	59	Carl Pickens	.50	.20
❑	60	Antonio London	.30	.10
❑	61	Courtney Hall	.30	.10
❑	62	Derrick Brooks	.75	.30
❑	63	Chris Boniol	.30	.10
❑	64	Jeff Lageman	.30	.10
❑	65	Roy Barker	.30	.10
❑	66	Devin Bush	.30	.10
❑	67	Aaron Glenn	.30	.10
❑	68	Wayne Simmons	.30	.10
❑	69	Steve Atwater	.30	.10
❑	70	Jimmie Jones	.30	.10
❑	71	Mark Carrier WR	.30	.10
❑	72	Chris Chandler	.50	.20
❑	73	Andy Harmon	.30	.10
❑	74	John Friesz	.30	.10
❑	75	Karim Abdul-Jabbar	.50	.20
❑	76	Levon Kirkland	.30	.10
❑	77	Torrance Small	.30	.10
❑	78	Harvey Williams	.30	.10
❑	79	Chris Calloway	.30	.10
❑	80	Vinny Testaverde	.50	.20
❑	81	Bryant Young	.30	.10
❑	82	Ray Buchanan	.30	.10
❑	83	Robert Smith	.50	.20
❑	84	Robert Brooks	.50	.20
❑	85	Ray Crockett	.30	.10
❑	86	Bennie Blades	.30	.10
❑	87	Mark Carrier DB	.30	.10
❑	88	Mike Tomczak	.30	.10
❑	89	Darick Holmes	.30	.10
❑	90	Drew Bledsoe	1.00	.40
❑	91	Darren Woodson	.30	.10
❑	92	Dan Wilkinson	.30	.10
❑	93	Charles Way	.30	.10
❑	94	Ray Farmer	.30	.10
❑	95	Marcus Allen	.75	.30
❑	96	Marco Coleman	.30	.10
❑	97	Zach Thomas	.75	.30
❑	98	Wesley Walls	.50	.20
❑	99	Frank Wycheck	.30	.10
❑	100	Troy Aikman	1.50	.60
❑	101	Clyde Simmons	.30	.10
❑	102	Courtney Hawkins	.30	.10
❑	103	Chuck Smith	.30	.10
❑	104	Neil O'Donnell	.50	.20
❑	105	Kevin Carter	.30	.10
❑	106	Chris Slade	.30	.10
❑	107	Jessie Armstead	.30	.10
❑	108	Sean Dawkins	.30	.10
❑	109	Robert Blackmon	.30	.10
❑	110	Kevin Smith	.30	.10
❑	111	Lonnie Johnson	.30	.10
❑	112	Craig Newsome	.30	.10
❑	113	Jonathan Ogden	.30	.10
❑	114	Chris Zorich	.30	.10
❑	115	Tim Brown	.75	.30
❑	116	Fred Barnett	.30	.10
❑	117	Michael Haynes	.30	.10
❑	118	Eric Hill	.30	.10
❑	119	Ronnie Harmon	.30	.10
❑	120	Sean Gilbert	.30	.10
❑	121	Derrick Alexander DE	.30	.10
❑	122	Derrick Thomas	.75	.30
❑	123	Tyrone Wheatley	.50	.20
❑	124	Cortez Kennedy	.30	.10
❑	125	Jeff George	.50	.20
❑	126	Chad Cota	.30	.10
❑	127	Gary Zimmerman	.30	.10
❑	128	Johnnie Morton	.50	.20
❑	129	Chad Brown	.30	.10
❑	130	Marvcus Patton	.30	.10
❑	131	James O.Stewart	.50	.20
❑	132	Terry Kirby	.50	.20
❑	133	Chris Mims	.30	.10
❑	134	William Thomas	.30	.10
❑	135	Steve Tasker	.30	.10
❑	136	Jason Belser	.30	.10
❑	137	Bryan Cox	.30	.10
❑	138	Jessie Tuggle	.30	.10
❑	139	Ashley Ambrose	.30	.10
❑	140	Mark Chmura	.50	.20
❑	141	Jeff Hostetler	.30	.10
❑	142	Rich Owens	.30	.10
❑	143	Willie Davis	.30	.10
❑	144	Hardy Nickerson	.30	.10
❑	145	Curtis Martin	1.00	.40
❑	146	Ken Norton	.30	.10
❑	147	Victor Green	.30	.10
❑	148	Anthony Miller	.30	.10
❑	149	John Kasay	.30	.10
❑	150	O.J. McDuffie	.50	.20
❑	151	Darren Perry	.30	.10
❑	152	Luther Elliss	.30	.10
❑	153	Greg Hill	.30	.10

❑ 154 John Randle .50 .20
❑ 155 Stephen Grant .30 .10
❑ 156 Leon Lett .30 .10
❑ 157 Darrien Gordon .30 .10
❑ 158 Ray Zellars .30 .10
❑ 159 Michael Jackson .50 .20
❑ 160 Leslie O'Neal .30 .10
❑ 161 Bruce Smith .50 .20
❑ 162 Santana Dotson .30 .10
❑ 163 Bobby Hebert .30 .10
❑ 164 Keith Hamilton .30 .10
❑ 165 Tony Boselli .30 .10
❑ 166 Alfred Williams .30 .10
❑ 167 Ty Detmer .50 .20
❑ 168 Chester McGlockton .30 .10
❑ 169 William Floyd .50 .20
❑ 170 Bruce Matthews .30 .10
❑ 171 Simeon Rice .50 .20
❑ 172 Scott Mitchell .50 .20
❑ 173 Ricardo McDonald .30 .10
❑ 174 Tyrone Poole .30 .10
❑ 175 Greg Lloyd .30 .10
❑ 176 Bruce Armstrong .30 .10
❑ 177 Erik Kramer .30 .10
❑ 178 Kimble Anders .50 .20
❑ 179 Lamar Smith .75 .30
❑ 180 Tony Tolbert .30 .10
❑ 181 Joe Aska .30 .10
❑ 182 Eric Allen .30 .10
❑ 183 Eric Turner .30 .10
❑ 184 Brad Johnson .75 .30
❑ 185 Tony Martin .50 .20
❑ 186 Mike Mamula .30 .10
❑ 187 Irving Spikes .30 .10
❑ 188 Keith Jackson .30 .10
❑ 189 Carlton Bailey .30 .10
❑ 190 Tyrone Braxton .30 .10
❑ 191 Chad Bratzke .30 .10
❑ 192 Adrian Murrell .50 .20
❑ 193 Roman Phifer .30 .10
❑ 194 Todd Collins .30 .10
❑ 195 Chris Warren .50 .20
❑ 196 Kevin Hardy .30 .10
❑ 197 Rick Mirer .30 .10
❑ 198 Cornelius Bennett .30 .10
❑ 199 Jimmy Hitchcock .30 .10
❑ 200 Michael Irvin .75 .30
❑ 201 Quentin Coryatt .30 .10
❑ 202 Reggie White .75 .30
❑ 203 Larry Centers .50 .20
❑ 204 Rodney Thomas .30 .10
❑ 205 Dana Stubblefield .30 .10
❑ 206 Rod Woodson .50 .20
❑ 207 Rhett Hall .30 .10
❑ 208 Steve Tovar .30 .10
❑ 209 Michael Westbrook .50 .20
❑ 210 Steve Wisniewski .30 .10
❑ 211 Carlester Crumpler .30 .10
❑ 212 Elvis Grbac .50 .20
❑ 213 Tim Bowens .30 .10
❑ 214 Robert Porcher .30 .10
❑ 215 John Carney .30 .10
❑ 216 Anthony Newman .30 .10
❑ 217 Earnest Byner .30 .10
❑ 218 Dewayne Washington .30 .10
❑ 219 Willie Green .30 .10
❑ 220 Terry Allen .75 .30
❑ 221 William Fuller .30 .10
❑ 222 Al Del Greco .30 .10
❑ 223 Trent Dilfer .75 .30
❑ 224 Michael Dean Perry .30 .10
❑ 225 Larry Allen .30 .10
❑ 226 Mark Bruener .30 .10
❑ 227 Clay Matthews .30 .10
❑ 228 Reuben Brown .30 .10
❑ 229 Edgar Bennett .50 .20
❑ 230 Neil Smith .50 .20
❑ 231 Ken Harvey .30 .10
❑ 232 Kyle Brady .30 .10
❑ 233 Corey Miller .30 .10
❑ 234 Tony Siragusa .30 .10
❑ 235 Todd Sauerbrun .30 .10
❑ 236 Daniel Stubbs .30 .10
❑ 237 Robb Thomas .30 .10
❑ 238 Jimmy Smith .50 .20
❑ 239 Marquez Pope .30 .10
❑ 240 Tim Biakabutuka .50 .20
❑ 241 Jamie Asher .30 .10
❑ 242 Steve McNair 1.00 .40
❑ 243 Harold Green .30 .10
❑ 244 Frank Sanders .50 .20
❑ 245 Joe Johnson .30 .10
❑ 246 Eric Bieniemy .30 .10
❑ 247 Kevin Turner .30 .10
❑ 248 Rickey Dudley .50 .20
❑ 249 Orlando Thomas .30 .10
❑ 250 Dan Marino 3.00 1.25
❑ 251 Deion Sanders .75 .30
❑ 252 Dan Williams .30 .10
❑ 253 Sam Gash .30 .10
❑ 254 Lonnie Marts .30 .10
❑ 255 Mo Lewis .30 .10
❑ 256 Charles Johnson .50 .20
❑ 257 Chris Jacke .30 .10
❑ 258 Keenan McCardell .50 .20
❑ 259 Donnell Woolford .30 .10
❑ 260 Terrance Shaw .30 .10
❑ 261 Jason Dunn .30 .10
❑ 262 Willie McGinest .30 .10
❑ 263 Ken Dilger .30 .10
❑ 264 Keith Lyle .30 .10
❑ 265 Antonio Langham .30 .10
❑ 266 Carlton Gray .30 .10
❑ 267 LeShon Johnson .30 .10
❑ 268 Thurman Thomas .75 .30
❑ 269 Jesse Campbell .30 .10
❑ 270 Carnell Lake .30 .10
❑ 271 Cris Dishman .30 .10
❑ 272 Kevin Williams .30 .10
❑ 273 Troy Brown .50 .20
❑ 274 William Roaf .30 .10
❑ 275 Terrell Davis 1.00 .40
❑ 276 Herman Moore .50 .20
❑ 277 Walt Harris .30 .10
❑ 278 Mark Collins .30 .10
❑ 279 Bert Emanuel .50 .20
❑ 280 Qadry Ismail .50 .20
❑ 281 Phil Hansen .30 .10
❑ 282 Steve Young 1.00 .40
❑ 283 Michael Sinclair .30 .10
❑ 284 Jeff Graham .30 .10
❑ 285 Sam Mills .30 .10
❑ 286 Terry McDaniel .30 .10
❑ 287 Eugene Robinson .30 .10
❑ 288 Tony Bennett .30 .10
❑ 289 Daryl Johnston .50 .20
❑ 290 Eric Swann .30 .10
❑ 291 Byron Bam Morris .30 .10
❑ 292 Thomas Lewis .30 .10
❑ 293 Terrell Fletcher .30 .10
❑ 294 Gus Frerotte .30 .10
❑ 295 Stanley Pritchett .30 .10
❑ 296 Mike Alstott .75 .30
❑ 297 Will Shields .30 .10
❑ 298 Errict Rhett .30 .10
❑ 299 Garrison Hearst .50 .20
❑ 300 Kerry Collins .75 .30
❑ 301 Darryll Lewis .30 .10
❑ 302 Chris T. Jones .30 .10
❑ 303 Yancey Thigpen .50 .20
❑ 304 Jackie Harris .30 .10
❑ 305 Steve Christie .30 .10
❑ 306 Gilbert Brown .50 .20
❑ 307 Terry Wooden .30 .10
❑ 308 Pete Mitchell .30 .10
❑ 309 Tim McDonald .30 .10
❑ 310 Jake Reed .50 .20
❑ 311 Ed McCaffrey .50 .20
❑ 312 Chris Doleman .30 .10
❑ 313 Eric Metcalf .50 .20
❑ 314 Ricky Reynolds .30 .10
❑ 315 David Sloan .30 .10
❑ 316 Marvin Washington .30 .10
❑ 317 Herschel Walker .50 .20
❑ 318 Michael Timpson .30 .10
❑ 319 Blaine Bishop .30 .10
❑ 320 Irv Smith .30 .10
❑ 321 Seth Joyner .30 .10
❑ 322 Terrell Buckley .30 .10
❑ 323 Michael Strahan .50 .20
❑ 324 Sam Adams .30 .10
❑ 325 Leslie Shepherd .30 .10
❑ 326 James Jett .50 .20
❑ 327 Anthony Pleasant .30 .10
❑ 328 Lee Woodall .30 .10
❑ 329 Shannon Sharpe .50 .20
❑ 330 Jamal Anderson .75 .30
❑ 331 Andre Hastings .30 .10
❑ 332 Troy Vincent .30 .10
❑ 333 Sean LaChapelle .30 .10
❑ 334 Winslow Oliver .30 .10
❑ 335 Sean Jones .30 .10
❑ 336 Darnay Scott .50 .20
❑ 337 Todd Lyght .30 .10
❑ 338 Leonard Russell .30 .10
❑ 339 Nate Newton .30 .10
❑ 340 Zack Crockett .30 .10
❑ 341 Amp Lee .30 .10
❑ 342 Bobby Engram .50 .20
❑ 343 Mike Hollis .30 .10
❑ 344 Rodney Hampton .50 .20
❑ 345 Mel Gray .30 .10
❑ 346 Van Malone .30 .10
❑ 347 Aaron Craver .30 .10
❑ 348 Jim Everett .30 .10
❑ 349 Trace Armstrong .30 .10
❑ 350 Pat Swilling .30 .10
❑ 351 Brent Jones .30 .10
❑ 352 Chris Spielman .30 .10
❑ 353 Brett Perriman .30 .10
❑ 354 Brian Kinchen .30 .10
❑ 355 Joey Galloway .50 .20
❑ 356 Henry Ellard .30 .10
❑ 357 Ben Coates .50 .20
❑ 358 Dorsey Levens .75 .30
❑ 359 Charlie Garner .50 .20
❑ 360 Erric Pegram .30 .10
❑ 361 Anthony Johnson .30 .10
❑ 362 Rashaan Salaam .30 .10
❑ 363 Jeff Blake .50 .20
❑ 364 Kent Graham .30 .10
❑ 365 Broderick Thomas .30 .10
❑ 366 Richmond Webb .30 .10
❑ 367 Alfred Pupunu .30 .10
❑ 368 Mark Stepnoski .30 .10
❑ 369 David Dunn .30 .10
❑ 370 Bobby Houston .30 .10
❑ 371 Anthony Parker .30 .10
❑ 372 Quinn Early .30 .10
❑ 373 LeRoy Butler .30 .10
❑ 374 Kurt Gouveia .30 .10
❑ 375 Greg Biekert .30 .10
❑ 376 Jim Harbaugh .50 .20
❑ 377 Eric Bjornson .30 .10
❑ 378 Craig Heyward .30 .10
❑ 379 Steve Bono .50 .20
❑ 380 Tony Banks .50 .20
❑ 381 John Mobley .30 .10
❑ 382 Irving Fryar .50 .20
❑ 383 Dermontti Dawson .30 .10
❑ 384 Eric Davis .30 .10
❑ 385 Natrone Means .50 .20
❑ 386 Jason Sehorn .50 .20
❑ 387 Michael McCrary .30 .10
❑ 388 Corwin Brown .30 .10
❑ 389 Kevin Glover .30 .10
❑ 390 Jerris McPhail .30 .10
❑ 391 Bobby Taylor .30 .10
❑ 392 Tony McGee .30 .10
❑ 393 Curtis Conway .50 .20

❑ 394	Napoleon Kaufman	.75	.30
❑ 395	Brian Blades	.30	.10
❑ 396	Richard Dent	.30	.10
❑ 397	Dave Brown	.30	.10
❑ 398	Stan Humphries	.50	.20
❑ 399	Stevon Moore	.30	.10
❑ 400	Brett Favre	3.00	1.50
❑ 401	Jerome Bettis	.75	.30
❑ 402	Darrin Smith	.30	.10
❑ 403	Chris Penn	.30	.10
❑ 404	Rob Moore	.50	.20
❑ 405	Micheal Barrow	.30	.10
❑ 406	Tony Brackens	.30	.10
❑ 407	Wayne Martin	.30	.10
❑ 408	Warren Moon	.75	.30
❑ 409	Jason Elam	.50	.20
❑ 410	J.J. Birden	.30	.10
❑ 411	Hugh Douglas	.30	.10
❑ 412	Lamar Lathon	.30	.10
❑ 413	John Kidd	.30	.10
❑ 414	Bryce Paup	.30	.10
❑ 415	Shawn Jefferson	.30	.10
❑ 416	Leeland McElroy SS	.30	.10
❑ 417	Elbert Shelley SS	.30	.10
❑ 418	Jermaine Lewis SS	.50	.20
❑ 419	Eric Moulds SS	.75	.30
❑ 420	Michael Bates SS	.30	.10
❑ 421	John Mangum SS	.30	.10
❑ 422	Corey Sawyer SS	.30	.10
❑ 423	Jim Schwantz SS RC	.30	.10
❑ 424	Rod Smith WR SS	.75	.30
❑ 425	Glyn Milburn SS	.30	.10
❑ 426	Desmond Howard SS	.50	.20
❑ 427	John Henry Mills SS RC	.30	.10
❑ 428	Cary Blanchard SS RC	.30	.10
❑ 429	Chris Hudson SS	.30	.10
❑ 430	Tamarick Vanover SS	.50	.20
❑ 431	Kirby Dar Dar SS RC	.50	.20
❑ 432	David Palmer SS	.30	.10
❑ 433	Dave Meggett SS	.30	.10
❑ 434	Tyrone Hughes SS	.30	.10
❑ 435	Amani Toomer SS	.50	.20
❑ 436	Wayne Chrebet SS	.50	.20
❑ 437	Carl Kidd RC SS	.30	.10
❑ 438	Derrick Witherspoon SS	.30	.10
❑ 439	Jahine Arnold SS	.30	.10
❑ 440	Andre Coleman SS	.30	.10
❑ 441	Jeff Wilkins SS	.30	.10
❑ 442	Jay Bellamy SS RC	.30	.10
❑ 443	Eddie Kennison SS	.50	.20
❑ 444	Nilo Silvan SS	.30	.10
❑ 445	Brian Mitchell SS	.30	.10
❑ 446	Garrison Hearst CL	.50	.20
❑ 447	Napoleon Kaufman CL	.75	.30
❑ 448	Brian Mitchell CL	.30	.10
❑ 449	Rodney Hampton CL	.30	.10
❑ 450	Edgar Bennett CL	.30	.10
❑ S1	Mark Chmura Sample	1.00	.40
❑ AU1	Reggie White AUTO	125.00	75.00

2001 Fleer Hot Prospects

❑	COMP.SET w/o SP's (100)	25.00	10.00
❑ 1	Aaron Brooks	1.00	.40
❑ 2	Tim Couch	.60	.25
❑ 3	Jeff George	.60	.25
❑ 4	Brett Favre	3.00	1.25
❑ 5	Donovan McNabb	1.25	.50
❑ 6	Ray Lucas	.40	.15
❑ 7	Doug Flutie	1.00	.40
❑ 8	Mark Brunell	1.00	.40
❑ 9	Steve McNair	1.00	.40
❑ 10	Trent Green	1.00	.40
❑ 11	Daunte Culpepper	1.00	.40
❑ 12	Rich Gannon	1.00	.40
❑ 13	Kurt Warner	2.00	.75
❑ 14	Brian Griese	1.00	.40
❑ 15	Kerry Collins	.60	.25
❑ 16	Vinny Testaverde	.60	.25
❑ 17	David Boston	1.00	.40
❑ 18	Peyton Manning	2.50	1.00
❑ 19	Keyshawn Johnson	1.00	.40
❑ 20	Tim Biakabutuka	.60	.25
❑ 22	Emmitt Smith	2.00	.75
❑ 23	Terry Glenn	.60	.25
❑ 24	Tony Gonzalez	.60	.25
❑ 25	Charlie Garner	.60	.25
❑ 26	Lamar Smith	.60	.25
❑ 27	Eddie George	1.00	.40
❑ 28	Fred Taylor	1.00	.40
❑ 29	Marvin Harrison	1.00	.40
❑ 30	Terrell Davis	1.00	.40
❑ 31	Marcus Robinson	1.00	.40
❑ 32	Edgerrin James	1.25	.50
❑ 33	Ed McCaffrey	1.00	.40
❑ 34	Ricky Williams	1.00	.40
❑ 36	Jerome Bettis	1.00	.40
❑ 37	Shaun Alexander	1.25	.50
❑ 38	Mike Anderson	1.00	.40
❑ 39	Keenan McCardell	.40	.15
❑ 40	Mike Alstott	1.00	.40
❑ 41	Terrell Fletcher	.40	.15
❑ 42	Kevin Johnson	.60	.25
❑ 43	Wesley Walls	.40	.15
❑ 44	Derrick Mason	.60	.25
❑ 45	Sammy Morris	.40	.15
❑ 46	Joey Galloway	.60	.25
❑ 47	Sylvester Morris	.40	.15
❑ 48	Stephen Davis	1.00	.40
❑ 49	Terrell Owens	1.00	.40
❑ 50	Troy Edwards	.40	.15
❑ 51	Amani Toomer	.60	.25
❑ 52	Ray Lewis	1.00	.40
❑ 53	Terance Mathis	.60	.25
❑ 54	Brian Urlacher	1.50	.60
❑ 55	Junior Seau	1.00	.40
❑ 56	Rocket Ismail	.60	.25
❑ 57	Wayne Chrebet	.60	.25
❑ 58	Peter Warrick	1.00	.40
❑ 59	Andre Rison	.60	.25
❑ 60	Desmond Howard	.40	.15
❑ 61	Eric Moulds	.60	.25
❑ 62	Jerry Rice	2.00	.75
❑ 63	Stephen Alexander	.40	.15
❑ 64	Isaac Bruce	1.00	.40
❑ 65	Travis Prentice	.40	.15
❑ 66	James Stewart	.60	.25
❑ 67	Jamal Anderson	1.00	.40
❑ 68	Ricky Watters	.40	.15
❑ 69	Jamal Lewis	1.50	.60
❑ 70	Priest Holmes	1.25	.50
❑ 71	Ahman Green	1.00	.40
❑ 72	Marshall Faulk	1.25	.50
❑ 73	Warrick Dunn	1.00	.40
❑ 74	Curtis Martin	1.00	.40
❑ 75	Corey Dillon	1.00	.40
❑ 76	Ron Dayne	1.00	.40
❑ 77	Thomas Jones	.60	.25
❑ 78	Duce Staley	1.00	.40
❑ 79	Tiki Barber	1.00	.40
❑ 80	Cris Carter	1.00	.40
❑ 81	Tim Brown	1.00	.40
❑ 82	Jimmy Smith	.60	.25
❑ 83	Elvis Grbac	.60	.25
❑ 84	Randy Moss	2.00	.75
❑ 85	Tim Dwight	1.00	.40
❑ 86	Antonio Freeman	1.00	.40
❑ 87	Muhsin Muhammad	.60	.25
❑ 88	Torry Holt	1.00	.40
❑ 89	Frank Wycheck	.40	.15
❑ 90	Jake Plummer	.60	.25
❑ 91	Brad Johnson	1.00	.40
❑ 92	Chris Chandler	.60	.25
❑ 93	Drew Bledsoe	1.25	.50
❑ 94	Rob Johnson	.60	.25
❑ 95	Matt Hasselbeck	.60	.25
❑ 96	Jon Kitna	.60	.25
❑ 97	Kordell Stewart	.60	.25
❑ 98	Charlie Batch	1.00	.40
❑ 99	Cade McNown	.40	.15
❑ 100	Jeff Garcia	1.00	.40
❑ 101	Quincy Morgan RC	3.00	1.25
❑ 102	Jesse Palmer RC	3.00	1.25
❑ 103	Reggie Wayne RC	6.00	2.50
❑ 104	Deuce McAllister RC	6.00	2.50
❑ 105	Chad Johnson RC	8.00	3.00
❑ 106	Chris Weinke RC	3.00	1.25
❑ 107	Michael Bennett RC	5.00	2.00
❑ 108	Rod Gardner RC	3.00	1.25
❑ 109	Michael Vick RC	20.00	10.00
❑ 110	Anthony Thomas RC	3.00	1.25
❑ 111	Santana Moss RC	5.00	2.00
❑ 112	Kevan Barlow RC	3.00	1.25
❑ 113	Koren Robinson RC	3.00	1.25
❑ 114	Rudi Johnson RC	6.00	2.50
❑ 115	Josh Heupel RC	3.00	1.25
❑ 116	James Jackson RC	3.00	1.25
❑ 117	Freddie Mitchell RC	3.00	1.25
❑ 118	LaDainian Tomlinson RC	15.00	7.50
❑ 119	Marques Tuiasosopo RC	3.00	1.25
❑ 120	Drew Brees RC	8.00	3.00
❑ 121	David Terrell RC	3.00	1.25
❑ 122	Chris Chambers RC	5.00	2.00
❑ 123	Mike McMahon RC	3.00	1.25
❑ 124	Robert Ferguson RC	3.00	1.25
❑ 125	Justin Smith RC	3.00	1.25
❑ 126	Leonard Davis RC	2.00	.75
❑ 127	Todd Heap RC	3.00	1.25
❑ 128	Dan Morgan RC	3.00	1.25
❑ 129	Gerard Warren RC	3.00	1.25
❑ 130	Travis Henry RC	3.00	1.25
❑ 131	Travis Minor RC	2.00	.75
❑ 132	Richard Seymour RC	3.00	1.25
❑ 133	Quincy Carter RC	3.00	1.25
❑ 134	Snoop Minnis RC	2.00	.75
❑ 135	Sage Rosenfels RC	3.00	1.25
❑ CL1	Checklist	.10	.02

2002 Fleer Hot Prospects

❑	COMP.SET w/o SP's (80)	25.00	10.00
❑ 1	Donovan McNabb	1.50	.60
❑ 2	Drew Brees	1.25	.50
❑ 3	Curtis Martin	1.25	.50
❑ 4	Priest Holmes	1.50	.60
❑ 5	Quincy Carter	.75	.30
❑ 6	Chris Weinke	.75	.30
❑ 7	Marshall Faulk	1.25	.50
❑ 8	Jake Plummer	.75	.30
❑ 9	Tom Brady	3.00	1.25

❑	10 Ahman Green	1.25	.50
❑	11 Brian Urlacher	2.00	.75
❑	12 Keyshawn Johnson	1.25	.50
❑	13 Jerome Bettis	1.25	.50
❑	14 Tiki Barber	1.25	.50
❑	15 Edgerrin James	1.50	.60
❑	16 Jamal Lewis	1.25	.50
❑	17 Terrell Owens	1.25	.50
❑	18 Joe Horn	.75	.30
❑	19 Daunte Culpepper	1.25	.50
❑	20 Terrell Davis	1.25	.50
❑	21 Fred Taylor	1.25	.50
❑	22 Emmitt Smith	3.00	1.25
❑	23 Jamal Anderson	.75	.30
❑	24 Garrison Hearst	.75	.30
❑	25 Chad Pennington	1.50	.60
❑	26 Michael Bennett	.75	.30
❑	27 James Allen	.75	.30
❑	28 Marty Booker	.50	.20
❑	29 Warren Sapp	.75	.30
❑	30 Jerry Rice	2.50	1.00
❑	31 Antowain Smith	.75	.30
❑	32 Marvin Harrison	1.25	.50
❑	33 Tim Couch	.75	.30
❑	34 Stephen Davis	.75	.30
❑	35 Kordell Stewart	.75	.30
❑	36 Tony Gonzalez	.75	.30
❑	37 Mike McMahon	1.25	.50
❑	38 Eric Moulds	.75	.30
❑	39 Kurt Warner	1.25	.50
❑	40 Ricky Williams	1.25	.50
❑	41 Michael Strahan	.75	.30
❑	42 Trent Green	.75	.30
❑	43 Brian Griese	1.25	.50
❑	44 David Boston	1.25	.50
❑	45 LaDainian Tomlinson	2.00	.75
❑	46 Tim Brown	1.25	.50
❑	47 Deuce McAllister	1.50	.60
❑	48 Jamie Sharper	.50	.20
❑	49 Rod Gardner	.75	.30
❑	50 Isaac Bruce	1.25	.50
❑	51 Freddie Mitchell	.75	.30
❑	52 Kerry Collins	.75	.30
❑	53 Mark Brunell	1.25	.50
❑	54 Corey Dillon	.75	.30
❑	55 Steve McNair	1.25	.50
❑	56 Aaron Brooks	1.25	.50
❑	57 Chris Chambers	1.25	.50
❑	58 Bill Schroeder	.75	.30
❑	59 Ray Lewis	1.25	.50
❑	60 Shaun Alexander	1.50	.60
❑	61 Kevin Johnson	.75	.30
❑	62 Michael Vick	4.00	1.50
❑	63 Jeff Garcia	1.25	.50
❑	64 Laveranues Coles	.75	.30
❑	65 Jimmy Smith	.75	.30
❑	66 Brett Favre	3.00	1.25
❑	67 Anthony Thomas	.75	.30
❑	68 Torry Holt	1.25	.50
❑	69 Duce Staley	1.25	.50
❑	70 Randy Moss	2.50	1.00
❑	71 Peyton Manning	2.50	1.00
❑	72 Peter Warrick	.75	.30
❑	73 Eddie George	1.25	.50
❑	74 Plaxico Burress	.75	.30
❑	75 Troy Brown	.75	.30
❑	76 Rod Smith	.75	.30
❑	77 Drew Bledsoe	1.50	.60
❑	78 Darrell Jackson	.75	.30
❑	79 Rich Gannon	1.25	.50
❑	80 Jay Fiedler	.75	.30
❑	81 David Carr/250 RC	40.00	15.00
❑	82 Andre Davis JSY RC	8.00	3.00
❑	83 Daniel Graham JSY RC	10.00	4.00
❑	84 Ron Johnson JSY RC	8.00	3.00
❑	85 Julius Peppers JSY RC	20.00	7.50
❑	86 Josh Reed JSY RC	10.00	4.00
❑	87 Travis Stephens JSY RC	8.00	3.00
❑	88 Mike Williams JSY RC	8.00	3.00
❑	89 Antonio Bryant JSY RC	10.00	4.00
❑	90 Eric Crouch JSY RC	10.00	4.00
❑	91 DeShaun Foster JSY RC	10.00	4.00
❑	92 Joey Harrington JSY RC	20.00	7.50
❑	93 Josh McCown JSY RC	15.00	6.00
❑	94 Patrick Ramsey JSY RC	12.00	5.00
❑	95 Jeremy Shockey JSY RC	25.00	10.00
❑	96 Marquise Walker JSY RC	8.00	3.00
❑	97 Reche Caldwell JSY RC	10.00	4.00
❑	98 Rohan Davey JSY RC	10.00	4.00
❑	99 Jabar Gaffney JSY RC	10.00	4.00
❑	100 David Garrard JSY RC	10.00	4.00
❑	101 Maurice Morris JSY RC	10.00	4.00
❑	102 Antwaan Randle El JSY RC	15.00	6.00
❑	103 Donte Stallworth JSY RC	20.00	7.50
❑	104 Roy Williams JSY RC	25.00	10.00
❑	105 Ladell Betts JSY RC	10.00	4.00
❑	106 Tim Carter JSY RC	8.00	3.00
❑	107 T.J. Duckett JSY RC	20.00	7.50
❑	108 William Green JSY RC	10.00	4.00
❑	109 Ashley Lelie JSY RC	20.00	7.50
❑	110 Clinton Portis JSY RC	25.00	10.00
❑	111 Cliff Russell JSY RC	8.00	3.00
❑	112 Javon Walker JSY RC	20.00	7.50

2003 Fleer Hot Prospects

❑	COMP.SET w/o SP's (80)	20.00	7.50
❑	1 Emmitt Smith	2.50	1.00
❑	2 Terrell Owens	1.00	.40
❑	3 Tiki Barber	1.00	.40
❑	4 Trent Green	.60	.25
❑	5 Quincy Morgan	.60	.25
❑	6 Eric Moulds	.60	.25
❑	7 Simeon Rice	.60	.25
❑	8 Hines Ward	1.00	.40
❑	9 Michael Bennett	.60	.25
❑	10 Donald Driver	.60	.25
❑	11 Stephen Davis	.60	.25
❑	12 Steve McNair	1.00	.40
❑	13 David Boston	.60	.25
❑	14 Deuce McAllister	1.00	.40
❑	15 Marvin Harrison	1.00	.40
❑	16 Peerless Price	.60	.25
❑	17 Matt Hasselbeck	.60	.25
❑	18 Jerry Rice	2.00	.75
❑	19 Junior Seau	1.00	.40
❑	20 Clinton Portis	1.50	.60
❑	21 Fred Taylor	1.00	.40
❑	22 William Green	.60	.25
❑	23 Warrick Dunn	.60	.25
❑	24 Koren Robinson	.60	.25
❑	25 Jeremy Shockey	1.50	.60
❑	26 Chris Chambers	1.00	.40
❑	27 Brett Favre	2.50	1.00
❑	28 Julius Peppers	1.00	.40
❑	29 Eddie George	.60	.25
❑	30 Todd Pinkston	.60	.25
❑	31 Tom Brady	2.50	1.00
❑	32 Edgerrin James	1.00	.40
❑	33 Chad Johnson	1.00	.40
❑	34 Laveranues Coles	.60	.25
❑	35 LaDainian Tomlinson	1.00	.40
❑	36 Priest Holmes	1.25	.50
❑	37 Shannon Sharpe	.60	.25
❑	38 Jamal Lewis	1.00	.40
❑	39 Warren Sapp	.60	.25
❑	40 Tim Brown	1.00	.40
❑	41 Kerry Collins	.60	.25
❑	42 Jimmy Smith	.60	.25
❑	43 Chad Hutchinson	.60	.25
❑	44 Marcel Shipp	.60	.25
❑	45 Jeff Garcia	1.00	.40
❑	46 Donovan McNabb	1.25	.50
❑	47 Randy Moss	1.50	.60
❑	48 Ahman Green	1.00	.40
❑	49 Travis Henry	.60	.25
❑	50 Brad Johnson	.60	.25
❑	51 Tommy Maddox	1.00	.40
❑	52 Aaron Brooks	1.00	.40
❑	53 Peyton Manning	1.50	.60
❑	54 Brian Urlacher	1.50	.60
❑	55 Rod Gardner	.60	.25
❑	56 Chad Pennington	1.25	.50
❑	57 Ricky Williams	1.00	.40
❑	58 James Stewart	.60	.25
❑	59 Todd Heap	.60	.25
❑	60 Marshall Faulk	1.00	.40
❑	61 Corey Dillon	.60	.25
❑	62 Michael Vick	2.50	1.00
❑	63 Shaun Alexander	1.00	.40
❑	64 Curtis Martin	1.00	.40
❑	65 Mark Brunell	.60	.25
❑	66 Joey Harrington	1.50	.60
❑	67 Drew Bledsoe	1.00	.40
❑	68 Keyshawn Johnson	1.00	.40
❑	69 Jerome Bettis	1.00	.40
❑	70 Daunte Culpepper	1.00	.40
❑	71 David Carr	1.50	.60
❑	72 Marty Booker	.60	.25
❑	73 Patrick Ramsey	1.00	.40
❑	74 Drew Brees	1.00	.40
❑	75 Donte Stallworth	1.00	.40
❑	76 Jake Plummer	.60	.25
❑	77 Ray Lewis	1.00	.40
❑	78 Kurt Warner	1.00	.40
❑	79 Rich Gannon	.60	.25
❑	80 Tony Gonzalez	.60	.25
❑	92 Dallas Clark JSY RC	8.00	3.00
❑	93 Terence Newman JSY RC	15.00	6.00
❑	94 Rex Grossman JSY RC	12.00	5.00
❑	95 Kelley Washington JSY RC	10.00	4.00
❑	96 Kyle Boller JSY RC	12.00	5.00
❑	91 Carson Palmer RC	30.00	12.50
❑	98 Charles Rogers JSY RC	8.00	3.00
❑	99 Chris Simms JSY RC	10.00	4.00
❑	100 Larry Johnson JSY RC	30.00	15.00
❑	101 Andre Johnson JSY RC	15.00	6.00
❑	102 Taylor Jacobs JSY RC	8.00	3.00
❑	103 Byron Leftwich JSY RC	25.00	10.00
❑	110 Tyrone Calico RC	6.00	2.50
❑	111 Billy McMullen RC	4.00	1.50
❑	112 Jerome McDougle RC	5.00	2.00
❑	113 Willis McGahee RC	12.00	5.00
❑	114 Anquan Boldin RC	12.00	5.00
❑	115 Artose Pinner RC	5.00	2.00
❑	116 Kevin Williams RC	5.00	2.00
❑	117 Bethel Johnson RC	5.00	2.00
❑	118 Quentin Griffin RC	5.00	2.00
❑	119 Nate Burleson RC	6.00	2.50
❑	120 DeWayne Robertson RC	5.00	2.00

2004 Fleer Hot Prospects

❑ COMP.SET w/o SP's (70) 20.00 7.50
❑ 71-94 AU JSY RC ODDS 1:20H, 1:840R
❑ 95-102 JSY RC ODDS 1:42H, 1:420R
❑ 95-102 JSY RC PRINT RUN 350 #'d SETS
❑ 103-112 ROOKIE ODDS 1:18H, 1:1440R
❑ 103-112 RC PRINT RUN 1000 SER. #'d SETS
❑ UNPRICED WHITE HOTS #'d OF 1

❑	1 Donovan McNabb	1.00	.40
❑	2 Charlie Garner	.50	.20
❑	3 Tim Rattay	.30	.10
❑	4 Drew Brees	.75	.30
❑	5 Jerry Rice	1.50	.60
❑	6 Aaron Brooks	.50	.20

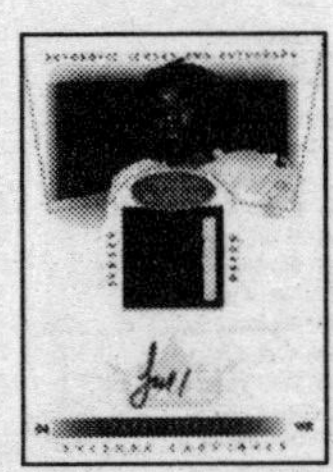

❑ 7 Chris Chambers .50 .20
❑ 8 Byron Leftwich 1.00 .40
❑ 9 Andre Johnson .75 .30
❑ 10 Edgerrin James .75 .30
❑ 11 Charles Rogers .50 .20
❑ 12 Quentin Griffin .75 .30
❑ 13 Carson Palmer 1.00 .40
❑ 14 Ray Lewis .75 .30
❑ 15 Clinton Portis .75 .30
❑ 16 Marc Bulger .75 .30
❑ 17 Matt Hasselbeck .50 .20
❑ 18 Plaxico Burress .50 .20
❑ 19 Priest Holmes 1.00 .40
❑ 20 David Carr .75 .30
❑ 21 Ahman Green .75 .30
❑ 22 Roy Williams S .50 .20
❑ 23 Travis Henry .50 .20
❑ 24 Michael Vick 1.50 .60
❑ 25 Eddie George .50 .20
❑ 26 Marshall Faulk .75 .30
❑ 27 Kevan Barlow .50 .20
❑ 28 Shaun Alexander .75 .30
❑ 29 Hines Ward .75 .30
❑ 30 Anquan Boldin .75 .30
❑ 31 Chad Pennington .75 .30
❑ 32 Randy Moss 1.00 .40
❑ 33 Fred Taylor .50 .20
❑ 34 Marvin Harrison .75 .30
❑ 35 Joey Harrington .75 .30
❑ 36 Rich Gannon .50 .20
❑ 37 Deuce McAllister .75 .30
❑ 38 Deion Branch .75 .30
❑ 39 Tony Gonzalez .50 .20
❑ 40 Brett Favre 2.00 .75
❑ 41 Keyshawn Johnson .50 .20
❑ 42 Lee Suggs .75 .30
❑ 43 Jake Delhomme .75 .30
❑ 44 Rex Grossman .75 .30
❑ 45 Drew Bledsoe .75 .30
❑ 46 Warrick Dunn .50 .20
❑ 47 Steve McNair .75 .30
❑ 48 Torry Holt .75 .30
❑ 49 Brian Westbrook .50 .20
❑ 50 Santana Moss .50 .20
❑ 51 Jeremy Shockey .75 .30
❑ 52 Daunte Culpepper .75 .30
❑ 53 Jeff Garcia .75 .30
❑ 54 Stephen Davis .50 .20
❑ 55 Eric Moulds .50 .20
❑ 56 Emmitt Smith 1.50 .60
❑ 57 Keenan McCardell .30 .10
❑ 58 LaDainian Tomlinson 1.00 .40
❑ 59 Terrell Owens .75 .30
❑ 60 Curtis Martin .75 .30
❑ 61 Joe Horn .50 .20
❑ 62 Tiki Barber .75 .30
❑ 63 Tom Brady 2.00 .75
❑ 64 Ricky Williams .75 .30
❑ 65 Peyton Manning 1.25 .50
❑ 66 Jake Plummer .50 .20
❑ 67 Chad Johnson .75 .30
❑ 68 Brian Urlacher 1.00 .40
❑ 69 Jamal Lewis .75 .30
❑ 70 Laveranues Coles .50 .20
❑ 71 Tatum Bell JSY AU/350 RC 80.00 40.00
❑ 72 B.Berrian JSY AU/344 RC 40.00 20.00
❑ 73 M.Clayton JSY AU/350 RC 80.00 40.00
❑ 74 Lee Evans JSY AU/350 RC 60.00 30.00
❑ 75 Fitzgerald JSY AU/140 RC 150.00 75.00
❑ 76 Henderson JSY AU/350 RC 30.00 15.00
❑ 77 D.Henson JSY AU/331 RC 40.00 20.00
❑ 78 St.Jackson JSY AU/300 RC 120.00 60.00
❑ 79 M.Jenkins JSY AU/349 RC 50.00 25.00
❑ 80 Greg Jones JSY AU/289 RC 50.00 25.00
❑ 81 Kev.Jones JSY AU/278 RC 120.00 60.00
❑ 82 J.Losman JSY AU/350 RC 100.00 50.00
❑ 83 Eli Manning JSY AU/350 RC 300.00 150.00
❑ 84 Chris Perry JSY AU/350 RC 50.00 20.00
❑ 85 Phil.Rivers JSY AU/350 RC 135.00 75.00
❑ 86 Roethlis.JSY AU/150 RC 500.00 250.00
❑ 87 Reg.Williams JSY AU/350 RC 60.00 25.00
❑ 88 Ro.Williams JSY AU/350 RC 120.00 50.00
❑ 89 Kell.Winslow JSY AU/50 RC 225.00 125.00
❑ 90 R.Woods JSY AU/350 RC 40.00 20.00
❑ 91 Jul.Jones JSY AU/350 RC 200.00 100.00
❑ 93 K.Colbert JSY AU/349 RC 50.00 25.00
❑ 94 M.Schaub JSY AU/120 RC 120.00 70.00
❑ 95 Cedric Cobbs JSY RC 15.00 6.00
❑ 96 Darius Watts JSY RC 15.00 6.00
❑ 97 DeAngelo Hall JSY RC 25.00 10.00
❑ 98 Derrick Hamilton JSY RC 12.00 5.00
❑ 99 Devard Darling JSY RC 15.00 6.00
❑ 100 Ben Troupe JSY RC 15.00 6.00
❑ 101 Mewelde Moore JSY RC 25.00 10.00
❑ 102 Ben Watson JSY RC 15.00 6.00
❑ 103 Sean Taylor RC 6.00 2.50
❑ 104 Ricky Ray RC 4.00 1.50
❑ 105 Carlos Francis RC 4.00 1.50
❑ 106 Samie Parker RC 5.00 2.00
❑ 107 Jerricho Cotchery RC 5.00 2.00
❑ 108 Ernest Wilford RC 5.00 2.00
❑ 109 Craig Krenzel RC 5.00 2.00
❑ 110 Robert Gallery RC 8.00 3.00
❑ 111 Dunta Robinson RC 5.00 2.00
❑ 112 Jonathan Vilma RC 5.00 2.00

2004 Fleer Inscribed

❑ COMP.SET w/o SP's (75) 25.00 10.00
❑ 76-100 RC ODDS: 1:12 HOB, 1:100 RET
❑ 76-100 RC PRINT RUN 750 SER.#'d SETS
❑ UNPRICED RED PRINT RUN 5 SETS

❑ 1 Terrell Owens 1.00 .40
❑ 2 David Carr 1.00 .40
❑ 3 Jerry Porter .60 .25
❑ 4 Charles Rogers .60 .25
❑ 5 Torry Holt 1.00 .40
❑ 6 Byron Leftwich 1.25 .50
❑ 7 Laveranues Coles .60 .25
❑ 8 Edgerrin James 1.00 .40
❑ 9 Brian Urlacher 1.25 .50
❑ 10 Hines Ward 1.00 .40
❑ 11 LaDainian Tomlinson 1.25 .50
❑ 12 Ahman Green 1.00 .40
❑ 13 Kevan Barlow .60 .25
❑ 14 Trent Green .60 .25
❑ 15 Deuce McAllister 1.00 .40
❑ 16 Lee Suggs 1.00 .40
❑ 17 Drew Brees 1.00 .40
❑ 18 Randy Moss 1.25 .50
❑ 19 Brandon Lloyd .60 .25
❑ 20 Jeff Garcia 1.00 .40
❑ 21 Roy Williams S .60 .25
❑ 22 Daunte Culpepper 1.00 .40
❑ 23 Matt Hasselbeck .60 .25
❑ 24 Keyshawn Johnson .60 .25
❑ 25 Michael Vick 2.00 .75
❑ 26 Shaun Alexander 1.00 .40
❑ 27 Chad Pennington 1.00 .40
❑ 28 Ashley Lelie .60 .25
❑ 29 Anquan Boldin 1.00 .40
❑ 30 Carson Palmer 1.25 .50
❑ 31 Jeremy Shockey 1.00 .40
❑ 32 Peerless Price .60 .25
❑ 33 Chad Johnson 1.00 .40
❑ 34 Tiki Barber 1.00 .40
❑ 35 Warrick Dunn .60 .25
❑ 36 Jamal Lewis 1.00 .40
❑ 37 Brian Westbrook .60 .25
❑ 38 Stephen Davis .60 .25
❑ 39 Steve McNair 1.00 .40
❑ 40 Donovan McNabb 1.25 .50
❑ 41 Fred Taylor .60 .25
❑ 42 Clinton Portis 1.00 .40
❑ 43 Santana Moss .60 .25
❑ 44 Rod Smith .60 .25
❑ 45 Josh McCown .60 .25
❑ 46 Ray Lewis 1.00 .40
❑ 47 Marshall Faulk 1.00 .40
❑ 48 Eric Moulds .60 .25
❑ 49 Jerry Rice 2.00 .75
❑ 50 Jake Delhomme 1.00 .40
❑ 51 Tony Gonzalez .60 .25
❑ 52 Aaron Brooks .60 .25
❑ 53 Randy McMichael .40 .15
❑ 54 David Boston .60 .25
❑ 55 Plaxico Burress .60 .25
❑ 56 Rich Gannon .60 .25
❑ 57 Brett Favre 2.50 1.00
❑ 58 Isaac Bruce .60 .25
❑ 59 Tom Brady 2.50 1.00
❑ 60 Priest Holmes 1.25 .50
❑ 61 Joe Horn .60 .25
❑ 62 Troy Brown .60 .25
❑ 63 Jake Plummer .60 .25
❑ 64 Derrick Brooks .60 .25
❑ 65 Marvin Harrison 1.00 .40
❑ 66 LaVar Arrington 2.00 .75
❑ 67 Drew Bledsoe 1.00 .40
❑ 68 Steve Smith 1.00 .40
❑ 69 Peyton Manning 1.50 .60
❑ 70 Rex Grossman 1.00 .40
❑ 71 Corey Dillon .60 .25
❑ 72 Mike Alstott .60 .25
❑ 73 Andre Johnson 1.00 .40
❑ 74 Joey Harrington 1.00 .40
❑ 75 Tyrone Calico .60 .25
❑ 76 Eli Manning RC 25.00 12.50
❑ 77 Larry Fitzgerald RC 15.00 6.00
❑ 78 Philip Rivers RC 15.00 7.50
❑ 79 Kellen Winslow RC 10.00 4.00
❑ 80 Roy Williams RC 12.00 5.00
❑ 81 Reggie Williams RC 6.00 2.50
❑ 82 Ben Roethlisberger RC 50.00 25.00
❑ 83 Lee Evans RC 6.00 2.50
❑ 84 Michael Clayton RC 10.00 4.00
❑ 85 J.P. Losman RC 10.00 4.00
❑ 86 Steven Jackson RC 15.00 6.00
❑ 87 Chris Perry RC 8.00 3.00
❑ 88 Michael Jenkins RC 5.00 2.00
❑ 89 Kevin Jones RC 15.00 6.00
❑ 90 Rashaun Woods RC 5.00 2.00
❑ 91 Ben Watson RC 5.00 2.00
❑ 92 Ben Troupe RC 5.00 2.00
❑ 93 Tatum Bell RC 10.00 4.00
❑ 94 Julius Jones RC 20.00 7.50
❑ 95 Devery Henderson RC 4.00 1.50
❑ 96 Darius Watts RC 5.00 2.00

❑ 97 Greg Jones RC 5.00 2.00
❑ 98 Keary Colbert RC 6.00 2.50
❑ 99 Derrick Hamilton RC 4.00 1.50
❑ 100 Bernard Berrian RC 5.00 2.00

2001 Fleer Premium

❑ COMP.SET w/o SP's (200) 25.00 10.00
❑ 1 Ricky Williams .60 .25
❑ 2 Dez White .25 .08
❑ 3 Jay Riemersma .25 .08
❑ 4 Derrick Mason .40 .15
❑ 5 Chad Lewis .25 .08
❑ 6 Shaun King .25 .08
❑ 7 Jevon Kearse .40 .15
❑ 8 Bobby Engram .25 .08
❑ 9 Warrick Dunn .60 .25
❑ 10 Randall Cunningham .60 .25
❑ 11 Stephen Alexander .25 .08
❑ 12 Jimmy Smith .40 .15
❑ 13 Az-Zahir Hakim .40 .15
❑ 14 Antonio Freeman .60 .25
❑ 15 Curtis Conway .40 .15
❑ 16 Tim Biakabutuka .40 .15
❑ 17 Peter Warrick .60 .25
❑ 18 Kurt Warner 1.25 .50
❑ 19 Brian Urlacher 1.00 .40
❑ 20 Rod Smith .40 .15
❑ 21 Frank Sanders .25 .08
❑ 22 Trevor Pryce .25 .08
❑ 23 Sammy Morris .25 .08
❑ 24 Cade McNown .25 .08
❑ 25 Keyshawn Johnson .60 .25
❑ 26 Tim Couch .40 .15
❑ 27 Dedric Ward .25 .08
❑ 28 Bill Schroeder .40 .15
❑ 29 John Randle .40 .15
❑ 30 Donovan McNabb .75 .30
❑ 31 Marvin Harrison .60 .25
❑ 32 Trent Dilfer .40 .15
❑ 33 David Boston .60 .25
❑ 34 Donnell Bennett .25 .08
❑ 35 Trace Armstrong .25 .08
❑ 36 Sam Adams .25 .08
❑ 37 Jeremiah Trotter .40 .15
❑ 38 Zach Thomas .60 .25
❑ 39 Shawn Jefferson .25 .08
❑ 40 J.J. Stokes .40 .15
❑ 41 Akili Smith .25 .08
❑ 42 Tony Siragusa .25 .08
❑ 43 William Roaf .25 .08
❑ 44 Muhsin Muhammad .40 .15
❑ 45 Terance Mathis .40 .15
❑ 46 Tee Martin .40 .15
❑ 47 Ray Lewis .60 .25
❑ 48 Matt Hasselbeck .40 .15
❑ 49 Todd Pinkston .25 .08
❑ 50 Rob Johnson .40 .15
❑ 51 Edgerrin James .75 .30
❑ 52 Rocket Ismail .40 .15
❑ 53 Trent Green .60 .25
❑ 54 Tim Dwight .60 .25
❑ 55 Anthony Becht .25 .08
❑ 56 Jessie Armstead .25 .08
❑ 57 Mike Anderson .60 .25
❑ 58 Jamal Anderson .60 .25
❑ 59 Anthony Wright .25 .08
❑ 60 Regan Upshaw .25 .08
❑ 61 John Holecek .25 .08
❑ 62 Shaun Alexander .75 .30
❑ 63 Troy Aikman 1.00 .40
❑ 64 Peter Boulware .25 .08
❑ 65 Hines Ward .60 .25
❑ 66 Michael Strahan .40 .15
❑ 67 Herman Moore .40 .15
❑ 68 Rich Gannon .60 .25
❑ 69 Ken Dilger .25 .08
❑ 70 Terrell Davis .60 .25
❑ 71 Terrence Wilkins .25 .08
❑ 72 Fred Taylor .60 .25
❑ 73 Napoleon Kaufman .25 .08
❑ 74 Tony Horne .25 .08
❑ 75 Ahman Green .60 .25
❑ 76 Jay Fiedler .60 .25
❑ 77 Albert Connell .25 .08
❑ 78 Charlie Batch .60 .25
❑ 79 James Allen .40 .15
❑ 80 Sylvester Morris .25 .08
❑ 81 Isaac Bruce .60 .25
❑ 82 Charles Woodson .40 .15
❑ 83 Lamar Smith .40 .15
❑ 84 Peyton Manning 1.50 .60
❑ 85 Sam Madison .25 .08
❑ 86 Olandis Gary .40 .15
❑ 87 Kevin Faulk .40 .15
❑ 88 Jeff Garcia .60 .25
❑ 89 JaJuan Dawson .25 .08
❑ 90 Sam Cowart .25 .08
❑ 91 David Sloan .25 .08
❑ 92 Bobby Shaw .25 .08
❑ 93 Travis Prentice .25 .08
❑ 94 Terrell Owens .60 .25
❑ 95 John Lynch .40 .15
❑ 96 Jim Harbaugh .40 .15
❑ 97 Brian Griese .60 .25
❑ 98 Jeff Graham .25 .08
❑ 99 La'Roi Glover .25 .08
❑ 100 Joey Galloway .40 .15
❑ 101 Wesley Walls .25 .08
❑ 102 Vinny Testaverde .40 .15
❑ 103 Jason Taylor .25 .08
❑ 104 Darnay Scott .25 .08
❑ 105 Samari Rolle .25 .08
❑ 106 Adrian Murrell .25 .08
❑ 107 Eric Moulds .40 .15
❑ 108 Keenan McCardell .25 .08
❑ 109 Donald Hayes .25 .08
❑ 110 Brett Favre 2.00 .75
❑ 111 Troy Edwards .25 .08
❑ 112 Ron Dayne .60 .25
❑ 113 Daunte Culpepper .60 .25
❑ 114 Chris Chandler .40 .15
❑ 115 Mark Brunell .60 .25
❑ 116 Courtney Brown .40 .15
❑ 117 Aaron Brooks .60 .25
❑ 118 Fred Beasley .25 .08
❑ 119 Mike Alstott .60 .25
❑ 120 Tyrone Wheatley .40 .15
❑ 121 R.Jay Soward .25 .08
❑ 122 Deion Sanders .60 .25
❑ 123 Jake Reed .40 .15
❑ 124 Jamal Lewis 1.00 .40
❑ 125 Tony Gonzalez .40 .15
❑ 126 Terrell Fletcher .25 .08
❑ 127 Wayne Chrebet .40 .15
❑ 128 Cris Carter .60 .25
❑ 129 Drew Bledsoe .75 .30
❑ 130 Tiki Barber .60 .25
❑ 131 Derrick Alexander .40 .15
❑ 132 Frank Wycheck .25 .08
❑ 133 Jerome Pathon .40 .15
❑ 134 Warren Sapp .40 .15
❑ 135 Joe Horn .40 .15
❑ 136 Ricky Watters .40 .15
❑ 137 Amani Toomer .40 .15
❑ 138 Bruce Smith .40 .15
❑ 139 Andre Rison .40 .15
❑ 140 J.R. Redmond .25 .08
❑ 141 Steve McNair .60 .25
❑ 142 Michael McCrary .25 .08
❑ 143 Ike Hilliard .40 .15
❑ 144 Charlie Garner .40 .15
❑ 145 Mark Bruener .25 .08
❑ 146 Emmitt Smith 1.25 .50
❑ 147 Darren Sharper .25 .08
❑ 148 Peerless Price .40 .15
❑ 149 Johnnie Morton .40 .15
❑ 150 Curtis Martin .60 .25
❑ 151 Joe Johnson .25 .08
❑ 152 MarTay Jenkins .25 .08
❑ 153 Priest Holmes .75 .30
❑ 154 Terry Glenn .40 .15
❑ 155 Oronde Gadsden .40 .15
❑ 156 Germane Crowell .25 .08
❑ 157 Steve Beuerlein .25 .08
❑ 158 Champ Bailey .40 .15
❑ 159 Troy Vincent .25 .08
❑ 160 James Stewart .40 .15
❑ 161 Jerry Rice 1.25 .50
❑ 162 Randy Moss 1.25 .50
❑ 163 Dave Moore .25 .08
❑ 164 Ed McCaffrey .60 .25
❑ 165 Thomas Jones .40 .15
❑ 166 Rickey Dudley .25 .08
❑ 167 Hugh Douglas .25 .08
❑ 168 Stephen Davis .60 .25
❑ 169 Kerry Collins .40 .15
❑ 170 Cam Cleeland .25 .08
❑ 171 Stephen Boyd .25 .08
❑ 172 Jerome Bettis .60 .25
❑ 173 Aeneas Williams .25 .08
❑ 174 Chad Pennington 1.00 .40
❑ 175 Dorsey Levens .40 .15
❑ 176 Desmond Howard .25 .08
❑ 177 Torry Holt .60 .25
❑ 178 Plaxico Burress .60 .25
❑ 179 Kevin Johnson .40 .15
❑ 180 Kyle Brady .25 .08
❑ 181 Jake Plummer .40 .15
❑ 182 Brad Johnson .60 .25
❑ 183 Eddie George .60 .25
❑ 184 Corey Dillon .60 .25
❑ 185 Curtis Enis .25 .08
❑ 186 Tim Brown .60 .25
❑ 187 Tony Boselli .25 .08
❑ 188 Duce Staley .60 .25
❑ 189 Junior Seau .60 .25
❑ 190 Marshall Faulk .75 .30
❑ 191 Kordell Stewart .40 .15
❑ 192 Corey Simon .40 .15
❑ 193 Shannon Sharpe .40 .15
❑ 194 Marcus Robinson .60 .25
❑ 195 Carl Pickens .25 .08
❑ 196 Doug Flutie .60 .25
❑ 197 Freddie Jones .25 .08
❑ 198 Patrick Jeffers .40 .15
❑ 199 Shawn Bryson .25 .08
❑ 200 Kevin Dyson .40 .15
❑ 201 David Terrell RC 5.00 2.00
❑ 202 Dan Morgan RC 5.00 2.00
❑ 203 Chris Weinke RC 5.00 2.00
❑ 204 Correll Buckhalter RC 6.00 2.50
❑ 205 Chad Johnson RC 12.00 5.00
❑ 206 LaDainian Tomlinson RC 25.00 12.50
❑ 207 Reggie Wayne RC 10.00 4.00
❑ 208 Tim Hasselbeck RC 5.00 2.00
❑ 209 Michael Vick RC 30.00 12.50
❑ 210 Heath Evans RC 3.00 1.25
❑ 211 Damione Lewis RC 3.00 1.25
❑ 212 Richard Seymour RC 5.00 2.00
❑ 213 Quincy Morgan RC 5.00 2.00
❑ 214 Drew Brees RC 12.00 5.00
❑ 215 Freddie Mitchell RC 5.00 2.00
❑ 216 Justin McCareins RC 5.00 2.00
❑ 217 Mike McMahon RC 5.00 2.00

❑ 218	Derrick Gibson RC	3.00	1.25
❑ 219	Rudi Johnson RC	10.00	4.00
❑ 220	Todd Heap RC	5.00	2.00
❑ 221	Josh Booty RC	5.00	2.00
❑ 222	Justin Smith RC	5.00	2.00
❑ 223	Marcus Stroud RC	5.00	2.00
❑ 224	Rod Gardner RC	5.00	2.00
❑ 225	Vinny Sutherland RC	3.00	1.25
❑ 226	Marques Tuiasosopo RC	5.00	2.00
❑ 227	Anthony Thomas RC	5.00	2.00
❑ 228	Bobby Newcombe RC	3.00	1.25
❑ 229	Michael Bennett RC	8.00	3.00
❑ 230	Snoop Minnis RC	3.00	1.25
❑ 231	Travis Minor RC	3.00	1.25
❑ 232	Travis Henry RC	5.00	2.00
❑ 233	Kevan Barlow RC	5.00	2.00
❑ 234	Gerard Warren RC	5.00	2.00
❑ 235	Sage Rosenfels RC	5.00	2.00
❑ 236	Chris Chambers RC	8.00	3.00
❑ 237	James Jackson RC	5.00	2.00
❑ 238	Deuce McAllister RC	10.00	4.00
❑ 239	Koren Robinson RC	5.00	2.00
❑ 240	Andre Carter RC	5.00	2.00
❑ 241	Santana Moss RC	8.00	3.00
❑ 242	LaMont Jordan RC	10.00	4.00
❑ 243	Ken-Yon Rambo RC	3.00	1.25
❑ 244	Jamal Reynolds RC	5.00	2.00
❑ 245	Fred Smoot RC	5.00	2.00
❑ 246	Robert Ferguson RC	5.00	2.00
❑ 247	Alex Bannister RC	3.00	1.25
❑ 248	Dan Alexander RC	5.00	2.00
❑ 249	Nate Clements RC	5.00	2.00
❑ 250	Quincy Carter RC	5.00	2.00

2002 Fleer Premium

❑	COMP.SET w/o SP's (160)	40.00	15.00
❑ 1	Kevin Dyson	.60	.25
❑ 2	Kerry Collins	.60	.25
❑ 3	Marty Booker	.60	.25
❑ 4	Curtis Conway	.40	.15
❑ 5	Drew Bledsoe	1.25	.50
❑ 6	Kurt Warner	1.00	.40
❑ 7	Hines Ward	1.00	.40
❑ 8	Terrell Owens	1.00	.40
❑ 9	Todd Pinkston	.60	.25
❑ 10	Eric Moulds	.60	.25
❑ 11	Quincy Morgan	.40	.15
❑ 12	Fred Taylor	1.00	.40
❑ 13	Santana Moss	1.00	.40
❑ 14	Peyton Manning	2.00	.75
❑ 15	Qadry Ismail	.60	.25
❑ 16	Mike McMahon	1.00	.40
❑ 17	David Patten	.40	.15
❑ 18	Wayne Chrebet	.60	.25
❑ 19	David Terrell	1.00	.40
❑ 20	Corey Bradford	.40	.15
❑ 21	Derrick Mason	.60	.25
❑ 22	Anthony Thomas	.60	.25
❑ 23	James Allen	.60	.25
❑ 24	Vinny Testaverde	.60	.25
❑ 25	Trent Green	.60	.25
❑ 26	Thomas Jones	.60	.25
❑ 27	Rocket Ismail	.60	.25
❑ 28	Duce Staley	1.00	.40
❑ 29	Drew Brees	1.00	.40
❑ 30	Chris Chandler	.60	.25
❑ 31	Kordell Stewart	.60	.25
❑ 32	Koren Robinson	.60	.25
❑ 33	Jon Kitna	.60	.25
❑ 34	Jamie Sharper	.40	.15
❑ 35	Germane Crowell	.40	.15
❑ 36	Lamar Smith	.60	.25
❑ 37	LaDainian Tomlinson	1.50	.60
❑ 38	Freddie Mitchell	.60	.25
❑ 39	Corey Dillon	.60	.25
❑ 40	Isaac Bruce	1.00	.40
❑ 41	James Thrash	.60	.25
❑ 42	Brian Griese	1.00	.40
❑ 43	Marvin Harrison	1.00	.40
❑ 44	Aaron Brooks	1.00	.40
❑ 45	Rich Gannon	1.00	.40
❑ 46	Mike Alstott	1.00	.40
❑ 47	Shannon Sharpe	.60	.25
❑ 48	Travis Henry	1.00	.40
❑ 49	Keyshawn Johnson	1.00	.40
❑ 50	Daunte Culpepper	1.00	.40
❑ 51	James Jackson	.40	.15
❑ 52	Justin McCareins	.60	.25
❑ 53	Quincy Carter	.60	.25
❑ 54	Stephen Davis	.60	.25
❑ 55	Joey Galloway	.60	.25
❑ 56	Joe Horn	.60	.25
❑ 57	Plaxico Burress	.60	.25
❑ 58	Brett Favre	2.50	1.00
❑ 59	Brian Urlacher	1.50	.60
❑ 60	David Boston	1.00	.40
❑ 61	Darrell Jackson	.60	.25
❑ 62	Trung Canidate	.60	.25
❑ 63	Shaun Alexander	1.25	.50
❑ 64	Steve McNair	1.00	.40
❑ 65	Doug Flutie	1.00	.40
❑ 66	LaMont Jordan	1.00	.40
❑ 67	Rod Smith	.60	.25
❑ 68	Marshall Faulk	1.00	.40
❑ 69	Tiki Barber	1.00	.40
❑ 70	James Stewart	.60	.25
❑ 71	Frank Wycheck	.40	.15
❑ 72	Peerless Price	.60	.25
❑ 73	Derrick Alexander	.60	.25
❑ 74	Charlie Garner	.60	.25
❑ 75	Peter Warrick	.60	.25
❑ 76	Warren Sapp	.60	.25
❑ 77	Kevan Barlow	.60	.25
❑ 78	Edgerrin James	1.25	.50
❑ 79	Willie Jackson	.40	.15
❑ 80	Keenan McCardell	.40	.15
❑ 81	Bill Schroeder	.40	.15
❑ 82	Curtis Martin	1.00	.40
❑ 83	Torry Holt	1.00	.40
❑ 84	Tony Gonzalez	.60	.25
❑ 85	Jeff Garcia	1.00	.40
❑ 86	Travis Taylor	.60	.25
❑ 87	Johnnie Morton	.60	.25
❑ 88	Tim Couch	.60	.25
❑ 89	Troy Brown	.60	.25
❑ 90	Emmitt Smith	2.50	1.00
❑ 91	Aeneas Williams	.40	.15
❑ 92	Rod Gardner	.60	.25
❑ 93	Brandon Stokley	.60	.25
❑ 94	Warrick Dunn	1.00	.40
❑ 95	Jay Riemersma	.40	.15
❑ 96	Kevin Johnson	.60	.25
❑ 97	Antowain Smith	.60	.25
❑ 98	James McKnight	.40	.15
❑ 99	Amani Toomer	.60	.25
❑ 100	Ricky Williams	1.00	.40
❑ 101	Priest Holmes	1.25	.50
❑ 102	Muhsin Muhammad	.60	.25
❑ 103	Jake Plummer	.60	.25
❑ 104	Marcus Robinson	.60	.25
❑ 105	Donovan McNabb	1.25	.50
❑ 106	Tom Brady	2.50	1.00
❑ 107	Jimmy Smith	.60	.25
❑ 108	Jamal Lewis	1.00	.40
❑ 109	Antonio Freeman	1.00	.40
❑ 110	Ron Dayne	.60	.25
❑ 111	Tim Brown	1.00	.40
❑ 112	Chris Chambers	1.00	.40
❑ 113	Garrison Hearst	.60	.25
❑ 114	Michael Vick	3.00	1.25
❑ 115	Snoop Minnis	.40	.15
❑ 116	Terrell Davis	1.00	.40
❑ 117	Ahman Green	1.00	.40
❑ 118	Donald Hayes	.40	.15
❑ 119	Jermaine Lewis	.40	.15
❑ 120	Chad Johnson	1.00	.40
❑ 121	Jay Fiedler	.60	.25
❑ 122	Randy Moss	2.00	.75
❑ 123	Wesley Walls	.40	.15
❑ 124	Eddie George	1.00	.40
❑ 125	Jerry Rice	2.00	.75
❑ 126	Michael Bennett	.60	.25
❑ 127	Jerome Bettis	1.00	.40
❑ 128	Mark Brunell	1.00	.40
❑ 129	Adam Vinatieri	1.00	.40
❑ 130	Ed McCaffrey	1.00	.40
❑ 131	Maurice Morris RC	5.00	2.00
❑ 132	Ron Johnson RC	4.00	1.50
❑ 133	Antwaan Randle El RC	8.00	3.00
❑ 134	Brian Westbrook RC	8.00	3.00
❑ 135	Julius Peppers RC	10.00	4.00
❑ 136	Travis Stephens RC	4.00	1.50
❑ 137	David Carr RC	12.00	5.00
❑ 138	Clinton Portis RC	15.00	6.00
❑ 139	Reche Caldwell RC	5.00	2.00
❑ 140	Tim Carter RC	4.00	1.50
❑ 141	Daniel Graham RC	5.00	2.00
❑ 142	Rohan Davey RC	5.00	2.00
❑ 143	T.J. Duckett RC	8.00	3.00
❑ 144	Luke Staley RC	4.00	1.50
❑ 145	Ashley Lelie RC	10.00	4.00
❑ 146	Josh Reed RC	5.00	2.00
❑ 147	Randy Fasani RC	4.00	1.50
❑ 148	Andre Davis RC	4.00	1.50
❑ 149	Joey Harrington RC	12.00	5.00
❑ 150	David Garrard RC	5.00	2.00
❑ 151	Ladell Betts RC	5.00	2.00
❑ 152	Donte Stallworth RC	10.00	4.00
❑ 153	Adrian Peterson RC	5.00	2.00
❑ 154	Lamar Gordon RC	5.00	2.00
❑ 155	Jonathan Wells RC	5.00	2.00
❑ 156	Jabar Gaffney RC	5.00	2.00
❑ 157	Patrick Ramsey RC	6.00	2.50
❑ 158	Roy Williams RC	12.00	5.00
❑ 159	Jeremy Shockey RC	15.00	6.00
❑ 160	Javon Walker RC	10.00	4.00
❑ 161	Marquise Walker RC	4.00	1.50
❑ 162	Antonio Bryant RC	5.00	2.00
❑ 163	Josh McCown RC	6.00	2.50
❑ 164	Najeh Davenport RC	5.00	2.00
❑ 165	William Green RC	5.00	2.00
❑ 166	Jerramy Stevens RC	5.00	2.00
❑ 167	DeShaun Foster RC	5.00	2.00
❑ 168	Cliff Russell RC	4.00	1.50
❑ 169	Kurt Kittner RC	4.00	1.50
❑ 170	Eric Crouch RC	5.00	2.00
❑ 171	Michael Pittman PP	.40	.15
❑ 172	Darnay Scott PP	.40	.15
❑ 173	Charles Woodson PP	.60	.25
❑ 174	Ty Law PP	.40	.15
❑ 175	Tony Boselli PP	.40	.15
❑ 176	Zach Thomas PP	1.00	.40
❑ 177	Trent Dilfer PP	.60	.25
❑ 178	Bubba Franks PP	.60	.25
❑ 179	Laveranues Coles PP	.60	.25
❑ 180	John Lynch PP	.60	.25
❑ 181	Kendrell Bell PP	1.00	.40
❑ 182	Mike Anderson PP	1.00	.40
❑ 183	Amos Zereoue PP	1.00	.40
❑ 184	Michael Strahan PP	.60	.25
❑ 185	Chad Lewis PP	.40	.15
❑ 186	Travis Minor PP	.40	.15
❑ 187	Jevon Kearse PP	.60	.25
❑ 188	Darren Sharper PP	.40	.15

- ❑ 189 Az-Zahir Hakim PP .40 .15
- ❑ 190 Ray Lewis PP 1.00 .40
- ❑ 191 Deuce McAllister PP 1.25 .50
- ❑ 192 Chris Weinke PP .60 .25
- ❑ 193 Desmond Howard PP .40 .15
- ❑ 194 Dominic Rhodes PP .60 .25
- ❑ 195 Joe Jurevicius PP .40 .15
- ❑ 196 Tim Dwight PP 1.00 .40
- ❑ 197 Jeff Zgonina PP .40 .15
- ❑ 198 Junior Seau PP 1.00 .40
- ❑ 199 Rosevelt Colvin PP RC 1.00 .40
- ❑ 200 Chad Pennington PP 1.25 .50

2000 Fleer Showcase

- ❑ COMP.SET w/o SP's (100) 25.00 10.00
- ❑ 1 Tim Couch .50 .20
- ❑ 2 Deion Sanders .75 .30
- ❑ 3 Darnay Scott .50 .20
- ❑ 4 Brett Favre 2.50 1.00
- ❑ 5 Mark Brunell .75 .30
- ❑ 6 Randy Moss 1.50 .60
- ❑ 7 Tyrone Wheatley .50 .20
- ❑ 8 Isaac Bruce .75 .30
- ❑ 9 Eddie George .75 .30
- ❑ 10 Troy Aikman 1.50 .60
- ❑ 11 Charlie Batch .75 .30
- ❑ 12 Marvin Harrison .75 .30
- ❑ 13 Terry Glenn .50 .20
- ❑ 14 Charles Johnson .50 .20
- ❑ 15 Jerry Rice 1.50 .60
- ❑ 16 Kurt Warner 1.50 .60
- ❑ 17 Kevin Johnson .75 .30
- ❑ 18 Jay Fiedler .75 .30
- ❑ 19 Vinny Testaverde .50 .20
- ❑ 20 Curtis Enis .30 .10
- ❑ 21 Elvis Grbac .50 .20
- ❑ 22 Kordell Stewart .50 .20
- ❑ 23 Jamal Anderson .75 .30
- ❑ 24 Dorsey Levens .50 .20
- ❑ 25 Derrick Mayes .50 .20
- ❑ 26 Marcus Robinson .75 .30
- ❑ 27 Cam Cleeland .30 .10
- ❑ 28 Charlie Garner .50 .20
- ❑ 29 Germane Crowell .30 .10
- ❑ 30 Cade McNown .30 .10
- ❑ 31 Tony Gonzalez .50 .20
- ❑ 32 Shaun King .30 .10
- ❑ 33 Wayne Chrebet .50 .20
- ❑ 34 Muhsin Muhammad .50 .20
- ❑ 35 Olandis Gary .75 .30
- ❑ 36 Ray Lewis .75 .30
- ❑ 37 Terrell Davis .75 .30
- ❑ 38 Steve Beuerlein .50 .20
- ❑ 39 James Stewart .50 .20
- ❑ 40 Jon Kitna .75 .30
- ❑ 41 Tim Biakabutuka .50 .20
- ❑ 42 Ryan Leaf .50 .20
- ❑ 43 Mike Alstott .75 .30
- ❑ 44 Yancey Thigpen .30 .10
- ❑ 45 Champ Bailey .50 .20
- ❑ 46 Peerless Price .50 .20
- ❑ 47 Ken Dilger .30 .10
- ❑ 48 Derrick Alexander .50 .20
- ❑ 49 Drew Bledsoe 1.00 .40
- ❑ 50 Jerome Bettis .75 .30
- ❑ 51 Jermaine Fazande .30 .10
- ❑ 52 Joey Galloway .50 .20
- ❑ 53 Jeff Blake .50 .20
- ❑ 54 Emmitt Smith 1.50 .60
- ❑ 55 Ricky Williams .75 .30
- ❑ 56 Marshall Faulk 1.25 .50
- ❑ 57 Stephen Davis .75 .30
- ❑ 58 Rob Johnson .50 .20
- ❑ 59 Brian Griese .75 .30
- ❑ 60 Damon Huard .75 .30
- ❑ 61 Jevon Kearse .75 .30
- ❑ 62 Doug Flutie .75 .30
- ❑ 63 Curtis Martin .75 .30
- ❑ 64 Torry Holt .75 .30
- ❑ 65 David Boston .75 .30
- ❑ 66 Cris Carter .75 .30
- ❑ 67 Jason Sehorn .30 .10
- ❑ 68 Keyshawn Johnson .75 .30
- ❑ 69 Chris Chandler .50 .20
- ❑ 70 Antonio Freeman .75 .30
- ❑ 71 Kerry Collins .50 .20
- ❑ 72 Akili Smith .30 .10
- ❑ 73 Troy Edwards .30 .10
- ❑ 74 Tim Dwight .75 .30
- ❑ 75 Donovan McNabb 1.25 .50
- ❑ 76 Tony Banks .50 .20
- ❑ 77 Ed McCaffrey .75 .30
- ❑ 78 Errict Rhett .30 .10
- ❑ 79 Fred Taylor .75 .30
- ❑ 80 Terrell Owens .75 .30
- ❑ 81 Steve McNair .75 .30
- ❑ 82 Rob Moore .50 .20
- ❑ 83 Jimmy Smith .50 .20
- ❑ 84 Daunte Culpepper 1.00 .40
- ❑ 85 Carl Pickens .50 .20
- ❑ 86 Moses Moreno .30 .10
- ❑ 87 Brad Johnson .75 .30
- ❑ 88 Jake Plummer .50 .20
- ❑ 89 Edgerrin James 1.25 .50
- ❑ 90 Zach Thomas .75 .30
- ❑ 91 Rich Gannon .75 .30
- ❑ 92 Warrick Dunn .75 .30
- ❑ 93 Shannon Sharpe .50 .20
- ❑ 94 Peyton Manning 2.00 .75
- ❑ 95 Keenan McCardell .50 .20
- ❑ 96 Tony Simmons .30 .10
- ❑ 97 Duce Staley .75 .30
- ❑ 98 Corey Dillon .75 .30
- ❑ 99 Tim Brown .75 .30
- ❑ 100 Ricky Watters .50 .20
- ❑ 101 Peter Warrick RC 10.00 4.00
- ❑ 102 Shaun Alexander RC 40.00 15.00
- ❑ 103 Anthony Becht RC 10.00 4.00
- ❑ 104 Courtney Brown RC 10.00 4.00
- ❑ 105 Plaxico Burress RC 20.00 7.50
- ❑ 106 Trung Canidate RC 8.00 3.00
- ❑ 107 Giovanni Carmazzi RC 8.00 3.00
- ❑ 108 Laveranues Coles RC 12.00 5.00
- ❑ 109 Ron Dayne RC 10.00 4.00
- ❑ 110 Reuben Droughns RC 12.00 5.00
- ❑ 111 Danny Farmer RC 8.00 3.00
- ❑ 112 Bubba Franks RC 10.00 4.00
- ❑ 113 Thomas Jones RC 15.00 6.00
- ❑ 114 Jamal Lewis RC 20.00 7.50
- ❑ 115 Sylvester Morris RC 8.00 3.00
- ❑ 116 Chad Pennington RC 20.00 7.50
- ❑ 117 Travis Prentice RC 8.00 3.00
- ❑ 118 J.R. Redmond RC 8.00 3.00
- ❑ 119 R.Jay Soward RC 8.00 3.00
- ❑ 120 Dez White RC 10.00 4.00
- ❑ 121 Sebastian Janikowski RC 5.00 2.00
- ❑ 122 Todd Pinkston RC 5.00 2.00
- ❑ 123 Marc Bulger RC 10.00 4.00
- ❑ 124 Ron Dugans RC 2.50 1.00
- ❑ 125 Joe Hamilton RC 4.00 1.50
- ❑ 126 Curtis Keaton RC 4.00 1.50
- ❑ 127 Tee Martin RC 5.00 2.00
- ❑ 128 Dennis Northcutt RC 5.00 2.00
- ❑ 129 Corey Simon RC 5.00 2.00
- ❑ 130 Chris Redman RC 4.00 1.50
- ❑ 131 Brian Urlacher RC 20.00 7.50
- ❑ 132 Travis Taylor RC 5.00 2.00
- ❑ 133 Michael Wiley RC 4.00 1.50
- ❑ 134 Tim Rattay RC 5.00 2.00
- ❑ 135 Jerry Porter RC 6.00 2.50
- ❑ 136 Tom Brady RC 80.00 40.00
- ❑ 137 Deon Dyer RC 4.00 1.50
- ❑ 138 Mareno Philyaw RC 2.50 1.00
- ❑ 139 Spergon Wynn RC 4.00 1.50
- ❑ 140 John Abraham RC 5.00 2.00
- ❑ 141 Ahmed Plummer RC 5.00 2.00
- ❑ 142 Chris Hovan RC 4.00 1.50
- ❑ 143 Rob Morris RC 4.00 1.50
- ❑ 144 Keith Bulluck RC 5.00 2.00
- ❑ 145 JaJuan Dawson RC 2.50 1.00
- ❑ 146 Chris Cole RC 4.00 1.50
- ❑ 147 Chafie Fields RC 2.50 1.00
- ❑ 148 Darrell Jackson RC 10.00 4.00
- ❑ 149 Marcus Knight RC 4.00 1.50
- ❑ 150 Gari Scott RC 2.50 1.00
- ❑ 151 Kwame Cavil RC 2.50 1.00
- ❑ 152 Frank Moreau RC 4.00 1.50
- ❑ 153 Doug Chapman RC 4.00 1.50
- ❑ 154 Erron Kinney RC 5.00 2.00
- ❑ 155 Ron Dixon RC 4.00 1.50
- ❑ 156 Ben Kelly RC 2.50 1.00
- ❑ 157 Bashir Yamini RC 2.50 1.00
- ❑ 158 Anthony Lucas RC 2.50 1.00
- ❑ 159 Avion Black RC 4.00 1.50
- ❑ 160 Ian Gold RC 4.00 1.50

2001 Fleer Showcase

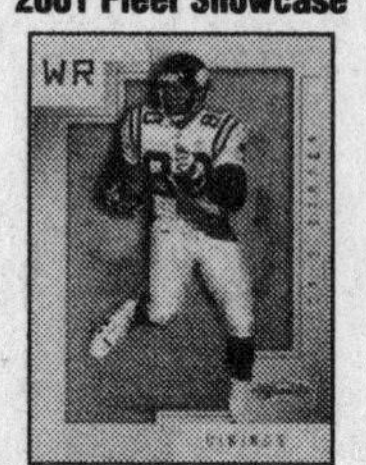

- ❑ COMP.SET w/o SP's (100) 25.00 10.00
- ❑ 1 Cris Carter 1.00 .40
- ❑ 2 Sylvester Morris .40 .15
- ❑ 3 Vinny Testaverde .60 .25
- ❑ 4 Jevon Kearse .60 .25
- ❑ 5 Terance Mathis .40 .15
- ❑ 6 Mike Anderson 1.00 .40
- ❑ 7 Aaron Brooks 1.00 .40
- ❑ 8 Jerry Rice 2.00 .75
- ❑ 9 Mike Alstott 1.00 .40
- ❑ 10 Jon Kitna .60 .25
- ❑ 11 Derrick Alexander .60 .25
- ❑ 12 Shaun Alexander 1.25 .50
- ❑ 13 Thomas Jones .60 .25
- ❑ 14 James Stewart .60 .25
- ❑ 15 Ron Dayne 1.00 .40
- ❑ 16 Az-Zahir Hakim .60 .25
- ❑ 17 Terrell Owens 1.00 .40
- ❑ 18 Travis Prentice .40 .15
- ❑ 19 Lamar Smith .60 .25
- ❑ 20 James Thrash .60 .25
- ❑ 21 Doug Flutie 1.00 .40
- ❑ 22 Derrick Mason .60 .25
- ❑ 23 Ray Lewis 1.00 .40
- ❑ 24 Ed McCaffrey 1.00 .40
- ❑ 25 Ricky Williams 1.00 .40
- ❑ 26 Tyrone Wheatley .60 .25
- ❑ 27 Chris Chandler .60 .25
- ❑ 28 Rod Smith .60 .25
- ❑ 29 Joe Horn .60 .25
- ❑ 30 Jerome Bettis 1.00 .40

❑ 31 Brian Urlacher 1.50 .60
❑ 32 Dorsey Levens .60 .25
❑ 33 Kordell Stewart .60 .25
❑ 34 Michael Westbrook .60 .25
❑ 35 Jamal Anderson 1.00 .40
❑ 36 Charlie Batch 1.00 .40
❑ 37 Kerry Collins .60 .25
❑ 38 Jake Plummer .60 .25
❑ 39 Robert Porcher .40 .15
❑ 40 Jason Sehorn .40 .15
❑ 41 Junior Seau 1.00 .40
❑ 42 Warren Sapp .60 .25
❑ 43 Champ Bailey .60 .25
❑ 44 Jamal Lewis 1.50 .60
❑ 45 Tony Banks .60 .25
❑ 46 Doug Chapman .40 .15
❑ 47 Stephen Davis 1.00 .40
❑ 48 Elvis Grbac .60 .25
❑ 49 Joey Galloway .60 .25
❑ 50 Terry Glenn .60 .25
❑ 51 Todd Pinkston .60 .25
❑ 52 JaJuan Dawson .40 .15
❑ 53 Zach Thomas 1.00 .40
❑ 54 Tim Couch .60 .25
❑ 55 Cade McNown .40 .15
❑ 56 Charlie Garner .60 .25
❑ 57 Jeff George .60 .25
❑ 58 Peerless Price .60 .25
❑ 59 Tony Gonzalez .60 .25
❑ 60 Rob Johnson .40 .15
❑ 61 Keenan McCardell .40 .15
❑ 62 Eric Moulds .60 .25
❑ 63 Jimmy Smith .60 .25
❑ 64 Jeff Garcia 1.00 .40
❑ 65 Rod Woodson .60 .25
❑ 66 Brian Griese 1.00 .40
❑ 67 Kevin Faulk .60 .25
❑ 68 Plaxico Burress 1.00 .40
❑ 69 Isaac Bruce 1.00 .40
❑ 70 Keyshawn Johnson 1.00 .40
❑ 71 Tim Biakabutuka .60 .25
❑ 72 Mark Brunell 1.00 .40
❑ 73 Wesley Walls .40 .15
❑ 74 Jerome Pathon .60 .25
❑ 75 Wayne Chrebet .60 .25
❑ 76 Muhsin Muhammad .60 .25
❑ 77 Marvin Harrison 1.00 .40
❑ 78 David Boston 1.00 .40
❑ 79 Germane Crowell .40 .15
❑ 80 Tiki Barber 1.00 .40
❑ 81 Laveranues Coles 1.00 .40
❑ 82 Tim Brown 1.00 .40
❑ 83 Matt Hasselbeck .60 .25
❑ 84 Brad Johnson 1.00 .40
❑ 85 Marcus Robinson 1.00 .40
❑ 86 Ahman Green 1.00 .40
❑ 87 Curtis Martin 1.00 .40
❑ 88 Peter Warrick 1.00 .40
❑ 89 Ray Lucas .40 .15
❑ 90 Duce Staley 1.00 .40
❑ 91 Darrell Jackson .40 .15
❑ 92 Steve McNair 1.00 .40
❑ 93 Rickey Dudley .40 .15
❑ 94 Jason Taylor .40 .15
❑ 95 Rich Gannon 1.00 .40
❑ 96 Torry Holt 1.00 .40
❑ 97 James Allen .60 .25
❑ 98 Antonio Freeman 1.00 .40
❑ 99 Trent Green .60 .25
❑ 100 Ricky Watters .60 .25
❑ 101 Corey Dillon AC 4.00 1.50
❑ 102 Emmitt Smith AC 8.00 3.00
❑ 103 Terrell Davis AC 4.00 1.50
❑ 104 Brett Favre AC 12.00 5.00
❑ 105 Peyton Manning AC 10.00 4.00
❑ 106 Edgerrin James AC 5.00 2.00
❑ 107 Fred Taylor AC 4.00 1.50
❑ 108 Daunte Culpepper AC 4.00 1.50
❑ 109 Randy Moss AC 8.00 3.00
❑ 110 Drew Bledsoe AC 5.00 2.00
❑ 111 Donovan McNabb AC 5.00 2.00
❑ 112 Kurt Warner AC 8.00 3.00
❑ 113 Marshall Faulk AC 5.00 2.00
❑ 114 Warrick Dunn AC 4.00 1.50
❑ 115 Eddie George AC 4.00 1.50
❑ 116 Michael Vick AC RC 100.00 40.00
❑ 117 David Terrell AC RC 15.00 6.00
❑ 118 Deuce McAllister AC RC 25.00 10.00
❑ 119 Koren Robinson AC RC 15.00 6.00
❑ 120 Rod Gardner AC RC 15.00 6.00
❑ 121 Santana Moss AC RC 25.00 10.00
❑ 122 Drew Brees AC RC 30.00 12.50
❑ 123 Chris Weinke AC RC 15.00 6.00
❑ 124 LaDainian Tomlinson AC RC 80.00 40.00
❑ 125 Freddie Mitchell AC RC 15.00 6.00
❑ 126 Chris Chambers RC 12.00 5.00
❑ 127 Reggie Wayne RC 15.00 6.00
❑ 128 Quincy Morgan RC 6.00 2.50
❑ 129 Rudi Johnson RC 15.00 6.00
❑ 130 Robert Ferguson RC 6.00 2.50
❑ 131 Todd Heap RC 6.00 2.50
❑ 132 Michael Bennett RC 12.00 5.00
❑ 133 Jesse Palmer RC 6.00 2.50
❑ 134 James Jackson RC 6.00 2.50
❑ 135 Chad Johnson RC 20.00 7.50
❑ 136 LaMont Jordan RC 15.00 6.00
❑ 137 Anthony Thomas RC 6.00 2.50
❑ 138 Travis Henry RC 6.00 2.50
❑ 139 Snoop Minnis RC 6.00 2.50
❑ 140 Marques Tuiasosopo RC 6.00 2.50
❑ 141 Travis Minor RC 6.00 2.50
❑ 142 Mike McMahon RC 6.00 2.50
❑ 143 Josh Heupel RC 6.00 2.50
❑ 144 Sage Rosenfels RC 6.00 2.50
❑ 145 Quincy Carter RC 6.00 2.50
❑ 146 Alge Crumpler RC 8.00 4.00
❑ 147 Kevan Barlow RC 6.00 2.50
❑ 148 Heath Evans RC 4.00 1.50
❑ 149 Correll Buckhalter RC 8.00 3.00
❑ 150 Justin McCareins RC 6.00 2.50
❑ 151 Reggie Germany RC 4.00 1.50
❑ 152 Vinny Sutherland RC 4.00 1.50
❑ 153 Scotty Anderson RC 4.00 1.50
❑ 154 Tim Hasselbeck RC 6.00 2.50
❑ 155 Alex Bannister RC 4.00 1.50
❑ 156 Andre Carter RC 6.00 2.50
❑ 157 Adam Archuleta RC 6.00 2.50
❑ 158 Ken-Yon Rambo RC 4.00 1.50
❑ 159 Gerard Warren RC 6.00 2.50
❑ 160 Justin Smith RC 6.00 2.50
❑ NNO Donovan McNabb AU/300 60.0025.00

2002 Fleer Showcase

❑ COMP.SET w/o SP's (125) 25.00 10.00
❑ 1 Kevin Johnson .60 .25
❑ 2 Chris Walsh .40 .15
❑ 3 Vinny Testaverde .60 .25
❑ 4 Kordell Stewart .60 .25
❑ 5 Chris Redman .40 .15
❑ 6 Johnnie Morton .60 .25
❑ 7 Tony Gonzalez .60 .25
❑ 8 Torry Holt 1.00 .40
❑ 9 Champ Bailey .60 .25
❑ 10 Eric Moulds .60 .25
❑ 11 Az-Zahir Hakim .40 .15
❑ 12 Mark Brunell 1.00 .40
❑ 13 Laveranues Coles .60 .25
❑ 14 Kevan Barlow .60 .25
❑ 15 Stephen Davis .60 .25
❑ 16 Benjamin Gay .60 .25
❑ 17 Randy Moss 2.00 .75
❑ 18 Hines Ward 1.00 .40
❑ 19 Brian Urlacher 1.50 .60
❑ 20 Dominic Rhodes .60 .25
❑ 21 David Patten .40 .15
❑ 22 Tim Brown 1.00 .40
❑ 23 Trent Dilfer .60 .25
❑ 24 David Boston 1.00 .40
❑ 25 Quincy Carter .60 .25
❑ 26 Daunte Culpepper 1.00 .40
❑ 27 Plaxico Burress .60 .25
❑ 28 Michael Pittman .40 .15
❑ 29 Joey Galloway .60 .25
❑ 30 Jason Taylor .40 .15
❑ 31 Drew Brees 1.00 .40
❑ 32 Jamal Anderson .60 .25
❑ 33 Dat Nguyen .40 .15
❑ 34 Chris Chambers 1.00 .40
❑ 35 Tiki Barber 1.00 .40
❑ 36 LaDainian Tomlinson 1.50 .60
❑ 37 Peter Warrick .60 .25
❑ 38 Bubba Franks .60 .25
❑ 39 Joe Horn .60 .25
❑ 40 Correll Buckhalter .60 .25
❑ 41 Mike Alstott 1.00 .40
❑ 42 Brian Finneran .40 .15
❑ 43 Troy Hambrick .40 .15
❑ 44 Zach Thomas 1.00 .40
❑ 45 Kerry Collins .60 .25
❑ 46 Junior Seau 1.00 .40
❑ 47 Alvis Whitted .40 .15
❑ 48 Terrell Davis 1.00 .40
❑ 49 Ricky Williams 1.00 .40
❑ 50 Curtis Conway .40 .15
❑ 51 Travis Taylor .60 .25
❑ 52 Brian Griese 1.00 .40
❑ 53 Sylvester Morris .40 .15
❑ 54 Amani Toomer .60 .25
❑ 55 Jeff Garcia 1.00 .40
❑ 56 Michael McCrary .40 .15
❑ 57 Ahman Green 1.00 .40
❑ 58 Trent Green .60 .25
❑ 59 Trung Canidate .60 .25
❑ 60 Jamal Lewis 1.00 .40
❑ 61 Larry Foster .40 .15
❑ 62 Priest Holmes 1.25 .50
❑ 63 Isaac Bruce 1.00 .40
❑ 64 Bruce Smith .40 .15
❑ 65 Darnay Scott .40 .15
❑ 66 Terry Glenn .60 .25
❑ 67 Darren Howard .40 .15
❑ 68 Hugh Douglas .40 .15
❑ 69 Milton Wynn .40 .15
❑ 70 Tim Couch .60 .25
❑ 71 Bill Schroeder .60 .25
❑ 72 Michael Strahan .60 .25
❑ 73 James Thrash .60 .25
❑ 74 Steve McNair 1.00 .40
❑ 75 Patrick Jeffers .40 .15
❑ 76 Marcus Pollard .40 .15
❑ 77 Willie McGinest .40 .15
❑ 78 Santana Moss 1.00 .40
❑ 79 Grant Wistrom .40 .15
❑ 80 Jim Miller .40 .15
❑ 81 Marvin Harrison 1.00 .40
❑ 82 Troy Brown .60 .25
❑ 83 Rich Gannon 1.00 .40
❑ 84 Shaun Alexander 1.25 .50
❑ 85 Jake Plummer .60 .25
❑ 86 Quincy Morgan .40 .15
❑ 87 Michael Bennett .60 .25
❑ 88 Jerome Bettis 1.00 .40
❑ 89 Marty Booker .40 .15
❑ 90 Trevor Insley .40 .15

- ❑ 91 Adam Vinatieri 1.00 .40
- ❑ 92 Charles Woodson .60 .25
- ❑ 93 Darrell Jackson .60 .25
- ❑ 94 Corey Dillon .60 .25
- ❑ 95 Corey Bradford .40 .15
- ❑ 96 Deuce McAllister 1.25 .50
- ❑ 97 Todd Pinkston .60 .25
- ❑ 98 Warren Sapp .60 .25
- ❑ 99 Alex Van Pelt .60 .25
- ❑ 100 Mike McMahon 1.00 .40
- ❑ 101 Fred Taylor 1.00 .40
- ❑ 102 Ron Dayne .60 .25
- ❑ 103 Ernie Conwell .40 .15
- ❑ 104 Rod Gardner .60 .25
- ❑ 105 Muhsin Muhammad .60 .25
- ❑ 106 Reggie Wayne 1.00 .40
- ❑ 107 Antowain Smith .60 .25
- ❑ 108 Chad Pennington 1.25 .50
- ❑ 109 Koren Robinson .60 .25
- ❑ 110 Travis Henry 1.00 .40
- ❑ 111 Ed McCaffrey 1.00 .40
- ❑ 112 Keenan McCardell .40 .15
- ❑ 113 Curtis Martin 1.00 .40
- ❑ 114 Bryant Young .40 .15
- ❑ 115 Derrick Mason .60 .25
- ❑ 116 Anthony Thomas .60 .25
- ❑ 117 Jermaine Lewis .40 .15
- ❑ 118 Aaron Brooks 1.00 .40
- ❑ 119 Charlie Garner .60 .25
- ❑ 120 Keyshawn Johnson 1.00 .40
- ❑ 121 Chris Weinke .60 .25
- ❑ 122 Rod Smith .60 .25
- ❑ 123 Jimmy Smith .60 .25
- ❑ 124 Terrell Owens 1.00 .40
- ❑ 125 Eddie George 1.00 .40
- ❑ 126 Tom Brady AC 10.00 4.00
- ❑ 127 Donovan McNabb AC 5.00 2.00
- ❑ 128 Kurt Warner AC 4.00 1.50
- ❑ 129 Peyton Manning AC 8.00 3.00
- ❑ 130 Marshall Faulk AC 4.00 1.50
- ❑ 131 Michael Vick AC 12.00 5.00
- ❑ 132 Emmitt Smith AC 10.00 4.00
- ❑ 133 Jerry Rice AC 8.00 3.00
- ❑ 134 Edgerrin James AC 5.00 2.00
- ❑ 135 Brett Favre AC 10.00 4.00
- ❑ 136 David Carr AC RC 25.00 10.00
- ❑ 137 Joey Harrington AC RC 25.00 10.00
- ❑ 138 Ashley Lelie AC RC 20.00 7.50
- ❑ 139 William Green AC RC 12.00 5.00
- ❑ 140 T.J. Duckett AC RC 20.00 7.50
- ❑ 141 Donte Stallworth AC RC 20.00 7.50
- ❑ 142 Ron Johnson RC 6.00 2.50
- ❑ 143 Jeremy Shockey RC 25.00 10.00
- ❑ 144 Daniel Graham RC 8.00 3.00
- ❑ 145 Reche Caldwell RC 8.00 3.00
- ❑ 146 Antonio Bryant RC 8.00 3.00
- ❑ 147 DeShaun Foster RC 8.00 3.00
- ❑ 148 Clinton Portis RC 25.00 10.00
- ❑ 149 Patrick Ramsey RC 10.00 4.00
- ❑ 150 Lamar Gordon RC 8.00 3.00
- ❑ 151 Josh Reed RC 8.00 3.00
- ❑ 152 Ladell Betts RC 8.00 3.00
- ❑ 153 Kurt Kittner RC 6.00 2.50
- ❑ 154 Jabar Gaffney RC 8.00 3.00
- ❑ 155 Josh McCown RC 10.00 4.00
- ❑ 156 Marquise Walker RC 6.00 2.50
- ❑ 157 Brian Westbrook RC 12.00 5.00
- ❑ 158 Andre Davis RC 6.00 2.50
- ❑ 159 David Garrard RC 8.00 3.00
- ❑ 160 Cliff Russell RC 6.00 2.50
- ❑ 161 Julius Peppers RC 15.00 6.00
- ❑ 162 Adrian Peterson RC 8.00 3.00
- ❑ 163 Antwaan Randle El RC 12.00 5.00
- ❑ 164 Javon Walker RC 15.00 6.00
- ❑ 165 Rohan Davey RC 8.00 3.00
- ❑ 166 Luke Staley RC 6.00 2.50

2003 Fleer Showcase

- ❑ COMP.SET w/o SP's (90) 25.00 10.00
- ❑ 1 Edgerrin James 1.00 .40

- ❑ 2 Donald Driver .60 .25
- ❑ 3 Drew Brees 1.00 .40
- ❑ 4 Corey Dillon .60 .25
- ❑ 5 Jerome Bettis 1.00 .40
- ❑ 6 Charlie Garner .60 .25
- ❑ 7 Eddie George .60 .25
- ❑ 8 Mark Brunell .60 .25
- ❑ 9 David Boston .60 .25
- ❑ 10 Todd Heap .60 .25
- ❑ 11 Terrell Owens 1.00 .40
- ❑ 12 Tommy Maddox 1.00 .40
- ❑ 13 Keyshawn Johnson 1.00 .40
- ❑ 14 Jamal Lewis 1.00 .40
- ❑ 15 Zach Thomas .60 .25
- ❑ 16 Isaac Bruce 1.00 .40
- ❑ 17 Michael Bennett .60 .25
- ❑ 18 Rod Smith .60 .25
- ❑ 19 Eric Moulds .60 .25
- ❑ 20 T.J Duckett .60 .25
- ❑ 21 Hines Ward 1.00 .40
- ❑ 22 Tiki Barber 1.00 .40
- ❑ 23 Julius Peppers 1.00 .40
- ❑ 24 Rich Gannon .60 .25
- ❑ 25 Rod Gardner .60 .25
- ❑ 26 Curtis Martin 1.00 .40
- ❑ 27 Donte Stallworth 1.00 .40
- ❑ 28 Anthony Thomas .60 .25
- ❑ 29 Warren Sapp .60 .25
- ❑ 30 Jake Plummer .60 .25
- ❑ 31 Patrick Ramsey 1.00 .40
- ❑ 32 Tai Streets .40 .15
- ❑ 33 Matt Hasselbeck .60 .25
- ❑ 34 James Stewart .60 .25
- ❑ 35 Chad Hutchinson .40 .15
- ❑ 36 Hugh Douglas .40 .15
- ❑ 37 Jimmy Smith .60 .25
- ❑ 38 Kerry Collins .60 .25
- ❑ 39 Junior Seau 1.00 .40
- ❑ 40 Ed McCaffrey .60 .25
- ❑ 41 Marshall Faulk 1.00 .40
- ❑ 42 Deuce McAllister 1.00 .40
- ❑ 43 Drew Bledsoe 1.00 .40
- ❑ 44 Brian Urlacher 1.50 .60
- ❑ 45 William Green .60 .25
- ❑ 46 Chris Chambers 1.00 .40
- ❑ 47 Daunte Culpepper 1.00 .40
- ❑ 48 Warrick Dunn .60 .25
- ❑ 49 Antwaan Randle El 1.00 .40
- ❑ 50 Joey Harrington 1.50 .60
- ❑ 51 Tim Brown 1.00 .40
- ❑ 52 Duce Staley .60 .25
- ❑ 53 Laveranues Coles .60 .25
- ❑ 54 Ray Lewis 1.00 .40
- ❑ 55 Marvin Harrison 1.00 .40
- ❑ 56 Tony Gonzalez .60 .25
- ❑ 57 Torry Holt 1.00 .40
- ❑ 58 Jeff Garcia 1.00 .40
- ❑ 59 Peerless Price .60 .25
- ❑ 60 Marcel Shipp .60 .25
- ❑ 61 Brian Finneran .40 .15
- ❑ 62 Fred Taylor 1.00 .40
- ❑ 63 Koren Robinson .40 .15
- ❑ 64 Shaun Alexander 1.00 .40
- ❑ 65 Plaxico Burress .60 .25
- ❑ 66 Ahman Green 1.00 .40
- ❑ 67 Simeon Rice .60 .25
- ❑ 68 Joe Horn .60 .25
- ❑ 69 Steve McNair 1.00 .40
- ❑ 70 Amani Toomer .60 .25
- ❑ 71 Kendrell Bell .60 .25
- ❑ 72 Marty Booker .60 .25
- ❑ 73 Stephen Davis .60 .25
- ❑ 74 David Carr 1.50 .60
- ❑ 75 Garrison Hearst .60 .25
- ❑ 76 Joey Galloway .60 .25
- ❑ 77 Aaron Brooks 1.00 .40
- ❑ 78 Mike Alstott 1.00 .40
- ❑ 79 Shannon Sharpe .60 .25
- ❑ 80 Derrick Mason .60 .25
- ❑ 81 Tim Couch .40 .15
- ❑ 82 Chad Johnson 1.00 .40
- ❑ 83 Jason Taylor .40 .15
- ❑ 84 Travis Henry .60 .25
- ❑ 85 Curtis Conway .40 .15
- ❑ 86 Peyton Manning 1.50 .60
- ❑ 87 Kurt Warner 1.00 .40
- ❑ 88 LaDainian Tomlinson 1.00 .40
- ❑ 89 Emmitt Smith 2.50 1.00
- ❑ 90 Priest Holmes 1.25 .50
- ❑ 91 Ricky Williams AC 5.00 2.00
- ❑ 92 Brett Favre AC 12.00 5.00
- ❑ 93 Clinton Portis AC 8.00 3.00
- ❑ 94 Randy Moss AC 8.00 3.00
- ❑ 95 Tom Brady AC 12.00 5.00
- ❑ 96 Chad Pennington AC 8.00 3.00
- ❑ 97 Michael Vick AC 15.00 6.00
- ❑ 98 Jeremy Shockey AC 10.00 4.00
- ❑ 99 Donovan McNabb AC 8.00 3.00
- ❑ 100 Jerry Rice AC 12.00 5.00
- ❑ 101 Carson Palmer AC/350 RC 50.0020.00
- ❑ 102 Lee Suggs AC/350 RC 25.00 10.00
- ❑ 103 Larry Johnson AC/350 RC 50.00 20.00
- ❑ 104 Taylor Jacobs AC/650 RC 5.00 2.00
- ❑ 105 Andre Johnson AC/350 RC 25.0010.00
- ❑ 106 Justin Fargas AC/650 RC 10.00 4.00
- ❑ 107 Charles Rogers AC/350 RC 20.007.50
- ❑ 108 Willis McGahee AC/650 RC 25.00 10.00
- ❑ 109 Byron Leftwich AC/350 RC 40.0015.00
- ❑ 110 Kyle Boller AC/650 RC 20.00 7.50
- ❑ 111 Bobby Wade RC 8.00 3.00
- ❑ 112 Brian St.Pierre RC 8.00 3.00
- ❑ 113 Doug Gabriel RC 8.00 3.00
- ❑ 114 Chris Brown RC 10.00 4.00
- ❑ 115 DeWayne Robertson RC 8.00 3.00
- ❑ 116 Anquan Boldin RC 20.00 7.50
- ❑ 117 Brandon Lloyd RC 10.00 4.00
- ❑ 118 Brad Banks RC 6.00 2.50
- ❑ 119 Dallas Clark RC 8.00 3.00
- ❑ 120 Artose Pinner RC 8.00 3.00
- ❑ 121 Dave Ragone RC 8.00 3.00
- ❑ 122 Arnaz Battle RC 8.00 3.00
- ❑ 123 Andrew Pinnock RC 6.00 2.50
- ❑ 124 Billy McMullen RC 6.00 2.50
- ❑ 125 Avon Cobourne RC 6.00 2.50
- ❑ 126 Terence Newman RC 15.00 6.00
- ❑ 127 Jimmy Kennedy RC 8.00 3.00
- ❑ 128 Terrell Suggs RC 12.00 5.00
- ❑ 129 Rex Grossman RC 12.00 5.00
- ❑ 130 Musa Smith RC 8.00 3.00
- ❑ 131 William Joseph RC 8.00 3.00
- ❑ 132 Tyrone Calico RC 10.00 4.00
- ❑ 133 Teyo Johnson RC 8.00 3.00
- ❑ 134 Onterrio Smith RC 8.00 3.00
- ❑ 135 Mike Doss RC 8.00 3.00
- ❑ 136 Kliff Kingsbury RC 6.00 2.50
- ❑ 137 Kelley Washington RC 8.00 3.00
- ❑ 138 Kareem Kelly RC 6.00 2.50
- ❑ 139 Jason Gesser RC 8.00 3.00
- ❑ 140 Chris Simms RC 12.00 5.00

2004 Fleer Showcase

- ❑ COMP.SET w/o SP's (100) 25.00 10.00
- ❑ 101-148 ROOKIE STATED ODDS 1:10H, 1:75R
- ❑ 101-148 ROOKIE PRINT RUN 599 SER.#'d SETS

❑ 1 Jamal Lewis	1.00	.40
❑ 2 Kevan Barlow	.60	.25
❑ 3 Travis Henry	.60	.25
❑ 4 Jon Kitna	.60	.25
❑ 5 David Boston	.60	.25
❑ 6 Andre Davis	.40	.15
❑ 7 Steve McNair	1.00	.40
❑ 8 Freddie Mitchell	.60	.25
❑ 9 Plaxico Burress	.60	.25
❑ 10 Jake Delhomme	1.00	.40
❑ 11 Andre Johnson	1.00	.40
❑ 12 T.J. Duckett	.60	.25
❑ 13 Ray Lewis	1.00	.40
❑ 14 Shaun Alexander	1.00	.40
❑ 15 Stephen Davis	.60	.25
❑ 16 Priest Holmes	1.25	.50
❑ 17 Edgerrin James	1.00	.40
❑ 18 Josh McCown	.60	.25
❑ 19 Jerry Rice	2.00	.75
❑ 20 Fred Taylor	.60	.25
❑ 21 Marty Booker	.60	.25
❑ 22 Eddie George	.60	.25
❑ 23 Jake Plummer	.60	.25
❑ 24 LaDainian Tomlinson	1.25	.50
❑ 25 David Carr	1.00	.40
❑ 26 Keenan McCardell	.40	.15
❑ 27 Jerry Porter	.60	.25
❑ 28 Drew Bledsoe	1.00	.40
❑ 29 Brian Dawkins	.60	.25
❑ 30 Curtis Martin	1.00	.40
❑ 31 Troy Brown	.60	.25
❑ 32 Peyton Manning	1.50	.60
❑ 33 Clinton Portis	1.00	.40
❑ 34 Brett Favre	2.50	1.00
❑ 35 Joey Harrington	1.00	.40
❑ 36 Tiki Barber	1.00	.40
❑ 37 Hines Ward	1.00	.40
❑ 38 Laveranues Coles	.60	.25
❑ 39 Deuce McAllister	1.00	.40
❑ 40 Kyle Boller	1.00	.40
❑ 41 Jeff Garcia	1.00	.40
❑ 42 Julius Peppers	1.00	.40
❑ 43 Chris Chambers	.60	.25
❑ 44 Willis McGahee	1.00	.40
❑ 45 Michael Vick	2.00	.75
❑ 46 Carson Palmer	1.25	.50
❑ 47 Ricky Williams	1.00	.40
❑ 48 Matt Hasselbeck	.60	.25
❑ 49 Anquan Boldin	1.00	.40
❑ 50 Tony Gonzalez	.60	.25
❑ 51 Marvin Harrison	1.00	.40
❑ 52 Santana Moss	.60	.25
❑ 53 Ahman Green	1.00	.40
❑ 54 Eric Moulds	.60	.25
❑ 55 Byron Leftwich	1.25	.50
❑ 56 Daunte Culpepper	1.00	.40
❑ 57 Terrell Owens	1.00	.40
❑ 58 Kerry Collins	.60	.25
❑ 59 Tommy Maddox	.60	.25
❑ 60 Chad Johnson	1.00	.40
❑ 61 Rich Gannon	.60	.25
❑ 62 Patrick Ramsey	.60	.25
❑ 63 Quincy Morgan	.60	.25
❑ 64 Koren Robinson	.60	.25
❑ 65 Deion Branch	1.00	.40
❑ 66 Rex Grossman	1.00	.40
❑ 67 Damerien McCants	.40	.15
❑ 68 Ashley Lelie	.60	.25
❑ 69 Roy Williams S	.60	.25
❑ 70 Michael Bennett	.60	.25
❑ 71 Domanick Davis	1.00	.40
❑ 72 Warren Sapp	.60	.25
❑ 73 Randy Moss	1.25	.50
❑ 74 Drew Brees	1.00	.40
❑ 75 Brian Westbrook	.60	.25
❑ 76 Kelly Holcomb	.60	.25
❑ 77 Jason Taylor	.40	.15
❑ 78 Charles Rogers	.60	.25
❑ 79 Marc Bulger	1.00	.40
❑ 80 Donald Driver	.60	.25
❑ 81 Trent Green	.60	.25
❑ 82 Peerless Price	.60	.25
❑ 83 Quincy Carter	.60	.25
❑ 84 Torry Holt	1.00	.40
❑ 85 Derrick Mason	.60	.25
❑ 86 Donte Stallworth	.60	.25
❑ 87 Derrick Brooks	.60	.25
❑ 88 Dre Bly	.40	.15
❑ 89 Antonio Bryant	.60	.25
❑ 90 DeShaun Foster	.60	.25
❑ 91 Emmitt Smith	2.00	.75
❑ 92 Chad Pennington	1.00	.40
❑ 93 Jeremy Shockey	1.00	.40
❑ 94 Aaron Brooks	.60	.25
❑ 95 Marshall Faulk	1.00	.40
❑ 96 Dante Hall	1.00	.40
❑ 97 Brian Urlacher	1.25	.50
❑ 98 Corey Dillon	.60	.25
❑ 99 Donovan McNabb	1.25	.50
❑ 100 Tom Brady	2.50	1.00
❑ 101 Derrick Strait RC	5.00	2.00
❑ 102 Michael Clayton RC	10.00	4.00
❑ 103 Larry Fitzgerald RC	15.00	6.00
❑ 104 Chris Gamble RC	6.00	2.50
❑ 105 Devery Henderson RC	4.00	1.50
❑ 106 Steven Jackson RC	15.00	6.00
❑ 107 Michael Jenkins RC	5.00	2.00
❑ 108 Greg Jones RC	5.00	2.00
❑ 109 Kevin Jones RC	15.00	6.00
❑ 110 Eli Manning RC	30.00	12.50
❑ 111 Chris Perry RC	8.00	3.00
❑ 112 Philip Rivers RC	15.00	7.50
❑ 113 Ben Roethlisberger RC	40.00	20.00
❑ 114 Bernard Berrian RC	5.00	2.00
❑ 115 Sean Taylor RC	6.00	2.50
❑ 116 Reggie Williams RC	6.00	2.50
❑ 117 Roy Williams RC	12.00	5.00
❑ 118 Kellen Winslow RC	10.00	4.00
❑ 119 Rashaun Woods RC	5.00	2.00
❑ 120 J.P. Losman RC	10.00	4.00
❑ 121 Will Poole RC	5.00	2.00
❑ 122 Will Smith RC	5.00	2.00
❑ 123 Devard Darling RC	5.00	2.00
❑ 124 Jonathan Vilma RC	5.00	2.00
❑ 125 Drew Henson RC	5.00	2.00
❑ 126 Michael Turner RC	5.00	2.00
❑ 127 Lee Evans RC	6.00	2.50
❑ 128 Ernest Wilford RC	5.00	2.00
❑ 129 Cedric Cobbs RC	5.00	2.00
❑ 130 Ricardo Colclough RC	5.00	2.00
❑ 131 Ryan Dinwiddie RC	4.00	1.50
❑ 132 DeAngelo Hall RC	6.00	2.50
❑ 133 Cody Pickett RC	5.00	2.00
❑ 134 Quincy Wilson RC	4.00	1.50
❑ 135 Ahmad Carroll RC	6.00	2.50
❑ 136 Robert Gallery RC	8.00	3.00
❑ 137 John Navarre RC	5.00	2.00
❑ 138 P.K. Sam RC	4.00	1.50
❑ 139 Jeff Smoker RC	5.00	2.00
❑ 140 Ben Troupe RC	5.00	2.00
❑ 141 Marquise Hill RC	4.00	1.50
❑ 142 D.J. Williams RC	6.00	2.50
❑ 143 Tommie Harris RC	5.00	2.00
❑ 144 Ben Watson RC	5.00	2.00
❑ 145 Tatum Bell RC	10.00	4.00
❑ 146 B.J. Symons RC	5.00	2.00
❑ 147 Matt Schaub RC	8.00	3.00
❑ 148 Casey Clausen RC	5.00	2.00
❑ 149 Jason Fife RC	2.50	1.00
❑ 150 Mike Williams No Ser.#	15.00	6.00

2004 Fleer Sweet Sigs

❑ COMP.SET w/o RC's (75)	15.00	6.00
❑ 76-100 RC ODDS 1:7 HOB, 1:50 RET		
❑ 76-100 RC PRINT RUN 999 SER.#'d SETS		
❑ 1 Brett Favre	2.00	.75
❑ 2 Daunte Culpepper	.75	.30
❑ 3 Marshall Faulk	.75	.30
❑ 4 Ashley Lelie	.50	.20
❑ 5 Rex Grossman	.75	.30
❑ 6 Jeff Garcia	.75	.30
❑ 7 Jake Plummer	.50	.20
❑ 8 Tony Gonzalez	.50	.20
❑ 9 Terrell Owens	.75	.30
❑ 10 Plaxico Burress	.50	.20
❑ 11 Michael Vick	1.50	.60
❑ 12 Carson Palmer	1.00	.40
❑ 13 Charles Rogers	.50	.20
❑ 14 Corey Dillon	.50	.20
❑ 15 Aaron Brooks	.50	.20
❑ 16 Torry Holt	.75	.30
❑ 17 Joey Galloway	.50	.20
❑ 18 Mark Brunell	.50	.20
❑ 19 Anquan Boldin	.75	.30
❑ 20 Domanick Davis	.75	.30
❑ 21 Edgerrin James	.75	.30
❑ 22 Hines Ward	.75	.30
❑ 23 Kyle Boller	.75	.30
❑ 24 Kurt Warner	.75	.30
❑ 25 Matt Hasselbeck	.50	.20
❑ 26 Chris Chambers	.50	.20
❑ 27 Deuce McAllister	.75	.30
❑ 28 Chad Pennington	.75	.30
❑ 29 Eddie George	.50	.20
❑ 30 Ray Lewis	.75	.30
❑ 31 Ahman Green	.75	.30
❑ 32 Marvin Harrison	.75	.30
❑ 33 Tiki Barber	.75	.30
❑ 34 Jerry Rice	1.50	.60
❑ 35 Emmitt Smith	1.50	.60
❑ 36 Chad Johnson	.75	.30
❑ 37 Roy Williams S	.50	.20
❑ 38 Peyton Manning	1.25	.50
❑ 39 Stephen Davis	.50	.20
❑ 40 Jamal Lewis	.75	.30
❑ 41 David Carr	.75	.30
❑ 42 A.J. Feeley	.75	.30
❑ 43 Jerry Porter	.50	.20
❑ 44 Willis McGahee	.75	.30
❑ 45 Quincy Morgan	.50	.20
❑ 46 Fred Taylor	.50	.20
❑ 47 Trent Green	.50	.20
❑ 48 Donovan McNabb	1.00	.40
❑ 49 Marc Bulger	.75	.30
❑ 50 LaVar Arrington	1.50	.60
❑ 51 Joey Harrington	.75	.30
❑ 52 Jake Delhomme	.75	.30

❑ 53	Jeremy Shockey	.75	.30
❑ 54	LaDainian Tomlinson	1.00	.40
❑ 55	Brian Urlacher	1.00	.40
❑ 56	Rudi Johnson	.50	.20
❑ 57	Shaun Alexander	.75	.30
❑ 58	Charlie Garner	.50	.20
❑ 59	Eric Moulds	.50	.20
❑ 60	Tom Brady	2.00	.75
❑ 61	Curtis Martin	.75	.30
❑ 62	Koren Robinson	.50	.20
❑ 63	Steve McNair	.75	.30
❑ 64	Travis Henry	.50	.20
❑ 65	Julius Peppers	.75	.30
❑ 66	Keyshawn Johnson	.50	.20
❑ 67	Andre Johnson	.75	.30
❑ 68	Priest Holmes	1.00	.40
❑ 69	Drew Brees	.75	.30
❑ 70	Rich Gannon	.50	.20
❑ 71	Randy Moss	1.00	.40
❑ 72	Peerless Price	.50	.20
❑ 73	Drew Bledsoe	.75	.30
❑ 74	Byron Leftwich	1.00	.40
❑ 75	Clinton Portis	.75	.30
❑ 76	Roy Williams RC	10.00	4.00
❑ 77	Eli Manning RC	25.00	10.00
❑ 78	Kevin Jones RC	12.00	5.00
❑ 79	Tatum Bell RC	8.00	3.00
❑ 80	DeAngelo Hall RC	5.00	2.00
❑ 81	Michael Clayton RC	8.00	3.00
❑ 82	Rashaun Woods RC	4.00	1.50
❑ 83	Darius Watts RC	4.00	1.50
❑ 84	J.P. Losman RC	8.00	3.00
❑ 85	Drew Henson RC	4.00	1.50
❑ 86	Philip Rivers RC	12.00	6.00
❑ 87	Ben Roethlisberger RC	30.00	15.00
❑ 88	Larry Fitzgerald RC	12.00	5.00
❑ 89	Chris Perry RC	6.00	2.50
❑ 90	Devery Henderson RC	3.00	1.25
❑ 91	Sean Taylor RC	5.00	2.00
❑ 92	Reggie Williams RC	5.00	2.00
❑ 93	Lee Evans RC	5.00	2.00
❑ 94	Julius Jones RC	15.00	6.00
❑ 95	Dunta Robinson RC	4.00	1.50
❑ 96	Michael Jenkins RC	4.00	1.50
❑ 97	Greg Jones RC	4.00	1.50
❑ 98	Kellen Winslow RC	8.00	3.00
❑ 99	Steven Jackson RC	12.00	5.00
❑ 100	Matt Schaub RC	6.00	2.50

1998 Fleer Tradition

❑	COMPLETE SET (250)	40.00	20.00
❑ 1	Brett Favre	2.00	.75
❑ 2	Barry Sanders	1.50	.60
❑ 3	John Elway	2.00	.75
❑ 4	Emmitt Smith	1.50	.60
❑ 5	Dan Marino	2.00	.75
❑ 6	Eddie George	.50	.20
❑ 7	Jerry Rice	1.00	.40
❑ 8	Jake Plummer	.50	.20
❑ 9	Joey Galloway	.30	.10
❑ 10	Mike Alstott	.50	.20
❑ 11	Brian Mitchell	.20	.07
❑ 12	Keyshawn Johnson	.50	.20
❑ 13	Jerald Moore	.20	.07
❑ 14	Randal Hill	.20	.07
❑ 15	Byron Hanspard	.20	.07
❑ 16	Jeff George	.30	.10
❑ 17	Terry Glenn	.50	.20
❑ 18	Jerome Bettis	.50	.20
❑ 19	Curtis Conway	.30	.10
❑ 20	Fred Lane	.20	.07
❑ 21	Isaac Bruce	.50	.20
❑ 22	Tiki Barber	.50	.20
❑ 23	Bobby Hoying	.30	.10
❑ 24	Marcus Allen	.50	.20
❑ 25	Dana Stubblefield	.20	.07
❑ 26	Peter Boulware	.20	.07
❑ 27	John Randle	.30	.10
❑ 28	Jason Sehorn	.30	.10
❑ 29	Rod Smith	.30	.10
❑ 30	Michael Sinclair	.20	.07
❑ 31	Marshall Faulk	.60	.25
❑ 32	Karl Williams	.20	.07
❑ 33	Kordell Stewart	.50	.20
❑ 34	Corey Dillon	.50	.20
❑ 35	Bryant Young	.20	.07
❑ 36	Charlie Garner	.30	.10
❑ 37	Andre Reed	.30	.10
❑ 38	Ray Buchanan	.20	.07
❑ 39	Brett Perriman	.20	.07
❑ 40	Leon Lett	.20	.07
❑ 41	Keenan McCardell	.30	.10
❑ 42	Eric Swann	.20	.07
❑ 43	Leslie Shepherd	.20	.07
❑ 44	Curtis Martin	.50	.20
❑ 45	Andre Rison	.30	.10
❑ 46	Keith Lyle	.20	.07
❑ 47	Rae Carruth	.20	.07
❑ 48	William Henderson	.30	.10
❑ 49	Sean Dawkins	.20	.07
❑ 50	Terrell Davis	.50	.20
❑ 51	Tim Brown	.50	.20
❑ 52	Willie McGinest	.20	.07
❑ 53	Jermaine Lewis	.30	.10
❑ 54	Ricky Watters	.30	.10
❑ 55	Freddie Jones	.20	.07
❑ 56	Robert Smith	.50	.20
❑ 57	Reidel Anthony	.30	.10
❑ 58	James Stewart	.30	.10
❑ 59	Earl Holmes RC	.50	.20
❑ 60	Dale Carter	.20	.07
❑ 61	Michael Irvin	.50	.20
❑ 62	Jason Taylor	.30	.10
❑ 63	Eric Metcalf	.20	.07
❑ 64	LeRoy Butler	.20	.07
❑ 65	Jamal Anderson	.50	.20
❑ 66	Jamie Asher	.20	.07
❑ 67	Chris Sanders	.20	.07
❑ 68	Warren Sapp	.30	.10
❑ 69	Ray Zellars	.20	.07
❑ 70	Carl Pickens	.30	.10
❑ 71	Garrison Hearst	.50	.20
❑ 72	Eddie Kennison	.30	.10
❑ 73	John Mobley	.20	.07
❑ 74	Rob Johnson	.30	.10
❑ 75	William Thomas	.20	.07
❑ 76	Drew Bledsoe	.75	.30
❑ 77	Micheal Barrow	.20	.07
❑ 78	Jim Harbaugh	.30	.10
❑ 79	Terry McDaniel	.20	.07
❑ 80	Johnnie Morton	.30	.10
❑ 81	Danny Kanell	.30	.10
❑ 82	Larry Centers	.20	.07
❑ 83	Courtney Hawkins	.20	.07
❑ 84	Tony Brackens	.20	.07
❑ 85	Tony Gonzalez	.50	.20
❑ 86	Aaron Glenn	.20	.07
❑ 87	Cris Carter	.50	.20
❑ 88	Chuck Smith	.20	.07
❑ 89	Tamarick Vanover	.20	.07
❑ 90	Karim Abdul-Jabbar	.50	.20
❑ 91	Bryant Westbrook	.20	.07
❑ 92	Mike Pritchard	.20	.07
❑ 93	Darren Woodson	.20	.07
❑ 94	Wesley Walls	.30	.10
❑ 95	Tony Banks	.30	.10
❑ 96	Michael Westbrook	.30	.10
❑ 97	Shannon Sharpe	.30	.10
❑ 98	Jeff Blake	.30	.10
❑ 99	Terrell Owens	.50	.20
❑ 100	Warrick Dunn	.50	.20
❑ 101	Levon Kirkland	.20	.07
❑ 102	Frank Wycheck	.20	.07
❑ 103	Gus Frerotte	.20	.07
❑ 104	Simeon Rice	.30	.10
❑ 105	Shawn Jefferson	.20	.07
❑ 106	Irving Fryar	.30	.10
❑ 107	Michael McCrary	.20	.07
❑ 108	Robert Brooks	.30	.10
❑ 109	Chris Chandler	.30	.10
❑ 110	Junior Seau	.50	.20
❑ 111	O.J. McDuffie	.30	.10
❑ 112	Glenn Foley	.30	.10
❑ 113	Darryl Williams	.20	.07
❑ 114	Elvis Grbac	.30	.10
❑ 115	Napoleon Kaufman	.50	.20
❑ 116	Anthony Miller	.20	.07
❑ 117	Troy Davis	.20	.07
❑ 118	Charles Way	.20	.07
❑ 119	Scott Mitchell	.30	.10
❑ 120	Ken Harvey	.20	.07
❑ 121	Tyrone Hughes	.20	.07
❑ 122	Mark Brunell	.50	.20
❑ 123	David Palmer	.20	.07
❑ 124	Rob Moore	.30	.10
❑ 125	Kerry Collins	.30	.10
❑ 126	Will Blackwell	.20	.07
❑ 127	Ray Crockett	.20	.07
❑ 128	Leslie O'Neal	.20	.07
❑ 129	Antowain Smith	.50	.20
❑ 130	Carlester Crumpler	.20	.07
❑ 131	Michael Jackson	.20	.07
❑ 132	Trent Dilfer	.50	.20
❑ 133	Dan Williams	.20	.07
❑ 134	Dorsey Levens	.50	.20
❑ 135	Ty Law	.30	.10
❑ 136	Rickey Dudley	.20	.07
❑ 137	Jessie Tuggle	.20	.07
❑ 138	Darrien Gordon	.20	.07
❑ 139	Kevin Turner	.20	.07
❑ 140	Willie Davis	.20	.07
❑ 141	Zach Thomas	.50	.20
❑ 142	Tony McGee	.20	.07
❑ 143	Dexter Coakley	.20	.07
❑ 144	Troy Brown	.30	.10
❑ 145	Leeland McElroy	.20	.07
❑ 146	Michael Strahan	.30	.10
❑ 147	Ken Dilger	.20	.07
❑ 148	Bryce Paup	.20	.07
❑ 149	Herman Moore	.30	.10
❑ 150	Reggie White	.50	.20
❑ 151	Dewayne Washington	.20	.07
❑ 152	Natrone Means	.30	.10
❑ 153	Ben Coates	.30	.10
❑ 154	Bert Emanuel	.30	.10
❑ 155	Steve Young	.60	.25
❑ 156	Jimmy Smith	.30	.10
❑ 157	Darrell Green	.30	.10
❑ 158	Troy Aikman	1.00	.40
❑ 159	Greg Hill	.20	.07
❑ 160	Raymont Harris	.20	.07
❑ 161	Troy Drayton	.20	.07
❑ 162	Stevon Moore	.20	.07
❑ 163	Warren Moon	.50	.20
❑ 164	Wayne Martin	.20	.07
❑ 165	Jason Gildon	.20	.07
❑ 166	Chris Calloway	.20	.07
❑ 167	Aeneas Williams	.20	.07
❑ 168	Michael Bates	.20	.07
❑ 169	Hugh Douglas	.20	.07
❑ 170	Brad Johnson	.50	.20
❑ 171	Bruce Smith	.30	.10
❑ 172	Neil Smith	.30	.10
❑ 173	James McKnight	.50	.20

❑ 174 Robert Porcher	.20	.07
❑ 175 Merton Hanks	.20	.07
❑ 176 Ki-Jana Carter	.20	.07
❑ 177 Mo Lewis	.20	.07
❑ 178 Chester McGlockton	.20	.07
❑ 179 Zack Crockett	.20	.07
❑ 180 Derrick Thomas	.50	.20
❑ 181 J.J. Stokes	.30	.10
❑ 182 Derrick Rodgers	.20	.07
❑ 183 Daryl Johnston	.30	.10
❑ 184 Chris Penn	.20	.07
❑ 185 Steve Atwater	.20	.07
❑ 186 Amp Lee	.20	.07
❑ 187 Frank Sanders	.30	.10
❑ 188 Chris Slade	.20	.07
❑ 189 Mark Chmura	.30	.10
❑ 190 Kimble Anders	.30	.10
❑ 191 Charles Johnson	.20	.07
❑ 192 William Floyd	.20	.07
❑ 193 Jay Graham	.20	.07
❑ 194 Hardy Nickerson	.20	.07
❑ 195 Terry Allen	.50	.20
❑ 196 James Jett	.30	.10
❑ 197 Jessie Armstead	.20	.07
❑ 198 Yancey Thigpen	.30	.10
❑ 199 Terance Mathis	.30	.10
❑ 200 Steve McNair	.50	.20
❑ 201 Wayne Chrebet	.50	.20
❑ 202 Jamir Miller	.20	.07
❑ 203 Duce Staley	.60	.25
❑ 204 Deion Sanders	.50	.20
❑ 205 Carnell Lake	.20	.07
❑ 206 Ed McCaffrey	.30	.10
❑ 207 Shawn Springs	.20	.07
❑ 208 Tony Martin	.30	.10
❑ 209 Jerris McPhail	.20	.07
❑ 210 Darnay Scott	.30	.10
❑ 211 Jake Reed	.30	.10
❑ 212 Adrian Murrell	.30	.10
❑ 213 Quinn Early	.20	.07
❑ 214 Marvin Harrison	.50	.20
❑ 215 Ryan McNeil	.20	.07
❑ 216 Derrick Alexander	.30	.10
❑ 217 Ray Lewis	.50	.20
❑ 218 Antonio Freeman	.50	.20
❑ 219 Dwayne Rudd	.20	.07
❑ 220 Muhsin Muhammad	.30	.10
❑ 221 Kevin Hardy	.20	.07
❑ 222 Andre Hastings	.20	.07
❑ 223 John Avery RC	.75	.30
❑ 224 Keith Brooking RC	1.25	.50
❑ 225 Kevin Dyson RC	1.25	.50
❑ 226 Robert Edwards RC	.75	.30
❑ 227 Greg Ellis RC	.50	.20
❑ 228 Curtis Enis RC	.50	.20
❑ 229 Terry Fair RC	.75	.30
❑ 230 Ahman Green RC	6.00	2.50
❑ 231 Jacquez Green RC	.75	.30
❑ 232 Brian Griese RC	3.00	1.25
❑ 233 Skip Hicks RC	.75	.30
❑ 234 Ryan Leaf RC	1.25	.50
❑ 235 Peyton Manning RC	15.00	6.00
❑ 236 R.W. McQuarters RC	.75	.30
❑ 237 Randy Moss RC	8.00	3.00
❑ 238 Marcus Nash RC	.50	.20
❑ 239 Anthony Simmons RC	.75	.30
❑ 240 Brian Simmons RC	.75	.30
❑ 241 Takeo Spikes RC	1.25	.50
❑ 242 Duane Starks RC	.50	.20
❑ 243 Fred Taylor RC	2.00	.75
❑ 244 Andre Wadsworth RC	.75	.30
❑ 245 Shaun Williams RC	.75	.30
❑ 246 Grant Wistrom RC	.75	.30
❑ 247 Charles Woodson RC	1.50	.60
❑ 248 Checklist	.20	.07
❑ 249 Checklist	.20	.07
❑ 250 Checklist	.20	.07

1999 Fleer Tradition

❑ COMPLETE SET (300)	40.00	20.00
❑ 1 Randy Moss	1.25	.50
❑ 2 Peyton Manning	1.50	.60
❑ 3 Barry Sanders	1.50	.60
❑ 4 Terrell Davis	.50	.20
❑ 5 Brett Favre	1.50	.60
❑ 6 Fred Taylor	.50	.20
❑ 7 Jake Plummer	.30	.10
❑ 8 John Elway	1.50	.60
❑ 9 Emmitt Smith	1.00	.40
❑ 10 Kerry Collins	.30	.10
❑ 11 Peter Boulware	.20	.07
❑ 12 Jamal Anderson	.50	.20
❑ 13 Doug Flutie	.50	.20
❑ 14 Michael Bates	.20	.07
❑ 15 Corey Dillon	.50	.20
❑ 16 Curtis Conway	.30	.10
❑ 17 Ty Detmer	.30	.10
❑ 18 Robert Brooks	.30	.10
❑ 19 Dale Carter	.20	.07
❑ 20 Charlie Batch	.50	.20
❑ 21 Ken Dilger	.20	.07
❑ 22 Troy Aikman	1.00	.40
❑ 23 Tavian Banks	.20	.07
❑ 24 Cris Carter	.50	.20
❑ 25 Derrick Alexander WR	.30	.10
❑ 26 Chris Bordano RC	.20	.07
❑ 27 Karim Abdul-Jabbar	.30	.10
❑ 28 Jessie Armstead	.20	.07
❑ 29 Drew Bledsoe	.60	.25
❑ 30 Brian Dawkins	.50	.20
❑ 31 Wayne Chrebet	.30	.10
❑ 32 Garrison Hearst	.30	.10
❑ 33 Eric Allen	.20	.07
❑ 34 Tony Banks	.30	.10
❑ 35 Jerome Bettis	.50	.20
❑ 36 Stephen Alexander	.20	.07
❑ 37 Rodney Harrison	.20	.07
❑ 38 Mike Alstott	.50	.20
❑ 39 Chad Brown	.20	.07
❑ 40 Johnny McWilliams	.20	.07
❑ 41 Kevin Dyson	.30	.10
❑ 42 Keith Brooking	.20	.07
❑ 43 Jim Harbaugh	.30	.10
❑ 44 Bobby Engram	.30	.10
❑ 45 John Holecek	.20	.07
❑ 46 Steve Beuerlein	.20	.07
❑ 47 Tony McGee	.20	.07
❑ 48 Greg Ellis	.20	.07
❑ 49 Corey Fuller	.20	.07
❑ 50 Stephen Boyd	.20	.07
❑ 51 Marshall Faulk	.60	.25
❑ 52 LeRoy Butler	.20	.07
❑ 53 Reggie Barlow	.20	.07
❑ 54 Randall Cunningham	.50	.20
❑ 55 Aeneas Williams	.20	.07
❑ 56 Kimble Anders	.30	.10
❑ 57 Cam Cleeland	.20	.07
❑ 58 John Avery	.20	.07
❑ 59 Gary Brown	.20	.07
❑ 60 Ben Coates	.30	.10
❑ 61 Koy Detmer	.20	.07
❑ 62 Bryan Cox	.20	.07
❑ 63 Edgar Bennett	.20	.07
❑ 64 Tim Brown	.50	.20
❑ 65 Isaac Bruce	.50	.20
❑ 66 Eddie George	.50	.20
❑ 67 Reidel Anthony	.30	.10
❑ 68 Charlie Jones	.20	.07
❑ 69 Terry Allen	.30	.10
❑ 70 Joey Galloway	.30	.10
❑ 71 Jamir Miller	.20	.07
❑ 72 Will Blackwell	.20	.07
❑ 73 Ray Buchanan	.20	.07
❑ 74 Priest Holmes	.75	.30
❑ 75 Michael Irvin	.30	.10
❑ 76 Jonathan Linton	.20	.07
❑ 77 Curtis Enis	.20	.07
❑ 78 Neil O'Donnell	.30	.10
❑ 79 Tim Biakabutuka	.30	.10
❑ 80 Terry Kirby	.20	.07
❑ 81 Germane Crowell	.20	.07
❑ 82 Jason Elam	.20	.07
❑ 83 Mark Chmura	.20	.07
❑ 84 Marvin Harrison	.50	.20
❑ 85 Jimmy Hitchcock	.20	.07
❑ 86 Tony Brackens	.20	.07
❑ 87 Sean Dawkins	.20	.07
❑ 88 Tony Gonzalez	.50	.20
❑ 89 Kent Graham	.20	.07
❑ 90 Oronde Gadsden	.30	.10
❑ 91 Hugh Douglas	.20	.07
❑ 92 Robert Edwards	.20	.07
❑ 93 R.W. McQuarters	.20	.07
❑ 94 Aaron Glenn	.20	.07
❑ 95 Kevin Carter	.20	.07
❑ 96 Rickey Dudley	.20	.07
❑ 97 Derrick Brooks	.50	.20
❑ 98 Mark Bruener	.20	.07
❑ 99 Darrell Green	.20	.07
❑ 100 Jessie Tuggle	.20	.07
❑ 101 Freddie Jones	.20	.07
❑ 102 Rob Moore	.30	.10
❑ 103 Ahman Green	.50	.20
❑ 104 Chris Chandler	.30	.10
❑ 105 Steve McNair	.50	.20
❑ 106 Kevin Greene	.20	.07
❑ 107 Jermaine Lewis	.30	.10
❑ 108 Erik Kramer	.20	.07
❑ 109 Eric Moulds	.50	.20
❑ 110 Terry Fair	.20	.07
❑ 111 Carl Pickens	.30	.10
❑ 112 La'Roi Glover RC		
❑ 113 Chris Spielman	.20	.07
❑ 114 Leroy Hoard	.20	.07
❑ 115 Mark Brunell	.50	.20
❑ 116 Patrick Jeffers RC	3.00	1.50
❑ 117 Elvis Grbac	.30	.10
❑ 118 Ike Hilliard	.20	.07
❑ 119 Sam Madison	.20	.07
❑ 120 Terrell Owens	.50	.20
❑ 121 Rich Gannon	.50	.20
❑ 122 Skip Hicks	.20	.07
❑ 123 Eric Green	.20	.07
❑ 124 Trent Dilfer	.30	.10
❑ 125 Terry Glenn	.50	.20
❑ 126 Trent Green	.50	.20
❑ 127 Charles Johnson	.20	.07
❑ 128 Adrian Murrell	.30	.10
❑ 129 Jason Gildon	.20	.07
❑ 130 Tim Dwight	.50	.20
❑ 131 Ryan Leaf	.50	.20
❑ 132 Rocket Ismail	.30	.10
❑ 133 Jon Kitna	.50	.20
❑ 134 Alonzo Mayes	.20	.07
❑ 135 Yancey Thigpen	.20	.07
❑ 136 David LaFleur	.20	.07
❑ 137 Ray Lewis	.50	.20
❑ 138 Herman Moore	.30	.10
❑ 139 Brian Griese	.50	.20
❑ 140 Antonio Freeman	.50	.20
❑ 141 Darnay Scott	.20	.07

❑ 142 Ed McDaniel .20 .07
❑ 143 Andre Reed .30 .10
❑ 144 Andre Hastings .20 .07
❑ 145 Chris Warren .20 .07
❑ 146 Kevin Hardy .20 .07
❑ 147 Joe Jurevicius .30 .10
❑ 148 Jerome Pathon .20 .07
❑ 149 Duce Staley .50 .20
❑ 150 Dan Marino 1.50 .60
❑ 151 Jerry Rice 1.00 .40
❑ 152 Byron Bam Morris .20 .07
❑ 153 Az-Zahir Hakim .20 .07
❑ 154 Ty Law .30 .10
❑ 155 Warrick Dunn .50 .20
❑ 156 Keyshawn Johnson .50 .20
❑ 157 Brian Mitchell .20 .07
❑ 158 James Jett .30 .10
❑ 159 Fred Lane .20 .07
❑ 160 Courtney Hawkins .20 .07
❑ 161 Andre Wadsworth .20 .07
❑ 162 Natrone Means .30 .10
❑ 163 Andrew Glover .20 .07
❑ 164 Anthony Simmons .20 .07
❑ 165 Leon Lett .20 .07
❑ 166 Frank Wycheck .20 .07
❑ 167 Barry Minter .20 .07
❑ 168 Michael McCrary .20 .07
❑ 169 Johnnie Morton .30 .10
❑ 170 Jay Riemersma .20 .07
❑ 171 Vonnie Holliday .20 .07
❑ 172 Brian Simmons .20 .07
❑ 173 Joe Johnson .20 .07
❑ 174 Ed McCaffrey .30 .10
❑ 175 Jason Sehorn .20 .07
❑ 176 Keenan McCardell .30 .10
❑ 177 Bobby Taylor .20 .07
❑ 178 Andre Rison .30 .10
❑ 179 Greg Hill .20 .07
❑ 180 O.J. McDuffie .30 .10
❑ 181 Darren Woodson .20 .07
❑ 182 Willie McGinest .20 .07
❑ 183 J.J. Stokes .30 .10
❑ 184 Leon Johnson .20 .07
❑ 185 Bert Emanuel .30 .10
❑ 186 Napoleon Kaufman .50 .20
❑ 187 Leslie Shepherd .20 .07
❑ 188 Levon Kirkland .20 .07
❑ 189 Simeon Rice .30 .10
❑ 190 Mikhael Ricks .20 .07
❑ 191 Robert Smith .50 .20
❑ 192 Michael Sinclair .20 .07
❑ 193 Muhsin Muhammad .30 .10
❑ 194 Duane Starks .20 .07
❑ 195 Terance Mathis .30 .10
❑ 196 Antowain Smith .50 .20
❑ 197 Tony Parrish .20 .07
❑ 198 Takeo Spikes .20 .07
❑ 199 Ernie Mills .20 .07
❑ 200 John Mobley .20 .07
❑ 202 Pete Mitchell .20 .07
❑ 203 Darick Holmes .20 .07
❑ 204 Derrick Thomas .50 .20
❑ 205 David Palmer .20 .07
❑ 206 Jason Taylor .20 .07
❑ 207 Sammy Knight .20 .07
❑ 208 Dwayne Rudd .20 .07
❑ 209 Lawyer Milloy .30 .10
❑ 210 Michael Strahan .30 .10
❑ 211 Mo Lewis .20 .07
❑ 212 William Thomas .20 .07
❑ 213 Darrell Russell .20 .07
❑ 214 Brad Johnson .50 .20
❑ 215 Kordell Stewart .30 .10
❑ 216 Robert Holcombe .20 .07
❑ 217 Junior Seau .50 .20
❑ 218 Jacquez Green .20 .07
❑ 219 Shawn Springs .20 .07
❑ 220 Michael Westbrook .30 .10
❑ 221 Rod Woodson .30 .10
❑ 222 Frank Sanders .30 .10
❑ 223 Bruce Smith .30 .10
❑ 224 Eugene Robinson .20 .07
❑ 225 Bill Romanowski .20 .07
❑ 226 Wesley Walls .30 .10
❑ 227 Jimmy Smith .30 .10
❑ 228 Deion Sanders .50 .20
❑ 229 Lamar Thomas .20 .07
❑ 230 Dorsey Levens .50 .20
❑ 231 Tony Simmons .20 .07
❑ 232 John Randle .30 .10
❑ 233 Curtis Martin .50 .20
❑ 234 Bryant Young .20 .07
❑ 235 Charles Woodson .50 .20
❑ 236 Charles Way .20 .07
❑ 237 Zach Thomas .50 .20
❑ 238 Ricky Proehl .20 .07
❑ 239 Ricky Watters .30 .10
❑ 240 Hardy Nickerson .20 .07
❑ 241 Shannon Sharpe .30 .10
❑ 242 O.J. Santiago .20 .07
❑ 243 Vinny Testaverde .30 .10
❑ 244 Roell Preston .20 .07
❑ 245 James Stewart .30 .10
❑ 246 Jake Reed .30 .10
❑ 247 Steve Young .60 .25
❑ 248 Shaun Williams .20 .07
❑ 249 Rod Smith .30 .10
❑ 250 Warren Sapp .30 .10
❑ 251 Champ Bailey RC 1.50 .60
❑ 252 Karsten Bailey RC .75 .30
❑ 253 D'Wayne Bates RC .75 .30
❑ 254 Michael Bishop RC 1.25 .50
❑ 255 David Boston RC 1.25 .50
❑ 256 Na Brown RC .75 .30
❑ 257 Fernando Bryant RC .75 .30
❑ 258 Shawn Bryson RC 1.25 .50
❑ 259 Darrin Chiaverini RC .75 .30
❑ 260 Chris Claiborne RC .40 .15
❑ 261 Mike Cloud RC .75 .30
❑ 262 Cecil Collins RC .40 .15
❑ 263 Tim Couch RC 1.25 .50
❑ 264 Scott Covington RC 1.25 .50
❑ 265 Daunte Culpepper RC 5.00 2.00
❑ 266 Antuan Edwards RC .40 .15
❑ 267 Troy Edwards RC .75 .30
❑ 268 Ebenezer Ekuban RC .75 .30
❑ 269 Kevin Faulk RC 1.25 .50
❑ 270 Jermaine Fazande RC .75 .30
❑ 271 Joe Germaine RC .75 .30
❑ 272 Martin Gramatica RC .40 .15
❑ 273 Torry Holt RC 3.00 1.25
❑ 274 Brock Huard RC 1.25 .50
❑ 275 Sedrick Irvin RC .40 .15
❑ 276 Sheldon Jackson RC .75 .30
❑ 277 Edgerrin James RC 5.00 2.00
❑ 278 James Johnson RC .75 .30
❑ 279 Kevin Johnson RC 1.25 .50
❑ 280 Malcolm Johnson RC .40 .15
❑ 281 Andy Katzenmoyer RC .75 .30
❑ 282 Jevon Kearse RC 2.00 .75
❑ 283 Patrick Kerney RC 1.25 .50
❑ 284 Shaun King RC .75 .30
❑ 285 Jim Kleinsasser RC 1.25 .50
❑ 286 Rob Konrad RC 1.25 .50
❑ 287 Chris McAlister RC .75 .30
❑ 288 Donovan McNabb RC 6.00 2.50
❑ 289 Cade McNown RC .75 .30
❑ 290 Dee Miller RC .40 .15
❑ 291 Joe Montgomery RC .75 .30
❑ 292 De'Mond Parker RC .40 .15
❑ 293 Peerless Price RC 1.25 .50
❑ 294 Akili Smith RC .75 .30
❑ 295 Justin Swift RC .40 .15
❑ 296 Jerame Tuman RC 1.25 .50
❑ 297 Ricky Williams RC 2.50 1.00
❑ 298 Antoine Winfield .75 .30
❑ 299 Craig Yeast RC .75 .30
❑ 300 Amos Zereoue RC 1.25 .50
❑ P6 Fred Taylor Promo 1.00 .40

2000 Fleer Tradition

❑ COMPLETE SET (400) 60.00 25.00
❑ 1 Kevin Johnson .50 .20
❑ 2 Chris Chandler .30 .10
❑ 3 Peerless Price .30 .10
❑ 4 Andre Rison .30 .10
❑ 5 Curtis Enis .20 .07
❑ 6 Tim Couch .30 .10
❑ 7 Brian Dawkins .50 .20
❑ 8 Akili Smith .20 .07
❑ 9 Kevin Faulk .30 .10
❑ 10 Joey Galloway .30 .10
❑ 11 Bill Romanowski .20 .07
❑ 12 Charlie Batch .50 .20
❑ 13 Terrence Wilkins .20 .07
❑ 14 Kevin Hardy .20 .07
❑ 15 Cade McNown .20 .07
❑ 16 Elvis Grbac .30 .10
❑ 17 Cris Carter .50 .20
❑ 18 Willie McGinest .20 .07
❑ 19 Michael Bishop .20 .07
❑ 20 Lee Woodall .20 .07
❑ 21 Jake Reed .30 .10
❑ 22 Bryan Cox .20 .07
❑ 23 Chris Sanders .20 .07
❑ 24 Tavian Banks .20 .07
❑ 25 Levon Kirkland .20 .07
❑ 26 James Hundon .20 .07
❑ 27 Junior Seau .50 .20
❑ 28 Darren Woodson .20 .07
❑ 29 Kevin Carter .20 .07
❑ 30 Joe Jurevicius .20 .07
❑ 31 John Lynch .30 .10
❑ 32 Steve McNair .50 .20
❑ 33 Jake Plummer .30 .10
❑ 34 Antonio Freeman .50 .20
❑ 35 Peter Boulware .20 .07
❑ 36 Brad Johnson .50 .20
❑ 37 Bobby Engram .30 .10
❑ 38 David Boston .50 .20
❑ 39 Jason Tucker .20 .07
❑ 40 Troy Brown .30 .10
❑ 41 Brian Griese .50 .20
❑ 42 Dorsey Levens .30 .10
❑ 43 Cornelius Bennett .20 .07
❑ 44 Donovan McNabb .75 .30
❑ 45 Rob Johnson .30 .10
❑ 46 Robert Smith .50 .20
❑ 47 Stanley Pritchett .20 .07
❑ 48 Tedy Bruschi .50 .20
❑ 49 Dan Marino 1.50 .60
❑ 50 Amani Toomer .30 .10
❑ 51 Aaron Glenn .20 .07
❑ 52 Rickey Dudley .20 .07
❑ 53 Tim Brown .50 .20
❑ 54 Jim Harbaugh .30 .10
❑ 55 Terrell Owens .50 .20
❑ 56 Jason Sehorn .20 .07
❑ 57 Cortez Kennedy .20 .07
❑ 58 London Fletcher RC .30 .10
❑ 59 Simeon Rice .30 .10
❑ 60 Shaun King .20 .07
❑ 61 Stephen Davis .50 .20

❑ 62 Andre Wadsworth .20 .07
❑ 63 Kyle Brady .20 .07
❑ 64 Priest Holmes .60 .25
❑ 65 Patrick Jeffers .50 .20
❑ 66 Barry Minter .20 .07
❑ 67 Curtis Martin .50 .20
❑ 68 Darrin Chiaverini .20 .07
❑ 69 Robert Thomas .20 .07
❑ 70 Samari Rolle .20 .07
❑ 71 Robert Porcher .20 .07
❑ 72 Jerry Rice 1.00 .40
❑ 73 Bill Schroeder .30 .10
❑ 74 Chad Bratzke .20 .07
❑ 75 Tony Brackens .20 .07
❑ 76 O.J. McDuffie .30 .10
❑ 77 John Randle .30 .10
❑ 78 Michael Pittman .20 .07
❑ 79 Drew Bledsoe .60 .25
❑ 80 Ike Hilliard .30 .10
❑ 81 Victor Green .20 .07
❑ 82 Duce Staley .50 .20
❑ 83 Bruce Smith .30 .10
❑ 84 Amos Zereoue .50 .20
❑ 85 Charlie Garner .30 .10
❑ 86 Shawn Springs .20 .07
❑ 87 Kurt Warner 1.00 .40
❑ 88 Eddie George .50 .20
❑ 89 Michael Westbrook .30 .10
❑ 90 Dexter Coakley .20 .07
❑ 91 Rob Moore .30 .10
❑ 92 Duane Starks .20 .07
❑ 93 Steve Beuerlein .30 .10
❑ 94 Marty Booker .30 .10
❑ 95 Karim Abdul-Jabbar .30 .10
❑ 96 Troy Aikman 1.00 .40
❑ 97 Germane Crowell .20 .07
❑ 98 Matt Hasselbeck .30 .10
❑ 99 E.G. Green .20 .07
❑ 100 Mark Brunell .50 .20
❑ 101 Tony Martin .30 .10
❑ 102 Darrell Green .20 .07
❑ 103 Ricky Williams .50 .20
❑ 104 Michael Strahan .30 .10
❑ 105 Vinny Testaverde .30 .10
❑ 106 Charles Johnson .30 .10
❑ 107 Hines Ward .50 .20
❑ 108 Bryant Young .20 .07
❑ 109 Mo Lewis .20 .07
❑ 110 Greg Clark .20 .07
❑ 111 Jon Kitna .50 .20
❑ 112 Jacquez Green .20 .07
❑ 113 Kevin Dyson .30 .10
❑ 114 Stephen Alexander .20 .07
❑ 115 Cam Cleeland .20 .07
❑ 116 Keith Poole .20 .07
❑ 117 Az-Zahir Hakim .30 .10
❑ 118 Tim Dwight .50 .20
❑ 119 Corey Bradford .20 .07
❑ 120 Carlos Emmons .20 .07
❑ 121 Trent Dilfer .30 .10
❑ 122 Lance Schulters .20 .07
❑ 123 Byron Hanspard .20 .07
❑ 124 Tim Biakabutuka .30 .10
❑ 125 Eddie Kennison .30 .10
❑ 126 Terry Kirby .20 .07
❑ 127 Mike McKenzie .20 .07
❑ 128 Fred Beasley .20 .07
❑ 129 Chad Brown .20 .07
❑ 130 Terrell Davis .50 .20
❑ 131 Herman Moore .30 .10
❑ 132 Vonnie Holliday .20 .07
❑ 133 Jim Miller .20 .07
❑ 134 Peyton Manning 1.25 .50
❑ 135 Derrick Alexander .30 .10
❑ 136 Oronde Gadsden .30 .10
❑ 137 Robert Griffith .20 .07
❑ 138 Troy Edwards .20 .07
❑ 139 Damon Huard .50 .20
❑ 140 Jessie Armstead .20 .07
❑ 141 Charles Woodson .30 .10
❑ 142 Troy Vincent .20 .07
❑ 143 Natrone Means .20 .07
❑ 144 Jeff Garcia .50 .20
❑ 145 Terry Glenn .30 .10
❑ 146 Marshall Faulk .60 .25
❑ 147 Pat Johnson .20 .07
❑ 148 Frank Wycheck .20 .07
❑ 149 Champ Bailey .30 .10
❑ 150 Jamal Anderson .50 .20
❑ 151 Doug Flutie .50 .20
❑ 152 Michael Bates .20 .07
❑ 153 Corey Dillon .50 .20
❑ 154 Keith McKenzie .20 .07
❑ 155 Orpheus Roye .20 .07
❑ 156 Olandis Gary .50 .20
❑ 157 Johnnie Morton .30 .10
❑ 158 Brett Favre 1.50 .60
❑ 159 Adrian Murrell .20 .07
❑ 160 Fred Taylor .50 .20
❑ 161 Tony Gonzalez .30 .10
❑ 162 Zach Thomas .50 .20
❑ 163 Randy Moss 1.00 .40
❑ 164 Marcus Robinson .50 .20
❑ 165 Tiki Barber .50 .20
❑ 166 Rich Gannon .50 .20
❑ 167 Jeremiah Trotter RC 1.50 .60
❑ 168 Jermaine Fazande .20 .07
❑ 169 Steve Young .60 .25
❑ 170 Isaac Bruce .50 .20
❑ 171 Warrick Dunn .50 .20
❑ 172 Yancey Thigpen .20 .07
❑ 173 Rod Smith .30 .10
❑ 174 Albert Connell .20 .07
❑ 175 Freddie Jones .20 .07
❑ 176 Terance Mathis .30 .10
❑ 177 Eric Moulds .50 .20
❑ 178 Brian Mitchell .20 .07
❑ 179 Wesley Walls .20 .07
❑ 180 Carl Pickens .30 .10
❑ 181 Errict Rhett .30 .10
❑ 182 Madre Hill .20 .07
❑ 183 Jason Elam .20 .07
❑ 184 Greg Ellis .20 .07
❑ 185 David Sloan .20 .07
❑ 186 Edgerrin James .75 .30
❑ 187 Jimmy Smith .30 .10
❑ 188 Tony Richardson RC .30 .10
❑ 189 James Hasty .20 .07
❑ 190 Sam Madison .20 .07
❑ 191 Tony Simmons .20 .07
❑ 192 Andre Hastings .20 .07
❑ 193 Keyshawn Johnson .50 .20
❑ 194 Na Brown .20 .07
❑ 195 Napoleon Kaufman .30 .10
❑ 196 Torrance Small .20 .07
❑ 197 Curtis Conway .30 .10
❑ 198 Jeff Graham .20 .07
❑ 199 Jason Hanson .20 .07
❑ 200 Derrick Mayes .30 .10
❑ 201 Torry Holt .50 .20
❑ 202 Warren Sapp .30 .10
❑ 203 Kimble Anders .20 .07
❑ 204 Blaine Bishop .20 .07
❑ 205 Leroy Hoard .20 .07
❑ 206 Larry Centers .20 .07
❑ 207 O.J. Santiago .20 .07
❑ 208 Antowain Smith .30 .10
❑ 209 Chuck Smith .20 .07
❑ 210 Takeo Spikes .20 .07
❑ 211 Rocket Ismail .30 .10
❑ 212 Ed McCaffrey .50 .20
❑ 213 Karsten Bailey .20 .07
❑ 214 Terry Fair .20 .07
❑ 215 Ken Dilger .20 .07
❑ 216 Jamie Martin .30 .10
❑ 217 Cris Dishman .20 .07
❑ 218 Jay Fiedler .30 .10
❑ 219 Lawyer Milloy .30 .10
❑ 220 Jake Delhomme RC 2.50 1.00
❑ 221 Wayne Chrebet .30 .10
❑ 222 Darrell Russell .20 .07
❑ 223 Christian Fauria .20 .07
❑ 224 Jerome Bettis .50 .20
❑ 225 Ryan Leaf .30 .10
❑ 226 Ricky Watters .30 .10
❑ 227 Keenan McCardell .30 .10
❑ 228 Grant Wistrom .20 .07
❑ 229 Jevon Kearse .50 .20
❑ 230 Frank Sanders .30 .10
❑ 231 Shannon Sharpe .30 .10
❑ 232 Jonathan Linton .20 .07
❑ 233 Alonzo Mayes .20 .07
❑ 234 Jason Garrett .20 .07
❑ 235 Kordell Stewart .30 .10
❑ 236 David LaFleur .20 .07
❑ 237 Kenny Bynum .20 .07
❑ 238 Byron Chamberlain .20 .07
❑ 239 Tyrone Davis .20 .07
❑ 240 Jerome Pathon .30 .10
❑ 241 Alvis Whitted .20 .07
❑ 242 Kevin Lockett .20 .07
❑ 243 Matthew Hatchette .20 .07
❑ 244 Rod Woodson .30 .10
❑ 245 Joe Horn .30 .10
❑ 246 Ronnie Powell .20 .07
❑ 247 Dedric Ward .20 .07
❑ 248 James Johnson .20 .07
❑ 249 James Jett .20 .07
❑ 250 Bobby Shaw RC .50 .20
❑ 251 J.J. Stokes .30 .10
❑ 252 Paul Shields RC .20 .07
❑ 253 Sean Dawkins .20 .07
❑ 254 Hardy Nickerson .20 .07
❑ 255 Stephen Boyd .20 .07
❑ 256 Chris Warren .20 .07
❑ 257 Kerry Collins .30 .10
❑ 258 Isaac Byrd .20 .07
❑ 259 Bobby Hoying .20 .07
❑ 260 Daunte Culpepper .60 .25
❑ 261 Moe Williams .30 .10
❑ 262 Kamil Loud .20 .07
❑ 263 Derrick Brooks .50 .20
❑ 264 Jay Riemersma .20 .07
❑ 265 Ray Lucas .30 .10
❑ 266 Jason Gildon .20 .07
❑ 267 James Stewart .30 .10
❑ 268 Marcellus Wiley .20 .07
❑ 269 Craig Yeast .20 .07
❑ 270 Michael Basnight .20 .07
❑ 271 Tyrone Wheatley .30 .10
❑ 272 Martin Gramatica .20 .07
❑ 273 Phillip Daniels RC .30 .10
❑ 274 Richard Huntley .20 .07
❑ 275 Muhsin Muhammad .30 .10
❑ 276 Todd Lyght .20 .07
❑ 277 Carlester Crumpler .20 .07
❑ 278 Jeff Lewis .20 .07
❑ 279 Jeff George .30 .10
❑ 280 Jeff Blake .30 .10
❑ 281 Michael McCrary .20 .07
❑ 282 Shawn Jefferson .20 .07
❑ 283 Mark Bruener .20 .07
❑ 284 Donnie Abraham .20 .07
❑ 285 Yatil Green .20 .07
❑ 286 Jermaine Lewis .20 .07
❑ 287 Rob Fredrickson .20 .07
❑ 288 Thurman Thomas .30 .10
❑ 289 Kent Graham .20 .07
❑ 290 Darnay Scott .30 .10
❑ 291 Tony Graziani .20 .07
❑ 292 Qadry Ismail .30 .10
❑ 293 Aeneas Williams .20 .07
❑ 294 Marvin Harrison .50 .20
❑ 295 Jimmy Hitchcock .20 .07
❑ 296 Bob Christian .20 .07
❑ 297 Pete Mitchell .20 .07
❑ 298 Mike Alstott .50 .20
❑ 299 Emmitt Smith 1.00 .40
❑ 300 Trevor Pryce .20 .07
❑ 301 Tony Banks .30 .10

❑ 302	Mikhael Ricks	.20	.07
❑ 303	Randall Cunningham	.50	.20
❑ 304	Thomas Jones RC	1.25	.50
❑ 305	Mark Simoneau RC	.60	.25
❑ 306	Jamal Lewis RC	2.00	.75
❑ 307	Kwame Cavil RC	.40	.15
❑ 308	Rashard Anderson RC	.60	.25
❑ 309	Brian Urlacher RC	3.00	1.25
❑ 310	Peter Warrick RC	.75	.30
❑ 311	Courtney Brown RC	.75	.30
❑ 312	Michael Wiley RC	.60	.25
❑ 313	Chris Cole RC	.60	.25
❑ 314	Reuben Droughns RC	1.00	.40
❑ 315	Bubba Franks RC	.75	.30
❑ 316	Rob Morris RC	.60	.25
❑ 317	R.Jay Soward RC	.60	.25
❑ 318	Sylvester Morris RC	.60	.25
❑ 319	Ben Kelly RC	.40	.15
❑ 320	Doug Chapman RC	.60	.25
❑ 321	J.R. Redmond RC	.60	.25
❑ 322	Darren Howard RC	.60	.25
❑ 323	Ron Dayne RC	.75	.30
❑ 324	Chad Pennington RC	2.00	.75
❑ 325	Jerry Porter RC	1.00	.40
❑ 326	Corey Simon RC	.75	.30
❑ 327	Plaxico Burress RC	1.50	.60
❑ 328	Trung Canidate RC	.60	.25
❑ 329	Rogers Beckett RC	.60	.25
❑ 330	Giovanni Carmazzi RC	.40	.15
❑ 331	Shaun Alexander RC	4.00	1.50
❑ 332	Joe Hamilton RC	.60	.25
❑ 333	Keith Bulluck RC	.75	.30
❑ 334	Todd Husak RC	.75	.30
❑ 335	D.Walker RC/R.Thompson RC	.60	.25
❑ 336	M.Philyaw RC/A.Midget RC	.40	.15
❑ 337	C.Redman RC/T.Taylor RC	.75	.30
❑ 338	Sam.Morris RC/A.Black RC	.60	.25
❑ 339	D.Grant RC/A.McKinley RC	.60	.25
❑ 340	D.White RC/F.Murphy RC	.75	.30
❑ 341	C.Keaton RC/R.Dugans RC	1.00	.40
❑ 342	Prentice RC/Northcutt RC	.60	.25
❑ 343	O.Grant RC/D.Goodrich RC	.40	.15
❑ 344	D.O'Neal RC/I.Gold RC	.75	.30
❑ 345	S.McDougle RC/B.Green RC	.40	.15
❑ 346	A.Lucas RC/N.Diggs RC	.60	.25
❑ 347	M.Washington RC/D.Kendra RC	.60	.25
❑ 348	T.Slaughter RC/S.Stith RC	.60	.25
❑ 349	W.Bartee RC/F.Moreau RC	.60	.25
❑ 350	D.Dyer RC/T.Wade RC	.60	.25
❑ 351	C.Hovan RC/T.Walters	.75	.30
❑ 352	T.Brady RC/Stachelski RC	20.00	7.50
❑ 353	M.Bulger RC/T.Smith RC	1.50	.60
❑ 354	C.Griffin RC/R.Dixon RC	.60	.25
❑ 355	L.Coles RC/A.Becht RC	.75	.30
❑ 356	Janikowski RC/Lechler RC	.75	.30
❑ 357	T.Pinkston RC/G.Scott RC	.75	.30
❑ 358	D.Farmer RC/T.Martin RC	.60	.25
❑ 359	B.Young RC/J.Shepherd RC	.60	.25
❑ 360	J.Seider RC/T.Gaylor RC	.60	.25
❑ 361	T.Rattay RC/C.Fields RC	.75	.30
❑ 362	D.Jackson RC/J.Williams RC	1.25	.50
❑ 363	N.Webster RC/J.Whalen RC	.40	.15
❑ 364	E.Kinney RC/C.Coleman RC	.75	.30
❑ 365	C.Samuels RC/L.Murray RC	.60	.25
❑ 366	Cardinals IA/Plummer	.30	.10
❑ 367	Falcons IA/Chandlr/Andrson	.30	.10
❑ 368	Ravens IA/Boulware	.20	.07
❑ 369	Bills IA/Flutie	.30	.10
❑ 370	Panthers IA/Beuerlein	.30	.10
❑ 371	Bears IA/McNown	.20	.07
❑ 372	Bengals IA/Dillon	.30	.10
❑ 373	Browns IA/Couch	.30	.10
❑ 374	Cowboys IA/Smith	.50	.20
❑ 375	Broncos IA/Gary	.30	.10
❑ 376	Lions IA/Batch	.30	.10
❑ 377	Packers IA/Levens	.30	.10
❑ 378	Colts IA/James	.60	.25
❑ 379	Jaguars IA/Brackens	.20	.07
❑ 380	Chiefs IA/Grbac	.20	.07
❑ 381	Dolphins IA/Marino	.75	.30
❑ 382	Vikings IA/Rob.Smith	.30	.10
❑ 383	Patriots IA/Bledsoe	.30	.10
❑ 384	Saints IA/Williams	.50	.20
❑ 385	Giants IA/Armstead	.20	.07
❑ 386	Jets IA/Martin	.30	.10
❑ 387	Raiders IA/Kaufman	.30	.10
❑ 388	Eagles IA/McNabb	.30	.10
❑ 389	Steelers IA/Bettis	.30	.10
❑ 390	Rams IA/Faulk	.50	.20
❑ 391	Chargers IA/Fazande	.20	.07
❑ 392	49ers IA/Garner	.30	.10
❑ 393	Seahawks IA/Kennedy	.20	.07
❑ 394	Buccaneers IA/Alstott	.30	.10
❑ 395	Titans IA/McNair	.30	.10
❑ 396	Redskins IA/S.Davis	.30	.10
❑ 397	Tim Couch CL	.30	.10
❑ 398	Peyton Manning CL	.60	.25
❑ 399	Kurt Warner CL	.50	.20
❑ 400	Randy Moss CL	.50	.20

2001 Fleer Tradition

❑	COMPLETE SET (450)	40.00	20.00
❑ 1	Thomas Jones	.40	.15
❑ 2	Bruce Smith	.25	.08
❑ 3	Marvin Harrison	.60	.25
❑ 4	Darrell Jackson	.60	.25
❑ 5	Trent Green	.60	.25
❑ 6	Wesley Walls	.25	.08
❑ 7	Jimmy Smith	.40	.15
❑ 8	Isaac Bruce	.60	.25
❑ 9	Jamal Anderson	.60	.25
❑ 10	Marty Booker	.25	.08
❑ 11	Elvis Grbac	.40	.15
❑ 12	Joe Jurevicius	.25	.08
❑ 13	Reidel Anthony	.25	.08
❑ 14	Darnay Scott	.25	.08
❑ 15	Oronde Gadsden	.40	.15
❑ 16	Shawn Bryson	.25	.08
❑ 17	Jonathan Ogden	.25	.08
❑ 18	Aaron Shea	.25	.08
❑ 19	Randy Moss	1.25	.50
❑ 20	Eddie George	.60	.25
❑ 21	Stephen Davis	.60	.25
❑ 22	Emmitt Smith	1.25	.50
❑ 23	Willie McGinest	.25	.08
❑ 24	Trent Dilfer	.40	.15
❑ 25	Peter Boulware	.25	.08
❑ 26	Rod Smith	.40	.15
❑ 27	Ricky Williams	.60	.25
❑ 28	Albert Connell	.25	.08
❑ 29	Robert Porcher	.25	.08
❑ 30	Jessie Armstead	.25	.08
❑ 31	Shane Matthews	.25	.08
❑ 32	Eric Moulds	.40	.15
❑ 33	Kurt Schulz	.25	.08
❑ 34	Richie Anderson	.25	.08
❑ 35	Ron Dugans	.25	.08
❑ 36	Steve Beuerlein	.40	.15
❑ 37	Darren Sharper	.25	.08
❑ 38	Andre Rison	.40	.15
❑ 39	Courtney Brown	.40	.15
❑ 40	Eddie Kennison	.40	.15
❑ 41	Ken Dilger	.25	.08
❑ 42	Charles Johnson	.25	.08
❑ 43	Dexter Coakley	.25	.08
❑ 44	Akili Smith	.25	.08
❑ 45	R.Jay Soward	.25	.08
❑ 46	Danny Farmer	.25	.08
❑ 47	Dez White	.25	.08
❑ 48	Olandis Gary	.40	.15
❑ 49	Wali Rainer	.25	.08
❑ 50	Derrick Alexander	.40	.15
❑ 51	Donnie Abraham	.25	.08
❑ 52	David Sloan	.25	.08
❑ 53	Larry Allen	.25	.08
❑ 54	Sam Madison	.25	.08
❑ 55	Troy Edwards	.25	.08
❑ 56	Ryan Longwell	.25	.08
❑ 57	Brian Griese	.60	.25
❑ 58	John Randle	.40	.15
❑ 59	Reggie Jones	.25	.08
❑ 60	Mike Peterson	.25	.08
❑ 61	Bill Romanowski	.25	.08
❑ 62	Kevin Faulk	.40	.15
❑ 63	Tai Streets	.25	.08
❑ 64	Tony Brackens	.25	.08
❑ 65	James Stewart	.40	.15
❑ 66	Joe Horn	.40	.15
❑ 67	Kurt Warner	1.25	.50
❑ 68	Eric Hicks RC	.25	.08
❑ 69	Bryan Westbrook	.25	.08
❑ 70	Tiki Barber	.60	.25
❑ 71	Frank Sanders	.25	.08
❑ 72	Olindo Mare	.25	.08
❑ 73	Bill Schroeder	.40	.15
❑ 74	Anthony Becht	.25	.08
❑ 75	Rob Johnson	.40	.15
❑ 76	Troy Brown	.40	.15
❑ 77	Chad Bratzke	.25	.08
❑ 78	Rickey Dudley	.25	.08
❑ 79	Doug Johnson	.25	.08
❑ 80	Joe Johnson	.25	.08
❑ 81	Keenan McCardell	.25	.08
❑ 82	Tim Brown	.60	.25
❑ 83	Blaine Bishop	.25	.08
❑ 84	Ron Dixon	.25	.08
❑ 85	Michael Cloud	.25	.08
❑ 86	Todd Pinkston	.25	.08
❑ 87	Shannon Sharpe	.40	.15
❑ 88	Marvin Jones	.25	.08
❑ 89	Zach Thomas	.60	.25
❑ 90	Kordell Stewart	.40	.15
❑ 91	Champ Bailey	.40	.15
❑ 92	Jacquez Green	.25	.08
❑ 93	Daunte Culpepper	.60	.25
❑ 94	Freddie Jones	.25	.08
❑ 95	Donald Hayes	.25	.08
❑ 96	Rich Gannon	.60	.25
❑ 97	Ty Law	.40	.15
❑ 98	Grant Wistrom	.25	.08
❑ 99	James Allen	.40	.15
❑ 100	Corey Simon	.40	.15
❑ 101	Jeff Blake	.40	.15
❑ 102	Bryant Young	.25	.08
❑ 103	Craig Yeast	.25	.08
❑ 104	Bobby Shaw	.25	.08
❑ 105	Kerry Collins	.40	.15
❑ 106	Brock Huard	.25	.08
❑ 107	JaJuan Dawson	.25	.08
❑ 108	Jeff Graham	.25	.08
❑ 109	Chad Pennington	1.00	.40
❑ 110	Jake Plummer	.40	.15
❑ 111	James McKnight	.40	.15
❑ 112	Terrell Owens	.60	.25
❑ 113	Mo Lewis	.25	.08
❑ 114	Jeremy McDaniel	.25	.08
❑ 115	Ed McCaffrey	.60	.25
❑ 116	Ricky Watters	.25	.08
❑ 117	Jerry Porter	.40	.15
❑ 118	Shawn Jefferson	.25	.08
❑ 119	Charlie Batch	.60	.25
❑ 120	Justin Watson	.25	.08
❑ 121	Donovan McNabb	.75	.30
❑ 122	Shaun King	.25	.08

❑	123	Brett Favre	2.00	.75
❑	124	Ronald McKinnon	.25	.08
❑	125	Richard Huntley	.25	.08
❑	126	Ray Lewis	.60	.25
❑	127	Jerome Pathon	.40	.15
❑	128	Sam Cowart	.25	.08
❑	129	Ryan Leaf	.40	.15
❑	130	Greg Clark	.25	.08
❑	131	Tony Boselli	.25	.08
❑	132	Frank Wycheck	.25	.08
❑	133	Charlie Garner	.40	.15
❑	134	Tony Siragusa	.25	.08
❑	135	Sylvester Morris	.25	.08
❑	136	Qadry Ismail	.40	.15
❑	137	Jon Kitna	.40	.15
❑	138	James Thrash	.40	.15
❑	139	Lamar Smith	.40	.15
❑	140	Brad Johnson	.60	.25
❑	141	London Fletcher	.25	.08
❑	142	Tim Biakabutuka	.40	.15
❑	143	Ed McDaniel	.25	.08
❑	144	Tony Parrish	.25	.08
❑	145	David Boston	.60	.25
❑	146	Brian Urlacher	1.00	.40
❑	147	Drew Bledsoe	.75	.30
❑	148	David Patten	.25	.08
❑	149	Marcellus Wiley	.25	.08
❑	150	Peter Warrick	.60	.25
❑	151	La'Roi Glover	.25	.08
❑	152	Troy Aikman	1.00	.40
❑	153	Chris Chandler	.40	.15
❑	154	Travis Prentice	.25	.08
❑	155	Ike Hilliard	.40	.15
❑	156	John Mobley	.25	.08
❑	157	Warren Sapp	.40	.15
❑	158	Joey Galloway	.40	.15
❑	159	Laveranues Coles	.60	.25
❑	160	Germane Crowell	.25	.08
❑	161	Jamal Lewis	1.00	.40
❑	162	Mike Anderson	.60	.25
❑	163	Charles Woodson	.40	.15
❑	164	Antonio Freeman	.60	.25
❑	165	Derrick Mason	.40	.15
❑	166	Chris Claiborne	.25	.08
❑	167	Brian Mitchell	.25	.08
❑	168	Mike Vanderjagt	.25	.08
❑	169	Rod Woodson	.40	.15
❑	170	Doug Chapman	.25	.08
❑	171	John Lynch	.40	.15
❑	172	Kevin Hardy	.25	.08
❑	173	Sam Shade	.25	.08
❑	174	Edgerrin James	.75	.30
❑	175	Brian Dawkins	.40	.15
❑	176	Donnie Edwards	.25	.08
❑	177	Patrick Jeffers	.40	.15
❑	178	Mark Brunell	.60	.25
❑	179	Junior Seau	.60	.25
❑	180	Trace Armstrong	.25	.08
❑	181	Marcus Robinson	.60	.25
❑	182	Tony Gonzalez	.40	.15
❑	183	J.J. Stokes	.40	.15
❑	184	Jake Reed	.40	.15
❑	185	Corey Dillon	.60	.25
❑	186	Jay Fiedler	.60	.25
❑	187	Christian Fauria	.25	.08
❑	188	Sammy Knight	.25	.08
❑	189	Kevin Johnson	.40	.15
❑	190	Matthew Hatchette	.25	.08
❑	191	Az-Zahir Hakim	.40	.15
❑	192	Keith Hamilton	.25	.08
❑	193	Darren Woodson	.25	.08
❑	194	Terry Glenn	.40	.15
❑	195	Simeon Rice	.40	.15
❑	196	Keyshawn Johnson	.60	.25
❑	197	Terrell Davis	.60	.25
❑	198	William Roaf	.25	.08
❑	199	Doug Flutie	.60	.25
❑	200	Kevin Carter	.25	.08
❑	201	Stephen Boyd	.25	.08
❑	202	Michael Strahan	.40	.15
❑	203	Ray Buchanan	.25	.08
❑	204	Tyrone Wheatley	.40	.15
❑	205	Jason Hanson	.25	.08
❑	206	Wayne Chrebet	.40	.15
❑	207	Samari Rolle	.25	.08
❑	208	Duce Staley	.60	.25
❑	209	Dorsey Levens	.40	.15
❑	210	Sebastian Janikowski	.25	.08
❑	211	Duane Starks	.25	.08
❑	212	Jason Gildon	.25	.08
❑	213	Terrence Wilkins	.25	.08
❑	214	Eric Allen	.25	.08
❑	215	Deion Sanders	.60	.25
❑	216	Curtis Conway	.40	.15
❑	217	Fred Taylor	.60	.25
❑	218	Troy Vincent	.25	.08
❑	219	Mike Minter RC	.40	.15
❑	220	Jeff Garcia	.60	.25
❑	221	Tony Richardson	.25	.08
❑	222	Jerome Bettis	.60	.25
❑	223	Chad Morton	.25	.08
❑	224	Tony Horne	.25	.08
❑	225	Dave Moore	.25	.08
❑	226	Victor Green	.25	.08
❑	227	Chris Sanders	.25	.08
❑	228	Marshall Faulk	.75	.30
❑	229	Cris Carter	.60	.25
❑	230	Rodney Harrison	.25	.08
❑	231	Tim Couch	.40	.15
❑	232	Antowain Smith	.40	.15
❑	233	Lawyer Milloy	.40	.15
❑	234	Lance Schulters	.25	.08
❑	235	Michael Wiley	.25	.08
❑	236	Steve McNair	.60	.25
❑	237	Aaron Brooks	.60	.25
❑	238	Anthony Simmons	.25	.08
❑	239	Dwayne Carswell	.25	.08
❑	240	Priest Holmes	.75	.30
❑	241	Amani Toomer	.40	.15
❑	242	Aeneas Williams	.25	.08
❑	243	MarTay Jenkins	.25	.08
❑	244	Jeff George	.40	.15
❑	245	Vinny Testaverde	.40	.15
❑	246	Peerless Price	.40	.15
❑	247	Bubba Franks	.40	.15
❑	248	Randall Cunningham	.60	.25
❑	249	Aaron Glenn	.25	.08
❑	250	Terance Mathis	.40	.15
❑	251	Peyton Manning	1.50	.60
❑	252	Terrell Buckley	.25	.08
❑	253	Greg Biekert	.25	.08
❑	254	Martin Gramatica	.25	.08
❑	255	Kyle Brady	.25	.08
❑	256	Johnnie Morton	.40	.15
❑	257	Jeremiah Trotter	.40	.15
❑	258	Travis Taylor	.40	.15
❑	259	Frank Moreau	.25	.08
❑	260	LeRoy Butler	.25	.08
❑	261	Plaxico Burress	.60	.25
❑	262	Randall Godfrey	.25	.08
❑	263	Jason Taylor	.25	.08
❑	264	Jeff Burris	.25	.08
❑	265	Jim Harbaugh	.40	.15
❑	266	Marco Coleman	.25	.08
❑	267	Robert Smith	.40	.15
❑	268	Mike Hollis	.25	.08
❑	269	Jerry Rice	1.25	.50
❑	270	Muhsin Muhammad	.40	.15
❑	271	J.R. Redmond	.25	.08
❑	272	Brian Walker	.25	.08
❑	273	Orlando Pace	.25	.08
❑	274	Cade McNown	.25	.08
❑	275	Darren Howard	.25	.08
❑	276	Ron Dayne	.60	.25
❑	277	Shaun Alexander	.75	.30
❑	278	Brandon Bennett	.25	.08
❑	279	Jason Sehorn	.25	.08
❑	280	Matt Hasselbeck	.40	.15
❑	281	Michael Pittman	.25	.08
❑	282	Dennis Northcutt	.40	.15
❑	283	Dedric Ward	.25	.08
❑	284	Curtis Martin	.60	.25
❑	285	Sammy Morris	.25	.08
❑	286	Rocket Ismail	.40	.15
❑	287	Jon Ritchie	.25	.08
❑	288	Shaun Ellis	.25	.08
❑	289	Tim Dwight	.60	.25
❑	290	Trevor Pryce	.25	.08
❑	291	Warrick Dunn	.60	.25
❑	292	Napoleon Kaufman	.40	.15
❑	293	Mike Alstott	.60	.25
❑	294	Herman Moore	.40	.15
❑	295	Chad Lewis	.25	.08
❑	296	Hugh Douglas	.25	.08
❑	297	Chris Redman	.25	.08
❑	298	Ahman Green	.60	.25
❑	299	Hines Ward	.60	.25
❑	300	Mark Bruener	.25	.08
❑	301	Jevon Kearse	.40	.15
❑	302	Jermaine Fazande	.25	.08
❑	303	Terrell Fletcher	.25	.08
❑	304	Torry Holt	.60	.25
❑	305	Chris McAlister	.25	.08
❑	306	Jason Elam	.25	.08
❑	307	Fred Beasley	.25	.08
❑	308	Frank Wycheck UH	.25	.08
❑	309	Michael McCrary UH	.25	.08
❑	310	Mark Brunell UH	.60	.25
❑	311	Tim Couch UH	.40	.15
❑	312	Takeo Spikes UH	.25	.08
❑	313	Jerome Bettis UH	.40	.15
❑	314	Zach Thomas UH	.60	.25
❑	315	Drew Bledsoe UH	.60	.25
❑	316	Wayne Chrebet UH	.25	.08
❑	317	Jay Riemersma UH	.25	.08
❑	318	Marvin Harrison UH	.40	.15
❑	319	Ed McCaffrey UH	.40	.15
❑	320	Tony Gonzalez UH	.25	.08
❑	321	Tim Brown UH	.40	.15
❑	322	Junior Seau UH	.40	.15
❑	323	Shawn Springs UH	.25	.08
❑	324	Troy Aikman UH	.40	.15
❑	325	Pat Tillman UH RC	20.00	10.00
❑	326	David Akers UH RC	.40	.15
❑	327	Michael Strahan UH	.40	.15
❑	328	Darrell Green UH	.25	.08
❑	329	Kurt Warner UH	.60	.25
❑	330	Jeff Garcia UH	.40	.15
❑	331	Aaron Brooks UH	.40	.15
❑	332	Jamal Anderson UH	.40	.15
❑	333	Brad Hoover UH	.25	.08
❑	334	Cris Carter UH	.40	.15
❑	335	Derrick Brooks UH	.60	.25
❑	336	Antonio Freeman UH	.40	.15
❑	337	Luther Elliss UH	.25	.08
❑	338	James Allen UH	.25	.08
❑	339	Arizona Cardinals TC	.40	.15
❑	340	Atlanta Falcons TC	.40	.15
❑	341	Baltimore Ravens TC	.25	.08
❑	342	Buffalo Bills TC	.25	.08
❑	343	Carolina Panthers TC	.25	.08
❑	344	Chicago Bears TC	.60	.25
❑	345	Cincinnati Bengals TC	.40	.15
❑	346	Cleveland Browns TC	.25	.08
❑	347	Cowboys TC/Emmitt	.60	.25
❑	348	Denver Broncos TC	.40	.15
❑	349	Detroit Lions TC	.25	.08
❑	350	Packers TC/Favre	1.00	.40
❑	351	Colts TC/James	.60	.25
❑	352	Jacksonville Jaguars TC	.60	.25
❑	353	Kansas City Chiefs TC	.25	.08
❑	354	Miami Dolphins TC	.40	.15
❑	355	Minnesota Vikings TC	.60	.25
❑	356	New England Patriots TC	.60	.25
❑	357	New Orleans Saints TC	.40	.15
❑	358	New York Giants TC	.40	.15
❑	359	New York Jets TC	.40	.15
❑	360	Oakland Raiders TC	.40	.15
❑	361	Philadelphia Eagles TC	.60	.25
❑	362	Pittsburgh Steelers TC	.40	.15

❑ 363 San Diego Chargers TC .25 .08
❑ 364 San Francisco 49ers TC .25 .08
❑ 365 Seattle Seahawks TC .25 .08
❑ 366 Rams TC/Warner .60 .25
❑ 367 Tampa Bay Buccaneers TC .40 .15
❑ 368 Tennessee Titans TC .40 .15
❑ 369 Washington Redskins TC .40 .15
❑ 370 Buffalo Bills TL .25 .08
❑ 371 Indianapolis Colts TL .60 .25
❑ 372 Miami Dolphins TL .25 .08
❑ 373 New England Patriots TL .40 .15
❑ 374 New York Jets TL .40 .15
❑ 375 Baltimore Ravens TL .40 .15
❑ 376 Cincinnati Bengals TL .25 .08
❑ 377 Cleveland Browns TL .25 .08
❑ 378 Jacksonville Jaguars TL .40 .15
❑ 379 Pittsburgh Steelers TL .40 .15
❑ 380 Tennessee Titans TL .40 .15
❑ 381 Denver Broncos TL .40 .15
❑ 382 Kansas City Chiefs TL .40 .15
❑ 383 Oakland Raiders TL .40 .15
❑ 384 San Diego Chargers TL .40 .15
❑ 385 Seattle Seahawks TL .25 .08
❑ 386 Arizona Cardinals TL .25 .08
❑ 387 Dallas Cowboys TL .60 .25
❑ 388 New York Giants TL .40 .15
❑ 389 Philadelphia Eagles TL .40 .15
❑ 390 Washington Redskins TL .40 .15
❑ 391 Chicago Bears TL .25 .08
❑ 392 Detroit Lions TL .25 .08
❑ 393 Green Bay Packers TL .60 .25
❑ 394 Minnesota Vikings TL .60 .25
❑ 395 Tampa Bay Buccaneers TL .40 .15
❑ 396 Atlanta Falcons TL .25 .08
❑ 397 Carolina Panthers TL .25 .08
❑ 398 New Orleans Saints TL .40 .15
❑ 399 San Francisco 49ersTL .40 .15
❑ 400 St. Louis Rams TL .60 .25
❑ 401 Michael Vick RC 8.00 4.00
❑ 402 Drew Brees RC 3.00 1.25
❑ 403 Michael Bennett RC 2.00 .75
❑ 404 David Terrell RC 1.25 .50
❑ 405 Deuce McAllister RC 2.50 1.00
❑ 406 Santana Moss RC 2.00 .75
❑ 407 Koren Robinson RC 1.25 .50
❑ 408 Chris Weinke RC 1.25 .50
❑ 409 Reggie Wayne RC 2.50 1.00
❑ 410 Rod Gardner RC 1.25 .50
❑ 411 James Jackson RC 1.25 .50
❑ 412 Travis Henry RC 1.25 .50
❑ 413 Josh Heupel RC 1.25 .50
❑ 414 LaDainian Tomlinson RC 6.00 3.00
❑ 415 Chad Johnson RC 3.00 1.25
❑ 416 Sage Rosenfels RC 1.25 .50
❑ 417 Quincy Morgan RC 1.25 .50
❑ 418 Ken-Yon Rambo RC .75 .30
❑ 419 LaMont Jordan RC 2.50 1.00
❑ 420 Anthony Thomas RC 1.25 .50
❑ 421 Dave Dickenson RC .75 .30
❑ 422 Travis Minor RC .75 .30
❑ 423 Kevan Barlow RC 1.25 .50
❑ 424 Chris Chambers RC 2.00 .75
❑ 425 Richard Seymour RC 1.25 .50
❑ 426 Gerard Warren RC 1.25 .50
❑ 427 Jamar Fletcher RC .75 .30
❑ 428 Freddie Mitchell RC 1.25 .50
❑ 429 Jamal Reynolds RC 1.25 .50
❑ 430 Marques Tuiasosopo RC 1.25 .50
❑ 431 Snoop Minnis RC .75 .30
❑ 432 Mike McMahon RC 1.25 .50
❑ 433 Robert Ferguson RC 1.25 .50
❑ 434 Ronney Daniels RC .50 .20
❑ 435 Rudi Johnson RC 2.50 1.00
❑ 436 Vinny Sutherland RC .75 .30
❑ 437 Josh Booty RC 1.25 .50
❑ 438 Reggie White RC .75 .30
❑ 439 Todd Heap RC 1.25 .50
❑ 440 Justin Smith RC 1.25 .50
❑ 441 Andre Carter RC 1.25 .50
❑ 442 Bobby Newcombe RC .75 .30
❑ 443 Alex Bannister RC .75 .30
❑ 444 Correll Buckhalter RC 1.50 .60
❑ 445 Quincy Carter RC 1.25 .50
❑ 446 Jesse Palmer RC 1.25 .50
❑ 447 Heath Evans RC .75 .30
❑ 448 Dan Morgan RC 1.25 .50
❑ 449 Justin McCareins RC 1.25 .50
❑ 450 Alge Crumpler RC 1.50 .60

2001 Fleer Tradition Glossy

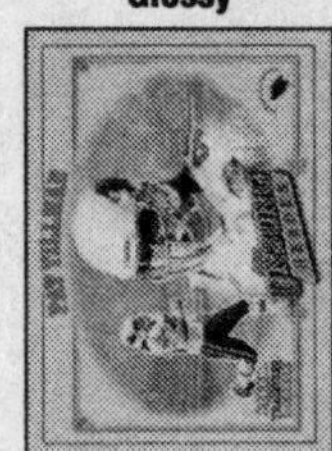

❑ COMP.SET w/o SP's (400) 40.00 20.00
❑ 1 Thomas Jones .50 .20
❑ 2 Bruce Smith .30 .10
❑ 3 Marvin Harrison .75 .30
❑ 4 Darrell Jackson .75 .30
❑ 5 Trent Green .75 .30
❑ 6 Wesley Walls .30 .10
❑ 7 Jimmy Smith .50 .20
❑ 8 Isaac Bruce .75 .30
❑ 9 Jamal Anderson .75 .30
❑ 10 Marty Booker .30 .10
❑ 11 Elvis Grbac .50 .20
❑ 12 Joe Jurevicius .30 .10
❑ 13 Reidel Anthony .30 .10
❑ 14 Darnay Scott .30 .10
❑ 15 Oronde Gadsden .50 .20
❑ 16 Shawn Bryson .30 .10
❑ 17 Jonathan Ogden .30 .10
❑ 18 Aaron Shea .30 .10
❑ 19 Randy Moss 1.50 .60
❑ 20 Eddie George .75 .30
❑ 21 Stephen Davis .75 .30
❑ 22 Emmitt Smith 1.50 .60
❑ 23 Willie McGinest .30 .10
❑ 24 Trent Dilfer .50 .20
❑ 25 Peter Boulware .30 .10
❑ 26 Rod Smith .50 .20
❑ 27 Ricky Williams .75 .30
❑ 28 Albert Connell .30 .10
❑ 29 Robert Porcher .30 .10
❑ 30 Jessie Armstead .30 .10
❑ 31 Shane Matthews .30 .10
❑ 32 Eric Moulds .50 .20
❑ 33 Kurt Schulz .30 .10
❑ 34 Richie Anderson .30 .10
❑ 35 Ron Dugans .30 .10
❑ 36 Steve Beuerlein .50 .20
❑ 37 Darren Sharper .30 .10
❑ 38 Andre Rison .50 .20
❑ 39 Courtney Brown .50 .20
❑ 40 Eddie Kennison .50 .20
❑ 41 Ken Dilger .30 .10
❑ 42 Charles Johnson .30 .10
❑ 43 Dexter Coakley .30 .10
❑ 44 Akili Smith .30 .10
❑ 45 R.Jay Soward .30 .10
❑ 46 Danny Farmer .30 .10
❑ 47 Dez White .30 .10
❑ 48 Olandis Gary .50 .20
❑ 49 Wali Rainer .30 .10
❑ 50 Derrick Alexander .50 .20
❑ 51 Donnie Abraham .30 .10
❑ 52 David Sloan .30 .10
❑ 53 Larry Allen .30 .10
❑ 54 Sam Madison .30 .10
❑ 55 Troy Edwards .30 .10
❑ 56 Ryan Longwell .30 .10
❑ 57 Brian Griese .75 .30
❑ 58 John Randle .50 .20
❑ 59 Reggie Jones .30 .10
❑ 60 Mike Peterson .30 .10
❑ 61 Bill Romanowski .30 .10
❑ 62 Kevin Faulk .50 .20
❑ 63 Tai Streets .30 .10
❑ 64 Tony Brackens .30 .10
❑ 65 James Stewart .50 .20
❑ 66 Joe Horn .50 .20
❑ 67 Kurt Warner 1.50 .60
❑ 68 Eric Hicks RC .30 .10
❑ 69 Bryan Westbrook .30 .10
❑ 70 Tiki Barber .75 .30
❑ 71 Frank Sanders .30 .10
❑ 72 Olindo Mare .30 .10
❑ 73 Bill Schroeder .50 .20
❑ 74 Anthony Becht .30 .10
❑ 75 Rob Johnson .50 .20
❑ 76 Troy Brown .50 .20
❑ 77 Chad Bratzke .30 .10
❑ 78 Rickey Dudley .30 .10
❑ 79 Doug Johnson .30 .10
❑ 80 Joe Johnson .30 .10
❑ 81 Keenan McCardell .30 .10
❑ 82 Tim Brown .75 .30
❑ 83 Blaine Bishop .30 .10
❑ 84 Ron Dixon .30 .10
❑ 85 Michael Cloud .30 .10
❑ 86 Todd Pinkston .30 .10
❑ 87 Shannon Sharpe .50 .20
❑ 88 Marvin Jones .30 .10
❑ 89 Zach Thomas .75 .30
❑ 90 Kordell Stewart .50 .20
❑ 91 Champ Bailey .50 .20
❑ 92 Jacquez Green .30 .10
❑ 93 Daunte Culpepper .75 .30
❑ 94 Freddie Jones .30 .10
❑ 95 Donald Hayes .30 .10
❑ 96 Rich Gannon .75 .30
❑ 97 Ty Law .50 .20
❑ 98 Grant Wistrom .30 .10
❑ 99 James Allen .50 .20
❑ 100 Corey Simon .50 .20
❑ 101 Jeff Blake .50 .20
❑ 102 Bryant Young .30 .10
❑ 103 Craig Yeast .30 .10
❑ 104 Bobby Shaw .30 .10
❑ 105 Kerry Collins .50 .20
❑ 106 Brock Huard .30 .10
❑ 107 JaJuan Dawson .30 .10
❑ 108 Jeff Graham .30 .10
❑ 109 Chad Pennington 1.25 .50
❑ 110 Jake Plummer .50 .20
❑ 111 James McKnight .50 .20
❑ 112 Terrell Owens .75 .30
❑ 113 Mo Lewis .30 .10
❑ 114 Jeremy McDaniel .30 .10
❑ 115 Ed McCaffrey .75 .30
❑ 116 Ricky Watters .30 .10
❑ 117 Jerry Porter .50 .20
❑ 118 Shawn Jefferson .30 .10
❑ 119 Charlie Batch .75 .30
❑ 120 Justin Watson .30 .10
❑ 121 Donovan McNabb 1.00 .40
❑ 122 Shaun King .30 .10
❑ 123 Brett Favre 2.50 1.00
❑ 124 Ronald McKinnon .30 .10
❑ 125 Richard Huntley .30 .10
❑ 126 Ray Lewis .75 .30
❑ 127 Jerome Pathon .50 .20
❑ 128 Sam Cowart .30 .10
❑ 129 Ryan Leaf .50 .20
❑ 130 Greg Clark .30 .10
❑ 131 Tony Boselli .30 .10
❑ 132 Frank Wycheck .30 .10

❑ 133 Charlie Garner .50 .20
❑ 134 Tony Siragusa .30 .10
❑ 135 Sylvester Morris .30 .10
❑ 136 Qadry Ismail .50 .20
❑ 137 Jon Kitna .50 .20
❑ 138 James Thrash .50 .20
❑ 139 Lamar Smith .50 .20
❑ 140 Brad Johnson .75 .30
❑ 141 London Fletcher .30 .10
❑ 142 Tim Biakabutuka .50 .20
❑ 143 Ed McDaniel .30 .10
❑ 144 Tony Parrish .30 .10
❑ 145 David Boston .75 .30
❑ 146 Brian Urlacher 1.25 .50
❑ 147 Drew Bledsoe 1.00 .40
❑ 148 David Patten .30 .10
❑ 149 Marcellus Wiley .30 .10
❑ 150 Peter Warrick .75 .30
❑ 151 La'Roi Glover .30 .10
❑ 152 Troy Aikman 1.25 .50
❑ 153 Chris Chandler .50 .20
❑ 154 Travis Prentice .30 .10
❑ 155 Ike Hilliard .50 .20
❑ 156 John Mobley .30 .10
❑ 157 Warren Sapp .50 .20
❑ 158 Joey Galloway .50 .20
❑ 159 Laveranues Coles .75 .30
❑ 160 Germane Crowell .30 .10
❑ 161 Jamal Lewis 1.25 .50
❑ 162 Mike Anderson .75 .30
❑ 163 Charles Woodson .50 .20
❑ 164 Antonio Freeman .75 .30
❑ 165 Derrick Mason .50 .20
❑ 166 Chris Claiborne .30 .10
❑ 167 Brian Mitchell .30 .10
❑ 168 Mike Vanderjagt .30 .10
❑ 169 Rod Woodson .50 .20
❑ 170 Doug Chapman .30 .10
❑ 171 John Lynch .50 .20
❑ 172 Kevin Hardy .30 .10
❑ 173 Sam Shade .30 .10
❑ 174 Edgerrin James 1.00 .40
❑ 175 Brian Dawkins .50 .20
❑ 176 Donnie Edwards .30 .10
❑ 177 Patrick Jeffers .50 .20
❑ 178 Mark Brunell .75 .30
❑ 179 Junior Seau .75 .30
❑ 180 Trace Armstrong .30 .10
❑ 181 Marcus Robinson .75 .30
❑ 182 Tony Gonzalez .50 .20
❑ 183 J.J. Stokes .50 .20
❑ 184 Jake Reed .50 .20
❑ 185 Corey Dillon .75 .30
❑ 186 Jay Fiedler .75 .30
❑ 187 Christian Fauria .30 .10
❑ 188 Sammy Knight .30 .10
❑ 189 Kevin Johnson .50 .20
❑ 190 Matthew Hatchette .30 .10
❑ 191 Az-Zahir Hakim .50 .20
❑ 192 Keith Hamilton .30 .10
❑ 193 Darren Woodson .30 .10
❑ 194 Terry Glenn .50 .20
❑ 195 Simeon Rice .50 .20
❑ 196 Keyshawn Johnson .75 .30
❑ 197 Terrell Davis .75 .30
❑ 198 William Roaf .30 .10
❑ 199 Doug Flutie .75 .30
❑ 200 Kevin Carter .30 .10
❑ 201 Stephen Boyd .30 .10
❑ 202 Michael Strahan .50 .20
❑ 203 Ray Buchanan .30 .10
❑ 204 Tyrone Wheatley .50 .20
❑ 205 Jason Hanson .30 .10
❑ 206 Wayne Chrebet .50 .20
❑ 207 Samari Rolle .30 .10
❑ 208 Duce Staley .75 .30
❑ 209 Dorsey Levens .50 .20
❑ 210 Sebastian Janikowski .30 .10
❑ 211 Duane Starks .30 .10
❑ 212 Jason Gildon .30 .10
❑ 213 Terrence Wilkins .30 .10
❑ 214 Eric Allen .30 .10
❑ 215 Deion Sanders .75 .30
❑ 216 Curtis Conway .50 .20
❑ 217 Fred Taylor .75 .30
❑ 218 Troy Vincent .30 .10
❑ 219 Mike Minter .50 .20
❑ 220 Jeff Garcia .75 .30
❑ 221 Tony Richardson .30 .10
❑ 222 Jerome Bettis .75 .30
❑ 223 Chad Morton .30 .10
❑ 224 Tony Horne .30 .10
❑ 225 Dave Moore .30 .10
❑ 226 Victor Green .30 .10
❑ 227 Chris Sanders .30 .10
❑ 228 Marshall Faulk 1.00 .40
❑ 229 Cris Carter .75 .30
❑ 230 Rodney Harrison .30 .10
❑ 231 Tim Couch .50 .20
❑ 232 Antowain Smith .50 .20
❑ 233 Lawyer Milloy .50 .20
❑ 234 Lance Schulters .30 .10
❑ 235 Michael Wiley .30 .10
❑ 236 Steve McNair .75 .30
❑ 237 Aaron Brooks .75 .30
❑ 238 Anthony Simmons .30 .10
❑ 239 Dwayne Carswell .30 .10
❑ 240 Priest Holmes 1.00 .40
❑ 241 Amani Toomer .50 .20
❑ 242 Aeneas Williams .30 .10
❑ 243 MarTay Jenkins .30 .10
❑ 244 Jeff George .50 .20
❑ 245 Vinny Testaverde .50 .20
❑ 246 Peerless Price .50 .20
❑ 247 Bubba Franks .50 .20
❑ 248 Randall Cunningham .75 .30
❑ 249 Aaron Glenn .30 .10
❑ 250 Terance Mathis .50 .20
❑ 251 Peyton Manning 2.00 .75
❑ 252 Terrell Buckley .30 .10
❑ 253 Greg Biekert .30 .10
❑ 254 Martin Gramatica .30 .10
❑ 255 Kyle Brady .30 .10
❑ 256 Johnnie Morton .50 .20
❑ 257 Jeremiah Trotter .50 .20
❑ 258 Travis Taylor .50 .20
❑ 259 Frank Moreau .30 .10
❑ 260 LeRoy Butler .30 .10
❑ 261 Plaxico Burress .75 .30
❑ 262 Randall Godfrey .30 .10
❑ 263 Jason Taylor .30 .10
❑ 264 Jeff Burris .30 .10
❑ 265 Jim Harbaugh .50 .20
❑ 266 Marco Coleman .30 .10
❑ 267 Robert Smith .50 .20
❑ 268 Mike Hollis .30 .10
❑ 269 Jerry Rice 1.50 .60
❑ 270 Muhsin Muhammad .50 .20
❑ 271 J.R. Redmond .30 .10
❑ 272 Brian Walker .30 .10
❑ 273 Orlando Pace .30 .10
❑ 274 Cade McNown .30 .10
❑ 275 Darren Howard .30 .10
❑ 276 Ron Dayne .75 .30
❑ 277 Shaun Alexander 1.00 .40
❑ 278 Brandon Bennett .30 .10
❑ 279 Jason Sehorn .30 .10
❑ 280 Matt Hasselbeck .50 .20
❑ 281 Michael Pittman .30 .10
❑ 282 Dennis Northcutt .50 .20
❑ 283 Dedric Ward .30 .10
❑ 284 Curtis Martin .75 .30
❑ 285 Sammy Morris .30 .10
❑ 286 Rocket Ismail .50 .20
❑ 287 Jon Ritchie .30 .10
❑ 288 Shaun Ellis .30 .10
❑ 289 Tim Dwight .75 .30
❑ 290 Trevor Pryce .30 .10
❑ 291 Warrick Dunn .75 .30
❑ 292 Napoleon Kaufman .50 .20
❑ 293 Mike Alstott .75 .30
❑ 294 Herman Moore .50 .20
❑ 295 Chad Lewis .30 .10
❑ 296 Hugh Douglas .30 .10
❑ 297 Chris Redman .30 .10
❑ 298 Ahman Green .75 .30
❑ 299 Hines Ward .75 .30
❑ 300 Mark Bruener .30 .10
❑ 301 Jevon Kearse .50 .20
❑ 302 Jermaine Fazande .30 .10
❑ 303 Terrell Fletcher .30 .10
❑ 304 Torry Holt .75 .30
❑ 305 Chris McAlister .30 .10
❑ 306 Jason Elam .30 .10
❑ 307 Fred Beasley .30 .10
❑ 308 Frank Wycheck UH .30 .10
❑ 309 Michael McCrary UH .30 .10
❑ 310 Mark Brunell UH .75 .30
❑ 311 Tim Couch UH .50 .20
❑ 312 Takeo Spikes UH .30 .10
❑ 313 Jerome Bettis UH .50 .20
❑ 314 Zach Thomas UH .75 .30
❑ 315 Drew Bledsoe UH .75 .30
❑ 316 Wayne Chrebet UH .30 .10
❑ 317 Jay Riemersma UH .30 .10
❑ 318 Marvin Harrison UH .50 .20
❑ 319 Ed McCaffrey UH .50 .20
❑ 320 Tony Gonzalez UH .30 .10
❑ 321 Tim Brown UH .50 .20
❑ 322 Junior Seau UH .50 .20
❑ 323 Shawn Springs UH .30 .10
❑ 324 Troy Aikman UH .75 .30
❑ 325 Pat Tillman UH RC 20.00 10.00
❑ 326 David Akers UH RC .50 .20
❑ 327 Michael Strahan UH .50 .20
❑ 328 Darrell Green UH .30 .10
❑ 329 Kurt Warner UH 1.00 .40
❑ 330 Jeff Garcia UH .50 .20
❑ 331 Aaron Brooks UH .50 .20
❑ 332 Jamal Anderson UH .50 .20
❑ 333 Brad Hoover UH .30 .10
❑ 334 Cris Carter UH .50 .20
❑ 335 Derrick Brooks UH .75 .30
❑ 336 Antonio Freeman UH .50 .20
❑ 337 Luther Elliss UH .30 .10
❑ 338 James Allen UH .30 .10
❑ 339 Arizona Cardinals TC .50 .20
❑ 340 Atlanta Falcons TC .50 .20
❑ 341 Baltimore Ravens TC .30 .10
❑ 342 Buffalo Bills TC .30 .10
❑ 343 Carolina Panthers TC .30 .10
❑ 344 Chicago Bears TC .75 .30
❑ 345 Cincinnati Bengals TC .50 .20
❑ 346 Cleveland Browns TC .30 .10
❑ 347 Cowboys TC/Emmitt .75 .30
❑ 348 Denver Broncos TC .50 .20
❑ 349 Detroit Lions TC .30 .10
❑ 350 Packers TC/Favre 1.25 .50
❑ 351 Colts TC/James .75 .30
❑ 352 Jacksonville Jaguars TC .75 .30
❑ 353 Kansas City Chiefs TC .30 .10
❑ 354 Miami Dolphins TC .50 .20
❑ 355 Minnesota Vikings TC .75 .30
❑ 356 New England Patriots TC .75 .30
❑ 357 New Orleans Saints TC .50 .20
❑ 358 New York Giants TC .50 .20
❑ 359 New York Jets TC .50 .20
❑ 360 Oakland Raiders TC .50 .20
❑ 361 Philadelphia Eagles TC .75 .30
❑ 362 Pittsburgh Steelers TC .50 .20
❑ 363 San Diego Chargers TC .30 .10
❑ 364 San Francisco 49ers TC .30 .10
❑ 365 Seattle Seahawks TC .30 .10
❑ 366 Rams TC/Warner .75 .30
❑ 367 Tampa Bay Buccaneers TC .50 .20
❑ 368 Tennessee Titans TC .50 .20
❑ 369 Washington Redskins TC .50 .20
❑ 370 Buffalo Bills TL .50 .20
❑ 371 Indianapolis Colts TL .75 .30
❑ 372 Miami Dolphins TL .30 .10

❑ 373	New England Patriots TL	.50	.20
❑ 374	New York Jets TL	.50	.20
❑ 375	Baltimore Ravens TL	.50	.20
❑ 376	Cincinnati Bengals TL	.30	.10
❑ 377	Cleveland Browns TL	.30	.10
❑ 378	Jacksonville Jaguars TL	.50	.20
❑ 379	Pittsburgh Steelers TL	.50	.20
❑ 380	Tennessee Titans TL	.50	.20
❑ 381	Denver Broncos TL	.50	.20
❑ 382	Kansas City Chiefs TL	.50	.20
❑ 383	Oakland Raiders TL	.50	.20
❑ 384	San Diego Chargers TL	.50	.20
❑ 385	Seattle Seahawks TL	.30	.10
❑ 386	Arizona Cardinals TL	.30	.10
❑ 387	Dallas Cowboys TL	.75	.30
❑ 388	New York Giants TL	.50	.20
❑ 389	Philadelphia Eagles TL	.50	.20
❑ 390	Washington Redskins TL	.50	.20
❑ 391	Chicago Bears TL	.30	.10
❑ 392	Detroit Lions TL	.30	.10
❑ 393	Green Bay Packers TL	.75	.30
❑ 394	Minnesota Vikings TL	.75	.30
❑ 395	Tampa Bay Buccaneers TL	.50	.20
❑ 396	Atlanta Falcons TL	.30	.10
❑ 397	Carolina Panthers TL	.30	.10
❑ 398	New Orleans Saints TL	.50	.20
❑ 399	San Francisco 49ersTL	.50	.20
❑ 400	St. Louis Rams TL	.75	.30
❑ 401	Michael Vick RC	30.00	15.00
❑ 402	Drew Brees RC	12.00	5.00
❑ 403	Michael Bennett RC	8.00	3.00
❑ 404	David Terrell RC	4.00	1.50
❑ 405	Deuce McAllister RC	10.00	4.00
❑ 406	Santana Moss RC	8.00	3.00
❑ 407	Koren Robinson RC	4.00	1.50
❑ 408	Chris Weinke RC	4.00	1.50
❑ 409	Reggie Wayne RC	10.00	4.00
❑ 410	Rod Gardner RC	4.00	1.50
❑ 411	James Jackson RC	4.00	1.50
❑ 412	Travis Henry RC	4.00	1.50
❑ 413	Josh Heupel RC	4.00	1.50
❑ 414	LaDainian Tomlinson RC	25.00	12.50
❑ 415	Chad Johnson RC	12.00	5.00
❑ 416	Sage Rosenfels RC	4.00	1.50
❑ 417	Quincy Morgan RC	4.00	1.50
❑ 418	Ken-Yon Rambo RC	3.00	1.25
❑ 419	LaMont Jordan RC	10.00	4.00
❑ 420	Anthony Thomas RC	4.00	1.50
❑ 421	Dave Dickenson RC	3.00	1.25
❑ 422	Travis Minor RC	3.00	1.25
❑ 423	Kevan Barlow RC	4.00	1.50
❑ 424	Chris Chambers RC	8.00	3.00
❑ 425	Richard Seymour RC	4.00	1.50
❑ 426	Gerard Warren RC	4.00	1.50
❑ 427	Jamar Fletcher RC	3.00	1.25
❑ 428	Freddie Mitchell RC	4.00	1.50
❑ 429	Jamal Reynolds RC	4.00	1.50
❑ 430	Marques Tuiasosopo RC	4.00	1.50
❑ 431	Snoop Minnis RC	3.00	1.25
❑ 432	Mike McMahon RC	4.00	1.50
❑ 433	Robert Ferguson RC	4.00	1.50
❑ 434	Ronney Daniels RC	3.00	1.25
❑ 435	Rudi Johnson RC	10.00	4.00
❑ 436	Vinny Sutherland RC	3.00	1.25
❑ 437	Josh Booty RC	4.00	1.50
❑ 438	Reggie White RC	3.00	1.25
❑ 439	Todd Heap RC	4.00	1.50
❑ 440	Justin Smith RC	4.00	1.50
❑ 441	Andre Carter RC	4.00	1.50
❑ 442	Bobby Newcombe RC	3.00	1.25
❑ 443	Alex Bannister RC	3.00	1.25
❑ 444	Correll Buckhalter RC	6.00	2.50
❑ 445	Quincy Carter RC	4.00	1.50
❑ 446	Jesse Palmer RC	4.00	1.50
❑ 447	Heath Evans RC	3.00	1.25
❑ 448	Dan Morgan RC	4.00	1.50
❑ 449	Justin McCareins RC	4.00	1.50
❑ 450	Alge Crumpler RC	5.00	2.00

2002 Fleer Tradition

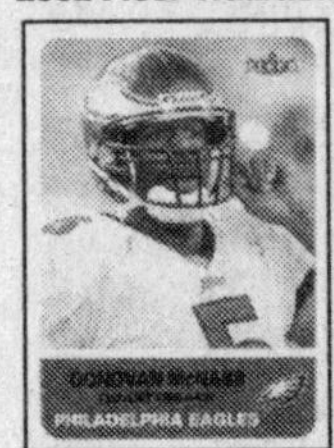

❑	COMPLETE SET (300)	80.00	30.00
❑ 1	Jeff Garcia	.60	.25
❑ 2	Brian Simmons	.25	.08
❑ 3	Kordell Stewart	.40	.15
❑ 4	Chris Weinke	.40	.15
❑ 5	Donovan McNabb	.75	.30
❑ 6	Antoine Winfield	.25	.08
❑ 7	Ray Lewis	.60	.25
❑ 8	Drew Brees	.60	.25
❑ 9	Frank Sanders	.25	.08
❑ 10	Rich Gannon	.60	.25
❑ 11	Jamal Anderson	.40	.15
❑ 12	Curtis Martin	.60	.25
❑ 13	Darrell Jackson	.40	.15
❑ 14	Micheal Barrow	.25	.08
❑ 15	Jeff Wilkins	.25	.08
❑ 16	Ricky Williams	.60	.25
❑ 17	Brad Johnson	.40	.15
❑ 18	Tedy Bruschi	.60	.25
❑ 19	Frank Wycheck	.25	.08
❑ 20	Byron Chamberlain	.25	.08
❑ 21	Terry Glenn	.25	.08
❑ 22	James McKnight	.25	.08
❑ 23	Thomas Jones	.40	.15
❑ 24	Jamie Sharper	.25	.08
❑ 25	Trent Green	.40	.15
❑ 26	Mike Rucker RC	1.00	.40
❑ 27	Mark Brunell	.60	.25
❑ 28	Takeo Spikes	.25	.08
❑ 29	Dominic Rhodes	.40	.15
❑ 30	Jim Miller	.25	.08
❑ 31	Corey Bradford	.25	.08
❑ 32	Jamir Miller	.25	.08
❑ 33	Johnnie Morton	.40	.15
❑ 34	Rocket Ismail	.40	.15
❑ 35	Mike Anderson	.60	.25
❑ 36	James Allen	.40	.15
❑ 37	Quincy Carter	.40	.15
❑ 38	Germane Crowell	.25	.08
❑ 39	Quincy Morgan	.25	.08
❑ 40	Kabeer Gbaja-Biamila	.40	.15
❑ 41	Reggie Wayne	.60	.25
❑ 42	Brian Urlacher	1.00	.40
❑ 43	Stacey Mack	.25	.08
❑ 44	Justin Smith	.25	.08
❑ 45	Snoop Minnis	.25	.08
❑ 46	Donald Hayes	.25	.08
❑ 47	Jay Fiedler	.40	.15
❑ 48	Nate Clements	.25	.08
❑ 49	Drew Bledsoe	.75	.30
❑ 50	Peter Boulware	.25	.08
❑ 51	Lawyer Milloy	.40	.15
❑ 52	Michael Pittman	.25	.08
❑ 53	Aaron Brooks	.60	.25
❑ 54	Maurice Smith	.40	.15
❑ 55	Ike Hilliard	.40	.15
❑ 56	Derrick Mason	.40	.15
❑ 57	LaMont Jordan	.60	.25
❑ 58	Charlie Garner	.40	.15
❑ 59	Mike Alstott	.60	.25
❑ 60	Freddie Mitchell	.40	.15
❑ 61	Isaac Bruce	.60	.25

❑ 62	Hines Ward	.60	.25
❑ 63	John Randle	.25	.08
❑ 64	Doug Flutie	.60	.25
❑ 65	Terrell Owens	.60	.25
❑ 66	Garrison Hearst	.40	.15
❑ 67	Rodney Harrison	.25	.08
❑ 68	Koren Robinson	.40	.15
❑ 69	Amos Zereoue	.60	.25
❑ 70	Aeneas Williams	.25	.08
❑ 71	Hugh Douglas	.25	.08
❑ 72	Jacquez Green	.25	.08
❑ 73	Sebastian Janikowski	.25	.08
❑ 74	Kevin Dyson	.40	.15
❑ 75	Terance Mathis	.25	.08
❑ 76	Vinny Testaverde	.40	.15
❑ 77	Kwamie Lassiter	.25	.08
❑ 78	Ron Dayne	.40	.15
❑ 79	Jonathan Ogden	.25	.08
❑ 80	Charlie Clemons RC	.25	.08
❑ 81	Peter Warrick	.40	.15
❑ 82	Adam Vinatieri	.60	.25
❑ 83	Ted Washington	.25	.08
❑ 84	Randy Moss	1.25	.50
❑ 85	Rosevelt Colvin RC	1.00	.40
❑ 86	Oronde Gadsden	.40	.15
❑ 87	Anthony Henry	.25	.08
❑ 88	Priest Holmes	.75	.30
❑ 89	Joey Galloway	.40	.15
❑ 90	Jimmy Smith	.40	.15
❑ 91	Bill Romanowski	.25	.08
❑ 92	Chris Claiborne	.40	.15
❑ 93	Marvin Harrison	.60	.25
❑ 94	Vonnie Holliday	.25	.08
❑ 95	Darren Sharper	.25	.08
❑ 96	Chad Bratzke	.25	.08
❑ 97	James Stewart	.40	.15
❑ 98	Fred Taylor	.60	.25
❑ 99	Jason Elam	.25	.08
❑ 100	Keyshawn Johnson	.60	.25
❑ 101	Dexter Coakley	.25	.08
❑ 102	Zach Thomas	.60	.25
❑ 103	Jamel White	.25	.08
❑ 104	Antowain Smith	.40	.15
❑ 105	Marty Booker	.25	.08
❑ 106	Deuce McAllister	.75	.30
❑ 107	Adam Archuleta	.25	.08
❑ 108	Rod Smith	.40	.15
❑ 109	Tony Boselli	.25	.08
❑ 110	Joe Johnson	.25	.08
❑ 111	Simeon Rice	.40	.15
❑ 112	Cory Schlesinger	.25	.08
❑ 113	La'Roi Glover	.25	.08
❑ 114	Tiki Barber	.60	.25
❑ 115	Michael Westbrook	.25	.08
❑ 116	Antonio Freeman	.60	.25
❑ 117	Kerry Collins	.40	.15
❑ 118	Laveranues Coles	.40	.15
❑ 119	Jay Feeley	.25	.08
❑ 120	Champ Bailey	.40	.15
❑ 121	Peyton Manning	1.25	.50
❑ 122	Chad Pennington	.75	.30
❑ 123	Anthony Dorsett	.25	.08
❑ 124	Jamal Lewis	.60	.25
❑ 125	Marcus Pollard	.25	.08
❑ 126	Charles Woodson	.40	.15
❑ 127	Duce Staley	.60	.25
❑ 128	Travis Henry	.60	.25
❑ 129	Tony Brackens	.25	.08
❑ 130	Jeremiah Trotter	.25	.08
❑ 131	Jerome Bettis	.60	.25
❑ 132	Chad Johnson	.60	.25
❑ 133	Lamar Smith	.40	.15
❑ 134	Joey Porter	.60	.25
❑ 135	Curtis Conway	.25	.08
❑ 136	David Terrell	.60	.25
❑ 137	Daunte Culpepper	.60	.25
❑ 138	Chris Fuamatu-Ma'afala	.25	.08
❑ 139	J.J. Stokes	.25	.08
❑ 140	Tim Couch	.40	.15
❑ 141	Ty Law	.40	.15

❑ 142	Vinny Sutherland	.25	.08
❑ 143	Trung Canidate	.40	.15
❑ 144	Larry Allen	.25	.08
❑ 145	Darren Howard	.25	.08
❑ 146	Ricky Watters	.40	.15
❑ 147	Grant Wistrom	.25	.08
❑ 148	Brian Griese	.60	.25
❑ 149	Jason Sehorn	.25	.08
❑ 150	Marshall Faulk	.60	.25
❑ 151	Martin Gramatica	.25	.08
❑ 152	Robert Porcher	.25	.08
❑ 153	Richie Anderson	.25	.08
❑ 154	Derrick Brooks	.60	.25
❑ 155	Jevon Kearse	.40	.15
❑ 156	Bill Schroeder	.40	.15
❑ 157	Marvin Jones	.25	.08
❑ 158	Eddie George	.60	.25
❑ 159	Keith Brooking	.25	.08
❑ 160	Ryan Longwell	.25	.08
❑ 161	Brian Dawkins	.40	.15
❑ 162	Chris Redman	.25	.08
❑ 163	Az-Zahir Hakim	.25	.08
❑ 164	James Thrash	.40	.15
❑ 165	Rob Johnson	.40	.15
❑ 166	Hardy Nickerson	.25	.08
❑ 167	Chad Scott	.25	.08
❑ 168	Jon Kitna	.40	.15
❑ 169	Donnie Edwards	.25	.08
❑ 170	Andre Carter	.25	.08
❑ 171	Warrick Holdman	.25	.08
❑ 172	Jason Taylor	.25	.08
❑ 173	Levon Kirkland	.25	.08
❑ 174	Mike Brown	.60	.25
❑ 175	David Patten	.25	.08
❑ 176	Kurt Warner	.60	.25
❑ 177	Fred Smoot	.25	.08
❑ 178	Dat Nguyen	.25	.08
❑ 179	Joe Horn	.40	.15
❑ 180	John Lynch	.40	.15
❑ 181	Troy Hambrick	.25	.08
❑ 182	John Carney	.25	.08
❑ 183	Wesley Walls	.25	.08
❑ 184	Deltha O'Neal	.25	.08
❑ 185	Joe Jurevicius	.25	.08
❑ 186	Steve McNair	.60	.25
❑ 187	Scotty Anderson	.25	.08
❑ 188	John Abraham	.40	.15
❑ 189	Stephen Davis	.40	.15
❑ 190	Nate Wayne	.25	.08
❑ 191	Corey Simon	.25	.08
❑ 192	Joel Makovicka	.25	.08
❑ 193	Rob Morris	.25	.08
❑ 194	Correll Buckhalter	.40	.15
❑ 195	Qadry Ismail	.40	.15
❑ 196	Keenan McCardell	.25	.08
❑ 197	Jason Gildon	.25	.08
❑ 198	Peerless Price	.40	.15
❑ 199	Tony Richardson	.25	.08
❑ 200	Kevan Barlow	.40	.15
❑ 201	Corey Dillon	.40	.15
❑ 202	Sam Madison	.25	.08
❑ 203	Chad Brown	.25	.08
❑ 204	Dez White	.25	.08
❑ 205	Troy Brown	.40	.15
❑ 206	Orlando Pace	.25	.08
❑ 207	Jermaine Lewis	.25	.08
❑ 208	Willie Jackson	.25	.08
❑ 209	Warrick Dunn	.60	.25
❑ 210	James Jackson	.25	.08
❑ 211	Sammy Knight	.25	.08
❑ 212	Ronde Barber	.25	.08
❑ 213	Ed McCaffrey	.60	.25
❑ 214	Amani Toomer	.40	.15
❑ 215	Rod Gardner	.40	.15
❑ 216	Mike McMahon	.60	.25
❑ 217	Wayne Chrebet	.40	.15
❑ 218	Jake Plummer	.40	.15
❑ 219	Bubba Franks	.40	.15
❑ 220	Shane Lechler	.40	.15
❑ 221	Travis Taylor	.40	.15
❑ 222	Edgerrin James	.75	.30
❑ 223	David Akers	.25	.08
❑ 224	Eric Moulds	.40	.15
❑ 225	Mike Vanderjagt	.25	.08
❑ 226	Kendrell Bell	.60	.25
❑ 227	Darnay Scott	.25	.08
❑ 228	Tony Gonzalez	.40	.15
❑ 229	Marcellus Wiley	.25	.08
❑ 230	Marcus Robinson	.40	.15
❑ 231	Muhsin Muhammad	.40	.15
❑ 232	Trent Dilfer	.40	.15
❑ 233	Kevin Johnson	.40	.15
❑ 234	Travis Minor	.25	.08
❑ 235	London Fletcher	.25	.08
❑ 236	Reggie Swinton	.25	.08
❑ 237	Michael Bennett	.40	.15
❑ 238	Brett Favre DD	1.50	.60
❑ 239	Terrell Davis DD	.60	.25
❑ 240	Emmitt Smith DD	1.50	.60
❑ 241	Shannon Sharpe DD	.40	.15
❑ 242	Cris Carter DD	.60	.25
❑ 243	Tim Brown DD	.60	.25
❑ 244	Jerry Rice DD	1.25	.50
❑ 245	Bruce Smith DD	.40	.15
❑ 246	Warren Sapp DD	.40	.15
❑ 247	Michael Strahan DD	.40	.15
❑ 248	Junior Seau DD	.60	.25
❑ 249	Darrell Green DD	.25	.08
❑ 250	Rod Woodson DD	.40	.15
❑ 251	David Boston BB	.60	.25
❑ 252	Michael Vick BB	2.00	.75
❑ 253	Anthony Thomas BB	.40	.15
❑ 254	Ahman Green BB	.60	.25
❑ 255	Chris Chambers BB	.60	.25
❑ 256	Tom Brady BB	1.50	.60
❑ 257	Plaxico Burress BB	.40	.15
❑ 258	LaDainian Tomlinson BB	1.00	.40
❑ 259	Shaun Alexander BB	.75	.30
❑ 260	Torry Holt BB	.60	.25
❑ 261	Julius Peppers RC	4.00	1.50
❑ 262	William Green RC	2.00	.75
❑ 263	Joey Harrington RC	5.00	2.00
❑ 264	Jabar Gaffney RC	2.00	.75
❑ 265	T.J. Duckett RC	3.00	1.25
❑ 266	Antwaan Randle El RC	3.00	1.25
❑ 267	Javon Walker RC	4.00	1.50
❑ 268	David Carr RC	5.00	2.00
❑ 269	DeShaun Foster RC	2.00	.75
❑ 270	Donte Stallworth RC	4.00	1.50
❑ 271	Antonio Bryant RC	2.00	.75
❑ 272	Clinton Portis RC	6.00	2.50
❑ 273	Josh Reed RC	2.00	.75
❑ 274	Ashley Lelie RC	4.00	1.50
❑ 275	Patrick Ramsey RC	2.50	1.00
❑ 276	J.Wells RC/A.Peterson RC	2.00	.75
❑ 277	Q.Jammer RC/R.Williams RC	5.00	2.00
❑ 278	J.Shockey RC/D.Graham RC	6.00	2.50
❑ 279	E.Crouch RC/Applewhite RC	2.00	.75
❑ 280	Buchanon RC/Sheppard RC	2.00	.75
❑ 281	K.Hill RC/D.Branch RC	4.00	1.50
❑ 282	R.Sims RC/W.Bryant RC	2.00	.75
❑ 283	J.Scobey RC/Westbrook RC	3.00	1.25
❑ 284	L.Betts RC/O.Easy RC	2.00	.75
❑ 285	A.Davis RC/D.Jones RC	1.50	.60
❑ 286	C.Russell RC/C.Taylor RC	2.00	.75
❑ 287	McAddley RC/J.McCown RC	2.50	1.00
❑ 288	D.Garrard RC/R.Davey RC	2.50	1.00
❑ 289	M.Walker RC/R.Johnson RC	1.50	.60
❑ 290	L.Staley RC/L.Gordon RC	2.00	.75
❑ 291	R.Caldwell RC/L.Mays RC	2.00	.75
❑ 292	R.Thomas RC/N.Harris RC	2.00	.75
❑ 293	M.Morris RC/J.Stevens RC	2.00	.75
❑ 294	K.Kittner RC/R.Fasani RC	1.50	.60
❑ 295	R.Calmus RC/J.Schifino RC	2.00	.75
❑ 296	T.Carter RC/F.Milons RC	1.50	.60
❑ 297	Wistrom RC/Stephens RC	2.00	.75
❑ 298	M.Williams RC/D.Freeney RC	2.50	1.00
❑ 299	Hendersn RC/Hayneswrth RC	2.00	.75
❑ 300	N.Davenport RC/C.Nall RC	2.00	.75

2003 Fleer Tradition

❑	COMPLETE SET (300)	40.00	15.00
❑ 1	Aaron Glenn	.25	.08
❑ 2	Jerry Rice	1.25	.50
❑ 3	Chad Hutchinson	.25	.08
❑ 4	Kris Jenkins	.25	.08
❑ 5	Ed Reed	.40	.15
❑ 6	Ed McCaffrey	.60	.25
❑ 7	Rod Gardner	.40	.15
❑ 8	Aaron Brooks	.60	.25
❑ 9	Chad Pennington	.75	.30
❑ 10	Jevon Kearse	.40	.15
❑ 11	Kurt Warner	.60	.25
❑ 12	Eddie George	.40	.15
❑ 13	Ron Dugans	.25	.08
❑ 14	Adam Vinatieri	.60	.25
❑ 15	Jimmy Smith	.40	.15
❑ 16	Chad Johnson	.60	.25
❑ 17	Kyle Brady	.25	.08
❑ 18	Eddie Kennison	.25	.08
❑ 19	Joe Jurevicius	.25	.08
❑ 20	Ronde Barber	.25	.08
❑ 21	Adam Archuleta	.25	.08
❑ 22	Champ Bailey	.40	.15
❑ 23	Joe Horn	.40	.15
❑ 24	Ladell Betts	.40	.15
❑ 25	Edgerrin James	.60	.25
❑ 26	Rosevelt Colvin	.25	.08
❑ 27	Ahman Green	.60	.25
❑ 28	Joey Porter	.60	.25
❑ 29	Charles Woodson	.40	.15
❑ 30	Lance Schulters	.25	.08
❑ 31	Edgerton Hartwell	.25	.08
❑ 32	Joey Galloway	.40	.15
❑ 33	Roy Williams	.60	.25
❑ 34	Al Wilson	.25	.08
❑ 35	Charlie Garner	.40	.15
❑ 36	John Lynch	.25	.08
❑ 37	La'Roi Glover	.25	.08
❑ 38	Emmitt Smith	1.50	.60
❑ 39	Ryan Longwell	.25	.08
❑ 40	Alge Crumpler	.40	.15
❑ 41	John Abraham	.25	.08
❑ 42	Chris Hovan	.25	.08
❑ 43	Laveranues Coles	.40	.15
❑ 44	Eric Hicks	.25	.08
❑ 45	Johnnie Morton	.40	.15
❑ 46	Sam Madison	.25	.08
❑ 47	Amani Toomer	.40	.15
❑ 48	Chris Redman	.25	.08
❑ 49	Jon Kitna	.40	.15
❑ 50	Leonard Little	.25	.08
❑ 51	Eric Moulds	.40	.15
❑ 52	Santana Moss	.40	.15
❑ 53	Amos Zereoue	.40	.15
❑ 54	Jonathan Wells	.25	.08
❑ 55	Chris Chambers	.60	.25
❑ 56	London Fletcher	.25	.08
❑ 57	Frank Wycheck	.25	.08
❑ 58	Josh McCown	.40	.15
❑ 59	Shannon Sharpe	.25	.08
❑ 60	Andre Carter	.25	.08
❑ 61	Corey Dillon	.40	.15

❑ 62 Josh Reed .40 .15
❑ 63 Marc Boerigter .40 .15
❑ 64 Fred Smoot .25 .08
❑ 65 Shaun Alexander .60 .25
❑ 66 Andre Davis .25 .08
❑ 67 Julian Peterson .25 .08
❑ 68 Corey Bradford .25 .08
❑ 69 Marc Bulger .60 .25
❑ 70 Fred Taylor .60 .25
❑ 71 Junior Seau .60 .25
❑ 72 Simeon Rice .40 .15
❑ 73 Anthony Thomas .40 .15
❑ 74 Correll Buckhalter .40 .15
❑ 75 Justin Smith .25 .08
❑ 76 Marcel Shipp .40 .15
❑ 77 Garrison Hearst .40 .15
❑ 78 Stacey Mack .25 .08
❑ 79 Antowain Smith .40 .15
❑ 80 Kabeer Gbaja-Biamila .40 .15
❑ 81 Curtis Martin .60 .25
❑ 82 Marcellus Wiley .25 .08
❑ 83 Gary Walker .25 .08
❑ 84 Kalimba Edwards .25 .08
❑ 85 Stephen Davis .40 .15
❑ 86 Antwaan Randle El .60 .25
❑ 87 Curtis Conway .25 .08
❑ 88 Keith Brooking .25 .08
❑ 89 Mark Word RC .25 .08
❑ 90 Greg Ellis .25 .08
❑ 91 Steve McNair .60 .25
❑ 92 Ashley Lelie .60 .25
❑ 93 Kelly Holcomb .40 .15
❑ 94 Darrell Jackson .40 .15
❑ 95 Mark Brunell .40 .15
❑ 96 Hugh Douglas .25 .08
❑ 97 Kendrell Bell .40 .15
❑ 98 Steve Smith .60 .25
❑ 99 Bill Schroeder .40 .15
❑ 100 Darren Howard .25 .08
❑ 101 Kevan Barlow .40 .15
❑ 102 Marshall Faulk .60 .25
❑ 103 Ike Hilliard .25 .08
❑ 104 T.J. Duckett .40 .15
❑ 105 Bobby Taylor .25 .08
❑ 106 Kevin Carter .25 .08
❑ 107 Darren Sharper .25 .08
❑ 108 Marty Booker .40 .15
❑ 109 Isaac Bruce .60 .25
❑ 110 Kevin Hardy .25 .08
❑ 111 Tai Streets .25 .08
❑ 112 Brad Johnson .40 .15
❑ 113 Daunte Culpepper .60 .25
❑ 114 Kevin Johnson .40 .15
❑ 115 Matt Hasselbeck .40 .15
❑ 116 Jabar Gaffney .40 .15
❑ 117 Takeo Spikes .25 .08
❑ 118 Brett Favre 1.50 .60
❑ 119 Keyshawn Johnson .60 .25
❑ 120 David Akers .25 .08
❑ 121 Maurice Morris .25 .08
❑ 122 Jake Delhomme .60 .25
❑ 123 Kordell Stewart .40 .15
❑ 124 Terrell Davis .60 .25
❑ 125 Brian Kelly .25 .08
❑ 126 David Terrell .40 .15
❑ 127 Koren Robinson .40 .15
❑ 128 Michael Strahan .40 .15
❑ 129 Jake Plummer .40 .15
❑ 130 Terrell Owens .60 .25
❑ 131 Brian Urlacher 1.00 .40
❑ 132 David Patten .25 .08
❑ 133 Michael Vick 1.50 .60
❑ 134 Jamal Lewis .60 .25
❑ 135 Terry Glenn .25 .08
❑ 136 Brian Simmons .25 .08
❑ 137 David Boston .40 .15
❑ 138 Michael Bennett .40 .15
❑ 139 James Stewart .40 .15
❑ 140 Tiki Barber .60 .25
❑ 141 Brian Griese .60 .25
❑ 142 Deion Branch .60 .25
❑ 143 Mike Peterson .25 .08
❑ 144 James Mungro .25 .08
❑ 145 Tim Couch .25 .08
❑ 146 Brian Dawkins .40 .15
❑ 147 Dennis Northcutt .40 .15
❑ 148 Mike Alstott .60 .25
❑ 149 James Thrash .25 .08
❑ 150 Tim Brown .60 .25
❑ 151 Brian Finneran .25 .08
❑ 152 Derrick Brooks .40 .15
❑ 153 Muhsin Muhammad .40 .15
❑ 154 Jason Elam .25 .08
❑ 155 Tim Dwight .40 .15
❑ 156 Bruce Smith .40 .15
❑ 157 Derrick Mason .40 .15
❑ 158 Napoleon Harris .25 .08
❑ 159 Jason Gildon .25 .08
❑ 160 Todd Heap .40 .15
❑ 161 Aaron Schobel .40 .15
❑ 162 Derrius Thompson .25 .08
❑ 163 Nate Clements .25 .08
❑ 164 Jason McAddley .25 .08
❑ 165 Todd Pinkston .40 .15
❑ 166 Bubba Franks .40 .15
❑ 167 Deuce McAllister .60 .25
❑ 168 Patrick Surtain .25 .08
❑ 169 Javon Walker .40 .15
❑ 170 Tom Brady 1.50 .60
❑ 171 Dexter Coakley .25 .08
❑ 172 Patrick Kerney .25 .08
❑ 173 Jay Fiedler .40 .15
❑ 174 Tommy Maddox .60 .25
❑ 175 Donald Driver .40 .15
❑ 176 Patrick Ramsey .60 .25
❑ 177 Olandis Gary .40 .15
❑ 178 Tony Gonzalez .40 .15
❑ 179 Donnie Edwards .25 .08
❑ 180 Peter Boulware .25 .08
❑ 181 Jeff Blake .25 .08
❑ 182 Torry Holt .60 .25
❑ 183 Donovan McNabb .75 .30
❑ 184 Peter Warrick .25 .08
❑ 185 Jeff Garcia .60 .25
❑ 186 Travis Henry .40 .15
❑ 187 Doug Jolley .25 .08
❑ 188 Peyton Manning 1.00 .40
❑ 189 Jerome Bettis .60 .25
❑ 190 Travis Taylor .40 .15
❑ 191 Drew Brees .60 .25
❑ 192 Phillip Buchanon .25 .08
❑ 193 Jerramy Stevens .25 .08
❑ 194 Trent Green .40 .15
❑ 195 Duce Staley .40 .15
❑ 196 Plaxico Burress .40 .15
❑ 197 Jerry Porter .40 .15
❑ 198 Trevor Pryce .25 .08
❑ 199 Dwight Freeney .40 .15
❑ 200 Quincy Morgan .40 .15
❑ 201 Troy Vincent .25 .08
❑ 202 Randy McMichael .40 .15
❑ 203 Troy Hambrick .25 .08
❑ 204 Randy Moss 1.00 .40
❑ 205 Troy Brown .40 .15
❑ 206 Ray Lewis .60 .25
❑ 207 Trung Canidate .40 .15
❑ 208 Raynoch Thompson .25 .08
❑ 209 Ty Law .40 .15
❑ 210 Reggie Wayne .40 .15
❑ 211 Warren Sapp .40 .15
❑ 212 Richard Seymour .25 .08
❑ 213 Warrick Dunn .40 .15
❑ 214 Robert Ferguson .25 .08
❑ 215 Wayne Chrebet .40 .15
❑ 216 Rod Coleman RC .60 .25
❑ 217 Will Allen .25 .08
❑ 218 Rod Woodson .40 .15
❑ 219 Zach Thomas .60 .25
❑ 220 Rod Smith .40 .15
❑ 221 Ricky Williams .60 .25
❑ 222 LaDainian Tomlinson .60 .25
❑ 223 Priest Holmes .75 .30
❑ 224 Rich Gannon .40 .15
❑ 225 Drew Bledsoe .60 .25
❑ 226 Kerry Collins .40 .15
❑ 227 Marvin Harrison .60 .25
❑ 228 Hines Ward .60 .25
❑ 229 Peerless Price .40 .15
❑ 230 Jason Taylor .25 .08
❑ 231 Jeremy Shockey 1.00 .40
❑ 232 Clinton Portis 1.00 .40
❑ 233 Antonio Bryant .40 .15
❑ 234 Donte Stallworth .60 .25
❑ 235 David Carr 1.00 .40
❑ 236 Joey Harrington 1.00 .40
❑ 237 William Green .40 .15
❑ 238 Julius Peppers .60 .25
❑ 239 Shipp/Thompson/Wilson .25 .08
❑ 240 Vick/Dunn/Finner/Brooking .75 .30
❑ 241 Lewis/Hartwell/Taylor/Reed .40 .15
❑ 242 Bled/Henry/Mould/Fletch .40 .15
❑ 243 Peppers/Smith/Muhammad .60 .25
❑ 244 Booker/Urlacher/Thomas .60 .25
❑ 245 Dillon/Smith/Johnson/Kitna .60 .25
❑ 246 Couch/Green/Morgan/Word .40 .15
❑ 247 Hutchinson/Galloway/Williams/Ellis .25 .08
❑ 248 Portis/Smith/Wilson .60 .25
❑ 249 Harring/Stew/Schr/Edwards .60 .25
❑ 250 Favre/Green/Driver/KGB .75 .30
❑ 251 Carr/Wells/Bradford/Glenn .60 .25
❑ 252 Mann/James/Harr/Freen .60 .25
❑ 253 Brunell/Taylor/Smith/McCree .25 .08
❑ 254 Green/Holmes/Kenn/Hicks .40 .15
❑ 255 Willms/Chamb/Thom/Tayl .60 .25
❑ 256 Culp/Benn/Moss/Williams .60 .25
❑ 257 Brady/Smith/Brown/Vina 1.00 .40
❑ 258 Brooks/McAllister/Horn/Howard .25 .08
❑ 259 Collins/Barber/Toomer/Strahan .60 .25
❑ 260 Pennington/Martin/Chrebet/Abraham .40 .15
❑ 261 Gannon/Garn/Rice/Woods .60 .25
❑ 262 McNabb/Staley/Pinkston/Taylor .40 .15
❑ 263 Maddox/Zereoue/Ward/ Gildon/Porter .40 .15
❑ 264 Brees/Tomlinson/Edwards .60 .25
❑ 265 Garcia/Hearst/Owens/Carter .40 .15
❑ 266 Hasselbeck/Alexander/ Robin/Tongue .25 .08
❑ 267 Bulger/Faulk/Holt/Little .60 .25
❑ 268 B.John/Key.John/S.Rice/Kelly .40 .15
❑ 269 McNair/George/Mason/Schulters .25 .08
❑ 270 Ramsey/Gardner/Smoot .25 .08
❑ 271 Carson Palmer RC 5.00 2.00
❑ 272 Kyle Boller RC 2.50 1.00
❑ 273 Byron Leftwich RC 4.00 1.50
❑ 274 Willis McGahee RC 3.00 1.25
❑ 275 Larry Johnson RC 5.00 2.50
❑ 276 Charles Rogers RC 1.25 .50
❑ 277 Andre Johnson RC 2.50 1.00
❑ 278 Bryant Johnson RC 1.25 .50
❑ 279 Rex Grossman RC 2.00 .75
❑ 280 Taylor Jacobs RC 1.00 .40
❑ 281 Rober RC/Sull RC/Will RC 1.25 .50
❑ 282 Jopp RC/Davis RC/Rag RC 2.50 1.00
❑ 283 Witt RC/Clark RC/Smith RC 1.25 .50
❑ 284 Edwds RC/Smith RC/Bail RC 1.25 .50
❑ 285 SuggsRC/BrownRC/SmithRC 2.00 .75
❑ 286 Griff RC/Pinn RC/Askew RC 1.25 .50
❑ 287 Farg RC/Gabr RC/Johns RC 1.25 .50
❑ 288 Kenn RC/Joseph RC/Warr RC 1.25 .50
❑ 289 Sug RC/Hayn RC/McDo RC 2.00 .75
❑ 290 Wash RC/Curt RC/Burles RC 1.50 .60
❑ 291 Wall RC/Dors RC/Simms RC 2.00 .75
❑ 292 Wade RC/Aik RC/Gage RC 1.25 .50
❑ 293 McCull RC/Sapp RC/Grah RC 1.00 .40
❑ 294 Kelly RC/Gard RC/Tolv RC 1.00 .40
❑ 295 Johns RC/Bold RC/Calic RC 3.00 1.25
❑ 296 Lloyd RC/McM RC/McD RC 2.00 .75
❑ 297 Kels RC/White RC/Doss RC 1.25 .50
❑ 298 Newm RC/Truf RC/Wool RC 2.50 1.00

❑ 299	Kings RC/Rom RC/St.P RC	1.25	.50
❑ 300	Pinn RC/Toef RC/Cobou RC	1.25	.50

2004 Fleer Tradition

❑	COMPLETE SET (360)	100.00	50.00
❑	COMP.SET w/o SP's (330)	30.00	15.00
❑	331-350 ROOKIE STATED ODDS 1:4 H/R		
❑	351-360 ROOKIE STATED ODDS 1:18H, 1:24R		
❑ 1	Dolphins TL	.40	.15
❑ 2	Bills TL	.40	.15
❑ 3	Patriots TL	.60	.25
❑ 4	Jets TL	.40	.15
❑ 5	Colts TL	.60	.25
❑ 6	Jaguars TL	.40	.15
❑ 7	Titans TL	.25	.08
❑ 8	Texans TL	.40	.15
❑ 9	Raiders TL	.60	.25
❑ 10	Broncos TL	.40	.15
❑ 11	Chiefs TL	.40	.15
❑ 12	Chargers TL	.50	.20
❑ 13	Steelers TL	.60	.25
❑ 14	Browns TL	.25	.08
❑ 15	Bengals TL	.40	.15
❑ 16	Ravens TL	.40	.15
❑ 17	Eagles TL	.40	.15
❑ 18	Giants TL	.40	.15
❑ 19	Redskins TL	.40	.15
❑ 20	Cowboys TL	.40	.15
❑ 21	Vikings TL	.60	.25
❑ 22	Packers TL	.75	.30
❑ 23	Bears TL	.60	.25
❑ 24	Lions TL	.40	.15
❑ 25	49ers TL	.40	.15
❑ 26	Rams TL	.40	.15
❑ 27	Seahawks TL	.40	.15
❑ 28	Cardinals TL	.25	.08
❑ 29	Panthers TL	.40	.15
❑ 30	BuccaneersTL	.25	.08
❑ 31	Falcons TL	.25	.08
❑ 32	Saints TL	.40	.15
❑ 33	Anquan Boldin	.60	.25
❑ 34	Michael Vick	1.25	.50
❑ 35	Kyle Boller	.60	.25
❑ 36	Aeneas Williams	.25	.08
❑ 37	Jake Delhomme	.60	.25
❑ 38	Rex Grossman	.60	.25
❑ 39	Carson Palmer	.75	.30
❑ 40	Quincy Morgan	.40	.15
❑ 41	Terry Glenn	.25	.08
❑ 42	Jake Plummer	.40	.15
❑ 43	Joey Harrington	.60	.25
❑ 44	Brett Favre	1.50	.60
❑ 45	Jeff Garcia	.60	.25
❑ 46	Peyton Manning	1.00	.40
❑ 47	Byron Leftwich	.75	.30
❑ 48	Trent Green	.40	.15
❑ 49	A.J. Feeley	.60	.25
❑ 50	Daunte Culpepper	.60	.25
❑ 51	Tom Brady	1.50	.60
❑ 52	Aaron Brooks	.40	.15
❑ 53	Kerry Collins	.40	.15
❑ 54	Chad Pennington	.60	.25
❑ 55	Rich Gannon	.40	.15
❑ 56	Donovan McNabb	.75	.30
❑ 57	Tommy Maddox	.40	.15
❑ 58	Drew Brees	.60	.25
❑ 59	Terrell Owens	.60	.25
❑ 60	Matt Hasselbeck	.40	.15
❑ 61	Kurt Warner	.60	.25
❑ 62	Brad Johnson	.40	.15
❑ 63	Jerome Bettis	.60	.25
❑ 64	Keith Bulluck	.25	.08
❑ 65	Rod Gardner	.40	.15
❑ 66	Eddie George	.40	.15
❑ 67	Warren Sapp	.40	.15
❑ 68	Marc Bulger	.60	.25
❑ 69	Shaun Alexander	.60	.25
❑ 70	Tai Streets	.25	.08
❑ 71	LaDainian Tomlinson	.75	.30
❑ 72	Steve McNair	.60	.25
❑ 73	Brian Westbrook	.40	.15
❑ 74	Jerry Rice	1.25	.50
❑ 75	Santana Moss	.40	.15
❑ 76	Moe Williams	.25	.08
❑ 77	Deuce McAllister	.60	.25
❑ 78	Adam Vinatieri	.60	.25
❑ 79	Randy Moss	.75	.30
❑ 80	Ricky Williams	.60	.25
❑ 81	Priest Holmes	.75	.30
❑ 82	Jimmy Smith	.40	.15
❑ 83	Edgerrin James	.60	.25
❑ 84	Andre Johnson	.60	.25
❑ 85	Ahman Green	.60	.25
❑ 86	Charles Rogers	.40	.15
❑ 87	Champ Bailey	.40	.15
❑ 88	Roy Williams S	.40	.15
❑ 89	Tim Couch	.25	.08
❑ 90	Corey Dillon	.40	.15
❑ 91	Thomas Jones	.40	.15
❑ 92	Stephen Davis	.40	.15
❑ 93	Travis Henry	.40	.15
❑ 94	Jamal Lewis	.60	.25
❑ 95	Warrick Dunn	.40	.15
❑ 96	Emmitt Smith	1.25	.50
❑ 97	Mark Brunell	.40	.15
❑ 98	Willis McGahee	.60	.25
❑ 99	Duce Staley	.40	.15
❑ 100	Lee Suggs	.60	.25
❑ 101	Rod Smith	.40	.15
❑ 102	Marvin Harrison	.60	.25
❑ 103	Larry Johnson	.75	.30
❑ 104	Michael Bennett	.40	.15
❑ 105	Donte Stallworth	.40	.15
❑ 106	DeShaun Foster	.40	.15
❑ 107	Hines Ward	.60	.25
❑ 108	T.J. Duckett	.40	.15
❑ 109	Brian Urlacher	.75	.30
❑ 110	Boss Bailey	.40	.15
❑ 111	Tim Brown	.60	.25
❑ 112	David Boston	.40	.15
❑ 113	Marshall Faulk	.60	.25
❑ 114	Jason Witten	.40	.15
❑ 115	Richard Seymour	.25	.08
❑ 116	Domanick Davis	.60	.25
❑ 117	Jon Kitna	.40	.15
❑ 118	Ray Lewis	.60	.25
❑ 119	Tedy Bruschi	.40	.15
❑ 120	Chris Chambers	.40	.15
❑ 121	Freddie Mitchell	.40	.15
❑ 122	Amani Toomer	.40	.15
❑ 123	Curtis Martin	.60	.25
❑ 124	Eric Moulds	.40	.15
❑ 125	Darrell Jackson	.40	.15
❑ 126	Clinton Portis	.60	.25
❑ 127	Jay Fiedler	.25	.08
❑ 128	Todd Heap	.40	.15
❑ 129	Dexter Jackson	.25	.08
❑ 130	James Jackson	.25	.08
❑ 131	Shannon Sharpe	.40	.15
❑ 132	Donald Driver	.40	.15
❑ 133	Billy Miller	.25	.08
❑ 134	Dante Hall	.60	.25
❑ 135	Onterrio Smith	.40	.15
❑ 136	Joe Horn	.40	.15
❑ 137	Shaun Ellis	.25	.08
❑ 138	L.J. Smith	.40	.15
❑ 139	Jerry Porter	.40	.15
❑ 140	Reggie Wayne	.40	.15
❑ 141	Derrick Brooks	.40	.15
❑ 142	Terrell Suggs	.40	.15
❑ 143	Randy McMichael	.25	.08
❑ 144	Mike Alstott	.40	.15
❑ 145	Nate Poole RC	.60	.25
❑ 146	Chris Brown	.60	.25
❑ 147	Torry Holt	.60	.25
❑ 148	Adewale Ogunleye	.40	.15
❑ 149	Peter Warrick	.40	.15
❑ 150	Alge Crumpler	.40	.15
❑ 151	Charlie Garner	.40	.15
❑ 152	Jeremy Shockey	.60	.25
❑ 153	Simeon Rice	.40	.15
❑ 154	Julian Peterson	.25	.08
❑ 155	Patrick Ramsey	.40	.15
❑ 156	Shawn Springs	.25	.08
❑ 157	Marcus Stroud	.25	.08
❑ 158	Keyshawn Johnson	.40	.15
❑ 159	Steve Smith	.60	.25
❑ 160	Ty Law	.40	.15
❑ 161	Derrick Mason	.40	.15
❑ 162	Josh Reed	.25	.08
❑ 163	Fred Smoot	.25	.08
❑ 164	Muhsin Muhammad	.40	.15
❑ 165	Justin Gage	.40	.15
❑ 166	Chad Johnson	.60	.25
❑ 167	Dennis Northcutt	.25	.08
❑ 168	Joey Galloway	.40	.15
❑ 169	Ashley Lelie	.40	.15
❑ 170	Casey Fitzsimmons	.25	.08
❑ 171	Dwight Freeney	.40	.15
❑ 172	Nick Barnett	.40	.15
❑ 173	LaBrandon Toefield	.25	.08
❑ 174	Jabar Gaffney	.40	.15
❑ 175	Tony Gonzalez	.40	.15
❑ 176	Zach Thomas	.60	.25
❑ 177	Nate Burleson	.60	.25
❑ 178	Deion Branch	.60	.25
❑ 179	Boo Williams	.25	.08
❑ 180	Michael Strahan	.40	.15
❑ 181	Anthony Becht	.25	.08
❑ 182	Charles Woodson	.40	.15
❑ 183	Sheldon Brown	.25	.08
❑ 184	Kendrell Bell	.40	.15
❑ 185	Kassim Osgood	.25	.08
❑ 186	Tony Parrish	.25	.08
❑ 187	Marcel Shipp	.40	.15
❑ 188	Bobby Engram	.25	.08
❑ 189	Keith Brooking	.25	.08
❑ 190	Isaac Bruce	.40	.15
❑ 191	Travis Taylor	.25	.08
❑ 192	Charles Lee	.25	.08
❑ 193	Takeo Spikes	.25	.08
❑ 194	Justin McCareins	.25	.08
❑ 195	Julius Peppers	.60	.25
❑ 196	LaVar Arrington	1.25	.50
❑ 197	Dez White	.40	.15
❑ 198	Rudi Johnson	.40	.15
❑ 199	Andre Davis	.25	.08
❑ 200	Quincy Carter	.40	.15
❑ 201	Quentin Griffin	.60	.25
❑ 202	Dallas Clark	.40	.15
❑ 203	Artose Pinner	.25	.08
❑ 204	Kevin Johnson	.25	.08
❑ 205	Kabeer Gbaja-Biamila	.40	.15
❑ 206	Marcus Coleman	.25	.08
❑ 207	Johnnie Morton	.40	.15
❑ 208	Jason Taylor	.25	.08
❑ 209	Kevin Williams	.25	.08
❑ 210	David Givens	.40	.15
❑ 211	Charles Grant	.25	.08
❑ 212	Ike Hilliard	.25	.08
❑ 213	Wayne Chrebet	.40	.15
❑ 214	Teyo Johnson	.25	.08
❑ 215	Brian Dawkins	.40	.15

❑ 216 Antwaan Randle El .60 .25
❑ 217 Eric Parker .25 .08
❑ 218 Josh McCown .40 .15
❑ 219 Tim Rattay .25 .08
❑ 220 Brian Finneran .25 .08
❑ 221 Chad Brown .25 .08
❑ 222 Ed Reed .40 .15
❑ 223 Dane Looker .40 .15
❑ 224 Aaron Schobel .40 .15
❑ 225 Joe Jurevicius .25 .08
❑ 226 Ricky Manning .25 .08
❑ 227 Jevon Kearse .40 .15
❑ 228 Laveranues Coles .40 .15
❑ 229 Kelley Washington .25 .08
❑ 230 William Green .40 .15
❑ 231 Terence Newman .40 .15
❑ 232 Bryant Johnson .25 .08
❑ 233 Peerless Price .40 .15
❑ 234 Peter Boulware .40 .15
❑ 235 Drew Bledsoe .60 .25
❑ 236 Kris Jenkins .25 .08
❑ 237 Marty Booker .40 .15
❑ 238 Matt Schobel .25 .08
❑ 239 Earl Little .25 .08
❑ 240 Antonio Bryant .40 .15
❑ 241 Al Wilson .25 .08
❑ 242 Dre Bly .25 .08
❑ 243 Javon Walker .40 .15
❑ 244 David Carr .60 .25
❑ 245 Mike Vanderjagt .25 .08
❑ 246 Fred Taylor .40 .15
❑ 247 Eddie Kennison .25 .08
❑ 248 Patrick Surtain .25 .08
❑ 249 Jim Kleinsasser .25 .08
❑ 250 Daniel Graham .25 .08
❑ 251 Jerome Pathon .25 .08
❑ 252 Tiki Barber .60 .25
❑ 253 John Abraham .25 .08
❑ 254 Justin Fargas .40 .15
❑ 255 Correll Buckhalter .40 .15
❑ 256 Plaxico Burress .40 .15
❑ 257 Quentin Jammer .25 .08
❑ 258 Kevan Barlow .40 .15
❑ 259 Koren Robinson .40 .15
❑ 260 Leonard Little .25 .08
❑ 261 John Lynch .40 .15
❑ 262 Tyrone Calico .40 .15
❑ 263 Taylor Jacobs .40 .15
❑ 264 Joey Porter .40 .15
❑ 265 Freddie Jones .25 .08
❑ 266 Marcus Pollard .25 .08
❑ 267 Mike Peterson .25 .08
❑ 268 Justin Griffith .25 .08
❑ 269 Shawn Bryson .25 .08
❑ 270 Will Allen .25 .08
❑ 271 Antonio Gates .60 .25
❑ 272 Chris McAlister .25 .08
❑ 273 Tony Hollings .25 .08
❑ 274 Cedrick Wilson .25 .08
❑ 275 Adam Archuleta .25 .08
❑ 276 London Fletcher .25 .08
❑ 277 Drew Bennett .40 .15
❑ 278 Rod Smart .25 .08
❑ 279 LaMont Jordan .60 .25
❑ 280 Jerry Azumah .25 .08
❑ 281 Bubba Franks .40 .15
❑ 282 Troy Edwards .25 .08
❑ 283 Willie McGinest .25 .08
❑ 284 Morten Andersen .25 .08
❑ 285 Dat Nguyen .25 .08
❑ 286 Samari Rolle .25 .08
❑ 287 Brian Simmons .25 .08
❑ 288 Chike Okeafor .25 .08
❑ 289 Rodney Harrison .25 .08
❑ 290 Jason Elam .25 .08
❑ 291 Tim Dwight .40 .15
❑ 292 Corey Bradford .25 .08
❑ 293 Charles Tillman .40 .15
❑ 294 Tim Carter .25 .08
❑ 295 Ahmed Plummer .25 .08
❑ 296 Troy Walters .25 .08
❑ 297 Michael Lewis .25 .08
❑ 298 Tory James .25 .08
❑ 299 Doug Flutie .60 .25
❑ 300 Az-Zahir Hakim .25 .08
❑ 301 Itula Mili .25 .08
❑ 302 Jamie Sharper .25 .08
❑ 303 Vonnie Holliday .25 .08
❑ 304 Brian Russell RC .60 .25
❑ 305 Bryan Gilmore .25 .08
❑ 306 Darren Sharper .25 .08
❑ 307 Kyle Brady .25 .08
❑ 308 David Tyree .25 .08
❑ 309 Andre Carter .25 .08
❑ 310 Lawyer Milloy .40 .15
❑ 311 David Terrell .40 .15
❑ 312 Richie Anderson .25 .08
❑ 313 Darren Howard .25 .08
❑ 314 Sebastian Janikowski .25 .08
❑ 315 Kimo von Oelhoffen .60 .25
❑ 316 Donnie Edwards .25 .08
❑ 317 Brandon Lloyd .40 .15
❑ 318 Robert Ferguson .25 .08
❑ 319 Derek Smith .25 .08
❑ 320 Anthony Thomas .40 .15
❑ 321 Ken Hamlin .25 .08
❑ 322 Ronde Barber .25 .08
❑ 323 Erron Kinney .25 .08
❑ 324 Tom Brady AW .60 .25
❑ 325 Peyton Manning AW .60 .25
❑ 326 Steve McNair AW .40 .15
❑ 327 Jamal Lewis AW .40 .15
❑ 328 Ray Lewis AW .40 .15
❑ 329 Anquan Boldin AW .25 .08
❑ 330 Terrell Suggs AW .25 .08
❑ 331 Eli Manning RC 10.00 5.00
❑ 332 Larry Fitzgerald RC 6.00 2.50
❑ 333 Ben Roethlisberger RC 20.00 10.00
❑ 334 Tatum Bell RC 4.00 1.50
❑ 335 Roy Williams RC 5.00 2.00
❑ 336 Drew Henson RC 2.00 .75
❑ 337 Philip Rivers RC 6.00 2.50
❑ 338 Rashaun Woods RC 2.00 .75
❑ 339 Kevin Jones RC 6.00 2.50
❑ 340 Sean Taylor RC 2.50 1.00
❑ 341 Steven Jackson RC 6.00 2.50
❑ 342 Kellen Winslow RC 4.00 1.50
❑ 343 Chris Perry RC 4.00 1.50
❑ 344 J.P. Losman RC 4.00 1.50
❑ 345 Greg Jones RC 2.00 .75
❑ 346 Reggie Williams RC 2.50 1.00
❑ 347 Michael Clayton RC 4.00 1.50
❑ 348 Jonathan Vilma RC 2.00 .75
❑ 349 Julius Jones RC 8.00 3.00
❑ 350 Michael Jenkins RC 2.00 .75
❑ 351 E.Manning/Rivers/Roethlis. 25.00 12.50
❑ 352 Fitzgerald/Re.Will/Ro.Will. 8.00 3.00
❑ 353 Evans RC/Berr.RC/Ham.RC 3.00 1.25
❑ 354 Ude.RC/Poole RC/Colb.RC 3.00 1.25
❑ 355 Gamb.RC/Rob.RC/Hall RC 3.00 1.25
❑ 356 Trou.RC/Wats.RC/Harts.RC 3.00 1.25
❑ 357 Darl.RC/Morant RC/Wilf.RC 3.00 1.25
❑ 358 McCo.RC/Pick.RC/Sch.RC 4.00 1.50
❑ 359 Bell/Turn.RC/Cobbs RC 5.00 2.00
❑ 360 Moore RC/Wils.RC/Kni.RC 3.00 1.25

2000 Greats of the Game

❑ COMP.SET w/o SP's (100) 40.00 20.00
❑ 1 Terry Bradshaw 1.50 .60
❑ 2 Paul Hornung .60 .25
❑ 3 Tony Dorsett .60 .25
❑ 4 L.C. Greenwood .40 .15
❑ 5 Ozzie Newsome .25 .08
❑ 6 Michael Irvin .40 .15
❑ 7 Art Donovan .40 .15
❑ 8 Don Maynard .40 .15
❑ 9 Bobby Mitchell .40 .15
❑ 10 Bob Lilly .40 .15
❑ 11 Earl Morrall .25 .08
❑ 12 Harvey Martin .25 .08 
❑ 13 Dan Fouts .60 .25
❑ 14 Joe Theismann .60 .25
❑ 15 Roger Staubach 1.50 .60
❑ 16 Otto Graham .40 .15
❑ 17 Cliff Branch .40 .15
❑ 18 Sonny Jurgensen .60 .25
❑ 19 Eric Dickerson .40 .15
❑ 20 Lee Roy Selmon .25 .08
❑ 21 Roger Craig .40 .15
❑ 22 Raymond Berry .40 .15
❑ 23 Bob Hayes .40 .15
❑ 24 Steve Largent .60 .25
❑ 25 Lenny Moore .40 .15
❑ 26 Chuck Bednarik .40 .15
❑ 27 Ken Stabler 1.25 .50
❑ 28 William Perry .40 .15
❑ 29 Joe Greene .60 .25
❑ 30 Joe Namath 1.50 .60
❑ 31 Jim Kelly .75 .30
❑ 32 Steve Young 1.25 .50
❑ 33 Randy White .40 .15
❑ 34 Lawrence Taylor .60 .25
❑ 35 Franco Harris .75 .30
❑ 36 Marcus Allen .60 .25
❑ 37 Mike Singletary .60 .25
❑ 38 Fran Tarkenton 1.25 .50
❑ 39 Mel Renfro .25 .08
❑ 40 Len Dawson .60 .25
❑ 41 Carl Eller .25 .08
❑ 42 Chuck Foreman .25 .08
❑ 43 Gino Marchetti .25 .08
❑ 44 Jim Marshall .25 .08
❑ 45 Jack Ham .40 .15
❑ 46 Mercury Morris .25 .08
❑ 47 Anthony Munoz .40 .15
❑ 48 Herschel Walker .40 .15
❑ 49 Drew Pearson .40 .15
❑ 50 John Elway 2.50 1.00
❑ 51 George Blanda .60 .25
❑ 52 Earl Campbell .60 .25
❑ 53 Bart Starr 2.00 .75
❑ 54 Dan Marino 2.50 1.00
❑ 55 Johnny Unitas 1.50 .60
❑ 56 Sammy Baugh .60 .25
❑ 57 Steve Van Buren .40 .15
❑ 58 Mel Blount .40 .15
❑ 59 Fred Biletnikoff .60 .25
❑ 60 John Brodie .25 .08
❑ 61 Daryle Lamonica .25 .08
❑ 62 James Lofton .25 .08
❑ 63 Ronnie Lott .40 .15
❑ 64 Gale Sayers 1.25 .50
❑ 65 Art Monk .40 .15
❑ 66 Jim Plunkett .40 .15
❑ 67 Charlie Joiner .25 .08
❑ 68 Deacon Jones .40 .15
❑ 69 Paul Warfield .60 .25
❑ 70 Jim Otto .25 .08
❑ 71 Billy Kilmer .40 .15
❑ 72 Archie Manning .40 .15
❑ 73 Alex Karras .40 .15
❑ 74 Tom Matte .25 .08
❑ 75 Jay Novacek .25 .08
❑ 76 Charley Taylor .40 .15

	Card	Player	Price	Price
❑	77	Sam Huff	.40	.15
❑	78	Jack Lambert	.60	.25
❑	79	Mike Ditka	.60	.25
❑	80	Frank Gifford	.60	.25
❑	81	Jim Thorpe	.60	.25
❑	82	Walter Payton	3.00	1.25
❑	83	Doak Walker	.60	.25
❑	84	Sid Luckman	.40	.15
❑	85	Bronko Nagurski	.60	.25
❑	86	Alan Ameche	.25	.08
❑	87	Merlin Olsen	.40	.15
❑	88	Dick Butkus	1.25	.50
❑	89	Elroy Hirsch	.40	.15
❑	90	Max McGee	.40	.15
❑	91	Ray Nitschke	.60	.25
❑	92	Phil Simms	.40	.15
❑	93	Vince Lombardi CC	1.25	.50
❑	94	Tom Landry CC	.75	.30
❑	95	Bill Walsh CC	.40	.15
❑	96	Mike Ditka CC	.60	.25
❑	97	Jimmy Johnson CC	.40	.15
❑	98	Chuck Noll CC	.40	.15
❑	99	Dan Reeves CC	.40	.15
❑	100	Don Shula CC	.60	.25
❑	101	Peter Warrick RC	8.00	3.00
❑	102	Thomas Jones RC	12.00	5.00
❑	103	Jamal Lewis RC	20.00	7.50
❑	104	Chad Pennington RC	20.00	7.50
❑	105	Chris Redman RC	6.00	2.50
❑	106	Ron Dayne RC	8.00	3.00
❑	107	Trung Canidate RC	6.00	2.50
❑	108	Shaun Alexander RC	40.00	15.00
❑	109	Plaxico Burress RC	15.00	6.00
❑	110	J.R. Redmond RC	6.00	2.50
❑	111	Travis Taylor RC	8.00	3.00
❑	112	Dez White RC	8.00	3.00
❑	113	Todd Pinkston RC	8.00	3.00
❑	114	Laveranues Coles RC	10.00	4.00
❑	115	Dennis Northcutt RC	8.00	3.00
❑	116	Jerry Porter RC	10.00	4.00
❑	117	R.Jay Soward RC	6.00	2.50
❑	118	Sylvester Morris RC	6.00	2.50
❑	119	Ron Dugans RC	6.00	2.50
❑	120	Travis Prentice RC	6.00	2.50
❑	121	Tee Martin RC	8.00	3.00
❑	122	James Williams RC	6.00	2.50
❑	123	Trevor Gaylor RC	6.00	2.50
❑	124	Shyrone Stith RC	6.00	2.50
❑	125	Frank Moreau RC	6.00	2.50
❑	126	Kwame Cavil RC	6.00	2.50
❑	127	Ron Dixon RC	6.00	2.50
❑	128	Darrell Jackson RC	15.00	6.00
❑	129	Sammy Morris RC	6.00	2.50
❑	130	JaJuan Dawson RC	6.00	2.50
❑	131	Doug Johnson RC	30.00	15.00
❑	132	Brian Urlacher RC	80.00	40.00
❑	133	Brad Hoover RC	30.00	15.00
❑	134	Mike Anderson AUTO RC	30.00	15.00

2004 Greats of the Game

	Card	Player	Price	Price
❑		COMP.SET w/o RC's (67)	40.00	15.00
❑		ROOKIE STATED ODDS: 1:15 HOB, 1:24 RET		
❑		ROOKIE PRINT RUN 999 SER.#'d SETS		
❑		CARDS #35/39/41 NOT PRICED		
❑	1	Jim Brown	3.00	1.25
❑	2	Jim Thorpe	2.00	.75
❑	3	Terry Bradshaw	3.00	1.25
❑	4	Fran Tarkenton	2.50	1.00
❑	5	Joe Namath	3.00	1.25
❑	6	Joe Montana	6.00	2.50
❑	7	George Rogers	1.00	.40
❑	8	Marcus Allen	2.00	.75
❑	9	Walter Payton	6.00	2.50
❑	10	Dick Butkus	3.00	1.25
❑	11	Dan Fouts	2.00	.75
❑	12	Kellen Winslow Sr.	1.50	.60
❑	13	Sammy Baugh	2.00	.75
❑	14	Bart Starr	4.00	1.50
❑	15	Steve Young	2.50	1.00
❑	16	Sid Luckman	2.00	.75
❑	17	Y.A. Tittle	2.00	.75
❑	18	Dan Marino	5.00	2.00
❑	19	Paul Hornung	2.00	.75
❑	20	John Elway	3.00	1.25
❑	21	Earl Campbell	2.00	.75
❑	22	Max McGee	1.50	.60
❑	23	Alan Ameche	1.00	.40
❑	24	Bronko Nagurski	2.00	.75
❑	25	Elroy Hirsch	1.50	.60
❑	26	Jack Lambert	2.50	1.00
❑	27	Sam Huff	1.50	.60
❑	28	Jay Novacek	1.50	.60
❑	29	Roger Staubach	3.00	1.25
❑	30	Bob Hayes	1.50	.60
❑	31	Ken Stabler	2.50	1.00
❑	32	Chuck Bednarik	1.50	.60
❑	33	Ronnie Lott	2.00	.75
❑	34	Steve Van Buren	1.50	.60
❑	36	Gale Sayers	2.50	1.00
❑	37	Jim Otto	1.00	.40
❑	38	Jim Plunkett	1.50	.60
❑	40	Don Maynard	1.50	.60
❑	42	Billy Sims	1.50	.60
❑	43	Franco Harris	2.50	1.00
❑	44	Tony Dorsett	2.00	.75
❑	45	Wilbert Montgomery	1.00	.40
❑	46	Eric Dickerson SP	4.00	1.50
❑	47	Jim Taylor	2.00	.75
❑	48	George Blanda	2.00	.75
❑	49	Cris Carter	2.00	.75
❑	50	Mike Quick	1.00	.40
❑	51	James Lofton	1.00	.40
❑	52	Lawrence Taylor	2.00	.75
❑	53	Roger Craig	2.00	.75
❑	54	Paul Warfield	1.50	.60
❑	55	Dan Pastorini	1.00	.40
❑	56	Ozzie Newsome	1.50	.60
❑	57	Charley Taylor	1.50	.60
❑	58	Deacon Jones	1.50	.60
❑	59	Bob Lilly	2.00	.75
❑	60	Mike Singletary	2.00	.75
❑	61	Warren Moon	1.50	.60
❑	62	Charles White	1.00	.40
❑	63	Bob Griese	2.00	.75
❑	64	Dwight Clark	1.50	.60
❑	65	Joe Greene	2.00	.75
❑	66	Dave Casper	1.00	.40
❑	67	Harold Carmichael	1.00	.40
❑	68	Drew Pearson	1.50	.60
❑	69	Tony Hill	1.00	.40
❑	70	Ray Nitschke	2.00	.75
❑	71	Eli Manning RC	20.00	10.00
❑	72	Philip Rivers RC	12.00	5.00
❑	73	Ben Roethlisberger RC	40.00	20.00
❑	74	Julius Jones RC	15.00	6.00
❑	75	Larry Fitzgerald RC	12.00	5.00
❑	76	Steven Jackson RC	12.00	5.00
❑	77	Kevin Jones RC	12.00	5.00
❑	78	Tatum Bell RC	8.00	3.00
❑	79	Rashaun Woods RC	4.00	1.50
❑	80	Roy Williams RC	10.00	4.00
❑	81	Lee Evans RC	5.00	2.00
❑	82	Michael Clayton RC	8.00	3.00
❑	83	J.P. Losman RC	8.00	3.00
❑	84	Drew Henson RC	4.00	1.50
❑	85	Kellen Winslow RC	8.00	3.00
❑	86	Chris Perry RC	6.00	2.50
❑	87	Reggie Williams RC	5.00	2.00
❑	88	Michael Jenkins RC	4.00	1.50
❑	89	Darius Watts RC	4.00	1.50
❑	90	Keary Colbert RC	5.00	2.00

2002 Gridiron Kings

	Card	Player	Price	Price
❑		COMPLETE SET (175)	150.00	90.00
❑		COMP.SET w/o SP's (100)	40.00	15.00
❑	1	David Boston	1.25	.50
❑	2	Jake Plummer	.75	.30
❑	3	Michael Vick	4.00	1.50
❑	4	Warrick Dunn	1.25	.50
❑	5	Jamal Lewis	1.25	.50
❑	6	Ray Lewis	1.25	.50
❑	7	Drew Bledsoe	1.50	.60
❑	8	Travis Henry	1.25	.50
❑	9	Eric Moulds	.75	.30
❑	10	Chris Weinke	.75	.30
❑	11	Lamar Smith	.75	.30
❑	12	Anthony Thomas	.75	.30
❑	13	Chris Chandler	.75	.30
❑	14	Brian Urlacher	2.00	.75
❑	15	Corey Dillon	.75	.30
❑	16	Peter Warrick	.75	.30
❑	17	Tim Couch	.75	.30
❑	18	James Jackson	.50	.20
❑	19	Kevin Johnson	.75	.30
❑	20	Quincy Carter	.75	.30
❑	21	Emmitt Smith	3.00	1.25
❑	22	Joey Galloway	.75	.30
❑	23	Brian Griese	1.25	.50
❑	24	Terrell Davis	1.25	.50
❑	25	Ed McCaffrey	1.25	.50
❑	26	Rod Smith	.75	.30
❑	27	Mike McMahon	1.25	.50
❑	28	Az-Zahir Hakim	.50	.20
❑	29	Germane Crowell	.50	.20
❑	30	Brett Favre	3.00	1.25
❑	31	Terry Glenn	.75	.30
❑	32	Ahman Green	1.25	.50
❑	33	James Allen	.75	.30
❑	34	Tony Simmons	.50	.20
❑	35	Peyton Manning	2.50	1.00
❑	36	Edgerrin James	1.50	.60
❑	37	Marvin Harrison	1.25	.50
❑	38	Dominic Rhodes	.75	.30
❑	39	Mark Brunell	1.25	.50
❑	40	Jimmy Smith	.75	.30
❑	41	Keenan McCardell	.50	.20
❑	42	Fred Taylor	1.25	.50
❑	43	Priest Holmes	1.50	.60
❑	44	Snoop Minnis	.50	.20
❑	45	Trent Green	.75	.30
❑	46	Tony Gonzalez	.75	.30
❑	47	Chris Chambers	1.25	.50
❑	48	Ricky Williams	1.25	.50
❑	49	Jay Fiedler	.75	.30
❑	50	Zach Thomas	1.25	.50
❑	51	Randy Moss	2.50	1.00
❑	52	Cris Carter	1.25	.50
❑	53	Daunte Culpepper	1.25	.50

No.	Player		
❑ 54	Michael Bennett	1.25	.50
❑ 55	Tom Brady	3.00	1.25
❑ 56	Antowain Smith	.75	.30
❑ 57	Troy Brown	.75	.30
❑ 58	Aaron Brooks	1.25	.50
❑ 59	Deuce McAllister	1.50	.60
❑ 60	Joe Horn	.75	.30
❑ 61	Kerry Collins	.75	.30
❑ 62	Ron Dayne	.75	.30
❑ 63	Michael Strahan	.75	.30
❑ 64	Vinny Testaverde	.75	.30
❑ 65	Curtis Martin	1.25	.50
❑ 66	Wayne Chrebet	.75	.30
❑ 67	Rich Gannon	1.25	.50
❑ 68	Tim Brown	1.25	.50
❑ 69	Jerry Rice	2.50	1.00
❑ 70	Charlie Garner	.75	.30
❑ 71	Donovan McNabb	1.50	.60
❑ 72	Duce Staley	1.25	.50
❑ 73	Freddie Mitchell	.75	.30
❑ 74	Kordell Stewart	.75	.30
❑ 75	Jerome Bettis	1.25	.50
❑ 76	Plaxico Burress	1.25	.50
❑ 77	Kendrell Bell	1.25	.50
❑ 78	LaDainian Tomlinson	2.00	.75
❑ 79	Drew Brees	1.25	.50
❑ 80	Doug Flutie	1.25	.50
❑ 81	Junior Seau	1.25	.50
❑ 82	Jeff Garcia	1.25	.50
❑ 83	Terrell Owens	1.25	.50
❑ 84	Garrison Hearst	.75	.30
❑ 85	Trent Dilfer	.75	.30
❑ 86	Shaun Alexander	1.50	.60
❑ 87	Koren Robinson	.75	.30
❑ 88	Marshall Faulk	1.25	.50
❑ 89	Kurt Warner	1.25	.50
❑ 90	Torry Holt	1.25	.50
❑ 91	Isaac Bruce	1.25	.50
❑ 92	Brad Johnson	.75	.30
❑ 93	Keyshawn Johnson	1.25	.50
❑ 94	Mike Alstott	1.25	.50
❑ 95	Warren Sapp	.75	.30
❑ 96	Steve McNair	1.25	.50
❑ 97	Eddie George	1.25	.50
❑ 98	Jevon Kearse	1.25	.50
❑ 99	Stephen Davis	.75	.30
❑ 100	Rod Gardner	.75	.30
❑ 101	David Carr RC	10.00	4.00
❑ 102	Joey Harrington RC	10.00	4.00
❑ 103	Patrick Ramsey RC	5.00	2.00
❑ 104	Josh McCown RC	5.00	2.00
❑ 105	David Garrard RC	4.00	1.50
❑ 106	Rohan Davey RC	4.00	1.50
❑ 107	Randy Fasani RC	3.00	1.25
❑ 108	Kurt Kittner RC	3.00	1.25
❑ 109	William Green RC	4.00	1.50
❑ 110	T.J. Duckett RC	6.00	2.50
❑ 111	DeShaun Foster RC	1.25	.50
❑ 112	Clinton Portis RC	12.00	5.00
❑ 113	Maurice Morris RC	4.00	1.50
❑ 114	Ladell Betts RC	4.00	1.50
❑ 115	Lamar Gordon RC	4.00	1.50
❑ 116	Brian Westbrook RC	6.00	2.50
❑ 117	Jonathan Wells RC	4.00	1.50
❑ 118	Travis Stephens RC	3.00	1.25
❑ 119	Josh Scobey RC	4.00	1.50
❑ 120	Donte Stallworth RC	8.00	3.00
❑ 121	Ashley Lelie RC	8.00	3.00
❑ 122	Javon Walker RC	8.00	3.00
❑ 123	Jabar Gaffney RC	4.00	1.50
❑ 124	Josh Reed RC	4.00	1.50
❑ 125	Tim Carter RC	3.00	1.25
❑ 126	Andre Davis RC	3.00	1.25
❑ 127	Reche Caldwell RC	4.00	1.50
❑ 128	Antwaan Randle El RC	6.00	2.50
❑ 129	Antonio Bryant RC	4.00	1.50
❑ 130	Deion Branch RC	8.00	3.00
❑ 131	Marquise Walker RC	3.00	1.25
❑ 132	Cliff Russell RC	3.00	1.25
❑ 133	Eric Crouch RC	4.00	1.50
❑ 134	Ron Johnson RC	3.00	1.25
❑ 135	Terry Charles RC	3.00	1.25
❑ 136	Jeremy Shockey RC	12.00	5.00
❑ 137	Daniel Graham RC	4.00	1.50
❑ 138	Julius Peppers RC	8.00	3.00
❑ 139	Dwight Freeney RC	5.00	2.00
❑ 140	Ryan Sims RC	4.00	1.50
❑ 141	John Henderson RC	4.00	1.50
❑ 142	Wendell Bryant RC	3.00	1.25
❑ 143	Albert Haynesworth RC	3.00	1.25
❑ 144	Quentin Jammer RC	4.00	1.50
❑ 145	Phillip Buchanon RC	4.00	1.50
❑ 146	Lito Sheppard RC	4.00	1.50
❑ 147	Roy Williams RC	10.00	4.00
❑ 148	Ed Reed RC	6.00	2.50
❑ 149	Napoleon Harris RC	4.00	1.50
❑ 150	Mike Williams RC	3.00	1.25
❑ 151	Art Monk	4.00	1.50
❑ 152	Barry Sanders	8.00	3.00
❑ 153	Bob Griese	5.00	2.00
❑ 154	Dan Marino	10.00	4.00
❑ 155	Dick Butkus	10.00	4.00
❑ 156	Earl Campbell	5.00	2.00
❑ 157	Eric Dickerson	5.00	2.00
❑ 158	Fran Tarkenton	5.00	2.00
❑ 159	Franco Harris	5.00	2.00
❑ 160	Herschel Walker	4.00	1.50
❑ 161	Joe Montana	15.00	6.00
❑ 162	Ronnie Lott	4.00	1.50
❑ 163	Joe Theismann	4.00	1.50
❑ 164	John Elway	10.00	4.00
❑ 165	John Riggins	5.00	2.00
❑ 166	Ken Stabler	6.00	2.50
❑ 167	Len Dawson	5.00	2.00
❑ 168	Marcus Allen	4.00	1.50
❑ 169	Mike Singletary	4.00	1.50
❑ 170	Roger Staubach	6.00	2.50
❑ 171	Walter Payton	12.00	5.00
❑ 172	Steve Largent	5.00	2.00
❑ 173	Terry Bradshaw	6.00	2.50
❑ 174	Thurman Thomas	4.00	1.50
❑ 175	Tony Dorsett	5.00	2.00

2003 Gridiron Kings

No.	Player		
❑	COMPLETE SET (175)	250.00	125.00
❑	COMP.SET w/o SP's (100)	30.00	12.50
❑ 1	David Boston	.75	.30
❑ 2	Marcel Shipp	.75	.30
❑ 3	Jake Plummer	.75	.30
❑ 4	Michael Vick	3.00	1.25
❑ 5	T.J. Duckett	.75	.30
❑ 6	Warrick Dunn	.75	.30
❑ 7	Ray Lewis	1.25	.50
❑ 8	Jamal Lewis	1.25	.50
❑ 9	Todd Heap	.75	.30
❑ 10	Drew Bledsoe	1.25	.50
❑ 11	Eric Moulds	.75	.30
❑ 12	Travis Henry	.75	.30
❑ 13	Julius Peppers	1.25	.50
❑ 14	Steve Smith	1.25	.50
❑ 15	Muhsin Muhammad	.75	.30
❑ 16	Anthony Thomas	.75	.30
❑ 17	David Terrell	.75	.30
❑ 18	Brian Urlacher	2.00	.75
❑ 19	Corey Dillon	.75	.30
❑ 20	Chad Johnson	1.25	.50
❑ 21	William Green	.75	.30
❑ 22	Tim Couch	.50	.20
❑ 23	Quincy Morgan	.75	.30
❑ 24	Roy Williams	1.25	.50
❑ 25	Emmitt Smith	3.00	1.25
❑ 26	Antonio Bryant	.75	.30
❑ 27	Clinton Portis	2.00	.75
❑ 28	Ashley Lelie	1.25	.50
❑ 29	Rod Smith	.75	.30
❑ 30	Brian Griese	1.25	.50
❑ 31	Joey Harrington	2.00	.75
❑ 32	James Stewart	.75	.30
❑ 33	Az-Zahir Hakim	.50	.20
❑ 34	Brett Favre	3.00	1.25
❑ 35	Ahman Green	1.25	.50
❑ 36	Donald Driver	.75	.30
❑ 37	Javon Walker	.75	.30
❑ 38	David Carr	2.00	.75
❑ 39	Jabar Gaffney	.75	.30
❑ 40	Jonathan Wells	.50	.20
❑ 41	Edgerrin James	1.25	.50
❑ 42	Marvin Harrison	1.25	.50
❑ 43	Peyton Manning	2.00	.75
❑ 44	Mark Brunell	.75	.30
❑ 45	Jimmy Smith	.75	.30
❑ 46	Fred Taylor	1.25	.50
❑ 47	Priest Holmes	1.50	.60
❑ 48	Tony Gonzalez	.75	.30
❑ 49	Trent Green	.75	.30
❑ 50	Jay Fiedler	.75	.30
❑ 51	Chris Chambers	1.25	.50
❑ 52	Zach Thomas	1.25	.50
❑ 53	Ricky Williams	1.25	.50
❑ 54	Randy Moss	2.00	.75
❑ 55	Daunte Culpepper	1.25	.50
❑ 56	Michael Bennett	.75	.30
❑ 57	Tom Brady	3.00	1.25
❑ 58	Deion Branch	1.25	.50
❑ 59	Antowain Smith	.50	.20
❑ 60	Donte Stallworth	1.25	.50
❑ 61	Deuce McAllister	1.25	.50
❑ 62	Aaron Brooks	1.25	.50
❑ 63	Kerry Collins	.75	.30
❑ 64	Jeremy Shockey	2.00	.75
❑ 65	Tiki Barber	1.25	.50
❑ 66	Curtis Martin	1.25	.50
❑ 67	Chad Pennington	1.50	.60
❑ 68	Santana Moss	.75	.30
❑ 69	Jerry Rice	2.50	1.00
❑ 70	Rich Gannon	.75	.30
❑ 71	Tim Brown	1.25	.50
❑ 72	Charlie Garner	.75	.30
❑ 73	Donovan McNabb	1.50	.60
❑ 74	Duce Staley	.75	.30
❑ 75	Antonio Freeman	.75	.30
❑ 76	Tommy Maddox	1.25	.50
❑ 77	Jerome Bettis	1.25	.50
❑ 78	Antwaan Randle El	1.25	.50
❑ 79	Plaxico Burress	.75	.30
❑ 80	LaDainian Tomlinson	1.25	.50
❑ 81	Junior Seau	1.25	.50
❑ 82	Drew Brees	1.25	.50
❑ 83	Terrell Owens	1.25	.50
❑ 84	Jeff Garcia	1.25	.50
❑ 85	Garrison Hearst	.75	.30
❑ 86	Koren Robinson	.75	.30
❑ 87	Shaun Alexander	1.25	.50
❑ 88	Trent Dilfer	.75	.30
❑ 89	Marshall Faulk	1.25	.50
❑ 90	Kurt Warner	1.25	.50
❑ 91	Isaac Bruce	1.25	.50
❑ 92	Brad Johnson	.75	.30
❑ 93	Keyshawn Johnson	1.25	.50
❑ 94	Warren Sapp	.75	.30
❑ 95	Steve McNair	1.25	.50
❑ 96	Derrick Mason	.75	.30
❑ 97	Eddie George	.75	.30
❑ 98	Bruce Smith	.75	.30

❑ 99 Rod Gardner .75 .30
❑ 100 Patrick Ramsey 1.25 .50
❑ 101 Carson Palmer RC 12.00 5.00
❑ 102 Byron Leftwich RC 10.00 4.00
❑ 103 Kyle Boller RC 6.00 2.50
❑ 104 Chris Simms RC 5.00 2.00
❑ 105 Dave Ragone RC 3.00 1.25
❑ 106 Rex Grossman RC 5.00 2.00
❑ 107 Brian St.Pierre RC 3.00 1.25
❑ 108 Kliff Kingsbury RC 2.50 1.00
❑ 109 Seneca Wallace RC 3.00 1.25
❑ 110 Larry Johnson RC 12.00 6.00
❑ 111 Lee Suggs RC 6.00 2.50
❑ 112 Justin Fargas RC 3.00 1.25
❑ 113 Onterrio Smith RC 3.00 1.25
❑ 114 Willis McGahee RC 8.00 3.00
❑ 115 Chris Brown RC 4.00 1.50
❑ 116 Musa Smith RC 3.00 1.25
❑ 117 Artose Pinner RC 3.00 1.25
❑ 118 Domanick Davis RC 5.00 2.00
❑ 119 Charles Rogers RC 3.00 1.25
❑ 120 Andre Johnson RC 6.00 2.50
❑ 121 Taylor Jacobs RC 2.50 1.00
❑ 122 Bryant Johnson RC 3.00 1.25
❑ 123 Kelley Washington RC 3.00 1.25
❑ 124 Brandon Lloyd RC 4.00 1.50
❑ 125 Tyrone Calico RC 4.00 1.50
❑ 126 Kevin Curtis RC 3.00 1.25
❑ 127 Bethel Johnson RC 3.00 1.25
❑ 128 Anquan Boldin RC 8.00 3.00
❑ 129 Nate Burleson RC 4.00 1.50
❑ 130 Jason Witten RC 5.00 2.00
❑ 131 Bennie Joppru RC 3.00 1.25
❑ 132 Teyo Johnson RC 3.00 1.25
❑ 133 Dallas Clark RC 3.00 1.25
❑ 134 Terrell Suggs RC 5.00 2.00
❑ 135 Chris Kelsay RC 3.00 1.25
❑ 136 Jerome McDougle RC 3.00 1.25
❑ 137 Michael Haynes RC 3.00 1.25
❑ 138 Calvin Pace RC 2.50 1.00
❑ 139 Jimmy Kennedy RC 3.00 1.25
❑ 140 Kevin Williams RC 3.00 1.25
❑ 141 DeWayne Robertson RC 3.00 1.25
❑ 142 William Joseph RC 3.00 1.25
❑ 143 Johnathan Sullivan RC 2.50 1.00
❑ 144 Boss Bailey RC 3.00 1.25
❑ 145 E.J. Henderson RC 3.00 1.25
❑ 146 Terence Newman RC 6.00 2.50
❑ 147 Marcus Trufant RC 3.00 1.25
❑ 148 Andre Woolfolk RC 3.00 1.25
❑ 149 Troy Polamalu RC 12.00 6.00
❑ 150 Mike Doss RC 3.00 1.25
❑ 151 Andre Reed 3.00 1.25
❑ 152 Bo Jackson 5.00 2.00
❑ 153 Dan Marino 10.00 4.00
❑ 154 Deacon Jones 3.00 1.25
❑ 155 Deion Sanders 4.00 1.50
❑ 156 Doak Walker 3.00 1.25
❑ 157 Don Maynard 3.00 1.25
❑ 158 Frank Gifford 3.00 1.25
❑ 159 Fred Biletnikoff 3.00 1.25
❑ 160 Gale Sayers 3.00 1.25
❑ 161 Jack Lambert 4.00 1.50
❑ 162 Jim Brown 4.00 1.50
❑ 163 Jim Kelly 5.00 2.00
❑ 164 Joe Greene 3.00 1.25
❑ 165 Joe Montana 12.00 5.00
❑ 166 John Elway 10.00 4.00
❑ 167 John Riggins 4.00 1.50
❑ 168 Johnny Unitas 3.00 1.25
❑ 169 Larry Csonka 3.00 1.25
❑ 170 Lawrence Taylor 3.00 1.25
❑ 171 Mike Ditka 3.00 1.25
❑ 172 Ozzie Newsome 3.00 1.25
❑ 173 Red Grange 3.00 1.25
❑ 174 Troy Aikman 5.00 2.00
❑ 175 Warren Moon 3.00 1.25

1948 Leaf

❑ COMPLETE SET (98) 6000.00 4500.00
❑ COMMON CARD (1-49) 30.00 20.00
❑ COMMON CARD (50-98) 175.00 100.00
❑ VAR (8B/12B/14B) 50.00 30.00
❑ WRAPPER (5-CENT) 160.00 110.00
❑ 1 Sid Luckman RC ! 400.00 250.00
❑ 2 Steve Suhey 30.00 20.00
❑ 3A Bull.Turner RB RC 135.00 75.00
❑ 3B Bull.Turner WB RC 175.00 100.00
❑ 4 Doak Walker RC 200.00 125.00
❑ 5 Levi Jackson RC 40.00 25.00
❑ 6 Bobby Layne RC 400.00 250.00
❑ 7 Bill Fischer 30.00 20.00
❑ 8A Vince Banonis BL 30.00 20.00
❑ 8B Vince Banonis WL 50.00 30.00
❑ 9 Tommy Thompson RC 40.00 25.00
❑ 10 Perry Moss 30.00 20.00
❑ 11 Terry Brennan RC 40.00 25.00
❑ 12A Bill Swiacki BL RC 30.00 20.00
❑ 12B Bill Swiacki WL RC 50.00 30.00
❑ 13A Johnny Lujack RC 200.00 125.00
❑ 13B Johnny Lujack RC ERR 300.00 175.00
❑ 14A Mal Kutner BL RC 30.00 20.00
❑ 14B Mal Kutner WL RC 50.00 30.00
❑ 15 Charlie Justice RC 90.00 50.00
❑ 16 Pete Pihos RC 150.00 90.00
❑ 17A K.Washington BL RC 55.00 35.00
❑ 17B K.Washington WL RC 80.00 50.00
❑ 18 Harry Gilmer RC 50.00 30.00
❑ 19A G.McAfee RC COR 150.00 90.00
❑ 19B G.McAfee RC ERR 200.00 125.00
❑ 20 George Taliaferro RC 40.00 25.00
❑ 21 Paul Christman RC 50.00 30.00
❑ 22 Steve Van Buren RC 250.00 150.00
❑ 23 Ken Kavanaugh RC 40.00 25.00
❑ 24 Jim Martin RC 40.00 25.00
❑ 25A Bud Angsman BL RC 40.00 25.00
❑ 25B Bud Angsman WL RC 60.00 35.00
❑ 26A Bob Waterfield BL RC 250.00 150.00
❑ 26B Bob Waterfield WL RC 450.00 300.00
❑ 27A Fred Davis YB 30.00 20.00
❑ 27B Fred Davis WB 50.00 30.00
❑ 28 Whitey Wistert RC 40.00 25.00
❑ 29 Charley Trippi RC 110.00 65.00
❑ 30 Paul Governali RC 40.00 25.00
❑ 31 Tom McWilliams 30.00 20.00
❑ 32 Leroy Zimmerman 30.00 20.00
❑ 33 Pat Harder RC UER 55.00 30.00
❑ 34 Sammy Baugh RC 600.00 400.00
❑ 35 Ted Fritsch Sr. RC 40.00 25.00
❑ 36 Bill Dudley RC 125.00 75.00
❑ 37 George Connor RC 100.00 50.00
❑ 38 Frank Dancewicz 30.00 20.00
❑ 39 Billy Dewell 30.00 20.00
❑ 40 John Nolan 30.00 20.00
❑ 41A Harry Szulborski YJ 30.00 20.00
❑ 41B Harry Szulborski OJ 50.00 30.00
❑ 42 Tex Coulter RC 40.00 25.00
❑ 43A Robert Nussbaumer MJ 30.00 20.00
❑ 43B Robert Nussbaumer RJ 50.00 30.00
❑ 44 Bob Mann 30.00 20.00
❑ 45 Jim White RC 30.00 20.00
❑ 46 Jack Jacobs 30.00 20.00
❑ 47 John Clement 30.00 20.00
❑ 48 Frank Reagan 30.00 20.00
❑ 49 Frank Tripucka RC 45.00 25.00
❑ 50 John Rauch RC 175.00 100.00
❑ 51 Mike Dimitro 175.00 100.00
❑ 52 Leo Nomellini RC 450.00 300.00
❑ 53 Charley Conerly RC 450.00 300.00
❑ 54 Chuck Bednarik RC 500.00 350.00
❑ 55 Chick Jagade 175.00 100.00
❑ 56 Bob Folsom RC 200.00 125.00
❑ 57 Gene Rossides RC 200.00 125.00
❑ 58 Art Weiner 175.00 100.00
❑ 59 Alex Sarkistian 175.00 100.00
❑ 60 Dick Harris Texas 175.00 100.00
❑ 61 Len Younce 175.00 100.00
❑ 62 Gene Derricotte 175.00 100.00
❑ 63 Roy Rebel Steiner 175.00 100.00
❑ 64 Frank Seno 175.00 100.00
❑ 65 Bob Hendren RC 175.00 100.00
❑ 66 Jack Cloud 175.00 100.00
❑ 67 Harrell Collins 175.00 100.00
❑ 68A Clyde LeForce RB RC 175.00 100.00
❑ 68B Clyde LeForce WB RC 200.00 125.00
❑ 69 Larry Joe 175.00 100.00
❑ 70 Phil O'Reilly 175.00 100.00
❑ 71 Paul Campbell 175.00 100.00
❑ 72 Ray Evans 175.00 100.00
❑ 73 Jackie Jensen RC UER 400.00 250.00
❑ 74 Russ Steger 175.00 100.00
❑ 75 Tony Minisi 175.00 100.00
❑ 76 Clayton Tonnemaker 175.00 100.00
❑ 77 George Savitsky 175.00 100.00
❑ 78 Clarence Self 175.00 100.00
❑ 79 Rod Franz 175.00 100.00
❑ 80 Jim Youle 175.00 100.00
❑ 81 Billy Bye 175.00 100.00
❑ 82 Fred Enke 175.00 100.00
❑ 83 Fred Folger 175.00 100.00
❑ 84 Jug Girard RC 200.00 125.00
❑ 85 Joe Scott 175.00 100.00
❑ 86 Bob Demoss 175.00 100.00
❑ 87 Dave Templeton 175.00 100.00
❑ 88 Herb Siegert 175.00 100.00
❑ 89 Bucky O'Conner 175.00 100.00
❑ 90 Joe Whisler 175.00 100.00
❑ 91 Leon Hart RC 250.00 150.00
❑ 92 Earl Banks 175.00 100.00
❑ 93 Frank Aschenbrenner 175.00 100.00
❑ 94 John Goldsberry RC 175.00 100.00
❑ 95 Porter Payne 175.00 100.00
❑ 96 Pete Perini 175.00 100.00
❑ 97 Jay Rhodemyre 175.00 100.00
❑ 98 Al DiMarco RC ! 250.00 125.00

1949 Leaf

❑ COMPLETE SET (49) 2200.00 1500.00
❑ WRAPPER (5-CENT) 300.00 250.00
❑ 1 Bob Hendren ! 80.00 40.00
❑ 2 Joe Scott 25.00 18.00
❑ 3 Frank Reagan 25.00 18.00
❑ 4 John Rauch 25.00 18.00
❑ 7 Bill Fischer 25.00 18.00
❑ 9 Elmer Bud Angsman 35.00 25.00
❑ 10 Billy Dewell 25.00 18.00
❑ 13 Tommy Thompson QB 35.00 25.00
❑ 15 Sid Luckman 125.00 75.00
❑ 16 Charley Trippi 55.00 35.00
❑ 17 Bob Mann 25.00 18.00
❑ 19 Paul Christman 35.00 25.00

❑ 22	Bill Dudley	55.00	35.00
❑ 23	Clyde LeForce	25.00	18.00
❑ 26	Sammy Baugh	300.00	200.00
❑ 28	Pete Pihos	70.00	50.00
❑ 31	Tex Coulter	35.00	25.00
❑ 32	Mal Kutner	35.00	25.00
❑ 35	Whitey Wistert	35.00	25.00
❑ 37	Ted Fritsch Sr.	35.00	25.00
❑ 38	Vince Banonis	25.00	18.00
❑ 39	Jim White	25.00	18.00
❑ 40	George Connor	55.00	35.00
❑ 41	George McAfee	55.00	35.00
❑ 43	Frank Tripucka	45.00	30.00
❑ 47	Fred Enke	25.00	18.00
❑ 49	Charley Conerly	100.00	60.00
❑ 51	Ken Kavanaugh	35.00	25.00
❑ 52	Bob Demoss	25.00	18.00
❑ 56	Johnny Lujack	100.00	60.00
❑ 57	Jim Youle	25.00	18.00
❑ 62	Harry Gilmer	35.00	25.00
❑ 65	Robert Nussbaumer	25.00	18.00
❑ 67	Bobby Layne	200.00	125.00
❑ 70	Herb Siegert	25.00	18.00
❑ 74	Tony Minisi	25.00	18.00
❑ 79	Steve Van Buren	150.00	90.00
❑ 81	Perry Moss	25.00	18.00
❑ 89	Bob Waterfield	125.00	75.00
❑ 90	Jack Jacobs	25.00	18.00
❑ 95	Kenny Washington	45.00	30.00
❑ 101	Pat Harder UER	35.00	25.00
❑ 110	Bill Swiacki	35.00	25.00
❑ 118	Fred Davis	25.00	18.00
❑ 126	Jay Rhodemyre	25.00	18.00
❑ 127	Frank Seno	25.00	18.00
❑ 134	Chuck Bednarik	175.00	110.00
❑ 144	George Savitsky	25.00	18.00
❑ 150	Bulldog Turner !	150.00	90.00

1996 Leaf

❑	COMPLETE SET (190)	20.00	7.50
❑ 1	Troy Aikman	1.00	.40
❑ 2	Ricky Watters	.20	.07
❑ 3	Robert Brooks	.40	.15
❑ 4	Ki-Jana Carter	.20	.07
❑ 5	Drew Bledsoe	.60	.25
❑ 6	Eric Swann	.10	.02
❑ 7	Hardy Nickerson	.10	.02
❑ 8	Tony Martin	.20	.07
❑ 9	Garrison Hearst	.20	.07
❑ 10	Bernie Parmalee	.10	.02
❑ 11	Neil Smith	.20	.07
❑ 12	Aaron Craver	.10	.02
❑ 13	Rashaan Salaam	.20	.07
❑ 14	Greg Hill	.20	.07
❑ 15	Charlie Garner	.20	.07
❑ 16	Kimble Anders	.20	.07
❑ 17	Steve McNair	.75	.30
❑ 18	Neil O'Donnell	.20	.07
❑ 19	Greg Lloyd	.20	.07
❑ 20	Warren Moon	.20	.07
❑ 21	Bernie Kosar	.10	.02
❑ 22	Derrick Thomas	.40	.15
❑ 23	Andre Hastings	.10	.02
❑ 24	Wayne Chrebet	.60	.25
❑ 25	Mark Seay	.10	.02
❑ 26	Eric Metcalf	.10	.02
❑ 27	Shawn Jefferson	.10	.02
❑ 28	Napoleon Kaufman	.40	.15
❑ 29	Steve Walsh	.10	.02
❑ 30	Derrick Alexander DE	.10	.02
❑ 31	Rodney Peete	.10	.02
❑ 32	Terance Mathis	.10	.02
❑ 33	Michael Westbrook	.40	.15
❑ 34	Kevin Carter	.10	.02
❑ 35	Aaron Hayden RC	.10	.02
❑ 36	J.J. Stokes	.40	.15
❑ 37	Andre Reed	.20	.07
❑ 38	Chris Warren	.20	.07
❑ 39	Jerry Rice	1.00	.40
❑ 40	Ben Coates	.20	.07
❑ 41	Reggie White	.40	.15
❑ 42	Joey Galloway	.40	.15
❑ 43	Sean Dawkins	.10	.02
❑ 44	Brett Favre	2.00	.75
❑ 45	Jeff George	.20	.07
❑ 46	Robert Smith	.20	.07
❑ 47	Ken Dilger	.20	.07
❑ 48	Larry Centers	.20	.07
❑ 49	Jackie Harris	.10	.02
❑ 50	Hugh Douglas	.20	.07
❑ 51	Herschel Walker	.20	.07
❑ 52	Kerry Collins	.40	.15
❑ 53	Michael Irvin	.40	.15
❑ 54	Willie McGinest	.10	.02
❑ 55	Herman Moore	.20	.07
❑ 56	Leroy Hoard	.10	.02
❑ 57	Scott Mitchell	.20	.07
❑ 58	Terrell Davis	.75	.30
❑ 59	Kevin Greene	.20	.07
❑ 60	Yancey Thigpen	.20	.07
❑ 61	Kevin Smith	.10	.02
❑ 62	Trent Dilfer	.40	.15
❑ 63	Cortez Kennedy	.10	.02
❑ 64	Carnell Lake	.10	.02
❑ 65	Quinn Early	.10	.02
❑ 66	Kyle Brady	.10	.02
❑ 67	Marshall Faulk	.50	.20
❑ 68	Fred Barnett	.10	.02
❑ 69	Quentin Coryatt	.10	.02
❑ 70	Dan Marino	2.00	.75
❑ 71	Junior Seau	.40	.15
❑ 72	Andre Coleman	.10	.02
❑ 73	Terry Kirby	.20	.07
❑ 74	Curtis Martin	.75	.30
❑ 75	Isaac Bruce	.40	.15
❑ 76	Mark Chmura	.20	.07
❑ 77	Edgar Bennett	.20	.07
❑ 78	Mario Bates	.20	.07
❑ 79	Eric Zeier	.10	.02
❑ 80	Adrian Murrell	.20	.07
❑ 81	Mark Brunell	.60	.25
❑ 82	Mark Rypien	.10	.02
❑ 83	Erric Pegram	.10	.02
❑ 84	Bryan Cox	.10	.02
❑ 85	Heath Shuler	.20	.07
❑ 86	Lake Dawson	.10	.02
❑ 87	O.J. McDuffie	.20	.07
❑ 88	Emmitt Smith	1.50	.60
❑ 89	Jim Harbaugh	.20	.07
❑ 90	Aaron Bailey	.10	.02
❑ 91	Jim Kelly	.40	.15
❑ 92	Rodney Hampton	.20	.07
❑ 93	Cris Carter	.40	.15
❑ 94	Henry Ellard	.10	.02
❑ 95	Darnay Scott	.20	.07
❑ 96	Daryl Johnston	.20	.07
❑ 97	Tamarick Vanover	.20	.07
❑ 98	Jeff Blake	.40	.15
❑ 99	Anthony Miller	.20	.07
❑ 100	Darren Woodson	.20	.07
❑ 101	Irving Fryar	.20	.07
❑ 102	Craig Heyward	.10	.02
❑ 103	Derek Loville	.10	.02
❑ 104	Ernie Mills	.10	.02
❑ 105	Brian Blades	.10	.02
❑ 106	Gus Frerotte	.20	.07
❑ 107	Alvin Harper	.10	.02
❑ 108	Tyrone Wheatley	.20	.07
❑ 109	John Elway	2.00	.75
❑ 110	Charles Haley	.20	.07
❑ 111	Terrell Fletcher	.10	.02
❑ 112	Vincent Brisby	.10	.02
❑ 113	Jerome Bettis	.40	.15
❑ 114	Barry Sanders	1.50	.60
❑ 115	Ken Norton Jr.	.10	.02
❑ 116	Sherman Williams	.10	.02
❑ 117	Antonio Freeman	.40	.15
❑ 118	Bert Emanuel	.20	.07
❑ 119	Marcus Allen	.40	.15
❑ 120	Stan Humphries	.20	.07
❑ 121	Chris Sanders	.20	.07
❑ 122	Jeff Graham	.10	.02
❑ 123	Jay Novacek	.10	.02
❑ 124	Aeneas Williams	.10	.02
❑ 125	Kordell Stewart	.40	.15
❑ 126	Steve Young	.75	.30
❑ 127	Jake Reed	.20	.07
❑ 128	Rick Mirer	.20	.07
❑ 129	Jeff Hostetler	.10	.02
❑ 130	Tim Brown	.40	.15
❑ 131	Shannon Sharpe	.20	.07
❑ 132	Dave Brown	.10	.02
❑ 133	Harvey Williams	.10	.02
❑ 134	Rodney Thomas	.10	.02
❑ 135	Frank Sanders	.20	.07
❑ 136	Brett Perriman	.10	.02
❑ 137	Steve Bono	.10	.02
❑ 138	Steve Atwater	.10	.02
❑ 139	Andre Rison	.20	.07
❑ 140	Orlando Thomas	.10	.02
❑ 141	Terry Allen	.20	.07
❑ 142	Carl Pickens	.20	.07
❑ 143	William Floyd	.20	.07
❑ 144	Bryce Paup	.10	.02
❑ 145	James O. Stewart	.20	.07
❑ 146	Eric Bjornson	.10	.02
❑ 147	Errict Rhett	.20	.07
❑ 148	Darick Holmes	.10	.02
❑ 149	Brian Mitchell	.10	.02
❑ 150	Brent Jones	.10	.02
❑ 151	Natrone Means	.20	.07
❑ 152	Rod Woodson	.20	.07
❑ 153	Bruce Smith	.20	.07
❑ 154	Deion Sanders	.60	.25
❑ 155	Kevin Williams	.10	.02
❑ 156	Erik Kramer	.10	.02
❑ 157	Jim Everett	.10	.02
❑ 158	Vinny Testaverde	.20	.07
❑ 159	Boomer Esiason	.20	.07
❑ 160	Leslie O'Neal	.10	.02
❑ 161	Curtis Conway	.40	.15
❑ 162	Thurman Thomas	.40	.15
❑ 163	Tony Brackens RC	.40	.15
❑ 164	Stepfret Williams RC	.20	.07
❑ 165	Alex Van Dyke RC	.20	.07
❑ 166	Cedric Jones RC	.10	.02
❑ 167	Stanley Pritchett RC	.20	.07
❑ 168	Willie Anderson RC	.10	.02
❑ 169	Regan Upshaw RC	.10	.02
❑ 170	Daryl Gardener RC	.10	.02
❑ 171	Alex Molden RC	.10	.02
❑ 172	John Mobley RC	.10	.02
❑ 173	Danny Kanell RC	.40	.15
❑ 174	Marco Battaglia RC	.10	.02
❑ 175	Simeon Rice RC	1.00	.40
❑ 176	Tony Banks RC	.40	.15
❑ 177	Stephen Davis RC	1.50	.60
❑ 178	Walt Harris RC	.10	.02
❑ 179	Amani Toomer RC	1.00	.40
❑ 180	Derrick Mayes RC	.40	.15
❑ 181	Jeff Lewis RC	.20	.07
❑ 182	Chris Darkins RC	.10	.02
❑ 183	Rickey Dudley RC	.40	.15
❑ 184	Jonathan Ogden RC	.40	.15

❑ 185 Mike Alstott RC 1.25 .50
❑ 186 Eric Moulds RC 1.50 .60
❑ 187 Karim Abdul-Jabbar RC .40 .15
❑ 188 Jerry Rice CL .40 .15
❑ 189 Dan Marino CL .40 .15
❑ 190 Emmitt Smith CL .40 .15

1997 Leaf

❑ COMPLETE SET (200) 25.00 10.00
❑ 1 Steve Young .75 .30
❑ 2 Brett Favre 2.50 1.00
❑ 3 Barry Sanders 2.00 .75
❑ 4 Drew Bledsoe .75 .30
❑ 5 Troy Aikman 1.25 .50
❑ 6 Kerry Collins .60 .25
❑ 7 Dan Marino 2.50 1.00
❑ 8 Jerry Rice 1.25 .50
❑ 9 John Elway 2.50 1.00
❑ 10 Emmitt Smith 2.00 .75
❑ 11 Tony Banks .40 .15
❑ 12 Gus Frerotte .25 .08
❑ 13 Elvis Grbac .40 .15
❑ 14 Neil O'Donnell .40 .15
❑ 15 Michael Irvin .60 .25
❑ 16 Marshall Faulk .75 .30
❑ 17 Todd Collins .25 .08
❑ 18 Scott Mitchell .40 .15
❑ 19 Trent Dilfer .60 .25
❑ 20 Rick Mirer .25 .08
❑ 21 Frank Sanders .40 .15
❑ 22 Larry Centers .40 .15
❑ 23 Brad Johnson .60 .25
❑ 24 Garrison Hearst .40 .15
❑ 25 Steve McNair .75 .30
❑ 26 Dorsey Levens .60 .25
❑ 27 Eric Metcalf .40 .15
❑ 28 Jeff George .40 .15
❑ 29 Rodney Hampton .40 .15
❑ 30 Michael Westbrook .40 .15
❑ 31 Cris Carter .60 .25
❑ 32 Heath Shuler .25 .08
❑ 33 Warren Moon .60 .25
❑ 34 Rod Woodson .40 .15
❑ 35 Ken Dilger .25 .08
❑ 36 Ben Coates .40 .15
❑ 37 Andre Reed .40 .15
❑ 38 Terrell Owens .75 .30
❑ 39 Jeff Blake .40 .15
❑ 40 Vinny Testaverde .40 .15
❑ 41 Robert Brooks .40 .15
❑ 42 Shannon Sharpe .40 .15
❑ 43 Terry Allen .60 .25
❑ 44 Terance Mathis .40 .15
❑ 45 Bobby Engram .40 .15
❑ 46 Rickey Dudley .40 .15
❑ 47 Alex Molden .25 .08
❑ 48 Lawrence Phillips .25 .08
❑ 49 Curtis Martin .75 .30
❑ 50 Jim Harbaugh .40 .15
❑ 51 Wayne Chrebet .60 .25
❑ 52 Quentin Coryatt .25 .08
❑ 53 Eddie George .60 .25
❑ 54 Michael Jackson .40 .15
❑ 55 Greg Lloyd .25 .08
❑ 56 Natrone Means .40 .15
❑ 57 Marcus Allen .60 .25
❑ 58 Desmond Howard .40 .15
❑ 59 Stan Humphries .40 .15
❑ 60 Reggie White .60 .25
❑ 61 Brett Perriman .25 .08
❑ 62 Warren Sapp .40 .15
❑ 63 Adrian Murrell .40 .15
❑ 64 Mark Brunell .75 .30
❑ 65 Carl Pickens .40 .15
❑ 66 Kordell Stewart .60 .25
❑ 67 Ricky Watters .40 .15
❑ 68 Tyrone Wheatley .40 .15
❑ 69 Stanley Pritchett .25 .08
❑ 70 Kevin Greene .40 .15
❑ 71 Karim Abdul-Jabbar .40 .15
❑ 72 Ki-Jana Carter .25 .08
❑ 73 Rashaan Salaam .25 .08
❑ 74 Simeon Rice .40 .15
❑ 75 Napoleon Kaufman .60 .25
❑ 76 Muhsin Muhammad .40 .15
❑ 77 Bruce Smith .40 .15
❑ 78 Eric Moulds .60 .25
❑ 79 O.J. McDuffie .40 .15
❑ 80 Danny Kanell .25 .08
❑ 81 Harvey Williams .25 .08
❑ 82 Greg Hill .25 .08
❑ 83 Terrell Davis .75 .30
❑ 84 Dan Wilkinson .25 .08
❑ 85 Yancey Thigpen .40 .15
❑ 86 Darrell Green .40 .15
❑ 87 Tamarick Vanover .40 .15
❑ 88 Mike Alstott .60 .25
❑ 89 Johnnie Morton .40 .15
❑ 90 Dale Carter .25 .08
❑ 91 Jerome Bettis .60 .25
❑ 92 James O.Stewart .40 .15
❑ 93 Irving Fryar .40 .15
❑ 94 Junior Seau .60 .25
❑ 95 Sean Dawkins .25 .08
❑ 96 J.J. Stokes .40 .15
❑ 97 Tim Biakabutuka .40 .15
❑ 98 Bert Emanuel .40 .15
❑ 99 Eddie Kennison .40 .15
❑ 100 Ray Zellars .25 .08
❑ 101 Dave Brown .25 .08
❑ 102 Leeland McElroy .25 .08
❑ 103 Chris Warren .40 .15
❑ 104 Byron Bam Morris .25 .08
❑ 105 Thurman Thomas .60 .25
❑ 106 Kyle Brady .25 .08
❑ 107 Anthony Miller .25 .08
❑ 108 Derrick Thomas .60 .25
❑ 109 Mark Chmura .40 .15
❑ 110 Deion Sanders .60 .25
❑ 111 Eric Swann .25 .08
❑ 112 Amani Toomer .40 .15
❑ 113 Raymont Harris .25 .08
❑ 114 Jake Reed .40 .15
❑ 115 Bryant Young .25 .08
❑ 116 Keenan McCardell .40 .15
❑ 117 Herman Moore .60 .25
❑ 118 Errict Rhett .25 .08
❑ 119 Henry Ellard .25 .08
❑ 120 Bobby Hoying .40 .15
❑ 121 Robert Smith .40 .15
❑ 122 Keyshawn Johnson .60 .25
❑ 123 Zach Thomas .60 .25
❑ 124 Charlie Garner .40 .15
❑ 125 Terry Kirby .40 .15
❑ 126 Darren Woodson .25 .08
❑ 127 Darnay Scott .40 .15
❑ 128 Chris Sanders .25 .08
❑ 129 Charles Johnson .40 .15
❑ 130 Joey Galloway .40 .15
❑ 131 Curtis Conway .40 .15
❑ 132 Isaac Bruce .60 .25
❑ 133 Bobby Taylor .25 .08
❑ 134 Jamal Anderson .60 .25
❑ 135 Ken Norton .25 .08
❑ 136 Darick Holmes .25 .08
❑ 137 Tony Brackens .25 .08
❑ 138 Tony Martin .40 .15
❑ 139 Antonio Freeman .60 .25
❑ 140 Neil Smith .40 .15
❑ 141 Terry Glenn .60 .25
❑ 142 Marvin Harrison .60 .25
❑ 143 Daryl Johnston .40 .15
❑ 144 Tim Brown .60 .25
❑ 145 Kimble Anders .40 .15
❑ 146 Derrick Alexander WR .40 .15
❑ 147 LeShon Johnson .25 .08
❑ 148 Anthony Johnson .25 .08
❑ 149 Leslie Shepherd .25 .08
❑ 150 Chris T. Jones .25 .08
❑ 151 Edgar Bennett .40 .15
❑ 152 Ty Detmer .40 .15
❑ 153 Ike Hilliard RC 1.00 .40
❑ 154 Jim Druckenmiller RC .40 .15
❑ 155 Warrick Dunn RC 1.50 .60
❑ 156 Yatil Green RC .40 .15
❑ 157 Reidel Anthony RC .60 .25
❑ 158 Antowain Smith RC 1.50 .60
❑ 159 Rae Carruth RC .25 .08
❑ 160 Tiki Barber RC 4.00 1.50
❑ 161 Byron Hanspard RC .40 .15
❑ 162 Jake Plummer RC 3.00 1.25
❑ 163 Joey Kent RC .60 .25
❑ 164 Corey Dillon RC 4.00 1.50
❑ 165 Kevin Lockett RC .40 .15
❑ 166 Will Blackwell RC .40 .15
❑ 167 Troy Davis RC .40 .15
❑ 168 James Farrior RC .60 .25
❑ 169 Danny Wuerffel RC .60 .25
❑ 170 Pat Barnes RC .60 .25
❑ 171 Darnell Autry RC .40 .15
❑ 172 Tom Knight RC .25 .08
❑ 173 David LaFleur RC .25 .08
❑ 174 Tony Gonzalez RC 2.00 .75
❑ 175 Kenny Holmes RC .60 .25
❑ 176 Reinard Wilson RC .40 .15
❑ 177 Renaldo Wynn RC .25 .08
❑ 178 Bryant Westbrook RC .25 .08
❑ 179 Darrell Russell RC .25 .08
❑ 180 Orlando Pace RC .60 .25
❑ 181 Shawn Springs RC .40 .15
❑ 182 Peter Boulware RC .60 .25
❑ 183 Dan Marino L 1.25 .50
❑ 184 Brett Favre L 1.25 .50
❑ 185 Emmitt Smith L 1.00 .40
❑ 186 Eddie George L .60 .25
❑ 187 Curtis Martin L .40 .15
❑ 188 Tim Brown L .40 .15
❑ 189 Mark Brunell L .60 .25
❑ 190 Isaac Bruce L .40 .15
❑ 191 Deion Sanders L .40 .15
❑ 192 John Elway L 1.25 .50
❑ 193 Jerry Rice L .60 .25
❑ 194 Barry Sanders L 1.00 .40
❑ 195 Herman Moore L .40 .15
❑ 196 Carl Pickens L .40 .15
❑ 197 Karim Abdul-Jabbar L .40 .15
❑ 198 Drew Bledsoe CL .60 .25
❑ 199 Troy Aikman CL .60 .25
❑ 200 Terrell Davis CL .60 .25

1999 Leaf Certified

❑ COMPLETE SET (225) 200.00 100.00
❑ COMP.SET w/o RCs 175) 40.00 15.00
❑ 1 Simeon Rice .60 .25
❑ 2 Frank Sanders .60 .25
❑ 3 Andre Wadsworth .40 .15
❑ 4 Larry Centers .40 .15
❑ 5 Byron Hanspard .40 .15
❑ 6 Terance Mathis .60 .25
❑ 7 O.J. Santiago .40 .15
❑ 8 Chris Calloway .40 .15
❑ 9 Michael Jackson .40 .15
❑ 10 Rod Woodson .60 .25
❑ 11 Pat Johnson .40 .15

❑	12	Rob Johnson	.60	.25
❑	13	Andre Reed	.60	.25
❑	14	Tim Biakabutuka	.60	.25
❑	15	Rae Carruth	.40	.15
❑	16	Fred Lane	.40	.15
❑	17	Muhsin Muhammad	.60	.25
❑	18	Wesley Walls	.60	.25
❑	19	Edgar Bennett	.40	.15
❑	20	Curtis Conway	.60	.25
❑	21	Bobby Engram	.60	.25
❑	22	Jeff Blake	.60	.25
❑	23	Darnay Scott	.40	.15
❑	24	Ty Detmer	.60	.25
❑	25	Sedrick Shaw	.40	.15
❑	26	Leslie Shepherd	.40	.15
❑	27	Terry Kirby	.40	.15
❑	28	Chris Warren	.40	.15
❑	29	Rocket Ismail	.60	.25
❑	30	Marcus Nash	.40	.15
❑	31	Neil Smith	.60	.25
❑	32	Bubby Brister	.40	.15
❑	33	Brian Griese	1.00	.40
❑	34	Germane Crowell	.40	.15
❑	35	Johnnie Morton	.60	.25
❑	36	Gus Frerotte	.40	.15
❑	37	Robert Brooks	.60	.25
❑	38	Mark Chmura	.40	.15
❑	39	Derrick Mayes	.40	.15
❑	40	Jerome Pathon	.40	.15
❑	41	Jimmy Smith	.60	.25
❑	42	James Stewart	.60	.25
❑	43	Tavian Banks	.40	.15
❑	44	Derrick Alexander WR	.60	.25
❑	45	Kimble Anders	.60	.25
❑	46	Elvis Grbac	.60	.25
❑	47	Derrick Thomas	1.00	.40
❑	48	Byron Bam Morris	.40	.15
❑	49	Tony Gonzalez	1.00	.40
❑	50	John Avery	.40	.15
❑	51	Tyrone Wheatley	.60	.25
❑	52	Zach Thomas	1.00	.40
❑	53	Lamar Thomas	.40	.15
❑	54	Jeff George	.60	.25
❑	55	John Randle	.60	.25
❑	56	Jake Reed	.60	.25
❑	57	Leroy Hoard	.40	.15
❑	58	Robert Edwards	.40	.15
❑	59	Ben Coates	.60	.25
❑	60	Tony Simmons	.40	.15
❑	61	Shawn Jefferson	.40	.15
❑	62	Eddie Kennison	.60	.25
❑	63	Lamar Smith	.60	.25
❑	64	Tiki Barber	1.00	.40
❑	65	Kerry Collins	.60	.25
❑	66	Ike Hilliard	.40	.15
❑	67	Gary Brown	.40	.15
❑	68	Joe Jurevicius	.60	.25
❑	69	Kent Graham	.40	.15
❑	70	Dedric Ward	.40	.15
❑	71	Terry Allen	.60	.25
❑	72	Neil O'Donnell	.60	.25
❑	73	Desmond Howard	.60	.25
❑	74	James Jett	.60	.25
❑	75	Jon Ritchie	.40	.15
❑	76	Rickey Dudley	.40	.15
❑	77	Charles Johnson	.40	.15
❑	78	Chris Fuamatu-Ma'afala	.40	.15
❑	79	Hines Ward	1.00	.40
❑	80	Ryan Leaf	1.00	.40
❑	81	Jim Harbaugh	.60	.25
❑	82	Junior Seau	1.00	.40
❑	83	Mikhael Ricks	.40	.15
❑	84	J.J. Stokes	.60	.25
❑	85	Ahman Green	1.00	.40
❑	86	Tony Banks	.60	.25
❑	87	Robert Holcombe	.40	.15
❑	88	Az-Zahir Hakim	.40	.15
❑	89	Greg Hill	.40	.15
❑	90	Trent Green	1.00	.40
❑	91	Eric Zeier	.40	.15
❑	92	Reidel Anthony	.60	.25
❑	93	Bert Emanuel	.60	.25
❑	94	Warren Sapp	.40	.15
❑	95	Kevin Dyson	.60	.25
❑	96	Yancey Thigpen	.40	.15
❑	97	Frank Wycheck	.40	.15
❑	98	Michael Westbrook	.60	.25
❑	99	Albert Connell	.40	.15
❑	100	Darrell Green	.40	.15
❑	101	Rob Moore	.60	.25
❑	102	Adrian Murrell	.60	.25
❑	103	Jake Plummer	1.00	.40
❑	104	Chris Chandler	.60	.25
❑	105	Jamal Anderson	1.00	.40
❑	106	Tim Dwight	1.00	.40
❑	107	Jermaine Lewis	1.00	.40
❑	108	Priest Holmes	2.50	1.00
❑	109	Bruce Smith	1.00	.40
❑	110	Eric Moulds	1.00	.40
❑	111	Antowain Smith	1.50	.60
❑	112	Curtis Enis	1.00	.40
❑	113	Corey Dillon	1.50	.60
❑	114	Michael Irvin	1.00	.40
❑	115	Ed McCaffrey	1.00	.40
❑	116	Shannon Sharpe	1.00	.40
❑	117	Terrell Davis	1.50	.60
❑	118	Charlie Batch	1.50	.60
❑	119	Antonio Freeman	1.00	.40
❑	120	Dorsey Levens	1.00	.40
❑	121	Marvin Harrison	1.50	.60
❑	122	Peyton Manning	5.00	2.00
❑	123	Keenan McCardell	1.00	.40
❑	124	Fred Taylor	1.50	.60
❑	125	Andre Rison	1.00	.40
❑	126	O.J. McDuffie	1.00	.40
❑	127	Karim Abdul-Jabbar	1.00	.40
❑	128	Randy Moss	4.00	1.50
❑	129	Terry Glenn	1.00	.40
❑	130	Vinny Testaverde	1.00	.40
❑	131	Keyshawn Johnson	1.00	.40
❑	132	Curtis Martin	1.00	.40
❑	133	Wayne Chrebet	1.00	.40
❑	134	Napoleon Kaufman	1.00	.40
❑	135	Charles Woodson	1.00	.40
❑	136	Duce Staley	1.50	.60
❑	137	Kordell Stewart	1.00	.40
❑	138	Terrell Owens	1.50	.60
❑	139	Ricky Watters	1.00	.40
❑	140	Joey Galloway	1.00	.40
❑	141	Jon Kitna	1.00	.40
❑	142	Isaac Bruce	1.50	.60
❑	143	Jacquez Green	1.00	.40
❑	144	Warrick Dunn	1.00	.40
❑	145	Mike Alstott	1.00	.40
❑	146	Trent Dilfer	1.00	.40
❑	147	Steve McNair	1.00	.40
❑	148	Eddie George	1.50	.60
❑	149	Skip Hicks	1.00	.40
❑	150	Brad Johnson	1.50	.60
❑	151	Doug Flutie	1.50	.60
❑	152	Thurman Thomas	1.00	.40
❑	153	Carl Pickens	1.00	.40
❑	154	Emmitt Smith	5.00	2.00
❑	155	Troy Aikman	5.00	2.00
❑	156	Deion Sanders	1.50	.60
❑	157	John Elway	8.00	3.00
❑	158	Rod Smith	1.00	.40
❑	159	Barry Sanders	8.00	3.00
❑	160	Herman Moore	1.50	.60
❑	161	Brett Favre	8.00	3.00
❑	162	Mark Brunell	1.50	.60
❑	163	Warren Moon	1.50	.60
❑	164	Dan Marino	8.00	3.00
❑	165	Randall Cunningham	1.50	.60
❑	166	Robert Smith	1.50	.60
❑	167	Cris Carter	1.50	.60
❑	168	Drew Bledsoe	3.00	1.25
❑	169	Tim Brown	1.50	.60
❑	170	Jerome Bettis	1.50	.60
❑	171	Natrone Means	1.00	.40
❑	172	Jerry Rice	5.00	2.00
❑	173	Steve Young	3.00	1.25
❑	174	Garrison Hearst	1.50	.60
❑	175	Marshall Faulk	3.00	1.25
❑	176	David Boston RC	5.00	2.00
❑	177	Jeff Paulk RC	2.00	.75
❑	178	Reginald Kelly RC	2.00	.75
❑	179	Scott Covington RC	5.00	2.00
❑	180	Chris McAlister RC	3.00	1.25
❑	181	Shawn Bryson RC	5.00	2.00
❑	182	Peerless Price RC	5.00	2.00
❑	183	Cade McNown RC	3.00	1.25
❑	184	Michael Bishop RC	5.00	2.00
❑	185	D'Wayne Bates RC	3.00	1.25
❑	186	Marty Booker RC	5.00	2.00
❑	187	Akili Smith RC	2.00	.75
❑	188	Craig Yeast RC	3.00	1.25
❑	189	Tim Couch RC	5.00	2.00
❑	190	Kevin Johnson RC	5.00	2.00
❑	191	Wane McGarity RC	2.00	.75
❑	192	Olandis Gary RC	5.00	2.00
❑	193	Travis McGriff RC	2.00	.75
❑	194	Sedrick Irvin RC	2.00	.75
❑	195	Chris Claiborne RC	2.00	.75
❑	196	De'Mond Parker RC	2.00	.75
❑	197	Dee Miller RC	2.00	.75
❑	198	Edgerrin James RC	15.00	6.00
❑	199	Mike Cloud RC	3.00	1.25
❑	200	Larry Parker RC	5.00	2.00
❑	201	Cecil Collins RC	2.00	.75
❑	202	James Johnson RC	3.00	1.25
❑	203	Rob Konrad RC	5.00	2.00
❑	204	Daunte Culpepper RC	15.00	6.00
❑	205	Jim Kleinsasser RC	5.00	2.00
❑	206	Kevin Faulk RC	5.00	2.00
❑	207	Andy Katzenmoyer RC	3.00	1.25
❑	208	Ricky Williams RC	8.00	3.00
❑	209	Joe Montgomery RC	3.00	1.25
❑	210	Sean Bennett RC	2.00	.75
❑	211	Dameane Douglas RC	5.00	2.00
❑	212	Donovan McNabb RC	20.00	7.50
❑	213	Na Brown RC	3.00	1.25
❑	214	Amos Zereoue RC	5.00	2.00
❑	215	Troy Edwards RC	3.00	1.25
❑	216	Jermaine Fazande RC	3.00	1.25
❑	217	Tai Streets RC	5.00	2.00
❑	218	Brock Huard RC	5.00	2.00
❑	219	Charlie Rogers RC	3.00	1.25
❑	220	Karsten Bailey RC	3.00	1.25
❑	221	Joe Germaine RC	3.00	1.25
❑	222	Torry Holt RC	10.00	4.00
❑	223	Shaun King RC	3.00	1.25
❑	224	Jevon Kearse RC	8.00	3.00
❑	225	Champ Bailey RC	6.00	2.50

2000 Leaf Certified

❑		COMP.SET w/o RC's (150)	40.00	15.00
❑	1	Frank Sanders	.40	.15
❑	2	Rob Moore	.60	.25
❑	3	Simeon Rice	.60	.25
❑	4	David Boston	1.00	.40
❑	5	Tim Dwight	1.00	.40
❑	6	Jamal Anderson	1.00	.40
❑	7	Chris Chandler	.40	.15

- ❑ 8 Terance Mathis .60 .25
- ❑ 9 Priest Holmes 1.25 .50
- ❑ 10 Rod Woodson .60 .25
- ❑ 11 Tony Banks .40 .15
- ❑ 12 Jermaine Lewis .40 .15
- ❑ 13 Shannon Sharpe .40 .15
- ❑ 14 Qadry Ismail .60 .25
- ❑ 15 Doug Flutie 1.00 .40
- ❑ 16 Antowain Smith .60 .25
- ❑ 17 Peerless Price .60 .25
- ❑ 18 Rob Johnson .40 .15
- ❑ 19 Muhsin Muhammad .60 .25
- ❑ 20 Wesley Walls .40 .15
- ❑ 21 Tim Biakabutuka .40 .15
- ❑ 22 Steve Beuerlein .40 .15
- ❑ 23 Patrick Jeffers .40 .15
- ❑ 24 Natrone Means .40 .15
- ❑ 25 Curtis Enis .40 .15
- ❑ 26 Bobby Engram .40 .15
- ❑ 27 Marcus Robinson 1.00 .40
- ❑ 28 Eddie Kennison .40 .15
- ❑ 29 Marty Booker .60 .25
- ❑ 30 Damay Scott .40 .15
- ❑ 31 Carl Pickens .40 .15
- ❑ 32 Karim Abdul-Jabbar .40 .15
- ❑ 33 Errict Rhett .40 .15
- ❑ 34 Darrin Chiaverini .40 .15
- ❑ 35 Randall Cunningham .40 .15
- ❑ 36 Michael Irvin .40 .15
- ❑ 37 Rocket Ismail .40 .15
- ❑ 38 Ed McCaffrey 1.00 .40
- ❑ 39 Rod Smith .40 .15
- ❑ 40 Herman Moore .60 .25
- ❑ 41 Johnnie Morton .40 .15
- ❑ 42 James Stewart .40 .15
- ❑ 43 Bill Schroeder .60 .25
- ❑ 44 Ahman Green 1.00 .40
- ❑ 45 Terrence Wilkins .40 .15
- ❑ 46 Keenan McCardell .40 .15
- ❑ 47 Derrick Alexander .40 .15
- ❑ 48 Elvis Grbac .40 .15
- ❑ 49 Tony Gonzalez .40 .15
- ❑ 50 O.J. McDuffie .40 .15
- ❑ 51 Tony Martin .40 .15
- ❑ 52 James Johnson .40 .15
- ❑ 53 Thurman Thomas .40 .15
- ❑ 54 Jay Fiedler 1.00 .40
- ❑ 55 Damon Huard .40 .15
- ❑ 56 Leroy Hoard .40 .15
- ❑ 57 Terry Glenn .60 .25
- ❑ 58 Kevin Faulk .40 .15
- ❑ 59 Jeff Blake .40 .15
- ❑ 60 Jake Reed .40 .15
- ❑ 61 Amani Toomer .40 .15
- ❑ 62 Kerry Collins .40 .15
- ❑ 63 Ike Hilliard .40 .15
- ❑ 64 Joe Montgomery .40 .15
- ❑ 65 Vinny Testaverde .40 .15
- ❑ 66 Wayne Chrebet .40 .15
- ❑ 67 Ray Lucas .60 .25
- ❑ 68 Napoleon Kaufman .60 .25
- ❑ 69 Charles Woodson .40 .15
- ❑ 70 Tyrone Wheatley .40 .15
- ❑ 71 Rich Gannon 1.00 .40
- ❑ 72 Duce Staley 1.00 .40
- ❑ 73 Kordell Stewart .60 .25
- ❑ 74 Jerome Bettis 1.00 .40
- ❑ 75 Troy Edwards .40 .15
- ❑ 76 Junior Seau 1.00 .40
- ❑ 77 Jim Harbaugh .40 .15
- ❑ 78 Curtis Conway .60 .25
- ❑ 79 Jermaine Fazande .40 .15
- ❑ 80 Terrell Owens 1.00 .40
- ❑ 81 Charlie Garner .60 .25
- ❑ 82 Garrison Hearst .40 .15
- ❑ 83 Jeff Garcia 1.00 .40
- ❑ 84 Derrick Mayes .40 .15
- ❑ 85 Az-Zahir Hakim .40 .15
- ❑ 86 Mike Alstott 1.00 .40
- ❑ 87 Warrick Dunn 1.00 .40
- ❑ 88 Jacquez Green .40 .15
- ❑ 89 Warren Sapp .40 .15
- ❑ 90 Yancey Thigpen .40 .15
- ❑ 91 Kevin Dyson .40 .15
- ❑ 92 Frank Wycheck .40 .15
- ❑ 93 Jevon Kearse 1.00 .40
- ❑ 94 Adrian Murrell .40 .15
- ❑ 95 Bruce Smith .40 .15
- ❑ 96 Michael Westbrook .40 .15
- ❑ 97 Albert Connell .40 .15
- ❑ 98 Champ Bailey .60 .25
- ❑ 99 Jeff George .40 .15
- ❑ 100 Deion Sanders 1.00 .40
- ❑ 101 Jake Plummer 1.00 .40
- ❑ 102 Eric Moulds 1.50 .60
- ❑ 103 Cade McNown .40 .15
- ❑ 104 Corey Dillon 1.50 .60
- ❑ 105 Akili Smith .60 .25
- ❑ 106 Tim Couch 1.00 .40
- ❑ 107 Kevin Johnson 1.50 .60
- ❑ 108 Emmitt Smith 3.00 1.25
- ❑ 109 Troy Aikman 3.00 1.25
- ❑ 110 Joey Galloway 1.00 .40
- ❑ 111 John Elway 5.00 2.00
- ❑ 112 Terrell Davis 1.00 .40
- ❑ 113 Olandis Gary 1.50 .60
- ❑ 114 Brian Griese 1.00 .40
- ❑ 115 Charlie Batch 1.50 .60
- ❑ 116 Barry Sanders 4.00 1.50
- ❑ 117 Germane Crowell .60 .25
- ❑ 118 Brett Favre 5.00 2.00
- ❑ 119 Dorsey Levens .60 .25
- ❑ 120 Antonio Freeman 1.50 .60
- ❑ 121 Peyton Manning 4.00 1.50
- ❑ 122 Edgerrin James 2.50 1.00
- ❑ 123 Marvin Harrison 1.50 .60
- ❑ 124 Mark Brunell 1.00 .40
- ❑ 125 Fred Taylor 1.00 .40
- ❑ 126 Jimmy Smith 1.00 .40
- ❑ 127 Dan Marino 5.00 2.00
- ❑ 128 Randy Moss 3.00 1.25
- ❑ 129 Daunte Culpepper 2.00 .75
- ❑ 130 Cris Carter 1.50 .60
- ❑ 131 Robert Smith 1.50 .60
- ❑ 132 Drew Bledsoe 2.00 .75
- ❑ 133 Ricky Williams 1.00 .40
- ❑ 134 Curtis Martin 1.50 .60
- ❑ 135 Tim Brown 1.50 .60
- ❑ 136 Donovan McNabb 2.50 1.00
- ❑ 137 Jerry Rice 3.00 1.25
- ❑ 138 Steve Young 2.00 .75
- ❑ 139 Jon Kitna 1.50 .60
- ❑ 140 Ricky Watters .60 .25
- ❑ 141 Kurt Warner 3.00 1.25
- ❑ 142 Marshall Faulk 2.00 .75
- ❑ 143 Torry Holt 1.50 .60
- ❑ 144 Isaac Bruce 1.50 .60
- ❑ 145 Shaun King .40 .15
- ❑ 146 Keyshawn Johnson 1.50 .60
- ❑ 147 Eddie George 1.00 .40
- ❑ 148 Steve McNair 1.50 .60
- ❑ 149 Stephen Davis 1.50 .60
- ❑ 150 Brad Johnson 1.50 .60
- ❑ 151 Rogers Beckett RC 4.00 1.50
- ❑ 152 Erik Flowers RC 4.00 1.50
- ❑ 153 Demario Brown RC 2.50 1.00
- ❑ 154 Doug Johnson RC 5.00 2.00
- ❑ 155 Deon Grant RC 4.00 1.50
- ❑ 156 Ian Gold RC 4.00 1.50
- ❑ 157 Brian Urlacher RC 20.00 7.50
- ❑ 158 Frank Murphy RC 2.50 1.00
- ❑ 159 James Whalen RC 2.50 1.00
- ❑ 160 JaJuan Dawson RC 2.50 1.00
- ❑ 161 William Bartee RC 4.00 1.50
- ❑ 162 Aaron Shea RC 1.00 .40
- ❑ 163 Deltha O'Neal RC 5.00 2.00
- ❑ 164 Jarious Jackson RC 4.00 1.50
- ❑ 165 Muneer Moore RC 2.50 1.00
- ❑ 166 Hank Poteat RC 4.00 1.50
- ❑ 167 Jacoby Shepherd RC 2.50 1.00
- ❑ 168 Ben Kelly RC 2.50 1.00
- ❑ 169 Orantes Grant RC 2.50 1.00
- ❑ 170 Chris Hovan RC 4.00 1.50
- ❑ 171 Leon Murray RC 2.50 1.00
- ❑ 172 Marc Bulger RC 10.00 4.00
- ❑ 173 Chad Morton RC 5.00 2.00
- ❑ 174 Na'il Diggs RC 4.00 1.50
- ❑ 175 Shaun Ellis RC 5.00 2.00
- ❑ 176 John Abraham RC 5.00 2.00
- ❑ 177 Fred Robbins RC 2.50 1.00
- ❑ 178 Marcus Knight RC 4.00 1.50
- ❑ 179 Thomas Hamner RC 2.50 1.00
- ❑ 180 Cornelius Griffin RC 4.00 1.50
- ❑ 181 Raynoch Thompson RC 4.00 1.50
- ❑ 182 Paul Smith RC 4.00 1.50
- ❑ 183 Ahmed Plummer RC 5.00 2.00
- ❑ 184 John Engelberger RC 4.00 1.50
- ❑ 185 Darren Howard RC 4.00 1.50
- ❑ 186 Corey Moore RC 2.50 1.00
- ❑ 187 Joe Hamilton RC 4.00 1.50
- ❑ 188 Rob Morris RC 4.00 1.50
- ❑ 189 Keith Bulluck RC 5.00 2.00
- ❑ 190 Todd Husak RC 5.00 2.00
- ❑ 191 Mareno Philyaw RC 3.00 1.25
- ❑ 192 Kwame Cavil RC 3.00 1.25
- ❑ 193 Sammy Morris RC 5.00 2.00
- ❑ 194 Avion Black RC 5.00 2.00
- ❑ 195 Bashir Yamini RC 3.00 1.25
- ❑ 196 Curtis Keaton RC 5.00 2.00
- ❑ 197 Mike Anderson RC 8.00 3.00
- ❑ 198 Bubba Franks RC 6.00 2.50
- ❑ 199 Anthony Lucas RC 3.00 1.25
- ❑ 200 Rondell Mealey RC 3.00 1.25
- ❑ 201 Terrelle Smith RC 5,00 2.00
- ❑ 202 Frank Moreau RC 5.00 2.00
- ❑ 203 Deon Dyer RC 5.00 2.00
- ❑ 204 Quinton Spotwood RC 3.00 1.25
- ❑ 205 Troy Walters RC 10.00 4.00
- ❑ 206 Doug Chapman RC 5.00 2.00
- ❑ 207 Tom Brady RC 80.00 40.00
- ❑ 208 Sherrod Gideon RC 3.00 1.25
- ❑ 209 Ron Dixon RC 5.00 2.00
- ❑ 210 Anthony Becht RC 6.00 2.50
- ❑ 211 James Williams RC 5.00 2.00
- ❑ 212 Sebastian Janikowski RC 6.00 2.50
- ❑ 213 Corey Simon RC 6.00 2.50
- ❑ 214 Gari Scott RC 3.00 1.25
- ❑ 215 Dante Hall RC 12.00 5.00
- ❑ 216 Tim Rattay RC 6.00 2.50
- ❑ 217 Chafie Fields RC 3.00 1.25
- ❑ 218 Trung Canidate RC 5.00 2.00
- ❑ 219 Chris Coleman RC 6.00 2.50
- ❑ 220 Erron Kinney RC 6.00 2.50
- ❑ 221 Thomas Jones RC 15.00 6.00
- ❑ 222 Travis Taylor RC 10.00 4.00
- ❑ 223 Chris Redman RC 8.00 3.00
- ❑ 224 Jamal Lewis RC 25.00 10.00
- ❑ 225 Dez White RC 10.00 4.00
- ❑ 226 Peter Warrick RC 10.00 4.00
- ❑ 227 Ron Dugans RC 8.00 3.00
- ❑ 228 Courtney Brown RC 10.00 4.00
- ❑ 229 Travis Prentice RC 8.00 3.00
- ❑ 230 Dennis Northcutt RC 10.00 4.00
- ❑ 231 Michael Wiley RC 8.00 3.00

❑ 232 Chris Cole RC 8.00 3.00
❑ 233 Reuben Droughns RC 12.00 5.00
❑ 234 R.Jay Soward RC 8.00 3.00
❑ 235 Shyrone Stith RC 8.00 3.00
❑ 236 Sylvester Morris RC 8.00 3.00
❑ 237 J.R. Redmond RC 8.00 3.00
❑ 238 Ron Dayne RC 10.00 4.00
❑ 239 Chad Pennington RC 25.00 10.00
❑ 240 Laveranues Coles RC 12.00 5.00
❑ 241 Jerry Porter RC 12.00 5.00
❑ 242 Todd Pinkston RC 10.00 4.00
❑ 243 Plaxico Burress RC 20.00 7.50
❑ 244 Danny Farmer RC 8.00 3.00
❑ 245 Tee Martin RC 10.00 4.00
❑ 246 Trevor Gaylor RC 8.00 3.00
❑ 247 Giovanni Carmazzi RC 8.00 3.00
❑ 248 Darrell Jackson RC 20.00 7.50
❑ 249 Shaun Alexander RC 50.00 20.00
❑ 250 Chris Samuels RC 8.00 3.00

2001 Leaf Certified Materials

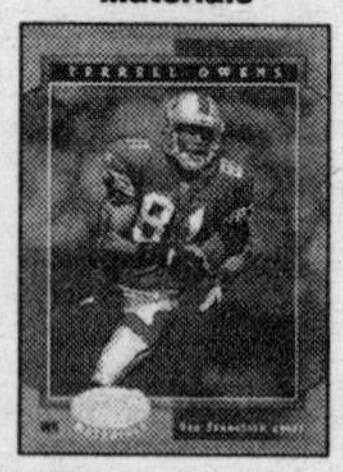

❑ COMP.SET w/o SPs (100) 30.00 12.50
❑ 1 Aaron Brooks 1.00 .40
❑ 2 Ahman Green 1.00 .40
❑ 3 Akili Smith .40 .15
❑ 4 Amani Toomer .60 .25
❑ 5 Antonio Freeman 1.00 .40
❑ 6 Barry Sanders 2.00 .75
❑ 7 Brad Johnson 1.00 .40
❑ 8 Brett Favre 3.00 1.25
❑ 9 Brian Griese 1.00 .40
❑ 10 Brian Urlacher 1.50 .60
❑ 11 Bruce Smith .40 .15
❑ 12 Cade McNown .40 .15
❑ 13 Chad Pennington 1.50 .60
❑ 14 Charlie Batch 1.00 .40
❑ 15 Charlie Garner .60 .25
❑ 16 Corey Dillon 1.00 .40
❑ 17 Cris Carter 1.00 .40
❑ 18 Curtis Martin 1.00 .40
❑ 19 Dan Marino 3.00 1.25
❑ 20 Darrell Jackson .40 .15
❑ 21 Daunte Culpepper 1.00 .40
❑ 22 David Boston 1.00 .40
❑ 23 Derrick Alexander .60 .25
❑ 24 Donovan McNabb 1.25 .50
❑ 25 Dorsey Levens .60 .25
❑ 26 Doug Flutie 1.00 .40
❑ 27 Drew Bledsoe 1.25 .50
❑ 28 Ed McCaffrey 1.00 .40
❑ 29 Eddie George 1.00 .40
❑ 30 Edgerrin James 1.25 .50
❑ 31 Elvis Grbac .60 .25
❑ 32 Emmitt Smith 2.00 .75
❑ 33 Eric Moulds 1.00 .40
❑ 34 Frank Wycheck .40 .15
❑ 35 Fred Taylor 1.00 .40
❑ 36 Ike Hilliard .60 .25
❑ 37 Isaac Bruce 1.00 .40
❑ 38 Jacquez Green .40 .15
❑ 39 Jake Plummer .60 .25
❑ 40 Jamal Anderson 1.00 .40
❑ 41 Jamal Lewis 1.50 .60
❑ 42 James Stewart .60 .25
❑ 43 Jay Fiedler 1.00 .40
❑ 44 Jeff Garcia 1.00 .40
❑ 45 Jeff George .60 .25
❑ 46 Jerome Bettis 1.00 .40
❑ 47 Jerry Rice 2.00 .75
❑ 48 Jevon Kearse .60 .25
❑ 49 Jimmy Smith .60 .25
❑ 50 Joe Horn .60 .25
❑ 51 Joey Galloway .60 .25
❑ 52 John Elway 3.00 1.25
❑ 53 Junior Seau 1.00 .40
❑ 54 Keenan McCardell .40 .15
❑ 55 Kerry Collins 1.00 .40
❑ 56 Keyshawn Johnson 1.00 .40
❑ 57 Kurt Warner 2.00 .75
❑ 58 Lamar Smith .60 .25
❑ 59 Laveranues Coles 1.00 .40
❑ 60 Marcus Robinson 1.00 .40
❑ 61 Mark Brunell 1.00 .40
❑ 62 Marshall Faulk 1.25 .50
❑ 63 Marvin Harrison 1.00 .40
❑ 64 Matt Hasselbeck .60 .25
❑ 65 Mike Alstott 1.00 .40
❑ 66 Mike Anderson 1.00 .40
❑ 67 Muhsin Muhammad .60 .25
❑ 68 Peter Warrick 1.00 .40
❑ 69 Peyton Manning 2.50 1.00
❑ 70 Plaxico Burress 1.00 .40
❑ 71 Randy Moss 2.00 .75
❑ 72 Ray Lewis 1.00 .40
❑ 73 Rich Gannon 1.00 .40
❑ 74 Ricky Watters .60 .25
❑ 75 Ricky Williams 1.00 .40
❑ 76 Rob Johnson 1.00 .40
❑ 77 Rod Smith .60 .25
❑ 78 Ron Dayne 1.00 .40
❑ 79 Shannon Sharpe .60 .25
❑ 80 Shaun Alexander 1.25 .50
❑ 81 Stephen Davis 1.00 .40
❑ 82 Steve McNair 1.00 .40
❑ 83 Steve Young 1.00 .40
❑ 84 Sylvester Morris .40 .15
❑ 85 Terrell Davis 1.00 .40
❑ 86 Terrell Owens 1.00 .40
❑ 87 Terry Glenn .60 .25
❑ 88 Thomas Jones .60 .25
❑ 89 Tiki Barber 1.00 .40
❑ 90 Tim Brown 1.00 .40
❑ 91 Tim Couch .60 .25
❑ 92 Tony Gonzalez .60 .25
❑ 93 Torry Holt 1.00 .40
❑ 94 Travis Taylor .60 .25
❑ 95 Troy Aikman 1.50 .60
❑ 96 Tyrone Wheatley .60 .25
❑ 97 Vinny Testaverde .60 .25
❑ 98 Warren Sapp .60 .25
❑ 99 Warrick Dunn 1.00 .40
❑ 100 Wayne Chrebet .60 .25
❑ 101 Chris Taylor RC 6.00 2.50
❑ 102 Ken-Yon Rambo RC 6.00 2.50
❑ 103 Correll Buckhalter RC 12.00 5.00
❑ 104 A.J. Feeley RC 10.00 4.00
❑ 105 Josh Booty RC 10.00 4.00
❑ 106 LaMont Jordan RC 25.00 10.00
❑ 107 Alge Crumpler RC 12.00 5.00
❑ 108 Jamal Reynolds RC 10.00 4.00
❑ 109 Nate Clements RC 10.00 4.00
❑ 110 Will Allen RC 6.00 2.50
❑ 111 Santana Moss FF RC 25.00 10.00
❑ 112 Chad Johnson FF RC 40.00 15.00
❑ 113 Chris Chambers FF RC 25.00 10.00
❑ 114 David Terrell FF RC 15.00 6.00
❑ 115 Freddie Mitchell FF RC 15.00 6.00
❑ 116 Koren Robinson FF RC 15.00 6.00
❑ 117 Quincy Morgan FF RC 15.00 6.00
❑ 118 Reggie Wayne FF RC 30.00 12.50
❑ 119 Robert Ferguson FF RC 15.00 6.00
❑ 120 Rod Gardner FF RC 15.00 6.00
❑ 121 Snoop Minnis FF RC 10.00 4.00
❑ 122 Josh Heupel FF RC 15.00 6.00
❑ 123 Anthony Thomas FF RC 15.00 6.00
❑ 124 Deuce McAllister FF RC 30.00 12.50
❑ 125 James Jackson FF RC 15.00 6.00
❑ 126 Travis Minor FF RC 10.00 4.00
❑ 127 Kevan Barlow FF RC 15.00 6.00
❑ 128 LaDain Tomlinson FF RC 60.00 30.00
❑ 129 Todd Heap FF RC 15.00 6.00
❑ 130 Michael Bennett FF RC 25.00 10.00
❑ 131 Rudi Johnson FF RC 30.00 12.50
❑ 132 Travis Henry FF RC 15.00 6.00
❑ 133 Michael Vick FF RC 80.00 30.00
❑ 134 Drew Brees FF RC 40.00 15.00
❑ 135 Chris Weinke FF RC 15.00 6.00
❑ 136 Quincy Carter FF RC 15.00 6.00
❑ 137 Mike McMahon FF RC 15.00 6.00
❑ 138 Jesse Palmer FF RC 15.00 6.00
❑ 139 Marq Tuiasosopo FF RC 15.00 6.00
❑ 140 Dan Morgan FF RC 15.00 6.00
❑ 141 Gerard Warren FF RC 15.00 6.00
❑ 142 Leonard Davis FF RC 10.00 4.00
❑ 143 Andre Carter FF RC 15.00 6.00
❑ 144 Justin Smith FF RC 15.00 6.00
❑ 145 Sage Rosenfels FF RC 15.00 6.00

2002 Leaf Certified

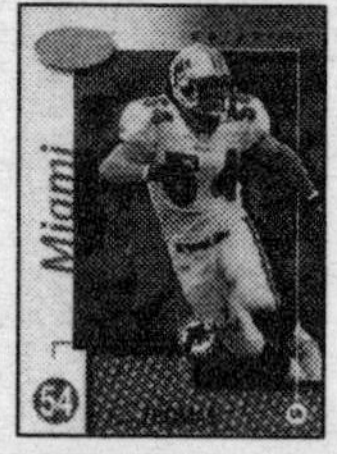

❑ COMP.SET w/o SP's (100) 25.00 10.00
❑ 1 David Boston 1.00 .40
❑ 2 Jake Plummer .60 .25
❑ 3 Michael Vick 3.00 1.25
❑ 4 Jamal Anderson .60 .25
❑ 5 Chris Redman .40 .15
❑ 6 Ray Lewis 1.00 .40
❑ 7 Eric Moulds .60 .25
❑ 8 Travis Henry 1.00 .40
❑ 9 Nate Clements .40 .15
❑ 10 Chris Weinke .60 .25
❑ 11 Muhsin Muhammad .60 .25
❑ 12 Wesley Walls .40 .15
❑ 13 Anthony Thomas .60 .25
❑ 14 Brian Urlacher 1.50 .60
❑ 15 Dez White .40 .15
❑ 16 Corey Dillon .60 .25
❑ 17 Peter Warrick .60 .25
❑ 18 Tim Couch .60 .25
❑ 19 Kevin Johnson .60 .25
❑ 20 James Jackson .40 .15
❑ 21 Emmitt Smith 2.50 1.00
❑ 22 Quincy Carter .60 .25
❑ 23 Brian Griese 1.00 .40
❑ 24 Ed McCaffrey 1.00 .40
❑ 25 Rod Smith .60 .25
❑ 26 Terrell Davis 1.00 .40
❑ 27 Mike Anderson 1.00 .40
❑ 28 Germane Crowell .40 .15
❑ 29 James Stewart .60 .25
❑ 30 Charlie Batch .60 .25
❑ 31 Antonio Freeman 1.00 .40
❑ 32 Brett Favre 2.50 1.00
❑ 33 Ahman Green 1.00 .40
❑ 34 LeRoy Butler .40 .15
❑ 35 Edgerrin James 1.25 .50
❑ 36 Marvin Harrison 1.00 .40
❑ 37 Peyton Manning 2.00 .75

❑ 38 Fred Taylor 1.00 .40
❑ 39 Jimmy Smith .60 .25
❑ 40 Mark Brunell 1.00 .40
❑ 41 Keenan McCardell .40 .15
❑ 42 Tony Gonzalez .60 .25
❑ 43 Priest Holmes 1.25 .50
❑ 44 Jay Fiedler .60 .25
❑ 45 Chris Chambers 1.00 .40
❑ 46 Zach Thomas 1.00 .40
❑ 47 Travis Minor .40 .15
❑ 48 Cris Carter 1.00 .40
❑ 49 Daunte Culpepper 1.00 .40
❑ 50 Randy Moss 2.00 .75
❑ 51 Drew Bledsoe 1.25 .50
❑ 52 Tom Brady 2.50 1.00
❑ 53 Antowain Smith .60 .25
❑ 54 Troy Brown .40 .15
❑ 55 Aaron Brooks 1.00 .40
❑ 56 Ricky Williams 1.00 .40
❑ 57 Ron Dayne .60 .25
❑ 58 Kerry Collins .60 .25
❑ 59 Michael Strahan .60 .25
❑ 60 Amani Toomer .60 .25
❑ 61 Chad Pennington 1.25 .50
❑ 62 Curtis Martin 1.00 .40
❑ 63 Vinny Testaverde .60 .25
❑ 64 Wayne Chrebet .60 .25
❑ 65 Charles Woodson .60 .25
❑ 66 Rich Gannon 1.00 .40
❑ 67 Tim Brown 1.00 .40
❑ 68 Jerry Rice 2.00 .75
❑ 69 Tyrone Wheatley .60 .25
❑ 70 Donovan McNabb 1.25 .50
❑ 71 Duce Staley 1.00 .40
❑ 72 Todd Pinkston .60 .25
❑ 73 Correll Buckhalter .60 .25
❑ 74 Jerome Bettis 1.00 .40
❑ 75 Kordell Stewart .60 .25
❑ 76 Plaxico Burress .60 .25
❑ 77 Hines Ward 1.00 .40
❑ 78 Junior Seau 1.00 .40
❑ 79 LaDainian Tomlinson 1.50 .60
❑ 80 Doug Flutie 1.00 .40
❑ 81 Terrell Owens 1.00 .40
❑ 82 Jeff Garcia 1.00 .40
❑ 83 Ricky Watters .60 .25
❑ 84 Shaun Alexander 1.25 .50
❑ 85 Koren Robinson .60 .25
❑ 86 Isaac Bruce 1.00 .40
❑ 87 Kurt Warner 1.00 .40
❑ 88 Marshall Faulk 1.00 .40
❑ 89 Torry Holt 1.00 .40
❑ 90 Keyshawn Johnson 1.00 .40
❑ 91 Mike Alstott 1.00 .40
❑ 92 Warren Sapp .60 .25
❑ 93 Brad Johnson .60 .25
❑ 94 Eddie George 1.00 .40
❑ 95 Jevon Kearse .60 .25
❑ 96 Steve McNair 1.00 .40
❑ 97 Derrick Mason .60 .25
❑ 98 Frank Wycheck .40 .15
❑ 99 Champ Bailey .60 .25
❑ 100 Stephen Davis .60 .25
❑ 101 Ladell Betts JSY RC 8.00 3.00
❑ 102 Antonio Bryant JSY RC 8.00 3.00
❑ 103 Reche Caldwell JSY RC 8.00 3.00
❑ 104 David Carr JSY RC 20.00 7.50
❑ 105 Tim Carter JSY RC 5.00 2.00
❑ 106 Eric Crouch JSY RC 8.00 3.00
❑ 107 Rohan Davey JSY RC 8.00 3.00
❑ 108 Andre Davis JSY RC 5.00 2.00
❑ 109 T.J. Duckett JSY RC 12.00 5.00
❑ 110 DeShaun Foster JSY RC 8.00 3.00
❑ 111 Jabar Gaffney JSY RC 8.00 3.00
❑ 112 Daniel Graham JSY RC 8.00 3.00
❑ 113 William Green FB RC 8.00 3.00
❑ 114 Joey Harrington JSY RC 20.00 7.50
❑ 115 David Garrard JSY RC 10.00 4.00
❑ 116 Ron Johnson JSY RC 5.00 2.00
❑ 117 Ashley Lelie JSY RC 15.00 6.00
❑ 118 Josh McCown JSY RC 10.00 4.00
❑ 119 Maurice Morris JSY RC 8.00 3.00
❑ 120 Julius Peppers JSY RC 15.00 6.00
❑ 121 Clinton Portis JSY RC 25.00 10.00
❑ 122 Patrick Ramsey JSY RC 10.00 4.00
❑ 123 Antwaan Randle El JSY RC 12.00 5.00
❑ 124 Josh Reed JSY RC 8.00 3.00
❑ 125 Cliff Russell JSY RC 5.00 2.00
❑ 126 Jeremy Shockey JSY RC 25.00 10.00
❑ 127 Donte Stallworth JSY RC 15.00 6.00
❑ 128 Travis Stephens JSY RC 5.00 2.00
❑ 129 Javon Walker JSY RC 15.00 6.00
❑ 130 Marquise Walker JSY RC 5.00 2.00
❑ 131 Roy Williams JSY RC 20.00 7.50
❑ 132 Mike Williams JSY RC 5.00 2.00

2003 Leaf Certified Materials

❑ COMP.SET w/o SP's (150) 30.00 12.50
❑ 1 Jake Plummer .60 .25
❑ 2 David Boston .60 .25
❑ 3 MarTay Jenkins .40 .15
❑ 4 Marcel Shipp .60 .25
❑ 5 Michael Vick 2.50 1.00
❑ 6 T.J. Duckett .60 .25
❑ 7 Chris Redman .40 .15
❑ 8 Ray Lewis 1.00 .40
❑ 9 Jamal Lewis 1.00 .40
❑ 10 Eric Moulds .60 .25
❑ 11 Nate Clements .40 .15
❑ 12 Travis Henry .60 .25
❑ 13 Drew Bledsoe 1.00 .40
❑ 14 Peerless Price .60 .25
❑ 15 Josh Reed .60 .25
❑ 16 Wesley Walls .40 .15
❑ 17 Muhsin Muhammad .60 .25
❑ 18 Julius Peppers 1.00 .40
❑ 19 Dez White .40 .15
❑ 20 Mike Brown .60 .25
❑ 21 Brian Urlacher 1.50 .60
❑ 22 Anthony Thomas .60 .25
❑ 23 David Terrell .60 .25
❑ 24 Corey Dillon .60 .25
❑ 25 Peter Warrick .60 .25
❑ 26 Josh McCown .60 .25
❑ 27 Dennis Northcutt .60 .25
❑ 28 Kevin Johnson .60 .25
❑ 29 Tim Couch .40 .15
❑ 30 Gerard Warren .40 .15
❑ 31 William Green .60 .25
❑ 32 Antonio Bryant .60 .25
❑ 33 Darren Woodson .40 .15
❑ 34 Emmitt Smith 2.50 1.00
❑ 35 Quincy Carter .60 .25
❑ 36 Roy Williams 1.00 .40
❑ 37 Brian Griese 1.00 .40
❑ 38 Ed McCaffrey 1.00 .40
❑ 39 Mike Anderson .60 .25
❑ 40 Rod Smith .60 .25
❑ 41 Clinton Portis 1.50 .60
❑ 42 Ashley Lelie 1.00 .40
❑ 43 Cory Schlesinger .40 .15
❑ 44 Germane Crowell .40 .15
❑ 45 James Stewart .60 .25
❑ 46 Scotty Anderson .40 .15
❑ 47 Joey Harrington 1.50 .60
❑ 48 Brett Favre 2.50 1.00
❑ 49 Terry Glenn .40 .15
❑ 50 Ahman Green 1.00 .40
❑ 51 Donald Driver .60 .25
❑ 52 Javon Walker .60 .25
❑ 53 David Carr 1.50 .60
❑ 54 Ron Dayne .40 .15
❑ 55 Terrell Davis 1.00 .40
❑ 56 Edgerrin James 1.00 .40
❑ 57 Marvin Harrison 1.00 .40
❑ 58 Peyton Manning 1.50 .60
❑ 59 Fred Taylor 1.00 .40
❑ 60 Jimmy Smith .60 .25
❑ 61 Kyle Brady .40 .15
❑ 62 Mark Brunell .60 .25
❑ 63 Tony Gonzalez .60 .25
❑ 64 Priest Holmes 1.25 .50
❑ 65 Trent Green .60 .25
❑ 66 Jason Taylor .40 .15
❑ 67 Jay Fiedler .60 .25
❑ 68 Zach Thomas 1.00 .40
❑ 69 Chris Chambers 1.00 .40
❑ 70 Ricky Williams 1.00 .40
❑ 71 Randy McMichael .60 .25
❑ 72 Daunte Culpepper 1.00 .40
❑ 73 Randy Moss 1.50 .60
❑ 74 Michael Bennett .60 .25
❑ 75 Ty Law .60 .25
❑ 76 Tom Brady 2.50 1.00
❑ 77 Troy Brown .60 .25
❑ 78 Antowain Smith .60 .25
❑ 79 Aaron Brooks 1.00 .40
❑ 80 Donte Stallworth 1.00 .40
❑ 81 Joe Horn .60 .25
❑ 82 Deuce McAllister 1.00 .40
❑ 83 Amani Toomer .60 .25
❑ 84 Kerry Collins .60 .25
❑ 85 Michael Strahan .60 .25
❑ 86 Tiki Barber 1.00 .40
❑ 87 Jeremy Shockey 1.50 .60
❑ 88 Chad Pennington 1.25 .50
❑ 89 Curtis Martin 1.00 .40
❑ 90 Laveranues Coles .60 .25
❑ 91 Vinny Testaverde .60 .25
❑ 92 Santana Moss .60 .25
❑ 93 Charles Woodson .60 .25
❑ 94 Sebastian Janikowski .40 .15
❑ 95 Tim Brown 1.00 .40
❑ 96 Rich Gannon .60 .25
❑ 97 Jerry Rice 2.00 .75
❑ 98 Donovan McNabb 1.25 .50
❑ 99 Duce Staley .60 .25
❑ 100 Todd Pinkston .40 .15
❑ 101 Chad Lewis .40 .15
❑ 102 A.J. Feeley .40 .15
❑ 103 Jerome Bettis 1.00 .40
❑ 104 Plaxico Burress .60 .25
❑ 105 Hines Ward 1.00 .40
❑ 106 Antwaan Randle El 1.00 .40
❑ 107 Kendrell Bell .60 .25
❑ 108 Junior Seau 1.00 .40
❑ 109 LaDainian Tomlinson 1.00 .40
❑ 110 Doug Flutie 1.00 .40
❑ 111 Drew Brees 1.00 .40
❑ 112 Terrell Owens 1.00 .40
❑ 113 Jeff Garcia 1.00 .40
❑ 114 Garrison Hearst .60 .25
❑ 115 Koren Robinson .60 .25
❑ 116 Shaun Alexander 1.00 .40
❑ 117 Isaac Bruce 1.00 .40
❑ 118 Kurt Warner 1.00 .40
❑ 119 Marshall Faulk 1.00 .40
❑ 120 Torry Holt 1.00 .40
❑ 121 Keyshawn Johnson 1.00 .40
❑ 122 Warren Sapp .60 .25
❑ 123 Mike Alstott 1.00 .40
❑ 124 Brad Johnson .60 .25
❑ 125 Eddie George .60 .25

❑ 126 Jevon Kearse .60 .25
❑ 127 Steve McNair 1.00 .40
❑ 128 Derrick Mason .60 .25
❑ 129 Keith Bulluck .40 .15
❑ 130 Champ Bailey .60 .25
❑ 131 Darrell Green .40 .15
❑ 132 Stephen Davis .60 .25
❑ 133 Rod Gardner .60 .25
❑ 134 Barry Sanders 2.50 1.00
❑ 135 Cris Carter 1.00 .40
❑ 136 Dan Marino 5.00 2.00
❑ 137 Deion Sanders 1.25 .50
❑ 138 Jim Kelly 2.00 .75
❑ 139 Joe Montana 6.00 2.50
❑ 140 John Elway 5.00 2.00
❑ 141 Marcus Allen 1.25 .50
❑ 142 Reggie White 1.00 .40
❑ 143 Sterling Sharpe 1.00 .40
❑ 144 Steve Young 1.50 .60
❑ 145 Thurman Thomas 1.00 .40
❑ 146 Troy Aikman 2.00 .75
❑ 147 Warren Moon 1.00 .40
❑ 148 Drew Bledsoe 1.00 .40
❑ 149 Jerry Rice 2.00 .75
❑ 150 Ricky Williams 1.00 .40
❑ 151 Carson Palmer JSY RC 30.00 12.50
❑ 152 Byron Leftwich JSY RC 25.00 10.00
❑ 153 Kyle Boller JSY RC 15.00 6.00
❑ 154 Rex Grossman JSY RC 12.00 5.00
❑ 155 Dave Ragone JSY RC 8.00 3.00
❑ 156 Kliff Kingsbury JSY RC 8.00 3.00
❑ 157 Seneca Wallace JSY RC 8.00 3.00
❑ 158 Larry Johnson JSY RC 30.00 15.00
❑ 159 Willis McGahee JSY RC 20.00 7.50
❑ 160 Justin Fargas JSY RC 8.00 3.00
❑ 161 Onterrio Smith JSY RC 8.00 3.00
❑ 162 Chris Brown JSY RC 10.00 4.00
❑ 163 Musa Smith JSY RC 8.00 3.00
❑ 164 Artose Pinner JSY RC 8.00 3.00
❑ 165 Andre Johnson JSY RC 15.00 6.00
❑ 166 Kelley Washington JSY RC 8.00 3.00
❑ 167 Taylor Jacobs JSY RC 8.00 3.00
❑ 168 Bryant Johnson JSY RC 8.00 3.00
❑ 169 Tyrone Calico JSY RC 10.00 4.00
❑ 170 Anquan Boldin JSY RC 20.00 7.50
❑ 171 Bethel Johnson JSY RC 8.00 3.00
❑ 172 Nate Burleson JSY RC 10.00 4.00
❑ 173 Kevin Curtis JSY RC 8.00 3.00
❑ 174 Dallas Clark JSY RC 8.00 3.00
❑ 175 Teyo Johnson JSY RC 8.00 3.00
❑ 176 Terrell Suggs JSY RC 12.00 5.00
❑ 177 DeWayne Robertson JSY RC 8.00 3.00
❑ 178 Brian St.Pierre JSY RC 8.00 3.00
❑ 179 Terence Newman JSY RC 15.00 6.00
❑ 180 Marcus Trufant JSY RC 8.00 3.00

2004 Leaf Certified Materials

❑ COMP.SET w/o SP's (150) 30.00 12.50
❑ 151-200 PRINT RUN 1000 SER.#'d SETS
❑ 201-233 PRINT RUN 1250 SER.#'d SETS
❑ UNPRICED MIRROR BLACK #'d OF 1
❑ UNPRICED MIRROR EMERALD #'d OF 5
❑ 1 Anquan Boldin 1.00 .40
❑ 2 Emmitt Smith 2.00 .75
❑ 3 Josh McCown .60 .25
❑ 4 Marcel Shipp .60 .25
❑ 5 Michael Vick 2.00 .75
❑ 6 Peerless Price .60 .25
❑ 7 T.J. Duckett .60 .25
❑ 8 Warrick Dunn .60 .25
❑ 9 Jamal Lewis 1.00 .40
❑ 10 Kyle Boller 1.00 .40
❑ 11 Ray Lewis 1.00 .40
❑ 12 Terrell Suggs .60 .25
❑ 13 Todd Heap .60 .25
❑ 14 Drew Bledsoe 1.00 .40
❑ 15 Eric Moulds .60 .25
❑ 16 Travis Henry .60 .25
❑ 17 Julius Peppers 1.00 .40
❑ 18 Muhsin Muhammad .60 .25
❑ 19 Stephen Davis .60 .25
❑ 20 Anthony Thomas .60 .25
❑ 21 Brian Urlacher 1.25 .50
❑ 22 Rex Grossman 1.00 .40
❑ 23 Chad Johnson 1.00 .40
❑ 24 Corey Dillon .60 .25
❑ 25 Peter Warrick .60 .25
❑ 26 Jeff Garcia 1.00 .40
❑ 27 Tim Couch .40 .15
❑ 28 William Green .60 .25
❑ 29 Antonio Bryant .60 .25
❑ 30 Keyshawn Johnson .60 .25
❑ 31 Quincy Carter .60 .25
❑ 32 Roy Williams S .60 .25
❑ 33 Terence Newman .60 .25
❑ 34 Ashley Lelie .60 .25
❑ 35 Ed McCaffrey .60 .25
❑ 36 Jake Plummer .60 .25
❑ 37 Mike Anderson .60 .25
❑ 38 Rod Smith .60 .25
❑ 39 Charles Rogers .60 .25
❑ 40 Joey Harrington 1.00 .40
❑ 41 Ahman Green 1.00 .40
❑ 42 Brett Favre 2.50 1.00
❑ 43 Donald Driver .60 .25
❑ 44 Javon Walker .60 .25
❑ 45 Robert Ferguson .40 .15
❑ 46 Andre Johnson 1.00 .40
❑ 47 David Carr 1.00 .40
❑ 48 Edgerrin James 1.00 .40
❑ 49 Marvin Harrison 1.00 .40
❑ 50 Peyton Manning 1.50 .60
❑ 51 Reggie Wayne .60 .25
❑ 52 Byron Leftwich 1.25 .50
❑ 53 Fred Taylor .60 .25
❑ 54 Jimmy Smith .60 .25
❑ 55 Dante Hall 1.00 .40
❑ 56 Priest Holmes 1.25 .50
❑ 57 Tony Gonzalez .60 .25
❑ 58 Trent Green .60 .25
❑ 59 A.J. Feeley 1.00 .40
❑ 60 Chris Chambers .60 .25
❑ 61 David Boston .60 .25
❑ 62 Jason Taylor .40 .15
❑ 63 Jay Fiedler .40 .15
❑ 64 Junior Seau 1.00 .40
❑ 65 Randy McMichael .40 .15
❑ 66 Ricky Williams 1.00 .40
❑ 67 Zach Thomas 1.00 .40
❑ 68 Daunte Culpepper 1.00 .40
❑ 69 Michael Bennett .60 .25
❑ 70 Randy Moss 1.25 .50
❑ 71 Tom Brady 2.50 1.00
❑ 72 Troy Brown .60 .25
❑ 73 Ty Law .60 .25
❑ 74 Aaron Brooks .60 .25
❑ 75 Deuce McAllister 1.00 .40
❑ 76 Donte Stallworth .60 .25
❑ 77 Amani Toomer .60 .25
❑ 78 Jeremy Shockey 1.00 .40
❑ 79 Kerry Collins .60 .25
❑ 80 Michael Strahan .60 .25
❑ 81 Tiki Barber 1.00 .40
❑ 82 Chad Pennington 1.00 .40
❑ 83 Curtis Martin 1.00 .40
❑ 84 Justin McCareins .40 .15
❑ 85 Santana Moss .60 .25
❑ 86 Charles Woodson .60 .25
❑ 87 Jerry Rice 2.00 .75
❑ 88 Rich Gannon .60 .25
❑ 89 Tim Brown 1.00 .40
❑ 90 Warren Sapp .60 .25
❑ 91 Correll Buckhalter .60 .25
❑ 92 Donovan McNabb 1.25 .50
❑ 93 Freddie Mitchell .60 .25
❑ 94 Jevon Kearse .60 .25
❑ 95 Terrell Owens 1.00 .40
❑ 96 Antwaan Randle El 1.00 .40
❑ 97 Duce Staley .60 .25
❑ 98 Hines Ward 1.00 .40
❑ 99 Jerome Bettis 1.00 .40
❑ 100 Plaxico Burress .60 .25
❑ 101 Doug Flutie 1.00 .40
❑ 102 LaDainian Tomlinson 1.25 .50
❑ 103 Koren Robinson .60 .25
❑ 104 Matt Hasselbeck .60 .25
❑ 105 Shaun Alexander 1.00 .40
❑ 106 Isaac Bruce .60 .25
❑ 107 Kurt Warner 1.00 .40
❑ 108 Marc Bulger 1.00 .40
❑ 109 Marshall Faulk 1.00 .40
❑ 110 Torry Holt 1.00 .40
❑ 111 Brad Johnson .60 .25
❑ 112 Mike Alstott .60 .25
❑ 113 Derrick Mason .60 .25
❑ 114 Drew Bennett .60 .25
❑ 115 Eddie George .60 .25
❑ 116 Frank Wycheck .40 .15
❑ 117 Keith Bulluck .40 .15
❑ 118 Steve McNair 1.00 .40
❑ 119 Tyrone Calico .60 .25
❑ 120 Clinton Portis 1.00 .40
❑ 121 LaVar Arrington 2.00 .75
❑ 122 Laveranues Coles .60 .25
❑ 123 Mark Brunell .60 .25
❑ 124 Patrick Ramsey .60 .25
❑ 125 Rod Gardner .60 .25
❑ 126 Jake Plummer FLB .60 .25
❑ 127 Thomas Jones FLB .60 .25
❑ 128 Priest Holmes FLB 1.25 .50
❑ 129 Jim Kelly FLB 2.00 .75
❑ 130 Doug Flutie FLB 1.00 .40
❑ 131 Walter Payton FLB 6.00 2.50
❑ 132 Troy Aikman FLB 2.50 1.00
❑ 133 John Elway FLB 4.00 1.50
❑ 134 Barry Sanders FLB 3.00 1.25
❑ 135 Mark Brunell FLB .60 .25
❑ 136 Earl Campbell FLB 1.50 .60
❑ 137 Joe Montana FLB 6.00 2.50
❑ 138 Dan Marino FLB 5.00 2.00
❑ 139 Curtis Martin FLB 1.00 .40
❑ 140 Drew Bledsoe FLB 1.00 .40
❑ 141 Ricky Williams FLB 1.00 .40
❑ 142 Junior Seau FLB 1.00 .40
❑ 143 Charlie Garner FLB .60 .25
❑ 144 Jerry Rice FLB 2.00 .75
❑ 145 Ahman Green FLB 1.00 .40
❑ 146 Jerome Bettis FLB 1.00 .40
❑ 147 Trent Green FLB .60 .25
❑ 148 Warrick Dunn FLB .60 .25
❑ 149 Deion Sanders FLB 1.50 .60
❑ 150 Stephen Davis FLB .60 .25
❑ 151 Adimchinobe Echemandu AU RC 10.00 4.00
❑ 152 Ahmad Carroll RC 8.00 3.00
❑ 153 Andy Hall AU RC 10.00 4.00
❑ 154 B.J. Johnson AU RC 10.00 4.00
❑ 155 B.J. Symons AU RC 15.00 6.00
❑ 156 Bradlee Van Pelt AU RC 30.00 15.00
❑ 157 Brandon Miree AU RC 10.00 4.00
❑ 158 Bruce Perry AU RC 15.00 6.00
❑ 159 Carlos Francis AU RC 10.00 4.00
❑ 160 Casey Bramlet AU RC 10.00 4.00

❑ 161 Chris Gamble RC 8.00 3.00
❑ 162 Clarence Moore AU RC 15.00 6.00
❑ 163 Cody Pickett AU RC 15.00 6.00
❑ 164 Craig Krenzel AU RC 15.00 6.00
❑ 165 D.J. Hackett RC 5.00 2.00
❑ 166 D.J. Williams RC 8.00 3.00
❑ 167 Derrick Ward AU RC 8.00 3.00
❑ 168 Drew Carter AU RC 15.00 6.00
❑ 169 Ernest Wilford RC 6.00 2.50
❑ 170 Drew Henson RC 6.00 2.50
❑ 171 Jamaar Taylor AU RC 15.00 6.00
❑ 172 Jared Lorenzen AU RC 10.00 4.00
❑ 173 Jarrett Payton AU RC 20.00 10.00
❑ 174 Jason Babin AU RC EXCH 15.00 6.00
❑ 175 Jeff Smoker AU RC 15.00 6.00
❑ 176 Jeris McIntyre AU RC 10.00 4.00
❑ 177 Jerricho Cotchery RC 6.00 2.50
❑ 178 Jim Sorgi AU RC 15.00 6.00
❑ 179 John Navarre AU RC 15.00 6.00
❑ 180 Patrick Crayton AU RC 15.00 6.00
❑ 181 Johnnie Morant RC 6.00 2.50
❑ 182 Sean Taylor RC 8.00 3.00
❑ 183 Jonathan Vilma RC 6.00 2.50
❑ 184 Josh Harris RC 6.00 2.50
❑ 185 Kenechi Udeze RC 8.00 3.00
❑ 186 Mark Jones AU RC 10.00 4.00
❑ 187 Matt Mauck AU RC 15.00 6.00
❑ 188 Maurice Mann AU RC 10.00 4.00
❑ 189 Michael Turner RC 6.00 2.50
❑ 190 P.K. Sam RC 5.00 2.00
❑ 191 Quincy Wilson RC 5.00 2.00
❑ 192 Ran Carthon AU RC 10.00 4.00
❑ 193 Ryan Krause AU RC 10.00 4.00
❑ 194 Samie Parker RC 6.00 2.50
❑ 195 Sloan Thomas AU RC 10.00 4.00
❑ 196 Tommie Harris RC 6.00 2.50
❑ 197 Triandos Luke AU RC 15.00 6.00
❑ 198 Troy Fleming AU RC 10.00 4.00
❑ 199 Vince Wilfork RC 8.00 3.00
❑ 200 Will Smith RC 6.00 2.50
❑ 201 Larry Fitzgerald JSY RC 20.00 7.50
❑ 202 DeAngelo Hall JSY RC 10.00 4.00
❑ 203 Matt Schaub JSY RC 10.00 4.00
❑ 204 Michael Jenkins JSY RC 8.00 3.00
❑ 205 Devard Darling JSY RC 8.00 3.00
❑ 206 J.P. Losman JSY RC 12.00 5.00
❑ 207 Lee Evans JSY RC 10.00 4.00
❑ 208 Keary Colbert JSY RC 10.00 4.00
❑ 209 Bernard Berrian JSY RC 8.00 3.00
❑ 210 Chris Perry JSY RC 10.00 4.00
❑ 211 Kellen Winslow JSY RC 12.00 5.00
❑ 212 Luke McCown JSY RC 8.00 3.00
❑ 213 Julius Jones JSY RC 25.00 10.00
❑ 214 Darius Watts JSY RC 8.00 3.00
❑ 215 Tatum Bell JSY RC 12.00 5.00
❑ 216 Kevin Jones JSY RC 20.00 7.50
❑ 217 Roy Williams JSY RC 15.00 6.00
❑ 218 Dunta Robinson JSY RC 8.00 3.00
❑ 219 Greg Jones JSY RC 10.00 4.00
❑ 220 Reggie Williams JSY RC 10.00 4.00
❑ 221 Mewelde Moore JSY RC 10.00 4.00
❑ 222 Ben Watson JSY RC 8.00 3.00
❑ 223 Cedric Cobbs JSY RC 8.00 3.00
❑ 224 Devery Henderson JSY RC 8.00 3.00
❑ 225 Eli Manning JSY RC 30.00 15.00
❑ 226 Robert Gallery JSY RC 10.00 4.00
❑ 227 Ben Roethlisberger JSY RC 50.00 25.00
❑ 228 Philip Rivers JSY RC 20.00 10.00
❑ 229 Derrick Hamilton JSY RC 8.00 3.00
❑ 230 Rashaun Woods JSY RC 8.00 3.00
❑ 231 Steven Jackson JSY RC 20.00 7.50
❑ 232 Michael Clayton JSY RC 12.00 5.00
❑ 233 Ben Troupe JSY RC 8.00 3.00

2005 Leaf Certified Materials

❑ COMPLETE SET (229)
❑ COMP.SET w/o RCs (150) 40.00 15.00
❑ 151-200 PRINT RUN 1000 SER.#'d SETS
❑ UNPRICED MIR.BLACK PRINT RUN 1 SET

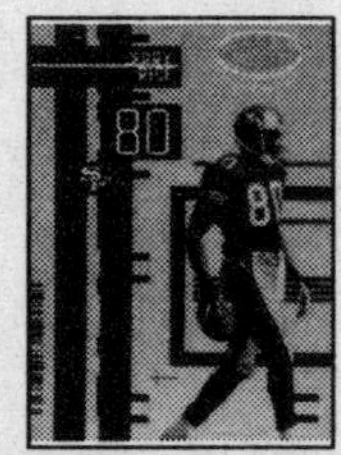

❑ UNPRICED MIR.EMERALD PRINT RUN 5 SETS
❑ 1 Anquan Boldin .60 .25
❑ 2 Josh McCown .60 .25
❑ 3 Larry Fitzgerald 1.00 .40
❑ 4 Michael Vick 1.50 .60
❑ 5 Peerless Price .50 .20
❑ 6 T.J. Duckett .60 .25
❑ 7 Warrick Dunn .60 .25
❑ 8 Jamal Lewis 1.00 .40
❑ 9 Kyle Boller .60 .25
❑ 10 Todd Heap .60 .25
❑ 11 Ray Lewis 1.00 .40
❑ 12 Terrell Suggs .60 .25
❑ 13 Drew Bledsoe 1.00 .40
❑ 14 Eric Moulds .60 .25
❑ 15 J.P. Losman 1.00 .40
❑ 16 Lee Evans .60 .25
❑ 17 Willis McGahee 1.00 .40
❑ 18 DeShaun Foster .60 .25
❑ 19 Jake Delhomme 1.00 .40
❑ 20 Steve Smith .60 .25
❑ 21 Brian Urlacher 1.00 .40
❑ 22 Rex Grossman .60 .25
❑ 23 Carson Palmer 1.00 .40
❑ 24 Chad Johnson 1.00 .40
❑ 25 Rudi Johnson .60 .25
❑ 26 Kellen Winslow Jr. 1.00 .40
❑ 27 Kelly Holcomb .50 .20
❑ 28 Lee Suggs .60 .25
❑ 29 William Green .50 .20
❑ 30 Julius Jones 1.25 .50
❑ 31 Keyshawn Johnson .60 .25
❑ 32 Roy Williams S .60 .25
❑ 33 Terence Newman .50 .20
❑ 34 Ashley Lelie .60 .25
❑ 35 Champ Bailey .60 .25
❑ 36 Darius Watts .60 .25
❑ 37 Jake Plummer .60 .25
❑ 38 Tatum Bell .60 .25
❑ 39 Charles Rogers .60 .25
❑ 40 Joey Harrington 1.00 .40
❑ 41 Kevin Jones 1.00 .40
❑ 42 Roy Williams WR 1.00 .40
❑ 43 Ahman Green 1.00 .40
❑ 44 Brett Favre 2.50 1.00
❑ 45 Javon Walker .60 .25
❑ 46 Robert Ferguson .50 .20
❑ 47 Andre Johnson .60 .25
❑ 48 David Carr 1.00 .40
❑ 49 Domanick Davis .60 .25
❑ 50 Dallas Clark .50 .20
❑ 51 Edgerrin James 1.00 .40
❑ 52 Marvin Harrison 1.00 .40
❑ 53 Peyton Manning 1.50 .60
❑ 54 Reggie Wayne .60 .25
❑ 55 Byron Leftwich 1.00 .40
❑ 56 Fred Taylor .60 .25
❑ 57 Jimmy Smith .60 .25
❑ 58 Reggie Williams .60 .25
❑ 59 Priest Holmes 1.00 .40
❑ 60 Tony Gonzalez .60 .25
❑ 61 Trent Green .60 .25
❑ 62 Chris Chambers .60 .25
❑ 63 Jason Taylor .50 .20
❑ 64 Junior Seau .60 .25
❑ 65 Zach Thomas 1.00 .40
❑ 66 Daunte Culpepper 1.00 .40
❑ 67 Michael Bennett .60 .25
❑ 68 Randy Moss 1.00 .40
❑ 69 Corey Dillon .60 .25
❑ 70 Tom Brady 2.50 1.00
❑ 71 Deion Branch .60 .25
❑ 72 Aaron Brooks .60 .25
❑ 73 Deuce McAllister 1.00 .40
❑ 74 Donte Stallworth .60 .25
❑ 75 Joe Horn .60 .25
❑ 76 Eli Manning 2.00 .75
❑ 77 Jeremy Shockey 1.00 .40
❑ 78 Michael Strahan .60 .25
❑ 79 Tiki Barber 1.00 .40
❑ 80 Anthony Becht .50 .20
❑ 81 Chad Pennington 1.00 .40
❑ 82 Curtis Martin 1.00 .40
❑ 83 Justin McCareins .50 .20
❑ 84 Laveranues Coles .60 .25
❑ 85 Santana Moss .60 .25
❑ 86 Shaun Ellis .50 .20
❑ 87 Jerry Porter .60 .25
❑ 88 Brian Westbrook .60 .25
❑ 89 Chad Lewis .50 .20
❑ 90 Donovan McNabb 1.25 .50
❑ 91 Freddie Mitchell .50 .20
❑ 92 Hugh Douglas .50 .20
❑ 93 Jevon Kearse .60 .25
❑ 94 Terrell Owens 1.00 .40
❑ 95 Todd Pinkston .50 .20
❑ 96 Antwaan Randle El .60 .25
❑ 97 Ben Roethlisberger 2.50 1.00
❑ 98 Duce Staley .60 .25
❑ 99 Hines Ward 1.00 .40
❑ 100 Jerome Bettis 1.00 .40
❑ 101 Antonio Gates 1.00 .40
❑ 102 Drew Brees 1.00 .40
❑ 103 LaDainian Tomlinson 1.25 .50
❑ 104 Kevan Barlow .60 .25
❑ 105 Darrell Jackson .60 .25
❑ 106 Koren Robinson .60 .25
❑ 107 Matt Hasselbeck .60 .25
❑ 108 Shaun Alexander 1.25 .50
❑ 109 Marc Bulger 1.00 .40
❑ 110 Steven Jackson 1.25 .50
❑ 111 Torry Holt 1.00 .40
❑ 112 Michael Clayton 1.00 .40
❑ 113 Chris Brown .60 .25
❑ 114 Drew Bennett .60 .25
❑ 115 Keith Bulluck .50 .20
❑ 116 Steve McNair 1.00 .40
❑ 117 Clinton Portis 1.00 .40
❑ 118 LaVar Arrington 1.00 .40
❑ 119 John Riggins 1.25 .50
❑ 120 Sean Taylor .60 .25
❑ 121 Jake Plummer .60 .25
❑ 122 Thomas Jones .60 .25
❑ 123 Doug Flutie 1.00 .40
❑ 124 Walter Payton 4.00 1.50
❑ 125 Corey Dillon .60 .25
❑ 126 Troy Aikman 1.50 .60
❑ 127 Terrell Davis 1.25 .50
❑ 128 Marshall Faulk 1.00 .40
❑ 129 Dan Marino 3.00 1.25
❑ 130 Thurman Thomas 1.00 .40
❑ 131 Warren Moon 1.00 .40
❑ 132 Curtis Martin 1.00 .40
❑ 133 Drew Bledsoe 1.00 .40
❑ 134 Kerry Collins .60 .25
❑ 135 Keyshawn Johnson .60 .25
❑ 136 A.J. Feeley .60 .25
❑ 137 Duce Staley .60 .25
❑ 138 Junior Seau .60 .25
❑ 139 Jerry Rice 2.00 .75
❑ 140 Steve Young 1.50 .60
❑ 141 Jerome Bettis 1.00 .40
❑ 142 Kurt Warner .60 .25

❑ 143 Trent Green .60 .25
❑ 144 Keyshawn Johnson .60 .25
❑ 145 Warren Sapp .60 .25
❑ 146 Warrick Dunn .60 .25
❑ 147 Jevon Kearse .60 .25
❑ 148 Deion Sanders 1.50 .60
❑ 149 Laveranues Coles .60 .25
❑ 150 Stephen Davis .60 .25
❑ 151 Cedric Benson RC 10.00 4.00
❑ 152 Mike Williams 10.00 4.00
❑ 153 DeMarcus Ware RC 8.00 3.00
❑ 154 Shawne Merriman RC 8.00 3.00
❑ 155 Thomas Davis RC 5.00 2.00
❑ 156 Derrick Johnson RC 8.00 3.00
❑ 157 Travis Johnson RC 4.00 1.50
❑ 158 David Pollack RC 5.00 2.00
❑ 159 Erasmus James RC 5.00 2.00
❑ 160 Marcus Spears RC 5.00 2.00
❑ 161 Fabian Washington RC 5.00 2.00
❑ 162 Aaron Rodgers RC 15.00 6.00
❑ 163 Marlin Jackson RC 5.00 2.00
❑ 164 Heath Miller RC 12.00 5.00
❑ 165 Matt Roth RC 5.00 2.00
❑ 166 Dan Cody RC 5.00 2.00
❑ 167 Bryant McFadden RC 5.00 2.00
❑ 168 Chris Henry RC 5.00 2.00
❑ 169 David Greene RC 5.00 2.00
❑ 170 Brandon Jones RC 5.00 2.00
❑ 171 Marion Barber RC 8.00 3.00
❑ 172 Brandon Jacobs RC 6.00 2.50
❑ 173 Jerome Mathis RC 5.00 2.00
❑ 174 Craphonso Thorpe RC 4.00 1.50
❑ 175 Alvin Pearman RC 5.00 2.00
❑ 176 Darren Sproles RC 5.00 2.00
❑ 177 Fred Gibson RC 4.00 1.50
❑ 178 Roydell Williams RC 5.00 2.00
❑ 179 Airese Currie RC 5.00 2.00
❑ 180 Damien Nash RC 4.00 1.50
❑ 181 Dan Orlovsky RC 6.00 2.50
❑ 182 Adrian McPherson RC 5.00 2.00
❑ 183 Larry Brackins RC 4.00 1.50
❑ 184 Rasheed Marshall RC 5.00 2.00
❑ 185 Cedric Houston RC 5.00 2.00
❑ 186 Chad Owens RC 5.00 2.00
❑ 187 Tab Perry RC 5.00 2.00
❑ 188 Dante Ridgeway RC 4.00 1.50
❑ 189 Craig Bragg RC 4.00 1.50
❑ 190 Deandra Cobb RC 4.00 1.50
❑ 191 Derek Anderson RC 5.00 2.00
❑ 192 Paris Warren RC 4.00 1.50
❑ 193 Lionel Gates RC 4.00 1.50
❑ 194 Anthony Davis RC 4.00 1.50
❑ 195 Ryan Fitzpatrick RC 8.00 3.00
❑ 196 J.R. Russell RC 4.00 1.50
❑ 197 Jason White RC 5.00 2.00
❑ 198 Kay-Jay Harris RC 4.00 1.50
❑ 199 T.A. McLendon RC 3.00 1.25
❑ 200 Taylor Stubblefield RC 3.00 1.25
❑ 201 Adam Jones JSY/1499 RC 8.00 3.00
❑ 202 Alex Smith QB JSY/499 RC 30.00 12.50
❑ 203 Andrew Walter JSY/1249 RC 10.00 4.00
❑ 204 Antrel Rolle JSY/999 RC 8.00 3.00
❑ 205 Braylon Edwards JSY/499 RC 25.00 10.00
❑ 206 Carnell Williams JSY/499 RC 40.00 15.00
❑ 207 Carlos Rogers JSY/1499 RC 10.00 4.00
❑ 208 Charlie Frye JSY/1499 RC 12.00 5.00
❑ 209 Ciatrick Fason JSY/1499 RC 8.00 3.00
❑ 210 Courtney Roby JSY/1249 RC 8.00 3.00
❑ 211 Eric Shelton JSY/999 RC 8.00 3.00
❑ 212 Frank Gore JSY/999 RC 10.00 4.00
❑ 213 J.J. Arrington JSY/499 RC 12.00 5.00
❑ 214 Kyle Orton JSY/1499 RC 10.00 4.00
❑ 215 Jason Campbell JSY/749 RC 12.00 5.00
❑ 216 Mark Bradley JSY/999 RC 8.00 3.00
❑ 217 Mark Clayton JSY/499 RC 12.00 5.00
❑ 218 Matt Jones JSY/749 RC 20.00 7.50
❑ 219 Maurice Clarett JSY/999 8.00 3.00
❑ 220 Reggie Brown JSY/999 RC 8.00 3.00
❑ 221 Roddy White JSY/749 RC 8.00 3.00
❑ 222 Ronnie Brown JSY/499 RC 25.00 10.00
❑ 223 Roscoe Parrish JSY/999 RC 8.00 3.00
❑ 224 Ryan Moats JSY/999 RC 8.00 3.00
❑ 225 Stefan LeFors JSY/1499 RC 8.00 3.00
❑ 226 Terrence Murphy JSY/1499 RC 8.00 3.00
❑ 227 Troy Williamson JSY/749 RC 12.00 5.00
❑ 228 Vernand Morency JSY/1499 RC 8.00 3.00
❑ 229 Vincent Jackson JSY/1499 RC 8.00 3.00

2000 Leaf Limited

❑ COMP.SET w/o SPs (200) 120.00 60.00
❑ 1 Ben Coates .50 .20
❑ 2 Joe Horn .75 .30
❑ 3 Jonathan Linton .50 .20
❑ 4 Derrick Mason .75 .30
❑ 5 Ray Lucas .75 .30
❑ 6 Brock Huard .75 .30
❑ 7 Frank Wycheck .50 .20
❑ 8 Michael Strahan .75 .30
❑ 9 Jessie Armstead .50 .20
❑ 10 Stephen Alexander .50 .20
❑ 11 Larry Centers .50 .20
❑ 12 Michael Pittman .50 .20
❑ 13 Priest Holmes 1.50 .60
❑ 14 Jermaine Lewis .75 .30
❑ 15 Jay Riemersma .50 .20
❑ 16 Wesley Walls .50 .20
❑ 17 Curtis Enis .50 .20
❑ 18 Bobby Engram .75 .30
❑ 19 Jim Miller .50 .20
❑ 20 Eddie Kennison .75 .30
❑ 21 Errict Rhett .50 .20
❑ 22 Chris Warren .50 .20
❑ 23 Byron Chamberlain .50 .20
❑ 24 Desmond Howard .50 .20
❑ 25 Lamar Smith .75 .30
❑ 26 Robert Porcher .50 .20
❑ 27 Corey Bradford .75 .30
❑ 28 Donald Driver 1.25 .50
❑ 29 Ahman Green 1.25 .50
❑ 30 Ken Dilger .50 .20
❑ 31 James McKnight .75 .30
❑ 32 Kimble Anders .50 .20
❑ 33 Zach Thomas 1.25 .50
❑ 34 James Johnson .50 .20
❑ 35 Lawyer Milloy .75 .30
❑ 36 Ty Law .75 .30
❑ 37 Willie McGinest .50 .20
❑ 38 Jason Sehorn .75 .30
❑ 39 Andre Rison .75 .30
❑ 40 Rickey Dudley .50 .20
❑ 41 Patrick Jeffers 1.25 .50
❑ 42 Darrell Russell .50 .20
❑ 43 Charles Johnson .75 .30
❑ 44 Michael Westbrook .75 .30
❑ 45 Levon Kirkland .50 .20
❑ 46 Ryan Leaf .75 .30
❑ 47 Sean Dawkins .50 .20
❑ 48 Todd Lyght .50 .20
❑ 49 Kevin Carter .50 .20
❑ 50 Neil O'Donnell .50 .20
❑ 51 Randall Cunningham 1.50 .60
❑ 52 Oronde Gadsden 1.00 .40
❑ 53 O.J. McDuffie 1.00 .40
❑ 54 Jake Reed 1.00 .40
❑ 55 Brian Mitchell .60 .25
❑ 56 Kordell Stewart 1.00 .40
❑ 57 Derrick Mayes 1.00 .40
❑ 58 Az-Zahir Hakim .60 .25
❑ 59 Jacquez Green .60 .25
❑ 60 Andre Reed 1.00 .40
❑ 61 Deion Sanders 1.50 .60
❑ 62 Frank Sanders 1.00 .40
❑ 63 Rob Moore 1.00 .40
❑ 64 Shawn Jefferson .60 .25
❑ 65 Pat Johnson .60 .25
❑ 66 Peter Boulware .60 .25
❑ 67 Donald Hayes .60 .25
❑ 68 Marty Booker 1.00 .40
❑ 69 Leslie Shepherd .60 .25
❑ 70 Jason Tucker .60 .25
❑ 71 Johnnie Morton 1.00 .40
❑ 72 Germane Crowell .60 .25
❑ 73 Herman Moore 1.00 .40
❑ 74 Bill Schroeder 1.00 .40
❑ 75 E.G. Green .60 .25
❑ 76 Jerome Pathon 1.00 .40
❑ 77 Tony Brackens .60 .25
❑ 78 Tony Richardson RC .60 .25
❑ 79 Sam Madison .60 .25
❑ 80 Jeff George 1.00 .40
❑ 81 Matthew Hatchette .60 .25
❑ 82 Kevin Faulk 1.00 .40
❑ 83 Jeff Blake 1.00 .40
❑ 84 Ike Hilliard 1.00 .40
❑ 85 Napoleon Kaufman 1.00 .40
❑ 86 Charles Woodson 1.00 .40
❑ 87 Na Brown .60 .25
❑ 88 Hines Ward 1.50 .60
❑ 89 Troy Edwards .60 .25
❑ 90 Curtis Conway 1.00 .40
❑ 91 Junior Seau 1.50 .60
❑ 92 Jim Harbaugh 1.00 .40
❑ 93 J.J. Stokes 1.00 .40
❑ 94 Jon Kitna 1.50 .60
❑ 95 Reidel Anthony .60 .25
❑ 96 Warrick Dunn 1.50 .60
❑ 97 Carl Pickens 1.00 .40
❑ 98 Yancey Thigpen .60 .25
❑ 99 Albert Connell .60 .25
❑ 100 Irving Fryar 1.00 .40
❑ 101 Qadry Ismail 1.25 .50
❑ 102 Shannon Sharpe 1.25 .50
❑ 103 Joey Galloway 1.25 .50
❑ 104 Ed McCaffrey 2.00 .75
❑ 105 Rod Smith 1.25 .50
❑ 106 Terrell Owens 2.00 .75
❑ 107 Warren Sapp 1.25 .50
❑ 108 Jevon Kearse 2.00 .75
❑ 109 Bruce Smith 1.25 .50
❑ 110 Champ Bailey 1.25 .50
❑ 111 David Boston 2.00 .75
❑ 112 Tim Dwight 2.00 .75
❑ 113 Terance Mathis 1.25 .50
❑ 114 Tony Banks 1.25 .50
❑ 115 Shawn Bryson .75 .30
❑ 116 Peerless Price 1.25 .50
❑ 117 Muhsin Muhammad 1.25 .50
❑ 118 Tim Biakabutuka 1.25 .50
❑ 119 Steve Beuerlein 1.25 .50
❑ 120 Corey Dillon 2.00 .75
❑ 121 Kevin Johnson 2.00 .75
❑ 122 Rocket Ismail 1.25 .50
❑ 123 Charlie Batch 2.00 .75
❑ 124 James Stewart 1.25 .50
❑ 125 Terrence Wilkins .75 .30
❑ 126 Keenan McCardell 1.25 .50
❑ 127 Mark Brunell 2.00 .75
❑ 128 Fred Taylor 2.00 .75
❑ 129 Derrick Alexander 1.25 .50
❑ 130 Tony Gonzalez 1.25 .50
❑ 131 Warren Moon 2.00 .75
❑ 132 Thurman Thomas 1.25 .50
❑ 133 Tony Martin 1.25 .50
❑ 134 Jay Fiedler 2.00 .75

❑ 135	John Randle	1.25	.50
❑ 136	Troy Brown	1.25	.50
❑ 137	Amani Toomer	1.25	.50
❑ 138	Kerry Collins	1.25	.50
❑ 139	Tiki Barber	2.00	.75
❑ 140	Wayne Chrebet	1.25	.50
❑ 141	Tyrone Wheatley	1.25	.50
❑ 142	Duce Staley	2.00	.75
❑ 143	Jermaine Fazande	.75	.30
❑ 144	Charlie Garner	1.25	.50
❑ 145	Torry Holt	2.00	.75
❑ 146	Mike Alstott	2.00	.75
❑ 147	Shaun King	.50	.20
❑ 148	Darrell Green	.75	.30
❑ 149	Brad Johnson	2.00	.75
❑ 150	Olandis Gary	2.00	.75
❑ 151	Jake Plummer	1.50	.60
❑ 152	Chris Chandler	1.50	.60
❑ 153	Jamal Anderson	2.50	1.00
❑ 154	Eric Moulds	2.50	1.00
❑ 155	Doug Flutie	2.50	1.00
❑ 156	Rob Johnson	1.50	.60
❑ 157	Marcus Robinson	2.50	1.00
❑ 158	Cade McNown	1.00	.40
❑ 159	Akili Smith	1.00	.40
❑ 160	Tim Couch	1.50	.60
❑ 161	Emmitt Smith	5.00	2.00
❑ 162	Troy Aikman	5.00	2.00
❑ 163	Brian Griese	2.50	1.00
❑ 164	John Elway	8.00	3.00
❑ 165	Terrell Davis	2.50	1.00
❑ 166	Dorsey Levens	1.50	.60
❑ 167	Antonio Freeman	2.50	1.00
❑ 168	Brett Favre	8.00	3.00
❑ 169	Marvin Harrison	2.50	1.00
❑ 170	Peyton Manning	6.00	2.50
❑ 171	Edgerrin James	4.00	1.50
❑ 172	Jimmy Smith	1.50	.60
❑ 173	Elvis Grbac	1.50	.60
❑ 174	Dan Marino	8.00	3.00
❑ 175	Randy Moss	5.00	2.00
❑ 176	Cris Carter	2.50	1.00
❑ 177	Robert Smith	2.50	1.00
❑ 178	Daunte Culpepper	3.00	1.25
❑ 179	Terry Glenn	1.50	.60
❑ 180	Drew Bledsoe	3.00	1.25
❑ 181	Ricky Williams	1.25	.50
❑ 182	Jake Delhomme RC	8.00	3.00
❑ 183	Curtis Martin	2.50	1.00
❑ 184	Vinny Testaverde	1.50	.60
❑ 185	Tim Brown	2.50	1.00
❑ 186	Rich Gannon	2.50	1.00
❑ 187	Donovan McNabb	3.00	1.25
❑ 188	Jerome Bettis	2.50	1.00
❑ 189	Bobby Shaw RC	2.50	1.00
❑ 190	Jerry Rice	5.00	2.00
❑ 191	Steve Young	3.00	1.25
❑ 192	Jeff Garcia	2.50	1.00
❑ 193	Ricky Watters	1.00	.40
❑ 194	Isaac Bruce	2.50	1.00
❑ 195	Marshall Faulk	3.00	1.25
❑ 196	Kurt Warner	5.00	2.00
❑ 197	Keyshawn Johnson	2.50	1.00
❑ 198	Eddie George	2.50	1.00
❑ 199	Steve McNair	2.50	1.00
❑ 200	Stephen Davis	2.50	1.00
❑ 201	Bobby Brooks RC	3.00	1.25
❑ 202	Cornelius Griffin RC	4.00	1.50
❑ 203	Danny Clark RC	4.00	1.50
❑ 204	Pat Dennis RC	3.00	1.25
❑ 205	Tommy Hendricks RC	5.00	2.00
❑ 206	Fred Jones RC	3.00	1.25
❑ 207	Isaiah Kacyvenski RC	3.00	1.25
❑ 208	Keith Miller RC	3.00	1.25
❑ 209	Andre O' Neal RC	3.00	1.25
❑ 210	Justin Snow RC	3.00	1.25
❑ 211	Armegis Spearman RC	4.00	1.50
❑ 212	Lester Towns RC	3.00	1.25
❑ 213	Antonio Wilson RC	3.00	1.25
❑ 214	Greg Wesley RC	5.00	2.00
❑ 215	Jabari Issa RC	3.00	1.25
❑ 216	Darwin Walker RC	3.00	1.25
❑ 217	Reggie Grimes RC	3.00	1.25
❑ 218	Rian Lindell RC	3.00	1.25
❑ 219	Chris Combs RC	3.00	1.25
❑ 220	Rashard Anderson RC	4.00	1.50
❑ 221	Erik Flowers RC	4.00	1.50
❑ 222	Corey Moore RC	3.00	1.25
❑ 223	Rob Meier RC	3.00	1.25
❑ 224	John Milem RC	3.00	1.25
❑ 225	Jeremiah Parker RC	3.00	1.25
❑ 226	Neil Rackers RC	5.00	2.00
❑ 227	Josh Taves RC	4.00	1.50
❑ 228	Mao Tosi RC	3.00	1.25
❑ 229	Gary Berry RC	3.00	1.25
❑ 230	Matt Bowen RC	3.00	1.25
❑ 231	Ralph Brown RC	3.00	1.25
❑ 232	Tony Darden RC	3.00	1.25
❑ 233	Arturo Freeman RC	3.00	1.25
❑ 234	David Gibson RC	3.00	1.25
❑ 235	Demario Brown RC	3.00	1.25
❑ 236	Deveron Harper RC	3.00	1.25
❑ 237	Johnnie Harris RC	3.00	1.25
❑ 238	Marcus Knight RC	4.00	1.50
❑ 239	Ronnie Heard RC	4.00	1.50
❑ 240	Eric Johnson RC	4.00	1.50
❑ 241	John Keith RC	3.00	1.25
❑ 242	Anthony Malbrough RC	3.00	1.25
❑ 243	Anthony Mitchell RC	3.00	1.25
❑ 244	Aric Morris RC	3.00	1.25
❑ 245	Bobby Myers RC	3.00	1.25
❑ 246	Erik Olson RC	3.00	1.25
❑ 247	Lewis Sanders RC	3.00	1.25
❑ 248	Tony Scott RC	3.00	1.25
❑ 249	David Terrell RC	3.00	1.25
❑ 250	Travares Tillman RC	3.00	1.25
❑ 251	David Stachelski RC	4.00	1.50
❑ 252	Darren Howard RC	5.00	2.00
❑ 253	Frank Chamberlin RC	4.00	1.50
❑ 254	Na'il Diggs RC	5.00	2.00
❑ 255	Orantes Grant RC	4.00	1.50
❑ 256	Barrett Green RC	4.00	1.50
❑ 257	Kory Minor RC	4.00	1.50
❑ 258	Deon Grant RC	5.00	2.00
❑ 259	Mark Simoneau RC	5.00	2.00
❑ 260	Raynoch Thompson RC	5.00	2.00
❑ 261	Kenyatta Wright RC	4.00	1.50
❑ 262	Marcus Bell LB RC	4.00	1.50
❑ 263	Jack Golden RC	4.00	1.50
❑ 264	Thomas Hamner RC	4.00	1.50
❑ 265	Sekou Sanyika RC	4.00	1.50
❑ 266	Marcus Washington RC	5.00	2.00
❑ 267	Tim Seder RC	5.00	2.00
❑ 268	Paul Edinger RC	6.00	2.50
❑ 269	Michael Boireau RC	4.00	1.50
❑ 270	Byron Frisch RC	4.00	1.50
❑ 271	Ketric Sanford RC	4.00	1.50
❑ 272	Frank Murphy RC	4.00	1.50
❑ 273	Robaire Smith RC	4.00	1.50
❑ 274	Adalius Thomas RC	5.00	2.00
❑ 275	William Bartee RC	5.00	2.00
❑ 276	Robert Bean RC	5.00	2.00
❑ 277	Tyrone Carter RC	6.00	2.50
❑ 278	Ike Charlton RC	4.00	1.50
❑ 279	Mario Edwards RC	5.00	2.00
❑ 280	Dwayne Goodrich RC	4.00	1.50
❑ 281	Michael Hawthorne RC	4.00	1.50
❑ 282	Kareem Larrimore RC	4.00	1.50
❑ 283	Mark Roman RC	5.00	2.00
❑ 284	Jacoby Shepherd RC	4.00	1.50
❑ 285	Jason Webster RC	4.00	1.50
❑ 286	Jimmy Wyrick RC	4.00	1.50
❑ 287	Rashidi Barnes RC	4.00	1.50
❑ 288	David Barrett RC	4.00	1.50
❑ 289	Ainsley Battles RC	4.00	1.50
❑ 290	Lamar Chapman RC	4.00	1.50
❑ 291	Todd Franz RC	4.00	1.50
❑ 292	Michael Green RC	4.00	1.50
❑ 293	Antwan Harris RC	4.00	1.50
❑ 294	Brandon Jennings RC	4.00	1.50
❑ 295	Darrick Vaughn RC	4.00	1.50
❑ 296	David Macklin RC	4.00	1.50
❑ 297	Bobby Brown RC	4.00	1.50
❑ 298	Reggie Stephens RC	4.00	1.50
❑ 299	Kenoy Kennedy RC	4.00	1.50
❑ 300	Raion Hill RC	4.00	1.50
❑ 301	Windrell Hayes RC	8.00	3.00
❑ 302	DaShon Polk RC	6.00	2.50
❑ 303	Tywan Mitchell RC	8.00	3.00
❑ 304	Casey Crawford RC	6.00	2.50
❑ 305	Hank Poteat RC	8.00	3.00
❑ 306	Mondriel Fulcher RC	6.00	2.50
❑ 307	Cory Geason RC	6.00	2.50
❑ 308	James Hill RC	6.00	2.50
❑ 309	Brian Jennings RC	6.00	2.50
❑ 310	John Jones RC	8.00	3.00
❑ 311	Anthony Lucas RC	6.00	2.50
❑ 312	Mike Leach RC	6.00	2.50
❑ 313	Dustin Lyman RC	6.00	2.50
❑ 314	Derek Rackley RC	6.00	2.50
❑ 315	Sebastian Janikowski RC	10.00	4.00
❑ 316	Brad St.Louis RC	6.00	2.50
❑ 317	Jay Tant RC	6.00	2.50
❑ 318	Austin Wheatley RC	6.00	2.50
❑ 319	Jermaine Wiggins RC	10.00	4.00
❑ 320	Todd Yoder RC	8.00	3.00
❑ 321	Deon Dyer RC	8.00	3.00
❑ 322	Jim Finn	6.00	2.50
❑ 323	Herbert Goodman RC	8.00	3.00
❑ 324	Mike Green RC	8.00	3.00
❑ 325	Dante Hall RC	20.00	7.50
❑ 326	Thabiti Davis RC	6.00	2.50
❑ 327	Kevin Houser RC	8.00	3.00
❑ 328	Jonas Lewis RC	6.00	2.50
❑ 329	Chad Morton RC	10.00	4.00
❑ 330	Patrick Pass RC	8.00	3.00
❑ 331	Maurice Smith RC	10.00	4.00
❑ 332	Paul Smith RC	8.00	3.00
❑ 333	Terrelle Smith RC	8.00	3.00
❑ 334	Craig Walendy RC	6.00	2.50
❑ 335	Jamel White RC	8.00	3.00
❑ 336	Jarious Jackson RC	8.00	3.00
❑ 337	Matt Lytle RC	8.00	3.00
❑ 338	Ron Powlus RC	10.00	4.00
❑ 339	Ian Gold RC	8.00	3.00
❑ 340	Brandon Short RC	8.00	3.00
❑ 341	T.J. Slaughter RC	6.00	2.50
❑ 342	Nate Webster RC	6.00	2.50
❑ 343	John Engelberger RC	8.00	3.00
❑ 344	Rogers Beckett RC	8.00	3.00
❑ 345	Mike Brown RC	15.00	6.00
❑ 346	Anthony Wright RC	12.00	5.00
❑ 347	Danny Farmer RC	8.00	3.00
❑ 348	Clint Stoerner RC	8.00	3.00
❑ 349	Julian Peterson RC	10.00	4.00
❑ 350	Ahmed Plummer RC	10.00	4.00
❑ 351	Avion Black RC	10.00	4.00
❑ 352	Kwame Cavil RC	8.00	3.00
❑ 353	Chris Cole RC	10.00	4.00
❑ 354	Chris Coleman RC	8.00	3.00
❑ 355	Trevor Gaylor RC	10.00	4.00
❑ 356	Damon Hodge RC	10.00	4.00
❑ 357	Darrell Jackson RC	25.00	10.00
❑ 358	Reggie Jones RC	8.00	3.00
❑ 359	Charles Lee RC	8.00	3.00
❑ 360	Jerry Porter RC	15.00	6.00
❑ 361	Bobby Shaw	10.00	4.00
❑ 362	Ron Dugans RC	8.00	3.00
❑ 363	James Williams RC	10.00	4.00
❑ 364	Bashir Yamini RC	8.00	3.00
❑ 365	Anthony Becht RC	12.00	5.00
❑ 366	Erron Kinney RC	12.00	5.00
❑ 367	Aaron Shea RC	10.00	4.00
❑ 368	Chris Samuels RC	10.00	4.00
❑ 369	Trung Canidate RC	10.00	4.00
❑ 370	Obafemi Ayanbadejo RC	10.00	4.00
❑ 371	Doug Chapman RC	10.00	4.00
❑ 372	Ronney Jenkins RC	10.00	4.00
❑ 373	Curtis Keaton RC	10.00	4.00
❑ 374	Kevin McDougal RC	10.00	4.00

❑ 375 Frank Moreau RC 10.00 4.00
❑ 376 Aaron Stecker RC 12.00 5.00
❑ 377 Shyrone Stith RC 10.00 4.00
❑ 378 Tom Brady RC 150.00 75.00
❑ 379 Giovanni Carmazzi RC 8.00 3.00
❑ 380 Joe Hamilton RC 10.00 4.00
❑ 381 Todd Husak RC 12.00 5.00
❑ 382 Doug Johnson RC 12.00 5.00
❑ 383 Tee Martin RC 12.00 5.00
❑ 384 Chad Pennington RC 60.00 25.00
❑ 385 Tim Rattay RC 12.00 5.00
❑ 386 Chris Redman RC 10.00 4.00
❑ 387 Billy Volek RC 20.00 7.50
❑ 388 Spergon Wynn RC 10.00 4.00
❑ 389 John Abraham RC 12.00 5.00
❑ 390 Keith Bulluck RC 12.00 5.00
❑ 391 Rob Morris RC 10.00 4.00
❑ 392 JaJuan Dawson RC 8.00 3.00
❑ 393 Chris Hovan RC 10.00 4.00
❑ 394 Shaun Ellis RC 12.00 5.00
❑ 395 Deltha O'Neal RC 12.00 5.00
❑ 396 Gari Scott RC 8.00 3.00
❑ 397 Dialleo Burks RC 8.00 3.00
❑ 398 Shockmain Davis RC 8.00 3.00
❑ 399 Brad Hoover RC 10.00 4.00
❑ 400 Brian Finneran RC 12.00 5.00
❑ 401 Sylvester Morris J/FB/750 RC 8.00 3.00
❑ 402 Denn Northcutt J/FB/500 RC 25.00 10.00
❑ 403 Todd Pinkston J/FB/100 RC 20.007.50
❑ 404 Larry Foster J/FB/500 RC 20.00 7.50
❑ 405 R.Jay Soward J/FB/1000 RC 12.005.00
❑ 406 Travis Taylor J/FB/250 RC 40.00 15.00
❑ 407 Peter Warrick J/FB/1000 RC 20.007.50
❑ 408 Dez White J/FB/1000 RC 20.00 7.50
❑ 409 Ron Dayne J/FB/1000 RC 20.00 7.50
❑ 410 Thomas Jones J/FB/500 RC 25.00 10.00
❑ 411 Jamal Lewis J/FB/1000 RC 30.0012.50
❑ 412 Sammy Morris J/FB/500 RC 20.007.50
❑ 413 Travis Prentice J/FB/500 RC 20.007.50
❑ 414 J.R. Redmond J/FB/250 RC 25.0010.00
❑ 415 Michael Wiley FB/1000 RC 12.00 5.00
❑ 416 Laver Coles J/FB/250 RC 40.00 15.00
❑ 417 Bubba Franks J/FB/500 RC 20.00 7.50
❑ 418 Mike Anderson J/FB/250 RC 40.00 20.00
❑ 419 Plaxico Burress J/FB/250 RC 60.00 25.00
❑ 420 Ron Dixon J/FB/1000 RC 12.00 5.00
❑ 421 Troy Walters J/FB/1000 RC 12.00 5.00
❑ 422 Sha Alexander J/FB/1000 RC 50.00 25.00
❑ 423 Brian Urlacher J/FB/1000 RC 40.00 15.00
❑ 424 Corey Simon J/FB/1000 RC 12.00 5.00
❑ 425 Courtney Brown J/FB/500 RC 25.00 10.00

2003 Leaf Limited

❑ COMP.SET w/o SP's (100) 250.00 100.00
❑ 1 Emmitt Smith 10.00 4.00
❑ 2 Michael Vick 10.00 4.00
❑ 3 Peerless Price 2.50 1.00
❑ 4 T.J. Duckett 2.50 1.00
❑ 5 Jamal Lewis 4.00 1.50
❑ 6 Drew Bledsoe 4.00 1.50
❑ 7 Eric Moulds 2.50 1.00
❑ 8 Travis Henry 2.50 1.00
❑ 9 Jim Kelly 8.00 3.00
❑ 10 Julius Peppers 4.00 1.50
❑ 11 Dick Butkus 6.00 2.50
❑ 12 Mike Singletary 4.00 1.50
❑ 13 Walter Payton 15.00 6.00
❑ 14 Anthony Thomas 2.50 1.00
❑ 15 Brian Urlacher 6.00 2.50
❑ 16 Marty Booker 2.50 1.00
❑ 17 Corey Dillon 2.50 1.00
❑ 18 Jim Thorpe 5.00 2.00
❑ 19 Jim Brown 10.00 4.00
❑ 20 Tim Couch 2.50 1.00
❑ 21 William Green 2.50 1.00
❑ 22 Deion Sanders 4.00 1.50
❑ 23 Michael Irvin 4.00 1.50
❑ 24 Roger Staubach 8.00 3.00
❑ 25 Troy Aikman 6.00 2.50
❑ 26 Tony Dorsett 6.00 2.50
❑ 27 Antonio Bryant 2.50 1.00
❑ 28 Clinton Portis 6.00 2.50
❑ 29 Jake Plummer 2.50 1.00
❑ 30 Rod Smith 2.50 1.00
❑ 31 Barry Sanders 8.00 3.00
❑ 32 Doak Walker 4.00 1.50
❑ 33 Joey Harrington 6.00 2.50
❑ 34 Bart Starr 8.00 3.00
❑ 35 Ahman Green 4.00 1.50
❑ 36 Brett Favre 10.00 4.00
❑ 37 Donald Driver 2.50 1.00
❑ 38 David Carr 6.00 2.50
❑ 39 Don Shula 5.00 2.00
❑ 40 Johnny Unitas 8.00 3.00
❑ 41 Edgerrin James 4.00 1.50
❑ 42 Marvin Harrison 4.00 1.50
❑ 43 Peyton Manning 6.00 2.50
❑ 44 Fred Taylor 4.00 1.50
❑ 45 Jimmy Smith 2.50 1.00
❑ 46 Mark Brunell 2.50 1.00
❑ 47 Marcus Allen 4.00 1.50
❑ 48 Priest Holmes 5.00 2.00
❑ 49 Tony Gonzalez 2.50 1.00
❑ 50 Trent Green 2.50 1.00
❑ 51 Dan Marino 12.00 5.00
❑ 52 Bob Griese 5.00 2.00
❑ 53 Chris Chambers 4.00 1.50
❑ 54 Ricky Williams 4.00 1.50
❑ 55 Fran Tarkenton 5.00 2.00
❑ 56 Daunte Culpepper 4.00 1.50
❑ 57 Michael Bennett 2.50 1.00
❑ 58 Randy Moss 6.00 2.50
❑ 59 Tom Brady 10.00 4.00
❑ 60 Aaron Brooks 4.00 1.50
❑ 61 Deuce McAllister 4.00 1.50
❑ 62 Donte Stallworth 4.00 1.50
❑ 63 Mark Bevaro 2.50 1.00
❑ 64 Jeremy Shockey 6.00 2.50
❑ 65 Kerry Collins 2.50 1.00
❑ 66 Tiki Barber 4.00 1.50
❑ 67 Joe Namath 8.00 3.00
❑ 68 Chad Pennington 5.00 2.00
❑ 69 Curtis Martin 4.00 1.50
❑ 70 Jerry Porter 2.50 1.00
❑ 71 Jerry Rice 8.00 3.00
❑ 72 Rich Gannon 2.50 1.00
❑ 73 Tim Brown 4.00 1.50
❑ 74 Donovan McNabb 5.00 2.00
❑ 75 Terry Bradshaw 8.00 3.00
❑ 76 Antwaan Randle El 4.00 1.50
❑ 77 Plaxico Burress 2.50 1.00
❑ 78 Tommy Maddox 4.00 1.50
❑ 79 David Boston 2.50 1.00
❑ 80 Drew Brees 4.00 1.50
❑ 81 LaDainian Tomlinson 4.00 1.50
❑ 82 Joe Montana 20.00 7.50
❑ 83 Steve Young 5.00 2.00
❑ 84 Jeff Garcia 4.00 1.50
❑ 85 Terrell Owens 4.00 1.50
❑ 86 Koren Robinson 2.50 1.00
❑ 87 Matt Hasselbeck 2.50 1.00
❑ 88 Shaun Alexander 4.00 1.50
❑ 89 Isaac Bruce 4.00 1.50
❑ 90 Kurt Warner 4.00 1.50
❑ 91 Marshall Faulk 4.00 1.50
❑ 92 Torry Holt 4.00 1.50
❑ 93 Brad Johnson 2.50 1.00
❑ 94 Keyshawn Johnson 4.00 1.50
❑ 95 Earl Campbell 4.00 1.50
❑ 96 Eddie George 2.50 1.00
❑ 97 Steve McNair 4.00 1.50
❑ 98 John Riggins 6.00 2.50
❑ 99 Laveranues Coles 2.50 1.00
❑ 100 Patrick Ramsey 4.00 1.50
❑ 101 LaTarence Dunbar RC 5.00 2.00
❑ 102 Sam Aiken RC 5.00 2.00
❑ 103 Bobby Wade RC 6.00 2.50
❑ 104 Justin Gage RC 6.00 2.50
❑ 105 Lee Suggs RC 12.00 5.00
❑ 106 Jason Witten RC 10.00 4.00
❑ 107 Quentin Griffin RC 6.00 2.50
❑ 108 Domanick Davis RC 10.00 4.00
❑ 109 LaBrandon Toefield RC 6.00 2.50
❑ 110 J.R. Tolver RC 5.00 2.00
❑ 111 Kliff Kingsbury RC 5.00 2.00
❑ 112 Talman Gardner RC 6.00 2.50
❑ 113 Teyo Johnson RC 6.00 2.50
❑ 114 Billy McMullen RC 5.00 2.00
❑ 115 L.J. Smith RC 6.00 2.50
❑ 116 Brian St.Pierre RC 6.00 2.50
❑ 117 Brandon Lloyd RC 8.00 3.00
❑ 118 Seneca Wallace RC 6.00 2.50
❑ 119 Kevin Curtis RC 6.00 2.50
❑ 120 Shaun McDonald RC 6.00 2.50
❑ 121 Terrell Suggs RC 10.00 4.00
❑ 122 Terence Newman RC 12.00 5.00
❑ 123 Tony Romo RC 6.00 2.50
❑ 124 DeWayne Robertson RC 6.00 2.50
❑ 125 Marcus Trufant RC 6.00 2.50
❑ 126 Artose Pinner AU RC 25.00 10.00
❑ 127 Bryant Johnson AU RC 25.00 10.00
❑ 128 Kelley Washington AU RC 25.0010.00
❑ 129 Dallas Clark AU RC 25.00 10.00
❑ 130 Onterrio Smith AU RC 25.00 10.00
❑ 131 Tony Hollings AU RC 25.00 10.00
❑ 132 Tyrone Calico AU RC 40.00 20.00
❑ 133 Carson Palmer AU RC 150.00 90.00
❑ 134 Byron Leftwich AU RC 100.00 50.00
❑ 135 Rex Grossman AU RC 50.00 20.00
❑ 136 Kyle Boller AU RC 60.00 25.00
❑ 137 Chris Simms AU RC 50.00 25.00
❑ 138 Dave Ragone AU RC 25.00 10.00
❑ 139 Ken Dorsey AU RC 25.00 10.00
❑ 140 Willis McGahee AU RC 80.00 40.00
❑ 141 Larry Johnson AU RC 150.00 90.00
❑ 142 Musa Smith AU RC 25.00 10.00
❑ 143 Chris Brown AU RC 30.00 12.50
❑ 144 Charles Rogers AU RC 25.00 10.00
❑ 145 Andre Johnson AU RC 60.00 35.00
❑ 146 Taylor Jacobs AU RC 25.00 10.00
❑ 147 Anquan Boldin AU RC 80.00 40.00
❑ 148 Bethel Johnson AU RC 25.00 10.00
❑ 149 Justin Fargas AU RC 25.00 10.00
❑ 150 Nate Burleson AU RC 30.00 12.50

2004 Leaf Limited

❑ 1-150 PRINT RUN 799 SER.#'d SETS
❑ 151-200 PRINT RUN 350 SER.#'d SETS

❑ 201-233 JSY AU PRINT RUN 150 SETS
❑ EXCH EXPIRATION: 7/1/2006
❑ 1 A.J. Feeley 4.00 1.50
❑ 2 Aaron Brooks 3.00 1.25
❑ 3 Ahman Green 4.00 1.50
❑ 4 Andre Johnson 4.00 1.50
❑ 5 Anquan Boldin 4.00 1.50
❑ 6 Antwaan Randle El 4.00 1.50
❑ 7 Ashley Lelie 3.00 1.25
❑ 8 Brad Johnson 3.00 1.25
❑ 9 Brett Favre 10.00 4.00
❑ 10 Brian Urlacher 5.00 2.00
❑ 11 Brian Westbrook 3.00 1.25
❑ 12 Byron Leftwich 5.00 2.00
❑ 13 Carson Palmer 5.00 2.00
❑ 14 Chad Johnson 4.00 1.50
❑ 15 Chad Pennington 4.00 1.50
❑ 16 Charlie Garner 3.00 1.25
❑ 17 Charles Rogers 3.00 1.25
❑ 18 Chris Brown 4.00 1.50
❑ 19 Chris Chambers 3.00 1.25
❑ 20 Clinton Portis 4.00 1.50
❑ 21 Corey Dillon 3.00 1.25
❑ 22 Deion Sanders 4.00 1.50
❑ 23 Curtis Martin 4.00 1.50
❑ 24 Daunte Culpepper 4.00 1.50
❑ 25 David Terrell 3.00 1.25
❑ 26 David Carr 4.00 1.50
❑ 27 Deion Branch 4.00 1.50
❑ 28 Derrick Mason 3.00 1.25
❑ 29 DeShaun Foster 3.00 1.25
❑ 30 Deuce McAllister 4.00 1.50
❑ 31 Domanick Davis 4.00 1.50
❑ 32 Donovan McNabb 5.00 2.00
❑ 33 Donte Stallworth 3.00 1.25
❑ 34 Drew Bledsoe 4.00 1.50
❑ 35 Duce Staley 3.00 1.25
❑ 36 Eddie George 3.00 1.25
❑ 37 Edgerrin James 4.00 1.50
❑ 38 Emmitt Smith 8.00 3.00
❑ 39 Eric Moulds 3.00 1.25
❑ 40 Fred Taylor 3.00 1.25
❑ 41 Hines Ward 4.00 1.50
❑ 42 Isaac Bruce 4.00 1.50
❑ 43 Jake Delhomme 4.00 1.50
❑ 44 Jake Plummer 3.00 1.25
❑ 45 Javon Walker 3.00 1.25
❑ 46 Jeff Garcia 4.00 1.50
❑ 47 Jeremy Shockey 4.00 1.50
❑ 48 Jerome Bettis 4.00 1.50
❑ 49 Jerry Porter 3.00 1.25
❑ 50 Jerry Rice 8.00 3.00
❑ 51 Jevon Kearse 3.00 1.25
❑ 52 Jimmy Smith 3.00 1.25
❑ 53 Joe Horn 3.00 1.25
❑ 54 Joey Harrington 4.00 1.50
❑ 55 Josh McCown 3.00 1.25
❑ 56 Kevan Barlow 3.00 1.25
❑ 57 Koren Robinson 3.00 1.25
❑ 58 Kyle Boller 4.00 1.50
❑ 59 LaDainian Tomlinson 5.00 2.00
❑ 60 LaVar Arrington 8.00 3.00
❑ 61 Laveranues Coles 3.00 1.25
❑ 62 Lee Suggs 4.00 1.50
❑ 63 Marc Bulger 4.00 1.50
❑ 64 Mark Brunell 3.00 1.25
❑ 65 Marshall Faulk 4.00 1.50
❑ 66 Marvin Harrison 4.00 1.50
❑ 67 Matt Hasselbeck 3.00 1.25
❑ 68 Michael Bennett 3.00 1.25
❑ 69 Michael Strahan 3.00 1.25
❑ 70 Michael Vick 8.00 3.00
❑ 71 Peerless Price 3.00 1.25
❑ 72 Peter Warrick 3.00 1.25
❑ 73 Peyton Manning 6.00 2.50
❑ 74 Priest Holmes 5.00 2.00
❑ 75 Quentin Griffin 4.00 1.50
❑ 76 Randy Moss 5.00 2.00
❑ 77 Ray Lewis 4.00 1.50
❑ 78 Rex Grossman 4.00 1.50
❑ 79 Lamar Gordon 2.50 1.00
❑ 80 Rod Smith 3.00 1.25
❑ 81 Roy Williams S 3.00 1.25
❑ 82 Rudi Johnson 3.00 1.25
❑ 83 Santana Moss 3.00 1.25
❑ 84 Shaun Alexander 4.00 1.50
❑ 85 Stephen Davis 3.00 1.25
❑ 86 Steve McNair 4.00 1.50
❑ 87 Steve Smith 4.00 1.50
❑ 88 T.J. Duckett 3.00 1.25
❑ 89 Terrell Owens 4.00 1.50
❑ 90 Thomas Jones 3.00 1.25
❑ 91 Tiki Barber 4.00 1.50
❑ 92 Tim Brown 4.00 1.50
❑ 93 Tom Brady 10.00 4.00
❑ 94 Tony Gonzalez 3.00 1.25
❑ 95 Torry Holt 4.00 1.50
❑ 96 Travis Henry 3.00 1.25
❑ 97 Trent Green 3.00 1.25
❑ 98 Warren Sapp 3.00 1.25
❑ 99 William Green 3.00 1.25
❑ 100 Willis McGahee 4.00 1.50
❑ 101 Barry Sanders 8.00 3.00
❑ 102 Bart Starr 10.00 4.00
❑ 103 Bo Jackson 8.00 3.00
❑ 104 Bob Griese 5.00 2.00
❑ 105 Bronko Nagurski 5.00 2.00
❑ 106 Dan Marino 12.00 5.00
❑ 107 Deion Sanders 8.00 3.00
❑ 108 Dick Butkus 8.00 3.00
❑ 109 Doak Walker 5.00 2.00
❑ 110 Don Maynard 4.00 1.50
❑ 111 Don Shula 5.00 2.00
❑ 112 Earl Campbell 5.00 2.00
❑ 113 Fran Tarkenton 6.00 2.50
❑ 114 Franco Harris 6.00 2.50
❑ 115 Fred Biletnikoff 5.00 2.00
❑ 116 Gale Sayers 6.00 2.50
❑ 117 Herman Edwards 4.00 1.50
❑ 118 Jim Brown 8.00 3.00
❑ 119 Jim Kelly 6.00 2.50
❑ 120 Jim Thorpe 5.00 2.00
❑ 121 Jimmy Johnson 4.00 1.50
❑ 122 Joe Greene 5.00 2.00
❑ 123 Joe Montana 15.00 6.00
❑ 124 Joe Namath 8.00 3.00
❑ 125 John Elway 8.00 3.00
❑ 126 John Riggins 6.00 2.50
❑ 127 Johnny Unitas 8.00 3.00
❑ 128 Larry Csonka 5.00 2.00
❑ 129 Lawrence Taylor 5.00 2.00
❑ 130 Marcus Allen 5.00 2.00
❑ 131 Mark Bavaro 3.00 1.25
❑ 132 Michael Irvin 5.00 2.00
❑ 133 Mike Ditka 5.00 2.00
❑ 134 Mike Singletary 5.00 2.00
❑ 135 Ozzie Newsome 4.00 1.50
❑ 136 Paul Warfield 4.00 1.50
❑ 137 Randall Cunningham 4.00 1.50
❑ 138 Ray Nitschke 5.00 2.00
❑ 139 Red Grange 6.00 2.50
❑ 140 Reggie White 5.00 2.00
❑ 141 Roger Staubach 8.00 3.00
❑ 142 Sterling Sharpe 4.00 1.50
❑ 143 Steve Largent 5.00 2.00
❑ 144 Terrell Davis 5.00 2.00
❑ 145 Terry Bradshaw 8.00 3.00
❑ 146 Thurman Thomas 4.00 1.50
❑ 147 Tony Dorsett 5.00 2.00
❑ 148 Troy Aikman 6.00 2.50
❑ 149 Walter Payton 15.00 6.00
❑ 150 Warren Moon 4.00 1.50
❑ 151 Ahmad Carroll RC 12.00 5.00
❑ 152 Andy Hall RC 8.00 3.00
❑ 153 Antwan Odom RC 10.00 4.00
❑ 154 B.J. Symons RC 10.00 4.00
❑ 155 Carlos Francis RC 8.00 3.00
❑ 156 Casey Bramlet RC 8.00 3.00
❑ 157 Chris Cooley RC 10.00 4.00
❑ 158 Chris Gamble RC 12.00 5.00
❑ 159 Clarence Moore RC 10.00 4.00
❑ 160 Cody Pickett RC 10.00 4.00
❑ 161 Courtney Watson RC 10.00 4.00
❑ 162 Craig Krenzel RC 10.00 4.00
❑ 163 D.J. Hackett RC 8.00 3.00
❑ 164 D.J. Williams RC 12.00 5.00
❑ 165 Derrick Strait RC 10.00 4.00
❑ 166 Dontarrious Thomas RC 10.00 4.00
❑ 167 Drew Henson RC 10.00 4.00
❑ 168 Ernest Wilford RC 10.00 4.00
❑ 169 Jamaar Taylor RC 10.00 4.00
❑ 170 Jason Babin RC 10.00 4.00
❑ 171 Jeff Smoker RC 10.00 4.00
❑ 172 Jerricho Cotchery RC 10.00 4.00
❑ 173 Jim Sorgi RC 10.00 4.00
❑ 174 Joey Thomas RC 10.00 4.00
❑ 175 John Navarre RC 10.00 4.00
❑ 176 Johnnie Morant RC 10.00 4.00
❑ 177 Jonathan Vilma RC 10.00 4.00
❑ 178 Josh Harris RC 10.00 4.00
❑ 179 Keiwan Ratliff RC 8.00 3.00
❑ 180 Kenechi Udeze RC 10.00 4.00
❑ 181 Kris Wilson RC 10.00 4.00
❑ 182 Marcus Tubbs RC 10.00 4.00
❑ 183 Marquise Hill RC 8.00 3.00
❑ 184 Matt Mauck RC 10.00 4.00
❑ 185 Maurice Mann RC 8.00 3.00
❑ 186 Michael Boulware RC 10.00 4.00
❑ 187 Michael Turner RC 10.00 4.00
❑ 188 P.K. Sam RC 8.00 3.00
❑ 189 Patrick Crayton RC 10.00 4.00
❑ 190 Ricardo Colclough RC 10.00 4.00
❑ 191 Richard Smith RC 8.00 3.00
❑ 192 Samie Parker RC 10.00 4.00
❑ 193 Sean Taylor RC 12.00 5.00
❑ 194 Teddy Lehman RC 10.00 4.00
❑ 195 Thomas Tapeh RC 8.00 3.00
❑ 196 Tommie Harris RC 10.00 4.00
❑ 197 Triandos Luke RC 10.00 4.00
❑ 198 Troy Fleming RC 8.00 3.00
❑ 199 Vince Wilfork RC 12.00 5.00
❑ 200 Will Smith RC 10.00 4.00
❑ 201 Larry Fitzgerald JSY AU RC 100.00 60.00
❑ 202 DeAngelo Hall JSY AU RC 40.00 15.00
❑ 203 Matt Schaub JSY AU RC 50.00 25.00
❑ 204 Michael Jenkins JSY AU RC 40.00 15.00
❑ 205 Devard Darling JSY AU RC 30.00 12.50
❑ 206 J.P. Losman JSY AU RC 80.00 30.00
❑ 207 Lee Evans JSY AU RC 40.00 20.00
❑ 208 Keary Colbert JSY AU RC 40.00 15.00
❑ 209 Bernard Berrian JSY AU RC 30.00 12.50
❑ 210 Chris Perry JSY AU RC 50.00 20.00
❑ 211 K.Winslow JSY AU RC EXCH 60.00 25.00
❑ 212 Luke McCown JSY AU RC 30.00 12.50
❑ 213 Julius Jones JSY AU RC 120.00 60.00
❑ 214 Darius Watts JSY AU RC 30.00 12.50
❑ 215 Tatum Bell JSY AU RC 60.00 25.00
❑ 216 Kevin Jones JSY AU RC 100.00 40.00
❑ 217 Roy Will.WR JSY AU RC 100.00 40.00
❑ 218 Dunta Robinson JSY AU RC 30.00 12.50
❑ 219 Greg Jones JSY AU RC 40.00 15.00
❑ 220 Reggie Williams JSY AU RC 40.00 20.00
❑ 221 Mewelde Moore JSY AU RC 40.00 15.00
❑ 222 Ben Watson JSY AU RC 30.00 12.50
❑ 223 Cedric Cobbs JSY AU RC 30.00 12.50
❑ 224 Devery Henderson JSY AU RC 25.00 10.00
❑ 225 Eli Manning JSY AU RC 200.00 100.00
❑ 226 Robert Gallery JSY AU RC 40.00 15.00
❑ 227 Roethlisberger JSY AU RC 350.00 200.00
❑ 228 Philip Rivers JSY AU RC 120.00 70.00
❑ 229 Derrick Hamilton JSY AU RC 25.00 10.00
❑ 230 Rashaun Woods JSY AU RC 30.00 12.50
❑ 231 Stev.Jackson JSY AU RC 100.00 40.00
❑ 232 Michael Clayton JSY AU RC 60.00 25.00
❑ 233 Ben Troupe JSY AU RC 30.00 12.50

2005 Leaf Limited

❑ 1-150 PRINT RUN 599 SER.#'d SETS
❑ 151-200 ROOKIE PRINT RUN 250 SER.#'d SETS
❑ 201-229 JSY AU PRINT RUN 100 SETS
❑ JSY AU EXCH EXPIRATION 6/1/2007
❑ UNPRICED PLATINUM SER.#'d TO 1

❑ 1	Anquan Boldin	3.00	1.25
❑ 2	Kurt Warner	3.00	1.25
❑ 3	Larry Fitzgerald	4.00	1.50
❑ 4	Alge Crumpler	3.00	1.25
❑ 5	Michael Vick	6.00	2.50
❑ 6	Warrick Dunn	3.00	1.25
❑ 7	Jamal Lewis	4.00	1.50
❑ 8	Kyle Boller	3.00	1.25
❑ 9	Ray Lewis	4.00	1.50
❑ 10	Derrick Mason	3.00	1.25
❑ 11	J.P. Losman	4.00	1.50
❑ 12	Lee Evans	3.00	1.25
❑ 13	Willis McGahee	4.00	1.50
❑ 14	DeShaun Foster	3.00	1.25
❑ 15	Jake Delhomme	4.00	1.50
❑ 16	Steve Smith	3.00	1.25
❑ 17	Brian Urlacher	4.00	1.50
❑ 18	Rex Grossman	3.00	1.25
❑ 19	Muhsin Muhammad	3.00	1.25
❑ 20	Carson Palmer	4.00	1.50
❑ 21	Chad Johnson	4.00	1.50
❑ 22	Rudi Johnson	3.00	1.25
❑ 23	Antonio Bryant	2.50	1.00
❑ 24	Lee Suggs	3.00	1.25
❑ 25	Trent Dilfer	3.00	1.25
❑ 26	Drew Bledsoe	4.00	1.50
❑ 27	Julius Jones	5.00	2.00
❑ 28	Keyshawn Johnson	3.00	1.25
❑ 29	Roy Williams S	3.00	1.25
❑ 30	Ashley Lelie	3.00	1.25
❑ 31	Jake Plummer	3.00	1.25
❑ 32	Tatum Bell	3.00	1.25
❑ 33	Rod Smith	3.00	1.25
❑ 34	Joey Harrington	4.00	1.50
❑ 35	Kevin Jones	4.00	1.50
❑ 36	Roy Williams WR	4.00	1.50
❑ 37	Ahman Green	4.00	1.50
❑ 38	Brett Favre	10.00	4.00
❑ 39	Javon Walker	3.00	1.25
❑ 40	Andre Johnson	3.00	1.25
❑ 41	David Carr	4.00	1.50
❑ 42	Domanick Davis	3.00	1.25
❑ 43	Edgerrin James	4.00	1.50
❑ 44	Marvin Harrison	4.00	1.50
❑ 45	Peyton Manning	6.00	2.50
❑ 46	Reggie Wayne	3.00	1.25
❑ 47	Byron Leftwich	4.00	1.50
❑ 48	Fred Taylor	3.00	1.25
❑ 49	Jimmy Smith	3.00	1.25
❑ 50	Priest Holmes	4.00	1.50
❑ 51	Tony Gonzalez	3.00	1.25
❑ 52	Trent Green	3.00	1.25
❑ 53	Chris Chambers	3.00	1.25
❑ 54	Ricky Williams	3.00	1.25
❑ 55	Daunte Culpepper	4.00	1.50
❑ 56	Nate Burleson	3.00	1.25
❑ 57	Michael Bennett	3.00	1.25
❑ 58	Corey Dillon	3.00	1.25
❑ 59	Deion Branch	3.00	1.25
❑ 60	Tom Brady	10.00	4.00
❑ 61	Aaron Brooks	3.00	1.25
❑ 62	Deuce McAllister	4.00	1.50
❑ 63	Joe Horn	3.00	1.25
❑ 64	Eli Manning	8.00	3.00
❑ 65	Jeremy Shockey	4.00	1.50
❑ 66	Plaxico Burress	3.00	1.25
❑ 67	Tiki Barber	4.00	1.50
❑ 68	Chad Pennington	4.00	1.50
❑ 69	Curtis Martin	4.00	1.50
❑ 70	Laveranues Coles	3.00	1.25
❑ 71	Kerry Collins	3.00	1.25
❑ 72	LaMont Jordan	4.00	1.50
❑ 73	Randy Moss	4.00	1.50
❑ 74	Brian Westbrook	3.00	1.25
❑ 75	Donovan McNabb	5.00	2.00
❑ 76	Terrell Owens	4.00	1.50
❑ 77	Ben Roethlisberger	10.00	4.00
❑ 78	Duce Staley	3.00	1.25
❑ 79	Hines Ward	4.00	1.50
❑ 80	Jerome Bettis	4.00	1.50
❑ 81	Antonio Gates	4.00	1.50
❑ 82	Drew Brees	4.00	1.50
❑ 83	LaDainian Tomlinson	5.00	2.00
❑ 84	Brandon Lloyd	2.50	1.00
❑ 85	Kevan Barlow	3.00	1.25
❑ 86	Darrell Jackson	3.00	1.25
❑ 87	Matt Hasselbeck	3.00	1.25
❑ 88	Shaun Alexander	5.00	2.00
❑ 89	Marc Bulger	4.00	1.50
❑ 90	Steven Jackson	5.00	2.00
❑ 91	Torry Holt	4.00	1.50
❑ 92	Brian Griese	3.00	1.25
❑ 93	Michael Clayton	4.00	1.50
❑ 94	Chris Brown	3.00	1.25
❑ 95	Drew Bennett	3.00	1.25
❑ 96	Steve McNair	4.00	1.50
❑ 97	Clinton Portis	4.00	1.50
❑ 98	LaVar Arrington	4.00	1.50
❑ 99	Patrick Ramsey	3.00	1.25
❑ 100	Santana Moss	3.00	1.25
❑ 101	Barry Sanders	8.00	3.00
❑ 102	Bart Starr	8.00	3.00
❑ 103	Bo Jackson	6.00	2.50
❑ 104	Brian Piccolo	6.00	2.50
❑ 105	Bob Griese	5.00	2.00
❑ 106	Dan Fouts	5.00	2.00
❑ 107	Dan Marino	10.00	4.00
❑ 108	Deacon Jones	4.00	1.50
❑ 109	Doak Walker	5.00	2.00
❑ 110	Don Maynard	4.00	1.50
❑ 111	Don Meredith	5.00	2.00
❑ 112	Don Shula	4.00	1.50
❑ 113	Earl Campbell	5.00	2.00
❑ 114	Eric Dickerson	4.00	1.50
❑ 115	Fran Tarkenton	6.00	2.50
❑ 116	Franco Harris	6.00	2.50
❑ 117	Gale Sayers	6.00	2.50
❑ 118	Jack Lambert	6.00	2.50
❑ 119	James Lofton	3.00	1.25
❑ 120	Jim Brown	8.00	3.00
❑ 121	Jim Kelly	6.00	2.50
❑ 122	Jim Thorpe	6.00	2.50
❑ 123	Joe Greene	5.00	2.00
❑ 124	Joe Montana	12.00	5.00
❑ 125	Joe Namath	6.00	2.50
❑ 126	John Elway	8.00	3.00
❑ 127	John Riggins	5.00	2.00
❑ 128	Johnny Unitas	8.00	3.00
❑ 129	Lawrence Taylor	5.00	2.00
❑ 130	Leroy Kelly	4.00	1.50
❑ 131	Marcus Allen	5.00	2.00
❑ 132	Michael Irvin	5.00	2.00
❑ 133	Mike Ditka	5.00	2.00
❑ 134	Mike Singletary	5.00	2.00
❑ 135	Ozzie Newsome	4.00	1.50
❑ 136	Paul Hornung	5.00	2.00
❑ 137	Paul Warfield	4.00	1.50
❑ 138	Randall Cunningham	4.00	1.50
❑ 139	Red Grange	6.00	2.50
❑ 140	Roger Staubach	8.00	3.00
❑ 141	Sammy Baugh	5.00	2.00
❑ 142	Sonny Jurgensen	4.00	1.50
❑ 143	Steve Largent	5.00	2.00
❑ 144	Steve Young	6.00	2.50
❑ 145	Terrell Davis	5.00	2.00
❑ 146	Terry Bradshaw	8.00	3.00
❑ 147	Tony Dorsett	4.00	1.50
❑ 148	Troy Aikman	6.00	2.50
❑ 149	Walter Payton	10.00	4.00
❑ 150	Warren Moon	5.00	2.00
❑ 151	Aaron Rodgers RC	25.00	10.00
❑ 152	Adrian McPherson RC	8.00	3.00
❑ 153	Airese Currie RC	8.00	3.00
❑ 154	Alvin Pearman RC	8.00	3.00
❑ 155	Anthony Davis RC	6.00	2.50
❑ 156	Brandon Jacobs RC	10.00	4.00
❑ 157	Brandon Jones RC	8.00	3.00
❑ 158	Cedric Benson RC	15.00	6.00
❑ 159	Cedric Houston RC	8.00	3.00
❑ 160	Chad Owens RC	8.00	3.00
❑ 161	Chris Henry RC	8.00	3.00
❑ 162	Nate Washington RC	6.00	2.50
❑ 163	Craig Bragg RC	6.00	2.50
❑ 164	Craphonso Thorpe RC	6.00	2.50
❑ 165	Damien Nash RC	6.00	2.50
❑ 166	Dan Orlovsky RC	10.00	4.00
❑ 167	Dante Ridgeway RC	6.00	2.50
❑ 168	Darren Sproles RC	8.00	3.00
❑ 169	David Greene RC	8.00	3.00
❑ 170	David Pollack RC	8.00	3.00
❑ 171	Deandra Cobb RC	6.00	2.50
❑ 172	DeMarcus Ware RC	12.00	5.00
❑ 173	Derek Anderson RC	8.00	3.00
❑ 174	Derrick Johnson RC	12.00	5.00
❑ 175	Erasmus James RC	8.00	3.00
❑ 176	Fabian Washington RC	8.00	3.00
❑ 177	Fred Gibson RC	6.00	2.50
❑ 178	Harry Williams RC	6.00	2.50
❑ 179	Heath Miller RC	20.00	7.50
❑ 180	J.R. Russell RC	6.00	2.50
❑ 181	James Kilian RC	8.00	3.00
❑ 182	Jerome Mathis RC	8.00	3.00
❑ 183	Larry Brackins RC	4.00	1.50
❑ 184	LeRon McCoy RC	6.00	2.50
❑ 185	Lionel Gates RC	6.00	2.50
❑ 186	Marcus Spears RC	8.00	3.00
❑ 187	Marion Barber RC	12.00	5.00
❑ 188	Marlin Jackson RC	8.00	3.00
❑ 189	Matt Cassel RC	12.00	5.00
❑ 190	Mike Williams	12.00	5.00
❑ 191	Noah Herron RC	8.00	3.00
❑ 192	Paris Warren RC	6.00	2.50
❑ 193	Rasheed Marshall RC	8.00	3.00
❑ 194	Roscoe Crosby RC	6.00	2.50
❑ 195	Roydell Williams RC	8.00	3.00
❑ 196	Ryan Fitzpatrick RC	12.00	5.00
❑ 197	Shawne Merriman RC	12.00	5.00
❑ 198	Tab Perry RC	8.00	3.00
❑ 199	Thomas Davis RC	8.00	3.00
❑ 200	Travis Johnson RC	6.00	2.50
❑ 201	Adam Jones JSY AU RC	30.00	12.50
❑ 202	Alex Smith QB JSY AU RC	100.00	50.00
❑ 203	Andrew Walter JSY AU RC	40.00	15.00
❑ 204	Antrel Rolle JSY AU RC	25.00	10.00
❑ 205	Braylon Edwards JSY AU RC	60.00	30.00
❑ 206	Carnell Williams JSY AU RC	120.00	60.00
❑ 207	C.Rogers JSY AU RC EXCH	30.00	15.00
❑ 208	Charlie Frye JSY AU RC	60.00	30.00
❑ 209	Ciatrick Fason JSY AU RC	25.00	10.00
❑ 210	Courtney Roby JSY AU RC	25.00	10.00
❑ 211	Eric Shelton JSY AU RC	25.00	10.00
❑ 212	Frank Gore JSY AU RC	30.00	12.50
❑ 213	J.J. Arrington JSY AU RC	40.00	20.00
❑ 214	Kyle Orton JSY AU RC	40.00	20.00
❑ 215	Jason Campbell JSY AU RC	60.00	30.00

❑ 216 Mark Bradley JSY AU RC 30.00 12.50
❑ 217 Mark Clayton JSY AU RC 30.00 12.50
❑ 218 Matt Jones JSY AU RC 60.00 35.00
❑ 219 Maurice Clarett JSY AU 25.00 10.00
❑ 220 Reggie Brown JSY AU RC 40.00 15.00
❑ 221 Ronnie Brown JSY AU RC 100.00 40.00
❑ 222 Roddy White JSY AU RC 25.00 10.00
❑ 223 Ryan Moats JSY AU RC 30.00 15.00
❑ 224 Roscoe Parrish JSY AU RC 25.00 10.00
❑ 225 Stefan LeFors JSY AU RC 25.00 10.00
❑ 226 Terrence Murphy JSY AU RC 25.00 10.00
❑ 227 Troy Williamson JSY AU RC 50.00 25.00
❑ 228 Vernand Morency JSY AU RC 20.00 7.50
❑ 229 Vincent Jackson JSY AU RC 25.00 10.00

1998 Leaf Rookies and Stars

❑ COMPLETE SET (300) 250.00 125.00
❑ 1 Keyshawn Johnson .60 .25
❑ 2 Marvin Harrison .60 .25
❑ 3 Eddie Kennison .40 .15
❑ 4 Bryant Young .25 .08
❑ 5 Darren Woodson .25 .08
❑ 6 Tyrone Wheatley .40 .15
❑ 7 Michael Westbrook .40 .15
❑ 8 Charles Way .25 .08
❑ 9 Ricky Watters .40 .15
❑ 10 Chris Warren .40 .15
❑ 11 Wesley Walls .40 .15
❑ 12 Tamarick Vanover .25 .08
❑ 13 Zach Thomas .60 .25
❑ 14 Derrick Thomas .60 .25
❑ 15 Yancey Thigpen .25 .08
❑ 16 Vinny Testaverde .40 .15
❑ 17 Dana Stubblefield .25 .08
❑ 18 J.J. Stokes .40 .15
❑ 19 James Stewart .40 .15
❑ 20 Jeff George .40 .15
❑ 21 John Randle .40 .15
❑ 22 Gary Brown .25 .08
❑ 23 Ed McCaffrey .40 .15
❑ 24 James Jett .40 .15
❑ 25 Rob Johnson .40 .15
❑ 26 Daryl Johnston .40 .15
❑ 27 Jermaine Lewis .40 .15
❑ 28 Tony Martin .40 .15
❑ 29 Derrick Mayes .40 .15
❑ 30 Keenan McCardell .40 .15
❑ 31 O.J. McDuffie .40 .15
❑ 32 Chris Chandler .40 .15
❑ 33 Doug Flutie .60 .25
❑ 34 Scott Mitchell .40 .15
❑ 35 Warren Moon .60 .25
❑ 36 Rob Moore .40 .15
❑ 37 Johnnie Morton .40 .15
❑ 38 Neil O'Donnell .40 .15
❑ 39 Rich Gannon .60 .25
❑ 40 Andre Reed .40 .15
❑ 41 Jake Reed .40 .15
❑ 42 Errict Rhett .40 .15
❑ 43 Simeon Rice .40 .15
❑ 44 Andre Rison .40 .15
❑ 45 Eric Moulds .60 .25
❑ 46 Frank Sanders .40 .15
❑ 47 Darnay Scott .40 .15
❑ 48 Junior Seau .60 .25
❑ 49 Shannon Sharpe .40 .15
❑ 50 Bruce Smith .40 .15
❑ 51 Jimmy Smith .40 .15
❑ 52 Robert Smith .60 .25
❑ 53 Derrick Alexander .40 .15
❑ 54 Kimble Anders .40 .15
❑ 55 Jamal Anderson .60 .25
❑ 56 Mario Bates .40 .15
❑ 57 Edgar Bennett .25 .08
❑ 58 Tim Biakabutuka .40 .15
❑ 59 Ki-Jana Carter .25 .08
❑ 60 Larry Centers .25 .08
❑ 61 Mark Chmura .40 .15
❑ 62 Wayne Chrebet .60 .25
❑ 63 Ben Coates .40 .15
❑ 64 Curtis Conway .40 .15
❑ 65 Randall Cunningham .60 .25
❑ 66 Rickey Dudley .25 .08
❑ 67 Bert Emanuel .40 .15
❑ 68 Bobby Engram .40 .15
❑ 69 William Floyd .25 .08
❑ 70 Irving Fryar .40 .15
❑ 71 Elvis Grbac .40 .15
❑ 72 Kevin Greene .40 .15
❑ 73 Jim Harbaugh .40 .15
❑ 74 Raymont Harris .25 .08
❑ 75 Garrison Hearst .60 .25
❑ 76 Greg Hill .25 .08
❑ 77 Desmond Howard .40 .15
❑ 78 Bobby Hoying .40 .15
❑ 79 Michael Jackson .25 .08
❑ 80 Terry Allen .60 .25
❑ 81 Jerome Bettis .60 .25
❑ 82 Jeff Blake .40 .15
❑ 83 Robert Brooks .40 .15
❑ 84 Tim Brown .60 .25
❑ 85 Isaac Bruce .60 .25
❑ 86 Cris Carter .60 .25
❑ 87 Ty Detmer .40 .15
❑ 88 Trent Dilfer .60 .25
❑ 89 Marshall Faulk .75 .30
❑ 90 Antonio Freeman .60 .25
❑ 91 Gus Frerotte .25 .08
❑ 92 Joey Galloway .40 .15
❑ 93 Michael Irvin .60 .25
❑ 94 Brad Johnson .60 .25
❑ 95 Danny Kanell .40 .15
❑ 96 Napoleon Kaufman .60 .25
❑ 97 Dorsey Levens .60 .25
❑ 98 Natrone Means .40 .15
❑ 99 Herman Moore .40 .15
❑ 100 Adrian Murrell .40 .15
❑ 101 Carl Pickens .40 .15
❑ 102 Rod Smith .40 .15
❑ 103 Thurman Thomas .60 .25
❑ 104 Reggie White .60 .25
❑ 105 Jim Druckenmiller .25 .08
❑ 106 Antowain Smith .60 .25
❑ 107 Reidel Anthony .40 .15
❑ 108 Ike Hilliard .40 .15
❑ 109 Rae Carruth .25 .08
❑ 110 Troy Davis .25 .08
❑ 111 Terance Mathis .40 .15
❑ 112 Brett Favre 2.50 1.00
❑ 113 Dan Marino 2.50 1.00
❑ 114 Emmitt Smith 2.00 .75
❑ 115 Barry Sanders 2.00 .75
❑ 116 Eddie George .60 .25
❑ 117 Drew Bledsoe 1.00 .40
❑ 118 Troy Aikman 1.25 .50
❑ 119 Terrell Davis .60 .25
❑ 120 John Elway 2.50 1.00
❑ 121 Mark Brunell .60 .25
❑ 122 Jerry Rice 1.25 .50
❑ 123 Kordell Stewart .60 .25
❑ 124 Steve McNair .60 .25
❑ 125 Curtis Martin .60 .25
❑ 126 Steve Young .75 .30
❑ 127 Kerry Collins .40 .15
❑ 128 Terry Glenn .60 .25
❑ 129 Deion Sanders .60 .25
❑ 130 Mike Alstott .60 .25
❑ 131 Tony Banks .40 .15
❑ 132 Karim Abdul-Jabbar .60 .25
❑ 133 Terrell Owens .60 .25
❑ 134 Yatil Green .25 .08
❑ 135 Tony Gonzalez .60 .25
❑ 136 Byron Hanspard .25 .08
❑ 137 David LaFleur .25 .08
❑ 138 Danny Wuerffel .40 .15
❑ 139 Tiki Barber .60 .25
❑ 140 Peter Boulware .25 .08
❑ 141 Will Blackwell .25 .08
❑ 142 Warrick Dunn .60 .25
❑ 143 Corey Dillon .60 .25
❑ 144 Jake Plummer .60 .25
❑ 145 Neil Smith .40 .15
❑ 146 Charles Johnson .25 .08
❑ 147 Fred Lane .25 .08
❑ 148 Dan Wilkinson .25 .08
❑ 149 Ken Norton Jr. .25 .08
❑ 150 Stephen Davis .25 .08
❑ 151 Gilbert Brown .25 .08
❑ 152 Kenny Bynum RC .25 .08
❑ 153 Derrick Cullors .25 .08
❑ 154 Charlie Garner .40 .15
❑ 155 Jeff Graham .25 .08
❑ 156 Warren Sapp .40 .15
❑ 157 Jerald Moore .25 .08
❑ 158 Sean Dawkins .25 .08
❑ 159 Charlie Jones .25 .08
❑ 160 Kevin Lockett .25 .08
❑ 161 James McKnight .60 .25
❑ 162 Chris Penn .25 .08
❑ 163 Leslie Shepherd .25 .08
❑ 164 Karl Williams .25 .08
❑ 165 Mark Bruener .25 .08
❑ 166 Ernie Conwell .25 .08
❑ 167 Ken Dilger .25 .08
❑ 168 Troy Drayton .25 .08
❑ 169 Freddie Jones .25 .08
❑ 170 Dale Carter .25 .08
❑ 171 Charles Woodson RC 8.00 3.00
❑ 172 Alonzo Mayes RC 2.50 1.00
❑ 173 Andre Wadsworth RC 4.00 1.50
❑ 174 Grant Wistrom RC 4.00 1.50
❑ 175 Greg Ellis RC 2.50 1.00
❑ 176 Chris Howard RC 2.50 1.00
❑ 177 Keith Brooking RC 6.00 2.50
❑ 178 Takeo Spikes RC 6.00 2.50
❑ 179 Anthony Simmons RC 4.00 1.50
❑ 180 Brian Simmons RC 4.00 1.50
❑ 181 Sam Cowart RC 4.00 1.50
❑ 182 Ken Oxendine RC 2.50 1.00
❑ 183 Vonnie Holliday RC 4.00 1.50
❑ 184 Terry Fair RC 4.00 1.50
❑ 185 Shaun Williams RC 4.00 1.50
❑ 186 Tremayne Stephens RC 2.50 1.00
❑ 187 Duane Starks RC 2.50 1.00
❑ 188 Jason Peter RC 2.50 1.00
❑ 189 Tebucky Jones RC 2.50 1.00
❑ 190 Donovin Darius RC 4.00 1.50
❑ 191 R.W. McQuarters RC 4.00 1.50
❑ 192 Corey Chavous RC 6.00 2.50
❑ 193 Cameron Cleeland RC 2.50 1.00
❑ 194 Stephen Alexander RC 4.00 1.50
❑ 195 Rod Rutledge RC 2.50 1.00
❑ 196 Scott Frost RC 2.50 1.00
❑ 197 Fred Beasley RC 2.50 1.00
❑ 198 Dorian Boose RC 2.50 1.00
❑ 199 Randy Moss RC 30.00 12.50
❑ 200 Jacquez Green RC 4.00 1.50
❑ 201 Marcus Nash RC 2.50 1.00
❑ 202 Hines Ward RC 25.00 12.50
❑ 203 Kevin Dyson RC 6.00 2.50
❑ 204 E.G. Green RC 4.00 1.50
❑ 205 Germane Crowell RC 4.00 1.50
❑ 206 Joe Jurevicius RC 6.00 2.50

❑ 207 Tony Simmons RC 4.00 1.50
❑ 208 Tim Dwight RC 6.00 2.50
❑ 209 Az-Zahir Hakim RC 6.00 2.50
❑ 210 Jerome Pathon RC 6.00 2.50
❑ 211 Pat Johnson RC 4.00 1.50
❑ 212 Mikhael Ricks RC 4.00 1.50
❑ 213 Donald Hayes RC 4.00 1.50
❑ 214 Jammi German RC 2.50 1.00
❑ 215 Larry Shannon RC 2.50 1.00
❑ 216 Brian Alford RC 2.50 1.00
❑ 217 Curtis Enis RC 2.50 1.00
❑ 218 Fred Taylor RC 10.00 4.00
❑ 219 Robert Edwards RC 4.00 1.50
❑ 220 Ahman Green RC 30.00 12.50
❑ 221 Tavian Banks RC 4.00 1.50
❑ 222 Skip Hicks RC 4.00 1.50
❑ 223 Robert Holcombe RC 4.00 1.50
❑ 224 John Avery RC 4.00 1.50
❑ 225 Chris Fuamatu-Ma'afala RC 4.00 1.50
❑ 226 Michael Pittman RC 8.00 4.00
❑ 227 Rashaan Shehee RC 4.00 1.50
❑ 228 Jonathan Linton RC 4.00 1.50
❑ 229 Jon Ritchie RC 4.00 1.50
❑ 230 Chris Floyd RC 2.50 1.00
❑ 231 Wilmont Perry RC 2.50 1.00
❑ 232 Raymond Priester RC 2.50 1.00
❑ 233 Peyton Manning RC 50.00 25.00
❑ 234 Ryan Leaf RC 6.00 2.50
❑ 235 Brian Griese RC 12.00 5.00
❑ 236 Jeff Ogden RC 6.00 2.50
❑ 237 Charlie Batch RC 6.00 2.50
❑ 238 Moses Moreno RC 2.50 1.00
❑ 239 Jonathan Quinn RC 6.00 2.50
❑ 240 Flozell Adams RC 2.50 1.00
❑ 241 Brett Favre PT 12.00 5.00
❑ 242 Dan Marino PT 12.00 5.00
❑ 243 Emmitt Smith PT 10.00 4.00
❑ 244 Barry Sanders PT 10.00 4.00
❑ 245 Eddie George PT 2.50 1.00
❑ 246 Drew Bledsoe PT 5.00 2.00
❑ 247 Troy Aikman PT 6.00 2.50
❑ 248 Terrell Davis PT 2.50 1.00
❑ 249 John Elway PT 12.00 5.00
❑ 250 Carl Pickens PT 2.50 1.00
❑ 251 Jerry Rice PT 6.00 2.50
❑ 252 Kordell Stewart PT 2.50 1.00
❑ 253 Steve McNair PT 2.50 1.00
❑ 254 Curtis Martin PT 2.50 1.00
❑ 255 Steve Young PT 4.00 1.50
❑ 256 Herman Moore PT 2.50 1.00
❑ 257 Dorsey Levens PT 2.50 1.00
❑ 258 Deion Sanders PT 2.50 1.00
❑ 259 Napoleon Kaufman PT 2.50 1.00
❑ 260 Warrick Dunn PT 2.50 1.00
❑ 261 Corey Dillon PT 2.50 1.00
❑ 262 Jerome Bettis PT 2.50 1.00
❑ 263 Tim Brown PT 2.50 1.00
❑ 264 Cris Carter PT 2.50 1.00
❑ 265 Antonio Freeman PT 2.50 1.00
❑ 266 Randy Moss PT 15.00 6.00
❑ 267 Curtis Enis PT 2.50 1.00
❑ 268 Fred Taylor PT 4.00 1.50
❑ 269 Robert Edwards PT 2.50 1.00
❑ 270 Peyton Manning PT 25.00 10.00
❑ 271 Barry Sanders TL 1.00 .40
❑ 272 Eddie George TL .40 .15
❑ 273 Troy Aikman TL .60 .25
❑ 274 Mark Brunell TL .60 .25
❑ 275 Kordell Stewart TL .60 .25
❑ 276 Tim Biakabutuka TL .25 .08
❑ 277 Terry Glenn TL .25 .08
❑ 278 Mike Alstott TL .25 .08
❑ 279 Tony Banks TL .25 .08
❑ 280 Karim Abdul-Jabbar TL .25 .08
❑ 281 Terrell Owens TL .40 .15
❑ 282 Byron Hanspard TL .25 .08
❑ 283 Jake Plummer TL .40 .15
❑ 284 Terry Allen TL .25 .08
❑ 285 Jeff Blake TL .25 .08
❑ 286 Brad Johnson TL .25 .08
❑ 287 Danny Kanell TL .25 .08
❑ 288 Natrone Means TL .25 .08
❑ 289 Rod Smith TL .25 .08
❑ 290 Thurman Thomas TL .25 .08
❑ 291 Reggie White TL .25 .08
❑ 292 Troy Davis TL .25 .08
❑ 293 Curtis Conway TL .25 .08
❑ 294 Irving Fryar TL .25 .08
❑ 295 Jim Harbaugh TL .25 .08
❑ 296 Andre Rison TL .25 .08
❑ 297 Ricky Watters TL .25 .08
❑ 298 Keyshawn Johnson TL .25 .08
❑ 299 Jeff George TL .25 .08
❑ 300 Marshall Faulk TL .60 .25

1999 Leaf Rookies and Stars

❑ COMPLETE SET (300) 150.00 75.00
❑ COMP.SET w/o SP's (200) 30.00 15.00
❑ 1 Frank Sanders .40 .15
❑ 2 Adrian Murrell .40 .15
❑ 3 Rob Moore .40 .15
❑ 4 Simeon Rice .40 .15
❑ 5 Michael Pittman .25 .08
❑ 6 Jake Plummer .40 .15
❑ 7 Chris Chandler .40 .15
❑ 8 Tim Dwight .40 .15
❑ 9 Chris Calloway .25 .08
❑ 10 Terance Mathis .40 .15
❑ 11 Jamal Anderson .60 .25
❑ 12 Byron Hanspard .25 .08
❑ 13 O.J. Santiago .25 .08
❑ 14 Ken Oxendine .25 .08
❑ 15 Priest Holmes 1.00 .40
❑ 16 Scott Mitchell .25 .08
❑ 17 Tony Banks .40 .15
❑ 18 Patrick Johnson .25 .08
❑ 19 Rod Woodson .40 .15
❑ 20 Jermaine Lewis .40 .15
❑ 21 Errict Rhett .40 .15
❑ 22 Stoney Case .25 .08
❑ 23 Andre Reed .40 .15
❑ 24 Eric Moulds .40 .15
❑ 25 Rob Johnson .40 .15
❑ 26 Doug Flutie .60 .25
❑ 27 Bruce Smith .40 .15
❑ 28 Jay Riemersma .25 .08
❑ 29 Antowain Smith .25 .08
❑ 30 Thurman Thomas .40 .15
❑ 31 Jonathan Linton .25 .08
❑ 32 Muhsin Muhammad .40 .15
❑ 33 Rae Carruth .25 .08
❑ 34 Wesley Walls .40 .15
❑ 35 Fred Lane .25 .08
❑ 36 Kevin Greene .25 .08
❑ 37 Tim Biakabutuka .40 .15
❑ 38 Curtis Enis .25 .08
❑ 39 Shane Matthews .40 .15
❑ 40 Bobby Engram .40 .15
❑ 41 Curtis Conway .40 .15
❑ 42 Marcus Robinson 1.25 .50
❑ 43 Darnay Scott .25 .08
❑ 44 Carl Pickens .40 .15
❑ 45 Corey Dillon .60 .25
❑ 46 Jeff Blake .40 .15
❑ 47 Terry Kirby .25 .08
❑ 48 Ty Detmer .40 .15
❑ 49 Leslie Shepherd .25 .08
❑ 50 Karim Abdul-Jabbar .40 .15
❑ 51 Emmitt Smith 1.25 .50
❑ 52 Deion Sanders .60 .25
❑ 53 Michael Irvin .40 .15
❑ 54 Rocket Ismail .40 .15
❑ 55 David LaFleur .25 .08
❑ 56 Troy Aikman 1.25 .50
❑ 57 Ed McCaffrey .40 .15
❑ 58 Rod Smith .40 .15
❑ 59 Shannon Sharpe .40 .15
❑ 60 Brian Griese .60 .25
❑ 61 John Elway 2.00 .75
❑ 62 Bubby Brister .25 .08
❑ 63 Neil Smith .40 .15
❑ 64 Terrell Davis .60 .25
❑ 65 John Avery .25 .08
❑ 66 Derek Loville .25 .08
❑ 67 Ron Rivers .25 .08
❑ 68 Herman Moore .40 .15
❑ 69 Johnnie Morton .40 .15
❑ 70 Charlie Batch .60 .25
❑ 71 Barry Sanders 2.00 .75
❑ 72 Germane Crowell .25 .08
❑ 73 Greg Hill .25 .08
❑ 74 Gus Frerotte .40 .15
❑ 75 Corey Bradford .25 .08
❑ 76 Dorsey Levens .60 .25
❑ 77 Antonio Freeman .60 .25
❑ 78 Mark Chmura .25 .08
❑ 79 Brett Favre 2.00 .75
❑ 80 Bill Schroeder .40 .15
❑ 81 Matt Hasselbeck .60 .25
❑ 82 E.G. Green .25 .08
❑ 83 Ken Dilger .25 .08
❑ 84 Jerome Pathon .25 .08
❑ 85 Marvin Harrison .60 .25
❑ 86 Peyton Manning 2.00 .75
❑ 87 Tavian Banks .25 .08
❑ 88 Keenan McCardell .40 .15
❑ 89 Mark Brunell .60 .25
❑ 90 Fred Taylor .60 .25
❑ 91 Jimmy Smith .40 .15
❑ 92 James Stewart .40 .15
❑ 93 Kyle Brady .25 .08
❑ 94 Derrick Thomas .60 .25
❑ 95 Rashaan Shehee .25 .08
❑ 96 Derrick Alexander WR .40 .15
❑ 97 Byron Bam Morris .25 .08
❑ 98 Andre Rison .40 .15
❑ 99 Elvis Grbac .40 .15
❑ 100 Tony Gonzalez .60 .25
❑ 101 Donnell Bennett .25 .08
❑ 102 Warren Moon .60 .25
❑ 103 Zach Thomas .60 .25
❑ 104 Oronde Gadsden .40 .15
❑ 105 Dan Marino 2.00 .75
❑ 106 O.J. McDuffie .40 .15
❑ 107 Tony Martin .40 .15
❑ 108 Randy Moss 1.50 .60
❑ 109 Cris Carter .60 .25
❑ 110 Robert Smith .60 .25
❑ 111 Randall Cunningham .60 .25
❑ 112 Jake Reed .40 .15
❑ 113 John Randle .40 .15
❑ 114 Leroy Hoard .25 .08
❑ 115 Jeff George .40 .15
❑ 116 Ty Law .40 .15
❑ 117 Shawn Jefferson .25 .08
❑ 118 Troy Brown .40 .15
❑ 119 Robert Edwards .25 .08
❑ 120 Tony Simmons .25 .08
❑ 121 Terry Glenn .60 .25
❑ 122 Ben Coates .40 .15
❑ 123 Drew Bledsoe .75 .30
❑ 124 Terry Allen .40 .15
❑ 125 Cameron Cleeland .25 .08

❑ 126 Eddie Kennison .40 .15
❑ 127 Amani Toomer .25 .08
❑ 128 Kerry Collins .40 .15
❑ 129 Joe Jurevicius .40 .15
❑ 130 Tiki Barber .60 .25
❑ 131 Ike Hilliard .25 .08
❑ 132 Michael Strahan .40 .15
❑ 133 Gary Brown .25 .08
❑ 134 Jason Sehorn .25 .08
❑ 135 Curtis Martin .60 .25
❑ 136 Vinny Testaverde .40 .15
❑ 137 Dedric Ward .25 .08
❑ 138 Keyshawn Johnson .60 .25
❑ 139 Wayne Chrebet .40 .15
❑ 140 Tyrone Wheatley .40 .15
❑ 141 Napoleon Kaufman .60 .25
❑ 142 Tim Brown .60 .25
❑ 143 Rickey Dudley .25 .08
❑ 144 Jon Ritchie .25 .08
❑ 145 James Jett .25 .08
❑ 146 Rich Gannon .60 .25
❑ 147 Charles Woodson .60 .25
❑ 148 Charles Johnson .25 .08
❑ 149 Duce Staley .60 .25
❑ 150 Will Blackwell .25 .08
❑ 151 Kordell Stewart .40 .15
❑ 152 Jerome Bettis .60 .25
❑ 153 Hines Ward .60 .25
❑ 154 Richard Huntley .40 .15
❑ 155 Natrone Means .40 .15
❑ 156 Mikhael Ricks .25 .08
❑ 157 Junior Seau .60 .25
❑ 158 Jim Harbaugh .40 .15
❑ 159 Ryan Leaf .60 .25
❑ 160 Erik Kramer .25 .08
❑ 161 Terrell Owens .60 .25
❑ 162 J.J. Stokes .40 .15
❑ 163 Lawrence Phillips .40 .15
❑ 164 Charlie Garner .40 .15
❑ 165 Jerry Rice 1.25 .50
❑ 166 Garrison Hearst .40 .15
❑ 167 Steve Young .75 .30
❑ 168 Derrick Mayes .40 .15
❑ 169 Ahman Green .60 .25
❑ 170 Joey Galloway .40 .15
❑ 171 Ricky Watters .40 .15
❑ 172 Jon Kitna .60 .25
❑ 173 Sean Dawkins .25 .08
❑ 174 Az-Zahir Hakim .25 .08
❑ 175 Robert Holcombe .25 .08
❑ 176 Isaac Bruce .60 .25
❑ 177 Amp Lee .25 .08
❑ 178 Marshall Faulk .75 .30
❑ 179 Trent Green .60 .25
❑ 180 Eric Zeier .40 .15
❑ 181 Bert Emanuel .40 .15
❑ 182 Jacquez Green .25 .08
❑ 183 Reidel Anthony .40 .15
❑ 184 Warren Sapp .25 .08
❑ 185 Mike Alstott .60 .25
❑ 186 Warrick Dunn .60 .25
❑ 187 Trent Dilfer .60 .25
❑ 188 Neil O'Donnell .40 .15
❑ 189 Eddie George .60 .25
❑ 190 Yancey Thigpen .25 .08
❑ 191 Steve McNair .60 .25
❑ 192 Kevin Dyson .40 .15
❑ 193 Frank Wycheck .25 .08
❑ 194 Stephen Davis .60 .25
❑ 195 Stephen Alexander .25 .08
❑ 196 Darrell Green .25 .08
❑ 197 Skip Hicks .25 .08
❑ 198 Brad Johnson .60 .25
❑ 199 Michael Westbrook .40 .15
❑ 200 Albert Connell .25 .08
❑ 201 David Boston RC 3.00 1.50
❑ 202 Joel Makovicka RC 3.00 1.50
❑ 203 Chris Greisen RC 2.50 1.25
❑ 204 Jeff Paulk RC 1.50 .75
❑ 205 Reginald Kelly RC 2.50 1.25
❑ 206 Chris McAlister RC 2.50 1.25
❑ 207 Brandon Stokley RC 4.00 1.50
❑ 208 Antoine Winfield RC 2.50 1.25
❑ 209 Bobby Collins RC 1.50 .75
❑ 210 Peerless Price RC 3.00 1.50
❑ 211 Shawn Bryson RC 3.00 1.50
❑ 212 Sheldon Jackson RC 2.50 1.25
❑ 213 Kamil Loud RC 1.50 .75
❑ 214 D'Wayne Bates RC 2.50 1.25
❑ 215 Jerry Azumah RC 2.50 1.25
❑ 216 Marty Booker RC 3.00 1.50
❑ 217 Cade McNown RC 2.50 1.25
❑ 218 James Allen RC 3.00 1.50
❑ 219 Nick Williams RC 2.50 1.25
❑ 220 Akili Smith RC 2.50 1.25
❑ 221 Craig Yeast RC 2.50 1.25
❑ 222 Damon Griffen RC 2.50 1.25
❑ 223 Scott Covington RC 3.00 1.50
❑ 224 Michael Basnight RC 1.50 .75
❑ 225 Ronnie Powell RC 1.50 .75
❑ 226 Rahim Abdullah RC 2.50 1.25
❑ 227 Tim Couch RC 3.00 1.50
❑ 228 Kevin Johnson RC 3.00 1.50
❑ 229 Darrin Chiaverini RC 2.50 1.25
❑ 230 Mark Campbell RC 2.50 1.25
❑ 231 Mike Lucky RC 2.50 1.25
❑ 232 Robert Thomas RC 2.50 1.25
❑ 233 Ebenezer Ekuban RC 2.50 1.25
❑ 234 Dat Nguyen RC 3.00 1.50
❑ 235 Wane McGarity RC 1.50 .75
❑ 236 Jason Tucker RC 2.50 1.25
❑ 237 Olandis Gary RC 3.00 1.50
❑ 238 Al Wilson RC 3.00 1.50
❑ 239 Travis McGriff RC 1.50 .75
❑ 240 Desmond Clark RC 3.00 1.50
❑ 241 Andre Cooper RC 1.50 .75
❑ 242 Chris Watson RC 1.50 .75
❑ 243 Sedrick Irvin RC 1.50 .75
❑ 244 Chris Claiborne RC 1.50 .75
❑ 245 Cory Sauter RC 1.50 .75
❑ 246 Brock Olivo RC 1.50 .75
❑ 247 De'Mond Parker RC 1.50 .75
❑ 248 Aaron Brooks RC 10.00 4.00
❑ 249 Antuan Edwards RC 2.50 1.25
❑ 250 Basil Mitchell RC 1.50 .75
❑ 251 Terrence Wilkins RC 2.50 1.25
❑ 252 Edgerrin James RC 15.00 6.00
❑ 253 Fernando Bryant RC 2.50 1.25
❑ 254 Mike Cloud RC 2.50 1.25
❑ 255 Larry Parker RC 3.00 1.50
❑ 256 Rob Konrad RC 3.00 1.50
❑ 257 Cecil Collins RC 1.50 .75
❑ 258 James Johnson RC 2.50 1.25
❑ 259 Jim Kleinsasser RC 3.00 1.50
❑ 260 Daunte Culpepper RC 15.00 6.00
❑ 261 Michael Bishop RC 3.00 1.50
❑ 262 Andy Katzenmoyer RC 2.50 1.25
❑ 263 Kevin Faulk RC 3.00 1.50
❑ 264 Brett Bech RC 1.50 .75
❑ 265 Ricky Williams RC 8.00 3.00
❑ 266 Sean Bennett RC 1.50 .75
❑ 267 Joe Montgomery RC 2.50 1.25
❑ 268 Dan Campbell RC 1.50 .75
❑ 269 Ray Lucas RC 3.00 1.50
❑ 270 Scott Dreisbach RC 2.50 1.25
❑ 271 Jed Weaver RC 1.50 .75
❑ 272 Dameane Douglas RC 2.50 1.25
❑ 273 Cecil Martin RC 2.50 1.25
❑ 274 Donovan McNabb RC 20.00 7.50
❑ 275 Na Brown RC 2.50 1.25
❑ 276 Jerame Tuman RC 3.00 1.50
❑ 277 Amos Zereoue RC 3.00 1.50
❑ 278 Troy Edwards RC 2.50 1.25
❑ 279 Jermaine Fazande RC 2.50 1.25
❑ 280 Steve Heiden RC 3.00 1.50
❑ 281 Jeff Garcia RC 20.00 7.50
❑ 282 Terry Jackson RC 2.50 1.25
❑ 283 Charlie Rogers RC 2.50 1.25
❑ 284 Brock Huard RC 3.00 1.50
❑ 285 Karsten Bailey RC 2.50 1.25
❑ 286 Lamar King RC 1.50 .75
❑ 287 Justin Watson RC 1.50 .75
❑ 288 Kurt Warner RC 20.00 7.50
❑ 289 Torry Holt RC 12.00 5.00
❑ 290 Joe Germaine RC 2.50 1.25
❑ 291 Dre' Bly RC 3.00 1.50
❑ 292 Martin Gramatica RC 1.50 .75
❑ 293 Rabih Abdullah RC 2.50 1.25
❑ 294 Shaun King RC 2.50 1.25
❑ 295 Anthony McFarland RC 2.50 1.25
❑ 296 Darnell McDonald RC 2.50 1.25
❑ 297 Kevin Daft RC 2.50 1.25
❑ 298 Jevon Kearse RC 8.00 3.00
❑ 299 Mike Sellers .25 .08
❑ 300 Champ Bailey RC 6.00 2.50

2000 Leaf Rookies and Stars

❑ COMP.SET w/o SP's (100) 15.00 6.00
❑ 1 Jake Plummer .40 .15
❑ 2 David Boston .60 .25
❑ 3 Tim Dwight .60 .25
❑ 4 Jamal Anderson .60 .25
❑ 5 Chris Chandler .40 .15
❑ 6 Tony Banks .40 .15
❑ 7 Qadry Ismail .40 .15
❑ 8 Eric Moulds .60 .25
❑ 9 Doug Flutie .60 .25
❑ 10 Lamar Smith .40 .15
❑ 11 Peerless Price .40 .15
❑ 12 Rob Johnson .40 .15
❑ 13 Reggie White .60 .25
❑ 14 Muhsin Muhammad .40 .15
❑ 15 Steve Beuerlein .40 .15
❑ 16 Cade McNown .25 .08
❑ 17 Derrick Alexander .40 .15
❑ 18 Marcus Robinson .60 .25
❑ 19 Corey Dillon .60 .25
❑ 20 Akili Smith .25 .08
❑ 21 Tim Couch .40 .15
❑ 22 Kevin Johnson .60 .25
❑ 23 Emmitt Smith 1.25 .50
❑ 24 Troy Aikman 1.25 .50
❑ 25 Joey Galloway .40 .15
❑ 26 Rocket Ismail .40 .15
❑ 27 John Elway 2.00 .75
❑ 28 Terrell Davis .60 .25
❑ 29 Brian Griese .60 .25
❑ 30 Olandis Gary .60 .25
❑ 31 Ed McCaffrey .60 .25
❑ 32 Rod Smith .40 .15
❑ 33 Barry Sanders 1.50 .60
❑ 34 Charlie Batch .60 .25
❑ 35 Germane Crowell .25 .08
❑ 36 James Stewart .40 .15
❑ 37 Brett Favre 2.00 .75
❑ 38 Dorsey Levens .40 .15
❑ 39 Antonio Freeman .60 .25
❑ 40 Peyton Manning 1.50 .60
❑ 41 Edgerrin James 1.00 .40
❑ 42 Marvin Harrison .60 .25
❑ 43 Fred Taylor .60 .25
❑ 44 Mark Brunell .60 .25
❑ 45 Jimmy Smith .40 .15

❑ 46	Elvis Grbac	.40	.15
❑ 47	Tony Gonzalez	.40	.15
❑ 48	Dan Marino	2.00	.75
❑ 49	Joe Horn	.40	.15
❑ 50	Jay Fiedler	.60	.25
❑ 51	James Allen	.40	.15
❑ 52	Randy Moss	1.25	.50
❑ 53	Daunte Culpepper	.75	.30
❑ 54	Cris Carter	.60	.25
❑ 55	Robert Smith	.60	.25
❑ 56	Drew Bledsoe	.75	.30
❑ 57	Terry Glenn	.60	.25
❑ 58	Ricky Williams	.60	.25
❑ 59	Amani Toomer	.40	.15
❑ 60	Kerry Collins	.40	.15
❑ 61	Curtis Martin	.60	.25
❑ 62	Vinny Testaverde	.40	.15
❑ 63	Wayne Chrebet	.40	.15
❑ 64	Tim Brown	.60	.25
❑ 65	Tyrone Wheatley	.40	.15
❑ 66	Rich Gannon	.60	.25
❑ 67	Donovan McNabb	1.00	.40
❑ 68	Duce Staley	.60	.25
❑ 69	Jerome Bettis	.60	.25
❑ 70	Donald Hayes	.25	.08
❑ 71	Junior Seau	.60	.25
❑ 72	Jermaine Fazande	.25	.08
❑ 73	Jerry Rice	1.25	.50
❑ 74	Steve Young	.75	.30
❑ 75	Terrell Owens	.60	.25
❑ 76	Charlie Garner	.40	.15
❑ 77	Jeff Garcia	.60	.25
❑ 78	Tim Biakabutuka	.40	.15
❑ 79	Tiki Barber	.60	.25
❑ 80	Ricky Watters	.40	.15
❑ 81	Kurt Warner	1.25	.50
❑ 82	Marshall Faulk	.75	.30
❑ 83	Isaac Bruce	.60	.25
❑ 84	Torry Holt	.60	.25
❑ 85	Mike Alstott	.60	.25
❑ 86	Warrick Dunn	.60	.25
❑ 87	Shaun King	.25	.08
❑ 88	Keyshawn Johnson	.60	.25
❑ 89	Warren Sapp	.40	.15
❑ 90	Eddie George	.60	.25
❑ 91	Jevon Kearse	.60	.25
❑ 92	Steve McNair	.60	.25
❑ 93	Carl Pickens	.40	.15
❑ 94	Deion Sanders	.60	.25
❑ 95	Stephen Davis	.60	.25
❑ 96	Brad Johnson	.60	.25
❑ 97	Bruce Smith	.40	.15
❑ 98	Michael Westbrook	.40	.15
❑ 99	Albert Connell	.25	.08
❑ 100	Jeff George	.40	.15
❑ 101	Thomas Jones RC	15.00	6.00
❑ 102	Bashir Yamini RC	5.00	2.00
❑ 103	Jamal Lewis RC	25.00	10.00
❑ 104	Travis Taylor RC	10.00	4.00
❑ 105	Chris Redman RC	8.00	3.00
❑ 106	Avion Black RC	8.00	3.00
❑ 107	Sammy Morris RC	8.00	3.00
❑ 108	Dez White RC	10.00	4.00
❑ 109	Peter Warrick RC	10.00	4.00
❑ 110	Ron Dugans RC	5.00	2.00
❑ 111	Curtis Keaton RC	8.00	3.00
❑ 112	Danny Farmer RC	8.00	3.00
❑ 113	Courtney Brown RC	10.00	4.00
❑ 114	Dennis Northcutt RC	10.00	4.00
❑ 115	Travis Prentice RC	8.00	3.00
❑ 116	JaJuan Dawson RC	5.00	2.00
❑ 117	Spergon Wynn RC	8.00	3.00
❑ 118	Michael Wiley RC	8.00	3.00
❑ 119	Chris Cole RC	8.00	3.00
❑ 120	Mike Anderson RC	12.00	5.00
❑ 121	Muneer Moore RC	5.00	2.00
❑ 122	Reuben Droughns RC	12.00	5.00
❑ 123	Bubba Franks RC	10.00	4.00
❑ 124	Anthony Lucas RC	5.00	2.00
❑ 125	Charles Lee RC	5.00	2.00
❑ 126	R.Jay Soward RC	8.00	3.00
❑ 127	Shyrone Stith RC	8.00	3.00
❑ 128	Sylvester Morris RC	8.00	3.00
❑ 129	Frank Moreau RC	8.00	3.00
❑ 130	Dante Hall RC	20.00	7.50
❑ 131	Doug Chapman RC	8.00	3.00
❑ 132	Troy Walters RC	10.00	4.00
❑ 133	J.R. Redmond RC	8.00	3.00
❑ 134	Tom Brady RC	120.00	60.00
❑ 135	Terrelle Smith RC	8.00	3.00
❑ 136	Chad Morton RC	10.00	4.00
❑ 137	Ron Dayne RC	10.00	4.00
❑ 138	Ron Dixon RC	8.00	3.00
❑ 139	Chad Pennington RC	25.00	10.00
❑ 140	Anthony Becht RC	10.00	4.00
❑ 141	Laveranues Coles RC	12.00	5.00
❑ 142	Windrell Hayes RC	8.00	3.00
❑ 143	Sebastian Janikowski RC	10.00	4.00
❑ 144	Jerry Porter RC	12.00	5.00
❑ 145	Corey Simon RC	10.00	4.00
❑ 146	Todd Pinkston RC	10.00	4.00
❑ 147	Gari Scott RC	5.00	2.00
❑ 148	Plaxico Burress RC	20.00	7.50
❑ 149	Tee Martin RC	10.00	4.00
❑ 150	Trevor Gaylor RC	8.00	3.00
❑ 151	Ronney Jenkins RC	8.00	3.00
❑ 152	Giovanni Carmazzi RC	5.00	2.00
❑ 153	Tim Rattay RC	10.00	4.00
❑ 154	Shaun Alexander RC	40.00	20.00
❑ 155	Darrell Jackson RC	15.00	6.00
❑ 156	James Williams RC	8.00	3.00
❑ 157	Trung Canidate RC	8.00	3.00
❑ 158	Joe Hamilton RC	8.00	3.00
❑ 159	Erron Kinney RC	10.00	4.00
❑ 160	Todd Husak RC	10.00	4.00
❑ 161	Raynoch Thompson RC	8.00	3.00
❑ 162	Darwin Walker RC	5.00	2.00
❑ 163	Jay Tant RC	5.00	2.00
❑ 164	Doug Johnson RC	10.00	4.00
❑ 165	Robert Bean RC	8.00	3.00
❑ 166	Mark Simoneau RC	8.00	3.00
❑ 167	John Jones RC	8.00	3.00
❑ 168	Obafemi Ayanbadejo RC	8.00	3.00
❑ 169	Mike Brown RC	15.00	6.00
❑ 170	Shockmain Davis RC	5.00	2.00
❑ 171	Erik Flowers RC	8.00	3.00
❑ 172	Corey Moore RC	5.00	2.00
❑ 173	Drew Haddad RC	5.00	2.00
❑ 174	Kwame Cavil RC	5.00	2.00
❑ 175	Pat Dennis RC	5.00	2.00
❑ 176	Rashard Anderson RC	8.00	3.00
❑ 177	Brian Finneran RC	10.00	4.00
❑ 178	Na'il Diggs RC	8.00	3.00
❑ 179	Marc Bulger RC	20.00	7.50
❑ 180	Mondriel Fulcher RC	5.00	2.00
❑ 181	Dwayne Carswell	5.00	2.00
❑ 182	Brian Urlacher RC	25.00	10.00
❑ 183	Paul Edinger RC	10.00	4.00
❑ 184	Karon Coleman RC	8.00	3.00
❑ 185	Aaron Shea RC	8.00	3.00
❑ 186	Fabien Bownes RC	5.00	2.00
❑ 187	Damon Hodge RC	8.00	3.00
❑ 188	Dwayne Goodrich RC	5.00	2.00
❑ 189	Clint Stoerner RC	8.00	3.00
❑ 190	James Whalen RC	5.00	2.00
❑ 191	Deltha O'Neal RC	10.00	4.00
❑ 192	Ian Gold RC	8.00	3.00
❑ 193	Kenoy Kennedy RC	5.00	2.00
❑ 194	Jarious Jackson RC	8.00	3.00
❑ 195	Leroy Fields RC	5.00	2.00
❑ 196	Barrett Green RC	5.00	2.00
❑ 197	Joey Jamison RC	5.00	2.00
❑ 198	Rondell Mealey RC	5.00	2.00
❑ 199	Rob Morris RC	8.00	3.00
❑ 200	Marcus Washington RC	8.00	3.00
❑ 201	Trevor Insley RC	5.00	2.00
❑ 202	Jamel White RC	8.00	3.00
❑ 203	Kevin McDougal RC	8.00	3.00
❑ 204	Ibn Green RC	5.00	2.00
❑ 205	T.J. Slaughter RC	5.00	2.00
❑ 206	Emanuel Smith RC	5.00	2.00
❑ 207	Herbert Goodman RC	8.00	3.00
❑ 208	William Bartee RC	8.00	3.00
❑ 209	Orantes Grant RC	5.00	2.00
❑ 210	Brad Hoover RC	8.00	3.00
❑ 211	Deon Dyer RC	8.00	3.00
❑ 212	Jonas Lewis RC	5.00	2.00
❑ 213	Chris Hovan RC	8.00	3.00
❑ 214	Fred Robbins RC	5.00	2.00
❑ 215	Michael Boireau RC	5.00	2.00
❑ 216	Giles Cole RC	5.00	2.00
❑ 217	Dave Stachelski RC	5.00	2.00
❑ 218	Patrick Pass RC	8.00	3.00
❑ 219	Darren Howard RC	8.00	3.00
❑ 220	Austin Wheatley RC	5.00	2.00
❑ 221	Kevin Houser RC	8.00	3.00
❑ 222	Rian Lindell RC	5.00	2.00
❑ 223	Jake Delhomme RC	50.00	20.00
❑ 224	Cornelius Griffin RC	8.00	3.00
❑ 225	Shaun Ellis RC	10.00	4.00
❑ 226	John Abraham RC	10.00	4.00
❑ 227	Travares Tillman RC	5.00	2.00
❑ 228	Julian Peterson RC	10.00	4.00
❑ 229	Marcus Knight RC	8.00	3.00
❑ 230	Thomas Hamner RC	5.00	2.00
❑ 231	Hank Poteat RC	8.00	3.00
❑ 232	Neil Rackers RC	10.00	4.00
❑ 233	Bobby Shaw RC	8.00	3.00
❑ 234	Rogers Beckett RC	8.00	3.00
❑ 235	Reggie Jones RC	5.00	2.00
❑ 236	Tim Seder RC	8.00	3.00
❑ 237	Durell Price RC	5.00	2.00
❑ 238	Ahmed Plummer RC	10.00	4.00
❑ 239	John Engelberger RC	8.00	3.00
❑ 240	Paul Smith RC	8.00	3.00
❑ 241	Chafie Fields RC	5.00	2.00
❑ 242	Kevin Feterik RC	5.00	2.00
❑ 243	Jacoby Shepherd RC	5.00	2.00
❑ 244	Nate Webster RC	5.00	2.00
❑ 245	Ketric Sanford RC	5.00	2.00
❑ 246	Tavarus Hogans RC	5.00	2.00
❑ 247	Keith Bulluck RC	10.00	4.00
❑ 248	Mike Green RC	8.00	3.00
❑ 249	Chris Coleman RC	10.00	4.00
❑ 250	Demario Brown RC	5.00	2.00
❑ 251	Billy Volek RC	15.00	6.00
❑ 252	Mareno Philyaw RC	5.00	2.00
❑ 253	Ethan Howell RC	5.00	2.00
❑ 254	Chris Samuels RC	8.00	3.00
❑ 255	Brandon Short RC	8.00	3.00
❑ 256	Maurice Smith RC	8.00	3.00
❑ 257	Frank Murphy RC	5.00	2.00
❑ 258	Darrick Vaughn RC	5.00	2.00
❑ 259	Payton Williams RC	5.00	2.00
❑ 260	JaJuan Seider RC	5.00	2.00
❑ 261	Antonio Banks EP RC	2.00	.75
❑ 262	Jonathan Brown EP RC	2.00	.75
❑ 263	Ontiwaun Carter EP RC	2.00	.75
❑ 264	Jeremaine Copeland EP	2.00	.75
❑ 265	Ralph Dawkins EP RC	3.00	1.25
❑ 266	Marques Douglas EP RC	2.00	.75
❑ 267	Kevin Drake EP RC	2.00	.75
❑ 268	Damon Dunn EP RC	3.00	1.25
❑ 269	Todd Floyd EP RC	2.00	.75
❑ 270	Tony Graziani EP	3.00	1.25
❑ 271	Derrick Ham EP RC	3.00	1.25
❑ 272	Duane Hawthorne EP RC	3.00	1.25
❑ 273	Alonzo Johnson EP RC	2.00	.75
❑ 274	Mark Kacmarynski EP RC	2.00	.75
❑ 275	Eric Kresser EP	2.00	.75
❑ 276	Jim Kubiak EP RC	3.00	1.25
❑ 277	Blaine McElmurry EP RC	2.00	.75
❑ 278	Scott Milanovich EP	3.00	1.25
❑ 279	Norman Miller EP RC	2.00	.75
❑ 280	Sean Morey EP RC	3.00	1.25
❑ 281	Jeff Ogden EP	3.00	1.25
❑ 282	Pepe Pearson EP RC	3.00	1.25
❑ 283	Ron Powlus EP RC	4.00	1.50
❑ 284	Jason Shelley EP RC	2.00	.75
❑ 285	Ben Snell EP RC	2.00	.75

❑ 286 Aaron Stecker EP RC 4.00 1.50
❑ 287 L.C. Stevens EP 2.00 .75
❑ 288 Mike Sutton EP RC 2.00 .75
❑ 289 Damian Vaughn EP RC 2.00 .75
❑ 290 Ted White EP 2.00 .75
❑ 291 Marcus Crandell EP RC 3.00 1.25
❑ 292 Darryl Daniel EP RC 3.00 1.25
❑ 293 Jesse Haynes EP 2.00 .75
❑ 294 Matt Lytle EP RC 3.00 1.25
❑ 295 Deon Mitchell EP RC 3.00 1.25
❑ 296 Kendrick Nord EP RC 2.00 .75
❑ 297 Ronnie Powell EP 2.00 .75
❑ 298 Selucio Sanford EP RC 3.00 1.25
❑ 299 Corey Thomas EP 2.00 .75
❑ 300 Vershan Jackson EP RC 2.00 .75
❑ 301 Michael Vick XRC 60.00 25.00
❑ 302 Drew Brees XRC 30.00 12.50
❑ 303 Quincy Carter XRC 12.00 5.00
❑ 304 Marques Tuiasosopa XRC 15.00 6.00
❑ 305 Chris Weinke XRC 10.00 4.00
❑ 306 LaDainian Tomlinson XRC 50.0025.00
❑ 307 Deuce McAllister XRC 25.00 10.00
❑ 308 Michael Bennett XRC 20.00 7.50
❑ 309 Anthony Thomas XRC 10.00 4.00
❑ 310 LaMont Jordan XRC 25.00 10.00
❑ 311 David Terrell XRC 12.00 5.00
❑ 312 Koren Robinson XRC 10.00 4.00
❑ 313 Rod Gardner XRC 15.00 6.00
❑ 314 Santana Moss XRC 20.00 7.50
❑ 315 Freddie Mitchell XRC 10.00 4.00
❑ 316 Gerard Warren XRC 10.00 4.00
❑ 317 Justin Smith XRC 10.00 4.00
❑ 318 Richard Seymour XRC 20.00 7.50
❑ 319 Andre Carter XRC 10.00 4.00
❑ 320 Jamal Reynolds XRC 10.00 4.00

2001 Leaf Rookies and Stars

❑ COMP.SET w/o SP's (100) 20.00 7.50
❑ 1 Aaron Brooks .60 .25
❑ 2 Ahman Green .60 .25
❑ 3 Antonio Freeman .60 .25
❑ 4 Brad Johnson .60 .25
❑ 5 Brett Favre 2.00 .75
❑ 6 Brian Griese .60 .25
❑ 7 Brian Urlacher 1.00 .40
❑ 8 Bruce Smith .25 .08
❑ 9 Cade McNown .25 .08
❑ 10 Chad Pennington 1.00 .40
❑ 11 Champ Bailey .40 .15
❑ 12 Charles Woodson .40 .15
❑ 13 Charlie Batch .60 .25
❑ 14 Charlie Garner .40 .15
❑ 15 Corey Dillon .60 .25
❑ 16 Cris Carter .60 .25
❑ 17 Curtis Martin .60 .25
❑ 18 Dan Marino 2.50 1.00
❑ 19 Daunte Culpepper .60 .25
❑ 20 David Boston .60 .25
❑ 21 Deion Sanders .60 .25
❑ 22 Donovan McNabb .75 .30
❑ 23 Doug Flutie .60 .25
❑ 24 Drew Bledsoe .75 .30
❑ 25 Duce Staley .60 .25
❑ 26 Ed McCaffrey .60 .25
❑ 27 Eddie George .60 .25
❑ 28 Edgerrin James .75 .30
❑ 29 Elvis Grbac .40 .15
❑ 30 Emmitt Smith 1.25 .50
❑ 31 Eric Moulds .40 .15
❑ 32 Fred Taylor .60 .25
❑ 33 Germane Crowell .25 .08
❑ 34 Ike Hilliard .40 .15
❑ 35 Isaac Bruce .60 .25
❑ 36 Jake Plummer .40 .15
❑ 37 Jamal Anderson .60 .25
❑ 38 Jamal Lewis 1.00 .40
❑ 39 James Allen .40 .15
❑ 40 James Stewart .40 .15
❑ 41 Jay Fiedler .60 .25
❑ 42 Jeff Garcia .60 .25
❑ 43 Jeff George .40 .15
❑ 44 Jeff Lewis .25 .08
❑ 45 Jerome Bettis .60 .25
❑ 46 Jerry Rice 1.25 .50
❑ 47 Jevon Kearse .40 .15
❑ 48 Jimmy Smith .40 .15
❑ 49 Joey Galloway .40 .15
❑ 50 John Elway 2.50 1.00
❑ 51 Junior Seau .60 .25
❑ 52 Keenan McCardell .25 .08
❑ 53 Kerry Collins .40 .15
❑ 54 Kevin Johnson .40 .15
❑ 55 Keyshawn Johnson .60 .25
❑ 56 Kordell Stewart .40 .15
❑ 57 Kurt Warner 1.25 .50
❑ 58 Lamar Smith .40 .15
❑ 59 Marcus Robinson .60 .25
❑ 60 Mark Brunell .60 .25
❑ 61 Marshall Faulk .75 .30
❑ 62 Marvin Harrison .60 .25
❑ 63 Matt Hasselbeck .40 .15
❑ 64 Mike Alstott .60 .25
❑ 65 Mike Anderson .60 .25
❑ 66 Muhsin Muhammad .40 .15
❑ 67 Peter Warrick .60 .25
❑ 68 Peyton Manning 1.50 .60
❑ 69 Priest Holmes .75 .30
❑ 70 Randy Moss 1.25 .50
❑ 71 Ray Lewis .60 .25
❑ 72 Rich Gannon .60 .25
❑ 73 Ricky Watters .40 .15
❑ 74 Ricky Williams .60 .25
❑ 75 Rob Johnson .40 .15
❑ 76 Rod Smith .40 .15
❑ 77 Ron Dayne .60 .25
❑ 78 Shannon Sharpe .40 .15
❑ 79 Shaun Alexander .75 .30
❑ 80 Stephen Davis .60 .25
❑ 81 Steve McNair .60 .25
❑ 82 Steve Young .75 .30
❑ 83 Sylvester Morris .25 .08
❑ 84 Terrell Davis .60 .25
❑ 85 Terrell Owens .60 .25
❑ 86 Thomas Jones .40 .15
❑ 87 Tim Brown .60 .25
❑ 88 Tim Couch .40 .15
❑ 89 Tony Banks .40 .15
❑ 90 Tony Gonzalez .40 .15
❑ 91 Torry Holt .60 .25
❑ 92 Travis Taylor .40 .15
❑ 93 Trent Green .60 .25
❑ 94 Troy Aikman 1.00 .40
❑ 95 Tyrone Wheatley .40 .15
❑ 96 Vinny Testaverde .40 .15
❑ 97 Warren Sapp .40 .15
❑ 98 Warrick Dunn .60 .25
❑ 99 Wayne Chrebet .40 .15
❑ 100 Zach Thomas .60 .25
❑ 101 A.J. Feeley RC 6.00 2.50
❑ 102 Josh Booty RC 6.00 2.50
❑ 103 Roderick Robinson RC 4.00 1.50
❑ 104 Renaldo Hill RC 4.00 1.50
❑ 105 Harold Blackmon RC 2.50 1.00
❑ 106 Rudi Johnson RC 10.00 4.00
❑ 107 Curtis Fuller RC 2.50 1.00
❑ 108 Dan Alexander RC 6.00 2.50
❑ 109 Anthony Thomas RPS 6.00 2.50
❑ 110 Travis Minor RPS 3.00 1.25
❑ 111 Heath Evans RC 4.00 1.50
❑ 112 Joe Walker RC 2.50 1.00
❑ 113 Moran Norris RC 2.50 1.00
❑ 114 Quincy Carter RPS 4.00 1.50
❑ 115 Michael Vick RPS 25.00 10.00
❑ 116 Vinny Sutherland RC 4.00 1.50
❑ 117 Scotty Anderson RC 4.00 1.50
❑ 118 Eddie Berlin RC 4.00 1.50
❑ 119 Jonathan Carter RC 4.00 1.50
❑ 120 Monty Beisel RC 6.00 2.50
❑ 121 T.J. Houshmandzadeh RC 6.00 2.50
❑ 122 Rodney Bailey RC 2.50 1.00
❑ 123 Reggie Germany RC 4.00 1.50
❑ 124 Ellis Wyms RC 2.50 1.00
❑ 125 Koren Robinson RPS 6.00 2.50
❑ 126 Antonio Pierce RC 8.00 3.00
❑ 127 Arnold Jackson RC 4.00 1.50
❑ 128 Andre Rone RC 2.50 1.00
❑ 129 Richard Newsome RC 2.50 1.00
❑ 130 Ifeanyi Ohalete RC 2.50 1.00
❑ 131 Dan O'Leary RC 4.00 1.50
❑ 132 Shad Meier RC 4.00 1.50
❑ 133 Jay Feeley RC 2.50 1.00
❑ 134 Brandon Manumaleuna RC 4.00 1.50
❑ 135 Riall Johnson RC 2.50 1.00
❑ 136 Snoop Minnis RPS 4.00 1.50
❑ 137 Jermaine Hampton RC 2.50 1.00
❑ 138 Johnny Huggins RC 2.50 1.00
❑ 139 Marcellus Rivers RC 4.00 1.50
❑ 140 Andre Carter RPS 6.00 2.50
❑ 141 Michael Stone RC 2.50 1.00
❑ 142 Tony Dixon RC 4.00 1.50
❑ 143 Bhawoh Jue RC 6.00 2.50
❑ 144 Will Peterson RC 4.00 1.50
❑ 145 Anthony Henry RC 6.00 2.50
❑ 146 Marques Tuiasosopo RPS 4.00 1.50
❑ 147 Reggie Swinton RC 4.00 1.50
❑ 148 Robert Carswell RC 2.50 1.00
❑ 149 Freddie Mitchell RPS 3.00 1.25
❑ 150 Idrees Bashir RC 2.50 1.00
❑ 151 James Boyd RC 2.50 1.00
❑ 152 Chris Chambers RPS 6.00 2.50
❑ 153 Aaron Schobel RC 6.00 2.50
❑ 154 Dominic Raiola RC 2.50 1.00
❑ 155 Derrick Burgess RC 6.00 2.50
❑ 156 DeLawrence Grant RC 2.50 1.00
❑ 157 Karon Riley RC 2.50 1.00
❑ 158 Cedric Scott RC 4.00 1.50
❑ 159 Patrick Washington RC 4.00 1.50
❑ 160 Eric Johnson RC 12.00 5.00
❑ 161 Tevita Ofahengaue RC 2.50 1.00
❑ 162 Chris Cooper RC 4.00 1.50
❑ 163 Fred Wakefield RC 4.00 1.50
❑ 164 Kenny Smith RC 4.00 1.50
❑ 165 Marcus Bell RC 4.00 1.50
❑ 166 Mario Fatafehi RC 4.00 1.50
❑ 167 Anthony Herron RC 2.50 1.00
❑ 168 Joe Tafoya RC 2.50 1.00
❑ 169 Morlon Greenwood RC 4.00 1.50
❑ 170 Orlando Huff RC 2.50 1.00
❑ 171 Carlos Polk RC 2.50 1.00
❑ 172 Edgerton Hartwell RC 2.50 1.00
❑ 173 Zeke Moreno RC 6.00 2.50
❑ 174 Alex Lincoln RC 4.00 1.50
❑ 175 Quinton Caver RC 4.00 1.50
❑ 176 Matt Stewart RC 2.50 1.00
❑ 177 Markus Steele RC 4.00 1.50
❑ 178 Dwight Smith RC 2.50 1.00
❑ 179 Reggie Wayne RPS 8.00 3.00
❑ 180 Jerametrius Butler RC 4.00 1.50
❑ 181 Jason Doering RC 2.50 1.00
❑ 182 John Howell RC 2.50 1.00
❑ 183 Alvin Porter RC 2.50 1.00
❑ 184 Eric Downing RC 2.50 1.00
❑ 185 John Nix RC 2.50 1.00

❑ 186 Tim Baker RC 2.50 1.00
❑ 187 Robert Garza RC 2.50 1.00
❑ 188 Randy Chevrier RC 2.50 1.00
❑ 189 Drew Brees RPS 10.00 4.00
❑ 190 Shawn Worthen RC 2.50 1.00
❑ 191 Drew Bennett RC 25.00 10.00
❑ 192 Marlon McCree RC 4.00 1.50
❑ 193 David Terrell RPS 4.00 1.50
❑ 194 Jeff Backus RC 4.00 1.50
❑ 195 Otis Leverette RC 2.50 1.00
❑ 196 Jason Glenn RC 6.00 2.50
❑ 197 Rashad Holman RC 2.50 1.00
❑ 198 T.J. Turner RC 2.50 1.00
❑ 199 Lynn Scott RC 6.00 2.50
❑ 200 Bill Gramatica RC 2.50 1.00
❑ 201 Michael Vick RC 50.00 20.00
❑ 202 Drew Brees RC 20.00 7.50
❑ 203 Quincy Carter RC 8.00 3.00
❑ 204 Jesse Palmer RC 8.00 3.00
❑ 205 Mike McMahon RC 8.00 3.00
❑ 206 Dave Dickenson RC 4.00 1.50
❑ 207 Jameel Cook RC 5.00 2.00
❑ 208 Marques Tuiasosopo RC 8.00 3.00
❑ 209 Chris Weinke RC 6.00 2.50
❑ 210 Sage Rosenfels RC 6.00 2.50
❑ 211 Josh Heupel RC 8.00 3.00
❑ 212 LaDainian Tomlinson RC 40.00 20.00
❑ 213 Michael Bennett RC 12.00 5.00
❑ 214 Anthony Thomas RC 8.00 3.00
❑ 215 Travis Henry RC 8.00 3.00
❑ 216 James Jackson RC 6.00 2.50
❑ 217 Correll Buckhalter RC 10.00 4.00
❑ 218 Derrick Blaylock RC 8.00 3.00
❑ 219 Dee Brown RC 8.00 3.00
❑ 220 LeVar Woods RC 5.00 2.00
❑ 221 Deuce McAllister RC 15.00 6.00
❑ 222 LaMont Jordan RC 15.00 6.00
❑ 223 Kevan Barlow RC 8.00 3.00
❑ 224 Travis Minor RC 5.00 2.00
❑ 225 David Terrell RC 8.00 3.00
❑ 226 Koren Robinson RC 8.00 3.00
❑ 227 Rod Gardner RC 8.00 3.00
❑ 228 Santana Moss RC 12.00 5.00
❑ 229 Freddie Mitchell RC 8.00 3.00
❑ 230 Reggie Wayne RC 1.00 6.00
❑ 231 Quincy Morgan RC 8.00 3.00
❑ 232 Chris Chambers RC 12.00 5.00
❑ 233 Steve Smith RC 20.00 10.00
❑ 234 Snoop Minnis RC 5.00 2.00
❑ 235 Justin McCareins RC 8.00 3.00
❑ 236 Onome Ojo RC 5.00 2.00
❑ 237 Damerien McCants RC 5.00 2.00
❑ 238 Mike McMahon RPS 3.00 1.25
❑ 239 Cedrick Wilson RC 8.00 3.00
❑ 240 Kevin Kasper RC 6.00 2.50
❑ 241 Chris Taylor RC 5.00 2.00
❑ 242 Ken-Yon Rambo RC 5.00 2.00
❑ 243 Richmond Flowers RC 5.00 2.00
❑ 244 Andre King RC 5.00 2.00
❑ 245 Boo Williams RC 5.00 2.00
❑ 246 Adrian Wilson RC 5.00 2.00
❑ 247 Cory Bird RC 8.00 3.00
❑ 248 Alex Bannister RC 5.00 2.00
❑ 249 Elvis Joseph RC 5.00 2.00
❑ 250 Chad Johnson RC 20.00 7.50
❑ 251 Robert Ferguson RC 8.00 3.00
❑ 252 David Martin RC 5.00 2.00
❑ 253 Quentin McCord RC 5.00 2.00
❑ 254 Todd Heap RC 8.00 3.00
❑ 255 Alge Crumpler RC 10.00 5.00
❑ 256 Nate Clements RC 8.00 3.00
❑ 257 Will Allen RC 5.00 2.00
❑ 258 Willie Middlebrooks RC 5.00 2.00
❑ 259 Fred Smoot RC 8.00 3.00
❑ 260 Andre Dyson RC 3.00 1.25
❑ 261 Gary Baxter RC 5.00 2.00
❑ 262 Jamar Fletcher RC 5.00 2.00
❑ 263 Ken Lucas RC 5.00 2.00
❑ 264 Tay Cody RC 3.00 1.25
❑ 265 Eric Kelly RC 3.00 1.25
❑ 266 Adam Archuleta RC 8.00 3.00
❑ 267 Derrick Gibson RC 5.00 2.00
❑ 268 Jarrod Cooper RC 8.00 3.00
❑ 269 Hakim Akbar RC 3.00 1.25
❑ 270 Tony Driver RC 5.00 2.00
❑ 271 Justin Smith RC 8.00 3.00
❑ 272 Andre Carter RC 8.00 3.00
❑ 273 Jamal Reynolds RC 8.00 3.00
❑ 274 Gerard Warren RC 8.00 3.00
❑ 275 Richard Seymour RC 8.00 3.00
❑ 276 Damione Lewis RC 5.00 2.00
❑ 277 Casey Hampton RC 5.00 2.00
❑ 278 Marcus Stroud RC 8.00 3.00
❑ 279 Benjamin Gay RC 6.00 2.50
❑ 280 Shaun Rogers RC 8.00 3.00
❑ 281 Dan Morgan RC 8.00 3.00
❑ 282 Kendrell Bell RC 12.00 5.00
❑ 283 Tommy Polley RC 8.00 3.00
❑ 284 Jamie Winborn RC 5.00 2.00
❑ 285 Sedrick Hodge RC 3.00 1.25
❑ 286 Torrance Marshall RC 8.00 3.00
❑ 287 Eric Westmoreland RC 5.00 2.00
❑ 288 Brian Allen RC 3.00 1.25
❑ 289 Brandon Spoon RC 8.00 3.00
❑ 290 Henry Burris RC 5.00 2.00
❑ 291 Leonard Davis RC 5.00 2.00
❑ 292 Kenyatta Walker RC 3.00 1.25
❑ 293 Cedric James RC 5.00 2.00
❑ 294 Sean Brewer RC 3.00 1.25
❑ 295 Jason Brookins RC 6.00 2.50
❑ 296 Kyle Vanden Bosch RC 8.00 3.00
❑ 297 Nick Goings RC 8.00 3.00
❑ 298 Kris Jenkins RC 8.00 3.00
❑ 299 Dominic Rhodes RC 8.00 3.00
❑ 300 Leonard Myers RC 3.00 1.25

2002 Leaf Rookies and Stars

❑ COMPLETE SET (300) 250.00 100.00
❑ COMP.SET w/o SP's (100) 25.00 10.00
❑ 1 Jake Plummer .50 .20
❑ 2 David Boston .75 .30
❑ 3 Thomas Jones .50 .20
❑ 4 Michael Vick 2.50 1.00
❑ 5 Warrick Dunn .75 .30
❑ 6 Jamal Lewis .75 .30
❑ 7 Chris Redman .30 .10
❑ 8 Ray Lewis .75 .30
❑ 9 Drew Bledsoe 1.00 .40
❑ 10 Travis Henry .75 .30
❑ 11 Eric Moulds .50 .20
❑ 12 Steve Smith .75 .30
❑ 13 Chris Weinke .50 .20
❑ 14 Lamar Smith .50 .20
❑ 15 Anthony Thomas .50 .20
❑ 16 David Terrell .75 .30
❑ 17 Brian Urlacher 1.25 .50
❑ 18 Corey Dillon .50 .20
❑ 19 Michael Westbrook .50 .20
❑ 20 Peter Warrick .50 .20
❑ 21 Tim Couch .50 .20
❑ 22 James Jackson .50 .20
❑ 23 Kevin Johnson .50 .20
❑ 24 Quincy Carter .50 .20
❑ 25 Joey Galloway .50 .20
❑ 26 Emmitt Smith 2.00 .75
❑ 27 Terrell Davis .75 .30
❑ 28 Brian Griese .75 .30
❑ 29 Ed McCaffrey .75 .30
❑ 30 Rod Smith .50 .20
❑ 31 Mike McMahon .75 .30
❑ 32 Germane Crowell .30 .10
❑ 33 Az-Zahir Hakim .30 .10
❑ 34 Terry Glenn .50 .20
❑ 35 Brett Favre 2.00 .75
❑ 36 Ahman Green .75 .30
❑ 37 James Allen .50 .20
❑ 38 Corey Bradford .30 .10
❑ 39 Peyton Manning 1.50 .60
❑ 40 Edgerrin James 1.00 .40
❑ 41 Marvin Harrison .75 .30
❑ 42 Qadry Ismail .50 .20
❑ 43 Fred Taylor .75 .30
❑ 44 Mark Brunell .75 .30
❑ 45 Jimmy Smith .50 .20
❑ 46 Priest Holmes 1.00 .40
❑ 47 Tony Gonzalez .50 .20
❑ 48 Trent Green .50 .20
❑ 49 Johnnie Morton .50 .20
❑ 50 Chris Chambers .75 .30
❑ 51 Ricky Williams .75 .30
❑ 52 Zach Thomas .75 .30
❑ 53 Randy Moss 1.50 .60
❑ 54 Michael Bennett .50 .20
❑ 55 Derrick Alexander .50 .20
❑ 56 Daunte Culpepper .75 .30
❑ 57 Tom Brady 2.00 .75
❑ 58 Troy Brown .50 .20
❑ 59 Antowain Smith .50 .20
❑ 60 Joe Horn .50 .20
❑ 61 Aaron Brooks .75 .30
❑ 62 Deuce McAllister 1.00 .40
❑ 63 Kerry Collins .50 .20
❑ 64 Amani Toomer .50 .20
❑ 65 Michael Strahan .50 .20
❑ 66 Laveranues Coles .50 .20
❑ 67 Vinny Testaverde .50 .20
❑ 68 Curtis Martin .75 .30
❑ 69 Rich Gannon .75 .30
❑ 70 Tim Brown .75 .30
❑ 71 Jerry Rice 1.50 .60
❑ 72 Donovan McNabb 1.00 .40
❑ 73 Freddie Mitchell .50 .20
❑ 74 Duce Staley .75 .30
❑ 75 Kordell Stewart .50 .20
❑ 76 Jerome Bettis .75 .30
❑ 77 Plaxico Burress .50 .20
❑ 78 Drew Brees .75 .30
❑ 79 LaDainian Tomlinson 1.25 .50
❑ 80 Junior Seau .75 .30
❑ 81 Jeff Garcia .75 .30
❑ 82 Garrison Hearst .50 .20
❑ 83 Terrell Owens .75 .30
❑ 84 Shaun Alexander 1.00 .40
❑ 85 Koren Robinson .50 .20
❑ 86 Kurt Warner .75 .30
❑ 87 Marshall Faulk .75 .30
❑ 88 Isaac Bruce .75 .30
❑ 89 Torry Holt .75 .30
❑ 90 Rob Johnson .50 .20
❑ 91 Brad Johnson .50 .20
❑ 92 Keyshawn Johnson .75 .30
❑ 93 Mike Alstott .75 .30
❑ 94 Eddie George .75 .30
❑ 95 Steve McNair .75 .30
❑ 96 Derrick Mason .50 .20
❑ 97 Jevon Kearse .50 .20
❑ 98 Stephen Davis .50 .20
❑ 99 Sage Rosenfels .30 .10
❑ 100 Rod Gardner .50 .20
❑ 101 Adrian Peterson RC 5.00 2.00
❑ 102 Nick Rolovich RC 4.00 1.50
❑ 103 Lew Thomas RC 2.50 1.00
❑ 104 David Carr RC 12.00 5.00

❑	105	Daryl Jones RC	4.00	1.50
❑	106	Brandon Doman RC	4.00	1.50
❑	107	Ed Reed RC	8.00	3.00
❑	108	Tellis Redmon RC	4.00	1.50
❑	109	Andra Davis RC	4.00	1.50
❑	110	Kendall Newson RC	2.50	1.00
❑	111	Joe Burns RC	4.00	1.50
❑	112	Maurice Morris RC	5.00	2.00
❑	113	Craig Nall RC	5.00	2.00
❑	114	Phillip Buchanon RC	5.00	2.00
❑	115	Mike Echols RC	2.50	1.00
❑	116	Terry Jones Jr. RC	4.00	1.50
❑	117	Anthony Weaver RC	4.00	1.50
❑	118	Jeb Putzier RC	5.00	2.00
❑	119	Tony Fisher RC	5.00	2.00
❑	120	Joey Harrington RC	12.00	5.00
❑	121	Lamar Gordon RC	5.00	2.00
❑	122	Tracey Wistrom RC	4.00	1.50
❑	123	Ashley Lelie RC	10.00	4.00
❑	124	Will Witherspoon RC	5.00	2.00
❑	125	Travis Stephens RC	4.00	1.50
❑	126	J.T. O'Sullivan RC	4.00	1.50
❑	127	Brian Westbrook RC	8.00	3.00
❑	128	James Mungro RC	5.00	2.00
❑	129	Lamont Thompson RC	4.00	1.50
❑	130	Jarrod Baxter RC	4.00	1.50
❑	131	Andre Lott RC	5.00	2.00
❑	132	Steve Bellisari RC	4.00	1.50
❑	133	David Garrard RC	5.00	2.00
❑	134	Michael Lewis RC	5.00	2.00
❑	135	James Allen RC	2.50	1.00
❑	136	Bryant McKinnie RC	4.00	1.50
❑	137	Marques Anderson RC	5.00	2.00
❑	138	Rohan Davey RC	5.00	2.00
❑	139	Kyle Johnson RC	2.50	1.00
❑	140	Dusty Bonner RC	2.50	1.00
❑	141	DeShaun Foster RC	5.00	2.00
❑	142	Chad Hutchinson RC	4.00	1.50
❑	143	Jack Brewer RC	4.00	1.50
❑	144	Eddie Freeman RC	2.50	1.00
❑	145	Seth Burford RC	4.00	1.50
❑	146	Roosevelt Williams RC	2.50	1.00
❑	147	Jamin Elliott RC	2.50	1.00
❑	148	Charles Grant RC	5.00	2.00
❑	149	Jeff Kelly RC	4.00	1.50
❑	150	Cliff Russell RC	4.00	1.50
❑	151	Josh Scobey RC	5.00	2.00
❑	152	Tank Williams RC	4.00	1.50
❑	153	Larry Tripplett RC	2.50	1.00
❑	154	Clinton Portis RC	15.00	6.00
❑	155	Javin Hunter RC	2.50	1.00
❑	156	Deveren Johnson RC	4.00	1.50
❑	157	Reche Caldwell RC	5.00	2.00
❑	158	Ronald Curry RC	5.00	2.00
❑	159	Chris Hope RC	5.00	2.00
❑	160	Damien Anderson RC	4.00	1.50
❑	161	Saleem Rasheed RC	5.00	2.00
❑	162	Albert Haynesworth RC	4.00	1.50
❑	163	Bryan Gilmore RC	4.00	1.50
❑	164	Wes Pate RC	2.50	1.00
❑	165	Deion Branch RC	10.00	5.00
❑	166	Ben Leber RC	5.00	2.00
❑	167	Andre Davis RC	4.00	1.50
❑	168	Darrell Hill RC	4.00	1.50
❑	169	Rodney Wright RC	2.50	1.00
❑	170	Demontray Carter RC	2.50	1.00
❑	171	Zak Kustok RC	5.00	2.00
❑	172	James Wofford RC	4.00	1.50
❑	173	David Priestley RC	4.00	1.50
❑	174	Donte Stallworth RC	10.00	4.00
❑	175	Marc Boerigter RC	8.00	3.00
❑	176	Freddie Milons RC	4.00	1.50
❑	177	John Simon RC	4.00	1.50
❑	178	Josh Norman RC	5.00	2.00
❑	179	Jabar Gaffney RC	5.00	2.00
❑	180	Doug Jolley RC	5.00	2.00
❑	181	Preston Parsons RC	2.50	1.00
❑	182	Chris Baker RC	4.00	1.50
❑	183	Javon Walker RC	10.00	4.00
❑	184	Justin Peelle RC	2.50	1.00
❑	185	Josh Reed RC	5.00	2.00
❑	186	Omar Easy RC	5.00	2.00
❑	187	Jerramy Stevens RC	5.00	2.00
❑	188	Shaun Hill RC	5.00	2.00
❑	189	David Thornton RC	2.50	1.00
❑	190	John Henderson RC	5.00	2.00
❑	191	Verron Haynes RC	5.00	2.00
❑	192	Dennis Johnson RC	2.50	1.00
❑	193	Napoleon Harris RC	5.00	2.00
❑	194	Jonathan Wells RC	5.00	2.00
❑	195	Howard Green RC	2.50	1.00
❑	196	Travis Fisher RC	5.00	2.00
❑	197	Anton Palepoi RC	2.50	1.00
❑	198	Ed Stansbury RC	2.50	1.00
❑	199	Josh McCown RC	6.00	2.50
❑	200	Alex Brown RC	5.00	2.00
❑	201	Joseph Jefferson RC	4.00	1.50
❑	202	Julius Peppers RC	10.00	4.00
❑	203	Larry Ned RC	4.00	1.50
❑	204	Rock Cartwright RC	6.00	2.50
❑	205	Kalimba Edwards RC	5.00	2.00
❑	206	Matt Schobel RC	4.00	1.50
❑	207	Maurice Jackson RC	2.50	1.00
❑	208	Kelly Campbell RC	4.00	1.50
❑	209	Mel Mitchell RC	4.00	1.50
❑	210	Ken Simonton RC	2.50	1.00
❑	211	Brian Allen RC	4.00	1.50
❑	212	Darnell Sanders RC	4.00	1.50
❑	213	Jesse Chatman RC	5.00	2.00
❑	214	Keyuo Craver RC	4.00	1.50
❑	215	Chester Taylor RC	5.00	2.00
❑	216	Kurt Kittner RC	4.00	1.50
❑	217	Derek Ross RC	4.00	1.50
❑	218	Charles Hill RC	2.50	1.00
❑	219	Jarvis Green RC	4.00	1.50
❑	220	Mike Jenkins RC	2.50	1.00
❑	221	Robert Royal RC	5.00	2.00
❑	222	Ladell Betts RC	5.00	2.00
❑	223	Antwoine Womack RC	4.00	1.50
❑	224	Raonall Smith RC	4.00	1.50
❑	225	Charles Stackhouse RC	4.00	1.50
❑	226	Quinn Gray RC	2.50	1.00
❑	227	Lito Sheppard RC	5.00	2.00
❑	228	Ryan Van Dyke RC	5.00	2.00
❑	229	Will Overstreet RC	2.50	1.00
❑	230	Leonard Henry RC	4.00	1.50
❑	231	Dorsett Davis RC	2.50	1.00
❑	232	Marquand Manuel RC	2.50	1.00
❑	233	Luke Staley RC	4.00	1.50
❑	234	Carlos Hall RC	5.00	2.00
❑	235	Marcus Brady RC	4.00	1.50
❑	236	Ryan Denney RC	4.00	1.50
❑	237	Eric McCoo RC	2.50	1.00
❑	238	Major Applewhite RC	5.00	2.00
❑	239	Adam Tate RC	2.50	1.00
❑	240	Marquise Walker RC	4.00	1.50
❑	241	John Flowers RC	2.50	1.00
❑	242	Levar Fisher RC	2.50	1.00
❑	243	Ricky Williams RC	4.00	1.50
❑	244	Mike Rumph RC	5.00	2.00
❑	245	Delvin Joyce RC	4.00	1.50
❑	246	Bryan Thomas RC	4.00	1.50
❑	247	Mike Williams RC	4.00	1.50
❑	248	Sam Brandon RC	4.00	1.50
❑	249	Eddie Drummond RC	4.00	1.50
❑	250	Najeh Davenport RC	5.00	2.00
❑	251	Brian Williams RC	2.50	1.00
❑	252	Scott Fujita RC	5.00	2.00
❑	253	Dwight Freeney RC	6.00	2.50
❑	254	Herb Haygood RC	2.50	1.00
❑	255	Patrick Ramsey RC	6.00	2.50
❑	256	Atnaf Harris RC	2.50	1.00
❑	257	Jason McAddley RC	4.00	1.50
❑	258	Pete Rebstock RC	2.50	1.00
❑	259	Quentin Jammer RC	5.00	2.00
❑	260	Luke Butkus RC	2.50	1.00
❑	261	Jeremy Allen RC	2.50	1.00
❑	262	Jake Schifino RC	4.00	1.50
❑	263	Randy Fasani RC	4.00	1.50
❑	264	Bryan Fletcher RC	2.50	1.00
❑	265	Jeremy Shockey RC	15.00	6.00
❑	266	Kevin Bentley RC	2.50	1.00
❑	267	Jon McGraw RC	2.50	1.00
❑	268	Robert Thomas RC	5.00	2.00
❑	269	Coy Wire RC	5.00	2.00
❑	270	Brian Poli-Dixon RC	4.00	1.50
❑	271	Willie Offord RC	4.00	1.50
❑	272	Rocky Calmus RC	5.00	2.00
❑	273	Sheldon Brown RC	5.00	2.00
❑	274	Terry Charles RC	4.00	1.50
❑	275	Ron Johnson RC	4.00	1.50
❑	276	Roy Williams RC	12.00	5.00
❑	277	Sam Simmons RC	2.50	1.00
❑	278	Andre Goodman RC	5.00	2.00
❑	279	Ryan Sims RC	5.00	2.00
❑	280	Antwaan Randle El RC	8.00	3.00
❑	281	Alan Harper RC	2.50	1.00
❑	282	Tavon Mason RC	2.50	1.00
❑	283	Kahlil Hill RC	4.00	1.50
❑	284	Antonio Bryant RC	5.00	2.00
❑	285	Akin Ayodele RC	2.50	1.00
❑	286	T.J. Duckett RC	8.00	3.00
❑	287	Kenyon Coleman RC	2.50	1.00
❑	288	Tim Carter RC	4.00	1.50
❑	289	Lamont Brightful RC	2.50	1.00
❑	290	Trev Faulk RC	2.50	1.00
❑	291	Randy McMichael RC	8.00	3.00
❑	292	Daniel Graham RC	5.00	2.00
❑	293	Wendell Bryant RC	2.50	1.00
❑	294	Jamar Martin RC	4.00	1.50
❑	295	Chris Luzar RC	4.00	1.50
❑	296	William Green RC	5.00	2.00
❑	297	Lee Mays RC	4.00	1.50
❑	298	Eric Crouch RC	5.00	2.00
❑	299	Steve Smith RC	2.50	1.00
❑	300	Woody Dantzler RC	4.00	1.50

2003 Leaf Rookies and Stars

❑		COMP.SET w/o SP's (100)	20.00	7.50
❑	1	Emmitt Smith	2.00	.75
❑	2	Michael Vick	2.00	.75
❑	3	Peerless Price	.50	.20
❑	4	T.J. Duckett	.50	.20
❑	5	Warrick Dunn	.50	.20
❑	6	Jamal Lewis	.75	.30
❑	7	Ray Lewis	.75	.30
❑	8	Drew Bledsoe	.75	.30
❑	9	Eric Moulds	.50	.20
❑	10	Josh Reed	.50	.20
❑	11	Travis Henry	.50	.20
❑	12	Julius Peppers	.75	.30
❑	13	Anthony Thomas	.50	.20
❑	14	Brian Urlacher	1.25	.50
❑	15	Marty Booker	.50	.20
❑	16	Kordell Stewart	.50	.20
❑	17	Corey Dillon	.50	.20
❑	18	Chad Johnson	.75	.30
❑	19	Tim Couch	.30	.10
❑	20	William Green	.50	.20
❑	21	Antonio Bryant	.50	.20
❑	22	Roy Williams	.75	.30
❑	23	Ashley Lelie	.75	.30
❑	24	Clinton Portis	1.25	.50

❑ 25	Ed McCaffrey	.75	.30
❑ 26	Jake Plummer	.50	.20
❑ 27	Rod Smith	.50	.20
❑ 28	Joey Harrington	1.25	.50
❑ 29	Ahman Green	.75	.30
❑ 30	Brett Favre	2.00	.75
❑ 31	Donald Driver	.50	.20
❑ 32	Javon Walker	.50	.20
❑ 33	David Carr	1.25	.50
❑ 34	Edgerrin James	.75	.30
❑ 35	Marvin Harrison	.75	.30
❑ 36	Peyton Manning	1.25	.50
❑ 37	Fred Taylor	.75	.30
❑ 38	Jimmy Smith	.50	.20
❑ 39	Mark Brunell	.50	.20
❑ 40	Priest Holmes	1.25	.50
❑ 41	Tony Gonzalez	.50	.20
❑ 42	Trent Green	.50	.20
❑ 43	Chris Chambers	.75	.30
❑ 44	Jay Fiedler	.50	.20
❑ 45	Junior Seau	.75	.30
❑ 46	Ricky Williams	.75	.30
❑ 47	Zach Thomas	.75	.30
❑ 48	Daunte Culpepper	.75	.30
❑ 49	Michael Bennett	.50	.20
❑ 50	Randy Moss	1.25	.50
❑ 51	Tom Brady	2.00	.75
❑ 52	Troy Brown	.50	.20
❑ 53	Aaron Brooks	.75	.30
❑ 54	Deuce McAllister	.75	.30
❑ 55	Donte Stallworth	.75	.30
❑ 56	Joe Horn	.50	.20
❑ 57	Jeremy Shockey	1.25	.50
❑ 58	Kerry Collins	.50	.20
❑ 59	Michael Strahan	.50	.20
❑ 60	Tiki Barber	.75	.30
❑ 61	Chad Pennington	1.00	.40
❑ 62	Curtis Martin	.75	.30
❑ 63	Santana Moss	.50	.20
❑ 64	Charles Woodson	.50	.20
❑ 65	Jerry Rice	1.50	.60
❑ 66	Rich Gannon	.50	.20
❑ 67	Tim Brown	.75	.30
❑ 68	Donovan McNabb	1.00	.40
❑ 69	Antwaan Randle El	.75	.30
❑ 70	Tommy Maddox	.75	.30
❑ 71	Jerome Bettis	.75	.30
❑ 72	Kendrell Bell	.50	.20
❑ 73	Plaxico Burress	.50	.20
❑ 74	David Boston	.50	.20
❑ 75	Drew Brees	.75	.30
❑ 76	LaDainian Tomlinson	.75	.30
❑ 77	Kevan Barlow	.50	.20
❑ 78	Jeff Garcia	.75	.30
❑ 79	Terrell Owens	.75	.30
❑ 80	Matt Hasselbeck	.50	.20
❑ 81	Koren Robinson	.50	.20
❑ 82	Shaun Alexander	.75	.30
❑ 83	Isaac Bruce	.75	.30
❑ 84	Kurt Warner	.75	.30
❑ 85	Marshall Faulk	.75	.30
❑ 86	Torry Holt	.75	.30
❑ 87	Brad Johnson	.50	.20
❑ 88	Keyshawn Johnson	.75	.30
❑ 89	Mike Alstott	.75	.30
❑ 90	Warren Sapp	.50	.20
❑ 91	Eddie George	.50	.20
❑ 92	Jevon Kearse	.50	.20
❑ 93	Steve McNair	.75	.30
❑ 94	Laveranues Coles	.50	.20
❑ 95	Rod Gardner	.50	.20
❑ 96	Patrick Ramsey	.75	.30
❑ 97	Boller/Suggs/Smith CL	.75	.30
❑ 98	R.Grossman/T.Jacobs CL	.75	.30
❑ 99	A.Boldin/B.Johnson CL	.75	.30
❑ 100	T.Calico/C.Brown CL	.75	.30
❑ 101	Charles Tillman RC	5.00	2.00
❑ 102	Justin Griffith RC	3.00	1.25
❑ 103	Ovie Mughelli RC	2.00	.75
❑ 104	Chris Edmonds RC	2.00	.75
❑ 105	Jeremi Johnson RC	3.00	1.25
❑ 106	Malaefou MacKenzie RC	2.00	.75
❑ 107	James Lynch RC	3.00	1.25
❑ 108	B.J. Askew RC	4.00	1.50
❑ 109	Andrew Pinnock RC	3.00	1.25
❑ 110	Chris Davis RC	3.00	1.25
❑ 111	Dan Curley RC	2.00	.75
❑ 112	Lenny Walls RC	3.00	1.25
❑ 113	Travis Fisher RC	2.00	.75
❑ 114	Ahmaad Galloway RC	3.00	1.25
❑ 115	Joe Smith RC	4.00	1.50
❑ 116	Reno Mahe RC	4.00	1.50
❑ 117	Torrie Cox RC	3.00	1.25
❑ 118	Kerry Carter RC	3.00	1.25
❑ 119	Dwone Hicks RC	2.00	.75
❑ 120	Cato June RC	4.00	1.50
❑ 121	Terry Pierce RC	3.00	1.25
❑ 122	Eddie Moore RC	3.00	1.25
❑ 123	Mike Seidman RC	2.00	.75
❑ 124	Michael Nattiel RC	4.00	1.50
❑ 125	Casey Fitzsimmons RC	4.00	1.50
❑ 126	George Wrighster RC	3.00	1.25
❑ 127	Mike Pinkard RC	2.00	.75
❑ 128	Donald Lee RC	3.00	1.25
❑ 129	Sean Berton RC	2.00	.75
❑ 130	Soloman Bates RC	2.00	.75
❑ 131	Zach Hilton RC	3.00	1.25
❑ 132	Antonio Gates RC	30.00	15.00
❑ 133	Aaron Walker RC	3.00	1.25
❑ 134	Richard Angulo RC	3.00	1.25
❑ 135	Will Heller RC	3.00	1.25
❑ 136	Theo Sanders RC	2.00	.75
❑ 137	Jimmy Farris RC	3.00	1.25
❑ 138	Ryan Nece RC	4.00	1.50
❑ 139	Antonio Brown RC	2.00	.75
❑ 140	Clarence Coleman RC	2.00	.75
❑ 141	Lawrence Hamilton RC	2.00	.75
❑ 142	C.J. Jones RC	2.00	.75
❑ 143	Frisman Jackson RC	4.00	1.50
❑ 144	Antonio Chatman RC	4.00	1.50
❑ 145	Rocky Boiman RC	3.00	1.25
❑ 146	Tron LaFavor RC	2.00	.75
❑ 147	Derick Armstrong RC	4.00	1.50
❑ 148	J.J. Moses RC	3.00	1.25
❑ 149	Aaron Moorehead RC	4.00	1.50
❑ 150	Brad Pyatt RC	3.00	1.25
❑ 151	Arland Bruce RC	2.00	.75
❑ 152	Chris Horn RC	2.00	.75
❑ 153	Kareem Kelly RC	3.00	1.25
❑ 154	Talman Gardner RC	4.00	1.50
❑ 155	David Tyree RC	3.00	1.25
❑ 156	Willie Ponder RC	2.00	.75
❑ 157	Greg Lewis RC	8.00	3.00
❑ 158	Eric Parker RC	4.00	1.50
❑ 159	Kassim Osgood RC	4.00	1.50
❑ 160	Jason Willis RC	2.00	.75
❑ 161	Akbar Gbaja-Biamila RC	4.00	1.50
❑ 162	Mike Furrey RC	6.00	2.50
❑ 163	Chris Kelsay RC	4.00	1.50
❑ 164	Cory Redding RC	3.00	1.25
❑ 165	Kenny Peterson RC	3.00	1.25
❑ 166	Osi Umenyiora RC	6.00	2.50
❑ 167	Tyler Brayton RC	4.00	1.50
❑ 168	DeWayne White RC	3.00	1.25
❑ 169	Kevin Williams RC	4.00	1.50
❑ 170	Dan Klecko RC	6.00	2.50
❑ 171	Johnathan Sullivan RC	3.00	1.25
❑ 172	William Joseph RC	4.00	1.50
❑ 173	Rien Long RC	2.00	.75
❑ 174	Angelo Crowell RC	3.00	1.25
❑ 175	Chaun Thompson RC	2.00	.75
❑ 176	Bradie James RC	4.00	1.50
❑ 177	Antwan Peek RC	3.00	1.25
❑ 178	Kawika Mitchell RC	3.00	1.25
❑ 179	Cie Grant RC	4.00	1.50
❑ 180	E.J. Henderson RC	4.00	1.50
❑ 181	Victor Hobson RC	4.00	1.50
❑ 182	Alonzo Jackson RC	3.00	1.25
❑ 183	Matt Wilhelm RC	4.00	1.50
❑ 184	Pisa Tinoisamoa RC	4.00	1.50
❑ 185	Ricky Manning RC	4.00	1.50
❑ 186	Dennis Weathersby RC	2.00	.75
❑ 187	Donald Strickland RC	2.00	.75
❑ 188	Asante Samuel RC	4.00	1.50
❑ 189	Eugene Wilson RC	4.00	1.50
❑ 190	Nnamdi Asomugha RC	3.00	1.25
❑ 191	Ike Taylor RC	8.00	3.00
❑ 192	Drayton Florence RC	2.00	.75
❑ 193	DeJuan Groce RC	4.00	1.50
❑ 194	Shane Walton RC	2.00	.75
❑ 195	Terrence Holt RC	3.00	1.25
❑ 196	Rashean Mathis RC	3.00	1.25
❑ 197	Julian Battle RC	3.00	1.25
❑ 198	Hanik Milligan RC	3.00	1.25
❑ 199	Terrence Kiel RC	4.00	1.50
❑ 200	David Kircus RC	3.00	1.25
❑ 201	Lee Suggs RC	12.00	5.00
❑ 202	Charles Rogers RC	6.00	2.50
❑ 203	Brandon Lloyd RC	8.00	3.00
❑ 204	Terrence Edwards RC	5.00	2.00
❑ 205	Tony Romo RC	6.00	2.50
❑ 206	Brooks Bollinger RC	6.00	2.50
❑ 207	Jerome McDougle RC	6.00	2.50
❑ 208	Jimmy Kennedy RC	6.00	2.50
❑ 209	Ken Dorsey RC	6.00	2.50
❑ 210	Kirk Farmer RC	3.00	1.25
❑ 211	Mike Doss RC	6.00	2.50
❑ 212	Chris Simms RC	10.00	4.00
❑ 213	Cecil Sapp RC	5.00	2.00
❑ 214	Justin Gage RC	6.00	2.50
❑ 215	Sam Aiken RC	5.00	2.00
❑ 216	Doug Gabriel RC	6.00	2.50
❑ 217	Jason Witten RC	10.00	4.00
❑ 218	Bennie Joppru RC	6.00	2.50
❑ 219	Jason Gesser RC	6.00	2.50
❑ 220	Brock Forsey RC	6.00	2.50
❑ 221	Quentin Griffin RC	6.00	2.50
❑ 222	Avon Cobourne RC	3.00	1.25
❑ 223	Domanick Davis RC	10.00	4.00
❑ 224	Boss Bailey RC	6.00	2.50
❑ 225	Tony Hollings RC	6.00	2.50
❑ 226	LaBrandon Toefield RC	6.00	2.50
❑ 227	Arlen Harris RC	6.00	2.50
❑ 228	Sultan McCullough RC	5.00	2.00
❑ 229	Visanthe Shiancoe RC	5.00	2.00
❑ 230	L.J. Smith RC	6.00	2.50
❑ 231	LaTarence Dunbar RC	5.00	2.00
❑ 232	Walter Young RC	3.00	1.25
❑ 233	Bobby Wade RC	6.00	2.50
❑ 234	Zuriel Smith RC	3.00	1.25
❑ 235	Adrian Madise RC	5.00	2.00
❑ 236	Ken Hamlin RC	6.00	2.50
❑ 237	Carl Ford RC	3.00	1.25
❑ 238	Cortez Hankton RC	5.00	2.00
❑ 239	J.R. Tolver RC	5.00	2.00
❑ 240	Keenan Howry RC	6.00	2.50
❑ 241	Billy McMullen RC	5.00	2.00
❑ 242	Arnaz Battle RC	6.00	2.50
❑ 243	Shaun McDonald RC	6.00	2.50
❑ 244	Andre Woolfolk RC	6.00	2.50
❑ 245	Sammy Davis RC	6.00	2.50
❑ 246	Calvin Pace RC	5.00	2.00
❑ 247	Michael Haynes RC	6.00	2.50
❑ 248	Ty Warren RC	6.00	2.50
❑ 249	Nick Barnett RC	10.00	4.00
❑ 250	Troy Polamalu RC	30.00	15.00
❑ 251	Carson Palmer JSY RC	30.00	12.50
❑ 252	Byron Leftwich JSY RC	25.00	10.00
❑ 253	Kyle Boller JSY RC	12.00	5.00
❑ 254	Rex Grossman JSY RC	10.00	4.00
❑ 255	Dave Ragone JSY RC	6.00	2.50
❑ 256	Brian St.Pierre JSY RC	6.00	2.50
❑ 257	Kliff Kingsbury JSY RC	6.00	2.50
❑ 258	Seneca Wallace JSY RC	6.00	2.50
❑ 259	Larry Johnson JSY RC	30.00	15.00
❑ 260	Willis McGahee JSY RC	15.00	6.00
❑ 261	Justin Fargas JSY RC	6.00	2.50
❑ 262	Onterrio Smith JSY RC	6.00	2.50
❑ 263	Chris Brown JSY RC	12.00	5.00
❑ 264	Musa Smith JSY RC	6.00	2.50

❑ 265 Artose Pinner JSY RC 6.00 2.50
❑ 266 Andre Johnson JSY RC 15.00 6.00
❑ 267 Kelley Washington JSY RC 8.00 3.00
❑ 268 Taylor Jacobs JSY RC 6.00 2.50
❑ 269 Bryant Johnson JSY RC 6.00 2.50
❑ 270 Tyrone Calico JSY RC 10.00 4.00
❑ 271 Anquan Boldin JSY RC 20.00 7.50
❑ 272 Bethel Johnson JSY RC 6.00 2.50
❑ 273 Nate Burleson JSY RC 8.00 3.00
❑ 274 Kevin Curtis JSY RC 6.00 2.50
❑ 275 Dallas Clark JSY RC 6.00 2.50
❑ 276 Teyo Johnson JSY RC 6.00 2.50
❑ 277 Terrell Suggs JSY RC 10.00 4.00
❑ 278 DeWayne Robertson JSY RC 6.00 2.50
❑ 279 Terence Newman JSY RC 12.00 5.00
❑ 280 Marcus Trufant JSY RC 6.00 2.50
❑ 281 C.Palmer/B.Leftwich JSY 30.00 12.50
❑ 282 K.Boller/D.Ragone JSY 10.00 4.00
❑ 283 R.Grossman/B.St.Pierre JSY 10.00 4.00
❑ 284 K.Kingsbury/S.Wallace JSY 10.00 4.00
❑ 285 L.Johnson/W.McGahee JSY 30.00 12.50
❑ 286 J.Fargas/O.Smith JSY 10.00 4.00
❑ 287 C.Brown/M.Smith JSY 12.00 5.00
❑ 288 A.Pinner/A.Johnson JSY 15.00 6.00
❑ 289 K.Washington/T.Jacobs JSY 10.00 4.00
❑ 290 B.Johnson/T.Calico JSY 12.00 5.00
❑ 291 A.Boldin/B.Johnson JSY 25.00 10.00
❑ 292 N.Burleson/K.Curtis JSY 12.00 5.00
❑ 293 D.Clark/T.Johnson JSY 10.00 4.00
❑ 294 T.Suggs/D.Robertson JSY 10.00 4.00
❑ 295 T.Newman/M.Trufant JSY 12.00 5.00

2004 Leaf Rookies and Stars

❑ COMP.SET w/o SP's (200) 60.00 30.00
❑ COMP.SET w/o RC's (100) 20.00 7.50
❑ 201-250 RC PRINT RUN 750 SER.#'d SETS
❑ 251-283 JSY PRINT RUN 750 SER.#'d SETS
❑ 284-299 PRINT RUN 500 SER.#'d SETS
❑ 1 Anquan Boldin .75 .30
❑ 2 Emmitt Smith 1.50 .60
❑ 3 Josh McCown .50 .20
❑ 4 Michael Vick 1.50 .60
❑ 5 Peerless Price .50 .20
❑ 6 T.J. Duckett .50 .20
❑ 7 Warrick Dunn .50 .20
❑ 8 Jamal Lewis .75 .30
❑ 9 Kyle Boller .75 .30
❑ 10 Ray Lewis .75 .30
❑ 11 Drew Bledsoe .75 .30
❑ 12 Eric Moulds .50 .20
❑ 13 Travis Henry .50 .20
❑ 14 Jake Delhomme .75 .30
❑ 15 Stephen Davis .50 .20
❑ 16 Steve Smith .75 .30
❑ 17 Brian Urlacher 1.00 .40
❑ 18 Rex Grossman .75 .30
❑ 19 Thomas Jones .50 .20
❑ 20 Carson Palmer 1.00 .40
❑ 21 Chad Johnson .75 .30
❑ 22 Rudi Johnson .50 .20
❑ 23 Jeff Garcia .75 .30
❑ 24 William Green .50 .20
❑ 25 Keyshawn Johnson .50 .20
❑ 26 Terence Newman .50 .20
❑ 27 Roy Williams S .50 .20
❑ 28 Jake Plummer .50 .20
❑ 29 Quentin Griffin .75 .30
❑ 30 Rod Smith .50 .20
❑ 31 Charles Rogers .50 .20
❑ 32 Joey Harrington .75 .30
❑ 33 Ahman Green .75 .30
❑ 34 Brett Favre 2.00 .75
❑ 35 Javon Walker .50 .20
❑ 36 Andre Johnson .75 .30
❑ 37 David Carr .75 .30
❑ 38 Domanick Davis .75 .30
❑ 39 Edgerrin James .75 .30
❑ 40 Marvin Harrison .75 .30
❑ 41 Peyton Manning 1.25 .50
❑ 42 Byron Leftwich 1.00 .40
❑ 43 Fred Taylor .50 .20
❑ 44 Jimmy Smith .50 .20
❑ 45 Priest Holmes 1.00 .40
❑ 46 Tony Gonzalez .50 .20
❑ 47 Trent Green .50 .20
❑ 48 A.J. Feeley .75 .30
❑ 49 Chris Chambers .50 .20
❑ 50 Deion Sanders 1.00 .40
❑ 51 Daunte Culpepper .75 .30
❑ 52 Michael Bennett .50 .20
❑ 53 Randy Moss 1.00 .40
❑ 54 Corey Dillon .50 .20
❑ 55 Deion Branch .75 .30
❑ 56 Tom Brady 2.00 .75
❑ 57 Aaron Brooks .50 .20
❑ 58 Deuce McAllister .75 .30
❑ 59 Joe Horn .50 .20
❑ 60 Jeremy Shockey .75 .30
❑ 61 Michael Strahan .50 .20
❑ 62 Tiki Barber .75 .30
❑ 63 Chad Pennington .75 .30
❑ 64 Curtis Martin .75 .30
❑ 65 Santana Moss .50 .20
❑ 66 Jerry Porter .50 .20
❑ 67 Jerry Rice 1.50 .60
❑ 68 Warren Sapp .50 .20
❑ 69 Donovan McNabb 1.00 .40
❑ 70 Jevon Kearse .50 .20
❑ 71 Terrell Owens .75 .30
❑ 72 Duce Staley .50 .20
❑ 73 Hines Ward .75 .30
❑ 74 Jerome Bettis .75 .30
❑ 75 LaDainian Tomlinson 1.00 .40
❑ 76 Kevan Barlow .50 .20
❑ 77 Tim Rattay .50 .20
❑ 78 Koren Robinson .50 .20
❑ 79 Matt Hasselbeck .50 .20
❑ 80 Shaun Alexander .75 .30
❑ 81 Isaac Bruce .50 .20
❑ 82 Marc Bulger .75 .30
❑ 83 Marshall Faulk .75 .30
❑ 84 Torry Holt .75 .30
❑ 85 Brad Johnson .50 .20
❑ 86 Derrick Brooks .50 .20
❑ 87 Chris Brown .75 .30
❑ 88 Derrick Mason .50 .20
❑ 89 Eddie George .50 .20
❑ 90 Steve McNair .75 .30
❑ 91 Clinton Portis .75 .30
❑ 92 LaVar Arrington 1.50 .60
❑ 93 Laveranues Coles .50 .20
❑ 94 Mark Brunell .50 .20
❑ 95 Hall/Schaub/Jenkins CL .75 .30
❑ 96 Losman/L.Evans CL 1.00 .40
❑ 97 Winslow Jr./L.McCown CL 1.50 .60
❑ 98 D.Watts/T.Bell CL .75 .30
❑ 99 K.Jones/Ro.Will. CL 2.00 .75
❑ 100 G.Jones/Re.Will. CL .75 .30
❑ 101 Darnell Dockett RC 3.00 1.25
❑ 102 Karlos Dansby RC 4.00 1.50
❑ 103 Larry Croom RC 3.00 1.25
❑ 104 Chad Lavalais RC 3.00 1.25
❑ 105 Demorrio Williams RC 4.00 1.50
❑ 106 B.J. Sams RC 4.00 1.50
❑ 107 Dwan Edwards RC 2.00 .75
❑ 108 Jason Peters RC 4.00 1.50
❑ 109 Shaud Williams RC 3.00 1.25
❑ 110 Tim Anderson RC 4.00 1.50
❑ 111 Tim Euhus RC 4.00 1.50
❑ 112 Michael Gaines RC 3.00 1.25
❑ 113 Rod Rutherford RC 3.00 1.25
❑ 114 Leon Joe RC 2.00 .75
❑ 115 Nathan Vasher RC 5.00 2.00
❑ 116 Caleb Miller RC 3.00 1.25
❑ 117 Jamall Broussard RC 2.00 .75
❑ 118 Keiwan Ratliff RC 3.00 1.25
❑ 119 Landon Johnson RC 3.00 1.25
❑ 120 Madieu Williams RC 3.00 1.25
❑ 121 Matthias Askew RC 3.00 1.25
❑ 122 Robert Geathers RC 3.00 1.25
❑ 123 Richard Alston RC 3.00 1.25
❑ 124 Bruce Thornton RC 2.00 .75
❑ 125 Patrick Crayton RC 4.00 1.50
❑ 126 Bradlee Van Pelt RC 6.00 2.50
❑ 127 Charlie Adams RC 2.00 .75
❑ 128 Nate Jackson RC 2.00 .75
❑ 129 Roc Alexander RC 2.00 .75
❑ 130 Romar Crenshaw RC 2.00 .75
❑ 131 Keith Smith RC 3.00 1.25
❑ 132 Joey Thomas RC 4.00 1.50
❑ 133 Kelvin Kight RC 2.00 .75
❑ 134 Scott McBrien RC 4.00 1.50
❑ 135 Andrae Thurman RC 2.00 .75
❑ 136 Derick Armstrong 3.00 1.25
❑ 137 Glenn Earl RC 3.00 1.25
❑ 138 Kendrick Starling RC 2.00 .75
❑ 139 Ben Hartsock RC 4.00 1.50
❑ 140 Gilbert Gardner RC 3.00 1.25
❑ 141 Jason David RC 4.00 1.50
❑ 142 Daryl Smith RC 4.00 1.50
❑ 143 Jared Allen RC 5.00 2.00
❑ 144 Jeris McIntyre RC 3.00 1.25
❑ 145 John Booth RC 3.00 1.25
❑ 146 Jonathan Smith RC 3.00 1.25
❑ 147 Junior Siavii RC 4.00 1.50
❑ 148 Keyaron Fox RC 3.00 1.25
❑ 149 Kris Wilson RC 4.00 1.50
❑ 150 Doug Easlick RC 3.00 1.25
❑ 151 Fred Russell RC 4.00 1.50
❑ 152 Tony Bua RC 3.00 1.25
❑ 153 Will Poole RC 4.00 1.50
❑ 154 Ben Nelson RC 2.00 .75
❑ 155 Brock Lesnar RC 5.00 2.00
❑ 156 Butchie Wallace RC 3.00 1.25
❑ 157 Darrion Scott RC 4.00 1.50
❑ 158 Dontarrious Thomas RC 4.00 1.50
❑ 159 Richard Owens RC 2.00 .75
❑ 160 Rod Davis RC 2.00 .75
❑ 161 Dexter Reid RC 2.00 .75
❑ 162 Kory Chapman RC 3.00 1.25
❑ 163 Marquise Hill RC 3.00 1.25
❑ 164 Courtney Watson RC 4.00 1.50
❑ 165 Mike Karney RC 3.00 1.25
❑ 166 Gibril Wilson RC 4.00 1.50
❑ 167 Reggie Torbor RC 3.00 1.25
❑ 168 Darrell McClover RC 3.00 1.25
❑ 169 Derrick Strait RC 4.00 1.50
❑ 170 Erik Coleman RC 4.00 1.50
❑ 171 Johnathan Reese RC 2.00 .75
❑ 172 Rashad Washington RC 3.00 1.25
❑ 173 Courtney Anderson RC 3.00 1.25
❑ 174 Stuart Schweigert RC 4.00 1.50
❑ 175 J.R. Reed RC 3.00 1.25
❑ 176 Justin Jenkins RC 3.00 1.25
❑ 177 Matt Ware RC 4.00 1.50
❑ 178 Nate Lawrie RC 3.00 1.25
❑ 179 Thomas Tapeh RC 3.00 1.25
❑ 180 Matt Kranchick RC 4.00 1.50
❑ 181 Willie Parker RC 20.00 10.00
❑ 182 Igor Olshansky RC 4.00 1.50
❑ 183 Ryan Krause RC 3.00 1.25
❑ 184 Shaun Phillips RC 3.00 1.25

❑ 185 Wes Welker RC 4.00 1.50
❑ 186 Richard Seigler RC 3.00 1.25
❑ 187 Shawntae Spencer RC 4.00 1.50
❑ 188 Marcus Tubbs RC 4.00 1.50
❑ 189 Niko Koutouvides RC 3.00 1.25
❑ 190 Brandon Chillar RC 3.00 1.25
❑ 191 Tony Hargrove RC 3.00 1.25
❑ 192 Mark Jones RC 3.00 1.25
❑ 193 Marquis Cooper RC 3.00 1.25
❑ 194 Antwan Odom RC 4.00 1.50
❑ 195 Michael Waddell RC 2.00 .75
❑ 196 Randy Starks RC 3.00 1.25
❑ 197 Rich Gardner RC 3.00 1.25
❑ 198 Travis Laboy RC 4.00 1.50
❑ 199 Vick King RC 3.00 1.25
❑ 200 Chris Cooley RC 4.00 1.50
❑ 201 Adimchinobe Echemandu RC 5.00 2.00
❑ 202 Ahmad Carroll RC 8.00 3.00
❑ 203 Andy Hall RC 5.00 2.00
❑ 204 B.J. Johnson RC 5.00 2.00
❑ 205 B.J. Symons RC 6.00 2.50
❑ 206 Brandon Miree RC 5.00 2.00
❑ 207 Bruce Perry RC 6.00 2.50
❑ 208 Carlos Francis RC 5.00 2.00
❑ 209 Casey Bramlet RC 5.00 2.00
❑ 210 Chris Gamble RC 8.00 3.00
❑ 211 Clarence Moore RC 6.00 2.50
❑ 212 Cody Pickett RC 6.00 2.50
❑ 213 Craig Krenzel RC 6.00 2.50
❑ 214 D.J. Hackett RC 5.00 2.00
❑ 215 D.J. Williams RC 8.00 3.00
❑ 216 Derrick Ward RC 3.00 1.25
❑ 217 Drew Carter RC 6.00 2.50
❑ 218 Drew Henson RC 6.00 2.50
❑ 219 Ernest Wilford RC 6.00 2.50
❑ 220 Jamaar Taylor RC 6.00 2.50
❑ 221 Jared Lorenzen RC 5.00 2.00
❑ 222 Jarrett Payton RC 8.00 3.00
❑ 223 Jason Babin RC 6.00 2.50
❑ 224 Jeff Smoker RC 6.00 2.50
❑ 225 Jerricho Cotchery RC 6.00 2.50
❑ 226 Jim Sorgi RC 6.00 2.50
❑ 227 John Navarre RC 6.00 2.50
❑ 228 Johnnie Morant RC 6.00 2.50
❑ 229 Jonathan Vilma RC 6.00 2.50
❑ 230 Josh Harris RC 6.00 2.50
❑ 231 Kenechi Udeze RC 6.00 2.50
❑ 232 Matt Mauck RC 6.00 2.50
❑ 233 Maurice Mann RC 5.00 2.00
❑ 234 Michael Turner RC 6.00 2.50
❑ 235 P.K. Sam RC 5.00 2.00
❑ 236 Quincy Wilson RC 5.00 2.00
❑ 237 Ran Carthon RC 5.00 2.00
❑ 238 Ricardo Colclough RC 6.00 2.50
❑ 239 Samie Parker RC 6.00 2.50
❑ 240 Sean Jones RC 5.00 2.00
❑ 241 Sean Taylor RC 8.00 3.00
❑ 242 Sloan Thomas RC 5.00 2.00
❑ 243 Tommie Harris RC 6.00 2.50
❑ 244 Triandos Luke RC 6.00 2.50
❑ 245 Troy Fleming RC 5.00 2.00
❑ 246 Vince Wilfork RC 8.00 3.00
❑ 247 Will Smith RC 6.00 2.50
❑ 248 Michael Boulware RC 6.00 2.50
❑ 249 Richard Smith RC 5.00 2.00
❑ 250 Teddy Lehman RC 6.00 2.50
❑ 251 Larry Fitzgerald JSY RC 20.00 7.50
❑ 252 DeAngelo Hall JSY RC 10.00 4.00
❑ 253 Matt Schaub JSY RC 10.00 4.00
❑ 254 Michael Jenkins JSY RC 8.00 3.00
❑ 255 Devard Darling JSY RC 8.00 3.00
❑ 256 J.P. Losman JSY RC 12.00 5.00
❑ 257 Lee Evans JSY RC 10.00 4.00
❑ 258 Keary Colbert JSY RC 10.00 4.00
❑ 259 Bernard Berrian JSY RC 8.00 3.00
❑ 260 Chris Perry JSY RC 10.00 4.00
❑ 261 Kellen Winslow Jr. JSY RC 12.00 5.00
❑ 262 Luke McCown JSY RC 8.00 3.00
❑ 263 Julius Jones JSY RC 25.00 10.00
❑ 264 Darius Watts JSY RC 8.00 3.00
❑ 265 Tatum Bell JSY RC 12.00 5.00
❑ 266 Kevin Jones JSY RC 20.00 7.50
❑ 267 Roy Williams JSY RC 15.00 6.00
❑ 268 Dunta Robinson JSY RC 8.00 3.00
❑ 269 Greg Jones JSY RC 8.00 3.00
❑ 270 Reggie Williams JSY RC 10.00 4.00
❑ 271 Mewelde Moore JSY RC 10.00 4.00
❑ 272 Ben Watson JSY RC 8.00 3.00
❑ 273 Cedric Cobbs JSY RC 8.00 3.00
❑ 274 Devery Henderson JSY RC 6.00 2.50
❑ 275 Eli Manning JSY RC 30.00 15.00
❑ 276 Robert Gallery JSY RC 10.00 4.00
❑ 277 Ben Roethlisberger JSY RC 50.00 25.00
❑ 278 Philip Rivers JSY RC 20.00 10.00
❑ 279 Derrick Hamilton JSY RC 6.00 2.50
❑ 280 Rashaun Woods JSY RC 8.00 3.00
❑ 281 Steven Jackson JSY RC 20.00 7.50
❑ 282 Michael Clayton JSY RC 12.00 5.00
❑ 283 Ben Troupe JSY RC 8.00 3.00
❑ 284 E.Manning/Rivers JSY 30.00 15.00
❑ 285 Fitzgerald/Ro.Williams JSY 20.00 7.50
❑ 286 Winslow Jr./G.Jones JSY 15.00 6.00
❑ 287 D.Hall/D.Robinson JSY 10.00 4.00
❑ 288 Re.Williams/Darling JSY 10.00 4.00
❑ 289 Roethlisberger/Losman JSY 50.00 25.00
❑ 290 Clayton/Henderson JSY 15.00 6.00
❑ 291 S.Jackson/Perry JSY 20.00 7.50
❑ 292 L.Evans/M.Jenkins JSY 12.00 5.00
❑ 293 R.Woods/T.Bell JSY 12.00 5.00
❑ 294 K.Jones/Berrian JSY 25.00 10.00
❑ 295 Watson/Troupe JSY 8.00 3.00
❑ 296 J.Jones/M.Moore JSY 25.00 10.00
❑ 297 M.Schaub/Hamilton JSY 12.00 5.00
❑ 298 L.McCown/Watts JSY 8.00 3.00
❑ 299 Colbert/Cobbs JSY 8.00 3.00

2005 Leaf Rookies and Stars

❑ COMP.SET w/o RC's (100) 20.00 7.50
❑ 201-250 RC PRINT RUN 799 SER.#'d SETS
❑ 251-279 JSY PRINT RUN 750 SER.#'d SETS
❑ 280-293 JSY DUAL PRINT RUN 500 SER.#'d SETS
❑ 1 Anquan Boldin .50 .20
❑ 2 Kurt Warner .50 .20
❑ 3 Larry Fitzgerald .75 .30
❑ 4 Michael Vick 1.25 .50
❑ 5 T.J. Duckett .50 .20
❑ 6 Warrick Dunn .50 .20
❑ 7 Jamal Lewis .75 .30
❑ 8 Kyle Boller .50 .20
❑ 9 Ray Lewis .75 .30
❑ 10 Derrick Mason .50 .20
❑ 11 J.P. Losman .75 .30
❑ 12 Lee Evans .50 .20
❑ 13 Willis McGahee .75 .30
❑ 14 DeShaun Foster .50 .20
❑ 15 Jake Delhomme .75 .30
❑ 16 Steve Smith .50 .20
❑ 17 Brian Urlacher .75 .30
❑ 18 Rex Grossman .50 .20
❑ 19 Muhsin Muhammad .50 .20
❑ 20 Carson Palmer .75 .30
❑ 21 Chad Johnson .75 .30
❑ 22 Rudi Johnson .50 .2
❑ 23 Lee Suggs .50 .2
❑ 24 Drew Bledsoe .75 .3
❑ 25 Julius Jones 1.00 .4
❑ 26 Keyshawn Johnson .50 .2
❑ 27 Roy Williams S .50 .2
❑ 28 Ashley Lelie .50 .2
❑ 29 Jake Plummer .50 .2
❑ 30 Rod Smith .50 .2
❑ 31 Tatum Bell .50 .2
❑ 32 Joey Harrington .75 .3
❑ 33 Kevin Jones .75 .3
❑ 34 Roy Williams WR .75 .3
❑ 35 Ahman Green .75 .3
❑ 36 Brett Favre 2.00 .7
❑ 37 Javon Walker .50 .2
❑ 38 Andre Johnson .50 .2
❑ 39 David Carr .75 .3
❑ 40 Domanick Davis .50 .2
❑ 41 Edgerrin James .75 .3
❑ 42 Marvin Harrison .75 .3
❑ 43 Peyton Manning 1.25 .5
❑ 44 Reggie Wayne .50 .2
❑ 45 Byron Leftwich .75 .3
❑ 46 Fred Taylor .50 .2
❑ 47 Jimmy Smith .50 .2
❑ 48 Priest Holmes .75 .3
❑ 49 Tony Gonzalez .50 .2
❑ 50 Trent Green .50 .2
❑ 51 Chris Chambers .50 .2
❑ 52 Daunte Culpepper .75 .3
❑ 53 Michael Bennett .50 .2
❑ 54 Nate Burleson .50 .2
❑ 55 Corey Dillon .50 .2
❑ 56 Deion Branch .50 .2
❑ 57 Tom Brady 2.00 .7
❑ 58 Aaron Brooks .50 .2
❑ 59 Deuce McAllister .75 .3
❑ 60 Joe Horn .50 .2
❑ 61 Eli Manning 1.50 .6
❑ 62 Jeremy Shockey .75 .3
❑ 63 Tiki Barber .75 .3
❑ 64 Plaxico Burress .50 .2
❑ 65 Chad Pennington .75 .3
❑ 66 Curtis Martin .75 .3
❑ 67 Laveranues Coles .50 .2
❑ 68 Jerry Porter .50 .2
❑ 69 Kerry Collins .50 .2
❑ 70 LaMont Jordan .75 .3
❑ 71 Randy Moss .75 .3
❑ 72 Brian Westbrook .50 .2
❑ 73 Donovan McNabb 1.00 .4
❑ 74 Terrell Owens .75 .3
❑ 75 Ben Roethlisberger 2.00 .7
❑ 76 Duce Staley .50 .2
❑ 77 Hines Ward .75 .3
❑ 78 Jerome Bettis .75 .3
❑ 79 Antonio Gates .75 .3
❑ 80 Drew Brees .75 .3
❑ 81 LaDainian Tomlinson 1.00 .4
❑ 82 Kevan Barlow .50 .2
❑ 83 Darrell Jackson .50 .2
❑ 84 Matt Hasselbeck .50 .2
❑ 85 Shaun Alexander 1.00 .4
❑ 86 Marc Bulger .75 .3
❑ 87 Steven Jackson 1.00 .4
❑ 88 Torry Holt .75 .3
❑ 89 Brian Griese .50 .2
❑ 90 Michael Clayton .75 .3
❑ 91 Chris Brown .50 .2
❑ 92 Drew Bennett .50 .2
❑ 93 Steve McNair .75 .3
❑ 94 Clinton Portis .75 .3
❑ 95 LaVar Arrington .75 .3
❑ 96 Santana Moss .50 .2
❑ 97 A.Smith QB CL/F.Gore 3.00 1.2
❑ 98 B.Edwards CL/C.Frye 2.00 .7
❑ 99 C.Fason CL/T.Williamson 1.25 .5
❑ 100 C.Rogers CL/J.Campbell 1.00 .4
❑ 101 Travis Johnson RC 4.00 1.5

❑ 102 Alex Smith TE RC 5.00 2.00
❑ 103 Channing Crowder RC 5.00 2.00
❑ 104 Craig Bragg RC 4.00 1.50
❑ 105 Darrent Williams RC 5.00 2.00
❑ 106 Derrick Wimbush RC 5.00 2.00
❑ 107 Josh Cribbs RC 5.00 2.00
❑ 108 Luis Castillo RC 5.00 2.00
❑ 109 Matt Roth RC 5.00 2.00
❑ 110 Mike Patterson RC 5.00 2.00
❑ 111 Fred Gibson RC 4.00 1.50
❑ 112 Marcus Spears RC 5.00 2.00
❑ 113 Brodney Pool RC 5.00 2.00
❑ 114 Barrett Ruud RC 5.00 2.00
❑ 115 Stanford Routt RC 4.00 1.50
❑ 116 Josh Bullocks RC 5.00 2.00
❑ 117 Kevin Burnett RC 5.00 2.00
❑ 118 Corey Webster RC 5.00 2.00
❑ 119 Lofa Tatupu RC 6.00 2.50
❑ 120 Mike Nugent RC 5.00 2.00
❑ 121 Jim Leonhard RC 8.00 3.00
❑ 122 Ronald Bartell RC 4.00 1.50
❑ 123 Nick Collins RC 5.00 2.00
❑ 124 Justin Miller RC 4.00 1.50
❑ 125 Jonathan Babineaux RC 4.00 1.50
❑ 126 Kelvin Hayden RC 4.00 1.50
❑ 127 Matt McCoy RC 4.00 1.50
❑ 128 Oshiomogho Atogwe RC 4.00 1.50
❑ 129 Stanley Wilson RC 4.00 1.50
❑ 130 Justin Tuck RC 5.00 2.00
❑ 131 Eric Green RC 2.50 1.00
❑ 132 Karl Paymah RC 8.00 3.00
❑ 133 Kirk Morrison RC 5.00 2.00
❑ 134 Dustin Fox RC 5.00 2.00
❑ 135 Alfred Fincher RC 4.00 1.50
❑ 136 Chris Henry RC 5.00 2.00
❑ 137 Ellis Hobbs RC 5.00 2.00
❑ 138 Scott Starks RC 4.00 1.50
❑ 139 Jordan Beck RC 4.00 1.50
❑ 140 Vincent Burns RC 4.00 1.50
❑ 141 Darryl Blackstock RC 4.00 1.50
❑ 142 Domonique Foxworth RC 5.00 2.00
❑ 143 Leroy Hill RC 5.00 2.00
❑ 144 Cedric Killings RC 4.00 1.50
❑ 145 Leonard Weaver RC 4.00 1.50
❑ 146 Sean Considine RC 5.00 2.00
❑ 147 Antonio Perkins RC 4.00 1.50
❑ 148 Travis Daniels RC 4.00 1.50
❑ 149 Vincent Fuller RC 4.00 1.50
❑ 150 Manuel White RC 4.00 1.50
❑ 151 Kerry Rhodes RC 5.00 2.00
❑ 152 Brady Poppinga RC 5.00 2.00
❑ 153 Chris Canty RC 5.00 2.00
❑ 154 James Sanders RC 5.00 2.00
❑ 155 Matt Giordano RC 5.00 2.00
❑ 156 Boomer Grigsby RC 6.00 2.50
❑ 157 Donte Nicholson RC 5.00 2.00
❑ 158 Jerome Collins RC 4.00 1.50
❑ 159 Trent Cole RC 5.00 2.00
❑ 160 Alphonso Hodge RC 2.50 1.00
❑ 161 Jonathan Welsh RC 4.00 1.50
❑ 162 Adam Seward RC 6.00 2.50
❑ 163 Robert McCune RC 4.00 1.50
❑ 164 Eric King RC 4.00 1.50
❑ 165 Gerald Sensabaugh RC 8.00 3.00
❑ 166 Justin Green RC 5.00 2.00
❑ 167 Jeb Huckeba RC 5.00 2.00
❑ 168 Michael Boley RC 4.00 1.50
❑ 169 Andre Maddox RC 4.00 1.50
❑ 170 Rian Wallace RC 4.00 1.50
❑ 171 Michael Hawkins RC 4.00 1.50
❑ 172 Lance Mitchell RC 4.00 1.50
❑ 173 Ryan Claridge RC 4.00 1.50
❑ 174 James Butler RC 4.00 1.50
❑ 175 Ryan Riddle RC 2.50 1.00
❑ 176 Bo Scaife RC 4.00 1.50
❑ 177 Chris Harris RC 10.00 4.00
❑ 178 C.C. Brown RC 4.00 1.50
❑ 179 Pat Thomas RC 4.00 1.50
❑ 180 Derrick Johnson CB RC 5.00 2.00
❑ 181 Joel Dreessen RC 4.00 1.50
❑ 182 Rick Razzano RC 5.00 2.00
❑ 183 Nehemiah Broughton RC 4.00 1.50
❑ 184 Marcus Maxwell RC 4.00 1.50
❑ 185 Harry Williams RC 4.00 1.50
❑ 186 Patrick Estes RC 4.00 1.50
❑ 187 Billy Bajema RC 4.00 1.50
❑ 188 Madison Hedgecock RC 5.00 2.00
❑ 189 Manuel Wright RC 5.00 2.00
❑ 190 Roscoe Crosby RC 4.00 1.50
❑ 191 Wesley Duke RC 5.00 2.00
❑ 192 Ronnie Cruz RC 4.00 1.50
❑ 193 Adam Bergen RC 5.00 2.00
❑ 194 B.J. Ward RC 4.00 1.50
❑ 195 Stephen Spach RC 4.00 1.50
❑ 196 Marviel Underwood RC 4.00 1.50
❑ 197 John Bronson RC 4.00 1.50
❑ 198 Zak Keasey RC 5.00 2.00
❑ 199 Gregg Guenther RC 4.00 1.50
❑ 200 Jerome Carter RC 4.00 1.50
❑ 201 Aaron Rodgers RC 20.00 7.50
❑ 202 Adrian McPherson RC 6.00 2.50
❑ 203 Alvin Pearman RC 6.00 2.50
❑ 204 Airese Currie RC 6.00 2.50
❑ 205 Anthony Davis RC 5.00 2.00
❑ 206 Brandon Jacobs RC 8.00 3.00
❑ 207 Brandon Jones RC 6.00 2.50
❑ 208 Bryant McFadden RC 6.00 2.50
❑ 209 Cedric Benson RC 12.00 5.00
❑ 210 Cedric Houston RC 6.00 2.50
❑ 211 Chad Owens RC 6.00 2.50
❑ 212 Chris Henry 6.00 2.50
❑ 213 Craphonso Thorpe RC 5.00 2.00
❑ 214 Damien Nash RC 5.00 2.00
❑ 215 Dan Cody RC 6.00 2.50
❑ 216 Dan Orlovsky RC 8.00 3.00
❑ 217 Dante Ridgeway RC 5.00 2.00
❑ 218 Darren Sproles RC 6.00 2.50
❑ 219 David Greene RC 6.00 2.50
❑ 220 David Pollack RC 6.00 2.50
❑ 221 Deandra Cobb RC 5.00 2.00
❑ 222 DeMarcus Ware RC 10.00 4.00
❑ 223 Derek Anderson RC 6.00 2.50
❑ 224 Derrick Johnson RC 10.00 4.00
❑ 225 Fabian Washington RC 6.00 2.50
❑ 226 Roydell Williams RC 6.00 2.50
❑ 227 Heath Miller RC 15.00 6.00
❑ 228 J.R. Russell RC 5.00 2.00
❑ 229 James Kilian RC 6.00 2.50
❑ 230 Jerome Mathis RC 6.00 2.50
❑ 231 Larry Brackins RC 5.00 2.00
❑ 232 LeRon McCoy RC 5.00 2.00
❑ 233 Lionel Gates RC 5.00 2.00
❑ 234 Marion Barber RC 10.00 4.00
❑ 235 Marlin Jackson RC 6.00 2.50
❑ 236 Matt Cassel RC 10.00 4.00
❑ 237 Mike Williams 12.00 5.00
❑ 238 Nate Washington RC 5.00 2.00
❑ 239 Noah Herron RC 6.00 2.50
❑ 240 Fred Amey RC 5.00 2.00
❑ 241 Paris Warren RC 5.00 2.00
❑ 242 Rasheed Marshall RC 6.00 2.50
❑ 243 Ryan Fitzpatrick RC 10.00 4.00
❑ 244 Shaun Cody RC 6.00 2.50
❑ 245 Shawne Merriman RC 10.00 4.00
❑ 246 Tab Perry RC 6.00 2.50
❑ 247 Thomas Davis RC 6.00 2.50
❑ 248 Tyson Thompson RC 8.00 3.00
❑ 249 Chris Carr RC 8.00 3.00
❑ 250 Odell Thurman RC 6.00 2.50
❑ 251 Adam Jones JSY RC 8.00 3.00
❑ 252 Alex Smith QB JSY RC 20.00 7.50
❑ 253 Andrew Walter JSY RC 10.00 4.00
❑ 254 Antrel Rolle JSY RC 8.00 3.00
❑ 255 Braylon Edwards JSY RC 15.00 6.00
❑ 256 Carlos Rogers JSY RC 10.00 4.00
❑ 257 Carnell Williams JSY RC 25.00 10.00
❑ 258 Charlie Frye JSY RC 12.00 5.00
❑ 259 Ciatrick Fason JSY RC 8.00 3.00
❑ 260 Courtney Roby JSY RC 8.00 3.00
❑ 261 Eric Shelton JSY RC 8.00 3.00
❑ 262 Frank Gore JSY RC 10.00 4.00
❑ 263 J.J. Arrington JSY RC 10.00 4.00
❑ 264 Jason Campbell JSY RC 10.00 4.00
❑ 265 Kyle Orton JSY RC 12.00 5.00
❑ 266 Mark Clayton JSY RC 10.00 4.00
❑ 267 Mark Bradley JSY RC 8.00 3.00
❑ 268 Matt Jones JSY RC 15.00 6.00
❑ 269 Maurice Clarett JSY 8.00 3.00
❑ 270 Reggie Brown JSY RC 8.00 3.00
❑ 271 Roddy White JSY RC 8.00 3.00
❑ 272 Ronnie Brown JSY RC 20.00 7.50
❑ 273 Roscoe Parrish JSY RC 6.00 2.50
❑ 274 Ryan Moats JSY RC 8.00 3.00
❑ 275 Stefan LeFors JSY RC 8.00 3.00
❑ 276 Terrence Murphy JSY RC 8.00 3.00
❑ 277 Troy Williamson JSY RC 12.00 5.00
❑ 278 Vernand Morency JSY RC 8.00 3.00
❑ 279 Vincent Jackson JSY RC 8.00 3.00
❑ 280 A.Smith QB J/J.Campbell J 25.00 10.00
❑ 281 R.Brown J/C.Williams J 30.00 12.50
❑ 282 B.Edwards J/T.Williamson J 20.00 7.50
❑ 283 A.Jones J/A.Rolle J 10.00 4.00
❑ 284 R.Parrish J/F.Gore J 12.00 5.00
❑ 285 C.Frye J/A.Walter J 15.00 6.00
❑ 286 J.Arrington J/E.Shelton J 12.00 5.00
❑ 287 C.Rogers J/K.Orton J 12.00 5.00
❑ 288 M.Clayton J/M.Bradley J 12.00 5.00
❑ 289 R.White J/Re.Brown J 10.00 4.00
❑ 290 T.Murphy J/C.Roby J 10.00 4.00
❑ 291 M.Clarett J/C.Fason J 10.00 4.00
❑ 292 R.Moats J/S.LeFors J 10.00 4.00
❑ 293 M.Jones J/V.Jackson J 15.00 6.00

1991 Pacific

❑ COMPLETE SET (660) 15.00 7.50
❑ COMP.SERIES 1 (550) 8.00 4.00
❑ COMP.FACT.SER.1 (550) 10.00 5.00
❑ COMP.SERIES 2 (110) 8.00 4.00
❑ COMP.FACT.SER.2 (110) 12.00 6.00
❑ COMP.CHECKLIST SET (5) 15.00 7.50
❑ 1 Deion Sanders .40 .15
❑ 2 Steve Broussard .05 .01
❑ 3 Aundray Bruce .05 .01
❑ 4 Rick Bryan .05 .01
❑ 5 John Rade .05 .01
❑ 6 Scott Case .05 .01
❑ 7 Tony Casillas .05 .01
❑ 8 Shawn Collins .05 .01
❑ 9 Darion Conner .05 .01
❑ 10 Tory Epps .05 .01
❑ 11 Bill Fralic .05 .01
❑ 12 Mike Gann .05 .01
❑ 13 Tim Green UER .05 .01
❑ 14 Chris Hinton .05 .01
❑ 15 Houston Hoover UER .05 .01
❑ 16 Chris Miller .10 .02
❑ 17 Andre Rison .10 .02
❑ 18 Mike Rozier .05 .01
❑ 19 Jessie Tuggle .05 .01
❑ 20 Don Beebe .05 .01
❑ 21 Ray Bentley .05 .01
❑ 22 Shane Conlan .05 .01
❑ 23 Kent Hull .05 .01
❑ 24 Mark Kelso .05 .01

❑ 25	James Lofton UER	.10	.02
❑ 26	Scott Norwood	.05	.01
❑ 27	Andre Reed	.10	.02
❑ 28	Leonard Smith	.05	.01
❑ 29	Bruce Smith	.25	.08
❑ 30	Leon Seals	.05	.01
❑ 31	Darryl Talley	.05	.01
❑ 32	Steve Tasker	.10	.02
❑ 33	Thurman Thomas	.25	.08
❑ 34	James Williams	.05	.01
❑ 35	Will Wolford	.05	.01
❑ 36	Frank Reich	.10	.02
❑ 37	Jeff Wright RC	.05	.01
❑ 38	Neal Anderson	.10	.02
❑ 39	Trace Armstrong	.05	.01
❑ 40	Johnny Bailey UER	.05	.01
❑ 41	Mark Bortz UER	.05	.01
❑ 42	Cap Boso RC	.05	.01
❑ 43	Kevin Butler	.05	.01
❑ 44	Mark Carrier DB	.10	.02
❑ 45	Jim Covert	.05	.01
❑ 46	Wendell Davis	.05	.01
❑ 47	Richard Dent	.10	.02
❑ 48	Shaun Gayle	.05	.01
❑ 49	Jim Harbaugh	.25	.08
❑ 50	Jay Hilgenberg	.05	.01
❑ 51	Brad Muster	.05	.01
❑ 52	William Perry	.10	.02
❑ 53	Mike Singletary UER	.10	.02
❑ 54	Peter Tom Willis	.05	.01
❑ 55	Donnell Woolford	.05	.01
❑ 56	Steve McMichael	.10	.02
❑ 57	Eric Ball	.05	.01
❑ 58	Lewis Billups	.05	.01
❑ 59	Jim Breech	.05	.01
❑ 60	James Brooks	.10	.02
❑ 61	Eddie Brown	.05	.01
❑ 62	Rickey Dixon	.05	.01
❑ 63	Boomer Esiason	.10	.02
❑ 64	James Francis	.05	.01
❑ 65	David Fulcher	.05	.01
❑ 66	David Grant	.05	.01
❑ 67	Harold Green UER	.05	.01
❑ 68	Rodney Holman	.05	.01
❑ 69	Stanford Jennings	.05	.01
❑ 70A	Tim Krumrie ERR	.50	.20
❑ 70B	Tim Krumrie COR	.30	.10
❑ 71	Tim McGee	.05	.01
❑ 72	Anthony Munoz	.10	.02
❑ 73	Mitchell Price RC	.05	.01
❑ 74	Eric Thomas	.05	.01
❑ 75	Ickey Woods	.05	.01
❑ 76	Mike Baab	.05	.01
❑ 77	Thane Gash	.05	.01
❑ 78	David Grayson	.05	.01
❑ 79	Mike Johnson	.05	.01
❑ 80	Reggie Langhorne	.05	.01
❑ 81	Kevin Mack	.05	.01
❑ 82	Clay Matthews	.10	.02
❑ 83A	Eric Metcalf ERR	.50	.20
❑ 83B	Eric Metcalf COR	.30	.10
❑ 84	Frank Minnifield	.05	.01
❑ 85	Mike Oliphant	.05	.01
❑ 86	Mike Pagel	.05	.01
❑ 87	John Talley	.05	.01
❑ 88	Lawyer Tillman	.05	.01
❑ 89	Gregg Rakoczy UER	.05	.01
❑ 90	Bryan Wagner	.05	.01
❑ 91	Rob Burnett RC	.10	.02
❑ 92	Tommie Agee	.05	.01
❑ 93	Troy Aikman UER	.75	.30
❑ 94A	Bill Bates ERR	.50	.20
❑ 94B	Bill Bates COR	.30	.10
❑ 95	Jack Del Rio	.10	.02
❑ 96	Issiac Holt UER	.05	.01
❑ 97	Michael Irvin	.25	.08
❑ 98	Jim Jeffcoat UER	.05	.01
❑ 99	Jimmie Jones	.05	.01
❑ 100	Kelvin Martin	.05	.01
❑ 101	Nate Newton	.10	.02
❑ 102	Danny Noonan	.05	.01
❑ 103	Ken Norton Jr.	.10	.02
❑ 104	Jay Novacek	.25	.08
❑ 105	Mike Saxon	.05	.01
❑ 106	Derrick Shepard	.05	.01
❑ 107	Emmitt Smith	2.50	1.00
❑ 108	Daniel Stubbs	.05	.01
❑ 109	Tony Tolbert	.05	.01
❑ 110	Alexander Wright	.05	.01
❑ 111	Steve Atwater	.05	.01
❑ 112	Melvin Bratton	.05	.01
❑ 113	Tyrone Braxton UER	.05	.01
❑ 114	Alphonso Carreker	.05	.01
❑ 115	John Elway	1.25	.50
❑ 116	Simon Fletcher	.05	.01
❑ 117	Bobby Humphrey	.05	.01
❑ 118	Mark Jackson	.05	.01
❑ 119	Vance Johnson	.05	.01
❑ 120	Greg Kragen UER	.05	.01
❑ 121	Karl Mecklenburg UER	.05	.01
❑ 122A	Orsen Mobley ERR	.50	.20
❑ 122B	Orson Mobley COR	.10	.02
❑ 123	Alton Montgomery	.05	.01
❑ 124	Ricky Nattiel	.05	.01
❑ 125	Steve Sewell	.05	.01
❑ 126	Shannon Sharpe	.50	.20
❑ 127	Dennis Smith	.05	.01
❑ 128A	Andre Townsend RC ERR	.50	.20
❑ 128B	Andre Townsend RC COR	.10	.02
❑ 129	Mike Horan	.05	.01
❑ 130	Jerry Ball	.05	.01
❑ 131	Bennie Blades	.05	.01
❑ 132	Lomas Brown	.05	.01
❑ 133	Jeff Campbell UER	.05	.01
❑ 134	Robert Clark	.05	.01
❑ 135	Michael Cofer	.05	.01
❑ 136	Dennis Gibson	.05	.01
❑ 137	Mel Gray	.10	.02
❑ 138	LeRoy Irvin UER	.05	.01
❑ 139	George Jamison RC	.05	.01
❑ 140	Richard Johnson	.05	.01
❑ 141	Eddie Murray	.05	.01
❑ 142	Dan Owens	.05	.01
❑ 143	Rodney Peete	.10	.02
❑ 144	Barry Sanders	1.25	.50
❑ 145	Chris Spielman	.10	.02
❑ 146	Marc Spindler	.05	.01
❑ 147	Andre Ware	.10	.02
❑ 148	William White	.05	.01
❑ 149	Tony Bennett	.10	.02
❑ 150	Robert Brown	.05	.01
❑ 151	LeRoy Butler	.10	.02
❑ 152	Anthony Dilweg	.05	.01
❑ 153	Michael Haddix	.05	.01
❑ 154	Ron Hallstrom	.05	.01
❑ 155	Tim Harris	.05	.01
❑ 156	Johnny Holland	.05	.01
❑ 157	Chris Jacke	.05	.01
❑ 158	Perry Kemp	.05	.01
❑ 159	Mark Lee	.05	.01
❑ 160	Don Majkowski	.05	.01
❑ 161	Tony Mandarich UER	.05	.01
❑ 162	Mark Murphy	.05	.01
❑ 163	Brian Noble	.05	.01
❑ 164	Shawn Patterson	.05	.01
❑ 165	Jeff Query	.05	.01
❑ 166	Sterling Sharpe	.25	.08
❑ 167	Darrell Thompson	.05	.01
❑ 168	Ed West	.05	.01
❑ 169	Ray Childress UER	.05	.01
❑ 170A	Cris Dishman RC ERR Chris	.10	.02
❑ 170B	Cris Dishman RC ERR/COR	.10	.02
❑ 170C	Cris Dishman RC COR	.10	.02
❑ 171	Curtis Duncan	.05	.01
❑ 172	William Fuller	.10	.02
❑ 173	Ernest Givins UER	.10	.02
❑ 174	Drew Hill	.05	.01
❑ 175A	Haywood Jeffires ERR	.25	.08
❑ 175B	Haywood Jeffires COR	.25	.08
❑ 176	Sean Jones	.10	.02
❑ 177	Lamar Lathon	.05	.01
❑ 178	Bruce Matthews	.10	.02
❑ 179	Bubba McDowell	.05	.01
❑ 180	Johnny Meads	.05	.01
❑ 181	Warren Moon UER	.25	.08
❑ 182	Mike Munchak	.10	.02
❑ 183	Allen Pinkett	.05	.01
❑ 184	Dean Steinkuhler UER	.05	.01
❑ 185	Lorenzo White UER	.05	.01
❑ 186A	John Grimsley ERR	.50	.20
❑ 186B	John Grimsley COR	.10	.02
❑ 187	Pat Beach	.05	.01
❑ 188	Albert Bentley	.05	.01
❑ 189	Dean Biasucci	.05	.01
❑ 190	Duane Bickett	.05	.01
❑ 191	Bill Brooks	.05	.01
❑ 192	Eugene Daniel	.05	.01
❑ 193	Jeff George	.25	.08
❑ 194	Jon Hand	.05	.01
❑ 195	Jeff Herrod	.05	.01
❑ 196A	Jessie Hester ERR Jesse	.30	.10
❑ 196B	Jessie Hester ERR	.10	.02
❑ 197	Mike Prior	.05	.01
❑ 198	Stacey Simmons	.05	.01
❑ 199	Rohn Stark	.05	.01
❑ 200	Pat Tomberlin	.05	.01
❑ 201	Clarence Verdin	.05	.01
❑ 202	Keith Taylor	.05	.01
❑ 203	Jack Trudeau	.05	.01
❑ 204	Chip Banks	.05	.01
❑ 205	John Alt	.05	.01
❑ 206	Deron Cherry	.05	.01
❑ 207	Steve DeBerg	.05	.01
❑ 208	Tim Grunhard	.05	.01
❑ 209	Albert Lewis	.05	.01
❑ 210	Nick Lowery UER	.05	.01
❑ 211	Bill Maas	.05	.01
❑ 212	Chris Martin	.05	.01
❑ 213	Todd McNair	.05	.01
❑ 214	Christian Okoye	.05	.01
❑ 215	Stephone Paige	.05	.01
❑ 216	Steve Pelluer	.05	.01
❑ 217	Kevin Porter	.05	.01
❑ 218	Kevin Ross	.05	.01
❑ 219	Dan Saleaumua	.05	.01
❑ 220	Neil Smith	.25	.08
❑ 221	David Szott UER	.05	.01
❑ 222	Derrick Thomas	.25	.08
❑ 223	Barry Word	.05	.01
❑ 224	Percy Snow	.05	.01
❑ 225	Marcus Allen	.25	.08
❑ 226	Eddie Anderson UER	.05	.01
❑ 227	Steve Beuerlein UER	.10	.02
❑ 228A	Tim Brown ERR NPO	.25	.08
❑ 228B	Tim Brown COR	.25	.08
❑ 229	Scott Davis	.05	.01
❑ 230	Mike Dyal	.05	.01
❑ 231	Mervyn Fernandez UER	.05	.01
❑ 232	Willie Gault UER	.05	.01
❑ 233	Ethan Horton UER	.05	.01
❑ 234	Bo Jackson UER	.30	.10
❑ 235	Howie Long	.25	.08
❑ 236	Terry McDaniel	.05	.01
❑ 237	Max Montoya	.05	.01
❑ 238	Don Mosebar	.05	.01
❑ 239	Jay Schroeder	.05	.01
❑ 240	Steve Smith	.05	.01
❑ 241	Greg Townsend	.05	.01
❑ 242	Aaron Wallace	.05	.01
❑ 243	Lionel Washington	.05	.01
❑ 244A	Steve Wisniewski ERR	.10	.02
❑ 244B	Steve Wisniewski ERR/COR	.75	.30
❑ 244C	Steve Wisniewski COR	.10	.02
❑ 245	Flipper Anderson	.05	.01
❑ 246	Latin Berry RC	.05	.01
❑ 247	Robert Delpino	.05	.01
❑ 248	Marcus Dupree	.05	.01
❑ 249	Henry Ellard	.10	.02
❑ 250	Jim Everett	.10	.02
❑ 251	Cleveland Gary	.05	.01

❑ 252 Jerry Gray .05 .01
❑ 253 Kevin Greene .10 .02
❑ 254 Pete Holohan UER .05 .01
❑ 255 Buford McGee .05 .01
❑ 256 Tom Newberry .05 .01
❑ 257A Irv Pankey ERR .50 .20
❑ 257B Irv Pankey COR .10 .02
❑ 258 Jackie Slater .05 .01
❑ 259 Doug Smith .05 .01
❑ 260 Frank Stams .05 .01
❑ 261 Michael Stewart .05 .01
❑ 262 Fred Strickland .05 .01
❑ 263 J.B. Brown UER .05 .01
❑ 264 Mark Clayton .10 .02
❑ 265 Jeff Cross .05 .01
❑ 266 Mark Dennis RC .05 .01
❑ 267 Mark Duper .10 .02
❑ 268 Ferrell Edmunds .05 .01
❑ 269 Dan Marino 1.25 .50
❑ 270 John Offerdahl .05 .01
❑ 271 Louis Oliver .05 .01
❑ 272 Tony Paige .05 .01
❑ 273 Reggie Roby .05 .01
❑ 274 Sammie Smith .05 .01
❑ 275 Keith Sims .05 .01
❑ 276 Brian Sochia .05 .01
❑ 277 Pete Stoyanovich .05 .01
❑ 278 Richmond Webb .05 .01
❑ 279 Jarvis Williams .05 .01
❑ 280 Tim McKyer .05 .01
❑ 281A Jim C. Jensen ERR .50 .20
❑ 281B Jim C. Jensen COR .10 .02
❑ 282 Scott Secules RC .05 .01
❑ 283 Ray Berry .05 .01
❑ 284 Joey Browner UER .05 .01
❑ 285 Anthony Carter .10 .02
❑ 286A Cris Carter ERR Chris .50 .20
❑ 286B Cris Carter ERR/COR Chris 1.50 .60
❑ 286C Cris Carter COR .50 .20
❑ 287 Chris Doleman .05 .01
❑ 288 Mark Dusbabek UER .05 .01
❑ 289 Hassan Jones .05 .01
❑ 290 Steve Jordan .05 .01
❑ 291 Carl Lee .05 .01
❑ 292 Kirk Lowdermilk .05 .01
❑ 293 Randall McDaniel .05 .01
❑ 294 Mike Merriweather .05 .01
❑ 295A Keith Millard UER .20 .07
❑ 295B Keith Millard COR 2.50 1.00
❑ 296 Al Noga UER .05 .01
❑ 297 Scott Studwell UER .05 .01
❑ 298 Henry Thomas .05 .01
❑ 299 Herschel Walker .10 .02
❑ 300 Gary Zimmerman .05 .01
❑ 301 Rich Gannon .25 .08
❑ 302 Wade Wilson UER .10 .02
❑ 303 Vincent Brown .05 .01
❑ 304 Marv Cook .05 .01
❑ 305 Hart Lee Dykes .05 .01
❑ 306 Irving Fryar .10 .02
❑ 307 Tommy Hodson UER .05 .01
❑ 308 Maurice Hurst .05 .01
❑ 309 Ronnie Lippett UER .05 .01
❑ 310 Fred Marion .05 .01
❑ 311 Greg McMurtry .05 .01
❑ 312 Johnny Rembert .05 .01
❑ 313 Chris Singleton .05 .01
❑ 314 Ed Reynolds .05 .01
❑ 315 Andre Tippett .05 .01
❑ 316 Garin Veris .05 .01
❑ 317 Brent Williams .05 .01
❑ 318A John Stephens ERR .10 .02
❑ 318B John Stephens ERR/COR .75 .30
❑ 318C John Stephens COR .10 .02
❑ 319 Sammy Martin .05 .01
❑ 320 Bruce Armstrong .05 .01
❑ 321A Morten Andersen ERR .30 .10
❑ 321B Morten Andersen ERR/COR .75 .30
❑ 321C Morten Andersen COR .10 .02
❑ 322 Gene Atkins UER .05 .01
❑ 323 Vince Buck .05 .01
❑ 324 John Fourcade .05 .01
❑ 325 Kevin Haverdink .05 .01
❑ 326 Bobby Hebert .05 .01
❑ 327 Craig Heyward .10 .02
❑ 328 Dalton Hilliard .05 .01
❑ 329 Rickey Jackson .05 .01
❑ 330A Vaughan Johnson ERR .20 .07
❑ 330B Vaughan Johnson COR 2.50 1.00
❑ 331 Eric Martin .05 .01
❑ 332 Wayne Martin .05 .01
❑ 333 Rueben Mayes UER .05 .01
❑ 334 Sam Mills .05 .01
❑ 335 Brett Perriman .25 .08
❑ 336 Pat Swilling .10 .02
❑ 337 Renaldo Turnbull .05 .01
❑ 338 Lonzell Hill .05 .01
❑ 339 Steve Walsh .05 .01
❑ 340 Carl Banks UER .05 .01
❑ 341 Mark Bavaro UER .05 .01
❑ 342 Maurice Carthon .05 .01
❑ 343 Pat Harlow RC .05 .01
❑ 344 Eric Dorsey .05 .01
❑ 345 John Elliott .05 .01
❑ 346 Rodney Hampton .25 .08
❑ 347 Jeff Hostetler .10 .02
❑ 348 Erik Howard UER .05 .01
❑ 349 Pepper Johnson .05 .01
❑ 350A Sean Landeta ERR .10 .02
❑ 350B Sean Landeta COR .50 .20
❑ 351 Leonard Marshall .05 .01
❑ 352 Dave Meggett .10 .02
❑ 353A Bart Oates ERR .10 .02
❑ 353B Bart Oates ERR/COR .75 .30
❑ 353C Bart Oates COR .10 .02
❑ 354 Gary Reasons .05 .01
❑ 355 Phil Simms .10 .02
❑ 356 Lawrence Taylor .25 .08
❑ 357 Reyna Thompson .05 .01
❑ 358 Brian Williams OL UER .05 .01
❑ 359 Matt Bahr .05 .01
❑ 360 Mark Ingram .10 .02
❑ 361 Brad Baxter .05 .01
❑ 362 Mark Boyer .05 .01
❑ 363 Dennis Byrd .05 .01
❑ 364 Dave Cadigan UER .05 .01
❑ 365 Kyle Clifton .05 .01
❑ 366 James Hasty .05 .01
❑ 367 Joe Kelly UER .05 .01
❑ 368 Jeff Lageman .05 .01
❑ 369 Pat Leahy UER .05 .01
❑ 370 Terance Mathis .10 .02
❑ 371 Erik McMillan .05 .01
❑ 372 Rob Moore .25 .08
❑ 373 Ken O'Brien .05 .01
❑ 374 Tony Stargell .05 .01
❑ 375 Jim Sweeney UER .05 .01
❑ 376 Al Toon .10 .02
❑ 377 Johnny Hector .05 .01
❑ 378 Jeff Criswell .05 .01
❑ 379 Mike Haight RC .05 .01
❑ 380 Troy Benson .05 .01
❑ 381 Eric Allen .05 .01
❑ 382 Fred Barnett .25 .08
❑ 383 Jerome Brown .05 .01
❑ 384 Keith Byars .05 .01
❑ 385 Randall Cunningham .25 .08
❑ 386 Byron Evans .05 .01
❑ 387 Wes Hopkins .05 .01
❑ 388 Keith Jackson .10 .02
❑ 389 Seth Joyner UER .10 .02
❑ 390 Bobby Wilson RC .05 .01
❑ 391 Heath Sherman .05 .01
❑ 392 Clyde Simmons UER .05 .01
❑ 393 Ben Smith .05 .01
❑ 394 Andre Waters .05 .01
❑ 395 Reggie White UER .25 .08
❑ 396 Calvin Williams .10 .02
❑ 397 Al Harris .05 .01
❑ 398 Anthony Toney .05 .01
❑ 399 Mike Quick .05 .01
❑ 400 Anthony Bell .05 .01
❑ 401 Rich Camarillo .05 .01
❑ 402 Roy Green .05 .01
❑ 403 Ken Harvey .10 .02
❑ 404 Eric Hill .05 .01
❑ 405 Garth Jax RC UER .05 .01
❑ 406 Ernie Jones .05 .01
❑ 407A Cedric Mack ERR .20 .07
❑ 407B Cedric Mack COR 2.50 1.00
❑ 408 Dexter Manley .05 .01
❑ 409 Tim McDonald .05 .01
❑ 410 Freddie Joe Nunn .05 .01
❑ 411 Ricky Proehl .05 .01
❑ 412 Moe Gardner RC .05 .01
❑ 413 Timm Rosenbach .05 .01
❑ 414 Luis Sharpe UER .05 .01
❑ 415 Vai Sikahema UER .05 .01
❑ 416 Anthony Thompson .05 .01
❑ 417 Ron Wolfley UER .05 .01
❑ 418 Lonnie Young .05 .01
❑ 419 Gary Anderson K .05 .01
❑ 420 Bubby Brister .05 .01
❑ 421 Thomas Everett .05 .01
❑ 422 Eric Green .05 .01
❑ 423 Delton Hall .05 .01
❑ 424 Bryan Hinkle .05 .01
❑ 425 Merril Hoge .05 .01
❑ 426 Carnell Lake .05 .01
❑ 427 Louis Lipps .05 .01
❑ 428 David Little .05 .01
❑ 429 Greg Lloyd .25 .08
❑ 430 Mike Mularkey .05 .01
❑ 431 Keith Willis UER .05 .01
❑ 432 Dwayne Woodruff .05 .01
❑ 433 Rod Woodson .25 .08
❑ 434 Tim Worley .05 .01
❑ 435 Warren Williams .05 .01
❑ 436 Terry Long UER .05 .01
❑ 437 Martin Bayless .05 .01
❑ 438 Jarrod Bunch RC .05 .01
❑ 439 Marion Butts .10 .02
❑ 440 Gill Byrd UER .05 .01
❑ 441 Arthur Cox .05 .01
❑ 442 John Friesz .25 .08
❑ 443 Leo Goeas .05 .01
❑ 444 Burt Grossman .05 .01
❑ 445 Courtney Hall UER .05 .01
❑ 446 Ronnie Harmon .05 .01
❑ 447 Nate Lewis RC .05 .01
❑ 448 Anthony Miller .10 .02
❑ 449 Leslie O'Neal .10 .02
❑ 450 Gary Plummer .05 .01
❑ 451 Junior Seau .25 .08
❑ 452 Billy Ray Smith .05 .01
❑ 453 Billy Joe Tolliver .05 .01
❑ 454 Broderick Thompson .05 .01
❑ 455 Lee Williams .05 .01
❑ 456 Michael Carter .05 .01
❑ 457 Mike Cofer .05 .01
❑ 458 Kevin Fagan .05 .01
❑ 459 Charles Haley .10 .02
❑ 460 Pierce Holt .05 .01
❑ 461 Johnnie Jackson UER RC .05 .01
❑ 462 Brent Jones .25 .08
❑ 463 Guy McIntyre .05 .01
❑ 464 Joe Montana 1.25 .50
❑ 465A Bubba Paris ERR .10 .02
❑ 465B Bubba Paris ERR/COR .50 .20
❑ 465C Bubba Paris COR .10 .02
❑ 466 Tom Rathman UER .05 .01
❑ 467 Jerry Rice UER .75 .30
❑ 468 Mike Sherrard .05 .01
❑ 469 John Taylor UER .10 .02
❑ 470 Steve Young .75 .30
❑ 471 Dennis Brown .05 .01
❑ 472 Dexter Carter .05 .01
❑ 473 Bill Romanowski .05 .01
❑ 474 Dave Waymer .05 .01
❑ 475 Robert Blackmon .05 .01

- ❑ 476 Derrick Fenner .05 .01
- ❑ 477 Nesby Glasgow UER .05 .01
- ❑ 478 Jacob Green .05 .01
- ❑ 479 Andy Heck .05 .01
- ❑ 480 Norm Johnson UER .05 .01
- ❑ 481 Tommy Kane .05 .01
- ❑ 482 Cortez Kennedy .25 .08
- ❑ 483A Dave Krieg ERR .20 .07
- ❑ 483B Dave Krieg COR 2.50 1.00
- ❑ 484 Bryan Millard .05 .01
- ❑ 485 Joe Nash .05 .01
- ❑ 486 Rufus Porter .05 .01
- ❑ 487 Eugene Robinson .05 .01
- ❑ 488 Mike Tice RC .05 .01
- ❑ 489 Chris Warren .25 .08
- ❑ 490 John L. Williams UER .05 .01
- ❑ 491 Terry Wooden .05 .01
- ❑ 492 Tony Woods .05 .01
- ❑ 493 Brian Blades .10 .02
- ❑ 494 Paul Skansi .05 .01
- ❑ 495 Gary Anderson RB .05 .01
- ❑ 496 Mark Carrier WR .25 .08
- ❑ 497 Chris Chandler .25 .08
- ❑ 498 Steve Christie .05 .01
- ❑ 499 Reggie Cobb .05 .01
- ❑ 500 Reuben Davis .05 .01
- ❑ 501 Willie Drewrey UER .05 .01
- ❑ 502 Randy Grimes .05 .01
- ❑ 503 Paul Gruber .05 .01
- ❑ 504 Wayne Haddix .05 .01
- ❑ 505 Ron Hall .05 .01
- ❑ 506 Harry Hamilton .05 .01
- ❑ 507 Bruce Hill .05 .01
- ❑ 508 Eugene Marve .05 .01
- ❑ 509 Keith McCants .05 .01
- ❑ 510 Winston Moss .05 .01
- ❑ 511 Kevin Murphy .05 .01
- ❑ 512 Mark Robinson .05 .01
- ❑ 513 Vinny Testaverde .10 .02
- ❑ 514 Broderick Thomas .05 .01
- ❑ 515A Jeff Bostic UER .10 .02
- ❑ 515B Jeff Bostic UER .10 .02
- ❑ 516 Todd Bowles .05 .01
- ❑ 517 Earnest Byner .05 .01
- ❑ 518 Gary Clark .25 .08
- ❑ 519 Craig Erickson RC .25 .08
- ❑ 520 Darryl Grant .05 .01
- ❑ 521 Darrell Green .05 .01
- ❑ 522 Russ Grimm .05 .01
- ❑ 523 Stan Humphries .25 .08
- ❑ 524 Joe Jacoby UER .05 .01
- ❑ 525 Jim Lachey .05 .01
- ❑ 526 Chip Lohmiller .05 .01
- ❑ 527 Charles Mann .05 .01
- ❑ 528 Wilber Marshall .05 .01
- ❑ 529A Art Monk .10 .02
- ❑ 529B Art Monk .10 .02
- ❑ 530 Tracy Rocker .05 .01
- ❑ 531 Mark Rypien .10 .02
- ❑ 532 Ricky Sanders UER .05 .01
- ❑ 533 Alvin Walton UER .05 .01
- ❑ 534 Todd Marinovich RC UER .05 .01
- ❑ 535 Mike Dumas RC .05 .01
- ❑ 536A Russell Maryland RC ERR .25 .08
- ❑ 536B Russell Maryland RC COR .25 .08
- ❑ 537 Eric Turner RC UER .10 .02
- ❑ 538 Ernie Mills RC .10 .02
- ❑ 539 Ed King RC .05 .01
- ❑ 540 Mike Stonebreaker .05 .01
- ❑ 541 Chris Zorich RC .25 .08
- ❑ 542A Mike Croel RC ERR .05 .01
- ❑ 542B Mike Croel RC COR .05 .01
- ❑ 543 Eric Moten RC .05 .01
- ❑ 544 Dan McGwire RC .05 .01
- ❑ 545 Keith Cash RC .05 .01
- ❑ 546 Kenny Walker RC UER .05 .01
- ❑ 547 Leroy Hoard UER .10 .02
- ❑ 548 Luis Cristobal UER .05 .01
- ❑ 549 Stacy Danley .05 .01
- ❑ 550 Todd Lyght RC .05 .01
- ❑ 551 Brett Favre RC 8.00 3.00
- ❑ 552 Mike Pritchard RC .25 .08
- ❑ 553 Moe Gardner .05 .01
- ❑ 554 Tim McKyer .05 .01
- ❑ 555 Erric Pegram RC .25 .08
- ❑ 556 Norm Johnson .05 .01
- ❑ 557 Bruce Pickens RC .05 .01
- ❑ 558 Henry Jones RC .10 .02
- ❑ 559 Phil Hansen RC .05 .01
- ❑ 560 Cornelius Bennett .10 .02
- ❑ 561 Stan Thomas .05 .01
- ❑ 562 Chris Zorich .10 .02
- ❑ 563 Anthony Morgan RC .05 .01
- ❑ 564 Darren Lewis RC .05 .01
- ❑ 565 Mike Stonebreaker .05 .01
- ❑ 566 Alfred Williams RC .05 .01
- ❑ 567 Lamar Rogers RC .05 .01
- ❑ 568 Erik Wilhelm RC UER .05 .01
- ❑ 569 Ed King .05 .01
- ❑ 570 Michael Jackson RC WR .25 .08
- ❑ 571 James Jones RC DT .05 .01
- ❑ 572 Russell Maryland .25 .08
- ❑ 573 Dixon Edwards RC .05 .01
- ❑ 574 Darrick Brownlow RC .05 .01
- ❑ 575 Larry Brown RC DB .10 .02
- ❑ 576 Mike Croel .05 .01
- ❑ 577 Keith Traylor RC .05 .01
- ❑ 578 Kenny Walker .05 .01
- ❑ 579 Reggie Johnson RC .05 .01
- ❑ 580 Herman Moore RC .25 .08
- ❑ 581 Kelvin Pritchett RC .10 .02
- ❑ 582 Kevin Scott RC .05 .01
- ❑ 583 Vinnie Clark RC .05 .01
- ❑ 584 Esera Tuaolo RC .05 .01
- ❑ 585 Don Davey .05 .01
- ❑ 586 Blair Kiel RC .05 .01
- ❑ 587 Mike Dumas .05 .01
- ❑ 588 Darryll Lewis RC .10 .02
- ❑ 589 John Flannery RC .05 .01
- ❑ 590 Kevin Donnalley RC .05 .01
- ❑ 591 Shane Curry .05 .01
- ❑ 592 Mark Vander Poel RC .05 .01
- ❑ 593 Dave McCloughan .05 .01
- ❑ 594 Mel Agee RC .05 .01
- ❑ 595 Kerry Cash RC .05 .01
- ❑ 596 Harvey Williams RC .25 .08
- ❑ 597 Joe Valerio .05 .01
- ❑ 598 Tim Barnett RC UER .05 .01
- ❑ 599 Todd Marinovich .10 .02
- ❑ 600 Nick Bell RC .05 .01
- ❑ 601 Roger Craig .10 .02
- ❑ 602 Ronnie Lott .10 .02
- ❑ 603 Mike Jones RC LB .05 .01
- ❑ 604 Todd Lyght .05 .01
- ❑ 605 Roman Phifer RC .05 .01
- ❑ 606 David Lang RC .05 .01
- ❑ 607 Aaron Craver RC .05 .01
- ❑ 608 Mark Higgs RC .05 .01
- ❑ 609 Chris Green .05 .01
- ❑ 610 Randy Baldwin RC .05 .01
- ❑ 611 Pat Harlow .05 .01
- ❑ 612 Leonard Russell RC .25 .08
- ❑ 613 Jerome Henderson RC .05 .01
- ❑ 614 Scott Zolak RC .05 .01
- ❑ 615 Jon Vaughn RC .05 .01
- ❑ 616 Harry Colon RC .05 .01
- ❑ 617 Wesley Carroll RC .05 .01
- ❑ 618 Quinn Early .10 .02
- ❑ 619 Reginald Jones RC .05 .01
- ❑ 620 Jarrod Bunch .05 .01
- ❑ 621 Kanavis McGhee RC .05 .01
- ❑ 622 Ed McCaffrey RC 2.00 .75
- ❑ 623 Browning Nagle RC .05 .01
- ❑ 624 Mo Lewis RC .10 .02
- ❑ 625 Blair Thomas .05 .01
- ❑ 626 Antone Davis RC .05 .01
- ❑ 627 Jim McMahon .10 .02
- ❑ 628 Scott Kowalkowski RC .05 .01
- ❑ 629 Brad Goebel RC .05 .01
- ❑ 630 William Thomas RC .05 .01
- ❑ 631 Eric Swann RC .25 .08
- ❑ 632 Mike Jones DE RC .05 .01
- ❑ 633 Aeneas Williams RC .25 .08
- ❑ 634 Dexter Davis RC .05 .01
- ❑ 635 Tom Tupa UER .05 .01
- ❑ 636 Johnny Johnson .05 .01
- ❑ 637 Randal Hill RC .10 .02
- ❑ 638 Jeff Graham RC WR .25 .08
- ❑ 639 Ernie Mills .05 .01
- ❑ 640 Adrian Cooper RC .05 .01
- ❑ 641 Stanley Richard RC .05 .01
- ❑ 642 Eric Bieniemy RC .05 .01
- ❑ 643 Eric Moten .05 .01
- ❑ 644 Shawn Jefferson RC .10 .02
- ❑ 645 Ted Washington RC .05 .01
- ❑ 646 John Johnson RC .05 .01
- ❑ 647 Dan McGwire .05 .01
- ❑ 648 Doug Thomas RC .05 .01
- ❑ 649 David Daniels RC .05 .01
- ❑ 650 John Kasay RC .10 .02
- ❑ 651 Jeff Kemp .05 .01
- ❑ 652 Charles McRae RC .05 .01
- ❑ 653 Lawrence Dawsey RC .10 .02
- ❑ 654 Robert Wilson RC .05 .01
- ❑ 655 Dexter Manley .05 .01
- ❑ 656 Chuck Weatherspoon .05 .01
- ❑ 657 Tim Ryan G RC .05 .01
- ❑ 658 Bobby Wilson .05 .01
- ❑ 659 Ricky Ervins RC .10 .02
- ❑ 660 Matt Millen .10 .02

1992 Pacific

- ❑ COMPLETE SET (660) 15.00 6.00
- ❑ COMP.FACT.SET (690) 25.00 10.00
- ❑ COMP.SERIES 1 (330) 8.00 3.00
- ❑ COMP.SERIES 2 (330) 8.00 3.00
- ❑ COMP.CHECKLIST SET (5) 3.00 1.50
- ❑ 1 Steve Broussard .05 .01
- ❑ 2 Darion Conner .05 .01
- ❑ 3 Tory Epps .05 .01
- ❑ 4 Michael Haynes .10 .02
- ❑ 5 Chris Hinton .05 .01
- ❑ 6 Mike Kenn .05 .01
- ❑ 7 Tim McKyer .05 .01
- ❑ 8 Chris Miller .10 .02
- ❑ 9 Erric Pegram .10 .02
- ❑ 10 Mike Pritchard .10 .02
- ❑ 11 Moe Gardner .05 .01
- ❑ 12 Tim Green .05 .01
- ❑ 13 Norm Johnson .05 .01
- ❑ 14 Don Beebe .05 .01
- ❑ 15 Cornelius Bennett .10 .02
- ❑ 16 Al Edwards .05 .01
- ❑ 17 Mark Kelso .05 .01
- ❑ 18 James Lofton .10 .02
- ❑ 19 Frank Reich .10 .02
- ❑ 20 Leon Seals .05 .01
- ❑ 21 Darryl Talley .05 .01
- ❑ 22 Thurman Thomas .25 .08
- ❑ 23 Kent Hull .05 .01
- ❑ 24 Jeff Wright .05 .01
- ❑ 25 Nate Odomes .05 .01
- ❑ 26 Carwell Gardner .05 .01
- ❑ 27 Neal Anderson .05 .01

❑ 28	Mark Carrier DB	.05	.01
❑ 29	Johnny Bailey	.05	.01
❑ 30	Jim Harbaugh	.25	.08
❑ 31	Jay Hilgenberg	.05	.01
❑ 32	William Perry	.10	.02
❑ 33	Wendell Davis	.05	.01
❑ 34	Donnell Woolford	.05	.01
❑ 35	Keith Van Horne	.05	.01
❑ 36	Shaun Gayle	.05	.01
❑ 37	Tom Waddle	.05	.01
❑ 38	Chris Zorich	.10	.02
❑ 39	Tom Thayer	.05	.01
❑ 40	Rickey Dixon	.05	.01
❑ 41	James Francis	.05	.01
❑ 42	David Fulcher	.05	.01
❑ 43	Reggie Rembert	.05	.01
❑ 44	Anthony Munoz	.10	.02
❑ 45	Harold Green	.05	.01
❑ 46	Mitchell Price	.05	.01
❑ 47	Rodney Holman	.05	.01
❑ 48	Bruce Kozerski	.05	.01
❑ 49	Bruce Reimers	.05	.01
❑ 50	Erik Wilhelm	.05	.01
❑ 51	Harlon Barnett	.05	.01
❑ 52	Mike Johnson	.05	.01
❑ 53	Brian Brennan	.05	.01
❑ 54	Ed King	.05	.01
❑ 55	Reggie Langhorne	.05	.01
❑ 56	James Jones DT	.05	.01
❑ 57	Mike Baab	.05	.01
❑ 58	Dan Fike	.05	.01
❑ 59	Frank Minnifield	.05	.01
❑ 60	Clay Matthews	.10	.02
❑ 61	Kevin Mack	.05	.01
❑ 62	Tony Casillas	.05	.01
❑ 63	Jay Novacek	.10	.02
❑ 64	Larry Brown DB	.05	.01
❑ 65	Michael Irvin	.25	.08
❑ 66	Jack Del Rio	.05	.01
❑ 67	Ken Willis	.05	.01
❑ 68	Emmitt Smith	1.50	.60
❑ 69	Alan Veingrad	.05	.01
❑ 70	John Gesek	.05	.01
❑ 71	Steve Beuerlein	.10	.02
❑ 72	Vinson Smith RC	.05	.01
❑ 73	Steve Atwater	.05	.01
❑ 74	Mike Croel	.05	.01
❑ 75	John Elway	1.25	.50
❑ 76	Gaston Green	.05	.01
❑ 77	Mike Horan	.05	.01
❑ 78	Vance Johnson	.05	.01
❑ 79	Karl Mecklenburg	.05	.01
❑ 80	Shannon Sharpe	.25	.08
❑ 81	David Treadwell	.05	.01
❑ 82	Kenny Walker	.05	.01
❑ 83	Greg Lewis	.05	.01
❑ 84	Shawn Moore	.05	.01
❑ 85	Alton Montgomery	.05	.01
❑ 86	Michael Young	.05	.01
❑ 87	Jerry Ball	.05	.01
❑ 88	Bennie Blades	.05	.01
❑ 89	Mel Gray	.10	.02
❑ 90	Herman Moore	.25	.08
❑ 91	Erik Kramer	.10	.02
❑ 92	Willie Green	.05	.01
❑ 93	George Jamison	.05	.01
❑ 94	Chris Spielman	.10	.02
❑ 95	Kelvin Pritchett	.05	.01
❑ 96	William White	.05	.01
❑ 97	Mike Utley	.10	.02
❑ 98	Tony Bennett	.05	.01
❑ 99	LeRoy Butler	.05	.01
❑ 100	Vinnie Clark	.05	.01
❑ 101	Ron Hallstrom	.05	.01
❑ 102	Chris Jacke	.05	.01
❑ 103	Tony Mandarich	.05	.01
❑ 104	Sterling Sharpe	.25	.08
❑ 105	Don Majkowski	.05	.01
❑ 106	Johnny Holland	.05	.01
❑ 107	Esera Tuaolo	.05	.01
❑ 108	Darrell Thompson	.05	.01
❑ 109	Bubba McDowell	.05	.01
❑ 110	Curtis Duncan	.05	.01
❑ 111	Lamar Lathon	.05	.01
❑ 112	Drew Hill	.05	.01
❑ 113	Bruce Matthews	.05	.01
❑ 114	Bo Orlando RC	.05	.01
❑ 115	Don Maggs	.05	.01
❑ 116	Lorenzo White	.05	.01
❑ 117	Ernest Givins	.10	.02
❑ 118	Tony Jones WR	.05	.01
❑ 119	Dean Steinkuhler	.05	.01
❑ 120	Dean Biasucci	.05	.01
❑ 121	Duane Bickett	.05	.01
❑ 122	Bill Brooks	.05	.01
❑ 123	Ken Clark	.05	.01
❑ 124	Jessie Hester	.05	.01
❑ 125	Anthony Johnson	.10	.02
❑ 126	Chip Banks	.05	.01
❑ 127	Mike Prior	.05	.01
❑ 128	Rohn Stark	.05	.01
❑ 129	Jeff Herrod	.05	.01
❑ 130	Clarence Verdin	.05	.01
❑ 131	Tim Manoa	.05	.01
❑ 132	Brian Baldinger RC	.05	.01
❑ 133	Tim Barnett	.05	.01
❑ 134	J.J. Birden	.05	.01
❑ 135	Deron Cherry	.05	.01
❑ 136	Steve DeBerg	.05	.01
❑ 137	Nick Lowery	.05	.01
❑ 138	Todd McNair	.05	.01
❑ 139	Christian Okoye	.05	.01
❑ 140	Mark Vlasic	.05	.01
❑ 141	Dan Saleaumua	.05	.01
❑ 142	Neil Smith	.25	.08
❑ 143	Robb Thomas	.05	.01
❑ 144	Eddie Anderson	.05	.01
❑ 145	Nick Bell	.05	.01
❑ 146	Tim Brown	.25	.08
❑ 147	Roger Craig	.10	.02
❑ 148	Jeff Gossett	.05	.01
❑ 149	Ethan Horton	.05	.01
❑ 150	Jamie Holland	.05	.01
❑ 151	Jeff Jaeger	.05	.01
❑ 152	Todd Marinovich	.05	.01
❑ 153	Marcus Allen	.25	.08
❑ 154	Steve Smith	.05	.01
❑ 155	Flipper Anderson	.05	.01
❑ 156	Robert Delpino	.05	.01
❑ 157	Cleveland Gary	.05	.01
❑ 158	Kevin Greene	.10	.02
❑ 159	Dale Hatcher	.05	.01
❑ 160	Duval Love	.05	.01
❑ 161	Ron Brown	.05	.01
❑ 162	Jackie Slater	.05	.01
❑ 163	Doug Smith	.05	.01
❑ 164	Aaron Cox	.05	.01
❑ 165	Larry Kelm	.05	.01
❑ 166	Mark Clayton	.10	.02
❑ 167	Louis Oliver	.05	.01
❑ 168	Mark Higgs	.05	.01
❑ 169	Aaron Craver	.05	.01
❑ 170	Sammie Smith	.05	.01
❑ 171	Tony Paige	.05	.01
❑ 172	Jeff Cross	.05	.01
❑ 173	David Griggs	.05	.01
❑ 174	Richmond Webb	.05	.01
❑ 175	Vestee Jackson	.05	.01
❑ 176	Jim C. Jensen	.05	.01
❑ 177	Anthony Carter	.10	.02
❑ 178	Cris Carter	.50	.20
❑ 179	Chris Doleman	.05	.01
❑ 180	Rich Gannon	.25	.08
❑ 181	Al Noga	.05	.01
❑ 182	Randall McDaniel	.05	.01
❑ 183	Todd Scott	.05	.01
❑ 184	Henry Thomas	.05	.01
❑ 185	Felix Wright	.05	.01
❑ 186	Gary Zimmerman	.05	.01
❑ 187	Herschel Walker	.10	.02
❑ 188	Vincent Brown	.05	.01
❑ 189	Harry Colon	.05	.01
❑ 190	Irving Fryar	.10	.02
❑ 191	Marv Cook	.05	.01
❑ 192	Leonard Russell	.10	.02
❑ 193	Hugh Millen	.05	.01
❑ 194	Pat Harlow	.05	.01
❑ 195	Jon Vaughn	.05	.01
❑ 196	Ben Coates RC	.75	.30
❑ 197	Johnny Rembert	.05	.01
❑ 198	Greg McMurtry	.05	.01
❑ 199	Morten Andersen	.05	.01
❑ 200	Tommy Barnhardt	.05	.01
❑ 201	Bobby Hebert	.05	.01
❑ 202	Dalton Hilliard	.05	.01
❑ 203	Sam Mills	.05	.01
❑ 204	Pat Swilling	.05	.01
❑ 205	Rickey Jackson	.05	.01
❑ 206	Stan Brock	.05	.01
❑ 207	Reginald Jones	.05	.01
❑ 208	Gill Fenerty	.05	.01
❑ 209	Eric Martin	.05	.01
❑ 210	Matt Bahr	.05	.01
❑ 211	Rodney Hampton	.10	.02
❑ 212	Jeff Hostetler	.10	.02
❑ 213	Pepper Johnson	.05	.01
❑ 214	Leonard Marshall	.05	.01
❑ 215	Doug Riesenberg	.05	.01
❑ 216	Stephen Baker	.05	.01
❑ 217	Mike Fox	.05	.01
❑ 218	Bart Oates	.05	.01
❑ 219	Everson Walls	.05	.01
❑ 220	Gary Reasons	.05	.01
❑ 221	Jeff Lageman	.05	.01
❑ 222	Joe Kelly	.05	.01
❑ 223	Mo Lewis	.05	.01
❑ 224	Tony Stargell	.05	.01
❑ 225	Jim Sweeney	.05	.01
❑ 226	Freeman McNeil	.10	.02
❑ 227	Brian Washington	.05	.01
❑ 228	Johnny Hector	.05	.01
❑ 229	Terance Mathis	.10	.02
❑ 230	Rob Moore	.10	.02
❑ 231	Brad Baxter	.05	.01
❑ 232	Eric Allen	.05	.01
❑ 233	Fred Barnett	.10	.02
❑ 234	Jerome Brown	.05	.01
❑ 235	Keith Byars	.05	.01
❑ 236	William Thomas	.05	.01
❑ 237	Jessie Small	.05	.01
❑ 238	Robert Drummond	.05	.01
❑ 239	Reggie White	.25	.08
❑ 240	James Joseph	.05	.01
❑ 241	Brad Goebel	.05	.01
❑ 242	Clyde Simmons	.05	.01
❑ 243	Rich Camarillo	.05	.01
❑ 244	Ken Harvey	.05	.01
❑ 245	Garth Jax	.05	.01
❑ 246	Johnny Johnson	.05	.01
❑ 247	Mike Jones	.05	.01
❑ 248	Ernie Jones	.05	.01
❑ 249	Tom Tupa	.05	.01
❑ 250	Ron Wolfley	.05	.01
❑ 251	Luis Sharpe	.05	.01
❑ 252	Eric Swann	.10	.02
❑ 253	Anthony Thompson	.05	.01
❑ 254	Gary Anderson K	.05	.01
❑ 255	Dermontti Dawson	.05	.01
❑ 256	Jeff Graham	.25	.08
❑ 257	Eric Green	.05	.01
❑ 258	Louis Lipps	.05	.01
❑ 259	Neil O'Donnell	.10	.02
❑ 260	Rod Woodson	.25	.08
❑ 261	Dwight Stone	.05	.01
❑ 262	Aaron Jones	.05	.01
❑ 263	Keith Willis	.05	.01
❑ 264	Ernie Mills	.05	.01
❑ 265	Martin Bayless	.05	.01
❑ 266	Rod Bernstine	.05	.01
❑ 267	John Carney	.05	.01

- ❑ 268 John Friesz .10 .02
- ❑ 269 Nate Lewis .05 .01
- ❑ 270 Shawn Jefferson .05 .01
- ❑ 271 Burt Grossman .05 .01
- ❑ 272 Eric Moten .05 .01
- ❑ 273 Gary Plummer .05 .01
- ❑ 274 Henry Rolling .05 .01
- ❑ 275 Steve Hendrickson RC .05 .01
- ❑ 276 Michael Carter .05 .01
- ❑ 277 Steve Bono RC .25 .08
- ❑ 278 Dexter Carter .05 .01
- ❑ 279 Mike Cofer .05 .01
- ❑ 280 Charles Haley .10 .02
- ❑ 281 Tom Rathman .05 .01
- ❑ 282 Guy McIntyre .05 .01
- ❑ 283 John Taylor .10 .02
- ❑ 284 Dave Waymer .05 .01
- ❑ 285 Steve Wallace .05 .01
- ❑ 286 Jamie Williams .05 .01
- ❑ 287 Brian Blades .10 .02
- ❑ 288 Jeff Bryant .05 .01
- ❑ 289 Grant Feasel .05 .01
- ❑ 290 Jacob Green .05 .01
- ❑ 291 Andy Heck .05 .01
- ❑ 292 Kelly Stouffer .05 .01
- ❑ 293 John Kasay .05 .01
- ❑ 294 Cortez Kennedy .10 .02
- ❑ 295 Bryan Millard .05 .01
- ❑ 296 Eugene Robinson .05 .01
- ❑ 297 Tony Woods .05 .01
- ❑ 298 Jesse Anderson UER .05 .01
- ❑ 299 Gary Anderson RB .05 .01
- ❑ 300 Mark Carrier WR .10 .02
- ❑ 301 Reggie Cobb .05 .01
- ❑ 302 Robert Wilson .05 .01
- ❑ 303 Jesse Solomon .05 .01
- ❑ 304 Broderick Thomas .05 .01
- ❑ 305 Lawrence Dawsey .10 .02
- ❑ 306 Charles McRae .05 .01
- ❑ 307 Paul Gruber .05 .01
- ❑ 308 Vinny Testaverde .10 .02
- ❑ 309 Brian Mitchell .10 .02
- ❑ 310 Darrell Green .05 .01
- ❑ 311 Art Monk .10 .02
- ❑ 312 Russ Grimm .05 .01
- ❑ 313 Mark Rypien .05 .01
- ❑ 314 Bobby Wilson .05 .01
- ❑ 315 Wilber Marshall .05 .01
- ❑ 316 Gerald Riggs .05 .01
- ❑ 317 Chip Lohmiller .05 .01
- ❑ 318 Joe Jacoby .05 .01
- ❑ 319 Martin Mayhew .05 .01
- ❑ 320 Amp Lee RC .05 .01
- ❑ 321 Terrell Buckley RC .05 .01
- ❑ 322 Tommy Vardell RC .05 .01
- ❑ 323 Ricardo McDonald RC .05 .01
- ❑ 324 Joe Bowden RC .05 .01
- ❑ 325 Darryl Williams RC .05 .01
- ❑ 326 Carlos Huerta .05 .01
- ❑ 327 Patrick Rowe RC .05 .01
- ❑ 328 Siran Stacy RC .05 .01
- ❑ 329 Dexter McNabb RC .05 .01
- ❑ 330 Willie Clay RC .05 .01
- ❑ 331 Oliver Barnett .05 .01
- ❑ 332 Aundray Bruce .05 .01
- ❑ 333 Ken Tippins RC .05 .01
- ❑ 334 Jessie Tuggle .05 .01
- ❑ 335 Brian Jordan .10 .02
- ❑ 336 Andre Rison .10 .02
- ❑ 337 Houston Hoover .05 .01
- ❑ 338 Bill Fralic .05 .01
- ❑ 339 Pat Chaffey RC .05 .01
- ❑ 340 Keith Jones .05 .01
- ❑ 341 Jamie Dukes RC .05 .01
- ❑ 342 Chris Mohr .05 .01
- ❑ 343 John Davis .05 .01
- ❑ 344 Ray Bentley .05 .01
- ❑ 345 Scott Norwood .05 .01
- ❑ 346 Shane Conlan .05 .01
- ❑ 347 Steve Tasker .10 .02
- ❑ 348 Will Wolford .05 .01
- ❑ 349 Gary Baldinger RC .05 .01
- ❑ 350 Kirby Jackson .05 .01
- ❑ 351 Jamie Mueller .05 .01
- ❑ 352 Pete Metzelaars .05 .01
- ❑ 353 Richard Dent .10 .02
- ❑ 354 Ron Rivera .05 .01
- ❑ 355 Jim Morrissey .05 .01
- ❑ 356 John Roper .05 .01
- ❑ 357 Steve McMichael .10 .02
- ❑ 358 Ron Morris .05 .01
- ❑ 359 Darren Lewis .05 .01
- ❑ 360 Anthony Morgan .05 .01
- ❑ 361 Stan Thomas .05 .01
- ❑ 362 James Thornton .05 .01
- ❑ 363 Brad Muster .05 .01
- ❑ 364 Tim Krumrie .05 .01
- ❑ 365 Lee Johnson .05 .01
- ❑ 366 Eric Ball .05 .01
- ❑ 367 Alonzo Mitz RC .05 .01
- ❑ 368 David Grant .05 .01
- ❑ 369 Lynn James .05 .01
- ❑ 370 Lewis Billups .05 .01
- ❑ 371 Jim Breech .05 .01
- ❑ 372 Alfred Williams .05 .01
- ❑ 373 Wayne Haddix .05 .01
- ❑ 374 Tim McGee .05 .01
- ❑ 375 Michael Jackson .10 .02
- ❑ 376 Leroy Hoard .10 .02
- ❑ 377 Tony Jones T .05 .01
- ❑ 378 Vince Newsome .05 .01
- ❑ 379 Todd Philcox RC .05 .01
- ❑ 380 Eric Metcalf .10 .02
- ❑ 381 John Rienstra .05 .01
- ❑ 382 Matt Stover .05 .01
- ❑ 383 Brian Hansen .05 .01
- ❑ 384 Joe Morris .05 .01
- ❑ 385 Anthony Pleasant .05 .01
- ❑ 386 Mark Stepnoski .05 .01
- ❑ 387 Erik Williams .05 .01
- ❑ 388 Jimmie Jones .05 .01
- ❑ 389 Kevin Gogan .05 .01
- ❑ 390 Manny Hendrix RC .05 .01
- ❑ 391 Issiac Holt .05 .01
- ❑ 392 Ken Norton .10 .02
- ❑ 393 Tommie Agee .05 .01
- ❑ 394 Alvin Harper .10 .02
- ❑ 395 Alexander Wright .05 .01
- ❑ 396 Mike Saxon .05 .01
- ❑ 397 Michael Brooks .05 .01
- ❑ 398 Bobby Humphrey .05 .01
- ❑ 399 Ken Lanier .05 .01
- ❑ 400 Steve Sewell .05 .01
- ❑ 401 Robert Perryman .05 .01
- ❑ 402 Wymon Henderson .05 .01
- ❑ 403 Keith Kartz .05 .01
- ❑ 404 Clarence Kay .05 .01
- ❑ 405 Keith Traylor .05 .01
- ❑ 406 Doug Widell .05 .01
- ❑ 407 Dennis Smith .05 .01
- ❑ 408 Marc Spindler .05 .01
- ❑ 409 Lomas Brown .05 .01
- ❑ 410 Robert Clark .05 .01
- ❑ 411 Eric Andolsek .05 .01
- ❑ 412 Mike Farr .05 .01
- ❑ 413 Ray Crockett .05 .01
- ❑ 414 Jeff Campbell .05 .01
- ❑ 415 Dan Owens .05 .01
- ❑ 416 Jim Arnold .05 .01
- ❑ 417 Barry Sanders 1.25 .50
- ❑ 418 Eddie Murray .05 .01
- ❑ 419 Vince Workman .05 .01
- ❑ 420 Ed West .05 .01
- ❑ 421 Charles Wilson .05 .01
- ❑ 422 Perry Kemp .05 .01
- ❑ 423 Chuck Cecil .05 .01
- ❑ 424 James Campen .05 .01
- ❑ 425 Robert Brown .05 .01
- ❑ 426 Brian Noble .05 .01
- ❑ 427 Rich Moran .05 .01
- ❑ 428 Vai Sikahema .05 .01
- ❑ 429 Allen Rice .05 .01
- ❑ 430 Haywood Jeffires .10 .02
- ❑ 431 Warren Moon .25 .08
- ❑ 432 Greg Montgomery .05 .01
- ❑ 433 Sean Jones .05 .01
- ❑ 434 Richard Johnson CB .05 .01
- ❑ 435 Al Smith .05 .01
- ❑ 436 Johnny Meads .05 .01
- ❑ 437 William Fuller .05 .01
- ❑ 438 Mike Munchak .10 .02
- ❑ 439 Ray Childress .05 .01
- ❑ 440 Cody Carlson .05 .01
- ❑ 441 Scott Radecic .05 .01
- ❑ 442 Quintus McDonald RC .05 .01
- ❑ 443 Eugene Daniel .05 .01
- ❑ 444 Mark Herrmann RC .05 .01
- ❑ 445 John Baylor RC .05 .01
- ❑ 446 Dave McCloughan .05 .01
- ❑ 447 Mark Vander Poel .05 .01
- ❑ 448 Randy Dixon .05 .01
- ❑ 449 Keith Taylor .05 .01
- ❑ 450 Alan Grant .05 .01
- ❑ 451 Tony Siragusa .05 .01
- ❑ 452 Rich Baldinger .05 .01
- ❑ 453 Derrick Thomas .25 .08
- ❑ 454 Bill Jones RC .05 .01
- ❑ 455 Troy Stradford .05 .01
- ❑ 456 Barry Word .05 .01
- ❑ 457 Tim Grunhard .05 .01
- ❑ 458 Chris Martin .05 .01
- ❑ 459 Jayice Pearson RC .05 .01
- ❑ 460 Dino Hackett .05 .01
- ❑ 461 David Lutz .05 .01
- ❑ 462 Albert Lewis .05 .01
- ❑ 463 Fred Jones RC .05 .01
- ❑ 464 Winston Moss .05 .01
- ❑ 465 Sam Graddy RC .05 .01
- ❑ 466 Steve Wisniewski .05 .01
- ❑ 467 Jay Schroeder .05 .01
- ❑ 468 Ronnie Lott .10 .02
- ❑ 469 Willie Gault .10 .02
- ❑ 470 Greg Townsend .05 .01
- ❑ 471 Max Montoya .05 .01
- ❑ 472 Howie Long .25 .08
- ❑ 473 Lionel Washington .05 .01
- ❑ 474 Riki Ellison .05 .01
- ❑ 475 Tom Newberry .05 .01
- ❑ 476 Damone Johnson .05 .01
- ❑ 477 Pat Terrell .05 .01
- ❑ 478 Marcus Dupree .05 .01
- ❑ 479 Todd Lyght .05 .01
- ❑ 480 Buford McGee .05 .01
- ❑ 481 Bern Brostek .05 .01
- ❑ 482 Jim Price .05 .01
- ❑ 483 Robert Young .05 .01
- ❑ 484 Tony Zendejas .05 .01
- ❑ 485 Robert Bailey RC .05 .01
- ❑ 486 Alvin Wright .05 .01
- ❑ 487 Pat Carter .05 .01
- ❑ 488 Pete Stoyanovich .05 .01
- ❑ 489 Reggie Roby .05 .01
- ❑ 490 Harry Galbreath .05 .01
- ❑ 491 Mike McGruder RC**/C .05 .01
- ❑ 492 J.B. Brown .05 .01
- ❑ 493 E.J. Junior .05 .01
- ❑ 494 Ferrell Edmunds .05 .01
- ❑ 495 Scott Secules .05 .01
- ❑ 496 Greg Baty RC .05 .01
- ❑ 497 Mike Iaquaniello .05 .01
- ❑ 498 Keith Sims .05 .01
- ❑ 499 John Randle .10 .02
- ❑ 500 Joey Browner .05 .01
- ❑ 501 Steve Jordan .05 .01
- ❑ 502 Darrin Nelson .05 .01
- ❑ 503 Audray McMillian .05 .01
- ❑ 504 Harry Newsome .05 .01
- ❑ 505 Hassan Jones .05 .01
- ❑ 506 Ray Berry .05 .01
- ❑ 507 Mike Merriweather .05 .01

❑ 508 Leo Lewis	.05	.01
❑ 509 Tim Irwin	.05	.01
❑ 510 Kirk Lowdermilk	.05	.01
❑ 511 Alfred Anderson	.05	.01
❑ 512 Michael Timpson RC	.05	.01
❑ 513 Jerome Henderson	.05	.01
❑ 514 Andre Tippett	.05	.01
❑ 515 Chris Singleton	.05	.01
❑ 516 John Stephens	.05	.01
❑ 517 Ronnie Lippett	.05	.01
❑ 518 Bruce Armstrong	.05	.01
❑ 519 Marion Hobby RC	.05	.01
❑ 520 Tim Goad	.05	.01
❑ 521 Mickey Washington RC	.05	.01
❑ 522 Fred Smerlas	.05	.01
❑ 523 Wayne Martin	.05	.01
❑ 524 Frank Warren	.05	.01
❑ 525 Floyd Turner	.05	.01
❑ 526 Wesley Carroll	.05	.01
❑ 527 Gene Atkins	.05	.01
❑ 528 Vaughan Johnson	.05	.01
❑ 529 Hoby Brenner	.05	.01
❑ 530 Renaldo Turnbull	.05	.01
❑ 531 Joel Hilgenberg	.05	.01
❑ 532 Craig Heyward	.10	.02
❑ 533 Vince Buck	.05	.01
❑ 534 Jim Dombrowski	.05	.01
❑ 535 Fred McAfee RC	.05	.01
❑ 536 Phil Simms	.10	.02
❑ 537 Lewis Tillman	.05	.01
❑ 538 John Elliott	.05	.01
❑ 539 Dave Meggett	.10	.02
❑ 540 Mark Collins	.05	.01
❑ 541 Ottis Anderson	.10	.02
❑ 542 Bobby Abrams RC	.05	.01
❑ 543 Sean Landeta	.05	.01
❑ 544 Brian Williams OL	.05	.01
❑ 545 Erik Howard	.05	.01
❑ 546 Mark Ingram	.05	.01
❑ 547 Kanavis McGhee	.05	.01
❑ 548 Kyle Clifton	.05	.01
❑ 549 Marvin Washington	.05	.01
❑ 550 Jeff Criswell	.05	.01
❑ 551 Dave Cadigan	.05	.01
❑ 552 Chris Burkett	.05	.01
❑ 553 Erik McMillan	.05	.01
❑ 554 James Hasty	.05	.01
❑ 555 Louie Aguiar RC	.05	.01
❑ 556 Troy Johnson RC	.05	.01
❑ 557 Troy Taylor RC	.05	.01
❑ 558 Pat Kelly RC	.05	.01
❑ 559 Heath Sherman	.05	.01
❑ 560 Roger Ruzek	.05	.01
❑ 561 Andre Waters	.05	.01
❑ 562 Izel Jenkins	.05	.01
❑ 563 Keith Jackson	.10	.02
❑ 564 Byron Evans	.05	.01
❑ 565 Wes Hopkins	.05	.01
❑ 566 Rich Miano	.05	.01
❑ 567 Seth Joyner	.05	.01
❑ 568 Thomas Sanders	.05	.01
❑ 569 David Alexander	.05	.01
❑ 570 Jeff Kemp	.05	.01
❑ 571 Jock Jones RC	.05	.01
❑ 572 Craig Patterson RC	.05	.01
❑ 573 Robert Massey	.05	.01
❑ 574 Bill Lewis	.05	.01
❑ 575 Freddie Joe Nunn	.05	.01
❑ 576 Aeneas Williams	.10	.02
❑ 577 John Jackson WR	.05	.01
❑ 578 Tim McDonald	.05	.01
❑ 579 Michael Zordich RC	.05	.01
❑ 580 Eric Hill	.05	.01
❑ 581 Lorenzo Lynch	.05	.01
❑ 582 Vernice Smith RC	.05	.01
❑ 583 Greg Lloyd	.10	.02
❑ 584 Carnell Lake	.05	.01
❑ 585 Hardy Nickerson	.10	.02
❑ 586 Delton Hall	.05	.01
❑ 587 Gerald Williams	.05	.01
❑ 588 Bryan Hinkle	.05	.01
❑ 589 Barry Foster	.10	.02
❑ 590 Bubby Brister	.10	.02
❑ 591 Rick Strom RC	.05	.01
❑ 592 David Little	.05	.01
❑ 593 Leroy Thompson RC	.05	.01
❑ 594 Eric Bieniemy	.05	.01
❑ 595 Courtney Hall	.05	.01
❑ 596 George Thornton	.05	.01
❑ 597 Donnie Elder	.05	.01
❑ 598 Billy Ray Smith	.05	.01
❑ 599 Gill Byrd	.05	.01
❑ 600 Marion Butts	.05	.01
❑ 601 Ronnie Harmon	.05	.01
❑ 602 Anthony Shelton	.05	.01
❑ 603 Mark May	.05	.01
❑ 604 Craig McEwen RC	.05	.01
❑ 605 Steve Young	.60	.25
❑ 606 Keith Henderson	.05	.01
❑ 607 Pierce Holt	.05	.01
❑ 608 Roy Foster	.05	.01
❑ 609 Don Griffin	.05	.01
❑ 610 Harry Sydney	.05	.01
❑ 611 Todd Bowles	.05	.01
❑ 612 Ted Washington	.05	.01
❑ 613 Johnnie Jackson	.05	.01
❑ 614 Jesse Sapolu	.05	.01
❑ 615 Brent Jones	.10	.02
❑ 616 Travis McNeal	.05	.01
❑ 617 Darrick Brilz RC	.05	.01
❑ 618 Terry Wooden	.05	.01
❑ 619 Tommy Kane	.05	.01
❑ 620 Nesby Glasgow	.05	.01
❑ 621 Dwayne Harper	.05	.01
❑ 622 Rick Tuten	.05	.01
❑ 623 Chris Warren	.10	.02
❑ 624 John L. Williams	.05	.01
❑ 625 Rufus Porter	.05	.01
❑ 626 David Daniels	.05	.01
❑ 627 Keith McCants	.05	.01
❑ 628 Reuben Davis	.05	.01
❑ 629 Mark Royals	.05	.01
❑ 630 Marty Carter RC	.05	.01
❑ 631 Ian Beckles	.05	.01
❑ 632 Ron Hall	.05	.01
❑ 633 Eugene Marve	.05	.01
❑ 634 Willie Drewrey	.05	.01
❑ 635 Tom McHale RC	.05	.01
❑ 636 Kevin Murphy	.05	.01
❑ 637 Robert Hardy RC	.05	.01
❑ 638 Ricky Sanders	.05	.01
❑ 639 Gary Clark	.10	.02
❑ 640 Andre Collins	.05	.01
❑ 641 Brad Edwards	.05	.01
❑ 642 Monte Coleman	.05	.01
❑ 643 Clarence Vaughn RC	.05	.01
❑ 644 Fred Stokes	.05	.01
❑ 645 Charles Mann	.05	.01
❑ 646 Earnest Byner	.05	.01
❑ 647 Jim Lachey	.05	.01
❑ 648 Jeff Bostic	.05	.01
❑ 649 Chris Mims RC	.05	.01
❑ 650 George Williams RC	.05	.01
❑ 651 Ed Cunningham RC	.05	.01
❑ 652 Tony Smith RC WR	.05	.01
❑ 653 Will Furrer RC	.05	.01
❑ 654 Matt Elliott RC	.05	.01
❑ 655 Mike Mooney RC	.05	.01
❑ 656 Eddie Blake RC	.05	.01
❑ 657 Leon Searcy RC	.05	.01
❑ 658 Kevin Turner RC	.05	.01
❑ 659 Keith Hamilton RC	.10	.02
❑ 660 Alan Haller RC	.05	.01

1993 Pacific

❑ COMPLETE SET (440)	20.00	10.00
❑ 1 Emmitt Smith	1.50	.60
❑ 2 Troy Aikman	.75	.30
❑ 3 Larry Brown DB	.05	.01
❑ 4 Tony Casillas	.05	.01
❑ 5 Thomas Everett	.05	.01
❑ 6 Alvin Harper	.10	.02
❑ 7 Michael Irvin	.25	.08
❑ 8 Charles Haley	.10	.02
❑ 9 Leon Lett RC	.10	.02
❑ 10 Kevin Smith	.10	.02
❑ 11 Robert Jones	.05	.01
❑ 12 Jimmy Smith	.25	.08
❑ 13 Derrick Gainer RC	.05	.01
❑ 14 Lin Elliott	.05	.01
❑ 15 William Thomas	.05	.01
❑ 16 Clyde Simmons	.05	.01
❑ 17 Seth Joyner	.05	.01
❑ 18 Randall Cunningham	.25	.08
❑ 19 Byron Evans	.05	.01
❑ 20 Fred Barnett	.10	.02
❑ 21 Calvin Williams	.10	.02
❑ 22 James Joseph	.05	.01
❑ 23 Heath Sherman	.05	.01
❑ 24 Siran Stacy	.05	.01
❑ 25 Andy Harmon	.10	.02
❑ 26 Eric Allen	.05	.01
❑ 27 Herschel Walker	.10	.02
❑ 28 Vai Sikahema	.05	.01
❑ 29 Earnest Byner	.05	.01
❑ 30 Jeff Bostic	.05	.01
❑ 31 Monte Coleman	.05	.01
❑ 32 Ricky Ervins	.05	.01
❑ 33 Darrell Green	.05	.01
❑ 34 Mark Schlereth	.05	.01
❑ 35 Mark Rypien	.05	.01
❑ 36 Art Monk	.10	.02
❑ 37 Brian Mitchell	.10	.02
❑ 38 Chip Lohmiller	.05	.01
❑ 39 Charles Mann	.05	.01
❑ 40 Shane Collins	.05	.01
❑ 41 Jim Lachey	.05	.01
❑ 42 Desmond Howard	.10	.02
❑ 43 Rodney Hampton	.10	.02
❑ 44 Dave Brown RC	.25	.08
❑ 45 Mark Collins	.05	.01
❑ 46 Jarrod Bunch	.05	.01
❑ 47 William Roberts	.05	.01
❑ 48 Sean Landeta	.05	.01
❑ 49 Lawrence Taylor	.25	.08
❑ 50 Ed McCaffrey	.25	.08
❑ 51 Bart Oates	.05	.01
❑ 52 Pepper Johnson	.05	.01
❑ 53 Eric Dorsey	.05	.01
❑ 54 Erik Howard	.05	.01
❑ 55 Phil Simms	.10	.02
❑ 56 Derek Brown TE	.05	.01
❑ 57 Johnny Bailey	.05	.01
❑ 58 Rich Camarillo	.05	.01
❑ 59 Larry Centers RC	.25	.08
❑ 60 Chris Chandler	.10	.02
❑ 61 Randal Hill	.05	.01
❑ 62 Ricky Proehl	.05	.01
❑ 63 Freddie Joe Nunn	.05	.01
❑ 64 Robert Massey	.05	.01
❑ 65 Aeneas Williams	.05	.01
❑ 66 Luis Sharpe	.05	.01
❑ 67 Eric Swann	.10	.02
❑ 68 Timm Rosenbach	.05	.01

❑	69	Anthony Edwards RC	.05	.01
❑	70	Greg Davis	.05	.01
❑	71	Terry Allen	.25	.08
❑	72	Anthony Carter	.10	.02
❑	73	Cris Carter	.25	.08
❑	74	Roger Craig	.10	.02
❑	75	Jack Del Rio	.05	.01
❑	76	Chris Doleman	.05	.01
❑	77	Rich Gannon	.25	.08
❑	78	Hassan Jones	.05	.01
❑	79	Steve Jordan	.05	.01
❑	80	Randall McDaniel	.05	.01
❑	81	Sean Salisbury	.05	.01
❑	82	Harry Newsome	.05	.01
❑	83	Carlos Jenkins	.05	.01
❑	84	Jake Reed	.25	.08
❑	85	Edgar Bennett	.25	.08
❑	86	Tony Bennett	.05	.01
❑	87	Terrell Buckley	.05	.01
❑	88	Ty Detmer	.25	.08
❑	89	Brett Favre	2.00	.75
❑	90	Chris Jacke	.05	.01
❑	91	Sterling Sharpe	.25	.08
❑	92	James Campen	.05	.01
❑	93	Brian Noble	.05	.01
❑	94	Lester Archambeau RC	.05	.01
❑	95	Harry Sydney	.05	.01
❑	96	Corey Harris	.05	.01
❑	97	Don Majkowski	.05	.01
❑	98	Ken Ruettgers	.05	.01
❑	99	Lomas Brown	.05	.01
❑	100	Jason Hanson	.05	.01
❑	101	Robert Porcher	.05	.01
❑	102	Chris Spielman	.10	.02
❑	103	Erik Kramer	.10	.02
❑	104	Tracy Scroggins	.05	.01
❑	105	Rodney Peete	.05	.01
❑	106	Barry Sanders	1.25	.50
❑	107	Herman Moore	.25	.08
❑	108	Brett Perriman	.25	.08
❑	109	Mel Gray	.10	.02
❑	110	Dennis Gibson	.05	.01
❑	111	Bennie Blades	.05	.01
❑	112	Andre Ware	.05	.01
❑	113	Gary Anderson RB	.05	.01
❑	114	Tyji Armstrong	.05	.01
❑	115	Reggie Cobb	.05	.01
❑	116	Marty Carter	.05	.01
❑	117	Lawrence Dawsey	.05	.01
❑	118	Steve DeBerg	.05	.01
❑	119	Ron Hall	.05	.01
❑	120	Courtney Hawkins	.05	.01
❑	121	Broderick Thomas	.05	.01
❑	122	Keith McCants	.05	.01
❑	123	Bruce Reimers	.05	.01
❑	124	Darrick Brownlow	.05	.01
❑	125	Mark Wheeler	.05	.01
❑	126	Ricky Reynolds	.05	.01
❑	127	Neal Anderson	.05	.01
❑	128	Trace Armstrong	.05	.01
❑	129	Mark Carrier DB	.05	.01
❑	130	Richard Dent	.10	.02
❑	131	Wendell Davis	.05	.01
❑	132	Darren Lewis	.05	.01
❑	133	Tom Waddle	.05	.01
❑	134	Jim Harbaugh	.25	.08
❑	135	Steve McMichael	.10	.02
❑	136	William Perry	.10	.02
❑	137	Alonzo Spellman	.05	.01
❑	138	John Roper	.05	.01
❑	139	Peter Tom Willis	.05	.01
❑	140	Dante Jones	.05	.01
❑	141	Harris Barton	.05	.01
❑	142	Michael Carter	.05	.01
❑	143	Eric Davis	.05	.01
❑	144	Dana Hall	.05	.01
❑	145	Amp Lee	.05	.01
❑	146	Don Griffin	.05	.01
❑	147	Jerry Rice	1.00	.40
❑	148	Ricky Watters	.25	.08
❑	149	Steve Young	.75	.30
❑	150	Bill Romanowski	.05	.01
❑	151	Klaus Wilmsmeyer	.05	.01
❑	152	Steve Bono	.10	.02
❑	153	Tom Rathman	.05	.01
❑	154	Odessa Turner	.05	.01
❑	155	Morten Andersen	.05	.01
❑	156	Richard Cooper	.05	.01
❑	157	Toi Cook	.05	.01
❑	158	Quinn Early	.10	.02
❑	159	Vaughn Dunbar	.05	.01
❑	160	Rickey Jackson	.05	.01
❑	161	Wayne Martin	.05	.01
❑	162	Hoby Brenner	.05	.01
❑	163	Joel Hilgenberg	.05	.01
❑	164	Mike Buck	.05	.01
❑	165	Torrance Small	.05	.01
❑	166	Eric Martin	.05	.01
❑	167	Vaughan Johnson	.05	.01
❑	168	Sam Mills	.05	.01
❑	169	Steve Broussard	.05	.01
❑	170	Darion Conner	.05	.01
❑	171	Drew Hill	.05	.01
❑	172	Chris Hinton	.05	.01
❑	173	Chris Miller	.10	.02
❑	174	Tim McKyer	.05	.01
❑	175	Norm Johnson	.05	.01
❑	176	Mike Pritchard	.10	.02
❑	177	Andre Rison	.10	.02
❑	178	Deion Sanders	.50	.20
❑	179	Tony Smith RB	.05	.01
❑	180	Bruce Pickens	.05	.01
❑	181	Michael Haynes	.10	.02
❑	182	Jessie Tuggle	.05	.01
❑	183	Marc Boutte	.05	.01
❑	184	Don Bracken	.05	.01
❑	185	Bern Brostek	.05	.01
❑	186	Henry Ellard	.10	.02
❑	187	Jim Everett	.10	.02
❑	188	Sean Gilbert	.10	.02
❑	189	Cleveland Gary	.05	.01
❑	190	Todd Kinchen	.05	.01
❑	191	Pat Terrell	.05	.01
❑	192	Jackie Slater	.05	.01
❑	193	David Lang	.05	.01
❑	194	Flipper Anderson	.05	.01
❑	195	Tony Zendejas	.05	.01
❑	196	Roman Phifer	.05	.01
❑	197	Steve Christie	.05	.01
❑	198	Cornelius Bennett	.10	.02
❑	199	Phil Hansen	.05	.01
❑	200	Don Beebe	.05	.01
❑	201	Mark Kelso	.05	.01
❑	202	Bruce Smith	.25	.08
❑	203	Darryl Talley	.05	.01
❑	204	Andre Reed	.10	.02
❑	205	Mike Lodish	.05	.01
❑	206	Jim Kelly	.25	.08
❑	207	Thurman Thomas	.25	.08
❑	208	Kenneth Davis	.05	.01
❑	209	Frank Reich	.10	.02
❑	210	Kent Hull	.05	.01
❑	211	Marco Coleman	.05	.01
❑	212	Bryan Cox	.05	.01
❑	213	Jeff Cross	.05	.01
❑	214	Mark Higgs	.05	.01
❑	215	Keith Jackson	.10	.02
❑	216	Scott Miller	.05	.01
❑	217	John Offerdahl	.05	.01
❑	218	Dan Marino	1.50	.60
❑	219	Keith Sims	.05	.01
❑	220	Chuck Klingbeil	.05	.01
❑	221	Troy Vincent	.05	.01
❑	222	Mike Williams RC WR	.05	.01
❑	223	Pete Stoyanovich	.05	.01
❑	224	J.B. Brown	.05	.01
❑	225	Ashley Ambrose	.05	.01
❑	226	Jason Belser RC	.05	.01
❑	227	Jeff George	.25	.08
❑	228	Quentin Coryatt	.10	.02
❑	229	Duane Bickett	.05	.01
❑	230	Steve Emtman	.05	.01
❑	231	Anthony Johnson	.10	.02
❑	232	Rohn Stark	.05	.01
❑	233	Jessie Hester	.05	.01
❑	234	Reggie Langhorne	.05	.01
❑	235	Clarence Verdin	.05	.01
❑	236	Dean Biasucci	.05	.01
❑	237	Jack Trudeau	.05	.01
❑	238	Tony Siragusa	.05	.01
❑	239	Chris Burkett	.05	.01
❑	240	Brad Baxter	.05	.01
❑	241	Rob Moore	.10	.02
❑	242	Browning Nagle	.05	.01
❑	243	Jim Sweeney	.05	.01
❑	244	Kurt Barber	.05	.01
❑	245	Siupeli Malamala RC	.05	.01
❑	246	Mike Brim	.05	.01
❑	247	Mo Lewis	.05	.01
❑	248	Johnny Mitchell	.05	.01
❑	249	Ken Whisenhunt RC	.05	.01
❑	250	James Hasty	.05	.01
❑	251	Kyle Clifton	.05	.01
❑	252	Terance Mathis	.10	.02
❑	253	Ray Agnew	.05	.01
❑	254	Eugene Chung	.05	.01
❑	255	Marv Cook	.05	.01
❑	256	Johnny Rembert	.05	.01
❑	257	Maurice Hurst	.05	.01
❑	258	Jon Vaughn	.05	.01
❑	259	Leonard Russell	.10	.02
❑	260	Pat Harlow	.05	.01
❑	261	Andre Tippett	.05	.01
❑	262	Michael Timpson	.05	.01
❑	263	Greg McMurtry	.05	.01
❑	264	Chris Singleton	.05	.01
❑	265	Reggie Redding RC	.05	.01
❑	266	Walter Stanley	.05	.01
❑	267	Gary Anderson K	.05	.01
❑	268	Merril Hoge	.05	.01
❑	269	Barry Foster	.10	.02
❑	270	Charles Davenport	.05	.01
❑	271	Jeff Graham	.10	.02
❑	272	Adrian Cooper	.05	.01
❑	273	David Little	.05	.01
❑	274	Neil O'Donnell	.25	.08
❑	275	Rod Woodson	.25	.08
❑	276	Ernie Mills	.05	.01
❑	277	Dwight Stone	.05	.01
❑	278	Darren Perry	.05	.01
❑	279	Dermontti Dawson	.05	.01
❑	280	Carlton Haselrig	.05	.01
❑	281	Pat Coleman	.05	.01
❑	282	Ernest Givins	.10	.02
❑	283	Warren Moon	.25	.08
❑	284	Haywood Jeffires	.10	.02
❑	285	Cody Carlson	.05	.01
❑	286	Ray Childress	.05	.01
❑	287	Bruce Matthews	.05	.01
❑	288	Webster Slaughter	.05	.01
❑	289	Bo Orlando	.05	.01
❑	290	Lorenzo White	.05	.01
❑	291	Eddie Robinson	.05	.01
❑	292	Bubba McDowell	.05	.01
❑	293	Bucky Richardson	.05	.01
❑	294	Sean Jones	.05	.01
❑	295	David Brandon	.05	.01
❑	296	Shawn Collins	.05	.01
❑	297	Lawyer Tillman	.05	.01
❑	298	Bob Dahl	.05	.01
❑	299	Kevin Mack	.05	.01
❑	300	Bernie Kosar	.10	.02
❑	301	Tommy Vardell	.05	.01
❑	302	Jay Hilgenberg	.05	.01
❑	303	Michael Dean Perry	.10	.02
❑	304	Michael Jackson	.10	.02
❑	305	Eric Metcalf	.10	.02
❑	306	Rico Smith RC	.05	.01
❑	307	Stevon Moore RC	.05	.01
❑	308	Leroy Hoard	.10	.02

❑ 309 Eric Ball .05 .01
❑ 310 Derrick Fenner .05 .01
❑ 311 James Francis .05 .01
❑ 312 Ricardo McDonald .05 .01
❑ 313 Tim Krumrie .05 .01
❑ 314 Carl Pickens .10 .02
❑ 315 David Klingler .05 .01
❑ 316 Donald Hollas RC .05 .01
❑ 317 Harold Green .05 .01
❑ 318 Daniel Stubbs .05 .01
❑ 319 Alfred Williams .05 .01
❑ 320 Darryl Williams .05 .01
❑ 321 Mike Arthur RC .05 .01
❑ 322 Leonard Wheeler .05 .01
❑ 323 Gill Byrd .05 .01
❑ 324 Eric Bieniemy .05 .01
❑ 325 Marion Butts .05 .01
❑ 326 John Carney .05 .01
❑ 327 Stan Humphries .10 .02
❑ 328 Ronnie Harmon .05 .01
❑ 329 Junior Seau .25 .08
❑ 330 Nate Lewis .05 .01
❑ 331 Harry Swayne .05 .01
❑ 332 Leslie O'Neal .10 .02
❑ 333 Eric Moten .05 .01
❑ 334 Blaise Winter RC .05 .01
❑ 335 Anthony Miller .10 .02
❑ 336 Gary Plummer .05 .01
❑ 337 Willie Davis .25 .08
❑ 338 J.J. Birden .05 .01
❑ 339 Tim Barnett .05 .01
❑ 340 Dave Krieg .10 .02
❑ 341 Barry Word .05 .01
❑ 342 Tracy Simien .05 .01
❑ 343 Christian Okoye .05 .01
❑ 344 Todd McNair .05 .01
❑ 345 Dan Saleaumua .05 .01
❑ 346 Derrick Thomas .25 .08
❑ 347 Harvey Williams .10 .02
❑ 348 Kimble Anders RC .25 .08
❑ 349 Tim Grunhard .05 .01
❑ 350 Tony Hargain RC UER .05 .01
❑ 351 Simon Fletcher .05 .01
❑ 352 John Elway 1.50 .60
❑ 353 Mike Croel .05 .01
❑ 354 Steve Atwater .05 .01
❑ 355 Tommy Maddox .25 .08
❑ 356 Karl Mecklenburg .05 .01
❑ 357 Shane Dronett .05 .01
❑ 358 Kenny Walker .05 .01
❑ 359 Reggie Rivers RC .05 .01
❑ 360 Cedric Tillman RC .05 .01
❑ 361 Arthur Marshall RC .05 .01
❑ 362 Greg Lewis .05 .01
❑ 363 Shannon Sharpe .25 .08
❑ 364 Doug Widell .05 .01
❑ 365 Todd Marinovich .05 .01
❑ 366 Nick Bell .05 .01
❑ 367 Eric Dickerson .10 .02
❑ 368 Max Montoya .05 .01
❑ 369 Winston Moss .05 .01
❑ 370 Howie Long .25 .08
❑ 371 Willie Gault .05 .01
❑ 372 Tim Brown .25 .08
❑ 373 Steve Smith .05 .01
❑ 374 Steve Wisniewski .05 .01
❑ 375 Alexander Wright .05 .01
❑ 376 Ethan Horton .05 .01
❑ 377 Napoleon McCallum .05 .01
❑ 378 Terry McDaniel .05 .01
❑ 379 Patrick Hunter .05 .01
❑ 380 Robert Blackmon .05 .01
❑ 381 John Kasay .05 .01
❑ 382 Cortez Kennedy .10 .02
❑ 383 Andy Heck .05 .01
❑ 384 Bill Hitchcock RC .05 .01
❑ 385 Rick Mirer RC .25 .08
❑ 386 Jeff Bryant .05 .01
❑ 387 Eugene Robinson .05 .01
❑ 388 John L. Williams .05 .01
❑ 389 Chris Warren .10 .02
❑ 390 Rufus Porter .05 .01
❑ 391 Joe Tofflemire RC .05 .01
❑ 392 Dan McGwire .05 .01
❑ 393 Boomer Esiason .10 .02
❑ 394 Brad Muster .05 .01
❑ 395 James Lofton .10 .02
❑ 396 Tim McGee .05 .01
❑ 397 Steve Beuerlein .10 .02
❑ 398 Gaston Green .05 .01
❑ 399 Bill Brooks .05 .01
❑ 400 Ronnie Lott .10 .02
❑ 401 Jay Schroeder .05 .01
❑ 402 Marcus Allen .25 .08
❑ 403 Kevin Greene .10 .02
❑ 404 Kirk Lowdermilk .05 .01
❑ 405 Hugh Millen .05 .01
❑ 406 Pat Swilling .05 .01
❑ 407 Bobby Hebert .05 .01
❑ 408 Carl Banks .05 .01
❑ 409 Jeff Hostetler .10 .02
❑ 410 Leonard Marshall .05 .01
❑ 411 Ken O'Brien .05 .01
❑ 412 Joe Montana 1.50 .60
❑ 413 Reggie White .25 .08
❑ 414 Gary Clark .10 .02
❑ 415 Johnny Johnson .05 .01
❑ 416 Tim McDonald .05 .01
❑ 417 Pierce Holt .05 .01
❑ 418 Gino Torretta RC .10 .02
❑ 419 Glyn Milburn RC .25 .08
❑ 420 O.J.McDuffie RC .25 .08
❑ 421 Coleman Rudolph RC .05 .01
❑ 422 Reggie Brooks RC .10 .02
❑ 423 Garrison Hearst RC .60 .25
❑ 424 Leonard Renfro RC .05 .01
❑ 425 Kevin Williams RC WR .25 .08
❑ 426 Demetrius DuBose RC .05 .01
❑ 427 Elvis Grbac RC 1.25 .50
❑ 428 Lincoln Kennedy RC .05 .01
❑ 429 Carlton Gray RC .05 .01
❑ 430 Micheal Barrow RC .25 .08
❑ 431 George Teague RC .10 .02
❑ 432 Curtis Conway RC .40 .15
❑ 433 Natrone Means RC .25 .08
❑ 434 Jerome Bettis RC 5.00 2.00
❑ 435 Drew Bledsoe RC 2.00 .75
❑ 436 Robert Smith RC 1.00 .40
❑ 437 Deon Figures RC .05 .01
❑ 438 Qadry Ismail RC .25 .08
❑ 439 Chris Slade RC .10 .02
❑ 440 Dana Stubblefield RC .25 .08

1994 Pacific

❑ COMPLETE SET (450) 30.00 15.00
❑ 1 Troy Aikman 1.00 .40
❑ 2 Charles Haley .10 .02
❑ 3 Alvin Harper .10 .02
❑ 4 Michael Irvin .25 .08
❑ 5 Jim Jeffcoat .05 .01
❑ 6 Daryl Johnston .10 .02
❑ 7 Robert Jones .05 .01
❑ 8 Brock Marion RC .25 .08
❑ 9 Russell Maryland .05 .01
❑ 10 Ken Norton .10 .02
❑ 11 Jay Novacek .10 .02
❑ 12 Emmitt Smith 1.50 .60
❑ 13 Kevin Smith .05 .01
❑ 14 Tony Tolbert .05 .01
❑ 15 Kevin Williams WR .10 .02
❑ 16 Don Beebe .05 .01
❑ 17 Cornelius Bennett .10 .02
❑ 18 Bill Brooks .05 .01
❑ 19 Steve Christie .05 .01
❑ 20 Russell Copeland .05 .01
❑ 21 Kenneth Davis .05 .01
❑ 22 Kent Hull .05 .01
❑ 23 Jim Kelly .25 .08
❑ 24 Pete Metzelaars .05 .01
❑ 25 Andre Reed .10 .02
❑ 26 Frank Reich .10 .02
❑ 27 Bruce Smith .25 .08
❑ 28 Darryl Talley .05 .01
❑ 29 Steve Tasker .10 .02
❑ 30 Thurman Thomas .25 .08
❑ 31 Steve Bono .10 .02
❑ 32 Dexter Carter .05 .01
❑ 33 Kevin Fagan .05 .01
❑ 34 Dana Hall .05 .01
❑ 35 Brent Jones .10 .02
❑ 36 Amp Lee .05 .01
❑ 37 Marc Logan .05 .01
❑ 38 Tim McDonald .05 .01
❑ 39 Guy McIntyre .05 .01
❑ 40 Tom Rathman .05 .01
❑ 41 Jerry Rice 1.00 .40
❑ 42 Dana Stubblefield .10 .02
❑ 43 Steve Wallace .05 .01
❑ 44 Ricky Watters .10 .02
❑ 45 Steve Young .75 .30
❑ 46 Marcus Allen .25 .08
❑ 47 Kimble Anders .10 .02
❑ 48 Tim Barnett .05 .01
❑ 49 J.J. Birden .05 .01
❑ 50 Dale Carter .05 .01
❑ 51 Jonathan Hayes .05 .01
❑ 52 Dave Krieg .10 .02
❑ 53 Albert Lewis .05 .01
❑ 54 Nick Lowery .05 .01
❑ 55 Joe Montana 2.00 .75
❑ 56 Neil Smith .10 .02
❑ 57 John Stephens .05 .01
❑ 58 Derrick Thomas .25 .08
❑ 59 Harvey Williams .10 .02
❑ 60 Micheal Barrow .05 .01
❑ 61 Gary Brown .05 .01
❑ 62 Cody Carlson .05 .01
❑ 63 Ray Childress .05 .01
❑ 64 Curtis Duncan .05 .01
❑ 65 Ernest Givins .10 .02
❑ 66 Haywood Jeffires .10 .02
❑ 67 Wilber Marshall .05 .01
❑ 68 Bubba McDowell .05 .01
❑ 69 Warren Moon .25 .08
❑ 70 Mike Munchak .10 .02
❑ 71 Marcus Robertson .05 .01
❑ 72 Webster Slaughter .05 .01
❑ 73 Gary Wellman RC .05 .01
❑ 74 Lorenzo White .05 .01
❑ 75 Ray Crockett .05 .01
❑ 76 Jason Hanson .05 .01
❑ 77 Rodney Holman .05 .01
❑ 78 George Jamison .05 .01
❑ 79 Erik Kramer .10 .02
❑ 80 Ryan McNeil .05 .01
❑ 81 Derrick Moore .05 .01
❑ 82 Herman Moore .25 .08
❑ 83 Rodney Peete .05 .01
❑ 84 Brett Perriman .10 .02
❑ 85 Barry Sanders 1.50 .60
❑ 86 Chris Spielman .10 .02
❑ 87 Pat Swilling .05 .01
❑ 88 Vernon Turner .05 .01
❑ 89 Andre Ware .05 .01

Card	Player	Mint	Ex
❑ 90	Michael Brooks	.05	.01
❑ 91	Dave Brown	.10	.02
❑ 92	Derek Brown TE	.05	.01
❑ 93	Jarrod Bunch	.05	.01
❑ 94	Chris Calloway	.05	.01
❑ 95	Kent Graham	.10	.02
❑ 96	Rodney Hampton	.10	.02
❑ 97	Mark Jackson	.05	.01
❑ 98	Ed McCaffrey	.25	.08
❑ 99	Dave Meggett	.05	.01
❑ 100	Aaron Pierce	.05	.01
❑ 101	Mike Sherrard	.05	.01
❑ 102	Phil Simms	.10	.02
❑ 103	Lewis Tillman	.05	.01
❑ 104	Eddie Anderson	.05	.01
❑ 105	Patrick Bates	.05	.01
❑ 106	Nick Bell	.05	.01
❑ 107	Tim Brown	.25	.08
❑ 108	Willie Gault	.05	.01
❑ 109	Jeff Gossett	.05	.01
❑ 110	Ethan Horton	.05	.01
❑ 111	Jeff Hostetler	.10	.02
❑ 112	Rocket Ismail	.10	.02
❑ 113	Chester McGlockton	.05	.01
❑ 114	Anthony Smith	.05	.01
❑ 115	Steve Smith	.05	.01
❑ 116	Greg Townsend	.05	.01
❑ 117	Steve Wisniewski	.05	.01
❑ 118	Alexander Wright	.05	.01
❑ 119	Steve Atwater	.05	.01
❑ 120	Rod Bernstine	.05	.01
❑ 121	Mike Croel	.05	.01
❑ 122	Shane Dronett	.05	.01
❑ 123	Jason Elam	.10	.02
❑ 124	John Elway	2.00	.75
❑ 125	Brian Habib	.05	.01
❑ 126	Rondell Jones	.05	.01
❑ 127	Tommy Maddox	.25	.08
❑ 128	Karl Mecklenburg	.05	.01
❑ 129	Glyn Milburn	.10	.02
❑ 130	Derek Russell	.05	.01
❑ 131	Shannon Sharpe	.10	.02
❑ 132	Dennis Smith	.05	.01
❑ 133	Edgar Bennett	.25	.08
❑ 134	Tony Bennett	.05	.01
❑ 135	Robert Brooks	.25	.08
❑ 136	Terrell Buckley	.05	.01
❑ 137	LeRoy Butler	.05	.01
❑ 138	Mark Clayton	.05	.01
❑ 139	Ty Detmer	.10	.02
❑ 140	Brett Favre	2.00	.75
❑ 141	John Jurkovic RC	.10	.02
❑ 142	Bryce Paup	.10	.02
❑ 143	Sterling Sharpe	.10	.02
❑ 144	George Teague	.05	.01
❑ 145	Darrell Thompson	.05	.01
❑ 146	Ed West	.05	.01
❑ 147	Reggie White	.25	.08
❑ 148	Terry Allen	.10	.02
❑ 149	Anthony Carter	.10	.02
❑ 150	Cris Carter	.50	.20
❑ 151	Roger Craig	.10	.02
❑ 152	Jack Del Rio	.05	.01
❑ 153	Chris Doleman	.05	.01
❑ 154	Scottie Graham RC	.10	.02
❑ 155	Eric Guliford RC	.05	.01
❑ 156	Qadry Ismail	.25	.08
❑ 157	Steve Jordan	.05	.01
❑ 158	Randall McDaniel	.05	.01
❑ 159	Jim McMahon	.10	.02
❑ 160	Audray McMillian	.05	.01
❑ 161	Sean Salisbury	.05	.01
❑ 162	Robert Smith	.25	.08
❑ 163	Henry Thomas	.05	.01
❑ 164	Gary Anderson K	.05	.01
❑ 165	Deon Figures	.05	.01
❑ 166	Barry Foster	.05	.01
❑ 167	Jeff Graham	.05	.01
❑ 168	Kevin Greene	.10	.02
❑ 169	Dave Hoffman	.05	.01
❑ 170	Merril Hoge	.05	.01
❑ 171	Gary Jones	.05	.01
❑ 172	Greg Lloyd	.10	.02
❑ 173	Ernie Mills	.05	.01
❑ 174	Neil O'Donnell	.25	.08
❑ 175	Darren Perry	.05	.01
❑ 176	Leon Searcy	.05	.01
❑ 177	Leroy Thompson	.05	.01
❑ 178	Willie Williams RC	.05	.01
❑ 179	Rod Woodson	.10	.02
❑ 180	Keith Byars	.05	.01
❑ 181	Marco Coleman	.05	.01
❑ 182	Bryan Cox	.05	.01
❑ 183	Irving Fryar	.10	.02
❑ 184	John Grimsley	.05	.01
❑ 185	Mark Higgs	.05	.01
❑ 186	Mark Ingram	.05	.01
❑ 187	Keith Jackson	.05	.01
❑ 188	Terry Kirby	.25	.08
❑ 189	Dan Marino	2.00	.75
❑ 190	O.J.McDuffie	.25	.08
❑ 191	Scott Mitchell	.10	.02
❑ 192	Pete Stoyanovich	.05	.01
❑ 193	Troy Vincent	.05	.01
❑ 194	Richmond Webb	.05	.01
❑ 195	Brad Baxter	.05	.01
❑ 196	Chris Burkett	.05	.01
❑ 197	Rob Carpenter WR	.05	.01
❑ 198	Boomer Esiason	.10	.02
❑ 199	Johnny Johnson	.05	.01
❑ 200	Jeff Lageman	.05	.01
❑ 201	Mo Lewis	.05	.01
❑ 202	Ronnie Lott	.10	.02
❑ 203	Leonard Marshall	.05	.01
❑ 204	Terance Mathis	.10	.02
❑ 205	Johnny Mitchell	.05	.01
❑ 206	Rob Moore	.10	.02
❑ 207	Anthony Prior	.05	.01
❑ 208	Blair Thomas	.05	.01
❑ 209	Brian Washington	.05	.01
❑ 210	Eric Bieniemy	.05	.01
❑ 211	Marion Butts	.05	.01
❑ 212	Gill Byrd	.05	.01
❑ 213	John Carney	.05	.01
❑ 214	Darren Carrington	.05	.01
❑ 215	John Friesz	.10	.02
❑ 216	Ronnie Harmon	.05	.01
❑ 217	Stan Humphries	.10	.02
❑ 218	Nate Lewis	.05	.01
❑ 219	Natrone Means	.25	.08
❑ 220	Anthony Miller	.10	.02
❑ 221	Chris Mims	.05	.01
❑ 222	Eric Moten	.05	.01
❑ 223	Leslie O'Neal	.05	.01
❑ 224	Junior Seau	.25	.08
❑ 225	Morten Andersen	.05	.01
❑ 226	Gene Atkins	.05	.01
❑ 227	Derek Brown RBK	.05	.01
❑ 228	Toi Cook	.05	.01
❑ 229	Vaughn Dunbar	.05	.01
❑ 230	Quinn Early	.10	.02
❑ 231	Reggie Freeman	.05	.01
❑ 232	Tyrone Hughes	.10	.02
❑ 233	Rickey Jackson	.05	.01
❑ 234	Eric Martin	.05	.01
❑ 235	Sam Mills	.05	.01
❑ 236	Brad Muster	.05	.01
❑ 237	Torrance Small	.05	.01
❑ 238	Irv Smith	.05	.01
❑ 239	Wade Wilson	.05	.01
❑ 240	Eric Allen	.05	.01
❑ 241	Victor Bailey	.05	.01
❑ 242	Fred Barnett	.10	.02
❑ 243	Mark Bavaro	.05	.01
❑ 244	Bubby Brister	.10	.02
❑ 245	Randall Cunningham	.25	.08
❑ 246	Antone Davis	.05	.01
❑ 247	Britt Hager RC	.05	.01
❑ 248	Vaughn Hebron	.05	.01
❑ 249	James Joseph	.05	.01
❑ 250	Seth Joyner	.05	.01
❑ 251	Rich Miano	.05	.01
❑ 252	Heath Sherman	.05	.01
❑ 253	Clyde Simmons	.05	.01
❑ 254	Herschel Walker	.10	.02
❑ 255	Calvin Williams	.10	.02
❑ 256	Jerry Ball	.05	.01
❑ 257	Mark Carrier WR	.10	.02
❑ 258	Michael Jackson	.10	.02
❑ 259	Mike Johnson	.05	.01
❑ 260	James Jones DT	.05	.01
❑ 261	Brian Kinchen	.05	.01
❑ 262	Clay Matthews	.05	.01
❑ 263	Eric Metcalf	.10	.02
❑ 264	Stevon Moore	.05	.01
❑ 265	Michael Dean Perry	.10	.02
❑ 266	Todd Philcox	.05	.01
❑ 267	Anthony Pleasant	.05	.01
❑ 268	Vinny Testaverde	.10	.02
❑ 269	Eric Turner	.05	.01
❑ 270	Tommy Vardell	.05	.01
❑ 271	Neal Anderson	.05	.01
❑ 272	Trace Armstrong	.05	.01
❑ 273	Mark Carrier DB	.05	.01
❑ 274	Bob Christian	.05	.01
❑ 275	Curtis Conway	.25	.08
❑ 276	Richard Dent	.10	.02
❑ 277	Robert Green	.05	.01
❑ 278	Jim Harbaugh	.25	.08
❑ 279	Craig Heyward	.10	.02
❑ 280	Terry Obee	.05	.01
❑ 281	Alonzo Spellman	.05	.01
❑ 282	Tom Waddle	.05	.01
❑ 283	Peter Tom Willis	.05	.01
❑ 284	Donnell Woolford	.05	.01
❑ 285	Tim Worley	.05	.01
❑ 286	Chris Zorich	.05	.01
❑ 287	Steve Broussard	.05	.01
❑ 288	Darion Conner	.05	.01
❑ 289	Jumpy Geathers	.05	.01
❑ 290	Michael Haynes	.10	.02
❑ 291	Bobby Hebert	.05	.01
❑ 292	Lincoln Kennedy	.05	.01
❑ 293	Chris Miller	.05	.01
❑ 294	David Mims RC	.05	.01
❑ 295	Erric Pegram	.05	.01
❑ 296	Mike Pritchard	.05	.01
❑ 297	Andre Rison	.10	.02
❑ 298	Deion Sanders	.50	.20
❑ 299	Chuck Smith	.05	.01
❑ 300	Tony Smith RB	.05	.01
❑ 301	Johnny Bailey	.05	.01
❑ 302	Steve Beuerlein	.10	.02
❑ 303	Chuck Cecil	.05	.01
❑ 304	Chris Chandler	.10	.02
❑ 305	Gary Clark	.10	.02
❑ 306	Rick Cunningham RC	.05	.01
❑ 307	Ken Harvey	.05	.01
❑ 308	Garrison Hearst	.25	.08
❑ 309	Randal Hill	.05	.01
❑ 310	Robert Massey	.05	.01
❑ 311	Ronald Moore	.05	.01
❑ 312	Ricky Proehl	.05	.01
❑ 313	Eric Swann	.10	.02
❑ 314	Aeneas Williams	.05	.01
❑ 315	Michael Bates	.05	.01
❑ 316	Brian Blades	.10	.02
❑ 317	Carlton Gray	.05	.01
❑ 318	Paul Green RC	.05	.01
❑ 319	Patrick Hunter	.05	.01
❑ 320	John Kasay	.05	.01
❑ 321	Cortez Kennedy	.10	.02
❑ 322	Kelvin Martin	.05	.01
❑ 323	Dan McGwire	.05	.01
❑ 324	Rick Mirer	.25	.08
❑ 325	Eugene Robinson	.05	.01
❑ 326	Rick Tuten	.05	.01
❑ 327	Chris Warren	.10	.02
❑ 328	John L. Williams	.05	.01
❑ 329	Reggie Cobb	.05	.01

❑ 330 Horace Copeland .05 .01
❑ 331 Lawrence Dawsey .05 .01
❑ 332 Santana Dotson .10 .02
❑ 333 Craig Erickson .05 .01
❑ 334 Ron Hall .05 .01
❑ 335 Courtney Hawkins .05 .01
❑ 336 Keith McCants .05 .01
❑ 337 Hardy Nickerson .10 .02
❑ 338 Mazio Royster RC .05 .01
❑ 339 Broderick Thomas .05 .01
❑ 340 Casey Weldon RC .25 .08
❑ 341 Mark Wheeler .05 .01
❑ 342 Vince Workman .05 .01
❑ 343 Flipper Anderson .05 .01
❑ 344 Jerome Bettis .50 .20
❑ 345 Richard Buchanan .05 .01
❑ 346 Shane Conlan .05 .01
❑ 347 Troy Drayton .05 .01
❑ 348 Henry Ellard .10 .02
❑ 349 Jim Everett .10 .02
❑ 350 Cleveland Gary .05 .01
❑ 351 Sean Gilbert .05 .01
❑ 352 David Lang .05 .01
❑ 353 Todd Lyght .05 .01
❑ 354 T.J. Rubley .05 .01
❑ 355 Jackie Slater .05 .01
❑ 356 Russell White .10 .02
❑ 357 Bruce Armstrong .05 .01
❑ 358 Drew Bledsoe .75 .30
❑ 359 Vincent Brisby .10 .02
❑ 360 Vincent Brown .05 .01
❑ 361 Ben Coates .10 .02
❑ 362 Marv Cook .05 .01
❑ 363 Ray Crittenden RC .05 .01
❑ 364 Corey Croom RC .05 .01
❑ 365 Pat Harlow .05 .01
❑ 366 Dion Lambert .05 .01
❑ 367 Greg McMurtry .05 .01
❑ 368 Leonard Russell .05 .01
❑ 369 Scott Secules .05 .01
❑ 370 Chris Slade .05 .01
❑ 371 Michael Timpson .05 .01
❑ 372 Kevin Turner .05 .01
❑ 373 Ashley Ambrose .05 .01
❑ 374 Dean Biasucci .05 .01
❑ 375 Duane Bickett .05 .01
❑ 376 Quentin Coryatt .05 .01
❑ 377 Rodney Culver .05 .01
❑ 378 Sean Dawkins RC .25 .08
❑ 379 Jeff George .25 .08
❑ 380 Jeff Herrod .05 .01
❑ 381 Jessie Hester .05 .01
❑ 382 Anthony Johnson .10 .02
❑ 383 Reggie Langhorne .05 .01
❑ 384 Roosevelt Potts .05 .01
❑ 385 William Schultz RC .05 .01
❑ 386 Rohn Stark .05 .01
❑ 387 Clarence Verdin .05 .01
❑ 388 Carl Banks .05 .01
❑ 389 Reggie Brooks .10 .02
❑ 390 Earnest Byner .05 .01
❑ 391 Tom Carter .05 .01
❑ 392 Cary Conklin .05 .01
❑ 393 Pat Eilers RC .05 .01
❑ 394 Ricky Ervins .05 .01
❑ 395 Rich Gannon .25 .08
❑ 396 Darrell Green .05 .01
❑ 397 Desmond Howard .10 .02
❑ 398 Chip Lohmiller .05 .01
❑ 399 Sterling Palmer RC .05 .01
❑ 400 Mark Rypien .05 .01
❑ 401 Ricky Sanders .05 .01
❑ 402 Johnny Thomas CB .05 .01
❑ 403 John Copeland .05 .01
❑ 404 Derrick Fenner .05 .01
❑ 405 Alex Gordon .05 .01
❑ 406 Harold Green .05 .01
❑ 407 Lance Gunn .05 .01
❑ 408 David Klingler .05 .01
❑ 409 Ricardo McDonald .05 .01
❑ 410 Tim McGee .05 .01
❑ 411 Reggie Rembert .05 .01
❑ 412 Patrick Robinson .05 .01
❑ 413 Jay Schroeder .05 .01
❑ 414 Erik Wilhelm .05 .01
❑ 415 Alfred Williams .05 .01
❑ 416 Darryl Williams .05 .01
❑ 417 Sam Adams RC .10 .02
❑ 418 Mario Bates RC .25 .08
❑ 419 James Bostic RC .25 .08
❑ 420 Bucky Brooks RC .05 .01
❑ 421 Jeff Burris RC .10 .02
❑ 422 Shante Carver RC .05 .01
❑ 423 Jeff Cothran RC .05 .01
❑ 424 Lake Dawson RC .10 .02
❑ 425 Trent Dilfer RC 1.25 .50
❑ 426 Marshall Faulk RC 5.00 2.00
❑ 427 Cory Fleming RC .05 .01
❑ 428 William Floyd RC .25 .08
❑ 429 Glenn Foley RC .25 .08
❑ 430 Rob Fredrickson RC .10 .02
❑ 431 Charlie Garner RC 1.25 .50
❑ 432 Greg Hill RC .25 .08
❑ 433 Charles Johnson RC .25 .08
❑ 434 Calvin Jones RC .05 .01
❑ 435 Jimmy Klingler RC .05 .01
❑ 436 Antonio Langham RC .10 .02
❑ 437 Kevin Lee RC .05 .01
❑ 438 Chuck Levy RC .05 .01
❑ 439 Willie McGinest RC .25 .08
❑ 440 Jamir Miller RC .10 .02
❑ 441 Johnnie Morton RC .50 .20
❑ 442 David Palmer RC .25 .08
❑ 443 Errict Rhett RC .25 .08
❑ 444 Corey Sawyer RC .10 .02
❑ 445 Darnay Scott RC .50 .20
❑ 446 Heath Shuler RC .25 .08
❑ 447 Lamar Smith RC 1.25 .50
❑ 448 Dan Wilkinson RC .10 .02
❑ 449 Bernard Williams RC .05 .01
❑ 450 Bryant Young RC .25 .08
❑ P1 Sterling Sharpe Promo .75 .30

1995 Pacific

❑ COMPLETE SET (450) 25.00 10.00
❑ 1 Randy Baldwin .10 .02
❑ 2 Tommy Barnhardt .10 .02
❑ 3 Tim McKyer .10 .02
❑ 4 Sam Mills .20 .07
❑ 5 Brian O'Neal .10 .02
❑ 6 Frank Reich .10 .02
❑ 7 Jack Trudeau .10 .02
❑ 8 Vernon Turner .10 .02
❑ 9 Kerry Collins RC 1.50 .60
❑ 10 Shawn King .10 .02
❑ 11 Steve Beuerlein .20 .07
❑ 12 Derek Brown TE .10 .02
❑ 13 Reggie Clark .10 .02
❑ 14 Reggie Cobb .10 .02
❑ 15 Desmond Howard .20 .07
❑ 16 Jeff Lageman .10 .02
❑ 17 Kelvin Pritchett .10 .02
❑ 18 Cedric Tillman .10 .02
❑ 19 Tony Boselli RC .30 .10
❑ 20 James O. Stewart RC 1.25 .50
❑ 21 Eric Davis .10 .02
❑ 22 William Floyd .20 .07
❑ 23 Elvis Grbac .30 .10
❑ 24 Brent Jones .10 .02
❑ 25 Ken Norton, Jr. .20 .07
❑ 26 Bart Oates .10 .02
❑ 27 Jerry Rice 1.00 .40
❑ 28 Deion Sanders .40 .15
❑ 29 John Taylor .10 .02
❑ 30 Adam Walker RC .10 .02
❑ 31 Steve Wallace .10 .02
❑ 32 Ricky Watters .20 .07
❑ 33 Lee Woodall .10 .02
❑ 34 Bryant Young .20 .07
❑ 35 Steve Young .75 .30
❑ 36 J.J. Stokes RC .30 .10
❑ 37 Troy Aikman 1.00 .40
❑ 38 Larry Allen .20 .07
❑ 39 Chris Boniol RC .10 .02
❑ 40 Lincoln Coleman .10 .02
❑ 41 Charles Haley .20 .07
❑ 42 Alvin Harper .10 .02
❑ 43 Chad Hennings .20 .07
❑ 44 Michael Irvin .30 .10
❑ 45 Daryl Johnston .20 .07
❑ 46 Leon Lett .10 .02
❑ 47 Nate Newton .20 .07
❑ 48 Jay Novacek .20 .07
❑ 49 Emmitt Smith 1.50 .60
❑ 50 James Washington .10 .02
❑ 51 Kevin Williams .20 .07
❑ 52 Sherman Williams RC .10 .02
❑ 53 Barry Foster .20 .07
❑ 54 Eric Green .10 .02
❑ 55 Kevin Greene .20 .07
❑ 56 Andre Hastings .20 .07
❑ 57 Charles Johnson .20 .07
❑ 58 Greg Lloyd .20 .07
❑ 59 Ernie Mills .10 .02
❑ 60 Byron Bam Morris .10 .02
❑ 61 Neil O'Donnell .20 .07
❑ 62 Darren Perry .10 .02
❑ 63 Yancey Thigpen RC .20 .07
❑ 64 Mike Tomczak .10 .02
❑ 65 John L. Williams .10 .02
❑ 66 Rod Woodson .20 .07
❑ 67 Mark Bruener RC .20 .07
❑ 68 Kordell Stewart RC 1.50 .60
❑ 69 Jeff Brohm RC .10 .02
❑ 70 Andre Coleman .10 .02
❑ 71 Reuben Davis .10 .02
❑ 72 Dennis Gibson .10 .02
❑ 73 Darrien Gordon .10 .02
❑ 74 Stan Humphries .20 .07
❑ 75 Shawn Jefferson .10 .02
❑ 76 Tony Martin .20 .07
❑ 77 Natrone Means .20 .07
❑ 78 Shannon Mitchell RC .10 .02
❑ 79 Leslie O'Neal .20 .07
❑ 80 Alfred Pupunu .10 .02
❑ 81 Stanley Richard .10 .02
❑ 82 Junior Seau .30 .10
❑ 83 Mark Seay .20 .07
❑ 84 Derrick Alexander WR .30 .10
❑ 85 Carl Banks .10 .02
❑ 86 Isaac Booth .10 .02
❑ 87 Rob Burnett .10 .02
❑ 88 Earnest Byner .10 .02
❑ 89 Steve Everitt .10 .02
❑ 90 Leroy Hoard .10 .02
❑ 91 Pepper Johnson .10 .02
❑ 92 Antonio Langham .10 .02
❑ 93 Eric Metcalf .20 .07

❑ 94	Anthony Pleasant	.10	.02
❑ 95	Frank Stams	.10	.02
❑ 96	Vinny Testaverde	.20	.07
❑ 97	Eric Turner	.10	.02
❑ 98	Mike Miller RC	.10	.02
❑ 99	Craig Powell RC	.10	.02
❑ 100	Gene Atkins	.10	.02
❑ 101	Aubrey Beavers	.10	.02
❑ 102	Tim Bowens	.10	.02
❑ 103	Keith Byars	.10	.02
❑ 104	Bryan Cox	.10	.02
❑ 105	Aaron Craver	.10	.02
❑ 106	Jeff Cross	.10	.02
❑ 107	Irving Fryar	.20	.07
❑ 108	Dan Marino	2.00	.75
❑ 109	O.J. McDuffie	.30	.10
❑ 110	Bernie Parmalee	.20	.07
❑ 111	James Saxon	.10	.02
❑ 112	Keith Sims	.10	.02
❑ 113	Irving Spikes	.20	.07
❑ 114	Pete Mitchell RC	.20	.07
❑ 115	Terry Allen	.20	.07
❑ 116	Cris Carter	.30	.10
❑ 117	Adrian Cooper	.10	.02
❑ 118	Bernard Dafney	.10	.02
❑ 119	Jack Del Rio	.10	.02
❑ 120	Vencie Glenn	.10	.02
❑ 121	Qadry Ismail	.20	.07
❑ 122	Carlos Jenkins	.10	.02
❑ 123	Andrew Jordan	.10	.02
❑ 124	Ed McDaniel	.10	.02
❑ 125	Warren Moon	.20	.07
❑ 126	David Palmer	.20	.07
❑ 127	John Randle	.20	.07
❑ 128	Jake Reed	.20	.07
❑ 129	Derrick Alexander DE RC	.10	.02
❑ 130	Chad May RC	.10	.02
❑ 131	Korey Stringer RC	.20	.07
❑ 132	Bruce Armstrong	.10	.02
❑ 133	Drew Bledsoe	.60	.25
❑ 134	Vincent Brisby	.10	.02
❑ 135	Troy Brown	.30	.10
❑ 136	Vincent Brown	.10	.02
❑ 137	Marion Butts	.10	.02
❑ 138	Ben Coates	.20	.07
❑ 139	Ray Crittenden	.10	.02
❑ 140	Maurice Hurst	.10	.02
❑ 141	Aaron Jones	.10	.02
❑ 142	Willie McGinest	.20	.07
❑ 143	Marty Moore RC	.30	.10
❑ 144	Mike Pitts	.10	.02
❑ 145	Leroy Thompson	.10	.02
❑ 146	Michael Timpson	.10	.02
❑ 147	Bennie Blades	.10	.02
❑ 148	Jocelyn Borgella	.10	.02
❑ 149	Anthony Carter	.20	.07
❑ 150	Willie Clay	.10	.02
❑ 151	Mel Gray	.10	.02
❑ 152	Mike Johnson	.10	.02
❑ 153	Dave Krieg	.10	.02
❑ 154	Robert Massey	.10	.02
❑ 155	Scott Mitchell	.20	.07
❑ 156	Herman Moore	.30	.10
❑ 157	Johnnie Morton	.20	.07
❑ 158	Barry Sanders	1.50	.60
❑ 159	Chris Spielman	.20	.07
❑ 160	Broderick Thomas	.10	.02
❑ 161	Cory Schlesinger RC	.20	.07
❑ 162	Marcus Allen	.30	.10
❑ 163	Donnell Bennett	.20	.07
❑ 164	J.J. Birden	.10	.02
❑ 165	Matt Blundin RC	.10	.02
❑ 166	Steve Bono	.20	.07
❑ 167	Dale Carter	.20	.07
❑ 168	Lake Dawson	.20	.07
❑ 169	Ron Dickerson	.10	.02
❑ 170	Lin Elliott	.10	.02
❑ 171	Jaime Fields	.10	.02
❑ 172	Greg Hill	.20	.07
❑ 173	Danan Hughes	.10	.02
❑ 174	Neil Smith	.20	.07
❑ 175	Steve Stenstrom RC	.10	.02
❑ 176	Edgar Bennett	.20	.07
❑ 177	Robert Brooks	.30	.10
❑ 178	Mark Brunell	.60	.25
❑ 179	Doug Evans RC	.30	.10
❑ 180	Brett Favre	2.00	.75
❑ 181	Corey Harris	.10	.02
❑ 182	LeShon Johnson	.20	.07
❑ 183	Sean Jones	.10	.02
❑ 184	Lenny McGill RC	.10	.02
❑ 185	Terry Mickens	.10	.02
❑ 186	Sterling Sharpe	.20	.07
❑ 187	Joe Sims	.10	.02
❑ 188	Darrell Thompson	.10	.02
❑ 189	Reggie White	.30	.10
❑ 190	Craig Newsome RC	.10	.02
❑ 191	Tim Brown	.30	.10
❑ 192	Vince Evans	.10	.02
❑ 193	Rob Fredrickson	.10	.02
❑ 194	Andrew Glover RC	.10	.02
❑ 195	Jeff Hostetler	.20	.07
❑ 196	Rocket Ismail	.20	.07
❑ 197	Jeff Jaeger	.10	.02
❑ 198	James Jett	.20	.07
❑ 199	Chester McGlockton	.20	.07
❑ 200	Don Mosebar	.10	.02
❑ 201	Tom Rathman	.10	.02
❑ 202	Harvey Williams	.10	.02
❑ 203	Steve Wisniewski	.10	.02
❑ 204	Alexander Wright	.10	.02
❑ 205	Napoleon Kaufman RC	1.25	.50
❑ 206	Trace Armstrong	.10	.02
❑ 207	Curtis Conway	.30	.10
❑ 208	Raymont Harris	.10	.02
❑ 209	Erik Kramer	.10	.02
❑ 210	Nate Lewis	.10	.02
❑ 211	Shane Matthews RC	.30	.10
❑ 212	John Thierry	.10	.02
❑ 213	Lewis Tillman	.10	.02
❑ 214	Tom Waddle	.10	.02
❑ 215	Steve Walsh	.10	.02
❑ 216	James Williams T RC	.10	.02
❑ 217	Donnell Woolford	.10	.02
❑ 218	Chris Zorich	.10	.02
❑ 219	Rashaan Salaam RC	.20	.07
❑ 220	John Booty	.10	.02
❑ 221	Michael Brooks	.10	.02
❑ 222	Dave Brown	.20	.07
❑ 223	Chris Calloway	.10	.02
❑ 224	Gary Downs	.10	.02
❑ 225	Kent Graham	.20	.07
❑ 226	Keith Hamilton	.10	.02
❑ 227	Rodney Hampton	.20	.07
❑ 228	Brian Kozlowski	.10	.02
❑ 229	Thomas Lewis	.20	.07
❑ 230	Dave Meggett	.10	.02
❑ 231	Aaron Pierce	.10	.02
❑ 232	Mike Sherrard	.10	.02
❑ 233	Phillippi Sparks	.10	.02
❑ 234	Tyrone Wheatley RC	1.25	.50
❑ 235	Trev Alberts	.10	.02
❑ 236	Aaron Bailey RC	.10	.02
❑ 237	Jason Belser	.10	.02
❑ 238	Tony Bennett	.10	.02
❑ 239	Kerry Cash	.10	.02
❑ 240	Marshall Faulk	1.25	.50
❑ 241	Stephen Grant	.10	.02
❑ 242	Jeff Herrod	.10	.02
❑ 243	Ronald Humphrey	.10	.02
❑ 244	Kirk Lowdermilk	.10	.02
❑ 245	Don Majkowski	.10	.02
❑ 246	Tony McCoy	.10	.02
❑ 247	Floyd Turner	.10	.02
❑ 248	Lamont Warren	.10	.02
❑ 249	Zack Crockett RC	.20	.07
❑ 250	Michael Bankston	.10	.02
❑ 251	Larry Centers	.20	.07
❑ 252	Gary Clark	.10	.02
❑ 253	Ed Cunningham	.10	.02
❑ 254	Garrison Hearst	.30	.10
❑ 255	Eric Hill	.10	.02
❑ 256	Terry Irving	.10	.02
❑ 257	Lorenzo Lynch	.10	.02
❑ 258	Jamir Miller	.10	.02
❑ 259	Ronald Moore	.10	.02
❑ 260	Terry Samuels	.10	.02
❑ 261	Jay Schroeder	.10	.02
❑ 262	Eric Swann	.20	.07
❑ 263	Aeneas Williams	.10	.02
❑ 264	Frank Sanders RC	.30	.10
❑ 265	Morten Andersen	.10	.02
❑ 266	Mario Bates	.20	.07
❑ 267	Derek Brown RBK	.10	.02
❑ 268	Darion Conner	.10	.02
❑ 269	Quinn Early	.20	.07
❑ 270	Jim Everett	.10	.02
❑ 271	Michael Haynes	.20	.07
❑ 272	Wayne Martin	.10	.02
❑ 273	Derrell Mitchell RC	.10	.02
❑ 274	Lorenzo Neal	.10	.02
❑ 275	Jimmy Spencer	.10	.02
❑ 276	Winfred Tubbs	.10	.02
❑ 277	Renaldo Turnbull	.10	.02
❑ 278	Jeff Uhlenhake	.10	.02
❑ 279	Steve Atwater	.10	.02
❑ 280	Keith Burns RC	.10	.02
❑ 281	Butler By'Not'e RC	.20	.07
❑ 282	Jeff Campbell	.10	.02
❑ 283	Derrick Clark RC	.10	.02
❑ 284	Shane Dronett	.10	.02
❑ 285	Jason Elam	.20	.07
❑ 286	John Elway	2.00	.75
❑ 287	Jerry Evans	.10	.02
❑ 288	Karl Mecklenburg	.10	.02
❑ 289	Glyn Milburn	.10	.02
❑ 290	Anthony Miller	.20	.07
❑ 291	Tom Rouen	.10	.02
❑ 292	Leonard Russell	.10	.02
❑ 293	Shannon Sharpe	.20	.07
❑ 294	Steve Russ RC	.10	.02
❑ 295	Mel Agee	.10	.02
❑ 296	Lester Archambeau	.10	.02
❑ 297	Bert Emanuel	.30	.10
❑ 298	Jeff George	.20	.07
❑ 299	Craig Heyward	.20	.07
❑ 300	Bobby Hebert	.10	.02
❑ 301	D.J. Johnson	.10	.02
❑ 302	Mike Kenn	.10	.02
❑ 303	Terance Mathis	.20	.07
❑ 304	Clay Matthews	.20	.07
❑ 305	Erric Pegram	.20	.07
❑ 306	Andre Rison	.20	.07
❑ 307	Chuck Smith	.10	.02
❑ 308	Jessie Tuggle	.10	.02
❑ 309	Lorenzo Styles RC	.10	.02
❑ 310	Cornelius Bennett	.20	.07
❑ 311	Bill Brooks	.10	.02
❑ 312	Jeff Burris	.10	.02
❑ 313	Carwell Gardner	.10	.02
❑ 314	Kent Hull	.10	.02
❑ 315	Yonel Jourdain	.10	.02
❑ 316	Jim Kelly	.30	.10
❑ 317	Vince Marrow	.10	.02
❑ 318	Pete Metzelaars	.10	.02
❑ 319	Andre Reed	.20	.07
❑ 320	Kurt Schulz RC	.10	.02
❑ 321	Bruce Smith	.30	.10
❑ 322	Darryl Talley	.10	.02
❑ 323	Matt Darby	.10	.02
❑ 324	Justin Armour RC	.10	.02
❑ 325	Todd Collins RC	.20	.07
❑ 326	David Alexander DE	.10	.02
❑ 327	Eric Allen	.10	.02

	Card	Hi	Lo
❑	328 Fred Barnett	.20	.07
❑	329 Randall Cunningham	.30	.10
❑	330 William Fuller	.10	.02
❑	331 Charlie Garner	.30	.10
❑	332 Vaughn Hebron	.10	.02
❑	333 James Joseph	.10	.02
❑	334 Bill Romanowski	.10	.02
❑	335 Ken Rose	.10	.02
❑	336 Jeff Snyder	.10	.02
❑	337 William Thomas	.10	.02
❑	338 Herschel Walker	.20	.07
❑	339 Calvin Williams	.20	.07
❑	340 Dave Barr RC	.10	.02
❑	341 Chidi Ahanotu	.10	.02
❑	342 Barney Bussey	.10	.02
❑	343 Horace Copeland	.10	.02
❑	344 Trent Dilfer	.30	.10
❑	345 Craig Erickson	.10	.02
❑	346 Paul Gruber	.10	.02
❑	347 Courtney Hawkins	.10	.02
❑	348 Lonnie Marts	.10	.02
❑	349 Martin Mayhew	.10	.02
❑	350 Hardy Nickerson	.10	.02
❑	351 Errict Rhett	.20	.07
❑	352 Lamar Thomas	.10	.02
❑	353 Charles Wilson	.10	.02
❑	354 Vince Workman	.10	.02
❑	355 Derrick Brooks RC	1.50	.60
❑	356 Warren Sapp RC	1.50	.60
❑	357 Sam Adams	.10	.02
❑	358 Michael Bates	.10	.02
❑	359 Brian Blades	.20	.07
❑	360 Carlton Gray	.10	.02
❑	361 Bill Hitchcock	.10	.02
❑	362 Cortez Kennedy	.20	.07
❑	363 Rick Mirer	.20	.07
❑	364 Eugene Robinson	.10	.02
❑	365 Michael Sinclair	.10	.02
❑	366 Steve Smith	.10	.02
❑	367 Bob Spitulski	.10	.02
❑	368 Rick Tuten	.10	.02
❑	369 Chris Warren	.20	.07
❑	370 Terrence Warren	.10	.02
❑	371 Christian Fauria RC	.20	.07
❑	372 Joey Galloway RC	1.50	.60
❑	373 Boomer Esiason	.20	.07
❑	374 Aaron Glenn	.10	.02
❑	375 Victor Green RC	.10	.02
❑	376 Johnny Johnson	.10	.02
❑	377 Mo Lewis	.10	.02
❑	378 Ronnie Lott	.20	.07
❑	379 Nick Lowery	.10	.02
❑	380 Johnny Mitchell	.10	.02
❑	381 Rob Moore	.20	.07
❑	382 Adrian Murrell	.20	.07
❑	383 Anthony Prior	.10	.02
❑	384 Brian Washington	.10	.02
❑	385 Matt Willig RC	.10	.02
❑	386 Kyle Brady RC	.30	.10
❑	387 Flipper Anderson	.10	.02
❑	388 Johnny Bailey	.10	.02
❑	389 Jerome Bettis	.30	.10
❑	390 Isaac Bruce	.50	.20
❑	391 Shane Conlan	.10	.02
❑	392 Troy Drayton	.10	.02
❑	393 D'Marco Farr	.10	.02
❑	394 Jessie Hester	.10	.02
❑	395 Todd Kinchen	.10	.02
❑	396 Ron Middleton	.10	.02
❑	397 Chris Miller	.10	.02
❑	398 Marquez Pope	.10	.02
❑	399 Robert Young	.10	.02
❑	400 Tony Zendejas	.10	.02
❑	401 Kevin Carter RC	.30	.10
❑	402 Reggie Brooks	.20	.07
❑	403 Tom Carter	.10	.02
❑	404 Andre Collins	.10	.02
❑	405 Pat Eilers	.10	.02
❑	406 Henry Ellard	.20	.07
❑	407 Ricky Ervins	.10	.02
❑	408 Gus Frerotte	.20	.07
❑	409 Ken Harvey	.10	.02
❑	410 Jim Lachey	.10	.02
❑	411 Brian Mitchell	.10	.02
❑	412 Reggie Roby	.10	.02
❑	413 Heath Shuler	.20	.07
❑	414 Tyronne Stowe	.10	.02
❑	415 Tydus Winans	.10	.02
❑	416 Cory Raymer RC	.10	.02
❑	417 Michael Westbrook RC	.30	.10
❑	418 Jeff Blake RC	.75	.30
❑	419 Steve Broussard	.10	.02
❑	420 Dave Cadigan	.10	.02
❑	421 Jeff Cothran	.10	.02
❑	422 Derrick Fenner	.10	.02
❑	423 James Francis	.10	.02
❑	424 Lee Johnson	.10	.02
❑	425 Louis Oliver	.10	.02
❑	426 Carl Pickens	.20	.07
❑	427 Jeff Query	.10	.02
❑	428 Corey Sawyer	.10	.02
❑	429 Darnay Scott	.20	.07
❑	430 Dan Wilkinson	.20	.07
❑	431 Alfred Williams	.10	.02
❑	432 Ki-Jana Carter RC	.30	.10
❑	433 David Dunn RC	.10	.02
❑	434 John Walsh RC	.10	.02
❑	435 Gary Brown	.10	.02
❑	436 Pat Carter	.10	.02
❑	437 Ray Childress	.10	.02
❑	438 Ernest Givins	.10	.02
❑	439 Haywood Jeffires	.10	.02
❑	440 Lamar Lathon	.10	.02
❑	441 Bruce Matthews	.10	.02
❑	442 Marcus Robertson	.10	.02
❑	443 Eddie Robinson	.10	.02
❑	444 Malcolm Seabron RC	.10	.02
❑	445 Webster Slaughter	.10	.02
❑	446 Al Smith	.10	.02
❑	447 Billy Joe Tolliver	.10	.02
❑	448 Lorenzo White	.10	.02
❑	449 Steve McNair RC	3.00	1.25
❑	450 Rodney Thomas RC	.20	.07
❑	P1 Natrone Means Promo	1.00	.40
❑	P1J Natrone Means Promo	1.00	.40

1996 Pacific

	Card	Hi	Lo
❑	COMPLETE SET (450)	40.00	20.00
❑	1 Jeff Feagles	.10	.02
❑	2 Rob Moore	.20	.07
❑	3 Clyde Simmons	.10	.02
❑	4 Mike Buck	.10	.02
❑	5 Aeneas Williams	.10	.02
❑	6 Simeon Rice RC	1.00	.40
❑	7 Garrison Hearst	.20	.07
❑	8 Eric Swann	.10	.02
❑	9 Dave Krieg	.10	.02
❑	10 Leeland McElroy RC	.20	.07
❑	11 Oscar McBride	.10	.02
❑	12 Frank Sanders	.20	.07
❑	13 Larry Centers	.20	.07
❑	14 Seth Joyner	.10	.02
❑	15 Stevie Anderson	.10	.02
❑	16 Craig Heyward	.10	.02
❑	17 Devin Bush	.10	.02
❑	18 Eric Metcalf	.10	.02
❑	19 Jeff George	.20	.07
❑	20 Richard Huntley RC	.20	.07
❑	21 Jamal Anderson RC	.50	.20
❑	22 Bert Emanuel	.20	.07
❑	23 Terance Mathis	.10	.02
❑	24 Roman Fortin	.10	.02
❑	25 Jessie Tuggle	.10	.02
❑	26 Morten Andersen	.10	.02
❑	27 Chris Doleman	.10	.02
❑	28 D.J. Johnson	.10	.02
❑	29 Kevin Ross	.10	.02
❑	30 Michael Jackson	.20	.07
❑	31 Eric Zeier	.10	.02
❑	32 Jonathan Ogden RC	.40	.15
❑	33 Eric Turner	.10	.02
❑	34 Andre Rison	.20	.07
❑	35 Lorenzo White	.10	.02
❑	36 Earnest Byner	.10	.02
❑	37 Derrick Alexander WR	.20	.07
❑	38 Brian Kinchen	.10	.02
❑	39 Anthony Pleasant	.10	.02
❑	40 Vinny Testaverde	.20	.07
❑	41 Pepper Johnson	.10	.02
❑	42 Frank Hartley	.10	.02
❑	43 Craig Powell	.10	.02
❑	44 Leroy Hoard	.10	.02
❑	45 Kent Hull	.10	.02
❑	46 Bryce Paup	.10	.02
❑	47 Andre Reed	.20	.07
❑	48 Darick Holmes	.10	.02
❑	49 Russell Copeland	.10	.02
❑	50 Jerry Ostroski	.10	.02
❑	51 Chris Green	.10	.02
❑	52 Eric Moulds RC	1.25	.50
❑	53 Justin Armour	.10	.02
❑	54 Jim Kelly	.40	.15
❑	55 Cornelius Bennett	.10	.02
❑	56 Steve Tasker	.10	.02
❑	57 Thurman Thomas	.40	.15
❑	58 Bruce Smith	.20	.07
❑	59 Todd Collins	.20	.07
❑	60 Shawn King	.10	.02
❑	61 Don Beebe	.10	.02
❑	62 John Kasay	.10	.02
❑	63 Tim McKyer	.10	.02
❑	64 Darion Conner	.10	.02
❑	65 Pete Metzelaars	.10	.02
❑	66 Derrick Moore	.10	.02
❑	67 Blake Brockermeyer	.10	.02
❑	68 Tim Biakabutuka RC	.40	.15
❑	69 Sam Mills	.10	.02
❑	70 Vince Workman	.10	.02
❑	71 Kerry Collins	.40	.15
❑	72 Carlton Bailey	.10	.02
❑	73 Mark Carrier WR	.10	.02
❑	74 Donnell Woolford	.10	.02
❑	75 Walt Harris RC	.10	.02
❑	76 John Thierry	.10	.02
❑	77 Al Fontenot RC	.10	.02
❑	78 Lewis Tillman	.10	.02
❑	79 Curtis Conway	.40	.15
❑	80 Chris Zorich	.10	.02
❑	81 Mark Carrier DB	.10	.02
❑	82 Bobby Engram RC	.40	.15
❑	83 Alonzo Spellman	.10	.02
❑	84 Rashaan Salaam	.20	.07
❑	85 Michael Timpson	.10	.02
❑	86 Nate Lewis	.10	.02
❑	87 James Williams T	.10	.02
❑	88 Jeff Graham	.10	.02
❑	89 Erik Kramer	.10	.02
❑	90 Willie Anderson	.10	.02

❑ 91 Tony McGee	.10	.02
❑ 92 Marco Battaglia	.10	.02
❑ 93 Dan Wilkinson	.10	.02
❑ 94 John Walsh	.10	.02
❑ 95 Eric Bieniemy	.10	.02
❑ 96 Ricardo McDonald	.10	.02
❑ 97 Carl Pickens	.20	.07
❑ 98 Kevin Sargent	.10	.02
❑ 99 David Dunn	.10	.02
❑ 100 Jeff Blake	.40	.15
❑ 101 Harold Green	.10	.02
❑ 102 James Francis	.10	.02
❑ 103 John Copeland	.10	.02
❑ 104 Darnay Scott	.20	.07
❑ 105 Darren Woodson	.20	.07
❑ 106 Jay Novacek	.10	.02
❑ 107 Charles Haley	.20	.07
❑ 108 Mark Tuinei	.10	.02
❑ 109 Michael Irvin	.40	.15
❑ 110 Troy Aikman	1.00	.40
❑ 111 Chris Boniol	.10	.02
❑ 112 Sherman Williams	.10	.02
❑ 113 Deion Sanders	.60	.25
❑ 114 Emmitt Smith	1.50	.60
❑ 115 Eric Bjornson	.10	.02
❑ 116 Nate Newton	.10	.02
❑ 117 Larry Allen	.10	.02
❑ 118 Kevin Williams	.10	.02
❑ 119 Leon Lett	.10	.02
❑ 120 John Mobley	.10	.02
❑ 121 Anthony Miller	.20	.07
❑ 122 Brian Habib	.10	.02
❑ 123 Aaron Craver	.10	.02
❑ 124 Glyn Milburn	.10	.02
❑ 125 Shannon Sharpe	.20	.07
❑ 126 Steve Atwater	.10	.02
❑ 127 Jason Elam	.20	.07
❑ 128 John Elway	2.00	.75
❑ 129 Reggie Rivers	.10	.02
❑ 130 Mike Pritchard	.10	.02
❑ 131 Vance Johnson	.10	.02
❑ 132 Terrell Davis	.75	.30
❑ 133 Tyrone Braxton	.10	.02
❑ 134 Ed McCaffrey	.20	.07
❑ 135 Brett Perriman	.10	.02
❑ 136 Chris Spielman	.10	.02
❑ 137 Luther Elliss	.10	.02
❑ 138 Johnnie Morton	.20	.07
❑ 139 Zefross Moss	.10	.02
❑ 140 Barry Sanders	1.50	.60
❑ 141 Lomas Brown	.10	.02
❑ 142 Cory Schlesinger	.10	.02
❑ 143 Jason Hanson	.10	.02
❑ 144 Kevin Glover	.10	.02
❑ 145 Ron Rivers RC	.20	.07
❑ 146 Aubrey Matthews	.10	.02
❑ 147 Reggie Brown LB RC	.10	.02
❑ 148 Herman Moore	.20	.07
❑ 149 Scott Mitchell	.20	.07
❑ 150 Brett Favre	2.00	.75
❑ 151 Sean Jones	.10	.02
❑ 152 LeRoy Butler	.10	.02
❑ 153 Mark Chmura	.20	.07
❑ 154 Derrick Mayes RC	.40	.15
❑ 155 Mark Ingram	.10	.02
❑ 156 Antonio Freeman	.40	.15
❑ 157 Chris Darkins RC	.10	.02
❑ 158 Robert Brooks	.40	.15
❑ 159 William Henderson	.40	.15
❑ 160 George Koonce	.10	.02
❑ 161 Craig Newsome	.10	.02
❑ 162 Darius Holland	.10	.02
❑ 163 George Teague	.10	.02
❑ 164 Edgar Bennett	.20	.07
❑ 165 Reggie White	.40	.15
❑ 166 Micheal Barrow	.10	.02
❑ 167 Mel Gray	.10	.02
❑ 168 Anthony Dorsett	.10	.02
❑ 169 Roderick Lewis	.10	.02
❑ 170 Henry Ford	.10	.02
❑ 171 Mark Stepnoski	.10	.02
❑ 172 Chris Sanders	.20	.07
❑ 173 Anthony Cook	.10	.02
❑ 174 Eddie Robinson	.10	.02
❑ 175 Steve McNair	.75	.30
❑ 176 Haywood Jeffires	.10	.02
❑ 177 Eddie George RC	1.25	.50
❑ 178 Marion Butts	.10	.02
❑ 179 Malcolm Seabron	.10	.02
❑ 180 Rodney Thomas	.10	.02
❑ 181 Ken Dilger	.20	.07
❑ 182 Zack Crockett	.10	.02
❑ 183 Tony Bennett	.10	.02
❑ 184 Quentin Coryatt	.10	.02
❑ 185 Marshall Faulk	.50	.20
❑ 186 Sean Dawkins	.10	.02
❑ 187 Jim Harbaugh	.20	.07
❑ 188 Eugene Daniel	.10	.02
❑ 189 Roosevelt Potts	.10	.02
❑ 190 Lamont Warren	.10	.02
❑ 191 Will Wolford	.10	.02
❑ 192 Tony Siragusa	.10	.02
❑ 193 Aaron Bailey	.10	.02
❑ 194 Trev Alberts	.10	.02
❑ 195 Kevin Hardy	.20	.07
❑ 196 Greg Spann	.10	.02
❑ 197 Steve Beuerlein	.20	.07
❑ 198 Steve Taneyhill	.10	.02
❑ 199 Vaughn Dunbar	.10	.02
❑ 200 Mark Brunell	.60	.25
❑ 201 Bernard Carter	.10	.02
❑ 202 James O. Stewart	.20	.07
❑ 203 Tony Boselli	.10	.02
❑ 204 Chris Doering	.10	.02
❑ 205 Willie Jackson	.20	.07
❑ 206 Tony Brackens RC	.40	.15
❑ 207 Ernest Givins	.10	.02
❑ 208 Le'Shai Maston	.10	.02
❑ 209 Pete Mitchell	.20	.07
❑ 210 Desmond Howard	.20	.07
❑ 211 Vinnie Clark	.10	.02
❑ 212 Jeff Lageman	.10	.02
❑ 213 Derrick Walker	.10	.02
❑ 214 Dan Saleaumua	.10	.02
❑ 215 Derrick Thomas	.40	.15
❑ 216 Neil Smith	.20	.07
❑ 217 Willie Davis	.10	.02
❑ 218 Mark Collins	.10	.02
❑ 219 Lake Dawson	.10	.02
❑ 220 Greg Hill	.20	.07
❑ 221 Anthony Davis	.10	.02
❑ 222 Kimble Anders	.20	.07
❑ 223 Webster Slaughter	.10	.02
❑ 224 Tamarick Vanover	.20	.07
❑ 225 Marcus Allen	.40	.15
❑ 226 Steve Bono	.10	.02
❑ 227 Will Shields	.10	.02
❑ 228 Karim Abdul-Jabbar RC	.40	.15
❑ 229 Tim Bowens	.10	.02
❑ 230 Keith Sims	.10	.02
❑ 231 Terry Kirby	.20	.07
❑ 232 Gene Atkins	.10	.02
❑ 233 Dan Marino	2.00	.75
❑ 234 Richmond Webb	.10	.02
❑ 235 Gary Clark	.10	.02
❑ 236 O.J. McDuffie	.20	.07
❑ 237 Marco Coleman	.10	.02
❑ 238 Bernie Parmalee	.10	.02
❑ 239 Randal Hill	.10	.02
❑ 240 Bryan Cox	.10	.02
❑ 241 Irving Fryar	.20	.07
❑ 242 Derrick Alexander DE	.10	.02
❑ 243 Qadry Ismail	.20	.07
❑ 244 Warren Moon	.20	.07
❑ 245 Cris Carter	.40	.15
❑ 246 Chad May	.10	.02
❑ 247 Robert Smith	.20	.07
❑ 248 Fuad Reveiz	.10	.02
❑ 249 Orlando Thomas	.10	.02
❑ 250 Chris Hinton	.10	.02
❑ 251 Jack Del Rio	.10	.02
❑ 252 Moe Williams RB RC	1.00	.40
❑ 253 Roy Barker	.10	.02
❑ 254 Jake Reed	.20	.07
❑ 255 Adrian Cooper	.10	.02
❑ 256 Curtis Martin	.75	.30
❑ 257 Ben Coates	.20	.07
❑ 258 Drew Bledsoe	.60	.25
❑ 259 Maurice Hurst	.10	.02
❑ 260 Troy Brown	.40	.15
❑ 261 Bruce Armstrong	.10	.02
❑ 262 Myron Guyton	.10	.02
❑ 263 Dave Meggett	.10	.02
❑ 264 Terry Glenn RC	1.00	.40
❑ 265 Chris Slade	.10	.02
❑ 266 Vincent Brisby	.10	.02
❑ 267 Willie McGinest	.10	.02
❑ 268 Vincent Brown	.10	.02
❑ 269 Will Moore	.10	.02
❑ 270 Jay Barker	.10	.02
❑ 271 Ray Zellars	.10	.02
❑ 272 Derek Brown RBK	.10	.02
❑ 273 William Roaf	.10	.02
❑ 274 Quinn Early	.10	.02
❑ 275 Michael Haynes	.10	.02
❑ 276 Rufus Porter	.10	.02
❑ 277 Renaldo Turnbull	.10	.02
❑ 278 Wayne Martin	.10	.02
❑ 279 Tyrone Hughes	.10	.02
❑ 280 Irv Smith	.10	.02
❑ 281 Eric Allen	.10	.02
❑ 282 Mark Fields	.10	.02
❑ 283 Mario Bates	.20	.07
❑ 284 Jim Everett	.10	.02
❑ 285 Vince Buck	.10	.02
❑ 286 Alex Molden RC	.10	.02
❑ 287 Tyrone Wheatley	.20	.07
❑ 288 Chris Calloway	.10	.02
❑ 289 Jessie Armstead	.10	.02
❑ 290 Arthur Marshall	.10	.02
❑ 291 Aaron Pierce	.10	.02
❑ 292 Dave Brown	.10	.02
❑ 293 Rodney Hampton	.20	.07
❑ 294 Jumbo Elliott	.10	.02
❑ 295 Mike Sherrard	.10	.02
❑ 296 Howard Cross	.10	.02
❑ 297 Michael Brooks	.10	.02
❑ 298 Herschel Walker	.20	.07
❑ 299 Danny Kanell RC	.40	.15
❑ 300 Keith Elias	.10	.02
❑ 301 Bobby Houston	.10	.02
❑ 302 Dexter Carter	.10	.02
❑ 303 Tony Casillas	.10	.02
❑ 304 Kyle Brady	.10	.02
❑ 305 Glenn Foley	.20	.07
❑ 306 Ronald Moore	.10	.02
❑ 307 Ryan Yarborough	.10	.02
❑ 308 Aaron Glenn	.10	.02
❑ 309 Adrian Murrell	.20	.07
❑ 310 Boomer Esiason	.20	.07
❑ 311 Kyle Clifton	.10	.02
❑ 312 Wayne Chrebet	.60	.25
❑ 313 Erik Howard	.10	.02
❑ 314 Keyshawn Johnson RC	1.00	.40
❑ 315 Marvin Washington	.10	.02
❑ 316 Johnny Mitchell	.10	.02
❑ 317 Alex Van Dyke RC	.20	.07
❑ 318 Billy Joe Hobert	.20	.07
❑ 319 Andrew Glover	.10	.02
❑ 320 Vince Evans	.10	.02
❑ 321 Chester McGlockton	.10	.02
❑ 322 Pat Swilling	.10	.02
❑ 323 Rocket Ismail	.10	.02
❑ 324 Eddie Anderson	.10	.02

- ❑ 325 Rickey Dudley RC .40 .15
- ❑ 326 Steve Wisniewski .10 .02
- ❑ 327 Harvey Williams .10 .02
- ❑ 328 Napoleon Kaufman .40 .15
- ❑ 329 Tim Brown .40 .15
- ❑ 330 Jeff Hostetler .10 .02
- ❑ 331 Anthony Smith .10 .02
- ❑ 332 Terry McDaniel .10 .02
- ❑ 333 Charlie Garner .20 .07
- ❑ 334 Ricky Watters .20 .07
- ❑ 335 Brian Dawkins RC 1.25 .50
- ❑ 336 Randall Cunningham .40 .15
- ❑ 337 Gary Anderson .10 .02
- ❑ 338 Calvin Williams .10 .02
- ❑ 339 Chris T. Jones .20 .07
- ❑ 340 Bobby Hoying RC .40 .15
- ❑ 341 William Fuller .10 .02
- ❑ 342 William Thomas .10 .02
- ❑ 343 Mike Mamula .10 .02
- ❑ 344 Fred Barnett .10 .02
- ❑ 345 Rodney Peete .10 .02
- ❑ 346 Mark McMillian .10 .02
- ❑ 347 Bobby Taylor .10 .02
- ❑ 348 Yancey Thigpen .20 .07
- ❑ 349 Neil O'Donnell .20 .07
- ❑ 350 Rod Woodson .20 .07
- ❑ 351 Kordell Stewart .40 .15
- ❑ 352 Dermontti Dawson .10 .02
- ❑ 353 Norm Johnson .10 .02
- ❑ 354 Ernie Mills .10 .02
- ❑ 355 Byron Bam Morris .10 .02
- ❑ 356 Mark Bruener .10 .02
- ❑ 357 Kevin Greene .20 .07
- ❑ 358 Greg Lloyd .20 .07
- ❑ 359 Andre Hastings .10 .02
- ❑ 360 Erric Pegram .10 .02
- ❑ 361 Carnell Lake .10 .02
- ❑ 362 Dwayne Harper .10 .02
- ❑ 363 Ronnie Harmon .10 .02
- ❑ 364 Leslie O'Neal .10 .02
- ❑ 365 John Carney .10 .02
- ❑ 366 Stan Humphries .20 .07
- ❑ 367 Brian Roche RC .10 .02
- ❑ 368 Terrell Fletcher .10 .02
- ❑ 369 Shaun Gayle .10 .02
- ❑ 370 Alfred Pupunu .10 .02
- ❑ 371 Shawn Jefferson .10 .02
- ❑ 372 Junior Seau .40 .15
- ❑ 373 Mark Seay .10 .02
- ❑ 374 Aaron Hayden .10 .02
- ❑ 375 Tony Martin .20 .07
- ❑ 376 Steve Young .75 .30
- ❑ 377 J.J. Stokes .40 .15
- ❑ 378 Jerry Rice 1.00 .40
- ❑ 379 Derek Loville .10 .02
- ❑ 380 Lee Woodall .10 .02
- ❑ 381 Terrell Owens RC 2.50 1.00
- ❑ 382 Elvis Grbac .20 .07
- ❑ 383 Ricky Ervins .10 .02
- ❑ 384 Eric Davis .10 .02
- ❑ 385 Dana Stubblefield .20 .07
- ❑ 386 Gary Plummer .10 .02
- ❑ 387 Tim McDonald .10 .02
- ❑ 388 William Floyd .20 .07
- ❑ 389 Ken Norton Jr. .10 .02
- ❑ 390 Merton Hanks .10 .02
- ❑ 391 Bart Oates .10 .02
- ❑ 392 Brent Jones .10 .02
- ❑ 393 Steve Broussard .10 .02
- ❑ 394 Robert Blackmon .10 .02
- ❑ 395 Rick Tuten .10 .02
- ❑ 396 Pete Kendall .10 .02
- ❑ 397 John Friesz .10 .02
- ❑ 398 Terry Wooden .10 .02
- ❑ 399 Rick Mirer .20 .07
- ❑ 400 Chris Warren .20 .07
- ❑ 401 Joey Galloway .40 .15
- ❑ 402 Howard Ballard .10 .02
- ❑ 403 Jason Kyle .10 .02
- ❑ 404 Kevin Mawae .10 .02
- ❑ 405 Mack Strong .40 .15
- ❑ 406 Reggie Brown RBK RC .10 .02
- ❑ 407 Cortez Kennedy .10 .02
- ❑ 408 Sean Gilbert .10 .02
- ❑ 409 J.T. Thomas .10 .02
- ❑ 410 Shane Conlan .10 .02
- ❑ 411 Johnny Bailey .10 .02
- ❑ 412 Mark Rypien .10 .02
- ❑ 413 Leonard Russell .10 .02
- ❑ 414 Troy Drayton .10 .02
- ❑ 415 Jerome Bettis .40 .15
- ❑ 416 Jessie Hester .10 .02
- ❑ 417 Isaac Bruce .40 .15
- ❑ 418 Roman Phifer .10 .02
- ❑ 419 Todd Kinchen .10 .02
- ❑ 420 Alexander Wright .10 .02
- ❑ 421 Marcus Jones RC .10 .02
- ❑ 422 Horace Copeland .10 .02
- ❑ 423 Eric Curry .10 .02
- ❑ 424 Courtney Hawkins .10 .02
- ❑ 425 Alvin Harper .10 .02
- ❑ 426 Derrick Brooks .40 .15
- ❑ 427 Errict Rhett .20 .07
- ❑ 428 Trent Dilfer .40 .15
- ❑ 429 Hardy Nickerson .10 .02
- ❑ 430 Brad Culpepper .10 .02
- ❑ 431 Warren Sapp .10 .02
- ❑ 432 Reggie Roby .10 .02
- ❑ 433 Santana Dotson .10 .02
- ❑ 434 Jerry Ellison .10 .02
- ❑ 435 Lawrence Dawsey .10 .02
- ❑ 436 Heath Shuler .20 .07
- ❑ 437 Stanley Richard .20 .07
- ❑ 438 Rod Stephens .10 .02
- ❑ 439 Stephen Davis RC 1.50 .60
- ❑ 440 Terry Allen .20 .07
- ❑ 441 Michael Westbrook .40 .15
- ❑ 442 Ken Harvey .10 .02
- ❑ 443 Coleman Bell .10 .02
- ❑ 444 Marvcus Patton .10 .02
- ❑ 445 Gus Frerotte .20 .07
- ❑ 446 Leslie Shepherd .10 .02
- ❑ 447 Tom Carter .10 .02
- ❑ 448 Brian Mitchell .10 .02
- ❑ 449 Darrell Green .10 .02
- ❑ 450A Tony Woods .10 .02
- ❑ 450B Chris Warren Promo .50 .20
- ❑ CW1 Chris Warren Promo 1.00 .40

1997 Pacific

- ❑ COMPLETE SET (450) 30.00 15.00
- ❑ 1 Lomas Brown .20 .07
- ❑ 2 Pat Carter .20 .07
- ❑ 3 Larry Centers .30 .10
- ❑ 4 Matt Darby .20 .07
- ❑ 5 Marcus Dowdell .20 .07
- ❑ 6 Aaron Graham .20 .07
- ❑ 7 Kent Graham .20 .07
- ❑ 8 LeShon Johnson .20 .07
- ❑ 9 Seth Joyner .20 .07
- ❑ 10 Leeland McElroy .20 .07
- ❑ 11 Rob Moore .30 .10
- ❑ 12 Simeon Rice .30 .10
- ❑ 13 Eric Swann .20 .07
- ❑ 14 Aeneas Williams .20 .07
- ❑ 15 Morten Andersen .20 .07
- ❑ 16 Jamal Anderson .50 .20
- ❑ 17 Lester Archambeau .20 .07
- ❑ 18 Cornelius Bennett .20 .07
- ❑ 19 J.J. Birden .20 .07
- ❑ 20 Antone Davis .20 .07
- ❑ 21 Bert Emanuel .30 .10
- ❑ 22 Travis Hall RC .20 .07
- ❑ 23 Bobby Hebert .20 .07
- ❑ 24 Craig Heyward .20 .07
- ❑ 25 Terance Mathis .30 .10
- ❑ 26 Tim McKyer .20 .07
- ❑ 27 Eric Metcalf .30 .10
- ❑ 28 Jessie Tuggle .20 .07
- ❑ 29 Derrick Alexander WR .30 .10
- ❑ 30 Orlando Brown .20 .07
- ❑ 31 Rob Burnett .20 .07
- ❑ 32 Earnest Byner .20 .07
- ❑ 33 Ray Ethridge .20 .07
- ❑ 34 Steve Everitt .20 .07
- ❑ 35 Carwell Gardner .20 .07
- ❑ 36 Michael Jackson .30 .10
- ❑ 37 Jermaine Lewis .50 .20
- ❑ 38 Stevon Moore .20 .07
- ❑ 39 Byron Bam Morris .20 .07
- ❑ 40 Jonathan Ogden .20 .07
- ❑ 41 Vinny Testaverde .30 .10
- ❑ 42 Todd Collins .20 .07
- ❑ 43 Russell Copeland .20 .07
- ❑ 44 Quinn Early .20 .07
- ❑ 45 John Fina .20 .07
- ❑ 46 Phil Hansen .20 .07
- ❑ 47 Eric Moulds .50 .20
- ❑ 48 Bryce Paup .20 .07
- ❑ 49 Andre Reed .30 .10
- ❑ 50 Kurt Schulz .20 .07
- ❑ 51 Bruce Smith .30 .10
- ❑ 52 Chris Spielman .20 .07
- ❑ 53 Steve Tasker .20 .07
- ❑ 54 Thurman Thomas .50 .20
- ❑ 55 Carlton Bailey .20 .07
- ❑ 56 Michael Bates .20 .07
- ❑ 57 Blake Brockermeyer .20 .07
- ❑ 58 Mark Carrier WR .20 .07
- ❑ 59 Kerry Collins .50 .20
- ❑ 60 Eric Davis .20 .07
- ❑ 61 Kevin Greene .30 .10
- ❑ 62 Rocket Ismail .30 .10
- ❑ 63 Anthony Johnson .20 .07
- ❑ 64 Shawn King .20 .07
- ❑ 65 Greg Kragen .20 .07
- ❑ 66 Sam Mills .20 .07
- ❑ 67 Tyrone Poole .20 .07
- ❑ 68 Wesley Walls .30 .10
- ❑ 69 Mark Carrier DB .20 .07
- ❑ 70 Curtis Conway .30 .10
- ❑ 71 Bobby Engram .30 .10
- ❑ 72 Jim Flanigan .20 .07
- ❑ 73 Al Fontenot .20 .07
- ❑ 74 Raymont Harris .20 .07
- ❑ 75 Walt Harris .20 .07
- ❑ 76 Andy Heck .20 .07
- ❑ 77 Dave Krieg .20 .07
- ❑ 78 Rashaan Salaam .20 .07
- ❑ 79 Vinson Smith .20 .07
- ❑ 80 Alonzo Spellman .20 .07
- ❑ 81 Michael Timpson .20 .07
- ❑ 82 James Williams .20 .07
- ❑ 83 Ashley Ambrose .20 .07
- ❑ 84 Eric Bieniemy .20 .07
- ❑ 85 Jeff Blake .30 .10
- ❑ 86 Ki-Jana Carter .20 .07
- ❑ 87 John Copeland .20 .07

❑	88	David Dunn	.20	.07
❑	89	Jeff Hill	.20	.07
❑	90	Ricardo McDonald	.20	.07
❑	91	Tony McGee	.20	.07
❑	92	Greg Myers	.20	.07
❑	93	Carl Pickens	.30	.10
❑	94	Corey Sawyer	.20	.07
❑	95	Darnay Scott	.30	.10
❑	96	Dan Wilkinson	.20	.07
❑	97	Troy Aikman	1.00	.40
❑	98	Larry Allen	.20	.07
❑	99	Eric Bjornson	.20	.07
❑	100	Ray Donaldson	.20	.07
❑	101	Michael Irvin	.50	.20
❑	102	Daryl Johnston	.30	.10
❑	103	Nate Newton	.20	.07
❑	104	Deion Sanders	.50	.20
❑	105	Jim Schwantz RC	.20	.07
❑	106	Emmitt Smith	1.50	.60
❑	107	Broderick Thomas	.20	.07
❑	108	Tony Tolbert	.20	.07
❑	109	Erik Williams	.20	.07
❑	110	Sherman Williams	.20	.07
❑	111	Darren Woodson	.20	.07
❑	112	Steve Atwater	.20	.07
❑	113	Aaron Craver	.20	.07
❑	114	Ray Crockett	.20	.07
❑	115	Terrell Davis	.60	.25
❑	116	Jason Elam	.30	.10
❑	117	John Elway	2.00	.75
❑	118	Todd Kinchen	.20	.07
❑	119	Ed McCaffrey	.30	.10
❑	120	Anthony Miller	.20	.07
❑	121	John Mobley	.20	.07
❑	122	Michael Dean Perry	.20	.07
❑	123	Reggie Rivers	.20	.07
❑	124	Shannon Sharpe	.30	.10
❑	125	Alfred Williams	.20	.07
❑	126	Reggie Brown LB	.30	.10
❑	127	Luther Elliss	.20	.07
❑	128	Kevin Glover	.20	.07
❑	129	Jason Hanson	.20	.07
❑	130	Pepper Johnson	.20	.07
❑	131	Glyn Milburn	.20	.07
❑	132	Scott Mitchell	.30	.10
❑	133	Herman Moore	.30	.10
❑	134	Johnnie Morton	.30	.10
❑	135	Brett Perriman	.20	.07
❑	136	Robert Porcher	.20	.07
❑	137	Ron Rivers	.20	.07
❑	138	Barry Sanders	1.50	.60
❑	139	Henry Thomas	.20	.07
❑	140	Don Beebe	.20	.07
❑	141	Edgar Bennett	.30	.10
❑	142	Robert Brooks	.30	.10
❑	143	LeRoy Butler	.20	.07
❑	144	Mark Chmura	.30	.10
❑	145	Brett Favre	2.00	.75
❑	146	Antonio Freeman	.50	.20
❑	147	Chris Jacke	.20	.07
❑	148	Travis Jervey	.30	.10
❑	149	Sean Jones	.20	.07
❑	150	Dorsey Levens	.50	.20
❑	151	John Michels	.20	.07
❑	152	Craig Newsome	.20	.07
❑	153	Eugene Robinson	.20	.07
❑	154	Reggie White	.50	.20
❑	155	Micheal Barrow	.20	.07
❑	156	Blaine Bishop	.20	.07
❑	157	Chris Chandler	.30	.10
❑	158	Anthony Cook	.20	.07
❑	159	Malcolm Floyd	.20	.07
❑	160	Eddie George	.50	.20
❑	161	Roderick Lewis	.20	.07
❑	162	Steve McNair	.60	.25
❑	163	John Henry Mills RC	.20	.07
❑	164	Derek Russell	.20	.07
❑	165	Chris Sanders	.20	.07
❑	166	Mark Stepnoski	.20	.07
❑	167	Frank Wycheck	.20	.07
❑	168	Robert Young	.20	.07
❑	169	Trev Alberts	.20	.07
❑	170	Aaron Bailey	.20	.07
❑	171	Tony Bennett	.20	.07
❑	172	Ray Buchanan	.20	.07
❑	173	Quentin Coryatt	.20	.07
❑	174	Eugene Daniel	.20	.07
❑	175	Sean Dawkins	.20	.07
❑	176	Ken Dilger	.20	.07
❑	177	Marshall Faulk	.60	.25
❑	178	Jim Harbaugh	.30	.10
❑	179	Marvin Harrison	.50	.20
❑	180	Paul Justin	.20	.07
❑	181	Lamont Warren	.20	.07
❑	182	Bernard Whittington	.20	.07
❑	183	Tony Boselli	.20	.07
❑	184	Tony Brackens	.20	.07
❑	185	Mark Brunell	.60	.25
❑	186	Brian DeMarco	.20	.07
❑	187	Rich Griffith	.20	.07
❑	188	Kevin Hardy	.20	.07
❑	189	Willie Jackson	.20	.07
❑	190	Jeff Lageman	.20	.07
❑	191	Keenan McCardell	.30	.10
❑	192	Natrone Means	.30	.10
❑	193	Pete Mitchell	.20	.07
❑	194	Joel Smeenge	.20	.07
❑	195	Jimmy Smith	.30	.10
❑	196	James O.Stewart	.30	.10
❑	197	Marcus Allen	.50	.20
❑	198	John Alt	.20	.07
❑	199	Kimble Anders	.30	.10
❑	200	Steve Bono	.30	.10
❑	201	Vaughn Booker	.20	.07
❑	202	Dale Carter	.20	.07
❑	203	Mark Collins	.20	.07
❑	204	Greg Hill	.20	.07
❑	205	Joe Horn	.50	.20
❑	206	Dan Saleaumua	.20	.07
❑	207	Will Shields	.20	.07
❑	208	Neil Smith	.30	.10
❑	209	Derrick Thomas	.50	.20
❑	210	Tamarick Vanover	.30	.10
❑	211	Karim Abdul-Jabbar	.30	.10
❑	212	Fred Barnett	.20	.07
❑	213	Tim Bowens	.20	.07
❑	214	Kirby Dar Dar RC	.30	.10
❑	215	Troy Drayton	.20	.07
❑	216	Craig Erickson	.20	.07
❑	217	Daryl Gardener	.20	.07
❑	218	Randal Hill	.20	.07
❑	219	Dan Marino	2.00	.75
❑	220	O.J. McDuffie	.30	.10
❑	221	Bernie Parmalee	.20	.07
❑	222	Stanley Pritchett	.20	.07
❑	223	Daniel Stubbs	.20	.07
❑	224	Zach Thomas	.50	.20
❑	225	Derrick Alexander DE	.20	.07
❑	226	Cris Carter	.50	.20
❑	227	Jeff Christy	.20	.07
❑	228	Qadry Ismail	.30	.10
❑	229	Brad Johnson	.50	.20
❑	230	Andrew Jordan	.20	.07
❑	231	Randall McDaniel	.20	.07
❑	232	David Palmer	.20	.07
❑	233	John Randle	.30	.10
❑	234	Jake Reed	.30	.10
❑	235	Scott Sisson	.20	.07
❑	236	Korey Stringer	.20	.07
❑	237	Darryl Talley	.20	.07
❑	238	Orlando Thomas	.20	.07
❑	239	Bruce Armstrong	.20	.07
❑	240	Drew Bledsoe	.60	.25
❑	241	Willie Clay	.20	.07
❑	242	Ben Coates	.30	.10
❑	243	Ferric Collons RC	.20	.07
❑	244	Terry Glenn	.50	.20
❑	245	Jerome Henderson	.20	.07
❑	246	Shawn Jefferson	.20	.07
❑	247	Dietrich Jells	.20	.07
❑	248	Ty Law	.30	.10
❑	249	Curtis Martin	.60	.25
❑	250	Willie McGinest	.20	.07
❑	251	Dave Meggett	.20	.07
❑	252	Lawyer Milloy	.30	.10
❑	253	Chris Slade	.20	.07
❑	254	Je'rod Cherry	.20	.07
❑	255	Jim Everett	.20	.07
❑	256	Mark Fields	.20	.07
❑	257	Michael Haynes	.20	.07
❑	258	Tyrone Hughes	.20	.07
❑	259	Haywood Jeffires	.20	.07
❑	260	Wayne Martin	.20	.07
❑	261	Mark McMillian	.20	.07
❑	262	Rufus Porter	.20	.07
❑	263	William Roaf	.20	.07
❑	264	Torrance Small	.20	.07
❑	265	Renaldo Turnbull	.20	.07
❑	266	Ray Zellars	.20	.07
❑	267	Jessie Armstead	.20	.07
❑	268	Chad Bratzke	.20	.07
❑	269	Dave Brown	.20	.07
❑	270	Chris Calloway	.20	.07
❑	271	Howard Cross	.20	.07
❑	272	Lawrence Dawsey	.20	.07
❑	273	Rodney Hampton	.30	.10
❑	274	Danny Kanell	.20	.07
❑	275	Arthur Marshall	.20	.07
❑	276	Aaron Pierce	.20	.07
❑	277	Phillippi Sparks	.20	.07
❑	278	Amani Toomer	.30	.10
❑	279	Charles Way	.20	.07
❑	280	Richie Anderson	.30	.10
❑	281	Fred Baxter	.20	.07
❑	282	Wayne Chrebet	.50	.20
❑	283	Kyle Clifton	.20	.07
❑	284	Jumbo Elliott	.20	.07
❑	285	Aaron Glenn	.20	.07
❑	286	Jeff Graham	.20	.07
❑	287	Bobby Hamilton RC	.20	.07
❑	288	Keyshawn Johnson	.50	.20
❑	289	Adrian Murrell	.30	.10
❑	290	Neil O'Donnell	.30	.10
❑	291	Webster Slaughter	.20	.07
❑	292	Alex Van Dyke	.20	.07
❑	293	Marvin Washington	.20	.07
❑	294	Joe Aska	.20	.07
❑	295	Jerry Ball	.20	.07
❑	296	Tim Brown	.50	.20
❑	297	Rickey Dudley	.30	.10
❑	298	Pat Harlow	.20	.07
❑	299	Nolan Harrison	.20	.07
❑	300	Billy Joe Hobert	.30	.10
❑	301	James Jett	.30	.10
❑	302	Napoleon Kaufman	.50	.20
❑	303	Lincoln Kennedy	.20	.07
❑	304	Albert Lewis	.20	.07
❑	305	Chester McGlockton	.20	.07
❑	306	Pat Swilling	.20	.07
❑	307	Steve Wisniewski	.20	.07
❑	308	Darion Conner	.20	.07
❑	309	Ty Detmer	.30	.10
❑	310	Jason Dunn	.20	.07
❑	311	Irving Fryar	.30	.10
❑	312	James Fuller	.20	.07
❑	313	William Fuller	.20	.07
❑	314	Charlie Garner	.30	.10
❑	315	Bobby Hoying	.30	.10
❑	316	Tom Hutton	.20	.07
❑	317	Chris T. Jones	.20	.07
❑	318	Mike Mamula	.20	.07
❑	319	Mark Seay	.20	.07
❑	320	Bobby Taylor	.20	.07
❑	321	Ricky Watters	.30	.10

❑ 322	Jahine Arnold	.20	.07
❑ 323	Jerome Bettis	.50	.20
❑ 324	Chad Brown	.20	.07
❑ 325	Mark Bruener	.20	.07
❑ 326	Andre Hastings	.20	.07
❑ 327	Norm Johnson	.20	.07
❑ 328	Levon Kirkland	.20	.07
❑ 329	Carnell Lake	.20	.07
❑ 330	Greg Lloyd	.20	.07
❑ 331	Ernie Mills	.20	.07
❑ 332	Orpheus Roye RC	.20	.07
❑ 333	Kordell Stewart	.50	.20
❑ 334	Yancey Thigpen	.30	.10
❑ 335	Mike Tomczak	.20	.07
❑ 336	Rod Woodson	.30	.10
❑ 337	Tony Banks	.30	.10
❑ 338	Bern Brostek	.20	.07
❑ 339	Isaac Bruce	.50	.20
❑ 340	Ernie Conwell	.20	.07
❑ 341	Keith Crawford	.20	.07
❑ 342	Wayne Gandy	.20	.07
❑ 343	Harold Green	.20	.07
❑ 344	Carlos Jenkins	.20	.07
❑ 345	Jimmie Jones	.20	.07
❑ 346	Eddie Kennison	.30	.10
❑ 347	Todd Lyght	.20	.07
❑ 348	Leslie O'Neal	.20	.07
❑ 349	Lawrence Phillips	.20	.07
❑ 350	Greg Robinson	.20	.07
❑ 351	Darren Bennett	.20	.07
❑ 352	Lewis Bush	.20	.07
❑ 353	Eric Castle	.20	.07
❑ 354	Terrell Fletcher	.20	.07
❑ 355	Darrien Gordon	.20	.07
❑ 356	Kurt Gouveia	.20	.07
❑ 357	Aaron Hayden	.20	.07
❑ 358	Stan Humphries	.30	.10
❑ 359	Tony Martin	.30	.10
❑ 360	Vaughn Parker RC	.20	.07
❑ 361	Brian Roche	.20	.07
❑ 362	Leonard Russell	.20	.07
❑ 363	Junior Seau	.50	.20
❑ 364	Roy Barker	.20	.07
❑ 365	Harris Barton	.20	.07
❑ 366	Dexter Carter	.20	.07
❑ 367	Chris Doleman	.20	.07
❑ 368	Tyronne Drakeford	.20	.07
❑ 369	Elvis Grbac	.30	.10
❑ 370	Derek Loville	.20	.07
❑ 371	Tim McDonald	.20	.07
❑ 372	Ken Norton	.20	.07
❑ 373	Terrell Owens	.60	.25
❑ 374	Gary Plummer	.20	.07
❑ 375	Jerry Rice	1.00	.40
❑ 376	Dana Stubblefield	.20	.07
❑ 377	Lee Woodall	.20	.07
❑ 378	Steve Young	.60	.25
❑ 379	Robert Blackmon	.20	.07
❑ 380	Brian Blades	.20	.07
❑ 381	Carlester Crumpler	.20	.07
❑ 382	Christian Fauria	.20	.07
❑ 383	John Friesz	.20	.07
❑ 384	Joey Galloway	.30	.10
❑ 385	Derrick Graham	.20	.07
❑ 386	Cortez Kennedy	.20	.07
❑ 387	Warren Moon	.50	.20
❑ 388	Winston Moss	.20	.07
❑ 389	Mike Pritchard	.20	.07
❑ 390	Michael Sinclair	.20	.07
❑ 391	Lamar Smith	.50	.20
❑ 392	Chris Warren	.30	.10
❑ 393	Chidi Ahanotu	.20	.07
❑ 394	Mike Alstott	.50	.20
❑ 395	Reggie Brooks	.20	.07
❑ 396	Trent Dilfer	.50	.20
❑ 397	Jerry Ellison	.20	.07
❑ 398	Paul Gruber	.20	.07
❑ 399	Alvin Harper	.20	.07
❑ 400	Courtney Hawkins	.20	.07
❑ 401	Dave Moore	.20	.07
❑ 402	Errict Rhett	.20	.07
❑ 403	Warren Sapp	.30	.10
❑ 404	Nilo Silvan	.20	.07
❑ 405	Regan Upshaw	.20	.07
❑ 406	Casey Weldon	.20	.07
❑ 407	Terry Allen	.50	.20
❑ 408	Jamie Asher	.20	.07
❑ 409	Bill Brooks	.20	.07
❑ 410	Tom Carter	.20	.07
❑ 411	Henry Ellard	.20	.07
❑ 412	Gus Frerotte	.20	.07
❑ 413	Darrell Green	.30	.10
❑ 414	Ken Harvey	.20	.07
❑ 415	Tre Johnson	.20	.07
❑ 416	Brian Mitchell	.20	.07
❑ 417	Rich Owens	.20	.07
❑ 418	Heath Shuler	.20	.07
❑ 419	Michael Westbrook	.30	.10
❑ 420	Tony Woods RC	.20	.07
❑ 421	Reidel Anthony RC	.50	.20
❑ 422	Darnell Autry RC	.30	.10
❑ 423	Tiki Barber RC	3.00	1.25
❑ 424	Pat Barnes RC	.50	.20
❑ 425	Terry Battle RC	.20	.07
❑ 426	Will Blackwell RC	.30	.10
❑ 427	Peter Boulware RC	.50	.20
❑ 428	Rae Carruth RC	.20	.07
❑ 429	Troy Davis RC	.30	.10
❑ 430	Jim Druckenmiller RC	.30	.10
❑ 431	Warrick Dunn RC	1.25	.50
❑ 432	Marc Edwards RC	.20	.07
❑ 433	James Farrior RC	.50	.20
❑ 434	Yatil Green RC	.30	.10
❑ 435	Byron Hanspard RC	.30	.10
❑ 436	Ike Hilliard RC	.75	.30
❑ 437	David LaFleur RC	.20	.07
❑ 438	Kevin Lockett RC	.30	.10
❑ 439	Sam Madison RC	.50	.20
❑ 440	Brian Manning RC	.30	.10
❑ 441	Orlando Pace RC	.50	.20
❑ 442	Jake Plummer RC	2.50	1.00
❑ 443	Chad Scott RC	.30	.10
❑ 444	Sedrick Shaw RC	.30	.10
❑ 445	Antowain Smith RC	1.25	.50
❑ 446	Shawn Springs RC	.30	.10
❑ 447	Ross Verba RC	.20	.07
❑ 448	Bryant Westbrook RC	.20	.07
❑ 449	Renaldo Wynn RC	.20	.07
❑ 450	Jimmy Johnson CO	.30	.10
❑ S1	Mark Brunell Sample	1.00	.40

1998 Pacific

❑	COMPLETE SET (450)	60.00	25.00
❑ 1	Mario Bates	.40	.15
❑ 2	Lomas Brown	.25	.08
❑ 3	Larry Centers	.25	.08
❑ 4	Chris Gedney	.25	.08
❑ 5	Terry Irving	.25	.08
❑ 6	Tom Knight	.25	.08
❑ 7	Eric Metcalf	.25	.08
❑ 8	Jamir Miller	.25	.08
❑ 9	Rob Moore	.40	.15
❑ 10	Joe Nedney	.25	.08
❑ 11	Jake Plummer	.60	.25
❑ 12	Simeon Rice	.40	.15
❑ 13	Frank Sanders	.40	.15
❑ 14	Eric Swann	.25	.08
❑ 15	Aeneas Williams	.25	.08
❑ 16	Morten Andersen	.25	.08
❑ 17	Jamal Anderson	.60	.25
❑ 18	Michael Booker	.25	.08
❑ 19	Keith Brooking RC	1.50	.60
❑ 20	Ray Buchanan	.25	.08
❑ 21	Devin Bush	.25	.08
❑ 22	Chris Chandler	.40	.15
❑ 23	Tony Graziani	.25	.08
❑ 24	Harold Green	.25	.08
❑ 25	Byron Hanspard	.25	.08
❑ 26	Todd Kinchen	.25	.08
❑ 27	Tony Martin	.40	.15
❑ 28	Terance Mathis	.40	.15
❑ 29	Eugene Robinson	.25	.08
❑ 30	O.J. Santiago	.25	.08
❑ 31	Chuck Smith	.25	.08
❑ 32	Jessie Tuggle	.25	.08
❑ 33	Bob Whitfield	.25	.08
❑ 34	Peter Boulware	.25	.08
❑ 35	Jay Graham	.25	.08
❑ 36	Eric Green	.25	.08
❑ 37	Jim Harbaugh	.40	.15
❑ 38	Michael Jackson	.25	.08
❑ 39	Jermaine Lewis	.40	.15
❑ 40	Ray Lewis	.60	.25
❑ 41	Michael McCrary	.25	.08
❑ 42	Stevon Moore	.25	.08
❑ 43	Jonathan Ogden	.25	.08
❑ 44	Errict Rhett	.40	.15
❑ 45	Matt Stover	.25	.08
❑ 46	Rod Woodson	.40	.15
❑ 47	Eric Zeier	.40	.15
❑ 48	Ruben Brown	.25	.08
❑ 49	Steve Christie	.25	.08
❑ 50	Quinn Early	.25	.08
❑ 51	John Fina	.25	.08
❑ 52	Doug Flutie	.60	.25
❑ 53	Phil Hansen	.25	.08
❑ 54	Lonnie Johnson	.25	.08
❑ 55	Rob Johnson	.40	.15
❑ 56	Henry Jones	.25	.08
❑ 57	Eric Moulds	.60	.25
❑ 58	Andre Reed	.40	.15
❑ 59	Antowain Smith	.60	.25
❑ 60	Bruce Smith	.40	.15
❑ 61	Thurman Thomas	.60	.25
❑ 62	Ted Washington	.25	.08
❑ 63	Michael Bates	.25	.08
❑ 64	Tim Biakabutuka	.40	.15
❑ 65	Blake Brockermeyer	.25	.08
❑ 66	Mark Carrier	.25	.08
❑ 67	Rae Carruth	.25	.08
❑ 68	Kerry Collins	.40	.15
❑ 69	Doug Evans	.25	.08
❑ 70	William Floyd	.25	.08
❑ 71	Sean Gilbert	.25	.08
❑ 72	Rocket Ismail	.25	.08
❑ 73	John Kasay	.25	.08
❑ 74	Fred Lane	.25	.08
❑ 75	Lamar Lathon	.25	.08
❑ 76	Muhsin Muhammad	.40	.15
❑ 77	Wesley Walls	.40	.15
❑ 78	Edgar Bennett	.25	.08
❑ 79	Tom Carter	.25	.08
❑ 80	Curtis Conway	.40	.15
❑ 81	Bobby Engram	.40	.15
❑ 82	Curtis Enis RC	.75	.30
❑ 83	Jim Flanigan	.25	.08
❑ 84	Walt Harris	.25	.08
❑ 85	Jeff Jaeger	.25	.08

❑ 86	Erik Kramer	.25	.08
❑ 87	John Mangum	.25	.08
❑ 88	Glyn Milburn	.25	.08
❑ 89	Barry Minter	.25	.08
❑ 90	Chris Penn	.25	.08
❑ 91	Todd Sauerbrun	.25	.08
❑ 92	James Williams	.25	.08
❑ 93	Ashley Ambrose	.25	.08
❑ 94	Willie Anderson	.25	.08
❑ 95	Eric Bieniemy	.25	.08
❑ 96	Jeff Blake	.40	.15
❑ 97	Ki-Jana Carter	.25	.08
❑ 98	John Copeland	.25	.08
❑ 99	Corey Dillon	.60	.25
❑ 100	Tony McGee	.25	.08
❑ 101	Neil O'Donnell	.40	.15
❑ 102	Carl Pickens	.40	.15
❑ 103	Kevin Sargent	.25	.08
❑ 104	Darnay Scott	.40	.15
❑ 105	Takeo Spikes RC	1.50	.60
❑ 106	Troy Aikman	1.25	.50
❑ 107	Larry Allen	.25	.08
❑ 108	Eric Bjornson	.25	.08
❑ 109	Billy Davis	.25	.08
❑ 110	Jason Garrett RC	.75	.30
❑ 111	Michael Irvin	.60	.25
❑ 112	Daryl Johnston	.40	.15
❑ 113	David LaFleur	.25	.08
❑ 114	Everett McIver	.25	.08
❑ 115	Ernie Mills	.25	.08
❑ 116	Nate Newton	.25	.08
❑ 117	Deion Sanders	.60	.25
❑ 118	Emmitt Smith	2.00	.75
❑ 119	Kevin Smith	.25	.08
❑ 120	Erik Williams	.25	.08
❑ 121	Steve Atwater	.25	.08
❑ 122	Tyrone Braxton	.25	.08
❑ 123	Ray Crockett	.25	.08
❑ 124	Terrell Davis	.60	.25
❑ 125	Jason Elam	.25	.08
❑ 126	John Elway	2.50	1.00
❑ 127	Willie Green	.25	.08
❑ 128	Brian Griese RC	3.00	1.25
❑ 129	Tony Jones	.25	.08
❑ 130	Ed McCaffrey	.40	.15
❑ 131	John Mobley	.25	.08
❑ 132	Tom Nalen	.25	.08
❑ 133	Marcus Nash RC	.75	.30
❑ 134	Bill Romanowski	.25	.08
❑ 135	Shannon Sharpe	.40	.15
❑ 136	Neil Smith	.40	.15
❑ 137	Rod Smith	.40	.15
❑ 138	Keith Traylor	.25	.08
❑ 139	Stephen Boyd	.25	.08
❑ 140	Mark Carrier DB	.25	.08
❑ 141	Charlie Batch RC	1.50	.60
❑ 142	Jason Hanson	.25	.08
❑ 143	Scott Mitchell	.40	.15
❑ 144	Herman Moore	.40	.15
❑ 145	Johnnie Morton	.40	.15
❑ 146	Robert Porcher	.25	.08
❑ 147	Ron Rivers	.25	.08
❑ 148	Barry Sanders	2.00	.75
❑ 149	Tracy Scroggins	.25	.08
❑ 150	David Sloan	.25	.08
❑ 151	Tommy Vardell	.25	.08
❑ 152	Kerwin Waldroup	.25	.08
❑ 153	Bryant Westbrook	.25	.08
❑ 154	Robert Brooks	.40	.15
❑ 155	Gilbert Brown	.25	.08
❑ 156	LeRoy Butler	.25	.08
❑ 157	Mark Chmura	.40	.15
❑ 158	Earl Dotson	.25	.08
❑ 159	Santana Dotson	.25	.08
❑ 160	Brett Favre	2.50	1.00
❑ 161	Antonio Freeman	.60	.25
❑ 162	Raymont Harris	.25	.08
❑ 163	William Henderson	.40	.15
❑ 164	Vonnie Holliday RC	1.25	.50
❑ 165	George Koonce	.25	.08
❑ 166	Dorsey Levens	.60	.25
❑ 167	Derrick Mayes	.40	.15
❑ 168	Craig Newsome	.25	.08
❑ 169	Ross Verba	.25	.08
❑ 170	Reggie White	.60	.25
❑ 171	Elijah Alexander	.25	.08
❑ 172	Aaron Bailey	.25	.08
❑ 173	Jason Belser	.25	.08
❑ 174	Robert Blackmon	.25	.08
❑ 175	Zack Crockett	.25	.08
❑ 176	Ken Dilger	.25	.08
❑ 177	Marshall Faulk	.75	.30
❑ 178	Tarik Glenn	.25	.08
❑ 179	Marvin Harrison	.60	.25
❑ 180	Tony Mandarich	.25	.08
❑ 181	Peyton Manning RC	15.00	6.00
❑ 182	Marcus Pollard	.25	.08
❑ 183	Lamont Warren	.25	.08
❑ 184	Tavian Banks RC	1.25	.50
❑ 185	Reggie Barlow	.25	.08
❑ 186	Tony Boselli	.25	.08
❑ 187	Tony Brackens	.25	.08
❑ 188	Mark Brunell	.60	.25
❑ 189	Kevin Hardy	.25	.08
❑ 190	Mike Hollis	.25	.08
❑ 191	Jeff Lageman	.25	.08
❑ 192	Keenan McCardell	.40	.15
❑ 193	Pete Mitchell	.25	.08
❑ 194	Bryce Paup	.25	.08
❑ 195	Leon Searcy	.25	.08
❑ 196	Jimmy Smith	.40	.15
❑ 197	James Stewart	.40	.15
❑ 198	Fred Taylor RC	2.50	1.00
❑ 199	Renaldo Wynn	.25	.08
❑ 200	Derrick Alexander WR	.40	.15
❑ 201	Kimble Anders	.40	.15
❑ 202	Donnell Bennett	.25	.08
❑ 203	Dale Carter	.25	.08
❑ 204	Anthony Davis	.25	.08
❑ 205	Rich Gannon	.60	.25
❑ 206	Tony Gonzalez	.60	.25
❑ 207	Elvis Grbac	.40	.15
❑ 208	James Hasty	.25	.08
❑ 209	Leslie O'Neal	.25	.08
❑ 210	Andre Rison	.40	.15
❑ 211	Rashaan Shehee RC	1.25	.50
❑ 212	Will Shields	.25	.08
❑ 213	Pete Stoyanovich	.25	.08
❑ 214	Derrick Thomas	.60	.25
❑ 215	Tamarick Vanover	.25	.08
❑ 216	Karim Abdul-Jabbar	.60	.25
❑ 217	Trace Armstrong	.25	.08
❑ 218	John Avery RC	1.25	.50
❑ 219	Tim Bowens	.25	.08
❑ 220	Terrell Buckley	.25	.08
❑ 221	Troy Drayton	.25	.08
❑ 222	Daryl Gardener	.25	.08
❑ 223	Damon Huard RC	8.00	3.00
❑ 224	Charles Jordan	.25	.08
❑ 225	Dan Marino	2.50	1.00
❑ 226	O.J. McDuffie	.40	.15
❑ 227	Bernie Parmalee	.25	.08
❑ 228	Stanley Pritchett	.25	.08
❑ 229	Derrick Rodgers	.25	.08
❑ 230	Lamar Thomas	.25	.08
❑ 231	Zach Thomas	.60	.25
❑ 232	Richmond Webb	.25	.08
❑ 233	Derrick Alexander DE	.25	.08
❑ 234	Jerry Ball	.25	.08
❑ 235	Cris Carter	.60	.25
❑ 236	Randall Cunningham	.60	.25
❑ 237	Charles Evans	.25	.08
❑ 238	Corey Fuller	.25	.08
❑ 239	Andrew Glover	.25	.08
❑ 240	Leroy Hoard	.25	.08
❑ 241	Brad Johnson	.60	.25
❑ 242	Ed McDaniel	.25	.08
❑ 243	Randall McDaniel	.25	.08
❑ 244	Randy Moss RC	10.00	4.00
❑ 245	John Randle	.40	.15
❑ 246	Jake Reed	.40	.15
❑ 247	Dwayne Rudd	.25	.08
❑ 248	Robert Smith	.60	.25
❑ 249	Bruce Armstrong	.25	.08
❑ 250	Drew Bledsoe	1.00	.40
❑ 251	Vincent Brisby	.25	.08
❑ 252	Tedy Bruschi	1.25	.50
❑ 253	Ben Coates	.40	.15
❑ 254	Derrick Cullors	.25	.08
❑ 255	Terry Glenn	.60	.25
❑ 256	Shawn Jefferson	.25	.08
❑ 257	Ted Johnson	.25	.08
❑ 258	Ty Law	.40	.15
❑ 259	Willie McGinest	.25	.08
❑ 260	Lawyer Milloy	.40	.15
❑ 261	Sedrick Shaw	.25	.08
❑ 262	Chris Slade	.25	.08
❑ 263	Troy Davis	.25	.08
❑ 264	Mark Fields	.25	.08
❑ 265	Andre Hastings	.25	.08
❑ 266	Billy Joe Hobert	.25	.08
❑ 267	Qadry Ismail	.40	.15
❑ 268	Tony Johnson	.25	.08
❑ 269	Sammy Knight RC	.60	.25
❑ 270	Wayne Martin	.25	.08
❑ 271	Chris Naeole	.25	.08
❑ 272	Keith Poole	.25	.08
❑ 273	William Roaf	.25	.08
❑ 274	Pio Sagapolutele	.25	.08
❑ 275	Danny Wuerffel	.40	.15
❑ 276	Ray Zellars	.25	.08
❑ 277	Jessie Armstead	.25	.08
❑ 278	Tiki Barber	.60	.25
❑ 279	Chris Calloway	.25	.08
❑ 280	Percy Ellsworth	.25	.08
❑ 281	Sam Games RC	.75	.30
❑ 282	Kent Graham	.25	.08
❑ 283	Ike Hilliard	.40	.15
❑ 284	Danny Kanell	.40	.15
❑ 285	Corey Miller	.25	.08
❑ 286	Phillippi Sparks	.25	.08
❑ 287	Michael Strahan	.40	.15
❑ 288	Amani Toomer	.40	.15
❑ 289	Charles Way	.25	.08
❑ 290	Tyrone Wheatley	.40	.15
❑ 291	Tito Wooten	.25	.08
❑ 292	Kyle Brady	.25	.08
❑ 293	Keith Byars	.25	.08
❑ 294	Wayne Chrebet	.60	.25
❑ 295	John Elliott	.25	.08
❑ 296	Glenn Foley	.40	.15
❑ 297	Aaron Glenn	.25	.08
❑ 298	Keyshawn Johnson	.60	.25
❑ 299	Curtis Martin	.60	.25
❑ 300	Otis Smith	.25	.08
❑ 301	Vinny Testaverde	.40	.15
❑ 302	Alex Van Dyke	.25	.08
❑ 303	Dedric Ward	.25	.08
❑ 304	Greg Biekert	.25	.08
❑ 305	Tim Brown	.60	.25
❑ 306	Rickey Dudley	.25	.08
❑ 307	Jeff George	.40	.15
❑ 308	Pat Harlow	.25	.08
❑ 309	Desmond Howard	.40	.15
❑ 310	James Jett	.40	.15
❑ 311	Napoleon Kaufman	.60	.25
❑ 312	Lincoln Kennedy	.25	.08
❑ 313	Russell Maryland	.25	.08
❑ 314	Darrell Russell	.25	.08
❑ 315	Eric Turner	.25	.08
❑ 316	Steve Wisniewski	.25	.08
❑ 317	Charles Woodson RC	2.00	.75
❑ 318	James Darling RC	.75	.30
❑ 319	Jason Dunn	.25	.08

❑ 320 Irving Fryar .40 .15
❑ 321 Charlie Garner .40 .15
❑ 322 Jeff Graham .25 .08
❑ 323 Bobby Hoying .40 .15
❑ 324 Chad Lewis .40 .15
❑ 325 Rodney Peete .25 .08
❑ 326 Freddie Solomon .25 .08
❑ 327 Duce Staley .75 .30
❑ 328 Bobby Taylor .25 .08
❑ 329 William Thomas .25 .08
❑ 330 Kevin Turner .25 .08
❑ 331 Troy Vincent .25 .08
❑ 332 Jerome Bettis .60 .25
❑ 333 Will Blackwell .25 .08
❑ 334 Mark Bruener .25 .08
❑ 335 Andre Coleman .25 .08
❑ 336 Dermontti Dawson .25 .08
❑ 337 Jason Gildon .25 .08
❑ 338 Courtney Hawkins .25 .08
❑ 339 Charles Johnson .25 .08
❑ 340 Levon Kirkland .25 .08
❑ 341 Carnell Lake .25 .08
❑ 342 Tim Lester .25 .08
❑ 343 Joel Steed .25 .08
❑ 344 Kordell Stewart .60 .25
❑ 345 Will Wolford .25 .08
❑ 346 Tony Banks .40 .15
❑ 347 Isaac Bruce .60 .25
❑ 348 Ernie Conwell .25 .08
❑ 349 D'Marco Farr .25 .08
❑ 350 Wayne Gandy .25 .08
❑ 351 Jerome Pathon RC 1.50 .60
❑ 352 Eddie Kennison .40 .15
❑ 353 Amp Lee .25 .08
❑ 354 Keith Lyle .25 .08
❑ 355 Ryan McNeil .25 .08
❑ 356 Jerald Moore .25 .08
❑ 357 Orlando Pace .25 .08
❑ 358 Roman Phifer .25 .08
❑ 359 David Thompson RC .75 .30
❑ 360 Darren Bennett .25 .08
❑ 361 John Carney .25 .08
❑ 362 Marco Coleman .25 .08
❑ 363 Terrell Fletcher .25 .08
❑ 364 William Fuller .25 .08
❑ 365 Charlie Jones .25 .08
❑ 366 Freddie Jones .25 .08
❑ 367 Ryan Leaf RC 1.50 .60
❑ 368 Natrone Means .40 .15
❑ 369 Junior Seau .60 .25
❑ 370 Terrance Shaw .25 .08
❑ 371 Tremayne Stephens RC .75 .30
❑ 372 Bryan Still .25 .08
❑ 373 Aaron Taylor .25 .08
❑ 374 Greg Clark .25 .08
❑ 375 Ty Detmer .40 .15
❑ 376 Jim Druckenmiller .25 .08
❑ 377 Marc Edwards .25 .08
❑ 378 Merton Hanks .25 .08
❑ 379 Garrison Hearst .60 .25
❑ 380 Chuck Levy .25 .08
❑ 381 Ken Norton .25 .08
❑ 382 Terrell Owens .60 .25
❑ 383 Marquez Pope .25 .08
❑ 384 Jerry Rice 1.25 .50
❑ 385 Irv Smith .25 .08
❑ 386 J.J. Stokes .40 .15
❑ 387 Iheanyi Uwaezuoke .25 .08
❑ 388 Bryant Young .25 .08
❑ 389 Steve Young .75 .30
❑ 390 Sam Adams .25 .08
❑ 391 Chad Brown .25 .08
❑ 392 Christian Fauria .25 .08
❑ 393 Joey Galloway .40 .15
❑ 394 Ahman Green RC 8.00 3.00
❑ 395 Walter Jones .25 .08
❑ 396 Cortez Kennedy .25 .08
❑ 397 Jon Kitna .60 .25
❑ 398 James McKnight .60 .25
❑ 399 Warren Moon .60 .25
❑ 400 Mike Pritchard .25 .08
❑ 401 Michael Sinclair .25 .08
❑ 402 Shawn Springs .25 .08
❑ 403 Ricky Watters .40 .15
❑ 404 Darryl Williams .25 .08
❑ 405 Mike Alstott .60 .25
❑ 406 Reidel Anthony .40 .15
❑ 407 Derrick Brooks .60 .25
❑ 408 Brad Culpepper .25 .08
❑ 409 Trent Dilfer .60 .25
❑ 410 Warrick Dunn .60 .25
❑ 411 Bert Emanuel .40 .15
❑ 412 Jacquez Green RC 1.25 .50
❑ 413 Paul Gruber .25 .08
❑ 414 Patrick Hape RC 1.25 .50
❑ 415 Dave Moore .25 .08
❑ 416 Hardy Nickerson .25 .08
❑ 417 Warren Sapp .40 .15
❑ 418 Robb Thomas .25 .08
❑ 419 Regan Upshaw .25 .08
❑ 420 Karl Williams .25 .08
❑ 421 Blaine Bishop .25 .08
❑ 422 Anthony Cook .25 .08
❑ 423 Willie Davis .25 .08
❑ 424 Al Del Greco .25 .08
❑ 425 Kevin Dyson .60 .25
❑ 426 Henry Ford .25 .08
❑ 427 Eddie George .60 .25
❑ 428 Jackie Harris .25 .08
❑ 429 Steve McNair .60 .25
❑ 430 Chris Sanders .25 .08
❑ 431 Mark Stepnoski .25 .08
❑ 432 Yancey Thigpen .25 .08
❑ 433 Barron Wortham .25 .08
❑ 434 Frank Wycheck .25 .08
❑ 435 Stephen Alexander RC 1.25 .50
❑ 436 Terry Allen .60 .25
❑ 437 Jamie Asher .25 .08
❑ 438 Bob Dahl .25 .08
❑ 439 Stephen Davis .25 .08
❑ 440 Cris Dishman .25 .08
❑ 441 Gus Frerotte .25 .08
❑ 442 Darrell Green .40 .15
❑ 443 Trent Green .75 .30
❑ 444 Ken Harvey .25 .08
❑ 445 Skip Hicks RC 1.25 .50
❑ 446 Jeff Hostetler .25 .08
❑ 447 Brian Mitchell .25 .08
❑ 448 Leslie Shepherd .25 .08
❑ 449 Michael Westbrook .40 .15
❑ 450 Dan Wilkinson .25 .08
❑ S1 Warrick Dunn Sample 1.00 .40

1999 Pacific

❑ COMPLETE SET (450) 80.00 30.00
❑ 1 Mario Bates .25 .08
❑ 2 Larry Centers .25 .08
❑ 3 Chris Gedney .25 .08
❑ 4 Kwamie Lassiter RC .60 .25
❑ 5 Johnny McWilliams .25 .08
❑ 6 Eric Metcalf .25 .08
❑ 7 Rob Moore .40 .15
❑ 8 Adrian Murrell .40 .15
❑ 9 Jake Plummer .40 .15
❑ 10 Simeon Rice .40 .15
❑ 11 Frank Sanders .40 .15
❑ 12 Andre Wadsworth .25 .08
❑ 13 Aeneas Williams .25 .08
❑ 14 M.Pittman/R.Anderson RC 1.25 .50
❑ 15 Morten Andersen .25 .08
❑ 16 Jamal Anderson .60 .25
❑ 17 Lester Archambeau .25 .08
❑ 18 Chris Chandler .40 .15
❑ 19 Bob Christian .25 .08
❑ 20 Steve DeBerg .25 .08
❑ 21 Tim Dwight .60 .25
❑ 22 Tony Martin .40 .15
❑ 23 Terance Mathis .40 .15
❑ 24 Eugene Robinson .25 .08
❑ 25 O.J. Santiago .25 .08
❑ 26 Chuck Smith .25 .08
❑ 27 Jessie Tuggle .25 .08
❑ 28 Jammi German/Ken Oxendine .25 .08
❑ 29 Peter Boulware .25 .08
❑ 30 Jay Graham .25 .08
❑ 31 Jim Harbaugh .40 .15
❑ 32 Priest Holmes 1.00 .40
❑ 33 Michael Jackson .25 .08
❑ 34 Jermaine Lewis .40 .15
❑ 35 Ray Lewis .60 .25
❑ 36 Michael McCrary .25 .08
❑ 37 Jonathan Ogden .25 .08
❑ 38 Errict Rhett .25 .08
❑ 39 James Roe RC 1.00 .40
❑ 40 Floyd Turner .25 .08
❑ 41 Rod Woodson .40 .15
❑ 42 Eric Zeier .25 .08
❑ 43 Wally Richardson/Patrick Johnson .25 .08
❑ 44 Ruben Brown .25 .08
❑ 45 Quinn Early .25 .08
❑ 46 Doug Flutie .60 .25
❑ 47 Sam Gash .25 .08
❑ 48 Phil Hansen .25 .08
❑ 49 Lonnie Johnson .25 .08
❑ 50 Rob Johnson .40 .15
❑ 51 Eric Moulds .60 .25
❑ 52 Andre Reed .40 .15
❑ 53 Jay Riemersma .25 .08
❑ 54 Antowain Smith .60 .25
❑ 55 Bruce Smith .40 .15
❑ 56 Thurman Thomas .40 .15
❑ 57 Ted Washington .25 .08
❑ 58 J.Linton/Kamil Loud RC 1.00 .40
❑ 59 Michael Bates .25 .08
❑ 60 Steve Beuerlein .25 .08
❑ 61 Tim Biakabutuka .40 .15
❑ 62 Mark Carrier WR .25 .08
❑ 63 Eric Davis .25 .08
❑ 64 William Floyd .25 .08
❑ 65 Sean Gilbert .25 .08
❑ 66 Kevin Greene .25 .08
❑ 67 Rocket Ismail .40 .15
❑ 68 Anthony Johnson .25 .08
❑ 69 Fred Lane .25 .08
❑ 70 Muhsin Muhammad .40 .15
❑ 71 Winslow Oliver .25 .08
❑ 72 Wesley Walls .40 .15
❑ 73 D.Craig RC/S.Matthews 1.50 .60
❑ 74 Edgar Bennett .25 .08
❑ 75 Curtis Conway .40 .15
❑ 76 Bobby Engram .40 .15
❑ 77 Curtis Enis .25 .08
❑ 78 Ty Hallock RC 1.00 .40
❑ 79 Walt Harris .25 .08
❑ 80 Jeff Jaeger .25 .08
❑ 81 Erik Kramer .25 .08
❑ 82 Glyn Milburn .25 .08

	#	Card	Mint	Ex
❑	83	Chris Penn	.25	.08
❑	84	Steve Stenstrom	.25	.08
❑	85	Ryan Wetnight	.25	.08
❑	86	James Allen RC/Moreno	1.50	.60
❑	87	Ashley Ambrose	.25	.08
❑	88	Brandon Bennett RC	1.00	.40
❑	89	Eric Bieniemy	.25	.08
❑	90	Jeff Blake	.40	.15
❑	91	Corey Dillon	.60	.25
❑	92	Paul Justin	.25	.08
❑	93	Eric Kresser RC	1.00	.40
❑	94	Tremain Mack	.25	.08
❑	95	Tony McGee	.25	.08
❑	96	Neil O'Donnell	.40	.15
❑	97	Carl Pickens	.40	.15
❑	98	Darnay Scott	.25	.08
❑	99	Takeo Spikes	.25	.08
❑	100	Ty Detmer	.25	.08
❑	101	Chris Gardocki	.25	.08
❑	102	Damon Gibson	.25	.08
❑	103	Antonio Langham	.25	.08
❑	104	Jerris McPhail	.25	.08
❑	105	Irv Smith	.25	.08
❑	106	Freddie Solomon	.25	.08
❑	107	S.Milanovich/Fred Brock RC	1.00	.40
❑	108	Troy Aikman	1.25	.50
❑	109	Larry Allen	.25	.08
❑	110	Eric Bjornson	.25	.08
❑	111	Billy Davis	.25	.08
❑	112	Michael Irvin	.40	.15
❑	113	David LaFleur	.25	.08
❑	114	Ernie Mills	.25	.08
❑	115	Nate Newton	.25	.08
❑	116	Deion Sanders	.60	.25
❑	117	Emmitt Smith	1.25	.50
❑	118	Chris Warren	.25	.08
❑	119	Bubby Brister	.40	.15
❑	120	Terrell Davis	.60	.25
❑	121	Jason Elam	.25	.08
❑	122	John Elway	2.00	.75
❑	123	Willie Green	.25	.08
❑	124	Howard Griffith	.25	.08
❑	125	Vaughn Hebron	.25	.08
❑	126	Ed McCaffrey	.40	.15
❑	127	John Mobley	.25	.08
❑	128	Bill Romanowski	.25	.08
❑	129	Shannon Sharpe	.40	.15
❑	130	Neil Smith	.40	.15
❑	131	Rod Smith	.40	.15
❑	132	Brian Griese/M.Nash	.60	.25
❑	133	Charlie Batch	.60	.25
❑	134	Stephen Boyd	.25	.08
❑	135	Mark Carrier DB	.25	.08
❑	136	Germane Crowell	.25	.08
❑	137	Terry Fair	.25	.08
❑	138	Jason Hanson	.25	.08
❑	139	Greg Jeffries RC	1.00	.40
❑	140	Herman Moore	.40	.15
❑	141	Johnnie Morton	.40	.15
❑	142	Robert Porcher	.25	.08
❑	143	Ron Rivers	.25	.08
❑	144	Barry Sanders	2.00	.75
❑	145	Tommy Vardell	.25	.08
❑	146	Bryant Westbrook	.25	.08
❑	147	Robert Brooks	.40	.15
❑	148	LeRoy Butler	.25	.08
❑	149	Mark Chmura	.25	.08
❑	150	Tyrone Davis	.25	.08
❑	151	Brett Favre	2.00	.75
❑	152	Antonio Freeman	.60	.25
❑	153	Raymont Harris	.25	.08
❑	154	Vonnie Holliday	.25	.08
❑	155	Darick Holmes	.25	.08
❑	156	Dorsey Levens	.60	.25
❑	157	Brian Manning	.25	.08
❑	158	Derrick Mayes	.25	.08
❑	159	Roell Preston	.25	.08
❑	160	Jeff Thomason	.25	.08
❑	161	Tyrone Williams	.25	.08
❑	162	C.Bradford/Michael Blair RC	1.50	.60
❑	163	Aaron Bailey	.25	.08
❑	164	Ken Dilger	.25	.08
❑	165	Marshall Faulk	.75	.30
❑	166	E.G. Green	.25	.08
❑	167	Marvin Harrison	.60	.25
❑	168	Craig Heyward	.25	.08
❑	169	Peyton Manning	2.00	.75
❑	170	Jerome Pathon	.40	.15
❑	171	Marcus Pollard	.25	.08
❑	172	Torrance Small	.25	.08
❑	173	Mike Vanderjagt	.25	.08
❑	174	Lamont Warren	.25	.08
❑	175	Tavian Banks	.25	.08
❑	176	Reggie Barlow	.25	.08
❑	177	Tony Boselli	.25	.08
❑	178	Tony Brackens	.25	.08
❑	179	Mark Brunell	.60	.25
❑	180	Kevin Hardy	.25	.08
❑	181	Damon Jones	.25	.08
❑	182	Jamie Martin	.60	.25
❑	183	Keenan McCardell	.40	.15
❑	184	Pete Mitchell	.25	.08
❑	185	Bryce Paup	.25	.08
❑	186	Jimmy Smith	.40	.15
❑	187	Fred Taylor	.60	.25
❑	188	Alvis Whitted/Chris Howard	.25	.08
❑	189	Derrick Alexander WR	.40	.15
❑	190	Kimble Anders	.40	.15
❑	191	Donnell Bennett	.25	.08
❑	192	Dale Carter	.25	.08
❑	193	Rich Gannon	.60	.25
❑	194	Tony Gonzalez	.60	.25
❑	195	Elvis Grbac	.40	.15
❑	196	Joe Horn	.40	.15
❑	197	Kevin Lockett	.25	.08
❑	198	Byron Bam Morris	.25	.08
❑	199	Andre Rison	.40	.15
❑	200	Derrick Thomas	.60	.25
❑	201	Tamarick Vanover	.25	.08
❑	202	Gregory Favors/Rashaan Shehee	.25	.08
❑	203	Karim Abdul-Jabbar	.40	.15
❑	204	Trace Armstrong	.25	.08
❑	205	John Avery	.25	.08
❑	206	Lorenzo Bromell RC	.60	.25
❑	207	Terrell Buckley	.25	.08
❑	208	Oronde Gadsden	.40	.15
❑	209	Sam Madison	.25	.08
❑	210	Dan Marino	2.00	.75
❑	211	O.J. McDuffie	.40	.15
❑	212	Ed Perry RC	.60	.25
❑	213	Jason Taylor	.25	.08
❑	214	Lamar Thomas	.25	.08
❑	215	Zach Thomas	.60	.25
❑	216	H.Lusk/Nate Jacquet RC	1.00	.40
❑	217	T.Doxzon RC/D.Huard	1.50	.60
❑	218	Gary Anderson	.25	.08
❑	219	Cris Carter	.60	.25
❑	220	Randall Cunningham	.60	.25
❑	221	Andrew Glover	.25	.08
❑	222	Matthew Hatchette	.25	.08
❑	223	Brad Johnson	.60	.25
❑	224	Ed McDaniel	.25	.08
❑	225	Randall McDaniel	.25	.08
❑	226	Randy Moss	1.50	.60
❑	227	David Palmer	.25	.08
❑	228	John Randle	.40	.15
❑	229	Jake Reed	.40	.15
❑	230	Robert Smith	.60	.25
❑	231	Todd Steussie	.25	.08
❑	232	S.Colinet RC/K.Mays	.25	.08
❑	233	Jay Fiedler RC/T.Bouman RC	6.00	2.50
❑	234	Drew Bledsoe	.75	.30
❑	235	Troy Brown	.40	.15
❑	236	Ben Coates	.40	.15
❑	237	Derrick Cullors	.25	.08
❑	238	Robert Edwards	.25	.08
❑	239	Terry Glenn	.60	.25
❑	240	Shawn Jefferson	.25	.08
❑	241	Ty Law	.40	.15
❑	242	Lawyer Milloy	.40	.15
❑	243	Lovett Purnell RC	1.00	.40
❑	244	Sedrick Shaw	.25	.08
❑	245	Tony Simmons	.25	.08
❑	246	Chris Slade	.25	.08
❑	247	R.Rutledge/Anth.Ladd RC	1.00	.40
❑	248	Chris Floyd/Harold Shaw	.25	.08
❑	249	Ink Aleaga RC	1.00	.40
❑	250	Cameron Cleeland	.25	.08
❑	251	Kerry Collins	.40	.15
❑	252	Troy Davis	.25	.08
❑	253	Sean Dawkins	.25	.08
❑	254	Mark Fields	.25	.08
❑	255	Andre Hastings	.25	.08
❑	256	Sammy Knight	.25	.08
❑	257	Keith Poole	.25	.08
❑	258	William Roaf	.25	.08
❑	259	Lamar Smith	.40	.15
❑	260	Danny Wuerffel	.25	.08
❑	261	Josh Wilcox RC/Brett Bech RC	1.00	.40
❑	262	Chris Bordano RC/W.Perry	1.00	.40
❑	263	Jessie Armstead	.25	.08
❑	264	Tiki Barber	.60	.25
❑	265	Chad Bratzke	.25	.08
❑	266	Gary Brown	.25	.08
❑	267	Chris Calloway	.25	.08
❑	268	Howard Cross	.25	.08
❑	269	Kent Graham	.25	.08
❑	270	Ike Hilliard	.25	.08
❑	271	Danny Kanell	.40	.15
❑	272	Michael Strahan	.40	.15
❑	273	Amani Toomer	.25	.08
❑	274	Charles Way	.25	.08
❑	275	Greg Comella RC/M.Cherry	1.50	.60
❑	276	Kyle Brady	.25	.08
❑	277	Keith Byars	.25	.08
❑	278	Chad Cascadden	.25	.08
❑	279	Wayne Chrebet	.40	.15
❑	280	Bryan Cox	.25	.08
❑	281	Glenn Foley	.40	.15
❑	282	Aaron Glenn	.25	.08
❑	283	Keyshawn Johnson	.60	.25
❑	284	Leon Johnson	.25	.08
❑	285	Mo Lewis	.25	.08
❑	286	Curtis Martin	.60	.25
❑	287	Otis Smith	.25	.08
❑	288	Vinny Testaverde	.40	.15
❑	289	Dedric Ward	.25	.08
❑	290	Tim Brown	.60	.25
❑	291	Rickey Dudley	.25	.08
❑	292	Jeff George	.40	.15
❑	293	Desmond Howard	.40	.15
❑	294	James Jett	.40	.15
❑	295	Lance Johnstone	.25	.08
❑	296	Randy Jordan	.25	.08
❑	297	Napoleon Kaufman	.60	.25
❑	298	Lincoln Kennedy	.25	.08
❑	299	Terry Mickens	.25	.08
❑	300	Darrell Russell	.25	.08
❑	301	Harvey Williams	.25	.08
❑	302	Ch.Woodson/Ritchie	.60	.25
❑	303	Rodney Williams/Jermaine Williams	.25	.08
❑	304	Koy Detmer	.25	.08
❑	305	Hugh Douglas	.25	.08
❑	306	Jason Dunn	.25	.08
❑	307	Irving Fryar	.40	.15
❑	308	Charlie Garner	.40	.15
❑	309	Jeff Graham	.25	.08
❑	310	Bobby Hoying	.40	.15
❑	311	Rodney Peete	.25	.08
❑	312	Allen Rossum	.25	.08
❑	313	Duce Staley	.60	.25
❑	314	William Thomas	.25	.08
❑	315	Kevin Turner	.25	.08
❑	316	K.Sinceno RC/C.Walker RC	1.00	.40

❑ 317 Jahine Arnold .25 .08
❑ 318 Jerome Bettis .60 .25
❑ 319 Will Blackwell .25 .08
❑ 320 Mark Bruener .25 .08
❑ 321 Dermontti Dawson .25 .08
❑ 322 Chris Fuamatu-Ma'afala .25 .08
❑ 323 Courtney Hawkins .25 .08
❑ 324 Richard Huntley .40 .15
❑ 325 Charles Johnson .25 .08
❑ 326 Levon Kirkland .25 .08
❑ 327 Kordell Stewart .40 .15
❑ 328 Hines Ward .60 .25
❑ 329 Dewayne Washington .25 .08
❑ 330 Tony Banks .40 .15
❑ 331 Steve Bono .25 .08
❑ 332 Isaac Bruce .60 .25
❑ 333 June Henley RC 1.25 .50
❑ 334 Robert Holcombe .25 .08
❑ 335 Mike Jones LB .25 .08
❑ 336 Eddie Kennison .40 .15
❑ 337 Amp Lee .25 .08
❑ 338 Jerald Moore .25 .08
❑ 339 Ricky Proehl .25 .08
❑ 340 J.T. Thomas .25 .08
❑ 341 Derrick Harris/Az-Zahir Hakim .40 .15
❑ 342 Roland Williams/Grant Wistrom .25 .08
❑ 343 Kurt Warner RC/T.Horne ! 12.00 5.00
❑ 344 Terrell Fletcher .25 .08
❑ 345 Greg Jackson .25 .08
❑ 346 Charlie Jones .25 .08
❑ 347 Freddie Jones .25 .08
❑ 348 Ryan Leaf .60 .25
❑ 349 Natrone Means .40 .15
❑ 350 Mikhael Ricks .25 .08
❑ 351 Junior Seau .60 .25
❑ 352 Bryan Still .25 .08
❑ 353 T.Stephens/R.Thelwell RC 1.25 .50
❑ 354 Greg Clark .25 .08
❑ 355 Marc Edwards .25 .08
❑ 356 Merton Hanks .25 .08
❑ 357 Garrison Hearst .40 .15
❑ 358 R.W. McQuarters .25 .08
❑ 359 Ken Norton Jr. .25 .08
❑ 360 Terrell Owens .60 .25
❑ 361 Jerry Rice 1.25 .50
❑ 362 J.J. Stokes .40 .15
❑ 363 Bryant Young .25 .08
❑ 364 Steve Young .75 .30
❑ 365 Chad Brown .25 .08
❑ 366 Christian Fauria .25 .08
❑ 367 Joey Galloway .40 .15
❑ 368 Ahman Green .60 .25
❑ 369 Cortez Kennedy .25 .08
❑ 370 Jon Kitna .60 .25
❑ 371 James McKnight .40 .15
❑ 372 Mike Pritchard .25 .08
❑ 373 Michael Sinclair .25 .08
❑ 374 Shawn Springs .25 .08
❑ 375 Ricky Watters .40 .15
❑ 376 Darryl Williams .25 .08
❑ 377 R.Wilson/K.Joseph RC 1.50 .60
❑ 378 Mike Alstott .60 .25
❑ 379 Reidel Anthony .40 .15
❑ 380 Derrick Brooks .60 .25
❑ 381 Trent Dilfer .60 .25
❑ 382 Warrick Dunn .60 .25
❑ 383 Bert Emanuel .40 .15
❑ 384 Jacquez Green .25 .08
❑ 385 Patrick Hape .25 .08
❑ 386 John Lynch .40 .15
❑ 387 Dave Moore .25 .08
❑ 388 Hardy Nickerson .25 .08
❑ 389 Warren Sapp .40 .15
❑ 390 Karl Williams .25 .08
❑ 391 Blaine Bishop .25 .08
❑ 392 Joe Bowden .25 .08
❑ 393 Isaac Byrd RC 1.00 .40
❑ 394 Willie Davis .25 .08
❑ 395 Al Del Greco .25 .08
❑ 396 Kevin Dyson .40 .15
❑ 397 Eddie George .60 .25
❑ 398 Jackie Harris .25 .08
❑ 399 Dave Krieg .25 .08
❑ 400 Steve McNair .60 .25
❑ 401 Michael Roan .25 .08
❑ 402 Yancey Thigpen .25 .08
❑ 403 Frank Wycheck .25 .08
❑ 404 Derrick Mason/Steve Matthews .40 .15
❑ 405 Stephen Alexander .25 .08
❑ 406 Terry Allen .40 .15
❑ 407 Jamie Asher .25 .08
❑ 408 Stephen Davis .60 .25
❑ 409 Darrell Green .25 .08
❑ 410 Trent Green .60 .25
❑ 411 Skip Hicks .25 .08
❑ 412 Brian Mitchell .25 .08
❑ 413 Leslie Shepherd .25 .08
❑ 414 Michael Westbrook .40 .15
❑ 415 T.Hardy/Rabih Abdullah RC 1.00 .40
❑ 416 C.Thomas RC/M.Quinn RC 1.00 .40
❑ 417 J.Quinn/Kelly Holcomb RC 8.00 3.00
❑ 418 Brian Alford/Blake Spence 1.00 .40
❑ 419 Andy Haase RC/Carlos King 1.00 .40
❑ 420 James Thrash RC/K.Hankton 1.50 .60
❑ 421 F.Beasley/Itula Mili RC 1.25 .50
❑ 422 Champ Bailey RC 2.00 .75
❑ 423 D'Wayne Bates RC 1.25 .50
❑ 424 Michael Bishop RC 1.50 .60
❑ 425 David Boston RC 1.50 .60
❑ 426 Shawn Bryson RC 1.50 .60
❑ 427 Tim Couch RC 1.50 .60
❑ 428 Scott Covington RC 1.50 .60
❑ 429 Daunte Culpepper RC 6.00 2.50
❑ 430 Autry Denson RC 1.25 .50
❑ 431 Troy Edwards RC 1.25 .50
❑ 432 Kevin Faulk RC 1.50 .60
❑ 433 Joe Germaine RC 1.25 .50
❑ 434 Torry Holt RC 4.00 1.50
❑ 435 Brock Huard RC 1.50 .60
❑ 436 Sedrick Irvin RC 1.00 .40
❑ 437 Edgerrin James RC 6.00 2.50
❑ 438 Andy Katzenmoyer RC 1.25 .50
❑ 439 Shaun King RC 1.25 .50
❑ 440 Rob Konrad RC 1.25 .50
❑ 441 Donovan McNabb RC 8.00 3.00
❑ 442 Cade McNown RC 1.25 .50
❑ 443 Billy Miller RC 1.00 .40
❑ 444 Dee Miller RC 1.00 .40
❑ 445 Sirr Parker RC 1.00 .40
❑ 446 Peerless Price RC 1.50 .60
❑ 447 Akili Smith RC 1.25 .50
❑ 448 Tai Streets RC 1.50 .60
❑ 449 Ricky Williams RC 3.00 1.25
❑ 450 Amos Zereoue RC 1.50 .60
❑ S1 Warrick Dunn Sample .60 .25

2000 Pacific

❑ COMPLETE SET (450) 60.00 25.00
❑ 1 Mario Bates .25 .08
❑ 2 David Boston .60 .25
❑ 3 Rob Fredrickson .25 .08
❑ 4 Terry Hardy .25 .08
❑ 5 Rob Moore .40 .15
❑ 6 Adrian Murrell .40 .15
❑ 7 Michael Pittman .25 .08
❑ 8 Jake Plummer .40 .15
❑ 9 Simeon Rice .40 .15
❑ 10 Frank Sanders .40 .15
❑ 11 Aeneas Williams .25 .08
❑ 12 M.Cody/A.McCullough .25 .08
❑ 13 D.McKinley RC/J.Makovicka .60 .25
❑ 14 Jamal Anderson .60 .25
❑ 15 Chris Calloway .25 .08
❑ 16 Chris Chandler .40 .15
❑ 17 Bob Christian .25 .08
❑ 18 Tim Dwight .60 .25
❑ 19 Jammi German .25 .08
❑ 20 Ronnie Harris .25 .08
❑ 21 Terance Mathis .40 .15
❑ 22 Ken Oxendine .25 .08
❑ 23 O.J. Santiago .25 .08
❑ 24 Bob Whitfield .25 .08
❑ 25 E.Baker/R.Kelly .25 .08
❑ 26 Justin Armour .25 .08
❑ 27 Tony Banks .40 .15
❑ 28 Peter Boulware .25 .08
❑ 29 Stoney Case .25 .08
❑ 30 Priest Holmes .75 .30
❑ 31 Qadry Ismail .40 .15
❑ 32 Patrick Johnson .25 .08
❑ 33 Michael McCrary .25 .08
❑ 34 Jonathan Ogden .25 .08
❑ 35 Errict Rhett .40 .15
❑ 36 Duane Starks .25 .08
❑ 37 Doug Flutie .60 .25
❑ 38 Rob Johnson .40 .15
❑ 39 Jonathan Linton .25 .08
❑ 40 Eric Moulds .60 .25
❑ 41 Peerless Price .40 .15
❑ 42 Andre Reed .40 .15
❑ 43 Jay Riemersma .25 .08
❑ 44 Antowain Smith .40 .15
❑ 45 Bruce Smith .40 .15
❑ 46 Thurman Thomas .40 .15
❑ 47 Kevin Williams .25 .08
❑ 48 B.Collins/S.Jackson .25 .08
❑ 49 Michael Bates .25 .08
❑ 50 Steve Beuerlein .40 .15
❑ 51 Tim Biakabutuka .40 .15
❑ 52 Antonio Edwards .25 .08
❑ 53 Donald Hayes .25 .08
❑ 54 Patrick Jeffers .60 .25
❑ 55 Anthony Johnson .25 .08
❑ 56 Jeff Lewis .25 .08
❑ 57 Eric Metcalf .25 .08
❑ 58 Muhsin Muhammad .40 .15
❑ 59 Jason Peter .25 .08
❑ 60 Wesley Walls .25 .08
❑ 61 John Allred .25 .08
❑ 62 Marty Booker .40 .15
❑ 63 Curtis Conway .40 .15
❑ 64 Bobby Engram .25 .08
❑ 65 Curtis Enis .25 .08
❑ 66 Shane Matthews .40 .15
❑ 67 Cade McNown .25 .08
❑ 68 Glyn Milburn .25 .08
❑ 69 Jim Miller .25 .08
❑ 70 Marcus Robinson .60 .25
❑ 71 Ryan Wetnight .25 .08
❑ 72 J.Allen/M.Brooks .40 .15
❑ 73 Jeff Blake .40 .15
❑ 74 Corey Dillon .60 .25
❑ 75 Rodney Heath RC .40 .15
❑ 76 Willie Jackson .25 .08
❑ 77 Tremain Mack .25 .08
❑ 78 Tony McGee .25 .08
❑ 79 Carl Pickens .40 .15
❑ 80 Darnay Scott .40 .15

	#	Player	Hi	Lo
❑	81	Akili Smith	.25	.08
❑	82	Takeo Spikes	.25	.08
❑	83	Craig Yeast	.25	.08
❑	84	M.Basnight/N.Williams	.25	.08
❑	85	Karim Abdul-Jabbar	.40	.15
❑	86	Darrin Chiaverini	.25	.08
❑	87	Tim Couch	.40	.15
❑	88	Marc Edwards	.25	.08
❑	89	Kevin Johnson	.60	.25
❑	90	Terry Kirby	.25	.08
❑	91	Daylon McCutcheon	.25	.08
❑	92	Jamir Miller	.25	.08
❑	93	Leslie Shepherd	.25	.08
❑	94	Irv Smith	.25	.08
❑	95	M.Campbell/J.Dearth	.25	.08
❑	96	Z.Davis RC/D.Dunn RC	.40	.15
❑	97	M.Hill/T.Saleh RC	.25	.08
❑	98	Troy Aikman	1.25	.50
❑	99	Eric Bjornson	.25	.08
❑	100	Dexter Coakley	.25	.08
❑	101	Greg Ellis	.25	.08
❑	102	Rocket Ismail	.40	.15
❑	103	David LaFleur	.25	.08
❑	104	Ernie Mills	.25	.08
❑	105	Jeff Ogden	.40	.15
❑	106	R.Neufeld RC/R.Thomas	.40	.15
❑	107	Deion Sanders	.60	.25
❑	108	Emmitt Smith	1.25	.50
❑	109	Chris Warren	.25	.08
❑	110	M.Lucky/J.Tucker	.25	.08
❑	111	Byron Chamberlain	.25	.08
❑	112	Terrell Davis	.60	.25
❑	113	Jason Elam	.25	.08
❑	114	Olandis Gary	.60	.25
❑	115	Brian Griese	.60	.25
❑	116	Ed McCaffrey	.60	.25
❑	117	Trevor Pryce	.25	.08
❑	118	Bill Romanowski	.25	.08
❑	119	Shannon Sharpe	.40	.15
❑	120	Rod Smith	.40	.15
❑	121	Al Wilson	.25	.08
❑	122	A.Cooper/C.Watson	.25	.08
❑	123	Charlie Batch	.60	.25
❑	124	Stephen Boyd	.25	.08
❑	125	Chris Claiborne	.25	.08
❑	126	Germane Crowell	.25	.08
❑	127	Terry Fair	.25	.08
❑	128	Gus Frerotte	.25	.08
❑	129	Jason Hanson	.25	.08
❑	130	Greg Hill	.25	.08
❑	131	Herman Moore	.40	.15
❑	132	Johnnie Morton	.40	.15
❑	133	Barry Sanders	1.50	.60
❑	134	David Sloan	.25	.08
❑	135	B.Olivo/C.Sauter	.25	.08
❑	136	Corey Bradford	.40	.15
❑	137	Tyrone Davis	.25	.08
❑	138	Brett Favre	2.00	.75
❑	139	Antonio Freeman	.60	.25
❑	140	Vonnie Holliday	.25	.08
❑	141	Dorsey Levens	.40	.15
❑	142	Keith McKenzie	.25	.08
❑	143	Mike McKenzie	.25	.08
❑	144	Bill Schroeder	.40	.15
❑	145	Jeff Thomason	.25	.08
❑	146	Frank Winters	.25	.08
❑	147	Cornelius Bennett	.25	.08
❑	148	Tony Blevins RC	.40	.15
❑	149	Chad Bratzke	.25	.08
❑	150	Ken Dilger	.25	.08
❑	151	Tarik Glenn	.25	.08
❑	152	E.G. Green	.25	.08
❑	153	Marvin Harrison	.60	.25
❑	154	Edgerrin James	1.00	.40
❑	155	Peyton Manning	1.50	.60
❑	156	Jerome Pathon	.40	.15
❑	157	Marcus Pollard	.25	.08
❑	158	Terrence Wilkins	.25	.08
❑	159	I.Jones RC/P.Shields RC	.60	.25
❑	160	Reggie Barlow	.25	.08
❑	161	Aaron Beasley	.25	.08
❑	162	Tony Boselli	.25	.08
❑	163	Tony Brackens	.25	.08
❑	164	Kyle Brady	.25	.08
❑	165	Mark Brunell	.60	.25
❑	166	Jay Fiedler	.60	.25
❑	167	Kevin Hardy	.25	.08
❑	168	Carnell Lake	.25	.08
❑	169	Keenan McCardell	.40	.15
❑	170	Jonathan Quinn	.25	.08
❑	171	Jimmy Smith	.40	.15
❑	172	James Stewart	.40	.15
❑	173	Fred Taylor	.60	.25
❑	174	L.Jackson RC/S.Mack	.60	.25
❑	175	Derrick Alexander	.40	.15
❑	176	Donnell Bennett	.25	.08
❑	177	Donnie Edwards	.25	.08
❑	178	Tony Gonzalez	.40	.15
❑	179	Elvis Grbac	.40	.15
❑	180	James Hasty	.25	.08
❑	181	Joe Horn	.40	.15
❑	182	Lonnie Johnson	.25	.08
❑	183	Kevin Lockett	.25	.08
❑	184	Larry Parker	.25	.08
❑	185	Tony Richardson RC	.40	.15
❑	186	Rashaan Shehee	.25	.08
❑	187	Tamarick Vanover	.25	.08
❑	188	Trace Armstrong	.25	.08
❑	189	Oronde Gadsden	.40	.15
❑	190	Damon Huard	.60	.25
❑	191	Nate Jacquet	.25	.08
❑	192	James Johnson	.25	.08
❑	193	Rob Konrad	.25	.08
❑	194	Sam Madison	.25	.08
❑	195	Dan Marino	2.00	.75
❑	196	Tony Martin	.40	.15
❑	197	O.J. McDuffie	.40	.15
❑	198	Stanley Pritchett	.25	.08
❑	199	Tim Ruddy	.25	.08
❑	200	Patrick Surtain	.25	.08
❑	201	Zach Thomas	.60	.25
❑	202	Cris Carter	.60	.25
❑	203	Duane Clemons	.25	.08
❑	204	Carlester Crumpler	.25	.08
❑	205	Daunte Culpepper	.75	.30
❑	206	Jeff George	.40	.15
❑	207	Matthew Hatchette	.25	.08
❑	208	Leroy Hoard	.25	.08
❑	209	Randy Moss	1.25	.50
❑	210	John Randle	.40	.15
❑	211	Jake Reed	.40	.15
❑	212	Robert Smith	.60	.25
❑	213	Robert Tate	.25	.08
❑	214	Terry Allen	.40	.15
❑	215	Bruce Armstrong	.25	.08
❑	216	Drew Bledsoe	.75	.30
❑	217	Ben Coates	.25	.08
❑	218	Kevin Faulk	.40	.15
❑	219	Terry Glenn	.40	.15
❑	220	Shawn Jefferson	.25	.08
❑	221	Andy Katzenmoyer	.25	.08
❑	222	Ty Law	.40	.15
❑	223	Willie McGinest	.25	.08
❑	224	Lawyer Milloy	.40	.15
❑	225	Tony Simmons	.25	.08
❑	226	M.Bishop/S.Morey RC	.40	.15
❑	227	Cameron Cleeland	.25	.08
❑	228	Troy Davis	.25	.08
❑	229	Jake Delhomme RC	2.50	1.00
❑	230	Andre Hastings	.25	.08
❑	231	Eddie Kennison	.40	.15
❑	232	Wilmont Perry	.25	.08
❑	233	Dino Philyaw	.25	.08
❑	234	Keith Poole	.25	.08
❑	235	William Roaf	.25	.08
❑	236	Billy Joe Tolliver	.25	.08
❑	237	Fred Weary	.25	.08
❑	238	Ricky Williams	.60	.25
❑	239	Franklin RC/M.Powell RC	.60	.25
❑	240	Jessie Armstead	.25	.08
❑	241	Tiki Barber	.60	.25
❑	242	Daniel Campbell	.25	.08
❑	243	Kerry Collins	.40	.15
❑	244	Percy Ellsworth	.25	.08
❑	245	Kent Graham	.25	.08
❑	246	Ike Hilliard	.40	.15
❑	247	Cedric Jones	.25	.08
❑	248	Bashir Levingston RC	.60	.25
❑	249	Pete Mitchell	.25	.08
❑	250	Michael Strahan	.40	.15
❑	251	Amani Toomer	.25	.08
❑	252	Charles Way	.25	.08
❑	253	Andre Weathers RC	.40	.15
❑	254	Richie Anderson	.40	.15
❑	255	Wayne Chrebet	.40	.15
❑	256	Marcus Coleman	.25	.08
❑	257	Bryan Cox	.25	.08
❑	258	Jason Fabini RC	.40	.15
❑	259	Robert Farmer RC	.60	.25
❑	260	Keyshawn Johnson	.60	.25
❑	261	Ray Lucas	.40	.15
❑	262	Curtis Martin	.60	.25
❑	263	Kevin Mawae	.25	.08
❑	264	Eric Ogbogu	.25	.08
❑	265	Bernie Parmalee	.25	.08
❑	266	Vinny Testaverde	.40	.15
❑	267	Dedric Ward	.25	.08
❑	268	Eric Barton RC	.40	.15
❑	269	Tim Brown	.60	.25
❑	270	Tony Bryant	.25	.08
❑	271	Rickey Dudley	.25	.08
❑	272	Rich Gannon	.60	.25
❑	273	Bobby Hoying	.40	.15
❑	274	James Jett	.25	.08
❑	275	Napoleon Kaufman	.40	.15
❑	276	Jon Ritchie	.25	.08
❑	277	Darrell Russell	.25	.08
❑	278	Kenny Shedd	.25	.08
❑	279	Marquis Walker RC	.40	.15
❑	280	Tyrone Wheatley	.40	.15
❑	281	Charles Woodson	.40	.15
❑	282	Luther Broughton RC	.40	.15
❑	283	Al Harris RC	.25	.08
❑	284	Greg Jefferson	.25	.08
❑	285	Dietrich Jells	.25	.08
❑	286	Charles Johnson	.40	.15
❑	287	Chad Lewis	.25	.08
❑	288	Mike Mamula	.25	.08
❑	289	Donovan McNabb	1.00	.40
❑	290	Doug Pederson	.25	.08
❑	291	Allen Rossum	.25	.08
❑	292	Torrance Small	.25	.08
❑	293	Duce Staley	.60	.25
❑	294	Jerome Bettis	.60	.25
❑	295	Kris Brown	.25	.08
❑	296	Mark Bruener	.25	.08
❑	297	Troy Edwards	.25	.08
❑	298	Jason Gildon	.25	.08
❑	299	Richard Huntley	.25	.08
❑	300	Bobby Shaw RC	.60	.25
❑	301	Scott Shields RC	.40	.15
❑	302	Kordell Stewart	.40	.15
❑	303	Hines Ward	.60	.25
❑	304	Amos Zereoue	.60	.25
❑	305	M.Cushing RC/J.Tuman	.40	.15
❑	306	P.Gonzalez/A.Wright RC	2.00	.75
❑	307	Isaac Bruce	.60	.25
❑	308	Kevin Carter	.25	.08
❑	309	Marshall Faulk	.75	.30
❑	310	London Fletcher RC	.40	.15
❑	311	Joe Germaine	.25	.08
❑	312	Az-Zahir Hakim	.40	.15
❑	313	Torry Holt	.60	.25
❑	314	Tony Horne	.25	.08

❑ 315 Mike Jones LB .25 .08
❑ 316 Dexter McCleon RC .60 .25
❑ 317 Orlando Pace .25 .08
❑ 318 Ricky Proehl .25 .08
❑ 319 Kurt Warner 1.25 .50
❑ 320 Roland Williams .25 .08
❑ 321 Grant Wistrom .25 .08
❑ 322 J.Hodgins RC/J.Watson .25 .08
❑ 323 Jermaine Fazande .25 .08
❑ 324 Jeff Graham .25 .08
❑ 325 Jim Harbaugh .40 .15
❑ 326 Raylee Johnson .25 .08
❑ 327 Charlie Jones .25 .08
❑ 328 Freddie Jones .25 .08
❑ 329 Natrone Means .25 .08
❑ 330 Chris Penn .25 .08
❑ 331 Mikhael Ricks .25 .08
❑ 332 Junior Seau .60 .25
❑ 333 R.Davis RC/R.Reed RC .40 .15
❑ 334 Fred Beasley .25 .08
❑ 335 Brentson Buckner .25 .08
❑ 336 Greg Clark .25 .08
❑ 337 Dave Fiore RC .25 .08
❑ 338 Charlie Garner .40 .15
❑ 339 Mark Harris RC .60 .25
❑ 340 Ramos McDonald RC .40 .15
❑ 341 Terrell Owens .60 .25
❑ 342 Jerry Rice 1.25 .50
❑ 343 Lance Schulters .25 .08
❑ 344 J.J. Stokes .40 .15
❑ 345 Bryant Young .25 .08
❑ 346 Steve Young .75 .30
❑ 347 Jeff Garcia .60 .25
❑ 348 Fabien Bownes RC .25 .08
❑ 349 Chad Brown .25 .08
❑ 350 Reggie Brown .25 .08
❑ 351 Sean Dawkins .25 .08
❑ 352 Christian Fauria .25 .08
❑ 353 Ahman Green .60 .25
❑ 354 Walter Jones .25 .08
❑ 355 Cortez Kennedy .25 .08
❑ 356 Jon Kitna .60 .25
❑ 357 Derrick Mayes .40 .15
❑ 358 Charlie Rogers .25 .08
❑ 359 Shawn Springs .25 .08
❑ 360 Ricky Watters .40 .15
❑ 361 Donne Abraham .25 .08
❑ 362 Mike Alstott .60 .25
❑ 363 Reidel Anthony .25 .08
❑ 364 Ronde Barber .25 .08
❑ 365 Derrick Brooks .60 .25
❑ 366 Warrick Dunn .60 .25
❑ 367 Jacquez Green .25 .08
❑ 368 Marcus Jones .25 .08
❑ 369 Shaun King .25 .08
❑ 370 John Lynch .40 .15
❑ 371 Warren Sapp .40 .15
❑ 372 Steve White RC .25 .08
❑ 373 M.Gramatica/K.McLeod RC .40 .15
❑ 374 Blaine Bishop .25 .08
❑ 375 Al Del Greco .25 .08
❑ 376 Kevin Dyson .40 .15
❑ 377 Eddie George .60 .25
❑ 378 Jevon Kearse .60 .25
❑ 379 Derrick Mason .40 .15
❑ 380 Bruce Matthews .25 .08
❑ 381 Steve McNair .60 .25
❑ 382 Neil O'Donnell .25 .08
❑ 383 Yancey Thigpen .25 .08
❑ 384 Frank Wycheck .25 .08
❑ 385 K.Daft/L.Brown .25 .08
❑ 386 Stephen Alexander .25 .08
❑ 387 Champ Bailey .40 .15
❑ 388 Larry Centers .25 .08
❑ 389 Marco Coleman .25 .08
❑ 390 Albert Connell .25 .08
❑ 391 Stephen Davis .60 .25
❑ 392 Irving Fryar .40 .15
❑ 393 Skip Hicks .25 .08
❑ 394 Brad Johnson .60 .25
❑ 395 Michael Westbrook .40 .15
❑ 396 O.Ayanbadejo RC/L.Gordon RC .40 .15
❑ 397 D.Driver/R.Powell .60 .25
❑ 398 T.Bouman/J.Brigham RC .60 .25
❑ 399 B.Huard/S.Bonner .25 .08
❑ 400 M.Sellers/S.George RC .40 .15
❑ 401 Shaun Alexander RC 6.00 2.50
❑ 402 LaVar Arrington RC 8.00 3.00
❑ 403 Tom Brady RC 20.00 10.00
❑ 404 Demario Brown RC .60 .25
❑ 405 Plaxico Burress RC 2.50 1.00
❑ 406 Trung Canidate RC 1.00 .40
❑ 407 Giovanni Carmazzi RC .60 .25
❑ 408 Kwame Cavil RC .60 .25
❑ 409 Chrys Chukwuma RC 1.25 .50
❑ 410 Ron Dayne RC 1.25 .50
❑ 411 Reuben Droughns RC 1.50 .60
❑ 412 Ron Dugans RC .60 .25
❑ 413 Deon Dyer RC 1.00 .40
❑ 414 Danny Farmer RC 1.00 .40
❑ 415 Chafie Fields RC .60 .25
❑ 416 Trevor Gaylor RC 1.00 .40
❑ 417 Sherrod Gideon RC .60 .25
❑ 418 Joey Goodspeed RC .60 .25
❑ 419 Joe Hamilton RC 1.00 .40
❑ 420 Tony Hartley RC .60 .25
❑ 421 Todd Husak RC 1.25 .50
❑ 422 Trevor Insley RC .60 .25
❑ 423 Thomas Jones RC 2.00 .75
❑ 424 Marcus Knight RC 1.00 .40
❑ 425 Jamal Lewis RC 3.00 1.25
❑ 426 Anthony Lucas RC 1.50 .60
❑ 427 Tee Martin RC 1.25 .50
❑ 428 Rondell Mealey RC .60 .25
❑ 429 Sylvester Morris RC 1.00 .40
❑ 430 Chad Morton RC 1.25 .50
❑ 431 Dennis Northcutt RC 1.25 .50
❑ 432 Chad Pennington RC 3.00 1.25
❑ 433 Rodnick Phillips RC .60 .25
❑ 434 Mareno Philyaw RC .60 .25
❑ 435 Jerry Porter RC 1.50 .60
❑ 436 Travis Prentice RC 1.00 .40
❑ 437 Tim Rattay RC 1.25 .50
❑ 438 Chris Redman RC 1.00 .40
❑ 439 J.R. Redmond RC 1.00 .40
❑ 440 Gari Scott RC .60 .25
❑ 441 Keith Smith RC .60 .25
❑ 442 Terrelle Smith RC 1.00 .40
❑ 443 R.Jay Soward RC 1.00 .40
❑ 444 Quinton Spotwood RC .60 .25
❑ 445 Shyrone Stith RC 1.00 .40
❑ 446 Travis Taylor RC 1.25 .50
❑ 447 Troy Walters RC 1.25 .50
❑ 448 Peter Warrick RC 1.25 .50
❑ 449 Dez White RC 1.25 .50
❑ 450 Michael Wiley RC 1.00 .40

2001 Pacific

❑ COMP.SET w/o SP's (450) 50.00 25.00
❑ 1 David Boston .60 .25
❑ 2 Mac Cody .25 .08
❑ 3 Chris Gedney .25 .08
❑ 4 Chris Greisen .25 .08
❑ 5 Terry Hardy .25 .08
❑ 6 MarTay Jenkins .25 .08
❑ 7 Thomas Jones .60 .25
❑ 8 Joel Makovicka .25 .08
❑ 9 Tywan Mitchell .25 .08
❑ 10 Rob Moore .40 .15
❑ 11 Michael Pittman .25 .08
❑ 12 Jake Plummer .40 .15
❑ 13 Frank Sanders .25 .08
❑ 14 Aeneas Williams .25 .08
❑ 15 Jamal Anderson .60 .25
❑ 16 Eugene Baker .25 .08
❑ 17 Chris Chandler .40 .15
❑ 18 Tim Dwight .60 .25
❑ 19 Brian Finneran .25 .08
❑ 20 Jammi German .25 .08
❑ 21 Shawn Jefferson .25 .08
❑ 22 Doug Johnson .25 .08
❑ 23 Danny Kanell .25 .08
❑ 24 Reggie Kelly .25 .08
❑ 25 Terance Mathis .40 .15
❑ 26 Derek Rackley .25 .08
❑ 27 Ron Rivers .25 .08
❑ 28 Maurice Smith .40 .15
❑ 29 Sam Adams .25 .08
❑ 30 Obafemi Ayanbadejo .25 .08
❑ 31 Tony Banks .40 .15
❑ 32 Trent Dilfer .40 .15
❑ 33 Sam Gash .25 .08
❑ 34 Priest Holmes .75 .30
❑ 35 Qadry Ismail .40 .15
❑ 36 Pat Johnson .25 .08
❑ 37 Jamal Lewis 1.00 .40
❑ 38 Jermaine Lewis .25 .08
❑ 39 Ray Lewis .60 .25
❑ 40 Chris Redman .25 .08
❑ 41 Shannon Sharpe .40 .15
❑ 42 Brandon Stokley .40 .15
❑ 43 Travis Taylor .40 .15
❑ 44 Shawn Bryson .25 .08
❑ 45 Kwame Cavil .25 .08
❑ 46 Sam Cowart .25 .08
❑ 47 Doug Flutie .60 .25
❑ 48 Rob Johnson .40 .15
❑ 49 Jonathan Linton .25 .08
❑ 50 Jeremy McDaniel .25 .08
❑ 51 Sammy Morris .25 .08
❑ 52 Eric Moulds .60 .25
❑ 53 Peerless Price .40 .15
❑ 54 Jay Riemersma .25 .08
❑ 55 Antowain Smith .40 .15
❑ 56 Chris Watson .25 .08
❑ 57 Marcellus Wiley .25 .08
❑ 58 Michael Bates .25 .08
❑ 59 Steve Beuerlein .40 .15
❑ 60 Tim Biakabutuka .40 .15
❑ 61 Isaac Byrd .25 .08
❑ 62 Dameyune Craig .25 .08
❑ 63 William Floyd .25 .08
❑ 64 Karl Hankton .25 .08
❑ 65 Donald Hayes .25 .08
❑ 66 Chris Hetherington RC .40 .15
❑ 67 Brad Hoover .25 .08
❑ 68 Patrick Jeffers .60 .25
❑ 69 Muhsin Muhammad .40 .15
❑ 70 Iheanyi Uwaezuoke .25 .08
❑ 71 Wesley Walls .25 .08
❑ 72 James Allen .40 .15
❑ 73 Marlon Barnes .25 .08
❑ 74 D'Wayne Bates .25 .08
❑ 75 Marty Booker .25 .08
❑ 76 Macey Brooks .25 .08
❑ 77 Bobby Engram .40 .15
❑ 78 Curtis Enis .25 .08
❑ 79 Mark Hartsell RC .40 .15
❑ 80 Eddie Kennison .25 .08

❑ 81	Shane Matthews	.25	.08
❑ 82	Cade McNown	.25	.08
❑ 83	Jim Miller	.25	.08
❑ 84	Marcus Robinson	.60	.25
❑ 85	Brian Urlacher	1.00	.40
❑ 86	Dez White	.25	.08
❑ 87	Brandon Bennett	.25	.08
❑ 88	Steve Bush RC	.40	.15
❑ 89	Corey Dillon	.60	.25
❑ 90	Ron Dugans	.25	.08
❑ 91	Danny Farmer	.25	.08
❑ 92	Damon Griffin	.25	.08
❑ 93	Clif Groce	.40	.15
❑ 94	Curtis Keaton	.25	.08
❑ 95	Scott Mitchell	.25	.08
❑ 96	Darnay Scott	.40	.15
❑ 97	Akili Smith	.25	.08
❑ 98	Peter Warrick	.60	.25
❑ 99	Nick Williams	.25	.08
❑ 100	Craig Yeast	.25	.08
❑ 101	Bobby Brown	.25	.08
❑ 102	Darrin Chiaverini	.25	.08
❑ 103	Tim Couch	.40	.15
❑ 104	JaJuan Dawson	.25	.08
❑ 105	Marc Edwards	.25	.08
❑ 106	Kevin Johnson	.40	.15
❑ 107	Dennis Northcutt	.40	.15
❑ 108	David Patten	.25	.08
❑ 109	Doug Pederson	.25	.08
❑ 110	Travis Prentice	.25	.08
❑ 111	Errict Rhett	.25	.08
❑ 112	Aaron Shea	.25	.08
❑ 113	Kevin Thompson	.25	.08
❑ 114	Jamel White	.25	.08
❑ 115	Spergon Wynn	.25	.08
❑ 116	Troy Aikman	1.00	.40
❑ 117	Chris Brazzell	.25	.08
❑ 118	Randall Cunningham	.60	.25
❑ 119	Jackie Harris	.25	.08
❑ 120	Damon Hodge	.25	.08
❑ 121	Rocket Ismail	.40	.15
❑ 122	David LaFleur	.25	.08
❑ 123	Wane McGarity	.25	.08
❑ 124	James McKnight	.40	.15
❑ 125	Emmitt Smith	1.25	.50
❑ 126	Clint Stoerner	.25	.08
❑ 127	Jason Tucker	.25	.08
❑ 128	Michael Wiley	.25	.08
❑ 129	Anthony Wright	.25	.08
❑ 130	Mike Anderson	.60	.25
❑ 131	Dwayne Carswell	.25	.08
❑ 132	Byron Chamberlain	.25	.08
❑ 133	Desmond Clark	.25	.08
❑ 134	Chris Cole	.25	.08
❑ 135	KaRon Coleman	.25	.08
❑ 136	Terrell Davis	.60	.25
❑ 137	Gus Frerotte	.40	.15
❑ 138	Olandis Gary	.60	.25
❑ 139	Brian Griese	.60	.25
❑ 140	Howard Griffith	.25	.08
❑ 141	Jarious Jackson	.40	.15
❑ 142	Ed McCaffrey	.60	.25
❑ 143	Scottie Montgomery RC	.40	.15
❑ 144	Rod Smith	.40	.15
❑ 145	Charlie Batch	.60	.25
❑ 146	Stoney Case	.25	.08
❑ 147	Germane Crowell	.25	.08
❑ 148	Larry Foster	.25	.08
❑ 149	Desmond Howard	.25	.08
❑ 150	Sedrick Irvin	.25	.08
❑ 151	Herman Moore	.40	.15
❑ 152	Johnnie Morton	.40	.15
❑ 153	Robert Porcher	.25	.08
❑ 154	Cory Sauter	.25	.08
❑ 155	Cory Schlesinger	.25	.08
❑ 156	David Sloan	.25	.08
❑ 157	Brian Stablein	.25	.08
❑ 158	James Stewart	.40	.15
❑ 159	Corey Bradford	.25	.08
❑ 160	Tyrone Davis	.25	.08
❑ 161	Donald Driver	.40	.15
❑ 162	Brett Favre	2.00	.75
❑ 163	Bubba Franks	.40	.15
❑ 164	Antonio Freeman	.60	.25
❑ 165	Herbert Goodman	.25	.08
❑ 166	Ahman Green	.60	.25
❑ 167	Matt Hasselbeck	.40	.15
❑ 168	William Henderson	.25	.08
❑ 169	Charles Lee	.25	.08
❑ 170	Dorsey Levens	.40	.15
❑ 171	Bill Schroeder	.40	.15
❑ 172	Darren Sharper	.25	.08
❑ 173	Matt Snider	.25	.08
❑ 174	Danny Wuerffel	.25	.08
❑ 175	Ken Dilger	.25	.08
❑ 176	Jim Finn	.25	.08
❑ 177	Lennox Gordon	.25	.08
❑ 178	E.G. Green	.25	.08
❑ 179	Marvin Harrison	.60	.25
❑ 180	Kelly Holcomb	.60	.25
❑ 181	Trevor Insley	.25	.08
❑ 182	Edgerrin James	.75	.30
❑ 183	Peyton Manning	1.50	.60
❑ 184	Kevin McDougal	.25	.08
❑ 185	Jerome Pathon	.40	.15
❑ 186	Marcus Pollard	.25	.08
❑ 187	Justin Snow	.25	.08
❑ 188	Terrence Wilkins	.25	.08
❑ 189	Reggie Barlow	.25	.08
❑ 190	Kyle Brady	.25	.08
❑ 191	Mark Brunell	.60	.25
❑ 192	Kevin Hardy	.25	.08
❑ 193	Anthony Johnson	.25	.08
❑ 194	Stacey Mack	.25	.08
❑ 195	Jamie Martin	.40	.15
❑ 196	Keenan McCardell	.25	.08
❑ 197	Daimon Shelton	.25	.08
❑ 198	Jimmy Smith	.40	.15
❑ 199	R.Jay Soward	.25	.08
❑ 200	Shyrone Stith	.25	.08
❑ 201	Fred Taylor	.60	.25
❑ 202	Alvis Whitted	.25	.08
❑ 203	Jermaine Williams	.25	.08
❑ 204	Derrick Alexander	.40	.15
❑ 205	Kimble Anders	.25	.08
❑ 206	Donnell Bennett	.25	.08
❑ 207	Mike Cloud	.25	.08
❑ 208	Todd Collins	.25	.08
❑ 209	Tony Gonzalez	.40	.15
❑ 210	Elvis Grbac	.40	.15
❑ 211	Dante Hall	.60	.25
❑ 212	Kevin Lockett	.25	.08
❑ 213	Warren Moon	.40	.15
❑ 214	Frank Moreau	.25	.08
❑ 215	Sylvester Morris	.25	.08
❑ 216	Larry Parker	.25	.08
❑ 217	Tony Richardson	.25	.08
❑ 218	Trace Armstrong	.25	.08
❑ 219	Autry Denson	.25	.08
❑ 220	Bert Emanuel	.25	.08
❑ 221	Jay Fiedler	.60	.25
❑ 222	Oronde Gadsden	.40	.15
❑ 223	Damon Huard	.60	.25
❑ 224	James Johnson	.25	.08
❑ 225	Rob Konrad	.25	.08
❑ 226	Tony Martin	.25	.08
❑ 227	O.J. McDuffie	.25	.08
❑ 228	Mike Quinn	.25	.08
❑ 229	Lamar Smith	.25	.08
❑ 230	Jason Taylor	.25	.08
❑ 231	Thurman Thomas	.40	.15
❑ 232	Zach Thomas	.60	.25
❑ 233	Todd Bouman	.40	.15
❑ 234	Bubby Brister	.25	.08
❑ 235	Cris Carter	.60	.25
❑ 236	Daunte Culpepper	.60	.25
❑ 237	John Davis RC	.40	.15
❑ 238	Robert Griffith	.25	.08
❑ 239	Matthew Hatchette	.25	.08
❑ 240	Jim Kleinsasser	.25	.08
❑ 241	Randy Moss	1.25	.50
❑ 242	John Randle	.25	.08
❑ 243	Robert Smith	.60	.25
❑ 244	Chris Walsh RC	.25	.08
❑ 245	Troy Walters	.25	.08
❑ 246	Moe Williams	.40	.15
❑ 247	Michael Bishop	.25	.08
❑ 248	Drew Bledsoe	.75	.30
❑ 249	Troy Brown	.40	.15
❑ 250	Tedy Bruschi	.50	.20
❑ 251	Tony Carter	.25	.08
❑ 252	Shockmain Davis	.25	.08
❑ 253	Kevin Faulk	.40	.15
❑ 254	Terry Glenn	.40	.15
❑ 255	Ty Law	.40	.15
❑ 256	Lawyer Milloy	.40	.15
❑ 257	J.R. Redmond	.25	.08
❑ 258	Harold Shaw	.25	.08
❑ 259	Tony Simmons	.25	.08
❑ 260	Jermaine Wiggins	.40	.15
❑ 261	Jeff Blake	.25	.08
❑ 262	Aaron Brooks	.60	.25
❑ 263	Cam Cleeland	.25	.08
❑ 264	Andrew Glover	.25	.08
❑ 265	La'Roi Glover	.25	.08
❑ 266	Joe Horn	.40	.15
❑ 267	Kevin Houser	.25	.08
❑ 268	Willie Jackson	.25	.08
❑ 269	Jerald Moore	.25	.08
❑ 270	Chad Morton	.25	.08
❑ 271	Keith Poole	.25	.08
❑ 272	Terrelle Smith	.25	.08
❑ 273	Ricky Williams	.60	.25
❑ 274	Robert Wilson	.25	.08
❑ 275	Jessie Armstead	.25	.08
❑ 276	Tiki Barber	.60	.25
❑ 277	Mike Cherry	.25	.08
❑ 278	Kerry Collins	.40	.15
❑ 279	Greg Comella	.25	.08
❑ 280	Thabiti Davis	.25	.08
❑ 281	Ron Dayne	.60	.25
❑ 282	Ron Dixon	.25	.08
❑ 283	Ike Hilliard	.25	.08
❑ 284	Joe Jurevicius	.25	.08
❑ 285	Jason Sehorn	.25	.08
❑ 286	Michael Strahan	.40	.15
❑ 287	Amani Toomer	.25	.08
❑ 288	Craig Walendy	.25	.08
❑ 289	Damon Washington RC	.40	.15
❑ 290	Richie Anderson	.25	.08
❑ 291	Anthony Becht	.25	.08
❑ 292	Wayne Chrebet	.40	.15
❑ 293	Laveranues Coles	.60	.25
❑ 294	Bryan Cox	.25	.08
❑ 295	Marvin Jones	.25	.08
❑ 296	Mo Lewis	.25	.08
❑ 297	Ray Lucas	.25	.08
❑ 298	Curtis Martin	.60	.25
❑ 299	Bernie Parmalee	.25	.08
❑ 300	Chad Pennington	1.00	.40
❑ 301	Jerald Sowell	.25	.08
❑ 302	Dwight Stone	.25	.08
❑ 303	Vinny Testaverde	.40	.15
❑ 304	Dedric Ward	.25	.08
❑ 305	Tim Brown	.60	.25
❑ 306	Zack Crockett	.25	.08
❑ 307	Scott Dreisbach	.25	.08
❑ 308	Rickey Dudley	.25	.08
❑ 309	David Dunn	.25	.08
❑ 310	Mondriel Fulcher	.25	.08
❑ 311	Rich Gannon	.60	.25
❑ 312	James Jett	.25	.08
❑ 313	Randy Jordan	.25	.08
❑ 314	Napoleon Kaufman	.40	.15

❑ 315 Rodney Peete .25 .08
❑ 316 Jerry Porter .40 .15
❑ 317 Andre Rison .40 .15
❑ 318 Tyrone Wheatley .25 .08
❑ 319 Charles Woodson .25 .08
❑ 320 Darnell Autry .25 .08
❑ 321 Na Brown .25 .08
❑ 322 Hugh Douglas .25 .08
❑ 323 Charles Johnson .25 .08
❑ 324 Chad Lewis .25 .08
❑ 325 Cecil Martin .25 .08
❑ 326 Donovan McNabb .75 .30
❑ 327 Brian Mitchell .25 .08
❑ 328 Todd Pinkston .25 .08
❑ 329 Ron Powlus .25 .08
❑ 330 Stanley Pritchett .25 .08
❑ 331 Torrance Small .25 .08
❑ 332 Duce Staley .60 .25
❑ 333 Troy Vincent .25 .08
❑ 334 Chris Warren .25 .08
❑ 335 Jerome Bettis .60 .25
❑ 336 Plaxico Burress .60 .25
❑ 337 Troy Edwards .25 .08
❑ 338 Chris Fuamatu-Ma'afala .25 .08
❑ 339 Cory Geason .25 .08
❑ 340 Kent Graham .25 .08
❑ 341 Courtney Hawkins .25 .08
❑ 342 Richard Huntley .25 .08
❑ 343 Tee Martin .40 .15
❑ 344 Bobby Shaw .25 .08
❑ 345 Kordell Stewart .40 .15
❑ 346 Hines Ward .60 .25
❑ 347 Destry Wright RC .40 .15
❑ 348 Amos Zereoue .60 .25
❑ 349 Isaac Bruce .60 .25
❑ 350 Trung Canidate .40 .15
❑ 351 Marshall Faulk .75 .30
❑ 352 London Fletcher .25 .08
❑ 353 Joe Germaine .25 .08
❑ 354 Trent Green .60 .25
❑ 355 Az-Zahir Hakim .25 .08
❑ 356 James Hodgins .25 .08
❑ 357 Robert Holcombe .25 .08
❑ 358 Torry Holt .60 .25
❑ 359 Tony Horne .25 .08
❑ 360 Ricky Proehl .25 .08
❑ 361 Chris Thomas RC .40 .15
❑ 362 Kurt Warner 1.25 .50
❑ 363 Justin Watson .25 .08
❑ 364 Kenny Bynum .25 .08
❑ 365 Robert Chancey .25 .08
❑ 366 Curtis Conway .40 .15
❑ 367 Jermaine Fazande .25 .08
❑ 368 Terrell Fletcher .25 .08
❑ 369 Trevor Gaylor .25 .08
❑ 370 Jeff Graham .25 .08
❑ 371 Jim Harbaugh .40 .15
❑ 372 Rodney Harrison .25 .08
❑ 373 Ronney Jenkins .25 .08
❑ 374 Freddie Jones .25 .08
❑ 375 Reggie Jones .25 .08
❑ 376 Ryan Leaf .40 .15
❑ 377 Junior Seau .60 .25
❑ 378 Fred Beasley .25 .08
❑ 379 Greg Clark .25 .08
❑ 380 Jeff Garcia .60 .25
❑ 381 Charlie Garner .40 .15
❑ 382 Terry Jackson .25 .08
❑ 383 Brian Jennings .25 .08
❑ 384 Travis Jervey .25 .08
❑ 385 Jonas Lewis .25 .08
❑ 386 Terrell Owens .60 .25
❑ 387 Jerry Rice 1.25 .50
❑ 388 Paul Smith .25 .08
❑ 389 J.J. Stokes .40 .15
❑ 390 Tai Streets .25 .08
❑ 391 Justin Swift .25 .08
❑ 392 Shaun Alexander .75 .30
❑ 393 Karsten Bailey .25 .08
❑ 394 Chad Brown .25 .08
❑ 395 Sean Dawkins .25 .08
❑ 396 Christian Fauria .25 .08
❑ 397 Brock Huard .25 .08
❑ 398 Darrell Jackson .25 .08
❑ 399 Jon Kitna .60 .25
❑ 400 Derrick Mayes .25 .08
❑ 401 Itula Mili .25 .08
❑ 402 Charlie Rogers .25 .08
❑ 403 Mack Strong .40 .15
❑ 404 Ricky Watters .25 .08
❑ 405 James Williams WR .25 .08
❑ 406 Rabih Abdullah .25 .08
❑ 407 Mike Alstott .60 .25
❑ 408 Reidel Anthony .25 .08
❑ 409 Derrick Brooks .60 .25
❑ 410 Warrick Dunn .60 .25
❑ 411 Jacquez Green .25 .08
❑ 412 Joe Hamilton .25 .08
❑ 413 Keyshawn Johnson .60 .25
❑ 414 Shaun King .25 .08
❑ 415 Charles Kirby RC .60 .25
❑ 416 Warren Sapp .40 .15
❑ 417 Aaron Stecker .25 .08
❑ 418 Todd Yoder .25 .08
❑ 419 Eric Zeier .25 .08
❑ 420 Chris Coleman .25 .08
❑ 421 Kevin Dyson .40 .15
❑ 422 Eddie George .60 .25
❑ 423 Jevon Kearse .40 .15
❑ 424 Erron Kinney .25 .08
❑ 425 Mike Leach .25 .08
❑ 426 Derrick Mason .40 .15
❑ 427 Steve McNair .60 .25
❑ 428 Lorenzo Neal .25 .08
❑ 429 Carl Pickens .40 .15
❑ 430 Chris Sanders .25 .08
❑ 431 Yancey Thigpen .25 .08
❑ 432 Rodney Thomas .25 .08
❑ 433 Frank Wycheck .25 .08
❑ 434 Stephen Alexander .25 .08
❑ 435 Champ Bailey .40 .15
❑ 436 Larry Centers .25 .08
❑ 437 Albert Connell .25 .08
❑ 438 Stephen Davis .60 .25
❑ 439 Zeron Flemister RC .40 .15
❑ 440 Irving Fryar .40 .15
❑ 441 Jeff George .40 .15
❑ 442 Skip Hicks .25 .08
❑ 443 Todd Husak .25 .08
❑ 444 Brad Johnson .40 .15
❑ 445 Adrian Murrell .25 .08
❑ 446 Deion Sanders .60 .25
❑ 447 Mike Sellers .25 .08
❑ 448 Derrius Thompson .25 .08
❑ 449 James Thrash .40 .15
❑ 450 Michael Westbrook .25 .08
❑ 451 Alex Bannister AU/1750 RC 10.00 4.00
❑ 452 Kevan Barlow AU/1500 RC 15.00 6.00
❑ 453 Drew Brees AU/1000 RC 40.00 20.00
❑ 454 Travis Henry AU/1500 RC 15.00 6.00
❑ 455 Chad Johnson AU/1750 RC 30.00 12.50
❑ 456 M.McMahon AU/1000 RC 10.00 4.00
❑ 457 B.Newcombe AU/1750 RC 12.00 5.00
❑ 458 Sage Rosenfels AU/1000 RC 20.00 7.50
❑ 459 LaDainian Tomlinson AU/1500 RC 75.00 40.00
❑ 460 Chris Weinke AU/1000 RC 12.00 5.00
❑ 461 Tay Cody RC 2.00 .75
❑ 462 Adam Archuleta RC 5.00 2.00
❑ 463 Will Allen RC 2.50 1.00
❑ 464 Moran Norris RC 2.00 .75
❑ 465 Tommy Polley RC 5.00 2.00
❑ 466 Ennis Davis RC 2.00 .75
❑ 467 Jamar Fletcher RC 2.50 1.00
❑ 468 Derrick Gibson RC 2.50 1.00
❑ 469 Sedrick Hodge RC 2.00 .75
❑ 470 Willie Howard RC 2.50 1.00
❑ 471 Steve Hutchinson RC 2.50 1.00
❑ 472 Michael Stone RC 2.00 .75
❑ 473 Vinny Sutherland/1750 RC 3.00 1.25
❑ 474 Joe Tafoya RC 2.00 .75
❑ 475 Maurice Williams RC 2.00 .75
❑ 476 Pork Chop Womack RC 2.00 .75
❑ 477 Chad Ward RC 2.00 .75
❑ 478 Scotty Anderson/1750 RC 3.00 1.25
❑ 479 Gary Baxter RC 2.50 1.00
❑ 480 M.Tuiasosopo/1000 RC 6.00 2.50
❑ 481 Tim Hasselbeck/1000 RC 6.00 2.50
❑ 482 Clevan Thomas RC 2.00 .75
❑ 483 Marcus Stroud RC 5.00 2.00
❑ 484 John Schlecht RC 2.00 .75
❑ 485 Brandon Spoon RC 5.00 2.00
❑ 486 Alex Lincoln RC 2.50 1.00
❑ 487 Anthony Thomas/1750 RC 4.00 1.50
❑ 488 Freddie Mitchell/1750 RC 4.00 1.50
❑ 489 Brian Allen RC 2.50 1.00
❑ 490 Zeke Moreno RC 5.00 2.00
❑ 491 Tony Driver RC 5.00 2.00
❑ 492 Kynan Forney RC 2.00 .75
❑ 493 Reggie Wayne/1750 RC 10.00 4.00
❑ 494 Larry Casher RC 2.50 1.00
❑ 495 Fred Wakefield RC 2.50 1.00
❑ 496 Jeff Backus RC 2.50 1.00
❑ 497 Jarrod Cooper RC 5.00 2.00
❑ 498 Heath Evans RC 5.00 2.00
❑ 499 James Jackson/1500 RC 3.00 1.25
❑ 500 Jabari Holloway RC 5.00 2.00
❑ 501 Quincy Morgan/1750 RC 4.00 1.50
❑ 502 Josh Booty/1000 RC 6.00 2.50
❑ 503 Ja'Mar Toombs RC 2.50 1.00
❑ 504 Jason McKinley/1000 RC 4.00 1.50
❑ 505 Reggie White/1500 RC 3.00 1.25
❑ 506 Todd Heap/1750 RC 4.00 1.50
❑ 507 Rudi Johnson/1500 RC 10.00 4.00
❑ 508 Snoop Minnis/1750 RC 3.00 1.25
❑ 509 David Terrell/1750 RC 4.00 1.50
❑ 510 Torrance Marshall RC 5.00 2.00
❑ 511 Michael Bennett/1500 RC 8.00 3.00
❑ 512 Chris Chambers/1750 RC 8.00 3.00
❑ 513 Ben Leard/1000 RC 4.00 1.50
❑ 514 Rod Gardner/1750 RC 4.00 1.50
❑ 515 Michael Vick/1000 RC 50.00 20.00
❑ 516 Josh Heupel/1000 RC 6.00 2.50
❑ 517 Jesse Palmer/1000 RC 6.00 2.50
❑ 518 Quincy Carter/1000 RC 6.00 2.50
❑ 519 A.J. Feeley/1000 RC 6.00 2.50
❑ 520 David Rivers/1000 RC 6.00 2.50
❑ 521 Deuce McAllister/1500 RC 12.00 5.00
❑ 522 LaMont Jordan/1500 RC 10.00 4.00
❑ 523 David Allen/1500 RC 8.00 3.00
❑ 524 Correll Buckhalter/1500 RC 12.00 5.00
❑ 525 Travis Minor/1500 6.00 2.50
❑ 526 Koren Robinson/1750 RC 4.00 1.50
❑ 527 Santana Moss/1750 RC 8.00 3.00
❑ 528 Robert Ferguson/1750 RC 4.00 1.50
❑ 529 T.J.Houshmndzdh/1750 RC 4.00 1.50
❑ 530 Cedrick Wilson/1750 RC 4.00 1.50

2002 Pacific

❑ COMPLETE SET (500) 100.00 50.00
❑ 1 David Boston .60 .25
❑ 2 Arnold Jackson .25 .08
❑ 3 MarTay Jenkins .25 .08
❑ 4 Thomas Jones .40 .15
❑ 5 Kwamie Lassiter .25 .08
❑ 6 Joel Makovicka .25 .08
❑ 7 Ronald McKinnon .25 .08
❑ 8 Tywan Mitchell .25 .08
❑ 9 Michael Pittman .25 .08
❑ 10 Jake Plummer .40 .15
❑ 11 Frank Sanders .25 .08
❑ 12 Kyle Vanden Bosch .25 .08
❑ 13 Jamal Anderson .40 .15
❑ 14 Keith Brooking .25 .08
❑ 15 Chris Chandler .40 .15
❑ 16 Bob Christian .25 .08
❑ 17 Alge Crumpler .40 .15
❑ 18 Brian Finneran .25 .08
❑ 19 Shawn Jefferson .25 .08
❑ 20 Patrick Kerney .25 .08
❑ 21 Terance Mathis .25 .08
❑ 22 Maurice Smith .40 .15
❑ 23 Rodney Thomas .25 .08
❑ 24 Darrick Vaughn .25 .08
❑ 25 Michael Vick 2.00 .75
❑ 26 Sam Adams .25 .08
❑ 27 Terry Allen .25 .08
❑ 28 Obafemi Ayanbadejo .25 .08
❑ 29 Peter Boulware .25 .08
❑ 30 Jason Brookins .25 .08
❑ 31 Randall Cunningham .60 .25
❑ 32 Elvis Grbac .40 .15
❑ 33 Todd Heap .25 .08
❑ 34 Qadry Ismail .40 .15
❑ 35 Jamal Lewis .60 .25
❑ 36 Ray Lewis .60 .25
❑ 37 Chris Redman .25 .08
❑ 38 Shannon Sharpe .40 .15
❑ 39 Brandon Stokley .40 .15
❑ 40 Travis Taylor .40 .15
❑ 41 Moe Williams .25 .08
❑ 42 Rod Woodson .40 .15
❑ 43 Shawn Bryson .25 .08
❑ 44 Larry Centers .25 .08
❑ 45 Nate Clements .25 .08
❑ 46 London Fletcher .25 .08
❑ 47 Reggie Germany .25 .08
❑ 48 Travis Henry .60 .25
❑ 49 Jeremy McDaniel .25 .08
❑ 50 Sammy Morris .25 .08
❑ 51 Eric Moulds .40 .15
❑ 52 Peerless Price .40 .15
❑ 53 Jay Riemersma .25 .08
❑ 54 Alex Van Pelt .25 .08
❑ 55 Tim Biakabutuka .25 .08
❑ 56 Isaac Byrd .25 .08
❑ 57 Doug Evans .25 .08
❑ 58 Donald Hayes .25 .08
❑ 59 Chris Hetherington .25 .08
❑ 60 Brad Hoover .25 .08
❑ 61 Richard Huntley .25 .08
❑ 62 Patrick Jeffers .25 .08
❑ 63 Matt Lytle .25 .08
❑ 64 Dan Morgan .25 .08
❑ 65 Muhsin Muhammad .40 .15
❑ 66 Mike Rucker RC 1.00 .40
❑ 67 Steve Smith .60 .25
❑ 68 Wesley Walls .25 .08
❑ 69 Chris Weinke .40 .15
❑ 70 James Allen .40 .15
❑ 71 Fred Baxter .25 .08
❑ 72 Marty Booker .25 .08
❑ 73 Mike Brown .60 .25
❑ 74 Rosevelt Colvin RC 1.00 .40
❑ 75 Phillip Daniels .25 .08
❑ 76 Leon Johnson .25 .08
❑ 77 Shane Matthews .25 .08
❑ 78 Jim Miller .25 .08
❑ 79 Tony Parrish .25 .08
❑ 80 Marcus Robinson .40 .15
❑ 81 David Terrell .60 .25
❑ 82 Anthony Thomas .40 .15
❑ 83 Brian Urlacher 1.00 .40
❑ 84 Ted Washington .25 .08
❑ 85 Dez White .25 .08
❑ 86 Brandon Bennett .25 .08
❑ 87 Corey Dillon .40 .15
❑ 88 Ron Dugans .25 .08
❑ 89 Danny Farmer .25 .08
❑ 90 T.J. Houshmandzadeh .40 .15
❑ 91 Chad Johnson .60 .25
❑ 92 Curtis Keaton .25 .08
❑ 93 Jon Kitna .40 .15
❑ 94 Tony McGee .25 .08
❑ 95 Lorenzo Neal .25 .08
❑ 96 Darnay Scott .25 .08
❑ 97 Akili Smith .25 .08
❑ 98 Justin Smith .25 .08
❑ 99 Takeo Spikes .25 .08
❑ 100 Peter Warrick .40 .15
❑ 101 Tim Couch .40 .15
❑ 102 JaJuan Dawson .25 .08
❑ 103 Benjamin Gay .40 .15
❑ 104 Anthony Henry .25 .08
❑ 105 James Jackson .25 .08
❑ 106 Kevin Johnson .40 .15
❑ 107 Andre King .25 .08
❑ 108 Jamir Miller .25 .08
❑ 109 Quincy Morgan .25 .08
❑ 110 Dennis Northcutt .25 .08
❑ 111 O.J. Santiago .25 .08
❑ 112 Jamel White .25 .08
❑ 113 Quincy Carter .40 .15
❑ 114 Darrin Chiaverini .60 .25
❑ 115 Dexter Coakley .25 .08
❑ 116 Joey Galloway .40 .15
❑ 117 Troy Hambrick .25 .08
❑ 118 Rocket Ismail .40 .15
❑ 119 Dat Nguyen .25 .08
❑ 120 Ken-Yon Rambo .25 .08
❑ 121 Emmitt Smith 1.50 .60
❑ 122 Reggie Swinton .25 .08
❑ 123 Robert Thomas .25 .08
❑ 124 Michael Wiley .25 .08
❑ 125 Anthony Wright .25 .08
❑ 126 Mike Anderson .60 .25
❑ 127 Dwayne Carswell .25 .08
❑ 128 Desmond Clark .25 .08
❑ 129 Chris Cole .25 .08
❑ 130 Terrell Davis .60 .25
❑ 131 Gus Frerotte .25 .08
❑ 132 Olandis Gary .40 .15
❑ 133 Brian Griese .60 .25
❑ 134 Kevin Kasper .25 .08
❑ 135 Ed McCaffrey .60 .25
❑ 136 Phil McGeoghan RC .40 .15
❑ 137 John Mobley .25 .08
❑ 138 Scottie Montgomery .25 .08
❑ 139 Deltha O'Neal .25 .08
❑ 140 Trevor Pryce .25 .08
❑ 141 Rod Smith .40 .15
❑ 142 Al Wilson .25 .08
❑ 143 Scotty Anderson .25 .08
❑ 144 Charlie Batch .40 .15
❑ 145 Aveion Cason .60 .25
❑ 146 Germane Crowell .25 .08
❑ 147 Reuben Droughns .60 .25
❑ 148 Bert Emanuel .25 .08
❑ 149 Larry Foster .25 .08
❑ 150 Az-Zahir Hakim .25 .08
❑ 151 Desmond Howard .25 .08
❑ 152 Mike McMahon .60 .25
❑ 153 Herman Moore .40 .15
❑ 154 Johnnie Morton .40 .15
❑ 155 Robert Porcher .25 .08
❑ 156 Cory Schlesinger .25 .08
❑ 157 David Sloan .25 .08
❑ 158 James Stewart .40 .15
❑ 159 Lamont Warren .25 .08
❑ 160 Donald Driver .40 .15
❑ 161 Brett Favre 1.50 .60
❑ 162 Bubba Franks .40 .15
❑ 163 Antonio Freeman .60 .25
❑ 164 Kabeer Gbaja-Biamila .40 .15
❑ 165 Terry Glenn .40 .15
❑ 166 Ahman Green .60 .25
❑ 167 William Henderson .25 .08
❑ 168 Dorsey Levens .40 .15
❑ 169 David Martin .25 .08
❑ 170 Rondell Mealey .25 .08
❑ 171 Bill Schroeder .40 .15
❑ 172 Darren Sharper .25 .08
❑ 173 Avion Black .25 .08
❑ 174 Tony Boselli .25 .08
❑ 175 Corey Bradford .25 .08
❑ 176 Marcus Coleman .25 .08
❑ 177 Leomont Evans .25 .08
❑ 178 Aaron Glenn .25 .08
❑ 179 Trevor Insley .25 .08
❑ 180 Jermaine Lewis .25 .08
❑ 181 Anthony Malbrough .25 .08
❑ 182 Frank Moreau .25 .08
❑ 183 Mike Quinn .25 .08
❑ 184 Charlie Rogers .25 .08
❑ 185 Jamie Sharper .25 .08
❑ 186 Matt Snider .25 .08
❑ 187 Gary Walker .25 .08
❑ 188 Kevin Williams RC .40 .15
❑ 189 Kailee Wong .25 .08
❑ 190 Chad Bratzke .25 .08
❑ 191 Ken Dilger .25 .08
❑ 192 Marvin Harrison .60 .25
❑ 193 Edgerrin James .75 .30
❑ 194 Kevin McDougal .25 .08
❑ 195 Rob Morris .25 .08
❑ 196 Jerome Pathon .25 .08
❑ 197 Marcus Pollard .25 .08
❑ 198 Dominic Rhodes .40 .15
❑ 199 Marcus Washington .25 .08
❑ 200 Reggie Wayne .60 .25
❑ 201 Terrence Wilkins .25 .08
❑ 202 Tony Brackens .25 .08
❑ 203 Kyle Brady .25 .08
❑ 204 Mark Brunell .60 .25
❑ 205 Donovin Darius .25 .08
❑ 206 Sean Dawkins .25 .08
❑ 207 Damon Gibson .25 .08
❑ 208 Elvis Joseph .25 .08
❑ 209 Stacey Mack .25 .08
❑ 210 Keenan McCardell .25 .08
❑ 211 Hardy Nickerson .25 .08
❑ 212 Jonathan Quinn .25 .08
❑ 213 Micah Ross RC .25 .08
❑ 214 Jimmy Smith .40 .15
❑ 215 Fred Taylor .60 .25
❑ 216 Patrick Washington .25 .08
❑ 217 Derrick Alexander .40 .15
❑ 218 Mike Cloud .25 .08
❑ 219 Donnie Edwards .25 .08
❑ 220 Tony Gonzalez .40 .15
❑ 221 Trent Green .40 .15
❑ 222 Dante Hall .60 .25
❑ 223 Priest Holmes .75 .30
❑ 224 Eddie Kennison .25 .08
❑ 225 Snoop Minnis .25 .08
❑ 226 Larry Parker .25 .08
❑ 227 Marvcus Patton .25 .08
❑ 228 Tony Richardson .25 .08
❑ 229 Mikhael Ricks .25 .08
❑ 230 Chris Chambers .60 .25
❑ 231 Jay Fiedler .40 .15
❑ 232 Oronde Gadsden .40 .15
❑ 233 Rob Konrad .25 .08

	No.	Player	Mint	Nr Mt
❑	234	Sam Madison	.25	.08
❑	235	Brock Marion	.25	.08
❑	236	James McKnight	.25	.08
❑	237	Travis Minor	.25	.08
❑	238	Jeff Ogden	.25	.08
❑	239	Lamar Smith	.40	.15
❑	240	Jason Taylor	.25	.08
❑	241	Zach Thomas	.60	.25
❑	242	Dedric Ward	.25	.08
❑	243	Ricky Williams	.60	.25
❑	244	Michael Bennett	.40	.15
❑	245	Todd Bouman	.25	.08
❑	246	Cris Carter	.60	.25
❑	247	Byron Chamberlain	.25	.08
❑	248	Doug Chapman	.25	.08
❑	249	Kenny Clark RC	.40	.15
❑	250	Daunte Culpepper	.60	.25
❑	251	Nate Jacquet	.25	.08
❑	252	Jim Kleinsasser	.25	.08
❑	253	Harold Morrow	.25	.08
❑	254	Randy Moss	1.25	.50
❑	255	Jake Reed	.25	.08
❑	256	Spergon Wynn	.25	.08
❑	257	Drew Bledsoe	.75	.30
❑	258	Tom Brady	1.50	.60
❑	259	Troy Brown	.40	.15
❑	260	Fred Coleman	.25	.08
❑	261	Marc Edwards	.25	.08
❑	262	Kevin Faulk	.40	.15
❑	263	Bobby Hamilton	.25	.08
❑	264	Ty Law	.40	.15
❑	265	Lawyer Milloy	.40	.15
❑	266	David Patten	.25	.08
❑	267	J.R. Redmond	.25	.08
❑	268	Antowain Smith	.40	.15
❑	269	Adam Vinatieri	.60	.25
❑	270	Jermaine Wiggins	.25	.08
❑	271	Aaron Brooks	.60	.25
❑	272	Cam Cleeland	.25	.08
❑	273	Charlie Clemons RC	.25	.08
❑	274	James Fenderson RC	.40	.15
❑	275	La'Roi Glover	.25	.08
❑	276	Joe Horn	.40	.15
❑	277	Willie Jackson	.25	.08
❑	278	Sammy Knight	.25	.08
❑	279	Michael Lewis	.25	.08
❑	280	Deuce McAllister	.75	.30
❑	281	Terrelle Smith	.25	.08
❑	282	Boo Williams	.25	.08
❑	283	Robert Wilson	.25	.08
❑	284	Tiki Barber	.60	.25
❑	285	Micheal Barrow	.25	.08
❑	286	Kerry Collins	.40	.15
❑	287	Greg Comella	.25	.08
❑	288	Thabiti Davis	.25	.08
❑	289	Ron Dayne	.40	.15
❑	290	Ron Dixon	.25	.08
❑	291	Ike Hilliard	.40	.15
❑	292	Joe Jurevicius	.25	.08
❑	293	Michael Strahan	.40	.15
❑	294	Amani Toomer	.40	.15
❑	295	Damon Washington	.25	.08
❑	296	John Abraham	.40	.15
❑	297	Richie Anderson	.25	.08
❑	298	Anthony Becht	.25	.08
❑	299	Wayne Chrebet	.40	.15
❑	300	Laveranues Coles	.40	.15
❑	301	James Farrior	.25	.08
❑	302	Marvin Jones	.25	.08
❑	303	LaMont Jordan	.60	.25
❑	304	Curtis Martin	.60	.25
❑	305	Santana Moss	.60	.25
❑	306	Chad Pennington	.75	.30
❑	307	Kevin Swayne	.25	.08
❑	308	Vinny Testaverde	.40	.15
❑	309	Craig Yeast	.25	.08
❑	310	Greg Biekert	.25	.08
❑	311	Tim Brown	.60	.25
❑	312	Zack Crockett	.25	.08
❑	313	Rich Gannon	.60	.25
❑	314	Charlie Garner	.40	.15
❑	315	Sebastian Janikowski	.25	.08
❑	316	Randy Jordan	.25	.08
❑	317	Terry Kirby	.25	.08
❑	318	Jerry Porter	.25	.08
❑	319	Jerry Rice	1.25	.50
❑	320	Jon Ritchie	.25	.08
❑	321	Tyrone Wheatley	.40	.15
❑	322	Roland Williams	.25	.08
❑	323	Charles Woodson	.40	.15
❑	324	Correll Buckhalter	.40	.15
❑	325	Brian Dawkins	.40	.15
❑	326	Hugh Douglas	.25	.08
❑	327	A.J. Feeley	.60	.25
❑	328	Chad Lewis	.25	.08
❑	329	Cecil Martin	.25	.08
❑	330	Brian Mitchell	.25	.08
❑	331	Freddie Mitchell	.40	.15
❑	332	Todd Pinkston	.40	.15
❑	333	Rod Smart RC	.25	.08
❑	334	Duce Staley	.60	.25
❑	335	James Thrash	.40	.15
❑	336	Jeremiah Trotter	.25	.08
❑	337	Troy Vincent	.25	.08
❑	338	Kendrell Bell	.60	.25
❑	339	Jerome Bettis	.60	.25
❑	340	Demetrius Brown RC	.40	.15
❑	341	Plaxico Burress	.40	.15
❑	342	Troy Edwards	.25	.08
❑	343	Chris Fuamatu-Ma'afala	.25	.08
❑	344	Jason Gildon	.25	.08
❑	345	Earl Holmes	.25	.08
❑	346	Joey Porter	.60	.25
❑	347	Chad Scott	.25	.08
❑	348	Bobby Shaw	.25	.08
❑	349	Kordell Stewart	.40	.15
❑	350	Hines Ward	.60	.25
❑	351	Amos Zereoue	.60	.25
❑	352	Adam Archuleta	.25	.08
❑	353	Dre' Bly	.25	.08
❑	354	Isaac Bruce	.60	.25
❑	355	Trung Canidate	.40	.15
❑	356	Ernie Conwell	.25	.08
❑	357	Marshall Faulk	.60	.25
❑	358	Torry Holt	.60	.25
❑	359	Leonard Little	.25	.08
❑	360	Yo Murphy	.25	.08
❑	361	Ricky Proehl	.25	.08
❑	362	Kurt Warner	.60	.25
❑	363	Aeneas Williams	.25	.08
❑	364	Drew Brees	.60	.25
❑	365	Curtis Conway	.25	.08
❑	366	Tim Dwight	.40	.15
❑	367	Terrell Fletcher	.25	.08
❑	368	Doug Flutie	.60	.25
❑	369	Jeff Graham	.25	.08
❑	370	Rodney Harrison	.25	.08
❑	371	Ronney Jenkins	.25	.08
❑	372	Raylee Johnson	.25	.08
❑	373	Freddie Jones	.25	.08
❑	374	Ryan McNeil	.25	.08
❑	375	Junior Seau	.60	.25
❑	376	LaDainian Tomlinson	1.00	.40
❑	377	Marcellus Wiley	.25	.08
❑	378	Kevan Barlow	.40	.15
❑	379	Fred Beasley	.25	.08
❑	380	Zack Bronson RC	.40	.15
❑	381	Andre Carter	.25	.08
❑	382	Jeff Garcia	.60	.25
❑	383	Garrison Hearst	.40	.15
❑	384	Terry Jackson	.25	.08
❑	385	Eric Johnson	.40	.15
❑	386	Saladin McCullough RC	.25	.08
❑	387	Terrell Owens	.60	.25
❑	388	Ahmed Plummer	.25	.08
❑	389	J.J. Stokes	.25	.08
❑	390	Tai Streets	.25	.08
❑	391	Vinny Sutherland	.25	.08
❑	392	Bryant Young	.25	.08
❑	393	Shaun Alexander	.75	.30
❑	394	Chad Brown	.25	.08
❑	395	Kerwin Cook RC	.40	.15
❑	396	Trent Dilfer	.40	.15
❑	397	Bobby Engram	.25	.08
❑	398	Christian Fauria	.25	.08
❑	399	Matt Hasselbeck	.40	.15
❑	400	Darrell Jackson	.40	.15
❑	401	John Randle	.25	.08
❑	402	Koren Robinson	.40	.15
❑	403	Anthony Simmons	.25	.08
❑	404	Mack Strong	.40	.15
❑	405	Ricky Watters	.25	.08
❑	406	James Williams WR	.25	.08
❑	407	Mike Alstott	.60	.25
❑	408	Ronde Barber	.25	.08
❑	409	Derrick Brooks	.60	.25
❑	410	Jameel Cook	.25	.08
❑	411	Warrick Dunn	.60	.25
❑	412	Jacquez Green	.25	.08
❑	413	Brad Johnson	.40	.15
❑	414	Keyshawn Johnson	.60	.25
❑	415	Rob Johnson	.40	.15
❑	416	John Lynch	.40	.15
❑	417	Dave Moore	.25	.08
❑	418	Warren Sapp	.40	.15
❑	419	Aaron Stecker	.25	.08
❑	420	Karl Williams	.25	.08
❑	421	Drew Bennett	.60	.25
❑	422	Eddie Berlin	.25	.08
❑	423	Rafael Cooper RC	.40	.15
❑	424	Kevin Dyson	.40	.15
❑	425	Eddie George	.60	.25
❑	426	Mike Green	.25	.08
❑	427	Skip Hicks	.25	.08
❑	428	Jevon Kearse	.40	.15
❑	429	Erron Kinney	.25	.08
❑	430	Derrick Mason	.40	.15
❑	431	Justin McCareins	.40	.15
❑	432	Steve McNair	.60	.25
❑	433	Neil O'Donnell	.25	.08
❑	434	Frank Wycheck	.25	.08
❑	435	Reidel Anthony	.25	.08
❑	436	Jessie Armstead	.25	.08
❑	437	Champ Bailey	.40	.15
❑	438	Tony Banks	.25	.08
❑	439	Michael Bates	.25	.08
❑	440	Donnell Bennett	.25	.08
❑	441	Ki-Jana Carter	.25	.08
❑	442	Stephen Davis	.40	.15
❑	443	Zeron Flemister	.25	.08
❑	444	Rod Gardner	.40	.15
❑	445	Kevin Lockett	.25	.08
❑	446	Eric Metcalf	.25	.08
❑	447	Sage Rosenfels	.25	.08
❑	448	Fred Smoot	.25	.08
❑	449	Michael Westbrook	.25	.08
❑	450	Danny Wuerffel	.25	.08
❑	451	Jason McAddley RC	1.50	.60
❑	452	Freddie Milons RC	1.50	.60
❑	453	Bryan Thomas RC	1.50	.60
❑	454	Levi Jones RC	1.50	.60
❑	455	William Green RC	2.00	.75
❑	456	Luke Staley RC	1.50	.60
❑	457	Daniel Graham RC	2.00	.75
❑	458	David Garrard RC	2.00	.75
❑	459	Reche Caldwell RC	2.00	.75
❑	460	Andra Davis RC	1.50	.60
❑	461	Lito Sheppard RC	2.00	.75
❑	462	Chris Hope RC	2.00	.75
❑	463	Javon Walker RC	4.00	1.50
❑	464	David Carr RC	5.00	2.00
❑	465	Alan Harper RC	1.00	.40
❑	466	Adrian Peterson RC	2.00	.75
❑	467	Kelly Campbell RC	1.50	.60

❑ 468	Ashley Lelie RC	4.00	1.50
❑ 469	Kurt Kittner RC	1.50	.60
❑ 470	Antwaan Randle El RC	3.00	1.25
❑ 471	Ladell Betts RC	2.00	.75
❑ 472	Josh Reed RC	2.00	.75
❑ 473	Clinton Portis RC	6.00	2.50
❑ 474	Ron Johnson RC	1.50	.60
❑ 475	Eric Crouch RC	2.00	.75
❑ 476	Tracey Wistrom RC	1.50	.60
❑ 477	David Neill RC	1.50	.60
❑ 478	Ronald Curry RC	2.00	.75
❑ 479	Lamar Gordon RC	2.00	.75
❑ 480	Damien Anderson RC	1.50	.60
❑ 481	Napoleon Harris RC	2.00	.75
❑ 482	Zak Kustok RC	2.00	.75
❑ 483	Rocky Calmus RC	2.00	.75
❑ 484	Roy Williams RC	5.00	2.00
❑ 485	Joey Harrington RC	5.00	2.00
❑ 486	Maurice Morris RC	2.00	.75
❑ 487	Antonio Bryant RC	2.00	.75
❑ 488	Josh McCown RC	2.50	1.00
❑ 489	John Henderson RC	2.00	.75
❑ 490	Quentin Jammer RC	2.00	.75
❑ 491	Mike Williams RC	1.50	.60
❑ 492	Patrick Ramsey RC	2.50	1.00
❑ 493	Kenyon Coleman RC	1.00	.40
❑ 494	DeShaun Foster RC	2.00	.75
❑ 495	Brian Poli-Dixon RC	1.50	.60
❑ 496	Cliff Russell RC	1.50	.60
❑ 497	Brian Westbrook RC	3.00	1.25
❑ 498	Andre Davis RC	1.50	.60
❑ 499	Larry Tripplett RC	1.00	.40
❑ 500	Lamont Thompson RC	1.50	.60
❑ 501	T.J. Duckett RC	3.00	1.25
❑ 502	Dameon Hunter RC	1.00	.40
❑ 503	Javin Hunter RC	1.00	.40
❑ 504	Tellis Redmon RC	1.50	.60
❑ 505	Chester Taylor RC	2.00	.75
❑ 506	Randy Fasani RC	1.50	.60
❑ 507	Julius Peppers RC	4.00	1.50
❑ 508	Jamin Elliott RC	1.00	.40
❑ 509	Chad Hutchinson RC	1.50	.60
❑ 510	Eddie Drummond RC	1.50	.60
❑ 511	Craig Nall RC	2.00	.75
❑ 512	Jabar Gaffney RC	2.00	.75
❑ 513	Jonathan Wells RC	2.00	.75
❑ 514	Shaun Hill RC	2.00	.75
❑ 515	Deion Branch RC	4.00	1.50
❑ 516	Rohan Davey RC	2.00	.75
❑ 517	J.T. O'Sullivan RC	1.50	.60
❑ 518	Tim Carter RC	1.50	.60
❑ 519	Daryl Jones RC	1.50	.60
❑ 520	Jeremy Shockey RC	6.00	2.50
❑ 521	Seth Burford RC	1.50	.60
❑ 522	Brandon Doman RC	1.50	.60
❑ 523	Jerramy Stevens RC	2.00	.75
❑ 524	Travis Stephens RC	1.50	.60
❑ 525	Marquise Walker RC	1.50	.60

1996 Pacific Dynagon

❑	COMPLETE SET (144)	60.00	25.00
❑ 1	Larry Centers	.75	.30
❑ 2	Garrison Hearst	.75	.30
❑ 3	Dave Krieg	.40	.15
❑ 4	Frank Sanders	.75	.30
❑ 5	Jeff George	.75	.30
❑ 6	Craig Heyward	.40	.15
❑ 7	Terance Mathis	.40	.15
❑ 8	Eric Metcalf	.40	.15
❑ 9	Todd Collins	.75	.30
❑ 10	Darick Holmes	.40	.15
❑ 11	Jim Kelly	1.50	.60
❑ 12	Eric Moulds RC	4.00	1.50
❑ 13	Bryce Paup	.40	.15
❑ 14	Thurman Thomas	1.50	.60
❑ 15	Tim Biakabutuka RC	1.50	.60
❑ 16	Blake Brockermeyer	.40	.15
❑ 17	Mark Carrier WR	.40	.15
❑ 18	Kerry Collins	1.50	.60
❑ 19	Derrick Moore	.40	.15
❑ 20	Bobby Engram RC	1.50	.60
❑ 21	Jeff Graham	.40	.15
❑ 22	Erik Kramer	.40	.15
❑ 23	Rashaan Salaam	.75	.30
❑ 24	Steve Stenstrom	.40	.15
❑ 25	Chris Zorich	.40	.15
❑ 26	Jeff Blake	1.50	.60
❑ 27	David Dunn	.40	.15
❑ 28	Carl Pickens	.75	.30
❑ 29	Darnay Scott	.75	.30
❑ 30	Earnest Byner	.40	.15
❑ 31	Leroy Hoard	.40	.15
❑ 32	Keenan McCardell	1.50	.60
❑ 33	Eric Zeier	.40	.15
❑ 34	Troy Aikman	3.00	1.25
❑ 35	Chris Boniol	.40	.15
❑ 36	Michael Irvin	1.50	.60
❑ 37	Daryl Johnston	.75	.30
❑ 38	Deion Sanders	2.00	.75
❑ 39	Emmitt Smith	5.00	2.00
❑ 40	Stepfret Williams	.40	.15
❑ 41	John Elway	6.00	2.50
❑ 42	Terrell Davis	2.50	1.00
❑ 43	Anthony Miller	.75	.30
❑ 44	Shannon Sharpe	.75	.30
❑ 45	Scott Mitchell	.75	.30
❑ 46	Herman Moore	.75	.30
❑ 47	Brett Perriman	.40	.15
❑ 48	Barry Sanders	5.00	2.00
❑ 49	Cory Schlesinger	.40	.15
❑ 50	Edgar Bennett	.75	.30
❑ 51	Robert Brooks	1.50	.60
❑ 52	Mark Chmura	.75	.30
❑ 53	Brett Favre	6.00	2.50
❑ 54	Reggie White	1.50	.60
❑ 55	Eddie George RC	4.00	1.50
❑ 56	Steve McNair	2.50	1.00
❑ 57	Chris Sanders	.75	.30
❑ 58	Rodney Thomas	.40	.15
❑ 59	Ben Bronson RC	.40	.15
❑ 60	Zack Crockett	.40	.15
❑ 61	Marshall Faulk	2.00	.75
❑ 62	Jim Harbaugh	.75	.30
❑ 63	Mark Brunell	2.00	.75
❑ 64	Kevin Hardy RC	1.50	.60
❑ 65	Willie Jackson	.75	.30
❑ 66	Pete Mitchell	.75	.30
❑ 67	James O.Stewart	.75	.30
❑ 68	Marcus Allen	1.50	.60
❑ 69	Steve Bono	.40	.15
❑ 70	Lake Dawson	.40	.15
❑ 71	Neil Smith	.75	.30
❑ 72	Tamarick Vanover	.75	.30
❑ 73	Irving Fryar	.75	.30
❑ 74	Terry Kirby	.75	.30
❑ 75	Dan Marino	6.00	2.50
❑ 76	O.J. McDuffie	.75	.30
❑ 77	Bernie Parmalee	.40	.15
❑ 78	Stanley Pritchett RC	.75	.30
❑ 79	Cris Carter	1.50	.60
❑ 80	Qadry Ismail	.75	.30
❑ 81	Chad May	.40	.15
❑ 82	Warren Moon	.75	.30
❑ 83	Robert Smith	.75	.30
❑ 84	Drew Bledsoe	2.00	.75
❑ 85	Ben Coates	.75	.30
❑ 86	Terry Glenn RC	3.00	1.25
❑ 87	Curtis Martin	2.50	1.00
❑ 88	Willie McGinest	.40	.15
❑ 89	Mario Bates	.75	.30
❑ 90	Jim Everett	.40	.15
❑ 91	Wayne Martin	.40	.15
❑ 92	Shane Pahukoa RC	.40	.15
❑ 93	Ray Zellars	.40	.15
❑ 94	Dave Brown	.40	.15
❑ 95	Chris Calloway	.40	.15
❑ 96	Rodney Hampton	.75	.30
❑ 97	Tyrone Wheatley	.75	.30
❑ 98	Wayne Chrebet	2.00	.75
❑ 99	Glenn Foley	.75	.30
❑ 100	Keyshawn Johnson RC	3.00	1.25
❑ 101	Adrian Murrell	.75	.30
❑ 102	Alex Van Dyke RC	.75	.30
❑ 103	Tim Brown	1.50	.60
❑ 104	Billy Joe Hobert	.75	.30
❑ 105	Rocket Ismail	.40	.15
❑ 106	Napoleon Kaufman	1.50	.60
❑ 107	Harvey Williams	.40	.15
❑ 108	Charlie Garner	.75	.30
❑ 109	Rodney Peete	.40	.15
❑ 110	Ricky Watters	.75	.30
❑ 111	Calvin Williams	.40	.15
❑ 112	Mark Bruener	.40	.15
❑ 113	Kevin Greene	.75	.30
❑ 114	Ernie Mills	.40	.15
❑ 115	Kordell Stewart	1.50	.60
❑ 116	Yancey Thigpen	.75	.30
❑ 117	Dave Barr	.40	.15
❑ 118	Jerome Bettis	1.50	.60
❑ 119	Isaac Bruce	1.50	.60
❑ 120	Lawrence Phillips RC	1.50	.60
❑ 121	J.T. Thomas	.40	.15
❑ 122	Ronnie Harmon	.40	.15
❑ 123	Aaron Hayden RC	.40	.15
❑ 124	Stan Humphries	.75	.30
❑ 125	Junior Seau	1.50	.60
❑ 126	William Floyd	.75	.30
❑ 127	Elvis Grbac	.75	.30
❑ 128	Jerry Rice	3.00	1.25
❑ 129	J.J. Stokes	1.50	.60
❑ 130	Steve Young	2.50	1.00
❑ 131	Joey Galloway	1.50	.60
❑ 132	Cortez Kennedy	.40	.15
❑ 133	Kevin Mawae	.40	.15
❑ 134	Rick Mirer	.75	.30
❑ 135	Chris Warren	.75	.30
❑ 136	Trent Dilfer	1.50	.60
❑ 137	Jerry Ellison	.40	.15
❑ 138	Alvin Harper	.40	.15
❑ 139	Errict Rhett	.75	.30
❑ 140	Terry Allen	.75	.30
❑ 141	Brian Mitchell	.40	.15
❑ 142	Gus Frerotte	.75	.30
❑ 143	Michael Westbrook	1.50	.60
❑ 144	Heath Shuler	.75	.30

1997 Pacific Dynagon

❑	COMPLETE SET (144)	80.00	40.00
❑ 1	Larry Centers	1.00	.40
❑ 2	Kent Graham	.60	.25
❑ 3	Leeland McElroy	.60	.25
❑ 4	Frank Sanders	1.00	.40
❑ 5	Jamal Anderson	1.25	.50
❑ 6	Bert Emanuel	1.00	.40
❑ 7	Bobby Hebert	.60	.25
❑ 8	Terance Mathis	1.00	.40
❑ 9	Eric Metcalf	1.00	.40
❑ 10	Derrick Alexander WR	1.00	.40

❑ 11	Earnest Byner	.60	.25
❑ 12	Michael Jackson	1.00	.40
❑ 13	Vinny Testaverde	1.00	.40
❑ 14	Quinn Early	.60	.25
❑ 15	Jim Kelly	1.25	.50
❑ 16	Eric Moulds	1.25	.50
❑ 17	Andre Reed	1.00	.40
❑ 18	Bruce Smith	1.00	.40
❑ 19	Thurman Thomas	1.25	.50
❑ 20	Tim Biakabutuka	1.00	.40
❑ 21	Mark Carrier WR	.60	.25
❑ 22	Kerry Collins	1.25	.50
❑ 23	Kevin Greene	1.00	.40
❑ 24	Anthony Johnson	.60	.25
❑ 25	Wesley Walls	1.00	.40
❑ 26	Curtis Conway	1.00	.40
❑ 27	Bobby Engram	1.00	.40
❑ 28	Raymont Harris	.60	.25
❑ 29	Dave Krieg	.60	.25
❑ 30	Rashaan Salaam	.60	.25
❑ 31	Jeff Blake	1.00	.40
❑ 32	Ki-Jana Carter	.60	.25
❑ 33	Garrison Hearst	1.00	.40
❑ 34	Carl Pickens	1.00	.40
❑ 35	Darnay Scott	1.00	.40
❑ 36	Troy Aikman	2.50	1.00
❑ 37	Chris Boniol	.60	.25
❑ 38	Michael Irvin	1.25	.50
❑ 39	Deion Sanders	1.25	.50
❑ 40	Emmitt Smith	4.00	1.50
❑ 41	Herschel Walker	1.00	.40
❑ 42	Terrell Davis	1.50	.60
❑ 43	John Elway	5.00	2.00
❑ 44	Ed McCaffrey	1.00	.40
❑ 45	Shannon Sharpe	1.00	.40
❑ 46	Alfred Williams	.60	.25
❑ 47	Scott Mitchell	1.00	.40
❑ 48	Herman Moore	1.00	.40
❑ 49	Brett Perriman	.60	.25
❑ 50	Barry Sanders	4.00	1.50
❑ 51	Edgar Bennett	1.00	.40
❑ 52	Robert Brooks	1.00	.40
❑ 53	Mark Chmura	1.00	.40
❑ 54	Brett Favre	5.00	2.00
❑ 55	Antonio Freeman	1.25	.50
❑ 56	Desmond Howard	1.00	.40
❑ 57	Reggie White	1.25	.50
❑ 58	Chris Chandler	1.00	.40
❑ 59	Eddie George	1.25	.50
❑ 60	James McKeehan	.60	.25
❑ 61	Steve McNair	1.50	.60
❑ 62	Chris Sanders	.60	.25
❑ 63	Sean Dawkins	.60	.25
❑ 64	Ken Dilger	.60	.25
❑ 65	Marshall Faulk	1.50	.60
❑ 66	Jim Harbaugh	1.00	.40
❑ 67	Marvin Harrison	1.25	.50
❑ 68	Tony Boselli	.60	.25
❑ 69	Mark Brunell	1.50	.60
❑ 70	Keenan McCardell	1.00	.40
❑ 71	Natrone Means	1.00	.40
❑ 72	Jimmy Smith	1.00	.40
❑ 73	Marcus Allen	1.25	.50
❑ 74	Kimble Anders	1.00	.40
❑ 75	Dale Carter	.60	.25
❑ 76	Greg Hill	.60	.25
❑ 77	Derrick Thomas	1.25	.50
❑ 78	Tamarick Vanover	1.00	.40
❑ 79	Karim Abdul-Jabbar	1.25	.50
❑ 80	Dan Marino	5.00	2.00
❑ 81	O.J. McDuffie	1.00	.40
❑ 82	Jerris McPhail	.60	.25
❑ 83	Zach Thomas	1.25	.50
❑ 84	Cris Carter	1.25	.50
❑ 85	Brad Johnson	1.25	.50
❑ 86	Jake Reed	1.00	.40
❑ 87	Robert Smith	1.00	.40
❑ 88	Drew Bledsoe	1.50	.60
❑ 89	Ben Coates	1.00	.40
❑ 90	Terry Glenn	1.25	.50
❑ 91	Curtis Martin	1.50	.60
❑ 92	Willie McGinest	.60	.25
❑ 93	Jim Everett	.60	.25
❑ 94	Michael Haynes	.60	.25
❑ 95	Haywood Jeffires	.60	.25
❑ 96	Ray Zellars	.60	.25
❑ 97	Dave Brown	.60	.25
❑ 98	Rodney Hampton	1.00	.40
❑ 99	Danny Kanell	1.00	.40
❑ 100	Thomas Lewis	.60	.25
❑ 101	Wayne Chrebet	1.25	.50
❑ 102	Keyshawn Johnson	1.25	.50
❑ 103	Adrian Murrell	1.00	.40
❑ 104	Neil O'Donnell	1.00	.40
❑ 105	Tim Brown	1.25	.50
❑ 106	Rickey Dudley	1.00	.40
❑ 107	Jeff Hostetler	.60	.25
❑ 108	Napoleon Kaufman	1.25	.50
❑ 109	Ty Detmer	1.00	.40
❑ 110	Jason Dunn	.60	.25
❑ 111	Irving Fryar	1.00	.40
❑ 112	Chris T. Jones	.60	.25
❑ 113	Ricky Watters	1.00	.40
❑ 114	Jerome Bettis	1.25	.50
❑ 115	Chad Brown	.60	.25
❑ 116	Kordell Stewart	1.25	.50
❑ 117	Mike Tomczak	.60	.25
❑ 118	Rod Woodson	1.00	.40
❑ 119	Tony Banks	1.00	.40
❑ 120	Isaac Bruce	1.25	.50
❑ 121	Eddie Kennison	1.00	.40
❑ 122	Lawrence Phillips	.60	.25
❑ 123	Terrell Fletcher	.60	.25
❑ 124	Stan Humphries	1.00	.40
❑ 125	Tony Martin	1.00	.40
❑ 126	Junior Seau	1.25	.50
❑ 127	Elvis Grbac	1.00	.40
❑ 128	Terrell Owens	1.50	.60
❑ 129	Ted Popson	.60	.25
❑ 130	Jerry Rice	2.50	1.00
❑ 131	Steve Young	1.50	.60
❑ 132	John Friesz	.60	.25
❑ 133	Joey Galloway	1.00	.40
❑ 134	Michael McCrary	.60	.25
❑ 135	Lamar Smith	1.25	.50
❑ 136	Chris Warren	1.00	.40
❑ 137	Mike Alstott	1.25	.50
❑ 138	Trent Dilfer	1.25	.50
❑ 139	Courtney Hawkins	.60	.25
❑ 140	Errict Rhett	.60	.25
❑ 141	Terry Allen	1.25	.50
❑ 142	Henry Ellard	.60	.25
❑ 143	Gus Frerotte	.60	.25
❑ 144	Leslie Shepherd	.60	.25
❑ C	Mark Brunell Sample	2.00	.75

2001 Pacific Dynagon

❑	COMP.SET w/o SP's (100)	40.00	15.00
❑ 1	David Boston	1.25	.50
❑ 2	Thomas Jones	.75	.30

❑ 3	Jake Plummer	.75	.30
❑ 4	Jamal Anderson	1.25	.50
❑ 5	Tim Dwight	1.25	.50
❑ 6	Elvis Grbac	.75	.30
❑ 7	Jamal Lewis	2.00	.75
❑ 8	Ray Lewis	1.25	.50
❑ 9	Shannon Sharpe	.75	.30
❑ 10	Rob Johnson	.75	.30
❑ 11	Eric Moulds	.75	.30
❑ 12	Peerless Price	.75	.30
❑ 13	Tim Biakabutuka	.75	.30
❑ 14	Patrick Jeffers	.75	.30
❑ 15	Muhsin Muhammad	.75	.30
❑ 16	James Allen	.75	.30
❑ 17	Cade McNown	.50	.20
❑ 18	Marcus Robinson	1.25	.50
❑ 19	Brian Urlacher	2.00	.75
❑ 20	Corey Dillon	1.25	.50
❑ 21	Akili Smith	.50	.20
❑ 22	Peter Warrick	1.25	.50
❑ 23	Tim Couch	.75	.30
❑ 24	Kevin Johnson	.75	.30
❑ 25	Randall Cunningham	1.25	.50
❑ 26	Emmitt Smith	2.50	1.00
❑ 27	Mike Anderson	1.25	.50
❑ 28	Terrell Davis	1.25	.50
❑ 29	Brian Griese	1.25	.50
❑ 30	Ed McCaffrey	1.25	.50
❑ 31	Rod Smith	.75	.30
❑ 32	Charlie Batch	1.25	.50
❑ 33	Johnnie Morton	.75	.30
❑ 34	James Stewart	.75	.30
❑ 35	Brett Favre	4.00	1.50
❑ 36	Antonio Freeman	1.25	.50
❑ 37	Ahman Green	1.25	.50
❑ 38	Marvin Harrison	1.25	.50
❑ 39	Edgerrin James	1.50	.60
❑ 40	Peyton Manning	3.00	1.25
❑ 41	Mark Brunell	1.25	.50
❑ 42	Keenan McCardell	.50	.20
❑ 43	Jimmy Smith	.75	.30
❑ 44	Fred Taylor	1.25	.50
❑ 45	Derrick Alexander	.75	.30
❑ 46	Tony Gonzalez	.75	.30
❑ 47	Sylvester Morris	.50	.20
❑ 48	Jay Fiedler	1.25	.50
❑ 49	Oronde Gadsden	.75	.30
❑ 50	Lamar Smith	.75	.30
❑ 51	Cris Carter	1.25	.50
❑ 52	Daunte Culpepper	1.25	.50
❑ 53	Randy Moss	2.50	1.00
❑ 54	Drew Bledsoe	1.50	.60
❑ 55	Terry Glenn	.50	.20
❑ 56	J.R. Redmond	.50	.20
❑ 57	Aaron Brooks	1.25	.50
❑ 58	Joe Horn	.75	.30
❑ 59	Ricky Williams	1.25	.50
❑ 60	Tiki Barber	1.25	.50
❑ 61	Kerry Collins	.75	.30
❑ 62	Ron Dayne	1.25	.50
❑ 63	Amani Toomer	.50	.20
❑ 64	Wayne Chrebet	.75	.30

Card		
65 Curtis Martin	1.25	.50
66 Vinny Testaverde	.75	.30
67 Tim Brown	1.25	.50
68 Rich Gannon	1.25	.50
69 Tyrone Wheatley	.75	.30
70 Charles Johnson	.50	.20
71 Donovan McNabb	1.50	.60
72 Duce Staley	1.25	.50
73 Jerome Bettis	1.25	.50
74 Plaxico Burress	1.25	.50
75 Kordell Stewart	.75	.30
76 Isaac Bruce	1.25	.50
77 Marshall Faulk	1.50	.60
78 Torry Holt	1.25	.50
79 Kurt Warner	2.50	1.00
80 Curtis Conway	.75	.30
81 Doug Flutie	1.25	.50
82 Jeff Garcia	1.25	.50
83 Charlie Garner	.75	.30
84 Terrell Owens	1.25	.50
85 Jerry Rice	2.50	1.00
86 Shaun Alexander	1.50	.60
87 Matt Hasselbeck	.75	.30
88 Darrell Jackson	1.25	.50
89 Mike Alstott	1.25	.50
90 Warrick Dunn	1.25	.50
91 Brad Johnson	1.25	.50
92 Keyshawn Johnson	1.25	.50
93 Shaun King	.50	.20
94 Eddie George	1.25	.50
95 Jevon Kearse	.75	.30
96 Derrick Mason	.75	.30
97 Steve McNair	1.25	.50
98 Stephen Davis	1.25	.50
99 Jeff George	.75	.30
100 Deion Sanders	1.25	.50
101 Michael Bennett AU RC	40.00	15.00
102 Drew Brees AU RC	80.00	40.00
103 Chris Chambers AU RC	30.00	15.00
104 LaMont Jordan AU RC	50.00	20.00
105 Deuce McAllister AU RC	60.00	30.00
106 Koren Robinson AU RC	25.00	10.00
107 David Terrell AU RC	25.00	12.50
108 LaDain Tomlinson AU RC	150.00	75.00
109 Marques Tuiasosopo AU RC	30.00	12.50
110 Michael Vick AU RC	200.00	100.00
111 Chris Weinke AU RC	25.00	10.00
112 Kevan Barlow AU RC	25.00	10.00
113 Josh Booty AU RC	20.00	7.50
114 Rod Gardner AU RC	25.00	10.00
115 Todd Heap AU RC	20.00	7.50
116 Travis Henry AU RC	25.00	10.00
117 James Jackson AU RC	20.00	7.50
118 Chad Johnson AU RC	80.00	40.00
119 Rudi Johnson AU RC	50.00	20.00
120 Ben Leard AU RC	12.00	5.00
121 Quincy Morgan AU RC	20.00	7.50
122 Snoop Minnis AU RC	12.00	5.00
123 Freddie Mitchell AU RC	20.00	7.50
124 Sage Rosenfels AU RC	20.00	7.50
125 Anthony Thomas AU RC	25.00	10.00
126 Reggie Wayne AU RC	40.00	20.00
127 Dan Alexander AU RC	12.00	5.00
128 Will Allen AU RC	10.00	4.00
129 Scotty Anderson AU RC	10.00	4.00
130 Adam Archuleta AU RC	12.00	5.00
131 Alex Bannister AU RC	10.00	4.00
133 Tay Cody AU RC	8.00	3.00
134 Tony Dixon AU RC	10.00	4.00
135 Heath Evans AU RC	10.00	4.00
137 Derrick Gibson AU RC	10.00	4.00
138 Edgerton Hartwell AU RC	8.00	3.00
139 Tim Hasselbeck AU RC	12.00	5.00
140 Jabari Holloway AU RC	10.00	4.00
141 Torrance Marshall AU RC	12.00	5.00
142 Jason McKinley AU RC	10.00	4.00
143 Mike McMahon AU RC	20.00	7.50
144 Bobby Newcombe AU RC	10.00	4.00
145 Moran Norris AU RC	8.00	3.00
146 Tommy Polley AU RC	12.00	5.00
147 Vinny Sutherland AU RC	10.00	4.00
149 Reggie White AU RC	10.00	4.00
150 Cedrick Wilson AU RC	20.00	7.50

1998 Pacific Omega

Card		
COMPLETE SET (250)	40.00	15.00
1 Larry Centers	.25	.08
2 Rob Moore	.40	.15
3 Michael Pittman RC	1.50	.75
4 Jake Plummer	.60	.25
5 Simeon Rice	.40	.15
6 Frank Sanders	.40	.15
7 Eric Swann	.25	.08
8 Morten Andersen	.25	.08
9 Jamal Anderson	.60	.25
10 Chris Chandler	.40	.15
11 Harold Green	.25	.08
12 Byron Hanspard	.25	.08
13 Terance Mathis	.40	.15
14 O.J. Santiago	.25	.08
15 Peter Boulware	.25	.08
16 Jay Graham	.25	.08
17 Eric Green	.25	.08
18 Michael Jackson	.25	.08
19 Jermaine Lewis	.40	.15
20 Ray Lewis	.60	.25
21 Jonathan Ogden	.25	.08
22 Eric Zeier	.40	.15
23 Steve Christie	.25	.08
24 Todd Collins	.25	.08
25 Quinn Early	.25	.08
26 Eric Moulds	.60	.25
27 Andre Reed	.40	.15
28 Antowain Smith	.60	.25
29 Bruce Smith	.40	.15
30 Thurman Thomas	.60	.25
31 Ted Washington	.25	.08
32 Michael Bates	.25	.08
33 Tim Biakabutuka	.40	.15
34 Mark Carrier	.25	.08
35 Rae Carruth	.25	.08
36 Kerry Collins	.40	.15
37 Kevin Greene	.40	.15
38 Fred Lane	.25	.08
39 Muhsin Muhammad	.40	.15
40 Wesley Walls	.40	.15
41 Curtis Conway	.40	.15
42 Bobby Engram	.40	.15
43 Curtis Enis RC	.50	.20
44 Walt Harris	.25	.08
45 Erik Kramer	.25	.08
46 Chris Penn	.25	.08
47 Ryan Wetnight RC	.25	.08
48 Jeff Blake	.40	.15
49 Ki-Jana Carter	.25	.08
50 John Copeland	.25	.08
51 Corey Dillon	.60	.25
52 Tony McGee	.25	.08
53 Carl Pickens	.40	.15
54 Darnay Scott	.40	.15
55 Takeo Spikes RC	1.25	.50
56 Troy Aikman	1.25	.50
57 Eric Bjornson	.25	.08
58 Greg Ellis RC	.50	.20
59 Michael Irvin	.60	.25
60 Daryl Johnston	.40	.15
61 David LaFleur	.25	.08
62 Deion Sanders	.60	.25
63 Emmitt Smith	2.00	.75
64 Herschel Walker	.40	.15
65 Nicky Sualua RC	.40	.15
66 Steve Atwater	.25	.08
67 Terrell Davis	.60	.25
68 John Elway	2.50	1.00
69 Brian Griese RC	2.50	1.00
70 Ed McCaffrey	.40	.15
71 John Mobley	.25	.08
72 Marcus Nash RC	.50	.20
73 Shannon Sharpe	.40	.15
74 Neil Smith	.40	.15
75 Rod Smith	.40	.15
76 Charlie Batch RC	1.25	.50
77 Germane Crowell RC	.75	.30
78 Jason Hanson	.25	.08
79 Scott Mitchell	.40	.15
80 Herman Moore	.40	.15
81 Johnnie Morton	.40	.15
82 Barry Sanders	2.00	.75
83 Tommy Vardell	.25	.08
84 Robert Brooks	.40	.15
85 Gilbert Brown	.25	.08
86 LeRoy Butler	.25	.08
87 Mark Chmura	.40	.15
88 Brett Favre	2.50	1.00
89 Antonio Freeman	.60	.25
90 William Henderson	.40	.15
91 Vonnie Holliday RC	.75	.30
92 Dorsey Levens	.60	.25
93 Reggie White	.60	.25
94 Aaron Bailey	.25	.08
95 Quentin Coryatt	.25	.08
96 Zack Crockett	.25	.08
97 Ken Dilger	.25	.08
98 Marshall Faulk	.75	.30
99 E.G. Green RC	.75	.30
100 Marvin Harrison	.60	.25
101 Peyton Manning RC	15.00	6.00
102 Jerome Pathon RC	1.25	.50
103 Tavian Banks RC	.75	.30
104 Tony Boselli	.25	.08
105 Tony Brackens	.25	.08
106 Mark Brunell	.60	.25
107 Kevin Hardy	.25	.08
108 Keenan McCardell	.40	.15
109 Pete Mitchell	.25	.08
110 Jimmy Smith	.40	.15
111 James Stewart	.40	.15
112 Fred Taylor RC	2.00	.75
113 Kimble Anders	.40	.15
114 Dale Carter	.25	.08
115 Tony Gonzalez	.60	.25
116 Elvis Grbac	.40	.15
117 Donnell Bennett	.25	.08
118 Andre Rison	.40	.15
119 Rashaan Shehee RC	.75	.30
120 Derrick Thomas	.60	.25
121 Tamarick Vanover	.25	.08
122 Karim Abdul-Jabbar	.60	.25
123 John Avery RC	.75	.30
124 Troy Drayton	.25	.08
125 John Dutton RC	.50	.20
126 Craig Erickson	.25	.08
127 Dan Marino	2.50	1.00
128 O.J. McDuffie	.40	.15
129 Jerris McPhail	.25	.08
130 Stanley Pritchett	.25	.08
131 Larry Shannon RC	.50	.20
132 Zach Thomas	.60	.25

❑ 133 Cris Carter .60 .25
❑ 134 Randall Cunningham .60 .25
❑ 135 Andrew Glover .25 .08
❑ 136 Brad Johnson .60 .25
❑ 137 Randall McDaniel .25 .08
❑ 138 David Palmer .25 .08
❑ 139 John Randle .40 .15
❑ 140 Jake Reed .40 .15
❑ 141 Robert Smith .60 .25
❑ 142 Drew Bledsoe 1.00 .40
❑ 143 Ben Coates .40 .15
❑ 144 Robert Edwards RC .75 .30
❑ 145 Terry Glenn .60 .25
❑ 146 Shawn Jefferson .25 .08
❑ 147 Willie McGinest .25 .08
❑ 148 Tony Simmons RC .75 .30
❑ 149 Chris Slade .25 .08
❑ 150 Troy Davis .25 .08
❑ 151 Mark Fields .25 .08
❑ 152 Andre Hastings .25 .08
❑ 153 Billy Joe Hobert .25 .08
❑ 154 William Roaf .25 .08
❑ 155 Heath Shuler .25 .08
❑ 156 Danny Wuerffel .40 .15
❑ 157 Ray Zellars .25 .08
❑ 158 Jessie Armstead .25 .08
❑ 159 Tiki Barber .60 .25
❑ 160 Chris Calloway .25 .08
❑ 161 Mike Cherry .25 .08
❑ 162 Danny Kanell .40 .15
❑ 163 Amani Toomer .40 .15
❑ 164 Charles Way .25 .08
❑ 165 Tyrone Wheatley .40 .15
❑ 166 Kyle Brady .25 .08
❑ 167 Wayne Chrebet .60 .25
❑ 168 Glenn Foley .40 .15
❑ 169 Scott Frost RC .50 .20
❑ 170 Keyshawn Johnson .60 .25
❑ 171 Leon Johnson .25 .08
❑ 172 Alex Van Dyke .25 .08
❑ 173 Dedric Ward .25 .08
❑ 174 Tim Brown .60 .25
❑ 175 Rickey Dudley .25 .08
❑ 176 Jeff George .40 .15
❑ 177 Desmond Howard .40 .15
❑ 178 James Jett .40 .15
❑ 179 Napoleon Kaufman .60 .25
❑ 180 Darrell Russell .25 .08
❑ 181 Charles Woodson RC 1.50 .60
❑ 182 Jason Dunn .25 .08
❑ 183 Irving Fryar .40 .15
❑ 184 Charlie Garner .40 .15
❑ 185 Bobby Hoying .40 .15
❑ 186 Chris T. Jones .25 .08
❑ 187 Michael Timpson .25 .08
❑ 188 Kevin Turner .25 .08
❑ 189 Jerome Bettis .60 .25
❑ 190 Will Blackwell .25 .08
❑ 191 Mark Bruener .25 .08
❑ 192 Charles Johnson .25 .08
❑ 193 George Jones .25 .08
❑ 194 Levon Kirkland .25 .08
❑ 195 Kordell Stewart .60 .25
❑ 196 Hines Ward RC 5.00 2.50
❑ 197 Tony Banks .40 .15
❑ 198 Isaac Bruce .60 .25
❑ 199 Ernie Conwell .25 .08
❑ 200 Robert Holcombe RC .75 .30
❑ 201 Eddie Kennison .40 .15
❑ 202 Amp Lee .25 .08
❑ 203 Orlando Pace .25 .08
❑ 204 Charlie Jones .25 .08
❑ 205 Freddie Jones .25 .08
❑ 206 Ryan Leaf RC 1.25 .50
❑ 207 Natrone Means .40 .15
❑ 208 Junior Seau .60 .25
❑ 209 Bryan Still .25 .08
❑ 210 Greg Clark .25 .08
❑ 211 Jim Druckenmiller .25 .08
❑ 212 Marc Edwards .25 .08
❑ 213 Garrison Hearst .60 .25
❑ 214 Terrell Owens .60 .25
❑ 215 Jerry Rice 1.25 .50
❑ 216 J.J. Stokes .40 .15
❑ 217 Bryant Young .25 .08
❑ 218 Steve Young .75 .30
❑ 219 Chad Brown .25 .08
❑ 220 Joey Galloway .40 .15
❑ 221 Cortez Kennedy .25 .08
❑ 222 Jon Kitna .60 .25
❑ 223 James McKnight .60 .25
❑ 224 Warren Moon .60 .25
❑ 225 Michael Sinclair .25 .08
❑ 226 Ricky Watters .40 .15
❑ 227 Mike Alstott .60 .25
❑ 228 Reidel Anthony .40 .15
❑ 229 Derrick Brooks .60 .25
❑ 230 Trent Dilfer .60 .25
❑ 231 Warrick Dunn .60 .25
❑ 232 Dave Moore .25 .08
❑ 233 Hardy Nickerson .25 .08
❑ 234 Warren Sapp .40 .15
❑ 235 Karl Williams .25 .08
❑ 236 Willie Davis .25 .08
❑ 237 Kevin Dyson RC 1.25 .50
❑ 238 Eddie George .60 .25
❑ 239 Derrick Mason .40 .15
❑ 240 Steve McNair .60 .25
❑ 241 Chris Sanders .25 .08
❑ 242 Frank Wycheck .25 .08
❑ 243 Terry Allen .60 .25
❑ 244 Jamie Asher .25 .08
❑ 245 Gus Frerotte .25 .08
❑ 246 Darrell Green .40 .15
❑ 247 Skip Hicks RC .75 .30
❑ 248 Brian Mitchell .25 .08
❑ 249 Leslie Shepherd .25 .08
❑ 250 Michael Westbrook .40 .15

1999 Pacific Omega

❑ COMPLETE SET (250) 40.00 20.00
❑ 1 Mario Bates .25 .08
❑ 2 David Boston RC 1.25 .50
❑ 3 Rob Moore .40 .15
❑ 4 Adrian Murrell .40 .15
❑ 5 Jake Plummer .40 .15
❑ 6 Frank Sanders .40 .15
❑ 7 Aeneas Williams .25 .08
❑ 8 J.Makovicka/L.Shelton RC 1.25 .50
❑ 9 Jamal Anderson .60 .25
❑ 10 Ray Buchanan .25 .08
❑ 11 Chris Chandler .40 .15
❑ 12 Tim Dwight .60 .25
❑ 13 Byron Hanspard .25 .08
❑ 14 Terance Mathis .40 .15
❑ 15 O.J. Santiago .25 .08
❑ 16 D.Kanell/C.Calloway .25 .08
❑ 17 Peter Boulware .25 .08
❑ 18 Priest Holmes 1.00 .40
❑ 19 Patrick Johnson .25 .08
❑ 20 Jermaine Lewis .40 .15
❑ 21 Ray Lewis .60 .25
❑ 22 Michael McCrary .25 .08
❑ 23 Jonathan Ogden .25 .08
❑ 24 T.Banks/S.Mitchell .25 .08
❑ 25 Doug Flutie .60 .25
❑ 26 Rob Johnson .40 .15
❑ 27 Eric Moulds .60 .25
❑ 28 Andre Reed .40 .15
❑ 29 Antowain Smith .60 .25
❑ 30 Bruce Smith .40 .15
❑ 31 Kevin Williams .25 .08
❑ 32 S.Bryson/P.Price RC 1.25 .50
❑ 33 Steve Beuerlein .25 .08
❑ 34 Tim Biakabutuka .40 .15
❑ 35 Rae Carruth .25 .08
❑ 36 Dameyune Craig RC 2.00 .75
❑ 37 William Floyd .25 .08
❑ 38 Kevin Greene .25 .08
❑ 39 Muhsin Muhammad .40 .15
❑ 40 Wesley Walls .40 .15
❑ 41 Edgar Bennett .25 .08
❑ 42 Robert Chancey RC 1.50 .60
❑ 43 Curtis Conway .40 .15
❑ 44 Bobby Engram .40 .15
❑ 45 Curtis Enis .25 .08
❑ 46 Cade McNown RC 1.00 .40
❑ 47 Ryan Wetnight .25 .08
❑ 48 D.Bates/Mar.Booker RC 1.25 .50
❑ 49 Jeff Blake .40 .15
❑ 50 Scott Covington RC 1.25 .50
❑ 51 Corey Dillon .60 .25
❑ 52 James Hundon .40 .15
❑ 53 Carl Pickens .40 .15
❑ 54 Darnay Scott .25 .08
❑ 55 Akili Smith RC 1.00 .40
❑ 56 Craig Yeast RC 1.00 .40
❑ 57 Tim Couch RC 1.25 .50
❑ 58 Ty Detmer .40 .15
❑ 59 Marc Edwards .25 .08
❑ 60 Kevin Johnson RC 1.25 .50
❑ 61 Terry Kirby .25 .08
❑ 62 Sedrick Shaw .25 .08
❑ 63 Leslie Shepherd .25 .08
❑ 64 Chiaverini/McCutcheon RC 1.00 .40
❑ 65 Troy Aikman 1.25 .50
❑ 66 Michael Irvin .40 .15
❑ 67 David LaFleur .25 .08
❑ 68 Wane McGarity RC .50 .20
❑ 69 Ernie Mills .25 .08
❑ 70 Deion Sanders .60 .25
❑ 71 Emmitt Smith 1.25 .50
❑ 72 R.Ismail/J.McKnight .40 .15
❑ 73 Bubby Brister .25 .08
❑ 74 Byron Chamberlain RC 1.00 .40
❑ 75 Terrell Davis .60 .25
❑ 76 Olandis Gary RC 1.25 .50
❑ 77 Brian Griese .60 .25
❑ 78 Ed McCaffrey .40 .15
❑ 79 Shannon Sharpe .40 .15
❑ 80 Rod Smith .40 .15
❑ 81 T.McGriff/A.Wilson RC .50 .20
❑ 82 Charlie Batch .60 .25
❑ 83 Chris Claiborne RC .50 .20
❑ 84 Germane Crowell .25 .08
❑ 85 Terry Fair .25 .08
❑ 86 Sedrick Irvin RC .50 .20
❑ 87 Herman Moore .40 .15
❑ 88 Johnnie Morton .40 .15
❑ 89 Barry Sanders 2.00 .75
❑ 90 Mark Chmura .25 .08
❑ 91 Brett Favre 2.00 .75
❑ 92 Antonio Freeman .60 .25
❑ 93 Desmond Howard .40 .15
❑ 94 Dorsey Levens .60 .25
❑ 95 Derrick Mayes .25 .08
❑ 96 Bill Schroeder .60 .25
❑ 97 A.Brooks/D.Miller RC 2.50 1.00

❑ 98 E.G. Green .25 .08
❑ 99 Marvin Harrison .60 .25
❑ 100 Edgerrin James RC 5.00 2.00
❑ 101 Peyton Manning 2.00 .75
❑ 102 Jerome Pathon .25 .08
❑ 103 Marcus Pollard .25 .08
❑ 104 Ken Dilger .25 .08
❑ 105 Derrick Alexander WR .40 .15
❑ 106 Reggie Barlow .25 .08
❑ 107 Tony Boselli .25 .08
❑ 108 Mark Brunell .60 .25
❑ 109 George Jones .25 .08
❑ 110 Keenan McCardell .40 .15
❑ 111 Jimmy Smith .40 .15
❑ 112 James Stewart .40 .15
❑ 113 Fred Taylor .60 .25
❑ 114 Kimble Anders .40 .15
❑ 115 Mike Cloud RC 1.00 .40
❑ 116 Tony Gonzalez .60 .25
❑ 117 Elvis Grbac .40 .15
❑ 118 Byron Bam Morris .25 .08
❑ 119 Andre Rison .40 .15
❑ 120 Derrick Thomas .60 .25
❑ 121 Karim Abdul-Jabbar .40 .15
❑ 122 Oronde Gadsden .40 .15
❑ 123 James Johnson RC 1.00 .40
❑ 124 Rob Konrad RC 1.25 .50
❑ 125 Dan Marino 2.00 .75
❑ 126 O.J. McDuffie .40 .15
❑ 127 Lamar Thomas .25 .08
❑ 128 Zach Thomas .60 .25
❑ 129 Cris Carter .60 .25
❑ 130 Daunte Culpepper RC 5.00 2.00
❑ 131 Randall Cunningham .60 .25
❑ 132 Matthew Hatchette .25 .08
❑ 133 Leroy Hoard .25 .08
❑ 134 David Palmer .25 .08
❑ 135 John Randle .40 .15
❑ 136 Randy Moss 1.50 .60
❑ 137 Robert Smith .60 .25
❑ 138 Drew Bledsoe .75 .30
❑ 139 Ben Coates .40 .15
❑ 140 Kevin Faulk RC 1.25 .50
❑ 141 Terry Glenn .60 .25
❑ 142 Shawn Jefferson .25 .08
❑ 143 Ty Law .40 .15
❑ 144 Tony Simmons .25 .08
❑ 145 Bishop RC/Katzenmoyer RC 1.25 .50
❑ 146 Cameron Cleeland .25 .08
❑ 147 Andre Hastings .25 .08
❑ 148 Billy Joe Hobert .25 .08
❑ 149 Joe Johnson .25 .08
❑ 150 Keith Poole .25 .08
❑ 151 William Roaf .25 .08
❑ 152 Billy Joe Tolliver .25 .08
❑ 153 Ricky Williams RC 2.50 1.00
❑ 154 Tiki Barber .60 .25
❑ 155 Gary Brown .25 .08
❑ 156 Kent Graham .25 .08
❑ 157 Ike Hilliard .25 .08
❑ 158 David Patten .40 .15
❑ 159 Jason Sehorn .25 .08
❑ 160 Amani Toomer .25 .08
❑ 161 Montgomery RC/Petit.RC 1.00 .40
❑ 162 Wayne Chrebet .40 .15
❑ 163 Bryan Cox .25 .08
❑ 164 Aaron Glenn .25 .08
❑ 165 Keyshawn Johnson .60 .25
❑ 166 Leon Johnson .25 .08
❑ 167 Curtis Martin .60 .25
❑ 168 Vinny Testaverde .40 .15
❑ 169 Dedric Ward .25 .08
❑ 170 Tim Brown .60 .25
❑ 171 Rickey Dudley .25 .08
❑ 172 James Jett .40 .15
❑ 173 Napoleon Kaufman .60 .25
❑ 174 Jon Ritchie .25 .08
❑ 175 Darrell Russell .25 .08
❑ 176 Charles Woodson .60 .25
❑ 177 R.Gannon/H.Shuler .60 .25
❑ 178 Hugh Douglas .25 .08
❑ 179 Donovan McNabb RC 6.00 2.50
❑ 180 Allen Rossum .25 .08
❑ 181 Duce Staley .40 .15
❑ 182 Kevin Turner .25 .08
❑ 183 C.Johnson/D.Pederson .25 .08
❑ 184 B.Gardner/C.Martin RC 1.25 .50
❑ 185 Jerome Bettis .60 .25
❑ 186 Mark Bruener .25 .08
❑ 187 Troy Edwards RC 1.00 .40
❑ 188 Courtney Hawkins .25 .08
❑ 189 Levon Kirkland .25 .08
❑ 190 Kordell Stewart .40 .15
❑ 191 Hines Ward .60 .25
❑ 192 M.Johnson/A.Zereoue RC 1.25 .50
❑ 193 Greg Clark .25 .08
❑ 194 Terrell Fletcher .25 .08
❑ 195 Charlie Jones .25 .08
❑ 196 Cecil Collins RC .50 .20
❑ 197 Natrone Means .40 .15
❑ 198 Mikhael Ricks .25 .08
❑ 199 Junior Seau .60 .25
❑ 200 Bryan Still .25 .08
❑ 201 Ryan Thelwell RC 1.00 .40
❑ 202 Garrison Hearst .40 .15
❑ 203 Terry Jackson RC 1.00 .40
❑ 204 R.W. McQuarters .25 .08
❑ 205 Terrell Owens .60 .25
❑ 206 Jerry Rice 1.25 .50
❑ 207 J.J. Stokes .40 .15
❑ 208 L.Phillips/T.Vardell .25 .08
❑ 209 Steve Young .75 .30
❑ 210 Karsten Bailey RC 1.00 .40
❑ 211 Chad Brown .25 .08
❑ 212 Christian Fauria .25 .08
❑ 213 Joey Galloway .40 .15
❑ 214 Ahman Green .60 .25
❑ 215 Brock Huard RC 1.25 .50
❑ 216 Cortez Kennedy .25 .08
❑ 217 Jon Kitna .60 .25
❑ 218 Ricky Watters .40 .15
❑ 219 Isaac Bruce .60 .25
❑ 220 Az-Zahir Hakim .25 .08
❑ 221 June Henley RC .25 .08
❑ 222 Greg Hill .25 .08
❑ 223 Torry Holt RC 3.00 1.25
❑ 224 Amp Lee .25 .08
❑ 225 Ricky Proehl .25 .08
❑ 226 M.Faulk/T.Green .75 .30
❑ 227 Mike Alstott .60 .25
❑ 228 Reidel Anthony .40 .15
❑ 229 Trent Dilfer .40 .15
❑ 230 Warrick Dunn .60 .25
❑ 231 Bert Emanuel .40 .15
❑ 232 Jacquez Green .25 .08
❑ 233 Warren Sapp .25 .08
❑ 234 Shaun King RC/McFar.RC 1.25 .50
❑ 235 Mike Archie RC .50 .20
❑ 236 Kevin Dyson .40 .15
❑ 237 Eddie George .60 .25
❑ 238 Derrick Mason .40 .15
❑ 239 Steve McNair .60 .25
❑ 240 Yancey Thigpen .25 .08
❑ 241 Frank Wycheck .25 .08
❑ 242 Jevon Kearse RC/Hall RC 2.00 .75
❑ 243 Stephen Alexander .25 .08
❑ 244 Champ Bailey RC 1.50 .60
❑ 245 Stephen Davis .60 .25
❑ 246 Skip Hicks .25 .08
❑ 247 James Thrash RC 1.25 .50
❑ 248 Michael Westbrook .40 .15
❑ 249 Dan Wilkinson .25 .08
❑ 250 B.Johnson/L.Centers .60 .25

2000 Pacific Omega

❑ COMP.SET w/o SP's (150) 20.00 7.50
❑ 1 David Boston .60 .25

❑ 2 Dave Brown .25 .08
❑ 3 Rob Moore .40 .15
❑ 4 Jake Plummer .40 .15
❑ 5 Simeon Rice .40 .15
❑ 6 Frank Sanders .40 .15
❑ 7 Jamal Anderson .60 .25
❑ 8 Chris Chandler .40 .15
❑ 9 Tim Dwight .60 .25
❑ 10 Terance Mathis .40 .15
❑ 11 Tony Banks .40 .15
❑ 12 Peter Boulware .25 .08
❑ 13 Priest Holmes .75 .30
❑ 14 Qadry Ismail .40 .15
❑ 15 Doug Flutie .60 .25
❑ 16 Rob Johnson .40 .15
❑ 17 Jonathan Linton .25 .08
❑ 18 Eric Moulds .60 .25
❑ 19 Peerless Price .40 .15
❑ 20 Antowain Smith .60 .25
❑ 21 Steve Beuerlein .25 .08
❑ 22 Tim Biakabutuka .40 .15
❑ 23 Patrick Jeffers .60 .25
❑ 24 Muhsin Muhammad .40 .15
❑ 25 Wesley Walls .40 .15
❑ 26 Bobby Engram .40 .15
❑ 27 Curtis Enis .25 .08
❑ 28 Cade McNown .25 .08
❑ 29 Marcus Robinson .60 .25
❑ 30 Willie Anderson .25 .08
❑ 31 Michael Basnight .25 .08
❑ 32 Corey Dillon .60 .25
❑ 33 Akili Smith .25 .08
❑ 34 Tim Couch .40 .15
❑ 35 Kevin Johnson .60 .25
❑ 36 Wali Rainer .25 .08
❑ 37 Troy Aikman 1.25 .50
❑ 38 Dexter Coakley .25 .08
❑ 39 Rocket Ismail .40 .15
❑ 40 Emmitt Smith 1.25 .50
❑ 41 Chris Warren .25 .08
❑ 42 Terrell Davis .60 .25
❑ 43 Olandis Gary .60 .25
❑ 44 Brian Griese .60 .25
❑ 45 Ed McCaffrey .60 .25
❑ 46 Rod Smith .40 .15
❑ 47 Charlie Batch .60 .25
❑ 48 Germane Crowell .25 .08
❑ 49 Herman Moore .40 .15
❑ 50 Johnnie Morton .40 .15
❑ 51 Barry Sanders 1.50 .60
❑ 52 Corey Bradford .40 .15
❑ 53 Brett Favre 2.00 .75
❑ 54 Antonio Freeman .60 .25
❑ 55 Dorsey Levens .40 .15
❑ 56 Bill Schroeder .40 .15
❑ 57 Ken Dilger .25 .08
❑ 58 Marvin Harrison .60 .25
❑ 59 Edgerrin James 1.00 .40
❑ 60 Peyton Manning 1.50 .60
❑ 61 Jerome Pathon .40 .15
❑ 62 Terrence Wilkins .25 .08
❑ 63 Mark Brunell .60 .25

❑ 64	Keenan McCardell	.40	.15
❑ 65	Jimmy Smith	.40	.15
❑ 66	Fred Taylor	.60	.25
❑ 67	Derrick Alexander	.40	.15
❑ 68	Donnell Bennett	.25	.08
❑ 69	Tony Gonzalez	.40	.15
❑ 70	Elvis Grbac	.40	.15
❑ 71	Tony Richardson RC	.25	.08
❑ 72	Oronde Gadsden	.40	.15
❑ 73	Damon Huard	.60	.25
❑ 74	James Johnson	.25	.08
❑ 75	Dan Marino	2.00	.75
❑ 76	Tony Martin	.40	.15
❑ 77	O.J. McDuffie	.40	.15
❑ 78	Cris Carter	.60	.25
❑ 79	Daunte Culpepper	.75	.30
❑ 80	Randy Moss	1.25	.50
❑ 81	Robert Smith	.60	.25
❑ 82	Drew Bledsoe	.75	.30
❑ 83	Kevin Faulk	.40	.15
❑ 84	Terry Glenn	.40	.15
❑ 85	P.J. Franklin RC	.40	.15
❑ 86	Keith Poole	.40	.15
❑ 87	Ricky Williams	.60	.25
❑ 88	Tiki Barber	.60	.25
❑ 89	Kerry Collins	.40	.15
❑ 90	Ike Hilliard	.40	.15
❑ 91	Amani Toomer	.40	.15
❑ 92	Wayne Chrebet	.40	.15
❑ 93	Ray Lucas	.40	.15
❑ 94	Curtis Martin	.60	.25
❑ 95	Vinny Testaverde	.40	.15
❑ 96	Tim Brown	.60	.25
❑ 97	Rich Gannon	.60	.25
❑ 98	James Jett	.25	.08
❑ 99	Napoleon Kaufman	.40	.15
❑ 100	Tyrone Wheatley	.40	.15
❑ 101	Charles Woodson	.40	.15
❑ 102	Brian Dawkins	.60	.25
❑ 103	Charles Johnson	.40	.15
❑ 104	Donovan McNabb	1.00	.40
❑ 105	Torrance Small	.25	.08
❑ 106	Duce Staley	.60	.25
❑ 107	Jerome Bettis	.60	.25
❑ 108	Troy Edwards	.25	.08
❑ 109	Richard Huntley	.25	.08
❑ 110	Kordell Stewart	.40	.15
❑ 111	Hines Ward	.60	.25
❑ 112	Isaac Bruce	.60	.25
❑ 113	Marshall Faulk	.75	.30
❑ 114	Az-Zahir Hakim	.40	.15
❑ 115	Torry Holt	.60	.25
❑ 116	Tony Horne	.25	.08
❑ 117	Kurt Warner	1.25	.50
❑ 118	Jermaine Fazande	.25	.08
❑ 119	Jeff Graham	.25	.08
❑ 120	Jim Harbaugh	.40	.15
❑ 121	Mikhael Ricks	.25	.08
❑ 122	Junior Seau	.60	.25
❑ 123	Jeff Garcia	.60	.25
❑ 124	Charlie Garner	.40	.15
❑ 125	Terrell Owens	.60	.25
❑ 126	Jerry Rice	1.25	.50
❑ 127	J.J. Stokes	.40	.15
❑ 128	Jon Kitna	.60	.25
❑ 129	Derrick Mayes	.40	.15
❑ 130	Charlie Rogers	.25	.08
❑ 131	Shawn Springs	.25	.08
❑ 132	Ricky Watters	.40	.15
❑ 133	Mike Alstott	.60	.25
❑ 134	Reidel Anthony	.25	.08
❑ 135	Warrick Dunn	.60	.25
❑ 136	Jacquez Green	.25	.08
❑ 137	Shaun King	.25	.08
❑ 138	Warren Sapp	.40	.15
❑ 139	Kevin Dyson	.40	.15
❑ 140	Eddie George	.60	.25
❑ 141	Jevon Kearse	.60	.25
❑ 142	Steve McNair	.60	.25
❑ 143	Yancey Thigpen	.25	.08
❑ 144	Frank Wycheck	.25	.08
❑ 145	Champ Bailey	.40	.15
❑ 146	Larry Centers	.25	.08
❑ 147	Albert Connell	.25	.08
❑ 148	Stephen Davis	.60	.25
❑ 149	Brad Johnson	.60	.25
❑ 150	Michael Westbrook	.40	.15
❑ 151	Thomas Jones RC	12.00	5.00
❑ 152	Jay Tant RC	4.00	1.50
❑ 153	Doug Johnson RC	8.00	3.00
❑ 154	Mareno Philyaw RC	4.00	1.50
❑ 155	Jamal Lewis RC	20.00	7.50
❑ 156	Chris Redman RC	6.00	2.50
❑ 157	Travis Taylor RC	8.00	3.00
❑ 158	Kwame Cavil RC	4.00	1.50
❑ 159	Corey Moore RC	4.00	1.50
❑ 160	Deon Grant RC	6.00	2.50
❑ 161	Frank Murphy RC	4.00	1.50
❑ 162	Dez White RC	8.00	3.00
❑ 163	Ron Dugans RC	4.00	1.50
❑ 164	Tony Hartley RC	4.00	1.50
❑ 165	Curtis Keaton RC	6.00	2.50
❑ 166	Peter Warrick RC	8.00	3.00
❑ 167	Courtney Brown RC	8.00	3.00
❑ 168	JaJuan Dawson RC	4.00	1.50
❑ 169	Dennis Northcutt RC	8.00	3.00
❑ 170	Travis Prentice RC	6.00	2.50
❑ 171	Aaron Shea RC	6.00	2.50
❑ 172	Michael Wiley RC	6.00	2.50
❑ 173	Chris Cole RC	6.00	2.50
❑ 174	Jarious Jackson RC	6.00	2.50
❑ 175	Deltha O'Neal RC	8.00	3.00
❑ 176	Reuben Droughns RC	8.00	3.00
❑ 177	Bubba Franks RC	8.00	3.00
❑ 178	Anthony Lucas RC	4.00	1.50
❑ 179	Rondell Mealey RC	4.00	1.50
❑ 180	Ibn Green RC	4.00	1.50
❑ 181	Kevin McDougal RC	6.00	2.50
❑ 182	R.Jay Soward RC	6.00	2.50
❑ 183	Shyrone Stith RC	6.00	2.50
❑ 184	Dante Hall RC	15.00	6.00
❑ 185	Frank Moreau RC	6.00	2.50
❑ 186	Sylvester Morris RC	6.00	2.50
❑ 187	Deon Dyer RC	6.00	2.50
❑ 188	Ben Kelly RC	4.00	1.50
❑ 189	Quinton Spotwood RC	4.00	1.50
❑ 190	Troy Walters RC	8.00	3.00
❑ 191	Tom Brady RC	80.00	40.00
❑ 192	J.R. Redmond RC	6.00	2.50
❑ 193	David Stachelski RC	4.00	1.50
❑ 194	Marc Bulger RC	15.00	6.00
❑ 195	Sherrod Gideon RC	4.00	1.50
❑ 196	Chad Morton RC	8.00	3.00
❑ 197	Ron Dayne RC	8.00	3.00
❑ 198	Anthony Becht RC	8.00	3.00
❑ 199	Laveranues Coles RC	10.00	4.00
❑ 200	Chad Pennington RC	20.00	7.50
❑ 201	Sebastian Janikowski RC	8.00	3.00
❑ 202	Marcus Knight RC	6.00	2.50
❑ 203	Jerry Porter RC	10.00	4.00
❑ 204	Todd Pinkston RC	8.00	3.00
❑ 205	Gari Scott RC	4.00	1.50
❑ 206	Plaxico Burress RC	15.00	6.00
❑ 207	Danny Farmer RC	6.00	2.50
❑ 208	Tee Martin RC	8.00	3.00
❑ 209	Hank Poteat RC	6.00	2.50
❑ 210	Trung Canidate RC	6.00	2.50
❑ 211	Patrick Batteaux RC	4.00	1.50
❑ 212	Trevor Gaylor RC	6.00	2.50
❑ 213	Ronney Jenkins RC	6.00	2.50
❑ 214	Terrence McCaskey RC	4.00	1.50
❑ 215	JaJuan Seider RC	4.00	1.50
❑ 216	Giovanni Carmazzi RC	4.00	1.50
❑ 217	Chafie Fields RC	4.00	1.50
❑ 218	Jonas Lewis RC	4.00	1.50
❑ 219	Tim Rattay RC	8.00	3.00
❑ 220	Shaun Alexander RC	40.00	15.00
❑ 221	Darrell Jackson RC	15.00	6.00
❑ 222	James Williams RC	6.00	2.50
❑ 223	Joe Hamilton RC	6.00	2.50
❑ 224	Erron Kinney RC	8.00	3.00
❑ 225	Todd Husak RC	8.00	3.00
❑ 226	P.Burress/D.Farmer	8.00	3.00
❑ 227	R.Dayne/J.Hamilton	3.00	1.25
❑ 228	P.Warrick/R.Dugans	4.00	1.50
❑ 229	T.Jones/C.Keaton	6.00	2.50
❑ 230	S.Alexander/R.Droughns	20.00	7.50
❑ 231	T.Taylor/D.Jackson	8.00	3.00
❑ 232	G.Carmazzi/T.Rattay	4.00	1.50
❑ 233	T.Canidate/J.R.Redmond	3.00	1.25
❑ 234	Syl.Morris/R.Soward	3.00	1.25
❑ 235	T.Prentice/T.Gaylor	3.00	1.25
❑ 236	T.Pinkston/S.Gideon	4.00	1.50
❑ 237	F.Murphy/D.White	4.00	1.50
❑ 238	C.Redman/T.Brady	50.00	20.00
❑ 239	J.Lewis/Tee Martin	10.00	4.00
❑ 240	R.Mealey/S.Stith	3.00	1.25
❑ 241	M.Wiley/C.Morton	3.00	1.25
❑ 242	L.Coles/S.Janikowski	4.00	1.50
❑ 243	T.Walters/T.Husak	4.00	1.50
❑ 244	M.Bulger/J.Porter	10.00	4.00
❑ 245	M.Philyaw/D.Johnson	4.00	1.50
❑ 246	D.Northcutt/C.Brown	4.00	1.50
❑ 247	J.Jackson/C.Cole	3.00	1.25
❑ 248	J.Dawson/G.Scott	2.00	.75
❑ 249	Q.Spotwood/C.Fields	2.00	.75
❑ 250	C.Pennington/J.Williams	10.00	4.00

1997 Pacific Philadelphia

❑	COMPLETE SET (330)	50.00	25.00
❑ 1	Kevin Butler	.20	.07
❑ 2	Larry Centers	.30	.10
❑ 3	Kent Graham	.20	.07
❑ 4	Leeland McElroy	.20	.07
❑ 5	Ronald McKinnon RC	.30	.10
❑ 6	Johnny McWilliams	.20	.07
❑ 7	Brad Otis	.20	.07
❑ 8	Frank Sanders	.30	.10
❑ 9	Rob Selby	.20	.07
❑ 10	Cedric Smith	.20	.07
❑ 11	Joe Staysniak	.20	.07
❑ 12	Cornelius Bennett	.20	.07
❑ 13	David Brandon	.20	.07
❑ 14	Tyrone Brown	.20	.07
❑ 15	John Burrough	.20	.07
❑ 16	Browning Nagle	.20	.07
❑ 17	Dan Owens	.20	.07
❑ 18	Anthony Phillips	.20	.07
❑ 19	Roell Preston	.20	.07
❑ 20	Darnell Walker	.20	.07
❑ 21	Bob Whitfield	.20	.07
❑ 22	Mike Zandofsky	.20	.07
❑ 23	Vashone Adams	.20	.07
❑ 24	Derrick Alexander WR	.30	.10
❑ 25	Harold Bishop	.20	.07
❑ 26	Jeff Blackshear	.20	.07
❑ 27	Donald Brady RC	.20	.07
❑ 28	Mike Frederick	.20	.07

❑ 29	Tim Goad	.20	.07
❑ 30	DeRon Jenkins	.20	.07
❑ 31	Ray Lewis	.75	.30
❑ 32	Rick Lyle	.20	.07
❑ 33	Byron Bam Morris	.20	.07
❑ 34	Chris Brantley	.20	.07
❑ 35	Jeff Burris	.20	.07
❑ 36	Todd Collins	.20	.07
❑ 37	Rob Coons	.20	.07
❑ 38	Corbin Lacina RC	.20	.07
❑ 39	Emanuel Martin	.20	.07
❑ 40	Marlo Perry	.20	.07
❑ 41	Shawn Price	.20	.07
❑ 42	Thomas Smith	.20	.07
❑ 43	Matt Stevens RC	.20	.07
❑ 44	Thurman Thomas	.50	.20
❑ 45	Jay Barker	.20	.07
❑ 46	Tim Biakabutuka	.30	.10
❑ 47	Kerry Collins	.50	.20
❑ 48	Matt Elliott	.20	.07
❑ 49	Howard Griffith	.20	.07
❑ 50	Anthony Johnson	.20	.07
❑ 51	John Kasay	.20	.07
❑ 52	Muhsin Muhammad	.30	.10
❑ 53	Winslow Oliver	.20	.07
❑ 54	Walter Rasby	.20	.07
❑ 55	Gerald Williams	.20	.07
❑ 56	Mark Butterfield	.20	.07
❑ 57	Bryan Cox	.20	.07
❑ 58	Mike Faulkerson	.20	.07
❑ 59	Paul Grasmanis	.20	.07
❑ 60	Robert Green	.20	.07
❑ 61	Jack Jackson	.20	.07
❑ 62	Bobby Neely	.20	.07
❑ 63	Todd Perry	.20	.07
❑ 64	Evan Pilgrim	.20	.07
❑ 65	Octus Polk	.20	.07
❑ 66	Rashaan Salaam	.20	.07
❑ 67	Willie Anderson	.20	.07
❑ 68	Jeff Blake	.30	.10
❑ 69	Scott Brumfield	.20	.07
❑ 70	Jeff Cothran	.20	.07
❑ 71	Gerald Dixon	.20	.07
❑ 72	Garrison Hearst	.30	.10
❑ 73	James Hundon RC	.50	.20
❑ 74	Brian Milne	.20	.07
❑ 75	Troy Sadowski	.20	.07
❑ 76	Tom Tumulty	.20	.07
❑ 77	Kimo von Oelhoffen RC	5.00	2.00
❑ 78	Troy Aikman	1.00	.40
❑ 79	Dale Hellestrae	.20	.07
❑ 80	Roger Harper	.20	.07
❑ 81	Michael Irvin	.50	.20
❑ 82	John Jett	.20	.07
❑ 83	Kelvin Martin	.20	.07
❑ 84	Deion Sanders	.50	.20
❑ 85	Darrin Smith	.20	.07
❑ 86	Emmitt Smith	1.50	.60
❑ 87	Herschel Walker	.30	.10
❑ 88	Charlie Williams	.20	.07
❑ 89	Glenn Cadrez	.20	.07
❑ 90	Dwayne Carswell RC	.50	.20
❑ 91	Terrell Davis	.60	.25
❑ 92	David Diaz-infante	.20	.07
❑ 93	John Elway	2.00	.75
❑ 94	Harald Hasselback	.20	.07
❑ 95	Tory James	.20	.07
❑ 96	Bill Musgrave	.20	.07
❑ 97	Ralph Tamm	.20	.07
❑ 98	Maa Tanuvasa RC	.20	.07
❑ 99	Gary Zimmerman	.20	.07
❑ 100	Shane Bonham	.20	.07
❑ 101	Stephen Boyd RC	.20	.07
❑ 102	Jeff Hartings RC	1.00	.40
❑ 103	Hessley Hempstead	.20	.07
❑ 104	Scott Kowalkowski	.20	.07
❑ 105	Herman Moore	.30	.10
❑ 106	Barry Sanders	1.50	.60
❑ 107	Tony Semple	.20	.07
❑ 108	Ryan Stewart	.20	.07
❑ 109	Mike Wells	.20	.07
❑ 110	Richard Woodley	.20	.07
❑ 111	Brett Favre	2.00	.75
❑ 112	Bernardo Harris RC	.30	.10
❑ 113	Keith McKenzie RC	.20	.07
❑ 114	Terry Mickens	.20	.07
❑ 115	Doug Pederson RC	.50	.20
❑ 116	Jeff Thomason RC	.20	.07
❑ 117	Adam Timmerman RC	.20	.07
❑ 118	Reggie White	.50	.20
❑ 119	Bruce Wilkerson	.20	.07
❑ 120	Gabe Wilkins RC	.20	.07
❑ 121	Tyrone Williams RC	.20	.07
❑ 122	Al Del Greco	.20	.07
❑ 123	Anthony Dorsett	.20	.07
❑ 124	Josh Evans	.20	.07
❑ 125	Eddie George	.50	.20
❑ 126	Lemanski Hall RC	.20	.07
❑ 127	Ronnie Harmon	.20	.07
❑ 128	Steve McNair	.60	.25
❑ 129	Michael Roan	.20	.07
❑ 130	Marcus Robertson	.20	.07
❑ 131	Jon Runyan	.20	.07
❑ 132	Chris Sanders	.20	.07
❑ 133	Kerwin Bell	.20	.07
❑ 134	Marshall Faulk	.60	.25
❑ 135	Clif Groce RC	.20	.07
❑ 136	Jim Harbaugh	.30	.10
❑ 137	Marvin Harrison	.50	.20
❑ 138	Eric Mahlum	.20	.07
❑ 139	Tony Mandarich	.20	.07
❑ 140	Dedric Mathis	.20	.07
❑ 141	Marcus Pollard RC	.20	.07
❑ 142	Scott Slutzker	.20	.07
❑ 143	Mark Stock	.20	.07
❑ 144	Bucky Brooks	.20	.07
❑ 145	Mark Brunell	.60	.25
❑ 146	Kendricke Bullard	.20	.07
❑ 147	Randy Jordan	.20	.07
❑ 148	Jeff Kopp	.20	.07
❑ 149	Le'Shai Maston	.20	.07
❑ 150	Keenan McCardell	.30	.10
❑ 151	Clyde Simmons	.20	.07
❑ 152	Jimmy Smith	.30	.10
❑ 153	Rich Tylski RC	.20	.07
❑ 154	Dave Widell	.20	.07
❑ 155	Marcus Allen	.50	.20
❑ 156	Keith Cash	.20	.07
❑ 157	Donnie Edwards	.30	.10
❑ 158	Trezelle Jenkins	.20	.07
❑ 159	Sean LaChapelle	.20	.07
❑ 160	Greg Manusky	.20	.07
❑ 161	Steve Matthews	.20	.07
❑ 162	Pellom McDaniels	.20	.07
❑ 163	Chris Penn	.20	.07
❑ 164	Danny Villa	.20	.07
❑ 165	Jerome Woods	.20	.07
❑ 166	Karim Abdul-Jabbar	.50	.20
❑ 167	John Bock	.20	.07
❑ 168	O.J. Brigance RC	.20	.07
❑ 169	Norman Hand RC	.20	.07
❑ 170	Anthony Harris	.20	.07
❑ 171	Larry Izzo RC	.20	.07
❑ 172	Charles Jordan	.20	.07
❑ 173	Dan Marino	2.00	.75
❑ 174	Everett McIver	.20	.07
❑ 175	Joe Nedney RC	.20	.07
❑ 176	Robert Wilson RC	.20	.07
❑ 177	David Dixon	.20	.07
❑ 178	Charles Evans	.20	.07
❑ 179	Hunter Goodwin RC	.20	.07
❑ 180	Ben Hanks	.20	.07
❑ 181	Warren Moon	.50	.20
❑ 182	Harold Morrow RC	.50	.20
❑ 183	Fernando Smith	.20	.07
❑ 184	Robert Smith	.30	.10
❑ 185	Sean Vanhorse	.20	.07
❑ 186	Jay Walker	.20	.07
❑ 187	Dewayne Washington	.20	.07
❑ 188	Moe Williams	.50	.20
❑ 189	Mike Bartrum	.20	.07
❑ 190	Drew Bledsoe	.60	.25
❑ 191	Troy Brown	.30	.10
❑ 192	Chad Eaton RC	.20	.07
❑ 193	Sam Gash	.20	.07
❑ 194	Mike Gisler	.20	.07
❑ 195	Curtis Martin	.60	.25
❑ 196	David Richards	.20	.07
❑ 197	Todd Rucci	.20	.07
❑ 198	Chris Sullivan	.20	.07
❑ 199	Adam Vinatieri RC	40.00	25.00
❑ 200	Doug Brien	.20	.07
❑ 201	Derek Brown RBK	.20	.07
❑ 202	Lee DeRamus	.20	.07
❑ 203	Jim Everett	.20	.07
❑ 204	Mercury Hayes	.20	.07
❑ 205	Joe Johnson	.20	.07
❑ 206	Henry Lusk RC	.20	.07
❑ 207	Andy McCollum	.20	.07
❑ 208	Alex Molden	.20	.07
❑ 209	Ray Zellars	.20	.07
❑ 210	Marcus Buckley	.20	.07
❑ 211	Doug Coleman RC	.20	.07
❑ 212	Percy Ellsworth RC	.20	.07
❑ 213	Rodney Hampton	.30	.10
❑ 214	Brian Saxton	.20	.07
❑ 215	Jason Sehorn	.30	.10
❑ 216	Stan White	.20	.07
❑ 217	Corey Widmer	.20	.07
❑ 218	Rodney Young	.20	.07
❑ 219	Rob Zatechka	.20	.07
❑ 220	Henry Bailey	.20	.07
❑ 221	Chad Cascadden RC	.20	.07
❑ 222	Wayne Chrebet	.50	.20
❑ 223	Tyrone Davis	.20	.07
❑ 224	Kwame Ellis	.20	.07
❑ 225	Glenn Foley	.30	.10
❑ 226	Erik Howard	.20	.07
❑ 227	Gary Jones S	.20	.07
❑ 228	Adrian Murrell	.30	.10
❑ 229	Marc Spindler	.20	.07
❑ 230	Lonnie Young	.20	.07
❑ 231	Eric Zomalt	.20	.07
❑ 232	Tim Brown	.50	.20
❑ 233	Aundray Bruce	.20	.07
❑ 234	Darren Carrington	.20	.07
❑ 235	Rick Cunningham	.20	.07
❑ 236	Rob Holmberg	.20	.07
❑ 237	Jeff Hostetler	.20	.07
❑ 238	Lorenzo Lynch	.20	.07
❑ 239	Barrett Robbins	.20	.07
❑ 240	Dan Turk	.20	.07
❑ 241	Harvey Williams	.20	.07
❑ 242	Brian Dawkins	.50	.20
❑ 243	Ty Detmer	.30	.10
❑ 244	Troy Drake	.20	.07
❑ 245	Rhett Hall	.20	.07
❑ 246	Joe Panos	.20	.07
❑ 247	Johnny Thomas	.20	.07
❑ 248	Kevin Turner	.20	.07
❑ 249	Ricky Watters	.30	.10
❑ 250	Derrick Witherspoon RC	.20	.07
❑ 251	Sylvester Wright	.20	.07
❑ 252	Jerome Bettis	.50	.20
❑ 253	Carlos Emmons RC	.20	.07
❑ 254	Jason Gildon	.20	.07
❑ 255	Jonathan Hayes	.20	.07
❑ 256	Kevin Henry	.20	.07
❑ 257	Jerry Olsavsky	.20	.07
❑ 258	Erric Pegram	.20	.07
❑ 259	Brendan Stai	.20	.07
❑ 260	Justin Strzelczyk	.20	.07
❑ 261	Mike Tomczak	.20	.07
❑ 262	Tony Banks	.30	.10

❑ 263 Hayward Clay .20 .07
❑ 264 Percell Gaskins .20 .07
❑ 265 Eddie Kennison .30 .10
❑ 266 Aaron Laing .20 .07
❑ 267 Keith Lyle .20 .07
❑ 268 Jamie Martin RC 2.50 1.00
❑ 269 Lawrence Phillips .20 .07
❑ 270 Zach Wiegert .20 .07
❑ 271 Toby Wright .20 .07
❑ 272 Darren Bennett .20 .07
❑ 273 Tony Berti .20 .07
❑ 274 Freddie Bradley .20 .07
❑ 275 Joe Cocozzo .20 .07
❑ 276 Andre Coleman .20 .07
❑ 277 Marco Coleman .20 .07
❑ 278 Rodney Harrison RC 1.00 .40
❑ 279 David Hendrix .20 .07
❑ 280 Leonard Russell .20 .07
❑ 281 Sean Salisbury .20 .07
❑ 282 Dennis Brown .20 .07
❑ 283 Chris Dalman .20 .07
❑ 284 Brent Jones .30 .10
❑ 285 Sean Manuel .20 .07
❑ 286 Marquez Pope .20 .07
❑ 287 Jerry Rice 1.00 .40
❑ 288 Kirk Scrafford .20 .07
❑ 289 Iheanyi Uwaezuoke .30 .10
❑ 290 Tommy Vardell .20 .07
❑ 291 Steve Young .60 .25
❑ 292 James Atkins .20 .07
❑ 293 T.J. Cunningham .20 .07
❑ 294 Stan Gelbaugh .20 .07
❑ 295 James Logan .20 .07
❑ 296 James McKnight RC 1.50 .60
❑ 297 Rick Mirer .20 .07
❑ 298 Todd Peterson .20 .07
❑ 299 Fred Thomas .20 .07
❑ 300 Rick Tuten .20 .07
❑ 301 Chris Warren .30 .10
❑ 302 Donnie Abraham RC .50 .20
❑ 303 Trent Dilfer .50 .20
❑ 304 Kenneth Gant .20 .07
❑ 305 Jeff Gooch .30 .10
❑ 306 Courtney Hawkins .20 .07
❑ 307 Tyoka Jackson RC .20 .07
❑ 308 Melvin Johnson S RC .20 .07
❑ 309 Lonnie Marts .20 .07
❑ 310 Hardy Nickerson .20 .07
❑ 311 Errict Rhett .20 .07
❑ 312 Terry Allen .50 .20
❑ 313 Flipper Anderson .20 .07
❑ 314 William Bell .20 .07
❑ 315 Scott Blanton .20 .07
❑ 316 Leomont Evans RC .20 .07
❑ 317 Gus Frerotte .20 .07
❑ 318 Darryl Morrison .20 .07
❑ 319 Matt Turk .20 .07
❑ 320 Jeff Uhlenhake .20 .07
❑ 321 Brian Walker RC .20 .07
❑ 322 Mark Brunell LL .50 .20
❑ 323 Barry Sanders LL .75 .30
❑ 324 Isaac Bruce LL .50 .20
❑ 325 Terry Allen LL .30 .10
❑ 326 Steve Young LL .50 .20
❑ 327 Jerry Rice LL .50 .20
❑ 328 Ricky Watters LL .30 .10
❑ 329 Kevin Greene LL .20 .07
❑ 330 Brett Favre LL 1.00 .40
❑ S1 Mark Brunell Sample 2.00 .75

1964 Philadelphia

❑ COMPLETE SET (198) 900.00 600.00
❑ WRAPPER (1-CENT) 40.00 30.00
❑ WRAPPER (5-CENT) 20.00 10.00
❑ 1 Raymond Berry ! 20.00 10.00
❑ 2 Tom Gilburg 2.50 1.25
❑ 3 John Mackey RC 30.00 18.00
❑ 4 Gino Marchetti 5.00 2.50

❑ 5 Jim Martin 2.50 1.25
❑ 6 Tom Matte RC 6.00 3.00
❑ 7 Jimmy Orr 3.00 1.50
❑ 8 Jim Parker 4.00 2.00
❑ 9 Bill Pellington 2.50 1.25
❑ 10 Alex Sandusky 2.50 1.25
❑ 11 Dick Szymanski 2.50 1.25
❑ 12 Johnny Unitas 45.00 25.00
❑ 13 Baltimore Colts 3.00 1.50
❑ 14 Colts Play/Don Shula 35.00 20.00
❑ 15 Doug Atkins 5.00 2.50
❑ 16 Ronnie Bull 2.50 1.25
❑ 17 Mike Ditka 40.00 25.00
❑ 18 Joe Fortunato 2.50 1.25
❑ 19 Willie Galimore 3.00 1.50
❑ 20 Joe Marconi 2.50 1.25
❑ 21 Bennie McRae RC 2.50 1.25
❑ 22 Johnny Morris 2.50 1.25
❑ 23 Richie Petitbon 2.50 1.25
❑ 24 Mike Pyle 2.50 1.25
❑ 25 Roosevelt Taylor RC 4.00 2.00
❑ 26 Bill Wade 3.00 1.50
❑ 27 Chicago Bears 3.00 1.50
❑ 28 Bears Play/George Halas 12.00 6.00
❑ 29 Johnny Brewer 2.50 1.25
❑ 30 Jim Brown 90.00 50.00
❑ 31 Gary Collins RC 8.00 4.00
❑ 32 Vince Costello 2.50 1.25
❑ 33 Galen Fiss 2.50 1.25
❑ 34 Bill Glass 2.50 1.25
❑ 35 Ernie Green RC 3.00 1.50
❑ 36 Rich Kreitling 2.50 1.25
❑ 37 John Morrow 2.50 1.25
❑ 38 Frank Ryan 3.00 1.50
❑ 39 Charlie Scales RC 2.50 1.25
❑ 40 Dick Schafrath RC 2.50 1.25
❑ 41 Cleveland Browns 3.00 1.50
❑ 42 Cleveland Browns Play 2.50 1.25
❑ 43 Don Bishop 2.50 1.25
❑ 44 Frank Clarke RC 3.00 1.50
❑ 45 Mike Connelly 2.50 1.25
❑ 46 Lee Folkins 2.50 1.25
❑ 47 Cornell Green RC 8.00 4.00
❑ 48 Bob Lilly 40.00 25.00
❑ 49 Amos Marsh 2.50 1.25
❑ 50 Tommy McDonald 5.00 2.50
❑ 51 Don Meredith 35.00 20.00
❑ 52 Pettis Norman RC 3.00 1.50
❑ 53 Don Perkins 4.00 2.00
❑ 54 Guy Reese 2.50 1.25
❑ 55 Dallas Cowboys 3.00 1.50
❑ 56 Cowboys Play/T.Landry 20.00 12.00
❑ 57 Terry Barr 2.50 1.25
❑ 58 Roger Brown 3.00 1.50
❑ 59 Gail Cogdill 2.50 1.25
❑ 60 John Gordy 2.50 1.25
❑ 61 Dick Lane 4.00 2.00
❑ 62 Yale Lary 4.00 2.00
❑ 63 Dan Lewis 2.50 1.25
❑ 64 Darris McCord 2.50 1.25
❑ 65 Earl Morrall 3.00 1.50
❑ 66 Joe Schmidt 5.00 2.50
❑ 67 Pat Studstill RC 3.00 1.50
❑ 68 Wayne Walker RC 3.00 1.50
❑ 69 Detroit Lions 3.00 1.50
❑ 70 Detroit Lions 2.50 1.25
❑ 71 Herb Adderley RC 35.00 20.00
❑ 72 Willie Davis DE RC 30.00 18.00
❑ 73 Forrest Gregg 5.00 2.50
❑ 74 Paul Hornung 35.00 20.00
❑ 75 Hank Jordan 5.00 2.50
❑ 76 Jerry Kramer 6.00 3.00
❑ 77 Tom Moore 3.00 1.50
❑ 78 Jim Ringo 5.00 2.50
❑ 79 Bart Starr 60.00 35.00
❑ 80 Jim Taylor 25.00 15.00
❑ 81 Jesse Whittenton RC 3.00 1.50
❑ 82 Willie Wood 8.00 4.00
❑ 83 Green Bay Packers 6.00 3.00
❑ 84 Packers Play/Lombardi 35.00 20.00
❑ 85 Jon Arnett 2.50 1.25
❑ 86 Pervis Atkins RC 2.50 1.25
❑ 87 Dick Bass 3.00 1.50
❑ 88 Carroll Dale 4.00 2.00
❑ 89 Roman Gabriel 6.00 3.00
❑ 90 Ed Meador 2.50 1.25
❑ 91 Merlin Olsen RC 50.00 30.00
❑ 92 Jack Pardee RC 4.00 2.00
❑ 93 Jim Phillips 2.50 1.25
❑ 94 Carver Shannon 2.50 1.25
❑ 95 Frank Varrichione 2.50 1.25
❑ 96 Danny Villanueva 2.50 1.25
❑ 97 Los Angeles Rams 3.00 1.50
❑ 98 Los Angeles Rams Play 2.50 1.25
❑ 99 Grady Alderman RC 3.00 1.50
❑ 100 Larry Bowie 2.50 1.25
❑ 101 Bill Brown RC 6.00 3.00
❑ 102 Paul Flatley RC 2.50 1.25
❑ 103 Rip Hawkins 2.50 1.25
❑ 104 Jim Marshall 8.00 4.00
❑ 105 Tommy Mason 3.00 1.50
❑ 106 Jim Prestel 2.50 1.25
❑ 107 Jerry Reichow 2.50 1.25
❑ 108 Ed Sharockman 2.50 1.25
❑ 109 Fran Tarkenton 35.00 20.00
❑ 110 Mick Tingelhoff RC 6.00 3.00
❑ 111 Minnesota Vikings 3.00 1.50
❑ 112 Vikings Play/Van Brock. 4.00 2.00
❑ 113 Erich Barnes 2.50 1.25
❑ 114 Roosevelt Brown 4.00 2.00
❑ 115 Don Chandler 2.50 1.25
❑ 116 Darrell Dess 2.50 1.25
❑ 117 Frank Gifford 35.00 20.00
❑ 118 Dick James 2.50 1.25
❑ 119 Jim Katcavage 2.50 1.25
❑ 120 John Lovetere 2.50 1.25
❑ 121 Dick Lynch RC 3.00 1.50
❑ 122 Jim Patton 2.50 1.25
❑ 123 Del Shofner 2.50 1.25
❑ 124 Y.A.Tittle 20.00 10.00
❑ 125 New York Giants 3.00 1.50
❑ 126 New York Giants Play 2.50 1.25
❑ 127 Sam Baker 2.50 1.25
❑ 128 Maxie Baughan 2.50 1.25
❑ 129 Timmy Brown 3.00 1.50
❑ 130 Mike Clark 2.50 1.25
❑ 131 Irv Cross RC 3.00 1.50
❑ 132 Ted Dean 2.50 1.25
❑ 133 Ron Goodwin 2.50 1.25
❑ 134 King Hill 2.50 1.25
❑ 135 Clarence Peaks 2.50 1.25
❑ 136 Pete Retzlaff 3.00 1.50
❑ 137 Jim Schrader 2.50 1.25
❑ 138 Norm Snead 3.00 1.50
❑ 139 Philadelphia Eagles 3.00 1.50
❑ 140 Philadelphia Eagles Play 2.50 1.25
❑ 141 Gary Ballman RC 2.50 1.25
❑ 142 Charley Bradshaw RC 2.50 1.25
❑ 143 Ed Brown 3.00 1.50
❑ 144 John Henry Johnson 4.00 2.00

❑ 145	Joe Krupa	2.50	1.25
❑ 146	Bill Mack	2.50	1.25
❑ 147	Lou Michaels	2.50	1.25
❑ 148	Buzz Nutter	2.50	1.25
❑ 149	Myron Pottios	2.50	1.25
❑ 150	John Reger	2.50	1.25
❑ 151	Mike Sandusky	2.50	1.25
❑ 152	Clendon Thomas	2.50	1.25
❑ 153	Pittsburgh Steelers	3.00	1.50
❑ 154	Pittsburgh Steelers Play	2.50	1.25
❑ 155	Kermit Alexander RC	3.00	1.50
❑ 156	Bernie Casey	3.00	1.50
❑ 157	Dan Colchico	2.50	1.25
❑ 158	Clyde Conner	2.50	1.25
❑ 159	Tommy Davis	2.50	1.25
❑ 160	Matt Hazeltine	2.50	1.25
❑ 161	Jim Johnson RC	20.00	10.00
❑ 162	Don Lisbon RC	2.50	1.25
❑ 163	Lamar McHan	2.50	1.25
❑ 164	Bob St.Clair	4.00	2.00
❑ 165	J.D. Smith	2.50	1.25
❑ 166	Abe Woodson	2.50	1.25
❑ 167	San Francisco 49ers	3.00	1.50
❑ 168	San Francisco 49ers Play	2.50	1.25
❑ 169	Garland Boyette UER	2.50	1.25
❑ 170	Bobby Joe Conrad	3.00	1.50
❑ 171	Bob DeMarco RC	2.50	1.25
❑ 172	Ken Gray RC	2.50	1.25
❑ 173	Jimmy Hill	2.50	1.25
❑ 174	Charlie Johnson	3.00	1.50
❑ 175	Ernie McMillan	2.50	1.25
❑ 176	Dale Meinert	2.50	1.25
❑ 177	Luke Owens	2.50	1.25
❑ 178	Sonny Randle	2.50	1.25
❑ 179	Joe Robb	2.50	1.25
❑ 180	Bill Stacy	2.50	1.25
❑ 181	St. Louis Cardinals	3.00	1.50
❑ 182	St. Louis Cardinals Play	2.50	1.25
❑ 183	Bill Barnes	2.50	1.25
❑ 184	Don Bosseler	2.50	1.25
❑ 185	Sam Huff	6.00	3.00
❑ 186	Sonny Jurgensen	20.00	10.00
❑ 187	Bob Khayat	2.50	1.25
❑ 188	Riley Mattson	2.50	1.25
❑ 189	Bobby Mitchell	6.00	3.00
❑ 190	John Nisby	2.50	1.25
❑ 191	Vince Promuto	2.50	1.25
❑ 192	Joe Rutgens	2.50	1.25
❑ 193	Lonnie Sanders	2.50	1.25
❑ 194	Jim Steffen	2.50	1.25
❑ 195	Washington Redskins	3.00	1.50
❑ 196	Washington Redskins Play	2.50	1.25
❑ 197	Checklist 1 UER !	30.00	18.00
❑ 198	Checklist 2 UER !	55.00	30.00

1965 Philadelphia

❑	COMPLETE SET (198)	800.00	500.00
❑	WRAPPER (5-CENT)	20.00	10.00
❑ 1	Colts Team !	15.00	7.50
❑ 2	Raymond Berry	10.00	5.00
❑ 3	Bob Boyd DB	2.00	1.00
❑ 4	Wendell Harris	2.00	1.00
❑ 5	Jerry Logan	2.00	1.00
❑ 6	Tony Lorick	2.00	1.00
❑ 7	Lou Michaels	2.00	1.00
❑ 8	Lenny Moore	8.00	4.00
❑ 9	Jimmy Orr	3.00	1.50
❑ 10	Jim Parker	4.00	2.00
❑ 11	Dick Szymanski	2.00	1.00
❑ 12	Johnny Unitas	40.00	25.00
❑ 13	Bob Vogel RC	2.00	1.00
❑ 14	Colts Play/Don Shula	20.00	12.00
❑ 15	Chicago Bears	3.00	1.50
❑ 16	Jon Arnett	2.00	1.00
❑ 17	Doug Atkins	5.00	2.50
❑ 18	Rudy Bukich RC	3.00	1.50
❑ 19	Mike Ditka	40.00	25.00
❑ 20	Dick Evey	2.00	1.00
❑ 21	Joe Fortunato	2.00	1.00
❑ 22	Bobby Joe Green RC	2.00	1.00
❑ 23	Johnny Morris	2.00	1.00
❑ 24	Mike Pyle	2.00	1.00
❑ 25	Roosevelt Taylor	3.00	1.50
❑ 26	Bill Wade	3.00	1.50
❑ 27	Bob Wetoska	2.00	1.00
❑ 28	Bears Play/George Halas	8.00	4.00
❑ 29	Cleveland Browns	3.00	1.50
❑ 30	Walter Beach	2.00	1.00
❑ 31	Jim Brown	80.00	50.00
❑ 32	Gary Collins	3.00	1.50
❑ 33	Bill Glass	2.00	1.00
❑ 34	Ernie Green	2.00	1.00
❑ 35	Jim Houston RC	2.00	1.00
❑ 36	Dick Modzelewski	2.00	1.00
❑ 37	Bernie Parrish	2.00	1.00
❑ 38	Walter Roberts	2.00	1.00
❑ 39	Frank Ryan	3.00	1.50
❑ 40	Dick Schafrath	2.00	1.00
❑ 41	Paul Warfield RC	90.00	50.00
❑ 42	Cleveland Browns	2.00	1.00
❑ 43	Dallas Cowboys	3.00	1.50
❑ 44	Frank Clarke	3.00	1.50
❑ 45	Mike Connelly	2.00	1.00
❑ 46	Buddy Dial	2.00	1.00
❑ 47	Bob Lilly	35.00	20.00
❑ 48	Tony Liscio RC	2.00	1.00
❑ 49	Tommy McDonald	5.00	2.50
❑ 50	Don Meredith	25.00	15.00
❑ 51	Pettis Norman	2.00	1.00
❑ 52	Don Perkins	4.00	2.00
❑ 53	Mel Renfro RC	40.00	25.00
❑ 54	Jim Ridlon	2.00	1.00
❑ 55	Jerry Tubbs	2.00	1.00
❑ 56	Cowboys Play/T.Landry	15.00	7.50
❑ 57	Detroit Lions	3.00	1.50
❑ 58	Terry Barr	2.00	1.00
❑ 59	Roger Brown	2.00	1.00
❑ 60	Gail Cogdill	2.00	1.00
❑ 61	Jim Gibbons	2.00	1.00
❑ 62	John Gordy	2.00	1.00
❑ 63	Yale Lary	4.00	2.00
❑ 64	Dick LeBeau RC	3.00	1.50
❑ 65	Earl Morrall	3.00	1.50
❑ 66	Nick Pietrosante	2.00	1.00
❑ 67	Pat Studstill	2.00	1.00
❑ 68	Wayne Walker	3.00	1.50
❑ 69	Tom Watkins	2.00	1.00
❑ 70	Detroit Lions	3.00	1.50
❑ 71	Green Bay Packers	6.00	3.00
❑ 72	Herb Adderley	8.00	4.00
❑ 73	Willie Davis DE	8.00	4.00
❑ 74	Boyd Dowler	4.00	2.00
❑ 75	Forrest Gregg	5.00	2.50
❑ 76	Paul Hornung	35.00	20.00
❑ 77	Hank Jordan	5.00	2.50
❑ 78	Tom Moore	3.00	1.50
❑ 79	Ray Nitschke	20.00	12.00
❑ 80	Elijah Pitts RC	8.00	4.00
❑ 81	Bart Starr	50.00	30.00
❑ 82	Jim Taylor	20.00	12.00
❑ 83	Willie Wood	6.00	3.00
❑ 84	Packers Play/Lombardi	20.00	12.00
❑ 85	Los Angeles Rams	3.00	1.50
❑ 86	Dick Bass	3.00	1.50
❑ 87	Roman Gabriel	5.00	2.50
❑ 88	Roosevelt Grier	4.00	2.00
❑ 89	Deacon Jones	10.00	5.00
❑ 90	Lamar Lundy RC	4.00	2.00
❑ 91	Marlin McKeever	2.00	1.00
❑ 92	Ed Meador	2.00	1.00
❑ 93	Bill Munson RC	4.00	2.00
❑ 94	Merlin Olsen	15.00	7.50
❑ 95	Bobby Smith	2.00	1.00
❑ 96	Frank Varrichione	2.00	1.00
❑ 97	Ben Wilson	2.00	1.00
❑ 98	Los Angeles Rams	2.00	1.00
❑ 99	Minnesota Vikings	3.00	1.50
❑ 100	Grady Alderman	2.00	1.00
❑ 101	Hal Bedsole RC	2.00	1.00
❑ 102	Bill Brown	3.00	1.50
❑ 103	Bill Butler	2.00	1.00
❑ 104	Fred Cox RC	3.00	1.50
❑ 105	Carl Eller RC	30.00	18.00
❑ 106	Paul Flatley	2.00	1.00
❑ 107	Jim Marshall	6.00	3.00
❑ 108	Tommy Mason	2.00	1.00
❑ 109	George Rose	2.00	1.00
❑ 110	Fran Tarkenton	25.00	15.00
❑ 111	Mick Tingelhoff	3.00	1.50
❑ 112	Vikings Play/Van Brock.	4.00	2.00
❑ 113	New York Giants	3.00	1.50
❑ 114	Erich Barnes	2.00	1.00
❑ 115	Roosevelt Brown	4.00	2.00
❑ 116	Clarence Childs	2.00	1.00
❑ 117	Jerry Hillebrand	2.00	1.00
❑ 118	Greg Larson RC	2.00	1.00
❑ 119	Dick Lynch	2.00	1.00
❑ 120	Joe Morrison RC	4.00	2.00
❑ 121	Lou Slaby	2.00	1.00
❑ 122	Aaron Thomas RC	2.00	1.00
❑ 123	Steve Thurlow	2.00	1.00
❑ 124	Ernie Wheelwright RC	2.00	1.00
❑ 125	Gary Wood RC	3.00	1.50
❑ 126	New York Giants	2.00	1.00
❑ 127	Philadelphia Eagles	3.00	1.50
❑ 128	Sam Baker	2.00	1.00
❑ 129	Maxie Baughan	2.00	1.00
❑ 130	Timmy Brown	3.00	1.50
❑ 131	Jack Concannon RC	2.00	1.00
❑ 132	Irv Cross	3.00	1.50
❑ 133	Earl Gros	2.00	1.00
❑ 134	Dave Lloyd	2.00	1.00
❑ 135	Floyd Peters RC	2.00	1.00
❑ 136	Nate Ramsey	2.00	1.00
❑ 137	Pete Retzlaff	3.00	1.50
❑ 138	Jim Ringo	4.00	2.00
❑ 139	Norm Snead	4.00	2.00
❑ 140	Philadelphia Eagles	2.00	1.00
❑ 141	Pittsburgh Steelers	3.00	1.50
❑ 142	John Baker	2.00	1.00
❑ 143	Gary Ballman	2.00	1.00
❑ 144	Charley Bradshaw	2.00	1.00
❑ 145	Ed Brown	2.00	1.00
❑ 146	Dick Haley	2.00	1.00
❑ 147	John Henry Johnson	4.00	2.00
❑ 148	Brady Keys	2.00	1.00
❑ 149	Ray Lemek	2.00	1.00
❑ 150	Ben McGee	2.00	1.00
❑ 151	Clarence Peaks	2.00	1.00
❑ 152	Myron Pottios	2.00	1.00
❑ 153	Clendon Thomas	2.00	1.00
❑ 154	Pittsburgh Steelers	2.00	1.00
❑ 155	St. Louis Cardinals	3.00	1.50
❑ 156	Jim Bakken RC	3.00	1.50
❑ 157	Joe Childress	2.00	1.00
❑ 158	Bobby Joe Conrad	3.00	1.50
❑ 159	Bob DeMarco	2.00	1.00
❑ 160	Pat Fischer RC	4.00	2.00

- ❑ 161 Irv Goode 2.00 1.00
- ❑ 162 Ken Gray 2.00 1.00
- ❑ 163 Charlie Johnson 3.00 1.50
- ❑ 164 Bill Koman 2.00 1.00
- ❑ 165 Dale Meinert 2.00 1.00
- ❑ 166 Jerry Stovall RC 3.00 1.50
- ❑ 167 Abe Woodson 2.00 1.00
- ❑ 168 St. Louis Cardinals 2.00 1.00
- ❑ 169 San Francisco 49ers 3.00 1.50
- ❑ 170 Kermit Alexander 2.00 1.00
- ❑ 171 John Brodie 10.00 5.00
- ❑ 172 Bernie Casey 3.00 1.50
- ❑ 173 John David Crow 3.00 1.50
- ❑ 174 Tommy Davis 2.00 1.00
- ❑ 175 Matt Hazeltine 2.00 1.00
- ❑ 176 Jim Johnson 4.00 2.00
- ❑ 177 Charlie Krueger RC 2.00 1.00
- ❑ 178 Roland Lakes 2.00 1.00
- ❑ 179 George Mira RC 3.00 1.50
- ❑ 180 Dave Parks RC 3.00 1.50
- ❑ 181 John Thomas RC 2.00 1.00
- ❑ 182 49ers Play/Christiansen 2.00 1.00
- ❑ 183 Washington Redskins 3.00 1.50
- ❑ 184 Pervis Atkins 2.00 1.00
- ❑ 185 Preston Carpenter 2.00 1.00
- ❑ 186 Angelo Coia 2.00 1.00
- ❑ 187 Sam Huff 6.00 3.00
- ❑ 188 Sonny Jurgensen 15.00 7.50
- ❑ 189 Paul Krause RC 20.00 12.00
- ❑ 190 Jim Martin 2.00 1.00
- ❑ 191 Bobby Mitchell 5.00 2.50
- ❑ 192 John Nisby 2.00 1.00
- ❑ 193 John Paluck 2.00 1.00
- ❑ 194 Vince Promuto 2.00 1.00
- ❑ 195 Charley Taylor RC 50.00 30.00
- ❑ 196 Washington Redskins 2.00 1.00
- ❑ 197 Checklist 1 ! 30.00 15.00
- ❑ 198 Checklist 2 UER ! 50.00 25.00

1966 Philadelphia

- ❑ COMPLETE SET (198) 900.00 600.00
- ❑ WRAPPER (5-CENT) 20.00 10.00
- ❑ 1 Falcons Insignia ! 12.00 6.00
- ❑ 2 Larry Benz 2.00 1.00
- ❑ 3 Dennis Claridge 2.00 1.00
- ❑ 4 Perry Lee Dunn 2.00 1.00
- ❑ 5 Dan Grimm 2.00 1.00
- ❑ 6 Alex Hawkins 2.00 1.00
- ❑ 7 Ralph Heck 2.00 1.00
- ❑ 8 Frank Lasky 2.00 1.00
- ❑ 9 Guy Reese 2.00 1.00
- ❑ 10 Bob Richards 2.00 1.00
- ❑ 11 Ron Smith RC 2.00 1.00
- ❑ 12 Ernie Wheelwright 2.00 1.00
- ❑ 13 Falcons Roster 3.00 1.50
- ❑ 14 Baltimore Colts 3.00 1.50
- ❑ 15 Raymond Berry 8.00 4.00
- ❑ 16 Bob Boyd DB 2.00 1.00
- ❑ 17 Jerry Logan 2.00 1.00
- ❑ 18 John Mackey 6.00 3.00
- ❑ 19 Tom Matte 4.00 2.00
- ❑ 20 Lou Michaels 2.00 1.00
- ❑ 21 Lenny Moore 8.00 4.00
- ❑ 22 Jimmy Orr 3.00 1.50
- ❑ 23 Jim Parker 4.00 2.00
- ❑ 24 Johnny Unitas 40.00 25.00
- ❑ 25 Bob Vogel 2.00 1.00
- ❑ 26 Colts Play/Moore/Parker 4.00 2.00
- ❑ 27 Chicago Bears 3.00 1.50
- ❑ 28 Doug Atkins 4.00 2.00
- ❑ 29 Rudy Bukich 2.00 1.00
- ❑ 30 Ronnie Bull 2.00 1.00
- ❑ 31 Dick Butkus RC ! 250.00 150.00
- ❑ 32 Mike Ditka 35.00 20.00
- ❑ 33 Joe Fortunato 2.00 1.00
- ❑ 34 Bobby Joe Green 2.00 1.00
- ❑ 35 Roger LeClerc 2.00 1.00
- ❑ 36 Johnny Morris 2.00 1.00
- ❑ 37 Mike Pyle 2.00 1.00
- ❑ 38 Gale Sayers RC ! 225.00 125.00
- ❑ 39 Bears Play/Gale Sayers 35.00 20.00
- ❑ 40 Cleveland Browns 3.00 1.50
- ❑ 41 Jim Brown 80.00 50.00
- ❑ 42 Gary Collins 3.00 1.50
- ❑ 43 Ross Fichtner 2.00 1.00
- ❑ 44 Ernie Green 2.00 1.00
- ❑ 45 Gene Hickerson RC 3.00 1.50
- ❑ 46 Jim Houston 2.00 1.00
- ❑ 47 John Morrow 2.00 1.00
- ❑ 48 Walter Roberts 2.00 1.00
- ❑ 49 Frank Ryan 3.00 1.50
- ❑ 50 Dick Schafrath 2.00 1.00
- ❑ 51 Paul Wiggin RC 2.00 1.00
- ❑ 52 Cleveland Browns 2.00 1.00
- ❑ 53 Dallas Cowboys 3.00 1.50
- ❑ 54 George Andrie RC UER 3.00 1.50
- ❑ 55 Frank Clarke 3.00 1.50
- ❑ 56 Mike Connelly 2.00 1.00
- ❑ 57 Cornell Green 4.00 2.00
- ❑ 58 Bob Hayes RC 50.00 30.00
- ❑ 59 Chuck Howley RC 18.00 10.00
- ❑ 60 Bob Lilly 20.00 12.00
- ❑ 61 Don Meredith 25.00 15.00
- ❑ 62 Don Perkins 3.00 1.50
- ❑ 63 Mel Renfro 15.00 7.50
- ❑ 64 Danny Villanueva 2.00 1.00
- ❑ 65 Dallas Cowboys 2.00 1.00
- ❑ 66 Detroit Lions 3.00 1.50
- ❑ 67 Roger Brown 2.00 1.00
- ❑ 68 John Gordy 2.00 1.00
- ❑ 69 Alex Karras 10.00 5.00
- ❑ 70 Dick LeBeau 2.00 1.00
- ❑ 71 Amos Marsh 2.00 1.00
- ❑ 72 Milt Plum 3.00 1.50
- ❑ 73 Bobby Smith 2.00 1.00
- ❑ 74 Wayne Rasmussen 2.00 1.00
- ❑ 75 Pat Studstill 2.00 1.00
- ❑ 76 Wayne Walker 2.00 1.00
- ❑ 77 Tom Watkins 2.00 1.00
- ❑ 78 Detroit Lions 2.00 1.00
- ❑ 79 Green Bay Packers 6.00 3.00
- ❑ 80 Herb Adderley 6.00 3.00
- ❑ 81 Lee Roy Caffey RC 4.00 2.00
- ❑ 82 Don Chandler 3.00 1.50
- ❑ 83 Willie Davis DE 6.00 3.00
- ❑ 84 Boyd Dowler 4.00 2.00
- ❑ 85 Forrest Gregg 4.00 2.00
- ❑ 86 Tom Moore 3.00 1.50
- ❑ 87 Ray Nitschke 15.00 7.50
- ❑ 88 Bart Starr 50.00 30.00
- ❑ 89 Jim Taylor 20.00 12.00
- ❑ 90 Willie Wood 6.00 3.00
- ❑ 91 Green Bay Packers 2.00 1.00
- ❑ 92 Los Angeles Rams 3.00 1.50
- ❑ 93 Willie Brown WR 2.00 1.00
- ❑ 94 Roman Gabriel/D.Bass 4.00 2.00
- ❑ 95 Bruce Gossett RC 3.00 1.50
- ❑ 96 Deacon Jones 6.00 3.00
- ❑ 97 Tommy McDonald 5.00 2.50
- ❑ 98 Marlin McKeever 2.00 1.00
- ❑ 99 Aaron Martin 2.00 1.00
- ❑ 100 Ed Meador 2.00 1.00
- ❑ 101 Bill Munson 3.00 1.50
- ❑ 102 Merlin Olsen 8.00 4.00
- ❑ 103 Jim Stiger 2.00 1.00
- ❑ 104 Rams Play/W.Brown 3.00 1.50
- ❑ 105 Minnesota Vikings 3.00 1.50
- ❑ 106 Grady Alderman 2.00 1.00
- ❑ 107 Bill Brown 3.00 1.50
- ❑ 108 Fred Cox 2.00 1.00
- ❑ 109 Paul Flatley 2.00 1.00
- ❑ 110 Rip Hawkins 2.00 1.00
- ❑ 111 Tommy Mason 2.00 1.00
- ❑ 112 Ed Sharockman 2.00 1.00
- ❑ 113 Gordon Smith 2.00 1.00
- ❑ 114 Fran Tarkenton 30.00 15.00
- ❑ 115 Mick Tingelhoff 3.00 1.50
- ❑ 116 Bobby Walden RC**/C 2.00 1.00
- ❑ 117 Minnesota Vikings 2.00 1.00
- ❑ 118 New York Giants 3.00 1.50
- ❑ 119 Roosevelt Brown 4.00 2.00
- ❑ 120 Henry Carr RC 3.00 1.50
- ❑ 121 Clarence Childs 2.00 1.00
- ❑ 122 Tucker Frederickson RC 3.00 1.50
- ❑ 123 Jerry Hillebrand 2.00 1.00
- ❑ 124 Greg Larson 2.00 1.00
- ❑ 125 Spider Lockhart RC 3.00 1.50
- ❑ 126 Dick Lynch 2.00 1.00
- ❑ 127 Earl Morrall/Scholtz 3.00 1.50
- ❑ 128 Joe Morrison 2.00 1.00
- ❑ 129 Steve Thurlow 2.00 1.00
- ❑ 130 New York Giants 2.00 1.00
- ❑ 131 Philadelphia Eagles 3.00 1.50
- ❑ 132 Sam Baker 2.00 1.00
- ❑ 133 Maxie Baughan 2.00 1.00
- ❑ 134 Bob Brown OT RC 12.00 6.00
- ❑ 135 Timmy Brown 3.00 1.50
- ❑ 136 Irv Cross 3.00 1.50
- ❑ 137 Earl Gros 2.00 1.00
- ❑ 138 Ray Poage 2.00 1.00
- ❑ 139 Nate Ramsey 2.00 1.00
- ❑ 140 Pete Retzlaff 3.00 1.50
- ❑ 141 Jim Ringo 4.00 2.00
- ❑ 142 Norm Snead 4.00 2.00
- ❑ 143 Philadelphia Eagles 2.00 1.00
- ❑ 144 Pittsburgh Steelers 3.00 1.50
- ❑ 145 Gary Ballman 2.00 1.00
- ❑ 146 Charley Bradshaw 2.00 1.00
- ❑ 147 Jim Butler 2.00 1.00
- ❑ 148 Mike Clark 2.00 1.00
- ❑ 149 Dick Hoak RC 2.00 1.00
- ❑ 150 Roy Jefferson RC 3.00 1.50
- ❑ 151 Frank Lambert 2.00 1.00
- ❑ 152 Mike Lind 2.00 1.00
- ❑ 153 Bill Nelsen RC 4.00 2.00
- ❑ 154 Clarence Peaks 2.00 1.00
- ❑ 155 Clendon Thomas 2.00 1.00
- ❑ 156 Pittsburgh Steelers 2.00 1.00
- ❑ 157 St. Louis Cardinals 3.00 1.50
- ❑ 158 Jim Bakken 2.00 1.00
- ❑ 159 Bobby Joe Conrad 3.00 1.50
- ❑ 160 Willis Crenshaw RC 2.00 1.00
- ❑ 161 Bob DeMarco 2.00 1.00
- ❑ 162 Pat Fischer 3.00 1.50
- ❑ 163 Charlie Johnson 3.00 1.50
- ❑ 164 Dale Meinert 2.00 1.00
- ❑ 165 Sonny Randle 2.00 1.00
- ❑ 166 Sam Silas RC 2.00 1.00
- ❑ 167 Bill Triplett 2.00 1.00
- ❑ 168 Larry Wilson 4.00 2.00
- ❑ 169 St. Louis Cardinals 2.00 1.00
- ❑ 170 San Francisco 49ers 3.00 1.50
- ❑ 171 Kermit Alexander 2.00 1.00
- ❑ 172 Bruce Bosley 2.00 1.00
- ❑ 173 John Brodie 6.00 3.00
- ❑ 174 Bernie Casey 3.00 1.50
- ❑ 175 John David Crow 4.00 2.00
- ❑ 176 Tommy Davis 2.00 1.00

❑ 177 Jim Johnson	4.00	2.00
❑ 178 Gary Lewis RC	2.00	1.00
❑ 179 Dave Parks	2.00	1.00
❑ 180 Walter Rock RC	3.00	1.50
❑ 181 Ken Willard RC	4.00	2.00
❑ 182 San Francisco 49ers	2.00	1.00
❑ 183 Washington Redskins	3.00	1.50
❑ 184 Rickie Harris	2.00	1.00
❑ 185 Sonny Jurgensen	8.00	4.00
❑ 186 Paul Krause	6.00	3.00
❑ 187 Bobby Mitchell	6.00	3.00
❑ 188 Vince Promuto	2.00	1.00
❑ 189 Pat Richter RC	2.00	1.00
❑ 190 Joe Rutgens	2.00	1.00
❑ 191 Johnny Sample	2.00	1.00
❑ 192 Lonnie Sanders	2.00	1.00
❑ 193 Jim Steffen	2.00	1.00
❑ 194 Charley Taylor	15.00	7.50
❑ 195 Washington Redskins	2.00	1.00
❑ 196 Referee Signals	3.00	1.50
❑ 197 Checklist 1 !	25.00	12.50
❑ 198 Checklist 2 UER !	50.00	25.00

1967 Philadelphia

❑ COMPLETE SET (198)	650.00	425.00
❑ WRAPPER (5-CENT)	20.00	10.00
❑ 1 Falcons Team !	10.00	5.00
❑ 2 Junior Coffey RC	3.00	1.50
❑ 3 Alex Hawkins	2.00	1.00
❑ 4 Randy Johnson RC	3.00	1.50
❑ 5 Lou Kirouac	2.00	1.00
❑ 6 Billy Martin RC	2.00	1.00
❑ 7 Tommy Nobis RC	20.00	10.00
❑ 8 Jerry Richardson RC	4.00	2.00
❑ 9 Marion Rushing	2.00	1.00
❑ 10 Ron Smith	2.00	1.00
❑ 11 Ernie Wheelwright UER	2.00	1.00
❑ 12 Atlanta Falcons	2.00	1.00
❑ 13 Baltimore Colts	3.00	1.50
❑ 14 Raymond Berry UER	7.00	3.50
❑ 15 Bob Boyd DB	2.00	1.00
❑ 16 Ordell Braase	2.00	1.00
❑ 17 Alvin Haymond RC	2.00	1.00
❑ 18 Tony Lorick	2.00	1.00
❑ 19 Lenny Lyles	2.00	1.00
❑ 20 John Mackey	5.00	2.50
❑ 21 Tom Matte	3.00	1.50
❑ 22 Lou Michaels	2.00	1.00
❑ 23 Johnny Unitas	40.00	25.00
❑ 24 Baltimore Colts	2.00	1.00
❑ 25 Chicago Bears	3.00	1.50
❑ 26 Rudy Bukich UER	2.00	1.00
❑ 27 Ronnie Bull	2.00	1.00
❑ 28 Dick Butkus	75.00	45.00
❑ 29 Mike Ditka	30.00	18.00
❑ 30 Dick Gordon RC	3.00	1.50
❑ 31 Roger LeClerc	2.00	1.00
❑ 32 Bennie McRae	2.00	1.00
❑ 33 Richie Petitbon	2.00	1.00
❑ 34 Mike Pyle	2.00	1.00
❑ 35 Gale Sayers	75.00	45.00
❑ 36 Chicago Bears	2.00	1.00
❑ 37 Cleveland Browns	3.00	1.50
❑ 38 Johnny Brewer	2.00	1.00
❑ 39 Gary Collins	3.00	1.50
❑ 40 Ross Fichtner	2.00	1.00
❑ 41 Ernie Green	2.00	1.00
❑ 42 Gene Hickerson	2.00	1.00
❑ 43 Leroy Kelly RC	40.00	25.00
❑ 44 Frank Ryan	3.00	1.50
❑ 45 Dick Schafrath	2.00	1.00
❑ 46 Paul Warfield	18.00	10.00
❑ 47 John Wooten	2.00	1.00
❑ 48 Cleveland Browns	2.00	1.00
❑ 49 Dallas Cowboys	3.00	1.50
❑ 50 George Andrie	2.00	1.00
❑ 51 Cornell Green	3.00	1.50
❑ 52 Bob Hayes	20.00	10.00
❑ 53 Chuck Howley	4.00	2.00
❑ 54 Lee Roy Jordan RC	20.00	12.00
❑ 55 Bob Lilly	15.00	7.50
❑ 56 Dave Manders RC	2.00	1.00
❑ 57 Don Meredith	25.00	15.00
❑ 58 Dan Reeves RC	30.00	18.00
❑ 59 Mel Renfro	6.00	3.00
❑ 60 Dallas Cowboys	3.00	1.50
❑ 61 Detroit Lions	3.00	1.50
❑ 62 Roger Brown	3.00	1.50
❑ 63 Gail Cogdill	2.00	1.00
❑ 64 John Gordy	2.00	1.00
❑ 65 Ron Kramer	2.00	1.00
❑ 66 Dick LeBeau	2.00	1.00
❑ 67 Mike Lucci RC	4.00	2.00
❑ 68 Amos Marsh	2.00	1.00
❑ 69 Tom Nowatzke	2.00	1.00
❑ 70 Pat Studstill	2.00	1.00
❑ 71 Karl Sweetan	2.00	1.00
❑ 72 Detroit Lions	2.00	1.00
❑ 73 Green Bay Packers	5.00	2.50
❑ 74 Herb Adderley UER	6.00	3.00
❑ 75 Lee Roy Caffey	3.00	1.50
❑ 76 Willie Davis DE	5.00	2.50
❑ 77 Forrest Gregg	4.00	2.00
❑ 78 Hank Jordan	4.00	2.00
❑ 79 Ray Nitschke	12.00	6.00
❑ 80 Dave Robinson RC	6.00	3.00
❑ 81 Bob Skoronski	3.00	1.50
❑ 82 Bart Starr	50.00	30.00
❑ 83 Willie Wood	5.00	2.50
❑ 84 Green Bay Packers	3.00	1.50
❑ 85 Los Angeles Rams	3.00	1.50
❑ 86 Dick Bass	3.00	1.50
❑ 87 Maxie Baughan	2.00	1.00
❑ 88 Roman Gabriel	4.00	2.00
❑ 89 Bruce Gossett	2.00	1.00
❑ 90 Deacon Jones	5.00	2.50
❑ 91 Tommy McDonald	5.00	2.50
❑ 92 Marlin McKeever	2.00	1.00
❑ 93 Tom Moore	2.00	1.00
❑ 94 Merlin Olsen	6.00	3.00
❑ 95 Clancy Williams	2.00	1.00
❑ 96 Los Angeles Rams	2.00	1.00
❑ 97 Minnesota Vikings	3.00	1.50
❑ 98 Grady Alderman	2.00	1.00
❑ 99 Bill Brown	3.00	1.50
❑ 100 Fred Cox	2.00	1.00
❑ 101 Paul Flatley	2.00	1.00
❑ 102 Dale Hackbart RC	2.00	1.00
❑ 103 Jim Marshall	4.00	2.00
❑ 104 Tommy Mason	2.00	1.00
❑ 105 Milt Sunde RC	2.00	1.00
❑ 106 Fran Tarkenton	20.00	10.00
❑ 107 Mick Tingelhoff	3.00	1.50
❑ 108 Minnesota Vikings	2.00	1.00
❑ 109 New York Giants	3.00	1.50
❑ 110 Henry Carr	2.00	1.00
❑ 111 Clarence Childs	2.00	1.00
❑ 112 Allen Jacobs	2.00	1.00
❑ 113 Homer Jones RC	3.00	1.50
❑ 114 Tom Kennedy	2.00	1.00
❑ 115 Spider Lockhart	2.00	1.00
❑ 116 Joe Morrison	2.00	1.00
❑ 117 Francis Peay	2.00	1.00
❑ 118 Jeff Smith LB	2.00	1.00
❑ 119 Aaron Thomas	2.00	1.00
❑ 120 New York Giants	2.00	1.00
❑ 121 Saints Insignia	3.00	1.50
❑ 122 Charley Bradshaw	2.00	1.00
❑ 123 Paul Hornung	25.00	12.50
❑ 124 Elbert Kimbrough	2.00	1.00
❑ 125 Earl Leggett RC	2.00	1.00
❑ 126 Obert Logan	2.00	1.00
❑ 127 Riley Mattson	2.00	1.00
❑ 128 John Morrow	2.00	1.00
❑ 129 Bob Scholtz	2.00	1.00
❑ 130 Dave Whitsell RC	2.00	1.00
❑ 131 Gary Wood	2.00	1.00
❑ 132 Saints Roster UER 121	3.00	1.50
❑ 133 Philadelphia Eagles	3.00	1.50
❑ 134 Sam Baker	2.00	1.00
❑ 135 Bob Brown OT	5.00	2.00
❑ 136 Timmy Brown	3.00	1.50
❑ 137 Earl Gros	2.00	1.00
❑ 138 Dave Lloyd	2.00	1.00
❑ 139 Floyd Peters	2.00	1.00
❑ 140 Pete Retzlaff	3.00	1.50
❑ 141 Joe Scarpati	2.00	1.00
❑ 142 Norm Snead	3.00	1.50
❑ 143 Jim Skaggs	2.00	1.00
❑ 144 Philadelphia Eagles	2.00	1.00
❑ 145 Pittsburgh Steelers	3.00	1.50
❑ 146 Bill Asbury	2.00	1.00
❑ 147 John Baker	2.00	1.00
❑ 148 Gary Ballman	2.00	1.00
❑ 149 Mike Clark	2.00	1.00
❑ 150 Riley Gunnels	2.00	1.00
❑ 151 John Hilton	2.00	1.00
❑ 152 Roy Jefferson	3.00	1.50
❑ 153 Brady Keys	2.00	1.00
❑ 154 Ben McGee	2.00	1.00
❑ 155 Bill Nelsen	3.00	1.50
❑ 156 Pittsburgh Steelers	2.00	1.00
❑ 157 St. Louis Cardinals	3.00	1.50
❑ 158 Jim Bakken	2.00	1.00
❑ 159 Bobby Joe Conrad	3.00	1.50
❑ 160 Ken Gray	2.00	1.00
❑ 161 Charlie Johnson	3.00	1.50
❑ 162 Joe Robb	2.00	1.00
❑ 163 Johnny Roland RC	3.00	1.50
❑ 164 Roy Shivers	2.00	1.00
❑ 165 Jackie Smith RC	15.00	7.50
❑ 166 Jerry Stovall	2.00	1.00
❑ 167 Larry Wilson	4.00	2.00
❑ 168 St. Louis Cardinals	2.00	1.00
❑ 169 San Francisco 49ers	3.00	1.50
❑ 170 Kermit Alexander	2.00	1.00
❑ 171 Bruce Bosley	2.00	1.00
❑ 172 John Brodie	6.00	3.00
❑ 173 Bernie Casey	3.00	1.50
❑ 174 Tommy Davis	2.00	1.00
❑ 175 Howard Mudd	2.00	1.00
❑ 176 Dave Parks	2.00	1.00
❑ 177 John Thomas	2.00	1.00
❑ 178 Dave Wilcox RC	10.00	5.00
❑ 179 Ken Willard	3.00	1.50
❑ 180 San Francisco 49ers	2.00	1.00
❑ 181 Washington Redskins	3.00	1.50
❑ 182 Charlie Gogolak RC	2.00	1.00
❑ 183 Chris Hanburger RC	5.00	2.50
❑ 184 Len Hauss RC	3.00	1.50
❑ 185 Sonny Jurgensen	7.00	3.50
❑ 186 Bobby Mitchell	5.00	2.50
❑ 187 Brig Owens	2.00	1.00
❑ 188 Jim Shorter	2.00	1.00
❑ 189 Jerry Smith RC	3.00	1.50
❑ 190 Charley Taylor	8.00	4.00
❑ 191 A.D. Whitfield	2.00	1.00
❑ 192 Washington Redskins	2.00	1.00

❑ 193 Browns Play/Leroy Kelly 6.00 3.00
❑ 194 New York Giants PC 2.00 1.00
❑ 195 Atlanta Falcons PC 2.00 1.00
❑ 196 Referee Signals 3.00 1.50
❑ 197 Checklist 1 ! 20.00 12.00
❑ 198 Checklist 2 UER ! 40.00 20.00

1991 Pinnacle

❑ COMPLETE SET (415) 20.00 7.50
❑ 1 Warren Moon .40 .15
❑ 2 Morten Andersen .10 .02
❑ 3 Rohn Stark .10 .02
❑ 4 Mark Bortz .10 .02
❑ 5 Mark Higgs RC .10 .02
❑ 6 Troy Aikman 2.00 .75
❑ 7 John Elway 3.00 1.25
❑ 8 Neal Anderson .20 .07
❑ 9 Chris Doleman .10 .02
❑ 10 Jay Schroeder .10 .02
❑ 11 Sterling Sharpe .40 .15
❑ 12 Steve DeBerg .10 .02
❑ 13 Ronnie Lott .20 .07
❑ 14 Sean Landeta .10 .02
❑ 15 Jim Everett .20 .07
❑ 16 Jim Breech .10 .02
❑ 17 Barry Foster .20 .07
❑ 18 Mike Merriweather .10 .02
❑ 19 Eric Metcalf .20 .07
❑ 20 Mark Carrier DB .20 .07
❑ 21 James Brooks .20 .07
❑ 22 Nate Odomes .10 .02
❑ 23 Rodney Hampton .40 .15
❑ 24 Chris Miller .20 .07
❑ 25 Roger Craig .20 .07
❑ 26 Louis Oliver .10 .02
❑ 27 Allen Pinkett .10 .02
❑ 28 Bubby Brister .10 .02
❑ 29 Reyna Thompson .10 .02
❑ 30 Issiac Holt .10 .02
❑ 31 Steve Broussard .10 .02
❑ 32 Christian Okoye .10 .02
❑ 33 Dave Meggett .20 .07
❑ 34 Andre Reed .20 .07
❑ 35 Shane Conlan .10 .02
❑ 36 Eric Ball .10 .02
❑ 37 Johnny Bailey .10 .02
❑ 38 Don Majkowski .10 .02
❑ 39 Gerald Williams .10 .02
❑ 40 Kevin Mack .10 .02
❑ 41 Jeff Herrod .10 .02
❑ 42 Emmitt Smith 6.00 2.50
❑ 43 Wendell Davis .10 .02
❑ 44 Lorenzo White .10 .02
❑ 45 Andre Rison .20 .07
❑ 46 Jerry Gray .10 .02
❑ 47 Dennis Smith .10 .02
❑ 48 Gaston Green .10 .02
❑ 49 Dermontti Dawson .10 .02
❑ 50 Jeff Hostetler .20 .07
❑ 51 Nick Lowery .10 .02
❑ 52 Merril Hoge .10 .02
❑ 53 Bobby Hebert .10 .02
❑ 54 Scott Case .10 .02
❑ 55 Jack Del Rio .20 .07
❑ 56 Cornelius Bennett .20 .07
❑ 57 Tony Mandarich .10 .02
❑ 58 Bill Brooks .10 .02
❑ 59 Jessie Tuggle .10 .02
❑ 60 Hugh Millen RC .10 .02
❑ 61 Tony Bennett .20 .07
❑ 62 Cris Dishman RC .10 .02
❑ 63 Darryl Henley RC .10 .02
❑ 64 Duane Bickett .10 .02
❑ 65 Jay Hilgenberg .10 .02
❑ 66 Joe Montana 3.00 1.25
❑ 67 Bill Fralic .10 .02
❑ 68 Sam Mills .10 .02
❑ 69 Bruce Armstrong .10 .02
❑ 70 Dan Marino 3.00 1.25
❑ 71 Jim Lachey .10 .02
❑ 72 Rod Woodson .40 .15
❑ 73 Simon Fletcher .10 .02
❑ 74 Bruce Matthews .20 .07
❑ 75 Howie Long .40 .15
❑ 76 John Friesz .40 .15
❑ 77 Karl Mecklenburg .10 .02
❑ 78 John L. Williams UER .10 .02
❑ 79 Rob Burnett RC .20 .07
❑ 80 Anthony Carter .20 .07
❑ 81 Henry Ellard .20 .07
❑ 82 Don Beebe .10 .02
❑ 83 Louis Lipps .10 .02
❑ 84 Greg McMurtry .10 .02
❑ 85 Will Wolford .10 .02
❑ 86 Eric Green .10 .02
❑ 87 Irving Fryar .20 .07
❑ 88 John Offerdahl .10 .02
❑ 89 John Alt .10 .02
❑ 90 Tom Tupa .10 .02
❑ 91 Don Mosebar .10 .02
❑ 92 Jeff George .50 .20
❑ 93 Vinny Testaverde .20 .07
❑ 94 Greg Townsend .10 .02
❑ 95 Derrick Fenner .10 .02
❑ 96 Brian Mitchell .20 .07
❑ 97 Herschel Walker .20 .07
❑ 98 Ricky Proehl .10 .02
❑ 99 Mark Clayton .20 .07
❑ 100 Derrick Thomas .40 .15
❑ 101 Jim Harbaugh .40 .15
❑ 102 Barry Word .10 .02
❑ 103 Jerry Rice 2.00 .75
❑ 104 Keith Byars .10 .02
❑ 105 Marion Butts .20 .07
❑ 106 Rich Moran .10 .02
❑ 107 Thurman Thomas .40 .15
❑ 108 Stephone Paige .10 .02
❑ 109 D.J. Johnson .10 .02
❑ 110 William Perry .20 .07
❑ 111 Haywood Jeffires .20 .07
❑ 112 Rodney Peete .20 .07
❑ 113 Andy Heck .10 .02
❑ 114 Kevin Ross .10 .02
❑ 115 Michael Carter .10 .02
❑ 116 Tim McKyer .10 .02
❑ 117 Kenneth Davis .10 .02
❑ 118 Richmond Webb .10 .02
❑ 119 Rich Camarillo .10 .02
❑ 120 James Francis .10 .02
❑ 121 Craig Heyward .20 .07
❑ 122 Hardy Nickerson .20 .07
❑ 123 Michael Brooks .10 .02
❑ 124 Fred Barnett .40 .15
❑ 125 Cris Carter 1.00 .40
❑ 126 Brian Jordan .20 .07
❑ 127 Pat Leahy .10 .02
❑ 128 Kevin Greene .20 .07
❑ 129 Trace Armstrong .10 .02
❑ 130 Eugene Lockhart .10 .02
❑ 131 Albert Lewis .10 .02
❑ 132 Ernie Jones .10 .02
❑ 133 Eric Martin .10 .02
❑ 134 Anthony Thompson .10 .02
❑ 135 Tim Krumrie .10 .02
❑ 136 James Lofton .20 .07
❑ 137 John Taylor .20 .07
❑ 138 Jeff Cross .10 .02
❑ 139 Tommy Kane .10 .02
❑ 140 Robb Thomas .10 .02
❑ 141 Gary Anderson K .10 .02
❑ 142 Mark Murphy .10 .02
❑ 143 Rickey Jackson .10 .02
❑ 144 Ken O'Brien .10 .02
❑ 145 Ernest Givins .20 .07
❑ 146 Jessie Hester .10 .02
❑ 147 Deion Sanders .75 .30
❑ 148 Keith Henderson RC .10 .02
❑ 149 Chris Singleton .10 .02
❑ 150 Rod Bernstine .10 .02
❑ 151 Quinn Early .20 .07
❑ 152 Boomer Esiason .20 .07
❑ 153 Mike Gann .10 .02
❑ 154 Dino Hackett .10 .02
❑ 155 Perry Kemp .10 .02
❑ 156 Mark Ingram .20 .07
❑ 157 Daryl Johnston .75 .30
❑ 158 Eugene Daniel .10 .02
❑ 159 Dalton Hilliard .10 .02
❑ 160 Rufus Porter .10 .02
❑ 161 Tunch Ilkin .10 .02
❑ 162 James Hasty .10 .02
❑ 163 Keith McKeller .10 .02
❑ 164 Heath Sherman .10 .02
❑ 165 Vai Sikahema .10 .02
❑ 166 Pat Terrell .10 .02
❑ 167 Anthony Munoz .20 .07
❑ 168 Brad Edwards RC .10 .02
❑ 169 Tom Rathman .10 .02
❑ 170 Steve McMichael .20 .07
❑ 171 Vaughan Johnson .10 .02
❑ 172 Nate Lewis RC .10 .02
❑ 173 Mark Rypien .20 .07
❑ 174 Rob Moore .50 .20
❑ 175 Tim Green .10 .02
❑ 176 Tony Casillas .10 .02
❑ 177 Jon Hand .10 .02
❑ 178 Todd McNair .10 .02
❑ 179 Toi Cook RC .10 .02
❑ 180 Eddie Brown .10 .02
❑ 181 Mark Jackson .10 .02
❑ 182 Pete Stoyanovich .10 .02
❑ 183 Bryce Paup RC .40 .15
❑ 184 Anthony Miller .20 .07
❑ 185 Dan Saleaumua .10 .02
❑ 186 Guy McIntyre .10 .02
❑ 187 Broderick Thomas .10 .02
❑ 188 Frank Warren .10 .02
❑ 189 Drew Hill .10 .02
❑ 190 Reggie White .40 .15
❑ 191 Chris Hinton .10 .02
❑ 192 David Little .10 .02
❑ 193 David Fulcher .10 .02
❑ 194 Clarence Verdin .10 .02
❑ 195 Junior Seau .60 .25
❑ 196 Blair Thomas .10 .02
❑ 197 Stan Brock .10 .02
❑ 198 Gary Clark .40 .15
❑ 199 Michael Irvin .40 .15
❑ 200 Ronnie Harmon .10 .02
❑ 201 Steve Young 2.00 .75
❑ 202 Brian Noble .10 .02
❑ 203 Dan Stryzinski .10 .02
❑ 204 Darryl Talley .10 .02
❑ 205 David Alexander .10 .02
❑ 206 Pat Swilling .20 .07
❑ 207 Gary Plummer .10 .02
❑ 208 Robert Delpino .10 .02
❑ 209 Norm Johnson .10 .02

❑ 210 Mike Singletary .20 .07
❑ 211 Anthony Johnson .40 .15
❑ 212 Eric Allen .10 .02
❑ 213 Gill Fenerty .10 .02
❑ 214 Neil Smith .40 .15
❑ 215 Joe Phillips .10 .02
❑ 216 Ottis Anderson .20 .07
❑ 217 LeRoy Butler .20 .07
❑ 218 Ray Childress .10 .02
❑ 219 Rodney Holman .10 .02
❑ 220 Kevin Fagan .10 .02
❑ 221 Bruce Smith .40 .15
❑ 222 Brad Muster .10 .02
❑ 223 Mike Horan .10 .02
❑ 224 Steve Atwater .10 .02
❑ 225 Rich Gannon .50 .20
❑ 226 Anthony Pleasant .10 .02
❑ 227 Steve Jordan .10 .02
❑ 228 Lomas Brown .10 .02
❑ 229 Jackie Slater .10 .02
❑ 230 Brad Baxter .10 .02
❑ 231 Joe Morris .10 .02
❑ 232 Marcus Allen .40 .15
❑ 233 Chris Warren .40 .15
❑ 234 Johnny Johnson .10 .02
❑ 235 Phil Simms .20 .07
❑ 236 Dave Krieg .20 .07
❑ 237 Jim McMahon .20 .07
❑ 238 Richard Dent .20 .07
❑ 239 John Washington RC .10 .02
❑ 240 Sammie Smith .10 .02
❑ 241 Brian Brennan .10 .02
❑ 242 Cortez Kennedy .40 .15
❑ 243 Tim McDonald .10 .02
❑ 244 Charles Haley .20 .07
❑ 245 Joey Browner .10 .02
❑ 246 Eddie Murray .10 .02
❑ 247 Bob Golic .10 .02
❑ 248 Myron Guyton .10 .02
❑ 249 Dennis Byrd .10 .02
❑ 250 Barry Sanders 3.00 1.25
❑ 251 Clay Matthews .20 .07
❑ 252 Pepper Johnson .10 .02
❑ 253 Eric Swann RC .40 .15
❑ 254 Lamar Lathon .10 .02
❑ 255 Andre Tippett .10 .02
❑ 256 Tom Newberry .10 .02
❑ 257 Kyle Clifton .10 .02
❑ 258 Leslie O'Neal .20 .07
❑ 259 Bubba McDowell .10 .02
❑ 260 Scott Davis .10 .02
❑ 261 Wilber Marshall .10 .02
❑ 262 Marv Cook .10 .02
❑ 263 Jeff Lageman .10 .02
❑ 264 Michael Young .10 .02
❑ 265 Gary Zimmerman .10 .02
❑ 266 Mike Munchak .20 .07
❑ 267 David Treadwell .10 .02
❑ 268 Steve Wisniewski .10 .02
❑ 269 Mark Duper .20 .07
❑ 270 Chris Spielman .20 .07
❑ 271 Brett Perriman .40 .15
❑ 272 Lionel Washington .10 .02
❑ 273 Lawrence Taylor .40 .15
❑ 274 Mark Collins .10 .02
❑ 275 Mark Carrier WR .40 .15
❑ 276 Paul Gruber .10 .02
❑ 277 Earnest Byner .10 .02
❑ 278 Andre Collins .10 .02
❑ 279 Reggie Cobb .10 .02
❑ 280 Art Monk .20 .07
❑ 281 Henry Jones RC .20 .07
❑ 282 Mike Pritchard RC .40 .15
❑ 283 Moe Gardner RC .10 .02
❑ 284 Chris Zorich RC .40 .15
❑ 285 Keith Traylor RC .10 .02
❑ 286 Mike Dumas RC .10 .02
❑ 287 Ed King RC .10 .02
❑ 288 Russell Maryland RC .40 .15
❑ 289 Alfred Williams RC .10 .02
❑ 290 Derek Russell RC .10 .02
❑ 291 Vinnie Clark RC .10 .02
❑ 292 Mike Croel RC .10 .02
❑ 293 Todd Marinovich RC .10 .02
❑ 294 Phil Hansen RC .10 .02
❑ 295 Aaron Craver RC .10 .02
❑ 296 Nick Bell RC .10 .02
❑ 297 Kenny Walker RC .10 .02
❑ 298 Roman Phifer RC .10 .02
❑ 299 Kanavis McGhee RC .10 .02
❑ 300 Ricky Ervins RC .20 .07
❑ 301 Jim Price RC .10 .02
❑ 302 John Johnson RC .10 .02
❑ 303 George Thornton RC .10 .02
❑ 304 Huey Richardson RC .10 .02
❑ 305 Harry Colon RC .10 .02
❑ 306 Antone Davis RC .10 .02
❑ 307 Todd Lyght RC .10 .02
❑ 308 Bryan Cox RC .40 .15
❑ 309 Brad Goebel RC .10 .02
❑ 310 Eric Moten RC .10 .02
❑ 311 John Kasay RC .20 .07
❑ 312 Esera Tuaolo RC .10 .02
❑ 313 Bobby Wilson RC .10 .02
❑ 314 Mo Lewis RC .20 .07
❑ 315 Harvey Williams RC .40 .15
❑ 316 Mike Stonebreaker .10 .02
❑ 317 Charles McRae RC .10 .02
❑ 318 John Flannery RC .10 .02
❑ 319 Ted Washington RC .10 .02
❑ 320 Stanley Richard RC .10 .02
❑ 321 Browning Nagle RC .10 .02
❑ 322 Ed McCaffrey RC 5.00 2.00
❑ 323 Jeff Graham RC WR .40 .15
❑ 324 Stan Thomas .10 .02
❑ 325 Lawrence Dawsey RC .20 .07
❑ 326 Eric Bieniemy RC .10 .02
❑ 327 Tim Barnett RC .10 .02
❑ 328 Erric Pegram RC .40 .15
❑ 329 Lamar Rogers RC .10 .02
❑ 330 Ernie Mills RC .20 .07
❑ 331 Pat Harlow RC .10 .02
❑ 332 Greg Lewis RC .10 .02
❑ 333 Jarrod Bunch RC .10 .02
❑ 334 Dan McGwire RC .10 .02
❑ 335 Randal Hill RC .20 .07
❑ 336 Leonard Russell RC .40 .15
❑ 337 Carnell Lake .10 .02
❑ 338 Brian Blades .20 .07
❑ 339 Darrell Green .10 .02
❑ 340 Bobby Humphrey .10 .02
❑ 341 Mervyn Fernandez .10 .02
❑ 342 Ricky Sanders .10 .02
❑ 343 Keith Jackson .20 .07
❑ 344 Carl Banks .10 .02
❑ 345 Gill Byrd .10 .02
❑ 346 Al Toon .20 .07
❑ 347 Stephen Baker .10 .02
❑ 348 Randall Cunningham .40 .15
❑ 349 Flipper Anderson .10 .02
❑ 350 Jay Novacek .40 .15
❑ 351 Steve Young/B.Smith HH .40 .15
❑ 352 Barry Sanders/Browner HH .75 .30
❑ 353 Joe Montana/M.Carrier HH .75 .30
❑ 354 Thurman Thomas/L.Taylor .20 .07
❑ 355 Jerry Rice/Darr.Green HH .50 .20
❑ 356 Warren Moon Tech .20 .07
❑ 357 Anthony Munoz TECH .10 .02
❑ 358 Barry Sanders Tech 1.25 .50
❑ 359 Jerry Rice Tech 1.25 .50
❑ 360 Joey Browner TECH .10 .02
❑ 361 Morten Andersen TECH .10 .02
❑ 362 Sean Landeta TECH .10 .02
❑ 363 Thurman Thomas GW .40 .15
❑ 364 Emmitt Smith GW 3.00 1.25
❑ 365 Gaston Green GW .10 .02
❑ 366 Barry Sanders GW 1.25 .50
❑ 367 Christian Okoye GW .10 .02
❑ 368 Earnest Byner GW .10 .02
❑ 369 Neal Anderson GW .10 .02
❑ 370 Herschel Walker GW .20 .07
❑ 371 Rodney Hampton GW .40 .15
❑ 372 Darryl Talley IDOL .10 .02
❑ 373 Mark Carrier IDOL .10 .02
❑ 374 Jim Breech IDOL .10 .02
❑ 375 R.Hampton/O.Anderson ID .10 .02
❑ 376 Kevin Mack IDOL .10 .02
❑ 377 S.Jordan/O.Robertson ID .10 .02
❑ 378 B.Esiason/B.Jones ID .10 .02
❑ 379 Steve DeBerg IDOL .20 .07
❑ 380 Al Toon IDOL .10 .02
❑ 381 Ronnie Lott/C.Taylor ID .20 .07
❑ 382 Henry Ellard IDOL .10 .02
❑ 383 Troy Aikman/Staubach ID 1.25 .50
❑ 384 T.Thomas/E.Campbell ID .40 .15
❑ 385 Dan Marino/Bradshaw ID 1.50 .60
❑ 386 Howie Long/Joe Greene ID .20 .07
❑ 387 Franco Harris IR .20 .07
❑ 388 Esera Tuaolo .10 .02
❑ 389 Super Bowl XXVI .10 .02
❑ 390 Charles Mann .10 .02
❑ 391 Kenny Walker Succeed .10 .02
❑ 392 Reggie Roby .10 .02
❑ 393 Bruce Pickens RC .10 .02
❑ 394 Ray Childress SIDE .10 .02
❑ 395 Karl Mecklenburg SIDE .10 .02
❑ 396 Dean Biasucci SIDE .10 .02
❑ 397 John Alt SIDE .10 .02
❑ 398 Marcus Allen SL .20 .07
❑ 399 John Offerdahl SIDE .10 .02
❑ 400 Richard Tardits RC SIDE .10 .02
❑ 401 Al Toon SIDE .10 .02
❑ 402 Joey Browner SIDE .10 .02
❑ 403 Spencer Tillman RC SIDE .10 .02
❑ 404 Jay Novacek SIDE .20 .07
❑ 405 Stephen Braggs SIDE .10 .02
❑ 406 Mike Tice RC SIDE .10 .02
❑ 407 Kevin Greene SIDE .20 .07
❑ 408 Reggie White SIDE .20 .07
❑ 409 Brian Noble SIDE .10 .02
❑ 410 Bart Oates SIDE .10 .02
❑ 411 Art Monk SIDE .20 .07
❑ 412 Ron Wolfley SIDE .10 .02
❑ 413 Louis Lipps SIDE .10 .02
❑ 414 Dante Jones RC SIDE .20 .07
❑ 415 Kenneth Davis SIDE .10 .02
❑ P1 Emmitt Smith Promo 25.00 12.50

1992 Pinnacle

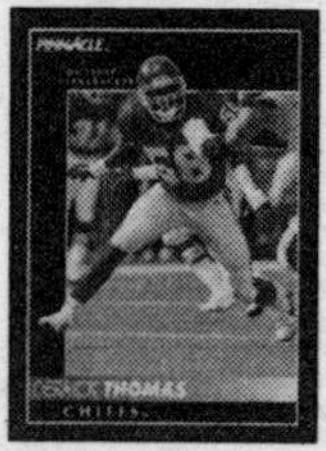

PINNACLE
DERRICK THOMAS
CHIEFS

❑ COMPLETE SET (360) 25.00 12.50
❑ 1 Reggie White .50 .20
❑ 2 Eric Green .15 .05
❑ 3 Craig Heyward .30 .10
❑ 4 Phil Simms .30 .10
❑ 5 Pepper Johnson .15 .05
❑ 6 Sean Landeta .15 .05
❑ 7 Dino Hackett .15 .05
❑ 8 Andre Ware .15 .05

Card	Mint	Exc
❑ 9 Ricky Nattiel	.15	.05
❑ 10 Jim Price	.15	.05
❑ 11 Jim Ritcher	.15	.05
❑ 12 Kelly Stouffer	.15	.05
❑ 13 Ray Crockett	.15	.05
❑ 14 Steve Tasker	.30	.10
❑ 15 Barry Sanders	3.00	1.25
❑ 16 Pat Swilling	.15	.05
❑ 17 Moe Gardner	.15	.05
❑ 18 Steve Young	2.00	.75
❑ 19 Chris Spielman	.30	.10
❑ 20 Richard Dent	.30	.10
❑ 21 Anthony Munoz	.30	.10
❑ 22 Thurman Thomas	.50	.20
❑ 23 Ricky Sanders	.15	.05
❑ 24 Steve Atwater	.15	.05
❑ 25 Tony Tolbert	.15	.05
❑ 26 Haywood Jeffires	.30	.10
❑ 27 Duane Bickett	.15	.05
❑ 28 Tim McDonald	.15	.05
❑ 29 Cris Carter	.75	.30
❑ 30 Derrick Thomas	.50	.20
❑ 31 Hugh Millen	.15	.05
❑ 32 Bart Oates	.15	.05
❑ 33 Darryl Talley	.15	.05
❑ 34 Marion Butts	.15	.05
❑ 35 Pete Stoyanovich	.15	.05
❑ 36 Ronnie Lott	.30	.10
❑ 37 Simon Fletcher	.15	.05
❑ 38 Morten Andersen	.15	.05
❑ 39 Clyde Simmons	.15	.05
❑ 40 Mark Rypien	.15	.05
❑ 41 Henry Ellard	.30	.10
❑ 42 Michael Irvin	.50	.20
❑ 43 Louis Lipps	.15	.05
❑ 44 John L. Williams	.15	.05
❑ 45 Broderick Thomas	.15	.05
❑ 46 Don Majkowski	.15	.05
❑ 47 William Perry	.30	.10
❑ 48 David Fulcher	.15	.05
❑ 49 Tony Bennett	.15	.05
❑ 50 Clay Matthews	.30	.10
❑ 51 Warren Moon	.50	.20
❑ 52 Bruce Armstrong	.15	.05
❑ 53 Bill Brooks	.15	.05
❑ 54 Greg Townsend	.15	.05
❑ 55 Steve Broussard	.15	.05
❑ 56 Mel Gray	.30	.10
❑ 57 Kevin Mack	.15	.05
❑ 58 Emmitt Smith	4.00	2.00
❑ 59 Mike Croel	.15	.05
❑ 60 Brian Mitchell	.30	.10
❑ 61 Bennie Blades	.15	.05
❑ 62 Carnell Lake	.15	.05
❑ 63 Cornelius Bennett	.30	.10
❑ 64 Darrell Thompson	.15	.05
❑ 65 Jessie Hester	.15	.05
❑ 66 Marv Cook	.15	.05
❑ 67 Tim Brown	.50	.20
❑ 68 Mark Duper	.15	.05
❑ 69 Robert Delpino	.15	.05
❑ 70 Eric Martin	.15	.05
❑ 71 Wendell Davis	.15	.05
❑ 72 Vaughan Johnson	.15	.05
❑ 73 Brian Blades	.30	.10
❑ 74 Ed King	.15	.05
❑ 75 Gaston Green	.15	.05
❑ 76 Christian Okoye	.15	.05
❑ 77 Rohn Stark	.15	.05
❑ 78 Kevin Greene	.30	.10
❑ 79 Jay Novacek	.30	.10
❑ 80 Chip Lohmiller	.15	.05
❑ 81 Cris Dishman	.15	.05
❑ 82 Ethan Horton	.15	.05
❑ 83 Pat Harlow	.15	.05
❑ 84 Mark Ingram	.15	.05
❑ 85 Mark Carrier DB	.15	.05
❑ 86 Sam Mills	.15	.05
❑ 87 Mark Higgs	.15	.05
❑ 88 Keith Jackson	.30	.10
❑ 89 Gary Anderson K	.15	.05
❑ 90 Ken Harvey	.15	.05
❑ 91 Anthony Carter	.30	.10
❑ 92 Randall McDaniel	.15	.05
❑ 93 Johnny Johnson	.15	.05
❑ 94 Shane Conlan	.15	.05
❑ 95 Sterling Sharpe	.50	.20
❑ 96 Guy McIntyre	.15	.05
❑ 97 Albert Lewis	.15	.05
❑ 98 Chris Doleman	.15	.05
❑ 99 Andre Rison	.30	.10
❑ 100 Bobby Hebert	.15	.05
❑ 101 Dan Owens	.15	.05
❑ 102 Rodney Hampton	.30	.10
❑ 103 Ernie Jones	.15	.05
❑ 104 Reggie Cobb	.15	.05
❑ 105 Wilber Marshall	.15	.05
❑ 106 Mike Munchak	.30	.10
❑ 107 Cortez Kennedy	.30	.10
❑ 108 Todd Lyght	.15	.05
❑ 109 Burt Grossman	.15	.05
❑ 110 Ferrell Edmunds	.15	.05
❑ 111 Jim Everett	.30	.10
❑ 112 Hardy Nickerson	.30	.10
❑ 113 Andre Tippett	.15	.05
❑ 114 Ronnie Harmon	.15	.05
❑ 115 Andre Waters	.15	.05
❑ 116 Ernest Givins	.30	.10
❑ 117 Eric Hill	.15	.05
❑ 118 Erric Pegram	.30	.10
❑ 119 Jarrod Bunch	.15	.05
❑ 120 Marcus Allen	.50	.20
❑ 121 Barry Foster	.30	.10
❑ 122 Kent Hull	.15	.05
❑ 123 Neal Anderson	.15	.05
❑ 124 Stephen Braggs	.15	.05
❑ 125 Nick Lowery	.15	.05
❑ 126 Jeff Hostetler	.30	.10
❑ 127 Michael Carter	.15	.05
❑ 128 Don Warren	.15	.05
❑ 129 Brad Baxter	.15	.05
❑ 130 John Taylor	.30	.10
❑ 131 Harold Green	.15	.05
❑ 132 Mike Merriweather	.15	.05
❑ 133 Gary Clark	.50	.20
❑ 134 Vince Buck	.15	.05
❑ 135 Dan Saleaumua	.15	.05
❑ 136 Gary Zimmerman	.15	.05
❑ 137 Richmond Webb	.15	.05
❑ 138 Art Monk	.30	.10
❑ 139 Mervyn Fernandez	.15	.05
❑ 140 Mark Jackson	.15	.05
❑ 141 Freddie Joe Nunn	.15	.05
❑ 142 Jeff Lageman	.15	.05
❑ 143 Kenny Walker	.15	.05
❑ 144 Mark Carrier WR	.30	.10
❑ 145 Jon Vaughn	.15	.05
❑ 146 Greg Davis	.15	.05
❑ 147 Bubby Brister	.15	.05
❑ 148 Mo Lewis	.15	.05
❑ 149 Howie Long	.50	.20
❑ 150 Rod Bernstine	.15	.05
❑ 151 Nick Bell	.15	.05
❑ 152 Terry Allen	.50	.20
❑ 153 William Fuller	.15	.05
❑ 154 Dexter Carter	.15	.05
❑ 155 Gene Atkins	.15	.05
❑ 156 Don Beebe	.15	.05
❑ 157 Mark Collins	.15	.05
❑ 158 Jerry Ball	.15	.05
❑ 159 Fred Barnett	.50	.20
❑ 160 Rodney Holman	.15	.05
❑ 161 Stephen Baker	.15	.05
❑ 162 Jeff Graham	.50	.20
❑ 163 Leonard Russell	.30	.10
❑ 164 Jeff Gossett	.15	.05
❑ 165 Vinny Testaverde	.30	.10
❑ 166 Maurice Hurst	.15	.05
❑ 167 Louis Oliver	.15	.05
❑ 168 Jim Morrissey	.15	.05
❑ 169 Greg Kragen	.15	.05
❑ 170 Andre Collins	.15	.05
❑ 171 Dave Meggett	.30	.10
❑ 172 Keith Henderson	.15	.05
❑ 173 Vince Newsome	.15	.05
❑ 174 Chris Hinton	.15	.05
❑ 175 James Hasty	.15	.05
❑ 176 John Offerdahl	.15	.05
❑ 177 Lomas Brown	.15	.05
❑ 178 Neil O'Donnell	.30	.10
❑ 179 Leonard Marshall	.15	.05
❑ 180 Bubba McDowell	.15	.05
❑ 181 Herman Moore	.50	.20
❑ 182 Rob Moore	.30	.10
❑ 183 Earnest Byner	.15	.05
❑ 184 Keith McCants	.15	.05
❑ 185 Floyd Turner	.15	.05
❑ 186 Steve Jordan	.15	.05
❑ 187 Nate Odomes	.15	.05
❑ 188 Jeff Herrod	.15	.05
❑ 189 Jim Harbaugh	.50	.20
❑ 190 Jessie Tuggle	.15	.05
❑ 191 Al Smith	.15	.05
❑ 192 Lawrence Dawsey	.30	.10
❑ 193 Steve Bono RC	.50	.20
❑ 194 Greg Lloyd	.30	.10
❑ 195 Steve Wisniewski	.15	.05
❑ 196 Larry Kelm	.15	.05
❑ 197 Tommy Kane	.15	.05
❑ 198 Mark Schlereth RC	.15	.05
❑ 199 Ray Childress	.15	.05
❑ 200 Vincent Brown	.15	.05
❑ 201 Rodney Peete	.30	.10
❑ 202 Dennis Smith	.15	.05
❑ 203 Bruce Matthews	.15	.05
❑ 204 Rickey Jackson	.15	.05
❑ 205 Eric Allen	.15	.05
❑ 206 Rich Camarillo	.15	.05
❑ 207 Jim Lachey	.15	.05
❑ 208 Kevin Ross	.15	.05
❑ 209 Irving Fryar	.30	.10
❑ 210 Mark Clayton	.30	.10
❑ 211 Keith Byars	.15	.05
❑ 212 John Elway	3.00	1.25
❑ 213 Harris Barton	.15	.05
❑ 214 Aeneas Williams	.30	.10
❑ 215 Rich Gannon	.50	.20
❑ 216 Toi Cook	.15	.05
❑ 217 Rod Woodson	.50	.20
❑ 218 Gary Anderson RB	.15	.05
❑ 219 Reggie Roby	.15	.05
❑ 220 Karl Mecklenburg	.15	.05
❑ 221 Rufus Porter	.15	.05
❑ 222 Jon Hand	.15	.05
❑ 223 Tim Barnett	.15	.05
❑ 224 Eric Swann	.30	.10
❑ 225 Eugene Robinson	.15	.05
❑ 226 Michael Young	.15	.05
❑ 227 Frank Warren	.15	.05
❑ 228 Mike Kenn	.15	.05
❑ 229 Tim Green	.15	.05
❑ 230 Barry Word	.15	.05
❑ 231 Mike Pritchard	.30	.10
❑ 232 John Kasay	.15	.05
❑ 233 Derek Russell	.15	.05
❑ 234 Jim Breech	.15	.05
❑ 235 Pierce Holt	.15	.05
❑ 236 Tim Krumrie	.15	.05
❑ 237 William Roberts	.15	.05
❑ 238 Erik Kramer	.30	.10
❑ 239 Brett Perriman	.50	.20
❑ 240 Reyna Thompson	.15	.05
❑ 241 Chris Miller	.30	.10
❑ 242 Drew Hill	.15	.05

❑ 243	Curtis Duncan	.15	.05
❑ 244	Seth Joyner	.15	.05
❑ 245	Ken Norton Jr.	.30	.10
❑ 246	Calvin Williams	.30	.10
❑ 247	James Joseph	.15	.05
❑ 248	Bennie Thompson RC	.15	.05
❑ 249	Tunch Ilkin	.15	.05
❑ 250	Brad Edwards	.15	.05
❑ 251	Jeff Jaeger	.15	.05
❑ 252	Gill Byrd	.15	.05
❑ 253	Jeff Feagles	.15	.05
❑ 254	Jamie Dukes RC	.15	.05
❑ 255	Greg McMurtry	.15	.05
❑ 256	Anthony Johnson	.30	.10
❑ 257	Lamar Lathon	.15	.05
❑ 258	John Roper	.15	.05
❑ 259	Lorenzo White	.15	.05
❑ 260	Brian Noble	.15	.05
❑ 261	Chris Singleton	.15	.05
❑ 262	Todd Marinovich	.15	.05
❑ 263	Jay Hilgenberg	.15	.05
❑ 264	Kyle Clifton	.15	.05
❑ 265	Tony Casillas	.15	.05
❑ 266	James Francis	.15	.05
❑ 267	Eddie Anderson	.15	.05
❑ 268	Tim Harris	.15	.05
❑ 269	James Lofton	.30	.10
❑ 270	Jay Schroeder	.15	.05
❑ 271	Ed West	.15	.05
❑ 272	Don Mosebar	.15	.05
❑ 273	Jackie Slater	.15	.05
❑ 274	Fred McAfee RC	.15	.05
❑ 275	Steve Sewell	.15	.05
❑ 276	Charles Mann	.15	.05
❑ 277	Ron Hall	.15	.05
❑ 278	Darrell Green	.15	.05
❑ 279	Jeff Cross	.15	.05
❑ 280	Jeff Wright	.15	.05
❑ 281	Issiac Holt	.15	.05
❑ 282	Dermontti Dawson	.15	.05
❑ 283	Michael Haynes	.30	.10
❑ 284	Tony Mandarich	.15	.05
❑ 285	Leroy Hoard	.30	.10
❑ 286	Darryl Henley	.15	.05
❑ 287	Tim McGee	.15	.05
❑ 288	Willie Gault	.30	.10
❑ 289	Dalton Hilliard	.15	.05
❑ 290	Tim McKyer	.15	.05
❑ 291	Tom Waddle	.15	.05
❑ 292	Eric Thomas	.15	.05
❑ 293	Herschel Walker	.30	.10
❑ 294	Donnell Woolford	.15	.05
❑ 295	James Brooks	.30	.10
❑ 296	Brad Muster	.15	.05
❑ 297	Brent Jones	.30	.10
❑ 298	Erik Howard	.15	.05
❑ 299	Alvin Harper	.30	.10
❑ 300	Joey Browner	.15	.05
❑ 301	Jack Del Rio	.15	.05
❑ 302	Cleveland Gary	.15	.05
❑ 303	Brett Favre	6.00	3.00
❑ 304	Freeman McNeil	.15	.05
❑ 305	Willie Green	.15	.05
❑ 306	Percy Snow	.15	.05
❑ 307	Neil Smith	.50	.20
❑ 308	Eric Bieniemy	.15	.05
❑ 309	Keith Traylor	.15	.05
❑ 310	Ernie Mills	.15	.05
❑ 311	Will Wolford	.15	.05
❑ 312	Robert Young	.15	.05
❑ 313	Anthony Smith	.15	.05
❑ 314	Robert Porcher RC	.50	.20
❑ 315	Leon Searcy RC	.15	.05
❑ 316	Amp Lee RC	.15	.05
❑ 317	Siran Stacy RC	.15	.05
❑ 318	Patrick Rowe RC	.15	.05
❑ 319	Chris Mims RC	.15	.05
❑ 320	Matt Elliott RC	.15	.05
❑ 321	Ricardo McDonald RC	.15	.05
❑ 322	Keith Hamilton RC	.30	.10
❑ 323	Edgar Bennett RC	.50	.20
❑ 324	Chris Hakel RC	.15	.05
❑ 325	Dexter McNabb RC	.15	.05
❑ 326	Rod Milstead RC	.15	.05
❑ 327	Joe Bowden RC	.15	.05
❑ 328	Brian Bollinger RC	.15	.05
❑ 329	Darryl Williams RC	.15	.05
❑ 330	Tommy Vardell RC	.15	.05
❑ 331	Glenn Parker SIDE	.15	.05
❑ 332	Herschel Walker SIDE	.15	.05
❑ 333	Mike Cofer SIDE	.15	.05
❑ 334	Mark Rypien SIDE	.15	.05
❑ 335	Andre Rison GW	.30	.10
❑ 336	Henry Ellard GW	.15	.05
❑ 337	Rob Moore GW	.15	.05
❑ 338	Fred Barnett GW	.15	.05
❑ 339	Mark Clayton GW	.15	.05
❑ 340	Eric Martin GW	.15	.05
❑ 341	Irving Fryar GW	.15	.05
❑ 342	Tim Brown GW	.30	.10
❑ 343	Sterling Sharpe GW	.30	.10
❑ 344	Gary Clark GW	.15	.05
❑ 345	John Mackey HOF	.15	.05
❑ 346	Lem Barney HOF	.15	.05
❑ 347	John Riggins HOF	.30	.10
❑ 348	Marion Butts IDOL	.15	.05
❑ 349	Jeff Lageman IDOL	.15	.05
❑ 350	Eric Green IDOL	.15	.05
❑ 351	Reggie White/Bob.Jones I	.30	.10
❑ 352	Marv Cook IDOL	.15	.05
❑ 353	John Elway/Staubach ID	1.25	.50
❑ 354	Steve Tasker IDOL	.15	.05
❑ 355	Nick Lowery IDOL	.15	.05
❑ 356	Mark Clayton/Warfield ID	.15	.05
❑ 357	Warren Moon/R.Gabriel ID	.30	.10
❑ 358	Eric Metcalf	.30	.10
❑ 359	Charles Haley	.30	.10
❑ 360	Terrell Buckley RC	.15	.05
❑ P1	Promo Panel	5.00	2.00

1993 Pinnacle

❑	COMPLETE SET (360)	20.00	7.50
❑ 1	Brett Favre	3.00	1.25
❑ 2	Tommy Vardell	.10	.02
❑ 3	Jarrod Bunch	.10	.02
❑ 4	Mike Croel	.10	.02
❑ 5	Morten Andersen	.10	.02
❑ 6	Barry Foster	.20	.07
❑ 7	Chris Spielman	.20	.07
❑ 8	Jim Jeffcoat	.10	.02
❑ 9	Ken Ruettgers	.10	.02
❑ 10	Cris Dishman	.10	.02
❑ 11	Ricky Watters	.40	.15
❑ 12	Alfred Williams	.10	.02
❑ 13	Mark Kelso	.10	.02
❑ 14	Moe Gardner	.10	.02
❑ 15	Terry Allen	.40	.15
❑ 16	Willie Gault	.10	.02
❑ 17	Bubba McDowell	.10	.02
❑ 18	Brian Mitchell	.20	.07
❑ 19	Karl Mecklenburg	.10	.02
❑ 20	Jim Everett	.20	.07
❑ 21	Bobby Humphrey	.10	.02
❑ 22	Tim Krumrie	.10	.02
❑ 23	Ken Norton Jr.	.20	.07
❑ 24	Wendell Davis	.10	.02
❑ 25	Brad Baxter	.10	.02
❑ 26	Mel Gray	.20	.07
❑ 27	Jon Vaughn	.10	.02
❑ 28	James Hasty	.10	.02
❑ 29	Chris Warren	.20	.07
❑ 30	Tim Harris	.10	.02
❑ 31	Eric Metcalf	.20	.07
❑ 32	Rob Moore	.20	.07
❑ 33	Charles Haley	.20	.07
❑ 34	Leonard Marshall	.10	.02
❑ 35	Jeff Graham	.20	.07
❑ 36	Eugene Robinson	.10	.02
❑ 37	Darryl Talley	.10	.02
❑ 38	Brent Jones	.20	.07
❑ 39	Reggie Roby	.10	.02
❑ 40	Bruce Armstrong	.10	.02
❑ 41	Audray McMillian	.10	.02
❑ 42	Bern Brostek	.10	.02
❑ 43	Tony Bennett	.10	.02
❑ 44	Albert Lewis	.10	.02
❑ 45	Derrick Thomas	.40	.15
❑ 46	Cris Carter	.40	.15
❑ 47	Richmond Webb	.10	.02
❑ 48	Sean Landeta	.10	.02
❑ 49	Cleveland Gary	.10	.02
❑ 50	Mark Carrier DB	.10	.02
❑ 51	Lawrence Dawsey	.10	.02
❑ 52	Lamar Lathon	.10	.02
❑ 53	Nick Bell	.10	.02
❑ 54	Curtis Duncan	.10	.02
❑ 55	Irving Fryar	.20	.07
❑ 56	Seth Joyner	.10	.02
❑ 57	Jay Novacek	.20	.07
❑ 58	John L. Williams	.10	.02
❑ 59	Amp Lee	.10	.02
❑ 60	Marion Butts	.10	.02
❑ 61	Clyde Simmons	.10	.02
❑ 62	Rich Gannon	.40	.15
❑ 63	Anthony Johnson	.20	.07
❑ 64	Dave Meggett	.10	.02
❑ 65	James Francis	.10	.02
❑ 66	Trace Armstrong	.10	.02
❑ 67	Mo Lewis	.10	.02
❑ 68	Cornelius Bennett	.20	.07
❑ 69	Mark Duper	.10	.02
❑ 70	Frank Reich	.20	.07
❑ 71	Eric Green	.10	.02
❑ 72	Bruce Matthews	.10	.02
❑ 73	Steve Broussard	.10	.02
❑ 74	Anthony Carter	.20	.07
❑ 75	Sterling Sharpe	.40	.15
❑ 76	Mike Kenn	.10	.02
❑ 77	Andre Rison	.20	.07
❑ 78	Todd Marinovich	.10	.02
❑ 79	Vincent Brown	.10	.02
❑ 80	Harold Green	.10	.02
❑ 81	Art Monk	.20	.07
❑ 82	Reggie Cobb	.10	.02
❑ 83	Johnny Johnson	.10	.02
❑ 84	Tommy Kane	.10	.02
❑ 85	Rohn Stark	.10	.02
❑ 86	Steve Tasker	.20	.07
❑ 87	Ronnie Harmon	.10	.02
❑ 88	Pepper Johnson	.10	.02
❑ 89	Hardy Nickerson	.20	.07
❑ 90	Alvin Harper	.20	.07
❑ 91	Louis Oliver	.10	.02
❑ 92	Rod Woodson	.40	.15
❑ 93	Sam Mills	.10	.02
❑ 94	Randall McDaniel	.10	.02
❑ 95	Johnny Holland	.10	.02
❑ 96	Jackie Slater	.10	.02

97	Don Mosebar	.10	.02
98	Andre Ware	.10	.02
99	Kelvin Martin	.10	.02
100	Emmitt Smith	2.50	1.00
101	Michael Brooks	.10	.02
102	Dan Saleaumua	.10	.02
103	John Elway	2.50	1.00
104	Henry Jones	.10	.02
105	William Perry	.20	.07
106	James Lofton	.20	.07
107	Camell Lake	.10	.02
108	Chip Lohmiller	.10	.02
109	Andre Tippett	.10	.02
110	Barry Word	.10	.02
111	Haywood Jeffires	.20	.07
112	Kenny Walker	.10	.02
113	John Randle	.20	.07
114	Donnell Woolford	.10	.02
115	Johnny Bailey	.10	.02
116	Marcus Allen	.40	.15
117	Mark Jackson	.10	.02
118	Ray Agnew	.10	.02
119	Gill Byrd	.10	.02
120	Kyle Clifton	.10	.02
121	Marv Cook	.10	.02
122	Jerry Ball	.10	.02
123	Steve Jordan	.10	.02
124	Shannon Sharpe	.40	.15
125	Brian Blades	.20	.07
126	Rodney Hampton	.20	.07
127	Bobby Hebert	.10	.02
128	Jessie Tuggle	.10	.02
129	Tom Newberry	.10	.02
130	Keith McCants	.10	.02
131	Richard Dent	.20	.07
132	Herman Moore	.40	.15
133	Michael Irvin	.40	.15
134	Ernest Givins	.20	.07
135	Mark Rypien	.10	.02
136	Leonard Russell	.20	.07
137	Reggie White	.40	.15
138	Thurman Thomas	.40	.15
139	Nick Lowery	.10	.02
140	Al Smith	.10	.02
141	Jackie Harris	.10	.02
142	Duane Bickett	.10	.02
143	Lawyer Tillman	.10	.02
144	Steve Wisniewski	.10	.02
145	Derrick Fenner	.10	.02
146	Harris Barton	.10	.02
147	Rich Camarillo	.10	.02
148	John Offerdahl	.10	.02
149	Mike Johnson	.10	.02
150	Ricky Reynolds	.10	.02
151	Fred Barnett	.20	.07
152	Nate Newton	.20	.07
153	Chris Doleman	.10	.02
154	Todd Scott	.10	.02
155	Tim McKyer	.10	.02
156	Ken Harvey	.10	.02
157	Jeff Feagles	.10	.02
158	Vince Workman	.10	.02
159	Bart Oates	.10	.02
160	Chris Miller	.20	.07
161	Pete Stoyanovich	.10	.02
162	Steve Wallace	.10	.02
163	Dermontti Dawson	.10	.02
164	Kenneth Davis	.10	.02
165	Mike Munchak	.20	.07
166	George Jamison	.10	.02
167	Christian Okoye	.10	.02
168	Chris Hinton	.10	.02
169	Vaughan Johnson	.10	.02
170	Gaston Green	.10	.02
171	Kevin Greene	.20	.07
172	Rob Burnett	.10	.02
173	Norm Johnson	.10	.02
174	Eric Hill	.10	.02
175	Lomas Brown	.10	.02
176	Chip Banks	.10	.02
177	Greg Townsend	.10	.02
178	David Fulcher	.10	.02
179	Gary Anderson RB	.10	.02
180	Brian Washington	.10	.02
181	Brett Perriman	.40	.15
182	Chris Chandler	.20	.07
183	Phil Hansen	.10	.02
184	Mark Clayton	.10	.02
185	Frank Warren	.10	.02
186	Tim Brown	.40	.15
187	Mark Stepnoski	.10	.02
188	Bryan Cox	.10	.02
189	Gary Zimmerman	.10	.02
190	Neil O'Donnell	.40	.15
191	Anthony Smith	.10	.02
192	Craig Heyward	.20	.07
193	Keith Byars	.10	.02
194	Sean Salisbury	.10	.02
195	Todd Lyght	.10	.02
196	Jessie Hester	.10	.02
197	Rufus Porter	.10	.02
198	Steve Christie	.10	.02
199	Nate Lewis	.10	.02
200	Barry Sanders	2.00	.75
201	Michael Haynes	.20	.07
202	John Taylor	.20	.07
203	John Friesz	.20	.07
204	William Fuller	.10	.02
205	Dennis Smith	.10	.02
206	Adrian Cooper	.10	.02
207	Henry Thomas	.10	.02
208	Gerald Williams	.10	.02
209	Chris Burkett	.10	.02
210	Broderick Thomas	.10	.02
211	Marvin Washington	.10	.02
212	Bennie Blades	.10	.02
213	Tony Casillas	.10	.02
214	Bubby Brister	.10	.02
215	Don Griffin	.10	.02
216	Jeff Cross	.10	.02
217	Derrick Walker	.10	.02
218	Lorenzo White	.10	.02
219	Ricky Sanders	.10	.02
220	Rickey Jackson	.10	.02
221	Simon Fletcher	.10	.02
222	Troy Vincent	.10	.02
223	Gary Clark	.20	.07
224	Stanley Richard	.10	.02
225	Dave Krieg	.20	.07
226	Warren Moon	.40	.15
227	Reggie Langhorne	.10	.02
228	Kent Hull	.10	.02
229	Ferrell Edmunds	.10	.02
230	Cortez Kennedy	.20	.07
231	Hugh Millen	.10	.02
232	Eugene Chung	.10	.02
233	Rodney Peete	.10	.02
234	Tom Waddle	.10	.02
235	David Klingler	.10	.02
236	Mark Carrier WR	.20	.07
237	Jay Schroeder	.10	.02
238	James Jones DT	.10	.02
239	Phil Simms	.20	.07
240	Steve Atwater	.10	.02
241	Jeff Herrod	.10	.02
242	Dale Carter	.10	.02
243	Glenn Cadrez RC	.10	.02
244	Wayne Martin	.10	.02
245	Willie Davis	.40	.15
246	Lawrence Taylor	.40	.15
247	Stan Humphries	.20	.07
248	Byron Evans	.10	.02
249	Wilber Marshall	.10	.02
250	Michael Bankston RC	.10	.02
251	Steve McMichael	.20	.07
252	Brad Edwards	.10	.02
253	Will Wolford	.10	.02
254	Paul Gruber	.10	.02
255	Steve Young	1.25	.50
256	Chuck Cecil	.10	.02
257	Pierce Holt	.10	.02
258	Anthony Miller	.20	.07
259	Carl Banks	.10	.02
260	Brad Muster	.10	.02
261	Clay Matthews	.20	.07
262	Rod Bernstine	.10	.02
263	Tim Barnett	.10	.02
264	Greg Lloyd	.20	.07
265	Sean Jones	.10	.02
266	J.J. Birden	.10	.02
267	Tim McDonald	.10	.02
268	Charles Mann	.10	.02
269	Bruce Smith	.40	.15
270	Sean Gilbert	.20	.07
271	Ricardo McDonald	.10	.02
272	Jeff Hostetler	.20	.07
273	Russell Maryland	.10	.02
274	Dave Brown RC	.40	.15
275	Ronnie Lott	.20	.07
276	Jim Kelly	.40	.15
277	Joe Montana	2.50	1.00
278	Eric Allen	.10	.02
279	Browning Nagle	.10	.02
280	Neal Anderson	.10	.02
281	Troy Aikman	1.25	.50
282	Ed McCaffrey	.40	.15
283	Robert Jones	.10	.02
284	Dalton Hilliard	.10	.02
285	Johnny Mitchell	.10	.02
286	Jay Hilgenberg	.10	.02
287	Eric Martin	.10	.02
288	Steve Emtman	.10	.02
289	Vaughn Dunbar	.10	.02
290	Mark Wheeler	.10	.02
291	Leslie O'Neal	.20	.07
292	Jerry Rice	1.50	.60
293	Neil Smith	.40	.15
294	Kerry Cash	.10	.02
295	Dan McGwire	.10	.02
296	Carl Pickens	.20	.07
297	Terrell Buckley	.10	.02
298	Randall Cunningham	.40	.15
299	Santana Dotson	.20	.07
300	Keith Jackson	.20	.07
301	Jim Lachey	.10	.02
302	Dan Marino	2.50	1.00
303	Lee Williams	.10	.02
304	Burt Grossman	.10	.02
305	Kevin Mack	.10	.02
306	Pat Swilling	.10	.02
307	Arthur Marshall RC	.10	.02
308	Jim Harbaugh	.40	.15
309	Kurt Barber	.10	.02
310	Harvey Williams	.20	.07
311	Ricky Ervins	.10	.02
312	Flipper Anderson	.10	.02
313	Bernie Kosar	.20	.07
314	Boomer Esiason	.20	.07
315	Deion Sanders	.75	.30
316	Ray Childress	.10	.02
317	Howie Long	.40	.15
318	Henry Ellard	.20	.07
319	Marco Coleman	.10	.02
320	Chris Mims	.10	.02
321	Quentin Coryatt	.20	.07
322	Jason Hanson	.10	.02
323	Ricky Proehl	.10	.02
324	Randal Hill	.10	.02
325	Vinny Testaverde	.20	.07
326	Jeff George	.40	.15
327	Junior Seau	.40	.15
328	Earnest Byner	.10	.02
329	Andre Reed	.20	.07
330	Phillippi Sparks	.10	.02

❑ 331 Kevin Ross .10 .02
❑ 332 Clarence Verdin .10 .02
❑ 333 Darryl Henley .10 .02
❑ 334 Dana Hall .10 .02
❑ 335 Greg McMurtry .10 .02
❑ 336 Ron Hall .10 .02
❑ 337 Darrell Green .10 .02
❑ 338 Carlton Bailey .10 .02
❑ 339 Irv Eatman .10 .02
❑ 340 Greg Kragen .10 .02
❑ 341 Wade Wilson .10 .02
❑ 342 Klaus Wilmsmeyer .10 .02
❑ 343 Derek Brown TE .10 .02
❑ 344 Erik Williams .10 .02
❑ 345 Jim McMahon .20 .07
❑ 346 Mike Sherrard .10 .02
❑ 347 Mark Bavaro .10 .02
❑ 348 Anthony Munoz .20 .07
❑ 349 Eric Dickerson .20 .07
❑ 350 Steve Beuerlein .20 .07
❑ 351 Tim McGee .10 .02
❑ 352 Terry McDaniel .10 .02
❑ 353 Dan Fouts HOF .10 .02
❑ 354 Chuck Noll HOF .20 .07
❑ 355 Bill Walsh RC HOF .20 .07
❑ 356 Larry Little HOF .10 .02
❑ 357 Todd Marinovich HH .10 .02
❑ 358 Jeff George HH .40 .15
❑ 359 Bernie Kosar HH .20 .07
❑ 360 Rob Moore HH .20 .07
❑ NNO Franco Harris AU/3000 25.00 12.50

1994 Pinnacle

❑ COMPLETE SET (270) 20.00 8.00
❑ 1 Deion Sanders .50 .20
❑ 2 Eric Metcalf .20 .07
❑ 3 Barry Sanders 2.00 .75
❑ 4 Ernest Givins .20 .07
❑ 5 Phil Simms .20 .07
❑ 6 Rod Woodson .20 .07
❑ 7 Michael Irvin .40 .15
❑ 8 Cortez Kennedy .20 .07
❑ 9 Eric Martin .10 .02
❑ 10 Jeff Hostetler .20 .07
❑ 11 Sterling Sharpe .20 .07
❑ 12 John Elway 2.50 1.00
❑ 13 Neal Anderson .10 .02
❑ 14 Terry Kirby .40 .15
❑ 15 Jim Everett .20 .07
❑ 16 Lawrence Dawsey .10 .02
❑ 17 Kelvin Martin .10 .02
❑ 18 Tim McGee .10 .02
❑ 19 Cris Carter .50 .20
❑ 20 Ronnie Harmon .10 .02
❑ 21 Jim Kelly .40 .15
❑ 22 Steve Young 1.00 .40
❑ 23 Johnny Johnson .10 .02
❑ 24 Sean Gilbert .10 .02
❑ 25 Brian Mitchell .10 .02
❑ 26 Carl Pickens .20 .07
❑ 27 Tim Brown .40 .15
❑ 28 Reggie Langhorne .10 .02
❑ 29 Webster Slaughter .10 .02
❑ 30 Alvin Harper .20 .07
❑ 31 Andre Rison .20 .07
❑ 32 Derrick Thomas .40 .15
❑ 33 Irving Fryar .20 .07
❑ 34 Vinny Testaverde .20 .07
❑ 35 Steve Beuerlein .20 .07
❑ 36 Brett Favre 2.50 1.00
❑ 37 Barry Foster .10 .02
❑ 38 Vaughan Johnson .10 .02
❑ 39 Carlton Bailey .10 .02
❑ 40 Steve Emtman .10 .02
❑ 41 Anthony Miller .20 .07
❑ 42 Jeff Cross .10 .02
❑ 43 Trace Armstrong .10 .02
❑ 44 Derek Russell .10 .02
❑ 45 Vincent Brisby .20 .07
❑ 46 Mark Jackson .10 .02
❑ 47 Eugene Robinson .10 .02
❑ 48 John Friesz .20 .07
❑ 49 Scott Mitchell .20 .07
❑ 50 Steve Atwater .10 .02
❑ 51 Ken Norton .20 .07
❑ 52 Vincent Brown .10 .02
❑ 53 Morten Andersen .10 .02
❑ 54 Gary Anderson K .10 .02
❑ 55 Eric Curry .10 .02
❑ 56 Henry Jones .10 .02
❑ 57 Flipper Anderson .10 .02
❑ 58 Pat Swilling .10 .02
❑ 59 Erric Pegram .10 .02
❑ 60 Bruce Matthews .10 .02
❑ 61 Willie Davis .20 .07
❑ 62 O.J.McDuffie .40 .15
❑ 63 Qadry Ismail .40 .15
❑ 64 Anthony Smith .10 .02
❑ 65 Eric Allen .10 .02
❑ 66 Marion Butts .10 .02
❑ 67 Chris Miller .10 .02
❑ 68 Terrell Buckley .10 .02
❑ 69 Thurman Thomas .40 .15
❑ 70 Roosevelt Potts .10 .02
❑ 71 Tony McGee .10 .02
❑ 72 Jason Hanson .10 .02
❑ 73 Victor Bailey .10 .02
❑ 74 Albert Lewis .10 .02
❑ 75 Nate Odomes .10 .02
❑ 76 Ben Coates .20 .07
❑ 77 Warren Moon .40 .15
❑ 78 Derek Brown RBK .10 .02
❑ 79 David Klingler .10 .02
❑ 80 Cleveland Gary .10 .02
❑ 81 Emmitt Smith 2.00 .75
❑ 82 Jay Novacek .20 .07
❑ 83 Dana Stubblefield .20 .07
❑ 84 Michael Brooks .10 .02
❑ 85 James Jett .10 .02
❑ 86 J.J. Birden .10 .02
❑ 87 William Fuller .10 .02
❑ 88 Glyn Milburn .20 .07
❑ 89 Tim Worley .10 .02
❑ 90 Brett Perriman .20 .07
❑ 91 Randall Cunningham .40 .15
❑ 92 Drew Bledsoe 1.00 .40
❑ 93 Jerome Bettis .60 .25
❑ 94 Boomer Esiason .20 .07
❑ 95 Garrison Hearst .40 .15
❑ 96 Bruce Smith .40 .15
❑ 97 Jackie Harris .10 .02
❑ 98 Jeff George .40 .15
❑ 99 Tom Waddle .10 .02
❑ 100 John Copeland .10 .02
❑ 101 Bobby Hebert .10 .02
❑ 102 Joe Montana 2.50 1.00
❑ 103 Herman Moore .40 .15
❑ 104 Rick Mirer .40 .15
❑ 105 Ricky Watters .20 .07
❑ 106 Neil O'Donnell .40 .15
❑ 107 Herschel Walker .20 .07
❑ 108 Rob Moore .20 .07
❑ 109 Reggie Brooks .20 .07
❑ 110 Tommy Vardell .10 .02
❑ 111 Eric Green .10 .02
❑ 112 Stan Humphries .20 .07
❑ 113 Greg Robinson .10 .02
❑ 114 Eric Swann .20 .07
❑ 115 Courtney Hawkins .10 .02
❑ 116 Andre Reed .20 .07
❑ 117 Steve McMichael .20 .07
❑ 118 Gary Brown .10 .02
❑ 119 Terry Allen .20 .07
❑ 120 Dan Marino 2.50 1.00
❑ 121 Gary Clark .20 .07
❑ 122 Chris Warren .20 .07
❑ 123 Pierce Holt .10 .02
❑ 124 Anthony Carter .20 .07
❑ 125 Quentin Coryatt .10 .02
❑ 126 Harold Green .10 .02
❑ 127 Leonard Russell .10 .02
❑ 128 Tim McDonald .10 .02
❑ 129 Chris Spielman .20 .07
❑ 130 Cody Carlson .10 .02
❑ 131 Ronald Moore .10 .02
❑ 132 Renaldo Turnbull .10 .02
❑ 133 Ronnie Lott .20 .07
❑ 134 Natrone Means .40 .15
❑ 135 Keith Byars .10 .02
❑ 136 Henry Ellard .20 .07
❑ 137 Steve Jordan .10 .02
❑ 138 Calvin Williams .20 .07
❑ 139 Brian Blades .20 .07
❑ 140 Michael Jackson .20 .07
❑ 141 Charles Haley .20 .07
❑ 142 Curtis Conway .40 .15
❑ 143 Nick Lowery .10 .02
❑ 144 Bill Brooks .10 .02
❑ 145 Michael Haynes .20 .07
❑ 146 Willie Green .10 .02
❑ 147 Duane Bickett .10 .02
❑ 148 Shannon Sharpe .20 .07
❑ 149 Ricky Proehl .10 .02
❑ 150 Troy Aikman 1.25 .50
❑ 151 Mike Sherrard .10 .02
❑ 152 Reggie Cobb .10 .02
❑ 153 Norm Johnson .10 .02
❑ 154 Neil Smith .20 .07
❑ 155 James Francis .10 .02
❑ 156 Greg McMurtry .10 .02
❑ 157 Greg Townsend .10 .02
❑ 158 Mel Gray .10 .02
❑ 159 Rocket Ismail .20 .07
❑ 160 Leslie O'Neal .10 .02
❑ 161 Johnny Mitchell .10 .02
❑ 162 Brent Jones .20 .07
❑ 163 Chris Doleman .10 .02
❑ 164 Seth Joyner .10 .02
❑ 165 Marco Coleman .10 .02
❑ 166 Mark Higgs .10 .02
❑ 167 John L. Williams .10 .02
❑ 168 Darrell Green .10 .02
❑ 169 Mark Carrier WR .20 .07
❑ 170 Reggie White .40 .15
❑ 171 Darryl Talley .10 .02
❑ 172 Russell Maryland .10 .02
❑ 173 Mark Collins .10 .02
❑ 174 Chris Jacke .10 .02
❑ 175 Richard Dent .20 .07
❑ 176 John Taylor .20 .07
❑ 177 Rodney Hampton .20 .07
❑ 178 Dwight Stone .10 .02
❑ 179 Cornelius Bennett .20 .07
❑ 180 Cris Dishman .10 .02
❑ 181 Jerry Rice 1.25 .50
❑ 182 Rod Bernstine .10 .02
❑ 183 Keith Hamilton .10 .02
❑ 184 Keith Jackson .10 .02

Card	Player	Mint	Nrmt
❑ 185	Craig Erickson	.10	.02
❑ 186	Marcus Allen	.40	.15
❑ 187	Marcus Robertson	.10	.02
❑ 188	Junior Seau	.40	.15
❑ 189	LeShon Johnson RC	.20	.07
❑ 190	Perry Klein RC	.10	.02
❑ 191	Bryant Young RC	.40	.15
❑ 192	Byron Bam Morris RC	.20	.07
❑ 193	Jeff Cothran RC	.10	.02
❑ 194	Lamar Smith RC	1.50	.60
❑ 195	Calvin Jones RC	.10	.02
❑ 196	James Bostic RC	.40	.15
❑ 197	Dan Wilkinson RC	.20	.07
❑ 198	Marshall Faulk RC	6.00	2.50
❑ 199	Heath Shuler RC	.40	.15
❑ 200	Willie McGinest RC	.40	.15
❑ 201	Trev Alberts RC	.20	.07
❑ 202	Trent Dilfer RC	1.50	.60
❑ 203	Sam Adams RC	.20	.07
❑ 204	Charles Johnson RC	.40	.15
❑ 205	Johnnie Morton RC	1.50	.60
❑ 206	Thomas Lewis RC	.20	.07
❑ 207	Greg Hill RC	.40	.15
❑ 208	William Floyd RC	.40	.15
❑ 209	Derrick Alexander WR RC	.40	.15
❑ 210	Darnay Scott RC	.75	.30
❑ 211	Lake Dawson RC	.20	.07
❑ 212	Errict Rhett RC	.40	.15
❑ 213	Kevin Lee RC	.10	.02
❑ 214	Chuck Levy RC	.10	.02
❑ 215	David Palmer RC	.40	.15
❑ 216	Ryan Yarborough RC	.10	.02
❑ 217	Charlie Garner RC	1.50	.60
❑ 218	Mario Bates RC	.40	.15
❑ 219	Jamir Miller RC	.20	.07
❑ 220	Bucky Brooks RC	.10	.02
❑ 221	Donnell Bennett RC	.40	.15
❑ 222	Kevin Greene	.20	.07
❑ 223	LeRoy Butler	.10	.02
❑ 224	Anthony Pleasant	.10	.02
❑ 225	Steve Christie	.10	.02
❑ 226	Bill Romanowski	.10	.02
❑ 227	Darren Carrington	.10	.02
❑ 228	Chester McGlockton	.10	.02
❑ 229	Jack Del Rio	.10	.02
❑ 230	Kevin Smith	.10	.02
❑ 231	Chris Zorich	.10	.02
❑ 232	Donnell Woolford	.10	.02
❑ 233	Tony Casillas	.10	.02
❑ 234	Terry McDaniel	.10	.02
❑ 235	Ray Childress	.10	.02
❑ 236	John Randle	.20	.07
❑ 237	Clyde Simmons	.10	.02
❑ 238	Dante Jones	.10	.02
❑ 239	Karl Mecklenburg	.10	.02
❑ 240	Daryl Johnston	.20	.07
❑ 241	Hardy Nickerson	.20	.07
❑ 242	Jeff Lageman	.10	.02
❑ 243	Lewis Tillman	.10	.02
❑ 244	Jim McMahon	.20	.07
❑ 245	Mike Pritchard	.10	.02
❑ 246	Harvey Williams	.20	.07
❑ 247	Sean Jones	.10	.02
❑ 248	Stevon Moore	.10	.02
❑ 249	Pete Metzelaars	.10	.02
❑ 250	Mike Johnson	.10	.02
❑ 251	Chris Slade	.10	.02
❑ 252	Jessie Hester	.10	.02
❑ 253	Louis Oliver	.10	.02
❑ 254	Ken Harvey	.10	.02
❑ 255	Bryan Cox	.10	.02
❑ 256	Erik Kramer	.20	.07
❑ 257	Andy Harmon	.10	.02
❑ 258	Rickey Jackson	.10	.02
❑ 259	Mark Carrier DB	.10	.02
❑ 260	Greg Lloyd	.20	.07
❑ 261	Robert Brooks	.40	.15
❑ 262	Dave Brown	.20	.07
❑ 263	Dennis Smith	.10	.02
❑ 264	Michael Dean Perry	.20	.07
❑ 265	Dan Saleaumua	.10	.02
❑ 266	Mo Lewis	.10	.02
❑ 267	AFC Checklist	.10	.02
❑ 268	AFC Checklist	.10	.02
❑ 269	NFC Checklist	.10	.02
❑ 270	NFC Checklist	.10	.02
❑ 271SP	Jerry Rice TD King SP	8.00	4.00
❑ NNO	Drew Bledsoe Pin.Passer	40.00	15.00

1995 Pinnacle

Card	Player	Mint	Nrmt
❑	COMPLETE SET (250)	20.00	8.00
❑ 1	Reggie White	.40	.15
❑ 2	Troy Aikman	1.00	.40
❑ 3	Willie Davis	.20	.07
❑ 4	Jerry Rice	1.00	.40
❑ 5	Bruce Smith	.40	.15
❑ 6	Keith Byars	.10	.02
❑ 7	Chris Warren	.20	.07
❑ 8	Erik Kramer	.10	.02
❑ 9	Leon Lett	.10	.02
❑ 10	Greg Lloyd	.20	.07
❑ 11	Jackie Harris	.10	.02
❑ 12	Irving Fryar	.20	.07
❑ 13	Rodney Hampton	.20	.07
❑ 14	Michael Irvin	.40	.15
❑ 15	Michael Haynes	.20	.07
❑ 16	Irving Spikes	.20	.07
❑ 17	Calvin Williams	.20	.07
❑ 18	Ken Norton Jr.	.20	.07
❑ 19	Herman Moore	.40	.15
❑ 20	Lewis Tillman	.10	.02
❑ 21	Cortez Kennedy	.20	.07
❑ 22	Dan Marino	2.00	.75
❑ 23	Erric Pegram	.20	.07
❑ 24	Tim Brown	.40	.15
❑ 25	Jeff Blake RC	.75	.30
❑ 26	Brett Favre	2.00	.75
❑ 27	Garrison Hearst	.40	.15
❑ 28	Ronnie Harmon	.10	.02
❑ 29	Qadry Ismail	.20	.07
❑ 30	Ben Coates	.20	.07
❑ 31	Deion Sanders	.60	.25
❑ 32	John Elway	2.00	.75
❑ 33	Natrone Means	.20	.07
❑ 34	Derrick Alexander WR	.40	.15
❑ 35	Craig Heyward	.20	.07
❑ 36	Jake Reed	.20	.07
❑ 37	Steve Walsh	.10	.02
❑ 38	John Randle	.20	.07
❑ 39	Barry Sanders	1.50	.60
❑ 40	Tydus Winans	.10	.02
❑ 41	Thomas Lewis	.20	.07
❑ 42	Jim Kelly	.40	.15
❑ 43	Gus Frerotte	.20	.07
❑ 44	Cris Carter	.40	.15
❑ 45	Kevin Williams WR	.20	.07
❑ 46	Dave Meggett	.10	.02
❑ 47	Pat Swilling	.10	.02
❑ 48	Neil O'Donnell	.20	.07
❑ 49	Terance Mathis	.20	.07
❑ 50	Desmond Howard	.20	.07
❑ 51	Bryant Young	.20	.07
❑ 52	Stan Humphries	.20	.07
❑ 53	Alvin Harper	.10	.02
❑ 54	Henry Ellard	.20	.07
❑ 55	Jessie Hester	.10	.02
❑ 56	Lorenzo White	.10	.02
❑ 57	John Friesz	.20	.07
❑ 58	Anthony Smith	.10	.02
❑ 59	Bert Emanuel	.40	.15
❑ 60	Gary Clark	.10	.02
❑ 61	Bill Brooks	.10	.02
❑ 62	Steve Young	.75	.30
❑ 63	Jerome Bettis	.40	.15
❑ 64	John Taylor	.10	.02
❑ 65	Ricky Proehl	.10	.02
❑ 66	Junior Seau	.40	.15
❑ 67	Bubby Brister	.10	.02
❑ 68	Neil Smith	.20	.07
❑ 69	Dan McGwire	.10	.02
❑ 70	Brett Perriman	.20	.07
❑ 71	Chris Spielman	.20	.07
❑ 72	Jeff George	.20	.07
❑ 73	Emmitt Smith	1.00	.40
❑ 74	Chris Penn	.10	.02
❑ 75	Derrick Fenner	.10	.02
❑ 76	Reggie Brooks	.20	.07
❑ 77	Chris Chandler	.20	.07
❑ 78	Rod Woodson	.20	.07
❑ 79	Isaac Bruce	.60	.25
❑ 80	Reggie Cobb	.10	.02
❑ 81	Bryce Paup	.20	.07
❑ 82	Warren Moon	.20	.07
❑ 83	Bryan Reeves	.10	.02
❑ 84	Lake Dawson	.20	.07
❑ 85	Larry Centers	.20	.07
❑ 86	Marshall Faulk	1.25	.50
❑ 87	Jim Harbaugh	.20	.07
❑ 88	Ray Childress	.10	.02
❑ 89	Eric Metcalf	.20	.07
❑ 90	Ernie Mills	.10	.02
❑ 91	Lamar Lathon	.10	.02
❑ 92	Errict Rhett	.20	.07
❑ 93	David Klingler	.20	.07
❑ 94	Vincent Brown	.10	.02
❑ 95	Andre Rison	.20	.07
❑ 96	Brian Mitchell	.10	.02
❑ 97	Mark Rypien	.10	.02
❑ 98	Eugene Robinson	.10	.02
❑ 99	Eric Green	.10	.02
❑ 100	Rocket Ismail	.20	.07
❑ 101	Flipper Anderson	.10	.02
❑ 102	Randall Cunningham	.40	.15
❑ 103	Ricky Watters	.20	.07
❑ 104	Amp Lee	.10	.02
❑ 105	Ernest Givins	.10	.02
❑ 106	Daryl Johnston	.20	.07
❑ 107	Dave Krieg	.10	.02
❑ 108	Dana Stubblefield	.20	.07
❑ 109	Torrance Small	.10	.02
❑ 110	Yancey Thigpen RC	.20	.07
❑ 111	Chester McGlockton	.20	.07
❑ 112	Craig Erickson	.10	.02
❑ 113	Herschel Walker	.20	.07
❑ 114	Mike Sherrard	.10	.02
❑ 115	Tony McGee	.10	.02
❑ 116	Adrian Murrell	.20	.07
❑ 117	Frank Reich	.10	.02
❑ 118	Hardy Nickerson	.10	.02
❑ 119	Andre Reed	.20	.07
❑ 120	Leonard Russell	.10	.02
❑ 121	Eric Allen	.10	.02
❑ 122	Jeff Hostetler	.20	.07
❑ 123	Barry Foster	.20	.07
❑ 124	Anthony Miller	.20	.07
❑ 125	Shawn Jefferson	.10	.02
❑ 126	Richie Anderson RC	.50	.20
❑ 127	Steve Bono	.20	.07

❑ 128 Seth Joyner .10 .02
❑ 129 Darnay Scott .20 .07
❑ 130 Johnny Mitchell .10 .02
❑ 131 Eric Swann .20 .07
❑ 132 Drew Bledsoe .60 .25
❑ 133 Marcus Allen .40 .15
❑ 134 Carl Pickens .20 .07
❑ 135 Michael Brooks .10 .02
❑ 136 John L. Williams .10 .02
❑ 137 Steve Beuerlein .20 .07
❑ 138 Robert Smith .40 .15
❑ 139 O.J. McDuffie .40 .15
❑ 140 Haywood Jeffires .10 .02
❑ 141 Aeneas Williams .10 .02
❑ 142 Rick Mirer .20 .07
❑ 143 William Floyd .20 .07
❑ 144 Fred Barnett .20 .07
❑ 145 Leroy Hoard .10 .02
❑ 146 Terry Kirby .20 .07
❑ 147 Boomer Esiason .20 .07
❑ 148 Ken Harvey .10 .02
❑ 149 Cleveland Gary .10 .02
❑ 150 Brian Blades .20 .07
❑ 151 Eric Turner .10 .02
❑ 152 Vinny Testaverde .20 .07
❑ 153 Ronald Moore UER .10 .02
❑ 154 Curtis Conway .40 .15
❑ 155 Johnnie Morton .20 .07
❑ 156 Kenneth Davis .10 .02
❑ 157 Scott Mitchell .20 .07
❑ 158 Sean Gilbert .20 .07
❑ 159 Shannon Sharpe .20 .07
❑ 160 Mark Seay .20 .07
❑ 161 Cornelius Bennett .20 .07
❑ 162 Heath Shuler .20 .07
❑ 163 Byron Bam Morris .10 .02
❑ 164 Robert Brooks .40 .15
❑ 165 Glyn Milburn .10 .02
❑ 166 Gary Brown .10 .02
❑ 167 Jim Everett .10 .02
❑ 168 Steve Atwater .10 .02
❑ 169 Darren Woodson .20 .07
❑ 170 Mark Ingram .10 .02
❑ 171 Donnell Woolford .10 .02
❑ 172 Trent Dilfer .40 .15
❑ 173 Charlie Garner .40 .15
❑ 174 Charles Johnson .20 .07
❑ 175 Mike Pritchard .10 .02
❑ 176 Derek Brown RBK .10 .02
❑ 177 Chris Miller .10 .02
❑ 178 Charles Haley .20 .07
❑ 179 J.J. Birden .10 .02
❑ 180 Jeff Graham .10 .02
❑ 181 Bernie Parmalee .20 .07
❑ 182 Mark Brunell .60 .25
❑ 183 Greg Hill .20 .07
❑ 184 Michael Timpson .10 .02
❑ 185 Terry Allen .20 .07
❑ 186 Ricky Ervins .10 .02
❑ 187 Dave Brown .20 .07
❑ 188 Dan Wilkinson .20 .07
❑ 189 Jay Novacek .20 .07
❑ 190 Harvey Williams .10 .02
❑ 191 Mario Bates .20 .07
❑ 192 Steve Young LAW .50 .20
❑ 193 Joe Montana 2.00 .75
❑ 194 Steve Young PP .50 .20
❑ 195 Troy Aikman PP .60 .25
❑ 196 Drew Bledsoe PP .40 .15
❑ 197 Dan Marino PP 1.00 .40
❑ 198 John Elway PP 1.00 .40
❑ 199 Brett Favre PP 1.00 .40
❑ 200 Heath Shuler PP .20 .07
❑ 201 Warren Moon PP .10 .02
❑ 202 Jim Kelly PP .40 .15
❑ 203 Jeff Hostetler PP .20 .07
❑ 204 Rick Mirer PP .20 .07
❑ 205 Dave Brown PP .20 .07
❑ 206 Randall Cunningham PP .20 .07
❑ 207 Neil O'Donnell PP .20 .07
❑ 208 Jim Everett PP .10 .02
❑ 209 Ki-Jana Carter RC .40 .15
❑ 210 Steve McNair RC 3.00 1.25
❑ 211 Michael Westbrook RC .40 .15
❑ 212 Kerry Collins RC 1.50 .60
❑ 213 Joey Galloway RC 1.50 .60
❑ 214 Kyle Brady RC .40 .15
❑ 215 J.J. Stokes RC .40 .15
❑ 216 Tyrone Wheatley RC 1.25 .50
❑ 217 Rashaan Salaam RC .20 .07
❑ 218 Napoleon Kaufman RC 1.25 .50
❑ 219 Frank Sanders RC .40 .15
❑ 220 Stoney Case RC .10 .02
❑ 221 Todd Collins RC .20 .07
❑ 222 Warren Sapp RC 1.50 .60
❑ 223 Sherman Williams RC .10 .02
❑ 224 Rob Johnson RC 1.00 .40
❑ 225 Mark Bruener RC .20 .07
❑ 226 Derrick Brooks RC 1.50 .60
❑ 227 Chad May RC .10 .02
❑ 228 James A.Stewart RC .10 .02
❑ 229 Ray Zellars RC .20 .07
❑ 230 Dave Barr RC .10 .02
❑ 231 Kordell Stewart RC 1.50 .60
❑ 232 Jimmy Oliver RC .10 .02
❑ 233 Tony Boselli RC .40 .15
❑ 234 James O. Stewart RC 1.25 .50
❑ 235 Derrick Alexander DE RC .10 .02
❑ 236 Lovell Pinkney RC .10 .02
❑ 237 John Walsh RC .10 .02
❑ 238 Tyrone Davis RC .10 .02
❑ 239 Joe Aska RC .10 .02
❑ 240 Korey Stringer RC .20 .07
❑ 241 Hugh Douglas RC .40 .15
❑ 242 Christian Fauria RC .20 .07
❑ 243 Terrell Fletcher RC .10 .02
❑ 244 Dan Marino CL .60 .25
❑ 245 Drew Bledsoe CL .40 .15
❑ 246 John Elway CL .40 .15
❑ 247 Emmitt Smith CL .50 .20
❑ 248 Steve Young CL .40 .15
❑ 249 Barry Sanders CL .60 .25
❑ 250 Jerry Rice/Seau CL .40 .15
❑ 251SP Deion Sanders SP 4.00 1.50

1996 Pinnacle

❑ COMPLETE SET (200) 20.00 8.00
❑ 1 Emmitt Smith 1.50 .60
❑ 2 Robert Brooks .40 .15
❑ 3 Joey Galloway .40 .15
❑ 4 Dan Marino 2.00 .75
❑ 5 Frank Sanders .20 .07
❑ 6 Cris Carter .40 .15
❑ 7 Jeff Blake .40 .15
❑ 8 Steve McNair .75 .30
❑ 9 Tamarick Vanover .20 .07
❑ 10 Andre Reed .20 .07
❑ 11 Junior Seau .40 .15
❑ 12 Alvin Harper .10 .02
❑ 13 Trent Dilfer .40 .15
❑ 14 Kordell Stewart .40 .15
❑ 15 Kyle Brady .10 .02
❑ 16 Charles Haley .20 .07
❑ 17 Greg Lloyd .20 .07
❑ 18 Mario Bates .20 .07
❑ 19 Shannon Sharpe .20 .07
❑ 20 Scott Mitchell .20 .07
❑ 21 Craig Heyward .10 .02
❑ 22 Marcus Allen .40 .15
❑ 23 Curtis Martin .75 .30
❑ 24 Drew Bledsoe .60 .25
❑ 25 Jerry Rice 1.00 .40
❑ 26 Charlie Garner .20 .07
❑ 27 Michael Irvin .40 .15
❑ 28 Curtis Conway .40 .15
❑ 29 Terrell Davis .75 .30
❑ 30 Jeff Hostetler .10 .02
❑ 31 Neil O'Donnell .20 .07
❑ 32 Errict Rhett .20 .07
❑ 33 Stan Humphries .20 .07
❑ 34 Jeff Graham .10 .02
❑ 35 Floyd Turner .10 .02
❑ 36 Vincent Brisby .10 .02
❑ 37 Steve Young .75 .30
❑ 38 Carl Pickens .20 .07
❑ 39 Terance Mathis .10 .02
❑ 40 Brett Favre 2.00 .75
❑ 41 Ki-Jana Carter .20 .07
❑ 42 Jim Everett .10 .02
❑ 43 Marshall Faulk .50 .20
❑ 44 William Floyd .20 .07
❑ 45 Deion Sanders .60 .25
❑ 46 Garrison Hearst .20 .07
❑ 47 Chris Sanders .20 .07
❑ 48 Isaac Bruce .40 .15
❑ 49 Natrone Means .20 .07
❑ 50 Troy Aikman 1.00 .40
❑ 51 Ben Coates .20 .07
❑ 52 Tony Martin .20 .07
❑ 53 Rod Woodson .20 .07
❑ 54 Edgar Bennett .20 .07
❑ 55 Eric Zeier .10 .02
❑ 56 Steve Bono .10 .02
❑ 57 Tim Brown .40 .15
❑ 58 Kevin Williams .10 .02
❑ 59 Erik Kramer .10 .02
❑ 60 Jim Kelly .40 .15
❑ 61 Larry Centers .20 .07
❑ 62 Terrell Fletcher .10 .02
❑ 63 Michael Westbrook .40 .15
❑ 64 Kerry Collins .40 .15
❑ 65 Jay Novacek .10 .02
❑ 66 J.J. Stokes .40 .15
❑ 67 John Elway 2.00 .75
❑ 68 Jim Harbaugh .20 .07
❑ 69 Aeneas Williams .10 .02
❑ 70 Tyrone Wheatley .20 .07
❑ 71 Chris Warren .20 .07
❑ 72 Rodney Thomas .10 .02
❑ 73 Jeff George .20 .07
❑ 74 Rick Mirer .20 .07
❑ 75 Yancey Thigpen .20 .07
❑ 76 Herman Moore .20 .07
❑ 77 Gus Frerotte .20 .07
❑ 78 Anthony Miller .20 .07
❑ 79 Ricky Watters .20 .07
❑ 80 Sherman Williams .10 .02
❑ 81 Hardy Nickerson .10 .02
❑ 82 Henry Ellard .10 .02
❑ 83 Aaron Craver .10 .02
❑ 84 Rodney Peete .10 .02
❑ 85 Eric Metcalf .10 .02
❑ 86 Brian Blades .10 .02
❑ 87 Rob Moore .20 .07
❑ 88 Kimble Anders .20 .07
❑ 89 Harvey Williams .10 .02
❑ 90 Thurman Thomas .40 .15
❑ 91 Dave Brown .10 .02

❑ 92	Terry Allen	.20	.07
❑ 93	Ken Norton Jr.	.10	.02
❑ 94	Reggie White	.40	.15
❑ 95	Mark Chmura	.20	.07
❑ 96	Bert Emanuel	.20	.07
❑ 97	Brett Perriman	.10	.02
❑ 98	Antonio Freeman	.40	.15
❑ 99	Brian Mitchell	.10	.02
❑ 100	Orlando Thomas	.10	.02
❑ 101	Aaron Hayden	.10	.02
❑ 102	Quinn Early	.10	.02
❑ 103	Lovell Pinkney	.10	.02
❑ 104	Napoleon Kaufman	.40	.15
❑ 105	Daryl Johnston	.20	.07
❑ 106	Steve Tasker	.10	.02
❑ 107	Brent Jones	.10	.02
❑ 108	Mark Brunell	.60	.25
❑ 109	Leslie O'Neal	.10	.02
❑ 110	Irving Fryar	.20	.07
❑ 111	Jim Miller	.40	.15
❑ 112	Sean Dawkins	.10	.02
❑ 113	Boomer Esiason	.20	.07
❑ 114	Heath Shuler	.20	.07
❑ 115	Bruce Smith	.20	.07
❑ 116	Russell Maryland	.10	.02
❑ 117	Jake Reed	.20	.07
❑ 118	O.J. McDuffie	.20	.07
❑ 119	Erik Williams	.10	.02
❑ 120	Willie McGinest	.10	.02
❑ 121	Terry Kirby	.20	.07
❑ 122	Fred Barnett	.10	.02
❑ 123	Andre Hastings	.10	.02
❑ 124	Dale Hellestrae	.10	.02
❑ 125	Darren Woodson	.20	.07
❑ 126	Steve Atwater	.10	.02
❑ 127	Quentin Coryatt	.10	.02
❑ 128	Derrick Thomas	.40	.15
❑ 129	Nate Newton	.10	.02
❑ 130	Kevin Greene	.20	.07
❑ 131	Barry Sanders	1.50	.60
❑ 132	Warren Moon	.20	.07
❑ 133	Rashaan Salaam	.20	.07
❑ 134	Rodney Hampton	.20	.07
❑ 135	James O.Stewart	.20	.07
❑ 136	Erric Pegram	.10	.02
❑ 137	Bryan Cox	.10	.02
❑ 138	Adrian Murrell	.20	.07
❑ 139	Robert Smith	.20	.07
❑ 140	Bernie Parmalee	.10	.02
❑ 141	Bryce Paup	.10	.02
❑ 142	Darick Holmes	.10	.02
❑ 143	Hugh Douglas	.20	.07
❑ 144	Ken Dilger	.20	.07
❑ 145	Derek Loville	.10	.02
❑ 146	Horace Copeland	.10	.02
❑ 147	Wayne Chrebet	.60	.25
❑ 148	Andre Coleman	.10	.02
❑ 149	Greg Hill	.20	.07
❑ 150	Eric Swann	.10	.02
❑ 151	Tyrone Hughes	.10	.02
❑ 152	Ernie Mills	.10	.02
❑ 153	Terry Glenn RC	1.25	.50
❑ 154	Cedric Jones RC	.10	.02
❑ 155	Leeland McElroy RC	.20	.07
❑ 156	Bobby Engram RC	.40	.15
❑ 157	Willie Anderson RC	.10	.02
❑ 158	Mike Alstott RC	1.25	.50
❑ 159	Alex Van Dyke RC	.20	.07
❑ 160	Jeff Lewis RC	.20	.07
❑ 161	Keyshawn Johnson RC	1.25	.50
❑ 162	Regan Upshaw RC	.10	.02
❑ 163	Eric Moulds RC	1.50	.60
❑ 164	Tim Biakabutuka RC	.40	.15
❑ 165	Kevin Hardy RC	.40	.15
❑ 166	Marvin Harrison RC	3.00	1.25
❑ 167	Karim Abdul-Jabbar RC	.40	.15
❑ 168	Tony Brackens RC	.40	.15
❑ 169	Stepfret Williams RC	.20	.07
❑ 170	Eddie George RC	1.50	.60
❑ 171	Lawrence Phillips RC	.40	.15
❑ 172	Danny Kanell RC	.40	.15
❑ 173	Derrick Mayes RC	.40	.15
❑ 174	Daryl Gardener RC	.10	.02
❑ 175	Jonathan Ogden RC	.40	.15
❑ 176	Alex Molden RC	.10	.02
❑ 177	Chris Darkins RC	.10	.02
❑ 178	Stephen Davis RC	2.00	.75
❑ 179	Rickey Dudley RC	.40	.15
❑ 180	Eddie Kennison RC	.40	.15
❑ 181	Simeon Rice RC	1.00	.40
❑ 182	Bobby Hoying RC	.40	.15
❑ 183	Troy Aikman BF6	.50	.20
❑ 184	Emmitt Smith BF6	1.00	.40
❑ 185	Michael Irvin BF6	.20	.07
❑ 186	Deion Sanders BF6	.40	.15
❑ 187	Daryl Johnston BF6	.20	.07
❑ 188	Jay Novacek BF6	.10	.02
❑ 189	Steve Young BF6	.40	.15
❑ 190	Jerry Rice BF6	.50	.20
❑ 191	J.J. Stokes BF6	.40	.15
❑ 192	Ken Norton BF6	.10	.02
❑ 193	William Floyd BF6	.20	.07
❑ 194	Brent Jones BF6	.10	.02
❑ 195	Dan Marino CL	.40	.15
❑ 196	Brett Favre CL	.40	.15
❑ 197	Emmitt Smith CL	.40	.15
❑ 198	Barry Sanders CL	.40	.15
❑ 199	ESmith/Mar/Fav/BSand CL	.40	.15
❑ 200	Brett Favre PackBack	2.00	.75

1997 Pinnacle

❑	COMPLETE SET (200)	20.00	7.50
❑ 1	Brett Favre	2.00	.75
❑ 2	Dan Marino	2.00	.75
❑ 3	Emmitt Smith	1.50	.60
❑ 4	Steve Young	.60	.25
❑ 5	Drew Bledsoe	.60	.25
❑ 6	Eddie George	.50	.20
❑ 7	Barry Sanders	1.50	.60
❑ 8	Jerry Rice	1.00	.40
❑ 9	John Elway	2.00	.75
❑ 10	Troy Aikman	1.00	.40
❑ 11	Kerry Collins	.50	.20
❑ 12	Rick Mirer	.20	.07
❑ 13	Jim Harbaugh	.30	.10
❑ 14	Elvis Grbac	.30	.10
❑ 15	Gus Frerotte	.20	.07
❑ 16	Neil O'Donnell	.30	.10
❑ 17	Jeff George	.30	.10
❑ 18	Kordell Stewart	.50	.20
❑ 19	Junior Seau	.50	.20
❑ 20	Vinny Testaverde	.30	.10
❑ 21	Terry Glenn	.50	.20
❑ 22	Anthony Johnson	.20	.07
❑ 23	Boomer Esiason	.30	.10
❑ 24	Terrell Owens	.60	.25
❑ 25	Natrone Means	.30	.10
❑ 26	Marcus Allen	.50	.20
❑ 27	James Jett	.30	.10
❑ 28	Chris T. Jones	.20	.07
❑ 29	Stan Humphries	.30	.10
❑ 30	Keith Byars	.20	.07
❑ 31	John Friesz	.20	.07
❑ 32	Mike Alstott	.50	.20
❑ 33	Eddie Kennison	.30	.10
❑ 34	Eric Moulds	.50	.20
❑ 35	Frank Sanders	.30	.10
❑ 36	Daryl Johnston	.30	.10
❑ 37	Cris Carter	.50	.20
❑ 38	Errict Rhett	.20	.07
❑ 39	Ben Coates	.30	.10
❑ 40	Shannon Sharpe	.30	.10
❑ 41	Jamal Anderson	.50	.20
❑ 42	Tim Biakabutuka	.30	.10
❑ 43	Jeff Blake	.30	.10
❑ 44	Michael Irvin	.50	.20
❑ 45	Terrell Davis	.60	.25
❑ 46	Byron Bam Morris	.20	.07
❑ 47	Rashaan Salaam	.20	.07
❑ 48	Adrian Murrell	.30	.10
❑ 49	Ty Detmer	.30	.10
❑ 50	Terry Allen	.50	.20
❑ 51	Mark Brunell	.60	.25
❑ 52	O.J. McDuffie	.30	.10
❑ 53	Willie McGinest	.20	.07
❑ 54	Chris Warren	.30	.10
❑ 55	Trent Dilfer	.50	.20
❑ 56	Jerome Bettis	.50	.20
❑ 57	Tamarick Vanover	.30	.10
❑ 58	Ki-Jana Carter	.20	.07
❑ 59	Ray Zellars	.20	.07
❑ 60	J.J. Stokes	.30	.10
❑ 61	Cornelius Bennett	.20	.07
❑ 62	Scott Mitchell	.30	.10
❑ 63	Tyrone Wheatley	.30	.10
❑ 64	Steve McNair	.60	.25
❑ 65	Tony Banks	.30	.10
❑ 66	James O.Stewart	.30	.10
❑ 67	Robert Smith	.30	.10
❑ 68	Thurman Thomas	.50	.20
❑ 69	Mark Chmura	.30	.10
❑ 70	Napoleon Kaufman	.50	.20
❑ 71	Ken Norton	.20	.07
❑ 72	Herschel Walker	.30	.10
❑ 73	Joey Galloway	.30	.10
❑ 74	Neil Smith	.30	.10
❑ 75	Simeon Rice	.30	.10
❑ 76	Michael Jackson	.30	.10
❑ 77	Muhsin Muhammad	.30	.10
❑ 78	Kevin Hardy	.20	.07
❑ 79	Irving Fryar	.30	.10
❑ 80	Jeff Hostetler	.20	.07
❑ 81	Eric Swann	.20	.07
❑ 82	Jim Everett	.20	.07
❑ 83	Karim Abdul-Jabbar	.50	.20
❑ 84	Garrison Hearst	.30	.10
❑ 85	Lawrence Phillips	.20	.07
❑ 86	Bryan Cox	.20	.07
❑ 87	Larry Centers	.30	.10
❑ 88	Wesley Walls	.30	.10
❑ 89	Curtis Conway	.30	.10
❑ 90	Darnay Scott	.30	.10
❑ 91	Anthony Miller	.20	.07
❑ 92	Edgar Bennett	.30	.10
❑ 93	Willie Green	.20	.07
❑ 94	Kent Graham	.20	.07
❑ 95	Dave Brown	.20	.07
❑ 96	Wayne Chrebet	.50	.20
❑ 97	Ricky Watters	.30	.10
❑ 98	Tony Martin	.30	.10
❑ 99	Warren Moon	.50	.20
❑ 100	Curtis Martin	.60	.25
❑ 101	Dorsey Levens	.50	.20
❑ 102	Jim Pyne	.20	.07
❑ 103	Antonio Freeman	.50	.20
❑ 104	Leeland McElroy	.20	.07
❑ 105	Isaac Bruce	.50	.20
❑ 106	Chris Sanders	.20	.07

❑ 107	Tim Brown	.50	.20
❑ 108	Greg Lloyd	.20	.07
❑ 109	Terrell Buckley	.20	.07
❑ 110	Deion Sanders	.50	.20
❑ 111	Carl Pickens	.30	.10
❑ 112	Bobby Engram	.30	.10
❑ 113	Andre Reed	.30	.10
❑ 114	Terance Mathis	.30	.10
❑ 115	Herman Moore	.30	.10
❑ 116	Robert Brooks	.30	.10
❑ 117	Ken Dilger	.20	.07
❑ 118	Keenan McCardell	.30	.10
❑ 119	Andre Hastings	.20	.07
❑ 120	Willie Davis	.20	.07
❑ 121	Bruce Smith	.30	.10
❑ 122	Rob Moore	.30	.10
❑ 123	Johnnie Morton	.30	.10
❑ 124	Sean Dawkins	.20	.07
❑ 125	Mario Bates	.20	.07
❑ 126	Henry Ellard	.20	.07
❑ 127	Derrick Alexander WR	.30	.10
❑ 128	Kevin Greene	.30	.10
❑ 129	Derrick Thomas	.50	.20
❑ 130	Rod Woodson	.30	.10
❑ 131	Rodney Hampton	.30	.10
❑ 132	Marshall Faulk	.60	.25
❑ 133	Michael Westbrook	.30	.10
❑ 134	Erik Kramer	.20	.07
❑ 135	Todd Collins	.20	.07
❑ 136	Bill Romanowski	.20	.07
❑ 137	Jake Reed	.30	.10
❑ 138	Heath Shuler	.20	.07
❑ 139	Keyshawn Johnson	.50	.20
❑ 140	Marvin Harrison	.50	.20
❑ 141	Andre Rison	.30	.10
❑ 142	Zach Thomas	.50	.20
❑ 143	Eric Metcalf	.30	.10
❑ 144	Amani Toomer	.30	.10
❑ 145	Desmond Howard	.30	.10
❑ 146	Jimmy Smith	.30	.10
❑ 147	Brad Johnson	.50	.20
❑ 148	Troy Vincent	.20	.07
❑ 149	Bryce Paup	.20	.07
❑ 150	Reggie White	.50	.20
❑ 151	Jake Plummer RC	2.50	1.00
❑ 152	Darnell Autry RC	.30	.10
❑ 153	Tiki Barber RC	3.00	1.25
❑ 154	Pat Barnes RC	.50	.20
❑ 155	Orlando Pace RC	.50	.20
❑ 156	Peter Boulware RC	.50	.20
❑ 157	Shawn Springs RC	.30	.10
❑ 158	Troy Davis RC	.30	.10
❑ 159	Ike Hilliard RC	.75	.30
❑ 160	Jim Druckenmiller RC	.30	.10
❑ 161	Warrick Dunn RC	1.25	.50
❑ 162	James Farrior RC	.50	.20
❑ 163	Tony Gonzalez RC	1.50	.60
❑ 164	Darrell Russell RC	.20	.07
❑ 165	Byron Hanspard RC	.30	.10
❑ 166	Corey Dillon RC	3.00	1.25
❑ 167	Kenny Holmes RC	.50	.20
❑ 168	Walter Jones RC	.50	.20
❑ 169	Danny Wuerffel RC	.50	.20
❑ 170	Tom Knight RC	.20	.07
❑ 171	David LaFleur RC	.20	.07
❑ 172	Kevin Lockett RC	.30	.10
❑ 173	Will Blackwell RC	.30	.10
❑ 174	Reidel Anthony RC	.50	.20
❑ 175	Dwayne Rudd RC	.50	.20
❑ 176	Yatil Green RC	.30	.10
❑ 177	Antowain Smith RC	1.25	.50
❑ 178	Rae Carruth RC	.20	.07
❑ 179	Bryant Westbrook RC	.20	.07
❑ 180	Reinard Wilson RC	.30	.10
❑ 181	Joey Kent RC	.50	.20
❑ 182	Renaldo Wynn RC	.20	.07
❑ 183	Brett Favre I	1.00	.40
❑ 184	Emmitt Smith I	.75	.30
❑ 185	Dan Marino I	1.00	.40
❑ 186	Troy Aikman I	.50	.20
❑ 187	Jerry Rice I	.50	.20
❑ 188	Drew Bledsoe I	.30	.10
❑ 189	Eddie George I	.50	.20
❑ 190	Terry Glenn I	.30	.10
❑ 191	John Elway I	1.00	.40
❑ 192	Steve Young I	.30	.10
❑ 193	Mark Brunell I	.50	.20
❑ 194	Barry Sanders I	.75	.30
❑ 195	Kerry Collins I	.30	.10
❑ 196	Curtis Martin I	.50	.20
❑ 197	Terrell Davis I	.50	.20
❑ 198	Bledsoe/KCollins/Marino CL	.50	.20
❑ 199	SYoung/Brunell/JGeorge CL	.20	.07
❑ 200	Aikman/Elway/Mirer CL	.20	.07

1997 Pinnacle Certified

❑	COMPLETE SET (150)	40.00	15.00
❑ 1	Emmitt Smith	3.00	1.25
❑ 2	Dan Marino	4.00	1.50
❑ 3	Brett Favre	4.00	1.50
❑ 4	Steve Young	1.25	.50
❑ 5	Kerry Collins	1.00	.40
❑ 6	Troy Aikman	2.00	.75
❑ 7	Drew Bledsoe	1.25	.50
❑ 8	Eddie George	1.00	.40
❑ 9	Jerry Rice	2.00	.75
❑ 10	John Elway	4.00	1.50
❑ 11	Barry Sanders	3.00	1.25
❑ 12	Mark Brunell	1.25	.50
❑ 13	Elvis Grbac	.60	.25
❑ 14	Tony Banks	.60	.25
❑ 15	Vinny Testaverde	.60	.25
❑ 16	Rick Mirer	.40	.15
❑ 17	Carl Pickens	.60	.25
❑ 18	Deion Sanders	1.00	.40
❑ 19	Terry Glenn	1.00	.40
❑ 20	Heath Shuler	.40	.15
❑ 21	Dave Brown	.40	.15
❑ 22	Keyshawn Johnson	1.00	.40
❑ 23	Jeff George	.60	.25
❑ 24	Ricky Watters	.60	.25
❑ 25	Kordell Stewart	1.00	.40
❑ 26	Junior Seau	1.00	.40
❑ 27	Terrell Owens	1.25	.50
❑ 28	Warren Moon	1.00	.40
❑ 29	Isaac Bruce	1.00	.40
❑ 30	Steve McNair	1.25	.50
❑ 31	Gus Frerotte	.40	.15
❑ 32	Trent Dilfer	1.00	.40
❑ 33	Shannon Sharpe	.60	.25
❑ 34	Scott Mitchell	.60	.25
❑ 35	Antonio Freeman	1.00	.40
❑ 36	Jim Harbaugh	.60	.25
❑ 37	Natrone Means	.60	.25
❑ 38	Marcus Allen	1.00	.40
❑ 39	Karim Abdul-Jabbar	.60	.25
❑ 40	Tim Biakabutuka	.60	.25
❑ 41	Jeff Blake	.60	.25
❑ 42	Michael Irvin	1.00	.40
❑ 43	Herschel Walker	.60	.25
❑ 44	Curtis Martin	1.25	.50
❑ 45	Eddie Kennison	.60	.25
❑ 46	Napoleon Kaufman	1.00	.40
❑ 47	Larry Centers	.60	.25
❑ 48	Jamal Anderson	1.00	.40
❑ 49	Derrick Alexander WR	.60	.25
❑ 50	Bruce Smith	.60	.25
❑ 51	Wesley Walls	.60	.25
❑ 52	Rod Smith WR	1.00	.40
❑ 53	Keenan McCardell	.60	.25
❑ 54	Robert Brooks	.60	.25
❑ 55	Willie Green	.40	.15
❑ 56	Jake Reed	.60	.25
❑ 57	Joey Galloway	.60	.25
❑ 58	Eric Metcalf	.60	.25
❑ 59	Chris Sanders	.40	.15
❑ 60	Jeff Hostetler	.40	.15
❑ 61	Kevin Greene	.60	.25
❑ 62	Frank Sanders	.60	.25
❑ 63	Dorsey Levens	1.00	.40
❑ 64	Sean Dawkins	.40	.15
❑ 65	Cris Carter	1.00	.40
❑ 66	Andre Hastings	.40	.15
❑ 67	Amani Toomer	.60	.25
❑ 68	Adrian Murrell	.60	.25
❑ 69	Ty Detmer	.60	.25
❑ 70	Yancey Thigpen	.60	.25
❑ 71	Jim Everett	.40	.15
❑ 72	Todd Collins	.40	.15
❑ 73	Curtis Conway	.60	.25
❑ 74	Herman Moore	.60	.25
❑ 75	Neil O'Donnell	.60	.25
❑ 76	Rod Woodson	.60	.25
❑ 77	Tony Martin	.60	.25
❑ 78	Kent Graham	.40	.15
❑ 79	Andre Reed	.60	.25
❑ 80	Reggie White	1.00	.40
❑ 81	Thurman Thomas	1.00	.40
❑ 82	Garrison Hearst	.60	.25
❑ 83	Chris Warren	.60	.25
❑ 84	Wayne Chrebet	1.00	.40
❑ 85	Chris T. Jones	.40	.15
❑ 86	Anthony Miller	.40	.15
❑ 87	Chris Chandler	.60	.25
❑ 88	Terrell Davis	1.25	.50
❑ 89	Mike Alstott	1.00	.40
❑ 90	Terry Allen	1.00	.40
❑ 91	Jerome Bettis	1.00	.40
❑ 92	Stan Humphries	.60	.25
❑ 93	Andre Rison	.60	.25
❑ 94	Marshall Faulk	1.25	.50
❑ 95	Erik Kramer	.40	.15
❑ 96	O.J. McDuffie	.60	.25
❑ 97	Robert Smith	.60	.25
❑ 98	Keith Byars	.40	.15
❑ 99	Rodney Hampton	.60	.25
❑ 100	Desmond Howard	.60	.25
❑ 101	Lawrence Phillips	.40	.15
❑ 102	Michael Westbrook	.60	.25
❑ 103	Johnnie Morton	.60	.25
❑ 104	Ben Coates	.60	.25
❑ 105	J.J. Stokes	.60	.25
❑ 106	Terance Mathis	.60	.25
❑ 107	Errict Rhett	.40	.15
❑ 108	Tim Brown	1.00	.40
❑ 109	Marvin Harrison	1.00	.40
❑ 110	Muhsin Muhammad	.60	.25
❑ 111	Byron Bam Morris	.40	.15
❑ 112	Mario Bates	.40	.15
❑ 113	Jimmy Smith	.60	.25
❑ 114	Irving Fryar	.60	.25
❑ 115	Tamarick Vanover	.60	.25
❑ 116	Brad Johnson	1.00	.40
❑ 117	Rashaan Salaam	.40	.15
❑ 118	Ki-Jana Carter	.40	.15
❑ 119	Tyrone Wheatley	.60	.25
❑ 120	John Friesz	.40	.15
❑ 121	Orlando Pace RC	1.25	.50

❑ 122 Jim Druckenmiller RC .60 .25
❑ 123 Byron Hanspard RC .60 .25
❑ 124 David LaFleur RC .30 .10
❑ 125 Reidel Anthony RC 1.25 .50
❑ 126 Antowain Smith RC 4.00 1.50
❑ 127 Bryant Westbrook RC .30 .10
❑ 128 Fred Lane RC .60 .25
❑ 129 Tiki Barber RC 8.00 3.00
❑ 130 Shawn Springs RC .60 .25
❑ 131 Ike Hilliard RC 2.50 1.00
❑ 132 James Farrior RC 1.25 .50
❑ 133 Darrell Russell RC .30 .10
❑ 134 Walter Jones RC 1.25 .50
❑ 135 Tom Knight RC .30 .10
❑ 136 Yatil Green RC .60 .25
❑ 137 Joey Kent RC .60 .25
❑ 138 Kevin Lockett RC .60 .25
❑ 139 Troy Davis RC .60 .25
❑ 140 Darnell Autry RC .60 .25
❑ 141 Pat Barnes RC 1.25 .50
❑ 142 Rae Carruth RC .30 .10
❑ 143 Will Blackwell RC .60 .25
❑ 144 Warrick Dunn RC 4.00 1.50
❑ 145 Corey Dillon RC 8.00 3.00
❑ 146 Dwayne Rudd RC 1.25 .50
❑ 147 Reinard Wilson RC .60 .25
❑ 148 Peter Boulware RC 1.25 .50
❑ 149 Tony Gonzalez RC 4.00 1.50
❑ 150 Danny Wuerffel RC 1.00 .40

1997 Pinnacle Inscriptions

❑ COMPLETE SET (50) 20.00 7.50
❑ 1 Mark Brunell 1.25 .50
❑ 2 Steve Young 1.25 .50
❑ 3 Rick Mirer .40 .15
❑ 4 Brett Favre 4.00 1.50
❑ 5 Tony Banks .60 .25
❑ 6 Elvis Grbac .60 .25
❑ 7 John Elway 4.00 1.50
❑ 8 Troy Aikman 2.00 .75
❑ 9 Neil O'Donnell .60 .25
❑ 10 Kordell Stewart 1.00 .40
❑ 11 Drew Bledsoe 1.25 .50
❑ 12 Kerry Collins 1.00 .40
❑ 13 Dan Marino 4.00 1.50
❑ 14 Jeff George .60 .25
❑ 15 Scott Mitchell .60 .25
❑ 16 Jim Harbaugh .60 .25
❑ 17 Dave Brown .40 .15
❑ 18 Jeff Blake .60 .25
❑ 19 Trent Dilfer 1.00 .40
❑ 20 Barry Sanders 3.00 1.25
❑ 21 Jerry Rice 2.00 .75
❑ 22 Emmitt Smith 3.00 1.25
❑ 23 Vinny Testaverde .60 .25
❑ 24 Warren Moon 1.00 .40
❑ 25 Junior Seau 1.00 .40
❑ 26 Gus Frerotte .40 .15
❑ 27 Heath Shuler .40 .15
❑ 28 Erik Kramer .40 .15
❑ 29 Boomer Esiason .60 .25
❑ 30 Jim Kelly 1.00 .40
❑ 31 Mark Brunell TNL 1.00 .40
❑ 32 Steve Young TNL 1.00 .40
❑ 33 Brett Favre TNL 2.50 1.00
❑ 34 Tony Banks TNL .60 .25
❑ 35 John Elway TNL 2.50 1.00
❑ 36 Troy Aikman TNL 1.25 .50
❑ 37 Kordell Stewart TNL 1.00 .40
❑ 38 Drew Bledsoe TNL 1.00 .40
❑ 39 Kerry Collins TNL .60 .25
❑ 40 Dan Marino TNL 2.50 1.00
❑ 41 Jim Harbaugh TNL .60 .25
❑ 42 Jeff Blake TNL .60 .25
❑ 43 Barry Sanders TNL 2.00 .75
❑ 44 Jerry Rice TNL 1.25 .50
❑ 45 Emmitt Smith TNL 2.00 .75
❑ 46 Rick Mirer TNL .40 .15
❑ 47 Jeff George TNL .40 .15
❑ 48 Neil O'Donnell TNL .60 .25
❑ 49 Elvis Grbac TNL .60 .25
❑ 50 Scott Mitchell TNL .40 .15
❑ P13 Dan Marino PROMO 2.50 1.00

1997 Pinnacle Inside

❑ COMPLETE SET (150) 20.00 7.50
❑ 1 Troy Aikman 1.00 .40
❑ 2 Dan Marino 2.00 .75
❑ 3 Barry Sanders 1.50 .60
❑ 4 Drew Bledsoe .60 .25
❑ 5 Kerry Collins .50 .20
❑ 6 Emmitt Smith 1.50 .60
❑ 7 Brett Favre 2.00 .75
❑ 8 John Elway 2.00 .75
❑ 9 Jerry Rice 1.00 .40
❑ 10 Mark Brunell .60 .25
❑ 11 Elvis Grbac .30 .10
❑ 12 Junior Seau .50 .20
❑ 13 Eddie George .50 .20
❑ 14 Steve Young .60 .25
❑ 15 Terrell Davis .60 .25
❑ 16 Thurman Thomas .50 .20
❑ 17 Deion Sanders .50 .20
❑ 18 Terrell Owens .60 .25
❑ 19 Neil O'Donnell .30 .10
❑ 20 Carl Pickens .30 .10
❑ 21 Marcus Allen .50 .20
❑ 22 Ricky Watters .30 .10
❑ 23 Vinny Testaverde .30 .10
❑ 24 Kordell Stewart .50 .20
❑ 25 Tony Banks .50 .20
❑ 26 Terry Glenn .50 .20
❑ 27 Todd Collins .20 .07
❑ 28 Robert Brooks .30 .10
❑ 29 Heath Shuler .20 .07
❑ 30 Shannon Sharpe .30 .10
❑ 31 Michael Westbrook .30 .10
❑ 32 Reggie White .50 .20
❑ 33 Brad Johnson .50 .20
❑ 34 Tamarick Vanover .30 .10
❑ 35 Larry Centers .30 .10
❑ 36 Terance Mathis .30 .10
❑ 37 Hardy Nickerson .20 .07
❑ 38 Jamal Anderson .50 .20
❑ 39 Kevin Hardy .20 .07
❑ 40 Stan Humphries .30 .10
❑ 41 Chris Warren .30 .10
❑ 42 Tim Brown .50 .20
❑ 43 Joey Galloway .30 .10
❑ 44 Boomer Esiason .30 .10
❑ 45 Jake Reed .30 .10
❑ 46 Kent Graham .20 .07
❑ 47 Marshall Faulk .60 .25
❑ 48 Sean Dawkins .20 .07
❑ 49 Dave Brown .20 .07
❑ 50 Willie Green .20 .07
❑ 51 Andre Hastings .20 .07
❑ 52 Erik Kramer .20 .07
❑ 53 Michael Irvin .50 .20
❑ 54 Gus Frerotte .20 .07
❑ 55 Winslow Oliver .20 .07
❑ 56 Jimmy Smith .30 .10
❑ 57 Derrick Alexander WR .30 .10
❑ 58 Adrian Murrell .30 .10
❑ 59 Ki-Jana Carter .20 .07
❑ 60 Garrison Hearst .30 .10
❑ 61 Chris Sanders .20 .07
❑ 62 Johnnie Morton .30 .10
❑ 63 Lawrence Phillips .20 .07
❑ 64 Bobby Engram .30 .10
❑ 65 Tim Biakabutuka .30 .10
❑ 66 Anthony Johnson .20 .07
❑ 67 Keyshawn Johnson .50 .20
❑ 68 Jeff George .30 .10
❑ 69 Errict Rhett .20 .07
❑ 70 Cris Carter .50 .20
❑ 71 Chris T. Jones .20 .07
❑ 72 Eric Moulds .50 .20
❑ 73 Rick Mirer .20 .07
❑ 74 Keenan McCardell .30 .10
❑ 75 Simeon Rice .30 .10
❑ 76 Eddie Kennison .30 .10
❑ 77 Herman Moore .30 .10
❑ 78 Jim Harbaugh .30 .10
❑ 79 Robert Smith .30 .10
❑ 80 Bruce Smith .30 .10
❑ 81 John Friesz .20 .07
❑ 82 Irving Fryar .30 .10
❑ 83 Edgar Bennett .30 .10
❑ 84 Ty Detmer .30 .10
❑ 85 Curtis Conway .30 .10
❑ 86 Napoleon Kaufman .50 .20
❑ 87 Tony Martin .30 .10
❑ 88 Amani Toomer .30 .10
❑ 89 Willie McGinest .20 .07
❑ 90 Daryl Johnston .30 .10
❑ 91 Stanley Pritchett .20 .07
❑ 92 Chris Chandler .30 .10
❑ 93 Natrone Means .30 .10
❑ 94 Kimble Anders .30 .10
❑ 95 Steve McNair .60 .25
❑ 96 Curtis Martin .60 .25
❑ 97 O.J. McDuffie .30 .10
❑ 98 Ben Coates .30 .10
❑ 99 Jerome Bettis .50 .20
❑ 100 Andre Reed .30 .10
❑ 101 Jeff Blake .30 .10
❑ 102 Wesley Walls .30 .10
❑ 103 Warren Moon .50 .20
❑ 104 Isaac Bruce .50 .20
❑ 105 Terry Allen .50 .20
❑ 106 Rodney Hampton .30 .10
❑ 107 Karim Abdul-Jabbar .50 .20
❑ 108 Marvin Harrison .50 .20
❑ 109 Dorsey Levens .50 .20
❑ 110 Rashaan Salaam .20 .07
❑ 111 Scott Mitchell .30 .10
❑ 112 Darnay Scott .30 .10
❑ 113 Aeneas Williams .20 .07
❑ 114 Trent Dilfer .50 .20
❑ 115 Antonio Freeman .50 .20

❑ 116	Jim Everett	.20	.07
❑ 117	Muhsin Muhammad	.30	.10
❑ 118	Rickey Dudley	.30	.10
❑ 119	Mike Alstott	.50	.20
❑ 120	Jim Druckenmiller RC	.30	.10
❑ 121	Tiki Barber RC	3.00	1.25
❑ 122	Ike Hilliard RC	.75	.30
❑ 123	Orlando Pace RC	.50	.20
❑ 124	Jake Plummer RC	2.50	1.00
❑ 125	Yatil Green RC	.30	.10
❑ 126	Byron Hanspard RC	.30	.10
❑ 127	James Farrior RC	.50	.20
❑ 128	Corey Dillon RC	3.00	1.25
❑ 129	Pat Barnes RC	.50	.20
❑ 130	Kenny Holmes RC	.50	.20
❑ 131	Rae Carruth RC	.20	.07
❑ 132	Danny Wuerffel RC	.50	.20
❑ 133	Darnell Autry RC	.30	.10
❑ 134	Reidel Anthony RC	.50	.20
❑ 135	Darrell Russell RC	.20	.07
❑ 136	Will Blackwell RC	.30	.10
❑ 137	Peter Boulware RC	.50	.20
❑ 138	Shawn Springs RC	.30	.10
❑ 139	Joey Kent RC	.50	.20
❑ 140	Troy Davis RC	.30	.10
❑ 141	Antowain Smith RC	1.25	.50
❑ 142	Walter Jones RC	.50	.20
❑ 143	Tony Gonzalez RC	1.50	.60
❑ 144	David LaFleur RC	.20	.07
❑ 145	Warrick Dunn RC	1.25	.50
❑ 146	Bryant Westbrook RC	.20	.07
❑ 147	Dwayne Rudd RC	.50	.20
❑ 148	Tom Knight RC	.20	.07
❑ 149	Kevin Lockett RC	.30	.10
❑ 150	Checklist	.20	.07
❑ P1	Troy Aikman Promo	1.00	.40
❑ P2	Dan Marino Promo	2.00	.75
❑ P7	Brett Favre Promo	2.00	.75

1997 Pinnacle Totally Certified Platinum Red

❑	COMPLETE SET (150)	150.00	60.00
❑ 1	Emmitt Smith	12.00	5.00
❑ 2	Dan Marino	15.00	6.00
❑ 3	Brett Favre	15.00	6.00
❑ 4	Steve Young	5.00	2.00
❑ 5	Kerry Collins	4.00	1.50
❑ 6	Troy Aikman	8.00	3.00
❑ 7	Drew Bledsoe	5.00	2.00
❑ 8	Eddie George	4.00	1.50
❑ 9	Jerry Rice	8.00	3.00
❑ 10	John Elway	15.00	6.00
❑ 11	Barry Sanders	12.00	5.00
❑ 12	Mark Brunell	5.00	2.00
❑ 13	Elvis Grbac	2.50	1.00
❑ 14	Tony Banks	2.50	1.00
❑ 15	Vinny Testaverde	2.50	1.00
❑ 16	Rick Mirer	1.50	.60
❑ 17	Carl Pickens	2.50	1.00
❑ 18	Deion Sanders	4.00	1.50
❑ 19	Terry Glenn	4.00	1.50
❑ 20	Heath Shuler	1.50	.60
❑ 21	Dave Brown	1.50	.60
❑ 22	Keyshawn Johnson	4.00	1.50
❑ 23	Jeff George	2.50	1.00
❑ 24	Ricky Watters	2.50	1.00
❑ 25	Kordell Stewart	4.00	1.50
❑ 26	Junior Seau	4.00	1.50
❑ 27	Terrell Owens	5.00	2.00
❑ 28	Warren Moon	4.00	1.50
❑ 29	Isaac Bruce	4.00	1.50
❑ 30	Steve McNair	5.00	2.00
❑ 31	Gus Frerotte	1.50	.60
❑ 32	Trent Dilfer	4.00	1.50
❑ 33	Shannon Sharpe	2.50	1.00
❑ 34	Scott Mitchell	2.50	1.00
❑ 35	Antonio Freeman	4.00	1.50
❑ 36	Jim Harbaugh	2.50	1.00
❑ 37	Natrone Means	2.50	1.00
❑ 38	Marcus Allen	4.00	1.50
❑ 39	Karim Abdul-Jabbar	4.00	1.50
❑ 40	Tim Biakabutuka	2.50	1.00
❑ 41	Jeff Blake	2.50	1.00
❑ 42	Michael Irvin	4.00	1.50
❑ 43	Herschel Walker	2.50	1.00
❑ 44	Curtis Martin	5.00	2.00
❑ 45	Eddie Kennison	2.50	1.00
❑ 46	Napoleon Kaufman	4.00	1.50
❑ 47	Larry Centers	2.50	1.00
❑ 48	Jamal Anderson	4.00	1.50
❑ 49	Derrick Alexander WR	2.50	1.00
❑ 50	Bruce Smith	2.50	1.00
❑ 51	Wesley Walls	2.50	1.00
❑ 52	Rod Smith WR	4.00	1.50
❑ 53	Keenan McCardell	2.50	1.00
❑ 54	Robert Brooks	2.50	1.00
❑ 55	Willie Green	1.50	.60
❑ 56	Jake Reed	2.50	1.00
❑ 57	Joey Galloway	2.50	1.00
❑ 58	Eric Metcalf	2.50	1.00
❑ 59	Chris Sanders	1.50	.60
❑ 60	Jeff Hostetler	1.50	.60
❑ 61	Kevin Greene	2.50	1.00
❑ 62	Frank Sanders	2.50	1.00
❑ 63	Dorsey Levens	4.00	1.50
❑ 64	Sean Dawkins	1.50	.60
❑ 65	Cris Carter	4.00	1.50
❑ 66	Andre Hastings	1.50	.60
❑ 67	Amani Toomer	2.50	1.00
❑ 68	Adrian Murrell	2.50	1.00
❑ 69	Ty Detmer	2.50	1.00
❑ 70	Yancey Thigpen	1.50	.60
❑ 71	Jim Everett	1.50	.60
❑ 72	Todd Collins	1.50	.60
❑ 73	Curtis Conway	2.50	1.00
❑ 74	Herman Moore	2.50	1.00
❑ 75	Neil O'Donnell	2.50	1.00
❑ 76	Rod Woodson	2.50	1.00
❑ 77	Tony Martin	2.50	1.00
❑ 78	Kent Graham	1.50	.60
❑ 79	Andre Reed	2.50	1.00
❑ 80	Reggie White	4.00	1.50
❑ 81	Thurman Thomas	4.00	1.50
❑ 82	Garrison Hearst	2.50	1.00
❑ 83	Chris Warren	2.50	1.00
❑ 84	Wayne Chrebet	4.00	1.50
❑ 85	Chris T. Jones	1.50	.60
❑ 86	Anthony Miller	1.50	.60
❑ 87	Chris Chandler	2.50	1.00
❑ 88	Terrell Davis	5.00	2.00
❑ 89	Mike Alstott	4.00	1.50
❑ 90	Terry Allen	4.00	1.50
❑ 91	Jerome Bettis	4.00	1.50
❑ 92	Stan Humphries	2.50	1.00
❑ 93	Andre Rison	2.50	1.00
❑ 94	Marshall Faulk	5.00	2.00
❑ 95	Erik Kramer	1.50	.60
❑ 96	O.J. McDuffie	2.50	1.00
❑ 97	Robert Smith	2.50	1.00
❑ 98	Keith Byars	1.50	.60
❑ 99	Rodney Hampton	2.50	1.00
❑ 100	Desmond Howard	2.50	1.00
❑ 101	Lawrence Phillips	1.50	.60
❑ 102	Michael Westbrook	2.50	1.00
❑ 103	Johnnie Morton	2.50	1.00
❑ 104	Ben Coates	2.50	1.00
❑ 105	J.J. Stokes	2.50	1.00
❑ 106	Terance Mathis	2.50	1.00
❑ 107	Errict Rhett	1.50	.60
❑ 108	Tim Brown	4.00	1.50
❑ 109	Marvin Harrison	4.00	1.50
❑ 110	Muhsin Muhammad	2.50	1.00
❑ 111	Byron Bam Morris	1.50	.60
❑ 112	Mario Bates	1.50	.60
❑ 113	Jimmy Smith	2.50	1.00
❑ 114	Irving Fryar	2.50	1.00
❑ 115	Tamarick Vanover	2.50	1.00
❑ 116	Brad Johnson	4.00	1.50
❑ 117	Rashaan Salaam	1.50	.60
❑ 118	Ki-Jana Carter	1.50	.60
❑ 119	Tyrone Wheatley	2.50	1.00
❑ 120	John Friesz	1.50	.60
❑ 121	Orlando Pace RC	4.00	1.50
❑ 122	Jim Druckenmiller RC	2.00	.75
❑ 123	Byron Hanspard RC	2.50	1.00
❑ 124	David LaFleur RC	1.00	.40
❑ 125	Reidel Anthony RC	4.00	1.50
❑ 126	Antowain Smith RC	10.00	4.00
❑ 127	Bryant Westbrook RC	1.00	.40
❑ 128	Fred Lane RC	2.00	.75
❑ 129	Tiki Barber RC	25.00	10.00
❑ 130	Shawn Springs RC	2.00	.75
❑ 131	Ike Hilliard RC	6.00	3.00
❑ 132	James Farrior RC	4.00	1.50
❑ 133	Darrell Russell RC	1.00	.40
❑ 134	Walter Jones RC	4.00	1.50
❑ 135	Tom Knight RC	1.00	.40
❑ 136	Yatil Green RC	2.00	.75
❑ 137	Joey Kent RC	2.00	.75
❑ 138	Kevin Lockett RC	2.00	.75
❑ 139	Troy Davis RC	2.00	.75
❑ 140	Darnell Autry RC	2.00	.75
❑ 141	Pat Barnes RC	4.00	1.50
❑ 142	Rae Carruth RC	1.00	.40
❑ 143	Will Blackwell RC	2.00	.75
❑ 144	Warrick Dunn RC	10.00	4.00
❑ 145	Corey Dillon RC	25.00	10.00
❑ 146	Dwayne Rudd RC	4.00	1.50
❑ 147	Reinard Wilson RC	2.00	.75
❑ 148	Peter Boulware RC	4.00	1.50
❑ 149	Tony Gonzalez RC	12.00	5.00
❑ 150	Danny Wuerffel RC	4.00	1.50

1992 Playoff

❑	COMPLETE SET (150)	25.00	10.00
❑ 1	Emmitt Smith	8.00	4.00
❑ 2	Steve Young	3.00	1.50
❑ 3	Jack Del Rio	.25	.08
❑ 4	Bobby Hebert	.25	.08
❑ 5	Shannon Sharpe	.75	.30
❑ 6	Gary Clark	.75	.30
❑ 7	Christian Okoye	.25	.08

❑ 8 Ernest Givins .40 .15
❑ 9 Mike Horan .25 .08
❑ 10 Dennis Gentry .25 .08
❑ 11 Michael Irvin .75 .30
❑ 12 Eric Floyd .25 .08
❑ 13 Brent Jones .40 .15
❑ 14 Anthony Carter .40 .15
❑ 15 Tony Martin .40 .15
❑ 16 Greg Lewis UER .25 .08
❑ 17 Todd McNair .25 .08
❑ 18 Earnest Byner .25 .08
❑ 19 Steve Beuerlein .40 .15
❑ 20 Roger Craig .40 .15
❑ 21 Mark Higgs .25 .08
❑ 22 Guy McIntyre .25 .08
❑ 23 Don Warren .25 .08
❑ 24 Alvin Harper .40 .15
❑ 25 Mark Jackson .25 .08
❑ 26 Chris Doleman .25 .08
❑ 27 Jesse Sapolu .25 .08
❑ 28 Tony Tolbert .25 .08
❑ 29 Wendell Davis .25 .08
❑ 30 Dan Saleaumua .25 .08
❑ 31 Jeff Bostic .25 .08
❑ 32 Jay Novacek .40 .15
❑ 33 Cris Carter 1.00 .40
❑ 34 Tony Paige .25 .08
❑ 35 Greg Kragen .25 .08
❑ 36 Jeff Dellenbach .25 .08
❑ 37 Keith DeLong .25 .08
❑ 38 Todd Scott .25 .08
❑ 39 Jeff Feagles .25 .08
❑ 40 Mike Saxon .25 .08
❑ 41 Martin Mayhew .25 .08
❑ 42 Steve Bono RC .75 .30
❑ 43 Willie Davis WR RC .40 .15
❑ 44 Mark Stepnoski .40 .15
❑ 45 Harry Newsome .25 .08
❑ 46 Thane Gash .25 .08
❑ 47 Gaston Green .25 .08
❑ 48 James Washington .25 .08
❑ 49 Kenny Walker .25 .08
❑ 50 Jeff Davidson RC .25 .08
❑ 51 Shane Conlan .25 .08
❑ 52 Richard Dent .40 .15
❑ 53 Haywood Jeffires .40 .15
❑ 54 Harry Galbreath .25 .08
❑ 55 Terry Allen .75 .30
❑ 56 Tommy Barnhardt .25 .08
❑ 57 Mike Golic .25 .08
❑ 58 Dalton Hilliard .25 .08
❑ 59 Danny Copeland .25 .08
❑ 60 Jerry Fontenot RC .25 .08
❑ 61 Kelvin Martin .25 .08
❑ 62 Mark Kelso .25 .08
❑ 63 Wymon Henderson .25 .08
❑ 64 Mark Rypien .25 .08
❑ 65 Bobby Humphrey .25 .08
❑ 66 Rich Gannon UER .75 .30
❑ 67 Darren Lewis .25 .08
❑ 68 Barry Foster .40 .15
❑ 69 Ken Norton Jr. .40 .15
❑ 70 James Lofton .40 .15
❑ 71 Trace Armstrong .25 .08
❑ 72 Vestee Jackson .25 .08
❑ 73 Clyde Simmons .25 .08
❑ 74 Brad Muster .25 .08
❑ 75 Cornelius Bennett .40 .15
❑ 76 Mike Merriweather .25 .08
❑ 77 John Elway 4.00 1.50
❑ 78 Herschel Walker .40 .15
❑ 79 Hassan Jones UER .25 .08
❑ 80 Jim Harbaugh .75 .30
❑ 81 Issiac Holt .25 .08
❑ 82 David Alexander .25 .08
❑ 83 Brian Mitchell .40 .15
❑ 84 Mark Tuinei .25 .08
❑ 85 Tom Rathman .25 .08
❑ 86 Reggie White .75 .30
❑ 87 William Perry .40 .15
❑ 88 Jeff Wright .25 .08
❑ 89 Keith Kartz .25 .08
❑ 90 Andre Waters .25 .08
❑ 91 Darryl Talley .25 .08
❑ 92 Morten Andersen .25 .08
❑ 93 Tom Waddle .25 .08
❑ 94 Felix Wright UER .25 .08
❑ 95 Keith Jackson .40 .15
❑ 96 Art Monk .40 .15
❑ 97 Seth Joyner .25 .08
❑ 98 Steve McMichael .40 .15
❑ 99 Thurman Thomas .75 .30
❑ 100 Warren Moon .75 .30
❑ 101 Tony Casillas .25 .08
❑ 102 Vance Johnson .25 .08
❑ 103 Doug Dawson RC .25 .08
❑ 104 Bill Maas .25 .08
❑ 105 Mark Clayton .40 .15
❑ 106 Hoby Brenner .25 .08
❑ 107 Gary Anderson K .25 .08
❑ 108 Marc Logan .25 .08
❑ 109 Ricky Sanders .25 .08
❑ 110 Vai Sikahema .25 .08
❑ 111 Neil Smith .75 .30
❑ 112 Cody Carlson .25 .08
❑ 113 Jimmie Jones .25 .08
❑ 114 Pat Swilling .25 .08
❑ 115 Neil O'Donnell .40 .15
❑ 116 Chip Lohmiller .25 .08
❑ 117 Mike Croel .25 .08
❑ 118 Pete Metzelaars .25 .08
❑ 119 Ray Childress .25 .08
❑ 120 Fred Banks .25 .08
❑ 121 Derek Kennard .25 .08
❑ 122 Daryl Johnston .75 .30
❑ 123 Lorenzo White UER .25 .08
❑ 124 Hardy Nickerson .40 .15
❑ 125 Derrick Thomas .75 .30
❑ 126 Steve Walsh .25 .08
❑ 127 Doug Widell .25 .08
❑ 128 Calvin Williams .40 .15
❑ 129 Tim Harris .25 .08
❑ 130 Rod Woodson .75 .30
❑ 131 Craig Heyward .40 .15
❑ 132 Barry Word .25 .08
❑ 133 Mark Duper .25 .08
❑ 134 Tim Johnson .25 .08
❑ 135 John Gesek .25 .08
❑ 136 Steve Jackson .25 .08
❑ 137 Dave Krieg .40 .15
❑ 138 Barry Sanders 4.00 1.50
❑ 139 Michael Haynes .40 .15
❑ 140 Eric Metcalf .40 .15
❑ 141 Stan Humphries .75 .30
❑ 142 Sterling Sharpe .75 .30
❑ 143 Todd Marinovich .25 .08
❑ 144 Rodney Hampton .40 .15
❑ 145 Rodney Peete .40 .15
❑ 146 Darryl Williams RC .25 .08
❑ 147 Darren Perry RC .25 .08
❑ 148 Terrell Buckley RC .25 .08
❑ 149 Amp Lee RC .25 .08
❑ 150 Ricky Watters .75 .30

1993 Playoff

❑ COMPLETE SET (315) 25.00 10.00
❑ 1 Troy Aikman 1.50 .60
❑ 2 Jerry Rice 2.00 .75
❑ 3 Keith Jackson .20 .07
❑ 4 Sean Gilbert .20 .07
❑ 5 Jim Kelly .40 .15
❑ 6 Junior Seau .40 .15
❑ 7 Deion Sanders 1.00 .40
❑ 8 Joe Montana 3.00 1.25
❑ 9 Terrell Buckley .10 .02
❑ 10 Emmitt Smith 3.00 1.25

❑ 11 Pete Stoyanovich .10 .02
❑ 12 Randall Cunningham .40 .15
❑ 13 Boomer Esiason .20 .07
❑ 14 Mike Saxon .10 .02
❑ 15 Chuck Cecil .10 .02
❑ 16 Vinny Testaverde .20 .07
❑ 17 Jeff Hostetler .20 .07
❑ 18 Mark Clayton .10 .02
❑ 19 Nick Bell .10 .02
❑ 20 Frank Reich .20 .07
❑ 21 Henry Ellard .20 .07
❑ 22 Andre Reed .20 .07
❑ 23 Mark Ingram .10 .02
❑ 24 Mike Brim .10 .02
❑ 25A Bernie Kosar ERR Kozar .20 .07
❑ 25B Bernie Kosar COR .20 .07
❑ 26 Jeff George .40 .15
❑ 27 Tommy Maddox .40 .15
❑ 28 Kent Graham RC .40 .15
❑ 29 David Klingler .10 .02
❑ 30 Robert Delpino .10 .02
❑ 31 Kevin Fagan .10 .02
❑ 32 Mark Bavaro .10 .02
❑ 33 Harold Green .10 .02
❑ 34 Shawn McCarthy .10 .02
❑ 35 Ricky Proehl .10 .02
❑ 36 Eugene Robinson .10 .02
❑ 37 Phil Simms .20 .07
❑ 38 David Lang .10 .02
❑ 39 Santana Dotson .20 .07
❑ 40 Brett Perriman .40 .15
❑ 41 Jim Harbaugh .40 .15
❑ 42 Keith Byars .10 .02
❑ 43 Quentin Coryatt .20 .07
❑ 44 Louis Oliver .10 .02
❑ 45 Howie Long .40 .15
❑ 46 Mike Sherrard .10 .02
❑ 47 Earnest Byner .10 .02
❑ 48 Neil Smith .40 .15
❑ 49 Audray McMillian .10 .02
❑ 50 Vaughn Dunbar .10 .02
❑ 51 Ronnie Lott .20 .07
❑ 52 Clyde Simmons .10 .02
❑ 53 Kevin Scott .10 .02
❑ 54 Bubby Brister .10 .02
❑ 55 Randal Hill .10 .02
❑ 56 Pat Swilling .10 .02
❑ 57 Steve Beuerlein .20 .07
❑ 58 Gary Clark .20 .07
❑ 59 Brian Noble .10 .02
❑ 60 Leslie O'Neal .20 .07
❑ 61 Vincent Brown .10 .02
❑ 62 Edgar Bennett .40 .15
❑ 63 Anthony Carter .20 .07
❑ 64 Glenn Cadrez RC UER .10 .02
❑ 65 Dalton Hilliard .10 .02
❑ 66 James Lofton .20 .07
❑ 67 Walter Stanley .10 .02
❑ 68 Tim Harris .10 .02
❑ 69 Carl Banks .10 .02
❑ 70 Andre Ware .10 .02
❑ 71 Karl Mecklenburg .10 .02

	No.	Player	Mint	Ex
❑	72	Russell Maryland	.10	.02
❑	73	Leroy Thompson	.10	.02
❑	74	Tommy Kane	.10	.02
❑	75	Dan Marino	3.00	1.25
❑	76	Darrell Fullington	.10	.02
❑	77	Jessie Tuggle	.10	.02
❑	78	Bruce Smith	.40	.15
❑	79	Neal Anderson	.10	.02
❑	80	Kevin Mack	.10	.02
❑	81	Shane Dronett	.10	.02
❑	82	Nick Lowery	.10	.02
❑	83	Sheldon White	.10	.02
❑	84	Flipper Anderson	.10	.02
❑	85	Jeff Herrod	.10	.02
❑	86	Dwight Stone	.10	.02
❑	87	Dave Krieg	.20	.07
❑	88	Bryan Cox	.10	.02
❑	89	Greg McMurtry	.10	.02
❑	90	Rickey Jackson	.10	.02
❑	91	Ernie Mills	.10	.02
❑	92	Browning Nagle	.10	.02
❑	93	John Taylor	.20	.07
❑	94	Eric Dickerson	.20	.07
❑	95	Johnny Holland	.10	.02
❑	96	Anthony Miller	.20	.07
❑	97	Fred Barnett	.20	.07
❑	98	Ricky Ervins UER	.10	.02
❑	99	Leonard Russell	.20	.07
❑	100	Lawrence Taylor	.40	.15
❑	101	Tony Casillas	.10	.02
❑	102	John Elway	3.00	1.25
❑	103	Bennie Blades	.10	.02
❑	104	Harry Sydney	.10	.02
❑	105	Bubba McDowell	.10	.02
❑	106	Todd McNair	.10	.02
❑	107	Steve Smith	.10	.02
❑	108	Jim Everett	.20	.07
❑	109	Bobby Humphrey	.10	.02
❑	110	Rich Gannon	.40	.15
❑	111	Marv Cook	.10	.02
❑	112	Wayne Martin	.10	.02
❑	113	Sean Landeta	.10	.02
❑	114	Brad Baxter UER	.10	.02
❑	115	Reggie White	.40	.15
❑	116	Johnny Johnson	.10	.02
❑	117	Jeff Graham	.20	.07
❑	118	Darren Carrington RC	.10	.02
❑	119	Ricky Watters	.40	.15
❑	120	Art Monk	.20	.07
❑	121	Cornelius Bennett	.20	.07
❑	122	Wade Wilson	.10	.02
❑	123	Daniel Stubbs	.10	.02
❑	124	Brad Muster	.10	.02
❑	125	Mike Tomczak	.10	.02
❑	126	Jay Novacek	.20	.07
❑	127	Shannon Sharpe	.40	.15
❑	128	Rodney Peete	.10	.02
❑	129	Daryl Johnston	.40	.15
❑	130	Warren Moon	.40	.15
❑	131	Willie Gault	.10	.02
❑	132	Tony Martin	.40	.15
❑	133	Terry Allen	.40	.15
❑	134	Hugh Millen	.10	.02
❑	135	Rob Moore	.20	.07
❑	136	Andy Harmon RC	.20	.07
❑	137	Kelvin Martin	.10	.02
❑	138	Rod Woodson	.40	.15
❑	139	Nate Lewis	.10	.02
❑	140	Darryl Talley	.10	.02
❑	141	Guy McIntyre	.10	.02
❑	142	John L. Williams	.10	.02
❑	143	Brad Edwards	.10	.02
❑	144	Trace Armstrong	.10	.02
❑	145	Kenneth Davis	.10	.02
❑	146	Clay Matthews	.20	.07
❑	147	Gaston Green	.10	.02
❑	148	Chris Spielman	.20	.07
❑	149	Cody Carlson	.10	.02
❑	150	Derrick Thomas	.40	.15
❑	151	Terry McDaniel	.10	.02
❑	152	Kevin Greene	.20	.07
❑	153	Roger Craig	.20	.07
❑	154	Craig Heyward	.20	.07
❑	155	Rodney Hampton	.20	.07
❑	156	Heath Sherman	.10	.02
❑	157	Mark Stepnoski	.10	.02
❑	158	Chris Chandler	.20	.07
❑	159	Rod Bernstine	.10	.02
❑	160	Pierce Holt	.10	.02
❑	161	Wilber Marshall	.10	.02
❑	162	Reggie Cobb	.10	.02
❑	163	Tom Rathman	.10	.02
❑	164	Michael Haynes	.20	.07
❑	165	Nate Odomes	.10	.02
❑	166	Tom Waddle	.10	.02
❑	167	Eric Ball	.10	.02
❑	168	Brett Favre UER	4.00	1.50
❑	169	Michael Jackson	.20	.07
❑	170	Lorenzo White	.10	.02
❑	171	Cleveland Gary	.10	.02
❑	172	Jay Schroeder	.10	.02
❑	173	Tony Paige	.10	.02
❑	174	Jack Del Rio	.10	.02
❑	175	Jon Vaughn	.10	.02
❑	176	Morten Andersen UER	.10	.02
❑	177	Chris Burkett	.10	.02
❑	178	Vai Sikahema	.10	.02
❑	179	Ronnie Harmon	.10	.02
❑	180	Amp Lee	.10	.02
❑	181	Chip Lohmiller	.10	.02
❑	182	Steve Broussard	.10	.02
❑	183	Don Beebe	.10	.02
❑	184	Tommy Vardell	.10	.02
❑	185	Keith Jennings	.10	.02
❑	186	Simon Fletcher	.10	.02
❑	187	Mel Gray	.20	.07
❑	188	Vince Workman	.10	.02
❑	189	Haywood Jeffires	.20	.07
❑	190	Barry Word	.10	.02
❑	191	Ethan Horton	.10	.02
❑	192	Mark Higgs	.10	.02
❑	193	Irving Fryar	.20	.07
❑	194	Charles Haley	.20	.07
❑	195	Steve Bono	.20	.07
❑	196	Mike Golic	.10	.02
❑	197	Gary Anderson K	.10	.02
❑	198	Sterling Sharpe	.40	.15
❑	199	Andre Tippett	.10	.02
❑	200	Thurman Thomas	.40	.15
❑	201	Chris Miller	.20	.07
❑	202	Henry Jones	.10	.02
❑	203	Mo Lewis	.10	.02
❑	204	Marion Butts	.10	.02
❑	205	Mike Johnson	.10	.02
❑	206	Alvin Harper	.20	.07
❑	207	Ray Childress	.10	.02
❑	208	Anthony Johnson	.20	.07
❑	209	Tony Bennett	.10	.02
❑	210	Anthony Newman RC	.10	.02
❑	211	Christian Okoye	.10	.02
❑	212	Marcus Allen	.40	.15
❑	213	Jackie Harris	.10	.02
❑	214	Mark Duper	.10	.02
❑	215	Cris Carter	.40	.15
❑	216	John Stephens	.10	.02
❑	217	Barry Sanders	2.50	1.00
❑	218A	H.Moore ERR Sherman	1.25	.50
❑	218B	Herman Moore COR	2.50	1.00
❑	219	Marvin Washington	.10	.02
❑	220	Calvin Williams	.20	.07
❑	221	John Randle	.20	.07
❑	222	Marco Coleman	.10	.02
❑	223	Eric Martin	.10	.02
❑	224	Dave Meggett	.10	.02
❑	225	Brian Washington	.10	.02
❑	226	Barry Foster	.20	.07
❑	227	Michael Zordich	.10	.02
❑	228	Stan Humphries	.20	.07
❑	229	Mike Cofer	.10	.02
❑	230	Chris Warren	.20	.07
❑	231	Keith McCants	.10	.02
❑	232	Mark Rypien	.10	.02
❑	233	James Francis	.10	.02
❑	234	Andre Rison	.20	.07
❑	235	William Perry	.20	.07
❑	236	Chip Banks	.10	.02
❑	237	Willie Davis	.40	.15
❑	238	Chris Doleman	.10	.02
❑	239	Tim Brown	.40	.15
❑	240	Darren Perry	.10	.02
❑	241	Johnny Bailey	.10	.02
❑	242	Ernest Givins	.20	.07
❑	243	John Carney	.10	.02
❑	244	Cortez Kennedy	.20	.07
❑	245	Lawrence Dawsey	.10	.02
❑	246	Martin Mayhew	.10	.02
❑	247	Shane Conlan	.10	.02
❑	248	J.J. Birden	.10	.02
❑	249	Quinn Early	.20	.07
❑	250	Michael Irvin	.40	.15
❑	251	Neil O'Donnell	.40	.15
❑	252	Stan Gelbaugh	.10	.02
❑	253	Drew Hill	.10	.02
❑	254	Wendell Davis	.10	.02
❑	255	Tim Johnson	.10	.02
❑	256	Seth Joyner	.10	.02
❑	257	Derrick Fenner	.10	.02
❑	258	Steve Young	1.50	.60
❑	259	Jackie Slater	.10	.02
❑	260	Eric Metcalf	.20	.07
❑	261	Rufus Porter	.10	.02
❑	262	Ken Norton Jr.	.20	.07
❑	263	Tim McDonald	.10	.02
❑	264	Mark Jackson	.10	.02
❑	265	Hardy Nickerson	.20	.07
❑	266	Anthony Munoz	.20	.07
❑	267	Mark Carrier WR	.20	.07
❑	268	Mike Pritchard	.20	.07
❑	269	Steve Emtman	.10	.02
❑	270	Ricky Sanders	.10	.02
❑	271	Robert Massey	.10	.02
❑	272	Pete Metzelaars	.10	.02
❑	273	Reggie Langhorne	.10	.02
❑	274	Tim McGee	.10	.02
❑	275	Reggie Rivers RC	.10	.02
❑	276	Jimmie Jones	.10	.02
❑	277	Lorenzo White TB	.10	.02
❑	278	Emmitt Smith TB	2.00	.75
❑	279	Thurman Thomas TB	.40	.15
❑	280	Barry Sanders TB	1.50	.60
❑	281	Rodney Hampton TB	.20	.07
❑	282	Barry Foster TB	.20	.07
❑	283	Troy Aikman PC	1.00	.40
❑	284	Michael Irvin PC	.20	.07
❑	285	Brett Favre PC	2.50	1.00
❑	286	Sterling Sharpe PC	.20	.07
❑	287	Steve Young PC	1.00	.40
❑	288	Jerry Rice PC	1.25	.50
❑	289	Stan Humphries PC	.20	.07
❑	290	Anthony Miller PC	.20	.07
❑	291	Dan Marino PC	2.00	.75
❑	292	Keith Jackson PC	.10	.02
❑	293	Patrick Bates RC	.10	.02
❑	294	Jerome Bettis RC	10.00	4.00
❑	295	Drew Bledsoe RC	6.00	2.50
❑	296	Tom Carter RC	.20	.07
❑	297	Curtis Conway RC	1.00	.40
❑	298	John Copeland RC	.20	.07
❑	299	Eric Curry RC	.10	.02
❑	300	Reggie Brooks RC	.20	.07
❑	301	Steve Everitt RC	.10	.02
❑	302	Deon Figures RC	.10	.02
❑	303	Garrison Hearst RC	2.00	.75
❑	304	Qadry Ismail RC UER	.40	.15

❑ 305 Marvin Jones RC	.10	.02
❑ 306 Lincoln Kennedy RC	.10	.02
❑ 307 O.J.McDuffie RC	.40	.15
❑ 308 Rick Mirer RC	.40	.15
❑ 309 Wayne Simmons RC	.10	.02
❑ 310 Irv Smith RC	.10	.02
❑ 311 Robert Smith RC	3.00	1.25
❑ 312 Dana Stubblefield RC	.40	.15
❑ 313 George Teague RC	.20	.07
❑ 314 Dan Williams RC	.10	.02
❑ 315 Kevin Williams RC WR	.40	.15
❑ NNO Santa Claus	2.00	.75

1994 Playoff

❑ COMPLETE SET (336)	30.00	12.50
❑ 1 Joe Montana	4.00	1.50
❑ 2 Derrick Thomas	.50	.20
❑ 3 Dan Marino	4.00	1.50
❑ 4 Cris Carter	.75	.30
❑ 5 Boomer Esiason	.30	.10
❑ 6 Bruce Smith	.50	.20
❑ 7 Andre Rison	.30	.10
❑ 8 Curtis Conway	.50	.20
❑ 9 Michael Irvin	.50	.20
❑ 10 Shannon Sharpe	.30	.10
❑ 11 Pat Swilling	.15	.05
❑ 12 John Parrella	.15	.05
❑ 13 Mel Gray	.15	.05
❑ 14 Ray Childress	.15	.05
❑ 15 Willie Davis	.30	.10
❑ 16 Rocket Ismail	.30	.10
❑ 17 Jim Everett	.30	.10
❑ 18 Mark Higgs	.15	.05
❑ 19 Trace Armstrong	.15	.05
❑ 20 Jim Kelly	.50	.20
❑ 21 Rob Burnett	.15	.05
❑ 22 Jay Novacek	.30	.10
❑ 23 Robert Delpino	.15	.05
❑ 24 Brett Perriman	.30	.10
❑ 25 Troy Aikman	2.00	.75
❑ 26 Reggie White	.50	.20
❑ 27 Lorenzo White	.15	.05
❑ 28 Bubba McDowell	.15	.05
❑ 29 Steve Emtman	.15	.05
❑ 30 Brett Favre	4.00	1.50
❑ 31 Derek Russell	.15	.05
❑ 32 Jeff Hostetler	.30	.10
❑ 33 Henry Ellard	.30	.10
❑ 34 Jack Del Rio	.15	.05
❑ 35 Mike Saxon	.15	.05
❑ 36 Rickey Jackson	.15	.05
❑ 37 Phil Simms	.30	.10
❑ 38 Quinn Early	.30	.10
❑ 39 Russell Copeland	.15	.05
❑ 40 Carl Pickens	.30	.10
❑ 41 Lance Gunn	.15	.05
❑ 42 Bernie Kosar	.30	.10
❑ 43 John Elway	4.00	1.50
❑ 44 George Teague	.15	.05
❑ 45 Nick Lowery	.15	.05
❑ 46 Haywood Jeffires	.30	.10
❑ 47 Will Shields	.15	.05

❑ 48 Daryl Johnston	.30	.10
❑ 49 Pete Metzelaars	.15	.05
❑ 50 Warren Moon	.50	.20
❑ 51 Cornelius Bennett	.30	.10
❑ 52 Vinny Testaverde	.30	.10
❑ 53 John Mangum RC	.15	.05
❑ 54 Tommy Vardell	.15	.05
❑ 55 Lincoln Coleman RC	.15	.05
❑ 56 Karl Mecklenburg	.15	.05
❑ 57 Jackie Harris	.15	.05
❑ 58 Curtis Duncan	.15	.05
❑ 59 Quentin Coryatt	.15	.05
❑ 60 Tim Brown	.50	.20
❑ 61 Irving Fryar	.30	.10
❑ 62 Sean Gilbert	.15	.05
❑ 63 Qadry Ismail	.50	.20
❑ 64 Irv Smith	.15	.05
❑ 65 Mark Jackson	.15	.05
❑ 66 Ronnie Lott	.30	.10
❑ 67 Henry Jones	.15	.05
❑ 68 Horace Copeland	.15	.05
❑ 69 John Copeland	.15	.05
❑ 70 Mark Carrier WR	.30	.10
❑ 71 Michael Jackson	.30	.10
❑ 72 Jason Elam	.30	.10
❑ 73 Rod Bernstine	.15	.05
❑ 74 Wayne Simmons	.15	.05
❑ 75 Cody Carlson	.15	.05
❑ 76 Alexander Wright	.15	.05
❑ 77 Shane Conlan	.15	.05
❑ 78 Keith Jackson	.15	.05
❑ 79 Sean Salisbury	.15	.05
❑ 80 Vaughan Johnson	.15	.05
❑ 81 Rob Moore	.30	.10
❑ 82 Andre Reed	.30	.10
❑ 83 David Klingler	.15	.05
❑ 84 Jim Harbaugh	.50	.20
❑ 85 John Jett RC	.15	.05
❑ 86 Sterling Sharpe	.30	.10
❑ 87 Webster Slaughter	.15	.05
❑ 88 J.J. Birden	.15	.05
❑ 89 O.J.McDuffie	.50	.20
❑ 90 Andre Tippett	.15	.05
❑ 91 Don Beebe	.15	.05
❑ 92 Mark Stepnoski	.15	.05
❑ 93 Neil Smith	.30	.10
❑ 94 Terry Kirby	.50	.20
❑ 95 Wade Wilson	.15	.05
❑ 96 Darryl Talley	.15	.05
❑ 97 Anthony Smith	.15	.05
❑ 98 Willie Roaf	.15	.05
❑ 99 Mo Lewis	.15	.05
❑ 100 James Washington	.15	.05
❑ 101 Nate Odomes	.15	.05
❑ 102 Chris Gedney	.15	.05
❑ 103 Joe Walter	.15	.05
❑ 104 Alvin Harper	.30	.10
❑ 105 Simon Fletcher	.15	.05
❑ 106 Rodney Peete	.15	.05
❑ 107 Terrell Buckley	.15	.05
❑ 108 Jeff George	.50	.20
❑ 109 James Jett	.15	.05
❑ 110 Tony Casillas	.15	.05
❑ 111 Marco Coleman	.15	.05
❑ 112 Anthony Carter	.30	.10
❑ 113 Lincoln Kennedy	.15	.05
❑ 114 Chris Calloway	.15	.05
❑ 115 Randall Cunningham	.50	.20
❑ 116 Steve Beuerlein	.30	.10
❑ 117 Neil O'Donnell	.50	.20
❑ 118 Stan Humphries	.30	.10
❑ 119 John Taylor	.30	.10
❑ 120 Cortez Kennedy	.30	.10
❑ 121 Santana Dotson	.30	.10
❑ 122 Thomas Smith	.15	.05
❑ 123 Kevin Williams WR	.30	.10
❑ 124 Andre Ware	.15	.05
❑ 125 Ethan Horton	.15	.05

❑ 126 Mike Sherrard	.15	.05
❑ 127 Fred Barnett	.30	.10
❑ 128 Ricky Proehl	.15	.05
❑ 129 Kevin Greene	.30	.10
❑ 130 John Carney	.15	.05
❑ 131 Tim McDonald	.15	.05
❑ 132 Rick Mirer	.50	.20
❑ 133 Blair Thomas	.15	.05
❑ 134 Hardy Nickerson	.30	.10
❑ 135 Heath Sherman	.15	.05
❑ 136 Andre Hastings	.30	.10
❑ 137 Randal Hill	.15	.05
❑ 138 Mike Cofer	.15	.05
❑ 139 Brian Blades	.30	.10
❑ 140 Earnest Byner	.15	.05
❑ 141 Bill Bates	.30	.10
❑ 142 Junior Seau	.50	.20
❑ 143 Johnny Bailey	.15	.05
❑ 144 Dwight Stone	.15	.05
❑ 145 Todd Kelly	.15	.05
❑ 146 Tyrone Montgomery	.15	.05
❑ 147 Herschel Walker	.30	.10
❑ 148 Gary Clark	.30	.10
❑ 149 Eric Green	.15	.05
❑ 150 Steve Young	1.50	.60
❑ 151 Anthony Miller	.30	.10
❑ 152 Dana Stubblefield	.30	.10
❑ 153 Dean Wells RC	.15	.05
❑ 154 Vincent Brisby	.30	.10
❑ 155 Chris Chandler	.30	.10
❑ 156 Clyde Simmons	.15	.05
❑ 157 Rod Woodson	.30	.10
❑ 158 Nate Lewis	.15	.05
❑ 159 Martin Harrison	.15	.05
❑ 160 Kelvin Martin	.15	.05
❑ 161 Craig Erickson	.15	.05
❑ 162 Johnny Mitchell	.15	.05
❑ 163 Calvin Williams	.30	.10
❑ 164 Deon Figures	.15	.05
❑ 165 Tom Rathman	.15	.05
❑ 166 Rick Hamilton	.15	.05
❑ 167 John L. Williams	.15	.05
❑ 168 Demetrius DuBose	.15	.05
❑ 169 Michael Brooks	.15	.05
❑ 170 Marion Butts	.15	.05
❑ 171 Brent Jones	.30	.10
❑ 172 Bobby Hebert	.15	.05
❑ 173 Brad Edwards	.15	.05
❑ 174 David Wyman	.15	.05
❑ 175 Herman Moore	.50	.20
❑ 176 LeRoy Butler	.15	.05
❑ 177 Reggie Langhorne	.15	.05
❑ 178 Dave Krieg	.30	.10
❑ 179 Patrick Bates	.15	.05
❑ 180 Erik Kramer	.30	.10
❑ 181 Troy Drayton	.15	.05
❑ 182 Dave Meggett	.15	.05
❑ 183 Eric Allen	.15	.05
❑ 184 Mark Bavaro	.15	.05
❑ 185 Leslie O'Neal	.15	.05
❑ 186 Jerry Rice	2.00	.75
❑ 187 Desmond Howard	.30	.10
❑ 188 Deion Sanders	.75	.30
❑ 189 Bill Maas	.15	.05
❑ 190 Frank Wycheck RC	2.00	.75
❑ 191 Ernest Givins	.30	.10
❑ 192 Terry McDaniel	.15	.05
❑ 193 Bryan Cox	.15	.05
❑ 194 Guy McIntyre	.15	.05
❑ 195 Pierce Holt	.15	.05
❑ 196 Fred Stokes	.15	.05
❑ 197 Mike Pritchard	.15	.05
❑ 198 Terry Obee	.15	.05
❑ 199 Mark Collins	.15	.05
❑ 200 Drew Bledsoe	1.25	.50
❑ 201 Barry Word	.15	.05
❑ 202 Derrick Lassic	.15	.05
❑ 203 Chris Spielman	.30	.10

❑ 204 John Jurkovic RC	.30	.10
❑ 205 Ken Norton Jr.	.30	.10
❑ 206 Dale Carter	.15	.05
❑ 207 Chris Doleman	.15	.05
❑ 208 Keith Hamilton	.15	.05
❑ 209 Andy Harmon	.15	.05
❑ 210 John Friesz	.30	.10
❑ 211 Steve Bono	.30	.10
❑ 212 Mark Rypien	.15	.05
❑ 213 Ricky Sanders	.15	.05
❑ 214 Michael Haynes	.30	.10
❑ 215 Todd McNair	.15	.05
❑ 216 Leon Lett	.15	.05
❑ 217 Scott Mitchell	.30	.10
❑ 218 Mike Morris RC	.15	.05
❑ 219 Darrin Smith	.15	.05
❑ 220 Jim McMahon	.30	.10
❑ 221 Garrison Hearst	.50	.20
❑ 222 Leroy Thompson	.15	.05
❑ 223 Darren Carrington	.15	.05
❑ 224 Pete Stoyanovich	.15	.05
❑ 225 Chris Miller	.15	.05
❑ 226 Bruce Smith SP	.30	.10
❑ 227 Simon Fletcher SP	.15	.05
❑ 228 Reggie White SP	.50	.20
❑ 229 Neil Smith SP	.30	.10
❑ 230 Chris Doleman SP	.15	.05
❑ 231 Keith Hamilton SP	.15	.05
❑ 232 Dana Stubblefield SP	.15	.05
❑ 233 Erric Pegram GA	.15	.05
❑ 234 Thurman Thomas GA	.50	.20
❑ 235 Lewis Tillman GA	.15	.05
❑ 236 Harold Green GA	.15	.05
❑ 237 Eric Metcalf GA	.30	.10
❑ 238 Emmitt Smith GA	3.00	1.25
❑ 239 Glyn Milburn GA	.30	.10
❑ 240 Barry Sanders GA	3.00	1.25
❑ 241 Edgar Bennett GA	.30	.10
❑ 242 Gary Brown GA	.15	.05
❑ 243 Roosevelt Potts GA	.15	.05
❑ 244 Marcus Allen GA	.50	.20
❑ 245 Greg Robinson GA	.15	.05
❑ 246 Jerome Bettis GA	.75	.30
❑ 247 Keith Byars GA	.15	.05
❑ 248 Robert Smith GA	.50	.20
❑ 249 Leonard Russell GA	.15	.05
❑ 250 Derek Brown RBK GA	.15	.05
❑ 251 Rodney Hampton GA	.30	.10
❑ 252 Johnny Johnson GA	.15	.05
❑ 253 Vaughn Hebron GA	.15	.05
❑ 254 Ronald Moore GA	.15	.05
❑ 255 Barry Foster GA	.15	.05
❑ 256 Natrone Means GA	.50	.20
❑ 257 Ricky Watters GA	.30	.10
❑ 258 Chris Warren GA	.50	.20
❑ 259 Vince Workman GA	.15	.05
❑ 260 Reggie Brooks GA	.15	.05
❑ 261 Carolina Panthers	.40	.15
❑ 262 Jacksonville Jaguars	.40	.15
❑ 263 Troy Aikman SB	1.00	.40
❑ 264 Barry Sanders SB	1.50	.60
❑ 265 Emmitt Smith SB	1.50	.60
❑ 266 Michael Irvin SB	.50	.20
❑ 267 Jerry Rice SB	1.00	.40
❑ 268 Shannon Sharpe SB	.30	.10
❑ 269 Bob Kratch SB	.15	.05
❑ 270 Howard Ballard SB	.15	.05
❑ 271 Erik Williams SB	.15	.05
❑ 272 Guy McIntyre SB	.15	.05
❑ 273 Kevin Williams WR SB	.30	.10
❑ 274 Mel Gray SB	.15	.05
❑ 275 Eddie Murray SB	.15	.05
❑ 276 Mark Stepnoski SB	.15	.05
❑ 277 Tommy Barnhardt SB	.15	.05
❑ 278 Derrick Thomas SB	.30	.10
❑ 279 Ken Norton Jr. SB	.30	.10
❑ 280 Chris Spielman SB	.15	.05
❑ 281 Deion Sanders SB	.50	.20
❑ 282 Mark Collins SB	.15	.05
❑ 283 Bruce Smith SB	.30	.10
❑ 284 Reggie White SB	.50	.20
❑ 285 Sean Gilbert SB	.15	.05
❑ 286 Cortez Kennedy SB	.30	.10
❑ 287 Steve Atwater SB	.15	.05
❑ 288 Tim McDonald SB	.15	.05
❑ 289 Jerome Bettis SB	.75	.30
❑ 290 Dana Stubblefield SB	.30	.10
❑ 291 Bert Emanuel RC	.50	.20
❑ 292 Jeff Burris RC	.30	.10
❑ 293 Bucky Brooks RC	.15	.05
❑ 294 Dan Wilkinson RC	.30	.10
❑ 295 Darnay Scott RC	1.00	.40
❑ 296 Derrick Alexander WR RC	.50	.20
❑ 297 Antonio Langham RC	.30	.10
❑ 298 Shante Carver RC	.15	.05
❑ 299 Shelby Hill RC	.15	.05
❑ 300 Larry Allen RC	.50	.20
❑ 301 Johnnie Morton RC	2.00	.75
❑ 302 Van Malone RC	.15	.05
❑ 303 Aaron Taylor RC	.15	.05
❑ 304 Marshall Faulk RC	6.00	2.50
❑ 305 Eric Mahlum RC	.15	.05
❑ 306 Trev Alberts RC	.30	.10
❑ 307 Greg Hill RC	.50	.20
❑ 308 Donnell Bennett RC	.50	.20
❑ 309 Rob Fredrickson RC	.30	.10
❑ 310 James Folston RC	.15	.05
❑ 311 Isaac Bruce RC	5.00	2.00
❑ 312 Tim Ruddy RC	.15	.05
❑ 313 Aubrey Beavers RC	.15	.05
❑ 314 David Palmer RC	.50	.20
❑ 315 Dewayne Washington RC	.30	.10
❑ 316 Willie McGinest RC	.50	.20
❑ 317 Mario Bates RC	.50	.20
❑ 318 Kevin Lee RC	.15	.05
❑ 319 Jason Sehorn RC	.75	.30
❑ 320 Thomas Randolph RC	.15	.05
❑ 321 Ryan Yarborough RC	.15	.05
❑ 322 Bernard Williams RC	.15	.05
❑ 323 Chuck Levy RC	.15	.05
❑ 324 Jamir Miller RC	.30	.10
❑ 325 Charles Johnson RC	.50	.20
❑ 326 Bryant Young RC	.50	.20
❑ 327 William Floyd RC	.50	.20
❑ 328 Kevin Mitchell RC	.15	.05
❑ 329 Sam Adams RC	.30	.10
❑ 330 Kevin Mawae RC	.50	.20
❑ 331 Errict Rhett RC	.50	.20
❑ 332 Trent Dilfer RC	1.50	.60
❑ 333 Heath Shuler RC	.50	.20
❑ 334 Aaron Glenn RC	.50	.20
❑ 335 Todd Steussie RC	.30	.10
❑ 336 Toby Wright RC	.15	.05
❑ NNO Gale Sayers Play.Club	4.00	1.50
❑ NNO Gale Sayers AUTO	60.00	25.00

1993 Playoff Contenders

❑ COMPLETE SET (150)	20.00	7.50
❑ 1 Brett Favre	3.00	1.50
❑ 2 Thurman Thomas	.40	.15
❑ 3 Barry Word	.10	.02
❑ 4 Herman Moore	.40	.15
❑ 5 Reggie Langhorne	.10	.02
❑ 6 Wilber Marshall	.10	.02
❑ 7 Ricky Watters	.40	.15
❑ 8 Marcus Allen	.40	.15
❑ 9 Jeff Hostetler	.20	.07
❑ 10 Steve Young	1.00	.40
❑ 11 Bobby Hebert	.10	.02
❑ 12 David Klingler	.10	.02
❑ 13 Craig Heyward	.20	.07
❑ 14 Andre Reed	.20	.07
❑ 15 Tommy Vardell	.10	.02
❑ 16 Anthony Carter	.20	.07
❑ 17 Mel Gray	.20	.07
❑ 18 Dan Marino	2.50	1.00
❑ 19 Haywood Jeffires	.20	.07
❑ 20 Joe Montana	2.50	1.00
❑ 21 Tim Brown	.40	.15
❑ 22 Jim McMahon	.20	.07
❑ 23 Scott Mitchell	.40	.15
❑ 24 Rickey Jackson	.10	.02
❑ 25 Troy Aikman	1.50	.60
❑ 26 Rodney Hampton	.20	.07
❑ 27 Fred Barnett	.20	.07
❑ 28 Gary Clark	.20	.07
❑ 29 Barry Foster	.20	.07
❑ 30 Brian Blades	.20	.07
❑ 31 Tim McDonald	.10	.02
❑ 32 Kelvin Martin	.10	.02
❑ 33 Henry Jones	.10	.02
❑ 34 Erric Pegram	.20	.07
❑ 35 Don Beebe	.10	.02
❑ 36 Eric Metcalf	.20	.07
❑ 37 Charles Haley	.20	.07
❑ 38 Robert Delpino	.10	.02
❑ 39 Leonard Russell UER	.20	.07
❑ 40 Jackie Harris	.10	.02
❑ 41 Ernest Givins	.20	.07
❑ 42 Willie Davis	.40	.15
❑ 43 Alexander Wright	.10	.02
❑ 44 Keith Byars	.10	.02
❑ 45 Dave Meggett	.10	.02
❑ 46 Johnny Johnson	.10	.02
❑ 47 Mark Bavaro	.10	.02
❑ 48 Seth Joyner	.10	.02
❑ 49 Junior Seau	.40	.15
❑ 50 Emmitt Smith	2.50	1.25
❑ 51 Shannon Sharpe	.40	.15
❑ 52 Rodney Peete	.10	.02
❑ 53 Andre Rison	.20	.07
❑ 54 Cornelius Bennett	.20	.07
❑ 55 Mark Carrier WR	.20	.07
❑ 56 Mark Clayton	.10	.02
❑ 57 Warren Moon	.40	.15
❑ 58 J.J. Birden	.10	.02
❑ 59 Howie Long	.40	.15
❑ 60 Irving Fryar	.20	.07
❑ 61 Mark Jackson	.10	.02
❑ 62 Eric Martin	.10	.02
❑ 63 Herschel Walker	.20	.07
❑ 64 Cortez Kennedy	.20	.07
❑ 65 Steve Beuerlein	.20	.07
❑ 66 Jim Kelly	.40	.15
❑ 67 Bernie Kosar Cowboys	.20	.07
❑ 68 Pat Swilling	.10	.02
❑ 69 Michael Irvin	.40	.15
❑ 70 Harvey Williams	.20	.07
❑ 71 Steve Smith	.10	.02
❑ 72 Wade Wilson	.10	.02
❑ 73 Phil Simms	.20	.07
❑ 74 Vinny Testaverde	.20	.07
❑ 75 Barry Sanders	2.50	1.00
❑ 76 Ken Norton Jr.	.20	.07
❑ 77 Rod Woodson	.40	.15
❑ 78 Webster Slaughter	.10	.02
❑ 79 Derrick Thomas	.40	.15
❑ 80 Mike Sherrard	.10	.02

❑ 81 Calvin Williams	.20	.07
❑ 82 Jay Novacek	.20	.07
❑ 83 Michael Brooks	.10	.02
❑ 84 Randall Cunningham	.40	.15
❑ 85 Chris Warren	.20	.07
❑ 86 Johnny Mitchell	.10	.02
❑ 87 Jim Harbaugh	.40	.15
❑ 88 Rod Bernstine	.10	.02
❑ 89 John Elway	2.50	1.00
❑ 90 Jerry Rice	1.50	.60
❑ 91 Brent Jones	.20	.07
❑ 92 Cris Carter	.40	.15
❑ 93 Alvin Harper	.20	.07
❑ 94 Horace Copeland RC	.20	.07
❑ 95 Rocket Ismail	.20	.07
❑ 96 Darrin Smith RC	.20	.07
❑ 97 Reggie Brooks RC	.20	.07
❑ 98 Demetrius DuBose RC	.10	.02
❑ 99 Eric Curry RC	.10	.02
❑ 100 Rick Mirer RC	.40	.15
❑ 101 Carlton Gray RC UER	.10	.02
❑ 102 Dana Stubblefield RC	.40	.15
❑ 103 Todd Kelly RC	.10	.02
❑ 104 Natrone Means RC	.40	.15
❑ 105 Darrien Gordon RC	.10	.02
❑ 106 Deon Figures RC	.10	.02
❑ 107 Garrison Hearst RC	1.25	.50
❑ 108 Ronald Moore RC	.20	.07
❑ 109 Leonard Renfro RC	.10	.02
❑ 110 Lester Holmes	.10	.02
❑ 111 Vaughn Hebron RC	.10	.02
❑ 112 Marvin Jones RC	.10	.02
❑ 113 Irv Smith RC	.10	.02
❑ 114 Willie Roaf RC	.20	.07
❑ 115 Derek Brown RC RBK	.20	.07
❑ 116 Vincent Brisby RC	.40	.15
❑ 117 Drew Bledsoe RC	4.00	1.50
❑ 118 Gino Torretta RC	.20	.07
❑ 119 Robert Smith RC	2.00	.75
❑ 120 Qadry Ismail RC	.40	.15
❑ 121 O.J.McDuffie RC	.40	.15
❑ 122 Terry Kirby RC	.40	.15
❑ 123 Troy Drayton RC	.20	.07
❑ 124 Jerome Bettis RC	6.00	2.50
❑ 125 Patrick Bates RC	.10	.02
❑ 126 Roosevelt Potts RC	.10	.02
❑ 127 Tom Carter RC	.20	.07
❑ 128 Patrick Robinson RC	.10	.02
❑ 129 Brad Hopkins RC	.10	.02
❑ 130 George Teague RC	.20	.07
❑ 131 Wayne Simmons RC	.10	.02
❑ 132 Mark Brunell RC	2.50	1.00
❑ 133 Ryan McNeil RC	.40	.15
❑ 134 Dan Williams RC	.10	.02
❑ 135 Glyn Milburn RC	.40	.15
❑ 136 Kevin Williams RC WR	.40	.15
❑ 137 Derrick Lassic RC	.10	.02
❑ 138 Steve Everitt RC	.10	.02
❑ 139 Lance Gunn RC	.10	.02
❑ 140 John Copeland RC	.20	.07
❑ 141 Curtis Conway RC	1.00	.40
❑ 142 Thomas Smith RC	.20	.07
❑ 143 Russell Copeland RC	.20	.07
❑ 144 Lincoln Kennedy RC	.10	.02
❑ 145 Boomer Esiason CL	.10	.02
❑ 146 Neil Smith CL	.10	.02
❑ 147 Jack Del Rio CL	.10	.02
❑ 148 Morten Andersen CL	.10	.02
❑ 149 Sterling Sharpe CL	.20	.07
❑ 150 Reggie White CL	.20	.07

1994 Playoff Contenders

❑ COMPLETE SET (120)	20.00	7.50
❑ 1 Drew Bledsoe	1.00	.40
❑ 2 Barry Sanders	2.50	1.00
❑ 3 Jerry Rice	1.50	.60
❑ 4 Rod Woodson	.20	.07
❑ 5 Irving Fryar	.20	.07

❑ 6 Charles Haley	.20	.07
❑ 7 Chris Warren	.20	.07
❑ 8 Craig Erickson	.10	.02
❑ 9 Eric Metcalf	.20	.07
❑ 10 Marcus Allen	.40	.15
❑ 11 Chris Miller	.10	.02
❑ 12 Andre Rison	.20	.07
❑ 13 Art Monk	.20	.07
❑ 14 Calvin Williams	.20	.07
❑ 15 Shannon Sharpe	.20	.07
❑ 16 Rodney Hampton	.20	.07
❑ 17 Marion Butts	.10	.02
❑ 18 John Jurkovic RC	.20	.07
❑ 19 Jim Kelly	.40	.15
❑ 20 Emmitt Smith	2.50	1.00
❑ 21 Jeff Hostetler	.20	.07
❑ 22 Barry Foster	.10	.02
❑ 23 Boomer Esiason	.20	.07
❑ 24 Jim Harbaugh	.40	.15
❑ 25 Joe Montana	3.00	1.25
❑ 26 Jeff George	.40	.15
❑ 27 Warren Moon	.40	.15
❑ 28 Steve Young	1.25	.50
❑ 29 Randall Cunningham	.40	.15
❑ 30 Shawn Jefferson	.10	.02
❑ 31 Cortez Kennedy	.20	.07
❑ 32 Reggie Brooks	.20	.07
❑ 33 Alvin Harper	.20	.07
❑ 34 Brent Jones	.20	.07
❑ 35 O.J.McDuffie	.40	.15
❑ 36 Jerome Bettis	.60	.25
❑ 37 Daryl Johnston	.20	.07
❑ 38 Herman Moore	.40	.15
❑ 39 Dave Meggett	.10	.02
❑ 40 Reggie White	.40	.15
❑ 41 Junior Seau	.40	.15
❑ 42 Dan Marino	3.00	1.25
❑ 43 Scott Mitchell	.20	.07
❑ 44 John Elway	3.00	1.25
❑ 45 Troy Aikman	1.50	.60
❑ 46 Terry Allen	.20	.07
❑ 47 David Klingler	.10	.02
❑ 48 Stan Humphries	.20	.07
❑ 49 Rick Mirer	.40	.15
❑ 50 Neil O'Donnell	.40	.15
❑ 51 Keith Jackson	.10	.02
❑ 52 Ricky Watters	.20	.07
❑ 53 Dave Brown	.20	.07
❑ 54 Neil Smith	.20	.07
❑ 55 Johnny Mitchell	.10	.02
❑ 56 Jackie Harris	.10	.02
❑ 57 Terry Kirby	.40	.15
❑ 58 Willie Davis	.20	.07
❑ 59 Rob Moore	.20	.07
❑ 60 Nate Newton	.10	.02
❑ 61 Deion Sanders	.75	.30
❑ 62 John Taylor	.20	.07
❑ 63 Sterling Sharpe	.20	.07
❑ 64 Natrone Means	.40	.15
❑ 65 Steve Beuerlein	.20	.07
❑ 66 Erik Kramer	.20	.07
❑ 67 Qadry Ismail	.40	.15
❑ 68 Johnny Johnson	.10	.02
❑ 69 Herschel Walker	.20	.07
❑ 70 Mark Stepnoski	.10	.02
❑ 71 Brett Favre	3.00	1.25
❑ 72 Dana Stubblefield	.20	.07
❑ 73 Bruce Smith	.40	.15
❑ 74 Leroy Hoard	.10	.02
❑ 75 Steve Walsh	.10	.02
❑ 76 Jay Novacek	.20	.07
❑ 77 Derrick Thomas	.40	.15
❑ 78 Keith Byars	.10	.02
❑ 79 Ben Coates	.20	.07
❑ 80 Lorenzo Neal	.10	.02
❑ 81 Ronnie Lott	.20	.07
❑ 82 Tim Brown	.40	.15
❑ 83 Michael Irvin	.40	.15
❑ 84 Ronald Moore	.10	.02
❑ 85 Andre Reed	.20	.07
❑ 86 James Jett	.10	.02
❑ 87 Curtis Conway	.40	.15
❑ 88 Bernie Parmalee RC	.40	.15
❑ 89 Keith Cash	.10	.02
❑ 90 Russell Copeland	.10	.02
❑ 91 Kevin Williams WR	.20	.07
❑ 92 Gary Brown	.10	.02
❑ 93 Thurman Thomas	.40	.15
❑ 94 Jamir Miller RC	.20	.07
❑ 95 Bert Emanuel RC	.40	.15
❑ 96 Bucky Brooks RC	.10	.02
❑ 97 Jeff Burris RC	.20	.07
❑ 98 Antonio Langham RC	.20	.07
❑ 99 Derrick Alexander WR RC	.40	.15
❑ 100 Dan Wilkinson RC	.20	.07
❑ 101 Shante Carver RC	.10	.02
❑ 102 Johnnie Morton RC	2.00	.75
❑ 103 LeShon Johnson RC	.20	.07
❑ 104 Marshall Faulk RC	6.00	2.50
❑ 105 Greg Hill RC	.40	.15
❑ 106 Lake Dawson RC	.20	.07
❑ 107 Irving Spikes RC	.20	.07
❑ 108 David Palmer RC	.40	.15
❑ 109 Willie McGinest RC	.40	.15
❑ 110 Joe Johnson RC	.10	.02
❑ 111 Aaron Glenn RC	.40	.15
❑ 112 Charlie Garner RC	1.50	.60
❑ 113 Charles Johnson RC	.40	.15
❑ 114 Byron Bam Morris RC	.20	.07
❑ 115 Bryant Young RC	.40	.15
❑ 116 William Floyd RC	.40	.15
❑ 117 Trent Dilfer RC	1.50	.60
❑ 118 Errict Rhett RC	.40	.15
❑ 119 Heath Shuler RC	.40	.15
❑ 120 Gus Frerotte RC	.40	.15

1995 Playoff Contenders

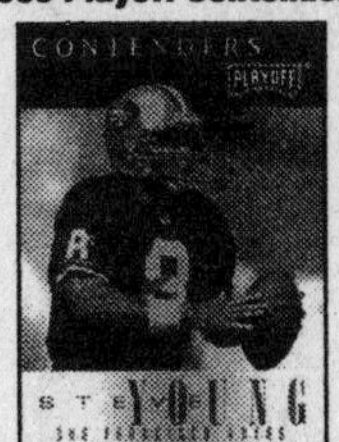

❑ COMPLETE SET (150)	25.00	10.00
❑ 1 Steve Young	1.00	.40
❑ 2 Jeff Blake RC	.75	.30
❑ 3 Rick Mirer	.20	.07
❑ 4 Brett Favre	2.50	1.25
❑ 5 Heath Shuler	.20	.07
❑ 6 Steve Bono	.20	.07

❑ 7 John Elway 2.50 1.00
❑ 8 Troy Aikman 1.25 .50
❑ 9 Rodney Peete .10 .02
❑ 10 Gus Frerotte .20 .07
❑ 11 Drew Bledsoe .75 .30
❑ 12 Jim Kelly .40 .15
❑ 13 Dan Marino 2.50 1.00
❑ 14 Errict Rhett .20 .07
❑ 15 Jeff Hostetler .20 .07
❑ 16 Erik Kramer .10 .02
❑ 17 Jim Everett .10 .02
❑ 18 Elvis Grbac .40 .15
❑ 19 Scott Mitchell .20 .07
❑ 20 Barry Sanders 2.00 .75
❑ 21 Deion Sanders .75 .30
❑ 22 Emmitt Smith 2.00 .75
❑ 23 Garrison Hearst .40 .15
❑ 24 Mario Bates .20 .07
❑ 25 Mark Brunell .75 .30
❑ 26 Robert Smith .40 .15
❑ 27 Rodney Hampton .20 .07
❑ 28 Marshall Faulk 1.50 .60
❑ 29 Greg Hill .20 .07
❑ 30 Bernie Parmalee .20 .07
❑ 31 Natrone Means .20 .07
❑ 32 Marcus Allen .40 .15
❑ 33 Byron Bam Morris .10 .02
❑ 34 Edgar Bennett .20 .07
❑ 35 Vincent Brisby .10 .02
❑ 36 Jerome Bettis .40 .15
❑ 37 Craig Heyward .20 .07
❑ 38 Anthony Miller .20 .07
❑ 39 Curtis Conway .40 .15
❑ 40 William Floyd .20 .07
❑ 41 Chris Warren .20 .07
❑ 42 Terry Kirby .20 .07
❑ 43 Herschel Walker .20 .07
❑ 44 Eric Metcalf .20 .07
❑ 45 Darnay Scott .20 .07
❑ 46 Jackie Harris .10 .02
❑ 47 Dana Stubblefield .20 .07
❑ 48 Daryl Johnston .20 .07
❑ 49 Dave Meggett .10 .02
❑ 50 Ricky Watters .20 .07
❑ 51 Ken Norton .20 .07
❑ 52 Boomer Esiason .20 .07
❑ 53 Lake Dawson .20 .07
❑ 54 Eric Green .10 .02
❑ 55 Junior Seau .40 .15
❑ 56 Yancey Thigpen RC .40 .15
❑ 57 James Jett .20 .07
❑ 58 Leonard Russell .10 .02
❑ 59 Brent Jones .10 .02
❑ 60 Trent Dilfer .40 .15
❑ 61 Terance Mathis .20 .07
❑ 62 Jeff George .20 .07
❑ 63 Alvin Harper .10 .02
❑ 64 Terry Allen .20 .07
❑ 65 Stan Humphries .20 .07
❑ 66 Robert Green .10 .02
❑ 67 Bryce Paup .20 .07
❑ 68 Tamarick Vanover RC .40 .15
❑ 69 Desmond Howard .20 .07
❑ 70 Derek Loville .10 .02
❑ 71 Dave Brown .20 .07
❑ 72 Carl Pickens .20 .07
❑ 73 Gary Clark .10 .02
❑ 74 Gary Brown .10 .02
❑ 75 Brett Perriman .20 .07
❑ 76 Charlie Garner .40 .15
❑ 77 Ben Coates .20 .07
❑ 78 Bruce Smith .40 .15
❑ 79 Erric Pegram .20 .07
❑ 80 Jerry Rice 1.25 .50
❑ 81 Tim Brown .40 .15
❑ 82 John Taylor .10 .02
❑ 83 Will Moore .10 .02
❑ 84 Jay Novacek .20 .07
❑ 85 Kevin Williams .20 .07
❑ 86 Rocket Ismail .20 .07
❑ 87 Robert Brooks .40 .15
❑ 88 Michael Irvin .40 .15
❑ 89 Mark Chmura .40 .15
❑ 90 Shannon Sharpe .20 .07
❑ 91 Henry Ellard .20 .07
❑ 92 Reggie White .40 .15
❑ 93 Isaac Bruce .75 .30
❑ 94 Charles Haley .20 .07
❑ 95 Jake Reed .20 .07
❑ 96 Pete Metzelaars .10 .02
❑ 97 Dave Krieg .10 .02
❑ 98 Tony Martin .20 .07
❑ 99 Charles Jordan RC .20 .07
❑ 100 Bert Emanuel .40 .15
❑ 101 Andre Rison .20 .07
❑ 102 Jeff Graham .10 .02
❑ 103 O.J. McDuffie .40 .15
❑ 104 Randall Cunningham .40 .15
❑ 105 Harvey Williams .10 .02
❑ 106 Cris Carter .40 .15
❑ 107 Irving Fryar .20 .07
❑ 108 Jim Harbaugh .20 .07
❑ 109 Bernie Kosar .10 .02
❑ 110 Charles Johnson .20 .07
❑ 111 Warren Moon .20 .07
❑ 112 Neil O'Donnell .20 .07
❑ 113 Fred Barnett .20 .07
❑ 114 Herman Moore .40 .15
❑ 115 Chris Miller .10 .02
❑ 116 Vinny Testaverde .20 .07
❑ 117 Craig Erickson .10 .02
❑ 118 Qadry Ismail .20 .07
❑ 119 Willie Davis .20 .07
❑ 120 Michael Jackson .20 .07
❑ 121 Stoney Case RC .40 .15
❑ 122 Frank Sanders RC .40 .15
❑ 123 Todd Collins RC .40 .15
❑ 124 Kerry Collins RC 1.50 .60
❑ 125 Sherman Williams RC .10 .02
❑ 126 Terrell Davis RC 2.50 1.00
❑ 127 Luther Elliss RC .10 .02
❑ 128 Steve McNair RC 3.00 1.25
❑ 129 Chris Sanders RC .40 .15
❑ 130 Ki-Jana Carter RC .40 .15
❑ 131 Rodney Thomas RC .40 .15
❑ 132 Tony Boselli RC .40 .15
❑ 133 Rob Johnson RC 1.00 .40
❑ 134 James O. Stewart RC 1.25 .50
❑ 135 Chad May RC .10 .02
❑ 136 Eric Bjornson RC .20 .07
❑ 137 Tyrone Wheatley RC 1.25 .50
❑ 138 Kyle Brady RC .40 .15
❑ 139 Curtis Martin RC 3.00 1.25
❑ 140 Eric Zeier RC .40 .15
❑ 141 Ray Zellars RC .20 .07
❑ 142 Napoleon Kaufman RC 1.25 .50
❑ 143 Mike Mamula RC .20 .07
❑ 144 Mark Bruener RC .20 .07
❑ 145 Kordell Stewart RC 1.50 .60
❑ 146 J.J. Stokes RC .40 .15
❑ 147 Joey Galloway RC 1.50 .60
❑ 148 Warren Sapp RC 1.50 .60
❑ 149 Michael Westbrook RC .40 .15
❑ 150 Rashaan Salaam RC .40 .15

1997 Playoff Contenders

❑ COMPLETE SET (150) 40.00 15.00
❑ 1 Kent Graham .40 .15
❑ 2 Leeland McElroy .40 .15
❑ 3 Rob Moore .60 .25
❑ 4 Frank Sanders .60 .25
❑ 5 Jake Plummer RC 5.00 2.00
❑ 6 Chris Chandler .60 .25
❑ 7 Bert Emanuel .60 .25
❑ 8 O.J. Santiago RC .60 .25
❑ 9 Byron Hanspard RC .60 .25 
❑ 10 Vinny Testaverde .60 .25
❑ 11 Michael Jackson .60 .25
❑ 12 Earnest Byner .40 .15
❑ 13 Jermaine Lewis 1.00 .40
❑ 14 Derrick Alexander WR .60 .25
❑ 15 Jay Graham RC .60 .25
❑ 16 Todd Collins .40 .15
❑ 17 Thurman Thomas 1.00 .40
❑ 18 Bruce Smith .60 .25
❑ 19 Andre Reed .60 .25
❑ 20 Quinn Early .40 .15
❑ 21 Antowain Smith RC 2.50 1.00
❑ 22 Kerry Collins 1.00 .40
❑ 23 Tim Biakabutuka .60 .25
❑ 24 Anthony Johnson .40 .15
❑ 25 Wesley Walls .60 .25
❑ 26 Fred Lane RC .60 .25
❑ 27 Rae Carruth RC .40 .15
❑ 28 Raymont Harris .40 .15
❑ 29 Rick Mirer .40 .15
❑ 30 Darnell Autry RC .60 .25
❑ 31 Jeff Blake .60 .25
❑ 32 Ki-Jana Carter .40 .15
❑ 33 Carl Pickens .60 .25
❑ 34 Darnay Scott .60 .25
❑ 35 Corey Dillon RC 6.00 2.50
❑ 36 Troy Aikman 2.00 .75
❑ 37 Emmitt Smith 3.00 1.25
❑ 38 Michael Irvin 1.00 .40
❑ 39 Deion Sanders 1.00 .40
❑ 40 Anthony Miller .40 .15
❑ 41 Eric Bjornson .40 .15
❑ 42 David LaFleur RC .40 .15
❑ 43 John Elway 4.00 1.50
❑ 44 Terrell Davis 1.25 .50
❑ 45 Shannon Sharpe .60 .25
❑ 46 Ed McCaffrey .60 .25
❑ 47 Rod Smith WR 1.00 .40
❑ 48 Scott Mitchell .60 .25
❑ 49 Barry Sanders 3.00 1.25
❑ 50 Herman Moore .60 .25
❑ 51 Brett Favre 4.00 1.50
❑ 52 Dorsey Levens 1.00 .40
❑ 53 William Henderson .60 .25
❑ 54 Derrick Mayes .60 .25
❑ 55 Antonio Freeman 1.00 .40
❑ 56 Robert Brooks .60 .25
❑ 57 Mark Chmura .60 .25
❑ 58 Reggie White 1.00 .40
❑ 59 Darren Sharper RC 1.00 .40
❑ 60 Jim Harbaugh .60 .25
❑ 61 Marshall Faulk 1.25 .50
❑ 62 Marvin Harrison 1.00 .40
❑ 63 Mark Brunell 1.25 .50
❑ 64 Natrone Means .60 .25
❑ 65 Jimmy Smith .60 .25
❑ 66 Keenan McCardell .60 .25
❑ 67 Elvis Grbac .60 .25
❑ 68 Greg Hill .40 .15
❑ 69 Marcus Allen 1.00 .40
❑ 70 Andre Rison .60 .25
❑ 71 Kimble Anders .60 .25

❑	72 Tony Gonzalez RC	3.00	1.25
❑	73 Pat Barnes RC	1.00	.40
❑	74 Dan Marino	4.00	1.50
❑	75 Karim Abdul-Jabbar	.60	.25
❑	76 Zach Thomas	1.00	.40
❑	77 O.J. McDuffie	.60	.25
❑	78 Brian Manning RC	.40	.15
❑	79 Brad Johnson	1.00	.40
❑	80 Cris Carter	1.00	.40
❑	81 Jake Reed	.60	.25
❑	82 Robert Smith	.60	.25
❑	83 Drew Bledsoe	1.25	.50
❑	84 Curtis Martin	1.25	.50
❑	85 Ben Coates	.60	.25
❑	86 Terry Glenn	1.00	.40
❑	87 Shawn Jefferson	.40	.15
❑	88 Heath Shuler	.40	.15
❑	89 Mario Bates	.40	.15
❑	90 Andre Hastings	.40	.15
❑	91 Troy Davis RC	.60	.25
❑	92 Danny Wuerffel RC	1.00	.40
❑	93 Dave Brown	.40	.15
❑	94 Chris Calloway	.40	.15
❑	95 Tiki Barber RC	6.00	2.50
❑	96 Mike Cherry RC	.40	.15
❑	97 Neil O'Donnell	.60	.25
❑	98 Keyshawn Johnson	1.00	.40
❑	99 Adrian Murrell	.60	.25
❑	100 Wayne Chrebet	1.00	.40
❑	101 Dedric Ward RC	.60	.25
❑	102 Leon Johnson RC	.60	.25
❑	103 Jeff George	.60	.25
❑	104 Napoleon Kaufman	1.00	.40
❑	105 Tim Brown	1.00	.40
❑	106 James Jett	.60	.25
❑	107 Ty Detmer	.60	.25
❑	108 Ricky Watters	.60	.25
❑	109 Irving Fryar	.60	.25
❑	110 Michael Timpson	.40	.15
❑	111 Chad Lewis RC	2.00	.75
❑	112 Kordell Stewart	1.00	.40
❑	113 Jerome Bettis	1.00	.40
❑	114 Charles Johnson	.60	.25
❑	115 George Jones RC	.60	.25
❑	116 Will Blackwell RC	.60	.25
❑	117 Stan Humphries	.60	.25
❑	118 Junior Seau	1.00	.40
❑	119 Freddie Jones RC	.60	.25
❑	120 Steve Young	1.25	.50
❑	121 Jerry Rice	2.00	.75
❑	122 Garrison Hearst	.60	.25
❑	123 William Floyd	.60	.25
❑	124 Terrell Owens	1.25	.50
❑	125 J.J. Stokes	.60	.25
❑	126 Marc Edwards RC	.40	.15
❑	127 Jim Druckenmiller RC	.60	.25
❑	128 Warren Moon	1.00	.40
❑	129 Chris Warren	.60	.25
❑	130 Joey Galloway	.60	.25
❑	131 Shawn Springs RC	.60	.25
❑	132 Tony Banks	.60	.25
❑	133 Lawrence Phillips	.40	.15
❑	134 Isaac Bruce	1.00	.40
❑	135 Eddie Kennison	.60	.25
❑	136 Orlando Pace RC	1.00	.40
❑	137 Trent Dilfer	1.00	.40
❑	138 Mike Alstott	1.00	.40
❑	139 Horace Copeland	.40	.15
❑	140 Jackie Harris	.40	.15
❑	141 Warrick Dunn RC	2.50	1.00
❑	142 Reidel Anthony RC	1.00	.40
❑	143 Steve McNair	1.25	.50
❑	144 Eddie George	1.00	.40
❑	145 Chris Sanders	.40	.15
❑	146 Gus Frerotte	.40	.15
❑	147 Terry Allen	1.00	.40
❑	148 Henry Ellard	.40	.15
❑	149 Leslie Shepherd	.40	.15
❑	150 Michael Westbrook	.60	.25
❑	S1 Terrell Davis Sample	2.00	.75

1998 Playoff Contenders Ticket

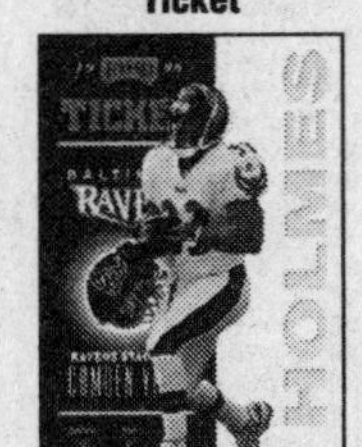

❑	COMP.SET w/o SPs (80)	60.00	25.00
❑	1 Rob Moore	1.25	.50
❑	2 Jake Plummer	2.00	.75
❑	3 Jamal Anderson	2.00	.75
❑	4 Terance Mathis	1.25	.50
❑	5 Priest Holmes RC	60.00	30.00
❑	6 Michael Jackson	.75	.30
❑	7 Eric Zeier	1.25	.50
❑	8 Andre Reed	1.25	.50
❑	9 Antowain Smith	2.00	.75
❑	10 Bruce Smith	1.25	.50
❑	11 Thurman Thomas	2.00	.75
❑	12 Rocket Ismail	.75	.30
❑	13 Wesley Walls	1.25	.50
❑	14 Curtis Conway	1.25	.50
❑	15 Jeff Blake	1.25	.50
❑	16 Corey Dillon	2.00	.75
❑	17 Carl Pickens	1.25	.50
❑	18 Troy Aikman	4.00	1.50
❑	19 Michael Irvin	2.00	.75
❑	20 Ernie Mills	.75	.30
❑	21 Deion Sanders	2.00	.75
❑	22 Emmitt Smith	6.00	2.50
❑	23 Terrell Davis	2.00	.75
❑	24 John Elway	8.00	3.00
❑	25 Neil Smith	1.25	.50
❑	26 Rod Smith WR	1.25	.50
❑	27 Herman Moore	1.25	.50
❑	28 Johnnie Morton	1.25	.50
❑	29 Barry Sanders	6.00	2.50
❑	30 Robert Brooks	1.25	.50
❑	31 Brett Favre	8.00	3.00
❑	32 Antonio Freeman	2.00	.75
❑	33 Dorsey Levens	2.00	.75
❑	34 Reggie White	2.00	.75
❑	35 Marshall Faulk	2.50	1.00
❑	36 Mark Brunell	2.00	.75
❑	37 Jimmy Smith	1.25	.50
❑	38 James Stewart	1.25	.50
❑	39 Donnell Bennett	.75	.30
❑	40 Andre Rison	1.25	.50
❑	41 Derrick Thomas	2.00	.75
❑	42 Karim Abdul-Jabbar	2.00	.75
❑	43 Dan Marino	8.00	3.00
❑	44 Cris Carter	2.00	.75
❑	45 Brad Johnson	2.00	.75
❑	46 Robert Smith	2.00	.75
❑	47 Drew Bledsoe	3.00	1.25
❑	48 Terry Glenn	2.00	.75
❑	49 Lamar Smith	1.25	.50
❑	50 Ike Hilliard	1.25	.50
❑	51 Danny Kanell	1.25	.50
❑	52 Wayne Chrebet	2.00	.75
❑	53 Keyshawn Johnson	2.00	.75
❑	54 Curtis Martin	2.00	.75
❑	55 Tim Brown	2.00	.75
❑	56 Rickey Dudley	.75	.30
❑	57 Jeff George	1.25	.50
❑	58 Napoleon Kaufman	2.00	.75
❑	59 Irving Fryar	1.25	.50
❑	60 Jerome Bettis	2.00	.75
❑	61 Charles Johnson	.75	.30
❑	62 Kordell Stewart	2.00	.75
❑	63 Natrone Means	1.25	.50
❑	64 Bryan Still	.75	.30
❑	65 Garrison Hearst	2.00	.75
❑	66 Jerry Rice	4.00	1.50
❑	67 Steve Young	2.50	1.00
❑	68 Joey Galloway	1.25	.50
❑	69 Warren Moon	2.00	.75
❑	70 Ricky Watters	1.25	.50
❑	71 Isaac Bruce	2.00	.75
❑	72 Mike Alstott	2.00	.75
❑	73 Reidel Anthony	1.25	.50
❑	74 Trent Dilfer	2.00	.75
❑	75 Warrick Dunn	2.00	.75
❑	76 Warren Sapp	1.25	.50
❑	77 Eddie George	2.00	.75
❑	78 Steve McNair	2.00	.75
❑	79 Terry Allen	2.00	.75
❑	80 Gus Frerotte	.75	.30
❑	81 Andre Wadsworth AUTO	25.00	10.00
❑	82 Tim Dwight AUTO	40.00	15.00
❑	83 Curtis Enis AUTO/400	40.00	15.00
❑	85 Charlie Batch AUTO	40.00	15.00
❑	86 Germane Crowell AUTO	25.00	10.00
❑	87 Pey.Manning AUTO/200	2500.00	1500.00
❑	88 Jerome Pathon AUTO	40.00	15.00
❑	89 Fred Taylor AUTO	80.00	40.00
❑	90 Tavian Banks AUTO	25.00	10.00
❑	92 Randy Moss AUTO/300	600.00	350.00
❑	93 Robert Edwards AUTO	25.00	10.00
❑	94 Hines Ward AUTO	250.00	125.00
❑	95 Ryan Leaf AUTO/200	60.00	25.00
❑	96 Mikhael Ricks AUTO	25.00	10.00
❑	97 Ahman Green AUTO	100.00	50.00
❑	98 Jacquez Green AUTO	25.00	10.00
❑	99 Kevin Dyson AUTO	40.00	15.00
❑	100 Skip Hicks AUTO	25.00	10.00
❑	103 C.Fuamatu-Ma'afala AU	25.00	10.00

1999 Playoff Contenders SSD

❑	COMPLETE SET (200)	2000.00	1000.00
❑	COMP.SET w/o RC/PT's (141)	60.00	25.00
❑	1 Randy Moss	5.00	2.00
❑	2 Randall Cunningham	2.00	.75
❑	3 Cris Carter	2.00	.75
❑	4 Robert Smith	2.00	.75
❑	5 Jake Reed	1.25	.50
❑	6 Albert Connell	.75	.30
❑	7 Jeff George	1.25	.50
❑	8 Brett Favre	6.00	2.50
❑	9 Antonio Freeman	2.00	.75
❑	10 Dorsey Levens	2.00	.75
❑	11 Mark Chmura	1.25	.50
❑	12 Mike Alstott	2.00	.75
❑	13 Warrick Dunn	2.00	.75
❑	14 Trent Dilfer	1.25	.50

❑ 15 Jacquez Green .75 .30
❑ 16 Reidel Anthony .75 .30
❑ 17 Warren Sapp 1.25 .50
❑ 18 Amani Toomer .75 .30
❑ 19 Curtis Enis .75 .30
❑ 20 Curtis Conway 1.25 .50
❑ 21 Bobby Engram 1.25 .50
❑ 22 Barry Sanders 6.00 2.50
❑ 23 Charlie Batch 2.00 .75
❑ 24 Herman Moore 1.25 .50
❑ 25 Johnnie Morton 1.25 .50
❑ 26 Greg Hill .75 .30
❑ 27 Germane Crowell .75 .30
❑ 28 Kerry Collins 1.25 .50
❑ 29 Ike Hilliard .75 .30
❑ 30 Joe Jurevicius 1.25 .50
❑ 31 Stephen Davis 2.00 .75
❑ 32 Brad Johnson 2.00 .75
❑ 33 Skip Hicks .75 .30
❑ 34 Michael Westbrook 1.25 .50
❑ 35 Jake Plummer 1.25 .50
❑ 36 Adrian Murrell .75 .30
❑ 37 Frank Sanders 1.25 .50
❑ 38 Rob Moore 1.25 .50
❑ 39 Gary Brown .75 .30
❑ 40 Duce Staley 2.00 .75
❑ 41 Charles Johnson 1.25 .50
❑ 42 Emmitt Smith 4.00 1.50
❑ 43 Troy Aikman 4.00 1.50
❑ 44 Michael Irvin 1.25 .50
❑ 45 Deion Sanders 2.00 .75
❑ 46 Rocket Ismail 1.25 .50
❑ 47 Jerry Rice 4.00 1.50
❑ 48 Terrell Owens 2.00 .75
❑ 49 Steve Young 2.50 1.00
❑ 50 Garrison Hearst 1.25 .50
❑ 51 J.J. Stokes 1.25 .50
❑ 52 Lawrence Phillips 1.25 .50
❑ 53 Jamal Anderson 2.00 .75
❑ 54 Chris Chandler 1.25 .50
❑ 55 Terance Mathis 1.25 .50
❑ 56 Tim Dwight 2.00 .75
❑ 57 Charlie Garner 1.25 .50
❑ 58 Chris Calloway 1.25 .50
❑ 59 Eddie Kennison 1.25 .50
❑ 60 Billy Joe Hobert .75 .30
❑ 61 Tim Biakabutuka 1.25 .50
❑ 62 Muhsin Muhammad 1.25 .50
❑ 63 Olandis Gary/1825 RC 25.00 10.00
❑ 64 Wesley Walls 1.25 .50
❑ 65 Isaac Bruce 2.00 .75
❑ 66 Marshall Faulk 2.50 1.00
❑ 67 Kordell Stewart 1.25 .50
❑ 68 Jerome Bettis 2.00 .75
❑ 69 Hines Ward 2.00 .75
❑ 70 Corey Dillon 2.00 .75
❑ 71 Carl Pickens 1.25 .50
❑ 72 Darnay Scott 1.25 .50
❑ 73 Steve McNair 2.00 .75
❑ 74 Eddie George 2.00 .75
❑ 75 Yancey Thigpen .75 .30
❑ 76 Kevin Dyson 1.25 .50
❑ 77 Fred Taylor 2.00 .75
❑ 78 Mark Brunell 2.00 .75
❑ 79 Jimmy Smith 1.25 .50
❑ 80 Keenan McCardell 1.25 .50
❑ 81 James Stewart 1.25 .50
❑ 82 Jermaine Lewis 1.25 .50
❑ 83 Priest Holmes 3.00 1.25
❑ 84 Stoney Case .75 .30
❑ 85 Errict Rhett 1.25 .50
❑ 86 Bill Schroeder 2.00 .75
❑ 87 Terry Kirby .75 .30
❑ 88 Leslie Shepherd .75 .30
❑ 89 Terrence Wilkins/825 RC 20.00 7.50
❑ 90 Dan Marino 6.00 2.50
❑ 91 O.J. McDuffie 1.25 .50
❑ 92 Karim Abdul-Jabbar 1.25 .50
❑ 93 Zach Thomas 2.00 .75
❑ 94 Terry Allen 1.25 .50
❑ 95 Tony Martin 1.25 .50
❑ 96 Drew Bledsoe 2.50 1.00
❑ 97 Terry Glenn 2.00 .75
❑ 98 Ben Coates 1.25 .50
❑ 99 Tony Simmons .75 .30
❑ 100 Curtis Martin 2.00 .75
❑ 101 Keyshawn Johnson 2.00 .75
❑ 102 Vinny Testaverde 1.25 .50
❑ 103 Wayne Chrebet 2.00 .75
❑ 104 Peyton Manning 6.00 2.50
❑ 105 Marvin Harrison 2.00 .75
❑ 106 E.G. Green .75 .30
❑ 107 Doug Flutie 2.00 .75
❑ 108 Thurman Thomas 1.25 .50
❑ 109 Andre Reed 1.25 .50
❑ 110 Eric Moulds 2.00 .75
❑ 111 Antowain Smith 2.00 .75
❑ 112 Bruce Smith 1.25 .50
❑ 113 Terrell Davis 2.00 .75
❑ 114 John Elway 6.00 2.50
❑ 115 Ed McCaffrey 1.25 .50
❑ 116 Rod Smith 1.25 .50
❑ 117 Shannon Sharpe 1.25 .50
❑ 118 Jeff Garcia AU/325 RC 100.00 50.00
❑ 119 Brian Griese 2.00 .75
❑ 120 Justin Watson/325 RC 25.00 10.00
❑ 121 Bubby Brister 1.25 .50
❑ 122 Ryan Leaf 2.00 .75
❑ 123 Natrone Means 1.25 .50
❑ 124 Mikhael Ricks .75 .30
❑ 125 Junior Seau 2.00 .75
❑ 126 Jim Harbaugh 1.25 .50
❑ 127 Andre Rison 1.25 .50
❑ 128 Elvis Grbac 1.25 .50
❑ 129 Bam Morris .75 .30
❑ 130 Rashaan Shehee .75 .30
❑ 131 Warren Moon 2.00 .75
❑ 132 Tony Gonzalez 2.00 .75
❑ 133 Derrick Alexander 1.25 .50
❑ 134 Jon Kitna 2.00 .75
❑ 135 Ricky Watters 1.25 .50
❑ 136 Joey Galloway 1.25 .50
❑ 137 Ahman Green 2.00 .75
❑ 138 Derrick Mayes 1.25 .50
❑ 139 Tyrone Wheatley 1.25 .50
❑ 140 Napoleon Kaufman 2.00 .75
❑ 141 Tim Brown 2.00 .75
❑ 142 Charles Woodson 2.00 .75
❑ 143 Rich Gannon 2.00 .75
❑ 144 Rickey Dudley .75 .30
❑ 145 Az-Zahir Hakim .75 .30
❑ 146 Kurt Warner AU/1825 RC 60.00 30.00
❑ 147 Sean Bennett AU/1325 RC 15.00 6.00
❑ 148 Bran.Stokley AU/1325 RC 30.00 15.00
❑ 149 Amos Zereoue AU/1325 RC 25.00 10.00
❑ 150 Brock Huard AU/1325 RC 25.00 10.00
❑ 151 Tim Couch AU/1025 RC 40.00 15.00
❑ 152 Ricky Williams AU/725 RC 100.00 40.00
❑ 153 Donov McNabb AU/525 RC 200.00 100.00
❑ 154 Edgerrin James AU/525 RC 175.00 100.00
❑ 155 Torry Holt AU/1025 RC 80.00 30.00
❑ 156 D.Culpepper AU/1025 RC 120.00 70.00
❑ 157 Akili Smith AU/1025 RC 20.00 7.50
❑ 158 Champ Bailey AU/1725 RC 30.00 12.50
❑ 159 Chris Claiborne AU/1825 RC 20.00 7.50
❑ 160A C McAlister No AU/1825 RC 15.00 6.00
❑ 160B Jason Tucker AU/1825 15.00 6.00
❑ 161 Troy Edwards AU/1225 RC 20.00 7.50
❑ 162 Jevon Kearse AU/325 RC 80.00 40.00
❑ 163 Darnell McDonald AU/1825 RC 20.00 7.50
❑ 164 David Boston AU/1025 RC 25.00 10.00
❑ 165 Peerless Price AU/1325 RC 30.00 12.50
❑ 166 C.Collins AU/1025 RC 15.00 6.00
❑ 167 Rob Konrad AU/1325 RC 20.00 7.50
❑ 168 Cade McNown AU/1025 RC 20.00 7.50
❑ 169 Shawn Bryson AU/1825 RC 20.00 7.50
❑ 170 Kevin Faulk AU/1325 RC 25.00 10.00
❑ 171 Corby Jones AU/1825 RC 15.00 6.00
❑ 172A Jam Johnson No AU/1325 RC 15.00 6.00
❑ 172B Patrick Jeffers AU/1325 25.00 10.00
❑ 173 Autry Denson AU/1825 RC 20.00 7.50
❑ 174 Sedrick Irvin AU/1825 RC 15.00 6.00
❑ 175 Michael Bishop AU/1825 RC 25.00 10.00
❑ 176 Joe Germaine AU/825 RC 25.00 10.00
❑ 177 De'Mond Parker AU/1325 RC 15.00 6.00
❑ 178A Shaun King No AU/1825 RC 15.00 6.00
❑ 178B Ray Lucas AU/1825 25.00 10.00
❑ 179 D'Wayne Bates AU/1825 RC 20.00 7.50
❑ 180 Tai Streets AU/1825 RC 25.00 10.00
❑ 181 Na Brown AU/1825 RC 20.00 7.50
❑ 182 Desmond Clark AU/1825 RC 20.00 7.50
❑ 183 Jim Kleinsasser AU/1825 RC 20.00 7.50
❑ 184 Kevin Johnson AU/1325 RC 25.00 10.00
❑ 185 Joe Montgomery AU/1325 RC 20.00 7.50
❑ 186 John Elway PT 10.00 4.00
❑ 187 Dan Marino PT 10.00 4.00
❑ 188 Jerry Rice PT 6.00 2.50
❑ 189 Barry Sanders PT 10.00 4.00
❑ 190 Steve Young PT 4.00 1.50
❑ 191 Doug Flutie PT 2.50 1.00
❑ 192 Troy Aikman PT 6.00 2.50
❑ 193 Drew Bledsoe PT 4.00 1.50
❑ 194 Brett Favre PT 10.00 4.00
❑ 195 Randall Cunningham PT 2.50 1.00
❑ 196 Terrell Davis PT 2.50 1.00
❑ 197 Kordell Stewart PT 2.50 1.00
❑ 198 Keyshawn Johnson PT 2.50 1.00
❑ 199 Jake Plummer PT 2.50 1.00
❑ 200 Peyton Manning PT 10.00 4.00
❑ 201 Jay Fiedler/1825 AU 25.00 10.00
❑ 202 Kevin Daft/325 AU 50.00 25.00

2000 Playoff Contenders

❑ COMP.SET w/o SP's (100) 20.00 7.50
❑ 1 David Boston .75 .30
❑ 2 Jake Plummer .50 .20
❑ 3 Chris Chandler .50 .20
❑ 4 Jamal Anderson .75 .30
❑ 5 Tim Dwight .75 .30
❑ 6 Qadry Ismail .50 .20
❑ 7 Tony Banks .50 .20
❑ 8 Lamar Smith .50 .20
❑ 9 Doug Flutie .75 .30
❑ 10 Eric Moulds .75 .30
❑ 11 Peerless Price .50 .20
❑ 12 Rob Johnson .50 .20
❑ 13 Muhsin Muhammad .50 .20
❑ 14 Reggie White .75 .30
❑ 15 Steve Beuerlein .50 .20
❑ 16 Cade McNown .30 .10
❑ 17 Derrick Alexander .50 .20
❑ 18 Marcus Robinson .50 .20
❑ 19 Akili Smith .30 .10
❑ 20 Corey Dillon .75 .30
❑ 21 Kevin Johnson .75 .30
❑ 22 Tim Couch .50 .20
❑ 23 Emmitt Smith 1.50 .60
❑ 24 Joey Galloway .50 .20

❑ 25 Rocket Ismail .50 .20
❑ 26 Troy Aikman 1.50 .60
❑ 27 Brian Griese .75 .30
❑ 28 Ed McCaffrey .75 .30
❑ 29 John Elway 2.50 1.00
❑ 30 Olandis Gary .75 .30
❑ 31 Rod Smith .50 .20
❑ 32 Terrell Davis .75 .30
❑ 33 Charlie Batch .75 .30
❑ 34 Germane Crowell .30 .10
❑ 35 James Stewart .50 .20
❑ 36 Barry Sanders 2.00 .75
❑ 37 Antonio Freeman .75 .30
❑ 38 Brett Favre 2.50 1.00
❑ 39 Dorsey Levens .50 .20
❑ 40 Edgerrin James 1.25 .50
❑ 41 Marvin Harrison .75 .30
❑ 42 Peyton Manning 2.00 .75
❑ 43 Fred Taylor .75 .30
❑ 44 Jimmy Smith .50 .20
❑ 45 Mark Brunell .75 .30
❑ 46 Elvis Grbac .50 .20
❑ 47 Tony Gonzalez .50 .20
❑ 48 Dan Marino 2.50 1.00
❑ 49 Joe Horn .50 .20
❑ 50 Jay Fiedler .75 .30
❑ 51 Thurman Thomas .50 .20
❑ 52 Cris Carter .75 .30
❑ 53 Daunte Culpepper 1.00 .40
❑ 54 Randy Moss 1.50 .60
❑ 55 Robert Smith .75 .30
❑ 56 Drew Bledsoe 1.00 .40
❑ 57 Terry Glenn .50 .20
❑ 58 Ricky Williams .75 .30
❑ 59 Amani Toomer .30 .10
❑ 60 Kerry Collins .50 .20
❑ 61 Curtis Martin .75 .30
❑ 62 Vinny Testaverde .50 .20
❑ 63 Wayne Chrebet .50 .20
❑ 64 Rich Gannon .75 .30
❑ 65 Tim Brown .75 .30
❑ 66 Tyrone Wheatley .50 .20
❑ 67 Donovan McNabb 1.25 .50
❑ 68 Duce Staley .75 .30
❑ 69 Jerome Bettis .75 .30
❑ 70 Jermaine Fazande .30 .10
❑ 71 Junior Seau .75 .30
❑ 72 Donald Hayes .30 .10
❑ 73 Charlie Garner .50 .20
❑ 74 Jeff Garcia .75 .30
❑ 75 Jerry Rice 1.50 .60
❑ 76 Steve Young 1.00 .40
❑ 77 Terrell Owens .75 .30
❑ 78 Tiki Barber .75 .30
❑ 79 Tim Biakabutuka .50 .20
❑ 80 Ricky Watters .50 .20
❑ 81 Isaac Bruce .75 .30
❑ 82 Kurt Warner 1.50 .60
❑ 83 Marshall Faulk 1.00 .40
❑ 84 Torry Holt .75 .30
❑ 85 Keyshawn Johnson .75 .30
❑ 86 Mike Alstott .75 .30
❑ 87 Shaun King .30 .10
❑ 88 Warren Sapp .50 .20
❑ 89 Warrick Dunn .75 .30
❑ 90 Eddie George .75 .30
❑ 91 Jevon Kearse .75 .30
❑ 92 Steve McNair .75 .30
❑ 93 Carl Pickens .50 .20
❑ 94 Albert Connell .30 .10
❑ 95 Brad Johnson .75 .30
❑ 96 Bruce Smith .50 .20
❑ 97 Deion Sanders .75 .30
❑ 98 Jeff George .50 .20
❑ 99 Michael Westbrook .50 .20
❑ 100 Stephen Davis .75 .30
❑ 101 Courtney Brown AU RC 80.00 30.00
❑ 102 Corey Simon AU RC 20.00 7.50
❑ 103 Brian Urlacher AU RC 60.00 35.00
❑ 104 Deon Grant AU RC 15.00 6.00
❑ 105 Peter Warrick AU RC 50.00 20.00
❑ 106 Jamal Lewis AU RC 50.00 25.00
❑ 107 Thomas Jones EXCH
❑ 108 Plaxico Burress AU RC 50.00 25.00
❑ 109 Travis Taylor AU RC 25.00 10.00
❑ 110 Ron Dayne AU RC 40.00 20.00
❑ 111 Bubba Franks AU RC 40.00 15.00
❑ 112 Chad Pennington AU RC 60.00 25.00
❑ 113 Shaun Alexander AU RC 150.00 75.00
❑ 114 Sylvester Morris AU RC 15.00 6.00
❑ 115 Mike Anderson AU RC 30.00 12.50
❑ 116 R.Jay Soward AU RC 15.00 6.00
❑ 117 Trung Canidate AU RC 15.00 6.00
❑ 118 Dennis Northcutt AU RC 20.00 7.50
❑ 119 Todd Pinkston AU RC 20.00 7.50
❑ 120 Jerry Porter AU RC 40.00 15.00
❑ 121 Travis Prentice AU RC 15.00 6.00
❑ 122 Giovanni Carmazzi AU RC 10.00 4.00
❑ 123 Ron Dugans AU RC 10.00 4.00
❑ 124 Dez White AU RC 20.00 7.50
❑ 125 Chris Cole AU RC 15.00 6.00
❑ 126 Ron Dixon AU RC 15.00 6.00
❑ 127 Chris Redman AU RC 15.00 6.00
❑ 128 J.R. Redmond AU RC 20.00 7.50
❑ 129 Laveranues Coles AU RC 30.00 12.50
❑ 130 JaJuan Dawson AU RC 10.00 4.00
❑ 131 Darrell Jackson AU RC 30.00 12.50
❑ 132 Reuben Droughns AU RC 30.00 12.50
❑ 133 Doug Chapman AU RC 15.00 6.00
❑ 134 Curtis Keaton AU RC 15.00 6.00
❑ 135 Gari Scott AU RC 10.00 4.00
❑ 136 Danny Farmer AU RC 15.00 6.00
❑ 137 Trevor Gaylor AU RC 15.00 6.00
❑ 138 Avion Black AU RC 15.00 6.00
❑ 139 Michael Wiley AU RC 15.00 6.00
❑ 140 Sammy Morris AU RC 15.00 6.00
❑ 141 Tee Martin AU RC 20.00 7.50
❑ 142 Troy Walters AU RC 20.00 7.50
❑ 143 Marc Bulger AU RC 50.00 20.00
❑ 144 Tom Brady AU RC 350.00 250.00
❑ 145 Todd Husak AU RC 20.00 7.50
❑ 146 Tim Rattay AU RC 25.00 10.00
❑ 147 Jarious Jackson AU RC 15.00 6.00
❑ 148 Joe Hamilton AU RC 15.00 6.00
❑ 149 Shyrone Stith AU RC 15.00 6.00
❑ 150 Kwame Cavil AU RC 10.00 4.00
❑ 151 Antonio Banks ET AU RC 6.00 2.50
❑ 152 Jonathan Brown ET AU RC 6.00 2.50
❑ 153 Ontiwaun Carter ET AU RC 6.00 2.50
❑ 154 Jeremaine Copeland ET 6.00 2.50
❑ 155 Ralph Dawkins ET AU RC 8.00 3.00
❑ 156 Marques Douglas ET AU RC 6.00 2.50
❑ 157 Kevin Drake ET AU RC 6.00 2.50
❑ 158 Damon Dunn ET AU RC 8.00 3.00
❑ 159 Todd Floyd ET AU RC 6.00 2.50
❑ 160 Tony Graziani ET AU 8.00 3.00
❑ 161 Derrick Ham ET EXCH
❑ 162 Duane Hawthorne ET AU RC 8.003.00
❑ 163 Alonzo Johnson ET AU RC 6.00 2.50
❑ 164 Mark Kacmarynski ET AU RC 6.002.50
❑ 165 Eric Kresser ET AU 6.00 2.50
❑ 166 Jim Kubiak ET AU RC 8.00 3.00
❑ 167 Blaine McElmurry ET AU RC 6.00 2.50
❑ 168 Scott Milanovich ET AU 10.00 4.00
❑ 169 Norman Miller ET AU RC 6.00 2.50
❑ 170 Sean Morey ET AU RC 8.00 3.00
❑ 171 Jeff Ogden ET AU 8.00 3.00
❑ 172 Pepe Pearson ET AU RC 8.00 3.00
❑ 173 Ron Powlus ET AU RC 10.00 4.00
❑ 174 Jason Shelley ET AU RC 8.00 3.00
❑ 175 Ben Snell ET AU RC 8.00 3.00
❑ 176 Aaron Stecker ET AU RC 8.00 3.00
❑ 177 L.C. Stevens ET AU 6.00 2.50
❑ 178 Mike Sutton ET AU RC 6.00 2.50
❑ 179 Damian Vaughn ET AU RC 6.00 2.50
❑ 180 Ted White ET AU 6.00 2.50
❑ 181 Marcus Crandell ET AU RC 8.00 3.00
❑ 182 Darryl Daniel ET AU RC 8.00 3.00
❑ 183 Jesse Haynes ET AU 6.00 2.50
❑ 184 Matt Lytle ET AU RC 8.00 3.00
❑ 185 Deon Mitchell ET AU RC 8.00 3.00
❑ 186 Kendrick Nord ET AU RC 6.00 2.50
❑ 187 Ronnie Powell EXCH
❑ 188 Selucio Sanford ET AU RC 8.00 3.00
❑ 189 Corey Thomas ET AU 6.00 2.50
❑ 190 Vershan Jackson ET AU RC 6.00 2.50
❑ 191 Jake Plummer PT 20.00 7.50
❑ 192 Jim Kelly PT AU 40.00 15.00
❑ 193 Bernie Kosar PT AU 40.00 15.00
❑ 194 Marvin Harrison PT AU 40.00 15.00
❑ 195 Fred Taylor PT EXCH
❑ 196 Kerry Collins PT AU 30.00 12.50
❑ 197 Kurt Warner PT AU 60.00 25.00
❑ 198 Jevon Kearse PT AU 30.00 12.50
❑ 199 Brad Johnson PT AU 30.00 12.50
❑ 200 Jeff George PT AU 30.00 12.50

2001 Playoff Contenders

❑ COMP.SET w/o SP's (100) 25.00 10.00
❑ 1 David Boston 1.00 .40
❑ 2 Jake Plummer .60 .25
❑ 3 Jamal Anderson 1.00 .40
❑ 4 Chris Chandler .60 .25
❑ 5 Elvis Grbac .60 .25
❑ 6 Brandon Stokley .60 .25
❑ 7 Travis Taylor .60 .25
❑ 8 Ray Lewis 1.00 .40
❑ 9 Rob Johnson .60 .25
❑ 10 Eric Moulds .60 .25
❑ 11 Tim Biakabutuka .60 .25
❑ 12 Muhsin Muhammad .60 .25
❑ 13 James Allen .60 .25
❑ 14 Brian Urlacher 1.50 .60
❑ 15 Peter Warrick 1.00 .40
❑ 16 Corey Dillon 1.00 .40
❑ 17 Tim Couch .60 .25
❑ 18 Kevin Johnson .60 .25
❑ 19 Rickey Dudley .40 .10
❑ 20 Emmitt Smith 2.00 .75
❑ 21 Joey Galloway .60 .25
❑ 22 Brian Griese 1.00 .40
❑ 23 Terrell Davis 1.00 .40
❑ 24 Mike Anderson 1.00 .40
❑ 25 Ed McCaffrey 1.00 .40
❑ 26 Rod Smith .60 .25
❑ 27 Charlie Batch 1.00 .40
❑ 28 James Stewart .60 .25
❑ 29 Germane Crowell .40 .10
❑ 30 Johnnie Morton .60 .25
❑ 31 Brett Favre 3.00 1.25
❑ 32 Ahman Green 1.00 .40
❑ 33 Antonio Freeman 1.00 .40
❑ 34 Peyton Manning 2.50 1.00
❑ 35 Edgerrin James 1.25 .50
❑ 36 Marvin Harrison 1.00 .40
❑ 37 Jerome Pathon .60 .25
❑ 38 Mark Brunell 1.00 .40
❑ 39 Fred Taylor 1.00 .40

❑ 40 Keenan McCardell	.40	.10
❑ 41 Jimmy Smith	.60	.25
❑ 42 Trent Green	1.00	.40
❑ 43 Priest Holmes	1.25	.50
❑ 44 Tony Gonzalez	.60	.25
❑ 45 Derrick Alexander	.60	.25
❑ 46 Jay Fiedler	1.00	.40
❑ 47 Lamar Smith	.60	.25
❑ 48 Zach Thomas	1.00	.40
❑ 49 Oronde Gadsden	.60	.25
❑ 50 Daunte Culpepper	1.00	.40
❑ 51 Randy Moss	2.00	.75
❑ 52 Cris Carter	1.00	.40
❑ 53 Drew Bledsoe	1.25	.50
❑ 54 J.R. Redmond	.40	.10
❑ 55 Troy Brown	.60	.25
❑ 56 Aaron Brooks	1.00	.40
❑ 57 Ricky Williams	1.00	.40
❑ 58 Joe Horn	.60	.25
❑ 59 Kerry Collins	.60	.25
❑ 60 Tiki Barber	1.00	.40
❑ 61 Ron Dayne	1.00	.40
❑ 62 Ike Hilliard	.60	.25
❑ 63 Vinny Testaverde	.60	.25
❑ 64 Curtis Martin	1.00	.40
❑ 65 Wayne Chrebet	.60	.25
❑ 66 Laveranues Coles	1.00	.40
❑ 67 Rich Gannon	1.00	.40
❑ 68 Tyrone Wheatley	.60	.25
❑ 69 Tim Brown	1.00	.40
❑ 70 Jerry Rice	2.00	.75
❑ 71 Donovan McNabb	1.25	.50
❑ 72 Duce Staley	1.00	.40
❑ 73 Todd Pinkston	.60	.25
❑ 74 Kordell Stewart	.60	.25
❑ 75 Jerome Bettis	1.00	.40
❑ 76 Plaxico Burress	1.00	.40
❑ 77 Doug Flutie	1.00	.40
❑ 78 Junior Seau	1.00	.40
❑ 79 Jeff Garcia	1.00	.40
❑ 80 Garrison Hearst	.60	.25
❑ 81 Terrell Owens	1.00	.40
❑ 82 Matt Hasselbeck	.60	.25
❑ 83 Ricky Watters	.60	.25
❑ 84 Shaun Alexander	1.25	.50
❑ 85 Darrell Jackson	1.00	.40
❑ 86 Kurt Warner	2.00	.75
❑ 87 Marshall Faulk	1.25	.50
❑ 88 Isaac Bruce	1.00	.40
❑ 89 Torry Holt	1.00	.40
❑ 90 Brad Johnson	1.00	.40
❑ 91 Keyshawn Johnson	1.00	.40
❑ 92 Warrick Dunn	1.00	.40
❑ 93 Warren Sapp	.60	.25
❑ 94 Steve McNair	1.00	.40
❑ 95 Eddie George	1.00	.40
❑ 96 Derrick Mason	.60	.25
❑ 97 Jevon Kearse	.60	.25
❑ 98 Stephen Davis	1.00	.40
❑ 99 Bruce Smith	.60	.25
❑ 100 Michael Westbrook	.60	.25
❑ 101 Adam Archuleta/50 RC	80.00	40.00
❑ 102 Alex Bannister AU RC	15.00	6.00
❑ 103 Alge Crumpler AU RC	30.00	15.00
❑ 104 Andre Carter AU/100 RC	50.00	25.00
❑ 105 Anthony Thomas AU/600 RC	25.00	10.00
❑ 106 Ben Leard AU RC	10.00	4.00
❑ 107 Bobby Newcombe AU RC	15.00	6.00
❑ 108 Brian Allen AU RC	10.00	4.00
❑ 109 Carlos Polk AU RC	10.00	4.00
❑ 110 Casey Hampton No Auto RC	25.00	10.00
❑ 111 Cedric Scott AU RC	10.00	4.00
❑ 112 Cedrick Wilson AU RC	30.00	15.00
❑ 113 Chad Johnson AU RC	125.00	75.00
❑ 114 Chris Chambers AU/170 RC	150.00	90.00
❑ 115 Chris Weinke AU/350 RC	30.00	15.00
❑ 116 Correll Buckhalter AU/590 RC	30.00	15.00
❑ 117 Damione Lewis AU RC	25.00	10.00
❑ 118 Dan Morgan AU RC	50.00	25.00
❑ 119 Daniel Guy AU RC	10.00	4.00
❑ 120 David Allen AU RC	10.00	4.00
❑ 121 David Terrell AU/500 RC	25.00	10.00
❑ 122 Ken Lucas AU/276 RC	10.00	4.00
❑ 123 Deu McAllister AU/500 RC	80.00	40.00
❑ 124 Drew Brees AU/500 RC	100.00	60.00
❑ 125 Eddie Berlin AU RC	10.00	4.00
❑ 126 Boo Williams AU/50 RC	60.00	30.00
❑ 127 Ennis Davis AU RC	10.00	4.00
❑ 128 Freddie Mitchell AU RC	25.00	10.00
❑ 129 Gary Baxter AU RC	15.00	6.00
❑ 130 Gerard Warren AU/200 RC	40.00	20.00
❑ 131 Hakim Akbar AU RC	10.00	4.00
❑ 132 Heath Evans AU RC	10.00	4.00
❑ 133 Jabari Holloway AU RC	15.00	6.00
❑ 134 Jamal Reynolds AU/500 RC	15.00	6.00
❑ 135 James Jackson AU RC	15.00	6.00
❑ 136 Jamie Winborn AU RC	10.00	4.00
❑ 137 Javon Green AU RC	10.00	4.00
❑ 138 Jesse Palmer AU RC	25.00	10.00
❑ 139 Dominic Rhodes AU/300 RC	60.00	35.00
❑ 140 Josh Heupel AU/150 RC	50.00	20.00
❑ 141 Justin Smith AU RC	15.00	6.00
❑ 142 Karon Riley AU RC	10.00	4.00
❑ 143 Keith Adams/50 RC	80.00	40.00
❑ 144 Kendrell Bell AU RC	40.00	15.00
❑ 145 Kenny Smith AU RC	15.00	6.00
❑ 146 Ken. Walker AU/50 RC	80.00	40.00
❑ 147 Ken-Yon Rambo AU RC	10.00	4.00
❑ 148 Kevan Barlow AU RC	40.00	15.00
❑ 149 Koren Robinson AU/400 RC	30.00	12.50
❑ 150 L.Tomlinson AU/600 RC	400.00	200.00
❑ 151 LaMont Jordan AU/50 RC	500.00	350.00
❑ 152 Leonard Davis/50 RC	80.00	40.00
❑ 153 Marcus Stroud AU RC	25.00	10.00
❑ 154 Marques Tuiasosopo AU RC	30.00	12.50
❑ 155 Snoop Minnis AU/295 RC	15.00	6.00
❑ 156 Michael Bennett AU/600 RC	40.00	15.00
❑ 157 Michael Vick AU/327 RC	400.00	200.00
❑ 158 Mike McMahon AU/529 RC	30.00	18.00
❑ 159 Moran Norris AU RC	10.00	4.00
❑ 160 Morlon Greenwood AU RC	10.00	4.00
❑ 161 Nate Clements/50 RC	80.00	40.00
❑ 162 Quincy Carter AU SP RC	150.00	60.00
❑ 163 Quincy Morgan AU RC	25.00	10.00
❑ 164 Jamar Fletcher/50 RC	80.00	40.00
❑ 165 Reggie Germany AU RC	10.00	4.00
❑ 166 Reggie Wayne AU/400 RC	80.00	50.00
❑ 167 Reggie White AU RC	10.00	4.00
❑ 168 Richard Seymour/50 RC	100.00	50.00
❑ 169 Robert Carswell/50 RC	60.00	30.00
❑ 170 Robert Ferguson AU RC	25.00	10.00
❑ 171 Rod Gardner AU/75 RC	150.00	75.00
❑ 172 Ronney Daniels AU RC	10.00	4.00
❑ 173 Rudi Johnson AU RC	75.00	40.00
❑ 174 Sage Rosenfels AU/400 RC	25.00	10.00
❑ 175 Santana Moss AU/500 RC	60.00	30.00
❑ 176 Shaun Rogers AU RC	25.00	10.00
❑ 177 Houshmandzadeh AU RC	30.00	15.00
❑ 178 Tim Hasselbeck AU RC	25.00	10.00
❑ 179 Todd Heap AU/169 RC	120.00	60.00
❑ 180 Tony Stewart AU RC	15.00	6.00
❑ 181 Torrance Marshall AU RC	15.00	6.00
❑ 182 Travis Henry AU/369 RC	25.00	10.00
❑ 183 Travis Minor AU RC	25.00	10.00
❑ 184 Vinny Sutherland AU RC	15.00	6.00
❑ 185 Will Allen AU RC	15.00	6.00
❑ 186 Willie Howard AU RC	10.00	4.00
❑ 187 W Middlebrooks/50 RC	60.00	30.00
❑ 188 Derrick Blaylock AU/200 RC	75.00	40.00
❑ 189 A.J. Feeley AU/200 RC	80.00	30.00
❑ 190 Steve Smith AU/300 RC	150.00	90.00
❑ 191 Onome Ojo AU/200 RC	15.00	6.00
❑ 192 Dee Brown AU/300 RC	25.00	10.00
❑ 193 Kevin Kasper AU/200 RC	25.00	10.00
❑ 194 Dave Dickenson AU/300 RC	25.00	10.00
❑ 195 Chris Barnes AU/200 RC	25.00	10.00
❑ 196 Scotty Anderson AU/300 RC	25.00	10.00
❑ 197 Chris Taylor AU/300 RC	15.00	6.00
❑ 198 Cedric James AU/300 SP RC	25.00	10.00
❑ 199 Justin McCareins AU/200 RC	50.00	20.00
❑ 200 Tommy Polley AU/200 RC	25.00	10.00

2002 Playoff Contenders

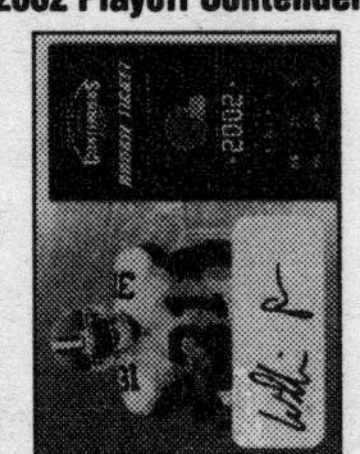

❑ COMP.SET w/o SP's (100)	25.00	10.00
❑ 1 Drew Bledsoe	1.25	.50
❑ 2 Travis Henry	1.00	.40
❑ 3 Eric Moulds	.60	.25
❑ 4 Chris Chambers	1.00	.40
❑ 5 Ricky Williams	1.00	.40
❑ 6 Zach Thomas	1.00	.40
❑ 7 Tom Brady	2.50	1.00
❑ 8 Antowain Smith	.60	.25
❑ 9 Troy Brown	.60	.25
❑ 10 Curtis Martin	1.00	.40
❑ 11 Vinny Testaverde	.60	.25
❑ 12 Chad Pennington	1.25	.50
❑ 13 Jeff Blake	.40	.15
❑ 14 Jamal Lewis	1.00	.40
❑ 15 Ray Lewis	1.00	.40
❑ 16 Michael Westbrook	.40	.15
❑ 17 Corey Dillon	.60	.25
❑ 18 Peter Warrick	.60	.25
❑ 19 Tim Couch	.60	.25
❑ 20 Quincy Morgan	.60	.25
❑ 21 Kevin Johnson	.60	.25
❑ 22 Kordell Stewart	.60	.25
❑ 23 Plaxico Burress	.60	.25
❑ 24 Jerome Bettis	1.00	.40
❑ 25 James Allen	.60	.25
❑ 26 Corey Bradford	.40	.15
❑ 27 Mark Brunell	1.00	.40
❑ 28 Fred Taylor	1.00	.40
❑ 29 Jimmy Smith	.60	.25
❑ 30 Peyton Manning	2.00	.75
❑ 31 Reggie Wayne	1.00	.40
❑ 32 Marvin Harrison	1.00	.40
❑ 33 Edgerrin James	1.25	.50
❑ 34 Steve McNair	1.00	.40
❑ 35 Eddie George	1.00	.40
❑ 36 Jevon Kearse	.60	.25
❑ 37 Derrick Mason	.60	.25
❑ 38 Brian Griese	1.00	.40
❑ 39 Terrell Davis	1.00	.40
❑ 40 Ed McCaffrey	1.00	.40
❑ 41 Rod Smith	.60	.25
❑ 42 Trent Green	.60	.25
❑ 43 Priest Holmes	1.25	.50
❑ 44 Johnnie Morton	.60	.25
❑ 45 Tony Gonzalez	.60	.25
❑ 46 Rich Gannon	1.00	.40
❑ 47 Tim Brown	1.00	.40
❑ 48 Jerry Rice	2.00	.75
❑ 49 Charlie Garner	.60	.25
❑ 50 Drew Brees	1.00	.40
❑ 51 LaDainian Tomlinson	1.50	.60
❑ 52 Junior Seau	1.00	.40
❑ 53 Quincy Carter	.60	.25
❑ 54 Emmitt Smith	2.50	1.00

❑ 55 Joey Galloway .60 .25
❑ 56 Kerry Collins .60 .25
❑ 57 Tiki Barber 1.00 .40
❑ 58 Michael Strahan .60 .25
❑ 59 Donovan McNabb 1.25 .50
❑ 60 Duce Staley 1.00 .40
❑ 61 Antonio Freeman 1.00 .40
❑ 62 Derrius Thompson .40 .15
❑ 63 Stephen Davis .60 .25
❑ 64 Rod Gardner .60 .25
❑ 65 Anthony Thomas .60 .25
❑ 66 Marty Booker .60 .25
❑ 67 Brian Urlacher 1.50 .60
❑ 68 James Stewart .60 .25
❑ 69 Az-Zahir Hakim .40 .15
❑ 70 Brett Favre 2.50 1.00
❑ 71 Ahman Green 1.00 .40
❑ 72 Donald Driver .60 .25
❑ 73 Daunte Culpepper 1.00 .40
❑ 74 Michael Bennett .60 .25
❑ 75 Randy Moss 2.00 .75
❑ 76 Michael Vick 3.00 1.25
❑ 77 Warrick Dunn 1.00 .40
❑ 78 Chris Weinke .60 .25
❑ 79 Lamar Smith .60 .25
❑ 80 Steve Smith 1.00 .40
❑ 81 Aaron Brooks 1.00 .40
❑ 82 Deuce McAllister 1.25 .50
❑ 83 Joe Horn .60 .25
❑ 84 Brad Johnson .60 .25
❑ 85 Keyshawn Johnson 1.00 .40
❑ 86 Mike Alstott 1.00 .40
❑ 87 Warren Sapp .60 .25
❑ 88 Jake Plummer .60 .25
❑ 89 Thomas Jones .60 .25
❑ 90 David Boston 1.00 .40
❑ 91 Kurt Warner 1.00 .40
❑ 92 Marshall Faulk 1.00 .40
❑ 93 Isaac Bruce 1.00 .40
❑ 94 Torry Holt 1.00 .40
❑ 95 Jeff Garcia 1.00 .40
❑ 96 Garrison Hearst .60 .25
❑ 97 Kevan Barlow .60 .25
❑ 98 Terrell Owens 1.00 .40
❑ 99 Trent Dilfer .60 .25
❑ 100 Shaun Alexander 1.25 .50
❑ 101 Adrian Peterson AU/360 RC 40.00 20.00
❑ 102 A.Haynesworth No Auto RC 30.00 12.50
❑ 103 Alex Brown AU/410 RC 40.00 20.00
❑ 104 Andra Davis AU/510 RC 15.00 6.00
❑ 105 Andre Davis AU/360 RC 30.00 12.50
❑ 106 Andre Lott AU/750 RC 15.00 6.00
❑ 107 Anthony Weaver AU/450 RC 15.00 6.00
❑ 108 Antonio Bryant AU/165 RC 80.00 50.00
❑ 109 Antw Randle El AU/135 RC 150.00 75.00
❑ 110 Ashley Lelie AU/360 RC 80.00 40.00
❑ 111 Brian Poli-Dixon AU/460 RC 20.00 7.50
❑ 112 Brian Westbrook AU/600 RC 60.00 30.00
❑ 113 Bryant McKinnie AU/600 RC 30.00 12.50
❑ 114 C Hutchinson AU/450 RC 20.00 7.50
❑ 115 Charles Grant AU/450 RC 20.00 7.50
❑ 116 Chester Taylor AU/315 RC 60.00 35.00
❑ 117 Cliff Russell AU/545 RC 20.00 7.50
❑ 118 Clinton Portis AU/360 RC 200.00 100.00
❑ 119 R.McMichael AU/400 RC 30.00 12.50
❑ 120 Damien Anderson AU/460 RC 15.00 6.00
❑ 121 Daniel Graham AU/185 RC 50.00 20.00
❑ 122 David Carr AU/250 RC 150.00 90.00
❑ 123 David Garrard AU/310 RC 60.00 35.00
❑ 124 Deion Branch AU/650 RC 50.00 20.00
❑ 125 John Simon AU/400 RC 20.00 7.50
❑ 126 DeShaun Foster AU/310 RC 80.00 40.00
❑ 127 Donte Stallworth AU/302 RC 60.00 25.00
❑ 128 Dwight Freeney AU/410 RC 60.00 35.00
❑ 129 Ed Reed AU/550 RC 50.00 25.00
❑ 130 Eric Crouch AU/280 RC 30.00 12.50
❑ 131 Freddie Milons AU/380 RC 20.00 7.50
❑ 132 Jabar Gaffney AU/315 RC 30.00 12.50
❑ 133 Javon Walker AU/435 RC 100.00 50.00
❑ 134 Jeremy Shockey AU/160 RC 200.00 100.00
❑ 135 Jerramy Stevens AU/250 RC 30.00 12.50
❑ 136 Joey Harrington AU/250 RC 120.00 60.00
❑ 137 John Henderson AU/560 RC 30.00 12.50
❑ 138 Jonathan Wells AU/485 RC 40.00 15.00
❑ 139 Josh McCown AU/595 RC 40.00 25.00
❑ 140 Josh Reed AU/290 RC 40.00 15.00
❑ 141 Josh Scobey AU/615 RC 15.00 6.00
❑ 142 Julius Peppers AU/40 RC 350.00 250.00
❑ 143 Kalimba Edwards AU/510 RC 20.00 7.50
❑ 144 Kelly Campbell AU/360 RC 30.00 12.50
❑ 145 Ken Simonton AU/650 RC 15.00 6.00
❑ 146 Keyuo Craver AU/850 RC 15.00 6.00
❑ 147 Kahlil Hill AU/850 RC 20.00 7.50
❑ 148 Kurt Kittner AU/235 RC 20.00 7.50
❑ 149 Ladell Betts AU/600 RC 30.00 12.50
❑ 150 Lamar Gordon AU/600 RC 30.00 12.50
❑ 151 Levar Fisher AU/760 RC 15.00 6.00
❑ 152 Lito Sheppard AU/410 RC 30.00 12.50
❑ 153 Luke Staley AU/360 RC 20.00 7.50
❑ 154 Marquise Walker AU/330 RC 30.00 12.50
❑ 155 Maurice Morris AU/153 RC 60.00 25.00
❑ 156 Mike Rumph AU/510 RC 30.00 12.50
❑ 157 Mike Williams AU/500 RC 20.00 7.50
❑ 158 Najeh Davenport AU/460 RC 30.00 12.50
❑ 159 Napoleon Harris AU/900 RC 20.00 7.50
❑ 160 Patrick Ramsey AU/575 RC 50.00 20.00
❑ 161 Buchanon No AU/310 RC 50.00 20.00
❑ 162 Quentin Jammer AU/300 RC 30.00 12.50
❑ 163 Randy Fasani AU/500 RC 20.00 7.50
❑ 164 Reche Caldwell AU/340 RC 30.00 12.50
❑ 165 Robert Thomas AU/460 RC 30.00 12.50
❑ 166 Rocky Calmus AU/385 RC 30.00 12.50
❑ 167 Rohan Davey AU/295 RC 50.00 25.00
❑ 168 Ron Johnson AU/385 RC 20.00 7.50
❑ 169 Roy Williams AU/250 RC 120.00 60.00
❑ 170 Ryan Sims No AU/360 RC 30.00 12.50
❑ 171 Tavon Mason AU/690 RC 15.00 6.00
❑ 172 Terry Charles AU/750 RC 15.00 6.00
❑ 173 T.J. Duckett AU/335 RC 40.00 15.00
❑ 174 Tim Carter AU/600 RC 20.00 7.50
❑ 175 Travis Stephens AU/170 RC 60.00 25.00
❑ 176 Trev Faulk AU/600 RC 15.00 6.00
❑ 177 Wendell Bryant AU/560 RC 15.00 6.00
❑ 178 William Green AU/317 RC 30.00 12.50
❑ 179 Woody Dantzler AU/185 RC 30.00 12.50
❑ 180 Tony Fisher AU/340 RC 30.00 12.50
❑ 181 Javin Hunter AU/400 RC 15.00 6.00
❑ 182 Daryl Jones AU/400 RC 20.00 7.50
❑ 183 Jesse Chatman AU/400 RC 30.00 12.50
❑ 184 J.T. O'Sullivan AU/340 RC 20.00 7.50
❑ 185 Josh Norman AU/340 RC 30.00 12.50
❑ 186 James Mungro AU/100 RC 100.00 40.00

2003 Playoff Contenders

❑ COMP.SET w/o SP's (100) 20.00 7.50
❑ UNPRICED CHAMPION.TICKET #'d TO 1
❑ 1 Roy Williams .75 .30
❑ 2 Antonio Bryant .50 .20
❑ 3 Jeremy Shockey 1.25 .50
❑ 4 Kerry Collins .50 .20
❑ 5 Tiki Barber .75 .30
❑ 6 Michael Strahan .50 .20
❑ 7 Donovan McNabb 1.00 .40
❑ 8 Duce Staley .50 .20
❑ 9 Todd Pinkston .50 .20
❑ 10 Patrick Ramsey .75 .30
❑ 11 Laveranues Coles .50 .20
❑ 12 Rod Gardner .50 .20
❑ 13 Drew Bledsoe .75 .30
❑ 14 Travis Henry .50 .20
❑ 15 Eric Moulds .50 .20
❑ 16 Josh Reed .50 .20
❑ 17 Ricky Williams .75 .30
❑ 18 Jay Fiedler .50 .20
❑ 19 Chris Chambers .75 .30
❑ 20 Zach Thomas .75 .30
❑ 21 Junior Seau .75 .30
❑ 22 Tom Brady 2.00 .75
❑ 23 Troy Brown .50 .20
❑ 24 Chad Pennington 1.00 .40
❑ 25 Curtis Martin .75 .30
❑ 26 Santana Moss .50 .20
❑ 27 Emmitt Smith 2.00 .75
❑ 28 Jeff Garcia .75 .30
❑ 29 Terrell Owens .75 .30
❑ 30 Kevan Barlow .50 .20
❑ 31 Shaun Alexander .75 .30
❑ 32 Matt Hasselbeck .50 .20
❑ 33 Koren Robinson .50 .20
❑ 34 Kurt Warner .75 .30
❑ 35 Marshall Faulk .75 .30
❑ 36 Torry Holt .75 .30
❑ 37 Isaac Bruce .75 .30
❑ 38 Clinton Portis 1.25 .50
❑ 39 Jake Plummer .50 .20
❑ 40 Rod Smith .50 .20
❑ 41 Ed McCaffrey .75 .30
❑ 42 Ashley Lelie .75 .30
❑ 43 Priest Holmes 1.00 .40
❑ 44 Trent Green .50 .20
❑ 45 Tony Gonzalez .50 .20
❑ 46 Jerry Rice 1.50 .60
❑ 47 Rich Gannon .50 .20
❑ 48 Tim Brown .75 .30
❑ 49 Jerry Porter .50 .20
❑ 50 Charles Woodson .50 .20
❑ 51 LaDainian Tomlinson .75 .30
❑ 52 Drew Brees .75 .30
❑ 53 David Boston .50 .20
❑ 54 Brian Urlacher 1.25 .50
❑ 55 Kordell Stewart .50 .20
❑ 56 Marty Booker .50 .20
❑ 57 Joey Harrington 1.25 .50
❑ 58 Brett Favre 2.00 .75
❑ 59 Ahman Green .75 .30
❑ 60 Donald Driver .50 .20
❑ 61 Javon Walker .50 .20
❑ 62 Randy Moss 1.25 .50
❑ 63 Daunte Culpepper .75 .30
❑ 64 Michael Bennett .50 .20
❑ 65 Jamal Lewis .75 .30
❑ 66 Ray Lewis .75 .30
❑ 67 Corey Dillon .50 .20
❑ 68 Chad Johnson .75 .30
❑ 69 William Green .50 .20
❑ 70 Tim Couch .30 .10
❑ 71 Quincy Morgan .50 .20
❑ 72 Plaxico Burress .50 .20
❑ 73 Tommy Maddox .75 .30
❑ 74 Hines Ward .75 .30
❑ 75 Antwaan Randle El .75 .30
❑ 76 Michael Vick 2.00 .75
❑ 77 Peerless Price .50 .20
❑ 78 Warrick Dunn .50 .20
❑ 79 T.J. Duckett .50 .20
❑ 80 Julius Peppers .75 .30
❑ 81 Stephen Davis .50 .20

❑ 82 Deuce McAllister .75 .30
❑ 83 Aaron Brooks .75 .30
❑ 84 Joe Horn .50 .20
❑ 85 Donte Stallworth .75 .30
❑ 86 Mike Alstott .75 .30
❑ 87 Brad Johnson .50 .20
❑ 88 Keyshawn Johnson .75 .30
❑ 89 Warren Sapp .50 .20
❑ 90 David Carr 1.25 .50
❑ 91 Jabar Gaffney .50 .20
❑ 92 Peyton Manning 1.25 .50
❑ 93 Edgerrin James .75 .30
❑ 94 Marvin Harrison .75 .30
❑ 95 Mark Brunell .50 .20
❑ 96 Fred Taylor .75 .30
❑ 97 Jimmy Smith .50 .20
❑ 98 Steve McNair .75 .30
❑ 99 Eddie George .50 .20
❑ 100 Jevon Kearse .50 .20
❑ 101 Lee Suggs AU/499 RC 50.00 20.00
❑ 102 Charles Rogers AU/204 RC 120.00 50.00
❑ 103 Brandon Lloyd AU/589 RC 50.0025.00
❑ 104 Terrence Edwards AU/399 RC 15.00 6.00
❑ 105 Mike Pinkard AU/849 RC 12.00 5.00
❑ 106 DeWayne White AU/524 RC 12.005.00
❑ 107 Jero McDougle AU/339 RC 20.00 7.50
❑ 108 Jimmy Kennedy AU/514 RC 20.007.50
❑ 109 William Joseph AU/764 RC 15.00 6.00
❑ 110 E.J. Henderson AU/774 RC 20.00 7.50
❑ 111 Mike Doss AU/574 RC 20.00 7.50
❑ 112A C.Simms Blk AU/310 RC 100.00 60.00
❑ 112B C.Simms Blu AU/79 RC 150.0075.00
❑ 113 Cecil Sapp AU/474 RC 15.00 6.00
❑ 114 Justin Gage AU/579 RC 20.00 7.50
❑ 115 Sam Aiken AU/664 RC 15.00 6.00
❑ 116 Doug Gabriel AU/389 RC 40.00 15.00
❑ 117 Jason Witten AU/599 RC 50.00 25.00
❑ 118 Bennie Joppru AU/449 RC 20.00 7.50
❑ 119 Chris Kelsay AU/864 RC 15.00 6.00
❑ 120 John.Sullivan/924 RC 10.00 4.00
❑ 121 Kevin Williams AU/764 RC 20.00 7.50
❑ 122 Rien Long AU/849 RC 12.00 5.00
❑ 123 Kenny Peterson/674 RC 15.00 6.00
❑ 124 Boss Bailey AU/564 RC 20.00 7.50
❑ 125 Denn Weathersby AU/774 RC 12.00 5.00
❑ 126A Car.Palmer Blk AU/36 RC 400.00 250.00
❑ 126B Car.Palmer Blu AU/158 RC 350.00 200.00
❑ 127 Byron Leftwich AU/169 RC 350.00 175.00
❑ 128 Kyle Boller AU/439 RC 60.00 25.00
❑ 129 Rex Grossman AU/494 RC 80.0040.00
❑ 130 Dave Ragone AU/344 RC 20.00 7.50
❑ 131 Brian St.Pierre AU/554 RC 15.00 6.00
❑ 132 Kliff Kingsbury AU/879 RC 20.00 7.50
❑ 133 Seneca Wallace AU/864 RC 20.007.50
❑ 134 Larry Johnson AU/344 RC 400.00 300.00
❑ 135 Will McGahee AU/369 RC 150.0075.00
❑ 136 Justin Fargas AU/354 RC 20.00 7.50
❑ 137 Onterrio Smith AU/414 RC 20.00 7.50
❑ 138 Chris Brown AU/279 RC 80.00 30.00
❑ 139 Musa Smith AU/379 RC 20.00 7.50
❑ 140 Artose Pinner AU/364 RC 30.00 12.50
❑ 141 Andre Johnson AU/199 RC 175.00 100.00
❑ 142 Kell Washington AU/472 RC 25.00 10.00
❑ 143 Taylor Jacobs AU/349 RC 15.00 6.00
❑ 144 Bryant Johnson AU/389 RC 20.00 7.50
❑ 145 Tyrone Calico AU/499 RC 25.00 10.00
❑ 146 Anquan Boldin AU/524 RC 80.00 30.00
❑ 147 Bethel Johnson AU/484 RC 30.0012.50
❑ 148 Nate Burleson AU/549 RC 50.0025.00
❑ 149 Kevin Curtis AU/455 RC 30.00 15.00
❑ 150 Dallas Clark AU/539 RC 30.00 15.00
❑ 151 Teyo Johnson AU/389 RC 20.00 7.50
❑ 152 Terrell Suggs AU/564 RC 30.00 15.00
❑ 153 DeWayne Robertson/689 RC 12.005.00
❑ 154 Terence Newman AU/364 RC 50.00 20.00
❑ 155 Marcus Trufant AU/739 RC 25.0010.00
❑ 156 Tony Romo AU/999 RC 20.00 7.50
❑ 157 Brooks Bollinger AU/974 RC 25.00 10.00
❑ 158 Ken Dorsey AU/774 RC 25.00 10.00
❑ 159 Kirk Farmer AU/999 RC 15.00 6.00
❑ 160 Jason Gesser AU/999 RC 15.00 6.00
❑ 161 Brock Forsey AU/999 RC 15.00 6.00
❑ 162 Quentin Griffin AU/999 RC 20.00 7.50
❑ 163 Avon Cobourne AU/974 RC 12.00 5.00
❑ 164 Domanick Davis AU/999 RC 40.00 15.00
❑ 165 Tony Hollings AU/974 RC 20.00 7.50
❑ 166 LaBran.Toefield AU/799 RC 20.007.50
❑ 167 Arlen Harris AU/974 RC 20.00 7.50
❑ 168 Sult McCullough AU/989 RC 15.006.00
❑ 169 Visant Shiancoe AU/999 RC 12.005.00
❑ 170 L.J. Smith AU/974 RC 20.00 7.50
❑ 171 LaTaren Dunbar AU/999 RC 12.005.00
❑ 172 Walter Young AU/889 RC 12.00 5.00
❑ 173 Bobby Wade AU/989 RC 15.00 6.00
❑ 174 Zuriel Smith AU/989 RC 12.00 5.00
❑ 175 Adrian Madise AU/999 RC 15.00 6.00
❑ 176 Ken Hamlin AU/989 RC 20.00 7.50
❑ 177 Carl Ford AU/999 RC 12.00 5.00
❑ 178 Cortez Hankton AU/989 RC 15.00 6.00
❑ 179 J.R. Tolver AU/889 RC 15.00 6.00
❑ 180 Keenan Howry AU/999 RC 15.00 6.00
❑ 181 Billy McMullen AU/899 RC 15.00 6.00
❑ 182 Arnaz Battle AU/989 RC 25.00 10.00
❑ 183 Shaun McDonald AU/899 RC 15.006.00
❑ 184 Andre Woolfolk AU/989 RC 15.006.00
❑ 185 Sammy Davis AU/999 RC 12.00 5.00
❑ 186 Calvin Pace AU/999 RC 12.00 5.00
❑ 187 Michael Haynes AU/999 RC 15.006.00
❑ 188 Ty Warren AU/999 RC 15.00 6.00
❑ 189 Nick Barnett AU/999 RC 40.00 15.00
❑ 190 Troy Polamalu AU/989 RC 135.00 75.00
❑ 191 Eric Parker AU/589 RC 25.00 10.00
❑ 192 Justin Griffith AU/589 RC 15.00 6.00
❑ 193 David Tyree AU/599 RC 15.00 6.00
❑ 194 Pisa Tinoisamoa/599 RC 20.00 7.50
❑ 195 Rashean Mathis AU/589 RC 12.005.00
❑ 196 Mike Sherman AU/574 RC 30.0012.50
❑ 197 Dave Wannstedt AU/574 RC 20.007.50
❑ 198 Dick Vermeil AU/574 RC 30.00 12.50
❑ 199 Tony Dungy AU/574 RC 30.00 12.50
❑ 200 Mike Martz AU/574 RC 20.00 7.50

2004 Playoff Contenders

❑ COMP.SET w/o SP's (100) 20.00 7.50
❑ EXCH EXPIRATION: 7/01/2006
❑ UNPRICED CHAMP.TICKET PRINT RUN 1
❑ AU PRINT RUNS ANNOUNCED BY PLAYOFF

❑ 1 Anquan Boldin .75 .30
❑ 2 Emmitt Smith 1.50 .60
❑ 3 Josh McCown .50 .20
❑ 4 Michael Vick 1.50 .60
❑ 5 Peerless Price .50 .20
❑ 6 T.J. Duckett .50 .20
❑ 7 Warrick Dunn .50 .20
❑ 8 Jamal Lewis .75 .30
❑ 9 Kyle Boller .75 .30
❑ 10 Ray Lewis .75 .30
❑ 11 Drew Bledsoe .75 .30
❑ 12 Eric Moulds .50 .20
❑ 13 Travis Henry .50 .20
❑ 14 Willis McGahee .75 .30
❑ 15 DeShaun Foster .50 .20
❑ 16 Jake Delhomme .75 .30
❑ 17 Stephen Davis .50 .20
❑ 18 Steve Smith .75 .30
❑ 19 Brian Urlacher 1.00 .40
❑ 20 Rex Grossman .75 .30
❑ 21 Thomas Jones .50 .20
❑ 22 Carson Palmer 1.00 .40
❑ 23 Chad Johnson .75 .30
❑ 24 Rudi Johnson .50 .20
❑ 25 Jeff Garcia .75 .30
❑ 26 Lee Suggs .75 .30
❑ 27 William Green .50 .20
❑ 28 Keyshawn Johnson .50 .20
❑ 29 Roy Williams S .50 .20
❑ 30 Eddie George .50 .20
❑ 31 Ashley Lelie .50 .20
❑ 32 Jake Plummer .50 .20
❑ 33 Quentin Griffin .75 .30
❑ 34 Rod Smith .50 .20
❑ 35 Charles Rogers .50 .20
❑ 36 Joey Harrington .75 .30
❑ 37 Ahman Green .75 .30
❑ 38 Brett Favre 2.00 .75
❑ 39 Javon Walker .50 .20
❑ 40 Andre Johnson .75 .30
❑ 41 David Carr .75 .30
❑ 42 Domanick Davis .75 .30
❑ 43 Edgerrin James .75 .30
❑ 44 Marvin Harrison .75 .30
❑ 45 Peyton Manning 1.25 .50
❑ 46 Byron Leftwich 1.00 .40
❑ 47 Fred Taylor .50 .20
❑ 48 Jimmy Smith .50 .20
❑ 49 Priest Holmes 1.00 .40
❑ 50 Tony Gonzalez .50 .20
❑ 51 Trent Green .50 .20
❑ 52 A.J. Feeley .75 .30
❑ 53 Chris Chambers .50 .20
❑ 54 Deion Sanders .75 .30
❑ 55 Daunte Culpepper .75 .30
❑ 56 Michael Bennett .50 .20
❑ 57 Randy Moss 1.00 .40
❑ 58 Corey Dillon .50 .20
❑ 59 Deion Branch .75 .30
❑ 60 Tom Brady 2.00 .75
❑ 61 Aaron Brooks .50 .20
❑ 62 Deuce McAllister .75 .30
❑ 63 Donte Stallworth .50 .20
❑ 64 Joe Horn .50 .20
❑ 65 Amani Toomer .50 .20
❑ 66 Jeremy Shockey .75 .30
❑ 67 Michael Strahan .50 .20
❑ 68 Tiki Barber .75 .30
❑ 69 Chad Pennington .75 .30
❑ 70 Curtis Martin .75 .30
❑ 71 Santana Moss .50 .20
❑ 72 Jerry Porter .50 .20
❑ 73 Jerry Rice 1.50 .60
❑ 74 Warren Sapp .50 .20
❑ 75 Brian Westbrook .50 .20
❑ 76 Donovan McNabb 1.00 .40
❑ 77 Jevon Kearse .50 .20
❑ 78 Terrell Owens .75 .30
❑ 79 Antwaan Randle El .75 .30
❑ 80 Hines Ward .75 .30
❑ 81 Jerome Bettis .75 .30
❑ 82 LaDainian Tomlinson 1.00 .40
❑ 83 Kevan Barlow .50 .20
❑ 84 Tim Rattay .50 .20
❑ 85 Koren Robinson .50 .20
❑ 86 Matt Hasselbeck .50 .20
❑ 87 Shaun Alexander .75 .30
❑ 88 Isaac Bruce .50 .20
❑ 89 Marc Bulger .75 .30
❑ 90 Marshall Faulk .75 .30

❑ 91 Torry Holt .75 .30
❑ 92 Brad Johnson .50 .20
❑ 93 Mike Alstott .50 .20
❑ 94 Chris Brown .75 .30
❑ 95 Derrick Mason .50 .20
❑ 96 Steve McNair .75 .30
❑ 97 Clinton Portis .75 .30
❑ 98 LaVar Arrington 1.50 .60
❑ 99 Laveranues Coles .50 .20
❑ 100 Mark Brunell .50 .20
❑ 101 Adimchinobe Echemandu AU RC 15.00 6.00
❑ 102 Ahmad Carroll AU/574* RC 25.00 10.00
❑ 103 Andy Hall AU RC 20.00 7.50
❑ 104 B.J. Johnson AU RC 15.00 6.00
❑ 105 B.J. Symons AU RC 20.00 7.50
❑ 106 Roethlisberger AU/541* RC 450.00 250.00
❑ 107 Ben Troupe AU/540* RC 25.00 10.00
❑ 108 Ben Watson AU/660* RC 25.00 10.00
❑ 109 Bernard Berrian AU/653* RC 20.00 7.50
❑ 110 Brandon Miree AU RC 15.00 6.00
❑ 111 Bruce Perry AU RC 20.00 7.50
❑ 112 Carlos Francis AU RC 20.00 7.50
❑ 113 Casey Bramlet AU RC 15.00 6.00
❑ 114 Cedric Cobbs AU/630* RC 25.00 10.00
❑ 115 Chris Gamble AU/490* RC 25.00 12.50
❑ 116 Chris Perry AU/478* RC 50.00 25.00
❑ 117 Clarence Moore AU RC 20.00 7.50
❑ 118 Cody Pickett AU RC 20.00 7.50
❑ 119 Craig Krenzel AU RC 20.00 7.50
❑ 120 D.J. Hackett AU/325* RC 30.00 15.00
❑ 121 D.J. Williams AU/490* RC 25.00 12.50
❑ 122 Darius Watts AU RC 20.00 7.50
❑ 123 DeAngelo Hall AU RC 30.00 12.50
❑ 124 Derrick Hamilton AU/373* RC 20.00 7.50
❑ 125 Derrick Ward AU RC 12.00 5.00
❑ 126 Devard Darling AU/325* RC 25.00 12.50
❑ 127 D.Henderson AU/475* RC 30.00 12.50
❑ 128 Drew Carter AU RC 20.00 7.50
❑ 129 Drew Henson AU/415* RC 30.00 12.50
❑ 130 D.Robinson AU/660* RC 25.00 10.00
❑ 131 Eli Manning AU/372* RC 300.00 150.00
❑ 132 Ernest Wilford AU/365* RC 35.00 20.00
❑ 133 Greg Jones AU/553* RC 40.00 20.00
❑ 134 J.P. Losman AU/358* RC 120.00 50.00
❑ 135 Jamaar Taylor AU RC 20.00 7.50
❑ 136 Jared Lorenzen AU RC 15.00 6.00
❑ 137 Jarrett Payton AU RC 30.00 15.00
❑ 138 Jason Babin AU RC 25.00 10.00
❑ 139 Jeff Smoker AU RC 20.00 7.50
❑ 140 J.Cotchery AU/325* RC 30.00 15.00
❑ 141 Jim Sorgi AU RC 20.00 7.50
❑ 142 John Navarre AU RC 20.00 7.50
❑ 143 Johnnie Morant AU/325* RC 30.00 15.00
❑ 144 Jonathan Vilma AU SP RC 30.00 12.50
❑ 145 Josh Harris AU/555* RC 20.00 7.50
❑ 146 Julius Jones AU/252* RC 250.00 125.00
❑ 147 Keary Colbert AU/495* RC 40.00 20.00
❑ 148 Kel.Winslow AU/135* RC 175.00 100.00
❑ 149 Kenechi Udeze AU/475* RC 25.00 12.50
❑ 150 Kevin Jones AU/327* RC 120.00 50.00
❑ 151 L.Fitzgerald AU/50* RC 750.00 400.00
❑ 152 Lee Evans AU/375* RC 50.00 25.00
❑ 153 Luke McCown AU/543* RC 25.00 10.00
❑ 154 Matt Mauck AU RC 20.00 7.50
❑ 155 Matt Schaub AU/367* RC 100.00 60.00
❑ 156 Maurice Mann AU RC 15.00 6.00
❑ 157 Mewelde Moore AU/435* RC 40.00 20.00
❑ 158 Michael Clayton AU/325* RC 100.00 40.00
❑ 159 Michael Jenkins AU/412* RC 40.00 20.00
❑ 160 Michael Turner AU/535* RC 30.00 15.00
❑ 161 P.K. Sam AU/300* RC 25.00 12.50
❑ 162 Philip Rivers AU/556* RC 150.00 90.00
❑ 163 Quincy Wilson AU/350* RC 25.00 12.50
❑ 164 Ran Carthon AU RC 15.00 6.00
❑ 165 Rashaun Woods AU RC 20.00 7.50
❑ 166 Re.Williams AU/336* RC 60.00 25.00
❑ 167 R.Colclough AU/640* RC 25.00 10.00
❑ 168 Robert Gallery AU/310* RC 40.00 15.00
❑ 169 Roy Williams AU/564* RC 100.00 40.00
❑ 170 Samie Parker AU/356* RC 30.00 12.50
❑ 171 Sean Jones AU RC 20.00 7.50
❑ 172 S.Taylor/575* RC No Auto 30.00 12.50
❑ 173 Sloan Thomas AU RC 15.00 6.00
❑ 174 Steven Jackson AU/333* RC 150.00 75.00
❑ 175 Tatum Bell AU/539* RC 100.00 50.00
❑ 176 Tommie Harris AU/365* RC 25.00 12.50
❑ 177 Triandos Luke AU RC 20.00 7.50
❑ 178 Troy Fleming AU RC 15.00 6.00
❑ 179 Vince Wilfork AU/315* RC 30.00 12.50
❑ 180 Will Smith AU/565* RC 20.00 7.50
❑ 181 Marcus Tubbs AU RC 20.00 7.50
❑ 182 Michael Boulware AU RC 20.00 7.50
❑ 183 Kris Wilson AU RC 20.00 7.50
❑ 184 Richard Smith AU RC 15.00 6.00
❑ 185 Teddy Lehman AU RC 20.00 7.50
❑ 186 Chris Cooley AU RC 30.00 15.00
❑ 187 Thomas Tapeh AU RC 15.00 6.00
❑ 188A Willie Parker Blk AU RC 120.00 60.00
❑ 188B Willie Parker Blu AU RC 225.00 150.00
❑ 189 Patrick Crayton AU RC 25.00 10.00
❑ 190 Kendrick Starling AU RC 15.00 6.00
❑ 191 B.J. Sams AU RC 20.00 7.50
❑ 192 Derick Armstrong AU EXCH 15.00 6.00
❑ 193 Wes Welker AU RC 20.00 7.50
❑ 194 Erik Coleman AU RC 20.00 7.50
❑ 195 Gibril Wilson AU RC 20.00 7.50
❑ 196 Andy Reid AU/335* RC 30.00 12.50
❑ 197 Brian Billick AU/585* RC 30.00 12.50
❑ 198 Jeff Fisher AU/585* RC 25.00 12.50
❑ 199 Jon Gruden AU/585* RC 25.00 12.50
❑ 200 Marvin Lewis AU/585* RC 25.00 12.50

2005 Playoff Contenders

❑ COMP.SET w/o RC's (100) 20.00 7.50
❑ AU PRINT RUNS ANNOUNCED BY PLAYOFF
❑ EXCH EXPIRATION: 8/1/2007
❑ UNPRICED CHAMPION.PRINT RUN 1 SET
❑ 1 Anquan Boldin .50 .20
❑ 2 Kurt Warner .50 .20
❑ 3 Larry Fitzgerald .75 .30
❑ 4 Michael Vick 1.25 .50
❑ 5 T.J. Duckett .50 .20
❑ 6 Warrick Dunn .50 .20
❑ 7 Derrick Mason .50 .20
❑ 8 Jamal Lewis .75 .30
❑ 9 Kyle Boller .50 .20
❑ 10 Ray Lewis .75 .30
❑ 11 J.P. Losman .75 .30
❑ 12 Lee Evans .50 .20
❑ 13 Willis McGahee .75 .30
❑ 14 DeShaun Foster .50 .20
❑ 15 Jake Delhomme .75 .30
❑ 16 Steve Smith .50 .20
❑ 17 Brian Urlacher .75 .30
❑ 18 Muhsin Muhammad .50 .20
❑ 19 Rex Grossman .50 .20
❑ 20 Carson Palmer .75 .30
❑ 21 Chad Johnson .75 .30
❑ 22 Rudi Johnson .50 .20
❑ 23 Lee Suggs .50 .20
❑ 24 Trent Dilfer .50 .20
❑ 25 Drew Bledsoe .75 .30
❑ 26 Jason Witten .50 .20
❑ 27 Julius Jones 1.00 .40
❑ 28 Keyshawn Johnson .50 .20
❑ 29 Ashley Lelie .50 .20
❑ 30 Jake Plummer .50 .20
❑ 31 Rod Smith .50 .20
❑ 32 Tatum Bell .50 .20
❑ 33 Joey Harrington .75 .30
❑ 34 Kevin Jones .75 .30
❑ 35 Roy Williams WR .75 .30
❑ 36 Ahman Green .75 .30
❑ 37 Brett Favre 2.00 .75
❑ 38 Javon Walker .50 .20
❑ 39 Andre Johnson .50 .20
❑ 40 David Carr .75 .30
❑ 41 Domanick Davis .50 .20
❑ 42 Edgerrin James .75 .30
❑ 43 Marvin Harrison .75 .30
❑ 44 Peyton Manning 1.25 .50
❑ 45 Reggie Wayne .50 .20
❑ 46 Byron Leftwich .75 .30
❑ 47 Fred Taylor .50 .20
❑ 48 Jimmy Smith .50 .20
❑ 49 Priest Holmes .75 .30
❑ 50 Tony Gonzalez .50 .20
❑ 51 Trent Green .50 .20
❑ 52 Chris Chambers .50 .20
❑ 53 Ricky Williams .50 .20
❑ 54 Daunte Culpepper .75 .30
❑ 55 Michael Bennett .50 .20
❑ 56 Nate Burleson .50 .20
❑ 57 Corey Dillon .50 .20
❑ 58 Deion Branch .50 .20
❑ 59 Tom Brady 2.00 .75
❑ 60 Aaron Brooks .50 .20
❑ 61 Deuce McAllister .75 .30
❑ 62 Joe Horn .50 .20
❑ 63 Eli Manning 1.50 .60
❑ 64 Jeremy Shockey .75 .30
❑ 65 Plaxico Burress .50 .20
❑ 66 Tiki Barber .75 .30
❑ 67 Chad Pennington .75 .30
❑ 68 Curtis Martin .75 .30
❑ 69 Laveranues Coles .50 .20
❑ 70 Kerry Collins .50 .20
❑ 71 LaMont Jordan .75 .30
❑ 72 Randy Moss .75 .30
❑ 73 Brian Westbrook .50 .20
❑ 74 Donovan McNabb 1.00 .40
❑ 75 Terrell Owens .75 .30
❑ 76 Ben Roethlisberger 2.00 .75
❑ 77 Duce Staley .50 .20
❑ 78 Hines Ward .75 .30
❑ 79 Jerome Bettis .75 .30
❑ 80 Antonio Gates .75 .30
❑ 81 Drew Brees .75 .30
❑ 82 LaDainian Tomlinson 1.00 .40
❑ 83 Brandon Lloyd .40 .15
❑ 84 Kevan Barlow .50 .20
❑ 85 Darrell Jackson .50 .20
❑ 86 Matt Hasselbeck .50 .20
❑ 87 Shaun Alexander 1.00 .40
❑ 88 Isaac Bruce .50 .20
❑ 89 Marc Bulger .75 .30
❑ 90 Steven Jackson 1.00 .40
❑ 91 Torry Holt .75 .30
❑ 92 Brian Griese .50 .20
❑ 93 Derrick Brooks .50 .20
❑ 94 Chris Brown .50 .20
❑ 95 Drew Bennett .50 .20
❑ 96 Steve McNair .75 .30
❑ 97 Travis Henry .50 .20
❑ 98 Clinton Portis .75 .30
❑ 99 LaVar Arrington .75 .30

❑ 100 Santana Moss .50 .20
❑ 101 Aaron Rodgers AU/530* RC 175.00 100.00
❑ 102 Adam Jones AU RC 20.00 7.50
❑ 103 Adrian McPherson AU/365* RC 40.00 20.00
❑ 104 Alvin Pearman AU RC EXCH 20.00 7.50
❑ 105 Airese Currie AU RC 20.00 7.50
❑ 106 Alex Smith QB AU/401* RC 200.00 100.00
❑ 107 Andrew Walter AU/99* RC 325.00 200.00
❑ 108 Anthony Davis AU/366* RC 30.00 15.00
❑ 109 Antrel Rolle AU RC 20.00 7.50
❑ 110 Brandon Jacobs AU RC 25.00 10.00
❑ 111 Brandon Jones AU RC 20.00 7.50
❑ 112 Braylon Edwards AU RC 100.00 50.00
❑ 113 Bryant McFadden AU/315* RC 40.00 20.00
❑ 114 Carlos Rogers AU RC EXCH 30.00 15.00
❑ 115 Carnell Williams AU/380* RC 225.00 125.00
❑ 116 Cedric Benson AU/289* RC 175.00 100.00
❑ 117 Houston AU/116* RC EX 250.00 125.00
❑ 118 Chad Owens AU RC 20.00 7.50
❑ 119 Charlie Frye AU RC 80.00 40.00
❑ 120 Chris Henry AU RC 40.00 20.00
❑ 121 Ciatrick Fason AU RC 20.00 7.50
❑ 122 Courtney Roby AU RC 20.00 7.50
❑ 123 Craig Bragg AU/425* RC 40.00 20.00
❑ 124 C.Thorpe AU/416* RC 40.00 20.00
❑ 125 Damien Nash AU RC 12.00 5.00
❑ 126 Dan Cody AU/315* RC 40.00 20.00
❑ 127 Dan Orlovsky AU RC 25.00 10.00
❑ 128 Dante Ridgeway AU/373* RC 30.00 15.00
❑ 129 Darren Sproles AU/454* RC 30.00 15.00
❑ 130 David Greene AU RC 25.00 10.00
❑ 131 David Pollack AU RC 20.00 7.50
❑ 132 Deandra Cobb AU/440* RC 30.00 15.00
❑ 133 DeMarcus Ware AU RC 30.00 12.50
❑ 134 Derek Anderson AU/450* RC 40.00 20.00
❑ 135 Derrick Johnson AU RC 40.00 15.00
❑ 136 Erasmus James AU RC EXCH 20.00 7.50
❑ 137 Eric Shelton AU RC 20.00 7.50
❑ 138 Washington AU RC EXCH 20.00 7.50
❑ 139 Frank Gore AU RC 40.00 15.00
❑ 140 F.Gibson AU/476* RC EXCH 50.00 20.00
❑ 141 Heath Miller AU/510* RC 80.00 40.00
❑ 142 J.J. Arrington AU/465* RC 50.00 25.00
❑ 143 J.R. Russell AU/489* RC 30.00 15.00
❑ 144 Jason Campbell AU RC 60.00 35.00
❑ 145 Jason White AU RC 15.00 6.00
❑ 146 Jerome Mathis AU/416* RC 30.00 15.00
❑ 147 Josh Davis AU RC 12.00 5.00
❑ 148 Kay-Jay Harris AU RC 12.00 5.00
❑ 149 Kyle Orton AU RC 40.00 15.00
❑ 150 Larry Brackins AU RC 12.00 5.00
❑ 151 Lionel Gates AU/241* RC 40.00 20.00
❑ 152 Marion Barber AU RC 40.00 20.00
❑ 153 Mark Bradley AU RC 25.00 10.00
❑ 154 Mark Clayton AU/494* RC 50.00 20.00
❑ 155 Marlin Jackson AU RC EXCH 20.00 7.50
❑ 156 Matt Jones AU/165* RC 175.00 100.00
❑ 157 Matt Roth AU RC 20.00 7.50
❑ 158 Maurice Clarett AU/89* 250.00 125.00
❑ 159 Mike Williams AU/73* 500.00 300.00
❑ 160 Paris Warren AU/241* RC 50.00 25.00
❑ 161 Rasheed Marshall AU RC 15.00 6.00
❑ 162 Reggie Brown AU/528* RC 50.00 25.00
❑ 163 Roddy White AU RC 20.00 7.50
❑ 164 Ronnie Brown AU/550* RC 175.00 100.00
❑ 165 Roscoe Parrish AU RC 20.00 7.50
❑ 166 Royd.Williams AU/491* RC 30.00 15.00
❑ 167 R.Fitzpatrick AU/284* RC 50.00 25.00
❑ 168 Ryan Moats AU RC 30.00 15.00
❑ 169 Shaun Cody AU RC 15.00 6.00
❑ 170 Shawne Merriman AU RC 40.00 20.00
❑ 171 Stefan LeFors AU RC 20.00 7.50
❑ 172 Steve Savoy AU RC 12.00 5.00
❑ 173 T.A. McLendon AU RC 12.00 5.00
❑ 174 Tab Perry AU RC 20.00 7.50
❑ 175 Taylor Stubblefield AU RC 12.00 5.00
❑ 176 Terrence Murphy AU RC 20.00 7.50
❑ 177 Thomas Davis AU RC 15.00 6.00
❑ 178 Travis Johnson AU RC 15.00 6.00
❑ 179 T.Williamson AU/402* RC 50.00 25.00
❑ 180 Vernand Morency AU RC 15.00 6.00
❑ 181 Vincent Jackson AU RC 20.00 7.50
❑ 182 Alex Smith TE AU RC 20.00 7.50
❑ 183 Channing Crowder AU RC 15.00 6.00
❑ 184 Darrent Williams AU RC 20.00 7.50
❑ 185 Derrick Wimbush AU RC 15.00 6.00
❑ 186 James Kilian AU RC 15.00 6.00
❑ 187 Josh Cribbs AU RC 15.00 6.00
❑ 188 LeRon McCoy AU RC 12.00 5.00
❑ 189 Luis Castillo AU RC 20.00 7.50
❑ 190 Matt Cassel AU RC 30.00 15.00
❑ 191 Mike Patterson AU RC 15.00 6.00
❑ 192 Nate Washington AU RC 20.00 7.50
❑ 193 Noah Herron AU RC 20.00 7.50
❑ 194 Fred Amey AU RC 15.00 6.00
❑ 195 Tyson Thompson AU RC 25.00 10.00
❑ 196 Mike Nugent AU RC 15.00 6.00
❑ 197 Odell Thurman AU RC 25.00 10.00
❑ 198 Chris Carr AU RC 20.00 7.50
❑ 199 Bo Scaife AU RC 15.00 6.00
❑ 200 Billy Bajema AU RC 12.00 5.00

2003 Playoff Hogg Heaven

❑ COMP.SET w/o SP's (150) 30.00 12.50
❑ 1 Emmitt Smith 2.50 1.00
❑ 2 Marcel Shipp .60 .25
❑ 3 Michael Vick 2.50 1.00
❑ 4 Warrick Dunn .60 .25
❑ 5 T.J. Duckett .60 .25
❑ 6 Peerless Price .60 .25
❑ 7 Brian Finneran .40 .15
❑ 8 Chris Redman .40 .15
❑ 9 Jamal Lewis 1.00 .40
❑ 10 Todd Heap .60 .25
❑ 11 Travis Taylor .60 .25
❑ 12 Ray Lewis 1.00 .40
❑ 13 Peter Boulware .40 .15
❑ 14 Ed Reed .60 .25
❑ 15 Drew Bledsoe 1.00 .40
❑ 16 Travis Henry .60 .25
❑ 17 Eric Moulds .60 .25
❑ 18 Josh Reed .60 .25
❑ 19 Takeo Spikes .40 .15
❑ 20 Julius Peppers 1.00 .40
❑ 21 Stephen Davis .60 .25
❑ 22 Muhsin Muhammad .60 .25
❑ 23 Wesley Walls .40 .15
❑ 24 Anthony Thomas .60 .25
❑ 25 Brian Urlacher 1.50 .60
❑ 26 Marty Booker .60 .25
❑ 27 Mike Brown .60 .25
❑ 28 Kordell Stewart .60 .25
❑ 29 Dez White .40 .15
❑ 30 Corey Dillon .60 .25
❑ 31 Chad Johnson 1.00 .40
❑ 32 Peter Warrick .60 .25
❑ 33 Tim Couch .40 .15
❑ 34 William Green .60 .25
❑ 35 Andre Davis .40 .15
❑ 36 Quincy Morgan .60 .25
❑ 37 Kevin Johnson .60 .25
❑ 38 Dennis Northcutt .40 .15
❑ 39 Antonio Bryant .60 .25
❑ 40 Terry Glenn .40 .15
❑ 41 Joey Galloway .60 .25
❑ 42 Roy Williams 1.00 .40
❑ 43 Darren Woodson .40 .15
❑ 44 Jake Plummer .60 .25
❑ 45 Clinton Portis 1.50 .60
❑ 46 Mike Anderson .60 .25
❑ 47 Rod Smith .60 .25
❑ 48 Ed McCaffrey .60 .25
❑ 49 Ashley Lelie 1.00 .40
❑ 50 Shannon Sharpe .60 .25
❑ 51 Al Wilson .40 .15
❑ 52 Joey Harrington 1.50 .60
❑ 53 James Stewart .60 .25
❑ 54 Brett Favre 2.50 1.00
❑ 55 Ahman Green 1.00 .40
❑ 56 Darren Sharper .40 .15
❑ 57 Donald Driver .60 .25
❑ 58 Javon Walker .60 .25
❑ 59 Robert Ferguson .40 .15
❑ 60 David Carr 1.50 .60
❑ 61 Jabar Gaffney .60 .25
❑ 62 Stacey Mack .40 .15
❑ 63 Marvin Harrison 1.00 .40
❑ 64 Peyton Manning 1.50 .60
❑ 65 Edgerrin James 1.00 .40
❑ 66 Reggie Wayne .60 .25
❑ 67 Fred Taylor 1.00 .40
❑ 68 Mark Brunell .60 .25
❑ 69 Jimmy Smith .60 .25
❑ 70 Hugh Douglas .40 .15
❑ 71 Priest Holmes 1.25 .50
❑ 72 Trent Green .60 .25
❑ 73 Tony Gonzalez .60 .25
❑ 74 Marc Boerigter .60 .25
❑ 75 Ricky Williams 1.00 .40
❑ 76 Jay Fiedler .60 .25
❑ 77 Chris Chambers 1.00 .40
❑ 78 Zach Thomas 1.00 .40
❑ 79 Jason Taylor .40 .15
❑ 80 Junior Seau 1.00 .40
❑ 81 Randy McMichael .60 .25
❑ 82 Patrick Surtain .40 .15
❑ 83 Randy Moss 1.50 .60
❑ 84 Michael Bennett .60 .25
❑ 85 Daunte Culpepper 1.00 .40
❑ 86 Tom Brady 2.50 1.00
❑ 87 Troy Brown .60 .25
❑ 88 Ty Law .60 .25
❑ 89 Aaron Brooks 1.00 .40
❑ 90 Deuce McAllister 1.00 .40
❑ 91 Donte Stallworth 1.00 .40
❑ 92 Joe Horn .60 .25
❑ 93 Michael Strahan .60 .25
❑ 94 Kerry Collins .60 .25
❑ 95 Tiki Barber 1.00 .40
❑ 96 Amani Toomer .60 .25
❑ 97 Jeremy Shockey 1.50 .60
❑ 98 Chad Pennington 1.25 .50
❑ 99 Curtis Martin 1.00 .40
❑ 100 Santana Moss .60 .25
❑ 101 Rich Gannon .60 .25
❑ 102 Jerry Rice 2.00 .75
❑ 103 Tim Brown 1.00 .40
❑ 104 Jerry Porter .60 .25
❑ 105 Charlie Garner .60 .25
❑ 106 Charles Woodson .60 .25
❑ 107 Donovan McNabb 1.25 .50
❑ 108 Duce Staley .60 .25
❑ 109 James Thrash .40 .15
❑ 110 Chad Lewis .40 .15
❑ 111 Troy Vincent .40 .15
❑ 112 Tommy Maddox 1.00 .40
❑ 113 Plaxico Burress .60 .25

❑ 114 Hines Ward 1.00 .40
❑ 115 Antwaan Randle El 1.00 .40
❑ 116 Jerome Bettis 1.00 .40
❑ 117 Kendrell Bell .60 .25
❑ 118 LaDainian Tomlinson 1.00 .40
❑ 119 Drew Brees 1.00 .40
❑ 120 David Boston .60 .25
❑ 121 Jeff Garcia 1.00 .40
❑ 122 Terrell Owens 1.00 .40
❑ 123 Tai Streets .60 .25
❑ 124 Kevan Barlow .60 .25
❑ 125 Matt Hasselbeck .60 .25
❑ 126 Koren Robinson .60 .25
❑ 127 Shaun Alexander 1.00 .40
❑ 128 Kurt Warner 1.00 .40
❑ 129 Marc Bulger 1.00 .40
❑ 130 Marshall Faulk 1.00 .40
❑ 131 Torry Holt 1.00 .40
❑ 132 Isaac Bruce 1.00 .40
❑ 133 Brad Johnson .60 .25
❑ 134 Keyshawn Johnson 1.00 .40
❑ 135 Warren Sapp .60 .25
❑ 136 Derrick Brooks .60 .25
❑ 137 John Lynch .60 .25
❑ 138 Michael Pittman .40 .15
❑ 139 Mike Alstott 1.00 .40
❑ 140 Steve McNair 1.00 .40
❑ 141 Eddie George .60 .25
❑ 142 Jevon Kearse .60 .25
❑ 143 Keith Bulluck .40 .15
❑ 144 Derrick Mason .60 .25
❑ 145 Patrick Ramsey 1.00 .40
❑ 146 Ladell Betts .60 .25
❑ 147 Laveranues Coles .60 .25
❑ 148 Rod Gardner .60 .25
❑ 149 Champ Bailey .60 .25
❑ 150 Bruce Smith .40 .15
❑ 151 Ken Dorsey RC 6.00 2.50
❑ 152 Lee Suggs RC 12.00 5.00
❑ 153 Domanick Davis RC 10.00 4.00
❑ 154 Quentin Griffin RC 6.00 2.50
❑ 155 LaBrandon Toefield RC 6.00 2.50
❑ 156 B.J. Askew RC 6.00 2.50
❑ 157 Jason Witten RC 10.00 4.00
❑ 158 Bennie Joppru RC 6.00 2.50
❑ 159 L.J. Smith RC 6.00 2.50
❑ 160 Billy McMullen RC 5.00 2.00
❑ 161 Shaun McDonald RC 6.00 2.50
❑ 162 Brandon Lloyd RC 8.00 3.00
❑ 163 Sam Aiken RC 5.00 2.00
❑ 164 Bobby Wade RC 6.00 2.50
❑ 165 Justin Gage RC 6.00 2.50
❑ 166 Doug Gabriel RC 6.00 2.50
❑ 167 David Kircus RC 5.00 2.00
❑ 168 Arnaz Battle RC 6.00 2.50
❑ 169 Kareem Kelly RC 5.00 2.00
❑ 170 Talman Gardner RC 6.00 2.50
❑ 171 Ryan Hoag RC 3.00 1.25
❑ 172 LaTarence Dunbar RC 5.00 2.00
❑ 173 Johnathan Sullivan RC 5.00 2.00
❑ 174 Kevin Williams RC 6.00 2.50
❑ 175 Jimmy Kennedy RC 8.00 3.00
❑ 176 Ty Warren RC 6.00 2.50
❑ 177 William Joseph RC 6.00 2.50
❑ 178 Michael Haynes RC 6.00 2.50
❑ 179 Jerome McDougle RC 6.00 2.50
❑ 180 Calvin Pace RC 3.00 1.25
❑ 181 Tyler Brayton RC 6.00 2.50
❑ 182 Chris Kelsay RC 6.00 2.50
❑ 183 DeWayne White RC 5.00 2.00
❑ 184 E.J. Henderson RC 6.00 2.50
❑ 185 Charles Rogers RC 6.00 2.50
❑ 186 Terry Pierce RC 5.00 2.00
❑ 187 Nick Barnett RC 10.00 4.00
❑ 188 Boss Bailey RC 6.00 2.50
❑ 189 Pisa Tinoisamoa RC 6.00 2.50
❑ 190 Chaun Thompson RC 3.00 1.25
❑ 191 Andre Woolfolk RC 6.00 2.50
❑ 192 Sammy Davis RC 6.00 2.50
❑ 193 Eugene Wilson RC 6.00 2.50
❑ 194 Drayton Florence RC 3.00 1.25
❑ 195 Ricky Manning RC 6.00 2.50
❑ 196 Donald Strickland RC 3.00 1.25
❑ 197 Dennis Weathersby RC 3.00 1.25
❑ 198 Troy Polamalu RC 25.00 12.50
❑ 199 Ken Hamlin RC 6.00 2.50
❑ 200 Mike Doss RC 6.00 2.50
❑ 201 Carson Palmer JSY RC 30.00 12.50
❑ 202 Byron Leftwich JSY RC 25.00 10.00
❑ 203 Kyle Boller JSY RC 15.00 6.00
❑ 204 Rex Grossman JSY RC 12.00 5.00
❑ 205 Andre Johnson JSY RC 15.00 6.00
❑ 206 Bryant Johnson JSY RC 8.00 3.00
❑ 207 Larry Johnson JSY RC 30.00 15.00
❑ 208 Taylor Jacobs JSY RC 6.00 2.50
❑ 209 Bethel Johnson JSY RC 8.00 3.00
❑ 210 Anquan Boldin JSY RC 20.00 7.50
❑ 211 Tyrone Calico JSY RC 10.00 4.00
❑ 212 Teyo Johnson JSY RC 8.00 3.00
❑ 213 Kelley Washington JSY RC 8.00 3.00
❑ 214 Musa Smith JSY RC 8.00 3.00
❑ 215 Chris Brown JSY RC 10.00 4.00
❑ 216 Justin Fargas JSY RC 8.00 3.00
❑ 217 Artose Pinner JSY RC 8.00 3.00
❑ 218 Onterrio Smith JSY RC 8.00 3.00
❑ 219 Brian St.Pierre JSY RC 8.00 3.00
❑ 220 Dave Ragone JSY RC 8.00 3.00
❑ 221 Dallas Clark JSY RC 8.00 3.00
❑ 222 Seneca Wallace JSY RC 8.00 3.00
❑ 223 Terrell Suggs JSY RC 12.00 5.00
❑ 224 Terence Newman JSY RC 15.00 6.00
❑ 225 DeWayne Robertson JSY RC 8.003.00
❑ 226 Marcus Trufant JSY RC 8.00 3.00
❑ 227 Kliff Kingsbury JSY RC 6.00 2.50
❑ 228 Kevin Curtis JSY RC 8.00 3.00
❑ 229 Willis McGahee JSY RC 20.00 7.50
❑ 230 Nate Burleson JSY RC 10.00 4.00

2004 Playoff Hogg Heaven

❑ COMP.SET w/o SP's (100) 30.00 12.50
❑ 101-150 RC PRINT RUN 750 SER.#'d SETS
❑ 151-180 RPH RC PRINT RUN 750 SER.#'d SETS
❑ 1 Anquan Boldin 1.00 .40
❑ 2 Emmitt Smith 2.00 .75
❑ 3 Josh McCown .60 .25
❑ 4 Michael Vick 2.00 .75
❑ 5 Peerless Price .60 .25
❑ 6 T.J. Duckett .60 .25
❑ 7 Jamal Lewis 1.00 .40
❑ 8 Kyle Boller 1.00 .40
❑ 9 Ray Lewis 1.00 .40
❑ 10 Terrell Owens 1.00 .40
❑ 11 Drew Bledsoe 1.00 .40
❑ 12 Eric Moulds .60 .25
❑ 13 Travis Henry .60 .25
❑ 14 Jake Delhomme 1.00 .40
❑ 15 Stephen Davis .60 .25
❑ 16 Steve Smith 1.00 .40
❑ 17 Anthony Thomas .60 .25
❑ 18 Brian Urlacher 1.25 .50
❑ 19 Rex Grossman 1.00 .40
❑ 20 Carson Palmer 1.25 .50
❑ 21 Chad Johnson 1.00 .40
❑ 22 Peter Warrick .60 .25
❑ 23 Rudi Johnson .60 .25
❑ 24 Andre Davis .40 .15
❑ 25 Lee Suggs 1.00 .40
❑ 26 Keyshawn Johnson .60 .25
❑ 27 Quincy Carter .60 .25
❑ 28 Roy Williams S .60 .25
❑ 29 Ashley Lelie .60 .25
❑ 30 Jake Plummer .60 .25
❑ 31 Rod Smith .60 .25
❑ 32 Charles Rogers .60 .25
❑ 33 Joey Harrington 1.00 .40
❑ 34 Ahman Green 1.00 .40
❑ 35 Brett Favre 2.50 1.00
❑ 36 Javon Walker .60 .25
❑ 37 Andre Johnson 1.00 .40
❑ 38 David Carr 1.00 .40
❑ 39 Domanick Davis 1.00 .40
❑ 40 Edgerrin James 1.00 .40
❑ 41 Marvin Harrison 1.00 .40
❑ 42 Peyton Manning 1.50 .60
❑ 43 Reggie Wayne .60 .25
❑ 44 Byron Leftwich 1.25 .50
❑ 45 Fred Taylor .60 .25
❑ 46 Jimmy Smith .60 .25
❑ 47 Priest Holmes 1.25 .50
❑ 48 Tony Gonzalez .60 .25
❑ 49 Trent Green .60 .25
❑ 50 A.J. Feeley 1.00 .40
❑ 51 Chris Chambers .60 .25
❑ 52 Ricky Williams 1.00 .40
❑ 53 Zach Thomas 1.00 .40
❑ 54 Daunte Culpepper 1.00 .40
❑ 55 Michael Bennett .60 .25
❑ 56 Randy Moss 1.25 .50
❑ 57 Deion Branch 1.00 .40
❑ 58 Tom Brady 2.50 1.00
❑ 59 Ty Law .60 .25
❑ 60 Aaron Brooks .60 .25
❑ 61 Deuce McAllister 1.00 .40
❑ 62 Joe Horn .60 .25
❑ 63 Jeremy Shockey 1.00 .40
❑ 64 Kerry Collins .60 .25
❑ 65 Michael Strahan .60 .25
❑ 66 Tiki Barber 1.00 .40
❑ 67 Chad Pennington 1.00 .40
❑ 68 Curtis Martin 1.00 .40
❑ 69 Santana Moss .60 .25
❑ 70 Jerry Rice 2.00 .75
❑ 71 Rich Gannon .60 .25
❑ 72 Tim Brown 1.00 .40
❑ 73 Brian Westbrook .60 .25
❑ 74 Donovan McNabb 1.25 .50
❑ 75 Jevon Kearse .60 .25
❑ 76 Hines Ward 1.00 .40
❑ 77 Jerome Bettis 1.00 .40
❑ 78 Kendrell Bell .60 .25
❑ 79 David Boston .60 .25
❑ 80 Drew Brees 1.00 .40
❑ 81 LaDainian Tomlinson 1.25 .50
❑ 82 Jeff Garcia 1.00 .40
❑ 83 Kevan Barlow .60 .25
❑ 84 Tim Rattay .40 .15
❑ 85 Koren Robinson .60 .25
❑ 86 Matt Hasselbeck .60 .25
❑ 87 Shaun Alexander 1.00 .40
❑ 88 Isaac Bruce .60 .25
❑ 89 Marc Bulger 1.00 .40
❑ 90 Marshall Faulk 1.00 .40
❑ 91 Torry Holt 1.00 .40
❑ 92 Brad Johnson .60 .25
❑ 93 Keenan McCardell .40 .15
❑ 94 Warren Sapp .60 .25

❑ 95 Derrick Mason .60 .25
❑ 96 Steve McNair 1.00 .40
❑ 97 Eddie George .60 .25
❑ 98 Clinton Portis 1.00 .40
❑ 99 Laveranues Coles .60 .25
❑ 100 Mark Brunell .60 .25
❑ 101 Adimchinobe Echemandu RC 5.00 2.00
❑ 102 Ahmad Carroll RC 8.00 3.00
❑ 103 Andy Hall RC 5.00 2.00
❑ 104 B.J. Symons RC 6.00 2.50
❑ 105 Bradlee Van Pelt RC 10.00 4.00
❑ 106 Brandon Miree RC 5.00 2.00
❑ 107 Bruce Perry RC 6.00 2.50
❑ 108 Carlos Francis RC 5.00 2.00
❑ 109 Casey Bramlet RC 5.00 2.00
❑ 110 Chris Gamble RC 8.00 3.00
❑ 111 Clarence Moore RC 6.00 2.50
❑ 112 Cody Pickett RC 6.00 2.50
❑ 113 Craig Krenzel RC 6.00 2.50
❑ 114 D.J. Hackett RC 5.00 2.00
❑ 115 D.J. Williams RC 8.00 3.00
❑ 116 Derrick Ward RC 3.00 1.25
❑ 117 Drew Carter RC 6.00 2.50
❑ 118 Ernest Wilford RC 6.00 2.50
❑ 119 Drew Henson RC 6.00 2.50
❑ 120 Jamaar Taylor RC 6.00 2.50
❑ 121 Jared Lorenzen RC 5.00 2.00
❑ 122 Jarrett Payton RC 8.00 3.00
❑ 123 Jason Babin RC 6.00 2.50
❑ 124 Jeff Smoker RC 6.00 2.50
❑ 125 Jeris McIntyre RC 5.00 2.00
❑ 126 Jerricho Cotchery RC 6.00 2.50
❑ 127 Jim Sorgi RC 6.00 2.50
❑ 128 John Navarre RC 6.00 2.50
❑ 129 Johnnie Morant RC 6.00 2.50
❑ 130 Sean Taylor RC 8.00 3.00
❑ 131 Jonathan Vilma RC 6.00 2.50
❑ 132 Josh Harris RC 6.00 2.50
❑ 133 Kenechi Udeze RC 6.00 2.50
❑ 134 Marcus Tubbs RC 6.00 2.50
❑ 135 Mark Jones RC 5.00 2.00
❑ 136 Matt Mauck RC 6.00 2.50
❑ 137 Maurice Mann RC 5.00 2.00
❑ 138 Michael Turner RC 6.00 2.50
❑ 139 P.K. Sam RC 5.00 2.00
❑ 140 Patrick Crayton RC 6.00 2.50
❑ 141 Quincy Wilson RC 5.00 2.00
❑ 142 Ran Carthon RC 5.00 2.00
❑ 143 Ryan Krause RC 5.00 2.00
❑ 144 Samie Parker RC 6.00 2.50
❑ 145 Sloan Thomas RC 5.00 2.00
❑ 146 Tommie Harris RC 6.00 2.50
❑ 147 Triandos Luke RC 6.00 2.50
❑ 148 Troy Fleming RC 5.00 2.00
❑ 149 Vince Wilfork RC 8.00 3.00
❑ 150 Will Smith RC 6.00 2.50
❑ 151 Larry Fitzgerald RPH RC 20.00 7.50
❑ 152 DeAngelo Hall RPH RC 8.00 3.00
❑ 153 Matt Schaub RPH RC 10.00 4.00
❑ 154 Michael Jenkins RPH RC 6.00 2.50
❑ 155 Devard Darling RPH RC 6.00 2.50
❑ 156 J.P. Losman RPH RC 12.00 5.00
❑ 157 Lee Evans RPH RC 8.00 3.00
❑ 158 Keary Colbert RPH RC 8.00 3.00
❑ 159 Bernard Berrian RPH RC 6.00 2.50
❑ 160 Chris Perry RPH RC 10.00 4.00
❑ 161 Kellen Winslow RPH RC 12.00 5.00
❑ 162 Luke McCown RPH RC 6.00 2.50
❑ 163 Julius Jones RPH RC 25.00 10.00
❑ 164 Darius Watts RPH RC 6.00 2.50
❑ 165 Tatum Bell RPH RC 12.00 5.00
❑ 166 Kevin Jones RPH RC 20.00 7.50
❑ 167 Roy Williams RPH RC 15.00 6.00
❑ 168 Greg Jones RPH RC 6.00 2.50
❑ 169 Reggie Williams RPH RC 8.00 3.00
❑ 170 Ben Watson RPH RC 6.00 2.50
❑ 171 Cedric Cobbs RPH RC 6.00 2.50
❑ 172 D.Henderson RPH RC 5.00 2.00
❑ 173 Eli Manning RPH RC 30.00 15.00
❑ 174 Roethlisberger RPH RC 50.00 25.00
❑ 175 Philip Rivers RPH RC 20.00 10.00
❑ 176 Derrick Hamilton RPH RC 5.00 2.00
❑ 177 Rashaun Woods RPH RC 6.00 2.50
❑ 178 Steven Jackson RPH RC 20.00 7.50
❑ 179 Michael Clayton RPH RC 12.00 5.00
❑ 180 Ben Troupe RPH RC 6.00 2.50

2001 Playoff Honors

❑ COMP.SET w/o SP's (100) 25.00 10.00
❑ 1 Rob Johnson .60 .25
❑ 2 Eric Moulds .60 .25
❑ 3 Marvin Harrison 1.00 .40
❑ 4 Edgerrin James 1.25 .50
❑ 5 Peyton Manning 2.50 1.00
❑ 6 Jay Fiedler 1.00 .40
❑ 7 Lamar Smith .60 .25
❑ 8 Zach Thomas 1.00 .40
❑ 9 Dan Marino 3.00 1.25
❑ 10 Drew Bledsoe 1.25 .50
❑ 11 Terry Glenn .60 .25
❑ 12 Wayne Chrebet .60 .25
❑ 13 Curtis Martin 1.00 .40
❑ 14 Chad Pennington 1.50 .60
❑ 15 Vinny Testaverde .60 .25
❑ 16 Corey Dillon 1.00 .40
❑ 17 Jon Kitna 1.00 .40
❑ 18 Akili Smith .40 .15
❑ 19 Peter Warrick 1.00 .40
❑ 20 Kevin Johnson .60 .25
❑ 21 Tim Couch .60 .25
❑ 22 Eddie George 1.00 .40
❑ 23 Steve McNair 1.00 .40
❑ 24 Jevon Kearse .60 .25
❑ 25 Jerome Bettis 1.00 .40
❑ 26 Kordell Stewart .60 .25
❑ 27 Plaxico Burress 1.00 .40
❑ 28 Mark Brunell 1.00 .40
❑ 29 Keenan McCardell .40 .15
❑ 30 Jimmy Smith .60 .25
❑ 31 Fred Taylor 1.00 .40
❑ 32 Elvis Grbac .60 .25
❑ 33 Jamal Lewis 1.50 .60
❑ 34 Ray Lewis 1.00 .40
❑ 35 Mike Anderson 1.00 .40
❑ 36 Terrell Davis 1.00 .40
❑ 37 John Elway 3.00 1.25
❑ 38 Brian Griese 1.00 .40
❑ 39 Ed McCaffrey 1.00 .40
❑ 40 Tony Gonzalez .60 .25
❑ 41 Trent Green 1.00 .40
❑ 42 Sylvester Morris .40 .15
❑ 43 Tim Brown 1.00 .40
❑ 44 Rich Gannon 1.00 .40
❑ 45 Charlie Garner .60 .25
❑ 46 Tyrone Wheatley .60 .25
❑ 47 Charles Woodson .60 .25
❑ 48 Tim Dwight 1.00 .40
❑ 49 Doug Flutie 1.00 .40
❑ 50 Junior Seau 1.00 .40
❑ 51 Shaun Alexander 1.25 .50
❑ 52 Matt Hasselbeck .60 .25
❑ 53 Ricky Watters .60 .25
❑ 54 Tony Banks .60 .25
❑ 55 Joey Galloway .60 .25
❑ 56 Emmitt Smith 2.00 .75
❑ 57 Troy Aikman 1.50 .60
❑ 58 Kerry Collins .60 .25
❑ 59 Ron Dayne 1.00 .40
❑ 60 Donovan McNabb 1.25 .50
❑ 61 Duce Staley 1.00 .40
❑ 62 David Boston 1.00 .40
❑ 63 Thomas Jones .60 .25
❑ 64 Jake Plummer .60 .25
❑ 65 Stephen Davis 1.00 .40
❑ 66 Jeff George .60 .25
❑ 67 Michael Westbrook .60 .25
❑ 68 Deion Sanders 1.00 .40
❑ 69 James Allen .60 .25
❑ 70 Cade McNown .40 .15
❑ 71 Marcus Robinson 1.00 .40
❑ 72 Brian Urlacher 1.50 .60
❑ 73 Germane Crowell .40 .15
❑ 74 Charlie Batch 1.00 .40
❑ 75 James Stewart .60 .25
❑ 76 Brett Favre 3.00 1.25
❑ 77 Antonio Freeman 1.00 .40
❑ 78 Ahman Green 1.00 .40
❑ 79 Cris Carter 1.00 .40
❑ 80 Daunte Culpepper 1.00 .40
❑ 81 Randy Moss 2.00 .75
❑ 82 Mike Alstott 1.00 .40
❑ 83 Warrick Dunn 1.00 .40
❑ 84 Brad Johnson 1.00 .40
❑ 85 Keyshawn Johnson 1.00 .40
❑ 86 Warren Sapp .60 .25
❑ 87 Jamal Anderson 1.00 .40
❑ 88 Chris Chandler .60 .25
❑ 89 Isaac Bruce 1.00 .40
❑ 90 Marshall Faulk 1.25 .50
❑ 91 Torry Holt 1.00 .40
❑ 92 Kurt Warner 2.00 .75
❑ 93 Aaron Brooks 1.00 .40
❑ 94 Albert Connell .40 .15
❑ 95 Ricky Williams 1.00 .40
❑ 96 Jeff Garcia 1.00 .40
❑ 97 Terrell Owens 1.00 .40
❑ 98 Steve Young 1.00 .40
❑ 99 Jerry Rice 2.00 .75
❑ 100 Jeff Lewis .40 .15
❑ 101 Rashard Casey RC 6.00 2.50
❑ 102 A.J. Feeley RC 10.00 4.00
❑ 103 Josh Booty RC 10.00 4.00
❑ 104 LaMont Jordan RC 20.00 7.50
❑ 105 Ben Leard RC 6.00 2.50
❑ 106 David Rivers RC 6.00 2.50
❑ 107 Tim Hasselbeck RC 10.00 4.00
❑ 108 Jason McKinley RC 6.00 2.50
❑ 109 Correll Buckhalter RC 12.00 5.00
❑ 110 Dan Alexander RC 10.00 4.00
❑ 111 Derrick Blaylock RC 10.00 4.00
❑ 112 Chris Barnes RC 6.00 2.50
❑ 113 Dee Brown RC 10.00 4.00
❑ 114 Derek Combs RC 6.00 2.50
❑ 115 David Allen RC 6.00 2.50
❑ 116 DeAngelo Evans RC 6.00 2.50
❑ 117 Reggie White RC 6.00 2.50
❑ 118 Heath Evans RC 6.00 2.50
❑ 119 George Layne RC 6.00 2.50
❑ 120 Moran Norris RC 4.00 1.50
❑ 121 Bhawoh Jue RC 10.00 4.00
❑ 122 Dustin McClintock RC 6.00 2.50
❑ 123 Ja'Mar Toombs RC 6.00 2.50
❑ 124 Steve Smith RC 25.00 12.50
❑ 125 Milton Wynn RC 6.00 2.50
❑ 126 Justin McCareins RC 10.00 4.00
❑ 127 Jarrod Cooper RC 10.00 4.00
❑ 128 Vinny Sutherland RC 6.00 2.50
❑ 129 Alex Bannister RC 6.00 2.50

❑ 130 Scotty Anderson RC	6.00	2.50
❑ 131 Onome Ojo RC	6.00	2.50
❑ 132 Damerien McCants RC	6.00	2.50
❑ 133 Eddie Berlin RC	6.00	2.50
❑ 134 Jonathan Carter RC	6.00	2.50
❑ 135 Bobby Newcombe RC	10.00	4.00
❑ 136 Cedrick Wilson RC	10.00	4.00
❑ 137 Kevin Kasper RC	10.00	4.00
❑ 138 Francis St. Paul RC	6.00	2.50
❑ 139 David Martin RC	6.00	2.50
❑ 140 T.J. Houshmandzadeh RC	10.00	4.00
❑ 141 John Capel RC	6.00	2.50
❑ 142 Reggie Germany RC	6.00	2.50
❑ 143 Chris Taylor RC	6.00	2.50
❑ 144 Ken-Yon Rambo RC	6.00	2.50
❑ 145 Richmond Flowers RC	6.00	2.50
❑ 146 Quentin McCord RC	6.00	2.50
❑ 147 Andre King RC	6.00	2.50
❑ 148 Boo Williams RC	6.00	2.50
❑ 149 Daniel Guy RC	4.00	1.50
❑ 150 Javon Green RC	6.00	2.50
❑ 151 Ronney Daniels RC	4.00	1.50
❑ 152 Alge Crumpler RC	12.00	6.00
❑ 153 Tony Driver RC	6.00	2.50
❑ 154 Shad Meier RC	6.00	2.50
❑ 155 Jabari Holloway RC	6.00	2.50
❑ 156 Ryan Pickett RC	4.00	1.50
❑ 157 Cedric James RC	6.00	2.50
❑ 158 Tony Stewart RC	10.00	4.00
❑ 159 Sean Brewer RC	4.00	1.50
❑ 160 Orlando Huff RC	4.00	1.50
❑ 161 Nate Clements RC	10.00	4.00
❑ 162 Will Allen RC	6.00	2.50
❑ 163 Willie Middlebrooks RC	6.00	2.50
❑ 164 Jamar Fletcher RC	6.00	2.50
❑ 165 Ken Lucas RC	6.00	2.50
❑ 166 Fred Smoot RC	10.00	4.00
❑ 167 Michael Stone RC	4.00	1.50
❑ 168 Tony Dixon RC	6.00	2.50
❑ 169 Andre Dyson RC	4.00	1.50
❑ 170 Gary Baxter RC	6.00	2.50
❑ 171 Adam Archuleta RC	10.00	4.00
❑ 172 Derrick Gibson RC	6.00	2.50
❑ 173 Edgerton Hartwell RC	4.00	1.50
❑ 174 Jamal Reynolds RC	10.00	4.00
❑ 175 Richard Seymour RC	10.00	4.00
❑ 176 Brandon Manumaleuna RC	6.00	2.50
❑ 177 Idrees Bashir RC	4.00	1.50
❑ 178 DeLawrence Grant RC	4.00	1.50
❑ 179 Karon Riley RC	4.00	1.50
❑ 180 Cedric Scott RC	6.00	2.50
❑ 181 Damione Lewis RC	6.00	2.50
❑ 182 Marcus Stroud RC	10.00	4.00
❑ 183 Casey Hampton RC	10.00	4.00
❑ 184 Willie Howard RC	6.00	2.50
❑ 185 Shaun Rogers RC	10.00	4.00
❑ 186 Kenny Smith RC	6.00	2.50
❑ 187 Marcus Bell DT RC	6.00	2.50
❑ 188 Mario Fatafehi RC	6.00	2.50
❑ 189 Kendrell Bell RC	12.00	5.00
❑ 190 Tommy Polley RC	10.00	4.00
❑ 191 Jamie Winborn RC	6.00	2.50
❑ 192 Sedrick Hodge RC	4.00	1.50
❑ 193 Torrance Marshall RC	10.00	4.00
❑ 194 Eric Westmoreland RC	6.00	2.50
❑ 195 Brian Allen RC	4.00	1.50
❑ 196 Morlon Greenwood RC	6.00	2.50
❑ 197 Brandon Spoon RC	10.00	4.00
❑ 198 Carlos Polk RC	4.00	1.50
❑ 199 Alex Lincoln RC	6.00	2.50
❑ 200 Keith Adams RC	4.00	1.50
❑ 201 Kevan Barlow JSY RC	10.00	4.00
❑ 202 Michael Bennett JSY RC	15.00	6.00
❑ 203 Drew Brees JSY RC	25.00	10.00
❑ 204 Quincy Carter JSY RC	10.00	4.00
❑ 205 Andre Carter JSY RC	10.00	4.00
❑ 206 Chris Chambers JSY RC	15.00	6.00
❑ 207 Robert Ferguson JSY RC	10.00	4.00
❑ 208 Rod Gardner JSY RC	10.00	4.00
❑ 210 Travis Henry JSY RC	10.00	4.00
❑ 212 Chad Johnson JSY RC	25.00	10.00
❑ 213 Rudi Johnson JSY RC	20.00	7.50
❑ 214 Sage Rosenfels JSY RC	10.00	4.00
❑ 215 Deuce McAllister JSY RC	20.00	7.50
❑ 216 Mike McMahon JSY RC	10.00	4.00
❑ 217 Snoop Minnis JSY RC	6.00	2.50
❑ 218 Travis Minor JSY RC	6.00	2.50
❑ 219 Freddie Mitchell JSY RC	10.00	4.00
❑ 220 Quincy Morgan JSY RC	10.00	4.00
❑ 222 Santana Moss JSY RC	15.00	6.00
❑ 223 Jesse Palmer JSY RC	10.00	4.00
❑ 224 Koren Robinson JSY RC	10.00	4.00
❑ 225 Josh Heupel JSY RC	10.00	4.00
❑ 226 Justin Smith JSY RC	10.00	4.00
❑ 227 David Terrell JSY RC	10.00	4.00
❑ 228 Anthony Thomas JSY RC	10.00	4.00
❑ 229 LaDainian Tomlinson JSY RC	40.00	20.00
❑ 230 Marques Tuiasosopo JSY RC	10.00	4.00
❑ 231 Michael Vick JSY RC	50.00	20.00
❑ 232 Gerard Warren JSY RC	10.00	4.00
❑ 233 Reggie Wayne JSY RC	20.00	7.50
❑ 234 Chris Weinke JSY RC	10.00	4.00
❑ 235 Leonard Davis JSY RC	6.00	2.50

2002 Playoff Honors

❑ COMP.SET w/o SP's (100)	25.00	10.00
❑ 1 David Boston	1.00	.40
❑ 2 Jake Plummer	.60	.25
❑ 3 Warrick Dunn	1.00	.40
❑ 4 Michael Vick	3.00	1.25
❑ 5 Jamal Lewis	1.00	.40
❑ 6 Chris Redman	.40	.15
❑ 7 Ray Lewis	1.00	.40
❑ 8 Drew Bledsoe	1.25	.50
❑ 9 Travis Henry	1.00	.40
❑ 10 Eric Moulds	.60	.25
❑ 11 Lamar Smith	.60	.25
❑ 12 Steve Smith	1.00	.40
❑ 13 Chris Weinke	.60	.25
❑ 14 Chris Chandler	.60	.25
❑ 15 David Terrell	1.00	.40
❑ 16 Anthony Thomas	.60	.25
❑ 17 Brian Urlacher	1.50	.60
❑ 18 Corey Dillon	.60	.25
❑ 19 Peter Warrick	.60	.25
❑ 20 Tim Couch	.60	.25
❑ 21 James Jackson	.40	.15
❑ 22 Kevin Johnson	.60	.25
❑ 23 Quincy Carter	.60	.25
❑ 24 Joey Galloway	.60	.25
❑ 25 Emmitt Smith	2.50	1.00
❑ 26 Terrell Davis	1.00	.40
❑ 27 Brian Griese	1.00	.40
❑ 28 Rod Smith	.60	.25
❑ 29 Germane Crowell	.40	.15
❑ 30 Az-Zahir Hakim	.40	.15
❑ 31 Mike McMahon	1.00	.40
❑ 32 Brett Favre	2.50	1.00
❑ 33 Terry Glenn	.60	.25
❑ 34 Ahman Green	1.00	.40
❑ 35 James Allen	.60	.25
❑ 36 Corey Bradford	.40	.15
❑ 37 Marvin Harrison	1.00	.40
❑ 38 Peyton Manning	2.00	.75
❑ 39 Edgerrin James	1.25	.50
❑ 40 Reggie Wayne	1.00	.40
❑ 41 Mark Brunell	1.00	.40
❑ 42 Fred Taylor	1.00	.40
❑ 43 Jimmy Smith	.60	.25
❑ 44 Tony Gonzalez	.60	.25
❑ 45 Trent Green	.60	.25
❑ 46 Priest Holmes	1.25	.50
❑ 47 Snoop Minnis	.40	.15
❑ 48 Chris Chambers	1.00	.40
❑ 49 Jay Fiedler	.60	.25
❑ 50 Ricky Williams	1.00	.40
❑ 51 Zach Thomas	1.00	.40
❑ 52 Randy Moss	2.00	.75
❑ 53 Daunte Culpepper	1.00	.40
❑ 54 Michael Bennett	.60	.25
❑ 55 Tom Brady	2.50	1.00
❑ 56 Troy Brown	.60	.25
❑ 57 Antowain Smith	.60	.25
❑ 58 Aaron Brooks	1.00	.40
❑ 59 Deuce McAllister	1.00	.40
❑ 60 Tiki Barber	1.00	.40
❑ 61 Kerry Collins	.60	.25
❑ 62 Amani Toomer	.60	.25
❑ 63 Michael Strahan	.60	.25
❑ 64 Curtis Martin	1.00	.40
❑ 65 Vinny Testaverde	.60	.25
❑ 66 Chad Pennington	1.25	.50
❑ 67 Laveranues Coles	.60	.25
❑ 68 Tim Brown	1.00	.40
❑ 69 Rich Gannon	1.00	.40
❑ 70 Jerry Rice	2.00	.75
❑ 71 Donovan McNabb	1.25	.50
❑ 72 Freddie Mitchell	.60	.25
❑ 73 Duce Staley	1.00	.40
❑ 74 Jerome Bettis	1.00	.40
❑ 75 Plaxico Burress	.60	.25
❑ 76 Kordell Stewart	.60	.25
❑ 77 Drew Brees	1.00	.40
❑ 78 Doug Flutie	1.00	.40
❑ 79 LaDainian Tomlinson	1.50	.60
❑ 80 Jeff Garcia	1.00	.40
❑ 81 Garrison Hearst	.60	.25
❑ 82 Terrell Owens	1.00	.40
❑ 83 Shaun Alexander	1.25	.50
❑ 84 Trent Dilfer	.60	.25
❑ 85 Koren Robinson	.60	.25
❑ 86 Isaac Bruce	1.00	.40
❑ 87 Marshall Faulk	1.00	.40
❑ 88 Torry Holt	1.00	.40
❑ 89 Kurt Warner	1.00	.40
❑ 90 Mike Alstott	1.00	.40
❑ 91 Brad Johnson	.60	.25
❑ 92 Keyshawn Johnson	1.00	.40
❑ 93 Keenan McCardell	.40	.15
❑ 94 Steve McNair	1.00	.40
❑ 95 Eddie George	1.00	.40
❑ 96 Jevon Kearse	.60	.25
❑ 97 Derrick Mason	.60	.25
❑ 98 Stephen Davis	.60	.25
❑ 99 Sage Rosenfels	.40	.15
❑ 100 Rod Gardner	.60	.25
❑ 101 Randy Fasani RC	5.00	2.00
❑ 102 Kurt Kittner RC	5.00	2.00
❑ 103 Brandon Doman RC	5.00	2.00
❑ 104 Craig Nall RC	6.00	2.50
❑ 105 J.T. O'Sullivan RC	5.00	2.00
❑ 106 Seth Burford RC	5.00	2.00
❑ 107 Jeff Kelly RC	5.00	2.00
❑ 108 Ronald Curry RC	6.00	2.50
❑ 109 Wes Pate RC	3.00	1.25
❑ 110 Chad Hutchinson RC	5.00	2.00
❑ 111 Major Applewhite RC	6.00	2.50
❑ 112 Preston Parsons RC	3.00	1.25

❑ 113	David Priestley RC	5.00	2.00
❑ 114	Lamar Gordon RC	6.00	2.50
❑ 115	Brian Westbrook RC	10.00	4.00
❑ 116	Jonathan Wells RC	6.00	2.50
❑ 117	Omar Easy RC	6.00	2.50
❑ 118	Verron Haynes RC	6.00	2.50
❑ 119	Josh Scobey RC	6.00	2.50
❑ 120	Larry Ned RC	5.00	2.00
❑ 121	Adrian Peterson RC	6.00	2.50
❑ 122	Brian Allen RC	5.00	2.00
❑ 123	Chester Taylor RC	6.00	2.50
❑ 124	Luke Staley RC	5.00	2.00
❑ 125	Antwoine Womack RC	5.00	2.00
❑ 126	Leonard Henry RC	5.00	2.00
❑ 127	Jesse Chatman RC	6.00	2.50
❑ 128	Damien Anderson RC	5.00	2.00
❑ 129	Eric McCoo RC	3.00	1.25
❑ 130	Tellis Redmon RC	5.00	2.00
❑ 131	Joe Burns RC	5.00	2.00
❑ 132	Delvon Flowers RC	5.00	2.00
❑ 133	Ken Simonton RC	3.00	1.25
❑ 134	Ricky Williams RC	5.00	2.00
❑ 135	Dicenzo Miller RC	3.00	1.25
❑ 136	James Mungro RC	6.00	2.50
❑ 137	Randy McMichael RC	10.00	4.00
❑ 138	Deion Branch RC	12.00	5.00
❑ 139	Terry Charles RC	5.00	2.00
❑ 140	Herb Haygood RC	3.00	1.25
❑ 141	Jason McAddley RC	5.00	2.00
❑ 142	Jake Schifino RC	5.00	2.00
❑ 143	Freddie Milons RC	5.00	2.00
❑ 144	Kahlil Hill RC	5.00	2.00
❑ 145	Lamont Brightful RC	3.00	1.25
❑ 146	Chris Luzar RC	5.00	2.00
❑ 147	Daryl Jones RC	5.00	2.00
❑ 148	Woody Dantzler RC	5.00	2.00
❑ 149	Kelly Campbell RC	5.00	2.00
❑ 150	Brian Poli-Dixon RC	5.00	2.00
❑ 151	Atrews Bell RC	3.00	1.25
❑ 152	Jarrod Baxter RC	5.00	2.00
❑ 153	Eddie Drummond RC	5.00	2.00
❑ 154	Jerramy Stevens RC	6.00	2.50
❑ 155	Doug Jolley RC	6.00	2.50
❑ 156	Jamar Martin RC	5.00	2.00
❑ 157	Najeh Davenport RC	6.00	2.50
❑ 158	Dwight Freeney RC	8.00	3.00
❑ 159	Bryan Thomas RC	5.00	2.00
❑ 160	Charles Grant RC	6.00	2.50
❑ 161	Kalimba Edwards RC	6.00	2.50
❑ 162	Ryan Denney RC	5.00	2.00
❑ 163	Will Overstreet RC	3.00	1.25
❑ 164	Dennis Johnson RC	3.00	1.25
❑ 165	Alex Brown RC	6.00	2.50
❑ 166	Kenyon Coleman RC	3.00	1.25
❑ 167	Ryan Sims RC	6.00	2.50
❑ 168	John Henderson RC	6.00	2.50
❑ 169	Wendell Bryant RC	3.00	1.25
❑ 170	Albert Haynesworth RC	5.00	2.00
❑ 171	Larry Tripplett RC	3.00	1.25
❑ 172	Eddie Freeman RC	3.00	1.25
❑ 173	Anthony Weaver RC	5.00	2.00
❑ 174	Quentin Jammer RC	6.00	2.50
❑ 175	Phillip Buchanon RC	6.00	2.50
❑ 176	Lito Sheppard RC	6.00	2.50
❑ 177	Mike Rumph RC	5.00	2.00
❑ 178	Roosevelt Williams RC	3.00	1.25
❑ 179	Derek Ross RC	5.00	2.00
❑ 180	Mike Echols RC	3.00	1.25
❑ 181	Keyou Craver RC	5.00	2.00
❑ 182	Ed Reed RC	10.00	4.00
❑ 183	Lamont Thompson RC	5.00	2.00
❑ 184	Tank Williams RC	5.00	2.00
❑ 185	Michael Lewis RC	6.00	2.50
❑ 186	Napoleon Harris RC	6.00	2.50
❑ 187	Robert Thomas RC	6.00	2.50
❑ 188	Raonall Smith RC	5.00	2.00
❑ 189	Levar Fisher RC	3.00	1.25
❑ 190	Rocky Calmus RC	6.00	2.50
❑ 191	Andra Davis RC	5.00	2.00
❑ 192	Nick Rolovich RC	5.00	2.00
❑ 193	Zak Kustok RC	6.00	2.50
❑ 194	Dusty Bonner RC	3.00	1.25
❑ 195	Tony Fisher RC	6.00	2.50
❑ 196	Sam Simmons RC	3.00	1.25
❑ 197	Lee Mays RC	5.00	2.00
❑ 198	Jamin Elliott RC	3.00	1.25
❑ 199	Javin Hunter RC	3.00	1.25
❑ 200	Kendall Newson RC	3.00	1.25
❑ 201	Ladell Betts JSY RC	10.00	4.00
❑ 202	Antonio Bryant JSY RC	10.00	4.00
❑ 203	Reche Caldwell JSY RC	10.00	4.00
❑ 204	David Carr JSY RC	25.00	10.00
❑ 205	Tim Carter JSY RC	8.00	3.00
❑ 206	Eric Crouch JSY RC	10.00	4.00
❑ 207	Rohan Davey JSY RC	10.00	4.00
❑ 208	Andre Davis JSY RC	8.00	3.00
❑ 209	T.J. Duckett JSY RC	15.00	6.00
❑ 210	DeShaun Foster JSY RC	10.00	4.00
❑ 211	Jabar Gaffney JSY RC	10.00	4.00
❑ 212	David Garrard JSY RC	12.00	5.00
❑ 213	Daniel Graham JSY RC	10.00	4.00
❑ 214	William Green JSY RC	10.00	4.00
❑ 215	Joey Harrington JSY RC	25.00	10.00
❑ 216	Ron Johnson JSY RC	8.00	3.00
❑ 217	Ashley Lelie JSY RC	20.00	7.50
❑ 218	Josh McCown JSY RC	12.00	5.00
❑ 219	Maurice Morris JSY RC	10.00	4.00
❑ 220	Julius Peppers JSY RC	20.00	7.50
❑ 221	Clinton Portis JSY RC	30.00	12.50
❑ 222	Patrick Ramsey JSY RC	12.00	5.00
❑ 223	Antwaan Randle El JSY RC	15.00	6.00
❑ 224	Josh Reed JSY RC	10.00	4.00
❑ 225	Cliff Russell JSY RC	8.00	3.00
❑ 226	Jeremy Shockey JSY RC	30.00	12.50
❑ 227	Donte Stallworth JSY RC	20.00	7.50
❑ 228	Travis Stephens JSY RC	8.00	3.00
❑ 229	Javon Walker JSY RC	20.00	10.00
❑ 230	Marquise Walker JSY RC	8.00	3.00
❑ 231	Roy Williams JSY RC	25.00	12.50
❑ 232	Mike Williams JSY RC	8.00	3.00
❑ RWH1	Payton/Smith JSY/250	120.00	50.00
❑ RWH1A	Payton/Smith AUTO/22	400.00	200.00

2003 Playoff Honors

❑	COMP.SET w/o SP's (100)	20.00	7.50
❑ 1	Aaron Brooks	1.00	.40
❑ 2	Ahman Green	1.00	.40
❑ 3	Amani Toomer	.60	.25
❑ 4	Anthony Thomas	.60	.25
❑ 5	Antonio Bryant	.60	.25
❑ 6	Antwaan Randle El	1.00	.40
❑ 7	Ashley Lelie	1.00	.40
❑ 8	Brad Johnson	.60	.25
❑ 9	Brett Favre	2.50	1.00
❑ 10	Brian Urlacher	1.50	.60
❑ 11	Bruce Smith	.60	.25
❑ 12	Chad Johnson	1.00	.40
❑ 13	Chad Pennington	1.25	.50
❑ 14	Charlie Garner	.60	.25
❑ 15	Chris Chambers	1.00	.40
❑ 16	Clinton Portis	1.50	.60
❑ 17	Corey Dillon	.60	.25
❑ 18	Curtis Martin	1.00	.40
❑ 19	Daunte Culpepper	1.00	.40
❑ 20	David Boston	.60	.25
❑ 21	David Carr	1.50	.60
❑ 22	Deuce McAllister	1.00	.40
❑ 23	Donald Driver	.60	.25
❑ 24	Donovan McNabb	1.25	.50
❑ 25	Donte Stallworth	1.00	.40
❑ 26	Drew Bledsoe	1.00	.40
❑ 27	Drew Brees	1.00	.40
❑ 28	Duce Staley	.60	.25
❑ 29	Ed McCaffrey	1.00	.40
❑ 30	Eddie George	.60	.25
❑ 31	Edgerrin James	1.00	.40
❑ 32	Emmitt Smith	2.50	1.00
❑ 33	Eric Moulds	.60	.25
❑ 34	Fred Taylor	1.00	.40
❑ 35	Garrison Hearst	.60	.25
❑ 36	Hines Ward	1.00	.40
❑ 37	Isaac Bruce	1.00	.40
❑ 38	Jabar Gaffney	.60	.25
❑ 39	Jake Plummer	.60	.25
❑ 40	Jamal Lewis	1.00	.40
❑ 41	Jay Fiedler	.60	.25
❑ 42	Jeff Garcia	1.00	.40
❑ 43	Jeremy Shockey	1.50	.60
❑ 44	Jerome Bettis	1.00	.40
❑ 45	Jerry Porter	.60	.25
❑ 46	Jerry Rice	2.00	.75
❑ 47	Jevon Kearse	.60	.25
❑ 48	Jimmy Smith	.60	.25
❑ 49	Joe Horn	.60	.25
❑ 50	Joey Harrington	1.50	.60
❑ 51	Josh Reed	.60	.25
❑ 52	Julius Peppers	1.00	.40
❑ 53	Kendrell Bell	.60	.25
❑ 54	Kerry Collins	.60	.25
❑ 55	Keyshawn Johnson	1.00	.40
❑ 56	Kordell Stewart	.60	.25
❑ 57	Koren Robinson	.60	.25
❑ 58	Kurt Warner	1.00	.40
❑ 59	LaDainian Tomlinson	1.00	.40
❑ 60	Laveranues Coles	.60	.25
❑ 61	Mark Brunell	.60	.25
❑ 62	Marshall Faulk	1.00	.40
❑ 63	Marvin Harrison	1.00	.40
❑ 64	Matt Hasselbeck	.60	.25
❑ 65	Michael Bennett	.60	.25
❑ 66	Michael Strahan	.60	.25
❑ 67	Michael Vick	2.50	1.00
❑ 68	Mike Alstott	1.00	.40
❑ 69	Patrick Ramsey	1.00	.40
❑ 70	Peerless Price	.60	.25
❑ 71	Peyton Manning	1.50	.60
❑ 72	Plaxico Burress	.60	.25
❑ 73	Priest Holmes	1.25	.50
❑ 74	Randy Moss	1.50	.60
❑ 75	Ray Lewis	1.00	.40
❑ 76	Rich Gannon	.60	.25
❑ 77	Ricky Williams	1.00	.40
❑ 78	Rod Gardner	.60	.25
❑ 79	Rod Smith	.60	.25
❑ 80	Roy Williams	1.00	.40
❑ 81	Shaun Alexander	1.00	.40
❑ 82	Stephen Davis	.60	.25
❑ 83	Steve McNair	1.00	.40
❑ 84	T.J. Duckett	.60	.25
❑ 85	Terrell Owens	1.00	.40
❑ 86	Tiki Barber	1.00	.40
❑ 87	Tim Brown	1.00	.40
❑ 88	Tim Couch	.40	.15
❑ 89	Todd Heap	.60	.25
❑ 90	Tom Brady	2.50	1.00
❑ 91	Tommy Maddox	1.00	.40
❑ 92	Tony Gonzalez	.60	.25

93	Torry Holt	1.00	.40
94	Travis Henry	.60	.25
95	Trent Green	.60	.25
96	Troy Brown	.60	.25
97	Warren Sapp	.60	.25
98	Warrick Dunn	.60	.25
99	William Green	.60	.25
100	Zach Thomas	1.00	.40
101	Chris Simms RC	8.00	3.00
102	Brooks Bollinger RC	5.00	2.00
103	Gibran Hamdan RC	2.50	1.00
104	Ken Dorsey RC	5.00	2.00
105	Jason Gesser RC	5.00	2.00
106	Brad Banks RC	4.00	1.50
107	Tony Romo RC	5.00	2.00
108	B.J. Askew RC	5.00	2.00
109	Domanick Davis RC	8.00	3.00
110	Lee Suggs RC	10.00	4.00
111	LaBrandon Toefield RC	5.00	2.00
112	Brock Forsey RC	5.00	2.00
113	Malaefou MacKenzie RC	2.50	1.00
114	Andrew Pinnock RC	4.00	1.50
115	Ahmaad Galloway RC	4.00	1.50
116	Tony Hollings RC	5.00	2.00
117	Charles Rogers RC	5.00	2.00
118	Billy McMullen RC	4.00	1.50
119	Shaun McDonald RC	5.00	2.00
120	Brandon Lloyd RC	6.00	2.50
121	Sam Aiken RC	4.00	1.50
122	Bobby Wade RC	5.00	2.00
123	Justin Gage RC	5.00	2.00
124	Adrian Madise RC	4.00	1.50
125	Jon Olinger RC	2.50	1.00
126	Doug Gabriel RC	5.00	2.00
127	J.R. Tolver RC	4.00	1.50
128	David Kircus RC	4.00	1.50
129	Zuriel Smith RC	2.50	1.00
130	LaTarence Dunbar RC	4.00	1.50
131	Arnaz Battle RC	5.00	2.00
132	Willie Ponder RC	2.50	1.00
133	Kareem Kelly RC	4.00	1.50
134	David Tyree RC	4.00	1.50
135	Keenan Howry RC	5.00	2.00
136	Taco Wallace RC	4.00	1.50
137	Walter Young RC	2.50	1.00
138	Talman Gardner RC	5.00	2.00
139	DeAndrew Rubin RC	2.50	1.00
140	Kevin Walter RC	4.00	1.50
141	Carl Ford RC	2.50	1.00
142	Travis Anglin RC	2.50	1.00
143	Ryan Hoag RC	2.50	1.00
144	Terrence Edwards RC	4.00	1.50
145	Bennie Joppru RC	5.00	2.00
146	L.J. Smith RC	5.00	2.00
147	Jason Witten RC	8.00	3.00
148	Andre Woolfolk RC	5.00	2.00
149	Nnamdi Asomugha RC	4.00	1.50
150	Troy Polamalu RC	15.00	7.50
151	Nate Hybl RC	10.00	4.00
152	Curt Anes RC	5.00	2.00
153	Avon Cobourne RC	5.00	2.00
154	Cecil Sapp RC	8.00	3.00
155	Casey Urlacher RC	10.00	4.00
156	Dwone Hicks RC	5.00	2.00
157	Jeremi Johnson RC	8.00	3.00
158	Kirk Farmer RC	8.00	3.00
159	James MacPherson RC	10.00	4.00
160	Chris Davis RC	8.00	3.00
161	Brandon Drumm RC	5.00	2.00
162	J.T. Wall RC	5.00	2.00
163	Casey Moore RC	8.00	3.00
164	Mike Seidman RC	5.00	2.00
165	Visanthe Shiancoe RC	8.00	3.00
166	George Wrighster RC	8.00	3.00
167	Dan Curley RC	5.00	2.00
168	Donald Lee RC	8.00	3.00
169	Aaron Walker RC	8.00	3.00
170	Trent Smith RC	5.00	2.00
171	Spencer Nead RC	8.00	3.00
172	Richard Angulo RC	8.00	3.00
173	Mike Pinkard RC	5.00	2.00
174	Johnathan Sullivan RC	8.00	3.00
175	Kevin Williams RC	10.00	4.00
176	Jimmy Kennedy RC	10.00	4.00
177	Ty Warren RC	10.00	4.00
178	William Joseph RC	10.00	4.00
179	Michael Haynes RC	10.00	4.00
180	Jerome McDougle RC	10.00	4.00
181	Calvin Pace RC	8.00	3.00
182	Tyler Brayton RC	10.00	4.00
183	Chris Kelsay RC	10.00	4.00
184	Osi Umenyiora RC	15.00	6.00
185	Alonzo Jackson RC	8.00	3.00
186	DeWayne White RC	8.00	3.00
187	Kenny Peterson RC	8.00	3.00
188	Nick Barnett RC	15.00	6.00
189	Boss Bailey RC	10.00	4.00
190	E.J. Henderson RC	10.00	4.00
191	Pisa Tinoisamoa RC	10.00	4.00
192	Sammy Davis RC	10.00	4.00
193	Charles Tillman RC	12.00	5.00
194	Eugene Wilson RC	10.00	4.00
195	Drayton Florence RC	5.00	2.00
196	Ricky Manning RC	10.00	4.00
197	Rashean Mathis RC	8.00	3.00
198	Ken Hamlin RC	10.00	4.00
199	Mike Doss RC	10.00	4.00
200	Julian Battle RC	8.00	3.00
201	Andre Johnson JSY RC	15.00	6.00
202	Anquan Boldin JSY RC	20.00	10.00
203	Artose Pinner JSY RC	8.00	3.00
204	Bethel Johnson JSY RC	8.00	3.00
205	Brian St.Pierre JSY RC	8.00	3.00
206	Bryant Johnson JSY RC	8.00	3.00
207	Byron Leftwich JSY RC	25.00	10.00
208	Carson Palmer JSY RC	30.00	12.50
209	Chris Brown JSY RC	10.00	4.00
210	Dallas Clark JSY RC	8.00	3.00
211	Dave Ragone JSY RC	8.00	3.00
212	DeWayne Robertson JSY RC	8.003.00	
213	Justin Fargas JSY RC	8.00	3.00
214	Kelley Washington JSY RC	8.00	3.00
215	Kevin Curtis JSY RC	8.00	3.00
216	Kliff Kingsbury JSY RC	6.00	2.50
217	Kyle Boller JSY RC	15.00	6.00
218	Larry Johnson JSY RC	30.00	15.00
219	Marcus Trufant JSY RC	8.00	3.00
220	Musa Smith JSY RC	8.00	3.00
221	Nate Burleson JSY RC	12.00	5.00
222	Onterrio Smith JSY RC	8.00	3.00
223	Rex Grossman JSY RC	12.00	5.00
224	Seneca Wallace JSY RC	8.00	3.00
225	Taylor Jacobs JSY RC	6.00	2.50
226	Terrell Suggs JSY RC	12.00	5.00
227	Terence Newman JSY RC	15.00	6.00
228	Teyo Johnson JSY RC	8.00	3.00
229	Tyrone Calico JSY RC	10.00	4.00
230	Willis McGahee JSY RC	20.00	7.50

2004 Playoff Honors

	COMP.SET w/o SP's (100)	20.00	7.50
	101-150 INSERTS IN HOBBY PACKS ONLY		
	101-150 RC PRINT RUN 750 #'d SETS		
	151-200 INSERTS IN RETAIL PACKS ONLY		
	151-200 RC PRINT RUN 425 #'d SETS		
	201-233 JSY RC PRINT RUN 750 #'d SETS		
1	Anquan Boldin	1.00	.40
2	Emmitt Smith	2.00	.75
3	Josh McCown	.60	.25
4	Michael Vick	2.00	.75
5	Peerless Price	.60	.25
6	T.J. Duckett	.60	.25
7	Warrick Dunn	.60	.25
8	Jamal Lewis	1.00	.40
9	Kyle Boller	1.00	.40
10	Ray Lewis	1.00	.40
11	Drew Bledsoe	1.00	.40
12	Eric Moulds	.60	.25
13	Travis Henry	.60	.25
14	DeShaun Foster	.60	.25
15	Jake Delhomme	1.00	.40
16	Steve Smith	1.00	.40
17	Stephen Davis	.60	.25
18	Brian Urlacher	1.25	.50
19	Rex Grossman	1.00	.40
20	Thomas Jones	.60	.25
21	Carson Palmer	1.25	.50
22	Chad Johnson	1.00	.40
23	Rudi Johnson	.60	.25
24	Jeff Garcia	1.00	.40
25	Lee Suggs	1.00	.40
26	Keyshawn Johnson	.60	.25
27	Quincy Carter	.60	.25
28	Roy Williams S	.60	.25
29	Jake Plummer	.60	.25
30	Quentin Griffin	1.00	.40
31	Rod Smith	.60	.25
32	Charles Rogers	.60	.25
33	Joey Harrington	1.00	.40
34	Ahman Green	1.00	.40
35	Brett Favre	2.50	1.00
36	Javon Walker	.60	.25
37	Andre Johnson	1.00	.40
38	David Carr	1.00	.40
39	Domanick Davis	1.00	.40
40	Edgerrin James	1.00	.40
41	Marvin Harrison	1.00	.40
42	Peyton Manning	1.50	.60
43	Byron Leftwich	1.25	.50
44	Fred Taylor	.60	.25
45	Jimmy Smith	.60	.25
46	Priest Holmes	1.25	.50
47	Tony Gonzalez	.60	.25
48	Trent Green	.60	.25
49	A.J. Feeley	1.00	.40
50	Chris Chambers	.60	.25
51	Ricky Williams	1.00	.40
52	Daunte Culpepper	1.00	.40
53	Michael Bennett	.60	.25
54	Randy Moss	1.25	.50
55	Corey Dillon	.60	.25
56	Deion Branch	1.00	.40
57	Tom Brady	2.50	1.00
58	Aaron Brooks	.60	.25
59	Deuce McAllister	1.00	.40
60	Joe Horn	.60	.25
61	Jeremy Shockey	1.00	.40
62	Michael Strahan	.60	.25
63	Tiki Barber	1.00	.40
64	Chad Pennington	1.00	.40
65	Curtis Martin	1.00	.40
66	Santana Moss	.60	.25
67	Jerry Rice	2.00	.75
68	Justin Fargas	.60	.25
69	Kerry Collins	.60	.25
70	Tim Brown	1.00	.40
71	Brian Westbrook	.60	.25

❑ 72	Donovan McNabb	1.25	.50
❑ 73	Jevon Kearse	.60	.25
❑ 74	Terrell Owens	1.00	.40
❑ 75	Duce Staley	.60	.25
❑ 76	Hines Ward	1.00	.40
❑ 77	Jerome Bettis	1.00	.40
❑ 78	Tommy Maddox	.60	.25
❑ 79	Drew Brees	1.00	.40
❑ 80	LaDainian Tomlinson	1.25	.50
❑ 81	Kevan Barlow	.60	.25
❑ 82	Tim Rattay	.40	.15
❑ 83	Koren Robinson	.60	.25
❑ 84	Matt Hasselbeck	.60	.25
❑ 85	Shaun Alexander	1.00	.40
❑ 86	Isaac Bruce	.60	.25
❑ 87	Marc Bulger	1.00	.40
❑ 88	Marshall Faulk	1.00	.40
❑ 89	Torry Holt	1.00	.40
❑ 90	Brad Johnson	.60	.25
❑ 91	Charlie Garner	.60	.25
❑ 92	Keenan McCardell	.40	.15
❑ 93	Chris Brown	1.00	.40
❑ 94	Derrick Mason	.60	.25
❑ 95	Eddie George	.60	.25
❑ 96	Steve McNair	1.00	.40
❑ 97	Clinton Portis	1.00	.40
❑ 98	LaVar Arrington	2.00	.75
❑ 99	Laveranues Coles	.60	.25
❑ 100	Mark Brunell	.60	.25
❑ 101	Drew Henson RC	5.00	2.00
❑ 102	Craig Krenzel RC	5.00	2.00
❑ 103	Andy Hall RC	4.00	1.50
❑ 104	Josh Harris RC	5.00	2.00
❑ 105	Jim Sorgi RC	5.00	2.00
❑ 106	Jeff Smoker RC	5.00	2.00
❑ 107	John Navarre RC	5.00	2.00
❑ 108	Cody Pickett RC	5.00	2.00
❑ 109	Casey Bramlet RC	4.00	1.50
❑ 110	Matt Mauck RC	5.00	2.00
❑ 111	B.J. Symons RC	5.00	2.00
❑ 112	Bradlee Van Pelt RC	10.00	4.00
❑ 113	Michael Turner RC	5.00	2.00
❑ 114	Troy Fleming RC	4.00	1.50
❑ 115	Adimchinobe Echemandu RC 4.001.50		
❑ 116	Quincy Wilson RC	4.00	1.50
❑ 117	Derrick Ward RC	2.50	1.00
❑ 118	Bruce Perry RC	5.00	2.00
❑ 119	Brandon Miree RC	4.00	1.50
❑ 120	Carlos Francis RC	4.00	1.50
❑ 121	Samie Parker RC	5.00	2.00
❑ 122	Jerricho Cotchery RC	5.00	2.00
❑ 123	Ernest Wilford RC	5.00	2.00
❑ 124	Johnnie Morant RC	5.00	2.00
❑ 125	Maurice Mann RC	4.00	1.50
❑ 126	D.J. Hackett RC	4.00	1.50
❑ 127	Drew Carter RC	5.00	2.00
❑ 128	P.K. Sam RC	4.00	1.50
❑ 129	Jamaar Taylor RC	5.00	2.00
❑ 130	Ryan Krause RC	4.00	1.50
❑ 131	Triandos Luke RC	5.00	2.00
❑ 132	Jeris McIntyre RC	4.00	1.50
❑ 133	Clarence Moore RC	5.00	2.00
❑ 134	Mark Jones RC	4.00	1.50
❑ 135	Sloan Thomas RC	4.00	1.50
❑ 136	Jonathan Smith RC	4.00	1.50
❑ 137	Patrick Crayton RC	5.00	2.00
❑ 138	Derek Abney RC	5.00	2.00
❑ 139	Kris Wilson RC	5.00	2.00
❑ 140	Sean Taylor RC	6.00	2.50
❑ 141	Jonathan Vilma RC	5.00	2.00
❑ 142	Tommie Harris RC	5.00	2.00
❑ 143	D.J. Williams RC	6.00	2.50
❑ 144	Will Smith RC	5.00	2.00
❑ 145	Kenechi Udeze RC	5.00	2.00
❑ 146	Vince Wilfork RC	6.00	2.50
❑ 147	Marcus Tubbs RC	5.00	2.00
❑ 148	Ahmad Carroll RC	6.00	2.50
❑ 149	Jason Babin RC	5.00	2.00
❑ 150	Chris Gamble RC	6.00	2.50
❑ 151	Willie Parker RC	30.00	15.00
❑ 152	Darnell Dockett RC	6.00	2.50
❑ 153	Nate Poole RC	4.00	1.50
❑ 154	Matt Kegel RC	8.00	3.00
❑ 155	Kendrick Starling RC	4.00	1.50
❑ 156	Tramon Douglas RC	4.00	1.50
❑ 157	Ryan Dinwiddie RC	6.00	2.50
❑ 158	Brian Gaither RC	4.00	1.50
❑ 159	Ran Carthon RC	6.00	2.50
❑ 160	Derick Armstrong	4.00	1.50
❑ 161	Chris Cooley RC	8.00	3.00
❑ 162	Casey Clausen RC	8.00	3.00
❑ 163	Omar Jenkins RC	4.00	1.50
❑ 164	Justin Jenkins RC	6.00	2.50
❑ 165	Wes Welker RC	8.00	3.00
❑ 166	Terrance Copper RC	6.00	2.50
❑ 167	Jarrett Payton RC	10.00	4.00
❑ 168	Zamir Cobb RC	8.00	3.00
❑ 169	Derrick Knight RC	6.00	2.50
❑ 170	Romby Bryant RC	4.00	1.50
❑ 171	Larry Croom RC	6.00	2.50
❑ 172	Thomas Tapeh RC	6.00	2.50
❑ 173	Brock Lesnar RC	8.00	3.00
❑ 174	Richard Smith RC	6.00	2.50
❑ 175	Ricky Ray RC	6.00	2.50
❑ 176	John Booth RC	4.00	1.50
❑ 177	Huey Whittaker RC	8.00	3.00
❑ 178	Fred Russell RC	8.00	3.00
❑ 179	Ben Hartsock RC	8.00	3.00
❑ 180	Tim Euhus RC	8.00	3.00
❑ 181	Ricardo Colclough RC	8.00	3.00
❑ 182	Keiwan Ratliff RC	6.00	2.50
❑ 183	Shawntae Spencer RC	8.00	3.00
❑ 184	Joey Thomas RC	8.00	3.00
❑ 185	Keith Smith RC	6.00	2.50
❑ 186	Derrick Strait RC	8.00	3.00
❑ 187	Jeremy LeSueur RC	6.00	2.50
❑ 188	Matt Ware RC	8.00	3.00
❑ 189	Rich Gardner RC	6.00	2.50
❑ 190	Daryl Smith RC	8.00	3.00
❑ 191	Dontarrious Thomas RC	8.00	3.00
❑ 192	Courtney Watson RC	8.00	3.00
❑ 193	Karlos Dansby RC	8.00	3.00
❑ 194	Teddy Lehman RC	8.00	3.00
❑ 195	Michael Boulware RC	8.00	3.00
❑ 196	Bob Sanders RC	15.00	6.00
❑ 197	Travis LaBoy RC	8.00	3.00
❑ 198	Antwan Odom RC	8.00	3.00
❑ 199	Marquise Hill RC	6.00	2.50
❑ 200	Terry Johnson RC	6.00	2.50
❑ 201	Larry Fitzgerald JSY RC	15.00	6.00
❑ 202	DeAngelo Hall JSY RC	8.00	3.00
❑ 203	Matt Schaub JSY RC	8.00	3.00
❑ 204	Michael Jenkins JSY RC	6.00	2.50
❑ 205	Devard Darling JSY RC	6.00	2.50
❑ 206	J.P. Losman JSY RC	10.00	4.00
❑ 207	Lee Evans JSY RC	8.00	3.00
❑ 208	Keary Colbert JSY RC	8.00	3.00
❑ 209	Bernard Berrian JSY RC	6.00	2.50
❑ 210	Chris Perry JSY RC	8.00	3.00
❑ 211	Kellen Winslow JSY RC	10.00	4.00
❑ 212	Luke McCown JSY RC	6.00	2.50
❑ 213	Julius Jones JSY RC	20.00	7.50
❑ 214	Darius Watts JSY RC	6.00	2.50
❑ 215	Tatum Bell JSY RC	10.00	4.00
❑ 216	Kevin Jones JSY RC	15.00	6.00
❑ 217	Roy Williams JSY RC	12.00	5.00
❑ 218	Dunta Robinson JSY RC	6.00	2.50
❑ 219	Greg Jones JSY RC	6.00	2.50
❑ 220	Reggie Williams JSY RC	8.00	3.00
❑ 221	Mewelde Moore JSY RC	8.00	3.00
❑ 222	Ben Watson JSY RC	6.00	2.50
❑ 223	Cedric Cobbs JSY RC	6.00	2.50
❑ 224	Devery Henderson JSY RC	5.00	2.00
❑ 225	Eli Manning JSY RC	25.00	10.00
❑ 226	Robert Gallery JSY RC	8.00	3.00
❑ 227	B.Roethlisberger JSY RC	40.00	20.00
❑ 227	Philip Rivers JSY RC	15.00	7.50
❑ 229	Derrick Hamilton JSY RC	5.00	2.00
❑ 230	Rashaun Woods JSY RC	6.00	2.50
❑ 231	Steven Jackson JSY RC	15.00	6.00
❑ 232	Michael Clayton JSY RC	10.00	4.00
❑ 233	Ben Troupe JSY RC	6.00	2.50

2005 Playoff Honors

❑ COMP.SET w/o SP's (100) 20.00 7.50

❑ 101-150 INSERTED IN HOBBY PACKS

❑ 101-150 PRINT RUN 699 SER.#'d SETS

❑ COMMON ROOKIE (151-200) 3.00 1.25

❑ ROOKIE SEMISTARS 151-200 5.00 2.00

❑ ROOKIE UNL.STARS 151-200 6.00 2.50

❑ 151-200 INSERTED IN RETAIL PACKS

❑ 151-200 PRINT RUN 399 SER.#'d SETS

❑ ROOKIE JSY PRINT RUN 750 SER.#'d SETS

❑ 1	Anquan Boldin	.60	.25
❑ 2	Larry Fitzgerald	1.00	.40
❑ 3	Kurt Warner	.60	.25
❑ 4	Michael Vick	1.50	.60
❑ 5	Alge Crumpler	.60	.25
❑ 6	Warrick Dunn	.60	.25
❑ 7	Jamal Lewis	1.00	.40
❑ 8	Kyle Boller	.60	.25
❑ 9	Ray Lewis	1.00	.40
❑ 10	Derrick Mason	.60	.25
❑ 11	Eric Moulds	.60	.25
❑ 12	J.P. Losman	1.00	.40
❑ 13	Willis McGahee	1.00	.40
❑ 14	Jake Delhomme	1.00	.40
❑ 15	Steve Smith	.60	.25
❑ 16	DeShaun Foster	.60	.25
❑ 17	Rex Grossman	.60	.25
❑ 18	Brian Urlacher	1.00	.40
❑ 19	Muhsin Muhammad	.60	.25
❑ 20	Carson Palmer	1.00	.40
❑ 21	Chad Johnson	1.00	.40
❑ 22	Rudi Johnson	.60	.25
❑ 23	Lee Suggs	.60	.25
❑ 24	Trent Dilfer	.60	.25
❑ 25	Reuben Droughns	.60	.25
❑ 26	Drew Bledsoe	1.00	.40
❑ 27	Julius Jones	1.25	.50
❑ 28	Keyshawn Johnson	.60	.25
❑ 29	Roy Williams S	.60	.25
❑ 30	Ashley Lelie	.60	.25
❑ 31	Jake Plummer	.60	.25
❑ 32	Rod Smith	.60	.25
❑ 33	Tatum Bell	.60	.25
❑ 34	Joey Harrington	1.00	.40
❑ 35	Kevin Jones	1.00	.40
❑ 36	Roy Williams WR	1.00	.40
❑ 37	Ahman Green	1.00	.40
❑ 38	Brett Favre	2.50	1.00
❑ 39	Javon Walker	.60	.25
❑ 40	Andre Johnson	.60	.25
❑ 41	David Carr	1.00	.40
❑ 42	Domanick Davis	.60	.25
❑ 43	Marvin Harrison	1.00	.40
❑ 44	Edgerrin James	1.00	.40

❑ 45 Peyton Manning 1.50 .60
❑ 46 Reggie Wayne .60 .25
❑ 47 Fred Taylor .60 .25
❑ 48 Byron Leftwich 1.00 .40
❑ 49 Jimmy Smith .60 .25
❑ 50 Priest Holmes 1.00 .40
❑ 51 Tony Gonzalez .60 .25
❑ 52 Trent Green .60 .25
❑ 53 A.J. Feeley .60 .25
❑ 54 Chris Chambers .60 .25
❑ 55 Daunte Culpepper 1.00 .40
❑ 56 Nate Burleson .60 .25
❑ 57 Michael Bennett .60 .25
❑ 58 Corey Dillon .60 .25
❑ 59 Deion Branch .60 .25
❑ 60 Tedy Bruschi .60 .25
❑ 61 Tom Brady 2.50 1.00
❑ 62 Aaron Brooks .60 .25
❑ 63 Deuce McAllister 1.00 .40
❑ 64 Joe Horn .60 .25
❑ 65 Eli Manning 2.00 .75
❑ 66 Tiki Barber 1.00 .40
❑ 67 Plaxico Burress .60 .25
❑ 68 Jeremy Shockey 1.00 .40
❑ 69 Chad Pennington 1.00 .40
❑ 70 Curtis Martin 1.00 .40
❑ 71 Laveranues Coles .60 .25
❑ 72 Kerry Collins .60 .25
❑ 73 Randy Moss 1.00 .40
❑ 74 LaMont Jordan 1.00 .40
❑ 75 Brian Westbrook .60 .25
❑ 76 Donovan McNabb 1.25 .50
❑ 77 Terrell Owens 1.00 .40
❑ 78 Ben Roethlisberger 2.50 1.00
❑ 79 Hines Ward 1.00 .40
❑ 80 Duce Staley .60 .25
❑ 81 Jerome Bettis 1.00 .40
❑ 82 Drew Brees 1.00 .40
❑ 83 LaDainian Tomlinson 1.25 .50
❑ 84 Antonio Gates 1.00 .40
❑ 85 Kevan Barlow .60 .25
❑ 86 Brandon Lloyd .50 .20
❑ 87 Darrell Jackson .60 .25
❑ 88 Matt Hasselbeck .60 .25
❑ 89 Shaun Alexander 1.25 .50
❑ 90 Marc Bulger 1.00 .40
❑ 91 Torry Holt 1.00 .40
❑ 92 Steven Jackson 1.25 .50
❑ 93 Brian Griese .60 .25
❑ 94 Michael Clayton 1.00 .40
❑ 95 Drew Bennett .60 .25
❑ 96 Steve McNair 1.00 .40
❑ 97 Chris Brown .60 .25
❑ 98 Clinton Portis 1.00 .40
❑ 99 LaVar Arrington 1.00 .40
❑ 100 Santana Moss .60 .25
❑ 101 Cedric Benson RC 10.00 4.00
❑ 102 Mike Williams 10.00 4.00
❑ 103 DeMarcus Ware RC 8.00 3.00
❑ 104 Shawne Merriman RC 8.00 3.00
❑ 105 Thomas Davis RC 5.00 2.00
❑ 106 Derrick Johnson RC 8.00 3.00
❑ 107 David Pollack RC 5.00 2.00
❑ 108 Erasmus James RC 5.00 2.00
❑ 109 Marcus Spears RC 5.00 2.00
❑ 110 Fabian Washington RC 5.00 2.00
❑ 111 Aaron Rodgers RC 15.00 6.00
❑ 112 Marlin Jackson RC 5.00 2.00
❑ 113 Heath Miller RC 12.00 5.00
❑ 114 Alex Smith TE RC 5.00 2.00
❑ 115 Chris Henry RC 5.00 2.00
❑ 116 David Greene RC 5.00 2.00
❑ 117 Brandon Jones RC 5.00 2.00
❑ 118 Marion Barber RC 8.00 3.00
❑ 119 Brandon Jacobs RC 6.00 2.50
❑ 120 Jerome Mathis RC 5.00 2.00
❑ 121 Craphonso Thorpe RC 4.00 1.50
❑ 122 Manuel White RC 4.00 1.50
❑ 123 Alvin Pearman RC 5.00 2.00
❑ 124 Darren Sproles RC 5.00 2.00
❑ 125 Fred Gibson RC 4.00 1.50
❑ 126 Roydell Williams RC 5.00 2.00
❑ 127 Airese Currie RC 5.00 2.00
❑ 128 Damien Nash RC 4.00 1.50
❑ 129 Dan Orlovsky RC 6.00 2.50
❑ 130 Adrian McPherson RC 5.00 2.00
❑ 131 Larry Brackins RC 4.00 1.50
❑ 132 Rasheed Marshall RC 5.00 2.00
❑ 133 Cedric Houston RC 5.00 2.00
❑ 134 Chad Owens RC 5.00 2.00
❑ 135 Tab Perry RC 5.00 2.00
❑ 136 Dante Ridgeway RC UER 4.00 1.50
❑ 137 Craig Bragg RC 4.00 1.50
❑ 138 Deandra Cobb RC 4.00 1.50
❑ 139 Derek Anderson RC 5.00 2.00
❑ 140 Travis Johnson RC 4.00 1.50
❑ 141 Paris Warren RC 4.00 1.50
❑ 142 LeRon McCoy RC 4.00 1.50
❑ 143 James Kilian RC 5.00 2.00
❑ 144 Matt Cassel RC 8.00 3.00
❑ 145 Lionel Gates RC 4.00 1.50
❑ 146 Harry Williams RC 4.00 1.50
❑ 147 Anthony Davis RC 4.00 1.50
❑ 148 Noah Herron RC 5.00 2.00
❑ 149 Ryan Fitzpatrick RC 8.00 3.00
❑ 150 J.R. Russell RC 4.00 1.50
❑ 151 Cole Magner RC 3.00 1.25
❑ 152 Luis Castillo RC 6.00 2.50
❑ 153 Mike Patterson RC 6.00 2.50
❑ 154 Brodney Pool RC 6.00 2.50
❑ 155 Barrett Ruud RC 6.00 2.50
❑ 156 Shaun Cody RC 6.00 2.50
❑ 157 Stanford Routt RC 5.00 2.00
❑ 158 Josh Bullocks RC 6.00 2.50
❑ 159 Kevin Burnett RC 6.00 2.50
❑ 160 Corey Webster RC 6.00 2.50
❑ 161 Lofa Tatupu RC 8.00 3.00
❑ 162 Matt Roth RC 6.00 2.50
❑ 163 Mike Nugent RC 6.00 2.50
❑ 164 Odell Thurman RC 6.00 2.50
❑ 165 Ronald Bartell RC 5.00 2.00
❑ 166 Nick Collins RC 6.00 2.50
❑ 167 Dan Cody RC 6.00 2.50
❑ 168 Darrent Williams RC 6.00 2.50
❑ 169 Justin Miller RC 5.00 2.00
❑ 170 Jerome Collins RC 5.00 2.00
❑ 171 Justin Green RC 6.00 2.50
❑ 172 Eric Green RC 3.00 1.25
❑ 173 Joel Dreessen RC 5.00 2.00
❑ 174 Bo Scaife RC 5.00 2.00
❑ 175 Antonio Perkins RC 5.00 2.00
❑ 176 Nehemiah Broughton RC 5.00 2.00
❑ 177 Patrick Estes RC 5.00 2.00
❑ 178 Billy Bajema RC 5.00 2.00
❑ 179 Madison Hedgecock RC 6.00 2.50
❑ 180 Roscoe Crosby RC 5.00 2.00
❑ 181 Kendrick Mosley RC 3.00 1.25
❑ 182 Tyson Thompson RC 10.00 4.00
❑ 183 Fred Amey RC 5.00 2.00
❑ 184 Brock Berlin RC 5.00 2.00
❑ 185 Gino Guidugli RC 3.00 1.25
❑ 186 Walter Reyes RC 5.00 2.00
❑ 187 Lydell Ross RC 5.00 2.00
❑ 188 Carlyle Holiday RC 5.00 2.00
❑ 189 Bryan Randall RC 5.00 2.00
❑ 190 Derrick Tinsley RC 5.00 2.00
❑ 191 Ryan Grant RC 6.00 2.50
❑ 192 Bobby Purify RC 5.00 2.00
❑ 193 Leonard Weaver RC 5.00 2.00
❑ 194 Vincent Fuller RC 5.00 2.00
❑ 195 Tony Brown RC 5.00 2.00
❑ 196 Zach Tuiasosopo RC 3.00 1.25
❑ 197 Craig Ochs RC 5.00 2.00
❑ 198 Ruvell Martin RC 5.00 2.00
❑ 199 Manuel Wright RC 6.00 2.50
❑ 200 Travis Daniels RC 5.00 2.00
❑ 201 Adam Jones JSY RC 8.00 3.00
❑ 202 Alex Smith QB JSY RC 20.00 7.50
❑ 203 Andrew Walter JSY RC 10.00 4.00
❑ 204 Antrel Rolle JSY RC 8.00 3.00
❑ 205 Braylon Edwards JSY RC 20.00 7.50
❑ 206 Carnell Williams JSY RC 25.00 10.00
❑ 207 Carlos Rogers JSY RC 10.00 4.00
❑ 208 Charlie Frye JSY RC 12.00 5.00
❑ 209 Ciatrick Fason JSY RC 8.00 3.00
❑ 210 Courtney Roby JSY RC 8.00 3.00
❑ 211 Eric Shelton JSY RC 8.00 3.00
❑ 212 Frank Gore JSY RC 10.00 4.00
❑ 213 J.J. Arrington JSY RC 10.00 4.00
❑ 214 Jason Campbell JSY RC 10.00 4.00
❑ 215 Kyle Orton JSY RC 10.00 4.00
❑ 216 Mark Bradley JSY RC 8.00 3.00
❑ 217 Mark Clayton JSY RC 10.00 4.00
❑ 218 Matt Jones JSY RC 15.00 6.00
❑ 219 Maurice Clarett JSY 8.00 3.00
❑ 220 Reggie Brown JSY RC 8.00 3.00
❑ 221 Ronnie Brown JSY RC 20.00 7.50
❑ 222 Roddy White JSY RC 8.00 3.00
❑ 223 Ryan Moats JSY RC 8.00 3.00
❑ 224 Roscoe Parrish JSY RC 8.00 3.00
❑ 225 Stefan LeFors JSY RC 8.00 3.00
❑ 226 Terrence Murphy JSY RC 8.00 3.00
❑ 227 Troy Williamson JSY RC 12.00 5.00
❑ 228 Vernand Morency JSY RC 8.00 3.00
❑ 229 Vincent Jackson JSY RC 8.00 3.00

1998 Playoff Momentum Hobby

❑ COMPLETE SET (250) 250.00 100.00
❑ 1 Jake Plummer 2.50 1.00
❑ 2 Eric Metcalf 1.00 .40
❑ 3 Adrian Murrell 1.50 .60
❑ 4 Larry Centers 1.00 .40
❑ 5 Frank Sanders 1.50 .60
❑ 6 Rob Moore 1.50 .60
❑ 7 Andre Wadsworth RC 4.00 1.50
❑ 8 Chris Chandler 1.50 .60
❑ 9 Jamal Anderson 2.50 1.00
❑ 10 Tony Martin 1.50 .60
❑ 11 Terance Mathis 1.50 .60
❑ 12 Tim Dwight RC 5.00 2.00
❑ 13 Jammi German RC 2.50 1.00
❑ 14 O.J. Santiago 1.00 .40
❑ 15 Jim Harbaugh 1.50 .60
❑ 16 Eric Zeier 1.50 .60
❑ 17 Duane Starks RC 2.50 1.00
❑ 18 Rod Woodson 1.50 .60
❑ 19 Errict Rhett 1.50 .60
❑ 20 Jay Graham 1.00 .40
❑ 21 Ray Lewis 2.50 1.00
❑ 22 Michael Jackson 1.00 .40
❑ 23 Jermaine Lewis 1.50 .60
❑ 24 Patrick Johnson RC 4.00 1.50
❑ 25 Eric Green 1.00 .40
❑ 26 Doug Flutie 2.50 1.00
❑ 27 Rob Johnson 1.50 .60
❑ 28 Antowain Smith 2.50 1.00
❑ 29 Thurman Thomas 2.50 1.00

❑ 30	Jonathan Linton RC	4.00	1.50
❑ 31	Bruce Smith	1.50	.60
❑ 32	Eric Moulds	2.50	1.00
❑ 33	Kevin Williams	1.00	.40
❑ 34	Andre Reed	1.50	.60
❑ 35	Steve Beuerlein	1.50	.60
❑ 36	Kerry Collins	1.50	.60
❑ 37	Anthony Johnson	1.00	.40
❑ 38	Fred Lane	1.00	.40
❑ 39	William Floyd	1.00	.40
❑ 40	Rocket Ismail	1.00	.40
❑ 41	Wesley Walls	1.50	.60
❑ 42	Muhsin Muhammad	1.50	.60
❑ 43	Rae Carruth	1.00	.40
❑ 44	Kevin Greene	1.50	.60
❑ 45	Greg Lloyd	1.00	.40
❑ 46	Moses Moreno RC	2.50	1.00
❑ 47	Erik Kramer	1.00	.40
❑ 48	Edgar Bennett	1.00	.40
❑ 49	Curtis Enis RC	2.50	1.00
❑ 50	Curtis Conway	1.50	.60
❑ 51	Bobby Engram	1.50	.60
❑ 52	Alonzo Mayes RC	2.50	1.00
❑ 53	Jeff Blake	1.50	.60
❑ 54	Neil O'Donnell	1.50	.60
❑ 55	Corey Dillon	2.50	1.00
❑ 56	Takeo Spikes RC	5.00	2.00
❑ 57	Carl Pickens	1.50	.60
❑ 58	Tony McGee	1.00	.40
❑ 59	Darnay Scott	1.50	.60
❑ 60	Troy Aikman	5.00	2.00
❑ 61	Deion Sanders	2.50	1.00
❑ 62	Emmitt Smith	8.00	3.00
❑ 63	Darren Woodson	1.00	.40
❑ 64	Chris Warren	1.50	.60
❑ 65	Daryl Johnston	1.50	.60
❑ 66	Ernie Mills	1.00	.40
❑ 67	Billy Davis	1.00	.40
❑ 68	Michael Irvin	2.50	1.00
❑ 69	David LaFleur	1.00	.40
❑ 70	John Elway	10.00	4.00
❑ 71	Brian Griese RC	10.00	4.00
❑ 72	Steve Atwater	1.00	.40
❑ 73	Terrell Davis	2.50	1.00
❑ 74	Rod Smith	1.50	.60
❑ 75	Marcus Nash RC	2.50	1.00
❑ 76	Shannon Sharpe	1.50	.60
❑ 77	Ed McCaffrey	1.50	.60
❑ 78	Neil Smith	1.50	.60
❑ 79	Charlie Batch RC	5.00	2.00
❑ 80	Germane Crowell RC	4.00	1.50
❑ 81	Scott Mitchell	1.50	.60
❑ 82	Barry Sanders	8.00	3.00
❑ 83	Terry Fair RC	4.00	1.50
❑ 84	Herman Moore	1.50	.60
❑ 85	Johnnie Morton	1.50	.60
❑ 86	Brett Favre	10.00	4.00
❑ 87	Rick Mirer	1.00	.40
❑ 88	Dorsey Levens	2.50	1.00
❑ 89	William Henderson	1.50	.60
❑ 90	Derrick Mayes	1.50	.60
❑ 91	Antonio Freeman	2.50	1.00
❑ 92	Robert Brooks	1.50	.60
❑ 93	Mark Chmura	1.50	.60
❑ 94	Vonnie Holliday RC	4.00	1.50
❑ 95	Reggie White	2.50	1.00
❑ 96	E.G. Green RC	4.00	1.50
❑ 97	Jerome Pathon RC	5.00	2.00
❑ 98	Peyton Manning RC	50.00	20.00
❑ 99	Marshall Faulk	3.00	1.25
❑ 100	Zack Crockett	1.00	.40
❑ 101	Ken Dilger	1.00	.40
❑ 102	Marvin Harrison	2.50	1.00
❑ 103	Mark Brunell	2.50	1.00
❑ 104	Jonathan Quinn RC	5.00	2.00
❑ 105	Tavian Banks RC	4.00	1.50
❑ 106	Fred Taylor RC	8.00	3.00
❑ 107	James Stewart	1.50	.60

❑ 108	Jimmy Smith	1.50	.60
❑ 109	Keenan McCardell	1.50	.60
❑ 110	Elvis Grbac	1.50	.60
❑ 111	Rich Gannon	2.50	1.00
❑ 112	Rashaan Shehee RC	4.00	1.50
❑ 113	Donnell Bennett	1.00	.40
❑ 114	Kimble Anders	1.50	.60
❑ 115	Derrick Thomas	2.50	1.00
❑ 116	Kevin Lockett	1.00	.40
❑ 117	Derrick Alexander WR	1.50	.60
❑ 118	Tony Gonzalez	2.50	1.00
❑ 119	Andre Rison	1.50	.60
❑ 120	Craig Erickson	1.00	.40
❑ 121	Dan Marino	10.00	4.00
❑ 122	John Avery RC	4.00	1.50
❑ 123	Karim Abdul-Jabbar	2.50	1.00
❑ 124	Zach Thomas	2.50	1.00
❑ 125	O.J. McDuffie	1.50	.60
❑ 126	Troy Drayton	1.00	.40
❑ 127	Randall Cunningham	2.50	1.00
❑ 128	Brad Johnson	2.50	1.00
❑ 129	Robert Smith	2.50	1.00
❑ 130	Cris Carter	2.50	1.00
❑ 131	Randy Moss RC	30.00	12.50
❑ 132	Jake Reed	1.50	.60
❑ 133	John Randle	1.50	.60
❑ 134	Drew Bledsoe	4.00	1.50
❑ 135	Tony Simmons RC	4.00	1.50
❑ 136	Sedrick Shaw	1.00	.40
❑ 137	Chris Floyd RC	2.50	1.00
❑ 138	Robert Edwards RC	4.00	1.50
❑ 139	Rod Rutledge RC	2.50	1.00
❑ 140	Shawn Jefferson	1.00	.40
❑ 141	Ben Coates	1.50	.60
❑ 142	Terry Glenn	2.50	1.00
❑ 143	Heath Shuler	1.00	.40
❑ 144	Danny Wuerffel	1.50	.60
❑ 145	Troy Davis	1.00	.40
❑ 146	Qadry Ismail	1.50	.60
❑ 147	Ray Zellars	1.00	.40
❑ 148	Lamar Smith	1.50	.60
❑ 149	Cameron Cleeland RC	2.50	1.00
❑ 150	Sean Dawkins	1.00	.40
❑ 151	Andre Hastings	1.00	.40
❑ 152	Danny Kanell	1.50	.60
❑ 153	Tiki Barber	2.50	1.00
❑ 154	Tyrone Wheatley	1.50	.60
❑ 155	Charles Way	1.00	.40
❑ 156	Gary Brown	1.00	.40
❑ 157	Shaun Williams RC	4.00	1.50
❑ 158	Chris Calloway	1.00	.40
❑ 159	Amani Toomer	1.50	.60
❑ 160	Brian Alford RC	2.50	1.00
❑ 161	Joe Jurevicius RC	5.00	2.00
❑ 162	Ike Hilliard	1.50	.60
❑ 163	Michael Strahan	1.50	.60
❑ 164	Glenn Foley	1.50	.60
❑ 165	Vinny Testaverde	1.50	.60
❑ 166	Keyshawn Johnson	2.50	1.00
❑ 167	Curtis Martin	2.50	1.00
❑ 168	Leon Johnson	1.00	.40
❑ 169	Keith Byars	1.00	.40
❑ 170	Wayne Chrebet	2.50	1.00
❑ 171	Kyle Brady	1.00	.40
❑ 172	Dedric Ward	1.00	.40
❑ 173	Jeff George	1.50	.60
❑ 174	Charles Woodson RC	10.00	4.00
❑ 175	Napoleon Kaufman	2.50	1.00
❑ 176	Jon Ritchie RC	4.00	1.50
❑ 177	Tim Brown	2.50	1.00
❑ 178	James Jett	1.50	.60
❑ 179	Rickey Dudley	1.00	.40
❑ 180	Bobby Hoying	1.50	.60
❑ 181	Duce Staley	3.00	1.25
❑ 182	Charlie Garner	1.50	.60
❑ 183	Irving Fryar	1.50	.60
❑ 184	Jeff Graham	1.00	.40
❑ 185	Jason Dunn	1.00	.40

❑ 186	Kordell Stewart	2.50	1.00
❑ 187	Jerome Bettis	2.50	1.00
❑ 188	Andre Coleman	1.00	.40
❑ 189	Chris Fuamatu-Ma'afala RC	4.00	1.50
❑ 190	Charles Johnson	1.00	.40
❑ 191	Hines Ward RC	20.00	10.00
❑ 192	Mark Bruener	1.00	.40
❑ 193	Courtney Hawkins	1.00	.40
❑ 194	Will Blackwell	1.00	.40
❑ 195	Levon Kirkland	1.00	.40
❑ 196	Mikhael Ricks RC	4.00	1.50
❑ 197	Ryan Leaf RC	5.00	2.00
❑ 198	Natrone Means	1.50	.60
❑ 199	Junior Seau	2.50	1.00
❑ 200	Bryan Still	1.00	.40
❑ 201	Freddie Jones	1.00	.40
❑ 202	Steve Young	3.00	1.25
❑ 203	Jim Druckenmiller	1.00	.40
❑ 204	Garrison Hearst	2.50	1.00
❑ 205	R.W. McQuarters RC	4.00	1.50
❑ 206	Merton Hanks	1.00	.40
❑ 207	Marc Edwards	1.00	.40
❑ 208	Jerry Rice	5.00	2.00
❑ 209	Terrell Owens	2.50	1.00
❑ 210	J.J. Stokes	1.50	.60
❑ 211	Tony Banks	1.50	.60
❑ 212	Robert Holcombe RC	4.00	1.50
❑ 213	Greg Hill	1.00	.40
❑ 214	Amp Lee	1.00	.40
❑ 215	Jerald Moore	1.00	.40
❑ 216	Isaac Bruce	2.50	1.00
❑ 217	Az-Zahir Hakim RC	5.00	2.00
❑ 218	Eddie Kennison	1.50	.60
❑ 219	Grant Wistrom RC	4.00	1.50
❑ 220	Warren Moon	2.50	1.00
❑ 221	Ahman Green RC	25.00	10.00
❑ 222	Steve Broussard	1.00	.40
❑ 223	Ricky Watters	1.50	.60
❑ 224	James McKnight	2.50	1.00
❑ 225	Joey Galloway	1.50	.60
❑ 226	Mike Pritchard	1.00	.40
❑ 227	Trent Dilfer	2.50	1.00
❑ 228	Warrick Dunn	2.50	1.00
❑ 229	Mike Alstott	2.50	1.00
❑ 230	John Lynch	1.50	.60
❑ 231	Jacquez Green RC	4.00	1.50
❑ 232	Reidel Anthony	1.50	.60
❑ 233	Bert Emanuel	1.50	.60
❑ 234	Warren Sapp	1.50	.60
❑ 235	Steve McNair	2.50	1.00
❑ 236	Eddie George	2.50	1.00
❑ 237	Chris Sanders	1.00	.40
❑ 238	Yancey Thigpen	1.00	.40
❑ 239	Willie Davis	1.00	.40
❑ 240	Kevin Dyson RC	5.00	2.00
❑ 241	Frank Wycheck	1.00	.40
❑ 242	Trent Green	2.50	1.00
❑ 243	Gus Frerotte	1.00	.40
❑ 244	Skip Hicks RC	4.00	1.50
❑ 245	Terry Allen	2.50	1.00
❑ 246	Stephen Davis	1.00	.40
❑ 247	Stephen Alexander RC	4.00	1.50
❑ 248	Michael Westbrook	1.50	.60
❑ 249	Dana Stubblefield SP	2.50	1.00
❑ 250	Dan Wilkinson SP	2.50	1.00

1999 Playoff Momentum SSD

❑	COMPLETE SET (200)	300.00	150.00
❑	COMP.SHORT SET (150)	100.00	50.00
❑ 1	Rob Moore	.50	.20
❑ 2	Adrian Murrell	.50	.20
❑ 3	Frank Sanders	.50	.20
❑ 4	Andre Wadsworth	.30	.10
❑ 5	Tim Dwight	.75	.30
❑ 6	Terance Mathis	.50	.20
❑ 7	Priest Holmes	1.25	.50
❑ 8	Jermaine Lewis	.50	.20

❑ 9 Scott Mitchell	.30	.10
❑ 10 Patrick Johnson	.30	.10
❑ 11 Tony Banks	.50	.20
❑ 12 Thurman Thomas	.50	.20
❑ 13 Andre Reed	.50	.20
❑ 14 Bruce Smith	.50	.20
❑ 15 Tim Biakabutuka	.50	.20
❑ 16 Muhsin Muhammad	.50	.20
❑ 17 Wesley Walls	.50	.20
❑ 18 Rae Carruth	.30	.10
❑ 19 Curtis Conway	.50	.20
❑ 20 Bobby Engram	.50	.20
❑ 21 Jeff Blake	.50	.20
❑ 22 Damay Scott	.30	.10
❑ 23 Ty Detmer	.50	.20
❑ 24 Leslie Shepherd	.30	.10
❑ 25 Sedrick Shaw	.30	.10
❑ 26 Michael Irvin	.50	.20
❑ 27 Rocket Ismail	.50	.20
❑ 28 Ed McCaffrey	.50	.20
❑ 29 Marcus Nash	.30	.10
❑ 30 Shannon Sharpe	.50	.20
❑ 31 Neil Smith	.50	.20
❑ 32 Rod Smith	.50	.20
❑ 33 Bubby Brister	.30	.10
❑ 34 Germane Crowell	.30	.10
❑ 35 Johnnie Morton	.50	.20
❑ 36 Bill Schroeder	.75	.30
❑ 37 Mark Chmura	.30	.10
❑ 38 Marvin Harrison	.75	.30
❑ 39 E.G. Green	.30	.10
❑ 40 Jerome Pathon	.30	.10
❑ 41 Keenan McCardell	.50	.20
❑ 42 Jimmy Smith	.50	.20
❑ 43 Kyle Brady	.30	.10
❑ 44 Tavian Banks	.30	.10
❑ 45 Warren Moon	.75	.30
❑ 46 Derrick Alexander WR	.50	.20
❑ 47 Elvis Grbac	.50	.20
❑ 48 Andre Rison	.50	.20
❑ 49 Byron Bam Morris	.30	.10
❑ 50 Rashaan Shehee	.30	.10
❑ 51 Karim Abdul-Jabbar	.50	.20
❑ 52 John Avery	.30	.10
❑ 53 Tony Martin	.50	.20
❑ 54 O.J. McDuffie	.50	.20
❑ 55 Oronde Gadsden	.50	.20
❑ 56 Robert Smith	.75	.30
❑ 57 Jeff George	.50	.20
❑ 58 Jake Reed	.50	.20
❑ 59 Leroy Hoard	.30	.10
❑ 60 Terry Allen	.50	.20
❑ 61 Terry Glenn	.75	.30
❑ 62 Ben Coates	.50	.20
❑ 63 Tony Simmons	.30	.10
❑ 64 Cameron Cleeland	.30	.10
❑ 65 Eddie Kennison	.50	.20
❑ 66 Billy Joe Hobert	.30	.10
❑ 67 Amani Toomer	.30	.10
❑ 68 Kerry Collins	.50	.20
❑ 69 Ike Hilliard	.30	.10
❑ 70 Gary Brown	.30	.10
❑ 71 Joe Jurevicius	.50	.20
❑ 72 Wayne Chrebet	.50	.20
❑ 73 Vinny Testaverde	.50	.20
❑ 74 Charles Woodson	.75	.30
❑ 75 James Jett	.50	.20
❑ 76 Charles Johnson	.30	.10
❑ 77 Duce Staley	.75	.30
❑ 78 Hines Ward	.75	.30
❑ 79 Jim Harbaugh	.50	.20
❑ 80 Ryan Leaf	.75	.30
❑ 81 Junior Seau	.75	.30
❑ 82 Mikhael Ricks	.30	.10
❑ 83 Garrison Hearst	.50	.20
❑ 84 J.J. Stokes	.50	.20
❑ 85 Lawrence Phillips	.50	.20
❑ 86 Derrick Mayes	.30	.10
❑ 87 Mike Pritchard	.30	.10
❑ 88 Ahman Green	.75	.30
❑ 89 Ricky Watters	.50	.20
❑ 90 Robert Holcombe	.30	.10
❑ 91 Isaac Bruce	.75	.30
❑ 92 Trent Dilfer	.50	.20
❑ 93 Reidel Anthony	.30	.10
❑ 94 Jacquez Green	.30	.10
❑ 95 Warren Sapp	.30	.10
❑ 96 Kevin Dyson	.50	.20
❑ 97 Yancey Thigpen	.30	.10
❑ 98 Stephen Davis	.75	.30
❑ 99 Irving Fryar	.50	.20
❑ 100 Michael Westbrook	.50	.20
❑ 101 Jake Plummer	.75	.30
❑ 102 Jamal Anderson	1.25	.50
❑ 103 Chris Chandler	.75	.30
❑ 104 Doug Flutie	.75	.30
❑ 105 Eric Moulds	1.25	.50
❑ 106 Antowain Smith	1.25	.50
❑ 107 Jonathan Linton	.50	.20
❑ 108 Curtis Enis	.50	.20
❑ 109 Corey Dillon	1.25	.50
❑ 110 Carl Pickens	.75	.30
❑ 111 Emmitt Smith	2.50	1.00
❑ 112 Troy Aikman	2.50	1.00
❑ 113 Deion Sanders	1.25	.50
❑ 114 John Elway	4.00	1.50
❑ 115 Terrell Davis	1.25	.50
❑ 116 Brian Griese	1.25	.50
❑ 117 Barry Sanders	4.00	1.50
❑ 118 Charlie Batch	.75	.30
❑ 119 Herman Moore	.75	.30
❑ 120 Brett Favre	4.00	1.50
❑ 121 Antonio Freeman	1.25	.50
❑ 122 Dorsey Levens	1.25	.50
❑ 123 Peyton Manning	4.00	1.50
❑ 124 Fred Taylor	1.25	.50
❑ 125 Mark Brunell	.75	.30
❑ 126 Dan Marino	4.00	1.50
❑ 127 Randy Moss	3.00	1.25
❑ 128 Cris Carter	1.25	.50
❑ 129 Randall Cunningham	1.25	.50
❑ 130 Drew Bledsoe	1.50	.60
❑ 131 Keyshawn Johnson	1.25	.50
❑ 132 Curtis Martin	1.25	.50
❑ 133 Tim Brown	1.25	.50
❑ 134 Napoleon Kaufman	1.25	.50
❑ 135 Kordell Stewart	.75	.30
❑ 136 Jerome Bettis	1.25	.50
❑ 137 Natrone Means	.75	.30
❑ 138 Jerry Rice	2.50	1.00
❑ 139 Steve Young	1.50	.60
❑ 140 Terrell Owens	1.25	.50
❑ 141 Joey Galloway	.75	.30
❑ 142 Jon Kitna	.75	.30
❑ 143 Marshall Faulk	1.50	.60
❑ 144 Kurt Warner RC	12.00	5.00
❑ 145 Warrick Dunn	1.25	.50
❑ 146 Mike Alstott	1.25	.50
❑ 147 Eddie George	.75	.30
❑ 148 Steve McNair	1.25	.50
❑ 149 Brad Johnson	1.25	.50
❑ 150 Skip Hicks	.50	.20
❑ 151 Tim Couch RC	5.00	2.00
❑ 152 Donovan McNabb RC	20.00	7.50
❑ 153 Akili Smith RC	.75	.30
❑ 154 Edgerrin James RC	15.00	6.00
❑ 155 Ricky Williams RC	8.00	3.00
❑ 156 Torry Holt RC	10.00	4.00
❑ 157 Champ Bailey RC	6.00	2.50
❑ 158 David Boston RC	5.00	2.00
❑ 159 Chris Claiborne RC	2.50	1.00
❑ 160 Chris McAlister RC	4.00	1.50
❑ 161 Daunte Culpepper RC	15.00	6.00
❑ 162 Cade McNown RC	4.00	1.50
❑ 163 Troy Edwards RC	4.00	1.50
❑ 164 Jevon Kearse RC	8.00	3.00
❑ 165 Kevin Johnson RC	5.00	2.00
❑ 166 James Johnson RC	4.00	1.50
❑ 167 Reginald Kelly RC	2.50	1.00
❑ 168 Rob Konrad RC	5.00	2.00
❑ 169 Jim Kleinsasser RC	5.00	2.00
❑ 170 Kevin Faulk RC	5.00	2.00
❑ 171 Joe Montgomery RC	4.00	1.50
❑ 172 Shaun King RC	4.00	1.50
❑ 173 Peerless Price RC	5.00	2.00
❑ 174 Mike Cloud RC	4.00	1.50
❑ 175 Jermaine Fazande RC	4.00	1.50
❑ 176 D'Wayne Bates RC	4.00	1.50
❑ 177 Brock Huard RC	5.00	2.00
❑ 178 Marty Booker RC	5.00	2.00
❑ 179 Karsten Bailey RC	4.00	1.50
❑ 180 Shawn Bryson RC	5.00	2.00
❑ 181 Jeff Paulk RC	2.50	1.00
❑ 182 Travis McGriff RC	2.50	1.00
❑ 183 Amos Zereoue RC	5.00	2.00
❑ 184 Craig Yeast RC	4.00	1.50
❑ 185 Joe Germaine RC	4.00	1.50
❑ 186 Dameane Douglas RC	4.00	1.50
❑ 187 Sedrick Irvin RC	2.50	1.00
❑ 188 Brandon Stokley RC	6.00	2.50
❑ 189 Larry Parker RC	5.00	2.00
❑ 190 Sean Bennett RC	2.50	1.00
❑ 191 Wane McGarity RC	2.50	1.00
❑ 192 Olandis Gary RC	5.00	2.00
❑ 193 Na Brown RC	4.00	1.50
❑ 194 Aaron Brooks RC	8.00	3.00
❑ 195 Cecil Collins RC	2.50	1.00
❑ 196 Darrin Chiaverini RC	4.00	1.50
❑ 197 Kevin Daft RC	4.00	1.50
❑ 198 Darnell McDonald RC	4.00	1.50
❑ 199 Joel Makovicka RC	5.00	2.00
❑ 200 Michael Bishop RC	5.00	2.00

2000 Playoff Momentum

❑ COMP.SET w/o SP's (100)	15.00	6.00
❑ 1 David Boston	.60	.25
❑ 2 Jake Plummer	.40	.15
❑ 3 Chris Chandler	.40	.15
❑ 4 Jamal Anderson	.60	.25
❑ 5 Tim Dwight	.60	.25
❑ 6 Qadry Ismail	.40	.15
❑ 7 Peerless Price	.40	.15

❑ 8	Antowain Smith	.40	.15
❑ 9	Eric Moulds	.60	.25
❑ 10	Rob Johnson	.40	.15
❑ 11	Natrone Means	.25	.08
❑ 12	Muhsin Muhammad	.40	.15
❑ 13	Steve Beuerlein	.40	.15
❑ 14	Patrick Jeffers	.60	.25
❑ 15	Curtis Enis	.25	.08
❑ 16	Cade McNown	.25	.08
❑ 17	Marcus Robinson	.60	.25
❑ 18	Corey Dillon	.60	.25
❑ 19	Akili Smith	.25	.08
❑ 20	Carl Pickens	.40	.15
❑ 21	Tim Couch	.40	.15
❑ 22	Kevin Johnson	.60	.25
❑ 23	Troy Aikman	1.25	.50
❑ 24	Emmitt Smith	1.25	.50
❑ 25	Joey Galloway	.40	.15
❑ 26	Rocket Ismail	.40	.15
❑ 27	Olandis Gary	.60	.25
❑ 28	John Elway	2.00	.75
❑ 29	Brian Griese	.60	.25
❑ 30	Ed McCaffrey	.60	.25
❑ 31	Terrell Davis	.60	.25
❑ 32	Charlie Batch	.60	.25
❑ 33	James Stewart	.40	.15
❑ 34	Germane Crowell	.25	.08
❑ 35	Barry Sanders	1.50	.60
❑ 36	Herman Moore	.40	.15
❑ 37	Antonio Freeman	.60	.25
❑ 38	Dorsey Levens	.40	.15
❑ 39	Brett Favre	2.00	.75
❑ 40	Edgerrin James	1.00	.40
❑ 41	Marvin Harrison	.60	.25
❑ 42	Peyton Manning	1.50	.60
❑ 43	Fred Taylor	.60	.25
❑ 44	Keenan McCardell	.40	.15
❑ 45	Mark Brunell	.60	.25
❑ 46	Jimmy Smith	.40	.15
❑ 47	Elvis Grbac	.40	.15
❑ 48	Tony Gonzalez	.40	.15
❑ 49	James Johnson	.25	.08
❑ 50	Dan Marino	2.00	.75
❑ 51	Thurman Thomas	.40	.15
❑ 52	Cris Carter	.60	.25
❑ 53	Robert Smith	.60	.25
❑ 54	Randy Moss	1.25	.50
❑ 55	Daunte Culpepper	.75	.30
❑ 56	Terry Glenn	.40	.15
❑ 57	Kevin Faulk	.40	.15
❑ 58	Drew Bledsoe	.75	.30
❑ 59	Ricky Williams	.60	.25
❑ 60	Amani Toomer	.40	.15
❑ 61	Kerry Collins	.40	.15
❑ 62	Vinny Testaverde	.40	.15
❑ 63	Curtis Martin	.60	.25
❑ 64	Rich Gannon	.60	.25
❑ 65	Tyrone Wheatley	.40	.15
❑ 66	Napoleon Kaufman	.40	.15
❑ 67	Tim Brown	.60	.25
❑ 68	Duce Staley	.60	.25
❑ 69	Donovan McNabb	1.00	.40
❑ 70	Kordell Stewart	.40	.15
❑ 71	Troy Edwards	.25	.08
❑ 72	Jerome Bettis	.60	.25
❑ 73	Jim Harbaugh	.40	.15
❑ 74	Jermaine Fazande	.25	.08
❑ 75	Steve Young	.75	.30
❑ 76	Charlie Garner	.40	.15
❑ 77	Terrell Owens	.60	.25
❑ 78	Jerry Rice	1.25	.50
❑ 79	Jeff Garcia	.60	.25
❑ 80	Ricky Watters	.40	.15
❑ 81	Jon Kitna	.60	.25
❑ 82	Marshall Faulk	.75	.30
❑ 83	Isaac Bruce	.60	.25
❑ 84	Torry Holt	.60	.25
❑ 85	Kurt Warner	1.25	.50
❑ 86	Keyshawn Johnson	.60	.25
❑ 87	Warrick Dunn	.60	.25
❑ 88	Mike Alstott	.60	.25
❑ 89	Warren Sapp	.40	.15
❑ 90	Shaun King	.25	.08
❑ 91	Eddie George	.60	.25
❑ 92	Steve McNair	.60	.25
❑ 93	Jevon Kearse	.60	.25
❑ 94	Bruce Smith	.40	.15
❑ 95	Deion Sanders	.60	.25
❑ 96	Albert Connell	.25	.08
❑ 97	Michael Westbrook	.40	.15
❑ 98	Brad Johnson	.60	.25
❑ 99	Jeff George	.40	.15
❑ 100	Stephen Davis	.60	.25
❑ 101	Peter Warrick RC	8.00	3.00
❑ 102	Jamal Lewis RC	20.00	7.50
❑ 103	Thomas Jones RC	12.00	5.00
❑ 104	Plaxico Burress RC	15.00	6.00
❑ 105	Travis Taylor RC	8.00	3.00
❑ 106	Ron Dayne RC	8.00	3.00
❑ 107	Bubba Franks RC	8.00	3.00
❑ 108	Sebastian Janikowski RC	8.00	3.00
❑ 109	Chad Pennington RC	20.00	7.50
❑ 110	Shaun Alexander RC	40.00	15.00
❑ 111	Sylvester Morris RC	6.00	2.50
❑ 112	Anthony Becht RC	8.00	3.00
❑ 113	R.Jay Soward RC	6.00	2.50
❑ 114	Trung Canidate RC	6.00	2.50
❑ 115	Dennis Northcutt RC	8.00	3.00
❑ 116	Todd Pinkston RC	8.00	3.00
❑ 117	Jerry Porter RC	10.00	4.00
❑ 118	Travis Prentice RC	6.00	2.50
❑ 119	Giovanni Carmazzi RC	4.00	1.50
❑ 120	Ron Dugans RC	4.00	1.50
❑ 121	Erron Kinney RC	8.00	3.00
❑ 122	Dez White RC	8.00	3.00
❑ 123	Chris Cole RC	6.00	2.50
❑ 124	Ron Dixon RC	6.00	2.50
❑ 125	Chris Redman RC	6.00	2.50
❑ 126	J.R. Redmond RC	6.00	2.50
❑ 127	Laveranues Coles RC	10.00	4.00
❑ 128	JaJuan Dawson RC	4.00	1.50
❑ 129	Darrell Jackson RC	15.00	6.00
❑ 130	Reuben Droughns RC	10.00	4.00
❑ 131	Doug Chapman RC	6.00	2.50
❑ 132	Terrelle Smith RC	6.00	2.50
❑ 133	Curtis Keaton RC	6.00	2.50
❑ 134	Gari Scott RC	4.00	1.50
❑ 135	Courtney Brown RC	8.00	3.00
❑ 136	Corey Simon RC	8.00	3.00
❑ 137	Brian Urlacher RC	30.00	12.50
❑ 138	Shaun Ellis RC	8.00	3.00
❑ 139	John Abraham RC	8.00	3.00
❑ 140	Deltha O'Neal RC	8.00	3.00
❑ 141	Rashard Anderson RC	6.00	2.50
❑ 142	Ahmed Plummer RC	8.00	3.00
❑ 143	Chris Hovan RC	6.00	2.50
❑ 144	Erik Flowers RC	6.00	2.50
❑ 145	Rob Morris RC	6.00	2.50
❑ 146	Keith Bulluck RC	8.00	3.00
❑ 147	Darren Howard RC	6.00	2.50
❑ 148	John Engelberger RC	6.00	2.50
❑ 149	Ian Gold RC	6.00	2.50
❑ 150	Raynoch Thompson RC	6.00	2.50
❑ 151	Cornelius Griffin RC	6.00	2.50
❑ 152	Rogers Beckett RC	6.00	2.50
❑ 153	Dwayne Goodrich RC	4.00	1.50
❑ 154	Barrett Green RC	4.00	1.50
❑ 155	Kevin Thompson RC	4.00	1.50
❑ 156	Ben Kelly RC	4.00	1.50
❑ 157	Danny Farmer RC	6.00	2.50
❑ 158	Aaron Shea RC	6.00	2.50
❑ 159	Trevor Gaylor RC	6.00	2.50
❑ 160	Mike Brown RC	12.00	5.00
❑ 161	Frank Moreau RC	6.00	2.50
❑ 162	Deon Dyer RC	6.00	2.50
❑ 163	Avion Black RC	6.00	2.50
❑ 164	Spergon Wynn RC	6.00	2.50
❑ 165	Billy Volek RC	12.00	5.00
❑ 166	Michael Wiley RC	6.00	2.50
❑ 167	Dante Hall RC	15.00	6.00
❑ 168	Ronney Jenkins RC	6.00	2.50
❑ 169	Sammy Morris RC	6.00	2.50
❑ 170	Kevin McDougal RC	6.00	2.50
❑ 171	Tee Martin RC	8.00	3.00
❑ 172	Troy Walters RC	8.00	3.00
❑ 173	Chad Morton RC	8.00	3.00
❑ 174	Jamel White RC	6.00	2.50
❑ 175	Shockmain Davis RC	4.00	1.50
❑ 176	Mario Edwards RC	6.00	2.50
❑ 177	Brandon Short RC	6.00	2.50
❑ 178	James Williams RC	6.00	2.50
❑ 179	Mike Anderson RC	10.00	4.00
❑ 180	Tom Brady RC	80.00	50.00
❑ 181	Na'il Diggs RC	6.00	2.50
❑ 182	Todd Husak RC	8.00	3.00
❑ 183	JaJuan Seider RC	4.00	1.50
❑ 184	Tim Rattay RC	8.00	3.00
❑ 185	Jarious Jackson RC	6.00	2.50
❑ 186	Joe Hamilton RC	6.00	2.50
❑ 187	Shyrone Stith RC	6.00	2.50
❑ 188	Mondriel Fulcher RC	4.00	1.50
❑ 189	Bashir Yamini RC	4.00	1.50
❑ 190	Herbert Goodman RC	6.00	2.50
❑ 191	Mike Green RC	6.00	2.50
❑ 192	Demario Brown RC	4.00	1.50
❑ 193	Charles Lee RC	4.00	1.50
❑ 194	Doug Johnson RC	8.00	3.00
❑ 195	Windrell Hayes RC	6.00	2.50
❑ 196	Julian Peterson RC	8.00	3.00
❑ 197	Kwame Cavil RC	4.00	1.50
❑ 198	Hank Poteat RC	6.00	2.50
❑ 199	Clint Stoerner RC	6.00	2.50
❑ 200	Mark Simoneau RC	6.00	2.50

1998 Playoff Prestige Hobby

❑	COMP.HOBBY SET (200)	100.00	40.00
❑ 1	John Elway	8.00	3.00
❑ 2	Steve Atwater	.75	.30
❑ 3	Terrell Davis	2.00	.75
❑ 4	Bill Romanowski	.75	.30
❑ 5	Rod Smith	1.25	.50
❑ 6	Shannon Sharpe	1.25	.50
❑ 7	Ed McCaffrey	1.25	.50
❑ 8	Neil Smith	1.25	.50
❑ 9	Brett Favre	8.00	3.00
❑ 10	Dorsey Levens	2.00	.75
❑ 11	LeRoy Butler	.75	.30
❑ 12	Antonio Freeman	2.00	.75
❑ 13	Robert Brooks	1.25	.50
❑ 14	Mark Chmura	1.25	.50
❑ 15	Gilbert Brown	.75	.30
❑ 16	Kordell Stewart	2.00	.75
❑ 17	Jerome Bettis	2.00	.75
❑ 18	Carnell Lake	.75	.30
❑ 19	Dermontti Dawson	.75	.30
❑ 20	Charles Johnson	.75	.30
❑ 21	Greg Lloyd	.75	.30

❑ 22 Levon Kirkland .75 .30
❑ 23 Steve Young 2.50 1.00
❑ 24 Jim Druckenmiller .75 .30
❑ 25 Garrison Hearst 2.00 .75
❑ 26 Merton Hanks .75 .30
❑ 27 Ken Norton .75 .30
❑ 28 Jerry Rice 4.00 1.50
❑ 29 Terrell Owens 2.00 .75
❑ 30 J.J. Stokes 1.25 .50
❑ 31 Trent Dilfer 2.00 .75
❑ 32 Warrick Dunn 2.00 .75
❑ 33 Mike Alstott 2.00 .75
❑ 34 Reidel Anthony 1.25 .50
❑ 35 Warren Sapp 1.25 .50
❑ 36 Elvis Grbac 1.25 .50
❑ 37 Kimble Anders 1.25 .50
❑ 38 Ted Popson .75 .30
❑ 39 Derrick Thomas 2.00 .75
❑ 40 Tony Gonzalez 2.00 .75
❑ 41 Andre Rison 1.25 .50
❑ 42 Derrick Alexander 1.25 .50
❑ 43 Brad Johnson 2.00 .75
❑ 44 Robert Smith 2.00 .75
❑ 45 Randall McDaniel .75 .30
❑ 46 Cris Carter 2.00 .75
❑ 47 Jake Reed 1.25 .50
❑ 48 John Randle 1.25 .50
❑ 49 Drew Bledsoe 3.00 1.25
❑ 50 Willie Clay .75 .30
❑ 51 Chris Slade .75 .30
❑ 52 Willie McGinest .75 .30
❑ 53 Shawn Jefferson .75 .30
❑ 54 Ben Coates 1.25 .50
❑ 55 Terry Glenn 2.00 .75
❑ 56 Jason Hanson .75 .30
❑ 57 Scott Mitchell 1.25 .50
❑ 58 Barry Sanders 6.00 2.50
❑ 59 Herman Moore 1.25 .50
❑ 60 Johnnie Morton 1.25 .50
❑ 61 Mark Brunell 2.00 .75
❑ 62 James Stewart 1.25 .50
❑ 63 Tony Boselli .75 .30
❑ 64 Jimmy Smith 1.25 .50
❑ 65 Keenan McCardell 1.25 .50
❑ 66 Dan Marino 8.00 3.00
❑ 67 Troy Drayton .75 .30
❑ 68 Bernie Parmalee .75 .30
❑ 69 Karim Abdul-Jabbar 2.00 .75
❑ 70 Zach Thomas 2.00 .75
❑ 71 O.J. McDuffie 1.25 .50
❑ 72 Tim Bowens .75 .30
❑ 73 Danny Kanell 1.25 .50
❑ 74 Tiki Barber 2.00 .75
❑ 75 Tyrone Wheatley 1.25 .50
❑ 76 Charles Way .75 .30
❑ 77 Jason Sehorn 1.25 .50
❑ 78 Ike Hilliard 1.25 .50
❑ 79 Michael Strahan 1.25 .50
❑ 80 Troy Aikman 4.00 1.50
❑ 81 Deion Sanders 2.00 .75
❑ 82 Emmitt Smith 6.00 2.50
❑ 83 Darren Woodson .75 .30
❑ 84 Daryl Johnston 1.25 .50
❑ 85 Michael Irvin 2.00 .75
❑ 86 David LaFleur .75 .30
❑ 87 Glenn Foley 1.25 .50
❑ 88 Neil O'Donnell 1.25 .50
❑ 89 Keyshawn Johnson 2.00 .75
❑ 90 Aaron Glenn .75 .30
❑ 91 Wayne Chrebet 2.00 .75
❑ 92 Curtis Martin 2.00 .75
❑ 93 Steve McNair 2.00 .75
❑ 94 Eddie George 2.00 .75
❑ 95 Bruce Matthews .75 .30
❑ 96 Frank Wycheck .75 .30
❑ 97 Yancey Thigpen .75 .30
❑ 98 Gus Frerotte .75 .30
❑ 99 Terry Allen 2.00 .75
❑ 100 Michael Westbrook 1.25 .50
❑ 101 Jamie Asher .75 .30
❑ 102 Marshall Faulk 2.50 1.00
❑ 103 Zack Crockett .75 .30
❑ 104 Ken Dilger .75 .30
❑ 105 Marvin Harrison 2.00 .75
❑ 106 Chris Chandler 1.25 .50
❑ 107 Byron Hanspard .75 .30
❑ 108 Jamal Anderson 2.00 .75
❑ 109 Terance Mathis 1.25 .50
❑ 110 Peter Boulware .75 .30
❑ 111 Michael Jackson .75 .30
❑ 112 Jim Harbaugh 1.25 .50
❑ 113 Errict Rhett 1.25 .50
❑ 114 Antowain Smith 2.00 .75
❑ 115 Thurman Thomas 2.00 .75
❑ 116 Bruce Smith 1.25 .50
❑ 117 Doug Flutie 2.00 .75
❑ 118 Rob Johnson 1.25 .50
❑ 119 Kerry Collins 1.25 .50
❑ 120 Fred Lane .75 .30
❑ 121 Wesley Walls 1.25 .50
❑ 122 William Floyd .75 .30
❑ 123 Kevin Greene 1.25 .50
❑ 124 Erik Kramer .75 .30
❑ 125 Darnell Autry .75 .30
❑ 126 Curtis Conway 1.25 .50
❑ 127 Edgar Bennett .75 .30
❑ 128 Jeff Blake 1.25 .50
❑ 129 Corey Dillon 2.00 .75
❑ 130 Carl Pickens 1.25 .50
❑ 131 Darnay Scott 1.25 .50
❑ 132 Jake Plummer 2.00 .75
❑ 133 Larry Centers .75 .30
❑ 134 Frank Sanders 1.25 .50
❑ 135 Rob Moore 1.25 .50
❑ 136 Adrian Murrell 1.25 .50
❑ 137 Troy Davis .75 .30
❑ 138 Ray Zellars .75 .30
❑ 139 Willie Roaf .75 .30
❑ 140 Andre Hastings .75 .30
❑ 141 Jeff George 1.25 .50
❑ 142 Napoleon Kaufman 2.00 .75
❑ 143 Desmond Howard 1.25 .50
❑ 144 Tim Brown 2.00 .75
❑ 145 James Jett 1.25 .50
❑ 146 Rickey Dudley .75 .30
❑ 147 Bobby Hoying 1.25 .50
❑ 148 Duce Staley 2.50 1.00
❑ 149 Charlie Garner 1.25 .50
❑ 150 Irving Fryar 1.25 .50
❑ 151 Chris T. Jones .75 .30
❑ 152 Tony Banks 1.25 .50
❑ 153 Craig Heyward .75 .30
❑ 154 Isaac Bruce 2.00 .75
❑ 155 Eddie Kennison 1.25 .50
❑ 156 Junior Seau 2.00 .75
❑ 157 Tony Martin 1.25 .50
❑ 158 Freddie Jones .75 .30
❑ 159 Natrone Means 1.25 .50
❑ 160 Warren Moon 2.00 .75
❑ 161 Steve Broussard .75 .30
❑ 162 Joey Galloway 1.25 .50
❑ 163 Brian Blades .75 .30
❑ 164 Ricky Watters 1.25 .50
❑ 165 Peyton Manning RC 25.00 10.00
❑ 166 Ryan Leaf RC 3.00 1.25
❑ 167 Andre Wadsworth RC 2.50 1.00
❑ 168 Charles Woodson RC 4.00 1.50
❑ 169 Curtis Enis RC 1.50 .60
❑ 170 Fred Taylor RC 5.00 2.00
❑ 171 Kevin Dyson RC 3.00 1.25
❑ 172 Robert Edwards RC 2.50 1.00
❑ 173 Randy Moss RC 15.00 6.00
❑ 174 R.W. McQuarters RC 2.50 1.00
❑ 175 John Avery RC 2.50 1.00
❑ 176 Marcus Nash RC 1.50 .60
❑ 177 Jerome Pathon RC 3.00 1.25
❑ 178 Jacquez Green RC 2.50 1.00
❑ 179 Robert Holcombe RC 2.50 1.00
❑ 180 Pat Johnson RC 2.50 1.00
❑ 181 Germane Crowell RC 2.50 1.00
❑ 182 Tony Simmons RC 2.50 1.00
❑ 183 Joe Jurevicius RC 3.00 1.25
❑ 184 Mikhael Ricks RC 2.50 1.00
❑ 185 Charlie Batch RC 3.00 1.25
❑ 186 Jon Ritchie RC 2.50 1.00
❑ 187 Scott Frost RC 1.50 .60
❑ 188 Skip Hicks RC 2.50 1.00
❑ 189 Brian Alford RC 1.50 .60
❑ 190 E.G. Green RC 2.50 1.00
❑ 191 Jammi German RC 1.50 .60
❑ 192 Ahman Green RC 12.00 5.00
❑ 193 Chris Floyd RC 1.50 .60
❑ 194 Larry Shannon RC 1.50 .60
❑ 195 Jonathan Quinn RC 3.00 1.25
❑ 196 Rashaan Shehee RC 2.50 1.00
❑ 197 Brian Griese RC 6.00 2.50
❑ 198 Hines Ward RC 10.00 5.00
❑ 199 Michael Pittman RC 4.00 2.00
❑ 200 Az-Zahir Hakim RC 3.00 1.25

1999 Playoff Prestige EXP

❑ COMPLETE SET (200) 50.00 25.00
❑ 1 Anthony McFarland RC 1.50 .60
❑ 2 Al Wilson RC 1.00 .40
❑ 3 Jevon Kearse RC 2.50 1.00
❑ 4 Aaron Brooks RC 3.00 1.25
❑ 5 Travis McGriff RC .75 .30
❑ 6 Jeff Paulk RC .75 .30
❑ 7 Shawn Bryson RC 1.50 .60
❑ 8 Karsten Bailey RC 1.00 .40
❑ 9 Mike Cloud RC 1.00 .40
❑ 10 James Johnson RC 1.00 .40
❑ 11 Tai Streets RC 1.50 .60
❑ 12 Jermaine Fazande RC 1.00 .40
❑ 13 Ebenezer Ekuban RC 1.00 .40
❑ 14 Joe Montgomery RC 1.00 .40
❑ 15 Craig Yeast RC 1.00 .40
❑ 16 Joe Germaine RC 1.00 .40
❑ 17 Andy Katzenmoyer RC 1.00 .40
❑ 18 Kevin Faulk RC 1.50 .60
❑ 19 Chris McAlister RC 1.00 .40
❑ 20 Sedrick Irvin RC .75 .30
❑ 21 Brock Huard RC 1.50 .60
❑ 22 Cade McNown RC 1.00 .40
❑ 23 Shaun King RC 1.00 .40
❑ 24 Amos Zereoue RC 1.50 .60
❑ 25 Dameane Douglas RC 1.00 .40
❑ 26 D'Wayne Bates RC 1.00 .40
❑ 27 Kevin Johnson RC 1.50 .60
❑ 28 Rob Konrad RC 1.50 .60
❑ 29 Troy Edwards RC 1.00 .40
❑ 30 Peerless Price RC 1.50 .60
❑ 31 Daunte Culpepper RC 6.00 2.50
❑ 32 Akili Smith RC 1.00 .40
❑ 33 David Boston RC 1.50 .60
❑ 34 Chris Claiborne RC .75 .30
❑ 35 Torry Holt RC 4.00 1.50

❑ 36	Champ Bailey RC	2.00	.75
❑ 37	Edgerrin James RC	6.00	2.50
❑ 38	Donovan McNabb RC	8.00	3.00
❑ 39	Ricky Williams RC	3.00	1.25
❑ 40	Tim Couch RC	1.50	.60
❑ 41	Charles Woodson RP	1.00	.40
❑ 42	Skip Hicks RP	.40	.15
❑ 43	Brian Griese RP	1.00	.40
❑ 44	Tim Dwight RP	1.00	.40
❑ 45	Ryan Leaf RP	.60	.25
❑ 46	Curtis Enis RP	.40	.15
❑ 47	Charlie Batch RP	1.00	.40
❑ 48	Fred Taylor RP	1.00	.40
❑ 49	Peyton Manning RP	1.50	.60
❑ 50	Randy Moss RP	1.25	.50
❑ 51	Jim Harbaugh	.60	.25
❑ 52	Warren Moon	1.00	.40
❑ 53	Jeff George	.60	.25
❑ 54	Rich Gannon	1.00	.40
❑ 55	Scott Mitchell	.40	.15
❑ 56	Kerry Collins	.60	.25
❑ 57	Brad Johnson	1.00	.40
❑ 58	Charles Johnson	.40	.15
❑ 59	Chris Calloway	.40	.15
❑ 60	Tyrone Wheatley	.60	.25
❑ 61	Michael Westbrook	.60	.25
❑ 62	Skip Hicks	.40	.15
❑ 63	Terry Allen	.60	.25
❑ 64	Albert Connell	.40	.15
❑ 65	Kevin Dyson	.60	.25
❑ 66	Frank Wycheck	.40	.15
❑ 67	Yancey Thigpen	.40	.15
❑ 68	Steve McNair	1.00	.40
❑ 69	Eddie George	1.00	.40
❑ 70	Eric Zeier	.40	.15
❑ 71	Jacquez Green	.40	.15
❑ 72	Reidel Anthony	.60	.25
❑ 73	Warren Sapp	.60	.25
❑ 74	Mike Alstott	1.00	.40
❑ 75	Warrick Dunn	1.00	.40
❑ 76	Trent Dilfer	.60	.25
❑ 77	Ahman Green	1.00	.40
❑ 78	Joey Galloway	.60	.25
❑ 79	Ricky Watters	.60	.25
❑ 80	Jon Kitna	1.00	.40
❑ 81	Amp Lee	.40	.15
❑ 82	Isaac Bruce	1.00	.40
❑ 83	Robert Holcombe	.40	.15
❑ 84	Greg Hill	.40	.15
❑ 85	Marshall Faulk	1.25	.50
❑ 86	Trent Green	1.00	.40
❑ 87	J.J. Stokes	.60	.25
❑ 88	Terrell Owens	1.00	.40
❑ 89	Jerry Rice	2.00	.75
❑ 90	Garrison Hearst	.60	.25
❑ 91	Steve Young	1.25	.50
❑ 92	Junior Seau	1.00	.40
❑ 93	Mikhael Ricks	.40	.15
❑ 94	Natrone Means	.60	.25
❑ 95	Ryan Leaf	1.00	.40
❑ 96	Courtney Hawkins	.40	.15
❑ 97	Chris Fuamatu-Ma'afala UER	.40	.15
❑ 98	Jerome Bettis	1.00	.40
❑ 99	Kordell Stewart	.60	.25
❑ 100	Bobby Hoying	.60	.25
❑ 101	Charlie Garner	.60	.25
❑ 102	Duce Staley	1.00	.40
❑ 103	Charles Woodson	1.00	.40
❑ 104	James Jett	.60	.25
❑ 105	Rickey Dudley	.40	.15
❑ 106	Tim Brown	1.00	.40
❑ 107	Napoleon Kaufman	1.00	.40
❑ 108	Wayne Chrebet	.60	.25
❑ 109	Keyshawn Johnson	1.00	.40
❑ 110	Vinny Testaverde	.60	.25
❑ 111	Curtis Martin	1.00	.40
❑ 112	Joe Jurevicius	.60	.25
❑ 113	Tiki Barber	1.00	.40

❑ 114	Ike Hilliard	.40	.15
❑ 115	Kent Graham	.40	.15
❑ 116	Gary Brown	.40	.15
❑ 117	Lamar Smith	.60	.25
❑ 118	Eddie Kennison	.60	.25
❑ 119	Cam Cleeland	.40	.15
❑ 120	Tony Simmons	.40	.15
❑ 121	Ben Coates	.60	.25
❑ 122	Darick Holmes	.40	.15
❑ 123	Terry Glenn	1.00	.40
❑ 124	Drew Bledsoe	1.25	.50
❑ 125	Leroy Hoard	.40	.15
❑ 126	Jake Reed	.60	.25
❑ 127	Randy Moss	2.50	1.00
❑ 128	Cris Carter	1.00	.40
❑ 129	Robert Smith	1.00	.40
❑ 130	Randall Cunningham	1.00	.40
❑ 131	Lamar Thomas	.40	.15
❑ 132	John Avery	.40	.15
❑ 133	O.J. McDuffie	.60	.25
❑ 134	Dan Marino	3.00	1.25
❑ 135	Karim Abdul-Jabbar	.60	.25
❑ 136	Rashaan Shehee	.40	.15
❑ 137	Derrick Alexander WR	.60	.25
❑ 138	Byron Bam Morris	.40	.15
❑ 139	Andre Rison	.60	.25
❑ 140	Elvis Grbac	.60	.25
❑ 141	Tavian Banks	.40	.15
❑ 142	Keenan McCardell	.60	.25
❑ 143	Jimmy Smith	.60	.25
❑ 144	Fred Taylor	1.00	.40
❑ 145	Mark Brunell	1.00	.40
❑ 146	Jerome Pathon	.40	.15
❑ 147	Marvin Harrison	1.00	.40
❑ 148	Peyton Manning	3.00	1.25
❑ 149	Robert Brooks	.60	.25
❑ 150	Mark Chmura	.40	.15
❑ 151	Antonio Freeman	1.00	.40
❑ 152	Dorsey Levens	1.00	.40
❑ 153	Brett Favre	3.00	1.25
❑ 154	Johnnie Morton	.60	.25
❑ 155	Germane Crowell	.40	.15
❑ 156	Barry Sanders	3.00	1.25
❑ 157	Herman Moore	.60	.25
❑ 158	Charlie Batch	1.00	.40
❑ 159	Marcus Nash	.40	.15
❑ 160	Shannon Sharpe	.60	.25
❑ 161	Rod Smith	.60	.25
❑ 162	Ed McCaffrey	.60	.25
❑ 163	Terrell Davis	1.00	.40
❑ 164	John Elway	3.00	1.25
❑ 165	Ernie Mills	.40	.15
❑ 166	Michael Irvin	.60	.25
❑ 167	Deion Sanders	1.00	.40
❑ 168	Emmitt Smith	2.00	.75
❑ 169	Troy Aikman	2.00	.75
❑ 170	Chris Spielman	.40	.15
❑ 171	Terry Kirby	.40	.15
❑ 172	Ty Detmer	.60	.25
❑ 173	Leslie Shepherd	.40	.15
❑ 174	Damay Scott	.40	.15
❑ 175	Jeff Blake	.60	.25
❑ 176	Carl Pickens	.60	.25
❑ 177	Corey Dillon	1.00	.40
❑ 178	Bobby Engram	.60	.25
❑ 179	Curtis Conway	.60	.25
❑ 180	Curtis Enis	.40	.15
❑ 181	Muhsin Muhammad	.60	.25
❑ 182	Steve Beuerlein	.40	.15
❑ 183	Tim Biakabutuka	.60	.25
❑ 184	Bruce Smith	.60	.25
❑ 185	Andre Reed	.60	.25
❑ 186	Thurman Thomas	.60	.25
❑ 187	Eric Moulds	1.00	.40
❑ 188	Antowain Smith	1.00	.40
❑ 189	Doug Flutie	1.00	.40
❑ 190	Jermaine Lewis	.60	.25
❑ 191	Priest Holmes	1.50	.60

❑ 192	O.J. Santiago	.40	.15
❑ 193	Tim Dwight	1.00	.40
❑ 194	Terance Mathis	.60	.25
❑ 195	Chris Chandler	.60	.25
❑ 196	Jamal Anderson	1.00	.40
❑ 197	Rob Moore	.60	.25
❑ 198	Frank Sanders	.60	.25
❑ 199	Adrian Murrell	.60	.25
❑ 200	Jake Plummer	.60	.25
❑ RR1	Barry Sanders RFR	20.00	7.50

1999 Playoff Prestige SSD

❑	COMPLETE SET (200)	150.00	75.00
❑	COMP.SET w/o SP's (150)	50.00	25.00
❑ 1	Jake Plummer	.75	.30
❑ 2	Adrian Murrell	.75	.30
❑ 3	Frank Sanders	.75	.30
❑ 4	Rob Moore	.75	.30
❑ 5	Jamal Anderson	1.25	.50
❑ 6	Chris Chandler	.75	.30
❑ 7	Terance Mathis	.75	.30
❑ 8	Tim Dwight	1.25	.50
❑ 9	O.J. Santiago	.50	.20
❑ 10	Priest Holmes	2.00	.75
❑ 11	Jermaine Lewis	.75	.30
❑ 12	Doug Flutie	1.25	.50
❑ 13	Antowain Smith	1.25	.50
❑ 14	Eric Moulds	1.25	.50
❑ 15	Thurman Thomas	.75	.30
❑ 16	Andre Reed	.75	.30
❑ 17	Bruce Smith	.75	.30
❑ 18	Tim Biakabutuka	.75	.30
❑ 19	Steve Beuerlein	.50	.20
❑ 20	Muhsin Muhammad	.75	.30
❑ 21	Curtis Enis	.50	.20
❑ 22	Curtis Conway	.75	.30
❑ 23	Bobby Engram	.75	.30
❑ 24	Corey Dillon	1.25	.50
❑ 25	Carl Pickens	.75	.30
❑ 26	Jeff Blake	.75	.30
❑ 27	Damay Scott	.50	.20
❑ 28	Leslie Shepherd	.50	.20
❑ 29	Ty Detmer	.75	.30
❑ 30	Terry Kirby	.50	.20
❑ 31	Chris Spielman	.50	.20
❑ 32	Troy Aikman	3.00	1.25
❑ 33	Emmitt Smith	3.00	1.25
❑ 34	Deion Sanders	1.25	.50
❑ 35	Michael Irvin	.75	.30
❑ 36	Ernie Mills	.50	.20
❑ 37	John Elway	5.00	2.00
❑ 38	Terrell Davis	1.25	.50
❑ 39	Ed McCaffrey	.75	.30
❑ 40	Rod Smith	.75	.30
❑ 41	Shannon Sharpe	.75	.30
❑ 42	Marcus Nash	.50	.20
❑ 43	Charlie Batch	1.25	.50
❑ 44	Herman Moore	.75	.30
❑ 45	Barry Sanders	5.00	2.00
❑ 46	Germane Crowell	.50	.20
❑ 47	Johnnie Morton	.75	.30

❑ 48	Brett Favre	5.00	2.00
❑ 49	Dorsey Levens	1.25	.50
❑ 50	Antonio Freeman	1.25	.50
❑ 51	Mark Chmura	.50	.20
❑ 52	Robert Brooks	.75	.30
❑ 53	Peyton Manning	5.00	2.00
❑ 54	Marvin Harrison	1.25	.50
❑ 55	Jerome Pathon	.50	.20
❑ 56	Mark Brunell	1.25	.50
❑ 57	Fred Taylor	1.25	.50
❑ 58	Jimmy Smith	.75	.30
❑ 59	Keenan McCardell	.75	.30
❑ 60	Tavian Banks	.50	.20
❑ 61	Elvis Grbac	.75	.30
❑ 62	Andre Rison	.75	.30
❑ 63	Byron Bam Morris	.50	.20
❑ 64	Derrick Alexander WR	.75	.30
❑ 65	Rashaan Shehee	.50	.20
❑ 66	Karim Abdul-Jabbar	.75	.30
❑ 67	Dan Marino	5.00	2.00
❑ 68	O.J. McDuffie	.75	.30
❑ 69	John Avery	.50	.20
❑ 70	Lamar Thomas	.50	.20
❑ 71	Randall Cunningham	1.25	.50
❑ 72	Robert Smith	1.25	.50
❑ 73	Cris Carter	1.25	.50
❑ 74	Randy Moss	4.00	1.50
❑ 75	Jake Reed	.75	.30
❑ 76	Leroy Hoard	.50	.20
❑ 77	Drew Bledsoe	2.00	.75
❑ 78	Terry Glenn	1.25	.50
❑ 79	Darick Holmes	.50	.20
❑ 80	Ben Coates	.75	.30
❑ 81	Tony Simmons	.50	.20
❑ 82	Cam Cleeland	.50	.20
❑ 83	Eddie Kennison	.75	.30
❑ 84	Lamar Smith	.75	.30
❑ 85	Gary Brown	.50	.20
❑ 86	Kent Graham	.50	.20
❑ 87	Ike Hilliard	.50	.20
❑ 88	Tiki Barber	1.25	.50
❑ 89	Joe Jurevicius	.75	.30
❑ 90	Curtis Martin	1.25	.50
❑ 91	Vinny Testaverde	.75	.30
❑ 92	Keyshawn Johnson	1.25	.50
❑ 93	Wayne Chrebet	.75	.30
❑ 94	Napoleon Kaufman	1.25	.50
❑ 95	Tim Brown	1.25	.50
❑ 96	Rickey Dudley	.50	.20
❑ 97	James Jett	.75	.30
❑ 98	Charles Woodson	1.25	.50
❑ 99	Duce Staley	1.25	.50
❑ 100	Charlie Garner	.75	.30
❑ 101	Bobby Hoying	.75	.30
❑ 102	Kordell Stewart	.75	.30
❑ 103	Jerome Bettis	1.25	.50
❑ 104	Chris Fuamatu-Ma'afala	.50	.20
❑ 105	Courtney Hawkins	.50	.20
❑ 106	Ryan Leaf	1.25	.50
❑ 107	Natrone Means	.75	.30
❑ 108	Mikhael Ricks	.50	.20
❑ 109	Junior Seau	1.25	.50
❑ 110	Steve Young	2.00	.75
❑ 111	Garrison Hearst	.75	.30
❑ 112	Jerry Rice	3.00	1.25
❑ 113	Terrell Owens	1.25	.50
❑ 114	J.J. Stokes	.75	.30
❑ 115	Trent Green	1.25	.50
❑ 116	Marshall Faulk	1.50	.60
❑ 117	Greg Hill	.50	.20
❑ 118	Robert Holcombe	.50	.20
❑ 119	Isaac Bruce	1.25	.50
❑ 120	Amp Lee	.50	.20
❑ 121	Jon Kitna	1.25	.50
❑ 122	Ricky Watters	.75	.30
❑ 123	Joey Galloway	.75	.30
❑ 124	Ahman Green	1.25	.50
❑ 125	Trent Dilfer	.75	.30
❑ 126	Warrick Dunn	1.25	.50
❑ 127	Mike Alstott	1.25	.50
❑ 128	Warren Sapp	.75	.30
❑ 129	Reidel Anthony	.75	.30
❑ 130	Jacquez Green	.50	.20
❑ 131	Eric Zeier	.50	.20
❑ 132	Eddie George	1.25	.50
❑ 133	Steve McNair	1.25	.50
❑ 134	Yancey Thigpen	.50	.20
❑ 135	Frank Wycheck	.50	.20
❑ 136	Kevin Dyson	.75	.30
❑ 137	Albert Connell	.50	.20
❑ 138	Terry Allen	.75	.30
❑ 139	Skip Hicks	.50	.20
❑ 140	Michael Westbrook	.75	.30
❑ 141	Tyrone Wheatley	.75	.30
❑ 142	Chris Calloway	.50	.20
❑ 143	Charles Johnson	.50	.20
❑ 144	Brad Johnson	1.25	.50
❑ 145	Kerry Collins	.75	.30
❑ 146	Scott Mitchell	.50	.20
❑ 147	Rich Gannon	1.25	.50
❑ 148	Jeff George	.75	.30
❑ 149	Warren Moon	1.25	.50
❑ 150	Jim Harbaugh	.75	.30
❑ 151	Randy Moss RP	6.00	2.50
❑ 152	Peyton Manning RP	8.00	3.00
❑ 153	Fred Taylor RP	2.50	1.00
❑ 154	Charlie Batch RP	2.50	1.00
❑ 155	Curtis Enis RP	1.50	.60
❑ 156	Ryan Leaf RP	1.50	.60
❑ 157	Tim Dwight RP	1.50	.60
❑ 158	Brian Griese RP	2.50	1.00
❑ 159	Skip Hicks RP	1.50	.60
❑ 160	Charles Woodson RP	2.50	1.00
❑ 161	Tim Couch RC	4.00	1.50
❑ 162	Ricky Williams RC	6.00	2.50
❑ 163	Donovan McNabb RC	15.00	6.00
❑ 164	Edgerrin James RC	12.00	5.00
❑ 165	Champ Bailey RC	5.00	2.00
❑ 166	Torry Holt RC	8.00	3.00
❑ 167	Chris Claiborne RC	2.00	.75
❑ 168	David Boston RC	4.00	1.50
❑ 169	Akili Smith RC	1.50	.60
❑ 170	Daunte Culpepper RC	12.00	5.00
❑ 171	Peerless Price RC	4.00	1.50
❑ 172	Troy Edwards RC	3.00	1.25
❑ 173	Rob Konrad RC	4.00	1.50
❑ 174	Kevin Johnson RC	4.00	1.50
❑ 175	D'Wayne Bates RC	3.00	1.25
❑ 176	Dameane Douglas RC	3.00	1.25
❑ 177	Amos Zereoue RC	4.00	1.50
❑ 178	Shaun King RC	3.00	1.25
❑ 179	Cade McNown RC	3.00	1.25
❑ 180	Brock Huard RC	4.00	1.50
❑ 181	Sedrick Irvin RC	2.00	.75
❑ 182	Chris McAlister RC	3.00	1.25
❑ 183	Kevin Faulk RC	4.00	1.50
❑ 184	Andy Katzenmoyer RC	3.00	1.25
❑ 185	Joe Germaine RC	3.00	1.25
❑ 186	Craig Yeast RC	3.00	1.25
❑ 187	Joe Montgomery RC	3.00	1.25
❑ 188	Ebenezer Ekuban RC	3.00	1.25
❑ 189	Jermaine Fazande RC	3.00	1.25
❑ 190	Tai Streets RC	4.00	1.50
❑ 191	James Johnson RC	3.00	1.25
❑ 192	Mike Cloud RC	3.00	1.25
❑ 193	Karsten Bailey RC	3.00	1.25
❑ 194	Shawn Bryson RC	4.00	1.50
❑ 195	Jeff Paulk RC	2.00	.75
❑ 196	Travis McGriff RC	2.00	.75
❑ 197	Aaron Brooks RC	6.00	2.50
❑ 198	Jevon Kearse RC	6.00	2.50
❑ 199	Al Wilson RC	3.00	1.25
❑ 200	Anthony McFarland RC	4.00	1.50

2000 Playoff Prestige

❑ COMPLETE SET (300)	350.00	175.00
❑ COMP.SET w/o SP's (200)	25.00	10.00

❑ 1	Frank Sanders	.40	.15
❑ 2	Rob Moore	.40	.15
❑ 3	Michael Pittman	.25	.08
❑ 4	Jake Plummer	.40	.15
❑ 5	David Boston	.60	.25
❑ 6	Chris Chandler	.40	.15
❑ 7	Tim Dwight	.60	.25
❑ 8	Shawn Jefferson	.25	.08
❑ 9	Terance Mathis	.40	.15
❑ 10	Jamal Anderson	.60	.25
❑ 11	Byron Hanspard	.25	.08
❑ 12	Ken Oxendine	.25	.08
❑ 13	Priest Holmes	.75	.30
❑ 14	Tony Banks	.40	.15
❑ 15	Shannon Sharpe	.40	.15
❑ 16	Rod Woodson	.40	.15
❑ 17	Jermaine Lewis	.40	.15
❑ 18	Qadry Ismail	.40	.15
❑ 19	Eric Moulds	.60	.25
❑ 20	Doug Flutie	.60	.25
❑ 21	Jay Riemersma	.25	.08
❑ 22	Antowain Smith	.40	.15
❑ 23	Jonathan Linton	.25	.08
❑ 24	Peerless Price	.40	.15
❑ 25	Rob Johnson	.40	.15
❑ 26	Muhsin Muhammad	.40	.15
❑ 27	Wesley Walls	.25	.08
❑ 28	Tim Biakabutuka	.40	.15
❑ 29	Steve Beuerlein	.40	.15
❑ 30	Patrick Jeffers	.60	.25
❑ 31	Natrone Means	.25	.08
❑ 32	Curtis Enis	.25	.08
❑ 33	Bobby Engram	.40	.15
❑ 34	Marcus Robinson	.60	.25
❑ 35	Marty Booker	.40	.15
❑ 36	Cade McNown	.25	.08
❑ 37	Darnay Scott	.40	.15
❑ 38	Carl Pickens	.40	.15
❑ 39	Corey Dillon	.60	.25
❑ 40	Akili Smith	.25	.08
❑ 41	Michael Basnight	.25	.08
❑ 42	Karim Abdul-Jabbar	.40	.15
❑ 43	Tim Couch	.40	.15
❑ 44	Kevin Johnson	.60	.25
❑ 45	Darrin Chiaverini	.25	.08
❑ 46	Errict Rhett	.40	.15
❑ 47	Emmitt Smith	1.25	.50
❑ 48	Deion Sanders	.60	.25
❑ 49	Michael Irvin	.40	.15
❑ 50	Rocket Ismail	.40	.15
❑ 51	Troy Aikman	1.25	.50
❑ 52	Jason Tucker	.25	.08
❑ 53	Joey Galloway	.40	.15
❑ 54	David LaFleur	.25	.08
❑ 55	Wane McGarity	.25	.08
❑ 56	Ed McCaffrey	.60	.25
❑ 57	Rod Smith	.40	.15
❑ 58	Brian Griese	.60	.25
❑ 59	John Elway	2.00	.75
❑ 60	Gus Frerotte	.25	.08
❑ 61	Neil Smith	.25	.08
❑ 62	Terrell Davis	.60	.25

❑ 63	Olandis Gary	.60	.25
❑ 64	Johnnie Morton	.40	.15
❑ 65	Charlie Batch	.60	.25
❑ 66	Barry Sanders	1.50	.60
❑ 67	James Stewart	.40	.15
❑ 68	Germane Crowell	.25	.08
❑ 69	Sedrick Irvin	.25	.08
❑ 70	Herman Moore	.40	.15
❑ 71	Corey Bradford	.40	.15
❑ 72	Dorsey Levens	.40	.15
❑ 73	Antonio Freeman	.60	.25
❑ 74	Brett Favre	2.00	.75
❑ 75	De'Mond Parker	.25	.08
❑ 76	Bill Schroeder	.40	.15
❑ 77	Donald Driver	.60	.25
❑ 78	E.G. Green	.25	.08
❑ 79	Marvin Harrison	.60	.25
❑ 80	Peyton Manning	1.50	.60
❑ 81	Terrence Wilkins	.25	.08
❑ 82	Edgerrin James	1.00	.40
❑ 83	Keenan McCardell	.40	.15
❑ 84	Mark Brunell	.60	.25
❑ 85	Fred Taylor	.60	.25
❑ 86	Jimmy Smith	.40	.15
❑ 87	Derrick Alexander	.40	.15
❑ 88	Andre Rison	.40	.15
❑ 89	Elvis Grbac	.40	.15
❑ 90	Tony Gonzalez	.40	.15
❑ 91	Donnell Bennett	.25	.08
❑ 92	Warren Moon	.60	.25
❑ 93	Kimble Anders	.25	.08
❑ 94	Tony Richardson RC	.40	.15
❑ 95	Jay Fiedler	.60	.25
❑ 96	Zach Thomas	.60	.25
❑ 97	Oronde Gadsden	.40	.15
❑ 98	Dan Marino	2.00	.75
❑ 99	O.J. McDuffie	.40	.15
❑ 100	Tony Martin	.40	.15
❑ 101	James Johnson	.25	.08
❑ 102	Rob Konrad	.25	.08
❑ 103	Damon Huard	.60	.25
❑ 104	Thurman Thomas	.40	.15
❑ 105	Randy Moss	1.25	.50
❑ 106	Cris Carter	.60	.25
❑ 107	Robert Smith	.60	.25
❑ 108	Randall Cunningham	.60	.25
❑ 109	John Randle	.40	.15
❑ 110	Leroy Hoard	.25	.08
❑ 111	Daunte Culpepper	.75	.30
❑ 112	Matthew Hatchette	.25	.08
❑ 113	Troy Brown	.40	.15
❑ 114	Tony Simmons	.25	.08
❑ 115	Terry Glenn	.40	.15
❑ 116	Ben Coates	.25	.08
❑ 117	Drew Bledsoe	.75	.30
❑ 118	Terry Allen	.40	.15
❑ 119	Kevin Faulk	.25	.08
❑ 120	Ricky Williams	.60	.25
❑ 121	Jake Delhomme RC	2.50	1.00
❑ 122	Jake Reed	.40	.15
❑ 123	Jeff Blake	.40	.15
❑ 124	Amani Toomer	.40	.15
❑ 125	Kerry Collins	.40	.15
❑ 126	Tiki Barber	.60	.25
❑ 127	Ike Hilliard	.40	.15
❑ 128	Joe Montgomery	.25	.08
❑ 129	Sean Bennett	.25	.08
❑ 130	Curtis Martin	.60	.25
❑ 131	Vinny Testaverde	.40	.15
❑ 132	Wayne Chrebet	.40	.15
❑ 133	Ray Lucas	.40	.15
❑ 134	Tyrone Wheatley	.40	.15
❑ 135	Napoleon Kaufman	.40	.15
❑ 136	Tim Brown	.60	.25
❑ 137	Rickey Dudley	.25	.08
❑ 138	James Jett	.25	.08
❑ 139	Rich Gannon	.60	.25
❑ 140	Charles Woodson	.40	.15
❑ 141	Duce Staley	.60	.25
❑ 142	Donovan McNabb	1.00	.40
❑ 143	Na Brown	.25	.08
❑ 144	Kordell Stewart	.40	.15
❑ 145	Jerome Bettis	.60	.25
❑ 146	Hines Ward	.60	.25
❑ 147	Troy Edwards	.25	.08
❑ 148	Curtis Conway	.40	.15
❑ 149	Junior Seau	.60	.25
❑ 150	Jim Harbaugh	.40	.15
❑ 151	Jermaine Fazande	.25	.08
❑ 152	Terrell Owens	.60	.25
❑ 153	J.J. Stokes	.40	.15
❑ 154	Charlie Garner	.40	.15
❑ 155	Jerry Rice	1.25	.50
❑ 156	Garrison Hearst	.40	.15
❑ 157	Steve Young	.75	.30
❑ 158	Jeff Garcia	.60	.25
❑ 159	Derrick Mayes	.40	.15
❑ 160	Ahman Green	.60	.25
❑ 161	Ricky Watters	.40	.15
❑ 162	Jon Kitna	.60	.25
❑ 163	Karsten Bailey	.25	.08
❑ 164	Sean Dawkins	.25	.08
❑ 165	Az-Zahir Hakim	.40	.15
❑ 166	Isaac Bruce	.60	.25
❑ 167	Marshall Faulk	.75	.30
❑ 168	Trent Green	.60	.25
❑ 169	Kurt Warner	1.25	.50
❑ 170	Torry Holt	.60	.25
❑ 171	Robert Holcombe	.25	.08
❑ 172	Kevin Carter	.25	.08
❑ 173	Keyshawn Johnson	.60	.25
❑ 174	Jacquez Green	.25	.08
❑ 175	Reidel Anthony	.25	.08
❑ 176	Warren Sapp	.40	.15
❑ 177	Mike Alstott	.60	.25
❑ 178	Warrick Dunn	.60	.25
❑ 179	Trent Dilfer	.40	.15
❑ 180	Shaun King	.25	.08
❑ 181	Neil O'Donnell	.25	.08
❑ 182	Eddie George	.60	.25
❑ 183	Yancey Thigpen	.25	.08
❑ 184	Steve McNair	.60	.25
❑ 185	Kevin Dyson	.40	.15
❑ 186	Frank Wycheck	.25	.08
❑ 187	Jevon Kearse	.60	.25
❑ 188	Adrian Murrell	.25	.08
❑ 189	Jeff George	.40	.15
❑ 190	Stephen Davis	.60	.25
❑ 191	Stephen Alexander	.25	.08
❑ 192	Darrell Green	.25	.08
❑ 193	Skip Hicks	.25	.08
❑ 194	Brad Johnson	.60	.25
❑ 195	Michael Westbrook	.40	.15
❑ 196	Albert Connell	.25	.08
❑ 197	Irving Fryar	.40	.15
❑ 198	Bruce Smith	.40	.15
❑ 199	Champ Bailey	.40	.15
❑ 200	Larry Centers	.25	.08
❑ 201	Jake Plummer PP	1.25	.50
❑ 202	Doug Flutie PP	1.25	.50
❑ 203	Eric Moulds PP	1.25	.50
❑ 204	Muhsin Muhammad PP	1.25	.50
❑ 205	Marcus Robinson PP	1.25	.50
❑ 206	Cade McNown PP	1.25	.50
❑ 207	Corey Dillon PP	1.25	.50
❑ 208	Tim Couch PP	1.25	.50
❑ 209	Kevin Johnson PP	1.25	.50
❑ 210	Emmitt Smith PP	3.00	1.25
❑ 211	Troy Aikman PP	3.00	1.25
❑ 212	Brian Griese PP	1.25	.50
❑ 213	Olandis Gary PP	1.25	.50
❑ 214	Germane Crowell PP	1.25	.50
❑ 215	Brett Favre PP	5.00	2.00
❑ 216	Charlie Batch PP	1.25	.50
❑ 217	Antonio Freeman PP	1.25	.50
❑ 218	Dorsey Levens PP	1.25	.50
❑ 219	Peyton Manning PP	4.00	1.50
❑ 220	Edgerrin James PP	2.50	1.00
❑ 221	Marvin Harrison PP	1.25	.50
❑ 222	Fred Taylor PP	1.25	.50
❑ 223	Mark Brunell PP	1.25	.50
❑ 224	Jimmy Smith PP	1.25	.50
❑ 225	Dan Marino PP	5.00	2.00
❑ 226	Randy Moss PP	3.00	1.25
❑ 227	Cris Carter PP	1.25	.50
❑ 228	Robert Smith PP	1.25	.50
❑ 229	Drew Bledsoe PP	2.00	.75
❑ 230	Terry Glenn PP	1.25	.50
❑ 231	Ricky Williams PP	1.25	.50
❑ 232	Amani Toomer PP	1.25	.50
❑ 233	Keyshawn Johnson PP	1.25	.50
❑ 234	Curtis Martin PP	1.25	.50
❑ 235	Ray Lucas PP	1.25	.50
❑ 236	Tim Brown PP	1.25	.50
❑ 237	Duce Staley PP	1.25	.50
❑ 238	Donovan McNabb PP	2.50	1.00
❑ 239	Jerry Rice PP	3.00	1.25
❑ 240	Jon Kitna PP	1.25	.50
❑ 241	Isaac Bruce PP	1.25	.50
❑ 242	Kurt Warner PP	3.00	1.25
❑ 243	Torry Holt PP	1.25	.50
❑ 244	Mike Alstott PP	1.25	.50
❑ 245	Marshall Faulk PP	2.00	.75
❑ 246	Shaun King PP	.25	.08
❑ 247	Eddie George PP	1.25	.50
❑ 248	Steve McNair PP	1.25	.50
❑ 249	Stephen Davis PP	1.25	.50
❑ 250	Brad Johnson PP	1.25	.50
❑ 251	Rondell Mealey RC	2.50	1.00
❑ 252	Peter Warrick RC	4.00	1.50
❑ 253	Courtney Brown RC	1.25	.50
❑ 254	Plaxico Burress RC	8.00	3.00
❑ 255	Corey Simon RC	1.25	.50
❑ 256	Thomas Jones RC	6.00	2.50
❑ 257	Travis Taylor RC	1.25	.50
❑ 258	Shaun Alexander RC	20.00	7.50
❑ 259	Chris Redman RC	1.25	.50
❑ 260	Chad Pennington RC	10.00	4.00
❑ 261	Jamal Lewis RC	10.00	4.00
❑ 262	Bubba Franks RC	4.00	1.50
❑ 263	Dez White RC	4.00	1.50
❑ 264	Ron Dayne RC	4.00	1.50
❑ 265	Sylvester Morris RC	3.00	1.25
❑ 266	R.Jay Soward RC	3.00	1.25
❑ 267	Sherrod Gideon RC	2.50	1.00
❑ 268	Travis Prentice RC	3.00	1.25
❑ 269	Darrell Jackson RC	8.00	3.00
❑ 270	Giovanni Carmazzi RC	2.50	1.00
❑ 271	Anthony Lucas RC	2.50	1.00
❑ 272	Danny Farmer RC	3.00	1.25
❑ 273	Dennis Northcutt RC	4.00	1.50
❑ 274	Troy Walters RC	4.00	1.50
❑ 275	Laveranues Coles RC	5.00	2.00
❑ 276	Tee Martin RC	4.00	1.50
❑ 277	J.R. Redmond RC	3.00	1.25
❑ 278	Jerry Porter RC	5.00	2.00
❑ 279	Sebastian Janikowski RC	4.00	1.50
❑ 280	Michael Wiley RC	3.00	1.25
❑ 281	Reuben Droughns RC	5.00	2.00
❑ 282	Trung Canidate RC	3.00	1.25
❑ 283	Shyrone Stith RC	3.00	1.25
❑ 284	Trevor Gaylor RC	3.00	1.25
❑ 285	Marc Bulger RC	8.00	3.00
❑ 286	Tom Brady RC	40.00	20.00
❑ 287	Todd Husak RC	4.00	1.50
❑ 288	Jarious Jackson RC	3.00	1.25
❑ 289	Terrelle Smith RC	3.00	1.25
❑ 290	Chad Morton RC	4.00	1.50
❑ 291	Chris Cole RC	4.00	1.50
❑ 292	Kwame Cavil RC	2.50	1.00
❑ 293	JaJuan Dawson RC	2.50	1.00
❑ 294	Curtis Keaton RC	3.00	1.25
❑ 295	Tim Rattay RC	4.00	1.50
❑ 296	Joe Hamilton RC	3.00	1.25

❑ 297 Gari Scott RC	2.50	1.00
❑ 298 Mike Anderson RC	5.00	2.00
❑ 299 Ron Dugans RC	2.50	1.00
❑ 300 Todd Pinkston RC	4.00	1.50

2002 Playoff Prestige

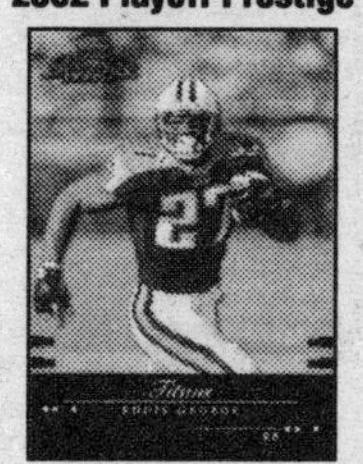

❑ COMP.SET w/o SP's (150)	40.00	15.00
❑ 1 David Boston	1.25	.50
❑ 2 MarTay Jenkins	.50	.20
❑ 3 Jake Plummer	.75	.30
❑ 4 Chris Chandler	.75	.30
❑ 5 Jamal Anderson	.75	.30
❑ 6 Michael Vick	4.00	1.50
❑ 7 Maurice Smith	.75	.30
❑ 8 Elvis Grbac	.75	.30
❑ 9 Jamal Lewis	1.25	.50
❑ 10 Todd Heap	.50	.20
❑ 11 Qadry Ismail	.75	.30
❑ 12 Shannon Sharpe	.75	.30
❑ 13 Ray Lewis	1.25	.50
❑ 14 Rod Woodson	.75	.30
❑ 15 Travis Henry	1.25	.50
❑ 16 Rob Johnson	.75	.30
❑ 17 Eric Moulds	.75	.30
❑ 18 Nate Clements	.50	.20
❑ 19 Donald Hayes	.50	.20
❑ 20 Muhsin Muhammad	.75	.30
❑ 21 Steve Smith	1.25	.50
❑ 22 Wesley Walls	.50	.20
❑ 23 Chris Weinke	.75	.30
❑ 24 James Allen	.75	.30
❑ 25 David Terrell	1.25	.50
❑ 26 Anthony Thomas	.75	.30
❑ 27 Dez White	.50	.20
❑ 28 Brian Urlacher	2.00	.75
❑ 29 Mike Brown	1.25	.50
❑ 30 Corey Dillon	.75	.30
❑ 31 Chad Johnson	1.25	.50
❑ 32 Peter Warrick	.75	.30
❑ 33 Justin Smith	.50	.20
❑ 34 Tim Couch	.75	.30
❑ 35 James Jackson	.50	.20
❑ 36 Quincy Morgan	.50	.20
❑ 37 Kevin Johnson	.75	.30
❑ 38 Gerard Warren	.50	.20
❑ 39 Anthony Henry	.50	.20
❑ 40 Quincy Carter	.75	.30
❑ 41 Joey Galloway	.75	.30
❑ 42 Rocket Ismail	.75	.30
❑ 43 Ryan Leaf	.75	.30
❑ 44 Emmitt Smith	3.00	1.25
❑ 45 Troy Hambrick	.50	.20
❑ 46 Mike Anderson	1.25	.50
❑ 47 Terrell Davis	1.25	.50
❑ 48 Brian Griese	1.25	.50
❑ 49 Rod Smith	.75	.30
❑ 50 Ed McCaffrey	1.25	.50
❑ 51 Charlie Batch	.75	.30
❑ 52 Johnnie Morton	.75	.30
❑ 53 Germane Crowell	.50	.20
❑ 54 James Stewart	.75	.30
❑ 55 Shaun Rogers	.50	.20
❑ 56 Brett Favre	3.00	1.25
❑ 57 Antonio Freeman	1.25	.50
❑ 58 Ahman Green	1.25	.50
❑ 59 Bill Schroeder	.75	.30
❑ 60 Kabeer Gbaja-Biamila	.75	.30
❑ 61 Marvin Harrison	1.25	.50
❑ 62 Terrence Wilkins	.50	.20
❑ 63 Dominic Rhodes	.75	.30
❑ 64 Reggie Wayne	1.25	.50
❑ 65 Edgerrin James	1.50	.60
❑ 66 Mark Brunell	1.25	.50
❑ 67 Keenan McCardell	.50	.20
❑ 68 Jimmy Smith	.75	.30
❑ 69 Fred Taylor	1.25	.50
❑ 70 Derrick Alexander	.75	.30
❑ 71 Tony Gonzalez	.75	.30
❑ 72 Trent Green	.75	.30
❑ 73 Priest Holmes	1.50	.60
❑ 74 Snoop Minnis	.50	.20
❑ 75 Chris Chambers	1.25	.50
❑ 76 Jay Fiedler	.75	.30
❑ 77 Travis Minor	.50	.20
❑ 78 Lamar Smith	.75	.30
❑ 79 Zach Thomas	1.25	.50
❑ 80 Michael Bennett	.75	.30
❑ 81 Cris Carter	1.25	.50
❑ 82 Daunte Culpepper	1.25	.50
❑ 83 Randy Moss	2.50	1.00
❑ 84 Drew Bledsoe	1.50	.60
❑ 85 Tom Brady	3.00	1.25
❑ 86 Troy Brown	.75	.30
❑ 87 Antowain Smith	.75	.30
❑ 88 Aaron Brooks	1.25	.50
❑ 89 Joe Horn	.75	.30
❑ 90 Deuce McAllister	1.50	.60
❑ 91 Ricky Williams	1.25	.50
❑ 92 Kerry Collins	.75	.30
❑ 93 Ron Dayne	.75	.30
❑ 94 Michael Strahan	.75	.30
❑ 95 Jason Sehorn	.50	.20
❑ 96 Wayne Chrebet	.75	.30
❑ 97 Laveranues Coles	.75	.30
❑ 98 LaMont Jordan	1.25	.50
❑ 99 Curtis Martin	1.25	.50
❑ 100 Santana Moss	1.25	.50
❑ 101 Vinny Testaverde	.75	.30
❑ 102 Tim Brown	1.25	.50
❑ 103 Jerry Porter	.50	.20
❑ 104 Jerry Rice	2.50	1.00
❑ 105 Charlie Garner	.75	.30
❑ 106 Tyrone Wheatley	.75	.30
❑ 107 Charles Woodson	.75	.30
❑ 108 Correll Buckhalter	.75	.30
❑ 109 Todd Pinkston	.75	.30
❑ 110 Freddie Mitchell	.75	.30
❑ 111 James Thrash	.75	.30
❑ 112 Duce Staley	1.25	.50
❑ 113 Jerome Bettis	1.25	.50
❑ 114 Plaxico Burress	.75	.30
❑ 115 Kordell Stewart	.75	.30
❑ 116 Hines Ward	1.25	.50
❑ 117 Kendrell Bell	1.25	.50
❑ 118 Drew Brees	1.25	.50
❑ 119 Curtis Conway	.50	.20
❑ 120 Doug Flutie	1.25	.50
❑ 121 LaDainian Tomlinson	2.00	.75
❑ 122 Junior Seau	1.25	.50
❑ 123 Kevan Barlow	.75	.30
❑ 124 Jeff Garcia	1.25	.50
❑ 125 Garrison Hearst	.75	.30
❑ 126 Terrell Owens	1.25	.50
❑ 127 Andre Carter	.50	.20
❑ 128 Shaun Alexander	1.50	.60
❑ 129 Matt Hasselbeck	.75	.30
❑ 130 Koren Robinson	.75	.30
❑ 131 Ricky Watters	.75	.30
❑ 132 Isaac Bruce	1.25	.50
❑ 133 Trung Canidate	.75	.30
❑ 134 Marshall Faulk	1.25	.50
❑ 135 Torry Holt	1.25	.50
❑ 136 Kurt Warner	1.25	.50
❑ 137 Mike Alstott	1.25	.50
❑ 138 Warrick Dunn	1.25	.50
❑ 139 Brad Johnson	.75	.30
❑ 140 Keyshawn Johnson	1.25	.50
❑ 141 Warren Sapp	.75	.30
❑ 142 Eddie George	1.25	.50
❑ 143 Derrick Mason	.75	.30
❑ 144 Steve McNair	1.25	.50
❑ 145 Jevon Kearse	.75	.30
❑ 146 Stephen Davis	.75	.30
❑ 147 Rod Gardner	.75	.30
❑ 148 Champ Bailey	.75	.30
❑ 149 Bruce Smith	.50	.20
❑ 150 Houston Texans	1.50	.60
❑ 151 David Carr RC	10.00	4.00
❑ 152 Julius Peppers RC	8.00	3.00
❑ 153 Joey Harrington RC	10.00	4.00
❑ 154 Quentin Jammer RC	4.00	1.50
❑ 155 Ryan Sims RC	4.00	1.50
❑ 156 Bryant McKinnie RC	3.00	1.25
❑ 157 Roy Williams RC	10.00	4.00
❑ 158 John Henderson RC	4.00	1.50
❑ 159 Dwight Freeney RC	5.00	2.00
❑ 160 Wendell Bryant RC	2.00	.75
❑ 161 Donte Stallworth RC	8.00	3.00
❑ 162 Jeremy Shockey RC	12.00	5.00
❑ 163 Albert Haynesworth RC	3.00	1.25
❑ 164 William Green RC	4.00	1.50
❑ 165 Phillip Buchanon RC	4.00	1.50
❑ 166 T.J. Duckett RC	6.00	2.50
❑ 167 Ashley Lelie RC	8.00	3.00
❑ 168 Javon Walker RC	8.00	3.00
❑ 169 Daniel Graham RC	4.00	1.50
❑ 170 Napoleon Harris RC	4.00	1.50
❑ 171 Lito Sheppard RC	4.00	1.50
❑ 172 Robert Thomas RC	4.00	1.50
❑ 173 Patrick Ramsey RC	5.00	2.00
❑ 174 Jabar Gaffney RC	4.00	1.50
❑ 175 DeShaun Foster RC	4.00	1.50
❑ 176 Kalimba Edwards RC	4.00	1.50
❑ 177 Josh Reed RC	4.00	1.50
❑ 178 Larry Tripplett RC	2.00	.75
❑ 179 Andre Davis RC	3.00	1.25
❑ 180 Reche Caldwell RC	4.00	1.50
❑ 181 Levar Fisher RC	2.00	.75
❑ 182 Clinton Portis RC	12.00	5.00
❑ 183 Anthony Weaver RC	3.00	1.25
❑ 184 Maurice Morris RC	4.00	1.50
❑ 185 Ladell Betts RC	4.00	1.50
❑ 186 Antwaan Randle El RC	6.00	2.50
❑ 187 Antonio Bryant RC	4.00	1.50
❑ 188 Rocky Calmus RC	4.00	1.50
❑ 189 Josh McCown RC	5.00	2.00
❑ 190 Lamar Gordon RC	4.00	1.50
❑ 191 Marquise Walker RC	3.00	1.25
❑ 192 Cliff Russell RC	3.00	1.25
❑ 193 Eric Crouch RC	4.00	1.50
❑ 194 Dennis Johnson RC	2.00	.75
❑ 195 Alex Brown RC	4.00	1.50
❑ 196 David Garrard RC	4.00	1.50
❑ 197 Rohan Davey RC	4.00	1.50
❑ 198 Alan Harper RC	2.00	.75
❑ 199 Ron Johnson RC	3.00	1.25
❑ 200 Andra Davis RC	3.00	1.25
❑ 201 Kurt Kittner RC	3.00	1.25
❑ 202 Freddie Milons RC	3.00	1.25
❑ 203 Adrian Peterson RC	4.00	1.50
❑ 204 Luke Staley RC	3.00	1.25
❑ 205 Tracey Wistrom RC	3.00	1.25
❑ 206 Woody Dantzler RC	3.00	1.25
❑ 207 Chad Hutchinson RC	3.00	1.25
❑ 208 Zak Kustok RC	4.00	1.50
❑ 209 Damien Anderson RC	3.00	1.25
❑ 210 James Mungro RC	4.00	1.50
❑ 211 Cortlen Johnson RC	2.00	.75

❑ 212 Demontray Carter RC 2.00 .75
❑ 213 Kelly Campbell RC 3.00 1.25
❑ 214 Brian Poli-Dixon RC 3.00 1.25
❑ 215 Mike Rumph RC 4.00 1.50
❑ 216 Najeh Davenport RC 4.00 1.50

2003 Playoff Prestige

❑ COMP.SET w/o SP's (150) 30.00 12.50
❑ 1 David Boston .75 .30
❑ 2 Thomas Jones .75 .30
❑ 3 Jake Plummer .75 .30
❑ 4 Marcel Shipp .75 .30
❑ 5 T.J. Duckett .75 .30
❑ 6 Warrick Dunn .75 .30
❑ 7 Michael Vick 3.00 1.25
❑ 8 Jeff Blake .50 .20
❑ 9 Todd Heap .75 .30
❑ 10 Jamal Lewis 1.25 .50
❑ 11 Ray Lewis 1.25 .50
❑ 12 Drew Bledsoe 1.25 .50
❑ 13 Travis Henry .75 .30
❑ 14 Eric Moulds .75 .30
❑ 15 Peerless Price .75 .30
❑ 16 Josh Reed .75 .30
❑ 17 DeShaun Foster .50 .20
❑ 18 Muhsin Muhammad .75 .30
❑ 19 Steve Smith 1.25 .50
❑ 20 Julius Peppers 1.25 .50
❑ 21 Marty Booker .75 .30
❑ 22 David Terrell .75 .30
❑ 23 Anthony Thomas .75 .30
❑ 24 Brian Urlacher 2.00 .75
❑ 25 Corey Dillon .75 .30
❑ 26 Chad Johnson 1.25 .50
❑ 27 Jon Kitna .75 .30
❑ 28 Peter Warrick .75 .30
❑ 29 Tim Couch .50 .20
❑ 30 Andre Davis .50 .20
❑ 31 William Green .75 .30
❑ 32 Quincy Morgan .75 .30
❑ 33 Dennis Northcutt .75 .30
❑ 34 Antonio Bryant .75 .30
❑ 35 Quincy Carter .75 .30
❑ 36 Troy Hambrick .50 .20
❑ 37 Chad Hutchinson .50 .20
❑ 38 Emmitt Smith 3.00 1.25
❑ 39 Roy Williams 1.25 .50
❑ 40 Brian Griese 1.25 .50
❑ 41 Ashley Lelie 1.25 .50
❑ 42 Ed McCaffrey .75 .30
❑ 43 Clinton Portis 2.00 .75
❑ 44 Rod Smith .75 .30
❑ 45 Germane Crowell .50 .20
❑ 46 Az-Zahir Hakim .50 .20
❑ 47 Joey Harrington 2.00 .75
❑ 48 James Stewart .75 .30
❑ 49 Donald Driver .75 .30
❑ 50 Brett Favre 3.00 1.25
❑ 51 Terry Glenn .50 .20
❑ 52 Ahman Green 1.25 .50
❑ 53 Javon Walker .75 .30
❑ 54 Corey Bradford .50 .20
❑ 55 David Carr 2.00 .75
❑ 56 Jabar Gaffney .75 .30
❑ 57 Jonathan Wells .50 .20
❑ 58 Marvin Harrison 1.25 .50
❑ 59 Edgerrin James 1.25 .50
❑ 60 Peyton Manning 2.00 .75
❑ 61 James Mungro .50 .20
❑ 62 Reggie Wayne .75 .30
❑ 63 Mark Brunell .75 .30
❑ 64 David Garrard .50 .20
❑ 65 Stacey Mack .50 .20
❑ 66 Jimmy Smith .75 .30
❑ 67 Fred Taylor 1.25 .50
❑ 68 Marc Boerigter .75 .30
❑ 69 Tony Gonzalez .75 .30
❑ 70 Trent Green .75 .30
❑ 71 Priest Holmes 1.50 .60
❑ 72 Eddie Kennison .50 .20
❑ 73 Cris Carter 1.25 .50
❑ 74 Chris Chambers 1.25 .50
❑ 75 Jay Fiedler .75 .30
❑ 76 Randy McMichael .75 .30
❑ 77 Zach Thomas .75 .30
❑ 78 Ricky Williams 1.25 .50
❑ 79 Michael Bennett .75 .30
❑ 80 Todd Bouman .50 .20
❑ 81 Daunte Culpepper 1.25 .50
❑ 82 Randy Moss 2.00 .75
❑ 83 Tom Brady 3.00 1.25
❑ 84 Deion Branch 1.25 .50
❑ 85 Troy Brown .75 .30
❑ 86 Kevin Faulk .50 .20
❑ 87 Antowain Smith .75 .30
❑ 88 Aaron Brooks 1.25 .50
❑ 89 Joe Horn .75 .30
❑ 90 Deuce McAllister 1.25 .50
❑ 91 Donte Stallworth 1.25 .50
❑ 92 Tiki Barber 1.25 .50
❑ 93 Kerry Collins .75 .30
❑ 94 Jeremy Shockey 2.00 .75
❑ 95 Michael Strahan .75 .30
❑ 96 Amani Toomer .75 .30
❑ 97 Laveranues Coles .75 .30
❑ 98 LaMont Jordan 1.25 .50
❑ 99 Curtis Martin 1.25 .50
❑ 100 Santana Moss .75 .30
❑ 101 Chad Pennington 1.50 .60
❑ 102 Tim Brown 1.25 .50
❑ 103 Rich Gannon .75 .30
❑ 104 Charlie Garner .75 .30
❑ 105 Jerry Rice 2.50 1.00
❑ 106 Charles Woodson .75 .30
❑ 107 Antonio Freeman .75 .30
❑ 108 Dorsey Levens .50 .20
❑ 109 Donovan McNabb 1.50 .60
❑ 110 Duce Staley .75 .30
❑ 111 James Thrash .50 .20
❑ 112 Jerome Bettis 1.25 .50
❑ 113 Plaxico Burress .75 .30
❑ 114 Tommy Maddox 1.25 .50
❑ 115 Antwaan Randle El 1.25 .50
❑ 116 Kordell Stewart .75 .30
❑ 117 Hines Ward 1.25 .50
❑ 118 Drew Brees 1.25 .50
❑ 119 Curtis Conway .50 .20
❑ 120 Junior Seau 1.25 .50
❑ 121 LaDainian Tomlinson 1.25 .50
❑ 122 Kevan Barlow .75 .30
❑ 123 Jeff Garcia 1.25 .50
❑ 124 Garrison Hearst .75 .30
❑ 125 Terrell Owens 1.25 .50
❑ 126 Shaun Alexander 1.25 .50
❑ 127 Trent Dilfer .75 .30
❑ 128 Darrell Jackson .75 .30
❑ 129 Maurice Morris .50 .20
❑ 130 Koren Robinson .50 .20
❑ 131 Isaac Bruce 1.25 .50
❑ 132 Marc Bulger 1.25 .50
❑ 133 Marshall Faulk 1.25 .50
❑ 134 Torry Holt 1.25 .50
❑ 135 Kurt Warner 1.25 .50
❑ 136 Mike Alstott 1.25 .50
❑ 137 Brad Johnson .75 .30
❑ 138 Keyshawn Johnson 1.25 .50
❑ 139 Dexter Jackson RC 1.25 .50
❑ 140 Warren Sapp .75 .30
❑ 141 Kevin Dyson .75 .30
❑ 142 Eddie George .75 .30
❑ 143 Jevon Kearse .75 .30
❑ 144 Derrick Mason .75 .30
❑ 145 Steve McNair 1.25 .50
❑ 146 Stephen Davis .75 .30
❑ 147 Rod Gardner .75 .30
❑ 148 Shane Matthews .50 .20
❑ 149 Patrick Ramsey 1.25 .50
❑ 150 Derrius Thompson .50 .20
❑ 151 Byron Leftwich RC 10.00 4.00
❑ 152 Carson Palmer RC 12.00 5.00
❑ 153 Chris Simms RC 5.00 2.00
❑ 154 Kliff Kingsbury RC 2.50 1.00
❑ 155 Dave Ragone RC 3.00 1.25
❑ 156 Jason Gesser RC 3.00 1.25
❑ 157 Ken Dorsey RC 3.00 1.25
❑ 158 Kyle Boller RC 6.00 2.50
❑ 159 Brad Banks RC 2.50 1.00
❑ 160 Rex Grossman RC 5.00 2.00
❑ 161 Seneca Wallace RC 3.00 1.25
❑ 162 Brian St.Pierre RC 3.00 1.25
❑ 163 Larry Johnson RC 12.00 6.00
❑ 164 Earnest Graham RC 2.50 1.00
❑ 165 Musa Smith RC 3.00 1.25
❑ 166 Lee Suggs RC 6.00 2.50
❑ 167 Willis McGahee RC 8.00 3.00
❑ 168 Onterrio Smith RC 3.00 1.25
❑ 170 Sultan McCullough RC 2.50 1.00
❑ 171 Chris Brown RC 4.00 1.50
❑ 172 Justin Fargas RC 3.00 1.25
❑ 173 Avon Cobourne RC 1.50 .60
❑ 174 Dahrran Diedrick RC 3.00 1.25
❑ 175 LaBrandon Toefield RC 3.00 1.25
❑ 176 Artose Pinner RC 3.00 1.25
❑ 177 Quentin Griffin RC 3.00 1.25
❑ 178 ReShard Lee RC 3.00 1.25
❑ 179 Andrew Pinnock RC 2.50 1.00
❑ 180 B.J. Askew RC 3.00 1.25
❑ 181 Andre Johnson RC 6.00 2.50
❑ 182 Brandon Lloyd RC 4.00 1.50
❑ 183 Bryant Johnson RC 3.00 1.25
❑ 184 Charles Rogers RC 3.00 1.25
❑ 185 Doug Gabriel RC 3.00 1.25
❑ 186 Justin Gage RC 3.00 1.25
❑ 187 Kareem Kelly RC 2.50 1.00
❑ 188 Kelley Washington RC 3.00 1.25
❑ 189 Taylor Jacobs RC 2.50 1.00
❑ 190 Terrence Edwards RC 2.50 1.00
❑ 191 Anquan Boldin RC 8.00 3.00
❑ 192 Billy McMullen RC 2.50 1.00
❑ 193 Talman Gardner RC 3.00 1.25
❑ 194 Arnaz Battle RC 3.00 1.25
❑ 195 Sam Aiken RC 2.50 1.00
❑ 196 Bobby Wade RC 3.00 1.25
❑ 197 Mike Bush RC 1.50 .60
❑ 198 Keenan Howry RC 3.00 1.25
❑ 199 Jerel Myers RC 1.50 .60
❑ 200 Dallas Clark RC 3.00 1.25
❑ 201 Mike Pinkard RC 1.50 .60
❑ 202 Teyo Johnson RC 3.00 1.25
❑ 203 Trent Smith RC 2.50 1.00
❑ 204 George Wrighster RC 2.50 1.00
❑ 205 Jason Witten RC 5.00 2.00
❑ 206 Cory Redding RC 2.50 1.00
❑ 207 DeWayne White RC 2.50 1.00
❑ 208 Jerome McDougle RC 3.00 1.25
❑ 209 Michael Haynes RC 3.00 1.25
❑ 210 Chris Kelsay RC 3.00 1.25
❑ 211 Calvin Pace RC 2.50 1.00

❑ 212 Kenny King RC	2.50	1.00
❑ 213 Jimmy Kennedy RC	3.00	1.25
❑ 214 William Joseph RC	3.00	1.25
❑ 215 DeWayne Robertson RC	3.00	1.25
❑ 216 Jarret Johnson RC	2.50	1.00
❑ 217 Rien Long RC	1.50	.60
❑ 218 Boss Bailey RC	3.00	1.25
❑ 219 Terrell Suggs RC	5.00	2.00
❑ 220 Terry Pierce RC	2.50	1.00
❑ 221 Bradie James RC	3.00	1.25
❑ 222 Angelo Crowell RC	2.50	1.00
❑ 223 Andre Woolfolk RC	3.00	1.25
❑ 224 Dennis Weathersby RC	1.50	.60
❑ 225 Marcus Trufant RC	3.00	1.25
❑ 226 Terence Newman RC	6.00	2.50
❑ 227 Ricky Manning RC	3.00	1.25
❑ 228 Mike Doss RC	3.00	1.25
❑ 229 Julian Battle RC	2.50	1.00
❑ 230 Rashean Mathis RC	2.50	1.00

2004 Playoff Prestige

❑ COMP.SET w/o RC's (150)	25.00	10.00
❑ 1 Anquan Boldin	1.00	.40
❑ 2 Emmitt Smith	2.00	.75
❑ 3 Jeff Blake	.40	.15
❑ 4 Marcel Shipp	.60	.25
❑ 5 Michael Vick	2.00	.75
❑ 6 Peerless Price	.60	.25
❑ 7 T.J. Duckett	.60	.25
❑ 8 Warrick Dunn	.60	.25
❑ 9 Ed Reed	.60	.25
❑ 10 Jamal Lewis	1.00	.40
❑ 11 Kyle Boller	1.00	.40
❑ 12 Ray Lewis	1.00	.40
❑ 13 Todd Heap	.60	.25
❑ 14 Drew Bledsoe	1.00	.40
❑ 15 Eric Moulds	.60	.25
❑ 16 Josh Reed	.40	.15
❑ 17 Travis Henry	.60	.25
❑ 18 DeShaun Foster	.60	.25
❑ 19 Stephen Davis	.60	.25
❑ 20 Jake Delhomme	1.00	.40
❑ 21 Julius Peppers	1.00	.40
❑ 22 Steve Smith	1.00	.40
❑ 23 Anthony Thomas	.60	.25
❑ 24 Brian Urlacher	1.25	.50
❑ 25 Marty Booker	.60	.25
❑ 26 Rex Grossman	1.00	.40
❑ 27 Chad Johnson	1.00	.40
❑ 28 Corey Dillon	.60	.25
❑ 29 Carson Palmer	1.25	.50
❑ 30 Peter Warrick	.60	.25
❑ 31 Rudi Johnson	.60	.25
❑ 32 Andre Davis	.40	.15
❑ 33 Quincy Morgan	.60	.25
❑ 34 William Green	.60	.25
❑ 35 Kelly Holcomb	.60	.25
❑ 36 Antonio Bryant	.60	.25
❑ 37 Quincy Carter	.60	.25
❑ 38 Roy Williams S	.60	.25
❑ 39 Terence Newman	.60	.25
❑ 40 Terry Glenn	.40	.15
❑ 41 Troy Hambrick	.40	.15
❑ 42 Ashley Lelie	.60	.25
❑ 43 Clinton Portis	1.00	.40
❑ 44 Rod Smith	.60	.25
❑ 45 Shannon Sharpe	.60	.25
❑ 46 Mike Anderson	.60	.25
❑ 47 Jake Plummer	.60	.25
❑ 48 Charles Rogers	.60	.25
❑ 49 Joey Harrington	1.00	.40
❑ 50 Ahman Green	1.00	.40
❑ 51 Brett Favre	2.50	1.00
❑ 52 Donald Driver	.60	.25
❑ 53 Javon Walker	.60	.25
❑ 54 Robert Ferguson	.40	.15
❑ 55 Andre Johnson	1.00	.40
❑ 56 David Carr	1.00	.40
❑ 57 Domanick Davis	1.00	.40
❑ 58 Jabar Gaffney	.60	.25
❑ 59 Dwight Freeney	.60	.25
❑ 60 Dallas Clark	.60	.25
❑ 61 Edgerrin James	1.00	.40
❑ 62 Marvin Harrison	1.00	.40
❑ 63 Peyton Manning	1.50	.60
❑ 64 Reggie Wayne	.60	.25
❑ 65 Byron Leftwich	1.25	.50
❑ 66 Fred Taylor	.60	.25
❑ 67 Jimmy Smith	.60	.25
❑ 68 Johnnie Morton	.60	.25
❑ 69 Priest Holmes	1.25	.50
❑ 70 Tony Gonzalez	.60	.25
❑ 71 Trent Green	.60	.25
❑ 72 Chris Chambers	.60	.25
❑ 73 Jay Fiedler	.40	.15
❑ 74 Randy McMichael	.40	.15
❑ 75 Ricky Williams	1.00	.40
❑ 76 Zach Thomas	1.00	.40
❑ 77 Daunte Culpepper	1.00	.40
❑ 78 Kelly Campbell	.40	.15
❑ 79 Michael Bennett	.60	.25
❑ 80 Moe Williams	.40	.15
❑ 81 Nate Burleson	1.00	.40
❑ 82 Randy Moss	1.25	.50
❑ 83 Deion Branch	1.00	.40
❑ 84 Kevin Faulk	.40	.15
❑ 85 Tom Brady	2.50	1.00
❑ 86 Troy Brown	.60	.25
❑ 87 Tedy Bruschi	.60	.25
❑ 88 Aaron Brooks	.60	.25
❑ 89 Deuce McAllister	1.00	.40
❑ 90 Donte Stallworth	.60	.25
❑ 91 Joe Horn	.60	.25
❑ 92 Amani Toomer	.60	.25
❑ 93 Ike Hilliard	.40	.15
❑ 94 Jeremy Shockey	1.00	.40
❑ 95 Kerry Collins	.60	.25
❑ 96 Michael Strahan	.60	.25
❑ 97 Tiki Barber	1.00	.40
❑ 98 Chad Pennington	1.00	.40
❑ 99 Curtis Martin	1.00	.40
❑ 100 LaMont Jordan	1.00	.40
❑ 101 Santana Moss	.60	.25
❑ 102 Charlie Garner	.60	.25
❑ 103 Jerry Porter	.60	.25
❑ 104 Jerry Rice	2.00	.75
❑ 105 Justin Fargas	.60	.25
❑ 106 Rich Gannon	.60	.25
❑ 107 Rod Woodson	.60	.25
❑ 108 Tim Brown	1.00	.40
❑ 109 Brian Westbrook	.60	.25
❑ 110 Correll Buckhalter	.60	.25
❑ 111 Donovan McNabb	1.25	.50
❑ 112 Freddie Mitchell	.60	.25
❑ 113 James Thrash	.40	.15
❑ 114 Amos Zereoue	.40	.15
❑ 115 Antwaan Randle El	1.00	.40
❑ 116 Hines Ward	1.00	.40
❑ 117 Joey Porter	.60	.25
❑ 118 Kendrell Bell	.60	.25
❑ 119 Plaxico Burress	.60	.25
❑ 120 David Boston	.60	.25
❑ 121 Drew Brees	1.00	.40
❑ 122 LaDainian Tomlinson	1.25	.50
❑ 123 Jeff Garcia	1.00	.40
❑ 124 Kevan Barlow	.60	.25
❑ 125 Tai Streets	.40	.15
❑ 126 Terrell Owens	1.00	.40
❑ 127 Tim Rattay	.40	.15
❑ 128 Darrell Jackson	.60	.25
❑ 129 Koren Robinson	.60	.25
❑ 130 Matt Hasselbeck	.60	.25
❑ 131 Shaun Alexander	1.00	.40
❑ 132 Isaac Bruce	.60	.25
❑ 133 Marc Bulger	1.00	.40
❑ 134 Marshall Faulk	1.00	.40
❑ 135 Torry Holt	1.00	.40
❑ 136 Brad Johnson	.60	.25
❑ 137 Derrick Brooks	.60	.25
❑ 138 Keenan McCardell	.40	.15
❑ 139 Keyshawn Johnson	.60	.25
❑ 140 Mike Alstott	.60	.25
❑ 141 Derrick Mason	.60	.25
❑ 142 Drew Bennett	.60	.25
❑ 143 Jevon Kearse	.60	.25
❑ 144 Justin McCareins	.40	.15
❑ 145 Steve McNair	1.00	.40
❑ 146 Tyrone Calico	.60	.25
❑ 147 Bruce Smith	.60	.25
❑ 148 Laveranues Coles	.60	.25
❑ 149 Patrick Ramsey	.60	.25
❑ 150 LaVar Arrington	2.00	.75
❑ 151 Eli Manning RC	12.00	6.00
❑ 152 Larry Fitzgerald RC	8.00	3.00
❑ 153 Philip Rivers RC	8.00	3.00
❑ 154 Sean Taylor RC	3.00	1.25
❑ 155 Kellen Winslow RC	5.00	2.00
❑ 156 Roy Williams RC	6.00	2.50
❑ 157 DeAngelo Hall RC	3.00	1.25
❑ 158 Reggie Williams RC	3.00	1.25
❑ 159 Ben Roethlisberger RC	15.00	7.50
❑ 160 Jonathan Vilma RC	2.50	1.00
❑ 161 Lee Evans RC	3.00	1.25
❑ 162 Tommie Harris RC	2.50	1.00
❑ 163 Michael Clayton RC	5.00	2.00
❑ 164 D.J. Williams SP RC	30.00	12.50
❑ 165 Will Smith RC	2.50	1.00
❑ 166 Kenechi Udeze RC	2.50	1.00
❑ 167 Vince Wilfork SP RC	30.00	12.50
❑ 168 J.P. Losman RC	5.00	2.00
❑ 169 Steven Jackson SP RC	50.00	25.00
❑ 170 Ahmad Carroll RC	3.00	1.25
❑ 171 Chris Perry RC	5.00	2.00
❑ 172 Jason Babin SP RC	30.00	15.00
❑ 173 Chris Gamble RC	3.00	1.25
❑ 174 Michael Jenkins RC	2.50	1.00
❑ 175 Kevin Jones RC	8.00	3.00
❑ 176 Rashaun Woods RC	2.50	1.00
❑ 177 Ben Watson RC	2.50	1.00
❑ 178 Karlos Dansby RC	2.50	1.00
❑ 179 Teddy Lehman RC	2.50	1.00
❑ 180 Ricardo Colclough SP RC	30.00	15.00
❑ 181 Daryl Smith RC	2.50	1.00
❑ 182 Ben Troupe RC	2.50	1.00
❑ 183 Tatum Bell RC	5.00	2.00
❑ 184 Julius Jones RC	10.00	4.00
❑ 185 Bob Sanders RC	5.00	2.00
❑ 186 Devery Henderson RC	2.00	.75
❑ 187 Dwan Edwards RC	1.25	.50
❑ 188 Michael Boulware RC	2.50	1.00
❑ 189 Darius Watts RC	2.50	1.00
❑ 190 Greg Jones RC	2.50	1.00
❑ 191 Antwan Odom RC	2.50	1.00
❑ 192 Sean Jones SP RC	25.00	10.00
❑ 193 Courtney Watson RC	2.50	1.00
❑ 194 Keary Colbert RC	3.00	1.25
❑ 195 Keith Smith RC	2.00	.75
❑ 196 Derrick Strait RC	2.50	1.00

❑ 197	Bernard Berrian RC	2.50	1.00
❑ 198	Devard Darling RC	2.50	1.00
❑ 199	Matt Schaub RC	4.00	1.50
❑ 200	Will Poole RC	2.50	1.00
❑ 201	Samie Parker RC	2.50	1.00
❑ 202	Luke McCown SP RC	30.00	15.00
❑ 203	Jerricho Cotchery RC	2.50	1.00
❑ 204	Mewelde Moore RC	3.00	1.25
❑ 205	Ernest Wilford RC	2.50	1.00
❑ 206	Cedric Cobbs SP RC	30.00	15.00
❑ 207	Johnnie Morant RC	2.50	1.00
❑ 208	Craig Krenzel RC	2.50	1.00
❑ 209	Michael Turner RC	2.50	1.00
❑ 210	D.J. Hackett RC	2.00	.75
❑ 211	P.K. Sam RC	2.00	.75
❑ 212	Josh Harris RC	2.50	1.00
❑ 213	Drew Henson RC	2.50	1.00
❑ 214	Jeff Smoker RC	2.50	1.00
❑ 215	John Navarre RC	2.50	1.00
❑ 216	Cody Pickett RC	2.50	1.00
❑ 217	Quincy Wilson RC	2.00	.75
❑ 218	Derek Abney RC	2.50	1.00
❑ 219	Maurice Clarett SP RC	25.00	10.00
❑ 220	Mike Williams SP RC	50.00	20.00
❑ 221	B.J. Johnson RC	2.00	.75
❑ 222	Brandon Everage RC	2.00	.75
❑ 223	Derek McCoy RC	2.00	.75
❑ 224	Jared Lorenzen RC	2.00	.75
❑ 225	Jarrett Payton RC	3.00	1.25
❑ 226	Jason Fife RC	2.00	.75
❑ 227	Robert Kent RC	1.25	.50

2005 Playoff Prestige

❑	COMP.SET w/o SP's (234)	100.00	50.00
❑	COMP.SET w/o RC's (150)	25.00	10.00
❑	ONE 151-244 DRAFT PICK PER PACK		
❑ 1	Anquan Boldin	.60	.25
❑ 2	Emmitt Smith	2.00	.75
❑ 3	Josh McCown	.60	.25
❑ 4	Larry Fitzgerald	1.00	.40
❑ 5	Michael Vick	1.50	.60
❑ 6	Peerless Price	.50	.20
❑ 7	Alge Crumpler	.60	.25
❑ 8	T.J. Duckett	.60	.25
❑ 9	Warrick Dunn	.60	.25
❑ 10	Ed Reed	.60	.25
❑ 11	Jamal Lewis	1.00	.40
❑ 12	Kyle Boller	.60	.25
❑ 13	Ray Lewis	1.00	.40
❑ 14	Todd Heap	.60	.25
❑ 15	Drew Bledsoe	1.00	.40
❑ 16	Eric Moulds	.60	.25
❑ 17	Lee Evans	.60	.25
❑ 18	Travis Henry	.60	.25
❑ 19	Willis McGahee	1.00	.40
❑ 20	Anthony Thomas	.60	.25
❑ 21	Brian Urlacher	1.00	.40
❑ 22	Rex Grossman	.60	.25
❑ 23	David Terrell	.60	.25
❑ 24	Thomas Jones	.60	.25
❑ 25	Carson Palmer	1.00	.40
❑ 26	Chad Johnson	1.00	.40
❑ 27	Peter Warrick	.50	.20
❑ 28	Rudi Johnson	.60	.25
❑ 29	Antonio Bryant	.50	.20
❑ 30	William Green	.50	.20
❑ 31	Jeff Garcia	.60	.25
❑ 32	Kellen Winslow	1.00	.40
❑ 33	Lee Suggs	.60	.25
❑ 34	Drew Henson	.60	.25
❑ 35	Julius Jones	1.25	.50
❑ 36	Jason Witten	.60	.25
❑ 37	Keyshawn Johnson	.60	.25
❑ 38	Roy Williams S	.60	.25
❑ 39	Ashley Lelie	.60	.25
❑ 40	Champ Bailey	.60	.25
❑ 41	Jake Plummer	.60	.25
❑ 42	Reuben Droughns	.60	.25
❑ 43	Rod Smith	.60	.25
❑ 44	Charles Rogers	.60	.25
❑ 45	Joey Harrington	1.00	.40
❑ 46	Kevin Jones	1.00	.40
❑ 47	Roy Williams WR	1.00	.40
❑ 48	Ahman Green	1.00	.40
❑ 49	Donald Driver	.60	.25
❑ 50	Javon Walker	.60	.25
❑ 51	Brett Favre	2.50	1.00
❑ 52	Andre Johnson	.60	.25
❑ 53	David Carr	1.00	.40
❑ 54	Domanick Davis	.60	.25
❑ 55	Jabar Gaffney	.50	.20
❑ 56	Edgerrin James	1.00	.40
❑ 57	Marvin Harrison	1.00	.40
❑ 58	Brandon Stokley	.60	.25
❑ 59	Peyton Manning	1.50	.60
❑ 60	Reggie Wayne	.60	.25
❑ 61	Byron Leftwich	1.00	.40
❑ 62	Fred Taylor	.60	.25
❑ 63	Jimmy Smith	.60	.25
❑ 64	Priest Holmes	1.00	.40
❑ 65	Tony Gonzalez	.60	.25
❑ 66	Johnnie Morton	.60	.25
❑ 67	Trent Green	.60	.25
❑ 68	Chris Chambers	.60	.25
❑ 69	Randy McMichael	.50	.20
❑ 70	A.J. Feeley	.60	.25
❑ 71	Zach Thomas	1.00	.40
❑ 72	Daunte Culpepper	1.00	.40
❑ 73	Marcus Robinson	.60	.25
❑ 74	Mewelde Moore	.60	.25
❑ 75	Nate Burleson	.60	.25
❑ 76	Onterrio Smith	.60	.25
❑ 77	Randy Moss	1.00	.40
❑ 78	Corey Dillon	.60	.25
❑ 79	Tom Brady	2.50	1.00
❑ 80	Deion Branch	.60	.25
❑ 81	Tedy Bruschi	.60	.25
❑ 82	David Givens	.60	.25
❑ 83	David Patten	.50	.20
❑ 84	Aaron Brooks	.60	.25
❑ 85	Deuce McAllister	1.00	.40
❑ 86	Donte Stallworth	.60	.25
❑ 87	Joe Horn	.60	.25
❑ 88	Eli Manning	2.00	.75
❑ 89	Jeremy Shockey	1.00	.40
❑ 90	Kurt Warner	.60	.25
❑ 91	Michael Strahan	.60	.25
❑ 92	Tiki Barber	1.00	.40
❑ 93	Amani Toomer	.60	.25
❑ 94	Chad Pennington	1.00	.40
❑ 95	Curtis Martin	1.00	.40
❑ 96	Santana Moss	.60	.25
❑ 97	Justin McCareins	.50	.20
❑ 98	Charles Woodson	.60	.25
❑ 99	Kerry Collins	.60	.25
❑ 100	Warren Sapp	.60	.25
❑ 101	Jerry Porter	.60	.25
❑ 102	Donovan McNabb	1.25	.50
❑ 103	Jevon Kearse	.60	.25
❑ 104	Terrell Owens	1.00	.40
❑ 105	Brian Westbrook	.60	.25
❑ 106	Todd Pinkston	.50	.20
❑ 107	Duce Staley	.60	.25
❑ 108	Hines Ward	1.00	.40
❑ 109	Jerome Bettis	1.00	.40
❑ 110	Joey Porter	.60	.25
❑ 111	Plaxico Burress	.60	.25
❑ 112	Ben Roethlisberger	2.50	1.00
❑ 113	Drew Brees	1.00	.40
❑ 114	LaDainian Tomlinson	1.25	.50
❑ 115	Keenan McCardell	.50	.20
❑ 116	Philip Rivers	1.00	.40
❑ 117	Antonio Gates	1.00	.40
❑ 118	Eric Johnson	.60	.25
❑ 119	Kevan Barlow	.60	.25
❑ 120	Brandon Lloyd	.50	.20
❑ 121	Tim Rattay	.50	.20
❑ 122	Darrell Jackson	.60	.25
❑ 123	Koren Robinson	.60	.25
❑ 124	Jerry Rice	2.00	.75
❑ 125	Matt Hasselbeck	.60	.25
❑ 126	Shaun Alexander	1.25	.50
❑ 127	Isaac Bruce	.60	.25
❑ 128	Marc Bulger	1.00	.40
❑ 129	Marshall Faulk	1.00	.40
❑ 130	Steven Jackson	1.25	.50
❑ 131	Torry Holt	1.00	.40
❑ 132	Derrick Brooks	.60	.25
❑ 133	Michael Clayton	1.00	.40
❑ 134	Michael Pittman	.50	.20
❑ 135	Chris Simms	.60	.25
❑ 136	Chris Brown	.60	.25
❑ 137	Derrick Mason	.60	.25
❑ 138	Drew Bennett	.60	.25
❑ 139	Steve McNair	1.00	.40
❑ 140	Clinton Portis	1.00	.40
❑ 141	LaVar Arrington	1.00	.40
❑ 142	Laveranues Coles	.60	.25
❑ 143	Patrick Ramsey	.60	.25
❑ 144	Rod Gardner	.60	.25
❑ 145	DeShaun Foster	.60	.25
❑ 146	Stephen Davis	.60	.25
❑ 147	Jake Delhomme	1.00	.40
❑ 148	Muhsin Muhammad	.60	.25
❑ 149	Steve Smith	.60	.25
❑ 150	Keary Colbert	.60	.25
❑ 151	Aaron Rodgers SP RC	50.00	20.00
❑ 152	Adrian McPherson SP RC	30.00	12.50
❑ 153	Alex Smith QB RC	10.00	4.00
❑ 154	Andrew Walter RC	4.00	1.50
❑ 155	Brock Berlin RC	2.00	.75
❑ 156	Charlie Frye SP RC	40.00	20.00
❑ 157	Chris Rix RC	2.00	.75
❑ 158	Dan Orlovsky RC	3.00	1.25
❑ 159	Darian Durant RC	2.50	1.00
❑ 160	David Greene RC	2.50	1.00
❑ 161	Derek Anderson RC	2.50	1.00
❑ 162	Gino Guidugli RC	1.25	.50
❑ 163	Jason Campbell RC	4.00	1.50
❑ 164	Jason White RC	2.50	1.00
❑ 165	Kyle Orton RC	4.00	1.50
❑ 166	Matt Jones SP RC	40.00	15.00
❑ 167	Ryan Fitzpatrick RC	4.00	1.50
❑ 168	Stefan LeFors RC	2.50	1.00
❑ 169	Timmy Chang RC	2.00	.75
❑ 170	Alvin Pearman RC	2.50	1.00
❑ 171	Anthony Davis RC	2.00	.75
❑ 172	Brandon Jacobs RC	3.00	1.25
❑ 173	Carnell Williams RC	12.00	5.00
❑ 174	Cedric Benson RC	5.00	2.00
❑ 175	Cedric Houston RC	2.50	1.00
❑ 176	Ciatrick Fason RC	2.50	1.00
❑ 177	Damien Nash RC	2.00	.75
❑ 178	Darren Sproles RC	2.50	1.00
❑ 179	Eric Shelton SP RC	25.00	10.00
❑ 180	Frank Gore SP RC	30.00	12.50
❑ 181	J.J. Arrington SP RC	30.00	12.50

❑ 182 Kay-Jay Harris RC	2.00	.75
❑ 183 Marion Barber RC	4.00	1.50
❑ 184 Ronnie Brown RC	8.00	3.00
❑ 185 Ryan Moats RC	2.50	1.00
❑ 186 T.A. McLendon RC	1.25	.50
❑ 187 Vernand Morency RC	2.50	1.00
❑ 188 Walter Reyes RC	2.00	.75
❑ 189 Braylon Edwards RC	8.00	3.00
❑ 190 Charles Frederick RC	2.00	.75
❑ 191 Chris Henry RC	2.50	1.00
❑ 192 Courtney Roby RC	2.50	1.00
❑ 193 Craig Bragg RC	2.00	.75
❑ 194 Craphonso Thorpe SP RC	20.00	7.50
❑ 195 Dante Ridgeway RC	2.00	.75
❑ 196 Fred Amey RC	2.00	.75
❑ 197 Fred Gibson RC	2.00	.75
❑ 198 J.R. Russell RC	2.00	.75
❑ 199 Jerome Mathis SP RC	25.00	10.00
❑ 200 Josh Davis RC	2.00	.75
❑ 201 Larry Brackins RC	1.25	.50
❑ 202 Mark Bradley RC	2.50	1.00
❑ 203 Mark Clayton SP RC	30.00	12.50
❑ 204 Mike Williams	6.00	2.50
❑ 205 Reggie Brown RC	2.50	1.00
❑ 206 Roddy White RC	2.50	1.00
❑ 207 Roscoe Parrish RC	2.50	1.00
❑ 208 Roydell Williams RC	2.50	1.00
❑ 209 Steve Savoy RC	1.25	.50
❑ 210 Tab Perry RC	2.50	1.00
❑ 211 Taylor Stubblefield RC	1.25	.50
❑ 212 Terrence Murphy RC	2.50	1.00
❑ 213 Troy Williamson RC	5.00	2.00
❑ 214 Vincent Jackson RC	2.50	1.00
❑ 215 Alex Smith TE RC	2.50	1.00
❑ 216 Heath Miller RC	6.00	2.50
❑ 217 Dan Cody RC	2.50	1.00
❑ 218 David Pollack RC	2.50	1.00
❑ 219 Erasmus James RC	2.50	1.00
❑ 220 Justin Tuck RC	2.50	1.00
❑ 221 Marcus Spears RC	2.50	1.00
❑ 222 Matt Roth RC	2.50	1.00
❑ 223 Anttaj Hawthorne RC	2.00	.75
❑ 224 Mike Patterson RC	2.50	1.00
❑ 225 Shaun Cody RC	2.50	1.00
❑ 226 Travis Johnson RC	2.00	.75
❑ 227 Channing Crowder RC	2.50	1.00
❑ 228 Darryl Blackstock RC	2.00	.75
❑ 229 DeMarcus Ware RC	4.00	1.50
❑ 230 Derrick Johnson RC	4.00	1.50
❑ 231 Kevin Burnett RC	2.50	1.00
❑ 232 Shawne Merriman RC	4.00	1.50
❑ 233 Adam Jones RC	2.50	1.00
❑ 234 Antrel Rolle RC	2.50	1.00
❑ 235 Brandon Browner RC	2.00	.75
❑ 236 Bryant McFadden RC	2.50	1.00
❑ 237 Carlos Rogers RC	3.00	1.25
❑ 238 Corey Webster RC	2.50	1.00
❑ 239 Fabian Washington RC	2.50	1.00
❑ 240 Justin Miller RC	2.00	.75
❑ 241 Marlin Jackson RC	2.50	1.00
❑ 242 Ernest Shazor RC	2.50	1.00
❑ 243 Josh Bullocks RC	2.50	1.00
❑ 244 Thomas Davis RC	2.50	1.00

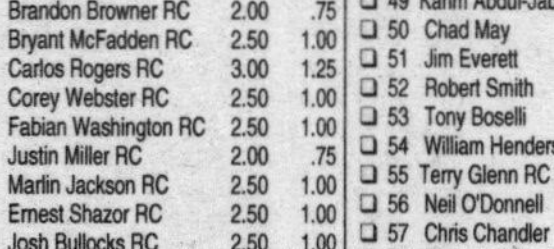

1996 Playoff Prime

❑ COMPLETE SET (200)	100.00	40.00
❑ COMP. BRONZE SET (100)	15.00	6.00
❑ 1 Brett Favre	3.00	1.25
❑ 2 Jerry Rice	1.50	.60
❑ 3 Troy Aikman	1.50	.60
❑ 4 Bruce Smith	.25	.08
❑ 5 Marshall Faulk	.60	.25
❑ 6 Erik Kramer	.10	.02
❑ 7 Carl Pickens	.25	.08
❑ 8 Anthony Miller	.25	.08
❑ 9 Cris Carter	.50	.20
❑ 10 Todd Kinchen	.10	.02
❑ 11 Stoney Case	.10	.02
❑ 12 Chris Calloway	.10	.02
❑ 13 Andre Rison	.25	.08
❑ 14 Bill Brooks	.10	.02
❑ 15 Shawn Jefferson	.10	.02
❑ 16 Eric Zeier	.10	.02
❑ 17 Yancey Thigpen	.25	.08
❑ 18 Edgar Bennett	.25	.08
❑ 19 Garrison Hearst	.25	.08
❑ 20 Daryl Johnston	.25	.08
❑ 21 Tyrone Wheatley	.25	.08
❑ 22 Darick Holmes	.10	.02
❑ 23 Dave Brown	.10	.02
❑ 24 Leeland McElroy RC	.25	.08
❑ 25 Craig Heyward	.10	.02
❑ 26 Kevin Hardy RC	.50	.20
❑ 27 Scott Mitchell	.25	.08
❑ 28 Willie Green	.10	.02
❑ 29 Vincent Brisby	.10	.02
❑ 30 Mike Tomczak	.10	.02
❑ 31 Luther Elliss	.10	.02
❑ 32 Mike Pritchard	.10	.02
❑ 33 Robert Green	.10	.02
❑ 34 Jeff Graham	.10	.02
❑ 35 Tamarick Vanover	.25	.08
❑ 36 William Floyd	.25	.08
❑ 37 Alvin Harper	.10	.02
❑ 38 Stan Humphries	.25	.08
❑ 39 Herman Moore	.25	.08
❑ 40 Tony Martin	.25	.08
❑ 41 Jonathan Ogden RC	.50	.20
❑ 42 Randall Cunningham	.50	.20
❑ 43 Chris Warren	.25	.08
❑ 44 Bobby Hebert	.10	.02
❑ 45 Jerome Bettis	.50	.20
❑ 46 Joey Galloway	.50	.20
❑ 47 Ernie Mills	.10	.02
❑ 48 Steve McNair	1.00	.40
❑ 49 Karim Abdul-Jabbar RC	.50	.20
❑ 50 Chad May	.10	.02
❑ 51 Jim Everett	.10	.02
❑ 52 Robert Smith	.25	.08
❑ 53 Tony Boselli	.10	.02
❑ 54 William Henderson	.50	.20
❑ 55 Terry Glenn RC UER	1.50	.60
❑ 56 Neil O'Donnell	.25	.08
❑ 57 Chris Chandler	.25	.08
❑ 58 Michael Jackson	.25	.08
❑ 59 Jason Dunn RC	.25	.08
❑ 60 James O. Stewart	.25	.08
❑ 61 Greg Hill	.25	.08
❑ 62 Mark Carrier WR	.10	.02
❑ 63 Bernie Parmalee	.10	.02
❑ 64 Chris Sanders	.25	.08
❑ 65 Jeff Hostetler	.10	.02
❑ 66 Eric Moulds RC	2.00	.75
❑ 67 James Jett	.25	.08
❑ 68 Henry Ellard	.10	.02
❑ 69 Mario Bates	.25	.08
❑ 70 Natrone Means	.25	.08
❑ 71 Bobby Engram RC	.50	.20
❑ 72 Christian Fauria	.10	.02
❑ 73 Gus Frerotte	.25	.08
❑ 74 Aaron Hayden	.10	.02
❑ 75 Reggie White	.50	.20
❑ 76 Dave Meggett	.10	.02
❑ 77 Harvey Williams	.10	.02
❑ 78 Terance Mathis	.10	.02
❑ 79 Byron Bam Morris	.10	.02
❑ 80 Trent Dilfer	.50	.20
❑ 81 Irving Fryar	.25	.08
❑ 82 Quinn Early	.10	.02
❑ 83 Lake Dawson	.10	.02
❑ 84 Todd Collins	.25	.08
❑ 85 Eric Metcalf	.10	.02
❑ 86 Tim Biakabutuka RC	.50	.20
❑ 87 Rob Johnson	.50	.20
❑ 88 Charlie Garner	.25	.08
❑ 89 Mike Mamula	.10	.02
❑ 90 Steve Walsh	.10	.02
❑ 91 Charles Haley	.25	.08
❑ 92 Mike Alstott RC	1.50	.60
❑ 93 Wayne Chrebet	.75	.30
❑ 94 Vinny Testaverde	.25	.08
❑ 95 Fred Barnett	.10	.02
❑ 96 Boomer Esiason	.25	.08
❑ 97 Zack Crockett	.10	.02
❑ 98 Kevin Williams	.10	.02
❑ 99 Eric Bieniemy	.10	.02
❑ 100 Bryan Cox	.10	.02
❑ 101 Larry Centers	1.00	.40
❑ 102 Jeff George	1.00	.40
❑ 103 Bryce Paup	1.00	.40
❑ 104 Kerry Collins	2.00	.75
❑ 105 Derrick Moore	.50	.20
❑ 106 Adrian Murrell	1.00	.40
❑ 107 Harold Green	.50	.20
❑ 108 Ki-Jana Carter	1.00	.40
❑ 109 Sherman Williams	.50	.20
❑ 110 Deion Sanders	4.00	2.00
❑ 111 Emmitt Smith	8.00	3.00
❑ 112 Shannon Sharpe	1.00	.40
❑ 113 Johnnie Morton	1.00	.40
❑ 114 Eddie Kennison RC	2.00	.75
❑ 115 Marvin Harrison RC	10.00	4.00
❑ 116 Amani Toomer RC	2.00	.75
❑ 117 Rickey Dudley RC	2.00	.75
❑ 118 Alex Van Dyke RC	1.00	.40
❑ 119 Dorsey Levens	2.00	.75
❑ 120 Antonio Freeman	2.00	.75
❑ 121 Willie Davis WR	1.00	.40
❑ 122 Lamont Warren	.50	.20
❑ 123 Sean Dawkins	.50	.20
❑ 124 Willie Jackson	1.00	.40
❑ 125 Kimble Anders	.50	.20
❑ 126 Dan Marino	10.00	4.00
❑ 127 Terry Kirby	1.00	.40
❑ 128 Amp Lee	.50	.20
❑ 129 Jake Reed	1.00	.40
❑ 130 Curtis Martin	4.00	1.50
❑ 131 Ray Zellars	.50	.20
❑ 132 Herschel Walker	1.00	.40
❑ 133 Mike Sherrard	.50	.20
❑ 134 Kyle Brady	1.00	.40
❑ 135 Rocket Ismail	1.00	.40
❑ 136 Ricky Watters	1.00	.40
❑ 137 Kordell Stewart	2.00	.75
❑ 138 Andre Hastings	.10	.02
❑ 139 Ronnie Harmon	.50	.20
❑ 140 Terrell Fletcher	.50	.20
❑ 141 J.J. Stokes	2.00	.75
❑ 142 Brent Jones	.50	.20
❑ 143 Tony McGee	.50	.20
❑ 144 Brian Blades	1.00	.40
❑ 145 Isaac Bruce	2.00	.75
❑ 146 Errict Rhett	1.00	.40
❑ 147 Warren Sapp	.50	.20
❑ 148 Horace Copeland	.50	.20
❑ 149 Heath Shuler	1.00	.40
❑ 150 Michael Westbrook	2.00	.75
❑ 151 Frank Sanders	1.50	.60

❑ 152	Rob Moore	1.50	.60
❑ 153	Bert Emanuel	1.50	.60
❑ 154	J.J. Birden	.75	.30
❑ 155	Thurman Thomas	2.50	1.00
❑ 156	Jim Kelly	2.50	1.00
❑ 157	Curtis Conway	1.50	.60
❑ 158	Damay Scott	1.50	.60
❑ 159	Jeff Blake	2.50	1.00
❑ 160	Jay Novacek	1.50	.60
❑ 161	Michael Irvin	2.50	1.00
❑ 162	John Elway	12.00	5.00
❑ 163	Terrell Davis	6.00	2.50
❑ 164	Barry Sanders	8.00	3.00
❑ 165	Brett Perriman	1.50	.60
❑ 166	Keyshawn Johnson RC	5.00	2.00
❑ 167	Eddie George RC	6.00	2.50
❑ 168	Derrick Mayes RC	2.50	1.00
❑ 169	Simeon Rice RC	6.00	2.50
❑ 170	Lawrence Phillips RC	1.50	.60
❑ 171	Robert Brooks	1.50	.60
❑ 172	Mark Chmura	1.50	.60
❑ 173	Rodney Thomas	.75	.30
❑ 174	Jim Harbaugh	1.50	.60
❑ 175	Ken Dilger	1.50	.60
❑ 176	Mark Brunell	5.00	2.00
❑ 177	Steve Bono	1.50	.60
❑ 178	Marcus Allen	2.50	1.00
❑ 179	O.J. McDuffie	1.50	.60
❑ 180	Eric Green	.75	.30
❑ 181	Warren Moon	2.50	1.00
❑ 182	Drew Bledsoe	5.00	2.00
❑ 183	Ben Coates	1.50	.60
❑ 184	Michael Haynes	1.50	.60
❑ 185	Rodney Hampton	1.50	.60
❑ 186	Rashaan Salaam	1.50	.60
❑ 187	Napoleon Kaufman	2.50	1.00
❑ 188	Tim Brown	2.50	1.00
❑ 189	Rodney Peete	.75	.30
❑ 190	Calvin Williams	.75	.30
❑ 191	Erric Pegram	1.50	.60
❑ 192	Mark Bruener	.75	.30
❑ 193	Junior Seau	2.50	1.00
❑ 194	Steve Young	6.00	2.50
❑ 195	Derek Loville	.75	.30
❑ 196	Rick Mirer	1.50	.60
❑ 197	Mark Rypien	.75	.30
❑ 198	Jackie Harris	.75	.30
❑ 199	Terry Allen	1.50	.60
❑ 200	Brian Mitchell	.75	.30

2002 Playoff Prime Signatures

❑ 1	Aaron Brooks	5.00	2.00
❑ 2	Brett Favre	12.00	5.00
❑ 3	Drew Bledsoe	6.00	2.50
❑ 4	Jake Plummer	3.00	1.25
❑ 5	Jeff Blake	2.00	.75
❑ 6	Jevon Kearse	3.00	1.25
❑ 7	Ricky Williams	5.00	2.00
❑ 8	Terrell Davis	6.00	2.50
❑ 9	Chris Chambers	5.00	2.00
❑ 10	Cris Carter	5.00	2.00
❑ 11	Emmitt Smith	12.00	5.00
❑ 12	Randall Cunningham	3.00	1.25
❑ 13	Corey Dillon	3.00	1.25
❑ 14	Brian Griese	5.00	2.00
❑ 15	Isaac Bruce	5.00	2.00
❑ 16	Koren Robinson	3.00	1.25
❑ 17	David Terrell	5.00	2.00
❑ 18	Mark Brunell	5.00	2.00
❑ 19	Eric Moulds	3.00	1.25
❑ 20	Kevan Barlow	3.00	1.25
❑ 21	David Boston	5.00	2.00
❑ 22	LaMont Jordan	5.00	2.00
❑ 23	Jimmy Smith	3.00	1.25
❑ 24	Marvin Harrison	5.00	2.00
❑ 25	Marcus Robinson	3.00	1.25
❑ 26	Ray Lewis	5.00	2.00
❑ 27	Mike Anderson	5.00	2.00
❑ 28	Randy Moss	10.00	4.00
❑ 29	Michael Bennett	3.00	1.25
❑ 30	Quincy Carter	3.00	1.25
❑ 31	Tim Brown	5.00	2.00
❑ 32	Michael Strahan	3.00	1.25
❑ 33	Tony Gonzalez	3.00	1.25
❑ 34	Santana Moss	5.00	2.00
❑ 35	Torry Holt	5.00	2.00
❑ 36	Anthony Thomas	3.00	1.25
❑ 37	Chris Weinke	3.00	1.25
❑ 38	Deuce McAllister	6.00	2.50
❑ 39	Drew Brees	5.00	2.00
❑ 40	Edgerrin James	6.00	2.50
❑ 41	Freddie Mitchell	3.00	1.25
❑ 42	James Jackson	2.00	.75
❑ 43	Kendrell Bell	5.00	2.00
❑ 44	LaDainian Tomlinson	8.00	3.00
❑ 45	Mike McMahon	5.00	2.00
❑ 46	Quincy Morgan	3.00	1.25
❑ 47	Robert Ferguson	2.00	.75
❑ 48	Steve Smith	5.00	2.00
❑ 49	Terrell Owens	5.00	2.00
❑ 50	Eddie George	5.00	2.00
❑ 51	Kurt Warner	5.00	2.00
❑ 52	Chad Johnson	5.00	2.00
❑ 53	Dan Marino	15.00	6.00
❑ 54	Jim Kelly	8.00	3.00
❑ 55	John Elway	15.00	6.00
❑ 56	Michael Irvin	5.00	2.00
❑ 57	Phil Simms	3.00	1.25
❑ 58	Steve Young	8.00	3.00
❑ 59	Troy Aikman	8.00	3.00
❑ 60	Warren Moon	5.00	2.00
❑ 61	Barry Sanders	8.00	3.00
❑ 62	Joe Montana	20.00	7.50
❑ 63	Joe Namath	6.00	2.50
❑ 64	Thurman Thomas	3.00	1.25
❑ 65	T.J. Duckett RC	25.00	10.00
❑ 66	William Green RC	12.00	5.00
❑ 67	Travis Stephens RC	10.00	4.00
❑ 68	Tim Carter RC	10.00	4.00
❑ 69	Terry Charles RC	10.00	4.00
❑ 70	Roy Williams RC	30.00	12.50
❑ 71	Marquise Walker RC	10.00	4.00
❑ 72	Rohan Davey RC	12.00	5.00
❑ 73	Quentin Jammer RC	12.00	5.00
❑ 74	Reche Caldwell RC	12.00	5.00
❑ 75	Maurice Morris RC	12.00	5.00
❑ 76	Woody Dantzler RC	10.00	4.00
❑ 77	Patrick Ramsey RC	15.00	6.00
❑ 78	Tavon Mason RC	6.00	2.50
❑ 79	Ladell Betts RC	12.00	5.00
❑ 80	Kahlil Hill RC	10.00	4.00
❑ 81	Josh Scobey RC	12.00	5.00
❑ 82	Brian Westbrook RC	20.00	7.50
❑ 83	Javon Walker RC	25.00	10.00
❑ 84	DeShaun Foster RC	12.00	5.00
❑ 85	Kelly Campbell RC	10.00	4.00
❑ 86	Ashley Lelie RC	25.00	10.00
❑ 87	Donte Stallworth RC	25.00	10.00
❑ 88	David Carr RC	40.00	15.00
❑ 89	Kurt Kittner RC	10.00	4.00
❑ 90	Clinton Portis RC	50.00	20.00
❑ 91	Josh Reed RC	12.00	5.00
❑ 92	Joey Harrington RC	40.00	15.00
❑ 93	Antwaan Randle El RC	20.00	7.50
❑ 94	Randy Fasani RC	10.00	4.00
❑ 95	Cliff Russell RC	10.00	4.00
❑ 96	John Henderson RC	12.00	5.00
❑ 97	Luke Staley RC	10.00	4.00
❑ 98	Antonio Bryant RC	12.00	5.00
❑ 99	Jonathan Wells RC	12.00	5.00
❑ 100	Chester Taylor RC	12.00	5.00
❑ 101	Lamar Gordon RC	12.00	5.00
❑ 102	Deion Branch RC	25.00	10.00
❑ 103	Josh McCown RC	15.00	6.00
❑ 104	Andre Davis RC	10.00	4.00
❑ 105	Freddie Milons RC	10.00	4.00
❑ 106	David Garrard RC	12.00	5.00
❑ 107	Chad Hutchinson RC	10.00	4.00
❑ 108	Jabar Gaffney RC	12.00	5.00
❑ 109	Eric Crouch RC	12.00	5.00
❑ 110	Albert Haynesworth RC	10.00	4.00
❑ NNO	Jeff Garcia TIN	5.00	2.00

2004 Playoff Prime Signatures

❑ 1	Anquan Boldin	4.00	1.50
❑ 2	Josh McCown	3.00	1.25
❑ 3	Alge Crumpler	3.00	1.25
❑ 4	Michael Vick	8.00	3.00
❑ 5	Jamal Lewis	4.00	1.50
❑ 6	Todd Heap	3.00	1.25
❑ 7	Jim Kelly	6.00	2.50
❑ 8	Thurman Thomas	4.00	1.50
❑ 9	Travis Henry	3.00	1.25
❑ 10	Jake Delhomme	4.00	1.50
❑ 11	Stephen Davis	3.00	1.25
❑ 12	Steve Smith	4.00	1.50
❑ 13	Brian Urlacher	5.00	2.00
❑ 14	Dick Butkus	6.00	2.50
❑ 15	Gale Sayers	6.00	2.50
❑ 16	Mike Ditka	5.00	2.00
❑ 17	Mike Singletary	5.00	2.00
❑ 18	Rex Grossman	4.00	1.50
❑ 19	Richard Dent	3.00	1.25
❑ 20	Chad Johnson	4.00	1.50
❑ 21	Rudi Johnson	3.00	1.25
❑ 22	Jim Brown	8.00	3.00
❑ 23	Lee Suggs	4.00	1.50
❑ 24	Ozzie Newsome	4.00	1.50
❑ 25	Paul Warfield	4.00	1.50
❑ 26	Quincy Morgan	3.00	1.25
❑ 27	William Green	3.00	1.25
❑ 28	Antonio Bryant	3.00	1.25
❑ 29	Herschel Walker	4.00	1.50
❑ 30	Jimmy Johnson	4.00	1.50
❑ 31	Keyshawn Johnson	3.00	1.25
❑ 32	Roger Staubach	8.00	3.00
❑ 33	Terence Newman	3.00	1.25
❑ 34	Tony Dorsett	5.00	2.00
❑ 35	Terrell Davis	4.00	1.50
❑ 36	Joey Harrington	4.00	1.50

❑ 37 Ahman Green 4.00 1.50
❑ 38 Javon Walker 3.00 1.25
❑ 39 Paul Hornung 5.00 2.00
❑ 40 Reggie White 5.00 2.00
❑ 41 Robert Ferguson 2.50 1.00
❑ 42 Sterling Sharpe 4.00 1.50
❑ 43 David Carr 4.00 1.50
❑ 44 Domanick Davis 4.00 1.50
❑ 45 Earl Campbell 5.00 2.00
❑ 46 Peyton Manning 6.00 2.50
❑ 47 Reggie Wayne 3.00 1.25
❑ 48 Dante Hall 4.00 1.50
❑ 49 Priest Holmes 5.00 2.00
❑ 50 Trent Green 3.00 1.25
❑ 51 A.J. Feeley 4.00 1.50
❑ 52 Don Shula 5.00 2.00
❑ 53 Chris Chambers 3.00 1.25
❑ 54 Travis Minor 2.50 1.00
❑ 55 Fran Tarkenton 6.00 2.50
❑ 56 Bill Belichick 5.00 2.00
❑ 57 Tom Brady 8.00 3.00
❑ 58 Aaron Brooks 3.00 1.25
❑ 59 Deuce McAllister 4.00 1.50
❑ 60 Boo Williams 2.50 1.00
❑ 61 Joe Horn 3.00 1.25
❑ 62 Lawrence Taylor 5.00 2.00
❑ 63 Mark Bavaro 2.50 1.00
❑ 64 Michael Strahan 3.00 1.25
❑ 65 Tiki Barber 4.00 1.50
❑ 66 Herman Edwards 4.00 1.50
❑ 67 Joe Namath 8.00 3.00
❑ 68 Justin McCareins 2.50 1.00
❑ 69 LaMont Jordan 4.00 1.50
❑ 70 Santana Moss 3.00 1.25
❑ 71 Bo Jackson 8.00 3.00
❑ 72 Fred Biletnikoff 5.00 2.00
❑ 73 George Blanda 5.00 2.00
❑ 74 Jim Plunkett 4.00 1.50
❑ 75 Marcus Allen 5.00 2.00
❑ 76 Barry Switzer 10.00 4.00
❑ 77 Correll Buckhalter 3.00 1.25
❑ 78 Donovan McNabb 5.00 2.00
❑ 79 Antwaan Randle El 4.00 1.50
❑ 80 Bill Cowher 5.00 2.00
❑ 81 Franco Harris 6.00 2.50
❑ 82 Jack Lambert 6.00 2.50
❑ 83 Joe Greene 5.00 2.00
❑ 84 Kendrell Bell 3.00 1.25
❑ 85 L.C. Greenwood 4.00 1.50
❑ 86 Mel Blount 4.00 1.50
❑ 87 Terry Bradshaw 8.00 3.00
❑ 88 LaDainian Tomlinson 5.00 2.00
❑ 89 Andre Carter 2.50 1.00
❑ 90 Bill Walsh 5.00 2.00
❑ 91 Shaun Alexander 4.00 1.50
❑ 92 Steve Largent 5.00 2.00
❑ 93 Matt Hasselbeck 3.00 1.25
❑ 94 Torry Holt 4.00 1.50
❑ 95 Clinton Portis 4.00 1.50
❑ 96 Laveranues Coles 3.00 1.25
❑ 97 Mark Brunell 3.00 1.25
❑ 98 Patrick Ramsey 3.00 1.25
❑ 99 Reuben Droughns 3.00 1.25
❑ 100 Sonny Jurgensen 4.00 1.50
❑ 101 Mauck AU RC/Luke AU RC 25.00 10.00
❑ 102 D.Wll AU RC/Miree AU RC 20.00 7.50
❑ 103 Frncs AU RC/Mmt AU RC 25.00 10.00
❑ 104 Vilma AU RC/Ward AU RC 25.00 10.00
❑ 105 Wlfrk AU RC/Sam AU RC 20.00 7.50
❑ 106 Srgi AU RC/Crthn AU RC 25.00 10.00
❑ 107 Flmng AU RC/Pytn AU RC 30.00 12.50
❑ 108 Bbin AU RC/Symns AU RC 25.00 10.00
❑ 109 J.Hrrs AU RC/Mre AU RC 25.00 10.00
❑ 110 M.Mnn AU RC/Brmlt AU RC 20.00 7.50
❑ 111 S.Jns AU RC/Eche.AU RC 20.00 7.50
❑ 112 A.Hll AU RC/B.Pry AU RC 25.00 10.00
❑ 113 J.Tylr AU RC/Lmzn AU RC 25.00 10.00
❑ 114 Gmble AU RC/Crtr AU RC 25.00 10.00
❑ 115 Hnsn AU RC/Kmzl AU RC 25.00 10.00
❑ 116 T.Hrrs AU RC/Crrll AU RC 25.00 10.00
❑ 117 Smkr AU RC/Hcktt AU RC 25.00 10.00
❑ 118 Wlfrd AU RC/Ctchry AU RC 25.00 10.00
❑ 119 W.Smth AU RC/Ude.AU RC 25.00 10.00
❑ 120 Prkr AU RC/Turner AU RC 25.00 10.00
❑ 121 Thom.AU RC/B.Jhn.AU RC 20.00 7.50
❑ 122 Nava.AU RC/Pick.AU RC 25.00 10.00
❑ 123 Colcl.AU RC/Q.Wil.AU RC 25.00 10.00
❑ 124 S.Taylor RC/Cooley AU RC 30.00 12.50
❑ 125 M.Boul.AU RC/Lehman RC 20.00 7.50
❑ 126 J.P. Losman AU RC 100.00 40.00
❑ 127 Lee Evans AU RC 60.00 30.00
❑ 128 Ben Watson AU RC 40.00 20.00
❑ 129 Cedric Cobbs AU RC 40.00 20.00
❑ 130 Devard Darling AU RC 40.00 20.00
❑ 131 Chris Perry AU RC 60.00 30.00
❑ 132 Kellen Winslow AU RC 80.00 30.00
❑ 133 Luke McCown AU RC 40.00 20.00
❑ 134 B.Roethlisberger AU RC 400.00 250.00
❑ 135 Dunta Robinson AU RC 50.00 25.00
❑ 136 Greg Jones AU RC 50.00 30.00
❑ 137 Reggie Williams AU RC 50.00 25.00
❑ 138 Ben Troupe AU RC 40.00 20.00
❑ 139 Tatum Bell AU RC 120.00 60.00
❑ 140 Darius Watts AU RC 40.00 20.00
❑ 141 Robert Gallery AU RC 50.00 25.00
❑ 142 Philip Rivers AU RC 175.00 100.00
❑ 143 Julius Jones AU RC 250.00 125.00
❑ 144 Eli Manning AU RC 350.00 200.00
❑ 145 Bernard Berrian AU RC 40.00 20.00
❑ 146 Roy Williams AU RC 120.00 60.00
❑ 147 Kevin Jones AU RC 120.00 60.00
❑ 148 Mewelde Moore AU RC 60.00 30.00
❑ 149 DeAngelo Hall AU RC 50.00 25.00
❑ 150 Michael Jenkins AU RC 50.00 25.00
❑ 151 Matt Schaub AU RC 100.00 60.00
❑ 152 Keary Colbert AU RC 60.00 25.00
❑ 153 Devery Henderson AU RC 30.00 15.00
❑ 154 Michael Clayton AU RC 80.00 30.00
❑ 155 Larry Fitzgerald AU RC 120.00 60.00
❑ 156 Rashaun Woods AU RC 40.00 20.00
❑ 157 Derrick Hamilton AU RC 40.00 20.00
❑ 158 Steven Jackson AU RC 150.00 75.00

1995 Pro Line

❑ COMPLETE SET (400) 20.00 8.00
❑ 1 Garrison Hearst .25 .08
❑ 2 Anthony Miller .10 .02
❑ 3 Brett Favre 1.50 .60
❑ 4 Jessie Hester .05 .01
❑ 5 Mike Fox .05 .01
❑ 6 Jeff Blake RC .60 .25
❑ 7 J.J. Birden .05 .01
❑ 8 Greg Jackson .05 .01
❑ 9 Leon Lett .05 .01
❑ 10 Bruce Matthews .05 .01
❑ 11 Andre Reed .10 .02
❑ 12 Joe Montana 1.50 .60
❑ 13 Craig Heyward .10 .02
❑ 14 Henry Ellard UER .10 .02
❑ 15 Chris Spielman .10 .02
❑ 16 Tony Woods .05 .01
❑ 17 Carl Banks .05 .01
❑ 18 Eric Zeier RC .25 .08
❑ 19 Michael Brooks .05 .01
❑ 20 Kevin Ross .05 .01
❑ 21 Qadry Ismail .10 .02
❑ 22 Mel Gray .05 .01
❑ 23 Ty Law RC 1.25 .50
❑ 24 Mark Collins .05 .01
❑ 25 Neil O'Donnell .10 .02
❑ 26 Ellis Johnson RC .05 .01
❑ 27 Rick Mirer .10 .02
❑ 28 Fred Barnett .10 .02
❑ 29 Mike Mamula RC .05 .01
❑ 30 Jim Jeffcoat .05 .01
❑ 31 Reggie Cobb .05 .01
❑ 32 Mark Carrier WR UER .10 .02
❑ 33 Darnay Scott .10 .02
❑ 34 Michael Jackson .10 .02
❑ 35 Terrell Buckley .05 .01
❑ 36 Nolan Harrison .05 .01
❑ 37 Thurman Thomas .25 .08
❑ 38 Anthony Smith .05 .01
❑ 39 Phillippi Sparks .05 .01
❑ 40 Cornelius Bennett .10 .02
❑ 41 Robert Young .05 .01
❑ 42 Pierce Holt .05 .01
❑ 43 Greg Lloyd .10 .02
❑ 44 Chad May RC .05 .01
❑ 45 Darrien Gordon .05 .01
❑ 46 Bryan Cox .05 .01
❑ 47 Junior Seau .25 .08
❑ 48 Al Smith .05 .01
❑ 49 Chris Slade .05 .01
❑ 50 Hardy Nickerson .05 .01
❑ 51 Brad Baxter .05 .01
❑ 52 Darryll Lewis .05 .01
❑ 53 Bryant Young .10 .02
❑ 54 Chris Warren .10 .02
❑ 55 Darion Conner .05 .01
❑ 56 Thomas Everett .05 .01
❑ 57 Charles Haley .10 .02
❑ 58 Chris Mims .05 .01
❑ 59 Sean Jones .05 .01
❑ 60 Tamarick Vanover RC .25 .08
❑ 61 Daryl Johnston .10 .02
❑ 62 Rashaan Salaam RC .10 .02
❑ 63 James Hasty .05 .01
❑ 64 Dante Jones .05 .01
❑ 65 Darren Perry UER .05 .01
❑ 66 Troy Drayton .05 .01
❑ 67 Mark Fields RC .25 .08
❑ 68 Brian Williams LB RC .05 .01
❑ 69 Steve Bono UER .10 .02
❑ 70 Eric Allen .05 .01
❑ 71 Chris Zorich .05 .01
❑ 72 Dave Brown .10 .02
❑ 73 Ken Norton Jr. .10 .02
❑ 74 Wayne Martin .05 .01
❑ 75 Mo Lewis .05 .01
❑ 76 Johnny Mitchell .05 .01
❑ 77 Todd Lyght .05 .01
❑ 78 Erric Pegram .10 .02
❑ 79 Kevin Greene .10 .02
❑ 80 Randal Hill .05 .01
❑ 81 Brett Perriman .10 .02
❑ 82 Mike Sherrard .05 .01
❑ 83 Curtis Conway .25 .08
❑ 84 Mark Tuinei .05 .01
❑ 85 Mark Seay .10 .02
❑ 86 Randy Baldwin .05 .01
❑ 87 Ricky Ervins .05 .01
❑ 88 Chester McGlockton .10 .02
❑ 89 Tyrone Wheatley RC 1.00 .40
❑ 90 Micheal Barrow UER .05 .01
❑ 91 Kenneth Davis .05 .01
❑ 92 Napoleon Kaufman RC 1.00 .40
❑ 93 Webster Slaughter .05 .01

❑ 94 Darren Woodson .10 .02
❑ 95 Pete Stoyanovich .05 .01
❑ 96 Jimmie Jones .05 .01
❑ 97 Craig Erickson .05 .01
❑ 98 Michael Westbrook RC .25 .08
❑ 99 Steve McNair RC 2.50 1.00
❑ 100 Errict Rhett .10 .02
❑ 101 Devin Bush RC .05 .01
❑ 102 Dewayne Washington .10 .02
❑ 103 Bart Oates .05 .01
❑ 104 Aaron Pierce .05 .01
❑ 105 Warren Sapp RC 1.25 .50
❑ 106 Eric Green .05 .01
❑ 107 Glyn Milburn .05 .01
❑ 108 Johnny Johnson .05 .01
❑ 109 Marshall Faulk 1.00 .40
❑ 110 William Thomas .05 .01
❑ 111 George Koonce .05 .01
❑ 112 Dana Stubblefield .10 .02
❑ 113 Steve Tovar .05 .01
❑ 114 Steve Israel .05 .01
❑ 115 Brent Williams .05 .01
❑ 116 Shane Conlan .05 .01
❑ 117 Winston Moss .05 .01
❑ 118 Nate Newton .10 .02
❑ 119 Michael Irvin .25 .08
❑ 120 Jeff Lageman .05 .01
❑ 121 Ki-Jana Carter RC .25 .08
❑ 122 Dan Marino 1.50 .60
❑ 123 Tony Casillas .05 .01
❑ 124 Kevin Carter RC .25 .08
❑ 125 Warren Moon .10 .02
❑ 126 Byron Bam Morris .05 .01
❑ 127 Ben Coates .10 .02
❑ 128 Michael Bankston .05 .01
❑ 129 Anthony Parker .05 .01
❑ 130 LeRoy Butler .05 .01
❑ 131 Tony Bennett .05 .01
❑ 132 Alvin Harper .05 .01
❑ 133 Tim Brown .25 .08
❑ 134 Tom Carter .05 .01
❑ 135 Lorenzo White .05 .01
❑ 136 Shane Dronett .05 .01
❑ 137 John Elliott UER .05 .01
❑ 138 Korey Stringer RC .10 .02
❑ 139 Jerry Rice .75 .30
❑ 140 Sherman Williams RC .05 .01
❑ 141 Kevin Turner .05 .01
❑ 142 Randall Cunningham .25 .08
❑ 143 Vinny Testaverde .10 .02
❑ 144 Tim Bowens .05 .01
❑ 145 Russell Maryland .05 .01
❑ 146 Chris Miller .05 .01
❑ 147 Vince Buck .05 .01
❑ 148 Willie Clay .05 .01
❑ 149 Jeff Graham .05 .01
❑ 150 Shannon Sharpe .10 .02
❑ 151 Carnell Lake .05 .01
❑ 152 Mark Bruener RC .10 .02
❑ 153 James Washington .05 .01
❑ 154 Pepper Johnson .05 .01
❑ 155 Bert Emanuel .25 .08
❑ 156 Mark Stepnoski .05 .01
❑ 157 Robert Jones .05 .01
❑ 158 Cris Dishman .05 .01
❑ 159 Henry Jones .05 .01
❑ 160 Henry Thomas .05 .01
❑ 161 John L. Williams .05 .01
❑ 162 Joe Cain .05 .01
❑ 163 Mike Johnson .05 .01
❑ 164 Merton Hanks .05 .01
❑ 165 Deion Sanders .40 .15
❑ 166 William Floyd .10 .02
❑ 167 Leroy Thompson .05 .01
❑ 168 Ray Childress .05 .01
❑ 169 Donnell Woolford .05 .01
❑ 170 Tony Siragusa .05 .01
❑ 171 Chad Brown .10 .02
❑ 172 Stanley Richard .05 .01
❑ 173 Rob Johnson RC .75 .30
❑ 174 Derrick Brooks RC 1.25 .50
❑ 175 Drew Bledsoe .50 .20
❑ 176 Maurice Hurst .05 .01
❑ 177 Ricky Watters .10 .02
❑ 178 Myron Guyton .05 .01
❑ 179 Ricky Proehl .05 .01
❑ 180 Haywood Jeffires .05 .01
❑ 181 Michael Strahan .25 .08
❑ 182 Charles Wilson .05 .01
❑ 183 Mark Carrier DB .05 .01
❑ 184 James O. Stewart RC 1.00 .40
❑ 185 Andy Harmon .05 .01
❑ 186 Ronnie Lott .10 .02
❑ 187 Clay Matthews .10 .02
❑ 188 John Carney .05 .01
❑ 189 Andre Rison .10 .02
❑ 190 Aeneas Williams .05 .01
❑ 191 Alexander Wright .05 .01
❑ 192 Desmond Howard .10 .02
❑ 193 Herman Moore .25 .08
❑ 194 Alfred Williams .05 .01
❑ 195 Tyrone Poole RC .25 .08
❑ 196 Darren Mickell .05 .01
❑ 197 Steve Young .60 .25
❑ 198 Roman Phifer .05 .01
❑ 199 Darrell Green .05 .01
❑ 200 Terry Wooden .05 .01
❑ 201 Chris Calloway .05 .01
❑ 202 Lewis Tillman .05 .01
❑ 203 Cris Carter .25 .08
❑ 204 Jim Everett .05 .01
❑ 205 Adrian Murrell .10 .02
❑ 206 Barry Sanders 1.25 .50
❑ 207 Mario Bates .10 .02
❑ 208 Shawn Lee .05 .01
❑ 209 Charles Mincy .05 .01
❑ 210 Kerry Collins RC 1.25 .50
❑ 211 Steve Walsh .05 .01
❑ 212 Chris Chandler .10 .02
❑ 213 Bennie Blades .05 .01
❑ 214 Kevin Williams WR .10 .02
❑ 215 Jim Kelly .25 .08
❑ 216 Marion Butts .05 .01
❑ 217 Jay Novacek .10 .02
❑ 218 Shawn Jefferson .05 .01
❑ 219 O.J. McDuffie .25 .08
❑ 220 Ray Seals .05 .01
❑ 221 Arthur Marshall .05 .01
❑ 222 Karl Mecklenburg .05 .01
❑ 223 Terance Mathis .10 .02
❑ 224 David Klingler .10 .02
❑ 225 Rod Woodson .10 .02
❑ 226 Quentin Coryatt .10 .02
❑ 227 Leroy Hoard .05 .01
❑ 228 Brian Blades .10 .02
❑ 229 Rob Moore .10 .02
❑ 230 Boomer Esiason .10 .02
❑ 231 Dave Krieg .05 .01
❑ 232 Sterling Sharpe .10 .02
❑ 233 Marcus Allen .25 .08
❑ 234 John Randle .10 .02
❑ 235 Craig Powell RC .05 .01
❑ 236 John Elway 1.50 .60
❑ 237 Mark Ingram .05 .01
❑ 238 Cortez Kennedy .10 .02
❑ 239 Brent Jones .05 .01
❑ 240 Ken Harvey .05 .01
❑ 241 Keenan McCardell .25 .08
❑ 242 Dan Wilkinson .10 .02
❑ 243 Don Beebe .05 .01
❑ 244 Jack Del Rio .05 .01
❑ 245 Byron Evans .05 .01
❑ 246 Ronald Moore .05 .01
❑ 247 Edgar Bennett .10 .02
❑ 248 William Fuller .05 .01
❑ 249 James Williams LB .05 .01
❑ 250 Neil Smith .10 .02
❑ 251 Sam Mills .10 .02
❑ 252 Willie McGinest .10 .02
❑ 253 Howard Cross .05 .01
❑ 254 Troy Aikman .75 .30
❑ 255 Herschel Walker .10 .02
❑ 256 Dale Carter .10 .02
❑ 257 Sean Dawkins .10 .02
❑ 258 Greg Hill .10 .02
❑ 259 Stan Humphries .10 .02
❑ 260 Erik Kramer .05 .01
❑ 261 Leslie O'Neal .10 .02
❑ 262 Trezelle Jenkins RC .05 .01
❑ 263 Antonio Langham .05 .01
❑ 264 Bryce Paup .10 .02
❑ 265 Jake Reed .10 .02
❑ 266 Richmond Webb .05 .01
❑ 267 Eric Davis .05 .01
❑ 268 Mark McMillian .05 .01
❑ 269 John Walsh RC .05 .01
❑ 270 Irving Fryar .10 .02
❑ 271 Rocket Ismail .10 .02
❑ 272 Phil Hansen .05 .01
❑ 273 J.J. Stokes RC .25 .08
❑ 274 Craig Newsome RC .05 .01
❑ 275 Leonard Russell .05 .01
❑ 276 Derrick Deese .05 .01
❑ 277 Broderick Thomas .05 .01
❑ 278 Bobby Houston .05 .01
❑ 279 Lamar Lathon .05 .01
❑ 280 Eugene Robinson .05 .01
❑ 281 Dan Saleaumua .05 .01
❑ 282 Kyle Brady RC .25 .08
❑ 283 John Taylor .05 .01
❑ 284 Tony Boselli RC .25 .08
❑ 285 Seth Joyner .05 .01
❑ 286 Steve Beuerlein .10 .02
❑ 287 Sam Adams .05 .01
❑ 288 Frank Reich .05 .01
❑ 289 Patrick Hunter .05 .01
❑ 290 Sean Gilbert .10 .02
❑ 291 Dermontti Dawson UER .10 .02
❑ 292 Shaun Gayle .05 .01
❑ 293 Vincent Brown .05 .01
❑ 294 Terry Kirby .10 .02
❑ 295 Courtney Hawkins .05 .01
❑ 296 Carl Pickens .10 .02
❑ 297 Luther Elliss RC .05 .01
❑ 298 Steve Atwater .05 .01
❑ 299 James Francis .05 .01
❑ 300 Rob Burnett .05 .01
❑ 301 Keith Hamilton .05 .01
❑ 302 Rob Fredrickson .05 .01
❑ 303 Jerome Bettis .25 .08
❑ 304 Emmitt Smith 1.25 .50
❑ 305 Clyde Simmons .05 .01
❑ 306 Reggie White .25 .08
❑ 307 Rodney Hampton .10 .02
❑ 308 Steve Emtman .05 .01
❑ 309 Hugh Douglas RC .25 .08
❑ 310 Bernie Parmalee .10 .02
❑ 311 Trent Dilfer .25 .08
❑ 312 Flipper Anderson .05 .01
❑ 313 Heath Shuler .10 .02
❑ 314 Rod Smith DB .10 .02
❑ 315 Ray Zellars RC .10 .02
❑ 316 Robert Brooks .25 .08
❑ 317 Lee Woodall .05 .01
❑ 318 Robert Porcher .05 .01
❑ 319 Todd Collins RC .10 .02
❑ 320 Willie Roaf .05 .01
❑ 321 Erik Williams .05 .01
❑ 322 Steve Wisniewski .05 .01
❑ 323 Derrick Alexander DE RC .05 .01
❑ 324 Frank Warren .05 .01
❑ 325 Kelvin Pritchett .05 .01
❑ 326 Dennis Gibson .05 .01
❑ 327 Jason Belser .05 .01

❑ 328 Vincent Brisby	.05	.01
❑ 329 Calvin Williams	.10	.02
❑ 330 Derek Brown RBK	.05	.01
❑ 331 Blake Brockermeyer	.05	.01
❑ 332 Jeff Herrod	.05	.01
❑ 333 Darryl Williams	.05	.01
❑ 334 Aaron Glenn	.05	.01
❑ 335 Eric Metcalf	.10	.02
❑ 336 Billy Milner RC	.05	.01
❑ 337 Terry McDaniel	.05	.01
❑ 338 Trace Armstrong	.05	.01
❑ 339 Yancey Thigpen RC	.10	.02
❑ 340 Jackie Harris	.05	.01
❑ 341 Jeff George	.10	.02
❑ 342 Darryl Talley	.05	.01
❑ 343 Marcus Robertson	.05	.01
❑ 344 Robert Massey	.05	.01
❑ 345 Jessie Tuggle	.05	.01
❑ 346 Scott Mitchell	.10	.02
❑ 347 Harvey Williams	.05	.01
❑ 348 Jack Jackson RC	.05	.01
❑ 349 Brian Mitchell	.05	.01
❑ 350 Lawrence Dawsey	.05	.01
❑ 351 Erik Howard	.05	.01
❑ 352 Quinn Early	.10	.02
❑ 353 Terry Allen	.10	.02
❑ 354 Simon Fletcher	.05	.01
❑ 355 Eric Turner	.05	.01
❑ 356 Natrone Means	.10	.02
❑ 357 Frank Sanders RC	.25	.08
❑ 358 Michael Timpson	.05	.01
❑ 359 Michael Haynes	.10	.02
❑ 360 Ruben Brown RC	.25	.08
❑ 361 Troy Vincent UER	.05	.01
❑ 362 Floyd Turner	.05	.01
❑ 363 Larry Centers	.10	.02
❑ 364 Eric Swann	.10	.02
❑ 365 Albert Lewis	.05	.01
❑ 366 Barry Foster	.10	.02
❑ 367 Michael Dean Perry	.05	.01
❑ 368 Jumpy Geathers UER	.05	.01
❑ 369 Kordell Stewart RC	1.25	.50
❑ 370 Chuck Smith	.05	.01
❑ 371 Lake Dawson	.10	.02
❑ 372 Terry Hoage	.05	.01
❑ 373 Jeff Cross	.05	.01
❑ 374 Tony McGee	.05	.01
❑ 375 Eric Curry	.05	.01
❑ 376 Harold Green	.05	.01
❑ 377 Eric Hill	.05	.01
❑ 378 Ray Buchanan	.05	.01
❑ 379 Willie Davis	.10	.02
❑ 380 Chris T.Jones RC	.05	.01
❑ 381 Martin Mayhew	.05	.01
❑ 382 Anthony Pleasant	.05	.01
❑ 383 Joey Galloway RC	1.25	.50
❑ 384 Anthony Morgan	.05	.01
❑ 385 Harlon Barnett	.05	.01
❑ 386 Bruce Smith	.25	.08
❑ 387 Jeff Hostetler	.10	.02
❑ 388 Randall McDaniel	.05	.01
❑ 389 Dave Meggett	.05	.01
❑ 390 Bill Romanowski	.05	.01
❑ 391 Gary Brown	.05	.01
❑ 392 Charles Johnson	.10	.02
❑ 393 Chris Doleman	.05	.01
❑ 394 Tony Martin	.10	.02
❑ 395 Raymont Harris	.05	.01
❑ 396 John Copeland	.05	.01
❑ 397 Emmitt Smith CL	.25	.08
❑ 398 Steve Young CL	.10	.02
❑ 399 Marshall Faulk CL	.50	.20
❑ 400 Ki-Jana Carter CL	.10	.02
❑ HP1 Marshall Faulk Sample	1.50	.60
❑ P1 Marshall Faulk Promo	1.50	.60
❑ P2 Jerome Bettis Natl. Promo	1.50	.60

1995 Pro Line Series 2

❑ COMPLETE SET (75)	15.00	6.00
❑ 1 Jim Kelly	.25	.08
❑ 2 Steve Walsh	.05	.01
❑ 3 Jeff Blake	.25	.08
❑ 4 Vinny Testaverde	.10	.02
❑ 5 Jeff Hostetler	.10	.02
❑ 6 Dan Marino	1.50	.60
❑ 7 Cris Carter	.25	.08
❑ 8 Drew Bledsoe	.50	.20
❑ 9 Jim Everett	.05	.01
❑ 10 Neil O'Donnell	.10	.02
❑ 11 Rodney Hampton	.10	.02
❑ 12 Troy Aikman	.75	.30
❑ 13 John Elway	1.50	.60
❑ 14 Barry Sanders	1.25	.50
❑ 15 Reggie White	.25	.08
❑ 16 Marshall Faulk	1.00	.40
❑ 17 Marcus Allen	.25	.08
❑ 18 James O. Stewart	.25	.08
❑ 19 Randall Cunningham	.25	.08
❑ 20 Natrone Means	.10	.02
❑ 21 Rick Mirer	.10	.02
❑ 22 Jerry Rice	.75	.30
❑ 23 Errict Rhett	.10	.02
❑ 24 Heath Shuler	.10	.02
❑ 25 Jerome Bettis	.25	.08
❑ 26 Garrison Hearst	.25	.08
❑ 27 Jeff George	.10	.02
❑ 28 Andre Reed	.10	.02
❑ 29 Warren Moon	.10	.02
❑ 30 Ben Coates	.10	.02
❑ 31 Mario Bates	.10	.02
❑ 32 Byron Bam Morris	.05	.01
❑ 33 Dave Brown	.10	.02
❑ 34 Emmitt Smith	1.25	.50
❑ 35 Anthony Miller	.10	.02
❑ 36 Herman Moore	.25	.08
❑ 37 Brett Favre	1.50	.60
❑ 38 Steve Bono	.10	.02
❑ 39 Stan Humphries	.10	.02
❑ 40 Steve Young	.60	.25
❑ 41 Trent Dilfer	.25	.08
❑ 42 Chris Miller	.05	.01
❑ 43 Herschel Walker	.10	.02
❑ 44 Michael Irvin	.25	.08
❑ 45 Junior Seau	.25	.08
❑ 46 Deion Sanders	.40	.15
❑ 47 William Floyd	.10	.02
❑ 48 Ki-Jana Carter	.10	.02
❑ 49 Kerry Collins	.40	.15
❑ 50 Steve McNair	.75	.30
❑ 51 Tony Boselli	.10	.02
❑ 52 Kyle Brady	.25	.08
❑ 53 Mike Mamula	.05	.01
❑ 54 Warren Sapp	.25	.08
❑ 55 J.J. Stokes	.10	.02
❑ 56 Joey Galloway	.40	.15
❑ 57 Hugh Douglas	.10	.02
❑ 58 Michael Westbrook	.25	.08
❑ 59 Napoleon Kaufman	.25	.08
❑ 60 Rashaan Salaam	.10	.02
❑ 61 Tyrone Wheatley	.25	.08
❑ 62 Terrell Fletcher RC	.05	.01
❑ 63 Eric Metcalf	.10	.02
❑ 64 Kevin Carter	.25	.08
❑ 65 Andre Rison	.10	.02
❑ 66 Eric Green	.05	.01
❑ 67 Dave Meggett	.05	.01
❑ 68 Ricky Watters	.10	.02
❑ 69 Steve Beuerlein	.10	.02
❑ 70 Craig Erickson	.05	.01
❑ 71 Michael Dean Perry	.05	.01
❑ 72 Alvin Harper	.05	.01
❑ 73 Rob Moore	.10	.02
❑ 74 Frank Reich	.05	.01
❑ 75 Checklist	.05	.01

1996 Pro Line

❑ COMPLETE SET (350)	25.00	10.00
❑ 1 Troy Aikman	1.00	.40
❑ 2 Steve Young	.75	.30
❑ 3 John Elway	2.00	.75
❑ 4 Jim Kelly	.40	.15
❑ 5 Dan Marino	2.00	.75
❑ 6 Brett Favre	2.00	.75
❑ 7 Kerry Collins	.40	.15
❑ 8 Jeff Blake	.40	.15
❑ 9 Stan Humphries	.20	.07
❑ 10 Steve Bono	.10	.02
❑ 11 Jeff George	.20	.07
❑ 12 Mark Brunell	.60	.25
❑ 13 Scott Mitchell	.20	.07
❑ 14 Steve McNair	.75	.30
❑ 15 Jeff Hostetler	.10	.02
❑ 16 Jim Everett	.10	.02
❑ 17 Rick Mirer	.20	.07
❑ 18 Boomer Esiason	.20	.07
❑ 19 Neil O'Donnell	.20	.07
❑ 20 Dave Brown	.10	.02
❑ 21 Erik Kramer	.10	.02
❑ 22 Trent Dilfer	.40	.15
❑ 23 Jim Harbaugh	.20	.07
❑ 24 Vinny Testaverde	.20	.07
❑ 25 Thurman Thomas	.40	.15
❑ 26 Rodney Peete	.10	.02
❑ 27 Gus Frerotte	.20	.07
❑ 28 Warren Moon	.20	.07
❑ 29 Eric Zeier	.10	.02
❑ 30 Randall Cunningham	.40	.15
❑ 31 Heath Shuler	.20	.07
❑ 32 John Friesz	.10	.02
❑ 33 Tommy Maddox	.40	.15
❑ 34 Glenn Foley	.20	.07
❑ 35 Drew Bledsoe	.60	.25
❑ 36 Kordell Stewart	.40	.15
❑ 37 Natrone Means	.20	.07
❑ 38 Errict Rhett	.20	.07
❑ 39 Rashaan Salaam	.20	.07
❑ 40 Emmitt Smith	1.50	.60
❑ 41 Larry Centers	.20	.07
❑ 42 Terrell Davis	.75	.30
❑ 43 Marshall Faulk	.50	.20

❑ 44 Rodney Hampton .20 .07
❑ 45 Byron Bam Morris .10 .02
❑ 46 Chris Warren .20 .07
❑ 47 Curtis Martin .75 .30
❑ 48 Ricky Watters .20 .07
❑ 49 Marcus Allen .40 .15
❑ 50 Barry Sanders 1.50 .60
❑ 51 Edgar Bennett .20 .07
❑ 52 Adrian Murrell .20 .07
❑ 53 James O. Stewart .20 .07
❑ 54 Leroy Hoard .10 .02
❑ 55 Jerome Bettis .40 .15
❑ 56 Craig Heyward .10 .02
❑ 57 Harvey Williams .10 .02
❑ 58 Bernie Parmalee .10 .02
❑ 59 Garrison Hearst .20 .07
❑ 60 Terry Allen .20 .07
❑ 61 Charlie Garner .20 .07
❑ 62 Dorsey Levens .40 .15
❑ 63 Derek Loville .10 .02
❑ 64 Greg Hill .20 .07
❑ 65 Derrick Moore .10 .02
❑ 66 Rodney Thomas .10 .02
❑ 67 Daryl Johnston .20 .07
❑ 68 Mario Bates .20 .07
❑ 69 Aaron Hayden RC .10 .02
❑ 70 Napoleon Kaufman .40 .15
❑ 71 Terry Kirby .20 .07
❑ 72 Glyn Milburn .10 .02
❑ 73 Robert Smith .20 .07
❑ 74 Ki-Jana Carter .20 .07
❑ 75 Tyrone Wheatley .20 .07
❑ 76 Erric Pegram .10 .02
❑ 77 Brian Mitchell .10 .02
❑ 78 Vaughn Dunbar .10 .02
❑ 79 Dave Meggett .10 .02
❑ 80 Scottie Graham .10 .02
❑ 81 Darick Holmes .10 .02
❑ 82 Marion Butts .10 .02
❑ 83 Harold Green .10 .02
❑ 84 Zack Crockett .10 .02
❑ 85 Amp Lee .10 .02
❑ 86 Lamont Warren .10 .02
❑ 87 Mark Chmura .20 .07
❑ 88 Irving Fryar .20 .07
❑ 89 Tim Brown .40 .15
❑ 90 Michael Irvin .40 .15
❑ 91 Tony Martin .20 .07
❑ 92 Alvin Harper .10 .02
❑ 93 Darnay Scott .20 .07
❑ 94 Eric Metcalf .10 .02
❑ 95 Michael Timpson .10 .02
❑ 96 Sean Dawkins .10 .02
❑ 97 Qadry Ismail .20 .07
❑ 98 Yancey Thigpen .20 .07
❑ 99 Joey Galloway .40 .15
❑ 100 Herman Moore .20 .07
❑ 101 J.J. Stokes .40 .15
❑ 102 Wayne Chrebet .60 .25
❑ 103 Ernest Givins .10 .02
❑ 104 Michael Jackson .20 .07
❑ 105 Henry Ellard .10 .02
❑ 106 Thomas Lewis .10 .02
❑ 107 Anthony Miller .20 .07
❑ 108 Terance Mathis .10 .02
❑ 109 Horace Copeland .10 .02
❑ 110 Rocket Ismail .10 .02
❑ 111 Quinn Early .10 .02
❑ 112 Haywood Jeffires .10 .02
❑ 113 Mark Carrier WR .10 .02
❑ 114 Brent Jones .10 .02
❑ 115 Ben Coates .20 .07
❑ 116 Ken Dilger .20 .07
❑ 117 Irv Smith .10 .02
❑ 118 Jay Novacek .10 .02
❑ 119 Tony McGee .10 .02
❑ 120 Troy Drayton .10 .02
❑ 121 Johnny Mitchell .10 .02
❑ 122 Rob Moore .20 .07
❑ 123 Kevin Williams WR .10 .02
❑ 124 O.J. McDuffie .20 .07
❑ 125 Carl Pickens .20 .07
❑ 126 Curtis Conway .40 .15
❑ 127 Ed McCaffrey .20 .07
❑ 128 Arthur Marshall .10 .02
❑ 129 Ernie Mills .10 .02
❑ 130 Cris Carter .40 .15
❑ 131 Isaac Bruce .40 .15
❑ 132 Brian Blades .10 .02
❑ 133 Michael Westbrook .40 .15
❑ 134 Andre Reed .20 .07
❑ 135 Andre Rison .20 .07
❑ 136 Brett Perriman .10 .02
❑ 137 Willie Jackson .20 .07
❑ 138 Ryan Yarborough .10 .02
❑ 139 Chris T. Jones .20 .07
❑ 140 Jerry Rice 1.00 .40
❑ 141 Lake Dawson .10 .02
❑ 142 Robert Brooks .40 .15
❑ 143 Vincent Brisby .10 .02
❑ 144 Desmond Howard .20 .07
❑ 145 Johnnie Morton .20 .07
❑ 146 Steve Tasker .10 .02
❑ 147 Ty Detmer .20 .07
❑ 148 Todd Kinchen .10 .02
❑ 149 Mike Sherrard .10 .02
❑ 150 Eric Green .10 .02
❑ 151 Mark Bruener .10 .02
❑ 152 Kyle Brady .10 .02
❑ 153 Frank Sanders .20 .07
❑ 154 Willie Green .10 .02
❑ 155 Jeff Graham .10 .02
❑ 156 Bert Emanuel .20 .07
❑ 157 Courtney Hawkins .10 .02
❑ 158 Mark Seay .10 .02
❑ 159 Chris Calloway .10 .02
❑ 160 John Taylor .10 .02
❑ 161 Fred Barnett .10 .02
❑ 162 Tamarick Vanover .20 .07
❑ 163 Keenan McCardell .40 .15
❑ 164 Bill Brooks .10 .02
❑ 165 Alexander Wright .10 .02
❑ 166 Jake Reed .20 .07
❑ 167 Floyd Turner .10 .02
❑ 168 Mike Pritchard .10 .02
❑ 169 Lawrence Dawsey .10 .02
❑ 170 Shawn Jefferson .10 .02
❑ 171 Michael Haynes .10 .02
❑ 172 Shannon Sharpe .20 .07
❑ 173 Jackie Harris .10 .02
❑ 174 Daryl Hobbs RC .10 .02
❑ 175 Chris Sanders .20 .07
❑ 176 Willie Davis .10 .02
❑ 177 Marco Coleman .10 .02
❑ 178 Pat Swilling .10 .02
❑ 179 Alonzo Spellman .10 .02
❑ 180 Simon Fletcher .10 .02
❑ 181 Sean Gilbert .10 .02
❑ 182 Tracy Scroggins .10 .02
❑ 183 Hugh Douglas .20 .07
❑ 184 Eric Swann .10 .02
❑ 185 Russell Maryland .10 .02
❑ 186 Warren Sapp .10 .02
❑ 187 Jim Flanigan .10 .02
❑ 188 Cortez Kennedy .10 .02
❑ 189 Andy Harmon .10 .02
❑ 190 Dan Saleaumua .10 .02
❑ 191 Kelvin Pritchett .10 .02
❑ 192 John Randle .20 .07
❑ 193 Dan Wilkinson .10 .02
❑ 194 Chester McGlockton .10 .02
❑ 195 Leon Lett .10 .02
❑ 196 Neil Smith .20 .07
❑ 197 Mike Mamula .10 .02
❑ 198 Mike Jones .10 .02
❑ 199 Reggie White .40 .15
❑ 200 Anthony Pleasant .10 .02
❑ 201 Phil Hansen .10 .02
❑ 202 Ray Seals .10 .02
❑ 203 Tony Bennett .10 .02
❑ 204 Leslie O'Neal .10 .02
❑ 205 Jeff Cross .10 .02
❑ 206 Anthony Cook .10 .02
❑ 207 Clyde Simmons .10 .02
❑ 208 Renaldo Turnbull .10 .02
❑ 209 Charles Haley .20 .07
❑ 210 John Copeland .10 .02
❑ 211 John Thierry .10 .02
❑ 212 Michael Strahan .20 .07
❑ 213 Jeff Lageman .10 .02
❑ 214 William Fuller .10 .02
❑ 215 Rickey Jackson .10 .02
❑ 216 Wayne Martin .10 .02
❑ 217 Steve Emtman .10 .02
❑ 218 Shawn Lee .10 .02
❑ 219 Chris Zorich .10 .02
❑ 220 Henry Thomas .10 .02
❑ 221 Dana Stubblefield .20 .07
❑ 222 D'Marco Farr .10 .02
❑ 223 Pierce Holt .10 .02
❑ 224 Sean Jones .10 .02
❑ 225 Robert Porcher .10 .02
❑ 226 Kevin Carter .10 .02
❑ 227 Chris Doleman .10 .02
❑ 228 Tony Tolbert .10 .02
❑ 229 Bruce Smith .20 .07
❑ 230 Marvin Washington .10 .02
❑ 231 Blaine Bishop .10 .02
❑ 232 Bryant Young .20 .07
❑ 233 Rob Burnett .10 .02
❑ 234 Lawrence Phillips RC .40 .15
❑ 235 Trev Alberts .10 .02
❑ 236 Eric Curry .10 .02
❑ 237 Anthony Smith .10 .02
❑ 238 Sam Mills .10 .02
❑ 239 Seth Joyner .10 .02
❑ 240 Quentin Coryatt .10 .02
❑ 241 Levon Kirkland .10 .02
❑ 242 Cornelius Bennett .10 .02
❑ 243 Chris Spielman .10 .02
❑ 244 Mo Lewis .10 .02
❑ 245 Lee Woodall .10 .02
❑ 246 Derrick Thomas .40 .15
❑ 247 Willie McGinest .10 .02
❑ 248 Terry Wooden .10 .02
❑ 249 Greg Lloyd .20 .07
❑ 250 Jack Del Rio .10 .02
❑ 251 Hardy Nickerson .10 .02
❑ 252 Micheal Barrow .10 .02
❑ 253 Lamar Lathon .10 .02
❑ 254 Bryan Cox .10 .02
❑ 255 Randy Kirk .10 .02
❑ 256 Jessie Tuggle .10 .02
❑ 257 Roman Phifer .10 .02
❑ 258 Ken Harvey .10 .02
❑ 259 Junior Seau .40 .15
❑ 260 Pepper Johnson .10 .02
❑ 261 Chris Slade .10 .02
❑ 262 Gary Plummer .10 .02
❑ 263 Wayne Simmons .10 .02
❑ 264 Bryce Paup .10 .02
❑ 265 William Thomas .10 .02
❑ 266 Kevin Greene .20 .07
❑ 267 Bobby Engram RC .40 .15
❑ 268 Ken Norton .10 .02
❑ 269 Eric Hill .10 .02
❑ 270 Darion Conner .10 .02
❑ 271 Tyrone Poole .10 .02
❑ 272 Cris Dishman .10 .02
❑ 273 Marcus Jones RC .10 .02
❑ 274 Rod Woodson .20 .07
❑ 275 Mark McMillian .10 .02
❑ 276 Dale Carter .10 .02
❑ 277 Darrell Green .10 .02

❑ 278	Donnell Woolford	.10	.02
❑ 279	Troy Vincent	.10	.02
❑ 280	Larry Brown	.10	.02
❑ 281	Aeneas Williams	.10	.02
❑ 282	Eric Allen	.10	.02
❑ 283	Ray Buchanan	.10	.02
❑ 284	Ty Law	.40	.15
❑ 285	Eric Davis	.10	.02
❑ 286	Todd Lyght	.10	.02
❑ 287	Terry McDaniel	.10	.02
❑ 288	Darryll Lewis	.10	.02
❑ 289	Deion Sanders	.60	.25
❑ 290	Phillippi Sparks	.10	.02
❑ 291	Bobby Taylor	.10	.02
❑ 292	Mark Collins	.10	.02
❑ 293	Steve Atwater	.10	.02
❑ 294	Stanley Richard	.20	.07
❑ 295	Stevon Moore	.10	.02
❑ 296	Bennie Blades	.10	.02
❑ 297	Tim McDonald	.10	.02
❑ 298	Shaun Gayle	.10	.02
❑ 299	Darren Woodson	.20	.07
❑ 300	Mark Carrier DB	.10	.02
❑ 301	Carnell Lake	.10	.02
❑ 302	James Washington	.10	.02
❑ 303	LeRoy Butler	.10	.02
❑ 304	Henry Jones	.10	.02
❑ 305	Darryl Williams	.10	.02
❑ 306	Darren Perry	.10	.02
❑ 307	Merton Hanks	.10	.02
❑ 308	Orlando Thomas	.10	.02
❑ 309	Eric Turner	.10	.02
❑ 310	Nate Newton	.10	.02
❑ 311	Steve Wisniewski	.10	.02
❑ 312	Derrick Deese	.10	.02
❑ 313	Larry Allen	.10	.02
❑ 314	Aaron Taylor	.10	.02
❑ 315	Blake Brockermeyer	.10	.02
❑ 316	William Roaf	.10	.02
❑ 317	Jumbo Elliott	.10	.02
❑ 318	Keyshawn Johnson RC	1.00	.40
❑ 319	Karim Abdul-Jabbar RC	.40	.15
❑ 320	Kevin Hardy RC	.40	.15
❑ 321	Duane Clemons RC	.10	.02
❑ 322	Jevon Langford RC	.10	.02
❑ 323	Mike Alstott RC	1.00	.40
❑ 324	Scott Greene RC	.10	.02
❑ 325	Derrick Mayes RC	.40	.15
❑ 326	Chris Doering RC	.10	.02
❑ 327	Amani Toomer RC	1.00	.40
❑ 328	Eric Moulds RC	1.25	.50
❑ 329	Alex Molden RC	.10	.02
❑ 330	Lawyer Milloy RC	.50	.20
❑ 331	Daryl Gardener RC	.10	.02
❑ 332	Randall Godfrey RC	.10	.02
❑ 333	Willie Anderson RC	.10	.02
❑ 334	Tony Banks RC	.40	.15
❑ 335	Jeff Lewis RC	.20	.07
❑ 336	Roman Oben RC	.10	.02
❑ 337	Andre Johnson RC	.10	.02
❑ 338	Brian Roche RC	.10	.02
❑ 339	Johnny McWilliams RC	.20	.07
❑ 340	Alex Van Dyke RC	.20	.07
❑ 341	Ray Mickens RC	.10	.02
❑ 342	Marvin Harrison RC	2.50	1.00
❑ 343	Terry Glenn RC	1.00	.40
❑ 344	Tim Biakabutuka RC	.40	.15
❑ 345	Simeon Rice RC	1.00	.40
❑ 346	Cedric Jones RC	.10	.02
❑ 347	Eddie George RC	1.25	.50
❑ 348	Drew Bledsoe CL	.40	.15
❑ 349	Emmitt Smith CL	.50	.20
❑ 350	Keyshawn Johnson CL	.40	.15

1997 Pro Line

❑	COMPLETE SET (300)	25.00	10.00
❑ 1	Larry Centers	.30	.10
❑ 2	Kent Graham	.20	.07

❑ 3	LeShon Johnson	.20	.07
❑ 4	Leeland McElroy	.20	.07
❑ 5	Rob Moore	.30	.10
❑ 6	Simeon Rice	.30	.10
❑ 7	Frank Sanders	.30	.10
❑ 8	Eric Swann	.20	.07
❑ 9	Aeneas Williams	.20	.07
❑ 10	Jamal Anderson	.50	.20
❑ 11	Cornelius Bennett	.20	.07
❑ 12	Ray Buchanan	.20	.07
❑ 13	Bert Emanuel	.30	.10
❑ 14	Terance Mathis	.30	.10
❑ 15	Eric Metcalf	.30	.10
❑ 16	Jessie Tuggle	.20	.07
❑ 17	Derrick Alexander WR	.30	.10
❑ 18	Earnest Byner	.20	.07
❑ 19	Michael Jackson	.30	.10
❑ 20	Antonio Langham	.20	.07
❑ 21	Ray Lewis	.75	.30
❑ 22	Byron Bam Morris	.20	.07
❑ 23	Jonathan Ogden	.20	.07
❑ 24	Vinny Testaverde	.30	.10
❑ 25	Eric Moulds	.50	.20
❑ 26	Todd Collins	.20	.07
❑ 27	Quinn Early	.20	.07
❑ 28	Phil Hansen	.20	.07
❑ 29	Darick Holmes	.20	.07
❑ 30	Bryce Paup	.20	.07
❑ 31	Andre Reed	.30	.10
❑ 32	Bruce Smith	.30	.10
❑ 33	Chris Spielman	.20	.07
❑ 34	Matt Stevens	.20	.07
❑ 35	Steve Tasker	.20	.07
❑ 36	Thurman Thomas	.50	.20
❑ 37	Mark Carrier WR	.20	.07
❑ 38	Kerry Collins	.50	.20
❑ 39	Tim Biakabutuka	.30	.10
❑ 40	Eric Davis	.20	.07
❑ 41	Kevin Greene	.30	.10
❑ 42	Anthony Johnson	.20	.07
❑ 43	Lamar Lathon	.20	.07
❑ 44	Sam Mills	.20	.07
❑ 45	Wesley Walls	.30	.10
❑ 46	Muhsin Muhammad	.30	.10
❑ 47	Mark Carrier DB	.20	.07
❑ 48	Curtis Conway	.30	.10
❑ 49	Bryan Cox	.20	.07
❑ 50	Bobby Engram	.30	.10
❑ 51	Raymont Harris	.20	.07
❑ 52	Walt Harris	.20	.07
❑ 53	Rick Mirer	.20	.07
❑ 54	Rashaan Salaam	.30	.10
❑ 55	Alonzo Spellman	.20	.07
❑ 56	Ashley Ambrose	.20	.07
❑ 57	Jeff Blake	.30	.10
❑ 58	Ki-Jana Carter	.20	.07
❑ 59	John Copeland	.20	.07
❑ 60	James Francis	.20	.07
❑ 61	Tony McGee	.20	.07
❑ 62	Carl Pickens	.30	.10
❑ 63	Darnay Scott	.30	.10
❑ 64	Steve Tovar	.20	.07

❑ 65	Dan Wilkinson	.20	.07
❑ 66	Troy Aikman	1.00	.40
❑ 67	Eric Bjornson	.20	.07
❑ 68	Michael Irvin	.50	.20
❑ 69	Daryl Johnston	.30	.10
❑ 70	Nate Newton	.20	.07
❑ 71	Deion Sanders	.50	.20
❑ 72	Emmitt Smith	1.50	.60
❑ 73	Kevin Smith	.20	.07
❑ 74	Kevin Williams	.20	.07
❑ 75	Darren Woodson	.20	.07
❑ 76	Mark Tuinei	.20	.07
❑ 77	Steve Atwater	.20	.07
❑ 78	Terrell Davis	.60	.25
❑ 79	John Elway	2.00	.75
❑ 80	Ed McCaffrey	.30	.10
❑ 81	Anthony Miller	.20	.07
❑ 82	John Mobley	.20	.07
❑ 83	Michael Dean Perry	.20	.07
❑ 84	Shannon Sharpe	.30	.10
❑ 85	Alfred Williams	.20	.07
❑ 86	Reggie Brown LB	.30	.10
❑ 87	Luther Elliss	.20	.07
❑ 88	Scott Mitchell	.30	.10
❑ 89	Herman Moore	.30	.10
❑ 90	Johnnie Morton	.30	.10
❑ 91	Brett Perriman	.20	.07
❑ 92	Robert Porcher	.20	.07
❑ 93	Barry Sanders	1.50	.60
❑ 94	Henry Thomas	.20	.07
❑ 95	Edgar Bennett	.30	.10
❑ 96	Robert Brooks	.30	.10
❑ 97	Gilbert Brown	.30	.10
❑ 98	LeRoy Butler	.20	.07
❑ 99	Mark Chmura	.30	.10
❑ 100	Brett Favre	2.00	.75
❑ 101	Santana Dotson	.20	.07
❑ 102	Antonio Freeman	.50	.20
❑ 103	Dorsey Levens	.50	.20
❑ 104	Wayne Simmons	.20	.07
❑ 105	Reggie White	.50	.20
❑ 106	Willie Davis	.20	.07
❑ 107	Eddie George	.50	.20
❑ 108	Darryll Lewis	.20	.07
❑ 109	Steve McNair	.60	.25
❑ 110	Marcus Robertson	.20	.07
❑ 111	Chris Sanders	.20	.07
❑ 112	Al Smith	.20	.07
❑ 113	Tony Bennett	.20	.07
❑ 114	Quentin Coryatt	.20	.07
❑ 115	Ken Dilger	.20	.07
❑ 116	Sean Dawkins	.20	.07
❑ 117	Marshall Faulk	.60	.25
❑ 118	Jim Harbaugh	.30	.10
❑ 119	Marvin Harrison	.50	.20
❑ 120	Jeff Herrod	.20	.07
❑ 121	Tony Boselli	.20	.07
❑ 122	Tony Brackens	.20	.07
❑ 123	Mark Brunell	.60	.25
❑ 124	Kevin Hardy	.20	.07
❑ 125	Jeff Lageman	.20	.07
❑ 126	Keenan McCardell	.30	.10
❑ 127	Natrone Means	.30	.10
❑ 128	Eddie Robinson	.20	.07
❑ 129	Jimmy Smith	.30	.10
❑ 130	James O.Stewart	.30	.10
❑ 131	Marcus Allen	.50	.20
❑ 132	Dale Carter	.20	.07
❑ 133	Mark Collins	.20	.07
❑ 134	Lake Dawson	.20	.07
❑ 135	Greg Hill	.20	.07
❑ 136	Sean LaChapelle	.20	.07
❑ 137	Chris Penn	.20	.07
❑ 138	Derrick Thomas	.50	.20
❑ 139	Tamarick Vanover	.30	.10
❑ 140	Elvis Grbac	.30	.10
❑ 141	Karim Abdul-Jabbar	.50	.20
❑ 142	Fred Barnett	.20	.07

❑ 143 Terrell Buckley .20 .07
❑ 144 Daryl Gardener .20 .07
❑ 145 Randal Hill .20 .07
❑ 146 Dan Marino 2.00 .75
❑ 147 O.J. McDuffie .30 .10
❑ 148 Jerris McPhail .20 .07
❑ 149 Zach Thomas .50 .20
❑ 150 Cris Carter .50 .20
❑ 151 Dixon Edwards .20 .07
❑ 152 Leroy Hoard .20 .07
❑ 153 Qadry Ismail .30 .10
❑ 154 Brad Johnson .50 .20
❑ 155 John Randle .30 .10
❑ 156 Jake Reed .30 .10
❑ 157 Robert Smith .30 .10
❑ 158 Orlando Thomas .20 .07
❑ 159 Dewayne Washington .20 .07
❑ 160 Drew Bledsoe .60 .25
❑ 161 Tedy Bruschi 1.00 .40
❑ 162 Willie Clay .20 .07
❑ 163 Ben Coates .30 .10
❑ 164 Terry Glenn .50 .20
❑ 165 Shawn Jefferson .20 .07
❑ 166 Ty Law .30 .10
❑ 167 Curtis Martin .60 .25
❑ 168 Willie McGinest .20 .07
❑ 169 Chris Slade .20 .07
❑ 170 Eric Allen .20 .07
❑ 171 Mario Bates .20 .07
❑ 172 Heath Shuler .20 .07
❑ 173 Michael Haynes .20 .07
❑ 174 Wayne Martin .20 .07
❑ 175 Torrance Small .20 .07
❑ 176 Dave Brown .20 .07
❑ 177 Chris Calloway .20 .07
❑ 178 Rodney Hampton .30 .10
❑ 179 Danny Kanell .30 .10
❑ 180 Thomas Lewis .20 .07
❑ 181 Jason Sehorn .30 .10
❑ 182 Amani Toomer .30 .10
❑ 183 Charles Way .30 .10
❑ 184 Tyrone Wheatley .30 .10
❑ 185 Wayne Chrebet .50 .20
❑ 186 Hugh Douglas .20 .07
❑ 187 Aaron Glenn .20 .07
❑ 188 Jeff Graham .20 .07
❑ 189 Keyshawn Johnson .50 .20
❑ 190 Mo Lewis .20 .07
❑ 191 Adrian Murrell .30 .10
❑ 192 Neil O'Donnell .30 .10
❑ 193 Tim Brown .50 .20
❑ 194 Rickey Dudley .30 .10
❑ 195 Jeff George .30 .10
❑ 196 Napoleon Kaufman .50 .20
❑ 197 Russell Maryland .20 .07
❑ 198 Terry McDaniel .20 .07
❑ 199 Chester McGlockton .20 .07
❑ 200 Desmond Howard .30 .10
❑ 201 Pat Swilling .20 .07
❑ 202 Ty Detmer .30 .10
❑ 203 Jason Dunn .20 .07
❑ 204 Ray Farmer .20 .07
❑ 205 Irving Fryar .30 .10
❑ 206 Chris T. Jones .20 .07
❑ 207 Bobby Taylor .20 .07
❑ 208 William Thomas .20 .07
❑ 209 Hollis Thomas RC .20 .07
❑ 210 Kevin Turner .20 .07
❑ 211 Ricky Watters .30 .10
❑ 212 Jerome Bettis .50 .20
❑ 213 Andre Hastings .20 .07
❑ 214 Charles Johnson .30 .10
❑ 215 Levon Kirkland .20 .07
❑ 216 Carnell Lake .20 .07
❑ 217 Greg Lloyd .20 .07
❑ 218 Darren Perry .20 .07
❑ 219 Kordell Stewart .50 .20
❑ 220 Rod Woodson .30 .10
❑ 221 Andre Coleman .20 .07
❑ 222 Marco Coleman .20 .07
❑ 223 Leonard Russell .20 .07
❑ 224 Stan Humphries .30 .10
❑ 225 Shawn Lee .20 .07
❑ 226 Tony Martin .30 .10
❑ 227 Chris Mims .20 .07
❑ 228 Junior Seau .50 .20
❑ 229 Chris Doleman .20 .07
❑ 230 William Floyd .30 .10
❑ 231 Merton Hanks .20 .07
❑ 232 Brent Jones .30 .10
❑ 233 Terry Kirby .30 .10
❑ 234 Ken Norton .20 .07
❑ 235 Terrell Owens .60 .25
❑ 236 Jerry Rice 1.00 .40
❑ 237 Bryant Young .20 .07
❑ 238 Steve Young .60 .25
❑ 239 Garrison Hearst .30 .10
❑ 240 Brian Blades .20 .07
❑ 241 Chad Brown .20 .07
❑ 242 John Friesz .20 .07
❑ 243 Joey Galloway .30 .10
❑ 244 Cortez Kennedy .20 .07
❑ 245 Chris Warren .30 .10
❑ 246 Darryl Williams .20 .07
❑ 247 Tony Banks .30 .10
❑ 248 Isaac Bruce .50 .20
❑ 249 Kevin Carter .20 .07
❑ 250 Eddie Kennison .30 .10
❑ 251 Todd Lyght .20 .07
❑ 252 Leslie O'Neal .20 .07
❑ 253 Anthony Parker .20 .07
❑ 254 Roman Phifer .20 .07
❑ 255 Lawrence Phillips .20 .07
❑ 256 Mike Alstott .50 .20
❑ 257 Derrick Brooks .50 .20
❑ 258 Trent Dilfer .50 .20
❑ 259 Jackie Harris .20 .07
❑ 260 Hardy Nickerson .20 .07
❑ 261 Errict Rhett .20 .07
❑ 262 Warren Sapp .30 .10
❑ 263 Terry Allen .50 .20
❑ 264 Jamie Asher .20 .07
❑ 265 Henry Ellard .20 .07
❑ 266 Gus Frerotte .20 .07
❑ 267 Sean Gilbert .20 .07
❑ 268 Darrell Green .30 .10
❑ 269 Ken Harvey .20 .07
❑ 270 Brian Mitchell .20 .07
❑ 271 Michael Westbrook .30 .10
❑ 272 Koy Detmer RC 1.00 .40
❑ 273 Yatil Green RC .30 .10
❑ 274 Troy Davis RC .30 .10
❑ 275 Darrell Russell RC .20 .07
❑ 276 Warrick Dunn RC 1.25 .50
❑ 277 David LaFleur RC .20 .07
❑ 278 Tony Gonzalez RC 1.50 .60
❑ 279 Jake Plummer RC 2.50 1.00
❑ 280 Antowain Smith RC 1.25 .50
❑ 281 Peter Boulware RC .50 .20
❑ 282 Shawn Springs RC .30 .10
❑ 283 Bryant Westbrook RC .20 .07
❑ 284 Rae Carruth RC .20 .07
❑ 285 Corey Dillon RC 3.00 1.25
❑ 286 Byron Hanspard RC .30 .10
❑ 287 Greg Jones RC .20 .07
❑ 288 Trevor Pryce RC .50 .20
❑ 289 Michael Booker RC .20 .07
❑ 290 Orlando Pace RC .50 .20
❑ 291 James Farrior RC .50 .20
❑ 292 Walter Jones RC .50 .20
❑ 293 Reinard Wilson RC .30 .10
❑ 294 Ike Hilliard RC .75 .30
❑ 295 Kenard Lang RC .30 .10
❑ 296 Reidel Anthony RC .50 .20
❑ 297 Brett Favre CL .50 .20
❑ 298 Kerry Collins CL .30 .10
❑ 299 Drew Bledsoe CL .30 .10
❑ 300 Terrell Davis CL .50 .20

1989 Pro Set

❑ COMPLETE SET (561) 25.00 10.00
❑ COMP.SERIES 1 (440) 6.00 3.00
❑ COMP.SERIES 2 (100) 20.00 10.00
❑ COMP.FINAL FACT.SET (21) 2.00 .75
❑ 1 Stacey Bailey .04 .01
❑ 2 Aundray Bruce RC .04 .01
❑ 3 Rick Bryan .04 .01
❑ 4 Bobby Butler .04 .01
❑ 5 Scott Case RC .04 .01
❑ 6 Tony Casillas .04 .01
❑ 7 Floyd Dixon .04 .01
❑ 8 Rick Donnelly .04 .01
❑ 9 Bill Fralic .04 .01
❑ 10 Mike Gann .04 .01
❑ 11 Mike Kenn .04 .01
❑ 12 Chris Miller RC .25 .08
❑ 13 John Rade .04 .01
❑ 14 Gerald Riggs UER .10 .02
❑ 15 John Settle RC .04 .01
❑ 16 Marion Campbell CO .04 .01
❑ 17 Cornelius Bennett .10 .02
❑ 18 Derrick Burroughs .04 .01
❑ 19 Shane Conlan .04 .01
❑ 20 Ronnie Harmon .10 .02
❑ 21 Kent Hull RC .04 .01
❑ 22 Jim Kelly .50 .20
❑ 23 Mark Kelso .04 .01
❑ 24 Pete Metzelaars .04 .01
❑ 25 Scott Norwood RC** .04 .01
❑ 26 Andre Reed .25 .08
❑ 27 Fred Smerlas .04 .01
❑ 28 Bruce Smith .25 .08
❑ 29 Leonard Smith .04 .01
❑ 30 Art Still .04 .01
❑ 31 Darryl Talley .10 .02
❑ 32 Thurman Thomas RC 1.00 .40
❑ 33 Will Wolford RC .04 .01
❑ 34 Marv Levy CO .04 .01
❑ 35 Neal Anderson .10 .02
❑ 36 Kevin Butler .04 .01
❑ 37 Jim Covert .04 .01
❑ 38 Richard Dent .10 .02
❑ 39 Dave Duerson .04 .01
❑ 40 Dennis Gentry .04 .01
❑ 41 Dan Hampton .10 .02
❑ 42 Jay Hilgenberg .04 .01
❑ 43 Dennis McKinnon UER .04 .01
❑ 44 Jim McMahon .10 .02
❑ 45 Steve McMichael .10 .02
❑ 46 Brad Muster RC .04 .01
❑ 47A William Perry ERR SP 6.00 2.50
❑ 47B Ron Morris RC .04 .01
❑ 48 Ron Rivera .04 .01
❑ 49 Vestee Jackson RC .04 .01
❑ 50 Mike Singletary .10 .02
❑ 51 Mike Tomczak .10 .02
❑ 52 Keith Van Horne RC .04 .01
❑ 53A Mike Ditka CO .25 .08

❑ 53B Mike Ditka CO HOF .25 .08
❑ 54 Lewis Billups .04 .01
❑ 55 James Brooks .10 .02
❑ 56 Eddie Brown .04 .01
❑ 57 Jason Buck RC .04 .01
❑ 58 Boomer Esiason .10 .02
❑ 59 David Fulcher .10 .02
❑ 60A Rodney Holman RC ERR .10 .02
❑ 60B Rodney Holman RC COR .25 .08
❑ 61 Reggie Williams .04 .01
❑ 62 Joe Kelly RC .04 .01
❑ 63 Tim Krumrie .04 .01
❑ 64 Tim McGee .04 .01
❑ 65 Max Montoya .04 .01
❑ 66 Anthony Munoz .10 .02
❑ 67 Jim Skow .04 .01
❑ 68 Eric Thomas RC .04 .01
❑ 69 Leon White .04 .01
❑ 70 Ickey Woods RC .10 .02
❑ 71 Carl Zander .04 .01
❑ 72 Sam Wyche CO .04 .01
❑ 73 Brian Brennan .04 .01
❑ 74 Earnest Byner .04 .01
❑ 75 Hanford Dixon .04 .01
❑ 76 Mike Pagel .04 .01
❑ 77 Bernie Kosar .10 .02
❑ 78 Reggie Langhorne RC .04 .01
❑ 79 Kevin Mack .04 .01
❑ 80 Clay Matthews .10 .02
❑ 81 Gerald McNeil .04 .01
❑ 82 Frank Minnifield .04 .01
❑ 83 Cody Risien .04 .01
❑ 84 Webster Slaughter .10 .02
❑ 85 Felix Wright .04 .01
❑ 86 Bud Carson CO UER .04 .01
❑ 87 Bill Bates .10 .02
❑ 88 Kevin Brooks .04 .01
❑ 89 Michael Irvin RC 1.25 .50
❑ 90 Jim Jeffcoat .04 .01
❑ 91 Ed Too Tall Jones .10 .02
❑ 92 Eugene Lockhart RC .04 .01
❑ 93 Nate Newton RC .10 .02
❑ 94 Danny Noonan .04 .01
❑ 95 Steve Pelluer .04 .01
❑ 96 Herschel Walker .10 .02
❑ 97 Everson Walls .04 .01
❑ 98 Jimmy Johnson RC CO .10 .02
❑ 99 Keith Bishop .04 .01
❑ 100A John Elway DRAFT 6.00 2.50
❑ 100B John Elway TRADE 2.00 .75
❑ 101 Simon Fletcher RC .04 .01
❑ 102 Mike Harden .04 .01
❑ 103 Mike Horan .04 .01
❑ 104 Mark Jackson .04 .01
❑ 105 Vance Johnson .10 .02
❑ 106 Rulon Jones .04 .01
❑ 107 Clarence Kay .04 .01
❑ 108 Karl Mecklenburg .04 .01
❑ 109 Ricky Nattiel .04 .01
❑ 110 Steve Sewell RC .04 .01
❑ 111 Dennis Smith .10 .02
❑ 112 Gerald Willhite .04 .01
❑ 113 Sammy Winder .04 .01
❑ 114 Dan Reeves CO .04 .01
❑ 115 Jim Arnold .04 .01
❑ 116 Jerry Ball RC .04 .01
❑ 117 Bennie Blades RC .04 .01
❑ 118 Lomas Brown .04 .01
❑ 119 Mike Cofer .04 .01
❑ 120 Garry James .04 .01
❑ 121 James Jones FB .04 .01
❑ 122 Chuck Long .04 .01
❑ 123 Pete Mandley .04 .01
❑ 124 Eddie Murray .04 .01
❑ 125 Chris Spielman RC .25 .08
❑ 126 Dennis Gibson .04 .01
❑ 127 Wayne Fontes CO .04 .01
❑ 128 John Anderson .04 .01
❑ 129 Brent Fullwood RC .04 .01
❑ 130 Mark Cannon .04 .01
❑ 131 Tim Harris .04 .01
❑ 132 Mark Lee .04 .01
❑ 133 Don Majkowski RC .10 .02
❑ 134 Mark Murphy .04 .01
❑ 135 Brian Noble .04 .01
❑ 136 Ken Ruettgers RC .04 .01
❑ 137 Johnny Holland .04 .01
❑ 138 Randy Wright .04 .01
❑ 139 Lindy Infante CO .04 .01
❑ 140 Steve Brown .04 .01
❑ 141 Ray Childress .04 .01
❑ 142 Jeff Donaldson .04 .01
❑ 143 Ernest Givins .10 .02
❑ 144 John Grimsley .04 .01
❑ 145 Alonzo Highsmith .04 .01
❑ 146 Drew Hill .04 .01
❑ 147 Robert Lyles .04 .01
❑ 148 Bruce Matthews RC .60 .25
❑ 149 Warren Moon .25 .08
❑ 150 Mike Munchak .10 .02
❑ 151 Allen Pinkett RC .04 .01
❑ 152 Mike Rozier .04 .01
❑ 153 Tony Zendejas .04 .01
❑ 154 Jerry Glanville CO .04 .01
❑ 155 Albert Bentley .04 .01
❑ 156 Dean Biasucci .04 .01
❑ 157 Duane Bickett .04 .01
❑ 158 Bill Brooks .10 .02
❑ 159 Chris Chandler RC 1.00 .40
❑ 160 Pat Beach .04 .01
❑ 161 Ray Donaldson .04 .01
❑ 162 Jon Hand .04 .01
❑ 163 Chris Hinton .04 .01
❑ 164 Rohn Stark .04 .01
❑ 165 Fredd Young .04 .01
❑ 166 Ron Meyer CO .04 .01
❑ 167 Lloyd Burruss .04 .01
❑ 168 Carlos Carson .04 .01
❑ 169 Deron Cherry .10 .02
❑ 170 Irv Eatman .04 .01
❑ 171 Dino Hackett .04 .01
❑ 172 Steve DeBerg .04 .01
❑ 173 Albert Lewis .04 .01
❑ 174 Nick Lowery .04 .01
❑ 175 Bill Maas .04 .01
❑ 176 Christian Okoye .04 .01
❑ 177 Stephone Paige .04 .01
❑ 178 Mark Adickes .04 .01
❑ 179 Kevin Ross RC .10 .02
❑ 180 Neil Smith RC .50 .20
❑ 181 M. Schottenheimer CO .04 .01
❑ 182 Marcus Allen .25 .08
❑ 183 Tim Brown RC 1.50 .60
❑ 184 Willie Gault .10 .02
❑ 185 Bo Jackson .30 .10
❑ 186 Howie Long .25 .08
❑ 187 Vann McElroy .04 .01
❑ 188 Matt Millen .10 .02
❑ 189 Don Mosebar RC .04 .01
❑ 190 Bill Pickel .04 .01
❑ 191 Jerry Robinson UER .04 .01
❑ 192 Jay Schroeder .04 .01
❑ 193A Stacey Toran .04 .01
❑ 193B Stacey Toran .50 .20
❑ 194 Mike Shanahan CO RC .10 .02
❑ 195 Greg Bell .04 .01
❑ 196 Ron Brown .04 .01
❑ 197 Aaron Cox RC .04 .01
❑ 198 Henry Ellard .25 .08
❑ 199 Jim Everett .10 .02
❑ 200 Jerry Gray .04 .01
❑ 201 Kevin Greene .25 .08
❑ 202 Pete Holohan .04 .01
❑ 203 LeRoy Irvin .04 .01
❑ 204 Mike Lansford .04 .01
❑ 205 Tom Newberry RC .04 .01
❑ 206 Mel Owens .04 .01
❑ 207 Jackie Slater .04 .01
❑ 208 Doug Smith .04 .01
❑ 209 Mike Wilcher .04 .01
❑ 210 John Robinson CO .04 .01
❑ 211 John Bosa .04 .01
❑ 212 Mark Brown .04 .01
❑ 213 Mark Clayton .10 .02
❑ 214A Ferrell Edmonds RC ERR .50 .20
❑ 214B Ferrell Edmunds RC COR .04 .01
❑ 215 Roy Foster .04 .01
❑ 216 Lorenzo Hampton .04 .01
❑ 217 Jim C.Jensen RC UER .04 .01
❑ 218 William Judson .04 .01
❑ 219 Eric Kumerow RC .04 .01
❑ 220 Dan Marino 2.00 .75
❑ 221 John Offerdahl .04 .01
❑ 222 Fuad Reveiz .04 .01
❑ 223 Reggie Roby .04 .01
❑ 224 Brian Sochia .04 .01
❑ 225 Don Shula CO RC .25 .08
❑ 226 Alfred Anderson .04 .01
❑ 227 Joey Browner .04 .01
❑ 228 Anthony Carter .10 .02
❑ 229 Chris Doleman .10 .02
❑ 230 Hassan Jones RC .04 .01
❑ 231 Steve Jordan .04 .01
❑ 232 Tommy Kramer .04 .01
❑ 233 Carl Lee RC .04 .01
❑ 234 Kirk Lowdermilk RC .04 .01
❑ 235 Randall McDaniel RC .25 .08
❑ 236 Doug Martin .04 .01
❑ 237 Keith Millard .04 .01
❑ 238 Darrin Nelson .04 .01
❑ 239 Jesse Solomon .04 .01
❑ 240 Scott Studwell .04 .01
❑ 241 Wade Wilson .10 .02
❑ 242 Gary Zimmerman .04 .01
❑ 243 Jerry Burns CO .04 .01
❑ 244 Bruce Armstrong RC .04 .01
❑ 245 Raymond Clayborn .04 .01
❑ 246 Reggie Dupard .04 .01
❑ 247 Tony Eason .04 .01
❑ 248 Sean Farrell .04 .01
❑ 249 Doug Flutie .75 .25
❑ 250 Brent Williams RC .04 .01
❑ 251 Roland James .04 .01
❑ 252 Ronnie Lippett .04 .01
❑ 253 Fred Marion .04 .01
❑ 254 Larry McGrew .04 .01
❑ 255 Stanley Morgan .04 .01
❑ 256 Johnny Rembert RC .04 .01
❑ 257 John Stephens RC .04 .01
❑ 258 Andre Tippett .04 .01
❑ 259 Garin Veris .04 .01
❑ 260A Raymond Berry CO .04 .01
❑ 260B Raymond Berry CO HOF .04 .01
❑ 261 Morten Andersen .04 .01
❑ 262 Hoby Brenner .04 .01
❑ 263 Stan Brock .04 .01
❑ 264 Brad Edelman .04 .01
❑ 265 Jumpy Geathers .04 .01
❑ 266A Bobby Hebert Passers .50 .20
❑ 266B Bobby Hebert Passes .04 .01
❑ 267 Craig Heyward RC .25 .08
❑ 268 Lonzell Hill .04 .01
❑ 269 Dalton Hilliard .04 .01
❑ 270 Rickey Jackson .10 .02
❑ 271 Steve Korte .04 .01
❑ 272 Eric Martin .04 .01
❑ 273 Rueben Mayes .04 .01
❑ 274 Sam Mills .10 .02
❑ 275 Brett Perriman RC .25 .08
❑ 276 Pat Swilling .10 .02
❑ 277 John Tice .04 .01
❑ 278 Jim Mora CO .04 .01
❑ 279 Eric Moore RC .04 .01
❑ 280 Carl Banks .04 .01

❑ 281 Mark Bavaro .10 .02
❑ 282 Maurice Carthon .04 .01
❑ 283 Mark Collins RC .04 .01
❑ 284 Erik Howard .04 .01
❑ 285 Terry Kinard .04 .01
❑ 286 Sean Landeta .04 .01
❑ 287 Lionel Manuel .04 .01
❑ 288 Leonard Marshall .04 .01
❑ 289 Joe Morris .04 .01
❑ 290 Bart Oates .04 .01
❑ 291 Phil Simms .10 .02
❑ 292 Lawrence Taylor .25 .08
❑ 293 Bill Parcells RC CO .10 .02
❑ 294 Dave Cadigan .04 .01
❑ 295 Kyle Clifton RC .04 .01
❑ 296 Alex Gordon .04 .01
❑ 297 James Hasty RC .04 .01
❑ 298 Johnny Hector .04 .01
❑ 299 Bobby Humphery .04 .01
❑ 300 Pat Leahy .04 .01
❑ 301 Marty Lyons .04 .01
❑ 302 Reggie McElroy RC .04 .01
❑ 303 Erik McMillan RC .04 .01
❑ 304 Freeman McNeil .04 .01
❑ 305 Ken O'Brien .04 .01
❑ 306 Pat Ryan .04 .01
❑ 307 Mickey Shuler .04 .01
❑ 308 Al Toon .10 .02
❑ 309 Jo Jo Townsell .04 .01
❑ 310 Roger Vick .04 .01
❑ 311 Joe Walton CO .04 .01
❑ 312 Jerome Brown .10 .02
❑ 313 Keith Byars .10 .02
❑ 314 Cris Carter RC 1.50 .60
❑ 315 Randall Cunningham .40 .15
❑ 316 Terry Hoage .04 .01
❑ 317 Wes Hopkins .04 .01
❑ 318 Keith Jackson RC .25 .08
❑ 319 Mike Quick .04 .01
❑ 320 Mike Reichenbach .04 .01
❑ 321 Dave Rimington .04 .01
❑ 322 John Teltschik .04 .01
❑ 323 Anthony Toney .04 .01
❑ 324 Andre Waters .04 .01
❑ 325 Reggie White .25 .08
❑ 326 Luis Zendejas .04 .01
❑ 327 Buddy Ryan CO .04 .01
❑ 328 Robert Awalt .04 .01
❑ 329 Tim McDonald RC .10 .02
❑ 330 Roy Green .10 .02
❑ 331 Neil Lomax .04 .01
❑ 332 Cedric Mack .04 .01
❑ 333 Stump Mitchell .04 .01
❑ 334 Niko Noga RC .04 .01
❑ 335 Jay Novacek RC .25 .08
❑ 336 Freddie Joe Nunn .04 .01
❑ 337 Luis Sharpe .04 .01
❑ 338 Vai Sikahema .04 .01
❑ 339 J.T. Smith .04 .01
❑ 340 Ron Wolfley .04 .01
❑ 341 Gene Stallings RC CO .10 .02
❑ 342 Gary Anderson K .04 .01
❑ 343 Bubby Brister RC .25 .08
❑ 344 Dermontti Dawson RC .10 .02
❑ 345 Thomas Everett RC .04 .01
❑ 346 Delton Hall RC .04 .01
❑ 347 Bryan Hinkle RC .04 .01
❑ 348 Merril Hoge RC .04 .01
❑ 349 Tunch Ilkin RC .04 .01
❑ 350 Aaron Jones RC .04 .01
❑ 351 Louis Lipps .10 .02
❑ 352 David Little .04 .01
❑ 353 Hardy Nickerson RC .25 .08
❑ 354 Rod Woodson RC .50 .20
❑ 355A Chuck Noll RC CO 1/3 .10 .02
❑ 355B Chuck Noll RC CO 1/2 .10 .02
❑ 356 Gary Anderson RB .04 .01
❑ 357 Rod Bernstine RC .04 .01
❑ 358 Gill Byrd .04 .01
❑ 359 Vencie Glenn .04 .01
❑ 360 Dennis McKnight .04 .01
❑ 361 Lionel James .04 .01
❑ 362 Mark Malone .04 .01
❑ 363A Anthony Miller RC 14.8 .25 .08
❑ 363B Anthony Miller RC 3 .25 .08
❑ 364 Ralf Mojsiejenko .04 .01
❑ 365 Leslie O'Neal .10 .02
❑ 366 Jamie Holland RC .04 .01
❑ 367 Lee Williams .04 .01
❑ 368 Dan Henning CO .04 .01
❑ 369 Harris Barton RC .04 .01
❑ 370 Michael Carter .04 .01
❑ 371 Mike Cofer RC K .04 .01
❑ 372 Roger Craig .25 .08
❑ 373 Riki Ellison RC .04 .01
❑ 374 Jim Fahnhorst .04 .01
❑ 375 John Frank .04 .01
❑ 376 Jeff Fuller .04 .01
❑ 377 Don Griffin .04 .01
❑ 378 Charles Haley .25 .08
❑ 379 Ronnie Lott .10 .02
❑ 380 Tim McKyer .04 .01
❑ 381 Joe Montana 2.00 .75
❑ 382 Tom Rathman .04 .01
❑ 383 Jerry Rice 1.50 .60
❑ 384 John Taylor RC .25 .08
❑ 385 Keena Turner .04 .01
❑ 386 Michael Walter .04 .01
❑ 387 Bubba Paris .04 .01
❑ 388 Steve Young 1.00 .40
❑ 389 George Seifert RC CO .10 .02
❑ 390 Brian Blades RC .25 .08
❑ 391A B.Bosworth Seattle .30 .10
❑ 391B B.Bosworth Seahawks .10 .02
❑ 392 Jeff Bryant .04 .01
❑ 393 Jacob Green .04 .01
❑ 394 Norm Johnson .04 .01
❑ 395 Dave Krieg .10 .02
❑ 396 Steve Largent .25 .08
❑ 397 Bryan Millard RC .04 .01
❑ 398 Paul Moyer .04 .01
❑ 399 Joe Nash .04 .01
❑ 400 Rufus Porter RC .04 .01
❑ 401 Eugene Robinson RC .04 .01
❑ 402 Bruce Scholtz .04 .01
❑ 403 Kelly Stouffer RC .04 .01
❑ 404A Curt Warner 1455 1.25 .50
❑ 404B Curt Warner 6074 .10 .02
❑ 405 John L.Williams .04 .01
❑ 406 Tony Woods RC .04 .01
❑ 407 David Wyman .04 .01
❑ 408 Chuck Knox CO .04 .01
❑ 409 Mark Carrier RC WR .25 .08
❑ 410 Randy Grimes .04 .01
❑ 411 Paul Gruber RC .04 .01
❑ 412 Harry Hamilton .04 .01
❑ 413 Ron Holmes .04 .01
❑ 414 Donald Igwebuike .04 .01
❑ 415 Dan Turk .04 .01
❑ 416 Ricky Reynolds .04 .01
❑ 417 Bruce Hill RC .04 .01
❑ 418 Lars Tate .04 .01
❑ 419 Vinny Testaverde .30 .10
❑ 420 James Wilder .04 .01
❑ 421 Ray Perkins CO .04 .01
❑ 422 Jeff Bostic .04 .01
❑ 423 Kelvin Bryant .04 .01
❑ 424 Gary Clark .25 .08
❑ 425 Monte Coleman .04 .01
❑ 426 Darrell Green .10 .02
❑ 427 Joe Jacoby .04 .01
❑ 428 Jim Lachey .04 .01
❑ 429 Charles Mann .04 .01
❑ 430 Dexter Manley .04 .01
❑ 431 Darryl Grant .04 .01
❑ 432 Mark May RC .04 .01
❑ 433 Art Monk .10 .02
❑ 434 Mark Rypien RC .25 .08
❑ 435 Ricky Sanders .04 .01
❑ 436 Alvin Walton RC .04 .01
❑ 437 Don Warren .04 .01
❑ 438 Jamie Morris .04 .01
❑ 439 Doug Williams .10 .02
❑ 440 Joe Gibbs RC CO .10 .02
❑ 441 Marcus Cotton .04 .01
❑ 442 Joel Williams .04 .01
❑ 443 Joe Devlin .04 .01
❑ 444 Robb Riddick .04 .01
❑ 445 William Perry .10 .02
❑ 446 Thomas Sanders RC .04 .01
❑ 447 Brian Blados .04 .01
❑ 448 Cris Collinsworth .10 .02
❑ 449 Stanford Jennings .04 .01
❑ 450 Barry Krauss UER .04 .01
❑ 451 Ozzie Newsome .10 .02
❑ 452 Mike Oliphant RC .04 .01
❑ 453 Tony Dorsett .25 .08
❑ 454 Bruce McNorton .04 .01
❑ 455 Eric Dickerson .10 .02
❑ 456 Keith Bostic .04 .01
❑ 457 Sam Clancy RC .04 .01
❑ 458 Jack Del Rio RC .25 .08
❑ 459 Mike Webster .10 .02
❑ 460 Bob Golic .04 .01
❑ 461 Otis Wilson .04 .01
❑ 462 Mike Haynes .10 .02
❑ 463 Greg Townsend .04 .01
❑ 464 Mark Duper .10 .02
❑ 465 E.J. Junior .04 .01
❑ 466 Troy Stradford .04 .01
❑ 467 Mike Merriweather .04 .01
❑ 468 Irving Fryar .25 .08
❑ 469 Vaughan Johnson RC** .04 .01
❑ 470 Pepper Johnson .04 .01
❑ 471 Gary Reasons RC .04 .01
❑ 472 Perry Williams RC .04 .01
❑ 473 Wesley Walker .04 .01
❑ 474 Anthony Bell RC .04 .01
❑ 475 Earl Ferrell .04 .01
❑ 476 Craig Wolfley .04 .01
❑ 477 Billy Ray Smith .04 .01
❑ 478A Jim McMahon NOTR .10 .02
❑ 478B Jim McMahon TR .10 .02
❑ 478C Jim McMahon 40.00 15.00
❑ 479 Eric Wright .04 .01
❑ 480A Earnest Byner NOTR .04 .01
❑ 480B Earnest Byner TR .30 .10
❑ 480C Earnest Byner 40.00 15.00
❑ 481 Russ Grimm .04 .01
❑ 482 Wilber Marshall .04 .01
❑ 483A Gerald Riggs .10 .02
❑ 483B Gerald Riggs .30 .10
❑ 483C Gerald Riggs 40.00 15.00
❑ 484 Brian Davis RC .04 .01
❑ 485 Shawn Collins RC .04 .01
❑ 486 Deion Sanders RC 2.00 .75
❑ 487 Trace Armstrong RC .04 .01
❑ 488 Donnell Woolford RC .10 .02
❑ 489 Eric Metcalf RC .25 .08
❑ 490 Troy Aikman RC 6.00 2.50
❑ 491 Steve Walsh RC .10 .02
❑ 492 Steve Atwater RC .25 .08
❑ 493 Bobby Humphrey RC .04 .01
❑ 494 Barry Sanders RC 8.00 3.00
❑ 495 Tony Mandarich RC .04 .01
❑ 496 David Williams RC .04 .01
❑ 497 Andre Rison RC UER 1.00 .40
❑ 498 Derrick Thomas RC 1.50 .60
❑ 499 Cleveland Gary RC .04 .01
❑ 500 Bill Hawkins RC .04 .01
❑ 501 Louis Oliver RC .10 .02
❑ 502 Sammie Smith RC .04 .01
❑ 503 Hart Lee Dykes RC .04 .01
❑ 504 Wayne Martin RC .04 .01

❑ 505 Brian Williams OL RC .04 .01
❑ 506 Jeff Lageman RC .10 .02
❑ 507 Eric Hill RC .04 .01
❑ 508 Joe Wolf RC .04 .01
❑ 509 Timm Rosenbach RC .04 .01
❑ 510 Tom Ricketts .04 .01
❑ 511 Tim Worley RC .04 .01
❑ 512 Burt Grossman RC .04 .01
❑ 513 Keith DeLong RC .04 .01
❑ 514 Andy Heck RC .04 .01
❑ 515 Broderick Thomas RC .25 .08
❑ 516 Don Beebe RC .25 .08
❑ 517 James Thornton RC .04 .01
❑ 518 Eric Kattus .04 .01
❑ 519 Bruce Kozerski RC .04 .01
❑ 520 Brian Washington RC .04 .01
❑ 521 Rodney Peete RC .50 .20
❑ 522 Erik Affholter RC .04 .01
❑ 523 Anthony Dilweg RC .04 .01
❑ 524 O'Brien Alston .04 .01
❑ 525 Mike Elkins .04 .01
❑ 526 Jonathan Hayes RC .04 .01
❑ 527 Terry McDaniel RC .04 .01
❑ 528 Frank Stams RC .04 .01
❑ 529 Darryl Ingram RC .04 .01
❑ 530 Henry Thomas .04 .01
❑ 531 Eric Coleman DB .04 .01
❑ 532 Sheldon White RC .04 .01
❑ 533 Eric Allen RC .25 .08
❑ 534 Robert Drummond .04 .01
❑ 535A G.Williams RC bal 10.00 5.00
❑ 535B G.Williams RC w/o scout .25 .08
❑ 535C G.Williams RC w/scout .04 .01
❑ 536 Billy Joe Tolliver RC .04 .01
❑ 537 Daniel Stubbs RC .04 .01
❑ 538 Wesley Walls RC .40 .15
❑ 539A James Jefferson RC*ERR .30 .10
❑ 539B James Jefferson RC*COR .04 .01
❑ 540 Tracy Rocker .04 .01
❑ 541 Art Shell CO .10 .02
❑ 542 Lemuel Stinson RC .04 .01
❑ 543 Tyrone Braxton RC UER .04 .01
❑ 544 David Treadwell RC .04 .01
❑ 545 Flipper Anderson RC .25 .08
❑ 546 Dave Meggett RC .25 .08
❑ 547 Lewis Tillman RC .04 .01
❑ 548 Carnell Lake RC .25 .08
❑ 549 Marion Butts RC .10 .02
❑ 550 Sterling Sharpe RC 1.00 .40
❑ 551 Ezra Johnson .04 .01
❑ 552 Clarence Verdin RC** .04 .01
❑ 553 Mervyn Fernandez RC**/C .04 .01
❑ 554 Ottis Anderson .10 .02
❑ 555 Gary Hogeboom .04 .01
❑ 556 Paul Palmer TR .04 .01
❑ 557 Jesse Solomon TR .04 .01
❑ 558 Chip Banks TR .04 .01
❑ 559 Steve Pelluer TR .04 .01
❑ 560 Darrin Nelson TR .04 .01
❑ 561 Herschel Walker TR .10 .02
❑ CC1 Pete Rozelle .50 .20

1990 Pro Set

❑ COMPLETE SET (801) 25.00 10.00
❑ COMP.SERIES 1 (377) 10.00 4.00
❑ COMP.SERIES 2 (392) 10.00 4.00
❑ COMP.FINAL SERIES (32) 4.00 1.50
❑ COMP.FINAL FACT. (32) 5.00 2.00
❑ 1A Ba.Sanders ROY Hawaii 80.00 30.00
❑ 1B Barry Sanders ROY .60 .25
❑ 2A Joe Montana POY 3521 ERR .50 .20
❑ 2B Joe Montana POY 3130 COR .50 .20
❑ 3 Lindy Infante UER .04 .01
❑ 4 Warren Moon MOY UER .25 .08
❑ 5 Keith Millard .04 .01
❑ 6 Derrick Thomas D.ROY .25 .08
❑ 7 Ottis Anderson .10 .02
❑ 8 Joe Montana LL UER .50 .20

❑ 9 Christian Okoye .04 .01
❑ 10 Thurman Thomas LL .25 .08
❑ 11 Mike Cofer .04 .01
❑ 12 Dalton Hilliard UER .04 .01
❑ 13 Sterling Sharpe LL .25 .08
❑ 14 Rich Camarillo .04 .01
❑ 15A Walter Stanley LL 87/8 .50 .20
❑ 15B Walter Stanley COR .04 .01
❑ 16 Rod Woodson .25 .08
❑ 17 Felix Wright .04 .01
❑ 18A Chris Doleman ERR .50 .20
❑ 18B Chris Doleman COR .50 .20
❑ 19A Andre Ware RC w/o strip .10 .02
❑ 19B Andre Ware RC w/stripe .10 .02
❑ 20A Mo Elewonibi RC .04 .01
❑ 20B Mo Elewonibi RC .04 .01
❑ 21A Percy Snow .50 .20
❑ 21B Percy Snow .04 .01
❑ 22A Anthony Thompson RC w/o .04 .01
❑ 22B Anthony Thompson RC w/ .04 .01
❑ 23 Buck Buchanan .04 .01
❑ 24 Bob Griese .10 .02
❑ 25A Franco Harris ERR .50 .20
❑ 25B Franco Harris COR .10 .02
❑ 26 Ted Hendricks .04 .01
❑ 27A Jack Lambert ERR .50 .20
❑ 27B Jack Lambert COR .50 .20
❑ 28 Tom Landry HOF .10 .02
❑ 29 Bob St.Clair .04 .01
❑ 30 Aundray Bruce UER .04 .01
❑ 31 Tony Casillas UER .04 .01
❑ 32 Shawn Collins .04 .01
❑ 33 Marcus Cotton .04 .01
❑ 34 Bill Fralic .04 .01
❑ 35 Chris Miller .10 .02
❑ 36 Deion Sanders UER .50 .20
❑ 37 John Settle .04 .01
❑ 38 Jerry Glanville CO .04 .01
❑ 39 Cornelius Bennett .10 .02
❑ 40 Jim Kelly .25 .08
❑ 41 Mark Kelso UER .04 .01
❑ 42 Scott Norwood .04 .01
❑ 43 Nate Odomes RC .10 .02
❑ 44 Scott Radecic .04 .01
❑ 45 Jim Ritcher RC .04 .01
❑ 46 Leonard Smith .04 .01
❑ 47 Darryl Talley .04 .01
❑ 48 Marv Levy CO .04 .01
❑ 49 Neal Anderson .10 .02
❑ 50 Kevin Butler .04 .01
❑ 51 Jim Covert .04 .01
❑ 52 Richard Dent .10 .02
❑ 53 Jay Hilgenberg .04 .01
❑ 54 Steve McMichael .10 .02
❑ 55 Ron Morris .04 .01
❑ 56 John Roper .04 .01
❑ 57 Mike Singletary .10 .02
❑ 58 Keith Van Horne .04 .01
❑ 59 Mike Ditka CO .25 .08
❑ 60 Lewis Billups .04 .01
❑ 61 Eddie Brown .04 .01
❑ 62 Jason Buck .04 .01

❑ 63A Rickey Dixon RC ERR .50 .20
❑ 63B Rickey Dixon RC COR .50 .20
❑ 64 Tim McGee .04 .01
❑ 65 Eric Thomas .04 .01
❑ 66 Ickey Woods .04 .01
❑ 67 Carl Zander .04 .01
❑ 68A Sam Wyche CO ERR .50 .20
❑ 68B Sam Wyche CO COR .50 .20
❑ 69 Paul Farren .04 .01
❑ 70 Thane Gash RC .04 .01
❑ 71 David Grayson .04 .01
❑ 72 Bernie Kosar .10 .02
❑ 73 Reggie Langhorne .04 .01
❑ 74 Eric Metcalf .25 .08
❑ 75A Ozzie Newsome ERR .50 .20
❑ 75B Ozzie Newsome COR .50 .20
❑ 75C Cody Risien SP .50 .20
❑ 76 Felix Wright .04 .01
❑ 77 Bud Carson CO .04 .01
❑ 78 Troy Aikman .75 .30
❑ 79 Michael Irvin .25 .08
❑ 80 Jim Jeffcoat .04 .01
❑ 81 Crawford Ker .04 .01
❑ 82 Eugene Lockhart .04 .01
❑ 83 Kelvin Martin RC .04 .01
❑ 84 Ken Norton Jr. RC .25 .08
❑ 85 Jimmy Johnson CO .10 .02
❑ 86 Steve Atwater .04 .01
❑ 87 Tyrone Braxton .04 .01
❑ 88 John Elway 1.25 .50
❑ 89 Simon Fletcher .04 .01
❑ 90 Ron Holmes .04 .01
❑ 91 Bobby Humphrey .04 .01
❑ 92 Vance Johnson .04 .01
❑ 93 Ricky Nattiel .04 .01
❑ 94 Dan Reeves CO .04 .01
❑ 95 Jim Arnold .04 .01
❑ 96 Jerry Ball .04 .01
❑ 97 Bennie Blades .04 .01
❑ 98 Lomas Brown .04 .01
❑ 99 Michael Cofer .04 .01
❑ 100 Richard Johnson .04 .01
❑ 101 Eddie Murray .04 .01
❑ 102 Barry Sanders 1.25 .50
❑ 103 Chris Spielman .25 .08
❑ 104 William White RC .04 .01
❑ 105 Eric Williams RC .04 .01
❑ 106 Wayne Fontes CO UER .04 .01
❑ 107 Brent Fullwood .04 .01
❑ 108 Ron Hallstrom RC .04 .01
❑ 109 Tim Harris .04 .01
❑ 110A Johnny Holland ERR .50 .20
❑ 110B Johnny Holland COR .50 .20
❑ 111A Perry Kemp ERR .50 .20
❑ 111B Perry Kemp COR .50 .20
❑ 112 Don Majkowski .04 .01
❑ 113 Mark Murphy .04 .01
❑ 114A Sterling Sharpe ERR Gle .25 .08
❑ 114B Sterling Sharpe COR Chi .50 .20
❑ 115 Ed West RC .04 .01
❑ 116 Lindy Infante CO .04 .01
❑ 117 Steve Brown .04 .01
❑ 118 Ray Childress .04 .01
❑ 119 Ernest Givins .10 .02
❑ 120 John Grimsley .04 .01
❑ 121 Alonzo Highsmith .04 .01
❑ 122 Drew Hill .04 .01
❑ 123 Bubba McDowell .04 .01
❑ 124 Dean Steinkuhler .04 .01
❑ 125 Lorenzo White FPSC .10 .02
❑ 126 Tony Zendejas .04 .01
❑ 127 Jack Pardee CO .04 .01
❑ 128 Albert Bentley .04 .01
❑ 129 Dean Biasucci .04 .01
❑ 130 Duane Bickett .04 .01
❑ 131 Bill Brooks .04 .01
❑ 132 Jon Hand .04 .01
❑ 133 Mike Prior .04 .01

❑ 134A	Andre Rison NOTR	.25	.08
❑ 134B	Andre Rison TR	.25	.08
❑ 134C	Andre Rison TR Lud/back	.25	.08
❑ 135	Rohn Stark	.04	.01
❑ 136	Donnell Thompson	.04	.01
❑ 137	Clarence Verdin	.04	.01
❑ 138	Fredd Young	.04	.01
❑ 139	Ron Meyer CO	.04	.01
❑ 140	John Alt RC	.04	.01
❑ 141	Steve DeBerg	.04	.01
❑ 142	Irv Eatman	.04	.01
❑ 143	Dino Hackett	.04	.01
❑ 144	Nick Lowery	.04	.01
❑ 145	Bill Maas	.04	.01
❑ 146	Stephone Paige	.04	.01
❑ 147	Neil Smith	.25	.08
❑ 148	M. Schottenheimer CO	.04	.01
❑ 149	Steve Beuerlein FPSC	.10	.02
❑ 150	Tim Brown	.25	.08
❑ 151	Mike Dyal	.04	.01
❑ 152A	Mervyn Fernandez ERR	.75	.30
❑ 152B	Mervyn Fernandez COR	.75	.30
❑ 153	Willie Gault	.10	.02
❑ 154	Bob Golic	.04	.01
❑ 155	Bo Jackson	.30	.10
❑ 156	Don Mosebar	.04	.01
❑ 157	Steve Smith	.04	.01
❑ 158	Greg Townsend	.04	.01
❑ 159	Bruce Wilkerson RC	.04	.01
❑ 160	Steve Wisniewski	.10	.02
❑ 161A	Art Shell CO ERR	.50	.20
❑ 161B	Art Shell CO COR	.50	.20
❑ 161C	Art Shell CO COR	.50	.20
❑ 162	Flipper Anderson	.04	.01
❑ 163	Greg Bell UER	.04	.01
❑ 164	Henry Ellard	.10	.02
❑ 165	Jim Everett	.10	.02
❑ 166	Jerry Gray	.04	.01
❑ 167	Kevin Greene	.10	.02
❑ 168	Pete Holohan	.04	.01
❑ 169	Larry Kelm RC	.04	.01
❑ 170	Tom Newberry	.04	.01
❑ 171	Vince Newsome RC	.04	.01
❑ 172	Irv Pankey	.04	.01
❑ 173	Jackie Slater	.04	.01
❑ 174	Fred Strickland RC	.04	.01
❑ 175	Mike Wilcher UER	.04	.01
❑ 176	John Robinson CO UER	.04	.01
❑ 177	Mark Clayton	.10	.02
❑ 178	Roy Foster	.04	.01
❑ 179	Harry Galbreath RC	.04	.01
❑ 180	Jim C. Jensen	.04	.01
❑ 181	Dan Marino	1.25	.50
❑ 182	Louis Oliver	.04	.01
❑ 183	Sammie Smith	.04	.01
❑ 184	Brian Sochia	.04	.01
❑ 185	Don Shula CO	.10	.02
❑ 186	Joey Browner	.04	.01
❑ 187	Anthony Carter	.10	.02
❑ 188	Chris Doleman	.04	.01
❑ 189	Steve Jordan	.04	.01
❑ 190	Carl Lee	.04	.01
❑ 191	Randall McDaniel	.10	.02
❑ 192	Mike Merriweather	.04	.01
❑ 193	Keith Millard	.04	.01
❑ 194	Al Noga	.04	.01
❑ 195	Scott Studwell	.04	.01
❑ 196	Henry Thomas	.04	.01
❑ 197	Herschel Walker	.10	.02
❑ 198	Wade Wilson	.10	.02
❑ 199	Gary Zimmerman	.04	.01
❑ 200	Jerry Burns CO	.04	.01
❑ 201	Vincent Brown RC	.04	.01
❑ 202	Hart Lee Dykes	.04	.01
❑ 203	Sean Farrell	.04	.01
❑ 204A	Fred Marion	.04	.01
❑ 204B	Fred Marion	.04	.01
❑ 205	Stanley Morgan UER	.04	.01
❑ 206	Eric Sievers RC	.04	.01
❑ 207	John Stephens	.04	.01
❑ 208	Andre Tippett	.04	.01
❑ 209	Rod Rust CO	.04	.01
❑ 210A	Morten Andersen ERR	.50	.20
❑ 210B	Morten Andersen COR	.50	.20
❑ 211	Brad Edelman	.04	.01
❑ 212	John Fourcade	.04	.01
❑ 213	Dalton Hilliard	.04	.01
❑ 214	Rickey Jackson	.10	.02
❑ 215	Vaughan Johnson	.04	.01
❑ 216A	Eric Martin ERR	.50	.20
❑ 216B	Eric Martin COR	.50	.20
❑ 217	Sam Mills	.10	.02
❑ 218	Pat Swilling UER	.10	.02
❑ 219	Frank Warren RC	.04	.01
❑ 220	Jim Wilks	.04	.01
❑ 221A	Jim Mora CO ERR	.50	.20
❑ 221B	Jim Mora CO COR	.50	.20
❑ 222	Raul Allegre	.04	.01
❑ 223	Carl Banks	.04	.01
❑ 224	John Elliott	.04	.01
❑ 225	Erik Howard	.04	.01
❑ 226	Pepper Johnson	.04	.01
❑ 227	Leonard Marshall UER	.04	.01
❑ 228	Dave Meggett	.10	.02
❑ 229	Bart Oates	.04	.01
❑ 230	Phil Simms	.10	.02
❑ 231	Lawrence Taylor	.25	.08
❑ 232	Bill Parcells CO	.10	.02
❑ 233	Troy Benson	.04	.01
❑ 234	Kyle Clifton UER	.04	.01
❑ 235	Johnny Hector	.04	.01
❑ 236	Jeff Lageman	.04	.01
❑ 237	Pat Leahy	.04	.01
❑ 238	Freeman McNeil	.04	.01
❑ 239	Ken O'Brien	.04	.01
❑ 240	Al Toon	.10	.02
❑ 241	Jo Jo Townsell	.04	.01
❑ 242	Bruce Coslet CO	.04	.01
❑ 243	Eric Allen	.04	.01
❑ 244	Jerome Brown	.04	.01
❑ 245	Keith Byars	.04	.01
❑ 246	Cris Carter	.50	.20
❑ 247	Randall Cunningham	.25	.08
❑ 248	Keith Jackson	.10	.02
❑ 249	Mike Quick	.04	.01
❑ 250	Clyde Simmons	.04	.01
❑ 251	Andre Waters	.04	.01
❑ 252	Reggie White	.25	.08
❑ 253	Buddy Ryan CO	.04	.01
❑ 254	Rich Camarillo	.04	.01
❑ 255	Earl Ferrell	.04	.01
❑ 256	Roy Green	.10	.02
❑ 257	Ken Harvey RC	.25	.08
❑ 258	Ernie Jones RC	.04	.01
❑ 259	Tim McDonald	.04	.01
❑ 260	Timm Rosenbach UER	.04	.01
❑ 261	Luis Sharpe	.04	.01
❑ 262	Vai Sikahema	.04	.01
❑ 263	J.T. Smith	.04	.01
❑ 264	Ron Wolfley UER	.04	.01
❑ 265	Joe Bugel CO	.04	.01
❑ 266	Gary Anderson K	.04	.01
❑ 267	Bubby Brister	.04	.01
❑ 268	Merril Hoge	.04	.01
❑ 269	Carnell Lake	.04	.01
❑ 270	Louis Lipps	.10	.02
❑ 271	David Little	.04	.01
❑ 272	Greg Lloyd	.25	.08
❑ 273	Keith Willis	.04	.01
❑ 274	Tim Worley	.04	.01
❑ 275	Chuck Noll CO	.10	.02
❑ 276	Marion Butts	.10	.02
❑ 277	Gill Byrd	.04	.01
❑ 278	Vencie Glenn UER	.04	.01
❑ 279	Burt Grossman	.04	.01
❑ 280	Gary Plummer	.04	.01
❑ 281	Billy Ray Smith	.04	.01
❑ 282	Billy Joe Tolliver	.04	.01
❑ 283	Dan Henning CO	.04	.01
❑ 284	Harris Barton	.04	.01
❑ 285	Michael Carter	.04	.01
❑ 286	Mike Cofer	.04	.01
❑ 287	Roger Craig	.10	.02
❑ 288	Don Griffin	.04	.01
❑ 289A	Charles Haley ERR	10.00	4.00
❑ 289B	Charles Haley COR 5 fum	.75	.30
❑ 290	Pierce Holt RC	.04	.01
❑ 291	Ronnie Lott	.10	.02
❑ 292	Guy McIntyre	.04	.01
❑ 293	Joe Montana	1.25	.50
❑ 294	Tom Rathman	.04	.01
❑ 295	Jerry Rice	.75	.30
❑ 296	Jesse Sapolu RC	.04	.01
❑ 297	John Taylor	.10	.02
❑ 298	Michael Walter	.04	.01
❑ 299	George Seifert CO	.10	.02
❑ 300	Jeff Bryant	.04	.01
❑ 301	Jacob Green	.04	.01
❑ 302	Norm Johnson UER	.04	.01
❑ 303	Bryan Millard	.04	.01
❑ 304	Joe Nash	.04	.01
❑ 305	Eugene Robinson	.04	.01
❑ 306	John L. Williams	.04	.01
❑ 307	David Wyman	.04	.01
❑ 308	Chuck Knox CO	.04	.01
❑ 309	Mark Carrier WR	.25	.08
❑ 310	Paul Gruber	.04	.01
❑ 311	Harry Hamilton	.04	.01
❑ 312	Bruce Hill	.04	.01
❑ 313	Donald Igwebuike	.04	.01
❑ 314	Kevin Murphy	.04	.01
❑ 315	Ervin Randle	.04	.01
❑ 316	Mark Robinson	.04	.01
❑ 317	Lars Tate	.04	.01
❑ 318	Vinny Testaverde	.10	.02
❑ 319A	Ray Perkins CO ERR	.75	.30
❑ 319B	Ray Perkins CO COR	.04	.01
❑ 320	Earnest Byner	.04	.01
❑ 321	Gary Clark	.25	.08
❑ 322	Darryl Grant	.04	.01
❑ 323	Darrell Green	.10	.02
❑ 324	Jim Lachey	.04	.01
❑ 325	Charles Mann	.04	.01
❑ 326	Wilber Marshall	.04	.01
❑ 327	Ralf Mojsiejenko	.04	.01
❑ 328	Art Monk	.10	.02
❑ 329	Gerald Riggs	.10	.02
❑ 330	Mark Rypien	.10	.02
❑ 331	Ricky Sanders	.04	.01
❑ 332	Alvin Walton	.04	.01
❑ 333	Joe Gibbs CO	.10	.02
❑ 334	Aloha Stadium	.04	.01
❑ 335	Brian Blades PB	.04	.01
❑ 336	James Brooks PB	.04	.01
❑ 337	Shane Conlan PB	.04	.01
❑ 338A	Eric Dickerson PB SP	3.00	1.25
❑ 338B	Lud Denny Promo	200.00	75.00
❑ 339	Ray Donaldson PB	.04	.01
❑ 340	Ferrell Edmunds PB	.04	.01
❑ 341	Boomer Esiason PB	.04	.01
❑ 342	David Fulcher PB	.04	.01
❑ 343A	Chris Hinton PB	.50	.20
❑ 343B	Chris Hinton PB	.04	.01
❑ 344	Rodney Holman PB	.04	.01
❑ 345	Kent Hull PB	.04	.01
❑ 346	Tunch Ilkin PB	.04	.01
❑ 347	Mike Johnson PB	.04	.01
❑ 348	Greg Kragen PB	.04	.01
❑ 349	Dave Krieg PB	.10	.02
❑ 350	Albert Lewis PB	.04	.01
❑ 351	Howie Long PB	.10	.02
❑ 352	Bruce Matthews PB	.04	.01
❑ 353	Clay Matthews PB	.04	.01
❑ 354	Erik McMillan PB	.04	.01

❑ 355 Karl Mecklenburg PB	.04	.01
❑ 356 Anthony Miller PB	.04	.01
❑ 357 Frank Minnifield PB	.04	.01
❑ 358 Max Montoya PB	.04	.01
❑ 359 Warren Moon PB	.25	.08
❑ 360 Mike Munchak PB	.04	.01
❑ 361 Anthony Munoz PB	.04	.01
❑ 362 John Offerdahl PB	.04	.01
❑ 363 Christian Okoye PB	.04	.01
❑ 364 Leslie O'Neal PB	.04	.01
❑ 365 Rufus Porter PB UER	.04	.01
❑ 366 Andre Reed PB	.10	.02
❑ 367 Johnny Rembert PB	.04	.01
❑ 368 Reggie Roby PB	.04	.01
❑ 369 Kevin Ross PB	.04	.01
❑ 370 Webster Slaughter PB	.04	.01
❑ 371 Bruce Smith PB	.10	.02
❑ 372 Dennis Smith PB	.04	.01
❑ 373 Derrick Thomas PB	.10	.02
❑ 374 Thurman Thomas PB	.25	.08
❑ 375 David Treadwell PB	.04	.01
❑ 376 Lee Williams PB	.04	.01
❑ 377 Rod Woodson PB	.10	.02
❑ 378 Bud Carson CO PB	.04	.01
❑ 379 Eric Allen PB	.04	.01
❑ 380 Neal Anderson PB	.10	.02
❑ 381 Jerry Ball PB	.04	.01
❑ 382 Joey Browner PB	.04	.01
❑ 383 Rich Camarillo PB	.04	.01
❑ 384 Mark Carrier WR PB	.04	.01
❑ 385 Roger Craig PB	.10	.02
❑ 386A Randall Cunningham PB	.50	.20
❑ 386B Randall Cunningham PB	.50	.20
❑ 387 Chris Doleman PB	.04	.01
❑ 388 Henry Ellard PB	.04	.01
❑ 389 Bill Fralic PB	.04	.01
❑ 390 Brent Fullwood PB	.04	.01
❑ 391 Jerry Gray PB	.04	.01
❑ 392 Kevin Greene PB	.10	.02
❑ 393 Tim Harris PB	.04	.01
❑ 394 Jay Hilgenberg PB	.04	.01
❑ 395 Dalton Hilliard PB	.04	.01
❑ 396 Keith Jackson PB	.10	.02
❑ 397 Vaughan Johnson PB	.04	.01
❑ 398 Steve Jordan PB	.04	.01
❑ 399 Carl Lee PB	.04	.01
❑ 400 Ronnie Lott PB	.10	.02
❑ 401 Don Majkowski PB	.04	.01
❑ 402 Charles Mann PB	.04	.01
❑ 403 Randall McDaniel PB	.04	.01
❑ 404 Tim McDonald PB	.04	.01
❑ 405 Guy McIntyre PB	.04	.01
❑ 406 Dave Meggett PB	.04	.01
❑ 407 Keith Millard PB	.04	.01
❑ 408 Joe Montana PB	.50	.20
❑ 409 Eddie Murray PB	.04	.01
❑ 410 Tom Newberry PB	.04	.01
❑ 411 Jerry Rice PB	.50	.20
❑ 412 Mark Rypien PB	.04	.01
❑ 413 Barry Sanders PB	.60	.25
❑ 414 Luis Sharpe PB	.04	.01
❑ 415 Sterling Sharpe PB	.04	.01
❑ 416 Mike Singletary PB	.10	.02
❑ 417 Jackie Slater PB	.04	.01
❑ 418 Doug Smith PB	.04	.01
❑ 419 Chris Spielman PB	.04	.01
❑ 420 Pat Swilling PB	.04	.01
❑ 421 John Taylor PB	.04	.01
❑ 422 Lawrence Taylor PB	.10	.02
❑ 423 Reggie White PB	.10	.02
❑ 424 Ron Wolfley PB	.04	.01
❑ 425 Gary Zimmerman PB	.04	.01
❑ 426 John Robinson CO PB	.04	.01
❑ 427 Scott Case UER	.04	.01
❑ 428 Mike Kenn	.04	.01
❑ 429 Mike Gann	.04	.01
❑ 430 Tim Green RC	.04	.01
❑ 431 Michael Haynes RC	.25	.08
❑ 432 Jessie Tuggle RC UER	.04	.01
❑ 433 John Rade	.04	.01
❑ 434 Andre Rison	.25	.08
❑ 435 Don Beebe	.10	.02
❑ 436 Ray Bentley	.04	.01
❑ 437 Shane Conlan	.04	.01
❑ 438 Kent Hull	.04	.01
❑ 439 Pete Metzelaars	.04	.01
❑ 440 Andre Reed UER	.25	.08
❑ 441 Frank Reich FPSC	.25	.08
❑ 442 Leon Seals RC	.04	.01
❑ 443 Bruce Smith	.25	.08
❑ 444 Thurman Thomas	.25	.08
❑ 445 Will Wolford	.04	.01
❑ 446 Trace Armstrong	.04	.01
❑ 447 Mark Bortz RC	.04	.01
❑ 448 Tom Thayer RC	.04	.01
❑ 449A Dan Hampton ERR	.50	.20
❑ 449B Dan Hampton COR	10.00	4.00
❑ 450 Shaun Gayle RC	.04	.01
❑ 451 Dennis Gentry	.04	.01
❑ 452 Jim Harbaugh	.25	.08
❑ 453 Vestee Jackson	.04	.01
❑ 454 Brad Muster	.04	.01
❑ 455 William Perry	.10	.02
❑ 456 Ron Rivera	.04	.01
❑ 457 James Thornton	.04	.01
❑ 458 Mike Tomczak	.10	.02
❑ 459 Donnell Woolford	.04	.01
❑ 460 Eric Ball	.04	.01
❑ 461 James Brooks	.10	.02
❑ 462 David Fulcher	.04	.01
❑ 463 Boomer Esiason	.10	.02
❑ 464 Rodney Holman	.04	.01
❑ 465 Bruce Kozerski	.04	.01
❑ 466 Tim Krumrie	.04	.01
❑ 467 Anthony Munoz	.10	.02
❑ 468 Brian Blados	.04	.01
❑ 469 Mike Baab	.04	.01
❑ 470 Brian Brennan	.04	.01
❑ 471 Raymond Clayborn	.04	.01
❑ 472 Mike Johnson	.04	.01
❑ 473 Kevin Mack	.04	.01
❑ 474 Clay Matthews	.10	.02
❑ 475 Frank Minnifield	.04	.01
❑ 476 Gregg Rakoczy RC	.04	.01
❑ 477 Webster Slaughter	.10	.02
❑ 478 James Dixon	.04	.01
❑ 479 Robert Awalt UER	.04	.01
❑ 480 Dennis McKinnon UER	.04	.01
❑ 481 Danny Noonan	.04	.01
❑ 482 Jesse Solomon	.04	.01
❑ 483 Daniel Stubbs UER	.04	.01
❑ 484 Steve Walsh	.10	.02
❑ 485 Michael Brooks RC	.04	.01
❑ 486 Mark Jackson	.04	.01
❑ 487 Greg Kragen	.04	.01
❑ 488 Ken Lanier RC	.04	.01
❑ 489 Karl Mecklenburg	.04	.01
❑ 490 Steve Sewell	.04	.01
❑ 491 Dennis Smith	.04	.01
❑ 492 David Treadwell	.04	.01
❑ 493 Michael Young RC	.04	.01
❑ 494 Robert Clark RC	.04	.01
❑ 495 Dennis Gibson	.04	.01
❑ 496A Kevin Glover RC C/G	.50	.20
❑ 496B Kevin Glover RC C	.04	.01
❑ 497 Mel Gray	.10	.02
❑ 498 Rodney Peete	.10	.02
❑ 499 Dave Brown DB	.04	.01
❑ 500 Jerry Holmes	.04	.01
❑ 501 Chris Jacke	.04	.01
❑ 502 Alan Veingrad	.04	.01
❑ 503 Mark Lee	.04	.01
❑ 504 Tony Mandarich	.04	.01
❑ 505 Brian Noble	.04	.01
❑ 506 Jeff Query	.04	.01
❑ 507 Ken Ruettgers	.04	.01
❑ 508 Patrick Allen	.04	.01
❑ 509 Curtis Duncan	.04	.01
❑ 510 William Fuller	.10	.02
❑ 511 Haywood Jeffires RC	.25	.08
❑ 512 Sean Jones	.10	.02
❑ 513 Terry Kinard	.04	.01
❑ 514 Bruce Matthews	.10	.02
❑ 515 Gerald McNeil	.04	.01
❑ 516 Greg Montgomery RC	.04	.01
❑ 517 Warren Moon	.25	.08
❑ 518 Mike Munchak	.10	.02
❑ 519 Allen Pinkett	.04	.01
❑ 520 Pat Beach	.04	.01
❑ 521 Eugene Daniel	.04	.01
❑ 522 Kevin Call	.04	.01
❑ 523 Ray Donaldson	.04	.01
❑ 524 Jeff Herrod RC	.04	.01
❑ 525 Keith Taylor	.04	.01
❑ 526 Jack Trudeau	.04	.01
❑ 527 Deron Cherry	.04	.01
❑ 528 Jeff Donaldson	.04	.01
❑ 529 Albert Lewis	.04	.01
❑ 530 Pete Mandley	.04	.01
❑ 531 Chris Martin RC	.04	.01
❑ 532 Christian Okoye	.04	.01
❑ 533 Steve Pelluer	.04	.01
❑ 534 Kevin Ross	.04	.01
❑ 535 Dan Saleaumua	.04	.01
❑ 536 Derrick Thomas	.25	.08
❑ 537 Mike Webster	.10	.02
❑ 538 Marcus Allen	.25	.08
❑ 539 Greg Bell	.04	.01
❑ 540 Thomas Benson	.04	.01
❑ 541 Ron Brown	.04	.01
❑ 542 Scott Davis	.04	.01
❑ 543 Riki Ellison	.04	.01
❑ 544 Jamie Holland	.04	.01
❑ 545 Howie Long	.25	.08
❑ 546 Terry McDaniel	.04	.01
❑ 547 Max Montoya	.04	.01
❑ 548 Jay Schroeder	.04	.01
❑ 549 Lionel Washington	.04	.01
❑ 550 Robert Delpino FPSC	.04	.01
❑ 551 Bobby Humphery	.04	.01
❑ 552 Mike Lansford	.04	.01
❑ 553 Michael Stewart RC	.04	.01
❑ 554 Doug Smith	.04	.01
❑ 555 Curt Warner	.04	.01
❑ 556 Alvin Wright RC	.04	.01
❑ 557 Jeff Cross	.04	.01
❑ 558 Jeff Dellenbach RC	.04	.01
❑ 559 Mark Duper	.10	.02
❑ 560 Ferrell Edmunds	.04	.01
❑ 561 Tim McKyer	.04	.01
❑ 562 John Offerdahl	.04	.01
❑ 563 Reggie Roby	.04	.01
❑ 564 Pete Stoyanovich	.04	.01
❑ 565 Alfred Anderson	.04	.01
❑ 566 Ray Berry	.04	.01
❑ 567 Rick Fenney	.04	.01
❑ 568 Rich Gannon RC	1.50	.60
❑ 569 Tim Irwin	.04	.01
❑ 570 Hassan Jones	.04	.01
❑ 571 Cris Carter	.50	.20
❑ 572 Kirk Lowdermilk	.04	.01
❑ 573 Reggie Rutland RC	.04	.01
❑ 574 Ken Stills	.04	.01
❑ 575 Bruce Armstrong	.04	.01
❑ 576 Irving Fryar	.10	.02
❑ 577 Roland James	.04	.01
❑ 578 Robert Perryman	.04	.01
❑ 579 Cedric Jones	.04	.01
❑ 580 Steve Grogan	.10	.02
❑ 581 Johnny Rembert	.04	.01
❑ 582 Ed Reynolds	.04	.01
❑ 583 Brent Williams	.04	.01
❑ 584 Marc Wilson	.04	.01
❑ 585 Hoby Brenner	.04	.01

❑ 586 Stan Brock	.04	.01
❑ 587 Jim Dombrowski RC	.04	.01
❑ 588 Joel Hilgenberg RC	.04	.01
❑ 589 Robert Massey	.04	.01
❑ 590 Floyd Turner FPSC	.04	.01
❑ 591 Ottis Anderson	.10	.02
❑ 592 Mark Bavaro	.04	.01
❑ 593 Maurice Carthon	.04	.01
❑ 594 Eric Dorsey RC	.04	.01
❑ 595 Myron Guyton	.04	.01
❑ 596 Jeff Hostetler RC	.25	.08
❑ 597 Sean Landeta	.04	.01
❑ 598 Lionel Manuel	.04	.01
❑ 599 Odessa Turner RC	.04	.01
❑ 600 Perry Williams	.04	.01
❑ 601 James Hasty	.04	.01
❑ 602 Erik McMillan	.04	.01
❑ 603 Alex Gordon UER	.04	.01
❑ 604 Ron Stallworth	.04	.01
❑ 605 Byron Evans RC	.04	.01
❑ 606 Ron Heller RC OT	.04	.01
❑ 607 Wes Hopkins	.04	.01
❑ 608 Mickey Shuler UER	.04	.01
❑ 609 Seth Joyner	.10	.02
❑ 610 Jim McMahon	.10	.02
❑ 611 Mike Pitts	.04	.01
❑ 612 Izel Jenkins RC	.04	.01
❑ 613 Anthony Bell	.04	.01
❑ 614 David Galloway	.04	.01
❑ 615 Eric Hill	.04	.01
❑ 616 Cedric Mack	.04	.01
❑ 617 Freddie Joe Nunn	.04	.01
❑ 618 Tootie Robbins	.04	.01
❑ 619 Tom Tupa RC	.04	.01
❑ 620 Joe Wolf	.04	.01
❑ 621 Dermontti Dawson	.10	.02
❑ 622 Thomas Everett	.04	.01
❑ 623 Tunch Ilkin	.04	.01
❑ 624 Hardy Nickerson	.10	.02
❑ 625 Gerald Williams RC	.04	.01
❑ 626 Rod Woodson	.25	.08
❑ 627A Rod Bernstine TE	.50	.20
❑ 627B Rod Bernstine RB	.04	.01
❑ 628 Courtney Hall	.04	.01
❑ 629 Ronnie Harmon	.10	.02
❑ 630A Anthony Miller WR	.25	.08
❑ 630B Anthony Miller WR-KR	.10	.02
❑ 631 Joe Phillips	.04	.01
❑ 632A Leslie O'Neal LB-DE	.50	.20
❑ 632B Leslie O'Neal LB	.15	.05
❑ 632C Leslie O'Neal COR	.10	.02
❑ 633A David Richards RC G-T	.15	.05
❑ 633B David Richards RC G	.15	.05
❑ 634 Mark Vlasic FPSC	.04	.01
❑ 635 Lee Williams	.04	.01
❑ 636 Chet Brooks	.04	.01
❑ 637 Keena Turner	.04	.01
❑ 638 Kevin Fagan RC	.04	.01
❑ 639 Brent Jones RC	.25	.08
❑ 640 Matt Millen	.10	.02
❑ 641 Bubba Paris	.04	.01
❑ 642 Bill Romanowski RC	1.00	.40
❑ 643 Fred Smerlas UER	.04	.01
❑ 644 Dave Waymer	.04	.01
❑ 645 Steve Young	.50	.20
❑ 646 Brian Blades	.10	.02
❑ 647 Andy Heck	.04	.01
❑ 648 Dave Krieg	.10	.02
❑ 649 Rufus Porter	.04	.01
❑ 650 Kelly Stouffer	.04	.01
❑ 651 Tony Woods	.04	.01
❑ 652 Gary Anderson RB	.04	.01
❑ 653 Reuben Davis	.04	.01
❑ 654 Randy Grimes	.04	.01
❑ 655 Ron Hall	.04	.01
❑ 656 Eugene Marve	.04	.01
❑ 657A Curt Jarvis ERR	.50	.20
❑ 657B Curt Jarvis COR	10.00	4.00
❑ 658 Ricky Reynolds	.04	.01
❑ 659 Broderick Thomas	.04	.01
❑ 660 Jeff Bostic	.04	.01
❑ 661 Todd Bowles RC	.04	.01
❑ 662 Ravin Caldwell	.04	.01
❑ 663 Russ Grimm UER	.04	.01
❑ 664 Joe Jacoby	.04	.01
❑ 665 Mark May	.04	.01
❑ 666 Walter Stanley	.04	.01
❑ 667 Don Warren	.04	.01
❑ 668 Stan Humphries RC	.25	.08
❑ 669A Jeff George Illinois SP	1.00	.40
❑ 669B Jeff George RC	.50	.20
❑ 670 Blair Thomas RC	.10	.02
❑ 671 Cortez Kennedy RC UER	.25	.08
❑ 672 Keith McCants RC	.04	.01
❑ 673 Junior Seau RC	1.25	.50
❑ 674 Mark Carrier RC DB	.25	.08
❑ 675 Andre Ware	.10	.02
❑ 676 Chris Singleton RC UER	.04	.01
❑ 677 Richmond Webb RC	.04	.01
❑ 678 Ray Agnew RC	.04	.01
❑ 679 Anthony Smith RC	.04	.01
❑ 680 James Francis RC	.04	.01
❑ 681 Percy Snow	.04	.01
❑ 682 Renaldo Turnbull RC	.04	.01
❑ 683 Lamar Lathon RC	.10	.02
❑ 684 James Williams DB RC	.04	.01
❑ 685 Emmitt Smith RC	5.00	2.00
❑ 686 Tony Bennett RC	.25	.08
❑ 687 Darrell Thompson RC	.04	.01
❑ 688 Steve Broussard RC	.04	.01
❑ 689 Eric Green RC	.10	.02
❑ 690 Ben Smith RC	.04	.01
❑ 691 Bern Brostek RC UER	.04	.01
❑ 692 Rodney Hampton RC	.25	.08
❑ 693 Dexter Carter RC	.04	.01
❑ 694 Rob Moore RC	.50	.20
❑ 695 Alexander Wright RC	.04	.01
❑ 696 Darion Conner RC	.10	.02
❑ 697 Reggie Rembert RC UER	.04	.01
❑ 698A Terry Wooden RC 90	.50	.20
❑ 698B Terry Wooden RC 51	.04	.01
❑ 699 Reggie Cobb RC	.04	.01
❑ 700 Anthony Thompson	.04	.01
❑ 701 Fred Washington RC	.04	.01
❑ 702 Ron Cox RC	.04	.01
❑ 703 Robert Blackmon RC	.04	.01
❑ 704 Dan Owens RC	.04	.01
❑ 705 Anthony Johnson RC	.25	.08
❑ 706 Aaron Wallace RC	.04	.01
❑ 707 Harold Green RC	.25	.08
❑ 708 Keith Sims RC	.04	.01
❑ 709 Tim Grunhard RC	.04	.01
❑ 710 Jeff Alm RC	.04	.01
❑ 711 Carwell Gardner RC	.04	.01
❑ 712 Kenny Davidson RC	.04	.01
❑ 713 Vince Buck RC	.04	.01
❑ 714 Leroy Hoard RC	.25	.08
❑ 715 Andre Collins RC	.04	.01
❑ 716 Dennis Brown RC	.04	.01
❑ 717 LeRoy Butler RC	.25	.08
❑ 718A Pat Terrell RC 41	.50	.20
❑ 718B Pat Terrell RC 37	.04	.01
❑ 719 Mike Bellamy RC	.04	.01
❑ 720 Mike Fox RC	.04	.01
❑ 721 Alton Montgomery RC	.04	.01
❑ 722 Eric Davis RC	.10	.02
❑ 723A Oliver Barnett RC DT	.50	.20
❑ 723B Oliver Barnett RC NT	.04	.01
❑ 724 Houston Hoover RC	.04	.01
❑ 725 Howard Ballard RC	.04	.01
❑ 726 Keith McKeller RC	.04	.01
❑ 727 Wendell Davis RC	.04	.01
❑ 728 Peter Tom Willis RC	.04	.01
❑ 729 Bernard Clark	.04	.01
❑ 730 Doug Widell RC	.04	.01
❑ 731 Eric Andolsek	.04	.01
❑ 732 Jeff Campbell RC	.04	.01
❑ 733 Marc Spindler RC	.04	.01
❑ 734 Keith Woodside	.04	.01
❑ 735 Willis Peguese RC	.04	.01
❑ 736 Frank Stams	.04	.01
❑ 737 Jeff Uhlenhake	.04	.01
❑ 738 Todd Kalis	.04	.01
❑ 739 Tommy Hodson RC UER	.04	.01
❑ 740 Greg McMurtry RC	.04	.01
❑ 741 Mike Buck RC	.04	.01
❑ 742 Kevin Haverdink UER	.04	.01
❑ 743A Johnny Bailey RC 46	.10	.02
❑ 743B Johnny Bailey RC 22	.10	.02
❑ 744A Eric Moore	.15	.05
❑ 744B Eric Moore	10.00	4.00
❑ 745 Tony Stargell RC	.04	.01
❑ 746 Fred Barnett RC	.25	.08
❑ 747 Walter Reeves	.04	.01
❑ 748 Derek Hill	.04	.01
❑ 749 Quinn Early	.25	.08
❑ 750 Ronald Lewis	.04	.01
❑ 751 Ken Clark RC	.04	.01
❑ 752 Garry Lewis RC	.04	.01
❑ 753 James Lofton	.10	.02
❑ 754 Steve Tasker UER	.25	.08
❑ 755 Jim Shofner CO	.04	.01
❑ 756 Jimmie Jones RC	.04	.01
❑ 757 Jay Novacek	.25	.08
❑ 758 Jessie Hester RC	.04	.01
❑ 759 Barry Word RC	.04	.01
❑ 760 Eddie Anderson RC	.04	.01
❑ 761 Cleveland Gary	.04	.01
❑ 762 Marcus Dupree RC	.04	.01
❑ 763 David Griggs RC	.04	.01
❑ 764 Rueben Mayes	.04	.01
❑ 765 Stephen Baker FPSC	.04	.01
❑ 766 Reyna Thompson RC UER	.04	.01
❑ 767 Everson Walls	.04	.01
❑ 768 Brad Baxter RC	.04	.01
❑ 769 Steve Walsh	.10	.02
❑ 770 Heath Sherman RC	.04	.01
❑ 771 Johnny Johnson RC	.10	.02
❑ 772A Dexter Manley ERR	30.00	15.00
❑ 772B Dexter Manley	.04	.01
❑ 773 Ricky Proehl RC	.25	.08
❑ 774 Frank Cornish	.04	.01
❑ 775 Tommy Kane RC	.04	.01
❑ 776 Derrick Fenner RC	.04	.01
❑ 777 Steve Christie RC	.04	.01
❑ 778 Wayne Haddix RC	.04	.01
❑ 779 Richard Williamson UER	.04	.01
❑ 780 Brian Mitchell RC	.25	.08
❑ 781 American Bowl/London	.04	.01
❑ 782 American Bowl/Berlin	.04	.01
❑ 783 American Bowl/Tokyo	.04	.01
❑ 784 American Bowl/Montreal	.04	.01
❑ 785A Berlin Wall	.75	.30
❑ 785B Berlin Wall	.75	.30
❑ 786 Al Davis NEWS	.04	.01
❑ 787 Falcons Back in Black	.04	.01
❑ 788 NFL Goes International	.04	.01
❑ 789 Overseas Appeal	.04	.01
❑ 790 Photo Contest	.04	.01
❑ 791 Photo Contest	.04	.01
❑ 792 Photo Contest	.04	.01
❑ 793 Photo Contest	.04	.01
❑ 794 Barry Sanders PHOTO	.50	.20
❑ 795 Photo Contest	.04	.01
❑ 796 Photo Contest	.04	.01
❑ 797 Photo Contest	.04	.01
❑ 798 Cris Carter PC	.04	.01
❑ 799 Ronnie Lott School	.10	.02
❑ 800D Mark Carrier DB D-ROY	.10	.02
❑ 800O Emmitt Smith O-ROY	1.50	.60
❑ 1990 Santa Claus SP	.50	.20
❑ CC2 Paul Tagliabue SP	.40	.15
❑ CC3 Joe Robbie Mem SP	.50	.20
❑ SC Super Pro SP	.50	.20

❑ SC4 Fred Washington UER	.04	.01
❑ SP1 Payne Stewart SP	1.00	.40
❑ NNO Lombardi HOLO/10000	60.00	25.00
❑ NNO Super Bowl XXIV Logo	.04	.01

1991 Pro Set

❑ COMPLETE SET (850)	20.00	8.00
❑ COMP.SERIES 1 (405)	8.00	3.00
❑ COMP.SERIES 2 (407)	8.00	3.00
❑ COMP.FINAL FACT. (38)	4.00	2.00
❑ 1D Mark Carrier DB D-ROY	.10	.02
❑ 1O Emmitt Smith O-ROY	1.25	.50
❑ 3 Joe Montana POY	.50	.20
❑ 4 Art Shell	.10	.02
❑ 5 Mike Singletary	.10	.02
❑ 6 Bruce Smith	.10	.02
❑ 7 Barry Word Comeback	.05	.01
❑ 8A Jim Kelly LL w/LOGO	.25	.08
❑ 8B Jim Kelly LL NO LOGO	.25	.08
❑ 8C Jim Kelly LL Reg NO LOGO	6.00	3.00
❑ 9 Warren Moon LL	.10	.02
❑ 10 Barry Sanders LL	.50	.20
❑ 11 Jerry Rice LL	.40	.15
❑ 12 Jay Novacek	.10	.02
❑ 13 Thurman Thomas LL	.10	.02
❑ 14 Nick Lowery	.05	.01
❑ 15 Mike Horan	.05	.01
❑ 16 Clarence Verdin	.05	.01
❑ 17 Kevin Clark LL RC	.05	.01
❑ 18 Mark Carrier DB LL	.10	.02
❑ 19A Derrick Thomas LL Bills	20.00	7.50
❑ 19B Derrick Thomas LL COR	.10	.02
❑ 20 Ottis Anderson ML	.10	.02
❑ 21 Roger Craig ML	.10	.02
❑ 22 Art Monk ML	.10	.02
❑ 23 Chuck Noll ML	.10	.02
❑ 24 Randall Cunningham ML	.10	.02
❑ 25 Dan Marino ML	.50	.20
❑ 26 49ers Road Record ML	.05	.01
❑ 27 Earl Campbell HOF	.05	.01
❑ 28 John Hannah HOF	.05	.01
❑ 29 Stan Jones HOF	.05	.01
❑ 30 Tex Schramm HOF	.05	.01
❑ 31 Jan Stenerud HOF	.05	.01
❑ 32 Russell Maryland RC TW	.10	.02
❑ 33 Chris Zorich RC TW	.10	.02
❑ 34 Darryll Lewis RC Thorpe	.10	.02
❑ 35 Alfred Williams RC TW	.05	.01
❑ 36 Rocket Ismail RC TW	1.00	.40
❑ 37 Ty Detmer RC HH	.40	.15
❑ 38 Andre Ware Heisman	.10	.02
❑ 39 Barry Sanders HH	.50	.20
❑ 40 Tim Brown HH	.10	.02
❑ 41 Vinny Testaverde HH	.10	.02
❑ 42 Bo Jackson HH	.30	.10
❑ 43 Mike Rozier HH	.05	.01
❑ 44 Herschel Walker HH	.10	.02
❑ 45 Marcus Allen HH	.10	.02
❑ 46A James Lofton SB	.10	.02
❑ 46B James Lofton SB	.10	.02
❑ 47A Bruce Smith SB black ink	.10	.02
❑ 47B Bruce Smith SB white ink	.10	.02
❑ 48 Myron Guyton SB	.05	.01
❑ 49 Stephen Baker SB	.05	.01
❑ 50 Mark Ingram SB UER	.05	.01
❑ 51 Ottis Anderson SB	.10	.02
❑ 52 Thurman Thomas SB	.25	.08
❑ 53 Matt Bahr SB	.05	.01
❑ 54 Scott Norwood SB	.05	.01
❑ 55 Stephen Baker	.05	.01
❑ 56 Carl Banks	.05	.01
❑ 57 Mark Collins	.05	.01
❑ 58 Steve DeOssie	.05	.01
❑ 59 Eric Dorsey	.05	.01
❑ 60 John Elliott	.05	.01
❑ 61 Myron Guyton	.05	.01
❑ 62 Rodney Hampton	.25	.08
❑ 63 Jeff Hostetler	.10	.02
❑ 64 Erik Howard	.05	.01
❑ 65 Mark Ingram	.10	.02
❑ 66 Greg Jackson RC	.05	.01
❑ 67 Leonard Marshall	.05	.01
❑ 68 Dave Meggett	.10	.02
❑ 69 Eric Moore	.05	.01
❑ 70 Bart Oates	.05	.01
❑ 71 Gary Reasons	.05	.01
❑ 72 Bill Parcells CO	.10	.02
❑ 73 Howard Ballard	.05	.01
❑ 74A Corn.Bennett w/LOGO	.25	.08
❑ 74B Corn.Bennett NO LOGO	.05	.01
❑ 75 Shane Conlan	.05	.01
❑ 76 Kent Hull	.05	.01
❑ 77 Kirby Jackson RC	.05	.01
❑ 78A Jim Kelly w/LOGO	.60	.25
❑ 78B Jim Kelly NO LOGO	.25	.08
❑ 79 Mark Kelso	.05	.01
❑ 80 Nate Odomes	.05	.01
❑ 81 Andre Reed	.10	.02
❑ 82 Jim Ritcher	.05	.01
❑ 83 Bruce Smith	.25	.08
❑ 84 Darryl Talley	.05	.01
❑ 85 Steve Tasker	.10	.02
❑ 86 Thurman Thomas	.25	.08
❑ 87 James Williams	.05	.01
❑ 88 Will Wolford	.05	.01
❑ 89 Jeff Wright RC UER	.05	.01
❑ 90 Marv Levy CO	.05	.01
❑ 91 Steve Broussard	.05	.01
❑ 92A Darion Conner ERR '99	10.00	4.00
❑ 92B Darion Conner COR	.25	.08
❑ 93 Bill Fralic	.05	.01
❑ 94 Tim Green	.05	.01
❑ 95 Michael Haynes	.25	.08
❑ 96 Chris Hinton	.05	.01
❑ 97 Chris Miller UER	.10	.02
❑ 98 Deion Sanders UER	.40	.15
❑ 99 Jerry Glanville CO	.05	.01
❑ 100 Kevin Butler	.05	.01
❑ 101 Mark Carrier DB	.10	.02
❑ 102 Jim Covert	.05	.01
❑ 103 Richard Dent	.10	.02
❑ 104 Jim Harbaugh	.25	.08
❑ 105 Brad Muster	.05	.01
❑ 106 Lemuel Stinson	.05	.01
❑ 107 Keith Van Horne	.05	.01
❑ 108 Mike Ditka CO UER	.25	.08
❑ 109 Lewis Billups	.05	.01
❑ 110 James Brooks	.10	.02
❑ 111 Boomer Esiason	.10	.02
❑ 112 James Francis	.05	.01
❑ 113 David Fulcher	.05	.01
❑ 114 Rodney Holman	.05	.01
❑ 115 Tim McGee	.05	.01
❑ 116 Anthony Munoz	.10	.02
❑ 117 Sam Wyche CO	.05	.01
❑ 118 Paul Farren	.05	.01
❑ 119 Thane Gash	.05	.01
❑ 120 Mike Johnson	.05	.01
❑ 121A Bernie Kosar w/LOGO	.10	.02
❑ 121B Bernie Kosar NO LOGO	.10	.02
❑ 122 Clay Matthews	.10	.02
❑ 123 Eric Metcalf	.10	.02
❑ 124 Frank Minnifield	.05	.01
❑ 125A Webster Slaughter	.10	.02
❑ 125B Webster Slaughter	.10	.02
❑ 126 Bill Belichick CO RC	1.50	.60
❑ 127 Tommie Agee	.05	.01
❑ 128 Troy Aikman	.75	.30
❑ 129 Jack Del Rio	.10	.02
❑ 130 John Gesek RC	.05	.01
❑ 131 Issiac Holt	.05	.01
❑ 132 Michael Irvin	.25	.08
❑ 133 Ken Norton	.10	.02
❑ 134 Daniel Stubbs	.05	.01
❑ 135 Jimmy Johnson CO	.10	.02
❑ 136 Steve Atwater	.05	.01
❑ 137 Michael Brooks	.05	.01
❑ 138 John Elway	1.25	.50
❑ 139 Wymon Henderson	.05	.01
❑ 140 Bobby Humphrey	.05	.01
❑ 141 Mark Jackson	.05	.01
❑ 142 Karl Mecklenburg	.05	.01
❑ 143 Doug Widell	.05	.01
❑ 144 Dan Reeves CO	.05	.01
❑ 145 Eric Andolsek	.05	.01
❑ 146 Jerry Ball	.05	.01
❑ 147 Bennie Blades	.05	.01
❑ 148 Lomas Brown	.05	.01
❑ 149 Robert Clark	.05	.01
❑ 150 Michael Cofer	.05	.01
❑ 151 Dan Owens	.05	.01
❑ 152 Rodney Peete	.10	.02
❑ 153 Wayne Fontes CO	.05	.01
❑ 154 Tim Harris	.05	.01
❑ 155 Johnny Holland	.05	.01
❑ 156 Don Majkowski	.05	.01
❑ 157 Tony Mandarich	.05	.01
❑ 158 Mark Murphy	.05	.01
❑ 159 Brian Noble	.05	.01
❑ 160 Jeff Query	.05	.01
❑ 161 Sterling Sharpe	.25	.08
❑ 162 Lindy Infante CO	.05	.01
❑ 163 Ray Childress	.05	.01
❑ 164 Ernest Givins	.10	.02
❑ 165 Richard Johnson CB	.05	.01
❑ 166 Bruce Matthews	.10	.02
❑ 167 Warren Moon	.25	.08
❑ 168 Mike Munchak	.10	.02
❑ 169 Al Smith	.05	.01
❑ 170 Lorenzo White	.05	.01
❑ 171 Jack Pardee CO	.05	.01
❑ 172 Albert Bentley	.05	.01
❑ 173 Duane Bickett	.05	.01
❑ 174 Bill Brooks	.05	.01
❑ 175A E.Dickerson w/LOGO	.40	.15
❑ 175B E.Dickerson NO LOGO 667	1.25	.50
❑ 175C E.Dickerson NO LOGO 677	.25	.08
❑ 176 Ray Donaldson	.05	.01
❑ 177 Jeff George	.25	.08
❑ 178 Jeff Herrod	.05	.01
❑ 179 Clarence Verdin	.05	.01
❑ 180 Ron Meyer CO	.05	.01
❑ 181 John Alt	.05	.01
❑ 182 Steve DeBerg	.05	.01
❑ 183 Albert Lewis	.05	.01
❑ 184 Nick Lowery UER	.05	.01
❑ 185 Christian Okoye	.05	.01
❑ 186 Stephone Paige	.05	.01
❑ 187 Kevin Porter	.05	.01
❑ 188 Derrick Thomas	.25	.08
❑ 189 Marty Schottenheimer CO	.05	.01
❑ 190 Willie Gault	.10	.02
❑ 191 Howie Long	.25	.08
❑ 192 Terry McDaniel	.05	.01
❑ 193 Jay Schroeder UER	.05	.01
❑ 194 Steve Smith	.05	.01
❑ 195 Greg Townsend	.05	.01
❑ 196 Lionel Washington	.05	.01

❑ 197 Steve Wisniewski UER .05 .01
❑ 198 Art Shell CO .10 .02
❑ 199 Henry Ellard .10 .02
❑ 200 Jim Everett .10 .02
❑ 201 Jerry Gray .05 .01
❑ 202 Kevin Greene .10 .02
❑ 203 Buford McGee .05 .01
❑ 204 Tom Newberry .05 .01
❑ 205 Frank Stams .05 .01
❑ 206 Alvin Wright .05 .01
❑ 207 John Robinson CO .05 .01
❑ 208 Jeff Cross .05 .01
❑ 209 Mark Duper .10 .02
❑ 210 Dan Marino 1.25 .50
❑ 211A Tim McKyer .10 .02
❑ 211B Tim McKyer TR .25 .08
❑ 212 John Offerdahl .05 .01
❑ 213 Sammie Smith .05 .01
❑ 214 Richmond Webb .05 .01
❑ 215 Jarvis Williams .05 .01
❑ 216 Don Shula CO .10 .02
❑ 217A D.Fullington ERR .10 .02
❑ 217B D.Fullington COR .10 .02
❑ 218 Tim Irwin .05 .01
❑ 219 Mike Merriweather .05 .01
❑ 220 Keith Millard .05 .01
❑ 221 Al Noga .05 .01
❑ 222 Henry Thomas .05 .01
❑ 223 Wade Wilson .10 .02
❑ 224 Gary Zimmerman .05 .01
❑ 225 Jerry Burns CO .05 .01
❑ 226 Bruce Armstrong .05 .01
❑ 227 Marv Cook FPSC .05 .01
❑ 228 Hart Lee Dykes .05 .01
❑ 229 Tommy Hodson .05 .01
❑ 230 Ronnie Lippett .05 .01
❑ 231 Ed Reynolds .05 .01
❑ 232 Chris Singleton .05 .01
❑ 233 John Stephens .05 .01
❑ 234 Dick MacPherson CO .05 .01
❑ 235 Stan Brock .05 .01
❑ 236 Craig Heyward .10 .02
❑ 237 Vaughan Johnson .05 .01
❑ 238 Robert Massey .05 .01
❑ 239 Brett Maxie .05 .01
❑ 240 Rueben Mayes .05 .01
❑ 241 Pat Swilling .10 .02
❑ 242 Renaldo Turnbull .05 .01
❑ 243 Jim Mora CO .05 .01
❑ 244 Kyle Clifton .05 .01
❑ 245 Jeff Criswell .05 .01
❑ 246 James Hasty .05 .01
❑ 247 Erik McMillan .05 .01
❑ 248 Scott Mersereau RC .05 .01
❑ 249 Ken O'Brien .05 .01
❑ 250A Blair Thomas w/LOGO .25 .08
❑ 250B Blair Thomas NO LOGO .10 .02
❑ 251 Al Toon .10 .02
❑ 252 Bruce Coslet CO .05 .01
❑ 253 Eric Allen .05 .01
❑ 254 Fred Barnett .25 .08
❑ 255 Keith Byars .05 .01
❑ 256 Randall Cunningham .25 .08
❑ 257 Seth Joyner .10 .02
❑ 258 Clyde Simmons .05 .01
❑ 259 Jessie Small .05 .01
❑ 260 Andre Waters .05 .01
❑ 261 Rich Kotite CO .05 .01
❑ 262 Roy Green .05 .01
❑ 263 Ernie Jones .05 .01
❑ 264 Tim McDonald .05 .01
❑ 265 Timm Rosenbach .05 .01
❑ 266 Rod Saddler .05 .01
❑ 267 Luis Sharpe .05 .01
❑ 268 Anthony Thompson UER .05 .01
❑ 269 Marcus Turner RC .05 .01
❑ 270 Joe Bugel CO .05 .01
❑ 271 Gary Anderson K .05 .01
❑ 272 Dermontti Dawson .05 .01
❑ 273 Eric Green .05 .01
❑ 274 Merril Hoge .05 .01
❑ 275 Tunch Ilkin .05 .01
❑ 276 D.J. Johnson .05 .01
❑ 277 Louis Lipps .05 .01
❑ 278 Rod Woodson .25 .08
❑ 279 Chuck Noll CO .10 .02
❑ 280 Martin Bayless .05 .01
❑ 281 Marion Butts UER .10 .02
❑ 282 Gill Byrd .05 .01
❑ 283 Burt Grossman .05 .01
❑ 284 Courtney Hall .05 .01
❑ 285 Anthony Miller .10 .02
❑ 286 Leslie O'Neal .10 .02
❑ 287 Billy Joe Tolliver .05 .01
❑ 288 Dan Henning CO .05 .01
❑ 289 Dexter Carter .05 .01
❑ 290 Michael Carter .05 .01
❑ 291 Kevin Fagan .05 .01
❑ 292 Pierce Holt .05 .01
❑ 293 Guy McIntyre .05 .01
❑ 294 Tom Rathman .05 .01
❑ 295 John Taylor .10 .02
❑ 296 Steve Young .75 .30
❑ 297 George Seifert CO .10 .02
❑ 298 Brian Blades .10 .02
❑ 299 Jeff Bryant .05 .01
❑ 300 Norm Johnson .05 .01
❑ 301 Tommy Kane .05 .01
❑ 302 Cortez Kennedy UER .25 .08
❑ 303 Bryan Millard .05 .01
❑ 304 John L. Williams .05 .01
❑ 305 David Wyman .05 .01
❑ 306A Chuck Knox CO w/LOGO .05 .01
❑ 306B Chuck Knox CO NO LOGO .50 .20
❑ 307 Gary Anderson RB .05 .01
❑ 308 Reggie Cobb .05 .01
❑ 309 Randy Grimes .05 .01
❑ 310 Harry Hamilton .05 .01
❑ 311 Bruce Hill .05 .01
❑ 312 Eugene Marve .05 .01
❑ 313 Ervin Randle .05 .01
❑ 314 Vinny Testaverde .10 .02
❑ 315 Richard Williamson CO .05 .01
❑ 316 Earnest Byner .05 .01
❑ 317 Gary Clark .25 .08
❑ 318A Andre Collins .10 .02
❑ 318B Andre Collins .10 .02
❑ 319 Darryl Grant .05 .01
❑ 320 Chip Lohmiller .05 .01
❑ 321 Martin Mayhew .05 .01
❑ 322 Mark Rypien .10 .02
❑ 323 Alvin Walton .05 .01
❑ 324 Joe Gibbs CO UER .10 .02
❑ 325 Jerry Glanville REP .05 .01
❑ 326A J.Elway REP LOGO 4.00 2.00
❑ 326B J.Elway REP NO LOGO 2.00 .75
❑ 327 Boomer Esiason REP .05 .01
❑ 328A Steve Tasker REP 4.00 2.00
❑ 328B Steve Tasker REP 2.00 .75
❑ 329 Jerry Rice REP .40 .15
❑ 330 Jeff Rutledge REP .05 .01
❑ 331 K.C. Defense REP .05 .01
❑ 332 49ers Streak REP .05 .01
❑ 333 Monday Meeting REP .05 .01
❑ 334A R.Cunningham w/LOGO .05 .01
❑ 334B R.Cunningham NO LOGO .05 .01
❑ 335A Bo/Barry REP w/LOGO .50 .20
❑ 335B Bo/Barry REP NO LOGO .50 .20
❑ 336 Lawrence Taylor REP .25 .08
❑ 337 Warren Moon REP .25 .08
❑ 338 Alan Grant REP .05 .01
❑ 339 Todd McNair REP .05 .01
❑ 340A Miami Dolphins REP .05 .01
❑ 340B Miami Dolphins REP .05 .01
❑ 341A Highest Scoring REP 4.00 2.00
❑ 341B Highest Scoring REP 2.00 .75
❑ 342 Matt Bahr REP .05 .01
❑ 343 Robert Tisch NEW .05 .01
❑ 344 Sam Jankovich NEW .05 .01
❑ 345 In-the-Grasp NEW .05 .01
❑ 346 Bo Jackson NEW .10 .02
❑ 347 NFL Teacher of the .05 .01
❑ 348 Ronnie Lott NEW .10 .02
❑ 349 Super Bowl XXV .10 .02
❑ 350 Whitney Houston RC NEW .05 .01
❑ 351 U.S. Troops in .05 .01
❑ 352 Art McNally OFF .05 .01
❑ 353 Dick Jorgensen OFF .05 .01
❑ 354 Jerry Seeman OFF .05 .01
❑ 355 Jim Tunney OFF .05 .01
❑ 356 Gerry Austin OFF .05 .01
❑ 357 Gene Barth OFF .05 .01
❑ 358 Red Cashion OFF .05 .01
❑ 359 Tom Dooley OFF .05 .01
❑ 360 Johnny Grier OFF .05 .01
❑ 361 Pat Haggerty OFF .05 .01
❑ 362 Dale Hamer OFF .05 .01
❑ 363 Dick Hantak OFF .05 .01
❑ 364 Jerry Markbreit OFF .05 .01
❑ 365 Gordon McCarter OFF .05 .01
❑ 366 Bob McElwee OFF .05 .01
❑ 367 Howard Roe OFF .05 .01
❑ 368 Tom White OFF .05 .01
❑ 369 Norm Schachter OFF .05 .01
❑ 370A Warren Moon Crack .25 .08
❑ 370B Warren Moon Crack .25 .08
❑ 371A Boomer Esiason .50 .20
❑ 371B Boomer Esiason .10 .02
❑ 372A Troy Aikman Str.ST .40 .15
❑ 372B Troy Aikman Str.LT .40 .15
❑ 373A Carl Banks .50 .20
❑ 373B Carl Banks .05 .01
❑ 374A Jim Everett .50 .20
❑ 374B Jim Everett .10 .02
❑ 375A Anth.Munoz dificul .10 .02
❑ 375B Anth.Munoz dificil .10 .02
❑ 375C Anth.Munoz large type .10 .02
❑ 375D Anth.Munoz Quedate .10 .02
❑ 376A Ray Childress 1.25 .50
❑ 376B Ray Childress .05 .01
❑ 377A Charles Mann 1.25 .50
❑ 377B Charles Mann .05 .01
❑ 378A Jackie Slater 1.25 .50
❑ 378B Jackie Slater .05 .01
❑ 379 Jerry Rice PB .40 .15
❑ 380 Andre Rison PB .10 .02
❑ 381 Jim Lachey NFC .05 .01
❑ 382 Jackie Slater NFC .05 .01
❑ 383 Randall McDaniel NFC .05 .01
❑ 384 Mark Bortz NFC .05 .01
❑ 385 Jay Hilgenberg NFC .05 .01
❑ 386 Keith Jackson NFC .05 .01
❑ 387 Joe Montana PB .50 .20
❑ 388 Barry Sanders PB .50 .20
❑ 389 Neal Anderson NFC .05 .01
❑ 390 Reggie White NFC .25 .08
❑ 391 Chris Doleman NFC .05 .01
❑ 392 Jerome Brown NFC .05 .01
❑ 393 Charles Haley NFC .05 .01
❑ 394 Lawrence Taylor PB .25 .08
❑ 395 Pepper Johnson NFC .05 .01
❑ 396 Mike Singletary NFC .10 .02
❑ 397 Darrell Green NFC .05 .01
❑ 398 Carl Lee NFC .05 .01
❑ 399 Joey Browner NFC .05 .01
❑ 400 Ronnie Lott NFC .10 .02
❑ 401 Sean Landeta NFC .05 .01
❑ 402 Morten Andersen NFC .05 .01
❑ 403 Mel Gray NFC .05 .01
❑ 404 Reyna Thompson NFC .05 .01
❑ 405 Jimmy Johnson CO NFC .10 .02
❑ 406 Andre Reed AFC .10 .02
❑ 407 Anthony Miller AFC .10 .02
❑ 408 Anthony Munoz AFC .10 .02

❑ 409 Bruce Armstrong AFC	.05	.01
❑ 410 Bruce Matthews AFC	.05	.01
❑ 411 Mike Munchak AFC	.05	.01
❑ 412 Kent Hull AFC	.05	.01
❑ 413 Rodney Holman AFC	.05	.01
❑ 414 Warren Moon PB	.25	.08
❑ 415 Thurman Thomas PB	.25	.08
❑ 416 Marion Butts AFC	.10	.02
❑ 417 Bruce Smith AFC	.10	.02
❑ 418 Greg Townsend AFC	.05	.01
❑ 419 Ray Childress AFC	.05	.01
❑ 420 Derrick Thomas PB	.25	.08
❑ 421 Leslie O'Neal AFC	.10	.02
❑ 422 John Offerdahl AFC	.05	.01
❑ 423 Shane Conlan AFC	.05	.01
❑ 424 Rod Woodson PB	.25	.08
❑ 425 Albert Lewis AFC	.05	.01
❑ 426 Steve Atwater AFC	.05	.01
❑ 427 David Fulcher AFC	.05	.01
❑ 428 Rohn Stark AFC	.05	.01
❑ 429 Nick Lowery AFC	.05	.01
❑ 430 Clarence Verdin AFC	.05	.01
❑ 431 Steve Tasker AFC	.05	.01
❑ 432 Art Shell CO AFC	.10	.02
❑ 433 Scott Case	.05	.01
❑ 434 Tory Epps UER	.05	.01
❑ 435 Mike Gann UER	.05	.01
❑ 436 Brian Jordan FPSC UER	.10	.02
❑ 437 Mike Kenn	.05	.01
❑ 438 John Rade	.05	.01
❑ 439 Andre Rison	.10	.02
❑ 440 Mike Rozier	.05	.01
❑ 441 Jessie Tuggle	.05	.01
❑ 442 Don Beebe	.05	.01
❑ 443 John Davis RC	.05	.01
❑ 444 James Lofton	.10	.02
❑ 445 Keith McKeller	.05	.01
❑ 446 Jamie Mueller	.05	.01
❑ 447 Scott Norwood	.05	.01
❑ 448 Frank Reich	.10	.02
❑ 449 Leon Seals	.05	.01
❑ 450 Leonard Smith	.05	.01
❑ 451 Neal Anderson	.10	.02
❑ 452 Trace Armstrong	.05	.01
❑ 453 Mark Bortz	.05	.01
❑ 454 Wendell Davis	.05	.01
❑ 455 Shaun Gayle	.05	.01
❑ 456 Jay Hilgenberg	.05	.01
❑ 457 Steve McMichael	.10	.02
❑ 458 Mike Singletary	.10	.02
❑ 459 Donnell Woolford	.05	.01
❑ 460 Jim Breech	.05	.01
❑ 461 Eddie Brown	.05	.01
❑ 462 Barney Bussey RC	.05	.01
❑ 463 Bruce Kozerski	.05	.01
❑ 464 Tim Krumrie	.05	.01
❑ 465 Bruce Reimers	.05	.01
❑ 466 Kevin Walker RC	.05	.01
❑ 467 Ickey Woods	.05	.01
❑ 468 Carl Zander UER	.05	.01
❑ 469 Mike Baab	.05	.01
❑ 470 Brian Brennan	.05	.01
❑ 471 Rob Burnett RC	.10	.02
❑ 472 Raymond Clayborn	.05	.01
❑ 473 Reggie Langhorne	.05	.01
❑ 474 Kevin Mack	.05	.01
❑ 475 Anthony Pleasant	.05	.01
❑ 476 Joe Morris	.05	.01
❑ 477 Dan Fike	.05	.01
❑ 478 Ray Horton	.05	.01
❑ 479 Jim Jeffcoat	.05	.01
❑ 480 Jimmie Jones	.05	.01
❑ 481 Kelvin Martin	.05	.01
❑ 482 Nate Newton	.10	.02
❑ 483 Danny Noonan	.05	.01
❑ 484 Jay Novacek	.25	.08
❑ 485 Emmitt Smith	2.50	1.00
❑ 486 James Washington RC	.05	.01

❑ 487 Simon Fletcher	.05	.01
❑ 488 Ron Holmes	.05	.01
❑ 489 Mike Horan	.05	.01
❑ 490 Vance Johnson	.05	.01
❑ 491 Keith Kartz	.05	.01
❑ 492 Greg Kragen	.05	.01
❑ 493 Ken Lanier	.05	.01
❑ 494 Warren Powers	.05	.01
❑ 495 Dennis Smith	.05	.01
❑ 496 Jeff Campbell	.05	.01
❑ 497 Ken Dallafior	.05	.01
❑ 498 Dennis Gibson	.05	.01
❑ 499 Kevin Glover	.05	.01
❑ 500 Mel Gray	.10	.02
❑ 501 Eddie Murray	.05	.01
❑ 502 Barry Sanders	1.25	.50
❑ 503 Chris Spielman	.10	.02
❑ 504 William White	.05	.01
❑ 505 Matt Brock RC	.05	.01
❑ 506 Robert Brown	.05	.01
❑ 507 LeRoy Butler	.10	.02
❑ 508 James Campen RC	.05	.01
❑ 509 Jerry Holmes	.05	.01
❑ 510 Perry Kemp	.05	.01
❑ 511 Ken Ruettgers	.05	.01
❑ 512 Scott Stephen RC	.05	.01
❑ 513 Ed West	.05	.01
❑ 514 Cris Dishman RC	.05	.01
❑ 515 Curtis Duncan	.05	.01
❑ 516 Drew Hill UER	.05	.01
❑ 517 Haywood Jeffires	.10	.02
❑ 518 Sean Jones	.10	.02
❑ 519 Lamar Lathon	.05	.01
❑ 520 Don Maggs	.05	.01
❑ 521 Bubba McDowell	.05	.01
❑ 522 Johnny Meads	.05	.01
❑ 523A Chip Banks ERR No Text	.50	.20
❑ 523B Chip Banks COR	.05	.01
❑ 524 Pat Beach	.05	.01
❑ 525 Sam Clancy	.05	.01
❑ 526 Eugene Daniel	.05	.01
❑ 527 Jon Hand	.05	.01
❑ 528 Jessie Hester	.05	.01
❑ 529A Mike Prior ERR No Text	.50	.20
❑ 529B Mike Prior COR	.05	.01
❑ 530 Keith Taylor	.05	.01
❑ 531 Donnell Thompson	.05	.01
❑ 532 Dino Hackett	.05	.01
❑ 533 David Lutz RC	.05	.01
❑ 534 Chris Martin	.05	.01
❑ 535 Kevin Ross	.05	.01
❑ 536 Dan Saleaumua	.05	.01
❑ 537 Neil Smith	.25	.08
❑ 538 Percy Snow	.05	.01
❑ 539 Robb Thomas	.05	.01
❑ 540 Barry Word	.05	.01
❑ 541 Marcus Allen	.25	.08
❑ 542 Eddie Anderson	.05	.01
❑ 543 Scott Davis	.05	.01
❑ 544 Mervyn Fernandez	.05	.01
❑ 545 Ethan Horton	.05	.01
❑ 546 Ronnie Lott	.10	.02
❑ 547 Don Mosebar	.05	.01
❑ 548 Jerry Robinson	.05	.01
❑ 549 Aaron Wallace	.05	.01
❑ 550 Flipper Anderson	.05	.01
❑ 551 Cleveland Gary	.05	.01
❑ 552 Damone Johnson RC	.05	.01
❑ 553 Duval Love RC	.05	.01
❑ 554 Irv Pankey	.05	.01
❑ 555 Mike Piel	.05	.01
❑ 556 Jackie Slater	.05	.01
❑ 557 Michael Stewart	.05	.01
❑ 558 Pat Terrell	.05	.01
❑ 559 J.B. Brown	.05	.01
❑ 560 Mark Clayton	.10	.02
❑ 561 Ferrell Edmunds	.05	.01
❑ 562 Harry Galbreath	.05	.01

❑ 563 David Griggs	.05	.01
❑ 564 Jim C. Jensen	.05	.01
❑ 565 Louis Oliver	.05	.01
❑ 566 Tony Paige	.05	.01
❑ 567 Keith Sims	.05	.01
❑ 568 Joey Browner	.05	.01
❑ 569 Anthony Carter	.10	.02
❑ 570 Chris Doleman	.05	.01
❑ 571 Rich Gannon UER	.25	.08
❑ 572 Hassan Jones	.05	.01
❑ 573 Steve Jordan	.05	.01
❑ 574 Carl Lee	.05	.01
❑ 575 Randall McDaniel	.05	.01
❑ 576 Herschel Walker	.10	.02
❑ 577 Ray Agnew	.05	.01
❑ 578 Vincent Brown	.05	.01
❑ 579 Irving Fryar	.10	.02
❑ 580 Tim Goad	.05	.01
❑ 581 Maurice Hurst	.05	.01
❑ 582 Fred Marion	.05	.01
❑ 583 Johnny Rembert	.05	.01
❑ 584 Andre Tippett	.05	.01
❑ 585 Brent Williams	.05	.01
❑ 586 Morten Andersen	.05	.01
❑ 587 Toi Cook RC	.05	.01
❑ 588 Jim Dombrowski	.05	.01
❑ 589 Dalton Hilliard	.05	.01
❑ 590 Rickey Jackson	.05	.01
❑ 591 Eric Martin	.05	.01
❑ 592 Sam Mills	.05	.01
❑ 593 Bobby Hebert	.05	.01
❑ 594 Steve Walsh	.05	.01
❑ 595 Ottis Anderson	.10	.02
❑ 596 Pepper Johnson	.05	.01
❑ 597 Bob Kratch RC	.05	.01
❑ 598 Sean Landeta	.05	.01
❑ 599 Doug Riesenberg	.05	.01
❑ 600 William Roberts	.05	.01
❑ 601 Phil Simms	.10	.02
❑ 602 Lawrence Taylor	.25	.08
❑ 603 Everson Walls	.05	.01
❑ 604 Brad Baxter	.05	.01
❑ 605 Dennis Byrd	.05	.01
❑ 606 Jeff Lageman	.05	.01
❑ 607 Pat Leahy	.05	.01
❑ 608 Rob Moore	.25	.08
❑ 609 Joe Mott	.05	.01
❑ 610 Tony Stargell	.05	.01
❑ 611 Brian Washington	.05	.01
❑ 612 Marvin Washington RC	.05	.01
❑ 613 David Alexander	.05	.01
❑ 614 Jerome Brown	.05	.01
❑ 615 Byron Evans	.05	.01
❑ 616 Ron Heller	.05	.01
❑ 617 Wes Hopkins	.05	.01
❑ 618 Keith Jackson	.10	.02
❑ 619 Heath Sherman	.05	.01
❑ 620 Reggie White	.25	.08
❑ 621 Calvin Williams	.10	.02
❑ 622 Ken Harvey	.10	.02
❑ 623 Eric Hill	.05	.01
❑ 624 Johnny Johnson	.05	.01
❑ 625 Freddie Joe Nunn	.05	.01
❑ 626 Ricky Proehl	.05	.01
❑ 627 Tootie Robbins	.05	.01
❑ 628 Jay Taylor	.05	.01
❑ 629 Tom Tupa	.05	.01
❑ 630 Jim Wahler RC	.05	.01
❑ 631 Bubby Brister	.05	.01
❑ 632 Thomas Everett	.05	.01
❑ 633 Bryan Hinkle	.05	.01
❑ 634 Carnell Lake	.05	.01
❑ 635 David Little	.05	.01
❑ 636 Hardy Nickerson	.10	.02
❑ 637 Gerald Williams	.05	.01
❑ 638 Keith Willis	.05	.01
❑ 639 Tim Worley	.05	.01
❑ 640 Rod Bernstine	.05	.01

❑ 641 Frank Cornish	.05	.01
❑ 642 Gary Plummer	.05	.01
❑ 643 Henry Rolling RC	.05	.01
❑ 644 Sam Seale	.05	.01
❑ 645 Junior Seau	.25	.08
❑ 646 Billy Ray Smith	.05	.01
❑ 647 Broderick Thompson	.05	.01
❑ 648 Derrick Walker RC	.05	.01
❑ 649 Todd Bowles	.05	.01
❑ 650 Don Griffin	.05	.01
❑ 651 Charles Haley	.10	.02
❑ 652 Brent Jones UER	.10	.02
❑ 653 Joe Montana	1.25	.50
❑ 654 Jerry Rice	.75	.30
❑ 655 Bill Romanowski	.05	.01
❑ 656 Michael Walter	.05	.01
❑ 657 Dave Waymer	.05	.01
❑ 658 Jeff Chadwick	.05	.01
❑ 659 Derrick Fenner	.05	.01
❑ 660 Nesby Glasgow	.05	.01
❑ 661 Jacob Green	.05	.01
❑ 662 Dwayne Harper RC	.05	.01
❑ 663 Andy Heck	.05	.01
❑ 664 Dave Krieg	.10	.02
❑ 665 Rufus Porter	.05	.01
❑ 666 Eugene Robinson	.05	.01
❑ 667 Mark Carrier WR	.25	.08
❑ 668 Steve Christie	.05	.01
❑ 669 Reuben Davis	.05	.01
❑ 670 Paul Gruber	.05	.01
❑ 671 Wayne Haddix	.05	.01
❑ 672 Ron Hall	.05	.01
❑ 673 Keith McCants UER	.05	.01
❑ 674 Ricky Reynolds	.05	.01
❑ 675 Mark Robinson	.05	.01
❑ 676 Jeff Bostic	.05	.01
❑ 677 Darrell Green	.05	.01
❑ 678 Markus Koch	.05	.01
❑ 679 Jim Lachey	.05	.01
❑ 680 Charles Mann	.05	.01
❑ 681 Wilber Marshall	.05	.01
❑ 682 Art Monk	.10	.02
❑ 683 Gerald Riggs	.05	.01
❑ 684 Ricky Sanders	.05	.01
❑ 685 Ray Handley NEW	.05	.01
❑ 686 NFL announces NEW	.05	.01
❑ 687 Miami gets NEW	.05	.01
❑ 688 Giants' George Young NEW	.05	.01
❑ 689 Five-millionth fan NEW	.05	.01
❑ 690 Sports Illustrated NEW	.05	.01
❑ 691 American Bowl NEW	.05	.01
❑ 692 American Bowl NEW	.05	.01
❑ 693 American Bowl NEW	.05	.01
❑ 694A Russell Maryland	.25	.08
❑ 694B Joe Ferguson LEG	.05	.01
❑ 695 Carl Hairston LEG	.10	.02
❑ 696 Dan Hampton LEG	.10	.02
❑ 697 Mike Haynes LEG	.05	.01
❑ 698 Marty Lyons LEG	.05	.01
❑ 699 Ozzie Newsome LEGEND	.10	.02
❑ 700 Scott Studwell LEG	.05	.01
❑ 701 Mike Webster LEG	.05	.01
❑ 702 Dwayne Woodruff LEG	.05	.01
❑ 703 Larry Kennan CO	.05	.01
❑ 704 Stan Gelbaugh RC LL	.10	.02
❑ 705 John Brantley LL	.05	.01
❑ 706 Danny Lockett LL	.05	.01
❑ 707 Anthony Parker RC LL	.10	.02
❑ 708 Dan Crossman LL	.05	.01
❑ 709 Eric Wilkerson LL	.05	.01
❑ 710 Judd Garrett RC LL	.05	.01
❑ 711 Tony Baker LL	.05	.01
❑ 712 Ran.Cunningham PHOTO	.05	.01
❑ 713 2nd Place BW PHOTO	.05	.01
❑ 714 3rd Place BW PHOTO	.05	.01
❑ 715 1st Place Color PHOTO	.05	.01
❑ 716 2nd Place Color PHOTO	.05	.01
❑ 717 3rd Place Color PHOTO	.05	.01

❑ 718 1st Place Color PHOTO	.05	.01
❑ 719 2nd Place Color PHOTO	.05	.01
❑ 720 3rd Place Color PHOTO	.05	.01
❑ 721 Ray Bentley	.05	.01
❑ 722 Earnest Byner	.05	.01
❑ 723 Bill Fralic	.05	.01
❑ 724 Joe Jacoby	.05	.01
❑ 725 Howie Long	.25	.08
❑ 726 Dan Marino THINK	.50	.20
❑ 727 Ron Rivera	.05	.01
❑ 728 Mike Singletary	.10	.02
❑ 729 Cornelius Bennett	.10	.02
❑ 730 Russell Maryland	.25	.08
❑ 731 Eric Turner RC	.10	.02
❑ 732 Bruce Pickens RC UER	.05	.01
❑ 733 Mike Croel RC	.05	.01
❑ 734 Todd Lyght RC	.05	.01
❑ 735 Eric Swann RC	.25	.08
❑ 736 Charles McRae RC	.05	.01
❑ 737 Antone Davis RC	.05	.01
❑ 738 Stanley Richard RC	.05	.01
❑ 739 Herman Moore RC	.25	.08
❑ 740 Pat Harlow RC	.05	.01
❑ 741 Alvin Harper RC	.25	.08
❑ 742 Mike Pritchard RC	.25	.08
❑ 743 Leonard Russell RC	.25	.08
❑ 744 Huey Richardson RC	.05	.01
❑ 745 Dan McGwire RC	.05	.01
❑ 746 Bobby Wilson RC	.05	.01
❑ 747 Alfred Williams	.05	.01
❑ 748 Vinnie Clark RC	.05	.01
❑ 749 Kelvin Pritchett RC	.10	.02
❑ 750 Harvey Williams RC	.25	.08
❑ 751 Stan Thomas	.05	.01
❑ 752 Randal Hill RC	.10	.02
❑ 753 Todd Marinovich RC	.05	.01
❑ 754 Ted Washington RC	.05	.01
❑ 755 Henry Jones RC	.10	.02
❑ 756 Jarrod Bunch RC	.05	.01
❑ 757 Mike Dumas RC	.05	.01
❑ 758 Ed King RC	.05	.01
❑ 759 Reggie Johnson RC	.05	.01
❑ 760 Roman Phifer RC	.05	.01
❑ 761 Mike Jones DE RC	.05	.01
❑ 762 Brett Favre RC	8.00	3.00
❑ 763 Browning Nagle RC	.05	.01
❑ 764 Esera Tuaolo RC	.05	.01
❑ 765 George Thornton RC	.05	.01
❑ 766 Dixon Edwards RC	.05	.01
❑ 767 Darryll Lewis	.10	.02
❑ 768 Eric Bieniemy RC	.05	.01
❑ 769 Shane Curry	.05	.01
❑ 770 Jerome Henderson RC	.05	.01
❑ 771 Wesley Carroll RC	.05	.01
❑ 772 Nick Bell RC	.05	.01
❑ 773 John Flannery RC	.05	.01
❑ 774 Ricky Watters RC	1.50	.60
❑ 775 Jeff Graham RC WR	.25	.08
❑ 776 Eric Moten RC	.05	.01
❑ 777 Jesse Campbell RC	.05	.01
❑ 778 Chris Zorich	.10	.02
❑ 779 Joe Valerio	.05	.01
❑ 780 Doug Thomas RC	.05	.01
❑ 781 Lamar Rogers RC UER	.05	.01
❑ 782 John Johnson RC	.05	.01
❑ 783 Phil Hansen RC	.05	.01
❑ 784 Kanavis McGhee RC	.05	.01
❑ 785 Calvin Stephens RC UER	.05	.01
❑ 786 James Jones RC DT	.05	.01
❑ 787 Reggie Barrett	.05	.01
❑ 788 Aeneas Williams RC	.25	.08
❑ 789 Aaron Craver RC	.05	.01
❑ 790 Keith Traylor RC	.05	.01
❑ 791 Godfrey Myles RC	.05	.01
❑ 792 Mo Lewis RC	.10	.02
❑ 793 James Richard RC	.05	.01
❑ 794 Carlos Jenkins RC	.05	.01
❑ 795 Lawrence Dawsey RC	.10	.02

❑ 796 Don Davey	.05	.01
❑ 797 Jake Reed RC	.50	.20
❑ 798 Dave McCloughan	.05	.01
❑ 799 Erik Williams RC	.10	.02
❑ 800 Steve Jackson RC	.05	.01
❑ 801 Bob Dahl	.05	.01
❑ 802 Ernie Mills RC	.10	.02
❑ 803 David Daniels RC	.05	.01
❑ 804 Rob Selby RC	.05	.01
❑ 805 Ricky Ervins RC	.10	.02
❑ 806 Tim Barnett RC	.05	.01
❑ 807 Chris Gardocki RC	.25	.08
❑ 808 Kevin Donnalley RC	.05	.01
❑ 809 Robert Wilson RC	.05	.01
❑ 810 Chuck Webb RC	.05	.01
❑ 811 Darryl Wren RC	.05	.01
❑ 812 Ed McCaffrey RC	2.00	.75
❑ 813 Shula's 300th Victory	.05	.01
❑ 814 Raiders-49ers sell	.05	.01
❑ 815 NFL International NEWS	.05	.01
❑ 816 Moe Gardner RC	.05	.01
❑ 817 Tim McKyer	.05	.01
❑ 818 Tom Waddle RC	.05	.01
❑ 819 Michael Jackson RC WR	.25	.08
❑ 820 Tony Casillas	.05	.01
❑ 821 Gaston Green	.05	.01
❑ 822 Kenny Walker RC	.05	.01
❑ 823 Willie Green RC	.05	.01
❑ 824 Erik Kramer RC	.25	.08
❑ 825 William Fuller	.10	.02
❑ 826 Allen Pinkett	.05	.01
❑ 827 Rick Venturi CO	.05	.01
❑ 828 Bill Maas	.05	.01
❑ 829 Jeff Jaeger	.05	.01
❑ 830 Robert Delpino	.05	.01
❑ 831 Mark Higgs RC	.05	.01
❑ 832 Reggie Roby	.05	.01
❑ 833 Terry Allen RC	1.50	.60
❑ 834 Cris Carter	.50	.20
❑ 835 John Randle RC	.60	.25
❑ 836 Hugh Millen RC	.05	.01
❑ 837 Jon Vaughn RC	.05	.01
❑ 838 Gill Fenerty	.05	.01
❑ 839 Floyd Turner	.05	.01
❑ 840 Irv Eatman	.05	.01
❑ 841 Lonnie Young	.05	.01
❑ 842 Jim McMahon	.10	.02
❑ 843 Randal Hill	.05	.01
❑ 844 Barry Foster FPSC	.10	.02
❑ 845 Neil O'Donnell RC	.25	.08
❑ 846 John Friesz FPSC	.25	.08
❑ 847 Broderick Thomas	.05	.01
❑ 848 Brian Mitchell	.10	.02
❑ 849 Mike Utley RC	.10	.02
❑ 850 Mike Croel ROY	.05	.01
❑ SC1 SB XXVI Theme Art	.25	.08
❑ SC3 Jim Thorpe Pioneer	.75	.30
❑ SC4 Otto Graham Pioneer	.75	.30
❑ SC5 Paul Brown Pioneer	.75	.30
❑ PSS1 Walter Payton	.50	.20
❑ PSS2 Red Grange	.50	.20
❑ MVPC25 Ottis Anderson	.25	.08
❑ AU336 L.Taylor REP AU/500	175.00	100.00
❑ AU394 L.Taylor PB AU/500	175.00	100.00
❑ AU699 O.Newsome AU/500	50.00	25.00
❑ AU824 Erik Kramer AU	50.00	25.00
❑ NNO Mini Pro Set Gazette	.25	.08
❑ NNO Pro Set Gazette	.25	.08
❑ NNO Santa Claus	.50	.20
❑ NNO Super Bowl XXV Art	.25	.08
❑ NNO Super Bowl XXV Logo	.25	.08

1991 Pro Set Platinum

❑ COMPLETE SET (315)	10.00	5.00
❑ COMP.SERIES 1 (150)	4.00	2.00
❑ COMP.SERIES 2 (165)	6.00	3.00
❑ 1 Chris Miller	.10	.02
❑ 2 Andre Rison	.25	.08

- 3 Tim Green .05 .01
- 4 Jessie Tuggle .05 .01
- 5 Thurman Thomas .25 .08
- 6 Darryl Talley .05 .01
- 7 Kent Hull .05 .01
- 8 Bruce Smith .25 .08
- 9 Shane Conlan .05 .01
- 10 Jim Harbaugh .25 .08
- 11 Neal Anderson .10 .02
- 12 Mark Bortz .05 .01
- 13 Richard Dent .10 .02
- 14 Steve McMichael .05 .01
- 15 James Brooks .05 .01
- 16 Boomer Esiason .10 .02
- 17 Tim Krumrie .05 .01
- 18 James Francis .05 .01
- 19 Lewis Billups .05 .01
- 20 Eric Metcalf .25 .08
- 21 Kevin Mack .05 .01
- 22 Clay Matthews .10 .02
- 23 Mike Johnson .05 .01
- 24 Troy Aikman .75 .30
- 25 Emmitt Smith 2.50 1.00
- 26 Daniel Stubbs .05 .01
- 27 Ken Norton .10 .02
- 28 John Elway 1.25 .50
- 29 Bobby Humphrey .05 .01
- 30 Simon Fletcher .05 .01
- 31 Karl Mecklenburg .05 .01
- 32 Rodney Peete .10 .02
- 33 Barry Sanders 1.25 .50
- 34 Michael Cofer .05 .01
- 35 Jerry Ball .05 .01
- 36 Sterling Sharpe .25 .08
- 37 Tony Mandarich .05 .01
- 38 Brian Noble .05 .01
- 39 Tim Harris .05 .01
- 40 Warren Moon .10 .02
- 41 Ernest Givins UER .10 .02
- 42 Mike Munchak .10 .02
- 43 Sean Jones .10 .02
- 44 Ray Childress .10 .02
- 45 Jeff George .25 .08
- 46 Albert Bentley .05 .01
- 47 Duane Bickett .05 .01
- 48 Steve DeBerg .10 .02
- 49 Christian Okoye .10 .02
- 50 Neil Smith .25 .08
- 51 Derrick Thomas .25 .08
- 52 Willie Gault .10 .02
- 53 Don Mosebar .05 .01
- 54 Howie Long .25 .08
- 55 Greg Townsend .05 .01
- 56 Terry McDaniel .10 .02
- 57 Jackie Slater .05 .01
- 58 Jim Everett .10 .02
- 59 Cleveland Gary .05 .01
- 60 Mike Piel .05 .01
- 61 Jerry Gray .05 .01
- 62 Dan Marino 1.25 .50
- 63 Sammie Smith .05 .01
- 64 Richmond Webb .05 .01

- ❑ 65 Louis Oliver .05 .01
- ❑ 66 Ferrell Edmunds .05 .01
- ❑ 67 Jeff Cross .05 .01
- ❑ 68 Wade Wilson .05 .01
- ❑ 69 Chris Doleman .10 .02
- ❑ 70 Joey Browner .05 .01
- ❑ 71 Keith Millard .05 .01
- ❑ 72 John Stephens .05 .01
- ❑ 73 Andre Tippett .05 .01
- ❑ 74 Brent Williams .05 .01
- ❑ 75 Craig Heyward .10 .02
- ❑ 76 Eric Martin .05 .01
- ❑ 77 Pat Swilling .10 .02
- ❑ 78 Sam Mills .10 .02
- ❑ 79 Jeff Hostetler .10 .02
- ❑ 80 Ottis Anderson .10 .02
- ❑ 81 Lawrence Taylor .25 .08
- ❑ 82 Pepper Johnson .05 .01
- ❑ 83 Blair Thomas .05 .01
- ❑ 84 Al Toon .10 .02
- ❑ 85 Ken O'Brien .05 .01
- ❑ 86 Erik McMillan .05 .01
- ❑ 87 Dennis Byrd .10 .02
- ❑ 88 Randall Cunningham .25 .08
- ❑ 89 Fred Barnett .25 .08
- ❑ 90 Seth Joyner .10 .02
- ❑ 91 Reggie White .25 .08
- ❑ 92 Timm Rosenbach .05 .01
- ❑ 93 Johnny Johnson .05 .01
- ❑ 94 Tim McDonald .05 .01
- ❑ 95 Freddie Joe Nunn .05 .01
- ❑ 96 Bubby Brister .10 .02
- ❑ 97 Gary Anderson K UER .05 .01
- ❑ 98 Merril Hoge .05 .01
- ❑ 99 Keith Willis .05 .01
- ❑ 100 Rod Woodson .25 .08
- ❑ 101 Billy Joe Tolliver .05 .01
- ❑ 102 Marion Butts .10 .02
- ❑ 103 Rod Bernstine .05 .01
- ❑ 104 Lee Williams .05 .01
- ❑ 105 Burt Grossman UER .05 .01
- ❑ 106 Tom Rathman .05 .01
- ❑ 107 John Taylor .10 .02
- ❑ 108 Michael Carter .05 .01
- ❑ 109 Guy McIntyre .05 .01
- ❑ 110 Pierce Holt .05 .01
- ❑ 111 John L. Williams .05 .01
- ❑ 112 Dave Krieg .10 .02
- ❑ 113 Bryan Millard .05 .01
- ❑ 114 Cortez Kennedy .25 .08
- ❑ 115 Derrick Fenner .05 .01
- ❑ 116 Vinny Testaverde .10 .02
- ❑ 117 Reggie Cobb .05 .01
- ❑ 118 Gary Anderson RB .05 .01
- ❑ 119 Bruce Hill .05 .01
- ❑ 120 Wayne Haddix .05 .01
- ❑ 121 Broderick Thomas .05 .01
- ❑ 122 Keith McCants .05 .01
- ❑ 123 Andre Collins .10 .02
- ❑ 124 Earnest Byner .05 .01
- ❑ 125 Jim Lachey .05 .01
- ❑ 126 Mark Rypien .10 .02
- ❑ 127 Charles Mann .05 .01
- ❑ 128 Nick Lowery .05 .01
- ❑ 129 Chip Lohmiller .05 .01
- ❑ 130 Mike Horan .05 .01
- ❑ 131 Rohn Stark .05 .01
- ❑ 132 Sean Landeta .05 .01
- ❑ 133 Clarence Verdin .05 .01
- ❑ 134 Johnny Bailey .05 .01
- ❑ 135 Herschel Walker .10 .02
- ❑ 136 Bo Jackson PP .30 .10
- ❑ 137 Dexter Carter PP .05 .01
- ❑ 138 Warren Moon PP .10 .02
- ❑ 139 Joe Montana PP 1.25 .50
- ❑ 140 Jerry Rice PP .75 .30
- ❑ 141 Deion Sanders PP .40 .15
- ❑ 142 Ronnie Lippett PP .05 .01

- ❑ 143 Terance Mathis .25 .08
- ❑ 144 Gaston Green PP .05 .01
- ❑ 145 Dean Biasucci PP .05 .01
- ❑ 146 Charles Haley PP .10 .02
- ❑ 147 Derrick Thomas PP .25 .08
- ❑ 148 Lawrence Taylor PP .10 .02
- ❑ 149 Art Shell CO PP .10 .02
- ❑ 150 Bill Parcells CO PP .10 .02
- ❑ 151 Steve Broussard .05 .01
- ❑ 152 Darion Conner .05 .01
- ❑ 153 Bill Fralic .05 .01
- ❑ 154 Mike Gann .05 .01
- ❑ 155 Tim McKyer .05 .01
- ❑ 156 Don Beebe UER .05 .01
- ❑ 157 Cornelius Bennett .10 .02
- ❑ 158 Andre Reed .25 .08
- ❑ 159 Leonard Smith .05 .01
- ❑ 160 Will Wolford .05 .01
- ❑ 161 Mark Carrier DB .10 .02
- ❑ 162 Wendell Davis .05 .01
- ❑ 163 Jay Hilgenberg .05 .01
- ❑ 164 Brad Muster .05 .01
- ❑ 165 Mike Singletary .10 .02
- ❑ 166 Eddie Brown .05 .01
- ❑ 167 David Fulcher .05 .01
- ❑ 168 Rodney Holman .05 .01
- ❑ 169 Anthony Munoz .10 .02
- ❑ 170 Craig Taylor RC .05 .01
- ❑ 171 Mike Baab .05 .01
- ❑ 172 David Grayson .05 .01
- ❑ 173 Reggie Langhorne .05 .01
- ❑ 174 Joe Morris .05 .01
- ❑ 175 Kevin Gogan RC .05 .01
- ❑ 176 Jack Del Rio .10 .02
- ❑ 177 Issiac Holt .05 .01
- ❑ 178 Michael Irvin .25 .08
- ❑ 179 Jay Novacek .25 .08
- ❑ 180 Steve Atwater .05 .01
- ❑ 181 Mark Jackson .05 .01
- ❑ 182 Ricky Nattiel .05 .01
- ❑ 183 Warren Powers .05 .01
- ❑ 184 Dennis Smith .05 .01
- ❑ 185 Bennie Blades .05 .01
- ❑ 186 Lomas Brown UER .05 .01
- ❑ 187 Robert Clark UER .05 .01
- ❑ 188 Mel Gray .10 .02
- ❑ 189 Chris Spielman .10 .02
- ❑ 190 Johnny Holland .05 .01
- ❑ 191 Don Majkowski .05 .01
- ❑ 192 Bryce Paup RC .25 .08
- ❑ 193 Darrell Thompson .05 .01
- ❑ 194 Ed West UER .05 .01
- ❑ 195 Cris Dishman RC .10 .02
- ❑ 196 Drew Hill .10 .02
- ❑ 197 Bruce Matthews .10 .02
- ❑ 198 Bubba McDowell .05 .01
- ❑ 199 Allen Pinkett .05 .01
- ❑ 200 Bill Brooks .10 .02
- ❑ 201 Jeff Herrod .05 .01
- ❑ 202 Anthony Johnson .10 .02
- ❑ 203 Mike Prior .05 .01
- ❑ 204 John Alt .05 .01
- ❑ 205 Stephone Paige .05 .01
- ❑ 206 Kevin Ross .05 .01
- ❑ 207 Dan Saleaumua .05 .01
- ❑ 208 Barry Word .05 .01
- ❑ 209 Marcus Allen .25 .08
- ❑ 210 Roger Craig .10 .02
- ❑ 211 Ronnie Lott .10 .02
- ❑ 212 Winston Moss .05 .01
- ❑ 213 Jay Schroeder .05 .01
- ❑ 214 Robert Delpino .05 .01
- ❑ 215 Henry Ellard .10 .02
- ❑ 216 Kevin Greene .10 .02
- ❑ 217 Tom Newberry .05 .01
- ❑ 218 Michael Stewart .05 .01
- ❑ 219 Mark Duper .10 .02
- ❑ 220 Mark Higgs RC .05 .01

❑ 221 John Offerdahl UER .05 .01
❑ 222 Keith Sims .05 .01
❑ 223 Anthony Carter .10 .02
❑ 224 Cris Carter .50 .20
❑ 225 Steve Jordan .05 .01
❑ 226 Randall McDaniel .05 .01
❑ 227 Al Noga .05 .01
❑ 228 Ray Agnew .05 .01
❑ 229 Bruce Armstrong .05 .01
❑ 230 Irving Fryar .10 .02
❑ 231 Greg McMurtry .05 .01
❑ 232 Chris Singleton .05 .01
❑ 233 Morten Andersen .05 .01
❑ 234 Vince Buck .05 .01
❑ 235 Gill Fenerty .05 .01
❑ 236 Rickey Jackson .10 .02
❑ 237 Vaughan Johnson .05 .01
❑ 238 Carl Banks .05 .01
❑ 239 Mark Collins .05 .01
❑ 240 Rodney Hampton .25 .08
❑ 241 Dave Meggett .10 .02
❑ 242 Bart Oates .05 .01
❑ 243 Kyle Clifton .05 .01
❑ 244 Jeff Lageman .10 .02
❑ 245 Freeman McNeil UER .10 .02
❑ 246 Rob Moore .25 .08
❑ 247 Eric Allen .05 .01
❑ 248 Keith Byars .10 .02
❑ 249 Keith Jackson .10 .02
❑ 250 Jim McMahon .10 .02
❑ 251 Andre Waters .05 .01
❑ 252 Ken Harvey .10 .02
❑ 253 Ernie Jones .05 .01
❑ 254 Luis Sharpe .05 .01
❑ 255 Anthony Thompson .05 .01
❑ 256 Tom Tupa .05 .01
❑ 257 Eric Green .10 .02
❑ 258 Barry Foster .10 .02
❑ 259 Bryan Hinkle .05 .01
❑ 260 Tunch Ilkin .05 .01
❑ 261 Louis Lipps .05 .01
❑ 262 Gill Byrd .05 .01
❑ 263 John Friesz .10 .02
❑ 264 Anthony Miller .10 .02
❑ 265 Junior Seau .25 .08
❑ 266 Ronnie Harmon .10 .02
❑ 267 Harris Barton .05 .01
❑ 268 Todd Bowles .05 .01
❑ 269 Don Griffin .05 .01
❑ 270 Bill Romanowski .05 .01
❑ 271 Steve Young .75 .30
❑ 272 Brian Blades .10 .02
❑ 273 Jacob Green .05 .01
❑ 274 Rufus Porter .05 .01
❑ 275 Eugene Robinson .05 .01
❑ 276 Mark Carrier WR .10 .02
❑ 277 Reuben Davis .05 .01
❑ 278 Paul Gruber .05 .01
❑ 279 Gary Clark .25 .08
❑ 280 Darrell Green .10 .02
❑ 281 Wilber Marshall .05 .01
❑ 282 Matt Millen .10 .02
❑ 283 Alvin Walton .05 .01
❑ 284 Joe Gibbs CO UER .10 .02
❑ 285 Don Shula CO UER .10 .02
❑ 286 Larry Brown RC DB .10 .02
❑ 287 Mike Croel RC .05 .01
❑ 288 Antone Davis RC .05 .01
❑ 289 Ricky Ervins RC UER .10 .02
❑ 290 Brett Favre RC 8.00 3.00
❑ 291 Pat Harlow RC .05 .01
❑ 292 Michael Jackson RC WR .25 .08
❑ 293 Henry Jones RC .10 .02
❑ 294 Aaron Craver RC .05 .01
❑ 295 Nick Bell RC .05 .01
❑ 296 Todd Lyght RC .10 .02
❑ 297 Todd Marinovich RC .05 .01
❑ 298 Russell Maryland RC .10 .02
❑ 299 Kanavis McGhee RC .05 .01
❑ 300 Dan McGwire RC .10 .02
❑ 301 Charles McRae RC .05 .01
❑ 302 Eric Moten RC .05 .01
❑ 303 Jerome Henderson RC .05 .01
❑ 304 Browning Nagle RC .05 .01
❑ 305 Mike Pritchard RC .25 .08
❑ 306 Stanley Richard RC .10 .02
❑ 307 Randal Hill RC .10 .02
❑ 308 Leonard Russell RC .10 .02
❑ 309 Eric Swann RC .10 .02
❑ 310 Phil Hansen RC .05 .01
❑ 311 Moe Gardner RC .05 .01
❑ 312 Jon Vaughn RC .05 .01
❑ 313 Aeneas Williams RC .25 .08
❑ 314 Alfred Williams RC .05 .01
❑ 315 Harvey Williams RC .25 .08
❑ PM1 Emmitt Smith Plat. 250.00 125.00
❑ PM2 Paul Brown Plat. 60.00 25.00

1992 Pro Set

❑ COMPLETE SET (700) 15.00 6.00
❑ COMP.SERIES 1 (400) 8.00 3.00
❑ COMP.SERIES 2 (300) 8.00 3.00
❑ 1 Mike Croel LL .04 .01
❑ 2 Thurman Thomas LL .25 .08
❑ 3 Wayne Fontes CO LL .04 .01
❑ 4 Anthony Munoz LL .10 .02
❑ 5 Steve Young LL .30 .10
❑ 6 Warren Moon LL .10 .02
❑ 7 Emmitt Smith LL .60 .25
❑ 8 Haywood Jeffires LL .04 .01
❑ 9 Marv Cook LL .04 .01
❑ 10 Michael Irvin LL .25 .08
❑ 11 Thurman Thomas LL .25 .08
❑ 12 Chip Lohmiller LL UER .04 .01
❑ 13 Barry Sanders LL .50 .20
❑ 14 Reggie Roby LL .04 .01
❑ 15 Mel Gray LL .04 .01
❑ 16 Ronnie Lott LL .10 .02
❑ 17 Pat Swilling LL .04 .01
❑ 18 Reggie White LL .10 .02
❑ 19 Haywood Jeffires ML .04 .01
❑ 20 Pat Leahy MILE .04 .01
❑ 21 James Lofton MILE .10 .02
❑ 22 Art Monk MILE .10 .02
❑ 23 Don Shula MILE .10 .02
❑ 24A Nick Lowery MILE ERR .04 .01
❑ 24B Nick Lowery MILE COR .04 .01
❑ 25 John Elway ML .50 .20
❑ 26 Chicago Bears MILE .04 .01
❑ 27 Marcus Allen MILE .10 .02
❑ 28 Terrell Buckley RC .04 .01
❑ 29 Amp Lee RC .04 .01
❑ 30 Chris Mims RC .04 .01
❑ 31 Leon Searcy RC .04 .01
❑ 32 Jimmy Smith RC 3.00 1.25
❑ 33 Siran Stacy RC .04 .01
❑ 34 Pete Gogolak INN .04 .01
❑ 35 Cheerleaders INN .04 .01
❑ 36 Houston Astrodome INN .04 .01
❑ 37 Week 1 REPLAY .04 .01
❑ 38 Week 2 REPLAY .04
❑ 39 Week 3 REPLAY .04
❑ 40 Week 4 REPLAY .04
❑ 41 Week 5 REPLAY .04
❑ 42 Week 6 REPLAY .04
❑ 43 Thurman Thomas REP .10
❑ 44 Week 8 REPLAY .04
❑ 45 Week 9 REPLAY UER .04
❑ 46 Week 10 REPLAY .04
❑ 47 Week 11 REPLAY .04
❑ 48 Week 12 REPLAY .04
❑ 49 M.Irvin/S.Beuerlein REP .10
❑ 50 Week 14 REPLAY .04
❑ 51 Week 15 REPLAY .04
❑ 52 Week 16 REPLAY .04
❑ 53 Week 17 REPLAY .04
❑ 54 AFC Wild Card REPLAY .04
❑ 55 AFC Wild Card REPLAY .04
❑ 56 NFC Wild Card REPLAY .04
❑ 57 NFC Wild Card REPLAY .04
❑ 58 AFC Divis. Playoff REPLAY .04
❑ 59 Thurman Thomas REP .10
❑ 60 Erik Kramer REP .04
❑ 61 NFC Divis. Playoff REPLAY .04
❑ 62 AFC Championship REPLAY .04
❑ 63 NFC Championship REPLAY .04
❑ 64 Super Bowl XXVI REPLAY .04
❑ 65 Super Bowl XXVI REPLAY .04
❑ 66 Super Bowl XXVI REPLAY .04
❑ 67 Super Bowl XXVI REPLAY .04
❑ 68 Super Bowl XXVI REPLAY .04
❑ 69 Thurman Thomas REP .10
❑ 70 Super Bowl XXVI REPLAY .04
❑ 71 Super Bowl XXVI REPLAY .04
❑ 72 Super Bowl XXVI REPLAY .04
❑ 73 Jeff Bostic .04
❑ 74 Earnest Byner .04
❑ 75 Gary Clark .25
❑ 76 Andre Collins .04
❑ 77 Darrell Green .04
❑ 78 Joe Jacoby .04
❑ 79 Jim Lachey .04
❑ 80 Chip Lohmiller .04
❑ 81 Charles Mann .04
❑ 82 Martin Mayhew .04
❑ 83 Matt Millen .10
❑ 84 Brian Mitchell .10
❑ 85 Art Monk .10
❑ 86 Gerald Riggs .04
❑ 87 Mark Rypien .04
❑ 88 Fred Stokes .04
❑ 89 Bobby Wilson .04
❑ 90 Joe Gibbs CO .10
❑ 91 Howard Ballard .04
❑ 92 Cornelius Bennett UER .10
❑ 93 Kenneth Davis .04
❑ 94 Al Edwards .04
❑ 95 Kent Hull .04
❑ 96 Kirby Jackson .04
❑ 97 Mark Kelso .04
❑ 98 James Lofton .10
❑ 99 Keith McKeller .04
❑ 100 Nate Odomes .04
❑ 101 Jim Ritcher .04
❑ 102 Leon Seals .04
❑ 103 Steve Tasker .10
❑ 104 Darryl Talley .04
❑ 105 Thurman Thomas .25
❑ 106 Will Wolford .04
❑ 107 Jeff Wright .04
❑ 108 Marv Levy CO .04
❑ 109 Darion Conner .04
❑ 110 Bill Fralic .04
❑ 111 Moe Gardner .04
❑ 112 Michael Haynes .10
❑ 113 Chris Miller .10
❑ 114 Erric Pegram .10
❑ 115 Bruce Pickens .04

❑ 116 Andre Rison .10 .02
❑ 117 Jerry Glanville CO .04 .01
❑ 118 Neal Anderson .04 .01
❑ 119 Trace Armstrong .04 .01
❑ 120 Wendell Davis .04 .01
❑ 121 Richard Dent .10 .02
❑ 122 Jay Hilgenberg .04 .01
❑ 123 Lemuel Stinson .04 .01
❑ 124 Stan Thomas .04 .01
❑ 125 Tom Waddle .04 .01
❑ 126 Mike Ditka CO .25 .08
❑ 127 James Brooks .10 .02
❑ 128 Eddie Brown .04 .01
❑ 129 David Fulcher .04 .01
❑ 130 Harold Green .04 .01
❑ 131 Tim Krumrie UER .04 .01
❑ 132 Anthony Munoz .10 .02
❑ 133 Craig Taylor .04 .01
❑ 134 Eric Thomas .04 .01
❑ 135 David Shula RC CO .04 .01
❑ 136 Mike Baab .04 .01
❑ 137 Brian Brennan .04 .01
❑ 138 Michael Jackson .10 .02
❑ 139 James Jones DT UER .04 .01
❑ 140 Ed King .04 .01
❑ 141 Clay Matthews .10 .02
❑ 142 Eric Metcalf .10 .02
❑ 143 Joe Morris .04 .01
❑ 144A Bill Belichick CO NPO .25 .08
❑ 144B Bill Belichick CO .25 .08
❑ 145 Steve Beuerlein .10 .02
❑ 146 Larry Brown DB .04 .01
❑ 147 Ray Horton .04 .01
❑ 148 Ken Norton .10 .02
❑ 149 Mike Saxon .04 .01
❑ 150 Emmitt Smith 1.50 .60
❑ 151 Mark Stepnoski .10 .02
❑ 152 Alexander Wright .04 .01
❑ 153 Jimmy Johnson CO .10 .02
❑ 154 Mike Croel .04 .01
❑ 155 John Elway 1.25 .50
❑ 156 Gaston Green .04 .01
❑ 157 Wymon Henderson .04 .01
❑ 158 Karl Mecklenburg UER .04 .01
❑ 159 Warren Powers .04 .01
❑ 160 Steve Sewell UER .04 .01
❑ 161 Doug Widell .04 .01
❑ 162 Dan Reeves CO .04 .01
❑ 163 Eric Andolsek .04 .01
❑ 164 Jerry Ball .04 .01
❑ 165 Bennie Blades .04 .01
❑ 166 Ray Crockett .04 .01
❑ 167 Willie Green .04 .01
❑ 168 Erik Kramer .10 .02
❑ 169 Barry Sanders 1.25 .50
❑ 170 Chris Spielman UER .04 .01
❑ 171 Wayne Fontes CO .04 .01
❑ 172 Vinnie Clark .04 .01
❑ 173 Tony Mandarich .04 .01
❑ 174 Brian Noble .04 .01
❑ 175 Bryce Paup .25 .08
❑ 176 Sterling Sharpe .25 .08
❑ 177 Darrell Thompson .04 .01
❑ 178 Esera Tuaolo UER .04 .01
❑ 179 Ed West .04 .01
❑ 180 Mike Holmgren RC CO .25 .08
❑ 181 Ray Childress .04 .01
❑ 182 Cris Dishman .04 .01
❑ 183 Curtis Duncan .04 .01
❑ 184 William Fuller .04 .01
❑ 185 Lamar Lathon .04 .01
❑ 186 Warren Moon .25 .08
❑ 187 Bo Orlando RC .04 .01
❑ 188 Lorenzo White .04 .01
❑ 189 Jack Pardee CO .04 .01
❑ 190 Chip Banks .04 .01
❑ 191 Dean Biasucci UER .04 .01
❑ 192 Bill Brooks .04 .01
❑ 193 Ray Donaldson .04 .01
❑ 194 Jeff Herrod .04 .01
❑ 195 Mike Prior .04 .01
❑ 196 Mark Vander Poel .04 .01
❑ 197 Clarence Verdin .04 .01
❑ 198 Ted Marchibroda CO .04 .01
❑ 199 John Alt .04 .01
❑ 200 Deron Cherry .04 .01
❑ 201 Steve DeBerg .04 .01
❑ 202 Nick Lowery .04 .01
❑ 203 Neil Smith .25 .08
❑ 204 Derrick Thomas .25 .08
❑ 205 Joe Valerio .04 .01
❑ 206 Barry Word .04 .01
❑ 207 M. Schottenheimer CO .04 .01
❑ 208 Marcus Allen .25 .08
❑ 209 Nick Bell .04 .01
❑ 210 Tim Brown .25 .08
❑ 211 Howie Long .25 .08
❑ 212 Ronnie Lott .10 .02
❑ 213 Todd Marinovich .04 .01
❑ 214 Greg Townsend .04 .01
❑ 215 Steve Wright .04 .01
❑ 216 Art Shell CO .10 .02
❑ 217 Flipper Anderson .04 .01
❑ 218 Robert Delpino .04 .01
❑ 219 Henry Ellard .10 .02
❑ 220 Kevin Greene .10 .02
❑ 221 Todd Lyght .04 .01
❑ 222 Tom Newberry .04 .01
❑ 223 Roman Phifer .04 .01
❑ 224 Michael Stewart .04 .01
❑ 225 Chuck Knox CO .04 .01
❑ 226 Aaron Craver .04 .01
❑ 227 Jeff Cross .04 .01
❑ 228 Mark Duper .04 .01
❑ 229 Ferrell Edmunds .04 .01
❑ 230 Jim C. Jensen .04 .01
❑ 231 Louis Oliver UER .04 .01
❑ 232 Reggie Roby .04 .01
❑ 233 Sammie Smith .04 .01
❑ 234 Don Shula CO .10 .02
❑ 235 Joey Browner .04 .01
❑ 236 Anthony Carter .10 .02
❑ 237 Chris Doleman .04 .01
❑ 238 Steve Jordan .04 .01
❑ 239 Kirk Lowdermilk .04 .01
❑ 240 Henry Thomas .04 .01
❑ 241 Herschel Walker .10 .02
❑ 242 Felix Wright .04 .01
❑ 243 Dennis Green CO RC .10 .02
❑ 244 Ray Agnew .04 .01
❑ 245 Marv Cook .04 .01
❑ 246 Irving Fryar UER .10 .02
❑ 247 Pat Harlow .04 .01
❑ 248 Hugh Millen .04 .01
❑ 249 Leonard Russell .10 .02
❑ 250 Andre Tippett .04 .01
❑ 251 Jon Vaughn .04 .01
❑ 252 Dick MacPherson CO .04 .01
❑ 253 Morten Andersen .04 .01
❑ 254 Bobby Hebert .04 .01
❑ 255 Joel Hilgenberg .04 .01
❑ 256 Vaughan Johnson .04 .01
❑ 257 Sam Mills .04 .01
❑ 258 Pat Swilling .04 .01
❑ 259 Floyd Turner .04 .01
❑ 260 Steve Walsh .04 .01
❑ 261 Jim Mora CO UER .04 .01
❑ 262 Stephen Baker .04 .01
❑ 263 Mark Collins .04 .01
❑ 264 Rodney Hampton .10 .02
❑ 265 Jeff Hostetler .10 .02
❑ 266 Erik Howard .04 .01
❑ 267 Sean Landeta .04 .01
❑ 268 Gary Reasons UER .04 .01
❑ 269 Everson Walls .04 .01
❑ 270 Ray Handley CO .04 .01
❑ 271 Louie Aguiar RC .04 .01
❑ 272 Brad Baxter .04 .01
❑ 273 Chris Burkett .04 .01
❑ 274 Irv Eatman .04 .01
❑ 275 Jeff Lageman .04 .01
❑ 276 Freeman McNeil .04 .01
❑ 277 Rob Moore .10 .02
❑ 278 Lonnie Young .04 .01
❑ 279 Bruce Coslet CO .04 .01
❑ 280 Jerome Brown .04 .01
❑ 281 Keith Byars .04 .01
❑ 282 Bruce Collie UER .04 .01
❑ 283 Keith Jackson .10 .02
❑ 284 James Joseph .04 .01
❑ 285 Seth Joyner .04 .01
❑ 286 Andre Waters .04 .01
❑ 287 Reggie White .25 .08
❑ 288 Rich Kotite CO .04 .01
❑ 289 Rich Camarillo .04 .01
❑ 290 Garth Jax .04 .01
❑ 291 Ernie Jones .04 .01
❑ 292 Tim McDonald .04 .01
❑ 293 Rod Saddler .04 .01
❑ 294 Anthony Thompson UER .04 .01
❑ 295 Tom Tupa UER .04 .01
❑ 296 Ron Wolfley .04 .01
❑ 297 Joe Bugel CO .04 .01
❑ 298 Gary Anderson K .04 .01
❑ 299 Jeff Graham .25 .08
❑ 300 Eric Green .04 .01
❑ 301 Bryan Hinkle .04 .01
❑ 302 Tunch Ilkin .04 .01
❑ 303 Louis Lipps .04 .01
❑ 304 Neil O'Donnell .10 .02
❑ 305 Rod Woodson .25 .08
❑ 306 Bill Cowher CO RC .75 .30
❑ 307 Eric Bieniemy .04 .01
❑ 308 Marion Butts .04 .01
❑ 309 John Friesz .10 .02
❑ 310 Courtney Hall .04 .01
❑ 311 Ronnie Harmon .04 .01
❑ 312 Henry Rolling .04 .01
❑ 313 Billy Ray Smith .04 .01
❑ 314 George Thornton .04 .01
❑ 315 Bobby Ross CO RC .04 .01
❑ 316 Todd Bowles .04 .01
❑ 317 Michael Carter .04 .01
❑ 318 Don Griffin .04 .01
❑ 319 Charles Haley .10 .02
❑ 320 Brent Jones .10 .02
❑ 321 John Taylor .10 .02
❑ 322 Ted Washington .04 .01
❑ 323 Steve Young .60 .25
❑ 324 George Seifert CO .10 .02
❑ 325 Brian Blades .10 .02
❑ 326 Jacob Green .04 .01
❑ 327 Patrick Hunter .04 .01
❑ 328 Tommy Kane .04 .01
❑ 329 Cortez Kennedy .10 .02
❑ 330 Dave Krieg .10 .02
❑ 331 Rufus Porter .04 .01
❑ 332 John L. Williams .04 .01
❑ 333 Tom Flores CO .04 .01
❑ 334 Gary Anderson RB .04 .01
❑ 335 Mark Carrier WR .10 .02
❑ 336 Reuben Davis .04 .01
❑ 337 Lawrence Dawsey .10 .02
❑ 338 Keith McCants UER .04 .01
❑ 339 Vinny Testaverde .10 .02
❑ 340 Broderick Thomas .04 .01
❑ 341 Robert Wilson .04 .01
❑ 342 Sam Wyche CO .04 .01
❑ 343 1991 Teacher of .04 .01
❑ 344 Owners Reject Instant .04 .01
❑ 345 NFL Experience .04 .01
❑ 346 Chuck Noll Retires .10 .02
❑ 347 Isaac Curtis .04 .01
❑ 348 Michael Irvin/D.Pearson .10 .02

❑ 349 Barry Sanders/B.Sims	.50	.20
❑ 350 Todd Marinovich/K.Stable	.04	.01
❑ 351 Leonard Russell/C.James	.10	.02
❑ 352 Bob Golic	.04	.01
❑ 353 Pat Harlow	.04	.01
❑ 354 Esera Tuaolo	.04	.01
❑ 355 Mark Schlereth RC Envir.	.04	.01
❑ 356 Trace Armstrong	.04	.01
❑ 357 Eric Bieniemy	.04	.01
❑ 358 Bill Romanowski	.04	.01
❑ 359 Irv Eatman	.04	.01
❑ 360 Jonathan Hayes	.04	.01
❑ 361 Atlanta Falcons	.04	.01
❑ 362 Chicago Bears	.04	.01
❑ 363 Dallas Cowboys	.04	.01
❑ 364 Detroit Lions	.04	.01
❑ 365 Green Bay Packers	.04	.01
❑ 366 Los Angeles Rams	.04	.01
❑ 367 Minnesota Vikings	.04	.01
❑ 368 New Orleans Saints UER	.04	.01
❑ 369 New York Giants	.04	.01
❑ 370 Philadelphia Eagles	.04	.01
❑ 371 Phoenix Cardinals	.04	.01
❑ 372 San Francisco 49ers	.04	.01
❑ 373 Tampa Bay Buccaneers	.04	.01
❑ 374 Washington Redskins	.04	.01
❑ 375 Steve Atwater PB UER	.04	.01
❑ 376 Cornelius Bennett PB	.10	.02
❑ 377 Tim Brown PB	.10	.02
❑ 378 Marion Butts PB	.04	.01
❑ 379 Ray Childress PB	.04	.01
❑ 380 Mark Clayton PB	.04	.01
❑ 381 Marv Cook PB	.04	.01
❑ 382 Cris Dishman PB	.04	.01
❑ 383 William Fuller PB	.04	.01
❑ 384 Gaston Green PB	.04	.01
❑ 385 Jeff Jaeger PB	.04	.01
❑ 386 Haywood Jeffires PB	.10	.02
❑ 387 James Lofton PB	.10	.02
❑ 388 Ronnie Lott PB	.10	.02
❑ 389 Karl Mecklenburg PB UER	.04	.01
❑ 390 Warren Moon PB	.10	.02
❑ 391 Anthony Munoz PB	.04	.01
❑ 392 Dennis Smith PB	.04	.01
❑ 393 Neil Smith PB	.10	.02
❑ 394 Darryl Talley PB	.04	.01
❑ 395 Derrick Thomas PB	.10	.02
❑ 396 Thurman Thomas PB	.10	.02
❑ 397 Greg Townsend PB	.04	.01
❑ 398 Richmond Webb PB	.04	.01
❑ 399 Rod Woodson PB	.10	.02
❑ 400 Dan Reeves CO PB	.04	.01
❑ 401 Troy Aikman PB	.40	.15
❑ 402 Eric Allen PB	.04	.01
❑ 403 Bennie Blades PB	.04	.01
❑ 404 Lomas Brown PB	.04	.01
❑ 405 Mark Carrier DB PB	.04	.01
❑ 406 Gary Clark PB	.10	.02
❑ 407 Mel Gray PB	.04	.01
❑ 408 Darrell Green PB	.04	.01
❑ 409 Michael Irvin PB	.25	.08
❑ 410 Vaughan Johnson PB	.04	.01
❑ 411 Seth Joyner PB	.04	.01
❑ 412 Jim Lachey PB	.04	.01
❑ 413 Chip Lohmiller PB	.04	.01
❑ 414 Charles Mann PB	.04	.01
❑ 415 Chris Miller PB	.10	.02
❑ 416 Sam Mills PB	.04	.01
❑ 417 Bart Oates PB	.04	.01
❑ 418 Jerry Rice PB	.40	.15
❑ 419 Andre Rison PB	.10	.02
❑ 420 Mark Rypien PB	.04	.01
❑ 421 Barry Sanders PB	.50	.20
❑ 422 Deion Sanders PB	.25	.08
❑ 423 Mark Schlereth PB	.04	.01
❑ 424 Mike Singletary PB	.04	.01
❑ 425 Emmitt Smith PB	.60	.25
❑ 426 Pat Swilling PB	.04	.01
❑ 427 Reggie White PB	.10	.02
❑ 428 Rick Bryan	.04	.01
❑ 429 Tim Green	.04	.01
❑ 430 Drew Hill	.04	.01
❑ 431 Norm Johnson	.04	.01
❑ 432 Keith Jones	.04	.01
❑ 433 Mike Pritchard	.10	.02
❑ 434 Deion Sanders	.50	.20
❑ 435 Tony Smith RC RB	.04	.01
❑ 436 Jessie Tuggle	.04	.01
❑ 437 Steve Christie	.04	.01
❑ 438 Shane Conlan	.04	.01
❑ 439 Matt Darby RC	.04	.01
❑ 440 John Fina RC	.04	.01
❑ 441 Henry Jones	.04	.01
❑ 442 Jim Kelly	.25	.08
❑ 443 Pete Metzelaars	.04	.01
❑ 444 Andre Reed	.10	.02
❑ 445 Bruce Smith	.25	.08
❑ 446 Troy Auzenne RC	.04	.01
❑ 447 Mark Carrier DB	.04	.01
❑ 448 Will Furrer RC	.04	.01
❑ 449 Jim Harbaugh	.25	.08
❑ 450 Brad Muster	.04	.01
❑ 451 Darren Lewis	.04	.01
❑ 452 Mike Singletary	.10	.02
❑ 453 Alonzo Spellman RC	.10	.02
❑ 454 Chris Zorich	.10	.02
❑ 455 Jim Breech	.04	.01
❑ 456 Boomer Esiason	.10	.02
❑ 457 Derrick Fenner	.04	.01
❑ 458 James Francis	.04	.01
❑ 459 David Klingler RC	.04	.01
❑ 460 Tim McGee	.04	.01
❑ 461 Carl Pickens RC	.25	.08
❑ 462 Alfred Williams	.04	.01
❑ 463 Darryl Williams RC	.04	.01
❑ 464 Mark Bavaro	.04	.01
❑ 465 Jay Hilgenberg	.04	.01
❑ 466 Leroy Hoard	.10	.02
❑ 467 Bernie Kosar	.10	.02
❑ 468 Michael Dean Perry	.10	.02
❑ 469 Todd Philcox RC	.04	.01
❑ 470 Patrick Rowe RC	.04	.01
❑ 471 Tommy Vardell RC	.04	.01
❑ 472 Everson Walls	.04	.01
❑ 473 Troy Aikman	.75	.30
❑ 474 Kenneth Gant RC	.04	.01
❑ 475 Charles Haley	.10	.02
❑ 476 Michael Irvin	.25	.08
❑ 477 Robert Jones RC	.04	.01
❑ 478 Russell Maryland	.04	.01
❑ 479 Jay Novacek	.10	.02
❑ 480 Kevin Smith RC DB	.04	.01
❑ 481 Tony Tolbert	.04	.01
❑ 482 Steve Atwater	.04	.01
❑ 483 Shane Dronett RC	.04	.01
❑ 484 Simon Fletcher	.04	.01
❑ 485 Greg Lewis	.04	.01
❑ 486 Tommy Maddox RC	2.00	.75
❑ 487 Shannon Sharpe	.25	.08
❑ 488 Dennis Smith	.04	.01
❑ 489 Sammie Smith	.04	.01
❑ 490 Kenny Walker	.04	.01
❑ 491 Lomas Brown	.04	.01
❑ 492 Mike Farr	.04	.01
❑ 493 Mel Gray	.10	.02
❑ 494 Jason Hanson RC	.10	.02
❑ 495 Herman Moore	.25	.08
❑ 496 Rodney Peete	.10	.02
❑ 497 Robert Porcher RC	.25	.08
❑ 498 Kelvin Pritchett	.04	.01
❑ 499 Andre Ware	.04	.01
❑ 500 Sanjay Beach RC	.04	.01
❑ 501 Edgar Bennett RC	.25	.08
❑ 502 Lewis Billups	.04	.01
❑ 503 Terrell Buckley	.04	.01
❑ 504 Ty Detmer	.25	.08
❑ 505 Brett Favre	2.50	1.25
❑ 506 Johnny Holland	.04	.01
❑ 507 Dexter McNabb RC	.04	.01
❑ 508 Vince Workman	.04	.01
❑ 509 Cody Carlson	.04	.01
❑ 510 Ernest Givins	.10	.02
❑ 511 Jerry Gray	.04	.01
❑ 512 Haywood Jeffires	.10	.02
❑ 513 Bruce Matthews	.04	.01
❑ 514 Bubba McDowell	.04	.01
❑ 515 Bucky Richardson RC	.04	.01
❑ 516 Webster Slaughter	.04	.01
❑ 517 Al Smith	.04	.01
❑ 518 Mel Agee	.04	.01
❑ 519 Ashley Ambrose RC	.25	.08
❑ 520 Kevin Call	.04	.01
❑ 521 Ken Clark	.04	.01
❑ 522 Quentin Coryatt RC	.04	.01
❑ 523 Steve Emtman RC	.04	.01
❑ 524 Jeff George	.25	.08
❑ 525 Jessie Hester	.04	.01
❑ 526 Anthony Johnson	.10	.02
❑ 527 Tim Barnett	.04	.01
❑ 528 Martin Bayless	.04	.01
❑ 529 J.J. Birden	.04	.01
❑ 530 Dale Carter RC	.10	.02
❑ 531 Dave Krieg	.10	.02
❑ 532 Albert Lewis	.04	.01
❑ 533 Nick Lowery	.04	.01
❑ 534 Christian Okoye	.04	.01
❑ 535 Harvey Williams	.25	.08
❑ 536 Aundray Bruce	.04	.01
❑ 537 Eric Dickerson	.10	.02
❑ 538 Willie Gault	.10	.02
❑ 539 Ethan Horton	.04	.01
❑ 540 Jeff Jaeger	.04	.01
❑ 541 Napoleon McCallum	.04	.01
❑ 542 Chester McGlockton RC	.10	.02
❑ 543 Steve Smith	.04	.01
❑ 544 Steve Wisniewski	.04	.01
❑ 545 Marc Boutte RC	.04	.01
❑ 546 Pat Carter	.04	.01
❑ 547 Jim Everett	.10	.02
❑ 548 Cleveland Gary	.04	.01
❑ 549 Sean Gilbert RC	.10	.02
❑ 550 Steve Israel RC	.04	.01
❑ 551 Todd Kinchen RC	.04	.01
❑ 552 Jackie Slater	.04	.01
❑ 553 Tony Zendejas	.04	.01
❑ 554 Robert Clark	.04	.01
❑ 555 Mark Clayton	.10	.02
❑ 556 Marco Coleman RC	.04	.01
❑ 557 Bryan Cox	.10	.02
❑ 558 Keith Jackson	.10	.02
❑ 559 Dan Marino	1.25	.50
❑ 560 John Offerdahl	.04	.01
❑ 561 Troy Vincent RC	.04	.01
❑ 562 Richmond Webb	.04	.01
❑ 563 Terry Allen	.25	.08
❑ 564 Cris Carter	.50	.20
❑ 565 Roger Craig	.10	.02
❑ 566 Rich Gannon	.25	.08
❑ 567 Hassan Jones	.04	.01
❑ 568 Randall McDaniel	.04	.01
❑ 569 Al Noga	.04	.01
❑ 570 Todd Scott	.04	.01
❑ 571 Van Waiters RC	.04	.01
❑ 572 Bruce Armstrong	.04	.01
❑ 573 Gene Chilton RC	.04	.01
❑ 574 Eugene Chung RC	.04	.01
❑ 575 Todd Collins RC	.04	.01
❑ 576 Hart Lee Dykes	.04	.01
❑ 577 David Howard RC	.04	.01
❑ 578 Eugene Lockhart	.04	.01
❑ 579 Greg McMurtry	.04	.01
❑ 580 Rod Smith DB RC	.04	.01
❑ 581 Gene Atkins	.04	.01
❑ 582 Vince Buck	.04	.01

❑ 583 Wesley Carroll	.04	.01
❑ 584 Jim Dombrowski	.04	.01
❑ 585 Vaughn Dunbar RC	.04	.01
❑ 586 Craig Heyward	.10	.02
❑ 587 Dalton Hilliard	.04	.01
❑ 588 Wayne Martin	.04	.01
❑ 589 Renaldo Turnbull	.04	.01
❑ 590 Carl Banks	.04	.01
❑ 591 Derek Brown RC TE	.04	.01
❑ 592 Jarrod Bunch	.04	.01
❑ 593 Mark Ingram	.04	.01
❑ 594 Ed McCaffrey	.30	.10
❑ 595 Phil Simms	.10	.02
❑ 596 Phillippi Sparks RC	.04	.01
❑ 597 Lawrence Taylor	.25	.08
❑ 598 Lewis Tillman	.04	.01
❑ 599 Kyle Clifton	.04	.01
❑ 600 Mo Lewis	.04	.01
❑ 601 Terance Mathis	.10	.02
❑ 602 Scott Mersereau	.04	.01
❑ 603 Johnny Mitchell RC	.04	.01
❑ 604 Browning Nagle	.04	.01
❑ 605 Ken O'Brien	.04	.01
❑ 606 Al Toon	.10	.02
❑ 607 Marvin Washington	.04	.01
❑ 608 Eric Allen	.04	.01
❑ 609 Fred Barnett	.25	.08
❑ 610 John Booty	.04	.01
❑ 611 Randall Cunningham	.25	.08
❑ 612 Rich Miano	.04	.01
❑ 613 Clyde Simmons	.04	.01
❑ 614 Siran Stacy	.04	.01
❑ 615 Herschel Walker	.10	.02
❑ 616 Calvin Williams	.10	.02
❑ 617 Chris Chandler	.25	.08
❑ 618 Randal Hill	.04	.01
❑ 619 Johnny Johnson	.04	.01
❑ 620 Lorenzo Lynch	.04	.01
❑ 621 Robert Massey	.04	.01
❑ 622 Ricky Proehl	.04	.01
❑ 623 Timm Rosenbach	.04	.01
❑ 624 Tony Sacca RC	.04	.01
❑ 625 Aeneas Williams UER	.10	.02
❑ 626 Bubby Brister	.04	.01
❑ 627 Barry Foster	.10	.02
❑ 628 Merril Hoge	.04	.01
❑ 629 D.J. Johnson	.04	.01
❑ 630 David Little	.04	.01
❑ 631 Greg Lloyd	.10	.02
❑ 632 Ernie Mills	.04	.01
❑ 633 Leon Searcy RC	.04	.01
❑ 634 Dwight Stone	.04	.01
❑ 635 Sam Anno RC	.04	.01
❑ 636 Burt Grossman	.04	.01
❑ 637 Stan Humphries	.25	.08
❑ 638 Nate Lewis	.04	.01
❑ 639 Anthony Miller	.10	.02
❑ 640 Chris Mims	.25	.08
❑ 641 Marquez Pope RC	.04	.01
❑ 642 Stanley Richard	.04	.01
❑ 643 Junior Seau	.25	.08
❑ 644 Brian Bollinger RC	.04	.01
❑ 645 Steve Bono RC	.25	.08
❑ 646 Dexter Carter	.04	.01
❑ 647 Dana Hall RC	.04	.01
❑ 648 Amp Lee	.04	.01
❑ 649 Joe Montana	1.25	.50
❑ 650 Tom Rathman	.04	.01
❑ 651 Jerry Rice	.75	.30
❑ 652 Ricky Watters	.25	.08
❑ 653 Robert Blackmon	.04	.01
❑ 654 John Kasay	.04	.01
❑ 655 Ronnie Lee RC	.04	.01
❑ 656 Dan McGwire	.04	.01
❑ 657 Ray Roberts RC	.04	.01
❑ 658 Kelly Stouffer	.04	.01
❑ 659 Chris Warren	.25	.08
❑ 660 Tony Woods	.04	.01

❑ 661 David Wyman	.04	.01
❑ 662 Reggie Cobb	.04	.01
❑ 663A Steve DeBerg ERR	.10	.02
❑ 663B Steve DeBerg COR	.10	.02
❑ 664 Santana Dotson RC	.10	.02
❑ 665 Willie Drewery	.04	.01
❑ 666 Paul Gruber	.04	.01
❑ 667 Ron Hall	.04	.01
❑ 668 Courtney Hawkins RC	.10	.02
❑ 669 Charles McRae	.04	.01
❑ 670 Ricky Reynolds	.04	.01
❑ 671 Monte Coleman	.04	.01
❑ 672 Brad Edwards	.04	.01
❑ 673 Jumpy Geathers UER	.04	.01
❑ 674 Kelly Goodburn	.04	.01
❑ 675 Kurt Gouveia	.04	.01
❑ 676 Chris Hakel RC	.04	.01
❑ 677 Wilber Marshall	.04	.01
❑ 678 Ricky Sanders	.04	.01
❑ 679 Mark Schlereth	.04	.01
❑ 680 Buffalo Bills	.04	.01
❑ 681 Cincinnati Bengals	.04	.01
❑ 682 Cleveland Browns	.04	.01
❑ 683 Denver Broncos	.04	.01
❑ 684 Houston Oilers	.04	.01
❑ 685 Indianapolis Colts	.04	.01
❑ 686 Tracy Simien SG	.04	.01
❑ 687 Los Angeles Raiders	.04	.01
❑ 688 Miami Dolphins	.04	.01
❑ 689 New England Patriots	.04	.01
❑ 690 New York Jets	.04	.01
❑ 691 Pittsburgh Steelers	.04	.01
❑ 692 San Diego Chargers	.04	.01
❑ 693 Seattle Seahawks	.04	.01
❑ 694 Play Smart	.04	.01
❑ 695 Hank Williams Jr. NEW	.04	.01
❑ 696 3 Brothers in NFL NEWS	.04	.01
❑ 697 Japan Bowl NEWS	.04	.01
❑ 698 Georgia Dome NEWS	.04	.01
❑ 699 Theme Art NEWS	.04	.01
❑ 700 Mark Rypien SB MVP NEW	.04	.01
❑ AU150 Emmitt Smith AU/1000	120.00	60.00
❑ AU168 Erik Kramer AU/1000	30.00	12.50
❑ NNO E.Smith Power Preview	.75	.30
❑ NNO Santa Claus	.50	.20
❑ SC5 Super Bowl XXVI Logo	.30	.10
❑ P1 Cover Card Promo	1.00	.40

1993 Pro Set

❑ COMPLETE SET (449)	15.00	6.00
❑ 1 Marco Coleman	.05	.01
❑ 2 Steve Young LL	.30	.10
❑ 3 Mike Holmgren	.10	.02
❑ 4 John Elway LL	.75	.30
❑ 5 Steve Young LL	.30	.10
❑ 6 Dan Marino LL	.75	.30
❑ 7 Emmitt Smith LL	.75	.30
❑ 8 Sterling Sharpe LL	.10	.02
❑ 9 Jay Novacek	.10	.02
❑ 10 Sterling Sharpe LL	.10	.02
❑ 11 Thurman Thomas LL	.10	.02
❑ 12 Pete Stoyanovich	.05	.01

❑ 13 Greg Montgomery	.05	.01
❑ 14 Johnny Bailey	.05	.01
❑ 15 Jon Vaughn	.05	.01
❑ 16 Audray McMillian	.05	.01
❑ 17 Clyde Simmons	.05	.01
❑ 18 Cortez Kennedy	.05	.01
❑ 19 AFC Wildcard	.05	.01
❑ 20 AFC Wildcard	.05	.01
❑ 21 NFC Wildcard	.05	.01
❑ 22 NFC Wildcard	.05	.01
❑ 23 AFC Divisional	.05	.01
❑ 24 Dan Marino REP	.75	.30
❑ 25 Troy Aikman REP	.50	.20
❑ 26 Ricky Watters REP	.10	.02
❑ 27 AFC Championship	.05	.01
❑ 28 NFC Championship	.05	.01
❑ 29 Super Bowl XXVIII Logo	.05	.01
❑ 30 Troy Aikman	.75	.30
❑ 31 Thomas Everett	.05	.01
❑ 32 Charles Haley	.10	.02
❑ 33 Alvin Harper	.10	.02
❑ 34 Michael Irvin	.25	.08
❑ 35 Robert Jones	.05	.01
❑ 36 Russell Maryland	.05	.01
❑ 37 Ken Norton	.10	.02
❑ 38 Jay Novacek	.10	.02
❑ 39 Emmitt Smith	1.50	.50
❑ 40 Darrin Smith RC	.10	.02
❑ 41 Mark Stepnoski	.05	.01
❑ 42 Kevin Williams RC WR	.25	.08
❑ 43 Daryl Johnston	.25	.08
❑ 44 Derrick Lassic RC	.05	.01
❑ 45 Don Beebe	.05	.01
❑ 46 Cornelius Bennett	.10	.02
❑ 47 Bill Brooks	.05	.01
❑ 48 Kenneth Davis	.05	.01
❑ 49 Jim Kelly	.25	.08
❑ 50 Andre Reed	.10	.02
❑ 51 Bruce Smith	.25	.08
❑ 52 Thomas Smith RC	.10	.02
❑ 53 Darryl Talley	.05	.01
❑ 54 Thurman Thomas	.25	.08
❑ 55 Russell Copeland RC	.10	.02
❑ 56 Steve Christie	.05	.01
❑ 57 Pete Metzelaars	.05	.01
❑ 58 Frank Reich	.10	.02
❑ 59 Henry Jones	.05	.01
❑ 60 Vinnie Clark	.05	.01
❑ 61 Eric Dickerson	.10	.02
❑ 62 Jumpy Geathers	.05	.01
❑ 63 Roger Harper RC	.05	.01
❑ 64 Michael Haynes	.10	.02
❑ 65 Bobby Hebert	.05	.01
❑ 66 Lincoln Kennedy RC	.05	.01
❑ 67 Chris Miller	.10	.02
❑ 68 Andre Rison	.10	.02
❑ 69 Deion Sanders	.50	.20
❑ 70 Jessie Tuggle	.05	.01
❑ 71 Ron George	.05	.01
❑ 72 Erric Pegram	.10	.02
❑ 73 Melvin Jenkins	.05	.01
❑ 74 Pierce Holt	.05	.01
❑ 75 Neal Anderson	.05	.01
❑ 76 Mark Carrier DB	.05	.01
❑ 77 Curtis Conway RC	.40	.15
❑ 78 Richard Dent	.10	.02
❑ 79 Jim Harbaugh	.25	.08
❑ 80 Craig Heyward	.10	.02
❑ 81 Darren Lewis	.05	.01
❑ 82 Alonzo Spellman	.05	.01
❑ 83 Tom Waddle	.05	.01
❑ 84 Wendell Davis	.05	.01
❑ 85 Chris Zorich	.05	.01
❑ 86 Carl Simpson RC	.05	.01
❑ 87 Chris Gedney RC	.05	.01
❑ 88 Trace Armstrong	.05	.01
❑ 89 Peter Tom Willis	.05	.01
❑ 90 John Copeland RC	.10	.02

❑ 91 Derrick Fenner .05 .01
❑ 92 James Francis .05 .01
❑ 93 Harold Green .05 .01
❑ 94 David Klingler .05 .01
❑ 95 Tim Krumrie .05 .01
❑ 96 Tony McGee RC .10 .02
❑ 97 Carl Pickens .10 .02
❑ 98 Alfred Williams .05 .01
❑ 99 Doug Pelfrey RC .05 .01
❑ 100 Lance Gunn RC .05 .01
❑ 101 Jay Schroeder .05 .01
❑ 102 Steve Tovar RC .05 .01
❑ 103 Jeff Query .05 .01
❑ 104 Ty Parten RC .05 .01
❑ 105 Jerry Ball .05 .01
❑ 106 Mark Carrier WR .10 .02
❑ 107 Rob Burnett .05 .01
❑ 108 Michael Jackson .10 .02
❑ 109 Mike Johnson .05 .01
❑ 110 Bernie Kosar .10 .02
❑ 111 Clay Matthews .10 .02
❑ 112 Eric Metcalf .10 .02
❑ 113 Michael Dean Perry .10 .02
❑ 114 Vinny Testaverde .10 .02
❑ 115 Eric Turner .05 .01
❑ 116 Tommy Vardell .05 .01
❑ 117 Leroy Hoard .10 .02
❑ 118 Steve Everitt RC .05 .01
❑ 119 Everson Walls .05 .01
❑ 120 Steve Atwater .05 .01
❑ 121 Rod Bernstine .05 .01
❑ 122 Mike Croel .05 .01
❑ 123 John Elway 1.50 .60
❑ 124 Simon Fletcher .05 .01
❑ 125 Glyn Milburn RC .25 .08
❑ 126 Reggie Rivers RC .05 .01
❑ 127 Shannon Sharpe .25 .08
❑ 128 Dennis Smith .05 .01
❑ 129 Dan Williams RC .05 .01
❑ 130 Rondell Jones RC .05 .01
❑ 131 Jason Elam RC .25 .08
❑ 132 Arthur Marshall RC .05 .01
❑ 133 Gary Zimmerman .05 .01
❑ 134 Karl Mecklenburg .05 .01
❑ 135 Bennie Blades .05 .01
❑ 136 Lomas Brown .05 .01
❑ 137 Bill Fralic .05 .01
❑ 138 Mel Gray .10 .02
❑ 139 Willie Green .05 .01
❑ 140 Ryan McNeil RC .25 .08
❑ 141 Rodney Peete .05 .01
❑ 142 Barry Sanders 1.25 .50
❑ 143 Chris Spielman .10 .02
❑ 144 Pat Swilling .05 .01
❑ 145 Andre Ware .05 .01
❑ 146 Herman Moore .25 .08
❑ 147 Tim McKyer .05 .01
❑ 148 Brett Perriman .25 .08
❑ 149 Antonio London RC .05 .01
❑ 150 Edgar Bennett .25 .08
❑ 151 Terrell Buckley .05 .01
❑ 152 Brett Favre 2.00 .75
❑ 153 Jackie Harris .05 .01
❑ 154 Johnny Holland .05 .01
❑ 155 Sterling Sharpe .25 .08
❑ 156 Tim Hauck .05 .01
❑ 157 George Teague RC .10 .02
❑ 158 Reggie White .25 .08
❑ 159 Mark Clayton .05 .01
❑ 160 Ty Detmer .25 .08
❑ 161 Wayne Simmons RC .05 .01
❑ 162 Mark Brunell RC 1.50 .60
❑ 163 Tony Bennett .05 .01
❑ 164 Brian Noble .05 .01
❑ 165 Cody Carlson .05 .01
❑ 166 Ray Childress .05 .01
❑ 167 Cris Dishman .05 .01
❑ 168 Curtis Duncan .05 .01
❑ 169 Brad Hopkins RC .05 .01
❑ 170 Haywood Jeffires .10 .02
❑ 171 Wilber Marshall .05 .01
❑ 172 Micheal Barrow RC UER .25 .08
❑ 173 Bubba McDowell .05 .01
❑ 174 Warren Moon .25 .08
❑ 175 Webster Slaughter .05 .01
❑ 176 Travis Hannah RC .05 .01
❑ 177 Lorenzo White .05 .01
❑ 178 Ernest Givins UER .10 .02
❑ 179 Keith McCants .05 .01
❑ 180 Kerry Cash .05 .01
❑ 181 Quentin Coryatt .10 .02
❑ 182 Kirk Lowdermilk .05 .01
❑ 183 Rodney Culver .05 .01
❑ 184 Rohn Stark .05 .01
❑ 185 Steve Emtman .05 .01
❑ 186 Jeff George .25 .08
❑ 187 Jeff Herrod .05 .01
❑ 188 Reggie Langhorne .05 .01
❑ 189 Roosevelt Potts RC .05 .01
❑ 190 Jack Trudeau .05 .01
❑ 191 Will Wolford .05 .01
❑ 192 Jessie Hester .05 .01
❑ 193 Anthony Johnson .10 .02
❑ 194 Ray Buchanan RC .25 .08
❑ 195 Dale Carter .05 .01
❑ 196 Willie Davis .25 .08
❑ 197 John Alt .05 .01
❑ 198 Joe Montana 1.50 .60
❑ 199 Will Shields RC .25 .08
❑ 200 Neil Smith .25 .08
❑ 201 Derrick Thomas .25 .08
❑ 202 Harvey Williams .10 .02
❑ 203 Marcus Allen .25 .08
❑ 204 J.J. Birden .05 .01
❑ 205 Tim Barnett .05 .01
❑ 206 Albert Lewis .05 .01
❑ 207 Nick Lowery .05 .01
❑ 208 Dave Krieg .10 .02
❑ 209 Keith Cash .05 .01
❑ 210 Patrick Bates RC .05 .01
❑ 211 Nick Bell .05 .01
❑ 212 Tim Brown .25 .08
❑ 213 Willie Gault .05 .01
❑ 214 Ethan Horton .05 .01
❑ 215 Jeff Hostetler .10 .02
❑ 216 Howie Long .25 .08
❑ 217 Greg Townsend .05 .01
❑ 218 Rocket Ismail .10 .02
❑ 219 Alexander Wright .05 .01
❑ 220 Greg Robinson RC .05 .01
❑ 221 Billy Joe Hobert RC .25 .08
❑ 222 Steve Wisniewski .05 .01
❑ 223 Steve Smith .05 .01
❑ 224 Vince Evans .05 .01
❑ 225 Flipper Anderson .05 .01
❑ 226 Jerome Bettis RC 4.00 1.50
❑ 227 Troy Drayton RC .10 .02
❑ 228 Henry Ellard .10 .02
❑ 229 Jim Everett .10 .02
❑ 230 Tony Zendejas .05 .01
❑ 231 Todd Lyght .05 .01
❑ 232 Todd Kinchen .05 .01
❑ 233 Jackie Slater .05 .01
❑ 234 Fred Stokes .05 .01
❑ 235 Russell White RC .10 .02
❑ 236 Cleveland Gary .05 .01
❑ 237 Sean LaChapelle RC .05 .01
❑ 238 Steve Israel .05 .01
❑ 239 Shane Conlan .05 .01
❑ 240 Keith Byars .05 .01
❑ 241 Marco Coleman .05 .01
❑ 242 Bryan Cox .05 .01
❑ 243 Irving Fryar .10 .02
❑ 244 Richmond Webb .05 .01
❑ 245 Mark Higgs .05 .01
❑ 246 Terry Kirby RC .25 .08
❑ 247 Mark Ingram .05 .01
❑ 248 John Offerdahl .05 .01
❑ 249 Keith Jackson .10 .02
❑ 250 Dan Marino 1.50 .60
❑ 251 O.J.McDuffie RC .25 .08
❑ 252 Louis Oliver .05 .01
❑ 253 Pete Stoyanovich .05 .01
❑ 254 Troy Vincent .05 .01
❑ 255 Anthony Carter .10 .02
❑ 256 Cris Carter .25 .08
❑ 257 Roger Craig .10 .02
❑ 258 Jack Del Rio .05 .01
❑ 259 Chris Doleman .05 .01
❑ 260 Barry Word .05 .01
❑ 261 Qadry Ismail RC .25 .08
❑ 262 Jim McMahon .10 .02
❑ 263 Robert Smith RC 1.25 .50
❑ 264 Fred Strickland .05 .01
❑ 265 Randall McDaniel .05 .01
❑ 266 Carl Lee .05 .01
❑ 267 Olanda Truitt RC UER .05 .01
❑ 268 Terry Allen .25 .08
❑ 269 Audray McMillian .05 .01
❑ 270 Drew Bledsoe RC 2.50 1.00
❑ 271 Eugene Chung .05 .01
❑ 272 Marv Cook .05 .01
❑ 273 Pat Harlow .05 .01
❑ 274 Greg McMurtry .05 .01
❑ 275 Leonard Russell .10 .02
❑ 276 Chris Slade RC .10 .02
❑ 277 Andre Tippett .05 .01
❑ 278 Vincent Brisby RC .25 .08
❑ 279 Ben Coates .50 .20
❑ 280 Sam Gash RC .25 .08
❑ 281 Bruce Armstrong .05 .01
❑ 282 Rod Smith DB .05 .01
❑ 283 Michael Timpson .05 .01
❑ 284 Scott Sisson RC .05 .01
❑ 285 Morten Andersen .05 .01
❑ 286 Reggie Freeman RC .05 .01
❑ 287 Dalton Hilliard .05 .01
❑ 288 Rickey Jackson .05 .01
❑ 289 Vaughan Johnson .05 .01
❑ 290 Eric Martin .05 .01
❑ 291 Sam Mills .05 .01
❑ 292 Brad Muster .05 .01
❑ 293 Willie Roaf RC .10 .02
❑ 294 Irv Smith RC .05 .01
❑ 295 Wade Wilson .05 .01
❑ 296 Derek Brown RC RBK .10 .02
❑ 297 Quinn Early .10 .02
❑ 298 Steve Walsh .05 .01
❑ 299 Renaldo Turnbull .05 .01
❑ 300 Jessie Armstead RC .10 .02
❑ 301 Carlton Bailey .05 .01
❑ 302 Michael Brooks .05 .01
❑ 303 Rodney Hampton .10 .02
❑ 304 Ed McCaffrey .25 .08
❑ 305 Dave Meggett .05 .01
❑ 306 Bart Oates .05 .01
❑ 307 Mike Sherrard .05 .01
❑ 308 Phil Simms .10 .02
❑ 309 Lawrence Taylor .25 .08
❑ 310 Mark Jackson .05 .01
❑ 311 Jarrod Bunch .05 .01
❑ 312 Howard Cross .05 .01
❑ 313 Michael Strahan RC 1.00 .40
❑ 314 Marcus Buckley RC .05 .01
❑ 315 Brad Baxter .05 .01
❑ 316 Adrian Murrell RC .25 .08
❑ 317 Boomer Esiason .10 .02
❑ 318 Johnny Johnson .05 .01
❑ 319 Marvin Jones RC .05 .01
❑ 320 Jeff Lageman .05 .01
❑ 321 Ronnie Lott .10 .02
❑ 322 Leonard Marshall .05 .01
❑ 323 Johnny Mitchell .05 .01
❑ 324 Rob Moore .10 .02

❑ 325 Browning Nagle .05 .01
❑ 326 Blair Thomas .05 .01
❑ 327 Brian Washington .05 .01
❑ 328 Terance Mathis .10 .02
❑ 329 Kyle Clifton .05 .01
❑ 330 Eric Allen .05 .01
❑ 331 Victor Bailey RC .05 .01
❑ 332 Fred Barnett .10 .02
❑ 333 Mark Bavaro .05 .01
❑ 334 Randall Cunningham .25 .08
❑ 335 Ken O'Brien .05 .01
❑ 336 Seth Joyner .05 .01
❑ 337 Leonard Renfro RC .05 .01
❑ 338 Heath Sherman .05 .01
❑ 339 Clyde Simmons .05 .01
❑ 340 Herschel Walker .10 .02
❑ 341 Calvin Williams .10 .02
❑ 342 Bubby Brister .05 .01
❑ 343 Vaughn Hebron RC .05 .01
❑ 344 Keith Millard .05 .01
❑ 345 Johnny Bailey .05 .01
❑ 346 Steve Beuerlein .10 .02
❑ 347 Chuck Cecil .05 .01
❑ 348 Larry Centers RC .25 .08
❑ 349 Chris Chandler .10 .02
❑ 350 Ernest Dye RC .05 .01
❑ 351 Garrison Hearst RC .75 .30
❑ 352 Randal Hill .05 .01
❑ 353 John Booty .05 .01
❑ 354 Gary Clark .10 .02
❑ 355 Ronald Moore RC .10 .02
❑ 356 Ricky Proehl .05 .01
❑ 357 Eric Swann .10 .02
❑ 358 Ken Harvey .05 .01
❑ 359 Ben Coleman RC .05 .01
❑ 360 Deon Figures RC .05 .01
❑ 361 Barry Foster .10 .02
❑ 362 Jeff Graham .10 .02
❑ 363 Eric Green .05 .01
❑ 364 Kevin Greene .10 .02
❑ 365 Andre Hastings RC .10 .02
❑ 366 Greg Lloyd .10 .02
❑ 367 Neil O'Donnell .25 .08
❑ 368 Dwight Stone .05 .01
❑ 369 Mike Tomczak .05 .01
❑ 370 Rod Woodson .25 .08
❑ 371 Chad Brown RC LB .10 .02
❑ 372 Ernie Mills .05 .01
❑ 373 Darren Perry .05 .01
❑ 374 Leon Searcy .05 .01
❑ 375 Marion Butts .05 .01
❑ 376 John Carney .05 .01
❑ 377 Ronnie Harmon .05 .01
❑ 378 Stan Humphries .10 .02
❑ 379 Nate Lewis .05 .01
❑ 380 Natrone Means RC .25 .08
❑ 381 Anthony Miller .10 .02
❑ 382 Chris Mims .05 .01
❑ 383 Leslie O'Neal .10 .02
❑ 384 Joe Cocozzo RC .05 .01
❑ 385 Junior Seau .25 .08
❑ 386 Jerrol Williams .05 .01
❑ 387 John Friesz .10 .02
❑ 388 Darrien Gordon RC .05 .01
❑ 389 Derrick Walker .05 .01
❑ 390 Dana Hall .05 .01
❑ 391 Brent Jones .10 .02
❑ 392 Todd Kelly RC .05 .01
❑ 393 Amp Lee .05 .01
❑ 394 Tim McDonald .05 .01
❑ 395 Jerry Rice 1.00 .40
❑ 396 Dana Stubblefield RC .25 .08
❑ 397 John Taylor .10 .02
❑ 398 Ricky Watters .25 .08
❑ 399 Steve Young .75 .30
❑ 400 Steve Bono .10 .02
❑ 401 Adrian Hardy .05 .01
❑ 402 Tom Rathman .05 .01
❑ 403 Elvis Grbac RC UER 1.50 .60
❑ 404 Bill Romanowski .05 .01
❑ 405 Brian Blades .10 .02
❑ 406 Ferrell Edmunds .05 .01
❑ 407 Carlton Gray RC .05 .01
❑ 408 Cortez Kennedy .10 .02
❑ 409 Kelvin Martin .05 .01
❑ 410 Dan McGwire .05 .01
❑ 411 Rick Mirer RC .25 .08
❑ 412 Rufus Porter .05 .01
❑ 413 Chris Warren .10 .02
❑ 414 Jon Vaughn .05 .01
❑ 415 John L. Williams .05 .01
❑ 416 Eugene Robinson .05 .01
❑ 417 Michael McCrary RC .10 .02
❑ 418 Michael Bates RC .05 .01
❑ 419 Stan Gelbaugh .05 .01
❑ 420 Reggie Cobb .05 .01
❑ 421 Eric Curry RC .05 .01
❑ 422 Lawrence Dawsey .05 .01
❑ 423 Santana Dotson .10 .02
❑ 424 Craig Erickson .10 .02
❑ 425 Ron Hall .05 .01
❑ 426 Courtney Hawkins .05 .01
❑ 427 Broderick Thomas .05 .01
❑ 428 Vince Workman .05 .01
❑ 429 Demetrius DuBose RC .05 .01
❑ 430 Lamar Thomas RC .05 .01
❑ 431 John Lynch RC .60 .25
❑ 432 Hardy Nickerson .10 .02
❑ 433 Horace Copeland RC .10 .02
❑ 434 Steve DeBerg .05 .01
❑ 435 Joe Jacoby .05 .01
❑ 436 Tom Carter RC .10 .02
❑ 437 Andre Collins .05 .01
❑ 438 Darrell Green .05 .01
❑ 439 Desmond Howard .10 .02
❑ 440 Chip Lohmiller .05 .01
❑ 441 Charles Mann .05 .01
❑ 442 Tim McGee .05 .01
❑ 443 Art Monk .10 .02
❑ 444 Mark Rypien .05 .01
❑ 445 Ricky Sanders .05 .01
❑ 446 Brian Mitchell .10 .02
❑ 447 Reggie Brooks RC .10 .02
❑ 448 Carl Banks .05 .01
❑ 449 Cary Conklin .05 .01
❑ NNO Santa Claus 1.50 .60

2000 Quantum Leaf

❑ COMPLETE SET (350) 150.00 60.00
❑ COMP.SET w/o SP's (300) 25.00 10.00
❑ COMP.ROOKIE UPDATE (31) 20.00 10.00
❑ 1 Frank Sanders .75 .30
❑ 2 Adrian Murrell .75 .30
❑ 3 Rob Moore .75 .30
❑ 4 Simeon Rice .75 .30
❑ 5 Michael Pittman .50 .20
❑ 6 Jake Plummer .75 .30
❑ 7 David Boston 1.25 .50
❑ 8 Mario Bates .50 .20
❑ 9 Chris Chandler .75 .30
❑ 10 Tim Dwight 1.25 .50
❑ 11 Chris Calloway .50 .20
❑ 12 Terance Mathis .75 .30
❑ 13 Jamal Anderson 1.25 .50
❑ 14 Byron Hanspard .50 .20
❑ 15 Ken Oxendine .50 .20
❑ 16 Tony Graziani .50 .20
❑ 17 Bob Christian .50 .20
❑ 18 Priest Holmes 1.50 .60
❑ 19 Tony Banks .75 .30
❑ 20 Patrick Johnson .50 .20
❑ 21 Rod Woodson .75 .30
❑ 22 Jermaine Lewis .50 .20
❑ 23 Errict Rhett .75 .30
❑ 24 Stoney Case .50 .20
❑ 25 Peter Boulware .50 .20
❑ 26 Qadry Ismail .75 .30
❑ 27 Brandon Stokley .75 .30
❑ 28 Andre Reed .75 .30
❑ 29 Eric Moulds 1.25 .50
❑ 30 Doug Flutie 1.25 .50
❑ 31 Bruce Smith .75 .30
❑ 32 Jay Riemersma .50 .20
❑ 33 Antowain Smith .75 .30
❑ 34 Thurman Thomas .75 .30
❑ 35 Jonathan Linton .50 .20
❑ 36 Peerless Price .75 .30
❑ 37 Rob Johnson .75 .30
❑ 38 Sam Gash .50 .20
❑ 39 Muhsin Muhammad .75 .30
❑ 40 Wesley Walls .50 .20
❑ 41 Fred Lane .50 .20
❑ 42 Kevin Greene .50 .20
❑ 43 Tim Biakabutuka .75 .30
❑ 44 Steve Beuerlein .75 .30
❑ 45 Donald Hayes .50 .20
❑ 46 Patrick Jeffers 1.25 .50
❑ 47 Curtis Enis .50 .20
❑ 48 Bobby Engram .50 .20
❑ 49 Curtis Conway .75 .30
❑ 50 Marcus Robinson 1.25 .50
❑ 51 Marty Booker .75 .30
❑ 52 Cade McNown .50 .20
❑ 53 Shane Matthews .75 .30
❑ 54 Jim Miller .50 .20
❑ 55 Darnay Scott .75 .30
❑ 56 Carl Pickens .75 .30
❑ 57 Corey Dillon 1.25 .50
❑ 58 Jeff Blake .75 .30
❑ 59 Akili Smith .50 .20
❑ 60 Michael Basnight .50 .20
❑ 61 Karim Abdul-Jabbar .75 .30
❑ 62 Tim Couch .75 .30
❑ 63 Kevin Johnson 1.25 .50
❑ 64 Terry Kirby .50 .20
❑ 65 Ty Detmer .75 .30
❑ 66 Leslie Shepherd .50 .20
❑ 67 Darrin Chiaverini .50 .20
❑ 68 Emmitt Smith 2.50 1.00
❑ 69 Deion Sanders 1.25 .50
❑ 70 Michael Irvin .75 .30
❑ 71 Rocket Ismail .75 .30
❑ 72 Troy Aikman 2.50 1.00
❑ 73 Daryl Johnston .75 .30
❑ 74 Chris Warren .50 .20
❑ 75 Jason Garrett .75 .30
❑ 76 Jason Tucker .50 .20
❑ 77 Lawyer Milloy .75 .30
❑ 78 Dexter Coakley .50 .20
❑ 79 Greg Ellis .50 .20
❑ 80 David LaFleur .50 .20
❑ 81 Todd Lyght .50 .20
❑ 82 Ernie Mills .50 .20
❑ 83 Wane McGarity .50 .20
❑ 84 Chris Brazzell RC .75 .30
❑ 85 Ed McCaffrey 1.25 .50
❑ 86 Rod Smith .75 .30
❑ 87 Shannon Sharpe .75 .30

❑ 88 Brian Griese 1.25 .50
❑ 89 John Elway 4.00 1.50
❑ 90 Neil Smith .75 .30
❑ 91 Terrell Davis 1.25 .50
❑ 92 Olandis Gary 1.25 .50
❑ 93 Derek Loville .50 .20
❑ 94 John Avery .50 .20
❑ 95 Bubby Brister .50 .20
❑ 96 Byron Chamberlain .50 .20
❑ 97 Dale Carter .50 .20
❑ 98 Johnnie Morton .75 .30
❑ 99 Charlie Batch 1.25 .50
❑ 100 Barry Sanders 3.00 1.25
❑ 101 Germane Crowell .50 .20
❑ 102 Gus Frerotte .50 .20
❑ 103 Desmond Howard .50 .20
❑ 104 Terry Fair .50 .20
❑ 105 Ron Rivers .50 .20
❑ 106 Greg Hill .50 .20
❑ 107 Sedrick Irvin .50 .20
❑ 108 David Sloan .50 .20
❑ 109 Herman Moore .75 .30
❑ 110 Robert Porcher .50 .20
❑ 111 Corey Bradford .75 .30
❑ 112 Dorsey Levens .75 .30
❑ 113 Antonio Freeman 1.25 .50
❑ 114 Brett Favre 4.00 1.50
❑ 115 De'Mond Parker .50 .20
❑ 116 Bill Schroeder .75 .30
❑ 117 Matt Hasselbeck .75 .30
❑ 118 Donald Driver 1.25 .50
❑ 119 Basil Mitchell .50 .20
❑ 120 E.G. Green .50 .20
❑ 121 Ken Dilger .50 .20
❑ 122 Marvin Harrison 1.25 .50
❑ 123 Peyton Manning 3.00 1.25
❑ 124 Terrence Wilkins .50 .20
❑ 125 Edgerrin James 2.00 .75
❑ 126 Jerome Pathon .75 .30
❑ 127 Marcus Pollard .50 .20
❑ 128 Keenan McCardell .75 .30
❑ 129 Mark Brunell 1.25 .50
❑ 130 Fred Taylor 1.25 .50
❑ 131 Jimmy Smith .75 .30
❑ 132 James Stewart .75 .30
❑ 133 Kyle Brady .50 .20
❑ 134 Tony Brackens .50 .20
❑ 135 Derrick Thomas 1.25 .50
❑ 136 Rashaan Shehee .50 .20
❑ 137 Derrick Alexander .75 .30
❑ 138 Bam Morris .50 .20
❑ 139 Andre Rison .75 .30
❑ 140 Elvis Grbac .75 .30
❑ 141 Tony Gonzalez .75 .30
❑ 142 Donnell Bennett .50 .20
❑ 143 Warren Moon 1.25 .50
❑ 144 Tamarick Vanover .50 .20
❑ 145 Kimble Anders .50 .20
❑ 146 Tony Richardson RC .75 .30
❑ 147 Zach Thomas 1.25 .50
❑ 148 Oronde Gadsden .75 .30
❑ 149 Dan Marino 4.00 1.50
❑ 150 O.J. McDuffie .75 .30
❑ 151 Tony Martin .75 .30
❑ 152 Cecil Collins .50 .20
❑ 153 James Johnson .50 .20
❑ 154 Rob Konrad .50 .20
❑ 155 Yatil Green .50 .20
❑ 156 Damon Huard 1.25 .50
❑ 157 Nate Jacquet .50 .20
❑ 158 Stanley Pritchett .50 .20
❑ 159 Sam Madison .50 .20
❑ 160 Randy Moss 2.50 1.00
❑ 161 Cris Carter 1.25 .50
❑ 162 Robert Smith 1.25 .50
❑ 163 Randall Cunningham 1.25 .50
❑ 164 Jake Reed .75 .30
❑ 165 John Randle .75 .30
❑ 166 Leroy Hoard .50 .20
❑ 167 Jeff George .75 .30
❑ 168 Daunte Culpepper 1.50 .60
❑ 169 Matthew Hatchette .50 .20
❑ 170 Robert Tate .50 .20
❑ 171 Ty Law .75 .30
❑ 172 Troy Brown .75 .30
❑ 173 Tony Simmons .50 .20
❑ 174 Terry Glenn .75 .30
❑ 175 Ben Coates .50 .20
❑ 176 Drew Bledsoe 1.50 .60
❑ 177 Terry Allen .75 .30
❑ 178 Kevin Faulk .75 .30
❑ 179 Shawn Jefferson .50 .20
❑ 180 Andy Katzenmoyer .50 .20
❑ 181 Willie McGinest .50 .20
❑ 182 Cameron Cleeland .50 .20
❑ 183 Eddie Kennison .75 .30
❑ 184 Ricky Williams 1.25 .50
❑ 185 Danny Wuerffel .50 .20
❑ 186 Brett Bech .50 .20
❑ 187 Billy Joe Hobert .50 .20
❑ 188 Jake Delhomme RC 5.00 2.00
❑ 189 Wilmont Perry .50 .20
❑ 190 Keith Poole .50 .20
❑ 191 Ashley Ambrose .50 .20
❑ 192 Amani Toomer .50 .20
❑ 193 Kerry Collins .75 .30
❑ 194 Tiki Barber 1.25 .50
❑ 195 Ike Hilliard .75 .30
❑ 196 Jason Sehorn .50 .20
❑ 197 Joe Montgomery .50 .20
❑ 198 Joe Jurevicius .50 .20
❑ 199 Michael Strahan .75 .30
❑ 200 Sean Bennett .50 .20
❑ 201 Jessie Armstead .50 .20
❑ 202 Pete Mitchell .50 .20
❑ 203 Curtis Martin 1.25 .50
❑ 204 Vinny Testaverde .75 .30
❑ 205 Keyshawn Johnson 1.25 .50
❑ 206 Wayne Chrebet .75 .30
❑ 207 Ray Lucas .75 .30
❑ 208 Tyrone Wheatley .75 .30
❑ 209 Napoleon Kaufman .75 .30
❑ 210 Tim Brown 1.25 .50
❑ 211 Rickey Dudley .50 .20
❑ 212 James Jett .50 .20
❑ 213 Rich Gannon 1.25 .50
❑ 214 Charles Woodson .75 .30
❑ 215 Zack Crockett .50 .20
❑ 216 Darrell Russell .50 .20
❑ 217 Duce Staley 1.25 .50
❑ 218 Donovan McNabb 2.00 .75
❑ 219 Charles Johnson .75 .30
❑ 220 Dameane Douglas .50 .20
❑ 221 Doug Pederson .50 .20
❑ 222 Torrance Small .50 .20
❑ 223 Troy Vincent .50 .20
❑ 224 Na Brown .50 .20
❑ 225 Kordell Stewart .75 .30
❑ 226 Jerome Bettis 1.25 .50
❑ 227 Hines Ward 1.25 .50
❑ 228 Troy Edwards .50 .20
❑ 229 Richard Huntley .50 .20
❑ 230 Mark Bruener .50 .20
❑ 231 Pete Gonzalez .50 .20
❑ 232 Levon Kirkland .50 .20
❑ 233 Bobby Shaw RC 1.25 .50
❑ 234 Amos Zereoue 1.25 .50
❑ 235 Natrone Means .50 .20
❑ 236 Junior Seau 1.25 .50
❑ 237 Jim Harbaugh .75 .30
❑ 238 Ryan Leaf .75 .30
❑ 239 Mikhael Ricks .50 .20
❑ 240 Jermaine Fazande .50 .20
❑ 241 Jeff Graham .50 .20
❑ 242 Tremayne Stephens .50 .20
❑ 243 Terrell Owens 1.25 .50
❑ 244 J.J. Stokes .75 .30
❑ 245 Charlie Garner .75 .30
❑ 246 Jerry Rice 2.50 1.00
❑ 247 Garrison Hearst .75 .30
❑ 248 Steve Young 1.50 .60
❑ 249 Jeff Garcia 1.25 .50
❑ 250 Fred Beasley .50 .20
❑ 251 Bryant Young .50 .20
❑ 252 Derrick Mayes .75 .30
❑ 253 Ahman Green 1.25 .50
❑ 254 Joey Galloway .75 .30
❑ 255 Ricky Watters .75 .30
❑ 256 Jon Kitna 1.25 .50
❑ 257 Sean Dawkins .50 .20
❑ 258 Sam Adams .50 .20
❑ 259 Christian Fauria .50 .20
❑ 260 Shawn Springs .50 .20
❑ 261 Az-Zahir Hakim .75 .30
❑ 262 Isaac Bruce 1.25 .50
❑ 263 Marshall Faulk 1.50 .60
❑ 264 Trent Green 1.25 .50
❑ 265 Kurt Warner 2.50 1.00
❑ 266 Torry Holt 1.25 .50
❑ 267 Robert Holcombe .50 .20
❑ 268 Kevin Carter .50 .20
❑ 269 Amp Lee .50 .20
❑ 270 Roland Williams .50 .20
❑ 271 Jacquez Green .50 .20
❑ 272 Reidel Anthony .50 .20
❑ 273 Warren Sapp .75 .30
❑ 274 Mike Alstott 1.25 .50
❑ 275 Warrick Dunn 1.25 .50
❑ 276 Trent Dilfer .75 .30
❑ 277 Shaun King .50 .20
❑ 278 Bert Emanuel .50 .20
❑ 279 Eric Zeier .50 .20
❑ 280 Neil O'Donnell .50 .20
❑ 281 Eddie George 1.25 .50
❑ 282 Yancey Thigpen .50 .20
❑ 283 Steve McNair 1.25 .50
❑ 284 Kevin Dyson .75 .30
❑ 285 Frank Wycheck .50 .20
❑ 286 Jevon Kearse 1.25 .50
❑ 287 Bruce Matthews .50 .20
❑ 288 Lorenzo Neal .50 .20
❑ 289 Stephen Davis 1.25 .50
❑ 290 Stephen Alexander .50 .20
❑ 291 Darrell Green .50 .20
❑ 292 Skip Hicks .50 .20
❑ 293 Brad Johnson 1.25 .50
❑ 294 Michael Westbrook .75 .30
❑ 295 Albert Connell .50 .20
❑ 296 Irving Fryar .75 .30
❑ 297 Champ Bailey .75 .30
❑ 298 Larry Centers .50 .20
❑ 299 Brian Mitchell .50 .20
❑ 300 James Thrash 1.25 .50
❑ 301 LaVar Arrington RC 10.00 5.00
❑ 302 Peter Warrick RC 2.50 1.00
❑ 303 Courtney Brown RC 2.50 1.00
❑ 304 Plaxico Burress RC 5.00 2.00
❑ 305 Corey Simon RC 2.50 1.00
❑ 306 Thomas Jones RC 4.00 1.50
❑ 307 Travis Taylor RC 2.50 1.00
❑ 308 Shaun Alexander RC 12.00 5.00
❑ 309 Chris Redman RC 2.00 .75
❑ 310 Chad Pennington RC 6.00 2.50
❑ 311 Jamal Lewis RC 6.00 2.50
❑ 312 Brian Urlacher RC 10.00 4.00
❑ 313 Keith Bulluck RC 2.50 1.00
❑ 314 Bubba Franks RC 2.50 1.00
❑ 315 Dez White RC 2.50 1.00
❑ 316 Ahmed Plummer RC 2.50 1.00
❑ 317 Ron Dayne RC 2.50 1.00
❑ 318 Shaun Ellis RC 2.50 1.00
❑ 319 Sylvester Morris RC 2.00 .75
❑ 320 Deltha O'Neal RC 2.50 1.00
❑ 321 R.Jay Soward RC 2.00 .75

- ❑ 322 Sherrod Gideon RC 1.50 .60
- ❑ 323 John Abraham RC 2.50 1.00
- ❑ 324 Travis Prentice RC 2.00 .75
- ❑ 325 Darrell Jackson RC 5.00 2.00
- ❑ 326 Giovanni Carmazzi RC 1.50 .60
- ❑ 327 Anthony Lucas RC 1.50 .60
- ❑ 328 Danny Farmer RC 2.00 .75
- ❑ 329 Dennis Northcutt RC 2.50 1.00
- ❑ 330 Troy Walters RC 2.50 1.00
- ❑ 331 Laveranues Coles RC 3.00 1.25
- ❑ 332 Tee Martin RC 2.50 1.00
- ❑ 333 J.R. Redmond RC 2.00 .75
- ❑ 334 Jerry Porter RC 3.00 1.25
- ❑ 335 Sebastian Janikowski RC 2.00 .75
- ❑ 336 Michael Wiley RC 2.00 .75
- ❑ 337 Reuben Droughns RC 2.00 .75
- ❑ 338 Trung Canidate RC 2.00 .75
- ❑ 339 Shyrone Stith RC 1.50 .60
- ❑ 340 Trevor Gaylor RC 1.50 .60
- ❑ 341 Rob Morris RC 2.50 1.00
- ❑ 342 Marc Bulger RC 5.00 2.00
- ❑ 343 Tom Brady RC 25.00 12.50
- ❑ 344 Todd Husak RC 2.50 1.00
- ❑ 345 Gari Scott RC 1.50 .60
- ❑ 346 Erron Kinney RC 2.50 1.00
- ❑ 347 Julian Peterson RC 2.50 1.00
- ❑ 348 Doug Chapman RC 2.00 .75
- ❑ 349 Ron Dugans RC 1.50 .60
- ❑ 350 Todd Pinkston RC 2.50 1.00
- ❑ 351 Deon Grant RC 1.25 .50
- ❑ 352 Na'il Diggs RC 1.25 .50
- ❑ 353 Raynoch Thompson RC 1.25 .50
- ❑ 354 Mario Edwards RC 1.25 .50
- ❑ 355 John Engelberger RC 1.25 .50
- ❑ 356 Dwayne Goodrich RC .75 .30
- ❑ 357 Ben Kelly RC .75 .30
- ❑ 358 Sekou Sanyika RC .75 .30
- ❑ 359 Brandon Short RC 1.25 .50
- ❑ 360 Jabari Issa RC .75 .30
- ❑ 361 Darwin Walker RC .75 .30
- ❑ 362 Jerry Johnson RC .75 .30
- ❑ 363 Robaire Smith RC .75 .30
- ❑ 364 Mark Roman RC 1.25 .50
- ❑ 365 Leonardo Carson RC .75 .30
- ❑ 366 Mark Simoneau RC 1.25 .50
- ❑ 367 Hank Poteat RC 1.25 .50
- ❑ 368 Darren Howard RC 1.25 .50
- ❑ 369 David Macklin RC .75 .30
- ❑ 370 Adalius Thomas RC 1.25 .50
- ❑ 371 Ralph Brown RC .75 .30
- ❑ 372 Mondriel Fulcher RC .75 .30
- ❑ 373 Sammy Morris RC 1.25 .50
- ❑ 374 Rondell Mealey RC .75 .30
- ❑ 375 Deon Dyer RC 1.25 .50
- ❑ 376 Mareno Philyaw RC .75 .30
- ❑ 377 Thomas Hamner RC .75 .30
- ❑ 378 Jarious Jackson RC 1.25 .50
- ❑ 379 Joe Hamilton RC 1.25 .50
- ❑ 380 Tim Rattay RC 2.00 .75
- ❑ 381 Chris Hovan RC 1.25 .50
- ❑ SB1 Kurt Warner MVP/1000 8.00 3.00
- ❑ SB1A Kurt Warner MVP AU/100 80.00 30.00
- ❑ NFL1 Kurt Warner MVP/1000 8.00 3.00
- ❑ NFL1A Kurt Warner MVP AU/100 80.00 30.00
- ❑ QLP10 Dan Marino Promo 3.00 1.50

2001 Quantum Leaf

- ❑ COMP.SET w/o SP's (200) 25.00 10.00
- ❑ COMP.ROOKIE UPDATE (36) 20.00 7.50
- ❑ 1 David Boston 1.00 .40
- ❑ 2 Frank Sanders .40 .15
- ❑ 3 Jake Plummer .60 .25
- ❑ 4 Michael Pittman .40 .15
- ❑ 5 Rob Moore .60 .25
- ❑ 6 Thomas Jones .60 .25
- ❑ 7 Chris Chandler .60 .25
- ❑ 8 Doug Johnson .40 .15

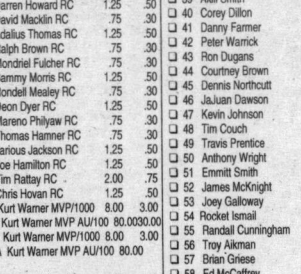

- ❑ 9 Jamal Anderson 1.00 .40
- ❑ 10 Tim Dwight 1.00 .40
- ❑ 11 Chris Redman .40 .15
- ❑ 12 Jamal Lewis 1.50 .60
- ❑ 13 Qadry Ismail .60 .25
- ❑ 14 Ray Lewis 1.00 .40
- ❑ 15 Rod Woodson .60 .25
- ❑ 16 Shannon Sharpe .60 .25
- ❑ 17 Travis Taylor .60 .25
- ❑ 18 Trent Dilfer .60 .25
- ❑ 19 Doug Flutie 1.00 .40
- ❑ 20 Eric Moulds .60 .25
- ❑ 21 Jay Riemersma .40 .15
- ❑ 22 Peerless Price .60 .25
- ❑ 23 Rob Johnson .60 .25
- ❑ 24 Sammy Morris .40 .15
- ❑ 25 Shawn Bryson .40 .15
- ❑ 26 Donald Hayes .40 .15
- ❑ 27 Muhsin Muhammad .60 .25
- ❑ 28 Patrick Jeffers .60 .25
- ❑ 29 Reggie White DE .60 .25
- ❑ 30 Steve Beuerlein .60 .25
- ❑ 31 Tim Biakabutuka .60 .25
- ❑ 32 Wesley Walls .40 .15
- ❑ 33 Brian Urlacher 1.50 .60
- ❑ 34 Cade McNown .40 .15
- ❑ 35 Dez White .40 .15
- ❑ 36 James Allen .60 .25
- ❑ 37 Marcus Robinson 1.00 .40
- ❑ 38 Marty Booker .40 .15
- ❑ 39 Akili Smith .40 .15
- ❑ 40 Corey Dillon 1.00 .40
- ❑ 41 Danny Farmer .40 .15
- ❑ 42 Peter Warrick 1.00 .40
- ❑ 43 Ron Dugans .40 .15
- ❑ 44 Courtney Brown .60 .25
- ❑ 45 Dennis Northcutt .60 .25
- ❑ 46 JaJuan Dawson .40 .15
- ❑ 47 Kevin Johnson .60 .25
- ❑ 48 Tim Couch .60 .25
- ❑ 49 Travis Prentice .40 .15
- ❑ 50 Anthony Wright .40 .15
- ❑ 51 Emmitt Smith 2.00 .75
- ❑ 52 James McKnight .60 .25
- ❑ 53 Joey Galloway .60 .25
- ❑ 54 Rocket Ismail .60 .25
- ❑ 55 Randall Cunningham 1.00 .40
- ❑ 56 Troy Aikman 1.50 .60
- ❑ 57 Brian Griese 1.00 .40
- ❑ 58 Ed McCaffrey 1.00 .40
- ❑ 59 Gus Frerotte .40 .15
- ❑ 60 John Elway 3.00 1.25
- ❑ 61 Mike Anderson 1.00 .40
- ❑ 62 Olandis Gary .60 .25
- ❑ 63 Rod Smith .60 .25
- ❑ 64 Terrell Davis 1.00 .40
- ❑ 65 Barry Sanders 2.00 .75
- ❑ 66 Charlie Batch 1.00 .40
- ❑ 67 Germane Crowell .40 .15
- ❑ 68 Herman Moore .60 .25
- ❑ 69 James Stewart .60 .25
- ❑ 70 Johnnie Morton .60 .25
- ❑ 71 Ahman Green 1.00 .40
- ❑ 72 Antonio Freeman 1.00 .40
- ❑ 73 Bill Schroeder .60 .25
- ❑ 74 Brett Favre 3.00 1.25
- ❑ 75 Dorsey Levens .60 .25
- ❑ 76 Matt Hasselbeck .60 .25
- ❑ 77 Edgerrin James 1.25 .50
- ❑ 78 Jerome Pathon .60 .25
- ❑ 79 Ken Dilger .40 .15
- ❑ 80 Marvin Harrison 1.00 .40
- ❑ 81 Peyton Manning 2.50 1.00
- ❑ 82 Fred Taylor 1.00 .40
- ❑ 83 Hardy Nickerson .40 .15
- ❑ 84 Jimmy Smith .60 .25
- ❑ 85 Keenan McCardell .40 .15
- ❑ 86 Mark Brunell 1.00 .40
- ❑ 87 Tony Brackens .40 .15
- ❑ 88 Derrick Alexander .60 .25
- ❑ 89 Elvis Grbac .60 .25
- ❑ 90 Sylvester Morris .40 .15
- ❑ 91 Tony Gonzalez .60 .25
- ❑ 92 Tony Richardson .40 .15
- ❑ 93 Warren Moon .60 .25
- ❑ 94 Dan Marino 3.00 1.25
- ❑ 95 Jay Fiedler 1.00 .40
- ❑ 96 Lamar Smith .60 .25
- ❑ 97 Oronde Gadsden .60 .25
- ❑ 98 Sam Madison .40 .15
- ❑ 99 Thurman Thomas .40 .15
- ❑ 100 Tony Martin .60 .25
- ❑ 101 Zach Thomas 1.00 .40
- ❑ 102 Cris Carter 1.00 .40
- ❑ 103 Daunte Culpepper 1.00 .40
- ❑ 104 John Randle .60 .25
- ❑ 105 Randy Moss 2.00 .75
- ❑ 106 Robert Smith .60 .25
- ❑ 107 Drew Bledsoe 1.25 .50
- ❑ 108 J.R. Redmond .40 .15
- ❑ 109 Kevin Faulk .60 .25
- ❑ 110 Michael Bishop .40 .15
- ❑ 111 Terry Glenn .60 .25
- ❑ 112 Troy Brown .60 .25
- ❑ 113 Aaron Brooks 1.00 .40
- ❑ 114 Jake Reed .60 .25
- ❑ 115 Jeff Blake .60 .25
- ❑ 116 Joe Horn .60 .25
- ❑ 117 La'Roi Glover .40 .15
- ❑ 118 Ricky Williams 1.00 .40
- ❑ 119 Willie Jackson .40 .15
- ❑ 120 Amani Toomer .40 .15
- ❑ 121 Ike Hilliard .60 .25
- ❑ 122 Jason Sehorn .40 .15
- ❑ 123 Kerry Collins .60 .25
- ❑ 124 Michael Strahan .60 .25
- ❑ 125 Ron Dayne 1.00 .40
- ❑ 126 Ron Dixon .40 .15
- ❑ 127 Tiki Barber 1.00 .40
- ❑ 128 Chad Pennington 1.50 .60
- ❑ 129 Curtis Martin 1.00 .40
- ❑ 130 Dedric Ward .40 .15
- ❑ 131 Laveranues Coles 1.00 .40
- ❑ 132 Vinny Testaverde .60 .25
- ❑ 133 Wayne Chrebet .60 .25
- ❑ 134 Charles Woodson .60 .25
- ❑ 135 Napoleon Kaufman .60 .25
- ❑ 136 Rich Gannon 1.00 .40
- ❑ 137 Tim Brown 1.00 .40
- ❑ 138 Tyrone Wheatley .60 .25
- ❑ 139 Charles Johnson .40 .15
- ❑ 140 Donovan McNabb 1.25 .50
- ❑ 141 Duce Staley 1.00 .40
- ❑ 142 Hugh Douglas .40 .15
- ❑ 143 Na Brown .40 .15
- ❑ 144 Todd Pinkston .40 .15
- ❑ 145 Bobby Shaw .40 .15
- ❑ 146 Hines Ward 1.00 .40
- ❑ 147 Jerome Bettis 1.00 .40
- ❑ 148 Kordell Stewart .60 .25

❑ 149 Levon Kirkland .40 .15
❑ 150 Plaxico Burress 1.00 .40
❑ 151 Richard Huntley .40 .15
❑ 152 Troy Edwards .40 .15
❑ 153 Jim Harbaugh .60 .25
❑ 154 Junior Seau 1.00 .40
❑ 155 Ryan Leaf .60 .25
❑ 156 Charlie Garner .60 .25
❑ 157 Jeff Garcia 1.00 .40
❑ 158 Jerry Rice 2.00 .75
❑ 159 Steve Young 1.25 .50
❑ 160 Terrell Owens 1.00 .40
❑ 161 Brock Huard .40 .15
❑ 162 Darrell Jackson 1.00 .40
❑ 163 Derrick Mayes .40 .15
❑ 164 Ricky Watters .60 .25
❑ 165 Shaun Alexander 1.25 .50
❑ 166 Az-Zahir Hakim .40 .15
❑ 167 Isaac Bruce 1.00 .40
❑ 168 Kurt Warner 2.00 .75
❑ 169 Marshall Faulk 1.25 .50
❑ 170 Torry Holt 1.00 .40
❑ 171 Trent Green 1.00 .40
❑ 172 Derrick Brooks 1.00 .40
❑ 173 Jacquez Green .40 .15
❑ 174 John Lynch .60 .25
❑ 175 Keyshawn Johnson 1.00 .40
❑ 176 Mike Alstott 1.00 .40
❑ 177 Reidel Anthony .40 .15
❑ 178 Shaun King .40 .15
❑ 179 Warren Sapp .60 .25
❑ 180 Warrick Dunn 1.00 .40
❑ 181 Carl Pickens .40 .15
❑ 182 Derrick Mason .60 .25
❑ 183 Eddie George 1.00 .40
❑ 184 Frank Wycheck .40 .15
❑ 185 Jevon Kearse .60 .25
❑ 186 Neil O'Donnell .40 .15
❑ 187 Steve McNair 1.00 .40
❑ 188 Yancey Thigpen .40 .15
❑ 189 Albert Connell .40 .15
❑ 190 Andre Reed .40 .15
❑ 191 Brad Johnson 1.00 .40
❑ 192 Bruce Smith .40 .15
❑ 193 Champ Bailey .60 .25
❑ 194 Darrell Green .40 .15
❑ 195 Deion Sanders 1.00 .40
❑ 196 Irving Fryar .60 .25
❑ 197 James Thrash .60 .25
❑ 198 Jeff George .60 .25
❑ 199 Michael Westbrook .60 .25
❑ 200 Stephen Davis 1.00 .40
❑ 201 Michael Vick RC 15.00 6.00
❑ 202 Drew Brees RC 5.00 2.00
❑ 203 Chris Weinke RC 2.00 .75
❑ 204 Sage Rosenfels RC 2.00 .75
❑ 205 Josh Heupel RC 2.00 .75
❑ 206 Marques Tuiasosopo RC 2.00 .75
❑ 207 Mike McMahon SP RC 40.00 15.00
❑ 208 Deuce McAllister SP RC 80.00 30.00
❑ 209 LaMont Jordan RC 4.00 1.50
❑ 210 LaDainian Tomlinson RC 12.00 6.00
❑ 211 James Jackson RC 2.00 .75
❑ 212 Anthony Thomas RC 2.00 .75
❑ 213 Travis Henry RC 2.00 .75
❑ 214 Travis Minor RC 1.25 .50
❑ 215 Rudi Johnson RC 4.00 1.50
❑ 216 Michael Bennett RC 3.00 1.25
❑ 217 Kevan Barlow RC 2.00 .75
❑ 218 Dan Alexander RC 1.25 .50
❑ 219 Correll Buckhalter SP RC 50.00 25.00
❑ 220 Moran Norris RC .75 .30
❑ 221 Jesse Palmer RC 2.00 .75
❑ 222 Heath Evans RC 1.25 .50
❑ 223 David Terrell SP RC 40.00 15.00
❑ 224 Santana Moss RC 3.00 1.25
❑ 225 Rod Gardner RC 2.00 .75
❑ 226 Quincy Morgan SP RC 50.00 20.00
❑ 227 Freddie Mitchell RC 2.00 .75
❑ 228 Reggie Wayne RC 4.00 1.50
❑ 229 Bobby Newcombe RC 1.25 .50
❑ 230 Casey Hampton RC 2.00 .75
❑ 231 Robert Ferguson RC 2.00 .75
❑ 232 Ken-Yon Rambo RC 1.25 .50
❑ 233 Alex Bannister RC 1.25 .50
❑ 234 Koren Robinson RC 2.00 .75
❑ 235 Chad Johnson RC 5.00 2.00
❑ 236 Chris Chambers RC 3.00 1.25
❑ 237 Snoop Minnis RC 1.25 .50
❑ 238 Vinny Sutherland RC 1.25 .50
❑ 239 Cedrick Wilson RC 2.00 .75
❑ 240 T.J. Houshmandzadeh RC 2.00 .75
❑ 241 Todd Heap RC 2.00 .75
❑ 242 Alge Crumpler RC 2.50 1.00
❑ 243 Jabari Holloway RC 1.25 .50
❑ 244 Tony Stewart RC 2.00 .75
❑ 245 Jamal Reynolds RC 2.00 .75
❑ 246 Andre Carter SP RC 40.00 15.00
❑ 247 Justin Smith SP RC 40.00 20.00
❑ 248 Richard Seymour RC 2.00 .75
❑ 249 Marcus Stroud RC 2.00 .75
❑ 250 Damione Lewis RC 1.25 .50
❑ 251 Gerard Warren SP RC 50.00 25.00
❑ 252 Tommy Polley SP RC 40.00 20.00
❑ 253 Dan Morgan RC 2.00 .75
❑ 254 Jamar Fletcher RC 1.25 .50
❑ 255 Ken Lucas RC 2.00 .75
❑ 256 Fred Smoot SP RC 40.00 15.00
❑ 257 Nate Clements RC 2.00 .75
❑ 258 Will Allen RC 1.25 .50
❑ 259 Derrick Gibson RC 1.25 .50
❑ 260 Adam Archuleta RC 2.00 .75
❑ 261 Karon Riley RC .75 .30
❑ 262 Cedric Scott RC 1.25 .50
❑ 263 Kenny Smith RC 1.25 .50
❑ 264 Willie Howard RC 1.25 .50
❑ 265 Shaun Rogers RC 2.00 .75
❑ 266 Ennis Davis RC .75 .30
❑ 267 Morlon Greenwood RC 1.25 .50
❑ 268 Gary Baxter RC 1.25 .50
❑ 269 Keith Adams RC .75 .30
❑ 270 Brian Allen RC .75 .30
❑ 271 Carlos Polk RC .75 .30
❑ 272 Torrance Marshall RC 2.00 .75
❑ 273 Jamie Winborn RC 1.25 .50
❑ 274 Hakim Akbar RC .75 .30
❑ 275 David Rivers RC 1.25 .50
❑ 276 Ben Leard RC 1.25 .50
❑ 277 Tim Hasselbeck RC 2.00 .75
❑ 278 DeAngelo Evans RC 1.25 .50
❑ 279 David Allen RC 1.25 .50
❑ 280 Reggie White RC 1.25 .50
❑ 281 Ja'Mar Toombs RC 1.25 .50
❑ 282 Dustin McClintock RC 1.25 .50
❑ 283 Boo Williams RC 1.25 .50
❑ 284 Ronney Daniels RC .75 .30
❑ 285 Daniel Guy RC .75 .30
❑ 286 Javon Green RC 1.25 .50
❑ 287 Marcellus Rivers RC 1.25 .50
❑ 288 Rashon Burns RC .75 .30
❑ 289 Jevaris Johnson RC .75 .30
❑ 290 David Warren RC .75 .30
❑ 291 John Capel RC 1.25 .50
❑ 292 Kendrell Bell RC 4.00 1.50
❑ 294 Willie Middlebrooks RC 1.25 .50
❑ 295 Reggie Germany RC 1.25 .50
❑ 296 Quincy Carter RC 2.00 .75

2004 Reflections

❑ COMP.SET w/o SP's (100) 40.00 15.00
❑ 201-294 RC PRINT RUN 1150 SER.#'d SETS
❑ OVERALL RC STATED ODDS 1:1
❑ 1 Emmitt Smith 3.00 1.25
❑ 2 Anquan Boldin 1.50 .60
❑ 3 Josh McCown 1.00 .40
❑ 4 Michael Vick 3.00 1.2
❑ 5 Peerless Price 1.00 .4
❑ 6 T.J. Duckett 1.00 .4
❑ 7 Todd Heap 1.00 .4
❑ 8 Jamal Lewis 1.50 .6
❑ 9 Kyle Boller 1.50 .6
❑ 10 Drew Bledsoe 1.50 .6
❑ 11 Travis Henry 1.00 .4
❑ 12 Eric Moulds 1.00 .4
❑ 13 Jake Delhomme 1.50 .6
❑ 14 Steve Smith 1.50 .6
❑ 15 Stephen Davis 1.00 .4
❑ 16 Rex Grossman 1.50 .6
❑ 17 Brian Urlacher 2.00 .7
❑ 18 Anthony Thomas 1.00 .4
❑ 19 Rudi Johnson 1.00 .40
❑ 20 Carson Palmer 2.00 .75
❑ 21 Chad Johnson 1.50 .60
❑ 22 Jeff Garcia 1.50 .60
❑ 23 Andre Davis .60 .25
❑ 24 Quincy Morgan 1.00 .40
❑ 25 Keyshawn Johnson 1.00 .40
❑ 26 Roy Williams S 1.00 .40
❑ 27 Quincy Carter 1.00 .40
❑ 28 Ashley Lelie 1.00 .40
❑ 29 Champ Bailey 1.00 .40
❑ 30 Jake Plummer 1.00 .40
❑ 31 Az-Zahir Hakim .60 .25
❑ 32 Joey Harrington 1.50 .60
❑ 33 Charles Rogers 1.00 .40
❑ 34 Javon Walker 1.00 .40
❑ 35 Ahman Green 1.50 .60
❑ 36 Brett Favre 4.00 1.50
❑ 37 Domanick Davis 1.50 .60
❑ 38 David Carr 1.50 .60
❑ 39 Andre Johnson 1.50 .60
❑ 40 Edgerrin James 1.50 .60
❑ 41 Marvin Harrison 1.50 .60
❑ 42 Dwight Freeney 1.00 .40
❑ 43 Peyton Manning 2.50 1.00
❑ 44 Fred Taylor 1.00 .40
❑ 45 Jimmy Smith 1.00 .40
❑ 46 Byron Leftwich 2.00 .75
❑ 47 Dante Hall 1.50 .60
❑ 48 Tony Gonzalez 1.00 .40
❑ 49 Trent Green 1.00 .40
❑ 50 Priest Holmes 2.00 .75
❑ 51 Zach Thomas 1.50 .60
❑ 52 A.J. Feeley 1.50 .60
❑ 53 Chris Chambers 1.00 .40
❑ 54 Ricky Williams 1.50 .60
❑ 55 Randy Moss 2.00 .75
❑ 56 Onterrio Smith 1.00 .40
❑ 57 Daunte Culpepper 1.50 .60
❑ 58 Tom Brady 4.00 1.50
❑ 59 Troy Brown 1.00 .40
❑ 60 Corey Dillon 1.00 .40
❑ 61 Donte Stallworth 1.00 .40
❑ 62 Deuce McAllister 1.50 .60
❑ 63 Aaron Brooks 1.00 .40
❑ 64 Amani Toomer 1.00 .40
❑ 65 Jeremy Shockey 1.50 .60

❑ 66 Michael Strahan 1.00 .40
❑ 67 Curtis Martin 1.50 .60
❑ 68 Chad Pennington 1.50 .60
❑ 69 Santana Moss 1.00 .40
❑ 70 Jerry Porter 1.00 .40
❑ 71 Jerry Rice 3.00 1.25
❑ 72 Rich Gannon 1.00 .40
❑ 73 Tim Brown 1.50 .60
❑ 74 Terrell Owens 1.50 .60
❑ 75 Brian Westbrook 1.00 .40
❑ 76 Donovan McNabb 2.00 .75
❑ 77 Tommy Maddox 1.00 .40
❑ 78 Hines Ward 1.50 .60
❑ 79 Duce Staley 1.00 .40
❑ 80 Donnie Edwards .60 .25
❑ 81 LaDainian Tomlinson 2.00 .75
❑ 82 Drew Brees 1.50 .60
❑ 83 Brandon Lloyd 1.00 .40
❑ 84 Tim Rattay .60 .25
❑ 85 Kevan Barlow 1.00 .40
❑ 86 Koren Robinson 1.00 .40
❑ 87 Shaun Alexander 1.50 .60
❑ 88 Matt Hasselbeck 1.00 .40
❑ 89 Torry Holt 1.50 .60
❑ 90 Marc Bulger 1.50 .60
❑ 91 Marshall Faulk 1.50 .60
❑ 92 Brad Johnson 1.00 .40
❑ 93 Keenan McCardell .60 .25
❑ 94 Charlie Garner 1.00 .40
❑ 95 Steve McNair 1.50 .60
❑ 96 Chris Brown 1.50 .60
❑ 97 Eddie George 1.00 .40
❑ 98 Mark Brunell 1.00 .40
❑ 99 Laveranues Coles 1.00 .40
❑ 100 Clinton Portis 1.50 .60
❑ 101 Kris Wilson/750 RC 6.00 2.50
❑ 102 Carlos Francis/750 RC 5.00 2.00
❑ 103 D.J. Williams/750 RC 8.00 3.00
❑ 104 Devery Henderson/450 RC 6.00 2.50
❑ 105 Craig Krenzel/750 RC 6.00 2.50
❑ 106 Jonathan Vilma/750 RC 6.00 2.50
❑ 107 Luke McCown/750 RC 6.00 2.50
❑ 108 Michael Turner/750 RC 6.00 2.50
❑ 109 Richard Seigler/750 RC 5.00 2.00
❑ 110 Stuart Schweigert/750 RC 6.00 2.50
❑ 111 Ben Watson/750 RC 6.00 2.50
❑ 112 Chris Perry/450 RC 12.00 5.00
❑ 113 Jason Fife/750 RC 5.00 2.00
❑ 114 Eli Manning/450 RC 40.00 20.00
❑ 115 Matt Kegel/750 RC 6.00 2.50
❑ 116 Kellen Winslow/450 RC 15.00 6.00
❑ 117 Chris Cooley/750 RC 6.00 2.50
❑ 118 Quincy Wilson/750 RC 5.00 2.00
❑ 119 Samie Parker/750 RC 6.00 2.50
❑ 120 Vince Wilfork/750 RC 8.00 3.00
❑ 121 Bernard Berrian/750 RC 6.00 2.50
❑ 122 Ahmad Carroll/750 RC 8.00 3.00
❑ 123 Derrick Hamilton/750 RC 5.00 2.00
❑ 124 Rich Gardner/750 RC 5.00 2.00
❑ 125 Jeff Smoker/750 RC 6.00 2.50
❑ 126 Kenechi Udeze/750 RC 6.00 2.50
❑ 127 Mewelde Moore/750 RC 8.00 3.00
❑ 128 Keyaron Fox/750 RC 5.00 2.00
❑ 129 Sean Jones/750 RC 5.00 2.00
❑ 130 Will Poole/750 RC 6.00 2.50
❑ 131 Travelle Wharton/750 RC 3.00 1.25
❑ 132 Demorrio Williams/750 RC 6.00 2.50
❑ 133 Jason Babin/750 RC 6.00 2.50
❑ 134 Ernest Wilford/750 RC 6.00 2.50
❑ 135 Jerricho Cotchery/750 RC 6.00 2.50
❑ 136 Kevin Jones/450 RC 25.00 10.00
❑ 137 Michael Boulware/750 RC 6.00 2.50
❑ 138 D.J. Hackett/750 RC 5.00 2.00
❑ 139 Sean Taylor/450 RC 10.00 4.00
❑ 140 Will Smith/750 RC 6.00 2.50
❑ 141 John Standeford/750 RC 5.00 2.00
❑ 142 Max Starks/750 RC 5.00 2.00
❑ 143 Cody Pickett/750 RC 6.00 2.50
❑ 144 Derrick Strait/750 RC 6.00 2.50
❑ 145 Greg Jones/450 RC 8.00 3.00
❑ 146 John Navarre/750 RC 6.00 2.50
❑ 147 Larry Fitzgerald/450 RC 25.00 10.00
❑ 148 Michael Clayton/450 RC 15.00 6.00
❑ 149 Rashaun Woods/450 RC 8.00 3.00
❑ 150 Shawn Andrews/750 RC 6.00 2.50
❑ 151 B.J. Symons/750 RC 6.00 2.50
❑ 152 Cedric Cobbs/450 RC 8.00 3.00
❑ 153 Darius Watts/750 RC 6.00 2.50
❑ 154 B.J. Johnson/750 RC 5.00 2.00
❑ 155 Ricardo Colclough/750 RC 6.00 2.50
❑ 156 Josh Harris/750 RC 6.00 2.50
❑ 157 Derek Abney/750 RC 6.00 2.50
❑ 158 Kendrick Starling/750 RC 3.00 1.25
❑ 159 Robert Gallery/450 RC 12.00 5.00
❑ 160 Tatum Bell/450 RC 15.00 6.00
❑ 161 Ben Hartsock/750 RC 6.00 2.50
❑ 162 Dwan Edwards/750 RC 3.00 1.25
❑ 163 Darnell Dockett/750 RC 5.00 2.00
❑ 164 Igor Olshansky/750 RC 6.00 2.50
❑ 165 Justin Smiley/750 RC 6.00 2.50
❑ 166 Julius Jones/450 RC 30.00 12.50
❑ 167 Matt Mauck/750 RC 6.00 2.50
❑ 168 Derek McCoy/750 RC 5.00 2.00
❑ 169 Chris Pittman/750 RC 6.00 2.50
❑ 170 Teddy Lehman/750 RC 6.00 2.50
❑ 171 Ben Troupe/450 RC 8.00 3.00
❑ 172 Chris Gamble/750 RC 8.00 3.00
❑ 173 DeAngelo Hall/750 RC 8.00 3.00
❑ 174 Dunta Robinson/750 RC 6.00 2.50
❑ 175 Jason Shivers/750 RC 5.00 2.00
❑ 176 Keary Colbert/450 RC 10.00 4.00
❑ 177 Jared Lorenzen/750 RC 5.00 2.00
❑ 178 Philip Rivers/450 RC 25.00 12.50
❑ 179 Roy Williams/450 RC 20.00 7.50
❑ 180 Bob Sanders/750 RC 12.00 5.00
❑ 181 Antwan Odom/750 RC 6.00 2.50
❑ 182 Josh Davis/750 RC 5.00 2.00
❑ 183 Courtney Watson/750 RC 6.00 2.50
❑ 184 Devard Darling/750 RC 6.00 2.50
❑ 185 J.P. Losman/450 RC 15.00 6.00
❑ 186 Johnnie Morant/750 RC 6.00 2.50
❑ 187 Lee Evans/450 RC 10.00 4.00
❑ 188 Michael Jenkins/450 RC 8.00 3.00
❑ 189 Reggie Williams/450 RC 10.00 4.00
❑ 190 Steven Jackson/450 RC 25.00 10.00
❑ 191 Roethlisberger/450 RC 60.00 30.00
❑ 192 P.K. Sam/750 RC 5.00 2.00
❑ 193 Derrick Knight/750 RC 5.00 2.00
❑ 194 Drew Henson/450 RC 8.00 3.00
❑ 195 Marquise Hill/750 RC 5.00 2.00
❑ 196 Karlos Dansby/750 RC 6.00 2.50
❑ 197 Matt Schaub/750 RC 10.00 4.00
❑ 198 Ben Utecht/750 RC 3.00 1.25
❑ 199 Darrion Scott/750 RC 6.00 2.50
❑ 200 Tommie Harris/750 RC 6.00 2.50
❑ 201 Andrae Thurman RC 3.00 1.25
❑ 202 Matt Kranchick RC 6.00 2.50
❑ 203 Shaun Phillips RC 5.00 2.00
❑ 204 Landon Johnson RC 5.00 2.00
❑ 205 Jeff Dugan RC 3.00 1.25
❑ 206 Wes Welker RC 6.00 2.50
❑ 207 Michael Gaines RC 5.00 2.00
❑ 208 Jamaar Taylor RC 6.00 2.50
❑ 209 Brandon Chillar RC 5.00 2.00
❑ 210 Jermaine Green RC 5.00 2.00
❑ 211 Triandos Luke RC 6.00 2.50
❑ 212 Brandon Miree RC 5.00 2.00
❑ 213 Dexter Reid RC 3.00 1.25
❑ 214 Isaac Hilton RC 5.00 2.00
❑ 215 Adrian Jones RC 5.00 2.00
❑ 216 Grant Wiley RC 5.00 2.00
❑ 217 Matt Cherry RC 3.00 1.25
❑ 218 Courtney Anderson RC 5.00 2.00
❑ 219 Antonio Smith RC 5.00 2.00
❑ 220 Sean Tufts RC 5.00 2.00
❑ 221 Johnny Lamar RC 6.00 2.50
❑ 222 Shawn Johnson RC 5.00 2.00
❑ 223 Jason Peters RC 6.00 2.50
❑ 224 Rodney Leisle RC 3.00 1.25
❑ 225 Lane Danielsen RC 6.00 2.50
❑ 226 Zack Abron RC 5.00 2.00
❑ 227 Romar Crenshaw RC 3.00 1.25
❑ 228 Keiwan Ratliff RC 5.00 2.00
❑ 229 Chad Lavalais RC 5.00 2.00
❑ 230 Jason Wright RC 5.00 2.00
❑ 231 Rayshun Reed RC 3.00 1.25
❑ 232 Patrick Crayton RC 6.00 2.50
❑ 233 Casey Bramlet RC 5.00 2.00
❑ 234 Nathaniel Adibi RC 6.00 2.50
❑ 235 Dontarrious Thomas RC 6.00 2.50
❑ 236 B.J. Sander RC 5.00 2.00
❑ 237 Ryan McGuffey RC 3.00 1.25
❑ 238 Shawntae Spencer RC 6.00 2.50
❑ 239 Amon Gordon RC 3.00 1.25
❑ 240 Vernon Carey RC 5.00 2.00
❑ 241 Stanford Samuels RC 5.00 2.00
❑ 242 Thomas Tapeh RC 5.00 2.00
❑ 243 Keith Smith RC 5.00 2.00
❑ 244 Casey Clausen RC 6.00 2.50
❑ 245 Jake Grove RC 3.00 1.25
❑ 246 Omar Nazel RC 5.00 2.00
❑ 247 Jammal Lord RC 6.00 2.50
❑ 248 Jeremy LeSueur RC 5.00 2.00
❑ 249 Daryl Smith RC 6.00 2.50
❑ 250 Nat Dorsey RC 3.00 1.25
❑ 251 Tim Anderson RC 6.00 2.50
❑ 252 Chris Snee RC 5.00 2.00
❑ 253 Sean Ryan RC 5.00 2.00
❑ 254 Tank Johnson RC 5.00 2.00
❑ 255 Marquis Cooper RC 5.00 2.00
❑ 256 Josh Scobee RC 3.00 1.25
❑ 257 Justin Jenkins RC 5.00 2.00
❑ 258 Nate Lawrie RC 5.00 2.00
❑ 259 Randy Starks RC 5.00 2.00
❑ 260 Caleb Miller RC 5.00 2.00
❑ 261 A.J. Ricker RC 3.00 1.25
❑ 262 Andy Hall RC 5.00 2.00
❑ 263 Troy Fleming RC 5.00 2.00
❑ 264 Matt Ware RC 6.00 2.50
❑ 265 Christian Ferrara RC 5.00 2.00
❑ 266 Stacy Andrews RC 5.00 2.00
❑ 267 Reggie Torbor RC 5.00 2.00
❑ 268 Jeris McIntyre RC 5.00 2.00
❑ 269 Jarrett Payton RC 8.00 3.00
❑ 270 Ronald Jones RC 3.00 1.25
❑ 271 Kelly Butler RC 5.00 2.00
❑ 272 Bryan Hickman RC 6.00 2.50
❑ 273 Chris Collins RC 5.00 2.00
❑ 274 Ryan Dinwiddie RC 5.00 2.00
❑ 275 Robert Geathers RC 5.00 2.00
❑ 276 Niko Koutouvides RC 5.00 2.00
❑ 277 Clarence Farmer RC 5.00 2.00
❑ 278 Jim Sorgi RC 6.00 2.50
❑ 279 Ran Carthon RC 5.00 2.00
❑ 280 Michael Waddell RC 3.00 1.25
❑ 281 Andrew Strojny RC 3.00 1.25
❑ 282 Sloan Thomas RC 5.00 2.00
❑ 283 Tim Euhus RC 6.00 2.50
❑ 284 Lawrence Richardson RC 6.00 2.50
❑ 285 Nate Kaeding RC 6.00 2.50
❑ 286 Ryan Krause RC 5.00 2.00
❑ 287 Derrick Ward RC 3.00 1.25
❑ 288 Nathan Vasher RC 8.00 3.00
❑ 289 Bobby McCray RC 5.00 2.00
❑ 290 Scott Rislov RC 6.00 2.50
❑ 291 Ryan Boschetti RC 3.00 1.25
❑ 292 Fred Russell RC 6.00 2.50
❑ 293 Von Hutchins RC 5.00 2.00
❑ 294 Derrick Crawford RC 3.00 1.25

2005 Reflections

❑ COMP.SET w/o SP's (100) 30.00 12.50
❑ 101-175 PRINT RUN 899 SER.#'d SETS
❑ 176-225 PRINT RUN 699 SER.#'d SETS

❑ 226-275 PRINT RUN 499 SER.#'d SETS
❑ 276-300 PRINT RUN 299 SER.#'d SETS
❑ OVERALL DRAFT PICK ODDS 1:3
❑ UNPRICED RAINBOW PRINT RUN 1 SET

❑	1	Larry Fitzgerald	1.25	.50
❑	2	Anquan Boldin	.75	.30
❑	3	Josh McCown	.75	.30
❑	4	Michael Vick	2.00	.75
❑	5	Warrick Dunn	.75	.30
❑	6	Peerless Price	.60	.25
❑	7	Ray Lewis	1.25	.50
❑	8	Jamal Lewis	1.25	.50
❑	9	Kyle Boller	.75	.30
❑	10	Derrick Mason	.75	.30
❑	11	J.P. Losman	1.25	.50
❑	12	Willis McGahee	1.25	.50
❑	13	Lee Evans	.75	.30
❑	14	Eric Moulds	.75	.30
❑	15	Jake Delhomme	1.25	.50
❑	16	Keary Colbert	.75	.30
❑	17	DeShaun Foster	.75	.30
❑	18	Brian Urlacher	1.25	.50
❑	19	Rex Grossman	.75	.30
❑	20	Muhsin Muhammad	.75	.30
❑	21	Carson Palmer	1.25	.50
❑	22	Rudi Johnson	.75	.30
❑	23	Chad Johnson	1.25	.50
❑	24	Julius Jones	1.50	.60
❑	25	Keyshawn Johnson	.75	.30
❑	26	Drew Bledsoe	1.25	.50
❑	27	Tatum Bell	.75	.30
❑	28	Jake Plummer	.75	.30
❑	29	Ashley Lelie	.75	.30
❑	30	Roy Williams WR	1.25	.50
❑	31	Kevin Jones	1.25	.50
❑	32	Jeff Garcia	.75	.30
❑	33	Brett Favre	3.00	1.25
❑	34	Ahman Green	1.25	.50
❑	35	Javon Walker	.75	.30
❑	36	David Carr	1.25	.50
❑	37	Andre Johnson	.75	.30
❑	38	Domanick Davis	.75	.30
❑	39	Peyton Manning	2.00	.75
❑	40	Reggie Wayne	.75	.30
❑	41	Edgerrin James	1.25	.50
❑	42	Marvin Harrison	1.25	.50
❑	43	Byron Leftwich	1.25	.50
❑	44	Fred Taylor	.75	.30
❑	45	Jimmy Smith	.75	.30
❑	46	Priest Holmes	1.25	.50
❑	47	Larry Johnson	1.25	.50
❑	48	Trent Green	.75	.30
❑	49	A.J. Feeley	.75	.30
❑	50	Chris Chambers	.75	.30
❑	51	Randy McMichael	.60	.25
❑	52	Daunte Culpepper	1.25	.50
❑	53	Onterrio Smith	.75	.30
❑	54	Nate Burleson	.75	.30
❑	55	Tom Brady	3.00	1.25
❑	56	Corey Dillon	.75	.30
❑	57	Deion Branch	.75	.30
❑	58	David Givens	.75	.30
❑	59	Aaron Brooks	.75	.30
❑	60	Deuce McAllister	1.25	.50
❑	61	Joe Horn	.75	.30
❑	62	Eli Manning	2.50	1.00
❑	63	Jeremy Shockey	1.25	.50
❑	64	Tiki Barber	1.25	.50
❑	65	Chad Pennington	1.25	.50
❑	66	Curtis Martin	1.25	.50
❑	67	Laveranues Coles	.75	.30
❑	68	Kerry Collins	.75	.30
❑	69	Jerry Porter	.75	.30
❑	70	Randy Moss	1.25	.50
❑	71	Donovan McNabb	1.50	.60
❑	72	Terrell Owens	1.25	.50
❑	73	Brian Dawkins	.75	.30
❑	74	Brian Westbrook	.75	.30
❑	75	Ben Roethlisberger	3.00	1.25
❑	76	Jerome Bettis	1.25	.50
❑	77	Hines Ward	1.25	.50
❑	78	Duce Staley	.75	.30
❑	79	Drew Brees	1.25	.50
❑	80	LaDainian Tomlinson	1.50	.60
❑	81	Antonio Gates	1.25	.50
❑	82	Tim Rattay	.60	.25
❑	83	Kevan Barlow	.75	.30
❑	84	Eric Johnson	.75	.30
❑	85	Shaun Alexander	1.50	.60
❑	86	Darrell Jackson	.75	.30
❑	87	Matt Hasselbeck	.75	.30
❑	88	Marc Bulger	1.25	.50
❑	89	Steven Jackson	1.50	.60
❑	90	Marshall Faulk	1.25	.50
❑	91	Torry Holt	1.25	.50
❑	92	Michael Pittman	.60	.25
❑	93	Brian Griese	.75	.30
❑	94	Michael Clayton	1.25	.50
❑	95	Steve McNair	1.25	.50
❑	96	Billy Volek	.75	.30
❑	97	Chris Brown	.75	.30
❑	98	Clinton Portis	1.25	.50
❑	99	Patrick Ramsey	.75	.30
❑	100	Santana Moss	.75	.30
❑	101	James Kilian RC	6.00	2.50
❑	102	Matt Cassel RC	10.00	4.00
❑	103	Keron Henry RC	3.00	1.25
❑	104	Adrian McPherson RC	6.00	2.50
❑	105	Marcus Randall RC	5.00	2.00
❑	106	Roydel Williams RC	6.00	2.50
❑	107	Dante Ridgeway RC	5.00	2.00
❑	108	Marcus Maxwell RC	5.00	2.00
❑	109	Paris Warren RC	5.00	2.00
❑	110	Courtney Roby RC	6.00	2.50
❑	111	Mark Bradley RC	6.00	2.50
❑	112	Brandon Jones RC	6.00	2.50
❑	113	Chase Lyman RC	5.00	2.00
❑	114	LeRon McCoy RC	5.00	2.00
❑	115	Adam Bergen RC	6.00	2.50
❑	116	Harry Williams RC	5.00	2.00
❑	117	Lance Moore RC	3.00	1.25
❑	118	Jason Anderson RC	5.00	2.00
❑	119	Lionel Gates RC	5.00	2.00
❑	120	Darrell Shropshire RC	5.00	2.00
❑	121	Will Matthews RC	5.00	2.00
❑	122	Noah Herron RC	6.00	2.50
❑	123	Jerome Collins RC	5.00	2.00
❑	124	Stanford Routt RC	5.00	2.00
❑	125	Nick Collins RC	6.00	2.50
❑	126	Maurice Clarett	6.00	2.50
❑	127	Kelvin Hayden RC	5.00	2.00
❑	128	Bo Scaife RC	5.00	2.00
❑	129	Eric King RC	5.00	2.00
❑	130	Kerry Rhodes RC	6.00	2.50
❑	131	Darrent Williams RC	6.00	2.50
❑	132	Stanley Wilson RC	5.00	2.00
❑	133	Nick Speegle RC	5.00	2.00
❑	134	Brodney Pool RC	6.00	2.50
❑	135	Ellis Hobbs RC	6.00	2.50
❑	136	Sean Considine RC	6.00	2.50
❑	137	Josh Bullocks RC	6.00	2.50
❑	138	Jovan Haye RC	5.00	2.00
❑	139	Jimmy Verdon RC	3.00	1.25
❑	140	Ryan Riddle RC	3.00	1.25
❑	141	Luis Castillo RC	6.00	2.50
❑	142	Jesse Lumsden RC	3.00	1.25
❑	143	David Baas RC	5.00	2.00
❑	144	Chris Spencer RC	6.00	2.50
❑	145	Jamaal Brown RC	6.00	2.50
❑	146	Marcus Lawrence RC	5.00	2.00
❑	147	Todd Mortensen RC	5.00	2.00
❑	148	Shane Boyd RC	3.00	1.25
❑	149	Darian Durant RC	6.00	2.50
❑	150	Chance Mock RC	3.00	1.25
❑	151	Damien Nash RC	5.00	2.00
❑	152	Deandra Cobb RC	5.00	2.00
❑	153	Jamaica Rector RC	3.00	1.25
❑	154	Carlyle Holiday RC	5.00	2.00
❑	155	Nehemiah Broughton RC	5.00	2.00
❑	156	Efrem Hill RC	5.00	2.00
❑	157	Dominic Robinson RC	3.00	1.25
❑	158	Rick Razzano RC	6.00	2.50
❑	159	Rasheed Marshall RC	6.00	2.50
❑	160	Lofa Tatupu RC	8.00	3.00
❑	161	Robert McCune RC	5.00	2.00
❑	162	Channing Crowder RC	6.00	2.50
❑	163	Ryan Claridge RC	5.00	2.00
❑	164	Fred Amey RC	5.00	2.00
❑	165	Jordan Beck RC	5.00	2.00
❑	166	Leroy Hill RC	6.00	2.50
❑	167	Travis Daniels RC	5.00	2.00
❑	168	Jerome Carter RC	5.00	2.00
❑	169	Chad Friehauf RC	5.00	2.00
❑	170	Scott Starks RC	5.00	2.00
❑	171	Marviel Underwood RC	5.00	2.00
❑	172	Domonique Foxworth RC	6.00	2.50
❑	173	Jon Goldsberry RC	6.00	2.50
❑	174	Jonathan Babineaux RC	5.00	2.00
❑	175	Sione Pouha RC	6.00	2.50
❑	176	Kerry Wright RC	5.00	2.00
❑	177	Jason White RC	6.00	2.50
❑	178	Matt Jones RC	15.00	6.00
❑	179	Gino Guidugli RC	3.00	1.25
❑	180	Timmy Chang RC	5.00	2.00
❑	181	Chris Rix RC	5.00	2.00
❑	182	Ryan Fitzpatrick RC	10.00	4.00
❑	183	Brock Berlin RC	5.00	2.00
❑	184	Bryan Randall RC	5.00	2.00
❑	185	Stefan LeFors RC	6.00	2.50
❑	186	Larry Brackins RC	5.00	2.00
❑	187	Charles Frederick RC	5.00	2.00
❑	188	J.R. Russell RC	5.00	2.00
❑	189	Vincent Jackson RC	6.00	2.50
❑	190	Josh Davis RC	5.00	2.00
❑	191	Chad Owens RC	6.00	2.50
❑	192	Airese Currie RC	6.00	2.50
❑	193	Chauncey Stovall RC	3.00	1.25
❑	194	Jovan Witherspoon RC	3.00	1.25
❑	195	Trent Cole RC	6.00	2.50
❑	196	Tab Perry RC	6.00	2.50
❑	197	Cedric Houston RC	6.00	2.50
❑	198	Brandon Jacobs RC	8.00	3.00
❑	199	Bobby Purify RC	5.00	2.00
❑	200	Marion Barber RC	10.00	4.00
❑	201	Alvin Pearman RC	6.00	2.50
❑	202	Madison Hedgecock RC	6.00	2.50
❑	203	Justin Green RC	6.00	2.50
❑	204	Manuel White RC	5.00	2.00
❑	205	Kevin Everett RC	6.00	2.50
❑	206	Matthew Tant RC	3.00	1.25
❑	207	Bryant McFadden RC	6.00	2.50
❑	208	Ryan Moats RC	6.00	2.50
❑	209	Fabian Washington RC	6.00	2.50
❑	210	Oshiomogho Atogwe RC	5.00	2.00
❑	211	Dustin Fox RC	6.00	2.50
❑	212	Shaun Cody RC	6.00	2.50
❑	213	Matt Roth RC	6.00	2.50

❑ 214	Vincent Burns RC	5.00	2.00
❑ 215	Bill Swancutt RC	5.00	2.00
❑ 216	Brady Poppinga RC	6.00	2.50
❑ 217	Logan Mankins RC	8.00	3.00
❑ 218	Michael Roos RC	3.00	1.25
❑ 219	Alfred Fincher RC	5.00	2.00
❑ 220	Darryl Blackstock RC	5.00	2.00
❑ 221	Jared Newberry RC	5.00	2.00
❑ 222	Khalif Barnes RC	5.00	2.00
❑ 223	Alex Barron RC	3.00	1.25
❑ 224	Patrick Estes RC	5.00	2.00
❑ 225	Elton Brown RC	3.00	1.25
❑ 226	David Greene RC	8.00	3.00
❑ 227	Dan Orlovsky RC	10.00	4.00
❑ 228	Derek Anderson RC	8.00	3.00
❑ 229	Kyle Orton RC	12.00	5.00
❑ 230	Chris Henry RC	8.00	3.00
❑ 231	Fred Gibson RC	6.00	2.50
❑ 232	Craphonso Thorpe RC	6.00	2.50
❑ 233	Terrence Murphy RC	8.00	3.00
❑ 234	Steve Savoy RC	4.00	1.50
❑ 235	Roscoe Parrish RC	8.00	3.00
❑ 236	Reggie Brown RC	8.00	3.00
❑ 237	Craig Bragg RC	6.00	2.50
❑ 238	Eric Shelton RC	8.00	3.00
❑ 239	T.A. McLendon RC	4.00	1.50
❑ 240	Walter Reyes RC	6.00	2.50
❑ 241	Anthony Davis RC	6.00	2.50
❑ 242	J.J. Arrington RC	10.00	4.00
❑ 243	Frank Gore RC	12.00	5.00
❑ 244	Alex Smith TE RC	8.00	3.00
❑ 245	Jeb Huckeba RC	8.00	3.00
❑ 246	Adam Jones RC	8.00	3.00
❑ 247	Brandon Browner RC	6.00	2.50
❑ 248	Carlos Rogers RC	10.00	4.00
❑ 249	Corey Webster RC	8.00	3.00
❑ 250	Justin Miller RC	6.00	2.50
❑ 251	Eric Green RC	4.00	1.50
❑ 252	Kurt Campbell RC	6.00	2.50
❑ 253	Ronald Bartell RC	6.00	2.50
❑ 254	Billy Bajema RC	6.00	2.50
❑ 255	Vincent Fuller RC	6.00	2.50
❑ 256	Donte Nicholson RC	8.00	3.00
❑ 257	Derrick Johnson RC	12.00	5.00
❑ 258	Mike Patterson RC	8.00	3.00
❑ 259	Anttaj Hawthorne RC	6.00	2.50
❑ 260	Erasmus James RC	8.00	3.00
❑ 261	David Pollack RC	8.00	3.00
❑ 262	Garrett Cross RC	4.00	1.50
❑ 263	Justin Tuck RC	8.00	3.00
❑ 264	DeMarcus Ware RC	12.00	5.00
❑ 265	Odell Thurman RC	8.00	3.00
❑ 266	Barrett Ruud RC	8.00	3.00
❑ 267	Lance Mitchell RC	6.00	2.50
❑ 268	Kevin Burnett RC	8.00	3.00
❑ 269	Daven Holly RC	6.00	2.50
❑ 270	James Butler RC	6.00	2.50
❑ 271	Kirk Morrison RC	8.00	3.00
❑ 272	Mike Nugent RC	8.00	3.00
❑ 273	Zach Tuiasosopo RC	4.00	1.50
❑ 274	Kay-Jay Harris RC	6.00	2.50
❑ 275	Darren Sproles RC	8.00	3.00
❑ 276	Ciatrick Fason RC	8.00	3.00
❑ 277	Charlie Frye RC	15.00	6.00
❑ 278	Vernand Morency RC	8.00	3.00
❑ 279	Jason Campbell RC	12.00	5.00
❑ 280	Antrel Rolle RC	8.00	3.00
❑ 281	Derrick Johnson RC	12.00	5.00
❑ 282	Shawne Merriman RC	12.00	5.00
❑ 283	Marlin Jackson RC	8.00	3.00
❑ 284	Jerome Mathis RC	8.00	3.00
❑ 285	Mike Williams	15.00	6.00
❑ 286	Dan Cody RC	8.00	3.00
❑ 287	Travis Johnson RC	8.00	3.00
❑ 288	Thomas Davis RC	8.00	3.00
❑ 289	Marcus Spears RC	8.00	3.00
❑ 290	Andrew Walter RC	12.00	5.00
❑ 291	Heath Miller RC	20.00	7.50
❑ 292	Mark Clayton RC	10.00	4.00
❑ 293	Troy Williamson RC	15.00	6.00
❑ 294	Roddy White RC	8.00	3.00
❑ 295	Braylon Edwards RC	25.00	10.00
❑ 296	Cedric Benson RC	15.00	6.00
❑ 297	Carnell Williams RC	40.00	20.00
❑ 298	Ronnie Brown RC	25.00	10.00
❑ 299	Alex Smith QB RC	30.00	12.50
❑ 300	Aaron Rodgers RC	25.00	10.00

1997 Revolution

❑	COMPLETE SET (150)	80.00	40.00
❑ 1	Larry Centers	.75	.30
❑ 2	Kent Graham	.50	.20
❑ 3	Leeland McElroy	.50	.20
❑ 4	Rob Moore	.75	.30
❑ 5	Jake Plummer RC	8.00	3.00
❑ 6	Jamal Anderson	1.25	.50
❑ 7	Bert Emanuel	.75	.30
❑ 8	Byron Hanspard RC	.75	.30
❑ 9	Terance Mathis	.75	.30
❑ 10	O.J. Santiago RC	.75	.30
❑ 11	Derrick Alexander WR	.75	.30
❑ 12	Peter Boulware RC	1.25	.50
❑ 13	Jay Graham RC	.75	.30
❑ 14	Michael Jackson	.75	.30
❑ 15	Vinny Testaverde	.75	.30
❑ 16	Todd Collins	.50	.20
❑ 17	Andre Reed	.75	.30
❑ 18	Jay Riemersma	.50	.20
❑ 19	Antowain Smith RC	4.00	1.50
❑ 20	Bruce Smith	.75	.30
❑ 21	Thurman Thomas	1.25	.50
❑ 22	Rae Carruth RC	.50	.20
❑ 23	Kerry Collins	1.25	.50
❑ 24	Anthony Johnson	.50	.20
❑ 25	Muhsin Muhammad	.75	.30
❑ 26	Wesley Walls	.75	.30
❑ 27	Curtis Conway	.75	.30
❑ 28	Bobby Engram	.75	.30
❑ 29	Raymont Harris	.50	.20
❑ 30	Rick Mirer	.50	.20
❑ 31	Rashaan Salaam	.50	.20
❑ 32	Jeff Blake	.75	.30
❑ 33	Corey Dillon RC	10.00	4.00
❑ 34	Carl Pickens	.75	.30
❑ 35	Darnay Scott	.75	.30
❑ 36	Troy Aikman	2.50	1.00
❑ 37	Michael Irvin	1.25	.50
❑ 38	Daryl Johnston	.75	.30
❑ 39	Deion Sanders	1.25	.50
❑ 40	Emmitt Smith	4.00	1.50
❑ 41	Terrell Davis	1.50	.60
❑ 42	John Elway	5.00	2.00
❑ 43	Ed McCaffrey	.75	.30
❑ 44	Shannon Sharpe	.75	.30
❑ 45	Neil Smith	.75	.30
❑ 46	Scott Mitchell	.75	.30
❑ 47	Herman Moore	.75	.30
❑ 48	Johnnie Morton	.75	.30
❑ 49	Barry Sanders	4.00	1.50
❑ 50	Robert Brooks	.75	.30
❑ 51	LeRoy Butler	.50	.20
❑ 52	Brett Favre	5.00	2.00
❑ 53	Antonio Freeman	1.25	.50
❑ 54	Dorsey Levens	1.25	.50
❑ 55	Reggie White	1.25	.50
❑ 56	Sean Dawkins	.50	.20
❑ 57	Ken Dilger	.50	.20
❑ 58	Marshall Faulk	1.50	.60
❑ 59	Jim Harbaugh	.75	.30
❑ 60	Marvin Harrison	1.25	.50
❑ 61	Mark Brunell	1.50	.60
❑ 62	Keenan McCardell	.75	.30
❑ 63	Natrone Means	.75	.30
❑ 64	Jimmy Smith	.75	.30
❑ 65	James O.Stewart	.75	.30
❑ 66	Marcus Allen	1.25	.50
❑ 67	Tony Gonzalez RC	5.00	2.00
❑ 68	Elvis Grbac	.75	.30
❑ 69	Greg Hill	.50	.20
❑ 70	Andre Rison	.75	.30
❑ 71	Karim Abdul-Jabbar	1.25	.50
❑ 72	Fred Barnett	.50	.20
❑ 73	Dan Marino	5.00	2.00
❑ 74	O.J. McDuffie	.75	.30
❑ 75	Irving Spikes	.50	.20
❑ 76	Cris Carter	1.25	.50
❑ 77	Matthew Hatchette RC	.75	.30
❑ 78	Brad Johnson	1.25	.50
❑ 79	Jake Reed	.75	.30
❑ 80	Robert Smith	.75	.30
❑ 81	Drew Bledsoe	1.50	.60
❑ 82	Ben Coates	.75	.30
❑ 83	Terry Glenn	1.25	.50
❑ 84	Curtis Martin	1.50	.60
❑ 85	Dave Meggett	.50	.20
❑ 86	Troy Davis RC	.75	.30
❑ 87	Andre Hastings	.50	.20
❑ 88	Heath Shuler	.50	.20
❑ 89	Irv Smith	.50	.20
❑ 90	Danny Wuerffel RC	1.25	.50
❑ 91	Ray Zellars	.50	.20
❑ 92	Tiki Barber RC	10.00	4.00
❑ 93	Dave Brown	.50	.20
❑ 94	Chris Calloway	.50	.20
❑ 95	Rodney Hampton	.75	.30
❑ 96	Amani Toomer	.75	.30
❑ 97	Wayne Chrebet	1.25	.50
❑ 98	Keyshawn Johnson	1.25	.50
❑ 99	Adrian Murrell	.75	.30
❑ 100	Neil O'Donnell	.75	.30
❑ 101	Dedric Ward RC	.75	.30
❑ 102	Tim Brown	1.25	.50
❑ 103	Rickey Dudley	.75	.30
❑ 104	Jeff George	.75	.30
❑ 105	Desmond Howard	.75	.30
❑ 106	Napoleon Kaufman	1.25	.50
❑ 107	Ty Detmer	.75	.30
❑ 108	Jason Dunn	.50	.20
❑ 109	Irving Fryar	.75	.30
❑ 110	Rodney Peete	.50	.20
❑ 111	Ricky Watters	.75	.30
❑ 112	Jerome Bettis	1.25	.50
❑ 113	Will Blackwell RC	.75	.30
❑ 114	Charles Johnson	.75	.30
❑ 115	Kordell Stewart	1.25	.50
❑ 116	Tony Banks	.75	.30
❑ 117	Isaac Bruce	1.25	.50
❑ 118	Ernie Conwell	.50	.20
❑ 119	Eddie Kennison	.75	.30
❑ 120	Lawrence Phillips	.50	.20
❑ 121	Stan Humphries	.75	.30
❑ 122	Tony Martin	.75	.30
❑ 123	Eric Metcalf	.75	.30
❑ 124	Junior Seau	1.25	.50
❑ 125	Jim Druckenmiller RC	.75	.30
❑ 126	Kevin Greene	.75	.30
❑ 127	Garrison Hearst	.75	.30
❑ 128	Terrell Owens	1.50	.60

❑ 129 Jerry Rice	2.50	1.00
❑ 130 J.J. Stokes	.75	.30
❑ 131 Rod Woodson	.75	.30
❑ 132 Steve Young	1.50	.60
❑ 133 Joey Galloway	.75	.30
❑ 134 Cortez Kennedy	.50	.20
❑ 135 Jon Kitna RC	6.00	2.50
❑ 136 Warren Moon	1.25	.50
❑ 137 Chris Warren	.75	.30
❑ 138 Mike Alstott	1.25	.50
❑ 139 Reidel Anthony RC	1.25	.50
❑ 140 Trent Dilfer	1.25	.50
❑ 141 Warrick Dunn RC	4.00	1.50
❑ 142 Willie Davis	.50	.20
❑ 143 Eddie George	1.25	.50
❑ 144 Steve McNair	1.50	.60
❑ 145 Chris Sanders	.50	.20
❑ 146 Terry Allen	1.25	.50
❑ 147 Jamie Asher	.50	.20
❑ 148 Henry Ellard	.50	.20
❑ 149 Gus Frerotte	.50	.20
❑ 150 Leslie Shepherd	.50	.20
❑ S1 Mark Brunell Sample	1.00	.40

1998 Revolution

❑ COMPLETE SET (150)	100.00	40.00
❑ 1 Larry Centers	.75	.30
❑ 2 Leeland McElroy	.75	.30
❑ 3 Rob Moore	1.25	.50
❑ 4 Jake Plummer	2.00	.75
❑ 5 Frank Sanders	1.25	.50
❑ 6 Jamal Anderson	2.00	.75
❑ 7 Chris Chandler	1.25	.50
❑ 8 Byron Hanspard	.75	.30
❑ 9 Jay Graham	.75	.30
❑ 10 Michael Jackson	.75	.30
❑ 11 Vinny Testaverde	1.25	.50
❑ 12 Eric Zeier	1.25	.50
❑ 13 Todd Collins	.75	.30
❑ 14 Quinn Early	.75	.30
❑ 15 Andre Reed	1.25	.50
❑ 16 Antowain Smith	2.00	.75
❑ 17 Bruce Smith	1.25	.50
❑ 18 Thurman Thomas	2.00	.75
❑ 19 Rae Carruth	.75	.30
❑ 20 Kerry Collins	1.25	.50
❑ 21 Wesley Walls	1.25	.50
❑ 22 Damell Autry	.75	.30
❑ 23 Curtis Conway	1.25	.50
❑ 24 Bobby Engram	1.25	.50
❑ 25 Curtis Enis RC	1.25	.50
❑ 26 Raymont Harris	.75	.30
❑ 27 Jeff Blake	1.25	.50
❑ 28 Corey Dillon	2.00	.75
❑ 29 Carl Pickens	1.25	.50
❑ 30 Damay Scott	1.25	.50
❑ 31 Troy Aikman	4.00	1.50
❑ 32 Michael Irvin	2.00	.75
❑ 33 Deion Sanders	2.00	.75
❑ 34 Emmitt Smith	6.00	2.50
❑ 35 Steve Atwater	.75	.30
❑ 36 Terrell Davis	2.00	.75
❑ 37 John Elway	8.00	3.00
❑ 38 Brian Griese RC	5.00	2.00
❑ 39 Ed McCaffrey	1.25	.50
❑ 40 Marcus Nash RC	1.25	.50
❑ 41 Shannon Sharpe	1.25	.50
❑ 42 Neil Smith	1.25	.50
❑ 43 Rod Smith	1.25	.50
❑ 44 Charlie Batch RC	2.50	1.00
❑ 45 Germane Crowell RC	2.00	.75
❑ 46 Scott Mitchell	1.25	.50
❑ 47 Herman Moore	1.25	.50
❑ 48 Barry Sanders	6.00	2.50
❑ 49 Robert Brooks	1.25	.50
❑ 50 Mark Chmura	1.25	.50
❑ 51 Brett Favre	8.00	3.00
❑ 52 Antonio Freeman	2.00	.75
❑ 53 Dorsey Levens	2.00	.75
❑ 54 Aaron Bailey	.75	.30
❑ 55 Ken Dilger	.75	.30
❑ 56 Marshall Faulk	2.50	1.00
❑ 57 Marvin Harrison	2.00	.75
❑ 58 Peyton Manning RC	25.00	10.00
❑ 59 Tavian Banks RC	2.00	.75
❑ 60 Tony Brackens	.75	.30
❑ 61 Mark Brunell	2.00	.75
❑ 62 Keenan McCardell	1.25	.50
❑ 63 Natrone Means	1.25	.50
❑ 64 Jimmy Smith	1.25	.50
❑ 65 James Stewart	1.25	.50
❑ 66 Fred Taylor RC	4.00	1.50
❑ 67 Tony Gonzalez	2.00	.75
❑ 68 Elvis Grbac	1.25	.50
❑ 69 Greg Hill	.75	.30
❑ 70 Andre Rison	1.25	.50
❑ 71 Derrick Thomas	2.00	.75
❑ 72 Karim Abdul-Jabbar	2.00	.75
❑ 73 John Avery RC	2.00	.75
❑ 74 Troy Drayton	.75	.30
❑ 75 Dan Marino	8.00	3.00
❑ 76 O.J. McDuffie	1.25	.50
❑ 77 Cris Carter	2.00	.75
❑ 78 Brad Johnson	2.00	.75
❑ 79 John Randle	1.25	.50
❑ 80 Jake Reed	1.25	.50
❑ 81 Robert Smith	2.00	.75
❑ 82 Drew Bledsoe	3.00	1.25
❑ 83 Ben Coates	1.25	.50
❑ 84 Robert Edwards RC	2.00	.75
❑ 85 Terry Glenn	2.00	.75
❑ 86 Tony Simmons RC	2.00	.75
❑ 87 Troy Davis	.75	.30
❑ 88 Heath Shuler	.75	.30
❑ 89 Danny Wuerffel	1.25	.50
❑ 90 Ray Zellars	.75	.30
❑ 91 Tiki Barber	2.00	.75
❑ 92 Joe Jurevicius RC	2.50	1.00
❑ 93 Danny Kanell	1.25	.50
❑ 94 Charles Way	.75	.30
❑ 95 Tyrone Wheatley	1.25	.50
❑ 96 Wayne Chrebet	2.00	.75
❑ 97 Glenn Foley	1.25	.50
❑ 98 Keyshawn Johnson	2.00	.75
❑ 99 Curtis Martin	2.00	.75
❑ 100 Tim Brown	2.00	.75
❑ 101 Rickey Dudley	.75	.30
❑ 102 Jeff George	1.25	.50
❑ 103 Desmond Howard	1.25	.50
❑ 104 Napoleon Kaufman	2.00	.75
❑ 105 Charles Woodson RC	3.00	1.25
❑ 106 Jason Dunn	.75	.30
❑ 107 Irving Fryar	1.25	.50
❑ 108 Charlie Garner	1.25	.50
❑ 109 Bobby Hoying	1.25	.50
❑ 110 Jerome Bettis	2.00	.75
❑ 111 Mark Bruener	.75	.30
❑ 112 Charles Johnson	.75	.30
❑ 113 Levon Kirkland	.75	.30
❑ 114 Kordell Stewart	2.00	.75
❑ 115 Hines Ward RC	10.00	5.00
❑ 116 Tony Banks	1.25	.50
❑ 117 Isaac Bruce	2.00	.75
❑ 118 Robert Holcombe RC	2.00	.75
❑ 119 Eddie Kennison	1.25	.50
❑ 120 Freddie Jones	.75	.30
❑ 121 Ryan Leaf RC	2.50	1.00
❑ 122 Tony Martin	1.25	.50
❑ 123 Junior Seau	2.00	.75
❑ 124 Jim Druckenmiller	.75	.30
❑ 125 Garrison Hearst	2.00	.75
❑ 126 Terrell Owens	2.00	.75
❑ 127 Jerry Rice	4.00	1.50
❑ 128 J.J. Stokes	1.25	.50
❑ 129 Steve Young	2.50	1.00
❑ 130 Joey Galloway	1.25	.50
❑ 131 Ahman Green RC	12.00	5.00
❑ 132 Cortez Kennedy	.75	.30
❑ 133 Jon Kitna	2.00	.75
❑ 134 James McKnight	2.00	.75
❑ 135 Warren Moon	2.00	.75
❑ 136 Mike Alstott	2.00	.75
❑ 137 Reidel Anthony	1.25	.50
❑ 138 Trent Dilfer	2.00	.75
❑ 139 Warrick Dunn	2.00	.75
❑ 140 Warren Sapp	1.25	.50
❑ 141 Kevin Dyson RC	2.50	1.00
❑ 142 Eddie George	2.00	.75
❑ 143 Steve McNair	2.00	.75
❑ 144 Chris Sanders	.75	.30
❑ 145 Frank Wycheck	.75	.30
❑ 146 Stephen Alexander RC	2.00	.75
❑ 147 Terry Allen	2.00	.75
❑ 148 Gus Frerotte	.75	.30
❑ 149 Skip Hicks RC	2.00	.75
❑ 150 Michael Westbrook	1.25	.50
❑ S1 Warrick Dunn Sample	1.00	.40

1999 Revolution

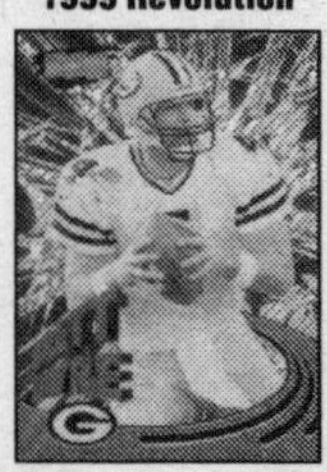

❑ COMPLETE SET (175)	100.00	50.00
❑ 1 David Boston RC	2.50	1.00
❑ 2 Joel Makovicka RC SP	3.00	1.25
❑ 3 Rob Moore	.75	.30
❑ 4 Adrian Murrell	.75	.30
❑ 5 Jake Plummer	.75	.30
❑ 6 Frank Sanders	.75	.30
❑ 7 Jamal Anderson	1.25	.50
❑ 8 Chris Chandler	.75	.30
❑ 9 Tim Dwight	1.25	.50
❑ 10 Terance Mathis	.75	.30
❑ 11 Jeff Paulk RC SP	1.50	.60
❑ 12 O.J. Santiago	.50	.20
❑ 13 Peter Boulware	.50	.20
❑ 14 Priest Holmes	2.00	.75
❑ 15 Michael Jackson	.50	.20
❑ 16 Jermaine Lewis	.75	.30
❑ 17 Doug Flutie	1.25	.50
❑ 18 Eric Moulds	1.25	.50
❑ 19 Peerless Price RC SP	3.00	1.25
❑ 20 Andre Reed	.75	.30
❑ 21 Antowain Smith	1.25	.50
❑ 22 Bruce Smith	.75	.30

❑ 23	Steve Beuerlein	.50	.20
❑ 24	Kevin Greene	.75	.30
❑ 25	Fred Lane	.50	.20
❑ 26	Muhsin Muhammad	.75	.30
❑ 27	Wesley Walls	.75	.30
❑ 28	Marty Booker RC SP	3.00	1.25
❑ 29	Curtis Conway	.75	.30
❑ 30	Bobby Engram	.75	.30
❑ 31	Curtis Enis	.50	.20
❑ 32	Erik Kramer	.50	.20
❑ 33	Cade McNown RC	2.00	.75
❑ 34	Scott Covington RC	2.50	1.00
❑ 35	Corey Dillon	1.25	.50
❑ 36	Carl Pickens	.75	.30
❑ 37	Darnay Scott	.50	.20
❑ 38	Akili Smith RC	2.00	.75
❑ 39	Craig Yeast RC SP	2.50	1.00
❑ 40	Darrin Chiaverini RC SP	2.50	1.00
❑ 41	Tim Couch RC	2.50	1.00
❑ 42	Ty Detmer	.75	.30
❑ 43	Kevin Johnson RC	2.50	1.00
❑ 44	Terry Kirby	.50	.20
❑ 45	Daylon McCutcheon RC SP	1.50	.60
❑ 46	Irv Smith	.50	.20
❑ 47	Troy Aikman	2.50	1.00
❑ 48	Michael Irvin	.75	.30
❑ 49	Wane McGarity RC SP	1.50	.60
❑ 50	Dat Nguyen RC SP	3.00	1.25
❑ 51	Deion Sanders	1.25	.50
❑ 52	Emmitt Smith	2.50	1.00
❑ 53	Terrell Davis	1.25	.50
❑ 54	John Elway	4.00	1.50
❑ 55	Brian Griese	1.25	.50
❑ 56	Ed McCaffrey	.75	.30
❑ 57	Travis McGriff RC SP	1.50	.60
❑ 58	Shannon Sharpe	.75	.30
❑ 59	Rod Smith WR	.75	.30
❑ 60	Charlie Batch	1.25	.50
❑ 61	Chris Claiborne RC	1.25	.50
❑ 62	Sedrick Irvin RC	1.25	.50
❑ 63	Herman Moore	.75	.30
❑ 64	Johnnie Morton	.75	.30
❑ 65	Barry Sanders	4.00	1.50
❑ 66	Aaron Brooks RC SP	6.00	2.50
❑ 67	Mark Chmura	.50	.20
❑ 68	Brett Favre	4.00	1.50
❑ 69	Antonio Freeman	1.25	.50
❑ 70	Dorsey Levens	1.25	.50
❑ 71	De'Mond Parker RC SP	1.50	.60
❑ 72	Marvin Harrison	1.25	.50
❑ 73	Edgerrin James RC	8.00	3.00
❑ 74	Peyton Manning	4.00	1.50
❑ 75	Jerome Pathon	.50	.20
❑ 76	Mike Peterson RC SP	2.50	1.00
❑ 77	Reggie Barlow	.50	.20
❑ 78	Mark Brunell	1.25	.50
❑ 79	Keenan McCardell	.75	.30
❑ 80	Jimmy Smith	.75	.30
❑ 81	Fred Taylor	1.25	.50
❑ 82	Mike Cloud RC	2.00	.75
❑ 83	Tony Gonzalez	1.25	.50
❑ 84	Elvis Grbac	.75	.30
❑ 85	Larry Parker RC SP	3.00	1.25
❑ 86	Andre Rison	.75	.30
❑ 87	Brian Shay RC SP	1.50	.60
❑ 88	Karim Abdul-Jabbar	.75	.30
❑ 89	Oronde Gadsden	.75	.30
❑ 90	James Johnson RC	2.00	.75
❑ 91	Rob Konrad RC	2.00	.75
❑ 92	Dan Marino	4.00	1.50
❑ 93	O.J. McDuffie	.75	.30
❑ 94	Cris Carter	1.25	.50
❑ 95	Daunte Culpepper RC	8.00	3.00
❑ 96	Randall Cunningham	1.25	.50
❑ 97	Jim Kleinsasser RC SP	2.50	1.00
❑ 98	Randy Moss	3.00	1.25
❑ 99	Jake Reed	.75	.30
❑ 100	Robert Smith	1.25	.50
❑ 101	Drew Bledsoe	1.50	.60
❑ 102	Ben Coates	.75	.30
❑ 103	Kevin Faulk RC	2.50	1.00
❑ 104	Terry Glenn	1.25	.50
❑ 105	Shawn Jefferson	.50	.20
❑ 106	Andy Katzenmoyer RC SP	2.50	1.00
❑ 107	Cameron Cleeland	.50	.20
❑ 108	Andre Hastings	.50	.20
❑ 109	Billy Joe Tolliver	.50	.20
❑ 110	Ricky Williams RC	4.00	1.50
❑ 111	Gary Brown	.50	.20
❑ 112	Kent Graham	.50	.20
❑ 113	Ike Hilliard	.50	.20
❑ 114	Joe Montgomery RC SP	2.50	1.00
❑ 115	Amani Toomer	.50	.20
❑ 116	Wayne Chrebet	.75	.30
❑ 117	Keyshawn Johnson	1.25	.50
❑ 118	Leon Johnson	.50	.20
❑ 119	Curtis Martin	1.25	.50
❑ 120	Vinny Testaverde	.75	.30
❑ 121	Dedric Ward	.50	.20
❑ 122	Tim Brown	1.25	.50
❑ 123	Dameane Douglas RC SP	3.00	1.25
❑ 124	Rickey Dudley	.50	.20
❑ 125	James Jett	.75	.30
❑ 126	Napoleon Kaufman	1.25	.50
❑ 127	Charles Woodson	1.25	.50
❑ 128	Na Brown RC SP	2.50	1.00
❑ 129	Cecil Martin RC SP	2.50	1.00
❑ 130	Donovan McNabb RC	10.00	4.00
❑ 131	Duce Staley	1.25	.50
❑ 132	Kevin Turner	.50	.20
❑ 133	Jerome Bettis	1.25	.50
❑ 134	Troy Edwards RC	2.00	.75
❑ 135	Courtney Hawkins	.50	.20
❑ 136	Malcolm Johnson RC SP	1.50	.60
❑ 137	Kordell Stewart	.75	.30
❑ 138	Jerame Tuman RC SP	3.00	1.25
❑ 139	Amos Zereoue RC	2.50	1.00
❑ 140	Isaac Bruce	1.25	.50
❑ 141	Joe Germaine RC	2.00	.75
❑ 142	Torry Holt RC SP	6.00	2.50
❑ 143	Amp Lee	.50	.20
❑ 144	Ricky Proehl	.50	.20
❑ 145	Freddie Jones	.50	.20
❑ 146	Ryan Leaf	1.25	.50
❑ 147	Natrone Means	.75	.30
❑ 148	Mikhael Ricks	.50	.20
❑ 149	Garrison Hearst	.75	.30
❑ 150	Terry Jackson RC SP	2.50	1.00
❑ 151	Terrell Owens	1.25	.50
❑ 152	Jerry Rice	2.50	1.00
❑ 153	J.J. Stokes	.75	.30
❑ 154	Steve Young	1.50	.60
❑ 155	Karsten Bailey RC	2.00	.75
❑ 156	Joey Galloway	.75	.30
❑ 157	Ahman Green	1.25	.50
❑ 158	Brock Huard RC	2.50	1.00
❑ 159	Jon Kitna	1.25	.50
❑ 160	Ricky Watters	.75	.30
❑ 161	Mike Alstott	1.25	.50
❑ 162	Reidel Anthony	.75	.30
❑ 163	Trent Dilfer	.75	.30
❑ 164	Warrick Dunn	1.25	.50
❑ 165	Shaun King RC	2.00	.75
❑ 166	Anthony McFarland RC	2.50	1.00
❑ 167	Kevin Dyson	.75	.30
❑ 168	Eddie George	1.25	.50
❑ 169	Darran Hall RC	1.25	.50
❑ 170	Steve McNair	1.25	.50
❑ 171	Frank Wycheck	.50	.20
❑ 172	Stephen Alexander	.50	.20
❑ 173	Champ Bailey RC	3.00	1.25
❑ 174	Skip Hicks	.50	.20
❑ 175	Michael Westbrook	.75	.30

2000 Revolution

❑	COMP.SET w/o SP's (100)	40.00	20.00
❑ 1	David Boston	1.25	.50
❑ 2	Jake Plummer	.75	.30
❑ 3	Frank Sanders	.75	.30
❑ 4	Jamal Anderson	1.25	.50
❑ 5	Chris Chandler	.75	.30
❑ 6	Tim Dwight	1.25	.50
❑ 7	Terance Mathis	.75	.30
❑ 8	Tony Banks	.75	.30
❑ 9	Qadry Ismail	.75	.30
❑ 10	Shannon Sharpe	.50	.20
❑ 11	Rob Johnson	.75	.30
❑ 12	Eric Moulds	1.25	.50
❑ 13	Peerless Price	.75	.30
❑ 14	Antowain Smith	.75	.30
❑ 15	Steve Beuerlein	.75	.30
❑ 16	Tim Biakabutuka	.75	.30
❑ 17	Muhsin Muhammad	.75	.30
❑ 18	Curtis Enis	.50	.20
❑ 19	Cade McNown	.50	.20
❑ 20	Marcus Robinson	1.25	.50
❑ 21	Corey Dillon	1.25	.50
❑ 22	Akili Smith	.50	.20
❑ 23	Tim Couch	.75	.30
❑ 24	Kevin Johnson	1.25	.50
❑ 25	Troy Aikman	2.50	1.00
❑ 26	Rocket Ismail	.75	.30
❑ 27	Emmitt Smith	2.50	1.00
❑ 28	Terrell Davis	1.25	.50
❑ 29	Brian Griese	1.25	.50
❑ 30	Ed McCaffrey	1.25	.50
❑ 31	Charlie Batch	1.25	.50
❑ 32	Herman Moore	.75	.30
❑ 33	James Stewart	.75	.30
❑ 34	Brett Favre	4.00	1.50
❑ 35	Antonio Freeman	1.25	.50
❑ 36	Dorsey Levens	.75	.30
❑ 37	Marvin Harrison	1.25	.50
❑ 38	Edgerrin James	2.00	.75
❑ 39	Peyton Manning	3.00	1.25
❑ 40	Terrence Wilkins	.50	.20
❑ 41	Mark Brunell	1.25	.50
❑ 42	Keenan McCardell	.75	.30
❑ 43	Jimmy Smith	.75	.30
❑ 44	Fred Taylor	1.25	.50
❑ 45	Derrick Alexander	.75	.30
❑ 46	Tony Gonzalez	.75	.30
❑ 47	Elvis Grbac	.75	.30
❑ 48	Damon Huard	1.25	.50
❑ 49	James Johnson	.50	.20
❑ 50	O.J. McDuffie	.75	.30
❑ 51	Cris Carter	1.25	.50
❑ 52	Daunte Culpepper	1.50	.60
❑ 53	Randy Moss	2.50	1.00
❑ 54	Robert Smith	1.25	.50
❑ 55	Drew Bledsoe	1.50	.60
❑ 56	Terry Glenn	.75	.30
❑ 57	Jeff Blake	.75	.30
❑ 58	Ricky Williams	1.25	.50
❑ 59	Tiki Barber	1.25	.50

❑ 60	Kerry Collins	.75	.30
❑ 61	Ike Hilliard	.75	.30
❑ 62	Amani Toomer	.50	.20
❑ 63	Wayne Chrebet	.75	.30
❑ 64	Curtis Martin	1.25	.50
❑ 65	Vinny Testaverde	.75	.30
❑ 66	Dedric Ward	.50	.20
❑ 67	Tim Brown	1.25	.50
❑ 68	Napoleon Kaufman	.75	.30
❑ 69	Tyrone Wheatley	.75	.30
❑ 70	Charles Johnson	.75	.30
❑ 71	Donovan McNabb	2.00	.75
❑ 72	Duce Staley	1.25	.50
❑ 73	Jerome Bettis	1.25	.50
❑ 74	Troy Edwards	.50	.20
❑ 75	Kordell Stewart	.75	.30
❑ 76	Isaac Bruce	1.25	.50
❑ 77	Marshall Faulk	1.50	.60
❑ 78	Az-Zahir Hakim	.50	.20
❑ 79	Torry Holt	1.25	.50
❑ 80	Kurt Warner	2.50	1.00
❑ 81	Curtis Conway	.75	.30
❑ 82	Jermaine Fazande	.50	.20
❑ 83	Ryan Leaf	.75	.30
❑ 84	Junior Seau	1.25	.50
❑ 85	Jeff Garcia	1.25	.50
❑ 86	Charlie Garner	.75	.30
❑ 87	Terrell Owens	1.25	.50
❑ 88	Jerry Rice	2.50	1.00
❑ 89	Jon Kitna	1.25	.50
❑ 90	Derrick Mayes	.75	.30
❑ 91	Ricky Watters	.75	.30
❑ 92	Mike Alstott	1.25	.50
❑ 93	Warrick Dunn	1.25	.50
❑ 94	Keyshawn Johnson	1.25	.50
❑ 95	Shaun King	.50	.20
❑ 96	Eddie George	1.25	.50
❑ 97	Jevon Kearse	1.25	.50
❑ 98	Steve McNair	1.25	.50
❑ 99	Stephen Davis	1.25	.50
❑ 100	Brad Johnson	1.25	.50
❑ 101	Thomas Jones RC	20.00	7.50
❑ 102	Doug Johnson RC	10.00	4.00
❑ 103	Jamal Lewis RC	25.00	10.00
❑ 104	Chris Redman RC	8.00	3.00
❑ 105	Travis Taylor RC	10.00	4.00
❑ 106	Troy Walters RC	10.00	4.00
❑ 107	Kwame Cavil RC	5.00	2.00
❑ 108	Sammy Morris RC	8.00	3.00
❑ 109	Dez White RC	10.00	4.00
❑ 110	Ron Dugans RC	5.00	2.00
❑ 111	Danny Farmer RC	8.00	3.00
❑ 112	Curtis Keaton RC	8.00	3.00
❑ 113	Peter Warrick RC	10.00	4.00
❑ 114	Dennis Northcutt RC	10.00	4.00
❑ 115	Travis Prentice RC	8.00	3.00
❑ 116	Kevin Thompson RC	5.00	2.00
❑ 117	Spergon Wynn RC	8.00	3.00
❑ 118	Michael Wiley RC	8.00	3.00
❑ 119	Mike Anderson RC	12.00	5.00
❑ 120	Chris Cole RC	8.00	3.00
❑ 121	Jarious Jackson RC	8.00	3.00
❑ 122	Charles Lee RC	5.00	2.00
❑ 123	Anthony Lucas RC	5.00	2.00
❑ 124	R.Jay Soward RC	8.00	3.00
❑ 125	Shyrone Stith RC	8.00	3.00
❑ 126	Sylvester Morris RC	8.00	3.00
❑ 127	Doug Chapman RC	8.00	3.00
❑ 128	Tom Brady RC	135.00	75.00
❑ 129	Gari Scott RC	5.00	2.00
❑ 130	J.R. Redmond RC	8.00	3.00
❑ 131	Ron Dayne RC	10.00	4.00
❑ 132	Ron Dixon RC	8.00	3.00
❑ 133	Laveranues Coles RC	12.00	5.00
❑ 134	Ronney Jenkins RC	8.00	3.00
❑ 135	Chad Pennington RC	25.00	10.00
❑ 136	Jerry Porter RC	12.00	5.00
❑ 137	Todd Pinkston RC	10.00	4.00
❑ 138	Plaxico Burress RC	20.00	7.50
❑ 139	Trung Canidate RC	8.00	3.00
❑ 140	Troy Walters RC	10.00	4.00
❑ 141	Giovanni Carmazzi RC	5.00	2.00
❑ 142	Tim Rattay RC	10.00	4.00
❑ 143	Shaun Alexander RC	40.00	20.00
❑ 144	Darrell Jackson RC	20.00	7.50
❑ 145	James Williams RC	8.00	3.00
❑ 146	Joe Hamilton RC	8.00	3.00
❑ 147	Aaron Stecker RC	10.00	4.00
❑ 148	Erron Kinney RC	10.00	4.00
❑ 149	Billy Volek RC	15.00	6.00
❑ 150	Todd Husak RC	10.00	4.00

1989 Score

❑	COMPLETE SET (330)	100.00	50.00
❑	COMP.FACT.SET (330)	100.00	50.00
❑ 1	Joe Montana	4.00	1.50
❑ 2	Bo Jackson	.60	.25
❑ 3	Boomer Esiason	.20	.07
❑ 4	Roger Craig	.50	.20
❑ 5	Ed Too Tall Jones	.20	.07
❑ 6	Phil Simms	.20	.07
❑ 7	Dan Hampton	.20	.07
❑ 8	John Settle RC	.10	.02
❑ 9	Bernie Kosar	.20	.07
❑ 10	Al Toon	.20	.07
❑ 11	Bubby Brister RC	1.00	.40
❑ 12	Mark Clayton	.20	.07
❑ 13	Dan Marino	4.00	1.50
❑ 14	Joe Morris	.10	.02
❑ 15	Warren Moon	.50	.20
❑ 16	Chuck Long	.10	.02
❑ 17	Mark Jackson	.10	.02
❑ 18	Michael Irvin RC	6.00	3.00
❑ 19	Bruce Smith	.50	.20
❑ 20	Anthony Carter	.20	.07
❑ 21	Charles Haley	.50	.20
❑ 22	Dave Duerson	.10	.02
❑ 23	Troy Stradford	.10	.02
❑ 24	Freeman McNeil	.10	.02
❑ 25	Jerry Gray	.10	.02
❑ 26	Bill Maas	.10	.02
❑ 27	Chris Chandler RC	5.00	2.00
❑ 28	Tom Newberry RC	.10	.02
❑ 29	Albert Lewis	.10	.02
❑ 30	Jay Schroeder	.10	.02
❑ 31	Dalton Hilliard	.10	.02
❑ 32	Tony Eason	.10	.02
❑ 33	Rick Donnelly UER	.10	.02
❑ 34	Herschel Walker	.20	.07
❑ 35	Wesley Walker	.10	.02
❑ 36	Chris Doleman	.20	.07
❑ 37	Pat Swilling	.20	.07
❑ 38	Joey Browner	.10	.02
❑ 39	Shane Conlan	.10	.02
❑ 40	Mike Tomczak	.20	.07
❑ 41	Webster Slaughter	.20	.07
❑ 42	Ray Donaldson	.10	.02
❑ 43	Christian Okoye	.10	.02
❑ 44	John Bosa	.10	.02
❑ 45	Aaron Cox RC	.10	.02
❑ 46	Bobby Hebert	.20	.07
❑ 47	Carl Banks	.10	.02
❑ 48	Jeff Fuller	.10	.02
❑ 49	Gerald Willhite	.10	.02
❑ 50	Mike Singletary	.20	.07
❑ 51	Stanley Morgan	.10	.02
❑ 52	Mark Bavaro	.20	.07
❑ 53	Mickey Shuler	.10	.02
❑ 54	Keith Millard	.10	.02
❑ 55	Andre Tippett	.10	.02
❑ 56	Vance Johnson	.20	.07
❑ 57	Bennie Blades RC	.20	.07
❑ 58	Tim Harris	.10	.02
❑ 59	Hanford Dixon	.10	.02
❑ 60	Chris Miller RC	1.00	.40
❑ 61	Cornelius Bennett	.50	.20
❑ 62	Neal Anderson	.20	.07
❑ 63	Ickey Woods RC UER	.50	.20
❑ 64	Gary Anderson RB	.10	.02
❑ 65	Vaughan Johnson RC	.10	.02
❑ 66	Ronnie Lippett	.10	.02
❑ 67	Mike Quick	.10	.02
❑ 68	Roy Green	.20	.07
❑ 69	Tim Krumrie	.10	.02
❑ 70	Mark Malone	.10	.02
❑ 71	James Jones FB	.10	.02
❑ 72	Cris Carter RC	12.00	5.00
❑ 73	Ricky Nattiel	.10	.02
❑ 74	Jim Arnold UER	.10	.02
❑ 75	Randall Cunningham	1.00	.40
❑ 76	John L.Williams	.10	.02
❑ 77	Paul Gruber RC	.10	.02
❑ 78	Rod Woodson RC	3.00	1.25
❑ 79	Ray Childress	.10	.02
❑ 80	Doug Williams	.20	.07
❑ 81	Deron Cherry	.20	.07
❑ 82	John Offerdahl	.10	.02
❑ 83	Louis Lipps	.20	.07
❑ 84	Neil Lomax	.10	.02
❑ 85	Wade Wilson	.20	.07
❑ 86	Tim Brown RC	12.00	5.00
❑ 87	Chris Hinton	.10	.02
❑ 88	Stump Mitchell	.10	.02
❑ 89	Tunch Ilkin RC	.10	.02
❑ 90	Steve Pelluer	.10	.02
❑ 91	Brian Noble	.10	.02
❑ 92	Reggie White	.50	.20
❑ 93	Aundray Bruce RC	.10	.02
❑ 94	Garry James	.10	.02
❑ 95	Drew Hill	.10	.02
❑ 96	Anthony Munoz	.20	.07
❑ 97	James Wilder	.10	.02
❑ 98	Dexter Manley	.10	.02
❑ 99	Lee Williams	.10	.02
❑ 100	Dave Krieg	.20	.07
❑ 101A	Keith Jackson RC 84	.50	.20
❑ 101B	Keith Jackson RC 88	.50	.20
❑ 102	Luis Sharpe	.10	.02
❑ 103	Kevin Greene	.50	.20
❑ 104	Duane Bickett	.10	.02
❑ 105	Mark Rypien RC	.50	.20
❑ 106	Curt Warner	.10	.02
❑ 107	Jacob Green	.10	.02
❑ 108	Gary Clark	.50	.20
❑ 109	Bruce Matthews RC	2.50	1.00
❑ 110	Bill Fralic	.10	.02
❑ 111	Bill Bates	.20	.07
❑ 112	Jeff Bryant	.10	.02
❑ 113	Charles Mann	.10	.02
❑ 114	Richard Dent	.20	.07
❑ 115	Bruce Hill RC	.10	.02
❑ 116	Mark May RC	.10	.02
❑ 117	Mark Collins RC	.10	.02
❑ 118	Ron Holmes	.10	.02
❑ 119	Scott Case RC	.10	.02
❑ 120	Tom Rathman	.10	.02
❑ 121	Dennis McKinnon	.10	.02
❑ 122A	Ricky Sanders ERR 46	.25	.08

❑ 122B Ricky Sanders COR 83 .50 .20
❑ 123 Michael Carter .10 .02
❑ 124 Ozzie Newsome .20 .07
❑ 125 Irving Fryar UER .20 .07
❑ 126A Ron Hall RC ERR .25 .08
❑ 126B Ron Hall RC COR .50 .20
❑ 127 Clay Matthews .20 .07
❑ 128 Leonard Marshall .10 .02
❑ 129 Kevin Mack .10 .02
❑ 130 Art Monk .20 .07
❑ 131 Garin Veris .10 .02
❑ 132 Steve Jordan .10 .02
❑ 133 Frank Minnifield .10 .02
❑ 134 Eddie Brown .10 .02
❑ 135 Stacey Bailey .10 .02
❑ 136 Rickey Jackson .20 .07
❑ 137 Henry Ellard .20 .07
❑ 138 Jim Burt .10 .02
❑ 139 Jerome Brown .20 .07
❑ 140 Rodney Holman RC .10 .02
❑ 141 Sammy Winder .10 .02
❑ 142 Marcus Cotton .10 .02
❑ 143 Jim Jeffcoat .10 .02
❑ 144 Rueben Mayes .10 .02
❑ 145 Jim McMahon .20 .07
❑ 146 Reggie Williams .10 .02
❑ 147 John Anderson .10 .02
❑ 148 Harris Barton RC .10 .02
❑ 149 Phillip Epps .10 .02
❑ 150 Jay Hilgenberg .10 .02
❑ 151 Earl Ferrell .10 .02
❑ 152 Andre Reed .50 .20
❑ 153 Dennis Gentry .10 .02
❑ 154 Max Montoya .10 .02
❑ 155 Darrin Nelson .10 .02
❑ 156 Jeff Chadwick .10 .02
❑ 157 James Brooks .20 .07
❑ 158 Keith Bishop .10 .02
❑ 159 Robert Awalt .10 .02
❑ 160 Marty Lyons .10 .02
❑ 161 Johnny Hector .10 .02
❑ 162 Tony Casillas .10 .02
❑ 163 Kyle Clifton RC .10 .02
❑ 164 Cody Risien .10 .02
❑ 165 Jamie Holland RC .10 .02
❑ 166 Merril Hoge RC .10 .02
❑ 167 Chris Spielman RC 1.00 .40
❑ 168 Carlos Carson .10 .02
❑ 169 Jerry Ball RC .10 .02
❑ 170 Don Majkowski RC .50 .20
❑ 171 Everson Walls .10 .02
❑ 172 Mike Rozier .10 .02
❑ 173 Matt Millen .20 .07
❑ 174 Karl Mecklenburg .10 .02
❑ 175 Paul Palmer .10 .02
❑ 176 Brian Blades RC UER .50 .20
❑ 177 Brent Fullwood RC .10 .02
❑ 178 Anthony Miller RC .50 .20
❑ 179 Brian Sochia .10 .02
❑ 180 Stephen Baker RC .10 .02
❑ 181 Jesse Solomon .10 .02
❑ 182 John Grimsley .10 .02
❑ 183 Timmy Newsome .10 .02
❑ 184 Steve Sewell RC .10 .02
❑ 185 Dean Biasucci .10 .02
❑ 186 Alonzo Highsmith .10 .02
❑ 187 Randy Grimes .10 .02
❑ 188A Mark Carrier RC WR ERR 1.00 .40
❑ 188B Mark Carrier RC WR COR 1.00 .40
❑ 189 Vann McElroy .10 .02
❑ 190 Greg Bell .10 .02
❑ 191 Quinn Early RC 1.00 .40
❑ 192 Lawrence Taylor .50 .20
❑ 193 Albert Bentley .10 .02
❑ 194 Ernest Givins .20 .07
❑ 195 Jackie Slater .10 .02
❑ 196 Jim Sweeney .10 .02
❑ 197 Freddie Joe Nunn .10 .02
❑ 198 Keith Byars .20 .07
❑ 199 Hardy Nickerson RC .50 .20
❑ 200 Steve Beuerlein RC 4.00 1.50
❑ 201 Bruce Armstrong RC .50 .20
❑ 202 Lionel Manuel .10 .02
❑ 203 J.T. Smith .10 .02
❑ 204 Mark Ingram RC .50 .20
❑ 205 Fred Smerlas .10 .02
❑ 206 Bryan Hinkle RC .10 .02
❑ 207 Steve McMichael .20 .07
❑ 208 Nick Lowery .10 .02
❑ 209 Jack Trudeau .10 .02
❑ 210 Lorenzo Hampton .10 .02
❑ 211 Thurman Thomas RC 6.00 3.00
❑ 212 Steve Young 1.50 .60
❑ 213 James Lofton .50 .20
❑ 214 Jim Covert .10 .02
❑ 215 Ronnie Lott .20 .07
❑ 216 Stephone Paige .10 .02
❑ 217 Mark Duper .20 .07
❑ 218A Willie Gault ERR 93 .25 .08
❑ 218B Willie Gault COR 83 .50 .20
❑ 219 Ken Ruettgers RC .10 .02
❑ 220 Kevin Ross RC .10 .02
❑ 221 Jerry Rice 3.00 1.50
❑ 222 Billy Ray Smith .10 .02
❑ 223 Jim Kelly 1.00 .40
❑ 224 Vinny Testaverde 1.00 .40
❑ 225 Steve Largent .50 .20
❑ 226 Warren Williams RC .10 .02
❑ 227 Morten Andersen .10 .02
❑ 228 Bill Brooks .20 .07
❑ 229 Reggie Langhorne RC .10 .02
❑ 230 Pepper Johnson .10 .02
❑ 231 Pat Leahy .10 .02
❑ 232 Fred Marion .10 .02
❑ 233 Gary Zimmerman .10 .02
❑ 234 Marcus Allen .50 .20
❑ 235 Gaston Green RC .10 .02
❑ 236 John Stephens RC .10 .02
❑ 237 Terry Kinard .10 .02
❑ 238 John Taylor RC .50 .20
❑ 239 Brian Bosworth .20 .07
❑ 240 Anthony Toney .10 .02
❑ 241 Ken O'Brien .10 .02
❑ 242 Howie Long .50 .20
❑ 243 Doug Flutie 2.50 1.00
❑ 244 Jim Everett .50 .20
❑ 245 Broderick Thomas RC .10 .02
❑ 246 Deion Sanders RC 12.00 5.00
❑ 247 Donnell Woolford RC .10 .02
❑ 248 Wayne Martin RC .10 .02
❑ 249 David Williams RC .10 .02
❑ 250 Bill Hawkins RC .10 .02
❑ 251 Eric Hill RC .10 .02
❑ 252 Burt Grossman RC .10 .02
❑ 253 Tracy Rocker .10 .02
❑ 254 Steve Wisniewski RC .50 .20
❑ 255 Jessie Small RC .10 .02
❑ 256 David Braxton .10 .02
❑ 257 Barry Sanders RC 40.00 15.00
❑ 258 Derrick Thomas RC 6.00 3.00
❑ 259 Eric Metcalf RC 1.00 .40
❑ 260 Keith DeLong RC .10 .02
❑ 261 Hart Lee Dykes RC .10 .02
❑ 262 Sammie Smith RC .10 .02
❑ 263 Steve Atwater RC .50 .20
❑ 264 Eric Ball RC .10 .02
❑ 265 Don Beebe RC .50 .20
❑ 266 Brian Williams OL RC .10 .02
❑ 267 Jeff Lageman RC .10 .02
❑ 268 Tim Worley RC .10 .02
❑ 269 Tony Mandarich RC .10 .02
❑ 270 Troy Aikman RC 30.00 12.50
❑ 271 Andy Heck RC .10 .02
❑ 272 Andre Rison RC 5.00 2.50
❑ 273 AFC Champ/Woods/Esiason .10 .02
❑ 274 NFC Champ/Joe Montana 1.00 .40
❑ 275 Joe Montana/Jerry Rice 2.00 .75
❑ 276 Rodney Carter .10 .02
❑ 277 Mark Jackson/V.Johnson/Nattiel .10 .02
❑ 278 John L. Williams .10 .02
❑ 279 Joe Montana/Jerry Rice 2.00 .75
❑ 280 Roy Green/Lomax .10 .02
❑ 281 Ran.Cunningham/K.Jackson .10 .02
❑ 282 Chris Doleman and .10 .02
❑ 283 Mark Duper and .10 .02
❑ 284 Bo Jackson/Marcus Allen .60 .25
❑ 285 Frank Minnifield AP .10 .02
❑ 286 Bruce Matthews AP .20 .07
❑ 287 Joey Browner AP .10 .02
❑ 288 Jay Hilgenberg AP .10 .02
❑ 289 Carl Lee RC AP .10 .02
❑ 290 Scott Norwood AP RC .10 .02
❑ 291 John Taylor AP .50 .20
❑ 292 Jerry Rice AP 1.50 .60
❑ 293A Keith Jackson AP 84 .50 .20
❑ 293B Keith Jackson AP 88 .50 .20
❑ 294 Gary Zimmerman AP .10 .02
❑ 295 Lawrence Taylor AP .50 .20
❑ 296 Reggie White AP .50 .20
❑ 297 Roger Craig AP .20 .07
❑ 298 Boomer Esiason AP .20 .07
❑ 299 Cornelius Bennett AP .20 .07
❑ 300 Mike Horan AP .10 .02
❑ 301 Deron Cherry AP .10 .02
❑ 302 Tom Newberry AP .10 .02
❑ 303 Mike Singletary AP .20 .07
❑ 304 Shane Conlan AP .10 .02
❑ 305A Tim Brown AP ERR 80 2.00 .75
❑ 305B Tim Brown AP COR 81 2.00 .75
❑ 306 Henry Ellard AP .20 .07
❑ 307 Bruce Smith AP .20 .07
❑ 308 Tim Krumrie AP .10 .02
❑ 309 Anthony Munoz AP .20 .07
❑ 310 Darrell Green SPD .10 .02
❑ 311 Anthony Miller SPD .50 .20
❑ 312 Wesley Walker SPEED .10 .02
❑ 313 Ron Brown SPEED .10 .02
❑ 314 Bo Jackson SPD .60 .25
❑ 315 Phillip Epps SPEED .10 .02
❑ 316A Eric Thomas RC SPD 31 .25 .08
❑ 316B Eric Thomas RC SPD 22 .50 .20
❑ 317 Herschel Walker SPD .20 .07
❑ 318 Jacob Green PRED .10 .02
❑ 319 Andre Tippett PRED .10 .02
❑ 320 Freddie Joe Nunn PRED .10 .02
❑ 321 Reggie White PRED .50 .20
❑ 322 Lawrence Taylor PRED .50 .20
❑ 323 Greg Townsend PRED .10 .02
❑ 324 Tim Harris PRED .10 .02
❑ 325 Bruce Smith PRED .20 .07
❑ 326 Tony Dorsett RB .50 .20
❑ 327 Steve Largent RB .50 .20
❑ 328 Tim Brown RB 2.00 .75
❑ 329 Joe Montana RB 1.50 .60
❑ 330 Tom Landry Tribute 1.00 .40

1989 Score Supplemental

❑ COMP.FACT.SET (110) 8.00 3.00
❑ 331S Herschel Walker .40 .15
❑ 332S Allen Pinkett RC .10 .02
❑ 333S Sterling Sharpe RC 3.00 1.25
❑ 334S Alvin Walton RC .10 .02
❑ 335S Frank Reich RC .40 .15
❑ 336S James Thornton RC .10 .02
❑ 337S David Fulcher .20 .07
❑ 338S Raul Allegre .10 .02
❑ 339S John Elway 4.00 2.00
❑ 340S Michael Cofer .10 .02
❑ 341S Jim Skow .10 .02
❑ 342S Steve DeBerg .10 .02
❑ 343S Mervyn Fernandez RC .10 .02
❑ 344S Mike Lansford .10 .02
❑ 345S Reggie Roby .10 .02
❑ 346S Raymond Clayborn .10 .02
❑ 347S Lonzell Hill .10 .02
❑ 348S Ottis Anderson .20 .07
❑ 349S Erik McMillan RC .10 .02
❑ 350S Al Harris RC .10 .02
❑ 351S Jack Del Rio RC .40 .15
❑ 352S Gary Anderson K .10 .02
❑ 353S Jim McMahon .20 .07
❑ 354S Keena Turner .10 .02
❑ 355S Tony Woods RC .10 .02
❑ 356S Donald Igwebuike .10 .02
❑ 357S Gerald Riggs .20 .07
❑ 358S Eddie Murray .10 .02
❑ 359S Dino Hackett .10 .02
❑ 360S Brad Muster RC .10 .02
❑ 361S Paul Palmer .10 .02
❑ 362S Jerry Robinson .10 .02
❑ 363S Simon Fletcher RC .20 .07
❑ 364S Tommy Kramer .10 .02
❑ 365S Jim C.Jensen RC .10 .02
❑ 366S Lorenzo White RC .40 .15
❑ 367S Fredd Young .10 .02
❑ 368S Ron Jaworski .10 .02
❑ 369S Mel Owens .10 .02
❑ 370S Dave Waymer .10 .02
❑ 371S Sean Landeta .10 .02
❑ 372S Sam Mills .20 .07
❑ 373S Todd Blackledge .10 .02
❑ 374S Jo Jo Townsell .10 .02
❑ 375S Ron Wolfley .10 .02
❑ 376S Ralf Mojsiejenko .10 .02
❑ 377S Eric Wright .10 .02
❑ 378S Nesby Glasgow .10 .02
❑ 379S Darryl Talley .20 .07
❑ 380S Eric Allen RC UER .40 .15
❑ 381S Dennis Smith .20 .07
❑ 382S John Tice .10 .02
❑ 383S Jesse Solomon .10 .02
❑ 384S Bo Jackson FB/BB 1.00 .40
❑ 385S Mike Merriweather .10 .02
❑ 386S Maurice Carthon .10 .02
❑ 387S David Grayson .10 .02
❑ 388S Wilber Marshall .10 .02
❑ 389S David Wyman .10 .02
❑ 390S Thomas Everett RC .10 .02
❑ 391S Alex Gordon .10 .02
❑ 392S D.J. Dozier .10 .02
❑ 393S Scott Radecic RC .10 .02
❑ 394S Eric Thomas .10 .02
❑ 395S Mike Gann .10 .02
❑ 396S William Perry .20 .07
❑ 397S Carl Hairston .10 .02
❑ 398S Billy Ard .10 .02
❑ 399S Donnell Thompson .10 .02
❑ 400S Mike Webster .20 .07
❑ 401S Scott Davis RC .10 .02
❑ 402S Sean Farrell .10 .02
❑ 403S Mike Golic RC .10 .02
❑ 404S Mike Kenn .10 .02
❑ 405S Keith Van Horne RC .10 .02
❑ 406S Bob Golic .10 .02
❑ 407S Neil Smith RC 2.00 .75
❑ 408S Dermontti Dawson RC .20 .07
❑ 409S Leslie O'Neal .20 .07
❑ 410S Matt Bahr .10 .02
❑ 411S Guy McIntyre RC .10 .02
❑ 412S Bryan Millard .10 .02
❑ 413S Joe Jacoby .10 .02
❑ 414S Rob Taylor RC .10 .02
❑ 415S Tony Zendejas .10 .02
❑ 416S Vai Sikahema .10 .02
❑ 417S Gary Reasons RC .10 .02
❑ 418S Shawn Collins RC .10 .02
❑ 419S Mark Green RC .10 .02
❑ 420S Courtney Hall RC .10 .02
❑ 421S Bobby Humphrey RC .10 .02
❑ 422S Myron Guyton RC .10 .02
❑ 423S Darryl Ingram RC .10 .02
❑ 424S Chris Jacke RC .10 .02
❑ 425S Keith Jones RC .10 .02
❑ 426S Robert Massey RC .10 .02
❑ 427S Bubba McDowell RC .40 .15
❑ 428S Dave Meggett RC .40 .15
❑ 429S Louis Oliver RC .20 .07
❑ 430S Danny Peebles .10 .02
❑ 431S Rodney Peete RC .75 .30
❑ 432S Jeff Query RC .10 .02
❑ 433S Timm Rosenbach RC UER .10 .02
❑ 434S Frank Stams RC .10 .02
❑ 435S Lawyer Tillman RC .10 .02
❑ 436S Billy Joe Tolliver RC .10 .02
❑ 437S Floyd Turner RC .20 .07
❑ 438S Steve Walsh RC .20 .07
❑ 439S Joe Wolf RC .10 .02
❑ 440S Trace Armstrong RC .10 .02

1990 Score

❑ COMPLETE SET (660) 15.00 6.00
❑ COMP.FACT.SET (665) 20.00 7.50
❑ 1 Joe Montana 1.25 .50
❑ 2 Christian Okoye .04 .01
❑ 3 Mike Singletary UER .10 .02
❑ 4 Jim Everett UER .10 .02
❑ 5 Phil Simms .10 .02
❑ 6 Brent Fullwood .04 .01
❑ 7 Bill Fralic .04 .01
❑ 8 Leslie O'Neal .10 .02
❑ 9 John Taylor .25 .08
❑ 10 Bo Jackson .30 .10
❑ 11 John Stephens .04 .01
❑ 12 Art Monk .10 .02
❑ 13 Dan Marino 1.25 .50
❑ 14 John Settle .04 .01
❑ 15 Don Majkowski .04 .01
❑ 16 Bruce Smith .25 .08
❑ 17 Brad Muster .04 .01
❑ 18 Jason Buck .04 .01
❑ 19 James Brooks .10 .02
❑ 20 Barry Sanders 1.25 .50
❑ 21 Troy Aikman .75 .30
❑ 22 Allen Pinkett .04 .01
❑ 23 Duane Bickett .04 .01
❑ 24 Kevin Ross .04 .01
❑ 25 John Elway 1.25 .50
❑ 26 Jeff Query .04 .01
❑ 27 Eddie Murray .04 .01
❑ 28 Richard Dent .10 .02
❑ 29 Lorenzo White .04 .01
❑ 30 Eric Metcalf .25 .08
❑ 31 Jeff Dellenbach RC .04 .01
❑ 32 Leon White .04 .01
❑ 33 Jim Jeffcoat .04 .01
❑ 34 Herschel Walker .10 .02
❑ 35 Mike Johnson UER .04 .01
❑ 36 Joe Phillips .04 .01
❑ 37 Willie Gault .10 .02
❑ 38 Keith Millard .04 .01
❑ 39 Fred Marion .04 .01
❑ 40 Boomer Esiason .10 .02
❑ 41 Dermontti Dawson .10 .02
❑ 42 Dino Hackett .04 .01
❑ 43 Reggie Roby .04 .01
❑ 44 Roger Vick .04 .01
❑ 45 Bobby Hebert .04 .01
❑ 46 Don Beebe .10 .02
❑ 47 Neal Anderson .10 .02
❑ 48 Johnny Holland .04 .01
❑ 49 Bobby Humphery .04 .01
❑ 50 Lawrence Taylor .25 .08
❑ 51 Billy Ray Smith .04 .01
❑ 52 Robert Perryman .04 .01
❑ 53 Gary Anderson K .04 .01
❑ 54 Raul Allegre .04 .01
❑ 55 Pat Swilling .10 .02
❑ 56 Chris Doleman .04 .01
❑ 57 Andre Reed .25 .08
❑ 58 Seth Joyner .10 .02
❑ 59 Bart Oates .04 .01
❑ 60 Bernie Kosar .10 .02
❑ 61 Dave Krieg .10 .02
❑ 62 Lars Tate .04 .01
❑ 63 Scott Norwood .04 .01
❑ 64 Kyle Clifton .04 .01
❑ 65 Alan Veingrad .04 .01
❑ 66 Gerald Riggs UER .10 .02
❑ 67 Tim Worley .04 .01
❑ 68 Rodney Holman .04 .01
❑ 69 Tony Zendejas .04 .01
❑ 70 Chris Miller .25 .08
❑ 71 Wilber Marshall .04 .01
❑ 72 Skip McClendon RC .04 .01
❑ 73 Jim Covert .04 .01
❑ 74 Sam Mills .10 .02
❑ 75 Chris Hinton .04 .01
❑ 76 Irv Eatman .04 .01
❑ 77 Bubba Paris UER .04 .01
❑ 78 John Elliott UER .04 .01
❑ 79 Thomas Everett .04 .01
❑ 80 Steve Smith .04 .01
❑ 81 Jackie Slater .04 .01
❑ 82 Kelvin Martin RC .04 .01
❑ 83 Jo Jo Townsell .04 .01
❑ 84 Jim C. Jensen .04 .01
❑ 85 Bobby Humphrey .04 .01
❑ 86 Mike Dyal .04 .01
❑ 87 Andre Rison UER .25 .08
❑ 88 Brian Sochia .04 .01
❑ 89 Greg Bell .04 .01
❑ 90 Dalton Hilliard .04 .01
❑ 91 Carl Banks .04 .01
❑ 92 Dennis Smith .04 .01
❑ 93 Bruce Matthews .10 .02
❑ 94 Charles Haley .10 .02
❑ 95 Deion Sanders UER .50 .20
❑ 96 Stephone Paige .04 .01
❑ 97 Marion Butts FSC .10 .02
❑ 98 Howie Long .25 .08
❑ 99 Donald Igwebuike .04 .01
❑ 100 Roger Craig UER .10 .02
❑ 101 Charles Mann .04 .01
❑ 102 Fredd Young .04 .01
❑ 103 Chris Jacke .04 .01

❑ 104 Scott Case .04 .01
❑ 105 Warren Moon .25 .08
❑ 106 Clyde Simmons .04 .01
❑ 107 Steve Atwater .04 .01
❑ 108 Morten Andersen .04 .01
❑ 109 Eugene Marve .04 .01
❑ 110 Thurman Thomas .25 .08
❑ 111 Carnell Lake .04 .01
❑ 112 Jim Kelly .25 .08
❑ 113 Stanford Jennings .04 .01
❑ 114 Jacob Green .04 .01
❑ 115 Karl Mecklenburg .04 .01
❑ 116 Ray Childress .04 .01
❑ 117 Erik McMillan .04 .01
❑ 118 Harry Newsome .04 .01
❑ 119 James Dixon .04 .01
❑ 120 Hassan Jones .04 .01
❑ 121 Eric Allen .04 .01
❑ 122 Felix Wright .04 .01
❑ 123 Merril Hoge .04 .01
❑ 124 Eric Ball .04 .01
❑ 125 Flipper Anderson FSC .04 .01
❑ 126 James Jefferson .04 .01
❑ 127 Tim McDonald .04 .01
❑ 128 Larry Kinnebrew .04 .01
❑ 129 Mark Collins .04 .01
❑ 130 Ickey Woods .04 .01
❑ 131 Jeff Donaldson UER .04 .01
❑ 132 Rich Camarillo .04 .01
❑ 133 Melvin Bratton RC .04 .01
❑ 134A Kevin Butler .35 .12
❑ 134B Kevin Butler .50 .20
❑ 135 Albert Bentley .04 .01
❑ 136A Vai Sikahema .35 .12
❑ 136B Vai Sikahema .50 .20
❑ 137 Todd McNair RC .04 .01
❑ 138 Alonzo Highsmith .04 .01
❑ 139 Brian Blades .10 .02
❑ 140 Jeff Lageman .04 .01
❑ 141 Eric Thomas .04 .01
❑ 142 Derek Hill .04 .01
❑ 143 Rick Fenney .04 .01
❑ 144 Herman Heard .04 .01
❑ 145 Steve Young .50 .20
❑ 146 Kent Hull .04 .01
❑ 147A Joey Browner face left .35 .12
❑ 147B Joey Browner straight .50 .20
❑ 148 Frank Minnifield .04 .01
❑ 149 Robert Massey .04 .01
❑ 150 Dave Meggett .10 .02
❑ 151 Bubba McDowell .04 .01
❑ 152 Rickey Dixon RC .04 .01
❑ 153 Ray Donaldson .04 .01
❑ 154 Alvin Walton .04 .01
❑ 155 Mike Cofer .04 .01
❑ 156 Darryl Talley .04 .01
❑ 157 A.J. Johnson .04 .01
❑ 158 Jerry Gray .04 .01
❑ 159 Keith Byars .04 .01
❑ 160 Andy Heck .04 .01
❑ 161 Mike Munchak .10 .02
❑ 162 Dennis Gentry .04 .01
❑ 163 Timm Rosenbach UER .04 .01
❑ 164 Randall McDaniel .10 .02
❑ 165 Pat Leahy .04 .01
❑ 166 Bubby Brister .04 .01
❑ 167 Aundray Bruce .04 .01
❑ 168 Bill Brooks .04 .01
❑ 169 Eddie Anderson RC .04 .01
❑ 170 Ronnie Lott .10 .02
❑ 171 Jay Hilgenberg .04 .01
❑ 172 Joe Nash .04 .01
❑ 173 Simon Fletcher .04 .01
❑ 174 Shane Conlan .04 .01
❑ 175 Sean Landeta .04 .01
❑ 176 John Alt RC .04 .01
❑ 177 Clay Matthews .10 .02
❑ 178 Anthony Munoz .10 .02
❑ 179 Pete Holohan .04 .01
❑ 180 Robert Awalt .04 .01
❑ 181 Rohn Stark .04 .01
❑ 182 Vance Johnson .04 .01
❑ 183 David Fulcher .04 .01
❑ 184 Robert Delpino FSC .04 .01
❑ 185 Drew Hill .04 .01
❑ 186 Reggie Langhorne UER .04 .01
❑ 187 Lonzell Hill .04 .01
❑ 188 Tom Rathman UER .04 .01
❑ 189 Greg Montgomery RC .04 .01
❑ 190 Leonard Smith .04 .01
❑ 191 Chris Spielman .25 .08
❑ 192 Tom Newberry .04 .01
❑ 193 Cris Carter .50 .20
❑ 194 Kevin Porter RC .04 .01
❑ 195 Donnell Thompson .04 .01
❑ 196 Vaughan Johnson .04 .01
❑ 197 Steve McMichael .10 .02
❑ 198 Jim Sweeney .04 .01
❑ 199 Rich Karlis UER .04 .01
❑ 200 Jerry Rice .75 .30
❑ 201 Dan Hampton UER .10 .02
❑ 202 Jim Lachey .04 .01
❑ 203 Reggie White .25 .08
❑ 204 Jerry Ball .04 .01
❑ 205 Russ Grimm .04 .01
❑ 206 Tim Green RC .04 .01
❑ 207 Shawn Collins .04 .01
❑ 208A R.Mojsiejenko Chargers .15 .05
❑ 208B R.Mojsiejenko Redskins .50 .20
❑ 209 Trace Armstrong .04 .01
❑ 210 Keith Jackson .10 .02
❑ 211 Jamie Holland .04 .01
❑ 212 Mark Clayton .10 .02
❑ 213 Jeff Cross .04 .01
❑ 214 Bob Gagliano .04 .01
❑ 215 Louis Oliver UER .04 .01
❑ 216 Jim Arnold .04 .01
❑ 217 Robert Clark RC .04 .01
❑ 218 Gill Byrd .04 .01
❑ 219 Rodney Peete .10 .02
❑ 220 Anthony Miller .25 .08
❑ 221 Steve Grogan .10 .02
❑ 222 Vince Newsome RC .04 .01
❑ 223 Thomas Benson .04 .01
❑ 224 Kevin Murphy .04 .01
❑ 225 Henry Ellard .10 .02
❑ 226 Richard Johnson .04 .01
❑ 227 Jim Skow .04 .01
❑ 228 Keith Jones .04 .01
❑ 229 Dave Brown DB .04 .01
❑ 230 Marcus Allen .25 .08
❑ 231 Steve Walsh .10 .02
❑ 232 Jim Harbaugh .25 .08
❑ 233 Mel Gray .10 .02
❑ 234 David Treadwell .04 .01
❑ 235 John Offerdahl .04 .01
❑ 236 Gary Reasons .04 .01
❑ 237 Tim Krumrie .04 .01
❑ 238 Dave Duerson .04 .01
❑ 239 Gary Clark UER .25 .08
❑ 240 Mark Jackson .04 .01
❑ 241 Mark Murphy .04 .01
❑ 242 Jerry Holmes .04 .01
❑ 243 Tim McGee .04 .01
❑ 244 Mike Tomczak .10 .02
❑ 245 Sterling Sharpe UER .25 .08
❑ 246 Bennie Blades .04 .01
❑ 247 Ken Harvey RC UER .25 .08
❑ 248 Ron Heller .04 .01
❑ 249 Louis Lipps .10 .02
❑ 250 Wade Wilson .10 .02
❑ 251 Freddie Joe Nunn .04 .01
❑ 252 Jerome Brown UER .04 .01
❑ 253 Myron Guyton .04 .01
❑ 254 Nate Odomes RC .10 .02
❑ 255 Rod Woodson .25 .08
❑ 256 Cornelius Bennett .10 .02
❑ 257 Keith Woodside .04 .01
❑ 258 Jeff Uhlenhake UER .04 .01
❑ 259 Harry Hamilton .04 .01
❑ 260 Mark Bavaro .04 .01
❑ 261 Vinny Testaverde .10 .02
❑ 262 Steve DeBerg .04 .01
❑ 263 Steve Wisniewski UER .10 .02
❑ 264 Pete Mandley .04 .01
❑ 265 Tim Harris .04 .01
❑ 266 Jack Trudeau .04 .01
❑ 267 Mark Kelso .04 .01
❑ 268 Brian Noble .04 .01
❑ 269 Jessie Tuggle RC .04 .01
❑ 270 Ken O'Brien .04 .01
❑ 271 David Little .04 .01
❑ 272 Pete Stoyanovich .04 .01
❑ 273 Odessa Turner RC .04 .01
❑ 274 Anthony Toney .04 .01
❑ 275 Tunch Ilkin .04 .01
❑ 276 Carl Lee .04 .01
❑ 277 Hart Lee Dykes .04 .01
❑ 278 Al Noga .04 .01
❑ 279 Greg Lloyd .25 .08
❑ 280 Billy Joe Tolliver .04 .01
❑ 281 Kirk Lowdermilk .04 .01
❑ 282 Earl Ferrell .04 .01
❑ 283 Eric Sievers RC .04 .01
❑ 284 Steve Jordan .04 .01
❑ 285 Burt Grossman .04 .01
❑ 286 Johnny Rembert .04 .01
❑ 287 Jeff Jaeger RC .04 .01
❑ 288 James Hasty .04 .01
❑ 289 Tony Mandarich DP .04 .01
❑ 290 Chris Singleton RC .04 .01
❑ 291 Lynn James RC .04 .01
❑ 292 Andre Ware RC .25 .08
❑ 293 Ray Agnew RC .04 .01
❑ 294 Joel Smeenge RC .04 .01
❑ 295 Marc Spindler RC .04 .01
❑ 296 Renaldo Turnbull RC .04 .01
❑ 297 Reggie Rembert RC .04 .01
❑ 298 Jeff Alm RC .04 .01
❑ 299 Cortez Kennedy RC .25 .08
❑ 300 Blair Thomas RC .10 .02
❑ 301 Pat Terrell RC .04 .01
❑ 302 Junior Seau RC 1.25 .50
❑ 303 Mo Elewonibi RC .04 .01
❑ 304 Tony Bennett RC .25 .08
❑ 305 Percy Snow RC .04 .01
❑ 306 Richmond Webb RC .04 .01
❑ 307 Rodney Hampton RC .25 .08
❑ 308 Barry Foster RC .25 .08
❑ 309 John Friesz RC .25 .08
❑ 310 Ben Smith RC .04 .01
❑ 311 Joe Montana HG .50 .20
❑ 312 Jim Everett HG .10 .02
❑ 313 Mark Rypien HG .10 .02
❑ 314 Phil Simms HG UER .10 .02
❑ 315 Don Majkowski HG .04 .01
❑ 316 Boomer Esiason HG .04 .01
❑ 317 Warren Moon HG Moon .25 .08
❑ 318 Jim Kelly HG .25 .08
❑ 319 Bernie Kosar HG UER .10 .02
❑ 320 Dan Marino HG UER .50 .20
❑ 321 Christian Okoye GF .04 .01
❑ 322 Thurman Thomas GF .25 .08
❑ 323 James Brooks GF .10 .02
❑ 324 Bobby Humphrey GF .04 .01
❑ 325 Barry Sanders GF .60 .25
❑ 326 Neal Anderson GF .04 .01
❑ 327 Dalton Hilliard GF .04 .01
❑ 328 Greg Bell GF .04 .01
❑ 329 Roger Craig GF UER .10 .02
❑ 330 Bo Jackson GF .30 .10
❑ 331 Don Warren .04 .01
❑ 332 Rufus Porter .04 .01
❑ 333 Sammie Smith .04 .01

❑	334	Lewis Tillman	.04	.01
❑	335	Michael Walter	.04	.01
❑	336	Marc Logan	.04	.01
❑	337	Ron Hallstrom RC	.04	.01
❑	338	Stanley Morgan	.04	.01
❑	339	Mark Robinson	.04	.01
❑	340	Frank Reich	.25	.08
❑	341	Chip Lohmiller FSC	.04	.01
❑	342	Steve Beuerlein	.10	.02
❑	343	John L. Williams	.04	.01
❑	344	Irving Fryar	.25	.08
❑	345	Anthony Carter	.10	.02
❑	346	Al Toon	.10	.02
❑	347	J.T. Smith	.04	.01
❑	348	Pierce Holt RC	.04	.01
❑	349	Ferrell Edmunds	.04	.01
❑	350	Mark Rypien	.10	.02
❑	351	Paul Gruber	.04	.01
❑	352	Ernest Givins	.10	.02
❑	353	Ervin Randle	.04	.01
❑	354	Guy McIntyre	.04	.01
❑	355	Webster Slaughter	.10	.02
❑	356	Reuben Davis	.04	.01
❑	357	Rickey Jackson	.10	.02
❑	358	Earnest Byner	.04	.01
❑	359	Eddie Brown	.04	.01
❑	360	Troy Stradford	.04	.01
❑	361	Pepper Johnson	.04	.01
❑	362	Ravin Caldwell	.04	.01
❑	363	Chris Mohr RC	.04	.01
❑	364	Jeff Bryant	.04	.01
❑	365	Bruce Collie	.04	.01
❑	366	Courtney Hall	.04	.01
❑	367	Jerry Olsavsky	.04	.01
❑	368	David Galloway	.04	.01
❑	369	Wes Hopkins	.04	.01
❑	370	Johnny Hector	.04	.01
❑	371	Clarence Verdin	.04	.01
❑	372	Nick Lowery	.04	.01
❑	373	Tim Brown	.25	.08
❑	374	Kevin Greene	.10	.02
❑	375	Leonard Marshall	.04	.01
❑	376	Roland James	.04	.01
❑	377	Scott Studwell	.04	.01
❑	378	Jarvis Williams	.04	.01
❑	379	Mike Saxon	.04	.01
❑	380	Kevin Mack	.04	.01
❑	381	Joe Kelly	.04	.01
❑	382	Tom Thayer RC	.04	.01
❑	383	Roy Green	.10	.02
❑	384	Michael Brooks RC	.04	.01
❑	385	Michael Cofer	.04	.01
❑	386	Ken Ruettgers	.04	.01
❑	387	Dean Steinkuhler	.04	.01
❑	388	Maurice Carthon	.04	.01
❑	389	Ricky Sanders	.04	.01
❑	390	Winston Moss RC	.04	.01
❑	391	Tony Woods	.04	.01
❑	392	Keith DeLong	.04	.01
❑	393	David Wyman	.04	.01
❑	394	Vencie Glenn	.04	.01
❑	395	Harris Barton	.04	.01
❑	396	Bryan Hinkle	.04	.01
❑	397	Derek Kennard	.04	.01
❑	398	Heath Sherman RC	.04	.01
❑	399	Troy Benson	.04	.01
❑	400	Gary Zimmerman	.04	.01
❑	401	Mark Duper	.10	.02
❑	402	Eugene Lockhart	.04	.01
❑	403	Tim Manoa	.04	.01
❑	404	Reggie Williams	.04	.01
❑	405	Mark Bortz RC	.04	.01
❑	406	Mike Kenn	.04	.01
❑	407	John Grimsley	.04	.01
❑	408	Bill Romanowski RC	1.00	.40
❑	409	Perry Kemp	.04	.01
❑	410	Norm Johnson	.04	.01
❑	411	Broderick Thomas	.04	.01
❑	412	Joe Wolf	.04	.01
❑	413	Andre Waters	.04	.01
❑	414	Jason Staurovsky	.04	.01
❑	415	Eric Martin	.04	.01
❑	416	Joe Prokop	.04	.01
❑	417	Steve Sewell	.04	.01
❑	418	Cedric Jones	.04	.01
❑	419	Alphonso Carreker	.04	.01
❑	420	Keith Willis	.04	.01
❑	421	Bobby Butler	.04	.01
❑	422	John Roper	.04	.01
❑	423	Tim Spencer	.04	.01
❑	424	Jesse Sapolu RC	.04	.01
❑	425	Ron Wolfley	.04	.01
❑	426	Doug Smith	.04	.01
❑	427	William Howard	.04	.01
❑	428	Keith Van Horne	.04	.01
❑	429	Tony Jordan	.04	.01
❑	430	Mervyn Fernandez	.04	.01
❑	431	Shaun Gayle RC	.04	.01
❑	432	Ricky Nattiel	.04	.01
❑	433	Albert Lewis	.04	.01
❑	434	Fred Banks RC	.04	.01
❑	435	Henry Thomas	.04	.01
❑	436	Chet Brooks	.04	.01
❑	437	Mark Ingram	.10	.02
❑	438	Jeff Gossett	.04	.01
❑	439	Mike Wilcher	.04	.01
❑	440	Deron Cherry UER	.04	.01
❑	441	Mike Rozier	.04	.01
❑	442	Jon Hand	.04	.01
❑	443	Ozzie Newsome	.10	.02
❑	444	Sammy Martin	.04	.01
❑	445	Luis Sharpe	.04	.01
❑	446	Lee Williams	.04	.01
❑	447	Chris Martin RC	.04	.01
❑	448	Kevin Fagan RC	.04	.01
❑	449	Gene Lang	.04	.01
❑	450	Greg Townsend	.04	.01
❑	451	Robert Lyles	.04	.01
❑	452	Eric Hill	.04	.01
❑	453	John Teltschik	.04	.01
❑	454	Vestee Jackson	.04	.01
❑	455	Bruce Reimers	.04	.01
❑	456	Butch Rolle RC	.04	.01
❑	457	Lawyer Tillman	.04	.01
❑	458	Andre Tippett	.04	.01
❑	459	James Thornton	.04	.01
❑	460	Randy Grimes	.04	.01
❑	461	Larry Roberts	.04	.01
❑	462	Ron Holmes	.04	.01
❑	463	Mike Wise DE	.04	.01
❑	464	Danny Copeland RC	.04	.01
❑	465	Bruce Wilkerson RC	.04	.01
❑	466	Mike Quick	.04	.01
❑	467	Mickey Shuler	.04	.01
❑	468	Mike Prior	.04	.01
❑	469	Ron Rivera	.04	.01
❑	470	Dean Biasucci	.04	.01
❑	471	Perry Williams	.04	.01
❑	472	Darren Comeaux UER	.04	.01
❑	473	Freeman McNeil	.04	.01
❑	474	Tyrone Braxton	.04	.01
❑	475	Jay Schroeder	.04	.01
❑	476	Naz Worthen	.04	.01
❑	477	Lionel Washington	.04	.01
❑	478	Carl Zander	.04	.01
❑	479	Al(Bubba) Baker	.10	.02
❑	480	Mike Merriweather	.04	.01
❑	481	Mike Gann	.04	.01
❑	482	Brent Williams	.04	.01
❑	483	Eugene Robinson	.04	.01
❑	484	Ray Horton	.04	.01
❑	485	Bruce Armstrong	.04	.01
❑	486	John Fourcade	.04	.01
❑	487	Lewis Billups	.04	.01
❑	488	Scott Davis	.04	.01
❑	489	Kenneth Sims	.04	.01
❑	490	Chris Chandler	.25	.08
❑	491	Mark Lee	.04	.01
❑	492	Johnny Meads	.04	.01
❑	493	Tim Irwin	.04	.01
❑	494	E.J. Junior	.04	.01
❑	495	Hardy Nickerson	.10	.02
❑	496	Rob McGovern	.04	.01
❑	497	Fred Strickland RC	.04	.01
❑	498	Reggie Rutland RC	.04	.01
❑	499	Mel Owens	.04	.01
❑	500	Derrick Thomas	.25	.08
❑	501	Jerrol Williams	.04	.01
❑	502	Maurice Hurst RC	.04	.01
❑	503	Larry Kelm RC	.04	.01
❑	504	Herman Fontenot	.04	.01
❑	505	Pat Beach	.04	.01
❑	506	Haywood Jeffires RC	.25	.08
❑	507	Neil Smith	.25	.08
❑	508	Cleveland Gary FSC	.04	.01
❑	509	William Perry	.10	.02
❑	510	Michael Carter	.04	.01
❑	511	Walker Lee Ashley	.04	.01
❑	512	Bob Golic	.04	.01
❑	513	Danny Villa RC	.04	.01
❑	514	Matt Millen	.10	.02
❑	515	Don Griffin	.04	.01
❑	516	Jonathan Hayes	.04	.01
❑	517	Gerald Williams RC	.04	.01
❑	518	Scott Fulhage	.04	.01
❑	519	Irv Pankey	.04	.01
❑	520	Randy Dixon RC	.04	.01
❑	521	Terry McDaniel	.04	.01
❑	522	Dan Saleaumua	.04	.01
❑	523	Darrin Nelson	.04	.01
❑	524	Leonard Griffin	.04	.01
❑	525	Michael Ball RC	.04	.01
❑	526	Ernie Jones RC	.04	.01
❑	527	Tony Eason UER	.04	.01
❑	528	Ed Reynolds	.04	.01
❑	529	Gary Hogeboom	.04	.01
❑	530	Don Mosebar	.04	.01
❑	531	Ottis Anderson	.10	.02
❑	532	Bucky Scribner	.04	.01
❑	533	Aaron Cox	.04	.01
❑	534	Sean Jones	.10	.02
❑	535	Doug Flutie	.50	.20
❑	536	Leo Lewis	.04	.01
❑	537	Art Still	.04	.01
❑	538	Matt Bahr	.04	.01
❑	539	Keena Turner	.04	.01
❑	540	Sammy Winder	.04	.01
❑	541	Mike Webster	.10	.02
❑	542	Doug Riesenberg RC	.04	.01
❑	543	Dan Fike	.04	.01
❑	544	Clarence Kay	.04	.01
❑	545	Jim Burt	.04	.01
❑	546	Mike Horan	.04	.01
❑	547	Al Harris	.04	.01
❑	548	Maury Buford	.04	.01
❑	549	Jerry Robinson	.04	.01
❑	550	Tracy Rocker	.04	.01
❑	551	Karl Mecklenburg CC	.04	.01
❑	552	Lawrence Taylor CC	.25	.08
❑	553	Derrick Thomas CC	.25	.08
❑	554	Mike Singletary CC	.10	.02
❑	555	Tim Harris CC	.04	.01
❑	556	Jerry Rice RM	.50	.20
❑	557	Art Monk RM	.10	.02
❑	558	Mark Carrier WR RM	.10	.02
❑	559	Andre Reed RM	.10	.02
❑	560	Sterling Sharpe RM	.25	.08
❑	561	Herschel Walker GF	.10	.02
❑	562	Ottis Anderson GF	.10	.02
❑	563	Randall Cunningham HG	.10	.02
❑	564	John Elway HG	.50	.20
❑	565	David Fulcher AP	.04	.01
❑	566	Ronnie Lott AP	.10	.02
❑	567	Jerry Gray AP	.04	.01

- ❑ 568 Albert Lewis AP .04 .01
- ❑ 569 Karl Mecklenburg AP .04 .01
- ❑ 570 Mike Singletary AP .10 .02
- ❑ 571 Lawrence Taylor AP .25 .08
- ❑ 572 Tim Harris AP .04 .01
- ❑ 573 Keith Millard AP .04 .01
- ❑ 574 Reggie White AP .25 .08
- ❑ 575 Chris Doleman AP .04 .01
- ❑ 576 Dave Meggett AP .10 .02
- ❑ 577 Rod Woodson AP .25 .08
- ❑ 578 Sean Landeta AP .04 .01
- ❑ 579 Eddie Murray AP .04 .01
- ❑ 580 Barry Sanders AP .60 .25
- ❑ 581 Christian Okoye AP .04 .01
- ❑ 582 Joe Montana AP .50 .20
- ❑ 583 Jay Hilgenberg AP .04 .01
- ❑ 584 Bruce Matthews AP .10 .02
- ❑ 585 Tom Newberry AP .04 .01
- ❑ 586 Gary Zimmerman AP .04 .01
- ❑ 587 Anthony Munoz AP .10 .02
- ❑ 588 Keith Jackson AP .10 .02
- ❑ 589 Sterling Sharpe AP .25 .08
- ❑ 590 Jerry Rice AP .50 .20
- ❑ 591 Bo Jackson RB .30 .10
- ❑ 592 Steve Largent RB .25 .08
- ❑ 593 Flipper Anderson RB .04 .01
- ❑ 594 Joe Montana RB .50 .20
- ❑ 595 Franco Harris HOF .10 .02
- ❑ 596 Bob St. Clair HOF .04 .01
- ❑ 597 Tom Landry HOF .10 .02
- ❑ 598 Jack Lambert HOF .10 .02
- ❑ 599 Ted Hendricks HOF .04 .01
- ❑ 600A Buck Buchanan HOF ERR 83 .10 .02
- ❑ 600B Buck Buchanan HOF COR 63 .10 .02
- ❑ 601 Bob Griese HOF .10 .02
- ❑ 602 Super Bowl Wrap .04 .01
- ❑ 603A Vince Lombardi w/o logo .20 .07
- ❑ 603B Vince Lombardi Curt.logo .20 .07
- ❑ 604 Mark Carrier WR UER .10 .02
- ❑ 605 Randall Cunningham .25 .08
- ❑ 606 Percy Snow C90 .04 .01
- ❑ 607 Andre Ware C90 .25 .08
- ❑ 608 Blair Thomas C90 .10 .02
- ❑ 609 Eric Green C90 .04 .01
- ❑ 610 Reggie Rembert C90 .04 .01
- ❑ 611 Richmond Webb C90 .04 .01
- ❑ 612 Bern Brostek C90 .04 .01
- ❑ 613 James Williams C90 .04 .01
- ❑ 614 Mark Carrier DB C90 .10 .02
- ❑ 615 Renaldo Turnbull C90 .04 .01
- ❑ 616 Cortez Kennedy C90 .10 .02
- ❑ 617 Keith McCants C90 .04 .01
- ❑ 618 Anthony Thompson RC .04 .01
- ❑ 619 LeRoy Butler RC .25 .08
- ❑ 620 Aaron Wallace RC .04 .01
- ❑ 621 Alexander Wright RC .04 .01
- ❑ 622 Keith McCants RC .04 .01
- ❑ 623 Jimmie Jones RC .04 .01
- ❑ 624 Anthony Johnson RC .25 .08
- ❑ 625 Fred Washington RC .04 .01
- ❑ 626 Mike Bellamy RC .04 .01
- ❑ 627 Mark Carrier DB RC .25 .08
- ❑ 628 Harold Green RC .25 .08
- ❑ 629 Eric Green RC .10 .02
- ❑ 630 Andre Collins RC .04 .01
- ❑ 631 Lamar Lathon RC .10 .02
- ❑ 632 Terry Wooden RC .04 .01
- ❑ 633 Jesse Anderson RC .04 .01
- ❑ 634 Jeff George RC .50 .20
- ❑ 635 Carwell Gardner RC .04 .01
- ❑ 636 Darrell Thompson RC .04 .01
- ❑ 637 Vince Buck RC .04 .01
- ❑ 638 Mike Jones TE RC .04 .01
- ❑ 639 Charles Arbuckle RC .04 .01
- ❑ 640 Dennis Brown RC .04 .01
- ❑ 641 James Williams DB RC .04 .01
- ❑ 642 Bern Brostek RC .04 .01
- ❑ 643 Darion Conner RC .10 .02
- ❑ 644 Mike Fox RC .04 .01
- ❑ 645 Cary Conklin RC .04 .01
- ❑ 646 Tim Grunhard RC .04 .01
- ❑ 647 Ron Cox RC .04 .01
- ❑ 648 Keith Sims RC .04 .01
- ❑ 649 Alton Montgomery RC .04 .01
- ❑ 650 Greg McMurtry RC .04 .01
- ❑ 651 Scott Mitchell RC .25 .08
- ❑ 652 Tim Ryan DE RC .04 .01
- ❑ 653 Jeff Mills RC .04 .01
- ❑ 654 Ricky Proehl RC .25 .08
- ❑ 655 Steve Broussard RC .04 .01
- ❑ 656 Peter Tom Willis RC .04 .01
- ❑ 657 Dexter Carter RC .04 .01
- ❑ 658 Tony Casillas .04 .01
- ❑ 659 Joe Morris .04 .01
- ❑ 660 Greg Kragen .04 .01
- ❑ B1 Matt Stover FF .25 .08
- ❑ B2 Demetrius Davis .04 .01
- ❑ B3 Ken McMichel .04 .01
- ❑ B4 Judd Garrett FF .04 .01
- ❑ B5 Elliott Searcy .04 .01

1990 Score Supplemental

- ❑ COMP.FACT.SET (110) 80.00 40.00
- ❑ 1T Marcus Dupree RC** .15 .05
- ❑ 2T Jerry Kauric .15 .05
- ❑ 3T Everson Walls .15 .05
- ❑ 4T Elliott Smith .15 .05
- ❑ 5T Donald Evans RC UER .30 .10
- ❑ 6T Jerry Holmes .15 .05
- ❑ 7T Dan Stryzinski RC .15 .05
- ❑ 8T Gerald McNeil .15 .05
- ❑ 9T Rick Tuten RC .15 .05
- ❑ 10T Mickey Shuler .15 .05
- ❑ 11T Jay Novacek .60 .25
- ❑ 12T Eric Williams RC .15 .05
- ❑ 13T Stanley Morgan .15 .05
- ❑ 14T Wayne Haddix RC .15 .05
- ❑ 15T Gary Anderson RB .15 .05
- ❑ 16T Stan Humphries RC .60 .25
- ❑ 17T Raymond Clayborn .15 .05
- ❑ 18T Mark Boyer RC .15 .05
- ❑ 19T Dave Waymer .15 .05
- ❑ 20T Andre Rison .60 .25
- ❑ 21T Daniel Stubbs .15 .05
- ❑ 22T Mike Rozier .15 .05
- ❑ 23T Damian Johnson .15 .05
- ❑ 24T Don Smith RBK RC .15 .05
- ❑ 25T Max Montoya .15 .05
- ❑ 26T Terry Kinard .15 .05
- ❑ 27T Herb Welch .15 .05
- ❑ 28T Cliff Odom .15 .05
- ❑ 29T John Kidd .15 .05
- ❑ 30T Barry Word RC .15 .05
- ❑ 31T Rich Karlis .15 .05
- ❑ 32T Mike Baab .15 .05
- ❑ 33T Ronnie Harmon .30 .10
- ❑ 34T Jeff Donaldson .15 .05
- ❑ 35T Riki Ellison .15 .05
- ❑ 36T Steve Walsh .30 .10
- ❑ 37T Bill Lewis RC .15 .05
- ❑ 38T Tim McKyer .15 .05
- ❑ 39T James Wilder .15 .05
- ❑ 40T Tony Paige .15 .05
- ❑ 41T Derrick Fenner RC .15 .05
- ❑ 42T Thane Gash RC .15 .05
- ❑ 43T Dave Duerson .15 .05
- ❑ 44T Clarence Weathers .15 .05
- ❑ 45T Matt Bahr .15 .05
- ❑ 46T Alonzo Highsmith .15 .05
- ❑ 47T Joe Kelly .15 .05
- ❑ 48T Chris Hinton .15 .05
- ❑ 49T Bobby Humphery .15 .05
- ❑ 50T Greg Bell .15 .05
- ❑ 51T Fred Smerlas .15 .05
- ❑ 52T Walter Stanley .15 .05
- ❑ 53T Jim Skow .15 .05
- ❑ 54T Renaldo Turnbull .15 .05
- ❑ 55T Bern Brostek .15 .05
- ❑ 56T Charles Wilson RC .15 .05
- ❑ 57T Keith McCants .15 .05
- ❑ 58T Alexander Wright .30 .10
- ❑ 59T Ian Beckles RC .15 .05
- ❑ 60T Eric Davis RC .30 .10
- ❑ 61T Chris Singleton .15 .05
- ❑ 62T Rob Moore RC 2.50 1.00
- ❑ 63T Darion Conner .30 .10
- ❑ 64T Tim Grunhard .15 .05
- ❑ 65T Junior Seau 6.00 2.50
- ❑ 66T Tony Stargell RC .15 .05
- ❑ 67T Anthony Thompson .15 .05
- ❑ 68T Cortez Kennedy .60 .25
- ❑ 69T Darrell Thompson .15 .05
- ❑ 70T Calvin Williams RC .60 .25
- ❑ 71T Rodney Hampton .60 .25
- ❑ 72T Terry Wooden .15 .05
- ❑ 73T Leo Goeas RC .15 .05
- ❑ 74T Ken Willis .15 .05
- ❑ 75T Ricky Proehl .60 .25
- ❑ 76T Steve Christie RC .15 .05
- ❑ 77T Andre Ware .60 .25
- ❑ 78T Jeff George 2.50 1.00
- ❑ 79T Walter Wilson .15 .05
- ❑ 80T Johnny Bailey RC .15 .05
- ❑ 81T Harold Green .30 .10
- ❑ 82T Mark Carrier DB .60 .25
- ❑ 83T Frank Cornish .15 .05
- ❑ 84T James Williams .15 .05
- ❑ 85T James Francis RC .15 .05
- ❑ 86T Percy Snow .15 .05
- ❑ 87T Anthony Johnson .60 .25
- ❑ 88T Tim Ryan DE .15 .05
- ❑ 89T Dan Owens RC .15 .05
- ❑ 90T Aaron Wallace RC .15 .05
- ❑ 91T Steve Broussard .15 .05
- ❑ 92T Eric Green .15 .05
- ❑ 93T Blair Thomas .30 .10
- ❑ 94T Robert Blackmon RC .15 .05
- ❑ 95T Alan Grant RC .15 .05
- ❑ 96T Andre Collins .15 .05
- ❑ 97T Dexter Carter .15 .05
- ❑ 98T Reggie Cobb RC .15 .05
- ❑ 99T Dennis Brown .15 .05
- ❑ 100T Kenny Davidson RC .15 .05
- ❑ 101T Emmitt Smith RC 60.00 30.00
- ❑ 102T Jeff Alm .15 .05
- ❑ 103T Alton Montgomery .15 .05
- ❑ 104T Tony Bennett .60 .25
- ❑ 105T Johnny Johnson RC .30 .10
- ❑ 106T Leroy Hoard RC .60 .25
- ❑ 107T Ray Agnew .15 .05
- ❑ 108T Richmond Webb .15 .05
- ❑ 109T Keith Sims .15 .05
- ❑ 110T Barry Foster .60 .25

1991 Score

- ❑ COMPLETE SET (686) 12.00 5.00
- ❑ COMP.FACT.SET (690) 20.00 7.50

❑ 1 Joe Montana 1.25 .50
❑ 2 Eric Allen .04 .01
❑ 3 Rohn Stark .04 .01
❑ 4 Frank Reich .10 .02
❑ 5 Derrick Thomas .25 .08
❑ 6 Mike Singletary .10 .02
❑ 7 Boomer Esiason .10 .02
❑ 8 Matt Millen .10 .02
❑ 9 Chris Spielman .10 .02
❑ 10 Gerald McNeil .04 .01
❑ 11 Nick Lowery .04 .01
❑ 12 Randall Cunningham .25 .08
❑ 13 Marion Butts .10 .02
❑ 14 Tim Brown .25 .08
❑ 15 Emmitt Smith 2.50 1.00
❑ 16 Rich Camarillo .04 .01
❑ 17 Mike Merriweather .04 .01
❑ 18 Derrick Fenner .04 .01
❑ 19 Clay Matthews .10 .02
❑ 20 Barry Sanders 1.25 .50
❑ 21 James Brooks .10 .02
❑ 22 Alton Montgomery .04 .01
❑ 23 Steve Atwater .04 .01
❑ 24 Ron Morris .04 .01
❑ 25 Brad Muster .04 .01
❑ 26 Andre Rison .10 .02
❑ 27 Brian Brennan .04 .01
❑ 28 Leonard Smith .04 .01
❑ 29 Kevin Butler .04 .01
❑ 30 Tim Harris .04 .01
❑ 31 Jay Novacek .25 .08
❑ 32 Eddie Murray .04 .01
❑ 33 Keith Woodside .04 .01
❑ 34 Ray Crockett RC .04 .01
❑ 35 Eugene Lockhart .04 .01
❑ 36 Bill Romanowski .04 .01
❑ 37 Eddie Brown .04 .01
❑ 38 Eugene Daniel .04 .01
❑ 39 Scott Fulhage .04 .01
❑ 40 Harold Green .10 .02
❑ 41 Mark Jackson .04 .01
❑ 42 Sterling Sharpe .25 .08
❑ 43 Mel Gray .10 .02
❑ 44 Jerry Holmes .04 .01
❑ 45 Allen Pinkett .04 .01
❑ 46 Warren Powers .04 .01
❑ 47 Rodney Peete .10 .02
❑ 48 Lorenzo White .04 .01
❑ 49 Dan Owens .04 .01
❑ 50 James Francis .04 .01
❑ 51 Ken Norton .10 .02
❑ 52 Ed West .04 .01
❑ 53 Andre Reed .10 .02
❑ 54 John Grimsley .04 .01
❑ 55 Michael Cofer .04 .01
❑ 56 Chris Doleman .04 .01
❑ 57 Pat Swilling .10 .02
❑ 58 Jessie Tuggle .04 .01
❑ 59 Mike Johnson .04 .01
❑ 60 Steve Walsh .04 .01
❑ 61 Sam Mills .04 .01
❑ 62 Don Mosebar .04 .01
❑ 63 Jay Hilgenberg .04 .01
❑ 64 Cleveland Gary .04 .01
❑ 65 Andre Tippett .04 .01
❑ 66 Tom Newberry .04 .01
❑ 67 Maurice Hurst .04 .01
❑ 68 Louis Oliver .04 .01
❑ 69 Fred Marion .04 .01
❑ 70 Christian Okoye .04 .01
❑ 71 Marv Cook FSC .04 .01
❑ 72 Darryl Talley .04 .01
❑ 73 Rick Fenney .04 .01
❑ 74 Kelvin Martin .04 .01
❑ 75 Howie Long .25 .08
❑ 76 Steve Wisniewski .04 .01
❑ 77 Karl Mecklenburg .04 .01
❑ 78 Dan Saleaumua .04 .01
❑ 79 Ray Childress .04 .01
❑ 80 Henry Ellard .10 .02
❑ 81 Ernest Givins UER .10 .02
❑ 82 Ferrell Edmunds .04 .01
❑ 83 Steve Jordan .04 .01
❑ 84 Tony Mandarich .04 .01
❑ 85 Eric Martin .04 .01
❑ 86 Rich Gannon FSC .25 .08
❑ 87 Irving Fryar .10 .02
❑ 88 Tom Rathman .04 .01
❑ 89 Dan Hampton .10 .02
❑ 90 Barry Word .04 .01
❑ 91 Kevin Greene .10 .02
❑ 92 Sean Landeta .04 .01
❑ 93 Trace Armstrong .04 .01
❑ 94 Dennis Byrd .04 .01
❑ 95 Timm Rosenbach .04 .01
❑ 96 Anthony Toney .04 .01
❑ 97 Tim Krumrie .04 .01
❑ 98 Jerry Ball .04 .01
❑ 99 Tim Green .04 .01
❑ 100 Bo Jackson .30 .10
❑ 101 Myron Guyton .04 .01
❑ 102 Mike Mularkey .04 .01
❑ 103 Jerry Gray .04 .01
❑ 104 Scott Stephen RC .04 .01
❑ 105 Anthony Bell .04 .01
❑ 106 Lomas Brown .04 .01
❑ 107 David Little .04 .01
❑ 108 Brad Baxter FSC .04 .01
❑ 109 Freddie Joe Nunn .04 .01
❑ 110 Dave Meggett .10 .02
❑ 111 Mark Rypien .10 .02
❑ 112 Warren Williams .04 .01
❑ 113 Ron Rivera .04 .01
❑ 114 Terance Mathis .10 .02
❑ 115 Anthony Munoz .10 .02
❑ 116 Jeff Bryant .04 .01
❑ 117 Issiac Holt .04 .01
❑ 118 Steve Sewell .04 .01
❑ 119 Tim Newton .04 .01
❑ 120 Emile Harry .04 .01
❑ 121 Gary Anderson K .04 .01
❑ 122 Mark Lee .04 .01
❑ 123 Alfred Anderson .04 .01
❑ 124 Anthony Blaylock .04 .01
❑ 125 Earnest Byner .04 .01
❑ 126 Bill Maas .04 .01
❑ 127 Keith Taylor .04 .01
❑ 128 Cliff Odom .04 .01
❑ 129 Bob Golic .04 .01
❑ 130 Bart Oates .04 .01
❑ 131 Jim Arnold .04 .01
❑ 132 Jeff Herrod .04 .01
❑ 133 Bruce Armstrong .04 .01
❑ 134 Craig Heyward .10 .02
❑ 135 Joey Browner .04 .01
❑ 136 Darren Comeaux .04 .01
❑ 137 Pat Beach .04 .01
❑ 138 Dalton Hilliard .04 .01
❑ 139 David Treadwell .04 .01
❑ 140 Gary Anderson RB .04 .01
❑ 141 Eugene Robinson .04 .01
❑ 142 Scott Case .04 .01
❑ 143 Paul Farren .04 .01
❑ 144 Gill Fenerty .04 .01
❑ 145 Tim Irwin .04 .01
❑ 146 Norm Johnson .04 .01
❑ 147 Willie Gault .10 .02
❑ 148 Clarence Verdin .04 .01
❑ 149 Jeff Uhlenhake .04 .01
❑ 150 Erik McMillan .04 .01
❑ 151 Kevin Ross .04 .01
❑ 152 Pepper Johnson .04 .01
❑ 153 Bryan Hinkle .04 .01
❑ 154 Gary Clark .25 .08
❑ 155 Robert Delpino .04 .01
❑ 156 Doug Smith .04 .01
❑ 157 Chris Martin .04 .01
❑ 158 Ray Berry .04 .01
❑ 159 Steve Christie .04 .01
❑ 160 Don Smith RB .04 .01
❑ 161 Greg McMurtry .04 .01
❑ 162 Jack Del Rio .10 .02
❑ 163 Floyd Dixon .04 .01
❑ 164 Buford McGee .04 .01
❑ 165 Brett Maxie .04 .01
❑ 166 Morten Andersen .04 .01
❑ 167 Kent Hull .04 .01
❑ 168 Skip McClendon .04 .01
❑ 169 Keith Sims .04 .01
❑ 170 Leonard Marshall .04 .01
❑ 171 Tony Woods .04 .01
❑ 172 Byron Evans .04 .01
❑ 173 Rob Burnett RC .10 .02
❑ 174 Tory Epps .04 .01
❑ 175 Toi Cook RC .04 .01
❑ 176 John Elliott .04 .01
❑ 177 Tommie Agee .04 .01
❑ 178 Keith Van Horne .04 .01
❑ 179 Dennis Smith .04 .01
❑ 180 James Lofton .10 .02
❑ 181 Art Monk .10 .02
❑ 182 Anthony Carter .10 .02
❑ 183 Louis Lipps .04 .01
❑ 184 Bruce Hill .04 .01
❑ 185 Michael Young .04 .01
❑ 186 Eric Green .04 .01
❑ 187 Barney Bussey RC .04 .01
❑ 188 Curtis Duncan .04 .01
❑ 189 Robert Awalt .04 .01
❑ 190 Johnny Johnson .04 .01
❑ 191 Jeff Cross .04 .01
❑ 192 Keith McKeller .04 .01
❑ 193 Robert Brown .04 .01
❑ 194 Vincent Brown .04 .01
❑ 195 Calvin Williams .10 .02
❑ 196 Sean Jones .10 .02
❑ 197 Willie Drewrey .04 .01
❑ 198 Bubba McDowell .04 .01
❑ 199 Al Noga .04 .01
❑ 200 Ronnie Lott .10 .02
❑ 201 Warren Moon .25 .08
❑ 202 Chris Hinton .04 .01
❑ 203 Jim Sweeney .04 .01
❑ 204 Wayne Haddix .04 .01
❑ 205 Tim Jorden RC .04 .01
❑ 206 Marvin Allen .04 .01
❑ 207 Jim Morrissey RC .04 .01
❑ 208 Ben Smith .04 .01
❑ 209 William White .04 .01
❑ 210 Jim C. Jensen .04 .01
❑ 211 Doug Reed .04 .01
❑ 212 Ethan Horton .04 .01
❑ 213 Chris Jacke .04 .01
❑ 214 Johnny Hector .04 .01
❑ 215 Drew Hill UER .04 .01
❑ 216 Roy Green .04 .01
❑ 217 Dean Steinkuhler .04 .01
❑ 218 Cedric Mack .04 .01

❑ 219 Chris Miller	.10	.02
❑ 220 Keith Byars	.04	.01
❑ 221 Lewis Billups	.04	.01
❑ 222 Roger Craig	.10	.02
❑ 223 Shaun Gayle	.04	.01
❑ 224 Mike Rozier	.04	.01
❑ 225 Troy Aikman	.75	.30
❑ 226 Bobby Humphrey	.04	.01
❑ 227 Eugene Marve	.04	.01
❑ 228 Michael Carter	.04	.01
❑ 229 Richard Johnson CB RC	.04	.01
❑ 230 Billy Joe Tolliver	.04	.01
❑ 231 Mark Murphy	.04	.01
❑ 232 John L. Williams	.04	.01
❑ 233 Ronnie Harmon	.04	.01
❑ 234 Thurman Thomas	.25	.08
❑ 235 Martin Mayhew	.04	.01
❑ 236 Richmond Webb	.04	.01
❑ 237 Gerald Riggs UER	.10	.02
❑ 238 Mike Prior	.04	.01
❑ 239 Mike Gann	.04	.01
❑ 240 Alvin Walton	.04	.01
❑ 241 Tim McGee	.04	.01
❑ 242 Bruce Matthews	.10	.02
❑ 243 Johnny Holland	.04	.01
❑ 244 Martin Bayless	.04	.01
❑ 245 Eric Metcalf	.10	.02
❑ 246 John Alt	.04	.01
❑ 247 Max Montoya	.04	.01
❑ 248 Rod Bernstine	.04	.01
❑ 249 Paul Gruber	.04	.01
❑ 250 Charles Haley	.10	.02
❑ 251 Scott Norwood	.04	.01
❑ 252 Michael Haddix	.04	.01
❑ 253 Ricky Sanders	.04	.01
❑ 254 Ervin Randle	.04	.01
❑ 255 Duane Bickett	.04	.01
❑ 256 Mike Munchak	.10	.02
❑ 257 Keith Jones	.04	.01
❑ 258 Riki Ellison	.04	.01
❑ 259 Vince Newsome	.04	.01
❑ 260 Lee Williams	.04	.01
❑ 261 Steve Smith	.04	.01
❑ 262 Sam Clancy	.04	.01
❑ 263 Pierce Holt	.04	.01
❑ 264 Jim Harbaugh	.25	.08
❑ 265 Dino Hackett	.04	.01
❑ 266 Andy Heck	.04	.01
❑ 267 Leo Goeas	.04	.01
❑ 268 Russ Grimm	.04	.01
❑ 269 Gill Byrd	.04	.01
❑ 270 Neal Anderson	.10	.02
❑ 271 Jackie Slater	.04	.01
❑ 272 Joe Nash	.04	.01
❑ 273 Todd Bowles	.04	.01
❑ 274 D.J. Dozier	.04	.01
❑ 275 Kevin Fagan	.04	.01
❑ 276 Don Warren	.04	.01
❑ 277 Jim Jeffcoat	.04	.01
❑ 278 Bruce Smith	.25	.08
❑ 279 Cortez Kennedy	.25	.08
❑ 280 Thane Gash	.04	.01
❑ 281 Perry Kemp	.04	.01
❑ 282 John Taylor	.10	.02
❑ 283 Stephone Paige	.04	.01
❑ 284 Paul Skansi	.04	.01
❑ 285 Shawn Collins	.04	.01
❑ 286 Mervyn Fernandez	.04	.01
❑ 287 Daniel Stubbs	.04	.01
❑ 288 Chip Lohmiller	.04	.01
❑ 289 Brian Blades	.10	.02
❑ 290 Mark Carrier WR	.25	.08
❑ 291 Carl Zander	.04	.01
❑ 292 David Wyman	.04	.01
❑ 293 Jeff Bostic	.04	.01
❑ 294 Irv Pankey	.04	.01
❑ 295 Keith Millard	.04	.01
❑ 296 Jamie Mueller	.04	.01
❑ 297 Bill Fralic	.04	.01
❑ 298 Wendell Davis FSC	.04	.01
❑ 299 Ken Clarke	.04	.01
❑ 300 Wymon Henderson	.04	.01
❑ 301 Jeff Campbell	.04	.01
❑ 302 Cody Carlson RC	.04	.01
❑ 303 Matt Brock RC	.04	.01
❑ 304 Maurice Carthon	.04	.01
❑ 305 Scott Mersereau RC	.04	.01
❑ 306 Steve Wright RC	.04	.01
❑ 307 J.B. Brown	.04	.01
❑ 308 Ricky Reynolds	.04	.01
❑ 309 Darryl Pollard	.04	.01
❑ 310 Donald Evans	.04	.01
❑ 311 Nick Bell RC	.04	.01
❑ 312 Pat Harlow RC	.04	.01
❑ 313 Dan McGwire RC	.04	.01
❑ 314 Mike Dumas RC	.04	.01
❑ 315 Mike Croel RC	.04	.01
❑ 316 Chris Smith RC	.04	.01
❑ 317 Kenny Walker RC	.04	.01
❑ 318 Todd Lyght RC	.04	.01
❑ 319 Mike Stonebreaker	.04	.01
❑ 320 Randall Cunningham 90	.10	.02
❑ 321 Terance Mathis 90	.25	.08
❑ 322 Gaston Green 90	.04	.01
❑ 323 Johnny Bailey 90	.04	.01
❑ 324 Donnie Elder 90	.04	.01
❑ 325 Dwight Stone 90 UER	.04	.01
❑ 326 J.J.Birden RC 90	.10	.02
❑ 327 Alexander Wright 90	.04	.01
❑ 328 Eric Metcalf 90	.10	.02
❑ 329 Andre Rison TL	.10	.02
❑ 330 Warren Moon TL UER	.10	.02
❑ 331 Steve Tasker DT	.04	.01
❑ 332 Mel Gray DT	.10	.02
❑ 333 Nick Lowery DT	.04	.01
❑ 334 Sean Landeta DT	.04	.01
❑ 335 David Fulcher DT	.04	.01
❑ 336 Joey Browner DT	.04	.01
❑ 337 Albert Lewis DT	.04	.01
❑ 338 Rod Woodson DT	.10	.02
❑ 339 Shane Conlan DT	.04	.01
❑ 340 Pepper Johnson DT	.04	.01
❑ 341 Chris Spielman DT	.04	.01
❑ 342 Derrick Thomas DT	.10	.02
❑ 343 Ray Childress DT	.04	.01
❑ 344 Reggie White DT	.10	.02
❑ 345 Bruce Smith DT	.10	.02
❑ 346 Darrell Green	.04	.01
❑ 347 Ray Bentley	.04	.01
❑ 348 Herschel Walker	.10	.02
❑ 349 Rodney Holman	.04	.01
❑ 350 Al Toon	.10	.02
❑ 351 Harry Hamilton	.04	.01
❑ 352 Albert Lewis	.04	.01
❑ 353 Renaldo Turnbull	.04	.01
❑ 354 Junior Seau	.25	.08
❑ 355 Merril Hoge	.04	.01
❑ 356 Shane Conlan	.04	.01
❑ 357 Jay Schroeder	.04	.01
❑ 358 Steve Broussard	.04	.01
❑ 359 Mark Bavaro	.04	.01
❑ 360 Jim Lachey	.04	.01
❑ 361 Greg Townsend	.04	.01
❑ 362 Dave Krieg	.10	.02
❑ 363 Jessie Hester	.04	.01
❑ 364 Steve Tasker	.10	.02
❑ 365 Ron Hall	.04	.01
❑ 366 Pat Leahy	.04	.01
❑ 367 Jim Everett	.10	.02
❑ 368 Felix Wright	.04	.01
❑ 369 Ricky Proehl	.04	.01
❑ 370 Anthony Miller	.10	.02
❑ 371 Keith Jackson	.10	.02
❑ 372 Pete Stoyanovich	.04	.01
❑ 373 Tommy Kane	.04	.01
❑ 374 Richard Johnson	.04	.01
❑ 375 Randall McDaniel	.04	.01
❑ 376 John Stephens	.04	.01
❑ 377 Haywood Jeffires	.10	.02
❑ 378 Rodney Hampton	.25	.08
❑ 379 Tim Grunhard	.04	.01
❑ 380 Jerry Rice	.75	.30
❑ 381 Ken Harvey	.10	.02
❑ 382 Vaughan Johnson	.04	.01
❑ 383 J.T. Smith	.04	.01
❑ 384 Carnell Lake	.04	.01
❑ 385 Dan Marino	1.25	.50
❑ 386 Kyle Clifton	.04	.01
❑ 387 Wilber Marshall	.04	.01
❑ 388 Pete Holohan	.04	.01
❑ 389 Gary Plummer	.04	.01
❑ 390 William Perry	.10	.02
❑ 391 Mark Robinson	.04	.01
❑ 392 Nate Odomes	.04	.01
❑ 393 Ickey Woods	.04	.01
❑ 394 Reyna Thompson	.04	.01
❑ 395 Deion Sanders	.40	.15
❑ 396 Harris Barton	.04	.01
❑ 397 Sammie Smith	.04	.01
❑ 398 Vinny Testaverde	.10	.02
❑ 399 Ray Donaldson	.04	.01
❑ 400 Tim McKyer	.04	.01
❑ 401 Nesby Glasgow	.04	.01
❑ 402 Brent Williams	.04	.01
❑ 403 Rob Moore	.25	.08
❑ 404 Bubby Brister	.04	.01
❑ 405 David Fulcher	.04	.01
❑ 406 Reggie Cobb	.04	.01
❑ 407 Jerome Brown	.04	.01
❑ 408 Erik Howard	.04	.01
❑ 409 Tony Paige	.04	.01
❑ 410 John Elway	1.25	.50
❑ 411 Charles Mann	.04	.01
❑ 412 Luis Sharpe	.04	.01
❑ 413 Hassan Jones	.04	.01
❑ 414 Frank Minnifield	.04	.01
❑ 415 Steve DeBerg	.04	.01
❑ 416 Mark Carrier DB	.10	.02
❑ 417 Brian Jordan FSC	.10	.02
❑ 418 Reggie Langhorne	.04	.01
❑ 419 Don Majkowski	.04	.01
❑ 420 Marcus Allen	.25	.08
❑ 421 Michael Brooks	.04	.01
❑ 422 Vai Sikahema	.04	.01
❑ 423 Dermontti Dawson	.04	.01
❑ 424 Jacob Green	.04	.01
❑ 425 Flipper Anderson	.04	.01
❑ 426 Bill Brooks	.04	.01
❑ 427 Keith McCants	.04	.01
❑ 428 Ken O'Brien	.04	.01
❑ 429 Fred Barnett FSC	.25	.08
❑ 430 Mark Duper	.10	.02
❑ 431 Mark Kelso	.04	.01
❑ 432 Leslie O'Neal	.10	.02
❑ 433 Ottis Anderson	.10	.02
❑ 434 Jesse Sapolu	.04	.01
❑ 435 Gary Zimmerman	.04	.01
❑ 436 Kevin Porter	.04	.01
❑ 437 Anthony Thompson	.04	.01
❑ 438 Robert Clark	.04	.01
❑ 439 Chris Warren	.25	.08
❑ 440 Gerald Williams	.04	.01
❑ 441 Jim Skow	.04	.01
❑ 442 Rick Donnelly	.04	.01
❑ 443 Guy McIntyre	.04	.01
❑ 444 Jeff Lageman	.04	.01
❑ 445 John Offerdahl	.04	.01
❑ 446 Clyde Simmons	.04	.01
❑ 447 John Kidd	.04	.01
❑ 448 Chip Banks	.04	.01
❑ 449 Johnny Meads	.04	.01
❑ 450 Rickey Jackson	.04	.01
❑ 451 Lee Johnson	.04	.01
❑ 452 Michael Irvin	.25	.08

❑ 453 Leon Seals .04 .01
❑ 454 Darrell Thompson .04 .01
❑ 455 Everson Walls .04 .01
❑ 456 LeRoy Butler .10 .02
❑ 457 Marcus Dupree .04 .01
❑ 458 Kirk Lowdermilk .04 .01
❑ 459 Chris Singleton .04 .01
❑ 460 Seth Joyner .10 .02
❑ 461 Rueben Mayes UER .04 .01
❑ 462 Ernie Jones .04 .01
❑ 463 Greg Kragen .04 .01
❑ 464 Bennie Blades .04 .01
❑ 465 Mark Bortz .04 .01
❑ 466 Tony Stargell .04 .01
❑ 467 Mike Cofer .04 .01
❑ 468 Randy Grimes .04 .01
❑ 469 Tim Worley .04 .01
❑ 470 Kevin Mack .04 .01
❑ 471 Wes Hopkins .04 .01
❑ 472 Will Wolford .04 .01
❑ 473 Sam Seale .04 .01
❑ 474 Jim Ritcher .04 .01
❑ 475 Jeff Hostetler FSC .25 .08
❑ 476 Mitchell Price RC .04 .01
❑ 477 Ken Lanier .04 .01
❑ 478 Naz Worthen .04 .01
❑ 479 Ed Reynolds .04 .01
❑ 480 Mark Clayton .10 .02
❑ 481 Matt Bahr .04 .01
❑ 482 Gary Reasons .04 .01
❑ 483 David Szott .04 .01
❑ 484 Barry Foster .10 .02
❑ 485 Bruce Reimers .04 .01
❑ 486 Dean Biasucci .04 .01
❑ 487 Cris Carter .50 .20
❑ 488 Albert Bentley .04 .01
❑ 489 Robert Massey .04 .01
❑ 490 Al Smith .04 .01
❑ 491 Greg Lloyd .25 .08
❑ 492 Steve McMichael UER .10 .02
❑ 493 Jeff Wright RC .04 .01
❑ 494 Scott Davis .04 .01
❑ 495 Freeman McNeil .04 .01
❑ 496 Simon Fletcher .04 .01
❑ 497 Terry McDaniel .04 .01
❑ 498 Heath Sherman .04 .01
❑ 499 Jeff Jaeger .04 .01
❑ 500 Mark Collins .04 .01
❑ 501 Tim Goad .04 .01
❑ 502 Jeff George .25 .08
❑ 503 Jimmie Jones .04 .01
❑ 504 Henry Thomas .04 .01
❑ 505 Steve Young .75 .30
❑ 506 William Roberts .04 .01
❑ 507 Neil Smith .25 .08
❑ 508 Mike Saxon .04 .01
❑ 509 Johnny Bailey .04 .01
❑ 510 Broderick Thomas .04 .01
❑ 511 Wade Wilson .10 .02
❑ 512 Hart Lee Dykes .04 .01
❑ 513 Hardy Nickerson .10 .02
❑ 514 Tim McDonald .04 .01
❑ 515 Frank Cornish .04 .01
❑ 516 Jarvis Williams .04 .01
❑ 517 Carl Lee .04 .01
❑ 518 Carl Banks .04 .01
❑ 519 Mike Golic .04 .01
❑ 520 Brian Noble .04 .01
❑ 521 James Hasty .04 .01
❑ 522 Bubba Paris .04 .01
❑ 523 Kevin Walker RC .04 .01
❑ 524 William Fuller .10 .02
❑ 525 Eddie Anderson .04 .01
❑ 526 Roger Ruzek .04 .01
❑ 527 Robert Blackmon .04 .01
❑ 528 Vince Buck .04 .01
❑ 529 Lawrence Taylor .25 .08
❑ 530 Reggie Roby .04 .01
❑ 531 Doug Riesenberg .04 .01
❑ 532 Joe Jacoby .04 .01
❑ 533 Kirby Jackson RC .04 .01
❑ 534 Robb Thomas .04 .01
❑ 535 Don Griffin .04 .01
❑ 536 Andre Waters .04 .01
❑ 537 Marc Logan .04 .01
❑ 538 James Thornton .04 .01
❑ 539 Ray Agnew .04 .01
❑ 540 Frank Stams .04 .01
❑ 541 Brett Perriman .25 .08
❑ 542 Andre Ware .10 .02
❑ 543 Kevin Haverdink .04 .01
❑ 544 Greg Jackson RC .04 .01
❑ 545 Tunch Ilkin .04 .01
❑ 546 Dexter Carter .04 .01
❑ 547 Rod Woodson .25 .08
❑ 548 Donnell Woolford .04 .01
❑ 549 Mark Boyer .04 .01
❑ 550 Jeff Query .04 .01
❑ 551 Burt Grossman .04 .01
❑ 552 Mike Kenn .04 .01
❑ 553 Richard Dent .10 .02
❑ 554 Gaston Green .04 .01
❑ 555 Phil Simms .10 .02
❑ 556 Brent Jones .25 .08
❑ 557 Ronnie Lippett .04 .01
❑ 558 Mike Horan .04 .01
❑ 559 Danny Noonan .04 .01
❑ 560 Reggie White .25 .08
❑ 561 Rufus Porter .04 .01
❑ 562 Aaron Wallace .04 .01
❑ 563 Vance Johnson .04 .01
❑ 564A Aaron Craver RC ERR .04 .01
❑ 564B Aaron Craver RC COR .04 .01
❑ 565A Russell Maryland RC ERR .25 .08
❑ 565B Russell Maryland RC COR .25 .08
❑ 566 Paul Justin RC .04 .01
❑ 567 Walter Dean .04 .01
❑ 568 Herman Moore RC .25 .08
❑ 569 Bill Musgrave RC .04 .01
❑ 570 Rob Carpenter RC WR .04 .01
❑ 571 Greg Lewis RC .04 .01
❑ 572 Ed King RC .04 .01
❑ 573 Ernie Mills RC .10 .02
❑ 574 Jake Reed RC .50 .20
❑ 575 Ricky Watters RC 1.50 .60
❑ 576 Derek Russell RC .04 .01
❑ 577 Shawn Moore RC .04 .01
❑ 578 Eric Bieniemy RC .04 .01
❑ 579 Chris Zorich RC .25 .08
❑ 580 Scott Miller .04 .01
❑ 581 Jarrod Bunch RC .04 .01
❑ 582 Ricky Ervins RC .10 .02
❑ 583 Browning Nagle RC .04 .01
❑ 584 Eric Turner RC .10 .02
❑ 585 William Thomas RC .04 .01
❑ 586 Stanley Richard RC .04 .01
❑ 587 Adrian Cooper RC .04 .01
❑ 588 Harvey Williams RC .25 .08
❑ 589 Alvin Harper RC .25 .08
❑ 590 John Carney .04 .01
❑ 591 Mark Vander Poel RC .04 .01
❑ 592 Mike Pritchard RC .25 .08
❑ 593 Eric Moten RC .04 .01
❑ 594 Moe Gardner RC .04 .01
❑ 595 Wesley Carroll RC .04 .01
❑ 596 Eric Swann RC .25 .08
❑ 597 Joe Kelly .04 .01
❑ 598 Steve Jackson RC .04 .01
❑ 599 Kelvin Pritchett RC .10 .02
❑ 600 Jesse Campbell RC .04 .01
❑ 601 Darryll Lewis RC UER .10 .02
❑ 602 Howard Griffith .04 .01
❑ 603 Blaise Bryant .04 .01
❑ 604 Vinnie Clark RC .04 .01
❑ 605 Mel Agee RC .04 .01
❑ 606 Bobby Wilson RC .04 .01
❑ 607 Kevin Donnalley RC .04 .01
❑ 608 Randal Hill RC .10 .02
❑ 609 Stan Thomas .04 .01
❑ 610 Mike Heldt .04 .01
❑ 611 Brett Favre RC 8.00 3.00
❑ 612 Lawrence Dawsey RC UER .10 .02
❑ 613 Dennis Gibson .04 .01
❑ 614 Dean Dingman .04 .01
❑ 615 Bruce Pickens RC .04 .01
❑ 616 Todd Marinovich RC .04 .01
❑ 617 Gene Atkins .04 .01
❑ 618 Marcus Dupree .04 .01
❑ 619 Warren Moon Man of Year .10 .02
❑ 620 Joe Montana TM .50 .20
❑ 621 Neal Anderson MVP .04 .01
❑ 622 James Brooks MVP .10 .02
❑ 623 Thurman Thomas TM .10 .02
❑ 624 Bobby Humphrey MVP .04 .01
❑ 625 Kevin Mack MVP .04 .01
❑ 626 Mark Carrier WR MVP .04 .01
❑ 627 Johnny Johnson TM .04 .01
❑ 628 Marion Butts MVP .10 .02
❑ 629 Steve DeBerg MVP .04 .01
❑ 630 Jeff George TM .10 .02
❑ 631 Troy Aikman TM .40 .15
❑ 632 Dan Marino TM .50 .20
❑ 633 Randall Cunningham TM .10 .02
❑ 634 Andre Rison TM .10 .02
❑ 635 Pepper Johnson MVP .04 .01
❑ 636 Pat Leahy MVP .04 .01
❑ 637 Barry Sanders TM .50 .20
❑ 638 Warren Moon TM .10 .02
❑ 639 Sterling Sharpe TM .04 .01
❑ 640 Bruce Armstrong MVP .04 .01
❑ 641 Bo Jackson TM .10 .02
❑ 642 Henry Ellard MVP .10 .02
❑ 643 Earnest Byner MVP .04 .01
❑ 644 Pat Swilling MVP .04 .01
❑ 645 John L. Williams MVP .04 .01
❑ 646 Rod Woodson TM .10 .02
❑ 647 Chris Doleman MVP .04 .01
❑ 648 Joey Browner CC .04 .01
❑ 649 Erik McMillan CC .04 .01
❑ 650 David Fulcher CC .04 .01
❑ 651A Ronnie Lott CC ERR .10 .02
❑ 651B Ronnie Lott CC COR .10 .02
❑ 652 Louis Oliver CC .04 .01
❑ 653 Mark Robinson CC .04 .01
❑ 654 Dennis Smith CC .04 .01
❑ 655 Reggie White SA ERR .10 .02
❑ 656 Charles Haley SA .04 .01
❑ 657 Leslie O'Neal SA .10 .02
❑ 658 Kevin Greene SA .10 .02
❑ 659 Dennis Byrd SA .04 .01
❑ 660 Bruce Smith SA .10 .02
❑ 661 Derrick Thomas SACK .10 .02
❑ 662 Steve DeBerg TL .04 .01
❑ 663 Barry Sanders TL .50 .20
❑ 664 Thurman Thomas TL .10 .02
❑ 665 Jerry Rice TL .40 .15
❑ 666 Derrick Thomas TL .10 .02
❑ 667 Bruce Smith TL .10 .02
❑ 668 Mark Carrier DB TL .04 .01
❑ 669 Richard Johnson CB TL .04 .01
❑ 670 Jan Stenerud HOF .04 .01
❑ 671 Stan Jones HOF .04 .01
❑ 672 John Hannah HOF .04 .01
❑ 673 Tex Schramm HOF .04 .01
❑ 674 Earl Campbell HOF .25 .08
❑ 675 Emmitt Smith/Carrier ROY .75 .30
❑ 676 Warren Moon DT .10 .02
❑ 677 Barry Sanders DT .50 .20
❑ 678 Thurman Thomas DT .25 .08
❑ 679 Andre Reed DT .10 .02
❑ 680 Andre Rison DT .10 .02
❑ 681 Keith Jackson DT .04 .01
❑ 682 Bruce Armstrong DT .04 .01
❑ 683 Jim Lachey DT .04 .01

❑ 684	Bruce Matthews DT	.04	.01
❑ 685	Mike Munchak DT	.04	.01
❑ 686	Don Mosebar DT	.04	.01
❑ B1	Jeff Hostetler BONUS SB	.25	.08
❑ B2	Matt Bahr SB	.04	.01
❑ B3	Ottis Anderson SB	.10	.02
❑ B4	Ottis Anderson SB	.10	.02

1991 Score Supplemental

❑	COMPLETE FACT.SET (110)	4.00	1.50
❑ 1T	Ronnie Lott	.10	.02
❑ 2T	Matt Millen	.10	.02
❑ 3T	Tim McKyer	.04	.01
❑ 4T	Vince Newsome	.04	.01
❑ 5T	Gaston Green	.04	.01
❑ 6T	Brett Perriman	.25	.08
❑ 7T	Roger Craig	.10	.02
❑ 8T	Pete Holohan	.04	.01
❑ 9T	Tony Zendejas	.04	.01
❑ 10T	Lee Williams	.04	.01
❑ 11T	Mike Stonebreaker	.04	.01
❑ 12T	Felix Wright	.04	.01
❑ 13T	Lonnie Young	.04	.01
❑ 14T	Hugh Millen RC	.04	.01
❑ 15T	Roy Green	.04	.01
❑ 16T	Greg Davis RC	.04	.01
❑ 17T	Dexter Manley	.04	.01
❑ 18T	Ted Washington RC	.04	.01
❑ 19T	Norm Johnson	.04	.01
❑ 20T	Joe Morris	.04	.01
❑ 21T	Robert Perryman	.04	.01
❑ 22T	Mike Iaquaniello RC UER	.04	.01
❑ 23T	Gerald Perry RC UER	.04	.01
❑ 24T	Zeke Mowatt	.04	.01
❑ 25T	Rich Miano RC	.04	.01
❑ 26T	Nick Bell	.04	.01
❑ 27T	Terry Orr RC	.04	.01
❑ 28T	Matt Stover RC	.25	.08
❑ 29T	Bubba Paris	.04	.01
❑ 30T	Ron Brown	.04	.01
❑ 31T	Don Davey	.04	.01
❑ 32T	Lee Rouson	.04	.01
❑ 33T	Terry Hoage UER	.04	.01
❑ 34T	Tony Covington	.04	.01
❑ 35T	John Rienstra	.04	.01
❑ 36T	Charles Dimry RC	.04	.01
❑ 37T	Todd Marinovich	.04	.01
❑ 38T	Winston Moss	.04	.01
❑ 39T	Vestee Jackson	.04	.01
❑ 40T	Brian Hansen	.04	.01
❑ 41T	Irv Eatman	.04	.01
❑ 42T	Jarrod Bunch	.04	.01
❑ 43T	Kanavis McGhee RC	.04	.01
❑ 44T	Vai Sikahema	.04	.01
❑ 45T	Charles McRae RC	.04	.01
❑ 46T	Quinn Early	.10	.02
❑ 47T	Jeff Faulkner RC	.04	.01
❑ 48T	William Frizzell RC	.04	.01
❑ 49T	John Booty	.04	.01
❑ 50T	Tim Harris	.04	.01
❑ 51T	Derek Russell	.04	.01
❑ 52T	John Flannery RC	.04	.01
❑ 53T	Tim Barnett RC	.04	.01
❑ 54T	Alfred Williams RC	.04	.01
❑ 55T	Dan McGwire	.04	.01
❑ 56T	Ernie Mills	.04	.01
❑ 57T	Stanley Richard	.04	.01
❑ 58T	Huey Richardson RC	.04	.01
❑ 59T	Jerome Henderson RC	.04	.01
❑ 60T	Bryan Cox RC	.25	.08
❑ 61T	Russell Maryland	.10	.02
❑ 62T	Reginald Jones RC	.04	.01
❑ 63T	Mo Lewis RC	.10	.02
❑ 64T	Moe Gardner	.04	.01
❑ 65T	Wesley Carroll	.04	.01
❑ 66T	Michael Jackson RC WR	.25	.08
❑ 67T	Shawn Jefferson RC	.10	.02
❑ 68T	Chris Zorich	.10	.02
❑ 69T	Kenny Walker	.04	.01
❑ 70T	Erric Pegram RC	.25	.08
❑ 71T	Alvin Harper	.25	.08
❑ 72T	Harry Colon RC	.04	.01
❑ 73T	Scott Miller	.04	.01
❑ 74T	Lawrence Dawsey	.10	.02
❑ 75T	Phil Hansen RC	.04	.01
❑ 76T	Roman Phifer RC	.04	.01
❑ 77T	Greg Lewis	.04	.01
❑ 78T	Merton Hanks RC	.25	.08
❑ 79T	James Jones RC DT	.04	.01
❑ 80T	Vinnie Clark	.04	.01
❑ 81T	R.J. Kors	.04	.01
❑ 82T	Mike Pritchard	.25	.08
❑ 83T	Stan Thomas	.04	.01
❑ 84T	Lamar Rogers RC	.04	.01
❑ 85T	Erik Williams RC	.10	.02
❑ 86T	Keith Traylor RC	.04	.01
❑ 87T	Mike Dumas	.04	.01
❑ 88T	Mel Agee	.04	.01
❑ 89T	Harvey Williams	.25	.08
❑ 90T	Todd Lyght	.04	.01
❑ 91T	Jake Reed	.40	.15
❑ 92T	Pat Harlow	.04	.01
❑ 93T	Antone Davis RC	.04	.01
❑ 94T	Aeneas Williams RC	.25	.08
❑ 95T	Eric Bieniemy	.04	.01
❑ 96T	John Kasay RC	.10	.02
❑ 97T	Robert Wilson RC	.04	.01
❑ 98T	Ricky Ervins	.10	.02
❑ 99T	Mike Croel	.04	.01
❑ 100T	David Lang RC	.04	.01
❑ 101T	Esera Tuaolo RC	.04	.01
❑ 102T	Randal Hill	.10	.02
❑ 103T	Jon Vaughn RC	.04	.01
❑ 104T	Dave McCloughan	.04	.01
❑ 105T	David Daniels RC	.04	.01
❑ 106T	Eric Moten	.04	.01
❑ 107T	Anthony Morgan RC	.04	.01
❑ 108T	Ed King	.04	.01
❑ 109T	Leonard Russell RC	.10	.02
❑ 110T	Aaron Craver	.04	.01

1992 Score

❑	COMPLETE SET (550)	25.00	12.50
❑ 1	Barry Sanders	2.00	.75
❑ 2	Pat Swilling	.05	.01
❑ 3	Moe Gardner	.05	.01
❑ 4	Steve Young	1.00	.40
❑ 5	Chris Spielman	.10	.02
❑ 6	Richard Dent	.10	.02
❑ 7	Anthony Munoz	.10	.02
❑ 8	Martin Mayhew	.05	.01
❑ 9	Terry McDaniel	.05	.01
❑ 10	Thurman Thomas	.25	.08
❑ 11	Ricky Sanders	.05	.01
❑ 12	Steve Atwater	.05	.01
❑ 13	Tony Tolbert	.05	.01
❑ 14	Vince Workman	.05	.01
❑ 15	Haywood Jeffires	.10	.02
❑ 16	Duane Bickett	.05	.01
❑ 17	Jeff Uhlenhake	.05	.01
❑ 18	Tim McDonald	.05	.01
❑ 19	Cris Carter	.50	.20
❑ 20	Derrick Thomas	.25	.08
❑ 21	Hugh Millen	.05	.01
❑ 22	Bart Oates	.05	.01
❑ 23	Eugene Robinson	.05	.01
❑ 24	Jerrol Williams	.05	.01
❑ 25	Reggie White	.25	.08
❑ 26	Marion Butts	.05	.01
❑ 27	Jim Sweeney	.05	.01
❑ 28	Tom Newberry	.05	.01
❑ 29	Pete Stoyanovich	.05	.01
❑ 30	Ronnie Lott	.10	.02
❑ 31	Simon Fletcher	.05	.01
❑ 32	Dino Hackett	.05	.01
❑ 33	Morten Andersen	.05	.01
❑ 34	Clyde Simmons	.05	.01
❑ 35	Mark Rypien	.05	.01
❑ 36	Greg Montgomery	.05	.01
❑ 37	Nate Lewis	.05	.01
❑ 38	Henry Ellard	.10	.02
❑ 39	Luis Sharpe	.05	.01
❑ 40	Michael Irvin	.25	.08
❑ 41	Louis Lipps	.05	.01
❑ 42	John L. Williams	.05	.01
❑ 43	Broderick Thomas	.05	.01
❑ 44	Michael Haynes	.10	.02
❑ 45	Don Majkowski	.05	.01
❑ 46	William Perry	.10	.02
❑ 47	David Fulcher	.05	.01
❑ 48	Tony Bennett	.05	.01
❑ 49	Clay Matthews	.10	.02
❑ 50	Warren Moon	.25	.08
❑ 51	Bruce Armstrong	.05	.01
❑ 52	Harry Newsome	.05	.01
❑ 53	Bill Brooks	.05	.01
❑ 54	Greg Townsend	.05	.01
❑ 55	Tom Rathman	.05	.01
❑ 56	Sean Landeta	.05	.01
❑ 57	Kyle Clifton	.05	.01
❑ 58	Steve Broussard	.05	.01
❑ 59	Mark Carrier WR	.10	.02
❑ 60	Mel Gray	.10	.02
❑ 61	Tim Krumrie	.05	.01
❑ 62	Rufus Porter	.05	.01
❑ 63	Kevin Mack	.05	.01
❑ 64	Todd Bowles	.05	.01
❑ 65	Emmitt Smith	2.50	1.25
❑ 66	Mike Croel	.05	.01
❑ 67	Brian Mitchell	.10	.02
❑ 68	Bennie Blades	.05	.01
❑ 69	Carnell Lake	.05	.01
❑ 70	Cornelius Bennett	.10	.02
❑ 71	Darrell Thompson	.05	.01
❑ 72	Wes Hopkins	.05	.01
❑ 73	Jessie Hester	.05	.01
❑ 74	Irv Eatman	.05	.01
❑ 75	Marv Cook	.05	.01
❑ 76	Tim Brown	.25	.08
❑ 77	Pepper Johnson	.05	.01
❑ 78	Mark Duper	.05	.01
❑ 79	Robert Delpino	.05	.01

❑ 80	Charles Mann	.05	.01
❑ 81	Brian Jordan	.10	.02
❑ 82	Wendell Davis	.05	.01
❑ 83	Lee Johnson	.05	.01
❑ 84	Ricky Reynolds	.05	.01
❑ 85	Vaughan Johnson	.05	.01
❑ 86	Brian Blades	.10	.02
❑ 87	Sam Seale	.05	.01
❑ 88	Ed King	.05	.01
❑ 89	Gaston Green	.05	.01
❑ 90	Christian Okoye	.05	.01
❑ 91	Chris Jacke	.05	.01
❑ 92	Rohn Stark	.05	.C1
❑ 93	Kevin Greene	.10	.02
❑ 94	Jay Novacek	.10	.02
❑ 95	Chip Lohmiller	.05	.01
❑ 96	Cris Dishman	.05	.01
❑ 97	Ethan Horton	.05	.01
❑ 98	Pat Harlow	.05	.01
❑ 99	Mark Ingram	.05	.01
❑ 100	Mark Carrier DB	.05	.01
❑ 101	Deron Cherry	.05	.01
❑ 102	Sam Mills	.05	.01
❑ 103	Mark Higgs	.05	.01
❑ 104	Keith Jackson	.10	.02
❑ 105	Steve Tasker	.10	.02
❑ 106	Ken Harvey	.05	.01
❑ 107	Bryan Hinkle	.05	.01
❑ 108	Anthony Carter	.10	.02
❑ 109	Johnny Hector	.05	.01
❑ 110	Randall McDaniel	.05	.01
❑ 111	Johnny Johnson	.05	.01
❑ 112	Shane Conlan	.05	.01
❑ 113	Ray Horton	.05	.01
❑ 114	Sterling Sharpe	.25	.08
❑ 115	Guy McIntyre	.05	.01
❑ 116	Tom Waddle	.05	.01
❑ 117	Albert Lewis	.05	.01
❑ 118	Riki Ellison	.05	.01
❑ 119	Chris Doleman	.05	.01
❑ 120	Andre Rison	.10	.02
❑ 121	Bobby Hebert	.05	.01
❑ 122	Dan Owens	.05	.01
❑ 123	Rodney Hampton	.10	.02
❑ 124	Ron Holmes	.05	.01
❑ 125	Ernie Jones	.05	.01
❑ 126	Michael Carter	.05	.01
❑ 127	Reggie Cobb	.05	.01
❑ 128	Esera Tuaolo	.05	.01
❑ 129	Wilber Marshall	.05	.01
❑ 130	Mike Munchak	.10	.02
❑ 131	Cortez Kennedy	.10	.02
❑ 132	Lamar Lathon	.05	.01
❑ 133	Todd Lyght	.05	.01
❑ 134	Jeff Feagles	.05	.01
❑ 135	Burt Grossman	.05	.01
❑ 136	Mike Cofer	.05	.01
❑ 137	Frank Warren	.05	.01
❑ 138	Jarvis Williams	.05	.01
❑ 139	Eddie Brown	.05	.01
❑ 140	John Elliott	.05	.01
❑ 141	Jim Everett	.10	.02
❑ 142	Hardy Nickerson	.10	.02
❑ 143	Eddie Murray	.05	.01
❑ 144	Andre Tippett	.05	.01
❑ 145	Heath Sherman	.05	.01
❑ 146	Ronnie Harmon	.05	.01
❑ 147	Eric Metcalf	.10	.02
❑ 148	Tony Martin	.10	.02
❑ 149	Chris Burkett	.05	.01
❑ 150	Andre Waters	.05	.01
❑ 151	Ray Donaldson	.05	.01
❑ 152	Paul Gruber	.05	.01
❑ 153	Chris Singleton	.05	.01
❑ 154	Clarence Kay	.05	.01
❑ 155	Ernest Givins	.10	.02
❑ 156	Eric Hill	.05	.01
❑ 157	Jesse Sapolu	.05	.01
❑ 158	Jack Del Rio	.05	.01
❑ 159	Erric Pegram	.10	.02
❑ 160	Joey Browner	.05	.01
❑ 161	Marcus Allen	.25	.08
❑ 162	Eric Moten	.05	.01
❑ 163	Donnell Thompson	.05	.01
❑ 164	Chuck Cecil	.05	.01
❑ 165	Matt Millen	.10	.02
❑ 166	Barry Foster	.10	.02
❑ 167	Kent Hull	.05	.01
❑ 168	Tony Jones WR	.05	.01
❑ 169	Mike Prior	.05	.01
❑ 170	Neal Anderson	.05	.01
❑ 171	Roger Craig	.10	.02
❑ 172	Felix Wright	.05	.01
❑ 173	James Francis	.05	.01
❑ 174	Eugene Lockhart	.05	.01
❑ 175	Dalton Hilliard	.05	.01
❑ 176	Nick Lowery	.05	.01
❑ 177	Tim McKyer	.05	.01
❑ 178	Lorenzo White	.05	.01
❑ 179	Jeff Hostetler	.10	.02
❑ 180	Jackie Harris RC	.25	.08
❑ 181	Ken Norton	.10	.02
❑ 182	Flipper Anderson	.05	.01
❑ 183	Don Warren	.05	.01
❑ 184	Brad Baxter	.05	.01
❑ 185	John Taylor	.10	.02
❑ 186	Harold Green	.05	.01
❑ 187	James Washington	.05	.01
❑ 188	Aaron Craver	.05	.01
❑ 189	Mike Merriweather	.05	.01
❑ 190	Gary Clark	.25	.08
❑ 191	Vince Buck	.05	.01
❑ 192	Cleveland Gary	.05	.01
❑ 193	Dan Saleaumua	.05	.01
❑ 194	Gary Zimmerman	.05	.01
❑ 195	Richmond Webb	.05	.01
❑ 196	Gary Plummer	.05	.01
❑ 197	Willie Green	.05	.01
❑ 198	Chris Warren	.25	.08
❑ 199	Mike Pritchard	.10	.02
❑ 200	Art Monk	.10	.02
❑ 201	Matt Stover	.05	.01
❑ 202	Tim Grunhard	.05	.01
❑ 203	Mervyn Fernandez	.05	.01
❑ 204	Mark Jackson	.05	.01
❑ 205	Freddie Joe Nunn	.05	.01
❑ 206	Stan Thomas	.05	.01
❑ 207	Keith McKeller	.05	.01
❑ 208	Jeff Lageman	.05	.01
❑ 209	Kenny Walker	.05	.01
❑ 210	Dave Krieg	.10	.02
❑ 211	Dean Biasucci	.05	.01
❑ 212	Herman Moore	.25	.08
❑ 213	Jon Vaughn	.05	.01
❑ 214	Howard Cross	.05	.01
❑ 215	Greg Davis	.05	.01
❑ 216	Bubby Brister	.05	.01
❑ 217	John Kasay	.05	.01
❑ 218	Ron Hall	.05	.01
❑ 219	Mo Lewis	.05	.01
❑ 220	Eric Green	.05	.01
❑ 221	Scott Case	.05	.01
❑ 222	Sean Jones	.05	.01
❑ 223	Winston Moss	.05	.01
❑ 224	Reggie Langhorne	.05	.01
❑ 225	Greg Lewis	.05	.01
❑ 226	Todd McNair	.05	.01
❑ 227	Rod Bernstine	.05	.01
❑ 228	Joe Jacoby	.05	.01
❑ 229	Brad Muster	.05	.01
❑ 230	Nick Bell	.05	.01
❑ 231	Terry Allen	.25	.08
❑ 232	Cliff Odom	.05	.01
❑ 233	Brian Hansen	.05	.01
❑ 234	William Fuller	.05	.01
❑ 235	Issiac Holt	.05	.01
❑ 236	Dexter Carter	.05	.01
❑ 237	Gene Atkins	.05	.01
❑ 238	Pat Beach	.05	.01
❑ 239	Tim McGee	.05	.01
❑ 240	Dermontti Dawson	.05	.01
❑ 241	Dan Fike	.05	.01
❑ 242	Don Beebe	.05	.01
❑ 243	Jeff Bostic	.05	.01
❑ 244	Mark Collins	.05	.01
❑ 245	Steve Sewell	.05	.01
❑ 246	Steve Walsh	.05	.01
❑ 247	Erik Kramer	.10	.02
❑ 248	Scott Norwood	.05	.01
❑ 249	Jesse Solomon	.05	.01
❑ 250	Jerry Ball	.05	.01
❑ 251	Eugene Daniel	.05	.01
❑ 252	Michael Stewart	.05	.01
❑ 253	Fred Barnett	.25	.08
❑ 254	Rodney Holman	.05	.01
❑ 255	Stephen Baker	.05	.01
❑ 256	Don Griffin	.05	.01
❑ 257	Will Wolford	.05	.01
❑ 258	Perry Kemp	.05	.01
❑ 259	Leonard Russell	.10	.02
❑ 260	Jeff Gossett	.05	.01
❑ 261	Dwayne Harper	.05	.01
❑ 262	Vinny Testaverde	.10	.02
❑ 263	Maurice Hurst	.05	.01
❑ 264	Tony Casillas	.05	.01
❑ 265	Louis Oliver	.05	.01
❑ 266	Jim Morrissey	.05	.01
❑ 267	Kenneth Davis	.05	.01
❑ 268	John Alt	.05	.01
❑ 269	Michael Zordich RC	.05	.01
❑ 270	Brian Brennan	.05	.01
❑ 271	Greg Kragen	.05	.01
❑ 272	Andre Collins	.05	.01
❑ 273	Dave Meggett	.10	.02
❑ 274	Scott Fulhage	.05	.01
❑ 275	Tony Zendejas	.05	.01
❑ 276	Herschel Walker	.10	.02
❑ 277	Keith Henderson	.05	.01
❑ 278	Johnny Bailey	.05	.01
❑ 279	Vince Newsome	.05	.01
❑ 280	Chris Hinton	.05	.01
❑ 281	Robert Blackmon	.05	.01
❑ 282	James Hasty	.05	.01
❑ 283	John Offerdahl	.05	.01
❑ 284	Wesley Carroll	.05	.01
❑ 285	Lomas Brown	.05	.01
❑ 286	Neil O'Donnell	.10	.02
❑ 287	Kevin Porter	.05	.01
❑ 288	Lionel Washington	.05	.01
❑ 289	Carlton Bailey RC	.05	.01
❑ 290	Leonard Marshall	.05	.01
❑ 291	John Carney	.05	.01
❑ 292	Bubba McDowell	.05	.01
❑ 293	Nate Newton	.05	.01
❑ 294	Dave Waymer	.05	.01
❑ 295	Rob Moore	.10	.02
❑ 296	Earnest Byner	.05	.01
❑ 297	Jason Staurovsky	.05	.01
❑ 298	Keith McCants	.05	.01
❑ 299	Floyd Turner	.05	.01
❑ 300	Steve Jordan	.05	.01
❑ 301	Nate Odomes	.05	.01
❑ 302	Gerald Riggs	.05	.01
❑ 303	Marvin Washington	.05	.01
❑ 304	Anthony Thompson	.05	.01
❑ 305	Steve DeBerg	.05	.01
❑ 306	Jim Harbaugh	.25	.08
❑ 307	Larry Brown DB	.05	.01
❑ 308	Roger Ruzek	.05	.01
❑ 309	Jessie Tuggle	.05	.01
❑ 310	Al Smith	.05	.01
❑ 311	Mark Kelso	.05	.01
❑ 312	Lawrence Dawsey	.10	.02
❑ 313	Steve Bono RC	.25	.08

❑	314	Greg Lloyd	.10	.02
❑	315	Steve Wisniewski	.05	.01
❑	316	Gill Fenerty	.05	.01
❑	317	Mark Stepnoski	.10	.02
❑	318	Derek Russell	.05	.01
❑	319	Chris Martin	.05	.01
❑	320	Shaun Gayle	.05	.01
❑	321	Bob Golic	.05	.01
❑	322	Larry Kelm	.05	.01
❑	323	Mike Brim RC	.05	.01
❑	324	Tommy Kane	.05	.01
❑	325	Mark Schlereth RC	.05	.01
❑	326	Ray Childress	.05	.01
❑	327	Richard Brown RC	.05	.01
❑	328	Vincent Brown	.05	.01
❑	329	Mike Farr UER	.05	.01
❑	330	Eric Swann	.10	.02
❑	331	Bill Fralic	.05	.01
❑	332	Rodney Peete	.10	.02
❑	333	Jerry Gray	.05	.01
❑	334	Ray Berry	.05	.01
❑	335	Dennis Smith	.05	.01
❑	336	Jeff Herrod	.05	.01
❑	337	Tony Mandarich	.05	.01
❑	338	Matt Bahr	.05	.01
❑	339	Mike Saxon	.05	.01
❑	340	Bruce Matthews	.05	.01
❑	341	Rickey Jackson	.05	.01
❑	342	Eric Allen	.05	.01
❑	343	Lonnie Young	.05	.01
❑	344	Steve McMichael	.10	.02
❑	345	Willie Gault	.10	.02
❑	346	Barry Word	.05	.01
❑	347	Rich Camarillo	.05	.01
❑	348	Bill Romanowski	.05	.01
❑	349	Jim Lachey	.05	.01
❑	350	Jim Ritcher	.05	.01
❑	351	Irving Fryar	.10	.02
❑	352	Gary Anderson K	.05	.01
❑	353	Henry Rolling	.05	.01
❑	354	Mark Bortz	.05	.01
❑	355	Mark Clayton	.10	.02
❑	356	Keith Woodside	.05	.01
❑	357	Jonathan Hayes	.05	.01
❑	358	Derrick Fenner	.05	.01
❑	359	Keith Byars	.05	.01
❑	360	Drew Hill	.05	.01
❑	361	Harris Barton	.05	.01
❑	362	John Kidd	.05	.01
❑	363	Aeneas Williams	.10	.02
❑	364	Brian Washington	.05	.01
❑	365	John Stephens	.05	.01
❑	366	Norm Johnson	.05	.01
❑	367	Darryl Henley	.05	.01
❑	368	William White	.05	.01
❑	369	Mark Murphy	.05	.01
❑	370	Myron Guyton	.05	.01
❑	371	Leon Seals	.05	.01
❑	372	Rich Gannon	.25	.08
❑	373	Toi Cook	.05	.01
❑	374	Anthony Johnson	.10	.02
❑	375	Rod Woodson	.25	.08
❑	376	Alexander Wright	.05	.01
❑	377	Kevin Butler	.05	.01
❑	378	Neil Smith	.25	.08
❑	379	Gary Anderson RB	.05	.01
❑	380	Reggie Roby	.05	.01
❑	381	Jeff Bryant	.05	.01
❑	382	Ray Crockett	.05	.01
❑	383	Richard Johnson CB	.05	.01
❑	384	Hassan Jones	.05	.01
❑	385	Karl Mecklenburg	.05	.01
❑	386	Jeff Jaeger	.05	.01
❑	387	Keith Willis	.05	.01
❑	388	Phil Simms	.10	.02
❑	389	Kevin Ross	.05	.01
❑	390	Chris Miller	.10	.02
❑	391	Brian Noble	.05	.01
❑	392	Jamie Dukes RC	.05	.01
❑	393	George Jamison	.05	.01
❑	394	Rickey Dixon	.05	.01
❑	395	Carl Lee	.05	.01
❑	396	Jon Hand	.05	.01
❑	397	Kirby Jackson	.05	.01
❑	398	Pat Terrell	.05	.01
❑	399	Howie Long	.25	.08
❑	400	Michael Young	.05	.01
❑	401	Keith Sims	.05	.01
❑	402	Tommy Barnhardt	.05	.01
❑	403	Greg McMurtry	.05	.01
❑	404	Keith Van Horne	.05	.01
❑	405	Seth Joyner	.05	.01
❑	406	Jim Jeffcoat	.05	.01
❑	407	Courtney Hall	.05	.01
❑	408	Tony Covington	.05	.01
❑	409	Jacob Green	.05	.01
❑	410	Charles Haley	.10	.02
❑	411	Darryl Talley	.05	.01
❑	412	Jeff Cross	.05	.01
❑	413	John Elway	2.00	.75
❑	414	Donald Evans	.05	.01
❑	415	Jackie Slater	.05	.01
❑	416	John Friesz	.10	.02
❑	417	Anthony Smith	.05	.01
❑	418	Gill Byrd	.05	.01
❑	419	Willie Drewrey	.05	.01
❑	420	Jay Hilgenberg	.05	.01
❑	421	David Treadwell	.05	.01
❑	422	Curtis Duncan	.05	.01
❑	423	Sammie Smith	.05	.01
❑	424	Henry Thomas	.05	.01
❑	425	James Lofton	.10	.02
❑	426	Fred Marion	.05	.01
❑	427	Bryce Paup	.25	.08
❑	428	Michael Timpson RC	.05	.01
❑	429	Reyna Thompson	.05	.01
❑	430	Mike Kenn	.05	.01
❑	431	Bill Maas	.05	.01
❑	432	Quinn Early	.10	.02
❑	433	Everson Walls	.05	.01
❑	434	Jimmie Jones	.05	.01
❑	435	Dwight Stone	.05	.01
❑	436	Harry Colon	.05	.01
❑	437	Don Mosebar	.05	.01
❑	438	Calvin Williams	.10	.02
❑	439	Tom Tupa	.05	.01
❑	440	Darrell Green	.05	.01
❑	441	Eric Thomas	.05	.01
❑	442	Terry Wooden	.05	.01
❑	443	Brett Perriman	.25	.08
❑	444	Todd Marinovich	.05	.01
❑	445	Jim Breech	.05	.01
❑	446	Eddie Anderson	.05	.01
❑	447	Jay Schroeder	.05	.01
❑	448	William Roberts	.05	.01
❑	449	Brad Edwards	.05	.01
❑	450	Tunch Ilkin	.05	.01
❑	451	Ivy Joe Hunter RC	.05	.01
❑	452	Robert Clark	.05	.01
❑	453	Tim Barnett	.05	.01
❑	454	Jarrod Bunch	.05	.01
❑	455	Tim Harris	.05	.01
❑	456	James Brooks	.10	.02
❑	457	Trace Armstrong	.05	.01
❑	458	Michael Brooks	.05	.01
❑	459	Andy Heck	.05	.01
❑	460	Greg Jackson	.05	.01
❑	461	Vance Johnson	.05	.01
❑	462	Kirk Lowdermilk	.05	.01
❑	463	Erik McMillan	.05	.01
❑	464	Scott Mersereau	.05	.01
❑	465	Jeff Wright	.05	.01
❑	466	Mike Tomczak	.05	.01
❑	467	David Alexander	.05	.01
❑	468	Bryan Millard	.05	.01
❑	469	John Randle	.10	.02
❑	470	Joel Hilgenberg	.05	.01
❑	471	Bennie Thompson RC	.05	.01
❑	472	Freeman McNeil	.05	.01
❑	473	Terry Orr RC	.05	.01
❑	474	Mike Horan	.05	.01
❑	475	Leroy Hoard	.10	.02
❑	476	Patrick Rowe RC	.05	.01
❑	477	Siran Stacy RC	.05	.01
❑	478	Amp Lee RC	.05	.01
❑	479	Eddie Blake RC	.05	.01
❑	480	Joe Bowden RC	.05	.01
❑	481	Rod Milstead RC	.05	.01
❑	482	Keith Hamilton RC	.10	.02
❑	483	Darryl Williams RC	.05	.01
❑	484	Robert Porcher RC	.25	.08
❑	485	Ed Cunningham RC	.05	.01
❑	486	Chris Mims RC	.05	.01
❑	487	Chris Hakel RC	.05	.01
❑	488	Jimmy Smith RC	4.00	1.50
❑	489	Todd Harrison RC	.05	.01
❑	490	Edgar Bennett RC	.25	.08
❑	491	Dexter McNabb RC	.05	.01
❑	492	Leon Searcy RC	.05	.01
❑	493	Tommy Vardell RC	.05	.01
❑	494	Terrell Buckley RC	.05	.01
❑	495	Kevin Turner RC	.05	.01
❑	496	Russ Campbell RC	.05	.01
❑	497	Torrance Small RC	.10	.02
❑	498	Nate Turner RC	.05	.01
❑	499	Cornelius Benton RC	.05	.01
❑	500	Matt Elliott RC	.05	.01
❑	501	Robert Stewart RC	.05	.01
❑	502	Muhammad Shamsid-Deen RC	.05	.01
❑	503	George Williams RC	.05	.01
❑	504	Pumpy Tudors RC	.05	.01
❑	505	Matt LaBounty RC	.05	.01
❑	506	Darryl Hardy RC	.05	.01
❑	507	Derrick Moore RC	.10	.02
❑	508	Willie Clay RC	.05	.01
❑	509	Bob Whitfield RC	.05	.01
❑	510	Ricardo McDonald RC	.05	.01
❑	511	Carlos Huerta RC	.05	.01
❑	512	Selwyn Jones RC	.05	.01
❑	513	Steve Gordon RC	.05	.01
❑	514	Bob Meeks RC	.05	.01
❑	515	Bennie Blades CC	.05	.01
❑	516	Andre Waters CC	.05	.01
❑	517	Bubba McDowell CC	.05	.01
❑	518	Kevin Porter CC	.05	.01
❑	519	Carnell Lake CC	.05	.01
❑	520	Leonard Russell ROY	.10	.02
❑	521	Mike Croel ROY	.05	.01
❑	522	Lawrence Dawsey ROY	.05	.01
❑	523	Moe Gardner ROY	.05	.01
❑	524	Steve Broussard LBM	.05	.01
❑	525	Dave Meggett LBM	.05	.01
❑	526	Darrell Green LBM	.05	.01
❑	527	Tony Jones WR LBM	.05	.01
❑	528	Barry Sanders LBM	1.00	.40
❑	529	Pat Swilling SA	.05	.01
❑	530	Reggie White SA	.10	.02
❑	531	William Fuller SA	.05	.01
❑	532	Simon Fletcher SA	.05	.01
❑	533	Derrick Thomas SA	.10	.02
❑	534	Mark Rypien MOY	.05	.01
❑	535	John Mackey HOF	.05	.01
❑	536	John Riggins HOF	.10	.02
❑	537	Lem Barney HOF	.05	.01
❑	538	Shawn McCarthy RC 90	.05	.01
❑	539	Al Edwards 90	.05	.01
❑	540	Alexander Wright 90	.05	.01
❑	541	Ray Crockett 90	.05	.01
❑	542	Steve Young/J.Taylor 90	.25	.08
❑	543	Nate Lewis 90	.05	.01
❑	544	Dexter Carter 90	.05	.01
❑	545	Reggie Rutland 90	.05	.01
❑	546	Jon Vaughn 90	.05	.01
❑	547	Chris Martin 90	.05	.01

❑ 548 Warren Moon HL .10 .02
❑ 549 Super Bowl Highlights .05 .01
❑ 550 Robb Thomas .05 .01
❑ NNO Dick Butkus Promo 8.00 4.00

1993 Score

❑ COMPLETE SET (440) 15.00 6.00
❑ 1 Barry Sanders 1.25 .50
❑ 2 Moe Gardner .05 .01
❑ 3 Ricky Watters .25 .08
❑ 4 Todd Lyght .05 .01
❑ 5 Rodney Hampton .10 .02
❑ 6 Curtis Duncan .05 .01
❑ 7 Barry Word .05 .01
❑ 8 Reggie Cobb .05 .01
❑ 9 Mike Kenn .05 .01
❑ 10 Michael Irvin .25 .08
❑ 11 Bryan Cox .05 .01
❑ 12 Chris Doleman .05 .01
❑ 13 Rod Woodson .25 .08
❑ 14 Emmitt Smith 1.50 .60
❑ 15 Pete Stoyanovich .05 .01
❑ 16 Steve Young .75 .30
❑ 17 Randall McDaniel .05 .01
❑ 18 Cortez Kennedy .10 .02
❑ 19 Mel Gray .10 .02
❑ 20 Barry Foster .10 .02
❑ 21 Tim Brown .25 .08
❑ 22 Todd McNair .05 .01
❑ 23 Anthony Johnson .10 .02
❑ 24 Nate Odomes .05 .01
❑ 25 Brett Favre 2.00 .75
❑ 26 Jack Del Rio .05 .01
❑ 27 Terry McDaniel .05 .01
❑ 28 Haywood Jeffires .10 .02
❑ 29 Jay Novacek .10 .02
❑ 30 Wilber Marshall .05 .01
❑ 31 Richmond Webb .05 .01
❑ 32 Steve Atwater .05 .01
❑ 33 James Lofton .10 .02
❑ 34 Harold Green .05 .01
❑ 35 Eric Metcalf .10 .02
❑ 36 Bruce Matthews .05 .01
❑ 37 Albert Lewis .05 .01
❑ 38 Jeff Herrod .05 .01
❑ 39 Vince Workman .05 .01
❑ 40 John Elway 1.50 .60
❑ 41 Brett Perriman .25 .08
❑ 42 Jon Vaughn .05 .01
❑ 43 Terry Allen .25 .08
❑ 44 Clyde Simmons .05 .01
❑ 45 Bennie Thompson .05 .01
❑ 46 Wendell Davis .05 .01
❑ 47 Bobby Hebert .05 .01
❑ 48 John Offerdahl .05 .01
❑ 49 Jeff Graham .10 .02
❑ 50 Steve Wisniewski .05 .01
❑ 51 Louis Oliver .05 .01
❑ 52 Rohn Stark .05 .01
❑ 53 Cleveland Gary .05 .01
❑ 54 John Randle .10 .02
❑ 55 Jim Everett .10 .02
❑ 56 Donnell Woolford .05 .01
❑ 57 Pepper Johnson .05 .01
❑ 58 Irving Fryar .10 .02
❑ 59 Greg Townsend .05 .01
❑ 60 Chris Burkett .05 .01
❑ 61 Johnny Johnson .05 .01
❑ 62 Ronnie Harmon .05 .01
❑ 63 Don Griffin .05 .01
❑ 64 Wayne Martin .05 .01
❑ 65 John L. Williams .05 .01
❑ 66 Brad Edwards .05 .01
❑ 67 Toi Cook .05 .01
❑ 68 Lawrence Dawsey .05 .01
❑ 69 Johnny Bailey .05 .01
❑ 70 Mike Brim .05 .01
❑ 71 Andre Rison .10 .02
❑ 72 Cornelius Bennett .10 .02
❑ 73 Brad Muster .05 .01
❑ 74 Broderick Thomas .05 .01
❑ 75 Tom Waddle .05 .01
❑ 76 Paul Gruber .05 .01
❑ 77 Jackie Harris .05 .01
❑ 78 Kenneth Davis .05 .01
❑ 79 Norm Johnson .05 .01
❑ 80 Jim Jeffcoat .05 .01
❑ 81 Chris Warren .10 .02
❑ 82 Greg Kragen .05 .01
❑ 83 Ricky Reynolds .05 .01
❑ 84 Hardy Nickerson .10 .02
❑ 85 Brian Mitchell .10 .02
❑ 86 Rufus Porter .05 .01
❑ 87 Greg Jackson .05 .01
❑ 88 Seth Joyner .05 .01
❑ 89 Tim Grunhard .05 .01
❑ 90 Tim Harris .05 .01
❑ 91 Sterling Sharpe .25 .08
❑ 92 Daniel Stubbs .05 .01
❑ 93 Rob Burnett .05 .01
❑ 94 Rich Camarillo .05 .01
❑ 95 Al Smith .05 .01
❑ 96 Thurman Thomas .25 .08
❑ 97 Morten Andersen .05 .01
❑ 98 Reggie White .25 .08
❑ 99 Gill Byrd .05 .01
❑ 100 Pierce Holt .05 .01
❑ 101 Tim McGee .05 .01
❑ 102 Rickey Jackson .05 .01
❑ 103 Vince Newsome .05 .01
❑ 104 Chris Spielman .10 .02
❑ 105 Tim McDonald .05 .01
❑ 106 James Francis .05 .01
❑ 107 Andre Tippett .05 .01
❑ 108 Sam Mills .05 .01
❑ 109 Hugh Millen .05 .01
❑ 110 Brad Baxter .05 .01
❑ 111 Ricky Sanders .05 .01
❑ 112 Marion Butts .05 .01
❑ 113 Fred Barnett .10 .02
❑ 114 Wade Wilson .05 .01
❑ 115 Dave Meggett .05 .01
❑ 116 Kevin Greene .10 .02
❑ 117 Reggie Langhorne .05 .01
❑ 118 Simon Fletcher .05 .01
❑ 119 Tommy Vardell .05 .01
❑ 120 Darion Conner .05 .01
❑ 121 Darren Lewis .05 .01
❑ 122 Charles Mann .05 .01
❑ 123 David Fulcher .05 .01
❑ 124 Tommy Kane .05 .01
❑ 125 Richard Brown .05 .01
❑ 126 Nate Lewis .05 .01
❑ 127 Tony Tolbert .05 .01
❑ 128 Greg Lloyd .10 .02
❑ 129 Herman Moore .25 .08
❑ 130 Robert Massey .05 .01
❑ 131 Chris Jacke .05 .01
❑ 132 Keith Byars .05 .01
❑ 133 William Fuller .05 .01
❑ 134 Rob Moore .10 .02
❑ 135 Duane Bickett .05 .01
❑ 136 Jarrod Bunch .05 .01
❑ 137 Ethan Horton .05 .01
❑ 138 Leonard Russell .10 .02
❑ 139 Darryl Henley .05 .01
❑ 140 Tony Bennett .05 .01
❑ 141 Harry Newsome .05 .01
❑ 142 Kelvin Martin .05 .01
❑ 143 Audray McMillian .05 .01
❑ 144 Chip Lohmiller .05 .01
❑ 145 Henry Jones .05 .01
❑ 146 Rod Bernstine .05 .01
❑ 147 Darryl Talley .05 .01
❑ 148 Clarence Verdin .05 .01
❑ 149 Derrick Thomas .25 .08
❑ 150 Raleigh McKenzie .05 .01
❑ 151 Phil Hansen .05 .01
❑ 152 Lin Elliott RC .05 .01
❑ 153 Chip Banks .05 .01
❑ 154 Shannon Sharpe .25 .08
❑ 155 David Williams .05 .01
❑ 156 Gaston Green .05 .01
❑ 157 Trace Armstrong .05 .01
❑ 158 Todd Scott .05 .01
❑ 159 Stan Humphries .10 .02
❑ 160 Christian Okoye .05 .01
❑ 161 Dennis Smith .05 .01
❑ 162 Derek Kennard .05 .01
❑ 163 Melvin Jenkins .05 .01
❑ 164 Tommy Barnhardt .05 .01
❑ 165 Eugene Robinson .05 .01
❑ 166 Tom Rathman .05 .01
❑ 167 Chris Chandler .10 .02
❑ 168 Steve Broussard .05 .01
❑ 169 Wymon Henderson .05 .01
❑ 170 Bryce Paup .10 .02
❑ 171 Kent Hull .05 .01
❑ 172 Willie Davis .25 .08
❑ 173 Richard Dent .10 .02
❑ 174 Rodney Peete .05 .01
❑ 175 Clay Matthews .10 .02
❑ 176 Erik Williams .05 .01
❑ 177 Mike Cofer .05 .01
❑ 178 Mark Kelso .05 .01
❑ 179 Kurt Gouveia .05 .01
❑ 180 Keith McCants .05 .01
❑ 181 Jim Arnold .05 .01
❑ 182 Sean Jones .05 .01
❑ 183 Chuck Cecil .05 .01
❑ 184 Mark Rypien .05 .01
❑ 185 William Perry .10 .02
❑ 186 Mark Jackson .05 .01
❑ 187 Jim Dombrowski .05 .01
❑ 188 Heath Sherman .05 .01
❑ 189 Bubba McDowell .05 .01
❑ 190 Fuad Reveiz .05 .01
❑ 191 Darren Perry .05 .01
❑ 192 Karl Mecklenburg .05 .01
❑ 193 Frank Reich .10 .02
❑ 194 Tony Casillas .05 .01
❑ 195 Jerry Ball .05 .01
❑ 196 Jessie Hester .05 .01
❑ 197 David Lang .05 .01
❑ 198 Sean Landeta .05 .01
❑ 199 Jerry Gray .05 .01
❑ 200 Mark Higgs .05 .01
❑ 201 Bruce Armstrong .05 .01
❑ 202 Vaughan Johnson .05 .01
❑ 203 Calvin Williams .10 .02
❑ 204 Leonard Marshall .05 .01
❑ 205 Mike Munchak .10 .02
❑ 206 Kevin Ross .05 .01
❑ 207 Daryl Johnston .25 .08
❑ 208 Jay Schroeder .05 .01
❑ 209 Mo Lewis .05 .01
❑ 210 Carlton Haselrig .05 .01
❑ 211 Cris Carter .25 .08

❑ 212 Marv Cook .05 .01
❑ 213 Mark Duper .05 .01
❑ 214 Jackie Slater .05 .01
❑ 215 Mike Prior .05 .01
❑ 216 Warren Moon .25 .08
❑ 217 Mike Saxon .05 .01
❑ 218 Derrick Fenner .05 .01
❑ 219 Brian Washington .05 .01
❑ 220 Jessie Tuggle .05 .01
❑ 221 Jeff Hostetler .10 .02
❑ 222 Deion Sanders .50 .20
❑ 223 Neal Anderson .05 .01
❑ 224 Kevin Mack .05 .01
❑ 225 Tommy Maddox .25 .08
❑ 226 Neil Smith .25 .08
❑ 227 Ronnie Lott .10 .02
❑ 228 Flipper Anderson .05 .01
❑ 229 Keith Jackson .10 .02
❑ 230 Pat Swilling .05 .01
❑ 231 Carl Banks .05 .01
❑ 232 Eric Allen .05 .01
❑ 233 Randal Hill .05 .01
❑ 234 Burt Grossman .05 .01
❑ 235 Jerry Rice 1.00 .40
❑ 236 Santana Dotson .10 .02
❑ 237 Andre Reed .10 .02
❑ 238 Troy Aikman .75 .30
❑ 239 Ray Childress .05 .01
❑ 240 Phil Simms .10 .02
❑ 241 Steve McMichael .10 .02
❑ 242 Browning Nagle .05 .01
❑ 243 Anthony Miller .10 .02
❑ 244 Earnest Byner .05 .01
❑ 245 Jay Hilgenberg .05 .01
❑ 246 Jeff George .25 .08
❑ 247 Marco Coleman .05 .01
❑ 248 Mark Carrier DB .05 .01
❑ 249 Howie Long .25 .08
❑ 250 Ed McCaffrey .25 .08
❑ 251 Jim Kelly .25 .08
❑ 252 Henry Ellard .10 .02
❑ 253 Joe Montana 1.50 .60
❑ 254 Dale Carter .05 .01
❑ 255 Boomer Esiason .10 .02
❑ 256 Gary Clark .10 .02
❑ 257 Carl Pickens .10 .02
❑ 258 Dave Krieg .10 .02
❑ 259 Russell Maryland .05 .01
❑ 260 Randall Cunningham .25 .08
❑ 261 Leslie O'Neal .10 .02
❑ 262 Vinny Testaverde .10 .02
❑ 263 Ricky Ervins .05 .01
❑ 264 Chris Mims .05 .01
❑ 265 Dan Marino 1.50 .60
❑ 266 Eric Martin .05 .01
❑ 267 Bruce Smith .25 .08
❑ 268 Jim Harbaugh .25 .08
❑ 269 Steve Emtman .05 .01
❑ 270 Ricky Proehl .05 .01
❑ 271 Vaughn Dunbar .05 .01
❑ 272 Junior Seau .25 .08
❑ 273 Sean Gilbert .10 .02
❑ 274 Jim Lachey .05 .01
❑ 275 Dalton Hilliard .05 .01
❑ 276 David Klingler .05 .01
❑ 277 Robert Jones .05 .01
❑ 278 David Treadwell .05 .01
❑ 279 Tracy Scroggins .05 .01
❑ 280 Terrell Buckley .05 .01
❑ 281 Quentin Coryatt .10 .02
❑ 282 Jason Hanson .05 .01
❑ 283 Shane Conlan .05 .01
❑ 284 Guy McIntyre .05 .01
❑ 285 Gary Zimmerman .05 .01
❑ 286 Marty Carter .05 .01
❑ 287 Jim Sweeney .05 .01
❑ 288 Arthur Marshall RC .05 .01
❑ 289 Eugene Chung .05 .01
❑ 290 Mike Pritchard .10 .02
❑ 291 Jim Ritcher .05 .01
❑ 292 Todd Marinovich .05 .01
❑ 293 Courtney Hall .05 .01
❑ 294 Mark Collins .05 .01
❑ 295 Troy Auzenne .05 .01
❑ 296 Aeneas Williams .05 .01
❑ 297 Andy Heck .05 .01
❑ 298 Shaun Gayle .05 .01
❑ 299 Kevin Fagan .05 .01
❑ 300 Carnell Lake .05 .01
❑ 301 Bernie Kosar .10 .02
❑ 302 Maurice Hurst .05 .01
❑ 303 Mike Merriweather .05 .01
❑ 304 Reggie Roby .05 .01
❑ 305 Darryl Williams .05 .01
❑ 306 Jerome Bettis RC 5.00 2.50
❑ 307 Curtis Conway RC .40 .15
❑ 308 Drew Bledsoe RC 2.50 1.00
❑ 309 John Copeland RC .10 .02
❑ 310 Eric Curry RC .05 .01
❑ 311 Lincoln Kennedy RC .05 .01
❑ 312 Dan Williams RC .05 .01
❑ 313 Patrick Bates RC .05 .01
❑ 314 Tom Carter RC .10 .02
❑ 315 Garrison Hearst RC .75 .30
❑ 316 Joel Hilgenberg .05 .01
❑ 317 Harris Barton .05 .01
❑ 318 Jeff Lageman .05 .01
❑ 319 Charles Mincy RC .05 .01
❑ 320 Ricardo McDonald .05 .01
❑ 321 Lorenzo White .05 .01
❑ 322 Troy Vincent .05 .01
❑ 323 Bennie Blades .05 .01
❑ 324 Dana Hall .05 .01
❑ 325 Ken Norton Jr. .10 .02
❑ 326 Will Wolford .05 .01
❑ 327 Neil O'Donnell .25 .08
❑ 328 Tracy Simien .05 .01
❑ 329 Darrell Green .05 .01
❑ 330 Kyle Clifton .05 .01
❑ 331 Elbert Shelley RC .05 .01
❑ 332 Jeff Wright .05 .01
❑ 333 Mike Johnson .05 .01
❑ 334 John Gesek .05 .01
❑ 335 Michael Brooks .05 .01
❑ 336 George Jamison .05 .01
❑ 337 Johnny Holland .05 .01
❑ 338 Lamar Lathon .05 .01
❑ 339 Bern Brostek .05 .01
❑ 340 Steve Jordan .05 .01
❑ 341 Gene Atkins .05 .01
❑ 342 Aaron Wallace .05 .01
❑ 343 Adrian Cooper .05 .01
❑ 344 Amp Lee .05 .01
❑ 345 Vincent Brown .05 .01
❑ 346 James Hasty .05 .01
❑ 347 Ron Hall .05 .01
❑ 348 Matt Elliott .05 .01
❑ 349 Tim Krumrie .05 .01
❑ 350 Mark Stepnoski .05 .01
❑ 351 Matt Stover .05 .01
❑ 352 James Washington .05 .01
❑ 353 Marc Spindler .05 .01
❑ 354 Frank Warren .05 .01
❑ 355 Vai Sikahema .05 .01
❑ 356 Dan Saleaumua .05 .01
❑ 357 Mark Clayton .05 .01
❑ 358 Brent Jones .10 .02
❑ 359 Andy Harmon RC .10 .02
❑ 360 Anthony Parker .05 .01
❑ 361 Chris Hinton .05 .01
❑ 362 Greg Montgomery .05 .01
❑ 363 Greg McMurtry .05 .01
❑ 364 Craig Heyward .10 .02
❑ 365 D.J. Johnson .05 .01
❑ 366 Bill Romanowski .05 .01
❑ 367 Steve Christie .05 .01
❑ 368 Art Monk .10 .02
❑ 369 Howard Ballard .05 .01
❑ 370 Andre Collins .05 .01
❑ 371 Alvin Harper .10 .02
❑ 372 Blaise Winter RC .05 .01
❑ 373 Al Del Greco .05 .01
❑ 374 Eric Green .05 .01
❑ 375 Chris Mohr .05 .01
❑ 376 Tom Newberry .05 .01
❑ 377 Cris Dishman .05 .01
❑ 378 Jumpy Geathers .05 .01
❑ 379 Don Mosebar .05 .01
❑ 380 Andre Ware .05 .01
❑ 381 Marvin Washington .05 .01
❑ 382 Bobby Humphrey .05 .01
❑ 383 Marc Logan .05 .01
❑ 384 Lomas Brown .05 .01
❑ 385 Steve Tasker .10 .02
❑ 386 Chris Miller .10 .02
❑ 387 Tony Paige .05 .01
❑ 388 Charles Haley .10 .02
❑ 389 Rich Moran .05 .01
❑ 390 Mike Sherrard .05 .01
❑ 391 Nick Lowery .05 .01
❑ 392 Henry Thomas .05 .01
❑ 393 Keith Sims .05 .01
❑ 394 Thomas Everett .05 .01
❑ 395 Steve Wallace .05 .01
❑ 396 John Carney .05 .01
❑ 397 Tim Johnson .05 .01
❑ 398 Jeff Gossett .05 .01
❑ 399 Anthony Smith .05 .01
❑ 400 Kelvin Pritchett .05 .01
❑ 401 Dermontti Dawson .05 .01
❑ 402 Alfred Williams .05 .01
❑ 403 Michael Haynes .10 .02
❑ 404 Bart Oates .05 .01
❑ 405 Ken Lanier .05 .01
❑ 406 Vencie Glenn .05 .01
❑ 407 John Taylor .10 .02
❑ 408 Nate Newton .10 .02
❑ 409 Mark Carrier WR .10 .02
❑ 410 Ken Harvey .05 .01
❑ 411 Troy Aikman SB .40 .15
❑ 412 Charles Haley SB .05 .01
❑ 413 Warren Moon/Jeffires DT .10 .02
❑ 414 Henry Jones DT .05 .01
❑ 415 Rickey Jackson DT .05 .01
❑ 416 Clyde Simmons DT .05 .01
❑ 417 Dale Carter ROY .05 .01
❑ 418 Carl Pickens ROY .10 .02
❑ 419 Vaughn Dunbar ROY .05 .01
❑ 420 Santana Dotson ROY .05 .01
❑ 421 Steve Emtman 90 .05 .01
❑ 422 Louis Oliver 90 .05 .01
❑ 423 Carl Pickens 90 .10 .02
❑ 424 Eddie Anderson 90 .05 .01
❑ 425 Deion Sanders 90 .25 .08
❑ 426 Jon Vaughn 90 .05 .01
❑ 427 Darren Lewis 90 .05 .01
❑ 428 Kevin Ross 90 .05 .01
❑ 429 David Brandon 90 .05 .01
❑ 430 Dave Meggett 90 .05 .01
❑ 431 Jerry Rice HL .50 .20
❑ 432 Sterling Sharpe HL .10 .02
❑ 433 Art Monk HL .05 .01
❑ 434 James Lofton HL .05 .01
❑ 435 Lawrence Taylor .10 .02
❑ 436 Bill Walsh RC HOF .10 .02
❑ 437 Chuck Noll HOF .10 .02
❑ 438 Dan Fouts HOF .05 .01
❑ 439 Larry Little HOF .05 .01
❑ 440 Steve Young MOY .40 .15
❑ NNO Dick Butkus AU/3000 40.00 25.00

1994 Score

❑ COMPLETE SET (330) 12.00 5.00
❑ 1 Barry Sanders 1.25 .50

❑ 2 Troy Aikman .75 .30
❑ 3 Sterling Sharpe .10 .02
❑ 4 Deion Sanders .50 .20
❑ 5 Bruce Smith .25 .08
❑ 6 Eric Metcalf .10 .02
❑ 7 John Elway 1.50 .60
❑ 8 Bruce Matthews .05 .01
❑ 9 Rickey Jackson .05 .01
❑ 10 Cortez Kennedy .10 .02
❑ 11 Jerry Rice .75 .30
❑ 12 Stanley Richard .05 .01
❑ 13 Rod Woodson .10 .02
❑ 14 Eric Swann .10 .02
❑ 15 Eric Allen .05 .01
❑ 16 Richard Dent .10 .02
❑ 17 Carl Pickens .10 .02
❑ 18 Rohn Stark .05 .01
❑ 19 Marcus Allen .25 .08
❑ 20 Steve Wisniewski .05 .01
❑ 21 Jerome Bettis .50 .20
❑ 22 Darrell Green .05 .01
❑ 23 Lawrence Dawsey .05 .01
❑ 24 Larry Centers .25 .08
❑ 25 Steve Jordan .05 .01
❑ 26 Johnny Johnson .05 .01
❑ 27 Phil Simms .10 .02
❑ 28 Bruce Armstrong .05 .01
❑ 29 Willie Roaf .05 .01
❑ 30 Andre Rison .10 .02
❑ 31 Henry Jones .05 .01
❑ 32 Warren Moon .25 .08
❑ 33 Sean Gilbert .05 .01
❑ 34 Ben Coates .10 .02
❑ 35 Seth Joyner .05 .01
❑ 36 Ronnie Harmon .05 .01
❑ 37 Quentin Coryatt .05 .01
❑ 38 Ricky Sanders .05 .01
❑ 39 Gerald Williams .05 .01
❑ 40 Emmitt Smith 1.00 .40
❑ 41 Jason Hanson .05 .01
❑ 42 Kevin Smith .05 .01
❑ 43 Irving Fryar .10 .02
❑ 44 Boomer Esiason .10 .02
❑ 45 Darryl Talley .05 .01
❑ 46 Paul Gruber .05 .01
❑ 47 Anthony Smith .05 .01
❑ 48 John Copeland .05 .01
❑ 49 Michael Jackson .10 .02
❑ 50 Shannon Sharpe .10 .02
❑ 51 Reggie White .25 .08
❑ 52 Andre Collins .05 .01
❑ 53 Jack Del Rio .05 .01
❑ 54 John Elliott .05 .01
❑ 55 Kevin Greene .10 .02
❑ 56 Steve Young .60 .25
❑ 57 Erric Pegram .05 .01
❑ 58 Donnell Woolford .05 .01
❑ 59 Darryl Williams .05 .01
❑ 60 Michael Irvin .25 .08
❑ 61 Mel Gray .05 .01
❑ 62 Greg Montgomery .05 .01
❑ 63 Neil Smith .10 .02
❑ 64 Andy Harmon .05 .01
❑ 65 Dan Marino 1.50 .60
❑ 66 Leonard Russell .05 .01
❑ 67 Joe Montana 1.50 .60
❑ 68 John Taylor .10 .02
❑ 69 Cris Dishman .05 .01
❑ 70 Cornelius Bennett .10 .02
❑ 71 Harold Green .05 .01
❑ 72 Anthony Pleasant .05 .01
❑ 73 Dennis Smith .05 .01
❑ 74 Bryce Paup .10 .02
❑ 75 Jeff George .25 .08
❑ 76 Henry Ellard .10 .02
❑ 77 Randall McDaniel .05 .01
❑ 78 Derek Brown RBK .05 .01
❑ 79 Johnny Mitchell .05 .01
❑ 80 Leroy Thompson .05 .01
❑ 81 Junior Seau .25 .08
❑ 82 Kelvin Martin .05 .01
❑ 83 Guy McIntyre .05 .01
❑ 84 Elbert Shelley .05 .01
❑ 85 Louis Oliver .05 .01
❑ 86 Tommy Vardell .05 .01
❑ 87 Jeff Herrod .05 .01
❑ 88 Edgar Bennett .25 .08
❑ 89 Reggie Langhorne .05 .01
❑ 90 Terry Kirby .25 .08
❑ 91 Marcus Robertson .05 .01
❑ 92 Mark Collins .05 .01
❑ 93 Calvin Williams .10 .02
❑ 94 Barry Foster .05 .01
❑ 95 Brent Jones .10 .02
❑ 96 Reggie Cobb .05 .01
❑ 97 Ray Childress .05 .01
❑ 98 Chris Miller .05 .01
❑ 99 John Carney .05 .01
❑ 100 Ricky Proehl .05 .01
❑ 101 Renaldo Turnbull .05 .01
❑ 102 John Randle .10 .02
❑ 103 Flipper Anderson .05 .01
❑ 104 Scottie Graham RC .10 .02
❑ 105 Webster Slaughter .05 .01
❑ 106 Tyrone Hughes .10 .02
❑ 107 Ken Norton Jr. .10 .02
❑ 108 Jim Kelly .25 .08
❑ 109 Michael Haynes .10 .02
❑ 110 Mark Carrier DB .05 .01
❑ 111 Eddie Murray .05 .01
❑ 112 Glyn Milburn .10 .02
❑ 113 Jackie Harris .05 .01
❑ 114 Dean Biasucci .05 .01
❑ 115 Tim Brown .25 .08
❑ 116 Mark Higgs .05 .01
❑ 117 Steve Emtman .05 .01
❑ 118 Clay Matthews .05 .01
❑ 119 Clyde Simmons .05 .01
❑ 120 Howard Ballard .05 .01
❑ 121 Ricky Watters .10 .02
❑ 122 William Fuller .05 .01
❑ 123 Robert Brooks .25 .08
❑ 124 Brian Blades .10 .02
❑ 125 Leslie O'Neal .05 .01
❑ 126 Gary Clark .10 .02
❑ 127 Jim Sweeney .05 .01
❑ 128 Vaughan Johnson .05 .01
❑ 129 Gary Brown .05 .01
❑ 130 Todd Lyght .05 .01
❑ 131 Nick Lowery .05 .01
❑ 132 Ernest Givins .10 .02
❑ 133 Lomas Brown .05 .01
❑ 134 Craig Erickson .05 .01
❑ 135 James Francis .05 .01
❑ 136 Andre Reed .10 .02
❑ 137 Jim Everett .10 .02
❑ 138 Nate Odomes .05 .01
❑ 139 Tom Waddle .05 .01
❑ 140 Stevon Moore .05 .01
❑ 141 Rod Bernstine .05 .01
❑ 142 Brett Favre 1.50 .60
❑ 143 Roosevelt Potts .05 .01
❑ 144 Chester McGlockton .05 .01
❑ 145 LeRoy Butler .05 .01
❑ 146 Charles Haley .10 .02
❑ 147 Rodney Hampton .10 .02
❑ 148 George Teague .05 .01
❑ 149 Gary Anderson K .05 .01
❑ 150 Mark Stepnoski .05 .01
❑ 151 Courtney Hawkins .05 .01
❑ 152 Tim Grunhard .05 .01
❑ 153 David Klingler .05 .01
❑ 154 Erik Williams .05 .01
❑ 155 Herman Moore .25 .08
❑ 156 Daryl Johnston .10 .02
❑ 157 Chris Zorich .05 .01
❑ 158 Shane Conlan .05 .01
❑ 159 Santana Dotson .10 .02
❑ 160 Sam Mills .05 .01
❑ 161 Ronnie Lott .10 .02
❑ 162 Jesse Sapolu .05 .01
❑ 163 Marion Butts .05 .01
❑ 164 Eugene Robinson .05 .01
❑ 165 Mark Schlereth .05 .01
❑ 166 John L. Williams .05 .01
❑ 167 Anthony Miller .10 .02
❑ 168 Rich Camarillo .05 .01
❑ 169 Jeff Lageman .05 .01
❑ 170 Michael Brooks .05 .01
❑ 171 Scott Mitchell .10 .02
❑ 172 Duane Bickett .05 .01
❑ 173 Willie Davis .10 .02
❑ 174 Maurice Hurst .05 .01
❑ 175 Brett Perriman .10 .02
❑ 176 Jay Novacek .10 .02
❑ 177 Terry Allen .10 .02
❑ 178 Pete Metzelaars .05 .01
❑ 179 Erik Kramer .10 .02
❑ 180 Neal Anderson .05 .01
❑ 181 Ethan Horton .05 .01
❑ 182 Tony Bennett .05 .01
❑ 183 Gary Zimmerman .05 .01
❑ 184 Jeff Hostetler .10 .02
❑ 185 Jeff Cross .05 .01
❑ 186 Vincent Brown .05 .01
❑ 187 Herschel Walker .10 .02
❑ 188 Courtney Hall .05 .01
❑ 189 Norm Johnson .05 .01
❑ 190 Hardy Nickerson .10 .02
❑ 191 Greg Townsend .05 .01
❑ 192 Mike Munchak .10 .02
❑ 193 Dante Jones .05 .01
❑ 194 Vinny Testaverde .10 .02
❑ 195 Vance Johnson .05 .01
❑ 196 Chris Jacke .05 .01
❑ 197 Will Wolford .05 .01
❑ 198 Terry McDaniel .05 .01
❑ 199 Bryan Cox .05 .01
❑ 200 Nate Newton .05 .01
❑ 201 Keith Byars .05 .01
❑ 202 Neil O'Donnell .25 .08
❑ 203 Harris Barton .05 .01
❑ 204 Thurman Thomas .25 .08
❑ 205 Jeff Query .05 .01
❑ 206 Russell Maryland .05 .01
❑ 207 Pat Swilling .05 .01
❑ 208 Haywood Jeffires .10 .02
❑ 209 John Alt .05 .01
❑ 210 O.J.McDuffie .25 .08
❑ 211 Keith Sims .05 .01
❑ 212 Eric Martin .05 .01
❑ 213 Kyle Clifton .05 .01
❑ 214 Luis Sharpe .05 .01
❑ 215 Thomas Everett .05 .01
❑ 216 Chris Warren .10 .02
❑ 217 Chris Doleman .05 .01
❑ 218 Tony Jones T .05 .01
❑ 219 Karl Mecklenburg .05 .01

- ❑ 220 Rob Moore .10 .02
- ❑ 221 Jessie Hester .05 .01
- ❑ 222 Jeff Jaeger .05 .01
- ❑ 223 Keith Jackson .05 .01
- ❑ 224 Mo Lewis .05 .01
- ❑ 225 Mike Horan .05 .01
- ❑ 226 Eric Green .05 .01
- ❑ 227 Jim Ritcher .05 .01
- ❑ 228 Eric Curry .05 .01
- ❑ 229 Stan Humphries .10 .02
- ❑ 230 Mike Johnson .05 .01
- ❑ 231 Alvin Harper .10 .02
- ❑ 232 Bennie Blades .05 .01
- ❑ 233 Cris Carter .50 .20
- ❑ 234 Morten Andersen .05 .01
- ❑ 235 Brian Washington .05 .01
- ❑ 236 Eric Hill .05 .01
- ❑ 237 Natrone Means .25 .08
- ❑ 238 Carlton Bailey .05 .01
- ❑ 239 Anthony Carter .10 .02
- ❑ 240 Jessie Tuggle .05 .01
- ❑ 241 Tim Irwin .05 .01
- ❑ 242 Mark Carrier WR .10 .02
- ❑ 243 Steve Atwater .05 .01
- ❑ 244 Sean Jones .05 .01
- ❑ 245 Bernie Kosar .10 .02
- ❑ 246 Richmond Webb .05 .01
- ❑ 247 Dave Meggett .05 .01
- ❑ 248 Vincent Brisby .10 .02
- ❑ 249 Fred Barnett .10 .02
- ❑ 250 Greg Lloyd .10 .02
- ❑ 251 Tim McDonald .05 .01
- ❑ 252 Mike Pritchard .05 .01
- ❑ 253 Greg Robinson .05 .01
- ❑ 254 Tony McGee .05 .01
- ❑ 255 Chris Spielman .10 .02
- ❑ 256 Keith Loneker RC .05 .01
- ❑ 257 Derrick Thomas .25 .08
- ❑ 258 Wayne Martin .05 .01
- ❑ 259 Art Monk .10 .02
- ❑ 260 Andy Heck .05 .01
- ❑ 261 Chip Lohmiller .05 .01
- ❑ 262 Simon Fletcher .05 .01
- ❑ 263 Ricky Reynolds .05 .01
- ❑ 264 Chris Hinton .05 .01
- ❑ 265 Ronald Moore .05 .01
- ❑ 266 Rocket Ismail .10 .02
- ❑ 267 Pete Stoyanovich .05 .01
- ❑ 268 Mark Jackson .05 .01
- ❑ 269 Randall Cunningham .25 .08
- ❑ 270 Dermontti Dawson .05 .01
- ❑ 271 Bill Romanowski .05 .01
- ❑ 272 Tim Johnson .05 .01
- ❑ 273 Steve Tasker .10 .02
- ❑ 274 Keith Hamilton .05 .01
- ❑ 275 Pierce Holt .05 .01
- ❑ 276 Heath Shuler RC .25 .08
- ❑ 277 Marshall Faulk RC 5.00 2.00
- ❑ 278 Charles Johnson RC .25 .08
- ❑ 279 Sam Adams RC .10 .02
- ❑ 280 Trev Alberts RC .10 .02
- ❑ 281 Derrick Alexander WR RC .25 .08
- ❑ 282 Bryant Young RC .25 .08
- ❑ 283 Greg Hill RC .25 .08
- ❑ 284 Darnay Scott RC .50 .20
- ❑ 285 Willie McGinest RC .25 .08
- ❑ 286 Thomas Randolph RC .05 .01
- ❑ 287 Errict Rhett RC .25 .08
- ❑ 288 Lamar Smith RC 1.25 .50
- ❑ 289 William Floyd RC .25 .08
- ❑ 290 Johnnie Morton RC .50 .20
- ❑ 291 Jamir Miller RC .10 .02
- ❑ 292 David Palmer RC .25 .08
- ❑ 293 Dan Wilkinson RC .10 .02
- ❑ 294 Trent Dilfer RC 1.25 .50
- ❑ 295 Antonio Langham RC .10 .02
- ❑ 296 Chuck Levy RC .05 .01
- ❑ 297 John Thierry RC .05 .01
- ❑ 298 Kevin Lee RC .05 .01
- ❑ 299 Aaron Glenn RC .25 .08
- ❑ 300 Charlie Garner RC 1.25 .50
- ❑ 301 Lonnie Johnson RC .05 .01
- ❑ 302 LeShon Johnson RC .10 .02
- ❑ 303 Thomas Lewis RC .10 .02
- ❑ 304 Ryan Yarborough RC .05 .01
- ❑ 305 Mario Bates RC .25 .08
- ❑ 306 Buffalo Bills TC .05 .01
- ❑ 307 Cincinnati Bengals TC .05 .01
- ❑ 308 Cleveland Browns TC .05 .01
- ❑ 309 Denver Broncos TC .05 .01
- ❑ 310 Houston Oilers TC .05 .01
- ❑ 311 Indianapolis Colts TC .05 .01
- ❑ 312 Kansas City Chiefs TC .05 .01
- ❑ 313 Los Angeles Raiders TC .05 .01
- ❑ 314 Miami Dolphins TC .05 .01
- ❑ 315 New England Patriots TC .05 .01
- ❑ 316 New York Jets TC .05 .01
- ❑ 317 Pittsburgh Steelers TC .05 .01
- ❑ 318 San Diego Charges TC .05 .01
- ❑ 319 Seattle Seahawks TC .05 .01
- ❑ 320 Garrison Hearst FF .25 .08
- ❑ 321 Drew Bledsoe FF .75 .30
- ❑ 322 Tyrone Hughes FF .10 .02
- ❑ 323 James Jett FF .05 .01
- ❑ 324 Tom Carter FF .05 .01
- ❑ 325 Reggie Brooks FF .05 .01
- ❑ 326 Dana Stubblefield FF .10 .02
- ❑ 327 Jerome Bettis FF .25 .08
- ❑ 328 Chris Slade FF .05 .01
- ❑ 329 Rick Mirer FF .25 .08
- ❑ 330 Emmitt Smith MVP .50 .20

1995 Score

- ❑ COMPLETE SET (275) 15.00 6.00
- ❑ 1 Steve Young .60 .25
- ❑ 2 Barry Sanders 1.25 .50
- ❑ 3 Jerry Rice .75 .30
- ❑ 4 Marshall Faulk 1.00 .40
- ❑ 5 Terance Mathis .10 .02
- ❑ 6 Rod Woodson .10 .02
- ❑ 7 Seth Joyner .05 .01
- ❑ 8 Michael Timpson .05 .01
- ❑ 9 Deion Sanders .50 .20
- ❑ 10 Emmitt Smith 1.25 .50
- ❑ 11 Cris Carter .25 .08
- ❑ 12 Jake Reed .10 .02
- ❑ 13 Reggie White .25 .08
- ❑ 14 Shannon Sharpe .10 .02
- ❑ 15 Troy Aikman .75 .30
- ❑ 16 Andre Reed .10 .02
- ❑ 17 Tyrone Hughes .10 .02
- ❑ 18 Sterling Sharpe .10 .02
- ❑ 19 Jerome Bettis .25 .08
- ❑ 20 Irving Fryar .10 .02
- ❑ 21 Warren Moon .10 .02
- ❑ 22 Ben Coates .10 .02
- ❑ 23 Frank Reich .05 .01
- ❑ 24 Henry Ellard .10 .02
- ❑ 25 Steve Atwater .05 .01
- ❑ 26 Willie Davis .10 .02
- ❑ 27 Michael Irvin .25 .08
- ❑ 28 Harvey Williams .05 .01
- ❑ 29 Aeneas Williams .05 .01
- ❑ 30 Errict Rhett .10 .02
- ❑ 31 Lorenzo White .05 .01
- ❑ 32 John Elway 1.50 .60
- ❑ 33 Rodney Hampton .10 .02
- ❑ 34 Webster Slaughter .05 .01
- ❑ 35 Eric Turner .05 .01
- ❑ 36 Dan Marino 1.50 .60
- ❑ 37 Daryl Johnston .10 .02
- ❑ 38 Bruce Smith .25 .08
- ❑ 39 Ronald Moore .05 .01
- ❑ 40 Larry Centers .10 .02
- ❑ 41 Curtis Conway .25 .08
- ❑ 42 Drew Bledsoe .50 .20
- ❑ 43 Quinn Early .10 .02
- ❑ 44 Marcus Allen .25 .08
- ❑ 45 Andre Rison .10 .02
- ❑ 46 Jeff Blake RC .50 .20
- ❑ 47 Barry Foster .10 .02
- ❑ 48 Antonio Langham .05 .01
- ❑ 49 Herman Moore .25 .08
- ❑ 50 Flipper Anderson .05 .01
- ❑ 51 Rick Mirer .10 .02
- ❑ 52 Jay Novacek .10 .02
- ❑ 53 Tim Bowens .05 .01
- ❑ 54 Carl Pickens .10 .02
- ❑ 55 Lewis Tillman .05 .01
- ❑ 56 Lawrence Dawsey .05 .01
- ❑ 57 Leroy Hoard .05 .01
- ❑ 58 Steve Broussard .05 .01
- ❑ 59 Dave Krieg .05 .01
- ❑ 60 John Taylor .05 .01
- ❑ 61 Johnny Mitchell .05 .01
- ❑ 62 Jessie Hester .05 .01
- ❑ 63 Johnny Bailey .05 .01
- ❑ 64 Brett Favre 1.50 .60
- ❑ 65 Bryce Paup .10 .02
- ❑ 66 J.J. Birden .05 .01
- ❑ 67 Steve Tasker .10 .02
- ❑ 68 Edgar Bennett .10 .02
- ❑ 69 Ray Buchanan .05 .01
- ❑ 70 Brent Jones .05 .01
- ❑ 71 Dave Meggett .05 .01
- ❑ 72 Jeff Graham .05 .01
- ❑ 73 Michael Brooks .05 .01
- ❑ 74 Ricky Ervins .05 .01
- ❑ 75 Chris Warren .10 .02
- ❑ 76 Natrone Means .10 .02
- ❑ 77 Tim Brown .25 .08
- ❑ 78 Jim Everett .05 .01
- ❑ 79 Chris Calloway .05 .01
- ❑ 80 John L. Williams .05 .01
- ❑ 81 Chris Chandler .10 .02
- ❑ 82 Tim McDonald .05 .01
- ❑ 83 Calvin Williams .10 .02
- ❑ 84 Tony McGee .05 .01
- ❑ 85 Erik Kramer .05 .01
- ❑ 86 Eric Green .05 .01
- ❑ 87 Nate Newton .10 .02
- ❑ 88 Leonard Russell .05 .01
- ❑ 89 Jeff George .10 .02
- ❑ 90 Raymont Harris .05 .01
- ❑ 91 Darnay Scott .10 .02
- ❑ 92 Brian Mitchell .05 .01
- ❑ 93 Craig Erickson .05 .01
- ❑ 94 Cortez Kennedy .10 .02
- ❑ 95 Derrick Alexander WR .25 .08
- ❑ 96 Charles Haley .10 .02
- ❑ 97 Randall Cunningham .25 .08
- ❑ 98 Haywood Jeffires .05 .01
- ❑ 99 Ronnie Harmon .05 .01
- ❑ 100 Dale Carter .10 .02
- ❑ 101 Dave Brown .10 .02
- ❑ 102 Michael Haynes .10 .02
- ❑ 103 Johnny Johnson .05 .01
- ❑ 104 William Floyd .10 .02

❑ 105 Jeff Hostetler .10 .02
❑ 106 Bernie Parmalee .10 .02
❑ 107 Mo Lewis .05 .01
❑ 108 Byron Bam Morris .05 .01
❑ 109 Vincent Brisby .05 .01
❑ 110 John Randle .10 .02
❑ 111 Steve Walsh .05 .01
❑ 112 Terry Allen .10 .02
❑ 113 Greg Lloyd .10 .02
❑ 114 Merton Hanks .05 .01
❑ 115 Mel Gray .05 .01
❑ 116 Jim Kelly .25 .08
❑ 117 Don Beebe .05 .01
❑ 118 Floyd Turner .05 .01
❑ 119 Neil Smith .10 .02
❑ 120 Keith Byars .05 .01
❑ 121 Rocket Ismail .10 .02
❑ 122 Leslie O'Neal .10 .02
❑ 123 Mike Sherrard .05 .01
❑ 124 Marion Butts .05 .01
❑ 125 Andre Coleman .05 .01
❑ 126 Charles Johnson .10 .02
❑ 127 Derrick Fenner .05 .01
❑ 128 Vinny Testaverde .10 .02
❑ 129 Chris Spielman .10 .02
❑ 130 Bert Emanuel .25 .08
❑ 131 Craig Heyward .10 .02
❑ 132 Anthony Miller .10 .02
❑ 133 Rob Moore .10 .02
❑ 134 Gary Brown .05 .01
❑ 135 David Klingler .10 .02
❑ 136 Sean Dawkins .10 .02
❑ 137 Terry McDaniel .05 .01
❑ 138 Fred Barnett .10 .02
❑ 139 Bryan Cox .05 .01
❑ 140 Andrew Jordan .05 .01
❑ 141 Leroy Thompson .05 .01
❑ 142 Richmond Webb .05 .01
❑ 143 Kimble Anders .10 .02
❑ 144 Mario Bates .10 .02
❑ 145 Irv Smith .05 .01
❑ 146 Carnell Lake .05 .01
❑ 147 Mark Seay .10 .02
❑ 148 Dana Stubblefield .10 .02
❑ 149 Kelvin Martin .05 .01
❑ 150 Pete Metzelaars .05 .01
❑ 151 Roosevelt Potts .05 .01
❑ 152 Bubby Brister .05 .01
❑ 153 Trent Dilfer .25 .08
❑ 154 Ricky Proehl .05 .01
❑ 155 Aaron Glenn .05 .01
❑ 156 Eric Metcalf .10 .02
❑ 157 Kevin Williams WR .10 .02
❑ 158 Charlie Garner .25 .08
❑ 159 Glyn Milburn .05 .01
❑ 160 Fuad Reveiz .05 .01
❑ 161 Brett Perriman .10 .02
❑ 162 Neil O'Donnell .10 .02
❑ 163 Tony Martin .10 .02
❑ 164 Sam Adams .05 .01
❑ 165 John Friesz .10 .02
❑ 166 Bryant Young .10 .02
❑ 167 Junior Seau .25 .08
❑ 168 Ken Harvey .05 .01
❑ 169 Bill Brooks .05 .01
❑ 170 Eugene Robinson .05 .01
❑ 171 Ricky Sanders .10 .02
❑ 172 Rodney Peete .05 .01
❑ 173 Boomer Esiason .10 .02
❑ 174 Reggie Roby .05 .01
❑ 175 Michael Jackson .10 .02
❑ 176 Gus Frerotte .10 .02
❑ 177 Terry Kirby .10 .02
❑ 178 Jessie Tuggle .05 .01
❑ 179 Courtney Hawkins .05 .01
❑ 180 Heath Shuler .10 .02
❑ 181 Jack Del Rio .05 .01
❑ 182 O.J. McDuffie .25 .08
❑ 183 Ricky Watters .10 .02
❑ 184 Willie Roaf .05 .01
❑ 185 Glenn Foley .05 .01
❑ 186 Blair Thomas .05 .01
❑ 187 Darren Woodson .10 .02
❑ 188 Kevin Greene .10 .02
❑ 189 Jeff Burris .05 .01
❑ 190 Jay Schroeder .05 .01
❑ 191 Stan Humphries .10 .02
❑ 192 Irving Spikes .10 .02
❑ 193 Jim Harbaugh .10 .02
❑ 194 Robert Brooks .25 .08
❑ 195 Greg Hill .10 .02
❑ 196 Herschel Walker .10 .02
❑ 197 Brian Blades .10 .02
❑ 198 Mark Ingram .05 .01
❑ 199 Kevin Turner .05 .01
❑ 200 Lake Dawson .10 .02
❑ 201 Alvin Harper .05 .01
❑ 202 Derek Brown RBK .05 .01
❑ 203 Qadry Ismail .10 .02
❑ 204 Reggie Brooks .10 .02
❑ 205 Steve Young SS .30 .10
❑ 206 Emmitt Smith SS .60 .25
❑ 207 Stan Humphries SS .05 .01
❑ 208 Barry Sanders SS .60 .25
❑ 209 Marshall Faulk SS .40 .15
❑ 210 Drew Bledsoe SS .25 .08
❑ 211 Jerry Rice SS .40 .15
❑ 212 Tim Brown SS .10 .02
❑ 213 Cris Carter SS .25 .08
❑ 214 Dan Marino SS .75 .30
❑ 215 Troy Aikman SS .40 .15
❑ 216 Jerome Bettis SS .10 .02
❑ 217 Deion Sanders SS .25 .08
❑ 218 Junior Seau SS .10 .02
❑ 219 John Elway SS .75 .30
❑ 220 Warren Moon SS .05 .01
❑ 221 Sterling Sharpe SS .10 .02
❑ 222 Marcus Allen SS .25 .08
❑ 223 Michael Irvin SS .10 .02
❑ 224 Brett Favre SS .75 .30
❑ 225 Rodney Hampton SS .05 .01
❑ 226 Dave Brown SS .10 .02
❑ 227 Ben Coates SS .10 .02
❑ 228 Jim Kelly SS .25 .08
❑ 229 Heath Shuler SS .10 .02
❑ 230 Herman Moore SS .25 .08
❑ 231 Jeff Hostetler SS .10 .02
❑ 232 Rick Mirer SS .10 .02
❑ 233 Byron Bam Morris SS .05 .01
❑ 234 Terance Mathis SS .05 .01
❑ 235 John Elway/B.Sanders CL .40 .15
❑ 236 Troy Aikman CL .05 .01
❑ 237 Jerry Rice CL .25 .08
❑ 238 Emmitt Smith CL .05 .01
❑ 239 Steve Young CL .25 .08
❑ 240 Drew Bledsoe CL .25 .08
❑ 241 Marshall Faulk CL .40 .15
❑ 242 Dan Marino CL .40 .15
❑ 243 Junior Seau CL .10 .02
❑ 244 Ray Zellars RC .10 .02
❑ 245 Rob Johnson RC .75 .30
❑ 246 Tony Boselli RC .25 .08
❑ 247 Kevin Carter RC .25 .08
❑ 248 Steve McNair RC 2.50 1.00
❑ 249 Tyrone Wheatley RC .75 .30
❑ 250 Steve Stenstrom RC .05 .01
❑ 251 Stoney Case RC .05 .01
❑ 252 Rodney Thomas RC .10 .02
❑ 253 Michael Westbrook RC .25 .08
❑ 254 Derrick Alexander DE RC .05 .01
❑ 255 Kyle Brady RC .25 .08
❑ 256 Kerry Collins RC 1.25 .50
❑ 257 Rashaan Salaam RC .10 .02
❑ 258 Frank Sanders RC .25 .08
❑ 259 John Walsh RC .05 .01
❑ 260 Sherman Williams RC .05 .01
❑ 261 Ki-Jana Carter RC .25 .08
❑ 262 Jack Jackson RC .05 .01
❑ 263 J.J. Stokes RC .25 .08
❑ 264 Kordell Stewart RC 1.25 .50
❑ 265 Dave Barr RC .05 .01
❑ 266 Eddie Goines RC .05 .01
❑ 267 Warren Sapp RC 1.25 .50
❑ 268 James O. Stewart RC .75 .30
❑ 269 Joey Galloway RC 1.25 .50
❑ 270 Tyrone Davis RC .05 .01
❑ 271 Napoleon Kaufman RC 1.00 .40
❑ 272 Mark Bruener RC .10 .02
❑ 273 Todd Collins RC .10 .02
❑ 274 Billy Williams RC .05 .01
❑ 275 James A.Stewart RC .05 .01
❑ P264 Kordell Stewart PROMO 2.50 1.00
❑ AD3 Steve Young 3.00 1.25

1996 Score

❑ COMPLETE SET (275) 20.00 7.50
❑ 1 Emmitt Smith 1.25 .50
❑ 2 Flipper Anderson .10 .02
❑ 3 Kordell Stewart .40 .15
❑ 4 Bruce Smith .20 .07
❑ 5 Marshall Faulk .50 .20
❑ 6 William Floyd .20 .07
❑ 7 Darren Woodson .20 .07
❑ 8 Lake Dawson .10 .02
❑ 9 Terry Allen .20 .07
❑ 10 Ki-Jana Carter .20 .07
❑ 11 Tony Boselli .10 .02
❑ 12 Christian Fauria .10 .02
❑ 13 Jeff George .20 .07
❑ 14 Dan Marino 1.50 .60
❑ 15 Rodney Thomas .10 .02
❑ 16 Anthony Miller .20 .07
❑ 17 Chris Sanders .20 .07
❑ 18 Natrone Means .20 .07
❑ 19 Curtis Conway .40 .15
❑ 20 Ben Coates .20 .07
❑ 21 Alvin Harper .10 .02
❑ 22 Frank Sanders .20 .07
❑ 23 Boomer Esiason .20 .07
❑ 24 Lovell Pinkney .10 .02
❑ 25 Troy Aikman .75 .30
❑ 26 Quinn Early .10 .02
❑ 27 Adrian Murrell .20 .07
❑ 28 Chris Spielman .10 .02
❑ 29 Tyrone Wheatley .20 .07
❑ 30 Tim Brown .40 .15
❑ 31 Erik Kramer .10 .02
❑ 32 Warren Moon .20 .07
❑ 33 Jimmy Oliver .10 .02
❑ 34 Herman Moore .20 .07
❑ 35 Quentin Coryatt .10 .02
❑ 36 Heath Shuler .20 .07
❑ 37 Jim Kelly .40 .15
❑ 38 Mike Morris .10 .02
❑ 39 Harvey Williams .10 .02
❑ 40 Vinny Testaverde .20 .07
❑ 41 Steve McNair .60 .25
❑ 42 Jerry Rice .75 .30

❑	43	Darick Holmes	.10	.02
❑	44	Kyle Brady	.10	.02
❑	45	Greg Lloyd	.20	.07
❑	46	Kerry Collins	.40	.15
❑	47	Willie McGinest	.10	.02
❑	48	Isaac Bruce	.40	.15
❑	49	Carnell Lake	.10	.02
❑	50	Charles Haley	.20	.07
❑	51	Troy Vincent	.10	.02
❑	52	Randall Cunningham	.40	.15
❑	53	Rashaan Salaam	.20	.07
❑	54	Willie Jackson	.20	.07
❑	55	Chris Warren	.20	.07
❑	56	Michael Irvin	.40	.15
❑	57	Mario Bates	.20	.07
❑	58	Warren Sapp	.10	.02
❑	59	John Elway	1.50	.60
❑	60	Shannon Sharpe	.20	.07
❑	61	Cornelius Bennett	.10	.02
❑	62	Robert Brooks	.40	.15
❑	63	Rodney Hampton	.20	.07
❑	64	Ken Norton Jr.	.10	.02
❑	65	Bryce Paup	.10	.02
❑	66	Eric Swann	.10	.02
❑	67	Rodney Peete	.10	.02
❑	68	Larry Centers	.20	.07
❑	69	Lamont Warren	.10	.02
❑	70	Jay Novacek	.10	.02
❑	71	Cris Carter	.40	.15
❑	72	Terrell Fletcher	.10	.02
❑	73	Andre Rison	.20	.07
❑	74	Ricky Watters	.20	.07
❑	75	Napoleon Kaufman	.40	.15
❑	76	Reggie White	.40	.15
❑	77	Yancey Thigpen	.20	.07
❑	78	Terry Kirby	.20	.07
❑	79	Deion Sanders	.40	.15
❑	80	Irving Fryar	.20	.07
❑	81	Marcus Allen	.40	.15
❑	82	Carl Pickens	.20	.07
❑	83	Drew Bledsoe	.50	.20
❑	84	Eric Metcalf	.10	.02
❑	85	Robert Smith	.20	.07
❑	86	Tamarick Vanover	.20	.07
❑	87	Henry Ellard	.10	.02
❑	88	Kevin Greene	.20	.07
❑	89	Mark Brunell	.50	.20
❑	90	Terrell Davis	.60	.25
❑	91	Brian Mitchell	.10	.02
❑	92	Aaron Bailey	.10	.02
❑	93	Rocket Ismail	.10	.02
❑	94	Dave Brown	.10	.02
❑	95	Rod Woodson	.20	.07
❑	96	Sean Gilbert	.10	.02
❑	97	Mark Seay	.10	.02
❑	98	Zack Crockett	.10	.02
❑	99	Scott Mitchell	.20	.07
❑	100	Erric Pegram	.10	.02
❑	101	David Palmer	.10	.02
❑	102	Vincent Brisby	.10	.02
❑	103	Brett Perriman	.10	.02
❑	104	Jim Everett	.10	.02
❑	105	Tony Martin	.20	.07
❑	106	Desmond Howard	.20	.07
❑	107	Stan Humphries	.20	.07
❑	108	Bill Brooks	.10	.02
❑	109	Neil Smith	.20	.07
❑	110	Michael Westbrook	.40	.15
❑	111	Herschel Walker	.20	.07
❑	112	Andre Coleman	.10	.02
❑	113	Derrick Alexander WR	.20	.07
❑	114	Jeff Blake	.40	.15
❑	115	Sherman Williams	.10	.02
❑	116	James O.Stewart	.20	.07
❑	117	Hardy Nickerson	.10	.02
❑	118	Elvis Grbac	.20	.07
❑	119	Brett Favre	1.50	.60
❑	120	Mike Sherrard	.10	.02
❑	121	Edgar Bennett	.20	.07
❑	122	Calvin Williams	.10	.02
❑	123	Brian Blades	.10	.02
❑	124	Jeff Graham	.10	.02
❑	125	Gary Brown	.10	.02
❑	126	Bernie Parmalee	.10	.02
❑	127	Kimble Anders	.20	.07
❑	128	Hugh Douglas	.20	.07
❑	129	James A.Stewart	.10	.02
❑	130	Eric Bjornson	.10	.02
❑	131	Ken Dilger	.20	.07
❑	132	Jerome Bettis	.40	.15
❑	133	Cortez Kennedy	.10	.02
❑	134	Bryan Cox	.10	.02
❑	135	Darnay Scott	.20	.07
❑	136	Bert Emanuel	.20	.07
❑	137	Steve Bono	.10	.02
❑	138	Charles Johnson	.10	.02
❑	139	Glyn Milburn	.10	.02
❑	140	Derrick Alexander DE	.10	.02
❑	141	Dave Meggett	.10	.02
❑	142	Trent Dilfer	.40	.15
❑	143	Eric Zeier	.10	.02
❑	144	Jim Harbaugh	.20	.07
❑	145	Antonio Freeman	.40	.15
❑	146	Orlando Thomas	.10	.02
❑	147	Russell Maryland	.10	.02
❑	148	Chad May	.10	.02
❑	149	Craig Heyward	.10	.02
❑	150	Aeneas Williams	.10	.02
❑	151	Kevin Williams WR	.10	.02
❑	152	Charlie Garner	.20	.07
❑	153	J.J. Stokes	.40	.15
❑	154	Stoney Case	.10	.02
❑	155	Mark Chmura	.20	.07
❑	156	Mark Bruener	.10	.02
❑	157	Derek Loville	.10	.02
❑	158	Justin Armour	.10	.02
❑	159	Brent Jones	.10	.02
❑	160	Aaron Craver	.10	.02
❑	161	Terance Mathis	.10	.02
❑	162	Chris Zorich	.10	.02
❑	163	Glenn Foley	.20	.07
❑	164	Johnny Mitchell	.10	.02
❑	165	Junior Seau	.40	.15
❑	166	Willie Davis	.10	.02
❑	167	Rick Mirer	.20	.07
❑	168	Mike Jones LB	.10	.02
❑	169	Greg Hill	.20	.07
❑	170	Steve Tasker	.10	.02
❑	171	Tony Bennett	.10	.02
❑	172	Jeff Hostetler	.10	.02
❑	173	Dave Krieg	.10	.02
❑	174	Mark Carrier WR	.10	.02
❑	175	Michael Haynes	.10	.02
❑	176	Chris Chandler	.20	.07
❑	177	Ernie Mills	.10	.02
❑	178	Jake Reed	.20	.07
❑	179	Errict Rhett	.20	.07
❑	180	Garrison Hearst	.20	.07
❑	181	Derrick Thomas	.40	.15
❑	182	Aaron Hayden RC	.10	.02
❑	183	Jackie Harris	.10	.02
❑	184	Curtis Martin	.60	.25
❑	185	Neil O'Donnell	.20	.07
❑	186	Derrick Moore	.10	.02
❑	187	Steve Young	.60	.25
❑	188	Pat Swilling	.10	.02
❑	189	Amp Lee	.10	.02
❑	190	Rob Johnson	.40	.15
❑	191	Todd Collins	.20	.07
❑	192	J.J. Birden	.10	.02
❑	193	O.J. McDuffie	.20	.07
❑	194	Shawn Jefferson	.10	.02
❑	195	Sean Dawkins	.10	.02
❑	196	Fred Barnett	.10	.02
❑	197	Roosevelt Potts	.10	.02
❑	198	Rob Moore	.20	.07
❑	199	Kevin Miniefield	.10	.02
❑	200	Barry Sanders	1.25	.50
❑	201	Floyd Turner	.10	.02
❑	202	Wayne Chrebet	.60	.25
❑	203	Andre Reed	.20	.07
❑	204	Tyrone Hughes	.10	.02
❑	205	Keenan McCardell	.40	.15
❑	206	Gus Frerotte	.20	.07
❑	207	Daryl Johnston	.20	.07
❑	208	Steve Broussard	.10	.02
❑	209	Steve Atwater	.10	.02
❑	210	Thurman Thomas	.40	.15
❑	211	Andre Hastings	.10	.02
❑	212	Joey Galloway	.40	.15
❑	213	Kevin Carter	.10	.02
❑	214	Keyshawn Johnson RC	1.00	.40
❑	215	Tony Brackens RC	.40	.15
❑	216	Stepfret Williams RC	.20	.07
❑	217	Mike Alstott RC	1.00	.40
❑	218	Terry Glenn RC	1.00	.40
❑	219	Tim Biakabutuka RC	.40	.15
❑	220	Eric Moulds RC	1.25	.50
❑	221	Jeff Lewis RC	.20	.07
❑	222	Bobby Engram RC	.40	.15
❑	223	Cedric Jones RC	.10	.02
❑	224	Stanley Pritchett RC	.20	.07
❑	225	Kevin Hardy RC	.40	.15
❑	226	Alex Van Dyke RC	.20	.07
❑	227	Willie Anderson RC	.10	.02
❑	228	Regan Upshaw RC	.10	.02
❑	229	Leeland McElroy RC	.20	.07
❑	230	Marvin Harrison RC	2.50	1.00
❑	231	Eddie George RC	1.25	.50
❑	232	Lawrence Phillips RC	.40	.15
❑	233	Daryl Gardener RC	.10	.02
❑	234	Alex Molden RC	.10	.02
❑	235	Derrick Mayes RC	.40	.15
❑	236	John Mobley RC	.10	.02
❑	237	Israel Ifeanyi RC	.10	.02
❑	238	Pete Kendall RC	.10	.02
❑	239	Danny Kanell RC	.40	.15
❑	240	Jonathan Ogden RC	.40	.15
❑	241	Reggie Brown LB RC	.10	.02
❑	242	Marcus Jones RC	.10	.02
❑	243	Jon Stark RC	.10	.02
❑	244	Barry Sanders SE	.60	.25
❑	245	Brett Favre SE	.75	.30
❑	246	John Elway SE	.75	.30
❑	247	Dan Marino SE	.75	.30
❑	248	Drew Bledsoe SE	.40	.15
❑	249	Michael Irvin SE	.20	.07
❑	250	Troy Aikman SE	.40	.15
❑	251	Emmitt Smith SE	.50	.20
❑	252	Steve Young SE	.40	.15
❑	253	Jerry Rice SE	.40	.15
❑	254	Jeff Blake SE	.20	.07
❑	255	Tim Brown SE	.20	.07
❑	256	Eric Metcalf SE	.10	.02
❑	257	Rodney Hampton SE	.10	.02
❑	258	Scott Mitchell SE	.10	.02
❑	259	Garrison Hearst SE	.20	.07
❑	260	Larry Centers SE	.20	.07
❑	261	Neil O'Donnell SE	.20	.07
❑	262	Orlando Thomas SE	.10	.02
❑	263	Hugh Douglas SE	.10	.02
❑	264	Bill Brooks SE	.10	.02
❑	265	Harvey Williams SE	.10	.02
❑	266	Charles Haley SE	.20	.07
❑	267	Greg Lloyd SE	.20	.07
❑	268	Daryl Johnston SE	.20	.07
❑	269	Dan Marino CL	.40	.15
❑	270	Jeff Blake CL	.20	.07
❑	271	John Elway CL	.40	.15
❑	272	Emmitt Smith CL	.40	.15
❑	273	Brett Favre CL	.40	.15
❑	274	Jerry Rice CL	.40	.15
❑	275	Five Star Players CL	.40	.15
❑	P1	Barry Sanders Promo	2.00	.75

1997 Score

❑ COMPLETE SET (330)	25.00	10.00
❑ 1 John Elway	2.00	.75
❑ 2 Drew Bledsoe	.60	.25
❑ 3 Brett Favre	2.00	.75
❑ 4 Emmitt Smith	1.50	.60
❑ 5 Kerry Collins	.50	.20
❑ 6 Jerry Rice	1.00	.40
❑ 7 Kordell Stewart	.50	.20
❑ 8 Barry Sanders	1.50	.60
❑ 9 Dan Marino	2.00	.75
❑ 10 Steve Young	.60	.25
❑ 11 Erik Kramer	.20	.07
❑ 12 Warren Moon	.50	.20
❑ 13 Chris Calloway	.20	.07
❑ 14 Doug Evans	.20	.07
❑ 15 Darren Woodson	.20	.07
❑ 16 Alonzo Spellman	.20	.07
❑ 17 Greg Hill	.20	.07
❑ 18 Aaron Craver	.20	.07
❑ 19 Jeff Hostetler	.20	.07
❑ 20 William Thomas	.20	.07
❑ 21 Marco Coleman	.20	.07
❑ 22 Wayne Simmons	.20	.07
❑ 23 Donnell Woolford	.20	.07
❑ 24 Vinny Testaverde	.30	.10
❑ 25 Ed McCaffrey	.30	.10
❑ 26 Jim Everett	.20	.07
❑ 27 Gilbert Brown	.30	.10
❑ 28 Jason Dunn	.20	.07
❑ 29 Stanley Pritchett	.20	.07
❑ 30 Joey Galloway	.30	.10
❑ 31 Amani Toomer	.30	.10
❑ 32 Chris Penn	.20	.07
❑ 33 Aeneas Williams	.20	.07
❑ 34 Bobby Taylor	.20	.07
❑ 35 Bryan Still	.20	.07
❑ 36 Ty Law	.30	.10
❑ 37 Shannon Sharpe	.30	.10
❑ 38 Marty Carter	.20	.07
❑ 39 Sam Mills	.20	.07
❑ 40 William Floyd	.30	.10
❑ 41 Brad Johnson	.50	.20
❑ 42 Sean Dawkins	.20	.07
❑ 43 Michael Irvin	.50	.20
❑ 44 Jeff George	.30	.10
❑ 45 Brent Jones	.30	.10
❑ 46 Mark Brunell	.60	.25
❑ 47 Rob Moore	.30	.10
❑ 48 Hardy Nickerson	.20	.07
❑ 49 Chris Chandler	.30	.10
❑ 50 Willie Anderson	.20	.07
❑ 51 Isaac Bruce	.50	.20
❑ 52 Natrone Means	.30	.10
❑ 53 Tony Banks	.30	.10
❑ 54 Marshall Faulk	.60	.25
❑ 55 Michael Westbrook	.30	.10
❑ 56 Bruce Smith	.30	.10
❑ 57 Jamal Anderson	.50	.20
❑ 58 Jackie Harris	.20	.07
❑ 59 Sean Gilbert	.20	.07
❑ 60 Ki-Jana Carter	.20	.07
❑ 61 Eric Moulds	.50	.20
❑ 62 James O.Stewart	.30	.10
❑ 63 Jeff Blake	.30	.10
❑ 64 O.J. McDuffie	.30	.10
❑ 65 Neil Smith	.30	.10
❑ 66 Kevin Smith	.20	.07
❑ 67 Terry Allen	.50	.20
❑ 68 Sean LaChapelle	.20	.07
❑ 69 Rashaan Salaam	.20	.07
❑ 70 Jeff Graham	.20	.07
❑ 71 Mark Carrier WR	.20	.07
❑ 72 Allen Aldridge	.20	.07
❑ 73 Keenan McCardell	.30	.10
❑ 74 Willie McGinest	.20	.07
❑ 75 Napoleon Kaufman	.50	.20
❑ 76 Jerris McPhail	.20	.07
❑ 77 Eric Swann	.20	.07
❑ 78 Kimble Anders	.30	.10
❑ 79 Charles Johnson	.30	.10
❑ 80 Bryan Cox	.20	.07
❑ 81 Johnnie Morton	.30	.10
❑ 82 Andre Rison	.30	.10
❑ 83 Corey Miller	.20	.07
❑ 84 Troy Drayton	.20	.07
❑ 85 Jim Harbaugh	.30	.10
❑ 86 Wesley Walls	.30	.10
❑ 87 Bryce Paup	.20	.07
❑ 88 Curtis Martin	.60	.25
❑ 89 Michael Sinclair	.20	.07
❑ 90 Chris T. Jones	.20	.07
❑ 91 Jake Reed	.30	.10
❑ 92 LeRoy Butler	.20	.07
❑ 93 Reggie Tongue	.20	.07
❑ 94 Bert Emanuel	.30	.10
❑ 95 Stan Humphries	.30	.10
❑ 96 Neil O'Donnell	.30	.10
❑ 97 Troy Vincent	.20	.07
❑ 98 Mike Alstott	.50	.20
❑ 99 Chad Cota	.20	.07
❑ 100 Marvin Harrison	.50	.20
❑ 101 Terrell Owens	.60	.25
❑ 102 Dave Brown	.20	.07
❑ 103 Harvey Williams	.20	.07
❑ 104 Desmond Howard	.30	.10
❑ 105 Carl Pickens	.30	.10
❑ 106 Kent Graham	.20	.07
❑ 107 Michael Bates	.20	.07
❑ 108 Terrell Davis	.60	.25
❑ 109 Marcus Allen	.50	.20
❑ 110 Ray Zellars	.20	.07
❑ 111 Chris Warren	.30	.10
❑ 112 Phillippi Sparks	.20	.07
❑ 113 Craig Erickson	.20	.07
❑ 114 Eddie George	.50	.20
❑ 115 Daryl Johnston	.30	.10
❑ 116 Ricky Watters	.30	.10
❑ 117 Tedy Bruschi	1.00	.40
❑ 118 Mike Mamula	.20	.07
❑ 119 Ken Harvey	.20	.07
❑ 120 John Randle	.30	.10
❑ 121 Mark Chmura	.30	.10
❑ 122 Sam Gash	.20	.07
❑ 123 John Kasay	.20	.07
❑ 124 Barry Minter	.20	.07
❑ 125 Raymont Harris	.20	.07
❑ 126 Derrick Thomas	.50	.20
❑ 127 Trent Dilfer	.50	.20
❑ 128 Carnell Lake	.20	.07
❑ 129 Brian Dawkins	.50	.20
❑ 130 Tyronne Drakeford	.20	.07
❑ 131 Daryl Gardener	.20	.07
❑ 132 Fred Strickland	.20	.07
❑ 133 Kevin Hardy	.20	.07
❑ 134 Winslow Oliver	.20	.07
❑ 135 Herman Moore	.30	.10
❑ 136 Keith Byars	.20	.07
❑ 137 Harold Green	.20	.07
❑ 138 Ty Detmer	.30	.10
❑ 139 Lamar Thomas	.20	.07
❑ 140 Elvis Grbac	.30	.10
❑ 141 Edgar Bennett	.30	.10
❑ 142 Cornelius Bennett	.20	.07
❑ 143 Tony Tolbert	.20	.07
❑ 144 James Hasty	.20	.07
❑ 145 Ben Coates	.30	.10
❑ 146 Errict Rhett	.20	.07
❑ 147 Jason Sehorn	.30	.10
❑ 148 Michael Jackson	.30	.10
❑ 149 John Mobley	.20	.07
❑ 150 Walt Harris	.20	.07
❑ 151 Terry Kirby	.30	.10
❑ 152 Devin Wyman	.20	.07
❑ 153 Ray Crockett	.20	.07
❑ 154 Quinn Early	.20	.07
❑ 155 Rodney Thomas	.20	.07
❑ 156 Mark Seay	.20	.07
❑ 157 Derrick Alexander WR	.30	.10
❑ 158 Lamar Lathon	.20	.07
❑ 159 Anthony Miller	.20	.07
❑ 160 Shawn Wooden RC	.20	.07
❑ 161 Antonio Freeman	.50	.20
❑ 162 Cortez Kennedy	.20	.07
❑ 163 Rickey Dudley	.30	.10
❑ 164 Tony Carter	.20	.07
❑ 165 Kevin Williams	.20	.07
❑ 166 Reggie White	.50	.20
❑ 167 Tim Bowens	.20	.07
❑ 168 Roy Barker	.20	.07
❑ 169 Adrian Murrell	.30	.10
❑ 170 Anthony Johnson	.20	.07
❑ 171 Terry Glenn	.50	.20
❑ 172 Jeff Lewis	.20	.07
❑ 173 Dorsey Levens	.50	.20
❑ 174 Willie Jackson	.20	.07
❑ 175 Willie Clay	.20	.07
❑ 176 Richmond Webb	.20	.07
❑ 177 Shawn Lee	.20	.07
❑ 178 Joe Aska	.20	.07
❑ 179 Rod Woodson	.30	.10
❑ 180 Jim Schwantz RC	.20	.07
❑ 181 Alfred Williams	.20	.07
❑ 182 Ferric Collons	.20	.07
❑ 183 Ken Norton Jr.	.20	.07
❑ 184 Rick Mirer	.20	.07
❑ 185 Leeland McElroy	.20	.07
❑ 186 Rodney Hampton	.30	.10
❑ 187 Ted Popson	.20	.07
❑ 188 Fred Barnett	.20	.07
❑ 189 Junior Seau	.50	.20
❑ 190 Micheal Barrow	.20	.07
❑ 191 Corey Widmer	.20	.07
❑ 192 Rodney Peete	.20	.07
❑ 193 Rod Smith WR	.50	.20
❑ 194 Muhsin Muhammad	.30	.10
❑ 195 Keith Jackson	.20	.07
❑ 196 Jimmy Smith	.30	.10
❑ 197 Dave Meggett	.20	.07
❑ 198 Lawrence Phillips	.20	.07
❑ 199 Chad Brown	.20	.07
❑ 200 Darrin Smith	.20	.07
❑ 201 Larry Centers	.30	.10
❑ 202 Kevin Greene	.30	.10
❑ 203 Sherman Williams	.20	.07
❑ 204 Chris Sanders	.20	.07
❑ 205 Shawn Jefferson	.20	.07
❑ 206 Thurman Thomas	.50	.20
❑ 207 Keyshawn Johnson	.50	.20
❑ 208 Bryant Young	.20	.07
❑ 209 Tim Biakabutuka	.30	.10
❑ 210 Troy Aikman	1.00	.40
❑ 211 Quentin Coryatt	.20	.07
❑ 212 Karim Abdul-Jabbar	.50	.20
❑ 213 Brian Blades	.20	.07
❑ 214 Ray Farmer	.20	.07
❑ 215 Simeon Rice	.30	.10

❑ 216 Tyrone Braxton .20 .07
❑ 217 Jerome Woods .20 .07
❑ 218 Charles Way .30 .10
❑ 219 Garrison Hearst .30 .10
❑ 220 Bobby Engram .30 .10
❑ 221 Billy Davis RC .20 .07
❑ 222 Ken Dilger .20 .07
❑ 223 Robert Smith .30 .10
❑ 224 John Friesz .20 .07
❑ 225 Charlie Garner .30 .10
❑ 226 Jerome Bettis .50 .20
❑ 227 Darnay Scott .30 .10
❑ 228 Terance Mathis .30 .10
❑ 229 Brian Williams LB .20 .07
❑ 230 Cris Carter .50 .20
❑ 231 Michael Haynes .20 .07
❑ 232 Cedric Jones .20 .07
❑ 233 Danny Kanell .30 .10
❑ 234 Deion Sanders .50 .20
❑ 235 Steve Atwater .20 .07
❑ 236 Jonathan Ogden .20 .07
❑ 237 Lake Dawson .20 .07
❑ 238 Eric Allen .20 .07
❑ 239 Eddie Kennison .30 .10
❑ 240 Irving Fryar .30 .10
❑ 241 Michael Strahan .30 .10
❑ 242 Steve McNair .60 .25
❑ 243 Terrell Buckley .20 .07
❑ 244 Merton Hanks .20 .07
❑ 245 Jessie Armstead .20 .07
❑ 246 Dana Stubblefield .20 .07
❑ 247 Brett Perriman .20 .07
❑ 248 Mark Collins .20 .07
❑ 249 Willie Roaf .20 .07
❑ 250 Gus Frerotte .20 .07
❑ 251 William Fuller .20 .07
❑ 252 Tamarick Vanover .30 .10
❑ 253 Scott Mitchell .30 .10
❑ 254 Eric Metcalf .30 .10
❑ 255 Herschel Walker .30 .10
❑ 256 Robert Brooks .30 .10
❑ 257 Zach Thomas .50 .20
❑ 258 Alvin Harper .20 .07
❑ 259 Wayne Chrebet .50 .20
❑ 260 Bill Romanowski .20 .07
❑ 261 Willie Green .20 .07
❑ 262 Dale Carter .20 .07
❑ 263 Chris Slade .20 .07
❑ 264 J.J. Stokes .30 .10
❑ 265 Tim Brown .50 .20
❑ 266 Eric Davis .20 .07
❑ 267 Mark Carrier DB .20 .07
❑ 268 Tony Martin .30 .10
❑ 269 Tyrone Wheatley .30 .10
❑ 270 Eugene Robinson .20 .07
❑ 271 Curtis Conway .30 .10
❑ 272 Michael Timpson .20 .07
❑ 273 Orlando Pace RC .50 .20
❑ 274 Tiki Barber RC 3.00 1.25
❑ 275 Byron Hanspard RC .30 .10
❑ 276 Warrick Dunn RC 1.25 .50
❑ 277 Rae Carruth RC .20 .07
❑ 278 Bryant Westbrook RC .20 .07
❑ 279 Antowain Smith RC 1.25 .50
❑ 280 Peter Boulware RC .50 .20
❑ 281 Reidel Anthony RC .50 .20
❑ 282 Troy Davis RC .30 .10
❑ 283 Jake Plummer RC 2.50 1.00
❑ 284 Chris Canty RC .20 .07
❑ 285 Dwayne Rudd RC .50 .20
❑ 286 Ike Hilliard RC .75 .30
❑ 287 Reinard Wilson RC .30 .10
❑ 288 Corey Dillon RC 3.00 1.25
❑ 289 Tony Gonzalez RC 1.50 .60
❑ 290 Darnell Autry RC .30 .10
❑ 291 Kevin Lockett RC .30 .10
❑ 292 Darrell Russell RC .20 .07
❑ 293 Jim Druckenmiller RC .30 .10
❑ 294 Shon Mitchell RC .20 .07
❑ 295 Joey Kent RC .50 .20
❑ 296 Shawn Springs RC .30 .10
❑ 297 James Farrior RC .50 .20
❑ 298 Sedrick Shaw RC .30 .10
❑ 299 Marcus Harris RC .20 .07
❑ 300 Danny Wuerffel RC .50 .20
❑ 301 Marc Edwards RC .20 .07
❑ 302 Michael Booker RC .20 .07
❑ 303 David LaFleur RC .20 .07
❑ 304 Mike Adams WR RC .20 .07
❑ 305 Pat Barnes RC .50 .20
❑ 306 George Jones RC .30 .10
❑ 307 Yatil Green RC .30 .10
❑ 308 Drew Bledsoe TBP .50 .20
❑ 309 Troy Aikman TBP .50 .20
❑ 310 Terrell Davis TBP .30 .10
❑ 311 Jim Everett TBP .20 .07
❑ 312 John Elway TBP 1.00 .40
❑ 313 Barry Sanders TBP .75 .30
❑ 314 Jim Harbaugh TBP .30 .10
❑ 315 Steve Young TBP .50 .20
❑ 316 Dan Marino TBP 1.00 .40
❑ 317 Michael Irvin TBP .50 .20
❑ 318 Emmitt Smith TBP .75 .30
❑ 319 Jeff Hostetler TBP .20 .07
❑ 320 Mark Brunell TBP .50 .20
❑ 321 Jeff Blake TBP .50 .20
❑ 322 Scott Mitchell TBP .20 .07
❑ 323 Boomer Esiason TBP .30 .10
❑ 324 Jerome Bettis TBP .50 .20
❑ 325 Warren Moon TBP .30 .10
❑ 326 Neil O'Donnell TBP .30 .10
❑ 327 Jim Kelly TBP .50 .20
❑ 328 Dan Marino CL .50 .20
❑ 329 John Elway CL .50 .20
❑ 330 Drew Bledsoe CL .30 .10
❑ P1 Troy Aikman Promo 1.00 .40
❑ P2 Brett Favre Promo 2.00 .75
❑ P3 Dan Marino Promo 2.00 .75
❑ P4 Barry Sanders Promo 1.50 .60

1998 Score

❑ COMPLETE SET (270) 40.00 15.00
❑ 1 John Elway 2.00 .75
❑ 2 Kordell Stewart .50 .20
❑ 3 Warrick Dunn .50 .20
❑ 4 Brad Johnson .50 .20
❑ 5 Kerry Collins .30 .10
❑ 6 Danny Kanell .30 .10
❑ 7 Emmitt Smith 1.50 .60
❑ 8 Jamal Anderson .50 .20
❑ 9 Jim Harbaugh .30 .10
❑ 10 Tony Martin .30 .10
❑ 11 Rod Smith .30 .10
❑ 12 Dorsey Levens .50 .20
❑ 13 Steve McNair .50 .20
❑ 14 Derrick Thomas .50 .20
❑ 15 Rob Moore .30 .10
❑ 16 Peter Boulware .20 .07
❑ 17 Terry Allen .50 .20
❑ 18 Joey Galloway .30 .10
❑ 19 Jerome Bettis .50 .20
❑ 20 Carl Pickens .30 .10
❑ 21 Napoleon Kaufman .50 .20
❑ 22 Troy Aikman 1.00 .40
❑ 23 Curtis Conway .30 .10
❑ 24 Adrian Murrell .30 .10
❑ 25 Elvis Grbac .30 .10
❑ 26 Garrison Hearst .50 .20
❑ 27 Chris Sanders .20 .07
❑ 28 Scott Mitchell .30 .10
❑ 29 Junior Seau .50 .20
❑ 30 Chris Chandler .30 .10
❑ 31 Kevin Hardy .20 .07
❑ 32 Terrell Davis .50 .20
❑ 33 Keyshawn Johnson .50 .20
❑ 34 Natrone Means .30 .10
❑ 35 Antowain Smith .50 .20
❑ 36 Jake Plummer .50 .20
❑ 37 Isaac Bruce .50 .20
❑ 38 Tony Banks .30 .10
❑ 39 Reidel Anthony .30 .10
❑ 40 Darren Woodson .20 .07
❑ 41 Corey Dillon .50 .20
❑ 42 Antonio Freeman .50 .20
❑ 43 Eddie George .50 .20
❑ 44 Yancey Thigpen .20 .07
❑ 45 Tim Brown .50 .20
❑ 46 Wayne Chrebet .50 .20
❑ 47 Andre Rison .30 .10
❑ 48 Michael Strahan .30 .10
❑ 49 Deion Sanders .50 .20
❑ 50 Eric Moulds .50 .20
❑ 51 Mark Brunell .50 .20
❑ 52 Rae Carruth .20 .07
❑ 53 Warren Sapp .30 .10
❑ 54 Mark Chmura .30 .10
❑ 55 Darrell Green .30 .10
❑ 56 Quinn Early .20 .07
❑ 57 Barry Sanders 1.50 .60
❑ 58 Neil O'Donnell .30 .10
❑ 59 Tony Brackens .20 .07
❑ 60 Willie Davis .20 .07
❑ 61 Shannon Sharpe .30 .10
❑ 62 Shawn Springs .20 .07
❑ 63 Tony Gonzalez .50 .20
❑ 64 Rodney Thomas .20 .07
❑ 65 Terance Mathis .30 .10
❑ 66 Brett Favre 2.00 .75
❑ 67 Eric Swann .20 .07
❑ 68 Kevin Turner .20 .07
❑ 69 Tyrone Wheatley .30 .10
❑ 70 Trent Dilfer .50 .20
❑ 71 Bryan Cox .20 .07
❑ 72 Lake Dawson .20 .07
❑ 73 Will Blackwell .20 .07
❑ 74 Fred Lane .20 .07
❑ 75 Ty Detmer .30 .10
❑ 76 Eddie Kennison .30 .10
❑ 77 Jimmy Smith .30 .10
❑ 78 Chris Calloway .20 .07
❑ 79 Shawn Jefferson .20 .07
❑ 80 Dan Marino 2.00 .75
❑ 81 LeRoy Butler .20 .07
❑ 82 William Roaf .20 .07
❑ 83 Rick Mirer .20 .07
❑ 84 Dermontti Dawson .20 .07
❑ 85 Errict Rhett .30 .10
❑ 86 Lamar Thomas .20 .07
❑ 87 Lamar Lathon .20 .07
❑ 88 John Randle .30 .10
❑ 89 Darryl Williams .20 .07
❑ 90 Keenan McCardell .30 .10
❑ 91 Erik Kramer .20 .07
❑ 92 Ken Dilger .20 .07
❑ 93 Dave Meggett .20 .07
❑ 94 Jeff Blake .30 .10
❑ 95 Ed McCaffrey .30 .10
❑ 96 Charles Johnson .20 .07

❑ 97	Irving Spikes	.20	.07
❑ 98	Mike Alstott	.50	.20
❑ 99	Vincent Brisby	.20	.07
❑ 100	Michael Westbrook	.30	.10
❑ 101	Rickey Dudley	.20	.07
❑ 102	Bert Emanuel	.30	.10
❑ 103	Daryl Johnston	.30	.10
❑ 104	Lawrence Phillips	.20	.07
❑ 105	Eric Bieniemy	.20	.07
❑ 106	Bryant Westbrook	.20	.07
❑ 107	Rob Johnson	.30	.10
❑ 108	Ray Zellars	.20	.07
❑ 109	Anthony Johnson	.20	.07
❑ 110	Reggie White	.50	.20
❑ 111	Wesley Walls	.30	.10
❑ 112	Amani Toomer	.30	.10
❑ 113	Gary Brown	.20	.07
❑ 114	Brian Blades	.20	.07
❑ 115	Alex Van Dyke	.20	.07
❑ 116	Michael Haynes	.20	.07
❑ 117	Jessie Armstead	.20	.07
❑ 118	James Jett	.30	.10
❑ 119	Troy Drayton	.20	.07
❑ 120	Craig Heyward	.20	.07
❑ 121	Steve Atwater	.20	.07
❑ 122	Tiki Barber	.50	.20
❑ 123	Karim Abdul-Jabbar	.50	.20
❑ 124	Kimble Anders	.30	.10
❑ 125	Frank Sanders	.30	.10
❑ 126	David Sloan	.20	.07
❑ 127	Andre Hastings	.20	.07
❑ 128	Vinny Testaverde	.30	.10
❑ 129	Robert Smith	.50	.20
❑ 130	Horace Copeland	.20	.07
❑ 131	Larry Centers	.20	.07
❑ 132	J.J. Stokes	.30	.10
❑ 133	Ike Hilliard	.30	.10
❑ 134	Muhsin Muhammad	.30	.10
❑ 135	Sean Dawkins	.20	.07
❑ 136	Raymont Harris	.20	.07
❑ 137	Lamar Smith	.30	.10
❑ 138	David Palmer	.20	.07
❑ 139	Steve Young	.60	.25
❑ 140	Bryan Still	.20	.07
❑ 141	Keith Byars	.20	.07
❑ 142	Cris Carter	.50	.20
❑ 143	Charlie Garner	.30	.10
❑ 144	Drew Bledsoe	.75	.30
❑ 145	Simeon Rice	.30	.10
❑ 146	Merton Hanks	.20	.07
❑ 147	Aeneas Williams	.20	.07
❑ 148	Rodney Hampton	.30	.10
❑ 149	Zach Thomas	.50	.20
❑ 150	Mark Bruener	.20	.07
❑ 151	Jason Dunn	.20	.07
❑ 152	Danny Wuerffel	.30	.10
❑ 153	Jim Druckenmiller	.20	.07
❑ 154	Greg Hill	.20	.07
❑ 155	Earnest Byner	.20	.07
❑ 156	Greg Lloyd	.20	.07
❑ 157	John Mobley	.20	.07
❑ 158	Tim Biakabutuka	.30	.10
❑ 159	Terrell Owens	.50	.20
❑ 160	O.J. McDuffie	.30	.10
❑ 161	Glenn Foley	.30	.10
❑ 162	Derrick Brooks	.50	.20
❑ 163	Dave Brown	.20	.07
❑ 164	Ki-Jana Carter	.20	.07
❑ 165	Bobby Hoying	.30	.10
❑ 166	Randal Hill	.20	.07
❑ 167	Michael Irvin	.50	.20
❑ 168	Bruce Smith	.30	.10
❑ 169	Troy Davis	.20	.07
❑ 170	Derrick Mayes	.30	.10
❑ 171	Henry Ellard	.30	.10
❑ 172	Dana Stubblefield	.20	.07
❑ 173	Willie McGinest	.20	.07
❑ 174	Leeland McElroy	.20	.07
❑ 175	Edgar Bennett	.20	.07
❑ 176	Robert Porcher	.20	.07
❑ 177	Randall Cunningham	.50	.20
❑ 178	Jim Everett	.20	.07
❑ 179	Jake Reed	.30	.10
❑ 180	Quentin Coryatt	.20	.07
❑ 181	William Floyd	.20	.07
❑ 182	Jason Sehorn	.30	.10
❑ 183	Carnell Lake	.20	.07
❑ 184	Dexter Coakley	.20	.07
❑ 185	Derrick Alexander WR	.30	.10
❑ 186	Johnnie Morton	.30	.10
❑ 187	Irving Fryar	.30	.10
❑ 188	Warren Moon	.50	.20
❑ 189	Todd Collins	.20	.07
❑ 190	Ken Norton Jr.	.20	.07
❑ 191	Terry Glenn	.50	.20
❑ 192	Rashaan Salaam	.20	.07
❑ 193	Jerry Rice	1.00	.40
❑ 194	James O.Stewart	.30	.10
❑ 195	David LaFleur	.20	.07
❑ 196	Eric Green	.20	.07
❑ 197	Gus Frerotte	.20	.07
❑ 198	Willie Green	.20	.07
❑ 199	Marshall Faulk	.60	.25
❑ 200	Brett Perriman	.20	.07
❑ 201	Darnay Scott	.30	.10
❑ 202	Marvin Harrison	.50	.20
❑ 203	Joe Aska	.20	.07
❑ 204	Darrien Gordon	.20	.07
❑ 205	Herman Moore	.30	.10
❑ 206	Curtis Martin	.50	.20
❑ 207	Derek Loville	.20	.07
❑ 208	Dale Carter	.20	.07
❑ 209	Heath Shuler	.20	.07
❑ 210	Jonathan Ogden	.20	.07
❑ 211	Leslie Shepherd	.20	.07
❑ 212	Tony Boselli	.20	.07
❑ 213	Eric Metcalf	.20	.07
❑ 214	Neil Smith	.30	.10
❑ 215	Anthony Miller	.20	.07
❑ 216	Jeff George	.30	.10
❑ 217	Charles Way	.20	.07
❑ 218	Mario Bates	.30	.10
❑ 219	Ben Coates	.30	.10
❑ 220	Michael Jackson	.20	.07
❑ 221	Thurman Thomas	.50	.20
❑ 222	Kyle Brady	.20	.07
❑ 223	Marcus Allen	.50	.20
❑ 224	Robert Brooks	.30	.10
❑ 225	Yatil Green	.20	.07
❑ 226	Byron Hanspard	.20	.07
❑ 227	Andre Reed	.30	.10
❑ 228	Chris Warren	.30	.10
❑ 229	Jackie Harris	.20	.07
❑ 230	Ricky Watters	.30	.10
❑ 231	Bobby Engram	.30	.10
❑ 232	Tamarick Vanover	.20	.07
❑ 233	Peyton Manning RC	15.00	6.00
❑ 234	Curtis Enis RC	.75	.30
❑ 235	Randy Moss RC	8.00	3.00
❑ 236	Charles Woodson RC	1.50	.60
❑ 237	Robert Edwards RC	1.00	.40
❑ 238	Jacquez Green RC	1.00	.40
❑ 239	Keith Brooking RC	1.50	.60
❑ 240	Jerome Pathon RC	1.50	.60
❑ 241	Kevin Dyson RC	1.50	.60
❑ 242	Fred Taylor RC	2.00	.75
❑ 243	Tavian Banks RC	1.00	.40
❑ 244	Marcus Nash RC	.75	.30
❑ 245	Brian Griese RC	2.50	1.00
❑ 246	Andre Wadsworth RC	1.00	.40
❑ 247	Ahman Green RC	6.00	2.50
❑ 248	Joe Jurevicius RC	1.50	.60
❑ 249	Germane Crowell RC	1.00	.40
❑ 250	Skip Hicks RC	1.00	.40
❑ 251	Ryan Leaf RC	1.50	.60
❑ 252	Hines Ward RC	6.00	2.50
❑ 253	John Elway OS	1.00	.40
❑ 254	Mark Brunell OS	.50	.20
❑ 255	Brett Favre OS	1.00	.40
❑ 256	Troy Aikman OS	.50	.20
❑ 257	Warrick Dunn OS	.30	.10
❑ 258	Barry Sanders OS	.75	.30
❑ 259	Eddie George OS	.50	.20
❑ 260	Kordell Stewart OS	.50	.20
❑ 261	Emmitt Smith OS	.75	.30
❑ 262	Steve Young OS	.50	.20
❑ 263	Terrell Davis OS	.50	.20
❑ 264	Dorsey Levens OS	.30	.10
❑ 265	Dan Marino OS	1.00	.40
❑ 266	Jerry Rice OS	.50	.20
❑ 267	Drew Bledsoe OS	.50	.20
❑ 268	Brett Favre CL	.60	.25
❑ 269	Barry Sanders CL	.50	.20
❑ 270	Terrell Davis CL	.50	.20
❑ 251AU	Ryan Leaf AUTO	40.00	15.00

1999 Score

❑	COMPLETE SET (275)	60.00	25.00
❑	COMP.SET w/o SP's (220)	15.00	6.00
❑ 1	Randy Moss	1.50	.60
❑ 2	Randall Cunningham	.60	.25
❑ 3	Cris Carter	.60	.25
❑ 4	Robert Smith	.60	.25
❑ 5	Jake Reed	.40	.15
❑ 6	Leroy Hoard	.25	.08
❑ 7	John Randle	.40	.15
❑ 8	Brett Favre	2.00	.75
❑ 9	Antonio Freeman	.60	.25
❑ 10	Dorsey Levens	.60	.25
❑ 11	Robert Brooks	.40	.15
❑ 12	Derrick Mayes	.40	.15
❑ 13	Mark Chmura	.40	.15
❑ 14	Darick Holmes	.25	.08
❑ 15	Vonnie Holliday	.25	.08
❑ 16	Mike Alstott	.60	.25
❑ 17	Warrick Dunn	.60	.25
❑ 18	Trent Dilfer	.40	.15
❑ 19	Jacquez Green	.25	.08
❑ 20	Reidel Anthony	.40	.15
❑ 21	Warren Sapp	.40	.15
❑ 22	Bert Emanuel	.40	.15
❑ 23	Curtis Enis	.25	.08
❑ 24	Curtis Conway	.40	.15
❑ 25	Bobby Engram	.40	.15
❑ 26	Erik Kramer	.40	.15
❑ 27	Moses Moreno	.25	.08
❑ 28	Edgar Bennett	.25	.08
❑ 29	Barry Sanders	2.00	.75
❑ 30	Charlie Batch	.60	.25
❑ 31	Herman Moore	.40	.15
❑ 32	Johnnie Morton	.40	.15
❑ 33	Germane Crowell	.25	.08
❑ 34	Terry Fair	.25	.08
❑ 35	Gary Brown	.25	.08
❑ 36	Kent Graham	.25	.08
❑ 37	Kerry Collins	.40	.15
❑ 38	Charles Way	.25	.08
❑ 39	Tiki Barber	.60	.25

❑ 40 Ike Hilliard .25 .08
❑ 41 Joe Jurevicius .40 .15
❑ 42 Michael Strahan .40 .15
❑ 43 Jason Sehorn .25 .08
❑ 44 Brad Johnson .60 .25
❑ 45 Terry Allen .40 .15
❑ 46 Skip Hicks .25 .08
❑ 47 Michael Westbrook .40 .15
❑ 48 Leslie Shepherd .25 .08
❑ 49 Stephen Alexander .25 .08
❑ 50 Albert Connell .25 .08
❑ 51 Darrell Green .40 .15
❑ 52 Jake Plummer .40 .15
❑ 53 Adrian Murrell .40 .15
❑ 54 Frank Sanders .40 .15
❑ 55 Rob Moore .40 .15
❑ 56 Larry Centers .25 .08
❑ 57 Simeon Rice .40 .15
❑ 58 Andre Wadsworth .25 .08
❑ 59 Duce Staley .60 .25
❑ 60 Charles Johnson .25 .08
❑ 61 Charlie Garner .40 .15
❑ 62 Bobby Hoying .40 .15
❑ 63 Daryl Johnston .40 .15
❑ 64 Emmitt Smith 1.25 .50
❑ 65 Troy Aikman 1.25 .50
❑ 66 Michael Irvin .40 .15
❑ 67 Deion Sanders .60 .25
❑ 68 Chris Warren .25 .08
❑ 69 Darren Woodson .25 .08
❑ 70 Rod Woodson .40 .15
❑ 71 Travis Jervey .25 .08
❑ 72 Jerry Rice 1.25 .50
❑ 73 Terrell Owens .60 .25
❑ 74 Steve Young .75 .30
❑ 75 Garrison Hearst .40 .15
❑ 76 J.J. Stokes .40 .15
❑ 77 Ken Norton .25 .08
❑ 78 R.W. McQuarters .25 .08
❑ 79 Bryant Young .25 .08
❑ 80 Jamal Anderson .60 .25
❑ 81 Chris Chandler .40 .15
❑ 82 Terance Mathis .40 .15
❑ 83 Tim Dwight .60 .25
❑ 84 O.J. Santiago .25 .08
❑ 85 Chris Calloway .25 .08
❑ 86 Keith Brooking .25 .08
❑ 87 Eddie Kennison .40 .15
❑ 88 Willie Roaf .25 .08
❑ 89 Cam Cleeland .25 .08
❑ 90 Lamar Smith .40 .15
❑ 91 Sean Dawkins .25 .08
❑ 92 Tim Biakabutuka .40 .15
❑ 93 Muhsin Muhammad .40 .15
❑ 94 Steve Beuerlein .25 .08
❑ 95 Rae Carruth .25 .08
❑ 96 Wesley Walls .40 .15
❑ 97 Kevin Greene .40 .15
❑ 98 Trent Green .60 .25
❑ 99 Tony Banks .40 .15
❑ 100 Greg Hill .25 .08
❑ 101 Robert Holcombe .25 .08
❑ 102 Isaac Bruce .60 .25
❑ 103 Amp Lee .25 .08
❑ 104 Az-Zahir Hakim .25 .08
❑ 105 Warren Moon .60 .25
❑ 106 Jeff George .40 .15
❑ 107 Rocket Ismail .40 .15
❑ 108 Kordell Stewart .40 .15
❑ 109 Jerome Bettis .60 .25
❑ 110 Courtney Hawkins .25 .08
❑ 111 Chris Fuamatu-Ma'afala .25 .08
❑ 112 Levon Kirkland .25 .08
❑ 113 Hines Ward .60 .25
❑ 114 Will Blackwell .25 .08
❑ 115 Corey Dillon .60 .25
❑ 116 Carl Pickens .40 .15
❑ 117 Neil O'Donnell .40 .15
❑ 118 Jeff Blake .40 .15
❑ 119 Darnay Scott .25 .08
❑ 120 Takeo Spikes .25 .08
❑ 121 Steve McNair .60 .25
❑ 122 Frank Wycheck .25 .08
❑ 123 Eddie George .60 .25
❑ 124 Chris Sanders .25 .08
❑ 125 Yancey Thigpen .25 .08
❑ 126 Kevin Dyson .40 .15
❑ 127 Blaine Bishop .25 .08
❑ 128 Fred Taylor .60 .25
❑ 129 Mark Brunell .60 .25
❑ 130 Jimmy Smith .40 .15
❑ 131 Keenan McCardell .40 .15
❑ 132 Kyle Brady .25 .08
❑ 133 Tavian Banks .25 .08
❑ 134 James Stewart .40 .15
❑ 135 Kevin Hardy .25 .08
❑ 136 Jonathan Quinn .25 .08
❑ 137 Jermaine Lewis .40 .15
❑ 138 Priest Holmes 1.00 .40
❑ 139 Scott Mitchell .40 .15
❑ 140 Eric Zeier .40 .15
❑ 141 Patrick Johnson .25 .08
❑ 142 Ray Lewis .60 .25
❑ 143 Terry Kirby .25 .08
❑ 144 Ty Detmer .25 .08
❑ 145 Irv Smith .25 .08
❑ 146 Chris Spielman .25 .08
❑ 147 Antonio Langham .25 .08
❑ 148 Dan Marino 2.00 .75
❑ 149 O.J. McDuffie .40 .15
❑ 150 Oronde Gadsden .40 .15
❑ 151 Karim Abdul-Jabbar .40 .15
❑ 152 Yatil Green .25 .08
❑ 153 Zach Thomas .60 .25
❑ 154 John Avery .25 .08
❑ 155 Lamar Thomas .25 .08
❑ 156 Drew Bledsoe .75 .30
❑ 157 Terry Glenn .60 .25
❑ 158 Ben Coates .40 .15
❑ 159 Shawn Jefferson .25 .08
❑ 160 Sedrick Shaw .25 .08
❑ 161 Tony Simmons .25 .08
❑ 162 Ty Law .40 .15
❑ 163 Robert Edwards .25 .08
❑ 164 Curtis Martin .60 .25
❑ 165 Keyshawn Johnson .60 .25
❑ 166 Vinny Testaverde .40 .15
❑ 167 Aaron Glenn .25 .08
❑ 168 Wayne Chrebet .40 .15
❑ 169 Dedric Ward .25 .08
❑ 170 Peyton Manning 2.00 .75
❑ 171 Marshall Faulk .75 .30
❑ 172 Marvin Harrison .60 .25
❑ 173 Jerome Pathon .25 .08
❑ 174 Ken Dilger .25 .08
❑ 175 E.G. Green .25 .08
❑ 176 Doug Flutie .60 .25
❑ 177 Thurman Thomas .40 .15
❑ 178 Andre Reed .40 .15
❑ 179 Eric Moulds .60 .25
❑ 180 Antowain Smith .60 .25
❑ 181 Bruce Smith .40 .15
❑ 182 Rob Johnson .40 .15
❑ 183 Terrell Davis .60 .25
❑ 184 John Elway 2.00 .75
❑ 185 Ed McCaffrey .40 .15
❑ 186 Rod Smith .40 .15
❑ 187 Shannon Sharpe .40 .15
❑ 188 Marcus Nash .25 .08
❑ 189 Brian Griese .60 .25
❑ 190 Neil Smith .40 .15
❑ 191 Bubby Brister .25 .08
❑ 192 Ryan Leaf .60 .25
❑ 193 Natrone Means .40 .15
❑ 194 Mikhael Ricks .25 .08
❑ 195 Junior Seau .60 .25
❑ 196 Jim Harbaugh .40 .15
❑ 197 Bryan Still .25 .08
❑ 198 Freddie Jones .25 .08
❑ 199 Andre Rison .40 .15
❑ 200 Elvis Grbac .40 .15
❑ 201 Byron Bam Morris .25 .08
❑ 202 Rashaan Shehee .25 .08
❑ 203 Kimble Anders .40 .15
❑ 204 Donnell Bennett .25 .08
❑ 205 Tony Gonzalez .60 .25
❑ 206 Derrick Alexander WR .40 .15
❑ 207 Jon Kitna .60 .25
❑ 208 Ricky Watters .40 .15
❑ 209 Joey Galloway .40 .15
❑ 210 Ahman Green .60 .25
❑ 211 Shawn Springs .25 .08
❑ 212 Michael Sinclair .25 .08
❑ 213 Napoleon Kaufman .60 .25
❑ 214 Tim Brown .60 .25
❑ 215 Charles Woodson .60 .25
❑ 216 Harvey Williams .25 .08
❑ 217 Jon Ritchie .25 .08
❑ 218 Rich Gannon .60 .25
❑ 219 Rickey Dudley .25 .08
❑ 220 James Jett .40 .15
❑ 221 Tim Couch RC 3.00 1.25
❑ 222 Ricky Williams RC 4.00 1.50
❑ 223 Donovan McNabb RC 10.00 4.00
❑ 224 Edgerrin James RC 8.00 3.00
❑ 225 Torry Holt RC 6.00 2.50
❑ 226 Daunte Culpepper RC 8.00 3.00
❑ 227 Akili Smith RC 2.00 .75
❑ 228 Champ Bailey RC 4.00 1.50
❑ 229 Chris Claiborne RC 1.25 .50
❑ 230 Chris McAlister RC 2.00 .75
❑ 231 Troy Edwards RC 2.00 .75
❑ 232 Jevon Kearse RC 5.00 2.00
❑ 233 Shaun King RC 2.00 .75
❑ 234 David Boston RC 3.00 1.25
❑ 235 Peerless Price RC 3.00 1.25
❑ 236 Cecil Collins RC 1.25 .50
❑ 237 Rob Konrad RC 2.00 .75
❑ 238 Cade McNown UER RC 2.00 .75
❑ 239 Shawn Bryson RC 3.00 1.25
❑ 240 Kevin Faulk RC 3.00 1.25
❑ 241 Scott Covington RC 3.00 1.25
❑ 242 James Johnson RC 2.00 .75
❑ 243 Mike Cloud RC 2.00 .75
❑ 244 Aaron Brooks RC 4.00 1.50
❑ 245 Sedrick Irvin RC 1.25 .50
❑ 246 Amos Zereoue RC 3.00 1.25
❑ 247 Jermaine Fazande RC 2.00 .75
❑ 248 Joe Germaine RC 2.00 .75
❑ 249 Brock Huard RC 3.00 1.25
❑ 250 Craig Yeast RC 2.00 .75
❑ 251 Travis McGriff RC 1.25 .50
❑ 252 D'Wayne Bates RC 2.00 .75
❑ 253 Na Brown RC 2.00 .75
❑ 254 Tai Streets RC 3.00 1.25
❑ 255 Andy Katzenmoyer RC 2.00 .75
❑ 256 Kevin Johnson RC 3.00 1.25
❑ 257 Joe Montgomery RC 2.00 .75
❑ 258 Karsten Bailey RC 2.00 .75
❑ 259 De'Mond Parker RC 1.25 .50
❑ 260 Reginald Kelly RC 1.25 .50
❑ 261 Eddie George AP 1.50 .60
❑ 262 Jamal Anderson AP 1.50 .60
❑ 263 Barry Sanders AP 6.00 2.50
❑ 264 Fred Taylor AP 1.50 .60
❑ 265 Keyshawn Johnson AP 1.50 .60
❑ 266 Jerry Rice AP 4.00 1.50
❑ 267 Doug Flutie AP 1.50 .60
❑ 268 Deion Sanders AP 1.50 .60
❑ 269 Randall Cunningham AP 1.50 .60
❑ 270 Steve Young AP 2.50 1.00
❑ 271 J.Elway/T.Davis GC 5.00 2.00
❑ 272 P.Manning/M.Faulk GC 5.00 2.00
❑ 273 B.Favre/A.Freeman GC 6.00 2.50

❑ 274	T.Aikman/E.Smith GC	4.00	1.50
❑ 275	C.Carter/R.Moss GC	4.00	1.50

1999 Score Supplemental

❑ COMPLETE SET (110)		25.00	10.00
❑ COMP.FACT.SET (110)		30.00	12.50
❑ S1	Chris Greisen RC	1.00	.40
❑ S2	Sherdrick Bonner RC	.60	.25
❑ S3	Joel Makovicka RC	1.50	.60
❑ S4	Andy McCullough RC	.60	.25
❑ S5	Jeff Paulk RC	.60	.25
❑ S6	Brandon Stokley RC	2.00	.75
❑ S7	Sheldon Jackson RC	1.00	.40
❑ S8	Bobby Collins RC	.60	.25
❑ S9	Kamil Loud RC	.60	.25
❑ S10	Antoine Winfield RC	1.00	.40
❑ S11	Jerry Azumah RC	1.00	.40
❑ S12	James Allen RC	1.50	.60
❑ S13	Nick Williams RC	1.00	.40
❑ S14	Michael Basnight RC	.60	.25
❑ S15	Damon Griffin RC	1.00	.40
❑ S16	Ronnie Powell RC	.60	.25
❑ S17	Darrin Chiaverini RC	1.00	.40
❑ S18	Mark Campbell RC	1.00	.40
❑ S19	Mike Lucky RC	1.00	.40
❑ S20	Wane McGarity RC	.60	.25
❑ S21	Jason Tucker RC	1.00	.40
❑ S22	Ebenezer Ekuban RC	1.00	.40
❑ S23	Robert Thomas RC	1.00	.40
❑ S24	Dat Nguyen RC	1.00	.40
❑ S25	Olandis Gary RC	1.50	.60
❑ S26	Desmond Clark RC	1.50	.60
❑ S27	Andre Cooper RC	.60	.25
❑ S28	Chris Watson RC	.60	.25
❑ S29	Al Wilson RC	1.50	.60
❑ S30	Cory Sauter RC	.60	.25
❑ S31	Brock Olivo RC	.60	.25
❑ S32	Basil Mitchell RC	.60	.25
❑ S33	Matt Snider RC	.60	.25
❑ S34	Antuan Edwards RC	1.00	.40
❑ S35	Mike McKenzie RC	1.00	.40
❑ S36	Terrence Wilkins RC	1.00	.40
❑ S37	Fernando Bryant RC	1.00	.40
❑ S38	Larry Parker RC	1.50	.60
❑ S39	Autry Denson RC	1.00	.40
❑ S40	Jim Kleinsasser RC	1.50	.60
❑ S41	Michael Bishop RC	1.50	.60
❑ S42	Andy Katzenmoyer	.25	.08
❑ S43	Brett Bech RC	.60	.25
❑ S44	Sean Bennett RC	.60	.25
❑ S45	Dan Campbell RC	.60	.25
❑ S46	Ray Lucas RC	1.50	.60
❑ S47	Scott Dreisbach RC	1.00	.40
❑ S48	Cecil Martin RC	1.00	.40
❑ S49	Dameane Douglas RC	1.00	.40
❑ S50	Jed Weaver RC	1.00	.40
❑ S51	Jerame Tuman RC	1.50	.60
❑ S52	Steve Heiden RC	1.50	.60
❑ S53	Jeff Garcia RC	4.00	1.50
❑ S54	Terry Jackson RC	1.00	.40
❑ S55	Charlie Rogers RC	1.00	.40
❑ S56	Lamar King RC	1.00	.40
❑ S57	Kurt Warner RC	8.00	3.00
❑ S58	Dre' Bly RC	1.50	.60
❑ S59	Justin Watson RC	.60	.25
❑ S60	Rabih Abdullah RC	1.00	.40
❑ S61	Martin Gramatica RC	.60	.25
❑ S62	Darnell McDonald RC	1.00	.40
❑ S63	Anthony McFarland RC	1.00	.40
❑ S64	Larry Brown TE RC	.60	.25
❑ S65	Kevin Daft RC	1.00	.40
❑ S66	Mike Sellers	.15	.05
❑ S67	Ken Oxendine	.15	.05
❑ S68	Errict Rhett	.25	.08
❑ S69	Stoney Case	.15	.05
❑ S70	Jonathan Linton	.15	.05
❑ S71	Marcus Robinson	1.00	.40
❑ S72	Shane Matthews	.25	.08
❑ S73	Cade McNown	1.00	.40
❑ S74	Akili Smith	.15	.05
❑ S75	Karim Abdul-Jabbar	.25	.08
❑ S76	Tim Couch	1.50	.60
❑ S77	Kevin Johnson	.40	.15
❑ S78	Ron Rivers	.15	.05
❑ S79	Bill Schroeder	.40	.15
❑ S80	Edgerrin James	2.50	1.00
❑ S81	Cecil Collins	.75	.30
❑ S82	Matthew Hatchette	.15	.05
❑ S83	Daunte Culpepper	2.50	1.00
❑ S84	Ricky Williams	1.25	.50
❑ S85	Tyrone Wheatley	.40	.15
❑ S86	Donovan McNabb	3.00	1.25
❑ S87	Marshall Faulk	.50	.20
❑ S88	Torry Holt	2.00	.75
❑ S89	Stephen Davis	.40	.15
❑ S90	Brad Johnson	.40	.15
❑ S91	Jake Plummer SS	.25	.08
❑ S92	Emmitt Smith SS	.75	.30
❑ S93	Troy Aikman SS	.75	.30
❑ S94	John Elway SS	1.25	.50
❑ S95	Terrell Davis SS	.40	.15
❑ S96	Barry Sanders SS	1.25	.50
❑ S97	Brett Favre SS	1.25	.50
❑ S98	Antonio Freeman SS	.40	.15
❑ S99	Peyton Manning SS	1.25	.50
❑ S100	Fred Taylor SS	.40	.15
❑ S101	Mark Brunell SS	.40	.15
❑ S102	Dan Marino SS	1.25	.50
❑ S103	Randy Moss SS	1.00	.40
❑ S104	Cris Carter SS	.40	.15
❑ S105	Drew Bledsoe SS	.50	.20
❑ S106	Terry Glenn SS	.40	.15
❑ S107	Keyshawn Johnson SS	.40	.15
❑ S108	Jerry Rice SS	.75	.30
❑ S109	Steve Young SS	.50	.20
❑ S110	Eddie George SS	.40	.15

2000 Score

❑ COMP.SET w/o SP's (220)		20.00	7.50
❑ 1	Michael Pittman	.25	.08
❑ 2	Jake Plummer	.40	.15
❑ 3	Rob Moore	.40	.15
❑ 4	David Boston	.60	.25
❑ 5	Frank Sanders	.40	.15
❑ 6	Jamal Anderson	.60	.25
❑ 7	Chris Chandler	.40	.15
❑ 8	Tim Dwight	.60	.25
❑ 9	Terance Mathis	.40	.15
❑ 10	Shawn Jefferson	.25	.08
❑ 11	Ashley Ambrose	.25	.08
❑ 12	Peter Boulware	.25	.08
❑ 13	Priest Holmes	.75	.30
❑ 14	Tony Banks	.40	.15
❑ 15	Qadry Ismail	.40	.15
❑ 16	Shannon Sharpe	.40	.15
❑ 17	Rod Woodson	.40	.15
❑ 18	Matt Stover	.25	.08
❑ 19	Michael McCrary	.25	.08
❑ 20	Doug Flutie	.60	.25
❑ 21	Rob Johnson	.40	.15
❑ 22	Eric Moulds	.60	.25
❑ 23	Peerless Price	.40	.15
❑ 24	Jonathan Linton	.25	.08
❑ 25	Antowain Smith	.40	.15
❑ 26	Jay Riemersma	.25	.08
❑ 27	Muhsin Muhammad	.40	.15
❑ 28	Tim Biakabutuka	.40	.15
❑ 29	Patrick Jeffers	.60	.25
❑ 30	Wesley Walls	.25	.08
❑ 31	Steve Beuerlein	.40	.15
❑ 32	John Kasay	.25	.08
❑ 33	Curtis Enis	.25	.08
❑ 34	Cade McNown	.25	.08
❑ 35	Marcus Robinson	.60	.25
❑ 36	Bobby Engram	.25	.08
❑ 37	Eddie Kennison	.25	.08
❑ 38	Akili Smith	.25	.08
❑ 39	Carl Pickens	.40	.15
❑ 40	Corey Dillon	.60	.25
❑ 41	Darnay Scott	.40	.15
❑ 42	Errict Rhett	.40	.15
❑ 43	Karim Abdul-Jabbar	.40	.15
❑ 44	Tim Couch	.40	.15
❑ 45	Kevin Johnson	.60	.25
❑ 46	Darrin Chiaverini	.25	.08
❑ 47	Terry Kirby	.25	.08
❑ 48	Jason Tucker	.25	.08
❑ 49	Rocket Ismail	.40	.15
❑ 50	Joey Galloway	.40	.15
❑ 51	Michael Irvin	.40	.15
❑ 52	Troy Aikman	1.25	.50
❑ 53	Emmitt Smith	1.25	.50
❑ 54	David LaFleur	.25	.08
❑ 55	Trevor Pryce	.25	.08
❑ 56	Brian Griese	.60	.25
❑ 57	Olandis Gary	.60	.25
❑ 58	Terrell Davis	.60	.25
❑ 59	Rod Smith	.40	.15
❑ 60	Ed McCaffrey	.60	.25
❑ 61	Gus Frerotte	.25	.08
❑ 62	Jason Elam	.25	.08
❑ 63	Kavika Pittman	.25	.08
❑ 64	James Stewart	.40	.15
❑ 65	Charlie Batch	.60	.25
❑ 66	Johnnie Morton	.40	.15
❑ 67	Herman Moore	.40	.15
❑ 68	Germane Crowell	.25	.08
❑ 69	Barry Sanders	1.50	.60
❑ 70	Chris Claiborne	.25	.08
❑ 71	Brett Favre	2.00	.75
❑ 72	Antonio Freeman	.60	.25
❑ 73	Dorsey Levens	.40	.15
❑ 74	De'Mond Parker	.25	.08
❑ 75	Corey Bradford	.40	.15
❑ 76	Basil Mitchell	.25	.08
❑ 77	Bill Schroeder	.40	.15
❑ 78	Peyton Manning	1.50	.60
❑ 79	Marvin Harrison	.60	.25
❑ 80	Terrence Wilkins	.25	.08
❑ 81	Edgerrin James	1.00	.40
❑ 82	E.G. Green	.25	.08
❑ 83	Chad Bratzke	.25	.08

84	Mark Brunell	.60	.25
85	Fred Taylor	.60	.25
86	Jimmy Smith	.40	.15
87	Keenan McCardell	.40	.15
88	Kevin Hardy	.25	.08
89	Aaron Beasley	.25	.08
90	Elvis Grbac	.40	.15
91	Derrick Alexander	.40	.15
92	Tony Gonzalez	.40	.15
93	Donnell Bennett	.25	.08
94	Warren Moon	.60	.25
95	Andre Rison	.40	.15
96	James Hasty	.25	.08
97	Dan Marino	2.00	.75
98	Thurman Thomas	.40	.15
99	James Johnson	.25	.08
100	O.J. McDuffie	.40	.15
101	Tony Martin	.40	.15
102	Oronde Gadsden	.40	.15
103	Zach Thomas	.60	.25
104	Sam Madison	.25	.08
105	Jay Fiedler	.60	.25
106	Damon Huard	.60	.25
107	Robert Smith	.60	.25
108	Leroy Hoard	.25	.08
109	Randy Moss	1.25	.50
110	Cris Carter	.60	.25
111	Daunte Culpepper	.75	.30
112	John Randle	.40	.15
113	Randall Cunningham	.60	.25
114	Gary Anderson	.25	.08
115	Drew Bledsoe DP	.75	.30
116	Terry Glenn	.40	.15
117	Kevin Faulk	.40	.15
118	Terry Allen SP	15.00	7.50
119	Adam Vinatieri	.60	.25
120	Ty Law	.40	.15
121	Lawyer Milloy	.40	.15
122	Troy Brown	.40	.15
123	Ben Coates	.25	.08
124	Cam Cleeland	.25	.08
125	Jeff Blake	.40	.15
126	Ricky Williams	.60	.25
127	Jake Reed	.40	.15
128	Jake Delhomme RC	2.50	1.00
129	Andrew Glover	.25	.08
130	Keith Poole	.25	.08
131	Joe Horn	.40	.15
132	Kerry Collins	.40	.15
133	Joe Montgomery	.25	.08
134	Sean Bennett	.25	.08
135	Amani Toomer	.25	.08
136	Ike Hilliard	.40	.15
137	Joe Jurevicius	.25	.08
138	Tiki Barber	.60	.25
139	Victor Green	.25	.08
140	Ray Lucas	.40	.15
141	Vinny Testaverde	.40	.15
142	Curtis Martin	.60	.25
143	Wayne Chrebet	.40	.15
144	Tyrone Wheatley	.40	.15
145	Rich Gannon	.60	.25
146	Napoleon Kaufman	.40	.15
147	Tim Brown	.25	.08
148	Rickey Dudley	.25	.08
149	Charles Woodson	.60	.25
150	James Jett	.25	.08
151	Duce Staley	.60	.25
152	Charles Johnson	.40	.15
153	Donovan McNabb	1.00	.40
154	Troy Vincent	.25	.08
155	Troy Edwards	.25	.08
156	Jerome Bettis	.60	.25
157	Kordell Stewart	.40	.15
158	Richard Huntley	.25	.08
159	Hines Ward	.60	.25
160	Levon Kirkland	.25	.08
161	Ryan Leaf	.40	.15
162	Jim Harbaugh	.40	.15
163	Jermaine Fazande	.25	.08
164	Natrone Means	.25	.08
165	Junior Seau	.60	.25
166	Curtis Conway	.40	.15
167	Freddie Jones	.25	.08
168	Jeff Graham	.25	.08
169	Terrell Owens	.60	.25
170	Jeff Garcia	.60	.25
171	Jerry Rice	1.25	.50
172	Steve Young	.75	.30
173	Garrison Hearst	.40	.15
174	Charlie Garner	.40	.15
175	Fred Beasley	.25	.08
176	Bryant Young	.25	.08
177	Derrick Mayes	.40	.15
178	Sean Dawkins	.25	.08
179	Jon Kitna	.60	.25
180	Ricky Watters	.40	.15
181	Charlie Rogers	.25	.08
182	Kurt Warner	1.25	.50
183	Marshall Faulk	.75	.30
184	Isaac Bruce	.60	.25
185	Az-Zahir Hakim	.40	.15
186	Trent Green	.60	.25
187	Jeff Wilkins	.25	.08
188	Torry Holt	.60	.25
189	London Fletcher RC	.40	.15
190	Robert Holcombe	.25	.08
191	Todd Lyght	.25	.08
192	Keyshawn Johnson	.60	.25
193	Derrick Brooks	.60	.25
194	Warren Sapp	.40	.15
195	Shaun King	.25	.08
196	Warrick Dunn	.60	.25
197	Mike Alstott	.60	.25
198	Jacquez Green	.25	.08
199	Reidel Anthony	.25	.08
200	Martin Gramatica	.25	.08
201	Donnie Abraham	.25	.08
202	Steve McNair	.60	.25
203	Eddie George	.60	.25
204	Jevon Kearse	.60	.25
205	Frank Wycheck	.25	.08
206	Kevin Dyson	.40	.15
207	Yancey Thigpen	.25	.08
208	Al Del Greco	.25	.08
209	Jeff George	.40	.15
210	Adrian Murrell	.40	.15
211	Brad Johnson	.60	.25
212	Stephen Davis	.60	.25
213	Stephen Alexander	.25	.08
214	Michael Westbrook	.40	.15
215	Darrell Green	.25	.08
216	Champ Bailey	.60	.25
217	Albert Connell	.25	.08
218	Larry Centers	.25	.08
219	Bruce Smith	.40	.15
220	Deion Sanders	.60	.25
221	Ricky Williams SS	.60	.25
222	Edgerrin James SS	1.00	.40
223	Tim Couch SS	.40	.15
224	Cade McNown SS	.30	.10
225	Olandis Gary SS	.75	.30
226	Torry Holt SS	.75	.30
227	Donovan McNabb SS	1.00	.40
228	Shaun King SS	.25	.08
229	Kevin Johnson SS	.75	.30
230	Kurt Warner SS	1.50	.60
231	Tony Gonzalez AP	.50	.20
232	Frank Wycheck AP	.30	.10
233	Eddie George AP	.75	.30
234	Mark Brunell AP	.75	.30
235	Corey Dillon AP	.75	.30
236	Peyton Manning AP	2.00	.75
237	Keyshawn Johnson AP	.75	.30
238	Rich Gannon AP	.75	.30
239	Terry Glenn AP	.50	.20
240	Tony Brackens AP	.30	.10
241	Edgerrin James AP	1.00	.40
242	Tim Brown AP	.75	.30
243	Michael Strahan AP	.50	.20
244	Kurt Warner AP	1.50	.60
245	Brad Johnson AP	.75	.30
246	Aeneas Williams AP	.30	.10
247	Marshall Faulk AP	1.00	.40
248	Dexter Coakley AP	.30	.10
249	Warren Sapp AP	.50	.20
250	Mike Alstott AP	.75	.30
251	David Sloan AP	.30	.10
252	Cris Carter AP	.75	.30
253	Muhsin Muhammad AP	.30	.10
254	Isaac Bruce AP	.75	.30
255	Wesley Walls AP	.30	.10
256	Steve Beuerlein LL	.50	.20
257	Kurt Warner LL	1.50	.60
258	Peyton Manning LL	2.00	.75
259	Brad Johnson LL	.75	.30
260	Edgerrin James LL	1.00	.40
261	Curtis Martin LL	.75	.30
262	Stephen Davis LL	.75	.30
263	Emmitt Smith LL	1.50	.60
264	Marvin Harrison LL	.75	.30
265	Jimmy Smith LL	.50	.20
266	Randy Moss LL	1.50	.60
267	Marcus Robinson LL	.75	.30
268	Kevin Carter LL	.30	.10
269	Simeon Rice LL	.50	.20
270	Robert Porcher LL	.30	.10
271	Jevon Kearse LL	.75	.30
272	Mike Vanderjagt LL	.30	.10
273	Olindo Mare LL	.30	.10
274	Todd Peterson LL	.30	.10
275	Mike Hollis LL	.30	.10
276	Mike Anderson RC/500	30.00	12.50
277	Peter Warrick RC	2.00	.75
278	Courtney Brown RC	.75	.30
279	Plaxico Burress RC	4.00	1.50
280	Corey Simon RC	.75	.30
281	Thomas Jones RC	3.00	1.25
282	Travis Taylor RC	.75	.30
283	Shaun Alexander RC	10.00	4.00
284	Patrick Pass RC/500	20.00	7.50
285	Chris Redman RC	.50	.20
286	Chad Pennington RC	5.00	2.00
287	Jamal Lewis RC	5.00	2.00
288	Brian Urlacher RC	8.00	3.00
289	Bubba Franks RC	2.00	.75
290	Dez White RC	2.00	.75
291	Frank Moreau RC/500	20.00	7.50
292	Ron Dayne RC	2.00	.75
293	Sylvester Morris RC	.50	.20
294	R.Jay Soward RC	1.50	.60
295	Curtis Keaton RC	1.50	.60
296	Spergon Wynn RC/500	20.00	7.50
297	Rondell Mealey RC	1.50	.60
298	Travis Prentice RC	1.50	.60
299	Darrell Jackson RC	4.00	1.50
300	Giovanni Carmazzi RC	1.50	.60
301	Anthony Lucas RC	1.50	.60
302	Danny Farmer RC	1.50	.60
303	Dennis Northcutt RC	2.00	.75
304	Troy Walters RC	2.00	.75
305	Laveranues Coles RC	2.50	1.00
306	Kwame Cavil RC	1.50	.60
307	Tee Martin RC	2.00	.75
308	J.R. Redmond RC	1.50	.60
309	Tim Rattay RC	2.00	.75
310	Jerry Porter RC	2.50	1.00
311	Michael Wiley RC	1.50	.60
312	Reuben Droughns RC	2.50	1.00
313	Trung Canidate RC	1.50	.60
314	Shyrone Stith RC	1.50	.60
315	Marc Bulger RC	4.00	1.50
316	Tom Brady RC	25.00	10.00
317	Doug Johnson RC	2.00	.75

❑ 318 Todd Husak RC	2.00	.75
❑ 319 Gari Scott RC	1.50	.60
❑ 320 Windrell Hayes RC/500	20.00	7.50
❑ 321 Chris Cole RC	1.50	.60
❑ 322 Sammy Morris RC	1.50	.60
❑ 323 Trevor Gaylor RC	1.50	.60
❑ 324 Jarious Jackson RC	1.50	.60
❑ 325 Doug Chapman RC/500	20.00	7.50
❑ 326 Ron Dugans RC	1.50	.60
❑ 327 Ron Dixon RC/500	20.00	7.50
❑ 328 Joe Hamilton RC	1.50	.60
❑ 329 Todd Pinkston RC	2.00	.75
❑ 330 Chad Morton RC	2.00	.75

2001 Score

❑ COMP.SET w/o SP's (220)	25.00	10.00
❑ 1 David Boston	.50	.20
❑ 2 Frank Sanders	.20	.07
❑ 3 Jake Plummer	.30	.10
❑ 4 Michael Pittman	.20	.07
❑ 5 Rob Moore	.30	.10
❑ 6 Thomas Jones	.30	.10
❑ 7 Chris Chandler	.30	.10
❑ 8 Doug Johnson	.20	.07
❑ 9 Jamal Anderson	.50	.20
❑ 10 Tim Dwight	.50	.20
❑ 11 Brandon Stokley	.30	.10
❑ 12 Chris Redman	.20	.07
❑ 13 Jamal Lewis	.75	.30
❑ 14 Qadry Ismail	.30	.10
❑ 15 Ray Lewis	.50	.20
❑ 16 Rod Woodson	.30	.10
❑ 17 Shannon Sharpe	.30	.10
❑ 18 Travis Taylor	.30	.10
❑ 19 Trent Dilfer	.30	.10
❑ 20 Elvis Grbac	.30	.10
❑ 21 Eric Moulds	.30	.10
❑ 22 Jay Riemersma	.20	.07
❑ 23 Peerless Price	.30	.10
❑ 24 Rob Johnson	.30	.10
❑ 25 Sam Cowart	.20	.07
❑ 26 Sammy Morris	.20	.07
❑ 27 Shawn Bryson	.20	.07
❑ 28 Donald Hayes	.20	.07
❑ 29 Muhsin Muhammad	.30	.10
❑ 30 Patrick Jeffers	.30	.10
❑ 31 Reggie White DE	.50	.20
❑ 32 Steve Beuerlein	.30	.10
❑ 33 Tim Biakabutuka	.30	.10
❑ 34 Wesley Walls	.20	.07
❑ 35 Brian Urlacher	.75	.30
❑ 36 Cade McNown	.20	.07
❑ 37 Dez White	.20	.07
❑ 38 James Allen	.30	.10
❑ 39 Marcus Robinson	.50	.20
❑ 40 Marty Booker	.20	.07
❑ 41 Akili Smith	.20	.07
❑ 42 Corey Dillon	.50	.20
❑ 43 Danny Farmer	.20	.07
❑ 44 Peter Warrick	.50	.20
❑ 45 Ron Dugans	.20	.07
❑ 46 Takeo Spikes	.20	.07
❑ 47 Courtney Brown	.30	.10
❑ 48 Dennis Northcutt	.30	.10
❑ 49 JaJuan Dawson	.20	.07
❑ 50 Kevin Johnson	.30	.10
❑ 51 Tim Couch	.30	.10
❑ 52 Travis Prentice	.20	.07
❑ 53 Anthony Wright	.20	.07
❑ 54 Emmitt Smith	1.00	.40
❑ 55 James McKnight	.30	.10
❑ 56 Joey Galloway	.30	.10
❑ 57 Rocket Ismail	.30	.10
❑ 58 Randall Cunningham	.50	.20
❑ 59 Troy Aikman	.75	.30
❑ 60 Brian Griese	.50	.20
❑ 61 Ed McCaffrey	.50	.20
❑ 62 Gus Frerotte	.20	.07
❑ 63 John Elway	1.50	.60
❑ 64 Mike Anderson	.50	.20
❑ 65 Olandis Gary	.30	.10
❑ 66 Rod Smith	.30	.10
❑ 67 Terrell Davis	.50	.20
❑ 68 Barry Sanders	1.00	.40
❑ 69 Charlie Batch	.50	.20
❑ 70 Germane Crowell	.20	.07
❑ 71 Herman Moore	.30	.10
❑ 72 James Stewart	.30	.10
❑ 73 Johnnie Morton	.30	.10
❑ 74 Robert Porcher	.20	.07
❑ 75 Jim Harbaugh	.30	.10
❑ 76 Ahman Green	.50	.20
❑ 77 Antonio Freeman	.50	.20
❑ 78 Bill Schroeder	.30	.10
❑ 79 Brett Favre	1.50	.60
❑ 80 Bubba Franks	.30	.10
❑ 81 Dorsey Levens	.30	.10
❑ 82 E.G. Green	.20	.07
❑ 83 Edgerrin James	.60	.25
❑ 84 Jerome Pathon	.30	.10
❑ 85 Ken Dilger	.20	.07
❑ 86 Marcus Pollard	.20	.07
❑ 87 Marvin Harrison	.50	.20
❑ 88 Peyton Manning	1.25	.50
❑ 89 Terrence Wilkins	.20	.07
❑ 90 Fred Taylor	.50	.20
❑ 91 Hardy Nickerson	.20	.07
❑ 92 Jimmy Smith	.30	.10
❑ 93 Keenan McCardell	.20	.07
❑ 94 Kyle Brady	.20	.07
❑ 95 Mark Brunell	.50	.20
❑ 96 Tony Brackens	.20	.07
❑ 97 Derrick Alexander	.30	.10
❑ 98 Sylvester Morris	.20	.07
❑ 99 Tony Gonzalez	.30	.10
❑ 100 Tony Richardson	.20	.07
❑ 101 Kimble Anders	.20	.07
❑ 102 Warren Moon	.50	.20
❑ 103 Dan Marino	1.50	.60
❑ 104 Jay Fiedler	.50	.20
❑ 105 Lamar Smith	.30	.10
❑ 106 O.J. McDuffie	.20	.07
❑ 107 Oronde Gadsden	.30	.10
❑ 108 Sam Madison	.20	.07
❑ 109 Thurman Thomas	.20	.07
❑ 110 Tony Martin	.20	.07
❑ 111 Zach Thomas	.50	.20
❑ 112 Cris Carter	.50	.20
❑ 113 Daunte Culpepper	.50	.20
❑ 114 Matthew Hatchette	.20	.07
❑ 115 Randy Moss	1.00	.40
❑ 116 Robert Smith	.50	.20
❑ 117 Drew Bledsoe	.60	.25
❑ 118 J.R. Redmond	.20	.07
❑ 119 Kevin Faulk	.30	.10
❑ 120 Michael Bishop	.20	.07
❑ 121 Terry Glenn	.30	.10
❑ 122 Troy Brown	.30	.10
❑ 123 Ty Law	.30	.10
❑ 124 Aaron Brooks	.50	.20
❑ 125 Darren Howard	.20	.07
❑ 126 Jake Reed	.30	.10
❑ 127 Jeff Blake	.30	.10
❑ 128 Joe Horn	.30	.10
❑ 129 La'Roi Glover	.20	.07
❑ 130 Ricky Williams	.50	.20
❑ 131 Willie Jackson	.20	.07
❑ 132 Albert Connell	.20	.07
❑ 133 Amani Toomer	.20	.07
❑ 134 Ike Hilliard	.30	.10
❑ 135 Jason Sehorn	.20	.07
❑ 136 Jessie Armstead	.20	.07
❑ 137 Kerry Collins	.30	.10
❑ 138 Michael Strahan	.30	.10
❑ 139 Ron Dayne	.50	.20
❑ 140 Ron Dixon	.20	.07
❑ 141 Tiki Barber	.50	.20
❑ 142 Anthony Becht	.20	.07
❑ 143 Chad Pennington	.75	.30
❑ 144 Curtis Martin	.50	.20
❑ 145 Dedric Ward	.20	.07
❑ 146 Laveranues Coles	.50	.20
❑ 147 Vinny Testaverde	.30	.10
❑ 148 Wayne Chrebet	.30	.10
❑ 149 Andre Rison	.30	.10
❑ 150 Charles Woodson	.30	.10
❑ 151 Darrell Russell	.20	.07
❑ 152 Napoleon Kaufman	.30	.10
❑ 153 Rich Gannon	.50	.20
❑ 154 Tim Brown	.50	.20
❑ 155 Tyrone Wheatley	.30	.10
❑ 156 Chad Lewis	.20	.07
❑ 157 Charles Johnson	.20	.07
❑ 158 Donovan McNabb	.60	.25
❑ 159 Duce Staley	.50	.20
❑ 160 Hugh Douglas	.20	.07
❑ 161 Na Brown	.20	.07
❑ 162 Todd Pinkston	.20	.07
❑ 163 James Thrash	.30	.10
❑ 164 Bobby Shaw	.20	.07
❑ 165 Hines Ward	.50	.20
❑ 166 Jerome Bettis	.50	.20
❑ 167 Kordell Stewart	.30	.10
❑ 168 Levon Kirkland	.20	.07
❑ 169 Plaxico Burress	.50	.20
❑ 170 Richard Huntley	.20	.07
❑ 171 Troy Edwards	.20	.07
❑ 172 Jeff Graham	.20	.07
❑ 173 Junior Seau	.50	.20
❑ 174 Doug Flutie	.50	.20
❑ 175 Charlie Garner	.30	.10
❑ 176 Jeff Garcia	.50	.20
❑ 177 Jerry Rice	1.00	.40
❑ 178 Steve Young	.50	.20
❑ 179 Terrell Owens	.50	.20
❑ 180 Brock Huard	.20	.07
❑ 181 Darrell Jackson	.50	.20
❑ 182 Derrick Mayes	.30	.10
❑ 183 Ricky Watters	.30	.10
❑ 184 Shaun Alexander	.60	.25
❑ 185 Matt Hasselbeck	.30	.10
❑ 186 John Randle	.30	.10
❑ 187 Az-Zahir Hakim	.20	.07
❑ 188 Isaac Bruce	.50	.20
❑ 189 Kurt Warner	1.00	.40
❑ 190 Marshall Faulk	.60	.25
❑ 191 Torry Holt	.50	.20
❑ 192 Trent Green	.50	.20
❑ 193 Derrick Brooks	.50	.20
❑ 194 Jacquez Green	.20	.07
❑ 195 John Lynch	.30	.10
❑ 196 Keyshawn Johnson	.50	.20
❑ 197 Mike Alstott	.50	.20
❑ 198 Reidel Anthony	.20	.07
❑ 199 Shaun King	.20	.07
❑ 200 Warren Sapp	.30	.10
❑ 201 Warrick Dunn	.50	.20
❑ 202 Ryan Leaf	.30	.10

❑ 203 Carl Pickens .20 .07
❑ 204 Derrick Mason .30 .10
❑ 205 Eddie George .50 .20
❑ 206 Frank Wycheck .20 .07
❑ 207 Jevon Kearse .30 .10
❑ 208 Neil O'Donnell .20 .07
❑ 209 Steve McNair .50 .20
❑ 210 Yancey Thigpen .20 .07
❑ 211 Andre Reed .30 .10
❑ 212 Brad Johnson .50 .20
❑ 213 Bruce Smith .30 .10
❑ 214 Champ Bailey .50 .20
❑ 215 Darrell Green .20 .07
❑ 216 Deion Sanders .50 .20
❑ 217 Irving Fryar .30 .10
❑ 218 Jeff George .30 .10
❑ 219 Michael Westbrook .30 .10
❑ 220 Stephen Davis .50 .20
❑ 221 Terrell Owens AP 1.00 .40
❑ 222 Peyton Manning AP 2.50 1.00
❑ 223 Stephen Davis AP 1.00 .40
❑ 224 Marvin Harrison AP 1.00 .40
❑ 225 Donovan McNabb AP 1.25 .50
❑ 226 Edgerrin James AP 1.25 .50
❑ 227 Eric Moulds AP .60 .25
❑ 228 Daunte Culpepper AP 1.00 .40
❑ 229 Eddie George AP 1.00 .40
❑ 230 Cris Carter AP 1.00 .40
❑ 231 Rich Gannon AP 1.00 .40
❑ 232 Jeff Garcia AP 1.00 .40
❑ 233 Jimmy Smith AP .60 .25
❑ 234 Tony Gonzalez AP .60 .25
❑ 235 Torry Holt AP 1.00 .40
❑ 236 Jevon Kearse AP .60 .25
❑ 237 Ray Lewis AP 1.00 .40
❑ 238 Warren Sapp AP .60 .25
❑ 239 Brian Urlacher AP 1.50 .60
❑ 240 Champ Bailey AP .60 .25
❑ 241 Peyton Manning LL 2.50 1.00
❑ 242 Jeff Garcia LL 1.00 .40
❑ 243 Elvis Grbac LL .60 .25
❑ 244 Daunte Culpepper LL 1.00 .40
❑ 245 Brett Favre LL 3.00 1.25
❑ 246 Edgerrin James LL 1.25 .50
❑ 247 Robert Smith LL .60 .25
❑ 248 Eddie George LL 1.00 .40
❑ 249 Mike Anderson LL 1.00 .40
❑ 250 Corey Dillon LL 1.00 .40
❑ 251 Torry Holt LL 1.00 .40
❑ 252 Rod Smith LL .60 .25
❑ 253 Isaac Bruce LL 1.00 .40
❑ 254 Terrell Owens LL 1.00 .40
❑ 255 Randy Moss LL 2.00 .75
❑ 256 La'Roi Glover LL .40 .15
❑ 257 Trace Armstrong LL .40 .15
❑ 258 Warren Sapp LL .60 .25
❑ 259 Hugh Douglas LL .40 .15
❑ 260 Jason Taylor LL .40 .15
❑ 261 Mike Anderson SS 1.00 .40
❑ 262 Jamal Lewis SS 1.25 .50
❑ 263 Sylvester Morris SS .40 .15
❑ 264 Darrell Jackson SS 1.00 .40
❑ 265 Peter Warrick SS 1.00 .40
❑ 266 Ron Dayne SS 1.00 .40
❑ 267 Shaun Alexander SS 1.25 .50
❑ 268 Plaxico Burress SS 1.00 .40
❑ 269 Brian Urlacher SS 1.50 .60
❑ 270 Courtney Brown SS .60 .25
❑ 271 Michael Vick RC 12.00 6.00
❑ 272 Drew Brees RC 5.00 2.00
❑ 273 Chris Weinke RC 1.00 .40
❑ 274 Quincy Carter RC 2.00 .75
❑ 275 Sage Rosenfels RC 1.00 .40
❑ 276 Josh Heupel RC 2.00 .75
❑ 277 David Rivers RC 1.25 .50
❑ 278 Ben Leard RC 1.25 .50
❑ 279 Marques Tuiasosopo RC 2.00 .75
❑ 280 Mike McMahon RC 2.00 .75
❑ 281 Deuce McAllister RC 4.00 1.50
❑ 282 LaMont Jordan RC 4.00 1.50
❑ 283 LaDainian Tomlinson RC 10.00 5.00
❑ 284 James Jackson RC 2.00 .75
❑ 285 Anthony Thomas RC 2.00 .75
❑ 286 Travis Henry RC 2.00 .75
❑ 287 Travis Minor RC 1.25 .50
❑ 288 Rudi Johnson RC 4.00 1.50
❑ 289 Michael Bennett RC 3.00 1.25
❑ 290 Kevan Barlow RC 2.00 .75
❑ 291 Reggie White RC 1.25 .50
❑ 292 Moran Norris RC .75 .30
❑ 293 Ja'Mar Toombs RC 1.25 .50
❑ 294 Heath Evans RC 1.25 .50
❑ 295 David Terrell RC 2.00 .75
❑ 296 Santana Moss RC 3.00 1.25
❑ 297 Rod Gardner RC 2.00 .75
❑ 298 Quincy Morgan RC 2.00 .75
❑ 299 Freddie Mitchell RC 2.00 .75
❑ 300 Boo Williams RC 1.25 .50
❑ 301 Reggie Wayne RC 4.00 1.50
❑ 302 Ronney Daniels RC .75 .30
❑ 303 Bobby Newcombe RC 1.25 .50
❑ 304 Vinny Sutherland RC 1.25 .50
❑ 305 Cedrick Wilson RC 2.00 .75
❑ 306 Robert Ferguson RC 2.00 .75
❑ 307 Ken-Yon Rambo RC 1.25 .50
❑ 308 Alex Bannister RC 1.25 .50
❑ 309 Koren Robinson RC 2.00 .75
❑ 310 Chad Johnson RC 5.00 2.00
❑ 311 Chris Chambers RC 3.00 1.25
❑ 312 Javon Green RC 1.25 .50
❑ 313 Snoop Minnis RC 1.25 .50
❑ 314 Scotty Anderson RC 1.25 .50
❑ 315 Todd Heap RC 2.00 .75
❑ 316 Alge Crumpler RC 2.50 1.00
❑ 317 Marcellus Rivers RC 1.25 .50
❑ 318 Rashon Burns RC .75 .30
❑ 319 Jamal Reynolds RC 2.00 .75
❑ 320 Andre Carter RC 2.00 .75
❑ 321 Justin Smith RC 2.00 .75
❑ 322 Gerard Warren RC 2.00 .75
❑ 323 Tommy Polley RC 2.00 .75
❑ 324 Dan Morgan RC 1.00 .40
❑ 325 Torrance Marshall RC 2.00 .75
❑ 326 Correll Buckhalter RC 2.50 1.00
❑ 327 Derrick Gibson RC 1.25 .50
❑ 328 Adam Archuleta RC 2.00 .75
❑ 329 Jamar Fletcher RC 1.25 .50
❑ 330 Nate Clements RC 2.00 .75

2002 Score

❑ COMPLETE SET (330) 50.00 20.00
❑ 1 David Boston .50 .20
❑ 2 Arnold Jackson .20 .07
❑ 3 MarTay Jenkins .20 .07
❑ 4 Thomas Jones .30 .10
❑ 5 Kwamie Lassiter .20 .07
❑ 6 Michael Pittman .20 .07
❑ 7 Jake Plummer .30 .10
❑ 8 Chris Chandler .30 .10
❑ 9 Alge Crumpler .30 .10
❑ 10 Terance Mathis .20 .07
❑ 11 Maurice Smith .30 .10
❑ 12 Ray Buchanan .20 .07
❑ 13 Jamal Anderson .30 .10
❑ 14 Keith Brooking .20 .07
❑ 15 Michael Vick 1.50 .60
❑ 16 Obafemi Ayanbadejo .20 .07
❑ 17 Jason Brookins .20 .07
❑ 18 Randall Cunningham .20 .07
❑ 19 Elvis Grbac .30 .10
❑ 20 Todd Heap .20 .07
❑ 21 Qadry Ismail .30 .10
❑ 22 Shannon Sharpe .30 .10
❑ 23 Travis Taylor .30 .10
❑ 24 Ray Lewis .50 .20
❑ 25 Jamal Lewis .50 .20
❑ 26 Larry Centers .20 .07
❑ 27 Rob Johnson .30 .10
❑ 28 Shawn Bryson .20 .07
❑ 29 Eric Moulds .30 .10
❑ 30 Peerless Price .30 .10
❑ 31 Nate Clements .20 .07
❑ 32 Travis Henry .50 .20
❑ 33 Isaac Byrd .20 .07
❑ 34 Nick Goings .20 .07
❑ 35 Donald Hayes .20 .07
❑ 36 Richard Huntley .20 .07
❑ 37 Muhsin Muhammad .30 .10
❑ 38 Steve Smith .50 .20
❑ 39 Wesley Walls .20 .07
❑ 40 Chris Weinke .30 .10
❑ 41 James Allen .30 .10
❑ 42 Marty Booker .20 .07
❑ 43 Jim Miller .20 .07
❑ 44 David Terrell .50 .20
❑ 45 Dez White .20 .07
❑ 46 Brian Urlacher .75 .30
❑ 47 Mike Brown .50 .20
❑ 48 Anthony Thomas .30 .10
❑ 49 T.J. Houshmandzadeh .30 .10
❑ 50 Chad Johnson .50 .20
❑ 51 Darnay Scott .20 .07
❑ 52 Peter Warrick .30 .10
❑ 53 Akili Smith .20 .07
❑ 54 Jon Kitna .30 .10
❑ 55 Justin Smith .20 .07
❑ 56 Corey Dillon .30 .10
❑ 57 Benjamin Gay .30 .10
❑ 58 Kevin Johnson .30 .10
❑ 59 Quincy Morgan .20 .07
❑ 60 James Jackson .20 .07
❑ 61 Anthony Henry .20 .07
❑ 62 Gerard Warren .20 .07
❑ 63 Jamir Miller .20 .07
❑ 64 Tim Couch .30 .10
❑ 65 Quincy Carter .30 .10
❑ 66 Joey Galloway .30 .10
❑ 67 Troy Hambrick .20 .07
❑ 68 Rocket Ismail .30 .10
❑ 69 Dexter Coakley .20 .07
❑ 70 Darren Woodson .20 .07
❑ 71 Emmitt Smith 1.25 .50
❑ 72 Mike Anderson .50 .20
❑ 73 Terrell Davis .50 .20
❑ 74 Kevin Kasper .20 .07
❑ 75 Rod Smith .30 .10
❑ 76 Ed McCaffrey .50 .20
❑ 77 Olandis Gary .30 .10
❑ 78 Dwayne Carswell .20 .07
❑ 79 Deltha O'Neal .20 .07
❑ 80 Brian Griese .50 .20
❑ 81 Scotty Anderson .20 .07
❑ 82 Johnnie Morton .30 .10
❑ 83 Cory Schlesinger .20 .07
❑ 84 James Stewart .30 .10
❑ 85 Shaun Rogers .20 .07
❑ 86 Mike McMahon .50 .20
❑ 87 Charlie Batch .30 .10

❑ 88 Robert Porcher .20 .07
❑ 89 Bubba Franks .30 .10
❑ 90 Robert Ferguson .20 .07
❑ 91 Antonio Freeman .50 .20
❑ 92 Ahman Green .50 .20
❑ 93 Bill Schroeder .30 .10
❑ 94 Kabeer Gbaja-Biamila .30 .10
❑ 95 Jamal Reynolds .20 .07
❑ 96 Darren Sharper .20 .07
❑ 97 Brett Favre 1.25 .50
❑ 98 Marvin Harrison .50 .20
❑ 99 Dominic Rhodes .30 .10
❑ 100 Edgerrin James .60 .25
❑ 101 Reggie Wayne .50 .20
❑ 102 Terrence Wilkins .20 .07
❑ 103 Ken Dilger .20 .07
❑ 104 Peyton Manning 1.00 .40
❑ 105 Elvis Joseph .20 .07
❑ 106 Stacey Mack .20 .07
❑ 107 Fred Taylor .50 .20
❑ 108 Keenan McCardell .20 .07
❑ 109 Jimmy Smith .30 .10
❑ 110 Mark Brunell .50 .20
❑ 111 Derrick Alexander .30 .10
❑ 112 Tony Gonzalez .30 .10
❑ 113 Trent Green .30 .10
❑ 114 Snoop Minnis .20 .07
❑ 115 Priest Holmes .60 .25
❑ 116 Chris Chambers .50 .20
❑ 117 Jay Fiedler .30 .10
❑ 118 Oronde Gadsden .30 .10
❑ 119 Travis Minor .20 .07
❑ 120 Lamar Smith .30 .10
❑ 121 Zach Thomas .50 .20
❑ 122 Michael Bennett .30 .10
❑ 123 Todd Bouman .20 .07
❑ 124 Cris Carter .50 .20
❑ 125 Byron Chamberlain .20 .07
❑ 126 Randy Moss 1.00 .40
❑ 127 Jake Reed .30 .10
❑ 128 Daunte Culpepper .50 .20
❑ 129 Drew Bledsoe .50 .20
❑ 130 Troy Brown .30 .10
❑ 131 David Patten .20 .07
❑ 132 J.R. Redmond .20 .07
❑ 133 Antowain Smith .30 .10
❑ 134 Ty Law .30 .10
❑ 135 Richard Seymour .20 .07
❑ 136 Adam Vinatieri .50 .20
❑ 137 Tom Brady 1.25 .50
❑ 138 Joe Horn .30 .10
❑ 139 Willie Jackson .20 .07
❑ 140 Deuce McAllister .60 .25
❑ 141 Boo Williams .20 .07
❑ 142 Ricky Williams .50 .20
❑ 143 La'Roi Glover .20 .07
❑ 144 Sammy Knight .20 .07
❑ 145 Aaron Brooks .50 .20
❑ 146 Tiki Barber .50 .20
❑ 147 Ron Dayne .30 .10
❑ 148 Ike Hilliard .30 .10
❑ 149 Amani Toomer .30 .10
❑ 150 Will Allen .20 .07
❑ 151 Michael Strahan .30 .10
❑ 152 Jason Sehorn .20 .07
❑ 153 Kerry Collins .30 .10
❑ 154 Anthony Becht .20 .07
❑ 155 Wayne Chrebet .30 .10
❑ 156 Laveranues Coles .30 .10
❑ 157 LaMont Jordan .50 .20
❑ 158 Santana Moss .50 .20
❑ 159 Chad Pennington .60 .25
❑ 160 John Abraham .30 .10
❑ 161 Vinny Testaverde .30 .10
❑ 162 Curtis Martin .50 .20
❑ 163 Tim Brown .50 .20
❑ 164 Rich Gannon .50 .20
❑ 165 Charlie Garner .30 .10
❑ 166 Jerry Porter .20 .07
❑ 167 Marques Tuiasosopo .30 .10
❑ 168 Tyrone Wheatley .30 .10
❑ 169 Charles Woodson .30 .10
❑ 170 Jerry Rice 1.00 .40
❑ 171 Correll Buckhalter .30 .10
❑ 172 Chad Lewis .20 .07
❑ 173 Brian Mitchell .20 .07
❑ 174 Freddie Mitchell .30 .10
❑ 175 Todd Pinkston .30 .10
❑ 176 Duce Staley .50 .20
❑ 177 Tony Stewart .20 .07
❑ 178 James Thrash .30 .10
❑ 179 Hugh Douglas .20 .07
❑ 180 Donovan McNabb .60 .25
❑ 181 Plaxico Burress .30 .10
❑ 182 Chris Fuamatu-Ma'afala .20 .07
❑ 183 Kordell Stewart .30 .10
❑ 184 Hines Ward .50 .20
❑ 185 Amos Zereoue .50 .20
❑ 186 Kendrell Bell .50 .20
❑ 187 Casey Hampton .20 .07
❑ 188 Jerome Bettis .50 .20
❑ 189 Drew Brees .50 .20
❑ 190 Curtis Conway .20 .07
❑ 191 Tim Dwight .30 .10
❑ 192 Doug Flutie .50 .20
❑ 193 Junior Seau .50 .20
❑ 194 Marcellus Wiley .20 .07
❑ 195 Ryan McNeil .20 .07
❑ 196 Jeff Graham .20 .07
❑ 197 LaDainian Tomlinson .75 .30
❑ 198 Kevan Barlow .30 .10
❑ 199 Garrison Hearst .30 .10
❑ 200 Eric Johnson .30 .10
❑ 201 Terrell Owens .50 .20
❑ 202 J.J. Stokes .30 .10
❑ 203 Andre Carter .20 .07
❑ 204 Jeff Garcia .50 .20
❑ 205 Trent Dilfer .30 .10
❑ 206 Matt Hasselbeck .30 .10
❑ 207 Darrell Jackson .30 .10
❑ 208 Koren Robinson .30 .10
❑ 209 Ricky Watters .30 .10
❑ 210 John Randle .20 .07
❑ 211 Shaun Alexander .60 .25
❑ 212 Isaac Bruce .50 .20
❑ 213 Trung Canidate .30 .10
❑ 214 Marshall Faulk .50 .20
❑ 215 Az-Zahir Hakim .20 .07
❑ 216 Torry Holt .50 .20
❑ 217 Yo Murphy .20 .07
❑ 218 Ricky Proehl .20 .07
❑ 219 Adam Archuleta .20 .07
❑ 220 Dre Bly .20 .07
❑ 221 London Fletcher .20 .07
❑ 222 Tommy Polley .20 .07
❑ 223 Aeneas Williams .20 .07
❑ 224 Kurt Warner .50 .20
❑ 225 Mike Alstott .50 .20
❑ 226 Warrick Dunn .50 .20
❑ 227 Jacquez Green .20 .07
❑ 228 Derrick Brooks .50 .20
❑ 229 John Lynch .30 .10
❑ 230 Warren Sapp .30 .10
❑ 231 Ronde Barber .20 .07
❑ 232 Brad Johnson .30 .10
❑ 233 Keyshawn Johnson .50 .20
❑ 234 Drew Bennett .50 .20
❑ 235 Kevin Dyson .30 .10
❑ 236 Eddie George .50 .20
❑ 237 Derrick Mason .30 .10
❑ 238 Justin McCareins .30 .10
❑ 239 Frank Wycheck .20 .07
❑ 240 Jevon Kearse .30 .10
❑ 241 Samari Rolle .20 .07
❑ 242 Steve McNair .50 .20
❑ 243 Tony Banks .20 .07
❑ 244 Stephen Davis .30 .10
❑ 245 Michael Westbrook .20 .07
❑ 246 Champ Bailey .30 .10
❑ 247 Darrell Green .20 .07
❑ 248 Bruce Smith .20 .07
❑ 249 Fred Smoot .20 .07
❑ 250 Rod Gardner .30 .10
❑ 251 David Carr RC 3.00 1.25
❑ 252 Joey Harrington RC 3.00 1.25
❑ 253 Patrick Ramsey RC 1.50 .60
❑ 254 Kurt Kittner RC .60 .25
❑ 255 Eric Crouch RC 1.25 .50
❑ 256 Josh McCown RC 1.50 .60
❑ 257 David Garrard RC 1.25 .50
❑ 258 Rohan Davey RC 1.25 .50
❑ 259 Ronald Curry RC 1.25 .50
❑ 260 Chad Hutchinson RC .60 .25
❑ 261 William Green RC 1.25 .50
❑ 262 T.J. Duckett RC 2.00 .75
❑ 263 Clinton Portis RC 4.00 1.50
❑ 264 DeShaun Foster RC 1.25 .50
❑ 265 Luke Staley RC .60 .25
❑ 266 Wes Pate RC .50 .20
❑ 267 Travis Stephens RC .60 .25
❑ 268 Adrian Peterson RC 1.25 .50
❑ 269 Zak Kustok RC 1.25 .50
❑ 270 Maurice Morris RC 1.25 .50
❑ 271 Lamar Gordon RC 1.25 .50
❑ 272 Chester Taylor RC 1.25 .50
❑ 273 Najeh Davenport RC 1.25 .50
❑ 274 Ladell Betts RC 1.25 .50
❑ 275 Ashley Lelie RC 2.50 1.00
❑ 276 Josh Reed RC 1.25 .50
❑ 277 Cliff Russell RC .60 .25
❑ 278 Javon Walker RC 2.50 1.00
❑ 279 Ron Johnson RC .60 .25
❑ 280 Antwaan Randle El RC 2.00 .75
❑ 281 Andre Davis RC .60 .25
❑ 282 Marquise Walker RC .60 .25
❑ 283 Kelly Campbell RC .60 .25
❑ 284 Tavon Mason RC .50 .20
❑ 285 Antonio Bryant RC 1.25 .50
❑ 286 Jabar Gaffney RC 1.25 .50
❑ 287 Donte Stallworth RC 2.50 1.00
❑ 288 Tim Carter RC .60 .25
❑ 289 Reche Caldwell RC 1.25 .50
❑ 290 Freddie Milons RC .60 .25
❑ 291 Brian Poli-Dixon RC .60 .25
❑ 292 Brian Westbrook RC 2.00 .75
❑ 293 Josh Scobey RC 1.25 .50
❑ 294 Jeremy Shockey RC 4.00 1.50
❑ 295 Daniel Graham RC 1.25 .50
❑ 296 Deion Branch RC 2.50 1.00
❑ 297 Julius Peppers RC 2.50 1.00
❑ 298 Kalimba Edwards RC 1.25 .50
❑ 299 Dwight Freeney RC 1.50 .60
❑ 300 Terry Charles RC .60 .25
❑ 301 Alex Brown RC 1.25 .50
❑ 302 Jason McAddley RC .60 .25
❑ 303 Michael Lewis RC 1.25 .50
❑ 304 Dennis Johnson RC .50 .20
❑ 305 Albert Haynesworth RC .60 .25
❑ 306 Ryan Sims RC 1.25 .50
❑ 307 Larry Tripplett RC .50 .20
❑ 308 Anthony Weaver RC .60 .25
❑ 309 Wendell Bryant RC .50 .20
❑ 310 John Henderson RC 1.25 .50
❑ 311 Alan Harper RC .50 .20
❑ 312 Napoleon Harris RC 1.25 .50
❑ 313 Bryan Thomas RC .60 .25
❑ 314 Andra Davis RC .60 .25
❑ 315 Levar Fisher RC .50 .20
❑ 316 Woody Dantzler RC .60 .25
❑ 317 Robert Thomas RC 1.25 .50
❑ 318 Quentin Jammer RC 1.25 .50
❑ 319 Lito Sheppard RC 1.25 .50
❑ 320 Travis Fisher RC 1.25 .50
❑ 321 Roy Williams RC 3.00 1.25

❑ 322	Phillip Buchanon RC	1.25	.50
❑ 323	Joseph Jefferson RC	.60	.25
❑ 324	Ed Reed RC	2.00	.75
❑ 325	Lamont Thompson RC	.60	.25
❑ 326	Raonall Smith RC	.60	.25
❑ 327	Mike Rumph RC	1.25	.50
❑ 328	Rocky Calmus RC	1.25	.50
❑ 329	Bryant McKinnie RC	.60	.25
❑ 330	Mike Williams RC	.60	.25

2003 Score

❑	COMPLETE SET (327)	50.00	20.00
❑ 1	Jeff Blake	.20	.08
❑ 2	Todd Heap	.30	.10
❑ 3	Ron Johnson	.20	.08
❑ 4	Jamal Lewis	.50	.20
❑ 5	Ray Lewis	.50	.20
❑ 6	Chris Redman	.20	.08
❑ 7	Ed Reed	.30	.10
❑ 8	Travis Taylor	.20	.08
❑ 9	Anthony Weaver	.20	.08
❑ 10	Drew Bledsoe	.50	.20
❑ 11	Larry Centers	.20	.08
❑ 12	Nate Clements	.20	.08
❑ 13	Travis Henry	.30	.10
❑ 14	Eric Moulds	.30	.10
❑ 15	Peerless Price	.30	.10
❑ 16	Josh Reed	.30	.10
❑ 17	Coy Wire	.20	.08
❑ 18	Corey Dillon	.30	.10
❑ 19	T.J. Houshmandzadeh	.20	.08
❑ 20	Chad Johnson	.50	.20
❑ 21	Jon Kitna	.30	.10
❑ 22	Lorenzo Neal	.20	.08
❑ 23	Peter Warrick	.30	.10
❑ 24	Nicolas Luchey RC	.20	.08
❑ 25	Tim Couch	.20	.08
❑ 26	Andre Davis	.20	.08
❑ 27	William Green	.30	.10
❑ 28	Kevin Johnson	.30	.10
❑ 29	Quincy Morgan	.30	.10
❑ 30	Dennis Northcutt	.30	.10
❑ 31	Jamel White	.20	.08
❑ 32	Mike Anderson	.30	.10
❑ 33	Steve Beuerlein	.20	.08
❑ 34	Jason Elam	.20	.08
❑ 35	Olandis Gary	.30	.10
❑ 36	Brian Griese	.50	.20
❑ 37	Ashley Lelie	.50	.20
❑ 38	Ed McCaffrey	.30	.10
❑ 39	Clinton Portis	.75	.30
❑ 40	Shannon Sharpe	.30	.10
❑ 41	Rod Smith	.30	.10
❑ 42	James Allen	.30	.10
❑ 43	Corey Bradford	.20	.08
❑ 44	David Carr	.75	.30
❑ 45	JaJuan Dawson	.20	.08
❑ 46	Jabar Gaffney	.30	.10
❑ 47	Aaron Glenn	.20	.08
❑ 48	Billy Miller	.20	.08
❑ 49	Jonathan Wells	.20	.08
❑ 50	Dwight Freeney	.30	.10
❑ 51	Marvin Harrison	.50	.20
❑ 52	Qadry Ismail	.30	.10
❑ 53	Edgerrin James	.50	.20
❑ 54	Peyton Manning	.75	.30
❑ 55	James Mungro	.20	.08
❑ 56	Marcus Pollard	.20	.08
❑ 57	Reggie Wayne	.30	.10
❑ 58	Kyle Brady	.20	.08
❑ 59	Mark Brunell	.30	.10
❑ 60	David Garrard	.20	.08
❑ 61	John Henderson	.20	.08
❑ 62	Stacey Mack	.20	.08
❑ 63	Jimmy Smith	.30	.10
❑ 64	Fred Taylor	.50	.20
❑ 65	Marc Boerigter	.30	.10
❑ 66	Tony Gonzalez	.30	.10
❑ 67	Trent Green	.30	.10
❑ 68	Priest Holmes	.60	.25
❑ 69	Eddie Kennison	.20	.08
❑ 70	Snoop Minnis	.20	.08
❑ 71	Johnnie Morton	.30	.10
❑ 72	Cris Carter	.50	.20
❑ 73	Chris Chambers	.50	.20
❑ 74	Robert Edwards	.20	.08
❑ 75	Jay Fiedler	.30	.10
❑ 76	Ray Lucas	.20	.08
❑ 77	Randy McMichael	.30	.10
❑ 78	Travis Minor	.20	.08
❑ 79	Zach Thomas	.30	.10
❑ 80	Ricky Williams	.50	.20
❑ 81	Tom Brady	1.25	.50
❑ 82	Deion Branch	.50	.20
❑ 83	Troy Brown	.30	.10
❑ 84	Tedy Bruschi	.50	.20
❑ 85	Kevin Faulk	.20	.08
❑ 86	Daniel Graham	.20	.08
❑ 87	David Patten	.20	.08
❑ 88	Antowain Smith	.30	.10
❑ 89	Adam Vinatieri	.50	.20
❑ 90	Donnie Abraham	.20	.08
❑ 91	Anthony Becht	.20	.08
❑ 92	Wayne Chrebet	.30	.10
❑ 93	Laveranues Coles	.30	.10
❑ 94	LaMont Jordan	.50	.20
❑ 95	Curtis Martin	.50	.20
❑ 96	Chad Morton	.20	.08
❑ 97	Santana Moss	.30	.10
❑ 98	Chad Pennington	.60	.25
❑ 99	Vinny Testaverde	.30	.10
❑ 100	Tim Brown	.50	.20
❑ 101	Phillip Buchanon	.20	.08
❑ 102	Rich Gannon	.30	.10
❑ 103	Charlie Garner	.30	.10
❑ 104	Doug Jolley	.20	.08
❑ 105	Jerry Porter	.30	.10
❑ 106	Jerry Rice	1.00	.40
❑ 107	Marques Tuiasosopo	.30	.10
❑ 108	Charles Woodson	.30	.10
❑ 109	Rod Woodson	.30	.10
❑ 110	Kendrell Bell	.30	.10
❑ 111	Jerome Bettis	.50	.20
❑ 112	Plaxico Burress	.30	.10
❑ 113	Tommy Maddox	.50	.20
❑ 114	Joey Porter	.50	.20
❑ 115	Antwaan Randle El	.50	.20
❑ 116	Kordell Stewart	.30	.10
❑ 117	Hines Ward	.50	.20
❑ 118	Amos Zereoue	.30	.10
❑ 119	Drew Brees	.50	.20
❑ 120	Reche Caldwell	.20	.08
❑ 121	Curtis Conway	.20	.08
❑ 122	Tim Dwight	.30	.10
❑ 123	Doug Flutie	.50	.20
❑ 124	Quentin Jammer	.20	.08
❑ 125	Ben Leber	.20	.08
❑ 126	Josh Norman	.20	.08
❑ 127	Junior Seau	.50	.20
❑ 128	LaDainian Tomlinson	.50	.20
❑ 129	Keith Bulluck	.20	.08
❑ 130	Rocky Calmus	.20	.08
❑ 131	Kevin Carter	.20	.08
❑ 132	Kevin Dyson	.30	.10
❑ 133	Eddie George	.30	.10
❑ 134	Albert Haynesworth	.20	.08
❑ 135	Jevon Kearse	.30	.10
❑ 136	Derrick Mason	.30	.10
❑ 137	Justin McCareins	.20	.08
❑ 138	Steve McNair	.50	.20
❑ 139	Frank Wycheck	.20	.08
❑ 140	David Boston	.30	.10
❑ 141	MarTay Jenkins	.20	.08
❑ 142	Freddie Jones	.20	.08
❑ 143	Thomas Jones	.30	.10
❑ 144	Jason McAddley	.20	.08
❑ 145	Josh McCown	.30	.10
❑ 146	Jake Plummer	.30	.10
❑ 147	Marcel Shipp	.30	.10
❑ 148	Alge Crumpler	.30	.10
❑ 149	T.J. Duckett	.30	.10
❑ 150	Warrick Dunn	.30	.10
❑ 151	Brian Finneran	.20	.08
❑ 152	Trevor Gaylor	.20	.08
❑ 153	Shawn Jefferson	.20	.08
❑ 154	Michael Vick	1.25	.50
❑ 155	Randy Fasani	.20	.08
❑ 156	DeShaun Foster	.20	.08
❑ 157	Muhsin Muhammad	.30	.10
❑ 158	Rodney Peete	.20	.08
❑ 159	Julius Peppers	.50	.20
❑ 160	Lamar Smith	.20	.08
❑ 161	Steve Smith	.50	.20
❑ 162	Chris Weinke	.30	.10
❑ 163	Wesley Walls	.20	.08
❑ 164	Marty Booker	.30	.10
❑ 165	Mike Brown	.30	.10
❑ 166	Chris Chandler	.20	.08
❑ 167	Jim Miller	.20	.08
❑ 168	Marcus Robinson	.30	.10
❑ 169	David Terrell	.30	.10
❑ 170	Anthony Thomas	.30	.10
❑ 171	Brian Urlacher	.75	.30
❑ 172	Dez White	.20	.08
❑ 173	Antonio Bryant	.30	.10
❑ 174	Quincy Carter	.30	.10
❑ 175	Dexter Coakley	.20	.08
❑ 176	Joey Galloway	.30	.10
❑ 177	La'Roi Glover	.20	.08
❑ 178	Troy Hambrick	.20	.08
❑ 179	Chad Hutchinson	.20	.08
❑ 180	Rocket Ismail	.30	.10
❑ 181	Emmitt Smith	1.25	.50
❑ 182	Roy Williams	.50	.20
❑ 183	Scotty Anderson	.20	.08
❑ 184	Germane Crowell	.20	.08
❑ 185	Az-Zahir Hakim	.20	.08
❑ 186	Joey Harrington	.75	.30
❑ 187	Cory Schlesinger	.20	.08
❑ 188	Bill Schroeder	.30	.10
❑ 189	James Stewart	.30	.10
❑ 190	Marques Anderson	.20	.08
❑ 191	Najeh Davenport	.20	.08
❑ 192	Donald Driver	.30	.10
❑ 193	Brett Favre	1.25	.50
❑ 194	Bubba Franks	.30	.10
❑ 195	Terry Glenn	.20	.08
❑ 196	Ahman Green	.50	.20
❑ 197	Darren Sharper	.20	.08
❑ 198	Javon Walker	.30	.10
❑ 199	D'Wayne Bates	.20	.08
❑ 200	Michael Bennett	.30	.10
❑ 201	Todd Bouman	.20	.08
❑ 202	Byron Chamberlain	.20	.08
❑ 203	Daunte Culpepper	.50	.20
❑ 204	Randy Moss	.75	.30
❑ 205	Kelly Campbell	.30	.10
❑ 206	Aaron Brooks	.50	.20

	#	Player	Hi	Lo
❑	207	Charles Grant	.20	.08
❑	208	Joe Horn	.30	.10
❑	209	Michael Lewis	.20	.08
❑	210	Deuce McAllister	.50	.20
❑	211	Jerome Pathon	.30	.10
❑	212	Donte Stallworth	.50	.20
❑	213	Boo Williams	.20	.08
❑	214	Tiki Barber	.50	.20
❑	215	Tim Carter	.30	.10
❑	216	Kerry Collins	.30	.10
❑	217	Ron Dayne	.20	.08
❑	218	Jesse Palmer	.20	.08
❑	219	Will Peterson	.20	.08
❑	220	Jason Sehorn	.20	.08
❑	221	Jeremy Shockey	.75	.30
❑	222	Michael Strahan	.30	.10
❑	223	Amani Toomer	.30	.10
❑	224	Koy Detmer	.20	.08
❑	225	Antonio Freeman	.30	.10
❑	226	Dorsey Levens	.20	.08
❑	227	Chad Lewis	.20	.08
❑	228	Donovan McNabb	.60	.25
❑	229	Freddie Mitchell	.30	.10
❑	230	Duce Staley	.30	.10
❑	231	James Thrash	.20	.08
❑	232	Brian Westbrook	.30	.10
❑	233	Kevan Barlow	.30	.10
❑	234	Andre Carter	.20	.08
❑	235	Jeff Garcia	.50	.20
❑	236	Garrison Hearst	.30	.10
❑	237	Eric Johnson	.30	.10
❑	238	Terrell Owens	.50	.20
❑	239	Jamal Robertson	.30	.10
❑	240	Tai Streets	.20	.08
❑	241	Shaun Alexander	.50	.20
❑	242	Trent Dilfer	.30	.10
❑	243	Bobby Engram	.20	.08
❑	244	Matt Hasselbeck	.30	.10
❑	245	Darrell Jackson	.30	.10
❑	246	Maurice Morris	.20	.08
❑	247	Koren Robinson	.20	.08
❑	248	Jerramy Stevens	.20	.08
❑	249	Isaac Bruce	.50	.20
❑	250	Marc Bulger	.50	.20
❑	251	Marshall Faulk	.50	.20
❑	252	Lamar Gordon	.20	.08
❑	253	Torry Holt	.50	.20
❑	254	Ricky Proehl	.20	.08
❑	255	Kurt Warner	.50	.20
❑	256	Aeneas Williams	.20	.08
❑	257	Mike Alstott	.50	.20
❑	258	Ken Dilger	.20	.08
❑	259	Brad Johnson	.30	.10
❑	260	Keyshawn Johnson	.50	.20
❑	261	Rob Johnson	.30	.10
❑	262	John Lynch	.30	.10
❑	263	Keenan McCardell	.20	.08
❑	264	Michael Pittman	.20	.08
❑	265	Warren Sapp	.30	.10
❑	266	Marquise Walker	.20	.08
❑	267	Champ Bailey	.30	.10
❑	268	Stephen Davis	.30	.10
❑	269	Rod Gardner	.30	.10
❑	270	Darrell Green	.20	.08
❑	271	Shane Matthews	.20	.08
❑	272	Damerien McCants	.20	.08
❑	273	Patrick Ramsey	.50	.20
❑	274	Bruce Smith	.30	.10
❑	275	Kenny Watson	.20	.08
❑	276	Carson Palmer RC	5.00	2.00
❑	277	Byron Leftwich RC	4.00	1.50
❑	278	Kyle Boller RC	2.50	1.00
❑	279	Chris Simms RC	2.00	.75
❑	280	Dave Ragone RC	1.25	.50
❑	281	Rex Grossman RC	2.00	.75
❑	282	Brian St.Pierre RC	1.25	.50
❑	283	Larry Johnson RC	5.00	2.50
❑	284	Lee Suggs RC	2.50	1.00
❑	285	Justin Fargas RC	1.25	.50
❑	286	Onterrio Smith RC	1.25	.50
❑	287	Willis McGahee RC	3.00	1.25
❑	288	Chris Brown RC	1.50	.60
❑	289	Musa Smith RC	1.25	.50
❑	290	Artose Pinner RC	1.25	.50
❑	291	Cecil Sapp RC	1.00	.40
❑	292	Derek Watson SP RC		
❑	293	LaBrandon Toefield RC	1.25	.50
❑	294	Charles Rogers RC	1.25	.50
❑	295	Andre Johnson RC	2.50	1.00
❑	296	Taylor Jacobs RC	1.00	.40
❑	297	Bryant Johnson RC	1.25	.50
❑	298	Kelley Washington RC	1.25	.50
❑	299	Brandon Lloyd RC	1.50	.60
❑	300	Justin Gage RC	1.25	.50
❑	301	Tyrone Calico RC	1.50	.60
❑	302	Kevin Curtis RC	1.25	.50
❑	303	Sam Aiken RC	1.00	.40
❑	304	Doug Gabriel RC	1.25	.50
❑	305	Talman Gardner RC	1.25	.50
❑	306	Jason Witten RC	2.00	.75
❑	307	Mike Pinkard RC	.60	.25
❑	308	Teyo Johnson RC	1.25	.50
❑	309	Bennie Joppru RC	1.25	.50
❑	310	Dallas Clark RC	1.25	.50
❑	311	Terrell Suggs RC	2.00	.75
❑	312	Chris Kelsay RC	1.25	.50
❑	313	Jerome McDougle RC	1.25	.50
❑	314	Andrew Williams RC	1.00	.40
❑	315	Michael Haynes RC	1.25	.50
❑	316	Jimmy Kennedy RC	1.25	.50
❑	317	Kevin Williams RC	1.25	.50
❑	318	Ken Dorsey RC	1.25	.50
❑	319	William Joseph RC	1.25	.50
❑	320	Kenny Peterson RC	1.00	.40
❑	321	Rien Long RC	.60	.25
❑	322	Boss Bailey RC	1.25	.50
❑	323	E.J. Henderson SP RC		
❑	324	Terence Newman RC	2.50	1.00
❑	325	Marcus Trufant RC	1.25	.50
❑	326	Andre Woolfolk RC	1.25	.50
❑	327	Dennis Weathersby RC	.60	.25
❑	328	Eugene Wilson SP RC		
❑	329	Mike Doss RC	1.25	.50
❑	330	Rashean Mathis RC	1.00	.40

2004 Score

	#	Player	Hi	Lo
❑		COMPLETE SET (440)	80.00	40.00
❑		ONE ROOKIE PER PACK		
❑	1	Emmitt Smith	1.00	.40
❑	2	Anquan Boldin	.50	.20
❑	3	Bryant Johnson	.20	.07
❑	4	Marcel Shipp	.30	.10
❑	5	Josh McCown	.30	.10
❑	6	Dexter Jackson	.20	.07
❑	7	Bertrand Berry	.20	.07
❑	8	Freddie Jones	.20	.07
❑	9	Duane Starks	.20	.07
❑	10	Michael Vick	1.00	.40
❑	11	T.J. Duckett	.30	.10
❑	12	Warrick Dunn	.30	.10
❑	13	Peerless Price	.30	.10
❑	14	Alge Crumpler	.30	.10
❑	15	Brian Finneran	.20	.07
❑	16	Jason Webster	.20	.07
❑	17	Dez White	.30	.10
❑	18	Keith Brooking	.20	.07
❑	19	Rod Coleman	.20	.07
❑	20	Jamal Lewis	.50	.20
❑	21	Kyle Boller	.50	.20
❑	22	Todd Heap	.30	.10
❑	23	Jonathan Ogden	.20	.07
❑	24	Travis Taylor	.20	.07
❑	25	Ray Lewis	.50	.20
❑	26	Peter Boulware	.30	.10
❑	27	Terrell Suggs	.30	.10
❑	28	Chris McAlister	.20	.07
❑	29	Ed Reed	.30	.10
❑	30	Drew Bledsoe	.50	.20
❑	31	Travis Henry	.30	.10
❑	32	Eric Moulds	.30	.10
❑	33	Josh Reed	.20	.07
❑	34	Willis McGahee	.50	.20
❑	35	Takeo Spikes	.20	.07
❑	36	Lawyer Milloy	.30	.10
❑	37	Troy Vincent	.20	.07
❑	38	Sam Adams	.20	.07
❑	39	Nate Clements	.20	.07
❑	40	Jake Delhomme	.50	.20
❑	41	Stephen Davis	.30	.10
❑	42	DeShaun Foster	.30	.10
❑	43	Muhsin Muhammad	.30	.10
❑	44	Steve Smith	.50	.20
❑	45	Ricky Proehl	.20	.07
❑	46	Julius Peppers	.50	.20
❑	47	Kris Jenkins	.20	.07
❑	48	Dan Morgan	.20	.07
❑	49	Ricky Manning	.20	.07
❑	50	Brad Hoover	.20	.07
❑	51	Carson Palmer	.60	.25
❑	52	Rudi Johnson	.30	.10
❑	53	Corey Dillon	.30	.10
❑	54	Chad Johnson	.50	.20
❑	55	Peter Warrick	.30	.10
❑	56	Kelley Washington	.20	.07
❑	57	Kevin Hardy	.20	.07
❑	58	Tory James	.20	.07
❑	59	Ickey Woods	.50	.20
❑	60	Anthony Thomas	.30	.10
❑	61	Thomas Jones	.30	.10
❑	62	Rex Grossman	.50	.20
❑	63	Marty Booker	.30	.10
❑	64	Justin Gage	.30	.10
❑	65	David Terrell	.30	.10
❑	66	Brian Urlacher	.60	.25
❑	67	Mike Brown	.20	.07
❑	68	Charles Tillman	.30	.10
❑	69	Jeff Garcia	.50	.20
❑	70	Lee Suggs	.50	.20
❑	71	William Green	.30	.10
❑	72	Kelly Holcomb	.30	.10
❑	73	Quincy Morgan	.30	.10
❑	74	Andre Davis	.20	.07
❑	75	Dennis Northcutt	.20	.07
❑	76	Gerard Warren	.20	.07
❑	77	Courtney Brown	.30	.10
❑	78	Joey Harrington	.50	.20
❑	79	Shawn Bryson	.20	.07
❑	80	Charles Rogers	.30	.10
❑	81	Mikhael Ricks	.20	.07
❑	82	Artose Pinner	.20	.07
❑	83	Az-Zahir Hakim	.20	.07
❑	84	Dre Bly	.20	.07
❑	85	Fernando Bryant	.20	.07
❑	86	Boss Bailey	.30	.10
❑	87	Tai Streets	.20	.07
❑	88	Jake Plummer	.30	.10
❑	89	Quentin Griffin	.50	.20
❑	90	Mike Anderson	.30	.10

❑	91	Garrison Hearst	.30	.10
❑	92	Rod Smith	.30	.10
❑	93	Ashley Lelie	.30	.10
❑	94	Shannon Sharpe	.30	.10
❑	95	Al Wilson	.20	.07
❑	96	Champ Bailey	.30	.10
❑	97	Jason Elam	.20	.07
❑	98	John Lynch	.30	.10
❑	99	Quincy Carter	.30	.10
❑	100	Antonio Bryant	.30	.10
❑	101	Terry Glenn	.20	.07
❑	102	Keyshawn Johnson	.30	.10
❑	103	Jason Witten	.30	.10
❑	104	La'Roi Glover	.20	.07
❑	105	Dat Nguyen	.20	.07
❑	106	Dexter Coakley	.20	.07
❑	107	Terence Newman	.30	.10
❑	108	Darren Woodson	.20	.07
❑	109	Roy Williams S	.30	.10
❑	110	Brett Favre	1.25	.50
❑	111	Ahman Green	.50	.20
❑	112	Najeh Davenport	.20	.07
❑	113	Donald Driver	.30	.10
❑	114	Robert Ferguson	.20	.07
❑	115	Javon Walker	.30	.10
❑	116	Bubba Franks	.30	.10
❑	117	Kabeer Gbaja-Biamila	.30	.10
❑	118	Darren Sharper	.20	.07
❑	119	Mike McKenzie	.20	.07
❑	120	Nick Barnett	.30	.10
❑	121	David Carr	.50	.20
❑	122	Domanick Davis	.50	.20
❑	123	Andre Johnson	.50	.20
❑	124	Corey Bradford	.20	.07
❑	125	Jabar Gaffney	.30	.10
❑	126	Billy Miller	.20	.07
❑	127	Gary Walker	.20	.07
❑	128	Jamie Sharper	.20	.07
❑	129	Aaron Glenn	.20	.07
❑	130	Robaire Smith	.20	.07
❑	131	Peyton Manning	.75	.30
❑	132	Edgerrin James	.50	.20
❑	133	Dominic Rhodes	.30	.10
❑	134	Marvin Harrison	.50	.20
❑	135	Reggie Wayne	.30	.10
❑	136	Brandon Stokley	.30	.10
❑	137	Marcus Pollard	.20	.07
❑	138	Dallas Clark	.30	.10
❑	139	Mike Vanderjagt	.20	.07
❑	140	Dwight Freeney	.30	.10
❑	141	Mike Doss	.20	.07
❑	142	Byron Leftwich	.60	.25
❑	143	Fred Taylor	.30	.10
❑	144	LaBrandon Toefield	.20	.07
❑	145	Jimmy Smith	.30	.10
❑	146	Kevin Johnson	.20	.07
❑	147	Marcus Stroud	.20	.07
❑	148	John Henderson	.20	.07
❑	149	Donovin Darius	.20	.07
❑	150	Deon Grant	.20	.07
❑	151	Rashean Mathis	.20	.07
❑	152	Trent Green	.30	.10
❑	153	Priest Holmes	.60	.25
❑	154	Johnnie Morton	.30	.10
❑	155	Eddie Kennison	.20	.07
❑	156	Marc Boerigter	.30	.10
❑	157	Tony Gonzalez	.30	.10
❑	158	Dante Hall	.50	.20
❑	159	Tony Richardson	.20	.07
❑	160	Gary Stills	.20	.07
❑	161	Daunte Culpepper	.50	.20
❑	162	Michael Bennett	.30	.10
❑	163	Moe Williams	.20	.07
❑	164	Onterrio Smith	.30	.10
❑	165	Jim Kleinsasser	.20	.07
❑	166	Antoine Winfield	.20	.07
❑	167	Nate Burleson	.50	.20
❑	168	Randy Moss	.60	.25
❑	169	Marcus Robinson	.30	.10
❑	170	Chris Hovan	.20	.07
❑	171	Brian Russell RC	.50	.20
❑	172	A.J. Feeley	.50	.20
❑	173	Jay Fiedler	.20	.07
❑	174	Ricky Williams	.50	.20
❑	175	Chris Chambers	.30	.10
❑	176	David Boston	.30	.10
❑	177	Randy McMichael	.20	.07
❑	178	Jason Taylor	.20	.07
❑	179	Adewale Ogunleye	.30	.10
❑	180	Zach Thomas	.50	.20
❑	181	Junior Seau	.50	.20
❑	182	Patrick Surtain	.20	.07
❑	183	Tom Brady	1.25	.50
❑	184	Kevin Faulk	.20	.07
❑	185	Troy Brown	.30	.10
❑	186	Deion Branch	.50	.20
❑	187	David Givens	.30	.10
❑	188	Bethel Johnson	.30	.10
❑	189	Richard Seymour	.20	.07
❑	190	Tedy Bruschi	.30	.10
❑	191	Ty Law	.30	.10
❑	192	Rodney Harrison	.20	.07
❑	193	Willie McGinest	.20	.07
❑	194	Adam Vinatieri	.50	.20
❑	195	Aaron Brooks	.30	.10
❑	196	Deuce McAllister	.50	.20
❑	197	Joe Horn	.30	.10
❑	198	Donte Stallworth	.30	.10
❑	199	Jerome Pathon	.20	.07
❑	200	Boo Williams	.20	.07
❑	201	Charles Grant	.20	.07
❑	202	Darren Howard	.20	.07
❑	203	Michael Lewis	.20	.07
❑	204	Johnathan Sullivan	.20	.07
❑	205	LeCharles Bentley RC	.20	.07
❑	206	Kerry Collins	.30	.10
❑	207	Tiki Barber	.50	.20
❑	208	Amani Toomer	.30	.10
❑	209	Ike Hilliard	.20	.07
❑	210	Tim Carter	.20	.07
❑	211	Jeremy Shockey	.50	.20
❑	212	Michael Strahan	.30	.10
❑	213	Will Allen	.20	.07
❑	214	Will Peterson	.20	.07
❑	215	William Joseph	.20	.07
❑	216	Chad Pennington	.50	.20
❑	217	Curtis Martin	.50	.20
❑	218	LaMont Jordan	.50	.20
❑	219	Santana Moss	.30	.10
❑	220	Justin McCareins	.20	.07
❑	221	Wayne Chrebet	.30	.10
❑	222	Anthony Becht	.20	.07
❑	223	Shaun Ellis	.20	.07
❑	224	John Abraham	.20	.07
❑	225	DeWayne Robertson	.20	.07
❑	226	Rich Gannon	.30	.10
❑	227	Justin Fargas	.30	.10
❑	228	Tyrone Wheatley	.20	.07
❑	229	Jerry Rice	1.00	.40
❑	230	Tim Brown	.50	.20
❑	231	Jerry Porter	.30	.10
❑	232	Teyo Johnson	.20	.07
❑	233	Charles Woodson	.30	.10
❑	234	Phillip Buchanon	.20	.07
❑	235	Rod Woodson	.30	.10
❑	236	Warren Sapp	.30	.10
❑	237	Donovan McNabb	.60	.25
❑	238	Brian Westbrook	.30	.10
❑	239	Correll Buckhalter	.30	.10
❑	240	Chad Lewis	.20	.07
❑	241	L.J. Smith	.30	.10
❑	242	Terrell Owens	.50	.20
❑	243	Todd Pinkston	.20	.07
❑	244	Freddie Mitchell	.30	.10
❑	245	Jevon Kearse	.30	.10
❑	246	Brian Dawkins	.30	.10
❑	247	Corey Simon	.30	.10
❑	248	Tommy Maddox	.30	.10
❑	249	Duce Staley	.30	.10
❑	250	Jerome Bettis	.50	.20
❑	251	Hines Ward	.50	.20
❑	252	Plaxico Burress	.30	.10
❑	253	Antwaan Randle El	.50	.20
❑	254	Kendrell Bell	.30	.10
❑	255	Joey Porter	.30	.10
❑	256	Alan Faneca	.50	.20
❑	257	Casey Hampton	.20	.07
❑	258	Drew Brees	.50	.20
❑	259	Doug Flutie	.50	.20
❑	260	LaDainian Tomlinson	.60	.25
❑	261	Reche Caldwell	.20	.07
❑	262	Tim Dwight	.30	.10
❑	263	Eric Parker	.20	.07
❑	264	Kevin Dyson	.20	.07
❑	265	Antonio Gates	.50	.20
❑	266	Quentin Jammer	.20	.07
❑	267	Zeke Moreno	.20	.07
❑	268	Tim Rattay	.20	.07
❑	269	Kevan Barlow	.30	.10
❑	270	Cedrick Wilson	.20	.07
❑	271	Brandon Lloyd	.30	.10
❑	272	Fred Beasley	.20	.07
❑	273	Andre Carter	.20	.07
❑	274	Julian Peterson	.20	.07
❑	275	Ahmed Plummer	.20	.07
❑	276	Tony Parrish	.20	.07
❑	277	Bryant Young	.20	.07
❑	278	Matt Hasselbeck	.30	.10
❑	279	Shaun Alexander	.50	.20
❑	280	Maurice Morris	.20	.07
❑	281	Koren Robinson	.30	.10
❑	282	Darrell Jackson	.30	.10
❑	283	Bobby Engram	.20	.07
❑	284	Grant Wistrom	.20	.07
❑	285	Chad Brown	.20	.07
❑	286	Marcus Trufant	.20	.07
❑	287	Bobby Taylor	.20	.07
❑	288	Marc Bulger	.50	.20
❑	289	Kurt Warner	.50	.20
❑	290	Marshall Faulk	.50	.20
❑	291	Lamar Gordon	.20	.07
❑	292	Torry Holt	.50	.20
❑	293	Isaac Bruce	.30	.10
❑	294	Leonard Little	.20	.07
❑	295	Aeneas Williams	.20	.07
❑	296	Orlando Pace	.20	.07
❑	297	Tommy Polley	.20	.07
❑	298	Pisa Tinoisamoa	.20	.07
❑	299	Brad Johnson	.30	.10
❑	300	Michael Pittman	.20	.07
❑	301	Charlie Garner	.30	.10
❑	302	Mike Alstott	.30	.10
❑	303	Keenan McCardell	.20	.07
❑	304	Joey Galloway	.30	.10
❑	305	Joe Jurevicius	.20	.07
❑	306	Anthony McFarland	.20	.07
❑	307	Derrick Brooks	.30	.10
❑	308	Ronde Barber	.20	.07
❑	309	Shelton Quarles	.20	.07
❑	310	Steve McNair	.50	.20
❑	311	Eddie George	.30	.10
❑	312	Chris Brown	.50	.20
❑	313	Derrick Mason	.30	.10
❑	314	Tyrone Calico	.30	.10
❑	315	Drew Bennett	.30	.10
❑	316	Kevin Carter	.20	.07
❑	317	Keith Bulluck	.20	.07
❑	318	Samari Rolle	.20	.07
❑	319	Albert Haynesworth	.20	.07
❑	320	Erron Kinney	.20	.07
❑	321	Mark Brunell	.30	.10
❑	322	Patrick Ramsey	.30	.10
❑	323	Laveranues Coles	.30	.10
❑	324	Rod Gardner	.30	.10

❑ 325 Darnerien McCants .20 .07
❑ 326 Clinton Portis .50 .20
❑ 327 LaVar Arrington 1.00 .40
❑ 328 Shawn Springs .20 .07
❑ 329 Fred Smoot .20 .07
❑ 330 James Thrash .20 .07
❑ 331 Marvin Harrison PB .30 .10
❑ 332 Steve McNair PB .30 .10
❑ 333 Ray Lewis PB .30 .10
❑ 334 Trent Green PB .20 .07
❑ 335 Peyton Manning PB .50 .20
❑ 336 Priest Holmes PB .50 .20
❑ 337 Clinton Portis PB .50 .20
❑ 338 Torry Holt PB .30 .10
❑ 339 Anquan Boldin PB .20 .07
❑ 340 Daunte Culpepper PB .30 .10
❑ 341 Ahman Green PB .30 .10
❑ 342 Brian Urlacher PB .50 .20
❑ 343 Donovan McNabb PB .50 .20
❑ 344 Marc Bulger PB .30 .10
❑ 345 Shaun Alexander PB .30 .10
❑ 346 Peyton Manning LL .50 .20
❑ 347 Daunte Culpepper LL .30 .10
❑ 348 Brett Favre LL .50 .20
❑ 349 Steve McNair LL .30 .10
❑ 350 Tom Brady LL .50 .20
❑ 351 Jamal Lewis LL .30 .10
❑ 352 Deuce McAllister LL .30 .10
❑ 353 Clinton Portis LL .50 .20
❑ 354 Ahman Green LL .30 .10
❑ 355 LaDainian Tomlinson LL .40 .15
❑ 356 Torry Holt LL .30 .10
❑ 357 Anquan Boldin LL .20 .07
❑ 358 Randy Moss LL .50 .20
❑ 359 Chad Johnson LL .30 .10
❑ 360 Marvin Harrison LL .30 .10
❑ 361 Peyton Manning HL .50 .20
❑ 362 Jamal Lewis HL .30 .10
❑ 363 Ray Lewis HL .30 .10
❑ 364 Anquan Boldin HL .20 .07
❑ 365 Terrell Suggs HL .20 .07
❑ 366 Jamal Lewis HL .30 .10
❑ 367 Priest Holmes HL .50 .20
❑ 368 Tom Brady HL .50 .20
❑ 369 Marc Bulger HL .30 .10
❑ 370 Steve McNair HL .30 .10
❑ 371 Eli Manning RC 8.00 3.00
❑ 372 Robert Gallery RC 2.00 .75
❑ 373 Larry Fitzgerald RC 4.00 1.50
❑ 374 Philip Rivers RC 4.00 1.50
❑ 375 Sean Taylor RC 1.50 .60
❑ 376 Kellen Winslow RC 2.50 1.00
❑ 377 Roy Williams RC 3.00 1.25
❑ 378 DeAngelo Hall RC 1.50 .60
❑ 379 Reggie Williams RC 1.50 .60
❑ 380 Dunta Robinson RC 1.25 .50
❑ 381 Ben Roethlisberger RC 15.00 7.50
❑ 382 Jonathan Vilma RC 1.25 .50
❑ 383 Lee Evans RC 1.50 .60
❑ 384 Tommie Harris RC 1.25 .50
❑ 385 Michael Clayton RC 2.50 1.00
❑ 386 D.J. Williams RC 1.50 .60
❑ 387 Will Smith RC 1.25 .50
❑ 388 Kenechi Udeze RC 1.25 .50
❑ 389 Vince Wilfork RC 1.50 .60
❑ 390 J.P. Losman RC 2.50 1.00
❑ 391 Marcus Tubbs RC 1.25 .50
❑ 392 Steven Jackson RC 4.00 1.50
❑ 393 Ahmad Carroll RC 1.50 .60
❑ 394 Chris Perry RC 2.00 .75
❑ 395 Jason Babin RC 1.25 .50
❑ 396 Chris Gamble RC 1.50 .60
❑ 397 Michael Jenkins RC 1.25 .50
❑ 398 Kevin Jones RC 4.00 1.50
❑ 399 Rashaun Woods RC 1.25 .50
❑ 400 Ben Watson RC 1.25 .50
❑ 401 Karlos Dansby RC 1.25 .50
❑ 402 Igor Olshansky RC 1.25 .50
❑ 403 Junior Siavii RC 1.25 .50
❑ 404 Teddy Lehman RC 1.25 .50
❑ 405 Ricardo Colclough RC 1.25 .50
❑ 406 Daryl Smith RC 1.25 .50
❑ 407 Ben Troupe RC 1.25 .50
❑ 408 Tatum Bell RC 2.50 1.00
❑ 409 Travis LaBoy RC 1.25 .50
❑ 410 Julius Jones RC 5.00 2.00
❑ 411 Mewelde Moore RC 1.50 .60
❑ 412 Drew Henson RC 1.25 .50
❑ 413 Dontarrious Thomas RC 1.25 .50
❑ 414 Keiwan Ratliff RC 1.00 .40
❑ 415 Devery Henderson RC 1.00 .40
❑ 416 Dwan Edwards RC .60 .25
❑ 417 Michael Boulware RC 1.25 .50
❑ 418 Darius Watts RC 1.25 .50
❑ 419 Greg Jones RC 1.25 .50
❑ 420 Madieu Williams RC 1.00 .40
❑ 421 Antwan Odom RC 1.25 .50
❑ 422 Shawntae Spencer RC 1.25 .50
❑ 423 Sean Jones RC 1.00 .40
❑ 424 Courtney Watson RC 1.25 .50
❑ 425 Kris Wilson RC 1.25 .50
❑ 426 Keary Colbert RC 1.50 .60
❑ 427 Marquise Hill RC 1.00 .40
❑ 428 Darnell Dockett RC 1.00 .40
❑ 429 Stuart Schweigert RC 1.25 .50
❑ 430 Ben Hartsock RC 1.25 .50
❑ 431 Joey Thomas RC 1.25 .50
❑ 432 Randy Starks RC 1.00 .40
❑ 433 Keith Smith RC 1.00 .40
❑ 434 Derrick Hamilton RC 1.00 .40
❑ 435 Bernard Berrian RC 1.25 .50
❑ 436 Chris Cooley RC 1.25 .50
❑ 437 Devard Darling RC 1.25 .50
❑ 438 Matt Schaub RC 2.00 .75
❑ 439 Luke McCown RC 1.25 .50
❑ 440 Cedric Cobbs RC 1.25 .50

2005 Score

❑ COMPLETE SET (385) 80.00 40.00
❑ ONE ROOKIE PER PACK
❑ 1 Anquan Boldin .30 .10
❑ 2 Bertrand Berry .25 .08
❑ 3 Bryant Johnson .25 .08
❑ 4 Darnell Dockett .25 .08
❑ 5 Freddie Jones .25 .08
❑ 6 Josh McCown .30 .10
❑ 7 Karlos Dansby .25 .08
❑ 8 Larry Fitzgerald .50 .20
❑ 9 Alge Crumpler .30 .10
❑ 10 DeAngelo Hall .30 .10
❑ 11 Keith Brooking .25 .08
❑ 12 Michael Jenkins .30 .10
❑ 13 Michael Vick .75 .30
❑ 14 Peerless Price .25 .08
❑ 15 Rod Coleman .25 .08
❑ 16 T.J. Duckett .30 .10
❑ 17 Warrick Dunn .30 .10
❑ 18 Chris McAlister .25 .08
❑ 19 Clarence Moore .25 .08
❑ 20 Ed Reed .30 .10
❑ 21 Jamal Lewis .50 .20
❑ 22 Jonathan Ogden .25 .08
❑ 23 Kyle Boller .30 .10
❑ 24 Peter Boulware .25 .08
❑ 25 Ray Lewis .50 .20
❑ 26 Terrell Suggs .30 .10
❑ 27 Todd Heap .30 .10
❑ 28 Drew Bledsoe .50 .20
❑ 29 Eric Moulds .30 .10
❑ 30 Josh Reed .25 .08
❑ 31 Lee Evans .30 .10
❑ 32 Nate Clements .25 .08
❑ 33 Takeo Spikes .25 .08
❑ 34 Travis Henry .30 .10
❑ 35 Willis McGahee .50 .20
❑ 36 Dan Morgan .25 .08
❑ 37 DeShaun Foster .30 .10
❑ 38 Jake Delhomme .50 .20
❑ 39 Julius Peppers .30 .10
❑ 40 Keary Colbert .30 .10
❑ 41 Kris Jenkins .25 .08
❑ 42 Muhsin Muhammad .30 .10
❑ 43 Nick Goings .25 .08
❑ 44 Stephen Davis .30 .10
❑ 45 Steve Smith .30 .10
❑ 46 Anthony Thomas .30 .10
❑ 47 Adewale Ogunleye .25 .08
❑ 48 Bernard Berrian .25 .08
❑ 49 Brian Urlacher .50 .20
❑ 50 David Terrell .30 .10
❑ 51 Mike Brown .25 .08
❑ 52 Rex Grossman .30 .10
❑ 53 Thomas Jones .30 .10
❑ 54 Tommie Harris .25 .08
❑ 55 Carson Palmer .50 .20
❑ 56 Chad Johnson .50 .20
❑ 57 Chris Perry .30 .10
❑ 58 Kelley Washington .25 .08
❑ 59 Madieu Williams .25 .08
❑ 60 Peter Warrick .25 .08
❑ 61 Rudi Johnson .30 .10
❑ 62 T.J. Houshmandzadeh .25 .08
❑ 63 Tory James .25 .08
❑ 64 Andre Davis .25 .08
❑ 65 Antonio Bryant .25 .08
❑ 66 Dennis Northcutt .25 .08
❑ 67 Gerard Warren .25 .08
❑ 68 Jeff Garcia .30 .10
❑ 69 Kellen Winslow Jr. .50 .20
❑ 70 Lee Suggs .30 .10
❑ 71 William Green .25 .08
❑ 72 Drew Henson .30 .10
❑ 73 Jason Witten .30 .10
❑ 74 Julius Jones .60 .25
❑ 75 Keyshawn Johnson .30 .10
❑ 76 La'Roi Glover .25 .08
❑ 77 J.P. Losman .50 .20
❑ 78 Roy Williams S .30 .10
❑ 79 Terence Newman .25 .08
❑ 80 Terry Glenn .25 .08
❑ 81 Al Wilson .25 .08
❑ 82 Ashley Lelie .30 .10
❑ 83 Champ Bailey .30 .10
❑ 84 D.J. Williams .25 .08
❑ 85 Jake Plummer .30 .10
❑ 86 Jason Elam .25 .08
❑ 87 John Lynch .30 .10
❑ 88 Reuben Droughns .30 .10
❑ 89 Rod Smith .30 .10
❑ 90 Tatum Bell .30 .10
❑ 91 Trent Dilfer .30 .10
❑ 92 Charles Rogers .30 .10
❑ 93 Dre' Bly .25 .08
❑ 94 Joey Harrington .50 .20
❑ 95 Kevin Jones .50 .20
❑ 96 Roy Williams WR .50 .20
❑ 97 Shawn Bryson .25 .08
❑ 98 Tai Streets .25 .08

❑ 99 Teddy Lehman .25 .08
❑ 100 Ahman Green .50 .20
❑ 101 Brett Favre 1.25 .50
❑ 102 Bubba Franks .30 .10
❑ 103 Darren Sharper .25 .08
❑ 104 Donald Driver .30 .10
❑ 105 Javon Walker .30 .10
❑ 106 Najeh Davenport .25 .08
❑ 107 Nick Barnett .25 .08
❑ 108 Robert Ferguson .25 .08
❑ 109 Aaron Glenn .25 .08
❑ 110 Andre Johnson .30 .10
❑ 111 Corey Bradford .25 .08
❑ 112 David Carr .50 .20
❑ 113 Domanick Davis .30 .10
❑ 114 Dunta Robinson .30 .10
❑ 115 Jabar Gaffney .25 .08
❑ 116 Jamie Sharper .25 .08
❑ 117 Jason Babin .25 .08
❑ 118 Brandon Stokley .30 .10
❑ 119 Dallas Clark .25 .08
❑ 120 Dwight Freeney .30 .10
❑ 121 Edgerrin James .50 .20
❑ 122 Marcus Pollard .25 .08
❑ 123 Marvin Harrison .50 .20
❑ 124 Peyton Manning .75 .30
❑ 125 Reggie Wayne .30 .10
❑ 126 Robert Mathis RC 1.00 .40
❑ 127 Byron Leftwich .50 .20
❑ 128 Daryl Smith .25 .08
❑ 129 Donovan Darius .25 .08
❑ 130 Ernest Wilford .25 .08
❑ 131 Fred Taylor .30 .10
❑ 132 Jimmy Smith .30 .10
❑ 133 John Henderson .25 .08
❑ 134 Marcus Stroud .25 .08
❑ 135 Reggie Williams .30 .10
❑ 136 Dante Hall .30 .10
❑ 137 Eddie Kennison .25 .08
❑ 138 Jared Allen .30 .10
❑ 139 Johnnie Morton .30 .10
❑ 140 Larry Johnson .50 .20
❑ 141 Priest Holmes .50 .20
❑ 142 Samie Parker .25 .08
❑ 143 Tony Gonzalez .30 .10
❑ 144 Trent Green .30 .10
❑ 145 A.J. Feeley .30 .10
❑ 146 Chris Chambers .30 .10
❑ 147 Jason Taylor .25 .08
❑ 148 Junior Seau .30 .10
❑ 149 Marty Booker .30 .10
❑ 150 Patrick Surtain .25 .08
❑ 151 Randy McMichael .25 .08
❑ 152 Sammy Morris .25 .08
❑ 153 Zach Thomas .50 .20
❑ 154 Daunte Culpepper .50 .20
❑ 155 Jim Kleinsasser .25 .08
❑ 156 Kelly Campbell .25 .08
❑ 157 Kevin Williams .25 .08
❑ 158 Marcus Robinson .30 .10
❑ 159 Mewelde Moore .30 .10
❑ 160 Michael Bennett .30 .10
❑ 161 Nate Burleson .30 .10
❑ 162 Onterrio Smith .30 .10
❑ 163 Randy Moss .50 .20
❑ 164 Adam Vinatieri .50 .20
❑ 165 Corey Dillon .30 .10
❑ 166 David Givens .30 .10
❑ 167 David Patten .25 .08
❑ 168 Deion Branch .30 .10
❑ 169 Mike Vrabel .30 .10
❑ 170 Richard Seymour .30 .10
❑ 171 Tedy Bruschi .30 .10
❑ 172 Tom Brady 1.25 .50
❑ 173 Troy Brown .30 .10
❑ 174 Ty Law .30 .10
❑ 175 Aaron Brooks .30 .10
❑ 176 Charles Grant .25 .08
❑ 177 Deuce McAllister .50 .20
❑ 178 Devery Henderson .25 .08
❑ 179 Donte Stallworth .30 .10
❑ 180 Jerome Pathon .25 .08
❑ 181 Joe Horn .30 .10
❑ 182 Will Smith .25 .08
❑ 183 Amani Toomer .30 .10
❑ 184 Eli Manning 1.00 .40
❑ 185 Gibril Wilson .25 .08
❑ 186 Ike Hilliard .30 .10
❑ 187 Jeremy Shockey .50 .20
❑ 188 Michael Strahan .30 .10
❑ 189 Tiki Barber .50 .20
❑ 190 Jamaar Taylor .25 .08
❑ 191 Tim Carter .25 .08
❑ 192 Chad Pennington .50 .20
❑ 193 DeWayne Robertson .25 .08
❑ 194 Curtis Martin .50 .20
❑ 195 John Abraham .25 .08
❑ 196 Jonathan Vilma .30 .10
❑ 197 Justin McCareins .25 .08
❑ 198 LaMont Jordan .50 .20
❑ 199 Santana Moss .30 .10
❑ 200 Shaun Ellis .25 .08
❑ 201 Wayne Chrebet .30 .10
❑ 202 Charles Woodson .30 .10
❑ 203 Doug Jolley .25 .08
❑ 204 Jerry Porter .30 .10
❑ 205 Justin Fargas .25 .08
❑ 206 Kerry Collins .30 .10
❑ 207 Robert Gallery .30 .10
❑ 208 Ronald Curry .30 .10
❑ 209 Sebastian Janikowski .25 .08
❑ 210 Tyrone Wheatley .25 .08
❑ 211 Warren Sapp .30 .10
❑ 212 Brian Dawkins .30 .10
❑ 213 Brian Westbrook .30 .10
❑ 214 Chad Lewis .25 .08
❑ 215 Corey Simon .25 .08
❑ 216 Donovan McNabb .60 .25
❑ 217 Freddie Mitchell .25 .08
❑ 218 Jevon Kearse .30 .10
❑ 219 L.J. Smith .25 .08
❑ 220 Lito Sheppard .25 .08
❑ 221 Terrell Owens .50 .20
❑ 222 Todd Pinkston .25 .08
❑ 223 Alan Faneca .50 .20
❑ 224 Antwaan Randle El .30 .10
❑ 225 Ben Roethlisberger 1.25 .50
❑ 226 Duce Staley .30 .10
❑ 227 Hines Ward .50 .20
❑ 228 James Farrior .25 .08
❑ 229 Jerome Bettis .50 .20
❑ 230 Joey Porter .30 .10
❑ 231 Kendrell Bell .30 .10
❑ 232 Plaxico Burress .30 .10
❑ 233 Troy Polamalu .75 .30
❑ 234 Antonio Gates .50 .20
❑ 235 Reche Caldwell .25 .08
❑ 236 Doug Flutie .50 .20
❑ 237 Drew Brees .50 .20
❑ 238 Eric Parker .25 .08
❑ 239 Keenan McCardell .25 .08
❑ 240 LaDainian Tomlinson .60 .25
❑ 241 Philip Rivers .50 .20
❑ 242 Quentin Jammer .25 .08
❑ 243 Tim Dwight .25 .08
❑ 244 Brandon Lloyd .25 .08
❑ 245 Bryant Young .25 .08
❑ 246 Cedrick Wilson .25 .08
❑ 247 Eric Johnson .30 .10
❑ 248 Julian Peterson .25 .08
❑ 249 Kevan Barlow .30 .10
❑ 250 Rashaun Woods .30 .10
❑ 251 Maurice Hicks RC .50 .20
❑ 252 Tim Rattay .25 .08
❑ 253 Bobby Engram .25 .08
❑ 254 Chad Brown .25 .08
❑ 255 Darrell Jackson .30 .10
❑ 256 Grant Wistrom .25 .08
❑ 257 Jerramy Stevens .25 .08
❑ 258 Koren Robinson .30 .10
❑ 259 Marcus Trufant .25 .08
❑ 260 Matt Hasselbeck .30 .10
❑ 261 Michael Boulware .25 .08
❑ 262 Shaun Alexander .60 .25
❑ 263 Isaac Bruce .30 .10
❑ 264 Leonard Little .25 .08
❑ 265 Marc Bulger .50 .20
❑ 266 Marshall Faulk .50 .20
❑ 267 Orlando Pace .25 .08
❑ 268 Pisa Tinoisamoa .25 .08
❑ 269 Shaun McDonald .25 .08
❑ 270 Steven Jackson .60 .25
❑ 271 Torry Holt .50 .20
❑ 272 Anthony McFarland .25 .08
❑ 273 Brian Griese .30 .10
❑ 274 Charlie Garner .30 .10
❑ 275 Derrick Brooks .30 .10
❑ 276 Joe Jurevicius .25 .08
❑ 277 Joey Galloway .30 .10
❑ 278 Michael Clayton .50 .20
❑ 279 Michael Pittman .25 .08
❑ 280 Mike Alstott .30 .10
❑ 281 Ronde Barber .25 .08
❑ 282 Albert Haynesworth .25 .08
❑ 283 Ben Troupe .25 .08
❑ 284 Billy Volek .30 .10
❑ 285 Chris Brown .30 .10
❑ 286 Derrick Mason .30 .10
❑ 287 Drew Bennett .30 .10
❑ 288 Keith Bulluck .25 .08
❑ 289 Kevin Carter .25 .08
❑ 290 Samari Rolle .25 .08
❑ 291 Steve McNair .50 .20
❑ 292 Tyrone Calico .30 .10
❑ 293 Chris Cooley .30 .10
❑ 294 Clinton Portis .50 .20
❑ 295 Fred Smoot .25 .08
❑ 296 LaVar Arrington .50 .20
❑ 297 Laveranues Coles .30 .10
❑ 298 Patrick Ramsey .30 .10
❑ 299 Rod Gardner .30 .10
❑ 300 Sean Taylor .30 .10
❑ 301 Michael Vick PB .50 .20
❑ 302 Daunte Culpepper PB .30 .10
❑ 303 Donovan McNabb PB .50 .20
❑ 304 Brian Westbrook PB .25 .08
❑ 305 Tiki Barber PB .30 .10
❑ 306 Ahman Green PB .30 .10
❑ 307 Joe Horn PB .25 .08
❑ 308 Javon Walker PB .25 .08
❑ 309 Torry Holt PB .30 .10
❑ 310 Muhsin Muhammad PB .25 .08
❑ 311 Jason Witten PB .25 .08
❑ 312 Alge Crumpler PB .25 .08
❑ 313 Peyton Manning PB .50 .20
❑ 314 Tom Brady PB .50 .20
❑ 315 Drew Brees PB .30 .10
❑ 316 LaDainian Tomlinson PB .50 .20
❑ 317 Rudi Johnson PB .25 .08
❑ 318 Jerome Bettis PB .30 .10
❑ 319 Marvin Harrison PB .30 .10
❑ 320 Hines Ward PB .30 .10
❑ 321 Andre Johnson PB .25 .08
❑ 322 Chad Johnson PB .30 .10
❑ 323 Tony Gonzalez PB .25 .08
❑ 324 Adam Vinatieri PB .30 .10
❑ 325 David Akers PB .25 .08
❑ 326 Takeo Spikes PB .25 .08
❑ 327 Joey Porter PB .25 .08
❑ 328 Tedy Bruschi PB .30 .10
❑ 329 Ed Reed PB .30 .10
❑ 330 Terrell Owens PB .30 .10
❑ 331 Alex Smith QB RC 4.00 1.50
❑ 332 Ronnie Brown RC 3.00 1.25

❑ 333 Braylon Edwards RC 3.00 1.25
❑ 334 Cedric Benson RC 2.00 .75
❑ 335 Carnell Williams RC 5.00 2.00
❑ 336 Adam Jones RC 1.00 .40
❑ 337 Troy Williamson RC 2.00 .75
❑ 338 Antrel Rolle RC 1.00 .40
❑ 339 Carlos Rogers RC 1.25 .50
❑ 340 Mike Williams 2.00 .75
❑ 341 DeMarcus Ware RC 1.50 .60
❑ 342 Shawne Merriman RC 1.50 .60
❑ 343 Thomas Davis RC 1.00 .40
❑ 344 Derrick Johnson RC 1.50 .60
❑ 345 Travis Johnson RC 1.00 .40
❑ 346 David Pollack RC 1.00 .40
❑ 347 Erasmus James RC 1.00 .40
❑ 348 Marcus Spears RC 1.00 .40
❑ 349 Matt Jones RC 2.50 1.00
❑ 350 Mark Clayton RC 1.25 .50
❑ 351 Fabian Washington RC 1.00 .40
❑ 352 Aaron Rodgers RC 3.00 1.25
❑ 353 Jason Campbell RC 1.50 .60
❑ 354 Roddy White RC 1.00 .40
❑ 355 Marlin Jackson RC 1.00 .40
❑ 356 Heath Miller RC 2.50 1.00
❑ 357 Mike Patterson RC 1.00 .40
❑ 358 Reggie Brown RC 1.00 .40
❑ 359 Shaun Cody RC 1.00 .40
❑ 360 Mark Bradley RC 1.00 .40
❑ 361 J.J. Arrington RC 1.25 .50
❑ 362 Dan Cody RC 1.00 .40
❑ 363 Eric Shelton RC 1.00 .40
❑ 364 Roscoe Parrish RC 1.00 .40
❑ 365 Terrence Murphy RC 1.00 .40
❑ 366 Vincent Jackson RC 1.00 .40
❑ 367 Frank Gore RC 1.50 .60
❑ 368 Charlie Frye RC 2.00 .75
❑ 369 Courtney Roby RC 1.00 .40
❑ 370 Andrew Walter RC 1.50 .60
❑ 371 Vernand Morency RC 1.00 .40
❑ 372 Ryan Moats RC 1.00 .40
❑ 373 Chris Henry RC 1.00 .40
❑ 374 David Greene RC 1.00 .40
❑ 375 Brandon Jones RC 1.00 .40
❑ 376 Maurice Clarett 1.00 .40
❑ 377 Kyle Orton RC 1.50 .60
❑ 378 Marion Barber RC 1.50 .60
❑ 379 Brandon Jacobs RC 1.25 .50
❑ 380 Ciatrick Fason RC 1.00 .40
❑ 381 Jerome Mathis RC 1.00 .40
❑ 382 Craphonso Thorpe RC 1.00 .40
❑ 383 Stefan LeFors RC 1.00 .40
❑ 384 Darren Sproles RC 1.00 .40
❑ 385 Fred Gibson RC 1.00 .40

2002 Score QBC Materials

❑ AUTOGRAPH CARDS TOO SCARCE TO PRICE
❑ 1 Donovan McNabb JSY 25.00 10.00
❑ 2 Jake Plummer JSY 10.00 4.00
❑ 3 Jeff Garcia JSY 12.00 5.00
❑ 4 Peyton Manning JSY 30.00 12.50
❑ 5 Rob Johnson JSY 10.00 4.00
❑ 6 Trent Dilfer JSY 10.00 4.00
❑ 7 Bernie Kosar JSY 10.00 4.00
❑ 8 Boomer Esiason JSY 12.00 5.00
❑ 9 Jim Everett JSY 10.00 4.00
❑ 10 Jim Kelly JSY 12.00 5.00
❑ 11 Steve Young JSY 20.00 7.50
❑ 12 Warren Moon JSY 12.00 5.00
❑ 13 Donovan McNabb FB 25.00 10.00
❑ 14 Jeff Garcia FB 12.00 5.00
❑ 15 Peyton Manning FB 30.00 12.50
❑ 16 Boomer Esiason FB 12.00 5.00
❑ 17 Jim Kelly FB 12.00 5.00
❑ 18 Steve Young FB 20.00 7.50
❑ 19 Warren Moon FB 12.00 5.00
❑ 20 Peyton Manning JSY 30.00 12.50
❑ 21 Doug Flutie JSY 15.00 6.00
❑ 22 Jeff Garcia JSY 12.00 5.00
❑ 23 Jake Plummer JSY 10.00 4.00
❑ 24 Aaron Brooks JSY 12.00 5.00
❑ 25 John Elway JSY 40.00 25.00
❑ 26 Boomer Esiason JSY 10.00 4.00
❑ 27 Warren Moon JSY 12.00 5.00
❑ 28 Jim Everett JSY 10.00 4.00
❑ 29 John Elway FB 40.00 25.00
❑ 30 Warren Moon FB 12.00 5.00
❑ 31 Jake Plummer FB 10.00 4.00
❑ 32 Peyton Manning FB 30.00 12.50
❑ 33 Jeff Garcia FB 12.00 5.00
❑ 34 Aaron Brooks FB 12.00 5.00
❑ 35 Doug Flutie FB 15.00 6.00
❑ 36 Boomer Esiason FB 12.00 5.00
❑ 37 Ken O'Brien JSY 8.00 3.00

2001 Score Select

❑ COMP.SET w/o SPs (220) 30.00 12.50
❑ 1 David Boston .75 .30
❑ 2 Frank Sanders .30 .10
❑ 3 Jake Plummer .50 .20
❑ 4 Michael Pittman .30 .10
❑ 5 Rob Moore .50 .20
❑ 6 Thomas Jones .50 .20
❑ 7 Chris Chandler .50 .20
❑ 8 Doug Johnson .30 .10
❑ 9 Jamal Anderson .75 .30
❑ 10 Tim Dwight .75 .30
❑ 11 Brandon Stokley .50 .20
❑ 12 Chris Redman .30 .10
❑ 13 Jamal Lewis 1.25 .50
❑ 14 Qadry Ismail .50 .20
❑ 15 Ray Lewis .75 .30
❑ 16 Rod Woodson .50 .20
❑ 17 Shannon Sharpe .50 .20
❑ 18 Travis Taylor .50 .20
❑ 19 Trent Dilfer .50 .20
❑ 20 Elvis Grbac .50 .20
❑ 21 Eric Moulds .50 .20
❑ 22 Jay Riemersma .30 .10
❑ 23 Peerless Price .50 .20
❑ 24 Rob Johnson .50 .20
❑ 25 Sam Cowart .30 .10
❑ 26 Sammy Morris .30 .10
❑ 27 Shawn Bryson .30 .10
❑ 28 Donald Hayes .30 .10
❑ 29 Muhsin Muhammad .50 .20
❑ 30 Patrick Jeffers .50 .20
❑ 31 Reggie White DE .75 .30
❑ 32 Steve Beuerlein .50 .20
❑ 33 Tim Biakabutuka .50 .20
❑ 34 Wesley Walls .30 .10
❑ 35 Brian Urlacher 1.25 .50
❑ 36 Cade McNown .30 .10
❑ 37 Dez White .30 .10
❑ 38 James Allen .50 .20
❑ 39 Marcus Robinson .75 .30
❑ 40 Marty Booker .30 .10
❑ 41 Akili Smith .30 .10
❑ 42 Corey Dillon .75 .30
❑ 43 Danny Farmer .30 .10
❑ 44 Peter Warrick .75 .30
❑ 45 Ron Dugans .30 .10
❑ 46 Takeo Spikes .30 .10
❑ 47 Courtney Brown .50 .20
❑ 48 Dennis Northcutt .50 .20
❑ 49 JaJuan Dawson .30 .10
❑ 50 Kevin Johnson .50 .20
❑ 51 Tim Couch .50 .20
❑ 52 Travis Prentice .30 .10
❑ 53 Anthony Wright .30 .10
❑ 54 Emmitt Smith 1.50 .60
❑ 55 James McKnight .50 .20
❑ 56 Joey Galloway .50 .20
❑ 57 Rocket Ismail .50 .20
❑ 58 Randall Cunningham .75 .30
❑ 59 Troy Aikman 1.25 .50
❑ 60 Brian Griese .75 .30
❑ 61 Ed McCaffrey .75 .30
❑ 62 Gus Frerotte .30 .10
❑ 63 John Elway 2.50 1.00
❑ 64 Mike Anderson .75 .30
❑ 65 Olandis Gary .50 .20
❑ 66 Rod Smith .50 .20
❑ 67 Terrell Davis .75 .30
❑ 68 Barry Sanders 1.50 .60
❑ 69 Charlie Batch .75 .30
❑ 70 Germane Crowell .30 .10
❑ 71 Herman Moore .50 .20
❑ 72 James Stewart .50 .20
❑ 73 Johnnie Morton .50 .20
❑ 74 Robert Porcher .30 .10
❑ 75 Jim Harbaugh .50 .20
❑ 76 Ahman Green .75 .30
❑ 77 Antonio Freeman .75 .30
❑ 78 Bill Schroeder .50 .20
❑ 79 Brett Favre 2.50 1.00
❑ 80 Bubba Franks .50 .20
❑ 81 Dorsey Levens .50 .20
❑ 82 E.G. Green .30 .10
❑ 83 Edgerrin James 1.00 .40
❑ 84 Jerome Pathon .50 .20
❑ 85 Ken Dilger .30 .10
❑ 86 Marcus Pollard .30 .10
❑ 87 Marvin Harrison .75 .30
❑ 88 Peyton Manning 2.00 .75
❑ 89 Terrence Wilkins .30 .10
❑ 90 Fred Taylor .75 .30
❑ 91 Hardy Nickerson .30 .10
❑ 92 Jimmy Smith .50 .20
❑ 93 Keenan McCardell .30 .10
❑ 94 Kyle Brady .30 .10
❑ 95 Mark Brunell .75 .30
❑ 96 Tony Brackens .30 .10
❑ 97 Derrick Alexander WR .50 .20
❑ 98 Sylvester Morris .30 .10
❑ 99 Tony Gonzalez .50 .20
❑ 100 Tony Richardson .30 .10
❑ 101 Kimble Anders .30 .10
❑ 102 Warren Moon .75 .30
❑ 103 Dan Marino 2.50 1.00
❑ 104 Jay Fiedler .75 .30

❑	105	Lamar Smith	.50	.20
❑	106	O.J. McDuffie	.30	.10
❑	107	Oronde Gadsden	.50	.20
❑	108	Sam Madison	.30	.10
❑	109	Thurman Thomas	.50	.20
❑	110	Tony Martin	.30	.10
❑	111	Zach Thomas	.75	.30
❑	112	Cris Carter	.75	.30
❑	113	Daunte Culpepper	.75	.30
❑	114	Matthew Hatchette	.30	.10
❑	115	Randy Moss	1.50	.60
❑	116	Robert Smith	.75	.30
❑	117	Drew Bledsoe	1.00	.40
❑	118	J.R. Redmond	.30	.10
❑	119	Kevin Faulk	.50	.20
❑	120	Michael Bishop	.30	.10
❑	121	Terry Glenn	.50	.20
❑	122	Troy Brown	.50	.20
❑	123	Ty Law	.50	.20
❑	124	Aaron Brooks	.75	.30
❑	125	Darren Howard	.30	.10
❑	126	Jake Reed	.50	.20
❑	127	Jeff Blake	.50	.20
❑	128	Joe Horn	.50	.20
❑	129	La'Roi Glover	.30	.10
❑	130	Ricky Williams	.75	.30
❑	131	Willie Jackson	.30	.10
❑	132	Albert Connell	.30	.10
❑	133	Amani Toomer	.50	.20
❑	134	Ike Hilliard	.50	.20
❑	135	Jason Sehorn	.30	.10
❑	136	Jessie Armstead	.30	.10
❑	137	Kerry Collins	.50	.20
❑	138	Michael Strahan	.50	.20
❑	139	Ron Dayne	.75	.30
❑	140	Ron Dixon	.30	.10
❑	141	Tiki Barber	.75	.30
❑	142	Anthony Becht	.30	.10
❑	143	Chad Pennington	1.25	.50
❑	144	Curtis Martin	.75	.30
❑	145	Dedric Ward	.30	.10
❑	146	Laveranues Coles	.75	.30
❑	147	Vinny Testaverde	.50	.20
❑	148	Wayne Chrebet	.50	.20
❑	149	Andre Rison	.50	.20
❑	150	Charles Woodson	.50	.20
❑	151	Darrell Russell	.30	.10
❑	152	Napoleon Kaufman	.50	.20
❑	153	Rich Gannon	.75	.30
❑	154	Tim Brown	.75	.30
❑	155	Tyrone Wheatley	.50	.20
❑	156	Chad Lewis	.30	.10
❑	157	Charles Johnson	.30	.10
❑	158	Donovan McNabb	1.00	.40
❑	159	Duce Staley	.75	.30
❑	160	Hugh Douglas	.30	.10
❑	161	Na Brown	.30	.10
❑	162	Todd Pinkston	.30	.10
❑	163	James Thrash	.50	.20
❑	164	Bobby Shaw	.30	.10
❑	165	Hines Ward	.75	.30
❑	166	Jerome Bettis	.75	.30
❑	167	Kordell Stewart	.50	.20
❑	168	Levon Kirkland	.30	.10
❑	169	Plaxico Burress	.75	.30
❑	170	Richard Huntley	.30	.10
❑	171	Troy Edwards	.30	.10
❑	172	Jeff Graham	.30	.10
❑	173	Junior Seau	.75	.30
❑	174	Doug Flutie	.75	.30
❑	175	Charlie Garner	.50	.20
❑	176	Jeff Garcia	.75	.30
❑	177	Jerry Rice	1.50	.60
❑	178	Steve Young	1.00	.40
❑	179	Terrell Owens	.75	.30
❑	180	Brock Huard	.30	.10
❑	181	Darrell Jackson	.75	.30
❑	182	Derrick Mayes	.30	.10
❑	183	Ricky Watters	.50	.20
❑	184	Shaun Alexander	1.00	.40
❑	185	Matt Hasselbeck	.50	.20
❑	186	John Randle	.50	.20
❑	187	Az-Zahir Hakim	.30	.10
❑	188	Isaac Bruce	.75	.30
❑	189	Kurt Warner	1.50	.60
❑	190	Marshall Faulk	1.00	.40
❑	191	Torry Holt	.75	.30
❑	192	Trent Green	.75	.30
❑	193	Derrick Brooks	.75	.30
❑	194	Jacquez Green	.30	.10
❑	195	John Lynch	.50	.20
❑	196	Keyshawn Johnson	.75	.30
❑	197	Mike Alstott	.75	.30
❑	198	Reidel Anthony	.30	.10
❑	199	Shaun King	.30	.10
❑	200	Warren Sapp	.50	.20
❑	201	Warrick Dunn	.75	.30
❑	202	Ryan Leaf	.50	.20
❑	203	Carl Pickens	.30	.10
❑	204	Derrick Mason	.50	.20
❑	205	Eddie George	.75	.30
❑	206	Frank Wycheck	.30	.10
❑	207	Jevon Kearse	.50	.20
❑	208	Neil O'Donnell	.30	.10
❑	209	Steve McNair	.75	.30
❑	210	Yancey Thigpen	.30	.10
❑	211	Andre Reed	.50	.20
❑	212	Brad Johnson	.75	.30
❑	213	Bruce Smith	.50	.20
❑	214	Champ Bailey	.75	.30
❑	215	Darrell Green	.30	.10
❑	216	Deion Sanders	.75	.30
❑	217	Irving Fryar	.50	.20
❑	218	Jeff George	.50	.20
❑	219	Michael Westbrook	.50	.20
❑	220	Stephen Davis	.75	.30
❑	221	Terrell Owens AP	2.00	.75
❑	222	Peyton Manning AP	6.00	2.50
❑	223	Stephen Davis AP	2.00	.75
❑	224	Marvin Harrison AP	2.00	.75
❑	225	Donovan McNabb AP	3.00	1.25
❑	226	Edgerrin James AP	3.00	1.25
❑	227	Eric Moulds AP	1.25	.50
❑	228	Daunte Culpepper AP	2.00	.75
❑	229	Eddie George AP	2.00	.75
❑	230	Cris Carter AP	2.00	.75
❑	231	Rich Gannon AP	2.00	.75
❑	232	Jeff Garcia AP	2.00	.75
❑	233	Jimmy Smith AP	1.25	.50
❑	234	Tony Gonzalez AP	1.25	.50
❑	235	Torry Holt AP	2.00	.75
❑	236	Jevon Kearse AP	1.25	.50
❑	237	Ray Lewis AP	2.00	.75
❑	238	Warren Sapp AP	1.25	.50
❑	239	Brian Urlacher AP	4.00	1.50
❑	240	Champ Bailey AP	1.25	.50
❑	241	Peyton Manning LL	6.00	2.50
❑	242	Jeff Garcia LL	2.00	.75
❑	243	Elvis Grbac LL	1.25	.50
❑	244	Daunte Culpepper LL	2.00	.75
❑	245	Brett Favre LL	8.00	3.00
❑	246	Edgerrin James LL	3.00	1.25
❑	247	Robert Smith LL	1.25	.50
❑	248	Eddie George LL	2.00	.75
❑	249	Mike Anderson LL	2.00	.75
❑	250	Corey Dillon LL	2.00	.75
❑	251	Torry Holt LL	2.00	.75
❑	252	Rod Smith LL	1.25	.50
❑	253	Isaac Bruce LL	2.00	.75
❑	254	Terrell Owens LL	2.00	.75
❑	255	Randy Moss LL	5.00	2.00
❑	256	La'Roi Glover LL	.75	.30
❑	257	Trace Armstrong LL	.75	.30
❑	258	Warren Sapp LL	1.25	.50
❑	259	Hugh Douglas LL	.75	.30
❑	260	Jason Taylor LL	.75	.30
❑	261	Mike Anderson SS	2.00	.75
❑	262	Jamal Lewis SS	3.00	1.25
❑	263	Sylvester Morris SS	.75	.30
❑	264	Darrell Jackson SS	2.00	.75
❑	265	Peter Warrick SS	2.00	.75
❑	266	Ron Dayne SS	2.00	.75
❑	267	Shaun Alexander SS	3.00	1.25
❑	268	Plaxico Burress SS	2.00	.75
❑	269	Brian Urlacher SS	4.00	1.50
❑	270	Courtney Brown SS	1.25	.50
❑	271	Michael Vick RC	60.00	25.00
❑	272	Drew Brees RC	30.00	12.50
❑	273	Chris Weinke RC	12.00	5.00
❑	274	Quincy Carter RC	12.00	5.00
❑	275	Sage Rosenfels RC	12.00	5.00
❑	276	Josh Heupel RC	12.00	5.00
❑	277	David Rivers RC	8.00	3.00
❑	278	Ben Leard RC	8.00	3.00
❑	279	Marques Tuiasosopo RC	12.00	5.00
❑	280	Mike McMahon RC	12.00	5.00
❑	281	Deuce McAllister RC	25.00	10.00
❑	282	LaMont Jordan RC	25.00	10.00
❑	283	LaDainian Tomlinson RC	50.00	25.00
❑	284	James Jackson RC	12.00	5.00
❑	285	Anthony Thomas RC	12.00	5.00
❑	286	Travis Henry RC	12.00	5.00
❑	287	Travis Minor RC	8.00	3.00
❑	288	Rudi Johnson RC	25.00	10.00
❑	289	Michael Bennett RC	20.00	7.50
❑	290	Kevan Barlow RC	12.00	5.00
❑	291	Reggie White RC	8.00	3.00
❑	292	Moran Norris RC	5.00	2.00
❑	293	Ja'Mar Toombs RC	8.00	3.00
❑	294	Heath Evans RC	8.00	3.00
❑	295	David Terrell RC	12.00	5.00
❑	296	Santana Moss RC	20.00	7.50
❑	297	Rod Gardner RC	12.00	5.00
❑	298	Quincy Morgan RC	12.00	5.00
❑	299	Freddie Mitchell RC	12.00	5.00
❑	300	Boo Williams RC	8.00	3.00
❑	301	Reggie Wayne RC	25.00	10.00
❑	302	Ronney Daniels RC	5.00	2.00
❑	303	Bobby Newcombe RC	8.00	3.00
❑	304	Vinny Sutherland RC	8.00	3.00
❑	305	Cedrick Wilson RC	12.00	5.00
❑	306	Robert Ferguson RC	12.00	5.00
❑	307	Ken-Yon Rambo RC	8.00	3.00
❑	308	Alex Bannister RC	8.00	3.00
❑	309	Koren Robinson RC	12.00	5.00
❑	310	Chad Johnson RC	30.00	12.50
❑	311	Chris Chambers RC	20.00	7.50
❑	312	Javon Green RC	8.00	3.00
❑	313	Snoop Minnis RC	8.00	3.00
❑	314	Scotty Anderson RC	8.00	3.00
❑	315	Todd Heap RC	12.00	5.00
❑	316	Alge Crumpler RC	15.00	7.50
❑	317	Marcellus Rivers RC	8.00	3.00
❑	318	Rashon Burns RC	5.00	2.00
❑	319	Jamal Reynolds RC	12.00	5.00
❑	320	Andre Carter RC	12.00	5.00
❑	321	Justin Smith RC	12.00	5.00
❑	322	Gerard Warren RC	12.00	5.00
❑	323	Tommy Polley RC	12.00	5.00
❑	324	Dan Morgan RC	12.00	5.00
❑	325	Torrance Marshall RC	12.00	5.00
❑	326	Correll Buckhalter RC	15.00	6.00
❑	327	Derrick Gibson RC	8.00	3.00
❑	328	Adam Archuleta RC	12.00	5.00
❑	329	Jamar Fletcher RC	8.00	3.00
❑	330	Nate Clements RC	12.00	5.00

1993 Select

❑		COMPLETE SET (200)	20.00	7.50
❑	1	Steve Young	2.00	.75
❑	2	Andre Reed	.40	.15
❑	3	Deion Sanders	1.25	.50
❑	4	Harold Green	.20	.07
❑	5	Wendell Davis	.20	.07

❑ 6 Mike Johnson	.20	.07
❑ 7 Troy Aikman	2.00	.75
❑ 8 Johnny Mitchell	.20	.07
❑ 9 Dale Carter	.20	.07
❑ 10 Bruce Matthews	.20	.07
❑ 11 Terrell Buckley	.20	.07
❑ 12 Steve Emtman	.20	.07
❑ 13 Neil Smith	.75	.30
❑ 14 Tim Brown	.75	.30
❑ 15 Chris Doleman	.20	.07
❑ 16 Dan Marino	4.00	1.50
❑ 17 Terry McDaniel	.20	.07
❑ 18 Neal Anderson	.20	.07
❑ 19 Phil Simms	.40	.15
❑ 20 Jeff Lageman	.20	.07
❑ 21 Jerry Rice	2.50	1.00
❑ 22 Dermontti Dawson	.20	.07
❑ 23 Reggie Cobb	.20	.07
❑ 24 Junior Seau	.75	.30
❑ 25 Darrell Green	.20	.07
❑ 26 Chris Warren	.40	.15
❑ 27 Randall Cunningham	.75	.30
❑ 28 Bruce Smith	.75	.30
❑ 29 Bryan Cox	.20	.07
❑ 30 David Klingler	.20	.07
❑ 31 Chip Lohmiller	.20	.07
❑ 32 Eric Metcalf	.40	.15
❑ 33 Ken Norton Jr.	.40	.15
❑ 34 John Elway	4.00	1.50
❑ 35 Harris Barton	.20	.07
❑ 36 Tim Barnett	.20	.07
❑ 37 Rodney Hampton	.40	.15
❑ 38 Desmond Howard	.40	.15
❑ 39 Tom Rathman	.20	.07
❑ 40 Derrick Thomas	.75	.30
❑ 41 Randal Hill	.20	.07
❑ 42 Steve Wisniewski	.20	.07
❑ 43 Brett Favre	5.00	2.00
❑ 44 Darryl Talley	.20	.07
❑ 45 Shane Conlan	.20	.07
❑ 46 Anthony Miller	.40	.15
❑ 47 Randall McDaniel	.20	.07
❑ 48 Rod Woodson	.75	.30
❑ 49 Eric Martin	.20	.07
❑ 50 Ronnie Lott	.40	.15
❑ 51 Chris Spielman	.40	.15
❑ 52 Vincent Brown	.20	.07
❑ 53 Donnell Woolford	.20	.07
❑ 54 Richmond Webb	.20	.07
❑ 55 Emmitt Smith	3.00	1.25
❑ 56 Haywood Jeffires	.40	.15
❑ 57 Jim Kelly	.75	.30
❑ 58 James Francis	.20	.07
❑ 59 Steve Wallace	.20	.07
❑ 60 Jarrod Bunch	.20	.07
❑ 61 Lawrence Dawsey	.20	.07
❑ 62 Steve Atwater	.20	.07
❑ 63 Art Monk	.40	.15
❑ 64 Eric Green	.20	.07
❑ 65 Lawrence Taylor	.75	.30
❑ 66 Ronnie Harmon	.20	.07
❑ 67 Fred Barnett	.40	.15
❑ 68 Cortez Kennedy	.40	.15
❑ 69 Mark Collins	.20	.07
❑ 70 Howie Long	.75	.30
❑ 71 Jackie Harris	.20	.07
❑ 72 Irving Fryar	.40	.15
❑ 73 Jim Everett	.40	.15
❑ 74 Troy Vincent	.20	.07
❑ 75 Cris Carter	.75	.30
❑ 76 Boomer Esiason	.40	.15
❑ 77 Sam Mills	.20	.07
❑ 78 Lorenzo White	.20	.07
❑ 79 Andre Rison	.40	.15
❑ 80 Quentin Coryatt	.40	.15
❑ 81 Steve McMichael	.40	.15
❑ 82 Nick Lowery	.20	.07
❑ 83 Michael Irvin	.75	.30
❑ 84 Thurman Thomas	.75	.30
❑ 85 Bill Romanowski	.20	.07
❑ 86 Carl Pickens	.40	.15
❑ 87 Tim McDonald	.20	.07
❑ 88 Bernie Kosar	.40	.15
❑ 89 Greg Lloyd	.40	.15
❑ 90 Barry Sanders	3.00	1.25
❑ 91 Shannon Sharpe	.75	.30
❑ 92 Henry Thomas	.20	.07
❑ 93 Barry Foster	.40	.15
❑ 94 Antone Davis	.20	.07
❑ 95 Stan Humphries	.40	.15
❑ 96 Eric Swann	.40	.15
❑ 97 Mike Pritchard	.40	.15
❑ 98 Reggie White	.75	.30
❑ 99 Jeff Hostetler	.40	.15
❑ 100 Flipper Anderson	.20	.07
❑ 101 Gary Clark	.40	.15
❑ 102 Morten Andersen	.20	.07
❑ 103 Leonard Russell	.40	.15
❑ 104 Chris Hinton	.20	.07
❑ 105 John Stephens	.20	.07
❑ 106 Byron Evans	.20	.07
❑ 107 Warren Moon	.75	.30
❑ 108 Marv Cook	.20	.07
❑ 109 Carlton Gray RC	.20	.07
❑ 110 Jay Novacek	.40	.15
❑ 111 Gary Anderson K	.20	.07
❑ 112 Andre Tippett	.20	.07
❑ 113 Cornelius Bennett	.40	.15
❑ 114 Clyde Simmons	.20	.07
❑ 115 Jeff George	.75	.30
❑ 116 Audray McMillian	.20	.07
❑ 117 Mark Carrier WR	.40	.15
❑ 118 Vaughan Johnson	.20	.07
❑ 119 Kevin Greene	.40	.15
❑ 120 John Taylor	.40	.15
❑ 121 Jerry Ball	.20	.07
❑ 122 Pat Swilling	.20	.07
❑ 123 George Teague RC	.40	.15
❑ 124 Ricky Reynolds	.20	.07
❑ 125 Marcus Allen	.75	.30
❑ 126 Henry Jones	.20	.07
❑ 127 Ricky Watters	.75	.30
❑ 128 Leon Searcy	.20	.07
❑ 129 Chris Miller	.40	.15
❑ 130 Jim Harbaugh	.75	.30
❑ 131 Luis Sharpe	.20	.07
❑ 132 Simon Fletcher	.20	.07
❑ 133 Eric Allen	.20	.07
❑ 134 Carlton Haselrig	.20	.07
❑ 135 Harvey Williams	.40	.15
❑ 136 Leslie O'Neal	.40	.15
❑ 137 Sterling Sharpe	.75	.30
❑ 138 Tim Harris	.20	.07
❑ 139 Mark Rypien	.20	.07
❑ 140 Harry Galbreath	.20	.07
❑ 141 Sean Gilbert	.40	.15
❑ 142 Keith Jackson	.40	.15
❑ 143 Mark Clayton	.20	.07
❑ 144 Guy McIntyre	.20	.07
❑ 145 Jessie Tuggle	.20	.07
❑ 146 Leonard Marshall	.20	.07
❑ 147 Willie Davis	.75	.30
❑ 148 Herman Moore	.75	.30
❑ 149 Charles Haley	.40	.15
❑ 150 Amp Lee	.20	.07
❑ 151 Gary Zimmerman	.20	.07
❑ 152 Bennie Blades	.20	.07
❑ 153 Pierce Holt	.20	.07
❑ 154 Edgar Bennett	.75	.30
❑ 155 Joe Montana	4.00	1.50
❑ 156 Ted Washington	.20	.07
❑ 157 Hardy Nickerson	.40	.15
❑ 158 Rohn Stark	.20	.07
❑ 159 Brent Jones	.40	.15
❑ 160 Eugene Robinson	.20	.07
❑ 161 Pepper Johnson	.20	.07
❑ 162 Dan Saleaumua	.20	.07
❑ 163 Seth Joyner	.20	.07
❑ 164 Bruce Armstrong	.20	.07
❑ 165 Mike Munchak	.40	.15
❑ 166 Drew Bledsoe RC	5.00	2.00
❑ 167 Curtis Conway RC	1.25	.50
❑ 168 Lincoln Kennedy RC	.20	.07
❑ 169 Dana Stubblefield RC	.75	.30
❑ 170 Wayne Simmons RC	.20	.07
❑ 171 Garrison Hearst RC	2.00	.75
❑ 172 Jerome Bettis RC	8.00	3.00
❑ 173 Eric Curry RC	.20	.07
❑ 174 Natrone Means RC	.75	.30
❑ 175 Glyn Milburn RC	.75	.30
❑ 176 Marvin Jones RC	.20	.07
❑ 177 O.J.McDuffie RC	.75	.30
❑ 178 Dan Williams RC	.20	.07
❑ 179 Rick Mirer RC	.75	.30
❑ 180 John Copeland RC	.40	.15
❑ 181 Willie Roaf RC	.40	.15
❑ 182 Patrick Bates RC	.20	.07
❑ 183 Troy Drayton RC	.40	.15
❑ 184 Vincent Brisby RC	.75	.30
❑ 185 Irv Smith RC	.20	.07
❑ 186 Marion Butts	.20	.07
❑ 187 Wayne Martin	.20	.07
❑ 188 Brian Blades	.40	.15
❑ 189 Mel Gray	.40	.15
❑ 190 Mark Stepnoski	.20	.07
❑ 191 Ernest Givins	.40	.15
❑ 192 Steve Tasker	.40	.15
❑ 193 Tim Grunhard	.20	.07
❑ 194 Stanley Richard	.20	.07
❑ 195 Jeff Wright	.20	.07
❑ 196 Rodney Peete	.20	.07
❑ 197 Tunch Ilkin	.20	.07
❑ 198 Rich Camarillo	.20	.07
❑ 199 Erik Williams	.20	.07
❑ 200 Pete Stoyanovich	.20	.07
❑ S21 Jerry Rice SAMPLE	2.50	1.00

1994 Select

❑ COMPLETE SET (225)	15.00	6.00
❑ 1 Emmitt Smith	2.50	1.00
❑ 2 Bruce Smith	.40	.15
❑ 3 Randall McDaniel	.10	.02

❑ 4 Drew Bledsoe 1.25 .50
❑ 5 Rod Woodson .20 .07
❑ 6 Richard Dent .20 .07
❑ 7 Norm Johnson .10 .02
❑ 8 Jim Everett .20 .07
❑ 9 Harold Green .10 .02
❑ 10 John Elway 3.00 1.25
❑ 11 Barry Sanders 2.50 1.00
❑ 12 Sterling Sharpe .20 .07
❑ 13 Marcus Robertson .10 .02
❑ 14 Steve Wisniewski .10 .02
❑ 15 Irving Fryar .20 .07
❑ 16 Tyrone Hughes .20 .07
❑ 17 Garrison Hearst .40 .15
❑ 18 Randall Cunningham .40 .15
❑ 19 Junior Seau .40 .15
❑ 20 Rick Mirer .40 .15
❑ 21 Jerry Rice 1.50 .60
❑ 22 Eric Metcalf .20 .07
❑ 23 Roosevelt Potts .10 .02
❑ 24 Neil Smith .20 .07
❑ 25 Jerome Bettis .75 .30
❑ 26 Keith Hamilton .10 .02
❑ 27 Hardy Nickerson .20 .07
❑ 28 Steve Tasker .20 .07
❑ 29 Johnny Johnson .10 .02
❑ 30 Tom Carter .10 .02
❑ 31 Andre Rison .20 .07
❑ 32 Cortez Kennedy .20 .07
❑ 33 Mark Carrier DB .10 .02
❑ 34 Shannon Sharpe .20 .07
❑ 35 Eric Swann .20 .07
❑ 36 Steve Young 1.25 .50
❑ 37 Johnny Mitchell .10 .02
❑ 38 Dermontti Dawson .10 .02
❑ 39 Mike Johnson .10 .02
❑ 40 Troy Aikman 1.50 .60
❑ 41 Pierce Holt .10 .02
❑ 42 Derrick Thomas .40 .15
❑ 43 Reggie Cobb .10 .02
❑ 44 Michael Jackson .20 .07
❑ 45 Lomas Brown .10 .02
❑ 46 Jeff Hostetler .20 .07
❑ 47 Pete Stoyanovich .10 .02
❑ 48 Reggie White .40 .15
❑ 49 Quentin Coryatt .10 .02
❑ 50 Cris Carter .75 .30
❑ 51 Sean Gilbert .10 .02
❑ 52 Chris Slade .10 .02
❑ 53 Ronnie Harmon .10 .02
❑ 54 Renaldo Turnbull .10 .02
❑ 55 Fred Barnett .20 .07
❑ 56 John Elliott .10 .02
❑ 57 Deion Sanders .75 .30
❑ 58 John Carney .10 .02
❑ 59 Louis Oliver .10 .02
❑ 60 Greg Lloyd .20 .07
❑ 61 Chris Hinton .10 .02
❑ 62 Ronald Moore .10 .02
❑ 63 Vincent Brown .10 .02
❑ 64 Tony McGee .10 .02
❑ 65 Erik Williams .10 .02
❑ 66 Thurman Thomas .40 .15
❑ 67 Neil O'Donnell .40 .15
❑ 68 Scott Mitchell .20 .07
❑ 69 Keith Byars .10 .02
❑ 70 Henry Ellard .20 .07
❑ 71 Chris Spielman .20 .07
❑ 72 LeRoy Butler .10 .02
❑ 73 Tim Brown .40 .15
❑ 74 Darrell Green .10 .02
❑ 75 Bruce Matthews .10 .02
❑ 76 Stan Humphries .20 .07
❑ 77 Will Wolford .10 .02
❑ 78 John Taylor .20 .07
❑ 79 Joe Montana 3.00 1.25
❑ 80 Chris Warren .20 .07
❑ 81 Michael Brooks .10 .02
❑ 82 Vance Johnson .10 .02
❑ 83 Rob Moore .20 .07
❑ 84 Herschel Walker .20 .07
❑ 85 Alvin Harper .20 .07
❑ 86 Wayne Martin .10 .02
❑ 87 Leslie O'Neal .10 .02
❑ 88 Flipper Anderson .10 .02
❑ 89 Tommy Vardell .10 .02
❑ 90 Mike Sherrard .10 .02
❑ 91 Chris Jacke .10 .02
❑ 92 Jim Kelly .40 .15
❑ 93 Jeff Graham .10 .02
❑ 94 Bryan Cox .10 .02
❑ 95 Michael Irvin .40 .15
❑ 96 Jeff Lageman .10 .02
❑ 97 Webster Slaughter .10 .02
❑ 98 Eugene Robinson .10 .02
❑ 99 Vencie Glenn .10 .02
❑ 100 Sean Jones .10 .02
❑ 101 Calvin Williams .20 .07
❑ 102 Jim Harbaugh .40 .15
❑ 103 Eric Curry .10 .02
❑ 104 Terry Allen .20 .07
❑ 105 Darryl Williams .10 .02
❑ 106 Gary Clark .20 .07
❑ 107 Marcus Allen .40 .15
❑ 108 Chip Lohmiller .10 .02
❑ 109 Vaughan Johnson .10 .02
❑ 110 Herman Moore .40 .15
❑ 111 Barry Foster .10 .02
❑ 112 Rocket Ismail .20 .07
❑ 113 Erric Pegram .10 .02
❑ 114 Anthony Miller .20 .07
❑ 115 Shane Conlan .10 .02
❑ 116 David Klingler .10 .02
❑ 117 Mark Collins .10 .02
❑ 118 Tony Bennett .10 .02
❑ 119 Donnell Woolford .10 .02
❑ 120 Reggie Brooks .20 .07
❑ 121 Sam Mills .10 .02
❑ 122 Greg Montgomery .10 .02
❑ 123 Kevin Greene .20 .07
❑ 124 Terry McDaniel .10 .02
❑ 125 Henry Jones .10 .02
❑ 126 Ricky Watters .20 .07
❑ 127 Dan Marino 3.00 1.25
❑ 128 Steve Atwater .10 .02
❑ 129 Ricky Proehl .10 .02
❑ 130 Ernest Givins .20 .07
❑ 131 John L. Williams .10 .02
❑ 132 John Randle .20 .07
❑ 133 Jay Novacek .20 .07
❑ 134 Boomer Esiason .20 .07
❑ 135 Jessie Hester .10 .02
❑ 136 Courtney Hawkins .10 .02
❑ 137 Ben Coates .20 .07
❑ 138 Stevon Moore .10 .02
❑ 139 Eric Allen .10 .02
❑ 140 Jessie Tuggle .10 .02
❑ 141 Marion Butts .10 .02
❑ 142 Brett Favre 3.00 1.25
❑ 143 Andre Reed .20 .07
❑ 144 Rodney Hampton .20 .07
❑ 145 Keith Sims .10 .02
❑ 146 Derek Brown RBK .10 .02
❑ 147 Eric Green .10 .02
❑ 148 Greg Robinson .10 .02
❑ 149 Nate Newton .10 .02
❑ 150 Mark Higgs .10 .02
❑ 151 Nick Lowery .10 .02
❑ 152 Craig Erickson .10 .02
❑ 153 Anthony Carter .20 .07
❑ 154 Simon Fletcher .10 .02
❑ 155 Ronnie Lott .20 .07
❑ 156 Gary Brown .10 .02
❑ 157 Brent Jones .20 .07
❑ 158 Jim Sweeney .10 .02
❑ 159 Robert Brooks .40 .15
❑ 160 Keith Jackson .10 .02
❑ 161 Daryl Johnston .20 .07
❑ 162 Tom Waddle .10 .02
❑ 163 Eric Martin .10 .02
❑ 164 Cornelius Bennett .20 .07
❑ 165 Tim McDonald .10 .02
❑ 166 Chris Doleman .10 .02
❑ 167 Gary Zimmerman .10 .02
❑ 168 Al Smith .10 .02
❑ 169 Mark Carrier WR .20 .07
❑ 170 Harris Barton .10 .02
❑ 171 Ray Childress .10 .02
❑ 172 Darryl Talley .10 .02
❑ 173 James Jett .10 .02
❑ 174 Mark Stepnoski .10 .02
❑ 175 Jeff Query .10 .02
❑ 176 Charles Haley .20 .07
❑ 177 Rod Bernstine .10 .02
❑ 178 Richmond Webb .10 .02
❑ 179 Rich Camarillo .10 .02
❑ 180 Pat Swilling .10 .02
❑ 181 Chris Miller .10 .02
❑ 182 Mike Pritchard .10 .02
❑ 183 Checklist NFC .10 .02
❑ 184 Natrone Means .40 .15
❑ 185 Erik Kramer .20 .07
❑ 186 Clyde Simmons .10 .02
❑ 187 Checklist AFC/NFC .10 .02
❑ 188 Warren Moon .40 .15
❑ 189 Michael Haynes .20 .07
❑ 190 Terry Kirby .40 .15
❑ 191 Brian Blades .20 .07
❑ 192 Haywood Jeffires .20 .07
❑ 193 Thomas Everett .10 .02
❑ 194 Morten Andersen .10 .02
❑ 195 Dana Stubblefield .20 .07
❑ 196 Ken Norton .20 .07
❑ 197 Art Monk .20 .07
❑ 198 Seth Joyner .10 .02
❑ 199 Heath Shuler RC .40 .15
❑ 200 Marshall Faulk RC 6.00 2.50
❑ 201 Charles Johnson RC .40 .15
❑ 202 Derrick Alexander WR RC .40 .15
❑ 203 Greg Hill RC .40 .15
❑ 204 Darnay Scott RC 1.00 .40
❑ 205 Willie McGinest RC .40 .15
❑ 206 Thomas Randolph RC .10 .02
❑ 207 Errict Rhett RC .40 .15
❑ 208 William Floyd RC .40 .15
❑ 209 Johnnie Morton RC 2.00 .75
❑ 210 David Palmer RC .40 .15
❑ 211 Dan Wilkinson RC .20 .07
❑ 212 Trent Dilfer RC 1.25 .50
❑ 213 Antonio Langham RC .20 .07
❑ 214 Chuck Levy RC .10 .02
❑ 215 John Thierry RC .10 .02
❑ 216 Kevin Lee RC .10 .02
❑ 217 Aaron Glenn RC .40 .15
❑ 218 Charlie Garner RC 1.50 .60
❑ 219 Jeff Burris RC .20 .07
❑ 220 LeShon Johnson RC .20 .07
❑ 221 Thomas Lewis RC .20 .07
❑ 222 Ryan Yarborough RC .10 .02
❑ 223 Mario Bates RC .40 .15
❑ 224 Checklist NFC/AFC .10 .02
❑ 225 Checklist AFC .10 .02
❑ SR1 Marshall Faulk SR 40.00 15.00
❑ SR2 Dan Wilkinson SR 8.00 3.00

1996 Select

❑ COMPLETE SET (200) 20.00 8.00
❑ 1 Troy Aikman 1.00 .40
❑ 2 Marshall Faulk .50 .20
❑ 3 Kordell Stewart .40 .15
❑ 4 Larry Centers .20 .07
❑ 5 Tamarick Vanover .20 .07
❑ 6 Ken Norton Jr. .10 .02
❑ 7 Steve Tasker .10 .02

❑ 8 Dan Marino 2.00 .75
❑ 9 Heath Shuler .20 .07
❑ 10 Anthony Miller .20 .07
❑ 11 Mario Bates .20 .07
❑ 12 Natrone Means .20 .07
❑ 13 Darren Woodson .20 .07
❑ 14 Chris Sanders .20 .07
❑ 15 Chris Warren .20 .07
❑ 16 Eric Metcalf .10 .02
❑ 17 Quentin Coryatt .10 .02
❑ 18 Jeff Hostetler .10 .02
❑ 19 Brett Favre 2.00 .75
❑ 20 Curtis Martin .75 .30
❑ 21 Floyd Turner .10 .02
❑ 22 Curtis Conway .40 .15
❑ 23 Orlando Thomas .10 .02
❑ 24 Lee Woodall .10 .02
❑ 25 Darick Holmes .10 .02
❑ 26 Marcus Allen .40 .15
❑ 27 Ricky Watters .20 .07
❑ 28 Herman Moore .20 .07
❑ 29 Rodney Hampton .20 .07
❑ 30 Alvin Harper .10 .02
❑ 31 Jeff Blake .40 .15
❑ 32 Wayne Chrebet .60 .25
❑ 33 Jerry Rice 1.00 .40
❑ 34 Dave Krieg .10 .02
❑ 35 Mark Brunell .60 .25
❑ 36 Terry Allen .20 .07
❑ 37 Emmitt Smith 1.50 .60
❑ 38 Bryan Cox .10 .02
❑ 39 Tony Martin .20 .07
❑ 40 John Elway 2.00 .75
❑ 41 Warren Moon .20 .07
❑ 42 Yancey Thigpen .20 .07
❑ 43 Jeff George .20 .07
❑ 44 Rodney Thomas .10 .02
❑ 45 Joey Galloway .40 .15
❑ 46 Jim Kelly .40 .15
❑ 47 Drew Bledsoe .60 .25
❑ 48 Greg Lloyd .20 .07
❑ 49 Michael Irvin .40 .15
❑ 50 Quinn Early .10 .02
❑ 51 Brent Jones .10 .02
❑ 52 Rashaan Salaam .20 .07
❑ 53 James O.Stewart .20 .07
❑ 54 Gus Frerotte .20 .07
❑ 55 Edgar Bennett .20 .07
❑ 56 Lamont Warren .10 .02
❑ 57 Napoleon Kaufman .40 .15
❑ 58 Kevin Williams .10 .02
❑ 59 Irving Fryar .20 .07
❑ 60 Trent Dilfer .40 .15
❑ 61 Eric Zeier .10 .02
❑ 62 Tyrone Wheatley .20 .07
❑ 63 Isaac Bruce .40 .15
❑ 64 Terrell Davis .75 .30
❑ 65 Lake Dawson .10 .02
❑ 66 Carnell Lake .10 .02
❑ 67 Kerry Collins .40 .15
❑ 68 Kyle Brady .10 .02
❑ 69 Rodney Peete .10 .02
❑ 70 Carl Pickens .20 .07
❑ 71 Robert Smith .20 .07
❑ 72 Rod Woodson .20 .07
❑ 73 Deion Sanders .60 .25
❑ 74 Sean Dawkins .10 .02
❑ 75 William Floyd .20 .07
❑ 76 Barry Sanders 1.50 .60
❑ 77 Ben Coates .20 .07
❑ 78 Neil O'Donnell .20 .07
❑ 79 Bill Brooks .10 .02
❑ 80 Steve Bono .10 .02
❑ 81 Jay Novacek .10 .02
❑ 82 Bernie Parmalee .10 .02
❑ 83 Derek Loville .10 .02
❑ 84 Frank Sanders .20 .07
❑ 85 Robert Brooks .40 .15
❑ 86 Jim Harbaugh .20 .07
❑ 87 Rick Mirer .20 .07
❑ 88 Craig Heyward .10 .02
❑ 89 Greg Hill .20 .07
❑ 90 Andre Coleman .10 .02
❑ 91 Shannon Sharpe .20 .07
❑ 92 Hugh Douglas .20 .07
❑ 93 Andre Hastings .10 .02
❑ 94 Bryce Paup .10 .02
❑ 95 Jim Everett .10 .02
❑ 96 Brian Mitchell .10 .02
❑ 97 Jeff Graham .10 .02
❑ 98 Steve McNair .75 .30
❑ 99 Charlie Garner .20 .07
❑ 100 Willie McGinest .10 .02
❑ 101 Harvey Williams .10 .02
❑ 102 Daryl Johnston .20 .07
❑ 103 Cris Carter .40 .15
❑ 104 J.J. Stokes .40 .15
❑ 105 Garrison Hearst .20 .07
❑ 106 Mark Chmura .20 .07
❑ 107 Derrick Thomas .40 .15
❑ 108 Errict Rhett .20 .07
❑ 109 Terance Mathis .10 .02
❑ 110 Dave Brown .10 .02
❑ 111 Erric Pegram .10 .02
❑ 112 Scott Mitchell .20 .07
❑ 113 Aaron Bailey .10 .02
❑ 114 Stan Humphries .20 .07
❑ 115 Bruce Smith .20 .07
❑ 116 Rob Johnson .40 .15
❑ 117 O.J. McDuffie .20 .07
❑ 118 Brian Blades .10 .02
❑ 119 Steve Atwater .10 .02
❑ 120 Tyrone Hughes .10 .02
❑ 121 Michael Westbrook .40 .15
❑ 122 Ki-Jana Carter .20 .07
❑ 123 Adrian Murrell .20 .07
❑ 124 Steve Young .75 .30
❑ 125 Charles Haley .20 .07
❑ 126 Vincent Brisby .10 .02
❑ 127 Jerome Bettis .40 .15
❑ 128 Erik Kramer .10 .02
❑ 129 Roosevelt Potts .10 .02
❑ 130 Tim Brown .40 .15
❑ 131 Reggie White .40 .15
❑ 132 Jake Reed .20 .07
❑ 133 Junior Seau .40 .15
❑ 134 Stoney Case .10 .02
❑ 135 Kimble Anders .20 .07
❑ 136 Brett Perriman .10 .02
❑ 137 Todd Collins .20 .07
❑ 138 Sherman Williams .10 .02
❑ 139 Hardy Nickerson .10 .02
❑ 140 Ernie Mills .10 .02
❑ 141 Glyn Milburn .10 .02
❑ 142 Terry Kirby .20 .07
❑ 143 Bert Emanuel .20 .07
❑ 144 Aeneas Williams .10 .02
❑ 145 Aaron Craver .10 .02
❑ 146 Jackie Harris .10 .02
❑ 147 Thurman Thomas .40 .15
❑ 148 Aaron Hayden RC .10 .02
❑ 149 Antonio Freeman .40 .15
❑ 150 Kevin Greene .20 .07
❑ 151 Kevin Hardy RC .40 .15
❑ 152 Eric Moulds RC 1.50 .60
❑ 153 Tim Biakabutuka RC .40 .15
❑ 154 Keyshawn Johnson RC 1.25 .50
❑ 155 Jeff Lewis RC .20 .07
❑ 156 Stepfret Williams RC .20 .07
❑ 157 Tony Brackens RC .40 .15
❑ 158 Mike Alstott RC 1.25 .50
❑ 159 Willie Anderson RC .10 .02
❑ 160 Marvin Harrison RC 3.00 1.25
❑ 161 Regan Upshaw RC .10 .02
❑ 162 Bobby Engram RC .40 .15
❑ 163 Leeland McElroy RC .20 .07
❑ 164 Alex Van Dyke RC .20 .07
❑ 165 Stanley Pritchett RC .20 .07
❑ 166 Cedric Jones RC .10 .02
❑ 167 Terry Glenn RC 1.25 .50
❑ 168 Eddie George RC 1.50 .60
❑ 169 Lawrence Phillips RC .40 .15
❑ 170 Jonathan Ogden RC .40 .15
❑ 171 Danny Kanell RC .40 .15
❑ 172 Alex Molden RC .10 .02
❑ 173 Daryl Gardener RC .10 .02
❑ 174 Derrick Mayes RC .40 .15
❑ 175 Marco Battaglia RC .10 .02
❑ 176 Jon Stark RC .10 .02
❑ 177 Karim Abdul-Jabbar RC .40 .15
❑ 178 Stephen Davis RC 2.00 .75
❑ 179 Rickey Dudley RC .40 .15
❑ 180 Eddie Kennison RC .40 .15
❑ 181 Barry Sanders FF .75 .30
❑ 182 Brett Favre FF 1.00 .40
❑ 183 John Elway FF 1.00 .40
❑ 184 Steve Young FF .40 .15
❑ 185 Michael Irvin FF .20 .07
❑ 186 Jerry Rice FF .50 .20
❑ 187 Emmitt Smith FF .75 .30
❑ 188 Isaac Bruce FF .40 .15
❑ 189 Chris Warren FF .20 .07
❑ 190 Errict Rhett FF .20 .07
❑ 191 Herman Moore FF .20 .07
❑ 192 Carl Pickens FF .20 .07
❑ 193 Cris Carter FF .40 .15
❑ 194 Terrell Davis FF .40 .15
❑ 195 Rodney Thomas FF .10 .02
❑ 196 Dan Marino CL .40 .15
❑ 197 Drew Bledsoe CL .20 .07
❑ 198 Emmitt Smith CL .40 .15
❑ 199 Jerry Rice CL .40 .15
❑ 200 Barry Sanders/Elway CL .40 .15

1995 Select Certified

❑ COMPLETE SET (135) 40.00 15.00
❑ 1 Marshall Faulk 4.00 1.50
❑ 2 Heath Shuler .50 .20
❑ 3 Garrison Hearst 1.00 .40
❑ 4 Errict Rhett .50 .20
❑ 5 Jeff George .50 .20
❑ 6 Jerome Bettis 1.00 .40

❑ 7 Jim Kelly 1.00 .40
❑ 8 Rick Mirer .50 .20
❑ 9 Willie Davis .50 .20
❑ 10 Steve Young 2.50 1.00
❑ 11 Erik Kramer .25 .08
❑ 12 Natrone Means .50 .20
❑ 13 Jeff Blake RC 3.00 1.25
❑ 14 Neil O'Donnell .50 .20
❑ 15 Andre Rison .50 .20
❑ 16 Randall Cunningham 1.00 .40
❑ 17 Emmitt Smith 5.00 2.00
❑ 18 Tim Brown 1.00 .40
❑ 19 Shannon Sharpe .50 .20
❑ 20 Boomer Esiason .50 .20
❑ 21 Barry Sanders 5.00 2.00
❑ 22 Rodney Hampton .50 .20
❑ 23 Robert Brooks 1.00 .40
❑ 24 Jim Everett .25 .08
❑ 25 Gary Brown .25 .08
❑ 26 Drew Bledsoe 1.25 .50
❑ 27 Desmond Howard .50 .20
❑ 28 Cris Carter 1.00 .40
❑ 29 Marcus Allen 1.00 .40
❑ 30 Dan Marino 6.00 2.50
❑ 31 Warren Moon .50 .20
❑ 32 Dave Krieg .25 .08
❑ 33 Ben Coates .50 .20
❑ 34 Terance Mathis .50 .20
❑ 35 Mario Bates .50 .20
❑ 36 Andre Reed .50 .20
❑ 37 Dave Brown .50 .20
❑ 38 Jeff Graham .25 .08
❑ 39 Johnny Mitchell .25 .08
❑ 40 Carl Pickens .50 .20
❑ 41 Jeff Hostetler .50 .20
❑ 42 Vinny Testaverde .50 .20
❑ 43 Ricky Watters .50 .20
❑ 44 Troy Aikman 3.00 1.25
❑ 45 Byron Bam Morris .25 .08
❑ 46 John Elway 6.00 2.50
❑ 47 Junior Seau 1.00 .40
❑ 48 Scott Mitchell .50 .20
❑ 49 Jerry Rice 3.00 1.25
❑ 50 Brett Favre 6.00 2.50
❑ 51 Chris Warren .50 .20
❑ 52 Chris Chandler .50 .20
❑ 53 Lorenzo White .25 .08
❑ 54 Craig Erickson .25 .08
❑ 55 Alvin Harper .25 .08
❑ 56 Steve Beuerlein .50 .20
❑ 57 Edgar Bennett .50 .20
❑ 58 Steve Bono .50 .20
❑ 59 Eric Green .25 .08
❑ 60 Jake Reed .50 .20
❑ 61 Terry Kirby .50 .20
❑ 62 Vincent Brisby .25 .08
❑ 63 Lake Dawson .50 .20
❑ 64 Torrance Small .25 .08
❑ 65 Mark Brunell 1.25 .50
❑ 66 Haywood Jeffires .25 .08
❑ 67 Flipper Anderson .25 .08
❑ 68 Ronald Moore .25 .08
❑ 69 LeShon Johnson .50 .20
❑ 70 Rocket Ismail .50 .20
❑ 71 Herman Moore 1.00 .40
❑ 72 Charlie Garner 1.00 .40
❑ 73 Anthony Miller .50 .20
❑ 74 Greg Lloyd .50 .20
❑ 75 Michael Irvin 1.00 .40
❑ 76 Stan Humphries .50 .20
❑ 77 Leroy Hoard .25 .08
❑ 78 Deion Sanders Mail Out 3.00 1.25
❑ 79 Darnay Scott .50 .20
❑ 80 Chris Miller .25 .08
❑ 81 Curtis Conway 1.00 .40
❑ 82 Trent Dilfer 1.00 .40
❑ 83 Bruce Smith 1.00 .40
❑ 84 Reggie Brooks .50 .20
❑ 85 Frank Reich .25 .08
❑ 86 Henry Ellard .50 .20
❑ 87 Eric Metcalf .50 .20
❑ 88 Sean Gilbert .50 .20
❑ 89 Larry Centers .50 .20
❑ 90 Ricky Ervins .25 .08
❑ 91 Craig Heyward .50 .20
❑ 92 Rod Woodson .50 .20
❑ 93 Steve Walsh .25 .08
❑ 94 Fred Barnett .50 .20
❑ 95 William Floyd .50 .20
❑ 96 Harvey Williams .25 .08
❑ 97 Greg Hill .50 .20
❑ 98 Irving Fryar .50 .20
❑ 99 Kevin Williams WR .50 .20
❑ 100 Herschel Walker .50 .20
❑ 101 Sean Dawkins .50 .20
❑ 102 Michael Haynes .50 .20
❑ 103 Reggie White 1.00 .40
❑ 104 Robert Smith 1.00 .40
❑ 105 Todd Collins RC 1.00 .40
❑ 106 Michael Westbrook RC 2.00 .75
❑ 107 Frank Sanders RC 2.00 .75
❑ 108 Christian Fauria RC 1.00 .40
❑ 109 Stoney Case RC .50 .20
❑ 110 Jimmy Oliver RC .50 .20
❑ 111 Mark Bruener RC 1.00 .40
❑ 112 Rodney Thomas RC 1.00 .40
❑ 113 Chris T.Jones RC .50 .20
❑ 114 James A.Stewart RC .50 .20
❑ 115 Kevin Carter RC 2.00 .75
❑ 116 Eric Zeier RC 2.00 .75
❑ 117 Curtis Martin RC 15.00 6.00
❑ 118 James O. Stewart RC 5.00 2.00
❑ 119 Joe Aska RC .50 .20
❑ 120 Ken Dilger RC 2.00 .75
❑ 121 Tyrone Wheatley RC 5.00 2.00
❑ 122 Ray Zellars RC 1.00 .40
❑ 123 Kyle Brady RC 2.00 .75
❑ 124 Chad May RC .50 .20
❑ 125 Napoleon Kaufman RC 5.00 2.00
❑ 126 Terrell Davis RC 12.00 5.00
❑ 127 Warren Sapp RC 6.00 2.50
❑ 128 Sherman Williams RC .50 .20
❑ 129 Kordell Stewart RC 8.00 3.00
❑ 130 Ki-Jana Carter RC 2.00 .75
❑ 131 Terrell Fletcher RC .50 .20
❑ 132 Rashaan Salaam RC 1.00 .40
❑ 133 J.J. Stokes RC 2.00 .75
❑ 134 Kerry Collins RC 8.00 3.00
❑ 135 Joey Galloway RC 8.00 3.00
❑ P7 Dan Marino Promo 5.00 2.00
❑ P10 Steve Young Promo 2.00 .75
❑ P44 Troy Aikman Promo 2.50 1.00

1996 Select Certified

❑ COMPLETE SET (125) 50.00 20.00
❑ 1 Isaac Bruce .75 .30
❑ 2 Rick Mirer .40 .15
❑ 3 Jake Reed .40 .15
❑ 4 Reggie White .75 .30
❑ 5 Harvey Williams .20 .07
❑ 6 Jim Everett .20 .07
❑ 7 Tony Martin .40 .15
❑ 8 Craig Heyward .20 .07
❑ 9 Tamarick Vanover .40 .15
❑ 10 Hugh Douglas .40 .15
❑ 11 Erik Kramer .20 .07
❑ 12 Charlie Garner .40 .15
❑ 13 Eric Pegram .20 .07
❑ 14 Scott Mitchell .40 .15
❑ 15 Michael Westbrook .75 .30
❑ 16 Robert Smith .40 .15
❑ 17 Kerry Collins .75 .30
❑ 18 Derek Loville .20 .07
❑ 19 Jeff Blake .75 .30
❑ 20 Terry Kirby .40 .15
❑ 21 Bruce Smith .40 .15
❑ 22 Stan Humphries .40 .15
❑ 23 Rodney Thomas .20 .07
❑ 24 Wayne Chrebet 1.00 .40
❑ 25 Napoleon Kaufman .75 .30
❑ 26 Marshall Faulk 1.00 .40
❑ 27 Emmitt Smith 3.00 1.25
❑ 28 Natrone Means .40 .15
❑ 29 Neil O'Donnell .40 .15
❑ 30 Warren Moon .40 .15
❑ 31 Junior Seau .75 .30
❑ 32 Chris Sanders .40 .15
❑ 33 Barry Sanders 3.00 1.25
❑ 34 Jeff Graham .20 .07
❑ 35 Kordell Stewart .75 .30
❑ 36 Jim Harbaugh .40 .15
❑ 37 Chris Warren .40 .15
❑ 38 Cris Carter .75 .30
❑ 39 J.J. Stokes .75 .30
❑ 40 Tyrone Wheatley .40 .15
❑ 41 Terrell Davis 1.50 .60
❑ 42 Mark Brunell 1.25 .50
❑ 43 Steve Young 1.50 .60
❑ 44 Rodney Hampton .40 .15
❑ 45 Drew Bledsoe 1.25 .50
❑ 46 Larry Centers .40 .15
❑ 47 Ken Norton Jr. .20 .07
❑ 48 Deion Sanders 1.25 .50
❑ 49 Alvin Harper .20 .07
❑ 50 Trent Dilfer .75 .30
❑ 51 Steve McNair 1.50 .60
❑ 52 Robert Brooks .75 .30
❑ 53 Edgar Bennett .40 .15
❑ 54 Troy Aikman 2.00 .75
❑ 55 Dan Marino 4.00 1.50
❑ 56 Steve Bono .20 .07
❑ 57 Marcus Allen .75 .30
❑ 58 Rodney Peete .20 .07
❑ 59 Ben Coates .40 .15
❑ 60 Yancey Thigpen .40 .15
❑ 61 Tim Brown .75 .30
❑ 62 Jerry Rice 2.00 .75
❑ 63 Quinn Early .20 .07
❑ 64 Ricky Watters .40 .15
❑ 65 Thurman Thomas .75 .30
❑ 66 Greg Lloyd .40 .15
❑ 67 Eric Metcalf .20 .07
❑ 68 Jeff George .40 .15
❑ 69 John Elway 4.00 1.50
❑ 70 Frank Sanders .40 .15
❑ 71 Curtis Conway .75 .30
❑ 72 Greg Hill .40 .15
❑ 73 Darick Holmes .20 .07
❑ 74 Herman Moore .40 .15
❑ 75 Carl Pickens .40 .15
❑ 76 Eric Zeier .20 .07
❑ 77 Curtis Martin 1.50 .60
❑ 78 Rashaan Salaam .40 .15
❑ 79 Joey Galloway .75 .30
❑ 80 Jeff Hostetler .20 .07
❑ 81 Jim Kelly .75 .30
❑ 82 Dave Brown .20 .07
❑ 83 Sean Dawkins .20 .07

❑ 84 Michael Irvin	.75	.30
❑ 85 Brett Favre	4.00	1.50
❑ 86 Cedric Jones RC	.25	.08
❑ 87 Jeff Lewis RC	.50	.20
❑ 88 Alex Van Dyke RC	.50	.20
❑ 89 Regan Upshaw RC	.25	.08
❑ 90 Karim Abdul-Jabbar RC	1.00	.40
❑ 91 Marvin Harrison RC	12.00	5.00
❑ 92 Stephen Davis RC	8.00	3.00
❑ 93 Terry Glenn RC	4.00	1.50
❑ 94 Kevin Hardy RC	1.00	.40
❑ 95 Stanley Pritchett RC	.25	.08
❑ 96 Willie Anderson RC	.25	.08
❑ 97 Lawrence Phillips RC	.50	.20
❑ 98 Bobby Hoying RC	1.00	.40
❑ 99 Amani Toomer RC	4.00	1.50
❑ 100 Eddie George RC	6.00	2.50
❑ 101 Stepfret Williams RC	.25	.08
❑ 102 Eric Moulds RC	5.00	2.00
❑ 103 Simeon Rice RC	2.50	1.00
❑ 104 John Mobley RC	.25	.08
❑ 105 Keyshawn Johnson RC	4.00	1.50
❑ 106 Daryl Gardener RC	.25	.08
❑ 107 Tony Banks RC	1.00	.40
❑ 108 Bobby Engram RC	1.00	.40
❑ 109 Jonathan Ogden RC	1.00	.40
❑ 110 Eddie Kennison RC	1.00	.40
❑ 111 Danny Kanell RC	1.00	.40
❑ 112 Tony Brackens RC	1.00	.40
❑ 113 Tim Biakabutuka RC	1.00	.40
❑ 114 Leeland McElroy RC	.50	.20
❑ 115 Rickey Dudley RC	1.00	.40
❑ 116 Troy Aikman SS	1.00	.40
❑ 117 Brett Favre SS	2.00	.75
❑ 118 Drew Bledsoe SS	.75	.30
❑ 119 Steve Young SS	.75	.30
❑ 120 Kerry Collins SS	.75	.30
❑ 121 John Elway SS	2.00	.75
❑ 122 Dan Marino SS	2.00	.75
❑ 123 Kordell Stewart SS	.75	.30
❑ 124 Jeff Blake SS	.40	.15
❑ 125 Jim Harbaugh SS	.40	.15

2000 SkyBox

❑ COMPLETE SET (300)	400.00	250.00
❑ COMP.SET w/o SPs (250)	30.00	12.50
❑ 1 Tim Couch	.40	.15
❑ 2 Edgerrin James	1.00	.40
❑ 3 Wesley Walls	.25	.08
❑ 4 Brian Griese	.60	.25
❑ 5 Herman Moore	.40	.15
❑ 6 Mark Brunell	.60	.25
❑ 7 John Randle	.40	.15
❑ 8 Victor Green	.25	.08
❑ 9 Michael Sinclair	.25	.08
❑ 10 Jevon Kearse	.60	.25
❑ 11 Peter Boulware	.25	.08
❑ 12 Kevin Johnson	.60	.25
❑ 13 Vonnie Holliday	.25	.08
❑ 14 Jason Taylor	.40	.15
❑ 15 Cam Cleeland	.25	.08
❑ 16 Jeff Graham	.25	.08
❑ 17 Jacquez Green	.25	.08
❑ 18 Chris McAlister	.25	.08
❑ 19 Takeo Spikes	.25	.08
❑ 20 Marvin Harrison	.60	.25
❑ 21 Jay Fiedler	.60	.25
❑ 22 Jake Reed	.40	.15
❑ 23 Jerry Rice	1.25	.50
❑ 24 Shaun King	.25	.08
❑ 25 Donovan McNabb	1.00	.40
❑ 26 David Boston	.60	.25
❑ 27 Curtis Enis	.25	.08
❑ 28 Olandis Gary	.60	.25
❑ 29 James Stewart	.40	.15
❑ 30 Jimmy Smith	.40	.15
❑ 31 Randy Moss	1.25	.50
❑ 32 Keyshawn Johnson	.60	.25
❑ 33 Kevin Carter	.25	.08
❑ 34 Stephen Davis	.60	.25
❑ 35 Jay Riemersma	.25	.08
❑ 36 Emmitt Smith	1.25	.50
❑ 37 E.G. Green	.25	.08
❑ 38 Dwayne Rudd	.25	.08
❑ 39 Michael Strahan	.40	.15
❑ 40 Troy Edwards	.25	.08
❑ 41 Derrick Mayes	.40	.15
❑ 42 Eddie George	.60	.25
❑ 43 Bruce Smith	.40	.15
❑ 44 Andre Wadsworth	.25	.08
❑ 45 Bobby Engram	.40	.15
❑ 46 Byron Chamberlain	.25	.08
❑ 47 Antonio Freeman	.60	.25
❑ 48 Hardy Nickerson	.25	.08
❑ 49 Terry Glenn	.40	.15
❑ 50 Wayne Chrebet	.40	.15
❑ 51 London Fletcher RC	.40	.15
❑ 52 Michael Westbrook	.40	.15
❑ 53 Rob Moore	.40	.15
❑ 54 Eddie Kennison	.40	.15
❑ 55 Ed McCaffrey	.60	.25
❑ 56 Dorsey Levens	.40	.15
❑ 57 Andre Rison	.40	.15
❑ 58 Willie McGinest	.25	.08
❑ 59 Tyrone Wheatley	.40	.15
❑ 60 Kurt Warner	1.25	.50
❑ 61 Stephen Alexander	.25	.08
❑ 62 Jessie Tuggle	.25	.08
❑ 63 Jim Miller	.25	.08
❑ 64 Luther Elliss	.25	.08
❑ 65 Bill Schroeder	.40	.15
❑ 66 Elvis Grbac	.40	.15
❑ 67 Ty Law	.40	.15
❑ 68 Tim Brown	.60	.25
❑ 69 Marshall Faulk	.75	.30
❑ 70 Champ Bailey	.40	.15
❑ 71 Charlie Batch	.60	.25
❑ 72 Steve Beuerlein	.40	.15
❑ 73 Rocket Ismail	.40	.15
❑ 74 Kevin Hardy	.25	.08
❑ 75 Zach Thomas	.60	.25
❑ 76 Aaron Glenn	.25	.08
❑ 77 Jerome Bettis	.60	.25
❑ 78 Chris Chandler	.40	.15
❑ 79 Marcus Robinson	.60	.25
❑ 80 Derrick Alexander	.40	.15
❑ 81 Drew Bledsoe	.75	.30
❑ 82 Charles Woodson	.40	.15
❑ 83 Isaac Bruce	.60	.25
❑ 84 Darrell Green	.25	.08
❑ 85 Tim Dwight	.60	.25
❑ 86 Darnay Scott	.40	.15
❑ 87 Chris Claiborne	.25	.08
❑ 88 Tony Gonzalez	.40	.15
❑ 89 Tony Simmons	.25	.08
❑ 90 Rich Gannon	.60	.25
❑ 91 Torry Holt	.60	.25
❑ 92 Jamal Anderson	.60	.25
❑ 93 Akili Smith	.25	.08
❑ 94 Germane Crowell	.25	.08
❑ 95 Lawyer Milloy	.40	.15
❑ 96 Napoleon Kaufman	.40	.15
❑ 97 Grant Wistrom	.25	.08
❑ 98 Terance Mathis	.40	.15
❑ 99 Karim Abdul-Jabbar	.40	.15
❑ 100 Kerry Collins	.40	.15
❑ 101 Troy Vincent	.25	.08
❑ 102 Jermaine Fazande	.25	.08
❑ 103 Warren Sapp	.40	.15
❑ 104 Tony Banks	.40	.15
❑ 105 Darrin Chiaverini	.25	.08
❑ 106 Corey Bradford	.40	.15
❑ 107 Tony Martin	.40	.15
❑ 108 Jeff Blake	.40	.15
❑ 109 Torrance Small	.25	.08
❑ 110 Freddie Jones	.25	.08
❑ 111 Warrick Dunn	.60	.25
❑ 112 Tim Biakabutuka	.40	.15
❑ 113 Rod Smith	.40	.15
❑ 114 Kyle Brady	.25	.08
❑ 115 Oronde Gadsden	.40	.15
❑ 116 Dedric Ward	.25	.08
❑ 117 Mikhael Ricks	.25	.08
❑ 118 Bryant Young	.25	.08
❑ 119 Michael Bates	.25	.08
❑ 120 Junior Seau	.60	.25
❑ 121 Bill Romanowski	.25	.08
❑ 122 Reggie Barlow	.25	.08
❑ 123 Jeff Garcia	.60	.25
❑ 124 Peerless Price	.40	.15
❑ 125 Jeff George	.40	.15
❑ 126 Cornelius Bennett	.25	.08
❑ 127 Amani Toomer	.40	.15
❑ 128 Charles Johnson	.40	.15
❑ 129 Cortez Kennedy	.25	.08
❑ 130 Samari Rolle	.25	.08
❑ 131 Eric Moulds	.60	.25
❑ 132 Joey Galloway	.40	.15
❑ 133 Peyton Manning	1.50	.60
❑ 134 Robert Smith	.60	.25
❑ 135 Jessie Armstead	.25	.08
❑ 136 Will Blackwell	.25	.08
❑ 137 Jon Kitna	.60	.25
❑ 138 Kevin Dyson	.40	.15
❑ 139 Jake Plummer	.40	.15
❑ 140 Cade McNown	.25	.08
❑ 141 Terrell Davis	.60	.25
❑ 142 Johnnie Morton	.40	.15
❑ 143 Fred Taylor	.60	.25
❑ 144 Ed McDaniel	.25	.08
❑ 145 Vinny Testaverde	.40	.15
❑ 146 Az-Zahir Hakim	.40	.15
❑ 147 Brad Johnson	.60	.25
❑ 148 Antowain Smith	.40	.15
❑ 149 Rob Konrad	.25	.08
❑ 150 Sam Cowart	.25	.08
❑ 151 Cris Carter	.60	.25
❑ 152 Jason Sehorn	.25	.08
❑ 153 Levon Kirkland	.25	.08
❑ 154 Shawn Springs	.25	.08
❑ 155 Frank Wycheck	.25	.08
❑ 156 Troy Aikman	1.25	.50
❑ 157 Keenan McCardell	.40	.15
❑ 158 Sam Madison	.25	.08
❑ 159 Curtis Martin	.60	.25
❑ 160 Hines Ward	.60	.25
❑ 161 Steve Young	.75	.30
❑ 162 Blaine Bishop	.25	.08
❑ 163 Shannon Sharpe	.40	.15
❑ 164 Michael Pittman	.25	.08
❑ 165 Brett Favre	2.00	.75
❑ 166 Damon Huard	.60	.25
❑ 167 Keith Poole	.25	.08
❑ 168 Curtis Conway	.40	.15
❑ 169 Derrick Brooks	.60	.25
❑ 170 Duce Staley	.60	.25
❑ 171 Rob Johnson	.40	.15
❑ 172 Pete Gonzalez	.25	.08

❑ 173 Ken Dilger .25 .08
❑ 174 Ike Hilliard .40 .15
❑ 175 Bobby Taylor .25 .08
❑ 176 Ricky Watters .40 .15
❑ 177 Steve McNair .60 .25
❑ 178 Pat Johnson .25 .08
❑ 179 Carl Pickens .40 .15
❑ 180 Terrence Wilkins .25 .08
❑ 181 Rashaan Shehee .25 .08
❑ 182 Ricky Williams .60 .25
❑ 183 James Jett .25 .08
❑ 184 Terrell Owens .60 .25
❑ 185 John Lynch .40 .15
❑ 186 Muhsin Muhammad .40 .15
❑ 187 Ryan McNeil .25 .08
❑ 188 Jerome Pathon .40 .15
❑ 189 Daunte Culpepper .75 .30
❑ 190 Joe Jurevicius .25 .08
❑ 191 Kordell Stewart .40 .15
❑ 192 Christian Fauria .25 .08
❑ 193 Yancey Thigpen .25 .08
❑ 194 Patrick Jeffers .60 .25
❑ 195 Corey Dillon .60 .25
❑ 196 Tamarick Vanover .25 .08
❑ 197 Doug Flutie .60 .25
❑ 198 Rickey Dudley .25 .08
❑ 199 Charlie Garner .40 .15
❑ 200 Mike Alstott .60 .25
❑ 201 Courtney Brown RC .75 .30
❑ 201H Courtney Brown SP 8.00 3.00
❑ 202 Peter Warrick RC .75 .30
❑ 202H Peter Warrick SP 8.00 3.00
❑ 203 Thomas Jones RC 1.25 .50
❑ 203H Thomas Jones SP 12.00 5.00
❑ 204 Sylvester Morris RC .50 .20
❑ 204H Sylvester Morris SP 5.00 2.00
❑ 205 Chad Pennington RC 2.00 .75
❑ 205H Chad Pennington SP 20.00 7.50
❑ 206 Ron Dayne RC .75 .30
❑ 206H Ron Dayne SP 8.00 3.00
❑ 207 Todd Pinkston RC .75 .30
❑ 207H Todd Pinkston SP 8.00 3.00
❑ 208 Todd Husak RC .75 .30
❑ 208H Todd Husak SP 8.00 3.00
❑ 209 Chris Redman RC .50 .20
❑ 209H Chris Redman SP 5.00 2.00
❑ 210 Jerry Porter RC 1.00 .40
❑ 210H Jerry Porter SP 10.00 4.00
❑ 211 Michael Wiley RC .50 .20
❑ 211H Michael Wiley SP 5.00 2.00
❑ 212 J.R. Redmond RC .50 .20
❑ 212H J.R. Redmond SP 5.00 2.00
❑ 213 Dennis Northcutt RC .75 .30
❑ 213H Dennis Northcutt SP 8.00 3.00
❑ 214 Gari Scott RC .30 .10
❑ 214H Gari Scott SP 3.00 1.25
❑ 215 Bashir Yamini RC .30 .10
❑ 215H Bashir Yamini SP 3.00 1.25
❑ 216 Danny Farmer RC .50 .20
❑ 216H Danny Farmer SP 5.00 2.00
❑ 217 Corey Simon RC .75 .30
❑ 217H Corey Simon SP 8.00 3.00
❑ 218 Plaxico Burress RC 1.50 .60
❑ 218H Plaxico Burress SP 15.00 6.00
❑ 219 Chad Morton RC .75 .30
❑ 219H Chad Morton SP 8.00 3.00
❑ 220 Bubba Franks RC .75 .30
❑ 220H Bubba Franks SP 8.00 3.00
❑ 221 Shaun Alexander RC 4.00 1.50
❑ 221H Shaun Alexander SP 30.00 12.50
❑ 222 Dez White RC .75 .30
❑ 222H Dez White SP 8.00 3.00
❑ 223 Mareno Philyaw RC .30 .10
❑ 223H Mareno Philyaw SP 3.00 1.25
❑ 224 Travis Taylor RC .75 .30
❑ 224H Travis Taylor SP .75 .30
❑ 225 Brian Urlacher RC 3.00 1.25
❑ 225H Brian Urlacher SP 25.00 10.00
❑ 226 Jamal Lewis RC 2.00 .75
❑ 226H Jamal Lewis SP 20.00 7.50
❑ 227 Sherrod Gideon RC .30 .10
❑ 227H Sherrod Gideon SP 3.00 1.25
❑ 228 Shyrone Stith RC .50 .20
❑ 228H Shyrone Stith SP 5.00 2.00
❑ 229 Chris Cole RC .50 .20
❑ 229H Chris Cole SP 5.00 2.00
❑ 230 Darrell Jackson RC 1.50 .60
❑ 230H Darrell Jackson SP 15.00 6.00
❑ 231 Quinton Spotwood RC .30 .10
❑ 231H Quinton Spotwood SP 3.00 1.25
❑ 232 Tee Martin RC .75 .30
❑ 232H Tee Martin SP 8.00 3.00
❑ 233 Tim Rattay RC .75 .30
❑ 233H Tim Rattay SP 8.00 3.00
❑ 234 Marc Bulger RC 1.50 .60
❑ 234H Marc Bulger SP 15.00 6.00
❑ 235 Doug Johnson RC .75 .30
❑ 235H Doug Johnson SP 8.00 3.00
❑ 236 Joe Hamilton RC .50 .20
❑ 236H Joe Hamilton SP 5.00 2.00
❑ 237 Trevor Gaylor RC .50 .20
❑ 237H Trevor Gaylor SP 5.00 2.00
❑ 238 Travis Prentice RC .50 .20
❑ 238H Travis Prentice SP 5.00 2.00
❑ 239 R.Jay Soward RC .50 .20
❑ 239H R.Jay Soward SP 5.00 2.00
❑ 240 Trung Canidate RC .50 .20
❑ 240H Trung Canidate SP 5.00 2.00
❑ 241 Giovanni Carmazzi RC .30 .10
❑ 241H Giovanni Carmazzi SP 3.00 1.25
❑ 242 Reuben Droughns RC 1.00 .40
❑ 242H Reuben Droughns SP 8.00 3.00
❑ 243 Curtis Keaton RC .50 .20
❑ 243H Curtis Keaton SP 5.00 2.00
❑ 244 Laveranues Coles RC 1.00 .40
❑ 244H Laveranues Coles SP 10.00 4.00
❑ 245 Ron Dugans RC .30 .10
❑ 245H Ron Dugans SP 3.00 1.25
❑ 246 Mike Anderson RC 1.00 .40
❑ 246H Mike Anderson SP 10.00 4.00
❑ 247 Anthony Becht RC .75 .30
❑ 247H Anthony Becht SP 8.00 3.00
❑ 248 Raynoch Thompson RC .50 .20
❑ 248H Raynoch Thompson SP 5.00 2.00
❑ 249 Rob Morris RC .75 .30
❑ 249H Rob Morris SP 8.00 3.00
❑ 250 Chafie Fields RC .30 .10
❑ 250H Chafie Fields SP 3.00 1.25
❑ P1 Tim Couch Promo 1.00 .40

1992 SkyBox Impact

❑ COMPLETE SET (350) 12.00 5.00
❑ 1 Jim Kelly .25 .08
❑ 2 Andre Rison .10 .02
❑ 3 Michael Dean Perry .10 .02
❑ 4 Herman Moore .25 .08
❑ 5 Fred McAfee RC .05 .01
❑ 6 Ricky Proehl .05 .01
❑ 7 Jim Everett .10 .02
❑ 8 Mark Carrier DB .05 .01
❑ 9 Eric Martin .05 .01
❑ 10 John Elway 1.25 .50
❑ 11 Michael Irvin .25 .08
❑ 12 Keith McCants .05 .01
❑ 13 Greg Lloyd .10 .02
❑ 14 Lawrence Taylor .25 .08
❑ 15 Mike Tomczak .05 .01
❑ 16 Cortez Kennedy .10 .02
❑ 17 William Fuller .05 .01
❑ 18 James Lofton .10 .02
❑ 19 Kevin Fagan .05 .01
❑ 20 Bill Brooks .05 .01
❑ 21 Roger Craig UER .10 .02
❑ 22 Jay Novacek .10 .02
❑ 23 Steve Sewell .05 .01
❑ 24 William Perry UER .10 .02
❑ 25 Jerry Rice .75 .30
❑ 26 James Joseph .05 .01
❑ 27 Timm Rosenbach .05 .01
❑ 28 Pat Terrell .05 .01
❑ 29 Jon Vaughn .05 .01
❑ 30 Steve Walsh .05 .01
❑ 31 James Hasty .05 .01
❑ 32 Dwight Stone .05 .01
❑ 33 Derrick Fenner UER .05 .01
❑ 34 Mark Bortz .05 .01
❑ 35 Dan Saleaumua .05 .01
❑ 36 Sammie Smith UER .05 .01
❑ 37 Antone Davis .05 .01
❑ 38 Steve Young .60 .25
❑ 39 Mike Baab .05 .01
❑ 40 Rick Fenney .05 .01
❑ 41 Chris Hinton .05 .01
❑ 42 Bart Oates .05 .01
❑ 43 Bryan Hinkle .05 .01
❑ 44 James Francis .05 .01
❑ 45 Ray Crockett .05 .01
❑ 46 Eric Dickerson .10 .02
❑ 47 Hart Lee Dykes .05 .01
❑ 48 Percy Snow .05 .01
❑ 49 Ron Hall .05 .01
❑ 50 Warren Moon .25 .08
❑ 51 Ed West .05 .01
❑ 52 Clarence Verdin .05 .01
❑ 53 Eugene Lockhart .05 .01
❑ 54 Andre Reed .10 .02
❑ 55 Kevin Ross .05 .01
❑ 56 Al Noga .05 .01
❑ 57 Wes Hopkins .05 .01
❑ 58 Rufus Porter .05 .01
❑ 59 Brian Mitchell .10 .02
❑ 60 Reggie Roby .05 .01
❑ 61 Rodney Peete .10 .02
❑ 62 Jeff Herrod .05 .01
❑ 63 Anthony Smith .05 .01
❑ 64 Brad Muster .05 .01
❑ 65 Jessie Tuggle .05 .01
❑ 66 Al Smith .05 .01
❑ 67 Jeff Hostetler .10 .02
❑ 68 John L. Williams .05 .01
❑ 69 Paul Gruber .05 .01
❑ 70 Cornelius Bennett .10 .02
❑ 71 William White .05 .01
❑ 72 Tom Rathman .05 .01
❑ 73 Boomer Esiason .10 .02
❑ 74 Neil Smith .25 .08
❑ 75 Sterling Sharpe .25 .08
❑ 76 James Jones DT .05 .01
❑ 77 David Treadwell .05 .01
❑ 78 Flipper Anderson .05 .01
❑ 79 Eric Allen .05 .01
❑ 80 Joe Jacoby .05 .01
❑ 81 Keith Sims .05 .01
❑ 82 Bubba McDowell .05 .01
❑ 83 Ronnie Lippett .05 .01
❑ 84 Cris Carter .50 .20
❑ 85 Chris Burkett .05 .01
❑ 86 Issiac Holt .05 .01

❑ 87 Duane Bickett .05 .01
❑ 88 Leslie O'Neal .10 .02
❑ 89 Gill Fenerty .05 .01
❑ 90 Pierce Holt .05 .01
❑ 91 Willie Drewrey .05 .01
❑ 92 Brian Blades .10 .02
❑ 93 Tony Martin .10 .02
❑ 94 Jessie Hester .05 .01
❑ 95 John Stephens .05 .01
❑ 96 Keith Willis UER .05 .01
❑ 97 Vai Sikahema UER .05 .01
❑ 98 Mark Higgs .05 .01
❑ 99 Steve McMichael .10 .02
❑ 100 Deion Sanders .50 .20
❑ 101 Marvin Washington .05 .01
❑ 102 Ken Norton .10 .02
❑ 103 Barry Word .05 .01
❑ 104 Sean Jones .05 .01
❑ 105 Ronnie Harmon .05 .01
❑ 106 Donnell Woolford .05 .01
❑ 107 Ray Agnew .05 .01
❑ 108 Lemuel Stinson .05 .01
❑ 109 Dennis Smith .05 .01
❑ 110 Lorenzo White .05 .01
❑ 111 Craig Heyward .10 .02
❑ 112 Jeff Query UER .05 .01
❑ 113 Gary Plummer .05 .01
❑ 114 John Taylor .10 .02
❑ 115 Rohn Stark .05 .01
❑ 116 Tom Waddle .05 .01
❑ 117 Jeff Cross .05 .01
❑ 118 Tim Green .05 .01
❑ 119 Anthony Munoz .10 .02
❑ 120 Mel Gray .10 .02
❑ 121 Ray Donaldson .05 .01
❑ 122 Dennis Byrd .05 .01
❑ 123 Carnell Lake .05 .01
❑ 124 Broderick Thomas .05 .01
❑ 125 Charles Mann .05 .01
❑ 126 Darion Conner .05 .01
❑ 127 John Roper .05 .01
❑ 128 Jack Del Rio UER .05 .01
❑ 129 Rickey Dixon .05 .01
❑ 130 Eddie Anderson .05 .01
❑ 131 Steve Broussard .05 .01
❑ 132 Michael Young .05 .01
❑ 133 Lamar Lathon .05 .01
❑ 134 Rickey Jackson .05 .01
❑ 135 Billy Ray Smith .05 .01
❑ 136 Tony Casillas .05 .01
❑ 137 Ickey Woods .05 .01
❑ 138 Ray Childress .05 .01
❑ 139 Vance Johnson .05 .01
❑ 140 Brett Perriman .25 .08
❑ 141 Calvin Williams .10 .02
❑ 142 Dino Hackett .05 .01
❑ 143 Jacob Green .05 .01
❑ 144 Robert Delpino .05 .01
❑ 145 Marv Cook .05 .01
❑ 146 Dwayne Harper .05 .01
❑ 147 Ricky Ervins .05 .01
❑ 148 Kelvin Martin .05 .01
❑ 149 Leroy Hoard .10 .02
❑ 150 Dan Marino 1.25 .50
❑ 151 Richard Johnson CB UER .05 .01
❑ 152 Henry Ellard .10 .02
❑ 153 Al Toon .10 .02
❑ 154 Dermontti Dawson .05 .01
❑ 155 Robert Blackmon .05 .01
❑ 156 Howie Long .25 .08
❑ 157 David Fulcher .05 .01
❑ 158 Mike Merriweather .05 .01
❑ 159 Gary Anderson K .05 .01
❑ 160 John Friesz .10 .02
❑ 161 Eugene Robinson .05 .01
❑ 162 Brad Baxter .05 .01
❑ 163 Bennie Blades .05 .01
❑ 164 Harold Green .05 .01
❑ 165 Ernest Givins .10 .02
❑ 166 Deron Cherry .05 .01
❑ 167 Carl Banks .05 .01
❑ 168 Keith Jackson .10 .02
❑ 169 Pat Leahy .05 .01
❑ 170 Alvin Harper .10 .02
❑ 171 David Little .05 .01
❑ 172 Anthony Carter .10 .02
❑ 173 Willie Gault .10 .02
❑ 174 Bruce Armstrong .05 .01
❑ 175 Junior Seau .25 .08
❑ 176 Eric Metcalf .10 .02
❑ 177 Tony Mandarich .05 .01
❑ 178 Ernie Jones .05 .01
❑ 179 Albert Bentley .05 .01
❑ 180 Mike Pritchard .10 .02
❑ 181 Bubby Brister .05 .01
❑ 182 Vaughan Johnson .05 .01
❑ 183 Robert Clark UER .05 .01
❑ 184 Lawrence Dawsey .10 .02
❑ 185 Eric Green .05 .01
❑ 186 Jay Schroeder .05 .01
❑ 187 Andre Tippett .05 .01
❑ 188 Vinny Testaverde .10 .02
❑ 189 Wendell Davis .05 .01
❑ 190 Russell Maryland .05 .01
❑ 191 Chris Singleton .05 .01
❑ 192 Ken O'Brien .05 .01
❑ 193 Merril Hoge .05 .01
❑ 194 Steve Bono RC .25 .08
❑ 195 Earnest Byner .05 .01
❑ 196 Mike Singletary .10 .02
❑ 197 Gaston Green .05 .01
❑ 198 Mark Carrier WR .10 .02
❑ 199 Harvey Williams .25 .08
❑ 200 Randall Cunningham .25 .08
❑ 201 Cris Dishman .05 .01
❑ 202 Greg Townsend .05 .01
❑ 203 Christian Okoye .05 .01
❑ 204 Sam Mills .05 .01
❑ 205 Kyle Clifton .05 .01
❑ 206 Jim Harbaugh .25 .08
❑ 207 Anthony Thompson .05 .01
❑ 208 Rob Moore .10 .02
❑ 209 Irving Fryar .10 .02
❑ 210 Derrick Thomas .25 .08
❑ 211 Chris Miller .10 .02
❑ 212 Doug Smith .05 .01
❑ 213 Michael Haynes .10 .02
❑ 214 Phil Simms .10 .02
❑ 215 Charles Haley .10 .02
❑ 216 Burt Grossman .05 .01
❑ 217 Rod Bernstine .05 .01
❑ 218 Louis Lipps .05 .01
❑ 219 Dan McGwire .05 .01
❑ 220 Ethan Horton .05 .01
❑ 221 Michael Carter .05 .01
❑ 222 Neil O'Donnell .10 .02
❑ 223 Anthony Miller .10 .02
❑ 224 Eric Swann .10 .02
❑ 225 Thurman Thomas .25 .08
❑ 226 Jeff George .25 .08
❑ 227 Joe Montana 1.25 .50
❑ 228 Leonard Marshall .05 .01
❑ 229 Haywood Jeffires .10 .02
❑ 230 Mark Clayton .10 .02
❑ 231 Chris Doleman .05 .01
❑ 232 Troy Aikman .75 .30
❑ 233 Gary Anderson RB .05 .01
❑ 234 Pat Swilling .05 .01
❑ 235 Ronnie Lott .10 .02
❑ 236 Brian Jordan .10 .02
❑ 237 Bruce Smith .25 .08
❑ 238 Tony Jones WR UER .05 .01
❑ 239 Tim McKyer .05 .01
❑ 240 Gary Clark .25 .08
❑ 241 Mitchell Price .05 .01
❑ 242 John Kasay .05 .01
❑ 243 Stephone Paige .05 .01
❑ 244 Jeff Wright .05 .01
❑ 245 Shannon Sharpe .25 .08
❑ 246 Keith Byars .05 .01
❑ 247 Charles Dimry .05 .01
❑ 248 Steve Smith .05 .01
❑ 249 Erric Pegram .10 .02
❑ 250 Bernie Kosar .10 .02
❑ 251 Peter Tom Willis .05 .01
❑ 252 Mark Ingram .05 .01
❑ 253 Keith McKeller .05 .01
❑ 254 Lewis Billups UER .05 .01
❑ 255 Alton Montgomery .05 .01
❑ 256 Jimmie Jones .05 .01
❑ 257 Brent Williams .05 .01
❑ 258 Gene Atkins .05 .01
❑ 259 Reggie Rutland .05 .01
❑ 260 Sam Seale UER .05 .01
❑ 261 Andre Ware .05 .01
❑ 262 Fred Barnett .25 .08
❑ 263 Randal Hill .05 .01
❑ 264 Patrick Hunter .05 .01
❑ 265 Johnny Rembert UER .05 .01
❑ 266 Monte Coleman .05 .01
❑ 267 Aaron Wallace .05 .01
❑ 268 Ferrell Edmunds .05 .01
❑ 269 Stan Thomas .05 .01
❑ 270 Robb Thomas .05 .01
❑ 271 Martin Bayless UER .05 .01
❑ 272 Dean Biasucci .05 .01
❑ 273 Keith Henderson .05 .01
❑ 274 Vinnie Clark .05 .01
❑ 275 Emmitt Smith 1.50 .60
❑ 276 Mark Rypien .05 .01
❑ 277 Michael Haynes TC .05 .01
❑ 278 Jim Kelly TC .10 .02
❑ 279 Tom Waddle TC .05 .01
❑ 280 Cincinnati Bengals CL .05 .01
❑ 281 Cleveland Browns CL .05 .01
❑ 282 Michael Irvin TC .10 .02
❑ 283 John Elway TC .50 .20
❑ 284 Detroit Lions CL .05 .01
❑ 285 Sterling Sharpe TC .10 .02
❑ 286 Warren Moon TC .10 .02
❑ 287 Jeff George TC .10 .02
❑ 288 Derrick Thomas TC .10 .02
❑ 289 Los Angeles Raiders CL .05 .01
❑ 290 Los Angeles Rams CL .05 .01
❑ 291 Dan Marino TC .50 .20
❑ 292 Cris Carter CL .25 .08
❑ 293 New England Patriots CL .05 .01
❑ 294 New Orleans Saints CL .05 .01
❑ 295 New York Giants CL .05 .01
❑ 296 New York Jets CL .05 .01
❑ 297 Philadelphia Eagles CL .05 .01
❑ 298 Phoenix Cardinals CL .05 .01
❑ 299 Pittsburgh Steelers CL .05 .01
❑ 300 San Diego Chargers CL .05 .01
❑ 301 Jerry Rice TC .50 .20
❑ 302 Seattle Seahawks CL .05 .01
❑ 303 Tampa Bay Buccaneers CL .05 .01
❑ 304 Mark Rypien TC .05 .01
❑ 305 Jim Kelly LL .10 .02
❑ 306 Steve Young LL .30 .10
❑ 307 Thurman Thomas LL .10 .02
❑ 308 Emmitt Smith LL .75 .30
❑ 309 Haywood Jeffires LL .05 .01
❑ 310 Michael Irvin LL .10 .02
❑ 311 William Fuller LL .05 .01
❑ 312 Pat Swilling LL .05 .01
❑ 313 Ronnie Lott LL .05 .01
❑ 314 Deion Sanders LL .25 .08
❑ 315 Cornelius Bennett HH .05 .01
❑ 316 David Fulcher HH .05 .01
❑ 317 Ronnie Lott HH .05 .01
❑ 318 Pat Swilling HH .05 .01
❑ 319 Lawrence Taylor HH .10 .02
❑ 320 Derrick Thomas HH .10 .02

Card	Price	Price
❑ 321 Steve Emtman RC	.05	.01
❑ 322 Carl Pickens RC	.25	.08
❑ 323 David Klingler RC	.05	.01
❑ 324 Dale Carter RC	.10	.02
❑ 325 Mike Gaddis RC	.05	.01
❑ 326 Quentin Coryatt RC	.05	.01
❑ 327 Darryl Williams RC	.05	.01
❑ 328 Jeremy Lincoln RC	.05	.01
❑ 329 Robert Jones RC	.05	.01
❑ 330 Bucky Richardson RC	.05	.01
❑ 331 Tony Brooks RC	.05	.01
❑ 332 Alonzo Spellman RC	.10	.02
❑ 333 Robert Brooks RC	.60	.25
❑ 334 Marco Coleman RC	.05	.01
❑ 335 Siran Stacy RC	.05	.01
❑ 336 Tommy Maddox RC	1.50	.60
❑ 337 Steve Israel RC	.05	.01
❑ 338 Vaughn Dunbar RC	.05	.01
❑ 339 Shane Collins RC	.05	.01
❑ 340 Kevin Smith RC DB	.05	.01
❑ 341 Chris Mims RC	.05	.01
❑ 342 Chester McGlockton UER RC	.10	.02
❑ 343 Tracy Scroggins RC	.05	.01
❑ 344 Howard Dinkins RC	.05	.01
❑ 345 Levon Kirkland RC	.05	.01
❑ 346 Terrell Buckley RC	.05	.01
❑ 347 Marquez Pope RC	.05	.01
❑ 348 Phillippi Sparks RC	.05	.01
❑ 349 Joe Bowden RC	.05	.01
❑ 350 Edgar Bennett RC	.25	.08
❑ SP1 Jim Kelly	8.00	3.00
❑ SP1AU Jim Kelly AUTO	40.00	15.00
❑ SP2AU Kelly/Magic AU/500	250.00	100.00

1993 SkyBox Impact

Card	Price	Price
❑ COMPLETE SET (400)	15.00	6.00
❑ 1 Steve Broussard	.05	.01
❑ 2 Michael Haynes	.10	.02
❑ 3 Tony Smith RB	.05	.01
❑ 4 Tory Epps	.05	.01
❑ 5 Chris Hinton	.05	.01
❑ 6 Bobby Hebert	.05	.01
❑ 7 Tim McKyer	.05	.01
❑ 8 Chris Miller	.10	.02
❑ 9 Bruce Pickens	.05	.01
❑ 10 Mike Pritchard	.10	.02
❑ 11 Andre Rison	.10	.02
❑ 12 Deion Sanders	.50	.20
❑ 13 Pierce Holt	.05	.01
❑ 14 Jessie Tuggle	.05	.01
❑ 15 Don Beebe	.05	.01
❑ 16 Cornelius Bennett	.10	.02
❑ 17 Kenneth Davis	.05	.01
❑ 18 Kent Hull	.05	.01
❑ 19 Jim Kelly	.25	.08
❑ 20 Mark Kelso	.05	.01
❑ 21 Keith McKeller UER	.05	.01
❑ 22 Andre Reed	.10	.02
❑ 23 Jim Ritcher	.05	.01
❑ 24 Bruce Smith	.25	.08
❑ 25 Thurman Thomas	.25	.08
❑ 26 Steve Christie	.05	.01
❑ 27 Darryl Talley UER	.05	.01
❑ 28 Pete Metzelaars	.05	.01
❑ 29 Steve Tasker	.10	.02
❑ 30 Henry Jones	.05	.01
❑ 31 Neal Anderson	.05	.01
❑ 32 Trace Armstrong	.05	.01
❑ 33 Mark Bortz	.05	.01
❑ 34 Mark Carrier DB	.05	.01
❑ 35 Wendell Davis	.05	.01
❑ 36 Richard Dent	.10	.02
❑ 37 Jim Harbaugh	.25	.08
❑ 38 Steve McMichael	.10	.02
❑ 39 Craig Heyward	.10	.02
❑ 40 William Perry	.10	.02
❑ 41 Donnell Woolford	.05	.01
❑ 42 Tom Waddle	.05	.01
❑ 43 Anthony Morgan	.05	.01
❑ 44 Jim Breech	.05	.01
❑ 45 David Klingler	.05	.01
❑ 46 Derrick Fenner	.05	.01
❑ 47 David Fulcher	.05	.01
❑ 48 James Francis	.05	.01
❑ 49 Harold Green	.05	.01
❑ 50 Carl Pickens	.10	.02
❑ 51 Jay Schroeder	.05	.01
❑ 52 Alex Gordon	.05	.01
❑ 53 Eric Ball	.05	.01
❑ 54 Eddie Brown	.05	.01
❑ 55 Jay Hilgenberg UER	.05	.01
❑ 56 Michael Jackson	.10	.02
❑ 57 Bernie Kosar	.10	.02
❑ 58 Kevin Mack	.05	.01
❑ 59 Eric Metcalf	.10	.02
❑ 60 Michael Dean Perry	.10	.02
❑ 61 Tommy Vardell	.05	.01
❑ 62 Leroy Hoard	.10	.02
❑ 63 Clay Matthews	.10	.02
❑ 64 Vinny Testaverde	.10	.02
❑ 65 Mark Carrier WR	.10	.02
❑ 66 Troy Aikman	.75	.30
❑ 67 Lin Elliott RC	.05	.01
❑ 68 Thomas Everett	.05	.01
❑ 69 Alvin Harper	.10	.02
❑ 70 Ray Horton	.05	.01
❑ 71 Michael Irvin	.25	.08
❑ 72 Russell Maryland	.05	.01
❑ 73 Jay Novacek	.10	.02
❑ 74 Emmitt Smith	1.50	.60
❑ 75 Tony Casillas	.05	.01
❑ 76 Robert Jones	.05	.01
❑ 77 Ken Norton Jr.	.10	.02
❑ 78 Daryl Johnston	.25	.08
❑ 79 Charles Haley	.10	.02
❑ 80 Leon Lett RC	.10	.02
❑ 81 Steve Atwater	.05	.01
❑ 82 Mike Croel	.05	.01
❑ 83 John Elway	1.50	.60
❑ 84 Simon Fletcher	.05	.01
❑ 85 Vance Johnson	.05	.01
❑ 86 Shannon Sharpe	.25	.08
❑ 87 Rod Bernstine	.05	.01
❑ 88 Robert Delpino	.05	.01
❑ 89 Karl Mecklenburg	.05	.01
❑ 90 Steve Sewell	.05	.01
❑ 91 Tommy Maddox UER	.25	.08
❑ 92 Arthur Marshall RC	.05	.01
❑ 93 Dennis Smith	.05	.01
❑ 94 Derek Russell	.05	.01
❑ 95 Bennie Blades	.05	.01
❑ 96 Michael Cofer	.05	.01
❑ 97 Willie Green	.05	.01
❑ 98 Herman Moore	.25	.08
❑ 99 Rodney Peete	.05	.01
❑ 100 Andre Ware	.05	.01
❑ 101 Barry Sanders UER	1.25	.50
❑ 102 Chris Spielman	.10	.02
❑ 103 Jason Hanson	.05	.01
❑ 104 Mel Gray	.10	.02
❑ 105 Pat Swilling	.05	.01
❑ 106 Bill Fralic	.05	.01
❑ 107 Rodney Holman	.05	.01
❑ 108 Brett Favre	2.00	.75
❑ 109 Sterling Sharpe	.25	.08
❑ 110 Reggie White	.25	.08
❑ 111 Terrell Buckley	.05	.01
❑ 112 Sanjay Beach	.05	.01
❑ 113 Tony Bennett	.05	.01
❑ 114 Jackie Harris	.05	.01
❑ 115 Bryce Paup	.10	.02
❑ 116 Shawn Patterson	.05	.01
❑ 117 John Stephens	.05	.01
❑ 118 Cris Dishman	.05	.01
❑ 119 Ernest Givins	.10	.02
❑ 120 Haywood Jeffires	.10	.02
❑ 121 Lamar Lathon	.05	.01
❑ 122 Warren Moon	.25	.08
❑ 123 Lorenzo White	.05	.01
❑ 124 Curtis Duncan	.05	.01
❑ 125 Webster Slaughter	.05	.01
❑ 126 Cody Carlson	.05	.01
❑ 127 Leonard Harris	.05	.01
❑ 128 Bruce Matthews	.05	.01
❑ 129 Ray Childress	.05	.01
❑ 130 Al Smith	.05	.01
❑ 131 Jeff George	.25	.08
❑ 132 Anthony Johnson	.10	.02
❑ 133 Steve Emtman	.05	.01
❑ 134 Quentin Coryatt	.10	.02
❑ 135 Rodney Culver	.05	.01
❑ 136 Jessie Hester	.05	.01
❑ 137 Aaron Cox	.05	.01
❑ 138 Clarence Verdin	.05	.01
❑ 139 Joe Montana	1.50	.60
❑ 140 Dave Krieg	.10	.02
❑ 141 Harvey Williams	.10	.02
❑ 142 Derrick Thomas	.25	.08
❑ 143 Barry Word	.05	.01
❑ 144 Christian Okoye	.05	.01
❑ 145 Nick Lowery	.05	.01
❑ 146 Dale Carter	.05	.01
❑ 147 Willie Davis	.25	.08
❑ 148 Tim Barnett	.05	.01
❑ 149 Neil Smith UER	.25	.08
❑ 150 Marcus Allen	.25	.08
❑ 151 Nick Bell	.05	.01
❑ 152 Tim Brown	.25	.08
❑ 153 Eric Dickerson	.10	.02
❑ 154 Willie Gault	.05	.01
❑ 155 Howie Long	.25	.08
❑ 156 Gaston Green	.05	.01
❑ 157 Chester McGlockton	.10	.02
❑ 158 Eddie Anderson	.05	.01
❑ 159 Ethan Horton	.05	.01
❑ 160 James Lofton	.10	.02
❑ 161 Jeff Hostetler	.10	.02
❑ 162 Terry McDaniel	.05	.01
❑ 163 Flipper Anderson	.05	.01
❑ 164 Shane Conlan	.05	.01
❑ 165 Jim Everett	.10	.02
❑ 166 Henry Ellard	.10	.02
❑ 167 Cleveland Gary	.05	.01
❑ 168 Todd Lyght	.05	.01
❑ 169 Sean Gilbert	.10	.02
❑ 170 Jim Price	.05	.01
❑ 171 Bill Hawkins	.05	.01
❑ 172 Mark Clayton	.05	.01
❑ 173 Mark Higgs	.05	.01
❑ 174 Dan Marino	1.50	.60
❑ 175 Louis Oliver	.05	.01
❑ 176 Reggie Roby	.05	.01
❑ 177 Bobby Humphrey	.05	.01
❑ 178 Troy Vincent	.05	.01
❑ 179 Marco Coleman	.05	.01
❑ 180 Aaron Craver	.05	.01
❑ 181 Keith Jackson	.10	.02
❑ 182 Mark Duper	.05	.01

Card	Player	Nrmt	Exc
❑ 183	Pete Stoyanovich	.05	.01
❑ 184	Irving Fryar	.10	.02
❑ 185	Bryan Cox	.05	.01
❑ 186	Terry Allen	.25	.08
❑ 187	Anthony Carter	.10	.02
❑ 188	Cris Carter	.25	.08
❑ 189	Chris Doleman	.05	.01
❑ 190	Rich Gannon	.25	.08
❑ 191	Sean Salisbury	.05	.01
❑ 192	Hassan Jones	.05	.01
❑ 193	Steve Jordan	.05	.01
❑ 194	Roger Craig	.10	.02
❑ 195	Todd Scott	.05	.01
❑ 196	Esera Tuaolo	.05	.01
❑ 197	Ray Agnew	.05	.01
❑ 198	Marv Cook	.05	.01
❑ 199	Tommy Hodson	.05	.01
❑ 200	Chris Singleton	.05	.01
❑ 201	Michael Timpson	.05	.01
❑ 202	Jon Vaughn ERR	.05	.01
❑ 203	Leonard Russell	.10	.02
❑ 204	Scott Zolak	.05	.01
❑ 205	Reyna Thompson	.05	.01
❑ 206	Andre Tippett	.05	.01
❑ 207	Morten Andersen UER	.05	.01
❑ 208	Wesley Carroll	.05	.01
❑ 209	Vince Buck	.05	.01
❑ 210	Rickey Jackson	.05	.01
❑ 211	Vaughan Johnson UER	.05	.01
❑ 212	Eric Martin	.05	.01
❑ 213	Sam Mills	.05	.01
❑ 214	Steve Walsh	.05	.01
❑ 215	Wade Wilson	.05	.01
❑ 216	Vaughn Dunbar	.05	.01
❑ 217	Brad Muster	.05	.01
❑ 218	Dalton Hilliard	.05	.01
❑ 219	Floyd Turner	.05	.01
❑ 220	Stephen Baker	.05	.01
❑ 221	Mark Jackson	.05	.01
❑ 222	Jarrod Bunch	.05	.01
❑ 223	Mark Collins	.05	.01
❑ 224	Rodney Hampton	.10	.02
❑ 225	Phil Simms	.10	.02
❑ 226	Pepper Johnson	.05	.01
❑ 227	Dave Meggett	.05	.01
❑ 228	Derek Brown TE	.05	.01
❑ 229	Mike Sherrard	.05	.01
❑ 230	Lawrence Taylor	.25	.08
❑ 231	Leonard Marshall	.05	.01
❑ 232	Brad Baxter	.05	.01
❑ 233	Dennis Byrd	.05	.01
❑ 234	Ronnie Lott	.10	.02
❑ 235	Boomer Esiason	.10	.02
❑ 236	Browning Nagle	.05	.01
❑ 237	Rob Moore	.10	.02
❑ 238	Jeff Lageman	.05	.01
❑ 239	Johnny Mitchell	.05	.01
❑ 240	Chris Burkett	.05	.01
❑ 241	Eric Thomas	.05	.01
❑ 242	Johnny Johnson	.05	.01
❑ 243	Eric Allen	.05	.01
❑ 244	Fred Barnett	.10	.02
❑ 245	Keith Byars	.05	.01
❑ 246	Randall Cunningham	.25	.08
❑ 247	Heath Sherman	.05	.01
❑ 248	Calvin Williams	.10	.02
❑ 249	Erik McMillan	.05	.01
❑ 250	Byron Evans	.05	.01
❑ 251	Seth Joyner	.05	.01
❑ 252	Vai Sikahema	.05	.01
❑ 253	Andre Waters	.05	.01
❑ 254	Tim Harris	.05	.01
❑ 255	Mark Bavaro	.05	.01
❑ 256	Clyde Simmons	.05	.01
❑ 257	Steve Beuerlein	.10	.02
❑ 258	Randal Hill	.05	.01
❑ 259	Ernie Jones	.05	.01
❑ 260	Robert Massey	.05	.01
❑ 261	Ricky Proehl UER	.05	.01
❑ 262	Aeneas Williams	.05	.01
❑ 263	Johnny Bailey	.05	.01
❑ 264	Chris Chandler UER	.10	.02
❑ 265	Anthony Thompson	.05	.01
❑ 266	Gary Clark	.10	.02
❑ 267	Chuck Cecil	.05	.01
❑ 268	Rich Camarillo	.05	.01
❑ 269	Neil O'Donnell	.25	.08
❑ 270	Gerald Williams	.05	.01
❑ 271	Greg Lloyd	.10	.02
❑ 272	Eric Green	.05	.01
❑ 273	Merril Hoge	.05	.01
❑ 274	Ernie Mills	.05	.01
❑ 275	Rod Woodson	.25	.08
❑ 276	Gary Anderson K	.05	.01
❑ 277	Barry Foster	.10	.02
❑ 278	Jeff Graham	.10	.02
❑ 279	Dwight Stone	.05	.01
❑ 280	Kevin Greene	.10	.02
❑ 281	Eric Bieniemy	.05	.01
❑ 282	Marion Butts	.05	.01
❑ 283	Gill Byrd	.05	.01
❑ 284	Stan Humphries	.10	.02
❑ 285	Anthony Miller	.10	.02
❑ 286	Leslie O'Neal	.10	.02
❑ 287	Junior Seau	.25	.08
❑ 288	Ronnie Harmon	.05	.01
❑ 289	Nate Lewis	.05	.01
❑ 290	John Kidd	.05	.01
❑ 291	Steve Young	.75	.30
❑ 292	John Taylor	.10	.02
❑ 293	Jerry Rice	1.00	.40
❑ 294	Tim McDonald	.05	.01
❑ 295	Brent Jones	.10	.02
❑ 296	Tom Rathman	.05	.01
❑ 297	Dexter Carter	.05	.01
❑ 298	Mike Cofer	.05	.01
❑ 299	Ricky Watters	.25	.08
❑ 300	Mervyn Fernandez	.05	.01
❑ 301	Amp Lee	.05	.01
❑ 302	Kevin Fagan	.05	.01
❑ 303	Roy Foster	.05	.01
❑ 304	Bill Romanowski	.05	.01
❑ 305	Brian Blades	.10	.02
❑ 306	John L. Williams	.05	.01
❑ 307	Tommy Kane	.05	.01
❑ 308	John Kasay	.05	.01
❑ 309	Chris Warren	.10	.02
❑ 310	Rufus Porter	.05	.01
❑ 311	Cortez Kennedy	.10	.02
❑ 312	Dan McGwire	.05	.01
❑ 313	Stan Gelbaugh	.05	.01
❑ 314	Kelvin Martin	.05	.01
❑ 315	Ferrell Edmunds	.05	.01
❑ 316	Eugene Robinson	.05	.01
❑ 317	Gary Anderson RB	.05	.01
❑ 318	Reggie Cobb	.05	.01
❑ 319	Lawrence Dawsey	.05	.01
❑ 320	Courtney Hawkins	.05	.01
❑ 321	Santana Dotson	.10	.02
❑ 322	Ron Hall	.05	.01
❑ 323	Keith McCants	.05	.01
❑ 324	Martin Mayhew	.05	.01
❑ 325	Anthony Munoz	.10	.02
❑ 326	Steve DeBerg	.05	.01
❑ 327	Vince Workman	.05	.01
❑ 328	Earnest Byner	.05	.01
❑ 329	Ricky Ervins	.05	.01
❑ 330	Jim Lachey	.05	.01
❑ 331	Chip Lohmiller	.05	.01
❑ 332	Ricky Sanders UER	.05	.01
❑ 333	Brad Edwards	.05	.01
❑ 334	Tim McGee	.05	.01
❑ 335	Darrell Green	.05	.01
❑ 336	Charles Mann	.05	.01
❑ 337	Wilber Marshall	.05	.01
❑ 338	Brian Mitchell	.10	.02
❑ 339	Art Monk	.10	.02
❑ 340	Mark Rypien	.05	.01
❑ 341	John Elway C83	.75	.30
❑ 342	Jim Kelly C83	.10	.02
❑ 343	Dan Marino C83	.75	.30
❑ 344	Eric Dickerson C83	.10	.02
❑ 345	Willie Gault C83	.05	.01
❑ 346	Ken O'Brien C83	.05	.01
❑ 347	Darrell Green C83	.05	.01
❑ 348	Richard Dent C83	.05	.01
❑ 349	Karl Mecklenburg C83	.05	.01
❑ 350	Henry Ellard C83	.05	.01
❑ 351	Roger Craig C83	.05	.01
❑ 352	Charles Mann C83	.05	.01
❑ 353	Checklist A UER	.05	.01
❑ 354	Checklist B UER	.05	.01
❑ 355	Checklist C UER	.05	.01
❑ 356	Checklist D UER	.05	.01
❑ 357	Checklist E UER	.05	.01
❑ 358	Checklist F UER	.05	.01
❑ 359	Checklist G UER	.05	.01
❑ 360	Rookies Checklist UER	.05	.01
❑ 361	Drew Bledsoe RC	2.50	1.00
❑ 362	Rick Mirer RC	.25	.08
❑ 363	Garrison Hearst RC	.75	.30
❑ 364	Marvin Jones RC	.05	.01
❑ 365	John Copeland RC	.10	.02
❑ 366	Eric Curry RC	.05	.01
❑ 367	Curtis Conway RC	.40	.15
❑ 368	Willie Roaf RC	.10	.02
❑ 369	Lincoln Kennedy RC	.05	.01
❑ 370	Jerome Bettis RC	4.00	1.50
❑ 371	Dan Williams RC	.05	.01
❑ 372	Patrick Bates RC	.05	.01
❑ 373	Brad Hopkins RC	.05	.01
❑ 374	Steve Everitt RC	.05	.01
❑ 375	Wayne Simmons RC	.05	.01
❑ 376	Tom Carter RC	.10	.02
❑ 377	Ernest Dye RC	.05	.01
❑ 378	Lester Holmes RC	.05	.01
❑ 379	Irv Smith RC	.05	.01
❑ 380	Robert Smith RC	1.25	.50
❑ 381	Darrien Gordon RC	.05	.01
❑ 382	Deon Figures RC	.05	.01
❑ 383	O.J.McDuffie RC	.25	.08
❑ 384	Dana Stubblefield RC	.25	.08
❑ 385	Todd Kelly RC	.05	.01
❑ 386	Thomas Smith RC	.10	.02
❑ 387	George Teague RC	.10	.02
❑ 388	Carlton Gray RC	.05	.01
❑ 389	Chris Slade RC	.10	.02
❑ 390	Ben Coleman RC	.05	.01
❑ 391	Ryan McNeil RC	.25	.08
❑ 392	Demetrius DuBose RC	.05	.01
❑ 393	Carl Simpson RC	.05	.01
❑ 394	Coleman Rudolph RC	.05	.01
❑ 395	Tony McGee RC	.10	.02
❑ 396	Roger Harper RC	.05	.01
❑ 397	Troy Drayton RC	.10	.02
❑ 398	Michael Strahan RC	1.00	.40
❑ 399	Natrone Means RC	.25	.08
❑ 400	Glyn Milburn RC	.25	.08

1994 SkyBox Impact

Card	Player	Nrmt	Exc
❑	COMPLETE SET (300)	15.00	6.00
❑ 1	Johnny Bailey	.05	.01
❑ 2	Steve Beuerlein	.10	.02
❑ 3	Gary Clark	.10	.02
❑ 4	Garrison Hearst	.25	.08
❑ 5	Ronald Moore	.05	.01
❑ 6	Ricky Proehl	.05	.01
❑ 7	Eric Swann	.10	.02
❑ 8	Aeneas Williams	.05	.01
❑ 9	Robert Massey	.05	.01
❑ 10	Chuck Cecil	.05	.01
❑ 11	Ken Harvey	.05	.01
❑ 12	Michael Haynes	.10	.02
❑ 13	Tony Smith RB	.05	.01

❑ 14 Bobby Hebert	.05	.01
❑ 15 Mike Pritchard	.05	.01
❑ 16 Andre Rison	.10	.02
❑ 17 Deion Sanders	.40	.15
❑ 18 Pierce Holt	.05	.01
❑ 19 Erric Pegram	.05	.01
❑ 20 Jessie Tuggle	.05	.01
❑ 21 Steve Broussard	.05	.01
❑ 22 Don Beebe	.05	.01
❑ 23 Cornelius Bennett	.10	.02
❑ 24 Kenneth Davis	.05	.01
❑ 25 Bill Brooks	.05	.01
❑ 26 Jim Kelly	.25	.08
❑ 27 Andre Reed	.10	.02
❑ 28 Bruce Smith	.25	.08
❑ 29 Darryl Talley	.05	.01
❑ 30 Thurman Thomas	.25	.08
❑ 31 Steve Tasker	.10	.02
❑ 32 Neal Anderson	.05	.01
❑ 33 Mark Carrier DB	.05	.01
❑ 34 Richard Dent	.10	.02
❑ 35 Jim Harbaugh	.25	.08
❑ 36 Chris Gedney	.05	.01
❑ 37 Tom Waddle	.05	.01
❑ 38 Curtis Conway	.25	.08
❑ 39 Dante Jones	.05	.01
❑ 40 Donnell Woolford	.05	.01
❑ 41 Tim Worley	.05	.01
❑ 42 John Copeland	.05	.01
❑ 43 David Klingler	.05	.01
❑ 44 Derrick Fenner	.05	.01
❑ 45 Harold Green	.05	.01
❑ 46 Carl Pickens	.10	.02
❑ 47 Tony McGee	.05	.01
❑ 48 Darryl Williams	.05	.01
❑ 49 Steve Everitt	.05	.01
❑ 50 Michael Jackson	.10	.02
❑ 51 Eric Metcalf	.10	.02
❑ 52 Tommy Vardell	.05	.01
❑ 53 Vinny Testaverde	.10	.02
❑ 54 Mark Carrier WR	.10	.02
❑ 55 Michael Dean Perry	.10	.02
❑ 56 Eric Turner	.05	.01
❑ 57 Troy Aikman	.75	.30
❑ 58 Alvin Harper	.10	.02
❑ 59 Michael Irvin	.25	.08
❑ 60 Leon Lett	.05	.01
❑ 61 Russell Maryland	.05	.01
❑ 62 Jay Novacek	.10	.02
❑ 63 Emmitt Smith	1.25	.50
❑ 64 Ken Norton	.10	.02
❑ 65 Charles Haley	.10	.02
❑ 66 Daryl Johnston	.10	.02
❑ 67 Kevin Smith	.05	.01
❑ 68 James Washington	.05	.01
❑ 69 Kevin Williams WR	.10	.02
❑ 70 Bernie Kosar	.10	.02
❑ 71 Mike Croel	.05	.01
❑ 72 John Elway	1.50	.60
❑ 73 Shannon Sharpe	.10	.02
❑ 74 Rod Bernstine	.05	.01
❑ 75 Simon Fletcher	.05	.01
❑ 76 Arthur Marshall	.05	.01
❑ 77 Glyn Milburn	.10	.02
❑ 78 Dennis Smith	.05	.01
❑ 79 Herman Moore	.25	.08
❑ 80 Rodney Peete	.05	.01
❑ 81 Barry Sanders	1.25	.50
❑ 82 Mel Gray	.05	.01
❑ 83 Erik Kramer	.10	.02
❑ 84 Pat Swilling	.05	.01
❑ 85 Willie Green	.05	.01
❑ 86 Chris Spielman	.10	.02
❑ 87 Robert Porcher	.05	.01
❑ 88 Derrick Moore	.05	.01
❑ 89 Edgar Bennett	.25	.08
❑ 90 Tony Bennett	.05	.01
❑ 91 LeRoy Butler	.05	.01
❑ 92 Brett Favre	1.50	.60
❑ 93 Jackie Harris	.05	.01
❑ 94 Sterling Sharpe	.10	.02
❑ 95 Darrell Thompson	.05	.01
❑ 96 Reggie White	.25	.08
❑ 97 Terrell Buckley	.05	.01
❑ 98 Cris Dishman	.05	.01
❑ 99 Ernest Givins	.10	.02
❑ 100 Haywood Jeffires	.10	.02
❑ 101 Warren Moon	.25	.08
❑ 102 Lorenzo White	.05	.01
❑ 103 Webster Slaughter	.05	.01
❑ 104 Ray Childress	.05	.01
❑ 105 Wilber Marshall	.05	.01
❑ 106 Gary Brown	.05	.01
❑ 107 Marcus Robertson	.05	.01
❑ 108 Sean Jones	.05	.01
❑ 109 Jeff George	.25	.08
❑ 110 Steve Emtman	.05	.01
❑ 111 Quentin Coryatt	.05	.01
❑ 112 Sean Dawkins RC	.25	.08
❑ 113 Jeff Herrod	.05	.01
❑ 114 Roosevelt Potts	.05	.01
❑ 115 Marcus Allen	.25	.08
❑ 116 Kimble Anders	.10	.02
❑ 117 Tim Barnett	.05	.01
❑ 118 J.J. Birden	.05	.01
❑ 119 Dale Carter	.05	.01
❑ 120 Willie Davis	.10	.02
❑ 121 Nick Lowery	.05	.01
❑ 122 Joe Montana	1.50	.60
❑ 123 Kevin Ross	.05	.01
❑ 124 Neil Smith	.10	.02
❑ 125 Derrick Thomas	.25	.08
❑ 126 Keith Cash	.05	.01
❑ 127 Tim Brown	.25	.08
❑ 128 Rocket Ismail	.10	.02
❑ 129 Ethan Horton	.05	.01
❑ 130 Jeff Hostetler	.10	.02
❑ 131 Patrick Bates	.05	.01
❑ 132 Terry McDaniel	.05	.01
❑ 133 Anthony Smith	.05	.01
❑ 134 Greg Robinson	.05	.01
❑ 135 James Jett	.05	.01
❑ 136 Alexander Wright	.05	.01
❑ 137 Flipper Anderson	.05	.01
❑ 138 Shane Conlan	.05	.01
❑ 139 Jim Everett	.10	.02
❑ 140 Henry Ellard	.10	.02
❑ 141 Jerome Bettis	.50	.20
❑ 142 Troy Drayton	.05	.01
❑ 143 Sean Gilbert	.05	.01
❑ 144 Chris Miller	.05	.01
❑ 145 Keith Byars	.05	.01
❑ 146 Marco Coleman	.05	.01
❑ 147 Bryan Cox	.05	.01
❑ 148 Irving Fryar	.10	.02
❑ 149 Mark Ingram	.05	.01
❑ 150 Keith Jackson	.05	.01
❑ 151 Terry Kirby	.25	.08
❑ 152 Dan Marino	1.50	.60
❑ 153 O.J.McDuffie	.25	.08
❑ 154 Scott Mitchell	.10	.02
❑ 155 Anthony Carter	.10	.02
❑ 156 Cris Carter	.40	.15
❑ 157 Chris Doleman	.05	.01
❑ 158 Steve Jordan	.05	.01
❑ 159 Qadry Ismail	.25	.08
❑ 160 Randall McDaniel	.05	.01
❑ 161 John Randle	.10	.02
❑ 162 Robert Smith	.25	.08
❑ 163 Henry Thomas	.05	.01
❑ 164 Terry Allen	.10	.02
❑ 165 Scottie Graham RC	.10	.02
❑ 166 Drew Bledsoe	.75	.30
❑ 167 Vincent Brown	.05	.01
❑ 168 Ben Coates	.10	.02
❑ 169 Leonard Russell	.05	.01
❑ 170 Andre Tippett	.05	.01
❑ 171 Vincent Brisby	.10	.02
❑ 172 Michael Timpson	.05	.01
❑ 173 Bruce Armstrong	.05	.01
❑ 174 Morten Andersen UER	.05	.01
❑ 175 Derek Brown RBK	.05	.01
❑ 176 Quinn Early	.10	.02
❑ 177 Rickey Jackson	.05	.01
❑ 178 Vaughan Johnson	.05	.01
❑ 179 Lorenzo Neal	.05	.01
❑ 180 Sam Mills	.05	.01
❑ 181 Irv Smith	.05	.01
❑ 182 Renaldo Turnbull	.05	.01
❑ 183 Wade Wilson	.05	.01
❑ 184 Willie Roaf	.05	.01
❑ 185 Michael Brooks	.05	.01
❑ 186 Mark Jackson	.05	.01
❑ 187 Rodney Hampton	.10	.02
❑ 188 Phil Simms	.10	.02
❑ 189 Dave Meggett	.05	.01
❑ 190 Mike Sherrard	.05	.01
❑ 191 Chris Calloway	.05	.01
❑ 192 Brad Baxter	.05	.01
❑ 193 Ronnie Lott	.10	.02
❑ 194 Boomer Esiason	.10	.02
❑ 195 Rob Moore	.10	.02
❑ 196 Johnny Johnson	.05	.01
❑ 197 Marvin Jones	.05	.01
❑ 198 Mo Lewis	.05	.01
❑ 199 Johnny Mitchell	.05	.01
❑ 200 Brian Washington	.05	.01
❑ 201 Eric Allen	.05	.01
❑ 202 Fred Barnett	.10	.02
❑ 203 Mark Bavaro	.05	.01
❑ 204 Randall Cunningham	.25	.08
❑ 205 Vaughn Hebron	.05	.01
❑ 206 Seth Joyner	.05	.01
❑ 207 Clyde Simmons	.05	.01
❑ 208 Herschel Walker	.10	.02
❑ 209 Calvin Williams	.10	.02
❑ 210 Neil O'Donnell	.25	.08
❑ 211 Eric Green	.05	.01
❑ 212 Leroy Thompson	.05	.01
❑ 213 Rod Woodson	.10	.02
❑ 214 Barry Foster	.05	.01
❑ 215 Jeff Graham	.05	.01
❑ 216 Kevin Greene	.10	.02
❑ 217 Deon Figures	.05	.01
❑ 218 Greg Lloyd	.10	.02
❑ 219 Marion Butts	.05	.01
❑ 220 Chris Mims	.05	.01
❑ 221 Eric Curry	.05	.01
❑ 222 Ronnie Harmon	.05	.01
❑ 223 Stan Humphries	.10	.02
❑ 224 Nate Lewis	.05	.01
❑ 225 Natrone Means	.25	.08
❑ 226 Anthony Miller	.10	.02
❑ 227 Leslie O'Neal	.05	.01
❑ 228 Junior Seau	.25	.08
❑ 229 Brent Jones	.10	.02
❑ 230 Tim McDonald	.05	.01
❑ 231 Tom Rathman	.05	.01

❑ 232 Jerry Rice	.75	.30
❑ 233 Dana Stubblefield	.10	.02
❑ 234 John Taylor	.10	.02
❑ 235 Ricky Watters	.10	.02
❑ 236 Steve Young	.60	.25
❑ 237 Amp Lee	.05	.01
❑ 238 Robert Blackmon	.05	.01
❑ 239 Brian Blades	.10	.02
❑ 240 Cortez Kennedy	.10	.02
❑ 241 Kelvin Martin	.05	.01
❑ 242 Rick Mirer	.25	.08
❑ 243 Eugene Robinson	.05	.01
❑ 244 Chris Warren	.10	.02
❑ 245 John L. Williams	.05	.01
❑ 246 Jon Vaughn	.05	.01
❑ 247 Reggie Cobb	.05	.01
❑ 248 Horace Copeland	.05	.01
❑ 249 Derrick Alexander WR RC	.25	.08
❑ 250 Santana Dotson	.10	.02
❑ 251 Craig Erickson	.05	.01
❑ 252 Courtney Hawkins	.05	.01
❑ 253 Hardy Nickerson	.10	.02
❑ 254 Vince Workman	.05	.01
❑ 255 Paul Gruber	.05	.01
❑ 256 Reggie Brooks	.10	.02
❑ 257 Tom Carter	.05	.01
❑ 258 Andre Collins	.05	.01
❑ 259 Darrell Green	.05	.01
❑ 260 Desmond Howard	.10	.02
❑ 261 Tim McGee	.05	.01
❑ 262 Brian Mitchell	.05	.01
❑ 263 Art Monk	.10	.02
❑ 264 John Friesz	.10	.02
❑ 265 Ricky Sanders	.05	.01
❑ 266 Checklist	.05	.01
❑ 267 Checklist	.05	.01
❑ 268 Checklist	.05	.01
❑ 269 Checklist	.05	.01
❑ 270 Checklist	.05	.01
❑ 271 Carolina Panthers	.15	.05
❑ 272 Jacksonville Jaguars	.15	.05
❑ 273 Dan Wilkinson RC	.10	.02
❑ 274 Marshall Faulk RC	5.00	2.00
❑ 275 Heath Shuler RC	.25	.08
❑ 276 Willie McGinest RC	.25	.08
❑ 277 Trev Alberts RC	.10	.02
❑ 278 Trent Dilfer RC	1.25	.50
❑ 279 Bryant Young RC	.25	.08
❑ 280 Sam Adams RC	.10	.02
❑ 281 Antonio Langham RC	.10	.02
❑ 282 Jamir Miller RC	.10	.02
❑ 283 John Thierry RC	.05	.01
❑ 284 Aaron Glenn RC	.25	.08
❑ 285 Joe Johnson RC	.05	.01
❑ 286 Bernard Williams RC	.05	.01
❑ 287 Wayne Gandy RC	.05	.01
❑ 288 Aaron Taylor RC	.05	.01
❑ 289 Charles Johnson RC	.25	.08
❑ 290 Dewayne Washington RC	.10	.02
❑ 291 Todd Steussie RC	.10	.02
❑ 292 Tim Bowens RC	.10	.02
❑ 293 Johnnie Morton RC	.50	.20
❑ 294 Rob Fredrickson RC	.10	.02
❑ 295 Shante Carver RC	.05	.01
❑ 296 Thomas Lewis RC	.10	.02
❑ 297 Greg Hill RC	.25	.08
❑ 298 Henry Ford RC	.05	.01
❑ 299 Jeff Burris RC	.10	.02
❑ 300 William Floyd RC	.25	.08
❑ NNO Carolina Panthers HOLO	20.00	7.50
❑ P1 Jim Kelly Promo	.75	.30

1995 SkyBox Impact

❑ COMPLETE SET (200)	15.00	6.00
❑ 1 Garrison Hearst	.25	.08
❑ 2 Ronald Moore	.05	.01
❑ 3 Eric Swann	.10	.02
❑ 4 Aeneas Williams	.05	.01

❑ 5 Jeff George	.10	.02
❑ 6 Craig Heyward	.10	.02
❑ 7 Terance Mathis	.10	.02
❑ 8 Andre Rison	.10	.02
❑ 9 Cornelius Bennett	.10	.02
❑ 10 Jim Kelly	.25	.08
❑ 11 Andre Reed	.10	.02
❑ 12 Bruce Smith	.25	.08
❑ 13 Thurman Thomas	.25	.08
❑ 14 Frank Reich	.05	.01
❑ 15 Lamar Lathon	.05	.01
❑ 16 Darion Conner	.05	.01
❑ 17 Randy Baldwin	.05	.01
❑ 18 Don Beebe	.05	.01
❑ 19 Mark Carrier DB	.05	.01
❑ 20 Jeff Graham	.05	.01
❑ 21 Raymont Harris	.05	.01
❑ 22 Alonzo Spellman	.05	.01
❑ 23 Lewis Tillman	.05	.01
❑ 24 Steve Walsh	.05	.01
❑ 25 Jeff Blake RC	.60	.25
❑ 26 Carl Pickens	.10	.02
❑ 27 Darnay Scott	.10	.02
❑ 28 Dan Wilkinson	.10	.02
❑ 29 Derrick Alexander WR	.25	.08
❑ 30 Leroy Hoard	.05	.01
❑ 31 Antonio Langham	.05	.01
❑ 32 Vinny Testaverde	.10	.02
❑ 33 Eric Turner	.05	.01
❑ 34 Troy Aikman	.75	.30
❑ 35 Charles Haley	.10	.02
❑ 36 Alvin Harper	.05	.01
❑ 37 Michael Irvin	.25	.08
❑ 38 Daryl Johnston	.10	.02
❑ 39 Jay Novacek	.10	.02
❑ 40 Leon Lett	.05	.01
❑ 41 Emmitt Smith	1.25	.50
❑ 42 John Elway	1.50	.60
❑ 43 Glyn Milburn	.05	.01
❑ 44 Anthony Miller	.10	.02
❑ 45 Leonard Russell	.05	.01
❑ 46 Shannon Sharpe	.10	.02
❑ 47 Scott Mitchell	.10	.02
❑ 48 Herman Moore	.25	.08
❑ 49 Barry Sanders	1.25	.50
❑ 50 Chris Spielman	.10	.02
❑ 51 Edgar Bennett	.10	.02
❑ 52 Robert Brooks	.25	.08
❑ 53 Brett Favre	1.50	.60
❑ 54 Bryce Paup	.10	.02
❑ 55 Sterling Sharpe	.10	.02
❑ 56 Reggie White	.25	.08
❑ 57 Ray Childress	.05	.01
❑ 58 Haywood Jeffires	.05	.01
❑ 59 Webster Slaughter	.05	.01
❑ 60 Lorenzo White	.05	.01
❑ 61 Trev Alberts	.05	.01
❑ 62 Quentin Coryatt	.10	.02
❑ 63 Sean Dawkins	.10	.02
❑ 64 Marshall Faulk	1.00	.40
❑ 65 Jeff Lageman	.05	.01
❑ 66 Steve Beuerlein	.10	.02
❑ 67 Desmond Howard	.10	.02
❑ 68 Kelvin Martin	.05	.01
❑ 69 Reggie Cobb	.05	.01
❑ 70 Marcus Allen	.25	.08
❑ 71 Greg Hill	.10	.02
❑ 72 Joe Montana	1.50	.60
❑ 73 Neil Smith	.10	.02
❑ 74 Derrick Thomas	.25	.08
❑ 75 Tim Brown	.25	.08
❑ 76 Rocket Ismail	.10	.02
❑ 77 Jeff Hostetler	.10	.02
❑ 78 Chester McGlockton	.10	.02
❑ 79 Harvey Williams	.05	.01
❑ 80 Tim Bowens	.05	.01
❑ 81 Irving Fryar	.10	.02
❑ 82 Keith Jackson	.05	.01
❑ 83 Terry Kirby	.10	.02
❑ 84 Dan Marino	1.50	.60
❑ 85 O.J. McDuffie	.25	.08
❑ 86 Bernie Parmalee	.10	.02
❑ 87 Terry Allen	.10	.02
❑ 88 Cris Carter	.25	.08
❑ 89 Qadry Ismail	.10	.02
❑ 90 Warren Moon	.10	.02
❑ 91 Jake Reed	.10	.02
❑ 92 Drew Bledsoe	.50	.20
❑ 93 Vincent Brisby	.05	.01
❑ 94 Ben Coates	.10	.02
❑ 95 Michael Timpson	.05	.01
❑ 96 Jim Everett	.05	.01
❑ 97 Michael Haynes	.10	.02
❑ 98 Willie Roaf	.05	.01
❑ 99 Michael Brooks	.05	.01
❑ 100 Dave Brown	.10	.02
❑ 101 Rodney Hampton	.10	.02
❑ 102 Thomas Lewis	.10	.02
❑ 103 Dave Meggett	.05	.01
❑ 104 Boomer Esiason	.10	.02
❑ 105 Johnny Johnson	.05	.01
❑ 106 Johnny Mitchell	.05	.01
❑ 107 Rob Moore	.10	.02
❑ 108 Fred Barnett	.10	.02
❑ 109 Randall Cunningham	.25	.08
❑ 110 Charlie Garner	.25	.08
❑ 111 Herschel Walker	.10	.02
❑ 112 Barry Foster	.10	.02
❑ 113 Eric Green	.05	.01
❑ 114 Charles Johnson	.10	.02
❑ 115 Greg Lloyd	.10	.02
❑ 116 Byron Bam Morris	.05	.01
❑ 117 Neil O'Donnell	.10	.02
❑ 118 Rod Woodson	.10	.02
❑ 119 Flipper Anderson	.05	.01
❑ 120 Jerome Bettis	.25	.08
❑ 121 Troy Drayton	.05	.01
❑ 122 Sean Gilbert	.10	.02
❑ 123 Ronnie Harmon	.05	.01
❑ 124 Stan Humphries	.10	.02
❑ 125 Shawn Jefferson	.05	.01
❑ 126 Natrone Means	.10	.02
❑ 127 Leslie O'Neal	.10	.02
❑ 128 Junior Seau	.25	.08
❑ 129 William Floyd	.10	.02
❑ 130 Brent Jones	.05	.01
❑ 131 Jerry Rice	.75	.30
❑ 132 Deion Sanders	.50	.20
❑ 133 Dana Stubblefield	.10	.02
❑ 134 Ricky Watters	.10	.02
❑ 135 Bryant Young	.10	.02
❑ 136 Steve Young	.60	.25
❑ 137 Brian Blades	.10	.02
❑ 138 Cortez Kennedy	.10	.02
❑ 139 Rick Mirer	.10	.02
❑ 140 Chris Warren	.10	.02
❑ 141 Horace Copeland	.05	.01
❑ 142 Trent Dilfer	.25	.08
❑ 143 Hardy Nickerson	.05	.01
❑ 144 Errict Rhett	.10	.02

❑ 145 Henry Ellard	.10	.02
❑ 146 Brian Mitchell	.05	.01
❑ 147 Heath Shuler	.10	.02
❑ 148 Tydus Winans	.05	.01
❑ 149 Steve Tasker	.10	.02
❑ 150 Jeff Burris	.05	.01
❑ 151 Tyrone Hughes	.10	.02
❑ 152 Mel Gray	.05	.01
❑ 153 Kevin Williams WR	.10	.02
❑ 154 Andre Coleman	.05	.01
❑ 155 Corey Sawyer	.05	.01
❑ 156 Darrien Gordon	.05	.01
❑ 157 Aaron Glenn	.05	.01
❑ 158 Eric Metcalf	.10	.02
❑ 159 Errict Rhett SS	.10	.02
❑ 160 Marshall Faulk SS	.40	.15
❑ 161 Darnay Scott SS	.10	.02
❑ 162 William Floyd SS	.05	.01
❑ 163 Charlie Garner SS	.10	.02
❑ 164 Heath Shuler SS	.10	.02
❑ 165 Trent Dilfer SS	.25	.08
❑ 166 Willie McGinest SS	.10	.02
❑ 167 Byron Bam Morris SS	.05	.01
❑ 168 Mario Bates SS	.10	.02
❑ 169 Ki-Jana Carter RC	.25	.08
❑ 170 Tony Boselli RC	.25	.08
❑ 171 Steve McNair RC	2.50	1.00
❑ 172 Michael Westbrook RC	.25	.08
❑ 173 Kerry Collins RC	1.25	.50
❑ 174 Kevin Carter RC	.25	.08
❑ 175 Mike Mamula RC	.05	.01
❑ 176 Joey Galloway RC	1.25	.50
❑ 177 Kyle Brady RC	.25	.08
❑ 178 J.J. Stokes RC	.25	.08
❑ 179 Warren Sapp RC	1.25	.50
❑ 180 Rob Johnson RC	.75	.30
❑ 181 Tyrone Wheatley RC	1.00	.40
❑ 182 Napoleon Kaufman RC	1.00	.40
❑ 183 James O. Stewart RC	1.00	.40
❑ 184 Dino Philyaw RC	.05	.01
❑ 185 Rashaan Salaam RC	.10	.02
❑ 186 Tyrone Poole RC	.25	.08
❑ 187 Ty Law RC	1.25	.50
❑ 188 Joe Aska RC	.05	.01
❑ 189 Mark Bruener RC	.10	.02
❑ 190 Derrick Brooks RC	1.25	.50
❑ 191 Jack Jackson RC	.05	.01
❑ 192 Ray Zellars RC	.10	.02
❑ 193 Eddie Goines RC	.05	.01
❑ 194 Chris Sanders RC	.10	.02
❑ 195 Charlie Simmons RC	.05	.01
❑ 196 Lee DeRamus RC	.05	.01
❑ 197 Frank Sanders RC	.25	.08
❑ 198 Rodney Thomas RC	.10	.02
❑ 199 Checklist A 1-128	.05	.01
❑ 200 Checklist B 129-200	.05	.01
❑ M1 Brett Favre SkyMotion	30.00	15.00
❑ M2 Brett Favre SkyMotion	30.00	15.00
❑ P1 Promo Sheet	2.50	1.00

1996 SkyBox Impact

❑ COMPLETE SET (200)	15.00	6.00
❑ 1 Garrison Hearst	.20	.07
❑ 2 Rob Moore	.20	.07
❑ 3 Frank Sanders	.20	.07
❑ 4 Eric Swann	.10	.02
❑ 5 Aeneas Williams	.10	.02
❑ 6 Bert Emanuel	.20	.07
❑ 7 Jeff George	.20	.07
❑ 8 Craig Heyward	.10	.02
❑ 9 Terance Mathis	.10	.02
❑ 10 Eric Metcalf	.10	.02
❑ 11 Leroy Hoard	.10	.02
❑ 12 Michael Jackson	.20	.07
❑ 13 Andre Rison	.20	.07
❑ 14 Vinny Testaverde	.20	.07
❑ 15 Eric Turner	.10	.02
❑ 16 Darick Holmes	.10	.02
❑ 17 Jim Kelly	.30	.10
❑ 18 Bryce Paup	.10	.02
❑ 19 Bruce Smith	.20	.07
❑ 20 Thurman Thomas	.30	.10
❑ 21 Mark Carrier WR	.10	.02
❑ 22 Kerry Collins	.30	.10
❑ 23 Derrick Moore	.10	.02
❑ 24 Tyrone Poole	.10	.02
❑ 25 Curtis Conway	.30	.10
❑ 26 Jeff Graham	.10	.02
❑ 27 Erik Kramer	.10	.02
❑ 28 Rashaan Salaam	.20	.07
❑ 29 Jeff Blake	.30	.10
❑ 30 Ki-Jana Carter	.20	.07
❑ 31 Carl Pickens	.20	.07
❑ 32 Darnay Scott	.20	.07
❑ 33 Troy Aikman	.75	.30
❑ 34 Charles Haley	.20	.07
❑ 35 Michael Irvin	.30	.10
❑ 36 Daryl Johnston	.20	.07
❑ 37 Jay Novacek	.10	.02
❑ 38 Deion Sanders	.40	.15
❑ 39 Emmitt Smith	1.25	.50
❑ 40 Steve Atwater	.10	.02
❑ 41 Terrell Davis	.60	.25
❑ 42 John Elway	1.50	.60
❑ 43 Anthony Miller	.20	.07
❑ 44 Shannon Sharpe	.20	.07
❑ 45 Scott Mitchell	.20	.07
❑ 46 Herman Moore	.20	.07
❑ 47 Brett Perriman	.10	.02
❑ 48 Barry Sanders	1.25	.50
❑ 49 Edgar Bennett	.20	.07
❑ 50 Robert Brooks	.30	.10
❑ 51 Mark Chmura	.20	.07
❑ 52 Brett Favre	1.50	.60
❑ 53 Reggie White	.30	.10
❑ 54 Mel Gray	.10	.02
❑ 55 Steve McNair	.60	.25
❑ 56 Chris Sanders	.20	.07
❑ 57 Rodney Thomas	.10	.02
❑ 58 Quentin Coryatt	.10	.02
❑ 59 Sean Dawkins	.10	.02
❑ 60 Ken Dilger	.20	.07
❑ 61 Marshall Faulk	.40	.15
❑ 62 Jim Harbaugh	.20	.07
❑ 63 Tony Boselli	.10	.02
❑ 64 Mark Brunell	.50	.20
❑ 65 Keenan McCardell	.30	.10
❑ 66 James O.Stewart	.20	.07
❑ 67 Marcus Allen	.30	.10
❑ 68 Steve Bono	.10	.02
❑ 69 Neil Smith	.20	.07
❑ 70 Derrick Thomas	.30	.10
❑ 71 Tamarick Vanover	.20	.07
❑ 72 Bryan Cox	.10	.02
❑ 73 Irving Fryar	.20	.07
❑ 74 Eric Green	.10	.02
❑ 75 Dan Marino	1.50	.60
❑ 76 O.J. McDuffie	.20	.07
❑ 77 Bernie Parmalee	.10	.02
❑ 78 Cris Carter	.30	.10
❑ 79 Qadry Ismail	.20	.07
❑ 80 Warren Moon	.20	.07
❑ 81 Jake Reed	.20	.07
❑ 82 Robert Smith	.20	.07
❑ 83 Drew Bledsoe	.50	.20
❑ 84 Ben Coates	.20	.07
❑ 85 Curtis Martin	.60	.25
❑ 86 Willie McGinest	.10	.02
❑ 87 Dave Meggett	.10	.02
❑ 88 Mario Bates	.20	.07
❑ 89 Quinn Early	.10	.02
❑ 90 Jim Everett	.10	.02
❑ 91 Michael Haynes	.10	.02
❑ 92 Renaldo Turnbull	.10	.02
❑ 93 Dave Brown	.10	.02
❑ 94 Rodney Hampton	.20	.07
❑ 95 Thomas Lewis	.10	.02
❑ 96 Phillippi Sparks	.10	.02
❑ 97 Tyrone Wheatley	.20	.07
❑ 98 Kyle Brady	.10	.02
❑ 99 Hugh Douglas	.20	.07
❑ 100 Mo Lewis	.10	.02
❑ 101 Adrian Murrell	.20	.07
❑ 102 Tim Brown	.30	.10
❑ 103 Jeff Hostetler	.10	.02
❑ 104 Rocket Ismail	.10	.02
❑ 105 Chester McGlockton	.10	.02
❑ 106 Harvey Williams	.10	.02
❑ 107 Fred Barnett	.10	.02
❑ 108 William Fuller	.10	.02
❑ 109 Charlie Garner	.20	.07
❑ 110 Rodney Peete	.10	.02
❑ 111 Ricky Watters	.20	.07
❑ 112 Calvin Williams	.10	.02
❑ 113 Byron Bam Morris	.10	.02
❑ 114 Neil O'Donnell	.20	.07
❑ 115 Erric Pegram	.10	.02
❑ 116 Kordell Stewart	.30	.10
❑ 117 Yancey Thigpen	.20	.07
❑ 118 Rod Woodson	.20	.07
❑ 119 Jerome Bettis	.30	.10
❑ 120 Isaac Bruce	.30	.10
❑ 121 Troy Drayton	.10	.02
❑ 122 Leslie O'Neal	.10	.02
❑ 123 Aaron Hayden RC	.10	.02
❑ 124 Stan Humphries	.20	.07
❑ 125 Natrone Means	.20	.07
❑ 126 Junior Seau	.30	.10
❑ 127 William Floyd	.20	.07
❑ 128 Brent Jones	.10	.02
❑ 129 Derek Loville	.10	.02
❑ 130 Ken Norton	.10	.02
❑ 131 Jerry Rice	.75	.30
❑ 132 J.J. Stokes	.30	.10
❑ 133 Steve Young	.60	.25
❑ 134 Brian Blades	.10	.02
❑ 135 Joey Galloway	.30	.10
❑ 136 Cortez Kennedy	.10	.02
❑ 137 Rick Mirer	.20	.07
❑ 138 Chris Warren	.20	.07
❑ 139 Trent Dilfer	.30	.10
❑ 140 Alvin Harper	.10	.02
❑ 141 Jackie Harris	.10	.02
❑ 142 Hardy Nickerson	.10	.02
❑ 143 Errict Rhett	.20	.07
❑ 144 Terry Allen	.20	.07
❑ 145 Henry Ellard	.10	.02
❑ 146 Brian Mitchell	.10	.02
❑ 147 Heath Shuler	.20	.07
❑ 148 Michael Westbrook	.30	.10
❑ 149 Karim Abdul-Jabbar RC	.30	.10
❑ 150 Mike Alstott RC	1.00	.40
❑ 151 Marco Battaglia RC	.10	.02
❑ 152 Tim Biakabutuka RC	.30	.10
❑ 153 Sean Boyd RC	.20	.07
❑ 154 Tony Brackens RC	.30	.10
❑ 155 Duane Clemons RC	.10	.02

❑ 156 Marcus Coleman RC	.10	.02
❑ 157 Chris Darkins RC	.10	.02
❑ 158 Rickey Dudley RC	.30	.10
❑ 159 Jason Dunn RC	.20	.07
❑ 160 Bobby Engram RC	.30	.10
❑ 161 Daryl Gardener RC	.10	.02
❑ 162 Eddie George RC	1.25	.50
❑ 163 Terry Glenn RC	1.00	.40
❑ 164 Kevin Hardy RC	.30	.10
❑ 165 Marvin Harrison RC	2.50	1.00
❑ 166 Dietrich Jells RC	.10	.02
❑ 167 DeRon Jenkins RC	.20	.07
❑ 168 Darrius Johnson RC	.10	.02
❑ 169 Keyshawn Johnson RC	1.00	.40
❑ 170 Lance Johnstone RC	.20	.07
❑ 171 Cedric Jones RC	.10	.02
❑ 172 Marcus Jones RC	.10	.02
❑ 173 Danny Kanell RC	.30	.10
❑ 174 Eddie Kennison RC	.30	.10
❑ 175 Jevon Langford RC	.10	.02
❑ 176 Markco Maddox RC	.20	.07
❑ 177 Derrick Mayes RC	.30	.10
❑ 178 Leeland McElroy RC	.20	.07
❑ 179 Dell McGee RC	.10	.02
❑ 180 Johnny McWilliams RC	.20	.07
❑ 181 Alex Molden RC	.10	.02
❑ 182 Eric Moulds RC	1.25	.50
❑ 183 Jonathan Ogden RC	.30	.10
❑ 184 Lawrence Phillips RC	.30	.10
❑ 185 Simeon Rice RC	.75	.30
❑ 186 Amani Toomer RC	1.00	.40
❑ 187 Regan Upshaw RC	.10	.02
❑ 188 Jerome Woods RC	.10	.02
❑ 189 Darrell Green I	.10	.02
❑ 190 Daryl Johnston I	.20	.07
❑ 191 Sam Mills I	.10	.02
❑ 192 Earnest Byner I	.10	.02
❑ 193 Herschel Walker I	.20	.07
❑ 194 Brett Favre Highlights	.30	.10
❑ 195 Brett Favre Highlights	.30	.10
❑ 196 Brett Favre Highlights	.30	.10
❑ 197 Brett Favre Highlights	.30	.10
❑ 198 Brett Favre Highlights	.30	.10
❑ 199 Checklist	.10	.02
❑ 200 Checklist	.10	.02
❑ BF1 Brett Favre SkyMotion	12.00	5.00
❑ BF1X Favre SkyMotion EXCH	1.00	.40
❑ BF2 Brett Favre SkyMint	30.00	12.50
❑ BF2X Favre SkyMint EXCH	1.00	.40
❑ P1 Promo Sheet	2.00	.75

1996 SkyBox Impact Rookies

❑ COMPLETE SET (150)	12.00	5.00
❑ 1 Leeland McElroy RC	.10	.02
❑ 2 Johnny McWilliams	.05	.01
❑ 3 Simeon Rice RC	.50	.20
❑ 4 DeRon Jenkins	.05	.01
❑ 5 Jermaine Lewis RC	.20	.07
❑ 6 Ray Lewis RC	2.00	.75
❑ 7 Jonathan Ogden	.20	.07
❑ 8 Eric Moulds RC UER 123	1.00	.40
❑ 9 Tim Biakabutuka RC	.20	.07
❑ 10 Muhsin Muhammad RC	.60	.25
❑ 11 Winslow Oliver	.05	.01
❑ 12 Bobby Engram RC	.20	.07
❑ 13 Walt Harris	.05	.01
❑ 14 Willie Anderson	.05	.01
❑ 15 Marco Battaglia	.05	.01
❑ 16 Jevon Langford	.05	.01
❑ 17 Kavika Pittman RC	.05	.01
❑ 18 Stepfret Williams	.05	.01
❑ 19 Tory James RC	.10	.02
❑ 20 Jeff Lewis RC	.10	.02
❑ 21 John Mobley	.05	.01
❑ 22 Detron Smith	.05	.01
❑ 23 Derrick Mayes RC	.20	.07
❑ 24 Eddie George RC	1.00	.40
❑ 25 Marvin Harrison RC	2.00	.75
❑ 26 Dedric Mathis	.05	.01
❑ 27 Tony Brackens RC	.20	.07
❑ 28 Kevin Hardy RC	.20	.07
❑ 29 Jerome Woods	.05	.01
❑ 30 Karim Abdul-Jabbar RC	.20	.07
❑ 31 Daryl Gardener	.05	.01
❑ 32 Jerris McPhail	.05	.01
❑ 33 Stanley Pritchett	.05	.01
❑ 34 Zach Thomas RC	.50	.20
❑ 35 Duane Clemons	.05	.01
❑ 36 Moe Williams RB RC	.50	.20
❑ 37 Tedy Bruschi RC	4.00	1.50
❑ 38 Terry Glenn RC	.75	.30
❑ 39 Alex Molden	.05	.01
❑ 40 Ricky Whittle	.05	.01
❑ 41 Cedric Jones	.05	.01
❑ 42 Danny Kanell RC	.20	.07
❑ 43 Amani Toomer RC	.75	.30
❑ 44 Marcus Coleman	.05	.01
❑ 45 Keyshawn Johnson RC	.75	.30
❑ 46 Ray Mickens	.05	.01
❑ 47 Alex Van Dyke RC	.10	.02
❑ 48 Rickey Dudley RC	.20	.07
❑ 49 Lance Johnstone	.10	.02
❑ 50 Brian Dawkins RC	1.00	.40
❑ 51 Jason Dunn	.05	.01
❑ 52 Ray Farmer	.05	.01
❑ 53 Bobby Hoying RC	.20	.07
❑ 54 Jermane Mayberry	.05	.01
❑ 55 Bryan Still RC	.10	.02
❑ 56 Tony Banks RC	.20	.07
❑ 57 Ernie Conwell	.05	.01
❑ 58 Eddie Kennison RC	.20	.07
❑ 59 Jerald Moore RC	.10	.02
❑ 60 Lawrence Phillips RC	.20	.07
❑ 61 Israel Ifeanyi	.05	.01
❑ 62 Terrell Owens RC	2.00	.75
❑ 63 Iheanyi Uwaezuoke RC	.20	.07
❑ 64 Mike Alstott RC	.75	.30
❑ 65 Marcus Jones	.05	.01
❑ 66 Nilo Silvan	.05	.01
❑ 67 Regan Upshaw	.05	.01
❑ 68 Stephen Davis RC	1.25	.50
❑ 69 Troy Aikman AIR	.50	.20
❑ 70 Terry Allen AIR	.10	.02
❑ 71 Edgar Bennett AIR	.10	.02
❑ 72 Jerome Bettis AIR	.10	.02
❑ 73 Drew Bledsoe AIR	.40	.15
❑ 74 Tim Brown AIR	.20	.07
❑ 75 Mark Brunell AIR	.40	.15
❑ 76 Cris Carter AIR	.20	.07
❑ 77 Kerry Collins AIR	.20	.07
❑ 78 Terrell Davis AIR	.40	.15
❑ 79 John Elway AIR	1.00	.40
❑ 80 Marshall Faulk AIR	.20	.07
❑ 81 Brett Favre AIR	1.00	.40
❑ 82 Joey Galloway AIR	.20	.07
❑ 83 Rodney Hampton AIR	.05	.01
❑ 84 Jim Harbaugh AIR	.10	.02
❑ 85 Michael Irvin AIR	.10	.02
❑ 86 Chris T. Jones AIR	.20	.07
❑ 87 Napoleon Kaufman AIR	.20	.07
❑ 88 Jim Kelly AIR	.20	.07
❑ 89 Dan Marino AIR	1.00	.40
❑ 90 Curtis Martin AIR	.40	.15
❑ 91 Terance Mathis AIR	.05	.01
❑ 92 Steve McNair AIR	.50	.15
❑ 93 Anthony Miller AIR	.10	.02
❑ 94 Scott Mitchell AIR	.05	.01
❑ 95 Herman Moore AIR	.10	.02
❑ 96 Brett Perriman AIR	.05	.01
❑ 97 Carl Pickens AIR	.10	.02
❑ 98 Jerry Rice AIR	.50	.20
❑ 99 Andre Rison AIR	.10	.02
❑ 100 Rashaan Salaam AIR	.10	.02
❑ 101 Barry Sanders AIR	.75	.30
❑ 102 Chris Sanders AIR	.10	.02
❑ 103 Deion Sanders AIR	.20	.07
❑ 104 Frank Sanders AIR	.10	.02
❑ 105 Bruce Smith AIR	.10	.02
❑ 106 Emmitt Smith AIR	.75	.30
❑ 107 Robert Smith AIR	.10	.02
❑ 108 Kordell Stewart AIR	.20	.07
❑ 109 J.J. Stokes AIR	.20	.07
❑ 110 Yancey Thigpen AIR	.10	.02
❑ 111 Thurman Thomas AIR	.10	.02
❑ 112 Eric Turner AIR	.05	.01
❑ 113 Tamarick Vanover AIR	.10	.02
❑ 114 Chris Warren AIR	.10	.02
❑ 115 Ricky Watters AIR	.10	.02
❑ 116 Michael Westbrook AIR	.20	.07
❑ 117 Reggie White AIR	.20	.07
❑ 118 Steve Young AIR	.40	.15
❑ 119 Jeff Blake AIR	.10	.02
❑ 120 Robert Brooks AIR	.10	.02
❑ 121 Isaac Bruce RS	.20	.07
❑ 122 Mark Chmura RS	.10	.02
❑ 123 Wayne Chrebet RS	.30	.10
❑ 124 Ben Coates RS	.10	.02
❑ 125 Ken Dilger RS	.10	.02
❑ 126 Bert Emanuel RS	.10	.02
❑ 127 Gus Frerotte RS	.10	.02
❑ 128 Kevin Greene RS	.10	.02
❑ 129 Erik Kramer RS	.05	.01
❑ 130 Greg Lloyd RS	.10	.02
❑ 131 Tony Martin RS	.05	.01
❑ 132 Brian Mitchell RS	.05	.01
❑ 133 Bryce Paup RS	.05	.01
❑ 134 Jake Reed RS	.10	.02
❑ 135 Errict Rhett RS	.10	.02
❑ 136 Yancey Thigpen RS	.10	.02
❑ 137 Tamarick Vanover RS	.10	.02
❑ 138 Chris Warren RS	.10	.02
❑ 139 Marcus Allen RS	.20	.07
❑ 140 Jerome Bettis RS	.20	.07
❑ 141 Tim Brown RRH	.20	.07
❑ 142 Mark Carrier RRH	.05	.01
❑ 143 Marshall Faulk RRH	.20	.07
❑ 144 Tyrone Hughes RRH	.05	.01
❑ 145 Dan Marino RRH	1.00	.40
❑ 146 Curtis Martin RRH	.40	.15
❑ 147 Barry Sanders RRH	.75	.30
❑ 148 Orlando Thomas RRH	.05	.01
❑ 149 Checklist (1-107) UER	.05	.01
❑ 150 Checklist (108-150/inserts)	.05	.01
❑ NNO Draft Exchange Card	1.00	.40

1997 SkyBox Impact

❑ COMPLETE SET (250)	15.00	6.00
❑ 1 Carl Pickens	.30	.10
❑ 2 Ray Lewis	.75	.30
❑ 3 Darrell Green	.30	.10
❑ 4 Brett Favre	2.00	.75
❑ 5 Todd Collins	.20	.07
❑ 6 Errict Rhett	.20	.07
❑ 7 John Elway	2.00	.75
❑ 8 Troy Aikman	1.00	.40
❑ 9 Steve McNair	.60	.25
❑ 10 Kordell Stewart	.50	.20

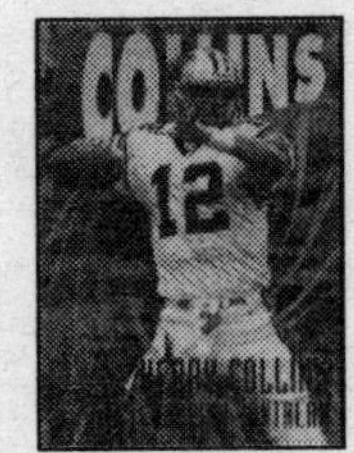

❑ 11 Drew Bledsoe .60 .25
❑ 12 Kerry Collins .50 .20
❑ 13 Dan Marino 2.00 .75
❑ 14 Ricky Watters .30 .10
❑ 15 Marvin Harrison .50 .20
❑ 16 Simeon Rice .30 .10
❑ 17 Qadry Ismail .30 .10
❑ 18 Andre Coleman .20 .07
❑ 19 Keyshawn Johnson .50 .20
❑ 20 Barry Sanders 1.50 .60
❑ 21 Rickey Dudley .30 .10
❑ 22 Emmitt Smith 1.50 .60
❑ 23 Erik Kramer .20 .07
❑ 24 Tony Boselli .20 .07
❑ 25 Steve Young .60 .25
❑ 26 Rod Woodson .30 .10
❑ 27 Eddie George .50 .20
❑ 28 Curtis Martin .60 .25
❑ 29 Amani Toomer .30 .10
❑ 30 Terrell Davis .60 .25
❑ 31 Jim Everett .20 .07
❑ 32 Marcus Allen .50 .20
❑ 33 Karim Abdul-Jabbar .50 .20
❑ 34 Thurman Thomas .50 .20
❑ 35 Cortez Kennedy .20 .07
❑ 36 Jerome Bettis .50 .20
❑ 37 Kevin Carter .20 .07
❑ 38 Gilbert Brown .30 .10
❑ 39 Bert Emanuel .30 .10
❑ 40 Kyle Brady .20 .07
❑ 41 Trent Dilfer .50 .20
❑ 42 Garrison Hearst .30 .10
❑ 43 Kevin Greene .30 .10
❑ 44 Bryan Cox .20 .07
❑ 45 Desmond Howard .30 .10
❑ 46 Larry Centers .30 .10
❑ 47 Quentin Coryatt .20 .07
❑ 48 Michael Jackson .30 .10
❑ 49 John Randle .30 .10
❑ 50 Mark Brunell .60 .25
❑ 51 William Thomas .20 .07
❑ 52 Glyn Milburn .20 .07
❑ 53 Mike Alstott .50 .20
❑ 54 Chris Spielman .20 .07
❑ 55 Junior Seau .50 .20
❑ 56 Brian Blades .20 .07
❑ 57 Lamar Lathon .20 .07
❑ 58 Derrick Thomas .50 .20
❑ 59 Dave Brown .20 .07
❑ 60 Frank Wycheck .20 .07
❑ 61 Chris Slade .20 .07
❑ 62 Neil Smith .30 .10
❑ 63 Ashley Ambrose .20 .07
❑ 64 Alex Molden .20 .07
❑ 65 Edgar Bennett .30 .10
❑ 66 Alvin Harper .20 .07
❑ 67 Jamal Anderson .50 .20
❑ 68 Eddie Kennison .30 .10
❑ 69 Ken Norton .20 .07
❑ 70 Zach Thomas .50 .20
❑ 71 Leeland McElroy .20 .07
❑ 72 Terry Allen .50 .20
❑ 73 Raymont Harris .20 .07
❑ 74 Ken Dilger .20 .07
❑ 75 Jason Dunn .20 .07
❑ 76 Robert Smith .30 .10
❑ 77 William Roaf .20 .07
❑ 78 Bruce Smith .30 .10
❑ 79 Vinny Testaverde .30 .10
❑ 80 Jerry Rice 1.00 .40
❑ 81 Tim Brown .50 .20
❑ 82 James O.Stewart .30 .10
❑ 83 Andre Reed .30 .10
❑ 84 Herman Moore .30 .10
❑ 85 Stan Humphries .30 .10
❑ 86 Chris Warren .30 .10
❑ 87 Tyrone Wheatley .30 .10
❑ 88 Michael Irvin .50 .20
❑ 89 Dan Wilkinson .20 .07
❑ 90 Tony Banks .30 .10
❑ 91 Chester McGlockton .20 .07
❑ 92 Reggie White .50 .20
❑ 93 Elvis Grbac .30 .10
❑ 94 Willie Davis .20 .07
❑ 95 Greg Lloyd .20 .07
❑ 96 Ben Coates .30 .10
❑ 97 Rashaan Salaam .20 .07
❑ 98 Eric Swann .20 .07
❑ 99 Hugh Douglas .20 .07
❑ 100 Henry Ellard .20 .07
❑ 101 Rod Smith WR .50 .20
❑ 102 Tim Biakabutuka .30 .10
❑ 103 Chad Brown .20 .07
❑ 104 Kevin Hardy .20 .07
❑ 105 Chris T. Jones .20 .07
❑ 106 Antonio Freeman .50 .20
❑ 107 Lamont Warren .20 .07
❑ 108 Derrick Alexander DE .20 .07
❑ 109 Brett Perriman .20 .07
❑ 110 Antonio Langham .20 .07
❑ 111 Eric Moulds .50 .20
❑ 112 O.J. McDuffie .30 .10
❑ 113 Eric Metcalf .30 .10
❑ 114 Ray Zellars .20 .07
❑ 115 Marco Coleman .20 .07
❑ 116 Terry Kirby .30 .10
❑ 117 Darren Woodson .20 .07
❑ 118 Charles Johnson .30 .10
❑ 119 Sam Mills .20 .07
❑ 120 Rodney Hampton .30 .10
❑ 121 Rick Mirer .20 .07
❑ 122 Derrick Brooks .50 .20
❑ 123 Greg Hill .20 .07
❑ 124 John Mobley .20 .07
❑ 125 Chris Sanders .20 .07
❑ 126 Kent Graham .20 .07
❑ 127 Michael Westbrook .30 .10
❑ 128 Harvey Williams .20 .07
❑ 129 Keenan McCardell .30 .10
❑ 130 Neil O'Donnell .30 .10
❑ 131 LeRoy Butler .20 .07
❑ 132 Willie McGinest .20 .07
❑ 133 Ki-Jana Carter .20 .07
❑ 134 Robert Jones .20 .07
❑ 135 Jim Harbaugh .30 .10
❑ 136 Wesley Walls .30 .10
❑ 137 Jackie Harris .20 .07
❑ 138 Jermaine Lewis .50 .20
❑ 139 Jake Reed .30 .10
❑ 140 John Friesz .20 .07
❑ 141 Jerris McPhail .20 .07
❑ 142 Charlie Garner .30 .10
❑ 143 Bryce Paup .20 .07
❑ 144 Tony Martin .30 .10
❑ 145 Shannon Sharpe .30 .10
❑ 146 Terrell Owens .60 .25
❑ 147 Curtis Conway .30 .10
❑ 148 Jamie Asher .20 .07
❑ 149 Lawrence Phillips .20 .07
❑ 150 Deion Sanders .50 .20
❑ 151 Frank Sanders .30 .10
❑ 152 Joey Galloway .30 .10
❑ 153 Mel Gray .20 .07
❑ 154 Robert Brooks .30 .10
❑ 155 Jeff George .30 .10
❑ 156 Michael Haynes .20 .07
❑ 157 Chris Chandler .30 .10
❑ 158 Adrian Murrell .30 .10
❑ 159 Tamarick Vanover .30 .10
❑ 160 Marshall Faulk .60 .25
❑ 161 Thomas Lewis .20 .07
❑ 162 Ty Detmer .30 .10
❑ 163 Darnay Scott .30 .10
❑ 164 Byron Bam Morris .20 .07
❑ 165 Scott Mitchell .30 .10
❑ 166 Brad Johnson .50 .20
❑ 167 Dave Meggett .20 .07
❑ 168 Bobby Engram .30 .10
❑ 169 Natrone Means .30 .10
❑ 170 Erric Pegram .20 .07
❑ 171 Leonard Russell .20 .07
❑ 172 Muhsin Muhammad .30 .10
❑ 173 Aeneas Williams .20 .07
❑ 174 Fred Barnett .20 .07
❑ 175 William Floyd .30 .10
❑ 176 Kimble Anders .30 .10
❑ 177 Darick Holmes .20 .07
❑ 178 Willie Green .20 .07
❑ 179 Rodney Thomas .20 .07
❑ 180 Derrick Alexander WR .30 .10
❑ 181 Sean Dawkins .20 .07
❑ 182 Dorsey Levens .50 .20
❑ 183 Napoleon Kaufman .50 .20
❑ 184 Mario Bates .20 .07
❑ 185 Yancey Thigpen .30 .10
❑ 186 Johnnie Morton .30 .10
❑ 187 Gus Frerotte .20 .07
❑ 188 Terance Mathis .30 .10
❑ 189 Tyrone Hughes .20 .07
❑ 190 Wayne Chrebet .50 .20
❑ 191 Tony Brackens .20 .07
❑ 192 Hardy Nickerson .20 .07
❑ 193 Daryl Johnston .30 .10
❑ 194 Irving Fryar .30 .10
❑ 195 Jeff Blake .30 .10
❑ 196 Charles Way .30 .10
❑ 197 Brian Mitchell .20 .07
❑ 198 Brent Jones .30 .10
❑ 199 Mark Chmura .30 .10
❑ 200 Terry Glenn .50 .20
❑ 201 Cris Carter .50 .20
❑ 202 Steve Atwater .20 .07
❑ 203 Rob Moore .30 .10
❑ 204 Anthony Johnson .20 .07
❑ 205 Warren Moon .50 .20
❑ 206 Darrien Gordon .20 .07
❑ 207 Isaac Bruce .50 .20
❑ 208 Reidel Anthony RC .50 .20
❑ 209 Darnell Autry RC .30 .10
❑ 210 Tiki Barber RC 3.00 1.25
❑ 211 Pat Barnes RC .50 .20
❑ 212 Terry Battle RC .20 .07
❑ 213 Michael Booker RC .20 .07
❑ 214 Peter Boulware RC .50 .20
❑ 215 Chris Canty RC .20 .07
❑ 216 Rae Carruth RC .20 .07
❑ 217 Troy Davis RC .30 .10
❑ 218 Corey Dillon RC 3.00 1.25
❑ 219 Jim Druckenmiller RC .30 .10
❑ 220 Warrick Dunn RC 1.25 .50
❑ 221 James Farrior RC .50 .20
❑ 222 Tarik Glenn RC .20 .07
❑ 223 Tony Gonzalez RC 1.50 .60
❑ 224 Yatil Green RC .30 .10
❑ 225 Byron Hanspard RC .30 .10
❑ 226 Ike Hilliard RC .75 .30
❑ 227 Kenny Holmes RC .50 .20
❑ 228 Walter Jones RC .50 .20

❑ 229 Tom Knight RC .20 .07
❑ 230 David LaFleur RC .20 .07
❑ 231 Kenard Lang RC .30 .10
❑ 232 Kevin Lockett RC .30 .10
❑ 233 Tremain Mack RC .20 .07
❑ 234 Sam Madison RC .50 .20
❑ 235 Chris Naeole RC .20 .07
❑ 236 Orlando Pace RC .50 .20
❑ 237 Jake Plummer RC 2.50 1.00
❑ 238 Dwayne Rudd RC .50 .20
❑ 239 Darrell Russell RC .20 .07
❑ 240 Jamie Sharper RC .30 .10
❑ 241 Sedrick Shaw RC .30 .10
❑ 242 Antowain Smith RC 1.25 .50
❑ 243 Shawn Springs RC .30 .10
❑ 244 Bryant Westbrook RC .20 .07
❑ 245 Reinard Wilson RC .30 .10
❑ 246 Danny Wuerffel RC .50 .20
❑ 247 Renaldo Wynn RC .20 .07
❑ 248 Checklist .20 .07
❑ 249 Checklist .20 .07
❑ 250 Checklist .20 .07
❑ S1 Karim Abdul-Jabbar Sample .30 .10
❑ S1AU Abdul-Jabb. AUTO/500 50.00 25.00

2003 SkyBox LE

❑ COMP.SET w/o SP's (60) 20.00 7.50
❑ 1 Emmitt Smith 2.00 .75
❑ 2 Eric Moulds .50 .20
❑ 3 William Green .50 .20
❑ 4 Clinton Portis 1.25 .50
❑ 5 Tony Gonzalez .50 .20
❑ 6 Aaron Brooks .75 .30
❑ 7 Chad Pennington 1.00 .40
❑ 8 Jerry Rice 1.50 .60
❑ 9 LaDainian Tomlinson .75 .30
❑ 10 Torry Holt .75 .30
❑ 11 Warren Sapp .50 .20
❑ 12 Steve McNair .75 .30
❑ 13 Marc Bulger .75 .30
❑ 14 Patrick Ramsey .75 .30
❑ 15 Peerless Price .50 .20
❑ 16 Jamal Lewis .75 .30
❑ 17 Rich Gannon .50 .20
❑ 18 Plaxico Burress .50 .20
❑ 19 Drew Brees .75 .30
❑ 20 Eddie George .50 .20
❑ 21 Ray Lewis .75 .30
❑ 22 Drew Bledsoe .75 .30
❑ 23 Antonio Bryant .50 .20
❑ 24 David Carr 1.25 .50
❑ 25 Priest Holmes 1.00 .40
❑ 26 Ricky Williams .75 .30
❑ 27 Peyton Manning 1.25 .50
❑ 28 Daunte Culpepper .75 .30
❑ 29 Jeremy Shockey 1.25 .50
❑ 30 Tiki Barber .75 .30
❑ 31 Koren Robinson .50 .20
❑ 32 Keyshawn Johnson .75 .30
❑ 33 Laveranues Coles .50 .20
❑ 34 Brian Urlacher 1.25 .50
❑ 35 Jake Plummer .50 .20
❑ 36 Edgerrin James .75 .30
❑ 37 Marvin Harrison .75 .30
❑ 38 Tom Brady 2.00 .75
❑ 39 Curtis Martin .75 .30
❑ 40 Donovan McNabb 1.00 .40
❑ 41 Hines Ward .75 .30
❑ 42 Charlie Garner .50 .20
❑ 43 Tommy Maddox .75 .30
❑ 44 Terrell Owens .75 .30
❑ 45 Shaun Alexander .75 .30
❑ 46 Ahman Green .75 .30
❑ 47 Fred Taylor .75 .30
❑ 48 Randy Moss 1.25 .50
❑ 49 Deuce McAllister .75 .30
❑ 50 Quincy Carter .50 .20
❑ 51 Jeff Garcia .75 .30
❑ 52 Marshall Faulk .75 .30
❑ 53 Dante Hall .75 .30
❑ 54 Michael Vick 2.00 .75
❑ 55 Stephen Davis .50 .20
❑ 56 Corey Dillon .50 .20
❑ 57 Travis Henry .50 .20
❑ 58 Chad Johnson .75 .30
❑ 59 Joey Harrington 1.25 .50
❑ 60 Brett Favre 2.00 .75
❑ 61 Bryant Johnson RC 25.00 12.50
❑ 62 Terence Newman RC 50.00 20.00
❑ 63 Labrandon Toefield RC 25.00 12.50
❑ 64 Visanthe Shiancoe RC 20.00 10.00
❑ 65 Josh Brown RC 40.00 15.00
❑ 66 Andre Woolfolk RC 25.00 12.50
❑ 67 Jeremi Johnson RC 20.00 10.00
❑ 68 Michael Doss RC 25.00 12.50
❑ 69 Talman Gardner RC 25.00 12.50
❑ 70 Arnaz Battle RC 25.00 12.50
❑ 71 Troy Polamalu RC 80.00 50.00
❑ 72 Brock Forsey RC 25.00 12.50
❑ 73 Domanick Davis RC 40.00 15.00
❑ 74 Onterrio Smith RC 25.00 12.50
❑ 75 Kassim Osgood RC 25.00 12.50
❑ 76 Asante Samuel RC 25.00 12.50
❑ 77 Terrell Suggs RC 40.00 20.00
❑ 78 Boss Bailey RC 25.00 12.50
❑ 79 Larry Johnson RC 80.00 50.00
❑ 80 Teyo Johnson RC 25.00 12.50
❑ 81 Chris Simms RC 40.00 15.00
❑ 82 Walter Young RC 20.00 10.00
❑ 83 Dave Ragone RC 25.00 12.50
❑ 84 E.J. Henderson RC 25.00 12.50
❑ 85 Billy McMullen RC 20.00 10.00
❑ 86 Taylor Jacobs RC 20.00 10.00
❑ 87 Sam Aiken RC 20.00 10.00
❑ 88 Avon Cobourne RC 20.00 10.00
❑ 89 J.R. Tolver RC 20.00 10.00
❑ 90 Doug Gabriel RC 25.00 12.50
❑ 91 Chris Brown RC 30.00 12.50
❑ 92 Musa Smith RC 25.00 12.50
❑ 93 Charles Rogers RC 25.00 12.50
❑ 94 Seth Marler RC 20.00 10.00
❑ 95 DeWayne Robertson RC 25.00 12.50
❑ 96 Shaun McDonald RC 25.00 12.50
❑ 97 Reno Mahe RC 25.00 12.50
❑ 98 Carson Palmer RC 80.00 40.00
❑ 99 Dallas Clark RC 25.00 12.50
❑ 100 Johnathan Sullivan RC 20.00 10.00
❑ 101 Brandon Lloyd RC 30.00 15.00
❑ 102 Ken Dorsey RC 25.00 12.50
❑ 103 Kelley Washington RC 25.00 12.50
❑ 104 Tony Hollings RC 25.00 12.50
❑ 105 Bethel Johnson RC 25.00 12.50
❑ 106 Antonio Gates RC 150.00 90.00
❑ 107 Tyler Brayton RC 25.00 12.50
❑ 108 Michael Haynes RC 25.00 12.50
❑ 109 Andre Johnson RC 50.00 20.00
❑ 110 Nate Burleson RC 30.00 12.50
❑ 111 Sammy Davis RC 25.00 12.50
❑ 112 Nick Barnett RC 40.00 20.00
❑ 113 Willis McGahee RC 60.00 30.00
❑ 114 Casey Fitzsimmons RC 25.00 12.50
❑ 115 Donald Lee RC 20.00 10.00
❑ 116 L.J. Smith RC 25.00 12.50
❑ 117 Tyrone Calico RC 30.00 15.00
❑ 118 Anquan Boldin RC 60.00 30.00
❑ 119 Jason Witten RC 40.00 20.00
❑ 120 George Wrighster RC 20.00 10.00
❑ 121 William Joseph RC 25.00 12.50
❑ 122 Kevin Curtis RC 25.00 12.50
❑ 123 Anthony Adams RC 20.00 10.00
❑ 124 Kyle Boller RC 50.00 20.00
❑ 125 Artose Pinner RC 25.00 12.50
❑ 126 Rashean Mathis RC 20.00 10.00
❑ 127 Justin Fargas RC 25.00 12.50
❑ 128 Pisa Tinoisamoa RC 25.00 12.50
❑ 129 Justin Griffith RC 20.00 10.00
❑ 130 Quentin Griffin RC 25.00 12.50
❑ 131 Cortez Hankton RC 20.00 10.00
❑ 132 B.J. Askew RC 25.00 12.50
❑ 133 Arlen Harris RC 25.00 12.50
❑ 134 Dan Klecko RC 25.00 12.50
❑ 135 Lee Suggs RC 50.00 20.00
❑ 136 Byron Leftwich RC 60.00 25.00
❑ 137 David Tyree RC 20.00 10.00
❑ 138 Aaron Walker RC 20.00 10.00
❑ 139 Marcus Trufant RC 25.00 12.50
❑ 140 Rex Grossman RC 40.00 15.00
❑ 141 Bennie Joppru RC 25.00 12.50
❑ 142 Kevin Williams RC 25.00 12.50
❑ 143 Jerome McDougle RC 25.00 12.50
❑ 144 Ken Hamlin RC 25.00 12.50
❑ 145 Zuriel Smith RC 20.00 10.00
❑ 146 Brooks Bollinger RC 25.00 12.50
❑ 147 Ike Taylor RC 30.00 12.50
❑ 148 Brad Pyatt RC 20.00 10.00
❑ 149 DeJuan Groce RC 25.00 12.50
❑ 150 Keenan Howry RC 25.00 12.50
❑ 151 Seneca Wallace RC 25.00 12.50
❑ 152 Richard Angulo RC 20.00 10.00
❑ 153 Jimmy Kennedy RC 25.00 12.50
❑ 154 Ty Warren RC 25.00 12.50
❑ 155 Nnamdi Asomugha RC 20.00 10.00
❑ 156 Chris Kelsay RC 25.00 12.50
❑ 157 Terry Pierce RC 20.00 10.00
❑ 158 Victor Hobson RC 25.00 12.50
❑ 159 Brian St.Pierre RC 25.00 12.50
❑ 160 Dewayne White RC 20.00 10.00

2004 SkyBox LE

❑ COMP.SET w/o SP's (60) 20.00 7.50
❑ ROOKIE STATED ODDS 1:29
❑ ROOKIE PRINT RUN 99 SER.#'d SETS
❑ UNPRICED EXEC.PURPLE #'d OF 1

❑ 1 Anquan Boldin .75 .30
❑ 2 Quincy Carter .50 .20
❑ 3 Chad Pennington .75 .30
❑ 4 Brett Favre 2.00 .75
❑ 5 Marc Bulger .75 .30
❑ 6 David Carr .75 .30
❑ 7 Byron Leftwich 1.00 .40
❑ 8 Hines Ward .75 .30

❑	9	Drew Bledsoe	.75	.30
❑	10	Domanick Davis	.75	.30
❑	11	Plaxico Burress	.50	.20
❑	12	Mark Brunell	.50	.20
❑	13	Terrell Owens	.75	.30
❑	14	Peyton Manning	1.25	.50
❑	15	Matt Hasselbeck	.50	.20
❑	16	Willis McGahee	.75	.30
❑	17	Fred Taylor	.50	.20
❑	18	Torry Holt	.75	.30
❑	19	Priest Holmes	1.00	.40
❑	20	Charlie Garner	.50	.20
❑	21	Brian Urlacher	1.00	.40
❑	22	Corey Dillon	.50	.20
❑	23	Daunte Culpepper	.75	.30
❑	24	Clinton Portis	.75	.30
❑	25	Chad Johnson	.75	.30
❑	26	Tom Brady	2.00	.75
❑	27	Deuce McAllister	.75	.30
❑	28	Randy Moss	1.00	.40
❑	29	A.J. Feeley	.75	.30
❑	30	Steve McNair	.75	.30
❑	31	Aaron Brooks	.50	.20
❑	32	Carson Palmer	1.00	.40
❑	33	Jeremy Shockey	.75	.30
❑	34	Emmitt Smith	1.50	.60
❑	35	Jeff Garcia	.75	.30
❑	36	Kurt Warner	.75	.30
❑	37	Andre Johnson	.75	.30
❑	38	LaDainian Tomlinson	1.00	.40
❑	39	Ray Lewis	.75	.30
❑	40	Charles Rogers	.50	.20
❑	41	Rich Gannon	.50	.20
❑	42	Jake Delhomme	.75	.30
❑	43	Marvin Harrison	.75	.30
❑	44	Shaun Alexander	.75	.30
❑	45	Ricky Williams	.75	.30
❑	46	Eddie George	.50	.20
❑	47	Edgerrin James	.75	.30
❑	48	Chris Chambers	.50	.20
❑	49	Jamal Lewis	.75	.30
❑	50	Joey Harrington	.75	.30
❑	51	Jerry Rice	1.50	.60
❑	52	Kyle Boller	.75	.30
❑	53	Ahman Green	.75	.30
❑	54	Donovan McNabb	1.00	.40
❑	55	Stephen Davis	.50	.20
❑	56	Tony Gonzalez	.50	.20
❑	57	Marshall Faulk	.75	.30
❑	58	Michael Vick	1.50	.60
❑	59	Jake Plummer	.50	.20
❑	60	Curtis Martin	.75	.30
❑	61	Eli Manning RC	50.00	20.00
❑	62	Robert Gallery RC	15.00	6.00
❑	63	Larry Fitzgerald RC	30.00	12.50
❑	64	Philip Rivers RC	30.00	15.00
❑	65	Sean Taylor RC	12.00	5.00
❑	66	Kellen Winslow RC	20.00	7.50
❑	67	Roy Williams RC	25.00	10.00
❑	68	DeAngelo Hall RC	12.00	5.00
❑	69	Reggie Williams RC	12.00	5.00
❑	70	Dunta Robinson RC	10.00	4.00
❑	71	Ben Roethlisberger RC	100.00	50.00
❑	72	Jonathan Vilma RC	10.00	4.00
❑	73	Lee Evans RC	12.00	5.00
❑	74	Tommie Harris RC	10.00	4.00
❑	75	Michael Clayton RC	20.00	7.50
❑	76	D.J. Williams RC	12.00	5.00
❑	77	Tim Euhus RC	10.00	4.00
❑	78	Kenechi Udeze RC	10.00	4.00
❑	79	Vince Wilfork RC	12.00	5.00
❑	80	J.P. Losman RC	20.00	7.50
❑	81	Jared Lorenzen RC	8.00	3.00
❑	82	Steven Jackson RC	30.00	12.50
❑	83	Ricky Ray RC	8.00	3.00
❑	84	Chris Perry RC	15.00	6.00
❑	85	Jason Babin RC	10.00	4.00
❑	86	Chris Gamble RC	12.00	5.00
❑	87	Michael Jenkins RC	10.00	4.00
❑	88	Kevin Jones RC	30.00	12.50
❑	89	Rashaun Woods RC	10.00	4.00
❑	90	Ben Watson RC	10.00	4.00
❑	91	Karlos Dansby RC	10.00	4.00
❑	92	Teddy Lehman RC	10.00	4.00
❑	93	Ben Troupe RC	10.00	4.00
❑	94	Tatum Bell RC	20.00	7.50
❑	95	Julius Jones RC	40.00	15.00
❑	96	Devery Henderson RC	8.00	3.00
❑	97	Drew Henson RC	10.00	4.00
❑	98	Darius Watts RC	10.00	4.00
❑	99	Greg Jones RC	10.00	4.00
❑	100	Luke McCown RC	10.00	4.00
❑	101	Keary Colbert RC	12.00	5.00
❑	102	Mewelde Moore RC	12.00	5.00
❑	103	Ben Hartsock RC	10.00	4.00
❑	104	Derrick Hamilton RC	8.00	3.00
❑	105	Bernard Berrian RC	10.00	4.00
❑	106	Chris Cooley RC	10.00	4.00
❑	107	Devard Darling RC	10.00	4.00
❑	108	Matt Schaub RC	15.00	6.00
❑	109	Carlos Francis RC	8.00	3.00
❑	110	Will Poole RC	10.00	4.00
❑	111	Samie Parker RC	10.00	4.00
❑	112	Derrick Knight RC	8.00	3.00
❑	113	Jerricho Cotchery RC	10.00	4.00
❑	114	Rod Rutherford RC	8.00	3.00
❑	115	Ernest Wilford RC	10.00	4.00
❑	116	Cedric Cobbs RC	10.00	4.00
❑	117	Johnnie Morant RC	10.00	4.00
❑	118	Craig Krenzel RC	10.00	4.00
❑	119	Maurice Mann RC	8.00	3.00
❑	120	Michael Turner RC	10.00	4.00
❑	121	Ryan Dinwiddie RC	8.00	3.00
❑	122	Drew Carter RC	10.00	4.00
❑	123	P.K. Sam RC	8.00	3.00
❑	124	Jamaar Taylor RC	10.00	4.00
❑	125	Ryan Krause RC	8.00	3.00
❑	126	Triandos Luke RC	10.00	4.00
❑	127	Andy Hall RC	8.00	3.00
❑	128	Josh Harris RC	10.00	4.00
❑	129	Jim Sorgi RC	10.00	4.00
❑	130	Jason Fife RC	8.00	3.00
❑	131	Clarence Moore RC	10.00	4.00
❑	132	Jeff Smoker RC	10.00	4.00
❑	133	John Navarre RC	10.00	4.00
❑	134	Justin Jenkins RC	8.00	3.00
❑	135	Adimchinobe Echemandu RC	8.00	3.00
❑	136	Jammal Lord RC	10.00	4.00
❑	137	Erik Jensen RC	8.00	3.00
❑	138	Cody Pickett RC	10.00	4.00
❑	139	Casey Bramlet RC	8.00	3.00
❑	140	Quincy Wilson RC	8.00	3.00
❑	141	Thomas Tapeh RC	8.00	3.00
❑	142	Matt Brandt RC	6.00	2.50
❑	143	Bruce Perry RC	10.00	4.00
❑	144	Mark Jones RC	8.00	3.00
❑	145	Keith Smith RC	8.00	3.00
❑	146	B.J. Symons RC	10.00	4.00
❑	147	Patrick Crayton RC	10.00	4.00
❑	148	Daryl Smith RC	10.00	4.00
❑	149	Demorrio Williams RC	10.00	4.00
❑	150	Casey Clausen RC	10.00	4.00
❑	151	Jarrett Payton RC	12.00	5.00
❑	152	Kris Wilson RC	10.00	4.00
❑	153	Renaldo Works RC	10.00	4.00
❑	154	Shawn Andrews RC	10.00	4.00
❑	155	Ricardo Colclough RC	10.00	4.00
❑	156	Travis LaBoy RC	10.00	4.00
❑	157	Bob Sanders RC	20.00	7.50
❑	158	Chad Lavalais RC	8.00	3.00
❑	159	Derrick Strait RC	10.00	4.00
❑	160	Darnell Dockett RC	8.00	3.00

1993 SkyBox Premium

❑		COMPLETE SET (270)	25.00	10.00
❑	1	Eric Martin	.10	.02
❑	2	Earnest Byner	.10	.02
❑	3	Ricky Proehl	.10	.02
❑	4	Mark Carrier WR	.20	.07
❑	5	Shannon Sharpe	.40	.15
❑	6	Anthony Thompson	.10	.02
❑	7	Drew Bledsoe RC	5.00	2.00
❑	8	Tom Carter RC	.20	.07
❑	9	Ryan McNeil RC	.40	.15
❑	10	Troy Aikman	1.50	.60
❑	11	Robert Jones	.10	.02
❑	12	Rodney Peete	.10	.02
❑	13	Wendell Davis	.10	.02
❑	14	Thurman Thomas	.40	.15
❑	15	John Stephens	.10	.02
❑	16	Rodney Hampton	.20	.07
❑	17	Eric Bieniemy	.10	.02
❑	18	Santana Dotson	.20	.07
❑	19	Jeff George	.40	.15
❑	20	John L. Williams	.10	.02
❑	21	Barry Word	.10	.02
❑	22	Chris Miller	.20	.07
❑	23	Jeff Hostetler	.20	.07
❑	24	Dwight Stone	.10	.02
❑	25	Brad Baxter	.10	.02
❑	26	Randall Cunningham	.40	.15
❑	27	Mark Higgs	.10	.02
❑	28	Vaughn Dunbar	.10	.02
❑	29	Ricky Ervins	.10	.02
❑	30	Johnny Bailey	.10	.02
❑	31	Michael Jackson	.20	.07
❑	32	Mike Croel	.10	.02
❑	33	Steve Young	1.50	.60
❑	34	Deon Figures RC	.10	.02
❑	35	Robert Smith RC	2.50	1.00
❑	36	Irv Smith RC	.10	.02
❑	37	Charles Haley	.20	.07
❑	38	Cris Dishman	.10	.02
❑	39	Barry Sanders	2.50	1.00
❑	40	Jim Harbaugh	.40	.15
❑	41	Darryl Talley	.10	.02
❑	42	Jackie Harris	.10	.02
❑	43	Phil Simms	.20	.07
❑	44	Marion Butts	.10	.02
❑	45	Anthony Munoz	.20	.07
❑	46	Steve Emtman	.10	.02
❑	47	Kelvin Martin	.10	.02
❑	48	Joe Montana	3.00	1.25
❑	49	Andre Rison	.20	.07
❑	50	Ethan Horton	.10	.02
❑	51	Kevin Greene	.20	.07
❑	52	Browning Nagle	.10	.02
❑	53	Tim Harris	.10	.02
❑	54	Keith Byars	.10	.02
❑	55	Terry Allen	.40	.15
❑	56	Chip Lohmiller	.10	.02
❑	57	Robert Massey	.10	.02
❑	58	Michael Dean Perry	.20	.07
❑	59	Tommy Maddox	.40	.15
❑	60	Jerry Rice	2.00	.75
❑	61	Lincoln Kennedy RC	.10	.02
❑	62	Jerome Bettis RC	8.00	3.00
❑	63	Coleman Rudolph RC	.10	.02

❑ 64 Emmitt Smith 3.00 1.50
❑ 65 Curtis Duncan .10 .02
❑ 66 Andre Ware .10 .02
❑ 67 Neal Anderson .10 .02
❑ 68 Jim Kelly .40 .15
❑ 69 Reggie White .40 .15
❑ 70 Dave Meggett .10 .02
❑ 71 Junior Seau .40 .15
❑ 72 Courtney Hawkins .10 .02
❑ 73 Clarence Verdin .10 .02
❑ 74 Tommy Kane .10 .02
❑ 75 Dale Carter .10 .02
❑ 76 Michael Haynes .20 .07
❑ 77 Willie Gault .10 .02
❑ 78 Eric Green .10 .02
❑ 79 Ronnie Lott .20 .07
❑ 80 Vai Sikahema .10 .02
❑ 81 Mark Ingram .10 .02
❑ 82 Anthony Carter .20 .07
❑ 83 Mark Rypien .10 .02
❑ 84 Gary Clark .20 .07
❑ 85 Bernie Kosar .20 .07
❑ 86 Cleveland Gary .10 .02
❑ 87 Tom Rathman .10 .02
❑ 88 Tony McGee RC .20 .07
❑ 89 Rick Mirer RC .40 .15
❑ 90 John Copeland RC .20 .07
❑ 91 Michael Irvin .40 .15
❑ 92 Wilber Marshall .10 .02
❑ 93 Mel Gray .20 .07
❑ 94 Craig Heyward .20 .07
❑ 95 Don Beebe .10 .02
❑ 96 Andre Tippett .10 .02
❑ 97 Derek Brown TE .10 .02
❑ 98 Ronnie Harmon .10 .02
❑ 99 Derrick Fenner .10 .02
❑ 100 Rodney Culver .10 .02
❑ 101 Cortez Kennedy .20 .07
❑ 102 Marcus Allen .40 .15
❑ 103 Steve Broussard .10 .02
❑ 104 Tim Brown .40 .15
❑ 105 Merril Hoge .10 .02
❑ 106 Chris Burkett .10 .02
❑ 107 Fred Barnett .20 .07
❑ 108 Dan Marino 3.00 1.25
❑ 109 Chris Doleman .10 .02
❑ 110 Art Monk .20 .07
❑ 111 Ernie Jones .10 .02
❑ 112 Jay Hilgenberg .10 .02
❑ 113 Jim Everett .20 .07
❑ 114 John Taylor .20 .07
❑ 115 Steve Everitt RC .10 .02
❑ 116 Carlton Gray RC .10 .02
❑ 117 Eric Curry RC .10 .02
❑ 118 Ken Norton Jr. .20 .07
❑ 119 Lorenzo White .10 .02
❑ 120 Pat Swilling .10 .02
❑ 121 William Perry .20 .07
❑ 122 Brett Favre 4.00 2.00
❑ 123 Jon Vaughn .10 .02
❑ 124 Mark Jackson .10 .02
❑ 125 Stan Humphries .20 .07
❑ 126 Harold Green .10 .02
❑ 127 Anthony Johnson .20 .07
❑ 128 Brian Blades .20 .07
❑ 129 Willie Davis .40 .15
❑ 130 Bobby Hebert .10 .02
❑ 131 Terry McDaniel .10 .02
❑ 132 Jeff Graham .20 .07
❑ 133 Jeff Lageman .10 .02
❑ 134 Andre Waters .10 .02
❑ 135 Steve Walsh .10 .02
❑ 136 Cris Carter .40 .15
❑ 137 Tim McGee .10 .02
❑ 138 Chuck Cecil .10 .02
❑ 139 John Elway 3.00 1.25
❑ 140 Todd Lyght .10 .02
❑ 141 Brent Jones .20 .07
❑ 142 Patrick Bates RC .10 .02
❑ 143 Darrien Gordon RC .10 .02
❑ 144 Michael Strahan RC 2.00 .75
❑ 145 Jay Novacek .20 .07
❑ 146 Warren Moon .40 .15
❑ 147 Rodney Holman .10 .02
❑ 148 Anthony Morgan .10 .02
❑ 149 Sterling Sharpe .40 .15
❑ 150 Leonard Russell .20 .07
❑ 151 Lawrence Taylor .40 .15
❑ 152 Leslie O'Neal .20 .07
❑ 153 Carl Pickens .20 .07
❑ 154 Aaron Cox .10 .02
❑ 155 Ferrell Edmunds .10 .02
❑ 156 Neil O'Donnell .40 .15
❑ 157 Tony Smith RB .10 .02
❑ 158 James Lofton .20 .07
❑ 159 George Teague RC .20 .07
❑ 160 Boomer Esiason .20 .07
❑ 161 Eric Allen .10 .02
❑ 162 Floyd Turner .10 .02
❑ 163 Esera Tuaolo .10 .02
❑ 164 Darrell Green .10 .02
❑ 165 Steve Beuerlein .20 .07
❑ 166 Vance Johnson .10 .02
❑ 167 Flipper Anderson .10 .02
❑ 168 Ricky Watters .40 .15
❑ 169 Marvin Jones RC .10 .02
❑ 170 Dana Stubblefield RC .40 .15
❑ 171 Willie Roaf RC .20 .07
❑ 172 Russell Maryland .10 .02
❑ 173 Ernest Givins .20 .07
❑ 174 Willie Green .10 .02
❑ 175 Bruce Smith .40 .15
❑ 176 Terrell Buckley .10 .02
❑ 177 Scott Zolak .10 .02
❑ 178 Mike Sherrard .10 .02
❑ 179 Lawrence Dawsey .10 .02
❑ 180 Jay Schroeder .10 .02
❑ 181 Quentin Coryatt .20 .07
❑ 182 Harvey Williams .20 .07
❑ 183 Natrone Means RC .40 .15
❑ 184 Eric Dickerson .20 .07
❑ 185 Gaston Green .10 .02
❑ 186 Thomas Smith RC .20 .07
❑ 187 Johnny Johnson .10 .02
❑ 188 Marco Coleman .10 .02
❑ 189 Wade Wilson .10 .02
❑ 190 Rich Gannon .40 .15
❑ 191 Brian Mitchell .20 .07
❑ 192 Eric Metcalf .20 .07
❑ 193 Robert Delpino .10 .02
❑ 194 Shane Conlan .10 .02
❑ 195 Dexter Carter .10 .02
❑ 196 Garrison Hearst RC 1.50 .60
❑ 197 Chris Slade RC .20 .07
❑ 198 Troy Drayton RC .20 .07
❑ 199 Lin Elliott .10 .02
❑ 200 Haywood Jeffires .20 .07
❑ 201 Herman Moore .40 .15
❑ 202 Cornelius Bennett .20 .07
❑ 203 Mark Clayton .10 .02
❑ 204 Marv Cook .10 .02
❑ 205 Stephen Baker .10 .02
❑ 206 Gary Anderson RB .10 .02
❑ 207 Eddie Brown .10 .02
❑ 208 Will Wolford .10 .02
❑ 209 Derrick Thomas .40 .15
❑ 210 Seth Joyner .10 .02
❑ 211 Mike Pritchard .20 .07
❑ 212 Rod Woodson .40 .15
❑ 213 Todd Kelly RC .10 .02
❑ 214 Rob Moore .20 .07
❑ 215 Keith Jackson .20 .07
❑ 216 Wesley Carroll .10 .02
❑ 217 Steve Jordan .10 .02
❑ 218 Ricky Sanders .10 .02
❑ 219 Tommy Vardell .10 .02
❑ 220 Rod Bernstine .10 .02
❑ 221 Henry Ellard .20 .07
❑ 222 Amp Lee .10 .02
❑ 223 O.J.McDuffie RC .40 .15
❑ 224 Carl Simpson RC .10 .02
❑ 225 Dan Williams RC .10 .02
❑ 226 Thomas Everett .10 .02
❑ 227 Webster Slaughter .10 .02
❑ 228 Trace Armstrong .10 .02
❑ 229 Kenneth Davis .10 .02
❑ 230 Tony Bennett .10 .02
❑ 231 Reyna Thompson .10 .02
❑ 232 Anthony Miller .20 .07
❑ 233 Reggie Cobb .10 .02
❑ 234 Mark Duper .10 .02
❑ 235 Chris Warren .20 .07
❑ 236 Christian Okoye .10 .02
❑ 237 Irving Fryar .20 .07
❑ 238 Deion Sanders .75 .30
❑ 239 Barry Foster .20 .07
❑ 240 Ernest Dye RC .10 .02
❑ 241 Calvin Williams .20 .07
❑ 242 Louis Oliver .10 .02
❑ 243 Dalton Hilliard .10 .02
❑ 244 Roger Craig .20 .07
❑ 245 Randal Hill .10 .02
❑ 246 Vinny Testaverde .20 .07
❑ 247 Steve Atwater .10 .02
❑ 248 Jim Price .10 .02
❑ 249 Martin Harrison RC .10 .02
❑ 250 Curtis Conway RC .75 .30
❑ 251 Demetrius DuBose RC .10 .02
❑ 252 Leonard Renfro RC .10 .02
❑ 253 Alvin Harper .20 .07
❑ 254 Leonard Harris .10 .02
❑ 255 Tom Waddle .10 .02
❑ 256 Andre Reed .20 .07
❑ 257 Sanjay Beach .10 .02
❑ 258 Michael Timpson .10 .02
❑ 259 Nate Lewis .10 .02
❑ 260 Steve DeBerg .10 .02
❑ 261 David Klingler .10 .02
❑ 262 Dan McGwire .10 .02
❑ 263 Dave Krieg .20 .07
❑ 264 Brad Muster .10 .02
❑ 265 Nick Bell .10 .02
❑ 266 Checklist 1 .10 .02
❑ 267 Checklist 2 .10 .02
❑ 268 Checklist 3 .10 .02
❑ 269 Checklist 4 .10 .02
❑ 270 Checklist 5 .10 .02
❑ P1 Promo Panel 2.00 .75
❑ P2 Promo Panel 2.00 .75

1994 SkyBox Premium

❑ COMPLETE SET (200) 20.00 7.50
❑ 1 Steve Beuerlein .15 .05
❑ 2 Gary Clark .15 .05
❑ 3 Garrison Hearst .30 .10
❑ 4 Ronald Moore .05 .01
❑ 5 Eric Swann .15 .05
❑ 6 Chuck Cecil .05 .01

❑	7 Seth Joyner	.05	.01
❑	8 Clyde Simmons	.05	.01
❑	9 Andre Rison	.15	.05
❑	10 Deion Sanders	.40	.15
❑	11 Erric Pegram	.05	.01
❑	12 Steve Broussard	.05	.01
❑	13 Chris Doleman	.05	.01
❑	14 Jeff George	.30	.10
❑	15 Cornelius Bennett	.15	.05
❑	16 Jim Kelly	.30	.10
❑	17 Andre Reed	.15	.05
❑	18 Bruce Smith	.30	.10
❑	19 Darryl Talley	.05	.01
❑	20 Thurman Thomas	.30	.10
❑	21 Mark Carrier DB	.05	.01
❑	22 Dante Jones	.05	.01
❑	23 Curtis Conway	.30	.10
❑	24 Tim Worley	.05	.01
❑	25 Erik Kramer	.15	.05
❑	26 John Copeland	.05	.01
❑	27 David Klingler	.05	.01
❑	28 Derrick Fenner	.05	.01
❑	29 Harold Green	.05	.01
❑	30 Carl Pickens	.15	.05
❑	31 Tony McGee	.05	.01
❑	32 Steve Everitt	.05	.01
❑	33 Michael Jackson	.15	.05
❑	34 Eric Metcalf	.15	.05
❑	35 Vinny Testaverde	.15	.05
❑	36 Michael Dean Perry	.15	.05
❑	37 Troy Aikman	1.25	.50
❑	38 Alvin Harper	.15	.05
❑	39 Michael Irvin	.30	.10
❑	40 Jay Novacek	.15	.05
❑	41 Emmitt Smith	2.00	.75
❑	42 Charles Haley	.15	.05
❑	43 Daryl Johnston	.15	.05
❑	44 Kevin Williams WR	.15	.05
❑	45 Rodney Peete	.05	.01
❑	46 John Elway	2.50	1.00
❑	47 Shannon Sharpe	.15	.05
❑	48 Rod Bernstine	.05	.01
❑	49 Glyn Milburn	.15	.05
❑	50 Mike Pritchard	.05	.01
❑	51 Anthony Miller	.15	.05
❑	52 Herman Moore	.30	.10
❑	53 Barry Sanders	2.00	.75
❑	54 Scott Mitchell	.15	.05
❑	55 Pat Swilling	.05	.01
❑	56 Willie Green	.05	.01
❑	57 Edgar Bennett	.30	.10
❑	58 Brett Favre	2.50	1.00
❑	59 Sterling Sharpe	.15	.05
❑	60 Reggie White	.30	.10
❑	61 Sean Jones	.05	.01
❑	62 Reggie Cobb	.05	.01
❑	63 Haywood Jeffires	.15	.05
❑	64 Lorenzo White	.05	.01
❑	65 Webster Slaughter	.05	.01
❑	66 Gary Brown	.05	.01
❑	67 Steve Emtman	.05	.01
❑	68 Quentin Coryatt	.05	.01
❑	69 Sean Dawkins RC	.30	.10
❑	70 Jim Harbaugh	.30	.10
❑	71 Tony Bennett	.05	.01
❑	72 Marcus Allen	.30	.10
❑	73 Steve Bono	.15	.05
❑	74 Dale Carter	.05	.01
❑	75 Joe Montana	2.50	1.00
❑	76 Neil Smith	.15	.05
❑	77 Derrick Thomas	.30	.10
❑	78 Keith Cash	.05	.01
❑	79 Tim Brown	.30	.10
❑	80 Rocket Ismail	.15	.05
❑	81 Jeff Hostetler	.15	.05
❑	82 Patrick Bates	.05	.01
❑	83 James Jett	.05	.01
❑	84 Jerome Bettis	.60	.25
❑	85 Chris Miller	.05	.01
❑	86 Marc Boutte	.05	.01
❑	87 Sean Gilbert	.05	.01
❑	88 Keith Jackson	.05	.01
❑	89 Terry Kirby	.30	.10
❑	90 Dan Marino	2.50	1.00
❑	91 Bryan Cox	.05	.01
❑	92 Bernie Kosar	.15	.05
❑	93 Qadry Ismail	.30	.10
❑	94 Robert Smith	.30	.10
❑	95 Terry Allen	.15	.05
❑	96 Scottie Graham RC	.15	.05
❑	97 Warren Moon	.30	.10
❑	98 Drew Bledsoe	1.00	.40
❑	99 Ben Coates	.15	.05
❑	100 Leonard Russell	.05	.01
❑	101 Vincent Brisby	.15	.05
❑	102 Marion Butts	.05	.01
❑	103 Morten Andersen	.05	.01
❑	104 Derek Brown RBK	.05	.01
❑	105 Michael Haynes	.15	.05
❑	106 Sam Mills	.05	.01
❑	107 Lorenzo Neal	.05	.01
❑	108 Willie Roaf	.05	.01
❑	109 Jim Everett	.15	.05
❑	110 Michael Brooks	.05	.01
❑	111 Rodney Hampton	.15	.05
❑	112 Dave Brown	.15	.05
❑	113 Dave Meggett	.05	.01
❑	114 Ronnie Lott	.15	.05
❑	115 Boomer Esiason	.15	.05
❑	116 Rob Moore	.15	.05
❑	117 Johnny Johnson	.05	.01
❑	118 Marvin Jones	.05	.01
❑	119 Johnny Mitchell	.05	.01
❑	120 Fred Barnett	.15	.05
❑	121 Randall Cunningham	.30	.10
❑	122 Herschel Walker	.15	.05
❑	123 Calvin Williams	.15	.05
❑	124 Neil O'Donnell	.30	.10
❑	125 Eric Green	.05	.01
❑	126 Leroy Thompson	.05	.01
❑	127 Rod Woodson	.15	.05
❑	128 Barry Foster	.05	.01
❑	129 Deon Figures	.05	.01
❑	130 John L. Williams	.05	.01
❑	131 Chris Mims	.05	.01
❑	132 Darrien Gordon	.05	.01
❑	133 Stan Humphries	.15	.05
❑	134 Natrone Means	.30	.10
❑	135 Junior Seau	.30	.10
❑	136 Brent Jones	.15	.05
❑	137 Jerry Rice	1.25	.50
❑	138 Dana Stubblefield	.15	.05
❑	139 John Taylor	.15	.05
❑	140 Ricky Watters	.15	.05
❑	141 Steve Young	1.00	.40
❑	142 Ken Norton Jr.	.15	.05
❑	143 Brian Blades	.15	.05
❑	144 Cortez Kennedy	.15	.05
❑	145 Kelvin Martin	.05	.01
❑	146 Rick Mirer	.30	.10
❑	147 Chris Warren	.15	.05
❑	148 Eric Curry	.05	.01
❑	149 Santana Dotson	.15	.05
❑	150 Craig Erickson	.05	.01
❑	151 Hardy Nickerson	.15	.05
❑	152 Paul Gruber	.05	.01
❑	153 Reggie Brooks	.15	.05
❑	154 Tom Carter	.05	.01
❑	155 Desmond Howard	.15	.05
❑	156 Ken Harvey	.05	.01
❑	157 Dan Wilkinson RC	.15	.05
❑	158 Marshall Faulk RC	5.00	2.00
❑	159 Heath Shuler RC	.30	.10
❑	160 Willie McGinest RC	.30	.10
❑	161 Trev Alberts RC	.15	.05
❑	162 Trent Dilfer RC	1.25	.50
❑	163 Bryant Young RC	.30	.10
❑	164 Sam Adams RC	.15	.05
❑	165 Antonio Langham RC	.15	.05
❑	166 Jamir Miller RC	.15	.05
❑	167 John Thierry RC	.05	.01
❑	168 Aaron Glenn RC	.30	.10
❑	169 Joe Johnson RC	.05	.01
❑	170 Bernard Williams RC	.05	.01
❑	171 Wayne Gandy RC	.05	.01
❑	172 Aaron Taylor RC	.05	.01
❑	173 Charles Johnson RC	.30	.10
❑	174 Dewayne Washington RC	.15	.05
❑	175 Todd Steussie RC	.15	.05
❑	176 Tim Bowens RC	.15	.05
❑	177 Johnnie Morton RC	1.25	.50
❑	178 Rob Fredrickson	.15	.05
❑	179 Shante Carver RC	.05	.01
❑	180 Thomas Lewis RC	.15	.05
❑	181 Greg Hill RC	.30	.10
❑	182 Henry Ford RC	.05	.01
❑	183 Jeff Burris RC	.15	.05
❑	184 William Floyd RC	.30	.10
❑	185 Derrick Alexander WR RC	.30	.10
❑	186 Glenn Foley RC	.30	.10
❑	187 Charlie Garner RC	1.25	.50
❑	188 Errict Rhett RC	.30	.10
❑	189 Chuck Levy RC	.05	.01
❑	190 Byron Bam Morris RC	.15	.05
❑	191 Donnell Bennett RC	.30	.10
❑	192 LeShon Johnson RC	.15	.05
❑	193 Mario Bates RC	.30	.10
❑	194 David Palmer RC	.30	.10
❑	195 Darnay Scott RC	.60	.25
❑	196 Lake Dawson RC	.15	.05
❑	197 Checklist	.05	.01
❑	198 Checklist	.05	.01
❑	199 Checklist	.05	.01
❑	200 Checklist for Inserts	.05	.01
❑	NNO NFL Anniv.Commemor.	.30	.10

1995 SkyBox Premium

❑	COMPLETE SET (200)	20.00	7.50
❑	1 Garrison Hearst	.40	.15
❑	2 Dave Krieg	.10	.02
❑	3 Rob Moore	.20	.07
❑	4 Eric Swann	.20	.07
❑	5 Larry Centers	.20	.07
❑	6 Jeff George	.20	.07
❑	7 Craig Heyward	.20	.07
❑	8 Terance Mathis	.20	.07
❑	9 Eric Metcalf	.20	.07
❑	10 Jim Kelly	.40	.15
❑	11 Andre Reed	.20	.07
❑	12 Bruce Smith	.40	.15
❑	13 Cornelius Bennett	.20	.07
❑	14 Randy Baldwin	.10	.02
❑	15 Don Beebe	.10	.02
❑	16 Barry Foster	.20	.07
❑	17 Lamar Lathon	.10	.02
❑	18 Frank Reich	.10	.02
❑	19 Jeff Graham	.10	.02
❑	20 Raymont Harris	.10	.02

❑	21	Lewis Tillman	.10	.02
❑	22	Michael Timpson	.10	.02
❑	23	Jeff Blake RC	1.00	.40
❑	24	Carl Pickens	.20	.07
❑	25	Darnay Scott	.20	.07
❑	26	Dan Wilkinson	.20	.07
❑	27	Derrick Alexander WR	.40	.15
❑	28	Leroy Hoard	.10	.02
❑	29	Antonio Langham	.10	.02
❑	30	Andre Rison	.20	.07
❑	31	Eric Turner	.10	.02
❑	32	Troy Aikman	1.25	.50
❑	33	Michael Irvin	.40	.15
❑	34	Daryl Johnston	.20	.07
❑	35	Emmitt Smith	2.00	.75
❑	36	John Elway	2.50	1.00
❑	37	Glyn Milburn	.10	.02
❑	38	Anthony Miller	.20	.07
❑	39	Shannon Sharpe	.20	.07
❑	40	Scott Mitchell	.20	.07
❑	41	Herman Moore	.40	.15
❑	42	Barry Sanders	2.00	.75
❑	43	Chris Spielman	.20	.07
❑	44	Edgar Bennett	.20	.07
❑	45	Robert Brooks	.40	.15
❑	46	Brett Favre	2.50	1.00
❑	47	Reggie White	.40	.15
❑	48	Mel Gray	.10	.02
❑	49	Haywood Jeffires	.10	.02
❑	50	Gary Brown	.10	.02
❑	51	Craig Erickson	.10	.02
❑	52	Quentin Coryatt	.20	.07
❑	53	Sean Dawkins	.20	.07
❑	54	Marshall Faulk	1.50	.60
❑	55	Steve Beuerlein	.20	.07
❑	56	Reggie Cobb	.10	.02
❑	57	Desmond Howard	.20	.07
❑	58	Ernest Givins	.10	.02
❑	59	Jeff Lageman	.10	.02
❑	60	Marcus Allen	.40	.15
❑	61	Steve Bono	.20	.07
❑	62	Greg Hill	.20	.07
❑	63	Willie Davis	.20	.07
❑	64	Tim Brown	.40	.15
❑	65	Rocket Ismail	.20	.07
❑	66	Jeff Hostetler	.20	.07
❑	67	Chester McGlockton	.20	.07
❑	68	Tim Bowens	.10	.02
❑	69	Irving Fryar	.20	.07
❑	70	Eric Green	.10	.02
❑	71	Terry Kirby	.20	.07
❑	72	Dan Marino	2.50	1.00
❑	73	O.J. McDuffie	.40	.15
❑	74	Bernie Parmalee	.20	.07
❑	75	Dewayne Washington	.20	.07
❑	76	Cris Carter	.40	.15
❑	77	Qadry Ismail	.20	.07
❑	78	Warren Moon	.20	.07
❑	79	Jake Reed	.20	.07
❑	80	Drew Bledsoe	.75	.30
❑	81	Vincent Brisby	.10	.02
❑	82	Ben Coates	.20	.07
❑	83	Dave Meggett	.10	.02
❑	84	Mario Bates	.20	.07
❑	85	Jim Everett	.10	.02
❑	86	Michael Haynes	.20	.07
❑	87	Tyrone Hughes	.20	.07
❑	88	Dave Brown	.20	.07
❑	89	Rodney Hampton	.20	.07
❑	90	Thomas Lewis	.20	.07
❑	91	Herschel Walker	.20	.07
❑	92	Mike Sherrard	.10	.02
❑	93	Boomer Esiason	.20	.07
❑	94	Aaron Glenn	.10	.02
❑	95	Johnny Johnson	.10	.02
❑	96	Johnny Mitchell	.10	.02
❑	97	Ronald Moore	.10	.02
❑	98	Fred Barnett	.20	.07
❑	99	Randall Cunningham	.40	.15
❑	100	Charlie Garner	.40	.15
❑	101	Ricky Watters	.20	.07
❑	102	Calvin Williams	.40	.15
❑	103	Charles Johnson	.20	.07
❑	104	Byron Bam Morris	.10	.02
❑	105	Neil O'Donnell	.20	.07
❑	106	Rod Woodson	.20	.07
❑	107	Jerome Bettis	.40	.15
❑	108	Troy Drayton	.10	.02
❑	109	Sean Gilbert	.20	.07
❑	110	Chris Miller	.10	.02
❑	111	Leonard Russell	.10	.02
❑	112	Ronnie Harmon	.10	.02
❑	113	Stan Humphries	.20	.07
❑	114	Shawn Jefferson	.10	.02
❑	115	Natrone Means	.20	.07
❑	116	Junior Seau	.40	.15
❑	117	William Floyd	.20	.07
❑	118	Brent Jones	.10	.02
❑	119	Jerry Rice	1.25	.50
❑	120	Deion Sanders	.75	.30
❑	121	Dana Stubblefield	.20	.07
❑	122	Bryant Young	.20	.07
❑	123	Steve Young	1.00	.40
❑	124	Brian Blades	.20	.07
❑	125	Cortez Kennedy	.20	.07
❑	126	Rick Mirer	.20	.07
❑	127	Ricky Proehl	.10	.02
❑	128	Chris Warren	.20	.07
❑	129	Horace Copeland	.10	.02
❑	130	Trent Dilfer	.40	.15
❑	131	Alvin Harper	.10	.02
❑	132	Jackie Harris	.10	.02
❑	133	Hardy Nickerson	.10	.02
❑	134	Errict Rhett	.20	.07
❑	135	Henry Ellard	.20	.07
❑	136	Brian Mitchell	.10	.02
❑	137	Heath Shuler	.20	.07
❑	138	Tydus Winans	.10	.02
❑	139	Brett Favre/Bledsoe	1.00	.40
❑	140	Marshall Faulk/Floyd	.60	.25
❑	141	Brett Favre/Dilfer	.75	.30
❑	142	Dan Marino/Favre	1.00	.40
❑	143	Errict Rhett/Dilfer	.40	.15
❑	144	Jerry Rice/Turner	.50	.20
❑	145	Andre Rison/E.Turner	.20	.07
❑	146	Barry Sanders/Meggett	.60	.25
❑	147	Emmitt Smith/Johnston	.60	.25
❑	148	Steve Young/Favre	1.00	.40
❑	149	Emmitt Smith/Rhett	.60	.25
❑	150	Marshall Faulk/B.Sanders	.75	.30
❑	151	Jerry Rice/D.Scott	.50	.20
❑	152	William Floyd/Johnston	.20	.07
❑	153	Dan Marino/Dilfer	.75	.30
❑	154	John Elway/Shuler	.75	.30
❑	155	Byron Bam Morris/Means	.10	.02
❑	156	Dan Wilkinson/R.White	.20	.07
❑	157	Mario Bates/Hampton	.20	.07
❑	158	Junior Seau/M.Jones	.40	.15
❑	159	Ki-Jana Carter RC	.40	.15
❑	160	Tony Boselli RC	.40	.15
❑	161	Steve McNair RC	4.00	1.50
❑	162	Michael Westbrook RC	.40	.15
❑	163	Kerry Collins RC	2.00	.75
❑	164	Kevin Carter RC	.40	.15
❑	165	Mike Mamula RC	.10	.02
❑	166	Joey Galloway RC	2.00	.75
❑	167	Kyle Brady RC	.40	.15
❑	168	J.J. Stokes RC	.40	.15
❑	169	Warren Sapp RC	2.00	.75
❑	170	Rob Johnson RC	1.25	.50
❑	171	Tyrone Wheatley RC	1.50	.60
❑	172	Napoleon Kaufman RC	1.50	.60
❑	173	James O. Stewart RC	1.50	.60
❑	174	Joe Aska RC	.10	.02
❑	175	Rashaan Salaam RC	.20	.07
❑	176	Tyrone Poole RC	.40	.15
❑	177	Ty Law RC	2.00	.75
❑	178	Dino Philyaw RC	.10	.02
❑	179	Mark Bruener RC	.20	.07
❑	180	Derrick Brooks RC	2.00	.75
❑	181	Jack Jackson RC	.10	.02
❑	182	Ray Zellars RC	.20	.07
❑	183	Eddie Goines RC	.10	.02
❑	184	Chris Sanders RC	.20	.07
❑	185	Charlie Simmons RC	.10	.02
❑	186	Lee DeRamus RC	.10	.02
❑	187	Frank Sanders RC	.40	.15
❑	188	Rodney Thomas RC	.20	.07
❑	189	Steve Stenstrom RC	.10	.02
❑	190	Stoney Case RC	.10	.02
❑	191	Tyrone Davis RC	.10	.02
❑	192	Kordell Stewart RC	2.00	.75
❑	193	Christian Fauria RC	.20	.07
❑	194	Todd Collins RC	.20	.07
❑	195	Sherman Williams RC	.10	.02
❑	196	Lovell Pinkney RC	.10	.02
❑	197	Eric Zeier RC	.40	.15
❑	198	Zack Crockett RC	.20	.07
❑	199	Checklist A	.10	.02
❑	200	Checklist B	.10	.02
❑	AU36	John Elway AUTO	150.00	75.00
❑	P1	Promo Sheet	2.00	.75
❑	AU46	Brett Favre AUTO/250	250.00	125.00

1996 SkyBox Premium

❑		COMPLETE SET (250)	20.00	7.50
❑	1	Larry Centers	.25	.08
❑	2	Boomer Esiason	.25	.08
❑	3	Garrison Hearst	.25	.08
❑	4	Rob Moore	.25	.08
❑	5	Frank Sanders	.25	.08
❑	6	Eric Swann	.10	.02
❑	7	Bert Emanuel	.25	.08
❑	8	Jeff George	.25	.08
❑	9	Craig Heyward	.10	.02
❑	10	Terance Mathis	.10	.02
❑	11	Eric Metcalf	.10	.02
❑	12	Derrick Alexander WR	.25	.08
❑	13	Leroy Hoard	.10	.02
❑	14	Michael Jackson	.25	.08
❑	15	Vinny Testaverde	.25	.08
❑	16	Eric Turner	.10	.02
❑	17	Darick Holmes	.10	.02
❑	18	Jim Kelly	.50	.20
❑	19	Bryce Paup	.10	.02
❑	20	Andre Reed	.25	.08
❑	21	Bruce Smith	.25	.08
❑	22	Thurman Thomas	.50	.20
❑	23	Tim Tindale RC	.10	.02
❑	24	Mark Carrier WR	.10	.02
❑	25	Kerry Collins	.50	.20
❑	26	Willie Green	.10	.02
❑	27	Kevin Greene	.25	.08
❑	28	Tyrone Poole	.10	.02
❑	29	Curtis Conway	.50	.20
❑	30	Bryan Cox	.10	.02
❑	31	Erik Kramer	.10	.02
❑	32	Nate Lewis	.10	.02

❑ 33	Rashaan Salaam	.25	.08
❑ 34	Alonzo Spellman	.10	.02
❑ 35	Michael Timpson	.10	.02
❑ 36	Jeff Blake	.50	.20
❑ 37	Ki-Jana Carter	.25	.08
❑ 38	David Dunn	.10	.02
❑ 39	Carl Pickens	.25	.08
❑ 40	Darnay Scott	.25	.08
❑ 41	Troy Aikman	1.25	.50
❑ 42	Charles Haley	.25	.08
❑ 43	Michael Irvin	.50	.20
❑ 44	Daryl Johnston	.25	.08
❑ 45	Jay Novacek	.10	.02
❑ 46	Deion Sanders	.75	.30
❑ 47	Emmitt Smith	2.00	.75
❑ 48	Kevin Williams	.10	.02
❑ 49	Steve Atwater	.10	.02
❑ 50	Terrell Davis	1.00	.40
❑ 51	John Elway	2.50	1.00
❑ 52	Anthony Miller	.25	.08
❑ 53	Shannon Sharpe	.25	.08
❑ 54	Mike Sherrard	.10	.02
❑ 55	Scott Mitchell	.25	.08
❑ 56	Herman Moore	.25	.08
❑ 57	Johnnie Morton	.25	.08
❑ 58	Brett Perriman	.10	.02
❑ 59	Barry Sanders	2.00	.75
❑ 60	Edgar Bennett	.25	.08
❑ 61	Robert Brooks	.50	.20
❑ 62	Mark Chmura	.25	.08
❑ 63	Brett Favre	2.50	1.00
❑ 64	Antonio Freeman	.50	.20
❑ 65	Keith Jackson	.10	.02
❑ 66	Reggie White	.50	.20
❑ 67	Chris Chandler	.25	.08
❑ 68	Mel Gray	.10	.02
❑ 69	Steve McNair	1.00	.40
❑ 70	Chris Sanders	.25	.08
❑ 71	Rodney Thomas	.10	.02
❑ 72	Quentin Coryatt	.10	.02
❑ 73	Sean Dawkins	.10	.02
❑ 74	Ken Dilger	.25	.08
❑ 75	Marshall Faulk	.60	.25
❑ 76	Jim Harbaugh	.25	.08
❑ 77	Lamont Warren	.10	.02
❑ 78	Tony Boselli	.10	.02
❑ 79	Mark Brunell	.75	.30
❑ 80	Willie Jackson	.25	.08
❑ 81	Natrone Means	.25	.08
❑ 82	James O.Stewart	.25	.08
❑ 83	Marcus Allen	.50	.20
❑ 84	Kimble Anders	.25	.08
❑ 85	Steve Bono	.10	.02
❑ 86	Lake Dawson	.10	.02
❑ 87	Neil Smith	.25	.08
❑ 88	Derrick Thomas	.50	.20
❑ 89	Tamarick Vanover	.25	.08
❑ 90	Fred Barnett	.10	.02
❑ 91	Terry Kirby	.25	.08
❑ 92	Dan Marino	2.50	1.00
❑ 93	O.J. McDuffie	.25	.08
❑ 94	Bernie Parmalee	.10	.02
❑ 95	Richmond Webb	.10	.02
❑ 96	Cris Carter	.50	.20
❑ 97	Scottie Graham	.10	.02
❑ 98	Qadry Ismail	.25	.08
❑ 99	Warren Moon	.25	.08
❑ 100	Jake Reed	.25	.08
❑ 101	Robert Smith	.25	.08
❑ 102	Drew Bledsoe	.75	.30
❑ 103	Vincent Brisby	.10	.02
❑ 104	Ben Coates	.25	.08
❑ 105	Curtis Martin	1.00	.40
❑ 106	Dave Meggett	.10	.02
❑ 107	Chris Slade	.10	.02
❑ 108	Mario Bates	.25	.08
❑ 109	Jim Everett	.10	.02
❑ 110	Michael Haynes	.10	.02

❑ 111	Tyrone Hughes	.10	.02
❑ 112	Renaldo Turnbull	.10	.02
❑ 113	Dave Brown	.10	.02
❑ 114	Chris Calloway	.10	.02
❑ 115	Rodney Hampton	.25	.08
❑ 116	Thomas Lewis	.10	.02
❑ 117	Tyrone Wheatley	.25	.08
❑ 118	Kyle Brady	.10	.02
❑ 119	Hugh Douglas	.25	.08
❑ 120	Aaron Glenn	.10	.02
❑ 121	Jeff Graham	.10	.02
❑ 122	Adrian Murrell	.25	.08
❑ 123	Neil O'Donnell	.25	.08
❑ 124	Tim Brown	.50	.20
❑ 125	Nolan Harrison	.10	.02
❑ 126	Billy Joe Hobert	.25	.08
❑ 127	Jeff Hostetler	.10	.02
❑ 128	Napoleon Kaufman	.50	.20
❑ 129	Chester McGlockton	.10	.02
❑ 130	Harvey Williams	.10	.02
❑ 131	Charlie Garner	.25	.08
❑ 132	Andy Harmon	.10	.02
❑ 133	Chris T. Jones	.25	.08
❑ 134	Mike Mamula	.10	.02
❑ 135	Rodney Peete	.10	.02
❑ 136	Bobby Taylor	.10	.02
❑ 137	Ricky Watters	.25	.08
❑ 138	Jerome Bettis	.50	.20
❑ 139	Greg Lloyd	.25	.08
❑ 140	Jim Miller	.50	.20
❑ 141	Ernie Mills	.10	.02
❑ 142	Kordell Stewart	.50	.20
❑ 143	Yancey Thigpen	.25	.08
❑ 144	Rod Woodson	.25	.08
❑ 145	Andre Coleman	.10	.02
❑ 146	Terrell Fletcher	.10	.02
❑ 147	Aaron Hayden RC	.10	.02
❑ 148	Stan Humphries	.25	.08
❑ 149	Junior Seau	.50	.20
❑ 150	Isaac Bruce	.50	.20
❑ 151	Kevin Carter	.10	.02
❑ 152	Todd Kinchen	.10	.02
❑ 153	Leslie O'Neal	.10	.02
❑ 154	Steve Walsh	.10	.02
❑ 155	William Floyd	.25	.08
❑ 156	Merton Hanks	.10	.02
❑ 157	Brent Jones	.10	.02
❑ 158	Derek Loville	.10	.02
❑ 159	Ken Norton	.10	.02
❑ 160	Jerry Rice	1.25	.50
❑ 161	J.J. Stokes	.50	.20
❑ 162	Steve Young	1.00	.40
❑ 163	Brian Blades	.10	.02
❑ 164	Christian Fauria	.10	.02
❑ 165	Joey Galloway	.50	.20
❑ 166	Rick Mirer	.25	.08
❑ 167	Chris Warren	.25	.08
❑ 168	Trent Dilfer	.50	.20
❑ 169	Alvin Harper	.10	.02
❑ 170	Jackie Harris	.10	.02
❑ 171	Hardy Nickerson	.10	.02
❑ 172	Errict Rhett	.25	.08
❑ 173	Terry Allen	.25	.08
❑ 174	Henry Ellard	.10	.02
❑ 175	Gus Frerotte	.25	.08
❑ 176	Brian Mitchell	.10	.02
❑ 177	Heath Shuler	.25	.08
❑ 178	Michael Westbrook	.50	.20
❑ 179	Karim Abdul-Jabbar RC	.50	.20
❑ 180	Mike Alstott RC	1.25	.50
❑ 181	Willie Anderson RC	.10	.02
❑ 182	Marco Battaglia RC	.10	.02
❑ 183	Tim Biakabutuka RC	.50	.20
❑ 184	Tony Brackens RC	.50	.20
❑ 185	Duane Clemons RC	.10	.02
❑ 186	Marcus Coleman RC	.10	.02
❑ 187	Ernie Conwell RC	.10	.02
❑ 188	Chris Darkins RC	.10	.02

❑ 189	Stephen Davis RC	2.00	.75
❑ 190	Brian Dawkins RC	1.50	.60
❑ 191	Rickey Dudley RC	.50	.20
❑ 192	Jason Dunn RC	.25	.08
❑ 193	Bobby Engram RC	.50	.20
❑ 194	Daryl Gardener RC	.10	.02
❑ 195	Eddie George RC	1.50	.60
❑ 196	Terry Glenn RC	1.25	.50
❑ 197	Kevin Hardy RC	.50	.20
❑ 198	Walt Harris RC	.10	.02
❑ 199	Marvin Harrison RC	3.00	1.25
❑ 200	Bobby Hoying RC	.50	.20
❑ 201	Israel Ifeanyi RC	.10	.02
❑ 202	DeRon Jenkins RC	.10	.02
❑ 203	Keyshawn Johnson RC	1.25	.50
❑ 204	Lance Johnstone RC	.25	.08
❑ 205	Cedric Jones RC	.10	.02
❑ 206	Marcus Jones RC	.10	.02
❑ 207	Eddie Kennison RC	.50	.20
❑ 208	Jevon Langford RC	.10	.02
❑ 209	Dedric Mathis RC	.10	.02
❑ 210	Jermane Mayberry RC	.10	.02
❑ 211	Leeland McElroy RC	.25	.08
❑ 212	Johnny McWilliams RC	.25	.08
❑ 213	Ray Mickens RC	.10	.02
❑ 214	John Mobley RC	.10	.02
❑ 215	Jerald Moore RC	.25	.08
❑ 216	Eric Moulds RC	1.50	.60
❑ 217	Muhsin Muhammad RC	1.00	.40
❑ 218	Jonathan Ogden RC	.50	.20
❑ 219	Lawrence Phillips RC	.50	.20
❑ 220	Kavika Pittman RC	.10	.02
❑ 221	Stanley Pritchett RC	.25	.08
❑ 222	Simeon Rice RC	1.25	.50
❑ 223	Detron Smith RC	.10	.02
❑ 224	Bryan Still RC	.25	.08
❑ 225	Amani Toomer RC	1.25	.50
❑ 226	Regan Upshaw RC	.10	.02
❑ 227	Alex Van Dyke RC	.25	.08
❑ 228	Stepfret Williams RC	.25	.08
❑ 229	Coryatt/McGlockton/ Pickens/Brooks	.25	.08
❑ 230	D.Crtr/E.Bnn/Blds/Hrst	.50	.20
❑ 231	Means/Mirer/Bettis/R.Smith	.25	.08
❑ 232	McDffie/Cnwy/Faulk/G.Hill	.50	.20
❑ 233	Shuler/Dilfer/Floyd/C.Johnson	.25	.08
❑ 234	Rhett/Dawkins/Bates/K.Carter	.25	.08
❑ 235	K.Cllns/McNair/Gallo./Salm	.50	.20
❑ 236	Stokes/Westb./Brdy/K.Stw.	.50	.20
❑ 237	K.Johnson/E.George/McElroy/ Phillips	.25	.08
❑ 238	Engram/Dudley/Moulds/ Biakabutuka	.25	.08
❑ 239	K.Stewart/Q.Coryatt	.50	.20
❑ 240	Panorama Nov.26, 1995	.25	.08
❑ 241	Panorama Nov.12, 1995	.10	.02
❑ 242	Panorama Dec.9, 1995	.10	.02
❑ 243	Panorama Sept.17, 1995	.25	.08
❑ 244	Panorama Oct.29, 1995	.10	.02
❑ 245	Panorama Oct.15, 1995	.10	.02
❑ 246	Panorama Dec.31, 1995	.50	.20
❑ 247	Panorama Jan.14, 1996	.10	.02
❑ 248	Panorama Nov.19, 1995	.25	.08
❑ 249	Checklist Card 1	.10	.02
❑ 250	Checklist Card 2	.10	.02
❑ P1	Promo Sheet/Favre/McElroy/KStew/QCory	2.50	1.00

1997 SkyBox Premium

❑	COMPLETE SET (250)	30.00	12.50
❑ 1	Brett Favre	2.50	1.25
❑ 2	Michael Bates	.25	.08
❑ 3	Jeff Graham	.25	.08
❑ 4	Terry Glenn	.60	.25
❑ 5	Stephen Davis	.60	.25
❑ 6	Wesley Walls	.40	.15
❑ 7	Barry Sanders	2.00	.75
❑ 8	Chris Sanders	.25	.08
❑ 9	O.J. McDuffie	.40	.15
❑ 10	Ken Dilger	.25	.08

	#	Player	Mint	Ex
❑	11	Kimble Anders	.40	.15
❑	12	Keenan McCardell	.40	.15
❑	13	Ki-Jana Carter	.25	.08
❑	14	Gary Brown	.25	.08
❑	15	Andre Rison	.40	.15
❑	16	Edgar Bennett	.40	.15
❑	17	Jerome Bettis	.60	.25
❑	18	Ted Johnson	.25	.08
❑	19	John Friesz	.25	.08
❑	20	Tony Brackens	.25	.08
❑	21	Bryan Cox	.25	.08
❑	22	Eric Moulds	.60	.25
❑	23	Johnnie Morton	.40	.15
❑	24	Brad Johnson	.60	.25
❑	25	Byron Bam Morris	.25	.08
❑	26	Anthony Johnson	.25	.08
❑	27	Jim Harbaugh	.40	.15
❑	28	Keyshawn Johnson	.60	.25
❑	29	Cary Blanchard	.25	.08
❑	30	Curtis Conway	.40	.15
❑	31	Herschel Walker	.40	.15
❑	32	Thurman Thomas	.60	.25
❑	33	Frank Sanders	.40	.15
❑	34	Lawrence Phillips	.25	.08
❑	35	Scottie Graham	.25	.08
❑	36	Jim Everett	.25	.08
❑	37	Dale Carter	.25	.08
❑	38	Ashley Ambrose	.25	.08
❑	39	Mark Chmura	.40	.15
❑	40	James O.Stewart	.40	.15
❑	41	John Mobley	.25	.08
❑	42	Terrell Davis	.75	.30
❑	43	Ben Coates	.40	.15
❑	44	Jeff George	.40	.15
❑	45	Ty Detmer	.40	.15
❑	46	Isaac Bruce	.60	.25
❑	47	Chris Warren	.40	.15
❑	48	Steve Walsh	.25	.08
❑	49	Bruce Smith	.40	.15
❑	50	Cris Carter	.60	.25
❑	51	Jamal Anderson	.60	.25
❑	52	Tim Biakabutuka	.40	.15
❑	53	Steve Young	.75	.30
❑	54	Eric Turner	.25	.08
❑	55	Jessie Tuggle	.25	.08
❑	56	Chris T. Jones	.25	.08
❑	57	Daryl Johnston	.40	.15
❑	58	Randall Cunningham	.60	.25
❑	59	Trent Dilfer	.60	.25
❑	60	Mark Brunell	.75	.30
❑	61	Warren Moon	.60	.25
❑	62	Terry Kirby	.40	.15
❑	63	Eddie George	.60	.25
❑	64	Neil Smith	.40	.15
❑	65	Gilbert Brown	.40	.15
❑	66	Emmitt Smith	2.00	.75
❑	67	Chad Brown	.25	.08
❑	68	Jamie Asher	.25	.08
❑	69	Willie McGinest	.25	.08
❑	70	Tim Brown	.60	.25
❑	71	Quentin Coryatt	.25	.08
❑	72	Mario Bates	.25	.08
❑	73	Fred Barnett	.25	.08
❑	74	Hugh Douglas	.25	.08
❑	75	Eric Swann	.25	.08
❑	76	Chris Chandler	.40	.15
❑	77	Larry Centers	.40	.15
❑	78	Vinny Testaverde	.40	.15
❑	79	Jermaine Lewis	.60	.25
❑	80	Junior Seau	.60	.25
❑	81	Kevin Greene	.40	.15
❑	82	Ricky Watters	.40	.15
❑	83	Billy Davis RC	.25	.08
❑	84	Michael Westbrook	.40	.15
❑	85	Charles Way	.40	.15
❑	86	Andre Reed	.40	.15
❑	87	Darrell Green	.40	.15
❑	88	Troy Aikman	1.25	.50
❑	89	Jim Pyne	.25	.08
❑	90	Dan Marino	2.50	1.00
❑	91	Elvis Grbac	.40	.15
❑	92	Mel Gray	.25	.08
❑	93	Marcus Allen	.60	.25
❑	94	Terry Allen	.60	.25
❑	95	Karim Abdul-Jabbar	.60	.25
❑	96	Rick Mirer	.25	.08
❑	97	Bert Emanuel	.40	.15
❑	98	John Elway	2.50	1.00
❑	99	Tony Martin	.40	.15
❑	100	Zach Thomas	.60	.25
❑	101	Harvey Williams	.25	.08
❑	102	Jason Sehorn	.40	.15
❑	103	Lawyer Milloy	.40	.15
❑	104	Thomas Lewis	.25	.08
❑	105	Michael Irvin	.60	.25
❑	106	James Hundon RC	.60	.25
❑	107	Willie Green	.25	.08
❑	108	Bobby Engram	.40	.15
❑	109	Mike Alstott	.60	.25
❑	110	Greg Lloyd	.25	.08
❑	111	Shannon Sharpe	.40	.15
❑	112	Desmond Howard	.40	.15
❑	113	Jason Elam	.40	.15
❑	114	Qadry Ismail	.40	.15
❑	115	William Thomas	.25	.08
❑	116	Marshall Faulk	.75	.30
❑	117	Tyrone Wheatley	.40	.15
❑	118	Tommy Vardell	.25	.08
❑	119	Rashaan Salaam	.25	.08
❑	120	Brian Mitchell	.25	.08
❑	121	Terance Mathis	.40	.15
❑	122	Dorsey Levens	.60	.25
❑	123	Todd Collins	.25	.08
❑	124	Derrick Alexander WR	.40	.15
❑	125	Stan Humphries	.40	.15
❑	126	Kordell Stewart	.60	.25
❑	127	Kent Graham	.25	.08
❑	128	Yancey Thigpen	.40	.15
❑	129	Bryan Still	.25	.08
❑	130	Carl Pickens	.40	.15
❑	131	Ray Lewis	1.00	.40
❑	132	Curtis Martin	.75	.30
❑	133	Kerry Collins	.60	.25
❑	134	Ed McCaffrey	.40	.15
❑	135	Darick Holmes	.25	.08
❑	136	Glyn Milburn	.25	.08
❑	137	Rickey Dudley	.40	.15
❑	138	Terrell Owens	.75	.30
❑	139	Kevin Williams	.25	.08
❑	140	Reggie White	.60	.25
❑	141	Darnay Scott	.40	.15
❑	142	Brett Perriman	.25	.08
❑	143	Neil O'Donnell	.40	.15
❑	144	Natrone Means	.40	.15
❑	145	Jerris McPhail	.25	.08
❑	146	Lamar Lathon	.25	.08
❑	147	Michael Jackson	.40	.15
❑	148	Simeon Rice	.40	.15
❑	149	Greg Hill	.25	.08
❑	150	Erik Kramer	.25	.08
❑	151	Quinn Early	.25	.08
❑	152	Tamarick Vanover	.40	.15
❑	153	Derrick Thomas	.60	.25
❑	154	Nilo Silvan	.25	.08
❑	155	Deion Sanders	.60	.25
❑	156	Lorenzo Neal	.25	.08
❑	157	Steve McNair	.75	.30
❑	158	Levon Kirkland	.25	.08
❑	159	Bobby Hebert	.25	.08
❑	160	William Floyd	.40	.15
❑	161	Leeland McElroy	.25	.08
❑	162	Chester McGlockton	.25	.08
❑	163	Michael Haynes	.25	.08
❑	164	Aeneas Williams	.25	.08
❑	165	Hardy Nickerson	.25	.08
❑	166	Ray Zellars	.25	.08
❑	167	Iheanyi Uwaezuoke	.40	.15
❑	168	Chris Slade	.25	.08
❑	169	Herman Moore	.40	.15
❑	170	Rob Moore	.40	.15
❑	171	Andre Hastings	.25	.08
❑	172	Antonio Freeman	.60	.25
❑	173	Tony Boselli	.25	.08
❑	174	Drew Bledsoe	.75	.30
❑	175	Sam Mills	.25	.08
❑	176	Robert Smith	.40	.15
❑	177	Jimmy Smith	.40	.15
❑	178	Alex Molden	.25	.08
❑	179	Joey Galloway	.40	.15
❑	180	Irving Fryar	.40	.15
❑	181	Wayne Chrebet	.60	.25
❑	182	Dave Brown	.25	.08
❑	183	Robert Brooks	.40	.15
❑	184	Tony Banks	.40	.15
❑	185	Eric Metcalf	.40	.15
❑	186	Napoleon Kaufman	.60	.25
❑	187	Frank Wycheck	.25	.08
❑	188	Donnell Woolford	.25	.08
❑	189	Kevin Turner	.25	.08
❑	190	Eddie Kennison	.40	.15
❑	191	Cortez Kennedy	.25	.08
❑	192	Raymont Harris	.25	.08
❑	193	Ronnie Harmon	.25	.08
❑	194	Kevin Hardy	.25	.08
❑	195	Gus Frerotte	.25	.08
❑	196	Marvin Harrison	.60	.25
❑	197	Jeff Blake	.40	.15
❑	198	Mike Tomczak	.25	.08
❑	199	William Roaf	.25	.08
❑	200	Jerry Rice	1.25	.50
❑	201	Jake Reed	.40	.15
❑	202	Ken Norton	.25	.08
❑	203	Errict Rhett	.25	.08
❑	204	Adrian Murrell	.40	.15
❑	205	Rodney Hampton	.40	.15
❑	206	Scott Mitchell	.40	.15
❑	207	Jason Dunn	.25	.08
❑	208	Mike Adams RC	.25	.08
❑	209	John Allred RC	.25	.08
❑	210	Reidel Anthony RC	.60	.25
❑	211	Darnell Autry RC	.40	.15
❑	212	Tiki Barber RC	4.00	1.50
❑	213	Will Blackwell RC	.40	.15
❑	214	Peter Boulware RC	.60	.25
❑	215	Macey Brooks RC	.60	.25
❑	216	Rae Carruth RC	.25	.08
❑	217	Troy Davis RC	.40	.15
❑	218	Corey Dillon RC	4.00	1.50
❑	219	Jim Druckenmiller RC	.40	.15
❑	220	Warrick Dunn RC	1.50	.60
❑	221	Marc Edwards RC	.25	.08
❑	222	James Farrior RC	.60	.25
❑	223	Tony Gonzalez RC	2.00	.75
❑	224	Jay Graham RC	.40	.15
❑	225	Yatil Green RC	.40	.15
❑	226	Byron Hanspard RC	.40	.15
❑	227	Ike Hilliard RC	.75	.30
❑	228	Leon Johnson RC	.40	.15

❑ 229 Damon Jones RC	.25	.08
❑ 230 Freddie Jones RC	.40	.15
❑ 231 Joey Kent RC	.60	.25
❑ 232 David LaFleur RC	.25	.08
❑ 233 Kevin Lockett RC	.40	.15
❑ 234 Sam Madison RC	.60	.25
❑ 235 Brian Manning RC	.25	.08
❑ 236 Ronnie McAda RC	.25	.08
❑ 237 Orlando Pace RC	.60	.25
❑ 238 Jake Plummer RC	3.00	1.25
❑ 239 Keith Poole RC	.60	.25
❑ 240 Darrell Russell RC	.25	.08
❑ 241 Sedrick Shaw RC	.40	.15
❑ 242 Antowain Smith RC	1.50	.60
❑ 243 Shawn Springs RC	.40	.15
❑ 244 Duce Staley RC	5.00	2.00
❑ 245 Dedric Ward RC	.40	.15
❑ 246 Bryant Westbrook RC	.25	.08
❑ 247 Danny Wuerffel RC	.60	.25
❑ 248 Checklist	.25	.08
❑ 249 Checklist	.25	.08
❑ 250 Checklist	.25	.08
❑ S1 Terrell Davis Sample	2.00	.75

1998 SkyBox Premium

❑ COMPLETE SET (250)	80.00	30.00
❑ 1 John Elway	2.50	1.00
❑ 2 Drew Bledsoe	1.00	.40
❑ 3 Antonio Freeman	.60	.25
❑ 4 Merton Hanks	.25	.08
❑ 5 James Jett	.40	.15
❑ 6 Ricky Proehl	.25	.08
❑ 7 Deion Sanders	.60	.25
❑ 8 Frank Sanders	.40	.15
❑ 9 Bruce Smith	.40	.15
❑ 10 Tiki Barber	.60	.25
❑ 11 Isaac Bruce	.60	.25
❑ 12 Mark Brunell	.60	.25
❑ 13 Quinn Early	.25	.08
❑ 14 Terry Glenn	.60	.25
❑ 15 Darrien Gordon	.25	.08
❑ 16 Keith Byars	.25	.08
❑ 17 Terrell Davis	.60	.25
❑ 18 Charlie Garner	.40	.15
❑ 19 Eddie Kennison	.40	.15
❑ 20 Keenan McCardell	.40	.15
❑ 21 Eric Moulds	.60	.25
❑ 22 Jimmy Smith	.40	.15
❑ 23 Reidel Anthony	.40	.15
❑ 24 Rae Carruth	.25	.08
❑ 25 Michael Irvin	.60	.25
❑ 26 Dorsey Levens	.60	.25
❑ 27 Derrick Mayes	.40	.15
❑ 28 Adrian Murrell	.40	.15
❑ 29 Dwayne Rudd	.25	.08
❑ 30 Leslie Shepherd	.25	.08
❑ 31 Jamal Anderson	.60	.25
❑ 32 Robert Brooks	.40	.15
❑ 33 Sean Dawkins	.25	.08
❑ 34 Cris Dishman	.25	.08
❑ 35 Rickey Dudley	.25	.08
❑ 36 Bobby Engram	.40	.15
❑ 37 Chester McGlockton	.25	.08
❑ 38 Terrell Owens	.60	.25
❑ 39 Wayne Chrebet	.60	.25
❑ 40 Dexter Coakley	.25	.08
❑ 41 Kerry Collins	.40	.15
❑ 42 Trent Dilfer	.60	.25
❑ 43 Bobby Hoying	.40	.15
❑ 44 Glyn Milburn	.25	.08
❑ 45 Rob Moore	.40	.15
❑ 46 Jake Reed	.40	.15
❑ 47 Dana Stubblefield	.25	.08
❑ 48 Reggie White	.60	.25
❑ 49 Natrone Means	.40	.15
❑ 50 Troy Aikman	1.25	.50
❑ 51 Aaron Bailey	.25	.08
❑ 52 William Floyd	.25	.08
❑ 53 Eric Metcalf	.25	.08
❑ 54 Warrick Dunn	.60	.25
❑ 55 Chad Lewis	.40	.15
❑ 56 Curtis Martin	.60	.25
❑ 57 Tony Martin	.40	.15
❑ 58 John Randle	.40	.15
❑ 59 Jeff Burris	.25	.08
❑ 60 Larry Centers	.25	.08
❑ 61 Bert Emanuel	.40	.15
❑ 62 Sean Gilbert	.25	.08
❑ 63 David Palmer	.25	.08
❑ 64 Eric Bieniemy	.25	.08
❑ 65 Peter Boulware	.25	.08
❑ 66 Charles Johnson	.25	.08
❑ 67 Jerris McPhail	.25	.08
❑ 68 Scott Mitchell	.40	.15
❑ 69 Chris Sanders	.25	.08
❑ 70 Ken Dilger	.25	.08
❑ 71 Brad Johnson	.60	.25
❑ 72 Danny Kanell	.40	.15
❑ 73 Fred Lane	.25	.08
❑ 74 Warren Sapp	.40	.15
❑ 75 Carl Pickens	.40	.15
❑ 76 Cris Carter	.60	.25
❑ 77 Marshall Faulk	.75	.30
❑ 78 Keyshawn Johnson	.60	.25
❑ 79 Tony McGee	.25	.08
❑ 80 Muhsin Muhammad	.40	.15
❑ 81 Kordell Stewart	.60	.25
❑ 82 Karl Williams	.25	.08
❑ 83 Willie Davis	.25	.08
❑ 84 David Dunn	.25	.08
❑ 85 Marvin Harrison	.60	.25
❑ 86 Michael Jackson	.25	.08
❑ 87 John Mobley	.25	.08
❑ 88 Shawn Springs	.25	.08
❑ 89 Wesley Walls	.40	.15
❑ 90 Jermaine Lewis	.40	.15
❑ 91 Ed McCaffrey	.40	.15
❑ 92 Chris Calloway	.25	.08
❑ 93 Lamont Warren	.25	.08
❑ 94 Ricky Watters	.40	.15
❑ 95 Tony Banks	.40	.15
❑ 96 Tony Brackens	.25	.08
❑ 97 Gary Brown	.25	.08
❑ 98 Howard Griffith	.25	.08
❑ 99 Ray Lewis	.60	.25
❑ 100 Jeff Blake	.40	.15
❑ 101 Charlie Jones	.25	.08
❑ 102 Glenn Foley	.40	.15
❑ 103 Jay Graham	.25	.08
❑ 104 James McKnight	.60	.25
❑ 105 Steve McNair	.60	.25
❑ 106 Chad Scott	.25	.08
❑ 107 Rod Smith WR	.40	.15
❑ 108 Jason Taylor	.40	.15
❑ 109 Corey Dillon	.60	.25
❑ 110 Eddie George	.60	.25
❑ 111 Jim Harbaugh	.40	.15
❑ 112 Warren Moon	.60	.25
❑ 113 Shannon Sharpe	.40	.15
❑ 114 Darnell Autry	.25	.08
❑ 115 Brett Favre	2.50	1.25
❑ 116 Jeff George	.40	.15
❑ 117 Tony Gonzalez	.60	.25
❑ 118 Garrison Hearst	.60	.25
❑ 119 Randal Hill	.25	.08
❑ 120 Eric Swann	.25	.08
❑ 121 Jamie Asher	.25	.08
❑ 122 Tim Brown	.60	.25
❑ 123 Stephen Davis	.25	.08
❑ 124 Chris Chandler	.40	.15
❑ 125 Jerry Rice	1.25	.50
❑ 126 Troy Davis	.25	.08
❑ 127 Ronnie Harmon	.25	.08
❑ 128 Andre Rison	.40	.15
❑ 129 Duce Staley	.75	.30
❑ 130 Charles Way	.25	.08
❑ 131 Bryant Westbrook	.25	.08
❑ 132 Mike Alstott	.60	.25
❑ 133 Gus Frerotte	.25	.08
❑ 134 Travis Jervey	.40	.15
❑ 135 Daryl Johnston	.40	.15
❑ 136 Jake Plummer	.60	.25
❑ 137 Junior Seau	.60	.25
❑ 138 Robert Smith	.60	.25
❑ 139 Thurman Thomas	.60	.25
❑ 140 Karim Abdul-Jabbar	.60	.25
❑ 141 Jerome Bettis	.60	.25
❑ 142 Byron Hanspard	.25	.08
❑ 143 Raymont Harris	.25	.08
❑ 144 Willie McGinest	.25	.08
❑ 145 Barry Sanders	2.00	.75
❑ 146 Irv Smith	.25	.08
❑ 147 Michael Strahan	.40	.15
❑ 148 Frank Wycheck	.25	.08
❑ 149 Steve Broussard	.25	.08
❑ 150 Joey Galloway	.40	.15
❑ 151 Courtney Hawkins	.25	.08
❑ 152 O.J. McDuffie	.40	.15
❑ 153 Herman Moore	.40	.15
❑ 154 Chris Penn	.25	.08
❑ 155 O.J. Santiago	.25	.08
❑ 156 Yancey Thigpen	.25	.08
❑ 157 Jason Sehorn	.40	.15
❑ 158 Ben Coates	.40	.15
❑ 159 Ernie Conwell	.25	.08
❑ 160 Dale Carter	.25	.08
❑ 161 Jeff Graham	.25	.08
❑ 162 Rob Johnson	.40	.15
❑ 163 Damon Jones	.25	.08
❑ 164 Mark Chmura	.40	.15
❑ 165 Curtis Conway	.40	.15
❑ 166 Elvis Grbac	.40	.15
❑ 167 Andre Hastings	.25	.08
❑ 168 Terry Kirby	.25	.08
❑ 169 Aeneas Williams	.25	.08
❑ 170 Derrick Alexander WR	.40	.15
❑ 171 Troy Brown	.40	.15
❑ 172 Irving Fryar	.40	.15
❑ 173 Jerald Moore	.25	.08
❑ 174 Andre Reed	.40	.15
❑ 175 James Stewart	.40	.15
❑ 176 Chris Warren	.40	.15
❑ 177 Will Blackwell	.25	.08
❑ 178 Erik Kramer	.25	.08
❑ 179 Dan Marino	2.50	1.00
❑ 180 Terance Mathis	.40	.15
❑ 181 Johnnie Morton	.40	.15
❑ 182 J.J. Stokes	.40	.15
❑ 183 Rodney Thomas	.25	.08
❑ 184 Steve Young	.75	.30
❑ 185 Kimble Anders	.40	.15
❑ 186 Napoleon Kaufman	.60	.25
❑ 187 Orlando Pace	.25	.08
❑ 188 Antowain Smith	.60	.25
❑ 189 Emmitt Smith	2.00	.75
❑ 190 Terry Allen	.60	.25
❑ 191 Mark Bruener	.25	.08
❑ 192 Rodney Harrison	.40	.15

	Card	Hi	Lo
❑	193 Billy Joe Hobert	.25	.08
❑	194 Leon Johnson	.25	.08
❑	195 Freddie Jones	.25	.08
❑	196 John Elway OFA	1.00	.40
❑	197 Brett Favre/Atwater OFA	.75	.30
❑	198 Brett Favre/Atwater OFA	.75	.30
❑	199 D.Levens/Traylor OFA	.40	.15
❑	200 Packers/Broncos OFA	.60	.25
❑	201 M.Chmura/Braxton OFA	.25	.08
❑	202 Atwater/Levens/Roman. OFA	.40	.15
❑	203 R.Brooks/R.Crockett OFA	.40	.15
❑	204 Tim McKyer OFA	.25	.08
❑	205 Allen Aldridge OFA	.25	.08
❑	206 T.Davis/R.Smith OFA	.60	.25
❑	207 Bill Romanowski OFA	.25	.08
❑	208 Elway/R.Smith/McCaff.OFA	1.00	.40
❑	209 Ray Crockett OFA	.25	.08
❑	210 John Elway OFA	1.00	.40
❑	211 Robert Edwards RC	2.50	1.00
❑	212 Roland Williams RC	2.00	.75
❑	213 Joe Jurevicius RC	4.00	1.50
❑	214 Wilmont Perry RC	2.00	.75
❑	215 Robert Holcombe RC	2.50	1.00
❑	216 Larry Shannon RC	2.00	.75
❑	217 Skip Hicks RC	2.50	1.00
❑	218 Pat Johnson RC	2.50	1.00
❑	219 Pat Palmer RC	2.00	.75
❑	220 John Dutton RC	2.00	.75
❑	221 Az-Zahir Hakim RC	4.00	1.50
❑	222 Mikhael Ricks RC	2.50	1.00
❑	223 Rashaan Shehee RC	2.50	1.00
❑	224 Ryan Leaf RC	4.00	1.50
❑	225 Alvis Whitted RC	2.50	1.00
❑	226 Marcus Nash RC	2.00	.75
❑	227 Fred Taylor RC	6.00	2.50
❑	228 Hines Ward RC	15.00	7.50
❑	229 Chris Fuamatu-Ma'afala RC	2.50	1.00
❑	230 Jerome Pathon RC	4.00	1.50
❑	231 Peyton Manning RC	40.00	15.00
❑	232 Charles Woodson RC	5.00	2.00
❑	233 Jon Ritchie RC	2.50	1.00
❑	234 Scott Frost RC	2.00	.75
❑	235 John Avery RC	2.50	1.00
❑	236 Jonathan Linton RC	2.50	1.00
❑	237 Jacquez Green RC	2.50	1.00
❑	238 Andre Wadsworth RC	2.50	1.00
❑	239 Cam Quayle RC	2.00	.75
❑	240 Randy Moss RC	25.00	10.00
❑	241 Raymond Priester RC	2.00	.75
❑	242 Donald Hayes RC	2.50	1.00
❑	243 Brian Griese RC	8.00	3.00
❑	244 Brian Alford RC	2.00	.75
❑	245 Kevin Dyson RC	4.00	1.50
❑	246 Jammi German RC	2.00	.75
❑	247 Cameron Cleeland RC	2.00	.75
❑	248 Curtis Enis RC	2.00	.75
❑	249 Terry Hardy RC	2.00	.75
❑	250 Tony Simmons RC	2.50	1.00
❑	NNO Checklist Card	.25	.08
❑	P136 Jake Plummer Promo	1.50	.60

1999 SkyBox Premium

	Card	Hi	Lo
❑	COMPLETE SET (290)	300.00	150.00
❑	COMP.SET w/o SPs (250)	50.00	25.00
❑	1 Randy Moss	1.50	.60
❑	2 Jamie Asher	.25	.08
❑	3 Joey Galloway	.40	.15
❑	4 Kent Graham	.25	.08
❑	5 Leslie Shepherd	.25	.08
❑	6 Levon Kirkland	.25	.08
❑	7 Marcus Pollard	.25	.08
❑	8 O.J. McDuffie	.40	.15
❑	9 Bill Romanowski	.25	.08
❑	10 Priest Holmes	1.00	.40
❑	11 Tim Biakabutuka	.40	.15
❑	12 Duce Staley	.60	.25
❑	13 Isaac Bruce	.60	.25
❑	14 Jay Riemersma	.25	.08
❑	15 Karim Abdul-Jabbar	.40	.15
❑	16 Kevin Dyson	.40	.15
❑	17 Rickey Dudley	.25	.08
❑	18 Rocket Ismail	.40	.15
❑	19 Billy Davis	.25	.08
❑	20 James Jett	.40	.15
❑	21 Jerome Bettis	.60	.25
❑	22 Michael McCrary	.25	.08
❑	23 Michael Westbrook	.40	.15
❑	24 Oronde Gadsden	.40	.15
❑	25 Brad Johnson	.60	.25
❑	26 Shawn Springs	.25	.08
❑	27 Cris Carter	.60	.25
❑	28 Ed McCaffrey	.40	.15
❑	29 Gary Brown	.25	.08
❑	30 Hines Ward	.60	.25
❑	31 Hugh Douglas	.25	.08
❑	32 Jamir Miller	.25	.08
❑	33 Michael Bates	.25	.08
❑	34 Peyton Manning	2.00	.75
❑	35 Tony Banks	.40	.15
❑	36 Charles Way	.25	.08
❑	37 Charlie Batch	.60	.25
❑	38 Jake Reed	.40	.15
❑	39 Mark Brunell	.60	.25
❑	40 Skip Hicks	.25	.08
❑	41 Steve Young	.75	.30
❑	42 Wesley Walls	.40	.15
❑	43 Antonio Langham	.25	.08
❑	44 Antowain Smith	.60	.25
❑	45 Brian Griese	.60	.25
❑	46 Jessie Armstead	.25	.08
❑	47 Thurman Thomas	.40	.15
❑	48 Jeff George	.40	.15
❑	49 Jessie Tuggle	.25	.08
❑	50 Jim Harbaugh	.40	.15
❑	51 Marvin Harrison	.60	.25
❑	52 Randall Cunningham	.60	.25
❑	53 Stephen Alexander	.25	.08
❑	54 Tiki Barber	.60	.25
❑	55 Billy Joe Tolliver	.25	.08
❑	56 Bruce Smith	.40	.15
❑	57 Eddie George	.60	.25
❑	58 Eugene Robinson	.25	.08
❑	59 John Elway	2.00	.75
❑	60 Kent Dilger	.25	.08
❑	61 Rodney Harrison	.25	.08
❑	62 Ty Detmer	.40	.15
❑	63 Andre Reed	.40	.15
❑	64 Dorsey Levens	.60	.25
❑	65 Eddie Kennison	.40	.15
❑	66 Freddie Jones	.25	.08
❑	67 Jacquez Green	.25	.08
❑	68 Jason Elam	.25	.08
❑	69 Marc Edwards	.25	.08
❑	70 Terance Mathis	.40	.15
❑	71 Alonzo Mayes	.25	.08
❑	72 Andre Wadsworth	.25	.08
❑	73 Barry Sanders	2.00	.75
❑	74 Derrick Alexander	.25	.08
❑	75 Garrison Hearst	.40	.15
❑	76 Leon Johnson	.25	.08
❑	77 Mike Alstott	.60	.25
❑	78 Shawn Jefferson	.25	.08
❑	79 Andre Hastings	.25	.08
❑	80 Eric Moulds	.60	.25
❑	81 Ryan Leaf	.60	.25
❑	82 Takeo Spikes	.25	.08
❑	83 Terrell Davis	.60	.25
❑	84 Tim Dwight	.60	.25
❑	85 Trent Dilfer	.40	.15
❑	86 Vonnie Holliday	.25	.08
❑	87 Antonio Freeman	.60	.25
❑	88 Carl Pickens	.40	.15
❑	89 Chris Chandler	.40	.15
❑	90 Dale Carter	.25	.08
❑	91 La'Roi Glover RC	.60	.25
❑	92 Natrone Means	.40	.15
❑	93 Reidel Anthony	.40	.15
❑	94 Brett Favre	2.00	.75
❑	95 Bubby Brister	.25	.08
❑	96 Cameron Cleeland	.25	.08
❑	97 Chris Calloway	.25	.08
❑	98 Corey Dillon	.60	.25
❑	99 Greg Hill	.25	.08
❑	100 Vinny Testaverde	.40	.15
❑	101 Trent Green	.60	.25
❑	102 Sam Gash	.25	.08
❑	103 Mikhael Ricks	.25	.08
❑	104 Emmitt Smith	1.25	.50
❑	105 Doug Flutie	.60	.25
❑	106 Deion Sanders	.60	.25
❑	107 Charles Johnson	.25	.08
❑	108 Byron Bam Morris	.25	.08
❑	109 Andre Rison	.40	.15
❑	110 Doug Pederson	.25	.08
❑	111 Marshall Faulk	.75	.30
❑	112 Tim Brown	.60	.25
❑	113 Warren Sapp	.25	.08
❑	114 Bryan Still	.25	.08
❑	115 Chris Penn	.25	.08
❑	116 Jamal Anderson	.60	.25
❑	117 Keyshawn Johnson	.60	.25
❑	118 Ricky Proehl	.25	.08
❑	119 Robert Brooks	.40	.15
❑	120 Tony Gonzalez	.60	.25
❑	121 Ty Law	.40	.15
❑	122 Elvis Grbac	.40	.15
❑	123 Jeff Blake	.40	.15
❑	124 Mark Chmura	.25	.08
❑	125 Junior Seau	.60	.25
❑	126 Mo Lewis	.25	.08
❑	127 Ray Buchanan	.25	.08
❑	128 Robert Holcombe	.25	.08
❑	129 Tony Simmons	.25	.08
❑	130 David Palmer	.25	.08
❑	131 Ike Hilliard	.25	.08
❑	132 Mike Vanderjagt	.25	.08
❑	133 Rae Carruth	.25	.08
❑	134 Sean Dawkins	.25	.08
❑	135 Shannon Sharpe	.40	.15
❑	136 Curtis Conway	.40	.15
❑	137 Darrell Green	.25	.08
❑	138 Germane Crowell	.25	.08
❑	139 J.J. Stokes	.40	.15
❑	140 Kevin Hardy	.25	.08
❑	141 Rob Moore	.40	.15
❑	142 Robert Smith	.60	.25
❑	143 Wayne Chrebet	.40	.15
❑	144 Yancey Thigpen	.25	.08
❑	145 Jerome Pathon	.25	.08
❑	146 John Mobley	.25	.08
❑	147 Kerry Collins	.40	.15
❑	148 Peter Boulware	.25	.08
❑	149 Matthew Hatchette	.25	.08
❑	150 Kordell Stewart	.40	.15
❑	151 Koy Detmer	.25	.08
❑	152 Sedrick Shaw	.25	.08
❑	153 Steve Beuerlein	.25	.08
❑	154 Zach Thomas	.60	.25

❑ 155 Adrian Murrell	.40	.15
❑ 156 Bobby Engram	.40	.15
❑ 157 Bryan Cox	.25	.08
❑ 158 Drew Bledsoe	.75	.30
❑ 159 Jerry Rice	1.25	.50
❑ 160 Keenan McCardell	.40	.15
❑ 161 Steve McNair	.60	.25
❑ 162 Terry Fair	.25	.08
❑ 163 Derrick Brooks	.60	.25
❑ 164 Eric Green	.25	.08
❑ 165 Erik Kramer	.25	.08
❑ 166 Frank Sanders	.40	.15
❑ 167 Fred Taylor	.60	.25
❑ 168 Johnnie Morton	.40	.15
❑ 169 R.W. McQuarters	.25	.08
❑ 170 Terry Glenn	.60	.25
❑ 171 Frank Wycheck	.25	.08
❑ 172 John Avery	.25	.08
❑ 173 Kevin Turner	.25	.08
❑ 174 Larry Centers	.25	.08
❑ 175 Michael Irvin	.40	.15
❑ 176 Rich Gannon	.60	.25
❑ 177 Ricky Watters	.40	.15
❑ 178 Rodney Thomas	.25	.08
❑ 179 Scott Mitchell	.25	.08
❑ 180 Chad Brown	.25	.08
❑ 181 John Randle	.40	.15
❑ 182 Michael Strahan	.40	.15
❑ 183 Muhsin Muhammad	.40	.15
❑ 184 Reggie Barlow	.25	.08
❑ 185 Rod Smith	.40	.15
❑ 186 Dan Marino	2.00	.75
❑ 187 Dexter Coakley	.25	.08
❑ 188 Jermaine Lewis	.40	.15
❑ 189 Jon Kitna	.60	.25
❑ 190 Napoleon Kaufman	.60	.25
❑ 191 Will Blackwell	.25	.08
❑ 192 Aaron Glenn	.25	.08
❑ 193 Ben Coates	.40	.15
❑ 194 Curtis Enis	.25	.08
❑ 195 Herman Moore	.40	.15
❑ 196 Jake Plummer	.40	.15
❑ 197 Jimmy Smith	.40	.15
❑ 198 Terrell Owens	.60	.25
❑ 199 Warrick Dunn	.60	.25
❑ 200 Charles Woodson	.60	.25
❑ 201 Ahman Green	.60	.25
❑ 202 Mark Bruener	.25	.08
❑ 203 Ray Lewis	.60	.25
❑ 204 Tony Martin	.40	.15
❑ 205 Troy Aikman	1.25	.50
❑ 206 Curtis Martin	.60	.25
❑ 207 Darnay Scott	.25	.08
❑ 208 Derrick Mayes	.25	.08
❑ 209 Keith Poole	.25	.08
❑ 210 Warren Moon	.60	.25
❑ 211 Chris Claiborne RC	.50	.20
❑ 211S Chris Claiborne SP	1.50	.60
❑ 212 Ricky Williams RC	2.50	1.00
❑ 212S Ricky Williams SP	8.00	3.00
❑ 213 Tim Couch RC	1.25	.50
❑ 213S Tim Couch SP	4.00	1.50
❑ 214 Champ Bailey RC	1.50	.60
❑ 214S Champ Bailey SP	5.00	2.00
❑ 215 Torry Holt RC	3.00	1.25
❑ 215S Torry Holt SP	10.00	4.00
❑ 216 Donovan McNabb RC	6.00	2.50
❑ 216S Donovan McNabb SP	20.00	7.50
❑ 217 David Boston RC	1.25	.50
❑ 217S David Boston SP	4.00	1.50
❑ 218 Chris McAlister RC	.75	.30
❑ 218S Chris McAlister SP	2.50	1.00
❑ 219 Michael Bishop RC	1.25	.50
❑ 219S Michael Bishop SP	4.00	1.50
❑ 220 Daunte Culpepper RC	5.00	2.00
❑ 220S Daunte Culpepper SP	15.00	6.00
❑ 221 Joe Germaine RC	.75	.30
❑ 221S Joe Germaine SP	2.50	1.00
❑ 222 Edgerrin James RC	5.00	2.00
❑ 222S Edgerrin James SP	15.00	6.00
❑ 223 Jevon Kearse RC	2.00	.75
❑ 223S Jevon Kearse SP	6.00	2.50
❑ 224 Ebenezer Ekuban RC	.75	.30
❑ 224S Ebenezer Ekuban SP	2.50	1.00
❑ 225 Scott Covington RC	1.25	.50
❑ 225S Scott Covington SP	4.00	1.50
❑ 226 Aaron Brooks RC	2.50	1.00
❑ 226S Aaron Brooks SP	8.00	3.00
❑ 227 Cecil Collins RC	.50	.20
❑ 227S Cecil Collins SP	1.50	.60
❑ 228 Akili Smith RC	.75	.30
❑ 228S Akili Smith SP	2.50	1.00
❑ 229 Shaun King RC	.75	.30
❑ 229S Shaun King SP	2.50	1.00
❑ 230 Chad Plummer RC	.50	.20
❑ 230S Chad Plummer SP	1.50	.60
❑ 231 Peerless Price RC	1.25	.50
❑ 231S Peerless Price SP	4.00	1.50
❑ 232 Antoine Winfield RC	.75	.30
❑ 232S Antoine Winfield SP	2.50	1.00
❑ 233 Antuan Edwards RC	.50	.20
❑ 233S Antuan Edwards SP	1.50	.60
❑ 234 Rob Konrad RC	1.25	.50
❑ 234S Rob Konrad SP	4.00	1.50
❑ 235 Troy Edwards RC	.75	.30
❑ 235S Troy Edwards SP	2.50	1.00
❑ 236 Terry Jackson RC	.75	.30
❑ 236S Terry Jackson SP	2.50	1.00
❑ 237 Jim Kleinsasser RC	1.25	.50
❑ 237S Jim Kleinsasser SP	4.00	1.50
❑ 238 Joe Montgomery RC	.75	.30
❑ 238S Joe Montgomery SP	2.50	1.00
❑ 239 Desmond Clark RC	1.25	.50
❑ 239S Desmond Clark SP	4.00	1.50
❑ 240 Lamar King RC	.50	.20
❑ 240S Lamar King SP	1.50	.60
❑ 241 Dameane Douglas RC	.75	.30
❑ 241S Dameane Douglas SP	2.50	1.00
❑ 242 Martin Gramatica RC	.50	.20
❑ 242S Martin Gramatica SP	1.50	.60
❑ 243 Jim Finn RC	.50	.20
❑ 243S Jim Finn SP	1.50	.60
❑ 244 Andy Katzenmoyer RC	.75	.30
❑ 244S Andy Katzenmoyer SP	2.50	1.00
❑ 245 Dee Miller RC	.50	.20
❑ 245S Dee Miller SP	1.50	.60
❑ 246 D'Wayne Bates RC	.75	.30
❑ 246S D'Wayne Bates SP	2.50	1.00
❑ 247 Amos Zereoue RC	1.25	.50
❑ 247S Amos Zereoue SP	4.00	1.50
❑ 248 Karsten Bailey RC	.75	.30
❑ 248S Karsten Bailey SP	2.50	1.00
❑ 249 Kevin Johnson RC	1.25	.50
❑ 249S Kevin Johnson SP	4.00	1.50
❑ 250 Cade McNown RC	.75	.30
❑ 250S Cade McNown SP	2.50	1.00

1993 SP

❑ COMPLETE SET (270)	60.00	25.00
❑ 1 Curtis Conway FOIL RC	4.00	1.50
❑ 2 John Copeland FOIL RC	.75	.30
❑ 3 Kevin Williams RC WR FOIL	1.50	.60
❑ 4 Dan Williams FOIL RC	.75	.30
❑ 5 Patrick Bates FOIL RC	.75	.30
❑ 6 Jerome Bettis FOIL RC	25.00	15.00
❑ 7 O.J.McDuffie FOIL RC	3.00	1.25
❑ 8 Robert Smith FOIL RC	8.00	3.00
❑ 9 Drew Bledsoe FOIL RC	30.00	12.50
❑ 10 Irv Smith FOIL RC	.75	.30
❑ 11 Marvin Jones FOIL RC	.75	.30
❑ 12 Victor Bailey FOIL RC	.75	.30
❑ 13 Garrison Hearst FOIL RC	8.00	3.00
❑ 14 Natrone Means FOIL RC	3.00	1.25
❑ 15 Todd Kelly FOIL RC	.75	.30
❑ 16 Rick Mirer FOIL RC	3.00	1.25
❑ 17 Eric Curry FOIL RC	.75	.30
❑ 18 Reggie Brooks FOIL RC	1.50	.60
❑ 19 Eric Dickerson	.50	.20
❑ 20 Roger Harper RC	.30	.10
❑ 21 Michael Haynes	.50	.20
❑ 22 Bobby Hebert	.30	.10
❑ 23 Lincoln Kennedy RC	.30	.10
❑ 24 Chris Miller	.50	.20
❑ 25 Mike Pritchard	.50	.20
❑ 26 Andre Rison	.50	.20
❑ 27 Deion Sanders	1.50	.60
❑ 28 Cornelius Bennett	.50	.20
❑ 29 Kenneth Davis	.30	.10
❑ 30 Henry Jones	.30	.10
❑ 31 Jim Kelly	1.00	.40
❑ 32 John Parrella RC	.30	.10
❑ 33 Andre Reed	.50	.20
❑ 34 Bruce Smith	1.00	.40
❑ 35 Thomas Smith RC	.50	.20
❑ 36 Thurman Thomas	1.00	.40
❑ 37 Neal Anderson	.30	.10
❑ 38 Myron Baker RC	.30	.10
❑ 39 Mark Carrier DB	.30	.10
❑ 40 Richard Dent	.50	.20
❑ 41 Chris Gedney RC	.30	.10
❑ 42 Jim Harbaugh	1.00	.40
❑ 43 Craig Heyward	.50	.20
❑ 44 Carl Simpson RC	.30	.10
❑ 45 Alonzo Spellman	.30	.10
❑ 46 Derrick Fenner	.30	.10
❑ 47 Harold Green	.30	.10
❑ 48 David Klingler	.30	.10
❑ 49 Ricardo McDonald	.30	.10
❑ 50 Tony McGee RC	.50	.20
❑ 51 Carl Pickens	.50	.20
❑ 52 Steve Tovar RC	.30	.10
❑ 53 Alfred Williams	.30	.10
❑ 54 Darryl Williams	.30	.10
❑ 55 Jerry Ball	.30	.10
❑ 56 Mike Caldwell RC	.30	.10
❑ 57 Mark Carrier WR	.50	.20
❑ 58 Steve Everitt RC	.30	.10
❑ 59 Dan Footman RC	.30	.10
❑ 60 Pepper Johnson	.30	.10
❑ 61 Bernie Kosar	.50	.20
❑ 62 Eric Metcalf	.50	.20
❑ 63 Michael Dean Perry	.50	.20
❑ 64 Troy Aikman	2.50	1.25
❑ 65 Charles Haley	.50	.20
❑ 66 Michael Irvin	1.00	.40
❑ 67 Robert Jones	.30	.10
❑ 68 Derrick Lassic RC	.30	.10
❑ 69 Russell Maryland	.30	.10
❑ 70 Ken Norton Jr.	.50	.20
❑ 71 Darrin Smith RC	.50	.20
❑ 72 Emmitt Smith	5.00	2.50
❑ 73 Steve Atwater	.30	.10
❑ 74 Rod Bernstine	.30	.10
❑ 75 Jason Elam RC	1.00	.40
❑ 76 John Elway	5.00	2.00
❑ 77 Simon Fletcher	.30	.10
❑ 78 Tommy Maddox	1.00	.40
❑ 79 Glyn Milburn RC	1.00	.40

❑ 80 Derek Russell .30 .10
❑ 81 Shannon Sharpe 1.00 .40
❑ 82 Bennie Blades .30 .10
❑ 83 Willie Green .30 .10
❑ 84 Antonio London RC .30 .10
❑ 85 Ryan McNeil RC 1.00 .40
❑ 86 Herman Moore 1.00 .40
❑ 87 Rodney Peete .30 .10
❑ 88 Barry Sanders 4.00 1.50
❑ 89 Chris Spielman .50 .20
❑ 90 Pat Swilling .30 .10
❑ 91 Mark Brunell RC 15.00 6.00
❑ 92 Terrell Buckley .30 .10
❑ 93 Brett Favre 6.00 3.00
❑ 94 Jackie Harris .30 .10
❑ 95 Sterling Sharpe 1.00 .40
❑ 96 John Stephens .30 .10
❑ 97 Wayne Simmons RC .30 .10
❑ 98 George Teague RC .50 .20
❑ 99 Reggie White 1.00 .40
❑ 100 Micheal Barrow RC 1.00 .40
❑ 101 Cody Carlson .30 .10
❑ 102 Ray Childress .30 .10
❑ 103 Brad Hopkins RC .30 .10
❑ 104 Haywood Jeffires .50 .20
❑ 105 Wilber Marshall .30 .10
❑ 106 Warren Moon 1.00 .40
❑ 107 Webster Slaughter .30 .10
❑ 108 Lorenzo White .30 .10
❑ 109 John Baylor .30 .10
❑ 110 Duane Bickett .30 .10
❑ 111 Quentin Coryatt .50 .20
❑ 112 Steve Emtman .30 .10
❑ 113 Jeff George 1.00 .40
❑ 114 Jessie Hester .30 .10
❑ 115 Anthony Johnson .50 .20
❑ 116 Reggie Langhorne .30 .10
❑ 117 Roosevelt Potts RC .30 .10
❑ 118 Marcus Allen 1.00 .40
❑ 119 J.J. Birden .30 .10
❑ 120 Willie Davis 1.00 .40
❑ 121 Jaime Fields RC .30 .10
❑ 122 Joe Montana 5.00 2.00
❑ 123 Will Shields RC 1.00 .40
❑ 124 Neil Smith 1.00 .40
❑ 125 Derrick Thomas 1.00 .40
❑ 126 Harvey Williams .50 .20
❑ 127 Tim Brown 1.00 .40
❑ 128 Billy Joe Hobert RC 1.00 .40
❑ 129 Jeff Hostetler .50 .20
❑ 130 Ethan Horton .30 .10
❑ 131 Rocket Ismail .50 .20
❑ 132 Howie Long 1.00 .40
❑ 133 Terry McDaniel .30 .10
❑ 134 Greg Robinson RC .30 .10
❑ 135 Anthony Smith .30 .10
❑ 136 Flipper Anderson .30 .10
❑ 137 Marc Boutte .30 .10
❑ 138 Shane Conlan .30 .10
❑ 139 Troy Drayton RC .50 .20
❑ 140 Henry Ellard .50 .20
❑ 141 Jim Everett .50 .20
❑ 142 Cleveland Gary .30 .10
❑ 143 Sean Gilbert .50 .20
❑ 144 Robert Young .30 .10
❑ 145 Marco Coleman .30 .10
❑ 146 Bryan Cox .30 .10
❑ 147 Irving Fryar .50 .20
❑ 148 Keith Jackson .50 .20
❑ 149 Terry Kirby RC 1.00 .40
❑ 150 Dan Marino 5.00 2.00
❑ 151 Scott Mitchell 1.00 .40
❑ 152 Louis Oliver .30 .10
❑ 153 Troy Vincent .30 .10
❑ 154 Anthony Carter .50 .20
❑ 155 Cris Carter 1.00 .40
❑ 156 Roger Craig .50 .20
❑ 157 Chris Doleman .30 .10
❑ 158 Qadry Ismail RC 2.00 .75
❑ 159 Steve Jordan .30 .10
❑ 160 Randall McDaniel .30 .10
❑ 161 Audray McMillian .30 .10
❑ 162 Barry Word .30 .10
❑ 163 Vincent Brown .30 .10
❑ 164 Marv Cook .30 .10
❑ 165 Sam Gash RC 1.00 .40
❑ 166 Pat Harlow .30 .10
❑ 167 Greg McMurtry .30 .10
❑ 168 Todd Rucci RC .30 .10
❑ 169 Leonard Russell .50 .20
❑ 170 Scott Sisson RC .30 .10
❑ 171 Chris Slade RC .50 .20
❑ 172 Morten Andersen .30 .10
❑ 173 Derek Brown RC RBK .50 .20
❑ 174 Reggie Freeman RC .30 .10
❑ 175 Rickey Jackson .30 .10
❑ 176 Eric Martin .30 .10
❑ 177 Wayne Martin .30 .10
❑ 178 Brad Muster .30 .10
❑ 179 Willie Roaf RC .50 .20
❑ 180 Renaldo Turnbull .30 .10
❑ 181 Derek Brown TE .30 .10
❑ 182 Marcus Buckley RC .30 .10
❑ 183 Jarrod Bunch .30 .10
❑ 184 Rodney Hampton .50 .20
❑ 185 Ed McCaffrey 1.00 .40
❑ 186 Kanavis McGhee .30 .10
❑ 187 Mike Sherrard .30 .10
❑ 188 Phil Simms .50 .20
❑ 189 Lawrence Taylor 1.00 .40
❑ 190 Kurt Barber .30 .10
❑ 191 Boomer Esiason .50 .20
❑ 192 Johnny Johnson .30 .10
❑ 193 Ronnie Lott .50 .20
❑ 194 Johnny Mitchell .30 .10
❑ 195 Rob Moore .50 .20
❑ 196 Adrian Murrell RC 1.00 .40
❑ 197 Browning Nagle .30 .10
❑ 198 Marvin Washington .30 .10
❑ 199 Eric Allen .30 .10
❑ 200 Fred Barnett .50 .20
❑ 201 Randall Cunningham 1.00 .40
❑ 202 Byron Evans .30 .10
❑ 203 Tim Harris .30 .10
❑ 204 Seth Joyner .30 .10
❑ 205 Leonard Renfro RC .30 .10
❑ 206 Heath Sherman .30 .10
❑ 207 Clyde Simmons .30 .10
❑ 208 Johnny Bailey .30 .10
❑ 209 Steve Beuerlein .50 .20
❑ 210 Chuck Cecil .30 .10
❑ 211 Larry Centers RC 1.00 .40
❑ 212 Gary Clark .50 .20
❑ 213 Ernest Dye RC .30 .10
❑ 214 Ken Harvey .30 .10
❑ 215 Randal Hill .30 .10
❑ 216 Ricky Proehl .30 .10
❑ 217 Deon Figures RC .30 .10
❑ 218 Barry Foster .50 .20
❑ 219 Eric Green .30 .10
❑ 220 Kevin Greene .50 .20
❑ 221 Carlton Haselrig .30 .10
❑ 222 Andre Hastings RC .50 .20
❑ 223 Greg Lloyd .50 .20
❑ 224 Neil O'Donnell 1.00 .40
❑ 225 Rod Woodson 1.00 .40
❑ 226 Marion Butts .30 .10
❑ 227 Darren Carrington RC .30 .10
❑ 228 Darrien Gordon RC .30 .10
❑ 229 Ronnie Harmon .30 .10
❑ 230 Stan Humphries .50 .20
❑ 231 Anthony Miller .50 .20
❑ 232 Chris Mims .30 .10
❑ 233 Leslie O'Neal .50 .20
❑ 234 Junior Seau 1.00 .40
❑ 235 Dana Hall .30 .10
❑ 236 Adrian Hardy .30 .10
❑ 237 Brent Jones .50 .20
❑ 238 Tim McDonald .30 .10
❑ 239 Tom Rathman .30 .10
❑ 240 Jerry Rice 3.00 1.50
❑ 241 Dana Stubblefield RC 1.00 .40
❑ 242 Ricky Watters 1.00 .40
❑ 243 Steve Young 2.50 1.25
❑ 244 Brian Blades .50 .20
❑ 245 Ferrell Edmunds .30 .10
❑ 246 Carlton Gray RC .30 .10
❑ 247 Cortez Kennedy .50 .20
❑ 248 Kelvin Martin .30 .10
❑ 249 Dan McGwire .30 .10
❑ 250 Jon Vaughn .30 .10
❑ 251 Chris Warren .50 .20
❑ 252 John L. Williams .30 .10
❑ 253 Reggie Cobb .30 .10
❑ 254 Horace Copeland RC .50 .20
❑ 255 Lawrence Dawsey .30 .10
❑ 256 Demetrius DuBose RC .30 .10
❑ 257 Craig Erickson .50 .20
❑ 258 Courtney Hawkins .30 .10
❑ 259 John Lynch RC 8.00 3.00
❑ 260 Hardy Nickerson .50 .20
❑ 261 Lamar Thomas RC .30 .10
❑ 262 Carl Banks .30 .10
❑ 263 Tom Carter RC .50 .20
❑ 264 Brad Edwards .30 .10
❑ 265 Kurt Gouveia .30 .10
❑ 266 Desmond Howard .50 .20
❑ 267 Charles Mann .30 .10
❑ 268 Art Monk .50 .20
❑ 269 Mark Rypien .30 .10
❑ 270 Ricky Sanders .30 .10
❑ P1 Joe Montana Promo 5.00 2.00

1994 SP

❑ COMPLETE SET (200) 50.00 25.00
❑ 1 Dan Wilkinson FOIL RC 1.25 .50
❑ 2 Heath Shuler FOIL RC .75 .30
❑ 3 Marshall Faulk FOIL RC 20.00 7.50
❑ 4 Willie McGinest FOIL RC 2.00 .75
❑ 5 Trent Dilfer FOIL RC 5.00 2.00
❑ 6 Bryant Young FOIL RC 1.25 .50
❑ 7 Antonio Langham FOIL RC .40 .15
❑ 8 John Thierry FOIL RC .40 .15
❑ 9 Aaron Glenn FOIL RC 1.25 .50
❑ 10 Charles Johnson FOIL RC 1.25 .50
❑ 11 Dewayne Washington FOIL RC .40 .15
❑ 12 Johnnie Morton FOIL RC 3.00 1.25
❑ 13 Greg Hill FOIL RC .75 .30
❑ 14 William Floyd FOIL RC .75 .30
❑ 15 Derrick Alexander WR FOIL RC 1.25.50
❑ 16 Darnay Scott FOIL RC 1.25 .50
❑ 17 Errict Rhett FOIL RC 1.25 .50
❑ 18 Charlie Garner FOIL RC 3.00 1.25
❑ 19 Thomas Lewis FOIL RC .40 .15
❑ 20 David Palmer FOIL RC 1.25 .50
❑ 21 Andre Reed .30 .10
❑ 22 Thurman Thomas .50 .20
❑ 23 Bruce Smith .50 .20

❑ 24 Jim Kelly	.50	.20
❑ 25 Cornelius Bennett	.30	.10
❑ 26 Bucky Brooks RC	.15	.05
❑ 27 Jeff Burris RC	.30	.10
❑ 28 Jim Harbaugh	.50	.20
❑ 29 Tony Bennett	.15	.05
❑ 30 Quentin Coryatt	.15	.05
❑ 31 Floyd Turner	.15	.05
❑ 32 Roosevelt Potts	.15	.05
❑ 33 Jeff Herrod	.15	.05
❑ 34 Irving Fryar	.30	.10
❑ 35 Bryan Cox	.15	.05
❑ 36 Dan Marino	4.00	1.50
❑ 37 Terry Kirby	.50	.20
❑ 38 Michael Stewart	.15	.05
❑ 39 Bernie Kosar	.30	.10
❑ 40 Aubrey Beavers RC	.15	.05
❑ 41 Vincent Brisby	.30	.10
❑ 42 Ben Coates	.30	.10
❑ 43 Drew Bledsoe	2.00	.75
❑ 44 Marion Butts	.15	.05
❑ 45 Chris Slade	.15	.05
❑ 46 Michael Timpson	.15	.05
❑ 47 Ray Crittenden RC	.15	.05
❑ 48 Rob Moore	.30	.10
❑ 49 Johnny Mitchell	.15	.05
❑ 50 Art Monk	.30	.10
❑ 51 Boomer Esiason	.30	.10
❑ 52 Ronnie Lott	.30	.10
❑ 53 Ryan Yarborough RC	.15	.05
❑ 54 Carl Pickens	.30	.10
❑ 55 David Klingler	.15	.05
❑ 56 Harold Green	.15	.05
❑ 57 John Copeland	.15	.05
❑ 58 Louis Oliver	.15	.05
❑ 59 Corey Sawyer	.30	.10
❑ 60 Michael Jackson	.30	.10
❑ 61 Mark Rypien	.15	.05
❑ 62 Vinny Testaverde	.30	.10
❑ 63 Eric Metcalf	.30	.10
❑ 64 Eric Turner	.15	.05
❑ 65 Haywood Jeffires	.30	.10
❑ 66 Micheal Barrow	.15	.05
❑ 67 Cody Carlson	.15	.05
❑ 68 Gary Brown	.15	.05
❑ 69 Bucky Richardson	.15	.05
❑ 70 Al Smith	.15	.05
❑ 71 Eric Green	.15	.05
❑ 72 Neil O'Donnell	.50	.20
❑ 73 Barry Foster	.15	.05
❑ 74 Greg Lloyd	.30	.10
❑ 75 Rod Woodson	.30	.10
❑ 76 Byron Bam Morris RC	.30	.10
❑ 77 John L. Williams	.15	.05
❑ 78 Anthony Miller	.30	.10
❑ 79 Mike Pritchard	.15	.05
❑ 80 John Elway	4.00	1.50
❑ 81 Shannon Sharpe	.30	.10
❑ 82 Steve Atwater	.15	.05
❑ 83 Simon Fletcher	.15	.05
❑ 84 Glyn Milburn	.30	.10
❑ 85 Mark Collins	.15	.05
❑ 86 Keith Cash	.15	.05
❑ 87 Willie Davis	.30	.10
❑ 88 Joe Montana	4.00	1.50
❑ 89 Marcus Allen	.50	.20
❑ 90 Neil Smith	.30	.10
❑ 91 Derrick Thomas	.50	.20
❑ 92 Tim Brown	.50	.20
❑ 93 Jeff Hostetler	.30	.10
❑ 94 Terry McDaniel	.15	.05
❑ 95 Rocket Ismail	.30	.10
❑ 96 Rob Fredrickson RC	.30	.10
❑ 97 Harvey Williams	.30	.10
❑ 98 Steve Wisniewski	.15	.05
❑ 99 Stan Humphries	.30	.10
❑ 100 Natrone Means	.50	.20
❑ 101 Leslie O'Neal	.15	.05
❑ 102 Junior Seau	.50	.20
❑ 103 Ronnie Harmon	.15	.05
❑ 104 Shawn Jefferson	.15	.05
❑ 105 Howard Ballard	.15	.05
❑ 106 Rick Mirer	.50	.20
❑ 107 Cortez Kennedy	.30	.10
❑ 108 Chris Warren	.30	.10
❑ 109 Brian Blades	.30	.10
❑ 110 Sam Adams RC	.30	.10
❑ 111 Gary Clark	.30	.10
❑ 112 Steve Beuerlein	.30	.10
❑ 113 Ronald Moore	.15	.05
❑ 114 Eric Swann	.30	.10
❑ 115 Clyde Simmons	.15	.05
❑ 116 Seth Joyner	.15	.05
❑ 117 Troy Aikman	2.00	.75
❑ 118 Charles Haley	.30	.10
❑ 119 Alvin Harper	.30	.10
❑ 120 Michael Irvin	.50	.20
❑ 121 Daryl Johnston	.30	.10
❑ 122 Emmitt Smith	3.00	1.25
❑ 123 Shante Carver RC	.15	.05
❑ 124 Dave Brown	.30	.10
❑ 125 Rodney Hampton	.30	.10
❑ 126 Dave Meggett	.15	.05
❑ 127 Chris Calloway	.15	.05
❑ 128 Mike Sherrard	.15	.05
❑ 129 Carlton Bailey	.15	.05
❑ 130 Randall Cunningham	.50	.20
❑ 131 William Fuller	.15	.05
❑ 132 Eric Allen	.15	.05
❑ 133 Calvin Williams	.30	.10
❑ 134 Herschel Walker	.30	.10
❑ 135 Bernard Williams RC	.15	.05
❑ 136 Henry Ellard	.30	.10
❑ 137 Ethan Horton	.15	.05
❑ 138 Desmond Howard	.30	.10
❑ 139 Reggie Brooks	.30	.10
❑ 140 John Friesz	.30	.10
❑ 141 Tom Carter	.15	.05
❑ 142 Terry Allen	.30	.10
❑ 143 Adrian Cooper	.15	.05
❑ 144 Qadry Ismail	.50	.20
❑ 145 Warren Moon	.50	.20
❑ 146 Henry Thomas	.15	.05
❑ 147 Todd Steussie RC	.30	.10
❑ 148 Cris Carter	.75	.30
❑ 149 Andy Heck	.15	.05
❑ 150 Curtis Conway	.50	.20
❑ 151 Erik Kramer	.30	.10
❑ 152 Lewis Tillman	.15	.05
❑ 153 Dante Jones	.15	.05
❑ 154 Alonzo Spellman	.15	.05
❑ 155 Herman Moore	.50	.20
❑ 156 Broderick Thomas	.15	.05
❑ 157 Scott Mitchell	.30	.10
❑ 158 Barry Sanders	3.00	1.25
❑ 159 Chris Spielman	.30	.10
❑ 160 Pat Swilling	.15	.05
❑ 161 Bennie Blades	.15	.05
❑ 162 Sterling Sharpe	.30	.10
❑ 163 Brett Favre	4.00	1.50
❑ 164 Reggie Cobb	.15	.05
❑ 165 Reggie White	.50	.20
❑ 166 Sean Jones	.15	.05
❑ 167 George Teague	.15	.05
❑ 168 LeShon Johnson RC	.30	.10
❑ 169 Courtney Hawkins	.15	.05
❑ 170 Jackie Harris	.15	.05
❑ 171 Craig Erickson	.15	.05
❑ 172 Santana Dotson	.30	.10
❑ 173 Eric Curry	.15	.05
❑ 174 Hardy Nickerson	.30	.10
❑ 175 Derek Brown RBK	.15	.05
❑ 176 Jim Everett	.30	.10
❑ 177 Michael Haynes	.30	.10
❑ 178 Tyrone Hughes	.30	.10
❑ 179 Wayne Martin	.15	.05
❑ 180 Willie Roaf	.15	.05
❑ 181 Irv Smith	.15	.05
❑ 182 Jeff George	.50	.20
❑ 183 Andre Rison	.30	.10
❑ 184 Erric Pegram	.15	.05
❑ 185 Bert Emanuel RC	1.00	.40
❑ 186 Chris Doleman	.15	.05
❑ 187 Ron George	.15	.05
❑ 188 Chris Miller	.15	.05
❑ 189 Troy Drayton	.15	.05
❑ 190 Chris Chandler	.30	.10
❑ 191 Jerome Bettis	1.00	.40
❑ 192 Jimmie Jones	.15	.05
❑ 193 Sean Gilbert	.15	.05
❑ 194 Jerry Rice	2.00	.75
❑ 195 Brent Jones	.30	.10
❑ 196 Deion Sanders	1.00	.40
❑ 197 Steve Young	1.50	.60
❑ 198 Ricky Watters	.30	.10
❑ 199 Dana Stubblefield	.30	.10
❑ 200 Ken Norton Jr.	.30	.10
❑ RB1 Dan Marino RB	25.00	10.00
❑ RB2 Jerry Rice RB	25.00	12.50
❑ P16 Joe Montana Promo	4.00	1.50

1995 SP

❑ COMPLETE SET (200)	50.00	20.00
❑ 1 Ki-Jana Carter FOIL RC	2.00	.75
❑ 2 Eric Zeier FOIL RC	2.00	.75
❑ 3 Steve McNair FOIL RC	12.00	5.00
❑ 4 Michael Westbrook FOIL RC	2.00	.75
❑ 5 Kerry Collins FOIL RC	6.00	2.50
❑ 6 Joey Galloway FOIL RC	5.00	2.00
❑ 7 Kevin Carter FOIL RC	2.00	.75
❑ 8 Mike Mamula RC	.50	.20
❑ 9 Kyle Brady FOIL RC	2.00	.75
❑ 10 J.J. Stokes FOIL RC	2.00	.75
❑ 11 Tyrone Poole RC	2.00	.75
❑ 12 Rashaan Salaam FOIL RC	1.00	.40
❑ 13 Sherman Williams FOIL RC	.50	.20
❑ 14 Luther Elliss RC	.50	.20
❑ 15 James O. Stewart FOIL RC	4.00	1.50
❑ 16 Tamarick Vanover FOIL RC	2.00	.75
❑ 17 Napoleon Kaufman FOIL RC	4.00	1.50
❑ 18 Curtis Martin FOIL RC	12.00	6.00
❑ 19 Tyrone Wheatley FOIL RC	4.00	1.50
❑ 20 Frank Sanders FOIL RC	2.00	.75
❑ 21 Devin Bush	.20	.07
❑ 22 Terance Mathis	.40	.15
❑ 23 Bert Emanuel	.75	.30
❑ 24 Eric Metcalf	.40	.15
❑ 25 Craig Heyward	.40	.15
❑ 26 Jeff George	.40	.15
❑ 27 Mark Carrier WR	.40	.15
❑ 28 Pete Metzelaars	.20	.07
❑ 29 Frank Reich	.20	.07
❑ 30 Sam Mills	.40	.15
❑ 31 John Kasay	.20	.07
❑ 32 Willie Green	.40	.15
❑ 33 Jeff Graham	.20	.07
❑ 34 Curtis Conway	.75	.30
❑ 35 Steve Walsh	.20	.07

☐	36 Erik Kramer	.20	.07
☐	37 Michael Timpson	.20	.07
☐	38 Mark Carrier DB	.20	.07
☐	39 Troy Aikman	2.00	.75
☐	40 Michael Irvin	.75	.30
☐	41 Charles Haley	.40	.15
☐	42 Deion Sanders	1.25	.50
☐	43 Jay Novacek	.40	.15
☐	44 Emmitt Smith	3.00	1.25
☐	45 Herman Moore	.75	.30
☐	46 Scott Mitchell UER	.40	.15
☐	47 Bennie Blades	.20	.07
☐	48 Johnnie Morton	.40	.15
☐	49 Chris Spielman	.40	.15
☐	50 Barry Sanders	3.00	1.25
☐	51 Edgar Bennett	.40	.15
☐	52 Reggie White	.75	.30
☐	53 Sean Jones	.20	.07
☐	54 Mark Ingram	.20	.07
☐	55 Robert Brooks	.75	.30
☐	56 Brett Favre	4.00	1.50
☐	57 Lovell Pinkney RC	.50	.20
☐	58 Chris Miller	.20	.07
☐	59 Isaac Bruce	1.25	.50
☐	60 Roman Phifer	.20	.07
☐	61 Sean Gilbert	.40	.15
☐	62 Jerome Bettis	.75	.30
☐	63 Derrick Alexander DE RC	.50	.20
☐	64 Cris Carter	.75	.30
☐	65 Jake Reed	.40	.15
☐	66 Robert Smith	.75	.30
☐	67 David Palmer	.40	.15
☐	68 Warren Moon	.40	.15
☐	69 Ray Zellars RC	1.00	.40
☐	70 Jim Everett	.20	.07
☐	71 Michael Haynes	.40	.15
☐	72 Quinn Early	.40	.15
☐	73 Willie Roaf	.20	.07
☐	74 Mario Bates	.40	.15
☐	75 Mike Sherrard	.20	.07
☐	76 Chris Calloway	.20	.07
☐	77 Dave Brown	.40	.15
☐	78 Thomas Lewis	.40	.15
☐	79 Herschel Walker	.40	.15
☐	80 Rodney Hampton	.40	.15
☐	81 Fred Barnett	.40	.15
☐	82 Calvin Williams	.40	.15
☐	83 Randall Cunningham	.75	.30
☐	84 Charlie Garner	.75	.30
☐	85 Bobby Taylor RC	3.00	1.25
☐	86 Ricky Watters	.40	.15
☐	87 Dave Krieg	.20	.07
☐	88 Rob Moore	.40	.15
☐	89 Eric Swann	.40	.15
☐	90 Clyde Simmons	.20	.07
☐	91 Seth Joyner	.20	.07
☐	92 Garrison Hearst	.75	.30
☐	93 Jerry Rice	2.00	.75
☐	94 Bryant Young	.40	.15
☐	95 Brent Jones	.20	.07
☐	96 Ken Norton	.40	.15
☐	97 William Floyd	.40	.15
☐	98 Steve Young	1.50	.60
☐	99 Warren Sapp RC	5.00	2.00
☐	100 Trent Dilfer	.75	.30
☐	101 Alvin Harper	.20	.07
☐	102 Hardy Nickerson	.20	.07
☐	103 Derrick Brooks RC	5.00	2.00
☐	104 Errict Rhett	.40	.15
☐	105 Henry Ellard	.40	.15
☐	106 Ken Harvey	.20	.07
☐	107 Gus Frerotte	.40	.15
☐	108 Brian Mitchell	.20	.07
☐	109 Terry Allen	.40	.15
☐	110 Heath Shuler	.40	.15
☐	111 Jim Kelly	.75	.30
☐	112 Andre Reed	.40	.15
☐	113 Bruce Smith	.75	.30
☐	114 Darick Holmes RC	1.00	.40
☐	115 Bryce Paup	.40	.15
☐	116 Cornelius Bennett	.40	.15
☐	117 Carl Pickens	.40	.15
☐	118 Darnay Scott	.40	.15
☐	119 Jeff Blake RC	2.00	.75
☐	120 Steve Tovar	.20	.07
☐	121 Tony McGee	.20	.07
☐	122 Dan Wilkinson	.40	.15
☐	123 Craig Powell RC	.20	.07
☐	124 Vinny Testaverde	.40	.15
☐	125 Eric Turner	.20	.07
☐	126 Leroy Hoard	.20	.07
☐	127 Lorenzo White	.20	.07
☐	128 Andre Rison	.40	.15
☐	129 Shannon Sharpe	.40	.15
☐	130 Terrell Davis RC	10.00	4.00
☐	131 Anthony Miller	.40	.15
☐	132 Mike Pritchard	.20	.07
☐	133 Steve Atwater	.20	.07
☐	134 John Elway	4.00	1.50
☐	135 Haywood Jeffires	.20	.07
☐	136 Gary Brown	.20	.07
☐	137 Al Smith	.20	.07
☐	138 Rodney Thomas RC	1.00	.40
☐	139 Chris Chandler	.40	.15
☐	140 Mel Gray	.20	.07
☐	141 Craig Erickson	.20	.07
☐	142 Sean Dawkins	.40	.15
☐	143 Ken Dilger RC	2.00	.75
☐	144 Ellis Johnson RC	.50	.20
☐	145 Quentin Coryatt	.40	.15
☐	146 Marshall Faulk	2.50	1.00
☐	147 Tony Boselli RC	2.00	.75
☐	148 Rob Johnson RC	3.00	1.25
☐	149 Desmond Howard	.40	.15
☐	150 Steve Beuerlein	.40	.15
☐	151 Reggie Cobb	.20	.07
☐	152 Jeff Lageman	.20	.07
☐	153 Willie Davis	.40	.15
☐	154 Marcus Allen	.75	.30
☐	155 Neil Smith	.40	.15
☐	156 Greg Hill	.40	.15
☐	157 Steve Bono	.40	.15
☐	158 Derrick Thomas	.75	.30
☐	159 Jeff Hostetler	.40	.15
☐	160 Harvey Williams	.20	.07
☐	161 Rocket Ismail	.40	.15
☐	162 Chester McGlockton	.40	.15
☐	163 Terry McDaniel	.20	.07
☐	164 Tim Brown	.75	.30
☐	165 Terry Kirby	.40	.15
☐	166 Irving Fryar	.40	.15
☐	167 O.J. McDuffie	.75	.30
☐	168 Bryan Cox	.20	.07
☐	169 Eric Green	.20	.07
☐	170 Dan Marino	4.00	1.50
☐	171 Ben Coates	.40	.15
☐	172 Vincent Brisby	.20	.07
☐	173 Chris Slade	.20	.07
☐	174 Ty Law RC	4.00	1.50
☐	175 Vincent Brown	.20	.07
☐	176 Drew Bledsoe	1.25	.50
☐	177 Johnny Mitchell	.20	.07
☐	178 Boomer Esiason	.40	.15
☐	179 Wayne Chrebet RC	6.00	3.00
☐	180 Mo Lewis	.20	.07
☐	181 Ronald Moore	.20	.07
☐	182 Aaron Glenn	.20	.07
☐	183 Mark Bruener RC	1.00	.40
☐	184 Neil O'Donnell	.40	.15
☐	185 Charles Johnson	.40	.15
☐	186 Greg Lloyd	.40	.15
☐	187 Rod Woodson	.40	.15
☐	188 Byron Bam Morris	.20	.07
☐	189 Terrell Fletcher RC	.50	.20
☐	190 Terrance Shaw RC UER	.50	.20
☐	191 Stan Humphries	.40	.15
☐	192 Junior Seau	.75	.30
☐	193 Leslie O'Neal	.40	.15
☐	194 Natrone Means	.40	.15
☐	195 Christian Fauria RC	1.00	.40
☐	196 Rick Mirer	.40	.15
☐	197 Sam Adams	.20	.07
☐	198 Cortez Kennedy	.40	.15
☐	199 Eugene Robinson	.20	.07
☐	200 Chris Warren	.40	.15
☐	DM1 Dan Marino Tribute	20.00	7.50
☐	JM1 Joe Montana Salute	20.00	7.50
☐	JMAP Joe Montana Promo	4.00	1.50
☐	NNO Dan Marino TRI Jumbo	25.00	10.00
☐	NNO Joe Montana SAL Jumbo	25.00	10.00
☐	P113 Dan Marino Promo	3.00	1.25

1995 SP Championship

☐	COMPLETE SET (225)	50.00	20.00
☐	1 Frank Sanders RC	.75	.30
☐	2 Stoney Case RC	.20	.07
☐	3 Lorenzo Styles RC	.20	.07
☐	4 Todd Collins RC	.40	.15
☐	5 Darick Holmes RC	.40	.15
☐	6 Brian DeMarco RC	.20	.07
☐	7 Tyrone Poole RC	.75	.30
☐	8 Kerry Collins RC	3.00	1.25
☐	9 Rashaan Salaam RC	.40	.15
☐	10 Steve Stenstrom RC	.20	.07
☐	11 Ki-Jana Carter RC	.75	.30
☐	12 Eric Zeier RC	.75	.30
☐	13 Sherman Williams RC	.20	.07
☐	14 Terrell Davis RC	5.00	2.00
☐	15 David Dunn RC	.20	.07
☐	16 Luther Elliss RC	.20	.07
☐	17 Craig Newsome RC	.20	.07
☐	18 Antonio Freeman RC	2.00	.75
☐	19 Steve McNair RC	6.00	2.50
☐	20 Anthony Cook RC	.20	.07
☐	21 Rodney Thomas RC	.40	.15
☐	22 Ellis Johnson RC	.20	.07
☐	23 Ken Dilger RC	.75	.30
☐	24 James O. Stewart RC	2.00	.75
☐	25 Pete Mitchell RC	.40	.15
☐	26 Tamarick Vanover RC	.75	.30
☐	27 Orlando Thomas RC	.20	.07
☐	28 Corey Fuller RC	.20	.07
☐	29 Curtis Martin RC	6.00	2.50
☐	30 Ty Law RC	2.50	1.00
☐	31 Roell Preston RC	.30	.10
☐	32 Mark Fields RC	.75	.30
☐	33 Tyrone Wheatley RC	2.00	.75
☐	34 Kyle Brady RC	.75	.30
☐	35 Napoleon Kaufman RC	2.50	1.00
☐	36 Kordell Stewart RC	3.00	1.25
☐	37 Mark Bruener RC	.40	.15
☐	38 Terrance Shaw RC	.20	.07
☐	39 Terrell Fletcher RC	.20	.07
☐	40 J.J. Stokes RC	.75	.30
☐	41 Christian Fauria RC	.40	.15
☐	42 Joey Galloway RC	3.00	1.25
☐	43 Kevin Carter RC	.75	.30
☐	44 Warren Sapp RC	3.00	1.25

45	Michael Westbrook RC	.75	.30
46	Clyde Simmons	.15	.05
47	Rob Moore	.30	.10
48	Seth Joyner	.15	.05
49	Dave Krieg	.15	.05
50	Garrison Hearst	.50	.20
51	Aeneas Williams	.15	.05
52	Terance Mathis	.30	.10
53	Bert Emanuel	.50	.20
54	Chris Doleman	.15	.05
55	Craig Heyward	.30	.10
56	Jeff George	.30	.10
57	Eric Metcalf	.30	.10
58	Jim Kelly	.50	.20
59	Andre Reed	.30	.10
60	Russell Copeland	.15	.05
61	Bruce Smith	.50	.20
62	Cornelius Bennett	.30	.10
63	Jeff Burris	.15	.05
64	Mark Carrier WR	.30	.10
65	Pete Metzelaars	.15	.05
66	Frank Reich	.15	.05
67	Sam Mills	.30	.10
68	John Kasay	.15	.05
69	Willie Green	.30	.10
70	Curtis Conway	.50	.20
71	Erik Kramer	.15	.05
72	Donnell Woolford	.15	.05
73	Mark Carrier DB	.15	.05
74	Jeff Graham	.15	.05
75	Raymont Harris	.15	.05
76	Carl Pickens	.30	.10
77	Darnay Scott	.30	.10
78	Jeff Blake RC	1.25	.50
79	Dan Wilkinson	.30	.10
80	Tony McGee	.15	.05
81	Eric Bieniemy	.15	.05
82	Vinny Testaverde	.30	.10
83	Eric Turner	.15	.05
84	Leroy Hoard	.15	.05
85	Lorenzo White	.15	.05
86	Antonio Langham	.15	.05
87	Andre Rison	.30	.10
88	Troy Aikman	1.50	.60
89	Michael Irvin	.50	.20
90	Charles Haley	.30	.10
91	Daryl Johnston	.30	.10
92	Jay Novacek	.30	.10
93	Emmitt Smith	2.50	1.00
94	Shannon Sharpe	.30	.10
95	Anthony Miller	.30	.10
96	Mike Pritchard	.15	.05
97	Glyn Milburn	.15	.05
98	Simon Fletcher	.15	.05
99	John Elway	3.00	1.25
100	Henry Thomas	.15	.05
101	Herman Moore	.50	.20
102	Scott Mitchell	.30	.10
103	Bennie Blades	.15	.05
104	Chris Spielman	.30	.10
105	Barry Sanders	2.50	1.00
106	Mark Ingram	.15	.05
107	Edgar Bennett	.30	.10
108	Reggie White	.50	.20
109	Sean Jones	.15	.05
110	Robert Brooks	.50	.20
111	Brett Favre	3.00	1.25
112	Chris Chandler	.30	.10
113	Haywood Jeffires	.15	.05
114	Gary Brown	.15	.05
115	Al Smith	.15	.05
116	Ray Childress	.15	.05
117	Mel Gray	.15	.05
118	Jim Harbaugh	.30	.10
119	Sean Dawkins	.30	.10
120	Roosevelt Potts	.15	.05
121	Marshall Faulk	2.00	.75
122	Tony Bennett	.15	.05
123	Quentin Coryatt	.30	.10
124	Desmond Howard	.30	.10
125	Tony Boselli	.50	.20
126	Steve Beuerlein	.30	.10
127	Jeff Lageman	.15	.05
128	Rob Johnson RC	2.00	.75
129	Ernest Givins	.15	.05
130	Willie Davis	.30	.10
131	Marcus Allen	.50	.20
132	Neil Smith	.30	.10
133	Greg Hill	.30	.10
134	Steve Bono	.30	.10
135	Lake Dawson	.30	.10
136	Dan Marino	3.00	1.25
137	Terry Kirby	.30	.10
138	Irving Fryar	.30	.10
139	O.J. McDuffie	.50	.20
140	Bryan Cox	.15	.05
141	Eric Green	.15	.05
142	Cris Carter	.50	.20
143	Robert Smith	.50	.20
144	John Randle	.30	.10
145	Jake Reed	.30	.10
146	Dewayne Washington	.30	.10
147	Warren Moon	.30	.10
148	Dave Meggett	.15	.05
149	Ben Coates	.30	.10
150	Vincent Brisby	.15	.05
151	Willie McGinest	.30	.10
152	Chris Slade	.15	.05
153	Drew Bledsoe	1.00	.40
154	Eric Allen	.15	.05
155	Mario Bates	.30	.10
156	Jim Everett	.15	.05
157	Renaldo Turnbull	.15	.05
158	Tyrone Hughes	.30	.10
159	Michael Haynes	.30	.10
160	Mike Sherrard	.15	.05
161	Dave Brown	.30	.10
162	Chris Calloway	.15	.05
163	Keith Hamilton	.15	.05
164	Rodney Hampton	.30	.10
165	Herschel Walker	.30	.10
166	Adrian Murrell	.30	.10
167	Johnny Mitchell	.15	.05
168	Boomer Esiason	.30	.10
169	Mo Lewis	.15	.05
170	Brad Baxter	.15	.05
171	Aaron Glenn	.15	.05
172	Jeff Hostetler	.30	.10
173	Harvey Williams	.15	.05
174	Tim Brown	.50	.20
175	Terry McDaniel	.15	.05
176	Pat Swilling	.15	.05
177	Rocket Ismail	.30	.10
178	Randall Cunningham	.50	.20
179	Calvin Williams	.30	.10
180	Ricky Watters	.30	.10
181	Charlie Garner	.50	.20
182	Fred Barnett	.30	.10
183	Rodney Peete	.15	.05
184	Neil O'Donnell	.30	.10
185	Charles Johnson	.30	.10
186	Rod Woodson	.30	.10
187	Byron Bam Morris	.15	.05
188	Kevin Greene	.30	.10
189	Greg Lloyd	.30	.10
190	Chris Miller	.15	.05
191	Isaac Bruce	.75	.30
192	Roman Phifer	.15	.05
193	Jerome Bettis	.50	.20
194	Carlos Jenkins	.15	.05
195	Troy Drayton	.15	.05
196	Andre Coleman	.15	.05
197	Natrone Means	.30	.10
198	Leslie O'Neal	.30	.10
199	Junior Seau	.50	.20
200	Tony Martin	.30	.10
201	Stan Humphries	.30	.10
202	Steve Young	1.25	.50
203	Jerry Rice	1.50	.60
204	Brent Jones	.15	.05
205	Dana Stubblefield	.30	.10
206	Lee Woodall	.15	.05
207	Merton Hanks	.15	.05
208	Rick Mirer	.30	.10
209	Brian Blades	.30	.10
210	Chris Warren	.30	.10
211	Sam Adams	.15	.05
212	Cortez Kennedy	.30	.10
213	Eugene Robinson	.15	.05
214	Alvin Harper	.15	.05
215	Trent Dilfer	.50	.20
216	Hardy Nickerson	.15	.05
217	Errict Rhett	.30	.10
218	Eric Curry	.15	.05
219	Jackie Harris	.15	.05
220	Henry Ellard	.30	.10
221	Terry Allen	.30	.10
222	Brian Mitchell	.15	.05
223	Ken Harvey	.15	.05
224	Gus Frerotte	.30	.10
225	Heath Shuler	.30	.10
P116	Joe Montana Promo	3.00	1.25

1996 SP

	COMPLETE SET (188)	100.00	40.00
1	Keyshawn Johnson RC	8.00	4.00
2	Kevin Hardy RC	.75	.30
3	Simeon Rice RC	3.00	1.25
4	Jonathan Ogden RC	1.25	.50
5	Eddie George RC	10.00	4.00
6	Terry Glenn RC	6.00	2.50
7	Terrell Owens RC	20.00	12.00
8	Tim Biakabutuka RC	2.00	.75
9	Lawrence Phillips RC	.75	.30
10	Alex Molden RC	.40	.15
11	Regan Upshaw RC	.40	.15
12	Rickey Dudley RC	1.25	.50
13	Duane Clemons RC	.40	.15
14	John Mobley RC	.75	.30
15	Eddie Kennison RC	2.00	.75
16	Karim Abdul-Jabbar RC	1.25	.50
17	Eric Moulds RC	8.00	3.00
18	Marvin Harrison RC	20.00	10.00
19	Stepfret Williams RC	.40	.15
20	Stephen Davis RC	12.00	5.00
21	Deion Sanders	1.25	.50
22	Emmitt Smith	3.00	1.25
23	Troy Aikman	2.00	.75
24	Michael Irvin	.75	.30
25	Herschel Walker	.40	.15
26	Kavika Pittman RC	.20	.07
27	Andre Hastings	.20	.07
28	Jerome Bettis	.75	.30
29	Mike Tomczak	.20	.07
30	Kordell Stewart	.75	.30
31	Charles Johnson	.20	.07
32	Greg Lloyd	.40	.15
33	Brett Favre	4.00	1.50

❑ 34 Mark Chmura	.40	.15
❑ 35 Edgar Bennett	.40	.15
❑ 36 Robert Brooks	.40	.15
❑ 37 Craig Newsome	.20	.07
❑ 38 Reggie White	.75	.30
❑ 39 Jim Harbaugh	.40	.15
❑ 40 Marshall Faulk	1.00	.40
❑ 41 Sean Dawkins	.20	.07
❑ 42 Quentin Coryatt	.20	.07
❑ 43 Ray Buchanan	.20	.07
❑ 44 Ken Dilger	.40	.15
❑ 45 Jerry Rice	2.00	.75
❑ 46 J.J. Stokes	.75	.30
❑ 47 Steve Young	1.50	.60
❑ 48 Derek Loville	.20	.07
❑ 49 Terry Kirby	.40	.15
❑ 50 Ken Norton	.20	.07
❑ 51 Tamarick Vanover	.40	.15
❑ 52 Marcus Allen	.75	.30
❑ 53 Steve Bono	.20	.07
❑ 54 Neil Smith	.40	.15
❑ 55 Derrick Thomas	.75	.30
❑ 56 Dale Carter	.20	.07
❑ 57 Terance Mathis	.20	.07
❑ 58 Eric Metcalf	.20	.07
❑ 59 Jamal Anderson RC	1.50	.60
❑ 60 Bert Emanuel	.40	.15
❑ 61 Craig Heyward	.20	.07
❑ 62 Cornelius Bennett	.20	.07
❑ 63 Tony Martin	.40	.15
❑ 64 Stan Humphries	.40	.15
❑ 65 Andre Coleman	.20	.07
❑ 66 Junior Seau	.75	.30
❑ 67 Terrell Fletcher	.20	.07
❑ 68 John Carney	.20	.07
❑ 69 Charlie Jones RC	.40	.15
❑ 70 Ricky Watters	.40	.15
❑ 71 Charlie Garner	.40	.15
❑ 72 Bobby Hoying RC	.75	.30
❑ 73 Jason Dunn RC	.40	.15
❑ 74 Bobby Taylor	.20	.07
❑ 75 Irving Fryar	.40	.15
❑ 76 Jim Kelly	.75	.30
❑ 77 Thurman Thomas	.75	.30
❑ 78 Bruce Smith	.40	.15
❑ 79 Bryce Paup	.20	.07
❑ 80 Darick Holmes	.20	.07
❑ 81 Andre Reed	.40	.15
❑ 82 Glyn Milburn	.20	.07
❑ 83 Brett Perriman	.20	.07
❑ 84 Herman Moore	.40	.15
❑ 85 Scott Mitchell	.40	.15
❑ 86 Barry Sanders	3.00	1.25
❑ 87 Johnnie Morton	.40	.15
❑ 88 Dan Marino	4.00	1.50
❑ 89 O.J. McDuffie	.40	.15
❑ 90 Stanley Pritchett RC	.20	.07
❑ 91 Zach Thomas RC	4.00	1.50
❑ 92 Daryl Gardener RC	.20	.07
❑ 93 Rashaan Salaam	.40	.15
❑ 94 Erik Kramer	.20	.07
❑ 95 Curtis Conway	.75	.30
❑ 96 Bobby Engram RC	.75	.30
❑ 97 Walt Harris RC	.20	.07
❑ 98 Bryan Cox	.20	.07
❑ 99 John Elway	4.00	1.50
❑ 100 Terrell Davis	1.50	.60
❑ 101 Anthony Miller	.40	.15
❑ 102 Shannon Sharpe	.40	.15
❑ 103 Tory James RC	.75	.30
❑ 104 Jeff Lewis RC	.40	.15
❑ 105 Joey Galloway	.75	.30
❑ 106 Chris Warren	.40	.15
❑ 107 Rick Mirer	.40	.15
❑ 108 Cortez Kennedy	.20	.07
❑ 109 Michael Sinclair	.20	.07
❑ 110 John Friesz	.20	.07
❑ 111 Warren Moon	.40	.15
❑ 112 Cris Carter	.75	.30
❑ 113 Jake Reed	.40	.15
❑ 114 Robert Smith	.40	.15
❑ 115 John Randle	.40	.15
❑ 116 Orlando Thomas	.20	.07
❑ 117 Jeff Hostetler	.20	.07
❑ 118 Tim Brown	.75	.30
❑ 119 Joe Aska	.20	.07
❑ 120 Napoleon Kaufman	.75	.30
❑ 121 Terry McDaniel	.20	.07
❑ 122 Harvey Williams	.20	.07
❑ 123 Trent Dilfer	.75	.30
❑ 124 Reggie Brooks	.20	.07
❑ 125 Alvin Harper	.20	.07
❑ 126 Mike Alstott RC	5.00	2.00
❑ 127 Hardy Nickerson	.20	.07
❑ 128 Mario Bates	.40	.15
❑ 129 Jim Everett	.20	.07
❑ 130 Tyrone Hughes	.20	.07
❑ 131 Michael Haynes	.20	.07
❑ 132 Eric Allen	.20	.07
❑ 133 Isaac Bruce	.75	.30
❑ 134 Kevin Carter	.20	.07
❑ 135 Leslie O'Neal	.20	.07
❑ 136 Tony Banks RC	.75	.30
❑ 137 Chris Chandler	.40	.15
❑ 138 Steve McNair	1.50	.60
❑ 139 Chris Sanders	.40	.15
❑ 140 Ronnie Harmon	.20	.07
❑ 141 Willie Davis	.20	.07
❑ 142 Michael Westbrook	.75	.30
❑ 143 Terry Allen	.40	.15
❑ 144 Brian Mitchell	.20	.07
❑ 145 Henry Ellard	.20	.07
❑ 146 Gus Frerotte	.40	.15
❑ 147 Kerry Collins	.75	.30
❑ 148 Sam Mills	.20	.07
❑ 149 Wesley Walls	.40	.15
❑ 150 Kevin Greene	.40	.15
❑ 151 Muhsin Muhammad RC	4.00	1.50
❑ 152 Winslow Oliver	.20	.07
❑ 153 Jeff Blake	.75	.30
❑ 154 Carl Pickens	.40	.15
❑ 155 Darnay Scott	.40	.15
❑ 156 Garrison Hearst	.40	.15
❑ 157 Marco Battaglia RC	.20	.07
❑ 158 Drew Bledsoe	1.25	.50
❑ 159 Curtis Martin	1.50	.60
❑ 160 Shawn Jefferson	.20	.07
❑ 161 Ben Coates	.40	.15
❑ 162 Lawyer Milloy RC	2.50	1.00
❑ 163 Tyrone Wheatley	.40	.15
❑ 164 Rodney Hampton	.40	.15
❑ 165 Chris Calloway	.20	.07
❑ 166 Dave Brown	.20	.07
❑ 167 Amani Toomer RC	5.00	2.00
❑ 168 Vinny Testaverde	.40	.15
❑ 169 Michael Jackson	.40	.15
❑ 170 Eric Turner	.20	.07
❑ 171 DeRon Jenkins	.20	.07
❑ 172 Jermaine Lewis RC	.75	.30
❑ 173 Frank Sanders	.40	.15
❑ 174 Rob Moore	.40	.15
❑ 175 Kent Graham	.20	.07
❑ 176 Leeland McElroy RC	.40	.15
❑ 177 Larry Centers	.40	.15
❑ 178 Eric Swann	.20	.07
❑ 179 Mark Brunell	1.25	.50
❑ 180 Willie Jackson	.40	.15
❑ 181 James O. Stewart	.40	.15
❑ 182 Natrone Means	.40	.15
❑ 183 Tony Brackens RC	.75	.30
❑ 184 Adrian Murrell	.40	.15
❑ 185 Neil O'Donnell	.40	.15
❑ 186 Hugh Douglas	.40	.15
❑ 187 Wayne Chrebet	1.00	.40
❑ 188 Alex Van Dyke RC	.40	.15
❑ SP13 Dan Marino Promo	3.00	1.25

1997 SP Authentic

❑ COMPLETE SET (198)	150.00	75.00
❑ 1 Orlando Pace RC	2.00	.75
❑ 2 Darrell Russell RC	.50	.20
❑ 3 Shawn Springs RC	1.00	.40
❑ 4 Peter Boulware RC	4.00	1.50
❑ 5 Bryant Westbrook RC	1.00	.40
❑ 6 Walter Jones RC	2.00	.75
❑ 7 Ike Hilliard RC	4.00	1.50
❑ 8 James Farrior RC	3.00	1.25
❑ 9 Tom Knight RC	.50	.20
❑ 10 Warrick Dunn RC	20.00	7.50
❑ 11 Tony Gonzalez RC	20.00	7.50
❑ 12 Reinard Wilson RC	1.00	.40
❑ 13 Yatil Green RC	1.00	.40
❑ 14 Reidel Anthony RC	2.00	.75
❑ 15 Kenny Holmes RC	.50	.20
❑ 16 Dwayne Rudd RC	.50	.20
❑ 17 Renaldo Wynn RC	.50	.20
❑ 18 David LaFleur RC	.50	.20
❑ 19 Antowain Smith RC	12.00	6.00
❑ 20 Jim Druckenmiller RC	1.00	.40
❑ 21 Rae Carruth RC	.50	.20
❑ 22 Byron Hanspard RC	1.00	.40
❑ 23 Jake Plummer RC	25.00	10.00
❑ 24 Joey Kent RC	1.00	.40
❑ 25 Corey Dillon RC	25.00	10.00
❑ 26 Danny Wuerffel RC	5.00	2.00
❑ 27 Will Blackwell RC	.50	.20
❑ 28 Troy Davis RC	1.00	.40
❑ 29 Darnell Autry RC	1.00	.40
❑ 30 Pat Barnes RC	1.00	.40
❑ 31 Kent Graham	.50	.20
❑ 32 Simeon Rice	.75	.30
❑ 33 Frank Sanders	.75	.30
❑ 34 Rob Moore	.75	.30
❑ 35 Eric Swann	.50	.20
❑ 36 Chris Chandler	.75	.30
❑ 37 Jamal Anderson	1.25	.50
❑ 38 Terance Mathis	.75	.30
❑ 39 Bert Emanuel	.75	.30
❑ 40 Michael Booker	.50	.20
❑ 41 Vinny Testaverde	.75	.30
❑ 42 Byron Bam Morris	.50	.20
❑ 43 Michael Jackson	.75	.30
❑ 44 Derrick Alexander WR	.75	.30
❑ 45 Jamie Sharper RC	2.00	.75
❑ 46 Kim Herring RC	.50	.20
❑ 47 Todd Collins	.50	.20
❑ 48 Thurman Thomas	1.25	.50
❑ 49 Andre Reed	.75	.30
❑ 50 Quinn Early	.50	.20
❑ 51 Bryce Paup	.50	.20
❑ 52 Lonnie Johnson	.50	.20
❑ 53 Kerry Collins	1.25	.50
❑ 54 Anthony Johnson	.50	.20
❑ 55 Tim Biakabutuka	.75	.30
❑ 56 Muhsin Muhammad	.75	.30
❑ 57 Sam Mills	.50	.20
❑ 58 Wesley Walls	.75	.30
❑ 59 Rick Mirer	.50	.20

❑ 60	Raymont Harris	.50	.20
❑ 61	Curtis Conway	.75	.30
❑ 62	Bobby Engram	.75	.30
❑ 63	Bryan Cox	.50	.20
❑ 64	John Allred RC	.50	.20
❑ 65	Jeff Blake	.75	.30
❑ 66	Ki-Jana Carter	.50	.20
❑ 67	Darnay Scott	.75	.30
❑ 68	Carl Pickens	.75	.30
❑ 69	Dan Wilkinson	.50	.20
❑ 70	Troy Aikman	2.50	1.25
❑ 71	Emmitt Smith	4.00	2.00
❑ 72	Michael Irvin	1.25	.50
❑ 73	Deion Sanders	1.25	.50
❑ 74	Anthony Miller	.50	.20
❑ 75	Antonio Anderson RC	.50	.20
❑ 76	John Elway	5.00	2.00
❑ 77	Terrell Davis	1.50	.60
❑ 78	Rod Smith WR	1.25	.50
❑ 79	Shannon Sharpe	.75	.30
❑ 80	Neil Smith	.75	.30
❑ 81	Trevor Pryce RC	2.00	.75
❑ 82	Scott Mitchell	.75	.30
❑ 83	Barry Sanders	4.00	1.50
❑ 84	Herman Moore	.75	.30
❑ 85	Johnnie Morton	.75	.30
❑ 86	Matt Russell RC	.50	.20
❑ 87	Brett Favre	5.00	2.50
❑ 88	Edgar Bennett	.75	.30
❑ 89	Robert Brooks	.75	.30
❑ 90	Antonio Freeman	1.25	.50
❑ 91	Reggie White	1.25	.50
❑ 92	Craig Newsome	.50	.20
❑ 93	Jim Harbaugh	.75	.30
❑ 94	Marshall Faulk	1.50	.60
❑ 95	Sean Dawkins	.50	.20
❑ 96	Marvin Harrison	1.25	.50
❑ 97	Quentin Coryatt	.50	.20
❑ 98	Tarik Glenn RC	.50	.20
❑ 99	Mark Brunell	1.50	.60
❑ 100	Natrone Means	.75	.30
❑ 101	Keenan McCardell	.75	.30
❑ 102	Jimmy Smith	.75	.30
❑ 103	Tony Brackens	.50	.20
❑ 104	Kevin Hardy	.50	.20
❑ 105	Elvis Grbac	.75	.30
❑ 106	Marcus Allen	1.25	.50
❑ 107	Greg Hill	.50	.20
❑ 108	Derrick Thomas	1.25	.50
❑ 109	Dale Carter	.50	.20
❑ 110	Dan Marino	5.00	2.00
❑ 111	Karim Abdul-Jabbar	.75	.30
❑ 112	Brian Manning RC	.50	.20
❑ 113	Daryl Gardener	.50	.20
❑ 114	Troy Drayton	.50	.20
❑ 115	Zach Thomas	1.25	.50
❑ 116	Jason Taylor RC	12.00	5.00
❑ 117	Brad Johnson	1.25	.50
❑ 118	Robert Smith	.75	.30
❑ 119	John Randle	.75	.30
❑ 120	Cris Carter	1.25	.50
❑ 121	Jake Reed	.75	.30
❑ 122	Randall Cunningham	1.25	.50
❑ 123	Drew Bledsoe	1.50	.60
❑ 124	Curtis Martin	1.50	.60
❑ 125	Terry Glenn	1.25	.50
❑ 126	Willie McGinest	.50	.20
❑ 127	Chris Canty RC	.50	.20
❑ 128	Sedrick Shaw RC	1.00	.40
❑ 129	Heath Shuler	.50	.20
❑ 130	Mario Bates	.50	.20
❑ 131	Ray Zellars	.50	.20
❑ 132	Andre Hastings	.50	.20
❑ 133	Dave Brown	.50	.20
❑ 134	Tyrone Wheatley	.75	.30
❑ 135	Rodney Hampton	.75	.30
❑ 136	Chris Calloway	.50	.20
❑ 137	Tiki Barber RC	40.00	20.00
❑ 138	Neil O'Donnell	.75	.30
❑ 139	Adrian Murrell	.75	.30
❑ 140	Wayne Chrebet	1.25	.50
❑ 141	Keyshawn Johnson	1.25	.50
❑ 142	Hugh Douglas	.50	.20
❑ 143	Jeff George	.75	.30
❑ 144	Napoleon Kaufman	1.25	.50
❑ 145	Tim Brown	1.25	.50
❑ 146	Desmond Howard	.75	.30
❑ 147	Rickey Dudley	.75	.30
❑ 148	Terry McDaniel	.50	.20
❑ 149	Ty Detmer	.75	.30
❑ 150	Ricky Watters	.75	.30
❑ 151	Chris T. Jones	.50	.20
❑ 152	Irving Fryar	.75	.30
❑ 153	Mike Mamula	.50	.20
❑ 154	Jon Harris RC	.50	.20
❑ 155	Kordell Stewart	1.25	.50
❑ 156	Jerome Bettis	1.25	.50
❑ 157	Charles Johnson	.75	.30
❑ 158	Greg Lloyd	.50	.20
❑ 159	George Jones RC	.50	.20
❑ 160	Terrell Fletcher	.50	.20
❑ 161	Stan Humphries	.75	.30
❑ 162	Tony Martin	.75	.30
❑ 163	Eric Metcalf	.75	.30
❑ 164	Junior Seau	1.25	.50
❑ 165	Rod Woodson	.75	.30
❑ 166	Steve Young	1.50	.60
❑ 167	Terry Kirby	.75	.30
❑ 168	Garrison Hearst	.75	.30
❑ 169	Jerry Rice	2.50	1.25
❑ 170	Ken Norton	.50	.20
❑ 171	Kevin Greene	.75	.30
❑ 172	Lamar Smith	1.25	.50
❑ 173	Warren Moon	1.25	.50
❑ 174	Chris Warren	.75	.30
❑ 175	Cortez Kennedy	.50	.20
❑ 176	Joey Galloway	.75	.30
❑ 177	Tony Banks	.75	.30
❑ 178	Isaac Bruce	1.25	.50
❑ 179	Eddie Kennison	.75	.30
❑ 180	Kevin Carter	.50	.20
❑ 181	Craig Heyward	.50	.20
❑ 182	Trent Dilfer	1.25	.50
❑ 183	Errict Rhett	.50	.20
❑ 184	Mike Alstott	1.25	.50
❑ 185	Hardy Nickerson	.50	.20
❑ 186	Ronde Barber RC	12.00	5.00
❑ 187	Steve McNair	1.50	.60
❑ 188	Eddie George	1.25	.50
❑ 189	Chris Sanders	.50	.20
❑ 190	Blaine Bishop	.50	.20
❑ 191	Derrick Mason RC	15.00	7.50
❑ 192	Gus Frerotte	.50	.20
❑ 193	Terry Allen	1.25	.50
❑ 194	Brian Mitchell	.50	.20
❑ 195	Alvin Harper	.50	.20
❑ 196	Jeff Hostetler	.50	.20
❑ 197	Leslie Shepherd	.50	.20
❑ 198	Stephen Davis	1.25	.50
❑ A1	Aikman Audio Blue	4.00	1.50
❑ A2	Aikman Audio Pro Bowl	10.00	4.00
❑ A3	Aikman Audio White/500	30.00	15.00

1998 SP Authentic

❑	COMP.SET w/o SP's (84)	40.00	20.00
❑	*HAND NUMBERED RCs: .5X TO .8X		
❑ 1	Andre Wadsworth RC	25.00	10.00
❑ 2	Corey Chavous RC	40.00	15.00
❑ 3	Keith Brooking RC	40.00	15.00
❑ 4	Duane Starks RC	15.00	7.50
❑ 5	Pat Johnson RC	25.00	10.00
❑ 6	Jason Peter RC	15.00	7.50
❑ 7	Curtis Enis RC	15.00	7.50
❑ 8	Takeo Spikes RC	40.00	15.00
❑ 9	Greg Ellis RC	15.00	7.50
❑ 10	Marcus Nash RC	15.00	7.50
❑ 11	Brian Griese RC	50.00	20.00
❑ 12	Germane Crowell RC	25.00	10.00
❑ 13	Vonnie Holliday RC	25.00	10.00
❑ 14	Peyton Manning RC	800.00	450.00
❑ 15	Jerome Pathon RC	25.00	10.00
❑ 16	Fred Taylor RC	50.00	20.00
❑ 17	John Avery RC	25.00	10.00
❑ 18	Randy Moss RC	250.00	125.00
❑ 19	Robert Edwards RC	15.00	7.50
❑ 20	Tony Simmons RC	25.00	10.00
❑ 21	Shaun Williams RC	25.00	10.00
❑ 22	Joe Jurevicius RC	40.00	15.00
❑ 23	Charles Woodson RC	50.00	20.00
❑ 24	Tra Thomas RC	15.00	7.50
❑ 25	Grant Wistrom RC	25.00	10.00
❑ 26	Ryan Leaf RC	40.00	15.00
❑ 27	Ahman Green RC	80.00	30.00
❑ 28	Jacquez Green RC	25.00	10.00
❑ 29	Kevin Dyson RC	40.00	15.00
❑ 30	Stephen Alexander RC	25.00	10.00
❑ 31	John Elway TW	20.00	7.50
❑ 32	Jerry Rice TW	12.00	5.00
❑ 33	Emmitt Smith TW	20.00	7.50
❑ 34	Steve Young TW	8.00	3.00
❑ 35	Jerome Bettis TW	6.00	2.50
❑ 36	Deion Sanders TW	6.00	2.50
❑ 37	Andre Rison TW	4.00	1.50
❑ 38	Warren Moon TW	6.00	2.50
❑ 39	Mark Brunell TW	6.00	2.50
❑ 40	Ricky Watters TW	4.00	1.50
❑ 41	Dan Marino TW	25.00	10.00
❑ 42	Brett Favre TW	25.00	10.00
❑ 43	Jake Plummer	1.00	.40
❑ 44	Adrian Murrell	.60	.25
❑ 45	Eric Swann	.40	.15
❑ 46	Jamal Anderson	1.00	.40
❑ 47	Chris Chandler	.60	.25
❑ 48	Jim Harbaugh	.60	.25
❑ 49	Michael Jackson	.40	.15
❑ 50	Jermaine Lewis	.60	.25
❑ 51	Rob Johnson	.60	.25
❑ 52	Antowain Smith	1.00	.40
❑ 53	Thurman Thomas	1.00	.40
❑ 54	Kerry Collins	.60	.25
❑ 55	Fred Lane	.40	.15
❑ 56	Rae Carruth	.40	.15
❑ 57	Erik Kramer	.40	.15
❑ 58	Curtis Conway	.60	.25
❑ 59	Corey Dillon	1.00	.40
❑ 60	Neil O'Donnell	.60	.25
❑ 61	Carl Pickens	.60	.25
❑ 62	Troy Aikman	2.00	.75
❑ 63	Emmitt Smith	3.00	1.25
❑ 64	Deion Sanders	1.00	.40
❑ 65	Terrell Davis	1.00	.40
❑ 66	John Elway	4.00	1.50
❑ 67	Rod Smith	.60	.25
❑ 68	Scott Mitchell	.60	.25
❑ 69	Barry Sanders	3.00	1.25
❑ 70	Herman Moore	.60	.25
❑ 71	Brett Favre	4.00	1.50

❑ 72 Dorsey Levens	1.00	.40
❑ 73 Antonio Freeman	1.00	.40
❑ 74 Marshall Faulk	1.25	.50
❑ 75 Marvin Harrison	1.00	.40
❑ 76 Mark Brunell	1.00	.40
❑ 77 Keenan McCardell	.60	.25
❑ 78 Jimmy Smith	.60	.25
❑ 79 Andre Rison	.60	.25
❑ 80 Elvis Grbac	.60	.25
❑ 81 Derrick Alexander	.60	.25
❑ 82 Dan Marino	4.00	1.50
❑ 83 Karim Abdul-Jabbar	1.00	.40
❑ 84 O.J. McDuffie	.60	.25
❑ 85 Brad Johnson	1.00	.40
❑ 86 Cris Carter	1.00	.40
❑ 87 Robert Smith	1.00	.40
❑ 88 Drew Bledsoe	1.50	.60
❑ 89 Terry Glenn	1.00	.40
❑ 90 Ben Coates	.60	.25
❑ 91 Lamar Smith	.60	.25
❑ 92 Danny Wuerffel	.60	.25
❑ 93 Tiki Barber	1.00	.40
❑ 94 Danny Kanell	.60	.25
❑ 95 Ike Hilliard	.60	.25
❑ 96 Curtis Martin	1.00	.40
❑ 97 Keyshawn Johnson	1.00	.40
❑ 98 Glenn Foley	.60	.25
❑ 99 Jeff George	.60	.25
❑ 100 Tim Brown	1.00	.40
❑ 101 Napoleon Kaufman	1.00	.40
❑ 102 Bobby Hoying	.60	.25
❑ 103 Charlie Garner	.60	.25
❑ 104 Irving Fryar	.60	.25
❑ 105 Kordell Stewart	1.00	.40
❑ 106 Jerome Bettis	1.00	.40
❑ 107 Charles Johnson	.40	.15
❑ 108 Tony Banks	.60	.25
❑ 109 Isaac Bruce	1.00	.40
❑ 110 Natrone Means	.60	.25
❑ 111 Junior Seau	1.00	.40
❑ 112 Steve Young	1.25	.50
❑ 113 Jerry Rice	2.00	.75
❑ 114 Garrison Hearst	1.00	.40
❑ 115 Ricky Watters	.60	.25
❑ 116 Warren Moon	1.00	.40
❑ 117 Joey Galloway	.60	.25
❑ 118 Trent Dilfer	1.00	.40
❑ 119 Warrick Dunn	1.25	.50
❑ 120 Mike Alstott	1.00	.40
❑ 121 Steve McNair	1.00	.40
❑ 122 Eddie George	1.00	.40
❑ 123 Yancey Thigpen	.40	.15
❑ 124 Gus Frerotte	.40	.15
❑ 125 Terry Allen	1.00	.40
❑ 126 Michael Westbrook	.60	.25
❑ AE13 Dan Marino SAMPLE	2.00	.75

1999 SP Authentic

❑ COMP.SET w/o SPs (90)	35.00	15.00
❑ *HAND NUMBERED RCs: .5X TO .8X		
❑ 1 Jake Plummer	.60	.25
❑ 2 Adrian Murrell	.60	.25
❑ 3 Frank Sanders	.60	.25
❑ 4 Jamal Anderson	1.00	.40
❑ 5 Chris Chandler	.60	.25
❑ 6 Terance Mathis	.60	.25
❑ 7 Priest Holmes	1.50	.60
❑ 8 Jermaine Lewis	.60	.25
❑ 9 Antowain Smith	1.00	.40
❑ 10 Doug Flutie	1.00	.40
❑ 11 Eric Moulds	1.00	.40
❑ 12 Muhsin Muhammad	.60	.25
❑ 13 Tim Biakabutuka	.60	.25
❑ 14 Wesley Walls	.60	.25
❑ 15 Curtis Enis	.40	.15
❑ 16 Bobby Engram	.60	.25
❑ 17 Corey Dillon	1.00	.40
❑ 18 Darnay Scott	.60	.25
❑ 19 Terry Kirby	.40	.15
❑ 20 Ty Detmer	.60	.25
❑ 21 Troy Aikman	2.00	.75
❑ 22 Michael Irvin	.60	.25
❑ 23 Emmitt Smith	2.00	.75
❑ 24 Terrell Davis	1.00	.40
❑ 25 Brian Griese	1.00	.40
❑ 26 Rod Smith	.60	.25
❑ 27 Shannon Sharpe	.60	.25
❑ 28 Barry Sanders	3.00	1.25
❑ 29 Charlie Batch	1.00	.40
❑ 30 Herman Moore	.60	.25
❑ 31 Johnnie Morton	.60	.25
❑ 32 Brett Favre	3.00	1.25
❑ 33 Antonio Freeman	1.00	.40
❑ 34 Dorsey Levens	1.00	.40
❑ 35 Mark Chmura	.60	.25
❑ 36 Peyton Manning	3.00	1.25
❑ 37 Marvin Harrison	1.00	.40
❑ 38 Mark Brunell	1.00	.40
❑ 39 Fred Taylor	1.00	.40
❑ 40 Jimmy Smith	.60	.25
❑ 41 Elvis Grbac	.60	.25
❑ 42 Andre Rison	.60	.25
❑ 43 Dan Marino	3.00	1.25
❑ 44 O.J. McDuffie	.60	.25
❑ 45 Yatil Green	.40	.15
❑ 46 Randall Cunningham	1.00	.40
❑ 47 Randy Moss	3.00	1.25
❑ 48 Robert Smith	1.00	.40
❑ 49 Cris Carter	1.00	.40
❑ 50 Drew Bledsoe	1.25	.50
❑ 51 Ben Coates	.40	.15
❑ 52 Terry Glenn	1.00	.40
❑ 53 Eddie Kennison	.60	.25
❑ 54 Cam Cleeland	.40	.15
❑ 55 Ike Hilliard	.60	.25
❑ 56 Gary Brown	.40	.15
❑ 57 Kerry Collins	.60	.25
❑ 58 Vinny Testaverde	.60	.25
❑ 59 Keyshawn Johnson	1.00	.40
❑ 60 Wayne Chrebet	1.00	.40
❑ 61 Curtis Martin	1.00	.40
❑ 62 Tim Brown	1.00	.40
❑ 63 Napoleon Kaufman	1.00	.40
❑ 64 Charles Woodson	1.00	.40
❑ 65 Duce Staley	1.00	.40
❑ 66 Charles Johnson	.60	.25
❑ 67 Kordell Stewart	.60	.25
❑ 68 Jerome Bettis	1.00	.40
❑ 69 Marshall Faulk	1.25	.50
❑ 70 Isaac Bruce	1.00	.40
❑ 71 Trent Green	1.00	.40
❑ 72 Jim Harbaugh	.60	.25
❑ 73 Junior Seau	1.00	.40
❑ 74 Natrone Means	.60	.25
❑ 75 Steve Young	1.25	.50
❑ 76 Jerry Rice	2.00	.75
❑ 77 Terrell Owens	1.00	.40
❑ 78 Lawrence Phillips	.60	.25
❑ 79 Joey Galloway	.60	.25
❑ 80 Ricky Watters	.60	.25
❑ 81 Jon Kitna	1.00	.40
❑ 82 Warrick Dunn	1.00	.40
❑ 83 Trent Dilfer	.60	.25
❑ 84 Mike Alstott	1.00	.40
❑ 85 Eddie George	1.00	.40
❑ 86 Steve McNair	1.00	.40
❑ 87 Yancey Thigpen	.40	.15
❑ 88 Brad Johnson	1.00	.40
❑ 89 Skip Hicks	.40	.15
❑ 90 Michael Westbrook	.60	.25
❑ 91 Ricky Williams RC	50.00	25.00
❑ 92 Tim Couch RC	25.00	10.00
❑ 93 Akili Smith RC	20.00	7.50
❑ 94 Edgerrin James RC	80.00	50.00
❑ 95 Donovan McNabb RC	100.00	50.00
❑ 96 Torry Holt RC	60.00	30.00
❑ 97 Cade McNown RC	20.00	7.50
❑ 98 Shaun King RC	20.00	7.50
❑ 99 Daunte Culpepper RC	80.00	40.00
❑ 100 Brock Huard RC	25.00	10.00
❑ 101 Chris Claiborne RC	12.00	5.00
❑ 102 James Johnson RC	20.00	7.50
❑ 103 Rob Konrad RC	25.00	10.00
❑ 104 Peerless Price RC	25.00	10.00
❑ 105 Kevin Faulk RC	25.00	10.00
❑ 106 Andy Katzenmoyer RC	20.00	7.50
❑ 107 Troy Edwards RC	20.00	7.50
❑ 108 Kevin Johnson RC	25.00	10.00
❑ 109 Mike Cloud RC	20.00	7.50
❑ 110 David Boston RC	25.00	10.00
❑ 111 Champ Bailey RC	30.00	12.50
❑ 112 D'Wayne Bates RC	20.00	7.50
❑ 113 Joe Germaine RC	20.00	7.50
❑ 114 Antoine Winfield RC	20.00	7.50
❑ 115 Fernando Bryant RC	20.00	7.50
❑ 116 Jevon Kearse RC	40.00	15.00
❑ 117 Chris McAlister RC	20.00	7.50
❑ 118 Brandon Stokley RC	30.00	12.50
❑ 119 Karsten Bailey RC	20.00	7.50
❑ 120 Daylon McCutcheon RC	20.00	7.50
❑ 121 Jermaine Fazande RC	20.00	7.50
❑ 122 Joel Makovicka RC	25.00	10.00
❑ 123 Ebenezer Ekuban RC	20.00	7.50
❑ 124 Joe Montgomery RC	20.00	7.50
❑ 125 Sean Bennett RC	12.00	5.00
❑ 126 Na Brown RC	20.00	7.50
❑ 127 De'Mond Parker RC	12.00	5.00
❑ 128 Sedrick Irvin RC	12.00	5.00
❑ 129 Terry Jackson RC	20.00	7.50
❑ 130 Jeff Paulk RC	12.00	5.00
❑ 131 Cecil Collins RC	12.00	5.00
❑ 132 Bobby Collins RC	12.00	5.00
❑ 133 Amos Zereoue RC	25.00	10.00
❑ 134 Travis McGriff RC	12.00	5.00
❑ 135 Larry Parker RC	25.00	10.00
❑ 136 Wane McGarity RC	12.00	5.00
❑ 137 Cecil Martin RC	20.00	7.50
❑ 138 Al Wilson RC	20.00	7.50
❑ 139 Jim Kleinsasser RC	20.00	7.50
❑ 140 Dat Nguyen RC	20.00	7.50
❑ 141 Marty Booker RC	25.00	10.00
❑ 142 Reginald Kelly RC	12.00	5.00
❑ 143 Scott Covington RC	25.00	10.00
❑ 144 Antuan Edwards RC	20.00	7.50
❑ 145 Craig Yeast RC	20.00	7.50
❑ WPA W.Payton AU/100	400.00	250.00
❑ WPSP W.Payton Jsy AU/34	1000.00	700.00

2000 SP Authentic

❑ COMP.SET w/o SP's (90)	15.00	6.00
❑ 1 Jake Plummer	.60	.25
❑ 2 David Boston	1.00	.40
❑ 3 Frank Sanders	.60	.25
❑ 4 Chris Chandler	.60	.25
❑ 5 Jamal Anderson	1.00	.40
❑ 6 Shawn Jefferson	.40	.15
❑ 7 Tony Banks	.60	.25

❑ 8	Shannon Sharpe	.60	.25
❑ 9	Rob Johnson	.60	.25
❑ 10	Antowain Smith	.60	.25
❑ 11	Muhsin Muhammad	.60	.25
❑ 12	Steve Beuerlein	.60	.25
❑ 13	Cade McNown	.40	.15
❑ 14	Curtis Enis	.40	.15
❑ 15	Marcus Robinson	1.00	.40
❑ 16	Akili Smith	.40	.15
❑ 17	Corey Dillon	1.00	.40
❑ 18	Tim Couch	.60	.25
❑ 19	Kevin Johnson	1.00	.40
❑ 20	Errict Rhett	.40	.15
❑ 21	Troy Aikman	2.00	.75
❑ 22	Emmitt Smith	2.50	1.00
❑ 23	Rocket Ismail	.60	.25
❑ 24	Joey Galloway	.60	.25
❑ 25	Terrell Davis	1.00	.40
❑ 26	Olandis Gary	1.00	.40
❑ 27	Ed McCaffrey	1.00	.40
❑ 28	Brian Griese	1.00	.40
❑ 29	Charlie Batch	1.00	.40
❑ 30	Germane Crowell	.40	.15
❑ 31	James O. Stewart	.60	.25
❑ 32	Brett Favre	3.00	1.25
❑ 33	Antonio Freeman	1.00	.40
❑ 34	Dorsey Levens	.60	.25
❑ 35	Peyton Manning	2.50	1.00
❑ 36	Edgerrin James	1.50	.60
❑ 37	Marvin Harrison	1.00	.40
❑ 38	Mark Brunell	1.00	.40
❑ 39	Fred Taylor	1.00	.40
❑ 40	Jimmy Smith	.60	.25
❑ 41	Elvis Grbac	.60	.25
❑ 42	Tony Gonzalez	.60	.25
❑ 43	James Johnson	.40	.15
❑ 44	Oronde Gadsden	.60	.25
❑ 45	Damon Huard	1.00	.40
❑ 46	Randy Moss	2.00	.75
❑ 47	Cris Carter	1.00	.40
❑ 48	Daunte Culpepper	1.25	.50
❑ 49	Drew Bledsoe	1.25	.50
❑ 50	Terry Glenn	.60	.25
❑ 51	Ricky Williams	1.00	.40
❑ 52	Jeff Blake	.60	.25
❑ 53	Keith Poole	.40	.15
❑ 54	Kerry Collins	.60	.25
❑ 55	Amani Toomer	.60	.25
❑ 56	Ike Hilliard	.60	.25
❑ 57	Wayne Chrebet	.60	.25
❑ 58	Curtis Martin	1.00	.40
❑ 59	Vinny Testaverde	.60	.25
❑ 60	Tim Brown	1.00	.40
❑ 61	Rich Gannon	1.00	.40
❑ 62	Tyrone Wheatley	.60	.25
❑ 63	Duce Staley	1.00	.40
❑ 64	Donovan McNabb	1.50	.60
❑ 65	Troy Edwards	.40	.15
❑ 66	Jerome Bettis	1.00	.40
❑ 67	Kordell Stewart	.60	.25
❑ 68	Marshall Faulk	1.25	.50
❑ 69	Kurt Warner	1.50	.60
❑ 70	Isaac Bruce	1.00	.40
❑ 71	Torry Holt	1.00	.40
❑ 72	Ryan Leaf	.60	.25
❑ 73	Jim Harbaugh	.60	.25
❑ 74	Jermaine Fazande	.40	.15
❑ 75	Jerry Rice	2.00	.75
❑ 76	Terrell Owens	1.00	.40
❑ 77	Jeff Garcia	1.00	.40
❑ 78	Ricky Watters	.60	.25
❑ 79	Jon Kitna	1.00	.40
❑ 80	Derrick Mayes	.60	.25
❑ 81	Shaun King	.40	.15
❑ 82	Mike Alstott	1.00	.40
❑ 83	Keyshawn Johnson	1.00	.40
❑ 84	Warrick Dunn	1.00	.40
❑ 85	Eddie George	1.00	.40
❑ 86	Steve McNair	1.00	.40
❑ 87	Jevon Kearse	1.00	.40
❑ 88	Brad Johnson	1.00	.40
❑ 89	Stephen Davis	1.00	.40
❑ 90	Michael Westbrook	.60	.25
❑ 91	Anthony Lucas RC	10.00	4.00
❑ 92	Avion Black RC	15.00	6.00
❑ 93	Dante Hall RC	40.00	15.00
❑ 94	Darrell Jackson RC	30.00	12.50
❑ 95	Deltha O'Neal RC	20.00	7.50
❑ 96	Erron Kinney RC	20.00	7.50
❑ 97	Doug Chapman RC	15.00	6.00
❑ 98	Frank Murphy RC	10.00	4.00
❑ 99	Gari Scott RC	10.00	4.00
❑ 100	Giovanni Carmazzi RC	10.00	4.00
❑ 101	JaJuan Dawson RC	10.00	4.00
❑ 102	Jarious Jackson RC	15.00	6.00
❑ 103	Rashard Anderson RC	15.00	6.00
❑ 104	Michael Wiley RC	15.00	6.00
❑ 105	Spergon Wynn RC	15.00	6.00
❑ 106	Muneer Moore RC	10.00	4.00
❑ 107	Ahmed Plummer RC	20.00	7.50
❑ 108	Chad Morton RC	20.00	7.50
❑ 109	Rob Morris RC	15.00	6.00
❑ 110	Ron Dixon RC	15.00	6.00
❑ 111	Rondell Mealey RC	10.00	4.00
❑ 112	Sebastian Janikowski RC	20.00	7.50
❑ 113	Shaun Ellis RC	20.00	7.50
❑ 114	Rogers Beckett RC	15.00	6.00
❑ 115	Shyrone Stith RC	15.00	6.00
❑ 116	Tim Rattay RC	25.00	10.00
❑ 117	Todd Husak RC	20.00	7.50
❑ 118	Tom Brady RC	800.00	600.00
❑ 119	Trevor Gaylor RC	15.00	6.00
❑ 120	Windrell Hayes RC	15.00	6.00
❑ 121	Anthony Becht RC	20.00	7.50
❑ 122	Brian Urlacher RC	80.00	40.00
❑ 123	Bubba Franks RC	20.00	7.50
❑ 124	Chad Pennington RC	80.00	30.00
❑ 125	Chris Redman RC	15.00	6.00
❑ 126	Corey Simon RC	20.00	7.50
❑ 127	Curtis Keaton RC	15.00	6.00
❑ 128	Danny Farmer RC	15.00	6.00
❑ 129	Dennis Northcutt RC	20.00	7.50
❑ 130	Dez White RC	20.00	7.50
❑ 131	J.R. Redmond RC	15.00	6.00
❑ 132	Jamal Lewis RC	80.00	30.00
❑ 133	Jerry Porter RC	50.00	30.00
❑ 134	Joe Hamilton RC	15.00	6.00
❑ 135	Laveranues Coles RC	40.00	15.00
❑ 136	R.Jay Soward RC	15.00	6.00
❑ 137	Reuben Droughns RC	40.00	15.00
❑ 138	Ron Dayne RC	30.00	12.50
❑ 139	Ron Dugans RC	10.00	4.00
❑ 140	Shaun Alexander RC	175.00	100.00
❑ 141	Sylvester Morris RC	15.00	6.00
❑ 142	Tee Martin RC	20.00	7.50
❑ 143	Thomas Jones RC	40.00	15.00
❑ 144	Todd Pinkston RC	20.00	7.50
❑ 145	Travis Prentice RC	15.00	6.00
❑ 146	Travis Taylor RC	20.00	7.50
❑ 147	Trung Canidate RC	15.00	6.00
❑ 148	Courtney Brown RC	20.00	7.50
❑ 149	Plaxico Burress RC	50.00	20.00
❑ 150	Peter Warrick RC	20.00	7.50
❑ 151	Billy Volek RC	50.00	20.00
❑ 152	Bobby Shaw RC	10.00	4.00
❑ 153	Brad Hoover RC	15.00	6.00
❑ 154	Brian Finneran RC	20.00	7.50
❑ 155	Charles Lee RC	10.00	4.00
❑ 156	Chris Cole RC	10.00	4.00
❑ 157	Clint Stoerner RC	15.00	6.00
❑ 158	Doug Johnson RC	20.00	7.50
❑ 159	Frank Moreau RC	15.00	6.00
❑ 160	Jake Delhomme RC	60.00	35.00
❑ 161	KaRon Coleman RC	10.00	4.00
❑ 162	Kevin McDougal RC	10.00	4.00
❑ 163	Larry Foster RC	10.00	4.00
❑ 164	Mike Anderson RC	30.00	12.50
❑ 165	Patrick Pass RC	10.00	4.00
❑ 166	Reggie Jones RC	10.00	4.00
❑ 167	Sammy Morris RC	15.00	6.00
❑ 168	Shockmain Davis RC	10.00	4.00
❑ 169	Terrelle Smith RC	10.00	4.00
❑ 170	Ronney Jenkins RC	10.00	4.00
❑ 171	Troy Walters RC	15.00	6.00

2001 SP Authentic

❑	COMP.SET w/o SP's (90)	20.00	7.50
❑	*SINGLE COLOR SWATCH: .3X TO .8X		
❑ 1	Jake Plummer	.60	.25
❑ 2	Thomas Jones	.60	.25
❑ 3	Frank Sanders	.40	.15
❑ 4	Jamal Anderson	1.00	.40
❑ 5	Chris Chandler	.60	.25
❑ 6	Tony Martin	.60	.25
❑ 7	Jamal Lewis	1.25	.50
❑ 8	Elvis Grbac	.60	.25
❑ 9	Travis Taylor	.60	.25
❑ 10	Peerless Price	.60	.25
❑ 11	Rob Johnson	.60	.25
❑ 12	Eric Moulds	.60	.25
❑ 13	Muhsin Muhammad	.60	.25
❑ 14	Isaac Byrd	.40	.15
❑ 15	Wesley Walls	.40	.15
❑ 16	James Allen	.60	.25
❑ 17	Marcus Robinson	1.00	.40
❑ 18	Brian Urlacher	1.25	.50
❑ 19	Jon Kitna	.60	.25
❑ 20	Peter Warrick	1.00	.40
❑ 21	Corey Dillon	1.00	.40
❑ 22	Kevin Johnson	.60	.25
❑ 23	JaJuan Dawson	.40	.15
❑ 24	Tim Couch	.60	.25
❑ 25	Rocket Ismail	.60	.25
❑ 26	Emmitt Smith	2.00	.75
❑ 27	Joey Galloway	.60	.25
❑ 28	Terrell Davis	1.00	.40
❑ 29	Mike Anderson	1.00	.40
❑ 30	Brian Griese	1.00	.40
❑ 31	Ed McCaffrey	1.00	.40
❑ 32	Charlie Batch	1.00	.40
❑ 33	James O. Stewart	.60	.25

❑	34	Johnnie Morton	.60	.25
❑	35	Brett Favre	3.00	1.25
❑	36	Antonio Freeman	1.00	.40
❑	37	Bill Schroeder	.40	.15
❑	38	Ahman Green	1.00	.40
❑	39	Peyton Manning	2.50	1.00
❑	40	Edgerrin James	1.25	.50
❑	41	Marvin Harrison	1.00	.40
❑	42	Mark Brunell	1.00	.40
❑	43	Fred Taylor	1.00	.40
❑	44	Jimmy Smith	.60	.25
❑	45	Tony Gonzalez	.60	.25
❑	46	Trent Green	1.00	.40
❑	47	Oronde Gadsden	.60	.25
❑	48	Jay Fiedler	1.00	.40
❑	49	Lamar Smith	.60	.25
❑	50	Randy Moss	2.00	.75
❑	51	Cris Carter	1.00	.40
❑	52	Daunte Culpepper	1.00	.40
❑	53	Drew Bledsoe	1.25	.50
❑	54	Terry Glenn	.60	.25
❑	55	Antowain Smith	.60	.25
❑	56	Ricky Williams	1.00	.40
❑	57	Joe Horn	.60	.25
❑	58	Aaron Brooks	1.00	.40
❑	59	Kerry Collins	.60	.25
❑	60	Tiki Barber	1.00	.40
❑	61	Ron Dayne	1.00	.40
❑	62	Vinny Testaverde	.60	.25
❑	63	Wayne Chrebet	.60	.25
❑	64	Curtis Martin	1.00	.40
❑	65	Tim Brown	1.00	.40
❑	66	Rich Gannon	1.00	.40
❑	67	Jerry Rice	2.00	.75
❑	68	Duce Staley	1.00	.40
❑	69	Donovan McNabb	1.25	.50
❑	70	Kordell Stewart	.60	.25
❑	71	Jerome Bettis	1.00	.40
❑	72	Marshall Faulk	1.25	.50
❑	73	Kurt Warner	1.50	.60
❑	74	Isaac Bruce	1.00	.40
❑	75	Doug Flutie	1.00	.40
❑	76	Junior Seau	1.00	.40
❑	77	Jeff Garcia	1.00	.40
❑	78	Garrison Hearst	.60	.25
❑	79	Terrell Owens	1.00	.40
❑	80	Ricky Watters	.60	.25
❑	81	Matt Hasselbeck	.60	.25
❑	82	Brad Johnson	1.00	.40
❑	83	Warrick Dunn	1.00	.40
❑	84	Mike Alstott	1.00	.40
❑	85	Kevin Dyson	.60	.25
❑	86	Eddie George	1.00	.40
❑	87	Steve McNair	1.00	.40
❑	88	Champ Bailey	.60	.25
❑	89	Michael Westbrook	.60	.25
❑	90	Stephen Davis	1.00	.40
❑	91	Michael Vick JSY AU RC	1500.00	750.00
❑	92	Rod Gardner JSY AU RC	100.00	50.00
❑	93	Freddie Mitchell JSY AU RC	80.00	30.00
❑	94	Koren Robinson JSY/500 RC	50.00	20.00
❑	95	David Terrell JSY/500 RC	40.00	15.00
❑	96	Michael Bennett JSY RC	60.00	25.00
❑	97	Robert Ferguson JSY RC	40.00	15.00
❑	98	Deuce McAllister JSY RC	100.00	50.00
❑	99	Travis Henry JSY RC	30.00	12.50
❑	100	Andre Carter JSY RC	25.00	10.00
❑	101	Drew Brees JSY RC	120.00	60.00
❑	102	Santana Moss JSY/500 RC	80.00	50.00
❑	103	Chris Weinke JSY/390 RC	40.00	15.00
❑	104	Chad Johnson JSY/160 RC	400.00	250.00
❑	105	Reggie Wayne JSY RC	100.00	50.00
❑	106	Kevan Barlow JSY/500 RC	60.00	25.00
❑	107	Chr Chambers JSY/500 RC	80.00	40.00
❑	108	Todd Heap JSY/500 RC	80.00	40.00
❑	109	A Thomas JSY/500 RC	40.00	15.00
❑	110	James Jackson JSY/500 RC	25.00	10.00
❑	111	Rudi Johnson JSY/500 RC	120.00	60.00
❑	112	Mike McMahon JSY RC	40.00	15.00
❑	113	Josh Heupel JSY RC	40.00	15.00
❑	114	Travis Minor JSY/500 RC	50.00	20.00
❑	115	Quincy Morgan JSY/500 RC	40.00	20.00
❑	116	Dan Morgan JSY/500 RC	40.00	20.00
❑	117	Jesse Palmer JSY/500 RC	50.00	20.00
❑	118	Sage Rosenfels JSY/300 RC	60.00	30.00
❑	119	Marq Tuiasosopo JSY RC	25.00	10.00
❑	120	L.Tomlinson JSY/500 RC	500.00	350.00
❑	123	Alge Crumpler AU RC	30.00	15.00
❑	124	Arnold Jackson AU RC	20.00	7.50
❑	125	Bobby Newcombe AU RC	20.00	7.50
❑	126	Brand Manumaleuna AU RC	20.00	7.50
❑	127	Cedrick Wilson AU RC	35.00	20.00
❑	128	Brian Allen AU RC	15.00	6.00
❑	129	Dee Brown AU RC	25.00	10.00
❑	130	Damerien McCants AU RC	20.00	7.50
❑	131	Dave Dickenson AU RC	20.00	7.50
❑	132	Derrick Blaylock AU RC	40.00	20.00
❑	133	Eddie Berlin AU RC	20.00	7.50
❑	134	Francis St.Paul AU RC	20.00	7.50
❑	135	Jamar Fletcher AU RC	20.00	7.50
❑	136	Josh Booty AU RC	25.00	10.00
❑	137	Scotty Anderson AU RC	20.00	7.50
❑	138	Ken-Yon Rambo AU RC	20.00	7.50
❑	139	Kenyatta Walker AU RC	15.00	6.00
❑	140	Kevin Kasper AU RC	30.00	12.50
❑	141	Snoop Minnis AU RC	20.00	7.50
❑	142	Houshmandzadeh AU RC	40.00	20.00
❑	143	Quincy Carter AU RC	40.00	15.00
❑	144	Ronney Daniels AU RC	15.00	6.00
❑	145	Sedrick Hodge AU RC	15.00	6.00
❑	146	Steve Smith AU RC	135.00	75.00
❑	147	Tim Hasselbeck AU RC	25.00	10.00
❑	148	Vinny Sutherland AU RC	20.00	7.50
❑	149	Richard Seymour AU RC	60.00	30.00
❑	150	Jamie Winborn AU	20.00	7.50
❑	151	Gerard Warren RC	12.00	5.00
❑	152	Justin Smith RC	12.00	5.00
❑	153	David Martin RC	10.00	4.00
❑	154	Jamal Reynolds RC	12.00	5.00
❑	155	Dominic Rhodes RC	12.00	5.00
❑	156	Nate Clements RC	12.00	5.00
❑	157	Michael Lewis RC	12.00	5.00
❑	158	Andre King RC	10.00	4.00
❑	159	Benjamin Gay RC	12.00	5.00
❑	160	Correll Buckhalter RC	30.00	15.00
❑	161	Roderick Robinson RC	10.00	4.00
❑	162	Moran Norris RC	8.00	3.00
❑	163	Onome Ojo RC	10.00	4.00
❑	164	Will Allen RC	10.00	4.00
❑	165	Jonathan Carter RC	10.00	4.00
❑	166	LaMont Jordan RC	75.00	40.00
❑	167	DeLawrence Grant RC	8.00	3.00
❑	168	Derrick Gibson RC	10.00	4.00
❑	169	A.J. Feeley RC	20.00	7.50
❑	170	Tim Baker RC	8.00	3.00
❑	171	Kendrell Bell RC	25.00	12.50
❑	172	Zeke Moreno RC	12.00	5.00
❑	173	Carlos Polk RC	8.00	3.00
❑	174	Ken Lucas RC	10.00	4.00
❑	175	Heath Evans RC	10.00	4.00
❑	176	Elvis Joseph RC	10.00	4.00
❑	177	Damione Lewis RC	10.00	4.00
❑	178	Tommy Polley RC	12.00	5.00
❑	179	Fred Smoot RC	12.00	5.00
❑	180	Jason Brookins RC	12.00	5.00
❑	181	Nick Goings RC	12.00	5.00
❑	182	Drew Bennett RC	25.00	10.00
❑	183	Justin McCareins RC	20.00	7.50
❑	184	Kabeer Gbaja-Biamila RC	25.00	10.00
❑	185	Edgerton Hartwell RC	8.00	3.00
❑	186	Robert Carswell RC	8.00	3.00
❑	187	Aaron Schobel RC	12.00	5.00
❑	188	Dan Alexander RC	12.00	5.00
❑	189	Jamie Winborn RC	10.00	4.00
❑	190	Karon Riley RC	8.00	3.00
❑	EG	Eddie George SAMPLE	3.00	1.50

2002 SP Authentic

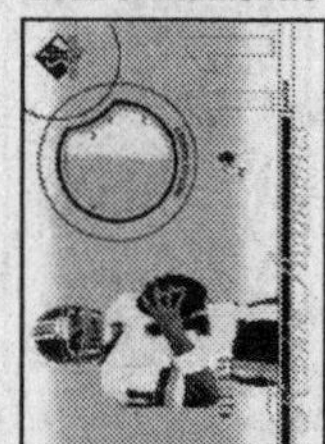

❑		COMP.SET w/o SP's (90)	25.00	10.00
❑	1	Tom Brady	2.00	.75
❑	2	Antowain Smith	.60	.25
❑	3	Troy Brown	.60	.25
❑	4	Kurt Warner	1.00	.40
❑	5	Marshall Faulk	1.00	.40
❑	6	Isaac Bruce	1.00	.40
❑	7	Kordell Stewart	.60	.25
❑	8	Jerome Bettis	1.00	.40
❑	9	Plaxico Burress	.60	.25
❑	10	Hines Ward	1.00	.40
❑	11	Donovan McNabb	1.25	.50
❑	12	Duce Staley	1.00	.40
❑	13	Dorsey Levens	.60	.25
❑	14	Antonio Freeman	1.00	.40
❑	15	Jerry Rice	2.00	.75
❑	16	Rich Gannon	1.00	.40
❑	17	Tim Brown	1.00	.40
❑	18	Jim Miller	.60	.25
❑	19	Marty Booker	.60	.25
❑	20	Brian Urlacher	1.25	.50
❑	21	Jamal Lewis	1.00	.40
❑	22	Chris Redman	.40	.15
❑	23	Ray Lewis	1.00	.40
❑	24	Brett Favre	2.50	1.00
❑	25	Ahman Green	1.00	.40
❑	26	Terry Glenn	.60	.25
❑	27	Keyshawn Johnson	1.00	.40
❑	28	Keenan McCardell	.40	.15
❑	29	Michael Pittman	.40	.15
❑	30	Curtis Martin	1.00	.40
❑	31	Vinny Testaverde	.60	.25
❑	32	Chad Pennington	1.25	.50
❑	33	Wayne Chrebet	.60	.25
❑	34	Terrell Owens	1.00	.40
❑	35	Garrison Hearst	.60	.25
❑	36	Jay Fiedler	.60	.25
❑	37	Ricky Williams	1.00	.40
❑	38	Chris Chambers	1.00	.40
❑	39	Shaun Alexander	1.25	.50
❑	40	Darrell Jackson	.60	.25
❑	41	Drew Bledsoe	1.25	.50
❑	42	Travis Henry	1.00	.40
❑	43	Eric Moulds	.60	.25
❑	44	Stephen Davis	.60	.25
❑	45	Rod Gardner	.60	.25
❑	46	Brian Griese	1.00	.40
❑	47	Olandis Gary	.60	.25
❑	48	Shannon Sharpe	.60	.25
❑	49	Tim Couch	.60	.25
❑	50	Kevin Johnson	.60	.25
❑	51	Steve McNair	1.00	.40
❑	52	Eddie George	1.00	.40
❑	53	Aaron Brooks	1.00	.40
❑	54	Deuce McAllister	1.25	.50
❑	55	Joe Horn	.60	.25
❑	56	Michael Vick	2.50	1.00
❑	57	Warrick Dunn	1.00	.40
❑	58	Kerry Collins	.60	.25
❑	59	Tiki Barber	1.00	.40

❑ 60 Amani Toomer .60 .25
❑ 61 Jake Plummer .60 .25
❑ 62 David Boston 1.00 .40
❑ 63 Thomas Jones .60 .25
❑ 64 Edgerrin James 1.25 .50
❑ 65 Marvin Harrison 1.00 .40
❑ 66 Mark Brunell 1.00 .40
❑ 67 Jimmy Smith .60 .25
❑ 68 Fred Taylor 1.00 .40
❑ 69 Corey Dillon .60 .25
❑ 70 Jon Kitna .60 .25
❑ 71 Michael Westbrook .40 .15
❑ 72 Trent Green .60 .25
❑ 73 Priest Holmes 1.25 .50
❑ 74 Tony Gonzalez .60 .25
❑ 75 Daunte Culpepper 1.00 .40
❑ 76 Michael Bennett .60 .25
❑ 77 Randy Moss 1.50 .60
❑ 78 Drew Brees 1.00 .40
❑ 79 Curtis Conway .40 .15
❑ 80 Junior Seau 1.00 .40
❑ 81 Quincy Carter .60 .25
❑ 82 Emmitt Smith 2.50 1.00
❑ 83 Joey Galloway .60 .25
❑ 84 Cory Schlesinger .40 .15
❑ 85 James Stewart .60 .25
❑ 86 Az-Zahir Hakim .40 .15
❑ 87 Rodney Peete .60 .25
❑ 88 Lamar Smith .60 .25
❑ 89 Corey Bradford .40 .15
❑ 90 Jermaine Lewis .40 .15
❑ 91 Peyton Manning AU 100.00 50.00
❑ 92 Anthony Thomas AU 25.00 12.50
❑ 93 LaDainian Tomlinson AU 50.00 30.00
❑ 94 Jeff Garcia AU 25.00 10.00
❑ 95 Kurt Warner SC 3.00 1.25
❑ 96 Brett Favre SC 8.00 3.00
❑ 97 Michael Vick SC 10.00 4.00
❑ 98 Donovan McNabb SC 4.00 1.50
❑ 99 Daunte Culpepper SC 3.00 1.25
❑ 100 Tom Brady SC 8.00 3.00
❑ 101 Drew Brees SC 3.00 1.25
❑ 102 Kordell Stewart SC 2.00 .75
❑ 103 Steve McNair SC 3.00 1.25
❑ 104 Peyton Manning SC 6.00 2.50
❑ 105 Mark Brunell SC 3.00 1.25
❑ 106 Jeff Garcia SC 3.00 1.25
❑ 107 Aaron Brooks SC 3.00 1.25
❑ 108 Rich Gannon SC 3.00 1.25
❑ 109 Tim Couch SC 2.00 .75
❑ 110 Jake Plummer SC 3.00 1.25
❑ 111 Drew Bledsoe SC 4.00 1.50
❑ 112 Brian Griese SC 3.00 1.25
❑ 113 Quincy Carter SC 2.00 .75
❑ 114 Vinny Testaverde SC 2.00 .75
❑ 115 Chad Pennington SC 4.00 1.50
❑ 116 Brad Johnson SC 2.00 .75
❑ 117 Trent Dilfer SC 2.00 .75
❑ 118 Jim Miller SC 2.00 .75
❑ 119 Tommy Maddox SC 8.00 3.00
❑ 120 Trent Green SC 2.00 .75
❑ 121 Rodney Peete SC 2.00 .75
❑ 122 Jay Fiedler SC 2.00 .75
❑ 123 Kerry Collins SC 2.00 .75
❑ 124 Chris Redman SC 2.00 .75
❑ 125 Marshall Faulk SS 4.00 1.50
❑ 126 Donovan McNabb SS 5.00 2.00
❑ 127 Michael Vick SS 12.00 5.00
❑ 128 Brett Favre SS 10.00 4.00
❑ 129 Peyton Manning SS 8.00 3.00
❑ 130 Kurt Warner SS 4.00 1.50
❑ 131 Curtis Martin SS 4.00 1.50
❑ 132 Randy Moss SS 8.00 3.00
❑ 133 Edgerrin James SS 5.00 2.00
❑ 134 Jerome Bettis SS 4.00 1.50
❑ 135 Emmitt Smith SS 10.00 4.00
❑ 136 LaDainian Tomlinson SS 6.00 2.50
❑ 137 Jeff Garcia SS 4.00 1.50
❑ 138 Kordell Stewart SS 2.50 1.00
❑ 139 Anthony Thomas SS 2.50 1.00
❑ 140 Tom Brady SS 10.00 4.00
❑ 141 Daunte Culpepper SS 4.00 1.50
❑ 142 Drew Bledsoe SS 5.00 2.00
❑ 143 Ricky Williams SS 4.00 1.50
❑ 144 Warrick Dunn SS 4.00 1.50
❑ 145 Steve McNair SS 4.00 1.50
❑ 146 Rich Gannon SS 4.00 1.50
❑ 147 Jake Plummer SS 2.50 1.00
❑ 148 Jerry Rice SS 8.00 3.00
❑ 149 Mark Brunell SS 4.00 1.50
❑ 150 Brian Griese SS 4.00 1.50
❑ 151 Eddie George SS 4.00 1.50
❑ 152 Tim Couch SS 2.50 1.00
❑ 153 Keyshawn Johnson SS 4.00 1.50
❑ 154 Shannon Sharpe SS 2.50 1.00
❑ 155 Phillip Buchanon RC 12.00 5.00
❑ 156 Brian Allen RC 10.00 4.00
❑ 157 Brian Westbrook RC 40.00 20.00
❑ 158 Lito Sheppard RC 12.00 5.00
❑ 159 Daryl Jones RC 10.00 4.00
❑ 160 Javin Hunter RC 6.00 2.50
❑ 161 Derrick Lewis RC 6.00 2.50
❑ 162 Javon Walker RC 30.00 15.00
❑ 163 Tank Williams RC 10.00 4.00
❑ 164 Shaun Hill RC 12.00 5.00
❑ 165 Napoleon Harris RC 12.00 5.00
❑ 166 Herb Haygood RC 6.00 2.50
❑ 167 Jake Schifino RC 10.00 4.00
❑ 168 Quentin Jammer RC 12.00 5.00
❑ 169 Jason McAddley RC 10.00 4.00
❑ 170 Jerramy Stevens RC 12.00 5.00
❑ 171 Jesse Chatman RC 12.00 5.00
❑ 172 Larry Ned RC 10.00 4.00
❑ 173 Najeh Davenport RC 12.00 5.00
❑ 174 Lamont Thompson RC 10.00 4.00
❑ 175 Darrell Hill RC 10.00 4.00
❑ 176 Ryan Sims RC 12.00 5.00
❑ 177 Ryan Denney RC 10.00 4.00
❑ 178 Jamin Elliott RC 6.00 2.50
❑ 179 Sam Simmons RC 6.00 2.50
❑ 180 Seth Burford RC 10.00 4.00
❑ 181 Tellis Redmon RC 10.00 4.00
❑ 182 Ben Leber RC 12.00 5.00
❑ 183 Kendall Newson RC 6.00 2.50
❑ 184 Marques Anderson RC 12.00 5.00
❑ 185 Adrian Peterson AU RC 20.00 7.50
❑ 186 Haynesworth AU RC EXCH
❑ 187 Antwoine Womack AU RC 20.00 7.50
❑ 188 Brandon Doman AU RC 20.00 7.50
❑ 189 Craig Nall AU RC 30.00 12.50
❑ 190 Chad Hutchinson AU RC 20.00 7.50
❑ 191 Chester Taylor AU RC 40.00 25.00
❑ 192 Damien Anderson AU RC 20.00 7.50
❑ 193 Deion Branch AU RC 50.00 25.00
❑ 194 Dusty Bonner AU RC 15.00 6.00
❑ 195 Ed Reed AU RC 50.00 20.00
❑ 196 Eric McCoo AU RC 15.00 6.00
❑ 197 J.T. O'Sullivan AU RC 20.00 7.50
❑ 198 Kalimba Edwards AU RC 25.00 10.00
❑ 199 Jonathan Wells AU RC 25.00 10.00
❑ 200 Josh Scobey AU RC 20.00 7.50
❑ 201 Kelly Campbell AU RC 30.00 15.00
❑ 202 Kurt Kittner AU RC 20.00 7.50
❑ 203 Lamar Gordon AU RC 25.00 10.00
❑ 204 Lee Mays AU RC 20.00 7.50
❑ 205 Leonard Henry AU RC 20.00 7.50
❑ 206 Luke Staley AU RC 20.00 7.50
❑ 207 Justin Peelle AU RC 15.00 6.00
❑ 208 Randy Fasani AU RC 20.00 7.50
❑ 209 Ricky Williams AU RC 25.00 10.00
❑ 210 Ronald Curry AU RC 30.00 15.00
❑ 211 Travis Stephens AU RC 20.00 7.50
❑ 212 Wendell Bryant AU RC 15.00 6.00
❑ 213 Woody Dantzler AU RC 20.00 7.50
❑ 214 Kahlil Hill AU RC 20.00 7.50
❑ 215 Donte Stallworth JSY RC 50.00 25.00
❑ 216 Joe Harrington AU/280 RC 200.00 100.00
❑ 217 Cliff Russell JSY RC 30.00 12.50
❑ 218 Clinton Portis JSY RC 100.00 50.00
❑ 219 Daniel Graham JSY RC 40.00 15.00
❑ 220 David Garrard JSY RC 60.00 30.00
❑ 221 DeShaun Foster JSY RC 60.00 30.00
❑ 222 Julius Peppers JSY RC 50.00 25.00
❑ 223 Jeremy Shockey JSY RC 60.00 30.00
❑ 224 Patrick Ramsey JSY RC 50.00 30.00
❑ 225 Josh Reed JSY RC 30.00 12.50
❑ 226 LaDell Betts JSY RC 30.00 12.50
❑ 227 Mike Williams JSY/350 RC 30.0012.50
❑ 228 Reche Caldwell JSY RC 30.00 12.50
❑ 229 Rohan Davey JSY RC 30.00 12.50
❑ 230 Ron Johnson JSY RC 30.00 12.50
❑ 231 Roy Williams JSY/350 RC 100.0050.00
❑ 232 T.J. Duckett JSY RC 40.00 15.00
❑ 233 Tim Carter JSY RC 30.00 12.50
❑ 234 William Green JSY RC 30.00 12.50
❑ 235 Randle El JSY AU RC 135.00 75.00
❑ 237 David Carr JSY AU RC 250.00 125.00
❑ 238 Andre Davis JSY AU RC 60.00 25.00
❑ 239 Eric Crouch JSY AU RC 50.00 20.00
❑ 240 Antonio Bryant JSY AU RC 80.0030.00
❑ 241 Jabar Gaffney JSY AU RC 60.00 25.00
❑ 242 Marquise Walker JSY AU RC 60.00 25.00
❑ 243 Maurice Morris JSY AU RC 60.0030.00
❑ 244 Josh McCown JSY AU RC 100.0040.00
❑ AP1 Walter Payton AU/34 400.00 250.00
❑ SW1 Walter Payton JSY/150 120.00 50.00
❑ SW1 W.Payton Gold JSY/34 200.00 100.00
❑ SCPS Payt/Smith JSY/250 120.00 60.00
❑ SCPSG Payt/Smith Gld JSY/34 300.00 175.00

2003 SP Authentic

❑ COMP.SET w/o SP's (90) 20.00 7.50
❑ 1 Donovan McNabb 1.25 .50
❑ 2 Tim Couch .40 .15
❑ 3 Joey Harrington 1.25 .50
❑ 4 Brett Favre 2.50 1.00
❑ 5 Jeff Garcia 1.00 .40
❑ 6 Kerry Collins .60 .25
❑ 7 Michael Vick 2.00 .75
❑ 8 David Carr 1.25 .50
❑ 9 Steve McNair 1.00 .40
❑ 10 Chad Pennington 1.25 .50
❑ 11 Patrick Ramsey 1.00 .40
❑ 12 Rich Gannon .60 .25
❑ 13 Kurt Warner 1.00 .40
❑ 14 Brad Johnson .60 .25
❑ 15 Jay Fiedler .60 .25
❑ 16 Jake Plummer .60 .25
❑ 17 Mark Brunell .60 .25
❑ 18 Peyton Manning 1.50 .60
❑ 19 Brian Griese 1.00 .40
❑ 20 Kordell Stewart .60 .25
❑ 21 Kelly Holcomb .60 .25
❑ 22 Josh McCown .60 .25
❑ 23 Matt Hasselbeck .60 .25
❑ 24 Marc Bulger 1.00 .40
❑ 25 Chris Redman .40 .15
❑ 26 Rodney Peete .60 .25

27	Jake Delhomme	1.00	.40
28	Jon Kitna	.60	.25
29	Trent Green	.60	.25
30	Quincy Carter	.60	.25
31	Chad Hutchinson	.40	.15
32	Edgerrin James	1.00	.40
33	Deuce McAllister	1.00	.40
34	Ricky Williams	1.00	.40
35	Priest Holmes	1.25	.50
36	Curtis Martin	1.00	.40
37	Shaun Alexander	1.00	.40
38	Eddie George	.60	.25
39	Marshall Faulk	1.00	.40
40	Garrison Hearst	.60	.25
41	Ahman Green	1.00	.40
42	Corey Dillon	.60	.25
43	Jamal Lewis	1.00	.40
44	William Green	.60	.25
45	Travis Henry	.60	.25
46	Mike Alstott	1.00	.40
47	Amos Zereoue	.60	.25
48	Stephen Davis	.60	.25
49	Duce Staley	.60	.25
50	Fred Taylor	1.00	.40
51	Anthony Thomas	.60	.25
52	Charlie Garner	.60	.25
53	Kevan Barlow	.60	.25
54	Brian Urlacher	1.25	.50
55	Junior Seau	1.00	.40
56	Zach Thomas	1.00	.40
57	Ray Lewis	1.00	.40
58	Jerry Porter	.60	.25
59	Marty Booker	.60	.25
60	Javon Walker	.60	.25
61	Donald Driver	.60	.25
62	Amani Toomer	.60	.25
63	Peerless Price	.60	.25
64	Santana Moss	.60	.25
65	Laveranues Coles	.60	.25
66	Troy Brown	.60	.25
67	Chris Chambers	1.00	.40
68	Rod Smith	.60	.25
69	Ashley Lelie	1.00	.40
70	Plaxico Burress	.60	.25
71	Keyshawn Johnson	1.00	.40
72	Isaac Bruce	1.00	.40
73	Torry Holt	1.00	.40
74	Koren Robinson	.60	.25
75	Derrick Mason	.60	.25
76	Kevin Johnson	.60	.25
77	Andre' Davis	.40	.15
78	Antonio Bryant	.60	.25
79	Eric Moulds	.60	.25
80	Jerry Rice	2.00	.75
81	Tim Brown	1.00	.40
82	Antwaan Randle El	1.00	.40
83	Donte Stallworth	1.00	.40
84	Randy Moss	1.50	.60
85	Chad Johnson	1.00	.40
86	Hines Ward	1.00	.40
87	Rod Gardner	.60	.25
88	Marvin Harrison	1.00	.40
89	David Boston	.60	.25
90	Julius Peppers	1.00	.40
91	Dewayne White RC	5.00	2.00
92	Casey Fitzsimmons RC	6.00	2.50
93	Aaron Moorehead RC	6.00	2.50
94	Jimmy Farris RC	5.00	2.00
95	Eric Parker RC	6.00	2.50
96	Michael Haynes RC	6.00	2.50
97	J.J. Moses RC	5.00	2.00
98	Ken Hamlin RC	6.00	2.50
99	William Joseph RC	6.00	2.50
100	Alonzo Jackson RC	5.00	2.00
101	Tyler Brayton RC	6.00	2.50
102	Eddie Moore RC	5.00	2.00
103	Cleo Lemon RC	12.00	5.00
104	Arlen Harris RC	6.00	2.50
105	Cortez Hankton RC	5.00	2.00
106	Angelo Crowell RC	5.00	2.00
107	Johnathan Sullivan RC	5.00	2.00
108	Pisa Tinoisamoa RC	6.00	2.50
109	Boss Bailey RC	6.00	2.50
110	Tommy Jones RC	3.00	1.25
111	E.J. Henderson RC	6.00	2.50
112	Jimmy Kennedy RC	6.00	2.50
113	Nnamdi Asomugha RC	5.00	2.00
114	Hanik Milligan RC	5.00	2.00
115	Sammy Davis RC	6.00	2.50
116	Drayton Florence RC	3.00	1.25
117	Andre Woolfolk RC	6.00	2.50
118	Dennis Weathersby RC	3.00	1.25
119	Mike Doss RC	6.00	2.50
120	Troy Polamalu RC	30.00	15.00
121	Clinton Portis SS	6.00	2.50
122	Daunte Culpepper SS	5.00	2.00
123	Jeremy Shockey SS	6.00	2.50
124	Drew Brees SS	5.00	2.00
125	Marshall Faulk SS	5.00	2.00
126	Emmitt Smith SS	10.00	4.00
127	Terrell Owens SS	5.00	2.00
128	Ricky Williams SS	5.00	2.00
129	Deuce McAllister SS	5.00	2.00
130	Ahman Green SS	5.00	2.00
131	Chad Pennington SS	5.00	2.00
132	Plaxico Burress SS	5.00	2.00
133	Steve McNair SS	5.00	2.00
134	Keyshawn Johnson SS	5.00	2.00
135	Jeff Garcia SS	5.00	2.00
136	Drew Bledsoe SS	5.00	2.00
137	Jerry Rice SS	8.00	3.00
138	Randy Moss SS	6.00	2.50
139	David Carr SS	6.00	2.50
140	Joey Harrington SS	6.00	2.50
141	Michael Vick SS	10.00	4.00
142	Tom Brady SS	10.00	4.00
143	Brian Urlacher SS	6.00	2.50
144	Brett Favre SS	10.00	4.00
145	Kurt Warner SS	5.00	2.00
146	LaDainian Tomlinson SS	5.00	2.00
147	Aaron Brooks SS	5.00	2.00
148	Edgerrin James SS	5.00	2.00
149	Peyton Manning SS	6.00	2.50
150	Donovan McNabb SS	5.00	2.00
151	Jason Gesser RC	12.00	5.00
152	Ken Dorsey RC	12.00	5.00
153	Jason Johnson RC	6.00	2.50
154	Avon Cobourne RC	6.00	2.50
155	Andrew Pinnock RC	10.00	4.00
156	Kirk Farmer RC	6.00	2.50
157	Reno Mahe RC	12.00	5.00
158	Lon Sheriff RC	6.00	2.50
159	Marquel Blackwell RC	6.00	2.50
160	Quentin Griffin RC	12.00	5.00
161	Rashean Mathis RC	10.00	4.00
162	Lee Suggs RC	30.00	15.00
163	Jeremi Johnson RC	10.00	4.00
164	Ovie Mughelli RC	6.00	2.50
165	Nick Barnett RC	20.00	10.00
166	Brock Forsey RC	12.00	5.00
167	Malaefou MacKenzie RC	6.00	2.50
168	Ahmaad Galloway RC	10.00	4.00
169	Cecil Sapp RC	10.00	4.00
170	Kerry Carter RC	10.00	4.00
171	Dahrran Diedrick RC	12.00	5.00
171A	Terrence Edwards RC	10.00	4.00
172	Joffrey Reynolds RC	6.00	2.50
173	Sultan McCullough RC	10.00	4.00
174	Brandon Drumm RC	6.00	2.50
175	Casey Moore RC	10.00	4.00
176	Gerald Hayes RC	6.00	2.50
178	Jamal Burke RC	6.00	2.50
179	Antonio Chatman RC	12.00	5.00
180	Reggie Newhouse RC	10.00	4.00
181	Chris Horn RC	6.00	2.50
182	Denero Marriott RC	6.00	2.50
183	DeAndrew Rubin RC	6.00	2.50
184	Taco Wallace RC	10.00	4.00
185	Doug Gabriel RC	12.00	5.00
186	Willie Ponder RC	6.00	2.50
187	David Tyree RC	10.00	4.00
188	Kevin Walter RC	10.00	4.00
189	Zuriel Smith RC	6.00	2.50
190	Keenan Howry RC	12.00	5.00
191	C.J. Jones RC	6.00	2.50
192	Arnaz Battle RC	12.00	5.00
193	Walter Young RC	6.00	2.50
194	Anthony Adams RC	10.00	4.00
195	Jerome McDougle RC	12.00	5.00
196	Will Heller RC	10.00	4.00
197	Cecil Moore RC	6.00	2.50
198	Mike Seidman RC	6.00	2.50
199	Jason Witten RC	20.00	10.00
200	L.J. Smith RC	12.00	5.00
201	Bennie Joppru RC	12.00	5.00
202	Donald Lee RC	10.00	4.00
203	Aaron Walker RC	10.00	4.00
204	Antonio Brown RC	6.00	2.50
205	George Wrighster RC	10.00	4.00
206	Danny Curley RC	6.00	2.50
207	Mike Banks RC	6.00	2.50
208	Mike Pinkard RC	6.00	2.50
209	Ryan Hoag RC	6.00	2.50
210	Brad Pyatt RC	10.00	4.00
211	Charles Rogers RC	12.00	5.00
212	Chris Simms AU/250 RC	175.00	100.00
213	Nate Hybl AU RC	20.00	7.50
214	Brandon Lloyd AU RC	50.00	25.00
215	ReShard Lee AU RC	20.00	7.50
216	Dwone Hicks AU RC	12.00	5.00
217	Tony Romo AU RC	30.00	15.00
218	Brett Engemann AU RC	12.00	5.00
219	Nick Maddox AU RC	12.00	5.00
220	James MacPherson AU RC	12.00	5.00
221	Juston Wood AU RC	12.00	5.00
222	Adrian Madise AU RC	15.00	6.00
223	Shaun McDonald AU RC	20.00	7.50
224	Carl Ford AU RC	12.00	5.00
225	Vishante Shiancoe AU RC	15.00	6.00
226	Gibran Hamdan AU RC	12.00	5.00
227	Brooks Bollinger AU RC	25.00	10.00
228	B.J. Askew AU RC	20.00	7.50
229	Domanick Davis AU RC	30.00	12.50
230	LaBrandon Toefield AU RC	20.00	7.50
231	Bobby Wade AU RC	20.00	7.50
232	Justin Gage AU RC	20.00	7.50
233	Billy McMullen AU RC	15.00	6.00
234	David Kircus AU RC	15.00	6.00
235	J.R. Tolver AU RC	15.00	6.00
236	Sam Aiken AU RC	15.00	6.00
237	LaTarence Dunbar AU RC	15.00	6.00
238	Kassim Osgood AU RC	20.00	7.50
239	Tony Hollings AU RC	20.00	7.50
240	Justin Griffith AU RC	15.00	6.00
241	Brian St.Pierre JSY RC	30.00	12.50
242	Kevin Curtis JSY RC	40.00	20.00
243	Dallas Clark JSY RC	30.00	12.50
244	Willis McGahee JSY RC	120.00	60.00
245	Terence Newman JSY RC	30.00	15.00
246	Justin Fargas JSY AU RC	60.00	25.00
247	Artose Pinner JSY RC	30.00	12.50
248	Kelley Washington JSY RC	30.00	15.00
249	DeWayne Robertson JSY RC	25.00	10.00
250	Nate Burleson JSY RC	50.00	25.00
251	Kliff Kingsbury JSY RC	25.00	10.00
252	Bethel Johnson JSY RC	30.00	12.50
253	Anquan Boldin JSY RC	60.00	30.00
254	Bryant Johnson JSY AU RC	60.00	25.00
255	Terrell Suggs JSY AU RC	80.00	40.00
256	Musa Smith JSY RC	30.00	12.50
257	Chris Brown JSY RC	40.00	15.00
258	Marcus Trufant JSY RC	30.00	12.50
259	Teyo Johnson JSY RC	30.00	12.50
260	Tyrone Calico JSY RC	40.00	20.00

❑ 261 Dave Ragone JSY AU RC 60.00 25.00
❑ 262 Kyle Boller JSY AU RC 100.00 50.00
❑ 263 Onterrio Smith JSY AU RC 60.00 25.00
❑ 264 Rex Grossman JSY RC 80.00 50.00
❑ 265 Larry Johnson JSY RC 250.00 125.00
❑ 266 Seneca Wallace JSY AU RC 80.00 50.00
❑ 268 Taylor Jacobs JSY AU RC 60.00 25.00
❑ 269 Byron Leftwich JSY AU RC 500.00 250.00
❑ 270 Carson Palmer JSY AU RC 650.00 350.00

2004 SP Authentic

❑ COMP.SET w/o SP's (90) 25.00 10.00
❑ 91-150 RC PRINT RUN 1199 SER.#'d SETS
❑ 151-185 AU RC PRINT RUN 990 SER.#'d SETS
❑ 186-200 JSY AU RC PRINT RUN 799
❑ 201-206 JSY AU RC PRINT RUN 499
❑ 207-216 JSY AU RC PRINT RUN 299
❑ EXCH EXPIRATION: 12/15/2007
❑ 1 Josh McCown .60 .25
❑ 2 Anquan Boldin 1.00 .40
❑ 3 Michael Vick 2.00 .75
❑ 4 Peerless Price .60 .25
❑ 5 Todd Heap .60 .25
❑ 6 Kyle Boller 1.00 .40
❑ 7 Jamal Lewis 1.00 .40
❑ 8 Drew Bledsoe 1.00 .40
❑ 9 Travis Henry .60 .25
❑ 10 Eric Moulds .60 .25
❑ 11 Steve Smith 1.00 .40
❑ 12 Stephen Davis .60 .25
❑ 13 Jake Delhomme 1.00 .40
❑ 14 Rex Grossman 1.00 .40
❑ 15 Brian Urlacher 1.25 .50
❑ 16 Thomas Jones .60 .25
❑ 17 Chad Johnson 1.00 .40
❑ 18 Rudi Johnson .60 .25
❑ 19 Carson Palmer 1.25 .50
❑ 20 William Green .60 .25
❑ 21 Andre Davis .40 .15
❑ 22 Jeff Garcia 1.00 .40
❑ 23 Roy Williams S .60 .25
❑ 24 Eddie George .60 .25
❑ 25 Keyshawn Johnson .60 .25
❑ 26 Ashley Lelie .60 .25
❑ 27 Jake Plummer .60 .25
❑ 28 Champ Bailey .60 .25
❑ 29 Charles Rogers .60 .25
❑ 30 Joey Harrington 1.00 .40
❑ 31 Ahman Green 1.00 .40
❑ 32 Brett Favre 2.50 1.00
❑ 33 Javon Walker .60 .25
❑ 34 David Carr 1.00 .40
❑ 35 Domanick Davis 1.00 .40
❑ 36 Andre Johnson 1.00 .40
❑ 37 Marvin Harrison 1.00 .40
❑ 38 Edgerrin James 1.00 .40
❑ 39 Peyton Manning 1.50 .60
❑ 40 Byron Leftwich 1.25 .50
❑ 41 Fred Taylor .60 .25
❑ 42 Trent Green .60 .25
❑ 43 Tony Gonzalez .60 .25
❑ 44 Priest Holmes 1.25 .50
❑ 45 Ricky Williams 1.00 .40
❑ 46 Chris Chambers .60 .25
❑ 47 Jay Fiedler .40 .15
❑ 48 Daunte Culpepper 1.00 .40
❑ 49 Randy Moss 1.25 .50
❑ 50 Onterrio Smith .60 .25
❑ 51 Tom Brady 2.50 1.00
❑ 52 Troy Brown .60 .25
❑ 53 Corey Dillon .60 .25
❑ 54 Deuce McAllister 1.00 .40
❑ 55 Aaron Brooks .60 .25
❑ 56 Joe Horn .60 .25
❑ 57 Amani Toomer .60 .25
❑ 58 Kurt Warner 1.00 .40
❑ 59 Jeremy Shockey 1.00 .40
❑ 60 Chad Pennington 1.00 .40
❑ 61 Santana Moss .60 .25
❑ 62 Curtis Martin 1.00 .40
❑ 63 Rich Gannon .60 .25
❑ 64 Jerry Rice 2.00 .75
❑ 65 Jerry Porter .60 .25
❑ 66 Terrell Owens 1.00 .40
❑ 67 Jevon Kearse .60 .25
❑ 68 Donovan McNabb 1.25 .50
❑ 69 Hines Ward 1.00 .40
❑ 70 Plaxico Burress .60 .25
❑ 71 Tommy Maddox .60 .25
❑ 72 Drew Brees 1.00 .40
❑ 73 LaDainian Tomlinson 1.25 .50
❑ 74 Tim Rattay .40 .15
❑ 75 Brandon Lloyd .60 .25
❑ 76 Kevan Barlow .60 .25
❑ 77 Shaun Alexander 1.00 .40
❑ 78 Koren Robinson .60 .25
❑ 79 Matt Hasselbeck .60 .25
❑ 80 Marshall Faulk 1.00 .40
❑ 81 Torry Holt 1.00 .40
❑ 82 Marc Bulger 1.00 .40
❑ 83 Brad Johnson .60 .25
❑ 84 Joey Galloway .60 .25
❑ 85 Steve McNair 1.00 .40
❑ 86 Derrick Mason .60 .25
❑ 87 Chris Brown 1.00 .40
❑ 88 Mark Brunell .60 .25
❑ 89 Laveranues Coles .60 .25
❑ 90 Clinton Portis 1.00 .40
❑ 91 Triandos Luke RC 8.00 3.00
❑ 92 Keith Smith RC 6.00 2.50
❑ 93 Shaun Phillips RC 6.00 2.50
❑ 94 D.J. Williams RC 10.00 4.00
❑ 95 Keiwan Ratliff RC 6.00 2.50
❑ 96 Madieu Williams RC 6.00 2.50
❑ 97 Chris Cooley RC 8.00 3.00
❑ 98 Stuart Schweigert RC 8.00 3.00
❑ 99 Sloan Thomas RC 6.00 2.50
❑ 100 Chad Lavalais RC 6.00 2.50
❑ 101 Jared Allen RC 15.00 6.00
❑ 102 Brian Jones RC 6.00 2.50
❑ 103 Matt Ware RC 8.00 3.00
❑ 104 Daryl Smith RC 8.00 3.00
❑ 105 J.R. Reed RC 6.00 2.50
❑ 106 D.J. Hackett RC 6.00 2.50
❑ 107 Jeris McIntyre RC 6.00 2.50
❑ 108 Dexter Reid RC 4.00 1.50
❑ 109 Courtney Anderson RC 6.00 2.50
❑ 110 Courtney Watson RC 8.00 3.00
❑ 111 Larry Croom RC 6.00 2.50
❑ 112 Jonathan Smith RC 6.00 2.50
❑ 113 Vernon Carey RC 6.00 2.50
❑ 114 Michael Gaines RC 6.00 2.50
❑ 115 Chris Snee RC 6.00 2.50
❑ 116 Nathan Vasher RC 10.00 4.00
❑ 117 Teddy Lehman RC 8.00 3.00
❑ 118 Marcus Tubbs RC 8.00 3.00
❑ 119 Ben Utecht RC 4.00 1.50
❑ 120 Maurice Mann RC 6.00 2.50
❑ 121 Thomas Tapeh RC 6.00 2.50
❑ 122 Will Allen RC 8.00 3.00
❑ 123 Demorrio Williams RC 8.00 3.00
❑ 124 Ran Carthon RC 6.00 2.50
❑ 125 Tim Euhus RC 8.00 3.00
❑ 126 Bradlee Van Pelt RC 12.00 5.00
❑ 127 Patrick Crayton RC 8.00 3.00
❑ 128 Ryan Krause RC 6.00 2.50
❑ 129 Joey Thomas RC 8.00 3.00
❑ 130 Antwan Odom RC 8.00 3.00
❑ 131 Karlos Dansby RC 8.00 3.00
❑ 132 Junior Siavii RC 8.00 3.00
❑ 133 Jamaar Taylor RC 8.00 3.00
❑ 134 Kendrick Starling RC 4.00 1.50
❑ 135 Wes Welker RC 8.00 3.00
❑ 136 Igor Olshansky RC 8.00 3.00
❑ 137 Mark Jones RC 6.00 2.50
❑ 138 Bruce Thornton RC 4.00 1.50
❑ 139 Michael Boulware RC 8.00 3.00
❑ 140 Matt Mauck RC 8.00 3.00
❑ 141 Clarence Moore RC 8.00 3.00
❑ 142 Derrick Strait RC 8.00 3.00
❑ 143 Jarrett Payton RC 10.00 4.00
❑ 144 Dontarrious Thomas RC 8.00 3.00
❑ 145 Shawntae Spencer RC 8.00 3.00
❑ 146 Bob Sanders RC 20.00 10.00
❑ 147 Darnell Dockett RC 6.00 2.50
❑ 148 Sean Taylor RC 10.00 4.00
❑ 149 Jason Babin RC 8.00 3.00
❑ 150 Ricardo Colclough RC 8.00 3.00
❑ 151 Brandon Chillar AU RC 15.00 6.00
❑ 152 Clarence Farmer AU RC 15.00 6.00
❑ 153 B.J. Symons AU RC 20.00 7.50
❑ 154 John Navarre AU RC 20.00 7.50
❑ 155 P.K. Sam AU RC EXCH 20.00 7.50
❑ 156 Casey Clausen AU RC 20.00 7.50
❑ 157 Drew Henson AU RC 20.00 7.50
❑ 158 Kris Wilson AU RC 20.00 7.50
❑ 159 Vince Wilfork AU RC 25.00 10.00
❑ 160 Michael Turner AU RC 20.00 7.50
❑ 161 Jonathan Vilma AU RC 30.00 12.50
❑ 162 Samie Parker AU RC 20.00 7.50
❑ 163 B.J. Sams AU RC 20.00 7.50
❑ 164 A.Echemandu AU RC 15.00 6.00
❑ 165 Ernest Wilford AU RC 20.00 7.50
❑ 166 Troy Fleming AU RC 20.00 7.50
❑ 167 Tommie Harris AU RC 20.00 7.50
❑ 168 Jammal Lord AU RC 20.00 7.50
❑ 169 Kenechi Udeze AU RC 20.00 7.50
❑ 170 Chris Gamble AU RC 25.00 10.00
❑ 171 Carlos Francis AU RC 15.00 6.00
❑ 172 Mewelde Moore AU RC 30.00 15.00
❑ 173 Jared Lorenzen AU RC 15.00 6.00
❑ 174 Jeff Smoker AU RC 20.00 7.50
❑ 175 Ben Hartsock AU RC 20.00 7.50
❑ 176 Jerricho Cotchery AU RC 20.00 7.50
❑ 177 Josh Harris AU RC 20.00 7.50
❑ 178 Cody Pickett AU RC 20.00 7.50
❑ 179 Quincy Wilson AU RC 15.00 6.00
❑ 180 Will Smith AU RC EXCH 20.00 7.50
❑ 181 Ahmad Carroll AU RC 25.00 10.00
❑ 182 B.J. Johnson AU RC 15.00 6.00
❑ 183 Dunta Robinson AU RC 25.00 10.00
❑ 184 Craig Krenzel AU RC 20.00 7.50
❑ 185 Johnnie Morant AU RC 20.00 7.50
❑ 186 Cedric Cobbs JSY AU RC 50.00 20.00
❑ 187 Matt Schaub JSY AU RC 150.00 90.00
❑ 188 Bernard Berrian JSY AU RC 50.00 20.00
❑ 189 Devard Darling JSY AU RC 50.00 20.00
❑ 190 Ben Watson JSY AU RC 60.00 30.00
❑ 191 Darius Watts JSY AU RC 50.00 20.00
❑ 192 DeAngelo Hall JSY AU RC 60.00 30.00
❑ 193 Ben Troupe JSY AU RC 50.00 20.00
❑ 194 Mich Jenkins JSY AU RC 80.00 30.00
❑ 195 Keary Colbert JSY AU RC 60.00 25.00
❑ 196 Robert Gallery JSY AU RC 60.00 25.00
❑ 197 Greg Jones JSY AU RC 75.00 40.00
❑ 198 Mich.Clayton JSY AU RC 100.00 40.00
❑ 199 Luke McCown JSY AU RC 50.00 20.00

❑ 200 Derrick Hamilton JSY AU RC 50.00 20.00
❑ 201 Ras.Woods JSY AU RC 50.00 20.00
❑ 202 Chris Perry JSY AU RC 100.00 50.00
❑ 203 D.Henderson JSY AU RC 60.00 30.00
❑ 204 Tatum Bell JSY AU RC 150.00 75.00
❑ 205 Lee Evans JSY AU RC 100.00 50.00
❑ 206 J.P. Losman JSY AU RC 150.00 75.00
❑ 207 Kel.Winslow JSY AU RC 120.00 60.00
❑ 208 Reg.Williams JSY AU RC 100.00 50.00
❑ 209 Julius Jones JSY AU RC 350.00 175.00
❑ 210 S.Jackson JSY AU RC 300.00 150.00
❑ 211 Kevin Jones JSY AU RC 300.00 150.00
❑ 212 Roy Williams JSY AU RC 250.00 125.00
❑ 213 Roethlisberger JSY AU RC 750.00 500.00
❑ 214 Philip Rivers JSY AU RC 400.00 250.00
❑ 215 L.Fitzgerald JSY AU RC 325.00 200.00
❑ 216 Eli Manning JSY AU RC 650.00 400.00

2005 SP Authentic

❑ COMP.SET w/o RC's (90) 25.00 10.00
❑ 91-180 PRINT RUN 750 SER.#'d SETS
❑ 181-220/254-257 PRINT RUN 850 SER.#'d SETS
❑ 221-253 PRINT RUN 99-899 SER.#'d SETS
❑ UNPRICED NFL LOGO PATCHES #'d TO 1
❑ EXCH EXPIRATION:12/20/2008
❑ 1 Kurt Warner .60 .25
❑ 2 Larry Fitzgerald 1.00 .40
❑ 3 Anquan Boldin .60 .25
❑ 4 Michael Vick 1.50 .60
❑ 5 Alge Crumpler .60 .25
❑ 6 Warrick Dunn .60 .25
❑ 7 Kyle Boller .60 .25
❑ 8 Jamal Lewis 1.00 .40
❑ 9 J.P. Losman 1.00 .40
❑ 10 Willis McGahee 1.00 .40
❑ 11 Lee Evans .60 .25
❑ 12 Jake Delhomme 1.00 .40
❑ 13 DeShaun Foster .60 .25
❑ 14 Muhsin Muhammad .60 .25
❑ 15 Walter Payton 4.00 1.50
❑ 16 Brian Urlacher 1.00 .40
❑ 17 Carson Palmer 1.00 .40
❑ 18 Rudi Johnson .60 .25
❑ 19 Chad Johnson 1.00 .40
❑ 20 Lee Suggs .60 .25
❑ 21 Antonio Bryant .50 .20
❑ 22 Julius Jones 1.25 .50
❑ 23 Drew Bledsoe 1.00 .40
❑ 24 Keyshawn Johnson .60 .25
❑ 25 Tatum Bell .60 .25
❑ 26 Jake Plummer .60 .25
❑ 27 Roy Williams WR 1.00 .40
❑ 28 Kevin Jones 1.00 .40
❑ 29 Jeff Garcia .60 .25
❑ 30 Brett Favre 2.50 1.00
❑ 31 Ahman Green 1.00 .40
❑ 32 Javon Walker .60 .25
❑ 33 David Carr 1.00 .40
❑ 34 Andre Johnson .60 .25
❑ 35 Domanick Davis .60 .25
❑ 36 Peyton Manning 1.50 .60
❑ 37 Edgerrin James 1.00 .40
❑ 38 Reggie Wayne .60 .25
❑ 39 Byron Leftwich 1.00 .40
❑ 40 Fred Taylor .60 .25
❑ 41 Jimmy Smith .60 .25
❑ 42 Priest Holmes 1.00 .40
❑ 43 Larry Johnson 1.00 .40
❑ 44 Trent Green .60 .25
❑ 45 Randy McMichael .50 .20
❑ 46 Chris Chambers .60 .25
❑ 47 Ricky Williams .60 .25
❑ 48 Daunte Culpepper 1.00 .40
❑ 49 Nate Burleson .60 .25
❑ 50 Tom Brady 2.50 1.00
❑ 51 Corey Dillon .60 .25
❑ 52 David Givens .60 .25
❑ 53 Aaron Brooks .60 .25
❑ 54 Deuce McAllister 1.00 .40
❑ 55 Joe Horn .60 .25
❑ 56 Eli Manning 2.00 .75
❑ 57 Jeremy Shockey 1.00 .40
❑ 58 Tiki Barber 1.00 .40
❑ 59 Chad Pennington 1.00 .40
❑ 60 Santana Moss .60 .25
❑ 61 Curtis Martin 1.00 .40
❑ 62 Randy Moss 1.00 .40
❑ 63 LaMont Jordan 1.00 .40
❑ 64 Kerry Collins .60 .25
❑ 65 Donovan McNabb 1.25 .50
❑ 66 Brian Westbrook .60 .25
❑ 67 Terrell Owens 1.00 .40
❑ 68 Ben Roethlisberger 2.50 1.00
❑ 69 Hines Ward 1.00 .40
❑ 70 Jerome Bettis 1.00 .40
❑ 71 Drew Brees 1.00 .40
❑ 72 Antonio Gates 1.00 .40
❑ 73 LaDainian Tomlinson 1.25 .50
❑ 74 Kevan Barlow .60 .25
❑ 75 Brandon Lloyd .50 .20
❑ 76 Matt Hasselbeck .60 .25
❑ 77 Shaun Alexander 1.25 .50
❑ 78 Darrell Jackson .60 .25
❑ 79 Marc Bulger 1.00 .40
❑ 80 Steven Jackson 1.25 .50
❑ 81 Torry Holt 1.00 .40
❑ 82 Brian Griese .60 .25
❑ 83 Michael Clayton 1.00 .40
❑ 84 Michael Pittman .50 .20
❑ 85 Steve McNair 1.00 .40
❑ 86 Drew Bennett .60 .25
❑ 87 Chris Brown .60 .25
❑ 88 Clinton Portis 1.00 .40
❑ 89 Patrick Ramsey .60 .25
❑ 90 Laveranues Coles .60 .25
❑ 91 Nehemiah Broughton RC 6.00 2.50
❑ 92 Madison Hedgecock RC 8.00 3.00
❑ 93 Damien Nash RC 6.00 2.50
❑ 94 Michael Boley RC 6.00 2.50
❑ 95 Lionel Gates RC 6.00 2.50
❑ 96 Noah Herron RC 8.00 3.00
❑ 97 Bo Scaife RC 6.00 2.50
❑ 98 Joel Dreessen RC 6.00 2.50
❑ 99 Rasheed Marshall RC 8.00 3.00
❑ 100 Andre Maddox RC 6.00 2.50
❑ 101 Tab Perry RC 8.00 3.00
❑ 102 Dante Ridgeway RC 6.00 2.50
❑ 103 Patrick Estes RC 6.00 2.50
❑ 104 Billy Bajema RC 6.00 2.50
❑ 105 Paris Warren RC 6.00 2.50
❑ 106 LeRon McCoy RC 6.00 2.50
❑ 107 Adam Bergen RC 8.00 3.00
❑ 108 Manuel White RC 6.00 2.50
❑ 109 Stephen Spach RC 6.00 2.50
❑ 110 Donte Nicholson RC 8.00 3.00
❑ 111 Brodney Pool RC 8.00 3.00
❑ 112 Stanford Routt RC 6.00 2.50
❑ 113 Josh Bullocks RC 8.00 3.00
❑ 114 Ronald Bartell RC 6.00 2.50
❑ 115 Nick Collins RC 8.00 3.00
❑ 116 Darrent Williams RC 8.00 3.00
❑ 117 Justin Miller RC 6.00 2.50
❑ 118 Kelvin Hayden RC 6.00 2.50
❑ 119 Bryant McFadden RC 8.00 3.00
❑ 120 Oshiomogho Atogwe RC 6.00 2.50
❑ 121 Stanley Wilson RC 6.00 2.50
❑ 122 Eric Green RC 4.00 1.50
❑ 123 Michael Hawkins RC 6.00 2.50
❑ 124 Marcus Spears RC 8.00 3.00
❑ 125 Ellis Hobbs RC 8.00 3.00
❑ 126 Scott Starks RC 6.00 2.50
❑ 127 Domonique Foxworth RC 8.00 3.00
❑ 128 Sean Considine RC 8.00 3.00
❑ 129 James Sanders RC 8.00 3.00
❑ 130 Travis Daniels RC 6.00 2.50
❑ 131 Vincent Fuller RC 6.00 2.50
❑ 132 Marviel Underwood RC 6.00 2.50
❑ 133 Jerome Carter RC 6.00 2.50
❑ 134 Kerry Rhodes RC 8.00 3.00
❑ 135 Fred Amey RC 6.00 2.50
❑ 136 Eric King RC 6.00 2.50
❑ 137 Derrick Johnson CB RC 8.00 3.00
❑ 138 Luis Castillo RC 8.00 3.00
❑ 139 Shaun Cody RC 8.00 3.00
❑ 140 Matt Roth RC 8.00 3.00
❑ 141 Jonathan Babineaux RC 6.00 2.50
❑ 142 Justin Tuck RC 8.00 3.00
❑ 143 Sione Pouha RC 8.00 3.00
❑ 144 Daven Holly RC 8.00 3.00
❑ 145 Vincent Burns RC 6.00 2.50
❑ 146 Derrick Johnson RC 12.00 5.00
❑ 147 Lofa Tatupu RC 12.00 5.00
❑ 148 Odell Thurman RC 8.00 3.00
❑ 149 Rick Razzano RC 8.00 3.00
❑ 150 Channing Crowder RC 8.00 3.00
❑ 151 Kirk Morrison RC 8.00 3.00
❑ 152 Alfred Fincher RC 6.00 2.50
❑ 153 Jordan Beck RC 6.00 2.50
❑ 154 Darryl Blackstock RC 6.00 2.50
❑ 155 Leroy Hill RC 8.00 3.00
❑ 156 Jammal Brown RC 8.00 3.00
❑ 157 Alex Barron RC 4.00 1.50
❑ 158 Chris Spencer RC 8.00 3.00
❑ 159 Logan Mankins RC 10.00 4.00
❑ 160 David Baas RC 6.00 2.50
❑ 161 Michael Roos RC 4.00 1.50
❑ 162 Kurt Campbell RC 6.00 2.50
❑ 163 Khalif Barnes RC 6.00 2.50
❑ 164 Antonio Perkins RC 6.00 2.50
❑ 165 Vonta Leach RC 8.00 3.00
❑ 166 Brady Poppinga RC 8.00 3.00
❑ 167 Trent Cole RC 8.00 3.00
❑ 168 Dave Rayner RC 6.00 2.50
❑ 169 Bill Swancutt RC 6.00 2.50
❑ 170 Eric Moore RC 6.00 2.50
❑ 171 Justin Green RC 8.00 3.00
❑ 172 Shaun Suisham RC 6.00 2.50
❑ 173 C.J. Mosley RC 6.00 2.50
❑ 174 Ryan Riddle RC 4.00 1.50
❑ 175 Darrell Shropshire RC 6.00 2.50
❑ 176 Boomer Grigsby RC 10.00 4.00
❑ 177 Rian Wallace RC 6.00 2.50
❑ 178 Lance Mitchell RC 6.00 2.50
❑ 179 Nick Speegle RC 6.00 2.50
❑ 180 Tyson Thompson RC 10.00 4.00
❑ 181 Dan Orlovsky AU RC 20.00 7.50
❑ 182 Anthony Davis AU RC 12.00 5.00
❑ 183 Kay-Jay Harris AU RC 12.00 5.00
❑ 184 Walter Reyes AU RC 12.00 5.00
❑ 185 Darren Sproles AU RC 15.00 6.00
❑ 186 Marlin Jackson AU RC 15.00 6.00
❑ 187 Corey Webster AU RC 15.00 6.00
❑ 188 Marion Barber AU RC 30.00 12.50
❑ 189 Chris Henry AU RC EXCH 20.00 7.50
❑ 190 Derek Anderson AU RC 15.00 6.00
❑ 191 David Pollack AU RC EXCH 20.00 7.50
❑ 192 Anttaj Hawthorne AU RC 12.00 5.00

❑ 193 David Greene AU RC 20.00 7.50
❑ 194 Erasmus James AU RC 15.00 6.00
❑ 195 Ryan Fitzpatrick AU RC 25.00 10.00
❑ 196 Derrick Johnson AU 25.00 10.00
❑ 197 Barrett Ruud AU RC 15.00 6.00
❑ 198 Kevin Burnett AU RC 15.00 6.00
❑ 199 C.Houston AU RC EXCH 20.00 10.00
❑ 200 J.R. Russell AU RC 12.00 5.00
❑ 201 Larry Brackins AU RC 12.00 5.00
❑ 202 Thomas Davis AU RC 15.00 6.00
❑ 203 Fred Gibson AU RC 12.00 5.00
❑ 204 Craphonso Thorpe AU RC 12.00 5.00
❑ 205 Brandon Jacobs AU RC 20.00 7.50
❑ 206 Taylor Stubblefield AU RC 10.00 4.00
❑ 207 Shawne Merriman AU RC 40.00 20.00
❑ 208 Travis Johnson AU RC 12.00 5.00
❑ 209 Adrian McPherson AU RC 15.00 6.00
❑ 210 Brandon Jones AU RC 15.00 6.00
❑ 211 Jerome Mathis AU RC 15.00 6.00
❑ 212 Alex Smith TE AU RC 15.00 6.00
❑ 213 Fabian Washington AU RC 15.00 6.00
❑ 214 Mike Nugent AU RC 15.00 6.00
❑ 215 Chase Lyman AU RC 12.00 5.00
❑ 216 Roydell Williams AU RC 15.00 6.00
❑ 217 Matt Cassel AU RC 30.00 15.00
❑ 218 Alvin Pearman AU RC 15.00 6.00
❑ 219 DeMarcus Ware AU RC 25.00 10.00
❑ 220 Mike Patterson AU RC 15.00 6.00
❑ 221 C.Roby JSY/899 AU RC 50.00 20.00
❑ 222 E.Shelton JSY/899 AU RC 50.00 20.00
❑ 223 S.LeFors JSY/899 AU RC 50.00 20.00
❑ 224 Frank Gore JSY/899 AU RC 80.00 40.00
❑ 225 Ryan Moats JSY/899 AU RC 80.00 40.00
❑ 226 A.Walter JSY/899 AU RC 80.00 40.00
❑ 227 A.Jones JSY/899 AU RC 50.00 20.00
❑ 228 C.Rogers JSY/699 AU RC 50.00 20.00
❑ 229 T.Murphy JSY/899 AU RC 50.00 20.00
❑ 230 Kyle Orton JSY/699 AU RC 60.00 30.00
❑ 231 C.Fason JSY/699 AU RC 60.00 25.00
❑ 232 V.Morency JSY/699 AU RC 40.00 15.00
❑ 233 R.Parrish JSY/699 AU RC 60.00 30.00
❑ 234 V.Jackson JSY/699 AU RC 60.00 30.00
❑ 235 M.Bradley JSY/699 AU RC 60.00 30.00
❑ 236 Re.Brown JSY/599 AU RC 80.00 40.00
❑ 237 Ro.White JSY/499 AU RC 50.00 20.00
❑ 238 M.Clayton JSY/499 AU RC 100.00 50.00
❑ 239 Antrel Rolle JSY/499 AU RC 50.00 20.00
❑ 240 Maurice Clarett JSY/499 AU 50.00 20.00
❑ 241 J.Arrington JSY/699 AU RC 60.00 25.00
❑ 242 Matt Jones JSY/399 AU RC 150.00 75.00
❑ 243 Ro.Brown JSY/299 AU RC 350.00 200.00
❑ 244 C.Frye JSY/499 AU RC 135.00 75.00
❑ 245 J.Campbell JSY/299 AU RC 250.00 150.00
❑ 246 T.Willmsn JSY/299 AU RC 120.00 60.00
❑ 247 B.Edwrd JSY/299 AU RC 200.00 100.00
❑ 248 A.Smith QB JSY/299 AU RC 300.00 175.00
❑ 249 C.Wllms JSY/299 AU RC 400.00 200.00
❑ 250 Miller JSY/299 AU RC EX 200.00 100.00
❑ 251 Benson JSY/99 AU RC EX 400.00 250.00
❑ 252 Rodgers JSY/99 AU RC EX 600.00 400.00
❑ 253 M.Williams JSY/99 AU 350.00 200.00
❑ 254 Chris Carr AU RC 20.00 7.50
❑ 255 Deandra Cobb AU RC 12.00 5.00
❑ 256 James Kilian AU RC 15.00 6.00
❑ 257 Airese Currie AU RC 15.00 6.00

2001 SP Game Used Edition

❑ COMP.SET w/o SP's (90) 100.00 50.00
❑ 1 Jake Plummer 1.50 .60
❑ 2 David Boston 2.50 1.00
❑ 3 Frank Sanders 1.00 .40
❑ 4 Jamal Anderson 2.50 1.00
❑ 5 Doug Johnson 1.00 .40
❑ 6 Shawn Jefferson 1.00 .40
❑ 7 Jamal Lewis 4.00 1.50
❑ 8 Shannon Sharpe 1.50 .60
❑ 9 Qadry Ismail 1.50 .60

❑ 10 Shawn Bryson 1.00 .40
❑ 11 Rob Johnson 1.50 .60
❑ 12 Eric Moulds 1.50 .60
❑ 13 Muhsin Muhammad 1.50 .60
❑ 14 Brad Hoover 1.00 .40
❑ 15 Tim Biakabutuka 1.50 .60
❑ 16 Cade McNown 1.00 .40
❑ 17 Marcus Robinson 2.50 1.00
❑ 18 Brian Urlacher 4.00 1.50
❑ 19 Akili Smith 1.00 .40
❑ 20 Peter Warrick 2.50 1.00
❑ 21 Corey Dillon 2.50 1.00
❑ 22 Kevin Johnson 1.50 .60
❑ 23 Rickey Dudley 1.00 .40
❑ 24 Tim Couch 1.50 .60
❑ 25 Tony Banks 1.00 .40
❑ 26 Emmitt Smith 5.00 2.00
❑ 27 Carl Pickens 1.00 .40
❑ 28 Terrell Davis 2.50 1.00
❑ 29 Mike Anderson 2.50 1.00
❑ 30 Brian Griese 2.50 1.00
❑ 31 Ed McCaffrey 2.50 1.00
❑ 32 Charlie Batch 2.50 1.00
❑ 33 Germane Crowell 1.00 .40
❑ 34 James O. Stewart 1.50 .60
❑ 35 Brett Favre 8.00 3.00
❑ 36 Antonio Freeman 2.50 1.00
❑ 37 Ahman Green 2.50 1.00
❑ 38 Peyton Manning 6.00 2.50
❑ 39 Edgerrin James 3.00 1.25
❑ 40 Marvin Harrison 2.50 1.00
❑ 41 Mark Brunell 2.50 1.00
❑ 42 Fred Taylor 2.50 1.00
❑ 43 Jimmy Smith 1.50 .60
❑ 44 Tony Gonzalez 1.50 .60
❑ 45 Derrick Alexander 1.50 .60
❑ 46 Oronde Gadsden 1.50 .60
❑ 47 Ray Lucas 1.00 .40
❑ 48 Lamar Smith 1.50 .60
❑ 49 Randy Moss 5.00 2.00
❑ 50 Cris Carter 2.50 1.00
❑ 51 Daunte Culpepper 2.50 1.00
❑ 52 Drew Bledsoe 3.00 1.25
❑ 53 Terry Glenn 1.50 .60
❑ 54 Ricky Williams 2.50 1.00
❑ 55 Jeff Blake 1.50 .60
❑ 56 Joe Horn 1.50 .60
❑ 57 Aaron Brooks 2.50 1.00
❑ 58 Kerry Collins 1.50 .60
❑ 59 Tiki Barber 2.50 1.00
❑ 60 Ron Dayne 2.50 1.00
❑ 61 Vinny Testaverde 1.50 .60
❑ 62 Wayne Chrebet 1.50 .60
❑ 63 Curtis Martin 2.50 1.00
❑ 64 Tim Brown 2.50 1.00
❑ 65 Rich Gannon 2.50 1.00
❑ 66 Tyrone Wheatley 1.50 .60
❑ 67 Duce Staley 2.50 1.00
❑ 68 Donovan McNabb 3.00 1.25
❑ 69 Kordell Stewart 1.50 .60
❑ 70 Jerome Bettis 2.50 1.00
❑ 71 Marshall Faulk 3.00 1.25
❑ 72 Kurt Warner 5.00 2.00
❑ 73 Isaac Bruce 2.50 1.00
❑ 74 Doug Flutie 2.50 1.00
❑ 75 Curtis Conway 1.50 .60
❑ 76 Jeff Garcia 2.50 1.00
❑ 77 Jerry Rice 5.00 2.00
❑ 78 Charlie Garner 1.50 .60
❑ 79 Terrell Owens 2.50 1.00
❑ 80 Ricky Watters 1.00 .40
❑ 81 Matt Hasselbeck 1.50 .60
❑ 82 Levon Kirkland 1.00 .40
❑ 83 Keyshawn Johnson 2.50 1.00
❑ 84 Brad Johnson 2.50 1.00
❑ 85 Mike Alstott 2.50 1.00
❑ 86 Eddie George 2.50 1.00
❑ 87 Steve McNair 2.50 1.00
❑ 88 Jeff George 1.50 .60
❑ 89 Michael Westbrook 2.50 1.00
❑ 90 Stephen Davis 2.50 1.00
❑ 91 Michael Vick JSY RC 80.00 40.00
❑ 92 Chris Weinke JSY RC 15.00 6.00
❑ 93 Drew Brees JSY RC 40.00 20.00
❑ 94 Deuce McAllister JSY RC 30.00 12.50
❑ 95 Michael Bennett JSY RC 25.00 10.00
❑ 96 LaDain Tomlinson JSY RC 60.00 30.00
❑ 97 Kevan Barlow JSY RC 15.00 6.00
❑ 98 Travis Minor JSY RC 12.00 5.00
❑ 99 Rudi Johnson JSY RC 30.00 12.50
❑ 100 Todd Heap JSY RC 15.00 6.00
❑ 101 Freddie Mitchell JSY RC 15.00 6.00
❑ 102 Santana Moss JSY RC 25.00 10.00
❑ 103 Reggie Wayne JSY RC 30.00 12.50
❑ 104 Koren Robinson JSY RC 15.00 6.00
❑ 105 Josh Heupel JSY RC 15.00 6.00
❑ 106 Rod Gardner JSY RC 15.00 6.00
❑ 107 Quincy Morgan JSY RC 15.00 6.00
❑ 108 Chad Johnson JSY RC 40.00 15.00
❑ 109 Dan Morgan JSY RC 15.00 6.00
❑ 110 Gerard Warren JSY RC 15.00 6.00
❑ 111 Chris Chambers JSY RC 25.00 10.00
❑ 112 James Jackson JSY RC 15.00 6.00
❑ 113 Jesse Palmer JSY RC 15.00 6.00
❑ 114 Sage Rosenfels JSY RC 15.00 6.00
❑ 115 Mike McMahon JSY RC 15.00 6.00
❑ 116 Marques Tuiasosopo JSY RC 15.00 6.00
❑ 117 Robert Ferguson JSY RC 15.00 6.00
❑ 118 Travis Henry JSY RC 15.00 6.00
❑ 119 Richard Seymour JSY RC 15.00 6.00
❑ 120 Andre Carter JSY RC 15.00 6.00
❑ 121 LaMont Jordan RC 15.00 6.00
❑ 122 Vinny Sutherland RC 5.00 2.00
❑ 123 Nate Clements RC 8.00 3.00
❑ 124 David Terrell RC 8.00 3.00
❑ 125 A.J. Feeley RC 8.00 3.00
❑ 126 David Rivers RC 5.00 2.00
❑ 127 Snoop Minnis RC 5.00 2.00
❑ 128 Josh Booty RC 8.00 3.00
❑ 129 Correll Buckhalter RC 10.00 4.00
❑ 130 Will Allen RC 5.00 2.00
❑ 131 Dan Alexander RC 8.00 3.00
❑ 132 Leonard Davis RC 5.00 2.00
❑ 133 Anthony Thomas RC 8.00 3.00
❑ 134 Alge Crumpler RC 10.00 5.00
❑ 135 Jamal Reynolds RC 8.00 3.00
❑ 136 Ken-Yon Rambo RC 5.00 2.00
❑ 137 Bobby Newcombe RC 5.00 2.00
❑ 138 Alex Bannister RC 5.00 2.00
❑ 139 Jabari Holloway RC 5.00 2.00
❑ 140 Jamar Fletcher RC 5.00 2.00
❑ 141 Adam Archuleta RC 8.00 3.00
❑ 142 Heath Evans RC 5.00 2.00
❑ 143 Scotty Anderson RC 5.00 2.00
❑ 144 Moran Norris RC 3.00 1.25
❑ 145 Justin Smith RC 8.00 3.00
❑ 146 Quincy Carter RC 8.00 3.00
❑ 147 Ronney Daniels RC 3.00 1.25
❑ 148 Ben Leard RC 5.00 2.00
❑ 149 Fred Smoot RC 8.00 3.00
❑ 150 Milton Wynn RC 5.00 2.00

2003 SP Game Used Edition

❑	COMP.SET w/o SP's (90)	60.00	30.00
❑ 1	Chad Hutchinson	1.25	.50
❑ 2	Quincy Carter	2.00	.75
❑ 3	Joey Galloway	2.00	.75
❑ 4	Kerry Collins	2.00	.75
❑ 5	Jeremy Shockey	5.00	2.00
❑ 6	Amani Toomer	2.00	.75
❑ 7	A.J. Feeley	2.00	.75
❑ 8	Duce Staley	2.00	.75
❑ 9	Dorsey Levens	1.25	.50
❑ 10	Ladell Betts	2.00	.75
❑ 11	Patrick Ramsey	3.00	1.25
❑ 12	Anthony Thomas	2.00	.75
❑ 13	Marty Booker	2.00	.75
❑ 14	Brian Urlacher	5.00	2.00
❑ 15	Joey Harrington	5.00	2.00
❑ 16	James Stewart	2.00	.75
❑ 17	Az-Zahir Hakim	1.25	.50
❑ 18	Donald Driver	2.00	.75
❑ 19	Javon Walker	2.00	.75
❑ 20	Kordell Stewart	2.00	.75
❑ 21	Randy Moss	5.00	2.00
❑ 22	Shaun Hill	1.25	.50
❑ 23	Brian Finneran	1.25	.50
❑ 24	T.J. Duckett	2.00	.75
❑ 25	Warrick Dunn	2.00	.75
❑ 26	Rodney Peete	1.25	.50
❑ 27	Stephen Davis	2.00	.75
❑ 28	Muhsin Muhammad	2.00	.75
❑ 29	Aaron Brooks	3.00	1.25
❑ 30	Deuce McAllister	3.00	1.25
❑ 31	Joe Horn	2.00	.75
❑ 32	Keyshawn Johnson	3.00	1.25
❑ 33	Brad Johnson	2.00	.75
❑ 34	Keenan McCardell	1.25	.50
❑ 35	Jake Plummer	2.00	.75
❑ 36	Josh McCown	2.00	.75
❑ 37	Thomas Jones	2.00	.75
❑ 38	Tai Streets	1.25	.50
❑ 39	Kevan Barlow	2.00	.75
❑ 40	Garrison Hearst	2.00	.75
❑ 41	Maurice Morris	1.25	.50
❑ 42	Matt Hasselbeck	2.00	.75
❑ 43	Koren Robinson	2.00	.75
❑ 44	Marc Bulger	3.00	1.25
❑ 45	Trung Canidate	2.00	.75
❑ 46	Emmitt Smith	8.00	3.00
❑ 47	Alex Van Pelt	1.25	.50
❑ 48	Travis Henry	2.00	.75
❑ 49	Eric Moulds	2.00	.75
❑ 50	Jason Taylor	1.25	.50
❑ 51	Jay Fiedler	2.00	.75
❑ 52	Randy McMichael	2.00	.75
❑ 53	Tom Brady	8.00	3.00
❑ 54	Antowain Smith	2.00	.75
❑ 55	Troy Brown	2.00	.75
❑ 56	Curtis Martin	3.00	1.25
❑ 57	Vinny Testaverde	2.00	.75
❑ 58	Santana Moss	2.00	.75
❑ 59	Jamal Lewis	3.00	1.25
❑ 60	Chris Redman	1.25	.50
❑ 61	Ray Lewis	3.00	1.25
❑ 62	Jon Kitna	2.00	.75
❑ 63	Peter Warrick	2.00	.75
❑ 64	Kelly Holcomb	2.00	.75
❑ 65	William Green	2.00	.75
❑ 66	Kevin Johnson	2.00	.75
❑ 67	Amos Zereoue	2.00	.75
❑ 68	Tommy Maddox	3.00	1.25
❑ 69	Hines Ward	3.00	1.25
❑ 70	Corey Bradford	1.25	.50
❑ 71	Jonathan Wells	1.25	.50
❑ 72	Jabar Gaffney	2.00	.75
❑ 73	Edgerrin James	3.00	1.25
❑ 74	David Garrard	1.25	.50
❑ 75	Mark Brunell	2.00	.75
❑ 76	Jimmy Smith	2.00	.75
❑ 77	Steve McNair	3.00	1.25
❑ 78	Kevin Dyson	2.00	.75
❑ 79	Terrell Davis	3.00	1.25
❑ 80	Shannon Sharpe	2.00	.75
❑ 81	Rod Smith	2.00	.75
❑ 82	Trent Green	2.00	.75
❑ 83	Priest Holmes	4.00	1.50
❑ 84	Tony Gonzalez	2.00	.75
❑ 85	Jerry Rice	6.00	2.50
❑ 86	Charlie Garner	2.00	.75
❑ 87	Jerry Porter	2.00	.75
❑ 88	Reche Caldwell	1.25	.50
❑ 89	Tim Dwight	2.00	.75
❑ 90	Junior Seau	3.00	1.25
❑ 91	Carson Palmer RC	50.00	20.00
❑ 92	Byron Leftwich RC	40.00	15.00
❑ 93	Dave Ragone RC	12.00	5.00
❑ 94	Kyle Boller RC	25.00	10.00
❑ 95	Rex Grossman RC	20.00	7.50
❑ 96	Chris Simms RC	20.00	7.50
❑ 97	Kliff Kingsbury RC	10.00	4.00
❑ 98	Jason Gesser RC	12.00	5.00
❑ 99	Brad Banks RC	10.00	4.00
❑ 100	Ken Dorsey RC	12.00	5.00
❑ 101	Juston Wood RC	6.00	2.50
❑ 102	Brian St.Pierre RC	12.00	5.00
❑ 103	Domanick Davis RC	20.00	7.50
❑ 104	Quentin Griffin RC	12.00	5.00
❑ 105	B.J. Askew RC	12.00	5.00
❑ 106	Onterrio Smith RC	12.00	5.00
❑ 107	Seneca Wallace RC	12.00	5.00
❑ 108	Artose Pinner RC	12.00	5.00
❑ 109	Justin Fargas RC	12.00	5.00
❑ 110	Chris Brown RC	15.00	6.00
❑ 111	Willis McGahee RC	30.00	12.50
❑ 112	Larry Johnson RC	50.00	25.00
❑ 113	Lee Suggs RC	25.00	10.00
❑ 114	Billy McMullen RC	10.00	4.00
❑ 115	Sultan McCullough RC	10.00	4.00
❑ 116	Musa Smith RC	12.00	5.00
❑ 117	Earnest Graham RC	10.00	4.00
❑ 118	Antwone Savage RC	6.00	2.50
❑ 119	Kirk Farmer RC	6.00	2.50
❑ 120	Kareem Kelly RC	10.00	4.00
❑ 121	J.R. Tolver RC	10.00	4.00
❑ 122	Tyrone Calico RC	15.00	6.00
❑ 123	Kevin Curtis RC	12.00	5.00
❑ 124	Bobby Wade RC	12.00	5.00
❑ 125	Justin Gage RC	12.00	5.00
❑ 126	Bryant Johnson RC	12.00	5.00
❑ 127	Doug Gabriel RC	12.00	5.00
❑ 128	Teyo Johnson RC	12.00	5.00
❑ 129	Brandon Lloyd RC	15.00	6.00
❑ 130	Kelley Washington RC	12.00	5.00
❑ 131	Talman Gardner RC	12.00	5.00
❑ 132	Anquan Boldin RC	30.00	12.50
❑ 133	Taylor Jacobs RC	10.00	4.00
❑ 134	Andre Johnson RC	25.00	10.00
❑ 135	Charles Rogers RC	12.00	5.00
❑ 136	Antonio Bryant JSY	12.00	5.00
❑ 137	Donovan McNabb JSY/99	30.00	15.00
❑ 138	Rod Gardner JSY	8.00	3.00
❑ 139	Ahman Green JSY	12.00	5.00
❑ 140	Brett Favre JSY/99	40.00	15.00
❑ 141	Daunte Culpepper JSY	12.00	5.00
❑ 142	Michael Bennett JSY	12.00	5.00
❑ 143	Michael Vick JSY/99	50.00	20.00
❑ 144	Jeff Garcia JSY	15.00	6.00
❑ 145	Terrell Owens JSY	12.00	5.00
❑ 146	Shaun Alexander JSY	12.00	5.00
❑ 147	Torry Holt JSY	12.00	5.00
❑ 148	Isaac Bruce JSY	10.00	4.00
❑ 149	Marshall Faulk JSY/99	20.00	7.50
❑ 150	Kurt Warner JSY/99	25.00	10.00
❑ 151	Drew Bledsoe JSY	12.00	5.00
❑ 152	Josh Reed JSY	10.00	4.00
❑ 153	Peerless Price JSY	10.00	4.00
❑ 154	David Boston JSY	10.00	4.00
❑ 155	Ricky Williams JSY/99	25.00	10.00
❑ 156	Chris Chambers JSY	12.00	5.00
❑ 157	Wayne Chrebet JSY	10.00	4.00
❑ 158	Chad Pennington JSY/99	25.00	12.50
❑ 159	Laveranues Coles JSY	10.00	4.00
❑ 160	Corey Dillon JSY	10.00	4.00
❑ 161	Tim Couch JSY	8.00	3.00
❑ 162	Jerome Bettis JSY	12.00	5.00
❑ 163	Plaxico Burress JSY	12.00	5.00
❑ 164	Antwaan Randle El JSY	12.00	5.00
❑ 165	David Carr JSY/99	30.00	15.00
❑ 166	Marvin Harrison JSY	10.00	4.00
❑ 167	Peyton Manning JSY	15.00	6.00
❑ 168	Fred Taylor JSY	10.00	4.00
❑ 169	Eddie George JSY	10.00	4.00
❑ 170	Clinton Portis JSY/99	30.00	15.00
❑ 171	Ashley Lelie JSY	10.00	4.00
❑ 172	Rich Gannon JSY	12.00	5.00
❑ 173	Phillip Buchanon JSY	10.00	4.00
❑ 174	Tim Brown JSY	12.00	5.00
❑ 175	LaDainian Tomlinson JSY	12.00	5.00
❑ 176	Drew Brees JSY/99	30.00	15.00
❑ 177	Jason Johnson RC	6.00	2.50
❑ 178	Sam Aiken RC	10.00	4.00
❑ 179	Nate Burleson RC	15.00	6.00
❑ 180	Tony Romo RC	12.00	5.00
❑ 181	Arnaz Battle RC	12.00	5.00

2004 SP Game Used Edition

❑ ROOKIE STATED ODDS 1:4

❑ ROOKIE PRINT RUN 425 SER.#'d SETS

❑ 1	Anquan Boldin	3.00	1.25
❑ 2	Marcel Shipp	2.00	.75
❑ 3	Josh McCown	2.00	.75
❑ 4	Michael Vick	6.00	2.50
❑ 5	T.J. Duckett	2.00	.75
❑ 6	Peerless Price	2.00	.75
❑ 7	Jamal Lewis	3.00	1.25
❑ 8	Todd Heap	2.00	.75
❑ 9	Kyle Boller	3.00	1.25
❑ 10	Drew Bledsoe	3.00	1.25
❑ 11	Travis Henry	2.00	.75

❑ 12 Eric Moulds 2.00 .75
❑ 13 Jake Delhomme 3.00 1.25
❑ 14 Stephen Davis 2.00 .75
❑ 15 Julius Peppers 3.00 1.25
❑ 16 Anthony Thomas 2.00 .75
❑ 17 Rex Grossman 3.00 1.25
❑ 18 Brian Urlacher 4.00 1.50
❑ 19 Carson Palmer 4.00 1.50
❑ 20 Chad Johnson 3.00 1.25
❑ 21 Rudi Johnson 2.00 .75
❑ 22 Jeff Garcia 3.00 1.25
❑ 23 Dennis Northcutt 1.25 .50
❑ 24 Andre Davis 1.25 .50
❑ 25 Quincy Carter 2.00 .75
❑ 26 Roy Williams S 2.00 .75
❑ 27 Keyshawn Johnson 2.00 .75
❑ 28 Quentin Griffin 3.00 1.25
❑ 29 Jake Plummer 2.00 .75
❑ 30 Ashley Lelie 2.00 .75
❑ 31 Shannon Sharpe 2.00 .75
❑ 32 Joey Harrington 3.00 1.25
❑ 33 Charles Rogers 2.00 .75
❑ 34 Az-Zahir Hakim 1.25 .50
❑ 35 Brett Favre 8.00 3.00
❑ 36 Javon Walker 2.00 .75
❑ 37 Ahman Green 3.00 1.25
❑ 38 Andre Johnson 3.00 1.25
❑ 39 David Carr 3.00 1.25
❑ 40 Domanick Davis 3.00 1.25
❑ 41 Peyton Manning 5.00 2.00
❑ 42 Edgerrin James 3.00 1.25
❑ 43 Marvin Harrison 3.00 1.25
❑ 44 Byron Leftwich 4.00 1.50
❑ 45 Fred Taylor 2.00 .75
❑ 46 Jimmy Smith 2.00 .75
❑ 47 Priest Holmes 4.00 1.50
❑ 48 Trent Green 2.00 .75
❑ 49 Dante Hall 3.00 1.25
❑ 50 Tony Gonzalez 2.00 .75
❑ 51 Ricky Williams 3.00 1.25
❑ 52 Jay Fiedler 1.25 .50
❑ 53 Chris Chambers 2.00 .75
❑ 54 Randy Moss 4.00 1.50
❑ 55 Daunte Culpepper 3.00 1.25
❑ 56 Moe Williams 1.25 .50
❑ 57 Tom Brady 8.00 3.00
❑ 58 Deion Branch 3.00 1.25
❑ 59 Corey Dillon 2.00 .75
❑ 60 Deuce McAllister 3.00 1.25
❑ 61 Aaron Brooks 2.00 .75
❑ 62 Joe Horn 2.00 .75
❑ 63 Jeremy Shockey 3.00 1.25
❑ 64 Amani Toomer 2.00 .75
❑ 65 Michael Strahan 2.00 .75
❑ 66 Curtis Martin 3.00 1.25
❑ 67 Chad Pennington 3.00 1.25
❑ 68 Santana Moss 2.00 .75
❑ 69 Jerry Rice 6.00 2.50
❑ 70 Tim Brown 3.00 1.25
❑ 71 Jerry Porter 2.00 .75
❑ 72 Donovan McNabb 4.00 1.50
❑ 73 Brian Westbrook 2.00 .75
❑ 74 Terrell Owens 3.00 1.25
❑ 75 Hines Ward 3.00 1.25
❑ 76 Plaxico Burress 2.00 .75
❑ 77 Duce Staley 2.00 .75
❑ 78 LaDainian Tomlinson 4.00 1.50
❑ 79 Quentin Jammer 1.25 .50
❑ 80 Drew Brees 3.00 1.25
❑ 81 Brandon Lloyd 2.00 .75
❑ 82 Kevan Barlow 2.00 .75
❑ 83 Tim Rattay 1.25 .50
❑ 84 Matt Hasselbeck 2.00 .75
❑ 85 Shaun Alexander 3.00 1.25
❑ 86 Darrell Jackson 2.00 .75
❑ 87 Marc Bulger 3.00 1.25
❑ 88 Torry Holt 3.00 1.25
❑ 89 Marshall Faulk 3.00 1.25
❑ 90 Isaac Bruce 2.00 .75
❑ 91 Brad Johnson 2.00 .75
❑ 92 Derrick Brooks 2.00 .75
❑ 93 Warren Sapp 2.00 .75
❑ 94 Steve McNair 3.00 1.25
❑ 95 Derrick Mason 2.00 .75
❑ 96 Eddie George 2.00 .75
❑ 97 Clinton Portis 3.00 1.25
❑ 98 Mark Brunell 2.00 .75
❑ 99 Laveranues Coles 2.00 .75
❑ 100 LaVar Arrington 6.00 2.50
❑ 101 Ben Troupe RC 12.00 5.00
❑ 102 Chris Gamble RC 15.00 6.00
❑ 103 DeAngelo Hall RC 15.00 6.00
❑ 104 Dunta Robinson RC 12.00 5.00
❑ 105 Jason Shivers RC 6.00 2.50
❑ 106 Keary Colbert RC 15.00 6.00
❑ 107 Craig Krenzel RC 12.00 5.00
❑ 108 Philip Rivers RC 40.00 20.00
❑ 109 Roy Williams RC 30.00 12.50
❑ 110 Will Allen RC 12.00 5.00
❑ 111 Bob Sanders RC 25.00 10.00
❑ 112 Kris Wilson RC 12.00 5.00
❑ 113 D.J. Williams RC 15.00 6.00
❑ 114 Devery Henderson RC 10.00 4.00
❑ 115 Carlos Francis RC 10.00 4.00
❑ 116 Jonathan Vilma RC 12.00 5.00
❑ 117 Luke McCown RC 12.00 5.00
❑ 118 Michael Turner RC 12.00 5.00
❑ 119 Richard Seigler RC 10.00 4.00
❑ 120 Jared Lorenzen RC 10.00 4.00
❑ 121 P.K. Sam RC 10.00 4.00
❑ 122 Justin Smiley RC 12.00 5.00
❑ 123 Marquise Hill RC 10.00 4.00
❑ 124 Ernest Wilford RC 12.00 5.00
❑ 125 Jerricho Cotchery RC 12.00 5.00
❑ 126 Kevin Jones RC 40.00 20.00
❑ 127 Michael Boulware RC 12.00 5.00
❑ 128 Jarrett Payton RC 15.00 6.00
❑ 129 Sean Taylor RC 15.00 6.00
❑ 130 Will Smith RC 12.00 5.00
❑ 131 Bernard Berrian RC 12.00 5.00
❑ 132 Ahmad Carroll RC 15.00 6.00
❑ 133 Derrick Hamilton RC 10.00 4.00
❑ 134 Dwan Edwards RC 6.00 2.50
❑ 135 Jeff Smoker RC 12.00 5.00
❑ 136 Kenechi Udeze RC 15.00 6.00
❑ 137 Mewelde Moore RC 20.00 7.50
❑ 138 Joey Thomas RC 12.00 5.00
❑ 139 Sean Jones RC 10.00 4.00
❑ 140 Will Poole RC 12.00 5.00
❑ 141 Casey Clausen RC 12.00 5.00
❑ 142 Stuart Schweigert RC 12.00 5.00
❑ 143 Cody Pickett RC 12.00 5.00
❑ 144 Derrick Strait RC 12.00 5.00
❑ 145 Greg Jones RC 12.00 5.00
❑ 146 John Navarre RC 12.00 5.00
❑ 147 Larry Fitzgerald RC 40.00 15.00
❑ 148 Michael Clayton RC 25.00 10.00
❑ 149 Rashaun Woods RC 12.00 5.00
❑ 150 Shawn Andrews RC 12.00 5.00
❑ 151 B.J. Symons RC 12.00 5.00
❑ 152 Cedric Cobbs RC 12.00 5.00
❑ 153 Darius Watts RC 12.00 5.00
❑ 154 B.J. Johnson RC 10.00 4.00
❑ 155 Max Starks RC 10.00 4.00
❑ 156 Josh Harris RC 12.00 5.00
❑ 157 Kendrick Starling RC 6.00 2.50
❑ 158 Brandon Miree RC 10.00 4.00
❑ 159 Robert Gallery RC 20.00 7.50
❑ 160 Tatum Bell RC 25.00 10.00
❑ 161 Ben Hartsock RC 12.00 5.00
❑ 162 Derek Abney RC 12.00 5.00
❑ 163 Ricardo Colclough RC 12.00 5.00
❑ 164 Justin Jenkins RC 10.00 4.00
❑ 165 Chris Cooley RC 12.00 5.00
❑ 166 Julius Jones RC 50.00 20.00
❑ 167 Matt Mauck RC 12.00 5.00
❑ 168 Vernon Carey RC 10.00 4.00
❑ 169 John Standeford RC 10.00 4.00
❑ 170 Teddy Lehman RC 12.00 5.00
❑ 171 Ben Roethlisberger RC 120.00 60.00
❑ 172 Ben Utecht RC 6.00 2.50
❑ 173 D.J. Hackett RC 10.00 4.00
❑ 174 Drew Henson RC 12.00 5.00
❑ 175 Rich Gardner RC 10.00 4.00
❑ 176 Karlos Dansby RC 12.00 5.00
❑ 177 Matt Schaub RC 20.00 7.50
❑ 178 Darrion Scott RC 12.00 5.00
❑ 179 Keyaron Fox RC 10.00 4.00
❑ 180 Tommie Harris RC 12.00 5.00
❑ 181 Ben Watson RC 12.00 5.00
❑ 182 Chris Perry RC 20.00 7.50
❑ 183 Travelle Wharton RC 6.00 2.50
❑ 184 Eli Manning RC 100.00 50.00
❑ 185 Demorrio Williams RC 12.00 5.00
❑ 186 Kellen Winslow RC 25.00 10.00
❑ 187 Jason Babin RC 12.00 5.00
❑ 188 Quincy Wilson RC 10.00 4.00
❑ 189 Samie Parker RC 12.00 5.00
❑ 190 Vince Wilfork RC 12.00 5.00
❑ 191 Antwan Odom RC 12.00 5.00
❑ 192 Josh Davis RC 10.00 4.00
❑ 193 Courtney Watson RC 12.00 5.00
❑ 194 Devard Darling RC 12.00 5.00
❑ 195 J.P. Losman RC 25.00 10.00
❑ 196 Johnnie Morant RC 12.00 5.00
❑ 197 Lee Evans RC 15.00 6.00
❑ 198 Michael Jenkins RC 12.00 5.00
❑ 199 Reggie Williams RC 15.00 6.00
❑ 200 Steven Jackson RC 40.00 15.00

2002 SP Legendary Cuts

❑ COMP.SET w/o SP's (90) 40.00 15.00
❑ 1 Tom Brady 3.00 1.25
❑ 2 Antowain Smith .75 .30
❑ 3 Troy Brown .75 .30
❑ 4 Drew Bledsoe 1.50 .60
❑ 5 Travis Henry 1.25 .50
❑ 6 Eric Moulds .75 .30
❑ 7 Ricky Williams 1.25 .50
❑ 8 Jay Fiedler .75 .30
❑ 9 Chris Chambers 1.25 .50
❑ 10 Curtis Martin 1.25 .50
❑ 11 Chad Pennington 1.50 .60
❑ 12 Wayne Chrebet .75 .30
❑ 13 Jerome Bettis 1.25 .50
❑ 14 Tommy Maddox 3.00 1.25
❑ 15 Hines Ward 1.25 .50
❑ 16 Tim Couch .75 .30
❑ 17 Kevin Johnson .75 .30
❑ 18 Jamal Lewis 1.25 .50
❑ 19 Chris Redman .50 .20
❑ 20 Corey Dillon .75 .30
❑ 21 Michael Westbrook .50 .20
❑ 22 Peyton Manning 2.50 1.00
❑ 23 Edgerrin James 1.50 .60
❑ 24 Marvin Harrison 1.25 .50
❑ 25 Qadry Ismail .75 .30
❑ 26 Mark Brunell 1.25 .50

	No.	Player		
❑	27	Jimmy Smith	.75	.30
❑	28	Stacey Mack	.50	.20
❑	29	Fred Taylor	1.25	.50
❑	30	Steve McNair	1.25	.50
❑	31	Eddie George	1.25	.50
❑	32	Kevin Dyson	.75	.30
❑	33	James Allen	.75	.30
❑	34	Corey Bradford	.50	.20
❑	35	Shannon Sharpe	.75	.30
❑	36	Brian Griese	1.25	.50
❑	37	Ed McCaffrey	1.25	.50
❑	38	Jerry Rice	2.50	1.00
❑	39	Rich Gannon	1.25	.50
❑	40	Tim Brown	1.25	.50
❑	41	Trent Green	.75	.30
❑	42	Priest Holmes	1.50	.60
❑	43	Tony Gonzalez	.75	.30
❑	44	LaDainian Tomlinson	2.00	.75
❑	45	Drew Brees	1.25	.50
❑	46	Curtis Conway	.50	.20
❑	47	Donovan McNabb	1.50	.60
❑	48	Duce Staley	1.25	.50
❑	49	Antonio Freeman	1.25	.50
❑	50	James Thrash	.75	.30
❑	51	Kerry Collins	.75	.30
❑	52	Tiki Barber	1.25	.50
❑	53	Amani Toomer	.75	.30
❑	54	Emmitt Smith	3.00	1.25
❑	55	Quincy Carter	.75	.30
❑	56	Joey Galloway	.75	.30
❑	57	Stephen Davis	.75	.30
❑	58	Champ Bailey	.75	.30
❑	59	Anthony Thomas	.75	.30
❑	60	Jim Miller	.75	.30
❑	61	Brian Urlacher	2.00	.75
❑	62	Brett Favre	3.00	1.25
❑	63	Ahman Green	1.25	.50
❑	64	Robert Ferguson	.50	.20
❑	65	Randy Moss	2.50	1.00
❑	66	Daunte Culpepper	1.25	.50
❑	67	Moe Williams	.50	.20
❑	68	James Stewart	.75	.30
❑	69	Az-Zahir Hakim	.50	.20
❑	70	Keyshawn Johnson	1.25	.50
❑	71	Brad Johnson	.75	.30
❑	72	Mike Alstott	1.25	.50
❑	73	Michael Vick	4.00	1.50
❑	74	Warrick Dunn	1.25	.50
❑	75	Shawn Jefferson	.50	.20
❑	76	Aaron Brooks	1.25	.50
❑	77	Deuce McAllister	1.50	.60
❑	78	Joe Horn	.75	.30
❑	79	Rodney Peete	.75	.30
❑	80	Steve Smith	1.25	.50
❑	81	Terrell Owens	1.25	.50
❑	82	Jeff Garcia	1.25	.50
❑	83	Garrison Hearst	.75	.30
❑	84	Kurt Warner	1.25	.50
❑	85	Marshall Faulk	1.25	.50
❑	86	Torry Holt	1.25	.50
❑	87	Jake Plummer	.75	.30
❑	88	David Boston	1.25	.50
❑	89	Shaun Alexander	1.50	.60
❑	90	Trent Dilfer	.75	.30
❑	91	Tom Brady VM	5.00	2.00
❑	92	Michael Vick VM	6.00	2.50
❑	93	LaDainian Tomlinson VM	3.00	1.25
❑	94	Rich Gannon VM	2.00	.75
❑	95	Randy Moss VM	4.00	1.50
❑	96	Aaron Brooks VM	2.00	.75
❑	97	Mark Brunell VM	2.00	.75
❑	98	Jeff Garcia VM	2.00	.75
❑	99	Ahman Green VM	2.00	.75
❑	100	Shaun Alexander VM	2.50	1.00
❑	101	Ricky Williams TG	2.50	1.00
❑	102	Bruce Smith TG	1.50	.60
❑	103	Curtis Martin TG	2.50	1.00
❑	104	Brian Urlacher TG	4.00	1.50
❑	105	Jerome Bettis TG	2.50	1.00
❑	106	Ray Lewis TG	2.50	1.00
❑	107	Edgerrin James TG	3.00	1.25
❑	108	Junior Seau TG	2.50	1.00
❑	109	Priest Holmes TG	3.00	1.25
❑	110	Warren Sapp TG	1.50	.60
❑	111	Emmitt Smith RI	10.00	4.00
❑	112	Jerry Rice RI	8.00	3.00
❑	113	Brett Favre RI	10.00	4.00
❑	114	Marshall Faulk RI	4.00	1.50
❑	115	Drew Bledsoe RI	5.00	2.00
❑	116	Tim Brown RI	4.00	1.50
❑	117	Donovan McNabb RI	5.00	2.00
❑	118	Peyton Manning RI	8.00	3.00
❑	119	Kurt Warner RI	4.00	1.50
❑	120	Shannon Sharpe RI	2.50	1.00
❑	121	Andre Davis RC	8.00	3.00
❑	122	Antonio Bryant RC	8.00	3.00
❑	123	Antwaan Randle El RC	12.00	5.00
❑	124	Ashley Lelie RC	15.00	6.00
❑	125	Ben Leber RC	8.00	3.00
❑	126	Chad Hutchinson RC	8.00	3.00
❑	127	Clinton Portis RC	25.00	10.00
❑	128	David Carr RC	20.00	7.50
❑	129	Deion Branch RC	15.00	6.00
❑	130	DeShaun Foster RC	8.00	3.00
❑	131	Donte Stallworth RC	15.00	6.00
❑	132	Jabar Gaffney RC	8.00	3.00
❑	133	Javon Walker RC	15.00	6.00
❑	134	Jeremy Shockey RC	25.00	10.00
❑	135	Joey Harrington RC	20.00	7.50
❑	136	Josh McCown RC	10.00	4.00
❑	137	Josh Reed RC	8.00	3.00
❑	138	Julius Peppers RC	15.00	6.00
❑	139	Marquise Walker RC	8.00	3.00
❑	140	Maurice Morris RC	8.00	3.00
❑	141	Patrick Ramsey RC	10.00	4.00
❑	142	Quentin Jammer RC	8.00	3.00
❑	143	Randy Fasani RC	8.00	3.00
❑	144	Reche Caldwell RC	8.00	3.00
❑	145	Rohan Davey RC	8.00	3.00
❑	146	Ron Johnson RC	8.00	3.00
❑	147	Roy Williams RC	20.00	7.50
❑	148	T.J. Duckett RC	12.00	5.00
❑	149	Travis Stephens RC	8.00	3.00
❑	150	William Green RC	8.00	3.00
❑	151	Albert Haynesworth RC	4.00	1.50
❑	152	Alex Brown RC	5.00	2.00
❑	153	Andra Davis RC	4.00	1.50
❑	154	Andre Gurode RC	4.00	1.50
❑	155	Anthony Weaver RC	4.00	1.50
❑	156	Brandon Doman RC	4.00	1.50
❑	157	Brian Westbrook RC	8.00	3.00
❑	158	Brian Williams RC	2.50	1.00
❑	159	Lamont Brightful RC	2.50	1.00
❑	160	Charles Grant RC	5.00	2.00
❑	161	Chester Taylor RC	5.00	2.00
❑	162	Cliff Russell RC	4.00	1.50
❑	163	Daniel Graham RC	5.00	2.00
❑	164	David Garrard RC	5.00	2.00
❑	165	James Mungro RC	5.00	2.00
❑	166	Dennis Johnson RC	2.50	1.00
❑	167	Derek Ross RC	4.00	1.50
❑	168	Dwight Freeney RC	6.00	2.50
❑	169	Ed Reed RC	8.00	3.00
❑	170	Carlos Hall RC	5.00	2.00
❑	171	Jarrod Baxter RC	4.00	1.50
❑	172	Jason McAddley RC	4.00	1.50
❑	173	Jerramy Stevens RC	5.00	2.00
❑	174	Jesse Chatman RC	5.00	2.00
❑	175	John Henderson RC	5.00	2.00
❑	176	Jon McGraw RC	2.50	1.00
❑	177	Jonathan Wells RC	5.00	2.00
❑	178	Justin Peelle RC	2.50	1.00
❑	179	Kalimba Edwards RC	5.00	2.00
❑	180	Keyou Craver RC	4.00	1.50
❑	181	Kurt Kittner RC	4.00	1.50
❑	182	LaDell Betts RC	5.00	2.00
❑	183	Lamar Gordon RC	5.00	2.00
❑	184	Lamont Thompson RC	4.00	1.50
❑	185	Larry Tripplett RC	2.50	1.00
❑	186	Randy McMichael RC	8.00	3.00
❑	187	Lito Sheppard RC	5.00	2.00
❑	188	Marques Anderson RC	5.00	2.00
❑	189	Michael Lewis RC	5.00	2.00
❑	190	Mike Pearson RC	2.50	1.00
❑	191	Mike Rumph RC	5.00	2.00
❑	192	Najeh Davenport RC	5.00	2.00
❑	193	Napoleon Harris RC	5.00	2.00
❑	194	Phillip Buchanon RC	5.00	2.00
❑	195	Quinn Gray RC	2.50	1.00
❑	196	Raonall Smith RC	4.00	1.50
❑	197	Ricky Williams RC	4.00	1.50
❑	198	Robert Thomas RC	5.00	2.00
❑	199	Rocky Calmus RC	5.00	2.00
❑	200	Ryan Denney RC	4.00	1.50
❑	201	Ryan Sims RC	5.00	2.00
❑	202	Jamal Robertson RC	4.00	1.50
❑	203	Shaun Hill RC	5.00	2.00
❑	204	Tank Williams RC	4.00	1.50
❑	205	Tellis Redmon RC	4.00	1.50
❑	206	Tim Carter RC	4.00	1.50
❑	207	Tony Fisher RC	5.00	2.00
❑	208	Travis Fisher RC	5.00	2.00
❑	209	Verron Haynes RC	5.00	2.00
❑	210	Wendell Bryant RC	2.50	1.00

1999 SP Signature

	No.	Player		
❑		COMPLETE SET (180)	400.00	200.00
❑		COMP.SET w/o SP's (170)	100.00	50.00
❑	1	Jake Plummer	1.00	.40
❑	2	Mario Bates	.60	.25
❑	3	Adrian Murrell	1.00	.40
❑	4	Jamal Anderson	1.50	.60
❑	5	Chris Chandler	1.00	.40
❑	6	Bob Christian	.60	.25
❑	7	O.J. Santiago	.60	.25
❑	8	Jim Harbaugh	1.00	.40
❑	9	Priest Holmes	2.50	1.00
❑	10	Ray Lewis	1.50	.60
❑	11	Michael Jackson	.60	.25
❑	12	Tony Siragusa	.60	.25
❑	13	Doug Flutie	1.50	.60
❑	14	Antowain Smith	1.50	.60
❑	15	Eric Moulds	1.50	.60
❑	16	William Floyd	.60	.25
❑	17	Fred Lane	.60	.25
❑	18	Muhsin Muhammad	1.00	.40
❑	19	Bobby Engram	1.00	.40
❑	20	Curtis Enis	.60	.25
❑	21	Curtis Conway	1.00	.40
❑	22	Corey Dillon	1.50	.60
❑	23	Carl Pickens	1.00	.40
❑	24	Ashley Ambrose	.60	.25
❑	25	Darnay Scott	.60	.25
❑	26	Troy Aikman	3.00	1.25
❑	27	Jason Garrett	.60	.25
❑	28	Emmitt Smith	3.00	1.25
❑	29	Deion Sanders	1.50	.60
❑	30	John Elway	5.00	2.00

❑ 31	Terrell Davis	1.50	.60
❑ 32	Ed McCaffrey	1.00	.40
❑ 33	John Mobley	.60	.25
❑ 34	Maa Tanuvasa	.60	.25
❑ 35	Ray Crockett	.60	.25
❑ 36	Barry Sanders	5.00	2.00
❑ 37	Herman Moore	1.00	.40
❑ 38	Charlie Batch	1.50	.60
❑ 39	Robert Porcher	.60	.25
❑ 40	Tommy Vardell	.60	.25
❑ 41	Brett Favre	5.00	2.00
❑ 42	Antonio Freeman	1.50	.60
❑ 43	Darick Holmes	.60	.25
❑ 44	Robert Brooks	1.00	.40
❑ 45	Peyton Manning	6.00	2.50
❑ 46	Marshall Faulk	2.00	.75
❑ 47	Torrance Small	.60	.25
❑ 48	Lamont Warren	.60	.25
❑ 49	Zack Crockett	.60	.25
❑ 50	Mark Brunell	1.50	.60
❑ 51	Pete Mitchell	.60	.25
❑ 52	Fred Taylor	1.50	.60
❑ 53	Jimmy Smith	1.00	.40
❑ 54	Andre Rison	1.00	.40
❑ 55	Rich Gannon	1.50	.60
❑ 56	Donnell Bennett	.60	.25
❑ 57	Dan Marino	5.00	2.00
❑ 58	Karim Abdul-Jabbar	1.00	.40
❑ 59	Troy Drayton	.60	.25
❑ 60	Jason Taylor	.60	.25
❑ 61	Cris Carter	1.50	.60
❑ 62	Randy Moss	5.00	2.00
❑ 63	Robert Smith	1.50	.60
❑ 64	Leroy Hoard	.60	.25
❑ 65	Randall Cunningham	1.50	.60
❑ 66	Derrick Alexander DE	.60	.25
❑ 67	Drew Bledsoe	2.00	.75
❑ 68	Robert Edwards	.60	.25
❑ 69	Willie McGinest	.60	.25
❑ 70	Chris Slade	.60	.25
❑ 71	Terry Glenn	1.50	.60
❑ 72	Ty Law	1.00	.40
❑ 73	Kerry Collins	1.00	.40
❑ 74	Sean Dawkins	.60	.25
❑ 75	Cam Cleeland	.60	.25
❑ 76	Sammy Knight	.60	.25
❑ 77	Danny Kanell	.60	.25
❑ 78	Gary Brown	.60	.25
❑ 79	Chris Calloway	1.00	.40
❑ 80	Curtis Martin	1.50	.60
❑ 81	Keyshawn Johnson	1.50	.60
❑ 82	Vinny Testaverde	1.00	.40
❑ 83	Leon Johnson	.60	.25
❑ 84	Kyle Brady	.60	.25
❑ 85	Tim Brown	1.50	.60
❑ 86	Jeff George	1.00	.40
❑ 87	Rickey Dudley	.60	.25
❑ 88	Napoleon Kaufman	1.50	.60
❑ 89	James Jett	1.00	.40
❑ 90	Harvey Williams	.60	.25
❑ 91	Koy Detmer	.60	.25
❑ 92	Duce Staley	1.50	.60
❑ 93	Charlie Garner	1.00	.40
❑ 94	Jerome Bettis	1.50	.60
❑ 95	Kordell Stewart	1.00	.40
❑ 96	Courtney Hawkins	.60	.25
❑ 97	Hines Ward	1.50	.60
❑ 98	Isaac Bruce	1.50	.60
❑ 99	Tony Banks	1.00	.40
❑ 100	Greg Hill	.60	.25
❑ 101	Keith Lyle	.60	.25
❑ 102	Ryan Leaf	1.50	.60
❑ 103	Craig Whelihan	.60	.25
❑ 104	Charlie Jones	.60	.25
❑ 105	Junior Seau	1.50	.60
❑ 106	Natrone Means	1.00	.40
❑ 107	Rodney Harrison	.60	.25
❑ 108	Steve Young	2.00	.75
❑ 109	Garrison Hearst	1.00	.40
❑ 110	Jerry Rice	3.00	1.25
❑ 111	Chris Doleman	.60	.25
❑ 112	Roy Barker	.60	.25
❑ 113	Ricky Watters	1.00	.40
❑ 114	Jon Kitna	1.50	.60
❑ 115	Joey Galloway	1.00	.40
❑ 116	Chad Brown	.60	.25
❑ 117	Michael Sinclair	.60	.25
❑ 118	Warrick Dunn	1.50	.60
❑ 119	Mike Alstott	1.50	.60
❑ 120	Bert Emanuel	1.00	.40
❑ 121	Hardy Nickerson	.60	.25
❑ 122	Eddie George	1.50	.60
❑ 123	Steve McNair	1.50	.60
❑ 124	Yancey Thigpen	.60	.25
❑ 125	Frank Wycheck	.60	.25
❑ 126	Jackie Harris	.60	.25
❑ 127	Terry Allen	1.00	.40
❑ 128	Trent Green	1.50	.60
❑ 129	Jamie Asher	.60	.25
❑ 130	Brian Mitchell	.60	.25
❑ 131	Lance Alworth	1.50	.60
❑ 132	Fred Biletnikoff	1.50	.60
❑ 133	Mel Blount	.60	.25
❑ 134	Cliff Branch	.60	.25
❑ 135	Harold Carmichael	.60	.25
❑ 136	Larry Csonka	1.50	.60
❑ 137	Eric Dickerson	.60	.25
❑ 138	Randy Gradishar	.60	.25
❑ 139	Joe Greene	1.50	.60
❑ 140	Jack Ham	1.00	.40
❑ 141	Ted Hendricks	.60	.25
❑ 142	Charlie Joiner	.60	.25
❑ 143	Ed Jones	.60	.25
❑ 144	Billy Kilmer	.60	.25
❑ 145	Paul Krause	.60	.25
❑ 146	James Lofton	.60	.25
❑ 147	Archie Manning	1.00	.40
❑ 148	Don Maynard	.60	.25
❑ 149	Ozzie Newsome	.60	.25
❑ 150	Jim Otto	.60	.25
❑ 151	Lee Roy Selmon	.60	.25
❑ 152	Billy Sims	.60	.25
❑ 153	Mike Singletary	1.00	.40
❑ 154	Ken Stabler	1.50	.60
❑ 155	John Stallworth	1.00	.40
❑ 156	Roger Staubach	2.00	.75
❑ 157	Charley Taylor	.60	.25
❑ 158	Paul Warfield	1.50	.60
❑ 159	Kellen Winslow	.60	.25
❑ 160	Jack Youngblood	.60	.25
❑ 161	Bill Bergey	.60	.25
❑ 162	Raymond Berry	1.00	.40
❑ 163	Chuck Howley	.60	.25
❑ 164	Rocky Bleier	1.00	.40
❑ 165	Russ Francis	.60	.25
❑ 166	Drew Pearson	.60	.25
❑ 167	Mercury Morris	.60	.25
❑ 168	Dick Anderson	.60	.25
❑ 169	Earl Morrall	.60	.25
❑ 170	Jim Hart	.60	.25
❑ 171	Ricky Williams RC	12.00	5.00
❑ 172	Cade McNown RC	10.00	4.00
❑ 173	Tim Couch RC	12.00	5.00
❑ 174	Daunte Culpepper RC	25.00	10.00
❑ 175	Akili Smith RC	12.00	5.00
❑ 176	Brock Huard RC	12.00	5.00
❑ 177	Donovan McNabb RC	30.00	12.50
❑ 178	Michael Bishop RC	10.00	4.00
❑ 179	Shaun King RC	10.00	4.00
❑ 180	Torry Holt RC	20.00	7.50

2003 SP Signature

❑ 1	Michael Vick	12.00	5.00
❑ 2	Aaron Brooks	5.00	2.00
❑ 3	Jim Brown	10.00	4.00
❑ 4	Steve Young	6.00	2.50
❑ 5	Jeff Garcia	5.00	2.00
❑ 6	Warren Moon	5.00	2.00
❑ 7	John Elway	15.00	6.00
❑ 8	Troy Aikman	8.00	3.00
❑ 9	Drew Brees	5.00	2.00
❑ 10	Chad Pennington	6.00	2.50
❑ 11	Fran Tarkenton	6.00	2.50
❑ 12	Joe Namath	10.00	4.00
❑ 13	Dan Marino	15.00	6.00
❑ 14	Terry Bradshaw	15.00	6.00
❑ 15	Edgerrin James	5.00	2.00
❑ 16	Joe Montana	20.00	7.50
❑ 17	Ken Stabler	10.00	4.00
❑ 18	Peyton Manning	8.00	3.00
❑ 19	Johnny Unitas	12.00	5.00
❑ 20	Barry Sanders	8.00	3.00
❑ 21	Jim Kelly	10.00	4.00
❑ 22	Michael Bennett	3.00	1.25
❑ 23	Phil Simms	8.00	3.00
❑ 24	David Carr	8.00	3.00
❑ 25	Deuce McAllister	5.00	2.00
❑ 26	Clinton Portis	8.00	3.00
❑ 27	Brad Johnson	3.00	1.25
❑ 28	Tim Couch	2.00	.75
❑ 29	Archie Manning	5.00	2.00
❑ 30	Ahman Green	5.00	2.00
❑ 31	Priest Holmes	6.00	2.50
❑ 32	Marcus Allen	6.00	2.50
❑ 33	Ricky Williams	5.00	2.00
❑ 34	Walter Payton	20.00	7.50
❑ 35	Anthony Thomas	3.00	1.25
❑ 36	Eddie George	3.00	1.25
❑ 37	Shaun Alexander	5.00	2.00
❑ 38	Rich Gannon	3.00	1.25
❑ 39	Jay Fiedler	3.00	1.25
❑ 40	Travis Henry	3.00	1.25
❑ 41	Chad Johnson	5.00	2.00
❑ 42	Eric Moulds	3.00	1.25
❑ 43	Julius Peppers		
❑ 44	John Riggins	6.00	2.50
❑ 45	Antonio Bryant	3.00	1.25
❑ 46	Laveranues Coles	3.00	1.25
❑ 47	Josh McCown	3.00	1.25
❑ 48	Matt Hasselbeck	3.00	1.25
❑ 49	William Green	3.00	1.25
❑ 50	Peerless Price	3.00	1.25
❑ 51	Kerry Collins	3.00	1.25
❑ 52	Zach Thomas	3.00	1.25
❑ 53	Bruiser Kinard	5.00	2.00
❑ 54	Brian Urlacher	8.00	3.00
❑ 55	Junior Seau	5.00	2.00
❑ 56	Jamal Lewis	5.00	2.00
❑ 57	Duce Staley	3.00	1.25
❑ 58	Chris Redman	2.00	.75
❑ 59	Kordell Stewart	3.00	1.25
❑ 60	Chad Hutchinson	2.00	.75
❑ 61	Kevan Barlow	3.00	1.25
❑ 62	Charlie Garner	3.00	1.25
❑ 63	Fred Taylor	5.00	2.00
❑ 64	Jerome Bettis	5.00	2.00
❑ 65	Donte Stallworth	5.00	2.00
❑ 66	Rod Smith	3.00	1.25

❑	67 Antwaan Randle El	5.00	2.00
❑	68 Brian Griese	5.00	2.00
❑	69 Corey Dillon	3.00	1.25
❑	70 Chris Chambers	5.00	2.00
❑	71 Steve McNair	5.00	2.00
❑	72 Jake Plummer	3.00	1.25
❑	73 Keyshawn Johnson	5.00	2.00
❑	74 Marvin Harrison	5.00	2.00
❑	75 Plaxico Burress	3.00	1.25
❑	76 Tim Brown	5.00	2.00
❑	77 Mark Brunell	3.00	1.25
❑	78 Curtis Martin	5.00	2.00
❑	79 Cal Hubbard	5.00	2.00
❑	80 Isaac Bruce	5.00	2.00
❑	81 Terrell Owens	5.00	2.00
❑	82 Santana Moss	3.00	1.25
❑	83 Tommy Maddox	5.00	2.00
❑	84 Randy Moss	8.00	3.00
❑	85 Drew Bledsoe	5.00	2.00
❑	86 Az-Zahir Hakim	2.00	.75
❑	87 Rod Gardner	3.00	1.25
❑	88 Tom Brady	12.00	5.00
❑	89 David Boston	3.00	1.25
❑	90 Trent Green	3.00	1.25
❑	91 Jeremy Shockey	8.00	3.00
❑	92 Daunte Culpepper	5.00	2.00
❑	93 Emmitt Smith	12.00	5.00
❑	94 Jerry Rice	10.00	4.00
❑	95 LaDainian Tomlinson	5.00	2.00
❑	96 Marshall Faulk	5.00	2.00
❑	97 Kurt Warner	5.00	2.00
❑	98 Brett Favre	12.00	5.00
❑	99 Doak Walker	8.00	3.00
❑	100 Donovan McNabb	6.00	2.50
❑	101 Ken Dorsey RC	8.00	3.00
❑	102 Kirk Farmer RC	4.00	1.50
❑	103 Nate Hybl RC	8.00	3.00
❑	104 Marquel Blackwell RC	4.00	1.50
❑	105 Brett Engemann RC	4.00	1.50
❑	106 Tony Romo RC	8.00	3.00
❑	107 Derick Armstrong RC	8.00	3.00
❑	108 Lon Sheriff RC	4.00	1.50
❑	109 Casey Moore RC	6.00	2.50
❑	110 Jason Gesser RC	8.00	3.00
❑	111 Brock Forsey RC	10.00	4.00
❑	112 Willis McGahee RC	20.00	7.50
❑	113 Nick Maddox RC	4.00	1.50
❑	114 LaBrandon Toefield RC	8.00	3.00
❑	115 Kareem Kelly RC	6.00	2.50
❑	116 Malaefou MacKenzie RC	4.00	1.50
❑	117 Troy Polamalu RC	30.00	15.00
❑	118 Terence Newman RC	15.00	6.00
❑	119 Marcus Trufant RC	8.00	3.00
❑	120 Terrell Suggs RC	12.00	5.00
❑	121 DeWayne Robertson RC	8.00	3.00
❑	122 Justin Griffith RC	6.00	2.50
❑	123 Lee Suggs RC	15.00	6.00
❑	124 Bryant Johnson RC	8.00	3.00
❑	125 Andre Woolfolk RC	8.00	3.00
❑	126 Cedric Henry RC	4.00	1.50
❑	127 Billy McMullen RC	6.00	2.50
❑	128 Charles Rogers RC	8.00	3.00
❑	129 David Kircus RC	6.00	2.50
❑	130 Jerome McDougle RC	8.00	3.00
❑	131 Ryan Hoag RC	4.00	1.50
❑	132 Mike Pinkard RC	4.00	1.50
❑	133 Shaun McDonald RC	8.00	3.00
❑	134 Bobby Wade RC	8.00	3.00
❑	135 Kassim Osgood RC	8.00	3.00
❑	136 Ovie Mughelli RC	4.00	1.50
❑	137 Doug Gabriel RC	8.00	3.00
❑	138 Aaron Walker RC	6.00	2.50
❑	139 Brandon Lloyd RC	10.00	4.00
❑	140 Donald Lee RC	6.00	2.50
❑	141 George Wrighster RC	6.00	2.50
❑	142 Antwone Savage RC	4.00	1.50
❑	143 Keenan Howry RC	8.00	3.00
❑	144 Kevin Walter RC	6.00	2.50
❑	145 Gerald Hayes RC	4.00	1.50
❑	146 Walter Young RC	4.00	1.50
❑	147 Casey Fitzsimmons RC	8.00	3.00
❑	148 Vishante Shiancoe RC	6.00	2.50
❑	149 Lance Briggs RC	10.00	4.00
❑	150 Zuriel Smith RC	4.00	1.50
❑	151 Terrence Edwards RC	6.00	2.50
❑	152 Arnaz Battle RC	8.00	3.00
❑	153 DeAndrew Rubin RC	4.00	1.50
❑	154 Pisa Tinoisamoa RC	8.00	3.00
❑	155 David Tyree RC	6.00	2.50
❑	156 Bradie James RC	8.00	3.00
❑	157 Anquan Boldin RC	20.00	7.50
❑	158 Kevin Curtis RC	8.00	3.00
❑	159 Taylor Jacobs RC	6.00	2.50
❑	160 Cato June RC	8.00	3.00
❑	161 Jason Witten RC	12.00	5.00
❑	162 Mike Seidman RC	4.00	1.50
❑	163 Dallas Clark RC	10.00	4.00
❑	164 Gibran Hamdan RC	4.00	1.50
❑	165 Kliff Kingsbury RC	6.00	2.50
❑	166 Brooks Bollinger RC	8.00	3.00
❑	167 Nick Barnett RC	12.00	5.00
❑	168 Rex Grossman RC	12.00	5.00
❑	169 Byron Leftwich RC	25.00	10.00
❑	170 Kyle Boller RC	15.00	6.00
❑	171 Chris Brown RC	12.00	5.00
❑	172 Carl Ford RC	5.00	2.00
❑	173 Kelley Washington RC	10.00	4.00
❑	174 Charles Tillman RC	12.00	5.00
❑	175 Ken Hamlin RC	10.00	4.00
❑	176 Bennie Joppru RC	10.00	4.00
❑	177 Nate Burleson RC	12.00	5.00
❑	178 Boss Bailey RC	10.00	4.00
❑	179 LaTarence Dunbar RC	8.00	3.00
❑	180 Adrian Madise RC	8.00	3.00
❑	181 J.R. Tolver RC	8.00	3.00
❑	182 Tyrone Calico RC	12.00	5.00
❑	183 Justin Gage RC	10.00	4.00
❑	184 Teyo Johnson RC	10.00	4.00
❑	185 B.J. Askew RC	10.00	4.00
❑	186 Sam Aiken RC	8.00	3.00
❑	187 Andre Johnson RC	15.00	6.00
❑	188 Bethel Johnson RC	10.00	4.00
❑	189 Artose Pinner RC	10.00	4.00
❑	190 Quentin Griffin RC	10.00	4.00
❑	191 Musa Smith RC	10.00	4.00
❑	192 Larry Johnson RC	30.00	15.00
❑	193 Onterrio Smith RC	10.00	4.00
❑	194 Justin Fargas RC	10.00	4.00
❑	195 Dwone Hicks RC	5.00	2.00
❑	196 Brian St.Pierre RC	10.00	4.00
❑	197 Dave Ragone RC	10.00	4.00
❑	198 Seneca Wallace RC	10.00	4.00
❑	199 Chris Simms RC	12.00	5.00
❑	200 Carson Palmer RC	30.00	15.00

1999 Sports Illustrated

❑	COMPLETE SET (150)	75.00	40.00
❑	1 Bart Starr MVP	.75	.30
❑	2 Bart Starr MVP	.75	.30
❑	3 Joe Namath MVP	.75	.30
❑	4 Len Dawson MVP	.50	.20
❑	5 Chuck Howley MVP	.30	.10
❑	6 Roger Staubach MVP	.75	.30
❑	7 Jake Scott MVP	.30	.10
❑	8 Larry Csonka MVP	.50	.20
❑	9 Franco Harris MVP	.50	.20
❑	10 Fred Biletnikoff MVP	.50	.20
❑	11 H.Martin/R.White MVP	.30	.10
❑	12 Terry Bradshaw MVP	.75	.30
❑	13 Terry Bradshaw MVP	.75	.30
❑	14 Jim Plunkett MVP	.30	.10
❑	15 Joe Montana MVP	.75	.30
❑	16 Marcus Allen MVP	.50	.20
❑	17 Joe Montana MVP	.75	.30
❑	18 Richard Dent MVP	.50	.20
❑	19 Phil Simms MVP	.30	.10
❑	20 Doug Williams MVP	.30	.10
❑	21 Jerry Rice MVP	.75	.30
❑	22 Joe Montana MVP	.75	.30
❑	23 Ottis Anderson MVP	.30	.10
❑	24 Mark Rypien MVP	.30	.10
❑	25 Troy Aikman MVP	.75	.30
❑	26 Emmitt Smith MVP	1.25	.50
❑	27 Steve Young MVP	.75	.30
❑	28 Larry Brown MVP	.30	.10
❑	29 Desmond Howard MVP	.50	.20
❑	30 Terrell Davis MVP	.75	.30
❑	31 Y.A. Tittle	.75	.30
❑	32 Paul Hornung	.50	.20
❑	33 Gale Sayers	.50	.20
❑	34 Garo Yepremian	.30	.10
❑	35 Bert Jones	.30	.10
❑	36 Joe Washington	.30	.10
❑	37 Joe Theismann	.30	.10
❑	38 Roger Craig	.30	.10
❑	39 Mike Singletary	.30	.10
❑	40 Bobby Bell	.30	.10
❑	41 Ken Houston	.30	.10
❑	42 Lenny Moore	.30	.10
❑	43 Mark Moseley	.30	.10
❑	44 Chuck Bednarik	.30	.10
❑	45 Ted Hendricks	.30	.10
❑	46 Steve Largent	.75	.30
❑	47 Bob Lilly	.30	.10
❑	48 Don Maynard	.30	.10
❑	49 John Mackey	.30	.10
❑	50 Anthony Munoz	.30	.10
❑	51 Bobby Mitchell	.30	.10
❑	52 Jim Brown	.75	.30
❑	53 Otto Graham	.50	.20
❑	54 Earl Morrall	.30	.10
❑	55 Danny White	.30	.10
❑	56 Karim Abdul-Jabbar	.50	.20
❑	57 Charlie Garner	.50	.20
❑	58 Jeff Blake	.50	.20
❑	59 Reggie White	.75	.30
❑	60 Derrick Thomas	.75	.30
❑	61 Duce Staley	.75	.30
❑	62 Tim Brown	.75	.30
❑	63 Elvis Grbac	.50	.20
❑	64 Tony Banks	.50	.20
❑	65 Rob Johnson	.50	.20
❑	66 Danny Kanell	.30	.10
❑	67 Marshall Faulk	1.00	.40
❑	68 Warrick Dunn	.75	.30
❑	69 Dan Marino	3.00	1.25
❑	70 Jimmy Smith	.50	.20
❑	71 John Elway	3.00	1.25
❑	72 Charles Way	.30	.10
❑	73 Ricky Watters	.50	.20
❑	74 Terry Glenn	.75	.30
❑	75 Bobby Hoying	.50	.20
❑	76 Curtis Martin	.75	.30
❑	77 Trent Dilfer	.50	.20
❑	78 Emmitt Smith	2.50	1.00
❑	79 Irving Fryar	.50	.20
❑	80 Troy Aikman	1.50	.60
❑	81 Barry Sanders	2.50	1.00

❑ 82 Brett Favre	3.00	1.25
❑ 83 Robert Smith	.75	.30
❑ 84 Dorsey Levens	.75	.30
❑ 85 Cris Carter	.75	.30
❑ 86 Jeff George	.50	.20
❑ 87 Jerome Bettis	.75	.30
❑ 88 Warren Moon	.75	.30
❑ 89 Steve Young	1.00	.40
❑ 90 Fred Lane	.30	.10
❑ 91 Jerry Rice	1.50	.60
❑ 92 Natrone Means	.50	.20
❑ 93 Mike Alstott	.75	.30
❑ 94 Kordell Stewart	.50	.20
❑ 95 Jake Plummer	.50	.20
❑ 96 Jamal Anderson	.75	.30
❑ 97 Corey Dillon	1.00	.40
❑ 98 Deion Sanders	.75	.30
❑ 99 Mark Brunell	.75	.30
❑ 100 Garrison Hearst	.50	.20
❑ 101 Andre Rison	.50	.20
❑ 102 Antowain Smith	.75	.30
❑ 103 Drew Bledsoe	1.25	.50
❑ 104 Eddie George	.75	.30
❑ 105 Keyshawn Johnson	.75	.30
❑ 106 Isaac Bruce	.75	.30
❑ 107 Rob Moore	.50	.20
❑ 108 Steve McNair	.75	.30
❑ 109 Terrell Davis	.75	.30
❑ 110 Carl Pickens	.50	.20
❑ 111 Wayne Chrebet	.50	.20
❑ 112 Kerry Collins	.50	.20
❑ 113 Eric Metcalf	.30	.10
❑ 114 Joey Galloway	.50	.20
❑ 115 Shannon Sharpe	.50	.20
❑ 116 Robert Brooks	.50	.20
❑ 117 Glenn Foley	.50	.20
❑ 118 Yancey Thigpen	.30	.10
❑ 119 Frank Sanders	.50	.20
❑ 120 Herman Moore	.50	.20
❑ 121 Antonio Freeman	.75	.30
❑ 122 Michael Irvin	.50	.20
❑ 123 Brad Johnson	.75	.30
❑ 124 James Stewart	.50	.20
❑ 125 Jim Harbaugh	.50	.20
❑ 126 Peyton Manning FF	8.00	3.00
❑ 127 Ryan Leaf FF	1.00	.40
❑ 128 Curtis Enis FF	.60	.25
❑ 129 Fred Taylor FF	2.00	.75
❑ 130 Randy Moss FF	6.00	2.50
❑ 131 John Avery FF	.60	.25
❑ 132 Charles Woodson FF	2.00	.75
❑ 133 Robert Edwards FF	.60	.25
❑ 134 Charlie Batch FF	2.00	.75
❑ 135 Brian Griese FF	2.00	.75
❑ 136 Skip Hicks FF	.60	.25
❑ 137 Jacquez Green FF	.60	.25
❑ 138 Robert Holcombe FF	.60	.25
❑ 139 Kevin Dyson FF	2.00	.75
❑ 140 Rodney Williams FF	.60	.25
❑ 141 Ahman Green FF	2.00	.75
❑ 142 Tavian Banks FF	1.00	.40
❑ 143 Donald Hayes FF	1.00	.40
❑ 144 Tony Simmons FF	1.00	.40
❑ 145 Pat Johnson FF	1.00	.40
❑ 146 Marcus Nash FF	.60	.25
❑ 147 Germane Crowell FF	.60	.25
❑ 148 R.W. McQuarters FF	.60	.25
❑ 149 Jonathan Quinn FF	2.00	.75
❑ 150 Andre Wadsworth FF	.60	.25
❑ P35 Gale Sayers Promo	3.00	1.25

1996 SPx

❑ COMPLETE SET (50)	25.00	10.00
❑ 1 Frank Sanders	1.00	.40
❑ 2 Terance Mathis	.50	.20
❑ 3 Todd Collins	1.00	.40
❑ 4 Kerry Collins	2.00	.75
❑ 5 Carl Pickens	1.00	.40
❑ 6 Darnay Scott	1.00	.40
❑ 7 Ki-Jana Carter	1.00	.40
❑ 8 Eric Zeier	.50	.20
❑ 9 Andre Rison	1.00	.40
❑ 10 Sherman Williams	.50	.20
❑ 11 Troy Aikman	4.00	1.50
❑ 12 Michael Irvin	2.00	.75
❑ 13 Emmitt Smith	6.00	2.50
❑ 14 Shannon Sharpe	1.00	.40
❑ 15 John Elway	8.00	3.00
❑ 16 Barry Sanders	6.00	2.50
❑ 17 Brett Favre	8.00	3.00
❑ 18 Rodney Thomas	.50	.20
❑ 19 Marshall Faulk	2.50	1.00
❑ 20 James O.Stewart	1.00	.40
❑ 21 Greg Hill	1.00	.40
❑ 22 Tamarick Vanover	1.00	.40
❑ 23 Dan Marino	8.00	3.00
❑ 24 Cris Carter	2.00	.75
❑ 25 Warren Moon	1.00	.40
❑ 26 Drew Bledsoe	2.50	1.00
❑ 27 Ben Coates	1.00	.40
❑ 28 Curtis Martin	3.00	1.25
❑ 29 Mario Bates	1.00	.40
❑ 30 Tyrone Wheatley	1.00	.40
❑ 31 Rodney Hampton	1.00	.40
❑ 32 Kyle Brady	.50	.20
❑ 33 Jeff Hostetler	.50	.20
❑ 34 Napoleon Kaufman	2.00	.75
❑ 35 Tim Brown	2.00	.75
❑ 36 Charles Johnson	.50	.20
❑ 37 Rod Woodson	1.00	.40
❑ 38 Natrone Means	1.00	.40
❑ 39 J.J. Stokes	2.00	.75
❑ 40 Steve Young	4.00	1.50
❑ 41 Brent Jones	.50	.20
❑ 42 Jerry Rice	4.00	1.50
❑ 43 Joe Montana	8.00	3.00
❑ 44 Rick Mirer	1.00	.40
❑ 45 Chris Warren	1.00	.40
❑ 46 Joey Galloway	2.00	.75
❑ 47 Isaac Bruce	2.00	.75
❑ 48 Jerome Bettis	2.00	.75
❑ 49 Errict Rhett	1.00	.40
❑ 50 Michael Westbrook	2.00	.75
❑ UDT13 Dan Marino RB	15.00	6.00
❑ UDT13 D.Marino RB AU	120.00	60.00
❑ UDT19 Joe Montana Tribute	15.00	6.00
❑ UDT19 J.Montana TRI AU	100.00	40.00
❑ P1 Dan Marino Promo	5.00	2.00
❑ P2 Joe Montana Promo	5.00	2.00

1997 SPx

❑ COMPLETE SET (50)	30.00	12.50
❑ 1 Jerry Rice	4.00	1.50
❑ 2 Steve Young	2.50	1.00
❑ 3 Karim Abdul-Jabbar	2.00	.75
❑ 4 Dan Marino	8.00	3.00
❑ 5 Bobby Engram	1.25	.50
❑ 6 Rashaan Salaam	.75	.30
❑ 7 Marvin Harrison	2.00	.75
❑ 8 Jim Harbaugh	1.25	.50
❑ 9 Marshall Faulk	2.50	1.00
❑ 10 Eric Moulds	2.00	.75
❑ 11 Thurman Thomas	2.00	.75
❑ 12 Tamarick Vanover	1.25	.50
❑ 13 Steve Bono	1.25	.50
❑ 14 Warren Moon	2.00	.75
❑ 15 Cris Carter	2.00	.75
❑ 16 Carl Pickens	1.25	.50
❑ 17 Ki-Jana Carter	.75	.30
❑ 18 Jeff Blake	1.25	.50
❑ 19 Tim Biakabutuka	1.25	.50
❑ 20 Kerry Collins	2.00	.75
❑ 21 Leeland McElroy	.75	.30
❑ 22 Simeon Rice	1.25	.50
❑ 23 John Elway	8.00	3.00
❑ 24 Terrell Davis	2.50	1.00
❑ 25 Jeff Lewis	.75	.30
❑ 26 Terry Glenn	2.00	.75
❑ 27 Curtis Martin	2.50	1.00
❑ 28 Drew Bledsoe	2.50	1.00
❑ 29 Lawrence Phillips	.75	.30
❑ 30 Isaac Bruce	2.00	.75
❑ 31 Eddie Kennison	1.25	.50
❑ 32 Keyshawn Johnson	2.00	.75
❑ 33 Stepfret Williams	.75	.30
❑ 34 Emmitt Smith	6.00	2.50
❑ 35 Troy Aikman	4.00	1.50
❑ 36 Deion Sanders	2.00	.75
❑ 37 Joey Galloway	1.25	.50
❑ 38 Rick Mirer	.75	.30
❑ 39 Rickey Dudley	1.25	.50
❑ 40 Jeff Hostetler	.75	.30
❑ 41 Junior Seau	2.00	.75
❑ 42 Derrick Mayes	1.25	.50
❑ 43 Brett Favre	8.00	3.00
❑ 44 Edgar Bennett	1.25	.50
❑ 45 Barry Sanders	6.00	2.50
❑ 46 Herman Moore	1.25	.50
❑ 47 Kordell Stewart	2.00	.75
❑ 48 Jerome Bettis	2.00	.75
❑ 49 Eddie George	2.00	.75
❑ 50 Steve McNair	2.50	1.00
❑ P80 Jerry Rice Promo	3.00	1.25

1998 SPx

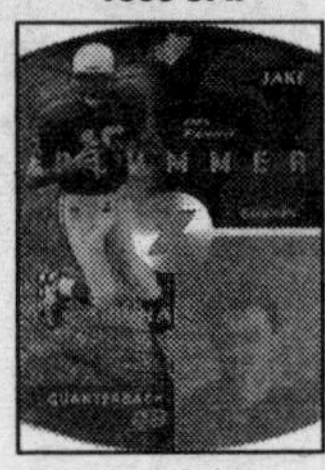

❑ COMPLETE SET (50)	80.00	30.00
❑ 1 Jake Plummer	2.00	.75
❑ 2 Byron Hanspard	.75	.30
❑ 3 Vinny Testaverde	1.25	.50
❑ 4 Antowain Smith	2.00	.75
❑ 5 Kerry Collins	1.25	.50
❑ 6 Rae Carruth	.75	.30
❑ 7 Darnell Autry	.75	.30
❑ 8 Rick Mirer	.75	.30
❑ 9 Jeff Blake	1.25	.50
❑ 10 Carl Pickens	1.25	.50
❑ 11 Troy Aikman	4.00	1.50
❑ 12 Emmitt Smith	6.00	3.00
❑ 13 Deion Sanders	2.00	.75
❑ 14 John Elway	8.00	3.00
❑ 15 Terrell Davis	2.00	.75
❑ 16 Herman Moore	1.25	.50
❑ 17 Barry Sanders	6.00	2.50
❑ 18 Brett Favre	8.00	3.00
❑ 19 Reggie White	2.00	.75
❑ 20 Marshall Faulk	2.50	1.00
❑ 21 Mark Brunell	2.00	.75
❑ 22 Elvis Grbac	1.25	.50
❑ 23 Marcus Allen	2.00	.75
❑ 24 Karim Abdul-Jabbar	2.00	.75
❑ 25 Dan Marino	8.00	3.00
❑ 26 Cris Carter	2.00	.75
❑ 27 Drew Bledsoe	3.00	1.25
❑ 28 Curtis Martin	2.00	.75
❑ 29 Heath Shuler	.75	.30
❑ 30 Ike Hilliard	1.25	.50
❑ 31 Keyshawn Johnson	2.00	.75
❑ 32 Jeff George	1.25	.50
❑ 33 Napoleon Kaufman	2.00	.75
❑ 34 Darrell Russell	.75	.30
❑ 35 Ricky Watters	1.25	.50
❑ 36 Kordell Stewart	2.00	.75
❑ 37 Jerome Bettis	2.00	.75
❑ 38 Junior Seau	2.00	.75
❑ 39 Steve Young	2.50	1.00
❑ 40 Jerry Rice	4.00	2.00
❑ 41 Joey Galloway	1.25	.50
❑ 42 Chris Warren	1.25	.50
❑ 43 Orlando Pace	.75	.30
❑ 44 Isaac Bruce	2.00	.75
❑ 45 Tony Banks	1.25	.50
❑ 46 Trent Dilfer	2.00	.75
❑ 47 Warrick Dunn	2.00	.75
❑ 48 Steve McNair	2.00	.75
❑ 49 Eddie George	2.00	.75
❑ 50 Terry Allen	2.00	.75

1998 SPx Finite

❑ COMP.SERIES 1 (190)	750.00	400.00
❑ COMP.SERIES 2 (180)	750.00	400.00
❑ 1 Jake Plummer	2.50	1.00
❑ 2 Eric Swann	1.00	.40
❑ 3 Rob Moore	1.50	.60
❑ 4 Jamal Anderson	2.50	1.00
❑ 5 Byron Hanspard	1.00	.40
❑ 6 Cornelius Bennett	1.00	.40
❑ 7 Michael Jackson	1.00	.40
❑ 8 Peter Boulware	1.00	.40
❑ 9 Jermaine Lewis	1.50	.60
❑ 10 Antowain Smith	2.50	1.00
❑ 11 Bruce Smith	1.50	.60
❑ 12 Bryce Paup	1.00	.40
❑ 13 Rae Carruth	1.00	.40
❑ 14 Michael Bates	1.00	.40
❑ 15 Fred Lane	1.00	.40
❑ 16 Darnell Autry	1.50	.60
❑ 17 Curtis Conway	1.50	.60
❑ 18 Erik Kramer	1.00	.40
❑ 19 Corey Dillon	2.50	1.00
❑ 20 Darnay Scott	1.50	.60
❑ 21 Reinard Wilson	1.00	.40
❑ 22 Troy Aikman	5.00	2.00
❑ 23 David LaFleur	1.00	.40
❑ 24 Emmitt Smith	8.00	3.00
❑ 25 John Elway	10.00	4.00
❑ 26 John Mobley	1.00	.40
❑ 27 Terrell Davis	2.50	1.00
❑ 28 Rod Smith	1.50	.60
❑ 29 Bryant Westbrook	1.00	.40
❑ 30 Scott Mitchell	1.50	.60
❑ 31 Barry Sanders	8.00	3.00
❑ 32 Dorsey Levens	2.50	1.00
❑ 33 Antonio Freeman	2.50	1.00
❑ 34 Reggie White	2.50	1.00
❑ 35 Marshall Faulk	3.00	1.25
❑ 36 Marvin Harrison	2.50	1.00
❑ 37 Ken Dilger	1.00	.40
❑ 38 Mark Brunell	2.50	1.00
❑ 39 Keenan McCardell	1.50	.60
❑ 40 Renaldo Wynn	1.00	.40
❑ 41 Marcus Allen	2.50	1.00
❑ 42 Elvis Grbac	1.50	.60
❑ 43 Andre Rison	1.50	.60
❑ 44 Yatil Green	1.00	.40
❑ 45 Zach Thomas	2.50	1.00
❑ 46 Karim Abdul-Jabbar	2.50	1.00
❑ 47 John Randle	1.50	.60
❑ 48 Brad Johnson	2.50	1.00
❑ 49 Jake Reed	1.50	.60
❑ 50 Danny Wuerffel	1.50	.60
❑ 51 Andre Hastings	1.00	.40
❑ 52 Drew Bledsoe	4.00	1.50
❑ 53 Terry Glenn	2.50	1.00
❑ 54 Ty Law	1.50	.60
❑ 55 Danny Kanell	1.50	.60
❑ 56 Tiki Barber	2.50	1.00
❑ 57 Jessie Armstead	1.00	.40
❑ 58 Glenn Foley	1.50	.60
❑ 59 James Farrior	1.00	.40
❑ 60 Wayne Chrebet	2.50	1.00
❑ 61 Tim Brown	2.50	1.00
❑ 62 Napoleon Kaufman	2.50	1.00
❑ 63 Darrell Russell	1.00	.40
❑ 64 Bobby Hoying	1.50	.60
❑ 65 Irving Fryar	1.50	.60
❑ 66 Charlie Garner	1.50	.60
❑ 67 Will Blackwell	1.00	.40
❑ 68 Kordell Stewart	2.50	1.00
❑ 69 Levon Kirkland	1.00	.40
❑ 70 Tony Banks	1.50	.60
❑ 71 Ryan McNeil	1.00	.40
❑ 72 Isaac Bruce	2.50	1.00
❑ 73 Tony Martin	1.50	.60
❑ 74 Junior Seau	2.50	1.00
❑ 75 Natrone Means	1.50	.60
❑ 76 Jerry Rice	5.00	2.00
❑ 77 Garrison Hearst	2.50	1.00
❑ 78 Terrell Owens	2.50	1.00
❑ 79 Warren Moon	2.50	1.00
❑ 80 Joey Galloway	1.50	.60
❑ 81 Chad Brown	1.00	.40
❑ 82 Warrick Dunn	2.50	1.00
❑ 83 Mike Alstott	2.50	1.00
❑ 84 Hardy Nickerson	1.00	.40
❑ 85 Steve McNair	2.50	1.00
❑ 86 Chris Sanders	1.00	.40
❑ 87 Darryll Lewis	1.00	.40
❑ 88 Gus Frerotte	1.00	.40
❑ 89 Terry Allen	2.50	1.00
❑ 90 Chris Dishman	1.00	.40
❑ 91 Kordell Stewart PM	3.00	1.25
❑ 92 Jerry Rice PM	6.00	2.50
❑ 93 Michael Irvin PM	3.00	1.25
❑ 94 Brett Favre PM	12.00	5.00
❑ 95 Jeff George PM	2.00	.75
❑ 96 Joey Galloway PM	2.00	.75
❑ 97 John Elway PM	12.00	5.00
❑ 98 Troy Aikman PM	6.00	2.50
❑ 99 Steve Young PM	4.00	1.50
❑ 100 Andre Rison PM	2.00	.75
❑ 101 Ben Coates PM	2.00	.75
❑ 102 Robert Brooks PM	2.00	.75
❑ 103 Dan Marino PM	12.00	5.00
❑ 104 Isaac Bruce PM	3.00	1.25
❑ 105 Junior Seau PM	3.00	1.25
❑ 106 Jake Plummer PM	3.00	1.25
❑ 107 Curtis Conway PM	2.00	.75
❑ 108 Jeff Blake PM	2.00	.75
❑ 109 Rod Smith PM	2.00	.75
❑ 110 Barry Sanders PM	10.00	4.00
❑ 111 Deion Sanders PM	3.00	1.25
❑ 112 Drew Bledsoe PM	5.00	2.00
❑ 113 Emmitt Smith PM	10.00	4.00
❑ 114 Herman Moore PM	2.00	.75
❑ 115 Dorsey Levens PM	3.00	1.25
❑ 116 Jimmy Smith PM	2.00	.75
❑ 117 Tony Martin PM	1.25	.50
❑ 118 Carl Pickens PM	2.00	.75
❑ 119 Keyshawn Johnson PM	3.00	1.25
❑ 120 Cris Carter PM	3.00	1.25
❑ 121 Warrick Dunn YM	5.00	2.00
❑ 122 Marshall Faulk YM	6.00	2.50
❑ 123 Trent Dilfer YM	5.00	2.00
❑ 124 Napoleon Kaufman YM	5.00	2.00
❑ 125 Corey Dillon YM	5.00	2.00
❑ 126 Darrell Russell YM	2.00	.75
❑ 127 Danny Kanell YM	3.00	1.25
❑ 128 Reidel Anthony YM	3.00	1.25
❑ 129 Steve McNair YM	5.00	2.00
❑ 130 Ike Hilliard YM	3.00	1.25
❑ 131 Tony Banks YM	3.00	1.25
❑ 132 Yatil Green YM	2.00	.75
❑ 133 J.J. Stokes YM	3.00	1.25
❑ 134 Fred Lane YM	2.00	.75
❑ 135 Bryant Westbrook YM	2.00	.75
❑ 136 Jake Plummer YM	5.00	2.00
❑ 137 Byron Hanspard YM	2.00	.75
❑ 138 Rae Carruth YM	2.00	.75
❑ 139 Keyshawn Johnson YM	5.00	2.00
❑ 140 Jim Druckenmiller YM	2.00	.75
❑ 141 Amani Toomer YM	3.00	1.25
❑ 142 Troy Davis YM	2.00	.75
❑ 143 Antowain Smith YM	5.00	2.00
❑ 144 Shawn Springs YM	2.00	.75
❑ 145 Rickey Dudley YM	2.00	.75
❑ 146 Terry Glenn YM	5.00	2.00
❑ 147 Johnnie Morton YM	3.00	1.25
❑ 148 David LaFleur YM	2.00	.75
❑ 149 Eddie Kennison YM	3.00	1.25
❑ 150 Bobby Hoying YM	3.00	1.25
❑ 151 Junior Seau PE	6.00	2.50
❑ 152 Shannon Sharpe PE	4.00	1.50
❑ 153 Bruce Smith PE	4.00	1.50
❑ 154 Brett Favre PE	20.00	7.50
❑ 155 Emmitt Smith PE	15.00	6.00
❑ 156 Keenan McCardell PE	2.50	1.00
❑ 157 Kordell Stewart PE	6.00	2.50
❑ 158 Troy Aikman PE	10.00	4.00
❑ 159 Steve Young PE	6.00	2.50
❑ 160 Tim Brown PE	6.00	2.50
❑ 161 Eddie George PE	6.00	2.50
❑ 162 Herman Moore PE	4.00	1.50
❑ 163 Dan Marino PE	20.00	7.50

❑ 164 Dorsey Levens PE 6.00 2.50
❑ 165 Jerry Rice PE 10.00 4.00
❑ 166 Warren Sapp PE 4.00 1.50
❑ 167 Robert Smith PE 6.00 2.50
❑ 168 Mark Brunell PE 6.00 2.50
❑ 169 Terrell Davis PE 6.00 2.50
❑ 170 Jerome Bettis PE 6.00 2.50
❑ 171 Dan Marino HG 30.00 12.50
❑ 172 Barry Sanders HG 25.00 10.00
❑ 173 Marcus Allen HG 8.00 3.00
❑ 174 Brett Favre HG 30.00 12.50
❑ 175 Warrick Dunn HG 8.00 3.00
❑ 176 Eddie George HG 8.00 3.00
❑ 177 John Elway HG 30.00 12.50
❑ 178 Troy Aikman HG 15.00 6.00
❑ 179 Cris Carter HG 8.00 3.00
❑ 180 Terrell Davis HG 8.00 3.00
❑ 181 Peyton Manning RC 300.00 150.00
❑ 182 Ryan Leaf RC 25.00 12.50
❑ 183 Andre Wadsworth RC 20.00 10.00
❑ 184 Charles Woodson RC 30.00 15.00
❑ 185 Curtis Enis RC 15.00 7.50
❑ 186 Grant Wistrom RC 20.00 10.00
❑ 187 Fred Taylor RC 40.00 15.00
❑ 188 Takeo Spikes RC 25.00 12.50
❑ 189 Kevin Dyson RC 25.00 12.50
❑ 190 Robert Edwards RC 20.00 10.00
❑ 191 Adrian Murrell 1.00 .40
❑ 192 Simeon Rice 1.00 .40
❑ 193 Frank Sanders 1.00 .40
❑ 194 Chris Chandler 1.00 .40
❑ 195 Terance Mathis 1.00 .40
❑ 196 Keith Brooking RC 1.50 .60
❑ 197 Jim Harbaugh 1.00 .40
❑ 198 Errict Rhett 1.00 .40
❑ 199 Pat Johnson RC 2.50 1.00
❑ 200 Rob Johnson 1.00 .40
❑ 201 Andre Reed 1.00 .40
❑ 202 Thurman Thomas 1.50 .60
❑ 203 Kerry Collins 1.00 .40
❑ 204 William Floyd .60 .25
❑ 205 Sean Gilbert .60 .25
❑ 206 Bobby Engram 1.00 .40
❑ 207 Edgar Bennett 1.00 .40
❑ 208 Walt Harris 1.00 .40
❑ 209 Carl Pickens 1.00 .40
❑ 210 Neil O'Donnell 1.00 .40
❑ 211 Tony McGee .60 .25
❑ 212 Deion Sanders 1.50 .60
❑ 213 Michael Irvin 1.50 .60
❑ 214 Greg Ellis RC 1.25 .50
❑ 215 Shannon Sharpe 1.00 .40
❑ 216 Neil Smith 1.00 .40
❑ 217 Marcus Nash RC 1.25 .50
❑ 218 Brian Griese RC 30.00 12.50
❑ 219 Johnnie Morton 1.00 .40
❑ 220 Herman Moore 1.50 .60
❑ 221 Charlie Batch RC 20.00 7.50
❑ 222 Robert Brooks 1.00 .40
❑ 223 Mark Chmura 1.00 .40
❑ 224 Brett Favre 6.00 2.50
❑ 225 Jerome Pathon RC 5.00 2.00
❑ 226 Zack Crockett .60 .25
❑ 227 Dan Footman .60 .25
❑ 228 Jimmy Smith 1.00 .40
❑ 229 Bryce Paup .60 .25
❑ 230 James Stewart 1.00 .40
❑ 231 Derrick Thomas 1.50 .60
❑ 232 Derrick Alexander 1.00 .40
❑ 233 Tony Gonzalez 1.50 .60
❑ 234 Dan Marino 6.00 2.50
❑ 235 O.J. McDuffie 1.00 .40
❑ 236 Troy Drayton .60 .25
❑ 237 Cris Carter 1.50 .60
❑ 238 Robert Smith 1.50 .60
❑ 239 Randy Moss RC 80.00 30.00
❑ 240 Lamar Smith 1.00 .40
❑ 241 Sean Dawkins .60 .25
❑ 242 Alex Molden .60 .25
❑ 243 Ben Coates 1.00 .40
❑ 244 Ted Johnson .60 .25
❑ 245 Sedrick Shaw .60 .25
❑ 246 Ike Hilliard 1.00 .40
❑ 247 Jason Sehorn 1.00 .40
❑ 248 Michael Strahan 1.00 .40
❑ 249 Keyshawn Johnson 1.50 .60
❑ 250 Curtis Martin 1.50 .60
❑ 251 Jeff George 1.00 .40
❑ 252 Rickey Dudley .60 .25
❑ 253 James Jett 1.00 .40
❑ 254 Bobby Taylor 1.00 .40
❑ 255 Rodney Peete 1.00 .40
❑ 256 William Thomas 1.00 .40
❑ 257 Jerome Bettis 1.50 .60
❑ 258 Charles Johnson .60 .25
❑ 259 Chris Fuamatu-Ma'afala RC 2.50 1.00
❑ 260 Eddie Kennison 1.00 .40
❑ 261 Az-Zahir Hakim RC 5.00 2.00
❑ 262 Robert Holcombe RC 2.50 1.00
❑ 263 Bryan Still .60 .25
❑ 264 Mikhael Ricks RC 2.50 1.00
❑ 265 Charlie Jones .60 .25
❑ 266 J.J. Stokes 1.00 .40
❑ 267 Marc Edwards .60 .25
❑ 268 Steve Young 2.00 .75
❑ 269 Ricky Watters 1.00 .40
❑ 270 Cortez Kennedy .60 .25
❑ 271 Shawn Springs .60 .25
❑ 272 Trent Dilfer 1.50 .60
❑ 273 Warren Sapp 1.00 .40
❑ 274 Reidel Anthony 1.00 .40
❑ 275 Yancey Thigpen .60 .25
❑ 276 Chris Sanders .60 .25
❑ 277 Eddie George 1.50 .60
❑ 278 Leslie Shepherd .60 .25
❑ 279 Skip Hicks RC 2.50 1.00
❑ 280 Dana Stubblefield .60 .25
❑ 281 John Elway ET 8.00 3.00
❑ 282 Brett Favre ET 8.00 3.00
❑ 283 Junior Seau ET 2.00 .75
❑ 284 Barry Sanders ET 6.00 2.50
❑ 285 Jerry Rice ET 4.00 1.50
❑ 286 Antonio Freeman ET 2.00 .75
❑ 287 Peyton Manning ET 30.00 12.50
❑ 288 Warrick Dunn ET 2.00 .75
❑ 289 Steve Young ET 2.50 1.00
❑ 290 Dan Marino ET 8.00 3.00
❑ 291 Jerome Bettis ET 2.00 .75
❑ 292 Ryan Leaf ET 2.00 .75
❑ 293 Deion Sanders ET 2.00 .75
❑ 294 Eddie George ET 2.00 .75
❑ 295 Joey Galloway ET 1.25 .50
❑ 296 Troy Aikman ET 4.00 1.50
❑ 297 Andre Wadsworth ET 1.25 .50
❑ 298 Terrell Davis ET 2.00 .75
❑ 299 Steve McNair ET 2.00 .75
❑ 300 Jake Plummer ET 2.00 .75
❑ 301 Emmitt Smith ET 6.00 2.50
❑ 302 Isaac Bruce ET 2.00 .75
❑ 303 Kordell Stewart ET 2.00 .75
❑ 304 Dorsey Levens ET 2.00 .75
❑ 305 Antowain Smith ET 2.00 .75
❑ 306 Drew Bledsoe ET 3.00 1.25
❑ 307 Marshall Faulk ET 2.50 1.00
❑ 308 Herman Moore ET 1.25 .50
❑ 309 Mark Brunell ET 2.00 .75
❑ 310 Charles Woodson ET 5.00 2.00
❑ 311 Peyton Manning NS 30.00 12.50
❑ 312 Curtis Enis NS 1.50 .60
❑ 313 Terry Fair NS RC 2.50 1.00
❑ 314 Andre Wadsworth NS 2.50 1.00
❑ 315 Anthony Simmons NS RC 2.50 1.00
❑ 316 Jacquez Green NS RC 8.00 3.00
❑ 317 Takeo Spikes NS 5.00 2.00
❑ 318 Vonnie Holliday NS RC 8.00 3.00
❑ 319 Kyle Turley NS RC 5.00 2.00
❑ 320 Keith Brooking NS 5.00 2.00
❑ 321 Randy Moss NS 20.00 7.50
❑ 322 Shaun Williams NS RC 2.50 1.00
❑ 323 Greg Ellis NS 1.50 .60
❑ 324 Mikhael Ricks NS 2.50 1.00
❑ 325 Charles Woodson NS 8.00 3.00
❑ 326 Corey Chavous NS RC 5.00 2.00
❑ 327 Stephen Alexander NS RC 8.00 3.00
❑ 328 Marcus Nash NS 1.50 .60
❑ 329 Tra Thomas NS RC 2.50 1.00
❑ 330 Duane Starks NS RC 5.00 2.00
❑ 331 John Avery NS RC 2.50 1.00
❑ 332 Kevin Dyson NS 5.00 2.00
❑ 333 Fred Taylor NS 10.00 4.00
❑ 334 Grant Wistrom NS 2.50 1.00
❑ 335 Ryan Leaf NS 5.00 2.00
❑ 336 Robert Edwards NS 2.50 1.00
❑ 337 Jason Peter NS RC 2.50 1.00
❑ 338 Brian Griese NS 12.00 5.00
❑ 339 Charlie Batch NS 5.00 2.00
❑ 340 Pat Johnson NS 2.50 1.00
❑ 341 John Elway SS 15.00 6.00
❑ 342 Curtis Enis SS 1.50 .60
❑ 343 Antonio Freeman SS 4.00 1.50
❑ 344 Mark Brunell SS 4.00 1.50
❑ 345 Robert Edwards SS 2.50 1.00
❑ 346 Ryan Leaf SS 4.00 1.50
❑ 347 Steve Young SS 5.00 2.00
❑ 348 Jerome Bettis SS 4.00 1.50
❑ 349 Antowain Smith SS 4.00 1.50
❑ 350 Tim Brown SS 4.00 1.50
❑ 351 Peyton Manning SS 30.00 12.50
❑ 352 Troy Aikman SS 8.00 3.00
❑ 353 Natrone Means SS 2.50 1.00
❑ 354 Dan Marino SS 15.00 6.00
❑ 355 Junior Seau SS 1.50 .60
❑ 356 Brad Johnson SS 4.00 1.50
❑ 357 Jerry Rice SS 8.00 3.00
❑ 358 Drew Bledsoe SS 6.00 2.50
❑ 359 Fred Taylor SS 8.00 3.00
❑ 360 Emmitt Smith SS 12.00 5.00
❑ 361 Terrell Davis UV 8.00 3.00
❑ 362 Kordell Stewart UV 6.00 2.50
❑ 363 Barry Sanders UV 20.00 7.50
❑ 364 Jake Plummer UV 6.00 2.50
❑ 365 Brett Favre UV 25.00 10.00
❑ 366 Curtis Enis UV 6.00 2.50
❑ 367 Eddie George UV 6.00 2.50
❑ 368 Napoleon Kaufman UV 6.00 2.50
❑ 369 Randy Moss UV 40.00 15.00
❑ 370 Warrick Dunn UV 6.00 2.50
❑ S8 Troy Aikman Sample 1.00 .40
❑ S234 Dan Marino Sample 2.00 .75

1999 SPx

❑ COMPLETE SET (135) 2000.00 1000.00
❑ COMP.SET w/o SP's (90) 25.00 12.50
❑ *HAND NUMBERED RCs: .5X TO .8X

❑ 1 Jake Plummer 1.00 .40
❑ 2 Adrian Murrell 1.00 .40
❑ 3 Frank Sanders 1.00 .40

❑ 4	Jamal Anderson	1.50	.60
❑ 5	Chris Chandler	1.00	.40
❑ 6	Terance Mathis	1.00	.40
❑ 7	Tony Banks	1.00	.40
❑ 8	Priest Holmes	2.50	1.00
❑ 9	Jermaine Lewis	1.00	.40
❑ 10	Antowain Smith	1.50	.60
❑ 11	Doug Flutie	1.50	.60
❑ 12	Eric Moulds	1.50	.60
❑ 13	Tim Biakabutuka	1.00	.40
❑ 14	Steve Beuerlein	1.00	.40
❑ 15	Muhsin Muhammad	1.00	.40
❑ 16	Bobby Engram	1.00	.40
❑ 17	Curtis Conway	1.00	.40
❑ 18	Curtis Enis	.60	.25
❑ 19	Corey Dillon	1.50	.60
❑ 20	Jeff Blake	1.00	.40
❑ 21	Carl Pickens	1.00	.40
❑ 22	Ty Detmer	1.00	.40
❑ 23	Terry Kirby	.60	.25
❑ 24	Leslie Shepherd	.60	.25
❑ 25	Troy Aikman	3.00	1.25
❑ 26	Emmitt Smith	3.00	1.25
❑ 27	Deion Sanders	1.50	.60
❑ 28	Terrell Davis	1.50	.60
❑ 29	Rod Smith	1.00	.40
❑ 30	Bubby Brister	1.00	.40
❑ 31	Barry Sanders	5.00	2.00
❑ 32	Herman Moore	1.00	.40
❑ 33	Charlie Batch	1.50	.60
❑ 34	Brett Favre	5.00	2.00
❑ 35	Antonio Freeman	1.50	.60
❑ 36	Dorsey Levens	1.50	.60
❑ 37	Peyton Manning	5.00	2.00
❑ 38	Marvin Harrison	1.50	.60
❑ 39	Jerome Pathon	.60	.25
❑ 40	Mark Brunell	1.50	.60
❑ 41	Jimmy Smith	1.00	.40
❑ 42	Fred Taylor	1.50	.60
❑ 43	Elvis Grbac	1.00	.40
❑ 44	Andre Rison	1.00	.40
❑ 45	Warren Moon	1.50	.60
❑ 46	Dan Marino	5.00	2.00
❑ 47	Karim Abdul-Jabbar	1.00	.40
❑ 48	O.J. McDuffie	1.00	.40
❑ 49	Randall Cunningham	1.50	.60
❑ 50	Robert Smith	1.50	.60
❑ 51	Randy Moss	4.00	1.50
❑ 52	Drew Bledsoe	2.00	.75
❑ 53	Terry Glenn	1.50	.60
❑ 54	Tony Simmons	.60	.25
❑ 55	Danny Wuerffel	.60	.25
❑ 56	Cam Cleeland	.60	.25
❑ 57	Kerry Collins	1.00	.40
❑ 58	Gary Brown	.60	.25
❑ 59	Ike Hilliard	.60	.25
❑ 60	Vinny Testaverde	1.00	.40
❑ 61	Curtis Martin	1.50	.60
❑ 62	Keyshawn Johnson	1.50	.60
❑ 63	Rich Gannon	1.50	.60
❑ 64	Napoleon Kaufman	1.50	.60
❑ 65	Tim Brown	1.50	.60
❑ 66	Duce Staley	1.50	.60
❑ 67	Doug Pederson	.60	.25
❑ 68	Charles Johnson	.60	.25
❑ 69	Kordell Stewart	1.00	.40
❑ 70	Jerome Bettis	1.50	.60
❑ 71	Trent Green	1.50	.60
❑ 72	Marshall Faulk	2.00	.75
❑ 73	Ryan Leaf	1.50	.60
❑ 74	Natrone Means	1.00	.40
❑ 75	Jim Harbaugh	1.00	.40
❑ 76	Steve Young	2.00	.75
❑ 77	Garrison Hearst	1.00	.40
❑ 78	Jerry Rice	3.00	1.25
❑ 79	Terrell Owens	1.50	.60
❑ 80	Ricky Watters	1.00	.40
❑ 81	Joey Galloway	1.00	.40
❑ 82	Jon Kitna	1.50	.60
❑ 83	Warrick Dunn	1.50	.60
❑ 84	Trent Dilfer	1.00	.40
❑ 85	Mike Alstott	1.50	.60
❑ 86	Steve McNair	1.50	.60
❑ 87	Eddie George	1.50	.60
❑ 88	Yancey Thigpen	.60	.25
❑ 89	Skip Hicks	.60	.25
❑ 90	Michael Westbrook	1.00	.40
❑ 91	Amos Zereoue RC	15.00	6.00
❑ 92	Chris Claiborne AU RC	25.00	10.00
❑ 93	Scott Covington RC	15.00	6.00
❑ 94	Jeff Paulk RC	10.00	4.00
❑ 95	Brandon Stokley AU RC	40.00	15.00
❑ 96	Antoine Winfield RC	12.00	5.00
❑ 97	Reginald Kelly RC	10.00	4.00
❑ 98	Jermaine Fazande AU RC	15.00	6.00
❑ 99	Andy Katzenmoyer RC	12.00	5.00
❑ 100	Craig Yeast RC	12.00	5.00
❑ 101	Joe Montgomery RC	12.00	5.00
❑ 102	Darrin Chiaverini RC	12.00	5.00
❑ 103	Travis McGriff RC	10.00	4.00
❑ 104	Jevon Kearse RC	30.00	12.50
❑ 105	Joel Makovicka AU RC	15.00	6.00
❑ 106	Aaron Brooks RC	25.00	10.00
❑ 107	Chris McAlister RC	12.00	5.00
❑ 108	Jim Kleinsasser RC	15.00	6.00
❑ 109	Ebenezer Ekuban RC	12.00	5.00
❑ 110	Karsten Bailey RC	12.00	5.00
❑ 111	Sedrick Irvin AU RC	12.00	5.00
❑ 112	D'Wayne Bates AU RC	12.00	5.00
❑ 113	Joe Germaine AU RC	15.00	6.00
❑ 114	Cecil Collins AU RC	15.00	6.00
❑ 115	Mike Cloud RC	12.00	5.00
❑ 116	James Johnson RC	12.00	5.00
❑ 117	Champ Bailey AU RC	40.00	15.00
❑ 118	Rob Konrad RC	15.00	6.00
❑ 119	Peerless Price AU RC	30.00	12.50
❑ 120	Kevin Faulk AU RC	25.00	10.00
❑ 121	Dameane Douglas RC	10.00	4.00
❑ 122	Kevin Johnson AU RC	15.00	6.00
❑ 123	Troy Edwards AU RC	25.00	10.00
❑ 124	Edgerrin James AU RC	135.00	75.00
❑ 125	David Boston AU RC	25.00	10.00
❑ 126	Michael Bishop AU RC	25.00	10.00
❑ 127	Shaun King AU RC SP	80.00	30.00
❑ 127X	Shaun King EXCH	10.00	4.00
❑ 128	Brock Huard AU RC	15.00	6.00
❑ 129	Torry Holt AU RC	60.00	25.00
❑ 130	Cade McNown AU/500 RC	50.00	20.00
❑ 131	Tim Couch AU/500 RC	80.00	30.00
❑ 132	Donovan McNabb AU RC	150.00	75.00
❑ 132X	Donovan McNabb EXCH	5.00	2.00
❑ 133	Akili Smith AU/500 RC	50.00	20.00
❑ 134	D.Culpepper AU/500 RC	350.00	200.00
❑ 135	Ricky Williams AU/500 RC	120.00	60.00
❑ S8	Troy Aikman Sample	2.00	.75

2000 SPx

❑	COMP.SET w/o SP's (90)	20.00	7.50
❑ 1	Jake Plummer	.60	.25
❑ 2	David Boston	1.00	.40
❑ 3	Frank Sanders	.60	.25
❑ 4	Chris Chandler	.60	.25
❑ 5	Jamal Anderson	1.00	.40
❑ 6	Shawn Jefferson	.40	.15
❑ 7	Qadry Ismail	.60	.25
❑ 8	Tony Banks	.60	.25
❑ 9	Shannon Sharpe	.60	.25
❑ 10	Rob Johnson	.60	.25
❑ 11	Eric Moulds	1.00	.40
❑ 12	Muhsin Muhammad	.60	.25
❑ 13	Steve Beuerlein	.40	.15
❑ 14	Cade McNown	.40	.15
❑ 15	Marcus Robinson	1.00	.40
❑ 16	Akili Smith	.40	.15
❑ 17	Corey Dillon	1.00	.40
❑ 18	Darnay Scott	.60	.25
❑ 19	Tim Couch	.60	.25
❑ 20	Kevin Johnson	1.00	.40
❑ 21	Errict Rhett	.40	.15
❑ 22	Troy Aikman	2.00	.75
❑ 23	Emmitt Smith	2.00	.75
❑ 24	Joey Galloway	.60	.25
❑ 25	Terrell Davis	1.00	.40
❑ 26	Olandis Gary	1.00	.40
❑ 27	Brian Griese	1.00	.40
❑ 28	Charlie Batch	1.00	.40
❑ 29	Germane Crowell	.40	.15
❑ 30	James Stewart	.60	.25
❑ 31	Brett Favre	3.00	1.25
❑ 32	Antonio Freeman	1.00	.40
❑ 33	Dorsey Levens	.60	.25
❑ 34	Peyton Manning	2.50	1.00
❑ 35	Edgerrin James	1.50	.60
❑ 36	Marvin Harrison	1.00	.40
❑ 37	Mark Brunell	1.00	.40
❑ 38	Fred Taylor	1.00	.40
❑ 39	Jimmy Smith	.60	.25
❑ 40	Keenan McCardell	.60	.25
❑ 41	Elvis Grbac	.60	.25
❑ 42	Tony Gonzalez	.60	.25
❑ 43	Tony Martin	.60	.25
❑ 44	Jay Fiedler	1.00	.40
❑ 45	Damon Huard	1.00	.40
❑ 46	Randy Moss	2.00	.75
❑ 47	Robert Smith	1.00	.40
❑ 48	Cris Carter	1.00	.40
❑ 49	Daunte Culpepper	1.25	.50
❑ 50	Drew Bledsoe	1.25	.50
❑ 51	Terry Glenn	.60	.25
❑ 52	Ricky Williams	1.00	.40
❑ 53	Jeff Blake	.60	.25
❑ 54	Keith Poole	.40	.15
❑ 55	Kerry Collins	.60	.25
❑ 56	Amani Toomer	.60	.25
❑ 57	Ike Hilliard	.60	.25
❑ 58	Ray Lucas	.60	.25
❑ 59	Curtis Martin	1.00	.40
❑ 60	Vinny Testaverde	.60	.25
❑ 61	Tim Brown	1.00	.40
❑ 62	Rich Gannon	1.00	.40
❑ 63	Tyrone Wheatley	.60	.25
❑ 64	Napoleon Kaufman	.60	.25
❑ 65	Duce Staley	1.00	.40
❑ 66	Donovan McNabb	1.50	.60
❑ 67	Troy Edwards	.40	.15
❑ 68	Jerome Bettis	1.00	.40
❑ 69	Kordell Stewart	.60	.25
❑ 70	Marshall Faulk	1.25	.50
❑ 71	Kurt Warner	1.50	.60
❑ 72	Isaac Bruce	1.00	.40
❑ 73	Torry Holt	1.00	.40
❑ 74	Ryan Leaf	.60	.25
❑ 75	Jim Harbaugh	.60	.25
❑ 76	Jerry Rice	2.00	.75
❑ 77	Terrell Owens	1.00	.40
❑ 78	Jeff Garcia	1.00	.40
❑ 79	Ricky Watters	.60	.25
❑ 80	Jon Kitna	1.00	.40

❑ 81	Derrick Mayes	.60	.25
❑ 82	Shaun King	.40	.15
❑ 83	Mike Alstott	1.00	.40
❑ 84	Keyshawn Johnson	1.00	.40
❑ 85	Eddie George	1.00	.40
❑ 86	Steve McNair	1.00	.40
❑ 87	Jevon Kearse	1.00	.40
❑ 88	Brad Johnson	1.00	.40
❑ 89	Stephen Davis	1.00	.40
❑ 90	Michael Westbrook	.60	.25
❑ 91	Anthony Lucas RC	8.00	3.00
❑ 92	Avion Black RC	12.00	5.00
❑ 93	Corey Moore RC	8.00	3.00
❑ 94	Chris Cole RC	12.00	5.00
❑ 95	Chris Hovan RC	12.00	5.00
❑ 96	Dante Hall RC	30.00	12.50
❑ 97	Darrell Jackson RC	30.00	12.50
❑ 98	Deltha O'Neal RC	15.00	6.00
❑ 99	Doug Chapman RC	12.00	5.00
❑ 100	Doug Johnson RC	15.00	6.00
❑ 101	Erron Kinney RC	15.00	6.00
❑ 102	Frank Moreau RC	12.00	5.00
❑ 103	Patrick Pass RC	12.00	5.00
❑ 104	Gari Scott RC	8.00	3.00
❑ 105	Giovanni Carmazzi RC	8.00	3.00
❑ 106	JaJuan Dawson RC	8.00	3.00
❑ 107	James Williams RC	12.00	5.00
❑ 108	Jarious Jackson RC	12.00	5.00
❑ 109	John Abraham RC	20.00	7.50
❑ 110	Keith Bulluck RC	15.00	6.00
❑ 111	Jonas Lewis RC	8.00	3.00
❑ 112	Mike Green RC	12.00	5.00
❑ 113	Ronney Jenkins RC	12.00	5.00
❑ 114	Michael Wiley RC	12.00	5.00
❑ 115	Mike Anderson RC	20.00	10.00
❑ 116	Mareno Philyaw RC	8.00	3.00
❑ 117	Muneer Moore RC	8.00	3.00
❑ 118	Paul Smith RC	12.00	5.00
❑ 119	Raynoch Thompson RC	12.00	5.00
❑ 120	Rob Morris RC	12.00	5.00
❑ 121	Ron Dixon RC	12.00	5.00
❑ 122	Rondell Mealey RC	8.00	3.00
❑ 123	Sebastian Janikowski RC	15.00	6.00
❑ 124	Shaun Ellis RC	15.00	6.00
❑ 125	Charles Lee RC	12.00	5.00
❑ 126	Shyrone Stith RC	12.00	5.00
❑ 127	Thomas Hamner RC	8.00	3.00
❑ 128	Tim Rattay RC	20.00	7.50
❑ 129	Todd Husak RC	15.00	6.00
❑ 130	Tom Brady RC	300.00	150.00
❑ 131	Trevor Gaylor RC	12.00	5.00
❑ 132	Windrell Hayes RC	12.00	5.00
❑ 133	Anthony Becht JSY AU RC	25.00	10.00
❑ 134	Brian Urlacher JSY AU RC	80.00	40.00
❑ 135	Bubba Franks JSY AU RC	30.00	12.50
❑ 136	C Pennington JSY AU RC	50.00	25.00
❑ 137	Chr Redman JSY AU RC	25.00	10.00
❑ 138	Corey Simon JSY AU RC	30.00	12.50
❑ 139	Curtis Keaton JSY AU RC	25.00	10.00
❑ 140	Danny Farmer JSY AU RC	25.00	10.00
❑ 141	Den Northcutt JSY AU RC	30.00	12.50
❑ 142	Dez White JSY AU RC	30.00	12.50
❑ 143	J.R. Redmond JSY AU SP RC	25.00	10.00
❑ 144	Jamal Lewis JSY AU RC	60.00	25.00
❑ 145	Jerry Porter JSY AU RC	50.00	20.00
❑ 146	Joe Hamilton EXCH	3.00	1.25
❑ 147	Laver Coles JSY AU RC	40.00	15.00
❑ 148	R.Jay Soward JSY AU RC	25.00	10.00
❑ 149	Reu Droughns JSY AU RC	40.00	15.00
❑ 150	Ron Dayne JSY AU RC	40.00	20.00
❑ 151	Ron Dugans JSY AU RC	20.00	7.50
❑ 152	Sha Alexander JSY AU RC	150.00	90.00
❑ 153	Sylvester Morris JSY AU RC	25.00	10.00
❑ 154	Tee Martin JSY AU RC	30.00	12.50
❑ 155	Thomas Jones JSY AU RC SP	175.00	100.00
❑ 156	Todd Pinkston JSY AU RC	30.00	12.50
❑ 157	Travis Prentice JSY AU RC	25.00	10.00
❑ 158	Travis Taylor JSY AU SP RC	40.00	15.00
❑ 159	Trung Canidate JSY AU RC	25.00	10.00
❑ 160	Courtney Brown JSY AU RC	30.00	12.50
❑ 161	Peter Warrick JSY AU RC	30.00	12.50
❑ 162	Plaxico Burress JSY AU RC	100.00	60.00
❑ S1	Peyton Manning Sample	4.00	1.50

2001 SPx

❑	COMP.SET w/o SP's (90)	20.00	7.50
❑ 1	Jake Plummer	.60	.25
❑ 2	David Boston	1.00	.40
❑ 3	Jamal Anderson	1.00	.40
❑ 4	Chris Chandler	.60	.25
❑ 5	Tony Martin	.60	.25
❑ 6	Elvis Grbac	.60	.25
❑ 7	Qadry Ismail	.60	.25
❑ 8	Ray Lewis	1.00	.40
❑ 9	Rob Johnson	.60	.25
❑ 10	Shawn Bryson	.40	.15
❑ 11	Eric Moulds	.60	.25
❑ 12	Tim Biakabutuka	.60	.25
❑ 13	Jeff Lewis	.40	.15
❑ 14	Muhsin Muhammad	.60	.25
❑ 15	Shane Matthews	.40	.15
❑ 16	Marcus Robinson	1.00	.40
❑ 17	Brian Urlacher	1.50	.60
❑ 18	Jon Kitna	.40	.15
❑ 19	Peter Warrick	1.00	.40
❑ 20	Corey Dillon	1.00	.40
❑ 21	Tim Couch	.60	.25
❑ 22	Travis Prentice	.40	.15
❑ 23	Kevin Johnson	.60	.25
❑ 24	Rocket Ismail	.60	.25
❑ 25	Emmitt Smith	2.00	.75
❑ 26	Joey Galloway	.60	.25
❑ 27	Terrell Davis	1.00	.40
❑ 28	Brian Griese	1.00	.40
❑ 29	Rod Smith	.60	.25
❑ 30	Ed McCaffrey	1.00	.40
❑ 31	Charlie Batch	1.00	.40
❑ 32	Germane Crowell	.40	.15
❑ 33	James O. Stewart	.60	.25
❑ 34	Brett Favre	3.00	1.25
❑ 35	Antonio Freeman	1.00	.40
❑ 36	Ahman Green	1.00	.40
❑ 37	Peyton Manning	2.50	1.00
❑ 38	Edgerrin James	1.25	.50
❑ 39	Marvin Harrison	1.00	.40
❑ 40	Mark Brunell	1.00	.40
❑ 41	Fred Taylor	1.00	.40
❑ 42	Jimmy Smith	.60	.25
❑ 43	Tony Gonzalez	.60	.25
❑ 44	Trent Green	1.00	.40
❑ 45	Priest Holmes	1.25	.50
❑ 46	Lamar Smith	.60	.25
❑ 47	Jay Fiedler	1.00	.40
❑ 48	Oronde Gadsden	.60	.25
❑ 49	Daunte Culpepper	1.00	.40
❑ 50	Randy Moss	2.00	.75
❑ 51	Cris Carter	1.00	.40
❑ 52	Drew Bledsoe	1.25	.50
❑ 53	Troy Brown	.60	.25
❑ 54	Ricky Williams	1.00	.40
❑ 55	Joe Horn	.60	.25
❑ 56	Aaron Brooks	1.00	.40
❑ 57	Albert Connell	.40	.15
❑ 58	Kerry Collins	.60	.25
❑ 59	Tiki Barber	1.00	.40
❑ 60	Ron Dayne	1.00	.40
❑ 61	Vinny Testaverde	.60	.25
❑ 62	Wayne Chrebet	.60	.25
❑ 63	Curtis Martin	1.00	.40
❑ 64	Tim Brown	1.00	.40
❑ 65	Jerry Rice	2.00	.75
❑ 66	Rich Gannon	1.00	.40
❑ 67	Duce Staley	1.00	.40
❑ 68	Donovan McNabb	1.25	.50
❑ 69	Kordell Stewart	.60	.25
❑ 70	Jerome Bettis	1.00	.40
❑ 71	Marshall Faulk	1.25	.50
❑ 72	Kurt Warner	2.00	.75
❑ 73	Isaac Bruce	1.00	.40
❑ 74	Torry Holt	1.00	.40
❑ 75	Doug Flutie	1.00	.40
❑ 76	Junior Seau	1.00	.40
❑ 77	Jeff Garcia	1.00	.40
❑ 78	Garrison Hearst	.60	.25
❑ 79	Terrell Owens	1.00	.40
❑ 80	Ricky Watters	.60	.25
❑ 81	Matt Hasselbeck	.60	.25
❑ 82	Brad Johnson	1.00	.40
❑ 83	Keyshawn Johnson	1.00	.40
❑ 84	Warrick Dunn	1.00	.40
❑ 85	Mike Alstott	1.00	.40
❑ 86	Kevin Dyson	.60	.25
❑ 87	Eddie George	1.00	.40
❑ 88	Steve McNair	1.00	.40
❑ 89	Michael Westbrook	.60	.25
❑ 90	Stephen Davis	1.00	.40
❑ 91B	D McAllister JSY AU/250 RC	100.00	50.00
❑ 91G	D McAllister JSY AU/250 RC	100.00	50.00
❑ 92B	Fr Mitchell JSY AU/250 RC	30.00	12.50
❑ 92G	Fr Mitchell JSY AU/250 RC	30.00	12.50
❑ 93B	Koren Robinson/999 RC	10.00	4.00
❑ 93G	Koren Robinson/999 RC	10.00	4.00
❑ 94B	David Terrell/999 RC	10.00	4.00
❑ 94G	David Terrell/999 RC	10.00	4.00
❑ 95B	M Vick JSY AU/250 RC	300.00	150.00
❑ 95G	M Vick JSY AU/250 RC	300.00	150.00
❑ 96B	M Bennett JSY AU/550 RC	40.00	15.00
❑ 96G	M Bennett JSY AU/550 RC	40.00	15.00
❑ 97B	Robert Ferguson/999 RC	10.00	4.00
❑ 97G	Robert Ferguson/999 RC	10.00	4.00
❑ 98B	Rod Gardner/999 RC	10.00	4.00
❑ 98G	Rod Gardner/999 RC	10.00	4.00
❑ 99B	Travis Henry JSY AU/550 RC	30.00	12.50
❑ 99G	Travis Henry JSY AU/550 RC	30.00	12.50
❑ 100B	C Johnson JSY AU/550 RC	100.00	60.00
❑ 100G	C Johnson JSY AU/550 RC	100.00	60.00
❑ 101B	Drew Brees JSY AU/250 RC	150.00	75.00
❑ 101G	Drew Brees JSY AU/250 RC	150.00	75.00
❑ 102B	S Moss JSY AU/550 RC	50.00	30.00
❑ 102G	S Moss JSY AU/550 RC	50.00	30.00
❑ 103B	C Weinke JSY AU/550 RC	25.00	10.00
❑ 103G	C Weinke JSY AU/550 RC	25.00	10.00
❑ 104B	R Seymour JSY AU/900 RC	40.00	20.00
❑ 104G	R Seymour JSY AU/900 RC	40.00	20.00
❑ 105B	Reggie Wayne/999 RC	25.00	10.00
❑ 105G	Reggie Wayne/999 RC	25.00	10.00
❑ 106B	K Barlow JSY AU/550 RC	30.00	12.50
❑ 106G	K Barlow JSY AU/550 RC	30.00	12.50
❑ 107B	Chambers JSY AU/900 RC	50.00	25.00
❑ 107G	Chambers JSY AU/900 RC	50.00	25.00
❑ 108B	Todd Heap JSY AU/900 RC	30.00	12.50
❑ 108G	Todd Heap JSY AU/900 RC	30.00	12.50
❑ 109B	A Thomas JSY AU/550 RC	30.00	12.50
❑ 109G	A Thomas JSY AU/550 RC	30.00	12.50
❑ 110B	J Jackson JSY AU/550 RC	25.00	10.00
❑ 110G	J Jackson JSY AU/550 RC	25.00	10.00
❑ 111B	R Johnson JSY AU/900 RC	60.00	30.00
❑ 111G	R Johnson JSY AU/900 RC	60.00	30.00

❑ 112B McMahon JSY AU/900 RC 25.00 10.00
❑ 112G M McMahon JSY AU/900 RC 25.00 10.00
❑ 113 Josh Heupel JSY AU/900 40.00 20.00
❑ 114B T Minor JSY AU/900 RC 25.00 10.00
❑ 114G T Minor JSY AU/900 RC 25.00 10.00
❑ 115B Quincy Morgan/999 RC 10.00 4.00
❑ 115G Quincy Morgan/999 RC 10.00 4.00
❑ 116B D Morgan JSY AU/900 RC 20.00 10.00
❑ 116G D Morgan JSY AU/900 RC 20.00 10.00
❑ 117B J Palmer JSY AU/900 RC 25.00 10.00
❑ 117G J Palmer JSY AU/900 RC 25.00 10.00
❑ 118B S Rosenfels JSY AU/900 RC 25.00 10.00
❑ 118G S Rosenfels JSY AU/900 RC 25.00 10.00
❑ 119B Tuiasosopo JSY AU/900 RC 30.00 12.50
❑ 119G Tuiasosopo JSY AU/900 RC 30.00 12.50
❑ 120B Damerien McCants/999 RC 6.00 2.50
❑ 120G Damerien McCants/999 RC 6.00 2.50
❑ 121B Snoop Minnis/999 RC 6.00 2.50
❑ 121G Snoop Minnis/999 RC 6.00 2.50
❑ 122B L Tomlinson JSY/250 RC 175.00 100.00
❑ 122G L Tomlinson JSY/250 RC 175.00 100.00
❑ 123B Quincy Carter/999 RC 10.00 4.00
❑ 123G Quincy Carter/999 RC 10.00 4.00
❑ 124B Arnold Jackson/999 RC 6.00 2.50
❑ 124G Arnold Jackson/999 RC 6.00 2.50
❑ 125B Justin McCareins/999 RC 10.00 4.00
❑ 125G Justin McCareins/999 RC 10.00 4.00
❑ 126B Eddie Berlin/999 RC 6.00 2.50
❑ 126G Eddie Berlin/999 RC 6.00 2.50
❑ 127B Quentin McCord/999 RC 6.00 2.50
❑ 127G Quentin McCord/999 RC 6.00 2.50
❑ 128B Vinny Sutherland/999 RC 6.00 2.50
❑ 128G Vinny Sutherland/999 RC 6.00 2.50
❑ 129B Willie Middlebrooks/999 RC 6.00 2.50
❑ 129G Willie Middlebrooks/999 RC 6.00 2.50
❑ 130B Dan Alexander/999 RC 10.00 4.00
❑ 130G Dan Alexander/999 RC 10.00 4.00
❑ 131B Dee Brown/999 RC 10.00 4.00
❑ 131G Dee Brown/999 RC 10.00 4.00
❑ 132B Andre Carter/999 RC 10.00 4.00
❑ 132G Andre Carter/999 RC 10.00 4.00
❑ 133B Justin Smith/999 RC 10.00 4.00
❑ 133G Justin Smith/999 RC 10.00 4.00
❑ 134B Houshmandzadeh/999 RC 10.00 4.00
❑ 134G Houshmandzadeh/999 RC 10.00 4.00
❑ 135B Andre King/999 RC 6.00 2.50
❑ 135G Andre King/999 RC 6.00 2.50
❑ 136B Nick Goings/999 RC 10.00 4.00
❑ 136G Nick Goings/999 RC 10.00 4.00
❑ 137B Scotty Anderson/999 RC 6.00 2.50
❑ 137G Scotty Anderson/999 RC 6.00 2.50
❑ 138B David Martin/999 RC 6.00 2.50
❑ 138G David Martin/999 RC 6.00 2.50
❑ 139B Derrick Blaylock/999 RC 12.00 5.00
❑ 139G Derrick Blaylock/999 RC 12.00 5.00
❑ 140B Onome Ojo/999 RC 6.00 2.50
❑ 140G Onome Ojo/999 RC 6.00 2.50
❑ 141B Jonathan Carter/999 RC 6.00 2.50
❑ 141G Jonathan Carter/999 RC 6.00 2.50
❑ 142B LaMont Jordan/999 RC 20.00 7.50
❑ 142G LaMont Jordan/999 RC 20.00 7.50
❑ 143B Dominic Rhodes/999 RC 10.00 4.00
❑ 143G Dominic Rhodes/999 RC 10.00 4.00
❑ 145B A.J. Feeley/999 RC 10.00 4.00
❑ 145G A.J. Feeley/999 RC 10.00 4.00
❑ 146B Correll Buckhalter/999 RC 12.00 5.00
❑ 146G Correll Buckhalter/999 RC 12.00 5.00
❑ 147B Steve Smith/999 RC 25.00 12.50
❑ 147G Steve Smith/999 RC 25.00 12.50
❑ 148B Dave Dickenson/999 RC 6.00 2.50
❑ 148G Dave Dickenson/999 RC 6.00 2.50
❑ 149B Cedrick Wilson/999 RC 10.00 4.00
❑ 149G Cedrick Wilson/999 RC 10.00 4.00
❑ 150B Jamie Winborn/999 RC 6.00 2.50
❑ 150G Jamie Winborn/999 RC 6.00 2.50
❑ 151B Alex Bannister/999 RC 6.00 2.50
❑ 151G Alex Bannister/999 RC 6.00 2.50
❑ 152B Heath Evans/999 RC 6.00 2.50
❑ 152G Heath Evans/999 RC 6.00 2.50
❑ 153B Josh Booty/999 RC 10.00 4.00
❑ 153G Josh Booty/999 RC 10.00 4.00
❑ 154B Adam Archuleta/999 RC 10.00 4.00
❑ 154G Adam Archuleta/999 RC 10.00 4.00
❑ 155B Francis St.Paul/999 RC 6.00 2.50
❑ 155G Francis St.Paul/999 RC 6.00 2.50
❑ 156B Andre Dyson/999 RC 4.00 1.50
❑ 156G Andre Dyson/999 RC 4.00 1.50
❑ RM Randy Moss SAMPLE 2.00 .75

2002 SPx

❑ COMP.SET w/o SP's (90) 20.00 7.50
❑ 1 Drew Bledsoe 1.25 .50
❑ 2 Peerless Price .60 .25
❑ 3 Travis Henry 1.00 .40
❑ 4 Ricky Williams 1.00 .40
❑ 5 Jay Fiedler .60 .25
❑ 6 Tom Brady 2.50 1.00
❑ 7 Troy Brown .60 .25
❑ 8 Antowain Smith .60 .25
❑ 9 Santana Moss 1.00 .40
❑ 10 Curtis Martin 1.00 .40
❑ 11 Vinny Testaverde .60 .25
❑ 12 Jamal Lewis 1.00 .40
❑ 13 Chris Redman .40 .15
❑ 14 Travis Taylor .60 .25
❑ 15 Corey Dillon .60 .25
❑ 16 T.J. Houshmandzadeh .60 .25
❑ 17 Peter Warrick .60 .25
❑ 18 Courtney Brown .60 .25
❑ 19 Kevin Johnson .60 .25
❑ 20 Tim Couch .60 .25
❑ 21 Hines Ward 1.00 .40
❑ 22 Jerome Bettis 1.00 .40
❑ 23 Kordell Stewart .60 .25
❑ 24 Corey Bradford .40 .15
❑ 25 Jermaine Lewis .40 .15
❑ 26 Edgerrin James 1.25 .50
❑ 27 Marvin Harrison 1.00 .40
❑ 28 Peyton Manning 2.00 .75
❑ 29 Jimmy Smith .60 .25
❑ 30 Mark Brunell 1.00 .40
❑ 31 Fred Taylor 1.00 .40
❑ 32 Eddie George 1.00 .40
❑ 33 Steve McNair 1.00 .40
❑ 34 Brian Griese 1.00 .40
❑ 35 Shannon Sharpe .60 .25
❑ 36 Rod Smith .60 .25
❑ 37 Trent Green .60 .25
❑ 38 Johnnie Morton .60 .25
❑ 39 Priest Holmes 1.25 .50
❑ 40 Jerry Rice 2.00 .75
❑ 41 Rich Gannon 1.00 .40
❑ 42 Tim Brown 1.00 .40
❑ 43 Drew Brees 1.00 .40
❑ 44 Junior Seau 1.00 .40
❑ 45 LaDainian Tomlinson 1.50 .60
❑ 46 Emmitt Smith 2.50 1.00
❑ 47 Quincy Carter .60 .25
❑ 48 Rocket Ismail .60 .25
❑ 49 Amani Toomer .60 .25
❑ 50 Kerry Collins .60 .25
❑ 51 Ron Dayne .60 .25
❑ 52 Donovan McNabb 1.25 .50
❑ 53 Duce Staley 1.00 .40
❑ 54 Antonio Freeman 1.00 .40
❑ 55 Rod Gardner .60 .25
❑ 56 Stephen Davis .60 .25
❑ 57 Brian Urlacher 1.50 .60
❑ 58 Anthony Thomas .60 .25
❑ 59 Jim Miller .60 .25
❑ 60 Marty Booker .60 .25
❑ 61 Az-Zahir Hakim .40 .15
❑ 62 James Stewart .60 .25
❑ 63 Ahman Green 1.00 .40
❑ 64 Brett Favre 2.50 1.00
❑ 65 Robert Ferguson .40 .15
❑ 66 Terry Glenn .60 .25
❑ 67 Randy Moss 2.00 .75
❑ 68 Daunte Culpepper 1.00 .40
❑ 69 Michael Bennett .60 .25
❑ 70 Michael Vick 3.00 1.25
❑ 71 Warrick Dunn 1.00 .40
❑ 72 Rodney Peete .60 .25
❑ 73 Muhsin Muhammad .60 .25
❑ 74 Aaron Brooks 1.00 .40
❑ 75 Deuce McAllister 1.25 .50
❑ 76 Keyshawn Johnson 1.00 .40
❑ 77 Michael Pittman .40 .15
❑ 78 Brad Johnson .60 .25
❑ 79 Thomas Jones .60 .25
❑ 80 David Boston 1.00 .40
❑ 81 Jake Plummer .60 .25
❑ 82 Terrell Owens 1.00 .40
❑ 83 Garrison Hearst .60 .25
❑ 84 Jeff Garcia 1.00 .40
❑ 85 Darrell Jackson .60 .25
❑ 86 Shaun Alexander 1.25 .50
❑ 87 Trent Dilfer .60 .25
❑ 88 Isaac Bruce 1.00 .40
❑ 89 Kurt Warner 1.00 .40
❑ 90 Marshall Faulk 1.00 .40
❑ 91 Saleem Rasheed RC 10.00 4.00
❑ 92 Jason McAddley RC 8.00 3.00
❑ 93 Brandon Doman RC 8.00 3.00
❑ 94 Mike Rumph RC 10.00 4.00
❑ 95 Wendell Bryant RC 5.00 2.00
❑ 96 Bryan Thomas RC 8.00 3.00
❑ 97 Anthony Weaver RC 8.00 3.00
❑ 98 Chester Taylor RC 10.00 4.00
❑ 99 Ed Reed RC 15.00 6.00
❑ 100 Lamar Gordon RC 10.00 4.00
❑ 101 Tellis Redmon RC 8.00 3.00
❑ 102 Ben Leber RC 10.00 4.00
❑ 103 Javin Hunter RC 5.00 2.00
❑ 104 Javon Walker RC 20.00 7.50
❑ 105 Shaun Hill RC 10.00 4.00
❑ 106 Raonall Smith RC 8.00 3.00
❑ 107 Darrell Hill RC 8.00 3.00
❑ 108 Kalimba Edwards RC 10.00 4.00
❑ 109 Robert Thomas RC 10.00 4.00
❑ 110 Craig Nall RC 10.00 4.00
❑ 111 Marques Anderson RC 10.00 4.00
❑ 112 Najeh Davenport RC 10.00 4.00
❑ 113 Jonathan Wells RC 10.00 4.00
❑ 114 Dwight Freeney RC 12.00 5.00
❑ 115 Larry Tripplett RC 5.00 2.00
❑ 116 T.J. Duckett RC 15.00 6.00
❑ 117 John Henderson RC 10.00 4.00
❑ 118 Albert Haynesworth RC 8.00 3.00
❑ 119 Tank Williams RC 8.00 3.00
❑ 120 Ryan Sims RC 10.00 4.00
❑ 121 Leonard Henry RC 8.00 3.00
❑ 122 Clinton Portis RC 50.00 20.00
❑ 123 Josh Reed RC 10.00 4.00
❑ 124 Chad Hutchinson RC 8.00 3.00
❑ 125 Deion Branch RC 20.00 10.00
❑ 126 Rocky Calmus RC 10.00 4.00
❑ 127 Donte Stallworth RC 20.00 7.50

❑ 128 Daryl Jones RC	8.00	3.00
❑ 129 Joey Harrington RC	30.00	12.50
❑ 130 Napoleon Harris RC	10.00	4.00
❑ 131 Phillip Buchanon RC	10.00	4.00
❑ 132 Patrick Ramsey RC	12.00	5.00
❑ 133 Brian Westbrook RC	20.00	10.00
❑ 134 Freddie Milons RC	8.00	3.00
❑ 135 Lito Sheppard RC	10.00	4.00
❑ 136 Michael Lewis RC	10.00	4.00
❑ 137 Jamin Elliott RC	5.00	2.00
❑ 138 Lee Mays RC	10.00	4.00
❑ 139 Verron Haynes RC	10.00	4.00
❑ 140 Jesse Chatman RC	10.00	4.00
❑ 141 Quentin Jammer RC	10.00	4.00
❑ 142 Seth Burford RC	8.00	3.00
❑ 143 Julius Peppers RC	20.00	7.50
❑ 144 William Green RC	10.00	4.00
❑ 145 DeShaun Foster RC	10.00	4.00
❑ 146 Daniel Graham RC	10.00	4.00
❑ 147 David Garrard RC	10.00	4.00
❑ 148 Reche Caldwell RC	10.00	4.00
❑ 149 Randy Fasani RC	8.00	3.00
❑ 150 J.T. O'Sullivan RC	8.00	3.00
❑ 151 Josh McCown JSY AU RC	40.00	20.00
❑ 152 Kurt Kittner JSY AU RC	20.00	7.50
❑ 153 Kahlil Hill JSY AU RC	15.00	6.00
❑ 154 Ladell Betts JSY AU RC	25.00	10.00
❑ 155 Ron Johnson JSY AU RC	15.00	6.00
❑ 156 Maurice Morris JSY AU RC	20.00	7.50
❑ 157 Andre Davis JSY AU RC	30.00	12.50
❑ 158 Antonio Bryant JSY AU RC	30.00	12.50
❑ 159 Roy Williams JSY AU RC	60.00	25.00
❑ 160 Lam Thompson JSY AU RC	15.00	6.00
❑ 161 Cliff Russell JSY AU RC	15.00	6.00
❑ 162 Woody Dantzler JSY AU RC	15.00	6.00
❑ 163 Travis Stephens JSY AU RC	15.00	6.00
❑ 164 Tony Fisher JSY AU RC	25.00	10.00
❑ 165 Eric McCoo JSY AU RC	15.00	6.00
❑ 166 Eric Crouch JSY AU RC	25.00	10.00
❑ 167 Rohan Davey JSY AU RC	20.00	7.50
❑ 168 Marquise Walker JSY AU RC	15.00	6.00
❑ 169 Jeremy Shockey JSY RC	50.00	20.00
❑ 170 Tim Carter JSY AU RC	20.00	7.50
❑ 171 Atrews Bell JSY AU RC	15.00	6.00
❑ 172 Ant Randle El JSY AU RC	60.00	30.00
❑ 173 Ricky Williams JSY AU RC	40.00	15.00
❑ 174 Mike Williams JSY AU	15.00	6.00
❑ 175 Adrian Peterson JSY AU RC	25.00	10.00
❑ 176 Jab Gaffney JSY AU/650 RC	30.00	12.50
❑ 177 Ashley Lelie JSY AU/250 RC	80.00	30.00
❑ 178 David Carr JSY AU/250 RC	120.00	60.00

2003 SPx

❑ COMP.SET w/o SP's (110)	25.00	10.00
❑ 1 Peyton Manning	1.50	.60
❑ 2 Aaron Brooks	1.00	.40
❑ 3 Joey Harrington	1.50	.60
❑ 4 Tim Couch	.40	.15
❑ 5 Jeff Garcia	1.00	.40
❑ 6 Jay Fiedler	.60	.25
❑ 7 Chad Hutchinson	.40	.15
❑ 8 Tommy Maddox	1.00	.40
❑ 9 Drew Brees	1.00	.40
❑ 10 Trent Green	.60	.25
❑ 11 Patrick Ramsey	1.00	.40
❑ 12 Daunte Culpepper	1.00	.40
❑ 13 Kurt Warner	1.00	.40
❑ 14 Brad Johnson	.60	.25
❑ 15 Rich Gannon	.60	.25
❑ 16 Jake Plummer	.60	.25
❑ 17 Steve McNair	1.00	.40
❑ 18 Mark Brunell	.60	.25
❑ 19 Drew Bledsoe	1.00	.40
❑ 20 Kordell Stewart	.60	.25
❑ 21 Kelly Holcomb	.60	.25
❑ 22 Josh McCown	.60	.25
❑ 23 Matt Hasselbeck	.60	.25
❑ 24 Marc Bulger	1.00	.40
❑ 25 Chris Redman	.40	.15
❑ 26 Rodney Peete	.60	.25
❑ 27 Jake Delhomme	1.00	.40
❑ 28 Jon Kitna	.60	.25
❑ 29 Kerry Collins	.60	.25
❑ 30 Quincy Carter	.60	.25
❑ 31 Ricky Williams	1.00	.40
❑ 32 Clinton Portis	1.50	.60
❑ 33 Deuce McAllister	1.00	.40
❑ 34 Ahman Green	1.00	.40
❑ 35 Priest Holmes	1.25	.50
❑ 36 Curtis Martin	1.00	.40
❑ 37 Michael Bennett	.60	.25
❑ 38 Eddie George	.60	.25
❑ 39 Marshall Faulk	1.00	.40
❑ 40 Garrison Hearst	.60	.25
❑ 41 Shaun Alexander	1.00	.40
❑ 42 Corey Dillon	.60	.25
❑ 43 Jamal Lewis	1.00	.40
❑ 44 William Green	.60	.25
❑ 45 Travis Henry	.60	.25
❑ 46 Randy Moss	1.50	.60
❑ 47 Terrell Owens	1.00	.40
❑ 48 Peerless Price	.60	.25
❑ 49 David Boston	.60	.25
❑ 50 Eric Moulds	.60	.25
❑ 51 Marvin Harrison	1.00	.40
❑ 52 Laveranues Coles	.60	.25
❑ 53 Santana Moss	.60	.25
❑ 54 Troy Brown	.60	.25
❑ 55 Chris Chambers	1.00	.40
❑ 56 Tim Brown	1.00	.40
❑ 57 Rod Smith	.60	.25
❑ 58 Hines Ward	1.00	.40
❑ 59 Keyshawn Johnson	1.00	.40
❑ 60 Isaac Bruce	1.00	.40
❑ 61 Torry Holt	1.00	.40
❑ 62 Koren Robinson	.60	.25
❑ 63 Chad Johnson	1.00	.40
❑ 64 Derrick Mason	.60	.25
❑ 65 Antonio Bryant	.60	.25
❑ 66 Kevin Johnson	.60	.25
❑ 67 Todd Heap	.60	.25
❑ 68 Tony Gonzalez	.60	.25
❑ 69 Jeremy Shockey	1.50	.60
❑ 70 Brian Urlacher	1.50	.60
❑ 71 Emmitt Smith/500	20.00	7.50
❑ 72 Edgerrin James/500	10.00	4.00
❑ 73 LaDainian Tomlinson/500	8.00	3.00
❑ 74 Brett Favre/500	20.00	7.50
❑ 75 Donovan McNabb/500	10.00	4.00
❑ 76 Tom Brady/500	20.00	7.50
❑ 77 Michael Vick/500	20.00	7.50
❑ 78 David Carr/500	12.00	5.00
❑ 79 Jerry Rice/500	15.00	6.00
❑ 80 Chad Pennington/500	10.00	4.00
❑ 81 Joey Harrington XCT	1.50	.60
❑ 82 Clinton Portis XCT	1.50	.60
❑ 83 Jeremy Shockey XCT	1.50	.60
❑ 84 David Boston XCT	.60	.25
❑ 85 Marshall Faulk XCT	1.00	.40
❑ 86 Emmitt Smith XCT	2.50	1.00
❑ 87 Terrell Owens XCT	1.00	.40
❑ 88 Randy Moss XCT	1.50	.60
❑ 89 Deuce McAllister XCT	1.00	.40
❑ 90 Ahman Green XCT	1.00	.40
❑ 91 Peerless Price XCT	.60	.25
❑ 92 Plaxico Burress XCT	.60	.25
❑ 93 Marvin Harrison XCT	1.00	.40
❑ 94 Keyshawn Johnson XCT	1.00	.40
❑ 95 Laveranues Coles XCT	.60	.25
❑ 96 Drew Bledsoe XCT	1.00	.40
❑ 97 Eric Moulds XCT	.60	.25
❑ 98 Chad Pennington XCT	1.25	.50
❑ 99 Jerry Rice XCT	2.00	.75
❑ 100 David Carr XCT	1.50	.60
❑ 101 Michael Vick XCT	2.50	1.00
❑ 102 Tom Brady XCT	2.50	1.00
❑ 103 Donovan McNabb XCT	1.25	.50
❑ 104 Brett Favre XCT	2.50	1.00
❑ 105 Kurt Warner XCT	1.00	.40
❑ 106 LaDainian Tomlinson XCT	1.00	.40
❑ 107 Drew Brees XCT	1.00	.40
❑ 108 Edgerrin James XCT	1.00	.40
❑ 109 Peyton Manning XCT	1.50	.60
❑ 110 Ricky Williams XCT	1.00	.40
❑ 111 Brooks Bollinger RC	10.00	4.00
❑ 112 Gibran Hamden RC	5.00	2.00
❑ 113 Jason Johnson RC	5.00	2.00
❑ 114 Tony Romo RC	10.00	4.00
❑ 115 Juston Wood RC	5.00	2.00
❑ 116 Kirk Farmer RC	5.00	2.00
❑ 117 Kliff Kingsbury RC	8.00	3.00
❑ 118 Jason Gesser RC	10.00	4.00
❑ 119 Brad Banks RC	8.00	3.00
❑ 120 Rob Adamson RC	5.00	2.00
❑ 121 Ken Dorsey RC	10.00	4.00
❑ 122 Curt Anes RC	5.00	2.00
❑ 123 George Wrighster RC	8.00	3.00
❑ 124 Brett Engemann RC	5.00	2.00
❑ 125 Aaron Walker RC	8.00	3.00
❑ 126 Nate Hybl RC	10.00	4.00
❑ 127 Chris Simms RC	15.00	6.00
❑ 128 Marquel Blackwell RC	5.00	2.00
❑ 129 Domanick Davis RC	15.00	6.00
❑ 130 Quentin Griffin RC	10.00	4.00
❑ 131 B.J. Askew RC	10.00	4.00
❑ 132 Earnest Graham RC	8.00	3.00
❑ 133 Sultan McCullough RC	8.00	3.00
❑ 134 Dahrran Diedrick RC	10.00	4.00
❑ 135 Cecil Sapp RC	8.00	3.00
❑ 136 LaBrandon Toefield RC	10.00	4.00
❑ 137 ReShard Lee RC	10.00	4.00
❑ 138 Dwone Hicks RC	5.00	2.00
❑ 139 Brock Forsey RC	10.00	4.00
❑ 140 Bethel Johnson RC	10.00	4.00
❑ 141 Andrew Pinnock RC	8.00	3.00
❑ 142 Ahmaad Galloway RC	8.00	3.00
❑ 143 J.T. Wall RC	5.00	2.00
❑ 144 Tom Lopienski RC	8.00	3.00
❑ 145 Justin Griffith RC	8.00	3.00
❑ 146 Lee Suggs RC	20.00	7.50
❑ 147 Nick Maddox RC	5.00	2.00
❑ 148 Jeremi Johnson RC	8.00	3.00
❑ 149 Doug Gabriel RC	10.00	4.00
❑ 150 Bobby Wade RC	10.00	4.00
❑ 151 Justin Gage RC	10.00	4.00
❑ 152 Arnaz Battle RC	10.00	4.00
❑ 153 Brandon Lloyd RC	12.00	5.00
❑ 154 Talman Gardner RC	10.00	4.00
❑ 155 Kareem Kelly RC	8.00	3.00
❑ 156 Billy McMullen RC	8.00	3.00
❑ 157 Antwone Savage RC	5.00	2.00
❑ 158 J.R. Tolver RC	8.00	3.00
❑ 159 Kassim Osgood RC	10.00	4.00
❑ 160 Shaun McDonald RC	10.00	4.00
❑ 161 Sam Aiken RC	8.00	3.00
❑ 162 Adrian Madise RC	8.00	3.00
❑ 163 Charles Rogers RC	10.00	4.00
❑ 164 David Kircus RC	8.00	3.00

❑	165	Zuriel Smith RC	5.00	2.00
❑	166	LaTarence Dunbar RC	8.00	3.00
❑	167	Willie Ponder RC	8.00	3.00
❑	168	David Tyree RC	5.00	2.00
❑	169	Kevin Walter RC	8.00	3.00
❑	170	Keenan Howry RC	10.00	4.00
❑	171	Walter Young RC	5.00	2.00
❑	172	DeAndrew Rubin RC	5.00	2.00
❑	173	Carl Ford RC	5.00	2.00
❑	174	Taco Wallace RC	8.00	3.00
❑	175	Travis Anglin RC	5.00	2.00
❑	176	Ryan Hoag RC	5.00	2.00
❑	177	Ronald Bellamy RC	8.00	3.00
❑	178	Terrence Edwards RC	8.00	3.00
❑	179	Jerel Myers RC	5.00	2.00
❑	180	Mike Bush RC	8.00	3.00
❑	181	Dan Curley RC	5.00	2.00
❑	182	Carl Morris RC	5.00	2.00
❑	183	Reggie Newhouse RC	8.00	3.00
❑	184	Troy Polamalu RC	35.00	20.00
❑	185	Cecil Moore RC	5.00	2.00
❑	186	Bennie Joppru RC	10.00	4.00
❑	187	Donald Lee RC	8.00	3.00
❑	188	Jason Witten RC	15.00	6.00
❑	189	Mike Seidman RC	5.00	2.00
❑	190	Vishante Shiancoe RC	8.00	3.00
❑	191	Anquan Boldin JSY AU RC	50.00	20.00
❑	192	Kyle Boller JSY AU/450 RC	50.00	20.00
❑	193	Chris Brown JSY AU RC	40.00	15.00
❑	194	Nate Burleson JSY AU RC	40.00	15.00
❑	195	Tyro Calico JSY AU/450 RC	50.00	20.00
❑	196	Dallas Clark JSY AU RC	40.00	15.00
❑	197	Kevin Curtis JSY AU RC	40.00	15.00
❑	198	Kliff Kingsbury JSY AU RC	25.00	10.00
❑	199	Justin Fargas JSY AU RC	30.00	12.50
❑	200	Grossman JSY AU/450 RC	100.00	50.00
❑	201	Taylor Jacobs JSY AU RC	25.00	10.00
❑	202	An Johnson JSY AU/250 RC	150.00	75.00
❑	203	Malae MacKenzie JSY AU RC	15.00	6.00
❑	204	Bryant Johnson JSY AU RC	30.00	12.50
❑	205	Larry Johnson JSY AU RC	200.00	125.00
❑	206	T Johnson JSY AU/450 RC	50.00	25.00
❑	207	Leftwich JSY AU/250 RC	250.00	125.00
❑	208	McGahee JSY AU/450 RC	150.00	75.00
❑	210	C.Palmer JSY AU/250 RC	350.00	250.00
❑	211	Artose Pinner JSY AU RC	30.00	12.50
❑	212	Dave Ragone JSY AU RC	30.00	12.50
❑	213	Terrell Suggs JSY AU RC	40.00	15.00
❑	215	Onterio Smith JSY AU RC	30.00	12.50
❑	216	Musa Smith JSY AU RC	30.00	12.50
❑	217	Brian St.Pierre JSY AU RC	30.00	12.50
❑	218	Marcus Trufant JSY AU RC	30.00	12.50
❑	219	Seneca Wallace JSY AU RC	30.00	12.50
❑	220	Kell Washington JSY AU RC	30.00	12.50

2004 SPx

❑ COMP.SET w/o SP's (100) 30.00 15.00
❑ 101-165 RC PRINT RUN 1650 SER.#'d SETS
❑ 166-190 RC PRINT RUN 799 SER.#'d SETS
❑ 191-221 JSY AU RC #'d TO 1499 UNLESS NOTED

❑	1	Anquan Boldin	1.00	.40
❑	2	Marcel Shipp	.60	.25
❑	3	Josh McCown	.60	.25
❑	4	Peerless Price	.60	.25
❑	5	Michael Vick	2.00	.75
❑	6	T.J. Duckett	.60	.25
❑	7	Kyle Boller	1.00	.40
❑	8	Todd Heap	.60	.25
❑	9	Jamal Lewis	1.00	.40
❑	10	Travis Henry	.60	.25
❑	11	Drew Bledsoe	1.00	.40
❑	12	Eric Moulds	.60	.25
❑	13	Jake Delhomme	1.00	.40
❑	14	Steve Smith	1.00	.40
❑	15	Stephen Davis	.60	.25
❑	16	Brian Urlacher	1.25	.50
❑	17	Rex Grossman	1.00	.40
❑	18	Thomas Jones	.60	.25
❑	19	Chad Johnson	1.00	.40
❑	20	Carson Palmer	1.25	.50
❑	21	Rudi Johnson	.60	.25
❑	22	William Green	.60	.25
❑	23	Jeff Garcia	1.00	.40
❑	24	Andre Davis	.40	.15
❑	25	Roy Williams S	.60	.25
❑	26	Eddie George	.60	.25
❑	27	Keyshawn Johnson	.60	.25
❑	28	Jake Plummer	.60	.25
❑	29	Ashley Lelie	.60	.25
❑	30	Quentin Griffin	1.00	.40
❑	31	Charles Rogers	.60	.25
❑	32	Olandis Gary	.40	.15
❑	33	Joey Harrington	1.00	.40
❑	34	Brett Favre	2.50	1.00
❑	35	Javon Walker	.60	.25
❑	36	Ahman Green	1.00	.40
❑	37	Andre Johnson	1.00	.40
❑	38	Domanick Davis	1.00	.40
❑	39	David Carr	1.00	.40
❑	40	Peyton Manning	1.50	.60
❑	41	Edgerrin James	1.00	.40
❑	42	Marvin Harrison	1.00	.40
❑	43	Byron Leftwich	1.25	.50
❑	44	Jimmy Smith	.60	.25
❑	45	Fred Taylor	.60	.25
❑	46	Trent Green	.60	.25
❑	47	Priest Holmes	1.25	.50
❑	48	Dante Hall	1.00	.40
❑	49	Tony Gonzalez	.60	.25
❑	50	A.J. Feeley	1.00	.40
❑	51	Marty Booker	.60	.25
❑	52	Chris Chambers	.60	.25
❑	53	Zach Thomas	1.00	.40
❑	54	Randy Moss	1.25	.50
❑	55	Daunte Culpepper	1.00	.40
❑	56	Onterrio Smith	.60	.25
❑	57	Troy Brown	.60	.25
❑	58	Corey Dillon	.60	.25
❑	59	Tom Brady	2.50	1.00
❑	60	Deuce McAllister	1.00	.40
❑	61	Joe Horn	.60	.25
❑	62	Aaron Brooks	.60	.25
❑	63	Jeremy Shockey	1.00	.40
❑	64	Kurt Warner	1.00	.40
❑	65	Tiki Barber	1.00	.40
❑	66	Chad Pennington	1.00	.40
❑	67	Curtis Martin	1.00	.40
❑	68	Santana Moss	.60	.25
❑	69	Rich Gannon	.60	.25
❑	70	Jerry Rice	2.00	.75
❑	71	Warren Sapp	.60	.25
❑	72	Donovan McNabb	1.25	.50
❑	73	Terrell Owens	1.00	.40
❑	74	Jevon Kearse	.60	.25
❑	75	Brian Westbrook	.60	.25
❑	76	Hines Ward	1.00	.40
❑	77	Duce Staley	.60	.25
❑	78	Tommy Maddox	.60	.25
❑	79	LaDainian Tomlinson	1.25	.50
❑	80	Drew Brees	1.00	.40
❑	81	Tim Rattay	.40	.15
❑	82	Kevan Barlow	.60	.25
❑	83	Brandon Lloyd	.60	.25
❑	84	Shaun Alexander	1.00	.40
❑	85	Matt Hasselbeck	.60	.25
❑	86	Koren Robinson	.60	.25
❑	87	Marc Bulger	1.00	.40
❑	88	Marshall Faulk	1.00	.40
❑	89	Torry Holt	1.00	.40
❑	90	Isaac Bruce	.60	.25
❑	91	Brad Johnson	.60	.25
❑	92	Keenan McCardell	.40	.15
❑	93	Derrick Brooks	.60	.25
❑	94	Steve McNair	1.00	.40
❑	95	Chris Brown	1.00	.40
❑	96	Derrick Mason	.60	.25
❑	97	Clinton Portis	1.00	.40
❑	98	Mark Brunell	.60	.25
❑	99	Laveranues Coles	.60	.25
❑	100	LaVar Arrington	2.00	.75
❑	101	B.J. Johnson RC	8.00	3.00
❑	102	Craig Krenzel RC	10.00	4.00
❑	103	Will Smith RC	10.00	4.00
❑	104	Jamaar Taylor RC	10.00	4.00
❑	105	Tommie Harris RC	10.00	4.00
❑	106	Shawn Andrews RC	10.00	4.00
❑	107	Kendrick Starling RC	5.00	2.00
❑	108	Jeris McIntyre RC	8.00	3.00
❑	109	Jason Babin RC	10.00	4.00
❑	110	Marcus Tubbs RC	10.00	4.00
❑	111	Triandos Luke RC	10.00	4.00
❑	112	Karlos Dansby RC	10.00	4.00
❑	113	Vernon Carey RC	8.00	3.00
❑	114	Ryan Krause RC	8.00	3.00
❑	115	Daryl Smith RC	10.00	4.00
❑	116	Ricardo Colclough RC	10.00	4.00
❑	117	Michael Boulware RC	10.00	4.00
❑	118	Chris Cooley RC	10.00	4.00
❑	119	Tank Johnson RC	8.00	3.00
❑	120	Marquise Hill RC	8.00	3.00
❑	121	Teddy Lehman RC	10.00	4.00
❑	122	Antwan Odom RC	10.00	4.00
❑	123	Sean Jones RC	8.00	3.00
❑	124	Junior Siavii RC	10.00	4.00
❑	125	Joey Thomas RC	10.00	4.00
❑	126	Shawntae Spencer RC	10.00	4.00
❑	127	Dontarrious Thomas RC	10.00	4.00
❑	128	Travis LaBoy RC	10.00	4.00
❑	129	Justin Jenkins RC	8.00	3.00
❑	130	Dwan Edwards RC	5.00	2.00
❑	131	Derrick Strait RC	10.00	4.00
❑	132	Matt Ware RC	10.00	4.00
❑	133	Jared Lorenzen RC	8.00	3.00
❑	134	Demorrio Williams RC	10.00	4.00
❑	135	Bob Sanders RC	20.00	10.00
❑	136	Justin Smiley RC	10.00	4.00
❑	137	Casey Bramlet RC	8.00	3.00
❑	138	Jake Grove RC	5.00	2.00
❑	139	Thomas Tapeh RC	8.00	3.00
❑	140	Igor Olshansky RC	10.00	4.00
❑	141	Stuart Schweigert RC	10.00	4.00
❑	142	Cody Pickett RC	10.00	4.00
❑	143	Derrick Ward RC	5.00	2.00
❑	144	Gilbert Gardner RC	8.00	3.00
❑	145	D.J. Hackett RC	8.00	3.00
❑	146	Marquis Cooper RC	8.00	3.00
❑	147	Courtney Watson RC	10.00	4.00
❑	148	Jim Sorgi RC	10.00	4.00
❑	149	Caleb Miller RC	8.00	3.00
❑	150	Casey Clausen RC	10.00	4.00
❑	151	Jammal Lord RC	10.00	4.00
❑	152	Sloan Thomas RC	8.00	3.00
❑	153	Keyaron Fox RC	8.00	3.00
❑	154	Adimchinobe Echemandu RC	8.00	3.00
❑	155	Ryan Dinwiddie RC	8.00	3.00
❑	156	Kris Wilson RC	10.00	4.00

❑ 157 D.J. Williams RC 12.00 5.00
❑ 158 Tim Euhus RC 10.00 4.00
❑ 159 Bradlee Van Pelt RC 15.00 6.00
❑ 160 Keiwan Ratliff RC 8.00 3.00
❑ 161 Darnell Dockett RC 8.00 3.00
❑ 162 Troy Fleming RC 8.00 3.00
❑ 163 Tramon Douglas RC 5.00 2.00
❑ 164 Jeremy LeSueur RC 8.00 3.00
❑ 165 Matt Mauck RC 10.00 4.00
❑ 166 Sean Taylor RC 12.00 5.00
❑ 167 B.J. Symons RC 12.00 5.00
❑ 168 Quincy Wilson RC 10.00 4.00
❑ 169 Ernest Wilford RC 12.00 5.00
❑ 170 Jerricho Cotchery RC 12.00 5.00
❑ 171 Michael Turner RC 12.00 5.00
❑ 172 Samie Parker RC 12.00 5.00
❑ 173 Andy Hall RC 10.00 4.00
❑ 174 Keith Smith RC 10.00 4.00
❑ 175 Josh Harris RC 12.00 5.00
❑ 176 Maurice Mann RC 10.00 4.00
❑ 177 Jonathan Vilma RC 12.00 5.00
❑ 178 Jeff Smoker RC 12.00 5.00
❑ 179 Ben Hartsock RC 12.00 5.00
❑ 180 Chris Gamble RC 15.00 6.00
❑ 181 Derrick Hamilton RC 10.00 4.00
❑ 182 John Navarre RC 12.00 5.00
❑ 183 P.K. Sam RC 10.00 4.00
❑ 184 Kenechi Udeze RC 12.00 5.00
❑ 185 Mewelde Moore RC 15.00 6.00
❑ 186 Carlos Francis RC 10.00 4.00
❑ 187 Dunta Robinson RC 12.00 5.00
❑ 188 Johnnie Morant RC 12.00 5.00
❑ 189 Ahmad Carroll RC 15.00 6.00
❑ 190 Vince Wilfork RC 15.00 6.00
❑ 191 Tatum Bell JSY AU RC 40.00 15.00
❑ 192 Cedric Cobbs JSY AU RC 20.00 7.50
❑ 193 Darius Watts JSY AU RC 20.00 7.50
❑ 194 Jul.Jones JSY AU/375 RC 150.00 75.00
❑ 195 Robert Gallery JSY AU RC 25.00 10.00
❑ 196 DeAngelo Hall JSY AU RC 30.00 12.50
❑ 197 Ben Watson JSY AU RC 20.00 7.50
❑ 198 Ben Troupe JSY AU RC 20.00 7.50
❑ 199 Matt Schaub JSY AU RC 35.00 20.00
❑ 200 Michael Jenkins JSY AU RC 25.00 12.50
❑ 201 Luke McCown JSY AU RC 20.00 7.50
❑ 202 Devery Henderson JSY AU RC 15.00 6.00
❑ 203 Bernard Berrian JSY AU RC 20.00 7.50
❑ 204 Keary Colbert JSY AU RC 25.00 10.00
❑ 205 Devard Darling JSY AU RC 25.00 10.00
❑ 206 Lee Evans JSY AU RC 30.00 15.00
❑ 207 Greg Jones JSY AU RC 25.00 12.50
❑ 208 Mich.Clayton JSY AU RC 40.00 15.00
❑ 209 Re.Williams JSY AU RC 25.00 10.00
❑ 210 C.Perry JSY AU/799 RC 30.00 12.50
❑ 211 Rash.Woods JSY AU RC 20.00 7.50
❑ 212 J.P. Losman JSY AU RC 40.00 15.00
❑ 213 Kevin Jones JSY AU RC 50.00 20.00
❑ 214 K.Winslow JSY AU/375 RC 50.00 25.00
❑ 215 S.Jackson JSY AU/375 RC 120.00 60.00
❑ 216 Hamilton JSY AU RC EXCH 15.00 6.00
❑ 217 Ro.Will.JSY AU/375 RC 100.00 40.00
❑ 218 P.Rivers JSY AU/375 RC 125.00 75.00
❑ 219 Fitzgerald JSY AU/100 RC 300.00 150.00
❑ 220 Roethlis.JSY AU/375 RC 450.00 250.00
❑ 221 Manning JSY AU/375 RC 350.00 200.00

2005 SPx

❑ COMP.SET w/o SP's (100) 30.00 15.00
❑ 101-170 RC PRINT RUN 1199 SER.#'d SETS
❑ 171-200 RC PRINT RUN 499 SER.#'d SETS
❑ EXCH EXPIRATION: 10/25/2008
❑ JSY AU RC PRINT RUN 1275 UNLESS NOTED
❑ UNPRICED NFL LOGO AUTOS #'d OF 1
❑ 1 Larry Fitzgerald 1.00 .40
❑ 2 Anquan Boldin .60 .25

❑ 3 Josh McCown .60 .25
❑ 4 Michael Vick 1.50 .60
❑ 5 Alge Crumpler .60 .25
❑ 6 Peerless Price .50 .20
❑ 7 Ray Lewis 1.00 .40
❑ 8 Jamal Lewis 1.00 .40
❑ 9 Kyle Boller .60 .25
❑ 10 J.P. Losman 1.00 .40
❑ 11 Willis McGahee 1.00 .40
❑ 12 Eric Moulds .60 .25
❑ 13 Jake Delhomme 1.00 .40
❑ 14 DeShaun Foster .60 .25
❑ 15 Steve Smith .60 .25
❑ 16 Brian Urlacher 1.00 .40
❑ 17 Rex Grossman .60 .25
❑ 18 Muhsin Muhammad .60 .25
❑ 19 Carson Palmer 1.00 .40
❑ 20 Rudi Johnson .60 .25
❑ 21 Chad Johnson 1.00 .40
❑ 22 Julius Jones 1.25 .50
❑ 23 Keyshawn Johnson .60 .25
❑ 24 Roy Williams S .60 .25
❑ 25 Tatum Bell .60 .25
❑ 26 Jake Plummer .60 .25
❑ 27 Ashley Lelie .60 .25
❑ 28 Roy Williams WR 1.00 .40
❑ 29 Kevin Jones 1.00 .40
❑ 30 Joey Harrington 1.00 .40
❑ 31 Brett Favre 2.50 1.00
❑ 32 Ahman Green 1.00 .40
❑ 33 Javon Walker .60 .25
❑ 34 David Carr 1.00 .40
❑ 35 Andre Johnson .60 .25
❑ 36 Domanick Davis .60 .25
❑ 37 Peyton Manning 1.50 .60
❑ 38 Reggie Wayne .60 .25
❑ 39 Edgerrin James 1.00 .40
❑ 40 Marvin Harrison 1.00 .40
❑ 41 Byron Leftwich 1.00 .40
❑ 42 Fred Taylor .60 .25
❑ 43 Jimmy Smith .60 .25
❑ 44 Priest Holmes 1.00 .40
❑ 45 Larry Johnson 1.00 .40
❑ 46 Trent Green .60 .25
❑ 47 A.J. Feeley .60 .25
❑ 48 Chris Chambers .60 .25
❑ 49 Randy McMichael .50 .20
❑ 50 Daunte Culpepper 1.00 .40
❑ 51 Nate Burleson .60 .25
❑ 52 Michael Bennett .60 .25
❑ 53 Tom Brady 2.50 1.00
❑ 54 Corey Dillon .60 .25
❑ 55 Deion Branch .60 .25
❑ 56 David Givens .60 .25
❑ 57 Aaron Brooks .60 .25
❑ 58 Deuce McAllister 1.00 .40
❑ 59 Joe Horn .60 .25
❑ 60 Eli Manning 2.00 .75
❑ 61 Jeremy Shockey 1.00 .40
❑ 62 Tiki Barber 1.00 .40
❑ 63 Chad Pennington 1.00 .40
❑ 64 Curtis Martin 1.00 .40
❑ 65 Laveranues Coles .60 .25
❑ 66 Kerry Collins .60 .25
❑ 67 Jerry Porter .60 .25
❑ 68 Randy Moss 1.00 .40
❑ 69 Donovan McNabb 1.25 .50
❑ 70 Terrell Owens 1.00 .40
❑ 71 Brian Dawkins .60 .25
❑ 72 Brian Westbrook .60 .25
❑ 73 Ben Roethlisberger 2.50 1.00
❑ 74 Jerome Bettis 1.00 .40
❑ 75 Hines Ward 1.00 .40
❑ 76 Duce Staley .60 .25
❑ 77 Drew Brees 1.00 .40
❑ 78 LaDainian Tomlinson 1.25 .50
❑ 79 Antonio Gates 1.00 .40
❑ 80 Eric Parker .50 .20
❑ 81 Tim Rattay .50 .20
❑ 82 Kevan Barlow .60 .25
❑ 83 Eric Johnson .60 .25
❑ 84 Shaun Alexander 1.25 .50
❑ 85 Darrell Jackson .60 .25
❑ 86 Matt Hasselbeck .60 .25
❑ 87 Marc Bulger 1.00 .40
❑ 88 Steven Jackson 1.25 .50
❑ 89 Marshall Faulk 1.00 .40
❑ 90 Torry Holt 1.00 .40
❑ 91 Michael Pittman .50 .20
❑ 92 Brian Griese .60 .25
❑ 93 Michael Clayton 1.00 .40
❑ 94 Steve McNair 1.00 .40
❑ 95 Drew Bennett .60 .25
❑ 96 Billy Volek .60 .25
❑ 97 Chris Brown .60 .25
❑ 98 Clinton Portis 1.00 .40
❑ 99 Patrick Ramsey .60 .25
❑ 100 Santana Moss .60 .25
❑ 101 Matt Jones RC 20.00 7.50
❑ 102 Jonathan Babineaux RC 6.00 2.50
❑ 103 Darrent Williams RC 8.00 3.00
❑ 104 Timmy Chang RC 6.00 2.50
❑ 105 Kelvin Hayden RC 6.00 2.50
❑ 106 Paris Warren RC 6.00 2.50
❑ 107 Stanley Wilson RC 6.00 2.50
❑ 108 Walter Reyes RC 6.00 2.50
❑ 109 Roydell Williams RC 8.00 3.00
❑ 110 Chase Lyman RC 6.00 2.50
❑ 111 Anthony Davis RC 6.00 2.50
❑ 112 Rasheed Marshall RC 8.00 3.00
❑ 113 Jerome Carter RC 6.00 2.50
❑ 114 Mike Nugent RC 8.00 3.00
❑ 115 Brodney Pool RC 8.00 3.00
❑ 116 Sean Considine RC 8.00 3.00
❑ 117 Chris Rix RC 6.00 2.50
❑ 118 Donte Nicholson RC 8.00 3.00
❑ 119 Dustin Fox RC 8.00 3.00
❑ 120 Oshiomogho Atogwe RC 6.00 2.50
❑ 121 Vincent Fuller RC 6.00 2.50
❑ 122 Josh Bullocks RC 8.00 3.00
❑ 123 Ronald Bartell RC 6.00 2.50
❑ 124 Brock Berlin RC 6.00 2.50
❑ 125 Fabian Washington RC 8.00 3.00
❑ 126 Domonique Foxworth RC 8.00 3.00
❑ 127 Bryant McFadden RC 8.00 3.00
❑ 128 Marlin Jackson RC 8.00 3.00
❑ 129 Eric Green RC 4.00 1.50
❑ 130 Justin Miller RC 6.00 2.50
❑ 131 Lofa Tatupu RC 10.00 4.00
❑ 132 Justin Tuck RC 8.00 3.00
❑ 133 Kurt Campbell RC 6.00 2.50
❑ 134 Darryl Blackstock RC 6.00 2.50
❑ 135 Kevin Burnett RC 8.00 3.00
❑ 136 Marviel Underwood RC 6.00 2.50
❑ 137 Kirk Morrison RC 8.00 3.00
❑ 138 Alfred Fincher RC 6.00 2.50
❑ 139 Lance Mitchell RC 6.00 2.50
❑ 140 Barrett Ruud RC 8.00 3.00
❑ 141 David Pollack RC 8.00 3.00
❑ 142 Bill Swancutt RC 6.00 2.50

❑ 143 DeMarcus Ware RC 12.00 5.00
❑ 144 Steve Savoy RC 4.00 1.50
❑ 145 Matt Roth RC 8.00 3.00
❑ 146 Shaun Cody RC 8.00 3.00
❑ 147 Dan Cody RC 8.00 3.00
❑ 148 Jordan Beck RC 6.00 2.50
❑ 149 Kevin Everett RC 8.00 3.00
❑ 150 Anttaj Hawthorne RC 6.00 2.50
❑ 151 Mike Patterson RC 8.00 3.00
❑ 152 Jerome Collins RC 6.00 2.50
❑ 153 Dante Ridgeway RC 6.00 2.50
❑ 154 Bryan Randall RC 6.00 2.50
❑ 155 Marcus Maxwell RC 6.00 2.50
❑ 156 Airese Currie RC 8.00 3.00
❑ 157 Chad Owens RC 8.00 3.00
❑ 158 Brandon Jacobs RC 10.00 4.00
❑ 159 Manuel White RC 6.00 2.50
❑ 160 Ellis Hobbs RC 8.00 3.00
❑ 161 Lionel Gates RC 6.00 2.50
❑ 162 Ryan Fitzpatrick RC 12.00 5.00
❑ 163 Noah Herron RC 8.00 3.00
❑ 164 Kay-Jay Harris RC 6.00 2.50
❑ 165 T.A. McLendon RC 4.00 1.50
❑ 166 Kerry Rhodes RC 8.00 3.00
❑ 167 Nick Collins RC 8.00 3.00
❑ 168 Eric Moore RC 6.00 2.50
❑ 169 Harry Williams RC 6.00 2.50
❑ 170 Luis Castillo RC 8.00 3.00
❑ 171 James Kilian RC 10.00 4.00
❑ 172 Matt Cassel RC 15.00 6.00
❑ 173 Alvin Pearman RC 10.00 4.00
❑ 174 Dan Orlovsky RC 12.00 5.00
❑ 175 Damien Nash RC 8.00 3.00
❑ 176 Jason White RC 10.00 4.00
❑ 177 Craig Bragg RC 8.00 3.00
❑ 178 Craphonso Thorpe RC 8.00 3.00
❑ 179 Derrick Johnson RC 15.00 6.00
❑ 180 Derek Anderson RC 10.00 4.00
❑ 181 Darren Sproles RC 10.00 4.00
❑ 182 Cedric Houston RC 10.00 4.00
❑ 183 Jerome Mathis RC 10.00 4.00
❑ 184 Larry Brackins RC 8.00 3.00
❑ 185 Fred Gibson RC 8.00 3.00
❑ 186 J.R. Russell RC 8.00 3.00
❑ 187 Alex Smith TE RC 10.00 4.00
❑ 188 Deandra Cobb RC 8.00 3.00
❑ 189 Tab Perry RC 10.00 4.00
❑ 190 Travis Johnson RC 8.00 3.00
❑ 191A Marion Barber RC 15.00 6.00
❑ 191B Andrew Walter JSY AU RC 40.00 15.00
❑ 192A Erasmus James RC 10.00 4.00
❑ 192B V.Morency JSY AU RC 25.00 10.00
❑ 193A Marcus Spears RC 8.00 3.00
❑ 193B Antrel Rolle JSY AU RC 25.00 10.00
❑ 194A Channing Crowder RC 10.00 4.00
❑ 194B Adam Jones JSY AU RC 25.00 10.00
❑ 195A Odell Thurman RC 8.00 3.00
❑ 195B M.Clarett JSY AU/250 50.00 25.00
❑ 196A Shawne Merriman RC 15.00 6.00
❑ 196B Mark Bradley JSY AU RC 25.00 10.00
❑ 197A Adrian McPherson RC 10.00 4.00
❑ 197B Eric Shelton JSY AU RC 25.00 10.00
❑ 198A Chris Henry RC 10.00 4.00
❑ 198B Kyle Orton JSY AU RC 40.00 20.00
❑ 199A Thomas Davis RC 10.00 4.00
❑ 199B Ryan Moats JSY AU RC 25.00 12.50
❑ 200A Corey Webster RC 10.00 4.00
❑ 200B Frank Gore JSY AU RC 30.00 15.00
❑ 201 J.J. Arrington JSY AU RC 40.00 15.00
❑ 202 M.Will.JSY AU/250 EXCH 150.00 75.00
❑ 203 V.Jackson JSY AU RC 25.00 10.00
❑ 204 Stefan LeFors JSY AU RC 25.00 10.00
❑ 205 D.Greene JSY AU RC EXCH 25.00 10.00
❑ 206 T.Murphy JSY AU RC 25.00 10.00
❑ 207 Courtney Roby JSY AU RC 25.00 10.00
❑ 208 Carlos Rogers JSY AU RC 30.00 12.50
❑ 209 Charlie Frye JSY AU RC 50.00 30.00
❑ 210 Mark Clayton JSY AU RC 30.00 12.50
❑ 211 Roddy White JSY AU RC 25.00 10.00
❑ 212 Jason Campbell JSY AU RC 40.00 25.00
❑ 213 Roscoe Parrish JSY AU RC 25.00 10.00
❑ 214 Reggie Brown JSY AU RC 30.00 15.00
❑ 215 H.Miller JSY AU RC EXCH 60.00 35.00
❑ 216 Williamson JSY AU/250 RC 100.00 50.00
❑ 217 Ciatrick Fason JSY AU RC 25.00 10.00
❑ 218 Benson JSY AU/150 RC EX 300.00 175.00
❑ 219 B.Edwards JSY AU/250 RC 150.00 75.00
❑ 220 Ro.Brown JSY AU/250 RC 250.00 125.00
❑ 221 C.Williams JSY AU/250 RC 350.00 200.00
❑ 222 A.Smith QB JSY AU/250 RC 250.00 125.00
❑ 223 A.Rodgers JSY AU/250 RC 225.00 125.00

1991 Stadium Club

❑ COMPLETE SET (500) 60.00 30.00
❑ 1 Pepper Johnson .20 .07
❑ 2 Emmitt Smith 5.00 2.00
❑ 3 Deion Sanders 1.50 .60
❑ 4 Andre Collins .20 .07
❑ 5 Eric Metcalf .40 .15
❑ 6 Richard Dent .40 .15
❑ 7 Eric Martin .20 .07
❑ 8 Marcus Allen .75 .30
❑ 9 Gary Anderson K .20 .07
❑ 10 Joey Browner .20 .07
❑ 11 Lorenzo White .20 .07
❑ 12 Bruce Smith .75 .30
❑ 13 Mark Boyer .20 .07
❑ 14 Mike Piel .20 .07
❑ 15 Albert Bentley .20 .07
❑ 16 Bennie Blades .20 .07
❑ 17 Jason Staurovsky .20 .07
❑ 18 Anthony Toney .20 .07
❑ 19 Dave Krieg .40 .15
❑ 20 Harvey Williams RC .75 .30
❑ 21 Bubba Paris .20 .07
❑ 22 Tim McGee .20 .07
❑ 23 Brian Noble .20 .07
❑ 24 Vinny Testaverde .40 .15
❑ 25 Doug Widell .20 .07
❑ 26 John Jackson WR RC .20 .07
❑ 27 Marion Butts .40 .15
❑ 28 Deron Cherry .20 .07
❑ 29 Don Warren .20 .07
❑ 30 Rod Woodson .75 .30
❑ 31 Mike Baab .20 .07
❑ 32 Greg Jackson RC .20 .07
❑ 33 Jerry Robinson .20 .07
❑ 34 Dalton Hilliard .20 .07
❑ 35 Brian Jordan .40 .15
❑ 36 James Thornton UER .20 .07
❑ 37 Michael Irvin .75 .30
❑ 38 Billy Joe Tolliver .20 .07
❑ 39 Jeff Herrod .20 .07
❑ 40 Scott Norwood .20 .07
❑ 41 Ferrell Edmunds .20 .07
❑ 42 Andre Waters .20 .07
❑ 43 Kevin Glover .20 .07
❑ 44 Ray Berry .20 .07
❑ 45 Timm Rosenbach .20 .07
❑ 46 Reuben Davis .20 .07
❑ 47 Charles Wilson .20 .07
❑ 48 Todd Marinovich RC .20 .07
❑ 49 Harris Barton .20 .07
❑ 50 Jim Breech .20 .07
❑ 51 Ron Holmes .20 .07
❑ 52 Chris Singleton .20 .07
❑ 53 Pat Leahy .20 .07
❑ 54 Tom Newberry .20 .07
❑ 55 Greg Montgomery .20 .07
❑ 56 Robert Blackmon .20 .07
❑ 57 Jay Hilgenberg .20 .07
❑ 58 Rodney Hampton .75 .30
❑ 59 Brett Perriman .75 .30
❑ 60 Ricky Watters RC 6.00 2.50
❑ 61 Howie Long .75 .30
❑ 62 Frank Cornish .20 .07
❑ 63 Chris Miller .40 .15
❑ 64 Keith Taylor .20 .07
❑ 65 Tony Paige .20 .07
❑ 66 Gary Zimmerman .20 .07
❑ 67 Mark Royals RC .20 .07
❑ 68 Ernie Jones .20 .07
❑ 69 David Grant .20 .07
❑ 70 Shane Conlan .20 .07
❑ 71 Jerry Rice 2.50 1.00
❑ 72 Christian Okoye .20 .07
❑ 73 Eddie Murray .20 .07
❑ 74 Reggie White .75 .30
❑ 75 Jeff Graham RC WR 1.00 .40
❑ 76 Mark Jackson .20 .07
❑ 77 David Grayson .20 .07
❑ 78 Dan Stryzinski .20 .07
❑ 79 Sterling Sharpe .75 .30
❑ 80 Cleveland Gary .20 .07
❑ 81 Johnny Meads .20 .07
❑ 82 Howard Cross .20 .07
❑ 83 Ken O'Brien .20 .07
❑ 84 Brian Blades .40 .15
❑ 85 Ethan Horton .20 .07
❑ 86 Bruce Armstrong .20 .07
❑ 87 James Washington RC .20 .07
❑ 88 Eugene Daniel .20 .07
❑ 89 James Lofton .40 .15
❑ 90 Louis Oliver .20 .07
❑ 91 Boomer Esiason .40 .15
❑ 92 Seth Joyner .40 .15
❑ 93 Mark Carrier WR .75 .30
❑ 94 Brett Favre RC UER 50.00 25.00
❑ 95 Lee Williams .20 .07
❑ 96 Neal Anderson .40 .15
❑ 97 Brent Jones .75 .30
❑ 98 John Alt .20 .07
❑ 99 Rodney Peete .40 .15
❑ 100 Steve Broussard .20 .07
❑ 101 Cedric Mack .20 .07
❑ 102 Pat Swilling .40 .15
❑ 103 Stan Humphries .75 .30
❑ 104 Darrell Thompson .20 .07
❑ 105 Reggie Langhorne .20 .07
❑ 106 Kenny Davidson .20 .07
❑ 107 Jim Everett .40 .15
❑ 108 Keith Millard .20 .07
❑ 109 Garry Lewis .20 .07
❑ 110 Jeff Hostetler .40 .15
❑ 111 Lamar Lathon .20 .07
❑ 112 Johnny Bailey .20 .07
❑ 113 Cornelius Bennett .40 .15
❑ 114 Travis McNeal .20 .07
❑ 115 Jeff Lageman .20 .07
❑ 116 Nick Bell RC .20 .07
❑ 117 Calvin Williams .40 .15
❑ 118 Shawn Lee RC .20 .07
❑ 119 Anthony Munoz .40 .15
❑ 120 Jay Novacek .75 .30
❑ 121 Kevin Fagan .20 .07
❑ 122 Leo Goeas .20 .07
❑ 123 Vance Johnson .20 .07
❑ 124 Brent Williams .20 .07

❑ 125 Clarence Verdin .20 .07
❑ 126 Luis Sharpe .20 .07
❑ 127 Darrell Green .20 .07
❑ 128 Barry Word .20 .07
❑ 129 Steve Walsh .20 .07
❑ 130 Bryan Hinkle .20 .07
❑ 131 Ed West .20 .07
❑ 132 Jeff Campbell .20 .07
❑ 133 Dennis Byrd .20 .07
❑ 134 Nate Odomes .20 .07
❑ 135 Trace Armstrong .20 .07
❑ 136 Jarvis Williams .20 .07
❑ 137 Warren Moon .75 .30
❑ 138 Eric Moten RC .20 .07
❑ 139 Tony Woods .20 .07
❑ 140 Phil Simms .40 .15
❑ 141 Ricky Reynolds .20 .07
❑ 142 Frank Stams .20 .07
❑ 143 Kevin Mack .20 .07
❑ 144 Wade Wilson .40 .15
❑ 145 Shawn Collins .20 .07
❑ 146 Roger Craig .40 .15
❑ 147 Jeff Feagles RC .20 .07
❑ 148 Norm Johnson .20 .07
❑ 149 Terance Mathis .40 .15
❑ 150 Reggie Cobb .20 .07
❑ 151 Chip Banks .20 .07
❑ 152 Darryl Pollard .20 .07
❑ 153 Karl Mecklenburg .20 .07
❑ 154 Ricky Proehl .20 .07
❑ 155 Pete Stoyanovich .20 .07
❑ 156 John Stephens .20 .07
❑ 157 Ron Morris .20 .07
❑ 158 Steve DeBerg .20 .07
❑ 159 Mike Munchak .40 .15
❑ 160 Brett Maxie .20 .07
❑ 161 Don Beebe .20 .07
❑ 162 Martin Mayhew .20 .07
❑ 163 Merril Hoge .20 .07
❑ 164 Kelvin Pritchett RC .40 .15
❑ 165 Jim Jeffcoat .20 .07
❑ 166 Myron Guyton .20 .07
❑ 167 Ickey Woods .20 .07
❑ 168 Andre Ware .40 .15
❑ 169 Gary Plummer .20 .07
❑ 170 Henry Ellard .40 .15
❑ 171 Scott Davis .20 .07
❑ 172 Randall McDaniel .20 .07
❑ 173 Randal Hill RC .40 .15
❑ 174 Anthony Bell .20 .07
❑ 175 Gary Anderson RB .20 .07
❑ 176 Byron Evans .20 .07
❑ 177 Tony Mandarich .20 .07
❑ 178 Jeff George 1.00 .40
❑ 179 Art Monk .40 .15
❑ 180 Mike Kenn .20 .07
❑ 181 Sean Landeta .20 .07
❑ 182 Shaun Gayle .20 .07
❑ 183 Michael Carter .20 .07
❑ 184 Robb Thomas .20 .07
❑ 185 Richmond Webb .20 .07
❑ 186 Carnell Lake .20 .07
❑ 187 Rueben Mayes .20 .07
❑ 188 Issiac Holt .20 .07
❑ 189 Leon Seals .20 .07
❑ 190 Al Smith .20 .07
❑ 191 Steve Atwater .20 .07
❑ 192 Greg McMurtry .20 .07
❑ 193 Al Toon .40 .15
❑ 194 Cortez Kennedy .75 .30
❑ 195 Gill Byrd .20 .07
❑ 196 Carl Zander .20 .07
❑ 197 Robert Brown .20 .07
❑ 198 Buford McGee .20 .07
❑ 199 Mervyn Fernandez .20 .07
❑ 200 Mike Dumas RC .20 .07
❑ 201 Rob Burnett RC .40 .15
❑ 202 Brian Mitchell .40 .15
❑ 203 Randall Cunningham .75 .30
❑ 204 Sammie Smith .20 .07
❑ 205 Ken Clarke .20 .07
❑ 206 Floyd Dixon .20 .07
❑ 207 Ken Norton .40 .15
❑ 208 Tony Siragusa RC .40 .15
❑ 209 Louis Lipps .20 .07
❑ 210 Chris Martin .20 .07
❑ 211 Jamie Mueller .20 .07
❑ 212 Dave Waymer .20 .07
❑ 213 Donnell Woolford .20 .07
❑ 214 Paul Gruber .20 .07
❑ 215 Ken Harvey .40 .15
❑ 216 Henry Jones RC .40 .15
❑ 217 Tommy Barnhardt RC .20 .07
❑ 218 Arthur Cox .20 .07
❑ 219 Pat Terrell .20 .07
❑ 220 Curtis Duncan .20 .07
❑ 221 Jeff Jaeger .20 .07
❑ 222 Scott Stephen RC .20 .07
❑ 223 Rob Moore 1.00 .40
❑ 224 Chris Hinton .20 .07
❑ 225 Marv Cook .20 .07
❑ 226 Patrick Hunter RC .20 .07
❑ 227 Earnest Byner .20 .07
❑ 228 Troy Aikman 3.00 1.25
❑ 229 Kevin Walker RC .20 .07
❑ 230 Keith Jackson .40 .15
❑ 231 Russell Maryland RC .75 .30
❑ 232 Charles Haley .40 .15
❑ 233 Nick Lowery .20 .07
❑ 234 Erik Howard .20 .07
❑ 235 Leonard Smith .20 .07
❑ 236 Tim Irwin .20 .07
❑ 237 Simon Fletcher .20 .07
❑ 238 Thomas Everett .20 .07
❑ 239 Reggie Roby .20 .07
❑ 240 Leroy Hoard .40 .15
❑ 241 Wayne Haddix .20 .07
❑ 242 Gary Clark .75 .30
❑ 243 Eric Andolsek .20 .07
❑ 244 Jim Wahler RC .20 .07
❑ 245 Vaughan Johnson .20 .07
❑ 246 Kevin Butler .20 .07
❑ 247 Steve Tasker .40 .15
❑ 248 LeRoy Butler .40 .15
❑ 249 Darion Conner .20 .07
❑ 250 Eric Turner RC .40 .15
❑ 251 Kevin Ross .20 .07
❑ 252 Stephen Baker .20 .07
❑ 253 Harold Green .40 .15
❑ 254 Rohn Stark .20 .07
❑ 255 Joe Nash .20 .07
❑ 256 Jesse Sapolu .20 .07
❑ 257 Willie Gault .40 .15
❑ 258 Jerome Brown .20 .07
❑ 259 Ken Willis .20 .07
❑ 260 Courtney Hall .20 .07
❑ 261 Hart Lee Dykes .20 .07
❑ 262 William Fuller .40 .15
❑ 263 Stan Thomas .20 .07
❑ 264 Dan Marino 4.00 1.50
❑ 265 Ron Cox .20 .07
❑ 266 Eric Green .20 .07
❑ 267 Anthony Carter .40 .15
❑ 268 Jerry Ball .20 .07
❑ 269 Ron Hall .20 .07
❑ 270 Dennis Smith .20 .07
❑ 271 Eric Hill .20 .07
❑ 272 Dan McGwire RC .20 .07
❑ 273 Lewis Billups UER .20 .07
❑ 274 Rickey Jackson .20 .07
❑ 275 Jim Sweeney .20 .07
❑ 276 Pat Beach .20 .07
❑ 277 Kevin Porter .20 .07
❑ 278 Mike Sherrard .20 .07
❑ 279 Andy Heck .20 .07
❑ 280 Ron Brown .20 .07
❑ 281 Lawrence Taylor .75 .30
❑ 282 Anthony Pleasant .20 .07
❑ 283 Wes Hopkins .20 .07
❑ 284 Jim Lachey .20 .07
❑ 285 Tim Harris .20 .07
❑ 286 Tory Epps .20 .07
❑ 287 Wendell Davis .20 .07
❑ 288 Bubba McDowell .20 .07
❑ 289 Bubby Brister .20 .07
❑ 290 Chris Zorich RC .75 .30
❑ 291 Mike Merriweather .20 .07
❑ 292 Burt Grossman .20 .07
❑ 293 Erik McMillan .20 .07
❑ 294 John Elway 4.00 1.50
❑ 295 Toi Cook RC .20 .07
❑ 296 Tom Rathman .20 .07
❑ 297 Matt Bahr .20 .07
❑ 298 Chris Spielman .40 .15
❑ 299 F.J.Nunn w/Aikman/Emmitt .40 .15
❑ 300 Jim C. Jensen .20 .07
❑ 301 David Fulcher UER .20 .07
❑ 302 Tommy Hodson .20 .07
❑ 303 Stephone Paige .20 .07
❑ 304 Greg Townsend .20 .07
❑ 305 Dean Biasucci .20 .07
❑ 306 Jimmie Jones .20 .07
❑ 307 Eugene Marve .20 .07
❑ 308 Flipper Anderson .20 .07
❑ 309 Darryl Talley .20 .07
❑ 310 Mike Croel RC .20 .07
❑ 311 Thane Gash .20 .07
❑ 312 Perry Kemp .20 .07
❑ 313 Heath Sherman .20 .07
❑ 314 Mike Singletary .40 .15
❑ 315 Chip Lohmiller .20 .07
❑ 316 Tunch Ilkin .20 .07
❑ 317 Junior Seau 1.25 .50
❑ 318 Mike Gann .20 .07
❑ 319 Tim McDonald .20 .07
❑ 320 Kyle Clifton .20 .07
❑ 321 Dan Owens .20 .07
❑ 322 Tim Grunhard .20 .07
❑ 323 Stan Brock .20 .07
❑ 324 Rodney Holman .20 .07
❑ 325 Mark Ingram .40 .15
❑ 326 Browning Nagle RC .20 .07
❑ 327 Joe Montana 5.00 2.00
❑ 328 Carl Lee .20 .07
❑ 329 John L. Williams .20 .07
❑ 330 David Griggs .20 .07
❑ 331 Clarence Kay .20 .07
❑ 332 Irving Fryar .40 .15
❑ 333 Doug Smith DT RC** .40 .15
❑ 334 Kent Hull .20 .07
❑ 335 Mike Wilcher .20 .07
❑ 336 Ray Donaldson .20 .07
❑ 337 Mark Carrier DB UER .20 .07
❑ 338 Kelvin Martin .20 .07
❑ 339 Keith Byars .20 .07
❑ 340 Wilber Marshall .20 .07
❑ 341 Ronnie Lott .40 .15
❑ 342 Blair Thomas .20 .07
❑ 343 Ronnie Harmon .20 .07
❑ 344 Brian Brennan .20 .07
❑ 345 Charles McRae RC .20 .07
❑ 346 Michael Cofer .20 .07
❑ 347 Keith Willis .20 .07
❑ 348 Bruce Kozerski .20 .07
❑ 349 Dave Meggett .40 .15
❑ 350 John Taylor .40 .15
❑ 351 Johnny Holland .20 .07
❑ 352 Steve Christie .20 .07
❑ 353 Ricky Ervins RC .40 .15
❑ 354 Robert Massey .20 .07
❑ 355 Derrick Thomas .75 .30
❑ 356 Tommy Kane .20 .07
❑ 357 Melvin Bratton .20 .07
❑ 358 Bruce Matthews .40 .15

Card		
❑ 359 Mark Duper	.40	.15
❑ 360 Jeff Wright RC	.20	.07
❑ 361 Barry Sanders	4.00	1.50
❑ 362 Chuck Webb RC	.20	.07
❑ 363 Darryl Grant	.20	.07
❑ 364 William Roberts	.20	.07
❑ 365 Reggie Rutland	.20	.07
❑ 366 Clay Matthews	.40	.15
❑ 367 Anthony Miller	.40	.15
❑ 368 Mike Prior	.20	.07
❑ 369 Jessie Tuggle	.20	.07
❑ 370 Brad Muster	.20	.07
❑ 371 Jay Schroeder	.20	.07
❑ 372 Greg Lloyd	.75	.30
❑ 373 Mike Cofer	.20	.07
❑ 374 James Brooks	.40	.15
❑ 375 Danny Noonan UER	.20	.07
❑ 376 Latin Berry RC	.20	.07
❑ 377 Brad Baxter	.20	.07
❑ 378 Godfrey Myles RC	.20	.07
❑ 379 Morten Andersen	.20	.07
❑ 380 Keith Woodside	.20	.07
❑ 381 Bobby Humphrey	.20	.07
❑ 382 Mike Golic	.20	.07
❑ 383 Keith McCants	.20	.07
❑ 384 Anthony Thompson	.20	.07
❑ 385 Mark Clayton	.40	.15
❑ 386 Neil Smith	.75	.30
❑ 387 Bryan Millard	.20	.07
❑ 388 Mel Gray UER	.40	.15
❑ 389 Ernest Givins	.40	.15
❑ 390 Reyna Thompson	.20	.07
❑ 391 Eric Bieniemy RC	.20	.07
❑ 392 Jon Hand	.20	.07
❑ 393 Mark Rypien	.40	.15
❑ 394 Bill Romanowski	.20	.07
❑ 395 Thurman Thomas	.75	.30
❑ 396 Jim Harbaugh	.75	.30
❑ 397 Don Mosebar	.20	.07
❑ 398 Andre Rison	.40	.15
❑ 399 Mike Johnson	.20	.07
❑ 400 Dermontti Dawson	.20	.07
❑ 401 Herschel Walker	.40	.15
❑ 402 Joe Prokop	.20	.07
❑ 403 Eddie Brown	.20	.07
❑ 404 Nate Newton	.40	.15
❑ 405 Damone Johnson RC	.20	.07
❑ 406 Jessie Hester	.20	.07
❑ 407 Jim Arnold	.20	.07
❑ 408 Ray Agnew	.20	.07
❑ 409 Michael Brooks	.20	.07
❑ 410 Keith Sims	.20	.07
❑ 411 Carl Banks	.20	.07
❑ 412 Jonathan Hayes	.20	.07
❑ 413 Richard Johnson CB RC	.20	.07
❑ 414 Darryll Lewis RC	.40	.15
❑ 415 Jeff Bryant	.20	.07
❑ 416 Leslie O'Neal	.40	.15
❑ 417 Andre Reed	.40	.15
❑ 418 Charles Mann	.20	.07
❑ 419 Keith DeLong	.20	.07
❑ 420 Bruce Hill	.20	.07
❑ 421 Matt Brock RC	.20	.07
❑ 422 Johnny Johnson	.20	.07
❑ 423 Mark Bortz	.20	.07
❑ 424 Ben Smith	.20	.07
❑ 425 Jeff Cross	.20	.07
❑ 426 Irv Pankey	.20	.07
❑ 427 Hassan Jones	.20	.07
❑ 428 Andre Tippett	.20	.07
❑ 429 Tim Worley	.20	.07
❑ 430 Daniel Stubbs	.20	.07
❑ 431 Max Montoya	.20	.07
❑ 432 Jumbo Elliott	.20	.07
❑ 433 Duane Bickett	.20	.07
❑ 434 Nate Lewis RC	.20	.07
❑ 435 Leonard Russell RC	.75	.30
❑ 436 Hoby Brenner	.20	.07
❑ 437 Ricky Sanders	.20	.07
❑ 438 Pierce Holt	.20	.07
❑ 439 Derrick Fenner	.20	.07
❑ 440 Drew Hill	.20	.07
❑ 441 Will Wolford	.20	.07
❑ 442 Albert Lewis	.20	.07
❑ 443 James Francis	.20	.07
❑ 444 Chris Jacke	.20	.07
❑ 445 Mike Farr	.20	.07
❑ 446 Stephen Braggs	.20	.07
❑ 447 Michael Haynes	.75	.30
❑ 448 Freeman McNeil UER	.20	.07
❑ 449 Kevin Donnalley RC	.20	.07
❑ 450 John Offerdahl	.20	.07
❑ 451 Eric Allen	.20	.07
❑ 452 Keith McKeller	.20	.07
❑ 453 Kevin Greene	.40	.15
❑ 454 Ronnie Lippett	.20	.07
❑ 455 Ray Childress	.20	.07
❑ 456 Mike Saxon	.20	.07
❑ 457 Mark Robinson	.20	.07
❑ 458 Greg Kragen	.20	.07
❑ 459 Steve Jordan	.20	.07
❑ 460 John Johnson RC	.20	.07
❑ 461 Sam Mills	.20	.07
❑ 462 Bo Jackson	1.00	.40
❑ 463 Mark Collins	.20	.07
❑ 464 Percy Snow	.20	.07
❑ 465 Jeff Bostic	.20	.07
❑ 466 Jacob Green	.20	.07
❑ 467 Dexter Carter	.20	.07
❑ 468 Rich Camarillo	.20	.07
❑ 469 Bill Brooks	.20	.07
❑ 470 John Carney	.20	.07
❑ 471 Don Majkowski	.20	.07
❑ 472 Ralph Tamm RC	.20	.07
❑ 473 Fred Barnett	.75	.30
❑ 474 Jim Covert	.20	.07
❑ 475 Kenneth Davis	.20	.07
❑ 476 Jerry Gray	.20	.07
❑ 477 Broderick Thomas	.20	.07
❑ 478 Chris Doleman	.20	.07
❑ 479 Haywood Jeffires	.40	.15
❑ 480 Craig Heyward	.40	.15
❑ 481 Markus Koch	.20	.07
❑ 482 Tim Krumrie	.20	.07
❑ 483 Robert Clark	.20	.07
❑ 484 Mike Rozier	.20	.07
❑ 485 Danny Villa	.20	.07
❑ 486 Gerald Williams	.20	.07
❑ 487 Steve Wisniewski	.20	.07
❑ 488 J.B. Brown	.20	.07
❑ 489 Eugene Robinson	.20	.07
❑ 490 Ottis Anderson	.40	.15
❑ 491 Tony Stargell	.20	.07
❑ 492 Jack Del Rio	.40	.15
❑ 493 Lamar Rogers RC	.20	.07
❑ 494 Ricky Nattiel	.20	.07
❑ 495 Dan Saleaumua	.20	.07
❑ 496 Checklist 1-100	.20	.07
❑ 497 Checklist 101-200	.20	.07
❑ 498 Checklist 201-300	.20	.07
❑ 499 Checklist 301-400	.20	.07
❑ 500 Checklist 401-500	.20	.07

1992 Stadium Club

Card		
❑ COMPLETE SET (700)	150.00	75.00
❑ COMP.SERIES 1 (300)	15.00	6.00
❑ COMP.SERIES 2 (300)	15.00	6.00
❑ COMP.HIGH SER.(100)	120.00	60.00
❑ 1 Mark Rypien	.08	.02
❑ 2 Carlton Bailey RC	.08	.02
❑ 3 Kevin Glover	.08	.02
❑ 4 Vance Johnson	.08	.02
❑ 5 Jim Jeffcoat	.08	.02
❑ 6 Dan Saleaumua	.08	.02
❑ 7 Darion Conner	.08	.02
❑ 8 Don Maggs	.08	.02
❑ 9 Richard Dent	.15	.05
❑ 10 Mark Murphy	.08	.02
❑ 11 Wesley Carroll	.08	.02
❑ 12 Chris Burkett	.08	.02
❑ 13 Steve Wallace	.08	.02
❑ 14 Jacob Green	.08	.02
❑ 15 Roger Ruzek	.08	.02
❑ 16 J.B. Brown	.08	.02
❑ 17 Dave Meggett	.15	.05
❑ 18 D.J. Johnson	.08	.02
❑ 19 Rich Gannon	.30	.10
❑ 20 Kevin Mack	.08	.02
❑ 21A Reggie Cobb ERR	.08	.02
❑ 21B Reggie Cobb COR	.08	.02
❑ 22 Nate Lewis	.08	.02
❑ 23 Doug Smith	.08	.02
❑ 24 Irving Fryar	.15	.05
❑ 25 Anthony Thompson	.08	.02
❑ 26 Duane Bickett	.08	.02
❑ 27 Don Majkowski	.08	.02
❑ 28 Mark Schlereth RC	.08	.02
❑ 29 Melvin Jenkins	.08	.02
❑ 30 Michael Haynes	.15	.05
❑ 31 Greg Lewis	.08	.02
❑ 32 Kenneth Davis	.08	.02
❑ 33 Derrick Thomas	.30	.10
❑ 34 David Williams	.08	.02
❑ 35 Neal Anderson	.08	.02
❑ 36 Andre Collins	.08	.02
❑ 37 Jesse Solomon	.08	.02
❑ 38 Barry Sanders	2.50	1.00
❑ 39 Jeff Gossett	.08	.02
❑ 40 Rickey Jackson	.08	.02
❑ 41 Ray Berry	.08	.02
❑ 42 Leroy Hoard	.15	.05
❑ 43 Eric Thomas	.08	.02
❑ 44 Brian Washington	.08	.02
❑ 45 Pat Terrell	.08	.02
❑ 46 Eugene Robinson	.08	.02
❑ 47 Luis Sharpe	.08	.02
❑ 48 Jerome Brown	.08	.02
❑ 49 Mark Collins	.08	.02
❑ 50 Johnny Holland	.08	.02
❑ 51 Tony Paige	.08	.02
❑ 52 Willie Green	.08	.02
❑ 53 Steve Atwater	.08	.02
❑ 54 Brad Muster	.08	.02
❑ 55 Cris Dishman	.08	.02
❑ 56 Eddie Anderson	.08	.02
❑ 57 Sam Mills	.08	.02
❑ 58 Donald Evans	.08	.02
❑ 59 Jon Vaughn	.08	.02
❑ 60 Marion Butts	.08	.02
❑ 61 Rodney Holman	.08	.02
❑ 62 Dwayne White RC	.08	.02
❑ 63 Martin Mayhew	.08	.02
❑ 64 Jonathan Hayes	.08	.02
❑ 65 Andre Rison	.15	.05
❑ 66 Calvin Williams	.15	.05
❑ 67 James Washington	.08	.02
❑ 68 Tim Harris	.08	.02
❑ 69 Jim Ritcher	.08	.02

❑ 70 Johnny Johnson .08 .02
❑ 71 John Offerdahl .08 .02
❑ 72 Herschel Walker .15 .05
❑ 73 Perry Kemp .08 .02
❑ 74 Erik Howard .08 .02
❑ 75 Lamar Lathon .08 .02
❑ 76 Greg Kragen .08 .02
❑ 77 Jay Schroeder .08 .02
❑ 78 Jim Arnold .08 .02
❑ 79 Chris Miller .15 .05
❑ 80 Deron Cherry .08 .02
❑ 81 Jim Harbaugh .30 .10
❑ 82 Gill Fenerty .08 .02
❑ 83 Fred Stokes .08 .02
❑ 84 Roman Phifer .08 .02
❑ 85 Clyde Simmons .08 .02
❑ 86 Vince Newsome .08 .02
❑ 87 Lawrence Dawsey .15 .05
❑ 88 Eddie Brown .08 .02
❑ 89 Greg Montgomery .08 .02
❑ 90 Jeff Lageman .08 .02
❑ 91 Terry Wooden .08 .02
❑ 92 Nate Newton .08 .02
❑ 93 David Richards .08 .02
❑ 94 Derek Russell .08 .02
❑ 95 Steve Jordan .08 .02
❑ 96 Hugh Millen .08 .02
❑ 97 Mark Duper .08 .02
❑ 98 Sean Landeta .08 .02
❑ 99 James Thornton .08 .02
❑ 100 Darrell Green .08 .02
❑ 101 Harris Barton .08 .02
❑ 102 John Alt .08 .02
❑ 103 Mike Farr .08 .02
❑ 104 Bob Golic .08 .02
❑ 105 Gene Atkins .08 .02
❑ 106 Gary Anderson K .08 .02
❑ 107 Norm Johnson .08 .02
❑ 108 Eugene Daniel .08 .02
❑ 109 Kent Hull .08 .02
❑ 110 John Elway 2.50 1.00
❑ 111 Rich Camarillo .08 .02
❑ 112 Charles Wilson .08 .02
❑ 113 Matt Bahr .08 .02
❑ 114 Mark Carrier WR .15 .05
❑ 115 Richmond Webb .08 .02
❑ 116 Charles Mann .08 .02
❑ 117 Tim McGee .08 .02
❑ 118 Wes Hopkins .08 .02
❑ 119 Mo Lewis .08 .02
❑ 120 Warren Moon .30 .10
❑ 121 Damone Johnson .08 .02
❑ 122 Kevin Gogan .08 .02
❑ 123 Joey Browner .08 .02
❑ 124 Tommy Kane .08 .02
❑ 125 Vincent Brown .08 .02
❑ 126 Barry Word .08 .02
❑ 127 Michael Brooks .08 .02
❑ 128 Jumbo Elliott .08 .02
❑ 129 Marcus Allen .30 .10
❑ 130 Tom Waddle .08 .02
❑ 131 Jim Dombrowski .08 .02
❑ 132 Aeneas Williams .15 .05
❑ 133 Clay Matthews .15 .05
❑ 134 Thurman Thomas .30 .10
❑ 135 Dean Biasucci .08 .02
❑ 136 Moe Gardner .08 .02
❑ 137 James Campen .08 .02
❑ 138 Tim Johnson .08 .02
❑ 139 Erik Kramer .15 .05
❑ 140 Keith McCants .08 .02
❑ 141 John Carney .08 .02
❑ 142 Tunch Ilkin .08 .02
❑ 143 Louis Oliver .08 .02
❑ 144 Bill Maas .08 .02
❑ 145 Wendell Davis .08 .02
❑ 146 Pepper Johnson .08 .02
❑ 147 Howie Long .30 .10
❑ 148 Brett Maxie .08 .02
❑ 149 Tony Casillas .08 .02
❑ 150 Michael Carter .08 .02
❑ 151 Byron Evans .08 .02
❑ 152 Lorenzo White .08 .02
❑ 153 Larry Kelm .08 .02
❑ 154 Andy Heck .08 .02
❑ 155 Harry Newsome .08 .02
❑ 156 Chris Singleton .08 .02
❑ 157 Mike Kenn .08 .02
❑ 158 Jeff Faulkner .08 .02
❑ 159 Ken Lanier .08 .02
❑ 160 Darryl Talley .08 .02
❑ 161 Louie Aguiar RC .08 .02
❑ 162 Danny Copeland .08 .02
❑ 163 Kevin Porter .08 .02
❑ 164 Trace Armstrong .08 .02
❑ 165 Dermontti Dawson .08 .02
❑ 166 Fred McAfee RC .08 .02
❑ 167 Ronnie Lott .15 .05
❑ 168 Tony Mandarich .08 .02
❑ 169 Howard Cross .08 .02
❑ 170 Vestee Jackson .08 .02
❑ 171 Jeff Herrod .08 .02
❑ 172 Randy Hilliard RC .08 .02
❑ 173 Robert Wilson .08 .02
❑ 174 Joe Walter RC .08 .02
❑ 175 Chris Spielman .15 .05
❑ 176 Darryl Henley .08 .02
❑ 177 Jay Hilgenberg .08 .02
❑ 178 John Kidd .08 .02
❑ 179 Doug Widell .08 .02
❑ 180 Seth Joyner .08 .02
❑ 181 Nick Bell .08 .02
❑ 182 Don Griffin .08 .02
❑ 183 Johnny Meads .08 .02
❑ 184 Jeff Bostic .08 .02
❑ 185 Johnny Hector .08 .02
❑ 186 Jessie Tuggle .08 .02
❑ 187 Robb Thomas .08 .02
❑ 188 Shane Conlan .08 .02
❑ 189 Michael Zordich RC .08 .02
❑ 190 Emmitt Smith 3.00 1.50
❑ 191 Robert Blackmon .08 .02
❑ 192 Carl Lee .08 .02
❑ 193 Harry Galbreath .08 .02
❑ 194 Ed King .08 .02
❑ 195 Stan Thomas .08 .02
❑ 196 Andre Waters .08 .02
❑ 197 Pat Harlow .08 .02
❑ 198 Zefross Moss .08 .02
❑ 199 Bobby Hebert .08 .02
❑ 200 Doug Riesenberg .08 .02
❑ 201 Mike Croel .08 .02
❑ 202 Jeff Jaeger .08 .02
❑ 203 Gary Plummer .08 .02
❑ 204 Chris Jacke .08 .02
❑ 205 Neil O'Donnell .15 .05
❑ 206 Mark Bortz .08 .02
❑ 207 Tim Barnett .08 .02
❑ 208 Jerry Ball .08 .02
❑ 209 Chip Lohmiller .08 .02
❑ 210 Jim Everett .15 .05
❑ 211 Tim McKyer .08 .02
❑ 212 Aaron Craver .08 .02
❑ 213 John L. Williams .08 .02
❑ 214 Simon Fletcher .08 .02
❑ 215 Walter Reeves .08 .02
❑ 216 Terance Mathis .15 .05
❑ 217 Mike Pitts .08 .02
❑ 218 Bruce Matthews .08 .02
❑ 219 Howard Ballard .08 .02
❑ 220 Leonard Russell .15 .05
❑ 221 Michael Stewart .08 .02
❑ 222 Mike Merriweather .08 .02
❑ 223 Ricky Sanders .08 .02
❑ 224 Ray Horton .08 .02
❑ 225 Michael Jackson .15 .05
❑ 226 Bill Romanowski .08 .02
❑ 227 Steve McMichael UER .15 .05
❑ 228 Chris Martin .08 .02
❑ 229 Tim Green .08 .02
❑ 230 Karl Mecklenburg .08 .02
❑ 231 Felix Wright .08 .02
❑ 232 Charles McRae .08 .02
❑ 233 Pete Stoyanovich .08 .02
❑ 234 Stephen Baker .08 .02
❑ 235 Herman Moore .30 .10
❑ 236 Terry McDaniel .08 .02
❑ 237 Dalton Hilliard .08 .02
❑ 238 Gill Byrd .08 .02
❑ 239 Leon Seals .08 .02
❑ 240 Rod Woodson .30 .10
❑ 241 Curtis Duncan .08 .02
❑ 242 Keith Jackson .15 .05
❑ 243 Mark Stepnoski .15 .05
❑ 244 Art Monk .15 .05
❑ 245 Matt Stover .08 .02
❑ 246 John Roper .08 .02
❑ 247 Rodney Hampton .15 .05
❑ 248 Steve Wisniewski .08 .02
❑ 249 Bryan Millard .08 .02
❑ 250 Todd Lyght .08 .02
❑ 251 Marvin Washington .08 .02
❑ 252 Eric Swann .15 .05
❑ 253 Bruce Kozerski .08 .02
❑ 254 Jon Hand .08 .02
❑ 255 Scott Fulhage .08 .02
❑ 256 Chuck Cecil .08 .02
❑ 257 Eric Martin .08 .02
❑ 258 Eric Metcalf .15 .05
❑ 259 T.J. Turner .08 .02
❑ 260 Kirk Lowdermilk .08 .02
❑ 261 Keith McKeller .08 .02
❑ 262 Wymon Henderson .08 .02
❑ 263 David Alexander .08 .02
❑ 264 George Jamison .08 .02
❑ 265 Ken Norton Jr. .15 .05
❑ 266 Jim Lachey .08 .02
❑ 267 Bo Orlando RC .08 .02
❑ 268 Nick Lowery .08 .02
❑ 269 Keith Van Horne .08 .02
❑ 270 Dwight Stone .08 .02
❑ 271 Keith DeLong .08 .02
❑ 272 James Francis .08 .02
❑ 273 Greg McMurtry .08 .02
❑ 274 Ethan Horton .08 .02
❑ 275 Stan Brock .08 .02
❑ 276 Ken Harvey .08 .02
❑ 277 Ronnie Harmon .08 .02
❑ 278 Mike Pritchard .15 .05
❑ 279 Kyle Clifton .08 .02
❑ 280 Anthony Johnson .15 .05
❑ 281 Esera Tuaolo .08 .02
❑ 282 Vernon Turner .08 .02
❑ 283 David Griggs .08 .02
❑ 284 Dino Hackett .08 .02
❑ 285 Carwell Gardner .08 .02
❑ 286 Ron Hall .08 .02
❑ 287 Reggie White .30 .10
❑ 288 Checklist 1-100 .08 .02
❑ 289 Checklist 101-200 .08 .02
❑ 290 Checklist 201-300 .08 .02
❑ 291 Mark Clayton MC .08 .02
❑ 292 Pat Swilling MC .08 .02
❑ 293 Ernest Givins MC .08 .02
❑ 294 Broderick Thomas MC .08 .02
❑ 295 John Friesz MC .08 .02
❑ 296 Cornelius Bennett MC .08 .02
❑ 297 Anthony Carter MC .15 .05
❑ 298 Earnest Byner MC .08 .02
❑ 299 Michael Irvin MC .30 .10
❑ 300 Cortez Kennedy MC .08 .02
❑ 301 Barry Sanders MC 1.50 .60
❑ 302 Mike Croel MC .08 .02
❑ 303 Emmitt Smith MC 2.00 .75

❑ 304 Leonard Russell MC .08 .02
❑ 305 Neal Anderson MC .08 .02
❑ 306 Derrick Thomas MC .15 .05
❑ 307 Mark Rypien MC .08 .02
❑ 308 Reggie White MC .15 .05
❑ 309 Rod Woodson MC .15 .05
❑ 310 Rodney Hampton MC .15 .05
❑ 311 Camell Lake .08 .02
❑ 312 Robert Delpino .08 .02
❑ 313 Brian Blades .15 .05
❑ 314 Marc Spindler .08 .02
❑ 315 Scott Norwood .08 .02
❑ 316 Frank Warren .08 .02
❑ 317 David Treadwell .08 .02
❑ 318 Steve Broussard .08 .02
❑ 319 Lorenzo Lynch .08 .02
❑ 320 Ray Agnew .08 .02
❑ 321 Derrick Walker .08 .02
❑ 322 Vinson Smith RC .08 .02
❑ 323 Gary Clark .30 .10
❑ 324 Charles Haley .15 .05
❑ 325 Keith Byars .08 .02
❑ 326 Winston Moss .08 .02
❑ 327 Paul McJulien RC UER .08 .02
❑ 328 Tony Covington .08 .02
❑ 329 Mark Carrier DB .08 .02
❑ 330 Mark Tuinei .08 .02
❑ 331 Tracy Simien RC .08 .02
❑ 332 Jeff Wright .08 .02
❑ 333 Bryan Cox .15 .05
❑ 334 Lonnie Young .08 .02
❑ 335 Clarence Verdin .08 .02
❑ 336 Dan Fike .08 .02
❑ 337 Steve Sewell .08 .02
❑ 338 Gary Zimmerman .08 .02
❑ 339 Barney Bussey .08 .02
❑ 340 William Perry .15 .05
❑ 341 Jeff Hostetler .15 .05
❑ 342 Doug Smith .08 .02
❑ 343 Cleveland Gary .08 .02
❑ 344 Todd Marinovich .08 .02
❑ 345 Rich Moran .08 .02
❑ 346 Tony Woods .08 .02
❑ 347 Vaughan Johnson .08 .02
❑ 348 Marv Cook .08 .02
❑ 349 Pierce Holt .08 .02
❑ 350 Gerald Williams .08 .02
❑ 351 Kevin Butler .08 .02
❑ 352 William White .08 .02
❑ 353 Henry Rolling .08 .02
❑ 354 James Joseph .08 .02
❑ 355 Vinny Testaverde .15 .05
❑ 356 Scott Radecic .08 .02
❑ 357 Lee Johnson .08 .02
❑ 358 Steve Tasker .15 .05
❑ 359 David Lutz .08 .02
❑ 360 Audray McMillian UER .08 .02
❑ 361 Brad Baxter .08 .02
❑ 362 Mark Dennis .08 .02
❑ 363 Eric Pegram .15 .05
❑ 364 Sean Jones .08 .02
❑ 365 William Roberts .08 .02
❑ 366 Steve Young 1.00 .40
❑ 367 Joe Jacoby .08 .02
❑ 368 Richard Brown RC .08 .02
❑ 369 Keith Kartz .08 .02
❑ 370 Freddie Joe Nunn .08 .02
❑ 371 Darren Comeaux .08 .02
❑ 372 Larry Brown DB .08 .02
❑ 373 Haywood Jeffires .15 .05
❑ 374 Tom Newberry .08 .02
❑ 375 Steve Bono RC .30 .10
❑ 376 Kevin Ross .08 .02
❑ 377 Kelvin Pritchett .08 .02
❑ 378 Jessie Hester .08 .02
❑ 379 Mitchell Price .08 .02
❑ 380 Barry Foster .15 .05
❑ 381 Reyna Thompson .08 .02
❑ 382 Cris Carter .75 .30
❑ 383 Lemuel Stinson .08 .02
❑ 384 Rod Bernstine .08 .02
❑ 385 James Lofton .15 .05
❑ 386 Kevin Murphy .08 .02
❑ 387 Greg Townsend .08 .02
❑ 388 Edgar Bennett RC .30 .10
❑ 389 Rob Moore .15 .05
❑ 390 Eugene Lockhart .08 .02
❑ 391 Bern Brostek .08 .02
❑ 392 Craig Heyward .15 .05
❑ 393 Ferrell Edmunds .08 .02
❑ 394 John Kasay .08 .02
❑ 395 Jesse Sapolu .08 .02
❑ 396 Jim Breech .08 .02
❑ 397 Neil Smith .30 .10
❑ 398 Bryce Paup .30 .10
❑ 399 Tony Tolbert .08 .02
❑ 400 Bubby Brister .08 .02
❑ 401 Dennis Smith .08 .02
❑ 402 Dan Owens .08 .02
❑ 403 Steve Beuerlein .15 .05
❑ 404 Rick Tuten .08 .02
❑ 405 Eric Allen .08 .02
❑ 406 Eric Hill .08 .02
❑ 407 Don Warren .08 .02
❑ 408 Greg Jackson .08 .02
❑ 409 Chris Doleman .08 .02
❑ 410 Anthony Munoz .15 .05
❑ 411 Michael Young .08 .02
❑ 412 Cornelius Bennett .15 .05
❑ 413 Ray Childress .08 .02
❑ 414 Kevin Call .08 .02
❑ 415 Burt Grossman .08 .02
❑ 416 Scott Miller .08 .02
❑ 417 Tim Newton .08 .02
❑ 418 Robert Young .08 .02
❑ 419 Tommy Vardell RC .08 .02
❑ 420 Michael Walter .08 .02
❑ 421 Chris Port RC .08 .02
❑ 422 Carlton Haselrig RC .08 .02
❑ 423 Rodney Peete .15 .05
❑ 424 Scott Stephen .08 .02
❑ 425 Chris Warren .30 .10
❑ 426 Scott Galbraith RC .08 .02
❑ 427 Fuad Reveiz UER .08 .02
❑ 428 Irv Eatman .08 .02
❑ 429 David Szott .08 .02
❑ 430 Brent Williams .08 .02
❑ 431 Mike Horan .08 .02
❑ 432 Brent Jones .15 .05
❑ 433 Paul Gruber .08 .02
❑ 434 Carlos Huerta .08 .02
❑ 435 Scott Case .08 .02
❑ 436 Greg Davis .08 .02
❑ 437 Ken Clarke .08 .02
❑ 438 Alfred Williams .08 .02
❑ 439 Jim C. Jensen .08 .02
❑ 440 Louis Lipps .08 .02
❑ 441 Larry Roberts .08 .02
❑ 442 James Jones DT .08 .02
❑ 443 Don Mosebar .08 .02
❑ 444 Quinn Early .15 .05
❑ 445 Robert Brown .08 .02
❑ 446 Tom Thayer .08 .02
❑ 447 Michael Irvin .30 .10
❑ 448 Jarrod Bunch .08 .02
❑ 449 Riki Ellison .08 .02
❑ 450 Joe Phillips .08 .02
❑ 451 Ernest Givins .15 .05
❑ 452 Glenn Parker .08 .02
❑ 453 Brett Perriman UER .30 .10
❑ 454 Jayice Pearson RC .08 .02
❑ 455 Mark Jackson .08 .02
❑ 456 Siran Stacy RC .08 .02
❑ 457 Rufus Porter .08 .02
❑ 458 Michael Ball .08 .02
❑ 459 Craig Taylor .08 .02
❑ 460 George Thomas RC .08 .02
❑ 461 Alvin Wright .08 .02
❑ 462 Ron Hallstrom .08 .02
❑ 463 Mike Mooney RC .08 .02
❑ 464 Dexter Carter .08 .02
❑ 465 Marty Carter RC .08 .02
❑ 466 Pat Swilling .08 .02
❑ 467 Mike Golic .08 .02
❑ 468 Reggie Roby .08 .02
❑ 469 Randall McDaniel .08 .02
❑ 470 John Stephens .08 .02
❑ 471 Ricardo McDonald RC .08 .02
❑ 472 Wilber Marshall .08 .02
❑ 473 Jim Sweeney .08 .02
❑ 474 Ernie Jones .08 .02
❑ 475 Bennie Blades .08 .02
❑ 476 Don Beebe .08 .02
❑ 477 Grant Feasel .08 .02
❑ 478 Ernie Mills .08 .02
❑ 479 Tony Jones T .08 .02
❑ 480 Jeff Uhlenhake .08 .02
❑ 481 Gaston Green .08 .02
❑ 482 John Taylor .15 .05
❑ 483 Anthony Smith .08 .02
❑ 484 Tony Bennett .08 .02
❑ 485 David Brandon RC .08 .02
❑ 486 Shawn Jefferson .08 .02
❑ 487 Christian Okoye .08 .02
❑ 488 Leonard Marshall .08 .02
❑ 489 Jay Novacek .15 .05
❑ 490 Harold Green .08 .02
❑ 491 Bubba McDowell .08 .02
❑ 492 Gary Anderson RB .08 .02
❑ 493 Terrell Buckley RC .08 .02
❑ 494 Jamie Dukes RC .08 .02
❑ 495 Morten Andersen .08 .02
❑ 496 Henry Thomas .08 .02
❑ 497 Bill Lewis .08 .02
❑ 498 Jeff Cross .08 .02
❑ 499 Hardy Nickerson .15 .05
❑ 500 Henry Ellard .15 .05
❑ 501 Joe Bowden RC .08 .02
❑ 502 Brian Noble .08 .02
❑ 503 Mike Cofer .08 .02
❑ 504 Jeff Bryant .08 .02
❑ 505 Lomas Brown .08 .02
❑ 506 Chip Banks .08 .02
❑ 507 Keith Traylor .08 .02
❑ 508 Mark Kelso .08 .02
❑ 509 Dexter McNabb RC .08 .02
❑ 510 Gene Chilton RC .08 .02
❑ 511 George Thornton .08 .02
❑ 512 Jeff Criswell .08 .02
❑ 513 Brad Edwards .08 .02
❑ 514 Ron Heller .08 .02
❑ 515 Tim Brown .30 .10
❑ 516 Keith Hamilton RC .15 .05
❑ 517 Mark Higgs .08 .02
❑ 518 Tommy Barnhardt .08 .02
❑ 519 Brian Jordan .15 .05
❑ 520 Ray Crockett .08 .02
❑ 521 Karl Wilson .08 .02
❑ 522 Ricky Reynolds .08 .02
❑ 523 Max Montoya .08 .02
❑ 524 David Little .08 .02
❑ 525 Alonzo Mitz RC .08 .02
❑ 526 Darryll Lewis .08 .02
❑ 527 Keith Henderson .08 .02
❑ 528 LeRoy Butler .08 .02
❑ 529 Rob Burnett .08 .02
❑ 530 Chris Chandler .30 .10
❑ 531 Maury Buford .08 .02
❑ 532 Mark Ingram .08 .02
❑ 533 Mike Saxon .08 .02
❑ 534 Bill Fralic .08 .02
❑ 535 Craig Patterson RC .08 .02
❑ 536 John Randle .15 .05
❑ 537 Dwayne Harper .08 .02

❑ 538 Chris Hakel RC .08 .02
❑ 539 Maurice Hurst .08 .02
❑ 540 Warren Powers UER .08 .02
❑ 541 Will Wolford .08 .02
❑ 542 Dennis Gibson .08 .02
❑ 543 Jackie Slater .08 .02
❑ 544 Floyd Turner .08 .02
❑ 545 Guy McIntyre .08 .02
❑ 546 Eric Green .08 .02
❑ 547 Rohn Stark .08 .02
❑ 548 William Fuller .08 .02
❑ 549 Alvin Harper .15 .05
❑ 550 Mark Clayton .15 .05
❑ 551 Natu Tuatagaloa RC .08 .02
❑ 552 Fred Barnett .30 .10
❑ 553 Bob Whitfield RC .08 .02
❑ 554 Courtney Hall .08 .02
❑ 555 Brian Mitchell .15 .05
❑ 556 Patrick Hunter .08 .02
❑ 557 Rick Bryan .08 .02
❑ 558 Anthony Carter .15 .05
❑ 559 Jim Wahler .08 .02
❑ 560 Joe Morris .08 .02
❑ 561 Tony Zendejas .08 .02
❑ 562 Mervyn Fernandez .08 .02
❑ 563 Jamie Williams .08 .02
❑ 564 Darrell Thompson .08 .02
❑ 565 Adrian Cooper .08 .02
❑ 566 Chris Goode .08 .02
❑ 567 Jeff Davidson RC .08 .02
❑ 568 James Hasty .08 .02
❑ 569 Chris Mims RC .08 .02
❑ 570 Ray Seals RC .08 .02
❑ 571 Myron Guyton .08 .02
❑ 572 Todd McNair .08 .02
❑ 573 Andre Tippett .08 .02
❑ 574 Kirby Jackson .08 .02
❑ 575 Mel Gray .15 .05
❑ 576 Stephone Paige .08 .02
❑ 577 Scott Davis .08 .02
❑ 578 John Gesek .08 .02
❑ 579 Earnest Byner .08 .02
❑ 580 John Friesz .15 .05
❑ 581 Al Smith .08 .02
❑ 582 Flipper Anderson .08 .02
❑ 583 Amp Lee RC .08 .02
❑ 584 Greg Lloyd .15 .05
❑ 585 Cortez Kennedy .15 .05
❑ 586 Keith Sims .08 .02
❑ 587 Terry Allen .30 .10
❑ 588 David Fulcher .08 .02
❑ 589 Chris Hinton .08 .02
❑ 590 Tim McDonald .08 .02
❑ 591 Bruce Armstrong .08 .02
❑ 592 Sterling Sharpe .30 .10
❑ 593 Tom Rathman .08 .02
❑ 594 Bill Brooks .08 .02
❑ 595 Broderick Thomas .08 .02
❑ 596 Jim Wilks .08 .02
❑ 597 Tyrone Braxton UER .08 .02
❑ 598 Checklist 301-400 UER .08 .02
❑ 599 Checklist 401-500 .08 .02
❑ 600 Checklist 501-600 .08 .02
❑ 601 Andre Reed MC .75 .30
❑ 602 Troy Aikman MC 4.00 2.00
❑ 603 Dan Marino MC 6.00 2.50
❑ 604 Randall Cunningham MC .75 .30
❑ 605 Jim Kelly MC 1.50 .60
❑ 606 Deion Sanders MC 2.00 .75
❑ 607 Junior Seau MC 1.50 .60
❑ 608 Jerry Rice MC 4.00 2.00
❑ 609 Bruce Smith MC .75 .30
❑ 610 Lawrence Taylor MC 1.50 .60
❑ 611 Todd Collins RC .50 .20
❑ 612 Ty Detmer 1.50 .60
❑ 613 Browning Nagle .50 .20
❑ 614 Tony Sacca RC UER .50 .20
❑ 615 Boomer Esiason .75 .30
❑ 616 Billy Joe Tolliver .50 .20
❑ 617 Leslie O'Neal .75 .30
❑ 618 Mark Wheeler RC .50 .20
❑ 619 Eric Dickerson .75 .30
❑ 620 Phil Simms .75 .30
❑ 621 Troy Vincent RC .50 .20
❑ 622 Jason Hanson RC .75 .30
❑ 623 Andre Reed .75 .30
❑ 624 Russell Maryland .50 .20
❑ 625 Steve Emtman RC .50 .20
❑ 626 Sean Gilbert RC .75 .30
❑ 627 Dana Hall RC .50 .20
❑ 628 Dan McGwire .50 .20
❑ 629 Lewis Billups .50 .20
❑ 630 Darryl Williams RC .50 .20
❑ 631 Dwayne Sabb RC .50 .20
❑ 632 Mark Royals .50 .20
❑ 633 Cary Conklin .50 .20
❑ 634 Al Toon .75 .30
❑ 635 Junior Seau 1.50 .60
❑ 636 Greg Skrepenak RC UER 68 .50 .20
❑ 637 Deion Sanders 3.00 1.50
❑ 638 Steve DeOssie .50 .20
❑ 639 Randall Cunningham 1.50 .60
❑ 640 Jim Kelly 1.50 .60
❑ 641 Michael Brandon RC .50 .20
❑ 642 Clayton Holmes RC .50 .20
❑ 643 Webster Slaughter .50 .20
❑ 644 Ricky Proehl .50 .20
❑ 645 Jerry Rice 5.00 2.50
❑ 646 Carl Banks .50 .20
❑ 647 J.J.Birden .50 .20
❑ 648 Tracy Scroggins RC .50 .20
❑ 649 Alonzo Spellman RC .75 .30
❑ 650 Joe Montana 8.00 3.00
❑ 651 Courtney Hawkins RC .75 .30
❑ 652 Corey Widmer RC .50 .20
❑ 653 Robert Brooks RC 4.00 1.50
❑ 654 Darren Woodson RC 1.50 .60
❑ 655 Derrick Fenner .50 .20
❑ 656 Steve Christie .50 .20
❑ 657 Chester McGlockton RC .75 .30
❑ 658 Steve Israel RC .50 .20
❑ 659 Robert Harris RC .50 .20
❑ 660 Dan Marino 8.00 3.00
❑ 661 Ed McCaffrey 5.00 2.00
❑ 662 Johnny Mitchell RC .50 .20
❑ 663 Timm Rosenbach .50 .20
❑ 664 Anthony Miller .75 .30
❑ 665 Merril Hoge .50 .20
❑ 666 Eugene Chung RC .50 .20
❑ 667 Rueben Mayes .50 .20
❑ 668 Martin Bayless .50 .20
❑ 669 Ashley Ambrose RC 1.50 .60
❑ 670 Michael Cofer UER .50 .20
❑ 671 Shane Dronett RC .50 .20
❑ 672 Bernie Kosar .75 .30
❑ 673 Mike Singletary .75 .30
❑ 674 Mike Lodish RC .50 .20
❑ 675 Phillippi Sparks RC .50 .20
❑ 676 Joel Steed RC .50 .20
❑ 677 Kevin Fagan .50 .20
❑ 678 Randal Hill .50 .20
❑ 679 Ken O'Brien .50 .20
❑ 680 Lawrence Taylor 1.50 .60
❑ 681 Harvey Williams 1.50 .60
❑ 682 Quentin Coryatt RC .50 .20
❑ 683 Brett Favre 100.00 60.00
❑ 684 Robert Jones RC .50 .20
❑ 685 Michael Dean Perry .75 .30
❑ 686 Bruce Smith 1.50 .60
❑ 687 Troy Auzenne RC .50 .20
❑ 688 Thomas McLemore RC .50 .20
❑ 689 Dale Carter RC .75 .30
❑ 690 Marc Boutte RC .50 .20
❑ 691 Jeff George 1.50 .60
❑ 692 Dion Lambert RC .50 .20
❑ 693 Vaughn Dunbar RC .50 .20
❑ 694 Derek Brown TE RC .50 .20
❑ 695 Troy Aikman 5.00 2.50
❑ 696 John Fina RC .50 .20
❑ 697 Kevin Smith RC DB .50 .20
❑ 698 Corey Miller RC .50 .20
❑ 699 Lance Olberding RC .50 .20
❑ 700 Checklist 601-700 UER .50 .20
❑ P1 Promo Sheet Natl. 10.00 4.00
❑ P2 Promo Sheet Diam.Day 12.00 5.00

1993 Stadium Club

❑ COMPLETE SET (550) 40.00 15.00
❑ COMP.SERIES 1 (250) 25.00 10.00
❑ COMP.SERIES 2 (250) 15.00 6.00
❑ COMP.HIGH SERIES (50) 8.00 4.00
❑ COMP.HIGH FACT.SET (51) 12.00 5.00
❑ 1 Sterling Sharpe .20 .07
❑ 2 Chris Burkett .10 .02
❑ 3 Santana Dotson .20 .07
❑ 4 Michael Jackson .20 .07
❑ 5 Neal Anderson .10 .02
❑ 6 Bryan Cox .10 .02
❑ 7 Dennis Gibson .10 .02
❑ 8 Jeff Graham .20 .07
❑ 9 Roger Ruzek .10 .02
❑ 10 Duane Bickett .10 .02
❑ 11 Charles Mann .10 .02
❑ 12 Tommy Maddox .40 .15
❑ 13 Vaughn Dunbar .10 .02
❑ 14 Gary Plummer .10 .02
❑ 15 Chris Miller .20 .07
❑ 16 Chris Warren .20 .07
❑ 17 Alvin Harper .20 .07
❑ 18 Eric Dickerson .20 .07
❑ 19 Mike Jones .10 .02
❑ 20 Ernest Givins .20 .07
❑ 21 Natrone Means RC .40 .15
❑ 22 Doug Riesenberg .10 .02
❑ 23 Barry Word .10 .02
❑ 24 Sean Salisbury .10 .02
❑ 25 Derrick Fenner .10 .02
❑ 26 David Howard .10 .02
❑ 27 Mark Kelso .10 .02
❑ 28 Todd Lyght .10 .02
❑ 29 Dana Hall .10 .02
❑ 30 Eric Metcalf .20 .07
❑ 31 Jason Hanson .10 .02
❑ 32 Dwight Stone .10 .02
❑ 33 Johnny Mitchell .10 .02
❑ 34 Reggie Roby .10 .02
❑ 35 Terrell Buckley .10 .02
❑ 36 Steve McMichael .20 .07
❑ 37 Marty Carter .10 .02
❑ 38 Seth Joyner .10 .02
❑ 39 Rohn Stark .10 .02
❑ 40 Eric Curry RC .10 .02
❑ 41 Tommy Barnhardt .10 .02
❑ 42 Karl Mecklenburg .10 .02
❑ 43 Darion Conner .10 .02
❑ 44 Ronnie Harmon .10 .02
❑ 45 Cortez Kennedy .20 .07
❑ 46 Tim Brown .40 .15

❑ 47 Bill Lewis	.10	.02
❑ 48 Randall McDaniel	.10	.02
❑ 49 Curtis Duncan	.10	.02
❑ 50 Troy Aikman	1.50	.60
❑ 51 David Klingler	.10	.02
❑ 52 Brent Jones	.20	.07
❑ 53 Dave Krieg	.20	.07
❑ 54 Bruce Smith	.40	.15
❑ 55 Vincent Brown	.10	.02
❑ 56 O.J.McDuffie RC	.40	.15
❑ 57 Cleveland Gary	.10	.02
❑ 58 Larry Centers RC	.40	.15
❑ 59 Pepper Johnson	.10	.02
❑ 60 Dan Marino	3.00	1.25
❑ 61 Robert Porcher	.10	.02
❑ 62 Jim Harbaugh	.40	.15
❑ 63 Sam Mills	.10	.02
❑ 64 Gary Anderson RB	.10	.02
❑ 65 Neil O'Donnell	.20	.07
❑ 66 Keith Byars	.10	.02
❑ 67 Jeff Herrod	.10	.02
❑ 68 Marion Butts	.10	.02
❑ 69 Terry McDaniel	.10	.02
❑ 70 John Elway	3.00	1.25
❑ 71 Steve Broussard	.10	.02
❑ 72 Kelvin Martin	.10	.02
❑ 73 Tom Carter RC	.20	.07
❑ 74 Bryce Paup	.20	.07
❑ 75 Jim Kelly UER	.20	.07
❑ 76 Bill Romanowski	.10	.02
❑ 77 Andre Collins	.10	.02
❑ 78 Mike Farr	.10	.02
❑ 79 Henry Ellard	.20	.07
❑ 80 Dale Carter	.10	.02
❑ 81 Johnny Bailey	.10	.02
❑ 82 Garrison Hearst RC	1.50	.60
❑ 83 Brent Williams	.10	.02
❑ 84 Ricardo McDonald	.10	.02
❑ 85 Emmitt Smith	3.00	1.50
❑ 86 Vai Sikahema	.10	.02
❑ 87 Jackie Harris	.10	.02
❑ 88 Alonzo Spellman	.10	.02
❑ 89 Mark Wheeler	.10	.02
❑ 90 Dalton Hilliard	.10	.02
❑ 91 Mark Higgs	.10	.02
❑ 92 Aaron Wallace	.10	.02
❑ 93 Earnest Byner	.10	.02
❑ 94 Stanley Richard	.10	.02
❑ 95 Cris Carter	.40	.15
❑ 96 Bobby Houston RC	.10	.02
❑ 97 Craig Heyward	.20	.07
❑ 98 Bernie Kosar	.20	.07
❑ 99 Mike Croel	.10	.02
❑ 100 Deion Sanders	1.00	.40
❑ 101 Warren Moon	.20	.07
❑ 102 Christian Okoye	.10	.02
❑ 103 Ricky Watters	.40	.15
❑ 104 Eric Swann	.20	.07
❑ 105 Rodney Hampton	.20	.07
❑ 106 Daryl Johnston	.20	.07
❑ 107 Andre Reed	.20	.07
❑ 108 Jerome Bettis RC	8.00	4.00
❑ 109 Eugene Daniel	.10	.02
❑ 110 Leonard Russell	.20	.07
❑ 111 Darryl Williams	.10	.02
❑ 112 Rod Woodson	.40	.15
❑ 113 Boomer Esiason	.20	.07
❑ 114 James Hasty	.10	.02
❑ 115 Marc Boutte	.10	.02
❑ 116 Tom Waddle	.10	.02
❑ 117 Lawrence Dawsey	.10	.02
❑ 118 Mark Collins	.10	.02
❑ 119 Willie Gault	.10	.02
❑ 120 Barry Sanders	2.50	1.00
❑ 121 Leroy Hoard	.20	.07
❑ 122 Anthony Munoz	.20	.07
❑ 123 Jesse Sapolu	.10	.02
❑ 124 Art Monk	.20	.07
❑ 125 Randal Hill	.10	.02
❑ 126 John Offerdahl	.10	.02
❑ 127 Carlos Jenkins	.10	.02
❑ 128 Al Smith	.10	.02
❑ 129 Michael Irvin	.40	.15
❑ 130 Kenneth Davis	.10	.02
❑ 131 Curtis Conway RC	.75	.30
❑ 132 Steve Atwater	.10	.02
❑ 133 Neil Smith	.40	.15
❑ 134 Steve Everitt RC	.10	.02
❑ 135 Chris Mims	.10	.02
❑ 136 Rickey Jackson	.10	.02
❑ 137 Edgar Bennett	.40	.15
❑ 138 Mike Pritchard	.20	.07
❑ 139 Richard Dent	.20	.07
❑ 140 Barry Foster	.20	.07
❑ 141 Eugene Robinson	.10	.02
❑ 142 Jackie Slater	.10	.02
❑ 143 Paul Gruber	.10	.02
❑ 144 Rob Moore	.20	.07
❑ 145 Robert Smith RC	2.50	1.00
❑ 146 Lorenzo White	.10	.02
❑ 147 Tommy Vardell	.10	.02
❑ 148 Dave Meggett	.10	.02
❑ 149 Vince Workman	.10	.02
❑ 150 Terry Allen	.40	.15
❑ 151 Howie Long	.40	.15
❑ 152 Charles Haley	.20	.07
❑ 153 Pete Metzelaars	.10	.02
❑ 154 John Copeland RC	.20	.07
❑ 155 Aeneas Williams	.10	.02
❑ 156 Ricky Sanders	.10	.02
❑ 157 Andre Ware	.10	.02
❑ 158 Tony Paige	.10	.02
❑ 159 Jerome Henderson	.10	.02
❑ 160 Harold Green	.10	.02
❑ 161 Wymon Henderson	.10	.02
❑ 162 Andre Rison	.20	.07
❑ 163 Donald Evans	.10	.02
❑ 164 Todd Scott	.10	.02
❑ 165 Steve Emtman	.10	.02
❑ 166 William Fuller	.10	.02
❑ 167 Michael Dean Perry	.20	.07
❑ 168 Randall Cunningham	.40	.15
❑ 169 Toi Cook	.10	.02
❑ 170 Browning Nagle	.10	.02
❑ 171 Darryl Henley	.10	.02
❑ 172 George Teague RC	.20	.07
❑ 173 Derrick Thomas	.40	.15
❑ 174 Jay Novacek	.20	.07
❑ 175 Mark Carrier DB	.10	.02
❑ 176 Kevin Fagan	.10	.02
❑ 177 Nate Lewis	.10	.02
❑ 178 Courtney Hawkins	.10	.02
❑ 179 Robert Blackmon	.10	.02
❑ 180 Rick Mirer RC	.40	.15
❑ 181 Mike Lodish	.10	.02
❑ 182 Jarrod Bunch	.10	.02
❑ 183 Anthony Smith	.10	.02
❑ 184 Brian Noble	.10	.02
❑ 185 Eric Bieniemy	.10	.02
❑ 186 Keith Jackson	.20	.07
❑ 187 Eric Martin	.10	.02
❑ 188 Vance Johnson	.10	.02
❑ 189 Kevin Mack	.10	.02
❑ 190 Rich Camarillo	.10	.02
❑ 191 Ashley Ambrose	.10	.02
❑ 192 Ray Childress	.10	.02
❑ 193 Jim Arnold	.10	.02
❑ 194 Ricky Ervins	.10	.02
❑ 195 Gary Anderson K	.10	.02
❑ 196 Eric Allen	.10	.02
❑ 197 Roger Craig	.20	.07
❑ 198 Jon Vaughn	.10	.02
❑ 199 Tim McDonald	.10	.02
❑ 200 Broderick Thomas	.10	.02
❑ 201 Jessie Tuggle	.10	.02
❑ 202 Alonzo Mitz	.10	.02
❑ 203 Harvey Williams	.20	.07
❑ 204 Russell Maryland	.10	.02
❑ 205 Marvin Washington	.10	.02
❑ 206 Jim Everett	.20	.07
❑ 207 Trace Armstrong	.10	.02
❑ 208 Steve Young	1.50	.60
❑ 209 Tony Woods	.10	.02
❑ 210 Brett Favre	4.00	2.00
❑ 211 Nate Odomes	.10	.02
❑ 212 Ricky Proehl	.10	.02
❑ 213 Jim Dombrowski	.10	.02
❑ 214 Anthony Carter	.20	.07
❑ 215 Tracy Simien	.10	.02
❑ 216 Clay Matthews	.20	.07
❑ 217 Patrick Bates RC	.10	.02
❑ 218 Jeff George	.40	.15
❑ 219 David Fulcher	.10	.02
❑ 220 Phil Simms	.20	.07
❑ 221 Eugene Chung	.10	.02
❑ 222 Reggie Cobb	.10	.02
❑ 223 Jim Sweeney	.10	.02
❑ 224 Greg Lloyd	.20	.07
❑ 225 Sean Jones	.10	.02
❑ 226 Marvin Jones RC	.10	.02
❑ 227 Bill Brooks	.10	.02
❑ 228 Moe Gardner	.10	.02
❑ 229 Louis Oliver	.10	.02
❑ 230 Flipper Anderson	.10	.02
❑ 231 Marc Spindler	.10	.02
❑ 232 Jerry Rice	2.00	.75
❑ 233 Chip Lohmiller	.10	.02
❑ 234 Nolan Harrison	.10	.02
❑ 235 Heath Sherman	.10	.02
❑ 236 Reyna Thompson	.10	.02
❑ 237 Derrick Walker	.10	.02
❑ 238 Rufus Porter	.10	.02
❑ 239 Checklist 1-125	.10	.02
❑ 240 Checklist 126-250	.10	.02
❑ 241 John Elway MC	1.50	.60
❑ 242 Troy Aikman MC	.75	.30
❑ 243 Steve Emtman MC	.10	.02
❑ 244 Ricky Watters MC	.20	.07
❑ 245 Barry Foster MC	.10	.02
❑ 246 Dan Marino MC	1.50	.60
❑ 247 Reggie White MC	.20	.07
❑ 248 Thurman Thomas MC	.20	.07
❑ 249 Broderick Thomas MC	.10	.02
❑ 250 Joe Montana MC	1.50	.60
❑ 251 Tim Goad	.10	.02
❑ 252 Joe Nash	.10	.02
❑ 253 Anthony Johnson	.20	.07
❑ 254 Carl Pickens	.20	.07
❑ 255 Steve Beuerlein	.20	.07
❑ 256 Anthony Newman	.10	.02
❑ 257 Corey Miller	.10	.02
❑ 258 Steve DeBerg	.10	.02
❑ 259 Johnny Holland	.10	.02
❑ 260 Jerry Ball	.10	.02
❑ 261 Siupeli Malamala RC	.10	.02
❑ 262 Steve Wisniewski	.10	.02
❑ 263 Kelvin Pritchett	.10	.02
❑ 264 Chris Gardocki	.10	.02
❑ 265 Henry Thomas	.10	.02
❑ 266 Arthur Marshall RC	.10	.02
❑ 267 Quinn Early	.20	.07
❑ 268 Jonathan Hayes	.10	.02
❑ 269 Eric Pegram	.20	.07
❑ 270 Clyde Simmons	.10	.02
❑ 271 Eric Moten	.10	.02
❑ 272 Brian Mitchell	.20	.07
❑ 273 Adrian Cooper	.10	.02
❑ 274 Gaston Green	.10	.02
❑ 275 John Taylor	.20	.07
❑ 276 Jeff Uhlenhake	.10	.02
❑ 277 Phil Hansen	.10	.02
❑ 278A Kev.Williams RC WR ERR	.40	.15
❑ 278B Kev.Williams RC WR COR	.40	.15
❑ 279 Robert Massey	.10	.02

❑ 280A Drew Bledsoe RC ERR 10.00 4.00
❑ 280B Drew Bledsoe RC COR 5.00 2.00
❑ 281 Walter Reeves .10 .02
❑ 282A Carlton Gray RC ERR .25 .08
❑ 282B Carlton Gray RC COR .15 .05
❑ 283 Derek Brown TE .10 .02
❑ 284 Martin Mayhew .10 .02
❑ 285 Sean Gilbert .20 .07
❑ 286 Jessie Hester .10 .02
❑ 287 Mark Clayton .10 .02
❑ 288 Blair Thomas .10 .02
❑ 289 J.J. Birden .10 .02
❑ 290 Shannon Sharpe .40 .15
❑ 291 Richard Fain RC .10 .02
❑ 292 Gene Atkins .10 .02
❑ 293 Burt Grossman .10 .02
❑ 294 Chris Doleman .10 .02
❑ 295 Pat Swilling .10 .02
❑ 296 Mike Kenn .10 .02
❑ 297 Merril Hoge .10 .02
❑ 298 Don Mosebar .10 .02
❑ 299 Kevin Smith .20 .07
❑ 300 Darrell Green .10 .02
❑ 301A Dan Footman RC ERR .25 .08
❑ 301B Dan Footman RC COR .15 .05
❑ 302 Vestee Jackson .10 .02
❑ 303 Carwell Gardner .10 .02
❑ 304 Amp Lee .10 .02
❑ 305 Bruce Matthews .10 .02
❑ 306 Antone Davis .10 .02
❑ 307 Dean Biasucci .10 .02
❑ 308 Maurice Hurst .10 .02
❑ 309 John Kasay .10 .02
❑ 310 Lawrence Taylor .20 .07
❑ 311 Ken Harvey .10 .02
❑ 312 Willie Davis .20 .07
❑ 313 Tony Bennett .10 .02
❑ 314 Jay Schroeder .10 .02
❑ 315 Darren Perry .10 .02
❑ 316A Troy Drayton RC ERR .25 .08
❑ 316B Troy Drayton RC COR .15 .05
❑ 317A Dan Williams RC ERR .25 .08
❑ 317B Dan Williams RC COR .15 .05
❑ 318 Michael Haynes .20 .07
❑ 319 Renaldo Turnbull .10 .02
❑ 320 Junior Seau .40 .15
❑ 321 Ray Crockett .10 .02
❑ 322 Will Furrer .10 .02
❑ 323 Byron Evans .10 .02
❑ 324 Jim McMahon .20 .07
❑ 325 Robert Jones .10 .02
❑ 326 Eric Davis .10 .02
❑ 327 Jeff Cross .10 .02
❑ 328 Kyle Clifton .10 .02
❑ 329 Haywood Jeffires .20 .07
❑ 330 Jeff Hostetler .20 .07
❑ 331 Darryl Talley .10 .02
❑ 332 Keith McCants .10 .02
❑ 333 Mo Lewis .10 .02
❑ 334 Matt Stover .10 .02
❑ 335 Ferrell Edmunds .10 .02
❑ 336 Matt Brock .10 .02
❑ 337 Ernie Mills .10 .02
❑ 338 Shane Dronett .10 .02
❑ 339 Brad Muster .10 .02
❑ 340 Jesse Solomon .10 .02
❑ 341 John Randle .20 .07
❑ 342 Chris Spielman .20 .07
❑ 343 David Whitmore .10 .02
❑ 344 Glenn Parker .10 .02
❑ 345 Marco Coleman .10 .02
❑ 346 Kenneth Gant .10 .02
❑ 347 Cris Dishman .10 .02
❑ 348 Kenny Walker .10 .02
❑ 349A Roosevelt Potts RC ERR .25 .08
❑ 349B Roosevelt Potts RC COR .15 .05
❑ 350 Reggie White .40 .15
❑ 351 Gerald Robinson .10 .02
❑ 352 Mark Rypien .10 .02
❑ 353 Stan Humphries .20 .07
❑ 354 Chris Singleton .10 .02
❑ 355 Herschel Walker .20 .07
❑ 356 Ron Hall .10 .02
❑ 357 Ethan Horton .10 .02
❑ 358 Anthony Pleasant .10 .02
❑ 359A Thomas Smith RC ERR .25 .08
❑ 359B Thomas Smith RC COR .15 .05
❑ 360 Audray McMillian .10 .02
❑ 361 D.J. Johnson .10 .02
❑ 362 Ron Heller .10 .02
❑ 363 Bern Brostek .10 .02
❑ 364 Ronnie Lott .20 .07
❑ 365 Reggie Johnson .10 .02
❑ 366 Lin Elliott .10 .02
❑ 367 Lemuel Stinson .10 .02
❑ 368 William White .10 .02
❑ 369 Ernie Jones .10 .02
❑ 370 Tom Rathman .10 .02
❑ 371 Tommy Kane .10 .02
❑ 372 David Brandon .10 .02
❑ 373 Lee Johnson .10 .02
❑ 374 Wade Wilson .10 .02
❑ 375 Nick Lowery .10 .02
❑ 376 Bubba McDowell .10 .02
❑ 377A Wayne Simmons RC ERR .25 .08
❑ 377B Wayne Simmons RC COR .15 .05
❑ 378 Calvin Williams .20 .07
❑ 379 Courtney Hall .10 .02
❑ 380 Troy Vincent .10 .02
❑ 381 Tim McGee .10 .02
❑ 382 Russell Freeman RC .10 .02
❑ 383 Steve Tasker .20 .07
❑ 384A Michael Strahan RC ERR 2.00 .75
❑ 384B Michael Strahan RC COR 2.00 .75
❑ 385 Greg Skrepenak .10 .02
❑ 386 Jake Reed .20 .07
❑ 387 Pete Stoyanovich .10 .02
❑ 388 Levon Kirkland .10 .02
❑ 389 Mel Gray .20 .07
❑ 390 Brian Washington .10 .02
❑ 391 Don Griffin .10 .02
❑ 392 Desmond Howard .20 .07
❑ 393 Luis Sharpe .10 .02
❑ 394 Mike Johnson .10 .02
❑ 395 Andre Tippett .10 .02
❑ 396 Donnell Woolford .10 .02
❑ 397A Demetrius DuBose RC ERR .25 .08
❑ 397B Demetrius DuBose RC COR .15 .05
❑ 398 Pat Terrell .10 .02
❑ 399 Todd McNair .10 .02
❑ 400 Ken Norton .20 .07
❑ 401 Keith Hamilton .10 .02
❑ 402 Andy Heck .10 .02
❑ 403 Jeff Gossett .10 .02
❑ 404 Dexter McNabb .10 .02
❑ 405 Richmond Webb .10 .02
❑ 406 Irving Fryar .20 .07
❑ 407 Brian Hansen .10 .02
❑ 408 David Little .10 .02
❑ 409A Glyn Milburn RC ERR .40 .15
❑ 409B Glyn Milburn RC COR .20 .07
❑ 410 Doug Dawson .10 .02
❑ 411 Scott Mersereau .10 .02
❑ 412 Don Beebe .10 .02
❑ 413 Vaughan Johnson .10 .02
❑ 414 Jack Del Rio .10 .02
❑ 415A Darrien Gordon RC ERR .25 .08
❑ 415B Darrien Gordon RC COR .15 .05
❑ 416 Mark Schlereth .10 .02
❑ 417 Lomas Brown .10 .02
❑ 418 William Thomas .10 .02
❑ 419 James Francis .10 .02
❑ 420 Quentin Coryatt .20 .07
❑ 421 Tyji Armstrong .10 .02
❑ 422 Hugh Millen .10 .02
❑ 423 Adrian White RC .10 .02
❑ 424 Eddie Anderson .10 .02
❑ 425 Mark Ingram .10 .02
❑ 426 Ken O'Brien .10 .02
❑ 427 Simon Fletcher .10 .02
❑ 428 Tim McKyer .10 .02
❑ 429 Leonard Marshall .10 .02
❑ 430 Eric Green .10 .02
❑ 431 Leonard Harris .10 .02
❑ 432 Darin Jordan RC .10 .02
❑ 433 Erik Howard .10 .02
❑ 434 David Lang .10 .02
❑ 435 Eric Turner .10 .02
❑ 436 Michael Cofer .10 .02
❑ 437 Jeff Bryant .10 .02
❑ 438 Charles McRae .10 .02
❑ 439 Henry Jones .10 .02
❑ 440 Joe Montana 3.00 1.25
❑ 441 Morten Andersen .10 .02
❑ 442 Jeff Jaeger .10 .02
❑ 443 Leslie O'Neal .20 .07
❑ 444 LeRoy Butler .10 .02
❑ 445 Steve Jordan .10 .02
❑ 446 Brad Edwards .10 .02
❑ 447 J.B. Brown .10 .02
❑ 448 Kerry Cash .10 .02
❑ 449 Mark Tuinei .10 .02
❑ 450 Rodney Peete .10 .02
❑ 451 Sheldon White .10 .02
❑ 452 Wesley Carroll .10 .02
❑ 453 Brad Baxter .10 .02
❑ 454 Mike Pitts .10 .02
❑ 455 Greg Montgomery .10 .02
❑ 456 Kenny Davidson .10 .02
❑ 457 Scott Fulhage .10 .02
❑ 458 Greg Townsend .10 .02
❑ 459 Rod Bernstine .10 .02
❑ 460 Gary Clark .20 .07
❑ 461 Hardy Nickerson .20 .07
❑ 462 Sean Landeta .10 .02
❑ 463 Rob Burnett .10 .02
❑ 464 Fred Barnett .20 .07
❑ 465 John L. Williams .10 .02
❑ 466 Anthony Miller .20 .07
❑ 467 Roman Phifer .10 .02
❑ 468 Rich Moran .10 .02
❑ 469A Willie Roaf RC ERR .25 .08
❑ 469B Willie Roaf RC COR .15 .05
❑ 470 William Perry .20 .07
❑ 471 Marcus Allen .40 .15
❑ 472 Carl Lee .10 .02
❑ 473 Kurt Gouveia .10 .02
❑ 474 Jarvis Williams .10 .02
❑ 475 Alfred Williams .10 .02
❑ 476 Mark Stepnoski .10 .02
❑ 477 Steve Wallace .10 .02
❑ 478 Pat Harlow .10 .02
❑ 479 Chip Banks .10 .02
❑ 480 Cornelius Bennett .20 .07
❑ 481A Ryan McNeil RC ERR .15 .05
❑ 481B Ryan McNeil RC COR .40 .15
❑ 482 Norm Johnson .10 .02
❑ 483 Dermontti Dawson .10 .02
❑ 484 Dwayne White .10 .02
❑ 485 Derek Russell .10 .02
❑ 486 Lionel Washington .10 .02
❑ 487 Eric Hill .10 .02
❑ 488 Micheal Barrow RC .40 .15
❑ 489 Checklist 251-375 UER .10 .02
❑ 490 Checklist 376-500 UER .10 .02
❑ 491 Emmitt Smith MC 1.50 .60
❑ 492 Derrick Thomas MC .20 .07
❑ 493 Deion Sanders MC .40 .15
❑ 494 Randall Cunningham MC .20 .07
❑ 495 Sterling Sharpe MC .20 .07
❑ 496 Barry Sanders MC 1.25 .50
❑ 497 Thurman Thomas MC .20 .07
❑ 498 Brett Favre MC 2.00 .75
❑ 499 Vaughan Johnson MC .10 .02
❑ 500 Steve Young MC .75 .30
❑ 501 Marvin Jones MC .10 .02
❑ 502 Reggie Brooks RC MC .20 .07
❑ 503 Eric Curry MC .10 .02
❑ 504 Drew Bledsoe MC 2.00 .75
❑ 505 Glyn Milburn MC .20 .07
❑ 506 Jerome Bettis MC 4.00 1.50
❑ 507 Robert Smith MC 1.00 .40
❑ 508 Dana Stubblefield RC MC .40 .15
❑ 509 Tom Carter MC .20 .07
❑ 510 Rick Mirer MC .40 .15
❑ 511 Russell Copeland RC .20 .07
❑ 512 Deon Figures RC .10 .02
❑ 513 Tony McGee RC .20 .07
❑ 514 Derrick Lassic RC .10 .02
❑ 515 Everett Lindsay RC .10 .02
❑ 516 Derek Brown RC RBK .10 .02
❑ 517 Harold Alexander RC .10 .02
❑ 518 Tom Scott OL RC .10 .02
❑ 519 Elvis Grbac RC 3.00 1.25
❑ 520 Terry Kirby RC .40 .15
❑ 521 Doug Pelfrey RC .10 .02

❑ 522 Horace Copeland RC .20 .07
❑ 523 Irv Smith RC .10 .02
❑ 524 Lincoln Kennedy RC .10 .02
❑ 525 Jason Elam RC .40 .15
❑ 526 Qadry Ismail RC .40 .15
❑ 527 Artie Smith RC .10 .02
❑ 528 Tyrone Hughes RC .20 .07
❑ 529 Lance Gunn RC .10 .02
❑ 530 Vincent Brisby RC .40 .15
❑ 531 Patrick Robinson RC .10 .02
❑ 532 Rocket Ismail .20 .07
❑ 533 Willie Beamon RC .10 .02
❑ 534 Vaughn Hebron RC .10 .02
❑ 535 Darren Drozdov RC .40 .15
❑ 536 James Jett RC .40 .15
❑ 537 Michael Bates RC .10 .02
❑ 538 Tom Rouen RC .10 .02
❑ 539 Michael Husted RC .10 .02
❑ 540 Greg Robinson RC .10 .02
❑ 541 Carl Banks .10 .02
❑ 542 Kevin Greene .20 .07
❑ 543 Scott Mitchell .40 .15
❑ 544 Michael Brooks .10 .02
❑ 545 Shane Conlan .10 .02
❑ 546 Vinny Testaverde .20 .07
❑ 547 Robert Delpino .10 .02
❑ 548 Bill Fralic .10 .02
❑ 549 Carlton Bailey .10 .02
❑ 550 Johnny Johnson .10 .02
❑ NNO Jerry Rice RB 10.00 4.00
❑ P1 Promo Sheet 5.00 2.00

1994 Stadium Club

❑ COMPLETE SET (630) 60.00 25.00
❑ COMP.SERIES 1 (270) 25.00 10.00
❑ COMP.SERIES 2 (270) 25.00 10.00
❑ COMP.HIGH SERIES (90) 10.00 5.00
❑ 1 Dan Wilkinson RC .20 .07
❑ 2 Chip Lohmiller .10 .02
❑ 3 Roosevelt Potts .10 .02
❑ 4 Martin Mayhew .10 .02
❑ 5 Shane Conlan .10 .02
❑ 6 Sam Adams RC .20 .07
❑ 7 Mike Kenn .10 .02
❑ 8 Tim Goad .10 .02
❑ 9 Tony Jones T .10 .02
❑ 10 Ronald Moore .10 .02
❑ 11 Mark Bortz .10 .02
❑ 12 Darren Carrington .10 .02
❑ 13 Eric Martin .10 .02
❑ 14 Eric Allen .10 .02
❑ 15 Aaron Glenn RC .40 .15
❑ 16 Bryan Cox .10 .02
❑ 17 Levon Kirkland .10 .02
❑ 18 Qadry Ismail .40 .15
❑ 19 Shane Dronett .10 .02
❑ 20 Chris Spielman .20 .07
❑ 21 Rob Fredrickson RC .20 .07
❑ 22 Wayne Simmons .10 .02
❑ 23 Glenn Montgomery .10 .02
❑ 24 Jason Sehorn RC .60 .25
❑ 25 Nick Lowery .10 .02
❑ 26 Dennis Brown .10 .02
❑ 27 Kenneth Davis .10 .02
❑ 28 Shante Carver RC .10 .02
❑ 29 Ryan Yarborough RC .10 .02
❑ 30 Cortez Kennedy .20 .07
❑ 31 Anthony Pleasant .10 .02
❑ 32 Jessie Tuggle .10 .02
❑ 33 Herschel Walker .20 .07
❑ 34 Andre Collins .10 .02
❑ 35 William Floyd RC .40 .15
❑ 36 Harold Green .10 .02
❑ 37 Courtney Hawkins .10 .02
❑ 38 Curtis Conway .40 .15
❑ 39 Ben Coates .20 .07
❑ 40 Natrone Means .40 .15
❑ 41 Eric Hill .10 .02
❑ 42 Keith Kartz .10 .02
❑ 43 Alexander Wright .10 .02
❑ 44 Willie Roaf .10 .02
❑ 45 Vencie Glenn .10 .02
❑ 46 Ronnie Lott .20 .07
❑ 47 George Koonce .10 .02
❑ 48 Rod Woodson .20 .07
❑ 49 Tim Grunhard .10 .02
❑ 50 Cody Carlson .10 .02
❑ 51 Bryant Young RC .40 .15
❑ 52 Jay Novacek .20 .07
❑ 53 Darryl Talley .10 .02
❑ 54 Harry Colon .10 .02
❑ 55 Dave Meggett .10 .02
❑ 56 Aubrey Beavers RC .10 .02
❑ 57 James Folston .10 .02
❑ 58 Willie Davis .20 .07
❑ 59 Jason Elam .20 .07
❑ 60 Eric Metcalf .20 .07
❑ 61 Bruce Armstrong .10 .02
❑ 62 Ron Heller .10 .02
❑ 63 LeRoy Butler .10 .02
❑ 64 Terry Obee .10 .02
❑ 65 Kurt Gouveia .10 .02
❑ 66 Pierce Holt .10 .02
❑ 67 David Alexander .10 .02
❑ 68 Deral Boykin .10 .02
❑ 69 Carl Pickens .20 .07
❑ 70 Broderick Thomas .10 .02
❑ 71 Barry Sanders CT 1.25 .50
❑ 72 Qadry Ismail CT .40 .15
❑ 73 Thurman Thomas CT .40 .15
❑ 74 Junior Seau .40 .15
❑ 75 Vinny Testaverde .20 .07
❑ 76 Tyrone Hughes .20 .07
❑ 77 Nate Newton .10 .02
❑ 78 Eric Swann .20 .07
❑ 79 Brad Baxter .10 .02
❑ 80 Dana Stubblefield .20 .07
❑ 81 Jumbo Elliott .10 .02
❑ 82 Steve Wisniewski .10 .02
❑ 83 Eddie Robinson .10 .02
❑ 84 Isaac Davis .10 .02
❑ 85 Cris Carter .60 .25
❑ 86 Mel Gray .10 .02
❑ 87 Cornelius Bennett .20 .07
❑ 88 Neil O'Donnell .40 .15
❑ 89 Jon Hand .10 .02
❑ 90 John Elway 3.00 1.25
❑ 91 Bill Hitchcock .10 .02
❑ 92 Neil Smith .20 .07
❑ 93 Joe Johnson RC .10 .02
❑ 94 Edgar Bennett .40 .15
❑ 95 Vincent Brown .10 .02
❑ 96 Tommy Vardell .10 .02
❑ 97 Donnell Woolford .10 .02
❑ 98 Lincoln Kennedy .10 .02
❑ 99 O.J.McDuffie .40 .15
❑ 100 Heath Shuler RC .40 .15
❑ 101 Jerry Rice BO .75 .30
❑ 102 Erik Williams BO .10 .02
❑ 103 Randall McDaniel BO .10 .02
❑ 104 Dermontti Dawson BO .10 .02
❑ 105 Nate Newton BO .10 .02
❑ 106 Harris Barton BO .10 .02
❑ 107 Shannon Sharpe BO .20 .07
❑ 108 Sterling Sharpe BO .20 .07
❑ 109 Steve Young BO .60 .25
❑ 110 Emmitt Smith BO 1.25 .50
❑ 111 Thurman Thomas BO .40 .15
❑ 112 Kyle Clifton .10 .02
❑ 113 Desmond Howard .20 .07
❑ 114 Quinn Early .20 .07
❑ 115 David Klingler .10 .02
❑ 116 Bern Brostek .10 .02
❑ 117 Gary Clark .20 .07
❑ 118 Courtney Hall .10 .02
❑ 119 Joe King .10 .02
❑ 120 Quentin Coryatt .10 .02
❑ 121 Johnnie Morton RC 2.00 .75
❑ 122 Andre Reed .20 .07
❑ 123 Eric Davis .10 .02
❑ 124 Jack Del Rio .10 .02
❑ 125 Greg Lloyd .20 .07
❑ 126 Bubba McDowell .10 .02
❑ 127 Mark Jackson .10 .02
❑ 128 Jeff Jaeger .10 .02
❑ 129 Chris Warren .20 .07
❑ 130 Tom Waddle .10 .02
❑ 131 Tony Smith RB .10 .02
❑ 132 Todd Collins .10 .02
❑ 133 Mark Bavaro .10 .02
❑ 134 Joe Phillips .10 .02
❑ 135 Chris Jacke .10 .02
❑ 136 Glyn Milburn .20 .07
❑ 137 Keith Jackson .10 .02
❑ 138 Steve Tovar .10 .02
❑ 139 Tim Johnson .10 .02
❑ 140 Brian Washington .10 .02
❑ 141 Troy Drayton .10 .02
❑ 142 Dewayne Washington RC .20 .07
❑ 143 Erik Williams .10 .02
❑ 144 Eric Turner .10 .02
❑ 145 John Taylor .20 .07
❑ 146 Richard Cooper .10 .02
❑ 147 Van Malone .10 .02
❑ 148 Tim Ruddy RC .10 .02
❑ 149 Henry Jones .10 .02
❑ 150 Tim Brown .40 .15
❑ 151 Stan Humphries .20 .07
❑ 152 Harry Newsome .10 .02
❑ 153 Craig Erickson .10 .02
❑ 154 Gary Anderson K .10 .02
❑ 155 Ray Childress .10 .02
❑ 156 Howard Cross .10 .02
❑ 157 Heath Sherman .10 .02
❑ 158 Terrell Buckley .10 .02
❑ 159 J.B. Brown .10 .02
❑ 160 Joe Montana 3.00 1.25
❑ 161 David Wyman .10 .02
❑ 162 Norm Johnson .10 .02
❑ 163 Rod Stephens .10 .02
❑ 164 Willie McGinest RC .40 .15
❑ 165 Barry Sanders 2.50 1.00
❑ 166 Marc Logan .10 .02
❑ 167 Anthony Newman .10 .02
❑ 168 Russell Maryland .10 .02
❑ 169 Luis Sharpe .10 .02
❑ 170 Jim Kelly .40 .15
❑ 171 Tre Johnson RC .10 .02
❑ 172 Johnny Mitchell .10 .02
❑ 173 David Palmer RC .40 .15
❑ 174 Bob Dahl .10 .02
❑ 175 Aaron Wallace .10 .02
❑ 176 Chris Gardocki .10 .02
❑ 177 Hardy Nickerson .20 .07
❑ 178 Jeff Query .10 .02
❑ 179 Leslie O'Neal .10 .02
❑ 180 Kevin Greene .20 .07
❑ 181 Alonzo Spellman .10 .02
❑ 182 Reggie Brooks .20 .07
❑ 183 Dana Stubblefield .20 .07
❑ 184 Tyrone Hughes .20 .07
❑ 185 Drew Bledsoe GE .40 .15
❑ 186 Ronald Moore GE .10 .02
❑ 187 Jason Elam GE .10 .02
❑ 188 Rick Mirer GE .40 .15
❑ 189 Willie Roaf GE .10 .02
❑ 190 Jerome Bettis GE .40 .15
❑ 191 Brad Hopkins .10 .02
❑ 192 Derek Brown RBK .10 .02
❑ 193 Nolan Harrison .10 .02
❑ 194 John Randle .20 .07
❑ 195 Carlton Bailey .10 .02
❑ 196 Kevin Williams WR .20 .07
❑ 197 Greg Hill RC .40 .15
❑ 198 Mark McMillian .10 .02
❑ 199 Brad Edwards .10 .02
❑ 200 Dan Marino 3.00 1.25
❑ 201 Ricky Watters .20 .07
❑ 202 George Teague .10 .02
❑ 203 Steve Beuerlein .20 .07
❑ 204 Jeff Burris RC .20 .07
❑ 205 Steve Atwater .10 .02
❑ 206 John Thierry RC .10 .02

❑ 207 Patrick Hunter	.10	.02
❑ 208 Wayne Gandy	.10	.02
❑ 209 Derrick Moore	.10	.02
❑ 210 Phil Simms	.20	.07
❑ 211 Kirk Lowdermilk	.10	.02
❑ 212 Patrick Robinson	.10	.02
❑ 213 Kevin Mitchell	.10	.02
❑ 214 Jonathan Hayes	.10	.02
❑ 215 Michael Dean Perry	.20	.07
❑ 216 John Fina	.10	.02
❑ 217 Anthony Smith	.10	.02
❑ 218 Paul Gruber	.10	.02
❑ 219 Carnell Lake	.10	.02
❑ 220 Carl Lee	.10	.02
❑ 221 Steve Christie	.10	.02
❑ 222 Greg Montgomery	.10	.02
❑ 223 Reggie Brooks	.20	.07
❑ 224 Derrick Thomas	.40	.15
❑ 225 Eric Metcalf	.20	.07
❑ 226 Michael Haynes	.20	.07
❑ 227 Bobby Hebert	.10	.02
❑ 228 Tyrone Hughes	.20	.07
❑ 229 Donald Frank	.10	.02
❑ 230 Vaughan Johnson	.10	.02
❑ 231 Eric Thomas	.10	.02
❑ 232 Ernest Givins	.20	.07
❑ 233 Charles Haley	.20	.07
❑ 234 Darrell Green	.10	.02
❑ 235 Harold Alexander	.10	.02
❑ 236 Dwayne Sabb	.10	.02
❑ 237 Harris Barton	.10	.02
❑ 238 Randall Cunningham	.40	.15
❑ 239 Ray Buchanan	.10	.02
❑ 240 Sterling Sharpe	.20	.07
❑ 241 Chris Mims	.10	.02
❑ 242 Mark Carrier DB	.10	.02
❑ 243 Ricky Proehl	.10	.02
❑ 244 Michael Brooks	.10	.02
❑ 245 Sean Gilbert	.10	.02
❑ 246 David Lutz	.10	.02
❑ 247 Kelvin Martin	.10	.02
❑ 248 Scottie Graham RC	.20	.07
❑ 249 Irving Fryar	.20	.07
❑ 250 Ricardo McDonald	.10	.02
❑ 251 Marvcus Patton	.10	.02
❑ 252 Errict Rhett RC	.40	.15
❑ 253 Winston Moss	.10	.02
❑ 254 Rod Bernstine	.10	.02
❑ 255 Terry Wooden	.10	.02
❑ 256 Antonio Langham RC	.20	.07
❑ 257 Tommy Barnhardt	.10	.02
❑ 258 Marvin Washington	.10	.02
❑ 259 Bo Orlando	.10	.02
❑ 260 Marcus Allen	.40	.15
❑ 261 Mario Bates RC	.40	.15
❑ 262 Marco Coleman	.10	.02
❑ 263 Doug Riesenberg	.10	.02
❑ 264 Jesse Sapolu	.10	.02
❑ 265 Dermontti Dawson	.10	.02
❑ 266 Fernando Smith RC	.10	.02
❑ 267 David Szott	.10	.02
❑ 268 Steve Christie	.10	.02
❑ 269 Bruce Matthews	.10	.02
❑ 270 Michael Irvin	.40	.15
❑ 271 Seth Joyner	.10	.02
❑ 272 Santana Dotson	.20	.07
❑ 273 Vincent Brisby	.20	.07
❑ 274 Rohn Stark	.10	.02
❑ 275 John Copeland	.10	.02
❑ 276 Toby Wright	.10	.02
❑ 277 David Griggs	.10	.02
❑ 278 Aaron Taylor	.10	.02
❑ 279 Chris Doleman	.10	.02
❑ 280 Reggie Brooks	.20	.07
❑ 281 Flipper Anderson	.10	.02
❑ 282 Alvin Harper	.20	.07
❑ 283 Chris Hinton	.10	.02
❑ 284 Kelvin Pritchett	.10	.02
❑ 285 Russell Copeland	.10	.02
❑ 286 Dwight Stone	.10	.02
❑ 287 Jeff Gossett	.10	.02
❑ 288 Larry Allen RC	.40	.15
❑ 289 Kevin Mawae RC	.40	.15
❑ 290 Mark Collins	.10	.02
❑ 291 Chris Zorich	.10	.02
❑ 292 Vince Buck	.10	.02
❑ 293 Gene Atkins	.10	.02
❑ 294 Webster Slaughter	.10	.02
❑ 295 Steve Young	1.25	.50
❑ 296 Dan Williams	.10	.02
❑ 297 Jessie Armstead	.10	.02
❑ 298 Victor Bailey	.10	.02
❑ 299 John Carney	.10	.02
❑ 300 Emmitt Smith	2.50	1.00
❑ 301 Bucky Brooks RC	.10	.02
❑ 302 Mo Lewis	.10	.02
❑ 303 Eugene Daniel	.10	.02
❑ 304 Tyji Armstrong	.10	.02
❑ 305 Eugene Chung	.10	.02
❑ 306 Rocket Ismail	.20	.07
❑ 307 Sean Jones	.10	.02
❑ 308 Rick Cunningham	.10	.02
❑ 309 Ken Harvey	.10	.02
❑ 310 Jeff George	.40	.15
❑ 311 Jon Vaughn	.10	.02
❑ 312 Roy Barker RC	.10	.02
❑ 313 Micheal Barrow	.10	.02
❑ 314 Ryan McNeil	.10	.02
❑ 315 Pete Stoyanovich	.10	.02
❑ 316 Darryl Williams	.10	.02
❑ 317 Renaldo Turnbull	.10	.02
❑ 318 Eric Green	.10	.02
❑ 319 Nate Lewis	.10	.02
❑ 320 Mike Flores	.10	.02
❑ 321 Derek Russell	.10	.02
❑ 322 Marcus Spears RC	.10	.02
❑ 323 Corey Miller	.10	.02
❑ 324 Derrick Thomas	.40	.15
❑ 325 Steve Everitt	.10	.02
❑ 326 Brent Jones	.20	.07
❑ 327 Marshall Faulk RC	6.00	2.50
❑ 328 Don Beebe	.10	.02
❑ 329 Harry Swayne	.10	.02
❑ 330 Boomer Esiason	.20	.07
❑ 331 Don Mosebar	.10	.02
❑ 332 Isaac Bruce RC	5.00	2.00
❑ 333 Rickey Jackson	.10	.02
❑ 334 Daryl Johnston	.20	.07
❑ 335 Lorenzo Lynch	.10	.02
❑ 336 Brian Blades	.20	.07
❑ 337 Michael Timpson	.10	.02
❑ 338 Reggie Cobb	.10	.02
❑ 339 Joe Walter	.10	.02
❑ 340 Barry Foster	.10	.02
❑ 341 Richmond Webb	.10	.02
❑ 342 Pat Swilling	.10	.02
❑ 343 Shaun Gayle	.10	.02
❑ 344 Reggie Roby	.10	.02
❑ 345 Chris Calloway	.10	.02
❑ 346 Doug Dawson	.10	.02
❑ 347 Rob Burnett	.10	.02
❑ 348 Dana Hall	.10	.02
❑ 349 Horace Copeland	.10	.02
❑ 350 Shannon Sharpe	.20	.07
❑ 351 Rich Miano	.10	.02
❑ 352 Henry Thomas	.10	.02
❑ 353 Dan Saleaumua	.10	.02
❑ 354 Kevin Ross	.10	.02
❑ 355 Morten Andersen	.10	.02
❑ 356 Anthony Blaylock	.10	.02
❑ 357 Stanley Richard	.10	.02
❑ 358 Albert Lewis	.10	.02
❑ 359 Darren Woodson	.20	.07
❑ 360 Drew Bledsoe	1.00	.40
❑ 361 Eric Mahlum	.10	.02
❑ 362 Trent Dilfer RC	1.50	.60
❑ 363 William Roberts	.10	.02
❑ 364 Robert Brooks	.40	.15
❑ 365 Jason Hanson	.10	.02
❑ 366 Troy Vincent	.10	.02
❑ 367 William Thomas	.10	.02
❑ 368 Lonnie Johnson RC	.10	.02
❑ 369 Jamir Miller RC	.20	.07
❑ 370 Michael Jackson	.20	.07
❑ 371 Charlie Ward CT RC	.40	.15
❑ 372 Shannon Sharpe CT	.20	.07
❑ 373 Jackie Slater CT	.10	.02
❑ 374 Steve Young CT	.60	.25
❑ 375 Bobby Wilson	.10	.02
❑ 376 Paul Frase	.10	.02
❑ 377 Dale Carter	.10	.02
❑ 378 Robert Delpino	.10	.02
❑ 379 Bert Emanuel RC	.40	.15
❑ 380 Rick Mirer	.40	.15
❑ 381 Carlos Jenkins	.10	.02
❑ 382 Gary Brown	.10	.02
❑ 383 Doug Pelfrey	.10	.02
❑ 384 Dexter Carter	.10	.02
❑ 385 Chris Miller	.10	.02
❑ 386 Charles Johnson RC	.40	.15
❑ 387 James Joseph	.10	.02
❑ 388 Darrin Smith	.10	.02
❑ 389 James Jett	.10	.02
❑ 390 Junior Seau	.40	.15
❑ 391 Chris Slade	.10	.02
❑ 392 Jim Harbaugh	.40	.15
❑ 393 Herman Moore	.40	.15
❑ 394 Thomas Randolph RC	.10	.02
❑ 395 Lamar Thomas	.10	.02
❑ 396 Reggie Rivers	.10	.02
❑ 397 Larry Centers	.40	.15
❑ 398 Chad Brown	.10	.02
❑ 399 Terry Kirby	.40	.15
❑ 400 Bruce Smith	.40	.15
❑ 401 Keenan McCardell RC	2.00	.75
❑ 402 Tim McDonald	.10	.02
❑ 403 Robert Smith	.40	.15
❑ 404 Matt Brock	.10	.02
❑ 405 Tony McGee	.10	.02
❑ 406 Ethan Horton	.10	.02
❑ 407 Michael Haynes	.20	.07
❑ 408 Steve Jackson	.10	.02
❑ 409 Erik Kramer	.20	.07
❑ 410 Jerome Bettis	.60	.25
❑ 411 D.J. Johnson	.10	.02
❑ 412 John Alt	.10	.02
❑ 413 Jeff Lageman	.10	.02
❑ 414 Rick Tuten	.10	.02
❑ 415 Jeff Robinson	.10	.02
❑ 416 Kevin Lee RC	.10	.02
❑ 417 Thomas Lewis RC	.20	.07
❑ 418 Kerry Cash	.10	.02
❑ 419 Chuck Levy RC	.10	.02
❑ 420 Mark Ingram	.10	.02
❑ 421 Dennis Gibson	.10	.02
❑ 422 Tyronne Drakeford	.10	.02
❑ 423 James Washington	.10	.02
❑ 424 Dante Jones	.10	.02
❑ 425 Eugene Robinson	.10	.02
❑ 426 Johnny Johnson	.10	.02
❑ 427 Brian Mitchell	.10	.02
❑ 428 Charles Mincy	.10	.02
❑ 429 Mark Carrier WR	.20	.07
❑ 430 Vince Workman	.10	.02
❑ 431 James Francis	.10	.02
❑ 432 Clay Matthews	.10	.02
❑ 433 Randall McDaniel	.10	.02
❑ 434 Brad Ottis	.10	.02
❑ 435 Bruce Smith	.40	.15
❑ 436 Cortez Kennedy BD	.10	.02
❑ 437 John Randle BD	.20	.07
❑ 438 Neil Smith BD	.20	.07
❑ 439 Cornelius Bennett BD	.20	.07
❑ 440 Junior Seau BD	.20	.07
❑ 441 Derrick Thomas BD	.20	.07
❑ 442 Rod Woodson BD	.20	.07
❑ 443 Terry McDaniel BD	.10	.02
❑ 444 Tim McDonald BD	.10	.02
❑ 445 Mark Carrier DB BD	.10	.02
❑ 446 Irv Smith	.10	.02
❑ 447 Steve Wallace	.10	.02
❑ 448 Cris Dishman	.10	.02
❑ 449 Bill Brooks	.10	.02
❑ 450 Jeff Hostetler	.20	.07
❑ 451 Brentson Buckner RC	.10	.02
❑ 452 Ken Ruettgers	.10	.02
❑ 453 Marc Boutte	.10	.02
❑ 454 John Offerdahl	.10	.02
❑ 455 Allen Aldridge	.10	.02
❑ 456 Steve Emtman	.10	.02
❑ 457 Andre Rison	.20	.07
❑ 458 Shawn Jefferson	.10	.02
❑ 459 Todd Steussie RC	.20	.07
❑ 460 Scott Mitchell	.20	.07
❑ 461 Tom Carter	.10	.02
❑ 462 Donnell Bennett RC	.40	.15
❑ 463 James Jones DT	.10	.02
❑ 464 Antone Davis	.10	.02
❑ 465 Jim Everett	.20	.07
❑ 466 Tony Tolbert	.10	.02
❑ 467 Merril Hoge	.10	.02

❑ 468 Michael Bates .10 .02
❑ 469 Phil Hansen .10 .02
❑ 470 Rodney Hampton .20 .07
❑ 471 Aeneas Williams .10 .02
❑ 472 Al Del Greco .10 .02
❑ 473 Todd Lyght .10 .02
❑ 474 Joel Steed .10 .02
❑ 475 Merton Hanks .20 .07
❑ 476 Tony Stargell .10 .02
❑ 477 Greg Robinson .10 .02
❑ 478 Roger Duffy .10 .02
❑ 479 Simon Fletcher .10 .02
❑ 480 Reggie White .40 .15
❑ 481 Lee Johnson .10 .02
❑ 482 Wayne Martin .10 .02
❑ 483 Thurman Thomas .40 .15
❑ 484 Warren Moon .40 .15
❑ 485 Sam Rogers RC .10 .02
❑ 486 Erric Pegram .10 .02
❑ 487 Will Wolford .10 .02
❑ 488 Duane Young .10 .02
❑ 489 Keith Hamilton .10 .02
❑ 490 Haywood Jeffires .20 .07
❑ 491 Trace Armstrong .10 .02
❑ 492 J.J. Birden .10 .02
❑ 493 Ricky Ervins .10 .02
❑ 494 Robert Blackmon .10 .02
❑ 495 William Perry .20 .07
❑ 496 Robert Massey .10 .02
❑ 497 Jim Jeffcoat .10 .02
❑ 498 Pat Harlow .10 .02
❑ 499 Jeff Cross .10 .02
❑ 500 Jerry Rice 1.50 .60
❑ 501 Darnay Scott RC 1.00 .40
❑ 502 Clyde Simmons .10 .02
❑ 503 Henry Rolling .10 .02
❑ 504 James Hasty .10 .02
❑ 505 Leroy Thompson .10 .02
❑ 506 Darrell Thompson .10 .02
❑ 507 Tim Bowens RC .20 .07
❑ 508 Gerald Perry .10 .02
❑ 509 Mike Croel .10 .02
❑ 510 Sam Mills .10 .02
❑ 511 Steve Young RZ .60 .25
❑ 512 Hardy Nickerson RZ .20 .07
❑ 513 Cris Carter RZ .20 .07
❑ 514 Boomer Esiason RZ .10 .02
❑ 515 Bruce Smith RZ .20 .07
❑ 516 Emmitt Smith RZ 1.25 .50
❑ 517 Eugene Robinson RZ .10 .02
❑ 518 Gary Brown RZ .10 .02
❑ 519 Jerry Rice RZ .75 .30
❑ 520 Troy Aikman RZ .75 .30
❑ 521 Marcus Allen RZ .20 .07
❑ 522 Junior Seau RZ .20 .07
❑ 523 Sterling Sharpe RZ .20 .07
❑ 524 Dana Stubblefield RZ .20 .07
❑ 525 Tom Carter RZ .10 .02
❑ 526 Pete Metzelaars .10 .02
❑ 527 Russell Freeman .10 .02
❑ 528 Keith Cash .10 .02
❑ 529 Willie Drewrey .10 .02
❑ 530 Randal Hill .10 .02
❑ 531 Pepper Johnson .10 .02
❑ 532 Rob Moore .20 .07
❑ 533 Todd Kelly .10 .02
❑ 534 Keith Byars .10 .02
❑ 535 Mike Fox .10 .02
❑ 536 Brett Favre 3.00 1.25
❑ 537 Terry McDaniel .10 .02
❑ 538 Darren Perry .10 .02
❑ 539 Maurice Hurst .10 .02
❑ 540 Troy Aikman 1.50 .60
❑ 541 Junior Seau .40 .15
❑ 542 Steve Broussard .10 .02
❑ 543 Lorenzo White .10 .02
❑ 544 Terry McDaniel .10 .02
❑ 545 Henry Thomas .10 .02
❑ 546 Tyrone Hughes .20 .07
❑ 547 Mark Collins .10 .02
❑ 548 Gary Anderson K .10 .02
❑ 549 Darrell Green .10 .02
❑ 550 Jerry Rice 1.25 .50
❑ 551 Cornelius Bennett .20 .07
❑ 552 Aeneas Williams .10 .02
❑ 553 Eric Metcalf .20 .07
❑ 554 Jumbo Elliott .10 .02
❑ 555 Mo Lewis .10 .02
❑ 556 Darren Carrington .10 .02
❑ 557 Kevin Greene .20 .07
❑ 558 John Elway 2.50 1.00
❑ 559 Eugene Robinson .10 .02
❑ 560 Drew Bledsoe .75 .30
❑ 561 Fred Barnett .20 .07
❑ 562 Bernie Parmalee RC .40 .15
❑ 563 Bryce Paup .20 .07
❑ 564 Donnell Woolford .10 .02
❑ 565 Terance Mathis .20 .07
❑ 566 Santana Dotson .20 .07
❑ 567 Randall McDaniel .10 .02
❑ 568 Stanley Richard .10 .02
❑ 569 Brian Blades .20 .07
❑ 570 Jerome Bettis .50 .20
❑ 571 Neil Smith .20 .07
❑ 572 Andre Reed .20 .07
❑ 573 Michael Bankston .10 .02
❑ 574 Dana Stubblefield .20 .07
❑ 575 Rod Woodson .20 .07
❑ 576 Ken Harvey .10 .02
❑ 577 Andre Rison .20 .07
❑ 578 Darion Conner .10 .02
❑ 579 Michael Strahan .40 .15
❑ 580 Barry Sanders 2.00 .75
❑ 581 Pepper Johnson .10 .02
❑ 582 Lewis Tillman .10 .02
❑ 583 Jeff George .40 .15
❑ 584 Michael Haynes .20 .07
❑ 585 Herschel Walker .20 .07
❑ 586 Tim Brown .40 .15
❑ 587 Jim Kelly .40 .15
❑ 588 Ricky Watters .20 .07
❑ 589 Randall Cunningham .40 .15
❑ 590 Troy Aikman 1.25 .50
❑ 591 Ken Norton Jr. .20 .07
❑ 592 Cortez Kennedy .20 .07
❑ 593 Ricky Ervins .10 .02
❑ 594 Cris Carter .50 .20
❑ 595 Sterling Sharpe .20 .07
❑ 596 John Randle .20 .07
❑ 597 Shannon Sharpe .20 .07
❑ 598 Ray Crittenden RC .10 .02
❑ 599 Barry Foster .10 .02
❑ 600 Deion Sanders .60 .25
❑ 601 Seth Joyner .10 .02
❑ 602 Chris Warren .20 .07
❑ 603 Tom Rathman .10 .02
❑ 604 Brett Favre 2.50 1.00
❑ 605 Marshall Faulk 2.00 .75
❑ 606 Terry Allen .20 .07
❑ 607 Ben Coates .20 .07
❑ 608 Brian Washington .10 .02
❑ 609 Henry Ellard .20 .07
❑ 610 Dave Meggett .10 .02
❑ 611 Stan Humphries .20 .07
❑ 612 Warren Moon .40 .15
❑ 613 Marcus Allen .40 .15
❑ 614 Ed McDaniel .10 .02
❑ 615 Joe Montana 2.50 1.00
❑ 616 Jeff Hostetler .20 .07
❑ 617 Johnny Johnson .10 .02
❑ 618 Andre Coleman RC .10 .02
❑ 619 Willie Davis .20 .07
❑ 620 Rick Mirer .40 .15
❑ 621 Dan Marino 2.50 1.00
❑ 622 Rob Moore .20 .07
❑ 623 Byron Bam Morris RC .20 .07
❑ 624 Natrone Means .40 .15
❑ 625 Steve Young .75 .30
❑ 626 Jim Everett .20 .07
❑ 627 Michael Brooks .10 .02
❑ 628 Dermontti Dawson .10 .02
❑ 629 Reggie White .40 .15
❑ 630 Emmitt Smith 1.50 .60
❑ O Micheal Barrow TSC 4.00 2.00
❑ NNO Checklist Card 1 .10 .02
❑ NNO Checklist Card 2 .10 .02
❑ NNO Checklist Card 3 .10 .02

1995 Stadium Club

❑ COMPLETE SET (450) 60.00 25.00
❑ COMP.SERIES 1 (225) 30.00 12.50
❑ COMP.SERIES 2 (225) 30.00 12.50
❑ 1 Steve Young 1.25 .50
❑ 2 Stan Humphries .20 .07

❑ 3 Chris Boniol RC .10 .02
❑ 4 Darren Perry .10 .02
❑ 5 Vinny Testaverde .20 .07
❑ 6 Aubrey Beavers .10 .02
❑ 7 Dewayne Washington .20 .07
❑ 8 Marion Butts .10 .02
❑ 9 George Koonce .10 .02
❑ 10 Joe Cain .10 .02
❑ 11 Mike Johnson .10 .02
❑ 12 Dale Carter .20 .07
❑ 13 Greg Biekert .10 .02
❑ 14 Aaron Pierce .10 .02
❑ 15 Aeneas Williams .10 .02
❑ 16 Stephen Grant RC .10 .02
❑ 17 Henry Jones .10 .02
❑ 18 James Williams LB .10 .02
❑ 19 Andy Harmon .10 .02
❑ 20 Anthony Miller .20 .07
❑ 21 Kevin Ross .10 .02
❑ 22 Erik Howard .10 .02
❑ 23 Brian Blades .20 .07
❑ 24 Trent Dilfer .40 .15
❑ 25 Roman Phifer .10 .02
❑ 26 Bruce Kozerski .10 .02
❑ 27 Henry Ellard .20 .07
❑ 28 Rich Camarillo .10 .02
❑ 29 Richmond Webb .10 .02
❑ 30 George Teague .10 .02
❑ 31 Antonio Langham .10 .02
❑ 32 Barry Foster .20 .07
❑ 33 Bruce Armstrong .10 .02
❑ 34 Tim McDonald .10 .02
❑ 35 James Harris DE .10 .02
❑ 36 Lomas Brown .10 .02
❑ 37 Jay Novacek .20 .07
❑ 38 John Thierry .10 .02
❑ 39 John Elliott .10 .02
❑ 40 Terry McDaniel .10 .02
❑ 41 Shawn Lee .10 .02
❑ 42 Shane Dronett .10 .02
❑ 43 Cornelius Bennett .20 .07
❑ 44 Steve Bono .20 .07
❑ 45 Byron Evans .10 .02
❑ 46 Eugene Robinson .10 .02
❑ 47 Tony Bennett .10 .02
❑ 48 Michael Bankston .10 .02
❑ 49 Willie Roaf .10 .02
❑ 50 Bobby Houston .10 .02
❑ 51 Ken Harvey .10 .02
❑ 52 Bruce Matthews .10 .02
❑ 53 Lincoln Kennedy .10 .02
❑ 54 Todd Lyght .10 .02
❑ 55 Paul Gruber .10 .02
❑ 56 Corey Sawyer .10 .02
❑ 57 Myron Guyton .10 .02
❑ 58 John Jackson T .10 .02
❑ 59 Sean Jones .10 .02
❑ 60 Pepper Johnson .10 .02
❑ 61 Steve Walsh .10 .02
❑ 62 Corey Miller .10 .02
❑ 63 Fuad Reveiz .10 .02
❑ 64 Rickey Jackson .10 .02
❑ 65 Scott Mitchell .20 .07
❑ 66 Michael Irvin .40 .15
❑ 67 Andre Reed .20 .07
❑ 68 Mark Seay .20 .07
❑ 69 Keith Byars .10 .02
❑ 70 Marcus Allen .40 .15
❑ 71 Shannon Sharpe .20 .07
❑ 72 Eric Hill .10 .02

❑ 73 James Washington .10 .02
❑ 74 Greg Jackson .10 .02
❑ 75 Chris Warren .20 .07
❑ 76 Will Wolford .10 .02
❑ 77 Anthony Smith .10 .02
❑ 78 Cris Dishman .10 .02
❑ 79 Carl Pickens .20 .07
❑ 80 Tyrone Hughes .20 .07
❑ 81 Chris Miller .10 .02
❑ 82 Clay Matthews .20 .07
❑ 83 Lonnie Marts .10 .02
❑ 84 Jerome Henderson .10 .02
❑ 85 Ben Coates .20 .07
❑ 86 Deon Figures .10 .02
❑ 87 Anthony Pleasant .10 .02
❑ 88 Guy McIntyre .10 .02
❑ 89 Jake Reed .20 .07
❑ 90 Rodney Hampton .20 .07
❑ 91 Santana Dotson .10 .02
❑ 92 Jeff Blackshear .10 .02
❑ 93 Willie Clay .10 .02
❑ 94 Nate Newton .20 .07
❑ 95 Bucky Brooks .10 .02
❑ 96 Lamar Lathon .10 .02
❑ 97 Tim Grunhard .10 .02
❑ 98 Harris Barton .10 .02
❑ 99 Brian Mitchell .10 .02
❑ 100 Natrone Means .20 .07
❑ 101 Sean Dawkins .20 .07
❑ 102 Chris Slade .10 .02
❑ 103 Tom Rathman .10 .02
❑ 104 Fred Barnett .20 .07
❑ 105 Gary Brown .10 .02
❑ 106 Leonard Russell .10 .02
❑ 107 Alfred Williams .10 .02
❑ 108 Kelvin Martin .10 .02
❑ 109 Alexander Wright .10 .02
❑ 110 O.J. McDuffie .40 .15
❑ 111 Mario Bates .20 .07
❑ 112 Tony Casillas .10 .02
❑ 113 Michael Timpson .10 .02
❑ 114 Robert Brooks .40 .15
❑ 115 Rob Burnett .10 .02
❑ 116 Mark Collins .10 .02
❑ 117 Chris Calloway .10 .02
❑ 118 Courtney Hawkins .10 .02
❑ 119 Marvcus Patton .10 .02
❑ 120 Greg Lloyd .20 .07
❑ 121 Ryan McNeil .10 .02
❑ 122 Gary Plummer .10 .02
❑ 123 Dwayne Sabb .10 .02
❑ 124 Jessie Hester .10 .02
❑ 125 Terance Mathis .20 .07
❑ 126 Steve Atwater .10 .02
❑ 127 Lorenzo Lynch .10 .02
❑ 128 James Francis .10 .02
❑ 129 John Fina .10 .02
❑ 130 Emmitt Smith 2.50 1.25
❑ 131 Bryan Cox .10 .02
❑ 132 Robert Blackmon .10 .02
❑ 133 Kenny Davidson .10 .02
❑ 134 Eugene Daniel .10 .02
❑ 135 Vince Buck .10 .02
❑ 136 Leslie O'Neal .20 .07
❑ 137 James Jett .20 .07
❑ 138 Johnny Johnson .10 .02
❑ 139 Michael Zordich .10 .02
❑ 140 Warren Moon .20 .07
❑ 141 William White .10 .02
❑ 142 Carl Banks .10 .02
❑ 143 Marty Carter .10 .02
❑ 144 Keith Hamilton .10 .02
❑ 145 Alvin Harper .10 .02
❑ 146 Corey Harris .10 .02
❑ 147 Elijah Alexander RC .10 .02
❑ 148 Darrell Green .10 .02
❑ 149 Yancey Thigpen RC .20 .07
❑ 150 Deion Sanders 1.00 .40
❑ 151 Burt Grossman .10 .02
❑ 152 J.B. Brown .10 .02
❑ 153 Johnny Bailey .10 .02
❑ 154 Harvey Williams .10 .02
❑ 155 Jeff Blake RC 1.00 .40
❑ 156 Al Smith .10 .02
❑ 157 Chris Doleman .10 .02
❑ 158 Garrison Hearst .40 .15
❑ 159 Bryce Paup .20 .07
❑ 160 Herman Moore .40 .15
❑ 161 Cortez Kennedy .20 .07
❑ 162 Marquez Pope .10 .02
❑ 163 Quinn Early .20 .07
❑ 164 Broderick Thomas .10 .02
❑ 165 Jeff Herrod .10 .02
❑ 166 Robert Jones .10 .02
❑ 167 Mo Lewis .10 .02
❑ 168 Ray Crittenden .10 .02
❑ 169 Raymont Harris .10 .02
❑ 170 Bruce Smith .40 .15
❑ 171 Dana Stubblefield .20 .07
❑ 172 Charles Haley .20 .07
❑ 173 Charles Johnson .20 .07
❑ 174 Shawn Jefferson .10 .02
❑ 175 Leroy Hoard .10 .02
❑ 176 Bernie Parmalee .20 .07
❑ 177 Scottie Graham .20 .07
❑ 178 Edgar Bennett .20 .07
❑ 179 Aubrey Matthews .10 .02
❑ 180 Don Beebe .10 .02
❑ 181 Eric Swann EC SP .30 .10
❑ 182 Jeff George EC SP .30 .10
❑ 183 Jim Kelly EC SP .60 .25
❑ 184 Sam Mills EC SP .30 .10
❑ 185 Mark Carrier DB EC SP .20 .07
❑ 186 Dan Wilkinson EC SP .30 .10
❑ 187 Eric Turner EC SP .20 .07
❑ 188 Troy Aikman EC SP 2.00 .75
❑ 189 John Elway EC SP 4.00 1.50
❑ 190 Barry Sanders EC SP 3.00 1.25
❑ 191 Brett Favre EC SP 4.00 2.00
❑ 192 Micheal Barrow EC SP .20 .07
❑ 193 Marshall Faulk EC SP 2.50 1.00
❑ 194 Steve Beuerlein EC SP .30 .10
❑ 195 Neil Smith EC SP .30 .10
❑ 196 Jeff Hostetler EC SP .30 .10
❑ 197 Jerome Bettis EC SP .60 .25
❑ 198 Dan Marino EC SP 4.00 1.50
❑ 199 Cris Carter EC SP .60 .25
❑ 200 Drew Bledsoe EC SP 1.00 .40
❑ 201 Jim Everett EC SP .20 .07
❑ 202 Dave Brown EC SP .30 .10
❑ 203 Boomer Esiason EC SP .30 .10
❑ 204 Randall Cunningham EC SP .30 .10
❑ 205 Rod Woodson EC SP .30 .10
❑ 206 Junior Seau EC SP .60 .25
❑ 207 Jerry Rice EC SP 2.00 .75
❑ 208 Rick Mirer EC SP .30 .10
❑ 209 Errict Rhett EC SP .30 .10
❑ 210 Heath Shuler EC SP .30 .10
❑ 211 Bobby Taylor SP RC .60 .25
❑ 212 Jesse James SP RC .20 .07
❑ 213 Devin Bush SP RC .20 .07
❑ 214 Luther Elliss SP RC .20 .07
❑ 215 Kerry Collins RC SP 2.00 .75
❑ 216 Derr.Alexander DE SP RC .20 .07
❑ 217 Rashaan Salaam RC SP .30 .10
❑ 218 J.J. Stokes RC SP .60 .25
❑ 219 Todd Collins RC SP .30 .10
❑ 220 Ki-Jana Carter RC SP .60 .25
❑ 221 Kyle Brady RC SP .60 .25
❑ 222 Kevin Carter RC SP .60 .25
❑ 223 Tony Boselli RC SP .60 .25
❑ 224 Scott Gragg SP RC .20 .07
❑ 225 Warren Sapp RC SP 2.00 .75
❑ 226 Ricky Reynolds .10 .02
❑ 227 Roosevelt Potts .10 .02
❑ 228 Jessie Tuggle .10 .02
❑ 229 Anthony Newman .10 .02
❑ 230 Randall Cunningham .40 .15
❑ 231 Jason Elam .20 .07
❑ 232 Darnay Scott .20 .07
❑ 233 Tom Carter .10 .02
❑ 234 Micheal Barrow .10 .02
❑ 235 Steve Tasker .20 .07
❑ 236 Howard Cross .10 .02
❑ 237 Charles Wilson .10 .02
❑ 238 Rob Fredrickson .10 .02
❑ 239 Russell Maryland .10 .02
❑ 240 Dan Marino 3.00 1.25
❑ 241 Rafael Robinson .10 .02
❑ 242 Ed McDaniel .10 .02
❑ 243 Brett Perriman .20 .07
❑ 244 Chuck Levy .10 .02
❑ 245 Errict Rhett .20 .07
❑ 246 Tracy Simien .10 .02
❑ 247 Steve Everitt .10 .02
❑ 248 John Jurkovic .10 .02
❑ 249 Johnny Mitchell .10 .02
❑ 250 Mark Carrier DB .10 .02
❑ 251 Merton Hanks .10 .02
❑ 252 Joe Johnson .10 .02
❑ 253 Andre Coleman .10 .02
❑ 254 Ray Buchanan .10 .02
❑ 255 Jeff George .20 .07
❑ 256 Shane Conlan .10 .02
❑ 257 Gus Frerotte .20 .07
❑ 258 Doug Pelfrey .10 .02
❑ 259 Glenn Montgomery .10 .02
❑ 260 John Elway 3.00 1.25
❑ 261 Larry Centers .20 .07
❑ 262 Calvin Williams .20 .07
❑ 263 Gene Atkins .10 .02
❑ 264 Tim Brown .40 .15
❑ 265 Leon Lett .10 .02
❑ 266 Martin Mayhew .10 .02
❑ 267 Arthur Marshall .10 .02
❑ 268 Maurice Hurst .10 .02
❑ 269 Greg Hill .20 .07
❑ 270 Junior Seau .40 .15
❑ 271 Rick Mirer .20 .07
❑ 272 Jack Del Rio .10 .02
❑ 273 Lewis Tillman .10 .02
❑ 274 Renaldo Turnbull .10 .02
❑ 275 Dan Footman .10 .02
❑ 276 John Taylor .10 .02
❑ 277 Russell Copeland .10 .02
❑ 278 Tracy Scroggins .10 .02
❑ 279 Lou Benfatti .10 .02
❑ 280 Rod Woodson .20 .07
❑ 281 Troy Drayton .10 .02
❑ 282 Quentin Coryatt .20 .07
❑ 283 Craig Heyward .20 .07
❑ 284 Jeff Cross .10 .02
❑ 285 Hardy Nickerson .10 .02
❑ 286 Dorsey Levens .75 .30
❑ 287 Derek Russell .10 .02
❑ 288 Seth Joyner .10 .02
❑ 289 Kimble Anders .20 .07
❑ 290 Drew Bledsoe .75 .30
❑ 291 Bryant Young .20 .07
❑ 292 Chris Zorich .10 .02
❑ 293 Michael Strahan .40 .15
❑ 294 Kevin Greene .20 .07
❑ 295 Aaron Glenn .10 .02
❑ 296 Jimmy Spencer RC .10 .02
❑ 297 Eric Turner .10 .02
❑ 298 William Thomas .10 .02
❑ 299 Dan Wilkinson .20 .07
❑ 300 Troy Aikman 1.50 .60
❑ 301 Terry Wooden .10 .02
❑ 302 Heath Shuler .20 .07
❑ 303 Jeff Burris .10 .02
❑ 304 Mark Stepnoski .10 .02
❑ 305 Chris Mims .10 .02
❑ 306 Todd Steussie .10 .02
❑ 307 Johnnie Morton .20 .07
❑ 308 Darryl Talley .10 .02
❑ 309 Nolan Harrison .10 .02
❑ 310 Dave Brown .20 .07
❑ 311 Brent Jones .10 .02
❑ 312 Curtis Conway .40 .15
❑ 313 Ronald Humphrey .10 .02
❑ 314 Richie Anderson RC .50 .20
❑ 315 Jim Everett .10 .02
❑ 316 Willie Davis .20 .07
❑ 317 Ed Cunningham .10 .02
❑ 318 Willie McGinest .20 .07
❑ 319 Sean Gilbert .20 .07
❑ 320 Brett Favre 3.00 1.50
❑ 321 Bennie Thompson .10 .02
❑ 322 Neil O'Donnell .20 .07
❑ 323 Vince Workman .10 .02
❑ 324 Terry Kirby .20 .07
❑ 325 Simon Fletcher .10 .02
❑ 326 Ricardo McDonald .10 .02
❑ 327 Duane Young .10 .02
❑ 328 Jim Harbaugh .20 .07
❑ 329 D.J. Johnson .10 .02
❑ 330 Boomer Esiason .20 .07
❑ 331 Donnell Woolford .10 .02
❑ 332 Mike Sherrard .10 .02
❑ 333 Tyrone Legette .10 .02

❑ 334 Larry Brown DB .10 .02
❑ 335 William Floyd .20 .07
❑ 336 Reggie Brooks .20 .07
❑ 337 Patrick Bates .10 .02
❑ 338 Jim Jeffcoat .10 .02
❑ 339 Ray Childress .10 .02
❑ 340 Cris Carter .40 .15
❑ 341 Charlie Garner .40 .15
❑ 342 Bill Hitchcock .10 .02
❑ 343 Levon Kirkland .10 .02
❑ 344 Robert Porcher .10 .02
❑ 345 Darryl Williams .10 .02
❑ 346 Vincent Brisby .10 .02
❑ 347 Kenyon Rasheed .10 .02
❑ 348 Floyd Turner .10 .02
❑ 349 Bob Whitfield .10 .02
❑ 350 Jerome Bettis .40 .15
❑ 351 Brad Baxter .10 .02
❑ 352 Darrin Smith .10 .02
❑ 353 Lamar Thomas .10 .02
❑ 354 Lorenzo Neal .10 .02
❑ 355 Erik Kramer .10 .02
❑ 356 Dwayne Harper .10 .02
❑ 357 Doug Evans RC .40 .15
❑ 358 Jeff Feagles .10 .02
❑ 359 Ray Crockett .10 .02
❑ 360 Neil Smith .20 .07
❑ 361 Troy Vincent .10 .02
❑ 362 Don Griffin .10 .02
❑ 363 Michael Brooks .10 .02
❑ 364 Carlton Gray .10 .02
❑ 365 Thomas Smith .10 .02
❑ 366 Ken Norton .20 .07
❑ 367 Tony McGee .10 .02
❑ 368 Eric Metcalf .20 .07
❑ 369 Mel Gray .10 .02
❑ 370 Barry Sanders 2.50 1.00
❑ 371 Rocket Ismail .20 .07
❑ 372 Chad Brown .20 .07
❑ 373 Qadry Ismail .20 .07
❑ 374 Anthony Prior .10 .02
❑ 375 Kevin Lee .10 .02
❑ 376 Robert Young .10 .02
❑ 377 Kevin Williams WR .20 .07
❑ 378 Tydus Winans .10 .02
❑ 379 Ricky Watters .20 .07
❑ 380 Jim Kelly .40 .15
❑ 381 Eric Swann .20 .07
❑ 382 Mike Pritchard .10 .02
❑ 383 Derek Brown RBK .10 .02
❑ 384 Dennis Gibson .10 .02
❑ 385 Byron Bam Morris .10 .02
❑ 386 Reggie White .40 .15
❑ 387 Jeff Graham .10 .02
❑ 388 Marshall Faulk 2.00 .75
❑ 389 Joe Phillips .10 .02
❑ 390 Jeff Hostetler .20 .07
❑ 391 Irving Fryar .20 .07
❑ 392 Stevon Moore .10 .02
❑ 393 Bert Emanuel .40 .15
❑ 394 Leon Searcy .10 .02
❑ 395 Robert Smith .40 .15
❑ 396 Michael Bates .10 .02
❑ 397 Thomas Lewis .20 .07
❑ 398 Joe Bowden .10 .02
❑ 399 Steve Tovar .10 .02
❑ 400 Jerry Rice 1.50 .60
❑ 401 Toby Wright .10 .02
❑ 402 Daryl Johnston .20 .07
❑ 403 Vincent Brown .10 .02
❑ 404 Marvin Washington .10 .02
❑ 405 Chris Spielman .20 .07
❑ 406 Willie Jackson ET SP .30 .10
❑ 407 Harry Boatswain ET SP .20 .07
❑ 408 Kelvin Pritchett ET SP .20 .07
❑ 409 Dave Widell ET SP .20 .07
❑ 410 Frank Reich ET SP .20 .07
❑ 411 Corey Mayfield ET SP RC .20 .07
❑ 412 Pete Metzelaars ET SP .20 .07
❑ 413 Keith Goganious ET SP .20 .07
❑ 414 John Kasay ET SP .20 .07
❑ 415 Ernest Givins ET SP .20 .07
❑ 416 Randy Baldwin ET SP .20 .07
❑ 417 Shawn Bouwens ET SP .20 .07
❑ 418 Mike Fox ET SP .20 .07
❑ 419 Mark Carrier WR ET SP .30 .10
❑ 420 Steve Beuerlein ET SP .30 .10
❑ 421 Steve Lofton ET SP .20 .07
❑ 422 Jeff Lageman ET SP .20 .07
❑ 423 Paul Butcher ET SP .20 .07
❑ 424 Mark Brunell ET SP 1.00 .40
❑ 425 Vernon Turner ET SP .20 .07
❑ 426 Tim McKyer ET SP .20 .07
❑ 427 James Williams ET SP .20 .07
❑ 428 Tommy Barnhardt ET SP .20 .07
❑ 429 Rogerick Green ET SP .20 .07
❑ 430 Desmond Howard ET SP .30 .10
❑ 431 Darion Conner ET SP .20 .07
❑ 432 Reggie Clark ET SP .20 .07
❑ 433 Eric Guliford ET SP .20 .07
❑ 434 Rob Johnson ET RC SP 1.25 .50
❑ 435 Sam Mills ET SP .30 .10
❑ 436 Kordell Stewart RC SP 2.00 .75
❑ 437 James O. Stewart RC SP 1.50 .60
❑ 438 Zach Wiegert SP .20 .07
❑ 439 Ellis Johnson RC SP .20 .07
❑ 440 Matt O'Dwyer RC SP .20 .07
❑ 441 Anthony Cook RC SP .20 .07
❑ 442 Ron Davis RC SP .20 .07
❑ 443 Chris Hudson RC SP .20 .07
❑ 444 Hugh Douglas RC SP .60 .25
❑ 445 Tyrone Poole RC SP .60 .25
❑ 446 Korey Stringer RC SP .30 .10
❑ 447 Ruben Brown RC SP .60 .25
❑ 448 Brian DeMarco RC SP .20 .07
❑ 449 Michael Westbrook RC SP .60 .25
❑ 450 Steve McNair RC SP 4.00 1.50

1996 Stadium Club

❑ COMPLETE SET (360) 60.00 30.00
❑ COMP.SERIES 1 (180) 30.00 15.00
❑ COMP.SERIES 2 (180) 30.00 15.00
❑ 1 Kyle Brady .10 .02
❑ 2 Mickey Washington .10 .02
❑ 3 Seth Joyner .10 .02
❑ 4 Vinny Testaverde .25 .08
❑ 5 Thomas Randolph .10 .02
❑ 6 Heath Shuler .25 .08
❑ 7 Ty Law .50 .20
❑ 8 Blake Brockermeyer .10 .02
❑ 9 Darryll Lewis .10 .02
❑ 10 Jeff Blake .50 .20
❑ 11 Tyrone Hughes .10 .02
❑ 12 Horace Copeland .10 .02
❑ 13 Roman Phifer .10 .02
❑ 14 Eugene Robinson .10 .02
❑ 15 Anthony Miller .25 .08
❑ 16 Robert Smith .25 .08
❑ 17 Chester McGlockton .10 .02
❑ 18 Marty Carter .10 .02
❑ 19 Scott Mitchell .25 .08
❑ 20 O.J. McDuffie .25 .08
❑ 21 Stan Humphries .25 .08
❑ 22 Eugene Daniel .10 .02
❑ 23 Devin Bush .10 .02
❑ 24 Darick Holmes .10 .02
❑ 25 Ricky Watters .25 .08
❑ 26 J.J. Stokes .50 .20
❑ 27 George Koonce .10 .02
❑ 28 Tamarick Vanover .25 .08
❑ 29 Yancey Thigpen .25 .08
❑ 30 Troy Aikman 1.25 .50
❑ 31 Rashaan Salaam .25 .08
❑ 32 Anthony Cook .10 .02
❑ 33 Tim McKyer .10 .02
❑ 34 Dale Carter .10 .02
❑ 35 Marvin Washington .10 .02
❑ 36 Terry Allen .25 .08
❑ 37 Keith Goganious .10 .02
❑ 38 Pepper Johnson .10 .02
❑ 39 Dave Brown .10 .02
❑ 40 Levon Kirkland .10 .02
❑ 41 Ken Dilger .25 .08
❑ 42 Harvey Williams .10 .02
❑ 43 Robert Blackmon .10 .02
❑ 44 Kevin Carter .10 .02
❑ 45 Warren Moon .25 .08
❑ 46 Allen Aldridge .10 .02
❑ 47 Terance Mathis .10 .02
❑ 48 Junior Seau .50 .20
❑ 49 William Fuller .10 .02
❑ 50 Lee Woodall .10 .02
❑ 51 Aeneas Williams .10 .02
❑ 52 Thomas Smith .10 .02
❑ 53 Chris Slade .10 .02
❑ 54 Eric Allen .10 .02
❑ 55 David Sloan .10 .02
❑ 56 Hardy Nickerson .10 .02
❑ 57 Michael Irvin .50 .20
❑ 58 Corey Sawyer .10 .02
❑ 59 Eric Green .10 .02
❑ 60 Reggie White .50 .20
❑ 61 Isaac Bruce .50 .20
❑ 62 Darrell Green .10 .02
❑ 63 Aaron Glenn .10 .02
❑ 64 Mark Brunell .75 .30
❑ 65 Mark Carrier WR .10 .02
❑ 66 Mel Gray .10 .02
❑ 67 Phillippi Sparks .10 .02
❑ 68 Ernie Mills .10 .02
❑ 69 Rick Mirer .25 .08
❑ 70 Neil Smith .25 .08
❑ 71 Terry McDaniel .10 .02
❑ 72 Terrell Davis 1.00 .40
❑ 73 Alonzo Spellman .10 .02
❑ 74 Jessie Tuggle .10 .02
❑ 75 Terry Kirby .25 .08
❑ 76 David Palmer .10 .02
❑ 77 Calvin Williams .10 .02
❑ 78 Shaun Gayle .10 .02
❑ 79 Bryant Young .25 .08
❑ 80 Jim Harbaugh .25 .08
❑ 81 Michael Jackson .25 .08
❑ 82 Dave Meggett .10 .02
❑ 83 Henry Thomas .10 .02
❑ 84 Jim Kelly .50 .20
❑ 85 Frank Sanders .25 .08
❑ 86 Daryl Johnston .25 .08
❑ 87 Alvin Harper .10 .02
❑ 88 John Copeland .10 .02
❑ 89 Mark Chmura .25 .08
❑ 90 Jim Everett .10 .02
❑ 91 Bobby Houston .10 .02
❑ 92 Willie Jackson .25 .08
❑ 93 Carlton Bailey .10 .02
❑ 94 Todd Lyght .10 .02
❑ 95 Ken Harvey .10 .02
❑ 96 Erric Pegram .10 .02
❑ 97 Anthony Smith .10 .02
❑ 98 Kimble Anders .25 .08
❑ 99 Steve McNair 1.00 .40
❑ 100 Jeff George .25 .08
❑ 101 Michael Timpson .10 .02
❑ 102 Brent Jones .10 .02
❑ 103 Mike Mamula .10 .02
❑ 104 Jeff Cross .10 .02
❑ 105 Craig Newsome .10 .02
❑ 106 Howard Cross .10 .02
❑ 107 Terry Wooden .10 .02
❑ 108 Randall McDaniel .10 .02
❑ 109 Andre Reed .25 .08
❑ 110 Steve Atwater .10 .02
❑ 111 Larry Centers .25 .08
❑ 112 Tony Bennett .10 .02
❑ 113 Drew Bledsoe .75 .30
❑ 114 Terrell Fletcher .10 .02
❑ 115 Warren Sapp .10 .02
❑ 116 Deion Sanders .75 .30
❑ 117 Bryce Paup .10 .02
❑ 118 Mario Bates .25 .08
❑ 119 Steve Tovar .10 .02
❑ 120 Barry Sanders 2.00 .75
❑ 121 Tony Boselli .10 .02

❑ 122 Micheal Barrow .10 .02
❑ 123 Sam Mills .10 .02
❑ 124 Tim Brown .50 .20
❑ 125 Darren Perry .10 .02
❑ 126 Brian Blades .10 .02
❑ 127 Tyrone Wheatley .25 .08
❑ 128 Derrick Thomas .50 .20
❑ 129 Edgar Bennett .25 .08
❑ 130 Cris Carter .50 .20
❑ 131 Stephen Grant .10 .02
❑ 132 Kevin Williams .10 .02
❑ 133 Darnay Scott .25 .08
❑ 134 Rod Stephens .10 .02
❑ 135 Ken Norton .10 .02
❑ 136 Tim Biakabutuka SP RC .50 .20
❑ 137 Willie Anderson SP RC .10 .02
❑ 138 Lawrence Phillips SP RC .50 .20
❑ 139 Jonathan Ogden SP RC .50 .20
❑ 140 Simeon Rice SP RC 1.25 .50
❑ 141 Alex Van Dyke SP RC .25 .08
❑ 142 Jerome Woods SP RC .10 .02
❑ 143 Eric Moulds SP RC 2.00 .75
❑ 144 Mike Alstott SP RC 1.50 .60
❑ 145 Marvin Harrison SP RC 4.00 1.50
❑ 146 Duane Clemons SP RC .10 .02
❑ 147 Regan Upshaw SP RC .10 .02
❑ 148 Eddie Kennison SP RC .50 .20
❑ 149 John Mobley SP RC .10 .02
❑ 150 Keyshawn Johnson SP RC 1.50 .60
❑ 151 Marco Battaglia SP RC .10 .02
❑ 152 Rickey Dudley SP RC .50 .20
❑ 153 Kevin Hardy SP RC .50 .20
❑ 154 Curtis Martin SM SP 1.00 .40
❑ 155 Dan Marino SM SP 2.50 1.00
❑ 156 Rashaan Salaam SM SP .25 .08
❑ 157 Joey Galloway SM SP .50 .20
❑ 158 John Elway SM SP 2.50 1.00
❑ 159 Marshall Faulk SM SP .60 .25
❑ 160 Jerry Rice SM SP 1.25 .50
❑ 161 Darren Bennett SM SP .10 .02
❑ 162 Tamarick Vanover SM SP .25 .08
❑ 163 Orlando Thomas SM SP .10 .02
❑ 164 Jim Kelly SM SP .50 .20
❑ 165 Larry Brown SM SP .10 .02
❑ 166 Erict Rhett SM SP .25 .08
❑ 167 Warren Moon SM SP .10 .02
❑ 168 Hugh Douglas SM SP .10 .02
❑ 169 Jim Everett SM SP .10 .02
❑ 170 AFC Championship Game SP .10 .02
❑ 171 Larry Centers SM SP .25 .08
❑ 172 Marcus Allen GM SP .50 .20
❑ 173 Morten Andersen GM SP .10 .02
❑ 174 Brett Favre GM SP 2.50 1.00
❑ 175 Jerry Rice GM SP 1.25 .50
❑ 176 Glyn Milburn GM SP .10 .02
❑ 177 Thurman Thomas GM SP .25 .08
❑ 178 Michael Irvin GM SP .25 .08
❑ 179 Barry Sanders GM SP 2.00 .75
❑ 180 Dan Marino GM SP 2.50 1.00
❑ 181 Joey Galloway .50 .20
❑ 182 Dwayne Harper .10 .02
❑ 183 Antonio Langham .10 .02
❑ 184 Chris Zorich .10 .02
❑ 185 Willie McGinest .10 .02
❑ 186 Wayne Chrebet .75 .30
❑ 187 Dermontti Dawson .10 .02
❑ 188 Charlie Garner .25 .08
❑ 189 Quentin Coryatt .10 .02
❑ 190 Rodney Hampton .25 .08
❑ 191 Kelvin Pritchett .10 .02
❑ 192 Willie Green .10 .02
❑ 193 Garrison Hearst .25 .08
❑ 194 Tracy Scroggins .10 .02
❑ 195 Rocket Ismail .10 .02
❑ 196 Michael Westbrook .50 .20
❑ 197 Troy Drayton .10 .02
❑ 198 Rob Fredrickson .10 .02
❑ 199 Sean Lumpkin .10 .02
❑ 200 John Elway 2.50 1.00
❑ 201 Bernie Parmalee .10 .02
❑ 202 Chris Chandler .25 .08
❑ 203 Lake Dawson .10 .02
❑ 204 Orlando Thomas .10 .02
❑ 205 Carl Pickens .25 .08
❑ 206 Kurt Schulz .10 .02
❑ 207 Clay Matthews .10 .02
❑ 208 Winston Moss .10 .02
❑ 209 Sean Dawkins .10 .02
❑ 210 Emmitt Smith 2.00 .75
❑ 211 Mark Carrier DB .10 .02
❑ 212 Clyde Simmons .10 .02
❑ 213 Derrick Brooks .50 .20
❑ 214 William Floyd .25 .08
❑ 215 Aaron Hayden .10 .02
❑ 216 Brian DeMarco .10 .02
❑ 217 Ben Coates .25 .08
❑ 218 Renaldo Turnbull .10 .02
❑ 219 Adrian Murrell .25 .08
❑ 220 Marcus Allen .50 .20
❑ 221 Brett Maxie .10 .02
❑ 222 Trev Alberts .10 .02
❑ 223 Darren Woodson .25 .08
❑ 224 Brian Mitchell .10 .02
❑ 225 Michael Haynes .10 .02
❑ 226 Sean Jones .10 .02
❑ 227 Eric Zeier .10 .02
❑ 228 Herman Moore .25 .08
❑ 229 Shane Conlan .10 .02
❑ 230 Chris Warren .25 .08
❑ 231 Dana Stubblefield .25 .08
❑ 232 Andre Coleman .10 .02
❑ 233 Kordell Stewart UER .50 .20
❑ 234 Ray Crockett .10 .02
❑ 235 Craig Heyward .10 .02
❑ 236 Mike Fox .10 .02
❑ 237 Derek Brown RBK .10 .02
❑ 238 Thomas Lewis .10 .02
❑ 239 Hugh Douglas .25 .08
❑ 240 Tom Carter .10 .02
❑ 241 Toby Wright .10 .02
❑ 242 Jason Belser .10 .02
❑ 243 Rodney Peete .10 .02
❑ 244 Napoleon Kaufman .50 .20
❑ 245 Merton Hanks .10 .02
❑ 246 Harry Colon .10 .02
❑ 247 Greg Hill .25 .08
❑ 248 Vincent Brisby .10 .02
❑ 249 Eric Hill .10 .02
❑ 250 Brett Favre 2.50 1.00
❑ 251 Leroy Hoard .10 .02
❑ 252 Eric Guliford .10 .02
❑ 253 Stanley Richard .25 .08
❑ 254 Carlos Jenkins .10 .02
❑ 255 D'Marco Farr .10 .02
❑ 256 Carlton Gray .10 .02
❑ 257 Derek Loville .10 .02
❑ 258 Ray Buchanan .10 .02
❑ 259 Jake Reed .25 .08
❑ 260 Dan Marino 2.50 1.00
❑ 261 Brad Baxter .10 .02
❑ 262 Pat Swilling .10 .02
❑ 263 Andy Harmon .10 .02
❑ 264 Harold Green .10 .02
❑ 265 Shannon Sharpe .25 .08
❑ 266 Erik Kramer .10 .02
❑ 267 Lamar Lathon .10 .02
❑ 268 Stevon Moore .10 .02
❑ 269 Tony Martin .25 .08
❑ 270 Bruce Smith .25 .08
❑ 271 James Washington .10 .02
❑ 272 Tyrone Poole .10 .02
❑ 273 Eric Swann .10 .02
❑ 274 Dexter Carter .10 .02
❑ 275 Greg Lloyd .25 .08
❑ 276 Michael Zordich .10 .02
❑ 277 Steve Wisniewski .10 .02
❑ 278 Chris Calloway .10 .02
❑ 279 Irv Smith .10 .02
❑ 280 Steve Young 1.00 .40
❑ 281 James O.Stewart .25 .08
❑ 282 Blaine Bishop .10 .02
❑ 283 Rob Moore .25 .08
❑ 284 Eric Metcalf .10 .02
❑ 285 Kerry Collins .50 .20
❑ 286 Dan Wilkinson .10 .02
❑ 287 Curtis Conway .50 .20
❑ 288 Jay Novacek .10 .02
❑ 289 Henry Ellard .10 .02
❑ 290 Curtis Martin 1.00 .40
❑ 291 Brett Perriman .10 .02
❑ 292 Jeff Lageman .10 .02
❑ 293 Trent Dilfer .50 .20
❑ 294 Cortez Kennedy .10 .02
❑ 295 Jeff Hostetler .10 .02
❑ 296 Mark Fields .10 .02
❑ 297 Qadry Ismail .25 .08
❑ 298 Steve Bono .10 .02
❑ 299 Tony Tolbert .10 .02
❑ 300 Jerry Rice 1.25 .50
❑ 301 Marvcus Patton .10 .02
❑ 302 Robert Brooks .50 .20
❑ 303 Terry Ray RC .10 .02
❑ 304 John Thierry .10 .02
❑ 305 Errict Rhett .25 .08
❑ 306 Ricardo McDonald .10 .02
❑ 307 Antonio London .10 .02
❑ 308 Lonnie Johnson .10 .02
❑ 309 Mark Collins .10 .02
❑ 310 Marshall Faulk .60 .25
❑ 311 Anthony Pleasant .10 .02
❑ 312 Howard Griffith .10 .02
❑ 313 Roosevelt Potts .10 .02
❑ 314 Jim Flanigan .10 .02
❑ 315 Omar Ellison RC .10 .02
❑ 316 Boomer Esiason SP .25 .08
❑ 317 Leslie O'Neal SP .10 .02
❑ 318 Jerome Bettis SP .50 .20
❑ 319 Larry Brown SP .10 .02
❑ 320 Neil O'Donnell SP .25 .08
❑ 321 Andre Rison SP .25 .08
❑ 322 Cornelius Bennett SP .10 .02
❑ 323 Quinn Early SP .10 .02
❑ 324 Bryan Cox SP .10 .02
❑ 325 Irving Fryar SP .25 .08
❑ 326 Eddie Robinson SP .10 .02
❑ 327 Chris Doleman SP .10 .02
❑ 328 Sean Gilbert SP .10 .02
❑ 329 Steve Walsh SP .10 .02
❑ 330 Kevin Greene SP .25 .08
❑ 331 Chris Spielman SP .10 .02
❑ 332 Jeff Graham SP .10 .02
❑ 333 Anthony Dorsett SP RC .10 .02
❑ 334 Amani Toomer SP RC 1.50 .60
❑ 335 Walt Harris SP RC .10 .02
❑ 336 Ray Mickens SP RC .10 .02
❑ 337 Danny Kanell SP RC .50 .20
❑ 338 Daryl Gardener SP RC .10 .02
❑ 339 Jonathan Ogden SP .25 .08
❑ 340 Eddie George SP RC 2.00 .75
❑ 341 Jeff Lewis SP RC .25 .08
❑ 342 Terrell Owens SP RC 4.00 1.50
❑ 343 Brian Dawkins SP RC 2.00 .75
❑ 344 Tim Biakabutuka SP .50 .20
❑ 345 Marvin Harrison SP 1.50 .60
❑ 346 Lawyer Milloy SP RC .60 .25
❑ 347 Eric Moulds SP .75 .30
❑ 348 Alex Van Dyke SP .25 .08
❑ 349 John Mobley SP .10 .02
❑ 350 Kevin Hardy SP .50 .20
❑ 351 Ray Lewis SP RC 5.00 2.00
❑ 352 Lawrence Phillips SP .50 .20
❑ 353 Stepfret Williams SP RC .25 .08
❑ 354 Bobby Engram SP RC .50 .20
❑ 355 Leeland McElroy SP RC .25 .08
❑ 356 Marco Battaglia SP .10 .02
❑ 357 Rickey Dudley SP .50 .20
❑ 358 Bobby Hoying SP RC .50 .20
❑ 359 Cedric Jones SP RC .10 .02
❑ 360 Keyshawn Johnson SP .50 .20
❑ P19 Scott Mitchell Prototype .50 .20
❑ P31 Rashaan Salaam Prototype .75 .30
❑ P56 Hardy Nickerson Prototype .50 .20
❑ NNO Checklist Card .10 .02

1997 Stadium Club

❑ COMPLETE SET (340) 60.00 25.00
❑ COMP.SERIES 1 (170) 30.00 15.00
❑ COMP.SERIES 2 (170) 30.00 15.00
❑ 1 Junior Seau .75 .30
❑ 2 Michael Irvin .75 .30
❑ 3 Marcus Allen .75 .30
❑ 4 Dale Carter .30 .10
❑ 5 Darnell Autry RC .50 .20
❑ 6 Isaac Bruce .75 .30
❑ 7 Darrell Green .50 .20
❑ 8 Joey Galloway .50 .20
❑ 9 Steve Atwater .30 .10
❑ 10 Kordell Stewart .75 .30
❑ 11 Tony Brackens .30 .10
❑ 12 Gus Frerotte .30 .10
❑ 13 Henry Ellard .30 .10

14	Charles Way	.50	.20
15	Jim Druckenmiller RC	.50	.20
16	Orlando Thomas	.30	.10
17	Terrell Davis	1.00	.40
18	Jim Schwantz	.30	.10
19	Derrick Thomas	.75	.30
20	Curtis Martin	1.00	.40
21	Deion Sanders	.75	.30
22	Bruce Smith	.50	.20
23	Jake Reed	.50	.20
24	Leeland McElroy	.30	.10
25	Jerome Bettis	.75	.30
26	Neil Smith	.50	.20
27	Terry Allen	.75	.30
28	Gilbert Brown	.50	.20
29	Steve McNair	1.00	.40
30	Kerry Collins	.75	.30
31	Thurman Thomas	.75	.30
32	Kenny Holmes RC	.75	.30
33	Karim Abdul-Jabbar	.75	.30
34	Steve Young	1.00	.40
35	Jerry Rice	1.50	.60
36	Jeff George	.50	.20
37	Errict Rhett	.30	.10
38	Mike Alstott	.75	.30
39	Tim Brown	.75	.30
40	Keyshawn Johnson	.75	.30
41	Jim Harbaugh	.50	.20
42	Kevin Hardy	.30	.10
43	Kevin Greene	.50	.20
44	Eric Metcalf	.50	.20
45	Troy Aikman	1.50	.60
46	Marshall Faulk	1.00	.40
47	Shannon Sharpe	.50	.20
48	Warren Moon	.75	.30
49	Mark Brunell	1.00	.40
50	Dan Marino	3.00	1.25
51	Byron Hanspard RC	.50	.20
52	Chris Chandler	.50	.20
53	Wayne Chrebet	.75	.30
54	Antonio Langham	.30	.10
55	Barry Sanders	2.50	1.00
56	Curtis Conway	.50	.20
57	Ricky Watters	.50	.20
58	William Thomas	.30	.10
59	Chris Warren	.50	.20
60	Terry Glenn	.75	.30
61	Peter Boulware RC	.75	.30
62	Chad Cota	.30	.10
63	Eddie Kennison	.50	.20
64	Lamar Smith	.75	.30
65	Brett Favre	3.00	1.50
66	Michael Westbrook	.50	.20
67	Larry Centers	.50	.20
68	Trent Dilfer	.75	.30
69	Stevon Moore	.30	.10
70	John Elway	3.00	1.25
71	Bryce Paup	.30	.10
72	Quentin Coryatt	.30	.10
73	Rashaan Salaam	.30	.10
74	Thomas Lewis	.30	.10
75	Drew Bledsoe	1.00	.40
76	Cris Carter	.75	.30
77	Joe Bowden	.30	.10
78	Allen Aldridge	.30	.10
79	Zach Thomas	.75	.30
80	Emmitt Smith	2.50	1.00
81	Daryl Johnston	.50	.20
82	Vinny Testaverde	.50	.20
83	James O.Stewart	.50	.20
84	Edgar Bennett	.50	.20
85	Shawn Springs RC	.50	.20
86	Elvis Grbac	.50	.20
87	Levon Kirkland	.30	.10
88	Jeff Graham	.30	.10
89	Terrell Fletcher	.30	.10
90	Eddie George	.75	.30
91	Jessie Tuggle	.30	.10
92	Terrell Owens	1.00	.40
93	Wayne Martin	.30	.10
94	Dwayne Harper	.30	.10
95	Mark Collins	.30	.10
96	Marvcus Patton	.30	.10
97	Napoleon Kaufman	.75	.30
98	Keenan McCardell	.50	.20
99	Ty Detmer	.50	.20
100	Reggie White	.75	.30
101	William Floyd	.50	.20
102	Scott Mitchell	.50	.20
103	Robert Blackmon	.30	.10
104	Dan Wilkinson	.30	.10
105	Warren Sapp	.50	.20
106	Dave Meggett	.30	.10
107	Brian Mitchell	.30	.10
108	Tyrone Poole	.30	.10
109	Derrick Alexander WR	.50	.20
110	David Palmer	.30	.10
111	James Farrior RC	.75	.30
112	Chad Brown	.30	.10
113	Marty Carter	.30	.10
114	Lawrence Phillips	.30	.10
115	Wesley Walls	.50	.20
116	John Friesz	.30	.10
117	Roman Phifer	.30	.10
118	Jason Sehorn	.50	.20
119	Henry Thomas	.30	.10
120	Natrone Means	.50	.20
121	Ty Law	.50	.20
122	Tony Gonzalez RC	3.00	1.25
123	Kevin Williams	.30	.10
124	Regan Upshaw	.30	.10
125	Antonio Freeman	.75	.30
126	Jessie Armstead	.30	.10
127	Pat Barnes RC	.75	.30
128	Charlie Garner	.50	.20
129	Irving Fryar	.50	.20
130	Rickey Dudley	.50	.20
131	Rodney Harrison RC	1.50	.60
132	Brent Jones	.50	.20
133	Neil O'Donnell	.50	.20
134	Darryll Lewis	.30	.10
135	Jason Belser	.30	.10
136	Mark Chmura	.50	.20
137	Seth Joyner	.30	.10
138	Herschel Walker	.50	.20
139	Santana Dotson	.30	.10
140	Carl Pickens	.50	.20
141	Terance Mathis	.50	.20
142	Walt Harris	.30	.10
143	John Mobley	.30	.10
144	Gabe Northern	.30	.10
145	Herman Moore	.50	.20
146	Michael Jackson	.50	.20
147	Chris Sanders	.30	.10
148	LeShon Johnson	.30	.10
149	Darrell Russell RC	.30	.10
150	Winslow Oliver	.30	.10
151	Tamarick Vanover	.50	.20
152	Tony Martin	.50	.20
153	Lamar Lathon	.30	.10
154	Ray Mickens	.30	.10
155	Derrick Brooks	.75	.30
156	Warrick Dunn RC	2.50	1.00
157	Tim McDonald	.30	.10
158	Keith Lyle	.30	.10
159	Terry McDaniel	.30	.10
160	Andre Hastings	.30	.10
161	Phillippi Sparks	.30	.10
162	Tedy Bruschi	1.50	.60
163	Bryant Westbrook RC	.30	.10
164	Victor Green	.30	.10
165	Jimmy Smith	.50	.20
166	Greg Biekert	.30	.10
167	Frank Sanders	.50	.20
168	Chris Doleman	.30	.10
169	Phil Hansen	.30	.10
170	Walter Jones RC	.75	.30
171	Mark Carrier WR	.30	.10
172	Greg Hill	.30	.10
173	Erik Kramer	.30	.10
174	Chris Spielman	.30	.10
175	Tom Knight RC	.30	.10
176	Sam Mills	.30	.10
177	Robert Smith	.50	.20
178	Dorsey Levens	.75	.30
179	Chris Slade	.30	.10
180	Troy Vincent	.30	.10
181	Mario Bates	.30	.10
182	Ed McCaffrey	.50	.20
183	Mike Mamula	.30	.10
184	Chad Hennings	.30	.10
185	Stan Humphries	.50	.20
186	Reinard Wilson RC	.50	.20
187	Kevin Carter	.30	.10
188	Qadry Ismail	.50	.20
189	Cortez Kennedy	.30	.10
190	Eric Swann	.30	.10
191	Corey Dillon RC	6.00	2.50
192	Renaldo Wynn	.30	.10
193	Bobby Hebert	.30	.10
194	Fred Barnett	.30	.10
195	Ray Lewis	1.25	.50
196	Robert Jones	.30	.10
197	Brian Williams	.30	.10
198	Willie McGinest	.30	.10
199	Jake Plummer RC	5.00	2.00
200	Aeneas Williams	.30	.10
201	Ashley Ambrose	.30	.10
202	Cornelius Bennett	.30	.10
203	Mo Lewis	.30	.10
204	James Hasty	.30	.10
205	Carnell Lake	.30	.10
206	Heath Shuler	.30	.10
207	Dana Stubblefield	.30	.10
208	Corey Miller	.30	.10
209	Ike Hilliard RC	1.25	.50
210	Bryant Young	.30	.10
211	Hardy Nickerson	.30	.10
212	Blaine Bishop	.30	.10
213	Marcus Robertson	.30	.10
214	Tony Bennett	.30	.10
215	Kent Graham	.30	.10
216	Steve Bono	.50	.20
217	Will Blackwell RC	.50	.20
218	Tyrone Braxton	.30	.10
219	Eric Moulds	.75	.30
220	Rod Woodson	.50	.20
221	Anthony Johnson	.30	.10
222	Willie Davis	.30	.10
223	Darrin Smith	.30	.10
224	Rick Mirer	.30	.10
225	Marvin Harrison	.75	.30
226	Terrell Buckley	.30	.10
227	Joe Aska	.30	.10
228	Yatil Green RC	.50	.20
229	William Fuller	.30	.10
230	Eddie Robinson	.30	.10
231	Brian Blades	.30	.10
232	Michael Sinclair	.30	.10
233	Ken Harvey	.30	.10
234	Harvey Williams	.30	.10
235	Simeon Rice	.50	.20
236	Chris T. Jones	.30	.10
237	Bert Emanuel	.50	.20
238	Corey Sawyer	.30	.10
239	Chris Calloway	.30	.10
240	Jeff Blake	.50	.20
241	Alonzo Spellman	.30	.10
242	Bryan Cox	.30	.10
243	Antowain Smith RC	2.50	1.00
244	Tim Biakabutuka	.50	.20
245	Ray Crockett	.30	.10
246	Dwayne Rudd	.30	.10
247	Glyn Milburn	.30	.10
248	Gary Plummer	.30	.10
249	O.J. McDuffie	.50	.20
250	Willie Clay	.30	.10
251	Jim Everett	.30	.10
252	Eugene Daniel	.30	.10
253	Corey Widmer	.30	.10
254	Mel Gray	.30	.10
255	Ken Norton	.30	.10
256	Johnnie Morton	.50	.20
257	Courtney Hawkins	.30	.10

❑ 258 Ricardo McDonald .30 .10
❑ 259 Todd Lyght .30 .10
❑ 260 Micheal Barrow .30 .10
❑ 261 Aaron Glenn .30 .10
❑ 262 Jeff Herrod .30 .10
❑ 263 Troy Davis RC .50 .20
❑ 264 Eric Hill .30 .10
❑ 265 Darrien Gordon .30 .10
❑ 266 Lake Dawson .30 .10
❑ 267 John Randle .50 .20
❑ 268 Henry Jones .30 .10
❑ 269 Mickey Washington .30 .10
❑ 270 Amani Toomer .50 .20
❑ 271 Steve Grant .30 .10
❑ 272 Adrian Murrell .50 .20
❑ 273 Derrick Witherspoon .30 .10
❑ 274 Albert Lewis .30 .10
❑ 275 Ben Coates .50 .20
❑ 276 Reidel Anthony RC .75 .30
❑ 277 Jim Schwantz .30 .10
❑ 278 Aaron Hayden .30 .10
❑ 279 Ryan McNeil .30 .10
❑ 280 LeRoy Butler .30 .10
❑ 281 Craig Newsome .30 .10
❑ 282 Bill Romanowski .30 .10
❑ 283 Michael Bankston .30 .10
❑ 284 Kevin Smith .30 .10
❑ 285 Byron Bam Morris .30 .10
❑ 286 Darnay Scott .50 .20
❑ 287 David LaFleur RC .30 .10
❑ 288 Randall Cunningham .75 .30
❑ 289 Eric Davis .30 .10
❑ 290 Todd Collins .30 .10
❑ 291 Steve Tovar .30 .10
❑ 292 Jermaine Lewis .75 .30
❑ 293 Alfred Williams .30 .10
❑ 294 Brad Johnson .75 .30
❑ 295 Charles Johnson .50 .20
❑ 296 Ted Johnson .30 .10
❑ 297 Merton Hanks .30 .10
❑ 298 Andre Coleman .30 .10
❑ 299 Keith Jackson .30 .10
❑ 300 Terry Kirby .50 .20
❑ 301 Tony Banks .50 .20
❑ 302 Terrance Shaw .30 .10
❑ 303 Bobby Engram .50 .20
❑ 304 Hugh Douglas .30 .10
❑ 305 Lawyer Milloy .50 .20
❑ 306 James Jett .50 .20
❑ 307 Joey Kent RC .75 .30
❑ 308 Rodney Hampton .50 .20
❑ 309 Dewayne Washington .30 .10
❑ 310 Kevin Lockett RC .50 .20
❑ 311 Ki-Jana Carter .30 .10
❑ 312 Jeff Lageman .30 .10
❑ 313 Don Beebe .30 .10
❑ 314 Willie Williams .30 .10
❑ 315 Tyrone Wheatley .50 .20
❑ 316 Leslie O'Neal .30 .10
❑ 317 Quinn Early .30 .10
❑ 318 Sean Gilbert .30 .10
❑ 319 Tim Bowens .30 .10
❑ 320 Sean Dawkins .30 .10
❑ 321 Ken Dilger .30 .10
❑ 322 George Koonce .30 .10
❑ 323 Jevon Langford .30 .10
❑ 324 Mike Caldwell .30 .10
❑ 325 Orlando Pace RC .75 .30
❑ 326 Garrison Hearst .50 .20
❑ 327 Mike Tomczak .30 .10
❑ 328 Rob Moore .50 .20
❑ 329 Andre Reed .50 .20
❑ 330 Kimble Anders .50 .20
❑ 331 Qadry Ismail .50 .20
❑ 332 Eric Allen .30 .10
❑ 333 Dave Brown .30 .10
❑ 334 Bennie Blades .30 .10
❑ 335 Jamal Anderson .75 .30
❑ 336 John Lynch .50 .20
❑ 337 Tyrone Hughes .30 .10
❑ 338 Ronnie Harmon .30 .10
❑ 339 Rae Carruth RC .30 .10
❑ 340 Robert Brooks .50 .20
❑ P1 Junior Seau Prototype .50 .20
❑ P20 Curtis Martin Prototype 1.00 .40
❑ P21 Deion Sanders Prototype .50 .20
❑ P30 Kerry Collins Prototype .75 .30
❑ P47 Shannon Sharpe Prototype .50 .20
❑ P84 Edgar Bennett Prototype .50 .20

1998 Stadium Club

❑ COMPLETE SET (195) 60.00 25.00
❑ 1 Barry Sanders 2.50 1.00
❑ 2 Tony Martin .50 .20
❑ 3 Fred Lane .30 .10
❑ 4 Darren Woodson .30 .10
❑ 5 Andre Reed .50 .20
❑ 6 Blaine Bishop .30 .10
❑ 7 Robert Brooks .50 .20
❑ 8 Tony Banks .50 .20
❑ 9 Charles Way .30 .10
❑ 10 Mark Brunell .75 .30
❑ 11 Darrell Green .50 .20
❑ 12 Aeneas Williams .30 .10
❑ 13 Rob Johnson .50 .20
❑ 14 Deion Sanders .75 .30
❑ 15 Marshall Faulk 1.00 .40
❑ 16 Stephen Boyd .30 .10
❑ 17 Adrian Murrell .50 .20
❑ 18 Wayne Chrebet .75 .30
❑ 19 Michael Sinclair .30 .10
❑ 20 Dan Marino 3.00 1.25
❑ 21 Willie Davis .30 .10
❑ 22 Chris Warren .50 .20
❑ 23 John Mobley .30 .10
❑ 24 Shannon Sharpe .50 .20
❑ 25 Thurman Thomas .75 .30
❑ 26 Corey Dillon .75 .30
❑ 27 Zach Thomas .75 .30
❑ 28 James Jett .50 .20
❑ 29 Eric Metcalf .30 .10
❑ 30 Drew Bledsoe 1.25 .50
❑ 31 Scott Greene .30 .10
❑ 32 Simeon Rice .50 .20
❑ 33 Robert Smith .75 .30
❑ 34 Keenan McCardell .50 .20
❑ 35 Jessie Armstead .30 .10
❑ 36 Jerry Rice 1.50 .60
❑ 37 Eric Green .30 .10
❑ 38 Terrell Owens .75 .30
❑ 39 Tim Brown .75 .30
❑ 40 Vinny Testaverde .50 .20
❑ 41 Brian Stablein .30 .10
❑ 42 Bert Emanuel .50 .20
❑ 43 Terry Glenn .75 .30
❑ 44 Chad Cota .30 .10
❑ 45 Jermaine Lewis .50 .20
❑ 46 Derrick Thomas .75 .30
❑ 47 O.J. McDuffie .50 .20
❑ 48 Frank Wycheck .30 .10
❑ 49 Steve Broussard .30 .10
❑ 50 Terrell Davis .75 .30
❑ 51 Eric Allen .30 .10
❑ 52 Napoleon Kaufman .75 .30
❑ 53 Dan Wilkinson .30 .10
❑ 54 Kerry Collins .50 .20
❑ 55 Frank Sanders .50 .20
❑ 56 Jeff Burris .30 .10
❑ 57 Michael Westbrook .50 .20
❑ 58 Michael McCrary .30 .10
❑ 59 Bobby Hoying .50 .20
❑ 60 Jerome Bettis .75 .30
❑ 61 Amp Lee .30 .10
❑ 62 Levon Kirkland .30 .10
❑ 63 Dana Stubblefield .30 .10
❑ 64 Terance Mathis .50 .20
❑ 65 Mark Chmura .50 .20
❑ 66 Bryant Westbrook .30 .10
❑ 67 Rod Smith .50 .20
❑ 68 Derrick Alexander .50 .20
❑ 69 Jason Taylor .50 .20
❑ 70 Eddie George .75 .30
❑ 71 Elvis Grbac .50 .20
❑ 72 Junior Seau .75 .30
❑ 73 Marvin Harrison .75 .30
❑ 74 Neil O'Donnell .50 .20
❑ 75 Johnnie Morton .50 .20
❑ 76 John Randle .50 .20
❑ 77 Danny Kanell .50 .20
❑ 78 Charlie Garner .50 .20
❑ 79 J.J. Stokes .50 .20
❑ 80 Troy Aikman 1.50 .60
❑ 81 Gus Frerotte .30 .10
❑ 82 Jake Plummer .75 .30
❑ 83 Andre Hastings .30 .10
❑ 84 Steve Atwater .30 .10
❑ 85 Larry Centers .30 .10
❑ 86 Kevin Hardy .30 .10
❑ 87 Willie McGinest .30 .10
❑ 88 Joey Galloway .50 .20
❑ 89 Charles Johnson .30 .10
❑ 90 Warrick Dunn .75 .30
❑ 91 Derrick Rodgers .30 .10
❑ 92 Aaron Glenn .30 .10
❑ 93 Shawn Jefferson .30 .10
❑ 94 Antonio Freeman .75 .30
❑ 95 Jake Reed .50 .20
❑ 96 Reidel Anthony .50 .20
❑ 97 Cris Dishman .30 .10
❑ 98 Jason Sehorn .50 .20
❑ 99 Herman Moore .50 .20
❑ 100 John Elway 3.00 1.25
❑ 101 Brad Johnson .75 .30
❑ 102 Jeff George .50 .20
❑ 103 Emmitt Smith 2.50 1.00
❑ 104 Steve McNair .75 .30
❑ 105 Ed McCaffrey .50 .20
❑ 106 Errict Rhett .50 .20
❑ 107 Dorsey Levens .75 .30
❑ 108 Michael Jackson .30 .10
❑ 109 Carl Pickens .50 .20
❑ 110 James Stewart .50 .20
❑ 111 Karim Abdul-Jabbar .75 .30
❑ 112 Jim Harbaugh .50 .20
❑ 113 Yancey Thigpen .30 .10
❑ 114 Chad Brown .30 .10
❑ 115 Chris Sanders .30 .10
❑ 116 Cris Carter .75 .30
❑ 117 Glenn Foley .50 .20
❑ 118 Ben Coates .50 .20
❑ 119 Jamal Anderson .75 .30
❑ 120 Steve Young 1.00 .40
❑ 121 Scott Mitchell .50 .20
❑ 122 Rob Moore .50 .20
❑ 123 Bobby Engram .50 .20
❑ 124 Rod Woodson .50 .20
❑ 125 Terry Allen .75 .30
❑ 126 Warren Sapp .50 .20
❑ 127 Irving Fryar .50 .20
❑ 128 Isaac Bruce .75 .30
❑ 129 Rae Carruth .30 .10
❑ 130 Sean Dawkins .30 .10
❑ 131 Andre Rison .50 .20
❑ 132 Kevin Greene .50 .20
❑ 133 Warren Moon .75 .30
❑ 134 Keyshawn Johnson .75 .30
❑ 135 Jay Graham .30 .10
❑ 136 Mike Alstott .75 .30
❑ 137 Peter Boulware .30 .10
❑ 138 Doug Evans .30 .10
❑ 139 Jimmy Smith .50 .20
❑ 140 Kordell Stewart .75 .30
❑ 141 Tamarick Vanover .30 .10
❑ 142 Chris Slade .30 .10
❑ 143 Freddie Jones .30 .10
❑ 144 Erik Kramer .30 .10
❑ 145 Ricky Watters .50 .20
❑ 146 Chris Chandler .50 .20
❑ 147 Garrison Hearst .75 .30
❑ 148 Trent Dilfer .75 .30
❑ 149 Bruce Smith .50 .20
❑ 150 Brett Favre 3.00 1.25
❑ 151 Will Blackwell .30 .10

❑ 152 Rickey Dudley	.30	.10
❑ 153 Natrone Means	.50	.20
❑ 154 Curtis Conway	.50	.20
❑ 155 Tony Gonzalez	.75	.30
❑ 156 Jeff Blake	.50	.20
❑ 157 Michael Irvin	.75	.30
❑ 158 Curtis Martin	.75	.30
❑ 159 Tim McDonald	.30	.10
❑ 160 Wesley Walls	.50	.20
❑ 161 Michael Strahan	.50	.20
❑ 162 Reggie White	.75	.30
❑ 163 Jeff Graham	.30	.10
❑ 164 Ray Lewis	.75	.30
❑ 165 Antowain Smith	.75	.30
❑ 166 Ryan Leaf RC	2.50	1.00
❑ 167 Jerome Pathon RC	2.50	1.00
❑ 168 Duane Starks RC	1.25	.50
❑ 169 Brian Simmons RC	2.00	.75
❑ 170 Pat Johnson RC	2.00	.75
❑ 171 Keith Brooking RC	2.50	1.00
❑ 172 Kevin Dyson RC	2.50	1.00
❑ 173 Robert Edwards RC	2.00	.75
❑ 174 Grant Wistrom RC	2.00	.75
❑ 175 Curtis Enis RC	1.25	.50
❑ 176 John Avery RC	2.00	.75
❑ 177 Jason Peter RC	1.25	.50
❑ 178 Brian Griese RC	5.00	2.00
❑ 179 Tavian Banks RC	2.00	.75
❑ 180 Andre Wadsworth RC	2.00	.75
❑ 181 Skip Hicks RC	2.00	.75
❑ 182 Hines Ward RC	10.00	6.00
❑ 183 Greg Ellis RC	1.25	.50
❑ 184 Robert Holcombe RC	2.00	.75
❑ 185 Joe Jurevicius RC	2.50	1.00
❑ 186 Takeo Spikes RC	2.50	1.00
❑ 187 Ahman Green RC	12.00	5.00
❑ 188 Jacquez Green RC	2.00	.75
❑ 189 Randy Moss RC	15.00	6.00
❑ 190 Charles Woodson RC	3.00	1.25
❑ 191 Fred Taylor RC	4.00	1.50
❑ 192 Marcus Nash RC	1.25	.50
❑ 193 Germane Crowell RC	2.00	.75
❑ 194 Tim Dwight RC	2.50	1.00
❑ 195 Peyton Manning RC	25.00	10.00

1999 Stadium Club

❑ COMPLETE SET (200)	60.00	25.00
❑ COMP.SET w/o SP's (175)	20.00	7.50
❑ UNPRICED 1/1 PRESS PLATES EXIST		
❑ FOUR DIFF.PP's PRODUCED PER CARD		
❑ 1 Dan Marino	2.50	1.00
❑ 2 Andre Reed	.50	.20
❑ 3 Michael Westbrook	.50	.20
❑ 4 Isaac Bruce	.75	.30
❑ 5 Curtis Martin	.75	.30
❑ 6 Courtney Hawkins	.30	.10
❑ 7 Charles Way	.30	.10
❑ 8 Terrell Owens	.75	.30
❑ 9 Warrick Dunn	.75	.30
❑ 10 Jake Plummer	.50	.20
❑ 11 Chad Brown	.30	.10
❑ 12 Yancey Thigpen	.30	.10
❑ 13 Lamar Thomas	.30	.10
❑ 14 Keenan McCardell	.50	.20
❑ 15 Shannon Sharpe	.50	.20
❑ 16 Robert Brooks	.50	.20
❑ 17 Cameron Cleeland	.30	.10
❑ 18 Derrick Thomas	.75	.30
❑ 19 Mark Brunell	.75	.30
❑ 20 Jamal Anderson	.75	.30
❑ 21 Germane Crowell	.30	.10
❑ 22 Rod Smith	.50	.20
❑ 23 Ty Law	.50	.20
❑ 24 Cris Carter	.75	.30
❑ 25 Terrell Davis	.75	.30
❑ 26 Takeo Spikes	.30	.10
❑ 27 Tim Biakabutuka	.50	.20
❑ 28 Jermaine Lewis	.50	.20
❑ 29 Adrian Murrell	.50	.20
❑ 30 Doug Flutie	.75	.30
❑ 31 Curtis Enis	.30	.10
❑ 32 Skip Hicks	.30	.10
❑ 33 Steve McNair	.75	.30
❑ 34 Charles Woodson	.75	.30
❑ 35 Jessie Armstead	.30	.10
❑ 36 Shawn Springs	.30	.10
❑ 37 Levon Kirkland	.30	.10
❑ 38 Freddie Jones	.30	.10
❑ 39 Warren Sapp	.30	.10
❑ 40 Emmitt Smith	1.50	.60
❑ 41 Reidel Anthony	.50	.20
❑ 42 Tony Simmons	.30	.10
❑ 43 Andre Hastings	.30	.10
❑ 44 Byron Bam Morris	.30	.10
❑ 45 Jimmy Smith	.50	.20
❑ 46 Antonio Freeman	.75	.30
❑ 47 Herman Moore	.50	.20
❑ 48 Muhsin Muhammad	.50	.20
❑ 49 Chris Chandler	.50	.20
❑ 50 John Elway	2.50	1.00
❑ 51 Aeneas Williams	.30	.10
❑ 52 Bobby Engram	.50	.20
❑ 53 Keith Poole	.30	.10
❑ 54 Zach Thomas	.75	.30
❑ 55 Mike Alstott	.75	.30
❑ 56 Junior Seau	.75	.30
❑ 57 Aaron Glenn	.30	.10
❑ 58 Darrell Green	.30	.10
❑ 59 Thurman Thomas	.50	.20
❑ 60 Troy Aikman	1.50	.60
❑ 61 Bill Romanowski	.30	.10
❑ 62 Wesley Walls	.50	.20
❑ 63 Andre Wadsworth	.30	.10
❑ 64 Robert Smith	.75	.30
❑ 65 Elvis Grbac	.50	.20
❑ 66 Terry Fair	.30	.10
❑ 67 Ben Coates	.50	.20
❑ 68 Bert Emanuel	.50	.20
❑ 69 Jacquez Green	.30	.10
❑ 70 Barry Sanders	2.50	1.00
❑ 71 James Jett	.50	.20
❑ 72 Gary Brown	.30	.10
❑ 73 Stephen Alexander	.30	.10
❑ 74 Wayne Chrebet	.50	.20
❑ 75 Drew Bledsoe	1.00	.40
❑ 76 John Lynch	.50	.20
❑ 77 Jake Reed	.50	.20
❑ 78 Marvin Harrison	.75	.30
❑ 79 Johnnie Morton	.50	.20
❑ 80 Brett Favre	2.50	1.00
❑ 81 Charlie Batch	.75	.30
❑ 82 Antowain Smith	.75	.30
❑ 83 Mikhael Ricks	.30	.10
❑ 84 Derrick Mayes	.30	.10
❑ 85 John Mobley	.30	.10
❑ 86 Ernie Mills	.30	.10
❑ 87 Jeff Blake	.50	.20
❑ 88 Curtis Conway	.50	.20
❑ 89 Bruce Smith	.50	.20
❑ 90 Peyton Manning	2.50	1.00
❑ 91 Tyrone Davis	.30	.10
❑ 92 Ray Buchanan	.30	.10
❑ 93 Tim Dwight	.75	.30
❑ 94 O.J. McDuffie	.50	.20
❑ 95 Vonnie Holliday	.30	.10
❑ 96 Jon Kitna	.75	.30
❑ 97 Trent Dilfer	.50	.20
❑ 98 Jerome Bettis	.75	.30
❑ 99 Dedric Ward	.30	.10
❑ 100 Fred Taylor	.75	.30
❑ 101 Ike Hilliard	.30	.10
❑ 102 Frank Wycheck	.30	.10
❑ 103 Eric Moulds	.75	.30
❑ 104 Rob Moore	.50	.20
❑ 105 Ed McCaffrey	.50	.20
❑ 106 Carl Pickens	.50	.20
❑ 107 Priest Holmes	1.25	.50
❑ 108 Kevin Hardy	.30	.10
❑ 109 Terry Glenn	.75	.30
❑ 110 Keyshawn Johnson	.75	.30
❑ 111 Karim Abdul-Jabbar	.50	.20
❑ 112 Stephen Boyd	.30	.10
❑ 113 Ahman Green	.75	.30
❑ 114 Duce Staley	.75	.30
❑ 115 Vinny Testaverde	.50	.20
❑ 116 Napoleon Kaufman	.75	.30
❑ 117 Frank Sanders	.50	.20
❑ 118 Peter Boulware	.30	.10
❑ 119 Kevin Greene	.30	.10
❑ 120 Steve Young	1.00	.40
❑ 121 Darnay Scott	.30	.10
❑ 122 Deion Sanders	.75	.30
❑ 123 Corey Dillon	.75	.30
❑ 124 Randall Cunningham	.75	.30
❑ 125 Eddie George	.75	.30
❑ 126 Derrick Alexander	.30	.10
❑ 127 Mark Chmura	.30	.10
❑ 128 Michael Sinclair	.30	.10
❑ 129 Rickey Dudley	.30	.10
❑ 130 Joey Galloway	.50	.20
❑ 131 Michael Strahan	.50	.20
❑ 132 Ricky Proehl	.30	.10
❑ 133 Natrone Means	.50	.20
❑ 134 Dorsey Levens	.75	.30
❑ 135 Andre Rison	.50	.20
❑ 136 Alonzo Mayes	.30	.10
❑ 137 John Randle	.50	.20
❑ 138 Terance Mathis	.50	.20
❑ 139 Rae Carruth	.30	.10
❑ 140 Jerry Rice	1.50	.60
❑ 141 Michael Irvin	.50	.20
❑ 142 Oronde Gadsden	.50	.20
❑ 143 Jerome Pathon	.30	.10
❑ 144 Ricky Watters	.50	.20
❑ 145 J.J. Stokes	.50	.20
❑ 146 Kordell Stewart	.50	.20
❑ 147 Tim Brown	.75	.30
❑ 148 Garrison Hearst	.50	.20
❑ 149 Tony Gonzalez	.75	.30
❑ 150 Randy Moss	2.00	.75
❑ 151 Daunte Culpepper RC	6.00	2.50
❑ 152 Amos Zereoue RC	2.00	.75
❑ 153 Champ Bailey RC	2.50	1.00
❑ 154 Peerless Price RC	2.00	.75
❑ 155 Edgerrin James RC	6.00	2.50
❑ 156 Joe Germaine RC	1.50	.60
❑ 157 David Boston RC	2.00	.75
❑ 158 Kevin Faulk RC	2.00	.75
❑ 159 Troy Edwards RC	1.50	.60
❑ 160 Akili Smith RC	1.50	.60
❑ 161 Kevin Johnson RC	2.00	.75
❑ 162 Rob Konrad RC	1.50	.60
❑ 163 Shaun King RC	1.50	.60
❑ 164 James Johnson RC	1.50	.60
❑ 165 Donovan McNabb RC	8.00	3.00
❑ 166 Torry Holt RC	4.00	1.50
❑ 167 Mike Cloud RC	1.50	.60
❑ 168 Sedrick Irvin RC	1.00	.40
❑ 169 Cade McNown RC	1.50	.60
❑ 170 Ricky Williams RC	3.00	1.25
❑ 171 Karsten Bailey RC	1.50	.60
❑ 172 Cecil Collins RC	1.00	.40
❑ 173 Brock Huard RC	2.00	.75
❑ 174 D'Wayne Bates RC	1.50	.60
❑ 175 Tim Couch RC	2.00	.75
❑ 176 Torrance Small	.30	.10
❑ 177 Warren Moon	.75	.30
❑ 178 Rocket Ismail	.50	.20
❑ 179 Marshall Faulk	1.00	.40
❑ 180 Trent Green	.75	.30
❑ 181 Sean Dawkins	.30	.10
❑ 182 Pete Mitchell	.30	.10
❑ 183 Jeff Graham	.30	.10
❑ 184 Eddie Kennison	.50	.20
❑ 185 Kerry Collins	.50	.20
❑ 186 Eric Green	.30	.10
❑ 187 Kyle Brady	.30	.10
❑ 188 Tony Martin	.50	.20
❑ 189 Jim Harbaugh	.50	.20
❑ 190 Erik Kramer	.30	.10
❑ 191 Steve Atwater	.30	.10
❑ 192 Chad Bratzke	.30	.10

❑ 193 Charles Johnson .30 .10
❑ 194 Damon Gibson .30 .10
❑ 195 Jeff George .50 .20
❑ 196 Scott Mitchell .30 .10
❑ 197 Terry Kirby .30 .10
❑ 198 Rich Gannon .75 .30
❑ 199 Chris Spielman .30 .10
❑ 200 Brad Johnson .75 .30
❑ PP4 Emmitt Smith PROMO 3.00 1.25

2000 Stadium Club

❑ COMPLETE SET (175) 50.00 20.00
❑ COMP.SET w/o SP's (150) 20.00 7.50
❑ 1 Peyton Manning 1.50 .60
❑ 2 Pete Mitchell .25 .08
❑ 3 Napoleon Kaufman .40 .15
❑ 4 Mikhael Ricks .25 .08
❑ 5 Mike Alstott .60 .25
❑ 6 Brad Johnson .60 .25
❑ 7 Tony Gonzalez .40 .15
❑ 8 Germane Crowell .25 .08
❑ 9 Marcus Robinson .60 .25
❑ 10 Stephen Davis .60 .25
❑ 11 Terance Mathis .40 .15
❑ 12 Jake Plummer .40 .15
❑ 13 Qadry Ismail .40 .15
❑ 14 Cade McNown .25 .08
❑ 15 Zach Thomas .60 .25
❑ 16 Curtis Martin .60 .25
❑ 17 Torrance Small .25 .08
❑ 18 Steve McNair .60 .25
❑ 19 Jim Harbaugh .40 .15
❑ 20 Keyshawn Johnson .60 .25
❑ 21 Antonio Freeman .60 .25
❑ 22 Ed McCaffrey .60 .25
❑ 23 Elvis Grbac .40 .15
❑ 24 Peerless Price .40 .15
❑ 25 Jerome Bettis .60 .25
❑ 26 Yancey Thigpen .25 .08
❑ 27 Jake Delhomme RC 2.50 1.00
❑ 28 Keith Poole .25 .08
❑ 29 Carl Pickens .40 .15
❑ 30 Jerry Rice 1.25 .50
❑ 31 Rob Moore .40 .15
❑ 32 Reidel Anthony .25 .08
❑ 33 Jimmy Smith .40 .15
❑ 34 Ray Lucas .40 .15
❑ 35 Troy Aikman 1.25 .50
❑ 36 Steve Beuerlein .40 .15
❑ 37 Charlie Batch .60 .25
❑ 38 Derrick Mayes .40 .15
❑ 39 Tim Brown .60 .25
❑ 40 Eddie George .60 .25
❑ 41 O.J. McDuffie .40 .15
❑ 42 Ike Hilliard .40 .15
❑ 43 Bill Schroeder .40 .15
❑ 44 Jim Miller .25 .08
❑ 45 Chris Chandler .40 .15
❑ 46 Fred Taylor .60 .25
❑ 47 Ricky Watters .40 .15
❑ 48 Tyrone Wheatley .40 .15
❑ 49 Bruce Smith .40 .15
❑ 50 Marshall Faulk .75 .30
❑ 51 Kevin Carter .25 .08
❑ 52 Champ Bailey .40 .15
❑ 53 Troy Edwards .25 .08
❑ 54 Doug Flutie .60 .25
❑ 55 Charles Johnson .40 .15
❑ 56 Michael Westbrook .40 .15
❑ 57 Frank Wycheck .25 .08
❑ 58 Drew Bledsoe .75 .30
❑ 59 Terrence Wilkins .25 .08
❑ 60 Ricky Williams .60 .25
❑ 61 Rod Smith .40 .15
❑ 62 Errict Rhett .40 .15
❑ 63 Vinny Testaverde .40 .15
❑ 64 Jacquez Green .25 .08
❑ 65 Curtis Conway .40 .15
❑ 66 Wayne Chrebet .40 .15
❑ 67 Albert Connell .25 .08
❑ 68 Kordell Stewart .40 .15
❑ 69 Bert Emanuel .25 .08
❑ 70 Randy Moss 1.25 .50
❑ 71 Akili Smith .25 .08
❑ 72 Brian Griese .60 .25
❑ 73 Frank Sanders .40 .15
❑ 74 Wesley Walls .25 .08
❑ 75 Michael Pittman .25 .08
❑ 76 Steve Young .75 .30
❑ 77 Jevon Kearse .60 .25
❑ 78 Az-Zahir Hakim .40 .15
❑ 79 James Stewart .40 .15
❑ 80 Brett Favre 2.00 .75
❑ 81 Dan Marino 2.00 .75
❑ 82 Joe Horn .40 .15
❑ 83 Mark Brunell .60 .25
❑ 84 Eddie Kennison .40 .15
❑ 85 Deion Sanders .60 .25
❑ 86 Priest Holmes .75 .30
❑ 87 Terry Glenn .40 .15
❑ 88 Olandis Gary .60 .25
❑ 89 Patrick Jeffers .60 .25
❑ 90 Emmitt Smith 1.25 .50
❑ 91 J.J. Stokes .40 .15
❑ 92 Warrick Dunn .60 .25
❑ 93 Damon Huard .60 .25
❑ 94 Herman Moore .40 .15
❑ 95 Corey Dillon .60 .25
❑ 96 Joey Galloway .40 .15
❑ 97 Jamal Anderson .60 .25
❑ 98 Junior Seau .60 .25
❑ 99 Robert Smith .60 .25
❑ 100 Edgerrin James 1.00 .40
❑ 101 Derrick Alexander .40 .15
❑ 102 Johnnie Morton .40 .15
❑ 103 Sean Dawkins .25 .08
❑ 104 Derrick Brooks .60 .25
❑ 105 Rickey Dudley .25 .08
❑ 106 Keenan McCardell .40 .15
❑ 107 Kerry Collins .40 .15
❑ 108 Kevin Johnson .60 .25
❑ 109 Eric Moulds .60 .25
❑ 110 Terrell Davis .60 .25
❑ 111 Shawn Jefferson .25 .08
❑ 112 Donovan McNabb 1.00 .40
❑ 113 Torry Holt .60 .25
❑ 114 Marvin Harrison .60 .25
❑ 115 Amani Toomer .40 .15
❑ 116 Tony Martin .40 .15
❑ 117 Curtis Enis .25 .08
❑ 118 Tiki Barber .60 .25
❑ 119 Freddie Jones .25 .08
❑ 120 Muhsin Muhammad .40 .15
❑ 121 Shaun King .25 .08
❑ 122 Isaac Bruce .60 .25
❑ 123 Duce Staley .60 .25
❑ 124 Hardy Nickerson .25 .08
❑ 125 Corey Bradford .40 .15
❑ 126 Kevin Hardy .25 .08
❑ 127 Hines Ward .60 .25
❑ 128 Charlie Garner .40 .15
❑ 129 Warren Sapp .40 .15
❑ 130 Tim Couch .40 .15
❑ 131 Kevin Dyson .40 .15
❑ 132 Rocket Ismail .40 .15
❑ 133 Tim Dwight .60 .25
❑ 134 Darnay Scott .40 .15
❑ 135 Jeff George .40 .15
❑ 136 Dorsey Levens .40 .15
❑ 137 Jeff Blake .40 .15
❑ 138 Jon Kitna .60 .25
❑ 139 Rich Gannon .60 .25
❑ 140 Cris Carter .60 .25
❑ 141 Jeff Graham .25 .08
❑ 142 James Johnson .25 .08
❑ 143 Tim Biakabutuka .40 .15
❑ 144 Bobby Engram .40 .15
❑ 145 Tony Banks .40 .15
❑ 146 Shannon Sharpe .40 .15
❑ 147 Antowain Smith .40 .15
❑ 148 Terrell Owens .60 .25
❑ 149 Rob Johnson .40 .15
❑ 150 Kurt Warner 1.25 .50
❑ 151 Thomas Jones RC 4.00 1.50
❑ 152 Chad Pennington RC 6.00 2.50
❑ 153 Ron Dayne RC 2.50 1.00
❑ 154 Tee Martin RC 2.50 1.00
❑ 155 Reuben Droughns RC 3.00 1.25
❑ 156 Jerry Porter RC 3.00 1.25
❑ 157 R.Jay Soward RC 2.00 .75
❑ 158 Sylvester Morris RC 2.00 .75
❑ 159 Todd Pinkston RC 2.50 1.00
❑ 160 Courtney Brown RC 2.50 1.00
❑ 161 Travis Taylor RC 2.50 1.00
❑ 162 Ron Dugans RC 2.00 .75
❑ 163 Laveranues Coles RC 3.00 1.25
❑ 164 Joe Hamilton RC 2.00 .75
❑ 165 Curtis Keaton RC 2.00 .75
❑ 166 Bubba Franks RC 2.50 1.00
❑ 167 Dennis Northcutt RC 2.50 1.00
❑ 168 Chris Redman RC 2.00 .75
❑ 169 Travis Prentice RC 2.00 .75
❑ 170 Shaun Alexander RC 12.00 5.00
❑ 171 Jamal Lewis RC 6.00 2.50
❑ 172 Peter Warrick RC 2.50 1.00
❑ 173 J.R. Redmond RC 2.00 .75
❑ 174 Trung Canidate RC 2.00 .75
❑ 175 Plaxico Burress RC 5.00 2.00

2001 Stadium Club

❑ COMPLETE SET (175) 120.00 60.00
❑ COMP.SET w/o SPs (125) 20.00 7.50
❑ 1 Peyton Manning 1.50 .60
❑ 2 Akili Smith .25 .08
❑ 3 Brian Griese .60 .25
❑ 4 Wayne Chrebet .40 .15
❑ 5 Oronde Gadsden .40 .15
❑ 6 Marvin Harrison .60 .25
❑ 7 Charles Johnson .25 .08
❑ 8 Jay Fiedler .60 .25
❑ 9 Kerry Collins .40 .15
❑ 10 Troy Aikman 1.00 .40
❑ 11 Donovan McNabb .75 .30
❑ 12 Ike Hilliard .40 .15
❑ 13 Warrick Dunn .60 .25
❑ 14 Derrick Alexander .40 .15
❑ 15 Jake Plummer .40 .15
❑ 16 Corey Dillon .60 .25
❑ 17 Ahman Green .60 .25
❑ 18 Keenan McCardell .25 .08
❑ 19 Derrick Mason .40 .15
❑ 20 Jerry Rice 1.25 .50
❑ 21 Emmitt Smith 1.25 .50
❑ 22 Dedric Ward .25 .08
❑ 23 Jamal Anderson .60 .25
❑ 24 Charlie Garner .40 .15
❑ 25 Vinny Testaverde .40 .15
❑ 26 Shaun Alexander .75 .30
❑ 27 Terry Glenn .40 .15
❑ 28 Cade McNown .25 .08
❑ 29 Germane Crowell .25 .08
❑ 30 Jeff Graham .25 .08
❑ 31 Rich Gannon .60 .25
❑ 32 Jevon Kearse .40 .15
❑ 33 Shannon Sharpe .40 .15

❑ 34	Marcus Robinson	.60	.25
❑ 35	Rod Smith	.40	.15
❑ 36	Curtis Martin	.60	.25
❑ 37	Robert Smith	.60	.25
❑ 38	Marshall Faulk	.75	.30
❑ 39	Tony Richardson	.25	.08
❑ 40	Travis Prentice	.25	.08
❑ 41	Edgerrin James	.75	.30
❑ 42	Duce Staley	.60	.25
❑ 43	Keyshawn Johnson	.60	.25
❑ 44	Joe Horn	.40	.15
❑ 45	Shawn Bryson	.25	.08
❑ 46	Ray Lewis	.60	.25
❑ 47	Fred Taylor	.60	.25
❑ 48	Jeff George	.40	.15
❑ 49	Sean Dawkins	.25	.08
❑ 50	Daunte Culpepper	.60	.25
❑ 51	Chris Chandler	.40	.15
❑ 52	Tim Couch	.40	.15
❑ 53	Trent Dilfer	.40	.15
❑ 54	Steve McNair	.60	.25
❑ 55	Kordell Stewart	.40	.15
❑ 56	Aaron Brooks	.60	.25
❑ 57	Michael Pittman	.25	.08
❑ 58	Bill Schroeder	.40	.15
❑ 59	Junior Seau	.60	.25
❑ 60	Kurt Warner	1.25	.50
❑ 61	Drew Bledsoe	.75	.30
❑ 62	Steve Beuerlein	.40	.15
❑ 63	Mike Anderson	.60	.25
❑ 64	Brad Johnson	.60	.25
❑ 65	Tim Brown	.60	.25
❑ 66	Qadry Ismail	.40	.15
❑ 67	Doug Flutie	.60	.25
❑ 68	Terrell Owens	.60	.25
❑ 69	Rocket Ismail	.40	.15
❑ 70	Charlie Batch	.60	.25
❑ 71	Jerome Pathon	.40	.15
❑ 72	Peter Warrick	.60	.25
❑ 73	Hines Ward	.60	.25
❑ 74	Ron Dayne	.60	.25
❑ 75	Lamar Smith	.40	.15
❑ 76	Amani Toomer	.40	.15
❑ 77	Joey Galloway	.40	.15
❑ 78	James Allen	.40	.15
❑ 79	Isaac Bruce	.60	.25
❑ 80	David Boston	.60	.25
❑ 81	James Thrash	.40	.15
❑ 82	Tony Gonzalez	.40	.15
❑ 83	Jason Taylor	.25	.08
❑ 84	Ricky Watters	.40	.15
❑ 85	Terance Mathis	.40	.15
❑ 86	Troy Brown	.40	.15
❑ 87	Mark Brunell	.60	.25
❑ 88	Rob Johnson	.40	.15
❑ 89	Freddie Jones	.25	.08
❑ 90	Eddie George	.60	.25
❑ 91	Tiki Barber	.60	.25
❑ 92	Donald Hayes	.25	.08
❑ 93	Muhsin Muhammad	.40	.15
❑ 94	Johnnie Morton	.40	.15
❑ 95	Warren Sapp	.40	.15
❑ 96	Bobby Shaw	.25	.08
❑ 97	Randy Moss	1.25	.50
❑ 98	Jerome Bettis	.60	.25
❑ 99	Antonio Freeman	.60	.25
❑ 100	Jamal Lewis	1.00	.40
❑ 101	Andre Rison	.40	.15
❑ 102	Kevin Faulk	.40	.15
❑ 103	Jon Kitna	.60	.25
❑ 104	Shawn Jefferson	.25	.08
❑ 105	Kevin Johnson	.40	.15
❑ 106	Torry Holt	.60	.25
❑ 107	Cris Carter	.60	.25
❑ 108	Chad Lewis	.25	.08
❑ 109	Stephen Davis	.60	.25
❑ 110	Jeff Blake	.40	.15
❑ 111	Elvis Grbac	.40	.15
❑ 112	Ed McCaffrey	.60	.25
❑ 113	Tim Biakabutuka	.40	.15
❑ 114	Trent Green	.60	.25
❑ 115	Jeff Garcia	.60	.25
❑ 116	Jacquez Green	.25	.08
❑ 117	Shaun King	.25	.08
❑ 118	Jimmy Smith	.40	.15
❑ 119	James Stewart	.40	.15
❑ 120	Brian Urlacher	1.00	.40
❑ 121	Tyrone Wheatley	.40	.15
❑ 122	J.R. Redmond	.25	.08
❑ 123	Eric Moulds	.40	.15
❑ 124	Ricky Williams	.60	.25
❑ 125	Brett Favre	2.00	.75
❑ 126	Koren Robinson RC	2.50	1.00
❑ 127	Richard Seymour RC	2.50	1.00
❑ 128	Jamal Reynolds RC	2.50	1.00
❑ 129	Kevin Kasper RC	2.50	1.00
❑ 130	LaMont Jordan RC	5.00	2.00
❑ 131	Reggie Wayne RC	5.00	2.00
❑ 132	Travis Henry RC	2.50	1.00
❑ 133	Alge Crumpler RC	3.00	1.25
❑ 134	Quincy Carter RC	2.50	1.00
❑ 135	Michael Bennett RC	4.00	1.50
❑ 136	Jamie Winborn RC	1.50	.60
❑ 137	Josh Heupel RC	2.50	1.00
❑ 138	Will Allen RC	1.50	.60
❑ 139	Scotty Anderson RC	1.50	.60
❑ 140	LaDainian Tomlinson RC	12.00	6.00
❑ 141	Freddie Mitchell RC	2.50	1.00
❑ 142	Gerard Warren RC	2.50	1.00
❑ 143	Chad Johnson RC	6.00	2.50
❑ 144	Todd Heap RC	2.50	1.00
❑ 145	Leonard Davis RC	1.50	.60
❑ 146	Kevan Barlow RC	2.50	1.00
❑ 147	Correll Buckhalter RC	3.00	1.25
❑ 148	Fred Smoot RC	2.50	1.00
❑ 149	Steve Smith RC	6.00	3.00
❑ 150	David Terrell RC	2.50	1.00
❑ 151	Chris Chambers RC	4.00	1.50
❑ 152	Mike McMahon RC	2.50	1.00
❑ 153	Rudi Johnson RC	5.00	2.00
❑ 154	Marques Tuiasosopo RC	2.50	1.00
❑ 155	Deuce McAllister RC	5.00	2.00
❑ 156	Marcus Stroud RC	2.50	1.00
❑ 157	Bobby Newcombe RC	1.50	.60
❑ 158	Rod Gardner RC	2.50	1.00
❑ 159	Drew Brees RC	6.00	2.50
❑ 160	Jesse Palmer RC	2.50	1.00
❑ 161	Derrick Gibson RC	1.50	.60
❑ 162	James Jackson RC	2.50	1.00
❑ 163	Dan Morgan RC	2.50	1.00
❑ 164	Michael Vick RC	15.00	6.00
❑ 165	Snoop Minnis RC	1.50	.60
❑ 166	Anthony Thomas RC	2.50	1.00
❑ 167	Andre Carter RC	2.50	1.00
❑ 168	Travis Minor RC	1.50	.60
❑ 169	Quincy Morgan RC	2.50	1.00
❑ 170	Justin Smith RC	2.50	1.00
❑ 171	Tay Cody RC	1.00	.40
❑ 172	Santana Moss RC	4.00	1.50
❑ 173	Sage Rosenfels RC	2.50	1.00
❑ 174	Robert Ferguson RC	2.50	1.00
❑ 175	Chris Weinke RC	2.50	1.00

2002 Stadium Club

❑	COMP.SET w/o SP's (125)	25.00	10.00
❑ 1	Randy Moss	1.25	.50
❑ 2	Kordell Stewart	.40	.15
❑ 3	Marvin Harrison	.60	.25
❑ 4	Chris Weinke	.40	.15
❑ 5	James Allen	.40	.15
❑ 6	Michael Pittman	.25	.08
❑ 7	Quincy Carter	.40	.15
❑ 8	Mike Anderson	.60	.25
❑ 9	Mike McMahon	.60	.25
❑ 10	Chris Chambers	.60	.25
❑ 11	Laveranues Coles	.40	.15
❑ 12	Curtis Conway	.25	.08
❑ 13	Brad Johnson	.40	.15
❑ 14	Shaun Alexander	.75	.30
❑ 15	Jerry Rice	1.25	.50
❑ 16	Rod Gardner	.40	.15
❑ 17	Derrick Mason	.40	.15
❑ 18	Tom Brady	1.50	.60
❑ 19	Jimmy Smith	.40	.15
❑ 20	Tim Couch	.40	.15
❑ 21	Jim Miller	.25	.08
❑ 22	Eric Moulds	.40	.15
❑ 23	Michael Vick	2.00	.75
❑ 24	Jon Kitna	.40	.15
❑ 25	Johnnie Morton	.40	.15
❑ 26	Priest Holmes	.75	.30
❑ 27	Aaron Brooks	.60	.25
❑ 28	Duce Staley	.60	.25
❑ 29	LaDainian Tomlinson	1.00	.40
❑ 30	Lamar Smith	.40	.15
❑ 31	Rod Smith	.40	.15
❑ 32	Richard Huntley	.25	.08
❑ 33	Antonio Freeman	.60	.25
❑ 34	Amani Toomer	.40	.15
❑ 35	Hines Ward	.60	.25
❑ 36	Marshall Faulk	.60	.25
❑ 37	Steve McNair	.60	.25
❑ 38	Tim Brown	.60	.25
❑ 39	Curtis Martin	.60	.25
❑ 40	Kevin Johnson	.40	.15
❑ 41	Rob Johnson	.40	.15
❑ 42	Qadry Ismail	.40	.15
❑ 43	Daunte Culpepper	.60	.25
❑ 44	Willie Jackson	.25	.08
❑ 45	Jeff Garcia	.60	.25
❑ 46	Matt Hasselbeck	.40	.15
❑ 47	Corey Bradford	.25	.08
❑ 48	Snoop Minnis	.25	.08
❑ 49	Ron Dayne	.40	.15
❑ 50	Peyton Manning	1.25	.50
❑ 51	Drew Bledsoe	.75	.30
❑ 52	Terry Glenn	.40	.15
❑ 53	Warrick Dunn	.60	.25
❑ 54	Mark Brunell	.60	.25
❑ 55	James Stewart	.40	.15
❑ 56	Muhsin Muhammad	.40	.15
❑ 57	Jake Plummer	.40	.15
❑ 58	Terance Mathis	.25	.08
❑ 59	Rocket Ismail	.40	.15
❑ 60	Joe Horn	.40	.15
❑ 61	Wayne Chrebet	.40	.15
❑ 62	James Thrash	.40	.15
❑ 63	Stephen Davis	.40	.15
❑ 64	Isaac Bruce	.60	.25
❑ 65	Peter Warrick	.40	.15
❑ 66	Anthony Thomas	.40	.15
❑ 67	Maurice Smith	.40	.15
❑ 68	Tony Gonzalez	.40	.15
❑ 69	Michael Bennett	.40	.15
❑ 70	Ike Hilliard	.40	.15
❑ 71	Plaxico Burress	.40	.15
❑ 72	Darrell Jackson	.40	.15
❑ 73	Kevan Barlow	.40	.15
❑ 74	Ray Lewis	.60	.25
❑ 75	Emmitt Smith	1.50	.60
❑ 76	Bill Schroeder	.40	.15
❑ 77	Az-Zahir Hakim	.25	.08
❑ 78	Troy Brown	.40	.15
❑ 79	Keyshawn Johnson	.60	.25
❑ 80	Tim Dwight	.40	.15
❑ 81	Peerless Price	.40	.15
❑ 82	Marty Booker	.25	.08
❑ 83	Terrell Davis	.60	.25
❑ 84	Dominic Rhodes	.40	.15
❑ 85	Jay Fiedler	.40	.15
❑ 86	Rich Gannon	.60	.25
❑ 87	Terrell Owens	.60	.25
❑ 88	Donald Hayes	.25	.08
❑ 89	Thomas Jones	.40	.15
❑ 90	Ricky Williams	.60	.25
❑ 91	Donovan McNabb	.75	.30
❑ 92	Eddie George	.60	.25
❑ 93	Germane Crowell	.25	.08
❑ 94	David Terrell	.60	.25
❑ 95	Alex Van Pelt	.25	.08
❑ 96	Antowain Smith	.40	.15
❑ 97	Jerome Bettis	.60	.25
❑ 98	Mike Alstott	.60	.25

❑	99 Doug Flutie	.60	.25
❑	100 Kurt Warner	.60	.25
❑	101 Cris Carter	.60	.25
❑	102 Oronde Gadsden	.40	.15
❑	103 Ahman Green	.60	.25
❑	104 Corey Dillon	.40	.15
❑	105 Marcus Robinson	.40	.15
❑	106 Shannon Sharpe	.40	.15
❑	107 Kerry Collins	.40	.15
❑	108 Garrison Hearst	.40	.15
❑	109 David Boston	.60	.25
❑	110 Travis Henry	.60	.25
❑	111 James Jackson	.25	.08
❑	112 Fred Taylor	.60	.25
❑	113 Edgerrin James	.75	.30
❑	114 Vinny Testaverde	.40	.15
❑	115 Todd Pinkston	.40	.15
❑	116 Koren Robinson	.40	.15
❑	117 Torry Holt	.60	.25
❑	118 Brian Griese	.60	.25
❑	119 Trent Green	.40	.15
❑	120 James McKnight	.25	.08
❑	121 Charlie Garner	.40	.15
❑	122 Tiki Barber	.60	.25
❑	123 Joey Galloway	.40	.15
❑	124 Quincy Morgan	.25	.08
❑	125 Brett Favre	1.50	.60
❑	126 Joey Harrington RC	8.00	3.00
❑	127 Ashley Lelie RC	6.00	2.50
❑	128 Terry Charles RC	2.50	1.00
❑	129 Charles Grant RC	3.00	1.25
❑	130 Levar Fisher RC	1.50	.60
❑	131 Larry Tripplett RC	1.50	.60
❑	132 Quentin Jammer RC	3.00	1.25
❑	133 Ron Johnson RC	2.50	1.00
❑	134 Maurice Morris RC	3.00	1.25
❑	135 Roy Williams RC	8.00	3.00
❑	136 Kurt Kittner RC	2.50	1.00
❑	137 Dennis Johnson RC	1.50	.60
❑	138 Seth Burford RC	2.50	1.00
❑	139 Michael Lewis RC	3.00	1.25
❑	140 William Green RC	3.00	1.25
❑	141 Rohan Davey RC	3.00	1.25
❑	142 Rocky Calmus RC	3.00	1.25
❑	143 Robert Thomas RC	3.00	1.25
❑	144 Travis Stephens RC	2.50	1.00
❑	145 Ladell Betts RC	3.00	1.25
❑	146 Daniel Graham RC	3.00	1.25
❑	147 Chester Taylor RC	3.00	1.25
❑	148 Tim Carter RC	2.50	1.00
❑	149 Lito Sheppard RC	3.00	1.25
❑	150 David Carr RC	8.00	3.00
❑	151 Alex Brown RC	3.00	1.25
❑	152 John Henderson RC	3.00	1.25
❑	153 Jamar Martin RC	2.50	1.00
❑	154 Raonall Smith RC	2.50	1.00
❑	155 Leonard Henry RC	2.50	1.00
❑	156 T.J. Duckett RC	5.00	2.00
❑	157 Patrick Ramsey RC	4.00	1.50
❑	158 Antwaan Randle El RC	5.00	2.00
❑	159 Luke Staley RC	2.50	1.00
❑	160 Jon McGraw RC	1.50	.60
❑	161 Phillip Buchanon RC	3.00	1.25
❑	162 Dwight Freeney RC	4.00	1.50
❑	163 Mike Rumph RC	3.00	1.25
❑	164 Albert Haynesworth RC	2.50	1.00
❑	165 Antonio Bryant RC	3.00	1.25
❑	166 Josh Reed RC	3.00	1.25
❑	167 Eric Crouch RC	3.00	1.25
❑	168 Reche Caldwell RC	3.00	1.25
❑	169 Adrian Peterson RC	3.00	1.25
❑	170 Jonathan Wells RC	3.00	1.25
❑	171 Wendell Bryant RC	1.50	.60
❑	172 Tellis Redmon RC	2.50	1.00
❑	173 Josh McCown RC	4.00	1.50
❑	174 DeShaun Foster RC	3.00	1.25
❑	175 Cliff Russell RC	2.50	1.00
❑	176 David Garrard RC	3.00	1.25
❑	177 Brian Westbrook RC	5.00	2.00
❑	178 Anthony Weaver RC	2.50	1.00
❑	179 Bryan Thomas RC	2.50	1.00
❑	180 Kalimba Edwards RC	3.00	1.25
❑	181 Javon Walker RC	6.00	2.50
❑	182 Marquise Walker RC	2.50	1.00
❑	183 Deion Branch RC	6.00	2.50
❑	184 Lamar Gordon RC	3.00	1.25
❑	185 Jeremy Shockey RC	10.00	4.00
❑	186 Clinton Portis RC	10.00	4.00
❑	187 Napoleon Harris RC	3.00	1.25
❑	188 Freddie Milons RC	2.50	1.00
❑	189 Julius Peppers RC	6.00	2.50
❑	190 Andre Davis RC	2.50	1.00
❑	191 Travis Fisher RC	3.00	1.25
❑	192 Chad Hutchinson RC	2.50	1.00
❑	193 Najeh Davenport RC	3.00	1.25
❑	194 Ed Reed RC	5.00	2.00
❑	195 Donte Stallworth RC	6.00	2.50
❑	196 Brandon Doman RC	2.50	1.00
❑	197 Zak Kustok RC	3.00	1.25
❑	198 Randy Fasani RC	2.50	1.00
❑	199 J.T. O'Sullivan RC	2.50	1.00
❑	200 Jabar Gaffney RC	3.00	1.25

1999 Stadium Club Chrome

❑	COMPLETE SET (150)	60.00	25.00
❑	1 Dan Marino	4.00	1.50
❑	2 Andre Reed	.75	.30
❑	3 Michael Westbrook	.75	.30
❑	4 Isaac Bruce	1.25	.50
❑	5 Curtis Martin	1.25	.50
❑	6 Terrell Owens	1.25	.50
❑	7 Warrick Dunn	1.25	.50
❑	8 Jake Plummer	.75	.30
❑	9 Chad Brown	.50	.20
❑	10 Yancey Thigpen	.75	.30
❑	11 Keenan McCardell	.75	.30
❑	12 Shannon Sharpe	.75	.30
❑	13 Cameron Cleeland	.50	.20
❑	14 Mark Brunell	1.25	.50
❑	15 Jamal Anderson	1.25	.50
❑	16 Germane Crowell	.50	.20
❑	17 Rod Smith	.75	.30
❑	18 Cris Carter	1.25	.50
❑	19 Terrell Davis	1.25	.50
❑	20 Tim Biakabutuka	.75	.30
❑	21 Jermaine Lewis	.75	.30
❑	22 Adrian Murrell	.75	.30
❑	23 Doug Flutie	1.25	.50
❑	24 Curtis Enis	.50	.20
❑	25 Skip Hicks	.50	.20
❑	26 Steve McNair	1.25	.50
❑	27 Charles Woodson	1.25	.50
❑	28 Freddie Jones	.50	.20
❑	29 Warren Sapp	.75	.30
❑	30 Emmitt Smith	2.50	1.00
❑	31 Reidel Anthony	.50	.20
❑	32 Tony Simmons	.50	.20
❑	33 Andre Hastings	.50	.20
❑	34 Byron Bam Morris	.50	.20
❑	35 Jimmy Smith	.75	.30
❑	36 Antonio Freeman	1.25	.50
❑	37 Herman Moore	.75	.30
❑	38 Muhsin Muhammad	.75	.30
❑	39 Chris Chandler	.75	.30
❑	40 John Elway	4.00	1.50
❑	41 Bobby Engram	.75	.30
❑	42 Keith Poole	.50	.20
❑	43 Mike Alstott	1.25	.50
❑	44 Junior Seau	1.25	.50
❑	45 Thurman Thomas	.75	.30
❑	46 Troy Aikman	2.50	1.00
❑	47 Wesley Walls	.75	.30
❑	48 Robert Smith	1.25	.50
❑	49 Elvis Grbac	.75	.30
❑	50 Ben Coates	.50	.20
❑	51 Bert Emanuel	.75	.30
❑	52 Jacquez Green	.50	.20
❑	53 Barry Sanders	4.00	1.50
❑	54 James Jett	.50	.20
❑	55 Gary Brown	.50	.20
❑	56 Stephen Alexander	.50	.20
❑	57 Wayne Chrebet	1.25	.50
❑	58 Drew Bledsoe	1.50	.60
❑	59 Jake Reed	.75	.30
❑	60 Marvin Harrison	1.25	.50
❑	61 Johnnie Morton	.75	.30
❑	62 Brett Favre	4.00	1.50
❑	63 Charlie Batch	1.25	.50
❑	64 Antowain Smith	1.25	.50
❑	65 Ernie Mills	.50	.20
❑	66 Jeff Blake	.75	.30
❑	67 Curtis Conway	.75	.30
❑	68 Bruce Smith	.75	.30
❑	69 Peyton Manning	4.00	1.50
❑	70 Tim Dwight	1.25	.50
❑	71 O.J. McDuffie	.75	.30
❑	72 Jon Kitna	1.25	.50
❑	73 Trent Dilfer	.75	.30
❑	74 Jerome Bettis	1.25	.50
❑	75 Dedric Ward	.50	.20
❑	76 Fred Taylor	1.25	.50
❑	77 Ike Hilliard	.75	.30
❑	78 Frank Wycheck	.50	.20
❑	79 Eric Moulds	1.25	.50
❑	80 Rob Moore	.75	.30
❑	81 Ed McCaffrey	.75	.30
❑	82 Carl Pickens	.75	.30
❑	83 Priest Holmes	2.00	.75
❑	84 Terry Glenn	1.25	.50
❑	85 Keyshawn Johnson	1.25	.50
❑	86 Karim Abdul-Jabbar	.75	.30
❑	87 Ahman Green	1.25	.50
❑	88 Duce Staley	1.25	.50
❑	89 Vinny Testaverde	.75	.30
❑	90 Napoleon Kaufman	1.25	.50
❑	91 Frank Sanders	.75	.30
❑	92 Steve Young	1.50	.60
❑	93 Darnay Scott	.75	.30
❑	94 Deion Sanders	1.25	.50
❑	95 Corey Dillon	1.25	.50
❑	96 Randall Cunningham	1.25	.50
❑	97 Eddie George	1.25	.50
❑	98 Derrick Alexander	.75	.30
❑	99 Mark Chmura	.75	.30
❑	100 Rickey Dudley	.50	.20
❑	101 Joey Galloway	.75	.30
❑	102 Ricky Proehl	.50	.20
❑	103 Natrone Means	.75	.30
❑	104 Dorsey Levens	1.25	.50
❑	105 Andre Rison	.75	.30
❑	106 John Randle	.75	.30
❑	107 Terance Mathis	.75	.30
❑	108 Rae Carruth	.50	.20
❑	109 Jerry Rice	2.50	1.00
❑	110 Michael Irvin	.75	.30
❑	111 Oronde Gadsden	.75	.30
❑	112 Jerome Pathon	.50	.20
❑	113 Ricky Watters	.75	.30
❑	114 J.J. Stokes	.75	.30
❑	115 Kordell Stewart	.75	.30
❑	116 Tim Brown	1.25	.50
❑	117 Tony Gonzalez	1.25	.50
❑	118 Randy Moss	3.00	1.25
❑	119 Daunte Culpepper RC	8.00	3.00
❑	120 Amos Zereoue RC	2.50	1.00
❑	121 Champ Bailey RC	3.00	1.25
❑	122 Peerless Price RC	2.50	1.00
❑	123 Edgerrin James RC	8.00	3.00
❑	124 Joe Germaine RC	2.00	.75
❑	125 David Boston RC	2.50	1.00
❑	126 Kevin Faulk RC	2.50	1.00
❑	127 Troy Edwards RC	2.00	.75
❑	128 Akili Smith RC	2.00	.75
❑	129 Kevin Johnson RC	2.50	1.00
❑	130 Rob Konrad RC	2.00	.75
❑	131 Shaun King RC	2.00	.75
❑	132 James Johnson RC	2.00	.75
❑	133 Donovan McNabb RC	10.00	4.00
❑	134 Torry Holt RC	5.00	2.00
❑	135 Mike Cloud RC	2.00	.75
❑	136 Sedrick Irvin RC	1.25	.50
❑	137 Cade McNown RC	2.00	.75

❑ 138 Ricky Williams RC 4.00 1.50
❑ 139 Karsten Bailey RC 2.00 .75
❑ 140 Cecil Collins RC 1.25 .50
❑ 141 Brock Huard RC 2.50 1.00
❑ 142 D'Wayne Bates RC 2.00 .75
❑ 143 Tim Couch RC 2.50 1.00
❑ 144 Rocket Ismail .75 .30
❑ 145 Marshall Faulk 1.50 .60
❑ 146 Trent Green 1.25 .50
❑ 147 Tony Martin .75 .30
❑ 148 Jim Harbaugh .75 .30
❑ 149 Rich Gannon 1.25 .50
❑ 150 Brad Johnson 1.25 .50

2002 Sweet Spot

❑ COMP.SET w/o SP's (90) 30.00 12.50
❑ 1 Aaron Brooks 1.25 .50
❑ 2 Tim Couch .75 .30
❑ 3 Jon Kitna .75 .30
❑ 4 Brett Favre 3.00 1.25
❑ 5 Donovan McNabb 1.50 .60
❑ 6 Jeff Garcia 1.25 .50
❑ 7 Michael Vick 4.00 1.50
❑ 8 Mark Brunell 1.25 .50
❑ 9 Steve McNair 1.25 .50
❑ 10 Kordell Stewart .75 .30
❑ 11 Drew Bledsoe 1.50 .60
❑ 12 Tom Brady 3.00 1.25
❑ 13 Kurt Warner 1.25 .50
❑ 14 Brian Griese 1.25 .50
❑ 15 Jim Miller .75 .30
❑ 16 Jake Plummer .75 .30
❑ 17 Quincy Carter .75 .30
❑ 18 Peyton Manning 2.50 1.00
❑ 19 Keyshawn Johnson 1.25 .50
❑ 20 Travis Henry 1.25 .50
❑ 21 LaDainian Tomlinson 2.00 .75
❑ 22 Emmitt Smith 3.00 1.25
❑ 23 Michael Bennett .75 .30
❑ 24 Duce Staley 1.25 .50
❑ 25 Thomas Jones .75 .30
❑ 26 Deuce McAllister 1.50 .60
❑ 27 Eddie George 1.25 .50
❑ 28 Marshall Faulk 1.25 .50
❑ 29 Curtis Martin 1.25 .50
❑ 30 Ahman Green 1.25 .50
❑ 31 Priest Holmes 1.50 .60
❑ 32 Edgerrin James 1.50 .60
❑ 33 Antowain Smith .75 .30
❑ 34 Ricky Williams 1.25 .50
❑ 35 Anthony Thomas .75 .30
❑ 36 Jerome Bettis 1.25 .50
❑ 37 Shaun Alexander 1.50 .60
❑ 38 Kerry Collins .75 .30
❑ 39 Drew Brees 1.25 .50
❑ 40 Chris Redman .50 .20
❑ 41 Marc Bulger 1.25 .50
❑ 42 Jay Fiedler .75 .30
❑ 43 Trent Green .75 .30
❑ 44 Daunte Culpepper 1.25 .50
❑ 45 Rich Gannon 1.25 .50
❑ 46 Rodney Peete .75 .30
❑ 47 Vinny Testaverde .75 .30
❑ 48 Stephen Davis .75 .30
❑ 49 James Allen .75 .30
❑ 50 Tiki Barber 1.25 .50
❑ 51 Ron Dayne .75 .30
❑ 52 Ray Lewis 1.25 .50
❑ 53 Corey Dillon .75 .30
❑ 54 Brian Urlacher 2.00 .75
❑ 55 Junior Seau 1.25 .50
❑ 56 Warrick Dunn 1.25 .50
❑ 57 Fred Taylor 1.25 .50
❑ 58 Jamal Lewis 1.25 .50
❑ 59 Trent Dilfer .75 .30
❑ 60 James Stewart .75 .30
❑ 61 David Patten .50 .20
❑ 62 Eric Moulds .75 .30
❑ 63 Isaac Bruce 1.25 .50
❑ 64 Troy Brown .75 .30
❑ 65 Terrell Owens 1.25 .50
❑ 66 Moe Williams .50 .20
❑ 67 Joe Horn .75 .30
❑ 68 Az-Zahir Hakim .50 .20
❑ 69 Jimmy Smith .75 .30
❑ 70 Michael Westbrook .50 .20
❑ 71 Olandis Gary .75 .30
❑ 72 Chris Chambers 1.25 .50
❑ 73 Kevin Johnson .75 .30
❑ 74 Joey Galloway .75 .30
❑ 75 Hines Ward 1.25 .50
❑ 76 Garrison Hearst .75 .30
❑ 77 Wayne Chrebet .75 .30
❑ 78 Muhsin Muhammad .75 .30
❑ 79 Rod Gardner .75 .30
❑ 80 Jerry Rice 2.50 1.00
❑ 81 Tim Brown 1.25 .50
❑ 82 Shannon Sharpe .75 .30
❑ 83 Terry Glenn .75 .30
❑ 84 Randy Moss 2.50 1.00
❑ 85 Corey Bradford .50 .20
❑ 86 Marty Booker .75 .30
❑ 87 Keenan McCardell .50 .20
❑ 88 Marvin Harrison 1.25 .50
❑ 89 David Boston 1.25 .50
❑ 90 Eddie Kennison .50 .20
❑ 91 Tim Carter RC 5.00 2.00
❑ 92 Joey Harrington RC 15.00 6.00
❑ 93 Patrick Ramsey RC 8.00 3.00
❑ 94 David Garrard RC 6.00 2.50
❑ 95 Donte Stallworth RC 12.00 5.00
❑ 96 Reche Caldwell RC 6.00 2.50
❑ 97 William Green RC 6.00 2.50
❑ 98 Josh Reed RC 6.00 2.50
❑ 99 DeShaun Foster RC 6.00 2.50
❑ 100 Jeremy Shockey RC 20.00 7.50
❑ 101 Mike Williams RC 5.00 2.00
❑ 102 Daniel Graham RC 6.00 2.50
❑ 103 Josh McCown RC 8.00 3.00
❑ 104 Javon Walker RC 12.00 5.00
❑ 105 Travis Stephens RC 5.00 2.00
❑ 106 Marquise Walker RC 5.00 2.00
❑ 107 T.J. Duckett RC 10.00 4.00
❑ 108 Damien Anderson RC 5.00 2.00
❑ 109 Quentin Jammer RC 6.00 2.50
❑ 110 Bryan Thomas RC 5.00 2.00
❑ 111 Chad Hutchinson RC 5.00 2.00
❑ 112 Brian Westbrook RC 10.00 4.00
❑ 113 Lamar Gordon RC 6.00 2.50
❑ 114 Deion Branch RC 12.00 5.00
❑ 115 Ed Reed RC 10.00 4.00
❑ 116 Jonathan Wells RC 6.00 2.50
❑ 117 Phillip Buchanon RC 6.00 2.50
❑ 118 Wendell Bryant RC 3.00 1.25
❑ 119 Kurt Kittner RC 5.00 2.00
❑ 120 Randy McMichael RC 10.00 4.00
❑ 121 Brandon Doman RC 5.00 2.00
❑ 122 Adrian Peterson RC 6.00 2.50
❑ 123 Ricky Williams RC 5.00 2.00
❑ 124 Seth Burford RC 5.00 2.00
❑ 125 Shaun Hill RC 6.00 2.50
❑ 126 Anthony Weaver RC 5.00 2.00
❑ 127 Freddie Milons RC 5.00 2.00
❑ 128 Darrell Hill RC 5.00 2.00
❑ 129 Daryl Jones RC 5.00 2.00
❑ 130 Chester Taylor RC 6.00 2.50
❑ 131 Najeh Davenport RC 6.00 2.50
❑ 132 Jason McAddley RC 5.00 2.00
❑ 133 Preston Parsons RC 3.00 1.25
❑ 134 Michael Lewis RC 6.00 2.50
❑ 135 Mike Rumph RC 6.00 2.50
❑ 136 Lamont Thompson RC 5.00 2.00
❑ 137 Dwight Freeney RC 8.00 3.00
❑ 138 Napoleon Harris RC 6.00 2.50
❑ 139 Tank Williams RC 5.00 2.00
❑ 140 Lee Mays RC 6.00 2.50
❑ 141 Robert Thomas RC 6.00 2.50
❑ 142 Tellis Redmon RC 5.00 2.00
❑ 143 Alex Brown RC 6.00 2.50
❑ 144 Ryan Sims RC 6.00 2.50
❑ 145 Larry Tripplett RC 3.00 1.25
❑ 146 Quinn Gray RC 3.00 1.25
❑ 147 Jesse Chatman RC 6.00 2.50
❑ 148 Jamin Elliott RC 3.00 1.25
❑ 149 Ben Leber RC 6.00 2.50
❑ 150 Lito Sheppard RC 6.00 2.50
❑ 151 Antonio Bryant AU/550 RC 25.00 12.50
❑ 152 Rohan Davey AU/550 RC 25.00 10.00
❑ 153 Randy Fasani AU/550 RC 15.00 6.00
❑ 154 J.T. O'Sullivan AU/550 RC 20.00 7.50
❑ 155 Ron Johnson AU/550 RC 15.00 6.00
❑ 156 Maurice Morris AU/550 RC 25.00 10.00
❑ 157 Kahlil Hill AU/550 RC 15.00 6.00
❑ 158 Ant Randle El AU/550 RC 30.00 15.00
❑ 159 Cliff Russell AU/550 RC 15.00 6.00
❑ 160 Ladell Betts AU/550 RC 20.00 7.50
❑ 161 David Carr AU/125 RC 120.00 50.00
❑ 162 Andre Davis AU/125 RC 30.00 12.50
❑ 163 Julius Peppers AU/125 80.00 40.00
❑ 164 Ashley Lelie AU/125 RC 60.00 30.00
❑ 165 Jabar Gaffney AU/125 RC 30.00 12.50
❑ 166 Clinton Portis AU/125 RC 150.00 75.00

2003 Sweet Spot

❑ COMP.SET w/o SP's (90) 30.00 12.50
❑ 1 Chad Pennington 1.50 .60
❑ 2 Aaron Brooks 1.25 .50
❑ 3 Joey Harrington 2.00 .75
❑ 4 Brett Favre 3.00 1.25
❑ 5 Donovan McNabb 1.50 .60
❑ 6 Jeff Garcia 1.25 .50
❑ 7 Michael Vick 3.00 1.25
❑ 8 David Carr 2.00 .75
❑ 9 Drew Brees 1.25 .50
❑ 10 Trent Green .75 .30
❑ 11 Patrick Ramsey 1.25 .50
❑ 12 Tom Brady 3.00 1.25
❑ 13 Kurt Warner 1.25 .50
❑ 14 Brad Johnson .75 .30
❑ 15 Brian Griese 1.25 .50
❑ 16 Jake Plummer .75 .30
❑ 17 Drew Bledsoe 1.25 .50
❑ 18 Peyton Manning 2.00 .75
❑ 19 Tim Couch .50 .20
❑ 20 Kordell Stewart .75 .30
❑ 21 Jay Fiedler .75 .30
❑ 22 Rich Gannon .75 .30
❑ 23 Josh McCown .75 .30
❑ 24 Matt Hasselbeck .75 .30
❑ 25 Tommy Maddox 1.25 .50
❑ 26 Rodney Peete .50 .20
❑ 27 Jake Delhomme 1.25 .50
❑ 28 Chris Redman .50 .20
❑ 29 Mark Brunell .75 .30
❑ 30 Marc Bulger 1.25 .50
❑ 31 Kelly Holcomb .75 .30
❑ 32 Chad Hutchinson .50 .20
❑ 33 Quincy Carter .75 .30
❑ 34 Steve McNair 1.25 .50
❑ 35 Marshall Faulk 1.25 .50
❑ 36 Deuce McAllister 1.25 .50
❑ 37 Emmitt Smith 3.00 1.25
❑ 38 LaDainian Tomlinson 1.25 .50
❑ 39 Kevan Barlow .75 .30
❑ 40 Michael Bennett .75 .30

❑ 41 Shaun Alexander 1.25 .50
❑ 42 Edgerrin James 1.25 .50
❑ 43 Ricky Williams 1.25 .50
❑ 44 Priest Holmes 1.50 .60
❑ 45 Ahman Green 1.25 .50
❑ 46 Curtis Martin 1.25 .50
❑ 47 Anthony Thomas .75 .30
❑ 48 Travis Henry .75 .30
❑ 49 Jerome Bettis 1.25 .50
❑ 50 Fred Taylor 1.25 .50
❑ 51 Corey Dillon .75 .30
❑ 52 Jamal Lewis 1.25 .50
❑ 53 William Green .75 .30
❑ 54 Brian Urlacher 2.00 .75
❑ 55 Junior Seau 1.25 .50
❑ 56 Ray Lewis 1.25 .50
❑ 57 Julius Peppers 1.25 .50
❑ 58 Terrell Owens 1.25 .50
❑ 59 David Boston .75 .30
❑ 60 Isaac Bruce 1.25 .50
❑ 61 Marvin Harrison 1.25 .50
❑ 62 Chris Chambers 1.25 .50
❑ 63 Chad Johnson 1.25 .50
❑ 64 Peter Warrick .75 .30
❑ 65 Peerless Price .75 .30
❑ 66 Antonio Bryant .75 .30
❑ 67 Laveranues Coles .75 .30
❑ 68 Rod Gardner .75 .30
❑ 69 Hines Ward 1.25 .50
❑ 70 Plaxico Burress .75 .30
❑ 71 Keyshawn Johnson 1.25 .50
❑ 72 Jabar Gaffney .75 .30
❑ 73 Eric Moulds .75 .30
❑ 74 Santana Moss .75 .30
❑ 75 Koren Robinson .75 .30
❑ 76 Jimmy Smith .75 .30
❑ 77 Donte Stallworth 1.25 .50
❑ 78 Kevin Johnson .75 .30
❑ 79 Quincy Morgan .75 .30
❑ 80 Jerry Rice 2.50 1.00
❑ 81 Tim Brown 1.25 .50
❑ 82 Rod Smith .75 .30
❑ 83 Ashley Lelie 1.25 .50
❑ 84 Randy Moss 2.00 .75
❑ 85 Torry Holt 1.25 .50
❑ 86 Troy Brown .75 .30
❑ 87 Donald Driver .75 .30
❑ 88 Todd Heap .75 .30
❑ 89 Tony Gonzalez .75 .30
❑ 90 Jeremy Shockey 2.00 .75
❑ 91 Casey Moore RC 5.00 2.00
❑ 92 Chris Crocker RC 4.00 1.50
❑ 93 Pisa Tinoisamoa RC 6.00 2.50
❑ 94 Nnamdi Asomugha RC 5.00 2.00
❑ 95 Tyler Brayton RC 6.00 2.50
❑ 96 Eddie Moore RC 5.00 2.00
❑ 97 Terrence Kiel RC 6.00 2.50
❑ 98 Casey Fitzsimmons RC 6.00 2.50
❑ 99 George Foster RC 4.00 1.50
❑ 100 J.J. Moses RC 5.00 2.00
❑ 101 Dan Klecko RC 6.00 2.50
❑ 102 Terry Pierce RC 5.00 2.00
❑ 103 Brad Pyatt RC 5.00 2.00
❑ 104 Boss Bailey RC 6.00 2.50
❑ 105 Michael Haynes RC 6.00 2.50
❑ 106 Jimmy Kennedy RC 6.00 2.50
❑ 107 Jerome McDougle RC 6.00 2.50
❑ 108 William Joseph RC 6.00 2.50
❑ 109 Visanthe Shiancoe RC 5.00 2.00
❑ 110 L.J. Smith RC 6.00 2.50
❑ 111 Avon Cobourne RC 4.00 1.50
❑ 112 Bennie Joppru RC 6.00 2.50
❑ 113 Ken Hamlin RC 6.00 2.50
❑ 114 Jeremi Johnson RC 5.00 2.00
❑ 115 Justin Griffith RC 5.00 2.00
❑ 116 Joffrey Reynolds RC 4.00 1.50
❑ 117 Kassim Osgood RC 6.00 2.50
❑ 118 Donald Lee RC 5.00 2.00
❑ 119 Denero Marriott RC 4.00 1.50
❑ 120 Jamal Burke RC 4.00 1.50
❑ 121 Michael Vick SS 25.00 10.00
❑ 122 Donovan McNabb SS 12.00 5.00
❑ 123 Jerry Rice SS 20.00 7.50
❑ 124 Brett Favre SS 25.00 10.00
❑ 125 Kurt Warner SS 10.00 4.00
❑ 126 Marshall Faulk SS 10.00 4.00
❑ 127 Ricky Williams SS 10.00 4.00
❑ 128 Emmitt Smith SS 25.00 10.00
❑ 129 Tom Brady SS 25.00 10.00
❑ 130 Randy Moss SS 15.00 6.00
❑ 131 LaDainian Tomlinson SS 10.00 4.00
❑ 132 Jeff Garcia SS 10.00 4.00
❑ 133 Brian Urlacher SS 15.00 6.00
❑ 134 Drew Bledsoe SS 10.00 4.00
❑ 135 Peyton Manning SS 15.00 6.00
❑ 136 Dave Ragone RC 8.00 3.00
❑ 137 Brian St.Pierre RC 8.00 3.00
❑ 138 Kliff Kingsbury RC 6.00 2.50
❑ 139 Marquel Blackwell RC 4.00 1.50
❑ 140 Brett Engemann RC 4.00 1.50
❑ 141 Kirk Farmer RC 4.00 1.50
❑ 142 Andrew Pinnock RC 6.00 2.50
❑ 143 Tony Romo RC 8.00 3.00
❑ 144 Nate Hybl RC 8.00 3.00
❑ 145 Ken Dorsey RC 8.00 3.00
❑ 146 Brock Forsey RC 8.00 3.00
❑ 147 Musa Smith RC 8.00 3.00
❑ 148 Domanick Davis RC 12.00 5.00
❑ 149 LaBrandon Toefield RC 8.00 3.00
❑ 150 B.J. Askew RC 8.00 3.00
❑ 151 Quentin Griffin RC 8.00 3.00
❑ 152 Ahmaad Galloway RC 6.00 2.50
❑ 153 Cecil Sapp RC 6.00 2.50
❑ 154 Justin Fargas RC 8.00 3.00
❑ 155 Sultan McCullough RC 6.00 2.50
❑ 156 Malaefou MacKenzie RC 4.00 1.50
❑ 157 Tom Lopienski RC 6.00 2.50
❑ 158 Lee Suggs RC 15.00 6.00
❑ 159 Richard Angulo RC 6.00 2.50
❑ 160 Dwone Hicks RC 4.00 1.50
❑ 161 Nate Burleson RC 10.00 4.00
❑ 162 Billy McMullen RC 6.00 2.50
❑ 163 David Tyree RC 6.00 2.50
❑ 164 Gerald Hayes RC 4.00 1.50
❑ 165 Anthony Adams RC 6.00 2.50
❑ 166 George Wrighster RC 6.00 2.50
❑ 167 Tyrone Calico RC 10.00 4.00
❑ 168 Shaun McDonald RC 8.00 3.00
❑ 169 Bobby Wade RC 8.00 3.00
❑ 170 Larry Johnson RC 30.00 15.00
❑ 171 Ryan Hoag RC 4.00 1.50
❑ 172 Doug Gabriel RC 8.00 3.00
❑ 173 Antonio Gates RC 50.00 30.00
❑ 174 Brandon Lloyd RC 10.00 4.00
❑ 175 Arnaz Battle RC 8.00 3.00
❑ 176 Kelley Washington RC 8.00 3.00
❑ 177 Antwone Savage RC 4.00 1.50
❑ 178 Keenan Howry RC 8.00 3.00
❑ 179 Adrian Madise RC 6.00 2.50
❑ 180 LaTarence Dunbar RC 6.00 2.50
❑ 181 Walter Young RC 4.00 1.50
❑ 182 Travaris Robinson RC 4.00 1.50
❑ 183 DeAndrew Rubin RC 4.00 1.50
❑ 184 Carl Ford RC 4.00 1.50
❑ 185 Zuriel Smith RC 4.00 1.50
❑ 186 Willie Ponder RC 5.00 2.00
❑ 187 Gibran Hamdan RC 5.00 2.00
❑ 188 Aaron Moorehead RC 10.00 4.00
❑ 189 Nick Barnett RC 15.00 6.00
❑ 190 Chris Brown RC 12.00 5.00
❑ 191 ReShard Lee RC 10.00 4.00
❑ 192 Anquan Boldin RC 25.00 10.00
❑ 193 Kevin Curtis RC 10.00 4.00
❑ 194 Taylor Jacobs RC 8.00 3.00
❑ 195 Sam Aiken RC 8.00 3.00
❑ 196 Aaron Walker RC 8.00 3.00
❑ 197 Mike Seidman RC 5.00 2.00
❑ 198 Jason Witten RC 15.00 6.00
❑ 199 Dallas Clark RC 10.00 4.00
❑ 200 Rashean Mathis RC 8.00 3.00
❑ 201 DeWayne Robertson RC 10.00 4.00
❑ 202 Johnathan Sullivan RC 8.00 3.00
❑ 203 Drayton Florence RC 5.00 2.00
❑ 204 Sammy Davis RC 10.00 4.00
❑ 205 Andre Woolfolk RC 10.00 4.00
❑ 206 Terence Newman RC 20.00 7.50
❑ 207 Mike Doss RC 10.00 4.00
❑ 208 Troy Polamalu RC 30.00 15.00
❑ 209 Terrell Suggs RC 15.00 6.00
❑ 210 Marcus Trufant RC 10.00 4.00
❑ 211 Seneca Wallace RC 15.00 6.00
❑ 212 Brooks Bollinger RC 15.00 6.00
❑ 213 Jason Gesser RC 15.00 6.00
❑ 214 Onterrio Smith RC 15.00 6.00
❑ 215 Artose Pinner RC 15.00 6.00
❑ 216 J.R. Tolver RC 12.00 5.00
❑ 217 Kerry Carter RC 12.00 5.00
❑ 218 Tony Hollings RC 15.00 6.00
❑ 219 Teyo Johnson RC 15.00 6.00
❑ 220 Bethel Johnson RC 15.00 6.00
❑ 221 Rex Grossman RC 30.00 12.50
❑ 222 Andre Johnson RC 40.00 15.00
❑ 223 Terrence Edwards RC 12.00 5.00
❑ 224 Willis McGahee RC 40.00 15.00
❑ 225 Charles Rogers RC 15.00 6.00
❑ 226 Chris Simms AU RC 50.00 30.00
❑ 227 Bryant Johnson AU RC 25.00 10.00
❑ 228 Byron Leftwich AU RC 80.00 30.00
❑ 229 Carson Palmer AU RC 120.00 70.00
❑ 230 Justin Gage AU RC 25.00 10.00
❑ 231 Kyle Boller AU RC 40.00 15.00

2004 Sweet Spot

❑ COMP.SET w/o SP's (100) 30.00 15.00
❑ 101-112 LEGENDS/2499 STATED ODDS 1:12
❑ 113-175 RC PRINT RUN 1299 SER.#'d SETS
❑ 176-210 RC PRINT RUN 999 SER.#'d SETS
❑ 211-230 RC PRINT RUN 499 SER.#'d SETS
❑ CARD #258 NOT RELEASED
❑ EXCH EXPIRATION: 1/7/2008
❑ 1 Anquan Boldin 1.25 .50
❑ 2 Emmitt Smith 2.50 1.00
❑ 3 Josh McCown .75 .30
❑ 4 Michael Vick 2.50 1.00
❑ 5 Warrick Dunn .75 .30
❑ 6 Peerless Price .75 .30
❑ 7 Jamal Lewis 1.25 .50
❑ 8 Deion Sanders 1.25 .50
❑ 9 Kyle Boller 1.25 .50
❑ 10 Drew Bledsoe 1.25 .50
❑ 11 Travis Henry .75 .30
❑ 12 Eric Moulds .75 .30
❑ 13 Jake Delhomme 1.25 .50
❑ 14 Stephen Davis .75 .30
❑ 15 Julius Peppers 1.25 .50
❑ 16 Thomas Jones .75 .30
❑ 17 Rex Grossman 1.25 .50
❑ 18 Brian Urlacher 1.50 .60
❑ 19 Carson Palmer 1.50 .60
❑ 20 Chad Johnson 1.25 .50
❑ 21 Rudi Johnson .75 .30
❑ 22 Jeff Garcia 1.25 .50
❑ 23 William Green .75 .30
❑ 24 Andre Davis .50 .20
❑ 25 Vinny Testaverde .75 .30
❑ 26 Eddie George .75 .30
❑ 27 Keyshawn Johnson .75 .30
❑ 28 Reuben Droughns .75 .30
❑ 29 Jake Plummer .75 .30
❑ 30 Ashley Lelie .75 .30
❑ 31 Rod Smith .75 .30
❑ 32 Joey Harrington 1.25 .50
❑ 33 Artose Pinner .50 .20
❑ 34 Az-Zahir Hakim .50 .20
❑ 35 Brett Favre 3.00 1.25
❑ 36 Javon Walker .75 .30
❑ 37 Ahman Green 1.25 .50
❑ 38 Andre Johnson 1.25 .50
❑ 39 David Carr 1.25 .50
❑ 40 Domanick Davis 1.25 .50
❑ 41 Peyton Manning 2.00 .75
❑ 42 Edgerrin James 1.25 .50
❑ 43 Marvin Harrison 1.25 .50

❑ 44 Byron Leftwich 1.50 .60
❑ 45 Fred Taylor .75 .30
❑ 46 Jimmy Smith .75 .30
❑ 47 Priest Holmes 1.50 .60
❑ 48 Trent Green .75 .30
❑ 49 Dante Hall 1.25 .50
❑ 50 Tony Gonzalez .75 .30
❑ 51 Randy McMichael .50 .20
❑ 52 Jay Fiedler .50 .20
❑ 53 Chris Chambers .75 .30
❑ 54 Randy Moss 1.50 .60
❑ 55 Daunte Culpepper 1.25 .50
❑ 56 Onterrio Smith .75 .30
❑ 57 Tom Brady 3.00 1.25
❑ 58 Deion Branch 1.25 .50
❑ 59 Corey Dillon .75 .30
❑ 60 Deuce McAllister 1.25 .50
❑ 61 Aaron Brooks .75 .30
❑ 62 Joe Horn .75 .30
❑ 63 Jeremy Shockey 1.25 .50
❑ 64 Tiki Barber 1.25 .50
❑ 65 Michael Strahan .75 .30
❑ 66 Curtis Martin 1.25 .50
❑ 67 Chad Pennington 1.25 .50
❑ 68 Santana Moss .75 .30
❑ 69 Charles Woodson .75 .30
❑ 70 Kerry Collins .75 .30
❑ 71 Warren Sapp .75 .30
❑ 72 Donovan McNabb 1.50 .60
❑ 73 Brian Westbrook .75 .30
❑ 74 Terrell Owens 1.25 .50
❑ 75 Hines Ward 1.25 .50
❑ 76 Plaxico Burress .75 .30
❑ 77 Duce Staley .75 .30
❑ 78 LaDainian Tomlinson 1.50 .60
❑ 79 Antonio Gates 1.25 .50
❑ 80 Drew Brees 1.25 .50
❑ 81 Eric Johnson .75 .30
❑ 82 Kevan Barlow .75 .30
❑ 83 Tim Rattay .50 .20
❑ 84 Matt Hasselbeck .75 .30
❑ 85 Shaun Alexander 1.25 .50
❑ 86 Jerry Rice 2.50 1.00
❑ 87 Marc Bulger 1.25 .50
❑ 88 Torry Holt 1.25 .50
❑ 89 Marshall Faulk 1.25 .50
❑ 90 Isaac Bruce .75 .30
❑ 91 Brad Johnson .75 .30
❑ 92 Derrick Brooks .75 .30
❑ 93 Joey Galloway .75 .30
❑ 94 Steve McNair 1.25 .50
❑ 95 Derrick Mason .75 .30
❑ 96 Chris Brown 1.25 .50
❑ 97 Clinton Portis 1.25 .50
❑ 98 Mark Brunell .75 .30
❑ 99 Laveranues Coles .75 .30
❑ 100 LaVar Arrington 2.50 1.00
❑ 101 Roger Staubach 8.00 3.00
❑ 102 Troy Aikman 6.00 2.50
❑ 103 John Elway 10.00 4.00
❑ 104 Barry Sanders 10.00 4.00
❑ 105 Fran Tarkenton 6.00 2.50
❑ 106 Archie Manning 6.00 2.50
❑ 107 Joe Namath 8.00 3.00
❑ 108 Ken Stabler 6.00 2.50
❑ 109 Howie Long 6.00 2.50
❑ 110 Kellen Winslow Sr. 5.00 2.00
❑ 111 Joe Montana 15.00 6.00
❑ 112 Joe Theismann 5.00 2.00
❑ 113 Darnell Dockett RC 6.00 2.50
❑ 114 Randy Starks RC 6.00 2.50
❑ 115 Rashad Baker RC 8.00 3.00
❑ 116 Tim Anderson RC 8.00 3.00
❑ 117 Darrion Scott RC 8.00 3.00
❑ 118 Courtney Watson RC 8.00 3.00
❑ 119 Gilbert Gardner RC 6.00 2.50
❑ 120 Marquis Cooper RC 6.00 2.50
❑ 121 Caleb Miller RC 6.00 2.50
❑ 122 Jeff Shoate RC 4.00 1.50
❑ 123 Keyaron Fox RC 6.00 2.50
❑ 124 Landon Johnson RC 6.00 2.50
❑ 125 Reggie Torbor RC 6.00 2.50
❑ 126 Demorrio Williams RC 8.00 3.00
❑ 127 Niko Koutouvides RC 6.00 2.50
❑ 128 Richard Seigler RC 6.00 2.50
❑ 129 Brandon Chillar RC 6.00 2.50
❑ 130 Nate Kaeding RC 8.00 3.00
❑ 131 Dave Ball RC 4.00 1.50
❑ 132 Josh Thomas RC 8.00 3.00
❑ 133 Josh Scobee RC 4.00 1.50
❑ 134 Wes Welker RC 8.00 3.00
❑ 135 Darrell McClover RC 6.00 2.50
❑ 136 Ben Utecht RC 4.00 1.50
❑ 137 Chris Snee RC 6.00 2.50
❑ 138 Jake Grove RC 4.00 1.50
❑ 139 Justin Smiley RC 8.00 3.00
❑ 140 Max Starks RC 6.00 2.50
❑ 141 Randall Gay RC 12.00 6.00
❑ 142 Charlie Anderson RC 4.00 1.50
❑ 143 Alain Kashama RC 8.00 3.00
❑ 144 Eric Edwards RC 10.00 4.00
❑ 145 Jacques Reeves RC 6.00 2.50
❑ 146 Jarrett Payton RC 10.00 4.00
❑ 147 Curtis Deloatch RC 6.00 2.50
❑ 148 Michael Gaines RC 6.00 2.50
❑ 149 Erik Jensen RC 6.00 2.50
❑ 150 Courtney Anderson RC 6.00 2.50
❑ 151 Bruce Thornton RC 4.00 1.50
❑ 152 Glenn Earl RC 6.00 2.50
❑ 153 Michael Waddell RC 4.00 1.50
❑ 154 J.R. Reed RC 6.00 2.50
❑ 155 Dwight Anderson RC 8.00 3.00
❑ 156 Von Hutchins RC 6.00 2.50
❑ 157 Travis LaBoy RC 8.00 3.00
❑ 158 Terry Johnson RC 6.00 2.50
❑ 159 Dwan Edwards RC 4.00 1.50
❑ 160 Colby Bockwoldt RC 8.00 3.00
❑ 161 Madieu Williams RC 6.00 2.50
❑ 162 Will Poole RC 8.00 3.00
❑ 163 Igor Olshansky RC 8.00 3.00
❑ 164 Michael Boulware RC 8.00 3.00
❑ 165 Shaun Phillips RC 6.00 2.50
❑ 166 Keith Smith RC 6.00 2.50
❑ 167 Will Smith RC 8.00 3.00
❑ 168 D.J. Williams RC 10.00 4.00
❑ 169 Derrick Strait RC 8.00 3.00
❑ 170 Karlos Dansby RC 8.00 3.00
❑ 171 Ricardo Colclough RC 8.00 3.00
❑ 172 Chad Lavalais RC 6.00 2.50
❑ 173 Teddy Lehman RC 8.00 3.00
❑ 174 Jim Sorgi RC 8.00 3.00
❑ 175 Bob Sanders RC 20.00 10.00
❑ 176 Sean Taylor RC 12.00 5.00
❑ 177 Marcus Tubbs RC 10.00 4.00
❑ 178 Daryl Smith RC 10.00 4.00
❑ 179 Bradlee Van Pelt RC 15.00 6.00
❑ 180 Shawntae Spencer RC 10.00 4.00
❑ 181 Nathan Vasher RC 12.00 5.00
❑ 182 Jared Allen RC 12.00 5.00
❑ 183 Rod Davis RC 5.00 2.00
❑ 184 Brian Jones RC 8.00 3.00
❑ 185 Will Allen RC 10.00 4.00
❑ 186 Antwan Odom RC 10.00 4.00
❑ 187 Vernon Carey RC 8.00 3.00
❑ 188 Mike Karney RC 8.00 3.00
❑ 189 Joey Thomas RC 10.00 4.00
❑ 190 Casey Bramlet RC 8.00 3.00
❑ 191 Keiwan Ratliff RC 8.00 3.00
❑ 192 Rich Gardner RC 8.00 3.00
❑ 193 Jason Babin RC 10.00 4.00
❑ 194 Dontarrious Thomas RC 10.00 4.00
❑ 195 Dexter Reid RC 5.00 2.00
❑ 196 Marquise Hill RC 8.00 3.00
❑ 197 Jonathan Smith RC 8.00 3.00
❑ 198 Larry Croom RC 8.00 3.00
❑ 199 Gibril Wilson RC 10.00 4.00
❑ 200 Erik Coleman RC 10.00 4.00
❑ 201 B.J. Sams RC 10.00 4.00
❑ 202 Bruce Perry RC 10.00 4.00
❑ 203 Brock Lesnar RC 15.00 6.00
❑ 204 Brandon Miree RC 8.00 3.00
❑ 205 Clarence Moore RC 10.00 4.00
❑ 206 Mark Jones RC 8.00 3.00
❑ 207 Patrick Crayton RC 10.00 4.00
❑ 208 Jeff Dugan RC 5.00 2.00
❑ 209 Sean Ryan RC 8.00 3.00
❑ 210 Sloan Thomas RC 8.00 3.00
❑ 211 Triandos Luke RC 12.00 5.00
❑ 212 Dexter Wynn RC 10.00 4.00
❑ 213 Matt Kranchick RC 12.00 5.00
❑ 214 Tim Euhus RC 12.00 5.00
❑ 215 Ryan Krause RC 10.00 4.00
❑ 216 Junior Siavii RC 12.00 5.00
❑ 217 Ran Carthon RC 10.00 4.00
❑ 218 Derrick Pope RC 10.00 4.00
❑ 219 Alex Lewis RC 12.00 5.00
❑ 220 Chris Cooley RC 12.00 5.00
❑ 221 Jamaar Taylor RC 12.00 5.00
❑ 222 Stuart Schweigert RC 12.00 5.00
❑ 223 Jason David RC 12.00 5.00
❑ 224 Maurice Mann RC 10.00 4.00
❑ 225 Robert Geathers RC 10.00 4.00
❑ 226 Matt Mauck RC 12.00 5.00
❑ 227 Jammal Lord RC 12.00 5.00
❑ 228 Travelle Wharton RC 6.00 2.50
❑ 229 D.J. Hackett RC 10.00 4.00
❑ 230 Thomas Tapeh RC 10.00 4.00
❑ 231 D.Robinson AU/699 RC EXCH 25.00 10.00
❑ 232 Ahmad Carroll AU/699 RC 25.00 10.00
❑ 233 Kenechi Udeze AU/699 RC 20.00 7.50
❑ 234 Tommie Harris AU/699 RC 20.00 7.50
❑ 235 Jonathan Vilma AU/699 RC 30.00 12.50
❑ 236 Vince Wilfork AU/699 RC 25.00 10.00
❑ 237 B.J. Symons AU/699 RC 20.00 7.50
❑ 238 B.J. Johnson AU/699 RC 15.00 6.00
❑ 239 Kris Wilson AU/699 RC 20.00 7.50
❑ 240 Josh Harris AU/699 RC 20.00 7.50
❑ 241 Troy Fleming AU/699 RC 15.00 6.00
❑ 242 J.Morant AU/699 RC 20.00 7.50
❑ 243 Craig Krenzel AU/699 RC 20.00 7.50
❑ 244 Q.Wilson AU/699 RC EXCH 15.00 6.00
❑ 245 P.K. Sam AU/699 RC 15.00 6.00
❑ 246 Michael Turner AU/699 RC 20.00 7.50
❑ 247 Carlos Francis AU/699 RC 20.00 7.50
❑ 248 Jared Lorenzen AU/699 RC 15.00 6.00
❑ 249 John Navarre AU/675 RC 20.00 7.50
❑ 250 Jeff Smoker AU/699 RC 20.00 7.50
❑ 251 Ernest Wilford AU/559 RC 20.00 7.50
❑ 252 Mew.Moore AU/699 RC 25.00 12.50
❑ 253 Chris Gamble AU/699 RC 25.00 10.00
❑ 254 Jerricho Cotchery AU/699 RC 20.00 7.50
❑ 255 Derrick Hamilton AU/699 RC 20.00 7.50
❑ 256 Samie Parker AU/699 RC 20.00 7.50
❑ 257 Cody Pickett AU/699 RC 25.00 10.00
❑ 259 Ben Hartsock AU/699 RC 20.00 7.50
❑ 260 Cedric Cobbs AU/699 RC 20.00 7.50
❑ 261 Matt Schaub AU/699 RC 40.00 15.00
❑ 262 Bernard Berrian AU/699 RC 20.00 7.50
❑ 263 Devard Darling AU/699 RC 20.00 7.50
❑ 264 Ben Watson AU/699 RC 20.00 7.50
❑ 265 Darius Watts AU/699 RC 20.00 7.50
❑ 266 DeAngelo Hall AU/399 RC 25.00 10.00
❑ 267 Ben Troupe AU/699 RC 20.00 7.50
❑ 268 Michael Jenkins AU/399 RC 25.00 10.00
❑ 269 Keary Colbert AU/699 RC 25.00 10.00
❑ 270 Robert Gallery AU/699 RC 25.00 10.00
❑ 271 Greg Jones AU/650 RC 25.00 12.50
❑ 272 Mic.Clayton AU/699 RC 50.00 20.00
❑ 273 Luke McCown AU/699 RC 20.00 7.50
❑ 274 Ras.Woods AU/699 RC 20.00 7.50
❑ 275 Reg.Williams AU/699 RC 25.00 10.00
❑ 276 Dev.Henderson AU/699 RC 15.00 6.00
❑ 277 Tatum Bell AU/699 RC 40.00 15.00
❑ 278 Lee Evans AU/350 RC 40.00 20.00
❑ 279 J.P. Losman AU/199 RC 60.00 30.00
❑ 280 Drew Henson AU/199 RC 40.00 15.00
❑ 281 Kel.Winslow AU/125 RC 60.00 30.00
❑ 282 Chris Perry AU/199 RC 50.00 20.00
❑ 283 Julius Jones AU/199 RC 120.00 60.00
❑ 284 Stev.Jackson AU/199 RC 100.00 50.00
❑ 285 Kevin Jones AU/199 RC 100.00 40.00
❑ 286 Roy Williams AU/149 RC 100.00 40.00
❑ 287 Roethlis AU/199 RC 250.00 125.00
❑ 288 Philip Rivers AU/199 RC 100.00 50.00
❑ 289 L.Fitzgerald AU/150 RC 100.00 50.00
❑ 290 Eli Manning AU/150 RC 200.00 100.00

2005 Sweet Spot

❑ COMP.SET w/o RCs (100) 30.00 15.00
❑ 101-142 PRINT RUN 899 SER.#'d SETS
❑ 143-182 PRINT RUN 699 SER.#'d SETS
❑ 183-222 PRINT RUN 499 SER.#'d SETS
❑ 223-242 PRINT RUN 299 SER.#'d SETS
❑ 285-302 PRINT RUN 899 SER.#'d SETS
❑ EXCH EXPIRATION: 12/9/2008
❑ 1 Larry Fitzgerald 1.25 .50
❑ 2 Anquan Boldin .75 .30
❑ 3 Kurt Warner .75 .30
❑ 4 Michael Vick 2.00 .75
❑ 5 T.J. Duckett .75 .30
❑ 6 Peerless Price .60 .25

❑ 7	Todd Heap	.75	.30
❑ 8	Jamal Lewis	1.25	.50
❑ 9	Kyle Boller	.75	.30
❑ 10	Derrick Mason	.75	.30
❑ 11	J.P. Losman	1.25	.50
❑ 12	Willis McGahee	1.25	.50
❑ 13	Lee Evans	.75	.30
❑ 14	Eric Moulds	.75	.30
❑ 15	Jake Delhomme	1.25	.50
❑ 16	Keary Colbert	.75	.30
❑ 17	DeShaun Foster	.75	.30
❑ 18	Brian Urlacher	1.25	.50
❑ 19	Rex Grossman	.75	.30
❑ 20	Muhsin Muhammad	.75	.30
❑ 21	Carson Palmer	1.25	.50
❑ 22	Rudi Johnson	.75	.30
❑ 23	Chad Johnson	1.25	.50
❑ 24	Julius Jones	1.50	.60
❑ 25	Keyshawn Johnson	.75	.30
❑ 26	Drew Bledsoe	1.25	.50
❑ 27	Tatum Bell	.75	.30
❑ 28	Jake Plummer	.75	.30
❑ 29	Ashley Lelie	.75	.30
❑ 30	Roy Williams WR	1.25	.50
❑ 31	Kevin Jones	1.25	.50
❑ 32	Joey Harrington	1.25	.50
❑ 33	Brett Favre	3.00	1.25
❑ 34	Ahman Green	1.25	.50
❑ 35	Javon Walker	.75	.30
❑ 36	David Carr	1.25	.50
❑ 37	Andre Johnson	.75	.30
❑ 38	Domanick Davis	.75	.30
❑ 39	Peyton Manning	2.00	.75
❑ 40	Reggie Wayne	.75	.30
❑ 41	Edgerrin James	1.25	.50
❑ 42	Marvin Harrison	1.25	.50
❑ 43	Byron Leftwich	1.25	.50
❑ 44	Fred Taylor	.75	.30
❑ 45	Jimmy Smith	.75	.30
❑ 46	Priest Holmes	1.25	.50
❑ 47	Tony Gonzalez	.75	.30
❑ 48	Trent Green	.75	.30
❑ 49	A.J. Feeley	.75	.30
❑ 50	Chris Chambers	.75	.30
❑ 51	Randy McMichael	.60	.25
❑ 52	Daunte Culpepper	1.25	.50
❑ 53	Michael Bennett	.75	.30
❑ 54	Nate Burleson	.75	.30
❑ 55	Tom Brady	3.00	1.25
❑ 56	Corey Dillon	.75	.30
❑ 57	Deion Branch	.75	.30
❑ 58	Richard Seymour	.60	.25
❑ 59	Aaron Brooks	.75	.30
❑ 60	Deuce McAllister	1.25	.50
❑ 61	Joe Horn	.75	.30
❑ 62	Eli Manning	2.50	1.00
❑ 63	Jeremy Shockey	1.25	.50
❑ 64	Tiki Barber	1.25	.50
❑ 65	Chad Pennington	1.25	.50
❑ 66	Curtis Martin	1.25	.50
❑ 67	Laveranues Coles	.75	.30
❑ 68	Kerry Collins	.75	.30
❑ 69	LaMont Jordan	1.25	.50
❑ 70	Randy Moss	1.25	.50
❑ 71	Donovan McNabb	1.50	.60
❑ 72	Terrell Owens	1.25	.50
❑ 73	Jeremiah Trotter	.60	.25
❑ 74	Brian Westbrook	.75	.30
❑ 75	Ben Roethlisberger	3.00	1.25
❑ 76	Willie Parker	10.00	4.00
❑ 77	Hines Ward	1.25	.50
❑ 78	Antwaan Randle El	.75	.30
❑ 79	Drew Brees	1.25	.50
❑ 80	LaDainian Tomlinson	1.50	.60
❑ 81	Antonio Gates	1.25	.50
❑ 82	Tim Rattay	.60	.25
❑ 83	Brandon Lloyd	.60	.25
❑ 84	Eric Johnson	.75	.30
❑ 85	Shaun Alexander	1.50	.60
❑ 86	Darrell Jackson	.75	.30
❑ 87	Matt Hasselbeck	.75	.30
❑ 88	Marc Bulger	1.25	.50
❑ 89	Steven Jackson	1.50	.60
❑ 90	Marshall Faulk	1.25	.50
❑ 91	Torry Holt	1.25	.50
❑ 92	Joey Galloway	.75	.30
❑ 93	Brian Griese	.75	.30
❑ 94	Michael Clayton	1.25	.50
❑ 95	Steve McNair	1.25	.50
❑ 96	Drew Bennett	.75	.30
❑ 97	Chris Brown	.75	.30
❑ 98	Clinton Portis	1.25	.50
❑ 99	Patrick Ramsey	.75	.30
❑ 100	Santana Moss	.75	.30
❑ 101	Antonio Perkins RC	5.00	2.00
❑ 102	James Sanders RC	6.00	2.50
❑ 103	Justin Green RC	6.00	2.50
❑ 104	Andre Maddox RC	5.00	2.00
❑ 105	C.C. Brown RC	5.00	2.00
❑ 106	Michael Hawkins RC	5.00	2.00
❑ 107	Deandra Cobb RC	5.00	2.00
❑ 108	Nehemiah Broughton RC	5.00	2.00
❑ 109	Madison Hedgecock RC	6.00	2.50
❑ 110	Paris Warren RC	5.00	2.00
❑ 111	Chris Harris RC	12.00	5.00
❑ 112	Matt Cassel RC	10.00	4.00
❑ 113	Justin Beriault RC	5.00	2.00
❑ 114	Roydell Williams RC	6.00	2.50
❑ 115	Alex Barron RC	3.00	1.25
❑ 116	Jammal Brown RC	6.00	2.50
❑ 117	Bo Scaife RC	5.00	2.00
❑ 118	Patrick Estes RC	5.00	2.00
❑ 119	Elton Brown RC	3.00	1.25
❑ 120	Rasheed Marshall RC	6.00	2.50
❑ 121	Jovan Haye RC	5.00	2.00
❑ 122	Nick Collins RC	6.00	2.50
❑ 123	Travis Daniels RC	5.00	2.00
❑ 124	Reynaldo Hill RC	8.00	3.00
❑ 125	Billy Bajema RC	5.00	2.00
❑ 126	Jim Leonhard RC	10.00	4.00
❑ 127	Boomer Grigsby RC	8.00	3.00
❑ 128	Chauncey Davis RC	6.00	2.50
❑ 129	David McMillan RC	10.00	4.00
❑ 130	Alfred Fincher RC	5.00	2.00
❑ 131	Kelvin Hayden RC	5.00	2.00
❑ 132	Kevin Burnett RC	6.00	2.50
❑ 133	Jonathan Welsh RC	5.00	2.00
❑ 134	Stanley Wilson RC	5.00	2.00
❑ 135	Stanford Routt RC	5.00	2.00
❑ 136	Kerry Rhodes RC	6.00	2.50
❑ 137	Ellis Hobbs RC	6.00	2.50
❑ 138	Darrent Williams RC	6.00	2.50
❑ 139	Eric King RC	5.00	2.00
❑ 140	Domonique Foxworth RC	6.00	2.50
❑ 141	Anthony Bryant RC	6.00	2.50
❑ 142	Scott Starks RC	5.00	2.00
❑ 143	Marviel Underwood RC	5.00	2.00
❑ 144	Mike Montgomery RC	8.00	3.00
❑ 145	Kevin Vickerson RC	10.00	4.00
❑ 146	Jerome Carter RC	5.00	2.00
❑ 147	Jay Ratliff RC	6.00	2.50
❑ 148	Damien Nash RC	5.00	2.00
❑ 149	Noah Herron RC	6.00	2.50
❑ 150	Jonathan Fanene RC	5.00	2.00
❑ 151	Chase Lyman RC	5.00	2.00
❑ 152	Adam Seward RC	10.00	4.00
❑ 153	Michael Boley RC	5.00	2.00
❑ 154	Pat Thomas RC	5.00	2.00
❑ 155	Evan Mathis RC	6.00	2.50
❑ 156	Derrick Johnson CB RC	6.00	2.50
❑ 157	Tab Perry RC	6.00	2.50
❑ 158	Joel Dreessen RC	5.00	2.00
❑ 159	Daven Holly RC	6.00	2.50
❑ 160	Brandon Jones RC	6.00	2.50
❑ 161	Dan Buenning RC	8.00	3.00
❑ 162	Kurt Campbell RC	5.00	2.00
❑ 163	Kerry Wright RC	5.00	2.00
❑ 164	Matt McCoy RC	5.00	2.00
❑ 165	Dave Rayner RC	5.00	2.00
❑ 166	Kirk Morrison RC	6.00	2.50
❑ 167	Lofa Tatupu RC	8.00	3.00
❑ 168	Bryant McFadden RC	6.00	2.50
❑ 169	Corey Webster RC	6.00	2.50
❑ 170	Eric Green RC	5.00	2.00
❑ 171	Fabian Washington RC	6.00	2.50
❑ 172	Donte Nicholson RC	6.00	2.50
❑ 173	Vonta Leach RC	6.00	2.50
❑ 174	Ronald Bartell RC	5.00	2.00
❑ 175	Sean Considine RC	6.00	2.50
❑ 176	Oshiomogho Atogwe RC	5.00	2.00
❑ 177	Ryan Grant RC	6.00	2.50
❑ 178	James Butler RC	5.00	2.00
❑ 179	Paul Ernster RC	5.00	2.00
❑ 180	Duke Preston RC	8.00	3.00
❑ 181	Mike Nugent RC	6.00	2.50
❑ 182	Sione Pouha RC	6.00	2.50
❑ 183	Geoff Hangartner RC	20.00	7.50
❑ 184	Justin Geisinger RC	20.00	7.50
❑ 185	Chris Kemoeatu RC	20.00	10.00
❑ 186	Ryan Fitzpatrick RC	12.00	5.00
❑ 187	Lionel Gates RC	6.00	2.50
❑ 188	Brandon Jacobs RC	10.00	4.00
❑ 189	Alvin Pearman RC	8.00	3.00
❑ 190	J.R. Russell RC	6.00	2.50
❑ 191	Manuel White RC	6.00	2.50
❑ 192	Tyson Thompson RC	10.00	4.00
❑ 193	Chad Owens RC	8.00	3.00
❑ 194	Dante Ridgeway RC	6.00	2.50
❑ 195	Stephen Spach RC	6.00	2.50
❑ 196	Scott Mruczkowski RC	15.00	6.00
❑ 197	Chris Carr RC	10.00	4.00
❑ 198	Jonathan Babineaux RC	6.00	2.50
❑ 199	Will Whitticker RC	15.00	6.00
❑ 200	Luis Castillo RC	8.00	3.00
❑ 201	Matt Roth RC	8.00	3.00
❑ 202	Shaun Cody RC	8.00	3.00
❑ 203	Justin Tuck RC	8.00	3.00
❑ 204	Vincent Burns RC	6.00	2.50
❑ 205	DeMarcus Ware RC	12.00	5.00
❑ 206	Bill Swancutt RC	6.00	2.50
❑ 207	Darryl Blackstock RC	6.00	2.50
❑ 208	Brady Poppinga RC	8.00	3.00
❑ 209	Leroy Hill RC	8.00	3.00
❑ 210	Ryan Claridge RC	6.00	2.50
❑ 211	Odell Thurman RC	8.00	3.00
❑ 212	Barrett Ruud RC	8.00	3.00
❑ 213	Lance Mitchell RC	6.00	2.50
❑ 214	Trent Cole RC	8.00	3.00
❑ 215	Jerome Mathis RC	8.00	3.00
❑ 216	Brandon Browner RC	6.00	2.50
❑ 217	Justin Miller RC	6.00	2.50
❑ 218	Thomas Davis RC	8.00	3.00
❑ 219	Brodney Pool RC	8.00	3.00
❑ 220	Dylan Gandy RC	6.00	2.50
❑ 221	Josh Bullocks RC	8.00	3.00
❑ 222	Vincent Fuller RC	6.00	2.50
❑ 223	Jordan Beck RC	6.00	2.50
❑ 224	Claude Terrell RC	20.00	7.50
❑ 225	Adrian McPherson RC	8.00	3.00
❑ 226	Jerome Collins RC	6.00	2.50
❑ 227	Cedric Houston RC	8.00	3.00
❑ 228	Daniel Loper RC	25.00	10.00
❑ 229	Adam Bergen RC	8.00	3.00
❑ 230	Jeb Huckeba RC	8.00	3.00
❑ 231	Eric Moore RC	6.00	2.50
❑ 232	Dan Cody RC	8.00	3.00
❑ 233	Alex Smith TE RC	8.00	3.00
❑ 234	Travis Johnson RC	6.00	2.50
❑ 235	Ryan Riddle RC	4.00	1.50
❑ 236	Mike Patterson RC	8.00	3.00
❑ 237	Darrell Shropshire RC	6.00	2.50
❑ 238	David Pollack RC	8.00	3.00
❑ 239	Marcus Spears RC	8.00	3.00
❑ 240	Shawne Merriman RC	12.00	5.00
❑ 241	Channing Crowder RC	8.00	3.00
❑ 242	Derrick Johnson RC	12.00	5.00
❑ 243	Kyle Orton AU/199 RC	40.00	15.00
❑ 244	David Greene AU/650 RC	20.00	7.50
❑ 245	Derek Anderson AU/650 RC	20.00	7.50
❑ 246	Dan Orlovsky AU/650 RC	25.00	10.00
❑ 247	Eric Shelton AU/650 RC	20.00	7.50
❑ 248	Stefan LeFors AU/650 RC	20.00	7.50
❑ 249	Reggie Brown AU/650 RC	25.00	10.00
❑ 250	Andrew Walter AU/650 RC	30.00	12.50

❑ 251 Mark Bradley AU/650 RC 20.00 7.50
❑ 252 Courtney Roby AU/650 RC 20.00 7.50
❑ 253 Vincent Jackson AU/650 RC 20.00 7.50
❑ 254 Terrence Murphy AU/650 RC 20.00 7.50
❑ 255 Marion Barber AU/650 RC 30.00 12.50
❑ 256 Frank Gore AU/650 RC 30.00 12.50
❑ 257 Chris Henry AU/650 RC 25.00 10.00
❑ 258 Heath Miller AU/650 RC 60.00 30.00
❑ 259 Arrington AU/650 RC EXCH 25.00 10.00
❑ 260 A.Rolle AU/650 RC EXCH 20.00 7.50
❑ 261 Fred Gibson AU/650 RC 15.00 6.00
❑ 262 Charlie Frye AU/650 RC 50.00 30.00
❑ 263 Adam Jones AU/650 RC 20.00 7.50
❑ 264 Ciatrick Fason AU/650 RC 20.00 7.50
❑ 265 Roscoe Parrish AU/650 RC 20.00 7.50
❑ 266 Erasmus James AU/650 RC 20.00 7.50
❑ 267 Carlos Rogers AU/650 RC 25.00 10.00
❑ 268 Ryan Moats AU/650 RC 25.00 10.00
❑ 269 Marlin Jackson AU/650 RC 20.00 7.50
❑ 270 Darren Sproles AU/650 RC 20.00 7.50
❑ 271 Maurice Clarett AU/199 25.00 10.00
❑ 272 Jason Campbell AU/199 RC 40.00 25.00
❑ 273 Vernand Morency AU/199 RC 20.00 7.50
❑ 274 M.Clayton AU/199 RC EX 40.00 20.00
❑ 275 Roddy White AU/650 RC 20.00 7.50
❑ 276 Williamson AU/199 RC 40.00 20.00
❑ 277 M.Williams AU/199 EXCH 40.00 20.00
❑ 278 B.Edwards AU/199 RC 80.00 40.00
❑ 279 Cedric Benson AU/199 RC 60.00 30.00
❑ 280 C.Williams AU/199 RC EX 120.00 60.00
❑ 281 Ronnie Brown AU/199 RC 100.00 50.00
❑ 282 Matt Jones AU/199 RC 60.00 30.00
❑ 283 Alex Smith QB AU/175 RC 100.00 50.00
❑ 284 Aaron Rodgers AU/199 RC 80.00 50.00
❑ 285 Rian Wallace RC 5.00 2.00
❑ 286 Nick Speegle RC 5.00 2.00
❑ 287 Chris Spencer RC 6.00 2.50
❑ 288 Logan Mankins RC 8.00 3.00
❑ 289 David Baas RC 5.00 2.00
❑ 290 Michael Roos RC 5.00 2.00
❑ 291 Khalif Barnes RC 5.00 2.00
❑ 292 Matt Giordano RC 6.00 2.50
❑ 293 Rick Razzano RC 6.00 2.50
❑ 294 Trai Essex RC 25.00 12.50
❑ 295 Roy Manning RC 20.00 10.00
❑ 296 Gerald Sensabaugh RC 8.00 3.00
❑ 297 Nick Kaczur RC 12.00 5.00
❑ 298 Ray Willis RC 6.00 2.50
❑ 299 Jason Brown RC 6.00 2.50
❑ 300 Frank Omiyale RC 5.00 2.00
❑ 301 Fred Amey RC 5.00 2.00
❑ 302 Reggie Hodges RC 5.00 2.00

2005 Throwback Threads

❑ COMP.SET w/o SP's (150) 25.00 10.00
❑ 151-200 ROOK.PRINT RUN 999 SER.#'d SETS
❑ ROOKIE JSY ODDS 1:15 HOB, 1:1337 RET

❑ 1 Anquan Boldin .50 .20
❑ 2 Bryant Johnson .40 .15
❑ 3 Josh McCown .50 .20
❑ 4 Larry Fitzgerald .75 .30
❑ 5 Michael Vick 1.25 .50
❑ 6 Warrick Dunn .50 .20
❑ 7 Peerless Price .40 .15
❑ 8 T.J. Duckett .50 .20
❑ 9 Alge Crumpler .50 .20
❑ 10 Jamal Lewis .75 .30
❑ 11 Kyle Boller .50 .20
❑ 12 Todd Heap .50 .20
❑ 13 Ray Lewis .75 .30
❑ 14 J.P. Losman .75 .30
❑ 15 Eric Moulds .50 .20
❑ 16 Josh Reed .40 .15
❑ 17 Lee Evans .50 .20
❑ 18 Willis McGahee .75 .30
❑ 19 DeShaun Foster .50 .20
❑ 20 Jake Delhomme .75 .30
❑ 21 Julius Peppers .50 .20
❑ 22 Muhsin Muhammad .50 .20
❑ 23 Stephen Davis .50 .20
❑ 24 Steve Smith .50 .20
❑ 25 Brian Urlacher .75 .30
❑ 26 David Terrell .50 .20
❑ 27 Rex Grossman .50 .20
❑ 28 Thomas Jones .50 .20
❑ 29 Carson Palmer .75 .30
❑ 30 Chad Johnson .75 .30
❑ 31 Peter Warrick .40 .15
❑ 32 Rudi Johnson .50 .20
❑ 33 Jeff Garcia .50 .20
❑ 34 Kelly Holcomb .40 .15
❑ 35 Kellen Winslow Jr. .75 .30
❑ 36 Lee Suggs .50 .20
❑ 37 William Green .40 .15
❑ 38 Julius Jones 1.00 .40
❑ 39 Drew Bledsoe .75 .30
❑ 40 Roy Williams S .50 .20
❑ 41 Keyshawn Johnson .50 .20
❑ 42 Terence Newman .40 .15
❑ 43 Ashley Lelie .50 .20
❑ 44 Rod Smith .50 .20
❑ 45 Tatum Bell .50 .20
❑ 46 Champ Bailey .50 .20
❑ 47 Darius Watts .50 .20
❑ 48 Jake Plummer .50 .20
❑ 49 Quentin Griffin .50 .20
❑ 50 Charles Rogers .50 .20
❑ 51 Joey Harrington .75 .30
❑ 52 Kevin Jones .75 .30
❑ 53 Roy Williams WR .75 .30
❑ 54 Ahman Green .75 .30
❑ 55 Brett Favre 2.00 .75
❑ 56 Javon Walker .50 .20
❑ 57 Nick Barnett .40 .15
❑ 58 Robert Ferguson .40 .15
❑ 59 Andre Johnson .50 .20
❑ 60 David Carr .75 .30
❑ 61 Domanick Davis .50 .20
❑ 62 Dallas Clark .40 .15
❑ 63 Edgerrin James .75 .30
❑ 64 Marvin Harrison .75 .30
❑ 65 Peyton Manning 1.25 .50
❑ 66 Reggie Wayne .50 .20
❑ 67 Byron Leftwich .75 .30
❑ 68 Jimmy Smith .50 .20
❑ 69 Fred Taylor .50 .20
❑ 70 Reggie Williams .50 .20
❑ 71 Dante Hall .50 .20
❑ 72 Priest Holmes .75 .30
❑ 73 Tony Gonzalez .50 .20
❑ 74 Trent Green .50 .20
❑ 75 Eddie Kennison .40 .15
❑ 76 Chris Chambers .50 .20
❑ 77 Junior Seau .50 .20
❑ 78 Randy McMichael .40 .15
❑ 79 Zach Thomas .75 .30
❑ 80 A.J. Feeley .50 .20
❑ 81 Daunte Culpepper .75 .30
❑ 82 Michael Bennett .50 .20
❑ 83 Nate Burleson .50 .20
❑ 84 Onterrio Smith .50 .20
❑ 85 Corey Dillon .50 .20
❑ 86 Bethel Johnson .40 .15
❑ 87 Deion Branch .50 .20
❑ 88 Tom Brady 2.00 .75
❑ 89 Ty Law .50 .20
❑ 90 Aaron Brooks .50 .20
❑ 91 Deuce McAllister .75 .30
❑ 92 Joe Horn .50 .20
❑ 93 Donte Stallworth .50 .20
❑ 94 Eli Manning 1.50 .60
❑ 95 Ike Hilliard .50 .20
❑ 96 Jeremy Shockey .75 .30
❑ 97 Michael Strahan .50 .20
❑ 98 Tiki Barber .75 .30
❑ 99 Anthony Becht .40 .15
❑ 100 Chad Pennington .75 .30
❑ 101 Curtis Martin .75 .30
❑ 102 John Abraham .40 .15
❑ 103 Justin McCareins .40 .15
❑ 104 Santana Moss .50 .20
❑ 105 Shaun Ellis .40 .15
❑ 106 Kerry Collins .50 .20
❑ 107 Randy Moss .75 .30
❑ 108 Jerry Porter .50 .20
❑ 109 Chad Lewis .40 .15
❑ 110 Donovan McNabb 1.00 .40
❑ 111 Freddie Mitchell .40 .15
❑ 112 Jevon Kearse .50 .20
❑ 113 Terrell Owens .75 .30
❑ 114 Brian Westbrook .50 .20
❑ 115 Antwaan Randle El .50 .20
❑ 116 Ben Roethlisberger 2.00 .75
❑ 117 Duce Staley .50 .20
❑ 118 Hines Ward .75 .30
❑ 119 Jerome Bettis .75 .30
❑ 120 Plaxico Burress .50 .20
❑ 121 Antonio Gates .75 .30
❑ 122 Drew Brees .75 .30
❑ 123 LaDainian Tomlinson 1.00 .40
❑ 124 Kevan Barlow .50 .20
❑ 125 Brandon Lloyd .40 .15
❑ 126 Darrell Jackson .50 .20
❑ 127 Koren Robinson .50 .20
❑ 128 Matt Hasselbeck .50 .20
❑ 129 Shaun Alexander 1.00 .40
❑ 130 Marc Bulger .75 .30
❑ 131 Isaac Bruce .50 .20
❑ 132 Marshall Faulk .75 .30
❑ 133 Steven Jackson 1.00 .40
❑ 134 Torry Holt .75 .30
❑ 135 Michael Clayton .75 .30
❑ 136 Brian Griese .50 .20
❑ 137 Derrick Brooks .50 .20
❑ 138 Mike Alstott .50 .20
❑ 139 Chris Brown .50 .20
❑ 140 Derrick Mason .50 .20
❑ 141 Keith Bulluck .40 .15
❑ 142 Steve McNair .75 .30
❑ 143 Tyrone Calico .50 .20
❑ 144 Drew Bennett .50 .20
❑ 145 Clinton Portis .75 .30
❑ 146 LaVar Arrington .75 .30
❑ 147 Sean Taylor .50 .20
❑ 148 Patrick Ramsey .50 .20
❑ 149 Laveranues Coles .50 .20
❑ 150 Rod Gardner .50 .20
❑ 151 Cedric Benson RC 10.00 4.00
❑ 152 DeMarcus Ware RC 8.00 3.00
❑ 153 Shawne Merriman RC 8.00 3.00
❑ 154 Thomas Davis RC 5.00 2.00
❑ 155 Derrick Johnson RC 8.00 3.00
❑ 156 Travis Johnson RC 4.00 1.50
❑ 157 David Pollack RC 5.00 2.00
❑ 158 Erasmus James RC 5.00 2.00
❑ 159 Marcus Spears RC 5.00 2.00
❑ 160 Fabian Washington RC 5.00 2.00
❑ 161 Marlin Jackson RC 5.00 2.00
❑ 162 Heath Miller RC 12.00 5.00
❑ 163 Shaun Cody RC 5.00 2.00
❑ 164 Dan Cody RC 5.00 2.00
❑ 165 Justin Miller RC 4.00 1.50
❑ 166 Chris Henry RC 5.00 2.00
❑ 167 David Greene RC 5.00 2.00
❑ 168 Brandon Jones RC 5.00 2.00
❑ 169 Marion Barber RC 8.00 3.00
❑ 170 Brandon Jacobs RC 6.00 2.50
❑ 171 Jerome Mathis RC 5.00 2.00
❑ 172 Craphonso Thorpe RC 4.00 1.50
❑ 173 Alvin Pearman RC 5.00 2.00
❑ 174 Darren Sproles RC 5.00 2.00
❑ 175 Fred Gibson RC 4.00 1.50
❑ 176 Roydell Williams RC 5.00 2.00
❑ 177 Airese Currie RC 5.00 2.00
❑ 178 Damien Nash RC 4.00 1.50
❑ 179 Dan Orlovsky RC 6.00 2.50
❑ 180 Adrian McPherson RC 5.00 2.00
❑ 181 Larry Brackins RC 4.00 1.50
❑ 182 Rasheed Marshall RC 5.00 2.00
❑ 183 Cedric Houston RC 5.00 2.00
❑ 184 Chad Owens RC 5.00 2.00
❑ 185 Tab Perry RC 5.00 2.00
❑ 186 Dante Ridgeway RC 4.00 1.50

❑ 187	Craig Bragg RC	4.00	1.50
❑ 188	Deandra Cobb RC	4.00	1.50
❑ 189	Derek Anderson RC	5.00	2.00
❑ 190	Marcus Maxwell RC	4.00	1.50
❑ 191	Paris Warren RC	4.00	1.50
❑ 192	Aaron Rodgers RC	15.00	6.00
❑ 193	James Kilian RC	5.00	2.00
❑ 194	Matt Cassel RC	8.00	3.00
❑ 195	Mike Williams	10.00	4.00
❑ 196	Lionel Gates RC	4.00	1.50
❑ 197	Anthony Davis RC	4.00	1.50
❑ 198	Noah Herron RC	5.00	2.00
❑ 199	Ryan Fitzpatrick RC	8.00	3.00
❑ 200	J.R. Russell RC	4.00	1.50
❑ 201	Adam Jones JSY RC	8.00	3.00
❑ 202	Alex Smith QB JSY RC	20.00	7.50
❑ 203	Antrel Rolle JSY RC	8.00	3.00
❑ 204	Andrew Walter JSY RC	10.00	4.00
❑ 205	Braylon Edwards JSY RC	15.00	6.00
❑ 206	Camell Williams JSY RC	25.00	12.50
❑ 207	Carlos Rogers JSY RC	10.00	4.00
❑ 208	Charlie Frye JSY RC	12.00	5.00
❑ 209	Ciatrick Fason JSY RC	8.00	3.00
❑ 210	Courtney Roby JSY RC	8.00	3.00
❑ 211	Eric Shelton JSY RC	8.00	3.00
❑ 212	Frank Gore JSY RC	10.00	4.00
❑ 213	J.J. Arrington JSY RC	10.00	4.00
❑ 214	Kyle Orton JSY RC	10.00	4.00
❑ 215	Jason Campbell JSY RC	10.00	4.00
❑ 216	Mark Bradley JSY RC	8.00	3.00
❑ 217	Mark Clayton JSY RC	10.00	4.00
❑ 218	Matt Jones JSY RC	15.00	6.00
❑ 219	Maurice Clarett JSY	8.00	3.00
❑ 220	Reggie Brown JSY RC	8.00	3.00
❑ 221	Ronnie Brown JSY RC	15.00	6.00
❑ 222	Roddy White JSY RC	8.00	3.00
❑ 223	Ryan Moats JSY RC	8.00	3.00
❑ 224	Roscoe Parrish JSY RC	8.00	3.00
❑ 225	Stefan LeFors JSY RC	8.00	3.00
❑ 226	Terrence Murphy JSY RC	8.00	3.00
❑ 227	Troy Williamson JSY RC	12.00	5.00
❑ 228	Vernand Morency JSY RC	8.00	3.00
❑ 229	Vincent Jackson JSY RC	8.00	3.00

1950 Topps Felt Backs

❑	COMPLETE SET (100)	7500.00	5000.00
❑	WRAPPER (1-CENT)	500.00	400.00
❑ 1	Lou Allen	60.00	35.00
❑ 2	Morris Bailey	60.00	35.00
❑ 3	George Bell	60.00	35.00
❑ 4	Lindy Berry HOR	60.00	35.00
❑ 5A	Mike Boldin Brn	60.00	35.00
❑ 5B	Mike Boldin Yel	100.00	60.00
❑ 6A	Bernie Botula Brn	60.00	35.00
❑ 6B	Bernie Botula Yel	100.00	60.00
❑ 7	Bob Bowlby	60.00	35.00
❑ 8	Bob Bucher	60.00	35.00
❑ 9A	Al Burnett Brn	60.00	35.00
❑ 9B	Al Burnett Yel	100.00	60.00
❑ 10	Don Burson	60.00	35.00
❑ 11	Paul Campbell	60.00	35.00
❑ 12	Herb Carey	60.00	35.00
❑ 13A	Bimbo Cecconi Brn	60.00	35.00
❑ 13B	Bimbo Cecconi Yel	100.00	60.00
❑ 14	Bill Chauncey	60.00	35.00
❑ 15	Dick Clark	60.00	35.00
❑ 16	Tom Coleman	60.00	35.00
❑ 17	Billy Conn	60.00	35.00
❑ 18	John Cox	60.00	35.00
❑ 19	Lou Creekmur RC	150.00	90.00
❑ 20	Richard Glen Davis RC	75.00	40.00
❑ 21	Warren Davis	60.00	35.00
❑ 22	Bob Deuber	60.00	35.00
❑ 23	Ray Dooney	60.00	35.00
❑ 24	Tom Dublinski	75.00	40.00
❑ 25	Jeff Fleischman	60.00	35.00
❑ 26	Jack Friedland	60.00	35.00
❑ 27	Bob Fuchs	60.00	35.00
❑ 28	Arnold Galiffa RC	75.00	40.00
❑ 29	Dick Gilman	60.00	35.00
❑ 30A	Frank Gitschier Brn	60.00	35.00
❑ 30B	Frank Gitschier Yel	100.00	60.00
❑ 31	Gene Glick	60.00	35.00
❑ 32	Bill Gregus	60.00	35.00
❑ 33	Harold Hagan	60.00	35.00
❑ 34	Charles Hall	60.00	35.00
❑ 35A	Leon Hart Brn	125.00	75.00
❑ 35B	Leon Hart Yel	200.00	125.00
❑ 36A	Bob Hester Brn	60.00	35.00
❑ 36B	Bob Hester Yel	100.00	60.00
❑ 37	George Hughes	60.00	35.00
❑ 38	Levi Jackson	75.00	40.00
❑ 39A	Jack Jensen Brn	200.00	125.00
❑ 39B	Jack Jensen Yel	300.00	175.00
❑ 40	Charlie Justice	150.00	90.00
❑ 41	Gary Kerkorian	60.00	35.00
❑ 42	Bernie Krueger	60.00	35.00
❑ 43	Bill Kuhn	60.00	35.00
❑ 44	Dean Laun	60.00	35.00
❑ 45	Chet Leach	60.00	35.00
❑ 46A	Bobby Lee Brn	60.00	35.00
❑ 46B	Bobby Lee Yel	100.00	60.00
❑ 47	Roger Lehew	60.00	35.00
❑ 48	Glenn Lippman	60.00	35.00
❑ 49	Melvin Lyle	60.00	35.00
❑ 50	Len Makowski	60.00	35.00
❑ 51A	Al Malekoff Brn	60.00	35.00
❑ 51B	Al Malekoff Yel	100.00	60.00
❑ 52A	Jim Martin Brn	75.00	40.00
❑ 52B	Jim Martin Yel	120.00	80.00
❑ 53	Frank Mataya	60.00	35.00
❑ 54A	Ray Mathews Brn RC	75.00	40.00
❑ 54B	Ray Mathews Yel RC	120.00	80.00
❑ 55A	Dick McKissack Brn	60.00	35.00
❑ 55B	Dick McKissack Yel	100.00	60.00
❑ 56	Frank Miller	60.00	35.00
❑ 57A	John Miller Brn	60.00	35.00
❑ 57B	John Miller Yel	100.00	60.00
❑ 58	Ed Modzelewski RC	75.00	40.00
❑ 59	Don Mouser	60.00	35.00
❑ 60	James Murphy	60.00	35.00
❑ 61A	Ray Nagle Brn	60.00	35.00
❑ 61B	Ray Nagle Yel	100.00	60.00
❑ 62	Leo Nomellini	250.00	150.00
❑ 63	James O'Day	60.00	35.00
❑ 64	Joe Paterno RC	1800.00	1200.00
❑ 65	Andy Pavich	60.00	35.00
❑ 66A	Pete Perini Brn	60.00	35.00
❑ 66B	Pete Perini Yel	100.00	60.00
❑ 67	Jim Powers	60.00	35.00
❑ 68	Dave Rakestraw	60.00	35.00
❑ 69	Herb Rich	60.00	35.00
❑ 70	Fran Rogel RC	60.00	35.00
❑ 71A	Darrell Royal Brn RC	300.00	175.00
❑ 71B	Darrell Royal Yel RC	450.00	300.00
❑ 72	Steve Sawle	60.00	35.00
❑ 73	Nick Sebek	60.00	35.00
❑ 74	Herb Seidell	60.00	35.00
❑ 75A	Charles Shaw Brn	60.00	35.00
❑ 75B	Charles Shaw Yel	100.00	60.00
❑ 76A	Emil Sitko Brn RC	75.00	40.00
❑ 76B	Emil Sitko Yel RC	120.00	80.00
❑ 77	Ed(Butch) Songin RC	75.00	40.00
❑ 78A	Mariano Stalloni Brn	60.00	35.00
❑ 78B	Mariano Stalloni Yel	100.00	60.00
❑ 79	Ernie Stautner RC	250.00	150.00
❑ 80	Don Stehley	60.00	35.00
❑ 81	Gil Stevenson	60.00	35.00
❑ 82	Bishop Strickland	60.00	35.00
❑ 83	Harry Szulborski	60.00	35.00
❑ 84A	Wally Teninga Brn	60.00	35.00
❑ 84B	Wally Teninga Yel	100.00	60.00
❑ 85	Clayton Tonnemaker	60.00	35.00
❑ 86A	Dan Towler Brn RC	150.00	90.00
❑ 86B	Dan Towler RC Yel	250.00	150.00
❑ 87A	Bert Turek Brn	60.00	35.00
❑ 87B	Bert Turek Yel	100.00	60.00
❑ 88	Harry Ulinski	60.00	35.00
❑ 89	Leon Van Billingham	60.00	35.00
❑ 90	Langdon Viracola	60.00	35.00
❑ 91	Leo Wagner	60.00	35.00
❑ 92A	Doak Walker Brn	350.00	200.00
❑ 92B	Doak Walker Yel	500.00	300.00
❑ 93	Jim Ward	60.00	35.00
❑ 94	Art Weiner	60.00	35.00
❑ 95	Dick Weiss	60.00	35.00
❑ 96	Froggie Williams	60.00	35.00
❑ 97	Robert (Red) Wilson	60.00	35.00
❑ 98	Roger Red Wilson	60.00	35.00
❑ 99	Carl Wren	60.00	35.00
❑ 100A	Pete Zinaich Brn	60.00	35.00
❑ 100B	Pete Zinaich Yel	100.00	60.00

1951 Topps Magic

❑	COMPLETE SET (75)	1100.00	800.00
❑	*BACK UNSCRATCHED: 1.5X TO 2.5X		
❑	WRAPPER (1-CENT)	200.00	150.00
❑	WRAPPER (5-CENT)	300.00	250.00
❑ 1	Jimmy Monahan RC	30.00	15.00
❑ 2	Bill Wade RC	50.00	30.00
❑ 3	Bill Reichardt	18.00	10.00
❑ 4	Babe Parilli RC	50.00	30.00
❑ 5	Billie Burkhalter	18.00	10.00
❑ 6	Ed Weber	18.00	10.00
❑ 7	Tom Scott	25.00	15.00
❑ 8	Frank Guthridge	18.00	10.00
❑ 9	John Karras	18.00	10.00
❑ 10	Vic Janowicz RC	150.00	80.00
❑ 11	Lloyd Hill	18.00	10.00
❑ 12	Jim Weatherall RC	25.00	15.00
❑ 13	Howard Hansen	18.00	10.00
❑ 14	Lou D'Achille	18.00	10.00
❑ 15	Johnny Turco	18.00	10.00
❑ 16	Jerrell Price	18.00	10.00
❑ 17	John Coatta	18.00	10.00
❑ 18	Bruce Patton	18.00	10.00
❑ 19	Marion Campbell RC	35.00	20.00
❑ 20	Blaine Earon	18.00	10.00
❑ 21	Dewey McConnell	18.00	10.00
❑ 22	Ray Beck	18.00	10.00
❑ 23	Jim Prewett	18.00	10.00
❑ 24	Bob Steele	18.00	10.00
❑ 25	Art Betts	18.00	10.00
❑ 26	Walt Trillhaase	18.00	10.00
❑ 27	Gil Bartosh	18.00	10.00
❑ 28	Bob Bestwick	18.00	10.00
❑ 29	Tom Rushing	18.00	10.00
❑ 30	Bert Rechichar RC	35.00	20.00
❑ 31	Bill Owens	18.00	10.00
❑ 32	Mike Goggins	18.00	10.00
❑ 33	John Petitbon	18.00	10.00
❑ 34	Byron Townsend	18.00	10.00
❑ 35	Ed Rotticci	18.00	10.00
❑ 36	Steve Wadiak	18.00	10.00
❑ 37	Bobby Marlow RC	25.00	15.00
❑ 38	Bill Fuchs	18.00	10.00
❑ 39	Ralph Staub	18.00	10.00
❑ 40	Bill Vesprini	18.00	10.00
❑ 41	Zack Jordan	18.00	10.00
❑ 42	Bob Smith RC	25.00	15.00
❑ 43	Charles Hanson	18.00	10.00
❑ 44	Glenn Smith	18.00	10.00
❑ 45	Armand Kitto	18.00	10.00
❑ 46	Vinnie Drake	18.00	10.00
❑ 47	Bill Putich RC	18.00	10.00

- ❑ 48 George Young RC 40.00 25.00
- ❑ 49 Don McRae 18.00 10.00
- ❑ 50 Frank Smith RC 18.00 10.00
- ❑ 51 Dick Hightower 18.00 10.00
- ❑ 52 Clyde Pickard 18.00 10.00
- ❑ 53 Bob Reynolds HB 25.00 15.00
- ❑ 54 Dick Gregory 18.00 10.00
- ❑ 55 Dale Samuels 18.00 10.00
- ❑ 56 Gale Galloway 18.00 10.00
- ❑ 57 Vic Pujo 18.00 10.00
- ❑ 58 Dave Waters 18.00 10.00
- ❑ 59 Joe Ernest 18.00 10.00
- ❑ 60 Elmer Costa 18.00 10.00
- ❑ 61 Nick Liotta 18.00 10.00
- ❑ 62 John Dottley 18.00 10.00
- ❑ 63 Hi Faubion 18.00 10.00
- ❑ 64 David Harr 18.00 10.00
- ❑ 65 Bill Matthews 18.00 10.00
- ❑ 66 Carroll McDonald 18.00 10.00
- ❑ 67 Dick Dewing 18.00 10.00
- ❑ 68 Joe Johnson RB 18.00 10.00
- ❑ 69 Arnold Burwitz 18.00 10.00
- ❑ 70 Ed Dobrowolski 18.00 10.00
- ❑ 71 Joe Dudeck 18.00 10.00
- ❑ 72 Johnny Bright RC 25.00 15.00
- ❑ 73 Harold Loehlein 18.00 10.00
- ❑ 74 Lawrence Hairston 18.00 10.00
- ❑ 75 Bob Carey RC 25.00 15.00

1955 Topps All-American

- ❑ COMPLETE SET (100) 3800.00 2800.00
- ❑ WRAPPER (1-CENT) 300.00 250.00
- ❑ WRAPPER (5-CENT) 250.00 200.00
- ❑ 1 Herman Hickman RC ! 125.00 65.00
- ❑ 2 John Kimbrough 18.00 10.00
- ❑ 3 Ed Weir 18.00 10.00
- ❑ 4 Emy Pinckert 18.00 10.00
- ❑ 5 Bobby Grayson 18.00 10.00
- ❑ 6 Nile Kinnick RC UER 125.00 75.00
- ❑ 7 Andy Bershak 18.00 10.00
- ❑ 8 George Cafego RC 18.00 10.00
- ❑ 9 Tom Hamilton SP 30.00 20.00
- ❑ 10 Bill Dudley 40.00 25.00
- ❑ 11 Bobby Dodd SP 30.00 20.00
- ❑ 12 Otto Graham 175.00 100.00
- ❑ 13 Aaron Rosenberg 18.00 10.00
- ❑ 14A Gay.Tinsley RC ERR 100.00 50.00
- ❑ 14B Gay.Tinsley RC COR 25.00 15.00
- ❑ 15 Ed Kaw SP 30.00 20.00
- ❑ 16 Knute Rockne 275.00 175.00
- ❑ 17 Bob Reynolds HB 18.00 10.00
- ❑ 18 Pudg.Heffelfinger RC SP 40.00 25.00
- ❑ 19 Bruce Smith 35.00 20.00
- ❑ 20 Sammy Baugh 200.00 125.00
- ❑ 21A W.White RC SP ERR 250.00 150.00
- ❑ 21B W.White RC SP COR 100.00 60.00
- ❑ 22 Brick Muller 18.00 10.00
- ❑ 23 Dick Kazmaier RC 25.00 15.00
- ❑ 24 Ken Strong 50.00 30.00
- ❑ 25 Casimir Myslinski SP 30.00 20.00
- ❑ 26 Larry Kelley RC SP 40.00 25.00
- ❑ 27 Red Grange UER 300.00 200.00
- ❑ 28 Mel Hein RC SP 75.00 40.00
- ❑ 29 Leo Nomellini SP 100.00 60.00
- ❑ 30 Wes Fesler 18.00 10.00
- ❑ 31 George Sauer Sr. RC 25.00 15.00
- ❑ 32 Hank Foldberg 18.00 10.00
- ❑ 33 Bob Higgins 18.00 10.00
- ❑ 34 Davey O'Brien RC 50.00 30.00
- ❑ 35 Tom Harmon RC SP 100.00 60.00
- ❑ 36 Turk Edwards SP 60.00 35.00
- ❑ 37 Jim Thorpe ! 400.00 275.00
- ❑ 38 Amos A. Stagg RC 75.00 40.00
- ❑ 39 Jerome Holland RC 25.00 15.00
- ❑ 40 Donn Moomaw 18.00 10.00
- ❑ 41 Joseph Alexander SP 30.00 20.00
- ❑ 42 Eddie Tryon RC SP 40.00 25.00
- ❑ 43 George Savitsky 18.00 10.00
- ❑ 44 Ed Garbisch 18.00 10.00
- ❑ 45 Elmer Oliphant 18.00 10.00
- ❑ 46 Arnold Lassman 18.00 10.00
- ❑ 47 Bo McMillin RC 25.00 15.00
- ❑ 48 Ed Widseth 18.00 10.00
- ❑ 49 Don Gordon Zimmerman 18.00 10.00
- ❑ 50 Ken Kavanaugh 25.00 15.00
- ❑ 51 Duane Purvis SP 30.00 20.00
- ❑ 52 Johnny Lujack 90.00 50.00
- ❑ 53 John F. Green 18.00 10.00
- ❑ 54 Edwin Dooley SP 30.00 20.00
- ❑ 55 Frank Merritt SP 30.00 20.00
- ❑ 56 Ernie Nevers RC 125.00 75.00
- ❑ 57 Vic Hanson SP 30.00 20.00
- ❑ 58 Ed Franco 18.00 10.00
- ❑ 59 Doc Blanchard RC 50.00 30.00
- ❑ 60 Dan Hill 18.00 10.00
- ❑ 61 Charles Brickley SP 30.00 20.00
- ❑ 62 Harry Newman 18.00 10.00
- ❑ 63 Charlie Justice 35.00 20.00
- ❑ 64 Benny Friedman RC 30.00 18.00
- ❑ 65 Joe Donchess SP 30.00 20.00
- ❑ 66 Bruiser Kinard RC 35.00 20.00
- ❑ 67 Frankie Albert 25.00 15.00
- ❑ 68 Four Horsemen RC SP 500.00 325.00
- ❑ 69 Frank Sinkwich RC 25.00 15.00
- ❑ 70 Bill Daddio 18.00 10.00
- ❑ 71 Bobby Wilson 18.00 10.00
- ❑ 72 Chub Peabody 18.00 10.00
- ❑ 73 Paul Governali 25.00 15.00
- ❑ 74 Gene McEver 18.00 10.00
- ❑ 75 Hugh Gallarneau 18.00 10.00
- ❑ 76 Angelo Bertelli RC 25.00 15.00
- ❑ 77 Bowden Wyatt SP 30.00 20.00
- ❑ 78 Jay Berwanger RC 35.00 20.00
- ❑ 79 Pug Lund 18.00 10.00
- ❑ 80 Bennie Oosterbaan 18.00 10.00
- ❑ 81 Cotton Warburton 18.00 10.00
- ❑ 82 Alex Wojciechowicz 35.00 20.00
- ❑ 83 Ted Coy SP 30.00 20.00
- ❑ 84 Ace Parker RC SP 50.00 30.00
- ❑ 85 Sid Luckman 150.00 90.00
- ❑ 86 Albie Booth SP 30.00 20.00
- ❑ 87 Adolph Schultz SP 30.00 20.00
- ❑ 88 Ralph Kercheval 18.00 10.00
- ❑ 89 Marshall Goldberg 25.00 15.00
- ❑ 90 Charlie O'Rourke 18.00 10.00
- ❑ 91 Bob Odell UER 18.00 10.00
- ❑ 92 Biggie Munn 18.00 10.00
- ❑ 93 Willie Heston SP 40.00 25.00
- ❑ 94 Joe Bernard SP 40.00 25.00
- ❑ 95 Chris Cagle SP 40.00 25.00
- ❑ 96 Bill Hollenback SP 40.00 25.00
- ❑ 97 Don Hutson RC SP 225.00 150.00
- ❑ 98 Beattie Feathers SP 100.00 60.00
- ❑ 99 Don Whitmire SP 40.00 25.00
- ❑ 100 Fats Henry RC SP ! 200.00 100.00

1956 Topps

- ❑ COMPLETE SET (120) 1800.00 1200.00
- ❑ WRAPPER (1-CENT) 250.00 200.00
- ❑ WRAPPER (5-CENT) 50.00 40.00
- ❑ 1 Johnny Carson SP ! 80.00 40.00
- ❑ 2 Gordy Soltau 6.00 3.50
- ❑ 3 Frank Varrichione 6.00 3.50
- ❑ 4 Eddie Bell 6.00 3.50
- ❑ 5 Alex Webster RC 12.00 6.00
- ❑ 6 Norm Van Brocklin 30.00 18.00
- ❑ 7 Green Bay Packers 25.00 15.00
- ❑ 8 Lou Creekmur 15.00 7.50
- ❑ 9 Lou Groza 25.00 15.00
- ❑ 10 Tom Bienemann SP 25.00 15.00
- ❑ 11 George Blanda 50.00 30.00
- ❑ 12 Alan Ameche 12.00 6.00
- ❑ 13 Vic Janowicz SP 45.00 25.00
- ❑ 14 Dick Moegle 8.00 4.00
- ❑ 15 Fran Rogel 6.00 3.50
- ❑ 16 Harold Giancanelli 6.00 3.50
- ❑ 17 Emlen Tunnell 15.00 7.50
- ❑ 18 Tank Younger 12.00 6.00
- ❑ 19 Billy Howton 8.00 4.00
- ❑ 20 Jack Christiansen 15.00 7.50
- ❑ 21 Darrel Brewster 6.00 3.50
- ❑ 22 Chicago Cardinals SP 100.00 60.00
- ❑ 23 Ed Brown 8.00 4.00
- ❑ 24 Joe Campanella 6.00 3.50
- ❑ 25 Leon Heath SP 22.00 12.00
- ❑ 26 San Francisco 49ers 18.00 10.00
- ❑ 27 Dick Flanagan 6.00 3.50
- ❑ 28 Chuck Bednarik 25.00 15.00
- ❑ 29 Kyle Rote 12.00 6.00
- ❑ 30 Les Richter 8.00 4.00
- ❑ 31 Howard Ferguson 6.00 3.50
- ❑ 32 Dorne Dibble 6.00 3.50
- ❑ 33 Kenny Konz 6.00 3.50
- ❑ 34 Dave Mann SP 25.00 15.00
- ❑ 35 Rick Casares 12.00 6.00
- ❑ 36 Art Donovan 30.00 18.00
- ❑ 37 Chuck Drazenovich SP 22.00 12.00
- ❑ 38 Joe Arenas 6.00 3.50
- ❑ 39 Lynn Chandnois 6.00 3.50
- ❑ 40 Philadelphia Eagles 18.00 10.00
- ❑ 41 Roosevelt Brown RC 35.00 20.00
- ❑ 42 Tom Fears 25.00 15.00
- ❑ 43 Gary Knafelc 6.00 3.50
- ❑ 44 Joe Schmidt RC 50.00 30.00
- ❑ 45 Cleveland Browns 18.00 10.00
- ❑ 46 Len Teeuws RC SP 25.00 15.00
- ❑ 47 Bill George RC 30.00 18.00
- ❑ 48 Baltimore Colts 18.00 10.00
- ❑ 49 Eddie LeBaron SP 45.00 25.00
- ❑ 50 Hugh McElhenny 30.00 18.00
- ❑ 51 Ted Marchibroda 12.00 6.00
- ❑ 52 Adrian Burk 6.00 3.50
- ❑ 53 Frank Gifford 60.00 35.00
- ❑ 54 Charley Toogood 6.00 3.50
- ❑ 55 Tobin Rote 8.00 4.00
- ❑ 56 Bill Stits 6.00 3.50
- ❑ 57 Don Colo 6.00 3.50
- ❑ 58 Ollie Matson SP 75.00 40.00
- ❑ 59 Harlon Hill 8.00 4.00
- ❑ 60 Lenny Moore RC ! 90.00 50.00
- ❑ 61 Wash.Redskins SP 90.00 50.00
- ❑ 62 Billy Wilson 6.00 3.50
- ❑ 63 Pittsburgh Steelers 18.00 10.00
- ❑ 64 Bob Pellegrini 6.00 3.50
- ❑ 65 Ken MacAfee E 6.00 3.50
- ❑ 66 Willard Sherman 6.00 3.50
- ❑ 67 Roger Zatkoff 6.00 3.50
- ❑ 68 Dave Middleton 6.00 3.50
- ❑ 69 Ray Renfro 8.00 4.00
- ❑ 70 Don Stonesifer SP 25.00 15.00
- ❑ 71 Stan Jones RC 30.00 18.00
- ❑ 72 Jim Mutscheller 6.00 3.50
- ❑ 73 Volney Peters SP 22.00 12.00
- ❑ 74 Leo Nomellini 20.00 12.00
- ❑ 75 Ray Mathews 6.00 3.50
- ❑ 76 Dick Bielski 6.00 3.50
- ❑ 77 Charley Conerly 25.00 15.00
- ❑ 78 Elroy Hirsch 30.00 18.00
- ❑ 79 Bill Forester RC 8.00 4.00
- ❑ 80 Jim Doran 6.00 3.50
- ❑ 81 Fred Morrison 6.00 3.50
- ❑ 82 Jack Simmons SP 25.00 15.00
- ❑ 83 Bill McColl 6.00 3.50
- ❑ 84 Bert Rechichar 6.00 3.50
- ❑ 85 Joe Scudero SP 22.00 12.00
- ❑ 86 Y.A.Tittle 50.00 30.00

- ❑ 87 Ernie Stautner 20.00 12.00
- ❑ 88 Norm Willey 6.00 3.50
- ❑ 89 Bob Schnelker 6.00 3.50
- ❑ 90 Dan Towler 12.00 6.00
- ❑ 91 John Martinkovic 6.00 3.50
- ❑ 92 Detroit Lions 18.00 10.00
- ❑ 93 George Ratterman 8.00 4.00
- ❑ 94 Chuck Ulrich SP 25.00 15.00
- ❑ 95 Bobby Watkins 6.00 3.50
- ❑ 96 Buddy Young 12.00 6.00
- ❑ 97 Billy Wells SP 22.00 12.00
- ❑ 98 Bob Toneff 6.00 3.50
- ❑ 99 Bill McPeak 6.00 3.50
- ❑ 100 Bobby Thomason 6.00 3.50
- ❑ 101 Roosevelt Grier RC 40.00 25.00
- ❑ 102 Ron Waller 6.00 3.50
- ❑ 103 Bobby Dillon 6.00 3.50
- ❑ 104 Leon Hart 12.00 6.00
- ❑ 105 Mike McCormack 15.00 7.50
- ❑ 106 John Olszewski SP 25.00 15.00
- ❑ 107 Bill Wightkin 6.00 3.50
- ❑ 108 George Shaw RC 8.00 4.00
- ❑ 109 Dale Atkeson SP 22.00 12.00
- ❑ 110 Joe Perry 25.00 15.00
- ❑ 111 Dale Dodrill 6.00 3.50
- ❑ 112 Tom Scott 6.00 3.50
- ❑ 113 New York Giants 18.00 10.00
- ❑ 114 Los Angeles Rams 18.00 10.00
- ❑ 115 Al Carmichael 6.00 3.50
- ❑ 116 Bobby Layne 50.00 30.00
- ❑ 117 Ed Modzelewski 6.00 3.50
- ❑ 118 Lamar McHan RC SP 25.00 15.00
- ❑ 119 Chicago Bears 18.00 10.00
- ❑ 120 Billy Vessels RC ! 40.00 20.00
- ❑ AD1 Lou Groza/Don Colo/Darrel Brewster 250.00 125.00
- ❑ NNO Checklist SP NNO! 400.00 250.00
- ❑ C1 Contest Card 1 ! 80.00 45.00
- ❑ C2 Contest Card 2 ! 80.00 45.00
- ❑ C3 Contest Card 3 ! 80.00 45.00
- ❑ CA Contest Card A ! 90.00 50.00
- ❑ CB Contest Card B ! 110.00 70.00

1957 Topps

- ❑ COMPLETE SET (154) 2200.00 1600.00
- ❑ COMMON CARD (1-88) 4.00 2.50
- ❑ COMMON CARD (89-154) 10.00 5.00
- ❑ WRAPPER (1-CENT) 50.00 30.00
- ❑ WRAPPER (5-CENT) 75.00 50.00
- ❑ 1 Eddie LeBaron ! 50.00 30.00
- ❑ 2 Pete Retzlaff RC 15.00 7.50
- ❑ 3 Mike McCormack 12.00 6.00
- ❑ 4 Lou Baldacci 4.00 2.50
- ❑ 5 Gino Marchetti 20.00 10.00
- ❑ 6 Leo Nomellini 20.00 10.00
- ❑ 7 Bobby Watkins 4.00 2.50
- ❑ 8 Dave Middleton 4.00 2.50
- ❑ 9 Bobby Dillon 4.00 2.50
- ❑ 10 Les Richter 6.00 3.50
- ❑ 11 Roosevelt Brown 20.00 10.00
- ❑ 12 Lavern Torgeson RC 4.00 2.50
- ❑ 13 Dick Bielski 4.00 2.50
- ❑ 14 Pat Summerall 20.00 10.00
- ❑ 15 Jack Butler RC 10.00 5.00
- ❑ 16 John Henry Johnson 15.00 7.50
- ❑ 17 Art Spinney 4.00 2.50
- ❑ 18 Bob St. Clair 12.00 6.00
- ❑ 19 Perry Jeter 4.00 2.50
- ❑ 20 Lou Creekmur 12.00 6.00
- ❑ 21 Dave Hanner 6.00 3.50
- ❑ 22 Norm Van Brocklin 30.00 18.00
- ❑ 23 Don Chandler RC 10.00 5.00
- ❑ 24 Al Dorow 4.00 2.50
- ❑ 25 Tom Scott 4.00 2.50
- ❑ 26 Ollie Matson 20.00 12.00
- ❑ 27 Fran Rogel 4.00 2.50
- ❑ 28 Lou Groza 25.00 15.00
- ❑ 29 Billy Vessels 6.00 3.50
- ❑ 30 Y.A.Tittle 40.00 25.00
- ❑ 31 George Blanda 40.00 25.00
- ❑ 32 Bobby Layne 40.00 25.00
- ❑ 33 Billy Howton 6.00 3.50
- ❑ 34 Bill Wade 10.00 5.00
- ❑ 35 Emlen Tunnell 15.00 7.50
- ❑ 36 Leo Elter 4.00 2.50
- ❑ 37 Clarence Peaks RC 6.00 3.50
- ❑ 38 Don Stonesifer 4.00 2.50
- ❑ 39 George Tarasovic 4.00 2.50
- ❑ 40 Darrel Brewster 4.00 2.50
- ❑ 41 Bert Rechichar 4.00 2.50
- ❑ 42 Billy Wilson 4.00 2.50
- ❑ 43 Ed Brown 6.00 3.50
- ❑ 44 Gene Gedman 4.00 2.50
- ❑ 45 Gary Knafelc 4.00 2.50
- ❑ 46 Elroy Hirsch 30.00 18.00
- ❑ 47 Don Heinrich 6.00 3.50
- ❑ 48 Gene Brito 4.00 2.50
- ❑ 49 Chuck Bednarik 25.00 15.00
- ❑ 50 Dave Mann 4.00 2.50
- ❑ 51 Bill McPeak 4.00 2.50
- ❑ 52 Kenny Konz 4.00 2.50
- ❑ 53 Alan Ameche 10.00 5.00
- ❑ 54 Gordy Soltau 4.00 2.50
- ❑ 55 Rick Casares 6.00 3.50
- ❑ 56 Charlie Ane 4.00 2.50
- ❑ 57 Al Carmichael 4.00 2.50
- ❑ 58A Willard Sherman ERR 300.00 175.00
- ❑ 58B Willard Sherman COR 4.00 2.50
- ❑ 59 Kyle Rote 10.00 5.00
- ❑ 60 Chuck Drazenovich 4.00 2.50
- ❑ 61 Bobby Walston 4.00 2.50
- ❑ 62 John Olszewski 4.00 2.50
- ❑ 63 Ray Mathews 4.00 2.50
- ❑ 64 Maurice Bassett 4.00 2.50
- ❑ 65 Art Donovan 25.00 15.00
- ❑ 66 Joe Arenas 4.00 2.50
- ❑ 67 Harlon Hill 6.00 3.50
- ❑ 68 Yale Lary 12.00 6.00
- ❑ 69 Bill Forester 6.00 3.50
- ❑ 70 Bob Boyd 4.00 2.50
- ❑ 71 Andy Robustelli 20.00 12.00
- ❑ 72 Sam Baker RC 6.00 3.50
- ❑ 73 Bob Pellegrini 4.00 2.50
- ❑ 74 Leo Sanford 4.00 2.50
- ❑ 75 Sid Watson 4.00 2.50
- ❑ 76 Ray Renfro 6.00 3.50
- ❑ 77 Carl Taseff 4.00 2.50
- ❑ 78 Clyde Conner 4.00 2.50
- ❑ 79 J.C. Caroline 4.00 2.50
- ❑ 80 Howard Cassady RC 15.00 7.50
- ❑ 81 Tobin Rote 6.00 3.50
- ❑ 82 Ron Waller 4.00 2.50
- ❑ 83 Jim Patton RC 6.00 3.50
- ❑ 84 Volney Peters 4.00 2.50
- ❑ 85 Dick Lane RC 50.00 30.00
- ❑ 86 Royce Womble 4.00 2.50
- ❑ 87 Duane Putnam RC 6.00 3.50
- ❑ 88 Frank Gifford ! 60.00 30.00
- ❑ 89 Steve Meilinger 10.00 5.00
- ❑ 90 Buck Lansford 10.00 5.00
- ❑ 91 Lindon Crow DP 8.00 4.00
- ❑ 92 Ernie Stautner DP 25.00 12.50
- ❑ 93 Preston Carpenter RC DP 8.00 4.00
- ❑ 94 Raymond Berry RC 135.00 75.00
- ❑ 95 Hugh McElhenny 30.00 18.00
- ❑ 96 Stan Jones 25.00 15.00
- ❑ 97 Dorne Dibble 10.00 5.00
- ❑ 98 Joe Scudero DP 8.00 4.00
- ❑ 99 Eddie Bell 10.00 5.00
- ❑ 100 Joe Childress DP 8.00 4.00
- ❑ 101 Elbert Nickel 12.00 6.00
- ❑ 102 Walt Michaels 12.00 6.00
- ❑ 103 Jim Mutscheller DP 8.00 4.00
- ❑ 104 Earl Morrall RC 50.00 30.00
- ❑ 105 Larry Strickland 10.00 5.00
- ❑ 106 Jack Christiansen 15.00 7.50
- ❑ 107 Fred Cone DP 8.00 4.00
- ❑ 108 Bud McFadin RC 12.00 6.00
- ❑ 109 Charley Conerly 30.00 18.00
- ❑ 110 Tom Runnels DP 8.00 4.00
- ❑ 111 Ken Keller DP 8.00 4.00
- ❑ 112 James Root 10.00 5.00
- ❑ 113 Ted Marchibroda DP 10.00 5.00
- ❑ 114 Don Paul DB 10.00 5.00
- ❑ 115 George Shaw 12.00 6.00
- ❑ 116 Dick Moegle 12.00 6.00
- ❑ 117 Don Bingham 10.00 5.00
- ❑ 118 Leon Hart 14.00 7.00
- ❑ 119 Bart Starr RC 450.00 300.00
- ❑ 120 Paul Miller DP 8.00 4.00
- ❑ 121 Alex Webster 12.00 6.00
- ❑ 122 Ray Wietecha DP 8.00 4.00
- ❑ 123 Johnny Carson 10.00 5.00
- ❑ 124 Tom. McDonald RC DP 30.00 18.00
- ❑ 125 Jerry Tubbs RC 12.00 6.00
- ❑ 126 Jack Scarbath 10.00 5.00
- ❑ 127 Ed Modzelewski DP 8.00 4.00
- ❑ 128 Lenny Moore 50.00 30.00
- ❑ 129 Joe Perry DP 25.00 15.00
- ❑ 130 Bill Wightkin 10.00 5.00
- ❑ 131 Jim Doran 10.00 5.00
- ❑ 132 Howard Ferguson UER 10.00 5.00
- ❑ 133 Tom Wilson 10.00 5.00
- ❑ 134 Dick James 10.00 5.00
- ❑ 135 Jimmy Harris 10.00 5.00
- ❑ 136 Chuck Ulrich 10.00 5.00
- ❑ 137 Lynn Chandnois 10.00 5.00
- ❑ 138 Johnny Unitas RC DP 450.00 300.00
- ❑ 139 Jim Ridlon DP 8.00 4.00
- ❑ 140 Zeke Bratkowski DP 10.00 5.00
- ❑ 141 Ray Krouse 10.00 5.00
- ❑ 142 John Martinkovic 10.00 5.00
- ❑ 143 Jim Cason DP 8.00 4.00
- ❑ 144 Ken MacAfee E 10.00 5.00
- ❑ 145 Sid Youngelman RC 12.00 6.00
- ❑ 146 Paul Larson 10.00 5.00
- ❑ 147 Len Ford 30.00 18.00
- ❑ 148 Bob Toneff DP 8.00 4.00
- ❑ 149 Ronnie Knox DP 8.00 4.00
- ❑ 150 Jim David RC 12.00 6.00
- ❑ 151 Paul Hornung RC 400.00 250.00
- ❑ 152 Tank Younger 14.00 7.00
- ❑ 153 Bill Svoboda DP 8.00 4.00
- ❑ 154 Fred Morrison ! 70.00 35.00
- ❑ AD1 Al Dorow/Harlon Hill/ Bert Rechich 600.00 350.00
- ❑ AD2 B.Watkins/ G.Marchetti/C.Peaks 600.00 350.00
- ❑ NNO1 Checklist Bazooka SP ! 750.00 500.00
- ❑ NNO2 Checklist Blony SP ! 750.00 500.00

1958 Topps

- ❑ COMPLETE SET (132) 1250.00 850.00
- ❑ WRAPPER (1-CENT) 60.00 35.00
- ❑ WRAPPER (5-CENT) 125.00 75.00
- ❑ 1 Gene Filipski RC ! 15.00 7.50
- ❑ 2 Bobby Layne 35.00 20.00
- ❑ 3 Joe Schmidt 12.00 6.00
- ❑ 4 Bill Barnes 4.00 2.00
- ❑ 5 Milt Plum RC 8.00 4.00
- ❑ 6 Billy Howton UER 5.00 2.50
- ❑ 7 Howard Cassady 5.00 2.50
- ❑ 8 Jim Dooley 4.00 2.00
- ❑ 9 Cleveland Browns 6.00 3.00
- ❑ 10 Lenny Moore 25.00 12.50
- ❑ 11 Darrel Brewster 4.00 2.00
- ❑ 12 Alan Ameche 8.00 4.00

❑ 13 Jim David 4.00 2.00
❑ 14 Jim Mutscheller 4.00 2.00
❑ 15 Andy Robustelli 10.00 5.00
❑ 16 Gino Marchetti 12.00 6.00
❑ 17 Ray Renfro 5.00 2.50
❑ 18 Yale Lary 8.00 4.00
❑ 19 Gary Glick 4.00 2.00
❑ 20 Jon Arnett RC 8.00 4.00
❑ 21 Bob Boyd 4.00 2.00
❑ 22 Johnny Unitas UER 135.00 75.00
❑ 23 Zeke Bratkowski 5.00 2.50
❑ 24 Sid Youngelman UER 4.00 2.00
❑ 25 Leo Elter 4.00 2.00
❑ 26 Kenny Konz 4.00 2.00
❑ 27 Washington Redskins 6.00 3.00
❑ 28 Carl Brettschneider 4.00 2.00
❑ 29 Chicago Bears 6.00 3.00
❑ 30 Alex Webster 5.00 2.50
❑ 31 Al Carmichael 4.00 2.00
❑ 32 Bobby Dillon 4.00 2.00
❑ 33 Steve Meilinger 4.00 2.00
❑ 34 Sam Baker 4.00 2.00
❑ 35 Chuck Bednarik 15.00 7.50
❑ 36 Bert Vic Zucco 4.00 2.00
❑ 37 George Tarasovic 4.00 2.00
❑ 38 Bill Wade 8.00 4.00
❑ 39 Dick Stanfel 5.00 2.50
❑ 40 Jerry Norton 4.00 2.00
❑ 41 San Francisco 49ers 6.00 3.00
❑ 42 Emlen Tunnell 10.00 5.00
❑ 43 Jim Doran 4.00 2.00
❑ 44 Ted Marchibroda 8.00 4.00
❑ 45 Chet Hanulak 4.00 2.00
❑ 46 Dale Dodrill 4.00 2.00
❑ 47 Johnny Carson 4.00 2.00
❑ 48 Dick Deschaine 4.00 2.00
❑ 49 Billy Wells UER 4.00 2.00
❑ 50 Larry Morris 4.00 2.00
❑ 51 Jack McClairen 4.00 2.00
❑ 52 Lou Groza 15.00 7.50
❑ 53 Rick Casares 5.00 2.50
❑ 54 Don Chandler 5.00 2.50
❑ 55 Duane Putnam 4.00 2.00
❑ 56 Gary Knafelc 4.00 2.00
❑ 57 Earl Morrall 10.00 5.00
❑ 58 Ron Kramer RC 5.00 2.50
❑ 59 Mike McCormack 8.00 4.00
❑ 60 Gern Nagler 4.00 2.00
❑ 61 New York Giants 6.00 3.00
❑ 62 Jim Brown RC ! 450.00 300.00
❑ 63 Joe Marconi RC 4.00 2.00
❑ 64 R.C. Owens RC UER 5.00 2.50
❑ 65 Jimmy Carr RC 5.00 2.50
❑ 66 Bart Starr UER 135.00 75.00
❑ 67 Tom Wilson 4.00 2.00
❑ 68 Lamar McHan 4.00 2.00
❑ 69 Chicago Cardinals 6.00 3.00
❑ 70 Jack Christiansen 8.00 4.00
❑ 71 Don McIlhenny RC 4.00 2.00
❑ 72 Ron Waller 4.00 2.00
❑ 73 Frank Gifford 50.00 25.00
❑ 74 Bert Rechichar 4.00 2.00
❑ 75 John Henry Johnson 10.00 5.00
❑ 76 Jack Butler 5.00 2.50
❑ 77 Frank Varrichione 4.00 2.00
❑ 78 Ray Mathews 4.00 2.00
❑ 79 Marv Matuszak UER 4.00 2.00
❑ 80 Harlon Hill UER 4.00 2.00
❑ 81 Lou Creekmur 8.00 4.00
❑ 82 Woodley Lewis UER 4.00 2.00
❑ 83 Don Heinrich 4.00 2.00
❑ 84 Charley Conerly 15.00 7.50
❑ 85 Los Angeles Rams 6.00 3.00
❑ 86 Y.A. Tittle 30.00 18.00
❑ 87 Bobby Walston 4.00 2.00
❑ 88 Earl Putman 4.00 2.00
❑ 89 Leo Nomellini 15.00 7.50
❑ 90 Sonny Jurgensen RC 100.00 60.00
❑ 91 Don Paul DB 4.00 2.00
❑ 92 Paige Cothren 4.00 2.00
❑ 93 Joe Perry 15.00 7.50
❑ 94 Tobin Rote 5.00 2.50
❑ 95 Billy Wilson 4.00 2.00
❑ 96 Green Bay Packers 6.00 3.00
❑ 97 Lavern Torgeson 4.00 2.00
❑ 98 Milt Davis 4.00 2.00
❑ 99 Larry Strickland 4.00 2.00
❑ 100 Matt Hazeltine RC 5.00 2.50
❑ 101 Walt Yowarsky 4.00 2.00
❑ 102 Roosevelt Brown 8.00 4.00
❑ 103 Jim Ringo 10.00 5.00
❑ 104 Joe Krupa 4.00 2.00
❑ 105 Les Richter 5.00 2.50
❑ 106 Art Donovan 20.00 12.00
❑ 107 John Olszewski 4.00 2.00
❑ 108 Ken Keller 4.00 2.00
❑ 109 Philadelphia Eagles 6.00 3.00
❑ 110 Baltimore Colts 6.00 3.00
❑ 111 Dick Bielski 4.00 2.00
❑ 112 Eddie LeBaron 8.00 4.00
❑ 113 Gene Brito 4.00 2.00
❑ 114 Willie Galimore RC 8.00 4.00
❑ 115 Detroit Lions 6.00 3.00
❑ 116 Pittsburgh Steelers 6.00 3.00
❑ 117 L.G. Dupre 5.00 2.50
❑ 118 Babe Parilli 5.00 2.50
❑ 119 Bill George 10.00 5.00
❑ 120 Raymond Berry 40.00 25.00
❑ 121 Jim Podoley UER 4.00 2.00
❑ 122 Hugh McElhenny 15.00 7.50
❑ 123 Ed Brown 5.00 2.50
❑ 124 Dick Moegle 5.00 2.50
❑ 125 Tom Scott 4.00 2.00
❑ 126 Tommy McDonald 12.00 6.00
❑ 127 Ollie Matson 20.00 10.00
❑ 128 Preston Carpenter 4.00 2.00
❑ 129 George Blanda 30.00 18.00
❑ 130 Gordy Soltau 4.00 2.00
❑ 131 Dick Nolan RC 5.00 2.50
❑ 132 Don Bosseler RC ! 20.00 10.00
❑ NNO Free Felt Initial Card 25.00 15.00

1959 Topps

❑ COMPLETE SET (176) 900.00 600.00
❑ COMMON CARD (1-88) 3.00 1.50
❑ COMMON CARD (89-176) 2.00 1.00
❑ WRAPPER (1-CENT) 90.00 50.00
❑ WRAPPER (1-CENT, REP) 80.00 50.00
❑ WRAPPER (5-CENT) 80.00 50.00
❑ 1 Johnny Unitas ! 150.00 90.00
❑ 2 Gene Brito 3.00 1.50
❑ 3 Detroit Lions 6.00 3.00
❑ 4 Max McGee RC 15.00 7.50
❑ 5 Hugh McElhenny 15.00 7.50
❑ 6 Joe Schmidt 8.00 4.00
❑ 7 Kyle Rote 6.00 3.00
❑ 8 Clarence Peaks 3.00 1.50
❑ 9 Pittsburgh Steelers 3.50 1.75
❑ 10 Jim Brown 150.00 90.00
❑ 11 Ray Mathews 3.00 1.50
❑ 12 Bobby Dillon 3.00 1.50
❑ 13 Joe Childress 3.00 1.50
❑ 14 Terry Barr RC 3.00 1.50
❑ 15 Del Shofner RC 4.00 2.00
❑ 16 Bob Pellegrini UER 3.00 1.50
❑ 17 Baltimore Colts 6.00 3.00
❑ 18 Preston Carpenter 3.00 1.50
❑ 19 Leo Nomellini 10.00 5.00
❑ 20 Frank Gifford 40.00 25.00
❑ 21 Charlie Ane 3.00 1.50
❑ 22 Jack Butler 3.00 1.50
❑ 23 Bart Starr 60.00 35.00
❑ 24 Chicago Cardinals 3.50 1.75
❑ 25 Bill Barnes 3.00 1.50
❑ 26 Walt Michaels 4.00 2.00
❑ 27 Clyde Conner UER 3.00 1.50
❑ 28 Paige Cothren 3.00 1.50
❑ 29 Roosevelt Grier 6.00 3.00
❑ 30 Alan Ameche 6.00 3.00
❑ 31 Philadelphia Eagles 6.00 3.00
❑ 32 Dick Nolan 4.00 2.00
❑ 33 R.C. Owens 4.00 2.00
❑ 34 Dale Dodrill 3.00 1.50
❑ 35 Gene Gedman 3.00 1.50
❑ 36 Gene Lipscomb RC 10.00 5.00
❑ 37 Ray Renfro 4.00 2.00
❑ 38 Cleveland Browns 3.50 1.75
❑ 39 Bill Forester 4.00 2.00
❑ 40 Bobby Layne 25.00 15.00
❑ 41 Pat Summerall 10.00 5.00
❑ 42 Jerry Mertens 3.00 1.50
❑ 43 Steve Myhra 3.00 1.50
❑ 44 John Henry Johnson 8.00 4.00
❑ 45 Woodley Lewis UER 3.00 1.50
❑ 46 Green Bay Packers 8.00 4.00
❑ 47 Don Owens UER 3.00 1.50
❑ 48 Ed Beatty 3.00 1.50
❑ 49 Don Chandler 3.00 1.50
❑ 50 Ollie Matson 12.00 6.00
❑ 51 Sam Huff RC 50.00 30.00
❑ 52 Tom Miner 3.00 1.50
❑ 53 New York Giants 3.50 1.75
❑ 54 Kenny Konz 3.00 1.50
❑ 55 Raymond Berry 20.00 10.00
❑ 56 Howard Ferguson UER 3.00 1.50
❑ 57 Chuck Ulrich 3.00 1.50
❑ 58 Bob St.Clair 6.00 3.00
❑ 59 Don Burroughs RC 3.00 1.50
❑ 60 Lou Groza 15.00 7.50
❑ 61 San Francisco 49ers 6.00 3.00
❑ 62 Andy Nelson 3.00 1.50
❑ 63 Harold Bradley 3.00 1.50
❑ 64 Dave Hanner 4.00 2.00
❑ 65 Charley Conerly 10.00 5.00
❑ 66 Gene Cronin RC 3.00 1.50
❑ 67 Duane Putnam 3.00 1.50
❑ 68 Baltimore Colts 3.50 1.75
❑ 69 Ernie Stautner 8.00 4.00
❑ 70 Jon Arnett 4.00 2.00
❑ 71 Ken Panfil 3.00 1.50
❑ 72 Matt Hazeltine 3.00 1.50
❑ 73 Harley Sewell 3.00 1.50
❑ 74 Mike McCormack 6.00 3.00
❑ 75 Jim Ringo 8.00 4.00
❑ 76 Los Angeles Rams 6.00 3.00
❑ 77 Bob Gain RC 3.00 1.50
❑ 78 Buzz Nutter 3.00 1.50
❑ 79 Jerry Norton 3.00 1.50
❑ 80 Joe Perry 12.00 6.00
❑ 81 Carl Brettschneider 3.00 1.50
❑ 82 Paul Hornung 60.00 30.00
❑ 83 Philadelphia Eagles 3.50 1.75
❑ 84 Les Richter 4.00 2.00
❑ 85 Howard Cassady 4.00 2.00
❑ 86 Art Donovan 15.00 7.50
❑ 87 Jim Patton 4.00 2.00
❑ 88 Pete Retzlaff 4.00 2.00
❑ 89 Jim Mutscheller 2.00 1.00
❑ 90 Zeke Bratkowski 3.00 1.50
❑ 91 Washington Redskins 4.00 2.00
❑ 92 Art Hunter 2.00 1.00
❑ 93 Gern Nagler 2.00 1.00
❑ 94 Chuck Weber 2.00 1.00
❑ 95 Lew Carpenter RC 3.00 1.50
❑ 96 Stan Jones 5.00 2.50
❑ 97 Ralph Guglielmi UER 3.00 1.50
❑ 98 Green Bay Packers 4.00 2.00
❑ 99 Ray Wietecha 2.00 1.00
❑ 100 Lenny Moore 12.00 6.00
❑ 101 Jim Ray Smith RC UER 3.00 1.50
❑ 102 Abe Woodson RC 3.00 1.50
❑ 103 Alex Karras RC 40.00 25.00
❑ 104 Chicago Bears 4.00 2.00
❑ 105 John David Crow RC 12.00 6.00
❑ 106 Joe Fortunato RC 2.00 1.00
❑ 107 Babe Parilli 3.00 1.50
❑ 108 Proverb Jacobs 2.00 1.00
❑ 109 Gino Marchetti 8.00 4.00
❑ 110 Bill Wade 3.00 1.50
❑ 111 San Francisco 49ers 3.00 1.50
❑ 112 Karl Rubke 2.00 1.00
❑ 113 Dave Middleton UER 2.00 1.00
❑ 114 Roosevelt Brown 5.00 2.50
❑ 115 John Olszewski 2.00 1.00

- ❑ 116 Jerry Kramer RC 30.00 18.00
- ❑ 117 King Hill RC 3.00 1.50
- ❑ 118 Chicago Cardinals 4.00 2.00
- ❑ 119 Frank Varrichione 2.00 1.00
- ❑ 120 Rick Casares 3.00 1.50
- ❑ 121 George Strugar 2.00 1.00
- ❑ 122 Bill Glass RC 3.00 1.50
- ❑ 123 Don Bosseler 2.00 1.00
- ❑ 124 John Reger 2.00 1.00
- ❑ 125 Jim Ninowski RC 2.00 1.00
- ❑ 126 Los Angeles Rams 3.00 1.50
- ❑ 127 Willard Sherman 2.00 1.00
- ❑ 128 Bob Schnelker 2.00 1.00
- ❑ 129 Ollie Spencer 2.00 1.00
- ❑ 130 Y.A.Tittle 25.00 15.00
- ❑ 131 Yale Lary 5.00 2.50
- ❑ 132 Jim Parker RC 25.00 12.50
- ❑ 133 New York Giants 4.00 2.00
- ❑ 134 Jim Schrader 2.00 1.00
- ❑ 135 M.C. Reynolds 2.00 1.00
- ❑ 136 Mike Sandusky 2.00 1.00
- ❑ 137 Ed Brown 3.00 1.50
- ❑ 138 Al Barry 2.00 1.00
- ❑ 139 Detroit Lions 3.00 1.50
- ❑ 140 Bobby Mitchell RC 35.00 20.00
- ❑ 141 Larry Morris 2.00 1.00
- ❑ 142 Jim Phillips RC 3.00 1.50
- ❑ 143 Jim David 2.00 1.00
- ❑ 144 Joe Krupa 2.00 1.00
- ❑ 145 Willie Galimore 3.00 1.50
- ❑ 146 Pittsburgh Steelers 4.00 2.00
- ❑ 147 Andy Robustelli 8.00 4.00
- ❑ 148 Billy Wilson 2.00 1.00
- ❑ 149 Leo Sanford 2.00 1.00
- ❑ 150 Eddie LeBaron 5.00 2.50
- ❑ 151 Bill McColl 2.00 1.00
- ❑ 152 Buck Lansford UER 2.00 1.00
- ❑ 153 Chicago Bears 3.00 1.50
- ❑ 154 Leo Sugar 2.00 1.00
- ❑ 155 Jim Taylor RC UER 35.00 20.00
- ❑ 156 Lindon Crow 2.00 1.00
- ❑ 157 Jack McClairen 2.00 1.00
- ❑ 158 Vince Costello RC UER 2.00 1.00
- ❑ 159 Stan Wallace 2.00 1.00
- ❑ 160 Mel Triplett RC 2.00 1.00
- ❑ 161 Cleveland Browns 4.00 2.00
- ❑ 162 Dan Currie RC 3.00 1.50
- ❑ 163 L.G. Dupre UER 3.00 1.50
- ❑ 164 John Morrow UER 2.00 1.00
- ❑ 165 Jim Podoley 2.00 1.00
- ❑ 166 Bruce Bosley RC 2.00 1.00
- ❑ 167 Harlon Hill 2.00 1.00
- ❑ 168 Washington Redskins 3.00 1.50
- ❑ 169 Junior Wren 2.00 1.00
- ❑ 170 Tobin Rote 3.00 1.50
- ❑ 171 Art Spinney 2.00 1.00
- ❑ 172 Chuck Drazenovich UER 2.00 1.00
- ❑ 173 Bobby Joe Conrad RC 3.00 1.50
- ❑ 174 Jesse Richardson 2.00 1.00
- ❑ 175 Sam Baker 2.00 1.00
- ❑ 176 Tom Tracy RC ! 8.00 4.00

1960 Topps

- ❑ COMPLETE SET (132) 600.00 400.00
- ❑ WRAPPER (1-CENT) 80.00 50.00
- ❑ WRAPPER (1-CENT, REP) 300.00 150.00
- ❑ WRAPPER (5-CENT) 80.00 50.00
- ❑ 1 Johnny Unitas ! 80.00 40.00
- ❑ 2 Alan Ameche 4.00 2.00
- ❑ 3 Lenny Moore 10.00 5.00
- ❑ 4 Raymond Berry 12.00 6.00
- ❑ 5 Jim Parker 8.00 4.00
- ❑ 6 George Preas 2.50 1.25
- ❑ 7 Art Spinney 2.50 1.25
- ❑ 8 Bill Pellington RC 3.00 1.50
- ❑ 9 Johnny Sample RC 3.00 1.50
- ❑ 10 Gene Lipscomb 3.00 1.50
- ❑ 11 Baltimore Colts 3.00 1.50
- ❑ 12 Ed Brown 3.00 1.50
- ❑ 13 Rick Casares 3.00 1.50
- ❑ 14 Willie Galimore 3.00 1.50
- ❑ 15 Jim Dooley 2.50 1.25
- ❑ 16 Harlon Hill UER 2.50 1.25
- ❑ 17 Stan Jones 4.00 2.00
- ❑ 18 Bill George 4.00 2.00
- ❑ 19 Erich Barnes RC 3.00 1.50
- ❑ 20 Doug Atkins 6.00 3.00
- ❑ 21 Chicago Bears 3.00 1.50
- ❑ 22 Milt Plum 3.00 1.50
- ❑ 23 Jim Brown 100.00 60.00
- ❑ 24 Sam Baker 2.50 1.25
- ❑ 25 Bobby Mitchell 10.00 5.00
- ❑ 26 Ray Renfro 3.00 1.50
- ❑ 27 Billy Howton 3.00 1.50
- ❑ 28 Jim Ray Smith 2.50 1.25
- ❑ 29 Jim Shofner RC 3.00 1.50
- ❑ 30 Bob Gain 2.50 1.25
- ❑ 31 Cleveland Browns 3.00 1.50
- ❑ 32 Don Heinrich 2.50 1.25
- ❑ 33 Ed Modzelewski UER 2.50 1.25
- ❑ 34 Fred Cone 2.50 1.25
- ❑ 35 L.G. Dupre 3.00 1.50
- ❑ 36 Dick Bielski 2.50 1.25
- ❑ 37 Charlie Ane UER 2.50 1.25
- ❑ 38 Jerry Tubbs 3.00 1.50
- ❑ 39 Doyle Nix 2.50 1.25
- ❑ 40 Ray Krouse 2.50 1.25
- ❑ 41 Earl Morrall 4.00 2.00
- ❑ 42 Howard Cassady 3.00 1.50
- ❑ 43 Dave Middleton 2.50 1.25
- ❑ 44 Jim Gibbons RC 3.00 1.50
- ❑ 45 Darris McCord 2.50 1.25
- ❑ 46 Joe Schmidt 6.00 3.00
- ❑ 47 Terry Barr 2.50 1.25
- ❑ 48 Yale Lary 4.00 2.00
- ❑ 49 Gil Mains 2.50 1.25
- ❑ 50 Detroit Lions 3.00 1.50
- ❑ 51 Bart Starr 45.00 30.00
- ❑ 52 Jim Taylor UER 8.00 4.00
- ❑ 53 Lew Carpenter 3.00 1.50
- ❑ 54 Paul Hornung 45.00 30.00
- ❑ 55 Max McGee 4.00 2.00
- ❑ 56 Forrest Gregg RC 40.00 25.00
- ❑ 57 Jim Ringo 5.00 2.50
- ❑ 58 Bill Forester 3.00 1.50
- ❑ 59 Dave Hanner 3.00 1.50
- ❑ 60 Green Bay Packers 8.00 4.00
- ❑ 61 Bill Wade 3.00 1.50
- ❑ 62 Frank Ryan RC 4.00 2.00
- ❑ 63 Ollie Matson 10.00 5.00
- ❑ 64 Jon Arnett 3.00 1.50
- ❑ 65 Del Shofner 3.00 1.50
- ❑ 66 Jim Phillips 2.50 1.25
- ❑ 67 Art Hunter 2.50 1.25
- ❑ 68 Les Richter 3.00 1.50
- ❑ 69 Lou Michaels RC 3.00 1.50
- ❑ 70 John Baker 2.50 1.25
- ❑ 71 Los Angeles Rams 3.00 1.50
- ❑ 72 Charley Conerly 8.00 4.00
- ❑ 73 Mel Triplett 2.50 1.25
- ❑ 74 Frank Gifford 35.00 20.00
- ❑ 75 Alex Webster 3.00 1.50
- ❑ 76 Bob Schnelker 2.50 1.25
- ❑ 77 Pat Summerall 8.00 4.00
- ❑ 78 Roosevelt Brown 4.00 2.00
- ❑ 79 Jim Patton 2.50 1.25
- ❑ 80 Sam Huff 20.00 10.00
- ❑ 81 Andy Robustelli 6.00 3.00
- ❑ 82 New York Giants 3.00 1.50
- ❑ 83 Clarence Peaks 2.50 1.25
- ❑ 84 Bill Barnes 2.50 1.25
- ❑ 85 Pete Retzlaff 3.00 1.50
- ❑ 86 Bobby Walston 2.50 1.25
- ❑ 87 Chuck Bednarik UER 8.00 4.00
- ❑ 88 Bob Pellegrini 2.50 1.25
- ❑ 89 Tom Brookshier RC 3.00 1.50
- ❑ 90 Marion Campbell 3.00 1.50
- ❑ 91 Jesse Richardson 2.50 1.25
- ❑ 92 Philadelphia Eagles 3.00 1.50
- ❑ 93 Bobby Layne 30.00 18.00
- ❑ 94 John Henry Johnson 6.00 3.00
- ❑ 95 Tom Tracy UER 3.00 1.50
- ❑ 96 Preston Carpenter 2.50 1.25
- ❑ 97 Frank Varrichione UER 2.50 1.25
- ❑ 98 John Nisby 2.50 1.25
- ❑ 99 Dean Derby 2.50 1.25
- ❑ 100 George Tarasovic 2.50 1.25
- ❑ 101 Ernie Stautner 5.00 2.50
- ❑ 102 Pittsburgh Steelers 3.00 1.50
- ❑ 103 King Hill 2.50 1.25
- ❑ 104 Mal Hammack 2.50 1.25
- ❑ 105 John David Crow 3.00 1.50
- ❑ 106 Bobby Joe Conrad 3.00 1.50
- ❑ 107 Woodley Lewis 2.50 1.25
- ❑ 108 Don Gillis 2.50 1.25
- ❑ 109 Carl Brettschneider 2.50 1.25
- ❑ 110 Leo Sugar 2.50 1.25
- ❑ 111 Frank Fuller 2.50 1.25
- ❑ 112 St. Louis Cardinals 3.00 1.50
- ❑ 113 Y.A.Tittle 30.00 18.00
- ❑ 114 Joe Perry 8.00 4.00
- ❑ 115 J.D.Smith RC 3.00 1.50
- ❑ 116 Hugh McElhenny 8.00 4.00
- ❑ 117 Billy Wilson 2.50 1.25
- ❑ 118 Bob St.Clair 4.00 2.00
- ❑ 119 Matt Hazeltine 2.50 1.25
- ❑ 120 Abe Woodson 2.50 1.25
- ❑ 121 Leo Nomellini 5.00 2.50
- ❑ 122 San Francisco 49ers 3.00 1.50
- ❑ 123 Ralph Guglielmi UER 2.50 1.25
- ❑ 124 Don Bosseler 2.50 1.25
- ❑ 125 John Olszewski 2.50 1.25
- ❑ 126 Bill Anderson UER 2.50 1.25
- ❑ 127 Joe Walton RC 3.00 1.50
- ❑ 128 Jim Schrader 2.50 1.25
- ❑ 129 Ralph Felton 2.50 1.25
- ❑ 130 Gary Glick 2.50 1.25
- ❑ 131 Bob Toneff 2.50 1.25
- ❑ 132 Redskins Team ! 30.00 18.00
- ❑ AD1 Alan Ameche/Paul Hornung/Tom Tracy 350.00 200.00
- ❑ AD2 Del Shofner/Milt Plum/Jim Patton 200.00 125.00
- ❑ AD3 Bob St.Clair/Jim Shofner/Gil Mains 200.00 125.00
- ❑ AD4 Tom Brookshier/Packers Team/George Preas 200.00 125.00

1961 Topps

- ❑ COMPLETE SET (198) 1000.00 650.00
- ❑ COMMON CARD (1-132) 2.50 1.25
- ❑ COMMON CARD (133-198) 3.00 1.50
- ❑ WRAPPER (1-CENT) 275.00 200.00
- ❑ WRAPPER (1-CENT, REP) 200.00 100.00
- ❑ WRAPPER (5-CENT) 100.00 60.00
- ❑ 1 Johnny Unitas ! 100.00 50.00
- ❑ 2 Lenny Moore 12.00 6.00
- ❑ 3 Alan Ameche 4.00 2.00
- ❑ 4 Raymond Berry 12.00 6.00
- ❑ 5 Jim Mutscheller 2.50 1.25
- ❑ 6 Jim Parker 5.00 2.50
- ❑ 7 Gino Marchetti 6.00 3.00
- ❑ 8 Gene Lipscomb 4.00 2.00
- ❑ 9 Baltimore Colts 3.00 1.50
- ❑ 10 Bill Wade 3.00 1.50

❑ 11 Johnny Morris RC	6.00	3.00
❑ 12 Rick Casares	3.00	1.50
❑ 13 Harlon Hill	2.50	1.25
❑ 14 Stan Jones	4.00	2.00
❑ 15 Doug Atkins	5.00	2.50
❑ 16 Bill George	4.00	2.00
❑ 17 J.C. Caroline	2.50	1.25
❑ 18 Chicago Bears	3.00	1.50
❑ 19 Eddie LeBaron IA	3.00	1.50
❑ 20 Eddie LeBaron	3.00	1.50
❑ 21 Don McIlhenny	2.50	1.25
❑ 22 L.G. Dupre	3.00	1.50
❑ 23 Jim Doran	2.50	1.25
❑ 24 Billy Howton	3.00	1.50
❑ 25 Buzz Guy	2.50	1.25
❑ 26 Jack Patera RC	2.50	1.25
❑ 27 Tom Franckhauser RC	2.50	1.25
❑ 28 Cowboys Team	15.00	7.50
❑ 29 Jim Ninowski	2.50	1.25
❑ 30 Dan Lewis RC	2.50	1.25
❑ 31 Nick Pietrosante RC	3.00	1.50
❑ 32 Gail Cogdill RC	3.00	1.50
❑ 33 Jim Gibbons	2.50	1.25
❑ 34 Jim Martin	2.50	1.25
❑ 35 Alex Karras	15.00	7.50
❑ 36 Joe Schmidt	5.00	2.50
❑ 37 Detroit Lions	3.00	1.50
❑ 38 Paul Hornung IA	18.00	9.00
❑ 39 Bart Starr	40.00	25.00
❑ 40 Paul Hornung	40.00	25.00
❑ 41 Jim Taylor	35.00	20.00
❑ 42 Max McGee	4.00	2.00
❑ 43 Boyd Dowler RC	8.00	4.00
❑ 44 Jim Ringo	5.00	2.50
❑ 45 Hank Jordan RC	30.00	18.00
❑ 46 Bill Forester	3.00	1.50
❑ 47 Green Bay Packers	15.00	7.50
❑ 48 Frank Ryan	3.00	1.50
❑ 49 Jon Arnett	3.00	1.50
❑ 50 Ollie Matson	8.00	4.00
❑ 51 Jim Phillips	2.50	1.25
❑ 52 Del Shofner	3.00	1.50
❑ 53 Art Hunter	2.50	1.25
❑ 54 Gene Brito	2.50	1.25
❑ 55 Lindon Crow	2.50	1.25
❑ 56 Los Angeles Rams	3.00	1.50
❑ 57 Johnny Unitas IA	25.00	15.00
❑ 58 Y.A.Tittle	30.00	18.00
❑ 59 John Brodie RC	40.00	25.00
❑ 60 J.D. Smith	2.50	1.25
❑ 61 R.C. Owens	3.00	1.50
❑ 62 Clyde Conner	2.50	1.25
❑ 63 Bob St.Clair	4.00	2.00
❑ 64 Leo Nomellini	6.00	3.00
❑ 65 Abe Woodson	2.50	1.25
❑ 66 San Francisco 49ers	3.00	1.50
❑ 67 Checklist Card	40.00	25.00
❑ 68 Milt Plum	3.00	1.50
❑ 69 Ray Renfro	3.00	1.50
❑ 70 Bobby Mitchell	8.00	4.00
❑ 71 Jim Brown	125.00	75.00
❑ 72 Mike McCormack	4.00	2.00
❑ 73 Jim Ray Smith	2.50	1.25
❑ 74 Sam Baker	2.50	1.25
❑ 75 Walt Michaels	3.00	1.50
❑ 76 Cleveland Browns	3.00	1.50
❑ 77 Jim Brown IA	35.00	20.00
❑ 78 George Shaw	2.50	1.25
❑ 79 Hugh McElhenny	8.00	4.00
❑ 80 Clancy Osborne	2.50	1.25
❑ 81 Dave Middleton	2.50	1.25
❑ 82 Frank Youso	2.50	1.25
❑ 83 Don Joyce	2.50	1.25
❑ 84 Ed Culpepper	2.50	1.25
❑ 85 Charley Conerly	8.00	4.00
❑ 86 Mel Triplett	2.50	1.25
❑ 87 Kyle Rote	3.00	1.50
❑ 88 Roosevelt Brown	4.00	2.00
❑ 89 Ray Wietecha	2.50	1.25
❑ 90 Andy Robustelli	5.00	2.50
❑ 91 Sam Huff	8.00	4.00
❑ 92 Jim Patton	2.50	1.25
❑ 93 New York Giants	3.00	1.50
❑ 94 Charley Conerly IA	6.00	3.00
❑ 95 Sonny Jurgensen	25.00	15.00
❑ 96 Tommy McDonald	5.00	2.50
❑ 97 Bill Barnes	2.50	1.25
❑ 98 Bobby Walston	2.50	1.25
❑ 99 Pete Retzlaff	3.00	1.50
❑ 100 Jim McCusker	2.50	1.25
❑ 101 Chuck Bednarik	8.00	4.00
❑ 102 Tom Brookshier	3.00	1.50
❑ 103 Philadelphia Eagles	3.00	1.50
❑ 104 Bobby Layne	30.00	18.00
❑ 105 John Henry Johnson	4.00	2.00
❑ 106 Tom Tracy	3.00	1.50
❑ 107 Buddy Dial RC	2.50	1.25
❑ 108 Jimmy Orr RC	4.00	2.00
❑ 109 Mike Sandusky	2.50	1.25
❑ 110 John Reger	2.50	1.25
❑ 111 Junior Wren	2.50	1.25
❑ 112 Pittsburgh Steelers	3.00	1.50
❑ 113 Bobby Layne IA	10.00	5.00
❑ 114 John Roach	2.50	1.25
❑ 115 Sam Etcheverry RC	3.00	1.50
❑ 116 John David Crow	3.00	1.50
❑ 117 Mal Hammack	2.50	1.25
❑ 118 Sonny Randle RC	3.00	1.50
❑ 119 Leo Sugar	2.50	1.25
❑ 120 Jerry Norton	2.50	1.25
❑ 121 St. Louis Cardinals	3.00	1.50
❑ 122 Checklist Card	50.00	30.00
❑ 123 Ralph Guglielmi	2.50	1.25
❑ 124 Dick James	2.50	1.25
❑ 125 Don Bosseler	2.50	1.25
❑ 126 Joe Walton	2.50	1.25
❑ 127 Bill Anderson	2.50	1.25
❑ 128 Vince Promuto RC	2.50	1.25
❑ 129 Bob Toneff	2.50	1.25
❑ 130 John Paluck	2.50	1.25
❑ 131 Washington Redskins	3.00	1.50
❑ 132 Milt Plum IA !	2.50	1.25
❑ 133 Abner Haynes !	8.00	4.00
❑ 134 Mel Branch UER	4.00	2.00
❑ 135 Jerry Cornelison UER	3.00	1.50
❑ 136 Bill Krisher	3.00	1.50
❑ 137 Paul Miller	3.00	1.50
❑ 138 Jack Spikes	4.00	2.00
❑ 139 Johnny Robinson RC	8.00	4.00
❑ 140 Cotton Davidson RC	4.00	2.00
❑ 141 Dave Smith RB	3.00	1.50
❑ 142 Bill Groman	3.00	1.50
❑ 143 Rich Michael	3.00	1.50
❑ 144 Mike Dukes	3.00	1.50
❑ 145 George Blanda	25.00	15.00
❑ 146 Billy Cannon	6.00	3.00
❑ 147 Dennit Morris	3.00	1.50
❑ 148 Jacky Lee UER	4.00	2.00
❑ 149 Al Dorow	3.00	1.50
❑ 150 Don Maynard RC	50.00	25.00
❑ 151 Art Powell RC	8.00	4.00
❑ 152 Sid Youngelman	3.00	1.50
❑ 153 Bob Mischak	3.00	1.50
❑ 154 Larry Grantham	3.00	1.50
❑ 155 Tom Saidock	3.00	1.50
❑ 156 Roger Donnahoo	3.00	1.50
❑ 157 Laverne Torczon	3.00	1.50
❑ 158 Archie Matsos RC	4.00	2.00
❑ 159 Elbert Dubenion	4.00	2.00
❑ 160 Wray Carlton RC	4.00	2.00
❑ 161 Rich McCabe	3.00	1.50
❑ 162 Ken Rice	3.00	1.50
❑ 163 Art Baker RC	3.00	1.50
❑ 164 Tom Rychlec	3.00	1.50
❑ 165 Mack Yoho	3.00	1.50
❑ 166 Jack Kemp	100.00	50.00
❑ 167 Paul Lowe	6.00	3.00
❑ 168 Ron Mix	10.00	5.00
❑ 169 Paul Maguire UER	6.00	3.00
❑ 170 Volney Peters	3.00	1.50
❑ 171 Ernie Wright RC	4.00	2.00
❑ 172 Ron Nery RC	3.00	1.50
❑ 173 Dave Kocourek RC	4.00	2.00
❑ 174 Jim Colclough	3.00	1.50
❑ 175 Babe Parilli	4.00	2.00
❑ 176 Billy Lott	3.00	1.50
❑ 177 Fred Bruney	3.00	1.50
❑ 178 Ross O'Hanley	3.00	1.50
❑ 179 Walt Cudzik	3.00	1.50
❑ 180 Charley Leo	3.00	1.50
❑ 181 Bob Dee	3.00	1.50
❑ 182 Jim Otto RC	40.00	25.00
❑ 183 Eddie Macon	3.00	1.50
❑ 184 Dick Christy	3.00	1.50
❑ 185 Alan Miller	3.00	1.50
❑ 186 Tom Flores RC	20.00	10.00
❑ 187 Joe Cannavino	3.00	1.50
❑ 188 Don Manoukian	3.00	1.50
❑ 189 Bob Coolbaugh	3.00	1.50
❑ 190 Lionel Taylor RC	8.00	4.00
❑ 191 Bud McFadin	3.00	1.50
❑ 192 Goose Gonsoulin RC	6.00	3.00
❑ 193 Frank Tripucka	4.00	2.00
❑ 194 Gene Mingo RC	4.00	2.00
❑ 195 Eldon Danenhauer	3.00	1.50
❑ 196 Bob McNamara	3.00	1.50
❑ 197 Dave Rolle UER	3.00	1.50
❑ 198 Checklist UER !	100.00	60.00
❑ AD1 Jim Martin/George Shaw/ Jim Ray Smith	200.00	125.00

1962 Topps

❑ COMPLETE SET (176)	2000.00	1200.00
❑ WRAPPER (1-CENT)	250.00	175.00
❑ WRAPPER (5-CENT,STARS)	50.00	25.00
❑ WRAPPER (5-CENT,BUCKS)	40.00	25.00
❑ 1 Johnny Unitas !	200.00	125.00
❑ 2 Lenny Moore	12.00	6.00
❑ 3 Alex Hawkins RC SP	10.00	5.00
❑ 4 Joe Perry	8.00	4.00
❑ 5 Raymond Berry SP	40.00	25.00
❑ 6 Steve Myhra	4.00	2.00
❑ 7 Tom Gilburg SP	8.00	4.00
❑ 8 Gino Marchetti	8.00	4.00
❑ 9 Bill Pellington	4.00	2.00
❑ 10 Andy Nelson	4.00	2.00
❑ 11 Wendell Harris SP	8.00	4.00
❑ 12 Baltimore Colts	6.00	3.00
❑ 13 Bill Wade SP	10.00	5.00
❑ 14 Willie Galimore	5.00	2.50
❑ 15 Johnny Morris SP	8.00	4.00
❑ 16 Rick Casares	5.00	2.50
❑ 17 Mike Ditka RC	225.00	125.00
❑ 18 Stan Jones	6.00	3.00
❑ 19 Roger LeClerc	4.00	2.00
❑ 20 Angelo Coia	4.00	2.00
❑ 21 Doug Atkins	7.00	3.50
❑ 22 Bill George	6.00	3.00
❑ 23 Richie Petitbon RC	5.00	2.50
❑ 24 Ronnie Bull RC SP	8.00	4.00
❑ 25 Chicago Bears	6.00	3.00
❑ 26 Howard Cassady	5.00	2.50
❑ 27 Ray Renfro SP	10.00	5.00
❑ 28 Jim Brown	175.00	100.00
❑ 29 Rich Kreitling	4.00	2.00
❑ 30 Jim Ray Smith	4.00	2.00
❑ 31 John Morrow	4.00	2.00
❑ 32 Lou Groza	15.00	7.50
❑ 33 Bob Gain	4.00	2.00
❑ 34 Bernie Parrish	4.00	2.00
❑ 35 Jim Shofner	4.00	2.00
❑ 36 Ernie Davis RC SP	150.00	90.00
❑ 37 Cleveland Browns	6.00	3.00
❑ 38 Eddie LeBaron	5.00	2.50
❑ 39 Don Meredith SP	100.00	60.00
❑ 40 J.W. Lockett SP	8.00	4.00
❑ 41 Don Perkins RC	10.00	5.00
❑ 42 Billy Howton	5.00	2.50
❑ 43 Dick Bielski	4.00	2.00
❑ 44 Mike Connelly RC	4.00	2.00
❑ 45 Jerry Tubbs SP	8.00	4.00
❑ 46 Don Bishop SP	8.00	4.00
❑ 47 Dick Moegle	4.00	2.00

❑ 48 Bobby Plummer SP 8.00 4.00
❑ 49 Cowboys Team 20.00 12.00
❑ 50 Milt Plum 5.00 2.50
❑ 51 Dan Lewis 4.00 2.00
❑ 52 Nick Pietrosante SP 8.00 4.00
❑ 53 Gail Cogdill 4.00 2.00
❑ 54 Jim Gibbons 4.00 2.00
❑ 55 Jim Martin 4.00 2.00
❑ 56 Yale Lary 6.00 3.00
❑ 57 Darris McCord 4.00 2.00
❑ 58 Alex Karras 25.00 15.00
❑ 59 Joe Schmidt 7.00 3.50
❑ 60 Dick Lane 6.00 3.00
❑ 61 John Lomakoski SP 8.00 4.00
❑ 62 Detroit Lions SP 18.00 10.00
❑ 63 Bart Starr SP 125.00 75.00
❑ 64 Paul Hornung SP 100.00 60.00
❑ 65 Tom Moore SP 12.00 6.00
❑ 66 Jim Taylor SP 50.00 30.00
❑ 67 Max McGee SP 12.00 6.00
❑ 68 Jim Ringo SP 15.00 7.50
❑ 69 Fuzzy Thurston RC SP 20.00 12.00
❑ 70 Forrest Gregg 7.00 3.50
❑ 71 Boyd Dowler 6.00 3.00
❑ 72 Hank Jordan SP 15.00 7.50
❑ 73 Bill Forester SP 10.00 5.00
❑ 74 Earl Gros SP 8.00 4.00
❑ 75 Packers Team SP 35.00 20.00
❑ 76 Checklist SP 80.00 45.00
❑ 77 Zeke Bratkowski SP 10.00 5.00
❑ 78 Jon Arnett SP 10.00 5.00
❑ 79 Ollie Matson SP 35.00 20.00
❑ 80 Dick Bass SP 10.00 5.00
❑ 81 Jim Phillips 4.00 2.00
❑ 82 Carroll Dale RC 5.00 2.50
❑ 83 Frank Varrichione 4.00 2.00
❑ 84 Art Hunter 4.00 2.00
❑ 85 Danny Villanueva RC 4.00 2.00
❑ 86 Les Richter SP 8.00 4.00
❑ 87 Lindon Crow 4.00 2.00
❑ 88 Roman Gabriel RC SP 60.00 35.00
❑ 89 Los Angeles Rams SP 18.00 10.00
❑ 90 Fran Tarkenton RC SP 225.00 125.00
❑ 91 Jerry Reichow SP 8.00 4.00
❑ 92 Hugh McElhenny SP 30.00 18.00
❑ 93 Mel Triplett SP 8.00 4.00
❑ 94 Tommy Mason RC SP 12.00 6.00
❑ 95 Dave Middleton SP 8.00 4.00
❑ 96 Frank Youso SP 8.00 4.00
❑ 97 Mike Mercer SP 8.00 4.00
❑ 98 Rip Hawkins SP 8.00 4.00
❑ 99 Cliff Livingston SP 8.00 4.00
❑ 100 Roy Winston RC SP 8.00 4.00
❑ 101 Vikings Team SP 25.00 15.00
❑ 102 Y.A.Tittle 40.00 25.00
❑ 103 Joe Walton 4.00 2.00
❑ 104 Frank Gifford 50.00 30.00
❑ 105 Alex Webster 5.00 2.50
❑ 106 Del Shofner 5.00 2.50
❑ 107 Don Chandler 4.00 2.00
❑ 108 Andy Robustelli 7.00 3.50
❑ 109 Jim Katcavage RC 5.00 2.50
❑ 110 Sam Huff SP 40.00 25.00
❑ 111 Erich Barnes 4.00 2.00
❑ 112 Jim Patton 4.00 2.00
❑ 113 Jerry Hillebrand SP 8.00 4.00
❑ 114 New York Giants 6.00 3.00
❑ 115 Sonny Jurgensen 40.00 25.00
❑ 116 Tommy McDonald 8.00 4.00
❑ 117 Ted Dean SP 8.00 4.00
❑ 118 Clarence Peaks 4.00 2.00
❑ 119 Bobby Walston 4.00 2.00
❑ 120 Pete Retzlaff SP 10.00 5.00
❑ 121 Jim Schrader SP 8.00 4.00
❑ 122 J.D. Smith T 4.00 2.00
❑ 123 King Hill 4.00 2.00
❑ 124 Maxie Baughan FTC 5.00 2.50
❑ 125 Pete Case SP 8.00 4.00
❑ 126 Philadelphia Eagles 6.00 3.00
❑ 127 Bobby Layne 40.00 25.00
❑ 128 Tom Tracy 5.00 2.50
❑ 129 John Henry Johnson 6.00 3.00
❑ 130 Buddy Dial SP 10.00 5.00
❑ 131 Preston Carpenter 4.00 2.00
❑ 132 Lou Michaels SP 8.00 4.00
❑ 133 Gene Lipscomb SP 10.00 5.00
❑ 134 Ernie Stautner SP 20.00 12.00
❑ 135 John Reger SP 8.00 4.00
❑ 136 Myron Pottios RC 4.00 2.00
❑ 137 Bob Ferguson SP 8.00 4.00
❑ 138 Pittsburgh Steelers SP 18.00 10.00
❑ 139 Sam Etcheverry 5.00 2.50
❑ 140 John David Crow SP 10.00 5.00
❑ 141 Bobby Joe Conrad SP 10.00 5.00
❑ 142 Prentice Gautt RC SP 8.00 4.00
❑ 143 Frank Mestnik 4.00 2.00
❑ 144 Sonny Randle 5.00 2.50
❑ 145 Gerry Perry UER 4.00 2.00
❑ 146 Jerry Norton 4.00 2.00
❑ 147 Jimmy Hill 4.00 2.00
❑ 148 Bill Stacy 4.00 2.00
❑ 149 Fate Echols SP 8.00 4.00
❑ 150 St. Louis Cardinals 6.00 3.00
❑ 151 Billy Kilmer RC 35.00 20.00
❑ 152 John Brodie 18.00 10.00
❑ 153 J.D. Smith RB 5.00 2.50
❑ 154 C.R. Roberts SP 8.00 4.00
❑ 155 Monty Stickles 4.00 2.00
❑ 156 Clyde Conner UER 4.00 2.00
❑ 157 Bob St.Clair 6.00 3.00
❑ 158 Tommy Davis RC 4.00 2.00
❑ 159 Leo Nomellini 8.00 4.00
❑ 160 Matt Hazeltine 4.00 2.00
❑ 161 Abe Woodson 4.00 2.00
❑ 162 Dave Baker 4.00 2.00
❑ 163 San Francisco 49ers 6.00 3.00
❑ 164 Norm Snead RC SP 30.00 18.00
❑ 165 Dick James 5.00 2.50
❑ 166 Bobby Mitchell 8.00 4.00
❑ 167 Sam Horner 4.00 2.00
❑ 168 Bill Barnes 4.00 2.00
❑ 169 Bill Anderson 4.00 2.00
❑ 170 Fred Dugan 4.00 2.00
❑ 171 John Aveni SP 8.00 4.00
❑ 172 Bob Toneff 4.00 2.00
❑ 173 Jim Kerr 4.00 2.00
❑ 174 Leroy Jackson SP 8.00 4.00
❑ 175 Washington Redskins 6.00 3.00
❑ 176 Checklist ! 100.00 60.00

1963 Topps

❑ COMPLETE SET (170) 1350.00 850.00
❑ WRAPPER (1-CENT) 450.00 300.00
❑ WRAPPER (5-CENT) 80.00 50.00
❑ 1 Johnny Unitas ! 135.00 75.00
❑ 2 Lenny Moore 8.00 4.00
❑ 3 Jimmy Orr 3.00 1.50
❑ 4 Raymond Berry 8.00 4.00
❑ 5 Jim Parker 5.00 2.50
❑ 6 Alex Sandusky 2.50 1.25
❑ 7 Dick Szymanski RC 2.50 1.25
❑ 8 Gino Marchetti 6.00 3.00
❑ 9 Billy Ray Smith RC 3.00 1.50
❑ 10 Bill Pellington 2.50 1.25
❑ 11 Bob Boyd RC DB 2.50 1.25
❑ 12 Baltimore Colts SP 10.00 5.00
❑ 13 Frank Ryan SP 8.00 4.00
❑ 14 Jim Brown SP 200.00 100.00
❑ 15 Ray Renfro SP 8.00 4.00
❑ 16 Rich Kreitling SP 6.00 3.50
❑ 17 Mike McCormack SP 10.00 5.00
❑ 18 Jim Ray Smith SP 6.00 3.50
❑ 19 Lou Groza SP 25.00 15.00
❑ 20 Bill Glass SP 6.00 3.50
❑ 21 Galen Fiss SP 6.00 3.50
❑ 22 Don Fleming RC SP 8.00 4.00
❑ 23 Bob Gain SP 6.00 3.50
❑ 24 Cleveland Browns SP 10.00 5.00
❑ 25 Milt Plum 3.00 1.50
❑ 26 Dan Lewis 2.50 1.25
❑ 27 Nick Pietrosante 2.50 1.25
❑ 28 Gail Cogdill 2.50 1.25
❑ 29 Harley Sewell 2.50 1.25
❑ 30 Jim Gibbons 2.50 1.25
❑ 31 Carl Brettschneider 2.50 1.25
❑ 32 Dick Lane 5.00 2.50
❑ 33 Yale Lary 5.00 2.50
❑ 34 Roger Brown RC 3.00 1.50
❑ 35 Joe Schmidt 6.00 3.00
❑ 36 Detroit Lions SP 10.00 5.00
❑ 37 Roman Gabriel 8.00 4.00
❑ 38 Zeke Bratkowski 3.00 1.50
❑ 39 Dick Bass 3.00 1.50
❑ 40 Jon Arnett 3.00 1.50
❑ 41 Jim Phillips 2.50 1.25
❑ 42 Frank Varrichione 2.50 1.25
❑ 43 Danny Villanueva 2.50 1.25
❑ 44 Deacon Jones RC 50.00 30.00
❑ 45 Lindon Crow 2.50 1.25
❑ 46 Marlin McKeever 2.50 1.25
❑ 47 Ed Meador RC 2.50 1.25
❑ 48 Los Angeles Rams 4.00 2.00
❑ 49 Y.A.Tittle SP 50.00 30.00
❑ 50 Del Shofner SP 6.00 3.50
❑ 51 Alex Webster SP 8.00 4.00
❑ 52 Phil King SP 6.00 3.50
❑ 53 Jack Stroud SP 6.00 3.50
❑ 54 Darrell Dess SP 6.00 3.50
❑ 55 Jim Katcavage SP 6.00 3.50
❑ 56 Roosevelt Grier SP 10.00 5.00
❑ 57 Erich Barnes SP 6.00 3.50
❑ 58 Jim Patton SP 6.00 3.50
❑ 59 Sam Huff SP 20.00 12.00
❑ 60 New York Giants 4.00 2.00
❑ 61 Bill Wade 3.00 1.50
❑ 62 Mike Ditka 60.00 35.00
❑ 63 Johnny Morris 2.50 1.25
❑ 64 Roger LeClerc 2.50 1.25
❑ 65 Roger Davis RC 2.50 1.25
❑ 66 Joe Marconi 2.50 1.25
❑ 67 Herman Lee 2.50 1.25
❑ 68 Doug Atkins 6.00 3.00
❑ 69 Joe Fortunato 2.50 1.25
❑ 70 Bill George 5.00 2.50
❑ 71 Richie Petitbon 3.00 1.50
❑ 72 Bears Team SP 10.00 5.00
❑ 73 Eddie LeBaron SP 10.00 5.00
❑ 74 Don Meredith SP 60.00 35.00
❑ 75 Don Perkins SP 10.00 5.00
❑ 76 Amos Marsh SP 6.00 3.50
❑ 77 Billy Howton SP 8.00 4.00
❑ 78 Andy Cvercko SP 6.00 3.50
❑ 79 Sam Baker SP 6.00 3.50
❑ 80 Jerry Tubbs SP 6.00 3.50
❑ 81 Don Bishop SP 6.00 3.50
❑ 82 Bob Lilly RC SP 175.00 100.00
❑ 83 Jerry Norton SP 6.00 3.50
❑ 84 Cowboys Team SP 20.00 12.00
❑ 85 Checklist 25.00 15.00
❑ 86 Bart Starr 75.00 40.00
❑ 87 Jim Taylor 30.00 18.00
❑ 88 Boyd Dowler 5.00 2.50
❑ 89 Forrest Gregg 6.00 3.00
❑ 90 Fuzzy Thurston 6.00 3.00
❑ 91 Jim Ringo 6.00 3.00
❑ 92 Ron Kramer 3.00 1.50
❑ 93 Hank Jordan 6.00 3.00
❑ 94 Bill Forester 3.00 1.50
❑ 95 Willie Wood RC 40.00 25.00
❑ 96 Ray Nitschke RC 125.00 75.00
❑ 97 Green Bay Packers 15.00 7.50
❑ 98 Fran Tarkenton 60.00 35.00
❑ 99 Tommy Mason 3.00 1.50
❑ 100 Mel Triplett 2.50 1.25
❑ 101 Jerry Reichow 2.50 1.25
❑ 102 Frank Youso 2.50 1.25
❑ 103 Hugh McElhenny 8.00 4.00
❑ 104 Gerald Huth 2.50 1.25
❑ 105 Ed Sharockman 2.50 1.25
❑ 106 Rip Hawkins 2.50 1.25
❑ 107 Jim Marshall RC 35.00 20.00
❑ 108 Jim Prestel 2.50 1.25
❑ 109 Minnesota Vikings 4.00 2.00

❑ 110	Sonny Jurgensen SP	25.00	15.00
❑ 111	Timmy Brown RC SP	10.00	5.00
❑ 112	Tommy McDonald SP	15.00	7.50
❑ 113	Clarence Peaks SP	6.00	3.50
❑ 114	Pete Retzlaff SP	8.00	4.00
❑ 115	Jim Schrader SP	6.00	3.50
❑ 116	Jim McCusker SP	6.00	3.50
❑ 117	Don Burroughs SP	6.00	3.50
❑ 118	Maxie Baughan SP	6.00	3.50
❑ 119	Riley Gunnels SP	6.00	3.50
❑ 120	Jimmy Carr SP	6.00	3.50
❑ 121	Philadelphia Eagles SP	10.00	5.00
❑ 122	Ed Brown SP	8.00	4.00
❑ 123	John H.Johnson SP	15.00	7.50
❑ 124	Buddy Dial SP	6.00	3.50
❑ 125	Bill Red Mack SP	6.00	3.50
❑ 126	Preston Carpenter SP	6.00	3.50
❑ 127	Ray Lemek SP	6.00	3.50
❑ 128	Buzz Nutter SP	6.00	3.50
❑ 129	Ernie Stautner SP	15.00	7.50
❑ 130	Lou Michaels SP	6.00	3.50
❑ 131	Clendon Thomas RC SP	6.00	3.50
❑ 132	Tom Bettis SP	6.00	3.50
❑ 133	Pittsburgh Steelers SP	10.00	5.00
❑ 134	John Brodie	8.00	4.00
❑ 135	J.D. Smith	2.50	1.25
❑ 136	Billy Kilmer	5.00	2.50
❑ 137	Bernie Casey RC	3.00	1.50
❑ 138	Tommy Davis	2.50	1.25
❑ 139	Ted Connolly	2.50	1.25
❑ 140	Bob St.Clair	5.00	2.50
❑ 141	Abe Woodson	2.50	1.25
❑ 142	Matt Hazeltine	2.50	1.25
❑ 143	Leo Nomellini	6.00	3.00
❑ 144	Dan Colchico	2.50	1.25
❑ 145	San Francisco 49ers SP	10.00	5.00
❑ 146	Charlie Johnson RC	8.00	4.00
❑ 147	John David Crow	3.00	1.50
❑ 148	Bobby Joe Conrad	3.00	1.50
❑ 149	Sonny Randle	2.50	1.25
❑ 150	Prentice Gautt	2.50	1.25
❑ 151	Taz Anderson	2.50	1.25
❑ 152	Ernie McMillan RC	3.00	1.50
❑ 153	Jimmy Hill	2.50	1.25
❑ 154	Bill Koman	2.50	1.25
❑ 155	Larry Wilson RC	20.00	12.00
❑ 156	Don Owens	2.50	1.25
❑ 157	St. Louis Cardinals SP	10.00	5.00
❑ 158	Norm Snead SP	10.00	5.00
❑ 159	Bobby Mitchell SP	15.00	7.50
❑ 160	Bill Barnes SP	6.00	3.50
❑ 161	Fred Dugan SP	6.00	3.50
❑ 162	Don Bosseler SP	6.00	3.50
❑ 163	John Nisby SP	6.00	3.50
❑ 164	Riley Mattson SP	6.00	3.50
❑ 165	Bob Toneff SP	6.00	3.50
❑ 166	Rod Breedlove SP	6.00	3.50
❑ 167	Dick James SP	6.00	3.50
❑ 168	Claude Crabb SP	6.00	3.50
❑ 169	Washington Redskins SP	10.00	5.00
❑ 170	Checklist UER !	50.00	30.00
❑ AD1	C.Johnson/Crow/Conrad	200.00	125.00

1964 Topps

❑	COMPLETE SET (176)	1500.00	1000.00
❑	WRAPPER (1-CENT)	40.00	30.00
❑	WRAPPER (5-CENT, PENN)	90.00	60.00
❑	WRAP. (5-CENT, 8-CARD)	150.00	90.00
❑ 1	Tommy Addison SP !	30.00	15.00
❑ 2	Houston Antwine RC	4.00	2.00
❑ 3	Nick Buoniconti	25.00	15.00
❑ 4	Ron Burton SP	10.00	5.00
❑ 5	Gino Cappelletti	5.00	2.50
❑ 6	Jim Colclough SP	6.00	3.00
❑ 7	Bob Dee SP	6.00	3.00
❑ 8	Larry Eisenhauer	4.00	2.00
❑ 9	Dick Felt SP	6.00	3.00
❑ 10	Larry Garron	4.00	2.00
❑ 11	Art Graham	4.00	2.00
❑ 12	Ron Hall DB	4.00	2.00
❑ 13	Charles Long	4.00	2.00
❑ 14	Don McKinnon	4.00	2.00
❑ 15	Don Oakes SP	6.00	3.00
❑ 16	Ross O'Hanley SP	6.00	3.00
❑ 17	Babe Parilli SP	10.00	5.00
❑ 18	Jesse Richardson SP	6.00	3.00
❑ 19	Jack Rudolph SP	6.00	3.00
❑ 20	Don Webb RC	4.00	2.00
❑ 21	Boston Patriots	6.00	3.00
❑ 22	Ray Abruzzese	4.00	2.00
❑ 23	Stew Barber RC	4.00	2.00
❑ 24	Dave Behrman	4.00	2.00
❑ 25	Al Bemiller	4.00	2.00
❑ 26	Elbert Dubenion SP	10.00	5.00
❑ 27	Jim Dunaway RC SP	6.00	3.00
❑ 28	Booker Edgerson SP	6.00	3.00
❑ 29	Cookie Gilchrist SP	25.00	15.00
❑ 30	Jack Kemp SP	120.00	60.00
❑ 31	Daryle Lamonica RC	75.00	40.00
❑ 32	Bill Miller	4.00	2.00
❑ 33	Herb Paterra RC	4.00	2.00
❑ 34	Ken Rice SP	6.00	3.00
❑ 35	Ed Rutkowski	4.00	2.00
❑ 36	George Saimes RC	4.00	2.00
❑ 37	Tom Sestak	4.00	2.00
❑ 38	Billy Shaw SP	15.00	7.50
❑ 39	Mike Stratton	5.00	2.50
❑ 40	Gene Sykes	4.00	2.00
❑ 41	John Tracey SP	6.00	3.00
❑ 42	Sid Youngelman SP	6.00	3.00
❑ 43	Buffalo Bills	6.00	3.00
❑ 44	Eldon Danenhauer SP	6.00	3.00
❑ 45	Jim Fraser SP	6.00	3.00
❑ 46	Chuck Gavin SP	6.00	3.00
❑ 47	Goose Gonsoulin SP	10.00	5.00
❑ 48	Ernie Barnes RC	4.00	2.00
❑ 49	Tom Janik	4.00	2.00
❑ 50	Billy Joe RC	5.00	2.50
❑ 51	Ike Lassiter RC	4.00	2.00
❑ 52	John McCormick QB SP	6.00	3.00
❑ 53	Bud McFadin SP	6.00	3.00
❑ 54	Gene Mingo SP	6.00	3.00
❑ 55	Charlie Mitchell	4.00	2.00
❑ 56	John Nocera SP	6.00	3.00
❑ 57	Tom Nomina	4.00	2.00
❑ 58	Harold Olson SP	6.00	3.00
❑ 59	Bob Scarpitto	4.00	2.00
❑ 60	John Sklopan	4.00	2.00
❑ 61	Mickey Slaughter	4.00	2.00
❑ 62	Don Stone	4.00	2.00
❑ 63	Jerry Sturm	4.00	2.00
❑ 64	Lionel Taylor SP	12.00	6.00
❑ 65	Broncos Team SP	20.00	10.00
❑ 66	Scott Appleton RC	4.00	2.00
❑ 67	Tony Banfield SP	6.00	3.00
❑ 68	George Blanda SP	75.00	40.00
❑ 69	Billy Cannon	6.00	3.00
❑ 70	Doug Cline SP	6.00	3.00
❑ 71	Gary Cutsinger SP	6.00	3.00
❑ 72	Willard Dewveall SP	6.00	3.00
❑ 73	Don Floyd SP	6.00	3.00
❑ 74	Freddy Glick SP	6.00	3.00
❑ 75	Charlie Hennigan SP	10.00	5.00
❑ 76	Ed Husmann SP	6.00	3.00
❑ 77	Bobby Jancik SP	6.00	3.00
❑ 78	Jacky Lee SP	10.00	5.00
❑ 79	Bob McLeod SP	6.00	3.00
❑ 80	Rich Michael SP	6.00	3.00
❑ 81	Larry Onesti RC	4.00	2.00
❑ 82	Checklist Card UER	60.00	30.00
❑ 83	Bob Schmidt SP	6.00	3.00
❑ 84	Walt Suggs SP	6.00	3.00
❑ 85	Bob Talamini SP	6.00	3.00
❑ 86	Charley Tolar SP	6.00	3.00
❑ 87	Don Trull RC	4.00	2.00
❑ 88	Houston Oilers	6.00	3.00
❑ 89	Fred Arbanas	4.00	2.00
❑ 90	Bobby Bell RC	40.00	25.00
❑ 91	Mel Branch SP	10.00	5.00
❑ 92	Buck Buchanan RC	40.00	25.00
❑ 93	Ed Budde RC	4.00	2.00
❑ 94	Chris Burford SP	10.00	5.00
❑ 95	Walt Corey RC	5.00	2.50
❑ 96	Len Dawson SP	75.00	40.00
❑ 97	Dave Grayson RC	4.00	2.00
❑ 98	Abner Haynes	6.00	3.00
❑ 99	Sherrill Headrick SP	10.00	5.00
❑ 100	E.J. Holub	4.00	2.00
❑ 101	Bobby Hunt RC	4.00	2.00
❑ 102	Frank Jackson SP	6.00	3.00
❑ 103	Curtis McClinton	5.00	2.50
❑ 104	Jerry Mays SP	10.00	5.00
❑ 105	Johnny Robinson SP	12.00	6.00
❑ 106	Jack Spikes SP	6.00	3.00
❑ 107	Smokey Stover SP	6.00	3.00
❑ 108	Jim Tyrer RC	8.00	4.00
❑ 109	Duane Wood SP	6.00	3.00
❑ 110	Kansas City Chiefs	6.00	3.00
❑ 111	Dick Christy SP	6.00	3.00
❑ 112	Dan Ficca SP	6.00	3.00
❑ 113	Larry Grantham	4.00	2.00
❑ 114	Curley Johnson SP	6.00	3.00
❑ 115	Gene Heeter	4.00	2.00
❑ 116	Jack Klotz	4.00	2.00
❑ 117	Pete Liske RC	5.00	2.50
❑ 118	Bob McAdam	4.00	2.00
❑ 119	Dee Mackey SP	6.00	3.00
❑ 120	Bill Mathis SP	10.00	5.00
❑ 121	Don Maynard	35.00	20.00
❑ 122	Dainard Paulson SP	6.00	3.00
❑ 123	Gerry Philbin RC	5.00	2.50
❑ 124	Mark Smolinski SP	6.00	3.00
❑ 125	Matt Snell RC	20.00	10.00
❑ 126	Mike Taliaferro	4.00	2.00
❑ 127	Bake Turner RC SP	10.00	5.00
❑ 128	Jeff Ware	4.00	2.00
❑ 129	Clyde Washington	4.00	2.00
❑ 130	Dick Wood RC	4.00	2.00
❑ 131	New York Jets	6.00	3.00
❑ 132	Dalva Allen SP	6.00	3.00
❑ 133	Dan Birdwell	4.00	2.00
❑ 134	Dave Costa RC	4.00	2.00
❑ 135	Dobie Craig	4.00	2.00
❑ 136	Clem Daniels	5.00	2.50
❑ 137	Cotton Davidson SP	10.00	5.00
❑ 138	Claude Gibson	4.00	2.00
❑ 139	Tom Flores SP	15.00	7.50
❑ 140	Wayne Hawkins SP	6.00	3.00
❑ 141	Ken Herock	4.00	2.00
❑ 142	Jon Jelacic SP	6.00	3.00
❑ 143	Joe Krakoski	4.00	2.00
❑ 144	Archie Matsos SP	6.00	3.00
❑ 145	Mike Mercer	4.00	2.00
❑ 146	Alan Miller SP	6.00	3.00
❑ 147	Bob Mischak SP	6.00	3.00
❑ 148	Jim Otto SP	30.00	18.00
❑ 149	Clancy Osborne SP	6.00	3.00
❑ 150	Art Powell SP	12.00	6.00
❑ 151	Bo Roberson	4.00	2.00
❑ 152	Fred Williamson SP	30.00	18.00
❑ 153	Oakland Raiders	6.00	3.00
❑ 154	Chuck Allen RC SP	10.00	5.00
❑ 155	Lance Alworth	50.00	30.00
❑ 156	George Blair	4.00	2.00
❑ 157	Earl Faison	4.00	2.00
❑ 158	Sam Gruneisen	4.00	2.00
❑ 159	John Hadl RC	40.00	25.00
❑ 160	Dick Harris SP	6.00	3.00
❑ 161	Emil Karas SP	6.00	3.00
❑ 162	Dave Kocourek SP	6.00	3.00
❑ 163	Ernie Ladd	8.00	4.00
❑ 164	Keith Lincoln	6.00	3.00
❑ 165	Paul Lowe SP	12.00	6.00
❑ 166	Charley McNeil	4.00	2.00
❑ 167	Jacque MacKinnon SP RC	6.00	3.00
❑ 168	Ron Mix SP	20.00	10.00
❑ 169	Don Norton SP	6.00	3.00
❑ 170	Don Rogers SP	6.00	3.00
❑ 171	Tobin Rote SP	10.00	5.00
❑ 172	Henry Schmidt SP RC	6.00	3.00
❑ 173	Bud Whitehead	4.00	2.00
❑ 174	Ernie Wright SP	10.00	5.00
❑ 175	San Diego Chargers	6.00	3.00
❑ 176	Checklist SP UER !	160.00	80.00

1965 Topps

❑ COMPLETE SET (176) 4000.00 2500.00
❑ WRAPPER (5-CENT) 150.00 90.00
❑ 1 Tommy Addison SP ! 35.00 20.00
❑ 2 Houston Antwine SP 12.00 7.00
❑ 3 Nick Buoniconti SP 30.00 18.00
❑ 4 Ron Burton SP 20.00 10.00
❑ 5 Gino Cappelletti SP 20.00 10.00
❑ 6 Jim Colclough 7.00 3.50
❑ 7 Bob Dee SP 12.00 7.00
❑ 8 Larry Eisenhauer 7.00 3.50
❑ 9 J.D. Garrett 7.00 3.50
❑ 10 Larry Garron 7.00 3.50
❑ 11 Art Graham SP 12.00 7.00
❑ 12 Ron Hall DB 7.00 3.50
❑ 13 Charles Long 7.00 3.50
❑ 14 Jon Morris RC 10.00 5.00
❑ 15 Billy Neighbors SP 12.00 7.00
❑ 16 Ross O'Hanley 7.00 3.50
❑ 17 Babe Parilli SP 20.00 10.00
❑ 18 Tony Romeo SP 12.00 7.00
❑ 19 Jack Rudolph SP 12.00 7.00
❑ 20 Bob Schmidt 7.00 3.50
❑ 21 Don Webb SP 12.00 7.00
❑ 22 Jim Whalen SP 12.00 7.00
❑ 23 Stew Barber 7.00 3.50
❑ 24 Glenn Bass SP 12.00 7.00
❑ 25 Al Bemiller SP 12.00 7.00
❑ 26 Wray Carlton SP 12.00 7.00
❑ 27 Tom Day 7.00 3.50
❑ 28 Elbert Dubenion SP 15.00 7.50
❑ 29 Jim Dunaway 7.00 3.50
❑ 30 Pete Gogolak RC SP 20.00 10.00
❑ 31 Dick Hudson SP 12.00 7.00
❑ 32 Harry Jacobs SP 12.00 7.00
❑ 33 Billy Joe SP 15.00 7.50
❑ 34 Tom Keating RC SP 12.00 7.00
❑ 35 Jack Kemp SP ! 150.00 75.00
❑ 36 Daryle Lamonica SP 50.00 30.00
❑ 37 Paul Maguire SP 20.00 10.00
❑ 38 Ron McDole RC SP 12.00 7.00
❑ 39 George Saimes SP 12.00 7.00
❑ 40 Tom Sestak SP 12.00 7.00
❑ 41 Billy Shaw SP 20.00 10.00
❑ 42 Mike Stratton SP 12.00 7.00
❑ 43 John Tracey SP 12.00 7.00
❑ 44 Ernie Warlick 7.00 3.50
❑ 45 Odell Barry 7.00 3.50
❑ 46 Willie Brown RC SP 100.00 60.00
❑ 47 Gerry Bussell SP 12.00 7.00
❑ 48 Eldon Danenhauer SP 12.00 7.00
❑ 49 Al Denson SP 12.00 7.00
❑ 50 Hewritt Dixon RC SP 15.00 7.50
❑ 51 Cookie Gilchrist SP 30.00 18.00
❑ 52 Goose Gonsoulin SP 15.00 7.50
❑ 53 Abner Haynes SP 20.00 10.00
❑ 54 Jerry Hopkins 7.00 3.50
❑ 55 Ray Jacobs SP 12.00 7.00
❑ 56 Jacky Lee SP 15.00 7.50
❑ 57 John McCormick QB 7.00 3.50
❑ 58 Bob McCullough SP 12.00 7.00
❑ 59 John McGeever 7.00 3.50
❑ 60 Charlie Mitchell SP 12.00 7.00
❑ 61 Jim Perkins SP 12.00 7.00
❑ 62 Bob Scarpitto SP 12.00 7.00
❑ 63 Mickey Slaughter SP 12.00 7.00
❑ 64 Jerry Sturm SP 12.00 7.00
❑ 65 Lionel Taylor SP 20.00 10.00
❑ 66 Scott Appleton SP 12.00 7.00
❑ 67 Johnny Baker SP 12.00 7.00
❑ 68 Sonny Bishop SP 12.00 7.00
❑ 69 George Blanda SP 125.00 75.00
❑ 70 Sid Blanks SP 12.00 7.00
❑ 71 Ode Burrell SP 12.00 7.00
❑ 72 Doug Cline SP 12.00 7.00
❑ 73 Willard Dewveall 7.00 3.50
❑ 74 Larry Elkins RC 7.00 3.50
❑ 75 Don Floyd SP 12.00 7.00
❑ 76 Freddy Glick 7.00 3.50
❑ 77 Tom Goode SP 12.00 7.00
❑ 78 Charlie Hennigan SP 20.00 10.00
❑ 79 Ed Husmann 7.00 3.50
❑ 80 Bobby Jancik SP 12.00 7.00
❑ 81 Bud McFadin SP 12.00 7.00
❑ 82 Bob McLeod SP 12.00 7.00
❑ 83 Jim Norton SP 12.00 7.00
❑ 84 Walt Suggs 7.00 3.50
❑ 85 Bob Talamini 7.00 3.50
❑ 86 Charley Tolar SP 12.00 7.00
❑ 87 Checklist SP ! 175.00 100.00
❑ 88 Don Trull SP 12.00 7.00
❑ 89 Fred Arbanas SP 12.00 7.00
❑ 90 Pete Beathard RC SP 12.00 7.00
❑ 91 Bobby Bell SP 40.00 25.00
❑ 92 Mel Branch SP 12.00 7.00
❑ 93 Tommy Brooker SP 12.00 7.00
❑ 94 Buck Buchanan SP 35.00 20.00
❑ 95 Ed Budde SP 12.00 7.00
❑ 96 Chris Burford SP 12.00 7.00
❑ 97 Walt Corey 7.00 3.50
❑ 98 Jerry Cornelison 7.00 3.50
❑ 99 Len Dawson SP 100.00 60.00
❑ 100 Jon Gilliam SP 12.00 7.00
❑ 101 Sherrill Headrick SP UER 12.00 7.00
❑ 102 Dave Hill SP 12.00 7.00
❑ 103 E.J. Holub SP 12.00 7.00
❑ 104 Bobby Hunt SP 12.00 7.00
❑ 105 Frank Jackson SP 12.00 7.00
❑ 106 Jerry Mays 10.00 5.00
❑ 107 Curtis McClinton SP 15.00 7.50
❑ 108 Bobby Ply SP 12.00 7.00
❑ 109 Johnny Robinson SP 15.00 7.50
❑ 110 Jim Tyrer SP 12.00 7.00
❑ 111 Bill Baird SP 12.00 7.00
❑ 112 Ralph Baker RC SP 12.00 7.00
❑ 113 Sam DeLuca SP 12.00 7.00
❑ 114 Larry Grantham SP 15.00 7.50
❑ 115 Gene Heeter SP 12.00 7.00
❑ 116 Winston Hill RC SP 20.00 10.00
❑ 117 John Huarte RC SP 30.00 18.00
❑ 118 Cosmo Iacavazzi SP 12.00 7.00
❑ 119 Curley Johnson SP 12.00 7.00
❑ 120 Dee Mackey UER 7.00 3.50
❑ 121 Don Maynard 50.00 30.00
❑ 122 Joe Namath RC SP ! 1600.00 1000.00
❑ 123 Dainard Paulson 7.00 3.50
❑ 124 Gerry Philbin SP 12.00 7.00
❑ 125 Sherman Plunkett RC SP 15.00 7.50
❑ 126 Mark Smolinski 7.00 3.50
❑ 127 Matt Snell SP 30.00 18.00
❑ 128 Mike Taliaferro SP 12.00 7.00
❑ 129 Bake Turner SP 12.00 7.00
❑ 130 Clyde Washington SP 12.00 7.00
❑ 131 Verlon Biggs RC SP 12.00 7.00
❑ 132 Dalva Allen 7.00 3.50
❑ 133 Fred Biletnikoff RC SP 225.00 150.00
❑ 134 Billy Cannon SP 20.00 10.00
❑ 135 Dave Costa SP 12.00 7.00
❑ 136 Clem Daniels SP 15.00 7.50
❑ 137 Ben Davidson RC SP 60.00 35.00
❑ 138 Cotton Davidson SP 15.00 7.50
❑ 139 Tom Flores SP 20.00 10.00
❑ 140 Claude Gibson 7.00 3.50
❑ 141 Wayne Hawkins 7.00 3.50
❑ 142 Archie Matsos SP 12.00 7.00
❑ 143 Mike Mercer SP 12.00 7.00
❑ 144 Bob Mischak SP 12.00 7.00
❑ 145 Jim Otto 30.00 18.00
❑ 146 Art Powell UER 10.00 5.00
❑ 147 Warren Powers DB SP 12.00 7.00
❑ 148 Ken Rice SP 12.00 7.00
❑ 149 Bo Roberson SP 12.00 7.00
❑ 150 Harry Schuh RC 7.00 3.50
❑ 151 Larry Todd SP 12.00 7.00
❑ 152 Fred Williamson SP 30.00 15.00
❑ 153 J.R. Williamson 7.00 3.50
❑ 154 Chuck Allen 10.00 5.00
❑ 155 Lance Alworth 75.00 50.00
❑ 156 Frank Buncom 7.00 3.50
❑ 157 Steve DeLong RC SP 12.00 7.00
❑ 158 Earl Faison SP 15.00 7.50
❑ 159 Kenny Graham SP 12.00 7.00
❑ 160 George Gross SP 12.00 7.00
❑ 161 John Hadl SP 35.00 20.00
❑ 162 Emil Karas SP 12.00 7.00
❑ 163 Dave Kocourek SP 12.00 7.00
❑ 164 Ernie Ladd SP 20.00 10.00
❑ 165 Keith Lincoln SP 20.00 10.00
❑ 166 Paul Lowe SP 20.00 10.00
❑ 167 Jacque MacKinnon 7.00 3.50
❑ 168 Ron Mix 20.00 12.00
❑ 169 Don Norton SP 12.00 7.00
❑ 170 Bob Petrich 7.00 3.50
❑ 171 Rick Redman SP 12.00 7.00
❑ 172 Pat Shea 7.00 3.50
❑ 173 Walt Sweeney RC SP 15.00 7.50
❑ 174 Dick Westmoreland RC 7.00 3.50
❑ 175 Ernie Wright SP 20.00 10.00
❑ 176 Checklist SP ! 225.00 125.00

1966 Topps

❑ COMPLETE SET (132) 1500.00 950.00
❑ WRAPPER (5-CENT) 60.00 30.00
❑ 1 Tommy Addison ! 20.00 10.00
❑ 2 Houston Antwine 5.00 3.00
❑ 3 Nick Buoniconti 10.00 5.00
❑ 4 Gino Cappelletti 7.00 3.50
❑ 5 Bob Dee 5.00 3.00
❑ 6 Larry Garron 5.00 3.00
❑ 7 Art Graham 5.00 3.00
❑ 8 Ron Hall DB 5.00 3.00
❑ 9 Charles Long 5.00 3.00
❑ 10 Jon Morris 5.00 3.00
❑ 11 Don Oakes 5.00 3.00
❑ 12 Babe Parilli 7.00 3.50
❑ 13 Don Webb 5.00 3.00
❑ 14 Jim Whalen 5.00 3.00
❑ 15 Funny Ring Checklist ! 300.00 200.00
❑ 16 Stew Barber 5.00 3.00
❑ 17 Glenn Bass 5.00 3.00
❑ 18 Dave Behrman 5.00 3.00
❑ 19 Al Bemiller 5.00 3.00
❑ 20 Butch Byrd RC 7.00 3.50
❑ 21 Wray Carlton 5.00 3.00
❑ 22 Tom Day 5.00 3.00
❑ 23 Elbert Dubenion 7.00 3.50
❑ 24 Jim Dunaway 5.00 3.00
❑ 25 Dick Hudson 5.00 3.00
❑ 26 Jack Kemp 150.00 75.00
❑ 27 Daryle Lamonica 20.00 12.00
❑ 28 Tom Sestak 5.00 3.00
❑ 29 Billy Shaw 10.00 5.00
❑ 30 Mike Stratton 5.00 3.00
❑ 31 Eldon Danenhauer 5.00 3.00
❑ 32 Cookie Gilchrist 10.00 5.00
❑ 33 Goose Gonsoulin 7.00 3.50
❑ 34 Wendell Hayes RC 10.00 5.00
❑ 35 Abner Haynes 10.00 5.00
❑ 36 Jerry Hopkins 5.00 3.00
❑ 37 Ray Jacobs 5.00 3.00
❑ 38 Charlie Janerette 5.00 3.00
❑ 39 Ray Kubala 5.00 3.00
❑ 40 John McCormick QB 5.00 3.00
❑ 41 Leroy Moore 5.00 3.00
❑ 42 Bob Scarpitto 5.00 3.00

❑ 43 Mickey Slaughter 5.00 3.00
❑ 44 Jerry Sturm 5.00 3.00
❑ 45 Lionel Taylor 10.00 5.00
❑ 46 Scott Appleton 5.00 3.00
❑ 47 Johnny Baker 5.00 3.00
❑ 48 George Blanda 35.00 20.00
❑ 49 Sid Blanks 5.00 3.00
❑ 50 Danny Brabham 5.00 3.00
❑ 51 Ode Burrell 5.00 3.00
❑ 52 Gary Cutsinger 5.00 3.00
❑ 53 Larry Elkins 5.00 3.00
❑ 54 Don Floyd 5.00 3.00
❑ 55 Willie Frazier RC 7.00 3.50
❑ 56 Freddy Glick 5.00 3.00
❑ 57 Charlie Hennigan 7.00 3.50
❑ 58 Bobby Jancik 5.00 3.00
❑ 59 Rich Michael 5.00 3.00
❑ 60 Don Trull 5.00 3.00
❑ 61 Checklist 55.00 30.00
❑ 62 Fred Arbanas 5.00 3.00
❑ 63 Pete Beathard 5.00 3.00
❑ 64 Bobby Bell 10.00 5.00
❑ 65 Ed Budde 5.00 3.00
❑ 66 Chris Burford 5.00 3.00
❑ 67 Len Dawson 40.00 25.00
❑ 68 Jon Gilliam 5.00 3.00
❑ 69 Sherrill Headrick 5.00 3.00
❑ 70 E.J. Holub UER 5.00 3.00
❑ 71 Bobby Hunt 5.00 3.00
❑ 72 Curtis McClinton 7.00 3.50
❑ 73 Jerry Mays 5.00 3.00
❑ 74 Johnny Robinson 7.00 3.50
❑ 75 Otis Taylor RC 25.00 15.00
❑ 76 Tom Erlandson 7.00 3.50
❑ 77 Norm Evans RC 10.00 5.00
❑ 78 Tom Goode 7.00 3.50
❑ 79 Mike Hudock 7.00 3.50
❑ 80 Frank Jackson 7.00 3.50
❑ 81 Billy Joe 7.00 3.50
❑ 82 Dave Kocourek 7.00 3.50
❑ 83 Bo Roberson 7.00 3.50
❑ 84 Jack Spikes 7.00 3.50
❑ 85 Jim Warren RC 7.00 3.50
❑ 86 Willie West RC 7.00 3.50
❑ 87 Dick Westmoreland 7.00 3.50
❑ 88 Eddie Wilson 7.00 3.50
❑ 89 Dick Wood 7.00 3.50
❑ 90 Verlon Biggs 7.00 3.50
❑ 91 Sam DeLuca 5.00 3.00
❑ 92 Winston Hill 5.00 3.00
❑ 93 Dee Mackey 5.00 3.00
❑ 94 Bill Mathis 5.00 3.00
❑ 95 Don Maynard 30.00 18.00
❑ 96 Joe Namath 250.00 150.00
❑ 97 Dainard Paulson 5.00 3.00
❑ 98 Gerry Philbin 7.00 3.50
❑ 99 Sherman Plunkett 5.00 3.00
❑ 100 Paul Rochester 5.00 3.00
❑ 101 George Sauer Jr. RC 15.00 7.50
❑ 102 Matt Snell 10.00 5.00
❑ 103 Jim Turner RC 7.00 3.50
❑ 104 Fred Biletnikoff UER 50.00 30.00
❑ 105 Bill Budness 5.00 3.00
❑ 106 Billy Cannon 10.00 5.00
❑ 107 Clem Daniels 7.00 3.50
❑ 108 Ben Davidson 15.00 7.50
❑ 109 Cotton Davidson 7.00 3.50
❑ 110 Claude Gibson 5.00 3.00
❑ 111 Wayne Hawkins 5.00 3.00
❑ 112 Ken Herock 5.00 3.00
❑ 113 Bob Mischak 5.00 3.00
❑ 114 Gus Otto 5.00 3.00
❑ 115 Jim Otto 20.00 12.00
❑ 116 Art Powell 10.00 5.00
❑ 117 Harry Schuh 5.00 3.00
❑ 118 Chuck Allen 5.00 3.00
❑ 119 Lance Alworth 40.00 25.00
❑ 120 Frank Buncom 5.00 3.00
❑ 121 Steve DeLong 5.00 3.00
❑ 122 John Farris 5.00 3.00
❑ 123 Kenny Graham 5.00 3.00
❑ 124 Sam Gruneisen 5.00 3.00
❑ 125 John Hadl 10.00 5.00
❑ 126 Walt Sweeney 5.00 3.00
❑ 127 Keith Lincoln 10.00 5.00
❑ 128 Ron Mix 10.00 5.00
❑ 129 Don Norton 5.00 3.00
❑ 130 Pat Shea 5.00 3.00
❑ 131 Ernie Wright 10.00 5.00
❑ 132 Checklist ! 100.00 50.00

1967 Topps

❑ COMPLETE SET (132) 700.00 400.00
❑ WRAPPER (5-CENT) 60.00 30.00
❑ 1 John Huarte ! 18.00 10.00
❑ 2 Babe Parilli 4.00 2.00
❑ 3 Gino Cappelletti 4.00 2.00
❑ 4 Larry Garron 3.00 1.50
❑ 5 Tommy Addison 3.00 1.50
❑ 6 Jon Morris 3.00 1.50
❑ 7 Houston Antwine 3.00 1.50
❑ 8 Don Oakes 3.00 1.50
❑ 9 Larry Eisenhauer 3.00 1.50
❑ 10 Jim Hunt 3.00 1.50
❑ 11 Jim Whalen 3.00 1.50
❑ 12 Art Graham 3.00 1.50
❑ 13 Nick Buoniconti 6.00 3.00
❑ 14 Bob Dee 3.00 1.50
❑ 15 Keith Lincoln 6.00 3.00
❑ 16 Tom Flores 4.00 2.00
❑ 17 Art Powell 4.00 2.00
❑ 18 Stew Barber 3.00 1.50
❑ 19 Wray Carlton 3.00 1.50
❑ 20 Elbert Dubenion 4.00 2.00
❑ 21 Jim Dunaway 3.00 1.50
❑ 22 Dick Hudson 3.00 1.50
❑ 23 Harry Jacobs 3.00 1.50
❑ 24 Jack Kemp 80.00 40.00
❑ 25 Ron McDole 3.00 1.50
❑ 26 George Saimes 3.00 1.50
❑ 27 Tom Sestak 3.00 1.50
❑ 28 Billy Shaw 6.00 3.00
❑ 29 Mike Stratton 3.00 1.50
❑ 30 Nemiah Wilson RC 3.00 1.50
❑ 31 John McCormick QB 3.00 1.50
❑ 32 Rex Mirich 3.00 1.50
❑ 33 Dave Costa 3.00 1.50
❑ 34 Goose Gonsoulin 4.00 2.00
❑ 35 Abner Haynes 6.00 3.00
❑ 36 Wendell Hayes 4.00 2.00
❑ 37 Archie Matsos 3.00 1.50
❑ 38 John Bramlett 3.00 1.50
❑ 39 Jerry Sturm 3.00 1.50
❑ 40 Max Leetzow 3.00 1.50
❑ 41 Bob Scarpitto 3.00 1.50
❑ 42 Lionel Taylor 6.00 3.00
❑ 43 Al Denson 3.00 1.50
❑ 44 Miller Farr RC 3.00 1.50
❑ 45 Don Trull 3.00 1.50
❑ 46 Jacky Lee 4.00 2.00
❑ 47 Bobby Jancik 3.00 1.50
❑ 48 Ode Burrell 3.00 1.50
❑ 49 Larry Elkins 3.00 1.50
❑ 50 W.K. Hicks 3.00 1.50
❑ 51 Sid Blanks 3.00 1.50
❑ 52 Jim Norton 3.00 1.50
❑ 53 Bobby Maples RC 3.00 1.50
❑ 54 Bob Talamini 3.00 1.50
❑ 55 Walt Suggs 3.00 1.50
❑ 56 Gary Cutsinger 3.00 1.50
❑ 57 Danny Brabham 3.00 1.50
❑ 58 Ernie Ladd 6.00 3.00
❑ 59 Checklist 50.00 25.00
❑ 60 Pete Beathard 3.00 1.50
❑ 61 Len Dawson 30.00 18.00
❑ 62 Bobby Hunt 3.00 1.50
❑ 63 Bert Coan 3.00 1.50
❑ 64 Curtis McClinton 4.00 2.00
❑ 65 Johnny Robinson 4.00 2.00
❑ 66 E.J. Holub 3.00 1.50
❑ 67 Jerry Mays 3.00 1.50
❑ 68 Jim Tyrer 4.00 2.00
❑ 69 Bobby Bell 6.00 3.00
❑ 70 Fred Arbanas 3.00 1.50
❑ 71 Buck Buchanan 6.00 3.00
❑ 72 Chris Burford 3.00 1.50
❑ 73 Otis Taylor 6.00 3.00
❑ 74 Cookie Gilchrist 8.00 4.00
❑ 75 Earl Faison 3.00 1.50
❑ 76 George Wilson Jr. 4.00 2.00
❑ 77 Rick Norton 3.00 1.50
❑ 78 Frank Jackson 4.00 2.00
❑ 79 Joe Auer 3.00 1.50
❑ 80 Willie West 3.00 1.50
❑ 81 Jim Warren 3.00 1.50
❑ 82 Wahoo McDaniel RC 50.00 30.00
❑ 83 Ernie Park 3.00 1.50
❑ 84 Billy Neighbors 3.00 1.50
❑ 85 Norm Evans 4.00 2.00
❑ 86 Tom Nomina 3.00 1.50
❑ 87 Rich Zecher 3.00 1.50
❑ 88 Dave Kocourek 3.00 1.50
❑ 89 Bill Baird 3.00 1.50
❑ 90 Ralph Baker 3.00 1.50
❑ 91 Verlon Biggs 3.00 1.50
❑ 92 Sam DeLuca 3.00 1.50
❑ 93 Larry Grantham 4.00 2.00
❑ 94 Jim Harris 3.00 1.50
❑ 95 Winston Hill 3.00 1.50
❑ 96 Bill Mathis 3.00 1.50
❑ 97 Don Maynard 20.00 12.00
❑ 98 Joe Namath 150.00 75.00
❑ 99 Gerry Philbin 4.00 2.00
❑ 100 Paul Rochester 3.00 1.50
❑ 101 George Sauer Jr. 4.00 2.00
❑ 102 Matt Snell 6.00 3.00
❑ 103 Daryle Lamonica 10.00 5.00
❑ 104 Glenn Bass 3.00 1.50
❑ 105 Jim Otto 6.00 3.00
❑ 106 Fred Biletnikoff 30.00 18.00
❑ 107 Cotton Davidson 4.00 2.00
❑ 108 Larry Todd 3.00 1.50
❑ 109 Billy Cannon 6.00 3.00
❑ 110 Clem Daniels 4.00 2.00
❑ 111 Dave Grayson 3.00 1.50
❑ 112 Kent McCloughan RC 3.00 1.50
❑ 113 Bob Svihus 3.00 1.50
❑ 114 Ike Lassiter 3.00 1.50
❑ 115 Harry Schuh 3.00 1.50
❑ 116 Ben Davidson 8.00 4.00
❑ 117 Tom Day 3.00 1.50
❑ 118 Scott Appleton 3.00 1.50
❑ 119 Steve Tensi RC 3.00 1.50
❑ 120 John Hadl 6.00 3.00
❑ 121 Paul Lowe 4.00 2.00
❑ 122 Jim Allison 3.00 1.50
❑ 123 Lance Alworth 35.00 20.00
❑ 124 Jacque MacKinnon 3.00 1.50
❑ 125 Ron Mix 6.00 3.00
❑ 126 Bob Petrich 3.00 1.50
❑ 127 Howard Kindig 3.00 1.50
❑ 128 Steve DeLong 3.00 1.50
❑ 129 Chuck Allen 3.00 1.50
❑ 130 Frank Buncom 3.00 1.50
❑ 131 Speedy Duncan RC 4.00 2.00
❑ 132 Checklist ! 70.00 35.00

1968 Topps

❑ COMPLETE SET (219) 550.00 350.00
❑ COMMON CARD (1-131) 1.50 .75
❑ COMMON CARD (132-219) 2.00 1.00
❑ WRAPPER (5-CENT, SER.1) 20.00 10.00
❑ WRAPPER (5-CENT, SER.2) 30.00 20.00
❑ 1 Bart Starr ! 40.00 25.00
❑ 2 Dick Bass 2.00 1.00
❑ 3 Grady Alderman 1.50 .75
❑ 4 Obert Logan 1.50 .75
❑ 5 Ernie Koy RC 2.00 1.00
❑ 6 Don Hultz 1.50 .75
❑ 7 Earl Gros 1.50 .75
❑ 8 Jim Bakken 1.50 .75
❑ 9 George Mira 2.00 1.00
❑ 10 Carl Kammerer 1.50 .75

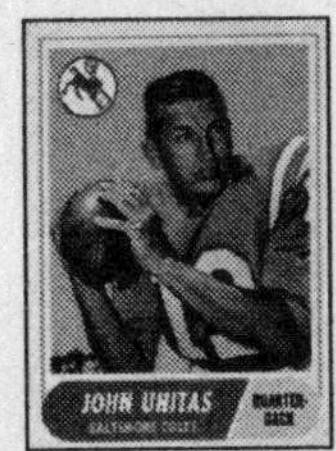

❑ 11 Willie Frazier 1.50 .75
❑ 12 Kent McCloughan UER 1.50 .75
❑ 13 George Sauer Jr. 2.00 1.00
❑ 14 Jack Clancy 1.50 .75
❑ 15 Jim Tyrer 2.00 1.00
❑ 16 Bobby Maples 1.50 .75
❑ 17 Bo Hickey 1.50 .75
❑ 18 Frank Buncom 1.50 .75
❑ 19 Keith Lincoln 2.00 1.00
❑ 20 Jim Whalen 1.50 .75
❑ 21 Junior Coffey 1.50 .75
❑ 22 Billy Ray Smith 1.50 .75
❑ 23 Johnny Morris 1.50 .75
❑ 24 Ernie Green 1.50 .75
❑ 25 Don Meredith 25.00 15.00
❑ 26 Wayne Walker 1.50 .75
❑ 27 Carroll Dale 2.00 1.00
❑ 28 Bernie Casey 2.00 1.00
❑ 29 Dave Osborn RC 2.00 1.00
❑ 30 Ray Poage 1.50 .75
❑ 31 Homer Jones 1.50 .75
❑ 32 Sam Baker 1.50 .75
❑ 33 Bill Saul 1.50 .75
❑ 34 Ken Willard 2.00 1.00
❑ 35 Bobby Mitchell 4.00 2.00
❑ 36 Gary Garrison RC 2.00 1.00
❑ 37 Billy Cannon 2.00 1.00
❑ 38 Ralph Baker 1.50 .75
❑ 39 Howard Twilley RC 4.00 2.00
❑ 40 Wendell Hayes 2.00 1.00
❑ 41 Jim Norton 1.50 .75
❑ 42 Tom Beer 1.50 .75
❑ 43 Chris Burford 1.50 .75
❑ 44 Stew Barber 1.50 .75
❑ 45 Leroy Mitchell UER 1.50 .75
❑ 46 Dan Grimm 1.50 .75
❑ 47 Jerry Logan 1.50 .75
❑ 48 Andy Livingston 1.50 .75
❑ 49 Paul Warfield 15.00 7.50
❑ 50 Don Perkins 3.00 1.50
❑ 51 Ron Kramer 1.50 .75
❑ 52 Bob Jeter RC 2.00 1.00
❑ 53 Les Josephson RC 2.00 1.00
❑ 54 Bobby Walden 1.50 .75
❑ 55 Checklist 15.00 7.50
❑ 56 Walter Roberts 1.50 .75
❑ 57 Henry Carr 1.50 .75
❑ 58 Gary Ballman 1.50 .75
❑ 59 J.R. Wilburn 1.50 .75
❑ 60 Jim Hart RC 10.00 5.00
❑ 61 Jim Johnson 3.00 1.50
❑ 62 Chris Hanburger 2.00 1.00
❑ 63 John Hadl 3.00 1.50
❑ 64 Hewritt Dixon 2.00 1.00
❑ 65 Joe Namath 80.00 50.00
❑ 66 Jim Warren 1.50 .75
❑ 67 Curtis McClinton 2.00 1.00
❑ 68 Bob Talamini 1.50 .75
❑ 69 Steve Tensi 1.50 .75
❑ 70 Dick Van Raaphorst UER 1.50 .75
❑ 71 Art Powell 2.00 1.00
❑ 72 Jim Nance RC 4.00 2.00
❑ 73 Bob Riggle 1.50 .75
❑ 74 John Mackey 5.00 2.50
❑ 75 Gale Sayers 40.00 25.00
❑ 76 Gene Hickerson 1.50 .75
❑ 77 Dan Reeves 10.00 5.00
❑ 78 Tom Nowatzke 1.50 .75
❑ 79 Elijah Pitts 3.00 1.50
❑ 80 Lamar Lundy 2.00 1.00
❑ 81 Paul Flatley 1.50 .75
❑ 82 Dave Whitsell 1.50 .75
❑ 83 Spider Lockhart 2.00 1.00
❑ 84 Dave Lloyd 1.50 .75
❑ 85 Roy Jefferson 2.00 1.00
❑ 86 Jackie Smith 6.00 3.00
❑ 87 John David Crow 2.00 1.00
❑ 88 Sonny Jurgensen 6.00 3.00
❑ 89 Ron Mix 3.00 1.50
❑ 90 Clem Daniels 2.00 1.00
❑ 91 Cornell Gordon 1.50 .75
❑ 92 Tom Goode 1.50 .75
❑ 93 Bobby Bell 3.00 1.50
❑ 94 Walt Suggs 1.50 .75
❑ 95 Eric Crabtree 1.50 .75
❑ 96 Sherrill Headrick 1.50 .75
❑ 97 Wray Carlton 1.50 .75
❑ 98 Gino Cappelletti 2.00 1.00
❑ 99 Tommy McDonald 4.00 2.00
❑ 100 Johnny Unitas 35.00 20.00
❑ 101 Richie Petitbon 1.50 .75
❑ 102 Erich Barnes 1.50 .75
❑ 103 Bob Hayes 8.00 4.00
❑ 104 Milt Plum 2.00 1.00
❑ 105 Boyd Dowler 2.00 1.00
❑ 106 Ed Meador 1.50 .75
❑ 107 Fred Cox 1.50 .75
❑ 108 Steve Stonebreaker RC 1.50 .75
❑ 109 Aaron Thomas 1.50 .75
❑ 110 Norm Snead 2.00 1.00
❑ 111 Paul Martha RC 1.50 .75
❑ 112 Jerry Stovall 1.50 .75
❑ 113 Kay McFarland 1.50 .75
❑ 114 Pat Richter 1.50 .75
❑ 115 Rick Redman 1.50 .75
❑ 116 Tom Keating 1.50 .75
❑ 117 Matt Snell 2.00 1.00
❑ 118 Dick Westmoreland 1.50 .75
❑ 119 Jerry Mays 1.50 .75
❑ 120 Sid Blanks 1.50 .75
❑ 121 Al Denson 1.50 .75
❑ 122 Bobby Hunt 1.50 .75
❑ 123 Mike Mercer 1.50 .75
❑ 124 Nick Buoniconti 3.00 1.50
❑ 125 Ron Vanderkelen RC 1.50 .75
❑ 126 Ordell Braase 1.50 .75
❑ 127 Dick Butkus 45.00 30.00
❑ 128 Gary Collins 2.00 1.00
❑ 129 Mel Renfro 6.00 3.00
❑ 130 Alex Karras 5.00 2.50
❑ 131 Herb Adderley ! 5.00 2.50
❑ 132 Roman Gabriel ! 4.00 2.00
❑ 133 Bill Brown 2.50 1.25
❑ 134 Kent Kramer 2.00 1.00
❑ 135 Tucker Frederickson 2.50 1.25
❑ 136 Nate Ramsey 2.00 1.00
❑ 137 Marv Woodson 2.00 1.00
❑ 138 Ken Gray 2.00 1.00
❑ 139 John Brodie 5.00 2.50
❑ 140 Jerry Smith 2.00 1.00
❑ 141 Brad Hubbert 2.00 1.00
❑ 142 George Blanda 20.00 10.00
❑ 143 Pete Lammons RC 2.00 1.00
❑ 144 Doug Moreau 2.00 1.00
❑ 145 E.J. Holub 2.00 1.00
❑ 146 Ode Burrell 2.00 1.00
❑ 147 Bob Scarpitto 2.00 1.00
❑ 148 Andre White 2.00 1.00
❑ 149 Jack Kemp 50.00 30.00
❑ 150 Art Graham 2.00 1.00
❑ 151 Tommy Nobis 6.00 3.00
❑ 152 Willie Richardson RC 2.50 1.25
❑ 153 Jack Concannon 2.00 1.00
❑ 154 Bill Glass 2.00 1.00
❑ 155 Craig Morton RC 10.00 5.00
❑ 156 Pat Studstill 2.00 1.00
❑ 157 Ray Nitschke 10.00 5.00
❑ 158 Roger Brown 2.00 1.00
❑ 159 Joe Kapp RC 5.00 2.50
❑ 160 Jim Taylor 15.00 7.50
❑ 161 Fran Tarkenton 20.00 10.00
❑ 162 Mike Ditka 30.00 18.00
❑ 163 Andy Russell RC 6.00 3.00
❑ 164 Larry Wilson 4.00 2.00
❑ 165 Tommy Davis 2.00 1.00
❑ 166 Paul Krause 4.00 2.00
❑ 167 Speedy Duncan 2.00 1.00
❑ 168 Fred Biletnikoff 15.00 7.50
❑ 169 Don Maynard 10.00 5.00
❑ 170 Frank Emanuel 2.00 1.00
❑ 171 Len Dawson 15.00 7.50
❑ 172 Miller Farr 2.00 1.00
❑ 173 Floyd Little RC 20.00 10.00
❑ 174 Lonnie Wright 2.00 1.00
❑ 175 Paul Costa 2.00 1.00
❑ 176 Don Trull 2.00 1.00
❑ 177 Jerry Simmons 2.00 1.00
❑ 178 Tom Matte 2.50 1.25
❑ 179 Bennie McRae 2.00 1.00
❑ 180 Jim Kanicki 2.00 1.00
❑ 181 Bob Lilly 15.00 7.50
❑ 182 Tom Watkins 2.00 1.00
❑ 183 Jim Grabowski RC 4.00 2.00
❑ 184 Jack Snow RC 4.00 2.00
❑ 185 Gary Cuozzo RC 2.50 1.25
❑ 186 Billy Kilmer 4.00 2.00
❑ 187 Jim Katcavage 2.00 1.00
❑ 188 Floyd Peters 2.00 1.00
❑ 189 Bill Nelsen 2.50 1.25
❑ 190 Bobby Joe Conrad 2.50 1.25
❑ 191 Kermit Alexander 2.00 1.00
❑ 192 Charley Taylor UER 6.00 3.00
❑ 193 Lance Alworth 20.00 10.00
❑ 194 Daryle Lamonica 5.00 2.50
❑ 195 Al Atkinson 2.00 1.00
❑ 196 Bob Griese RC 90.00 50.00
❑ 197 Buck Buchanan 4.00 2.00
❑ 198 Pete Beathard 2.00 1.00
❑ 199 Nemiah Wilson 2.00 1.00
❑ 200 Ernie Wright 2.00 1.00
❑ 201 George Saimes 2.00 1.00
❑ 202 John Charles 2.00 1.00
❑ 203 Randy Johnson 2.00 1.00
❑ 204 Tony Lorick 2.00 1.00
❑ 205 Dick Evey 2.00 1.00
❑ 206 Leroy Kelly 10.00 5.00
❑ 207 Lee Roy Jordan 6.00 3.00
❑ 208 Jim Gibbons 2.00 1.00
❑ 209 Donny Anderson RC 4.00 2.00
❑ 210 Maxie Baughan 2.00 1.00
❑ 211 Joe Morrison 2.00 1.00
❑ 212 Jim Snowden 2.00 1.00
❑ 213 Lenny Lyles 2.00 1.00
❑ 214 Bobby Joe Green 2.00 1.00
❑ 215 Frank Ryan 2.50 1.25
❑ 216 Cornell Green 2.50 1.25
❑ 217 Karl Sweetan 2.00 1.00
❑ 218 Dave Williams 2.00 1.00
❑ 219A Checklist Green ! 18.00 10.00
❑ 219B Checklist Blue ! 20.00 12.00

1969 Topps

❑ COMPLETE SET (263) 550.00 350.00
❑ COMMON CARD (1-132) 1.50 .75
❑ COMMON CARD (133-263) 2.00 1.00
❑ WRAPPER (5-CENT) 30.00 15.00
❑ 1 Leroy Kelly ! 20.00 10.00
❑ 2 Paul Flatley 1.50 .75
❑ 3 Jim Cadile 1.50 .75
❑ 4 Erich Barnes 1.50 .75
❑ 5 Willie Richardson 1.50 .75
❑ 6 Bob Hayes 5.00 2.50
❑ 7 Bob Jeter 1.50 .75
❑ 8 Jim Colclough 1.50 .75
❑ 9 Sherrill Headrick 1.50 .75
❑ 10 Jim Dunaway 1.50 .75

❑ 11 Bill Munson 2.00 1.00
❑ 12 Jack Pardee 2.00 1.00
❑ 13 Jim Lindsey 1.50 .75
❑ 14 Dave Whitsell 1.50 .75
❑ 15 Tucker Frederickson 1.50 .75
❑ 16 Alvin Haymond 2.00 1.00
❑ 17 Andy Russell 2.00 1.00
❑ 18 Tom Beer 1.50 .75
❑ 19 Bobby Maples 1.50 .75
❑ 20 Len Dawson 8.00 4.00
❑ 21 Willis Crenshaw 1.50 .75
❑ 22 Tommy Davis 1.50 .75
❑ 23 Rickie Harris 1.50 .75
❑ 24 Jerry Simmons 1.50 .75
❑ 25 Johnny Unitas 40.00 25.00
❑ 26 Brian Piccolo RC UER 80.00 50.00
❑ 27 Bob Matheson 1.50 .75
❑ 28 Howard Twilley 2.00 1.00
❑ 29 Jim Turner 2.00 1.00
❑ 30 Pete Banaszak RC 2.00 1.00
❑ 31 Lance Rentzel RC 2.00 1.00
❑ 32 Bill Triplett 1.50 .75
❑ 33 Boyd Dowler 2.00 1.00
❑ 34 Merlin Olsen 5.00 2.50
❑ 35 Joe Kapp 3.00 1.50
❑ 36 Dan Abramowicz RC 4.00 2.00
❑ 37 Spider Lockhart 2.00 1.00
❑ 38 Tom Day 1.50 .75
❑ 39 Art Graham 1.50 .75
❑ 40 Bob Cappadona 1.50 .75
❑ 41 Gary Ballman 1.50 .75
❑ 42 Clendon Thomas 1.50 .75
❑ 43 Jackie Smith 4.00 2.00
❑ 44 Dave Wilcox 3.00 1.50
❑ 45 Jerry Smith 1.50 .75
❑ 46 Dan Grimm 1.50 .75
❑ 47 Tom Matte 2.00 1.00
❑ 48 John Stofa 1.50 .75
❑ 49 Rex Mirich 1.50 .75
❑ 50 Miller Farr 1.50 .75
❑ 51 Gale Sayers 40.00 25.00
❑ 52 Bill Nelsen 2.00 1.00
❑ 53 Bob Lilly 6.00 3.00
❑ 54 Wayne Walker 1.50 .75
❑ 55 Ray Nitschke 5.00 2.50
❑ 56 Ed Meador 1.50 .75
❑ 57 Lonnie Warwick 1.50 .75
❑ 58 Wendell Hayes 1.50 .75
❑ 59 Dick Anderson RC 5.00 2.50
❑ 60 Don Maynard 6.00 3.00
❑ 61 Tony Lorick 1.50 .75
❑ 62 Pete Gogolak 1.50 .75
❑ 63 Nate Ramsey 1.50 .75
❑ 64 Dick Shiner 1.50 .75
❑ 65 Larry Wilson UER 3.00 1.50
❑ 66 Ken Willard 2.00 1.00
❑ 67 Charley Taylor 5.00 2.50
❑ 68 Billy Cannon 2.00 1.00
❑ 69 Lance Alworth 8.00 4.00
❑ 70 Jim Nance 2.00 1.00
❑ 71 Nick Rassas 1.50 .75
❑ 72 Lenny Lyles 1.50 .75
❑ 73 Bennie McRae 1.50 .75
❑ 74 Bill Glass 1.50 .75
❑ 75 Don Meredith 25.00 15.00
❑ 76 Dick LeBeau 1.50 .75
❑ 77 Carroll Dale 2.00 1.00
❑ 78 Ron McDole 1.50 .75
❑ 79 Charley King 1.50 .75
❑ 80 Checklist UER 15.00 7.50
❑ 81 Dick Bass 2.00 1.00
❑ 82 Roy Winston 1.50 .75
❑ 83 Don McCall 1.50 .75
❑ 84 Jim Katcavage 2.00 1.00
❑ 85 Norm Snead 2.00 1.00
❑ 86 Earl Gros 1.50 .75
❑ 87 Don Brumm 1.50 .75
❑ 88 Sonny Bishop 1.50 .75
❑ 89 Fred Arbanas 1.50 .75
❑ 90 Karl Noonan 1.50 .75
❑ 91 Dick Witcher 1.50 .75
❑ 92 Vince Promuto 1.50 .75
❑ 93 Tommy Nobis 4.00 2.00
❑ 94 Jerry Hill 1.50 .75
❑ 95 Ed O'Bradovich RC 1.50 .75
❑ 96 Ernie Kellerman 1.50 .75
❑ 97 Chuck Howley 2.00 1.00
❑ 98 Hewritt Dixon 1.50 .75
❑ 99 Ron Mix 3.00 1.50
❑ 100 Joe Namath 75.00 40.00
❑ 101 Billy Gambrell 1.50 .75
❑ 102 Elijah Pitts 2.00 1.00
❑ 103 Billy Truax RC 2.00 1.00
❑ 104 Ed Sharockman 1.50 .75
❑ 105 Doug Atkins 3.00 1.50
❑ 106 Greg Larson 1.50 .75
❑ 107 Israel Lang 1.50 .75
❑ 108 Houston Antwine 1.50 .75
❑ 109 Paul Guidry 1.50 .75
❑ 110 Al Denson 1.50 .75
❑ 111 Roy Jefferson 2.00 1.00
❑ 112 Chuck Latourette 1.50 .75
❑ 113 Jim Johnson 3.00 1.50
❑ 114 Bobby Mitchell 4.00 2.00
❑ 115 Randy Johnson 1.50 .75
❑ 116 Lou Michaels 1.50 .75
❑ 117 Rudy Kuechenberg 1.50 .75
❑ 118 Walt Suggs 1.50 .75
❑ 119 Goldie Sellers 1.50 .75
❑ 120 Larry Csonka RC ! 75.00 40.00
❑ 121 Jim Houston 1.50 .75
❑ 122 Craig Baynham 1.50 .75
❑ 123 Alex Karras 5.00 2.50
❑ 124 Jim Grabowski 2.00 1.00
❑ 125 Roman Gabriel 3.00 1.50
❑ 126 Larry Bowie 1.50 .75
❑ 127 Dave Parks 2.00 1.00
❑ 128 Ben Davidson 3.00 1.50
❑ 129 Steve DeLong 1.50 .75
❑ 130 Fred Hill 1.50 .75
❑ 131 Ernie Koy 2.00 1.00
❑ 132A Checklist no border ! 15.00 7.50
❑ 132B Checklist bordered ! 20.00 10.00
❑ 133 Dick Hoak 2.00 1.00
❑ 134 Larry Stallings RC 2.00 1.00
❑ 135 Clifton McNeil RC 2.00 1.00
❑ 136 Walter Rock 2.00 1.00
❑ 137 Billy Lothridge 2.00 1.00
❑ 138 Bob Vogel 2.00 1.00
❑ 139 Dick Butkus 40.00 25.00
❑ 140 Frank Ryan 2.50 1.25
❑ 141 Larry Garron 2.00 1.00
❑ 142 George Saimes 2.00 1.00
❑ 143 Frank Buncom 2.00 1.00
❑ 144 Don Perkins 2.50 1.25
❑ 145 Johnnie Robinson UER 2.00 1.00
❑ 146 Lee Roy Caffey 2.50 1.25
❑ 147 Bernie Casey 2.50 1.25
❑ 148 Billy Martin E 2.00 1.00
❑ 149 Gene Howard 2.00 1.00
❑ 150 Fran Tarkenton 20.00 10.00
❑ 151 Eric Crabtree 2.00 1.00
❑ 152 W.K. Hicks 2.00 1.00
❑ 153 Bobby Bell 4.00 2.00
❑ 154 Sam Baker 2.00 1.00
❑ 155 Marv Woodson 2.00 1.00
❑ 156 Dave Williams 2.00 1.00
❑ 157 Bruce Bosley UER 2.00 1.00
❑ 158 Carl Kammerer 2.00 1.00
❑ 159 Jim Burson 2.00 1.00
❑ 160 Roy Hilton 2.00 1.00
❑ 161 Bob Griese 25.00 15.00
❑ 162 Bob Talamini 2.00 1.00
❑ 163 Jim Otto 4.00 2.00
❑ 164 Ronnie Bull 2.00 1.00
❑ 165 Walter Johnson RC 2.00 1.00
❑ 166 Lee Roy Jordan 4.00 2.00
❑ 167 Mike Lucci 2.50 1.25
❑ 168 Willie Wood 4.00 2.00
❑ 169 Maxie Baughan 2.00 1.00
❑ 170 Bill Brown 2.50 1.25
❑ 171 John Hadl 4.00 2.00
❑ 172 Gino Cappelletti 2.50 1.25
❑ 173 George Butch Byrd 2.50 1.25
❑ 174 Steve Stonebreaker 2.00 1.00
❑ 175 Joe Morrison 2.00 1.00
❑ 176 Joe Scarpati 2.00 1.00
❑ 177 Bobby Walden 2.00 1.00
❑ 178 Roy Shivers 2.00 1.00
❑ 179 Kermit Alexander 2.00 1.00
❑ 180 Pat Richter 2.00 1.00
❑ 181 Pete Perreault 2.00 1.00
❑ 182 Pete Duranko 2.00 1.00
❑ 183 Leroy Mitchell 2.00 1.00
❑ 184 Jim Simon 2.00 1.00
❑ 185 Billy Ray Smith 2.00 1.00
❑ 186 Jack Concannon 2.00 1.00
❑ 187 Ben Davis 2.00 1.00
❑ 188 Mike Clark 2.00 1.00
❑ 189 Jim Gibbons 2.00 1.00
❑ 190 Dave Robinson 2.50 1.25
❑ 191 Otis Taylor 2.50 1.25
❑ 192 Nick Buoniconti 4.00 2.00
❑ 193 Matt Snell 2.50 1.25
❑ 194 Bruce Gossett 2.00 1.00
❑ 195 Mick Tingelhoff 2.50 1.25
❑ 196 Earl Leggett 2.00 1.00
❑ 197 Pete Case 2.00 1.00
❑ 198 Tom Woodeshick RC 2.00 1.00
❑ 199 Ken Kortas 2.00 1.00
❑ 200 Jim Hart 4.00 2.00
❑ 201 Fred Biletnikoff 10.00 5.00
❑ 202 Jacque MacKinnon 2.00 1.00
❑ 203 Jim Whalen 2.00 1.00
❑ 204 Matt Hazeltine 2.00 1.00
❑ 205 Charlie Gogolak 2.00 1.00
❑ 206 Ray Ogden 2.00 1.00
❑ 207 John Mackey 4.00 2.00
❑ 208 Roosevelt Taylor 2.00 1.00
❑ 209 Gene Hickerson 2.00 1.00
❑ 210 Dave Edwards RC 2.50 1.25
❑ 211 Tom Sestak 2.00 1.00
❑ 212 Ernie Wright 2.00 1.00
❑ 213 Dave Costa 2.00 1.00
❑ 214 Tom Vaughn 2.00 1.00
❑ 215 Bart Starr 35.00 20.00
❑ 216 Les Josephson 2.00 1.00
❑ 217 Fred Cox 2.00 1.00
❑ 218 Mike Tilleman 2.00 1.00
❑ 219 Darrell Dess 2.00 1.00
❑ 220 Dave Lloyd 2.00 1.00
❑ 221 Pete Beathard 2.00 1.00
❑ 222 Buck Buchanan 4.00 2.00
❑ 223 Frank Emanuel 2.00 1.00
❑ 224 Paul Martha 2.00 1.00
❑ 225 Johnny Roland 2.00 1.00
❑ 226 Gary Lewis 2.00 1.00
❑ 227 Sonny Jurgensen UER 6.00 3.00
❑ 228 Jim Butler 2.00 1.00
❑ 229 Mike Curtis RC 6.00 3.00
❑ 230 Richie Petitbon 2.00 1.00
❑ 231 George Sauer Jr. 2.50 1.25
❑ 232 George Blanda 20.00 10.00
❑ 233 Gary Garrison 2.00 1.00
❑ 234 Gary Collins 2.50 1.25
❑ 235 Craig Morton 4.00 2.00
❑ 236 Tom Nowatzke 2.00 1.00
❑ 237 Donny Anderson 2.50 1.25
❑ 238 Deacon Jones 4.00 2.00
❑ 239 Grady Alderman 2.00 1.00
❑ 240 Billy Kilmer 4.00 2.00
❑ 241 Mike Taliaferro 2.00 1.00
❑ 242 Stew Barber 2.00 1.00
❑ 243 Bobby Hunt 2.00 1.00
❑ 244 Homer Jones 2.00 1.00
❑ 245 Bob Brown OT 4.00 2.00
❑ 246 Bill Asbury 2.00 1.00
❑ 247 Charlie Johnson 2.50 1.25
❑ 248 Chris Hanburger 2.50 1.25
❑ 249 John Brodie 6.00 3.00
❑ 250 Earl Morrall 2.50 1.25
❑ 251 Floyd Little 5.00 2.50
❑ 252 Jerrel Wilson RC 2.00 1.00
❑ 253 Jim Keyes 2.00 1.00
❑ 254 Mel Renfro 4.00 2.00
❑ 255 Herb Adderley 4.00 2.00
❑ 256 Jack Snow 2.50 1.25
❑ 257 Charlie Durkee 2.00 1.00
❑ 258 Charlie Harper 2.00 1.00
❑ 259 J.R. Wilburn 2.00 1.00
❑ 260 Charlie Krueger 2.00 1.00
❑ 261 Pete Jacques 2.00 1.00
❑ 262 Gerry Philbin 2.00 1.00
❑ 263 Daryle Lamonica ! 10.00 5.00

1970 Topps

❑ COMPLETE SET (263) 475.00 300.00
❑ COMMON CARD (1-132) 1.00 .40
❑ COMMON CARD (133-263) 1.25 .50
❑ WRAPPER (10-CENT) 12.00 8.00
❑ 1 Len Dawson UER ! 20.00 12.00

❑	2	Doug Hart	1.00	.40
❑	3	Verlon Biggs	1.00	.40
❑	4	Ralph Neely RC	1.50	.60
❑	5	Harmon Wages	1.00	.40
❑	6	Dan Conners	1.00	.40
❑	7	Gino Cappelletti	1.50	.60
❑	8	Erich Barnes	1.00	.40
❑	9	Checklist	10.00	5.00
❑	10	Bob Griese	15.00	7.50
❑	11	Ed Flanagan	1.00	.40
❑	12	George Seals	1.00	.40
❑	13	Harry Jacobs	1.00	.40
❑	14	Mike Haffner	1.00	.40
❑	15	Bob Vogel	1.00	.40
❑	16	Bill Peterson	1.00	.40
❑	17	Spider Lockhart	1.00	.40
❑	18	Billy Truax	1.00	.40
❑	19	Jim Beirne	1.00	.40
❑	20	Leroy Kelly	6.00	3.00
❑	21	Dave Lloyd	1.00	.40
❑	22	Mike Tilleman	1.00	.40
❑	23	Gary Garrison	1.00	.40
❑	24	Larry Brown RC	8.00	4.00
❑	25	Jan Stenerud RC	12.00	6.00
❑	26	Rolf Krueger	1.00	.40
❑	27	Roland Lakes	1.00	.40
❑	28	Dick Hoak	1.00	.40
❑	29	Gene Washington Vik RC	2.50	1.25
❑	30	Bart Starr	20.00	10.00
❑	31	Dave Grayson	1.00	.40
❑	32	Jerry Rush	1.00	.40
❑	33	Len St. Jean	1.00	.40
❑	34	Randy Edmunds	1.00	.40
❑	35	Matt Snell	1.50	.60
❑	36	Paul Costa	1.00	.40
❑	37	Mike Pyle	1.00	.40
❑	38	Roy Hilton	1.00	.40
❑	39	Steve Tensi	1.00	.40
❑	40	Tommy Nobis	2.50	1.25
❑	41	Pete Case	1.00	.40
❑	42	Andy Rice	1.00	.40
❑	43	Elvin Bethea RC	8.00	4.00
❑	44	Jack Snow	1.50	.60
❑	45	Mel Renfro	2.50	1.25
❑	46	Andy Livingston	1.00	.40
❑	47	Gary Ballman	1.00	.40
❑	48	Bob DeMarco	1.00	.40
❑	49	Steve DeLong	1.00	.40
❑	50	Daryle Lamonica	4.00	2.00
❑	51	Jim Lynch RC	1.00	.40
❑	52	Mel Farr RC	1.00	.40
❑	53	Bob Long RC	1.00	.40
❑	54	John Elliott	1.00	.40
❑	55	Ray Nitschke	5.00	2.50
❑	56	Jim Shorter	1.00	.40
❑	57	Dave Wilcox	2.50	1.25
❑	58	Eric Crabtree	1.00	.40
❑	59	Alan Page RC	30.00	15.00
❑	60	Jim Nance	1.50	.60
❑	61	Glen Ray Hines	1.00	.40
❑	62	John Mackey	2.50	1.25
❑	63	Ron McDole	1.00	.40
❑	64	Tom Beier	1.00	.40
❑	65	Bill Nelsen	1.50	.60
❑	66	Paul Flatley	1.00	.40
❑	67	Sam Brunelli	1.00	.40
❑	68	Jack Pardee	1.50	.60
❑	69	Brig Owens	1.00	.40
❑	70	Gale Sayers	25.00	12.50
❑	71	Lee Roy Jordan	2.50	1.25
❑	72	Harold Jackson RC	5.00	2.50
❑	73	John Hadl	2.50	1.25
❑	74	Dave Parks	1.00	.40
❑	75	Lem Barney RC	14.00	7.00
❑	76	Johnny Roland	1.00	.40
❑	77	Ed Budde	1.00	.40
❑	78	Ben McGee	1.00	.40
❑	79	Ken Bowman	1.00	.40
❑	80	Fran Tarkenton	15.00	7.50
❑	81	G.Washington 49er RC	5.00	2.50
❑	82	Larry Grantham	1.00	.40
❑	83	Bill Brown	1.50	.60
❑	84	John Charles	1.00	.40
❑	85	Fred Biletnikoff	7.00	3.50
❑	86	Royce Berry	1.00	.40
❑	87	Bob Lilly	5.00	2.50
❑	88	Earl Morrall	1.50	.60
❑	89	Jerry LeVias RC	1.50	.60
❑	90	O.J. Simpson RC	80.00	40.00
❑	91	Mike Howell	1.00	.40
❑	92	Ken Gray	1.00	.40
❑	93	Chris Hanburger	1.00	.40
❑	94	Larry Seiple RC	1.00	.40
❑	95	Rich Jackson RC	1.00	.40
❑	96	Rockne Freitas	1.00	.40
❑	97	Dick Post RC	1.50	.60
❑	98	Ben Hawkins RC	1.00	.40
❑	99	Ken Reaves	1.00	.40
❑	100	Roman Gabriel	2.50	1.25
❑	101	Dave Rowe	1.00	.40
❑	102	Dave Robinson	1.00	.40
❑	103	Otis Taylor	1.50	.60
❑	104	Jim Turner	1.00	.40
❑	105	Joe Morrison	1.00	.40
❑	106	Dick Evey	1.00	.40
❑	107	Ray Mansfield	1.00	.40
❑	108	Grady Alderman	1.00	.40
❑	109	Bruce Gossett	1.00	.40
❑	110	Bob Trumpy RC	4.00	2.00
❑	111	Jim Hunt	1.00	.40
❑	112	Larry Stallings	1.00	.40
❑	113A	Lance Rentzel Red	1.50	.60
❑	113B	Lance Rentzel Black	1.50	.60
❑	114	Bubba Smith RC	25.00	12.50
❑	115	Norm Snead	1.50	.60
❑	116	Jim Otto	2.50	1.25
❑	117	Bo Scott RC	1.00	.40
❑	118	Rick Redman	1.00	.40
❑	119	George Butch Byrd	1.00	.40
❑	120	George Webster RC	1.50	.60
❑	121	Chuck Walton RC	1.00	.40
❑	122	Dave Costa	1.00	.40
❑	123	Al Dodd	1.00	.40
❑	124	Len Hauss	1.00	.40
❑	125	Deacon Jones	2.50	1.25
❑	126	Randy Johnson	1.00	.40
❑	127	Ralph Heck	1.00	.40
❑	128	Emerson Boozer RC	1.50	.60
❑	129	Johnny Robinson	1.50	.60
❑	130	John Brodie	5.00	2.50
❑	131	Gale Gillingham RC	1.00	.40
❑	132	Checklist DP	6.00	3.00
❑	133	Chuck Walker	1.25	.50
❑	134	Bennie McRae	1.25	.50
❑	135	Paul Warfield	7.00	3.50
❑	136	Dan Darragh	1.25	.50
❑	137	Paul Robinson RC	1.25	.50
❑	138	Ed Philpott	1.25	.50
❑	139	Craig Morton	3.00	1.50
❑	140	Tom Dempsey RC	2.00	.75
❑	141	Al Nelson	1.25	.50
❑	142	Tom Matte	2.00	.75
❑	143	Dick Schafrath	1.25	.50
❑	144	Willie Brown	4.00	2.00
❑	145	Charley Taylor UER	5.00	2.50
❑	146	John Huard	1.25	.50
❑	147	Dave Osborn	1.25	.50
❑	148	Gene Mingo	1.25	.50
❑	149	Larry Hand	1.25	.50
❑	150	Joe Namath	50.00	25.00
❑	151	Tom Mack RC	10.00	5.00
❑	152	Kenny Graham	1.25	.50
❑	153	Don Herrmann	1.25	.50
❑	154	Bobby Bell	3.00	1.50
❑	155	Hoyle Granger	1.25	.50
❑	156	Claude Humphrey RC	2.00	.75
❑	157	Clifton McNeil	1.25	.50
❑	158	Mick Tingelhoff	2.00	.75
❑	159	Don Horn RC	1.25	.50
❑	160	Larry Wilson	3.00	1.50
❑	161	Tom Neville	1.25	.50
❑	162	Larry Csonka	20.00	10.00
❑	163	Doug Buffone RC	1.25	.50
❑	164	Cornell Green	2.00	.75
❑	165	Haven Moses RC	2.00	.75
❑	166	Billy Kilmer	3.00	1.50
❑	167	Tim Rossovich RC	1.25	.50
❑	168	Bill Bergey RC	4.00	2.00
❑	169	Gary Collins	2.00	.75
❑	170	Floyd Little	3.00	1.50
❑	171	Tom Keating	1.25	.50
❑	172	Pat Fischer	1.25	.50
❑	173	Walt Sweeney	1.25	.50
❑	174	Greg Larson	1.25	.50
❑	175	Carl Eller	3.00	1.50
❑	176	George Sauer Jr.	2.00	.75
❑	177	Jim Hart	3.00	1.50
❑	178	Bob Brown OT	3.00	1.50
❑	179	Mike Garrett RC	2.00	.75
❑	180	Johnny Unitas	25.00	15.00
❑	181	Tom Regner	1.25	.50
❑	182	Bob Jeter	1.25	.50
❑	183	Gail Cogdill	1.25	.50
❑	184	Earl Gros	1.25	.50
❑	185	Dennis Partee	1.25	.50
❑	186	Charlie Krueger	1.25	.50
❑	187	Martin Baccaglio	1.25	.50
❑	188	Charles Long	1.25	.50
❑	189	Bob Hayes	4.00	2.00
❑	190	Dick Butkus	25.00	12.50
❑	191	Al Bemiller	1.25	.50
❑	192	Dick Westmoreland	1.25	.50
❑	193	Joe Scarpati	1.25	.50
❑	194	Ron Snidow	1.25	.50
❑	195	Earl McCullouch RC	1.25	.50
❑	196	Jake Kupp	1.25	.50
❑	197	Bob Lurtsema	1.25	.50
❑	198	Mike Current	1.25	.50
❑	199	Charlie Smith RB	1.25	.50
❑	200	Sonny Jurgensen	6.00	3.00
❑	201	Mike Curtis	2.00	.75
❑	202	Aaron Brown RC	1.25	.50
❑	203	Richie Petitbon	1.25	.50
❑	204	Walt Suggs	1.25	.50
❑	205	Roy Jefferson	1.25	.50
❑	206	Russ Washington RC	1.25	.50
❑	207	Woody Peoples RC	1.25	.50
❑	208	Dave Williams	1.25	.50
❑	209	John Zook RC	1.25	.50
❑	210	Tom Woodeshick	1.25	.50
❑	211	Howard Fest	1.25	.50
❑	212	Jack Concannon	1.25	.50
❑	213	Jim Marshall	3.00	1.50
❑	214	Jon Morris	1.25	.50
❑	215	Dan Abramowicz	2.00	.75
❑	216	Paul Martha	1.25	.50
❑	217	Ken Willard	1.25	.50
❑	218	Walter Rock	1.25	.50
❑	219	Garland Boyette	1.25	.50
❑	220	Buck Buchanan	3.00	1.50
❑	221	Bill Munson	2.00	.75
❑	222	David Lee RC	1.25	.50
❑	223	Karl Noonan	1.25	.50
❑	224	Harry Schuh	1.25	.50
❑	225	Jackie Smith	3.00	1.50
❑	226	Gerry Philbin	1.25	.50
❑	227	Ernie Koy	1.25	.50
❑	228	Chuck Howley	2.00	.75
❑	229	Billy Shaw	3.00	1.50
❑	230	Jerry Hillebrand	1.25	.50
❑	231	Bill Thompson RC	2.00	.75
❑	232	Carroll Dale	2.00	.75
❑	233	Gene Hickerson	1.25	.50
❑	234	Jim Butler	1.25	.50
❑	235	Greg Cook RC	1.25	.50
❑	236	Lee Roy Caffey	1.25	.50
❑	237	Merlin Olsen	4.00	2.00
❑	238	Fred Cox	1.25	.50
❑	239	Nate Ramsey	1.25	.50
❑	240	Lance Alworth	7.00	3.50
❑	241	Chuck Hinton	1.25	.50
❑	242	Jerry Smith	1.25	.50
❑	243	Tony Baker FB	1.25	.50
❑	244	Nick Buoniconti	3.00	1.50

❑ 245	Jim Johnson	3.00	1.50
❑ 246	Willie Richardson	1.25	.50
❑ 247	Fred Dryer RC	10.00	5.00
❑ 248	Bobby Maples	1.25	.50
❑ 249	Alex Karras	4.00	2.00
❑ 250	Joe Kapp	2.00	.75
❑ 251	Ben Davidson	3.00	1.50
❑ 252	Mike Stratton	1.25	.50
❑ 253	Les Josephson	1.25	.50
❑ 254	Don Maynard	6.00	3.00
❑ 255	Houston Antwine	1.25	.50
❑ 256	Mac Percival RC	1.25	.50
❑ 257	George Goeddeke	1.25	.50
❑ 258	Homer Jones	1.25	.50
❑ 259	Bob Berry	1.25	.50
❑ 260A	Calvin Hill RC Red	15.00	7.50
❑ 260B	Calvin Hill RC Black	20.00	10.00
❑ 261	Willie Wood	3.00	1.50
❑ 262	Ed Weisacosky	1.25	.50
❑ 263	Jim Tyrer !	3.00	1.50

1971 Topps

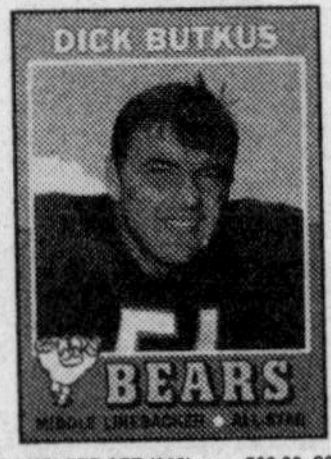

❑	COMPLETE SET (263)	500.00	300.00
❑	COMMON CARD (1-132)	.75	.30
❑	COMMON CARD (133-263)	1.00	.40
❑ 1	Johnny Unitas !	30.00	15.00
❑ 2	Jim Butler	.75	.30
❑ 3	Marty Schottenheimer RC	12.00	6.00
❑ 4	Joe O'Donnell	.75	.30
❑ 5	Tom Dempsey	1.25	.50
❑ 6	Chuck Allen	.75	.30
❑ 7	Ernie Kellerman	.75	.30
❑ 8	Walt Garrison RC	2.00	.75
❑ 9	Bill Van Heusen	.75	.30
❑ 10	Lance Alworth	8.00	4.00
❑ 11	Greg Landry RC	2.00	.75
❑ 12	Larry Krause	.75	.30
❑ 13	Buck Buchanan	2.00	.75
❑ 14	Roy Gerela RC	1.25	.50
❑ 15	Clifton McNeil	.75	.30
❑ 16	Bob Brown OT	2.00	.75
❑ 17	Lloyd Mumphord	.75	.30
❑ 18	Gary Cuozzo	.75	.30
❑ 19	Don Maynard	5.00	2.50
❑ 20	Larry Wilson	2.00	.75
❑ 21	Charlie Smith RB	.75	.30
❑ 22	Ken Avery	.75	.30
❑ 23	Billy Walik	.75	.30
❑ 24	Jim Johnson	2.00	.75
❑ 25	Dick Butkus	25.00	12.50
❑ 26	Charley Taylor UER	4.00	2.00
❑ 27	Checklist UER	8.00	4.00
❑ 28	Lionel Aldridge RC	.75	.30
❑ 29	Billy Lothridge	.75	.30
❑ 30	Terry Hanratty RC	1.25	.50
❑ 31	Lee Roy Jordan	2.00	.75
❑ 32	Rick Volk RC	.75	.30
❑ 33	Howard Kindig	.75	.30
❑ 34	Carl Garrett RC	.75	.30
❑ 35	Bobby Bell	2.00	.75
❑ 36	Gene Hickerson	.75	.30
❑ 37	Dave Parks	.75	.30
❑ 38	Paul Martha	.75	.30
❑ 39	George Blanda	15.00	7.50
❑ 40	Tom Woodeshick	.75	.30
❑ 41	Alex Karras	3.00	1.50
❑ 42	Rick Redman	.75	.30
❑ 43	Zeke Moore	.75	.30
❑ 44	Jack Snow	1.25	.50
❑ 45	Larry Csonka	15.00	7.50
❑ 46	Karl Kassulke	.75	.30
❑ 47	Jim Hart	2.00	.75
❑ 48	Al Atkinson	.75	.30
❑ 49	Horst Muhlmann RC	.75	.30
❑ 50	Sonny Jurgensen	5.00	2.50
❑ 51	Ron Johnson RC	1.25	.50
❑ 52	Cas Banaszek	.75	.30
❑ 53	Bubba Smith	8.00	4.00
❑ 54	Bobby Douglass RC	1.25	.50
❑ 55	Willie Wood	2.00	.75
❑ 56	Bake Turner	.75	.30
❑ 57	Mike Morgan LB	.75	.30
❑ 58	George Butch Byrd	1.25	.50
❑ 59	Don Horn	.75	.30
❑ 60	Tommy Nobis	2.00	.75
❑ 61	Jan Stenerud	4.00	2.00
❑ 62	Altie Taylor RC	.75	.30
❑ 63	Gary Pettigrew	.75	.30
❑ 64	Spike Jones RC	.75	.30
❑ 65	Duane Thomas RC	2.00	.75
❑ 66	Marty Domres RC	.75	.30
❑ 67	Dick Anderson	1.25	.50
❑ 68	Ken Iman	.75	.30
❑ 69	Miller Farr	.75	.30
❑ 70	Daryle Lamonica	3.00	1.50
❑ 71	Alan Page	12.00	6.00
❑ 72	Pat Matson	.75	.30
❑ 73	Emerson Boozer	.75	.30
❑ 74	Pat Fischer	.75	.30
❑ 75	Gary Collins	1.25	.50
❑ 76	John Fuqua RC	1.25	.50
❑ 77	Bruce Gossett	.75	.30
❑ 78	Ed O'Bradovich	.75	.30
❑ 79	Bob Tucker RC	1.25	.50
❑ 80	Mike Curtis	1.25	.50
❑ 81	Rich Jackson	.75	.30
❑ 82	Tom Janik	.75	.30
❑ 83	Gale Gillingham	.75	.30
❑ 84	Jim Mitchell TE	.75	.30
❑ 85	Charlie Johnson	1.25	.50
❑ 86	Edgar Chandler	.75	.30
❑ 87	Cyril Pinder	.75	.30
❑ 88	Johnny Robinson	1.25	.50
❑ 89	Ralph Neely	.75	.30
❑ 90	Dan Abramowicz	.75	.30
❑ 91	Mercury Morris RC	5.00	2.50
❑ 92	Steve DeLong	.75	.30
❑ 93	Larry Stallings	.75	.30
❑ 94	Tom Mack	2.00	.75
❑ 95	Hewritt Dixon	.75	.30
❑ 96	Fred Cox	.75	.30
❑ 97	Chris Hanburger	.75	.30
❑ 98	Gerry Philbin	.75	.30
❑ 99	Ernie Wright	.75	.30
❑ 100	John Brodie	4.00	2.00
❑ 101	Tucker Frederickson	.75	.30
❑ 102	Bobby Walden	.75	.30
❑ 103	Dick Gordon	.75	.30
❑ 104	Walter Johnson	.75	.30
❑ 105	Mike Lucci	1.25	.50
❑ 106	Checklist DP	6.00	3.00
❑ 107	Ron Berger	.75	.30
❑ 108	Dan Sullivan	.75	.30
❑ 109	George Kunz RC	.75	.30
❑ 110	Floyd Little	2.00	.75
❑ 111	Zeke Bratkowski	1.25	.50
❑ 112	Haven Moses	1.25	.50
❑ 113	Ken Houston RC	15.00	7.50
❑ 114	Willie Lanier RC	15.00	7.50
❑ 115	Larry Brown	2.00	.75
❑ 116	Tim Rossovich	.75	.30
❑ 117	Errol Linden	.75	.30
❑ 118	Mel Renfro	2.00	.75
❑ 119	Mike Garrett	.75	.30
❑ 120	Fran Tarkenton	15.00	7.50
❑ 121	Garo Yepremian RC	2.00	.75
❑ 122	Glen Condren	.75	.30
❑ 123	Johnny Roland	.75	.30
❑ 124	Dave Herman	.75	.30
❑ 125	Merlin Olsen	3.00	1.50
❑ 126	Doug Buffone	.75	.30
❑ 127	Earl McCullouch	.75	.30
❑ 128	Spider Lockhart	.75	.30
❑ 129	Ken Willard	.75	.30
❑ 130	Gene Washington Vik	.75	.30
❑ 131	Mike Phipps RC	1.25	.50
❑ 132	Andy Russell	1.25	.50
❑ 133	Ray Nitschke !	4.00	2.00
❑ 134	Jerry Logan	1.00	.40
❑ 135	MacArthur Lane RC	1.50	.60
❑ 136	Jim Turner	1.00	.40
❑ 137	Kent McCloughan	1.00	.40
❑ 138	Paul Guidry	1.00	.40
❑ 139	Otis Taylor	1.50	.60
❑ 140	Virgil Carter RC	1.00	.40
❑ 141	Joe Dawkins	1.00	.40
❑ 142	Steve Preece	1.00	.40
❑ 143	Mike Bragg RC	1.00	.40
❑ 144	Bob Lilly	5.00	2.50
❑ 145	Joe Kapp	1.50	.60
❑ 146	Al Dodd	1.00	.40
❑ 147	Nick Buoniconti	2.50	1.25
❑ 148	Speedy Duncan	1.00	.40
❑ 149	Cedrick Hardman RC	1.00	.40
❑ 150	Gale Sayers	25.00	12.50
❑ 151	Jim Otto	2.50	1.25
❑ 152	Billy Truax	1.00	.40
❑ 153	John Elliott	1.00	.40
❑ 154	Dick LeBeau	1.00	.40
❑ 155	Bill Bergey	1.50	.60
❑ 156	Terry Bradshaw RC !	200.00	125.00
❑ 157	Leroy Kelly	6.00	3.00
❑ 158	Paul Krause	2.50	1.25
❑ 159	Ted Vactor	1.00	.40
❑ 160	Bob Griese	15.00	7.50
❑ 161	Ernie McMillan	1.00	.40
❑ 162	Donny Anderson	1.50	.60
❑ 163	John Pitts	1.00	.40
❑ 164	Dave Costa	1.00	.40
❑ 165	Gene Washington 49er	1.50	.60
❑ 166	John Zook	1.00	.40
❑ 167	Pete Gogolak	1.00	.40
❑ 168	Erich Barnes	1.00	.40
❑ 169	Alvin Reed	1.00	.40
❑ 170	Jim Nance	1.50	.60
❑ 171	Craig Morton	2.50	1.25
❑ 172	Gary Garrison	1.00	.40
❑ 173	Joe Scarpati	1.00	.40
❑ 174	Adrian Young UER	1.00	.40
❑ 175	John Mackey	2.50	1.25
❑ 176	Mac Percival	1.00	.40
❑ 177	Preston Pearson RC	4.00	2.00
❑ 178	Fred Biletnikoff	8.00	4.00
❑ 179	Mike Battle RC	1.00	.40
❑ 180	Len Dawson	8.00	4.00
❑ 181	Les Josephson	1.00	.40
❑ 182	Royce Berry	1.00	.40
❑ 183	Herman Weaver	1.00	.40
❑ 184	Norm Snead	1.50	.60
❑ 185	Sam Brunelli	1.00	.40
❑ 186	Jim Kiick RC	5.00	2.50
❑ 187	Austin Denney	1.00	.40
❑ 188	Roger Wehrli RC	1.50	.60
❑ 189	Dave Wilcox	2.50	1.25
❑ 190	Bob Hayes	2.50	1.25
❑ 191	Joe Morrison	1.00	.40
❑ 192	Manny Sistrunk	1.00	.40
❑ 193	Don Cockroft RC	1.00	.40
❑ 194	Lee Bouggess	1.00	.40
❑ 195	Bob Berry	1.00	.40
❑ 196	Ron Sellers	1.00	.40
❑ 197	George Webster	1.00	.40
❑ 198	Hoyle Granger	1.00	.40
❑ 199	Bob Vogel	1.00	.40
❑ 200	Bart Starr	20.00	10.00
❑ 201	Mike Mercer	1.00	.40
❑ 202	Dave Smith WR	1.00	.40
❑ 203	Lee Roy Caffey	1.00	.40
❑ 204	Mick Tingelhoff	1.50	.60
❑ 205	Matt Snell	1.50	.60
❑ 206	Jim Tyrer	1.00	.40
❑ 207	Willie Brown	2.50	1.25
❑ 208	Bob Johnson RC	1.00	.40
❑ 209	Deacon Jones	2.50	1.25
❑ 210	Charlie Sanders RC	1.50	.60
❑ 211	Jake Scott RC	6.00	3.00
❑ 212	Bob Anderson RC	1.00	.40
❑ 213	Charlie Krueger	1.00	.40
❑ 214	Jim Bakken	1.00	.40
❑ 215	Harold Jackson	1.50	.60
❑ 216	Bill Brundige	1.00	.40
❑ 217	Calvin Hill	5.00	2.50
❑ 218	Claude Humphrey	1.00	.40

❑ 219	Glen Ray Hines	1.00	.40
❑ 220	Bill Nelsen	1.50	.60
❑ 221	Roy Hilton	1.00	.40
❑ 222	Don Herrmann	1.00	.40
❑ 223	John Bramlett	1.00	.40
❑ 224	Ken Ellis	1.00	.40
❑ 225	Dave Osborn	1.50	.60
❑ 226	Edd Hargett RC	1.00	.40
❑ 227	Gene Mingo	1.00	.40
❑ 228	Larry Grantham	1.00	.40
❑ 229	Dick Post	1.00	.40
❑ 230	Roman Gabriel	2.50	1.25
❑ 231	Mike Eischeid	1.00	.40
❑ 232	Jim Lynch	1.00	.40
❑ 233	Lemar Parrish RC	1.50	.60
❑ 234	Cecil Turner	1.00	.40
❑ 235	Dennis Shaw RC	1.00	.40
❑ 236	Mel Farr	1.00	.40
❑ 237	Curt Knight	1.00	.40
❑ 238	Chuck Howley	1.50	.60
❑ 239	Bruce Taylor RC	1.00	.40
❑ 240	Jerry LeVias	1.00	.40
❑ 241	Bob Lurtsema	1.00	.40
❑ 242	Earl Morrall	1.50	.60
❑ 243	Kermit Alexander	1.00	.40
❑ 244	Jackie Smith	2.50	1.25
❑ 245	Joe Greene RC	50.00	30.00
❑ 246	Harmon Wages	1.00	.40
❑ 247	Errol Mann	1.00	.40
❑ 248	Mike McCoy DT RC	1.00	.40
❑ 249	Milt Morin RC	1.00	.40
❑ 250	Joe Namath	60.00	35.00
❑ 251	Jackie Burkett	1.00	.40
❑ 252	Steve Chomyszak	1.00	.40
❑ 253	Ed Sharockman	1.00	.40
❑ 254	Robert Holmes RC	1.00	.40
❑ 255	John Hadl	2.50	1.25
❑ 256	Cornell Gordon	1.00	.40
❑ 257	Mark Moseley RC	1.50	.60
❑ 258	Gus Otto	1.00	.40
❑ 259	Mike Taliaferro	1.00	.40
❑ 260	O.J.Simpson	25.00	12.50
❑ 261	Paul Warfield	8.00	4.00
❑ 262	Jack Concannon	1.00	.40
❑ 263	Tom Matte !	2.50	1.25

1972 Topps

❑	COMPLETE SET (351)	2200.00	1500.00
❑	COMMON CARD (1-132)	.50	.25
❑	COMMON CARD (133-263)	.60	.30
❑	COMMON CARD (264-351)	18.00	10.00
❑	WRAPPER (10-CENT)	10.00	6.00
❑	WRAPPER SER.3 (10-CENT)	20.00	15.00
❑ 1	L.Csonka/Litt/Hubb LL	4.00	2.00
❑ 2	NFC Rushing Leaders	.50	.25
❑ 3	B.Griese/Dawson/Cart LL	2.00	.75
❑ 4	R.Staubach/Lan/Kil LL	5.00	2.50
❑ 5	AFC Receiving Leaders	1.00	.40
❑ 6	NFC Receiving Leaders	.50	.25
❑ 7	Yepre/Stener/O'Brien LL	.50	.25
❑ 8	NFC Scoring Leaders	.50	.25
❑ 9	Jim Kiick	2.00	.75
❑ 10	Otis Taylor	1.00	.40
❑ 11	Bobby Joe Green	.50	.25
❑ 12	Ken Ellis	.50	.25
❑ 13	John Riggins RC	20.00	10.00
❑ 14	Dave Parks	.50	.25
❑ 15	John Hadl	2.00	.75
❑ 16	Ron Hornsby	.50	.25
❑ 17	Chip Myers RC	.50	.25
❑ 18	Billy Kilmer	2.00	.75
❑ 19	Fred Hoaglin	.50	.25
❑ 20	Carl Eller	2.00	.75
❑ 21	Steve Zabel	.50	.25
❑ 22	Vic Washington RC	.50	.25
❑ 23	Len St. Jean	.50	.25
❑ 24	Bill Thompson	.50	.25
❑ 25	Steve Owens RC	2.00	.75
❑ 26	Ken Burrough RC	1.00	.40
❑ 27	Mike Clark	.50	.25
❑ 28	Willie Brown	2.00	.75
❑ 29	Checklist	6.00	3.00
❑ 30	Marlin Briscoe RC	.50	.25
❑ 31	Jerry Logan	.50	.25
❑ 32	Donny Anderson	1.00	.40
❑ 33	Rich McGeorge	.50	.25
❑ 34	Charlie Durkee	.50	.25
❑ 35	Willie Lanier	4.00	2.00
❑ 36	Chris Farasopoulos	.50	.25
❑ 37	Ron Shanklin RC	.50	.25
❑ 38	Forrest Blue RC	.50	.25
❑ 39	Ken Reaves	.50	.25
❑ 40	Roman Gabriel	2.00	.75
❑ 41	Mac Percival	.50	.25
❑ 42	Lem Barney	3.00	1.50
❑ 43	Nick Buoniconti	2.00	.75
❑ 44	Charlie Gogolak	.50	.25
❑ 45	Bill Bradley RC	1.00	.40
❑ 46	Joe Jones DE	.50	.25
❑ 47	Dave Williams	.50	.25
❑ 48	Pete Athas	.50	.25
❑ 49	Virgil Carter	.50	.25
❑ 50	Floyd Little	2.00	.75
❑ 51	Curt Knight	.50	.25
❑ 52	Bobby Maples	.50	.25
❑ 53	Charlie West	.50	.25
❑ 54	Marv Hubbard RC	1.00	.40
❑ 55	Archie Manning RC	20.00	10.00
❑ 56	Jim O'Brien RC	1.00	.40
❑ 57	Wayne Patrick	.50	.25
❑ 58	Ken Bowman	.50	.25
❑ 59	Roger Wehrli	.50	.25
❑ 60	Charlie Sanders	.50	.25
❑ 61	Jan Stenerud	2.00	.75
❑ 62	Willie Ellison	.50	.25
❑ 63	Walt Sweeney	.50	.25
❑ 64	Ron Smith	.50	.25
❑ 65	Jim Plunkett RC	20.00	10.00
❑ 66	Herb Adderley UER	2.00	.75
❑ 67	Mike Reid RC	2.00	.75
❑ 68	Richard Caster RC	1.00	.40
❑ 69	Dave Wilcox	2.00	.75
❑ 70	Leroy Kelly	3.00	1.50
❑ 71	Bob Lee RC	.50	.25
❑ 72	Verlon Biggs	.50	.25
❑ 73	Henry Allison	.50	.25
❑ 74	Steve Ramsey	.50	.25
❑ 75	Claude Humphrey	1.00	.40
❑ 76	Bob Grim RC	.50	.25
❑ 77	John Fuqua	1.00	.40
❑ 78	Ken Houston	4.00	2.00
❑ 79	Checklist DP	5.00	2.50
❑ 80	Bob Griese	8.00	4.00
❑ 81	Lance Rentzel	1.00	.40
❑ 82	Ed Podolak RC	1.00	.40
❑ 83	Ike Hill	.50	.25
❑ 84	George Farmer	.50	.25
❑ 85	John Brockington RC	2.00	.75
❑ 86	Jim Otto	2.00	.75
❑ 87	Richard Neal	.50	.25
❑ 88	Jim Hart	2.00	.75
❑ 89	Bob Babich	.50	.25
❑ 90	Gene Washington 49er	1.00	.40
❑ 91	John Zook	.50	.25
❑ 92	Bobby Duhon	.50	.25
❑ 93	Ted Hendricks RC	15.00	7.50
❑ 94	Rockne Freitas	.50	.25
❑ 95	Larry Brown	2.00	.75
❑ 96	Mike Phipps	1.00	.40
❑ 97	Julius Adams	.50	.25
❑ 98	Dick Anderson	1.00	.40
❑ 99	Fred Willis	.50	.25
❑ 100	Joe Namath	35.00	20.00
❑ 101	L.C.Greenwood RC	15.00	7.50
❑ 102	Mark Nordquist	.50	.25
❑ 103	Robert Holmes	.50	.25
❑ 104	Ron Yary RC	5.00	2.00
❑ 105	Bob Hayes	2.00	.75
❑ 106	Lyle Alzado RC	15.00	7.50
❑ 107	Bob Berry	.50	.25
❑ 108	Phil Villapiano RC	1.00	.40
❑ 109	Dave Elmendorf	.50	.25
❑ 110	Gale Sayers	20.00	10.00
❑ 111	Jim Tyrer	.50	.25
❑ 112	Mel Gray RC	2.00	.75
❑ 113	Gerry Philbin	.50	.25
❑ 114	Bob James	.50	.25
❑ 115	Garo Yepremian	1.00	.40
❑ 116	Dave Robinson	1.00	.40
❑ 117	Jeff Queen	.50	.25
❑ 118	Norm Snead	1.00	.40
❑ 119	Jim Nance IA	1.00	.40
❑ 120	Terry Bradshaw IA	15.00	7.50
❑ 121	Jim Kiick IA	1.00	.40
❑ 122	Roger Staubach IA	20.00	12.00
❑ 123	Bo Scott IA	.50	.25
❑ 124	John Brodie IA	2.00	.75
❑ 125	Rick Volk IA	.50	.25
❑ 126	John Riggins IA	6.00	3.00
❑ 127	Bubba Smith IA	2.00	.75
❑ 128	Roman Gabriel IA	1.00	.40
❑ 129	Calvin Hill IA	1.00	.40
❑ 130	Bill Nelsen IA	.50	.25
❑ 131	Tom Matte IA	1.00	.40
❑ 132	Bob Griese IA	4.00	2.00
❑ 133	AFC Semi-Final	1.00	.40
❑ 134	NFC Semi-Final	1.00	.40
❑ 135	AFC Semi-Final	1.00	.40
❑ 136	NFC Semi-Final	1.00	.40
❑ 137	AFC Title Game/Unitas	3.00	1.50
❑ 138	NFC Title Game/Bob Lilly	2.00	.75
❑ 139	Super Bowl VI/Staubach	5.00	2.50
❑ 140	Larry Csonka	8.00	4.00
❑ 141	Rick Volk	.60	.30
❑ 142	Roy Jefferson	1.00	.40
❑ 143	Raymond Chester RC	1.00	.40
❑ 144	Bobby Douglass	.60	.30
❑ 145	Bob Lilly	5.00	2.50
❑ 146	Harold Jackson	1.00	.40
❑ 147	Pete Gogolak	.60	.30
❑ 148	Art Malone	.60	.30
❑ 149	Ed Flanagan	.60	.30
❑ 150	Terry Bradshaw	40.00	25.00
❑ 151	MacArthur Lane	1.00	.40
❑ 152	Jack Snow	1.00	.40
❑ 153	Al Beauchamp	.60	.30
❑ 154	Bob Anderson	.60	.30
❑ 155	Ted Kwalick RC	.60	.30
❑ 156	Dan Pastorini RC	2.00	.75
❑ 157	Emmitt Thomas RC	2.00	.75
❑ 158	Randy Vataha RC	.60	.30
❑ 159	Al Atkinson	.60	.30
❑ 160	O.J.Simpson	15.00	7.50
❑ 161	Jackie Smith	2.00	.75
❑ 162	Ernie Kellerman	.60	.30
❑ 163	Dennis Partee	.60	.30
❑ 164	Jake Kupp	.60	.30
❑ 165	Johnny Unitas	20.00	10.00
❑ 166	Clint Jones RC	.60	.30
❑ 167	Paul Warfield	6.00	3.00
❑ 168	Roland McDole	.60	.30
❑ 169	Daryle Lamonica	2.00	.75
❑ 170	Dick Butkus	15.00	7.50
❑ 171	Jim Butler	.60	.30
❑ 172	Mike McCoy DT	.60	.30
❑ 173	Dave Smith WR	.60	.30
❑ 174	Greg Landry	1.00	.40
❑ 175	Tom Dempsey	1.00	.40
❑ 176	John Charles	.60	.30
❑ 177	Bobby Bell	2.00	.75
❑ 178	Don Horn	.60	.30
❑ 179	Bob Trumpy	2.00	.75
❑ 180	Duane Thomas	1.00	.40
❑ 181	Merlin Olsen	3.00	1.50
❑ 182	Dave Herman	.60	.30
❑ 183	Jim Nance	1.00	.40
❑ 184	Pete Beathard	.60	.30
❑ 185	Bob Tucker	.60	.30
❑ 186	Gene Upshaw RC	15.00	7.50
❑ 187	Bo Scott	.60	.30
❑ 188	J.D.Hill RC	.60	.30
❑ 189	Bruce Gossett	.60	.30
❑ 190	Bubba Smith	4.00	2.00

❑ 191 Edd Hargett .60 .30
❑ 192 Gary Garrison .60 .30
❑ 193 Jake Scott 1.00 .40
❑ 194 Fred Cox .60 .30
❑ 195 Sonny Jurgensen 4.00 2.00
❑ 196 Greg Brezina RC .60 .30
❑ 197 Ed O'Bradovich .60 .30
❑ 198 John Rowser .60 .30
❑ 199 Altie Taylor UER .60 .30
❑ 200 Roger Staubach RC ! 175.00 100.00
❑ 201 Leroy Keyes RC .60 .30
❑ 202 Garland Boyette .60 .30
❑ 203 Tom Beer .60 .30
❑ 204 Buck Buchanan 2.00 .75
❑ 205 Larry Wilson 2.00 .75
❑ 206 Scott Hunter RC .60 .30
❑ 207 Ron Johnson .60 .30
❑ 208 Sam Brunelli .60 .30
❑ 209 Deacon Jones 2.00 .75
❑ 210 Fred Biletnikoff 6.00 3.00
❑ 211 Bill Nelsen 1.00 .40
❑ 212 George Nock .60 .30
❑ 213 Dan Abramowicz 1.00 .40
❑ 214 Irv Goode .60 .30
❑ 215 Isiah Robertson RC 1.00 .40
❑ 216 Tom Matte 1.00 .40
❑ 217 Pat Fischer .60 .30
❑ 218 Gene Washington Vik .60 .30
❑ 219 Paul Robinson .60 .30
❑ 220 John Brodie 4.00 2.00
❑ 221 Manny Fernandez RC 1.00 .40
❑ 222 Errol Mann .60 .30
❑ 223 Dick Gordon .60 .30
❑ 224 Calvin Hill 2.00 .75
❑ 225 Fran Tarkenton 12.00 6.00
❑ 226 Jim Turner .60 .30
❑ 227 Jim Mitchell TE .60 .30
❑ 228 Pete Liske .60 .30
❑ 229 Carl Garrett .60 .30
❑ 230 Joe Greene 20.00 10.00
❑ 231 Gale Gillingham .60 .30
❑ 232 Norm Bulaich RC 1.00 .40
❑ 233 Spider Lockhart .60 .30
❑ 234 Ken Willard .60 .30
❑ 235 George Blanda 12.00 6.00
❑ 236 Wayne Mulligan .60 .30
❑ 237 Dave Lewis .60 .30
❑ 238 Dennis Shaw .60 .30
❑ 239 Fair Hooker .60 .30
❑ 240 Larry Little RC 15.00 7.50
❑ 241 Mike Garrett .60 .30
❑ 242 Glen Ray Hines .60 .30
❑ 243 Myron Pottios .60 .30
❑ 244 Charlie Joiner RC 20.00 10.00
❑ 245 Len Dawson 6.00 3.00
❑ 246 W.K. Hicks .60 .30
❑ 247 Les Josephson .60 .30
❑ 248 Lance Alworth UER 6.00 3.00
❑ 249 Frank Nunley .60 .30
❑ 250 Mel Farr IA .60 .30
❑ 251 Johnny Unitas IA 8.00 4.00
❑ 252 George Farmer IA .60 .30
❑ 253 Duane Thomas IA 1.00 .40
❑ 254 John Hadl IA 2.00 .75
❑ 255 Vic Washington IA .60 .30
❑ 256 Don Horn IA .60 .30
❑ 257 L.C.Greenwood IA 2.00 .75
❑ 258 Bob Lee IA .60 .30
❑ 259 Larry Csonka IA 4.00 2.00
❑ 260 Mike McCoy DT IA .60 .30
❑ 261 Greg Landry IA 1.00 .40
❑ 262 Ray May IA .60 .30
❑ 263 Bobby Douglass IA .60 .30
❑ 264 Charlie Sanders AP ! 30.00 15.00
❑ 265 Ron Yary AP 30.00 15.00
❑ 266 Rayfield Wright AP 30.00 15.00
❑ 267 Larry Little AP 35.00 20.00
❑ 268 John Niland AP 30.00 15.00
❑ 269 Forrest Blue AP 30.00 15.00
❑ 270 Otis Taylor AP 30.00 15.00
❑ 271 Paul Warfield AP 50.00 30.00
❑ 272 Bob Griese AP 70.00 40.00
❑ 273 John Brockington AP 30.00 15.00
❑ 274 Floyd Little AP 30.00 15.00
❑ 275 Garo Yepremian AP 30.00 15.00
❑ 276 Jerrel Wilson AP 18.00 10.00
❑ 277 Carl Eller AP 30.00 15.00
❑ 278 Bubba Smith AP 40.00 25.00
❑ 279 Alan Page AP 40.00 25.00
❑ 280 Bob Lilly AP 60.00 30.00
❑ 281 Ted Hendricks AP 50.00 30.00
❑ 282 Dave Wilcox AP 30.00 15.00
❑ 283 Willie Lanier AP 35.00 20.00
❑ 284 Jim Johnson AP 30.00 15.00
❑ 285 Willie Brown AP 35.00 20.00
❑ 286 Bill Bradley AP 30.00 15.00
❑ 287 Ken Houston AP 35.00 20.00
❑ 288 Mel Farr 18.00 10.00
❑ 289 Kermit Alexander 18.00 10.00
❑ 290 John Gilliam RC 25.00 12.50
❑ 291 Steve Spurrier RC 100.00 50.00
❑ 292 Walter Johnson 18.00 10.00
❑ 293 Jack Pardee 25.00 12.50
❑ 294 Checklist UER 80.00 50.00
❑ 295 Winston Hill 18.00 10.00
❑ 296 Hugo Hollas 18.00 10.00
❑ 297 Ray May RC 18.00 10.00
❑ 298 Jim Bakken 18.00 10.00
❑ 299 Larry Carwell 18.00 10.00
❑ 300 Alan Page 50.00 30.00
❑ 301 Walt Garrison 25.00 12.50
❑ 302 Mike Lucci 25.00 12.50
❑ 303 Nemiah Wilson 18.00 10.00
❑ 304 Carroll Dale 25.00 12.50
❑ 305 Jim Kanicki 18.00 10.00
❑ 306 Preston Pearson 30.00 15.00
❑ 307 Lemar Parrish 25.00 12.50
❑ 308 Earl Morrall 25.00 12.50
❑ 309 Tommy Nobis 25.00 12.50
❑ 310 Rich Jackson 18.00 10.00
❑ 311 Doug Cunningham 18.00 10.00
❑ 312 Jim Marsalis 18.00 10.00
❑ 313 Jim Beirne 18.00 10.00
❑ 314 Tom McNeill 18.00 10.00
❑ 315 Milt Morin 18.00 10.00
❑ 316 Rayfield Wright RC 25.00 12.50
❑ 317 Jerry LeVias 25.00 12.50
❑ 318 Travis Williams RC 25.00 12.50
❑ 319 Edgar Chandler 18.00 10.00
❑ 320 Bob Wallace 18.00 10.00
❑ 321 Delles Howell 18.00 10.00
❑ 322 Emerson Boozer 25.00 12.50
❑ 323 George Atkinson RC 25.00 12.50
❑ 324 Mike Montler 18.00 10.00
❑ 325 Randy Johnson 18.00 10.00
❑ 326 Mike Curtis UER 25.00 12.50
❑ 327 Miller Farr 18.00 10.00
❑ 328 Horst Muhlmann 18.00 10.00
❑ 329 John Niland RC 25.00 12.50
❑ 330 Andy Russell 30.00 15.00
❑ 331 Mercury Morris 40.00 25.00
❑ 332 Jim Johnson 30.00 15.00
❑ 333 Jerrel Wilson 18.00 10.00
❑ 334 Charley Taylor 40.00 25.00
❑ 335 Dick LeBeau 18.00 10.00
❑ 336 Jim Marshall 30.00 15.00
❑ 337 Tom Mack 30.00 15.00
❑ 338 Steve Spurrier IA 60.00 30.00
❑ 339 Floyd Little IA 25.00 12.50
❑ 340 Len Dawson IA 40.00 25.00
❑ 341 Dick Butkus IA 70.00 40.00
❑ 342 Larry Brown IA 25.00 12.50
❑ 343 Joe Namath IA 175.00 100.00
❑ 344 Jim Turner IA 18.00 10.00
❑ 345 Doug Cunningham IA 18.00 10.00
❑ 346 Edd Hargett IA 18.00 10.00
❑ 347 Steve Owens IA 18.00 10.00
❑ 348 George Blanda IA 50.00 30.00
❑ 349 Ed Podolak IA 18.00 10.00
❑ 350 Rich Jackson IA 18.00 10.00
❑ 351 Ken Willard IA ! 40.00 25.00

1973 Topps

❑ COMPLETE SET (528) 400.00 200.00
❑ 1 Simpson/L.Brown LL 8.00 3.00
❑ 2 Passing Leaders 1.00 .40
❑ 3 Jackson/Biletnikoff LL 1.50 .60
❑ 4 Scoring Leaders .50 .25
❑ 5 Interception Leaders .50 .25
❑ 6 Punting Leaders .50 .25
❑ 7 Bob Trumpy 1.50 .60
❑ 8 Mel Tom .50 .25
❑ 9 Clarence Ellis .50 .25
❑ 10 John Niland .50 .25
❑ 11 Randy Jackson .50 .25
❑ 12 Greg Landry 1.50 .60
❑ 13 Cid Edwards .50 .25
❑ 14 Phil Olsen .50 .25
❑ 15 Terry Bradshaw 25.00 15.00
❑ 16 Al Cowlings RC 1.50 .60
❑ 17 Walker Gillette .50 .25
❑ 18 Bob Atkins .50 .25
❑ 19 Diron Talbert RC .50 .25
❑ 20 Jim Johnson 1.50 .60
❑ 21 Howard Twilley 1.00 .40
❑ 22 Dick Enderle .50 .25
❑ 23 Wayne Colman .50 .25
❑ 24 John Schmitt .50 .25
❑ 25 George Blanda 10.00 5.00
❑ 26 Milt Morin .50 .25
❑ 27 Mike Current .50 .25
❑ 28 Rex Kern RC .50 .25
❑ 29 MacArthur Lane 1.00 .40
❑ 30 Alan Page 3.00 1.50
❑ 31 Randy Vataha .50 .25
❑ 32 Jim Kearney .50 .25
❑ 33 Steve Smith T .50 .25
❑ 34 Ken Anderson RC 15.00 7.50
❑ 35 Calvin Hill 1.50 .60
❑ 36 Andy Maurer .50 .25
❑ 37 Joe Taylor .50 .25
❑ 38 Deacon Jones 1.50 .60
❑ 39 Mike Weger .50 .25
❑ 40 Roy Gerela 1.00 .40
❑ 41 Les Josephson .50 .25
❑ 42 Dave Washington .50 .25
❑ 43 Bill Curry RC 1.00 .40
❑ 44 Fred Heron .50 .25
❑ 45 John Brodie 3.00 1.50
❑ 46 Roy Winston .50 .25
❑ 47 Mike Bragg .50 .25
❑ 48 Mercury Morris 1.50 .60
❑ 49 Jim Files .50 .25
❑ 50 Gene Upshaw 3.00 1.50
❑ 51 Hugo Hollas .50 .25
❑ 52 Rod Sherman .50 .25
❑ 53 Ron Snidow .50 .25
❑ 54 Steve Tannen RC .50 .25
❑ 55 Jim Carter RC .50 .25
❑ 56 Lydell Mitchell RC 1.50 .60
❑ 57 Jack Rudnay RC .50 .25
❑ 58 Halvor Hagen .50 .25
❑ 59 Tom Dempsey 1.00 .40
❑ 60 Fran Tarkenton 10.00 5.00
❑ 61 Lance Alworth 5.00 2.50
❑ 62 Vern Holland .50 .25
❑ 63 Steve DeLong .50 .25
❑ 64 Art Malone .50 .25
❑ 65 Isiah Robertson 1.00 .40
❑ 66 Jerry Rush .50 .25
❑ 67 Bryant Salter .50 .25
❑ 68 Checklist 1-132 5.00 2.50
❑ 69 J.D. Hill .50 .25
❑ 70 Forrest Blue .50 .25
❑ 71 Myron Pottios .50 .25
❑ 72 Norm Thompson RC .50 .25
❑ 73 Paul Robinson .50 .25
❑ 74 Larry Grantham .50 .25
❑ 75 Manny Fernandez 1.00 .40
❑ 76 Kent Nix .50 .25
❑ 77 Art Shell RC 15.00 7.50
❑ 78 George Saimes .50 .25
❑ 79 Don Cockroft .50 .25
❑ 80 Bob Tucker 1.00 .40
❑ 81 Don McCauley RC .50 .25
❑ 82 Bob Brown DT .50 .25
❑ 83 Larry Carwell .50 .25
❑ 84 Mo Moorman .50 .25
❑ 85 John Gilliam 1.00 .40
❑ 86 Wade Key .50 .25
❑ 87 Ross Brupbacher .50 .25
❑ 88 Dave Lewis .50 .25
❑ 89 Franco Harris RC 50.00 25.00
❑ 90 Tom Mack 1.50 .60
❑ 91 Mike Tilleman .50 .25
❑ 92 Carl Mauck .50 .25
❑ 93 Larry Hand .50 .25
❑ 94 Dave Foley RC .50 .25
❑ 95 Frank Nunley .50 .25
❑ 96 John Charles .50 .25
❑ 97 Jim Bakken .50 .25

98	Pat Fischer	1.00	.40
99	Randy Rasmussen	.50	.25
100	Larry Csonka	6.00	3.00
101	Mike Siani RC	.50	.25
102	Tom Roussel	.50	.25
103	Clarence Scott RC	1.00	.40
104	Charlie Johnson	1.00	.40
105	Rick Volk	.50	.25
106	Willie Young	.50	.25
107	Emmitt Thomas	1.00	.40
108	Jon Morris	.50	.25
109	Clarence Williams	.50	.25
110	Rayfield Wright	1.00	.40
111	Norm Bulaich	.50	.25
112	Mike Eischeid	.50	.25
113	Speedy Thomas	.50	.25
114	Glen Holloway	.50	.25
115	Jack Ham RC	30.00	15.00
116	Jim Nettles	.50	.25
117	Errol Mann	.50	.25
118	John Mackey	1.50	.60
119	George Kunz	.50	.25
120	Bob James	.50	.25
121	Garland Boyette	.50	.25
122	Mel Phillips	.50	.25
123	Johnny Roland	.50	.25
124	Doug Swift	.50	.25
125	Archie Manning	4.00	2.00
126	Dave Herman	.50	.25
127	Carleton Oats	.50	.25
128	Bill Van Heusen	.50	.25
129	Rich Jackson	.50	.25
130	Len Hauss	1.00	.40
131	Billy Parks RC	.50	.25
132	Ray May	.50	.25
133	NFC Semi/Staubach	5.00	2.00
134	AFC Semi/Immac.Rec.	2.50	1.00
135	NFC Semi-Final	1.00	.40
136	AFC Semi/L.Csonka	2.00	.75
137	NFC Title Game/Kilmer	1.50	.60
138	AFC Title Game	1.00	.40
139	Super Bowl VII	1.50	.60
140	Dwight White RC	3.00	1.25
141	Jim Marsalis	.50	.25
142	Doug Van Horn	.50	.25
143	Al Matthews	.50	.25
144	Bob Windsor	.50	.25
145	Dave Hampton RC	.50	.25
146	Horst Muhlmann	.50	.25
147	Wally Hilgenberg RC	.50	.25
148	Ron Smith	.50	.25
149	Coy Bacon RC	1.00	.40
150	Winston Hill	.50	.25
151	Ron Jessie RC	1.00	.40
152	Ken Iman	.50	.25
153	Ron Saul	.50	.25
154	Jim Braxton RC	1.00	.40
155	Bubba Smith	2.50	1.25
156	Gary Cuozzo	1.00	.40
157	Charlie Krueger	1.00	.40
158	Tim Foley RC	1.00	.40
159	Lee Roy Jordan	1.50	.60
160	Bob Brown OT	1.50	.60
161	Margene Adkins	.50	.25
162	Ron Widby	.50	.25
163	Jim Houston	.50	.25
164	Joe Dawkins	.50	.25
165	L.C.Greenwood	4.00	2.00
166	Richmond Flowers RC	.50	.25
167	Curley Culp RC	1.50	.60
168	Len St. Jean	.50	.25
169	Walter Rock	.50	.25
170	Bill Bradley	1.00	.40
171	Ken Riley RC	1.50	.60
172	Rich Coady	.50	.25
173	Don Hansen	.50	.25
174	Lionel Aldridge	.50	.25
175	Don Maynard	4.00	2.00
176	Dave Osborn	1.00	.40
177	Jim Bailey	.50	.25
178	John Pitts	.50	.25
179	Dave Parks	.50	.25
180	Chester Marcol RC	.50	.25
181	Len Rohde	.50	.25
182	Jeff Staggs	.50	.25
183	Gene Hickerson	.50	.25
184	Charlie Evans	.50	.25
185	Mel Renfro	1.50	.60
186	Marvin Upshaw	.50	.25
187	George Atkinson	1.00	.40
188	Norm Evans	1.00	.40
189	Steve Ramsey	.50	.25
190	Dave Chapple	.50	.25
191	Gerry Mullins	.50	.25
192	John Didion	.50	.25
193	Bob Gladieux	.50	.25
194	Don Hultz	.50	.25
195	Mike Lucci	.50	.25
196	John Wilbur	.50	.25
197	George Farmer	.50	.25
198	Tommy Casanova RC	1.00	.40
199	Russ Washington	.50	.25
200	Claude Humphrey	1.50	.60
201	Pat Hughes	.50	.25
202	Zeke Moore	.50	.25
203	Chip Glass	.50	.25
204	Glenn Ressler	.50	.25
205	Willie Ellison	1.00	.40
206	John Leypoldt	.50	.25
207	Johnny Fuller	.50	.25
208	Bill Hayhoe	.50	.25
209	Ed Bell	.50	.25
210	Willie Brown	1.50	.60
211	Carl Eller	1.50	.60
212	Mark Nordquist	.50	.25
213	Larry Willingham	.50	.25
214	Nick Buoniconti	1.50	.60
215	John Hadl	1.50	.60
216	Jethro Pugh RC	1.50	.60
217	Leroy Mitchell	.50	.25
218	Billy Newsome	.50	.25
219	John McMakin	.50	.25
220	Larry Brown	1.50	.60
221	Clarence Scott RC	.50	.25
222	Paul Naumoff	.50	.25
223	Ted Fritsch Jr.	.50	.25
224	Checklist 133-264	5.00	2.50
225	Dan Pastorini	1.50	.60
226	Joe Beauchamp UER	.50	.25
227	Pat Matson	.50	.25
228	Tony McGee DT	.50	.25
229	Mike Phipps	1.00	.40
230	Harold Jackson	1.50	.60
231	Willie Williams	.50	.25
232	Spike Jones	.50	.25
233	Jim Tyrer	.50	.25
234	Roy Hilton	.50	.25
235	Phil Villapiano	1.00	.40
236	Charley Taylor UER	3.00	1.50
237	Malcolm Snider	.50	.25
238	Vic Washington	.50	.25
239	Grady Alderman	.50	.25
240	Dick Anderson	1.00	.40
241	Ron Yankowski	.50	.25
242	Billy Masters	.50	.25
243	Herb Adderley	1.50	.60
244	David Ray	.50	.25
245	John Riggins	8.00	4.00
246	Mike Wagner RC	1.50	.60
247	Don Morrison	.50	.25
248	Earl McCullouch	.50	.25
249	Dennis Wirgowski	.50	.25
250	Chris Hanburger	1.00	.40
251	Pat Sullivan RC	1.50	.60
252	Walt Sweeney	.50	.25
253	Willie Alexander	.50	.25
254	Doug Dressler	.50	.25
255	Walter Johnson	.50	.25
256	Ron Hornsby	.50	.25
257	Ben Hawkins	.50	.25
258	Donnie Green RC	.50	.25
259	Fred Hoaglin	.50	.25
260	Jerrel Wilson	.50	.25
261	Horace Jones	.50	.25
262	Woody Peoples	.50	.25
263	Jim Hill RC	.50	.25
264	John Fuqua	.50	.25
265	Donny Anderson KP	1.00	.40
266	Roman Gabriel KP	1.50	.60
267	Mike Garrett KP	1.00	.40
268	Rufus Mayes RC	.50	.25
269	Chip Myrtle	.50	.25
270	Bill Stanfill RC	1.00	.40
271	Clint Jones	.50	.25
272	Miller Farr	.50	.25
273	Harry Schuh	.50	.25
274	Bob Hayes	1.50	.60
275	Bobby Douglass	1.00	.40
276	Gus Hollomon	.50	.25
277	Del Williams	.50	.25
278	Julius Adams	.50	.25
279	Herman Weaver	.50	.25
280	Joe Greene	8.00	4.00
281	Wes Chesson	.50	.25
282	Charlie Harraway	.50	.25
283	Paul Guidry	.50	.25
284	Terry Owens	.50	.25
285	Jan Stenerud	1.50	.60
286	Pete Athas	.50	.25
287	Dale Lindsey	.50	.25
288	Jack Tatum RC	15.00	6.00
289	Floyd Little	1.50	.60
290	Bob Johnson	.50	.25
291	Tommy Hart RC	.50	.25
292	Tom Mitchell	.50	.25
293	Walt Patulski RC	.50	.25
294	Jim Skaggs	.50	.25
295	Bob Griese	6.00	3.00
296	Mike McCoy DT	.50	.25
297	Mel Gray	1.00	.40
298	Bobby Bryant	.50	.25
299	Blaine Nye RC	.50	.25
300	Dick Butkus	12.00	6.00
301	Charlie Cowan RC	.50	.25
302	Mark Lomas	.50	.25
303	Josh Ashton	.50	.25
304	Happy Feller	.50	.25
305	Ron Shanklin	.50	.25
306	Wayne Rasmussen	.50	.25
307	Jerry Smith	.50	.25
308	Ken Reaves	.50	.25
309	Ron East	.50	.25
310	Otis Taylor	1.50	.60
311	John Garlington	.50	.25
312	Lyle Alzado	4.00	2.00
313	Remi Prudhomme	.50	.25
314	Cornelius Johnson	.50	.25
315	Lemar Parrish	1.00	.40
316	Jim Kiick	1.50	.60
317	Steve Zabel	.50	.25
318	Alden Roche	.50	.25
319	Tom Blanchard	.50	.25
320	Fred Biletnikoff	4.00	2.00
321	Ralph Neely	1.00	.40
322	Dan Dierdorf RC	20.00	7.50
323	Richard Caster	1.00	.40
324	Gene Howard	.50	.25
325	Elvin Bethea	1.50	.60
326	Carl Garrett	1.00	.40
327	Ron Billingsley	.50	.25
328	Charlie West	.50	.25
329	Tom Neville	.50	.25
330	Ted Kwalick	1.00	.40
331	Rudy Redmond	.50	.25
332	Henry Davis	.50	.25
333	John Zook	.50	.25
334	Jim Turner	.50	.25
335	Len Dawson	5.00	2.50
336	Bob Chandler RC	1.00	.40
337	Al Beauchamp	.50	.25
338	Tom Matte	1.00	.40
339	Paul Laaveg	.50	.25
340	Ken Ellis	.50	.25
341	Jim Langer RC	10.00	5.00
342	Ron Porter	.50	.25
343	Jack Youngblood RC	15.00	7.50
344	Cornell Green	1.50	.60
345	Marv Hubbard	1.00	.40
346	Bruce Taylor	.50	.25
347	Sam Havrilak	.50	.25
348	Walt Sumner	.50	.25
349	Steve O'Neal	.50	.25
350	Ron Johnson	1.00	.40
351	Rockne Freitas	.50	.25
352	Larry Stallings	.50	.25
353	Jim Cadile	.50	.25
354	Ken Burrough	1.00	.40
355	Jim Plunkett	4.00	2.00
356	Dave Long	.50	.25
357	Ralph Anderson	.50	.25
358	Checklist 265-396	5.00	2.50

❑ 359 Gene Washington Vik 1.00 .40
❑ 360 Dave Wilcox 1.50 .60
❑ 361 Paul Smith .50 .25
❑ 362 Alvin Wyatt .50 .25
❑ 363 Charlie Smith RB .50 .25
❑ 364 Royce Berry .50 .25
❑ 365 Dave Elmendorf .50 .25
❑ 366 Scott Hunter 1.00 .40
❑ 367 Bob Kuechenberg RC 3.00 1.25
❑ 368 Pete Gogolak .50 .25
❑ 369 Dave Edwards .50 .25
❑ 370 Lem Barney 2.50 1.25
❑ 371 Verlon Biggs .50 .25
❑ 372 John Reaves RC .50 .25
❑ 373 Ed Podolak 1.00 .40
❑ 374 Chris Farasopoulos .50 .25
❑ 375 Gary Garrison .50 .25
❑ 376 Tom Funchess .50 .25
❑ 377 Bobby Joe Green .50 .25
❑ 378 Don Brumm .50 .25
❑ 379 Jim O'Brien .50 .25
❑ 380 Paul Krause 1.50 .60
❑ 381 Leroy Kelly 2.50 1.25
❑ 382 Ray Mansfield .50 .25
❑ 383 Dan Abramowicz 1.00 .40
❑ 384 John Outlaw RC .50 .25
❑ 385 Tommy Nobis 1.50 .60
❑ 386 Tom Domres .50 .25
❑ 387 Ken Willard .50 .25
❑ 388 Mike Stratton .50 .25
❑ 389 Fred Dryer 2.50 1.25
❑ 390 Jake Scott 1.50 .60
❑ 391 Rich Houston .50 .25
❑ 392 Virgil Carter .50 .25
❑ 393 Tody Smith .50 .25
❑ 394 Ernie Calloway .50 .25
❑ 395 Charlie Sanders 1.00 .40
❑ 396 Fred Willis .50 .25
❑ 397 Curt Knight .50 .25
❑ 398 Nemiah Wilson .50 .25
❑ 399 Carroll Dale 1.00 .40
❑ 400 Joe Namath 30.00 15.00
❑ 401 Wayne Mulligan .50 .25
❑ 402 Jim Harrison .50 .25
❑ 403 Tim Rossovich .50 .25
❑ 404 David Lee .50 .25
❑ 405 Frank Pitts .50 .25
❑ 406 Jim Marshall 1.50 .60
❑ 407 Bob Brown TE .50 .25
❑ 408 John Rowser .50 .25
❑ 409 Mike Montler .50 .25
❑ 410 Willie Lanier 1.50 .60
❑ 411 Bill Bell K .50 .25
❑ 412 Cedrick Hardman .50 .25
❑ 413 Bob Anderson .50 .25
❑ 414 Earl Morrall 1.50 .60
❑ 415 Ken Houston 1.50 .60
❑ 416 Jack Snow 1.00 .40
❑ 417 Dick Cunningham .50 .25
❑ 418 Greg Larson .50 .25
❑ 419 Mike Bass 1.00 .40
❑ 420 Mike Reid 1.50 .60
❑ 421 Walt Garrison 1.50 .60
❑ 422 Pete Liske .50 .25
❑ 423 Jim Yarbrough .50 .25
❑ 424 Rich McGeorge .50 .25
❑ 425 Bobby Howfield .50 .25
❑ 426 Pete Banaszak .50 .25
❑ 427 Willie Holman .50 .25
❑ 428 Dale Hackbart .50 .25
❑ 429 Fair Hooker .50 .25
❑ 430 Ted Hendricks 5.00 2.50
❑ 431 Mike Garrett 1.00 .40
❑ 432 Glen Ray Hines .50 .25
❑ 433 Fred Cox .50 .25
❑ 434 Bobby Walden .50 .25
❑ 435 Bobby Bell 1.50 .60
❑ 436 Dave Rowe .50 .25
❑ 437 Bob Berry .50 .25
❑ 438 Bill Thompson .50 .25
❑ 439 Jim Beirne .50 .25
❑ 440 Larry Little 3.00 1.50
❑ 441 Rocky Thompson .50 .25
❑ 442 Brig Owens .50 .25
❑ 443 Richard Neal .50 .25
❑ 444 Al Nelson .50 .25
❑ 445 Chip Myers .50 .25
❑ 446 Ken Bowman .50 .25
❑ 447 Jim Purnell .50 .25
❑ 448 Altie Taylor .50 .25
❑ 449 Linzy Cole .50 .25
❑ 450 Bob Lilly 5.00 2.50
❑ 451 Charlie Ford .50 .25
❑ 452 Milt Sunde .50 .25
❑ 453 Doug Wyatt .50 .25
❑ 454 Don Nottingham RC 1.00 .40
❑ 455 Johnny Unitas 15.00 7.50
❑ 456 Frank Lewis RC 1.00 .40
❑ 457 Roger Wehrli 1.00 .40
❑ 458 Jim Cheyunski .50 .25
❑ 459 Jerry Sherk RC 1.00 .40
❑ 460 Gene Washington 49er 1.00 .40
❑ 461 Jim Otto 1.50 .60
❑ 462 Ed Budde .50 .25
❑ 463 Jim Mitchell TE 1.00 .40
❑ 464 Emerson Boozer 1.00 .40
❑ 465 Garo Yepremian 1.50 .60
❑ 466 Pete Duranko .50 .25
❑ 467 Charlie Joiner 8.00 4.00
❑ 468 Spider Lockhart 1.00 .40
❑ 469 Marty Domres .50 .25
❑ 470 John Brockington 1.50 .60
❑ 471 Ed Flanagan .50 .25
❑ 472 Roy Jefferson 1.00 .40
❑ 473 Julian Fagan .50 .25
❑ 474 Bill Brown 1.00 .40
❑ 475 Roger Staubach 30.00 15.00
❑ 476 Jan White RC .50 .25
❑ 477 Pat Holmes .50 .25
❑ 478 Bob DeMarco .50 .25
❑ 479 Merlin Olsen 2.50 1.25
❑ 480 Andy Russell 1.50 .60
❑ 481 Steve Spurrier 20.00 10.00
❑ 482 Nate Ramsey .50 .25
❑ 483 Dennis Partee .50 .25
❑ 484 Jerry Simmons .50 .25
❑ 485 Donny Anderson 1.50 .60
❑ 486 Ralph Baker .50 .25
❑ 487 Ken Stabler RC ! 60.00 35.00
❑ 488 Ernie McMillan .50 .25
❑ 489 Ken Burrow .50 .25
❑ 490 Jack Gregory RC .50 .25
❑ 491 Larry Seiple 1.00 .40
❑ 492 Mick Tingelhoff 1.00 .40
❑ 493 Craig Morton 1.50 .60
❑ 494 Cecil Turner .50 .25
❑ 495 Steve Owens 1.50 .60
❑ 496 Rickie Harris .50 .25
❑ 497 Buck Buchanan 1.50 .60
❑ 498 Checklist 397-528 5.00 2.50
❑ 499 Billy Kilmer 1.50 .60
❑ 500 O.J.Simpson 15.00 7.50
❑ 501 Bruce Gossett .50 .25
❑ 502 Art Thoms RC .50 .25
❑ 503 Larry Kaminski .50 .25
❑ 504 Larry Smith RB .50 .25
❑ 505 Bruce Van Dyke .50 .25
❑ 506 Alvin Reed .50 .25
❑ 507 Delles Howell .50 .25
❑ 508 Leroy Keyes .50 .25
❑ 509 Bo Scott 1.00 .40
❑ 510 Ron Yary 1.50 .60
❑ 511 Paul Warfield 5.00 2.50
❑ 512 Mac Percival .50 .25
❑ 513 Essex Johnson .50 .25
❑ 514 Jackie Smith 1.50 .60
❑ 515 Norm Snead 1.50 .60
❑ 516 Charlie Stukes .50 .25
❑ 517 Reggie Rucker RC 1.00 .40
❑ 518 Bill Sandeman UER .50 .25
❑ 519 Mel Farr 1.00 .40
❑ 520 Raymond Chester 1.00 .40
❑ 521 Fred Carr RC 1.00 .40
❑ 522 Jerry LeVias 1.00 .40
❑ 523 Jim Strong .50 .25
❑ 524 Roland McDole .50 .25
❑ 525 Dennis Shaw .50 .25
❑ 526 Dave Manders .50 .25
❑ 527 Skip Vanderbundt .50 .25
❑ 528 Mike Sensibaugh RC ! 1.50 .60

1974 Topps

❑ COMPLETE SET (528) 300.00 175.00
❑ 1 O.J.Simpson RB UER 20.00 10.00
❑ 2 Blaine Nye .40 .20
❑ 3 Don Hansen .40 .20
❑ 4 Ken Bowman .40 .20
❑ 5 Carl Eller 1.50 .60
❑ 6 Jerry Smith .40 .20
❑ 7 Ed Podolak .40 .20
❑ 8 Mel Gray 1.50 .60
❑ 9 Pat Matson .40 .20
❑ 10 Floyd Little 1.50 .60
❑ 11 Frank Pitts .40 .20
❑ 12 Vern Den Herder RC .75 .30
❑ 13 John Fuqua .75 .30
❑ 14 Jack Tatum 2.00 .75
❑ 15 Winston Hill .40 .20
❑ 16 John Beasley .40 .20
❑ 17 David Lee .40 .20
❑ 18 Rich Coady .40 .20
❑ 19 Ken Willard .40 .20
❑ 20 Coy Bacon .75 .30
❑ 21 Ben Hawkins .40 .20
❑ 22 Paul Guidry .40 .20
❑ 23 Norm Snead HOR .75 .30
❑ 24 Jim Yarbrough .40 .20
❑ 25 Jack Reynolds RC 3.00 1.25
❑ 26 Josh Ashton .40 .20
❑ 27 Donnie Green .40 .20
❑ 28 Bob Hayes 1.50 .60
❑ 29 John Zook .40 .20
❑ 30 Bobby Bryant .40 .20
❑ 31 Scott Hunter .75 .30
❑ 32 Dan Dierdorf 6.00 3.00
❑ 33 Curt Knight .40 .20
❑ 34 Elmo Wright RC .40 .20
❑ 35 Essex Johnson .40 .20
❑ 36 Walt Sumner .40 .20
❑ 37 Marv Montgomery .40 .20
❑ 38 Tim Foley .75 .30
❑ 39 Mike Siani .40 .20
❑ 40 Joe Greene 6.00 3.00
❑ 41 Bobby Howfield .40 .20
❑ 42 Del Williams .40 .20
❑ 43 Don McCauley .40 .20
❑ 44 Randy Jackson .40 .20
❑ 45 Ron Smith .40 .20
❑ 46 Gene Washington 49er .75 .30
❑ 47 Po James .40 .20
❑ 48 Solomon Freelon .40 .20
❑ 49 Bob Windsor HOR .40 .20
❑ 50 John Hadl 1.50 .60
❑ 51 Greg Larson .40 .20
❑ 52 Steve Owens .75 .30
❑ 53 Jim Cheyunski .40 .20
❑ 54 Rayfield Wright .75 .30
❑ 55 Dave Hampton .40 .20
❑ 56 Ron Widby .40 .20
❑ 57 Milt Sunde .40 .20
❑ 58 Billy Kilmer 1.50 .60
❑ 59 Bobby Bell 1.50 .60
❑ 60 Jim Bakken .40 .20
❑ 61 Rufus Mayes .40 .20
❑ 62 Vic Washington .40 .20
❑ 63 Gene Washington Vik .75 .30
❑ 64 Clarence Scott .40 .20
❑ 65 Gene Upshaw 2.00 .75
❑ 66 Larry Seiple .75 .30
❑ 67 John McMakin .40 .20
❑ 68 Ralph Baker .40 .20
❑ 69 Lydell Mitchell .75 .30
❑ 70 Archie Manning 2.50 1.25
❑ 71 George Farmer .40 .20

❑ 72 Ron East	.40	.20
❑ 73 Al Nelson	.40	.20
❑ 74 Pat Hughes	.40	.20
❑ 75 Fred Willis	.40	.20
❑ 76 Larry Walton	.40	.20
❑ 77 Tom Neville	.40	.20
❑ 78 Ted Kwalick	.40	.20
❑ 79 Walt Patulski	.40	.20
❑ 80 John Niland	.40	.20
❑ 81 Ted Fritsch Jr.	.40	.20
❑ 82 Paul Krause	1.50	.60
❑ 83 Jack Snow	.75	.30
❑ 84 Mike Bass	.40	.20
❑ 85 Jim Tyrer	.40	.20
❑ 86 Ron Yankowski	.40	.20
❑ 87 Mike Phipps	.75	.30
❑ 88 Al Beauchamp	.40	.20
❑ 89 Riley Odoms RC	1.50	.60
❑ 90 MacArthur Lane	.40	.20
❑ 91 Art Thoms	.40	.20
❑ 92 Marlin Briscoe	.40	.20
❑ 93 Bruce Van Dyke	.40	.20
❑ 94 Tom Myers RC	.40	.20
❑ 95 Calvin Hill	1.50	.60
❑ 96 Bruce Laird	.40	.20
❑ 97 Tony McGee DT	.40	.20
❑ 98 Len Rohde	.40	.20
❑ 99 Tom McNeill	.40	.20
❑ 100 Delles Howell	.40	.20
❑ 101 Gary Garrison	.40	.20
❑ 102 Dan Goich	.40	.20
❑ 103 Len St. Jean	.40	.20
❑ 104 Zeke Moore	.40	.20
❑ 105 Ahmad Rashad RC	20.00	10.00
❑ 106 Mel Renfro	1.50	.60
❑ 107 Jim Mitchell TE	.40	.20
❑ 108 Ed Budde	.40	.20
❑ 109 Harry Schuh	.40	.20
❑ 110 Greg Pruitt RC	4.00	2.00
❑ 111 Ed Flanagan	.40	.20
❑ 112 Larry Stallings	.40	.20
❑ 113 Chuck Foreman RC	4.00	2.00
❑ 114 Royce Berry	.40	.20
❑ 115 Gale Gillingham	.40	.20
❑ 116 Charlie Johnson HOR	1.50	.60
❑ 117 Checklist 1-132 UER	4.00	2.00
❑ 118 Bill Butler	.40	.20
❑ 119 Roy Jefferson	.75	.30
❑ 120 Bobby Douglass	.75	.30
❑ 121 Harold Carmichael RC	12.00	6.00
❑ 122 George Kunz AP	.40	.20
❑ 123 Larry Little	2.00	.75
❑ 124 Forrest Blue AP	.40	.20
❑ 125 Ron Yary	1.50	.60
❑ 126 Tom Mack AP	1.50	.60
❑ 127 Bob Tucker AP	.75	.30
❑ 128 Paul Warfield	4.00	2.00
❑ 129 Fran Tarkenton	10.00	5.00
❑ 130 O.J.Simpson	12.00	6.00
❑ 131 Larry Csonka	6.00	3.00
❑ 132 Bruce Gossett AP	.40	.20
❑ 133 Bill Stanfill AP	.75	.30
❑ 134 Alan Page	2.50	1.25
❑ 135 Paul Smith AP	.40	.20
❑ 136 Claude Humphrey AP	.75	.30
❑ 137 Jack Ham	10.00	5.00
❑ 138 Lee Roy Jordan	1.50	.60
❑ 139 Phil Villapiano AP	.75	.30
❑ 140 Ken Ellis AP	.40	.20
❑ 141 Willie Brown	1.50	.60
❑ 142 Dick Anderson AP	.75	.30
❑ 143 Bill Bradley AP	.75	.30
❑ 144 Jerrel Wilson AP	.40	.20
❑ 145 Reggie Rucker	.75	.30
❑ 146 Marty Domres	.40	.20
❑ 147 Bob Kowalkowski	.40	.20
❑ 148 John Matuszak RC	6.00	2.50
❑ 149 Mike Adamle RC	.75	.30
❑ 150 Johnny Unitas	15.00	7.50
❑ 151 Charlie Ford	.40	.20
❑ 152 Bob Klein RC	.40	.20
❑ 153 Jim Merlo	.40	.20
❑ 154 Willie Young	.40	.20
❑ 155 Donny Anderson	.75	.30
❑ 156 Brig Owens	.40	.20
❑ 157 Bruce Jarvis	.40	.20
❑ 158 Ron Carpenter RC	.40	.20
❑ 159 Don Cockroft	.40	.20
❑ 160 Tommy Nobis	1.50	.60
❑ 161 Craig Morton	1.50	.60
❑ 162 Jon Staggers	.40	.20
❑ 163 Mike Eischeid	.40	.20
❑ 164 Jerry Sisemore RC	.40	.20
❑ 165 Cedrick Hardman	.40	.20
❑ 166 Bill Thompson	.75	.30
❑ 167 Jim Lynch	.75	.30
❑ 168 Bob Moore	.40	.20
❑ 169 Glen Edwards	.40	.20
❑ 170 Mercury Morris	1.50	.60
❑ 171 Julius Adams	.40	.20
❑ 172 Cotton Speyrer	.40	.20
❑ 173 Bill Munson	.75	.30
❑ 174 Benny Johnson	.40	.20
❑ 175 Burgess Owens RC	.40	.20
❑ 176 Cid Edwards	.40	.20
❑ 177 Doug Buffone	.40	.20
❑ 178 Charlie Cowan	.40	.20
❑ 179 Bob Newland	.40	.20
❑ 180 Ron Johnson	.75	.30
❑ 181 Bob Rowe	.40	.20
❑ 182 Len Hauss	.40	.20
❑ 183 Joe DeLamielleure RC	8.00	3.00
❑ 184 Sherman White RC	.40	.20
❑ 185 Fair Hooker	.40	.20
❑ 186 Nick Mike-Mayer	.40	.20
❑ 187 Ralph Neely	.40	.20
❑ 188 Rich McGeorge	.40	.20
❑ 189 Ed Marinaro RC	4.00	1.50
❑ 190 Dave Wilcox	1.50	.60
❑ 191 Joe Owens RC	.40	.20
❑ 192 Bill Van Heusen	.40	.20
❑ 193 Jim Kearney	.40	.20
❑ 194 Otis Sistrunk RC	1.50	.60
❑ 195 Ron Shanklin	.40	.20
❑ 196 Bill Lenkaitis	.40	.20
❑ 197 Tom Drougas	.40	.20
❑ 198 Larry Hand	.40	.20
❑ 199 Mack Alston	.40	.20
❑ 200 Bob Griese	6.00	3.00
❑ 201 Earlie Thomas	.40	.20
❑ 202 Carl Gersbach	.40	.20
❑ 203 Jim Harrison	.40	.20
❑ 204 Jake Kupp	.40	.20
❑ 205 Merlin Olsen	2.00	.75
❑ 206 Spider Lockhart	.75	.30
❑ 207 Walker Gillette	.40	.20
❑ 208 Verlon Biggs	.40	.20
❑ 209 Bob James	.40	.20
❑ 210 Bob Trumpy	1.50	.60
❑ 211 Jerry Sherk	.40	.20
❑ 212 Andy Maurer	.40	.20
❑ 213 Fred Carr	.40	.20
❑ 214 Mick Tingelhoff	.75	.30
❑ 215 Steve Spurrier	15.00	7.50
❑ 216 Richard Harris	.40	.20
❑ 217 Charlie Greer	.40	.20
❑ 218 Buck Buchanan	1.50	.60
❑ 219 Ray Guy RC	10.00	5.00
❑ 220 Franco Harris	12.00	6.00
❑ 221 Darryl Stingley RC	1.50	.60
❑ 222 Rex Kern	.40	.20
❑ 223 Toni Fritsch	.75	.30
❑ 224 Levi Johnson	.40	.20
❑ 225 Bob Kuechenberg	.75	.30
❑ 226 Elvin Bethea	1.50	.60
❑ 227 Al Woodall RC	.75	.30
❑ 228 Terry Owens	.40	.20
❑ 229 Bivian Lee	.40	.20
❑ 230 Dick Butkus	10.00	5.00
❑ 231 Jim Bertelsen RC	.75	.30
❑ 232 John Mendenhall RC	.40	.20
❑ 233 Conrad Dobler RC	1.50	.60
❑ 234 J.D. Hill	.75	.30
❑ 235 Ken Houston	1.50	.60
❑ 236 Dave Lewis	.40	.20
❑ 237 John Garlington	.40	.20
❑ 238 Bill Sandeman	.40	.20
❑ 239 Alden Roche	.40	.20
❑ 240 John Gilliam	.75	.30
❑ 241 Bruce Taylor	.40	.20
❑ 242 Vern Winfield	.40	.20
❑ 243 Bobby Maples	.40	.20
❑ 244 Wendell Hayes	.40	.20
❑ 245 George Blanda	8.00	4.00
❑ 246 Dwight White	.75	.30
❑ 247 Sandy Durko	.40	.20
❑ 248 Tom Mitchell	.40	.20
❑ 249 Chuck Walton	.40	.20
❑ 250 Bob Lilly	4.00	2.00
❑ 251 Doug Swift	.40	.20
❑ 252 Lynn Dickey RC	1.50	.60
❑ 253 Jerome Barkum RC	.40	.20
❑ 254 Clint Jones	.40	.20
❑ 255 Billy Newsome	.40	.20
❑ 256 Bob Asher	.40	.20
❑ 257 Joe Scibelli	.40	.20
❑ 258 Tom Blanchard	.40	.20
❑ 259 Norm Thompson	.40	.20
❑ 260 Larry Brown	1.50	.60
❑ 261 Paul Seymour	.40	.20
❑ 262 Checklist 133-264	4.00	2.00
❑ 263 Doug Dieken RC	.40	.20
❑ 264 Lemar Parrish	.75	.30
❑ 265 Bob Lee UER	.40	.20
❑ 266 Bob Brown DT	.40	.20
❑ 267 Roy Winston	.40	.20
❑ 268 Randy Beisler	.40	.20
❑ 269 Joe Dawkins	.40	.20
❑ 270 Tom Dempsey	.75	.30
❑ 271 Jack Rudnay	.40	.20
❑ 272 Art Shell	5.00	2.50
❑ 273 Mike Wagner	.75	.30
❑ 274 Rick Cash	.40	.20
❑ 275 Greg Landry	1.50	.60
❑ 276 Glenn Ressler	.40	.20
❑ 277 Billy Joe DuPree RC	3.00	1.25
❑ 278 Norm Evans	.40	.20
❑ 279 Billy Parks	.40	.20
❑ 280 John Riggins	6.00	3.00
❑ 281 Lionel Aldridge	.40	.20
❑ 282 Steve O'Neal	.40	.20
❑ 283 Craig Clemons	.40	.20
❑ 284 Willie Williams	.40	.20
❑ 285 Isiah Robertson	.75	.30
❑ 286 Dennis Shaw	.40	.20
❑ 287 Bill Brundige	.40	.20
❑ 288 John Leypoldt	.40	.20
❑ 289 John DeMarie	.40	.20
❑ 290 Mike Reid	1.50	.60
❑ 291 Greg Brezina	.40	.20
❑ 292 Willie Buchanon RC	.40	.20
❑ 293 Dave Osborn	.75	.30
❑ 294 Mel Phillips	.40	.20
❑ 295 Haven Moses	.75	.30
❑ 296 Wade Key	.40	.20
❑ 297 Marvin Upshaw	.40	.20
❑ 298 Ray Mansfield	.40	.20
❑ 299 Edgar Chandler	.40	.20
❑ 300 Marv Hubbard	.75	.30
❑ 301 Herman Weaver	.40	.20
❑ 302 Jim Bailey	.40	.20
❑ 303 D.D.Lewis RC	1.50	.60
❑ 304 Ken Burrough	.75	.30
❑ 305 Jake Scott	1.50	.60
❑ 306 Randy Rasmussen	.40	.20
❑ 307 Pettis Norman	.40	.20
❑ 308 Carl Johnson	.40	.20
❑ 309 Joe Taylor	.40	.20
❑ 310 Pete Gogolak	.40	.20
❑ 311 Tony Baker FB	.40	.20
❑ 312 John Richardson	.40	.20
❑ 313 Dave Robinson	.75	.30
❑ 314 Reggie McKenzie RC	1.50	.60
❑ 315 Isaac Curtis RC	1.50	.60
❑ 316 Thom Darden	.40	.20
❑ 317 Ken Reaves	.40	.20
❑ 318 Malcolm Snider	.40	.20
❑ 319 Jeff Siemon RC	.75	.30
❑ 320 Dan Abramowicz	.75	.30
❑ 321 Lyle Alzado	2.00	.75
❑ 322 John Reaves	.40	.20
❑ 323 Morris Stroud	.40	.20
❑ 324 Bobby Walden	.40	.20
❑ 325 Randy Vataha	.40	.20
❑ 326 Nemiah Wilson	.40	.20
❑ 327 Paul Naumoff	.40	.20
❑ 328 O.J.Simpson/Brock. LL	3.00	1.50
❑ 329 R.Staubach/Stabler LL	5.00	2.50
❑ 330 Harold Carmichael/Wil LL	1.50	.60
❑ 331 Scoring Leaders	.75	.30
❑ 332 Interception Leaders	.75	.30

❑	333	Punting Leaders	.75	.30
❑	334	Dennis Nelson	.40	.20
❑	335	Walt Garrison	.75	.30
❑	336	Tody Smith	.40	.20
❑	337	Ed Bell	.40	.20
❑	338	Bryant Salter	.40	.20
❑	339	Wayne Colman	.40	.20
❑	340	Garo Yepremian	.75	.30
❑	341	Bob Newton	.40	.20
❑	342	Vince Clements RC	.40	.20
❑	343	Ken Iman	.40	.20
❑	344	Jim Tolbert	.40	.20
❑	345	Chris Hanburger	.75	.30
❑	346	Dave Foley	.40	.20
❑	347	Tommy Casanova	.75	.30
❑	348	John James	.40	.20
❑	349	Clarence Williams	.40	.20
❑	350	Leroy Kelly	1.50	.60
❑	351	Stu Voigt RC	.75	.30
❑	352	Skip Vanderbundt	.40	.20
❑	353	Pete Duranko	.40	.20
❑	354	John Outlaw	.40	.20
❑	355	Jan Stenerud	1.50	.60
❑	356	Barry Pearson	.40	.20
❑	357	Brian Dowling RC	.40	.20
❑	358	Dan Conners	.40	.20
❑	359	Bob Bell	.40	.20
❑	360	Rick Volk	.40	.20
❑	361	Pat Toomay	.75	.30
❑	362	Bob Gresham	.40	.20
❑	363	John Schmitt	.40	.20
❑	364	Mel Rogers	.40	.20
❑	365	Manny Fernandez	.75	.30
❑	366	Ernie Jackson	.40	.20
❑	367	Gary Huff RC	.75	.30
❑	368	Bob Grim	.40	.20
❑	369	Ernie McMillan	.40	.20
❑	370	Dave Elmendorf	.40	.20
❑	371	Mike Bragg	.40	.20
❑	372	John Skorupan	.40	.20
❑	373	Howard Fest	.40	.20
❑	374	Jerry Tagge RC	.75	.30
❑	375	Art Malone	.40	.20
❑	376	Bob Babich	.40	.20
❑	377	Jim Marshall	1.50	.60
❑	378	Bob Hoskins	.40	.20
❑	379	Don Zimmerman	.40	.20
❑	380	Ray May	.40	.20
❑	381	Emmitt Thomas	.75	.30
❑	382	Terry Hanratty	.75	.30
❑	383	John Hannah RC	15.00	7.50
❑	384	George Atkinson	.40	.20
❑	385	Ted Hendricks	3.00	1.50
❑	386	Jim O'Brien	.40	.20
❑	387	Jethro Pugh	.75	.30
❑	388	Elbert Drungo	.40	.20
❑	389	Richard Caster	.75	.30
❑	390	Deacon Jones	1.50	.60
❑	391	Checklist 265-396	4.00	2.00
❑	392	Jess Phillips	.40	.20
❑	393	Garry Lyle UER	.40	.20
❑	394	Jim Files	.40	.20
❑	395	Jim Hart	1.50	.60
❑	396	Dave Chapple	.40	.20
❑	397	Jim Langer	2.00	.75
❑	398	John Wilbur	.40	.20
❑	399	Dwight Harrison	.40	.20
❑	400	John Brockington	.75	.30
❑	401	Ken Anderson	6.00	3.00
❑	402	Mike Tilleman	.40	.20
❑	403	Charlie Hall	.40	.20
❑	404	Tommy Hart	.40	.20
❑	405	Norm Bulaich	.75	.30
❑	406	Jim Turner	.40	.20
❑	407	Mo Moorman	.40	.20
❑	408	Ralph Anderson	.40	.20
❑	409	Jim Otto	1.50	.60
❑	410	Andy Russell	1.50	.60
❑	411	Glenn Doughty	.40	.20
❑	412	Altie Taylor	.40	.20
❑	413	Marv Bateman	.40	.20
❑	414	Willie Alexander	.40	.20
❑	415	Bill Zapalac RC	.40	.20
❑	416	Russ Washington	.40	.20
❑	417	Joe Federspiel	.40	.20
❑	418	Craig Cotton	.40	.20
❑	419	Randy Johnson	.40	.20
❑	420	Harold Jackson	1.50	.60
❑	421	Roger Wehrli	.75	.30
❑	422	Charlie Harraway	.40	.20
❑	423	Spike Jones	.40	.20
❑	424	Bob Johnson	.40	.20
❑	425	Mike McCoy DT	.40	.20
❑	426	Dennis Havig	.40	.20
❑	427	Bob McKay RC	.40	.20
❑	428	Steve Zabel	.40	.20
❑	429	Horace Jones	.40	.20
❑	430	Jim Johnson	1.50	.60
❑	431	Roy Gerela	.75	.30
❑	432	Tom Graham RC	.40	.20
❑	433	Curley Culp	.75	.30
❑	434	Ken Mendenhall	.40	.20
❑	435	Jim Plunkett	2.50	1.25
❑	436	Julian Fagan	.40	.20
❑	437	Mike Garrett	.75	.30
❑	438	Bobby Joe Green	.40	.20
❑	439	Jack Gregory	.40	.20
❑	440	Charlie Sanders	.75	.30
❑	441	Bill Curry	.75	.30
❑	442	Bob Pollard	.40	.20
❑	443	David Ray	.40	.20
❑	444	Terry Metcalf RC	3.00	1.50
❑	445	Pat Fischer	.75	.30
❑	446	Bob Chandler	.75	.30
❑	447	Bill Bergey	.75	.30
❑	448	Walter Johnson	.40	.20
❑	449	Charle Young RC	1.50	.60
❑	450	Chester Marcol	.40	.20
❑	451	Ken Stabler	20.00	10.00
❑	452	Preston Pearson	1.50	.60
❑	453	Mike Current	.40	.20
❑	454	Ron Bolton	.40	.20
❑	455	Mark Lomas	.40	.20
❑	456	Raymond Chester	.75	.30
❑	457	Jerry LeVias	.75	.30
❑	458	Skip Butler	.40	.20
❑	459	Mike Livingston RC	.40	.20
❑	460	AFC Semi-Final	.75	.30
❑	461	NFC Semi/Staubach	4.00	2.00
❑	462	Playoff Champs/Stabler	3.00	1.50
❑	463	SB VIII/Tarkenton	2.00	.75
❑	464	Wayne Mulligan	.40	.20
❑	465	Horst Muhlmann	.40	.20
❑	466	Milt Morin	.40	.20
❑	467	Don Parish	.40	.20
❑	468	Richard Neal	.40	.20
❑	469	Ron Jessie	.75	.30
❑	470	Terry Bradshaw	25.00	12.50
❑	471	Fred Dryer	1.50	.60
❑	472	Jim Carter	.40	.20
❑	473	Ken Burrow	.40	.20
❑	474	Wally Chambers RC	.75	.30
❑	475	Dan Pastorini	1.50	.60
❑	476	Don Morrison	.40	.20
❑	477	Carl Mauck	.40	.20
❑	478	Larry Cole RC	.75	.30
❑	479	Jim Kiick	1.50	.60
❑	480	Willie Lanier	1.50	.60
❑	481	Don Herrmann	.75	.30
❑	482	George Hunt	.40	.20
❑	483	Bob Howard RC	.40	.20
❑	484	Myron Pottios	.40	.20
❑	485	Jackie Smith	1.50	.60
❑	486	Vern Holland	.40	.20
❑	487	Jim Braxton	.40	.20
❑	488	Joe Reed	.40	.20
❑	489	Wally Hilgenberg	.40	.20
❑	490	Fred Biletnikoff	4.00	2.00
❑	491	Bob DeMarco	.40	.20
❑	492	Mark Nordquist	.40	.20
❑	493	Larry Brooks	.40	.20
❑	494	Pete Athas	.40	.20
❑	495	Emerson Boozer	.75	.30
❑	496	L.C.Greenwood	2.00	.75
❑	497	Rockne Freitas	.40	.20
❑	498	Checklist 397-528 UER	4.00	2.00
❑	499	Joe Schmiesing	.40	.20
❑	500	Roger Staubach	25.00	12.50
❑	501	Al Cowlings UER	.75	.30
❑	502	Sam Cunningham RC	1.50	.60
❑	503	Dennis Partee	.40	.20
❑	504	John Didion	.40	.20
❑	505	Nick Buoniconti	1.50	.60
❑	506	Carl Garrett	.75	.30
❑	507	Doug Van Horn	.40	.20
❑	508	Jamie Rivers	.40	.20
❑	509	Jack Youngblood	4.00	2.00
❑	510	Charley Taylor UER	2.50	1.25
❑	511	Ken Riley	1.50	.60
❑	512	Joe Ferguson RC	3.00	1.25
❑	513	Bill Lueck	.40	.20
❑	514	Ray Brown DB RC	.40	.20
❑	515	Fred Cox	.40	.20
❑	516	Joe Jones DE	.40	.20
❑	517	Larry Schreiber	.40	.20
❑	518	Dennis Wirgowski	.40	.20
❑	519	Leroy Mitchell	.40	.20
❑	520	Otis Taylor	1.50	.60
❑	521	Henry Davis	.40	.20
❑	522	Bruce Barnes	.40	.20
❑	523	Charlie Smith RB	.40	.20
❑	524	Bert Jones RC	5.00	2.00
❑	525	Lem Barney	2.00	.75
❑	526	John Fitzgerald RC	.40	.20
❑	527	Tom Funchess	.40	.20
❑	528	Steve Tannen	1.50	.60

1975 Topps

❑		COMPLETE SET (528)	300.00	175.00
❑	1	McCutcheon/Armstrong LL	1.50	.60
❑	2	Jurgensen/K.Anderson LL	1.50	.60
❑	3	Receiving Leaders	1.50	.60
❑	4	Scoring Leaders	.75	.30
❑	5	Interception Leaders	.75	.30
❑	6	Punting Leaders	1.50	.60
❑	7	George Blanda HL	5.00	2.50
❑	8	George Blanda	5.00	2.50
❑	9	Ralph Baker	.30	.15
❑	10	Don Woods	.30	.15
❑	11	Bob Asher	.30	.15
❑	12	Mel Blount RC	20.00	10.00
❑	13	Sam Cunningham	.75	.30
❑	14	Jackie Smith	1.50	.60
❑	15	Greg Landry	.75	.30
❑	16	Buck Buchanan	1.50	.60
❑	17	Haven Moses	.75	.30
❑	18	Clarence Ellis	.30	.15
❑	19	Jim Carter	.30	.15
❑	20	Charley Taylor UER	2.00	.75
❑	21	Jess Phillips	.30	.15
❑	22	Larry Seiple	.30	.15
❑	23	Doug Dieken	.30	.15
❑	24	Ron Saul	.30	.15
❑	25	Isaac Curtis	1.50	.60
❑	26	Gary Larsen RC	.30	.15
❑	27	Bruce Jarvis	.30	.15
❑	28	Steve Zabel	.30	.15
❑	29	John Mendenhall	.30	.15
❑	30	Rick Volk	.30	.15
❑	31	Checklist 1-132	4.00	2.00
❑	32	Dan Abramowicz	.75	.30
❑	33	Bubba Smith	1.50	.60
❑	34	David Ray	.30	.15
❑	35	Dan Dierdorf	4.00	2.00
❑	36	Randy Rasmussen	.30	.15
❑	37	Bob Howard	.30	.15
❑	38	Gary Huff	.75	.30
❑	39	Rocky Bleier RC	20.00	10.00
❑	40	Mel Gray	.75	.30
❑	41	Tony McGee DT	.30	.15
❑	42	Larry Hand	.30	.15
❑	43	Wendell Hayes	.30	.15
❑	44	Doug Wilkerson RC	.30	.15

45	Paul Smith	.30	.15
46	Dave Robinson	.75	.30
47	Bivian Lee	.30	.15
48	Jim Mandich RC	.75	.30
49	Greg Pruitt	1.50	.60
50	Dan Pastorini	1.50	.60
51	Ron Pritchard	.30	.15
52	Dan Conners	.30	.15
53	Fred Cox	.30	.15
54	Tony Greene	.30	.15
55	Craig Morton	1.50	.60
56	Jerry Sisemore	.30	.15
57	Glenn Doughty	.30	.15
58	Larry Schreiber	.30	.15
59	Charlie Waters RC	4.00	2.00
60	Jack Youngblood	1.50	.60
61	Bill Lenkaitis	.30	.15
62	Greg Brezina	.30	.15
63	Bob Pollard	.30	.15
64	Mack Alston	.30	.15
65	Drew Pearson RC	20.00	10.00
66	Charlie Stukes	.30	.15
67	Emerson Boozer	.75	.30
68	Dennis Partee	.30	.15
69	Bob Newton	.30	.15
70	Jack Tatum	1.50	.60
71	Frank Lewis	.30	.15
72	Bob Young	.30	.15
73	Julius Adams	.30	.15
74	Paul Naumoff	.30	.15
75	Otis Taylor	1.50	.60
76	Dave Hampton	.30	.15
77	Mike Current	.30	.15
78	Brig Owens	.30	.15
79	Bobby Scott	.30	.15
80	Harold Carmichael	3.00	1.50
81	Bill Stanfill	.30	.15
82	Bob Babich	.30	.15
83	Vic Washington	.30	.15
84	Mick Tingelhoff	.75	.30
85	Bob Trumpy	1.50	.60
86	Earl Edwards	.30	.15
87	Ron Hornsby	.30	.15
88	Don McCauley	.30	.15
89	Jim Johnson	1.50	.60
90	Andy Russell	.75	.30
91	Cornell Green	1.50	.60
92	Charlie Cowan	.30	.15
93	Jon Staggers	.30	.15
94	Billy Newsome	.30	.15
95	Willie Brown	1.50	.60
96	Carl Mauck	.30	.15
97	Doug Buffone	.30	.15
98	Preston Pearson	.75	.30
99	Jim Bakken	.30	.15
100	Bob Griese	5.00	2.50
101	Bob Windsor	.30	.15
102	Rockne Freitas	.30	.15
103	Jim Marsalis	.30	.15
104	Bill Thompson	.75	.30
105	Ken Burrow	.30	.15
106	Diron Talbert	.30	.15
107	Joe Federspiel	.30	.15
108	Norm Bulaich	.75	.30
109	Bob DeMarco	.30	.15
110	Tom Wittum	.30	.15
111	Larry Hefner	.30	.15
112	Tody Smith	.30	.15
113	Stu Voigt	.30	.15
114	Horst Muhlmann	.30	.15
115	Ahmad Rashad	6.00	3.00
116	Joe Dawkins	.30	.15
117	George Kunz	.30	.15
118	D.D.Lewis	.75	.30
119	Levi Johnson	.30	.15
120	Len Dawson	4.00	2.00
121	Jim Bertelsen	.30	.15
122	Ed Bell	.30	.15
123	Art Thoms	.30	.15
124	Joe Beauchamp	.30	.15
125	Jack Ham	6.00	3.00
126	Carl Garrett	.30	.15
127	Roger Finnie	.30	.15
128	Howard Twilley	.75	.30
129	Bruce Barnes	.30	.15
130	Nate Wright	.30	.15
131	Jerry Tagge	.30	.15
132	Floyd Little	1.50	.60
133	John Zook	.30	.15
134	Len Hauss	.30	.15
135	Archie Manning	1.50	.60
136	Po James	.30	.15
137	Walt Sumner	.30	.15
138	Randy Beisler	.30	.15
139	Willie Alexander	.30	.15
140	Garo Yepremian	.75	.30
141	Chip Myers	.30	.15
142	Jim Braxton	.30	.15
143	Doug Van Horn	.30	.15
144	Stan White	.30	.15
145	Roger Staubach	20.00	10.00
146	Herman Weaver	.30	.15
147	Marvin Upshaw	.30	.15
148	Bob Klein	.30	.15
149	Earlie Thomas	.30	.15
150	John Brockington	.75	.30
151	Mike Siani	.30	.15
152	Sam Davis RC	.30	.15
153	Mike Wagner	.75	.30
154	Larry Stallings	.30	.15
155	Wally Chambers	.30	.15
156	Randy Vataha	.30	.15
157	Jim Marshall	1.50	.60
158	Jim Turner	.30	.15
159	Walt Sweeney	.30	.15
160	Ken Anderson	4.00	2.00
161	Ray Brown DB	.30	.15
162	John Didion	.30	.15
163	Tom Dempsey	.30	.15
164	Clarence Scott	.30	.15
165	Gene Washington 49er	.75	.30
166	Willie Rodgers RC	.30	.15
167	Doug Swift	.30	.15
168	Rufus Mayes	.30	.15
169	Marv Bateman	.30	.15
170	Lydell Mitchell	.75	.30
171	Ron Smith	.30	.15
172	Bill Munson	.75	.30
173	Bob Grim	.30	.15
174	Ed Budde	.30	.15
175	Bob Lilly UER	4.00	2.00
176	Jim Youngblood RC	1.50	.60
177	Steve Tannen	.30	.15
178	Rich McGeorge	.30	.15
179	Jim Tyrer	.30	.15
180	Forrest Blue	.30	.15
181	Jerry LeVias	.75	.30
182	Joe Gilliam RC	1.50	.60
183	Jim Otis RC	.75	.30
184	Mel Tom	.30	.15
185	Paul Seymour	.30	.15
186	George Webster	.30	.15
187	Pete Duranko	.30	.15
188	Essex Johnson	.30	.15
189	Bob Lee	.75	.30
190	Gene Upshaw	1.50	.60
191	Tom Myers	.30	.15
192	Don Zimmerman	.30	.15
193	John Garlington	.30	.15
194	Skip Butler	.30	.15
195	Tom Mitchell	.30	.15
196	Jim Langer	1.50	.60
197	Ron Carpenter	.30	.15
198	Dave Foley	.30	.15
199	Bert Jones	1.50	.60
200	Larry Brown	.75	.30
201	Biletnikoff/C.Taylor AP	2.00	.75
202	All Pro Tackles	.30	.15
203	L.Little/T.Mack AP	1.50	.60
204	All Pro Centers	.30	.15
205	Hannah/Gillingham AP	1.50	.60
206	Dan Dierdorf/W.Hill AP	1.50	.60
207	All Pro Tight Ends	.75	.30
208	F.Tarkenton/Stabler AP	4.00	2.00
209	Simpson/McCutch. AP	3.00	1.50
210	All Pro Backs	.75	.30
211	All Pro Receivers	.75	.30
212	All Pro Kickers	.30	.15
213	Youngblood/Bethea AP	1.50	.60
214	All Pro Tackles	.75	.30
215	M.Olsen/M.Reid AP	1.50	.60
216	Carl Eller/L.Alzado AP	1.50	.60
217	Hendricks/Villapiano AP	1.50	.60
218	Willie Lanier/Jordan AP	1.50	.60
219	All Pro Linebackers	.75	.30
220	All Pro Cornerbacks	.30	.15
221	All Pro Cornerbacks	.30	.15
222	K.Houston/D.Anderson AP	.75	.30
223	Cliff Harris/J.Tatum AP	1.50	.60
224	All Pro Punters	.75	.30
225	All Pro Returners	.75	.30
226	Ted Kwalick	.30	.15
227	Spider Lockhart	.75	.30
228	Mike Livingston	.30	.15
229	Larry Cole	.30	.15
230	Gary Garrison	.30	.15
231	Larry Brooks	.30	.15
232	Bobby Howfield	.30	.15
233	Fred Carr	.30	.15
234	Norm Evans	.30	.15
235	Dwight White	.75	.30
236	Conrad Dobler	.75	.30
237	Garry Lyle	.30	.15
238	Darryl Stingley	1.50	.60
239	Tom Graham	.30	.15
240	Chuck Foreman	1.50	.60
241	Ken Riley	.75	.30
242	Don Morrison	.30	.15
243	Lynn Dickey	.75	.30
244	Don Cockroft	.30	.15
245	Claude Humphrey	.75	.30
246	John Skorupan	.30	.15
247	Raymond Chester	.75	.30
248	Cas Banaszek	.30	.15
249	Art Malone	.30	.15
250	Ed Flanagan	.30	.15
251	Checklist 133-264	4.00	2.00
252	Nemiah Wilson	.30	.15
253	Ron Jessie	.30	.15
254	Jim Lynch	.30	.15
255	Bob Tucker	.75	.30
256	Terry Owens	.30	.15
257	John Fitzgerald	.30	.15
258	Jack Snow	.75	.30
259	Garry Puetz	.30	.15
260	Mike Phipps	.75	.30
261	Al Matthews	.30	.15
262	Bob Kuechenberg	.30	.15
263	Ron Yankowski	.30	.15
264	Ron Shanklin	.30	.15
265	Bobby Douglass	.75	.30
266	Josh Ashton	.30	.15
267	Bill Van Heusen	.30	.15
268	Jeff Siemon	.30	.15
269	Bob Newland	.30	.15
270	Gale Gillingham	.30	.15
271	Zeke Moore	.30	.15
272	Mike Tilleman	.30	.15
273	John Leypoldt	.30	.15
274	Ken Mendenhall	.30	.15
275	Norm Snead	.75	.30
276	Bill Bradley	.75	.30
277	Jerry Smith	.30	.15
278	Clarence Davis	.30	.15
279	Jim Yarbrough	.30	.15
280	Lemar Parrish	.30	.15
281	Bobby Bell	1.50	.60
282	Lynn Swann RC UER !	60.00	30.00
283	John Hicks	.30	.15
284	Coy Bacon	.75	.30
285	Lee Roy Jordan	1.50	.60
286	Willie Buchanon	.30	.15
287	Al Woodall	.30	.15
288	Reggie Rucker	.75	.30
289	John Schmitt	.30	.15
290	Carl Eller	1.50	.60
291	Jake Scott	.75	.30
292	Donny Anderson	.75	.30
293	Charley Wade	.30	.15
294	John Tanner	.30	.15
295	Charlie Johnson	.75	.30
296	Tom Blanchard	.30	.15
297	Curley Culp	.75	.30
298	Jeff Van Note RC	.75	.30
299	Bob James	.30	.15
300	Franco Harris	8.00	4.00
301	Tim Berra	.75	.30
302	Bruce Gossett	.30	.15
303	Verlon Biggs	.30	.15
304	Bob Kowalkowski	.30	.15
305	Marv Hubbard	.30	.15

❑ 306 Ken Avery .30 .15
❑ 307 Mike Adamle .30 .15
❑ 308 Don Herrmann .30 .15
❑ 309 Chris Fletcher .30 .15
❑ 310 Roman Gabriel 1.50 .60
❑ 311 Billy Joe DuPree 1.50 .60
❑ 312 Fred Dryer 1.50 .60
❑ 313 John Riggins 5.00 2.50
❑ 314 Bob McKay .30 .15
❑ 315 Ted Hendricks 1.50 .60
❑ 316 Bobby Bryant .30 .15
❑ 317 Don Nottingham .30 .15
❑ 318 John Hannah 4.00 2.00
❑ 319 Rich Coady .30 .15
❑ 320 Phil Villapiano .75 .30
❑ 321 Jim Plunkett 1.50 .60
❑ 322 Lyle Alzado 1.50 .60
❑ 323 Ernie Jackson .30 .15
❑ 324 Billy Parks .30 .15
❑ 325 Willie Lanier 1.50 .60
❑ 326 John James .30 .15
❑ 327 Joe Ferguson .75 .30
❑ 328 Ernie Holmes RC 1.50 .60
❑ 329 Bruce Laird .30 .15
❑ 330 Chester Marcol .30 .15
❑ 331 Dave Wilcox 1.50 .60
❑ 332 Pat Fischer .75 .30
❑ 333 Steve Owens .75 .30
❑ 334 Royce Berry .30 .15
❑ 335 Russ Washington .30 .15
❑ 336 Walker Gillette .30 .15
❑ 337 Mark Nordquist .30 .15
❑ 338 James Harris RC 1.50 .60
❑ 339 Warren Koegel .30 .15
❑ 340 Emmitt Thomas .75 .30
❑ 341 Walt Garrison .75 .30
❑ 342 Thom Darden .30 .15
❑ 343 Mike Eischeid .30 .15
❑ 344 Ernie McMillan .30 .15
❑ 345 Nick Buoniconti 1.50 .60
❑ 346 George Farmer .30 .15
❑ 347 Sam Adams OL .30 .15
❑ 348 Larry Cipa .30 .15
❑ 349 Bob Moore .30 .15
❑ 350 Otis Armstrong RC 1.50 .60
❑ 351 George Blanda RB 3.00 1.50
❑ 352 Fred Cox RB .75 .30
❑ 353 Tom Dempsey RB .75 .30
❑ 354 Ken Houston RB 1.50 .60
❑ 355 O.J.Simpson RB 5.00 2.50
❑ 356 Ron Smith RB .75 .30
❑ 357 Bob Atkins .30 .15
❑ 358 Pat Sullivan .75 .30
❑ 359 Joe DeLamielleure 2.50 1.00
❑ 360 Lawr. McCutcheon RC 1.50 .60
❑ 361 David Lee .30 .15
❑ 362 Mike McCoy DT .30 .15
❑ 363 Skip Vanderbundt .30 .15
❑ 364 Mark Moseley .75 .30
❑ 365 Lem Barney 1.50 .60
❑ 366 Doug Dressler .30 .15
❑ 367 Dan Fouts RC 40.00 20.00
❑ 368 Bob Hyland .30 .15
❑ 369 John Outlaw .30 .15
❑ 370 Roy Gerela .30 .15
❑ 371 Isiah Robertson .75 .30
❑ 372 Jerome Barkum .30 .15
❑ 373 Ed Podolak .30 .15
❑ 374 Milt Morin .30 .15
❑ 375 John Niland .30 .15
❑ 376 Checklist 265-396 UER 4.00 2.00
❑ 377 Ken Iman .30 .15
❑ 378 Manny Fernandez .75 .30
❑ 379 Dave Gallagher .30 .15
❑ 380 Ken Stabler 15.00 7.50
❑ 381 Mack Herron .30 .15
❑ 382 Bill McClard .30 .15
❑ 383 Ray May .30 .15
❑ 384 Don Hansen .30 .15
❑ 385 Elvin Bethea 1.50 .60
❑ 386 Joe Scibelli .30 .15
❑ 387 Neal Craig .30 .15
❑ 388 Marty Domres .30 .15
❑ 389 Ken Ellis .30 .15
❑ 390 Charle Young .75 .30
❑ 391 Tommy Hart .30 .15
❑ 392 Moses Denson .30 .15
❑ 393 Larry Walton .30 .15
❑ 394 Dave Green .30 .15
❑ 395 Ron Johnson .75 .30
❑ 396 Ed Bradley RC .30 .15
❑ 397 J.T. Thomas .30 .15
❑ 398 Jim Bailey .30 .15
❑ 399 Barry Pearson .30 .15
❑ 400 Fran Tarkenton 8.00 4.00
❑ 401 Jack Rudnay .30 .15
❑ 402 Rayfield Wright .75 .30
❑ 403 Roger Wehrli .75 .30
❑ 404 Vern Den Herder .30 .15
❑ 405 Fred Biletnikoff 3.00 1.50
❑ 406 Ken Grandberry .30 .15
❑ 407 Bob Adams .30 .15
❑ 408 Jim Merlo .30 .15
❑ 409 John Pitts .30 .15
❑ 410 Dave Osborn .75 .30
❑ 411 Dennis Havig .30 .15
❑ 412 Bob Johnson .30 .15
❑ 413 Ken Burrough UER .75 .30
❑ 414 Jim Cheyunski .30 .15
❑ 415 MacArthur Lane .30 .15
❑ 416 Joe Theismann RC 25.00 12.50
❑ 417 Mike Boryla RC .30 .15
❑ 418 Bruce Taylor .30 .15
❑ 419 Chris Hanburger .75 .30
❑ 420 Tom Mack 1.50 .60
❑ 421 Errol Mann .30 .15
❑ 422 Jack Gregory .30 .15
❑ 423 Harrison Davis .30 .15
❑ 424 Burgess Owens .30 .15
❑ 425 Joe Greene 5.00 2.50
❑ 426 Morris Stroud .30 .15
❑ 427 John DeMarie .30 .15
❑ 428 Mel Renfro 1.50 .60
❑ 429 Cid Edwards .30 .15
❑ 430 Mike Reid 1.50 .60
❑ 431 Jack Mildren RC .30 .15
❑ 432 Jerry Simmons .30 .15
❑ 433 Ron Yary 1.50 .60
❑ 434 Howard Stevens .30 .15
❑ 435 Ray Guy 2.00 .75
❑ 436 Tommy Nobis 1.50 .60
❑ 437 Solomon Freelon .30 .15
❑ 438 J.D. Hill .75 .30
❑ 439 Toni Linhart .30 .15
❑ 440 Dick Anderson .75 .30
❑ 441 Guy Morriss .30 .15
❑ 442 Bob Hoskins .30 .15
❑ 443 John Hadl 1.50 .60
❑ 444 Roy Jefferson .30 .15
❑ 445 Charlie Sanders .75 .30
❑ 446 Pat Curran .30 .15
❑ 447 David Knight .30 .15
❑ 448 Bob Brown DT .30 .15
❑ 449 Pete Gogolak .30 .15
❑ 450 Terry Metcalf 1.50 .60
❑ 451 Bill Bergey 1.50 .60
❑ 452 Dan Abramowicz HL .75 .30
❑ 453 Otis Armstrong HL .75 .30
❑ 454 Cliff Branch HL 1.50 .60
❑ 455 John James HL .30 .15
❑ 456 Lydell Mitchell HL .75 .30
❑ 457 Lemar Parrish HL .75 .30
❑ 458 Ken Stabler HL 5.00 2.50
❑ 459 Lynn Swann HL 8.00 4.00
❑ 460 Emmitt Thomas HL .30 .15
❑ 461 Terry Bradshaw 20.00 10.00
❑ 462 Jerrel Wilson .30 .15
❑ 463 Walter Johnson .30 .15
❑ 464 Golden Richards .75 .30
❑ 465 Tommy Casanova .75 .30
❑ 466 Randy Jackson .30 .15
❑ 467 Ron Bolton .30 .15
❑ 468 Joe Owens .30 .15
❑ 469 Wally Hilgenberg .30 .15
❑ 470 Riley Odoms .75 .30
❑ 471 Otis Sistrunk .75 .30
❑ 472 Eddie Ray .30 .15
❑ 473 Reggie McKenzie .75 .30
❑ 474 Elbert Drungo .30 .15
❑ 475 Mercury Morris 1.50 .60
❑ 476 Dan Dickel .30 .15
❑ 477 Merritt Kersey .30 .15
❑ 478 Mike Holmes .30 .15
❑ 479 Clarence Williams .30 .15
❑ 480 Billy Kilmer 1.50 .60
❑ 481 Altie Taylor .30 .15
❑ 482 Dave Elmendorf .30 .15
❑ 483 Bob Rowe .30 .15
❑ 484 Pete Athas .30 .15
❑ 485 Winston Hill .30 .15
❑ 486 Bo Matthews .30 .15
❑ 487 Earl Thomas .30 .15
❑ 488 Jan Stenerud 1.50 .60
❑ 489 Steve Holden .30 .15
❑ 490 Cliff Harris RC 4.00 2.00
❑ 491 Boobie Clark RC .75 .30
❑ 492 Joe Taylor .30 .15
❑ 493 Tom Neville .30 .15
❑ 494 Wayne Colman .30 .15
❑ 495 Jim Mitchell TE .30 .15
❑ 496 Paul Krause 1.50 .60
❑ 497 Jim Otto 1.50 .60
❑ 498 John Rowser .30 .15
❑ 499 Larry Little 1.50 .60
❑ 500 O.J.Simpson 10.00 5.00
❑ 501 John Dutton RC 1.50 .60
❑ 502 Pat Hughes .30 .15
❑ 503 Malcolm Snider .30 .15
❑ 504 Fred Willis .30 .15
❑ 505 Harold Jackson 1.50 .60
❑ 506 Mike Bragg .30 .15
❑ 507 Jerry Sherk .75 .30
❑ 508 Mirro Roder .30 .15
❑ 509 Tom Sullivan .30 .15
❑ 510 Jim Hart 1.50 .60
❑ 511 Cedrick Hardman .30 .15
❑ 512 Blaine Nye .30 .15
❑ 513 Elmo Wright .30 .15
❑ 514 Herb Orvis .30 .15
❑ 515 Richard Caster .75 .30
❑ 516 Doug Kotar RC .30 .15
❑ 517 Checklist 397-528 4.00 2.00
❑ 518 Jesse Freitas .30 .15
❑ 519 Ken Houston 1.50 .60
❑ 520 Alan Page 1.50 .60
❑ 521 Tim Foley .75 .30
❑ 522 Bill Olds .30 .15
❑ 523 Bobby Maples .30 .15
❑ 524 Cliff Branch RC 15.00 7.50
❑ 525 Merlin Olsen 1.50 .60
❑ 526 AFC Champs/Brad./Harris 4.00 2.00
❑ 527 NFC Champs/Foreman 1.50 .60
❑ 528 Super Bowl IX/Bradshaw 5.00 2.50

1976 Topps

❑ COMPLETE SET (528) 350.00 200.00
❑ 1 George Blanda RB ! 5.00 2.50
❑ 2 Neal Colzie RB .75 .30
❑ 3 Chuck Foreman RB .75 .30
❑ 4 Jim Marshall RB .75 .30
❑ 5 Terry Metcalf RB .75 .30
❑ 6 O.J.Simpson RB 3.00 1.50
❑ 7 Fran Tarkenton RB 3.00 1.50
❑ 8 Charley Taylor RB 1.50 .60
❑ 9 Ernie Holmes .75 .30
❑ 10 Ken Anderson 1.50 .60
❑ 11 Bobby Bryant .30 .15
❑ 12 Jerry Smith .75 .30
❑ 13 David Lee .30 .15
❑ 14 Robert Newhouse RC 1.50 .60
❑ 15 Vern Den Herder .30 .15
❑ 16 John Hannah 1.50 .60
❑ 17 J.D. Hill .75 .30

❑ 18 James Harris .75 .30
❑ 19 Willie Buchanon .30 .15
❑ 20 Charle Young .75 .30
❑ 21 Jim Yarbrough .30 .15
❑ 22 Ronnie Coleman .30 .15
❑ 23 Don Cockroft .30 .15
❑ 24 Willie Lanier 1.50 .60
❑ 25 Fred Biletnikoff 3.00 1.50
❑ 26 Ron Yankowski .30 .15
❑ 27 Spider Lockhart .30 .15
❑ 28 Bob Johnson .30 .15
❑ 29 J.T. Thomas .30 .15
❑ 30 Ron Yary 1.50 .60
❑ 31 Brad Dusek RC .30 .15
❑ 32 Raymond Chester .75 .30
❑ 33 Larry Little 1.50 .60
❑ 34 Pat Leahy RC 1.50 .60
❑ 35 Steve Bartkowski RC 4.00 2.00
❑ 36 Tom Myers .30 .15
❑ 37 Bill Van Heusen .30 .15
❑ 38 Russ Washington .30 .15
❑ 39 Tom Sullivan .30 .15
❑ 40 Curley Culp .75 .30
❑ 41 Johnnie Gray .30 .15
❑ 42 Bob Klein .30 .15
❑ 43 Lem Barney 1.50 .60
❑ 44 Harvey Martin RC 6.00 3.00
❑ 45 Reggie Rucker .75 .30
❑ 46 Neil Clabo .30 .15
❑ 47 Ray Hamilton .30 .15
❑ 48 Joe Ferguson .75 .30
❑ 49 Ed Podolak .30 .15
❑ 50 Ray Guy 1.50 .60
❑ 51 Glen Edwards .30 .15
❑ 52 Jim LeClair .30 .15
❑ 53 Mike Barnes .30 .15
❑ 54 Nat Moore RC 1.50 .60
❑ 55 Billy Kilmer 1.50 .60
❑ 56 Larry Stallings .30 .15
❑ 57 Jack Gregory .30 .15
❑ 58 Steve Mike-Mayer .30 .15
❑ 59 Virgil Livers .30 .15
❑ 60 Jerry Sherk .75 .30
❑ 61 Guy Morriss .30 .15
❑ 62 Barty Smith .30 .15
❑ 63 Jerome Barkum .30 .15
❑ 64 Ira Gordon .30 .15
❑ 65 Paul Krause 1.50 .60
❑ 66 John McMakin .30 .15
❑ 67 Checklist 1-132 3.00 1.50
❑ 68 Charlie Johnson UER .75 .30
❑ 69 Tommy Nobis 1.50 .60
❑ 70 Lydell Mitchell .75 .30
❑ 71 Vern Holland .30 .15
❑ 72 Tim Foley .75 .30
❑ 73 Golden Richards .75 .30
❑ 74 Bryant Salter .30 .15
❑ 75 Terry Bradshaw 20.00 10.00
❑ 76 Ted Hendricks 1.50 .60
❑ 77 Rich Saul RC .30 .15
❑ 78 John Smith RC .30 .15
❑ 79 Altie Taylor .30 .15
❑ 80 Cedrick Hardman .30 .15
❑ 81 Ken Payne .30 .15
❑ 82 Zeke Moore .30 .15
❑ 83 Alvin Maxson .30 .15
❑ 84 Wally Hilgenberg .30 .15
❑ 85 John Niland .30 .15
❑ 86 Mike Sensibaugh .30 .15
❑ 87 Ron Johnson .75 .30
❑ 88 Winston Hill .30 .15
❑ 89 Charlie Joiner 4.00 2.00
❑ 90 Roger Wehrli .75 .30
❑ 91 Mike Bragg .30 .15
❑ 92 Dan Dickel .30 .15
❑ 93 Earl Morrall .75 .30
❑ 94 Pat Toomay .30 .15
❑ 95 Gary Garrison .30 .15
❑ 96 Ken Geddes .30 .15
❑ 97 Mike Current .30 .15
❑ 98 Bob Avellini RC .75 .30
❑ 99 Dave Pureifory .30 .15
❑ 100 Franco Harris 8.00 4.00
❑ 101 Randy Logan .30 .15
❑ 102 John Fitzgerald .30 .15
❑ 103 Gregg Bingham RC .75 .30
❑ 104 Jim Plunkett 1.50 .60
❑ 105 Carl Eller 1.50 .60
❑ 106 Larry Walton .30 .15
❑ 107 Clarence Scott .30 .15
❑ 108 Skip Vanderbundt .30 .15
❑ 109 Boobie Clark .75 .30
❑ 110 Tom Mack 1.50 .60
❑ 111 Bruce Laird .30 .15
❑ 112 Dave Dalby RC .30 .15
❑ 113 John Leypoldt .30 .15
❑ 114 Barry Pearson .30 .15
❑ 115 Larry Brown .75 .30
❑ 116 Jackie Smith 1.50 .60
❑ 117 Pat Hughes .30 .15
❑ 118 Al Woodall .30 .15
❑ 119 John Zook .30 .15
❑ 120 Jake Scott .75 .30
❑ 121 Rich Glover .30 .15
❑ 122 Ernie Jackson .30 .15
❑ 123 Otis Armstrong 1.50 .60
❑ 124 Bob Grim .30 .15
❑ 125 Jeff Siemon .75 .30
❑ 126 Harold Hart .30 .15
❑ 127 John DeMarie .30 .15
❑ 128 Dan Fouts 12.00 6.00
❑ 129 Jim Kearney .30 .15
❑ 130 John Dutton .75 .30
❑ 131 Calvin Hill 1.50 .60
❑ 132 Toni Fritsch .30 .15
❑ 133 Ron Jessie .30 .15
❑ 134 Don Nottingham .30 .15
❑ 135 Lemar Parrish .30 .15
❑ 136 Russ Francis RC 1.50 .60
❑ 137 Joe Reed .30 .15
❑ 138 C.L. Whittington .30 .15
❑ 139 Otis Sistrunk .75 .30
❑ 140 Lynn Swann 20.00 10.00
❑ 141 Jim Carter .30 .15
❑ 142 Mike Montler .30 .15
❑ 143 Walter Johnson .30 .15
❑ 144 Doug Kotar .30 .15
❑ 145 Roman Gabriel 1.50 .60
❑ 146 Billy Newsome .30 .15
❑ 147 Ed Bradley .30 .15
❑ 148 Walter Payton RC 250.00 125.00
❑ 149 Johnny Fuller .30 .15
❑ 150 Alan Page 1.50 .60
❑ 151 Frank Grant .30 .15
❑ 152 Dave Green .30 .15
❑ 153 Nelson Munsey .30 .15
❑ 154 Jim Mandich .30 .15
❑ 155 Lawrence McCutcheon 1.50 .60
❑ 156 Steve Ramsey .30 .15
❑ 157 Ed Flanagan .30 .15
❑ 158 Randy White RC 20.00 10.00
❑ 159 Gerry Mullins .30 .15
❑ 160 Jan Stenerud 1.50 .60
❑ 161 Steve Odom .30 .15
❑ 162 Roger Finnie .30 .15
❑ 163 Norm Snead .75 .30
❑ 164 Jeff Van Note .75 .30
❑ 165 Bill Bergey 1.50 .60
❑ 166 Allen Carter .30 .15
❑ 167 Steve Holden .30 .15
❑ 168 Sherman White .30 .15
❑ 169 Bob Berry .30 .15
❑ 170 Ken Houston 1.50 .60
❑ 171 Bill Olds .30 .15
❑ 172 Larry Seiple .30 .15
❑ 173 Cliff Branch 4.00 2.00
❑ 174 Reggie McKenzie .75 .30
❑ 175 Dan Pastorini 1.50 .60
❑ 176 Paul Naumoff .30 .15
❑ 177 Checklist 133-264 3.00 1.50
❑ 178 Durwood Keeton .30 .15
❑ 179 Earl Thomas .30 .15
❑ 180 L.C.Greenwood 1.50 .60
❑ 181 John Outlaw .30 .15
❑ 182 Frank Nunley .30 .15
❑ 183 Dave Jennings RC .75 .30
❑ 184 MacArthur Lane .30 .15
❑ 185 Chester Marcol .30 .15
❑ 186 J.J. Jones .30 .15
❑ 187 Tom DeLeone .30 .15
❑ 188 Steve Zabel .30 .15
❑ 189 Ken Johnson DT .30 .15
❑ 190 Rayfield Wright .75 .30
❑ 191 Brent McClanahan .30 .15
❑ 192 Pat Fischer .75 .30
❑ 193 Roger Carr RC .75 .30
❑ 194 Manny Fernandez .75 .30
❑ 195 Roy Gerela .30 .15
❑ 196 Dave Elmendorf .30 .15
❑ 197 Bob Kowalkowski .30 .15
❑ 198 Phil Villapiano .75 .30
❑ 199 Will Wynn .30 .15
❑ 200 Terry Metcalf 1.50 .60
❑ 201 Tarkenton/Anderson LL 2.00 .75
❑ 202 Receiving Leaders .75 .30
❑ 203 O.J.Simpson/J.Otis LL 2.50 1.25
❑ 204 Simpson/Foreman LL 2.50 1.25
❑ 205 M.Blount/P.Krause LL 1.50 .60
❑ 206 Punting Leaders .75 .30
❑ 207 Ken Ellis .30 .15
❑ 208 Ron Saul .30 .15
❑ 209 Toni Linhart .30 .15
❑ 210 Jim Langer 1.50 .60
❑ 211 Jeff Wright S .30 .15
❑ 212 Moses Denson .30 .15
❑ 213 Earl Edwards .30 .15
❑ 214 Walker Gillette .30 .15
❑ 215 Bob Trumpy .75 .30
❑ 216 Emmitt Thomas .75 .30
❑ 217 Lyle Alzado 1.50 .60
❑ 218 Carl Garrett .75 .30
❑ 219 Van Green .30 .15
❑ 220 Jack Lambert RC 35.00 20.00
❑ 221 Spike Jones .30 .15
❑ 222 John Hadl 1.50 .60
❑ 223 Billy Johnson RC 1.50 .60
❑ 224 Tony McGee DT .30 .15
❑ 225 Preston Pearson .75 .30
❑ 226 Isiah Robertson .75 .30
❑ 227 Errol Mann .30 .15
❑ 228 Paul Seal .30 .15
❑ 229 Roland Harper RC .30 .15
❑ 230 Ed White RC .75 .30
❑ 231 Joe Theismann 6.00 3.00
❑ 232 Jim Cheyunski .30 .15
❑ 233 Bill Stanfill .75 .30
❑ 234 Marv Hubbard .30 .15
❑ 235 Tommy Casanova .75 .30
❑ 236 Bob Hyland .30 .15
❑ 237 Jesse Freitas .30 .15
❑ 238 Norm Thompson .30 .15
❑ 239 Charlie Smith WR .30 .15
❑ 240 John James .30 .15
❑ 241 Alden Roche .30 .15
❑ 242 Gordon Jolley .30 .15
❑ 243 Larry Ely .30 .15
❑ 244 Richard Caster .30 .15
❑ 245 Joe Greene 5.00 2.00
❑ 246 Larry Schreiber .30 .15
❑ 247 Terry Schmidt .30 .15
❑ 248 Jerrel Wilson .30 .15
❑ 249 Marty Domres .30 .15
❑ 250 Isaac Curtis .75 .30
❑ 251 Harold McLinton .30 .15
❑ 252 Fred Dryer 1.50 .60
❑ 253 Bill Lenkaitis .30 .15
❑ 254 Don Hardeman .30 .15
❑ 255 Bob Griese 4.00 2.00
❑ 256 Oscar Roan RC .30 .15
❑ 257 Randy Gradishar RC 2.50 1.25
❑ 258 Bob Thomas RC .30 .15
❑ 259 Joe Owens .30 .15
❑ 260 Cliff Harris 1.50 .60
❑ 261 Frank Lewis .30 .15
❑ 262 Mike McCoy DT .30 .15
❑ 263 Rickey Young RC .30 .15
❑ 264 Brian Kelley RC .30 .15
❑ 265 Charlie Sanders .75 .30
❑ 266 Jim Hart 1.50 .60
❑ 267 Greg Gantt .30 .15
❑ 268 John Ward .30 .15
❑ 269 Al Beauchamp .30 .15
❑ 270 Jack Tatum 1.50 .60
❑ 271 Jim Lash .30 .15
❑ 272 Diron Talbert .30 .15
❑ 273 Checklist 265-396 3.00 1.50
❑ 274 Steve Spurrier 8.00 3.00
❑ 275 Greg Pruitt 1.50 .60
❑ 276 Jim Mitchell TE .30 .15
❑ 277 Jack Rudnay .30 .15
❑ 278 Freddie Solomon RC .75 .30

❑ 279 Frank LeMaster .30 .15
❑ 280 Wally Chambers .30 .15
❑ 281 Mike Collier .30 .15
❑ 282 Clarence Williams .30 .15
❑ 283 Mitch Hoopes .30 .15
❑ 284 Ron Bolton .30 .15
❑ 285 Harold Jackson 1.50 .60
❑ 286 Greg Landry .75 .30
❑ 287 Tony Greene .30 .15
❑ 288 Howard Stevens .30 .15
❑ 289 Roy Jefferson .30 .15
❑ 290 Jim Bakken .30 .15
❑ 291 Doug Sutherland .30 .15
❑ 292 Marvin Cobb RC .30 .15
❑ 293 Mack Alston .30 .15
❑ 294 Rod McNeill .30 .15
❑ 295 Gene Upshaw 1.50 .60
❑ 296 Dave Gallagher .30 .15
❑ 297 Larry Ball .30 .15
❑ 298 Ron Howard .30 .15
❑ 299 Don Strock RC 1.50 .60
❑ 300 O.J.Simpson 8.00 4.00
❑ 301 Ray Mansfield .30 .15
❑ 302 Larry Marshall .30 .15
❑ 303 Dick Himes .30 .15
❑ 304 Ray Wersching RC .30 .15
❑ 305 John Riggins 4.00 2.00
❑ 306 Bob Parsons .30 .15
❑ 307 Ray Brown DB .30 .15
❑ 308 Len Dawson 3.00 1.50
❑ 309 Andy Maurer .30 .15
❑ 310 Jack Youngblood 1.50 .60
❑ 311 Essex Johnson .30 .15
❑ 312 Stan White .30 .15
❑ 313 Drew Pearson 5.00 2.00
❑ 314 Rockne Freitas .30 .15
❑ 315 Mercury Morris 1.50 .60
❑ 316 Willie Alexander .30 .15
❑ 317 Paul Warfield 3.00 1.50
❑ 318 Bob Chandler .75 .30
❑ 319 Bobby Walden .30 .15
❑ 320 Riley Odoms .75 .30
❑ 321 Mike Boryla .30 .15
❑ 322 Bruce Van Dyke .30 .15
❑ 323 Pete Banaszak .30 .15
❑ 324 Darryl Stingley 1.50 .60
❑ 325 John Mendenhall .30 .15
❑ 326 Dan Dierdorf 2.00 .75
❑ 327 Bruce Taylor .30 .15
❑ 328 Don McCauley .30 .15
❑ 329 John Reaves UER .30 .15
❑ 330 Chris Hanburger .75 .30
❑ 331 NFC Champs/Staubach 3.00 1.50
❑ 332 AFC Champs/F.Harris 2.00 .75
❑ 333 Super Bowl X/Bradshaw 2.50 1.25
❑ 334 Godwin Turk .30 .15
❑ 335 Dick Anderson .75 .30
❑ 336 Woody Green .30 .15
❑ 337 Pat Curran .30 .15
❑ 338 Council Rudolph .30 .15
❑ 339 Joe Lavender .30 .15
❑ 340 John Gilliam .75 .30
❑ 341 Steve Furness RC .75 .30
❑ 342 D.D. Lewis .75 .30
❑ 343 Duane Carrell .30 .15
❑ 344 Jon Morris .30 .15
❑ 345 John Brockington .75 .30
❑ 346 Mike Phipps .75 .30
❑ 347 Lyle Blackwood RC .30 .15
❑ 348 Julius Adams .30 .15
❑ 349 Terry Hermeling .30 .15
❑ 350 Rolland Lawrence RC .30 .15
❑ 351 Glenn Doughty .30 .15
❑ 352 Doug Swift .30 .15
❑ 353 Mike Strachan .30 .15
❑ 354 Craig Morton 1.50 .60
❑ 355 George Blanda 5.00 2.50
❑ 356 Garry Puetz .30 .15
❑ 357 Carl Mauck .30 .15
❑ 358 Walt Patulski .30 .15
❑ 359 Stu Voigt .30 .15
❑ 360 Fred Carr .30 .15
❑ 361 Po James .30 .15
❑ 362 Otis Taylor 1.50 .60
❑ 363 Jeff West .30 .15
❑ 364 Gary Huff .75 .30
❑ 365 Dwight White .75 .30
❑ 366 Dan Ryczek .30 .15
❑ 367 Jon Keyworth RC .30 .15
❑ 368 Mel Renfro 1.50 .60
❑ 369 Bruce Coslet RC 1.50 .60
❑ 370 Len Hauss .30 .15
❑ 371 Rick Volk .30 .15
❑ 372 Howard Twilley .75 .30
❑ 373 Cullen Bryant RC .75 .30
❑ 374 Bob Babich .30 .15
❑ 375 Herman Weaver .30 .15
❑ 376 Steve Grogan RC 3.00 1.25
❑ 377 Bubba Smith 1.50 .60
❑ 378 Burgess Owens .30 .15
❑ 379 Al Matthews .30 .15
❑ 380 Art Shell 1.50 .60
❑ 381 Larry Brown .30 .15
❑ 382 Horst Muhlmann .30 .15
❑ 383 Ahmad Rashad 2.50 1.25
❑ 384 Bobby Maples .30 .15
❑ 385 Jim Marshall 1.50 .60
❑ 386 Joe Dawkins .30 .15
❑ 387 Dennis Partee .30 .15
❑ 388 Eddie McMillan RC .30 .15
❑ 389 Randy Johnson .30 .15
❑ 390 Bob Kuechenberg .30 .15
❑ 391 Rufus Mayes .30 .15
❑ 392 Lloyd Mumphord .30 .15
❑ 393 Ike Harris .30 .15
❑ 394 Dave Hampton .30 .15
❑ 395 Roger Staubach 20.00 10.00
❑ 396 Doug Buffone .30 .15
❑ 397 Howard Fest .30 .15
❑ 398 Wayne Mulligan .30 .15
❑ 399 Bill Bradley .75 .30
❑ 400 Chuck Foreman 1.50 .60
❑ 401 Jack Snow .75 .30
❑ 402 Bob Howard .30 .15
❑ 403 John Matuszak 1.50 .60
❑ 404 Bill Munson .75 .30
❑ 405 Andy Russell .75 .30
❑ 406 Skip Butler .30 .15
❑ 407 Hugh McKinnis .30 .15
❑ 408 Bob Penchion .30 .15
❑ 409 Mike Bass .30 .15
❑ 410 George Kunz .30 .15
❑ 411 Ron Pritchard .30 .15
❑ 412 Barry Smith .30 .15
❑ 413 Norm Bulaich .30 .15
❑ 414 Marv Bateman .30 .15
❑ 415 Ken Stabler 12.00 6.00
❑ 416 Conrad Dobler .75 .30
❑ 417 Bob Tucker .75 .30
❑ 418 Gene Washington 49er .75 .30
❑ 419 Ed Marinaro 1.50 .60
❑ 420 Jack Ham 4.00 2.00
❑ 421 Jim Turner .30 .15
❑ 422 Chris Fletcher .30 .15
❑ 423 Carl Barzilauskas .30 .15
❑ 424 Robert Brazile RC 1.50 .60
❑ 425 Harold Carmichael 2.00 .75
❑ 426 Ron Jaworski RC 5.00 2.00
❑ 427 Ed Too Tall Jones RC 20.00 10.00
❑ 428 Larry McCarren .30 .15
❑ 429 Mike Thomas RC .30 .15
❑ 430 Joe DeLamielleure 1.50 .60
❑ 431 Tom Blanchard .30 .15
❑ 432 Ron Carpenter .30 .15
❑ 433 Levi Johnson .30 .15
❑ 434 Sam Cunningham .75 .30
❑ 435 Garo Yepremian .75 .30
❑ 436 Mike Livingston .30 .15
❑ 437 Larry Csonka 4.00 2.00
❑ 438 Doug Dieken .75 .30
❑ 439 Bill Lueck .30 .15
❑ 440 Tom MacLeod .30 .15
❑ 441 Mick Tingelhoff .75 .30
❑ 442 Terry Hanratty .75 .30
❑ 443 Mike Siani .30 .15
❑ 444 Dwight Harrison .30 .15
❑ 445 Jim Otis .75 .30
❑ 446 Jack Reynolds .75 .30
❑ 447 Jean Fugett RC .75 .30
❑ 448 Dave Beverly .30 .15
❑ 449 Bernard Jackson RC .30 .15
❑ 450 Charley Taylor 2.00 .75
❑ 451 Atlanta Falcons CL 2.00 .75
❑ 452 Baltimore Colts CL 2.00 .75
❑ 453 Buffalo Bills CL 2.00 .75
❑ 454 Chicago Bears CL 2.00 .75
❑ 455 Cincinnati Bengals CL 2.00 .75
❑ 456 Cleveland Browns CL 2.00 .75
❑ 457 Dallas Cowboys CL 2.00 .75
❑ 458 Denver Broncos CL UER 2.00 .75
❑ 459 Detroit Lions CL 2.00 .75
❑ 460 Green Bay Packers CL 2.00 .75
❑ 461 Houston Oilers CL 2.00 .75
❑ 462 Kansas City Chiefs CL 2.00 .75
❑ 463 Los Angeles Rams CL 2.00 .75
❑ 464 Miami Dolphins CL 2.00 .75
❑ 465 Minnesota Vikings CL 2.00 .75
❑ 466 New England Patriots CL 2.00 .75
❑ 467 New Orleans Saints CL 2.00 .75
❑ 468 New York Giants CL 2.00 .75
❑ 469 New York Jets CL 2.00 .75
❑ 470 Oakland Raiders CL 2.00 .75
❑ 471 Philadelphia Eagles CL 2.00 .75
❑ 472 Pittsburgh Steelers CL 2.00 .75
❑ 473 St. Louis Cardinals CL 2.00 .75
❑ 474 San Diego Chargers CL 2.00 .75
❑ 475 San Francisco 49ers CL 2.00 .75
❑ 476 Seattle Seahawks CL 2.00 .75
❑ 477 Tampa Bay Buccaneers CL 2.00 .75
❑ 478 Washington Redskins CL 2.00 .75
❑ 479 Fred Cox .30 .15
❑ 480 Mel Blount 6.00 3.00
❑ 481 John Bunting RC .75 .30
❑ 482 Ken Mendenhall .30 .15
❑ 483 Will Harrell .30 .15
❑ 484 Marlin Briscoe .30 .15
❑ 485 Archie Manning 1.50 .60
❑ 486 Tody Smith .30 .15
❑ 487 George Hunt .30 .15
❑ 488 Roscoe Word .30 .15
❑ 489 Paul Seymour .30 .15
❑ 490 Lee Roy Jordan 1.50 .60
❑ 491 Chip Myers .30 .15
❑ 492 Norm Evans .30 .15
❑ 493 Jim Bertelsen .30 .15
❑ 494 Mark Moseley .75 .30
❑ 495 George Buehler .30 .15
❑ 496 Charlie Hall .30 .15
❑ 497 Marvin Upshaw .30 .15
❑ 498 Tom Banks RC .30 .15
❑ 499 Randy Vataha .30 .15
❑ 500 Fran Tarkenton 6.00 3.00
❑ 501 Mike Wagner .75 .30
❑ 502 Art Malone .30 .15
❑ 503 Fred Cook .30 .15
❑ 504 Rich McGeorge .30 .15
❑ 505 Ken Burrough .75 .30
❑ 506 Nick Mike-Mayer .30 .15
❑ 507 Checklist 397-528 3.00 1.50
❑ 508 Steve Owens .75 .30
❑ 509 Brad Van Pelt RC .30 .15
❑ 510 Ken Riley .75 .30
❑ 511 Art Thoms .30 .15
❑ 512 Ed Bell .30 .15
❑ 513 Tom Wittum .30 .15
❑ 514 Jim Braxton .30 .15
❑ 515 Nick Buoniconti 1.50 .60
❑ 516 Brian Sipe RC 6.00 2.50
❑ 517 Jim Lynch .30 .15
❑ 518 Prentice McCray .30 .15
❑ 519 Tom Dempsey .30 .15
❑ 520 Mel Gray .75 .30
❑ 521 Nate Wright .30 .15
❑ 522 Rocky Bleier 6.00 3.00
❑ 523 Dennis Johnson RC .30 .15
❑ 524 Jerry Sisemore .30 .15
❑ 525 Bert Jones .30 .15
❑ 526 Perry Smith .30 .15
❑ 527 Blaine Nye .30 .15
❑ 528 Bob Moore ! 1.50 .60

1977 Topps

❑ COMPLETE SET (528) 250.00 125.00
❑ 1 K.Stabler/J.Harris LL ! 2.50 1.25
❑ 2 Drew Pearson/M.Lane LL 1.00 .40
❑ 3 W.Payton/Simpson LL 10.00 5.00
❑ 4 Scoring Leaders .50 .20
❑ 5 Interception Leaders .50 .20
❑ 6 Punting Leaders .25 .10
❑ 7 Mike Phipps .50 .20
❑ 8 Rick Volk .25 .10

❑	9	Steve Furness	.50	.20
❑	10	Isaac Curtis	.50	.20
❑	11	Nate Wright	.50	.20
❑	12	Jean Fugett	.25	.10
❑	13	Ken Mendenhall	.25	.10
❑	14	Sam Adams OL	.25	.10
❑	15	Charlie Waters	1.00	.40
❑	16	Bill Stanfill	.25	.10
❑	17	John Holland	.25	.10
❑	18	Pat Haden RC	2.00	.75
❑	19	Bob Young	.25	.10
❑	20	Wally Chambers	.25	.10
❑	21	Lawrence Gaines	.25	.10
❑	22	Larry McCarren	.25	.10
❑	23	Horst Muhlmann	.25	.10
❑	24	Phil Villapiano	.50	.20
❑	25	Greg Pruitt	.50	.20
❑	26	Ron Howard	.25	.10
❑	27	Craig Morton	1.00	.40
❑	28	Rufus Mayes	.25	.10
❑	29	Lee Roy Selmon RC UER	12.00	6.00
❑	30	Ed White	.50	.20
❑	31	Harold McLinton	.25	.10
❑	32	Glenn Doughty	.25	.10
❑	33	Bob Kuechenberg	1.00	.40
❑	34	Duane Carrell	.25	.10
❑	35	Riley Odoms	.25	.10
❑	36	Bobby Scott	.25	.10
❑	37	Nick Mike-Mayer	.25	.10
❑	38	Bill Lenkaitis	.25	.10
❑	39	Roland Harper	.50	.20
❑	40	Tommy Hart	.25	.10
❑	41	Mike Sensibaugh	.25	.10
❑	42	Rusty Jackson	.25	.10
❑	43	Levi Johnson	.25	.10
❑	44	Mike McCoy DT	.25	.10
❑	45	Roger Staubach	20.00	10.00
❑	46	Fred Cox	.25	.10
❑	47	Bob Babich	.25	.10
❑	48	Reggie McKenzie	.50	.20
❑	49	Dave Jennings	.25	.10
❑	50	Mike Haynes RC	10.00	4.00
❑	51	Larry Brown	.50	.20
❑	52	Marvin Cobb	.25	.10
❑	53	Fred Cook	.25	.10
❑	54	Freddie Solomon	.50	.20
❑	55	John Riggins	2.50	1.25
❑	56	John Bunting	.50	.20
❑	57	Ray Wersching	.50	.20
❑	58	Mike Livingston	.25	.10
❑	59	Billy Johnson	.50	.20
❑	60	Mike Wagner	.25	.10
❑	61	Waymond Bryant	.25	.10
❑	62	Jim Otis	.50	.20
❑	63	Ed Galigher	.25	.10
❑	64	Randy Vataha	.25	.10
❑	65	Jim Zorn RC	4.00	1.50
❑	66	Jon Keyworth	.25	.10
❑	67	Checklist 1-132	2.00	.75
❑	68	Henry Childs	.25	.10
❑	69	Thom Darden	.25	.10
❑	70	George Kunz	.25	.10
❑	71	Lenvil Elliott	.25	.10
❑	72	Curtis Johnson	.25	.10
❑	73	Doug Van Horn	.25	.10
❑	74	Joe Theismann	4.00	2.00
❑	75	Dwight White	.50	.20
❑	76	Scott Laidlaw	.25	.10
❑	77	Monte Johnson	.25	.10
❑	78	Dave Beverly	.25	.10
❑	79	Jim Mitchell TE	.25	.10
❑	80	Jack Youngblood	1.00	.40
❑	81	Mel Gray	.50	.20
❑	82	Dwight Harrison	.25	.10
❑	83	John Hadl	.50	.20
❑	84	Matt Blair RC	1.00	.40
❑	85	Charlie Sanders	.25	.10
❑	86	Noah Jackson	.25	.10
❑	87	Ed Marinaro	.50	.20
❑	88	Bob Howard	.25	.10
❑	89	John McDaniel	.25	.10
❑	90	Dan Dierdorf	1.50	.60
❑	91	Mark Moseley	.50	.20
❑	92	Cleo Miller	.25	.10
❑	93	Andre Tillman	.25	.10
❑	94	Bruce Taylor	.25	.10
❑	95	Bert Jones	1.00	.40
❑	96	Anthony Davis RC	1.00	.40
❑	97	Don Goode	.25	.10
❑	98	Ray Rhodes RC	6.00	3.00
❑	99	Mike Webster RC	12.00	6.00
❑	100	O.J.Simpson	6.00	3.00
❑	101	Doug Plank RC	.25	.10
❑	102	Efren Herrera	.50	.20
❑	103	Charlie Smith WR	.25	.10
❑	104	Carlos Brown RC	1.00	.40
❑	105	Jim Marshall	1.00	.40
❑	106	Paul Naumoff	.25	.10
❑	107	Walter White	.25	.10
❑	108	John Cappelletti RC	3.00	1.25
❑	109	Chip Myers	.25	.10
❑	110	Ken Stabler	10.00	5.00
❑	111	Joe Ehrmann	.25	.10
❑	112	Rick Engles	.25	.10
❑	113	Jack Dolbin RC	.25	.10
❑	114	Ron Bolton	.25	.10
❑	115	Mike Thomas	.25	.10
❑	116	Mike Fuller	.25	.10
❑	117	John Hill	.25	.10
❑	118	Richard Todd RC	1.00	.40
❑	119	Duriel Harris RC	.50	.20
❑	120	John James	.25	.10
❑	121	Lionel Antoine	.25	.10
❑	122	John Skorupan	.25	.10
❑	123	Skip Butler	.25	.10
❑	124	Bob Tucker	.25	.10
❑	125	Paul Krause	1.00	.40
❑	126	Dave Hampton	.25	.10
❑	127	Tom Wittum	.25	.10
❑	128	Gary Huff	.50	.20
❑	129	Emmitt Thomas	.25	.10
❑	130	Drew Pearson	2.00	.75
❑	131	Ron Saul	.25	.10
❑	132	Steve Niehaus	.25	.10
❑	133	Fred Carr	1.00	.40
❑	134	Norm Bulaich	.25	.10
❑	135	Bob Trumpy	.50	.20
❑	136	Greg Landry	.50	.20
❑	137	George Buehler	.25	.10
❑	138	Reggie Rucker	.50	.20
❑	139	Julius Adams	.25	.10
❑	140	Jack Ham	2.50	1.25
❑	141	Wayne Morris RC	.25	.10
❑	142	Marv Bateman	.25	.10
❑	143	Bobby Maples	.25	.10
❑	144	Harold Carmichael	1.00	.40
❑	145	Bob Avellini	.50	.20
❑	146	Harry Carson RC	3.00	1.50
❑	147	Lawrence Pillers	.25	.10
❑	148	Ed Williams RC	.25	.10
❑	149	Dan Pastorini	.50	.20
❑	150	Ron Yary	1.00	.40
❑	151	Joe Lavender	.25	.10
❑	152	Pat McInally RC	.50	.20
❑	153	Lloyd Mumphord	.25	.10
❑	154	Cullen Bryant	.50	.20
❑	155	Willie Lanier	1.00	.40
❑	156	Gene Washington 49er	.50	.20
❑	157	Scott Hunter	.25	.10
❑	158	Jim Merlo	.25	.10
❑	159	Randy Grossman	.50	.20
❑	160	Blaine Nye	.25	.10
❑	161	Ike Harris	.25	.10
❑	162	Doug Dieken	.25	.10
❑	163	Guy Morriss	.25	.10
❑	164	Bob Parsons	.25	.10
❑	165	Steve Grogan	1.00	.40
❑	166	John Brockington	.50	.20
❑	167	Charlie Joiner	2.50	1.25
❑	168	Ron Carpenter	.25	.10
❑	169	Jeff Wright S	.25	.10
❑	170	Chris Hanburger	.25	.10
❑	171	Roosevelt Leaks RC	.50	.20
❑	172	Larry Little	1.00	.40
❑	173	John Matuszak	.50	.20
❑	174	Joe Ferguson	.50	.20
❑	175	Brad Van Pelt	.50	.20
❑	176	Dexter Bussey RC	.50	.20
❑	177	Steve Largent RC	40.00	20.00
❑	178	Dewey Selmon	.50	.20
❑	179	Randy Gradishar	1.00	.40
❑	180	Mel Blount	3.00	1.50
❑	181	Dan Neal	.25	.10
❑	182	Rich Szaro	.25	.10
❑	183	Mike Boryla	.25	.10
❑	184	Steve Jones	.25	.10
❑	185	Paul Warfield	2.50	1.25
❑	186	Greg Buttle RC	.25	.10
❑	187	Rich McGeorge	.25	.10
❑	188	Leon Gray RC	.50	.20
❑	189	John Shinners	.25	.10
❑	190	Toni Linhart	.25	.10
❑	191	Robert Miller	.25	.10
❑	192	Jake Scott	.25	.10
❑	193	Jon Morris	.25	.10
❑	194	Randy Crowder	.25	.10
❑	195	Lynn Swann UER	18.00	10.00
❑	196	Marsh White	.25	.10
❑	197	Rod Perry RC	1.00	.40
❑	198	Willie Hall	.25	.10
❑	199	Mike Hartenstine	.25	.10
❑	200	Jim Bakken	.25	.10
❑	201	Atlanta Falcons CL UER	1.25	.50
❑	202	Baltimore Colts CL	1.25	.50
❑	203	Buffalo Bills CL	1.25	.50
❑	204	Chicago Bears CL	1.25	.50
❑	205	Cincinnati Bengals CL	1.25	.50
❑	206	Cleveland Browns CL	1.25	.50
❑	207	Dallas Cowboys CL	1.25	.50
❑	208	Denver Broncos CL	1.25	.50
❑	209	Detroit Lions CL	1.25	.50
❑	210	Green Bay Packers CL	1.25	.50
❑	211	Houston Oilers CL	1.25	.50
❑	212	Kansas City Chiefs CL	1.25	.50
❑	213	Los Angeles Rams CL	1.25	.50
❑	214	Miami Dolphins CL	1.25	.50
❑	215	Minnesota Vikings CL	1.25	.50
❑	216	New England Patriots CL	1.25	.50
❑	217	New Orleans Saints CL	1.25	.50
❑	218	New York Giants CL	1.25	.50
❑	219	New York Jets CL	1.25	.50
❑	220	Oakland Raiders CL	1.25	.50
❑	221	Philadelphia Eagles CL	1.25	.50
❑	222	Pittsburgh Steelers CL	1.25	.50
❑	223	St. Louis Cardinals CL	1.25	.50
❑	224	San Diego Chargers CL	1.25	.50
❑	225	San Francisco 49ers CL	1.25	.50
❑	226	Seattle Seahawks CL	1.25	.50
❑	227	Tampa Bay Buccaneers CL	1.25	.50
❑	228	Washington Redskins CL	1.25	.50
❑	229	Sam Cunningham	.50	.20
❑	230	Alan Page	1.00	.40
❑	231	Eddie Brown S	.25	.10
❑	232	Stan White	.25	.10
❑	233	Vern Den Herder	.25	.10
❑	234	Clarence Davis	.25	.10
❑	235	Ken Anderson	1.00	.40
❑	236	Karl Chandler	.25	.10
❑	237	Will Harrell	.25	.10
❑	238	Clarence Scott	.25	.10
❑	239	Bo Rather	.25	.10
❑	240	Robert Brazile	.50	.20
❑	241	Bob Bell	.25	.10
❑	242	Rolland Lawrence	.25	.10
❑	243	Tom Sullivan	.25	.10
❑	244	Larry Brunson	.25	.10
❑	245	Terry Bradshaw	20.00	10.00
❑	246	Rich Saul	.25	.10
❑	247	Cleveland Elam	.25	.10
❑	248	Don Woods	.25	.10
❑	249	Bruce Laird	.25	.10
❑	250	Coy Bacon	.50	.20
❑	251	Russ Francis	1.00	.40
❑	252	Jim Braxton	.25	.10

❑ 253 Perry Smith .25 .10
❑ 254 Jerome Barkum .25 .10
❑ 255 Garo Yepremian .50 .20
❑ 256 Checklist 133-264 2.00 .75
❑ 257 Tony Galbreath RC .50 .20
❑ 258 Troy Archer .25 .10
❑ 259 Brian Sipe 1.00 .40
❑ 260 Billy Joe DuPree .50 .20
❑ 261 Bobby Walden .25 .10
❑ 262 Larry Marshall .25 .10
❑ 263 Ted Fritsch Jr. .25 .10
❑ 264 Larry Hand .25 .10
❑ 265 Tom Mack 1.00 .40
❑ 266 Ed Bradley .25 .10
❑ 267 Pat Leahy .50 .20
❑ 268 Louis Carter .25 .10
❑ 269 Archie Griffin RC 6.00 3.00
❑ 270 Art Shell 1.00 .40
❑ 271 Stu Voigt .25 .10
❑ 272 Prentice McCray .25 .10
❑ 273 MacArthur Lane .25 .10
❑ 274 Dan Fouts 6.00 3.00
❑ 275 Charle Young .50 .20
❑ 276 Wilbur Jackson RC .25 .10
❑ 277 John Hicks .25 .10
❑ 278 Nat Moore 1.00 .40
❑ 279 Virgil Livers .25 .10
❑ 280 Curley Culp .50 .20
❑ 281 Rocky Bleier 2.50 1.25
❑ 282 John Zook .25 .10
❑ 283 Tom DeLeone .25 .10
❑ 284 Danny White RC 10.00 5.00
❑ 285 Otis Armstrong .50 .20
❑ 286 Larry Walton .25 .10
❑ 287 Jim Carter .25 .10
❑ 288 Don McCauley .25 .10
❑ 289 Frank Grant .25 .10
❑ 290 Roger Wehrli .50 .20
❑ 291 Mick Tingelhoff .50 .20
❑ 292 Bernard Jackson .25 .10
❑ 293 Tom Owen RC .25 .10
❑ 294 Mike Esposito .25 .10
❑ 295 Fred Biletnikoff 2.50 1.25
❑ 296 Revie Sorey RC .25 .10
❑ 297 John McMakin .25 .10
❑ 298 Dan Ryczek .25 .10
❑ 299 Wayne Moore .25 .10
❑ 300 Franco Harris 4.00 2.00
❑ 301 Rick Upchurch RC 1.00 .40
❑ 302 Jim Stienke .25 .10
❑ 303 Charlie Davis .25 .10
❑ 304 Don Cockroft .25 .10
❑ 305 Ken Burrough .50 .20
❑ 306 Clark Gaines .25 .10
❑ 307 Bobby Douglass .25 .10
❑ 308 Ralph Perretta .25 .10
❑ 309 Wally Hilgenberg .25 .10
❑ 310 Monte Jackson RC .50 .20
❑ 311 Chris Bahr RC .50 .20
❑ 312 Jim Cheyunski .25 .10
❑ 313 Mike Patrick .25 .10
❑ 314 Ed Too Tall Jones 5.00 2.50
❑ 315 Bill Bradley .25 .10
❑ 316 Benny Malone .25 .10
❑ 317 Paul Seymour .25 .10
❑ 318 Jim Laslavic .25 .10
❑ 319 Frank Lewis .50 .20
❑ 320 Ray Guy 1.00 .40
❑ 321 Allan Ellis .25 .10
❑ 322 Conrad Dobler .50 .20
❑ 323 Chester Marcol .25 .10
❑ 324 Doug Kotar .25 .10
❑ 325 Lemar Parrish .50 .20
❑ 326 Steve Holden .25 .10
❑ 327 Jeff Van Note .50 .20
❑ 328 Howard Stevens .25 .10
❑ 329 Brad Dusek .50 .20
❑ 330 Joe DeLamielleure 1.00 .40
❑ 331 Jim Plunkett 1.00 .40
❑ 332 Checklist 265-396 2.00 .75
❑ 333 Lou Piccone .25 .10
❑ 334 Ray Hamilton .25 .10
❑ 335 Jan Stenerud 1.00 .40
❑ 336 Jeris White .25 .10
❑ 337 Sherman Smith RC .25 .10
❑ 338 Dave Green .25 .10
❑ 339 Terry Schmidt .25 .10
❑ 340 Sammie White RC 1.00 .40
❑ 341 Jon Kolb RC .25 .10
❑ 342 Randy White 8.00 4.00
❑ 343 Bob Klein .25 .10
❑ 344 Bob Kowalkowski .25 .10
❑ 345 Terry Metcalf .50 .20
❑ 346 Joe Danelo .25 .10
❑ 347 Ken Payne .25 .10
❑ 348 Neal Craig .25 .10
❑ 349 Dennis Johnson .25 .10
❑ 350 Bill Bergey .50 .20
❑ 351 Raymond Chester .25 .10
❑ 352 Bob Matheson .25 .10
❑ 353 Mike Kadish .25 .10
❑ 354 Mark Van Eeghen RC 1.00 .40
❑ 355 L.C.Greenwood 1.00 .40
❑ 356 Sam Hunt .25 .10
❑ 357 Darrell Austin .25 .10
❑ 358 Jim Turner .25 .10
❑ 359 Ahmad Rashad 2.00 .75
❑ 360 Walter Payton 40.00 15.00
❑ 361 Mark Arneson .25 .10
❑ 362 Jerrel Wilson .25 .10
❑ 363 Steve Bartkowski 1.00 .40
❑ 364 John Watson .25 .10
❑ 365 Ken Riley .50 .20
❑ 366 Gregg Bingham .25 .10
❑ 367 Golden Richards .50 .20
❑ 368 Clyde Powers .25 .10
❑ 369 Diron Talbert .25 .10
❑ 370 Lydell Mitchell .50 .20
❑ 371 Bob Jackson .25 .10
❑ 372 Jim Mandich .25 .10
❑ 373 Frank LeMaster .25 .10
❑ 374 Benny Ricardo .25 .10
❑ 375 Lawrence McCutcheon .50 .20
❑ 376 Lynn Dickey .50 .20
❑ 377 Phil Wise .25 .10
❑ 378 Tony McGee DT .25 .10
❑ 379 Norm Thompson .25 .10
❑ 380 Dave Casper RC 4.00 1.50
❑ 381 Glen Edwards .25 .10
❑ 382 Bob Thomas .25 .10
❑ 383 Bob Chandler .50 .20
❑ 384 Rickey Young .50 .20
❑ 385 Carl Eller 1.00 .40
❑ 386 Lyle Alzado 1.00 .40
❑ 387 John Leypoldt .25 .10
❑ 388 Gordon Bell .25 .10
❑ 389 Mike Bragg .25 .10
❑ 390 Jim Langer 1.00 .40
❑ 391 Vern Holland .25 .10
❑ 392 Nelson Munsey .25 .10
❑ 393 Mack Mitchell .25 .10
❑ 394 Tony Adams RC .25 .10
❑ 395 Preston Pearson .50 .20
❑ 396 Emanuel Zanders .25 .10
❑ 397 Vince Papale .25 .10
❑ 398 Joe Fields RC .50 .20
❑ 399 Craig Clemons .25 .10
❑ 400 Fran Tarkenton 5.00 2.50
❑ 401 Andy Johnson .25 .10
❑ 402 Willie Buchanon .25 .10
❑ 403 Pat Curran .25 .10
❑ 404 Ray Jarvis .25 .10
❑ 405 Joe Greene 2.50 1.25
❑ 406 Bill Simpson .25 .10
❑ 407 Ronnie Coleman .25 .10
❑ 408 J.K. McKay RC .50 .20
❑ 409 Pat Fischer .50 .20
❑ 410 John Dutton .50 .20
❑ 411 Boobie Clark .25 .10
❑ 412 Pat Tilley RC 1.00 .40
❑ 413 Don Strock .50 .20
❑ 414 Brian Kelley .25 .10
❑ 415 Gene Upshaw 1.00 .40
❑ 416 Mike Montler .25 .10
❑ 417 Checklist 397-528 2.00 .75
❑ 418 John Gilliam .25 .10
❑ 419 Brent McClanahan .25 .10
❑ 420 Jerry Sherk .25 .10
❑ 421 Roy Gerela .25 .10
❑ 422 Tim Fox .50 .20
❑ 423 John Ebersole .25 .10
❑ 424 James Scott RC .25 .10
❑ 425 Delvin Williams RC .50 .20
❑ 426 Spike Jones .25 .10
❑ 427 Harvey Martin 1.00 .4
❑ 428 Don Herrmann .25 .1
❑ 429 Calvin Hill .50 .2
❑ 430 Isiah Robertson .25 .1
❑ 431 Tony Greene .25 .10
❑ 432 Bob Johnson .25 .10
❑ 433 Lem Barney 1.00 .40
❑ 434 Eric Torkelson .25 .10
❑ 435 John Mendenhall .25 .10
❑ 436 Larry Seiple .50 .20
❑ 437 Art Kuehn .25 .10
❑ 438 John Vella .25 .10
❑ 439 Greg Latta .25 .10
❑ 440 Roger Carr .50 .20
❑ 441 Doug Sutherland .25 .10
❑ 442 Mike Kruczek .25 .10
❑ 443 Steve Zabel .25 .10
❑ 444 Mike Pruitt RC 1.00 .40
❑ 445 Harold Jackson .50 .20
❑ 446 George Jakowenko .25 .10
❑ 447 John Fitzgerald .25 .10
❑ 448 Carey Joyce .25 .10
❑ 449 Jim LeClair .25 .10
❑ 450 Ken Houston 1.00 .40
❑ 451 Steve Grogan RB .50 .20
❑ 452 Jim Marshall RB .50 .20
❑ 453 O.J.Simpson RB 2.50 1.25
❑ 454 Fran Tarkenton RB 3.00 1.50
❑ 455 Jim Zorn RB .50 .20
❑ 456 Robert Pratt .25 .10
❑ 457 Walker Gillette .25 .10
❑ 458 Charlie Hall .25 .10
❑ 459 Robert Newhouse .50 .20
❑ 460 John Hannah 1.00 .40
❑ 461 Ken Reaves .25 .10
❑ 462 Herman Weaver .25 .10
❑ 463 James Harris .50 .20
❑ 464 Howard Twilley .50 .20
❑ 465 Jeff Siemon .50 .20
❑ 466 John Outlaw .25 .10
❑ 467 Chuck Muncie RC 1.00 .40
❑ 468 Bob Moore .25 .10
❑ 469 Robert Woods .25 .10
❑ 470 Cliff Branch 2.00 .75
❑ 471 Johnnie Gray .25 .10
❑ 472 Don Hardeman .25 .10
❑ 473 Steve Ramsey .25 .10
❑ 474 Steve Mike-Mayer .25 .10
❑ 475 Gary Garrison .25 .10
❑ 476 Walter Johnson .25 .10
❑ 477 Neil Clabo .25 .10
❑ 478 Len Hauss .25 .10
❑ 479 Darryl Stingley .50 .20
❑ 480 Jack Lambert 8.00 4.00
❑ 481 Mike Adamle .50 .20
❑ 482 David Lee .25 .10
❑ 483 Tom Mullen .25 .10
❑ 484 Claude Humphrey .25 .10
❑ 485 Jim Hart 1.00 .40
❑ 486 Bobby Thompson RB .25 .10
❑ 487 Jack Rudnay .25 .10
❑ 488 Rich Sowells .25 .10
❑ 489 Reuben Gant .25 .10
❑ 490 Cliff Harris 1.00 .40
❑ 491 Bob Brown DT .25 .10
❑ 492 Don Nottingham .25 .10
❑ 493 Ron Jessie .25 .10
❑ 494 Otis Sistrunk .50 .20
❑ 495 Billy Kilmer .50 .20
❑ 496 Oscar Roan .25 .10
❑ 497 Bill Van Heusen .25 .10
❑ 498 Randy Logan .25 .10
❑ 499 John Smith .25 .10
❑ 500 Chuck Foreman .50 .20
❑ 501 J.T. Thomas .25 .10
❑ 502 Steve Schubert .25 .10
❑ 503 Mike Barnes .25 .10
❑ 504 J.V. Cain .25 .10
❑ 505 Larry Csonka 3.00 1.50
❑ 506 Elvin Bethea 1.00 .40
❑ 507 Ray Easterling .25 .10
❑ 508 Joe Reed .25 .10
❑ 509 Steve Odom .25 .10
❑ 510 Tommy Casanova .25 .10
❑ 511 Dave Dalby .25 .10
❑ 512 Richard Caster .25 .10
❑ 513 Fred Dryer 1.00 .40

❑ 514 Jeff Kinney	.25	.10
❑ 515 Bob Griese	3.00	1.50
❑ 516 Butch Johnson RC	1.00	.40
❑ 517 Gerald Irons	.25	.10
❑ 518 Don Calhoun	.25	.10
❑ 519 Jack Gregory	.25	.10
❑ 520 Tom Banks	.25	.10
❑ 521 Bobby Bryant	.25	.10
❑ 522 Reggie Harrison	.25	.10
❑ 523 Terry Hermeling	.25	.10
❑ 524 David Taylor	.25	.10
❑ 525 Brian Baschnagel RC	.50	.20
❑ 526 AFC Champ/Stabler	1.00	.40
❑ 527 NFC Championship	.50	.20
❑ 528 Super Bowl XI	1.00	.40

1978 Topps

❑ COMPLETE SET (528)	150.00	80.00
❑ 1 Gary Huff HL !	1.00	.40
❑ 2 Craig Morton HL	1.00	.40
❑ 3 Walter Payton HL	8.00	3.00
❑ 4 O.J.Simpson HL	2.00	.75
❑ 5 Fran Tarkenton HL	2.00	.75
❑ 6 Bob Thomas HL	.20	.07
❑ 7 Joe Pisarcik	.50	.20
❑ 8 Skip Thomas	.20	.07
❑ 9 Roosevelt Leaks	.20	.07
❑ 10 Ken Houston	1.00	.40
❑ 11 Tom Blanchard	.20	.07
❑ 12 Jim Turner	.20	.07
❑ 13 Tom DeLeone	.20	.07
❑ 14 Jim LeClair	.20	.07
❑ 15 Bob Avellini	.50	.20
❑ 16 Tony McGee DT	.20	.07
❑ 17 James Harris	.50	.20
❑ 18 Terry Nelson	.20	.07
❑ 19 Rocky Bleier	2.00	.75
❑ 20 Joe DeLamielleure	1.00	.40
❑ 21 Richard Caster	.20	.07
❑ 22 A.J.Duhe RC	1.00	.40
❑ 23 John Outlaw	.20	.07
❑ 24 Danny White	1.25	.50
❑ 25 Larry Csonka	2.50	1.00
❑ 26 David Hill RC	.50	.20
❑ 27 Mark Arneson	.20	.07
❑ 28 Jack Tatum	.50	.20
❑ 29 Norm Thompson	.20	.07
❑ 30 Sammie White	.50	.20
❑ 31 Dennis Johnson	.20	.07
❑ 32 Robin Earl	.20	.07
❑ 33 Don Cockroft	.20	.07
❑ 34 Bob Johnson	.20	.07
❑ 35 John Hannah	1.00	.40
❑ 36 Scott Hunter	.20	.07
❑ 37 Ken Burrough	.50	.20
❑ 38 Wilbur Jackson	.50	.20
❑ 39 Rich McGeorge	.20	.07
❑ 40 Lyle Alzado	1.00	.40
❑ 41 John Ebersole	.20	.07
❑ 42 Gary Green RC	.20	.07
❑ 43 Art Kuehn	.20	.07
❑ 44 Glen Edwards	.50	.20
❑ 45 Lawrence McCutcheon	.50	.20
❑ 46 Duriel Harris	.20	.07
❑ 47 Rich Szaro	.20	.07
❑ 48 Mike Washington	.20	.07
❑ 49 Stan White	.20	.07
❑ 50 Dave Casper	1.00	.40
❑ 51 Len Hauss	.20	.07
❑ 52 James Scott	.20	.07
❑ 53 Brian Sipe	1.00	.40
❑ 54 Gary Shirk	.20	.07
❑ 55 Archie Griffin	1.00	.40
❑ 56 Mike Patrick	.20	.07
❑ 57 Mario Clark	.20	.07
❑ 58 Jeff Siemon	.20	.07
❑ 59 Steve Mike-Mayer	.20	.07
❑ 60 Randy White	4.00	2.00
❑ 61 Darrell Austin	.20	.07
❑ 62 Tom Sullivan	.20	.07
❑ 63 Johnny Rodgers RC	1.00	.40
❑ 64 Ken Reaves	.20	.07
❑ 65 Terry Bradshaw	12.00	6.00
❑ 66 Fred Steinfort	.20	.07
❑ 67 Curley Culp	.50	.20
❑ 68 Ted Hendricks	1.00	.40
❑ 69 Raymond Chester	.20	.07
❑ 70 Jim Langer	1.00	.40
❑ 71 Calvin Hill	.50	.20
❑ 72 Mike Hartenstine	.20	.07
❑ 73 Gerald Irons	.20	.07
❑ 74 Billy Brooks	.50	.20
❑ 75 John Mendenhall	.20	.07
❑ 76 Andy Johnson	.20	.07
❑ 77 Tom Wittum	.20	.07
❑ 78 Lynn Dickey	.50	.20
❑ 79 Carl Eller	1.00	.40
❑ 80 Tom Mack	1.00	.40
❑ 81 Clark Gaines	.20	.07
❑ 82 Lem Barney	1.00	.40
❑ 83 Mike Montler	.20	.07
❑ 84 Jon Kolb	.20	.07
❑ 85 Bob Chandler	.50	.20
❑ 86 Robert Newhouse	.50	.20
❑ 87 Frank LeMaster	.20	.07
❑ 88 Jeff West	.20	.07
❑ 89 Lyle Blackwood	.50	.20
❑ 90 Gene Upshaw	1.00	.40
❑ 91 Frank Grant	.20	.07
❑ 92 Tom Hicks	.20	.07
❑ 93 Mike Pruitt	.50	.20
❑ 94 Chris Bahr	.20	.07
❑ 95 Russ Francis	.50	.20
❑ 96 Norris Thomas	.20	.07
❑ 97 Gary Barbaro RC	.50	.20
❑ 98 Jim Merlo	.20	.07
❑ 99 Karl Chandler	.20	.07
❑ 100 Fran Tarkenton	4.00	1.50
❑ 101 Abdul Salaam	.20	.07
❑ 102 Marv Kellum	.20	.07
❑ 103 Herman Weaver	.20	.07
❑ 104 Roy Gerela	.20	.07
❑ 105 Harold Jackson	.50	.20
❑ 106 Dewey Selmon	.50	.20
❑ 107 Checklist 1-132	1.00	.40
❑ 108 Clarence Davis	.20	.07
❑ 109 Robert Pratt	.20	.07
❑ 110 Harvey Martin	1.00	.40
❑ 111 Brad Dusek	.20	.07
❑ 112 Greg Latta	.20	.07
❑ 113 Tony Peters	.20	.07
❑ 114 Jim Braxton	.20	.07
❑ 115 Ken Riley	.50	.20
❑ 116 Steve Nelson	.20	.07
❑ 117 Rick Upchurch	.50	.20
❑ 118 Spike Jones	.20	.07
❑ 119 Doug Kotar	.20	.07
❑ 120 Bob Griese	2.50	1.00
❑ 121 Burgess Owens	.20	.07
❑ 122 Rolf Benirschke RC	.50	.20
❑ 123 Haskel Stanback RC	.20	.07
❑ 124 J.T. Thomas	.20	.07
❑ 125 Ahmad Rashad	1.50	.60
❑ 126 Rick Kane	.20	.07
❑ 127 Elvin Bethea	1.00	.40
❑ 128 Dave Dalby	.20	.07
❑ 129 Mike Barnes	.20	.07
❑ 130 Isiah Robertson	.20	.07
❑ 131 Jim Plunkett	1.00	.40
❑ 132 Allan Ellis	.20	.07
❑ 133 Mike Bragg	.20	.07
❑ 134 Bob Jackson	.20	.07
❑ 135 Coy Bacon	.20	.07
❑ 136 John Smith	.20	.07
❑ 137 Chuck Muncie	.50	.20
❑ 138 Johnnie Gray	.20	.07
❑ 139 Jimmy Robinson	.20	.07
❑ 140 Tom Banks	.20	.07
❑ 141 Marvin Powell RC	.20	.07
❑ 142 Jerrel Wilson	.20	.07
❑ 143 Ron Howard	.20	.07
❑ 144 Rob Lytle RC	.50	.20
❑ 145 L.C.Greenwood	1.00	.40
❑ 146 Morris Owens	.20	.07
❑ 147 Joe Reed	.20	.07
❑ 148 Mike Kadish	.20	.07
❑ 149 Phil Villapiano	.50	.20
❑ 150 Lydell Mitchell	.50	.20
❑ 151 Randy Logan	.20	.07
❑ 152 Mike Williams RC	.20	.07
❑ 153 Jeff Van Note	.50	.20
❑ 154 Steve Schubert	.20	.07
❑ 155 Billy Kilmer	.50	.20
❑ 156 Boobie Clark	.20	.07
❑ 157 Charlie Hall	.20	.07
❑ 158 Raymond Clayborn RC	1.00	.40
❑ 159 Jack Gregory	.20	.07
❑ 160 Cliff Harris	1.00	.40
❑ 161 Joe Fields	.20	.07
❑ 162 Don Nottingham	.20	.07
❑ 163 Ed White	.50	.20
❑ 164 Toni Fritsch	.20	.07
❑ 165 Jack Lambert	4.00	2.00
❑ 166 NFC Champs/Staubach	1.50	.60
❑ 167 AFC Champs/Lytle	.50	.20
❑ 168 Super Bowl XII/Dorsett	3.00	1.50
❑ 169 Neal Colzie RC	.20	.07
❑ 170 Cleveland Elam	.20	.07
❑ 171 David Lee	.20	.07
❑ 172 Jim Otis	.20	.07
❑ 173 Archie Manning	1.00	.40
❑ 174 Jim Carter	.20	.07
❑ 175 Jean Fugett	.20	.07
❑ 176 Willie Parker C	.20	.07
❑ 177 Haven Moses	.50	.20
❑ 178 Horace King RC	.20	.07
❑ 179 Bob Thomas	.20	.07
❑ 180 Monte Jackson	.20	.07
❑ 181 Steve Zabel	.20	.07
❑ 182 John Fitzgerald	.20	.07
❑ 183 Mike Livingston	.20	.07
❑ 184 Larry Poole	.20	.07
❑ 185 Isaac Curtis	.50	.20
❑ 186 Chuck Ramsey	.20	.07
❑ 187 Bob Klein	.20	.07
❑ 188 Ray Rhodes	1.00	.40
❑ 189 Otis Sistrunk	.50	.20
❑ 190 Bill Bergey	.50	.20
❑ 191 Sherman Smith	.50	.20
❑ 192 Dave Green	.20	.07
❑ 193 Carl Mauck	.20	.07
❑ 194 Reggie Harrison	.20	.07
❑ 195 Roger Carr	.50	.20
❑ 196 Steve Bartkowski	1.00	.40
❑ 197 Ray Wersching	.20	.07
❑ 198 Willie Buchanon	.20	.07
❑ 199 Neil Clabo	.20	.07
❑ 200 Walter Payton UER	25.00	12.50
❑ 201 Sam Adams OL	.20	.07
❑ 202 Larry Gordon	.20	.07
❑ 203 Pat Tilley	.50	.20
❑ 204 Mack Mitchell	.20	.07
❑ 205 Ken Anderson	1.00	.40
❑ 206 Scott Dierking	.20	.07
❑ 207 Jack Rudnay	.20	.07
❑ 208 Jim Stienke	.20	.07
❑ 209 Bill Simpson	.20	.07
❑ 210 Errol Mann	.20	.07
❑ 211 Bucky Dilts	.20	.07
❑ 212 Reuben Gant	.20	.07
❑ 213 Thomas Henderson RC	1.50	.60
❑ 214 Steve Furness	.50	.20
❑ 215 John Riggins	2.00	.75
❑ 216 Keith Krepfle RC	.20	.07
❑ 217 Fred Dean RC	.50	.20
❑ 218 Emanuel Zanders	.20	.07
❑ 219 Don Testerman	.20	.07
❑ 220 George Kunz	.20	.07
❑ 221 Darryl Stingley	.50	.20
❑ 222 Ken Sanders	.20	.07
❑ 223 Gary Huff	.20	.07
❑ 224 Gregg Bingham	.20	.07
❑ 225 Jerry Sherk	.20	.07

❑ 226 Doug Plank .20 .07
❑ 227 Ed Taylor .20 .07
❑ 228 Emery Moorehead .20 .07
❑ 229 Reggie Williams RC 1.00 .40
❑ 230 Claude Humphrey .20 .07
❑ 231 Randy Cross RC 2.00 .75
❑ 232 Jim Hart 1.00 .40
❑ 233 Bobby Bryant .20 .07
❑ 234 Larry Brown .20 .07
❑ 235 Mark Van Eeghen .50 .20
❑ 236 Terry Hermeling .20 .07
❑ 237 Steve Odom .20 .07
❑ 238 Jan Stenerud 1.00 .40
❑ 239 Andre Tillman .20 .07
❑ 240 Tom Jackson RC 5.00 2.00
❑ 241 Ken Mendenhall .20 .07
❑ 242 Tim Fox .20 .07
❑ 243 Don Herrmann .20 .07
❑ 244 Eddie McMillan .20 .07
❑ 245 Greg Pruitt .50 .20
❑ 246 J.K. McKay .20 .07
❑ 247 Larry Keller .20 .07
❑ 248 Dave Jennings .50 .20
❑ 249 Bo Harris .20 .07
❑ 250 Revie Sorey .20 .07
❑ 251 Tony Greene .20 .07
❑ 252 Butch Johnson .50 .20
❑ 253 Paul Naumoff .20 .07
❑ 254 Rickey Young .50 .20
❑ 255 Dwight White .50 .20
❑ 256 Joe Lavender .20 .07
❑ 257 Checklist 133-264 1.00 .40
❑ 258 Ronnie Coleman .20 .07
❑ 259 Charlie Smith WR .20 .07
❑ 260 Ray Guy 1.00 .40
❑ 261 David Taylor .20 .07
❑ 262 Bill Lenkaitis .20 .07
❑ 263 Jim Mitchell TE .20 .07
❑ 264 Delvin Williams .20 .07
❑ 265 Jack Youngblood 1.00 .40
❑ 266 Chuck Crist .20 .07
❑ 267 Richard Todd .50 .20
❑ 268 Dave Logan RC 1.00 .40
❑ 269 Rufus Mayes .20 .07
❑ 270 Brad Van Pelt .20 .07
❑ 271 Chester Marcol .20 .07
❑ 272 J.V. Cain .20 .07
❑ 273 Larry Seiple .20 .07
❑ 274 Brent McClanahan .20 .07
❑ 275 Mike Wagner .20 .07
❑ 276 Diron Talbert .20 .07
❑ 277 Brian Baschnagel .20 .07
❑ 278 Ed Podolak .20 .07
❑ 279 Don Goode .20 .07
❑ 280 John Dutton .50 .20
❑ 281 Don Calhoun .20 .07
❑ 282 Monte Johnson .20 .07
❑ 283 Ron Jessie .20 .07
❑ 284 Jon Morris .20 .07
❑ 285 Riley Odoms .20 .07
❑ 286 Marv Bateman .20 .07
❑ 287 Joe Klecko RC 1.00 .40
❑ 288 Oliver Davis .20 .07
❑ 289 John McDaniel .20 .07
❑ 290 Roger Staubach 12.00 6.00
❑ 291 Brian Kelley .20 .07
❑ 292 Mike Hogan .20 .07
❑ 293 John Leypoldt .20 .07
❑ 294 Jack Novak .20 .07
❑ 295 Joe Greene 2.00 .75
❑ 296 John Hill .20 .07
❑ 297 Danny Buggs .20 .07
❑ 298 Ted Albrecht .20 .07
❑ 299 Nelson Munsey .20 .07
❑ 300 Chuck Foreman .50 .20
❑ 301 Dan Pastorini .50 .20
❑ 302 Tommy Hart .20 .07
❑ 303 Dave Beverly .20 .07
❑ 304 Tony Reed RC .50 .20
❑ 305 Cliff Branch 1.50 .60
❑ 306 Clarence Duren .20 .07
❑ 307 Randy Rasmussen .20 .07
❑ 308 Oscar Roan .20 .07
❑ 309 Lenvil Elliott .20 .07
❑ 310 Dan Dierdorf 1.00 .40
❑ 311 Johnny Perkins .20 .07
❑ 312 Rafael Septien RC .50 .20
❑ 313 Terry Beeson .20 .07
❑ 314 Lee Roy Selmon 2.00 .75
❑ 315 Tony Dorsett RC 40.00 25.00
❑ 316 Greg Landry .50 .20
❑ 317 Jake Scott .20 .07
❑ 318 Dan Peiffer .20 .07
❑ 319 John Bunting .50 .20
❑ 320 John Stallworth RC 20.00 10.00
❑ 321 Bob Howard .20 .07
❑ 322 Larry Little 1.00 .40
❑ 323 Reggie McKenzie .50 .20
❑ 324 Duane Carrell .20 .07
❑ 325 Ed Simonini .20 .07
❑ 326 John Vella .20 .07
❑ 327 Wesley Walker RC 3.00 1.50
❑ 328 Jon Keyworth .20 .07
❑ 329 Ron Bolton .20 .07
❑ 330 Tommy Casanova .20 .07
❑ 331 R.Staubach/B.Griese LL 4.00 2.00
❑ 332 A.Rashad/Mitchell LL 1.00 .40
❑ 333 W.Payton/VanEeghenLL 3.00 1.25
❑ 334 W.Payton/E.Mann LL 3.00 1.25
❑ 335 Interception Leaders .20 .07
❑ 336 Punting Leaders .50 .20
❑ 337 Robert Brazile .50 .20
❑ 338 Charlie Joiner 1.50 .60
❑ 339 Joe Ferguson .50 .20
❑ 340 Bill Thompson .20 .07
❑ 341 Sam Cunningham .50 .20
❑ 342 Curtis Johnson .20 .07
❑ 343 Jim Marshall 1.00 .40
❑ 344 Charlie Sanders .20 .07
❑ 345 Willie Hall .20 .07
❑ 346 Pat Haden 1.00 .40
❑ 347 Jim Bakken .20 .07
❑ 348 Bruce Taylor .20 .07
❑ 349 Barty Smith .20 .07
❑ 350 Drew Pearson 1.50 .60
❑ 351 Mike Webster 2.50 1.00
❑ 352 Bobby Hammond .20 .07
❑ 353 Dave Mays .20 .07
❑ 354 Pat McInally .20 .07
❑ 355 Toni Linhart .20 .07
❑ 356 Larry Hand .20 .07
❑ 357 Ted Fritsch Jr. .20 .07
❑ 358 Larry Marshall .20 .07
❑ 359 Waymond Bryant .20 .07
❑ 360 Louie Kelcher RC .50 .20
❑ 361 Stanley Morgan RC 2.00 .75
❑ 362 Bruce Harper RC .50 .20
❑ 363 Bernard Jackson .20 .07
❑ 364 Walter White .20 .07
❑ 365 Ken Stabler 8.00 4.00
❑ 366 Fred Dryer 1.00 .40
❑ 367 Ike Harris .20 .07
❑ 368 Norm Bulaich .20 .07
❑ 369 Merv Krakau .20 .07
❑ 370 John James .20 .07
❑ 371 Bennie Cunningham RC .20 .07
❑ 372 Doug Van Horn .20 .07
❑ 373 Thom Darden .20 .07
❑ 374 Eddie Edwards RC .20 .07
❑ 375 Mike Thomas .20 .07
❑ 376 Fred Cook .20 .07
❑ 377 Mike Phipps .50 .20
❑ 378 Paul Krause 1.00 .40
❑ 379 Harold Carmichael 1.00 .40
❑ 380 Mike Haynes 1.00 .40
❑ 381 Wayne Morris .20 .07
❑ 382 Greg Buttle .20 .07
❑ 383 Jim Zorn 1.00 .40
❑ 384 Jack Dolbin .20 .07
❑ 385 Charlie Waters .50 .20
❑ 386 Dan Ryczek .20 .07
❑ 387 Joe Washington RC 1.00 .40
❑ 388 Checklist 265-396 1.00 .40
❑ 389 James Hunter .20 .07
❑ 390 Billy Johnson .50 .20
❑ 391 Jim Allen RC .20 .07
❑ 392 George Buehler .20 .07
❑ 393 Harry Carson 1.00 .40
❑ 394 Cleo Miller .20 .07
❑ 395 Gary Burley .20 .07
❑ 396 Mark Moseley .50 .20
❑ 397 Virgil Livers .20 .07
❑ 398 Joe Ehrmann .20 .07
❑ 399 Freddie Solomon .20 .07
❑ 400 O.J.Simpson 4.00 2.0
❑ 401 Julius Adams .20 .0
❑ 402 Artimus Parker .20 .0
❑ 403 Gene Washington 49er .50 .2
❑ 404 Herman Edwards .50 .2
❑ 405 Craig Morton 1.00 .4
❑ 406 Alan Page 1.00 .4
❑ 407 Larry McCarren .20 .0
❑ 408 Tony Galbreath .50 .2
❑ 409 Roman Gabriel 1.00 .4
❑ 410 Efren Herrera .20 .0
❑ 411 Jim Smith RC 1.00 .4
❑ 412 Bill Bryant .20 .0
❑ 413 Doug Dieken .20 .0
❑ 414 Marvin Cobb .20 .0
❑ 415 Fred Biletnikoff 2.00 .7
❑ 416 Joe Theismann 2.50 1.0
❑ 417 Roland Harper .20 .0
❑ 418 Derrel Luce .20 .0
❑ 419 Ralph Perretta .20 .0
❑ 420 Louis Wright RC 1.00 .4
❑ 421 Prentice McCray .20 .0
❑ 422 Garry Puetz .20 .0
❑ 423 Alfred Jenkins RC 1.00 .4
❑ 424 Paul Seymour .20 .0
❑ 425 Garo Yepremian .50 .2
❑ 426 Emmitt Thomas .20 .0
❑ 427 Dexter Bussey .20 .0
❑ 428 John Sanders .20 .0
❑ 429 Ed Too Tall Jones 2.00 .7
❑ 430 Ron Yary 1.00 .4
❑ 431 Frank Lewis .50 .2
❑ 432 Jerry Golsteyn .20 .0
❑ 433 Clarence Scott .20 .0
❑ 434 Pete Johnson RC 1.00 .4
❑ 435 Charle Young .50 .2
❑ 436 Harold McLinton .20 .0
❑ 437 Noah Jackson .20 .0
❑ 438 Bruce Laird .20 .0
❑ 439 John Matuszak .50 .2
❑ 440 Nat Moore .50 .2
❑ 441 Leon Gray .20 .07
❑ 442 Jerome Barkum .20 .07
❑ 443 Steve Largent 12.00 6.0
❑ 444 John Zook .20 .07
❑ 445 Preston Pearson .50 .20
❑ 446 Conrad Dobler .50 .20
❑ 447 Wilbur Summers .20 .07
❑ 448 Lou Piccone .20 .07
❑ 449 Ron Jaworski 1.00 .40
❑ 450 Jack Ham 1.50 .60
❑ 451 Mick Tingelhoff .50 .20
❑ 452 Clyde Powers .20 .07
❑ 453 John Cappelletti 1.00 .40
❑ 454 Dick Ambrose .20 .07
❑ 455 Lemar Parrish .20 .07
❑ 456 Ron Saul .20 .07
❑ 457 Bob Parsons .20 .07
❑ 458 Glenn Doughty .20 .07
❑ 459 Don Woods .20 .07
❑ 460 Art Shell 1.00 .40
❑ 461 Sam Hunt .20 .07
❑ 462 Lawrence Pillers .20 .07
❑ 463 Henry Childs .20 .07
❑ 464 Roger Wehrli .20 .07
❑ 465 Otis Armstrong .50 .20
❑ 466 Bob Baumhower RC 2.00 .75
❑ 467 Ray Jarvis .20 .07
❑ 468 Guy Morriss .20 .07
❑ 469 Matt Blair .50 .20
❑ 470 Billy Joe DuPree .50 .20
❑ 471 Roland Hooks .20 .07
❑ 472 Joe Danelo .20 .07
❑ 473 Reggie Rucker .50 .20
❑ 474 Vern Holland .20 .07
❑ 475 Mel Blount 1.50 .60
❑ 476 Eddie Brown S .20 .07
❑ 477 Bo Rather .20 .07
❑ 478 Don McCauley .20 .07
❑ 479 Glen Walker .20 .07
❑ 480 Randy Gradishar 1.00 .40
❑ 481 Dave Rowe .20 .07
❑ 482 Pat Leahy .50 .20
❑ 483 Mike Fuller .20 .07
❑ 484 David Lewis RC .20 .07
❑ 485 Steve Grogan 1.00 .40
❑ 486 Mel Gray .50 .20

❑	487 Eddie Payton RC	.50	.20
❑	488 Checklist 397-528	1.00	.40
❑	489 Stu Voigt	.20	.07
❑	490 Rolland Lawrence	.20	.07
❑	491 Nick Mike-Mayer	.20	.07
❑	492 Troy Archer	.20	.07
❑	493 Benny Malone	.20	.07
❑	494 Golden Richards	.50	.20
❑	495 Chris Hanburger	.20	.07
❑	496 Dwight Harrison	.20	.07
❑	497 Gary Fencik RC	1.00	.40
❑	498 Rich Saul	.20	.07
❑	499 Dan Fouts	4.00	2.00
❑	500 Franco Harris	4.00	2.00
❑	501 Atlanta Falcons TL	.75	.30
❑	502 Baltimore Colts TL	.75	.30
❑	503 Bills TL/O.J.Simpson	1.50	.60
❑	504 Bears TL/Walter Payton	2.00	.75
❑	505 Bengals TL/Reg.Williams	.75	.30
❑	506 Cleveland Browns TL	.75	.30
❑	507 Cowboys TL/T.Dorsett	2.50	1.00
❑	508 Denver Broncos TL	1.00	.40
❑	509 Detroit Lions TL	.75	.30
❑	510 Green Bay Packers TL	1.00	.40
❑	511 Houston Oilers TL	.75	.30
❑	512 Kansas City Chiefs TL	.75	.30
❑	513 Los Angeles Rams TL	.75	.30
❑	514 Miami Dolphins TL	1.00	.40
❑	515 Minnesota Vikings TL	.75	.30
❑	516 New England Patriots TL	.75	.30
❑	517 New Orleans Saints TL	.75	.30
❑	518 New York Giants TL	.75	.30
❑	519 Jets TL/Wesley Walker	.75	.30
❑	520 Oakland Raiders TL	1.00	.40
❑	521 Philadelphia Eagles TL	.75	.30
❑	522 Steelers TL/Harris/Blount	1.00	.40
❑	523 St.Louis Cardinals TL	.75	.30
❑	524 San Diego Chargers TL	1.00	.40
❑	525 San Francisco 49ers TL	.75	.30
❑	526 Seahawks TL/S.Largent	1.50	.60
❑	527 Tampa Bay Bucs TL	.75	.30
❑	528 Redskins TL/Ken Houston	1.00	.40

1979 Topps

❑	COMPLETE SET (528)	150.00	75.00
❑	1 Staubach/Bradshaw LL	8.00	4.00
❑	2 S.Largent/R.Young LL	1.00	.40
❑	3 E.Campbell/W.Payton LL	8.00	4.00
❑	4 Scoring Leaders	.20	.07
❑	5 Interception Leaders	.20	.07
❑	6 Punting Leaders	.20	.07
❑	7 Johnny Perkins	.20	.07
❑	8 Charles Phillips	.20	.07
❑	9 Derrel Luce	.20	.07
❑	10 John Riggins	1.25	.50
❑	11 Chester Marcol	.20	.07
❑	12 Bernard Jackson	.20	.07
❑	13 Dave Logan	.20	.07
❑	14 Bo Harris	.20	.07
❑	15 Alan Page	1.00	.40
❑	16 John Smith	.20	.07
❑	17 Dwight McDonald	.20	.07
❑	18 John Cappelletti	.50	.20
❑	19 Steelers TL/Harris/Dungy	1.00	.40
❑	20 Bill Bergey	.50	.20
❑	21 Jerome Barkum	.20	.07
❑	22 Larry Csonka	2.50	1.00
❑	23 Joe Ferguson	.50	.20
❑	24 Ed Too Tall Jones	1.25	.50
❑	25 Dave Jennings	.50	.20
❑	26 Horace King	.20	.07
❑	27 Steve Little	.50	.20
❑	28 Morris Bradshaw	.20	.07
❑	29 Joe Ehrmann	.20	.07
❑	30 Ahmad Rashad	1.00	.40
❑	31 Joe Lavender	.20	.07
❑	32 Dan Neal	.20	.07
❑	33 Johnny Evans	.20	.07
❑	34 Pete Johnson	.50	.20
❑	35 Mike Haynes	1.00	.40
❑	36 Tim Mazzetti	.20	.07
❑	37 Mike Barber RC	.20	.07
❑	38 49ers TL/O.J.Simpson	1.50	.60
❑	39 Bill Gregory	.20	.07
❑	40 Randy Gradishar	1.00	.40
❑	41 Richard Todd	.50	.20
❑	42 Henry Marshall	.20	.07
❑	43 John Hill	.20	.07
❑	44 Sidney Thornton	.20	.07
❑	45 Ron Jessie	.20	.07
❑	46 Bob Baumhower	.50	.20
❑	47 Johnnie Gray	.20	.07
❑	48 Doug Williams RC	6.00	3.00
❑	49 Don McCauley	.20	.07
❑	50 Ray Guy	.50	.20
❑	51 Bob Klein	.20	.07
❑	52 Golden Richards	.20	.07
❑	53 Mark Miller QB	.20	.07
❑	54 John Sanders	.20	.07
❑	55 Gary Burley	.20	.07
❑	56 Steve Nelson	.20	.07
❑	57 Buffalo Bills TL	.75	.30
❑	58 Bobby Bryant	.20	.07
❑	59 Rick Kane	.20	.07
❑	60 Larry Little	1.00	.40
❑	61 Ted Fritsch Jr.	.20	.07
❑	62 Larry Mallory	.20	.07
❑	63 Marvin Powell	.20	.07
❑	64 Jim Hart	1.00	.40
❑	65 Joe Greene	1.50	.60
❑	66 Walter White	.20	.07
❑	67 Gregg Bingham	.20	.07
❑	68 Errol Mann	.20	.07
❑	69 Bruce Laird	.20	.07
❑	70 Drew Pearson	1.00	.40
❑	71 Steve Bartkowski	1.00	.40
❑	72 Ted Albrecht	.20	.07
❑	73 Charlie Hall	.20	.07
❑	74 Pat McInally	.20	.07
❑	75 Bubba Baker RC	1.00	.40
❑	76 New England Pats TL	.75	.30
❑	77 Steve DeBerg RC	2.00	.75
❑	78 John Yarno	.20	.07
❑	79 Stu Voigt	.20	.07
❑	80 Frank Corral AP	.20	.07
❑	81 Troy Archer	.20	.07
❑	82 Bruce Harper	.20	.07
❑	83 Tom Jackson	1.50	.60
❑	84 Larry Brown	.50	.20
❑	85 Wilbert Montgomery RC	1.00	.40
❑	86 Butch Johnson	.50	.20
❑	87 Mike Kadish	.20	.07
❑	88 Ralph Perretta	.20	.07
❑	89 David Lee	.20	.07
❑	90 Mark Van Eeghen	.50	.20
❑	91 John McDaniel	.20	.07
❑	92 Gary Fencik	.50	.20
❑	93 Mack Mitchell	.20	.07
❑	94 Cincinnati Bengals TL/Jauron	1.00	.40
❑	95 Steve Grogan	1.00	.40
❑	96 Garo Yepremian	.50	.20
❑	97 Barty Smith	.20	.07
❑	98 Frank Reed	.20	.07
❑	99 Jim Clack	.20	.07
❑	100 Chuck Foreman	.50	.20
❑	101 Joe Klecko	1.00	.40
❑	102 Pat Tilley	.50	.20
❑	103 Conrad Dobler	.50	.20
❑	104 Craig Colquitt	.20	.07
❑	105 Dan Pastorini	.50	.20
❑	106 Rod Perry AP	.20	.07
❑	107 Nick Mike-Mayer	.20	.07
❑	108 John Matuszak	.50	.20
❑	109 David Taylor	.20	.07
❑	110 Billy Joe DuPree	.50	.20
❑	111 Harold McLinton	.20	.07
❑	112 Virgil Livers	.20	.07
❑	113 Cleveland Browns TL	.75	.30
❑	114 Checklist 1-132	1.00	.40
❑	115 Ken Anderson	1.00	.40
❑	116 Bill Lenkaitis	.20	.07
❑	117 Bucky Dilts	.20	.07
❑	118 Tony Greene	.20	.07
❑	119 Bobby Hammond	.20	.07
❑	120 Nat Moore	.50	.20
❑	121 Pat Leahy	.50	.20
❑	122 James Harris	.50	.20
❑	123 Lee Roy Selmon	1.25	.50
❑	124 Bennie Cunningham	.50	.20
❑	125 Matt Blair AP	.50	.20
❑	126 Jim Allen	.20	.07
❑	127 Alfred Jenkins	.50	.20
❑	128 Arthur Whittington	.20	.07
❑	129 Norm Thompson	.20	.07
❑	130 Pat Haden	1.00	.40
❑	131 Freddie Solomon	.20	.07
❑	132 Bears TL/W.Payton	2.00	.75
❑	133 Mark Moseley	.20	.07
❑	134 Cleo Miller	.20	.07
❑	135 Ross Browner RC	.50	.20
❑	136 Don Calhoun	.20	.07
❑	137 David Whitehurst	.20	.07
❑	138 Terry Beeson	.20	.07
❑	139 Ken Stone	.20	.07
❑	140 Brad Van Pelt AP	.20	.07
❑	141 Wesley Walker	1.00	.40
❑	142 Jan Stenerud	1.00	.40
❑	143 Henry Childs	.20	.07
❑	144 Otis Armstrong	1.00	.40
❑	145 Dwight White	.50	.20
❑	146 Steve Wilson	.20	.07
❑	147 Tom Skladany RC	.20	.07
❑	148 Lou Piccone	.20	.07
❑	149 Monte Johnson	.20	.07
❑	150 Joe Washington	.50	.20
❑	151 Eagles TL/W.Montgomery	.75	.30
❑	152 Fred Dean	.20	.07
❑	153 Rolland Lawrence	.20	.07
❑	154 Brian Baschnagel	.20	.07
❑	155 Joe Theismann	2.00	.75
❑	156 Marvin Cobb	.20	.07
❑	157 Dick Ambrose	.20	.07
❑	158 Mike Patrick	.20	.07
❑	159 Gary Shirk	.20	.07
❑	160 Tony Dorsett	12.00	6.00
❑	161 Greg Buttle	.20	.07
❑	162 A.J. Duhe	.50	.20
❑	163 Mick Tingelhoff	.50	.20
❑	164 Ken Burrough	.50	.20
❑	165 Mike Wagner	.20	.07
❑	166 AFC Champs/F.Harris	1.00	.40
❑	167 NFC Championship	.50	.20
❑	168 Super Bowl XIII/Harris	1.25	.50
❑	169 Raiders TL/Ted Hendricks	1.00	.40
❑	170 O.J.Simpson	4.00	1.50
❑	171 Doug Nettles	.20	.07
❑	172 Dan Dierdorf	1.00	.40
❑	173 Dave Beverly	.20	.07
❑	174 Jim Zorn	1.00	.40
❑	175 Mike Thomas	.20	.07
❑	176 John Outlaw	.20	.07
❑	177 Jim Turner	.20	.07
❑	178 Freddie Scott	.20	.07
❑	179 Mike Phipps	.50	.20
❑	180 Jack Youngblood	1.00	.40
❑	181 Sam Hunt	.20	.07
❑	182 Tony Hill RC	1.00	.40
❑	183 Gary Barbaro	.20	.07
❑	184 Archie Griffin	.50	.20
❑	185 Jerry Sherk	.20	.07
❑	186 Bobby Jackson	.20	.07
❑	187 Don Woods	.20	.07
❑	188 New York Giants TL	.75	.30
❑	189 Raymond Chester	.20	.07
❑	190 Joe DeLamielleure AP	1.00	.40
❑	191 Tony Galbreath	.50	.20
❑	192 Robert Brazile AP	.50	.20
❑	193 Neil O'Donoghue	.20	.07
❑	194 Mike Webster	1.00	.40
❑	195 Ed Simonini	.20	.07
❑	196 Benny Malone	.20	.07
❑	197 Tom Wittum	.20	.07
❑	198 Steve Largent	8.00	4.00

❑ 199 Tommy Hart .20 .07
❑ 200 Fran Tarkenton 3.00 1.50
❑ 201 Leon Gray AP .20 .07
❑ 202 Leroy Harris .20 .07
❑ 203 Eric Williams LB .20 .07
❑ 204 Thom Darden AP .20 .07
❑ 205 Ken Riley .50 .20
❑ 206 Clark Gaines .20 .07
❑ 207 Kansas City Chiefs TL .75 .30
❑ 208 Joe Danelo .20 .07
❑ 209 Glen Walker .20 .07
❑ 210 Art Shell 1.00 .40
❑ 211 Jon Keyworth .20 .07
❑ 212 Herman Edwards .20 .07
❑ 213 John Fitzgerald .20 .07
❑ 214 Jim Smith .50 .20
❑ 215 Coy Bacon .50 .20
❑ 216 Dennis Johnson RBK RC .20 .07
❑ 217 John Jefferson RC 3.00 1.50
❑ 218 Gary Weaver .20 .07
❑ 219 Tom Blanchard .20 .07
❑ 220 Bert Jones 1.00 .40
❑ 221 Stanley Morgan 1.00 .40
❑ 222 James Hunter .20 .07
❑ 223 Jim O'Bradovich .20 .07
❑ 224 Carl Mauck .20 .07
❑ 225 Chris Bahr .20 .07
❑ 226 Jets TL/Wesley Walker .75 .30
❑ 227 Roland Harper .20 .07
❑ 228 Randy Dean .20 .07
❑ 229 Bob Jackson .20 .07
❑ 230 Sammie White .50 .20
❑ 231 Mike Dawson .20 .07
❑ 232 Checklist 133-264 1.00 .40
❑ 233 Ken MacAfee RC .20 .07
❑ 234 Jon Kolb AP .20 .07
❑ 235 Willie Hall .20 .07
❑ 236 Ron Saul AP .20 .07
❑ 237 Haskel Stanback .20 .07
❑ 238 Zenon Andrusyshyn .20 .07
❑ 239 Norris Thomas .20 .07
❑ 240 Rick Upchurch .50 .20
❑ 241 Robert Pratt .20 .07
❑ 242 Julius Adams .20 .07
❑ 243 Rich McGeorge .20 .07
❑ 244 Seahawks TL/S.Largent 1.25 .50
❑ 245 Blair Bush RC .20 .07
❑ 246 Billy Johnson .50 .20
❑ 247 Randy Rasmussen .20 .07
❑ 248 Brian Kelley .20 .07
❑ 249 Mike Pruitt .50 .20
❑ 250 Harold Carmichael 1.00 .40
❑ 251 Mike Hartenstine .20 .07
❑ 252 Robert Newhouse .50 .20
❑ 253 Gary Danielson RC 1.00 .40
❑ 254 Mike Fuller .20 .07
❑ 255 L.C.Greenwood 1.00 .40
❑ 256 Lemar Parrish .20 .07
❑ 257 Ike Harris .20 .07
❑ 258 Ricky Bell RC 1.00 .40
❑ 259 Willie Parker C .20 .07
❑ 260 Gene Upshaw 1.00 .40
❑ 261 Glenn Doughty .20 .07
❑ 262 Steve Zabel .20 .07
❑ 263 Atlanta Falcons TL .75 .30
❑ 264 Ray Wersching .20 .07
❑ 265 Lawrence McCutcheon .50 .20
❑ 266 Willie Buchanon AP .20 .07
❑ 267 Matt Robinson .20 .07
❑ 268 Reggie Rucker .50 .20
❑ 269 Doug Van Horn .20 .07
❑ 270 Lydell Mitchell .50 .20
❑ 271 Vern Holland .20 .07
❑ 272 Eason Ramson .20 .07
❑ 273 Steve Towle .20 .07
❑ 274 Jim Marshall 1.00 .40
❑ 275 Mel Blount 1.25 .50
❑ 276 Bob Kuziel .20 .07
❑ 277 James Scott .20 .07
❑ 278 Tony Reed .20 .07
❑ 279 Dave Green .20 .07
❑ 280 Toni Linhart .20 .07
❑ 281 Andy Johnson .20 .07
❑ 282 Los Angeles Rams TL .75 .30
❑ 283 Phil Villapiano .50 .20
❑ 284 Dexter Bussey .20 .07
❑ 285 Craig Morton 1.00 .40
❑ 286 Guy Morriss .20 .07
❑ 287 Lawrence Pillers .20 .07
❑ 288 Gerald Irons .20 .07
❑ 289 Scott Perry .20 .07
❑ 290 Randy White 2.00 .75
❑ 291 Jack Gregory .20 .07
❑ 292 Bob Chandler .20 .07
❑ 293 Rich Szaro .20 .07
❑ 294 Sherman Smith .20 .07
❑ 295 Tom Banks AP .20 .07
❑ 296 Revie Sorey AP .20 .07
❑ 297 Ricky Thompson .20 .07
❑ 298 Ron Yary 1.00 .40
❑ 299 Lyle Blackwood .20 .07
❑ 300 Franco Harris 2.50 1.25
❑ 301 Oilers TL/E.Campbell 3.00 1.50
❑ 302 Scott Bull .20 .07
❑ 303 Dewey Selmon .50 .20
❑ 304 Jack Rudnay .20 .07
❑ 305 Fred Biletnikoff 2.00 .75
❑ 306 Jeff West .20 .07
❑ 307 Shafer Suggs .20 .07
❑ 308 Ozzie Newsome RC 12.00 6.00
❑ 309 Boobie Clark .20 .07
❑ 310 James Lofton RC 12.00 6.00
❑ 311 Joe Pisarcik .20 .07
❑ 312 Bill Simpson AP .20 .07
❑ 313 Haven Moses .50 .20
❑ 314 Jim Merlo .20 .07
❑ 315 Preston Pearson .50 .20
❑ 316 Larry Tearry .20 .07
❑ 317 Tom Dempsey .20 .07
❑ 318 Greg Latta .20 .07
❑ 319 Redskins TL/John Riggins 1.50 .60
❑ 320 Jack Ham 1.25 .50
❑ 321 Harold Jackson .50 .20
❑ 322 George Roberts .20 .07
❑ 323 Ron Jaworski 1.00 .40
❑ 324 Jim Otis .20 .07
❑ 325 Roger Carr .50 .20
❑ 326 Jack Tatum .50 .20
❑ 327 Derrick Gaffney .20 .07
❑ 328 Reggie Williams 1.00 .40
❑ 329 Doug Dieken .20 .07
❑ 330 Efren Herrera .20 .07
❑ 331 Earl Campbell RB 6.00 3.00
❑ 332 Tony Galbreath RB .20 .07
❑ 333 Bruce Harper RB .20 .07
❑ 334 John James RB .20 .07
❑ 335 Walter Payton RB 4.00 1.50
❑ 336 Rickey Young RB .20 .07
❑ 337 Jeff Van Note .50 .20
❑ 338 Chargers TL/J.Jefferson 1.00 .40
❑ 339 Stan Walters RC .20 .07
❑ 340 Louis Wright .50 .20
❑ 341 Horace Ivory .20 .07
❑ 342 Andre Tillman .20 .07
❑ 343 Greg Coleman RC .20 .07
❑ 344 Doug English RC 1.00 .40
❑ 345 Ted Hendricks 1.00 .40
❑ 346 Rich Saul .20 .07
❑ 347 Mel Gray .50 .20
❑ 348 Toni Fritsch .20 .07
❑ 349 Cornell Webster .20 .07
❑ 350 Ken Houston 1.00 .40
❑ 351 Ron Johnson DB RC .50 .20
❑ 352 Doug Kotar .20 .07
❑ 353 Brian Sipe 1.00 .40
❑ 354 Billy Brooks .20 .07
❑ 355 John Dutton .50 .20
❑ 356 Don Goode .20 .07
❑ 357 Detroit Lions TL .75 .30
❑ 358 Reuben Gant .20 .07
❑ 359 Bob Parsons .20 .07
❑ 360 Cliff Harris 1.00 .40
❑ 361 Raymond Clayborn .50 .20
❑ 362 Scott Dierking .20 .07
❑ 363 Bill Bryan .20 .07
❑ 364 Mike Livingston .20 .07
❑ 365 Otis Sistrunk .50 .20
❑ 366 Charle Young .50 .20
❑ 367 Keith Wortman .20 .07
❑ 368 Checklist 265-396 1.00 .40
❑ 369 Mike Michel .20 .07
❑ 370 Delvin Williams AP .20 .07
❑ 371 Steve Furness .50 .20
❑ 372 Emery Moorehead .20 .07
❑ 373 Clarence Scott .20 .07
❑ 374 Rufus Mayes .20 .07
❑ 375 Chris Hanburger .20 .07
❑ 376 Baltimore Colts TL .75 .30
❑ 377 Bob Avellini .50 .20
❑ 378 Jeff Siemon .20 .07
❑ 379 Roland Hooks .20 .07
❑ 380 Russ Francis .50 .20
❑ 381 Roger Wehrli .20 .07
❑ 382 Joe Fields .20 .07
❑ 383 Archie Manning 1.00 .40
❑ 384 Rob Lytle .20 .07
❑ 385 Thomas Henderson .50 .20
❑ 386 Morris Owens .20 .07
❑ 387 Dan Fouts 3.00 1.50
❑ 388 Chuck Crist .20 .07
❑ 389 Ed O'Neil .20 .07
❑ 390 Earl Campbell RC 30.00 15.00
❑ 391 Randy Grossman .20 .07
❑ 392 Monte Jackson .20 .07
❑ 393 John Mendenhall .20 .07
❑ 394 Miami Dolphins TL 1.00 .40
❑ 395 Isaac Curtis .50 .20
❑ 396 Mike Bragg .20 .07
❑ 397 Doug Plank .20 .07
❑ 398 Mike Barnes .20 .07
❑ 399 Calvin Hill .50 .20
❑ 400 Roger Staubach 10.00 5.00
❑ 401 Doug Beaudoin .20 .07
❑ 402 Chuck Ramsey .20 .07
❑ 403 Mike Hogan .20 .07
❑ 404 Mario Clark .20 .07
❑ 405 Riley Odoms .20 .07
❑ 406 Carl Eller 1.00 .40
❑ 407 Packers TL/J.Lofton 1.50 .60
❑ 408 Mark Arneson .20 .07
❑ 409 Vince Ferragamo RC 1.00 .40
❑ 410 Cleveland Elam .20 .07
❑ 411 Donnie Shell RC 4.00 1.50
❑ 412 Ray Rhodes 1.00 .40
❑ 413 Don Cockroft .20 .07
❑ 414 Don Bass .50 .20
❑ 415 Cliff Branch 1.00 .40
❑ 416 Diron Talbert .20 .07
❑ 417 Tom Hicks .20 .07
❑ 418 Roosevelt Leaks .20 .07
❑ 419 Charlie Joiner 1.00 .40
❑ 420 Lyle Alzado 1.00 .40
❑ 421 Sam Cunningham .50 .20
❑ 422 Larry Keller .20 .07
❑ 423 Jim Mitchell TE .20 .07
❑ 424 Randy Logan .20 .07
❑ 425 Jim Langer 1.00 .40
❑ 426 Gary Green .20 .07
❑ 427 Luther Blue .20 .07
❑ 428 Dennis Johnson .20 .07
❑ 429 Danny White 1.00 .40
❑ 430 Roy Gerela .20 .07
❑ 431 Jimmy Robinson .20 .07
❑ 432 Minnesota Vikings TL .75 .30
❑ 433 Oliver Davis .20 .07
❑ 434 Lenvil Elliott .20 .07
❑ 435 Willie Miller RC .20 .07
❑ 436 Brad Dusek .20 .07
❑ 437 Bob Thomas .20 .07
❑ 438 Ken Mendenhall .20 .07
❑ 439 Clarence Davis .20 .07
❑ 440 Bob Griese 2.50 1.00
❑ 441 Tony McGee DT .20 .07
❑ 442 Ed Taylor .20 .07
❑ 443 Ron Howard .20 .07
❑ 444 Wayne Morris .20 .07
❑ 445 Charlie Waters .50 .20
❑ 446 Rick Danmeier .20 .07
❑ 447 Paul Naumoff .20 .07
❑ 448 Keith Krepfle .20 .07
❑ 449 Rusty Jackson .20 .07
❑ 450 John Stallworth 4.00 2.00
❑ 451 New Orleans Saints TL .75 .30
❑ 452 Ron Mikolajczyk .20 .07
❑ 453 Fred Dryer 1.00 .40
❑ 454 Jim LeClair .20 .07
❑ 455 Greg Pruitt .50 .20
❑ 456 Jake Scott .20 .07
❑ 457 Steve Schubert .20 .07
❑ 458 George Kunz .20 .07
❑ 459 Mike Williams .20 .07

❑ 460 Dave Casper AP 1.00 .40
❑ 461 Sam Adams OL .20 .07
❑ 462 Abdul Salaam .20 .07
❑ 463 Terdell Middleton .50 .20
❑ 464 Mike Wood .20 .07
❑ 465 Bill Thompson AP .20 .07
❑ 466 Larry Gordon .20 .07
❑ 467 Benny Ricardo .20 .07
❑ 468 Reggie McKenzie .50 .20
❑ 469 Cowboys TL/T.Dorsett 1.50 .60
❑ 470 Rickey Young .50 .20
❑ 471 Charlie Smith WR .20 .07
❑ 472 Al Dixon .20 .07
❑ 473 Tom DeLeone .20 .07
❑ 474 Louis Breeden .50 .20
❑ 475 Jack Lambert 2.00 .75
❑ 476 Terry Hermeling .20 .07
❑ 477 J.K. McKay .20 .07
❑ 478 Stan White .20 .07
❑ 479 Terry Nelson .20 .07
❑ 480 Walter Payton 20.00 10.00
❑ 481 Dave Dalby .20 .07
❑ 482 Burgess Owens .20 .07
❑ 483 Rolf Benirschke .20 .07
❑ 484 Jack Dolbin .20 .07
❑ 485 John Hannah 1.00 .40
❑ 486 Checklist 397-528 1.00 .40
❑ 487 Greg Landry .50 .20
❑ 488 St. Louis Cardinals TL .75 .30
❑ 489 Paul Krause 1.00 .40
❑ 490 John James .20 .07
❑ 491 Merv Krakau .20 .07
❑ 492 Dan Doornink .20 .07
❑ 493 Curtis Johnson .20 .07
❑ 494 Rafael Septien .20 .07
❑ 495 Jean Fugett .20 .07
❑ 496 Frank LeMaster .20 .07
❑ 497 Allan Ellis .20 .07
❑ 498 Billy Waddy RC .50 .20
❑ 499 Hank Bauer .20 .07
❑ 500 Terry Bradshaw UER 10.00 5.00
❑ 501 Larry McCarren .20 .07
❑ 502 Fred Cook .20 .07
❑ 503 Chuck Muncie .50 .20
❑ 504 Herman Weaver .20 .07
❑ 505 Eddie Edwards .20 .07
❑ 506 Tony Peters .20 .07
❑ 507 Denver Broncos TL .75 .30
❑ 508 Jimbo Elrod .20 .07
❑ 509 David Hill .20 .07
❑ 510 Harvey Martin .50 .20
❑ 511 Terry Miller .50 .20
❑ 512 June Jones RC .50 .20
❑ 513 Randy Cross 1.00 .40
❑ 514 Duriel Harris .20 .07
❑ 515 Harry Carson 1.00 .40
❑ 516 Tim Fox .20 .07
❑ 517 John Zook .20 .07
❑ 518 Bob Tucker .20 .07
❑ 519 Kevin Long RC .20 .07
❑ 520 Ken Stabler 6.00 3.00
❑ 521 John Bunting .50 .20
❑ 522 Rocky Bleier 1.25 .50
❑ 523 Noah Jackson .20 .07
❑ 524 Cliff Parsley .20 .07
❑ 525 Louie Kelcher AP .50 .20
❑ 526 Bucs TL/Ricky Bell .75 .30
❑ 527 Bob Brudzinski RC .20 .07
❑ 528 Danny Buggs .20 .07

1980 Topps

❑ COMPLETE SET (528) 75.00 40.00
❑ 1 Ottis Anderson RB 1.00 .40
❑ 2 Harold Carmichael RB 1.00 .40
❑ 3 Dan Fouts RB 1.00 .40
❑ 4 Paul Krause RB .50 .20
❑ 5 Rick Upchurch RB .50 .20
❑ 6 Garo Yepremian RB .20 .07
❑ 7 Harold Jackson .50 .20
❑ 8 Mike Williams .20 .07
❑ 9 Calvin Hill .50 .20
❑ 10 Jack Ham 1.00 .40
❑ 11 Dan Melville .20 .07
❑ 12 Matt Robinson .20 .07
❑ 13 Billy Campfield .20 .07
❑ 14 Phil Tabor .20 .07
❑ 15 Randy Hughes UER .20 .07

❑ 16 Andre Tillman .20 .07
❑ 17 Isaac Curtis .50 .20
❑ 18 Charley Hannah .20 .07
❑ 19 Redskins TL/J.Riggins 1.00 .40
❑ 20 Jim Zorn .50 .20
❑ 21 Brian Baschnagel .20 .07
❑ 22 Jon Keyworth .20 .07
❑ 23 Phil Villapiano .20 .07
❑ 24 Richard Osborne .20 .07
❑ 25 Rich Saul AP .20 .07
❑ 26 Doug Beaudoin .20 .07
❑ 27 Cleveland Elam .20 .07
❑ 28 Charlie Joiner 1.00 .40
❑ 29 Dick Ambrose .20 .07
❑ 30 Mike Reinfeldt RC .20 .07
❑ 31 Matt Bahr RC 1.00 .40
❑ 32 Keith Krepfle .20 .07
❑ 33 Herb Scott .20 .07
❑ 34 Doug Kotar .20 .07
❑ 35 Bob Griese 1.50 .60
❑ 36 Jerry Butler RC 1.00 .40
❑ 37 Rolland Lawrence .20 .07
❑ 38 Gary Weaver .20 .07
❑ 39 Chiefs TL/J.T.Smith .50 .20
❑ 40 Chuck Muncie .50 .20
❑ 41 Mike Hartenstine .20 .07
❑ 42 Sammie White .50 .20
❑ 43 Ken Clark .20 .07
❑ 44 Clarence Harmon .20 .07
❑ 45 Bert Jones 1.00 .40
❑ 46 Mike Washington .20 .07
❑ 47 Joe Fields .20 .07
❑ 48 Mike Wood .20 .07
❑ 49 Oliver Davis .20 .07
❑ 50 Stan Walters AP .20 .07
❑ 51 Riley Odoms .20 .07
❑ 52 Steve Pisarkiewicz .20 .07
❑ 53 Tony Hill 1.00 .40
❑ 54 Scott Perry .20 .07
❑ 55 George Martin RC .20 .07
❑ 56 George Roberts .20 .07
❑ 57 Seahawks TL/S. Largent 1.00 .40
❑ 58 Billy Johnson .50 .20
❑ 59 Reuben Gant .20 .07
❑ 60 Dennis Harrah RC .20 .07
❑ 61 Rocky Bleier 1.00 .40
❑ 62 Sam Hunt .20 .07
❑ 63 Allan Ellis .20 .07
❑ 64 Ricky Thompson .20 .07
❑ 65 Ken Stabler 4.00 2.00
❑ 66 Dexter Bussey .20 .07
❑ 67 Ken Mendenhall .20 .07
❑ 68 Woodrow Lowe .20 .07
❑ 69 Thom Darden .20 .07
❑ 70 Randy White 1.50 .60
❑ 71 Ken MacAfee .20 .07
❑ 72 Ron Jaworski 1.00 .40
❑ 73 William Andrews RC 1.00 .40
❑ 74 Jimmy Robinson .20 .07
❑ 75 Roger Wehrli AP .20 .07
❑ 76 Dolphins TL/L.Csonka 1.00 .40
❑ 77 Jack Rudnay .20 .07
❑ 78 James Lofton 2.00 .75
❑ 79 Robert Brazile .50 .20
❑ 80 Russ Francis .50 .20
❑ 81 Ricky Bell 1.00 .40
❑ 82 Bob Avellini .50 .20
❑ 83 Bobby Jackson .20 .07
❑ 84 Mike Bragg .20 .07
❑ 85 Cliff Branch 1.00 .40
❑ 86 Blair Bush .20 .07
❑ 87 Sherman Smith .20 .07
❑ 88 Glen Edwards .20 .07
❑ 89 Don Cockroft .20 .07
❑ 90 Louis Wright .50 .20
❑ 91 Randy Grossman .20 .07
❑ 92 Carl Hairston RC 1.00 .40
❑ 93 Archie Manning 1.00 .40
❑ 94 New York Giants TL .50 .20
❑ 95 Preston Pearson .50 .20
❑ 96 Rusty Chambers .20 .07
❑ 97 Greg Coleman .20 .07
❑ 98 Charle Young .20 .07
❑ 99 Matt Cavanaugh RC .50 .20
❑ 100 Jesse Baker .20 .07
❑ 101 Doug Plank .20 .07
❑ 102 Checklist 1-132 .75 .30
❑ 103 Luther Bradley RC .20 .07
❑ 104 Bob Kuziel .20 .07
❑ 105 Craig Morton .50 .20
❑ 106 Sherman White .20 .07
❑ 107 Jim Breech RC .50 .20
❑ 108 Hank Bauer .20 .07
❑ 109 Tom Blanchard .20 .07
❑ 110 Ozzie Newsome 2.00 .75
❑ 111 Steve Furness .20 .07
❑ 112 Frank LeMaster .20 .07
❑ 113 Cowboys TL/T.Dorsett 1.00 .40
❑ 114 Doug Van Horn .20 .07
❑ 115 Delvin Williams .20 .07
❑ 116 Lyle Blackwood .20 .07
❑ 117 Derrick Gaffney .20 .07
❑ 118 Cornell Webster .20 .07
❑ 119 Sam Cunningham .50 .20
❑ 120 Jim Youngblood AP .50 .20
❑ 121 Bob Thomas .20 .07
❑ 122 Jack Thompson RC .50 .20
❑ 123 Randy Cross 1.00 .40
❑ 124 Karl Lorch RC .20 .07
❑ 125 Mel Gray .20 .07
❑ 126 John James .20 .07
❑ 127 Terdell Middleton .20 .07
❑ 128 Leroy Jones .20 .07
❑ 129 Tom DeLeone .20 .07
❑ 130 John Stallworth 1.50 .60
❑ 131 Jimmie Giles RC .50 .20
❑ 132 Philadelphia Eagles TL 1.00 .40
❑ 133 Gary Green .20 .07
❑ 134 John Dutton .50 .20
❑ 135 Harry Carson 1.00 .40
❑ 136 Bob Kuechenberg .50 .20
❑ 137 Ike Harris .20 .07
❑ 138 Tommy Kramer RC 1.00 .40
❑ 139 Sam Adams OL .20 .07
❑ 140 Doug English .50 .20
❑ 141 Steve Schubert .20 .07
❑ 142 Rusty Jackson .20 .07
❑ 143 Reese McCall .20 .07
❑ 144 Scott Dierking .20 .07
❑ 145 Ken Houston 1.00 .40
❑ 146 Bob Martin .20 .07
❑ 147 Sam McCullum .20 .07
❑ 148 Tom Banks .20 .07
❑ 149 Willie Buchanon .20 .07
❑ 150 Greg Pruitt .50 .20
❑ 151 Denver Broncos TL 1.00 .40
❑ 152 Don Smith RC .20 .07
❑ 153 Pete Johnson .50 .20
❑ 154 Charlie Smith WR .20 .07
❑ 155 Mel Blount 1.00 .40
❑ 156 John Mendenhall .20 .07
❑ 157 Danny White 1.00 .40
❑ 158 Jimmy Cefalo RC .50 .20
❑ 159 Richard Bishop AP .20 .07
❑ 160 Walter Payton 12.00 6.00
❑ 161 Dave Dalby .20 .07
❑ 162 Preston Dennard .20 .07
❑ 163 Johnnie Gray .20 .07
❑ 164 Russell Erxleben .20 .07
❑ 165 Toni Fritsch AP .20 .07
❑ 166 Terry Hermeling .20 .07
❑ 167 Roland Hooks .20 .07
❑ 168 Roger Carr .20 .07
❑ 169 San Diego Chargers TL 1.00 .40
❑ 170 Ottis Anderson RC 4.00 1.50
❑ 171 Brian Sipe 1.00 .40
❑ 172 Leonard Thompson .20 .07

❑ 173	Tony Reed	.20	.07
❑ 174	Bob Tucker	.20	.07
❑ 175	Joe Greene	1.00	.40
❑ 176	Jack Dolbin	.20	.07
❑ 177	Chuck Ramsey	.20	.07
❑ 178	Paul Hofer	.20	.07
❑ 179	Randy Logan	.20	.07
❑ 180	David Lewis AP	.20	.07
❑ 181	Duriel Harris	.20	.07
❑ 182	June Jones	.50	.20
❑ 183	Larry McCarren	.20	.07
❑ 184	Ken Johnson RB	.20	.07
❑ 185	Charlie Waters	.50	.20
❑ 186	Noah Jackson	.20	.07
❑ 187	Reggie Williams	.50	.20
❑ 188	New England Patriots TL	.50	.20
❑ 189	Carl Eller	1.00	.40
❑ 190	Ed White AP	.20	.07
❑ 191	Mario Clark	.20	.07
❑ 192	Roosevelt Leaks	.20	.07
❑ 193	Ted McKnight	.20	.07
❑ 194	Danny Buggs	.20	.07
❑ 195	Lester Hayes RC	2.00	.75
❑ 196	Clarence Scott	.20	.07
❑ 197	Saints TL/Wes Chandler	.50	.20
❑ 198	Richard Caster	.20	.07
❑ 199	Louie Giammona	.20	.07
❑ 200	Terry Bradshaw	8.00	3.00
❑ 201	Ed Newman	.20	.07
❑ 202	Fred Dryer	1.00	.40
❑ 203	Dennis Franks	.20	.07
❑ 204	Bob Breunig RC	.50	.20
❑ 205	Alan Page	1.00	.40
❑ 206	Earnest Gray RC	.20	.07
❑ 207	Vikings TL/A.Rashad	1.00	.40
❑ 208	Horace Ivory	.20	.07
❑ 209	Isaac Hagins	.20	.07
❑ 210	Gary Johnson AP	.20	.07
❑ 211	Kevin Long	.20	.07
❑ 212	Bill Thompson	.20	.07
❑ 213	Don Bass	.20	.07
❑ 214	George Starke RC	.20	.07
❑ 215	Efren Herrera	.20	.07
❑ 216	Theo Bell	.20	.07
❑ 217	Monte Jackson	.20	.07
❑ 218	Reggie McKenzie	.20	.07
❑ 219	Bucky Dilts	.20	.07
❑ 220	Lyle Alzado	1.00	.40
❑ 221	Tim Foley	.20	.07
❑ 222	Mark Arneson	.20	.07
❑ 223	Fred Quillan	.20	.07
❑ 224	Benny Ricardo	.20	.07
❑ 225	Phil Simms RC	12.00	6.00
❑ 226	Bears TL/Walter Payton	1.25	.50
❑ 227	Max Runager	.20	.07
❑ 228	Barty Smith	.20	.07
❑ 229	Jay Saldi	.50	.20
❑ 230	John Hannah	1.00	.40
❑ 231	Tim Wilson	.20	.07
❑ 232	Jeff Van Note	.20	.07
❑ 233	Henry Marshall	.20	.07
❑ 234	Diron Talbert	.20	.07
❑ 235	Garo Yepremian	.50	.20
❑ 236	Larry Brown	.20	.07
❑ 237	Clarence Williams RB	.20	.07
❑ 238	Burgess Owens	.20	.07
❑ 239	Vince Ferragamo	.50	.20
❑ 240	Rickey Young	.20	.07
❑ 241	Dave Logan	.20	.07
❑ 242	Larry Gordon	.20	.07
❑ 243	Terry Miller	.20	.07
❑ 244	Baltimore Colts TL	1.00	.40
❑ 245	Steve DeBerg	1.00	.40
❑ 246	Checklist 133-264	.75	.30
❑ 247	Greg Latta	.20	.07
❑ 248	Raymond Clayborn	.50	.20
❑ 249	Jim Clack	.20	.07
❑ 250	Drew Pearson	1.00	.40
❑ 251	John Bunting	.50	.20
❑ 252	Rob Lytle	.20	.07
❑ 253	Jim Hart	1.00	.40
❑ 254	John McDaniel	.20	.07
❑ 255	Dave Pear AP	.20	.07
❑ 256	Donnie Shell	1.00	.40
❑ 257	Dan Doornink	.20	.07
❑ 258	Wallace Francis RC	1.00	.40
❑ 259	Dave Beverly	.20	.07
❑ 260	Lee Roy Selmon	1.00	.40
❑ 261	Doug Dieken	.20	.07
❑ 262	Gary Davis	.20	.07
❑ 263	Bob Rush	.20	.07
❑ 264	Buffalo Bills TL	.50	.20
❑ 265	Greg Landry	.50	.20
❑ 266	Jan Stenerud	1.00	.40
❑ 267	Tom Hicks	.20	.07
❑ 268	Pat McInally	.20	.07
❑ 269	Tim Fox	.20	.07
❑ 270	Harvey Martin	.50	.20
❑ 271	Dan Lloyd	.20	.07
❑ 272	Mike Barber	.20	.07
❑ 273	Wendell Tyler RC	1.00	.40
❑ 274	Jeff Komlo	.20	.07
❑ 275	Wes Chandler RC	1.00	.40
❑ 276	Brad Dusek	.20	.07
❑ 277	Charlie Johnson NT	.20	.07
❑ 278	Dennis Swilley	.20	.07
❑ 279	Johnny Evans	.20	.07
❑ 280	Jack Lambert	1.50	.60
❑ 281	Vern Den Herder	.20	.07
❑ 282	Tampa Bay Bucs TL	1.00	.40
❑ 283	Bob Klein	.20	.07
❑ 284	Jim Turner	.20	.07
❑ 285	Marvin Powell AP	.50	.20
❑ 286	Aaron Kyle	.20	.07
❑ 287	Dan Neal	.20	.07
❑ 288	Wayne Morris	.20	.07
❑ 289	Steve Bartkowski	.50	.20
❑ 290	Dave Jennings AP	.50	.20
❑ 291	John Smith	.20	.07
❑ 292	Bill Gregory	.20	.07
❑ 293	Frank Lewis	.20	.07
❑ 294	Fred Cook	.20	.07
❑ 295	David Hill AP	.20	.07
❑ 296	Wade Key	.20	.07
❑ 297	Sidney Thornton	.20	.07
❑ 298	Charlie Hall	.20	.07
❑ 299	Joe Lavender	.20	.07
❑ 300	Tom Rafferty RC	.20	.07
❑ 301	Mike Renfro RC	.50	.20
❑ 302	Wilbur Jackson	.50	.20
❑ 303	Packers TL/J.Lofton	1.00	.40
❑ 304	Henry Childs	.20	.07
❑ 305	Russ Washington AP	.20	.07
❑ 306	Jim LeClair	.20	.07
❑ 307	Tommy Hart	.20	.07
❑ 308	Gary Barbaro	.20	.07
❑ 309	Billy Taylor	.20	.07
❑ 310	Ray Guy	.50	.20
❑ 311	Don Hasselbeck RC	.50	.20
❑ 312	Doug Williams	1.00	.40
❑ 313	Nick Mike-Mayer	.20	.07
❑ 314	Don McCauley	.20	.07
❑ 315	Wesley Walker	1.00	.40
❑ 316	Dan Dierdorf	1.00	.40
❑ 317	Dave Brown DB RC	.50	.20
❑ 318	Leroy Harris	.20	.07
❑ 319	Steelers TL/Harris/Lambrt	1.00	.40
❑ 320	Mark Moseley AP UER	.20	.07
❑ 321	Mark Dennard	.20	.07
❑ 322	Terry Nelson	.20	.07
❑ 323	Tom Jackson	1.00	.40
❑ 324	Rick Kane	.20	.07
❑ 325	Jerry Sherk	.20	.07
❑ 326	Ray Preston	.20	.07
❑ 327	Golden Richards	.20	.07
❑ 328	Randy Dean	.20	.07
❑ 329	Rick Danmeier	.20	.07
❑ 330	Tony Dorsett	6.00	3.00
❑ 331	R.Staubach/Fouts LL	3.00	1.50
❑ 332	Receiving Leaders	.50	.20
❑ 333	Sacks Leaders	1.00	.40
❑ 334	Scoring Leaders	1.00	.40
❑ 335	Interception Leaders	1.00	.40
❑ 336	Punting Leaders	1.00	.40
❑ 337	Freddie Solomon	.20	.07
❑ 338	Cincinnati Bengals TL/Jauron	1.00	.40
❑ 339	Ken Stone	.20	.07
❑ 340	Greg Buttle AP	.20	.07
❑ 341	Bob Baumhower	.50	.20
❑ 342	Billy Waddy	.20	.07
❑ 343	Cliff Parsley	.20	.07
❑ 344	Walter White	.20	.07
❑ 345	Mike Thomas	.20	.07
❑ 346	Neil O'Donoghue	.20	.07
❑ 347	Freddie Scott	.20	.07
❑ 348	Joe Ferguson	.50	.20
❑ 349	Doug Nettles	.20	.07
❑ 350	Mike Webster	1.00	.40
❑ 351	Ron Saul	.20	.07
❑ 352	Julius Adams	.20	.07
❑ 353	Rafael Septien	.20	.07
❑ 354	Cleo Miller	.20	.07
❑ 355	Keith Simpson AP	.20	.07
❑ 356	Johnny Perkins	.20	.07
❑ 357	Jerry Sisemore	.20	.07
❑ 358	Arthur Whittington	.20	.07
❑ 359	Cardinals TL/Anderson	1.00	.40
❑ 360	Rick Upchurch	.50	.20
❑ 361	Kim Bokamper RC	.20	.07
❑ 362	Roland Harper	.20	.07
❑ 363	Pat Leahy	.20	.07
❑ 364	Louis Breeden	.20	.07
❑ 365	John Jefferson	1.00	.40
❑ 366	Jerry Eckwood	.20	.07
❑ 367	David Whitehurst	.20	.07
❑ 368	Willie Parker C	.20	.07
❑ 369	Ed Simonini	.20	.07
❑ 370	Jack Youngblood	1.00	.40
❑ 371	Don Warren RC	1.00	.40
❑ 372	Andy Johnson	.20	.07
❑ 373	D.D. Lewis	.50	.20
❑ 374A	B.Reece RC ERR	1.00	.40
❑ 374B	Beasley Reece RC COR	.50	.20
❑ 375	L.C.Greenwood	1.00	.40
❑ 376	Cleveland Browns TL	.50	.20
❑ 377	Herman Edwards	.20	.07
❑ 378	Rob Carpenter RC RB	.20	.07
❑ 379	Herman Weaver	.20	.07
❑ 380	Gary Fencik	.20	.07
❑ 381	Don Strock	.50	.20
❑ 382	Art Shell	1.00	.40
❑ 383	Tim Mazzetti	.20	.07
❑ 384	Bruce Harper	.20	.07
❑ 385	Al (Bubba) Baker	.50	.20
❑ 386	Conrad Dobler	.20	.07
❑ 387	Stu Voigt	.20	.07
❑ 388	Ken Anderson	1.00	.40
❑ 389	Pat Tilley	.20	.07
❑ 390	John Riggins	1.00	.40
❑ 391	Checklist 265-396	.75	.30
❑ 392	Fred Dean	.20	.07
❑ 393	Benny Barnes RC	.20	.07
❑ 394	Los Angeles Rams TL	.50	.20
❑ 395	Brad Van Pelt	.20	.07
❑ 396	Eddie Hare	.20	.07
❑ 397	John Sciarra RC	.20	.07
❑ 398	Bob Jackson	.20	.07
❑ 399	John Yarno	.20	.07
❑ 400	Franco Harris	2.00	.75
❑ 401	Ray Wersching	.20	.07
❑ 402	Virgil Livers	.20	.07
❑ 403	Raymond Chester	.20	.07
❑ 404	Leon Gray	.20	.07
❑ 405	Richard Todd	.50	.20
❑ 406	Larry Little	1.00	.40
❑ 407	Ted Fritsch Jr.	.20	.07
❑ 408	Larry Mucker	.20	.07
❑ 409	Jim Allen	.20	.07
❑ 410	Randy Gradishar	1.00	.40
❑ 411	Atlanta Falcons TL	1.00	.40
❑ 412	Louie Kelcher	.50	.20
❑ 413	Robert Newhouse	.50	.20
❑ 414	Gary Shirk	.20	.07
❑ 415	Mike Haynes	1.00	.40
❑ 416	Craig Colquitt	.20	.07
❑ 417	Lou Piccone	.20	.07
❑ 418	Clay Matthews RC	2.50	1.00
❑ 419	Marvin Cobb	.20	.07
❑ 420	Harold Carmichael	1.00	.40
❑ 421	Uwe Von Schamann	.50	.20
❑ 422	Mike Phipps	.50	.20
❑ 423	Nolan Cromwell RC	1.00	.40
❑ 424	Glenn Doughty	.20	.07
❑ 425	Bob Young AP	.20	.07
❑ 426	Tony Galbreath	.20	.07
❑ 427	Luke Prestridge RC	.20	.07
❑ 428	Terry Beeson	.20	.07
❑ 429	Jack Tatum	.50	.20
❑ 430	Lemar Parrish AP	.20	.07
❑ 431	Chester Marcol	.20	.07
❑ 432	Houston Oilers TL	1.00	.40

❑ 433 John Fitzgerald	.20	.07
❑ 434 Gary Jeter RC	.50	.20
❑ 435 Steve Grogan	1.00	.40
❑ 436 Jon Kolb UER	.20	.07
❑ 437 Jim O'Bradovich UER	.20	.07
❑ 438 Gerald Irons	.20	.07
❑ 439 Jeff West	.20	.07
❑ 440 Wilbert Montgomery	.50	.20
❑ 441 Norris Thomas	.20	.07
❑ 442 James Scott	.20	.07
❑ 443 Curtis Brown	.20	.07
❑ 444 Ken Fantetti	.20	.07
❑ 445 Pat Haden	1.00	.40
❑ 446 Carl Mauck	.20	.07
❑ 447 Bruce Laird	.20	.07
❑ 448 Otis Armstrong	.20	.07
❑ 449 Gene Upshaw	1.00	.40
❑ 450 Steve Largent	6.00	3.00
❑ 451 Benny Malone	.20	.07
❑ 452 Steve Nelson	.20	.07
❑ 453 Mark Cotney	.20	.07
❑ 454 Joe Danelo	.20	.07
❑ 455 Billy Joe DuPree	.50	.20
❑ 456 Ron Johnson DB	.20	.07
❑ 457 Archie Griffin	.50	.20
❑ 458 Reggie Rucker	.20	.07
❑ 459 Claude Humphrey	.20	.07
❑ 460 Lydell Mitchell	.50	.20
❑ 461 Steve Towle	.20	.07
❑ 462 Revie Sorey	.20	.07
❑ 463 Tom Skladany	.20	.07
❑ 464 Clark Gaines	.20	.07
❑ 465 Frank Corral	.20	.07
❑ 466 Steve Fuller RC	.50	.20
❑ 467 Ahmad Rashad	1.00	.40
❑ 468 Oakland Raiders TL	1.00	.40
❑ 469 Brian Peets	.20	.07
❑ 470 Pat Donovan RC	.50	.20
❑ 471 Ken Burrough	.20	.07
❑ 472 Don Calhoun	.20	.07
❑ 473 Bill Bryan	.20	.07
❑ 474 Terry Jackson	.20	.07
❑ 475 Joe Theismann	1.25	.50
❑ 476 Jim Smith	.50	.20
❑ 477 Joe DeLamielleure	1.00	.40
❑ 478 Mike Pruitt AP	.50	.20
❑ 479 Steve Mike-Mayer	.20	.07
❑ 480 Bill Bergey	.50	.20
❑ 481 Mike Fuller	.20	.07
❑ 482 Bob Parsons	.20	.07
❑ 483 Billy Brooks	.20	.07
❑ 484 Jerome Barkum	.20	.07
❑ 485 Larry Csonka	1.50	.60
❑ 486 John Hill	.20	.07
❑ 487 Mike Dawson	.20	.07
❑ 488 Detroit Lions TL	.50	.20
❑ 489 Ted Hendricks	1.00	.40
❑ 490 Dan Pastorini	.50	.20
❑ 491 Stanley Morgan	1.00	.40
❑ 492 AFC Champs/Bleier	1.00	.40
❑ 493 NFC Champs/Ferragamo	.50	.20
❑ 494 Super Bowl XIV	1.00	.40
❑ 495 Dwight White	.50	.20
❑ 496 Haven Moses	.20	.07
❑ 497 Guy Morriss	.20	.07
❑ 498 Dewey Selmon	.50	.20
❑ 499 Dave Butz RC	1.00	.40
❑ 500 Chuck Foreman	.50	.20
❑ 501 Chris Bahr	.20	.07
❑ 502 Mark Miller QB	.20	.07
❑ 503 Tony Greene	.20	.07
❑ 504 Brian Kelley	.20	.07
❑ 505 Joe Washington	.50	.20
❑ 506 Butch Johnson	.50	.20
❑ 507 New York Jets TL	.50	.20
❑ 508 Steve Little	.20	.07
❑ 509 Checklist 397-528	.75	.30
❑ 510 Mark Van Eeghen	.20	.07
❑ 511 Gary Danielson	.50	.20
❑ 512 Manu Tuiasosopo	.20	.07
❑ 513 Paul Coffman RC	.50	.20
❑ 514 Cullen Bryant	.20	.07
❑ 515 Nat Moore	.50	.20
❑ 516 Bill Lenkaitis	.20	.07
❑ 517 Lynn Cain RC	.20	.07
❑ 518 Gregg Bingham	.20	.07
❑ 519 Ted Albrecht	.20	.07
❑ 520 Dan Fouts	2.00	.75
❑ 521 Bernard Jackson	.20	.07
❑ 522 Coy Bacon	.20	.07
❑ 523 Tony Franklin RC	.50	.20
❑ 524 Bo Harris	.20	.07
❑ 525 Bob Grupp AP	.20	.07
❑ 526 San Francisco 49ers TL	1.00	.40
❑ 527 Steve Wilson	.20	.07
❑ 528 Bennie Cunningham	.50	.20

1981 Topps

❑ COMPLETE SET (528)	200.00	100.00
❑ 1 Ron Jaworski/B.Sipe LL	.75	.30
❑ 2 K.Winslow/Cooper LL	.75	.30
❑ 3 Sack Leaders	.40	.15
❑ 4 Scoring Leaders	.15	.05
❑ 5 Interception Leaders	.40	.15
❑ 6 Punting Leaders	.15	.05
❑ 7 Don Calhoun	.15	.05
❑ 8 Jack Tatum	.40	.15
❑ 9 Reggie Rucker	.15	.05
❑ 10 Mike Webster	.75	.30
❑ 11 Vince Evans RC	.75	.30
❑ 12 Ottis Anderson SA	.75	.30
❑ 13 Leroy Harris	.15	.05
❑ 14 Gordon King	.15	.05
❑ 15 Harvey Martin	.40	.15
❑ 16 Johnny Lam Jones RC	.40	.15
❑ 17 Ken Greene	.15	.05
❑ 18 Frank Lewis	.15	.05
❑ 19 Seahawks TL/Largent	.75	.30
❑ 20 Lester Hayes	.75	.30
❑ 21 Uwe Von Schamann	.15	.05
❑ 22 Joe Washington	.15	.05
❑ 23 Louie Kelcher	.15	.05
❑ 24 Willie Miller	.15	.05
❑ 25 Steve Grogan	.75	.30
❑ 26 John Hill	.15	.05
❑ 27 Stan White	.15	.05
❑ 28 William Andrews SA	.40	.15
❑ 29 Clarence Scott	.15	.05
❑ 30 Leon Gray AP	.15	.05
❑ 31 Craig Colquitt	.15	.05
❑ 32 Doug Williams	.75	.30
❑ 33 Bob Breunig	.40	.15
❑ 34 Billy Taylor	.15	.05
❑ 35 Harold Carmichael	.75	.30
❑ 36 Ray Wersching	.15	.05
❑ 37 Dennis Johnson LB RC	.15	.05
❑ 38 Archie Griffin	.40	.15
❑ 39 Los Angeles Rams TL	.40	.15
❑ 40 Gary Fencik	.40	.15
❑ 41 Lynn Dickey	.15	.05
❑ 42 Steve Bartkowski SA	.40	.15
❑ 43 Art Shell	.75	.30
❑ 44 Wilbur Jackson	.15	.05
❑ 45 Frank Corral	.15	.05
❑ 46 Ted McKnight	.15	.05
❑ 47 Joe Klecko	.40	.15
❑ 48 Dan Doornink	.15	.05
❑ 49 Doug Dieken	.15	.05
❑ 50 Jerry Robinson RC	.40	.15
❑ 51 Wallace Francis	.15	.05
❑ 52 Dave Preston RC	.15	.05
❑ 53 Jay Saldi	.15	.05
❑ 54 Rush Brown	.15	.05
❑ 55 Phil Simms	3.00	1.50
❑ 56 Nick Mike-Mayer	.15	.05
❑ 57 Redskins TL/A.Monk	2.00	.75
❑ 58 Mike Renfro	.15	.05
❑ 59 Ted Brown SA	.15	.05
❑ 60 Steve Nelson	.15	.05
❑ 61 Sidney Thornton	.15	.05
❑ 62 Kent Hill	.15	.05
❑ 63 Don Bessillieu	.15	.05
❑ 64 Fred Cook	.15	.05
❑ 65 Raymond Chester	.15	.05
❑ 66 Rick Kane	.15	.05
❑ 67 Mike Fuller	.15	.05
❑ 68 Dewey Selmon	.40	.15
❑ 69 Charles White RC	.75	.30
❑ 70 Jeff Van Note	.15	.05
❑ 71 Robert Newhouse	.40	.15
❑ 72 Roynell Young RC	.15	.05
❑ 73 Lynn Cain SA	.15	.05
❑ 74 Mike Friede	.15	.05
❑ 75 Earl Cooper RC	.15	.05
❑ 76 New Orleans Saints TL	.40	.15
❑ 77 Rick Danmeier	.15	.05
❑ 78 Darrol Ray	.15	.05
❑ 79 Gregg Bingham	.15	.05
❑ 80 John Hannah	.75	.30
❑ 81 Jack Thompson	.40	.15
❑ 82 Rick Upchurch	.40	.15
❑ 83 Mike Butler	.15	.05
❑ 84 Don Warren	.15	.05
❑ 85 Mark Van Eeghen	.15	.05
❑ 86 J.T.Smith RC	.75	.30
❑ 87 Herman Weaver	.15	.05
❑ 88 Terry Bradshaw SA	2.00	.75
❑ 89 Charlie Hall	.15	.05
❑ 90 Donnie Shell	.75	.30
❑ 91 Ike Harris	.15	.05
❑ 92 Charlie Johnson NT	.15	.05
❑ 93 Rickey Watts	.15	.05
❑ 94 New England Patriots TL	.75	.30
❑ 95 Drew Pearson	.75	.30
❑ 96 Neil O'Donoghue	.15	.05
❑ 97 Conrad Dobler	.15	.05
❑ 98 Jewerl Thomas RC	.15	.05
❑ 99 Mike Barber	.15	.05
❑ 100 Billy Sims RC	3.00	1.25
❑ 101 Vern Den Herder	.15	.05
❑ 102 Greg Landry	.40	.15
❑ 103 Joe Cribbs SA	.40	.15
❑ 104 Mark Murphy S RC	.15	.05
❑ 105 Chuck Muncie	.40	.15
❑ 106 Alfred Jackson	.40	.15
❑ 107 Chris Bahr	.15	.05
❑ 108 Gordon Jones	.15	.05
❑ 109 Willie Harper RC	.15	.05
❑ 110 Dave Jennings	.15	.05
❑ 111 Bennie Cunningham	.15	.05
❑ 112 Jerry Sisemore	.15	.05
❑ 113 Cleveland Browns TL	.75	.30
❑ 114 Rickey Young	.15	.05
❑ 115 Ken Anderson	.75	.30
❑ 116 Randy Gradishar	.75	.30
❑ 117 Eddie Lee Ivery RC	.15	.05
❑ 118 Wesley Walker	.75	.30
❑ 119 Chuck Foreman	.40	.15
❑ 120 Nolan Cromwell UER	.40	.15
❑ 121 Curtis Dickey SA	.15	.05
❑ 122 Wayne Morris	.15	.05
❑ 123 Greg Stemrick	.15	.05
❑ 124 Coy Bacon	.15	.05
❑ 125 Jim Zorn	.40	.15
❑ 126 Henry Childs	.15	.05
❑ 127 Checklist 1-132	.75	.30
❑ 128 Len Walterscheid	.15	.05
❑ 129 Johnny Evans	.15	.05
❑ 130 Gary Barbaro	.15	.05
❑ 131 Jim Smith	.15	.05
❑ 132 New York Jets TL	.40	.15
❑ 133 Curtis Brown	.15	.05
❑ 134 D.D. Lewis	.15	.05
❑ 135 Jim Plunkett	.75	.30
❑ 136 Nat Moore	.40	.15
❑ 137 Don McCauley	.15	.05
❑ 138 Tony Dorsett SA	.75	.30
❑ 139 Julius Adams	.15	.05
❑ 140 Ahmad Rashad	.75	.30
❑ 141 Rich Saul	.15	.05
❑ 142 Ken Fantetti	.15	.05
❑ 143 Kenny Johnson	.15	.05
❑ 144 Clark Gaines	.15	.05

❑ 145 Mark Moseley .15 .05
❑ 146 Vernon Perry RC .15 .05
❑ 147 Jerry Eckwood .15 .05
❑ 148 Freddie Solomon .15 .05
❑ 149 Jerry Sherk .15 .05
❑ 150 Kellen Winslow RC 8.00 4.00
❑ 151 Packers TL/Lofton .75 .30
❑ 152 Ross Browner .15 .05
❑ 153 Dan Fouts SA .75 .30
❑ 154 Woody Peoples .15 .05
❑ 155 Jack Lambert 1.00 .40
❑ 156 Mike Dennis .15 .05
❑ 157 Rafael Septien .15 .05
❑ 158 Archie Manning .75 .30
❑ 159 Don Hasselbeck .15 .05
❑ 160 Alan Page .75 .30
❑ 161 Arthur Whittington .15 .05
❑ 162 Billy Waddy .15 .05
❑ 163 Horace Belton .15 .05
❑ 164 Luke Prestridge .15 .05
❑ 165 Joe Theismann .75 .30
❑ 166 Morris Towns .15 .05
❑ 167 Dave Brown DB .15 .05
❑ 168 Ezra Johnson .15 .05
❑ 169 Tampa Bay Bucs TL .15 .05
❑ 170 Joe DeLamielleure .75 .30
❑ 171 Earnest Gray SA .15 .05
❑ 172 Mike Thomas .15 .05
❑ 173 Jim Haslett RC 2.00 .75
❑ 174 David Woodley RC .40 .15
❑ 175 Al(Bubba) Baker .40 .15
❑ 176 Nesby Glasgow RC .15 .05
❑ 177 Pat Leahy .15 .05
❑ 178 Tom Brahaney .15 .05
❑ 179 Herman Edwards .15 .05
❑ 180 Junior Miller RC .15 .05
❑ 181 Richard Wood RC .15 .05
❑ 182 Lenvil Elliott .15 .05
❑ 183 Sammie White .40 .15
❑ 184 Russell Erxleben .15 .05
❑ 185 Ed Too Tall Jones .75 .30
❑ 186 Ray Guy SA .40 .15
❑ 187 Haven Moses .15 .05
❑ 188 New York Giants TL .40 .15
❑ 189 David Whitehurst .15 .05
❑ 190 John Jefferson .75 .30
❑ 191 Terry Beeson .15 .05
❑ 192 Dan Ross RC .40 .15
❑ 193 Dave Williams RB RC .15 .05
❑ 194 Art Monk RC 15.00 6.00
❑ 195 Roger Wehrli .15 .05
❑ 196 Ricky Feacher .15 .05
❑ 197 Miami Dolphins TL .75 .30
❑ 198 Carl Roaches RC .15 .05
❑ 199 Billy Campfield .15 .05
❑ 200 Ted Hendricks .75 .30
❑ 201 Fred Smerlas RC .75 .30
❑ 202 Walter Payton SA 3.00 1.25
❑ 203 Luther Bradley .15 .05
❑ 204 Herb Scott .15 .05
❑ 205 Jack Youngblood .75 .30
❑ 206 Danny Pittman .15 .05
❑ 207 Houston Oilers TL .40 .15
❑ 208 Vagas Ferguson RC .40 .15
❑ 209 Mark Dennard .15 .05
❑ 210 Lemar Parrish .15 .05
❑ 211 Bruce Harper .15 .05
❑ 212 Ed Simonini .15 .05
❑ 213 Nick Lowery RC .75 .30
❑ 214 Kevin House RC .40 .15
❑ 215 Mike Kenn RC .75 .30
❑ 216 Joe Montana RC 150.00 75.00
❑ 217 Joe Senser .15 .05
❑ 218 Lester Hayes SA .40 .15
❑ 219 Gene Upshaw .75 .30
❑ 220 Franco Harris 1.25 .50
❑ 221 Ron Bolton .15 .05
❑ 222 Charles Alexander RC .40 .15
❑ 223 Matt Robinson .15 .05
❑ 224 Ray Oldham .15 .05
❑ 225 George Martin .15 .05
❑ 226 Buffalo Bills TL .75 .30
❑ 227 Tony Franklin .15 .05
❑ 228 George Cumby .15 .05
❑ 229 Butch Johnson .40 .15
❑ 230 Mike Haynes .75 .30
❑ 231 Rob Carpenter .40 .15
❑ 232 Steve Fuller .40 .15
❑ 233 John Sawyer .15 .05
❑ 234 Kenny King SA .15 .05
❑ 235 Jack Ham .75 .30
❑ 236 Jimmy Rogers .15 .05
❑ 237 Bob Parsons .15 .05
❑ 238 Marty Lyons RC .75 .30
❑ 239 Pat Tilley .15 .05
❑ 240 Dennis Harrah .15 .05
❑ 241 Thom Darden .15 .05
❑ 242 Rolf Benirschke .15 .05
❑ 243 Gerald Small .15 .05
❑ 244 Atlanta Falcons TL .75 .30
❑ 245 Roger Carr .15 .05
❑ 246 Sherman White .15 .05
❑ 247 Ted Brown .15 .05
❑ 248 Matt Cavanaugh .40 .15
❑ 249 John Dutton .15 .05
❑ 250 Bill Bergey .40 .15
❑ 251 Jim Allen .15 .05
❑ 252 Mike Nelms SA .15 .05
❑ 253 Tom Blanchard .15 .05
❑ 254 Ricky Thompson .15 .05
❑ 255 John Matuszak .40 .15
❑ 256 Randy Grossman .15 .05
❑ 257 Ray Griffin RC .15 .05
❑ 258 Lynn Cain .15 .05
❑ 259 Checklist 133-264 .75 .30
❑ 260 Mike Pruitt .40 .15
❑ 261 Chris Ward RC .15 .05
❑ 262 Fred Steinfort .15 .05
❑ 263 James Owens .15 .05
❑ 264 Bears TL/Payton/Hampton 1.50 .60
❑ 265 Dan Fouts 1.50 .60
❑ 266 Arnold Morgado .15 .05
❑ 267 John Jefferson SA .75 .30
❑ 268 Bill Lenkaitis .15 .05
❑ 269 James Jones COW .15 .05
❑ 270 Brad Van Pelt .15 .05
❑ 271 Steve Largent 2.50 1.25
❑ 272 Elvin Bethea .75 .30
❑ 273 Cullen Bryant .15 .05
❑ 274 Gary Danielson .40 .15
❑ 275 Tony Galbreath .15 .05
❑ 276 Dave Butz .15 .05
❑ 277 Steve Mike-Mayer .15 .05
❑ 278 Ron Johnson DB .15 .05
❑ 279 Tom DeLeone .15 .05
❑ 280 Ron Jaworski .75 .30
❑ 281 Mel Gray .15 .05
❑ 282 San Diego Chargers TL .75 .30
❑ 283 Mark Brammer RC .15 .05
❑ 284 Alfred Jenkins SA .40 .15
❑ 285 Greg Buttle .15 .05
❑ 286 Randy Hughes .15 .05
❑ 287 Delvin Williams .15 .05
❑ 288 Brian Baschnagel .15 .05
❑ 289 Gary Jeter .15 .05
❑ 290 Stanley Morgan .75 .30
❑ 291 Gerry Ellis .15 .05
❑ 292 Al Richardson .15 .05
❑ 293 Jimmie Giles .40 .15
❑ 294 Dave Jennings SA .15 .05
❑ 295 Wilbert Montgomery .40 .15
❑ 296 Dave Pureifory .15 .05
❑ 297 Greg Hawthorne .15 .05
❑ 298 Dick Ambrose .15 .05
❑ 299 Terry Hermeling .15 .05
❑ 300 Danny White .75 .30
❑ 301 Ken Burrough .15 .05
❑ 302 Paul Hofer .15 .05
❑ 303 Denver Broncos TL .75 .30
❑ 304 Eddie Payton .40 .15
❑ 305 Isaac Curtis .40 .15
❑ 306 Benny Ricardo .15 .05
❑ 307 Riley Odoms .15 .05
❑ 308 Bob Chandler .15 .05
❑ 309 Larry Heater .15 .05
❑ 310 Art Still RC .75 .30
❑ 311 Harold Jackson .40 .15
❑ 312 Charlie Joiner SA .75 .30
❑ 313 Jeff Nixon .15 .05
❑ 314 Aundra Thompson .15 .05
❑ 315 Richard Todd .40 .15
❑ 316 Dan Hampton RC 3.00 1.25
❑ 317 Doug Marsh .15 .05
❑ 318 Louie Giammona .15 .05
❑ 319 49ers TL/Dwight Clark .75 .30
❑ 320 Manu Tuiasosopo .15 .05
❑ 321 Rich Milot .15 .05
❑ 322 Mike Guman RC .15 .05
❑ 323 Bob Kuechenberg .40 .15
❑ 324 Tom Skladany .15 .05
❑ 325 Dave Logan .15 .05
❑ 326 Bruce Laird .15 .05
❑ 327 James Jones COW SA .15 .05
❑ 328 Joe Danelo .15 .05
❑ 329 Kenny King RC .40 .15
❑ 330 Pat Donovan .15 .05
❑ 331 Earl Cooper RB .40 .15
❑ 332 John Jefferson RB .75 .30
❑ 333 Kenny King RB .40 .15
❑ 334 Rod Martin RB .40 .15
❑ 335 Jim Plunkett RB .75 .30
❑ 336 Bill Thompson RB .40 .15
❑ 337 John Cappelletti .40 .15
❑ 338 Lions TL/Billy Sims .75 .30
❑ 339 Don Smith .15 .05
❑ 340 Rod Perry .15 .05
❑ 341 David Lewis .15 .05
❑ 342 Mark Gastineau RC 1.00 .40
❑ 343 Steve Largent SA .75 .30
❑ 344 Charlie Young .15 .05
❑ 345 Toni Fritsch .15 .05
❑ 346 Matt Blair .40 .15
❑ 347 Don Bass .15 .05
❑ 348 Jim Jensen RC .40 .15
❑ 349 Karl Lorch .15 .05
❑ 350 Brian Sipe .40 .15
❑ 351 Theo Bell .15 .05
❑ 352 Sam Adams OL .15 .05
❑ 353 Paul Coffman .15 .05
❑ 354 Eric Harris .15 .05
❑ 355 Tony Hill .40 .15
❑ 356 J.T. Turner .15 .05
❑ 357 Frank LeMaster .15 .05
❑ 358 Jim Jodat .15 .05
❑ 359 Raiders TL/Hendricks .75 .30
❑ 360 Joe Cribbs RC .75 .30
❑ 361 James Lofton SA .75 .30
❑ 362 Dexter Bussey .15 .05
❑ 363 Bobby Jackson .15 .05
❑ 364 Steve DeBerg .75 .30
❑ 365 Ottis Anderson 1.00 .40
❑ 366 Tom Myers .15 .05
❑ 367 John James .15 .05
❑ 368 Reese McCall .15 .05
❑ 369 Jack Reynolds .40 .15
❑ 370 Gary Johnson .15 .05
❑ 371 Jimmy Cefalo .15 .05
❑ 372 Horace Ivory .15 .05
❑ 373 Garo Yepremian .15 .05
❑ 374 Brian Kelley .15 .05
❑ 375 Terry Bradshaw 6.00 2.50
❑ 376 Cowboys TL/Tony Dorsett .75 .30
❑ 377 Randy Logan .15 .05
❑ 378 Tim Wilson .15 .05
❑ 379 Archie Manning SA .75 .30
❑ 380 Revie Sorey .15 .05
❑ 381 Randy Holloway .15 .05
❑ 382 Henry Lawrence .15 .05
❑ 383 Pat McInally .15 .05
❑ 384 Kevin Long .15 .05
❑ 385 Louis Wright .40 .15
❑ 386 Leonard Thompson .15 .05
❑ 387 Jan Stenerud .40 .15
❑ 388 Raymond Butler RC .15 .05
❑ 389 Checklist 265-396 .75 .30
❑ 390 Steve Bartkowski .40 .15
❑ 391 Clarence Harmon .15 .05
❑ 392 Wilbert Montgomery SA .40 .15
❑ 393 Billy Joe DuPree .40 .15
❑ 394 Kansas City Chiefs TL .40 .15
❑ 395 Earnest Gray .15 .05
❑ 396 Ray Hamilton .15 .05
❑ 397 Brenard Wilson .15 .05
❑ 398 Calvin Hill .75 .30
❑ 399 Robin Cole .15 .05
❑ 400 Walter Payton 12.00 6.00
❑ 401 Jim Hart .75 .30
❑ 402 Ron Yary .75 .30
❑ 403 Cliff Branch .75 .30
❑ 404 Roland Hooks .15 .05
❑ 405 Ken Stabler 3.00 1.50

❑ 406 Chuck Ramsey .15 .05
❑ 407 Mike Nelms RC .15 .05
❑ 408 Ron Jaworski SA .40 .15
❑ 409 James Hunter .15 .05
❑ 410 Lee Roy Selmon .75 .30
❑ 411 Baltimore Colts TL .40 .15
❑ 412 Henry Marshall .15 .05
❑ 413 Preston Pearson .40 .15
❑ 414 Richard Bishop .15 .05
❑ 415 Greg Pruitt .40 .15
❑ 416 Matt Bahr .40 .15
❑ 417 Tom Mullady .15 .05
❑ 418 Glen Edwards .15 .05
❑ 419 Sam McCullum .15 .05
❑ 420 Stan Walters .15 .05
❑ 421 George Roberts .15 .05
❑ 422 Dwight Clark RC 5.00 2.00
❑ 423 Pat Thomas RC .15 .05
❑ 424 Bruce Harper SA .15 .05
❑ 425 Craig Morton .40 .15
❑ 426 Derrick Gaffney .15 .05
❑ 427 Pete Johnson .15 .05
❑ 428 Wes Chandler .75 .30
❑ 429 Burgess Owens .15 .05
❑ 430 James Lofton 2.00 .75
❑ 431 Tony Reed .15 .05
❑ 432 Vikings TL/A.Rashad .75 .30
❑ 433 Ron Springs RC .40 .15
❑ 434 Tim Fox .15 .05
❑ 435 Ozzie Newsome 2.00 .75
❑ 436 Steve Furness .15 .05
❑ 437 Will Lewis .15 .05
❑ 438 Mike Hartenstine .15 .05
❑ 439 John Bunting .15 .05
❑ 440 Eddie Murray RC .75 .30
❑ 441 Mike Pruitt SA .40 .15
❑ 442 Larry Swider .15 .05
❑ 443 Steve Freeman .15 .05
❑ 444 Bruce Hardy RC .15 .05
❑ 445 Pat Haden .40 .15
❑ 446 Curtis Dickey RC .15 .05
❑ 447 Doug Wilkerson .15 .05
❑ 448 Alfred Jenkins .40 .15
❑ 449 Dave Dalby .15 .05
❑ 450 Robert Brazile .15 .05
❑ 451 Bobby Hammond .15 .05
❑ 452 Raymond Clayborn .15 .05
❑ 453 Jim Miller P RC .15 .05
❑ 454 Roy Simmons .15 .05
❑ 455 Charlie Waters .40 .15
❑ 456 Ricky Bell .75 .30
❑ 457 Ahmad Rashad SA .75 .30
❑ 458 Don Cockroft .15 .05
❑ 459 Keith Krepfle .15 .05
❑ 460 Marvin Powell .15 .05
❑ 461 Tommy Kramer .75 .30
❑ 462 Jim LeClair .15 .05
❑ 463 Freddie Scott .15 .05
❑ 464 Rob Lytle .15 .05
❑ 465 Johnnie Gray .15 .05
❑ 466 Doug France RC .15 .05
❑ 467 Carlos Carson RC .40 .15
❑ 468 Cardinals TL/O.Anderson .75 .30
❑ 469 Efren Herrera .15 .05
❑ 470 Randy White 1.00 .40
❑ 471 Richard Caster .15 .05
❑ 472 Andy Johnson .15 .05
❑ 473 Billy Sims SA .75 .30
❑ 474 Joe Lavender .15 .05
❑ 475 Harry Carson .40 .15
❑ 476 John Stallworth 1.00 .40
❑ 477 Bob Thomas .15 .05
❑ 478 Keith Wright RC .15 .05
❑ 479 Ken Stone .15 .05
❑ 480 Carl Hairston .40 .15
❑ 481 Reggie McKenzie .15 .05
❑ 482 Bob Griese 1.50 .60
❑ 483 Mike Bragg .15 .05
❑ 484 Scott Dierking .15 .05
❑ 485 David Hill .15 .05
❑ 486 Brian Sipe SA .40 .15
❑ 487 Rod Martin RC .40 .15
❑ 488 Cincinnati Bengals TL .40 .15
❑ 489 Preston Dennard .15 .05
❑ 490 John Smith .15 .05
❑ 491 Mike Reinfeldt .15 .05
❑ 492 NFC Champs/Jaworski .75 .30
❑ 493 AFC Champs/Plunkett .75 .30
❑ 494 Super Bowl XV/J.Plunkett .75 .30
❑ 495 Joe Greene .75 .30
❑ 496 Charlie Joiner .75 .30
❑ 497 Rolland Lawrence .15 .05
❑ 498 Al(Bubba) Baker SA .40 .15
❑ 499 Brad Dusek .15 .05
❑ 500 Tony Dorsett 4.00 2.00
❑ 501 Robin Earl .15 .05
❑ 502 Theotis Brown RC .15 .05
❑ 503 Joe Ferguson .40 .15
❑ 504 Beasley Reece .15 .05
❑ 505 Lyle Alzado .75 .30
❑ 506 Tony Nathan RC .75 .30
❑ 507 Philadelphia Eagles TL .40 .15
❑ 508 Herb Orvis .15 .05
❑ 509 Clarence Williams RB .15 .05
❑ 510 Ray Guy .40 .15
❑ 511 Jeff Komlo .15 .05
❑ 512 Freddie Solomon SA .15 .05
❑ 513 Tim Mazzetti .15 .05
❑ 514 Elvis Peacock RC .15 .05
❑ 515 Russ Francis .40 .15
❑ 516 Roland Harper .15 .05
❑ 517 Checklist 397-528 .75 .30
❑ 518 Billy Johnson .40 .15
❑ 519 Dan Dierdorf .75 .30
❑ 520 Fred Dean .15 .05
❑ 521 Jerry Butler .15 .05
❑ 522 Ron Saul .15 .05
❑ 523 Charlie Smith WR .15 .05
❑ 524 Kellen Winslow SA 3.00 1.50
❑ 525 Bert Jones .75 .30
❑ 526 Steelers TL/Fr.Harris .75 .30
❑ 527 Duriel Harris .15 .05
❑ 528 William Andrews .75 .30

1982 Topps

❑ COMPLETE SET (528) 80.00 50.00
❑ 1 Ken Anderson RB .75 .30
❑ 2 Dan Fouts RB .75 .30
❑ 3 LeRoy Irvin RB .15 .05
❑ 4 Stump Mitchell RB .15 .05
❑ 5 George Rogers RB .75 .30
❑ 6 Dan Ross RB .15 .05
❑ 7 AFC Champs/K.Anderson .75 .30
❑ 8 NFC Champs/E.Cooper .75 .30
❑ 9 Super Bowl XVI/A.Munoz .75 .30
❑ 10 Baltimore Colts TL .15 .05
❑ 11 Raymond Butler .15 .05
❑ 12 Roger Carr .15 .05
❑ 13 Curtis Dickey .40 .15
❑ 14 Zachary Dixon .15 .05
❑ 15 Nesby Glasgow .15 .05
❑ 16 Bert Jones .75 .30
❑ 17 Bruce Laird .15 .05
❑ 18 Reese McCall .15 .05
❑ 19 Randy McMillan .15 .05
❑ 20 Ed Simonini .15 .05
❑ 21 Buffalo Bills TL .40 .15
❑ 22 Mark Brammer .15 .05
❑ 23 Curtis Brown .15 .05
❑ 24 Jerry Butler .15 .05
❑ 25 Mario Clark .15 .05
❑ 26 Joe Cribbs .40 .15
❑ 27 Joe Cribbs IA .40 .15
❑ 28 Joe Ferguson .40 .15
❑ 29 Jim Haslett .75 .30
❑ 30 Frank Lewis .15 .05
❑ 31 Frank Lewis IA .15 .05
❑ 32 Shane Nelson .15 .05
❑ 33 Charles Romes .15 .05
❑ 34 Bill Simpson .15 .05
❑ 35 Fred Smerlas .15 .05
❑ 36 Bengals TL/C.Collinswort .40 .15
❑ 37 Charles Alexander .15 .05
❑ 38 Ken Anderson .75 .30
❑ 39 Ken Anderson IA .75 .30
❑ 40 Jim Breech .15 .05
❑ 41 Jim Breech IA .15 .05
❑ 42 Louis Breeden .15 .05
❑ 43 Ross Browner .15 .05
❑ 44 Cris Collinsworth RC 2.00 .75
❑ 45 Cris Collinsworth IA .75 .30
❑ 46 Isaac Curtis .15 .05
❑ 47 Pete Johnson .15 .05
❑ 48 Pete Johnson IA .15 .05
❑ 49 Steve Kreider .15 .05
❑ 50 Pat McInally .15 .05
❑ 51 Anthony Munoz RC 8.00 4.00
❑ 52 Dan Ross .15 .05
❑ 53 David Verser RC .15 .05
❑ 54 Reggie Williams .40 .15
❑ 55 Browns TL/O.Newsome .40 .15
❑ 56 Lyle Alzado .75 .30
❑ 57 Dick Ambrose .15 .05
❑ 58 Ron Bolton .15 .05
❑ 59 Steve Cox .15 .05
❑ 60 Joe DeLamielleure .75 .30
❑ 61 Tom DeLeone .15 .05
❑ 62 Doug Dieken .15 .05
❑ 63 Ricky Feacher .15 .05
❑ 64 Don Goode .15 .05
❑ 65 Robert L.Jackson RC .15 .05
❑ 66 Dave Logan .15 .05
❑ 67 Ozzie Newsome 1.00 .40
❑ 68 Ozzie Newsome IA .75 .30
❑ 69 Greg Pruitt .40 .15
❑ 70 Mike Pruitt .40 .15
❑ 71 Mike Pruitt IA .40 .15
❑ 72 Reggie Rucker .15 .05
❑ 73 Clarence Scott .15 .05
❑ 74 Brian Sipe .40 .15
❑ 75 Charles White .40 .15
❑ 76 Denver Broncos TL .40 .15
❑ 77 Rubin Carter .15 .05
❑ 78 Steve Foley .15 .05
❑ 79 Randy Gradishar .40 .15
❑ 80 Tom Jackson .75 .30
❑ 81 Craig Morton .40 .15
❑ 82 Craig Morton IA .40 .15
❑ 83 Riley Odoms .15 .05
❑ 84 Rick Parros .15 .05
❑ 85 Dave Preston .15 .05
❑ 86 Tony Reed .15 .05
❑ 87 Bob Swenson RC .15 .05
❑ 88 Bill Thompson .15 .05
❑ 89 Rick Upchurch .40 .15
❑ 90 Steve Watson RC .40 .15
❑ 91 Steve Watson IA .15 .05
❑ 92 Houston Oilers TL .15 .05
❑ 93 Mike Barber .15 .05
❑ 94 Elvin Bethea .75 .30
❑ 95 Gregg Bingham .15 .05
❑ 96 Robert Brazile .15 .05
❑ 97 Ken Burrough .15 .05
❑ 98 Toni Fritsch .15 .05
❑ 99 Leon Gray .15 .05
❑ 100 Gifford Nielsen RC .40 .15
❑ 101 Vernon Perry .15 .05
❑ 102 Mike Reinfeldt .15 .05
❑ 103 Mike Renfro .15 .05
❑ 104 Carl Roaches .15 .05
❑ 105 Ken Stabler 2.00 .75
❑ 106 Greg Stemrick .15 .05
❑ 107 J.C. Wilson .15 .05
❑ 108 Tim Wilson .15 .05
❑ 109 Kansas City Chiefs TL .15 .05
❑ 110 Gary Barbaro .15 .05
❑ 111 Brad Budde RC .15 .05
❑ 112 Joe Delaney RC .75 .30
❑ 113 Joe Delaney IA .40 .15
❑ 114 Steve Fuller .15 .05
❑ 115 Gary Green .15 .05
❑ 116 James Hadnot .15 .05
❑ 117 Eric Harris .15 .05

❑ 118 Billy Jackson .15 .05
❑ 119 Bill Kenney RC .15 .05
❑ 120 Nick Lowery .75 .30
❑ 121 Nick Lowery IA .40 .15
❑ 122 Henry Marshall .15 .05
❑ 123 J.T.Smith .40 .15
❑ 124 Art Still .15 .05
❑ 125 Miami Dolphins TL .40 .15
❑ 126 Bob Baumhower .40 .15
❑ 127 Glenn Blackwood RC .15 .05
❑ 128 Jimmy Cefalo .15 .05
❑ 129 A.J. Duhe .40 .15
❑ 130 Andra Franklin RC .15 .05
❑ 131 Duriel Harris .15 .05
❑ 132 Nat Moore .40 .15
❑ 133 Tony Nathan .40 .15
❑ 134 Ed Newman .15 .05
❑ 135 Earnie Rhone .15 .05
❑ 136 Don Strock .15 .05
❑ 137 Tommy Vigorito .15 .05
❑ 138 Uwe Von Schamann .15 .05
❑ 139 Uwe Von Schamann IA .15 .05
❑ 140 David Woodley .40 .15
❑ 141 New England Pats TL .40 .15
❑ 142 Julius Adams .15 .05
❑ 143 Richard Bishop .15 .05
❑ 144 Matt Cavanaugh .15 .05
❑ 145 Raymond Clayborn .15 .05
❑ 146 Tony Collins RC .15 .05
❑ 147 Vagas Ferguson .15 .05
❑ 148 Tim Fox .15 .05
❑ 149 Steve Grogan .40 .15
❑ 150 John Hannah .75 .30
❑ 151 John Hannah IA .40 .15
❑ 152 Don Hasselbeck .15 .05
❑ 153 Mike Haynes .40 .15
❑ 154 Harold Jackson .40 .15
❑ 155 Andy Johnson .15 .05
❑ 156 Stanley Morgan .40 .15
❑ 157 Stanley Morgan IA .40 .15
❑ 158 Steve Nelson .15 .05
❑ 159 Rod Shoate .15 .05
❑ 160 Jets TL/F.McNeil .40 .15
❑ 161 Dan Alexander RC .15 .05
❑ 162 Mike Augustyniak .15 .05
❑ 163 Jerome Barkum .15 .05
❑ 164 Greg Buttle .15 .05
❑ 165 Scott Dierking .15 .05
❑ 166 Joe Fields .15 .05
❑ 167 Mark Gastineau .40 .15
❑ 168 Mark Gastineau IA .40 .15
❑ 169 Bruce Harper .15 .05
❑ 170 Johnny Lam Jones .15 .05
❑ 171 Joe Klecko .40 .15
❑ 172 Joe Klecko IA .40 .15
❑ 173 Pat Leahy .40 .15
❑ 174 Pat Leahy IA .15 .05
❑ 175 Marty Lyons .40 .15
❑ 176 Freeman McNeil RC .75 .30
❑ 177 Marvin Powell .15 .05
❑ 178 Chuck Ramsey .15 .05
❑ 179 Darrol Ray .15 .05
❑ 180 Abdul Salaam .15 .05
❑ 181 Richard Todd .40 .15
❑ 182 Richard Todd IA .40 .15
❑ 183 Wesley Walker .40 .15
❑ 184 Chris Ward .15 .05
❑ 185 Oakland Raiders TL .40 .15
❑ 186 Cliff Branch .75 .30
❑ 187 Bob Chandler .15 .05
❑ 188 Ray Guy .40 .15
❑ 189 Lester Hayes .40 .15
❑ 190 Ted Hendricks .75 .30
❑ 191 Monte Jackson .15 .05
❑ 192 Derrick Jensen .15 .05
❑ 193 Kenny King .15 .05
❑ 194 Rod Martin .15 .05
❑ 195 John Matuszak .40 .15
❑ 196 Matt Millen RC 1.50 .60
❑ 197 Derrick Ramsey .15 .05
❑ 198 Art Shell .75 .30
❑ 199 Mark Van Eeghen .15 .05
❑ 200 Arthur Whittington .15 .05
❑ 201 Marc Wilson RC .40 .15
❑ 202 Steelers TL/Fr.Harris .75 .30
❑ 203 Mel Blount .75 .30
❑ 204 Terry Bradshaw 5.00 2.00
❑ 205 Terry Bradshaw IA 1.25 .50
❑ 206 Craig Colquitt .15 .05
❑ 207 Bennie Cunningham .15 .05
❑ 208 Russell Davis RC .15 .05
❑ 209 Gary Dunn .15 .05
❑ 210 Jack Ham .75 .30
❑ 211 Franco Harris 1.00 .40
❑ 212 Franco Harris IA .75 .30
❑ 213 Jack Lambert .75 .30
❑ 214 Jack Lambert IA .75 .30
❑ 215 Mark Malone RC .75 .30
❑ 216 Frank Pollard RC .15 .05
❑ 217 Donnie Shell .75 .30
❑ 218 Jim Smith .15 .05
❑ 219 John Stallworth .75 .30
❑ 220 John Stallworth IA .75 .30
❑ 221 David Trout .15 .05
❑ 222 Mike Webster .75 .30
❑ 223 San Diego Chargers TL .75 .30
❑ 224 Rolf Benirschke .15 .05
❑ 225 Rolf Benirschke IA .15 .05
❑ 226 James Brooks RC .75 .30
❑ 227 Willie Buchanon .15 .05
❑ 228 Wes Chandler .75 .30
❑ 229 Wes Chandler IA .40 .15
❑ 230 Dan Fouts 1.00 .40
❑ 231 Dan Fouts IA .75 .30
❑ 232 Gary Johnson .15 .05
❑ 233 Charlie Joiner .75 .30
❑ 234 Charlie Joiner IA .75 .30
❑ 235 Louie Kelcher .15 .05
❑ 236 Chuck Muncie .40 .15
❑ 237 Chuck Muncie IA .15 .05
❑ 238 George Roberts .15 .05
❑ 239 Ed White .15 .05
❑ 240 Doug Wilkerson .15 .05
❑ 241 Kellen Winslow 2.00 .75
❑ 242 Kellen Winslow IA .75 .30
❑ 243 Seahawks TL/S.Largent .75 .30
❑ 244 Theotis Brown .15 .05
❑ 245 Dan Doornink .15 .05
❑ 246 John Harris .15 .05
❑ 247 Efren Herrera .15 .05
❑ 248 David Hughes .15 .05
❑ 249 Steve Largent 2.00 .75
❑ 250 Steve Largent IA .75 .30
❑ 251 Sam McCullum .15 .05
❑ 252 Sherman Smith .15 .05
❑ 253 Manu Tuiasosopo .15 .05
❑ 254 John Yarno .15 .05
❑ 255 Jim Zorn .40 .15
❑ 256 Jim Zorn IA .40 .15
❑ 257 J.Montana/Anderson LL 4.00 2.00
❑ 258 Kellen Winslow/Clark LL .75 .30
❑ 259 QB Sack Leaders .15 .05
❑ 260 Scoring Leaders .40 .15
❑ 261 Interception Leaders .40 .15
❑ 262 Punting Leaders .15 .05
❑ 263 Brothers: Bahr .15 .05
❑ 264 Brothers: Blackwood .40 .15
❑ 265 Brothers: Brock .15 .05
❑ 266 Brothers: Griffin .40 .15
❑ 267 Brothers: Hannah .75 .30
❑ 268 Brothers: Jackson .15 .05
❑ 269 Walter/Eddie Payton 1.00 .40
❑ 270 Brothers: Selmon .75 .30
❑ 271 Atlanta Falcons TL .40 .15
❑ 272 William Andrews .40 .15
❑ 273 William Andrews IA .40 .15
❑ 274 Steve Bartkowski .40 .15
❑ 275 Steve Bartkowski IA .40 .15
❑ 276 Bobby Butler RC .15 .05
❑ 277 Lynn Cain .15 .05
❑ 278 Wallace Francis .15 .05
❑ 279 Alfred Jackson .15 .05
❑ 280 John James .15 .05
❑ 281 Alfred Jenkins .15 .05
❑ 282 Alfred Jenkins IA .15 .05
❑ 283 Kenny Johnson .15 .05
❑ 284 Mike Kenn .75 .30
❑ 285 Fulton Kuykendall .15 .05
❑ 286 Mick Luckhurst RC .15 .05
❑ 287 Mick Luckhurst IA .15 .05
❑ 288 Junior Miller .15 .05
❑ 289 Al Richardson .15 .05
❑ 290 R.C.Thielemann RC .15 .05
❑ 291 Jeff Van Note .15 .05
❑ 292 Bears TL/Walter Payton .75 .30
❑ 293 Brian Baschnagel .15 .05
❑ 294 Robin Earl .15 .05
❑ 295 Vince Evans .40 .15
❑ 296 Gary Fencik .15 .05
❑ 297 Dan Hampton .75 .30
❑ 298 Noah Jackson .15 .05
❑ 299 Ken Margerum .15 .05
❑ 300 Jim Osborne .15 .05
❑ 301 Bob Parsons .15 .05
❑ 302 Walter Payton 10.00 4.00
❑ 303 Walter Payton IA 3.00 1.25
❑ 304 Revie Sorey .15 .05
❑ 305 Matt Suhey RC .75 .30
❑ 306 Rickey Watts .15 .05
❑ 307 Cowboys TL/Dorsett .75 .30
❑ 308 Bob Breunig .15 .05
❑ 309 Doug Cosbie RC .15 .05
❑ 310 Pat Donovan .15 .05
❑ 311 Tony Dorsett 1.50 .60
❑ 312 Tony Dorsett IA .75 .30
❑ 313 Michael Downs RC .15 .05
❑ 314 Billy Joe DuPree .40 .15
❑ 315 John Dutton .15 .05
❑ 316 Tony Hill .40 .15
❑ 317 Butch Johnson .40 .15
❑ 318 Ed Too Tall Jones .75 .30
❑ 319 James Jones COW .15 .05
❑ 320 Harvey Martin .40 .15
❑ 321 Drew Pearson .75 .30
❑ 322 Herb Scott .15 .05
❑ 323 Rafael Septien .15 .05
❑ 324 Rafael Septien IA .15 .05
❑ 325 Ron Springs .40 .15
❑ 326 Dennis Thurman RC .15 .05
❑ 327 Everson Walls RC .75 .30
❑ 328 Everson Walls IA .75 .30
❑ 329 Danny White .75 .30
❑ 330 Danny White IA .40 .15
❑ 331 Randy White .75 .30
❑ 332 Randy White IA .75 .30
❑ 333 Detroit Lions TL .40 .15
❑ 334 Jim Allen .15 .05
❑ 335 Al(Bubba) Baker .40 .15
❑ 336 Dexter Bussey .15 .05
❑ 337 Doug English .40 .15
❑ 338 Ken Fantetti .15 .05
❑ 339 William Gay .15 .05
❑ 340 David Hill .15 .05
❑ 341 Eric Hipple RC .15 .05
❑ 342 Rick Kane .15 .05
❑ 343 Eddie Murray .75 .30
❑ 344 Eddie Murray IA .40 .15
❑ 345 Ray Oldham .15 .05
❑ 346 Dave Pureifory .15 .05
❑ 347 Freddie Scott .15 .05
❑ 348 Freddie Scott IA .15 .05
❑ 349 Billy Sims .75 .30
❑ 350 Billy Sims IA .75 .30
❑ 351 Tom Skladany .15 .05
❑ 352 Leonard Thompson .15 .05
❑ 353 Stan White .15 .05
❑ 354 Packers TL/Lofton .75 .30
❑ 355 Paul Coffman .15 .05
❑ 356 George Cumby .15 .05
❑ 357 Lynn Dickey .15 .05
❑ 358 Lynn Dickey IA .15 .05
❑ 359 Gerry Ellis .15 .05
❑ 360 Maurice Harvey .15 .05
❑ 361 Harlan Huckleby .15 .05
❑ 362 John Jefferson .75 .30
❑ 363 Mark Lee RC .15 .05
❑ 364 James Lofton 1.00 .40
❑ 365 James Lofton IA .75 .30
❑ 366 Jan Stenerud .40 .15
❑ 367 Jan Stenerud IA .40 .15
❑ 368 Rich Wingo .15 .05
❑ 369 Los Angeles Rams TL .40 .15
❑ 370 Frank Corral .15 .05
❑ 371 Nolan Cromwell .40 .15
❑ 372 Nolan Cromwell IA .40 .15
❑ 373 Preston Dennard .15 .05
❑ 374 Mike Fanning .15 .05
❑ 375 Doug France .15 .05
❑ 376 Mike Guman .15 .05
❑ 377 Pat Haden .40 .15
❑ 378 Dennis Harrah .15 .05

	Card	Price 1	Price 2
❑	379 Drew Hill RC	.75	.30
❑	380 LeRoy Irvin RC	.15	.05
❑	381 Cody Jones	.15	.05
❑	382 Rod Perry	.15	.05
❑	383 Rich Saul	.15	.05
❑	384 Pat Thomas	.15	.05
❑	385 Wendell Tyler	.40	.15
❑	386 Wendell Tyler IA	.40	.15
❑	387 Billy Waddy	.15	.05
❑	388 Jack Youngblood	.75	.30
❑	389 Minnesota Vikings TL	.15	.05
❑	390 Matt Blair	.15	.05
❑	391 Ted Brown	.15	.05
❑	392 Ted Brown IA	.15	.05
❑	393 Rick Danmeier	.15	.05
❑	394 Tommy Kramer	.40	.15
❑	395 Mark Mullaney	.15	.05
❑	396 Eddie Payton	.15	.05
❑	397 Ahmad Rashad	.75	.30
❑	398 Joe Senser	.15	.05
❑	399 Joe Senser IA	.15	.05
❑	400 Sammie White	.40	.15
❑	401 Sammie White IA	.15	.05
❑	402 Ron Yary	.75	.30
❑	403 Rickey Young	.15	.05
❑	404 Saints TL/Ric.Jackson	.40	.15
❑	405 Russell Erxleben	.15	.05
❑	406 Elois Grooms	.15	.05
❑	407 Jack Holmes	.15	.05
❑	408 Archie Manning	.75	.30
❑	409 Derland Moore	.15	.05
❑	410 George Rogers RC	.75	.30
❑	411 George Rogers IA	.75	.30
❑	412 Toussaint Tyler	.15	.05
❑	413 Dave Waymer RC	.15	.05
❑	414 Wayne Wilson	.15	.05
❑	415 New York Giants TL	.15	.05
❑	416 Scott Brunner RC	.15	.05
❑	417 Rob Carpenter	.15	.05
❑	418 Harry Carson	.40	.15
❑	419 Bill Currier	.15	.05
❑	420 Joe Danelo	.15	.05
❑	421 Joe Danelo IA	.15	.05
❑	422 Mark Haynes RC	.15	.05
❑	423 Terry Jackson	.15	.05
❑	424 Dave Jennings	.15	.05
❑	425 Gary Jeter	.15	.05
❑	426 Brian Kelley	.15	.05
❑	427 George Martin	.15	.05
❑	428 Curtis McGriff	.15	.05
❑	429 Bill Neill	.15	.05
❑	430 Johnny Perkins	.15	.05
❑	431 Beasley Reece	.15	.05
❑	432 Gary Shirk	.15	.05
❑	433 Phil Simms	2.00	.75
❑	434 Lawrence Taylor RC	20.00	7.50
❑	435 Lawrence Taylor IA	10.00	4.00
❑	436 Brad Van Pelt	.15	.05
❑	437 Philadelphia Eagles TL	.40	.15
❑	438 John Bunting	.15	.05
❑	439 Billy Campfield	.15	.05
❑	440 Harold Carmichael	.75	.30
❑	441 Harold Carmichael IA	.75	.30
❑	442 Herman Edwards	.15	.05
❑	443 Tony Franklin	.15	.05
❑	444 Tony Franklin IA	.15	.05
❑	445 Carl Hairston	.15	.05
❑	446 Dennis Harrison	.15	.05
❑	447 Ron Jaworski	.75	.30
❑	448 Charlie Johnson NT	.15	.05
❑	449 Keith Krepfle	.15	.05
❑	450 Frank LeMaster	.15	.05
❑	451 Randy Logan	.15	.05
❑	452 Wilbert Montgomery	.40	.15
❑	453 Wilbert Montgomery IA	.40	.15
❑	454 Hubie Oliver	.15	.05
❑	455 Jerry Robinson	.15	.05
❑	456 Jerry Robinson IA	.15	.05
❑	457 Jerry Sisemore	.15	.05
❑	458 Charlie Smith WR	.15	.05
❑	459 Stan Walters	.15	.05
❑	460 Brenard Wilson	.15	.05
❑	461 Roynell Young	.15	.05
❑	462 Cardinals TL/O.Anderson	.40	.15
❑	463 Ottis Anderson	.75	.30
❑	464 Ottis Anderson IA	.75	.30
❑	465 Carl Birdsong	.15	.05
❑	466 Rush Brown	.15	.05
❑	467 Mel Gray	.40	.15
❑	468 Ken Greene	.15	.05
❑	469 Jim Hart	.75	.30
❑	470 E.J.Junior RC	.40	.15
❑	471 Neil Lomax RC	.75	.30
❑	472 Stump Mitchell RC	.75	.30
❑	473 Wayne Morris	.15	.05
❑	474 Neil O'Donoghue	.15	.05
❑	475 Pat Tilley	.15	.05
❑	476 Pat Tilley IA	.15	.05
❑	477 49ers TL/Dwight Clark	.40	.15
❑	478 Dwight Clark	.75	.30
❑	479 Dwight Clark IA	.75	.30
❑	480 Earl Cooper	.15	.05
❑	481 Randy Cross	.40	.15
❑	482 Johnny Davis RC	.15	.05
❑	483 Fred Dean	.15	.05
❑	484 Fred Dean IA	.15	.05
❑	485 Dwight Hicks RC	.75	.30
❑	486 Ronnie Lott RC	20.00	7.50
❑	487 Ronnie Lott IA	6.00	3.00
❑	488 Joe Montana	20.00	7.50
❑	489 Joe Montana IA	12.00	5.00
❑	490 Ricky Patton	.15	.05
❑	491 Jack Reynolds	.40	.15
❑	492 Freddie Solomon	.15	.05
❑	493 Ray Wersching	.15	.05
❑	494 Charle Young	.15	.05
❑	495 Tampa Bay Bucs TL	.40	.15
❑	496 Cedric Brown	.15	.05
❑	497 Neal Colzie	.15	.05
❑	498 Jerry Eckwood	.15	.05
❑	499 Jimmie Giles	.40	.15
❑	500 Hugh Green RC	.75	.30
❑	501 Kevin House	.15	.05
❑	502 Kevin House IA	.15	.05
❑	503 Cecil Johnson	.15	.05
❑	504 James Owens	.15	.05
❑	505 Lee Roy Selmon	.75	.30
❑	506 Mike Washington	.15	.05
❑	507 James Wilder RC	.40	.15
❑	508 Doug Williams	.40	.15
❑	509 Redskins TL/Monk	.75	.30
❑	510 Perry Brooks	.15	.05
❑	511 Dave Butz	.40	.15
❑	512 Wilbur Jackson	.15	.05
❑	513 Joe Lavender	.15	.05
❑	514 Terry Metcalf	.40	.15
❑	515 Art Monk	3.00	1.25
❑	516 Mark Moseley	.15	.05
❑	517 Mark Murphy	.15	.05
❑	518 Mike Nelms	.15	.05
❑	519 Lemar Parrish	.15	.05
❑	520 John Riggins	.75	.30
❑	521 Joe Theismann	.75	.30
❑	522 Ricky Thompson	.15	.05
❑	523 Don Warren UER	.15	.05
❑	524 Joe Washington	.40	.15
❑	525 Checklist 1-132	.50	.20
❑	526 Checklist 133-264	.50	.20
❑	527 Checklist 265-396	.50	.20
❑	528 Checklist 397-528	.50	.20

1983 Topps

	Card	Price 1	Price 2
❑	COMPLETE SET (396)	60.00	30.00
❑	1 Ken Anderson RB	.60	.25
❑	2 Tony Dorsett RB	.60	.25
❑	3 Dan Fouts RB	.60	.25
❑	4 Joe Montana RB	3.00	1.50
❑	5 Mark Moseley RB	.30	.10
❑	6 Mike Nelms RB	.10	.02
❑	7 Darrol Ray RB	.10	.02
❑	8 John Riggins RB	.60	.25
❑	9 Fulton Walker RB	.10	.02
❑	10 NFC Champs/Riggins	.60	.25
❑	11 AFC Championship	.30	.10
❑	12 Super Bowl XVII/J.Riggins	.10	.02
❑	13 Atlanta Falcons TL	.30	.10
❑	14 William Andrews DP	.30	.10
❑	15 Steve Bartkowski	.30	.10
❑	16 Bobby Butler	.10	.02
❑	17 Buddy Curry	.10	.02
❑	18 Alfred Jackson DP	.10	.02
❑	19 Alfred Jenkins	.10	.02
❑	20 Kenny Johnson	.10	.02
❑	21 Mike Kenn	.10	.02
❑	22 Mick Luckhurst	.10	.02
❑	23 Junior Miller	.10	.02
❑	24 Al Richardson	.10	.02
❑	25 Gerald Riggs RC DP	.30	.10
❑	26 R.C. Thielemann	.10	.02
❑	27 Jeff Van Note	.10	.02
❑	28 Bears TL/W.Payton	1.00	.40
❑	29 Brian Baschnagel	.10	.02
❑	30 Dan Hampton	.60	.25
❑	31 Mike Hartenstine	.10	.02
❑	32 Noah Jackson	.10	.02
❑	33 Jim McMahon RC	8.00	4.00
❑	34 Emery Moorehead DP	.10	.02
❑	35 Bob Parsons	.10	.02
❑	36 Walter Payton	6.00	3.00
❑	37 Terry Schmidt	.10	.02
❑	38 Mike Singletary RC	8.00	4.00
❑	39 Matt Suhey DP	.30	.10
❑	40 Rickey Watts DP	.10	.02
❑	41 Otis Wilson RC DP	.30	.10
❑	42 Cowboys TL/Tony Dorsett	.60	.25
❑	43 Bob Breunig	.30	.10
❑	44 Doug Cosbie	.10	.02
❑	45 Pat Donovan	.10	.02
❑	46 Tony Dorsett DP	1.00	.40
❑	47 Tony Hill	.30	.10
❑	48 Butch Johnson DP	.30	.10
❑	49 Ed Too Tall Jones DP	.60	.25
❑	50 Harvey Martin DP	.30	.10
❑	51 Drew Pearson	.60	.25
❑	52 Rafael Septien	.10	.02
❑	53 Ron Springs DP	.10	.02
❑	54 Dennis Thurman	.10	.02
❑	55 Everson Walls	.30	.10
❑	56 Danny White DP	.60	.25
❑	57 Randy White	.60	.25
❑	58 Detroit Lions TL	.30	.10
❑	59 Al(Bubba) Baker DP	.30	.10
❑	60 Dexter Bussey DP	.10	.02
❑	61 Gary Danielson DP	.10	.02
❑	62 Keith Dorney DP	.10	.02
❑	63 Doug English	.10	.02
❑	64 Ken Fantetti DP	.10	.02
❑	65 Alvin Hall DP	.10	.02
❑	66 David Hill DP	.10	.02
❑	67 Eric Hipple	.10	.02
❑	68 Eddie Murray DP	.30	.10
❑	69 Freddie Scott	.10	.02
❑	70 Billy Sims DP	.30	.10
❑	71 Tom Skladany DP	.10	.02
❑	72 Leonard Thompson DP	.10	.02
❑	73 Bobby Watkins	.10	.02
❑	74 Green Bay Packers TL	.10	.02
❑	75 John Anderson	.10	.02
❑	76 Paul Coffman	.10	.02
❑	77 Lynn Dickey	.10	.02
❑	78 Mike Douglass DP	.10	.02
❑	79 Eddie Lee Ivery	.10	.02
❑	80 John Jefferson DP	.60	.25
❑	81 Ezra Johnson	.10	.02
❑	82 Mark Lee	.10	.02
❑	83 James Lofton	.60	.25
❑	84 Larry McCarren	.10	.02
❑	85 Jan Stenerud DP	.30	.10
❑	86 Los Angeles Rams TL	.10	.02
❑	87 Bill Bain DP	.10	.02
❑	88 Nolan Cromwell	.30	.10
❑	89 Preston Dennard	.10	.02
❑	90 Vince Ferragamo DP	.30	.10

❑	91 Mike Guman	.10	.02
❑	92 Kent Hill	.10	.02
❑	93 Mike Lansford RC DP	.10	.02
❑	94 Rod Perry	.10	.02
❑	95 Pat Thomas DP	.10	.02
❑	96 Jack Youngblood	.60	.25
❑	97 Minnesota Vikings TL	.10	.02
❑	98 Matt Blair	.10	.02
❑	99 Ted Brown	.10	.02
❑	100 Greg Coleman	.10	.02
❑	101 Randy Holloway	.10	.02
❑	102 Tommy Kramer	.30	.10
❑	103 Doug Martin DP	.10	.02
❑	104 Mark Mullaney	.10	.02
❑	105 Joe Senser	.10	.02
❑	106 Willie Teal DP	.10	.02
❑	107 Sammie White	.30	.10
❑	108 Rickey Young	.10	.02
❑	109 New Orleans Saints TL	.30	.10
❑	110 Stan Brock RC	.10	.02
❑	111 Bruce Clark RC	.10	.02
❑	112 Russell Erxleben DP	.10	.02
❑	113 Russell Gary	.10	.02
❑	114 Jeff Groth DP	.10	.02
❑	115 John Hill DP	.10	.02
❑	116 Derland Moore	.10	.02
❑	117 George Rogers	.30	.10
❑	118 Ken Stabler	1.50	.60
❑	119 Wayne Wilson	.10	.02
❑	120 New York Giants TL	.10	.02
❑	121 Scott Brunner	.10	.02
❑	122 Rob Carpenter	.10	.02
❑	123 Harry Carson	.30	.10
❑	124 Joe Danelo DP	.10	.02
❑	125 Earnest Gray	.10	.02
❑	126 Mark Haynes DP	.30	.10
❑	127 Terry Jackson	.10	.02
❑	128 Dave Jennings	.10	.02
❑	129 Brian Kelley	.10	.02
❑	130 George Martin	.10	.02
❑	131 Tom Mullady	.10	.02
❑	132 Johnny Perkins	.10	.02
❑	133 Lawrence Taylor	5.00	2.00
❑	134 Brad Van Pelt	.10	.02
❑	135 Butch Woolfolk DP RC	.10	.02
❑	136 Philadelphia Eagles TL	.30	.10
❑	137 Harold Carmichael	.60	.25
❑	138 Herman Edwards	.10	.02
❑	139 Tony Franklin DP	.10	.02
❑	140 Carl Hairston DP	.10	.02
❑	141 Dennis Harrison DP	.10	.02
❑	142 Ron Jaworski DP	.30	.10
❑	143 Frank LeMaster	.10	.02
❑	144 Wilbert Montgomery DP	.30	.10
❑	145 Guy Morriss	.10	.02
❑	146 Jerry Robinson	.10	.02
❑	147 Max Runager	.10	.02
❑	148 Ron Smith DP RC	.10	.02
❑	149 John Spagnola	.10	.02
❑	150 Stan Walters DP	.10	.02
❑	151 Roynell Young DP	.10	.02
❑	152 Cardinals TL/O.Anderson	.30	.10
❑	153 Ottis Anderson	.60	.25
❑	154 Carl Birdsong	.10	.02
❑	155 Dan Dierdorf DP	.60	.25
❑	156 Roy Green RC	.60	.25
❑	157 Elois Grooms	.10	.02
❑	158 Neil Lomax DP	.30	.10
❑	159 Wayne Morris	.10	.02
❑	160 Tootie Robbins RC	.10	.02
❑	161 Luis Sharpe RC	.10	.02
❑	162 Pat Tilley	.10	.02
❑	163 San Francisco 49ers TL	.10	.02
❑	164 Dwight Clark	.60	.25
❑	165 Randy Cross	.30	.10
❑	166 Russ Francis	.30	.10
❑	167 Dwight Hicks	.10	.02
❑	168 Ronnie Lott	2.50	1.25
❑	169 Joe Montana DP	10.00	4.00
❑	170 Jeff Moore	.10	.02
❑	171 Renaldo Nehemiah RC DP	.60	.25
❑	172 Freddie Solomon	.10	.02
❑	173 Ray Wersching DP	.10	.02
❑	174 Tampa Bay Bucs TL	.10	.02
❑	175 Cedric Brown	.10	.02
❑	176 Bill Capece	.10	.02
❑	177 Neal Colzie	.10	.02
❑	178 Jimmie Giles	.10	.02
❑	179 Hugh Green	.30	.10
❑	180 Kevin House DP	.10	.02
❑	181 James Owens	.10	.02
❑	182 Lee Roy Selmon	.60	.25
❑	183 Mike Washington	.10	.02
❑	184 James Wilder	.10	.02
❑	185 Doug Williams DP	.30	.10
❑	186 Redskins TL/John Riggins	.60	.25
❑	187 Jeff Bostic RC DP	1.00	.40
❑	188 Charlie Brown RC	.30	.10
❑	189 Vernon Dean DP RC	.10	.02
❑	190 Joe Jacoby RC	1.00	.40
❑	191 Dexter Manley RC	.30	.10
❑	192 Rich Milot	.10	.02
❑	193 Art Monk DP	1.00	.40
❑	194 Mark Moseley DP	.10	.02
❑	195 Mike Nelms	.10	.02
❑	196 Neal Olkewicz DP	.10	.02
❑	197 Tony Peters	.10	.02
❑	198 John Riggins DP	.60	.25
❑	199 Joe Theismann	.60	.25
❑	200 Don Warren	.10	.02
❑	201 Jeris White DP	.10	.02
❑	202 J.Theismann/K.Anderson LL	.60	.25
❑	203 Receiving Leaders	.30	.10
❑	204 Tony Dorsett/F.McNeil LL	.60	.25
❑	205 M.Allen/W.Tyler LL	1.25	.50
❑	206 Interception Leaders	.30	.10
❑	207 Punting Leaders	.10	.02
❑	208 Baltimore Colts TL	.10	.02
❑	209 Matt Bouza	.10	.02
❑	210 Johnie Cooks RC DP	.10	.02
❑	211 Curtis Dickey	.10	.02
❑	212 Nesby Glasgow DP	.10	.02
❑	213 Derrick Hatchett	.10	.02
❑	214 Randy McMillan	.10	.02
❑	215 Mike Pagel RC	.30	.10
❑	216 Rohn Stark RC DP	.30	.10
❑	217 Donnell Thompson RC DP	.10	.02
❑	218 Leo Wisniewski DP	.10	.02
❑	219 Buffalo Bills TL	.30	.10
❑	220 Curtis Brown	.10	.02
❑	221 Jerry Butler	.10	.02
❑	222 Greg Cater DP	.10	.02
❑	223 Joe Cribbs	.30	.10
❑	224 Joe Ferguson	.30	.10
❑	225 Roosevelt Leaks	.10	.02
❑	226 Frank Lewis	.10	.02
❑	227 Eugene Marve RC	.10	.02
❑	228 Fred Smerlas DP	.10	.02
❑	229 Ben Williams DP	.10	.02
❑	230 Cincinnati Bengals TL	.10	.02
❑	231 Charles Alexander	.10	.02
❑	232 Ken Anderson DP	.60	.25
❑	233 Jim Breech DP	.10	.02
❑	234 Ross Browner	.10	.02
❑	235 Cris Collinsworth DP	.60	.25
❑	236 Isaac Curtis	.10	.02
❑	237 Pete Johnson	.10	.02
❑	238 Steve Kreider DP	.10	.02
❑	239 Max Montoya RC DP	.10	.02
❑	240 Anthony Munoz	1.00	.40
❑	241 Ken Riley	.10	.02
❑	242 Dan Ross	.10	.02
❑	243 Reggie Williams	.30	.10
❑	244 Cleveland Browns TL	.30	.10
❑	245 Chip Banks RC DP	.30	.10
❑	246 Tom Cousineau RC DP	.30	.10
❑	247 Joe DeLamielleure DP	.30	.10
❑	248 Doug Dieken DP	.10	.02
❑	249 Hanford Dixon RC	.10	.02
❑	250 Ricky Feacher DP	.10	.02
❑	251 Lawrence Johnson DP	.10	.02
❑	252 Dave Logan DP	.10	.02
❑	253 Paul McDonald DP	.10	.02
❑	254 Ozzie Newsome DP	.60	.25
❑	255 Mike Pruitt	.30	.10
❑	256 Clarence Scott DP	.10	.02
❑	257 Brian Sipe DP	.30	.10
❑	258 Dwight Walker DP	.10	.02
❑	259 Charles White	.30	.10
❑	260 Denver Broncos TL	.10	.02
❑	261 Steve DeBerg DP	.30	.10
❑	262 Randy Gradishar DP	.30	.10
❑	263 Rulon Jones RC DP	.10	.02
❑	264 Rich Karlis DP	.10	.02
❑	265 Don Latimer	.10	.02
❑	266 Rick Parros DP	.10	.02
❑	267 Luke Prestridge	.10	.02
❑	268 Rick Upchurch	.30	.10
❑	269 Steve Watson DP	.10	.02
❑	270 Gerald Willhite DP	.10	.02
❑	271 Houston Oilers TL	.10	.02
❑	272 Harold Bailey	.10	.02
❑	273 Jesse Baker DP	.10	.02
❑	274 Gregg Bingham DP	.10	.02
❑	275 Robert Brazile DP	.10	.02
❑	276 Donnie Craft	.10	.02
❑	277 Daryl Hunt	.10	.02
❑	278 Archie Manning DP	.30	.10
❑	279 Gifford Nielsen	.10	.02
❑	280 Mike Renfro	.10	.02
❑	281 Carl Roaches DP	.10	.02
❑	282 Kansas City Chiefs TL	.30	.10
❑	283 Gary Barbaro	.10	.02
❑	284 Joe Delaney	.10	.02
❑	285 Jeff Gossett RC	.60	.25
❑	286 Gary Green DP	.10	.02
❑	287 Eric Harris DP	.10	.02
❑	288 Billy Jackson DP	.10	.02
❑	289 Bill Kenney DP	.10	.02
❑	290 Nick Lowery	.60	.25
❑	291 Henry Marshall	.10	.02
❑	292 Art Still DP	.10	.02
❑	293 Raiders TL/M.Allen	2.00	.75
❑	294 Marcus Allen RC DP	15.00	6.00
❑	295 Lyle Alzado	.60	.25
❑	296 Chris Bahr DP	.10	.02
❑	297 Cliff Branch	.60	.25
❑	298 Todd Christensen RC	.75	.30
❑	299 Ray Guy	.30	.10
❑	300 Frank Hawkins DP	.10	.02
❑	301 Lester Hayes DP	.10	.02
❑	302 Ted Hendricks DP	.60	.25
❑	303 Kenny King DP	.10	.02
❑	304 Rod Martin	.10	.02
❑	305 Matt Millen DP	.60	.25
❑	306 Burgess Owens	.10	.02
❑	307 Jim Plunkett	.60	.25
❑	308 Miami Dolphins TL	.30	.10
❑	309 Bob Baumhower	.10	.02
❑	310 Glenn Blackwood	.10	.02
❑	311 Lyle Blackwood DP	.10	.02
❑	312 A.J. Duhe	.10	.02
❑	313 Andra Franklin	.10	.02
❑	314 Duriel Harris	.10	.02
❑	315 Bob Kuechenberg DP	.30	.10
❑	316 Don McNeal	.10	.02
❑	317 Tony Nathan	.30	.10
❑	318 Ed Newman	.10	.02
❑	319 Earnie Rhone DP	.10	.02
❑	320 Joe Rose DP	.10	.02
❑	321 Don Strock DP	.10	.02
❑	322 Uwe Von Schamann	.10	.02
❑	323 David Woodley DP	.30	.10
❑	324 New England Pats TL	.10	.02
❑	325 Julius Adams	.10	.02
❑	326 Pete Brock	.10	.02
❑	327 Rich Camarillo RC DP	.10	.02
❑	328 Tony Collins DP	.10	.02
❑	329 Steve Grogan	.30	.10
❑	330 John Hannah	.60	.25
❑	331 Don Hasselbeck	.10	.02
❑	332 Mike Haynes	.30	.10
❑	333 Roland James RC	.10	.02
❑	334A Stanley Morgan ERR IL	.60	.25
❑	334B Stanley Morgan COR	.30	.10
❑	335 Steve Nelson	.10	.02
❑	336 Kenneth Sims DP	.10	.02
❑	337 Mark Van Eeghen	.30	.10
❑	338 New York Jets TL	.30	.10
❑	339 Greg Buttle	.10	.02
❑	340 Joe Fields	.10	.02
❑	341 Mark Gastineau DP	.30	.10
❑	342 Bruce Harper	.10	.02
❑	343 Bobby Jackson	.10	.02
❑	344 Bobby Jones	.10	.02
❑	345 Johnny Lam Jones DP	.10	.02
❑	346 Joe Klecko	.30	.10
❑	347 Marty Lyons	.10	.02
❑	348 Freeman McNeil	.60	.25
❑	349 Lance Mehl RC	.10	.02
❑	350 Marvin Powell DP	.10	.02

Card		
❑ 351 Darrol Ray DP	.10	.02
❑ 352 Abdul Salaam	.10	.02
❑ 353 Richard Todd	.30	.10
❑ 354 Wesley Walker	.30	.10
❑ 355 Steelers TL/Franco Harris	.60	.25
❑ 356 Gary Anderson K RC DP	6.00	3.00
❑ 357 Mel Blount DP	.60	.25
❑ 358 Terry Bradshaw DP	1.50	.60
❑ 359 Larry Brown	.10	.02
❑ 360 Bennie Cunningham	.10	.02
❑ 361 Gary Dunn	.10	.02
❑ 362 Franco Harris	.75	.30
❑ 363 Jack Lambert	.60	.25
❑ 364 Frank Pollard	.10	.02
❑ 365 Donnie Shell	.30	.10
❑ 366 John Stallworth	.60	.25
❑ 367 Loren Toews	.10	.02
❑ 368 Mike Webster DP	.60	.25
❑ 369 Dwayne Woodruff RC	.10	.02
❑ 370 San Diego Chargers TL	.30	.10
❑ 371 Rolf Benirschke DP	.10	.02
❑ 372 James Brooks	.60	.25
❑ 373 Wes Chandler	.30	.10
❑ 374 Dan Fouts DP	.60	.25
❑ 375 Tim Fox	.10	.02
❑ 376 Gary Johnson	.10	.02
❑ 377 Charlie Joiner DP	.60	.25
❑ 378 Louie Kelcher	.10	.02
❑ 379 Chuck Muncie	.10	.02
❑ 380 Cliff Thrift	.10	.02
❑ 381 Doug Wilkerson	.10	.02
❑ 382 Kellen Winslow	.75	.30
❑ 383 Seattle Seahawks TL	.10	.02
❑ 384 Kenny Easley RC	.60	.25
❑ 385 Jacob Green RC	.30	.10
❑ 386 John Harris	.10	.02
❑ 387 Michael Jackson	.10	.02
❑ 388 Norm Johnson RC	.10	.02
❑ 389 Steve Largent	1.25	.50
❑ 390 Keith Simpson	.10	.02
❑ 391 Sherman Smith	.10	.02
❑ 392 Jeff West DP	.10	.02
❑ 393 Jim Zorn DP	.30	.10
❑ 394 Checklist 1-132	.50	.20
❑ 395 Checklist 133-264	.50	.20
❑ 396 Checklist 265-396	.50	.20

1984 Topps

Card		
❑ COMPLETE SET (396)	200.00	100.00
❑ COMP.FACT.SET (396)	300.00	175.00
❑ 1 Eric Dickerson RB	.50	.20
❑ 2 Ali Haji-Sheikh RB	.25	.08
❑ 3 Franco Harris RB	.50	.20
❑ 4 Mark Moseley RB	.25	.08
❑ 5 John Riggins RB	.50	.20
❑ 6 Jan Stenerud RB	.25	.08
❑ 7 AFC Champs/M.Allen	.50	.20
❑ 8 NFC Champs/Riggins	.25	.08
❑ 9 Super Bowl XVIII/Allen UER	.50	.20
❑ 10 Indianapolis Colts TL	.10	.02
❑ 11 Raul Allegre RC	.10	.02
❑ 12 Curtis Dickey	.25	.08
❑ 13 Ray Donaldson RC	.25	.08
❑ 14 Nesby Glasgow	.10	.02
❑ 15 Chris Hinton RC	.50	.20
❑ 16 Vernon Maxwell RC	.10	.02
❑ 17 Randy McMillan	.10	.02
❑ 18 Mike Pagel	.25	.08
❑ 19 Rohn Stark	.25	.08
❑ 20 Leo Wisniewski	.10	.02
❑ 21 Buffalo Bills TL	.25	.08
❑ 22 Jerry Butler	.10	.02
❑ 23 Joe Danelo	.10	.02
❑ 24 Joe Ferguson	.25	.08
❑ 25 Steve Freeman	.10	.02
❑ 26 Roosevelt Leaks	.25	.08
❑ 27 Frank Lewis	.10	.02
❑ 28 Eugene Marve	.10	.02
❑ 29 Booker Moore	.10	.02
❑ 30 Fred Smerlas	.10	.02
❑ 31 Ben Williams	.25	.08
❑ 32 Cincinnati Bengals TL	.25	.08
❑ 33 Charles Alexander	.10	.02
❑ 34 Ken Anderson	.50	.20
❑ 35 Ken Anderson IR	.50	.20
❑ 36 Jim Breech	.10	.02
❑ 37 Cris Collinsworth	.50	.20
❑ 38 Cris Collinsworth IR	.50	.20
❑ 39 Isaac Curtis	.25	.08
❑ 40 Eddie Edwards	.10	.02
❑ 41 Ray Horton RC	.10	.02
❑ 42 Pete Johnson	.25	.08
❑ 43 Steve Kreider	.10	.02
❑ 44 Max Montoya	.10	.02
❑ 45 Anthony Munoz	.50	.20
❑ 46 Reggie Williams	.25	.08
❑ 47 Cleveland Browns TL	.25	.08
❑ 48 Matt Bahr	.25	.08
❑ 49 Chip Banks	.10	.02
❑ 50 Tom Cousineau	.10	.02
❑ 51 Joe DeLamielleure	.50	.20
❑ 52 Doug Dieken	.10	.02
❑ 53 Bob Golic RC	.50	.20
❑ 54 Bobby Jones	.10	.02
❑ 55 Dave Logan	.10	.02
❑ 56 Clay Matthews	.50	.20
❑ 57 Paul McDonald	.10	.02
❑ 58 Ozzie Newsome	.50	.20
❑ 59 Ozzie Newsome IR	.50	.20
❑ 60 Mike Pruitt	.25	.08
❑ 61 Denver Broncos TL	.25	.08
❑ 62 Barney Chavous RC	.10	.02
❑ 63 John Elway RC !	80.00	30.00
❑ 64 Steve Foley	.10	.02
❑ 65 Tom Jackson	.50	.20
❑ 66 Rich Karlis	.10	.02
❑ 67 Luke Prestridge	.10	.02
❑ 68 Zach Thomas WR	.10	.02
❑ 69 Rick Upchurch	.25	.08
❑ 70 Steve Watson	.25	.08
❑ 71 Sammy Winder RC	.25	.08
❑ 72 Louis Wright	.25	.08
❑ 73 Houston Oilers TL	.10	.02
❑ 74 Jesse Baker	.10	.02
❑ 75 Gregg Bingham	.10	.02
❑ 76 Robert Brazile	.25	.08
❑ 77 Steve Brown RC	.10	.02
❑ 78 Chris Dressel	.10	.02
❑ 79 Doug France	.10	.02
❑ 80 Florian Kempf	.10	.02
❑ 81 Carl Roaches	.25	.08
❑ 82 Tim Smith WR RC	.25	.08
❑ 83 Willie Tullis	.10	.02
❑ 84 Kansas City Chiefs TL	.10	.02
❑ 85 Mike Bell RC	.10	.02
❑ 86 Theotis Brown	.10	.02
❑ 87 Carlos Carson	.50	.20
❑ 88 Carlos Carson IR	.25	.08
❑ 89 Deron Cherry RC	.25	.08
❑ 90 Gary Green	.10	.02
❑ 91 Billy Jackson	.10	.02
❑ 92 Bill Kenney	.25	.08
❑ 93 Bill Kenney IR	.25	.08
❑ 94 Nick Lowery	.50	.20
❑ 95 Henry Marshall	.10	.02
❑ 96 Art Still	.10	.02
❑ 97 Los Angeles Raiders TL	.25	.08
❑ 98 Marcus Allen	5.00	2.50
❑ 99 Marcus Allen IR	2.50	1.00
❑ 100 Lyle Alzado	.25	.08
❑ 101 Lyle Alzado IR	.25	.08
❑ 102 Chris Bahr	.10	.02
❑ 103 Malcolm Barnwell RC	.10	.02
❑ 104 Cliff Branch	.50	.20
❑ 105 Todd Christensen	.50	.20
❑ 106 Todd Christensen IR	.50	.20
❑ 107 Ray Guy	.50	.20
❑ 108 Frank Hawkins	.10	.02
❑ 109 Lester Hayes	.25	.08
❑ 110 Ted Hendricks	.50	.20
❑ 111 Howie Long RC	15.00	6.00
❑ 112 Rod Martin	.25	.08
❑ 113 Vann McElroy RC	.10	.02
❑ 114 Jim Plunkett	.50	.20
❑ 115 Greg Pruitt	.25	.08
❑ 116 Dolphins TL/M.Duper	.50	.20
❑ 117 Bob Baumhower	.10	.02
❑ 118 Doug Betters RC	.10	.02
❑ 119 A.J. Duhe	.10	.02
❑ 120 Mark Duper RC	.50	.20
❑ 121 Andra Franklin	.10	.02
❑ 122 William Judson	.10	.02
❑ 123 Dan Marino RC !	80.00	30.00
❑ 124 Dan Marino IR	12.00	5.00
❑ 125 Nat Moore	.25	.08
❑ 126 Ed Newman	.10	.02
❑ 127 Reggie Roby RC	.25	.08
❑ 128 Gerald Small	.10	.02
❑ 129 Dwight Stephenson RC	3.00	1.25
❑ 130 Uwe Von Schamann	.10	.02
❑ 131 New England Pats TL	.10	.02
❑ 132 Rich Camarillo	.25	.08
❑ 133 Tony Collins	.25	.08
❑ 134 Tony Collins IR	.10	.02
❑ 135 Bob Cryder	.10	.02
❑ 136 Steve Grogan	.25	.08
❑ 137 John Hannah	.50	.20
❑ 138 Brian Holloway RC	.10	.02
❑ 139 Roland James	.10	.02
❑ 140 Stanley Morgan	.25	.08
❑ 141 Rick Sanford	.10	.02
❑ 142 Mosi Tatupu RC	.10	.02
❑ 143 Andre Tippett RC	.50	.20
❑ 144 New York Jets TL	.25	.08
❑ 145 Jerome Barkum	.10	.02
❑ 146 Mark Gastineau	.25	.08
❑ 147 Mark Gastineau IR	.25	.08
❑ 148 Bruce Harper	.10	.02
❑ 149 Johnny Lam Jones	.10	.02
❑ 150 Joe Klecko	.25	.08
❑ 151 Pat Leahy	.10	.02
❑ 152 Freeman McNeil	.25	.08
❑ 153 Lance Mehl	.10	.02
❑ 154 Marvin Powell	.25	.08
❑ 155 Darrol Ray	.10	.02
❑ 156 Pat Ryan RC	.10	.02
❑ 157 Kirk Springs	.10	.02
❑ 158 Wesley Walker	.25	.08
❑ 159 Steelers TL/F.Harris	.50	.20
❑ 160 Walter Abercrombie RC	.25	.08
❑ 161 Gary Anderson K	.50	.20
❑ 162 Terry Bradshaw	2.00	.75
❑ 163 Craig Colquitt	.10	.02
❑ 164 Bennie Cunningham	.10	.02
❑ 165 Franco Harris	.50	.20
❑ 166 Franco Harris IR	.50	.20
❑ 167 Jack Lambert	.50	.20
❑ 168 Jack Lambert IR	.50	.20
❑ 169 Frank Pollard	.10	.02
❑ 170 Donnie Shell	.25	.08
❑ 171 Mike Webster	.25	.08
❑ 172 Keith Willis RC	.10	.02
❑ 173 Rick Woods	.10	.02
❑ 174 Chargers TL/K.Winslow	.50	.20
❑ 175 Rolf Benirschke	.10	.02
❑ 176 James Brooks	.25	.08
❑ 177 Maury Buford	.10	.02
❑ 178 Wes Chandler	.25	.08
❑ 179 Dan Fouts	.60	.25
❑ 180 Dan Fouts IR	.50	.20
❑ 181 Charlie Joiner	.50	.20
❑ 182 Linden King	.10	.02
❑ 183 Chuck Muncie	.25	.08
❑ 184 Billy Ray Smith RC	.50	.20
❑ 185 Danny Walters RC	.10	.02
❑ 186 Kellen Winslow	.60	.25
❑ 187 Kellen Winslow IR	.50	.20
❑ 188 Seahawks TL/C.Warner	.50	.20
❑ 189 Steve August	.10	.02
❑ 190 Dave Brown DB	.10	.02
❑ 191 Zachary Dixon	.10	.02
❑ 192 Kenny Easley	.25	.08
❑ 193 Jacob Green	.10	.02

❑ 194 Norm Johnson .25 .08
❑ 195 Dave Krieg RC 1.50 .60
❑ 196 Steve Largent 1.00 .40
❑ 197 Steve Largent IR .50 .20
❑ 198 Curt Warner RC .50 .20
❑ 199 Curt Warner IR .50 .20
❑ 200 Jeff West .10 .02
❑ 201 Charle Young .10 .02
❑ 202 D.Marino/Bartkow. LL 6.00 2.50
❑ 203 Receiving Leaders .25 .08
❑ 204 Eric Dickerson/Warner LL .50 .20
❑ 205 Scoring Leaders .10 .02
❑ 206 Interception Leaders .10 .02
❑ 207 Punting Leaders .10 .02
❑ 208 Atlanta Falcons TL .25 .08
❑ 209 William Andrews .25 .08
❑ 210 William Andrews IR .25 .08
❑ 211 Stacey Bailey RC .10 .02
❑ 212 Steve Bartkowski .50 .20
❑ 213 Steve Bartkowski IR .25 .08
❑ 214 Ralph Giacomarro .10 .02
❑ 215 Billy Johnson .25 .08
❑ 216 Mike Kenn .25 .08
❑ 217 Mick Luckhurst .10 .02
❑ 218 Gerald Riggs .50 .20
❑ 219 R.C. Thielemann .10 .02
❑ 220 Jeff Van Note .25 .08
❑ 221 Bears TL/W.Payton .75 .30
❑ 222 Jim Covert RC .50 .20
❑ 223 Leslie Frazier .10 .02
❑ 224 Willie Gault RC .50 .20
❑ 225 Mike Hartenstine .10 .02
❑ 226 Noah Jackson UER .10 .02
❑ 227 Jim McMahon 1.25 .50
❑ 228 Walter Payton 4.00 2.00
❑ 229 Walter Payton IR 1.25 .50
❑ 230 Mike Richardson RC .10 .02
❑ 231 Terry Schmidt .10 .02
❑ 232 Mike Singletary 1.25 .50
❑ 233 Matt Suhey .25 .08
❑ 234 Bob Thomas .10 .02
❑ 235 Cowboys TL/T.Dorsett .50 .20
❑ 236 Bob Breunig .10 .02
❑ 237 Doug Cosbie .25 .08
❑ 238 Tony Dorsett 1.00 .40
❑ 239 Tony Dorsett IR .50 .20
❑ 240 John Dutton .10 .02
❑ 241 Tony Hill .25 .08
❑ 242 Ed Too Tall Jones .50 .20
❑ 243 Drew Pearson .50 .20
❑ 244 Rafael Septien .10 .02
❑ 245 Ron Springs .25 .08
❑ 246 Dennis Thurman .10 .02
❑ 247 Everson Walls .10 .02
❑ 248 Danny White .50 .20
❑ 249 Randy White .50 .20
❑ 250 Detroit Lions TL .25 .08
❑ 251 Jeff Chadwick RC .25 .08
❑ 252 Garry Cobb .10 .02
❑ 253 Doug English .25 .08
❑ 254 William Gay .10 .02
❑ 255 Eric Hipple .25 .08
❑ 256 James Jones FB RC .25 .08
❑ 257 Bruce McNorton .10 .02
❑ 258 Eddie Murray .25 .08
❑ 259 Ulysses Norris .10 .02
❑ 260 Billy Sims .50 .20
❑ 261 Billy Sims IR .25 .08
❑ 262 Leonard Thompson .10 .02
❑ 263 Packers TL/J.Lofton .50 .20
❑ 264 John Anderson .10 .02
❑ 265 Paul Coffman .25 .08
❑ 266 Lynn Dickey .25 .08
❑ 267 Gerry Ellis .10 .02
❑ 268 John Jefferson .50 .20
❑ 269 John Jefferson IR .50 .20
❑ 270 Ezra Johnson .10 .02
❑ 271 Tim Lewis RC .10 .02
❑ 272 James Lofton .50 .20
❑ 273 James Lofton IR .50 .20
❑ 274 Larry McCarren .10 .02
❑ 275 Jan Stenerud .25 .08
❑ 276 Rams TL/E.Dickerson .50 .20
❑ 277 Mike Barber .10 .02
❑ 278 Jim Collins .10 .02
❑ 279 Nolan Cromwell .25 .08
❑ 280 Eric Dickerson RC 10.00 4.00
❑ 281 Eric Dickerson IR 2.00 .75
❑ 282 George Farmer South. .10 .02
❑ 283 Vince Ferragamo .25 .08
❑ 284 Kent Hill .10 .02
❑ 285 John Misko .10 .02
❑ 286 Jackie Slater RC 4.00 1.50
❑ 287 Jack Youngblood .25 .08
❑ 288 Minnesota Vikings TL .10 .02
❑ 289 Ted Brown .25 .08
❑ 290 Greg Coleman .10 .02
❑ 291 Steve Dils .10 .02
❑ 292 Tony Galbreath .10 .02
❑ 293 Tommy Kramer .25 .08
❑ 294 Doug Martin .10 .02
❑ 295 Darrin Nelson RC .25 .08
❑ 296 Benny Ricardo .10 .02
❑ 297 John Swain .10 .02
❑ 298 John Turner .10 .02
❑ 299 New Orleans Saints TL .25 .08
❑ 300 Morten Andersen RC 1.50 .60
❑ 301 Russell Erxleben .10 .02
❑ 302 Jeff Groth .10 .02
❑ 303 Rickey Jackson RC .50 .20
❑ 304 Johnnie Poe RC .10 .02
❑ 305 George Rogers .25 .08
❑ 306 Richard Todd .25 .08
❑ 307 Jim Wilks RC .10 .02
❑ 308 Dave Wilson RC .10 .02
❑ 309 Wayne Wilson .10 .02
❑ 310 New York Giants TL .10 .02
❑ 311 Leon Bright .10 .02
❑ 312 Scott Brunner .10 .02
❑ 313 Rob Carpenter .10 .02
❑ 314 Harry Carson .25 .08
❑ 315 Earnest Gray .10 .02
❑ 316 Ali Haji-Sheikh RC .10 .02
❑ 317 Mark Haynes .25 .08
❑ 318 Dave Jennings .10 .02
❑ 319 Brian Kelley .10 .02
❑ 320 Phil Simms .75 .30
❑ 321 Lawrence Taylor 3.00 1.50
❑ 322 Lawrence Taylor IR 1.50 .60
❑ 323 Brad Van Pelt .10 .02
❑ 324 Butch Woolfolk .10 .02
❑ 325 Eagles TL/M.Quick .25 .08
❑ 326 Harold Carmichael .25 .08
❑ 327 Herman Edwards .10 .02
❑ 328 Michael Haddix RC .10 .02
❑ 329 Dennis Harrison .10 .02
❑ 330 Ron Jaworski .25 .08
❑ 331 Wilbert Montgomery .25 .08
❑ 332 Hubie Oliver .10 .02
❑ 333 Mike Quick RC .50 .20
❑ 334 Jerry Robinson .10 .02
❑ 335 Max Runager .10 .02
❑ 336 Michael Williams .10 .02
❑ 337 Cardinals TL/O.Anderson .25 .08
❑ 338 Ottis Anderson .50 .20
❑ 339 Al(Bubba) Baker .25 .08
❑ 340 Carl Birdsong .10 .02
❑ 341 David Galloway .10 .02
❑ 342 Roy Green .25 .08
❑ 343 Roy Green IR .25 .08
❑ 344 Curtis Greer RC .10 .02
❑ 345 Neil Lomax .25 .08
❑ 346 Doug Marsh .10 .02
❑ 347 Stump Mitchell .25 .08
❑ 348 Lionel Washington RC .25 .08
❑ 349 49ers TL/D.Clark .25 .08
❑ 350 Dwaine Board .10 .02
❑ 351 Dwight Clark .50 .20
❑ 352 Dwight Clark IR .25 .08
❑ 353 Roger Craig RC ! 3.00 1.25
❑ 354 Fred Dean .25 .08
❑ 355 Fred Dean IR w/Marino .50 .20
❑ 356 Dwight Hicks .25 .08
❑ 357 Ronnie Lott 1.50 .60
❑ 358 Joe Montana 10.00 4.00
❑ 359 Joe Montana IR 3.00 1.50
❑ 360 Freddie Solomon .10 .02
❑ 361 Wendell Tyler .10 .02
❑ 362 Ray Wersching .10 .02
❑ 363 Eric Wright RC .25 .08
❑ 364 Tampa Bay Bucs TL .10 .02
❑ 365 Gerald Carter .10 .02
❑ 366 Hugh Green .25 .08
❑ 367 Kevin House .25 .08
❑ 368 Michael Morton RC .10
❑ 369 James Owens .10
❑ 370 Booker Reese .10
❑ 371 Lee Roy Selmon .50
❑ 372 Jack Thompson .25
❑ 373 James Wilder .25
❑ 374 Steve Wilson .10
❑ 375 Redskins TL/J.Riggins .50
❑ 376 Jeff Bostic .10
❑ 377 Charlie Brown .50
❑ 378 Charlie Brown IR .25
❑ 379 Dave Butz .25
❑ 380 Darrell Green RC 10.00 5
❑ 381 Russ Grimm RC 1.00
❑ 382 Joe Jacoby .25
❑ 383 Dexter Manley .25
❑ 384 Art Monk 1.00
❑ 385 Mark Moseley .25
❑ 386 Mark Murphy .10
❑ 387 Mike Nelms .10
❑ 388 John Riggins .50
❑ 389 John Riggins IR .50
❑ 390 Joe Theismann .50
❑ 391 Joe Theismann IR .50
❑ 392 Don Warren .25
❑ 393 Joe Washington .25
❑ 394 Checklist 1-132 .30
❑ 395 Checklist 133-264 .30
❑ 396 Checklist 265-396 .30

1984 Topps USFL

❑ COMP.FACT.SET (132) 250.00 150.
❑ COMPLETE SET (132) 250.00 125.
❑ 1 Luther Bradley 2.00 .
❑ 2 Frank Corral 2.00 .
❑ 3 Trumaine Johnson 2.00 .
❑ 4 Greg Landry 2.50 1.
❑ 5 Kit Lathrop 2.00 .
❑ 6 Kevin Long 2.00 .
❑ 7 Tim Spencer 2.00 .
❑ 8 Stan White 2.00 .
❑ 9 Buddy Aydelette 2.00 .
❑ 10 Tom Banks 2.00 .7
❑ 11 Fred Bohannon 2.00 .
❑ 12 Joe Cribbs 4.00 2.0
❑ 13 Joey Jones 2.00 .7
❑ 14 Scott Norwood XRC 2.50 1.
❑ 15 Jim Smith 2.50 1.
❑ 16 Cliff Stoudt 4.00 2.
❑ 17 Vince Evans 4.00 2.
❑ 18 Vagas Ferguson 2.00 .7
❑ 19 John Gillen 2.00 .7
❑ 20 Kris Haines 2.00 .7
❑ 21 Glenn Hyde 2.00 .7
❑ 22 Mark Keel 2.00 .7
❑ 23 Gary Lewis XRC 2.00 .7
❑ 24 Doug Plank 2.00 .7
❑ 25 Neil Balholm 2.00 .7
❑ 26 David Dumars 2.00 .7
❑ 27 David Martin XRC 2.00 .7
❑ 28 Craig Penrose 2.00 .7
❑ 29 Dave Stalls 2.00 .7
❑ 30 Harry Sydney XRC 2.00 .7
❑ 31 Vincent White 2.00 .7
❑ 32 George Yarno 2.00 .7
❑ 33 Kiki DeAyala 2.00 .7
❑ 34 Sam Harrell 2.00 .7
❑ 35 Mike Hawkins 2.00 .7
❑ 36 Jim Kelly XRC 80.00 40.0

❑ 37 Mark Rush	2.00	.75
❑ 38 Ricky Sanders XRC	6.00	3.00
❑ 39 Paul Bergmann	2.00	.75
❑ 40 Tom Dinkel	2.00	.75
❑ 41 Wyatt Henderson	2.00	.75
❑ 42 Vaughan Johnson XRC	2.50	1.25
❑ 43 Willie McClendon Geor.	2.00	.75
❑ 44 Matt Robinson	2.00	.75
❑ 45 George Achica	2.00	.75
❑ 46 Mark Adickes	2.00	.75
❑ 47 Howard Carson	2.00	.75
❑ 48 Kevin Nelson	2.00	.75
❑ 49 Jeff Partridge	2.00	.75
❑ 50 Jo Jo Townsell	2.50	1.25
❑ 51 Eddie Weaver	2.00	.75
❑ 52 Steve Young XRC	120.00	60.00
❑ 53 Derrick Crawford	2.00	.75
❑ 54 Walter Lewis	2.00	.75
❑ 55 Phil McKinnely	2.00	.75
❑ 56 Vic Minore	2.00	.75
❑ 57 Gary Shirk	2.00	.75
❑ 58 Reggie White XRC	60.00	30.00
❑ 59 Anthony Carter XRC	12.00	5.00
❑ 60 John Corker	2.00	.75
❑ 61 David Greenwood	2.00	.75
❑ 62 Bobby Hebert XRC	4.00	2.00
❑ 63 Derek Holloway	2.00	.75
❑ 64 Ken Lacy	2.00	.75
❑ 65 Tyrone McGriff	2.00	.75
❑ 66 Ray Pinney	2.00	.75
❑ 67 Gary Barbaro	2.00	.75
❑ 68 Sam Bowers	2.00	.75
❑ 69 Clarence Collins	2.00	.75
❑ 70 Willie Harper	2.00	.75
❑ 71 Jim LeClair	2.00	.75
❑ 72 Bobby Leopold XRC	2.00	.75
❑ 73 Brian Sipe	4.00	2.00
❑ 74 Herschel Walker XRC	25.00	12.50
❑ 75 Junior Ah You XRC	2.00	.75
❑ 76 Marcus Dupree XRC	6.00	2.50
❑ 77 Marcus Marek	2.00	.75
❑ 78 Tim Mazzetti	2.00	.75
❑ 79 Mike Robinson XRC	2.00	.75
❑ 80 Dan Ross	4.00	2.00
❑ 81 Mark Schellen	2.00	.75
❑ 82 Johnnie Walton	2.00	.75
❑ 83 Gordon Banks	2.00	.75
❑ 84 Fred Besana	2.00	.75
❑ 85 Dave Browning	2.00	.75
❑ 86 Eric Jordan	2.00	.75
❑ 87 Frank Manumaleuga	2.00	.75
❑ 88 Gary Plummer XRC	4.00	2.00
❑ 89 Stan Talley	2.00	.75
❑ 90 Arthur Whittington	2.00	.75
❑ 91 Terry Beeson	2.00	.75
❑ 92 Mel Gray	4.00	2.00
❑ 93 Mike Katolin	2.00	.75
❑ 94 Dewey McClain	2.00	.75
❑ 95 Sidney Thornton	2.00	.75
❑ 96 Doug Williams	4.00	2.00
❑ 97 Kelvin Bryant XRC	4.00	2.00
❑ 98 John Bunting	2.00	.75
❑ 99 Irv Eatman XRC	2.50	1.25
❑ 100 Scott Fitzkee	2.00	.75
❑ 101 Chuck Fusina	2.00	.75
❑ 102 Sean Landeta XRC	2.50	1.25
❑ 103 David Trout	2.00	.75
❑ 104 Scott Woerner	2.00	.75
❑ 105 Glenn Carano	2.00	.75
❑ 106 Ron Crosby	2.00	.75
❑ 107 Jerry Holmes	2.00	.75
❑ 108 Bruce Huther	2.00	.75
❑ 109 Mike Rozier XRC	4.00	2.00
❑ 110 Larry Swider	2.00	.75
❑ 111 Danny Buggs	2.00	.75
❑ 112 Putt Choate	2.00	.75
❑ 113 Rich Garza	2.00	.75
❑ 114 Joey Hackett	2.00	.75
❑ 115 Rick Neuheisel XRC	4.00	2.00
❑ 116 Mike St. Clair	2.00	.75
❑ 117 Gary Anderson XRC RB	4.00	2.00
❑ 118 Zenon Andrusyshyn	2.00	.75
❑ 119 Doug Beaudoin	2.00	.75
❑ 120 Mike Butler	2.00	.75
❑ 121 Willie Gillespie	2.00	.75
❑ 122 Fred Nordgren	2.00	.75
❑ 123 John Reaves	2.00	.75
❑ 124 Eric Truvillion	2.00	.75
❑ 125 Reggie Collier	2.00	.75
❑ 126 Mike Guess	2.00	.75
❑ 127 Mike Hohensee	2.00	.75
❑ 128 Craig James XRC	8.00	3.00
❑ 129 Eric Robinson	2.00	.75
❑ 130 Billy Taylor	2.00	.75
❑ 131 Joey Walters	2.00	.75
❑ 132 Checklist 1-132	2.50	1.25

1985 Topps

❑ COMPLETE SET (396)	60.00	35.00
❑ COMP.FACT.SET (396)	75.00	40.00
❑ 1 Mark Clayton RB	.50	.20
❑ 2 Eric Dickerson RB	.50	.20
❑ 3 Charlie Joiner RB	.50	.20
❑ 4 Dan Marino RB	6.00	3.00
❑ 5 Art Monk RB	.50	.20
❑ 6 Walter Payton RB	1.00	.40
❑ 7 NFC Champs/Suhey	.25	.08
❑ 8 AFC Championship	.25	.08
❑ 9 Super Bowl XIX	.25	.08
❑ 10 Atlanta Falcons TL	.10	.02
❑ 11 William Andrews	.25	.08
❑ 12 Stacey Bailey	.10	.02
❑ 13 Steve Bartkowski	.50	.20
❑ 14 Rick Bryan RC	.10	.02
❑ 15 Alfred Jackson	.10	.02
❑ 16 Kenny Johnson	.10	.02
❑ 17 Mike Kenn	.10	.02
❑ 18 Mike Pitts RC	.10	.02
❑ 19 Gerald Riggs	.25	.08
❑ 20 Sylvester Stamps	.10	.02
❑ 21 R.C. Thielemann	.10	.02
❑ 22 Bears TL/W.Payton	.75	.30
❑ 23 Todd Bell RC	.10	.02
❑ 24 Richard Dent RC	4.00	1.50
❑ 25 Gary Fencik	.25	.08
❑ 26 Dave Finzer	.10	.02
❑ 27 Leslie Frazier	.10	.02
❑ 28 Steve Fuller	.25	.08
❑ 29 Willie Gault	.50	.20
❑ 30 Dan Hampton	.50	.20
❑ 31 Jim McMahon	.75	.30
❑ 32 Steve McMichael RC	.50	.20
❑ 33 Walter Payton	4.00	1.50
❑ 34 Mike Singletary	.75	.30
❑ 35 Matt Suhey	.10	.02
❑ 36 Bob Thomas	.10	.02
❑ 37 Cowboys TL/Dorsett	.50	.20
❑ 38 Bill Bates RC	1.00	.40
❑ 39 Doug Cosbie	.25	.08
❑ 40 Tony Dorsett	.75	.30
❑ 41 Michael Downs	.10	.02
❑ 42 Mike Hegman RC UER	.10	.02
❑ 43 Tony Hill	.25	.08
❑ 44 Gary Hogeboom RC	.10	.02
❑ 45 Jim Jeffcoat RC	.50	.20
❑ 46 Ed Too Tall Jones	.50	.20
❑ 47 Mike Renfro	.10	.02
❑ 48 Rafael Septien	.10	.02
❑ 49 Dennis Thurman	.10	.02
❑ 50 Everson Walls	.25	.08
❑ 51 Danny White	.50	.20
❑ 52 Randy White	.50	.20
❑ 53 Detroit Lions TL	.10	.02
❑ 54 Jeff Chadwick	.10	.02
❑ 55 Michael Cofer RC	.10	.02
❑ 56 Gary Danielson	.10	.02
❑ 57 Keith Dorney	.10	.02
❑ 58 Doug English	.25	.08
❑ 59 William Gay	.10	.02
❑ 60 Ken Jenkins	.10	.02
❑ 61 James Jones FB	.25	.08
❑ 62 Eddie Murray	.25	.08
❑ 63 Billy Sims	.50	.20
❑ 64 Leonard Thompson	.10	.02
❑ 65 Bobby Watkins	.10	.02
❑ 66 Green Bay Packers TL	.25	.08
❑ 67 Paul Coffman	.10	.02
❑ 68 Lynn Dickey	.25	.08
❑ 69 Mike Douglass	.10	.02
❑ 70 Tom Flynn RC	.10	.02
❑ 71 Eddie Lee Ivery	.10	.02
❑ 72 Ezra Johnson	.10	.02
❑ 73 Mark Lee	.10	.02
❑ 74 Tim Lewis	.10	.02
❑ 75 James Lofton	.50	.20
❑ 76 Bucky Scribner	.10	.02
❑ 77 Rams TL/Dickerson	.50	.20
❑ 78 Nolan Cromwell	.25	.08
❑ 79 Eric Dickerson	1.25	.50
❑ 80 Henry Ellard RC	2.50	1.00
❑ 81 Kent Hill	.10	.02
❑ 82 LeRoy Irvin	.25	.08
❑ 83 Jeff Kemp RC	.25	.08
❑ 84 Mike Lansford	.10	.02
❑ 85 Barry Redden	.10	.02
❑ 86 Jackie Slater	.50	.20
❑ 87 Doug Smith C RC	.25	.08
❑ 88 Jack Youngblood	.25	.08
❑ 89 Minnesota Vikings TL	.10	.02
❑ 90 Alfred Anderson RC	.10	.02
❑ 91 Ted Brown	.25	.08
❑ 92 Greg Coleman	.10	.02
❑ 93 Tommy Hannon	.10	.02
❑ 94 Tommy Kramer	.25	.08
❑ 95 Leo Lewis RC	.25	.08
❑ 96 Doug Martin	.10	.02
❑ 97 Darrin Nelson	.25	.08
❑ 98 Jan Stenerud	.25	.08
❑ 99 Sammie White	.25	.08
❑ 100 New Orleans Saints TL	.10	.02
❑ 101 Morten Andersen	.50	.20
❑ 102 Hoby Brenner RC	.25	.08
❑ 103 Bruce Clark	.10	.02
❑ 104 Hokie Gajan	.10	.02
❑ 105 Brian Hansen RC	.10	.02
❑ 106 Rickey Jackson	.50	.20
❑ 107 George Rogers	.25	.08
❑ 108 Dave Wilson	.10	.02
❑ 109 Tyrone Young	.10	.02
❑ 110 New York Giants TL	.10	.02
❑ 111 Carl Banks RC	.50	.20
❑ 112 Jim Burt RC	.50	.20
❑ 113 Rob Carpenter	.10	.02
❑ 114 Harry Carson	.25	.08
❑ 115 Earnest Gray	.10	.02
❑ 116 Ali Haji-Sheikh	.10	.02
❑ 117 Mark Haynes	.25	.08
❑ 118 Bobby Johnson	.10	.02
❑ 119 Lionel Manuel RC	.25	.08
❑ 120 Joe Morris RC	.50	.20
❑ 121 Zeke Mowatt RC	.25	.08
❑ 122 Jeff Rutledge RC	.10	.02
❑ 123 Phil Simms	.50	.20
❑ 124 Lawrence Taylor	1.50	.60
❑ 125 Philadelphia Eagles TL	.10	.02
❑ 126 Greg Brown	.10	.02
❑ 127 Ray Ellis	.10	.02
❑ 128 Dennis Harrison	.10	.02
❑ 129 Wes Hopkins RC	.25	.08
❑ 130 Mike Horan RC	.10	.02
❑ 131 Kenny Jackson RC	.10	.02
❑ 132 Ron Jaworski	.25	.08
❑ 133 Paul McFadden	.10	.02
❑ 134 Wilbert Montgomery	.25	.08
❑ 135 Mike Quick	.50	.20
❑ 136 John Spagnola	.10	.02
❑ 137 St.Louis Cardinals TL	.10	.02
❑ 138 Ottis Anderson	.50	.20
❑ 139 Al(Bubba) Baker	.25	.08
❑ 140 Roy Green	.25	.08
❑ 141 Curtis Greer	.10	.02
❑ 142 E.J.Junior	.10	.02
❑ 143 Neil Lomax	.25	.08

❑	144	Stump Mitchell	.25	.08
❑	145	Neil O'Donoghue	.10	.02
❑	146	Pat Tilley	.10	.02
❑	147	Lionel Washington	.10	.02
❑	148	49ers TL/J.Montana	1.25	.50
❑	149	Dwaine Board	.10	.02
❑	150	Dwight Clark	.50	.20
❑	151	Roger Craig	1.00	.40
❑	152	Randy Cross	.25	.08
❑	153	Fred Dean	.25	.08
❑	154	Keith Fahnhorst RC	.10	.02
❑	155	Dwight Hicks	.10	.02
❑	156	Ronnie Lott	.50	.20
❑	157	Joe Montana	10.00	4.00
❑	158	Renaldo Nehemiah	.25	.08
❑	159	Fred Quillan	.10	.02
❑	160	Jack Reynolds	.10	.02
❑	161	Freddie Solomon	.10	.02
❑	162	Keena Turner RC	.10	.02
❑	163	Wendell Tyler	.10	.02
❑	164	Ray Wersching	.10	.02
❑	165	Carlton Williamson	.10	.02
❑	166	Tampa Bay Bucs TL	.25	.08
❑	167	Gerald Carter	.10	.02
❑	168	Mark Cotney	.10	.02
❑	169	Steve DeBerg	.50	.20
❑	170	Sean Farrell RC	.10	.02
❑	171	Hugh Green	.25	.08
❑	172	Kevin House	.25	.08
❑	173	David Logan	.10	.02
❑	174	Michael Morton	.10	.02
❑	175	Lee Roy Selmon	.50	.20
❑	176	James Wilder	.10	.02
❑	177	Redskins TL/J.Riggins	.50	.20
❑	178	Charlie Brown	.10	.02
❑	179	Monte Coleman RC	.25	.08
❑	180	Vernon Dean	.10	.02
❑	181	Darrell Green	.50	.20
❑	182	Russ Grimm	.25	.08
❑	183	Joe Jacoby	.25	.08
❑	184	Dexter Manley	.25	.08
❑	185	Art Monk	.50	.20
❑	186	Mark Moseley	.25	.08
❑	187	Calvin Muhammad	.10	.02
❑	188	Mike Nelms	.10	.02
❑	189	John Riggins	.50	.20
❑	190	Joe Theismann	.50	.20
❑	191	Joe Washington	.25	.08
❑	192	D.Marino/Montana LL	10.00	4.00
❑	193	Art Monk/O.Newsome LL	.25	.08
❑	194	E.Dickerson/Jackson LL	.50	.20
❑	195	Scoring Leaders	.10	.02
❑	196	Interception Leaders	.10	.02
❑	197	Punting Leaders	.10	.02
❑	198	Bills TL/Greg Bell	.10	.02
❑	199	Greg Bell RC	.25	.08
❑	200	Preston Dennard	.10	.02
❑	201	Joe Ferguson	.25	.08
❑	202	Byron Franklin	.10	.02
❑	203	Steve Freeman	.10	.02
❑	204	Jim Haslett	.25	.08
❑	205	Charles Romes	.10	.02
❑	206	Fred Smerlas	.10	.02
❑	207	Darryl Talley RC	.50	.20
❑	208	Van Williams	.10	.02
❑	209	Cincinnati Bengals TL	.25	.08
❑	210	Ken Anderson	.50	.20
❑	211	Jim Breech	.10	.02
❑	212	Louis Breeden	.10	.02
❑	213	James Brooks	.25	.08
❑	214	Ross Browner	.25	.08
❑	215	Eddie Edwards	.10	.02
❑	216	M.L. Harris	.10	.02
❑	217	Bobby Kemp	.10	.02
❑	218	Larry Kinnebrew RC	.10	.02
❑	219	Anthony Munoz	.50	.20
❑	220	Reggie Williams	.25	.08
❑	221	Cleveland Browns TL	.10	.02
❑	222	Matt Bahr	.25	.08
❑	223	Chip Banks	.10	.02
❑	224	Reggie Camp	.10	.02
❑	225	Tom Cousineau	.10	.02
❑	226	Joe DeLamielleure	.50	.20
❑	227	Ricky Feacher	.10	.02
❑	228	Boyce Green RC	.10	.02
❑	229	Al Gross	.10	.02
❑	230	Clay Matthews	.50	.20
❑	231	Paul McDonald	.10	.02
❑	232	Ozzie Newsome	.50	.20
❑	233	Mike Pruitt	.25	.08
❑	234	Don Rogers DB	.10	.02
❑	235	Broncos TL/J.Elway	2.50	1.00
❑	236	Rubin Carter	.10	.02
❑	237	Barney Chavous	.10	.02
❑	238	John Elway	12.00	5.00
❑	239	Steve Foley	.10	.02
❑	240	Mike Harden RC	.10	.02
❑	241	Tom Jackson	.50	.20
❑	242	Butch Johnson	.10	.02
❑	243	Rulon Jones	.10	.02
❑	244	Rich Karlis	.10	.02
❑	245	Steve Watson	.25	.08
❑	246	Gerald Willhite	.10	.02
❑	247	Sammy Winder	.25	.08
❑	248	Houston Oilers TL	.10	.02
❑	249	Jesse Baker	.10	.02
❑	250	Carter Hartwig	.10	.02
❑	251	Warren Moon RC	15.00	6.00
❑	252	Larry Moriarty RC	.10	.02
❑	253	Mike Munchak RC	1.50	.60
❑	254	Carl Roaches	.10	.02
❑	255	Tim Smith	.25	.08
❑	256	Willie Tullis	.10	.02
❑	257	Jamie Williams RC	.10	.02
❑	258	Indianapolis Colts TL	.10	.02
❑	259	Raymond Butler	.10	.02
❑	260	Johnie Cooks	.10	.02
❑	261	Eugene Daniel RC	.10	.02
❑	262	Curtis Dickey	.25	.08
❑	263	Chris Hinton	.25	.08
❑	264	Vernon Maxwell	.10	.02
❑	265	Randy McMillan	.10	.02
❑	266	Art Schlichter RC	.50	.20
❑	267	Rohn Stark	.25	.08
❑	268	Leo Wisniewski	.10	.02
❑	269	Kansas City Chiefs TL	.10	.02
❑	270	Jim Arnold	.10	.02
❑	271	Mike Bell	.10	.02
❑	272	Todd Blackledge RC	.25	.08
❑	273	Carlos Carson	.25	.08
❑	274	Deron Cherry	.25	.08
❑	275	Herman Heard RC	.10	.02
❑	276	Bill Kenney	.25	.08
❑	277	Nick Lowery	.50	.20
❑	278	Bill Maas RC	.10	.02
❑	279	Henry Marshall	.10	.02
❑	280	Art Still	.10	.02
❑	281	Raiders TL/M.Allen	.50	.20
❑	282	Marcus Allen	2.50	1.00
❑	283	Lyle Alzado	.25	.08
❑	284	Chris Bahr	.10	.02
❑	285	Malcolm Barnwell	.10	.02
❑	286	Cliff Branch	.50	.20
❑	287	Todd Christensen	.50	.20
❑	288	Ray Guy	.50	.20
❑	289	Lester Hayes	.25	.08
❑	290	Mike Haynes	.25	.08
❑	291	Henry Lawrence	.10	.02
❑	292	Howie Long	2.00	.75
❑	293	Rod Martin	.25	.08
❑	294	Vann McElroy	.10	.02
❑	295	Matt Millen	.25	.08
❑	296	Bill Pickel RC	.10	.02
❑	297	Jim Plunkett	.50	.20
❑	298	Dokie Williams RC	.10	.02
❑	299	Marc Wilson	.25	.08
❑	300	Dolphins TL/Duper	.25	.08
❑	301	Bob Baumhower	.10	.02
❑	302	Doug Betters	.10	.02
❑	303	Glenn Blackwood	.25	.08
❑	304	Lyle Blackwood	.25	.08
❑	305	Kim Bokamper	.10	.02
❑	306	Charles Bowser RC	.10	.02
❑	307	Jimmy Cefalo	.10	.02
❑	308	Mark Clayton RC	.75	.30
❑	309	A.J. Duhe	.10	.02
❑	310	Mark Duper	.50	.20
❑	311	Andra Franklin	.10	.02
❑	312	Bruce Hardy	.10	.02
❑	313	Pete Johnson	.25	.08
❑	314	Dan Marino	12.00	5.00
❑	315	Tony Nathan	.25	.08
❑	316	Ed Newman	.10	.02
❑	317	Reggie Roby	.50	.20
❑	318	Dwight Stephenson	1.00	.40
❑	319	Uwe Von Schamann	.10	.02
❑	320	New England Pats TL	.10	.02
❑	321	Raymond Clayborn	.25	.08
❑	322	Tony Collins	.25	.08
❑	323	Tony Eason RC	.50	.20
❑	324	Tony Franklin	.10	.02
❑	325	Irving Fryar RC	5.00	2.00
❑	326	John Hannah	.50	.20
❑	327	Brian Holloway	.10	.02
❑	328	Craig James RC	.75	.30
❑	329	Stanley Morgan	.25	.08
❑	330	Steve Nelson	.10	.02
❑	331	Derrick Ramsey	.10	.02
❑	332	Stephen Starring RC	.25	.08
❑	333	Mosi Tatupu	.10	.02
❑	334	Andre Tippett	.50	.20
❑	335	New York Jets TL	.25	.08
❑	336	Russell Carter RC	.10	.02
❑	337	Mark Gastineau	.25	.08
❑	338	Bruce Harper	.10	.02
❑	339	Bobby Humphery RC	.10	.02
❑	340	Johnny Lam Jones	.10	.02
❑	341	Joe Klecko	.25	.08
❑	342	Pat Leahy	.10	.02
❑	343	Marty Lyons	.25	.08
❑	344	Freeman McNeil	.25	.08
❑	345	Lance Mehl	.10	.02
❑	346	Ken O'Brien RC	.50	.20
❑	347	Marvin Powell	.10	.02
❑	348	Pat Ryan	.10	.02
❑	349	Mickey Shuler RC	.10	.02
❑	350	Wesley Walker	.25	.08
❑	351	Pittsburgh Steelers TL	.25	.08
❑	352	Walter Abercrombie	.10	.02
❑	353	Gary Anderson K	.25	.08
❑	354	Robin Cole	.10	.02
❑	355	Bennie Cunningham	.10	.02
❑	356	Rich Erenberg	.10	.02
❑	357	Jack Lambert	.50	.20
❑	358	Louis Lipps RC	.50	.20
❑	359	Mark Malone	.25	.08
❑	360	Mike Merriweather RC	.10	.02
❑	361	Frank Pollard	.10	.02
❑	362	Donnie Shell	.25	.08
❑	363	John Stallworth	.50	.20
❑	364	Sam Washington	.10	.02
❑	365	Mike Webster	.25	.08
❑	366	Dwayne Woodruff	.10	.02
❑	367	San Diego Chargers TL	.10	.02
❑	368	Rolf Benirschke	.10	.02
❑	369	Gill Byrd RC	.50	.20
❑	370	Wes Chandler	.25	.08
❑	371	Bobby Duckworth	.10	.02
❑	372	Dan Fouts	.50	.20
❑	373	Mike Green	.10	.02
❑	374	Pete Holohan RC	.10	.02
❑	375	Earnest Jackson RC	.25	.08
❑	376	Lionel James RC	.25	.08
❑	377	Charlie Joiner	.50	.20
❑	378	Billy Ray Smith	.25	.08
❑	379	Kellen Winslow	.50	.20
❑	380	Seattle Seahawks TL	.25	.08
❑	381	Dave Brown DB	.10	.02
❑	382	Jeff Bryant	.10	.02
❑	383	Dan Doornink	.10	.02
❑	384	Kenny Easley	.25	.08
❑	385	Jacob Green	.25	.08
❑	386	David Hughes	.10	.02
❑	387	Norm Johnson	.10	.02
❑	388	Dave Krieg	.50	.20
❑	389	Steve Largent	1.00	.40
❑	390	Joe Nash RC	.10	.02
❑	391	Daryl Turner RC	.10	.02
❑	392	Curt Warner	.50	.20
❑	393	Fredd Young RC	.25	.08
❑	394	Checklist 1-132	.25	.08
❑	395	Checklist 133-264	.25	.08
❑	396	Checklist 265-396	.25	.08

1985 Topps USFL

	Card		
❑	COMP.FACT.SET (132)	120.00	60.00
❑	COMPLETE SET (132)	120.00	60.00
❑	1 Case DeBruijn	.50	.20
❑	2 Mike Katolin	.50	.20
❑	3 Bruce Laird	.50	.20
❑	4 Kit Lathrop	.50	.20

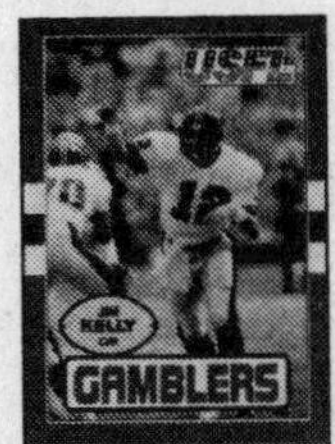

❑ 5 Kevin Long	.50	.20
❑ 6 Karl Lorch	.50	.20
❑ 7 Dave Tipton DT	.50	.20
❑ 8 Doug Williams	2.00	.75
❑ 9 Luis Zendejas XRC	.50	.20
❑ 10 Kelvin Bryant	1.00	.40
❑ 11 Willie Collier	.50	.20
❑ 12 Irv Eatman	.50	.20
❑ 13 Scott Fitzkee	.50	.20
❑ 14 William Fuller XRC	3.00	1.25
❑ 15 Chuck Fusina	.50	.20
❑ 16 Pete Kugler	.50	.20
❑ 17 Garcia Lane	.50	.20
❑ 18 Mike Lush	.50	.20
❑ 19 Sam Mills XRC	5.00	2.00
❑ 20 Buddy Aydelette	.50	.20
❑ 21 Joe Cribbs	2.00	.75
❑ 22 David Dumars	.50	.20
❑ 23 Robin Earl	.50	.20
❑ 24 Joey Jones	.50	.20
❑ 25 Leon Perry RB	.50	.20
❑ 26 Dave Pureifory	.50	.20
❑ 27 Bill Roe	.50	.20
❑ 28 Doug Smith DT XRC	2.00	.75
❑ 29 Cliff Stoudt	1.00	.40
❑ 30 Jeff Delaney	.50	.20
❑ 31 Vince Evans	1.00	.40
❑ 32 Leonard Harris XRC	.50	.20
❑ 33 Bill Johnson RB	.50	.20
❑ 34 Marc Lewis XRC	.50	.20
❑ 35 David Martin	.50	.20
❑ 36 Bruce Thornton	.50	.20
❑ 37 Craig Walls	.50	.20
❑ 38 Vincent White	.50	.20
❑ 39 Luther Bradley	.50	.20
❑ 40 Pete Catan	.50	.20
❑ 41 Kiki DeAyala	.50	.20
❑ 42 Toni Fritsch	.50	.20
❑ 43 Sam Harrell	.50	.20
❑ 44 Richard Johnson WR XRC	1.00	.40
❑ 45 Jim Kelly	20.00	10.00
❑ 46 Gerald McNeil XRC	.50	.20
❑ 47 Clarence Verdin XRC	2.00	.75
❑ 48 Dale Walters	.50	.20
❑ 49 Gary Clark XRC	6.00	2.50
❑ 50 Tom Dinkel	.50	.20
❑ 51 Mike Edwards LB	.50	.20
❑ 52 Brian Franco	.50	.20
❑ 53 Bob Gruber	.50	.20
❑ 54 Robbie Mahfouz	.50	.20
❑ 55 Mike Rozier	2.00	.75
❑ 56 Brian Sipe	1.00	.40
❑ 57 J.T. Turner	.50	.20
❑ 58 Howard Carson	.50	.20
❑ 59 Wymon Henderson XRC	.50	.20
❑ 60 Kevin Nelson	.50	.20
❑ 61 Jeff Partridge	.50	.20
❑ 62 Ben Rudolph	.50	.20
❑ 63 Jo Jo Townsell	1.00	.40
❑ 64 Eddie Weaver	.50	.20
❑ 65 Steve Young	30.00	15.00
❑ 66 Tony Zendejas XRC	1.00	.40
❑ 67 Mossy Cade	.50	.20
❑ 68 Leonard Coleman XRC	.50	.20
❑ 69 John Corker	.50	.20
❑ 70 Derrick Crawford	.50	.20
❑ 71 Art Kuehn	.50	.20
❑ 72 Walter Lewis	.50	.20
❑ 73 Tyrone McGriff	.50	.20
❑ 74 Tim Spencer	1.00	.40
❑ 75 Reggie White	25.00	12.50
❑ 76 Gizmo Williams XRC	2.00	.75
❑ 77 Sam Bowers	.50	.20
❑ 78 Maurice Carthon XRC	2.00	.75
❑ 79 Clarence Collins	.50	.20
❑ 80 Doug Flutie XRC	30.00	12.50
❑ 81 Freddie Gilbert DE	.50	.20
❑ 82 Kerry Justin	.50	.20
❑ 83 Dave Lapham	.50	.20
❑ 84 Rick Partridge	.50	.20
❑ 85 Roger Ruzek XRC	1.00	.40
❑ 86 Herschel Walker	8.00	3.00
❑ 87 Gordon Banks	.50	.20
❑ 88 Monte Bennett	.50	.20
❑ 89 Albert Bentley XRC	1.00	.40
❑ 90 Novo Bojovic	.50	.20
❑ 91 Dave Browning	.50	.20
❑ 92 Anthony Carter	2.00	.75
❑ 93 Bobby Hebert	2.00	.75
❑ 94 Ray Pinney	.50	.20
❑ 95 Stan Talley	.50	.20
❑ 96 Ruben Vaughan	.50	.20
❑ 97 Curtis Bledsoe	.50	.20
❑ 98 Reggie Collier	.50	.20
❑ 99 Jerry Doerger	.50	.20
❑ 100 Jerry Golsteyn	.50	.20
❑ 101 Bob Niziolek	.50	.20
❑ 102 Joel Patten	.50	.20
❑ 103 Ricky Simmons	.50	.20
❑ 104 Joey Walters	.50	.20
❑ 105 Marcus Dupree	1.00	.40
❑ 106 Jeff Gossett	1.00	.40
❑ 107 Frank Lockett	.50	.20
❑ 108 Marcus Marek	.50	.20
❑ 109 Kenny Neil	.50	.20
❑ 110 Robert Pennywell	.50	.20
❑ 111 Matt Robinson	.50	.20
❑ 112 Dan Ross	1.00	.40
❑ 113 Doug Woodward	.50	.20
❑ 114 Danny Buggs	.50	.20
❑ 115 Putt Choate	.50	.20
❑ 116 Greg Fields	.50	.20
❑ 117 Ken Hartley	.50	.20
❑ 118 Nick Mike-Mayer	.50	.20
❑ 119 Rick Neuheisel	2.00	.75
❑ 120 Peter Raeford	.50	.20
❑ 121 Gary Worthy	.50	.20
❑ 122 Gary Anderson RB	1.00	.40
❑ 123 Zenon Andrusyshyn	.50	.20
❑ 124 Greg Boone	.50	.20
❑ 125 Mike Butler	.50	.20
❑ 126 Mike Clark	.50	.20
❑ 127 Willie Gillespie	.50	.20
❑ 128 James Harrell	.50	.20
❑ 129 Marvin Harvey	.50	.20
❑ 130 John Reaves	1.00	.40
❑ 131 Eric Truvillion	.50	.20
❑ 132 Checklist 1-132	1.00	.40

1986 Topps

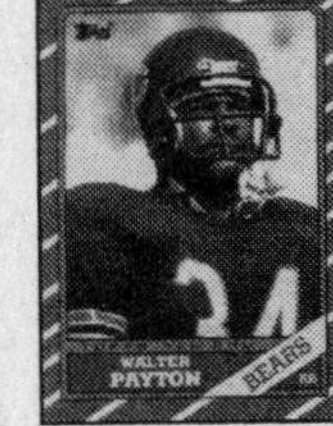

❑ COMPLETE SET (396)	120.00	60.00
❑ COMP.FACT.SET (396)	225.00	150.00
❑ 1 Marcus Allen RB	.75	.30
❑ 2 Eric Dickerson RB	.50	.20
❑ 3 Lionel James RB	.10	.02
❑ 4 Steve Largent RB	.50	.20
❑ 5 George Martin RB	.10	.02
❑ 6 Stephone Paige RB	.10	.02
❑ 7 Walter Payton RB	.75	.30
❑ 8 Super Bowl XX	.25	.08
❑ 9 Bears TL/W.Payton	.60	.25
❑ 10 Jim McMahon	.50	.20
❑ 11 Walter Payton	3.00	1.25
❑ 12 Matt Suhey	.10	.02
❑ 13 Willie Gault	.25	.08
❑ 14 Dennis McKinnon RC	.10	.02
❑ 15 Emery Moorehead	.10	.02
❑ 16 Jim Covert	.25	.08
❑ 17 Jay Hilgenberg RC	.50	.20
❑ 18 Kevin Butler RC	.25	.08
❑ 19 Richard Dent	.75	.30
❑ 20 William Perry RC	.50	.20
❑ 21 Steve McMichael	.50	.20
❑ 22 Dan Hampton	.50	.20
❑ 23 Otis Wilson	.10	.02
❑ 24 Mike Singletary	.60	.25
❑ 25 Wilber Marshall RC	.50	.20
❑ 26 Leslie Frazier	.10	.02
❑ 27 Dave Duerson RC	.10	.02
❑ 28 Gary Fencik	.10	.02
❑ 29 Patriots TL	.50	.20
❑ 30 Tony Eason	.10	.02
❑ 31 Steve Grogan	.25	.08
❑ 32 Craig James	.50	.20
❑ 33 Tony Collins	.10	.02
❑ 34 Irving Fryar	1.25	.50
❑ 35 Brian Holloway	.10	.02
❑ 36 John Hannah	.50	.20
❑ 37 Tony Franklin	.10	.02
❑ 38 Garin Veris RC	.10	.02
❑ 39 Andre Tippett	.25	.08
❑ 40 Steve Nelson	.10	.02
❑ 41 Raymond Clayborn	.10	.02
❑ 42 Fred Marion RC	.10	.02
❑ 43 Rich Camarillo	.10	.02
❑ 44 Dolphins TL/D.Marino	2.00	.75
❑ 45 Dan Marino	8.00	4.00
❑ 46 Tony Nathan	.25	.08
❑ 47 Ron Davenport RC	.10	.02
❑ 48 Mark Duper	.50	.20
❑ 49 Mark Clayton	.50	.20
❑ 50 Nat Moore	.25	.08
❑ 51 Bruce Hardy	.10	.02
❑ 52 Roy Foster	.10	.02
❑ 53 Dwight Stephenson	.75	.30
❑ 54 Fuad Reveiz RC	.25	.08
❑ 55 Bob Baumhower	.10	.02
❑ 56 Mike Charles	.10	.02
❑ 57 Hugh Green	.25	.08
❑ 58 Glenn Blackwood	.10	.02
❑ 59 Reggie Roby	.25	.08
❑ 60 Raiders TL/M.Allen	.50	.20
❑ 61 Marc Wilson	.10	.02
❑ 62 Marcus Allen	1.50	.60
❑ 63 Dokie Williams	.10	.02
❑ 64 Todd Christensen	.50	.20
❑ 65 Chris Bahr	.10	.02
❑ 66 Fulton Walker	.10	.02
❑ 67 Howie Long	1.25	.50
❑ 68 Bill Pickel	.10	.02
❑ 69 Ray Guy	.50	.20
❑ 70 Greg Townsend RC	.50	.20
❑ 71 Rod Martin	.25	.08
❑ 72 Matt Millen	.25	.08
❑ 73 Mike Haynes	.25	.08
❑ 74 Lester Hayes	.25	.08
❑ 75 Vann McElroy	.10	.02
❑ 76 Rams TL/ Dickerson	.50	.20
❑ 77 Dieter Brock RC	.25	.08
❑ 78 Eric Dickerson	.75	.30
❑ 79 Henry Ellard	1.00	.40
❑ 80 Ron Brown RC	.25	.08
❑ 81 Tony Hunter RC	.10	.02
❑ 82 Kent Hill AP	.10	.02
❑ 83 Doug Smith	.10	.02
❑ 84 Dennis Harrah	.10	.02
❑ 85 Jackie Slater	.50	.20
❑ 86 Mike Lansford	.10	.02
❑ 87 Gary Jeter	.10	.02
❑ 88 Mike Wilcher	.10	.02
❑ 89 Jim Collins	.10	.02
❑ 90 LeRoy Irvin	.25	.08
❑ 91 Gary Green	.10	.02
❑ 92 Nolan Cromwell	.25	.08
❑ 93 Dale Hatcher RC	.10	.02
❑ 94 Jets TL	.25	.08

Card			
❑ 95	Ken O'Brien	.50	.20
❑ 96	Freeman McNeil	.25	.08
❑ 97	Tony Paige RC	.10	.02
❑ 98	Johnny Lam Jones	.10	.02
❑ 99	Wesley Walker	.25	.08
❑ 100	Kurt Sohn	.10	.02
❑ 101	Al Toon RC	.50	.20
❑ 102	Mickey Shuler	.10	.02
❑ 103	Marvin Powell	.10	.02
❑ 104	Pat Leahy	.10	.02
❑ 105	Mark Gastineau	.25	.08
❑ 106	Joe Klecko	.25	.08
❑ 107	Marty Lyons	.10	.02
❑ 108	Lance Mehl	.10	.02
❑ 109	Bobby Jackson	.10	.02
❑ 110	Dave Jennings	.10	.02
❑ 111	Broncos TL	.25	.08
❑ 112	John Elway	8.00	4.00
❑ 113	Sammy Winder	.25	.08
❑ 114	Gerald Willhite	.10	.02
❑ 115	Steve Watson	.10	.02
❑ 116	Vance Johnson RC	.50	.20
❑ 117	Rich Karlis	.10	.02
❑ 118	Rulon Jones	.10	.02
❑ 119	Karl Mecklenburg RC	.50	.20
❑ 120	Louis Wright	.10	.02
❑ 121	Mike Harden	.10	.02
❑ 122	Dennis Smith RC	.50	.20
❑ 123	Steve Foley	.10	.02
❑ 124	Cowboys TL	.25	.08
❑ 125	Danny White	.50	.20
❑ 126	Tony Dorsett	.60	.25
❑ 127	Timmy Newsome	.10	.02
❑ 128	Mike Renfro	.10	.02
❑ 129	Tony Hill	.25	.08
❑ 130	Doug Cosbie	.25	.08
❑ 131	Rafael Septien	.10	.02
❑ 132	Ed Too Tall Jones	.50	.20
❑ 133	Randy White	.50	.20
❑ 134	Jim Jeffcoat	.50	.20
❑ 135	Everson Walls	.25	.08
❑ 136	Dennis Thurman	.10	.02
❑ 137	Giants TL	.25	.08
❑ 138	Phil Simms	.50	.20
❑ 139	Joe Morris	.50	.20
❑ 140	George Adams RC	.10	.02
❑ 141	Lionel Manuel	.25	.08
❑ 142	Bobby Johnson	.10	.02
❑ 143	Phil McConkey RC	.25	.08
❑ 144	Mark Bavaro RC	.50	.20
❑ 145	Zeke Mowatt	.10	.02
❑ 146	Brad Benson RC	.10	.02
❑ 147	Bart Oates RC	.25	.08
❑ 148	Leonard Marshall RC	.50	.20
❑ 149	Jim Burt	.25	.08
❑ 150	George Martin	.10	.02
❑ 151	Lawrence Taylor	1.25	.50
❑ 152	Harry Carson	.25	.08
❑ 153	Elvis Patterson RC	.10	.02
❑ 154	Sean Landeta RC	.25	.08
❑ 155	49ers TL/Roger Craig	.50	.20
❑ 156	Joe Montana	8.00	4.00
❑ 157	Roger Craig	.50	.20
❑ 158	Wendell Tyler	.10	.02
❑ 159	Carl Monroe	.10	.02
❑ 160	Dwight Clark	.25	.08
❑ 161	Jerry Rice RC !	80.00	40.00
❑ 162	Randy Cross	.25	.08
❑ 163	Keith Fahnhorst	.10	.02
❑ 164	Jeff Stover	.10	.02
❑ 165	Michael Carter RC	.10	.02
❑ 166	Dwaine Board	.10	.02
❑ 167	Eric Wright	.25	.08
❑ 168	Ronnie Lott	.75	.30
❑ 169	Carlton Williamson	.10	.02
❑ 170	Redskins TL	.25	.08
❑ 171	Joe Theismann	.50	.20
❑ 172	Jay Schroeder RC	.50	.20
❑ 173	George Rogers	.25	.08
❑ 174	Ken Jenkins	.10	.02
❑ 175	Art Monk	.50	.20
❑ 176	Gary Clark RC	2.00	.75
❑ 177	Joe Jacoby	.25	.08
❑ 178	Russ Grimm	.25	.08
❑ 179	Mark Moseley	.10	.02
❑ 180	Dexter Manley	.25	.08
❑ 181	Charles Mann RC	.50	.20
❑ 182	Vernon Dean	.10	.02
❑ 183	Raphel Cherry RC	.10	.02
❑ 184	Curtis Jordan	.10	.02
❑ 185	Browns TL/Kosar	.50	.20
❑ 186	Gary Danielson	.25	.08
❑ 187	Bernie Kosar RC	3.00	1.25
❑ 188	Kevin Mack RC	.50	.20
❑ 189	Earnest Byner RC	.75	.30
❑ 190	Glen Young	.10	.02
❑ 191	Ozzie Newsome	.50	.20
❑ 192	Mike Baab	.10	.02
❑ 193	Cody Risien	.25	.08
❑ 194	Bob Golic	.25	.08
❑ 195	Reggie Camp	.10	.02
❑ 196	Chip Banks	.25	.08
❑ 197	Tom Cousineau	.10	.02
❑ 198	Frank Minnifield RC	.10	.02
❑ 199	Al Gross	.10	.02
❑ 200	Seahawks TL	.25	.08
❑ 201	Dave Krieg	.50	.20
❑ 202	Curt Warner	.25	.08
❑ 203	Steve Largent	.60	.25
❑ 204	Norm Johnson	.10	.02
❑ 205	Daryl Turner	.10	.02
❑ 206	Jacob Green	.10	.02
❑ 207	Joe Nash	.10	.02
❑ 208	Jeff Bryant	.10	.02
❑ 209	Randy Edwards	.10	.02
❑ 210	Fredd Young	.10	.02
❑ 211	Kenny Easley	.10	.02
❑ 212	John Harris	.10	.02
❑ 213	Packers TL	.10	.02
❑ 214	Lynn Dickey	.25	.08
❑ 215	Gerry Ellis	.10	.02
❑ 216	Eddie Lee Ivery	.10	.02
❑ 217	Jessie Clark	.10	.02
❑ 218	James Lofton	.50	.20
❑ 219	Paul Coffman	.10	.02
❑ 220	Alphonso Carreker	.10	.02
❑ 221	Ezra Johnson	.10	.02
❑ 222	Mike Douglass	.10	.02
❑ 223	Tim Lewis	.10	.02
❑ 224	Mark Murphy RC CB	.10	.02
❑ 225	Joe Montana/K.O'Brien LL	1.00	.40
❑ 226	Receiving Leaders	.25	.08
❑ 227	Marcus Allen/G.Riggs LL	.50	.20
❑ 228	Scoring Leaders	.25	.08
❑ 229	Interception Leaders	.10	.02
❑ 230	Chargers TL/Dan Fouts	.50	.20
❑ 231	Dan Fouts	.50	.20
❑ 232	Lionel James	.10	.02
❑ 233	Gary Anderson RB RC	.50	.20
❑ 234	Tim Spencer RC	.25	.08
❑ 235	Wes Chandler	.25	.08
❑ 236	Charlie Joiner	.50	.20
❑ 237	Kellen Winslow	.50	.20
❑ 238	Jim Lachey RC	.50	.20
❑ 239	Bob Thomas	.10	.02
❑ 240	Jeffery Dale	.10	.02
❑ 241	Ralf Mojsiejenko	.10	.02
❑ 242	Lions TL	.10	.02
❑ 243	Eric Hipple	.10	.02
❑ 244	Billy Sims	.25	.08
❑ 245	James Jones FB	.10	.02
❑ 246	Pete Mandley RC	.10	.02
❑ 247	Leonard Thompson	.10	.02
❑ 248	Lomas Brown RC	.25	.08
❑ 249	Eddie Murray	.25	.08
❑ 250	Curtis Green	.10	.02
❑ 251	William Gay	.10	.02
❑ 252	Jimmy Williams	.10	.02
❑ 253	Bobby Watkins	.10	.02
❑ 254	Bengals TL/B.Esiason	.50	.20
❑ 255	Boomer Esiason RC	5.00	2.00
❑ 256	James Brooks	.25	.08
❑ 257	Larry Kinnebrew	.10	.02
❑ 258	Cris Collinsworth	.25	.08
❑ 259	Mike Martin	.10	.02
❑ 260	Eddie Brown RC	.50	.20
❑ 261	Anthony Munoz	.50	.20
❑ 262	Jim Breech	.10	.02
❑ 263	Ross Browner	.25	.08
❑ 264	Carl Zander	.10	.02
❑ 265	James Griffin	.10	.02
❑ 266	Robert Jackson	.10	.02
❑ 267	Pat McInally	.10	.02
❑ 268	Eagles TL	.50	.20
❑ 269	Ron Jaworski	.25	.0
❑ 270	Earnest Jackson	.25	.0
❑ 271	Mike Quick	.25	.0
❑ 272	John Spagnola	.10	.0
❑ 273	Mark Dennard	.10	.0
❑ 274	Paul McFadden	.10	.0
❑ 275	Reggie White RC	20.00	7.5
❑ 276	Greg Brown	.10	.0
❑ 277	Herman Edwards	.10	.0
❑ 278	Roynell Young	.10	.0
❑ 279	Wes Hopkins	.10	.0
❑ 280	Steelers TL	.25	.0
❑ 281	Mark Malone	.25	.0
❑ 282	Frank Pollard	.10	.0
❑ 283	Walter Abercrombie	.10	.0
❑ 284	Louis Lipps	.50	.2
❑ 285	John Stallworth	.50	.2
❑ 286	Mike Webster	.25	.0
❑ 287	Gary Anderson K	.25	.0
❑ 288	Keith Willis	.10	.0
❑ 289	Mike Merriweather	.10	.0
❑ 290	Dwayne Woodruff	.10	.0
❑ 291	Donnie Shell	.25	.0
❑ 292	Vikings TL	.25	.0
❑ 293	Tommy Kramer	.25	.0
❑ 294	Darrin Nelson	.10	.0
❑ 295	Ted Brown	.25	.0
❑ 296	Buster Rhymes	.10	.0
❑ 297	Anthony Carter RC	1.00	.4
❑ 298	Steve Jordan RC	.50	.2
❑ 299	Keith Millard RC	.50	.2
❑ 300	Joey Browner RC	.50	.2
❑ 301	John Turner	.10	.0
❑ 302	Greg Coleman	.10	.0
❑ 303	Chiefs TL	.10	.0
❑ 304	Bill Kenney	.10	.0
❑ 305	Herman Heard	.10	.0
❑ 306	Stephone Paige RC	.50	.2
❑ 307	Carlos Carson	.25	.08
❑ 308	Nick Lowery	.25	.08
❑ 309	Mike Bell	.10	.02
❑ 310	Bill Maas	.10	.02
❑ 311	Art Still	.10	.02
❑ 312	Albert Lewis RC	.50	.20
❑ 313	Deron Cherry	.25	.08
❑ 314	Colts TL	.10	.02
❑ 315	Mike Pagel	.10	.02
❑ 316	Randy McMillan	.10	.02
❑ 317	Albert Bentley RC	.25	.08
❑ 318	George Wonsley RC	.10	.02
❑ 319	Robbie Martin	.10	.02
❑ 320	Pat Beach	.10	.02
❑ 321	Chris Hinton	.25	.08
❑ 322	Duane Bickett RC	.50	.20
❑ 323	Eugene Daniel	.10	.02
❑ 324	Cliff Odom RC	.10	.02
❑ 325	Rohn Stark	.25	.08
❑ 326	Cardinals TL	.10	.02
❑ 327	Neil Lomax	.25	.08
❑ 328	Stump Mitchell	.25	.08
❑ 329	Ottis Anderson	.50	.20
❑ 330	J.T.Smith	.25	.08
❑ 331	Pat Tilley	.10	.02
❑ 332	Roy Green	.25	.08
❑ 333	Lance Smith RC	.10	.02
❑ 334	Curtis Greer	.10	.02
❑ 335	Freddie Joe Nunn RC	.25	.08
❑ 336	E.J. Junior	.25	.08
❑ 337	Lonnie Young RC	.10	.02
❑ 338	Saints TL	.10	.02
❑ 339	Bobby Hebert RC	.50	.20
❑ 340	Dave Wilson	.10	.02
❑ 341	Wayne Wilson	.10	.02
❑ 342	Hoby Brenner	.10	.02
❑ 343	Stan Brock	.25	.08
❑ 344	Morten Andersen	.50	.20
❑ 345	Bruce Clark	.10	.02
❑ 346	Rickey Jackson	.50	.20
❑ 347	Dave Waymer	.10	.02
❑ 348	Brian Hansen	.10	.02
❑ 349	Oilers TL/W.Moon	.50	.20
❑ 350	Warren Moon	3.00	1.50
❑ 351	Mike Rozier RC	.50	.20
❑ 352	Butch Woolfolk	.10	.02
❑ 353	Drew Hill	.50	.20
❑ 354	Willie Drewrey RC	.10	.02
❑ 355	Tim Smith	.25	.08

356	Mike Munchak	.50	.20
357	Ray Childress RC	.50	.20
358	Frank Bush	.10	.02
359	Steve Brown	.10	.02
360	Falcons TL	.10	.02
361	David Archer RC	.50	.20
362	Gerald Riggs	.25	.08
363	William Andrews	.25	.08
364	Billy Johnson	.25	.08
365	Arthur Cox	.10	.02
366	Mike Kenn	.10	.02
367	Bill Fralic RC	.25	.08
368	Mick Luckhurst	.10	.02
369	Rick Bryan	.10	.02
370	Bobby Butler	.10	.02
371	Rick Donnelly RC	.10	.02
372	Buccaneers TL	.10	.02
373	Steve DeBerg	.50	.20
374	Steve Young RC	20.00	10.00
375	James Wilder	.10	.02
376	Kevin House	.10	.02
377	Gerald Carter	.10	.02
378	Jimmie Giles	.25	.08
379	Sean Farrell	.10	.02
380	Donald Igwebuike	.10	.02
381	David Logan	.10	.02
382	Jeremiah Castille RC	.10	.02
383	Bills TL	.10	.02
384	Bruce Mathison RC	.10	.02
385	Joe Cribbs	.25	.08
386	Greg Bell	.25	.08
387	Jerry Butler	.10	.02
388	Andre Reed RC	6.00	2.50
389	Bruce Smith RC	5.00	2.00
390	Fred Smerlas	.10	.02
391	Darryl Talley	.50	.20
392	Jim Haslett	.25	.08
393	Charles Romes	.10	.02
394	Checklist 1-132	.20	.07
395	Checklist 133-264	.20	.07
396	Checklist 265-396	.20	.07

1987 Topps

	COMPLETE SET (396)	30.00	15.00
	COMP.FACT.SET (396)	60.00	30.00
1	Super Bowl XXI	.50	.20
2	Todd Christensen RB	.25	.08
3	Dave Jennings RB	.10	.02
4	Charlie Joiner RB	.50	.20
5	Steve Largent RB	.50	.20
6	Dan Marino RB	2.00	.75
7	Donnie Shell RB	.25	.08
8	Phil Simms RB	.50	.20
9	New York Giants TL	.25	.08
10	Phil Simms	.50	.20
11	Joe Morris	.25	.08
12	Maurice Carthon RC	.50	.20
13	Lee Rouson	.10	.02
14	Bobby Johnson	.10	.02
15	Lionel Manuel	.10	.02
16	Phil McConkey	.10	.02
17	Mark Bavaro	.50	.20
18	Zeke Mowatt	.10	.02
19	Raul Allegre	.10	.02
20	Sean Landeta	.10	.02
21	Brad Benson	.10	.02
22	Jim Burt	.10	.02
23	Leonard Marshall	.50	.20
24	Carl Banks	.50	.20
25	Harry Carson	.10	.02
26	Lawrence Taylor	.75	.30
27	Terry Kinard RC	.10	.02
28	Pepper Johnson RC	.50	.20
29	Erik Howard RC	.10	.02
30	Broncos TL	.10	.02
31	John Elway	6.00	2.50
32	Gerald Willhite	.10	.02
33	Sammy Winder	.25	.08
34	Ken Bell	.10	.02
35	Steve Watson	.10	.02
36	Rich Karlis	.10	.02
37	Keith Bishop	.10	.02
38	Rulon Jones	.10	.02
39	Karl Mecklenburg	.50	.20
40	Louis Wright	.10	.02
41	Mike Harden	.10	.02
42	Dennis Smith	.25	.08
43	Bears TL/W.Payton	.50	.20
44	Jim McMahon	.50	.20
45	Doug Flutie RC	12.00	6.00
46	Walter Payton	2.00	.75
47	Matt Suhey	.10	.02
48	Willie Gault	.25	.08
49	Dennis Gentry RC	.10	.02
50	Kevin Butler	.10	.02
51	Jim Covert	.10	.02
52	Jay Hilgenberg	.25	.08
53	Dan Hampton	.50	.20
54	Steve McMichael	.50	.20
55	William Perry	.50	.20
56	Richard Dent	.50	.20
57	Otis Wilson	.10	.02
58	Mike Singletary	.50	.20
59	Wilber Marshall	.50	.20
60	Mike Richardson	.10	.02
61	Dave Duerson	.10	.02
62	Gary Fencik	.10	.02
63	Redskins TL	.25	.08
64	Jay Schroeder	.25	.08
65	George Rogers	.25	.08
66	Kelvin Bryant RC	.25	.08
67	Ken Jenkins	.10	.02
68	Gary Clark	.50	.20
69	Art Monk	.50	.20
70	Clint Didier RC	.10	.02
71	Steve Cox	.10	.02
72	Joe Jacoby	.10	.02
73	Russ Grimm	.10	.02
74	Charles Mann	.25	.08
75	Dave Butz	.10	.02
76	Dexter Manley	.25	.08
77	Darrell Green	.50	.20
78	Curtis Jordan	.10	.02
79	Browns TL	.10	.02
80	Bernie Kosar	.50	.20
81	Curtis Dickey	.10	.02
82	Kevin Mack	.25	.08
83	Herman Fontenot	.10	.02
84	Brian Brennan RC	.10	.02
85	Ozzie Newsome	.50	.20
86	Jeff Gossett	.25	.08
87	Cody Risien	.10	.02
88	Reggie Camp	.10	.02
89	Bob Golic	.10	.02
90	Carl Hairston	.10	.02
91	Chip Banks	.10	.02
92	Frank Minnifield	.10	.02
93	Hanford Dixon	.10	.02
94	Gerald McNeil RC	.10	.02
95	Dave Puzzuoli	.10	.02
96	Patriots TL	.10	.02
97	Tony Eason	.25	.08
98	Craig James	.25	.08
99	Tony Collins	.25	.08
100	Mosi Tatupu	.10	.02
101	Stanley Morgan	.25	.08
102	Irving Fryar	.50	.20
103	Stephen Starring	.10	.02
104	Tony Franklin	.10	.02
105	Rich Camarillo	.10	.02
106	Garin Veris	.10	.02
107	Andre Tippett	.25	.08
108	Don Blackmon	.10	.02
109	Ronnie Lippett RC	.10	.02
110	Raymond Clayborn	.10	.02
111	49ers TL/R.Craig	.25	.08
112	Joe Montana	6.00	2.50
113	Roger Craig	.50	.20
114	Joe Cribbs	.25	.08
115	Jerry Rice	6.00	2.50
116	Dwight Clark	.25	.08
117	Ray Wersching	.10	.02
118	Max Runager	.10	.02
119	Jeff Stover	.10	.02
120	Dwaine Board	.10	.02
121	Tim McKyer RC	.25	.08
122	Don Griffin RC	.25	.08
123	Ronnie Lott	.50	.20
124	Tom Holmoe	.10	.02
125	Charles Haley RC	1.25	.50
126	Jets TL	.10	.02
127	Ken O'Brien	.25	.08
128	Pat Ryan	.10	.02
129	Freeman McNeil	.25	.08
130	Johnny Hector RC	.10	.02
131	Al Toon	.50	.20
132	Wesley Walker	.25	.08
133	Mickey Shuler	.10	.02
134	Pat Leahy	.10	.02
135	Mark Gastineau	.25	.08
136	Joe Klecko	.25	.08
137	Marty Lyons	.10	.02
138	Bob Crable	.10	.02
139	Lance Mehl	.10	.02
140	Dave Jennings	.10	.02
141	Harry Hamilton RC	.10	.02
142	Lester Lyles	.10	.02
143	Bobby Humphery UER	.10	.02
144	Rams TL/E.Dickerson	.50	.20
145	Jim Everett RC	2.00	.75
146	Eric Dickerson	.50	.20
147	Barry Redden	.10	.02
148	Ron Brown	.25	.08
149	Kevin House	.10	.02
150	Henry Ellard	.50	.20
151	Doug Smith	.10	.02
152	Dennis Harrah	.10	.02
153	Jackie Slater	.25	.08
154	Gary Jeter	.10	.02
155	Carl Ekern	.10	.02
156	Mike Wilcher	.10	.02
157	Jerry Gray RC	.10	.02
158	LeRoy Irvin	.10	.02
159	Nolan Cromwell	.25	.08
160	Chiefs TL	.10	.02
161	Bill Kenney	.10	.02
162	Stephone Paige	.25	.08
163	Henry Marshall	.10	.02
164	Carlos Carson	.10	.02
165	Nick Lowery	.25	.08
166	Irv Eatman RC	.10	.02
167	Brad Budde	.10	.02
168	Art Still	.10	.02
169	Bill Maas	.10	.02
170	Lloyd Burruss RC	.10	.02
171	Deron Cherry	.10	.02
172	Seahawks TL	.25	.08
173	Dave Krieg	.50	.20
174	Curt Warner	.25	.08
175	John L.Williams RC	.50	.20
176	Bobby Joe Edmonds RC	.25	.08
177	Steve Largent	.60	.25
178	Bruce Scholtz	.10	.02
179	Norm Johnson	.10	.02
180	Jacob Green	.10	.02
181	Fredd Young	.10	.02
182	Dave Brown DB	.10	.02
183	Kenny Easley	.10	.02
184	Bengals TL	.25	.08
185	Boomer Esiason	.50	.20
186	James Brooks	.25	.08
187	Larry Kinnebrew	.10	.02
188	Cris Collinsworth	.25	.08
189	Eddie Brown	.50	.20
190	Tim McGee RC	.50	.20
191	Jim Breech	.10	.02
192	Anthony Munoz	.50	.20
193	Max Montoya	.10	.02
194	Eddie Edwards	.10	.02
195	Ross Browner	.25	.08
196	Emanuel King	.10	.02
197	Louis Breeden	.10	.02
198	Vikings TL	.10	.02

Card		
❑ 199 Tommy Kramer	.25	.08
❑ 200 Darrin Nelson	.10	.02
❑ 201 Allen Rice	.10	.02
❑ 202 Anthony Carter	.50	.20
❑ 203 Leo Lewis	.10	.02
❑ 204 Steve Jordan	.50	.20
❑ 205 Chuck Nelson RC	.10	.02
❑ 206 Greg Coleman	.10	.02
❑ 207 Gary Zimmerman RC	.50	.20
❑ 208 Doug Martin	.10	.02
❑ 209 Keith Millard	.10	.02
❑ 210 Issiac Holt RC	.10	.02
❑ 211 Joey Browner	.25	.08
❑ 212 Rufus Bess	.10	.02
❑ 213 Raiders TL/M.Allen	.50	.20
❑ 214 Jim Plunkett	.50	.20
❑ 215 Marcus Allen	1.00	.40
❑ 216 Napoleon McCallum RC	.25	.08
❑ 217 Dokie Williams	.10	.02
❑ 218 Todd Christensen	.50	.20
❑ 219 Chris Bahr	.10	.02
❑ 220 Howie Long	.60	.25
❑ 221 Bill Pickel	.10	.02
❑ 222 Sean Jones RC	.75	.30
❑ 223 Lester Hayes	.25	.08
❑ 224 Mike Haynes	.25	.08
❑ 225 Vann McElroy	.10	.02
❑ 226 Fulton Walker	.10	.02
❑ 227 Dan Marino/T.Kramer LL	1.25	.50
❑ 228 J.Rice/Christensen LL	1.25	.50
❑ 229 Eric Dickerson/Warner LL	.50	.20
❑ 230 Scoring Leaders	.10	.02
❑ 231 Interception Leaders	.50	.20
❑ 232 Dolphins TL	.25	.08
❑ 233 Dan Marino	6.00	2.50
❑ 234 Lorenzo Hampton RC	.10	.02
❑ 235 Tony Nathan	.25	.08
❑ 236 Mark Duper	.50	.20
❑ 237 Mark Clayton	.50	.20
❑ 238 Nat Moore	.25	.08
❑ 239 Bruce Hardy	.10	.02
❑ 240 Reggie Roby	.25	.08
❑ 241 Roy Foster	.10	.02
❑ 242 Dwight Stephenson	.50	.20
❑ 243 Hugh Green	.10	.02
❑ 244 John Offerdahl RC	.50	.20
❑ 245 Mark Brown	.10	.02
❑ 246 Doug Betters	.10	.02
❑ 247 Bob Baumhower	.10	.02
❑ 248 Falcons TL	.10	.02
❑ 249 David Archer	.50	.20
❑ 250 Gerald Riggs	.25	.08
❑ 251 William Andrews	.25	.08
❑ 252 Charlie Brown	.10	.02
❑ 253 Arthur Cox	.10	.02
❑ 254 Rick Donnelly	.10	.02
❑ 255 Bill Fralic	.10	.02
❑ 256 Mike Gann RC	.10	.02
❑ 257 Rick Bryan	.10	.02
❑ 258 Bret Clark	.10	.02
❑ 259 Mike Pitts	.10	.02
❑ 260 Cowboys TL/T.Dorsett	.50	.20
❑ 261 Danny White	.50	.20
❑ 262 Steve Pelluer RC	.10	.02
❑ 263 Tony Dorsett UER	.50	.20
❑ 264 Herschel Walker RC	2.50	1.00
❑ 265 Timmy Newsome	.10	.02
❑ 266 Tony Hill	.25	.08
❑ 267 Mike Sherrard RC	.50	.20
❑ 268 Jim Jeffcoat	.50	.20
❑ 269 Ron Fellows	.10	.02
❑ 270 Bill Bates	.50	.20
❑ 271 Michael Downs	.10	.02
❑ 272 Saints TL/B.Hebert	.25	.08
❑ 273 Dave Wilson	.10	.02
❑ 274 Rueben Mayes RC UER	.10	.02
❑ 275 Hoby Brenner	.10	.02
❑ 276 Eric Martin RC	.50	.20
❑ 277 Morten Andersen	.25	.08
❑ 278 Brian Hansen	.10	.02
❑ 279 Rickey Jackson	.50	.20
❑ 280 Dave Waymer	.10	.02
❑ 281 Bruce Clark	.10	.02
❑ 282 Jumpy Geathers RC	.25	.08
❑ 283 Steelers TL	.25	.08
❑ 284 Mark Malone	.25	.08
❑ 285 Earnest Jackson	.10	.02
❑ 286 Walter Abercrombie	.10	.02
❑ 287 Louis Lipps	.25	.08
❑ 288 John Stallworth UER	.50	.20
❑ 289 Gary Anderson K	.10	.02
❑ 290 Keith Willis	.10	.02
❑ 291 Mike Merriweather	.10	.02
❑ 292 Lupe Sanchez	.10	.02
❑ 293 Donnie Shell	.25	.08
❑ 294 Eagles TL/K.Byars	.50	.20
❑ 295 Mike Reichenbach	.10	.02
❑ 296 Randall Cunningham RC	6.00	3.00
❑ 297 Keith Byars RC	.75	.30
❑ 298 Mike Quick	.25	.08
❑ 299 Kenny Jackson	.10	.02
❑ 300 John Teltschik RC	.10	.02
❑ 301 Reggie White	3.00	1.50
❑ 302 Ken Clarke	.10	.02
❑ 303 Greg Brown	.10	.02
❑ 304 Roynell Young	.10	.02
❑ 305 Andre Waters RC	.50	.20
❑ 306 Oilers TL/W.Moon	.50	.20
❑ 307 Warren Moon	1.50	.60
❑ 308 Mike Rozier	.25	.08
❑ 309 Drew Hill	.25	.08
❑ 310 Ernest Givins RC	.50	.20
❑ 311 Lee Johnson RC	.10	.02
❑ 312 Kent Hill	.10	.02
❑ 313 Dean Steinkuhler RC	.25	.08
❑ 314 Ray Childress	.50	.20
❑ 315 John Grimsley RC	.10	.02
❑ 316 Jesse Baker	.10	.02
❑ 317 Lions TL	.10	.02
❑ 318 Chuck Long RC	.25	.08
❑ 319 James Jones FB	.10	.02
❑ 320 Garry James	.10	.02
❑ 321 Jeff Chadwick	.10	.02
❑ 322 Leonard Thompson	.10	.02
❑ 323 Pete Mandley	.10	.02
❑ 324 Jimmie Giles	.25	.08
❑ 325 Herman Hunter	.10	.02
❑ 326 Keith Ferguson	.10	.02
❑ 327 Devon Mitchell	.10	.02
❑ 328 Cardinals TL	.10	.02
❑ 329 Neil Lomax	.25	.08
❑ 330 Stump Mitchell	.10	.02
❑ 331 Earl Ferrell	.10	.02
❑ 332 Vai Sikahema RC	.25	.08
❑ 333 Ron Wolfley RC	.10	.02
❑ 334 J.T.Smith	.25	.08
❑ 335 Roy Green	.25	.08
❑ 336 Al(Bubba) Baker	.10	.02
❑ 337 Freddie Joe Nunn	.10	.02
❑ 338 Cedric Mack	.10	.02
❑ 339 Chargers TL	.25	.08
❑ 340 Dan Fouts	.50	.20
❑ 341 Gary Anderson RB UER	.50	.20
❑ 342 Wes Chandler	.25	.08
❑ 343 Kellen Winslow	.50	.20
❑ 344 Ralf Mojsiejenko	.10	.02
❑ 345 Rolf Benirschke	.10	.02
❑ 346 Lee Williams RC	.25	.08
❑ 347 Leslie O'Neal RC	1.00	.40
❑ 348 Billy Ray Smith	.25	.08
❑ 349 Gill Byrd	.25	.08
❑ 350 Packers TL	.10	.02
❑ 351 Randy Wright	.10	.02
❑ 352 Kenneth Davis RC	.50	.20
❑ 353 Gerry Ellis	.10	.02
❑ 354 James Lofton	.50	.20
❑ 355 Phillip Epps RC	.10	.02
❑ 356 Walter Stanley RC	.10	.02
❑ 357 Eddie Lee Ivery	.10	.02
❑ 358 Tim Harris RC	.50	.20
❑ 359 Mark Lee UER	.10	.02
❑ 360 Mossy Cade	.10	.02
❑ 361 Bills TL/J.Kelly	1.00	.40
❑ 362 Jim Kelly RC	10.00	4.00
❑ 363 Robb Riddick RC	.10	.02
❑ 364 Greg Bell	.10	.02
❑ 365 Andre Reed	1.25	.50
❑ 366 Pete Metzelaars RC	.50	.20
❑ 367 Sean McNanie	.10	.02
❑ 368 Fred Smerlas	.10	.02
❑ 369 Bruce Smith	2.00	.75
❑ 370 Darryl Talley	.25	.08
❑ 371 Charles Romes	.10	.02
❑ 372 Colts TL	.10	.02
❑ 373 Jack Trudeau RC	.25	.08
❑ 374 Gary Hogeboom	.10	.02
❑ 375 Randy McMillan	.10	.02
❑ 376 Albert Bentley	.10	.02
❑ 377 Matt Bouza	.10	.02
❑ 378 Bill Brooks RC	1.00	.40
❑ 379 Rohn Stark	.10	.02
❑ 380 Chris Hinton	.10	.02
❑ 381 Ray Donaldson	.10	.02
❑ 382 Jon Hand RC	.10	.02
❑ 383 Buccaneers TL	.10	.02
❑ 384 Steve Young	5.00	2.00
❑ 385 James Wilder	.10	.02
❑ 386 Frank Garcia	.10	.02
❑ 387 Gerald Carter	.10	.02
❑ 388 Phil Freeman	.10	.02
❑ 389 Calvin Magee	.10	.02
❑ 390 Donald Igwebuike	.10	.02
❑ 391 David Logan	.10	.02
❑ 392 Jeff Davis	.10	.02
❑ 393 Chris Washington	.10	.02
❑ 394 Checklist 1-132	.10	.02
❑ 395 Checklist 133-264	.10	.02
❑ 396 Checklist 265-396	.10	.02

1988 Topps

Card		
❑ COMPLETE SET (396)	20.00	7.50
❑ COMP.FACT.SET (396)	30.00	15.00
❑ 1 Super Bowl XXII	.20	.07
❑ 2 Vencie Glenn RB	.05	.01
❑ 3 Steve Largent RB	.40	.15
❑ 4 Joe Montana RB	.75	.30
❑ 5 Walter Payton RB	.40	.15
❑ 6 Jerry Rice RB	.75	.30
❑ 7 Redskins TL	.20	.07
❑ 8 Doug Williams	.20	.07
❑ 9 George Rogers	.20	.07
❑ 10 Kelvin Bryant	.20	.07
❑ 11 Timmy Smith SR	.20	.07
❑ 12 Art Monk	.40	.15
❑ 13 Gary Clark	.40	.15
❑ 14 Ricky Sanders RC	.40	.15
❑ 15 Steve Cox	.05	.01
❑ 16 Joe Jacoby	.05	.01
❑ 17 Charles Mann	.20	.07
❑ 18 Dave Butz	.05	.01
❑ 19 Darrell Green	.20	.07
❑ 20 Dexter Manley	.05	.01
❑ 21 Barry Wilburn	.05	.01
❑ 22 Broncos TL	.05	.01
❑ 23 John Elway	2.00	.75
❑ 24 Sammy Winder	.05	.01
❑ 25 Vance Johnson	.20	.07
❑ 26 Mark Jackson RC	.40	.15
❑ 27 Ricky Nattiel RC	.05	.01
❑ 28 Clarence Kay	.05	.01
❑ 29 Rich Karlis	.05	.01
❑ 30 Keith Bishop	.05	.01
❑ 31 Mike Horan	.05	.01
❑ 32 Rulon Jones	.05	.01
❑ 33 Karl Mecklenburg	.20	.07
❑ 34 Jim Ryan	.05	.01
❑ 35 Mark Haynes	.20	.07
❑ 36 Mike Harden	.05	.01
❑ 37 49ers TL	.40	.15
❑ 38 Joe Montana	2.00	.75
❑ 39 Steve Young	1.00	.40
❑ 40 Roger Craig	.20	.07
❑ 41 Tom Rathman RC	.40	.15

❑ 42 Joe Cribbs .20 .07
❑ 43 Jerry Rice 2.00 .75
❑ 44 Mike Wilson RC .05 .01
❑ 45 Ron Heller TE RC .05 .01
❑ 46 Ray Wersching .05 .01
❑ 47 Michael Carter .05 .01
❑ 48 Dwaine Board .05 .01
❑ 49 Michael Walter .05 .01
❑ 50 Don Griffin .05 .01
❑ 51 Ronnie Lott .40 .15
❑ 52 Charles Haley .40 .15
❑ 53 Dana McLemore .05 .01
❑ 54 Saints TL .20 .07
❑ 55 Bobby Hebert .20 .07
❑ 56 Rueben Mayes .05 .01
❑ 57 Dalton Hilliard RC .05 .01
❑ 58 Eric Martin .20 .07
❑ 59 John Tice RC .05 .01
❑ 60 Brad Edelman .05 .01
❑ 61 Morten Andersen .20 .07
❑ 62 Brian Hansen .05 .01
❑ 63 Mel Gray RC .40 .15
❑ 64 Rickey Jackson .20 .07
❑ 65 Sam Mills RC .75 .30
❑ 66 Pat Swilling RC .40 .15
❑ 67 Dave Waymer .05 .01
❑ 68 Bears TL .20 .07
❑ 69 Jim McMahon .40 .15
❑ 70 Mike Tomczak RC .05 .01
❑ 71 Neal Anderson RC .40 .15
❑ 72 Willie Gault .20 .07
❑ 73 Dennis Gentry .05 .01
❑ 74 Dennis McKinnon .05 .01
❑ 75 Kevin Butler .05 .01
❑ 76 Jim Covert .05 .01
❑ 77 Jay Hilgenberg .05 .01
❑ 78 Steve McMichael .20 .07
❑ 79 William Perry .20 .07
❑ 80 Richard Dent .40 .15
❑ 81 Ron Rivera RC .05 .01
❑ 82 Mike Singletary .40 .15
❑ 83 Dan Hampton .40 .15
❑ 84 Dave Duerson .05 .01
❑ 85 Browns TL .20 .07
❑ 86 Bernie Kosar .40 .15
❑ 87 Earnest Byner .40 .15
❑ 88 Kevin Mack .20 .07
❑ 89 Webster Slaughter RC .40 .15
❑ 90 Gerald McNeil .05 .01
❑ 91 Brian Brennan .05 .01
❑ 92 Ozzie Newsome .40 .15
❑ 93 Cody Risien .05 .01
❑ 94 Bob Golic .05 .01
❑ 95 Carl Hairston .05 .01
❑ 96 Mike Johnson RC .05 .01
❑ 97 Clay Matthews .20 .07
❑ 98 Frank Minnifield .05 .01
❑ 99 Hanford Dixon .05 .01
❑ 100 Dave Puzzuoli .05 .01
❑ 101 Felix Wright RC .05 .01
❑ 102 Oilers TL/Moon .40 .15
❑ 103 Warren Moon .50 .20
❑ 104 Mike Rozier .05 .01
❑ 105 Alonzo Highsmith RC .20 .07
❑ 106 Drew Hill .20 .07
❑ 107 Ernest Givins .40 .15
❑ 108 Curtis Duncan RC .40 .15
❑ 109 Tony Zendejas RC .05 .01
❑ 110 Mike Munchak .40 .15
❑ 111 Kent Hill .05 .01
❑ 112 Ray Childress .20 .07
❑ 113 Al Smith RC .20 .07
❑ 114 Keith Bostic RC .05 .01
❑ 115 Jeff Donaldson .05 .01
❑ 116 Colts TL/Dickerson .40 .15
❑ 117 Jack Trudeau .05 .01
❑ 118 Eric Dickerson .40 .15
❑ 119 Albert Bentley .05 .01
❑ 120 Matt Bouza .05 .01
❑ 121 Bill Brooks .40 .15
❑ 122 Dean Biasucci RC .05 .01
❑ 123 Chris Hinton .05 .01
❑ 124 Ray Donaldson .05 .01
❑ 125 Ron Solt RC .05 .01
❑ 126 Donnell Thompson .05 .01
❑ 127 Barry Krauss RC .05 .01
❑ 128 Duane Bickett .05 .01
❑ 129 Mike Prior RC .05 .01
❑ 130 Seahawks TL .20 .07
❑ 131 Dave Krieg .20 .07
❑ 132 Curt Warner .20 .07
❑ 133 John L.Williams .40 .15
❑ 134 Bobby Joe Edmonds .05 .01
❑ 135 Steve Largent .40 .15
❑ 136 Raymond Butler .05 .01
❑ 137 Norm Johnson .05 .01
❑ 138 Ruben Rodriguez .05 .01
❑ 139 Blair Bush .05 .01
❑ 140 Jacob Green .05 .01
❑ 141 Joe Nash .05 .01
❑ 142 Jeff Bryant .05 .01
❑ 143 Fredd Young .05 .01
❑ 144 Brian Bosworth RC 1.50 .60
❑ 145 Kenny Easley .05 .01
❑ 146 Vikings TL .20 .07
❑ 147 Wade Wilson RC .40 .15
❑ 148 Tommy Kramer .20 .07
❑ 149 Darrin Nelson .05 .01
❑ 150 D.J.Dozier RC .20 .07
❑ 151 Anthony Carter .20 .07
❑ 152 Leo Lewis .05 .01
❑ 153 Steve Jordan .20 .07
❑ 154 Gary Zimmerman .05 .01
❑ 155 Chuck Nelson .05 .01
❑ 156 Henry Thomas RC .40 .15
❑ 157 Chris Doleman RC .40 .15
❑ 158 Scott Studwell RC .05 .01
❑ 159 Jesse Solomon RC .05 .01
❑ 160 Joey Browner .05 .01
❑ 161 Neal Guggemos .05 .01
❑ 162 Steelers TL .20 .07
❑ 163 Mark Malone .05 .01
❑ 164 Walter Abercrombie .05 .01
❑ 165 Earnest Jackson .05 .01
❑ 166 Frank Pollard .05 .01
❑ 167 Dwight Stone RC .20 .07
❑ 168 Gary Anderson K .05 .01
❑ 169 Harry Newsome RC .05 .01
❑ 170 Keith Willis .05 .01
❑ 171 Keith Gary .05 .01
❑ 172 David Little RC .20 .07
❑ 173 Mike Merriweather .05 .01
❑ 174 Dwayne Woodruff .05 .01
❑ 175 Patriots TL .40 .15
❑ 176 Steve Grogan .20 .07
❑ 177 Tony Eason .20 .07
❑ 178 Tony Collins .20 .07
❑ 179 Mosi Tatupu .05 .01
❑ 180 Stanley Morgan .20 .07
❑ 181 Irving Fryar .40 .15
❑ 182 Stephen Starring .05 .01
❑ 183 Tony Franklin .05 .01
❑ 184 Rich Camarillo .05 .01
❑ 185 Garin Veris .05 .01
❑ 186 Andre Tippett .20 .07
❑ 187 Ronnie Lippett .05 .01
❑ 188 Fred Marion .05 .01
❑ 189 Dolphins TL/D.Marino .75 .30
❑ 190 Dan Marino 2.00 .75
❑ 191 Troy Stradford RC .20 .07
❑ 192 Lorenzo Hampton .05 .01
❑ 193 Mark Duper .20 .07
❑ 194 Mark Clayton .20 .07
❑ 195 Reggie Roby .20 .07
❑ 196 Dwight Stephenson .40 .15
❑ 197 T.J. Turner RC .05 .01
❑ 198 John Bosa RC .05 .01
❑ 199 Jackie Shipp .05 .01
❑ 200 John Offerdahl .20 .07
❑ 201 Mark Brown .05 .01
❑ 202 Paul Lankford .05 .01
❑ 203 Chargers TL .40 .15
❑ 204 Tim Spencer .05 .01
❑ 205 Gary Anderson RB .20 .07
❑ 206 Curtis Adams .05 .01
❑ 207 Lionel James .05 .01
❑ 208 Chip Banks .05 .01
❑ 209 Kellen Winslow .40 .15
❑ 210 Ralf Mojsiejenko .05 .01
❑ 211 Jim Lachey .20 .07
❑ 212 Lee Williams .05 .01
❑ 213 Billy Ray Smith .05 .01
❑ 214 Vencie Glenn RC .20 .07
❑ 215 J.Montana/B.Kosar LL .50 .20
❑ 216 Receiving Leaders .20 .07
❑ 217 Eric Dickerson/C.White L .20 .07
❑ 218 Jerry Rice/J.Breech LL .40 .15
❑ 219 Interception Leaders .05 .01
❑ 220 Bills TL/Jim Kelly .40 .15
❑ 221 Jim Kelly .75 .30
❑ 222 Ronnie Harmon RC .40 .15
❑ 223 Robb Riddick .05 .01
❑ 224 Andre Reed .40 .15
❑ 225 Chris Burkett RC .05 .01
❑ 226 Pete Metzelaars .40 .15
❑ 227 Bruce Smith .50 .20
❑ 228 Darryl Talley .20 .07
❑ 229 Eugene Marve .05 .01
❑ 230 Cornelius Bennett RC .75 .30
❑ 231 Mark Kelso RC .05 .01
❑ 232 Shane Conlan RC .40 .15
❑ 233 Eagles TL/R.Cunningham .40 .15
❑ 234 Randall Cunningham 1.00 .40
❑ 235 Keith Byars .40 .15
❑ 236 Anthony Toney RC .05 .01
❑ 237 Mike Quick .20 .07
❑ 238 Kenny Jackson .05 .01
❑ 239 John Spagnola .05 .01
❑ 240 Paul McFadden .05 .01
❑ 241 Reggie White .60 .25
❑ 242 Ken Clarke .05 .01
❑ 243 Mike Pitts .05 .01
❑ 244 Clyde Simmons RC .40 .15
❑ 245 Seth Joyner RC .40 .15
❑ 246 Andre Waters .40 .15
❑ 247 Jerome Brown RC .40 .15
❑ 248 Cardinals TL .05 .01
❑ 249 Neil Lomax .20 .07
❑ 250 Stump Mitchell .05 .01
❑ 251 Earl Ferrell .05 .01
❑ 252 Vai Sikahema .05 .01
❑ 253 J.T. Smith .20 .07
❑ 254 Roy Green .20 .07
❑ 255 Robert Awalt RC .20 .07
❑ 256 Freddie Joe Nunn .05 .01
❑ 257 Leonard Smith RC .05 .01
❑ 258 Travis Curtis .05 .01
❑ 259 Cowboys TL/H.Walker .40 .15
❑ 260 Danny White .40 .15
❑ 261 Herschel Walker .40 .15
❑ 262 Tony Dorsett .40 .15
❑ 263 Doug Cosbie .05 .01
❑ 264 Roger Ruzek RC .20 .07
❑ 265 Darryl Clack .05 .01
❑ 266 Ed Too Tall Jones .40 .15
❑ 267 Jim Jeffcoat .05 .01
❑ 268 Everson Walls .05 .01
❑ 269 Bill Bates .20 .07
❑ 270 Michael Downs .05 .01
❑ 271 Giants TL .20 .07
❑ 272 Phil Simms .40 .15
❑ 273 Joe Morris .20 .07
❑ 274 Lee Rouson .05 .01
❑ 275 George Adams .05 .01
❑ 276 Lionel Manuel .05 .01
❑ 277 Mark Bavaro .20 .07
❑ 278 Raul Allegre .05 .01
❑ 279 Sean Landeta .05 .01
❑ 280 Erik Howard .05 .01
❑ 281 Leonard Marshall .20 .07
❑ 282 Carl Banks .20 .07
❑ 283 Pepper Johnson .20 .07
❑ 284 Harry Carson .20 .07
❑ 285 Lawrence Taylor .40 .15
❑ 286 Terry Kinard .05 .01
❑ 287 Rams TL/Everett .40 .15
❑ 288 Jim Everett .40 .15
❑ 289 Charles White .20 .07
❑ 290 Ron Brown .20 .07
❑ 291 Henry Ellard .40 .15
❑ 292 Mike Lansford .05 .01
❑ 293 Dale Hatcher .05 .01
❑ 294 Doug Smith .05 .01
❑ 295 Jackie Slater .20 .07
❑ 296 Jim Collins .05 .01
❑ 297 Jerry Gray .05 .01
❑ 298 LeRoy Irvin .05 .01
❑ 299 Nolan Cromwell .20 .07
❑ 300 Kevin Greene RC 1.25 .50
❑ 301 Jets TL .20 .07
❑ 302 Ken O'Brien .20 .07

❑ 303 Freeman McNeil .20 .07
❑ 304 Johnny Hector .05 .01
❑ 305 Al Toon .20 .07
❑ 306 JoJo Townsell RC .20 .07
❑ 307 Mickey Shuler .05 .01
❑ 308 Pat Leahy .05 .01
❑ 309 Roger Vick .05 .01
❑ 310 Alex Gordon RC .05 .01
❑ 311 Troy Benson .05 .01
❑ 312 Bob Crable .05 .01
❑ 313 Harry Hamilton .05 .01
❑ 314 Packers TL .05 .01
❑ 315 Randy Wright .05 .01
❑ 316 Kenneth Davis .20 .07
❑ 317 Phillip Epps .05 .01
❑ 318 Walter Stanley .05 .01
❑ 319 Frankie Neal .05 .01
❑ 320 Don Bracken .05 .01
❑ 321 Brian Noble RC .20 .07
❑ 322 Johnny Holland RC .20 .07
❑ 323 Tim Harris .20 .07
❑ 324 Mark Murphy .05 .01
❑ 325 Raiders TL/B.Jackson .50 .20
❑ 326 Marc Wilson .05 .01
❑ 327 Bo Jackson RC 5.00 2.00
❑ 328 Marcus Allen .40 .15
❑ 329 James Lofton .40 .15
❑ 330 Todd Christensen .20 .07
❑ 331 Chris Bahr .05 .01
❑ 332 Stan Talley .05 .01
❑ 333 Howie Long .40 .15
❑ 334 Sean Jones .40 .15
❑ 335 Matt Millen .20 .07
❑ 336 Stacey Toran .05 .01
❑ 337 Vann McElroy .05 .01
❑ 338 Greg Townsend .20 .07
❑ 339 Bengals TL/Esiason .40 .15
❑ 340 Boomer Esiason .40 .15
❑ 341 Larry Kinnebrew .05 .01
❑ 342 Stanford Jennings RC .05 .01
❑ 343 Eddie Brown .20 .07
❑ 344 Jim Breech .05 .01
❑ 345 Anthony Munoz .40 .15
❑ 346 Scott Fulhage RC .05 .01
❑ 347 Tim Krumrie RC .05 .01
❑ 348 Reggie Williams .20 .07
❑ 349 David Fulcher RC .05 .01
❑ 350 Buccaneers TL .05 .01
❑ 351 Frank Garcia .05 .01
❑ 352 Vinny Testaverde RC 4.00 1.50
❑ 353 James Wilder .05 .01
❑ 354 Jeff Smith RBK .05 .01
❑ 355 Gerald Carter .05 .01
❑ 356 Calvin Magee .05 .01
❑ 357 Donald Igwebuike .05 .01
❑ 358 Ron Holmes RC .05 .01
❑ 359 Chris Washington .05 .01
❑ 360 Ervin Randle .05 .01
❑ 361 Chiefs TL .05 .01
❑ 362 Bill Kenney .05 .01
❑ 363 Christian Okoye RC .40 .15
❑ 364 Paul Palmer .05 .01
❑ 365 Stephone Paige .20 .07
❑ 366 Carlos Carson .05 .01
❑ 367 Kelly Goodburn RC .05 .01
❑ 368 Bill Maas .05 .01
❑ 369 Mike Bell .05 .01
❑ 370 Dino Hackett RC .05 .01
❑ 371 Deron Cherry .05 .01
❑ 372 Lions TL .05 .01
❑ 373 Chuck Long .20 .07
❑ 374 Garry James .05 .01
❑ 375 James Jones FB .05 .01
❑ 376 Pete Mandley .05 .01
❑ 377 Gary Lee RC .05 .01
❑ 378 Eddie Murray .05 .01
❑ 379 Jim Arnold .05 .01
❑ 380 Dennis Gibson RC .05 .01
❑ 381 Michael Cofer LB .05 .01
❑ 382 James Griffin .05 .01
❑ 383 Falcons TL .05 .01
❑ 384 Scott Campbell .05 .01
❑ 385 Gerald Riggs .20 .07
❑ 386 Floyd Dixon RC .05 .01
❑ 387 Rick Donnelly .05 .01
❑ 388 Bill Fralic .20 .07
❑ 389 Major Everett .05 .01
❑ 390 Mike Gann .05 .01
❑ 391 Tony Casillas RC .20 .07
❑ 392 Rick Bryan .05 .01
❑ 393 John Rade RC .05 .01
❑ 394 Checklist 1-132 .05 .01
❑ 395 Checklist 133-264 .05 .01
❑ 396 Checklist 265-396 .05 .01

1989 Topps

❑ COMPLETE SET (396) 20.00 7.50
❑ COMP.FACT.SET (396) 25.00 10.00
❑ 1 Super Bowl XXIII/Montana .50 .20
❑ 2 Tim Brown RB .50 .20
❑ 3 Eric Dickerson RB .10 .02
❑ 4 Steve Largent RB .25 .08
❑ 5 Dan Marino RB .75 .30
❑ 6 49ers TL/Montana .50 .20
❑ 7 Jerry Rice 1.50 .60
❑ 8 Roger Craig .25 .08
❑ 9 Ronnie Lott .10 .02
❑ 10 Michael Carter .05 .01
❑ 11 Charles Haley .25 .08
❑ 12 Joe Montana 2.00 .75
❑ 13 John Taylor RC .10 .02
❑ 14 Michael Walter .05 .01
❑ 15 Mike Cofer K RC .05 .01
❑ 16 Tom Rathman .05 .01
❑ 17 Daniel Stubbs RC .05 .01
❑ 18 Keena Turner .05 .01
❑ 19 Tim McKyer .05 .01
❑ 20 Larry Roberts .05 .01
❑ 21 Jeff Fuller .05 .01
❑ 22 Bubba Paris .05 .01
❑ 23 Bengals Team UER .10 .02
❑ 24 Eddie Brown .05 .01
❑ 25 Boomer Esiason .10 .02
❑ 26 Tim Krumrie .05 .01
❑ 27 Ickey Woods RC .10 .02
❑ 28 Anthony Munoz .10 .02
❑ 29 Tim McGee .05 .01
❑ 30 Max Montoya .05 .01
❑ 31 David Grant .05 .01
❑ 32 Rodney Holman RC .05 .01
❑ 33 David Fulcher .10 .02
❑ 34 Jim Skow .05 .01
❑ 35 James Brooks .10 .02
❑ 36 Reggie Williams .05 .01
❑ 37 Eric Thomas RC .05 .01
❑ 38 Stanford Jennings .05 .01
❑ 39 Jim Breech .05 .01
❑ 40 Bills TL/Jim Kelly .25 .08
❑ 41 Shane Conlan .05 .01
❑ 42 Scott Norwood RC .05 .01
❑ 43 Cornelius Bennett .10 .02
❑ 44 Bruce Smith .25 .08
❑ 45 Thurman Thomas RC 1.00 .40
❑ 46 Jim Kelly .50 .20
❑ 47 John Kidd .05 .01
❑ 48 Kent Hull RC .05 .01
❑ 49 Art Still .05 .01
❑ 50 Fred Smerlas .05 .01
❑ 51A Derrick Burroughs .05 .01
❑ 51B Derrick Burroughs .05 .01
❑ 52 Andre Reed .25 .08
❑ 53 Robb Riddick .05 .01
❑ 54 Chris Burkett .05 .01
❑ 55 Ronnie Harmon .10 .02
❑ 56 Mark Kelso UER .05 .01
❑ 57 Bears Team .05 .01
❑ 58 Mike Singletary .10 .02
❑ 59 Jay Hilgenberg UER .05 .01
❑ 60 Richard Dent .10 .02
❑ 61 Ron Rivera .05 .01
❑ 62 Jim McMahon .10 .02
❑ 63 Mike Tomczak .10 .02
❑ 64 Neal Anderson .10 .02
❑ 65 Dennis Gentry .05 .01
❑ 66 Dan Hampton .10 .02
❑ 67 David Tate .05 .01
❑ 68 Thomas Sanders RC .05 .01
❑ 69 Steve McMichael .10 .02
❑ 70 Dennis McKinnon .05 .01
❑ 71 Brad Muster RC .05 .01
❑ 72 Vestee Jackson RC .05 .01
❑ 73 Dave Duerson .05 .01
❑ 74 Vikings Team .05 .01
❑ 75 Joey Browner .05 .01
❑ 76 Carl Lee RC .05 .01
❑ 77 Gary Zimmerman .05 .01
❑ 78 Hassan Jones RC .05 .01
❑ 79 Anthony Carter .10 .02
❑ 80 Ray Berry .05 .01
❑ 81 Steve Jordan .05 .01
❑ 82 Issiac Holt .05 .01
❑ 83 Wade Wilson .10 .02
❑ 84 Chris Doleman .10 .02
❑ 85 Alfred Anderson .05 .01
❑ 86 Keith Millard .05 .01
❑ 87 Darrin Nelson .05 .01
❑ 88 D.J. Dozier .05 .01
❑ 89 Scott Studwell .05 .01
❑ 90 Oilers Team .05 .01
❑ 91 Bruce Matthews RC .60 .25
❑ 92 Curtis Duncan .05 .01
❑ 93 Warren Moon .25 .08
❑ 94 Johnny Meads RC .05 .01
❑ 95 Drew Hill .05 .01
❑ 96 Alonzo Highsmith .05 .01
❑ 97 Mike Munchak .10 .02
❑ 98 Mike Rozier .05 .01
❑ 99 Tony Zendejas .05 .01
❑ 100 Jeff Donaldson .05 .01
❑ 101 Ray Childress .05 .01
❑ 102 Sean Jones .10 .02
❑ 103 Ernest Givins .10 .02
❑ 104 William Fuller RC .25 .08
❑ 105 Allen Pinkett RC .05 .01
❑ 106 Eagles TL/R.Cunningham .10 .02
❑ 107 Keith Jackson RC .25 .08
❑ 108 Reggie White .25 .08
❑ 109 Clyde Simmons .10 .02
❑ 110 John Teltschik .05 .01
❑ 111 Wes Hopkins .05 .01
❑ 112 Keith Byars .10 .02
❑ 113 Jerome Brown .10 .02
❑ 114 Mike Quick .05 .01
❑ 115 Randall Cunningham .40 .15
❑ 116 Anthony Toney .05 .01
❑ 117 Ron Johnson WR .05 .01
❑ 118 Terry Hoage .05 .01
❑ 119 Seth Joyner .10 .02
❑ 120 Eric Allen RC .25 .08
❑ 121 Cris Carter RC 1.50 .60
❑ 122 Rams Team .05 .01
❑ 123 Tom Newberry RC .05 .01
❑ 124 Pete Holohan .05 .01
❑ 125 Robert Delpino RC UER .05 .01
❑ 126 Carl Ekern .05 .01
❑ 127 Greg Bell .05 .01
❑ 128 Mike Lansford .05 .01
❑ 129 Jim Everett .10 .02
❑ 130 Mike Wilcher .05 .01
❑ 131 Jerry Gray .05 .01
❑ 132 Dale Hatcher .05 .01
❑ 133 Doug Smith .05 .01
❑ 134 Kevin Greene .25 .08
❑ 135 Jackie Slater .05 .01
❑ 136 Aaron Cox RC .05 .01
❑ 137 Henry Ellard .25 .08
❑ 138 Browns Team .10 .02
❑ 139 Frank Minnifield .05 .01
❑ 140 Webster Slaughter .10 .02
❑ 141 Bernie Kosar .10 .02
❑ 142 Charles Buchanan .05 .01
❑ 143 Clay Matthews .10 .02
❑ 144 Reggie Langhorne RC .05 .01

❑	145 Hanford Dixon	.05	.01
❑	146 Brian Brennan	.05	.01
❑	147 Earnest Byner	.05	.01
❑	148 Michael Dean Perry RC	.10	.02
❑	149 Kevin Mack	.05	.01
❑	150 Matt Bahr	.05	.01
❑	151 Ozzie Newsome	.10	.02
❑	152 Saints Team	.10	.02
❑	153 Morten Andersen	.05	.01
❑	154 Pat Swilling	.10	.02
❑	155 Sam Mills	.10	.02
❑	156 Lonzell Hill	.05	.01
❑	157 Dalton Hilliard	.05	.01
❑	158 Craig Heyward RC	.10	.02
❑	159 Vaughan Johnson RC	.05	.01
❑	160 Rueben Mayes	.05	.01
❑	161 Gene Atkins RC	.05	.01
❑	162 Bobby Hebert	.10	.02
❑	163 Rickey Jackson	.10	.02
❑	164 Eric Martin	.05	.01
❑	165 Giants Team	.05	.01
❑	166 Lawrence Taylor	.25	.08
❑	167 Bart Oates	.05	.01
❑	168 Carl Banks	.05	.01
❑	169 Eric Moore RC	.05	.01
❑	170 Sheldon White RC	.05	.01
❑	171 Mark Collins RC	.05	.01
❑	172 Phil Simms	.10	.02
❑	173 Jim Burt	.05	.01
❑	174 Stephen Baker RC	.10	.02
❑	175 Mark Bavaro	.10	.02
❑	176 Pepper Johnson	.05	.01
❑	177 Lionel Manuel	.05	.01
❑	178 Joe Morris	.05	.01
❑	179 Jumbo Elliott RC	.05	.01
❑	180 Gary Reasons RC	.05	.01
❑	181 Seahawks Team	.10	.02
❑	182 Brian Blades RC	.25	.08
❑	183 Steve Largent	.25	.08
❑	184 Rufus Porter RC	.05	.01
❑	185 Ruben Rodriguez	.05	.01
❑	186 Curt Warner	.05	.01
❑	187 Paul Moyer	.05	.01
❑	188 Dave Krieg	.10	.02
❑	189 Jacob Green	.05	.01
❑	190 John L.Williams	.05	.01
❑	191 Eugene Robinson RC	.05	.01
❑	192 Brian Bosworth	.10	.02
❑	193 Patriots Team	.05	.01
❑	194 John Stephens RC	.05	.01
❑	195 Robert Perryman RC	.05	.01
❑	196 Andre Tippett	.05	.01
❑	197 Fred Marion	.05	.01
❑	198 Doug Flutie	1.00	.40
❑	199 Stanley Morgan	.05	.01
❑	200 Johnny Rembert RC	.05	.01
❑	201 Tony Eason	.05	.01
❑	202 Marvin Allen	.05	.01
❑	203 Raymond Clayborn	.05	.01
❑	204 Irving Fryar	.25	.08
❑	205 Colts Team	.05	.01
❑	206 Eric Dickerson	.10	.02
❑	207 Chris Hinton	.05	.01
❑	208 Duane Bickett	.05	.01
❑	209 Chris Chandler RC	1.00	.40
❑	210 Jon Hand	.05	.01
❑	211 Ray Donaldson	.05	.01
❑	212 Dean Biasucci	.05	.01
❑	213 Bill Brooks	.10	.02
❑	214 Chris Goode RC	.05	.01
❑	215 Clarence Verdin RC	.05	.01
❑	216 Albert Bentley	.05	.01
❑	217 Passing Leaders	.10	.02
❑	218 Receiving Leaders	.10	.02
❑	219 Eric Dickerson/Walker LL	.10	.02
❑	220 Scoring Leaders	.05	.01
❑	221 Interception Leaders	.05	.01
❑	222 Jets Team	.05	.01
❑	223 Erik McMillan RC	.05	.01
❑	224 James Hasty RC	.05	.01
❑	225 Al Toon	.10	.02
❑	226 John Booty RC	.05	.01
❑	227 Johnny Hector	.05	.01
❑	228 Ken O'Brien	.05	.01
❑	229 Marty Lyons	.05	.01
❑	230 Mickey Shuler	.05	.01
❑	231 Robin Cole	.05	.01
❑	232 Freeman McNeil	.05	.01
❑	233 Marion Barber RC	.05	.01
❑	234 Jo Jo Townsell	.05	.01
❑	235 Wesley Walker	.05	.01
❑	236 Roger Vick	.05	.01
❑	237 Pat Leahy	.05	.01
❑	238 Broncos TL/Elway	.50	.20
❑	239 Mike Horan	.05	.01
❑	240 Tony Dorsett	.25	.08
❑	241 John Elway	2.00	.75
❑	242 Mark Jackson	.05	.01
❑	243 Sammy Winder	.05	.01
❑	244 Rich Karlis	.05	.01
❑	245 Vance Johnson	.10	.02
❑	246 Steve Sewell RC	.05	.01
❑	247 Karl Mecklenburg UER	.05	.01
❑	248 Rulon Jones	.05	.01
❑	249 Simon Fletcher RC	.05	.01
❑	250 Redskins Team	.10	.02
❑	251 Chip Lohmiller RC	.05	.01
❑	252 Jamie Morris	.05	.01
❑	253 Mark Rypien RC UER	.10	.02
❑	254 Barry Wilburn	.05	.01
❑	255 Mark May RC	.05	.01
❑	256 Wilber Marshall	.05	.01
❑	257 Charles Mann	.05	.01
❑	258 Gary Clark	.25	.08
❑	259 Doug Williams	.10	.02
❑	260 Art Monk	.10	.02
❑	261 Kelvin Bryant	.05	.01
❑	262 Dexter Manley	.05	.01
❑	263 Ricky Sanders	.05	.01
❑	264 Raiders Team	.25	.08
❑	265 Tim Brown RC	1.50	.60
❑	266 Jay Schroeder	.05	.01
❑	267 Marcus Allen	.25	.08
❑	268 Mike Haynes	.10	.02
❑	269 Bo Jackson	.30	.10
❑	270 Steve Beuerlein RC	.60	.25
❑	271 Vann McElroy	.05	.01
❑	272 Willie Gault	.10	.02
❑	273 Howie Long	.25	.08
❑	274 Greg Townsend	.05	.01
❑	275 Mike Wise DE	.05	.01
❑	276 Cardinals Team	.05	.01
❑	277 Luis Sharpe	.05	.01
❑	278 Scott Dill	.05	.01
❑	279 Vai Sikahema	.05	.01
❑	280 Ron Wolfley	.05	.01
❑	281 David Galloway	.05	.01
❑	282 Jay Novacek RC	.25	.08
❑	283 Neil Lomax	.05	.01
❑	284 Robert Awalt	.05	.01
❑	285 Cedric Mack	.05	.01
❑	286 Freddie Joe Nunn	.05	.01
❑	287 J.T. Smith	.05	.01
❑	288 Stump Mitchell	.05	.01
❑	289 Roy Green	.10	.02
❑	290 Dolphins TL/Marino	.50	.20
❑	291 Jarvis Williams RC	.05	.01
❑	292 Troy Stradford	.05	.01
❑	293 Dan Marino	2.00	.75
❑	294 T.J. Turner	.05	.01
❑	295 John Offerdahl	.05	.01
❑	296 Ferrell Edmunds RC	.05	.01
❑	297 Scott Schwedes	.05	.01
❑	298 Lorenzo Hampton	.05	.01
❑	299 Jim C.Jensen RC	.05	.01
❑	300 Brian Sochia	.05	.01
❑	301 Reggie Roby	.05	.01
❑	302 Mark Clayton	.10	.02
❑	303 Chargers Team	.05	.01
❑	304 Lee Williams	.05	.01
❑	305 Gary Plummer RC	.05	.01
❑	306 Gary Anderson RB	.05	.01
❑	307 Gill Byrd	.05	.01
❑	308 Jamie Holland RC	.05	.01
❑	309 Billy Ray Smith	.05	.01
❑	310 Lionel James	.05	.01
❑	311 Mark Vlasic RC	.05	.01
❑	312 Curtis Adams	.05	.01
❑	313 Anthony Miller RC	.25	.08
❑	314 Steelers Team	.05	.01
❑	315 Bubby Brister RC	.25	.08
❑	316 David Little	.05	.01
❑	317 Tunch Ilkin RC	.05	.01
❑	318 Louis Lipps	.10	.02
❑	319 Warren Williams RC	.05	.01
❑	320 Dwight Stone	.10	.02
❑	321 Merril Hoge RC	.05	.01
❑	322 Thomas Everett RC	.05	.01
❑	323 Rod Woodson RC	.50	.20
❑	324 Gary Anderson K	.05	.01
❑	325 Buccaneers Team	.05	.01
❑	326 Donnie Elder	.05	.01
❑	327 Vinny Testaverde	.30	.10
❑	328 Harry Hamilton	.05	.01
❑	329 James Wilder	.05	.01
❑	330 Lars Tate	.05	.01
❑	331 Mark Carrier RC WR	.25	.08
❑	332 Bruce Hill RC	.05	.01
❑	333 Paul Gruber RC	.05	.01
❑	334 Ricky Reynolds	.05	.01
❑	335 Eugene Marve	.05	.01
❑	336 Falcons Team	.05	.01
❑	337 Aundray Bruce RC	.05	.01
❑	338 John Rade	.05	.01
❑	339 Scott Case RC	.05	.01
❑	340 Robert Moore	.05	.01
❑	341 Chris Miller RC	.25	.08
❑	342 Gerald Riggs	.10	.02
❑	343 Gene Lang	.05	.01
❑	344 Marcus Cotton	.05	.01
❑	345 Rick Donnelly	.05	.01
❑	346 John Settle RC	.05	.01
❑	347 Bill Fralic	.05	.01
❑	348 Chiefs Team	.05	.01
❑	349 Steve DeBerg	.05	.01
❑	350 Mike Stensrud	.05	.01
❑	351 Dino Hackett	.05	.01
❑	352 Deron Cherry	.10	.02
❑	353 Christian Okoye	.05	.01
❑	354 Bill Maas	.05	.01
❑	355 Carlos Carson	.05	.01
❑	356 Albert Lewis	.05	.01
❑	357 Paul Palmer	.05	.01
❑	358 Nick Lowery	.05	.01
❑	359 Stephone Paige	.05	.01
❑	360 Lions Team	.05	.01
❑	361 Chris Spielman RC	.25	.08
❑	362 Jim Arnold	.05	.01
❑	363 Devon Mitchell	.05	.01
❑	364 Mike Cofer	.05	.01
❑	365 Bennie Blades RC	.05	.01
❑	366 James Jones FB	.05	.01
❑	367 Garry James	.05	.01
❑	368 Pete Mandley	.05	.01
❑	369 Keith Ferguson	.05	.01
❑	370 Dennis Gibson	.05	.01
❑	371 Packers Team UER	.05	.01
❑	372 Brent Fullwood RC	.05	.01
❑	373 Don Majkowski RC	.10	.02
❑	374 Tim Harris	.05	.01
❑	375 Keith Woodside RC	.05	.01
❑	376 Mark Murphy	.05	.01
❑	377 Dave Brown DB	.05	.01
❑	378 Perry Kemp RC	.05	.01
❑	379 Sterling Sharpe RC	.75	.30
❑	380 Chuck Cecil RC	.05	.01
❑	381 Walter Stanley	.05	.01
❑	382 Cowboys Team	.05	.01
❑	383 Michael Irvin RC	1.25	.50
❑	384 Bill Bates	.10	.02
❑	385 Herschel Walker	.25	.08
❑	386 Darryl Clack	.05	.01
❑	387 Danny Noonan	.05	.01
❑	388 Eugene Lockhart RC	.05	.01
❑	389 Ed Too Tall Jones	.10	.02
❑	390 Steve Pelluer	.05	.01
❑	391 Ray Alexander	.05	.01
❑	392 Nate Newton RC	.10	.02
❑	393 Garry Cobb	.05	.01
❑	394 Checklist 1-132	.05	.01
❑	395 Checklist 133-264	.05	.01
❑	396 Checklist 265-396	.05	.01

1989 Topps Traded

❑	COMP.FACT.SET (132)	15.00	6.00
❑	1T Eric Ball RC	.05	.01
❑	2T Tony Mandarich RC	.05	.01
❑	3T Shawn Collins RC	.05	.01
❑	4T Ray Bentley RC	.05	.01
❑	5T Tony Casillas	.05	.01
❑	6T Al Del Greco RC	.05	.01

❑ 7T Dan Saleaumua RC	.10	.02
❑ 8T Keith Bishop	.05	.01
❑ 9T Rodney Peete RC	.60	.25
❑ 10T Lorenzo White RC	.25	.08
❑ 11T Steve Smith RC	.10	.02
❑ 12T Pete Mandley	.05	.01
❑ 13T Mervyn Fernandez RC**/C	.05	.01
❑ 14T Flipper Anderson RC	.25	.08
❑ 15T Louis Oliver RC	.10	.02
❑ 16T Rick Fenney	.05	.01
❑ 17T Gary Jeter	.05	.01
❑ 18T Greg Cox	.05	.01
❑ 19T Bubba McDowell RC	.10	.02
❑ 20T Ron Heller	.05	.01
❑ 21T Tim McDonald RC	.05	.01
❑ 22T Jerrol Williams RC	.05	.01
❑ 23T Marion Butts RC	.10	.02
❑ 24T Steve Young	.75	.30
❑ 25T Mike Merriweather	.05	.01
❑ 26T Richard Johnson	.05	.01
❑ 27T Gerald Riggs	.10	.02
❑ 28T Dave Waymer	.05	.01
❑ 29T Issiac Holt	.05	.01
❑ 30T Deion Sanders RC	1.50	.60
❑ 31T Todd Blackledge	.05	.01
❑ 32T Jeff Cross RC	.05	.01
❑ 33T Steve Wisniewski RC	.10	.02
❑ 34T Ron Brown	.10	.02
❑ 35T Rod Bernstine RC	.05	.01
❑ 36T Jeff Uhlenhake RC	.05	.01
❑ 37T Donnell Woolford RC	.25	.08
❑ 38T Bob Gagliano RC	.05	.01
❑ 39T Ezra Johnson	.05	.01
❑ 40T Ron Jaworski	.05	.01
❑ 41T Lawyer Tillman RC	.05	.01
❑ 42T Lorenzo Lynch RC	.05	.01
❑ 43T Mike Alexander	.05	.01
❑ 44T Tim Worley RC	.05	.01
❑ 45T Guy Bingham	.05	.01
❑ 46T Cleveland Gary RC	.05	.01
❑ 47T Danny Peebles	.05	.01
❑ 48T Clarence Weathers RC	.05	.01
❑ 49T Jeff Lageman RC	.25	.08
❑ 50T Eric Metcalf RC	.25	.08
❑ 51T Myron Guyton RC	.05	.01
❑ 52T Steve Atwater RC	.05	.01
❑ 53T John Fourcade RC	.05	.01
❑ 54T Randall McDaniel RC	.25	.08
❑ 55T Al Noga RC	.05	.01
❑ 56T Sammie Smith RC	.10	.02
❑ 57T Jesse Solomon	.05	.01
❑ 58T Greg Kragen RC	.05	.01
❑ 59T Don Beebe RC	.25	.08
❑ 60T Hart Lee Dykes RC	.10	.02
❑ 61T Trace Armstrong RC	.10	.02
❑ 62T Steve Pelluer	.05	.01
❑ 63T Barry Krauss	.05	.01
❑ 64T Kevin Murphy RC	.05	.01
❑ 65T Steve Tasker RC	.25	.08
❑ 66T Jessie Small RC	.05	.01
❑ 67T Dave Meggett RC	.25	.08
❑ 68T Dean Hamel	.05	.01
❑ 69T Jim Covert	.05	.01
❑ 70T Troy Aikman RC	5.00	2.00
❑ 71T Raul Allegre	.05	.01
❑ 72T Chris Jacke RC	.10	.02
❑ 73T Leslie O'Neal	.10	.02
❑ 74T Keith Taylor RC	.05	.01
❑ 75T Steve Walsh RC	.25	.08
❑ 76T Tracy Rocker	.05	.01
❑ 77T Robert Massey RC	.10	.02
❑ 78T Bryan Wagner	.05	.01
❑ 79T Steve DeOssie	.05	.01
❑ 80T Carnell Lake RC	.25	.08
❑ 81T Frank Reich RC	.25	.08
❑ 82T Tyrone Braxton RC	.05	.01
❑ 83T Barry Sanders RC	6.00	2.50
❑ 84T Pete Stoyanovich RC	.10	.02
❑ 85T Paul Palmer	.05	.01
❑ 86T Billy Joe Tolliver RC	.05	.01
❑ 87T Eric Hill RC	.10	.02
❑ 88T Gerald McNeil	.05	.01
❑ 89T Bill Hawkins RC	.05	.01
❑ 90T Derrick Thomas RC	1.25	.50
❑ 91T Jim Harbaugh RC	.75	.30
❑ 92T Brian Williams OL RC	.05	.01
❑ 93T Jack Trudeau	.05	.01
❑ 94T Leonard Smith	.05	.01
❑ 95T Gary Hogeboom	.05	.01
❑ 96T A.J.Johnson RC	.05	.01
❑ 97T Jim McMahon	.10	.02
❑ 98T David Williams RC	.05	.01
❑ 99T Rohn Stark	.05	.01
❑ 100T Sean Landeta	.05	.01
❑ 101T Tim Johnson RC	.05	.01
❑ 102T Andre Rison RC	.75	.30
❑ 103T Earnest Byner	.10	.02
❑ 104T Don McPherson RC	.05	.01
❑ 105T Zefross Moss RC	.05	.01
❑ 106T Frank Stams RC	.05	.01
❑ 107T Courtney Hall RC	.10	.02
❑ 108T Marc Logan RC	.05	.01
❑ 109T James Lofton	.25	.08
❑ 110T Lewis Tillman RC	.10	.02
❑ 111T Irv Pankey RC	.05	.01
❑ 112T Ralf Mojsiejenko	.05	.01
❑ 113T Bobby Humphrey RC	.05	.01
❑ 114T Chris Burkett	.05	.01
❑ 115T Greg Lloyd RC	.25	.08
❑ 116T Matt Millen	.10	.02
❑ 117T Carl Zander	.05	.01
❑ 118T Wayne Martin RC	.25	.08
❑ 119T Mike Saxon	.05	.01
❑ 120T Herschel Walker	.10	.02
❑ 121T Andy Heck RC	.05	.01
❑ 122T Mark Robinson	.05	.01
❑ 123T Keith Van Horne RC	.05	.01
❑ 124T Ricky Hunley	.05	.01
❑ 125T Timm Rosenbach RC	.10	.02
❑ 126T Steve Grogan	.10	.02
❑ 127T Stephen Braggs RC	.05	.01
❑ 128T Terry Long	.05	.01
❑ 129T Evan Cooper	.05	.01
❑ 130T Robert Lyles	.05	.01
❑ 131T Mike Webster	.10	.02
❑ 132T Checklist 1-132	.05	.01

1990 Topps

❑ COMPLETE SET (528)	25.00	10.00
❑ COMP.FACT.SET (528)	30.00	12.50
❑ 1 Joe Montana RB	.50	.20
❑ 2 Flipper Anderson RB	.05	.01
❑ 3 Troy Aikman RB	.40	.15
❑ 4 Kevin Butler RB	.05	.01
❑ 5 Super Bowl XXIV	.05	.01
❑ 6 Dexter Carter RC	.05	.01
❑ 7 Matt Millen	.10	.02
❑ 8 Jerry Rice	.75	.30
❑ 9 Ronnie Lott	.10	.02
❑ 10 John Taylor	.10	.02
❑ 11 Guy McIntyre	.05	.01
❑ 12 Roger Craig	.10	.02
❑ 13 Joe Montana	1.25	.50
❑ 14 Brent Jones RC	.25	.08
❑ 15 Tom Rathman	.05	.01
❑ 16 Harris Barton	.05	.01
❑ 17 Charles Haley	.10	.02
❑ 18 Pierce Holt RC	.05	.01
❑ 19 Michael Carter	.05	.01
❑ 20 Chet Brooks	.05	.01
❑ 21 Eric Wright	.05	.01
❑ 22 Mike Cofer	.05	.01
❑ 23 Jim Fahnhorst	.05	.01
❑ 24 Keena Turner	.05	.01
❑ 25 Don Griffin	.05	.01
❑ 26 Kevin Fagan RC	.05	.01
❑ 27 Bubba Paris	.05	.01
❑ 28 Barry Sanders/C.Okoye LL	.50	.20
❑ 29 Steve Atwater	.05	.01
❑ 30 Tyrone Braxton	.05	.01
❑ 31 Ron Holmes	.05	.01
❑ 32 Bobby Humphrey	.05	.01
❑ 33 Greg Kragen	.05	.01
❑ 34 David Treadwell	.05	.01
❑ 35 Karl Mecklenburg	.05	.01
❑ 36 Dennis Smith	.05	.01
❑ 37 John Elway	1.25	.50
❑ 38 Vance Johnson	.05	.01
❑ 39 Simon Fletcher UER	.05	.01
❑ 40 Jim Juriga	.05	.01
❑ 41 Mark Jackson	.05	.01
❑ 42 Melvin Bratton RC	.05	.01
❑ 43 Wymon Henderson RC	.05	.01
❑ 44 Ken Bell	.05	.01
❑ 45 Sammy Winder	.05	.01
❑ 46 Alphonso Carreker	.05	.01
❑ 47 Orson Mobley RC	.05	.01
❑ 48 Rodney Hampton RC	.25	.08
❑ 49 Dave Meggett	.10	.02
❑ 50 Myron Guyton	.05	.01
❑ 51 Phil Simms	.10	.02
❑ 52 Lawrence Taylor	.25	.08
❑ 53 Carl Banks	.05	.01
❑ 54 Pepper Johnson	.05	.01
❑ 55 Leonard Marshall	.05	.01
❑ 56 Mark Collins	.05	.01
❑ 57 Erik Howard	.05	.01
❑ 58 Eric Dorsey RC	.05	.01
❑ 59 Ottis Anderson	.10	.02
❑ 60 Mark Bavaro	.05	.01
❑ 61 Odessa Turner RC	.05	.01
❑ 62 Gary Reasons	.05	.01
❑ 63 Maurice Carthon	.05	.01
❑ 64 Lionel Manuel	.05	.01
❑ 65 Sean Landeta	.05	.01
❑ 66 Perry Williams	.05	.01
❑ 67 Pat Terrell RC	.05	.01
❑ 68 Flipper Anderson	.05	.01
❑ 69 Jackie Slater	.05	.01
❑ 70 Tom Newberry	.05	.01
❑ 71 Jerry Gray	.05	.01
❑ 72 Henry Ellard	.10	.02
❑ 73 Doug Smith	.05	.01
❑ 74 Kevin Greene	.10	.02
❑ 75 Jim Everett	.10	.02
❑ 76 Mike Lansford	.05	.01
❑ 77 Greg Bell	.05	.01
❑ 78 Pete Holohan	.05	.01
❑ 79 Robert Delpino	.05	.01
❑ 80 Mike Wilcher	.05	.01
❑ 81 Mike Piel	.05	.01
❑ 82 Mel Owens	.05	.01
❑ 83 Michael Stewart RC	.05	.01
❑ 84 Ben Smith RC	.05	.01
❑ 85 Keith Jackson	.10	.02
❑ 86 Reggie White	.25	.08
❑ 87 Eric Allen	.05	.01
❑ 88 Jerome Brown	.05	.01
❑ 89 Robert Drummond	.05	.01
❑ 90 Anthony Toney	.05	.01
❑ 91 Keith Byars	.05	.01
❑ 92 Cris Carter	.50	.20
❑ 93 Randall Cunningham	.25	.08
❑ 94 Ron Johnson WR	.05	.01
❑ 95 Mike Quick	.05	.01
❑ 96 Clyde Simmons	.05	.01

97	Mike Pitts	.05	.01
98	Izel Jenkins RC	.05	.01
99	Seth Joyner	.10	.02
100	Mike Schad	.05	.01
101	Wes Hopkins	.05	.01
102	Kirk Lowdermilk	.05	.01
103	Rick Fenney	.05	.01
104	Randall McDaniel	.10	.02
105	Herschel Walker	.10	.02
106	Al Noga	.05	.01
107	Gary Zimmerman	.05	.01
108	Chris Doleman	.05	.01
109	Keith Millard	.05	.01
110	Carl Lee	.05	.01
111	Joey Browner	.05	.01
112	Steve Jordan	.05	.01
113	Reggie Rutland RC	.05	.01
114	Wade Wilson	.10	.02
115	Anthony Carter	.10	.02
116	Rich Karlis	.05	.01
117	Hassan Jones	.05	.01
118	Henry Thomas	.05	.01
119	Scott Studwell	.05	.01
120	Ralf Mojsiejenko	.05	.01
121	Earnest Byner	.05	.01
122	Gerald Riggs	.10	.02
123	Tracy Rocker	.05	.01
124	A.J. Johnson	.05	.01
125	Charles Mann	.05	.01
126	Art Monk	.10	.02
127	Ricky Sanders	.05	.01
128	Gary Clark	.25	.08
129	Jim Lachey	.05	.01
130	Martin Mayhew RC	.05	.01
131	Ravin Caldwell	.05	.01
132	Don Warren	.05	.01
133	Mark Rypien	.10	.02
134	Ed Simmons RC	.05	.01
135	Darryl Grant	.05	.01
136	Darrell Green	.10	.02
137	Chip Lohmiller	.05	.01
138	Tony Bennett RC	.25	.08
139	Tony Mandarich	.05	.01
140	Sterling Sharpe	.25	.08
141	Tim Harris	.05	.01
142	Don Majkowski	.05	.01
143	Rich Moran RC	.05	.01
144	Jeff Query	.05	.01
145	Brent Fullwood	.05	.01
146	Chris Jacke	.05	.01
147	Keith Woodside	.05	.01
148	Perry Kemp	.05	.01
149	Herman Fontenot	.05	.01
150	Dave Brown DB	.05	.01
151	Brian Noble	.05	.01
152	Johnny Holland	.05	.01
153	Mark Murphy	.05	.01
154	Bob Nelson NT	.05	.01
155	Darrell Thompson RC	.05	.01
156	Lawyer Tillman	.05	.01
157	Eric Metcalf	.25	.08
158	Webster Slaughter	.10	.02
159	Frank Minnifield	.05	.01
160	Brian Brennan	.05	.01
161	Thane Gash RC	.05	.01
162	Robert Banks DE	.05	.01
163	Bernie Kosar	.10	.02
164	David Grayson	.05	.01
165	Kevin Mack	.05	.01
166	Mike Johnson	.05	.01
167	Tim Manoa	.05	.01
168	Ozzie Newsome	.10	.02
169	Felix Wright	.05	.01
170	Al(Bubba) Baker	.10	.02
171	Reggie Langhorne	.05	.01
172	Clay Matthews	.10	.02
173	Andrew Stewart	.05	.01
174	Barry Foster RC	.25	.08
175	Tim Worley	.05	.01
176	Tim Johnson	.05	.01
177	Carnell Lake	.05	.01
178	Greg Lloyd	.25	.08
179	Rod Woodson	.25	.08
180	Tunch Ilkin	.05	.01
181	Dermontti Dawson	.10	.02
182	Gary Anderson K	.05	.01
183	Bubby Brister	.05	.01
184	Louis Lipps	.10	.02
185	Merril Hoge	.05	.01
186	Mike Mularkey	.05	.01
187	Derek Hill	.05	.01
188	Rodney Carter	.05	.01
189	Dwayne Woodruff	.05	.01
190	Keith Willis	.05	.01
191	Jerry Olsavsky	.05	.01
192	Mark Stock	.05	.01
193	Sacks Leaders	.05	.01
194	Leonard Smith	.05	.01
195	Darryl Talley	.05	.01
196	Mark Kelso	.05	.01
197	Kent Hull	.05	.01
198	Nate Odomes RC	.10	.02
199	Pete Metzelaars	.05	.01
200	Don Beebe	.10	.02
201	Ray Bentley	.05	.01
202	Steve Tasker	.10	.02
203	Scott Norwood	.05	.01
204	Andre Reed	.25	.08
205	Bruce Smith	.25	.08
206	Thurman Thomas	.25	.08
207	Jim Kelly	.25	.08
208	Cornelius Bennett	.10	.02
209	Shane Conlan	.05	.01
210	Larry Kinnebrew	.05	.01
211	Jeff Alm RC	.05	.01
212	Robert Lyles	.05	.01
213	Bubba McDowell	.05	.01
214	Mike Munchak	.10	.02
215	Bruce Matthews	.10	.02
216	Warren Moon	.25	.08
217	Drew Hill	.05	.01
218	Ray Childress	.05	.01
219	Steve Brown	.05	.01
220	Alonzo Highsmith	.05	.01
221	Allen Pinkett	.05	.01
222	Sean Jones	.10	.02
223	Johnny Meads	.05	.01
224	John Grimsley	.05	.01
225	Haywood Jeffires RC	.25	.08
226	Curtis Duncan	.05	.01
227	Greg Montgomery RC	.05	.01
228	Ernest Givins	.10	.02
229	Joe Montana/B.Esiason LL	.30	.10
230	Robert Massey	.05	.01
231	John Fourcade	.05	.01
232	Dalton Hilliard	.05	.01
233	Vaughan Johnson	.05	.01
234	Hoby Brenner	.05	.01
235	Pat Swilling	.10	.02
236	Kevin Haverdink	.05	.01
237	Bobby Hebert	.05	.01
238	Sam Mills	.10	.02
239	Eric Martin	.05	.01
240	Lonzell Hill	.05	.01
241	Steve Trapilo	.05	.01
242	Rickey Jackson	.10	.02
243	Craig Heyward	.10	.02
244	Rueben Mayes	.05	.01
245	Morten Andersen	.05	.01
246	Percy Snow RC	.05	.01
247	Pete Mandley	.05	.01
248	Derrick Thomas	.25	.08
249	Dan Saleaumua	.05	.01
250	Todd McNair RC	.05	.01
251	Leonard Griffin	.05	.01
252	Jonathan Hayes	.05	.01
253	Christian Okoye	.05	.01
254	Albert Lewis	.05	.01
255	Nick Lowery	.05	.01
256	Kevin Ross	.05	.01
257	Steve DeBerg UER	.05	.01
258	Stephone Paige	.05	.01
259	James Saxon RC	.05	.01
260	Herman Heard	.05	.01
261	Deron Cherry	.05	.01
262	Dino Hackett	.05	.01
263	Neil Smith	.25	.08
264	Steve Pelluer	.05	.01
265	Eric Thomas	.05	.01
266	Eric Ball	.05	.01
267	Leon White	.05	.01
268	Tim Krumrie	.05	.01
269	Jason Buck	.05	.01
270	Boomer Esiason	.10	.02
271	Carl Zander	.05	.01
272	Eddie Brown	.05	.01
273	David Fulcher	.05	.01
274	Tim McGee	.05	.01
275	James Brooks	.10	.02
276	Rickey Dixon RC	.05	.01
277	Ickey Woods	.05	.01
278	Anthony Munoz	.10	.02
279	Rodney Holman	.05	.01
280	Mike Alexander	.05	.01
281	Mervyn Fernandez	.05	.01
282	Steve Wisniewski	.10	.02
283	Steve Smith	.05	.01
284	Howie Long	.25	.08
285	Bo Jackson	.30	.10
286	Mike Dyal	.05	.01
287	Thomas Benson	.05	.01
288	Willie Gault	.10	.02
289	Marcus Allen	.25	.08
290	Greg Townsend	.05	.01
291	Steve Beuerlein	.10	.02
292	Scott Davis	.05	.01
293	Eddie Anderson RC	.05	.01
294	Terry McDaniel	.05	.01
295	Tim Brown	.25	.08
296	Bob Golic	.05	.01
297	Jeff Jaeger RC	.05	.01
298	Jeff George RC	.50	.20
299	Chip Banks	.05	.01
300	Andre Rison UER	.25	.08
301	Rohn Stark	.05	.01
302	Keith Taylor	.05	.01
303	Jack Trudeau	.05	.01
304	Chris Hinton	.05	.01
305	Ray Donaldson	.05	.01
306	Jeff Herrod RC	.05	.01
307	Clarence Verdin	.05	.01
308	Jon Hand	.05	.01
309	Bill Brooks	.05	.01
310	Albert Bentley	.05	.01
311	Mike Prior	.05	.01
312	Pat Beach	.05	.01
313	Eugene Daniel	.05	.01
314	Duane Bickett	.05	.01
315	Dean Biasucci	.05	.01
316	Richmond Webb RC	.05	.01
317	Jeff Cross	.05	.01
318	Louis Oliver	.05	.01
319	Sammie Smith	.05	.01
320	Pete Stoyanovich	.05	.01
321	John Offerdahl	.05	.01
322	Ferrell Edmunds	.05	.01
323	Dan Marino	1.25	.50
324	Andre Brown	.05	.01
325	Reggie Roby	.05	.01
326	Jarvis Williams	.05	.01
327	Roy Foster	.05	.01
328	Mark Clayton	.10	.02
329	Brian Sochia	.05	.01
330	Mark Duper	.10	.02
331	T.J. Turner	.05	.01
332	Jeff Uhlenhake	.05	.01
333	Jim C.Jensen	.05	.01
334	Cortez Kennedy RC	.25	.08
335	Andy Heck	.05	.01
336	Rufus Porter	.05	.01
337	Brian Blades	.10	.02
338	Dave Krieg	.10	.02
339	John L. Williams	.05	.01
340	David Wyman	.05	.01
341	Paul Skansi RC	.05	.01
342	Eugene Robinson	.05	.01
343	Joe Nash	.05	.01
344	Jacob Green	.05	.01
345	Jeff Bryant	.05	.01
346	Ruben Rodriguez	.05	.01
347	Norm Johnson	.05	.01
348	Darren Comeaux	.05	.01
349	Andre Ware RC	.10	.02
350	Richard Johnson	.05	.01
351	Rodney Peete	.10	.02
352	Barry Sanders	1.25	.50
353	Chris Spielman	.25	.08
354	Eddie Murray	.05	.01
355	Jerry Ball	.05	.01
356	Mel Gray	.10	.02
357	Eric Williams RC	.05	.01

❑	358	Robert Clark RC	.05	.01
❑	359	Jason Phillips	.05	.01
❑	360	Terry Taylor RC	.05	.01
❑	361	Bennie Blades	.05	.01
❑	362	Michael Cofer	.05	.01
❑	363	Jim Arnold	.05	.01
❑	364	Marc Spindler RC	.05	.01
❑	365	Jim Covert	.05	.01
❑	366	Jim Harbaugh	.25	.08
❑	367	Neal Anderson	.10	.02
❑	368	Mike Singletary	.10	.02
❑	369	John Roper	.05	.01
❑	370	Steve McMichael	.10	.02
❑	371	Dennis Gentry	.05	.01
❑	372	Brad Muster	.05	.01
❑	373	Ron Morris	.05	.01
❑	374	James Thornton	.05	.01
❑	375	Kevin Butler	.05	.01
❑	376	Richard Dent	.10	.02
❑	377	Dan Hampton	.10	.02
❑	378	Jay Hilgenberg	.05	.01
❑	379	Donnell Woolford	.05	.01
❑	380	Trace Armstrong	.05	.01
❑	381	Junior Seau RC	1.25	.50
❑	382	Rod Bernstine	.05	.01
❑	383	Marion Butts	.10	.02
❑	384	Burt Grossman	.05	.01
❑	385	Darrin Nelson	.05	.01
❑	386	Leslie O'Neal	.10	.02
❑	387	Billy Joe Tolliver	.05	.01
❑	388	Courtney Hall	.05	.01
❑	389	Lee Williams	.05	.01
❑	390	Anthony Miller	.25	.08
❑	391	Gill Byrd	.05	.01
❑	392	Wayne Walker WR	.05	.01
❑	393	Billy Ray Smith	.05	.01
❑	394	Vencie Glenn	.05	.01
❑	395	Tim Spencer	.05	.01
❑	396	Gary Plummer	.05	.01
❑	397	Arthur Cox	.05	.01
❑	398	Jamie Holland	.05	.01
❑	399	Keith McCants RC	.05	.01
❑	400	Kevin Murphy	.05	.01
❑	401	Danny Peebles	.05	.01
❑	402	Mark Robinson	.05	.01
❑	403	Broderick Thomas	.05	.01
❑	404	Ron Hall	.05	.01
❑	405	Mark Carrier WR	.25	.08
❑	406	Paul Gruber	.05	.01
❑	407	Vinny Testaverde	.10	.02
❑	408	Bruce Hill	.05	.01
❑	409	Lars Tate	.05	.01
❑	410	Harry Hamilton	.05	.01
❑	411	Ricky Reynolds	.05	.01
❑	412	Donald Igwebuike	.05	.01
❑	413	Reuben Davis	.05	.01
❑	414	William Howard	.05	.01
❑	415	Winston Moss RC	.05	.01
❑	416	Chris Singleton RC	.05	.01
❑	417	Hart Lee Dykes	.05	.01
❑	418	Steve Grogan	.10	.02
❑	419	Bruce Armstrong	.05	.01
❑	420	Robert Perryman	.05	.01
❑	421	Andre Tippett	.05	.01
❑	422	Sammy Martin	.05	.01
❑	423	Stanley Morgan	.05	.01
❑	424	Cedric Jones	.05	.01
❑	425	Sean Farrell	.05	.01
❑	426	Marc Wilson	.05	.01
❑	427	John Stephens	.05	.01
❑	428	Eric Sievers RC	.05	.01
❑	429	Maurice Hurst RC	.05	.01
❑	430	Johnny Rembert	.05	.01
❑	431	Jerry Rice/Andre Reed LL	.30	.10
❑	432	Eric Hill	.05	.01
❑	433	Gary Hogeboom	.05	.01
❑	434	Timm Rosenbach UER	.05	.01
❑	435	Tim McDonald	.05	.01
❑	436	Rich Camarillo	.05	.01
❑	437	Luis Sharpe	.05	.01
❑	438	J.T. Smith	.05	.01
❑	439	Roy Green	.10	.02
❑	440	Ernie Jones RC	.05	.01
❑	441	Robert Awalt	.05	.01
❑	442	Vai Sikahema	.05	.01
❑	443	Joe Wolf	.05	.01
❑	444	Stump Mitchell	.05	.01
❑	445	David Galloway	.05	.01
❑	446	Ron Wolfley	.05	.01
❑	447	Freddie Joe Nunn	.05	.01
❑	448	Blair Thomas RC	.10	.02
❑	449	Jeff Lageman	.05	.01
❑	450	Tony Eason	.05	.01
❑	451	Erik McMillan	.05	.01
❑	452	Jim Sweeney	.05	.01
❑	453	Ken O'Brien	.05	.01
❑	454	Johnny Hector	.05	.01
❑	455	Jo Jo Townsell	.05	.01
❑	456	Roger Vick	.05	.01
❑	457	James Hasty	.05	.01
❑	458	Dennis Byrd RC	.10	.02
❑	459	Ron Stallworth	.05	.01
❑	460	Mickey Shuler	.05	.01
❑	461	Bobby Humphery	.05	.01
❑	462	Kyle Clifton	.05	.01
❑	463	Al Toon	.10	.02
❑	464	Freeman McNeil	.05	.01
❑	465	Pat Leahy	.05	.01
❑	466	Scott Case	.05	.01
❑	467	Shawn Collins	.05	.01
❑	468	Floyd Dixon	.05	.01
❑	469	Deion Sanders	.50	.20
❑	470	Tony Casillas	.05	.01
❑	471	Michael Haynes RC	.25	.08
❑	472	Chris Miller	.25	.08
❑	473	John Settle	.05	.01
❑	474	Aundray Bruce	.05	.01
❑	475	Gene Lang	.05	.01
❑	476	Tim Gordon RC	.05	.01
❑	477	Scott Fulhage	.05	.01
❑	478	Bill Fralic	.05	.01
❑	479	Jessie Tuggle RC	.05	.01
❑	480	Marcus Cotton	.05	.01
❑	481	Steve Walsh	.10	.02
❑	482	Troy Aikman	.75	.30
❑	483	Ray Horton	.05	.01
❑	484	Tony Tolbert RC	.10	.02
❑	485	Steve Folsom	.05	.01
❑	486	Ken Norton Jr. RC	.25	.08
❑	487	Kelvin Martin RC	.05	.01
❑	488	Jack Del Rio	.10	.02
❑	489	Daryl Johnston RC	1.00	.40
❑	490	Bill Bates	.10	.02
❑	491	Jim Jeffcoat	.05	.01
❑	492	Vince Albritton	.05	.01
❑	493	Eugene Lockhart	.05	.01
❑	494	Mike Saxon	.05	.01
❑	495	James Dixon	.05	.01
❑	496	Willie Broughton	.05	.01
❑	497	Checklist 1-132	.05	.01
❑	498	Checklist 133-264	.05	.01
❑	499	Checklist 265-396	.05	.01
❑	500	Checklist 397-528	.05	.01
❑	501	Bears Team	.10	.02
❑	502	Bengals Team	.05	.01
❑	503	Bills Team	.05	.01
❑	504	Broncos Team	.05	.01
❑	505	Browns Team	.05	.01
❑	506	Buccaneers Team	.05	.01
❑	507	Cardinals Team	.05	.01
❑	508	Chargers Team	.05	.01
❑	509	Chiefs Team	.05	.01
❑	510	Colts Team	.05	.01
❑	511	Cowboys TL/Aikman	.30	.10
❑	512	Dolphins Team	.05	.01
❑	513	Eagles Team	.05	.01
❑	514	Falcons Team	.05	.01
❑	515	49ers TL/Montana/Craig	.30	.10
❑	516	Giants Team	.05	.01
❑	517	Jets Team	.05	.01
❑	518	Lions Team	.05	.01
❑	519	Oilers TL/Moon	.10	.02
❑	520	Packers Team	.05	.01
❑	521	Patriots Team	.05	.01
❑	522	Raiders TL/Bo Jackson	.10	.02
❑	523	Rams Team	.05	.01
❑	524	Redskins Team	.05	.01
❑	525	Saints Team	.05	.01
❑	526	Seahawks Team	.05	.01
❑	527	Steelers Team	.05	.01
❑	528	Vikings Team	.05	.01

1990 Topps Traded

❑		COMP.FACT.SET (132)	15.00	6.00
❑	1T	Gerald McNeil	.05	.01
❑	2T	Andre Rison	.25	.08
❑	3T	Steve Walsh	.25	.08
❑	4T	Lorenzo White	.10	.02
❑	5T	Max Montoya	.05	.01
❑	6T	William Roberts RC	.05	.01
❑	7T	Alonzo Highsmith	.05	.01
❑	8T	Chris Hinton	.10	.02
❑	9T	Stanley Morgan	.10	.02
❑	10T	Mickey Shuler	.05	.01
❑	11T	Bobby Humphery	.05	.01
❑	12T	Gary Anderson RB	.05	.01
❑	13T	Mike Tomczak	.10	.02
❑	14T	Anthony Pleasant RC	.10	.02
❑	15T	Walter Stanley	.05	.01
❑	16T	Greg Bell	.05	.01
❑	17T	Tony Martin RC	.75	.30
❑	18T	Terry Kinard	.05	.01
❑	19T	Cris Carter	.50	.20
❑	20T	James Wilder	.05	.01
❑	21T	Jerry Kauric	.05	.01
❑	22T	Irving Fryar	.25	.08
❑	23T	Ken Harvey RC	.25	.08
❑	24T	James Williams DB RC	.05	.01
❑	25T	Ron Cox RC	.05	.01
❑	26T	Andre Ware	.25	.08
❑	27T	Emmitt Smith RC	12.00	5.00
❑	28T	Junior Seau	.75	.30
❑	29T	Mark Carrier RC DB	.25	.08
❑	30T	Rodney Hampton	.25	.08
❑	31T	Rob Moore RC	.50	.20
❑	32T	Bern Brostek RC	.05	.01
❑	33T	Dexter Carter	.10	.02
❑	34T	Blair Thomas	.10	.02
❑	35T	Harold Green RC	.25	.08
❑	36T	Darrell Thompson	.05	.01
❑	37T	Eric Green RC	.25	.08
❑	38T	Renaldo Turnbull RC	.25	.08
❑	39T	Leroy Hoard RC	.25	.08
❑	40T	Anthony Thompson RC	.10	.02
❑	41T	Jeff George	.25	.08
❑	42T	Alexander Wright RC	.05	.01
❑	43T	Richmond Webb	.05	.01
❑	44T	Cortez Kennedy	.25	.08
❑	45T	Ray Agnew RC	.05	.01
❑	46T	Percy Snow	.05	.01
❑	47T	Chris Singleton	.05	.01
❑	48T	James Francis RC	.10	.02
❑	49T	Tony Bennett	.10	.02
❑	50T	Reggie Cobb RC	.10	.02
❑	51T	Barry Foster	.25	.08
❑	52T	Ben Smith	.05	.01
❑	53T	Anthony Smith RC	.25	.08
❑	54T	Steve Christie RC	.05	.01
❑	55T	Johnny Bailey RC	.10	.02
❑	56T	Alan Grant RC	.05	.01
❑	57T	Eric Floyd RC	.05	.01
❑	58T	Robert Blackmon RC	.05	.01
❑	59T	Brent Williams	.05	.01
❑	60T	Raymond Clayborn	.05	.01
❑	61T	Dave Duerson	.05	.01
❑	62T	Derrick Fenner RC	.10	.02
❑	63T	Ken Willis	.05	.01
❑	64T	Brad Baxter RC	.10	.02
❑	65T	Tony Paige	.05	.01
❑	66T	Jay Schroeder	.05	.01
❑	67T	Jim Breech	.05	.01

	Card	Player	Mint	Ex
❑	68T	Barry Word RC	.10	.02
❑	69T	Anthony Dilweg FTC	.05	.01
❑	70T	Rich Gannon RC	2.00	.75
❑	71T	Stan Humphries RC	.25	.08
❑	72T	Jay Novacek	.25	.08
❑	73T	Tommy Kane RC	.05	.01
❑	74T	Everson Walls	.05	.01
❑	75T	Mike Rozier	.10	.02
❑	76T	Robb Thomas	.05	.01
❑	77T	Terance Mathis RC	.75	.30
❑	78T	LeRoy Irvin	.05	.01
❑	79T	Jeff Donaldson	.05	.01
❑	80T	Ethan Horton RC	.10	.02
❑	81T	J.B.Brown RC	.05	.01
❑	82T	Joe Kelly	.05	.01
❑	83T	John Carney RC	.05	.01
❑	84T	Dan Stryzinski RC	.05	.01
❑	85T	John Kidd	.05	.01
❑	86T	Al Smith	.10	.02
❑	87T	Travis McNeal	.05	.01
❑	88T	Reyna Thompson RC	.05	.01
❑	89T	Rick Donnelly	.05	.01
❑	90T	Marv Cook RC	.10	.02
❑	91T	Mike Farr RC	.05	.01
❑	92T	Daniel Stubbs	.05	.01
❑	93T	Jeff Campbell RC	.05	.01
❑	94T	Tim McKyer	.05	.01
❑	95T	Ian Beckles RC	.05	.01
❑	96T	Lemuel Stinson	.05	.01
❑	97T	Frank Cornish	.05	.01
❑	98T	Riki Ellison	.05	.01
❑	99T	Jamie Mueller RC	.05	.01
❑	100T	Brian Hansen	.05	.01
❑	101T	Warren Powers RC	.05	.01
❑	102T	Howard Cross RC	.05	.01
❑	103T	Tim Grunhard RC	.05	.01
❑	104T	Johnny Johnson RC	.25	.08
❑	105T	Calvin Williams RC	.25	.08
❑	106T	Keith McCants	.05	.01
❑	107T	Lamar Lathon RC	.10	.02
❑	108T	Steve Broussard RC	.10	.02
❑	109T	Glenn Parker RC	.05	.01
❑	110T	Alton Montgomery RC	.05	.01
❑	111T	Jim McMahon	.10	.02
❑	112T	Aaron Wallace RC	.05	.01
❑	113T	Keith Sims RC	.05	.01
❑	114T	Ervin Randle	.05	.01
❑	115T	Walter Wilson	.05	.01
❑	116T	Terry Wooden RC	.05	.01
❑	117T	Bernard Clark	.05	.01
❑	118T	Tony Stargell RC	.05	.01
❑	119T	Jimmie Jones RC	.05	.01
❑	120T	Andre Collins RC	.10	.02
❑	121T	Ricky Proehl RC	.25	.08
❑	122T	Darion Conner RC	.10	.02
❑	123T	Jeff Rutledge	.05	.01
❑	124T	Heath Sherman RC	.10	.02
❑	125T	Tommie Agee RC	.05	.01
❑	126T	Tory Epps RC	.05	.01
❑	127T	Tommy Hodson RC	.05	.01
❑	128T	Jessie Hester RC	.05	.01
❑	129T	Alfred Oglesby RC	.05	.01
❑	130T	Chris Chandler	.25	.08
❑	131T	Fred Barnett RC	.25	.08
❑	132T	Checklist 1-132	.05	.01

1991 Topps

	Set	Mint	Ex
❑	COMPLETE SET (660)	20.00	10.00
❑	COMP.FACT.SET (660)	30.00	15.00

	Card	Player	Mint	Ex
❑	1	Super Bowl XXV	.05	.01
❑	2	Roger Craig HL	.10	.02
❑	3	Derrick Thomas HL	.10	.02
❑	4	Pete Stoyanovich HL	.05	.01
❑	5	Ottis Anderson HL	.10	.02
❑	6	Jerry Rice HL	.50	.20
❑	7	Warren Moon HL	.10	.02
❑	8	Warren Moon/J.Everett LL	.10	.02
❑	9	B.Sanders/T.Thomas LL	.40	.15
❑	10	J.Rice/H.Jeffires LL	.30	.10
❑	11	M.Carrier DB/R.Johnson DB LL	.05	.01
❑	12	Derrick Thomas/C.Haley L	.10	.02
❑	13	Jumbo Elliott	.05	.01
❑	14	Leonard Marshall	.05	.01
❑	15	William Roberts	.05	.01
❑	16	Lawrence Taylor	.25	.08
❑	17	Mark Ingram	.10	.02
❑	18	Rodney Hampton	.25	.08
❑	19	Carl Banks	.05	.01
❑	20	Ottis Anderson	.10	.02
❑	21	Mark Collins	.05	.01
❑	22	Pepper Johnson	.05	.01
❑	23	Dave Meggett	.10	.02
❑	24	Reyna Thompson	.05	.01
❑	25	Stephen Baker	.05	.01
❑	26	Mike Fox	.05	.01
❑	27	Maurice Carthon UER	.05	.01
❑	28	Jeff Hostetler	.25	.08
❑	29	Greg Jackson RC	.05	.01
❑	30	Sean Landeta	.05	.01
❑	31	Bart Oates	.05	.01
❑	32	Phil Simms	.10	.02
❑	33	Erik Howard	.05	.01
❑	34	Myron Guyton	.05	.01
❑	35	Mark Bavaro	.05	.01
❑	36	Jarrod Bunch RC	.05	.01
❑	37	Will Wolford	.05	.01
❑	38	Ray Bentley	.05	.01
❑	39	Nate Odomes	.05	.01
❑	40	Scott Norwood	.05	.01
❑	41	Darryl Talley	.05	.01
❑	42	Carwell Gardner	.05	.01
❑	43	James Lofton	.10	.02
❑	44	Shane Conlan	.05	.01
❑	45	Steve Tasker	.10	.02
❑	46	James Williams	.05	.01
❑	47	Kent Hull	.05	.01
❑	48	Al Edwards	.05	.01
❑	49	Frank Reich	.10	.02
❑	50	Leon Seals	.05	.01
❑	51	Keith McKeller	.05	.01
❑	52	Thurman Thomas	.25	.08
❑	53	Leonard Smith	.05	.01
❑	54	Andre Reed	.10	.02
❑	55	Kenneth Davis	.05	.01
❑	56	Jeff Wright RC	.05	.01
❑	57	Jamie Mueller	.05	.01
❑	58	Jim Ritcher	.05	.01
❑	59	Bruce Smith	.25	.08
❑	60	Ted Washington RC	.05	.01
❑	61	Guy McIntyre	.05	.01
❑	62	Michael Carter	.05	.01
❑	63	Pierce Holt	.05	.01
❑	64	Darryl Pollard	.05	.01
❑	65	Mike Sherrard	.05	.01
❑	66	Dexter Carter	.05	.01
❑	67	Bubba Paris	.05	.01
❑	68	Harry Sydney	.05	.01
❑	69	Tom Rathman	.05	.01
❑	70	Jesse Sapolu	.05	.01
❑	71	Mike Cofer	.05	.01
❑	72	Keith DeLong	.05	.01
❑	73	Joe Montana	1.25	.50
❑	74	Bill Romanowski	.05	.01
❑	75	John Taylor	.10	.02
❑	76	Brent Jones	.25	.08
❑	77	Harris Barton	.05	.01
❑	78	Charles Haley	.10	.02
❑	79	Eric Davis	.05	.01
❑	80	Kevin Fagan	.05	.01
❑	81	Jerry Rice	.75	.30
❑	82	Dave Waymer	.05	.01
❑	83	Todd Marinovich RC	.05	.01
❑	84	Steve Smith	.05	.01
❑	85	Tim Brown	.25	.08
❑	86	Ethan Horton	.05	.01
❑	87	Marcus Allen	.25	.08
❑	88	Terry McDaniel	.05	.01
❑	89	Thomas Benson	.05	.01
❑	90	Roger Craig	.10	.02
❑	91	Don Mosebar	.05	.01
❑	92	Aaron Wallace	.05	.01
❑	93	Eddie Anderson	.05	.01
❑	94	Willie Gault	.10	.02
❑	95	Howie Long	.25	.08
❑	96	Jay Schroeder	.05	.01
❑	97	Ronnie Lott	.10	.02
❑	98	Bob Golic	.05	.01
❑	99	Bo Jackson	.30	.10
❑	100	Max Montoya	.05	.01
❑	101	Scott Davis	.05	.01
❑	102	Greg Townsend	.05	.01
❑	103	Garry Lewis	.05	.01
❑	104	Mervyn Fernandez	.05	.01
❑	105	Steve Wisniewski UER	.05	.01
❑	106	Jeff Jaeger	.05	.01
❑	107	Nick Bell RC	.05	.01
❑	108	Mark Dennis RC	.05	.01
❑	109	Jarvis Williams	.05	.01
❑	110	Mark Clayton	.10	.02
❑	111	Harry Galbreath	.05	.01
❑	112	Dan Marino	1.25	.50
❑	113	Louis Oliver	.05	.01
❑	114	Pete Stoyanovich	.05	.01
❑	115	Ferrell Edmunds	.05	.01
❑	116	Jeff Cross	.05	.01
❑	117	Richmond Webb	.05	.01
❑	118	Jim C. Jensen	.05	.01
❑	119	Keith Sims	.05	.01
❑	120	Mark Duper	.10	.02
❑	121	Shawn Lee RC	.05	.01
❑	122	Reggie Roby	.05	.01
❑	123	Jeff Uhlenhake	.05	.01
❑	124	Sammie Smith	.05	.01
❑	125	John Offerdahl	.05	.01
❑	126	Hugh Green	.05	.01
❑	127	Tony Paige	.05	.01
❑	128	David Griggs	.05	.01
❑	129	J.B. Brown	.05	.01
❑	130	Harvey Williams RC	.25	.08
❑	131	John Alt	.05	.01
❑	132	Albert Lewis	.05	.01
❑	133	Robb Thomas	.05	.01
❑	134	Neil Smith	.25	.08
❑	135	Stephone Paige	.05	.01
❑	136	Nick Lowery	.05	.01
❑	137	Steve DeBerg	.05	.01
❑	138	Rich Baldinger RC	.05	.01
❑	139	Percy Snow	.05	.01
❑	140	Kevin Porter	.05	.01
❑	141	Chris Martin	.05	.01
❑	142	Deron Cherry	.05	.01
❑	143	Derrick Thomas	.25	.08
❑	144	Tim Grunhard	.05	.01
❑	145	Todd McNair	.05	.01
❑	146	David Szott	.05	.01
❑	147	Dan Saleaumua	.05	.01
❑	148	Jonathan Hayes	.05	.01
❑	149	Christian Okoye	.05	.01
❑	150	Dino Hackett	.05	.01
❑	151	Bryan Barker RC	.05	.01
❑	152	Kevin Ross	.05	.01
❑	153	Barry Word	.05	.01
❑	154	Stan Thomas	.05	.01
❑	155	Brad Muster	.05	.01
❑	156	Donnell Woolford	.05	.01
❑	157	Neal Anderson	.10	.02
❑	158	Jim Covert	.05	.01
❑	159	Jim Harbaugh	.25	.08
❑	160	Shaun Gayle	.05	.01
❑	161	William Perry	.10	.02
❑	162	Ron Morris	.05	.01
❑	163	Mark Bortz	.05	.01
❑	164	James Thornton	.05	.01
❑	165	Ron Rivera	.05	.01
❑	166	Kevin Butler	.05	.01
❑	167	Jay Hilgenberg	.05	.01
❑	168	Peter Tom Willis	.05	.01
❑	169	Johnny Bailey	.05	.01
❑	170	Ron Cox	.05	.01
❑	171	Keith Van Horne	.05	.01
❑	172	Mark Carrier DB	.10	.02
❑	173	Richard Dent	.10	.02
❑	174	Wendell Davis	.05	.01

❑	175	Trace Armstrong	.05	.01
❑	176	Mike Singletary	.10	.02
❑	177	Chris Zorich RC	.25	.08
❑	178	Gerald Riggs	.05	.01
❑	179	Jeff Bostic	.05	.01
❑	180	Kurt Gouveia RC	.05	.01
❑	181	Stan Humphries	.25	.08
❑	182	Chip Lohmiller	.05	.01
❑	183	Raleigh McKenzie RC	.05	.01
❑	184	Alvin Walton	.05	.01
❑	185	Earnest Byner	.05	.01
❑	186	Markus Koch	.05	.01
❑	187	Art Monk	.10	.02
❑	188	Ed Simmons	.05	.01
❑	189	Bobby Wilson RC	.05	.01
❑	190	Charles Mann	.05	.01
❑	191	Darrell Green	.05	.01
❑	192	Mark Rypien	.10	.02
❑	193	Ricky Sanders	.05	.01
❑	194	Jim Lachey	.05	.01
❑	195	Martin Mayhew	.05	.01
❑	196	Gary Clark	.25	.08
❑	197	Wilber Marshall	.05	.01
❑	198	Darryl Grant	.05	.01
❑	199	Don Warren	.05	.01
❑	200	Ricky Ervins RC UER	.10	.02
❑	201	Eric Allen	.05	.01
❑	202	Anthony Toney	.05	.01
❑	203	Ben Smith UER	.05	.01
❑	204	David Alexander	.05	.01
❑	205	Jerome Brown	.05	.01
❑	206	Mike Golic	.05	.01
❑	207	Roger Ruzek	.05	.01
❑	208	Andre Waters	.05	.01
❑	209	Fred Barnett	.25	.08
❑	210	Randall Cunningham	.25	.08
❑	211	Mike Schad	.05	.01
❑	212	Reggie White	.25	.08
❑	213	Mike Bellamy	.05	.01
❑	214	Jeff Feagles RC	.05	.01
❑	215	Wes Hopkins	.05	.01
❑	216	Clyde Simmons	.05	.01
❑	217	Keith Byars	.05	.01
❑	218	Seth Joyner	.10	.02
❑	219	Byron Evans	.05	.01
❑	220	Keith Jackson	.10	.02
❑	221	Calvin Williams	.10	.02
❑	222	Mike Dumas RC	.05	.01
❑	223	Ray Childress	.05	.01
❑	224	Ernest Givins	.10	.02
❑	225	Lamar Lathon	.05	.01
❑	226	Greg Montgomery	.05	.01
❑	227	Mike Munchak	.10	.02
❑	228	Al Smith	.05	.01
❑	229	Bubba McDowell	.05	.01
❑	230	Haywood Jeffires	.10	.02
❑	231	Drew Hill	.05	.01
❑	232	William Fuller	.10	.02
❑	233	Warren Moon	.25	.08
❑	234	Doug Smith DT RC	.10	.02
❑	235	Cris Dishman RC	.05	.01
❑	236	Teddy Garcia RC	.05	.01
❑	237	Richard Johnson CB RC	.05	.01
❑	238	Bruce Matthews	.10	.02
❑	239	Gerald McNeil	.05	.01
❑	240	Johnny Meads	.05	.01
❑	241	Curtis Duncan	.05	.01
❑	242	Sean Jones	.10	.02
❑	243	Lorenzo White	.05	.01
❑	244	Rob Carpenter RC WR	.05	.01
❑	245	Bruce Reimers	.05	.01
❑	246	Ickey Woods	.05	.01
❑	247	Lewis Billups	.05	.01
❑	248	Boomer Esiason	.10	.02
❑	249	Tim Krumrie	.05	.01
❑	250	David Fulcher	.05	.01
❑	251	Jim Breech	.05	.01
❑	252	Mitchell Price RC	.05	.01
❑	253	Carl Zander	.05	.01
❑	254	Barney Bussey RC	.05	.01
❑	255	Leon White	.05	.01
❑	256	Eddie Brown	.05	.01
❑	257	James Francis	.05	.01
❑	258	Harold Green	.10	.02
❑	259	Anthony Munoz	.10	.02
❑	260	James Brooks	.10	.02
❑	261	Kevin Walker RC UER	.05	.01
❑	262	Bruce Kozerski	.05	.01
❑	263	David Grant	.05	.01
❑	264	Tim McGee	.05	.01
❑	265	Rodney Holman	.05	.01
❑	266	Dan McGwire RC	.05	.01
❑	267	Andy Heck	.05	.01
❑	268	Dave Krieg	.10	.02
❑	269	David Wyman	.05	.01
❑	270	Robert Blackmon	.05	.01
❑	271	Grant Feasel	.05	.01
❑	272	Patrick Hunter RC	.05	.01
❑	273	Travis McNeal	.05	.01
❑	274	John L. Williams	.05	.01
❑	275	Tony Woods	.05	.01
❑	276	Derrick Fenner	.05	.01
❑	277	Jacob Green	.05	.01
❑	278	Brian Blades	.10	.02
❑	279	Eugene Robinson	.05	.01
❑	280	Terry Wooden	.05	.01
❑	281	Jeff Bryant	.05	.01
❑	282	Norm Johnson	.05	.01
❑	283	Joe Nash UER	.05	.01
❑	284	Rick Donnelly	.05	.01
❑	285	Chris Warren	.25	.08
❑	286	Tommy Kane	.05	.01
❑	287	Cortez Kennedy	.25	.08
❑	288	Ernie Mills RC	.10	.02
❑	289	Dermontti Dawson	.05	.01
❑	290	Tunch Ilkin	.05	.01
❑	291	Tim Worley	.05	.01
❑	292	David Little	.05	.01
❑	293	Gary Anderson K	.05	.01
❑	294	Chris Calloway	.05	.01
❑	295	Carnell Lake	.05	.01
❑	296	Dan Stryzinski	.05	.01
❑	297	Rod Woodson	.25	.08
❑	298	John Jackson T RC	.05	.01
❑	299	Bubby Brister	.05	.01
❑	300	Thomas Everett	.05	.01
❑	301	Merril Hoge	.05	.01
❑	302	Eric Green	.05	.01
❑	303	Greg Lloyd	.25	.08
❑	304	Gerald Williams	.05	.01
❑	305	Bryan Hinkle	.05	.01
❑	306	Keith Willis	.05	.01
❑	307	Louis Lipps	.05	.01
❑	308	Donald Evans	.05	.01
❑	309	D.J. Johnson	.05	.01
❑	310	Wesley Carroll RC	.05	.01
❑	311	Eric Martin	.05	.01
❑	312	Brett Maxie	.05	.01
❑	313	Rickey Jackson	.05	.01
❑	314	Robert Massey	.05	.01
❑	315	Pat Swilling	.10	.02
❑	316	Morten Andersen	.05	.01
❑	317	Toi Cook RC	.05	.01
❑	318	Sam Mills	.05	.01
❑	319	Steve Walsh	.05	.01
❑	320	Tommy Barnhardt RC	.05	.01
❑	321	Vince Buck	.05	.01
❑	322	Joel Hilgenberg	.05	.01
❑	323	Rueben Mayes	.05	.01
❑	324	Renaldo Turnbull	.05	.01
❑	325	Brett Perriman	.25	.08
❑	326	Vaughan Johnson	.05	.01
❑	327	Gill Fenerty	.05	.01
❑	328	Stan Brock	.05	.01
❑	329	Dalton Hilliard	.05	.01
❑	330	Hoby Brenner	.05	.01
❑	331	Craig Heyward	.10	.02
❑	332	Jon Hand	.05	.01
❑	333	Duane Bickett	.05	.01
❑	334	Jessie Hester	.05	.01
❑	335	Rohn Stark	.05	.01
❑	336	Zefross Moss	.05	.01
❑	337	Bill Brooks	.05	.01
❑	338	Clarence Verdin	.05	.01
❑	339	Mike Prior	.05	.01
❑	340	Chip Banks	.05	.01
❑	341	Dean Biasucci	.05	.01
❑	342	Ray Donaldson	.05	.01
❑	343	Jeff Herrod	.05	.01
❑	344	Donnell Thompson	.05	.01
❑	345	Chris Goode	.05	.01
❑	346	Eugene Daniel	.05	.01
❑	347	Pat Beach	.05	.01
❑	348	Keith Taylor	.05	.01
❑	349	Jeff George	.25	.08
❑	350	Tony Siragusa RC	.10	.02
❑	351	Randy Dixon	.05	.01
❑	352	Albert Bentley	.05	.01
❑	353	Russell Maryland RC	.25	.08
❑	354	Mike Saxon	.05	.01
❑	355	Godfrey Myles RC UER	.05	.01
❑	356	Mark Stepnoski RC	.10	.02
❑	357	James Washington RC	.05	.01
❑	358	Jay Novacek	.25	.08
❑	359	Kelvin Martin	.05	.01
❑	360	Emmitt Smith UER	2.50	1.00
❑	361	Jim Jeffcoat	.05	.01
❑	362	Alexander Wright	.05	.01
❑	363	James Dixon UER	.05	.01
❑	364	Alonzo Highsmith	.05	.01
❑	365	Daniel Stubbs	.05	.01
❑	366	Jack Del Rio	.10	.02
❑	367	Mark Tuinei RC	.05	.01
❑	368	Michael Irvin	.25	.08
❑	369	John Gesek RC	.05	.01
❑	370	Ken Willis	.05	.01
❑	371	Troy Aikman	.75	.30
❑	372	Jimmie Jones	.05	.01
❑	373	Nate Newton	.10	.02
❑	374	Issiac Holt	.05	.01
❑	375	Alvin Harper RC	.25	.08
❑	376	Todd Kalis	.05	.01
❑	377	Wade Wilson	.10	.02
❑	378	Joey Browner	.05	.01
❑	379	Chris Doleman	.05	.01
❑	380	Hassan Jones	.05	.01
❑	381	Henry Thomas	.05	.01
❑	382	Darrell Fullington	.05	.01
❑	383	Steve Jordan	.05	.01
❑	384	Gary Zimmerman	.05	.01
❑	385	Ray Berry	.05	.01
❑	386	Cris Carter	.50	.20
❑	387	Mike Merriweather	.05	.01
❑	388	Carl Lee	.05	.01
❑	389	Keith Millard	.05	.01
❑	390	Reggie Rutland	.05	.01
❑	391	Anthony Carter	.10	.02
❑	392	Mark Dusbabek	.05	.01
❑	393	Kirk Lowdermilk	.05	.01
❑	394	Al Noga UER	.05	.01
❑	395	Herschel Walker	.10	.02
❑	396	Randall McDaniel	.05	.01
❑	397	Herman Moore RC	.25	.08
❑	398	Eddie Murray	.05	.01
❑	399	Lomas Brown	.05	.01
❑	400	Marc Spindler	.05	.01
❑	401	Bennie Blades	.05	.01
❑	402	Kevin Glover	.05	.01
❑	403	Aubrey Matthews RC	.05	.01
❑	404	Michael Cofer	.05	.01
❑	405	Robert Clark	.05	.01
❑	406	Eric Andolsek	.05	.01
❑	407	William White	.05	.01
❑	408	Rodney Peete	.10	.02
❑	409	Mel Gray	.10	.02
❑	410	Jim Arnold	.05	.01
❑	411	Jeff Campbell	.05	.01
❑	412	Chris Spielman	.10	.02
❑	413	Jerry Ball	.05	.01
❑	414	Dan Owens	.05	.01
❑	415	Barry Sanders	1.25	.50
❑	416	Andre Ware	.10	.02
❑	417	Stanley Richard RC	.05	.01
❑	418	Gill Byrd	.05	.01
❑	419	John Kidd	.05	.01
❑	420	Sam Seale	.05	.01
❑	421	Gary Plummer	.05	.01
❑	422	Anthony Miller	.10	.02
❑	423	Ronnie Harmon	.05	.01
❑	424	Frank Cornish	.05	.01
❑	425	Marion Butts	.10	.02
❑	426	Leo Goeas	.05	.01
❑	427	Junior Seau	.25	.08
❑	428	Courtney Hall	.05	.01
❑	429	Leslie O'Neal	.10	.02
❑	430	Martin Bayless	.05	.01
❑	431	John Carney	.05	.01
❑	432	Lee Williams	.05	.01
❑	433	Arthur Cox	.05	.01
❑	434	Burt Grossman	.05	.01
❑	435	Nate Lewis RC	.05	.01

❑ 436 Rod Bernstine .05 .01
❑ 437 Henry Rolling RC .05 .01
❑ 438 Billy Joe Tolliver .05 .01
❑ 439 Vinnie Clark RC .05 .01
❑ 440 Brian Noble .05 .01
❑ 441 Charles Wilson .05 .01
❑ 442 Don Majkowski .05 .01
❑ 443 Tim Harris .05 .01
❑ 444 Scott Stephen RC .05 .01
❑ 445 Perry Kemp .05 .01
❑ 446 Darrell Thompson .05 .01
❑ 447 Chris Jacke .05 .01
❑ 448 Mark Murphy .05 .01
❑ 449 Ed West .05 .01
❑ 450 LeRoy Butler .10 .02
❑ 451 Keith Woodside .05 .01
❑ 452 Tony Bennett .10 .02
❑ 453 Mark Lee .05 .01
❑ 454 James Campen RC .05 .01
❑ 455 Robert Brown .05 .01
❑ 456 Sterling Sharpe .25 .08
❑ 457A T.Mandarich ERR Bronc. 2.50 1.25
❑ 457B T.Mandarich COR Packers .05 .01
❑ 458 Johnny Holland .05 .01
❑ 459 Matt Brock RC .05 .01
❑ 460A Esera Tuaolo RC ERR .05 .01
❑ 460B Esera Tuaolo RC COR .05 .01
❑ 461 Freeman McNeil .05 .01
❑ 462 Terance Mathis UER 460 .25 .08
❑ 463 Rob Moore .25 .08
❑ 464 Darrell Davis RC .05 .01
❑ 465 Chris Burkett .05 .01
❑ 466 Jeff Criswell .05 .01
❑ 467 Tony Stargell .05 .01
❑ 468 Ken O'Brien .05 .01
❑ 469 Erik McMillan .05 .01
❑ 470 Jeff Lageman UER .05 .01
❑ 471 Pat Leahy .05 .01
❑ 472 Dennis Byrd .05 .01
❑ 473 Jim Sweeney .05 .01
❑ 474 Brad Baxter .05 .01
❑ 475 Joe Kelly .05 .01
❑ 476 Al Toon .10 .02
❑ 477 Joe Prokop .05 .01
❑ 478 Mark Boyer .05 .01
❑ 479 Kyle Clifton .05 .01
❑ 480 James Hasty .05 .01
❑ 481 Browning Nagle RC .05 .01
❑ 482 Gary Anderson RB .05 .01
❑ 483 Mark Carrier WR .25 .08
❑ 484 Ricky Reynolds .05 .01
❑ 485 Bruce Hill .05 .01
❑ 486 Steve Christie .05 .01
❑ 487 Paul Gruber .05 .01
❑ 488 Jesse Anderson .05 .01
❑ 489 Reggie Cobb .05 .01
❑ 490 Harry Hamilton .05 .01
❑ 491 Vinny Testaverde .10 .02
❑ 492 Mark Royals RC .05 .01
❑ 493 Keith McCants .05 .01
❑ 494 Ron Hall .05 .01
❑ 495 Ian Beckles .05 .01
❑ 496 Mark Robinson .05 .01
❑ 497 Reuben Davis .05 .01
❑ 498 Wayne Haddix .05 .01
❑ 499 Kevin Murphy .05 .01
❑ 500 Eugene Marve .05 .01
❑ 501 Broderick Thomas .05 .01
❑ 502 Eric Swann RC UER .25 .08
❑ 503 Ernie Jones .05 .01
❑ 504 Rich Camarillo .05 .01
❑ 505 Tim McDonald .05 .01
❑ 506 Freddie Joe Nunn .05 .01
❑ 507 Tim Jorden RC .05 .01
❑ 508 Johnny Johnson .05 .01
❑ 509 Eric Hill .05 .01
❑ 510 Derek Kennard .05 .01
❑ 511 Ricky Proehl .05 .01
❑ 512 Bill Lewis .05 .01
❑ 513 Roy Green .05 .01
❑ 514 Anthony Bell .05 .01
❑ 515 Timm Rosenbach .05 .01
❑ 516 Jim Wahler RC .05 .01
❑ 517 Anthony Thompson .05 .01
❑ 518 Ken Harvey .10 .02
❑ 519 Luis Sharpe .05 .01
❑ 520 Walter Reeves .05 .01
❑ 521 Lonnie Young .05 .01
❑ 522 Rod Saddler .05 .01
❑ 523 Todd Lyght RC .05 .01
❑ 524 Alvin Wright .05 .01
❑ 525 Flipper Anderson .05 .01
❑ 526 Jackie Slater .05 .01
❑ 527 Damone Johnson RC .05 .01
❑ 528 Cleveland Gary .05 .01
❑ 529 Mike Piel .05 .01
❑ 530 Buford McGee .05 .01
❑ 531 Michael Stewart .05 .01
❑ 532 Jim Everett .10 .02
❑ 533 Mike Wilcher .05 .01
❑ 534 Irv Pankey .05 .01
❑ 535 Bern Brostek .05 .01
❑ 536 Henry Ellard .10 .02
❑ 537 Doug Smith .05 .01
❑ 538 Larry Kelm .05 .01
❑ 539 Pat Terrell .05 .01
❑ 540 Tom Newberry .05 .01
❑ 541 Jerry Gray .05 .01
❑ 542 Kevin Greene .10 .02
❑ 543 Duval Love RC .05 .01
❑ 544 Frank Stams .05 .01
❑ 545 Mike Croel RC .05 .01
❑ 546 Mark Jackson .05 .01
❑ 547 Greg Kragen .05 .01
❑ 548 Karl Mecklenburg .05 .01
❑ 549 Simon Fletcher .05 .01
❑ 550 Bobby Humphrey .05 .01
❑ 551 Ken Lanier .05 .01
❑ 552 Vance Johnson .05 .01
❑ 553 Ron Holmes .05 .01
❑ 554 John Elway 1.25 .50
❑ 555 Melvin Bratton .05 .01
❑ 556 Dennis Smith .05 .01
❑ 557 Ricky Nattiel .05 .01
❑ 558 Clarence Kay .05 .01
❑ 559 Michael Brooks .05 .01
❑ 560 Mike Horan .05 .01
❑ 561 Warren Powers .05 .01
❑ 562 Keith Kartz .05 .01
❑ 563 Shannon Sharpe .50 .20
❑ 564 Wymon Henderson .05 .01
❑ 565 Steve Atwater .05 .01
❑ 566 David Treadwell .05 .01
❑ 567 Bruce Pickens RC .05 .01
❑ 568 Jessie Tuggle .05 .01
❑ 569 Chris Hinton .05 .01
❑ 570 Keith Jones .05 .01
❑ 571 Bill Fralic .05 .01
❑ 572 Mike Rozier .05 .01
❑ 573 Scott Fulhage .05 .01
❑ 574 Floyd Dixon .05 .01
❑ 575 Andre Rison .10 .02
❑ 576 Darion Conner .05 .01
❑ 577 Brian Jordan .10 .02
❑ 578 Michael Haynes .25 .08
❑ 579 Oliver Barnett .05 .01
❑ 580 Shawn Collins .05 .01
❑ 581 Tim Green .05 .01
❑ 582 Deion Sanders .40 .15
❑ 583 Mike Kenn .05 .01
❑ 584 Mike Gann .05 .01
❑ 585 Chris Miller .10 .02
❑ 586 Tory Epps .05 .01
❑ 587 Steve Broussard .05 .01
❑ 588 Gary Wilkins .05 .01
❑ 589 Eric Turner RC .10 .02
❑ 590 Thane Gash .05 .01
❑ 591 Clay Matthews .10 .02
❑ 592 Mike Johnson .05 .01
❑ 593 Raymond Clayborn .05 .01
❑ 594 Leroy Hoard .10 .02
❑ 595 Reggie Langhorne .05 .01
❑ 596 Mike Baab .05 .01
❑ 597 Anthony Pleasant .05 .01
❑ 598 David Grayson .05 .01
❑ 599 Rob Burnett RC .10 .02
❑ 600 Frank Minnifield .05 .01
❑ 601 Gregg Rakoczy .05 .01
❑ 602 Eric Metcalf UER .25 .08
❑ 603 Paul Farren .05 .01
❑ 604 Brian Brennan .05 .01
❑ 605 Tony Jones T RC .05 .01
❑ 606 Stephen Braggs .05 .01
❑ 607 Kevin Mack .05 .01
❑ 608 Pat Harlow RC .05 .01
❑ 609 Marv Cook .05 .01
❑ 610 John Stephens .05 .01
❑ 611 Ed Reynolds .05 .01
❑ 612 Tim Goad .05 .01
❑ 613 Chris Singleton .05 .01
❑ 614 Bruce Armstrong .05 .01
❑ 615 Tommy Hodson .05 .01
❑ 616 Sammy Martin .05 .01
❑ 617 Andre Tippett .05 .01
❑ 618 Johnny Rembert .05 .01
❑ 619 Maurice Hurst .05 .01
❑ 620 Vincent Brown .05 .01
❑ 621 Ray Agnew .05 .01
❑ 622 Ronnie Lippett .05 .01
❑ 623 Greg McMurtry .05 .01
❑ 624 Brent Williams .05 .01
❑ 625 Jason Staurovsky .05 .01
❑ 626 Marvin Allen .05 .01
❑ 627 Hart Lee Dykes .05 .01
❑ 628 Atlanta Falcons .05 .01
❑ 629 Buffalo Bills .05 .01
❑ 630 Chicago Bears .10 .02
❑ 631 Cincinnati Bengals .05 .01
❑ 632 Cleveland Browns .05 .01
❑ 633 Dallas Cowboys .05 .01
❑ 634 Denver Broncos .05 .01
❑ 635 Detroit Lions .05 .01
❑ 636 Green Bay Packers .05 .01
❑ 637 Oilers TL/Warren Moon .10 .02
❑ 638 Colts TL/Jeff George .05 .01
❑ 639 Kansas City Chiefs .05 .01
❑ 640 Los Angeles Raiders .10 .02
❑ 641 Los Angeles Rams .05 .01
❑ 642 Miami Dolphins .05 .01
❑ 643 Minnesota Vikings .10 .02
❑ 644 New Eng. Patriots .05 .01
❑ 645 New Orleans Saints .05 .01
❑ 646 New York Giants .05 .01
❑ 647 New York Jets .05 .01
❑ 648 Eagles TL/R.Cunningham .05 .01
❑ 649 Phoenix Cardinals .05 .01
❑ 650 Pittsburgh Steelers .05 .01
❑ 651 San Diego Chargers .05 .01
❑ 652 San Francisco 49ers .05 .01
❑ 653 Seattle Seahawks .05 .01
❑ 654 Tampa Bay Buccaneers .05 .01
❑ 655 Washington Redskins .05 .01
❑ 656 Checklist 1-132 .05 .01
❑ 657 Checklist 132-264 .05 .01
❑ 658 Checklist 265-396 .05 .01
❑ 659 Checklist 397-528 .05 .01
❑ 660 Checklist 529-660 .05 .01

1992 Topps

❑ COMPLETE SET (759) 50.00 25.00
❑ COMP.FACT.SET (680) 80.00 40.00
❑ COMP.SERIES 1 (330) 20.00 10.00
❑ COMP.SERIES 2 (330) 20.00 10.00
❑ COMP.HIGH SER.(99) 10.00 5.00
❑ COMP.FACT.HIGH SET (113) 12.00 5.00
❑ 1 Tim McGee .05 .01
❑ 2 Rich Camarillo .05 .01
❑ 3 Anthony Johnson .10 .02
❑ 4 Larry Kelm .05 .01
❑ 5 Irving Fryar .10 .02
❑ 6 Joey Browner .05 .01
❑ 7 Michael Walter .05 .01
❑ 8 Cortez Kennedy .10 .02

❑ 9 Reyna Thompson .05 .01
❑ 10 John Friesz .10 .02
❑ 11 Leroy Hoard .10 .02
❑ 12 Steve McMichael .10 .02
❑ 13 Marvin Washington .05 .01
❑ 14 Clyde Simmons .05 .01
❑ 15 Stephone Paige .05 .01
❑ 16 Mike Utley .10 .02
❑ 17 Tunch Ilkin .05 .01
❑ 18 Lawrence Dawsey .10 .02
❑ 19 Vance Johnson .05 .01
❑ 20 Bryce Paup .25 .08
❑ 21 Jeff Wright .05 .01
❑ 22 Gill Fenerty .05 .01
❑ 23 Lamar Lathon .05 .01
❑ 24 Danny Copeland .05 .01
❑ 25 Marcus Allen .25 .08
❑ 26 Tim Green .05 .01
❑ 27 Pete Stoyanovich .05 .01
❑ 28 Alvin Harper .10 .02
❑ 29 Roy Foster .05 .01
❑ 30 Eugene Daniel .05 .01
❑ 31 Luis Sharpe .05 .01
❑ 32 Terry Wooden .05 .01
❑ 33 Jim Breech .05 .01
❑ 34 Randy Hilliard RC .05 .01
❑ 35 Roman Phifer .05 .01
❑ 36 Erik Howard .05 .01
❑ 37 Chris Singleton .05 .01
❑ 38 Matt Stover .05 .01
❑ 39 Tim Irwin .05 .01
❑ 40 Karl Mecklenburg .05 .01
❑ 41 Joe Phillips .05 .01
❑ 42 Bill Jones RC .05 .01
❑ 43 Mark Carrier DB .05 .01
❑ 44 George Jamison .05 .01
❑ 45 Rob Taylor .05 .01
❑ 46 Jeff Jaeger .05 .01
❑ 47 Don Majkowski .05 .01
❑ 48 Al Edwards .05 .01
❑ 49 Curtis Duncan .05 .01
❑ 50 Sam Mills .05 .01
❑ 51 Terance Mathis .10 .02
❑ 52 Brian Mitchell .10 .02
❑ 53 Mike Pritchard .10 .02
❑ 54 Calvin Williams .10 .02
❑ 55 Hardy Nickerson .10 .02
❑ 56 Nate Newton .05 .01
❑ 57 Steve Wallace .05 .01
❑ 58 John Offerdahl .05 .01
❑ 59 Aeneas Williams .10 .02
❑ 60 Lee Johnson .05 .01
❑ 61 Ricardo McDonald RC .05 .01
❑ 62 David Richards .05 .01
❑ 63 Paul Gruber .05 .01
❑ 64 Greg McMurtry .05 .01
❑ 65 Jay Hilgenberg .05 .01
❑ 66 Tim Grunhard .05 .01
❑ 67 Dwayne White RC .05 .01
❑ 68 Don Beebe .05 .01
❑ 69 Simon Fletcher .05 .01
❑ 70 Warren Moon .25 .08
❑ 71 Chris Jacke .05 .01
❑ 72 Steve Wisniewski UER .05 .01
❑ 73 Mike Cofer .05 .01
❑ 74 Tim Johnson UER .05 .01
❑ 75 T.J. Turner .05 .01
❑ 76 Scott Case .05 .01
❑ 77 Michael Jackson .10 .02
❑ 78 Jon Hand .05 .01
❑ 79 Stan Brock .05 .01
❑ 80 Robert Blackmon .05 .01
❑ 81 D.J. Johnson .05 .01
❑ 82 Damone Johnson .05 .01
❑ 83 Marc Spindler .05 .01
❑ 84 Larry Brown DB .05 .01
❑ 85 Ray Berry .05 .01
❑ 86 Andre Waters .05 .01
❑ 87 Carlos Huerta .05 .01
❑ 88 Brad Muster .05 .01
❑ 89 Chuck Cecil .05 .01
❑ 90 Nick Lowery .05 .01
❑ 91 Cornelius Bennett .10 .02
❑ 92 Jessie Tuggle .05 .01
❑ 93 Mark Schlereth RC .05 .01
❑ 94 Vestee Jackson .05 .01
❑ 95 Eric Bieniemy .05 .01
❑ 96 Jeff Hostetler .10 .02
❑ 97 Ken Lanier .05 .01
❑ 98 Wayne Haddix .05 .01
❑ 99 Lorenzo White .05 .01
❑ 100 Mervyn Fernandez .05 .01
❑ 101 Brent Williams .05 .01
❑ 102 Ian Beckles .05 .01
❑ 103 Harris Barton .05 .01
❑ 104 Edgar Bennett RC .25 .08
❑ 105 Mike Pitts .05 .01
❑ 106 Fuad Reveiz .05 .01
❑ 107 Vernon Turner .05 .01
❑ 108 Tracy Hayworth RC .05 .01
❑ 109 Checklist 1-110 .05 .01
❑ 110 Tom Waddle .05 .01
❑ 111 Fred Stokes .05 .01
❑ 112 Howard Ballard .05 .01
❑ 113 David Szott .05 .01
❑ 114 Tim McKyer .05 .01
❑ 115 Kyle Clifton .05 .01
❑ 116 Tony Bennett .05 .01
❑ 117 Joel Hilgenberg .05 .01
❑ 118 Dwayne Harper .05 .01
❑ 119 Mike Baab .05 .01
❑ 120 Mark Clayton .10 .02
❑ 121 Eric Swann .10 .02
❑ 122 Neil O'Donnell .10 .02
❑ 123 Mike Munchak .10 .02
❑ 124 Howie Long .25 .08
❑ 125 John Elway 1.25 .50
❑ 126 Joe Prokop .05 .01
❑ 127 Pepper Johnson .05 .01
❑ 128 Richard Dent .10 .02
❑ 129 Robert Porcher RC .25 .08
❑ 130 Earnest Byner .05 .01
❑ 131 Kent Hull .05 .01
❑ 132 Mike Merriweather .05 .01
❑ 133 Scott Fulhage .05 .01
❑ 134 Kevin Porter .05 .01
❑ 135 Tony Casillas .05 .01
❑ 136 Dean Biasucci .05 .01
❑ 137 Ben Smith .05 .01
❑ 138 Bruce Kozerski .05 .01
❑ 139 Jeff Campbell .05 .01
❑ 140 Kevin Greene .10 .02
❑ 141 Gary Plummer .05 .01
❑ 142 Vincent Brown .05 .01
❑ 143 Ron Hall .05 .01
❑ 144 Louie Aguiar RC .05 .01
❑ 145 Mark Duper .05 .01
❑ 146 Jesse Sapolu .05 .01
❑ 147 Jeff Gossett .05 .01
❑ 148 Brian Noble .05 .01
❑ 149 Derek Russell .05 .01
❑ 150 Carlton Bailey RC .05 .01
❑ 151 Kelly Goodburn .05 .01
❑ 152 Audray McMillian UER .05 .01
❑ 153 Neal Anderson .05 .01
❑ 154 Bill Maas .05 .01
❑ 155 Rickey Jackson .05 .01
❑ 156 Chris Miller .10 .02
❑ 157 Darren Comeaux .05 .01
❑ 158 David Williams .05 .01
❑ 159 Rich Gannon .25 .08
❑ 160 Kevin Mack .05 .01
❑ 161 Jim Arnold .05 .01
❑ 162 Reggie White .25 .08
❑ 163 Leonard Russell .10 .02
❑ 164 Doug Smith .05 .01
❑ 165 Tony Mandarich .05 .01
❑ 166 Greg Lloyd .10 .02
❑ 167 Jumbo Elliott .05 .01
❑ 168 Jonathan Hayes .05 .01
❑ 169 Jim Ritcher .05 .01
❑ 170 Mike Kenn .05 .01
❑ 171 James Washington .05 .01
❑ 172 Tim Harris .05 .01
❑ 173 James Thornton .05 .01
❑ 174 John Brandes RC .05 .01
❑ 175 Fred McAfee RC .05 .01
❑ 176 Henry Rolling .05 .01
❑ 177 Tony Paige .05 .01
❑ 178 Jay Schroeder .05 .01
❑ 179 Jeff Herrod .05 .01
❑ 180 Emmitt Smith 1.50 .60
❑ 181 Wymon Henderson .05 .01
❑ 182 Rob Moore .10 .02
❑ 183 Robert Wilson .05 .01
❑ 184 Michael Zordich RC .05 .01
❑ 185 Jim Harbaugh .25 .08
❑ 186 Vince Workman .05 .01
❑ 187 Ernest Givins .10 .02
❑ 188 Herschel Walker .10 .02
❑ 189 Dan Fike .05 .01
❑ 190 Seth Joyner .05 .01
❑ 191 Steve Young .60 .25
❑ 192 Dennis Gibson .05 .01
❑ 193 Darryl Talley .05 .01
❑ 194 Emile Harry .05 .01
❑ 195 Bill Fralic .05 .01
❑ 196 Michael Stewart .05 .01
❑ 197 James Francis .05 .01
❑ 198 Jerome Henderson .05 .01
❑ 199 John L. Williams .05 .01
❑ 200 Rod Woodson .25 .08
❑ 201 Mike Farr .05 .01
❑ 202 Greg Montgomery .05 .01
❑ 203 Andre Collins .05 .01
❑ 204 Scott Miller .05 .01
❑ 205 Clay Matthews .10 .02
❑ 206 Ethan Horton .05 .01
❑ 207 Rich Miano .05 .01
❑ 208 Chris Mims RC .05 .01
❑ 209 Anthony Morgan .05 .01
❑ 210 Rodney Hampton .10 .02
❑ 211 Chris Hinton .05 .01
❑ 212 Esera Tuaolo .05 .01
❑ 213 Shane Conlan .05 .01
❑ 214 John Carney .05 .01
❑ 215 Kenny Walker .05 .01
❑ 216 Scott Radecic .05 .01
❑ 217 Chris Martin .05 .01
❑ 218 Checklist 111-220 UER .05 .01
❑ 219 Wesley Carroll .05 .01
❑ 220 Bill Romanowski .05 .01
❑ 221 Reggie Cobb .05 .01
❑ 222 Alfred Anderson .05 .01
❑ 223 Cleveland Gary .05 .01
❑ 224 Eddie Blake RC .05 .01
❑ 225 Chris Spielman .10 .02
❑ 226 John Roper .05 .01
❑ 227 George Thomas RC .05 .01
❑ 228 Jeff Faulkner .05 .01
❑ 229 Chip Lohmiller UER .05 .01
❑ 230 Hugh Millen .05 .01
❑ 231 Ray Horton .05 .01
❑ 232 James Campen .05 .01
❑ 233 Howard Cross .05 .01
❑ 234 Keith McKeller .05 .01
❑ 235 Dino Hackett .05 .01
❑ 236 Jerome Brown .05 .01
❑ 237 Andy Heck .05 .01
❑ 238 Rodney Holman .05 .01
❑ 239 Bruce Matthews .05 .01
❑ 240 Jeff Lageman .05 .01
❑ 241 Bobby Hebert .05 .01
❑ 242 Gary Anderson K .05 .01
❑ 243 Mark Bortz .05 .01
❑ 244 Rich Moran .05 .01
❑ 245 Jeff Uhlenhake .05 .01
❑ 246 Ricky Sanders .05 .01
❑ 247 Clarence Kay .05 .01
❑ 248 Ed King .05 .01
❑ 249 Eddie Anderson .05 .01
❑ 250 Amp Lee RC .05 .01
❑ 251 Norm Johnson .05 .01
❑ 252 Michael Carter .05 .01
❑ 253 Felix Wright .05 .01
❑ 254 Leon Seals .05 .01
❑ 255 Nate Lewis .05 .01
❑ 256 Kevin Call .05 .01
❑ 257 Darryl Henley .05 .01
❑ 258 Jon Vaughn .05 .01
❑ 259 Matt Bahr .05 .01
❑ 260 Johnny Johnson .05 .01
❑ 261 Ken Norton .10 .02
❑ 262 Wendell Davis .05 .01
❑ 263 Eugene Robinson .05 .01
❑ 264 David Treadwell .05 .01
❑ 265 Michael Haynes .10 .02
❑ 266 Robb Thomas .05 .01
❑ 267 Nate Odomes .05 .01
❑ 268 Martin Mayhew .05 .01
❑ 269 Perry Kemp .05 .01

	Card	Price 1	Price 2
❑	270 Jerry Ball	.05	.01
❑	271 Tommy Vardell RC	.05	.01
❑	272 Ernie Mills	.05	.01
❑	273 Mo Lewis	.05	.01
❑	274 Roger Ruzek	.05	.01
❑	275 Steve Smith	.05	.01
❑	276 Bo Orlando RC	.05	.01
❑	277 Louis Oliver	.05	.01
❑	278 Toi Cook	.05	.01
❑	279 Eddie Brown	.05	.01
❑	280 Keith McCants	.05	.01
❑	281 Rob Burnett	.05	.01
❑	282 Keith DeLong	.05	.01
❑	283 Stan Thomas UER	.05	.01
❑	284 Robert Brown	.05	.01
❑	285 John Alt	.05	.01
❑	286 Randy Dixon	.05	.01
❑	287 Siran Stacy RC	.05	.01
❑	288 Ray Agnew	.05	.01
❑	289 Darion Conner	.05	.01
❑	290 Kirk Lowdermilk	.05	.01
❑	291 Greg Jackson	.05	.01
❑	292 Ken Harvey	.05	.01
❑	293 Jacob Green	.05	.01
❑	294 Mark Tuinei	.05	.01
❑	295 Mark Rypien	.05	.01
❑	296 Gerald Robinson RC	.05	.01
❑	297 Broderick Thompson	.05	.01
❑	298 Doug Widell	.05	.01
❑	299 Carwell Gardner	.05	.01
❑	300 Barry Sanders	1.25	.50
❑	301 Eric Metcalf	.10	.02
❑	302 Eric Thomas	.05	.01
❑	303 Terrell Buckley RC	.05	.01
❑	304 Byron Evans	.05	.01
❑	305 Johnny Hector	.05	.01
❑	306 Steve Broussard	.05	.01
❑	307 Gene Atkins	.05	.01
❑	308 Terry McDaniel	.05	.01
❑	309 Charles McRae	.05	.01
❑	310 Jim Lachey	.05	.01
❑	311 Pat Harlow	.05	.01
❑	312 Kevin Butler	.05	.01
❑	313 Scott Stephen	.05	.01
❑	314 Dermontti Dawson	.05	.01
❑	315 Johnny Meads	.05	.01
❑	316 Checklist 221-330	.05	.01
❑	317 Aaron Craver	.05	.01
❑	318 Michael Brooks	.05	.01
❑	319 Guy McIntyre	.05	.01
❑	320 Thurman Thomas	.25	.08
❑	321 Courtney Hall	.05	.01
❑	322 Dan Saleaumua	.05	.01
❑	323 Vinson Smith RC	.05	.01
❑	324 Steve Jordan	.05	.01
❑	325 Walter Reeves	.05	.01
❑	326 Erik Kramer	.10	.02
❑	327 Duane Bickett	.05	.01
❑	328 Tom Newberry	.05	.01
❑	329 John Kasay	.05	.01
❑	330 Dave Meggett	.10	.02
❑	331 Kevin Ross	.05	.01
❑	332 Keith Hamilton RC	.10	.02
❑	333 Dwight Stone	.05	.01
❑	334 Mel Gray	.10	.02
❑	335 Harry Galbreath	.05	.01
❑	336 William Perry	.10	.02
❑	337 Brian Blades	.10	.02
❑	338 Randall McDaniel	.05	.01
❑	339 Pat Coleman RC	.05	.01
❑	340 Michael Irvin	.25	.08
❑	341 Checklist 331-440	.05	.01
❑	342 Chris Mohr	.05	.01
❑	343 Greg Davis	.05	.01
❑	344 Dave Cadigan	.05	.01
❑	345 Art Monk	.10	.02
❑	346 Tim Goad	.05	.01
❑	347 Vinnie Clark	.05	.01
❑	348 David Fulcher	.05	.01
❑	349 Craig Heyward	.10	.02
❑	350 Ronnie Lott	.10	.02
❑	351 Dexter Carter	.05	.01
❑	352 Mark Jackson	.05	.01
❑	353 Brian Jordan	.10	.02
❑	354 Ray Donaldson	.05	.01
❑	355 Jim Price	.05	.01
❑	356 Rod Bernstine	.05	.01
❑	357 Tony Mayberry RC	.05	.01
❑	358 Richard Brown RC	.05	.01
❑	359 David Alexander	.05	.01
❑	360 Haywood Jeffires	.10	.02
❑	361 Henry Thomas	.05	.01
❑	362 Jeff Graham	.25	.08
❑	363 Don Warren	.05	.01
❑	364 Scott Davis	.05	.01
❑	365 Harlon Barnett	.05	.01
❑	366 Mark Collins	.05	.01
❑	367 Rick Tuten	.05	.01
❑	368 Lonnie Marts RC	.05	.01
❑	369 Dennis Smith	.05	.01
❑	370 Steve Tasker	.10	.02
❑	371 Robert Massey	.05	.01
❑	372 Ricky Reynolds	.05	.01
❑	373 Alvin Wright	.05	.01
❑	374 Kelvin Martin	.05	.01
❑	375 Vince Buck	.05	.01
❑	376 John Kidd	.05	.01
❑	377 William White	.05	.01
❑	378 Bryan Cox	.10	.02
❑	379 Jamie Dukes RC	.05	.01
❑	380 Anthony Munoz	.10	.02
❑	381 Mark Gunn RC	.05	.01
❑	382 Keith Henderson	.05	.01
❑	383 Charles Wilson	.05	.01
❑	384 Shawn McCarthy RC	.05	.01
❑	385 Ernie Jones	.05	.01
❑	386 Nick Bell	.05	.01
❑	387 Derrick Walker	.05	.01
❑	388 Mark Stepnoski	.10	.02
❑	389 Broderick Thomas	.05	.01
❑	390 Reggie Roby	.05	.01
❑	391 Bubba McDowell	.05	.01
❑	392 Eric Martin	.05	.01
❑	393 Toby Caston RC	.05	.01
❑	394 Bern Brostek	.05	.01
❑	395 Christian Okoye	.05	.01
❑	396 Frank Minnifield	.05	.01
❑	397 Mike Golic	.05	.01
❑	398 Grant Feasel	.05	.01
❑	399 Michael Ball	.05	.01
❑	400 Mike Croel	.05	.01
❑	401 Maury Buford	.05	.01
❑	402 Jeff Bostic UER	.05	.01
❑	403 Sean Landeta	.05	.01
❑	404 Terry Allen	.25	.08
❑	405 Donald Evans	.05	.01
❑	406 Don Mosebar	.05	.01
❑	407 D.J. Dozier	.05	.01
❑	408 Bruce Pickens	.05	.01
❑	409 Jim Dombrowski	.05	.01
❑	410 Deron Cherry	.05	.01
❑	411 Richard Johnson CB	.05	.01
❑	412 Alexander Wright	.05	.01
❑	413 Tom Rathman	.05	.01
❑	414 Mark Dennis	.05	.01
❑	415 Phil Hansen	.05	.01
❑	416 Lonnie Young	.05	.01
❑	417 Burt Grossman	.05	.01
❑	418 Tony Covington	.05	.01
❑	419 John Stephens	.05	.01
❑	420 Jim Everett	.10	.02
❑	421 Johnny Holland	.05	.01
❑	422 Mike Barber RC WR	.05	.01
❑	423 Carl Lee	.05	.01
❑	424 Craig Patterson RC	.05	.01
❑	425 Greg Townsend	.05	.01
❑	426 Brett Perriman	.25	.08
❑	427 Morten Andersen	.05	.01
❑	428 John Gesek	.05	.01
❑	429 Bryan Barker	.05	.01
❑	430 John Taylor	.10	.02
❑	431 Donnell Woolford	.05	.01
❑	432 Ron Holmes	.05	.01
❑	433 Lee Williams	.05	.01
❑	434 Alfred Oglesby	.05	.01
❑	435 Jarrod Bunch	.05	.01
❑	436 Carlton Haselrig RC	.05	.01
❑	437 Rufus Porter	.05	.01
❑	438 Rohn Stark	.05	.01
❑	439 Tony Jones T	.05	.01
❑	440 Andre Rison	.10	.02
❑	441 Eric Hill	.05	.01
❑	442 Jesse Solomon	.05	.01
❑	443 Jackie Slater	.05	.01
❑	444 Donnie Elder	.05	.01
❑	445 Brett Maxie	.05	.01
❑	446 Max Montoya	.05	.01
❑	447 Will Wolford	.05	.01
❑	448 Craig Taylor	.05	.01
❑	449 Jimmie Jones	.05	.01
❑	450 Anthony Carter	.10	.02
❑	451 Brian Bollinger RC	.05	.01
❑	452 Checklist 441-550	.05	.01
❑	453 Brad Edwards	.05	.01
❑	454 Gene Chilton RC	.05	.01
❑	455 Eric Allen	.05	.01
❑	456 William Roberts	.05	.01
❑	457 Eric Green	.05	.01
❑	458 Irv Eatman	.05	.01
❑	459 Derrick Thomas	.25	.08
❑	460 Tommy Kane	.05	.01
❑	461 LeRoy Butler	.05	.01
❑	462 Oliver Barnett	.05	.01
❑	463 Anthony Smith	.05	.01
❑	464 Cris Dishman	.05	.01
❑	465 Pat Terrell	.05	.01
❑	466 Greg Kragen	.05	.01
❑	467 Rodney Peete	.10	.02
❑	468 Willie Drewrey	.05	.01
❑	469 Jim Wilks	.05	.01
❑	470 Vince Newsome	.05	.01
❑	471 Chris Gardocki	.05	.01
❑	472 Chris Chandler	.25	.08
❑	473 George Thornton	.05	.01
❑	474 Albert Lewis	.05	.01
❑	475 Kevin Glover	.05	.01
❑	476 Joe Bowden RC	.05	.01
❑	477 Harry Sydney	.05	.01
❑	478 Bob Golic	.05	.01
❑	479 Tony Zendejas	.05	.01
❑	480 Brad Baxter	.05	.01
❑	481 Steve Beuerlein	.10	.02
❑	482 Mark Higgs	.05	.01
❑	483 Drew Hill	.05	.01
❑	484 Bryan Millard	.05	.01
❑	485 Mark Kelso	.05	.01
❑	486 David Grant	.05	.01
❑	487 Gary Zimmerman	.05	.01
❑	488 Leonard Marshall	.05	.01
❑	489 Keith Jackson	.10	.02
❑	490 Sterling Sharpe	.25	.08
❑	491 Ferrell Edmunds	.05	.01
❑	492 Wilber Marshall	.05	.01
❑	493 Charles Haley	.10	.02
❑	494 Riki Ellison	.05	.01
❑	495 Bill Brooks	.05	.01
❑	496 Bill Hawkins	.05	.01
❑	497 Erik Williams	.05	.01
❑	498 Leon Searcy RC	.05	.01
❑	499 Mike Horan	.05	.01
❑	500 Pat Swilling	.05	.01
❑	501 Maurice Hurst	.05	.01
❑	502 William Fuller	.05	.01
❑	503 Tim Newton	.05	.01
❑	504 Lorenzo Lynch	.05	.01
❑	505 Tim Barnett	.05	.01
❑	506 Tom Thayer	.05	.01
❑	507 Chris Burkett	.05	.01
❑	508 Ronnie Harmon	.05	.01
❑	509 James Brooks	.10	.02
❑	510 Bennie Blades	.05	.01
❑	511 Roger Craig	.10	.02
❑	512 Tony Woods	.05	.01
❑	513 Greg Lewis	.05	.01
❑	514 Erric Pegram	.10	.02
❑	515 Elvis Patterson	.05	.01
❑	516 Jeff Cross	.05	.01
❑	517 Myron Guyton	.05	.01
❑	518 Jay Novacek	.10	.02
❑	519 Leo Barker RC	.05	.01
❑	520 Keith Byars	.05	.01
❑	521 Dalton Hilliard	.05	.01
❑	522 Ted Washington	.05	.01
❑	523 Dexter McNabb RC	.05	.01
❑	524 Frank Reich	.10	.02
❑	525 Henry Ellard	.10	.02
❑	526 Barry Foster	.10	.02
❑	527 Barry Word	.05	.01
❑	528 Gary Anderson RB	.05	.01
❑	529 Reggie Rutland	.05	.01
❑	530 Stephen Baker	.05	.01

	Card	Price 1	Price 2
❑	531 John Flannery	.05	.01
❑	532 Steve Wright	.05	.01
❑	533 Eric Sanders	.05	.01
❑	534 Bob Whitfield RC	.05	.01
❑	535 Gaston Green	.05	.01
❑	536 Anthony Pleasant	.05	.01
❑	537 Jeff Bryant	.05	.01
❑	538 Jarvis Williams	.05	.01
❑	539 Jim Morrissey	.05	.01
❑	540 Andre Tippett	.05	.01
❑	541 Gill Byrd	.05	.01
❑	542 Raleigh McKenzie	.05	.01
❑	543 Jim Sweeney	.05	.01
❑	544 David Lutz	.05	.01
❑	545 Wayne Martin	.05	.01
❑	546 Karl Wilson	.05	.01
❑	547 Pierce Holt	.05	.01
❑	548 Doug Smith	.05	.01
❑	549 Nolan Harrison RC	.05	.01
❑	550 Freddie Joe Nunn	.05	.01
❑	551 Eric Moore	.05	.01
❑	552 Cris Carter	.50	.20
❑	553 Kevin Gogan	.05	.01
❑	554 Harold Green	.05	.01
❑	555 Kenneth Davis	.05	.01
❑	556 Travis McNeal	.05	.01
❑	557 Jim C. Jensen	.05	.01
❑	558 Willie Green	.05	.01
❑	559 Scott Galbraith RC	.05	.01
❑	560 Louis Lipps	.05	.01
❑	561 Matt Brock	.05	.01
❑	562 Mike Prior	.05	.01
❑	563 Checklist 551-660	.05	.01
❑	564 Robert Delpino	.05	.01
❑	565 Vinny Testaverde	.10	.02
❑	566 Willie Gault	.10	.02
❑	567 Quinn Early	.10	.02
❑	568 Eric Moten	.05	.01
❑	569 Lance Smith	.05	.01
❑	570 Darrell Green	.05	.01
❑	571 Moe Gardner	.05	.01
❑	572 Steve Atwater	.05	.01
❑	573 Ray Childress	.05	.01
❑	574 Dave Krieg	.10	.02
❑	575 Bruce Armstrong	.05	.01
❑	576 Fred Barnett	.25	.08
❑	577 Don Griffin	.05	.01
❑	578 David Brandon RC	.05	.01
❑	579 Robert Young	.05	.01
❑	580 Keith Van Horne	.05	.01
❑	581 Jeff Criswell	.05	.01
❑	582 Lewis Tillman	.05	.01
❑	583 Bubby Brister	.05	.01
❑	584 Aaron Wallace	.05	.01
❑	585 Chris Doleman	.05	.01
❑	586 Marty Carter RC	.05	.01
❑	587 Chris Warren	.25	.08
❑	588 David Griggs	.05	.01
❑	589 Darrell Thompson	.05	.01
❑	590 Marion Butts	.05	.01
❑	591 Scott Norwood	.05	.01
❑	592 Lomas Brown	.05	.01
❑	593 Daryl Johnston	.25	.08
❑	594 Alonzo Mitz RC	.05	.01
❑	595 Tommy Barnhardt	.05	.01
❑	596 Tim Jorden	.05	.01
❑	597 Neil Smith	.25	.08
❑	598 Todd Marinovich	.05	.01
❑	599 Sean Jones	.05	.01
❑	600 Clarence Verdin	.05	.01
❑	601 Trace Armstrong	.05	.01
❑	602 Steve Bono RC	.25	.08
❑	603 Mark Ingram	.05	.01
❑	604 Flipper Anderson	.05	.01
❑	605 James Jones DT	.05	.01
❑	606 Al Noga	.05	.01
❑	607 Rick Bryan	.05	.01
❑	608 Eugene Lockhart	.05	.01
❑	609 Charles Mann	.05	.01
❑	610 James Hasty	.05	.01
❑	611 Jeff Feagles	.05	.01
❑	612 Tim Brown	.25	.08
❑	613 David Little	.05	.01
❑	614 Keith Sims	.05	.01
❑	615 Kevin Murphy	.05	.01
❑	616 Ray Crockett	.05	.01
❑	617 Jim Jeffcoat	.05	.01
❑	618 Patrick Hunter	.05	.01
❑	619 Keith Kartz	.05	.01
❑	620 Peter Tom Willis	.05	.01
❑	621 Vaughan Johnson	.05	.01
❑	622 Shawn Jefferson	.05	.01
❑	623 Anthony Thompson	.05	.01
❑	624 John Rienstra	.05	.01
❑	625 Don Maggs	.05	.01
❑	626 Todd Lyght	.05	.01
❑	627 Brent Jones	.10	.02
❑	628 Todd McNair	.05	.01
❑	629 Winston Moss	.05	.01
❑	630 Mark Carrier WR	.10	.02
❑	631 Dan Owens	.05	.01
❑	632 Sammie Smith UER	.05	.01
❑	633 James Lofton	.10	.02
❑	634 Paul McJulien RC	.05	.01
❑	635 Tony Tolbert	.05	.01
❑	636 Carnell Lake	.05	.01
❑	637 Gary Clark	.25	.08
❑	638 Brian Washington	.05	.01
❑	639 Jessie Hester	.05	.01
❑	640 Doug Riesenberg	.05	.01
❑	641 Joe Walter RC	.05	.01
❑	642 John Rade	.05	.01
❑	643 Wes Hopkins	.05	.01
❑	644 Kelly Stouffer	.05	.01
❑	645 Marv Cook	.05	.01
❑	646 Ken Clarke	.05	.01
❑	647 Bobby Humphrey UER	.05	.01
❑	648 Tim McDonald	.05	.01
❑	649 Donald Frank RC	.05	.01
❑	650 Richmond Webb	.05	.01
❑	651 Lemuel Stinson	.05	.01
❑	652 Merton Hanks	.10	.02
❑	653 Frank Warren	.05	.01
❑	654 Thomas Benson	.05	.01
❑	655 Al Smith	.05	.01
❑	656 Steve DeBerg	.05	.01
❑	657 Jayice Pearson RC	.05	.01
❑	658 Joe Morris	.05	.01
❑	659 Fred Strickland	.05	.01
❑	660 Kelvin Pritchett	.05	.01
❑	661 Lewis Billups	.05	.01
❑	662 Todd Collins RC	.05	.01
❑	663 Corey Miller RC	.05	.01
❑	664 Levon Kirkland RC	.05	.01
❑	665 Jerry Rice	.75	.30
❑	666 Mike Lodish RC	.05	.01
❑	667 Chuck Smith RC	.05	.01
❑	668 Lance Olberding RC	.05	.01
❑	669 Kevin Smith RC DB	.05	.01
❑	670 Dale Carter RC	.10	.02
❑	671 Sean Gilbert RC	.10	.02
❑	672 Ken O'Brien	.05	.01
❑	673 Ricky Proehl	.05	.01
❑	674 Junior Seau	.25	.08
❑	675 Courtney Hawkins RC	.10	.02
❑	676 Eddie Robinson RC	.05	.01
❑	677 Tommy Jeter RC	.05	.01
❑	678 Jeff George	.25	.08
❑	679 Cary Conklin	.05	.01
❑	680 Rueben Mayes	.05	.01
❑	681 Sean Lumpkin RC	.05	.01
❑	682 Dan Marino	1.25	.50
❑	683 Ed McDaniel RC	.05	.01
❑	684 Greg Skrepenak RC	.05	.01
❑	685 Tracy Scroggins RC	.05	.01
❑	686 Tommy Maddox RC	2.00	.75
❑	687 Mike Singletary	.10	.02
❑	688 Patrick Rowe RC	.05	.01
❑	689 Phillippi Sparks RC	.05	.01
❑	690 Joel Steed RC	.05	.01
❑	691 Kevin Fagan	.05	.01
❑	692 Deion Sanders	.50	.20
❑	693 Bruce Smith	.25	.08
❑	694 David Klingler RC	.05	.01
❑	695 Clayton Holmes RC	.05	.01
❑	696 Brett Favre	6.00	2.50
❑	697 Marc Boutte RC	.05	.01
❑	698 Dwayne Sabb RC	.05	.01
❑	699 Ed McCaffrey	.30	.10
❑	700 Randall Cunningham	.25	.08
❑	701 Quentin Coryatt RC	.05	.01
❑	702 Bernie Kosar	.10	.02
❑	703 Vaughn Dunbar RC	.05	.01
❑	704 Browning Nagle	.05	.01
❑	705 Mark Wheeler RC	.05	.01
❑	706 Paul Siever RC	.05	.01
❑	707 Anthony Miller	.10	.02
❑	708 Corey Widmer RC	.05	.01
❑	709 Eric Dickerson	.10	.02
❑	710 Martin Bayless	.05	.01
❑	711 Jason Hanson RC	.10	.02
❑	712 Michael Dean Perry	.10	.02
❑	713 Billy Joe Tolliver UER	.05	.01
❑	714 Chad Hennings RC	.10	.02
❑	715 Bucky Richardson RC	.05	.01
❑	716 Steve Israel RC	.05	.01
❑	717 Robert Harris RC	.05	.01
❑	718 Timm Rosenbach	.05	.01
❑	719 Joe Montana	1.25	.50
❑	720 Derek Brown TE RC	.05	.01
❑	721 Robert Brooks RC	.75	.30
❑	722 Boomer Esiason	.10	.02
❑	723 Troy Auzenne RC	.05	.01
❑	724 John Fina RC	.05	.01
❑	725 Chris Crooms RC	.05	.01
❑	726 Eugene Chung RC	.05	.01
❑	727 Darren Woodson RC	.25	.08
❑	728 Leslie O'Neal	.10	.02
❑	729 Dan McGwire	.05	.01
❑	730 Al Toon	.10	.02
❑	731 Michael Brandon RC	.05	.01
❑	732 Steve DeOssie	.05	.01
❑	733 Jim Kelly	.25	.08
❑	734 Webster Slaughter	.05	.01
❑	735 Tony Smith RBK RC	.05	.01
❑	736 Shane Collins RC	.05	.01
❑	737 Randal Hill	.05	.01
❑	738 Chris Holder RC	.05	.01
❑	739 Russell Maryland	.05	.01
❑	740 Carl Pickens RC	.25	.08
❑	741 Andre Reed	.10	.02
❑	742 Steve Emtman RC	.05	.01
❑	743 Carl Banks	.05	.01
❑	744 Troy Aikman	.75	.30
❑	745 Mark Royals	.05	.01
❑	746 J.J.Birden	.05	.01
❑	747 Michael Cofer	.05	.01
❑	748 Darryl Ashmore RC	.05	.01
❑	749 Dion Lambert RC	.05	.01
❑	750 Phil Simms	.10	.02
❑	751 Reggie E.White RC	.05	.01
❑	752 Harvey Williams	.25	.08
❑	753 Ty Detmer	.25	.08
❑	754 Tony Brooks RC	.05	.01
❑	755 Steve Christie	.05	.01
❑	756 Lawrence Taylor	.25	.08
❑	757 Merril Hoge	.05	.01
❑	758 Robert Jones RC	.05	.01
❑	759 Checklist 661-759	.05	.01

1993 Topps

	Card	Price 1	Price 2
❑	COMPLETE SET (660)	40.00	20.00
❑	COMP.FACT.SET (673)	80.00	50.00
❑	COMP.SERIES 1 (330)	15.00	6.00
❑	COMP.SERIES 2 (330)	10.00	5.00
❑	1 Art Monk RB	.05	.01
❑	2 Jerry Rice RB	.50	.20
❑	3 Stanley Richard	.05	.01
❑	4 Ron Hall	.05	.01
❑	5 Daryl Johnston	.25	.08
❑	6 Wendell Davis	.05	.01
❑	7 Vaughn Dunbar	.05	.01
❑	8 Mike Jones	.05	.01

❑ 9 Anthony Johnson .10 .02
❑ 10 Chris Miller .10 .02
❑ 11 Kyle Clifton .05 .01
❑ 12 Curtis Conway RC .40 .15
❑ 13 Lionel Washington .05 .01
❑ 14 Reggie Johnson .05 .01
❑ 15 David Little .05 .01
❑ 16 Nick Lowery .05 .01
❑ 17 Darryl Williams .05 .01
❑ 18 Brent Jones .10 .02
❑ 19 Bruce Matthews .05 .01
❑ 20 Heath Sherman .05 .01
❑ 21 John Kasay UER .05 .01
❑ 22 Troy Drayton RC .10 .02
❑ 23 Eric Metcalf .10 .02
❑ 24 Andre Tippett .05 .01
❑ 25 Rodney Hampton .10 .02
❑ 26 Henry Jones .05 .01
❑ 27 Jim Everett .10 .02
❑ 28 Steve Jordan .05 .01
❑ 29 LeRoy Butler .05 .01
❑ 30 Troy Vincent .05 .01
❑ 31 Nate Lewis .05 .01
❑ 32 Rickey Jackson .05 .01
❑ 33 Darion Conner .05 .01
❑ 34 Tom Carter RC .10 .02
❑ 35 Jeff George .25 .08
❑ 36 Larry Centers RC .25 .08
❑ 37 Reggie Cobb .05 .01
❑ 38 Mike Saxon .05 .01
❑ 39 Brad Baxter .05 .01
❑ 40 Reggie White .25 .08
❑ 41 Haywood Jeffires .10 .02
❑ 42 Alfred Williams .05 .01
❑ 43 Aaron Wallace .05 .01
❑ 44 Tracy Simien .05 .01
❑ 45 Pat Harlow .05 .01
❑ 46 D.J. Johnson .05 .01
❑ 47 Don Griffin .05 .01
❑ 48 Flipper Anderson .05 .01
❑ 49 Keith Kartz .05 .01
❑ 50 Bernie Kosar .10 .02
❑ 51 Kent Hull .05 .01
❑ 52 Erik Howard .05 .01
❑ 53 Pierce Holt .05 .01
❑ 54 Dwayne Harper .05 .01
❑ 55 Bennie Blades .05 .01
❑ 56 Mark Duper .05 .01
❑ 57 Brian Noble .05 .01
❑ 58 Jeff Feagles .05 .01
❑ 59 Michael Haynes .10 .02
❑ 60 Junior Seau .25 .08
❑ 61 Gary Anderson RB .05 .01
❑ 62 Jon Hand .05 .01
❑ 63 Lin Elliott RC .05 .01
❑ 64 Dana Stubblefield RC .25 .08
❑ 65 Vaughan Johnson .05 .01
❑ 66 Mo Lewis .05 .01
❑ 67 Aeneas Williams .05 .01
❑ 68 David Fulcher .05 .01
❑ 69 Chip Lohmiller .05 .01
❑ 70 Greg Townsend .05 .01
❑ 71 Simon Fletcher .05 .01
❑ 72 Sean Salisbury .05 .01
❑ 73 Christian Okoye .05 .01
❑ 74 Jim Arnold .05 .01
❑ 75 Bruce Smith .25 .08
❑ 76 Fred Barnett .10 .02
❑ 77 Bill Romanowski .05 .01
❑ 78 Dermontti Dawson .05 .01
❑ 79 Bern Brostek .05 .01
❑ 80 Warren Moon .25 .08
❑ 81 Bill Fralic .05 .01
❑ 82 Lomas Brown FP .05 .01
❑ 83 Duane Bickett FP .05 .01
❑ 84 Neil Smith FP .10 .02
❑ 85 Reggie White FP .10 .02
❑ 86 Tim McDonald FP .05 .01
❑ 87 Leslie O'Neal FP .05 .01
❑ 88 Steve Young FP .40 .15
❑ 89 Paul Gruber FP .05 .01
❑ 90 Wilber Marshall FP .05 .01
❑ 91 Trace Armstrong .05 .01
❑ 92 Bobby Houston RC .05 .01
❑ 93 George Thornton .05 .01
❑ 94 Keith McCants .05 .01
❑ 95 Ricky Sanders .05 .01
❑ 96 Jackie Harris .05 .01
❑ 97 Todd Marinovich .05 .01
❑ 98 Henry Thomas .05 .01
❑ 99 Jeff Wright .05 .01
❑ 100 John Elway 1.50 .60
❑ 101 Garrison Hearst RC .75 .30
❑ 102 Roy Foster .05 .01
❑ 103 David Lang .05 .01
❑ 104 Matt Stover .05 .01
❑ 105 Lawrence Taylor .25 .08
❑ 106 Pete Stoyanovich .05 .01
❑ 107 Jessie Tuggle .05 .01
❑ 108 William White .05 .01
❑ 109 Andy Harmon RC .10 .02
❑ 110 John L. Williams .05 .01
❑ 111 Jon Vaughn .05 .01
❑ 112 John Alt .05 .01
❑ 113 Chris Jacke .05 .01
❑ 114 Jim Breech .05 .01
❑ 115 Eric Martin .05 .01
❑ 116 Derrick Walker .05 .01
❑ 117 Ricky Ervins .05 .01
❑ 118 Roger Craig .10 .02
❑ 119 Jeff Gossett .05 .01
❑ 120 Emmitt Smith 1.50 .60
❑ 121 Bob Whitfield .05 .01
❑ 122 Alonzo Spellman .05 .01
❑ 123 David Klingler .05 .01
❑ 124 Tommy Maddox .25 .08
❑ 125 Robert Porcher .05 .01
❑ 126 Edgar Bennett .25 .08
❑ 127 Harvey Williams .10 .02
❑ 128 Dave Brown RC .25 .08
❑ 129 Johnny Mitchell .05 .01
❑ 130 Drew Bledsoe RC 2.50 1.00
❑ 131 Zefross Moss .05 .01
❑ 132 Nate Odomes .05 .01
❑ 133 Rufus Porter .05 .01
❑ 134 Jackie Slater .05 .01
❑ 135 Steve Young .75 .30
❑ 136 Chris Calloway .10 .02
❑ 137 Steve Atwater .05 .01
❑ 138 Mark Carrier DB .05 .01
❑ 139 Marvin Washington .05 .01
❑ 140 Barry Foster .10 .02
❑ 141 Ricky Reynolds .05 .01
❑ 142 Bubba McDowell .05 .01
❑ 143 Dan Footman RC .05 .01
❑ 144 Richmond Webb .05 .01
❑ 145 Mike Pritchard .10 .02
❑ 146 Chris Spielman .10 .02
❑ 147 Dave Krieg .10 .02
❑ 148 Nick Bell .05 .01
❑ 149 Vincent Brown .05 .01
❑ 150 Seth Joyner .05 .01
❑ 151 Tommy Kane .05 .01
❑ 152 Carlton Gray RC .05 .01
❑ 153 Harry Newsome .05 .01
❑ 154 Rohn Stark .05 .01
❑ 155 Shannon Sharpe .25 .08
❑ 156 Charles Haley .10 .02
❑ 157 Cornelius Bennett .10 .02
❑ 158 Doug Riesenberg .05 .01
❑ 159 Amp Lee .05 .01
❑ 160 Sterling Sharpe UER .25 .08
❑ 161 Alonzo Mitz .05 .01
❑ 162 Pat Terrell .05 .01
❑ 163 Mark Schlereth .05 .01
❑ 164 Gary Anderson K .05 .01
❑ 165 Quinn Early .10 .02
❑ 166 Jerome Bettis RC 5.00 2.50
❑ 167 Lawrence Dawsey .05 .01
❑ 168 Derrick Thomas .25 .08
❑ 169 Rodney Peete .05 .01
❑ 170 Jim Kelly .25 .08
❑ 171 Deion Sanders TL .25 .08
❑ 172 Richard Dent TL .05 .01
❑ 173 Emmitt Smith TL .75 .30
❑ 174 Barry Sanders TL .60 .25
❑ 175 Sterling Sharpe TL .10 .02
❑ 176 Cleveland Gary TL .05 .01
❑ 177 Terry Allen TL .10 .02
❑ 178 Vaughan Johnson TL .05 .01
❑ 179 Rodney Hampton TL .05 .01
❑ 180 Randall Cunningham TL .10 .02
❑ 181 Ricky Proehl TL .05 .01
❑ 182 Jerry Rice TL .50 .20
❑ 183 Reggie Cobb TL .05 .01
❑ 184 Earnest Byner TL .05 .01
❑ 185 Jeff Lageman .05 .01
❑ 186 Carlos Jenkins .05 .01
❑ 187 G.Hearst/Dye/Moore/Cole. .40 .15
❑ 188 Todd Lyght .05 .01
❑ 189 Carl Simpson RC .05 .01
❑ 190 Barry Sanders 1.25 .50
❑ 191 Jim Harbaugh .25 .08
❑ 192 Roger Ruzek .05 .01
❑ 193 Brent Williams .05 .01
❑ 194 Chip Banks .05 .01
❑ 195 Mike Croel .05 .01
❑ 196 Marion Butts .05 .01
❑ 197 James Washington .05 .01
❑ 198 John Offerdahl .05 .01
❑ 199 Tom Rathman .05 .01
❑ 200 Joe Montana 1.50 .60
❑ 201 Pepper Johnson .05 .01
❑ 202 Cris Dishman .05 .01
❑ 203 Adrian White RC .05 .01
❑ 204 Reggie Brooks RC .10 .02
❑ 205 Cortez Kennedy .10 .02
❑ 206 Robert Massey .05 .01
❑ 207 Toi Cook .05 .01
❑ 208 Harry Sydney .05 .01
❑ 209 Lincoln Kennedy RC .05 .01
❑ 210 Randall McDaniel .05 .01
❑ 211 Eugene Daniel .05 .01
❑ 212 Rob Burnett .05 .01
❑ 213 Steve Broussard .05 .01
❑ 214 Brian Washington .05 .01
❑ 215 Leonard Renfro RC .05 .01
❑ 216 Audray McMillian LL .05 .01
❑ 217 Sterling Sharpe/Miller L .05 .01
❑ 218 Clyde Simmons LL .05 .01
❑ 219 Emmitt Smith/B.Foster LL .40 .15
❑ 220 Steve Young/W.Moon LL .25 .08
❑ 221 Mel Gray .10 .02
❑ 222 Luis Sharpe .05 .01
❑ 223 Eric Moten .05 .01
❑ 224 Albert Lewis .05 .01
❑ 225 Alvin Harper .10 .02
❑ 226 Steve Wallace .05 .01
❑ 227 Mark Higgs .05 .01
❑ 228 Eugene Lockhart .05 .01
❑ 229 Sean Jones .05 .01
❑ 230 J.Lynch RC/Thom/DuBose .60 .25
❑ 231 Jimmy Williams .05 .01
❑ 232 Demetrius DuBose RC .05 .01
❑ 233 John Roper .05 .01
❑ 234 Keith Hamilton .05 .01
❑ 235 Donald Evans .05 .01
❑ 236 Kenneth Davis .05 .01
❑ 237 John Copeland RC .10 .02
❑ 238 Leonard Russell .10 .02
❑ 239 Ken Harvey .05 .01
❑ 240 Dale Carter .05 .01
❑ 241 Anthony Pleasant .05 .01
❑ 242 Darrell Green .05 .01
❑ 243 Natrone Means RC .25 .08
❑ 244 Rob Moore .10 .02
❑ 245 Chris Doleman .05 .01
❑ 246 J.B. Brown .05 .01
❑ 247 Ray Crockett .05 .01
❑ 248 John Taylor .10 .02
❑ 249 Russell Maryland .05 .01
❑ 250 Brett Favre 2.00 .75
❑ 251 Carl Pickens .10 .02
❑ 252 Andy Heck .05 .01
❑ 253 Jerome Henderson .05 .01
❑ 254 Deion Sanders .50 .20
❑ 255 Steve Emtman .05 .01
❑ 256 Calvin Williams .10 .02
❑ 257 Sean Gilbert .10 .02
❑ 258 Don Beebe .05 .01
❑ 259 Robert Smith RC 1.25 .50
❑ 260 Robert Blackmon .05 .01
❑ 261 Jim Kelly TL .10 .02
❑ 262 Harold Green TL UER .05 .01
❑ 263 Clay Matthews TL .05 .01
❑ 264 John Elway TL .75 .30
❑ 265 Warren Moon TL .10 .02
❑ 266 Jeff George TL .10 .02
❑ 267 Derrick Thomas TL .10 .02
❑ 268 Howie Long TL .05 .01
❑ 269 Dan Marino TL .75 .30

❑	270	Jon Vaughn TL	.05	.01
❑	271	Chris Burkett TL	.05	.01
❑	272	Barry Foster TL	.05	.01
❑	273	Marion Butts TL	.05	.01
❑	274	Chris Warren TL	.05	.01
❑	275	M.Strahan RC/M.Buck.	1.00	.40
❑	276	Tony Casillas	.05	.01
❑	277	Jarrod Bunch	.05	.01
❑	278	Eric Green	.05	.01
❑	279	Stan Brock	.05	.01
❑	280	Chester McGlockton	.10	.02
❑	281	Ricky Watters	.25	.08
❑	282	Dan Saleaumua	.05	.01
❑	283	Rich Camarillo	.05	.01
❑	284	Cris Carter	.25	.08
❑	285	Rick Mirer RC	.25	.08
❑	286	Matt Brock	.05	.01
❑	287	Burt Grossman	.05	.01
❑	288	Andre Collins	.05	.01
❑	289	Mark Jackson	.05	.01
❑	290	Dan Marino	1.50	.60
❑	291	Cornelius Bennett FG	.05	.01
❑	292	Steve Atwater FG	.05	.01
❑	293	Bryan Cox FG	.05	.01
❑	294	Sam Mills FG	.05	.01
❑	295	Pepper Johnson FG	.05	.01
❑	296	Seth Joyner FG	.05	.01
❑	297	Chris Spielman FG	.05	.01
❑	298	Junior Seau FG	.10	.02
❑	299	Cortez Kennedy FG	.05	.01
❑	300	Broderick Thomas FG	.05	.01
❑	301	Todd McNair	.05	.01
❑	302	Nate Newton	.10	.02
❑	303	Michael Walter	.05	.01
❑	304	Clyde Simmons	.05	.01
❑	305	Ernie Mills	.05	.01
❑	306	Steve Wisniewski	.05	.01
❑	307	Coleman Rudolph RC	.05	.01
❑	308	Thurman Thomas	.25	.08
❑	309	Reggie Roby	.05	.01
❑	310	Eric Swann	.10	.02
❑	311	Mark Wheeler	.05	.01
❑	312	Jeff Herrod	.05	.01
❑	313	Leroy Hoard	.10	.02
❑	314	Patrick Bates RC	.05	.01
❑	315	Earnest Byner	.05	.01
❑	316	Dave Meggett	.05	.01
❑	317	George Teague RC	.10	.02
❑	318	Ray Childress	.05	.01
❑	319	Mike Kenn	.05	.01
❑	320	Jason Hanson	.05	.01
❑	321	Gary Clark	.10	.02
❑	322	Chris Gardocki	.05	.01
❑	323	Ken Norton	.10	.02
❑	324	Eric Curry RC	.05	.01
❑	325	Byron Evans	.05	.01
❑	326	O.J.McDuffie RC	.25	.08
❑	327	Dwight Stone	.05	.01
❑	328	Tommy Barnhardt	.05	.01
❑	329	Checklist 1-165	.05	.01
❑	330	Checklist 166-329	.05	.01
❑	331	Erik Williams	.05	.01
❑	332	Phil Hansen	.05	.01
❑	333	Martin Harrison RC	.05	.01
❑	334	Mark Ingram	.05	.01
❑	335	Mark Rypien	.05	.01
❑	336	Anthony Miller	.10	.02
❑	337	Antone Davis	.05	.01
❑	338	Mike Munchak	.10	.02
❑	339	Wayne Martin	.05	.01
❑	340	Joe Montana	1.50	.60
❑	341	Deon Figures RC	.05	.01
❑	342	Ed McDaniel	.05	.01
❑	343	Chris Burkett	.05	.01
❑	344	Tony Smith RB	.05	.01
❑	345	James Lofton	.10	.02
❑	346	Courtney Hawkins	.05	.01
❑	347	Dennis Smith	.05	.01
❑	348	Anthony Morgan	.05	.01
❑	349	Chris Goode	.05	.01
❑	350	Phil Simms	.10	.02
❑	351	Patrick Hunter	.05	.01
❑	352	Brett Perriman	.25	.08
❑	353	Corey Miller	.05	.01
❑	354	Harry Galbreath	.05	.01
❑	355	Mark Carrier WR	.10	.02
❑	356	Troy Drayton	.10	.02
❑	357	Greg Davis	.05	.01
❑	358	Tim Krumrie	.05	.01
❑	359	Tim McDonald	.05	.01
❑	360	Webster Slaughter	.05	.01
❑	361	Steve Christie	.05	.01
❑	362	Courtney Hall	.05	.01
❑	363	Charles Mann	.05	.01
❑	364	Vestee Jackson	.05	.01
❑	365	Robert Jones	.05	.01
❑	366	Rich Miano	.05	.01
❑	367	Morten Andersen	.05	.01
❑	368	Jeff Graham	.10	.02
❑	369	Martin Mayhew	.05	.01
❑	370	Anthony Carter	.10	.02
❑	371	Greg Kragen	.05	.01
❑	372	Ron Cox	.05	.01
❑	373	Perry Williams	.05	.01
❑	374	Willie Gault	.05	.01
❑	375	Chris Warren	.10	.02
❑	376	Reyna Thompson	.05	.01
❑	377	Bennie Thompson	.05	.01
❑	378	Kevin Mack	.05	.01
❑	379	Clarence Verdin	.05	.01
❑	380	Marc Boutte	.05	.01
❑	381	Marvin Jones RC	.05	.01
❑	382	Greg Jackson	.05	.01
❑	383	Steve Bono	.10	.02
❑	384	Terrell Buckley	.05	.01
❑	385	Garrison Hearst	.25	.08
❑	386	Mike Brim	.05	.01
❑	387	Jesse Sapolu	.05	.01
❑	388	Carl Lee	.05	.01
❑	389	Jeff Cross	.05	.01
❑	390	Karl Mecklenburg	.05	.01
❑	391	Chad Hennings	.05	.01
❑	392	Oliver Barnett	.05	.01
❑	393	Dalton Hilliard	.05	.01
❑	394	Broderick Thompson	.05	.01
❑	395	Rocket Ismail	.10	.02
❑	396	John Kidd	.05	.01
❑	397	Eddie Anderson	.05	.01
❑	398	Lamar Lathon	.05	.01
❑	399	Darren Perry	.05	.01
❑	400	Drew Bledsoe	1.25	.50
❑	401	Ferrell Edmunds	.05	.01
❑	402	Lomas Brown	.05	.01
❑	403	Drew Hill	.05	.01
❑	404	David Whitmore	.05	.01
❑	405	Mike Johnson	.05	.01
❑	406	Paul Gruber	.05	.01
❑	407	Kirk Lowdermilk	.05	.01
❑	408	Curtis Conway	.25	.08
❑	409	Bryce Paup	.10	.02
❑	410	Boomer Esiason	.10	.02
❑	411	Jay Schroeder	.05	.01
❑	412	Anthony Newman	.05	.01
❑	413	Ernie Jones	.05	.01
❑	414	Carlton Bailey	.05	.01
❑	415	Kenneth Gant	.05	.01
❑	416	Todd Scott	.05	.01
❑	417	Anthony Smith	.05	.01
❑	418	Erik McMillan	.05	.01
❑	419	Ronnie Harmon	.05	.01
❑	420	Andre Reed	.10	.02
❑	421	Wymon Henderson	.05	.01
❑	422	Carnell Lake	.05	.01
❑	423	Al Noga	.05	.01
❑	424	Curtis Duncan	.05	.01
❑	425	Mike Gann	.05	.01
❑	426	Eugene Robinson	.05	.01
❑	427	Scott Mersereau	.05	.01
❑	428	Chris Singleton	.05	.01
❑	429	Gerald Robinson	.05	.01
❑	430	Pat Swilling	.05	.01
❑	431	Ed McCaffrey	.25	.08
❑	432	Neal Anderson	.05	.01
❑	433	Joe Phillips	.05	.01
❑	434	Jerry Ball	.05	.01
❑	435	Tyronne Stowe	.05	.01
❑	436	Dana Stubblefield	.25	.08
❑	437	Eric Curry	.05	.01
❑	438	Derrick Fenner	.05	.01
❑	439	Mark Clayton	.05	.01
❑	440	Quentin Coryatt	.10	.02
❑	441	Willie Roaf RC	.10	.02
❑	442	Ernest Dye	.05	.01
❑	443	Jeff Jaeger	.05	.01
❑	444	Stan Humphries	.10	.02
❑	445	Johnny Johnson	.05	.01
❑	446	Larry Brown DB	.05	.01
❑	447	Kurt Gouveia	.05	.01
❑	448	Qadry Ismail RC	.25	.08
❑	449	Dan Footman	.05	.01
❑	450	Tom Waddle	.05	.01
❑	451	Kelvin Martin	.05	.01
❑	452	Kanavis McGhee	.05	.01
❑	453	Herman Moore	.25	.08
❑	454	Jesse Solomon	.05	.01
❑	455	Shane Conlan	.05	.01
❑	456	Joel Steed	.05	.01
❑	457	Charles Arbuckle	.05	.01
❑	458	Shane Dronett	.05	.01
❑	459	Steve Tasker	.10	.02
❑	460	Herschel Walker	.10	.02
❑	461	Willie Davis	.25	.08
❑	462	Al Smith	.05	.01
❑	463	O.J.McDuffie	.25	.08
❑	464	Kevin Fagan	.05	.01
❑	465	Hardy Nickerson	.10	.02
❑	466	Leonard Marshall	.05	.01
❑	467	John Baylor	.05	.01
❑	468	Jay Novacek	.10	.02
❑	469	Wayne Simmons RC	.05	.01
❑	470	Tommy Vardell	.05	.01
❑	471	Cleveland Gary	.05	.01
❑	472	Mark Collins	.05	.01
❑	473	Craig Heyward	.10	.02
❑	474	John Copeland UER	.10	.02
❑	475	Jeff Hostetler	.10	.02
❑	476	Brian Mitchell	.10	.02
❑	477	Natrone Means	.25	.08
❑	478	Brad Muster	.05	.01
❑	479	David Lutz	.05	.01
❑	480	Andre Rison	.10	.02
❑	481	Michael Zordich	.05	.01
❑	482	Jim McMahon	.10	.02
❑	483	Carlton Gray	.05	.01
❑	484	Chris Mohr	.05	.01
❑	485	Ernest Givins	.10	.02
❑	486	Tony Tolbert	.05	.01
❑	487	Vai Sikahema	.05	.01
❑	488	Larry Webster	.05	.01
❑	489	James Hasty	.05	.01
❑	490	Reggie White	.25	.08
❑	491	Reggie Rivers RC	.05	.01
❑	492	Roman Phifer	.05	.01
❑	493	Levon Kirkland	.05	.01
❑	494	Demetrius DuBose	.05	.01
❑	495	William Perry	.10	.02
❑	496	Clay Matthews	.10	.02
❑	497	Aaron Jones	.05	.01
❑	498	Jack Trudeau	.05	.01
❑	499	Michael Brooks	.05	.01
❑	500	Jerry Rice	1.00	.40
❑	501	Lonnie Marts	.05	.01
❑	502	Tim McGee	.05	.01
❑	503	Kelvin Pritchett	.05	.01
❑	504	Bobby Hebert	.05	.01
❑	505	Audray McMillian	.05	.01
❑	506	Chuck Cecil	.05	.01
❑	507	Leonard Renfro	.05	.01
❑	508	Ethan Horton	.05	.01
❑	509	Kevin Smith	.10	.02
❑	510	Louis Oliver	.05	.01
❑	511	John Stephens	.05	.01
❑	512	Browning Nagle	.05	.01
❑	513	Ricardo McDonald	.05	.01
❑	514	Leslie O'Neal	.10	.02
❑	515	Lorenzo White	.05	.01
❑	516	Thomas Smith RC	.10	.02
❑	517	Tony Woods	.05	.01
❑	518	Darryl Henley	.05	.01
❑	519	Robert Delpino	.05	.01
❑	520	Rod Woodson	.25	.08
❑	521	Phillippi Sparks	.05	.01
❑	522	Jessie Hester	.05	.01
❑	523	Shaun Gayle	.05	.01
❑	524	Brad Edwards	.05	.01
❑	525	Randall Cunningham	.25	.08
❑	526	Marv Cook	.05	.01
❑	527	Dennis Gibson	.05	.01
❑	528	Eric Pegram	.10	.02
❑	529	Terry McDaniel	.05	.01
❑	530	Troy Aikman	.75	.30

❑ 531 Irving Fryar	.10	.02
❑ 532 Blair Thomas	.05	.01
❑ 533 Jim Wilks	.05	.01
❑ 534 Michael Jackson	.10	.02
❑ 535 Eric Davis	.05	.01
❑ 536 James Campen	.05	.01
❑ 537 Steve Beuerlein	.10	.02
❑ 538 Robert Smith	.50	.20
❑ 539 J.J. Birden	.05	.01
❑ 540 Broderick Thomas	.05	.01
❑ 541 Darryl Talley	.05	.01
❑ 542 Russell Freeman RC	.05	.01
❑ 543 David Alexander	.05	.01
❑ 544 Chris Mims	.05	.01
❑ 545 Coleman Rudolph	.05	.01
❑ 546 Steve McMichael	.10	.02
❑ 547 David Williams	.05	.01
❑ 548 Chris Hinton	.05	.01
❑ 549 Jim Jeffcoat	.05	.01
❑ 550 Howie Long	.25	.08
❑ 551 Roosevelt Potts RC	.05	.01
❑ 552 Bryan Cox	.05	.01
❑ 553 David Richards UER	.05	.01
❑ 554 Reggie Brooks	.10	.02
❑ 555 Neil O'Donnell	.25	.08
❑ 556 Irv Smith RC	.05	.01
❑ 557 Henry Ellard	.10	.02
❑ 558 Steve DeBerg	.05	.01
❑ 559 Jim Sweeney	.05	.01
❑ 560 Harold Green	.05	.01
❑ 561 Darrell Thompson	.05	.01
❑ 562 Vinny Testaverde	.10	.02
❑ 563 Bubby Brister	.05	.01
❑ 564 Sean Landeta	.05	.01
❑ 565 Neil Smith	.25	.08
❑ 566 Craig Erickson	.10	.02
❑ 567 Jim Ritcher	.05	.01
❑ 568 Don Mosebar	.05	.01
❑ 569 John Gesek	.05	.01
❑ 570 Gary Plummer	.05	.01
❑ 571 Norm Johnson	.05	.01
❑ 572 Ron Heller	.05	.01
❑ 573 Carl Simpson	.05	.01
❑ 574 Greg Montgomery	.05	.01
❑ 575 Dana Hall	.05	.01
❑ 576 Vencie Glenn	.05	.01
❑ 577 Dean Biasucci	.05	.01
❑ 578 Rod Bernstine UER	.05	.01
❑ 579 Randal Hill	.05	.01
❑ 580 Sam Mills	.05	.01
❑ 581 Santana Dotson	.10	.02
❑ 582 Greg Lloyd	.10	.02
❑ 583 Eric Thomas	.05	.01
❑ 584 Henry Rolling	.05	.01
❑ 585 Tony Bennett	.05	.01
❑ 586 Sheldon White	.05	.01
❑ 587 Mark Kelso	.05	.01
❑ 588 Marc Spindler	.05	.01
❑ 589 Greg McMurtry	.05	.01
❑ 590 Art Monk	.10	.02
❑ 591 Marco Coleman	.05	.01
❑ 592 Tony Jones T	.05	.01
❑ 593 Melvin Jenkins	.05	.01
❑ 594 Kevin Ross	.05	.01
❑ 595 William Fuller	.05	.01
❑ 596 James Joseph	.05	.01
❑ 597 Lamar McGriggs RC	.05	.01
❑ 598 Gill Byrd	.05	.01
❑ 599 Alexander Wright	.05	.01
❑ 600 Rick Mirer	.25	.08
❑ 601 Richard Dent	.10	.02
❑ 602 Thomas Everett	.05	.01
❑ 603 Jack Del Rio	.05	.01
❑ 604 Jerome Bettis	2.50	1.00
❑ 605 Ronnie Lott	.10	.02
❑ 606 Marty Carter	.05	.01
❑ 607 Arthur Marshall RC	.05	.01
❑ 608 Lee Johnson	.05	.01
❑ 609 Bruce Armstrong	.05	.01
❑ 610 Ricky Proehl	.05	.01
❑ 611 Will Wolford	.05	.01
❑ 612 Mike Prior	.05	.01
❑ 613 George Jamison	.05	.01
❑ 614 Gene Atkins	.05	.01
❑ 615 Merril Hoge	.05	.01
❑ 616 Desmond Howard	.10	.02
❑ 617 Jarvis Williams	.05	.01
❑ 618 Marcus Allen	.25	.08
❑ 619 Gary Brown	.05	.01
❑ 620 Bill Brooks	.05	.01
❑ 621 Eric Allen	.05	.01
❑ 622 Todd Kelly	.05	.01
❑ 623 Michael Dean Perry	.10	.02
❑ 624 David Braxton	.05	.01
❑ 625 Mike Sherrard	.05	.01
❑ 626 Jeff Bryant	.05	.01
❑ 627 Eric Bieniemy	.05	.01
❑ 628 Tim Brown	.25	.08
❑ 629 Troy Auzenne	.05	.01
❑ 630 Michael Irvin	.25	.08
❑ 631 Maurice Hurst	.05	.01
❑ 632 Duane Bickett	.05	.01
❑ 633 George Teague	.10	.02
❑ 634 Vince Workman	.05	.01
❑ 635 Renaldo Turnbull	.05	.01
❑ 636 Johnny Bailey	.05	.01
❑ 637 Dan Williams RC	.05	.01
❑ 638 James Thornton	.05	.01
❑ 639 Terry Allen	.25	.08
❑ 640 Kevin Greene	.10	.02
❑ 641 Tony Zendejas	.05	.01
❑ 642 Scott Kowalkowski RC	.05	.01
❑ 643 Jeff Query UER	.05	.01
❑ 644 Brian Blades	.10	.02
❑ 645 Keith Jackson	.10	.02
❑ 646 Monte Coleman	.05	.01
❑ 647 Guy McIntyre	.05	.01
❑ 648 Barry Word	.05	.01
❑ 649 Steve Everitt RC	.05	.01
❑ 650 Patrick Bates	.05	.01
❑ 651 Marcus Robertson RC	.05	.01
❑ 652 John Carney	.05	.01
❑ 653 Derek Brown TE	.05	.01
❑ 654 Carwell Gardner	.05	.01
❑ 655 Moe Gardner	.05	.01
❑ 656 Andre Ware	.05	.01
❑ 657 Keith Van Horne	.05	.01
❑ 658 Hugh Millen	.05	.01
❑ 659 Checklist 330-495	.05	.01
❑ 660 Checklist 496-660	.05	.01

1994 Topps

❑ COMPLETE SET (660)	80.00	40.00
❑ COMP.FACT.SET	80.00	45.00
❑ COMP.SERIES 1 (330)	25.00	12.50
❑ COMP.SERIES 2 (330)	25.00	12.50
❑ 1 Emmitt Smith	1.50	.60
❑ 2 Russell Copeland	.05	.01
❑ 3 Jesse Sapolu	.05	.01
❑ 4 David Szott	.05	.01
❑ 5 Rodney Hampton	.10	.02
❑ 6 Bubba McDowell	.05	.01
❑ 7 Bryce Paup	.10	.02
❑ 8 Winston Moss	.05	.01
❑ 9 Brett Perriman	.10	.02
❑ 10 Rod Woodson	.10	.02
❑ 11 John Randle	.10	.02
❑ 12 David Wyman	.05	.01
❑ 13 Jeff Cross	.05	.01
❑ 14 Richard Cooper	.05	.01
❑ 15 Johnny Mitchell	.05	.01
❑ 16 David Alexander	.05	.01
❑ 17 Ronnie Harmon	.05	.01
❑ 18 Tyronne Stowe UER	.05	.01
❑ 19 Chris Zorich	.05	.01
❑ 20 Rob Burnett	.05	.01
❑ 21 Harold Alexander	.05	.01
❑ 22 Rod Stephens	.05	.01
❑ 23 Mark Wheeler	.05	.01
❑ 24 Dwayne Sabb	.05	.01
❑ 25 Troy Drayton	.05	.01
❑ 26 Kurt Gouveia	.05	.01
❑ 27 Warren Moon	.25	.08
❑ 28 Jeff Query	.05	.01
❑ 29 Chuck Levy RC	.05	.01
❑ 30 Bruce Smith	.25	.08
❑ 31 Doug Riesenberg	.05	.01
❑ 32 Willie Drewrey	.05	.01
❑ 33 Nate Newton UER	.05	.01
❑ 34 James Jett	.05	.01
❑ 35 George Teague	.05	.01
❑ 36 Marc Spindler	.05	.01
❑ 37 Jack Del Rio	.05	.01
❑ 38 Dale Carter	.05	.01
❑ 39 Steve Atwater	.05	.01
❑ 40 Herschel Walker	.10	.02
❑ 41 James Hasty	.05	.01
❑ 42 Seth Joyner	.05	.01
❑ 43 Keith Jackson	.05	.01
❑ 44 Tommy Vardell	.05	.01
❑ 45 Antonio Langham RC	.10	.02
❑ 46 Derek Brown RBK	.05	.01
❑ 47 John Wojciechowski	.05	.01
❑ 48 Horace Copeland	.05	.01
❑ 49 Luis Sharpe	.05	.01
❑ 50 Pat Harlow	.05	.01
❑ 51 David Palmer RC	.25	.08
❑ 52 Tony Smith RB	.05	.01
❑ 53 Tim Johnson	.05	.01
❑ 54 Anthony Newman	.05	.01
❑ 55 Terry Wooden	.05	.01
❑ 56 Derrick Fenner	.05	.01
❑ 57 Mike Fox	.05	.01
❑ 58 Brad Hopkins	.05	.01
❑ 59 Daryl Johnston UER	.10	.02
❑ 60 Steve Young	.75	.30
❑ 61 Scottie Graham RC	.10	.02
❑ 62 Nolan Harrison	.05	.01
❑ 63 David Richards	.05	.01
❑ 64 Chris Mohr	.05	.01
❑ 65 Hardy Nickerson	.10	.02
❑ 66 Heath Sherman	.05	.01
❑ 67 Irving Fryar	.10	.02
❑ 68 Ray Buchanan UER	.05	.01
❑ 69 Jay Taylor	.05	.01
❑ 70 Shannon Sharpe	.10	.02
❑ 71 Vinny Testaverde	.10	.02
❑ 72 Renaldo Turnbull	.05	.01
❑ 73 Dwight Stone	.05	.01
❑ 74 Willie McGinest RC	.25	.08
❑ 75 Darrell Green	.05	.01
❑ 76 Kyle Clifton	.05	.01
❑ 77 Leo Goeas	.05	.01
❑ 78 Ken Ruettgers	.05	.01
❑ 79 Craig Heyward	.10	.02
❑ 80 Andre Rison	.10	.02
❑ 81 Chris Mims	.05	.01
❑ 82 Gary Clark	.10	.02
❑ 83 Ricardo McDonald	.05	.01
❑ 84 Patrick Hunter	.05	.01
❑ 85 Bruce Matthews	.05	.01
❑ 86 Russell Maryland	.05	.01
❑ 87 Gary Anderson K	.05	.01
❑ 88 Brad Edwards	.05	.01
❑ 89 Carlton Bailey	.05	.01
❑ 90 Qadry Ismail	.25	.08
❑ 91 Terry McDaniel	.05	.01
❑ 92 Willie Green	.05	.01
❑ 93 Cornelius Bennett	.10	.02
❑ 94 Paul Gruber	.05	.01
❑ 95 Pete Stoyanovich	.05	.01
❑ 96 Merton Hanks	.10	.02
❑ 97 Tre Johnson RC	.05	.01
❑ 98 Jonathan Hayes	.05	.01
❑ 99 Jason Elam	.10	.02
❑ 100 Jerome Bettis	.50	.20
❑ 101 Ronnie Lott	.10	.02
❑ 102 Maurice Hurst	.05	.01
❑ 103 Kirk Lowdermilk	.05	.01
❑ 104 Tony Jones T	.05	.01
❑ 105 Steve Beuerlein	.10	.02
❑ 106 Isaac Davis RC	.05	.01
❑ 107 Vaughan Johnson	.05	.01

❑ 108	Terrell Buckley	.05	.01
❑ 109	Pierce Holt	.05	.01
❑ 110	Alonzo Spellman	.05	.01
❑ 111	Patrick Robinson	.05	.01
❑ 112	Cortez Kennedy	.10	.02
❑ 113	Kevin Williams WR	.10	.02
❑ 114	Danny Copeland	.05	.01
❑ 115	Chris Doleman	.05	.01
❑ 116	Jerry Rice LL	.50	.20
❑ 117	Neil Smith LL	.10	.02
❑ 118	Emmitt Smith LL	.75	.30
❑ 119	E.Robinson/Odomes LL	.05	.01
❑ 120	Steve Young LL	.25	.08
❑ 121	Carnell Lake	.05	.01
❑ 122	Ernest Givins UER	.10	.02
❑ 123	Henry Jones	.05	.01
❑ 124	Michael Brooks	.05	.01
❑ 125	Jason Hanson	.05	.01
❑ 126	Andy Harmon	.05	.01
❑ 127	Errict Rhett RC	.25	.08
❑ 128	Harris Barton	.05	.01
❑ 129	Greg Robinson	.05	.01
❑ 130	Derrick Thomas	.25	.08
❑ 131	Keith Kartz	.05	.01
❑ 132	Lincoln Kennedy	.05	.01
❑ 133	Leslie O'Neal	.05	.01
❑ 134	Tim Goad	.05	.01
❑ 135	Rohn Stark	.05	.01
❑ 136	O.J.McDuffie	.25	.08
❑ 137	Donnell Woolford	.05	.01
❑ 138	Jamir Miller RC	.10	.02
❑ 139	Eric Thomas UER	.05	.01
❑ 140	Willie Roaf	.05	.01
❑ 141	Wayne Gandy RC	.05	.01
❑ 142	Mike Brim	.05	.01
❑ 143	Kelvin Martin	.05	.01
❑ 144	Edgar Bennett	.25	.08
❑ 145	Michael Dean Perry	.10	.02
❑ 146	Shante Carver RC	.05	.01
❑ 147	Jessie Armstead UER	.05	.01
❑ 148	Mo Elewonibi	.05	.01
❑ 149	Dana Stubblefield	.10	.02
❑ 150	Cody Carlson	.05	.01
❑ 151	Vencie Glenn	.05	.01
❑ 152	Levon Kirkland	.05	.01
❑ 153	Derrick Moore	.05	.01
❑ 154	John Fina	.05	.01
❑ 155	Jeff Hostetler	.10	.02
❑ 156	Courtney Hawkins	.05	.01
❑ 157	Todd Collins	.05	.01
❑ 158	Neil Smith	.10	.02
❑ 159	Simon Fletcher	.05	.01
❑ 160	Dan Marino	2.00	.75
❑ 161	Sam Adams RC	.10	.02
❑ 162	Marvin Washington	.05	.01
❑ 163	John Copeland	.05	.01
❑ 164	Eugene Robinson	.05	.01
❑ 165	Mark Carrier DB	.05	.01
❑ 166	Mike Kenn	.05	.01
❑ 167	Tyrone Hughes	.10	.02
❑ 168	Darren Carrington	.05	.01
❑ 169	Shane Conlan	.05	.01
❑ 170	Ricky Proehl	.05	.01
❑ 171	Jeff Herrod	.05	.01
❑ 172	Mark Carrier WR	.10	.02
❑ 173	George Koonce	.05	.01
❑ 174	Desmond Howard	.10	.02
❑ 175	Dave Meggett	.05	.01
❑ 176	Charles Haley	.10	.02
❑ 177	Steve Wisniewski	.05	.01
❑ 178	Dermontti Dawson	.05	.01
❑ 179	Tim McDonald	.05	.01
❑ 180	Broderick Thomas	.05	.01
❑ 181	Bernard Dafney	.05	.01
❑ 182	Bo Orlando	.05	.01
❑ 183	Andre Reed	.10	.02
❑ 184	Randall Cunningham	.25	.08
❑ 185	Chris Spielman	.10	.02
❑ 186	Keith Byars	.05	.01
❑ 187	Ben Coates	.10	.02
❑ 188	Tracy Simien	.05	.01
❑ 189	Carl Pickens	.10	.02
❑ 190	Reggie White	.25	.08
❑ 191	Norm Johnson	.05	.01
❑ 192	Brian Washington	.05	.01
❑ 193	Stan Humphries	.10	.02
❑ 194	Fred Stokes	.05	.01
❑ 195	Dan Williams	.05	.01
❑ 196	John Elway TOG	.75	.30
❑ 197	Eric Allen TOG	.05	.01
❑ 198	Hardy Nickerson TOG	.10	.02
❑ 199	Jerome Bettis TOG	.25	.08
❑ 200	Troy Aikman TOG	.50	.20
❑ 201	Thurman Thomas TOG	.10	.02
❑ 202	Cornelius Bennett TOG UER	.10	.02
❑ 203	Michael Irvin TOG	.10	.02
❑ 204	Jim Kelly TOG	.10	.02
❑ 205	Junior Seau TOG	.10	.02
❑ 206	Heath Shuler RC UER	.25	.08
❑ 207	Howard Cross UER	.05	.01
❑ 208	Pat Swilling	.05	.01
❑ 209	Pete Metzelaars	.05	.01
❑ 210	Tony McGee	.05	.01
❑ 211	Neil O'Donnell	.25	.08
❑ 212	Eugene Chung	.05	.01
❑ 213	J.B. Brown	.05	.01
❑ 214	Marcus Allen	.25	.08
❑ 215	Harry Newsome	.05	.01
❑ 216	Greg Hill RC	.25	.08
❑ 217	Ryan Yarborough	.05	.01
❑ 218	Marty Carter	.05	.01
❑ 219	Bern Brostek	.05	.01
❑ 220	Boomer Esiason	.10	.02
❑ 221	Vince Buck	.05	.01
❑ 222	Jim Jeffcoat	.05	.01
❑ 223	Bob Dahl	.05	.01
❑ 224	Marion Butts	.05	.01
❑ 225	Ronald Moore	.05	.01
❑ 226	Robert Blackmon	.05	.01
❑ 227	Curtis Conway	.25	.08
❑ 228	Jon Hand	.05	.01
❑ 229	Shane Dronett	.05	.01
❑ 230	Erik Williams UER	.05	.01
❑ 231	Dennis Brown	.05	.01
❑ 232	Ray Childress	.05	.01
❑ 233	Johnnie Morton RC	.50	.20
❑ 234	Kent Hull	.05	.01
❑ 235	John Elliott	.05	.01
❑ 236	Ron Heller	.05	.01
❑ 237	J.J. Birden	.05	.01
❑ 238	Thomas Randolph RC	.05	.01
❑ 239	Chip Lohmiller	.05	.01
❑ 240	Tim Brown	.25	.08
❑ 241	Steve Tovar	.05	.01
❑ 242	Moe Gardner	.05	.01
❑ 243	Vincent Brown	.05	.01
❑ 244	Tony Zendejas	.05	.01
❑ 245	Eric Allen	.05	.01
❑ 246	Joe King RC	.05	.01
❑ 247	Mo Lewis	.05	.01
❑ 248	Rod Bernstine	.05	.01
❑ 249	Tom Waddle	.05	.01
❑ 250	Junior Seau	.25	.08
❑ 251	Eric Metcalf	.10	.02
❑ 252	Cris Carter	.50	.20
❑ 253	Bill Hitchcock	.05	.01
❑ 254	Zefross Moss	.05	.01
❑ 255	Morten Andersen	.05	.01
❑ 256	Keith Rucker RC	.05	.01
❑ 257	Chris Jacke	.05	.01
❑ 258	Richmond Webb	.05	.01
❑ 259	Herman Moore	.25	.08
❑ 260	Phil Simms	.10	.02
❑ 261	Mark Tuinei	.05	.01
❑ 262	Don Beebe	.05	.01
❑ 263	Marc Logan	.05	.01
❑ 264	Willie Davis	.10	.02
❑ 265	David Klingler	.05	.01
❑ 266	Martin Mayhew UER	.05	.01
❑ 267	Mark Bavaro	.05	.01
❑ 268	Greg Lloyd	.10	.02
❑ 269	Al Del Greco	.05	.01
❑ 270	Reggie Brooks	.10	.02
❑ 271	Greg Townsend	.05	.01
❑ 272	Rohn Stark CAL	.05	.01
❑ 273	Marcus Allen CAL	.10	.02
❑ 274	Ronnie Lott CAL	.10	.02
❑ 275	Dan Marino CAL	.75	.30
❑ 276	Sean Gilbert	.05	.01
❑ 277	LeRoy Butler	.05	.01
❑ 278	Troy Auzenne	.05	.01
❑ 279	Eric Swann	.10	.02
❑ 280	Quentin Coryatt	.05	.01
❑ 281	Anthony Pleasant	.05	.01
❑ 282	Brad Baxter	.05	.01
❑ 283	Carl Lee	.05	.01
❑ 284	Courtney Hall	.05	.01
❑ 285	Quinn Early	.10	.02
❑ 286	Eddie Robinson	.05	.01
❑ 287	Marco Coleman	.05	.01
❑ 288	Harold Green	.05	.01
❑ 289	Santana Dotson	.10	.02
❑ 290	Robert Porcher	.05	.01
❑ 291	Joe Phillips	.05	.01
❑ 292	Mark McMillian	.05	.01
❑ 293	Eric Davis	.05	.01
❑ 294	Mark Jackson	.05	.01
❑ 295	Darryl Talley	.05	.01
❑ 296	Curtis Duncan	.05	.01
❑ 297	Bruce Armstrong	.05	.01
❑ 298	Eric Hill	.05	.01
❑ 299	Andre Collins	.05	.01
❑ 300	Jay Novacek	.10	.02
❑ 301	Roosevelt Potts	.05	.01
❑ 302	Eric Martin	.05	.01
❑ 303	Chris Warren	.10	.02
❑ 304	Deral Boykin RC	.05	.01
❑ 305	Jessie Tuggle	.05	.01
❑ 306	Glyn Milburn	.10	.02
❑ 307	Terry Obee	.05	.01
❑ 308	Eric Turner	.05	.01
❑ 309	Dewayne Washington RC	.10	.02
❑ 310	Sterling Sharpe	.10	.02
❑ 311	Jeff Gossett	.05	.01
❑ 312	John Carney	.05	.01
❑ 313	Aaron Glenn RC	.25	.08
❑ 314	Nick Lowery	.05	.01
❑ 315	Thurman Thomas	.25	.08
❑ 316	Troy Aikman MG	.50	.20
❑ 317	Thurman Thomas MG	.10	.02
❑ 318	Michael Irvin MG	.10	.02
❑ 319	Steve Beuerlein MG	.10	.02
❑ 320	Jerry Rice	1.00	.40
❑ 321	Alexander Wright	.05	.01
❑ 322	Michael Bates	.05	.01
❑ 323	Greg Davis	.05	.01
❑ 324	Mark Bortz	.05	.01
❑ 325	Kevin Greene	.10	.02
❑ 326	Wayne Simmons	.05	.01
❑ 327	Wayne Martin	.05	.01
❑ 328	Michael Irvin UER	.25	.08
❑ 329	Checklist Card	.05	.01
❑ 330	Checklist Card	.05	.01
❑ 331	Doug Pelfrey	.05	.01
❑ 332	Myron Guyton	.05	.01
❑ 333	Howard Ballard	.05	.01
❑ 334	Ricky Ervins	.05	.01
❑ 335	Steve Emtman	.05	.01
❑ 336	Eric Curry	.05	.01
❑ 337	Bert Emanuel RC	.25	.08
❑ 338	Darryl Ashmore	.05	.01
❑ 339	Stevon Moore	.05	.01
❑ 340	Garrison Hearst	.25	.08
❑ 341	Vance Johnson	.05	.01
❑ 342	Anthony Johnson	.10	.02
❑ 343	Merril Hoge	.05	.01
❑ 344	William Thomas	.05	.01
❑ 345	Scott Mitchell	.10	.02
❑ 346	Jim Everett	.10	.02
❑ 347	Ray Crockett	.05	.01
❑ 348	Bryan Cox	.05	.01
❑ 349	Charles Johnson RC	.25	.08
❑ 350	Randall McDaniel	.05	.01
❑ 351	Micheal Barrow	.05	.01
❑ 352	Darrell Thompson	.05	.01
❑ 353	Kevin Gogan	.05	.01
❑ 354	Brad Daluiso	.05	.01
❑ 355	Mark Collins	.05	.01
❑ 356	Bryant Young RC	.25	.08
❑ 357	Steve Christie	.05	.01
❑ 358	Derek Kennard	.05	.01
❑ 359	Jon Vaughn	.05	.01
❑ 360	Drew Bledsoe 3X	.75	.30
❑ 361	Randy Baldwin	.05	.01
❑ 362	Kevin Ross	.05	.01
❑ 363	Reuben Davis	.05	.01
❑ 364	Chris Miller	.05	.01
❑ 365	Tim McGee	.05	.01
❑ 366	Tony Woods	.05	.01
❑ 367	Dean Biasucci	.05	.01
❑ 368	George Jamison	.05	.01

❑	369	Lorenzo Lynch	.05	.01
❑	370	Johnny Johnson	.05	.01
❑	371	Greg Kragen	.05	.01
❑	372	Vinson Smith	.05	.01
❑	373	Vince Workman	.05	.01
❑	374	Allen Aldridge	.05	.01
❑	375	Terry Kirby	.25	.08
❑	376	Mario Bates RC	.25	.08
❑	377	Dixon Edwards	.05	.01
❑	378	Leon Searcy	.05	.01
❑	379	Eric Guliford RC	.05	.01
❑	380	Gary Brown	.05	.01
❑	381	Phil Hansen	.05	.01
❑	382	Keith Hamilton	.05	.01
❑	383	John Alt	.05	.01
❑	384	John Taylor	.10	.02
❑	385	Reggie Cobb	.05	.01
❑	386	Rob Fredrickson RC	.10	.02
❑	387	Pepper Johnson	.05	.01
❑	388	Kevin Lee RC	.05	.01
❑	389	Stanley Richard	.05	.01
❑	390	Jackie Slater	.05	.01
❑	391	Darrick Brilz	.05	.01
❑	392	John Gesek	.05	.01
❑	393	Kelvin Pritchett	.05	.01
❑	394	Aeneas Williams	.05	.01
❑	395	Henry Ford	.05	.01
❑	396	Eric Mahlum	.05	.01
❑	397	Tom Rouen	.05	.01
❑	398	Vinnie Clark	.05	.01
❑	399	Jim Sweeney	.05	.01
❑	400	Troy Aikman	1.00	.40
❑	401	Toi Cook	.05	.01
❑	402	Dan Saleaumua	.05	.01
❑	403	Andy Heck	.05	.01
❑	404	Deon Figures	.05	.01
❑	405	Henry Thomas	.05	.01
❑	406	Glenn Montgomery	.05	.01
❑	407	Trent Dilfer RC	1.00	.40
❑	408	Eddie Murray	.05	.01
❑	409	Gene Atkins	.05	.01
❑	410	Mike Sherrard	.05	.01
❑	411	Don Mosebar	.05	.01
❑	412	Thomas Smith	.05	.01
❑	413	Ken Norton Jr.	.10	.02
❑	414	Robert Brooks	.25	.08
❑	415	Jeff Lageman	.05	.01
❑	416	Tony Siragusa	.05	.01
❑	417	Brian Blades	.10	.02
❑	418	Matt Stover	.05	.01
❑	419	Jesse Solomon	.05	.01
❑	420	Reggie Roby	.05	.01
❑	421	Shawn Jefferson	.05	.01
❑	422	Marc Boutte	.05	.01
❑	423	William White	.05	.01
❑	424	Clyde Simmons	.05	.01
❑	425	Anthony Miller	.10	.02
❑	426	Brent Jones	.10	.02
❑	427	Tim Grunhard	.05	.01
❑	428	Alfred Williams	.05	.01
❑	429	Roy Barker RC	.05	.01
❑	430	Dante Jones	.05	.01
❑	431	Leroy Thompson	.05	.01
❑	432	Marcus Robertson	.05	.01
❑	433	Thomas Lewis RC	.10	.02
❑	434	Sean Jones	.05	.01
❑	435	Michael Haynes	.10	.02
❑	436	Albert Lewis	.05	.01
❑	437	Tim Bowens RC	.10	.02
❑	438	Marvcus Patton	.05	.01
❑	439	Rich Miano	.05	.01
❑	440	Craig Erickson	.05	.01
❑	441	Larry Allen RC	.25	.08
❑	442	Fernando Smith	.05	.01
❑	443	D.J. Johnson	.05	.01
❑	444	Leonard Russell	.05	.01
❑	445	Marshall Faulk RC	5.00	2.00
❑	446	Najee Mustafaa	.05	.01
❑	447	Brian Hansen	.05	.01
❑	448	Isaac Bruce RC	4.00	2.00
❑	449	Kevin Scott	.05	.01
❑	450	Natrone Means UER	.25	.08
❑	451	Tracy Rogers RC	.05	.01
❑	452	Mike Croel	.05	.01
❑	453	Anthony Edwards	.05	.01
❑	454	Brentson Buckner RC	.05	.01
❑	455	Tom Carter	.05	.01
❑	456	Burt Grossman	.05	.01
❑	457	Jimmy Spencer RC	.05	.01
❑	458	Rocket Ismail	.10	.02
❑	459	Fred Strickland	.05	.01
❑	460	Jeff Burris RC	.10	.02
❑	461	Adrian Hardy	.05	.01
❑	462	Lamar McGriggs	.05	.01
❑	463	Webster Slaughter	.05	.01
❑	464	Demetrius DuBose	.05	.01
❑	465	Dave Brown	.10	.02
❑	466	Kenneth Gant	.05	.01
❑	467	Erik Kramer	.10	.02
❑	468	Mark Ingram	.05	.01
❑	469	Roman Phifer	.05	.01
❑	470	Steve Young	.50	.20
❑	471	Nick Lowery	.05	.01
❑	472	Irving Fryar	.10	.02
❑	473	Art Monk	.10	.02
❑	474	Mel Gray	.05	.01
❑	475	Reggie White	.25	.08
❑	476	Eric Ball	.05	.01
❑	477	Dwayne Harper	.05	.01
❑	478	Will Shields	.05	.01
❑	479	Roger Harper	.05	.01
❑	480	Rick Mirer	.25	.08
❑	481	Vincent Brisby	.10	.02
❑	482	John Jurkovic RC	.10	.02
❑	483	Michael Jackson	.10	.02
❑	484	Ed Cunningham	.05	.01
❑	485	Brad Ottis	.05	.01
❑	486	Sterling Palmer RC	.05	.01
❑	487	Tony Bennett	.05	.01
❑	488	Mike Pritchard	.05	.01
❑	489	Bucky Brooks RC	.05	.01
❑	490	Troy Vincent	.05	.01
❑	491	Eric Green	.05	.01
❑	492	Van Malone	.05	.01
❑	493	Marcus Spears RC	.05	.01
❑	494	Brian Williams OL	.05	.01
❑	495	Robert Smith	.25	.08
❑	496	Haywood Jeffires	.10	.02
❑	497	Darrin Smith	.05	.01
❑	498	Tommy Barnhardt	.05	.01
❑	499	Anthony Smith	.05	.01
❑	500	Ricky Watters	.10	.02
❑	501	Antone Davis	.05	.01
❑	502	David Braxton	.05	.01
❑	503	Donnell Bennett RC	.25	.08
❑	504	Donald Evans	.05	.01
❑	505	Lewis Tillman	.05	.01
❑	506	Lance Smith	.05	.01
❑	507	Aaron Taylor	.05	.01
❑	508	Ricky Sanders	.05	.01
❑	509	Dennis Smith	.05	.01
❑	510	Barry Foster	.05	.01
❑	511	Stan Brock	.05	.01
❑	512	Henry Rolling	.05	.01
❑	513	Walter Reeves	.05	.01
❑	514	John Booty	.05	.01
❑	515	Kenneth Davis	.05	.01
❑	516	Cris Dishman	.05	.01
❑	517	Bill Lewis	.05	.01
❑	518	Jeff Bryant	.05	.01
❑	519	Brian Mitchell	.05	.01
❑	520	Joe Montana	2.00	.75
❑	521	Keith Sims	.05	.01
❑	522	Harry Colon	.05	.01
❑	523	Leon Lett	.05	.01
❑	524	Carlos Jenkins	.05	.01
❑	525	Victor Bailey	.05	.01
❑	526	Harvey Williams	.10	.02
❑	527	Irv Smith	.05	.01
❑	528	Jason Sehorn RC	.40	.15
❑	529	John Thierry RC	.05	.01
❑	530	Brett Favre	2.00	.75
❑	531	Sean Dawkins RC	.25	.08
❑	532	Erric Pegram	.05	.01
❑	533	Jimmy Williams	.05	.01
❑	534	Michael Timpson	.05	.01
❑	535	Flipper Anderson	.05	.01
❑	536	John Parrella	.05	.01
❑	537	Freddie Joe Nunn	.05	.01
❑	538	Doug Dawson	.05	.01
❑	539	Michael Stewart	.05	.01
❑	540	John Elway	2.00	.75
❑	541	Ronnie Lott	.10	.02
❑	542	Barry Sanders TOG	.75	.30
❑	543	Andre Reed TOG	.10	.02
❑	544	Deion Sanders TOG	.25	.08
❑	545	Dan Marino TOG	.75	.30
❑	546	Carlton Bailey TOG	.05	.01
❑	547	Emmitt Smith TOG	.75	.30
❑	548	Alvin Harper TOG	.10	.02
❑	549	Eric Metcalf TOG	.10	.02
❑	550	Jerry Rice TOG	.50	.20
❑	551	Derrick Thomas TOG	.25	.08
❑	552	Mark Collins TOG	.05	.01
❑	553	Eric Turner TOG	.05	.01
❑	554	Sterling Sharpe TOG	.10	.02
❑	555	Steve Young TOG	.25	.08
❑	556	Darnay Scott RC	.50	.20
❑	557	Joel Steed	.05	.01
❑	558	Dennis Gibson	.05	.01
❑	559	Charles Mincy	.05	.01
❑	560	Rickey Jackson	.05	.01
❑	561	Dave Cadigan	.05	.01
❑	562	Rick Tuten	.05	.01
❑	563	Mike Caldwell	.05	.01
❑	564	Todd Steussie RC	.10	.02
❑	565	Kevin Smith	.05	.01
❑	566	Arthur Marshall	.05	.01
❑	567	Aaron Wallace	.05	.01
❑	568	Calvin Williams	.10	.02
❑	569	Todd Kelly	.05	.01
❑	570	Barry Sanders	1.50	.60
❑	571	Shaun Gayle	.05	.01
❑	572	Will Wolford	.05	.01
❑	573	Ethan Horton	.05	.01
❑	574	Chris Slade	.05	.01
❑	575	Jeff Wright	.05	.01
❑	576	Toby Wright	.05	.01
❑	577	Lamar Thomas	.05	.01
❑	578	Chris Singleton	.05	.01
❑	579	Ed West	.05	.01
❑	580	Jeff George	.25	.08
❑	581	Kevin Mitchell	.05	.01
❑	582	Chad Brown	.05	.01
❑	583	Rich Camarillo	.05	.01
❑	584	Gary Zimmerman	.05	.01
❑	585	Randal Hill	.05	.01
❑	586	Keith Cash	.05	.01
❑	587	Sam Mills	.05	.01
❑	588	Shawn Lee	.05	.01
❑	589	Kent Graham	.10	.02
❑	590	Steve Everitt	.05	.01
❑	591	Rob Moore	.10	.02
❑	592	Kevin Mawae RC	.25	.08
❑	593	Jerry Ball	.05	.01
❑	594	Larry Brown DB	.05	.01
❑	595	Tim Krumrie	.05	.01
❑	596	Aubrey Beavers RC	.05	.01
❑	597	Chris Hinton	.05	.01
❑	598	Greg Montgomery	.05	.01
❑	599	Jimmie Jones	.05	.01
❑	600	Jim Kelly	.25	.08
❑	601	Joe Johnson RC	.05	.01
❑	602	Tim Irwin	.05	.01
❑	603	Steve Jackson	.05	.01
❑	604	James Williams RC LB	.05	.01
❑	605	Blair Thomas	.05	.01
❑	606	Danan Hughes	.05	.01
❑	607	Russell Freeman	.05	.01
❑	608	Andre Hastings	.10	.02
❑	609	Ken Harvey	.05	.01
❑	610	Jim Harbaugh	.25	.08
❑	611	Emmitt Smith MG	.75	.30
❑	612	Andre Rison MG	.10	.02
❑	613	Steve Young MG	.25	.08
❑	614	Anthony Miller MG	.05	.01
❑	615	Barry Sanders MG	.75	.30
❑	616	Bernie Kosar	.10	.02
❑	617	Chris Gardocki	.05	.01
❑	618	William Floyd RC	.25	.08
❑	619	Matt Brock	.05	.01
❑	620	Dan Wilkinson RC	.10	.02
❑	621	Tony Meola RC	.10	.02
❑	622	Tony Tolbert	.05	.01
❑	623	Mike Zandofsky	.05	.01
❑	624	William Fuller	.05	.01
❑	625	Steve Jordan	.05	.01
❑	626	Mike Johnson	.05	.01
❑	627	Ferrell Edmunds	.05	.01
❑	628	Gene Williams	.05	.01
❑	629	Willie Beamon	.05	.01

❑ 630	Gerald Perry	.05	.01
❑ 631	John Baylor	.05	.01
❑ 632	Carwell Gardner	.05	.01
❑ 633	Thomas Everett	.05	.01
❑ 634	Lamar Lathon	.05	.01
❑ 635	Michael Bankston	.05	.01
❑ 636	Ray Crittenden RC	.05	.01
❑ 637	Kimble Anders	.10	.02
❑ 638	Robert Delpino	.05	.01
❑ 639	Darren Perry	.05	.01
❑ 640	Byron Evans	.05	.01
❑ 641	Mark Higgs	.05	.01
❑ 642	Lorenzo Neal	.05	.01
❑ 643	Henry Ellard	.10	.02
❑ 644	Trace Armstrong	.05	.01
❑ 645	Greg McMurtry	.05	.01
❑ 646	Steve McMichael	.10	.02
❑ 647	Terance Mathis	.10	.02
❑ 648	Eric Bieniemy	.05	.01
❑ 649	Bobby Houston	.05	.01
❑ 650	Alvin Harper	.10	.02
❑ 651	James Folston RC	.05	.01
❑ 652	Mel Gray	.05	.01
❑ 653	Adrian Cooper	.05	.01
❑ 654	Dexter Carter	.05	.01
❑ 655	Don Griffin	.05	.01
❑ 656	Corey Widmer	.05	.01
❑ 657	Lee Johnson	.05	.01
❑ 658	Nate Odomes	.05	.01
❑ 659	Checklist Card	.05	.01
❑ 660	Checklist Card	.05	.01
❑ P1	Promo Sheet	4.00	1.50
❑ P2	Promo Sheet Special Effects	4.00	1.50

1995 Topps

❑	COMPLETE SET (468)	40.00	15.00
❑	COMP.FACT.SET (478)	50.00	25.00
❑	COMP.SERIES 1 (248)	20.00	7.50
❑	COMP.SERIES 2 (220)	20.00	7.50
❑ 1	Barry Sanders TYC	.75	.30
❑ 2	Chris Warren TYC	.20	.07
❑ 3	Jerry Rice TYC	.50	.20
❑ 4	Emmitt Smith TYC	.75	.30
❑ 5	Henry Ellard TYC	.20	.07
❑ 6	Natrone Means TYC	.20	.07
❑ 7	Terance Mathis TYC	.20	.07
❑ 8	Tim Brown TYC	.20	.07
❑ 9	Andre Reed TYC	.20	.07
❑ 10	Marshall Faulk TYC	.60	.25
❑ 11	Irving Fryar TYC	.20	.07
❑ 12	Cris Carter TYC	.30	.10
❑ 13	Michael Irvin TYC	.30	.10
❑ 14	Jake Reed TYC	.20	.07
❑ 15	Ben Coates TYC	.20	.07
❑ 16	Herman Moore TYC	.30	.10
❑ 17	Carl Pickens TYC	.20	.07
❑ 18	Fred Barnett TYC	.20	.07
❑ 19	Sterling Sharpe TYC	.20	.07
❑ 20	Anthony Miller TYC	.20	.07
❑ 21	Thurman Thomas TYC	.30	.10
❑ 22	Andre Rison TYC	.20	.07
❑ 23	Brian Blades TYC	.20	.07
❑ 24	Rodney Hampton TYC	.20	.07
❑ 25	Terry Allen TYC	.20	.07
❑ 26	Jerome Bettis TYC	.30	.10
❑ 27	Errict Rhett TYC	.20	.07
❑ 28	Rob Moore TYC	.20	.07
❑ 29	Shannon Sharpe TYC	.20	.07
❑ 30	Drew Bledsoe TYC	.30	.10
❑ 31	Dan Marino TYC	1.00	.40
❑ 32	Warren Moon TYC	.20	.07
❑ 33	Steve Young TYC	.40	.15
❑ 34	Brett Favre TYC	1.00	.40
❑ 35	Jim Everett TYC	.10	.02
❑ 36	Jeff George TYC	.20	.07
❑ 37	John Elway TYC	1.00	.40
❑ 38	Jeff Hostetler TYC	.20	.07
❑ 39	Randall Cunningham TYC	.30	.10
❑ 40	Stan Humphries TYC	.20	.07
❑ 41	Jim Kelly TYC	.30	.10
❑ 42	Tommy Barnhardt	.10	.02
❑ 43	Bob Whitfield	.10	.02
❑ 44	William Thomas	.10	.02
❑ 45	Glyn Milburn	.10	.02
❑ 46	Steve Christie	.10	.02
❑ 47	Kevin Mawae	.10	.02
❑ 48	Vencie Glenn	.10	.02
❑ 49	Eric Curry	.10	.02
❑ 50	Jeff Hostetler	.20	.07
❑ 51	Tyronne Stowe	.10	.02
❑ 52	Steve Jackson	.10	.02
❑ 53	Ben Coleman	.10	.02
❑ 54	Brad Baxter	.10	.02
❑ 55	Darryl Williams	.10	.02
❑ 56	Troy Drayton	.10	.02
❑ 57	George Teague	.10	.02
❑ 58	Calvin Williams	.20	.07
❑ 59	Jeff Cross	.10	.02
❑ 60	Leroy Hoard	.10	.02
❑ 61	John Carney	.10	.02
❑ 62	Daryl Johnston	.20	.07
❑ 63	Jim Jeffcoat	.10	.02
❑ 64	Matt Stover	.10	.02
❑ 65	LeRoy Butler	.10	.02
❑ 66	Curtis Conway	.30	.10
❑ 67	O.J. McDuffie	.30	.10
❑ 68	Robert Massey	.10	.02
❑ 69	Ed McDaniel	.10	.02
❑ 70	William Floyd	.20	.07
❑ 71	Willie Davis	.20	.07
❑ 72	William Roberts	.10	.02
❑ 73	Chester McGlockton	.20	.07
❑ 74	D.J. Johnson	.10	.02
❑ 75	Rondell Jones	.10	.02
❑ 76	Morten Andersen	.10	.02
❑ 77	Glenn Parker	.10	.02
❑ 78	William Fuller	.10	.02
❑ 79	Ray Buchanan	.10	.02
❑ 80	Maurice Hurst	.10	.02
❑ 81	Wayne Gandy	.10	.02
❑ 82	Marcus Turner	.10	.02
❑ 83	Greg Davis	.10	.02
❑ 84	Terry Wooden	.10	.02
❑ 85	Thomas Everett	.10	.02
❑ 86	Steve Broussard	.10	.02
❑ 87	Tom Carter	.10	.02
❑ 88	Glenn Montgomery	.10	.02
❑ 89	Larry Allen	.20	.07
❑ 90	Donnell Woolford	.10	.02
❑ 91	John Alt	.10	.02
❑ 92	Phil Hansen	.10	.02
❑ 93	Seth Joyner	.10	.02
❑ 94	Michael Brooks	.10	.02
❑ 95	Randall McDaniel	.10	.02
❑ 96	Tydus Winans	.10	.02
❑ 97	Rob Fredrickson	.10	.02
❑ 98	Ray Crockett	.10	.02
❑ 99	Courtney Hall	.10	.02
❑ 100	Merton Hanks	.10	.02
❑ 101	Aaron Glenn	.10	.02
❑ 102	Roosevelt Potts	.10	.02
❑ 103	Leon Lett	.10	.02
❑ 104	Jessie Tuggle	.10	.02
❑ 105	Martin Mayhew	.10	.02
❑ 106	Willie Roaf	.10	.02
❑ 107	Todd Lyght	.10	.02
❑ 108	Ernest Givins	.10	.02
❑ 109	Tony McGee	.10	.02
❑ 110	Barry Sanders	1.50	.60
❑ 111	Dermontti Dawson	.20	.07
❑ 112	Rick Tuten	.10	.02
❑ 113	Vincent Brisby	.10	.02
❑ 114	Charlie Garner	.30	.10
❑ 115	Irving Fryar	.20	.07
❑ 116	Stevon Moore	.10	.02
❑ 117	Matt Darby	.10	.02
❑ 118	Howard Cross	.10	.02
❑ 119	John Gesek	.10	.02
❑ 120	Jack Del Rio	.10	.02
❑ 121	Marcus Allen	.30	.10
❑ 122	Torrance Small	.10	.02
❑ 123	Chris Mims	.10	.02
❑ 124	Don Mosebar	.10	.02
❑ 125	Carl Pickens	.20	.07
❑ 126	Tom Rouen	.10	.02
❑ 127	Garrison Hearst	.30	.10
❑ 128	Charles Johnson	.20	.07
❑ 129	Derek Brown RBK	.10	.02
❑ 130	Troy Aikman	1.00	.40
❑ 131	Troy Vincent	.10	.02
❑ 132	Ken Ruettgers	.10	.02
❑ 133	Michael Jackson	.20	.07
❑ 134	Dennis Gibson	.10	.02
❑ 135	Brett Perriman	.20	.07
❑ 136	Jeff Graham	.10	.02
❑ 137	Chad Brown	.20	.07
❑ 138	Ken Norton Jr.	.20	.07
❑ 139	Chris Slade	.10	.02
❑ 140	Dave Brown	.20	.07
❑ 141	Bert Emanuel	.30	.10
❑ 142	Renaldo Turnbull	.10	.02
❑ 143	Jim Harbaugh	.20	.07
❑ 144	Micheal Barrow	.10	.02
❑ 145	Vincent Brown	.10	.02
❑ 146	Bryant Young	.20	.07
❑ 147	Boomer Esiason	.20	.07
❑ 148	Sean Gilbert	.20	.07
❑ 149	Greg Truitt	.10	.02
❑ 150	Rod Woodson	.20	.07
❑ 151	Robert Porcher	.10	.02
❑ 152	Joe Phillips	.10	.02
❑ 153	Gary Zimmerman	.10	.02
❑ 154	Bruce Smith	.30	.10
❑ 155	Randall Cunningham	.30	.10
❑ 156	Fred Strickland	.10	.02
❑ 157	Derrick Alexander WR	.30	.10
❑ 158	James Williams LB	.10	.02
❑ 159	Scott Dill	.10	.02
❑ 160	Tim Bowens	.10	.02
❑ 161	Floyd Turner	.10	.02
❑ 162	Ronnie Harmon	.10	.02
❑ 163	Wayne Martin	.10	.02
❑ 164	John Randle	.20	.07
❑ 165	Larry Centers	.20	.07
❑ 166	Larry Brown DB	.10	.02
❑ 167	Albert Lewis	.10	.02
❑ 168	Michael Strahan	.30	.10
❑ 169	Reggie Brooks	.20	.07
❑ 170	Craig Heyward	.20	.07
❑ 171	Pat Harlow	.10	.02
❑ 172	Eugene Robinson	.10	.02
❑ 173	Shane Conlan	.10	.02
❑ 174	Bennie Blades	.10	.02
❑ 175	Neil O'Donnell	.20	.07
❑ 176	Steve Tovar	.10	.02
❑ 177	Donald Evans	.10	.02
❑ 178	Brent Jones	.10	.02
❑ 179	Ray Childress	.10	.02
❑ 180	Reggie White	.30	.10
❑ 181	David Alexander	.10	.02
❑ 182	Greg Hill	.20	.07
❑ 183	Vinny Testaverde	.20	.07
❑ 184	Jeff Burris	.10	.02
❑ 185	Hardy Nickerson	.10	.02
❑ 186	Terry Kirby	.20	.07
❑ 187	Kirk Lowdermilk	.10	.02
❑ 188	Eric Swann	.20	.07
❑ 189	Chris Zorich	.10	.02
❑ 190	Simon Fletcher	.10	.02
❑ 191	Qadry Ismail	.20	.07
❑ 192	Heath Shuler	.20	.07
❑ 193	Michael Haynes	.20	.07
❑ 194	Mike Sherrard	.10	.02
❑ 195	Nolan Harrison	.10	.02
❑ 196	Marcus Robertson	.10	.02
❑ 197	Kevin Williams WR	.20	.07
❑ 198	Moe Gardner	.10	.02
❑ 199	Rick Mirer	.20	.07
❑ 200	Junior Seau	.30	.10
❑ 201	Byron Bam Morris	.10	.02
❑ 202	Willie McGinest	.20	.07
❑ 203	Chris Spielman	.20	.07
❑ 204	Darnay Scott	.20	.07

205	Jesse Sapolu	.10	.02
206	Marvin Washington	.10	.02
207	Anthony Newman	.10	.02
208	Cortez Kennedy	.20	.07
209	Quentin Coryatt	.20	.07
210	Neil Smith	.20	.07
211	Keith Sims	.10	.02
212	Sean Jones	.10	.02
213	Tony Jones T	.10	.02
214	Lewis Tillman	.10	.02
215	Darren Woodson	.20	.07
216	Jason Hanson	.10	.02
217	John Taylor	.10	.02
218	Shawn Lee	.10	.02
219	Kevin Greene	.20	.07
220	Jerry Rice	1.00	.40
221	Ki-Jana Carter RC	.30	.10
222	Tony Boselli RC	.30	.10
223	Michael Westbrook RC	.30	.10
224	Kerry Collins RC	1.25	.50
225	Kevin Carter RC	.30	.10
226	Kyle Brady RC	.30	.10
227	J.J. Stokes RC	.30	.10
228	Derrick Alexander DE RC	.10	.02
229	Warren Sapp RC	1.50	.60
230	Ruben Brown RC	.30	.10
231	Hugh Douglas RC	.30	.10
232	Luther Elliss RC	.10	.02
233	Rashaan Salaam RC	.20	.07
234	Tyrone Poole RC	.30	.10
235	Korey Stringer RC	.20	.07
236	Devin Bush RC	.10	.02
237	Cory Raymer RC	.10	.02
238	Zach Wiegert RC	.10	.02
239	Ron Davis RC	.10	.02
240	Todd Collins RC	.20	.07
241	Bobby Taylor RC	.30	.10
242	Patrick Riley RC	.10	.02
243	Scott Gragg	.10	.02
244	Marvcus Patton	.10	.02
245	Alvin Harper	.10	.02
246	Ricky Watters	.20	.07
247	Checklist 1	.10	.02
248	Checklist 2	.10	.02
249	Terance Mathis	.20	.07
250	Mark Carrier DB	.10	.02
251	Elijah Alexander	.10	.02
252	George Koonce	.10	.02
253	Tony Bennett	.10	.02
254	Steve Wisniewski	.10	.02
255	Bernie Parmalee	.20	.07
256	Dwayne Sabb	.10	.02
257	Lorenzo Neal	.10	.02
258	Corey Miller	.10	.02
259	Fred Barnett	.20	.07
260	Greg Lloyd	.20	.07
261	Robert Blackmon	.10	.02
262	Ken Harvey	.10	.02
263	Eric Hill	.10	.02
264	Russell Copeland	.10	.02
265	Jeff Blake RC	.75	.30
266	Carl Banks	.10	.02
267	Jay Novacek	.20	.07
268	Mel Gray	.10	.02
269	Kimble Anders	.20	.07
270	Cris Carter	.30	.10
271	Johnny Mitchell	.10	.02
272	Shawn Jefferson	.10	.02
273	Doug Brien	.10	.02
274	Sean Landeta	.10	.02
275	Scott Mitchell	.20	.07
276	Charles Wilson	.10	.02
277	Anthony Smith	.10	.02
278	Anthony Miller	.20	.07
279	Steve Walsh	.10	.02
280	Drew Bledsoe	.60	.25
281	Jamir Miller	.10	.02
282	Robert Brooks	.30	.10
283	Sean Lumpkin	.10	.02
284	Bryan Cox	.10	.02
285	Byron Evans	.10	.02
286	Chris Doleman	.10	.02
287	Anthony Pleasant	.10	.02
288	Stephen Grant RC	.10	.02
289	Doug Riesenberg	.10	.02
290	Natrone Means	.20	.07
291	Henry Thomas	.10	.02
292	Mike Pritchard	.10	.02
293	Courtney Hawkins	.10	.02
294	Bill Bates	.20	.07
295	Jerome Bettis	.30	.10
296	Russell Maryland	.10	.02
297	Stanley Richard	.10	.02
298	William White	.10	.02
299	Dan Wilkinson	.20	.07
300	Steve Young	.75	.30
301	Gary Brown	.10	.02
302	Jake Reed	.20	.07
303	Carlton Gray	.10	.02
304	Levon Kirkland	.10	.02
305	Shannon Sharpe	.20	.07
306	Luis Sharpe	.10	.02
307	Marshall Faulk	1.25	.50
308	Stan Humphries	.20	.07
309	Chris Calloway	.10	.02
310	Tim Brown	.30	.10
311	Steve Everitt	.10	.02
312	Raymont Harris	.10	.02
313	Tim McDonald	.10	.02
314	Trent Dilfer	.30	.10
315	Jim Everett	.10	.02
316	Ray Crittenden	.10	.02
317	Jim Kelly	.30	.10
318	Andre Reed	.20	.07
319	Chris Miller	.10	.02
320	Bobby Houston	.10	.02
321	Charles Haley	.20	.07
322	James Francis	.10	.02
323	Bernard Williams	.10	.02
324	Michael Bates	.10	.02
325	Brian Mitchell	.10	.02
326	Mike Johnson	.10	.02
327	Eric Bieniemy	.10	.02
328	Aubrey Beavers	.10	.02
329	Dale Carter	.20	.07
330	Emmitt Smith	1.50	.60
331	Darren Perry	.10	.02
332	Marquez Pope	.10	.02
333	Clyde Simmons	.10	.02
334	Corey Croom	.10	.02
335	Thomas Randolph	.10	.02
336	Harvey Williams	.10	.02
337	Michael Timpson	.10	.02
338	Eugene Daniel	.10	.02
339	Shane Dronett	.10	.02
340	Eric Turner	.10	.02
341	Eric Metcalf	.20	.07
342	Leslie O'Neal	.20	.07
343	Mark Wheeler	.10	.02
344	Mark Pike	.10	.02
345	Brett Favre	2.00	.75
346	Johnny Bailey	.10	.02
347	Henry Ellard	.20	.07
348	Chris Gardocki	.10	.02
349	Henry Jones	.10	.02
350	Dan Marino	2.00	.75
351	Lake Dawson	.20	.07
352	Mark McMillian	.10	.02
353	Deion Sanders	.60	.25
354	Antonio London	.10	.02
355	Cris Dishman	.10	.02
356	Ricardo McDonald	.10	.02
357	Dexter Carter	.10	.02
358	Kevin Smith	.10	.02
359	Yancey Thigpen RC	.20	.07
360	Chris Warren	.20	.07
361	Quinn Early	.20	.07
362	John Mangum	.10	.02
363	Santana Dotson	.10	.02
364	Rocket Ismail	.20	.07
365	Aeneas Williams	.10	.02
366	Dan Williams	.10	.02
367	Sean Dawkins	.20	.07
368	Pepper Johnson	.10	.02
369	Roman Phifer	.10	.02
370	Rodney Hampton	.20	.07
371	Darrell Green	.10	.02
372	Michael Zordich	.10	.02
373	Andre Coleman	.10	.02
374	Wayne Simmons	.10	.02
375	Michael Irvin	.30	.10
376	Clay Matthews	.20	.07
377	Dewayne Washington	.20	.07
378	Keith Byars	.10	.02
379	Todd Collins LB	.30	.10
380	Mark Collins	.10	.02
381	Joel Steed	.10	.02
382	Bart Oates	.10	.02
383	Al Smith	.10	.02
384	Rafael Robinson	.10	.02
385	Mo Lewis	.10	.02
386	Aubrey Matthews	.10	.02
387	Corey Sawyer	.10	.02
388	Bucky Brooks	.10	.02
389	Erik Kramer	.10	.02
390	Tyrone Hughes	.20	.07
391	Terry McDaniel	.10	.02
392	Craig Erickson	.10	.02
393	Mike Flores	.10	.02
394	Harry Swayne	.10	.02
395	Irving Spikes	.20	.07
396	Lorenzo Lynch	.10	.02
397	Antonio Langham	.10	.02
398	Edgar Bennett	.20	.07
399	Thomas Lewis	.20	.07
400	John Elway	2.00	.75
401	Jeff George	.20	.07
402	Errict Rhett	.20	.07
403	Bill Romanowski	.10	.02
404	Alexander Wright	.10	.02
405	Warren Moon	.20	.07
406	Eddie Robinson	.10	.02
407	John Copeland	.10	.02
408	Robert Jones	.10	.02
409	Steve Bono	.20	.07
410	Cornelius Bennett	.20	.07
411	Ben Coates	.20	.07
412	Dana Stubblefield	.20	.07
413	Darryl Talley	.10	.02
414	Brian Blades	.20	.07
415	Herman Moore	.30	.10
416	Nick Lowery	.10	.02
417	Donnell Bennett	.20	.07
418	Van Malone	.10	.02
419	Pete Stoyanovich	.10	.02
420	Joe Montana	2.00	.75
421	Steve Young	.50	.20
422	Steve Young	.50	.20
423	Steve Young	.50	.20
424	Steve Young	.50	.20
425	Steve Young	.50	.20
426	Rod Stephens	.10	.02
427	Ellis Johnson RC UER	.10	.02
428	Kordell Stewart RC	1.25	.50
429	James O. Stewart RC	1.00	.40
430	Steve McNair RC	2.50	1.00
431	Brian DeMarco	.20	.07
432	Matt O'Dwyer	.10	.02
433	Lorenzo Styles RC	.10	.02
434	Anthony Cook RC	.10	.02
435	Jesse James	.10	.02
436	Darryl Pounds RC	.10	.02
437	Derrick Graham	.10	.02
438	Vernon Turner	.10	.02
439	Carlton Bailey	.10	.02
440	Darion Conner	.10	.02
441	Randy Baldwin	.10	.02
442	Tim McKyer	.10	.02
443	Sam Mills	.20	.07
444	Bob Christian	.10	.02
445	Steve Lofton	.10	.02
446	Lamar Lathon	.10	.02
447	Tony Smith RB	.10	.02
448	Don Beebe	.10	.02
449	Barry Foster	.20	.07
450	Frank Reich	.10	.02
451	Pete Metzelaars	.10	.02
452	Reggie Cobb	.10	.02
453	Jeff Lageman	.10	.02
454	Derek Brown TE	.10	.02
455	Desmond Howard	.20	.07
456	Vinnie Clark	.10	.02
457	Keith Goganious	.10	.02
458	Shawn Bouwens	.10	.02
459	Rob Johnson RC	.75	.30
460	Steve Beuerlein	.20	.07
461	Mark Brunell	.60	.25
462	Harry Colon	.10	.02
463	Chris Hudson	.10	.02
464	Darren Carrington	.10	.02
465	Ernest Givins	.10	.02

❑ 466 Kelvin Pritchett .10 .02
❑ 467 Checklist (249-358) .10 .02
❑ 468 Checklist (358-468) .10 .02

1996 Topps

❑ COMPLETE SET (440) 40.00 20.00
❑ COMP.FACT.SET (448) 60.00 35.00
❑ COMP.CER.FACT.SET (445) 40.00 20.00
❑ 1 Troy Aikman 1.00 .40
❑ 2 Kevin Greene .20 .07
❑ 3 Robert Brooks .30 .10
❑ 4 Eugene Daniel .10 .02
❑ 5 Rodney Peete .10 .02
❑ 6 James Hasty .10 .02
❑ 7 Tim McDonald .10 .02
❑ 8 Darick Holmes .10 .02
❑ 9 Morten Andersen .10 .02
❑ 10 Junior Seau .30 .10
❑ 11 Brett Perriman .10 .02
❑ 12 Eric Green .10 .02
❑ 13 Jim Flanigan .10 .02
❑ 14 Cortez Kennedy .10 .02
❑ 15 Orlando Thomas .10 .02
❑ 16 Anthony Miller .20 .07
❑ 17 Sean Gilbert .10 .02
❑ 18 Rob Fredrickson .10 .02
❑ 19 Willie Green .10 .02
❑ 20 Jeff Blake .30 .10
❑ 21 Trent Dilfer .30 .10
❑ 22 Chris Chandler .20 .07
❑ 23 Renaldo Turnbull .10 .02
❑ 24 Dave Meggett .10 .02
❑ 25 Heath Shuler .20 .07
❑ 26 Michael Jackson .20 .07
❑ 27 Thomas Randolph .10 .02
❑ 28 Keith Goganious .10 .02
❑ 29 Seth Joyner .10 .02
❑ 30 Wayne Chrebet .60 .25
❑ 31 Craig Newsome .10 .02
❑ 32 William Fuller .10 .02
❑ 33 Merton Hanks .10 .02
❑ 34 Dale Carter .10 .02
❑ 35 Quentin Coryatt .10 .02
❑ 36 Robert Jones .10 .02
❑ 37 Eric Metcalf .10 .02
❑ 38 Byron Bam Morris .10 .02
❑ 39 Bill Brooks .10 .02
❑ 40 Barry Sanders 1.50 .60
❑ 41 Michael Haynes .10 .02
❑ 42 Joey Galloway .30 .10
❑ 43 Robert Smith .20 .07
❑ 44 John Thierry .10 .02
❑ 45 Bryan Cox .10 .02
❑ 46 Anthony Parker .10 .02
❑ 47 Harvey Williams .10 .02
❑ 48 Terrell Davis .75 .30
❑ 49 Darnay Scott .20 .07
❑ 50 Kerry Collins .30 .10
❑ 51 Cris Dishman .10 .02
❑ 52 Dwayne Harper .10 .02
❑ 53 Warren Sapp .10 .02
❑ 54 Will Moore .10 .02
❑ 55 Earnest Byner .10 .02
❑ 56 Aaron Glenn .10 .02
❑ 57 Michael Westbrook .30 .10
❑ 58 Vencie Glenn .10 .02
❑ 59 Rob Moore .20 .07
❑ 60 Mark Brunell .60 .25
❑ 61 Craig Heyward .10 .02
❑ 62 Eric Allen .10 .02
❑ 63 Bill Romanowski .10 .02
❑ 64 Dana Stubblefield .20 .07
❑ 65 Steve Bono .10 .02
❑ 66 George Koonce .10 .02
❑ 67 Larry Brown .10 .02
❑ 68 Warren Moon .20 .07
❑ 69 Erric Pegram .10 .02
❑ 70 Jim Kelly .30 .10
❑ 71 Jason Belser .10 .02
❑ 72 Henry Thomas .10 .02
❑ 73 Mark Carrier DB .10 .02
❑ 74 Terry Wooden .10 .02
❑ 75 Terry McDaniel .10 .02
❑ 76 O.J. McDuffie .20 .07
❑ 77 Dan Wilkinson .10 .02
❑ 78 Blake Brockermeyer .10 .02
❑ 79 Micheal Barrow .10 .02
❑ 80 Dave Brown .10 .02
❑ 81 Todd Lyght .10 .02
❑ 82 Henry Ellard .10 .02
❑ 83 Jeff Lageman .10 .02
❑ 84 Anthony Pleasant .10 .02
❑ 85 Aeneas Williams .10 .02
❑ 86 Vincent Brisby .10 .02
❑ 87 Terrell Fletcher .10 .02
❑ 88 Brad Baxter .10 .02
❑ 89 Shannon Sharpe .20 .07
❑ 90 Errict Rhett .20 .07
❑ 91 Michael Zordich .10 .02
❑ 92 Dan Saleaumua .10 .02
❑ 93 Devin Bush .10 .02
❑ 94 Wayne Simmons .10 .02
❑ 95 Tyrone Hughes .10 .02
❑ 96 John Randle .20 .07
❑ 97 Tony Tolbert .10 .02
❑ 98 Yancey Thigpen .20 .07
❑ 99 J.J. Stokes .30 .10
❑ 100 Marshall Faulk .40 .15
❑ 101 Barry Minter .10 .02
❑ 102 Glenn Foley .20 .07
❑ 103 Chester McGlockton .10 .02
❑ 104 Carlton Gray .10 .02
❑ 105 Terry Kirby .20 .07
❑ 106 Darryll Lewis .10 .02
❑ 107 Thomas Smith .10 .02
❑ 108 Mike Fox .10 .02
❑ 109 Antonio Langham .10 .02
❑ 110 Drew Bledsoe .60 .25
❑ 111 Troy Drayton .10 .02
❑ 112 Marvcus Patton .10 .02
❑ 113 Tyrone Wheatley .20 .07
❑ 114 Desmond Howard .20 .07
❑ 115 Johnny Mitchell .10 .02
❑ 116 Dave Krieg .10 .02
❑ 117 Natrone Means .20 .07
❑ 118 Herman Moore .20 .07
❑ 119 Darren Woodson .20 .07
❑ 120 Ricky Watters .20 .07
❑ 121 Emmitt Smith TYC .75 .30
❑ 122 Barry Sanders TYC .75 .30
❑ 123 Curtis Martin TYC .30 .10
❑ 124 Chris Warren TYC .20 .07
❑ 125 Terry Allen TYC .20 .07
❑ 126 Ricky Watters TYC .20 .07
❑ 127 Errict Rhett TYC .20 .07
❑ 128 Rodney Hampton TYC .10 .02
❑ 129 Terrell Davis TYC .30 .10
❑ 130 Harvey Williams TYC .10 .02
❑ 131 Craig Heyward TYC .10 .02
❑ 132 Marshall Faulk TYC .30 .10
❑ 133 Rashaan Salaam TYC .20 .07
❑ 134 Garrison Hearst TYC .20 .07
❑ 135 Edgar Bennett TYC .20 .07
❑ 136 Thurman Thomas TYC .20 .07
❑ 137 Brian Washington .10 .02
❑ 138 Derek Loville .10 .02
❑ 139 Curtis Conway .30 .10
❑ 140 Isaac Bruce .30 .10
❑ 141 Ricardo McDonald .10 .02
❑ 142 Bruce Armstrong .10 .02
❑ 143 Will Wolford .10 .02
❑ 144 Thurman Thomas .30 .10
❑ 145 Mel Gray .10 .02
❑ 146 Napoleon Kaufman .30 .10
❑ 147 Terry Allen .20 .07
❑ 148 Chris Calloway .10 .02
❑ 149 Harry Colon .10 .02
❑ 150 Pepper Johnson .10 .02
❑ 151 Marco Coleman .10 .02
❑ 152 Shawn Jefferson .10 .02
❑ 153 Larry Centers .20 .07
❑ 154 Lamar Lathon .10 .02
❑ 155 Mark Chmura .20 .07
❑ 156 Dermontti Dawson .10 .02
❑ 157 Alvin Harper .10 .02
❑ 158 Randall McDaniel .10 .02
❑ 159 Allen Aldridge .10 .02
❑ 160 Chris Warren .20 .07
❑ 161 Jessie Tuggle .10 .02
❑ 162 Sean Lumpkin .10 .02
❑ 163 Bobby Houston .10 .02
❑ 164 Dexter Carter .10 .02
❑ 165 Erik Kramer .10 .02
❑ 166 Brock Marion .10 .02
❑ 167 Toby Wright .10 .02
❑ 168 John Copeland .10 .02
❑ 169 Sean Dawkins .10 .02
❑ 170 Tim Brown .30 .10
❑ 171 Darion Conner .10 .02
❑ 172 Aaron Hayden RC .10 .02
❑ 173 Charlie Garner .20 .07
❑ 174 Anthony Cook .10 .02
❑ 175 Derrick Thomas .30 .10
❑ 176 Willie McGinest .10 .02
❑ 177 Thomas Lewis .10 .02
❑ 178 Sherman Williams .10 .02
❑ 179 Cornelius Bennett .10 .02
❑ 180 Frank Sanders .30 .10
❑ 181 Leroy Hoard .10 .02
❑ 182 Bernie Parmalee .10 .02
❑ 183 Sterling Palmer .10 .02
❑ 184 Kelvin Pritchett .10 .02
❑ 185 Kordell Stewart .30 .10
❑ 186 Brent Jones .10 .02
❑ 187 Robert Blackmon .10 .02
❑ 188 Adrian Murrell .20 .07
❑ 189 Edgar Bennett .20 .07
❑ 190 Rashaan Salaam .20 .07
❑ 191 Ellis Johnson .10 .02
❑ 192 Andre Coleman .10 .02
❑ 193 Will Shields .10 .02
❑ 194 Derrick Brooks .30 .10
❑ 195 Carl Pickens .20 .07
❑ 196 Carlton Bailey .10 .02
❑ 197 Terance Mathis .20 .07
❑ 198 Carlos Jenkins .10 .02
❑ 199 Derrick Alexander .10 .02
❑ 200 Deion Sanders .60 .25
❑ 201 Glyn Milburn .10 .02
❑ 202 Chris Sanders .20 .07
❑ 203 Rocket Ismail .10 .02
❑ 204 Fred Barnett .10 .02
❑ 205 Quinn Early .10 .02
❑ 206 Henry Jones .10 .02
❑ 207 Herschel Walker .20 .07
❑ 208 James Washington .10 .02
❑ 209 Lee Woodall .10 .02
❑ 210 Neil Smith .20 .07
❑ 211 Tony Bennett .10 .02
❑ 212 Ernie Mills .10 .02
❑ 213 Clyde Simmons .10 .02
❑ 214 Chris Slade .10 .02
❑ 215 Tony Boselli .10 .02
❑ 216 Ryan McNeil .10 .02
❑ 217 Rob Burnett .10 .02
❑ 218 Stan Humphries .20 .07
❑ 219 Rick Mirer .20 .07
❑ 220 Troy Vincent .10 .02
❑ 221 Sean Jones .10 .02
❑ 222 Marty Carter .10 .02
❑ 223 Boomer Esiason .20 .07
❑ 224 Charles Haley .20 .07
❑ 225 Sam Mills .10 .02
❑ 226 Greg Biekert .10 .02
❑ 227 Bryant Young .20 .07
❑ 228 Ken Dilger .20 .07
❑ 229 Levon Kirkland .10 .02
❑ 230 Brian Mitchell .10 .02
❑ 231 Hardy Nickerson .10 .02
❑ 232 Elvis Grbac .20 .07
❑ 233 Kurt Schulz .10 .02
❑ 234 Chris Doleman .10 .02
❑ 235 Tamarick Vanover .20 .07

❑ 236	Jesse Campbell	.10	.02
❑ 237	William Thomas	.10	.02
❑ 238	Shane Conlan	.10	.02
❑ 239	Jason Elam	.20	.07
❑ 240	Steve McNair	.75	.30
❑ 241	Jerry Rice TYC	.50	.20
❑ 242	Isaac Bruce TYC	.30	.10
❑ 243	Herman Moore TYC	.20	.07
❑ 244	Michael Irvin TYC	.20	.07
❑ 245	Robert Brooks TYC	.30	.10
❑ 246	Brett Perriman TYC	.10	.02
❑ 247	Cris Carter TYC	.30	.10
❑ 248	Tim Brown TYC	.20	.07
❑ 249	Yancey Thigpen TYC	.20	.07
❑ 250	Jeff Graham TYC	.10	.02
❑ 251	Carl Pickens TYC	.20	.07
❑ 252	Tony Martin TYC	.10	.02
❑ 253	Eric Metcalf TYC	.10	.02
❑ 254	Jake Reed TYC	.20	.07
❑ 255	Quinn Early TYC	.10	.02
❑ 256	Anthony Miller TYC	.20	.07
❑ 257	Joey Galloway TYC	.30	.10
❑ 258	Bert Emanuel TYC	.20	.07
❑ 259	Terance Mathis TYC	.10	.02
❑ 260	Curtis Conway TYC	.20	.07
❑ 261	Henry Ellard TYC	.10	.02
❑ 262	Mark Carrier TYC	.10	.02
❑ 263	Brian Blades TYC	.10	.02
❑ 264	William Roaf	.10	.02
❑ 265	Ed McDaniel	.10	.02
❑ 266	Nate Newton	.10	.02
❑ 267	Brett Maxie	.10	.02
❑ 268	Anthony Smith	.10	.02
❑ 269	Mickey Washington	.10	.02
❑ 270	Jerry Rice	1.00	.40
❑ 271	Shaun Gayle	.10	.02
❑ 272	Gilbert Brown RC	.30	.10
❑ 273	Mark Bruener	.10	.02
❑ 274	Eugene Robinson	.10	.02
❑ 275	Marvin Washington	.10	.02
❑ 276	Keith Sims	.10	.02
❑ 277	Ashley Ambrose	.10	.02
❑ 278	Garrison Hearst	.20	.07
❑ 279	Donnell Woolford	.10	.02
❑ 280	Cris Carter	.30	.10
❑ 281	Curtis Martin	.75	.30
❑ 282	Scott Mitchell	.20	.07
❑ 283	Stevon Moore	.10	.02
❑ 284	Roman Phifer	.10	.02
❑ 285	Ken Harvey	.10	.02
❑ 286	Rodney Hampton	.20	.07
❑ 287	Willie Davis	.10	.02
❑ 288	Yonel Jourdain	.10	.02
❑ 289	Brian DeMarco	.10	.02
❑ 290	Reggie White	.30	.10
❑ 291	Kevin Williams	.10	.02
❑ 292	Gary Plummer	.10	.02
❑ 293	Terrance Shaw	.10	.02
❑ 294	Calvin Williams	.10	.02
❑ 295	Eddie Robinson	.10	.02
❑ 296	Tony McGee	.10	.02
❑ 297	Clay Matthews	.10	.02
❑ 298	Joe Cain	.10	.02
❑ 299	Tim McKyer	.10	.02
❑ 300	Greg Lloyd	.20	.07
❑ 301	Steve Wisniewski	.10	.02
❑ 302	Ray Buchanan	.10	.02
❑ 303	Lake Dawson	.10	.02
❑ 304	Kevin Carter	.10	.02
❑ 305	Phillippi Sparks	.10	.02
❑ 306	Emmitt Smith	1.50	.60
❑ 307	Ruben Brown	.10	.02
❑ 308	Tom Carter	.10	.02
❑ 309	William Floyd	.20	.07
❑ 310	Jim Everett	.10	.02
❑ 311	Vincent Brown	.10	.02
❑ 312	Dennis Gibson	.10	.02
❑ 313	Lorenzo Lynch	.10	.02
❑ 314	Corey Harris	.10	.02
❑ 315	James O.Stewart	.20	.07
❑ 316	Kyle Brady	.10	.02
❑ 317	Irving Fryar	.20	.07
❑ 318	Jake Reed	.20	.07
❑ 319	Vinny Testaverde	.20	.07
❑ 320	John Elway	2.00	.75
❑ 321	Tracy Scroggins	.10	.02
❑ 322	Chris Spielman	.10	.02

❑ 323	Horace Copeland	.10	.02
❑ 324	Chris Zorich	.10	.02
❑ 325	Mike Mamula	.10	.02
❑ 326	Henry Ford	.10	.02
❑ 327	Steve Walsh	.10	.02
❑ 328	Stanley Richard	.20	.07
❑ 329	Mike Jones	.10	.02
❑ 330	Jim Harbaugh	.20	.07
❑ 331	Darren Perry	.10	.02
❑ 332	Ken Norton	.10	.02
❑ 333	Kimble Anders	.20	.07
❑ 334	Harold Green	.10	.02
❑ 335	Tyrone Poole	.10	.02
❑ 336	Mark Fields	.10	.02
❑ 337	Darren Bennett	.10	.02
❑ 338	Mike Sherrard	.10	.02
❑ 339	Terry Ray RC	.10	.02
❑ 340	Bruce Smith	.20	.07
❑ 341	Daryl Johnston	.20	.07
❑ 342	Vinnie Clark	.10	.02
❑ 343	Mike Caldwell	.10	.02
❑ 344	Vinson Smith	.10	.02
❑ 345	Mo Lewis	.10	.02
❑ 346	Brian Blades	.10	.02
❑ 347	Rod Stephens	.10	.02
❑ 348	David Palmer	.10	.02
❑ 349	Blaine Bishop	.10	.02
❑ 350	Jeff George	.20	.07
❑ 351	George Teague	.10	.02
❑ 352	Jeff Hostetler	.10	.02
❑ 353	Michael Strahan	.20	.07
❑ 354	Eric Davis	.10	.02
❑ 355	Jerome Bettis	.30	.10
❑ 356	Irv Smith	.10	.02
❑ 357	Jeff Herrod	.10	.02
❑ 358	Jay Novacek	.10	.02
❑ 359	Bryce Paup	.10	.02
❑ 360	Neil O'Donnell	.20	.07
❑ 361	Eric Swann	.10	.02
❑ 362	Corey Sawyer	.10	.02
❑ 363	Ty Law	.30	.10
❑ 364	Bo Orlando	.10	.02
❑ 365	Marcus Allen	.30	.10
❑ 366	Mark McMillian	.10	.02
❑ 367	Mark Carrier WR	.10	.02
❑ 368	Jackie Harris	.10	.02
❑ 369	Steve Atwater	.10	.02
❑ 370	Steve Young	.75	.30
❑ 371	Brett Favre TYC	1.00	.40
❑ 372	Scott Mitchell TYC	.10	.02
❑ 373	Warren Moon TYC	.10	.02
❑ 374	Jeff George TYC	.20	.07
❑ 375	Jim Everett TYC	.10	.02
❑ 376	John Elway TYC	1.00	.40
❑ 377	Erik Kramer TYC	.10	.02
❑ 378	Jeff Blake TYC	.20	.07
❑ 379	Dan Marino TYC	1.00	.40
❑ 380	Dave Krieg TYC	.10	.02
❑ 381	Drew Bledsoe TYC	.30	.10
❑ 382	Stan Humphries TYC	.10	.02
❑ 383	Troy Aikman TYC	.50	.20
❑ 384	Steve Young TYC	.30	.10
❑ 385	Jim Kelly TYC	.30	.10
❑ 386	Steve Bono TYC	.10	.02
❑ 387	David Sloan	.10	.02
❑ 388	Jeff Graham	.10	.02
❑ 389	Hugh Douglas	.20	.07
❑ 390	Dan Marino	2.00	.75
❑ 391	Winston Moss	.10	.02
❑ 392	Darrell Green	.10	.02
❑ 393	Mark Stepnoski	.10	.02
❑ 394	Bert Emanuel	.20	.07
❑ 395	Eric Zeier	.10	.02
❑ 396	Willie Jackson	.20	.07
❑ 397	Qadry Ismail	.20	.07
❑ 398	Michael Brooks	.10	.02
❑ 399	D'Marco Farr	.10	.02
❑ 400	Brett Favre	2.00	.75
❑ 401	Carnell Lake	.10	.02
❑ 402	Pat Swilling	.10	.02
❑ 403	Stephen Grant	.10	.02
❑ 404	Steve Tasker	.10	.02
❑ 405	Ben Coates	.20	.07
❑ 406	Steve Tovar	.10	.02
❑ 407	Tony Martin	.20	.07
❑ 408	Greg Hill	.20	.07
❑ 409	Eric Guliford	.10	.02

❑ 410	Michael Irvin	.30	.10
❑ 411	Eric Hill	.10	.02
❑ 412	Mario Bates	.20	.07
❑ 413	Brian Stablein RC	.10	.02
❑ 414	Marcus Jones RC	.10	.02
❑ 415	Reggie Brown LB RC	.10	.02
❑ 416	Lawrence Phillips RC	.30	.10
❑ 417	Alex Van Dyke RC	.20	.07
❑ 418	Daryl Gardener RC	.10	.02
❑ 419	Mike Alstott RC	1.00	.40
❑ 420	Kevin Hardy RC	.30	.10
❑ 421	Rickey Dudley RC	.30	.10
❑ 422	Jerome Woods RC	.10	.02
❑ 423	Eric Moulds RC	1.25	.50
❑ 424	Cedric Jones RC	.10	.02
❑ 425	Simeon Rice RC	.75	.30
❑ 426	Marvin Harrison RC	2.50	1.00
❑ 427	Tim Biakabutuka RC	.30	.10
❑ 428	Duane Clemons RC	.10	.02
❑ 429	Alex Molden RC	.10	.02
❑ 430	Keyshawn Johnson RC	1.00	.40
❑ 431	Willie Anderson RC	.10	.02
❑ 432	John Mobley RC	.10	.02
❑ 433	Leeland McElroy RC	.20	.07
❑ 434	Regan Upshaw RC	.10	.02
❑ 435	Eddie George RC	1.25	.50
❑ 436	Jonathan Ogden RC	.30	.10
❑ 437	Eddie Kennison RC	.30	.10
❑ 438	Jermane Mayberry RC	.10	.02
❑ 439	Checklist 1 of 2	.10	.02
❑ 440	Checklist 2 of 2	.10	.02
❑ P1	Joe Namath/Steve Young Promo	15.00	7.50
❑ P1R	Joe Namath Promo Steve Young	20.00	10.00

1997 Topps

❑	COMPLETE SET (415)	40.00	20.00
❑	COMP.FACT.SET (424)	70.00	40.00
❑ 1	Brett Favre	2.00	.75
❑ 2	Lawyer Milloy	.30	.10
❑ 3	Tim Biakabutuka	.30	.10
❑ 4	Clyde Simmons	.20	.07
❑ 5	Deion Sanders	.50	.20
❑ 6	Anthony Miller	.20	.07
❑ 7	Marquez Pope	.20	.07
❑ 8	Mike Tomczak	.20	.07
❑ 9	William Thomas	.20	.07
❑ 10	Marshall Faulk	.60	.25
❑ 11	John Randle	.30	.10
❑ 12	Jim Kelly	.50	.20
❑ 13	Steve Bono	.30	.10
❑ 14	Rod Stephens	.20	.07
❑ 15	Stan Humphries	.20	.07
❑ 16	Terrell Buckley	.20	.07
❑ 17	Ki-Jana Carter	.20	.07
❑ 18	Marcus Robertson	.20	.07
❑ 19	Corey Harris	.20	.07
❑ 20	Rashaan Salaam	.20	.07
❑ 21	Rickey Dudley	.30	.10
❑ 22	Jamir Miller	.20	.07
❑ 23	Martin Mayhew	.20	.07
❑ 24	Jason Sehorn	.30	.10
❑ 25	Isaac Bruce	.50	.20
❑ 26	Johnnie Morton	.30	.10
❑ 27	Antonio Langham	.20	.07
❑ 28	Cornelius Bennett	.20	.07
❑ 29	Joe Johnson	.20	.07
❑ 30	Keyshawn Johnson	.50	.20
❑ 31	Willie Green	.20	.07

No.	Player	Mint	NRMT
❏ 32	Craig Newsome	.20	.07
❏ 33	Brock Marion	.20	.07
❏ 34	Corey Fuller	.20	.07
❏ 35	Ben Coates	.30	.10
❏ 36	Ty Detmer	.30	.10
❏ 37	Charles Johnson	.30	.10
❏ 38	Willie Jackson	.20	.07
❏ 39	Tyronne Drakeford	.20	.07
❏ 40	Gus Frerotte	.20	.07
❏ 41	Robert Blackmon	.20	.07
❏ 42	Andre Coleman	.20	.07
❏ 43	Mario Bates	.20	.07
❏ 44	Chris Calloway	.20	.07
❏ 45	Terry McDaniel	.20	.07
❏ 46	Anthony Davis	.20	.07
❏ 47	Stanley Pritchett	.20	.07
❏ 48	Ray Buchanan	.20	.07
❏ 49	Chris Chandler	.30	.10
❏ 50	Ashley Ambrose	.20	.07
❏ 51	Tyrone Braxton	.20	.07
❏ 52	Pepper Johnson	.20	.07
❏ 53	Frank Sanders	.30	.10
❏ 54	Clay Matthews	.20	.07
❏ 55	Bruce Smith	.30	.10
❏ 56	Jermaine Lewis	.50	.20
❏ 57	Mark Carrier WR UER	.20	.07
❏ 58	Jeff Graham	.20	.07
❏ 59	Keith Lyle	.20	.07
❏ 60	Trent Dilfer	.50	.20
❏ 61	Trace Armstrong	.20	.07
❏ 62	Jeff Herrod	.20	.07
❏ 63	Tyrone Wheatley	.30	.10
❏ 64	Torrance Small	.20	.07
❏ 65	Chris Warren	.30	.10
❏ 66	Terry Kirby	.30	.10
❏ 67	Erric Pegram	.20	.07
❏ 68	Sean Gilbert	.20	.07
❏ 69	Greg Biekert	.20	.07
❏ 70	Ricky Watters	.30	.10
❏ 71	Chris Hudson	.20	.07
❏ 72	Tamarick Vanover	.30	.10
❏ 73	Orlando Thomas	.20	.07
❏ 74	Jimmy Spencer	.20	.07
❏ 75	John Mobley	.20	.07
❏ 76	Henry Thomas	.20	.07
❏ 77	Santana Dotson	.20	.07
❏ 78	Boomer Esiason	.30	.10
❏ 79	Bobby Hebert	.20	.07
❏ 80	Kerry Collins	.50	.20
❏ 81	Bobby Engram	.30	.10
❏ 82	Kevin Smith	.20	.07
❏ 83	Rick Mirer	.20	.07
❏ 84	Ted Johnson	.20	.07
❏ 85	Derrick Alexander WR	.30	.10
❏ 86	Hugh Douglas	.20	.07
❏ 87	Rodney Harrison RC	1.00	.40
❏ 88	Roman Phifer	.20	.07
❏ 89	Warren Moon	.50	.20
❏ 90	Thurman Thomas	.50	.20
❏ 91	Michael McCrary	.20	.07
❏ 92	Dana Stubblefield	.20	.07
❏ 93	Andre Hastings UER	.20	.07
❏ 94	William Fuller	.20	.07
❏ 95	Jeff Hostetler	.20	.07
❏ 96	Danny Kanell	.20	.07
❏ 97	Mark Fields	.20	.07
❏ 98	Eddie Robinson	.20	.07
❏ 99	Daryl Gardener	.20	.07
❏ 100	Drew Bledsoe	.60	.25
❏ 101	Winslow Oliver	.20	.07
❏ 102	Raymont Harris	.20	.07
❏ 103	LeShon Johnson	.20	.07
❏ 104	Byron Bam Morris	.20	.07
❏ 105	Herman Moore	.30	.10
❏ 106	Keith Jackson	.20	.07
❏ 107	Chris Penn	.20	.07
❏ 108	Robert Griffith RC	.20	.07
❏ 109	Jeff Burris	.20	.07
❏ 110	Troy Aikman	1.00	.40
❏ 111	Allen Aldridge	.20	.07
❏ 112	Mel Gray	.20	.07
❏ 113	Aaron Bailey	.20	.07
❏ 114	Michael Strahan	.30	.10
❏ 115	Adrian Murrell	.30	.10
❏ 116	Chris Mims	.20	.07
❏ 117	Robert Jones	.20	.07
❏ 118	Derrick Brooks	.50	.20
❏ 119	Tom Carter	.20	.07
❏ 120	Carl Pickens	.30	.10
❏ 121	Tony Brackens	.20	.07
❏ 122	O.J. McDuffie	.30	.10
❏ 123	Napoleon Kaufman	.50	.20
❏ 124	Chris T. Jones	.20	.07
❏ 125	Kordell Stewart	.50	.20
❏ 126	Ray Zellars	.20	.07
❏ 127	Jessie Tuggle	.20	.07
❏ 128	Greg Kragen	.20	.07
❏ 129	Brett Perriman	.20	.07
❏ 130	Steve Young	.60	.25
❏ 131	Willie Clay	.20	.07
❏ 132	Kimble Anders	.30	.10
❏ 133	Eugene Daniel	.20	.07
❏ 134	Jevon Langford	.20	.07
❏ 135	Shannon Sharpe	.30	.10
❏ 136	Wayne Simmons	.20	.07
❏ 137	Leeland McElroy	.20	.07
❏ 138	Mike Caldwell	.20	.07
❏ 139	Eric Moulds	.50	.20
❏ 140	Eddie George	.50	.20
❏ 141	Jamal Anderson	.50	.20
❏ 142	Michael Timpson	.20	.07
❏ 143	Tony Tolbert	.20	.07
❏ 144	Robert Smith	.30	.10
❏ 145	Mike Alstott	.50	.20
❏ 146	Gary Jones	.20	.07
❏ 147	Terrance Shaw	.20	.07
❏ 148	Carlton Gray	.20	.07
❏ 149	Kevin Carter	.20	.07
❏ 150	Darrell Green	.30	.10
❏ 151	David Dunn	.20	.07
❏ 152	Ken Norton	.20	.07
❏ 153	Chad Brown	.20	.07
❏ 154	Pat Swilling	.20	.07
❏ 155	Irving Fryar	.30	.10
❏ 156	Michael Haynes	.20	.07
❏ 157	Shawn Jefferson	.20	.07
❏ 158	Stephen Grant	.20	.07
❏ 159	James O.Stewart	.30	.10
❏ 160	Derrick Thomas	.50	.20
❏ 161	Tim Bowens	.20	.07
❏ 162	Dixon Edwards	.20	.07
❏ 163	Micheal Barrow	.20	.07
❏ 164	Antonio Freeman	.50	.20
❏ 165	Terrell Davis	.60	.25
❏ 166	Henry Ellard	.30	.10
❏ 167	Daryl Johnston	.30	.10
❏ 168	Bryan Cox	.20	.07
❏ 169	Chad Cota	.20	.07
❏ 170	Vinny Testaverde	.30	.10
❏ 171	Andre Reed	.30	.10
❏ 172	Larry Centers	.30	.10
❏ 173	Craig Heyward	.20	.07
❏ 174	Glyn Milburn	.20	.07
❏ 175	Hardy Nickerson	.20	.07
❏ 176	Corey Miller	.20	.07
❏ 177	Bobby Houston	.20	.07
❏ 178	Marco Coleman	.20	.07
❏ 179	Winston Moss	.20	.07
❏ 180	Tony Banks	.30	.10
❏ 181	Jeff Lageman	.20	.07
❏ 182	Jason Belser	.20	.07
❏ 183	James Jett	.30	.10
❏ 184	Wayne Martin	.20	.07
❏ 185	Dave Meggett	.20	.07
❏ 186	Terrell Owens	.60	.25
❏ 187	Willie Williams	.20	.07
❏ 188	Eric Turner	.20	.07
❏ 189	Chuck Smith	.20	.07
❏ 190	Simeon Rice	.30	.10
❏ 191	Kevin Greene	.30	.10
❏ 192	Lance Johnstone	.20	.07
❏ 193	Marty Carter	.20	.07
❏ 194	Ricardo McDonald	.20	.07
❏ 195	Michael Irvin	.50	.20
❏ 196	George Koonce	.20	.07
❏ 197	Robert Porcher	.20	.07
❏ 198	Mark Collins	.20	.07
❏ 199	Louis Oliver	.20	.07
❏ 200	John Elway	2.00	.75
❏ 201	Jake Reed	.30	.10
❏ 202	Rodney Hampton	.30	.10
❏ 203	Aaron Glenn	.20	.07
❏ 204	Mike Mamula	.20	.07
❏ 205	Terry Allen	.50	.20
❏ 206	John Lynch	.30	.10
❏ 207	Todd Lyght	.20	.07
❏ 208	Dean Wells	.20	.07
❏ 209	Aaron Hayden	.20	.07
❏ 210	Blaine Bishop	.20	.07
❏ 211	Bert Emanuel	.30	.10
❏ 212	Mark Carrier DB UER	.20	.07
❏ 213	Dale Carter	.20	.07
❏ 214	Jimmy Smith	.30	.10
❏ 215	Jim Harbaugh	.30	.10
❏ 216	Jeff George	.30	.10
❏ 217	Anthony Newman	.20	.07
❏ 218	Ty Law	.30	.10
❏ 219	Brent Jones	.20	.07
❏ 220	Emmitt Smith	1.50	.60
❏ 221	Bennie Blades	.20	.07
❏ 222	Alfred Williams	.20	.07
❏ 223	Eugene Robinson	.20	.07
❏ 224	Fred Barnett	.20	.07
❏ 225	Errict Rhett	.20	.07
❏ 226	Leslie O'Neal	.20	.07
❏ 227	Michael Sinclair	.20	.07
❏ 228	Marvcus Patton	.20	.07
❏ 229	Darrien Gordon	.20	.07
❏ 230	Jerome Bettis	.50	.20
❏ 231	Troy Vincent	.20	.07
❏ 232	Ray Mickens	.20	.07
❏ 233	Lonnie Johnson	.20	.07
❏ 234	Charles Way	.20	.07
❏ 235	Chris Sanders	.20	.07
❏ 236	Bracy Walker	.20	.07
❏ 237	Dave Krieg UER	.20	.07
❏ 238	Kent Graham	.20	.07
❏ 239	Ray Lewis	.75	.30
❏ 240	Cris Carter	.50	.20
❏ 241	Elvis Grbac	.30	.10
❏ 242	Eric Davis	.20	.07
❏ 243	Harvey Williams	.20	.07
❏ 244	Eric Allen	.20	.07
❏ 245	Bryant Young	.20	.07
❏ 246	Terrell Fletcher	.20	.07
❏ 247	Darren Perry	.20	.07
❏ 248	Ken Harvey	.20	.07
❏ 249	Marvin Washington	.20	.07
❏ 250	Marcus Allen	.50	.20
❏ 251	Darrin Smith	.20	.07
❏ 252	James Francis	.20	.07
❏ 253	Michael Jackson	.30	.10
❏ 254	Ryan McNeil	.20	.07
❏ 255	Mark Chmura	.30	.10
❏ 256	Keenan McCardell	.30	.10
❏ 257	Tony Bennett	.20	.07
❏ 258	Irving Spikes	.20	.07
❏ 259	Jason Dunn	.20	.07
❏ 260	Joey Galloway	.30	.10
❏ 261	Eddie Kennison	.30	.10
❏ 262	Lonnie Marts	.20	.07
❏ 263	Thomas Lewis	.20	.07
❏ 264	Tedy Bruschi	1.00	.40
❏ 265	Steve Atwater	.20	.07
❏ 266	Dorsey Levens	.50	.20
❏ 267	Kurt Schulz	.20	.07
❏ 268	Rob Moore	.30	.10
❏ 269	Walt Harris	.20	.07
❏ 270	Steve McNair	.60	.25
❏ 271	Bill Romanowski	.20	.07
❏ 272	Sean Dawkins	.20	.07
❏ 273	Don Beebe	.20	.07
❏ 274	Fernando Smith	.20	.07
❏ 275	Willie McGinest	.20	.07
❏ 276	Levon Kirkland	.20	.07
❏ 277	Tony Martin	.30	.10
❏ 278	Warren Sapp	.30	.10
❏ 279	Lamar Smith	.50	.20
❏ 280	Mark Brunell	.60	.25
❏ 281	Jim Everett	.20	.07
❏ 282	Victor Green	.20	.07
❏ 283	Mike Jones	.20	.07
❏ 284	Charlie Garner	.30	.10
❏ 285	Karim Abdul-Jabbar	.30	.10
❏ 286	Michael Westbrook	.30	.10
❏ 287	Lawrence Phillips	.20	.07
❏ 288	Amani Toomer	.30	.10
❏ 289	Neil Smith	.30	.10
❏ 290	Barry Sanders	1.50	.60
❏ 291	Willie Davis	.20	.07
❏ 292	Bo Orlando	.20	.07

❑ 293 Alonzo Spellman .20 .07
❑ 294 Eric Hill .20 .07
❑ 295 Wesley Walls .30 .10
❑ 296 Todd Collins .20 .07
❑ 297 Stevon Moore .20 .07
❑ 298 Eric Metcalf .30 .10
❑ 299 Darren Woodson .20 .07
❑ 300 Jerry Rice 1.00 .40
❑ 301 Scott Mitchell .30 .10
❑ 302 Ray Crockett .20 .07
❑ 303 Jim Schwantz RC UER .20 .07
❑ 304 Steve Tovar .20 .07
❑ 305 Terance Mathis .30 .10
❑ 306 Earnest Byner .20 .07
❑ 307 Chris Spielman .20 .07
❑ 308 Curtis Conway .30 .10
❑ 309 Cris Dishman .20 .07
❑ 310 Marvin Harrison .50 .20
❑ 311 Sam Mills .20 .07
❑ 312 Brent Alexander RC .20 .07
❑ 313 Shawn Wooden RC .20 .07
❑ 314 Dewayne Washington .20 .07
❑ 315 Terry Glenn .50 .20
❑ 316 Winfred Tubbs .20 .07
❑ 317 Dave Brown .20 .07
❑ 318 Neil O'Donnell .30 .10
❑ 319 Anthony Parker .20 .07
❑ 320 Junior Seau .50 .20
❑ 321 Brian Mitchell .20 .07
❑ 322 Regan Upshaw .20 .07
❑ 323 Darryl Williams .20 .07
❑ 324 Chris Doleman .20 .07
❑ 325 Rod Woodson .30 .10
❑ 326 Derrick Witherspoon .20 .07
❑ 327 Chester McGlockton .20 .07
❑ 328 Mickey Washington .20 .07
❑ 329 Greg Hill .20 .07
❑ 330 Reggie White .50 .20
❑ 331 John Copeland .20 .07
❑ 332 Doug Evans .20 .07
❑ 333 Lamar Lathon .20 .07
❑ 334 Mark Maddox .20 .07
❑ 335 Natrone Means .30 .10
❑ 336 Corey Widmer .20 .07
❑ 337 Terry Wooden .20 .07
❑ 338 Merton Hanks .20 .07
❑ 339 Cortez Kennedy .20 .07
❑ 340 Tyrone Hughes .20 .07
❑ 341 Tim Brown .50 .20
❑ 342 John Jurkovic .20 .07
❑ 343 Carnell Lake .20 .07
❑ 344 Stanley Richard .20 .07
❑ 345 Darryll Lewis .20 .07
❑ 346 Dan Wilkinson .20 .07
❑ 347 Broderick Thomas .20 .07
❑ 348 Brian Williams .20 .07
❑ 349 Eric Swann .20 .07
❑ 350 Dan Marino 2.00 .75
❑ 351 Anthony Johnson .20 .07
❑ 352 Joe Cain .20 .07
❑ 353 Quinn Early .20 .07
❑ 354 Seth Joyner .20 .07
❑ 355 Garrison Hearst .30 .10
❑ 356 Edgar Bennett .30 .10
❑ 357 Brian Washington .20 .07
❑ 358 Kevin Hardy .20 .07
❑ 359 Quentin Coryatt .20 .07
❑ 360 Tim McDonald .20 .07
❑ 361 Brian Blades .20 .07
❑ 362 Courtney Hawkins .20 .07
❑ 363 Ray Farmer .20 .07
❑ 364 Jessie Armstead .20 .07
❑ 365 Curtis Martin .60 .25
❑ 366 Zach Thomas .50 .20
❑ 367 Frank Wycheck .30 .10
❑ 368 Darnay Scott .30 .10
❑ 369 Percy Ellsworth RC .20 .07
❑ 370 Desmond Howard .30 .10
❑ 371 Aeneas Williams .20 .07
❑ 372 Bryce Paup .20 .07
❑ 373 Michael Bates .20 .07
❑ 374 Brad Johnson .50 .20
❑ 375 Jeff Blake .30 .10
❑ 376 Donnell Woolford UER .20 .07
❑ 377 Mo Lewis .20 .07
❑ 378 Phillippi Sparks .20 .07
❑ 379 Michael Bankston .20 .07
❑ 380 LeRoy Butler .20 .07
❑ 381 Tyrone Poole .20 .07
❑ 382 Wayne Chrebet .50 .20
❑ 383 Chris Slade .20 .07
❑ 384 Checklist 1 (1-208) .20 .07
❑ 385 Checklist 2 (209-415) .20 .07
❑ 386 Will Blackwell RC SP .30 .10
❑ 387 Tom Knight RC SP .20 .07
❑ 388 Darnell Autry RC SP .50 .20
❑ 389 Bryant Westbrook RC SP .20 .07
❑ 390 David LaFleur RC SP .30 .10
❑ 391 Antowain Smith RC SP 2.50 1.00
❑ 392 Kevin Lockett RC SP .50 .20
❑ 393 Rae Carruth RC SP .30 .10
❑ 394 Renaldo Wynn RC SP .30 .10
❑ 395 Jim Druckenmiller RC SP .50 .20
❑ 396 Kenny Holmes RC SP .75 .30
❑ 397 Shawn Springs RC SP .50 .20
❑ 398 Troy Davis RC SP .50 .20
❑ 399 Dwayne Rudd RC SP .75 .30
❑ 400 Orlando Pace RC SP .75 .30
❑ 401 Byron Hanspard RC SP .50 .20
❑ 402 Corey Dillon RC SP 6.00 2.50
❑ 403 Walter Jones RC SP .75 .30
❑ 404 Reidel Anthony RC SP .75 .30
❑ 405 Peter Boulware RC SP .75 .30
❑ 406 Reinard Wilson RC SP .50 .20
❑ 407 Pat Barnes RC SP .75 .30
❑ 408 Yatil Green RC SP .75 .30
❑ 409 Joey Kent RC SP .75 .30
❑ 410 Ike Hilliard RC SP 1.50 .60
❑ 411 Jake Plummer SP RC 5.00 2.00
❑ 412 Darrell Russell RC SP .30 .10
❑ 413 James Farrior RC SP .75 .30
❑ 414 Tony Gonzalez RC SP 3.00 1.25
❑ 415 Warrick Dunn RC SP 2.50 1.00
❑ P40 Gus Frerotte PROMO .25 .10
❑ P170 Vinny Testaverde PROMO .25 .10
❑ P240 Cris Carter PROMO .40 .15
❑ P250 Marcus Allen PROMO .40 .15
❑ P285 Karim Abdul-Jabbar PROMO .25 .10
❑ P356 Edgar Bennett PROMO .25 .10

1998 Topps

❑ COMPLETE SET (360) 60.00 30.00
❑ COMP.FACT.SET (365) 90.00 50.00
❑ 1 Barry Sanders 1.50 .60
❑ 2 Derrick Rodgers .20 .07
❑ 3 Chris Calloway .20 .07
❑ 4 Bruce Armstrong .20 .07
❑ 5 Horace Copeland .20 .07
❑ 6 Chad Brown .20 .07
❑ 7 Ken Harvey .20 .07
❑ 8 Levon Kirkland .20 .07
❑ 9 Glenn Foley .30 .10
❑ 10 Corey Dillon .50 .20
❑ 11 Sean Dawkins .20 .07
❑ 12 Curtis Conway .30 .10
❑ 13 Chris Chandler .30 .10
❑ 14 Kerry Collins .30 .10
❑ 15 Jonathan Ogden .20 .07
❑ 16 Sam Shade .20 .07
❑ 17 Vaughn Hebron .20 .07
❑ 18 Quentin Coryatt .20 .07
❑ 19 Jerris McPhail .20 .07
❑ 20 Warrick Dunn .50 .20
❑ 21 Wayne Martin .20 .07
❑ 22 Chad Lewis .30 .10
❑ 23 Danny Kanell .30 .10
❑ 24 Shawn Springs .20 .07
❑ 25 Emmitt Smith 1.50 .60
❑ 26 Todd Lyght .20 .07
❑ 27 Donnie Edwards .20 .07
❑ 28 Charlie Jones .20 .07
❑ 29 Willie McGinest .20 .07
❑ 30 Steve Young .60 .25
❑ 31 Darrell Russell .20 .07
❑ 32 Gary Anderson .20 .07
❑ 33 Stanley Richard .20 .07
❑ 34 Leslie O'Neal .20 .07
❑ 35 Dermontti Dawson .20 .07
❑ 36 Jeff Brady .20 .07
❑ 37 Kimble Anders .30 .10
❑ 38 Glyn Milburn .20 .07
❑ 39 Greg Hill .20 .07
❑ 40 Freddie Jones .20 .07
❑ 41 Bobby Engram .30 .10
❑ 42 Aeneas Williams .20 .07
❑ 43 Antowain Smith .50 .20
❑ 44 Reggie White .50 .20
❑ 45 Rae Carruth .20 .07
❑ 46 Leon Johnson .20 .07
❑ 47 Bryant Young .20 .07
❑ 48 Jamie Asher .20 .07
❑ 49 Hardy Nickerson .20 .07
❑ 50 Jerome Bettis .50 .20
❑ 51 Michael Strahan .30 .10
❑ 52 John Randle .30 .10
❑ 53 Kevin Hardy .20 .07
❑ 54 Eric Bjornson .20 .07
❑ 55 Morten Andersen UER .20 .07
❑ 56 Larry Centers .20 .07
❑ 57 Bryce Paup .20 .07
❑ 58 John Mobley .20 .07
❑ 59 Michael Bates .20 .07
❑ 60 Tim Brown .50 .20
❑ 61 Doug Evans .20 .07
❑ 62 Will Shields .20 .07
❑ 63 Jeff Graham .20 .07
❑ 64 Henry Jones .20 .07
❑ 65 Steve Broussard .20 .07
❑ 66 Blaine Bishop .20 .07
❑ 67 Ernie Conwell .20 .07
❑ 68 Heath Shuler .20 .07
❑ 69 Eric Metcalf .20 .07
❑ 70 Terry Glenn .50 .20
❑ 71 James Hasty .20 .07
❑ 72 Robert Porcher .20 .07
❑ 73 Keenan McCardell .30 .10
❑ 74 Tyrone Hughes .20 .07
❑ 75 Troy Aikman 1.00 .40
❑ 76 Peter Boulware .20 .07
❑ 77 Rob Johnson .30 .10
❑ 78 Erik Kramer .20 .07
❑ 79 Kevin Smith .20 .07
❑ 80 Andre Rison .30 .10
❑ 81 Jim Harbaugh .30 .10
❑ 82 Chris Hudson .20 .07
❑ 83 Ray Zellars .20 .07
❑ 84 Jeff George .30 .10
❑ 85 Willie Davis .20 .07
❑ 86 Jason Gildon .20 .07
❑ 87 Robert Brooks .30 .10
❑ 88 Chad Cota .20 .07
❑ 89 Simeon Rice .30 .10
❑ 90 Mark Brunell .50 .20
❑ 91 Jay Graham .20 .07
❑ 92 Scott Greene .20 .07
❑ 93 Jeff Blake .30 .10
❑ 94 Jason Belser .20 .07
❑ 95 Derrick Alexander DE .20 .07
❑ 96 Ty Law .30 .10
❑ 97 Charles Johnson .20 .07
❑ 98 James Jett .30 .10
❑ 99 Darrell Green .30 .10
❑ 100 Brett Favre 2.00 .75
❑ 101 George Jones .20 .07
❑ 102 Derrick Mason .30 .10
❑ 103 Sam Adams .20 .07
❑ 104 Lawrence Phillips .20 .07
❑ 105 Randal Hill .20 .07
❑ 106 John Mangum .20 .07
❑ 107 Natrone Means .30 .10
❑ 108 Bill Romanowski .20 .07
❑ 109 Terance Mathis .30 .10
❑ 110 Bruce Smith .30 .10

❑	111	Pete Mitchell	.20	.07
❑	112	Duane Clemons	.20	.07
❑	113	Willie Clay	.20	.07
❑	114	Eric Allen	.20	.07
❑	115	Troy Drayton	.20	.07
❑	116	Derrick Thomas	.50	.20
❑	117	Charles Way	.20	.07
❑	118	Wayne Chrebet	.50	.20
❑	119	Bobby Hoying	.30	.10
❑	120	Michael Jackson	.20	.07
❑	121	Gary Zimmerman	.20	.07
❑	122	Yancey Thigpen	.20	.07
❑	123	Dana Stubblefield	.20	.07
❑	124	Keith Lyle	.20	.07
❑	125	Marco Coleman	.20	.07
❑	126	Karl Williams	.20	.07
❑	127	Stephen Davis	.20	.07
❑	128	Chris Sanders	.20	.07
❑	129	Cris Dishman	.20	.07
❑	130	Jake Plummer	.50	.20
❑	131	Darryl Williams	.20	.07
❑	132	Merton Hanks	.20	.07
❑	133	Torrance Small	.20	.07
❑	134	Aaron Glenn	.20	.07
❑	135	Chester McGlockton	.20	.07
❑	136	William Thomas	.20	.07
❑	137	Kordell Stewart	.50	.20
❑	138	Jason Taylor	.30	.10
❑	139	Lake Dawson	.20	.07
❑	140	Carl Pickens	.30	.10
❑	141	Eugene Robinson	.20	.07
❑	142	Ed McCaffrey	.30	.10
❑	143	Lamar Lathon	.20	.07
❑	144	Ray Buchanan	.20	.07
❑	145	Thurman Thomas	.50	.20
❑	146	Andre Reed	.30	.10
❑	147	Wesley Walls	.30	.10
❑	148	Rob Moore	.30	.10
❑	149	Darren Woodson	.20	.07
❑	150	Eddie George	.50	.20
❑	151	Michael Irvin	.50	.20
❑	152	Johnnie Morton	.30	.10
❑	153	Ken Dilger	.20	.07
❑	154	Tony Boselli	.20	.07
❑	155	Randall McDaniel	.20	.07
❑	156	Mark Fields	.20	.07
❑	157	Phillippi Sparks	.20	.07
❑	158	Troy Davis	.20	.07
❑	159	Troy Vincent	.20	.07
❑	160	Cris Carter	.50	.20
❑	161	Amp Lee	.20	.07
❑	162	Will Blackwell	.20	.07
❑	163	Chad Scott	.20	.07
❑	164	Henry Ellard	.30	.10
❑	165	Robert Jones	.20	.07
❑	166	Garrison Hearst	.50	.20
❑	167	James McKnight	.50	.20
❑	168	Rodney Harrison	.30	.10
❑	169	Adrian Murrell	.30	.10
❑	170	Rod Smith WR	.30	.10
❑	171	Desmond Howard	.30	.10
❑	172	Ben Coates	.30	.10
❑	173	David Palmer	.20	.07
❑	174	Zach Thomas	.50	.20
❑	175	Dale Carter	.20	.07
❑	176	Mark Chmura	.30	.10
❑	177	Elvis Grbac	.30	.10
❑	178	Jason Hanson	.20	.07
❑	179	Walt Harris	.20	.07
❑	180	Ricky Watters	.30	.10
❑	181	Ray Lewis	.50	.20
❑	182	Lonnie Johnson	.20	.07
❑	183	Marvin Harrison	.50	.20
❑	184	Dorsey Levens	.50	.20
❑	185	Tony Gonzalez	.50	.20
❑	186	Andre Hastings	.20	.07
❑	187	Kevin Turner	.20	.07
❑	188	Mo Lewis	.20	.07
❑	189	Jason Sehorn	.30	.10
❑	190	Drew Bledsoe	.75	.30
❑	191	Michael Sinclair	.20	.07
❑	192	William Floyd	.20	.07
❑	193	Kenny Holmes	.20	.07
❑	194	Marvcus Patton	.20	.07
❑	195	Warren Sapp	.30	.10
❑	196	Junior Seau	.50	.20
❑	197	Ryan McNeil	.20	.07
❑	198	Tyrone Wheatley	.30	.10
❑	199	Robert Smith	.50	.20
❑	200	Terrell Davis	.50	.20
❑	201	Brett Perriman	.20	.07
❑	202	Tamarick Vanover	.20	.07
❑	203	Stephen Boyd	.20	.07
❑	204	Zack Crockett	.20	.07
❑	205	Sherman Williams	.20	.07
❑	206	Neil Smith	.30	.10
❑	207	Jermaine Lewis	.30	.10
❑	208	Kevin Williams	.20	.07
❑	209	Byron Hanspard	.20	.07
❑	210	Warren Moon	.50	.20
❑	211	Tony McGee	.20	.07
❑	212	Raymont Harris	.20	.07
❑	213	Eric Davis	.20	.07
❑	214	Darrien Gordon	.20	.07
❑	215	James Stewart	.30	.10
❑	216	Derrick Mayes	.30	.10
❑	217	Brad Johnson	.50	.20
❑	218	Karim Abdul-Jabbar UER	.50	.20
❑	219	Hugh Douglas	.20	.07
❑	220	Terry Allen	.50	.20
❑	221	Rhett Hall	.20	.07
❑	222	Terrell Fletcher	.20	.07
❑	223	Carnell Lake	.20	.07
❑	224	Darryll Lewis	.20	.07
❑	225	Chris Slade	.20	.07
❑	226	Michael Westbrook	.30	.10
❑	227	Willie Williams	.20	.07
❑	228	Tony Banks	.30	.10
❑	229	Keyshawn Johnson	.50	.20
❑	230	Mike Alstott	.50	.20
❑	231	Tiki Barber	.50	.20
❑	232	Jake Reed	.30	.10
❑	233	Eric Swann	.20	.07
❑	234	Eric Moulds	.50	.20
❑	235	Vinny Testaverde	.30	.10
❑	236	Jessie Tuggle	.20	.07
❑	237	Ryan Wetnight RC	.20	.07
❑	238	Tyrone Poole	.20	.07
❑	239	Bryant Westbrook	.20	.07
❑	240	Steve McNair	.50	.20
❑	241	Jimmy Smith	.30	.10
❑	242	Dewayne Washington	.20	.07
❑	243	Robert Harris	.20	.07
❑	244	Rod Woodson	.30	.10
❑	245	Reidel Anthony	.30	.10
❑	246	Jessie Armstead	.20	.07
❑	247	O.J. McDuffie	.30	.10
❑	248	Carlton Gray	.20	.07
❑	249	LeRoy Butler	.20	.07
❑	250	Jerry Rice	1.00	.40
❑	251	Frank Sanders	.30	.10
❑	252	Todd Collins	.20	.07
❑	253	Fred Lane	.20	.07
❑	254	David Dunn	.20	.07
❑	255	Micheal Barrow	.20	.07
❑	256	Luther Elliss	.20	.07
❑	257	Scott Mitchell	.30	.10
❑	258	Dave Meggett	.20	.07
❑	259	Rickey Dudley	.20	.07
❑	260	Isaac Bruce	.50	.20
❑	261	Tony Martin	.30	.10
❑	262	Leslie Shepherd	.20	.07
❑	263	Derrick Brooks	.50	.20
❑	264	Greg Lloyd	.20	.07
❑	265	Terrell Buckley	.20	.07
❑	266	Antonio Freeman	.50	.20
❑	267	Tony Brackens	.20	.07
❑	268	Mark McMillian	.20	.07
❑	269	Dexter Coakley	.20	.07
❑	270	Dan Marino	2.00	.75
❑	271	Bryan Cox	.20	.07
❑	272	Leeland McElroy	.20	.07
❑	273	Jeff Burris	.20	.07
❑	274	Eric Green	.20	.07
❑	275	Darnay Scott	.30	.10
❑	276	Greg Clark	.20	.07
❑	277	Mario Bates	.30	.10
❑	278	Eric Turner	.20	.07
❑	279	Neil O'Donnell	.30	.10
❑	280	Herman Moore	.30	.10
❑	281	Gary Brown	.20	.07
❑	282	Terrell Owens	.50	.20
❑	283	Frank Wycheck	.20	.07
❑	284	Trent Dilfer	.50	.20
❑	285	Curtis Martin	.50	.20
❑	286	Ricky Proehl	.20	.07
❑	287	Steve Atwater	.20	.07
❑	288	Aaron Bailey	.20	.07
❑	289	William Henderson	.30	.10
❑	290	Marcus Allen	.50	.20
❑	291	Tom Knight	.20	.07
❑	292	Quinn Early	.20	.07
❑	293	Michael McCrary	.20	.07
❑	294	Bert Emanuel	.30	.10
❑	295	Tom Carter	.20	.07
❑	296	Kevin Glover	.20	.07
❑	297	Marshall Faulk	.60	.25
❑	298	Harvey Williams	.20	.07
❑	299	Chris Warren	.30	.10
❑	300	John Elway	2.00	.75
❑	301	Eddie Kennison	.30	.10
❑	302	Gus Frerotte	.20	.07
❑	303	Regan Upshaw	.20	.07
❑	304	Kevin Gogan	.20	.07
❑	305	Napoleon Kaufman	.50	.20
❑	306	Charlie Garner	.30	.10
❑	307	Shawn Jefferson	.20	.07
❑	308	Tommy Vardell	.20	.07
❑	309	Mike Hollis	.20	.07
❑	310	Irving Fryar	.30	.10
❑	311	Shannon Sharpe	.30	.10
❑	312	Byron Bam Morris	.20	.07
❑	313	Jamal Anderson	.50	.20
❑	314	Chris Gedney	.20	.07
❑	315	Chris Spielman	.20	.07
❑	316	Derrick Alexander WR	.30	.10
❑	317	O.J. Santiago	.20	.07
❑	318	Anthony Miller	.20	.07
❑	319	Ki-Jana Carter	.20	.07
❑	320	Deion Sanders	.50	.20
❑	321	Joey Galloway	.30	.10
❑	322	J.J. Stokes	.30	.10
❑	323	Rodney Thomas	.20	.07
❑	324	John Lynch	.30	.10
❑	325	Mike Pritchard	.20	.07
❑	326	Terrance Shaw	.20	.07
❑	327	Ted Johnson	.20	.07
❑	328	Ashley Ambrose	.20	.07
❑	329	Checklist 1	.20	.07
❑	330	Checklist 2	.20	.07
❑	331	Jerome Pathon RC	2.50	1.00
❑	332	Ryan Leaf RC	2.50	1.00
❑	333	Duane Starks RC	1.25	.50
❑	334	Brian Simmons RC	2.00	.75
❑	335	Keith Brooking RC	2.50	1.00
❑	336	Robert Edwards RC	2.00	.75
❑	337	Curtis Enis RC	1.25	.50
❑	338	John Avery RC	2.00	.75
❑	339	Fred Taylor RC	4.00	1.50
❑	340	Germane Crowell RC	2.00	.75
❑	341	Hines Ward RC	10.00	6.00
❑	342	Marcus Nash RC	1.25	.50
❑	343	Jacquez Green RC	2.00	.75
❑	344	Joe Jurevicius RC	2.50	1.00
❑	345	Greg Ellis RC	1.25	.50
❑	346	Brian Griese RC	5.00	2.00
❑	347	Tavian Banks RC	2.00	.75
❑	348	Robert Holcombe RC	2.00	.75
❑	349	Skip Hicks RC	2.00	.75
❑	350	Ahman Green RC	12.00	5.00
❑	351	Takeo Spikes RC	2.50	1.00
❑	352	Randy Moss RC	15.00	6.00
❑	353	Andre Wadsworth RC	2.00	.75
❑	354	Jason Peter RC	1.25	.50
❑	355	Grant Wistrom RC	2.00	.75
❑	356	Charles Woodson RC	3.00	1.25
❑	357	Kevin Dyson RC	2.50	1.00
❑	358	Pat Johnson RC	2.00	.75
❑	359	Tim Dwight RC	2.50	1.00
❑	360	Peyton Manning RC	25.00	10.00
❑	P1	Robert Tisch	5.00	2.00

1999 Topps

❑		COMPLETE SET (357)	50.00	20.00
❑		COMP.SET w/o SP's (330)	20.00	10.00
❑	1	Terrell Davis	.60	.25
❑	2	Adrian Murrell	.40	.15
❑	3	Ernie Mills	.25	.08
❑	4	Jimmy Hitchcock	.25	.08
❑	5	Charlie Garner	.40	.15
❑	6	Blaine Bishop	.25	.08

❑ 7 Junior Seau .60 .25
❑ 8 Andre Rison .40 .15
❑ 9 Jake Reed .40 .15
❑ 10 Cris Carter .60 .25
❑ 11 Torrance Small .25 .08
❑ 12 Ronald McKinnon .25 .08
❑ 13 Tyrone Davis .25 .08
❑ 14 Warren Moon .60 .25
❑ 15 Joe Johnson .25 .08
❑ 16 Bert Emanuel .40 .15
❑ 17 Brad Culpepper .25 .08
❑ 18 Henry Jones .25 .08
❑ 19 Jonathan Ogden .25 .08
❑ 20 Terrell Owens .60 .25
❑ 21 Derrick Mason .40 .15
❑ 22 Jon Ritchie .25 .08
❑ 23 Eric Metcalf .25 .08
❑ 24 Kevin Carter .25 .08
❑ 25 Fred Taylor .60 .25
❑ 26 DeWayne Washington .25 .08
❑ 27 William Thomas .25 .08
❑ 28 Rocket Ismail .40 .15
❑ 29 Jason Taylor .25 .08
❑ 30 Doug Flutie .60 .25
❑ 31 Michael Sinclair .25 .08
❑ 32 Yancey Thigpen .25 .08
❑ 33 Darnay Scott .25 .08
❑ 34 Amani Toomer .25 .08
❑ 35 Edgar Bennett .25 .08
❑ 36 LeRoy Butler .25 .08
❑ 37 Jessie Tuggle .25 .08
❑ 38 Andrew Glover .25 .08
❑ 39 Tim McDonald .25 .08
❑ 40 Marshall Faulk .75 .30
❑ 41 Ray Mickens .25 .08
❑ 42 Kimble Anders .40 .15
❑ 43 Trent Green .60 .25
❑ 44 Dermontti Dawson .25 .08
❑ 45 Greg Ellis .25 .08
❑ 46 Hugh Douglas .25 .08
❑ 47 Amp Lee .25 .08
❑ 48 Lamar Thomas .25 .08
❑ 49 Curtis Conway .40 .15
❑ 50 Emmitt Smith 1.25 .50
❑ 51 Elvis Grbac .40 .15
❑ 52 Tony Simmons .25 .08
❑ 53 Darrin Smith .25 .08
❑ 54 Donovin Darius .25 .08
❑ 55 Corey Chavous .25 .08
❑ 56 Phillippi Sparks .25 .08
❑ 57 Luther Elliss .25 .08
❑ 58 Tim Dwight .60 .25
❑ 59 Andre Hastings .25 .08
❑ 60 Dan Marino 2.00 .75
❑ 61 Micheal Barrow .25 .08
❑ 62 Corey Fuller .25 .08
❑ 63 Bill Romanowski .25 .08
❑ 64 Derrick Rodgers .40 .15
❑ 65 Natrone Means .40 .15
❑ 66 Peter Boulware .25 .08
❑ 67 Brian Mitchell .25 .08
❑ 68 Cornelius Bennett .25 .08
❑ 69 Dedric Ward .25 .08
❑ 70 Drew Bledsoe .75 .30
❑ 71 Freddie Jones .25 .08
❑ 72 Derrick Thomas .60 .25
❑ 73 Willie Davis .25 .08
❑ 74 Larry Centers .25 .08
❑ 75 Mark Brunell .60 .25
❑ 76 Chuck Smith .25 .08
❑ 77 Desmond Howard .40 .15
❑ 78 Sedrick Shaw .25 .08
❑ 79 Tiki Barber .60 .25
❑ 80 Curtis Martin .60 .25
❑ 81 Barry Minter .25 .08
❑ 82 Skip Hicks .25 .08
❑ 83 O.J. Santiago .25 .08
❑ 84 Ed McCaffrey .40 .15
❑ 85 Terrell Buckley .25 .08
❑ 86 Charlie Jones .25 .08
❑ 87 Pete Mitchell .25 .08
❑ 88 La'Roi Glover RC .60 .25
❑ 89 Eric Davis .25 .08
❑ 90 John Elway 2.00 .75
❑ 91 Kavika Pittman .25 .08
❑ 92 Fred Lane .25 .08
❑ 93 Warren Sapp .25 .08
❑ 94 Lorenzo Bromell RC .60 .25
❑ 95 Lawyer Milloy .40 .15
❑ 96 Aeneas Williams .25 .08
❑ 97 Michael McCrary .25 .08
❑ 98 Rickey Dudley .25 .08
❑ 99 Bryce Paup .25 .08
❑ 100 Jamal Anderson .60 .25
❑ 101 D'Marco Farr .25 .08
❑ 102 Johnnie Morton .40 .15
❑ 103 Jeff Graham .25 .08
❑ 104 Sam Cowart .25 .08
❑ 105 Bryant Young .25 .08
❑ 106 Jermaine Lewis .40 .15
❑ 107 Chad Bratzke .25 .08
❑ 108 Jeff Burris .25 .08
❑ 109 Roell Preston .25 .08
❑ 110 Vinny Testaverde .40 .15
❑ 111 Ruben Brown .25 .08
❑ 112 Darryll Lewis .25 .08
❑ 113 Billy Davis .25 .08
❑ 114 Bryant Westbrook .25 .08
❑ 115 Stephen Alexander .25 .08
❑ 116 Terrell Fletcher .25 .08
❑ 117 Terry Glenn .60 .25
❑ 118 Rod Smith .40 .15
❑ 119 Carl Pickens .40 .15
❑ 120 Tim Brown .60 .25
❑ 121 Mikhael Ricks .25 .08
❑ 122 Jason Gildon .25 .08
❑ 123 Charles Way .25 .08
❑ 124 Rob Moore .40 .15
❑ 125 Jerome Bettis .60 .25
❑ 126 Kerry Collins .40 .15
❑ 127 Bruce Smith .40 .15
❑ 128 James Hasty .25 .08
❑ 129 Ken Norton Jr. .25 .08
❑ 130 Charles Woodson .60 .25
❑ 131 Tony McGee .25 .08
❑ 132 Kevin Turner .25 .08
❑ 133 Jerome Pathon .25 .08
❑ 134 Garrison Hearst .40 .15
❑ 135 Craig Newsome .25 .08
❑ 136 Hardy Nickerson .25 .08
❑ 137 Ray Lewis .60 .25
❑ 138 Derrick Alexander .25 .08
❑ 139 Phil Hansen .25 .08
❑ 140 Joey Galloway .40 .15
❑ 141 Oronde Gadsden .40 .15
❑ 142 Herman Moore .40 .15
❑ 143 Bobby Taylor .25 .08
❑ 144 Mario Bates .25 .08
❑ 145 Kevin Dyson .40 .15
❑ 146 Aaron Glenn .25 .08
❑ 147 Ed McDaniel .25 .08
❑ 148 Terry Allen .40 .15
❑ 149 Ike Hilliard .25 .08
❑ 150 Steve Young .75 .30
❑ 151 Eugene Robinson .25 .08
❑ 152 John Mobley .25 .08
❑ 153 Kevin Hardy .25 .08
❑ 154 Lance Johnstone .25 .08
❑ 155 Willie McGinest .25 .08
❑ 156 Gary Anderson .25 .08
❑ 157 Dexter Coakley .25 .08
❑ 158 Mark Fields .25 .08
❑ 159 Steve McNair .60 .25
❑ 160 Corey Dillon .60 .25
❑ 161 Zach Thomas .60 .25
❑ 162 Kent Graham .25 .08
❑ 163 Tony Parrish .25 .08
❑ 164 Sam Gash .25 .08
❑ 165 Kyle Brady .25 .08
❑ 166 Donnell Bennett .25 .08
❑ 167 Tony Martin .40 .15
❑ 168 Michael Bates .25 .08
❑ 169 Bobby Engram .40 .15
❑ 170 Jimmy Smith .40 .15
❑ 171 Vonnie Holliday .25 .08
❑ 172 Simeon Rice .40 .15
❑ 173 Kevin Greene .25 .08
❑ 174 Mike Alstott .60 .25
❑ 175 Eddie George .60 .25
❑ 176 Michael Jackson .25 .08
❑ 177 Neil O'Donnell .40 .15
❑ 178 Sean Dawkins .25 .08
❑ 179 Courtney Hawkins .25 .08
❑ 180 Michael Irvin .40 .15
❑ 181 Thurman Thomas .40 .15
❑ 182 Cam Cleeland .25 .08
❑ 183 Ellis Johnson .25 .08
❑ 184 Will Blackwell .25 .08
❑ 185 Ty Law .40 .15
❑ 186 Merton Hanks .25 .08
❑ 187 Dan Wilkinson .25 .08
❑ 188 Andre Wadsworth .25 .08
❑ 189 Troy Vincent .25 .08
❑ 190 Frank Sanders .40 .15
❑ 191 Stephen Boyd .25 .08
❑ 192 Jason Elam .25 .08
❑ 193 Kordell Stewart .40 .15
❑ 194 Ted Johnson .25 .08
❑ 195 Glyn Milburn .25 .08
❑ 196 Gary Brown .25 .08
❑ 197 Travis Hall .25 .08
❑ 198 John Randle .40 .15
❑ 199 Jay Riemersma .25 .08
❑ 200 Barry Sanders 2.00 .75
❑ 201 Chris Spielman .25 .08
❑ 202 Rod Woodson .40 .15
❑ 203 Darrell Russell .25 .08
❑ 204 Tony Boselli .25 .08
❑ 205 Darren Woodson .25 .08
❑ 206 Muhsin Muhammad .40 .15
❑ 207 Jim Harbaugh .40 .15
❑ 208 Isaac Bruce .60 .25
❑ 209 Mo Lewis .25 .08
❑ 210 Dorsey Levens .60 .25
❑ 211 Frank Wycheck .25 .08
❑ 212 Napoleon Kaufman .60 .25
❑ 213 Walt Harris .25 .08
❑ 214 Leon Lett .25 .08
❑ 215 Karim Abdul-Jabbar .40 .15
❑ 216 Carnell Lake .25 .08
❑ 217 Byron Bam Morris .25 .08
❑ 218 John Avery .25 .08
❑ 219 Chris Slade .25 .08
❑ 220 Robert Smith .60 .25
❑ 221 Mike Pritchard .25 .08
❑ 222 Ty Detmer .40 .15
❑ 223 Randall Cunningham .60 .25
❑ 224 Alonzo Mayes .25 .08
❑ 225 Jake Plummer .40 .15
❑ 226 Derrick Mayes .25 .08
❑ 227 Jeff Brady .25 .08
❑ 228 John Lynch .40 .15
❑ 229 Steve Atwater .25 .08
❑ 230 Warrick Dunn .60 .25
❑ 231 Shawn Jefferson .25 .08
❑ 232 Erik Kramer .25 .08
❑ 233 Ken Dilger .25 .08
❑ 234 Ryan Leaf .60 .25
❑ 235 Ray Buchanan .25 .08
❑ 236 Kevin Williams .25 .08
❑ 237 Ricky Watters .40 .15
❑ 238 Dwayne Rudd .25 .08
❑ 239 Duce Staley .60 .25
❑ 240 Charlie Batch .60 .25
❑ 241 Tim Biakabutuka .40 .15
❑ 242 Tony Gonzalez .60 .25
❑ 243 Bryan Still .25 .08
❑ 244 Donnie Edwards .25 .08
❑ 245 Troy Aikman 1.25 .50
❑ 246 Tony Banks .40 .15
❑ 247 Curtis Enis .25 .08
❑ 248 Chris Chandler .40 .15
❑ 249 James Jett .40 .15
❑ 250 Brett Favre 2.00 .75

❑ 251	Keith Poole	.25	.08
❑ 252	Ricky Proehl	.25	.08
❑ 253	Shannon Sharpe	.40	.15
❑ 254	Robert Jones	.25	.08
❑ 255	Chad Brown	.25	.08
❑ 256	Ben Coates	.40	.15
❑ 257	Jacquez Green	.25	.08
❑ 258	Jessie Armstead	.25	.08
❑ 259	Dale Carter	.25	.08
❑ 260	Antowain Smith	.60	.25
❑ 261	Mark Chmura	.25	.08
❑ 262	Michael Westbrook	.40	.15
❑ 263	Marvin Harrison	.60	.25
❑ 264	Darrien Gordon	.25	.08
❑ 265	Rodney Harrison	.25	.08
❑ 266	Charles Johnson	.25	.08
❑ 267	Roman Phifer	.25	.08
❑ 268	Reidel Anthony	.40	.15
❑ 269	Jerry Rice	1.25	.50
❑ 270	Eric Moulds	.60	.25
❑ 271	Robert Porcher	.25	.08
❑ 272	Deion Sanders	.60	.25
❑ 273	Germane Crowell	.25	.08
❑ 274	Randy Moss	1.50	.60
❑ 275	Antonio Freeman	.60	.25
❑ 276	Trent Dilfer	.40	.15
❑ 277	Eric Turner	.25	.08
❑ 278	Jeff George	.40	.15
❑ 279	Levon Kirkland	.25	.08
❑ 280	O.J. McDuffie	.40	.15
❑ 281	Takeo Spikes	.25	.08
❑ 282	Jim Flanigan	.25	.08
❑ 283	Chris Warren	.25	.08
❑ 284	J.J. Stokes	.40	.15
❑ 285	Bryan Cox	.25	.08
❑ 286	Sam Madison	.25	.08
❑ 287	Priest Holmes	1.00	.40
❑ 288	Keenan McCardell	.40	.15
❑ 289	Michael Strahan	.40	.15
❑ 290	Robert Edwards	.25	.08
❑ 291	Tommy Vardell	.25	.08
❑ 292	Wayne Chrebet	.40	.15
❑ 293	Chris Calloway	.25	.08
❑ 294	Wesley Walls	.40	.15
❑ 295	Derrick Brooks	.60	.25
❑ 296	Trace Armstrong	.25	.08
❑ 297	Brian Simmons	.25	.08
❑ 298	Darrell Green	.25	.08
❑ 299	Robert Brooks	.40	.15
❑ 300	Peyton Manning	2.00	.75
❑ 301	Dana Stubblefield	.25	.08
❑ 302	Shawn Springs	.25	.08
❑ 303	Leslie Shepherd	.25	.08
❑ 304	Ken Harvey	.25	.08
❑ 305	Jon Kitna	.60	.25
❑ 306	Terance Mathis	.40	.15
❑ 307	Andre Reed	.40	.15
❑ 308	Jackie Harris	.25	.08
❑ 309	Rich Gannon	.60	.25
❑ 310	Keyshawn Johnson	.60	.25
❑ 311	Victor Green	.25	.08
❑ 312	Eric Allen	.25	.08
❑ 313	Terry Fair	.25	.08
❑ 314	Jason Elam SH	.25	.08
❑ 315	Garrison Hearst SH	.40	.15
❑ 316	Jake Plummer SH	.40	.15
❑ 317	Randall Cunningham SH	.60	.25
❑ 318	Randy Moss SH	.75	.30
❑ 319	Jamal Anderson SH	.60	.25
❑ 320	John Elway SH	1.00	.40
❑ 321	Doug Flutie SH	.40	.15
❑ 322	Emmitt Smith SH	.75	.30
❑ 323	Terrell Davis SH	.60	.25
❑ 324	Jerris McPhail	.25	.08
❑ 325	Damon Gibson	.25	.08
❑ 326	Jim Pyne	.25	.08
❑ 327	Antonio Langham	.25	.08
❑ 328	Freddie Solomon	.25	.08
❑ 329	Ricky Williams RC	4.00	1.50
❑ 330	Daunte Culpepper RC	8.00	3.00
❑ 331	Chris Claiborne RC	1.25	.50
❑ 332	Amos Zereoue RC	2.50	1.00
❑ 333	Chris McAlister RC	2.00	.75
❑ 334	Kevin Faulk RC	2.50	1.00
❑ 335	James Johnson RC	2.00	.75
❑ 336	Mike Cloud RC	2.00	.75
❑ 337	Jevon Kearse RC	4.00	1.50
❑ 338	Akili Smith RC	2.00	.75
❑ 339	Edgerrin James RC	8.00	3.00
❑ 340	Cecil Collins RC	1.25	.50
❑ 341	Donovan McNabb RC	10.00	4.00
❑ 342	Kevin Johnson RC	2.50	1.00
❑ 343	Torry Holt RC	5.00	2.00
❑ 344	Rob Konrad RC	1.25	.50
❑ 345	Tim Couch RC	2.50	1.00
❑ 346	David Boston RC	2.50	1.00
❑ 347	Karsten Bailey RC	2.00	.75
❑ 348	Troy Edwards RC	2.00	.75
❑ 349	Sedrick Irvin RC	1.25	.50
❑ 350	Shaun King RC	2.00	.75
❑ 351	Peerless Price RC	2.50	1.00
❑ 352	Brock Huard RC	2.50	1.00
❑ 353	Cade McNown RC	2.00	.75
❑ 354	Champ Bailey RC	3.00	1.25
❑ 355	D'Wayne Bates RC	2.00	.75
❑ 356	Checklist Card	.25	.08
❑ 357	Checklist Card	.25	.08

2000 Topps

❑ COMPLETE SET (400)	60.00	25.00
❑ COMP.SET w/o SP's (360)	20.00	7.50
❑ SBMVP STATED ODDS 1:1287 HTA		

❑ 1	Kurt Warner	1.25	.50
❑ 2	Darrell Russell	.25	.08
❑ 3	Tai Streets	.25	.08
❑ 4	Bryant Young	.25	.08
❑ 5	Kent Graham	.25	.08
❑ 6	Shawn Jefferson	.25	.08
❑ 7	Wesley Walls	.25	.08
❑ 8	Jessie Armstead	.25	.08
❑ 9	Dedric Ward	.25	.08
❑ 10	Emmitt Smith	1.25	.50
❑ 11	James Stewart	.40	.15
❑ 12	Frank Sanders	.25	.08
❑ 13	Ray Buchanan	.25	.08
❑ 14	Olindo Mare	.25	.08
❑ 15	Andre Reed	.40	.15
❑ 16	Curtis Conway	.40	.15
❑ 17	Patrick Jeffers	.60	.25
❑ 18	Greg Hill	.25	.08
❑ 19	John Unitas	.60	.25
❑ 20	Brett Favre	2.00	.75
❑ 21	Jerome Pathon	.40	.15
❑ 22	Jason Tucker	.25	.08
❑ 23	Charles Johnson	.40	.15
❑ 24	Brian Mitchell	.25	.08
❑ 25	Billy Miller	.25	.08
❑ 26	Jay Fiedler	.60	.25
❑ 27	Marcus Pollard	.25	.08
❑ 28	De'Mond Parker	.25	.08
❑ 29	Leslie Shepherd	.25	.08
❑ 30	Fred Taylor	.60	.25
❑ 31	Michael Pittman	.25	.08
❑ 32	Ricky Watters	.40	.15
❑ 33	Derrick Brooks	.60	.25
❑ 34	Junior Seau	.60	.25
❑ 35	Troy Vincent	.25	.08
❑ 36	Eric Allen	.25	.08
❑ 37	Pete Mitchell	.25	.08
❑ 38	Tony Simmons	.25	.08
❑ 39	Az-Zahir Hakim	.40	.15
❑ 40	Dan Marino	2.00	.75
❑ 41	Mac Cody	.25	.08
❑ 42	Scott Dreisbach	.25	.08
❑ 43	Al Wilson	.25	.08
❑ 44	Luther Broughton RC	.40	.15
❑ 45	Wane McGarity	.25	.08
❑ 46	Stephen Boyd	.25	.08
❑ 47	Michael Strahan	.40	.15
❑ 48	Chris Chandler	.40	.15
❑ 49	Tony Martin	.40	.15
❑ 50	Edgerrin James	1.00	.40
❑ 51	John Randle	.40	.15
❑ 52	Warrick Dunn	.60	.25
❑ 53	Elvis Grbac	.40	.15
❑ 54	Champ Bailey	.40	.15
❑ 55	Kyle Brady	.25	.08
❑ 56	John Lynch	.40	.15
❑ 57	Kevin Carter	.25	.08
❑ 58	Mike Pritchard	.25	.08
❑ 59	Deon Mitchell RC	.40	.15
❑ 60	Randy Moss	1.25	.50
❑ 61	Jermaine Fazande	.25	.08
❑ 62	Donovan McNabb	1.00	.40
❑ 63	Richard Huntley	.25	.08
❑ 64	Rich Gannon	.60	.25
❑ 65	Aaron Glenn	.25	.08
❑ 66	Amani Toomer	.25	.08
❑ 67	Andre Hastings	.25	.08
❑ 68	Ricky Williams	.60	.25
❑ 69	Sam Madison	.25	.08
❑ 70	Drew Bledsoe	.75	.30
❑ 71	Eric Moulds	.60	.25
❑ 72	Justin Armour	.25	.08
❑ 73	Jamal Anderson	.60	.25
❑ 74	Mario Bates	.25	.08
❑ 75	Sam Gash	.25	.08
❑ 76	Macey Brooks	.25	.08
❑ 77	Tremain Mack	.25	.08
❑ 78	David LaFleur	.25	.08
❑ 79	Dexter Coakley	.25	.08
❑ 80	Cris Carter	.60	.25
❑ 81	Byron Chamberlain	.25	.08
❑ 82	David Sloan	.25	.08
❑ 83	Mike Devlin RC	.25	.08
❑ 84	Jimmy Smith	.40	.15
❑ 85	Derrick Alexander	.40	.15
❑ 86	Damon Huard	.60	.25
❑ 87	Jake Reed	.40	.15
❑ 88	Darrell Green	.25	.08
❑ 89	Derrick Mason	.40	.15
❑ 90	Curtis Martin	.60	.25
❑ 91	Donnie Abraham	.25	.08
❑ 92	D'Marco Farr	.25	.08
❑ 93	Ahman Green	.60	.25
❑ 94	Shane Matthews	.40	.15
❑ 95	Torrance Small	.25	.08
❑ 96	Duce Staley	.60	.25
❑ 97	Jon Ritchie	.25	.08
❑ 98	Victor Green	.25	.08
❑ 99	Kerry Collins	.40	.15
❑ 100	Peyton Manning	1.50	.60
❑ 101	Ben Coates	.25	.08
❑ 102	Thurman Thomas	.40	.15
❑ 103	Cornelius Bennett	.25	.08
❑ 104	Terance Mathis	.40	.15
❑ 105	Adrian Murrell	.40	.15
❑ 106	Donald Hayes	.25	.08
❑ 107	Terry Kirby	.25	.08
❑ 108	James Allen	.40	.15
❑ 109	Ty Law	.40	.15
❑ 110	Tim Brown	.60	.25
❑ 111	Chad Bratzke	.25	.08
❑ 112	Deion Sanders	.60	.25
❑ 113	James Johnson	.25	.08
❑ 114	Tony Richardson RC	.40	.15
❑ 115	Tony Brackens	.25	.08
❑ 116	Ken Dilger	.25	.08
❑ 117	Albert Connell	.25	.08
❑ 118	Neil O'Donnell	.25	.08
❑ 119	Selucio Sanford EP RC	.60	.25
❑ 120	Steve Young	.75	.30
❑ 121	Tony Horne	.25	.08
❑ 122	Charlie Rogers	.25	.08
❑ 123	J.J. Stokes	.40	.15
❑ 124	Kenny Bynum	.25	.08
❑ 125	Jeff Graham	.25	.08
❑ 126	Ike Hilliard	.40	.15
❑ 127	Ray Lucas	.40	.15
❑ 128	Terry Glenn	.40	.15
❑ 129	Rickey Dudley	.25	.08
❑ 130	Joey Galloway	.40	.15

❑ 131 Brian Dawkins .60 .25
❑ 132 Rob Moore .40 .15
❑ 133 Bob Christian .25 .08
❑ 134 Anthony Wright RC 2.00 .75
❑ 135 Antowain Smith .40 .15
❑ 136 Kevin Johnson .60 .25
❑ 137 Scott Covington .25 .08
❑ 138 D'Wayne Bates .25 .08
❑ 139 Sam Cowart .25 .08
❑ 140 Isaac Bruce .60 .25
❑ 141 Tony McGee .25 .08
❑ 142 Dale Carter .25 .08
❑ 143 Matt Hasselbeck .40 .15
❑ 144 Torry Holt .60 .25
❑ 145 Daunte Culpepper .75 .30
❑ 146 Yatil Green .25 .08
❑ 147 Chris Howard .25 .08
❑ 148 Irving Fryar .40 .15
❑ 149 Derrick Mayes .40 .15
❑ 150 Warren Sapp .40 .15
❑ 151 Ricky Proehl .25 .08
❑ 152 Eric Kresser EP .50 .20
❑ 153 Jeff Garcia .60 .25
❑ 154 Freddie Jones .25 .08
❑ 155 Mike Cloud .25 .08
❑ 156 Wayne Chrebet .40 .15
❑ 157 Joe Montgomery .25 .08
❑ 158 Shannon Sharpe .40 .15
❑ 159 Eddie Kennison .25 .08
❑ 160 Eddie George .60 .25
❑ 161 Jay Riemersma .25 .08
❑ 162 Peter Boulware .25 .08
❑ 163 Aeneas Williams .25 .08
❑ 164 Jim Miller .25 .08
❑ 165 Jamir Miller .25 .08
❑ 166 Tim Biakabutuka .40 .15
❑ 167 Kordell Stewart .40 .15
❑ 168 Charlie Garner .40 .15
❑ 169 Germane Crowell .25 .08
❑ 170 Stephen Davis .60 .25
❑ 171 Jeff George .40 .15
❑ 172 Mark Brunell .60 .25
❑ 173 Stephen Alexander .25 .08
❑ 174 Mike Alstott .60 .25
❑ 175 Terry Allen .40 .15
❑ 176 Ed McCaffrey .60 .25
❑ 177 Bobby Engram .25 .08
❑ 178 Andre Cooper .25 .08
❑ 179 Kevin Faulk .25 .08
❑ 180 Errict Rhett .40 .15
❑ 181 Jammi German .25 .08
❑ 182 Oronde Gadsden .40 .15
❑ 183 Jevon Kearse .60 .25
❑ 184 Herman Moore .40 .15
❑ 185 Terrence Wilkins .25 .08
❑ 186 Rocket Ismail .40 .15
❑ 187 Patrick Johnson .25 .08
❑ 188 Simeon Rice .40 .15
❑ 189 Mo Lewis .25 .08
❑ 190 Qadry Ismail .40 .15
❑ 191 Terry Jackson .25 .08
❑ 192 Rashaan Shehee .25 .08
❑ 193 Charles Woodson .40 .15
❑ 194 Akili Smith .25 .08
❑ 195 Yancey Thigpen .25 .08
❑ 196 Michael Westbrook .40 .15
❑ 197 Donnell Bennett .25 .08
❑ 198 Sedrick Irvin .25 .08
❑ 199 Keenan McCardell .40 .15
❑ 200 Marshall Faulk .75 .30
❑ 201 Jeff Blake .40 .15
❑ 202 Rob Johnson .40 .15
❑ 203 Vinny Testaverde .40 .15
❑ 204 Andy Katzenmoyer .25 .08
❑ 205 Michael Basnight .25 .08
❑ 206 Lance Schulters .25 .08
❑ 207 Shaun King .25 .08
❑ 208 Bill Schroeder .40 .15
❑ 209 Skip Hicks .25 .08
❑ 210 Jake Plummer .40 .15
❑ 211 Leroy Hoard .25 .08
❑ 212 Reggie Barlow .25 .08
❑ 213 E.G. Green .25 .08
❑ 214 Fred Lane .25 .08
❑ 215 Antonio Freeman .60 .25
❑ 216 Grant Wistrom .25 .08
❑ 217 Kevin Dyson .40 .15
❑ 218 Mikhael Ricks .25 .08
❑ 219 Rod Woodson .40 .15
❑ 220 Tim Dwight .60 .25
❑ 221 Darnay Scott .40 .15
❑ 222 Curtis Enis .25 .08
❑ 223 Sean Bennett .25 .08
❑ 224 Napoleon Kaufman .40 .15
❑ 225 Jonathan Linton .25 .08
❑ 226 Jim Harbaugh .40 .15
❑ 227 Hardy Nickerson .25 .08
❑ 228 Todd Lyght .25 .08
❑ 229 Dorsey Levens .40 .15
❑ 230 Steve Beuerlein .40 .15
❑ 231 Marty Booker .40 .15
❑ 232 Andre Wadsworth .25 .08
❑ 233 James Hasty .25 .08
❑ 234 Shawn Bryson .25 .08
❑ 235 Larry Centers .25 .08
❑ 236 Charlie Batch .60 .25
❑ 237 Steve McNair .60 .25
❑ 238 Darrin Chiaverini .25 .08
❑ 239 Jerome Bettis .60 .25
❑ 240 Muhsin Muhammad .40 .15
❑ 241 Terrell Fletcher .25 .08
❑ 242 Jon Kitna .60 .25
❑ 243 Frank Wycheck .25 .08
❑ 244 Tony Gonzalez .40 .15
❑ 245 Ron Rivers .25 .08
❑ 246 Olandis Gary .60 .25
❑ 247 Jermaine Lewis .25 .08
❑ 248 Joe Jurevicius .25 .08
❑ 249 Richie Anderson .40 .15
❑ 250 Marcus Robinson .60 .25
❑ 251 Shawn Springs .25 .08
❑ 252 William Floyd .25 .08
❑ 253 Bobby Shaw RC .60 .25
❑ 254 Glyn Milburn .25 .08
❑ 255 Brian Griese .60 .25
❑ 256 Donnie Edwards .25 .08
❑ 257 Joe Horn .40 .15
❑ 258 Cameron Cleeland .25 .08
❑ 259 Glenn Foley .25 .08
❑ 260 Corey Dillon .60 .25
❑ 261 Troy Brown .40 .15
❑ 262 Stoney Case .25 .08
❑ 263 Kevin Williams .25 .08
❑ 264 London Fletcher RC .40 .15
❑ 265 O.J. McDuffie .40 .15
❑ 266 Jonathan Quinn .25 .08
❑ 267 Trent Dilfer .40 .15
❑ 268 Dameyune Craig .25 .08
❑ 269 Terrell Owens .60 .25
❑ 270 Tim Couch .40 .15
❑ 271 Dameane Douglas .25 .08
❑ 272 Moses Moreno .25 .08
❑ 273 Bruce Smith .40 .15
❑ 274 Peerless Price .40 .15
❑ 275 Sam Gamer .25 .08
❑ 276 Natrone Means .25 .08
❑ 277 Na Brown .25 .08
❑ 278 Dave Moore .25 .08
❑ 279 Chris Sanders .25 .08
❑ 280 Troy Aikman 1.25 .50
❑ 281 Cecil Collins .25 .08
❑ 282 Matthew Hatchette .25 .08
❑ 283 Bill Romanowski .25 .08
❑ 284 Basil Mitchell .25 .08
❑ 285 Tony Banks .40 .15
❑ 286 Jake Delhomme RC 2.50 1.00
❑ 287 Keyshawn Johnson .60 .25
❑ 288 Dexter McCleon RC .60 .25
❑ 289 Corey Bradford .40 .15
❑ 290 Terrell Davis .60 .25
❑ 291 Johnnie Morton .40 .15
❑ 292 Kevin Lockett .25 .08
❑ 293 Robert Smith .60 .25
❑ 294 Jeff Lewis .25 .08
❑ 295 Wali Rainer .25 .08
❑ 296 Troy Edwards .25 .08
❑ 297 Keith Poole .25 .08
❑ 298 Priest Holmes .75 .30
❑ 299 David Boston .60 .25
❑ 300 Marvin Harrison .60 .25
❑ 301 Levon Kirkland .25 .08
❑ 302 Robert Holcombe .25 .08
❑ 303 Autry Denson .25 .08
❑ 304 Kevin Hardy .25 .08
❑ 305 Rod Smith .40 .15
❑ 306 Robert Porcher .25 .08
❑ 307 Cade McNown .25 .08
❑ 308 Craig Yeast .25 .08
❑ 309 Doug Flutie .60 .25
❑ 310 Jerry Rice 1.25 .50
❑ 311 Brad Johnson .60 .25
❑ 312 Tiki Barber .60 .25
❑ 313 Will Blackwell .25 .08
❑ 314 Sean Dawkins .25 .08
❑ 315 Jacquez Green .25 .08
❑ 316 Zach Thomas .60 .25
❑ 317 Gus Frerotte .25 .08
❑ 318 Chris Warren .25 .08
❑ 319 Carl Pickens .40 .15
❑ 320 Tyrone Wheatley HL .25 .08
❑ 321 Kurt Warner HL .60 .25
❑ 322 Dan Marino HL 1.00 .40
❑ 323 Cris Carter HL .40 .15
❑ 324 Brett Favre HL 1.00 .40
❑ 325 Marshall Faulk HL .60 .25
❑ 326 Jevon Kearse HL .40 .15
❑ 327 Edgerrin James HL .60 .25
❑ 328 Emmitt Smith HL .60 .25
❑ 329 Andre Reed HL .25 .08
❑ 330 K.Dyson/F.Wycheck HL .25 .08
❑ 331 Olindo Mare MM .25 .08
❑ 332 Marcus Coleman MM .25 .08
❑ 333 James Johnson MM .25 .08
❑ 334 Ray Lucas MM .40 .15
❑ 335 Dedric Ward MM .25 .08
❑ 336 Richie Cunningham MM .25 .08
❑ 337 James Hasty MM .25 .08
❑ 338 Sedrick Shaw MM .25 .08
❑ 339 Kurt Warner MM .60 .25
❑ 340 Marshall Faulk MM .60 .25
❑ 341 Brian Shay EP .50 .20
❑ 342 L.C. Stevens EP .50 .20
❑ 343 Corey Thomas EP .50 .20
❑ 344 Scott Milanovich EP .60 .25
❑ 345 Pat Barnes EP .60 .25
❑ 346 Danny Wuerffel EP .60 .25
❑ 347 Kevin Daft EP .50 .20
❑ 348 Ron Powlus EP RC 1.00 .40
❑ 349 Tony Graziani EP .60 .25
❑ 350 Norman Miller EP RC .50 .20
❑ 351 Cory Sauter EP .50 .20
❑ 352 Marcus Crandell EP RC .60 .25
❑ 353 Sean Morey EP RC .60 .25
❑ 354 Jeff Ogden EP .60 .25
❑ 355 Ted White EP .50 .20
❑ 356 Jim Kubiak EP RC .60 .25
❑ 357 Aaron Stecker EP RC 1.00 .40
❑ 358 Ronnie Powell EP .50 .20
❑ 359 Matt Lytle EP RC .60 .25
❑ 360 Kendrick Nord EP RC .50 .20
❑ 361 Tim Rattay RC 2.50 1.00
❑ 362 Rob Morris RC 2.50 1.00
❑ 363 Chris Samuels RC 2.00 .75
❑ 364 Todd Husak RC 2.50 1.00
❑ 365 Ahmed Plummer RC 2.50 1.00
❑ 366 Frank Murphy RC 2.00 .75
❑ 367 Michael Wiley RC 2.50 1.00
❑ 368 Giovanni Carmazzi RC 2.00 .75
❑ 369 Anthony Becht RC 2.50 1.00
❑ 370 John Abraham RC 2.50 1.00
❑ 371 Shaun Alexander RC 12.00 5.00
❑ 372 Thomas Jones RC 4.00 1.50
❑ 373 Courtney Brown RC 1.00 .40
❑ 374 Curtis Keaton RC 2.00 .75
❑ 375 Jerry Porter RC 3.00 1.25
❑ 376 Corey Simon RC 1.00 .40
❑ 377 Dez White RC 2.50 1.00
❑ 378 Jamal Lewis RC 6.00 2.50
❑ 379 Ron Dayne RC 2.50 1.00
❑ 380 R.Jay Soward RC 2.50 1.00
❑ 381 Tee Martin RC 2.50 1.00
❑ 382 Shaun Ellis RC 2.50 1.00
❑ 383 Brian Urlacher RC 10.00 4.00
❑ 384 Reuben Droughns RC 4.00 1.50
❑ 385 Travis Taylor RC 1.00 .40
❑ 386 Plaxico Burress RC 5.00 2.00
❑ 387 Chad Pennington RC 6.00 2.50
❑ 388 Sylvester Morris RC 2.50 1.00
❑ 389 Ron Dugans RC 2.00 .75
❑ 390 Joe Hamilton RC 2.50 1.00
❑ 391 Chris Redman RC .60 .25

❑ 392 Trung Canidate RC 2.50 1.00
❑ 393 J.R. Redmond RC 2.50 1.00
❑ 394 Danny Farmer RC 2.50 1.00
❑ 395 Todd Pinkston RC 2.50 1.00
❑ 396 Dennis Northcutt RC 2.50 1.00
❑ 397 Laveranues Coles RC 3.00 1.25
❑ 398 Bubba Franks RC 2.50 1.00
❑ 399 Travis Prentice RC 2.50 1.00
❑ 400 Peter Warrick RC 2.50 1.00
❑ SBMVP Kurt Warner FB AU 120.00 50.00

2001 Topps

❑ COMPLETE SET (385) 60.00 25.00
❑ 1 Marshall Faulk .75 .30
❑ 2 Lawyer Milloy .40 .15
❑ 3 Rich Gannon .60 .25
❑ 4 Rod Smith .40 .15
❑ 5 David Boston .60 .25
❑ 6 Jeremy McDaniel .25 .08
❑ 7 Joey Galloway .40 .15
❑ 8 Ron Dixon .25 .08
❑ 9 Terrell Fletcher .25 .08
❑ 10 Deion Sanders .60 .25
❑ 11 Jevon Kearse .40 .15
❑ 12 Charles Woodson .40 .15
❑ 13 Brian Walker .25 .08
❑ 14 Mike Peterson .25 .08
❑ 15 Marcus Robinson .60 .25
❑ 16 Duane Starks .25 .08
❑ 17 KaRon Coleman .25 .08
❑ 18 Randy Moss 1.25 .50
❑ 19 Reggie Jones .25 .08
❑ 20 Derrick Brooks .60 .25
❑ 21 Eddie George .60 .25
❑ 22 Wayne Chrebet .40 .15
❑ 23 Kevin Hardy .25 .08
❑ 24 Bill Schroeder .40 .15
❑ 25 Doug Flutie .60 .25
❑ 26 Tim Dwight .60 .25
❑ 27 Eddie Kennison .40 .15
❑ 28 Reggie Kelly .25 .08
❑ 29 Ricky Watters .40 .15
❑ 30 Stephen Alexander .25 .08
❑ 31 Az-Zahir Hakim .25 .08
❑ 32 Henri Crockett .25 .08
❑ 33 Joe Horn .40 .15
❑ 34 Danny Farmer .25 .08
❑ 35 Shannon Sharpe .40 .15
❑ 36 Brad Hoover .25 .08
❑ 37 David Patten .25 .08
❑ 38 Kevin Faulk .40 .15
❑ 39 Freddie Jones .25 .08
❑ 40 Michael Westbrook .40 .15
❑ 41 Jacquez Green .25 .08
❑ 42 Torrance Small .25 .08
❑ 43 Terrence Wilkins .25 .08
❑ 44 Brett Favre 2.00 .75
❑ 45 Tony Banks .40 .15
❑ 46 Johnnie Morton .40 .15
❑ 47 Jimmy Smith .40 .15
❑ 48 Jerry Rice 1.25 .50
❑ 49 Jeff George .40 .15
❑ 50 Ray Lewis .60 .25
❑ 51 Joe Johnson .25 .08
❑ 52 Rocket Ismail .40 .15
❑ 53 Muhsin Muhammad .40 .15
❑ 54 Ken Dilger .25 .08
❑ 55 Ike Hilliard .40 .15
❑ 56 Joey Porter RC 4.00 1.50
❑ 57 Shaun Alexander .75 .30
❑ 58 Jeff Garcia .60 .25
❑ 59 Jay Fiedler .60 .25
❑ 60 Wane McGarity .25 .08
❑ 61 Steve Beuerlein .25 .08
❑ 62 Tywan Mitchell .25 .08
❑ 63 Travis Prentice .25 .08
❑ 64 Robert Griffith .25 .08
❑ 65 Napoleon Kaufman .25 .08
❑ 66 Randall Godfrey .25 .08
❑ 67 Junior Seau .60 .25
❑ 68 Willie Jackson .25 .08
❑ 69 Larry Foster .25 .08
❑ 70 Brandon Stokley .40 .15
❑ 71 Hugh Douglas .25 .08
❑ 72 James Thrash .40 .15
❑ 73 Vinny Testaverde .40 .15
❑ 74 Leslie Shepherd .25 .08
❑ 75 Terrell Davis .60 .25
❑ 76 Jake Plummer .40 .15
❑ 77 Corey Dillon .60 .25
❑ 78 Ron Dayne .60 .25
❑ 79 Brock Huard .25 .08
❑ 80 Todd Husak .25 .08
❑ 81 Richard Huntley .25 .08
❑ 82 Shaun Ellis .25 .08
❑ 83 Kyle Brady .25 .08
❑ 84 Corey Bradford .25 .08
❑ 85 Eric Moulds .40 .15
❑ 86 Brian Finneran .25 .08
❑ 87 Antonio Freeman .60 .25
❑ 88 Terry Glenn .25 .08
❑ 89 Tai Streets .25 .08
❑ 90 Chris Sanders .25 .08
❑ 91 Sylvester Morris .25 .08
❑ 92 Peter Warrick .60 .25
❑ 93 Chris Greisen .25 .08
❑ 94 Cade McNown .25 .08
❑ 95 Jerome Pathon .40 .15
❑ 96 John Randle .25 .08
❑ 97 Curtis Conway .40 .15
❑ 98 Keyshawn Johnson .60 .25
❑ 99 Trent Green .60 .25
❑ 100 Mike Anderson .60 .25
❑ 101 Jeff Blake .40 .15
❑ 102 Tee Martin .40 .15
❑ 103 Darrell Jackson .60 .25
❑ 104 Mark Brunell .60 .25
❑ 105 Charlie Batch .60 .25
❑ 106 Wesley Walls .25 .08
❑ 107 Edgerrin James .75 .30
❑ 108 Robert Wilson .25 .08
❑ 109 Donovan McNabb .75 .30
❑ 110 Champ Bailey .40 .15
❑ 111 Isaac Bruce .60 .25
❑ 112 Michael Strahan .40 .15
❑ 113 Donnie Edwards .25 .08
❑ 114 Randall Cunningham .60 .25
❑ 115 Germane Crowell .25 .08
❑ 116 Jermaine Lewis .25 .08
❑ 117 Dennis McKinley .25 .08
❑ 118 Ryan Leaf .40 .15
❑ 119 Samari Rolle .25 .08
❑ 120 Daunte Culpepper .60 .25
❑ 121 Tim Couch .40 .15
❑ 122 Greg Biekert .25 .08
❑ 123 Warrick Dunn .60 .25
❑ 124 Richie Anderson .25 .08
❑ 125 Trace Armstrong .25 .08
❑ 126 Bernardo Harris .25 .08
❑ 127 Kwame Cavil .25 .08
❑ 128 James Allen .40 .15
❑ 129 Anthony Becht .25 .08
❑ 130 Tiki Barber .60 .25
❑ 131 Brad Johnson .60 .25
❑ 132 Tyrone Wheatley .40 .15
❑ 133 Kurt Warner 1.25 .50
❑ 134 Desmond Howard .25 .08
❑ 135 Thomas Jones .40 .15
❑ 136 Peyton Manning 1.50 .60
❑ 137 Tony Richardson .25 .08
❑ 138 Chris Chandler .40 .15
❑ 139 Plaxico Burress .60 .25
❑ 140 J.R. Redmond .25 .08
❑ 141 Fred Taylor .60 .25
❑ 142 Akili Smith .25 .08
❑ 143 Sammy Morris .25 .08
❑ 144 Jessie Armstead .25 .08
❑ 145 Charlie Garner .40 .15
❑ 146 Steve McNair .60 .25
❑ 147 Charles Johnson .25 .08
❑ 148 Troy Aikman 1.00 .40
❑ 149 Kevin Johnson .40 .15
❑ 150 Brian Urlacher 1.00 .40
❑ 151 Travis Taylor .40 .15
❑ 152 Aaron Shea .25 .08
❑ 153 Mike Cloud .25 .08
❑ 154 Donald Driver .40 .15
❑ 155 Chad Pennington 1.00 .40
❑ 156 Troy Edwards .25 .08
❑ 157 Reidel Anthony .25 .08
❑ 158 Michael Bishop .25 .08
❑ 159 Mo Lewis .25 .08
❑ 160 Damon Huard .25 .08
❑ 161 James McKnight .40 .15
❑ 162 Craig Yeast .25 .08
❑ 163 Michael Pittman .25 .08
❑ 164 Robert Smith .40 .15
❑ 165 Terrelle Smith .25 .08
❑ 166 Jeremiah Trotter .40 .15
❑ 167 Amani Toomer .25 .08
❑ 168 JaJuan Dawson .25 .08
❑ 169 Tim Biakabutuka .40 .15
❑ 170 Oronde Gadsden .40 .15
❑ 171 Ray Lucas .25 .08
❑ 172 Jermaine Fazande .25 .08
❑ 173 Todd Bouman .40 .15
❑ 174 Frank Wycheck .25 .08
❑ 175 Hines Ward .60 .25
❑ 176 Ahman Green .60 .25
❑ 177 Kaseem Sinceno .25 .08
❑ 178 Jamal Anderson .60 .25
❑ 179 Jay Riemersma .25 .08
❑ 180 Jarious Jackson .40 .15
❑ 181 Andre Rison .40 .15
❑ 182 Jerome Bettis .60 .25
❑ 183 Blaine Bishop .25 .08
❑ 184 Dorsey Levens .25 .08
❑ 185 James Stewart .40 .15
❑ 186 Chad Lewis .25 .08
❑ 187 Justin Watson .25 .08
❑ 188 Warren Sapp .40 .15
❑ 189 Rod Woodson .40 .15
❑ 190 Ricky Williams .60 .25
❑ 191 Marty Booker .25 .08
❑ 192 MarTay Jenkins .25 .08
❑ 193 Peerless Price .40 .15
❑ 194 Tony Gonzalez .40 .15
❑ 195 Jon Kitna .40 .15
❑ 196 Stephen Davis .60 .25
❑ 197 Curtis Martin .60 .25
❑ 198 Matt Hasselbeck .40 .15
❑ 199 Pat Johnson .25 .08
❑ 200 Emmitt Smith 1.25 .50
❑ 201 Doug Johnson .25 .08
❑ 202 Autry Denson .25 .08
❑ 203 Troy Brown .40 .15
❑ 204 Jeff Graham .25 .08
❑ 205 Corey Simon .40 .15
❑ 206 Jamel White .25 .08
❑ 207 Jeff Lewis .25 .08
❑ 208 Frank Sanders .25 .08
❑ 209 Al Wilson .25 .08
❑ 210 Jason Sehorn .25 .08
❑ 211 Shaun King .25 .08
❑ 212 Torry Holt .60 .25
❑ 213 Kordell Stewart .40 .15
❑ 214 Keenan McCardell .25 .08
❑ 215 Dedric Ward .25 .08
❑ 216 Michael Wiley .25 .08
❑ 217 Rob Johnson .40 .15
❑ 218 Jamal Lewis 1.00 .40
❑ 219 Herman Moore .40 .15
❑ 220 Ron Dugans .25 .08
❑ 221 Jason Taylor .25 .08
❑ 222 Charles Lee .25 .08
❑ 223 J.J. Stokes .40 .15
❑ 224 Albert Connell .25 .08
❑ 225 Keith Poole .25 .08
❑ 226 Elvis Grbac .40 .15
❑ 227 Shawn Jefferson .25 .08
❑ 228 Jackie Harris .25 .08
❑ 229 Derrick Alexander .40 .15
❑ 230 Darnell Autry .25 .08

❑ 231	Bobby Shaw	.25	.08
❑ 232	Aaron Brooks	.60	.25
❑ 233	Cris Carter	.60	.25
❑ 234	Desmond Clark	.25	.08
❑ 235	Spergon Wynn	.25	.08
❑ 236	Qadry Ismail	.40	.15
❑ 237	Sam Cowart	.25	.08
❑ 238	Zach Thomas	.60	.25
❑ 239	Drew Bledsoe	.75	.30
❑ 240	Ronney Jenkins	.25	.08
❑ 241	Keith Mitchell RC	.25	.08
❑ 242	Laveranues Coles	.60	.25
❑ 243	Marcus Pollard	.25	.08
❑ 244	Darren Sharper	.25	.08
❑ 245	Donald Hayes	.25	.08
❑ 246	Brian Griese	.60	.25
❑ 247	Frank Moreau	.25	.08
❑ 248	Bruce Smith	.25	.08
❑ 249	Fred Beasley	.25	.08
❑ 250	Mike Alstott	.60	.25
❑ 251	Trent Dilfer	.40	.15
❑ 252	Terance Mathis	.40	.15
❑ 253	Shawn Bryson	.25	.08
❑ 254	Dennis Northcutt	.40	.15
❑ 255	Brandon Bennett	.25	.08
❑ 256	Stacey Mack	.25	.08
❑ 257	Tim Brown	.60	.25
❑ 258	Duce Staley	.60	.25
❑ 259	Sean Dawkins	.25	.08
❑ 260	Ricky Proehl	.25	.08
❑ 261	Chris Fuamatu-ma'afala	.25	.08
❑ 262	La'Roi Glover	.25	.08
❑ 263	Bubba Franks	.40	.15
❑ 264	Kevin Lockett	.25	.08
❑ 265	Lamar Smith	.40	.15
❑ 266	Priest Holmes	.75	.30
❑ 267	Macey Brooks	.25	.08
❑ 268	Anthony Wright	.25	.08
❑ 269	Ed McCaffrey	.60	.25
❑ 270	Joe Jurevicius	.25	.08
❑ 271	Terrell Owens	.60	.25
❑ 272	Tony Simmons	.25	.08
❑ 273	Itula Mili	.25	.08
❑ 274	Chad Morton	.25	.08
❑ 275	Marvin Harrison	.60	.25
❑ 276	Jason Gildon	.25	.08
❑ 277	Derrick Mason	.40	.15
❑ 278	Greg Clark	.25	.08
❑ 279	Casey Crawford	.25	.08
❑ 280	Kerry Collins	.40	.15
❑ 281	Terrell Owens	.60	.25
❑ 282	Marshall Faulk	.60	.25
❑ 283	Mike Anderson	.40	.15
❑ 284	Cris Carter	.40	.15
❑ 285	Corey Dillon	.40	.15
❑ 286	Daunte Culpepper	.60	.25
❑ 287	Peyton Manning	.75	.30
❑ 288	Torry Holt	.60	.25
❑ 289	Marvin Harrison	.40	.15
❑ 290	Edgerrin James	.75	.30
❑ 291	Takeo Spikes	.25	.08
❑ 292	John Lynch	.40	.15
❑ 293	Sam Madison	.25	.08
❑ 294	Stephen Boyd	.25	.08
❑ 295	Tony Siragusa	.25	.08
❑ 296	Robert Porcher	.25	.08
❑ 297	Donnell Bennett	.25	.08
❑ 298	Hardy Nickerson	.25	.08
❑ 299	Jonathan Quinn	.25	.08
❑ 300	Rob Morris	.25	.08
❑ 301	E.G. Green	.25	.08
❑ 302	David Sloan	.25	.08
❑ 303	Jason Tucker	.25	.08
❑ 304	Darrin Chiaverini	.25	.08
❑ 305	Wali Rainer	.25	.08
❑ 306	Jerry Azumah	.25	.08
❑ 307	Jonathan Linton	.25	.08
❑ 308	Dameyune Craig	.25	.08
❑ 309	Courtney Brown	.25	.08
❑ 310	Jammi German	.25	.08
❑ 311	Michael Vick RC	8.00	4.00
❑ 312	Jamar Fletcher RC	.75	.30
❑ 313	Will Allen RC	.75	.30
❑ 314	Jamal Reynolds RC	1.25	.50
❑ 315	Quincy Morgan RC	1.25	.50
❑ 316	Eric Kelly RC	.50	.20
❑ 317	Michael Stone RC	.50	.20
❑ 318	Rod Gardner RC	1.25	.50
❑ 319	Ken-Yon Rambo RC	.75	.30
❑ 320	Eric Westmoreland RC	.75	.30
❑ 321	Steve Smith RC	3.00	1.50
❑ 322	George Layne RC	.75	.30
❑ 323	Justin McCareins RC	1.25	.50
❑ 324	Adam Archuleta RC	1.25	.50
❑ 325	Justin Smith RC	1.25	.50
❑ 326	David Terrell RC	1.25	.50
❑ 327	Correll Buckhalter RC	1.50	.60
❑ 328	Drew Brees RC	3.00	1.25
❑ 329	Chris Barnes RC	.75	.30
❑ 330	Santana Moss RC	2.00	.75
❑ 331	Josh Heupel RC	1.25	.50
❑ 332	Cedrick Wilson RC	1.25	.50
❑ 333	Gerard Warren RC	1.25	.50
❑ 334	Jamie Henderson RC	.75	.30
❑ 335	Onomo Ojo RC	.75	.30
❑ 336	Marcus Stroud RC	1.25	.50
❑ 337	Quincy Carter RC	1.25	.50
❑ 338	Koren Robinson RC	1.25	.50
❑ 339	Ryan Pickett RC	.50	.20
❑ 340	Chad Johnson RC	3.00	1.25
❑ 341	Nate Clements RC	1.25	.50
❑ 342	Jesse Palmer RC	1.25	.50
❑ 343	Snoop Minnis RC	.75	.30
❑ 344	Reggie Wayne RC	2.50	1.00
❑ 345	Kevin Kasper RC	1.25	.50
❑ 346	Will Peterson RC	.75	.30
❑ 347	Marques Tuiasosopo RC	1.25	.50
❑ 348	Sage Rosenfels RC	1.25	.50
❑ 349	Dan Alexander RC	1.25	.50
❑ 350	LaDainian Tomlinson RC	6.00	3.00
❑ 351	Dan Morgan RC	1.25	.50
❑ 352	Scotty Anderson RC	.75	.30
❑ 353	Deuce McAllister RC	2.50	1.00
❑ 354	Todd Heap RC	1.25	.50
❑ 355	Tony Dixon RC	.75	.30
❑ 356	Chris Chambers RC	2.00	.75
❑ 357	Eddie Berlin RC	.75	.30
❑ 358	Anthony Thomas RC	1.25	.50
❑ 359	James Jackson RC	1.25	.50
❑ 360	Richard Seymour RC	1.25	.50
❑ 361	Andre Carter RC	1.25	.50
❑ 362	Bobby Newcombe RC	.75	.30
❑ 363	Robert Ferguson RC	1.25	.50
❑ 364	Jonathan Carter RC	.75	.30
❑ 365	Damione Lewis RC	.75	.30
❑ 366	Damerien McCants RC	.75	.30
❑ 367	Tim Hasselbeck RC	1.25	.50
❑ 368	Derrick Gibson RC	.75	.30
❑ 369	Rudi Johnson RC	2.50	1.00
❑ 370	Alge Crumpler RC	1.50	.60
❑ 371	Derrick Blaylock RC	1.25	.50
❑ 372	Moran Norris RC	.50	.20
❑ 373	Travis Minor RC	.75	.30
❑ 374	LaMont Jordan RC	2.50	1.00
❑ 375	Kevan Barlow RC	1.25	.50
❑ 376	Freddie Mitchell RC	1.25	.50
❑ 377	Shaun Rogers RC	1.25	.50
❑ 378	Tay Cody RC	.50	.20
❑ 379	Travis Henry RC	1.25	.50
❑ 380	Chris Weinke RC	1.25	.50
❑ 381	Willie Middlebrooks RC	.75	.30
❑ 382	Rashard Casey RC	.75	.30
❑ 383	Mike McMahon RC	1.25	.50
❑ 384	Michael Bennett RC	2.00	.75
❑ 385	Jabari Holloway RC	.75	.30
❑ SBMVP	Ray Lewis FB AU	175.00	100.00

2002 Topps

❑	COMPLETE SET (385)	50.00	20.00
❑ 1	Kurt Warner	.60	.25
❑ 2	Jeff Graham	.25	.08
❑ 3	Todd Bouman	.25	.08
❑ 4	Duce Staley	.60	.25
❑ 5	Jon Kitna	.40	.15
❑ 6	Shannon Sharpe	.40	.15
❑ 7	Darrell Jackson	.40	.15
❑ 8	Michael Pittman	.25	.08
❑ 9	Tony Gonzalez	.40	.15
❑ 10	Wayne Chrebet	.40	.15
❑ 11	Jevon Kearse	.40	.15
❑ 12	Bill Schroeder	.40	.15
❑ 13	Jeremy McDaniel	.25	.08
❑ 14	Todd Pinkston	.40	.15
❑ 15	Maurice Smith	.40	.15
❑ 16	Charlie Batch	.40	.15
❑ 17	Olandis Gary	.40	.15
❑ 18	Ron Dugans	.25	.08
❑ 19	Brian Urlacher	1.00	.40
❑ 20	Amani Toomer	.40	.15
❑ 21	Tim Couch	.40	.15
❑ 22	Derrick Brooks	.60	.25
❑ 23	Frank Sanders	.25	.08
❑ 24	James Williams	.25	.08
❑ 25	Lamar Smith	.40	.15
❑ 26	Darrick Vaughn	.25	.08
❑ 27	Cris Carter	.60	.25
❑ 28	Roland Williams	.25	.08
❑ 29	Bobby Shaw	.25	.08
❑ 30	Jerome Pathon	.40	.15
❑ 31	Rod Woodson	.40	.15
❑ 32	Ronney Jenkins	.25	.08
❑ 33	Chris Chandler	.40	.15
❑ 34	Dez White	.25	.08
❑ 35	Rod Smith	.40	.15
❑ 36	Troy Brown	.40	.15
❑ 37	JaJuan Dawson	.25	.08
❑ 38	Reidel Anthony	.25	.08
❑ 39	Mike Green	.25	.08
❑ 40	Steve Smith	.60	.25
❑ 41	Willie Jackson	.25	.08
❑ 42	MarTay Jenkins	.25	.08
❑ 43	Reggie Germany	.25	.08
❑ 44	Desmond Howard	.25	.08
❑ 45	Fred Taylor	.60	.25
❑ 46	Scotty Anderson	.25	.08
❑ 47	John Lynch	.40	.15
❑ 48	Amos Zereoue	.60	.25
❑ 49	Darnay Scott	.25	.08
❑ 50	Anthony Thomas	.40	.15
❑ 51	Jeff Garcia	.60	.25
❑ 52	Charlie Garner	.40	.15
❑ 53	Drew Bledsoe	.60	.25
❑ 54	Donnie Edwards	.25	.08
❑ 55	Corey Bradford	.25	.08
❑ 56	Desmond Clark	.25	.08
❑ 57	Courtney Brown	.40	.15
❑ 58	Wesley Walls	.25	.08
❑ 59	Chad Brown	.25	.08
❑ 60	Shawn Jefferson	.25	.08
❑ 61	Corey Dillon	.40	.15
❑ 62	Johnnie Morton	.40	.15
❑ 63	Marcus Pollard	.25	.08
❑ 64	Jason Taylor	.25	.08
❑ 65	Kevin Faulk	.40	.15
❑ 66	Shane Matthews	.25	.08
❑ 67	Hines Ward	.60	.25
❑ 68	Garrison Hearst	.40	.15
❑ 69	Trung Canidate	.40	.15
❑ 70	Tony Banks	.25	.08
❑ 71	Matt Hasselbeck	.40	.15
❑ 72	Correll Buckhalter	.40	.15
❑ 73	Ron Dayne	.40	.15
❑ 74	Zach Thomas	.60	.25
❑ 75	Emmitt Smith	1.50	.60
❑ 76	Peter Warrick	.40	.15
❑ 77	Rob Johnson	.40	.15
❑ 78	Michael Strahan	.40	.15
❑ 79	Ray Lewis	.60	.25
❑ 80	Jamir Miller	.25	.08
❑ 81	Brian Griese	.60	.25
❑ 82	Stacey Mack	.25	.08
❑ 83	Michael Bennett	.40	.15
❑ 84	Ricky Williams	1.00	.40
❑ 85	Jamal Lewis	.60	.25

❑	86	Doug Flutie	.60	.25
❑	87	Jonathan Quinn	.25	.08
❑	88	Mike Alstott	.60	.25
❑	89	Samari Rolle	.25	.08
❑	90	LaMont Jordan	.60	.25
❑	91	Dominic Rhodes	.40	.15
❑	92	Quincy Carter	.40	.15
❑	93	Marcus Robinson	.40	.15
❑	94	Travis Henry	.60	.25
❑	95	Jason Brookins	.25	.08
❑	96	Nick Goings	.25	.08
❑	97	Brian Finneran	.25	.08
❑	98	Dorsey Levens	.40	.15
❑	99	Reggie Swinton	.25	.08
❑	100	Chris Chambers	.60	.25
❑	101	Kordell Stewart	.40	.15
❑	102	Tai Streets	.25	.08
❑	103	Chris Redman	.25	.08
❑	104	Jacquez Green	.25	.08
❑	105	Rod Gardner	.40	.15
❑	106	Kevin Kasper	.25	.08
❑	107	Anthony Henry	.25	.08
❑	108	Dan Morgan	.25	.08
❑	109	Ronald McKinnon	.25	.08
❑	110	Qadry Ismail	.40	.15
❑	111	Chad Johnson	.60	.25
❑	112	James Stewart	.40	.15
❑	113	Terrence Wilkins	.25	.08
❑	114	Joey Galloway	.40	.15
❑	115	Deuce McAllister	.75	.30
❑	116	Joe Jurevicius	.25	.08
❑	117	Tyrone Wheatley	.40	.15
❑	118	Jason Gildon	.25	.08
❑	119	LaDainian Tomlinson	1.00	.40
❑	120	Grant Wistrom	.25	.08
❑	121	Eddie George	.60	.25
❑	122	Laveranues Coles	.40	.15
❑	123	Antowain Smith	.40	.15
❑	124	Larry Parker	.25	.08
❑	125	Bubba Franks	.40	.15
❑	126	Troy Hambrick	.25	.08
❑	127	Jamal Reynolds	.25	.08
❑	128	Doug Chapman	.25	.08
❑	129	Freddie Mitchell	.40	.15
❑	130	Tim Dwight	.40	.15
❑	131	Erron Kinney	.25	.08
❑	132	James Allen	.40	.15
❑	133	Eric Moulds	.40	.15
❑	134	Keenan McCardell	.25	.08
❑	135	David Sloan	.25	.08
❑	136	Dennis Northcutt	.40	.15
❑	137	Kevan Barlow	.40	.15
❑	138	Bobby Engram	.25	.08
❑	139	Champ Bailey	.40	.15
❑	140	Donald Hayes	.25	.08
❑	141	Brandon Bennett	.25	.08
❑	142	Deltha O'Neal	.25	.08
❑	143	James Jackson	.25	.08
❑	144	Shaun Rogers	.25	.08
❑	145	Joe Johnson	.25	.08
❑	146	Ricky Watters	.40	.15
❑	147	Warrick Dunn	.60	.25
❑	148	Steve McNair	.60	.25
❑	149	Marvin Harrison	.60	.25
❑	150	Kendrell Bell	.60	.25
❑	151	Jim Miller	.25	.08
❑	152	Terry Allen	.25	.08
❑	153	Jake Plummer	.40	.15
❑	154	James McKnight	.25	.08
❑	155	Curtis Martin	.60	.25
❑	156	Keyshawn Johnson	.60	.25
❑	157	Kevin Lockett	.25	.08
❑	158	Jeremiah Trotter	.25	.08
❑	159	Derrick Alexander	.40	.15
❑	160	Brandon Stokley	.40	.15
❑	161	J.J. Stokes	.40	.15
❑	162	Drew Bennett	.60	.25
❑	163	Drew Brees	.60	.25
❑	164	Tim Brown	.60	.25
❑	165	Daunte Culpepper	.60	.25
❑	166	Rocket Ismail	.40	.15
❑	167	Alex Van Pelt	.40	.15
❑	168	Arnold Jackson	.25	.08
❑	169	Oronde Gadsden	.40	.15
❑	170	Isaac Bruce	.60	.25
❑	171	Warren Sapp	.40	.15
❑	172	Michael Westbrook	.25	.08
❑	173	John Abraham	.40	.15
❑	174	Jessie Armstead	.25	.08
❑	175	Brock Marion	.25	.08
❑	176	Brett Favre	1.50	.60
❑	177	Benjamin Gay	.40	.15
❑	178	Muhsin Muhammad	.40	.15
❑	179	Reggie Wayne	.60	.25
❑	180	Kailee Wong	.25	.08
❑	181	Rich Gannon	.60	.25
❑	182	Chris Fuamatu-Ma'afala	.25	.08
❑	183	Shaun Alexander	.75	.30
❑	184	Kevin Dyson	.40	.15
❑	185	Kwamie Lassiter	.25	.08
❑	186	Elvis Joseph	.25	.08
❑	187	Trent Dilfer	.40	.15
❑	188	Marty Booker	.25	.08
❑	189	Travis Taylor	.40	.15
❑	190	Michael Vick	2.00	.75
❑	191	Mike McMahon	.60	.25
❑	192	Jay Fiedler	.40	.15
❑	193	Zack Bronson	.25	.08
❑	194	Derrick Mason	.40	.15
❑	195	Anthony Becht	.25	.08
❑	196	Ahman Green	.60	.25
❑	197	Alge Crumpler	.40	.15
❑	198	Thomas Jones	.40	.15
❑	199	Tiki Barber	.60	.25
❑	200	Donovan McNabb	.75	.30
❑	201	Andre Carter	.25	.08
❑	202	Stephen Davis	.40	.15
❑	203	Troy Edwards	.25	.08
❑	204	Lawyer Milloy	.40	.15
❑	205	Peyton Manning	1.25	.50
❑	206	James Farrior	.25	.08
❑	207	Gerard Warren	.25	.08
❑	208	Peerless Price	.40	.15
❑	209	Avion Black	.25	.08
❑	210	Marcellus Wiley	.25	.08
❑	211	Torry Holt	.60	.25
❑	212	A.J. Feeley	.60	.25
❑	213	Travis Minor	.25	.08
❑	214	Darren Sharper	.25	.08
❑	215	Jerry Porter	.25	.08
❑	216	Randall Cunningham	.25	.08
❑	217	Chris Weinke	.40	.15
❑	218	Mike Anderson	.60	.25
❑	219	Snoop Minnis	.25	.08
❑	220	David Martin	.25	.08
❑	221	Vinny Sutherland	.25	.08
❑	222	Ki-Jana Carter	.25	.08
❑	223	Kevin Swayne	.25	.08
❑	224	Mark Brunell	.60	.25
❑	225	Quincy Morgan	.25	.08
❑	226	David Terrell	.60	.25
❑	227	Terance Mathis	.25	.08
❑	228	Frank Wycheck	.25	.08
❑	229	Az-Zahir Hakim	.25	.08
❑	230	Freddie Jones	.25	.08
❑	231	Jerry Rice	1.25	.50
❑	232	Ike Hilliard	.40	.15
❑	233	Terrell Davis	.60	.25
❑	234	Shawn Bryson	.25	.08
❑	235	David Boston	.60	.25
❑	236	Edgerrin James	.75	.30
❑	237	Trent Green	.40	.15
❑	238	Charlie Rogers	.25	.08
❑	239	Vinny Testaverde	.40	.15
❑	240	Koren Robinson	.40	.15
❑	241	Ronde Barber	.25	.08
❑	242	Dwayne Carswell	.25	.08
❑	243	Dedric Ward	.25	.08
❑	244	Richard Huntley	.25	.08
❑	245	Jamal Anderson	.40	.15
❑	246	Ryan Leaf	.40	.15
❑	247	Priest Holmes	.75	.30
❑	248	Tom Brady	1.50	.60
❑	249	Charles Woodson	.40	.15
❑	250	Jerome Bettis	.60	.25
❑	251	Tommy Polley	.25	.08
❑	252	Anthony Wright	.25	.08
❑	253	Chad Pennington	.75	.30
❑	254	David Patten	.25	.08
❑	255	Antonio Freeman	.60	.25
❑	256	Jamel White	.25	.08
❑	257	Jermaine Lewis	.25	.08
❑	258	Aaron Brooks	.60	.25
❑	259	Ron Dixon	.25	.08
❑	260	James Thrash	.40	.15
❑	261	Junior Seau	.60	.25
❑	262	Byron Chamberlain	.25	.08
❑	263	Ed McCaffrey	.60	.25
❑	264	Nate Clements	.25	.08
❑	265	Tony Martin	.40	.15
❑	266	Germane Crowell	.25	.08
❑	267	Terrell Owens	.60	.25
❑	268	Marshall Faulk	.60	.25
❑	269	Dat Nguyen	.25	.08
❑	270	Elvis Grbac	.40	.15
❑	271	Dante Hall	.60	.25
❑	272	Sylvester Morris	.25	.08
❑	273	Mike Brown	.60	.25
❑	274	Kevin Johnson	.40	.15
❑	275	Jimmy Smith	.40	.15
❑	276	Randy Moss	1.25	.50
❑	277	Kerry Collins	.40	.15
❑	278	Santana Moss	.60	.25
❑	279	Plaxico Burress	.40	.15
❑	280	Brad Johnson	.40	.15
❑	281	Curtis Conway	.25	.08
❑	282	Eric Johnson	.40	.15
❑	283	Joe Horn	.40	.15
❑	284	Peter Boulware	.25	.08
❑	285	Larry Foster	.25	.08
❑	286	Nate Jacquet	.25	.08
❑	287	Terry Glenn	.40	.15
❑	288	Jarious Jackson	.25	.08
❑	289	Hugh Douglas	.25	.08
❑	290	Chad Lewis	.25	.08
❑	291	Ahman Green WW	.40	.15
❑	292	Peyton Manning WW	.60	.25
❑	293	Kurt Warner WW	.40	.15
❑	294	Daunte Culpepper WW	.60	.25
❑	295	Tom Brady WW	.75	.30
❑	296	Rod Gardner WW	.25	.08
❑	297	Corey Dillon WW	.40	.15
❑	298	Priest Holmes WW	.50	.20
❑	299	Shaun Alexander WW	.50	.20
❑	300	Randy Moss WW	.60	.25
❑	301	Eric Moulds WW	.25	.08
❑	302	Brett Favre WW	.75	.30
❑	303	Todd Bouman WW	.25	.08
❑	304	Dominic Rhodes WW	.40	.15
❑	305	Marvin Harrison WW	.40	.15
❑	306	Torry Holt WW	.60	.25
❑	307	Derrick Mason WW	.25	.08
❑	308	Jerry Rice WW	.60	.25
❑	309	Donovan McNabb WW	.40	.15
❑	310	Marshall Faulk WW	.40	.15
❑	311	David Carr RC	3.00	1.25
❑	312	Quentin Jammer RC	1.25	.50
❑	313	Mike Williams RC	1.00	.40
❑	314	Rocky Calmus RC	1.25	.50
❑	315	Travis Fisher RC	1.25	.50
❑	316	Dwight Freeney RC	1.50	.60
❑	317	Jeremy Shockey RC	4.00	1.50
❑	318	Marquise Walker RC	1.00	.40
❑	319	Eric Crouch RC	1.25	.50
❑	320	DeShaun Foster RC	1.25	.50
❑	321	Roy Williams RC	3.00	1.25
❑	322	Andre Davis RC	1.00	.40
❑	323	Alex Brown RC	1.25	.50
❑	324	Michael Lewis RC	1.25	.50
❑	325	Terry Charles RC	1.00	.40
❑	326	Clinton Portis RC	4.00	1.50
❑	327	Dennis Johnson RC	.60	.25
❑	328	Lito Sheppard RC	1.25	.50
❑	329	Ryan Sims RC	1.25	.50
❑	330	Raonall Smith RC	1.00	.40
❑	331	Albert Haynesworth RC	1.00	.40
❑	332	Eddie Freeman RC	.60	.25
❑	333	Levi Jones RC	1.00	.40
❑	334	Josh McCown RC	1.50	.60
❑	335	Cliff Russell RC	1.00	.40
❑	336	Maurice Morris RC	1.25	.50
❑	337	Antwaan Randle El RC	2.00	.75
❑	338	Ladell Betts RC	1.25	.50
❑	339	Daniel Graham RC	1.25	.50
❑	340	David Garrard RC	1.25	.50
❑	341	Antonio Bryant RC	1.25	.50
❑	342	Patrick Ramsey RC	1.50	.60
❑	343	Kelly Campbell RC	1.00	.40
❑	344	Will Overstreet RC	.60	.25
❑	345	Ryan Denney RC	1.00	.40
❑	346	John Henderson RC	1.25	.50

❑ 347 Freddie Milons RC 1.00 .40
❑ 348 Tim Carter RC 1.00 .40
❑ 349 Kurt Kittner RC 1.00 .40
❑ 350 Joey Harrington RC 3.00 1.25
❑ 351 Ricky Williams RC 1.25 .50
❑ 352 Bryant McKinnie RC 1.00 .40
❑ 353 Ed Reed RC 2.00 .75
❑ 354 Josh Reed RC 1.25 .50
❑ 355 Seth Burford RC 1.00 .40
❑ 356 Javon Walker RC 2.50 1.00
❑ 357 Jamar Martin RC 1.00 .40
❑ 358 Leonard Henry RC 1.00 .40
❑ 359 Julius Peppers RC 2.50 1.00
❑ 360 Jabar Gaffney RC 1.25 .50
❑ 361 Kalimba Edwards RC 1.25 .50
❑ 362 Napoleon Harris RC 1.25 .50
❑ 363 Ashley Lelie RC 2.50 1.00
❑ 364 Anthony Weaver RC 1.00 .40
❑ 365 Bryan Thomas RC 1.00 .40
❑ 366 Wendell Bryant RC .60 .25
❑ 367 Damien Anderson RC 1.00 .40
❑ 368 Travis Stephens RC 1.00 .40
❑ 369 Rohan Davey RC 1.25 .50
❑ 370 Mike Pearson RC .60 .25
❑ 371 Marc Colombo RC .60 .25
❑ 372 Phillip Buchanon RC 1.25 .50
❑ 373 T.J. Duckett RC 2.00 .75
❑ 374 Ron Johnson RC 1.00 .40
❑ 375 Larry Tripplett RC .60 .25
❑ 376 Randy Fasani RC 1.00 .40
❑ 377 Keyuo Craver RC 1.00 .40
❑ 378 Marquand Manuel RC .60 .25
❑ 379 Jonathan Wells RC 1.25 .50
❑ 380 Reche Caldwell RC 1.25 .50
❑ 381 Luke Staley RC 1.00 .40
❑ 382 Donte Stallworth RC 2.50 1.00
❑ 383 Levar Fisher RC .60 .25
❑ 384 Lamar Gordon RC 1.25 .50
❑ 385 William Green RC 1.25 .50
❑ SBMVP Tom Brady FB AU/150 500.00 300.00

2003 Topps

❑ COMPLETE SET (385) 60.00 25.00
❑ 1 Michael Vick 1.50 .60
❑ 2 Wesley Walls .25 .08
❑ 3 Josh Reed .40 .15
❑ 4 Josh McCown .40 .15
❑ 5 James Stewart .40 .15
❑ 6 Deltha O'Neal .25 .08
❑ 7 Quincy Morgan .40 .15
❑ 8 Tony Fisher .25 .08
❑ 9 Corey Bradford .25 .08
❑ 10 Byron Chamberlain .25 .08
❑ 11 James McKnight .25 .08
❑ 12 Fred Taylor .60 .25
❑ 13 David Patten .25 .08
❑ 14 Jerome Bettis .60 .25
❑ 15 Jerry Porter .40 .15
❑ 16 Anthony Becht .25 .08
❑ 17 Steve McNair .60 .25
❑ 18 Stephen Davis .40 .15
❑ 19 Terrence Wilkins .25 .08
❑ 20 Jamie Martin .25 .08
❑ 21 Tai Streets .25 .08
❑ 22 Frank Wycheck .25 .08
❑ 23 Sammy Knight .25 .08
❑ 24 Marcus Pollard .25 .08
❑ 25 Jamie Sharper .25 .08
❑ 26 T.J. Houshmandzadeh .25 .08
❑ 27 Javin Hunter .25 .08
❑ 28 Alge Crumpler .40 .15
❑ 29 Chris Weinke .40 .15
❑ 30 David Terrell .40 .15
❑ 31 Troy Hambrick .25 .08
❑ 32 Bubba Franks .40 .15
❑ 33 Todd Bouman .25 .08
❑ 34 Trent Green .40 .15
❑ 35 Mark Brunell .40 .15
❑ 36 James Thrash .25 .08
❑ 37 Donnie Edwards .25 .08
❑ 38 Mike Alstott .60 .25
❑ 39 Bobby Engram .25 .08
❑ 40 Deuce McAllister .60 .25
❑ 41 Santana Moss .40 .15
❑ 42 Kordell Stewart .40 .15
❑ 43 Jason Taylor .25 .08
❑ 44 Corey Dillon .40 .15
❑ 45 Damien Anderson .25 .08
❑ 46 Rodney Peete .25 .08
❑ 47 Jeff Blake .25 .08
❑ 48 Mike McMahon .40 .15
❑ 49 Ed McCaffrey .60 .25
❑ 50 Priest Holmes .75 .30
❑ 51 Moe Williams .25 .08
❑ 52 Brian Dawkins .40 .15
❑ 53 Tim Brown .60 .25
❑ 54 Curtis Martin .60 .25
❑ 55 Charles Stackhouse .25 .08
❑ 56 Derrius Thompson .25 .08
❑ 57 John Simon .25 .08
❑ 58 Joe Jurevicius .25 .08
❑ 59 Jonathan Wells .25 .08
❑ 60 William Green .40 .15
❑ 61 Ken-Yon Rambo .25 .08
❑ 62 Frank Sanders .25 .08
❑ 63 Chester Taylor .25 .08
❑ 64 Keith Brooking .25 .08
❑ 65 Bill Schroeder .40 .15
❑ 66 Travis Minor .25 .08
❑ 67 Eric Parker RC .60 .25
❑ 68 Phillip Buchanon .25 .08
❑ 69 Amos Zereoue .40 .15
❑ 70 Warren Sapp .40 .15
❑ 71 Ladell Betts .40 .15
❑ 72 Lamar Gordon .25 .08
❑ 73 Koren Robinson .25 .08
❑ 74 Ron Dayne .25 .08
❑ 75 Donovan McNabb .75 .30
❑ 76 Edgerrin James .60 .25
❑ 77 Stacey Mack .25 .08
❑ 78 Justin Smith .25 .08
❑ 79 Kelly Holcomb .40 .15
❑ 80 Thomas Jones .40 .15
❑ 81 Randy McMichael .40 .15
❑ 82 Daunte Culpepper .60 .25
❑ 83 Tommy Maddox .60 .25
❑ 84 Tyrone Wheatley .25 .08
❑ 85 Kevin Dyson .40 .15
❑ 86 Rod Gardner .40 .15
❑ 87 Wayne Chrebet .40 .15
❑ 88 Marc Boerigter .40 .15
❑ 89 Darnay Scott .25 .08
❑ 90 T.J. Duckett .40 .15
❑ 91 Marcel Shipp .40 .15
❑ 92 Ross Tucker .25 .08
❑ 93 Drew Bledsoe .60 .25
❑ 94 Scotty Anderson .25 .08
❑ 95 Rod Smith .40 .15
❑ 96 Jim Kleinsasser .25 .08
❑ 97 Peyton Manning 1.00 .40
❑ 98 Junior Seau .60 .25
❑ 99 Darrell Jackson .40 .15
❑ 100 Brett Favre 1.50 .60
❑ 101 Ashley Lelie .60 .25
❑ 102 Jajuan Dawson .25 .08
❑ 103 Kyle Brady .25 .08
❑ 104 Kevin Faulk .25 .08
❑ 105 Jeremy Shockey 1.00 .40
❑ 106 Hines Ward .60 .25
❑ 107 Jeff Garcia .60 .25
❑ 108 Shane Matthews .25 .08
❑ 109 Jevon Kearse .40 .15
❑ 110 Eddie Kennison .25 .08
❑ 111 Quincy Carter .40 .15
❑ 112 Brian Urlacher 1.00 .40
❑ 113 Charlie Rogers .25 .08
❑ 114 Robert Ferguson .25 .08
❑ 115 Christian Fauria .25 .08
❑ 116 Brian Westbrook .40 .15
❑ 117 Antwaan Randle El .60 .25
❑ 118 Eddie George .40 .15
❑ 119 Derrick Brooks .40 .15
❑ 120 Isaac Bruce .60 .25
❑ 121 Joe Horn .40 .15
❑ 122 Jermaine Lewis .25 .08
❑ 123 Jon Kitna .40 .15
❑ 124 David Boston .40 .15
❑ 125 Todd Heap .40 .15
❑ 126 Lamar Smith .25 .08
❑ 127 Marcus Robinson .40 .15
❑ 128 Germane Crowell .25 .08
❑ 129 Kevin Johnson .40 .15
❑ 130 Cris Carter .60 .25
❑ 131 Drew Brees .60 .25
❑ 132 Champ Bailey .40 .15
❑ 133 Brian Finneran .25 .08
❑ 134 Mike Anderson .60 .25
❑ 135 Derek Ross .25 .08
❑ 136 Javon Walker .40 .15
❑ 137 D'Wayne Bates .25 .08
❑ 138 Chad Lewis .25 .08
❑ 139 Charlie Garner .40 .15
❑ 140 Laveranues Coles .40 .15
❑ 141 Ron Dixon .25 .08
❑ 142 Rob Johnson .40 .15
❑ 143 Shaun Alexander .60 .25
❑ 144 Kevan Barlow .40 .15
❑ 145 Aaron Brooks .60 .25
❑ 146 Jay Foreman .25 .08
❑ 147 Mike Peterson .25 .08
❑ 148 Brandon Bennett .25 .08
❑ 149 Jake Plummer .40 .15
❑ 150 Emmitt Smith 1.50 .60
❑ 151 Mikhael Ricks .25 .08
❑ 152 Terry Glenn .25 .08
❑ 153 Michael Bennett .40 .15
❑ 154 Deion Branch .60 .25
❑ 155 Justin McCareins .25 .08
❑ 156 Keyshawn Johnson .60 .25
❑ 157 Marc Bulger .60 .25
❑ 158 Matt Hasselbeck .40 .15
❑ 159 Garrison Hearst .40 .15
❑ 160 Jamel White .25 .08
❑ 161 Doug Johnson .25 .08
❑ 162 Larry Centers .25 .08
❑ 163 Dee Brown .25 .08
❑ 164 Dez White .25 .08
❑ 165 Brian Griese .60 .25
❑ 166 Johnnie Morton .40 .15
❑ 167 Oronde Gadsden .25 .08
❑ 168 Chad Morton .25 .08
❑ 169 Rod Woodson .40 .15
❑ 170 Ricky Proehl .25 .08
❑ 171 Tim Dwight .40 .15
❑ 172 Patrick Ramsey .60 .25
❑ 173 Donald Driver .40 .15
❑ 174 Joey Harrington 1.00 .40
❑ 175 Ricky Williams .60 .25
❑ 176 David Givens .60 .25
❑ 177 Antonio Freeman .40 .15
❑ 178 Dwight Freeney .40 .15
❑ 179 Jabar Gaffney .40 .15
❑ 180 Leon Johnson .25 .08
❑ 181 Freddie Jones .25 .08
❑ 182 Ron Johnson .25 .08
❑ 183 Duce Staley .40 .15
❑ 184 Charles Woodson .40 .15
❑ 185 Trung Canidate .40 .15
❑ 186 Jerome Pathon .25 .08
❑ 187 Jimmy Smith .40 .15
❑ 188 Reggie Wayne .40 .15
❑ 189 Chad Johnson .60 .25
❑ 190 Steve Beuerlein .25 .08
❑ 191 Joey Galloway .40 .15
❑ 192 Chris Walsh .25 .08
❑ 193 Ty Law .40 .15
❑ 194 Ike Hilliard .25 .08
❑ 195 Curtis Conway .25 .08
❑ 196 Kenny Watson .25 .08
❑ 197 Brad Johnson .40 .15
❑ 198 Shawn Jefferson .25 .08
❑ 199 Jamal Lewis .60 .25

❑ 200 Terrell Owens .60 .25
❑ 201 Todd Pinkston .40 .15
❑ 202 Maurice Morris .25 .08
❑ 203 Dante Hall .60 .25
❑ 204 Jeremiah Trotter UER .25 .08
❑ 205 Keenan McCardell .25 .08
❑ 206 Antonio Bryant .40 .15
❑ 207 Trevor Gaylor .25 .08
❑ 208 Eric Moulds .40 .15
❑ 209 Jim Miller .25 .08
❑ 210 Kabeer Gbaja-Biamila .40 .15
❑ 211 James Mungro .25 .08
❑ 212 Troy Brown .40 .15
❑ 213 J.J. Stokes .40 .15
❑ 214 Rich Gannon .40 .15
❑ 215 Chad Pennington .75 .30
❑ 216 Michael Strahan .40 .15
❑ 217 David Garrard .25 .08
❑ 218 Chris Chambers .60 .25
❑ 219 Antowain Smith .40 .15
❑ 220 Olandis Gary .40 .15
❑ 221 Jason McAddley .25 .08
❑ 222 Brandon Stokley .40 .15
❑ 223 Derrick Alexander .25 .08
❑ 224 Hugh Douglas .25 .08
❑ 225 Danny Wuerffel .25 .08
❑ 226 Derrick Mason .40 .15
❑ 227 Michael Pittman .25 .08
❑ 228 Torry Holt .60 .25
❑ 229 Bobby Shaw .25 .08
❑ 230 Tony Gonzalez .40 .15
❑ 231 Ed Hartwell .25 .08
❑ 232 Kris Mangum RC .40 .15
❑ 233 Martay Jenkins .25 .08
❑ 234 Marty Booker .40 .15
❑ 235 London Fletcher .25 .08
❑ 236 Shannon Sharpe .40 .15
❑ 237 Zach Thomas .60 .25
❑ 238 Plaxico Burress .60 .25
❑ 239 Trent Dilfer .40 .15
❑ 240 Kurt Warner .60 .25
❑ 241 Vinny Testaverde .40 .15
❑ 242 Al Wilson .25 .08
❑ 243 Chris Redman .25 .08
❑ 244 Warrick Dunn .40 .15
❑ 245 Jay Fiedler .40 .15
❑ 246 A.J. Feeley .25 .08
❑ 247 LaMont Jordan .60 .25
❑ 248 Kerry Collins .40 .15
❑ 249 Michael Lewis .25 .08
❑ 250 Jerry Rice 1.25 .50
❑ 251 Simeon Rice .40 .15
❑ 252 Reche Caldwell .25 .08
❑ 253 Randy Moss 1.00 .40
❑ 254 Az-Zahir Hakim .25 .08
❑ 255 Nate Wayne .25 .08
❑ 256 James Allen .40 .15
❑ 257 Qadry Ismail .40 .15
❑ 258 Tom Brady 1.50 .60
❑ 259 Brian Kelly .25 .08
❑ 260 Ray Lucas .25 .08
❑ 261 Amani Toomer .40 .15
❑ 262 Travis Henry .40 .15
❑ 263 Chris Chandler .25 .08
❑ 264 Peter Warrick .40 .15
❑ 265 Ray Lewis .60 .25
❑ 266 Sam Cowart .25 .08
❑ 267 Donte Stallworth .60 .25
❑ 268 David Carr 1.00 .40
❑ 269 Andre Davis .25 .08
❑ 270 Jake Delhomme .60 .25
❑ 271 Travis Taylor .40 .15
❑ 272 Steve Smith .60 .25
❑ 273 Tiki Barber .60 .25
❑ 274 Chad Hutchinson .25 .08
❑ 275 Marshall Faulk .60 .25
❑ 276 Chris Claiborne .25 .08
❑ 277 Billy Miller .25 .08
❑ 278 Peerless Price .40 .15
❑ 279 Ed Reed .40 .15
❑ 280 Ahman Green .60 .25
❑ 281 Roy Williams .60 .25
❑ 282 Dennis Northcutt .25 .08
❑ 283 Julius Peppers .60 .25
❑ 284 John Davis .25 .08
❑ 285 LaDainian Tomlinson .60 .25
❑ 286 Muhsin Muhammad .40 .15
❑ 287 Tim Couch .25 .08
❑ 288 Clinton Portis 1.00 .40
❑ 289 Anthony Thomas .40 .15
❑ 290 Marvin Harrison .60 .25
❑ 291 Priest Holmes WW .40 .15
❑ 292 Drew Bledsoe WW .40 .15
❑ 293 Tom Brady WW .60 .25
❑ 294 Shaun Alexander WW .25 .08
❑ 295 Brett Favre WW .60 .25
❑ 296 Travis Henry WW .25 .08
❑ 297 Marshall Faulk WW .40 .15
❑ 298 Terrell Owens WW .25 .08
❑ 299 Jeff Garcia WW .25 .08
❑ 300 Plaxico Burress WW .25 .08
❑ 301 Donovan McNabb WW .40 .15
❑ 302 Ricky Williams WW .40 .15
❑ 303 Michael Vick WW .75 .30
❑ 304 Steve Smith WW .40 .15
❑ 305 Marvin Harrison WW .25 .08
❑ 306 Chad Pennington WW .40 .15
❑ 307 Jeremy Shockey WW .60 .25
❑ 308 Tommy Maddox WW .25 .08
❑ 309 Steve McNair WW .25 .08
❑ 310 Rich Gannon WW .25 .08
❑ 311 Carson Palmer RC 6.00 2.50
❑ 312 Keenan Howry RC 1.25 .50
❑ 313 Michael Haynes RC 1.25 .50
❑ 314 Terrell Suggs RC 2.00 .75
❑ 315 Rashean Mathis RC 1.00 .40
❑ 316 Chris Kelsay RC 1.25 .50
❑ 317 Brad Banks RC 1.00 .40
❑ 318 Jordan Gross RC 1.00 .40
❑ 319 Lee Suggs RC 2.50 1.00
❑ 320 Kliff Kingsbury RC 1.00 .40
❑ 321 William Joseph RC 1.25 .50
❑ 322 Kelley Washington RC 1.25 .50
❑ 323 Jerome McDougle RC 1.25 .50
❑ 324 Osi Umenyiora RC 2.00 .75
❑ 325 Chris Simms RC 2.00 .75
❑ 326 Alonzo Jackson RC 1.00 .40
❑ 327 L.J. Smith RC 1.25 .50
❑ 328 Mike Doss RC 1.25 .50
❑ 329 Bobby Wade RC 1.25 .50
❑ 330 Ken Hamlin RC 1.25 .50
❑ 331 Brandon Lloyd RC 1.50 .60
❑ 332 Justin Fargas RC 1.25 .50
❑ 333 DeWayne Robertson RC 1.25 .50
❑ 334 Bryant Johnson RC 1.25 .50
❑ 335 Boss Bailey RC 1.25 .50
❑ 336 Onterrio Smith RC 1.25 .50
❑ 337 Doug Gabriel RC 1.25 .50
❑ 338 Jimmy Kennedy RC 1.25 .50
❑ 339 B.J. Askew RC 1.25 .50
❑ 340 Taylor Jacobs RC 1.00 .40
❑ 341 Dallas Clark RC 1.25 .50
❑ 342 DeWayne White RC 1.00 .40
❑ 343 Amaz Battle RC 1.25 .50
❑ 344 Kareem Kelly RC 1.00 .40
❑ 345 Terry Pierce RC 1.00 .40
❑ 346 Billy McMullen RC 1.00 .40
❑ 347 Talman Gardner RC 1.25 .50
❑ 348 Anquan Boldin RC 3.00 1.25
❑ 349 Travis Anglin RC .60 .25
❑ 350 Byron Leftwich RC 4.00 1.50
❑ 351 Marcus Trufant RC 1.25 .50
❑ 352 Sam Aiken RC 1.00 .40
❑ 353 LaBrandon Toefield RC 1.25 .50
❑ 354 J.R. Tolver RC 1.00 .40
❑ 355 Charles Rogers RC 1.25 .50
❑ 356 Chaun Thompson RC .60 .25
❑ 357 Chris Brown RC 1.50 .60
❑ 358 Justin Gage RC 1.25 .50
❑ 359 Kevin Williams RC 1.25 .50
❑ 360 Willis McGahee RC 3.00 1.25
❑ 361 Victor Hobson RC 1.25 .50
❑ 362 Brian St.Pierre RC 1.25 .50
❑ 363 Nate Burleson RC 2.00 .75
❑ 364 Calvin Pace RC 1.00 .40
❑ 365 Larry Johnson RC 6.00 2.50
❑ 366 Andre Woolfolk RC 1.25 .50
❑ 367 Tyrone Calico RC 1.50 .60
❑ 368 Seneca Wallace RC 1.25 .50
❑ 369 Domanick Davis RC 2.00 .75
❑ 370 Rex Grossman RC 2.00 .75
❑ 371 Artose Pinner RC 1.25 .50
❑ 372 Jason Witten RC 2.00 .75
❑ 373 Bennie Joppru RC 1.25 .50
❑ 374 Bethel Johnson RC 1.25 .50
❑ 375 Kyle Boller RC 2.50 1.00
❑ 376 Shaun McDonald RC 1.25 .50
❑ 377 Musa Smith RC 1.25 .50
❑ 378 Ken Dorsey RC 1.25 .50
❑ 379 Johnathan Sullivan RC 1.00 .40
❑ 380 Andre Johnson RC 2.50 1.00
❑ 381 Nick Barnett RC 2.00 .75
❑ 382 Teyo Johnson RC 1.25 .50
❑ 383 Terence Newman RC 2.50 1.00
❑ 384 Kevin Curtis RC 1.25 .50
❑ 385 Dave Ragone RC 1.25 .50
❑ MVP Dex.Jackson FB AU/250 60.00 25.00

2004 Topps

❑ COMPLETE SET (385) 60.00 30.00
❑ RH38 STATED ODDS 1:36 H/HTA/R
❑ RH38A ODDS 1:13,494H, 1:3895HTA
❑ SBMVP ODDS
1:35,787H,1:10,710HTA,1:33,984R
❑ 1 Peyton Manning 1.00 .40
❑ 2 Curtis Conway .25 .08
❑ 3 Tim Brown .60 .25
❑ 4 David Givens .40 .15
❑ 5 Dorsey Levens .25 .08
❑ 6 Jamal Robertson .25 .08
❑ 7 Doug Flutie .60 .25
❑ 8 Lamar Gordon .25 .08
❑ 9 Leonard Little .25 .08
❑ 10 Patrick Ramsey .40 .15
❑ 11 Justin McCareins .25 .08
❑ 12 Charles Lee .25 .08
❑ 13 Matt Hasselbeck .40 .15
❑ 14 Chris Chambers .40 .15
❑ 15 Derrick Blaylock .40 .15
❑ 16 Shannon Sharpe .40 .15
❑ 17 Bubba Franks .40 .15
❑ 18 London Fletcher .25 .08
❑ 19 Eric Moulds .40 .15
❑ 20 Anquan Boldin .60 .25
❑ 21 Brian Urlacher .75 .30
❑ 22 Stephen Davis .40 .15
❑ 23 Mikhael Ricks .25 .08
❑ 24 Jason Taylor .25 .08
❑ 25 Michael Vick 1.25 .50
❑ 26 Dante Hall .60 .25
❑ 27 Marcus Pollard .25 .08
❑ 28 Rick Mirer .25 .08
❑ 29 David Tyree .25 .08
❑ 30 Chad Pennington .60 .25
❑ 31 Kevan Barlow .40 .15
❑ 32 James Farrior .25 .08
❑ 33 James Thrash .25 .08
❑ 34 Damerien McCants .25 .08
❑ 35 L.J. Smith .40 .15
❑ 36 Tommy Maddox .40 .15
❑ 37 Tedy Bruschi .40 .15
❑ 38 Moe Williams .25 .08
❑ 39 Todd Bouman .25 .08
❑ 40 Domanick Davis .60 .25
❑ 41 Dwight Freeney .40 .15
❑ 42 Kyle Brady .25 .08
❑ 43 LaVar Arrington 1.25 .50
❑ 44 Troy Hambrick .25 .08
❑ 45 Jake Plummer .40 .15
❑ 46 Freddie Jones .25 .08
❑ 47 Chester Taylor .25 .08
❑ 48 Willis McGahee .60 .25
❑ 49 Bobby Wade .25 .08

❑ 50 Steve McNair .60 .25
❑ 51 Joe Jurevicius .25 .08
❑ 52 Ladell Betts .25 .08
❑ 53 LaMont Jordan .60 .25
❑ 54 Kerry Collins .40 .15
❑ 55 Hines Ward .60 .25
❑ 56 Scott Fujita .25 .08
❑ 57 Kevin Johnson .25 .08
❑ 58 Troy Brown .40 .15
❑ 59 Jerome Pathon .25 .08
❑ 60 Andre Johnson .60 .25
❑ 61 DeShaun Foster .40 .15
❑ 62 Terrell Suggs .40 .15
❑ 63 Marcel Shipp .40 .15
❑ 64 Allen Rossum .25 .08
❑ 65 Kyle Boller .60 .25
❑ 66 Terence Newman .40 .15
❑ 67 Javon Walker .40 .15
❑ 68 Shawn Bryson .25 .08
❑ 69 Travis Minor .25 .08
❑ 70 Terrell Owens .60 .25
❑ 71 Kassim Osgood .25 .08
❑ 72 Bobby Engram .25 .08
❑ 73 Drew Bennett .40 .15
❑ 74 Rock Cartwright .25 .08
❑ 75 Ahman Green .60 .25
❑ 76 Steve Beuerlein .25 .08
❑ 77 Takeo Spikes .25 .08
❑ 78 Dez White .40 .15
❑ 79 Tim Couch .25 .08
❑ 80 Travis Henry .40 .15
❑ 81 T.J. Duckett .40 .15
❑ 82 LaBrandon Toefield .25 .08
❑ 83 Randy McMichael .25 .08
❑ 84 Jonathan Carter .25 .08
❑ 85 Jerry Rice 1.25 .50
❑ 86 Maurice Morris .25 .08
❑ 87 Kurt Warner .60 .25
❑ 88 Josh Scobey .25 .08
❑ 89 Travis Taylor .25 .08
❑ 90 Fred Taylor .40 .15
❑ 91 Zach Thomas .60 .25
❑ 92 Kelly Campbell .25 .08
❑ 93 Tim Carter .25 .08
❑ 94 Marques Tuiasosopo .40 .15
❑ 95 Laveranues Coles .40 .15
❑ 96 Chris Brown .60 .25
❑ 97 Thomas Jones .40 .15
❑ 98 Dane Looker .40 .15
❑ 99 Ross Tucker .25 .08
❑ 100 Priest Holmes .75 .30
❑ 101 Troy Walters .25 .08
❑ 102 Jamie Sharper .25 .08
❑ 103 Quincy Morgan .40 .15
❑ 104 Aveion Cason .25 .08
❑ 105 Joey Galloway .40 .15
❑ 106 Bill Schroeder .25 .08
❑ 107 Tony Fisher .25 .08
❑ 108 Adewale Ogunleye .40 .15
❑ 109 Justin Fargas .40 .15
❑ 110 Daunte Culpepper .60 .25
❑ 111 Donnie Edwards .25 .08
❑ 112 Jed Weaver .25 .08
❑ 113 Arlen Harris .25 .08
❑ 114 Keenan McCardell .25 .08
❑ 115 Chad Johnson .60 .25
❑ 116 Marty Booker .40 .15
❑ 117 Anthony Wright .25 .08
❑ 118 Brian Finneran .25 .08
❑ 119 Robert Ferguson .25 .08
❑ 120 Ricky Williams .60 .25
❑ 121 Shaun Ellis .25 .08
❑ 122 Brian Westbrook .40 .15
❑ 123 Sam Cowart .25 .08
❑ 124 Tim Rattay .25 .08
❑ 125 LaDainian Tomlinson .75 .30
❑ 126 Simeon Rice .40 .15
❑ 127 Jason Witten .40 .15
❑ 128 Lee Suggs .60 .25
❑ 129 Keith Brooking .25 .08
❑ 130 Rex Grossman .60 .25
❑ 131 Kelley Washington .25 .08
❑ 132 Antonio Bryant .40 .15
❑ 133 Dallas Clark .40 .15
❑ 134 Stacey Mack .25 .08
❑ 135 Charles Rogers .40 .15
❑ 136 Donte' Stallworth .40 .15
❑ 137 Deion Branch .60 .25
❑ 138 Nate Burleson .60 .25
❑ 139 Ike Hilliard .25 .08
❑ 140 Randy Moss .75 .30
❑ 141 Michael Strahan .40 .15
❑ 142 John Abraham .25 .08
❑ 143 Tim Dwight .40 .15
❑ 144 Isaac Bruce .40 .15
❑ 145 Brad Johnson .40 .15
❑ 146 Trung Canidate .25 .08
❑ 147 Warrick Dunn .40 .15
❑ 148 Josh McCown .40 .15
❑ 149 Muhsin Muhammad .40 .15
❑ 150 Donovan McNabb .75 .30
❑ 151 Tai Streets .25 .08
❑ 152 Antonio Gates .60 .25
❑ 153 Antwaan Randle El .60 .25
❑ 154 Doug Jolley .25 .08
❑ 155 Shaun Alexander .60 .25
❑ 156 William Green .40 .15
❑ 157 Carson Palmer .75 .30
❑ 158 Quentin Griffin .60 .25
❑ 159 Az-Zahir Hakim .25 .08
❑ 160 Edgerrin James .60 .25
❑ 161 Gus Frerotte .25 .08
❑ 162 Brandon Lloyd .40 .15
❑ 163 Brian Griese .40 .15
❑ 164 Boo Williams .25 .08
❑ 165 Santana Moss .40 .15
❑ 166 Tyrone Wheatley .25 .08
❑ 167 Eric Parker .25 .08
❑ 168 Amos Zereoue .25 .08
❑ 169 Itula Mili .25 .08
❑ 170 Marshall Faulk .60 .25
❑ 171 Tyrone Calico .40 .15
❑ 172 Tim Hasselbeck .25 .08
❑ 173 Anthony Becht .25 .08
❑ 174 Larry Johnson .75 .30
❑ 175 Marvin Harrison .60 .25
❑ 176 Tony Gonzalez .40 .15
❑ 177 Wayne Chrebet .40 .15
❑ 178 Mike Barrow .25 .08
❑ 179 Bethel Johnson .40 .15
❑ 180 Deuce McAllister .60 .25
❑ 181 Drew Brees .60 .25
❑ 182 Teyo Johnson .25 .08
❑ 183 Garrison Hearst .40 .15
❑ 184 Todd Pinkston .25 .08
❑ 185 Jeff Garcia .60 .25
❑ 186 Darrell Jackson .40 .15
❑ 187 Billy Volek .60 .25
❑ 188 Ray Lewis .60 .25
❑ 189 Ricky Proehl .25 .08
❑ 190 Rudi Johnson .40 .15
❑ 191 Emmitt Smith 1.25 .50
❑ 192 Cedrick Wilson .25 .08
❑ 193 Julius Peppers .60 .25
❑ 194 Peter Warrick .40 .15
❑ 195 Trent Green .40 .15
❑ 196 Derrius Thompson .25 .08
❑ 197 Onterrio Smith .40 .15
❑ 198 Jerome Bettis .60 .25
❑ 199 Keyshawn Johnson .40 .15
❑ 200 Jamal Lewis .60 .25
❑ 201 Alge Crumpler .40 .15
❑ 202 Justin Gage .40 .15
❑ 203 Mike Rucker .25 .08
❑ 204 Michael Bennett .40 .15
❑ 205 Jimmy Smith .40 .15
❑ 206 Ricky Williams TT .25 .08
❑ 207 Corey Bradford .25 .08
❑ 208 Jerry Porter .40 .15
❑ 209 Erron Kinney .25 .08
❑ 210 Marc Bulger .60 .25
❑ 211 Jeff Blake .25 .08
❑ 212 Terry Jones .25 .08
❑ 213 Kordell Stewart .40 .15
❑ 214 Andra Davis .25 .08
❑ 215 David Carr .60 .25
❑ 216 Nick Barnett .40 .15
❑ 217 Mark Brunell .40 .15
❑ 218 Daniel Graham .25 .08
❑ 219 Jim Kleinsasser .25 .08
❑ 220 Aaron Brooks .40 .15
❑ 221 Plaxico Burress .40 .15
❑ 222 Correll Buckhalter .40 .15
❑ 223 Jevon Kearse .40 .15
❑ 224 Michael Pittman .25 .08
❑ 225 Clinton Portis .60 .25
❑ 226 Corey Dillon .40 .15
❑ 227 Steve Smith .60 .25
❑ 228 David Thornton .25 .08
❑ 229 Eddie Kennison .25 .08
❑ 230 Amani Toomer .40 .15
❑ 231 Artose Pinner .25 .08
❑ 232 Kelly Holcomb .40 .15
❑ 233 Jay Fiedler .25 .08
❑ 234 Ernie Conwell .25 .08
❑ 235 Torry Holt .60 .25
❑ 236 Eddie George .40 .15
❑ 237 Jeremy Shockey .60 .25
❑ 238 Troy Edwards .25 .08
❑ 239 Antowain Smith .40 .15
❑ 240 Jon Kitna .40 .15
❑ 241 Bryant Johnson .25 .08
❑ 242 Todd Heap .40 .15
❑ 243 Doug Johnson .25 .08
❑ 244 Ashley Lelie .40 .15
❑ 245 Byron Leftwich .75 .30
❑ 246 Shawn Barber .25 .08
❑ 247 Duce Staley .40 .15
❑ 248 Rod Gardner .40 .15
❑ 249 Warren Sapp .40 .15
❑ 250 Brett Favre 1.50 .60
❑ 251 Olandis Gary .25 .08
❑ 252 Reggie Wayne .40 .15
❑ 253 Billy Miller .25 .08
❑ 254 Johnnie Morton .40 .15
❑ 255 Joe Horn .40 .15
❑ 256 Curtis Martin .60 .25
❑ 257 Freddie Mitchell .40 .15
❑ 258 Charlie Garner .40 .15
❑ 259 Marcus Robinson .40 .15
❑ 260 Derrick Mason .40 .15
❑ 261 Bobby Shaw .25 .08
❑ 262 Desmond Clark .25 .08
❑ 263 James Jackson .25 .08
❑ 264 Josh Reed .25 .08
❑ 265 David Boston .40 .15
❑ 266 Drew Bledsoe .60 .25
❑ 267 Brock Forsey .25 .08
❑ 268 Dat Nguyen .25 .08
❑ 269 Mike Anderson .40 .15
❑ 270 Anthony Thomas .40 .15
❑ 271 Najeh Davenport .25 .08
❑ 272 Jabar Gaffney .40 .15
❑ 273 Tiki Barber .60 .25
❑ 274 Rich Gannon .40 .15
❑ 275 Tom Brady 1.50 .60
❑ 276 Terry Glenn .25 .08
❑ 277 Dennis Northcutt .25 .08
❑ 278 A.J. Feeley .60 .25
❑ 279 Peerless Price .40 .15
❑ 280 Jake Delhomme .60 .25
❑ 281 Kevin Faulk .25 .08
❑ 282 Quincy Carter .40 .15
❑ 283 Andre' Davis .25 .08
❑ 284 Tony Hollings .25 .08
❑ 285 Joey Harrington .60 .25
❑ 286 Richie Anderson .25 .08
❑ 287 Donald Driver .40 .15
❑ 288 Koren Robinson .40 .15
❑ 289 Tony Banks .25 .08
❑ 290 Rod Smith .40 .15
❑ 291 Anquan Boldin WW .25 .08
❑ 292 Jamal Lewis WW .40 .15
❑ 293 Priest Holmes WW .60 .25
❑ 294 Peyton Manning WW .60 .25
❑ 295 Marvin Harrison WW .40 .15
❑ 296 Steve McNair WW .40 .15
❑ 297 Travis Henry WW .25 .08
❑ 298 Torry Holt WW .40 .15
❑ 299 Tom Brady WW .60 .25
❑ 300 Ahman Green WW .40 .15
❑ 301 Donovan McNabb WW .60 .25
❑ 302 Deuce McAllister WW .40 .15
❑ 303 Domanick Davis WW .40 .15
❑ 304 Clinton Portis WW .60 .25
❑ 305 Rudi Johnson WW .25 .08
❑ 306 Brett Favre WW .60 .25
❑ 307 LaDainian Tomlinson WW .50 .20
❑ 308 Steve Smith WW .40 .15
❑ 309 Edgerrin James WW .40 .15
❑ 310 Ty Law WW .25 .08

❑ 311 Ben Roethlisberger RC 20.00 7.50
❑ 312 Ahmad Carroll RC 2.00 .75
❑ 313 Johnnie Morant RC 1.50 .60
❑ 314 Greg Jones RC 1.50 .60
❑ 315 Michael Clayton RC 3.00 1.25
❑ 316 Josh Harris RC 1.50 .60
❑ 317 Tatum Bell RC 3.00 1.25
❑ 318 Robert Gallery RC 2.50 1.00
❑ 319 B.J. Symons RC 1.50 .60
❑ 320 Roy Williams RC 4.00 1.50
❑ 321 DeAngelo Hall RC 2.00 .75
❑ 322 Jeff Smoker RC 1.50 .60
❑ 323 Lee Evans RC 2.00 .75
❑ 324 Michael Jenkins RC 1.50 .60
❑ 325 Steven Jackson RC 5.00 2.00
❑ 326 Will Smith RC 1.50 .60
❑ 327 Vince Wilfork RC 2.00 .75
❑ 328 Ben Troupe RC 1.50 .60
❑ 329 Chris Gamble RC 2.00 .75
❑ 330 Kevin Jones RC 5.00 2.00
❑ 331 Jonathan Vilma RC 1.50 .60
❑ 332 Dontarrious Thomas RC 1.50 .60
❑ 333 Michael Boulware RC 1.50 .60
❑ 334 Meweide Moore RC 2.00 .75
❑ 335 Drew Henson RC 1.50 .60
❑ 336 D.J. Williams RC 2.00 .75
❑ 337 Ernest Wilford RC 1.50 .60
❑ 338 John Navarre RC 1.50 .60
❑ 339 Jerricho Cotchery RC 1.50 .60
❑ 340 Derrick Hamilton RC 1.25 .50
❑ 341 Carlos Francis RC 1.25 .50
❑ 342 Ben Watson RC 1.50 .60
❑ 343 Reggie Williams RC 2.00 .75
❑ 344 Devard Darling RC 1.50 .60
❑ 345 Chris Perry RC 2.50 1.00
❑ 346 Derrick Strait RC 1.50 .60
❑ 347 Sean Taylor RC 2.00 .75
❑ 348 Michael Turner RC 1.50 .60
❑ 349 Keary Colbert RC 2.00 .75
❑ 350 Eli Manning RC 10.00 4.00
❑ 351 Julius Jones RC 6.00 2.50
❑ 352 Jason Babin RC 1.50 .60
❑ 353 Cody Pickett RC 1.50 .60
❑ 354 Kenechi Udeze RC 1.50 .60
❑ 355 Rashaun Woods RC 1.50 .60
❑ 356 Matt Schaub RC 2.50 1.00
❑ 357 Tommie Harris RC 1.50 .60
❑ 358 Dwan Edwards RC .75 .30
❑ 359 Shawn Andrews RC 1.50 .60
❑ 360 Larry Fitzgerald RC 5.00 2.00
❑ 361 P.K. Sam RC 1.25 .50
❑ 362 Teddy Lehman RC 1.50 .60
❑ 363 Darius Watts RC 1.50 .60
❑ 364 D.J. Hackett RC 1.25 .50
❑ 365 Cedric Cobbs RC 1.50 .60
❑ 366 Antwan Odom RC 1.50 .60
❑ 367 Marquise Hill RC 1.25 .50
❑ 368 Luke McCown RC 1.50 .60
❑ 369 Triandos Luke RC 1.50 .60
❑ 370 Kellen Winslow RC 3.00 1.25
❑ 371 Derek Abney RC 1.50 .60
❑ 372 Chris Cooley RC 1.50 .60
❑ 373 Dunta Robinson RC 1.50 .60
❑ 374 Sean Jones RC 1.25 .50
❑ 375 Philip Rivers RC 5.00 2.00
❑ 376 Craig Krenzel RC 1.50 .60
❑ 377 Daryl Smith RC 1.50 .60
❑ 378 Samie Parker RC 1.50 .60
❑ 379 Ben Hartsock RC 1.50 .60
❑ 380 J.P. Losman RC 3.00 1.25
❑ 381 Karlos Dansby RC 1.50 .60
❑ 382 Ricardo Colclough RC 1.50 .60
❑ 383 Bernard Berrian RC 1.50 .60
❑ 384 Junior Siavii RC 1.50 .60
❑ 385 Devery Henderson RC 1.25 .50
❑ TB38 Tom Brady RH 6.00 2.50
❑ RHTBR2 Tom Brady RH AU 350.00 250.00
❑ SBMVP Tom Brady FB AU/99 500.00 300.00

2005 Topps

❑ COMP.COWBOYS SET (445) 60.00 30.00
❑ COMP.EAGLES SET (445) 60.00 30.00
❑ COMP.FACT.SET (445) 60.00 30.00
❑ COMP.PACKERS SET (445) 60.00 30.00
❑ COMP.RAIDERS SET (445) 60.00 30.00
❑ COMP.SB XL SET (445) 75.00 50.00
❑ COMPLETE SET (440) 60.00 30.00

❑ RH39 STATED ODDS 1:275 HOB/HTA/RET
❑ RH39A 1:62,233H, 1:15,547HTA, 1:51,346R
❑ SBMVP 1:27,629H, 1:7774HTA, 1:43,632R
❑ UNPRICED PLATINUM PRINT RUN 1 SET
❑ 1 Brian Westbrook .40 .15
❑ 2 Tim Rattay .30 .10
❑ 3 Domanick Davis .40 .15
❑ 4 Lee Suggs .40 .15
❑ 5 Keith Brooking .30 .10
❑ 6 Rex Grossman .40 .15
❑ 7 Chad Johnson .60 .25
❑ 8 Willis McGahee .60 .25
❑ 9 Eli Manning 1.25 .50
❑ 10 Tom Brady 1.50 .60
❑ 11 Ray Lewis .60 .25
❑ 12 Terence Newman .30 .10
❑ 13 Daunte Culpepper .60 .25
❑ 14 Marvin Harrison .60 .25
❑ 15 Greg Jones .30 .10
❑ 16 Anquan Boldin .40 .15
❑ 17 Julius Peppers .40 .15
❑ 18 Kevin Jones .60 .25
❑ 19 Javon Walker .40 .15
❑ 20 Michael Lewis .30 .10
❑ 21 Jamaar Taylor .30 .10
❑ 22 Hines Ward .60 .25
❑ 23 Drew Brees .60 .25
❑ 24 Marcus Trufant .30 .10
❑ 25 Derrick Brooks .40 .15
❑ 26 Sean Taylor .40 .15
❑ 27 Derrius Thompson .30 .10
❑ 28 Nick Barnett .30 .10
❑ 29 Dante Hall .40 .15
❑ 30 Mike Cloud .30 .10
❑ 31 Jake Plummer .40 .15
❑ 32 Donte Stallworth .40 .15
❑ 33 Shaun Ellis .30 .10
❑ 34 Jeremy Shockey .60 .25
❑ 35 Teyo Johnson .30 .10
❑ 36 Adam Archuleta .30 .10
❑ 37 Darius Watts .40 .15
❑ 38 Michael Pittman .30 .10
❑ 39 Drew Bennett .40 .15
❑ 40 Aaron Stecker .30 .10
❑ 41 Artose Pinner .30 .10
❑ 42 Dane Looker .30 .10
❑ 43 Jeff Garcia .40 .15
❑ 44 Travis Taylor .30 .10
❑ 45 Najeh Davenport .30 .10
❑ 46 Walter Jones .30 .10
❑ 47 Donnie Edwards .30 .10
❑ 48 Terrell Owens .60 .25
❑ 49 Matt Birk .30 .10
❑ 50 Chris Baker .30 .10
❑ 51 Brandon Lloyd .30 .10
❑ 52 Marshall Faulk .60 .25
❑ 53 Jonathan Vilma .40 .15
❑ 54 Dallas Clark .30 .10
❑ 55 David Carr .60 .25
❑ 56 Jerricho Cotchery .30 .10
❑ 57 Deuce McAllister .60 .25
❑ 58 Donald Driver .40 .15
❑ 59 Jeff Smoker .40 .15
❑ 60 Champ Bailey .40 .15
❑ 61 Jason Witten .40 .15
❑ 62 T.J. Houshmandzadeh .30 .10
❑ 63 Jay Fiedler .30 .10
❑ 64 Philip Rivers .60 .25
❑ 65 Jake Delhomme .60 .25
❑ 66 Terrence McGee RC .60 .25
❑ 67 Chester Taylor .40 .15
❑ 68 Tommy Maddox .30 .10
❑ 69 Bryant Johnson .30 .10
❑ 70 Justin Gage .30 .10
❑ 71 Troy Hambrick .30 .10
❑ 72 Kerry Collins .40 .15
❑ 73 Jeb Putzier .30 .10
❑ 74 Keary Colbert .40 .15
❑ 75 Jason Elam .30 .10
❑ 76 Jerramy Stevens .30 .10
❑ 77 Clinton Portis .60 .25
❑ 78 Sam Aiken .30 .10
❑ 79 Trent Green .40 .15
❑ 80 Dat Nguyen .30 .10
❑ 81 Ladell Betts .30 .10
❑ 82 Peter Warrick .30 .10
❑ 83 Dominic Rhodes .30 .10
❑ 84 Jason Taylor .30 .10
❑ 85 Antwaan Randle El .40 .15
❑ 86 Michael Jenkins .40 .15
❑ 87 Adam Vinatieri .60 .25
❑ 88 Mark Brunell .40 .15
❑ 89 Brian Finneran .30 .10
❑ 90 Ernie Conwell .30 .10
❑ 91 Chad Pennington .60 .25
❑ 92 Dan Morgan .30 .10
❑ 93 Kelly Holcomb .30 .10
❑ 94 Ronde Barber .30 .10
❑ 95 Torry Holt .60 .25
❑ 96 Bubba Franks .40 .15
❑ 97 Keyshawn Johnson .40 .15
❑ 98 J.P. Losman .60 .25
❑ 99 Ed Reed .40 .15
❑ 100 Chris McAlister .30 .10
❑ 101 Jamie Sharper .30 .10
❑ 102 Chad Lewis .30 .10
❑ 103 Chris Brown .40 .15
❑ 104 Marc Boerigter .40 .15
❑ 105 Zach Thomas .60 .25
❑ 106 Byron Leftwich .60 .25
❑ 107 Tatum Bell .40 .15
❑ 108 Tai Streets .30 .10
❑ 109 Tory James .30 .10
❑ 110 Cedrick Wilson .30 .10
❑ 111 Darrell Jackson .40 .15
❑ 112 Ben Roethlisberger 1.50 .60
❑ 113 Quentin Jammer .30 .10
❑ 114 Maurice Morris .30 .10
❑ 115 Simeon Rice .40 .15
❑ 116 Tyrone Calico .40 .15
❑ 117 Patrick Ramsey .40 .15
❑ 118 Marcus Robinson .40 .15
❑ 119 Reggie Wayne .40 .15
❑ 120 Kevin Faulk .30 .10
❑ 121 Nate Burleson .40 .15
❑ 122 Aaron Brooks .40 .15
❑ 123 Willie Roaf .30 .10
❑ 124 Fred Taylor .40 .15
❑ 125 Dwight Freeney .40 .15
❑ 126 Olin Kreutz .30 .10
❑ 127 Dunta Robinson .40 .15
❑ 128 Warren Sapp .40 .15
❑ 129 Chris Perry .40 .15
❑ 130 Desmond Clark .30 .10
❑ 131 Takeo Spikes .30 .10
❑ 132 B.J. Sams .30 .10
❑ 133 Bertrand Berry .30 .10
❑ 134 Drew Henson .40 .15
❑ 135 Robert Ferguson .30 .10
❑ 136 Julius Jones .75 .30
❑ 137 Jeremiah Trotter .30 .10
❑ 138 Chris Simms .40 .15
❑ 139 Darnerien McCants .30 .10
❑ 140 Robert Gallery .40 .15
❑ 141 Michael Strahan .40 .15
❑ 142 Reggie Williams .40 .15
❑ 143 Tony Gonzalez .40 .15
❑ 144 Priest Holmes .60 .25
❑ 145 Luke McCown .30 .10
❑ 146 Allen Rossum .30 .10
❑ 147 Eric Moulds .40 .15
❑ 148 Jonathan Wells .30 .10
❑ 149 Randy McMichael .30 .10
❑ 150 John Abraham .30 .10
❑ 151 Doug Gabriel .30 .10
❑ 152 Tiki Barber .60 .25

❑ 153 Marcel Shipp .30 .10
❑ 154 LaDainian Tomlinson .75 .30
❑ 155 Richard Seymour .40 .15
❑ 156 Mike Vanderjagt .30 .10
❑ 157 Roy Williams WR .60 .25
❑ 158 William Green .30 .10
❑ 159 DeAngelo Hall .40 .15
❑ 160 Josh McCown .40 .15
❑ 161 Terrell Suggs .40 .15
❑ 162 Brian Dawkins .40 .15
❑ 163 Lee Evans .40 .15
❑ 164 Nick Goings .30 .10
❑ 165 Carson Palmer .60 .25
❑ 166 Charles Woodson .40 .15
❑ 167 Keenan McCardell .30 .10
❑ 168 Kevan Barlow .40 .15
❑ 169 Matt Hasselbeck .40 .15
❑ 170 Steven Jackson .75 .30
❑ 171 Ben Troupe .30 .10
❑ 172 Jamal Lewis .60 .25
❑ 173 Sammy Morris .30 .10
❑ 174 Troy Polamalu 1.00 .40
❑ 175 Donovan McNabb .75 .30
❑ 176 Curtis Martin .60 .25
❑ 177 David Givens .40 .15
❑ 178 Kenechi Udeze .30 .10
❑ 179 A.J. Feeley .40 .15
❑ 180 Eddie Kennison .30 .10
❑ 181 LaBrandon Toefield .30 .10
❑ 182 Jabar Gaffney .30 .10
❑ 183 Bethel Johnson .30 .10
❑ 184 Eddie Drummond .30 .10
❑ 185 Rod Smith .40 .15
❑ 186 La'Roi Glover .30 .10
❑ 187 Onterrio Smith .40 .15
❑ 188 Antonio Bryant .30 .10
❑ 189 Lee Mays .30 .10
❑ 190 Michael Vick 1.00 .40
❑ 191 Samie Parker .30 .10
❑ 192 London Fletcher .30 .10
❑ 193 DeShaun Foster .40 .15
❑ 194 Rashaun Woods .40 .15
❑ 195 Marc Bulger .60 .25
❑ 196 Adrian Peterson .30 .10
❑ 197 Justin McCareins .30 .10
❑ 198 Corey Dillon .40 .15
❑ 199 James Farrior .30 .10
❑ 200 Antonio Gates .60 .25
❑ 201 Todd Pinkston .30 .10
❑ 202 Randy Hymes .30 .10
❑ 203 Peyton Manning 1.00 .40
❑ 204 Ahman Green .60 .25
❑ 205 Charles Rogers .40 .15
❑ 206 John Lynch .40 .15
❑ 207 Larry Fitzgerald .60 .25
❑ 208 Jonathan Ogden .30 .10
❑ 209 Michael Bennett .40 .15
❑ 210 DeWayne Robertson .30 .10
❑ 211 Justin Fargas .30 .10
❑ 212 Duce Staley .40 .15
❑ 213 Koren Robinson .40 .15
❑ 214 Billy Volek .40 .15
❑ 215 Laveranues Coles .40 .15
❑ 216 Michael Clayton .60 .25
❑ 217 Amani Toomer .40 .15
❑ 218 Thomas Jones .40 .15
❑ 219 Todd Heap .40 .15
❑ 220 Ken Lucas .30 .10
❑ 221 Donovin Darius .30 .10
❑ 222 Ashley Lelie .40 .15
❑ 223 Warrick Dunn .40 .15
❑ 224 Doug Jolley .30 .10
❑ 225 Jimmy Smith .40 .15
❑ 226 Quentin Griffin .40 .15
❑ 227 Isaac Bruce .40 .15
❑ 228 Ronald Curry .40 .15
❑ 229 Corey Bradford .30 .10
❑ 230 LaVar Arrington .60 .25
❑ 231 William Henderson .30 .10
❑ 232 Brandon Stokley .40 .15
❑ 233 Alge Crumpler .40 .15
❑ 234 Joe Horn .40 .15
❑ 235 Bernard Berrian .30 .10
❑ 236 Michael Boulware .30 .10
❑ 237 Brett Favre 1.50 .60
❑ 238 Dennis Northcutt .30 .10
❑ 239 Muhsin Muhammad .40 .15
❑ 240 Shawn Springs .30 .10
❑ 241 Kelly Campbell .30 .10
❑ 242 Johnnie Morton .40 .15
❑ 243 Derrick Blaylock .30 .10
❑ 244 Chris Chambers .40 .15
❑ 245 Joey Harrington .60 .25
❑ 246 Brian Urlacher .60 .25
❑ 247 T.J. Duckett .40 .15
❑ 248 Quincy Morgan .30 .10
❑ 249 Darren Sharper .30 .10
❑ 250 L.J. Smith .30 .10
❑ 251 Steve McNair .60 .25
❑ 252 Eric Parker .30 .10
❑ 253 Jerome Bettis .60 .25
❑ 254 LaMont Jordan .60 .25
❑ 255 Tedy Bruschi .40 .15
❑ 256 Ernest Wilford .30 .10
❑ 257 Reuben Droughns .40 .15
❑ 258 Lito Sheppard .30 .10
❑ 259 Steve Smith .40 .15
❑ 260 Shaun Alexander .75 .30
❑ 261 Kevin Curtis .40 .15
❑ 262 Drew Bledsoe .60 .25
❑ 263 Derrick Mason .40 .15
❑ 264 Jevon Kearse .40 .15
❑ 265 Jerry Porter .40 .15
❑ 266 Edgerrin James .60 .25
❑ 267 Santana Moss .40 .15
❑ 268 Kyle Boller .40 .15
❑ 269 Travis Henry .40 .15
❑ 270 Stephen Davis .40 .15
❑ 271 Gibril Wilson .30 .10
❑ 272 Plaxico Burress .40 .15
❑ 273 Deion Branch .40 .15
❑ 274 Larry Johnson .60 .25
❑ 275 Rudi Johnson .40 .15
❑ 276 Andre Johnson .40 .15
❑ 277 David Akers .30 .10
❑ 278 Randy Moss .60 .25
❑ 279 Roy Williams S .40 .15
❑ 280 Antoine Winfield .30 .10
❑ 281 Antonio Pierce .30 .10
❑ 282 Keith Bulluck .30 .10
❑ 283 Correll Buckhalter .40 .15
❑ 284 Troy Vincent .30 .10
❑ 285 D.J. Williams .30 .10
❑ 286 Matt Schaub .40 .15
❑ 287 Clarence Moore .30 .10
❑ 288 Billy Miller .30 .10
❑ 289 Terrence Holt .30 .10
❑ 290 Tony Hollings .30 .10
❑ 291 E.J. Henderson .30 .10
❑ 292 Fred Smoot .30 .10
❑ 293 Patrick Crayton .30 .10
❑ 294 Mike Alstott .40 .15
❑ 295 Mewelde Moore .40 .15
❑ 296 Shawn Bryson .30 .10
❑ 297 David Garrard .30 .10
❑ 298 Kurt Warner .40 .15
❑ 299 Nate Clements .30 .10
❑ 300 Kellen Winslow .60 .25
❑ 301 Eric Johnson .40 .15
❑ 302 Peerless Price .30 .10
❑ 303 Joey Galloway .40 .15
❑ 304 Sebastian Janikowski .30 .10
❑ 305 Jason McAddley .30 .10
❑ 306 Chris Gamble .40 .15
❑ 307 Brian Griese .40 .15
❑ 308 Greg Lewis .60 .25
❑ 309 Wes Welker .30 .10
❑ 310 Jesse Chatman .30 .10
❑ 311 Curtis Martin LL .40 .15
❑ 312 Daunte Culpepper LL .40 .15
❑ 313 Muhsin Muhammad LL .30 .10
❑ 314 Shaun Alexander LL .60 .25
❑ 315 Trent Green LL .30 .10
❑ 316 Joe Horn LL .30 .10
❑ 317 Corey Dillon LL .30 .10
❑ 318 Peyton Manning LL .60 .25
❑ 319 Javon Walker LL .30 .10
❑ 320 Edgerrin James LL .40 .15
❑ 321 Jake Scott GM .30 .10
❑ 322 John Elway GM 1.00 .40
❑ 323 Dwight Clark GM .40 .15
❑ 324 Lawrence Taylor GM .60 .25
❑ 325 Joe Namath GM .75 .30
❑ 326 Richard Dent GM .40 .15
❑ 327 Peyton Manning GM .60 .25
❑ 328 Don Maynard GM .30 .10
❑ 329 Joe Greene GM .60 .25
❑ 330 Roger Staubach GM .75 .30
❑ 331 Daunte Culpepper AP .40 .15
❑ 332 Peyton Manning AP .60 .25
❑ 333 Tiki Barber AP .40 .15
❑ 334 Antonio Gates AP .40 .15
❑ 335 Marvin Harrison AP .40 .15
❑ 336 Lito Sheppard AP .30 .10
❑ 337 LaDainian Tomlinson AP .60 .25
❑ 338 Muhsin Muhammad AP .30 .10
❑ 339 Allen Rossum AP .30 .10
❑ 340 Dwight Freeney AP .40 .15
❑ 341 Jerome Bettis AP .40 .15
❑ 342 Alge Crumpler AP .30 .10
❑ 343 Ed Reed AP .30 .10
❑ 344 Ronde Barber AP .30 .10
❑ 345 Takeo Spikes AP .30 .10
❑ 346 Rudi Johnson AP .30 .10
❑ 347 Adam Vinatieri AP .40 .15
❑ 348 Torry Holt AP .40 .15
❑ 349 Chad Johnson AP .40 .15
❑ 350 Brian Westbrook AP .30 .10
❑ 351 Michael Vick AP .60 .25
❑ 352 Tom Brady AP .60 .25
❑ 353 Donovan McNabb AP .60 .25
❑ 354 Ahman Green AP .40 .15
❑ 355 Andre Johnson AP .30 .10
❑ 356 Drew Brees AP .40 .15
❑ 357 Hines Ward AP .40 .15
❑ 358 Deion Branch PH .30 .10
❑ 359 Philadelphia Eagles PH .60 .25
❑ 360 Tom Brady PH .60 .25
❑ 361 Taylor Stubblefield RC .75 .30
❑ 362 Dan Cody RC 1.50 .60
❑ 363 Ryan Claridge RC 1.25 .50
❑ 364 David Pollack RC 1.50 .60
❑ 365 Craig Bragg RC 1.25 .50
❑ 366 Alvin Pearman RC 1.50 .60
❑ 367 Marcus Maxwell RC 1.25 .50
❑ 368 Brock Berlin RC 1.25 .50
❑ 369 Khalif Barnes RC 1.25 .50
❑ 370 Eric King RC 1.25 .50
❑ 371 Alex Smith TE RC 1.50 .60
❑ 372 Dante Ridgeway RC 1.25 .50
❑ 373 Shaun Cody RC 1.50 .60
❑ 374 Donte Nicholson RC 1.50 .60
❑ 375 DeMarcus Ware RC 2.50 1.00
❑ 376 Lionel Gates RC 1.25 .50
❑ 377 Fabian Washington RC 1.50 .60
❑ 378 Brandon Jacobs RC 2.00 .75
❑ 379 Noah Herron RC 1.50 .60
❑ 380 Derrick Johnson RC 2.50 1.00
❑ 381 J.R. Russell RC 1.25 .50
❑ 382 Adrian McPherson RC 1.50 .60
❑ 383 Marcus Spears RC 1.50 .60
❑ 384 Justin Miller RC 1.25 .50
❑ 385 Marion Barber RC 2.50 1.00
❑ 386 Anthony Davis RC 1.25 .50
❑ 387 Chad Owens RC 1.50 .60
❑ 388 Craphonso Thorpe RC 1.25 .50
❑ 389 Travis Johnson RC 1.25 .50
❑ 390 Erasmus James RC 1.50 .60
❑ 391 Mike Patterson RC 1.50 .60
❑ 392 Alphonso Hodge RC .75 .30
❑ 393 Airese Currie RC 1.50 .60
❑ 394 Justin Tuck RC 1.50 .60
❑ 395 Dan Orlovsky RC 2.00 .75
❑ 396 Thomas Davis RC 1.50 .60
❑ 397 Derek Anderson RC 1.50 .60
❑ 398 Matt Roth RC 1.50 .60
❑ 399 Darryl Blackstock RC 1.25 .50
❑ 400 Chris Henry RC 1.50 .60
❑ 401 Rasheed Marshall RC 1.50 .60
❑ 402 Anttaj Hawthorne RC 1.25 .50
❑ 403 Bryant McFadden RC 1.50 .60
❑ 404 Darren Sproles RC 1.50 .60
❑ 405 Oshiomogho Atogwe RC 1.25 .50
❑ 406 Fred Gibson RC 1.25 .50
❑ 407 J.J. Arrington RC 2.00 .75
❑ 408 Cedric Benson RC 3.00 1.25
❑ 409 Mark Bradley RC 1.50 .60
❑ 410 Reggie Brown RC 1.50 .60
❑ 411 Ronnie Brown RC 5.00 2.00
❑ 412 Jason Campbell RC 2.50 1.00
❑ 413 Maurice Clarett 1.50 .60

❑ 414 Mark Clayton RC 2.00 .75
❑ 415 Braylon Edwards RC 5.00 2.00
❑ 416 Ciatrick Fason RC 1.50 .60
❑ 417 Charlie Frye RC 3.00 1.25
❑ 418 Frank Gore RC 2.50 1.00
❑ 419 David Greene RC 1.50 .60
❑ 420 Vincent Jackson RC 1.50 .60
❑ 421 Adam Jones RC 1.50 .60
❑ 422 Matt Jones RC 4.00 1.50
❑ 423 Stefan LeFors RC 1.50 .60
❑ 424 Heath Miller RC 4.00 1.50
❑ 425 Ryan Moats RC 1.50 .60
❑ 426 Vernand Morency RC 1.50 .60
❑ 427 Terrence Murphy RC 1.50 .60
❑ 428 Kyle Orton RC 2.50 1.00
❑ 429 Roscoe Parrish RC 1.50 .60
❑ 430 Courtney Roby RC 1.50 .60
❑ 431 Aaron Rodgers RC 5.00 2.00
❑ 432 Carlos Rogers RC 2.00 .75
❑ 433 Antrel Rolle RC 1.50 .60
❑ 434 Eric Shelton RC 1.50 .60
❑ 435 Alex Smith QB RC 6.00 2.50
❑ 436 Andrew Walter RC 2.50 1.00
❑ 437 Roddy White RC 1.50 .60
❑ 438 Carnell Williams RC 8.00 3.00
❑ 439 Mike Williams 3.00 1.25
❑ 440 Troy Williamson RC 3.00 1.25
❑ RHDB Deion Branch RH 5.00 2.00
❑ RHDBA Deion Branch RH AU 350.00 200.00
❑ SBMVP D.Branch FB AU/200 150.00 75.00

2003 Topps All American

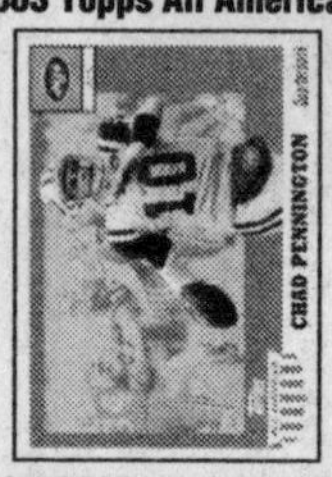

❑ COMPLETE SET (150) 100.00 50.00
❑ COMP.SET w/o SP's (100) 25.00 10.00
❑ 1 Marvin Harrison 1.25 .50
❑ 2 Tiki Barber 1.25 .50
❑ 3 Jamal Lewis 1.25 .50
❑ 4 Tim Couch .75 .30
❑ 5 Michael Bennett .75 .30
❑ 6 Brad Johnson .75 .30
❑ 7 Garrison Hearst .75 .30
❑ 8 Plaxico Burress .75 .30
❑ 9 Rod Gardner .75 .30
❑ 10 Charlie Garner .75 .30
❑ 11 Chad Pennington 1.50 .60
❑ 12 Brian Griese 1.25 .50
❑ 13 Julius Peppers 1.25 .50
❑ 14 David Boston .75 .30
❑ 15 Anthony Thomas .75 .30
❑ 16 Ahman Green 1.25 .50
❑ 17 Fred Taylor 1.25 .50
❑ 18 Joe Horn .75 .30
❑ 19 Joey Galloway .75 .30
❑ 20 Eddie George .75 .30
❑ 21 Jeff Garcia 1.25 .50
❑ 22 Hines Ward 1.25 .50
❑ 23 Kurt Warner 1.25 .50
❑ 24 Marty Booker .75 .30
❑ 25 Joey Harrington 2.00 .75
❑ 26 Jay Fiedler .75 .30
❑ 27 Troy Brown .75 .30
❑ 28 David Carr 2.00 .75
❑ 29 Eric Moulds .75 .30
❑ 30 Michael Vick 3.00 1.25
❑ 31 Keyshawn Johnson 1.25 .50
❑ 32 Torry Holt 1.25 .50
❑ 33 LaDainian Tomlinson 1.25 .50
❑ 34 Duce Staley .75 .30
❑ 35 Curtis Martin 1.25 .50
❑ 36 Stephen Davis .75 .30
❑ 37 Jim Miller .50 .20
❑ 38 Travis Taylor .50 .20
❑ 39 Jimmy Smith .75 .30
❑ 40 Trent Green .75 .30
❑ 41 Tom Brady 3.00 1.25
❑ 42 Randy Moss 2.00 .75
❑ 43 Clinton Portis 2.00 .75
❑ 44 Emmitt Smith 3.00 1.25
❑ 45 Steve McNair 1.25 .50
❑ 46 Shaun Alexander 1.25 .50
❑ 47 Jerome Bettis 1.25 .50
❑ 48 Rich Gannon .75 .30
❑ 49 William Green .75 .30
❑ 50 Priest Holmes 1.50 .60
❑ 51 James Stewart .75 .30
❑ 52 Warrick Dunn .75 .30
❑ 53 Jake Plummer .75 .30
❑ 54 Antowain Smith .75 .30
❑ 55 Peyton Manning 2.00 .75
❑ 56 Deuce McAllister 1.25 .50
❑ 57 Jeremy Shockey 2.00 .75
❑ 58 Darrell Jackson .75 .30
❑ 59 Derrick Mason .75 .30
❑ 60 Terrell Owens 1.25 .50
❑ 61 Laveranues Coles .75 .30
❑ 62 Amani Toomer .75 .30
❑ 63 Tony Gonzalez .75 .30
❑ 64 Corey Bradford .50 .20
❑ 65 Donald Driver .75 .30
❑ 66 Rod Smith .75 .30
❑ 67 Chad Johnson 1.25 .50
❑ 68 Travis Henry .75 .30
❑ 69 Mark Brunell .75 .30
❑ 70 Edgerrin James 1.25 .50
❑ 71 Jerry Rice 2.50 1.00
❑ 72 Aaron Brooks 1.25 .50
❑ 73 Marshall Faulk 1.25 .50
❑ 74 Curtis Conway .50 .20
❑ 75 Tommy Maddox 1.25 .50
❑ 76 Isaac Bruce 1.25 .50
❑ 77 Matt Hasselbeck .75 .30
❑ 78 Muhsin Muhammad .75 .30
❑ 79 Drew Bledsoe 1.25 .50
❑ 80 Ricky Williams 1.25 .50
❑ 81 Daunte Culpepper 1.25 .50
❑ 82 Chad Hutchinson .50 .20
❑ 83 Brian Urlacher 2.00 .75
❑ 84 Drew Brees 1.25 .50
❑ 85 Corey Dillon .75 .30
❑ 86 Chris Chambers 1.25 .50
❑ 87 Peerless Price .75 .30
❑ 88 Kerry Collins .75 .30
❑ 89 Donovan McNabb 1.50 .60
❑ 90 Brett Favre 3.00 1.25
❑ 91 Patrick Ramsey 1.25 .50
❑ 92 T.J. Duckett .75 .30
❑ 93 Derrick Brooks .75 .30
❑ 94 Jon Kitna .75 .30
❑ 95 Jerry Porter .75 .30
❑ 96 Todd Pinkston .75 .30
❑ 97 Tai Streets .50 .20
❑ 98 Ray Lewis 1.25 .50
❑ 99 Michael Pittman .50 .20
❑ 100 Brian Finneran .50 .20
❑ 101 Carson Palmer RC 12.00 5.00
❑ 102 Terrell Suggs RC 5.00 2.00
❑ 103 Boss Bailey RC 3.00 1.25
❑ 104 Justin Gage RC 3.00 1.25
❑ 105 Bobby Wade RC 3.00 1.25
❑ 106 Larry Johnson RC 12.00 6.00
❑ 107 Ken Dorsey RC 3.00 1.25
❑ 108 Quentin Griffin RC 3.00 1.25
❑ 109 Musa Smith RC 3.00 1.25
❑ 110 Chris Simms RC 5.00 2.00
❑ 111 Michael Haynes RC 3.00 1.25
❑ 112 Charles Rogers RC 3.00 1.25
❑ 113 Kliff Kingsbury RC 2.50 1.00
❑ 114 Jerome McDougle RC 3.00 1.25
❑ 115 ReShard Lee RC 3.00 1.25
❑ 116 Chris Brown RC 4.00 1.50
❑ 117 Bryant Johnson RC 3.00 1.25
❑ 118 Teyo Johnson RC 3.00 1.25
❑ 119 Talman Gardner RC 3.00 1.25
❑ 120 Brian St.Pierre RC 3.00 1.25
❑ 121 Onterrio Smith RC 3.00 1.25
❑ 122 Marcus Trufant RC 3.00 1.25
❑ 123 Earnest Graham RC 2.50 1.00
❑ 124 Kareem Kelly RC 2.50 1.00
❑ 125 Jason Witten RC 5.00 2.00
❑ 126 Brandon Lloyd RC 4.00 1.50
❑ 127 Anquan Boldin RC 8.00 3.00
❑ 128 Lee Suggs RC 5.00 2.00
❑ 129 Terry Pierce RC 2.50 1.00
❑ 130 Dallas Clark RC 3.00 1.25
❑ 131 Kelley Washington RC 3.00 1.25
❑ 132 Seneca Wallace RC 3.00 1.25
❑ 133 Domanick Davis RC 5.00 2.00
❑ 134 Terrence Edwards RC 2.50 1.00
❑ 135 Dave Ragone RC 3.00 1.25
❑ 136 Andre Johnson RC 6.00 2.50
❑ 137 Taylor Jacobs RC 2.50 1.00
❑ 138 Kyle Boller RC 6.00 2.50
❑ 139 Willis McGahee RC 8.00 3.00
❑ 140 Byron Leftwich RC 10.00 4.00
❑ 141 Sam Aiken RC 2.50 1.00
❑ 142 Bennie Joppru RC 3.00 1.25
❑ 143 Justin Fargas RC 3.00 1.25
❑ 144 Avon Cobourne RC 2.50 1.00
❑ 145 Rex Grossman RC 5.00 2.00
❑ 146 LaBrandon Toefield RC 3.00 1.25
❑ 147 Tyrone Calico RC 4.00 1.50
❑ 148 Brad Banks RC 2.50 1.00
❑ 149 Terence Newman RC 6.00 2.50
❑ 150 Jimmy Kennedy RC 3.00 1.25

2005 Topps All American

❑ COMPLETE SET (91) 40.00 15.00
❑ UNPRICED PRINT PLATE PRINT RUN 1 SET
❑ ES5 STATED ODDS 1:1220 HOB/RET
❑ ES5C STATED ODDS 1:27,245 HOB/RET
❑ 1 Dan Fouts 1.25 .50
❑ 2 Kellen Winslow 1.00 .40
❑ 3 Marty Lyons 1.25 .50
❑ 4 Alan Page 1.00 .40
❑ 5 Carl Eller .75 .30
❑ 6 Jake Scott .75 .30
❑ 7 William Perry 1.00 .40
❑ 8 Joe Montana 4.00 1.50
❑ 9 Fred Biletnikoff 1.25 .50
❑ 10 Dave Casper 1.00 .40
❑ 11 Earl Campbell 1.25 .50
❑ 12 Mark May .75 .30
❑ 13 Joe Greene 1.25 .50
❑ 14 Ozzie Newsome 1.00 .40
❑ 15 Joe Namath 3.00 1.25
❑ 16 Ted Hendricks .75 .30
❑ 17 Lawrence Taylor 1.25 .50
❑ 18 Randy Gradishar 1.00 .40
❑ 19 Reggie McKenzie .75 .30
❑ 20 Dave Foley 1.25 .50
❑ 21 Mike Montler ERR .75 .30
❑ 22 Merlin Olsen 1.00 .40
❑ 23 John David Crow .75 .30
❑ 24 Paul Hornung 1.50 .60
❑ 25 Jim Brown 2.00 .75
❑ 26 Bob Lilly 1.00 .40
❑ 27 Mel Renfro .75 .30
❑ 28 Dick Butkus 2.00 .75
❑ 29 Roger Staubach 2.00 .75
❑ 30 Gale Sayers 1.50 .60
❑ 31 Bob Griese 1.25 .50
❑ 32 Dick Anderson .75 .30
❑ 33 Jim Plunkett 1.00 .40
❑ 34 Johnny Rodgers 1.25 .50

❑ 35	Ed Marinaro	.75	.30
❑ 36	Greg Pruitt	1.25	.50
❑ 37	Johnny Musso	1.25	.50
❑ 38	Johnny Majors	1.00	.40
❑ 39	Bert Jones	.75	.30
❑ 40	Steve Bartkowski	1.00	.40
❑ 41	John Cappelletti	1.00	.40
❑ 42	Archie Griffin	1.25	.50
❑ 43	Randy White	1.00	.40
❑ 44	Tommy Kramer	.75	.30
❑ 45	Mike Singletary	1.25	.50
❑ 46	Tony Dorsett	1.25	.50
❑ 47	Tony Franklin	.75	.30
❑ 48	John Jefferson	.75	.30
❑ 49	Billy Sims	1.25	.50
❑ 50	Charles White	1.00	.40
❑ 51	Herschel Walker	1.00	.40
❑ 52	Ronnie Lott	1.25	.50
❑ 53	Anthony Carter	1.00	.40
❑ 54	Jim McMahon	1.25	.50
❑ 55	Marcus Allen	1.50	.60
❑ 56	John Elway	2.50	1.00
❑ 57	Mike Rozier	1.25	.50
❑ 58	Irving Fryar	1.25	.50
❑ 59	Bo Jackson	2.00	.75
❑ 60	Eric Dickerson	1.00	.40
❑ 61	Kenny Easley	.75	.30
❑ 62	Bruce Matthews	.75	.30
❑ 63	Alex Karras	1.00	.40
❑ 64	Bubba Smith	.75	.30
❑ 65	Chuck Long	1.00	.40
❑ 66	Lorenzo White	.75	.30
❑ 67	Cris Carter	1.25	.50
❑ 68	Brad Muster	.75	.30
❑ 69	D.J. Dozier	1.00	.40
❑ 70	Craig Heyward	.75	.30
❑ 71	Chris Spielman	1.25	.50
❑ 72	Chuck Cecil	.75	.30
❑ 73	Hart Lee Dykes	.75	.30
❑ 74	Tony Mandarich	.75	.30
❑ 75	Barry Sanders	2.00	.75
❑ 76	Troy Aikman	1.50	.60
❑ 77	Andre Ware	.75	.30
❑ 78	Desmond Howard	1.25	.50
❑ 79	Gino Torretta	.75	.30
❑ 80	Charlie Ward	.75	.30
❑ 81	Danny Wuerffel	1.00	.40
❑ 82	Tommie Frazier	1.25	.50
❑ 83	Ty Detmer	.75	.30
❑ 84	Wendell Davis	.75	.30
❑ 85	Jay Novacek	1.00	.40
❑ 86	Keith Byars	1.00	.40
❑ 87	Steve Spurrier	1.25	.50
❑ 88	Earl Morrall	1.00	.40
❑ 89	Anthony Davis	.75	.30
❑ 90	Brad Van Pelt	.75	.30
❑ 91	Roland James	.75	.30
❑ ES5	Elvis Presley Shirt/500	80.00	50.00
❑ ES5C	Elvis Shirt Chr/25	200.00	125.00

1996 Topps Chrome

❑	COMPLETE SET (165)	100.00	40.00
❑ 1	Troy Aikman	2.50	1.00
❑ 2	Kevin Greene	.50	.20
❑ 3	Robert Brooks	1.00	.40
❑ 4	Junior Seau	1.00	.40
❑ 5	Brett Perriman	.20	.07
❑ 6	Cortez Kennedy	.20	.07
❑ 7	Orlando Thomas	.20	.07
❑ 8	Anthony Miller	.50	.20
❑ 9	Jeff Blake	1.00	.40
❑ 10	Trent Dilfer	1.00	.40
❑ 11	Heath Shuler	.50	.20
❑ 12	Michael Jackson	.50	.20
❑ 13	Merton Hanks	.20	.07
❑ 14	Dale Carter	.20	.07
❑ 15	Eric Metcalf	.20	.07
❑ 16	Barry Sanders	4.00	1.50
❑ 17	Joey Galloway	1.00	.40
❑ 18	Bryan Cox	.20	.07
❑ 19	Harvey Williams	.20	.07
❑ 20	Terrell Davis	1.50	.60
❑ 21	Darnay Scott	.50	.20
❑ 22	Kerry Collins	1.00	.40
❑ 23	Warren Sapp	.20	.07
❑ 24	Michael Westbrook	1.00	.40
❑ 25	Mark Brunell	1.50	.60
❑ 26	Craig Heyward	.20	.07
❑ 27	Eric Allen	.20	.07
❑ 28	Dana Stubblefield	.50	.20
❑ 29	Steve Bono	.20	.07
❑ 30	Larry Brown	.20	.07
❑ 31	Warren Moon	.50	.20
❑ 32	Jim Kelly	1.00	.40
❑ 33	Terry McDaniel	.20	.07
❑ 34	Dan Wilkinson	.20	.07
❑ 35	Dave Brown	.20	.07
❑ 36	Todd Lyght	.20	.07
❑ 37	Aeneas Williams	.20	.07
❑ 38	Shannon Sharpe	.50	.20
❑ 39	Errict Rhett	.50	.20
❑ 40	Yancey Thigpen	.50	.20
❑ 41	J.J. Stokes	1.00	.40
❑ 42	Marshall Faulk	1.25	.50
❑ 43	Chester McGlockton	.20	.07
❑ 44	Darryll Lewis	.20	.07
❑ 45	Drew Bledsoe	1.50	.60
❑ 46	Tyrone Wheatley	.50	.20
❑ 47	Herman Moore	.50	.20
❑ 48	Darren Woodson	.50	.20
❑ 49	Ricky Watters	.50	.20
❑ 50	Emmitt Smith TYC	1.50	.60
❑ 51	Barry Sanders TYC	1.50	.60
❑ 52	Curtis Martin TYC	1.00	.40
❑ 53	Chris Warren TYC	.50	.20
❑ 54	Errict Rhett TYC	.50	.20
❑ 55	Rodney Hampton TYC	.20	.07
❑ 56	Terrell Davis TYC	1.00	.40
❑ 57	Marshall Faulk TYC	1.00	.40
❑ 58	Rashaan Salaam TYC	.50	.20
❑ 59	Curtis Conway	1.00	.40
❑ 60	Isaac Bruce	1.00	.40
❑ 61	Thurman Thomas	1.00	.40
❑ 62	Terry Allen	.50	.20
❑ 63	Lamar Lathon	.20	.07
❑ 64	Mark Chmura	.50	.20
❑ 65	Chris Warren	.50	.20
❑ 66	Jessie Tuggle	.20	.07
❑ 67	Erik Kramer	.20	.07
❑ 68	Tim Brown	1.00	.40
❑ 69	Derrick Thomas	1.00	.40
❑ 70	Willie McGinest	.20	.07
❑ 71	Frank Sanders	.50	.20
❑ 72	Bernie Parmalee	.20	.07
❑ 73	Kordell Stewart	1.00	.40
❑ 74	Brent Jones	.20	.07
❑ 75	Edgar Bennett	.50	.20
❑ 76	Rashaan Salaam	.50	.20
❑ 77	Carl Pickens	.50	.20
❑ 78	Terance Mathis	.20	.07
❑ 79	Deion Sanders	1.25	.50
❑ 80	Glyn Milburn	.20	.07
❑ 81	Lee Woodall	.20	.07
❑ 82	Neil Smith	.50	.20
❑ 83	Stan Humphries	.50	.20
❑ 84	Rick Mirer	.50	.20
❑ 85	Troy Vincent	.20	.07
❑ 86	Sam Mills	.20	.07
❑ 87	Brian Mitchell	.20	.07
❑ 88	Hardy Nickerson	.20	.07
❑ 89	Tamarick Vanover	.50	.20
❑ 90	Steve McNair	1.50	.60
❑ 91	Jerry Rice TYC	1.00	.40
❑ 92	Isaac Bruce TYC	1.00	.40
❑ 93	Herman Moore TYC	.50	.20
❑ 94	Cris Carter TYC	1.00	.40
❑ 95	Tim Brown TYC	.50	.20
❑ 96	Carl Pickens TYC	.50	.20
❑ 97	Joey Galloway TYC	1.00	.40
❑ 98	Jerry Rice	2.50	1.00
❑ 99	Cris Carter	1.00	.40
❑ 100	Curtis Martin	1.50	.60
❑ 101	Scott Mitchell	.50	.20
❑ 102	Ken Harvey	.20	.07
❑ 103	Rodney Hampton	.50	.20
❑ 104	Reggie White	1.00	.40
❑ 105	Eddie Robinson	.20	.07
❑ 106	Greg Lloyd	.50	.20
❑ 107	Phillippi Sparks	.20	.07
❑ 108	Emmitt Smith	4.00	1.50
❑ 109	Tom Carter	.20	.07
❑ 110	Jim Everett	.20	.07
❑ 111	James O.Stewart	.50	.20
❑ 112	Kyle Brady	.20	.07
❑ 113	Irving Fryar	.50	.20
❑ 114	Vinny Testaverde	.50	.20
❑ 115	John Elway	5.00	2.00
❑ 116	Chris Spielman	.20	.07
❑ 117	Mike Mamula	.20	.07
❑ 118	Jim Harbaugh	.50	.20
❑ 119	Ken Norton	.20	.07
❑ 120	Bruce Smith	.50	.20
❑ 121	Daryl Johnston	.50	.20
❑ 122	Blaine Bishop	.20	.07
❑ 123	Jeff George	.50	.20
❑ 124	Jeff Hostetler	.20	.07
❑ 125	Jerome Bettis	1.00	.40
❑ 126	Jay Novacek	.20	.07
❑ 127	Bryce Paup	.20	.07
❑ 128	Neil O'Donnell	.50	.20
❑ 129	Marcus Allen	1.00	.40
❑ 130	Steve Young	1.50	.60
❑ 131	Brett Favre TYC	2.00	.75
❑ 132	Scott Mitchell TYC	.20	.07
❑ 133	John Elway TYC	2.00	.75
❑ 134	Jeff Blake TYC	.50	.20
❑ 135	Dan Marino TYC	2.00	.75
❑ 136	Drew Bledsoe TYC	1.00	.40
❑ 137	Troy Aikman TYC	1.00	.40
❑ 138	Steve Young TYC	1.00	.40
❑ 139	Jim Kelly TYC	1.00	.40
❑ 140	Jeff Graham	.20	.07
❑ 141	Hugh Douglas	.50	.20
❑ 142	Dan Marino	5.00	2.00
❑ 143	Darrell Green	.20	.07
❑ 144	Eric Zeier	.20	.07
❑ 145	Brett Favre	5.00	2.00
❑ 146	Carnell Lake	.20	.07
❑ 147	Ben Coates	.50	.20
❑ 148	Tony Martin	.50	.20
❑ 149	Michael Irvin	1.00	.40
❑ 150	Lawrence Phillips RC	1.00	.40
❑ 151	Alex Van Dyke RC	1.50	.60
❑ 152	Kevin Hardy RC	1.50	.60
❑ 153	Rickey Dudley RC	5.00	2.00
❑ 154	Eric Moulds RC	10.00	5.00
❑ 155	Simeon Rice RC	4.00	1.50
❑ 156	Marvin Harrison RC	30.00	15.00
❑ 157	Tim Biakabutuka RC	4.00	1.50
❑ 158	Duane Clemons RC	1.00	.40
❑ 159	Keyshawn Johnson RC	12.00	5.00
❑ 160	John Mobley RC	1.50	.60
❑ 161	Leeland McElroy RC	1.50	.60
❑ 162	Eddie George RC	12.00	6.00
❑ 163	Jonathan Ogden RC	2.00	.75
❑ 164	Eddie Kennison RC	5.00	2.00
❑ 165	Checklist	.20	.07

1997 Topps Chrome

❑	COMPLETE SET (165)	60.00	30.00
❑ 1	Brett Favre	6.00	2.50
❑ 2	Tim Biakabutuka	1.00	.40
❑ 3	Deion Sanders	1.50	.60
❑ 4	Marshall Faulk	2.00	.75
❑ 5	John Randle	1.00	.40
❑ 6	Stan Humphries	1.00	.40
❑ 7	Ki-Jana Carter	.60	.25
❑ 8	Rashaan Salaam	.60	.25
❑ 9	Rickey Dudley	1.00	.40
❑ 10	Isaac Bruce	1.50	.60
❑ 11	Keyshawn Johnson	1.50	.60
❑ 12	Ben Coates	1.00	.40
❑ 13	Ty Detmer	1.00	.40

❑ 14	Gus Frerotte	.60	.25
❑ 15	Mario Bates	.60	.25
❑ 16	Chris Calloway	.60	.25
❑ 17	Frank Sanders	1.00	.40
❑ 18	Bruce Smith	1.00	.40
❑ 19	Jeff Graham	.60	.25
❑ 20	Trent Dilfer	1.50	.60
❑ 21	Tyrone Wheatley	1.00	.40
❑ 22	Chris Warren	1.00	.40
❑ 23	Terry Kirby	1.00	.40
❑ 24	Tony Gonzalez RC	8.00	3.00
❑ 25	Ricky Watters	1.00	.40
❑ 26	Tamarick Vanover	1.00	.40
❑ 27	Kerry Collins	1.50	.60
❑ 28	Bobby Engram	1.00	.40
❑ 29	Derrick Alexander WR	1.00	.40
❑ 30	Hugh Douglas	.60	.25
❑ 31	Thurman Thomas	1.50	.60
❑ 32	Drew Bledsoe	2.00	.75
❑ 33	LeShon Johnson	.60	.25
❑ 34	Byron Bam Morris	.60	.25
❑ 35	Herman Moore	1.00	.40
❑ 36	Troy Aikman	3.00	1.25
❑ 37	Mel Gray	.60	.25
❑ 38	Adrian Murrell	1.00	.40
❑ 39	Carl Pickens	1.00	.40
❑ 40	Tony Brackens	.60	.25
❑ 41	O.J. McDuffie	1.00	.40
❑ 42	Napoleon Kaufman	1.50	.60
❑ 43	Chris T. Jones	.60	.25
❑ 44	Kordell Stewart	1.50	.60
❑ 45	Steve Young	2.00	.75
❑ 46	Shannon Sharpe	1.00	.40
❑ 47	Leeland McElroy	.60	.25
❑ 48	Eric Moulds	1.50	.60
❑ 49	Eddie George	1.50	.60
❑ 50	Jamal Anderson	1.50	.60
❑ 51	Robert Smith	1.00	.40
❑ 52	Mike Alstott	1.50	.60
❑ 53	Darrell Green	1.00	.40
❑ 54	Irving Fryar	1.00	.40
❑ 55	Derrick Thomas	1.50	.60
❑ 56	Antonio Freeman	1.50	.60
❑ 57	Terrell Davis	2.00	.75
❑ 58	Henry Ellard	.60	.25
❑ 59	Daryl Johnston	1.00	.40
❑ 60	Bryan Cox	.60	.25
❑ 61	Vinny Testaverde	1.00	.40
❑ 62	Andre Reed	1.00	.40
❑ 63	Larry Centers	1.00	.40
❑ 64	Hardy Nickerson	.60	.25
❑ 65	Tony Banks	1.00	.40
❑ 66	Dave Meggett	.60	.25
❑ 67	Simeon Rice	1.00	.40
❑ 68	Warrick Dunn RC	6.00	2.50
❑ 69	Michael Irvin	1.50	.60
❑ 70	John Elway	6.00	2.50
❑ 71	Jake Reed	1.00	.40
❑ 72	Rodney Hampton	1.00	.40
❑ 73	Aaron Glenn	.60	.25
❑ 74	Terry Allen	1.50	.60
❑ 75	Blaine Bishop	.60	.25
❑ 76	Bert Emanuel	1.00	.40
❑ 77	Mark Carrier WR	.60	.25
❑ 78	Jimmy Smith	1.00	.40
❑ 79	Jim Harbaugh	1.00	.40
❑ 80	Brent Jones	1.00	.40
❑ 81	Emmitt Smith	5.00	2.00
❑ 82	Fred Barnett	.60	.25
❑ 83	Errict Rhett	.60	.25
❑ 84	Michael Sinclair	.60	.25
❑ 85	Jerome Bettis	1.50	.60
❑ 86	Chris Sanders	.60	.25
❑ 87	Kent Graham	.60	.25
❑ 88	Cris Carter	1.50	.60
❑ 89	Harvey Williams	.60	.25
❑ 90	Eric Allen	.60	.25
❑ 91	Bryant Young	.60	.25
❑ 92	Marcus Allen	1.50	.60
❑ 93	Michael Jackson	1.00	.40
❑ 94	Mark Chmura	1.00	.40
❑ 95	Keenan McCardell	1.00	.40
❑ 96	Joey Galloway	1.00	.40
❑ 97	Eddie Kennison	1.00	.40
❑ 98	Steve Atwater	.60	.25
❑ 99	Dorsey Levens	1.50	.60
❑ 100	Rob Moore	1.00	.40
❑ 101	Steve McNair	2.00	.75
❑ 102	Sean Dawkins	.60	.25
❑ 103	Don Beebe	.60	.25
❑ 104	Willie McGinest	.60	.25
❑ 105	Tony Martin	1.00	.40
❑ 106	Mark Brunell	2.00	.75
❑ 107	Karim Abdul-Jabbar	1.50	.60
❑ 108	Michael Westbrook	1.00	.40
❑ 109	Lawrence Phillips	.60	.25
❑ 110	Barry Sanders	5.00	2.00
❑ 111	Willie Davis	.60	.25
❑ 112	Wesley Walls	1.00	.40
❑ 113	Todd Collins	.60	.25
❑ 114	Jerry Rice	3.00	1.25
❑ 115	Scott Mitchell	1.00	.40
❑ 116	Terance Mathis	1.00	.40
❑ 117	Chris Spielman	.60	.25
❑ 118	Curtis Conway	1.00	.40
❑ 119	Marvin Harrison	1.50	.60
❑ 120	Terry Glenn	1.50	.60
❑ 121	Dave Brown	.60	.25
❑ 122	Neil O'Donnell	1.00	.40
❑ 123	Junior Seau	1.50	.60
❑ 124	Reggie White	1.50	.60
❑ 125	Lamar Lathon	.60	.25
❑ 126	Natrone Means	1.00	.40
❑ 127	Tim Brown	1.50	.60
❑ 128	Eric Swann	.60	.25
❑ 129	Dan Marino	6.00	2.50
❑ 130	Anthony Johnson	.60	.25
❑ 131	Edgar Bennett	1.00	.40
❑ 132	Kevin Hardy	.60	.25
❑ 133	Brian Blades	.60	.25
❑ 134	Curtis Martin	2.00	.75
❑ 135	Zach Thomas	1.50	.60
❑ 136	Darnay Scott	1.00	.40
❑ 137	Desmond Howard	1.00	.40
❑ 138	Aeneas Williams	.60	.25
❑ 139	Bryce Paup	.60	.25
❑ 140	Brad Johnson	1.50	.60
❑ 141	Jeff Blake	1.00	.40
❑ 142	Wayne Chrebet	1.50	.60
❑ 143	Will Blackwell RC	1.25	.50
❑ 144	Tom Knight RC	.60	.25
❑ 145	Darnell Autry RC	1.00	.40
❑ 146	Bryant Westbrook RC	.60	.25
❑ 147	David LaFleur RC	.75	.30
❑ 148	Antowain Smith RC	8.00	3.00
❑ 149	Rae Carruth RC	.75	.30
❑ 150	Jim Druckenmiller RC	1.00	.40
❑ 151	Shawn Springs RC	.75	.30
❑ 152	Troy Davis RC	1.25	.50
❑ 153	Orlando Pace RC	2.00	.75
❑ 154	Byron Hanspard RC	1.25	.50
❑ 155	Corey Dillon RC	20.00	7.50
❑ 156	Reidel Anthony RC	2.00	.75
❑ 157	Peter Boulware RC	2.00	.75
❑ 158	Reinard Wilson RC	1.25	.50
❑ 159	Pat Barnes RC	2.00	.75
❑ 160	Joey Kent RC	2.00	.75
❑ 161	Ike Hilliard RC	3.00	1.25
❑ 162	Jake Plummer RC	15.00	6.00
❑ 163	Darrell Russell RC	.75	.30
❑ 164	Checklist Card	.60	.25
❑ 165	Checklist Card	.60	.25

1998 Topps Chrome

❑	COMPLETE SET (165)	120.00	50.00
❑ 1	Barry Sanders	4.00	1.50
❑ 2	Duane Starks RC	2.00	.75
❑ 3	J.J. Stokes	.75	.30
❑ 4	Joey Galloway	.75	.30
❑ 5	Deion Sanders	1.25	.50
❑ 6	Anthony Miller	.50	.20
❑ 7	Jamal Anderson	1.25	.50
❑ 8	Shannon Sharpe	.75	.30
❑ 9	Irving Fryar	.75	.30
❑ 10	Curtis Martin	1.25	.50
❑ 11	Shawn Jefferson	.50	.20
❑ 12	Charlie Garner	.75	.30
❑ 13	Robert Edwards RC	3.00	1.25
❑ 14	Napoleon Kaufman	1.25	.50
❑ 15	Gus Frerotte	.50	.20
❑ 16	John Elway	5.00	2.00
❑ 17	Jerome Pathon RC	4.00	1.50
❑ 18	Marshall Faulk	1.50	.60
❑ 19	Michael McCrary	.50	.20
❑ 20	Marcus Allen	1.25	.50
❑ 21	Trent Dilfer	1.25	.50
❑ 22	Frank Wycheck	.50	.20
❑ 23	Terrell Owens	1.25	.50
❑ 24	Herman Moore	.75	.30
❑ 25	Neil O'Donnell	.75	.30
❑ 26	Darnay Scott	.75	.30
❑ 27	Keith Brooking RC	4.00	1.50
❑ 28	Eric Green	.50	.20
❑ 29	Dan Marino	5.00	2.00
❑ 30	Antonio Freeman	1.25	.50
❑ 31	Tony Martin	.75	.30
❑ 32	Isaac Bruce	1.25	.50
❑ 33	Rickey Dudley	.50	.20
❑ 34	Scott Mitchell	.75	.30
❑ 35	Randy Moss RC	25.00	10.00
❑ 36	Fred Lane	.50	.20
❑ 37	Frank Sanders	.75	.30
❑ 38	Jerry Rice	2.50	1.00
❑ 39	O.J. McDuffie	.75	.30
❑ 40	Jessie Armstead	.50	.20
❑ 41	Reidel Anthony	.75	.30
❑ 42	Steve McNair	1.25	.50
❑ 43	Jake Reed	.75	.30
❑ 44	Charles Woodson RC	5.00	2.00
❑ 45	Tiki Barber	1.25	.50
❑ 46	Mike Alstott	1.25	.50
❑ 47	Keyshawn Johnson	1.25	.50
❑ 48	Tony Banks	.75	.30
❑ 49	Michael Westbrook	.75	.30
❑ 50	Chris Slade	.50	.20
❑ 51	Terry Allen	1.25	.50
❑ 52	Karim Abdul-Jabbar	1.25	.50
❑ 53	Brad Johnson	1.25	.50
❑ 54	Tony McGee	.50	.20
❑ 55	Kevin Dyson RC	4.00	1.50
❑ 56	Warren Moon	1.25	.50
❑ 57	Byron Hanspard	.50	.20
❑ 58	Jermaine Lewis	.75	.30
❑ 59	Neil Smith	.75	.30
❑ 60	Tamarick Vanover	.50	.20
❑ 61	Terrell Davis	1.25	.50
❑ 62	Robert Smith	1.25	.50
❑ 63	Junior Seau	1.25	.50
❑ 64	Warren Sapp	.75	.30
❑ 65	Michael Sinclair	.50	.20
❑ 66	Ryan Leaf RC	4.00	1.50
❑ 67	Drew Bledsoe	2.00	.75
❑ 68	Jason Sehorn	.75	.30
❑ 69	Andre Hastings	.50	.20
❑ 70	Tony Gonzalez	1.25	.50
❑ 71	Dorsey Levens	1.25	.50
❑ 72	Ray Lewis	1.25	.50

❑ 73	Grant Wistrom RC	3.00	1.25
❑ 74	Elvis Grbac	.75	.30
❑ 75	Mark Chmura	.75	.30
❑ 76	Zach Thomas	1.25	.50
❑ 77	Ben Coates	.75	.30
❑ 78	Rod Smith WR	.75	.30
❑ 79	Andre Wadsworth RC	3.00	1.25
❑ 80	Garrison Hearst	1.25	.50
❑ 81	Will Blackwell	.50	.20
❑ 82	Cris Carter	1.25	.50
❑ 83	Mark Fields	.50	.20
❑ 84	Ken Dilger	.50	.20
❑ 85	Johnnie Morton	.75	.30
❑ 86	Michael Irvin	1.25	.50
❑ 87	Eddie George	1.25	.50
❑ 88	Rob Moore	.75	.30
❑ 89	Takeo Spikes RC	4.00	1.50
❑ 90	Wesley Walls	.75	.30
❑ 91	Andre Reed	.75	.30
❑ 92	Thurman Thomas	1.25	.50
❑ 93	Ed McCaffrey	.75	.30
❑ 94	Carl Pickens	.75	.30
❑ 95	Jason Taylor	.75	.30
❑ 96	Kordell Stewart	1.25	.50
❑ 97	Greg Ellis RC	2.00	.75
❑ 98	Aaron Glenn	.50	.20
❑ 99	Jake Plummer	1.25	.50
❑ 100	Checklist	.50	.20
❑ 101	Chris Sanders	.50	.20
❑ 102	Michael Jackson	.50	.20
❑ 103	Bobby Hoying	.75	.30
❑ 104	Wayne Chrebet	1.25	.50
❑ 105	Charles Way	.50	.20
❑ 106	Derrick Thomas	1.25	.50
❑ 107	Troy Drayton	.50	.20
❑ 108	Robert Holcombe RC	3.00	1.25
❑ 109	Pete Mitchell	.50	.20
❑ 110	Bruce Smith	.75	.30
❑ 111	Terance Mathis	.75	.30
❑ 112	Lawrence Phillips	.50	.20
❑ 113	Brett Favre	5.00	2.00
❑ 114	Darrell Green	.75	.30
❑ 115	Charles Johnson	.50	.20
❑ 116	Jeff Blake	.75	.30
❑ 117	Mark Brunell	1.25	.50
❑ 118	Simeon Rice	.75	.30
❑ 119	Robert Brooks	.75	.30
❑ 120	Jacquez Green RC	3.00	1.25
❑ 121	Willie Davis	.50	.20
❑ 122	Jeff George	.75	.30
❑ 123	Andre Rison	.75	.30
❑ 124	Erik Kramer	.50	.20
❑ 125	Peter Boulware	.50	.20
❑ 126	Marcus Nash RC	2.00	.75
❑ 127	Troy Aikman	2.50	1.00
❑ 128	Keenan McCardell	.75	.30
❑ 129	Bryant Westbrook	.50	.20
❑ 130	Terry Glenn	1.25	.50
❑ 131	Blaine Bishop	.50	.20
❑ 132	Tim Brown	1.25	.50
❑ 133	Brian Griese RC	8.00	3.00
❑ 134	John Mobley	.50	.20
❑ 135	Larry Centers	.50	.20
❑ 136	Eric Bjornson	.50	.20
❑ 137	Kevin Hardy	.50	.20
❑ 138	John Randle	.75	.30
❑ 139	Michael Strahan	.75	.30
❑ 140	Jerome Bettis	1.25	.50
❑ 141	Rae Carruth	.50	.20
❑ 142	Reggie White	1.25	.50
❑ 143	Antowain Smith	1.25	.50
❑ 144	Aeneas Williams	.50	.20
❑ 145	Bobby Engram	.75	.30
❑ 146	Germane Crowell RC	3.00	1.25
❑ 147	Freddie Jones	.50	.20
❑ 148	Kimble Anders	.75	.30
❑ 149	Steve Young	1.50	.60
❑ 150	Willie McGinest	.50	.20
❑ 151	Emmitt Smith	4.00	1.50
❑ 152	Fred Taylor RC	6.00	2.50
❑ 153	Danny Kanell	.75	.30
❑ 154	Warrick Dunn	1.25	.50
❑ 155	Kerry Collins	.75	.30
❑ 156	Chris Chandler	.75	.30
❑ 157	Curtis Conway	.75	.30
❑ 158	Curtis Enis RC	2.00	.75
❑ 159	Corey Dillon	1.25	.50
❑ 160	Glenn Foley	.75	.30
❑ 161	Marvin Harrison	1.25	.50
❑ 162	Chad Brown	.50	.20
❑ 163	Derrick Rodgers	.50	.20
❑ 164	Levon Kirkland	.50	.20
❑ 165	Peyton Manning RC	40.00	20.00

1999 Topps Chrome

❑	COMPLETE SET (165)	150.00	60.00
❑	COMP.SET w/o SP's (135)	50.00	25.00
❑ 1	Randy Moss	3.00	1.25
❑ 2	Keyshawn Johnson	1.25	.50
❑ 3	Priest Holmes	2.00	.75
❑ 4	Warren Moon	1.25	.50
❑ 5	Joey Galloway	.75	.30
❑ 6	Zach Thomas	1.25	.50
❑ 7	Cam Cleeland	.50	.20
❑ 8	Jim Harbaugh	.75	.30
❑ 9	Napoleon Kaufman	1.25	.50
❑ 10	Fred Taylor	1.25	.50
❑ 11	Mark Brunell	1.25	.50
❑ 12	Shannon Sharpe	.75	.30
❑ 13	Jacquez Green	.50	.20
❑ 14	Adrian Murrell	.75	.30
❑ 15	Cris Carter	1.25	.50
❑ 16	Jerome Pathon	.50	.20
❑ 17	Drew Bledsoe	1.50	.60
❑ 18	Curtis Martin	1.25	.50
❑ 19	Johnnie Morton	.75	.30
❑ 20	Doug Flutie	1.25	.50
❑ 21	Carl Pickens	.75	.30
❑ 22	Jerome Bettis	1.25	.50
❑ 23	Derrick Alexander	.50	.20
❑ 24	Antowain Smith	1.25	.50
❑ 25	Barry Sanders	4.00	1.50
❑ 26	Reidel Anthony	.75	.30
❑ 27	Wayne Chrebet	.75	.30
❑ 28	Terance Mathis	.75	.30
❑ 29	Shawn Springs	.50	.20
❑ 30	Emmitt Smith	2.50	1.00
❑ 31	Robert Smith	1.25	.50
❑ 32	Charles Johnson	.50	.20
❑ 33	Mike Alstott	1.25	.50
❑ 34	Ike Hilliard	.50	.20
❑ 35	Ricky Watters	.75	.30
❑ 36	Charles Woodson	1.25	.50
❑ 37	Rod Smith	.75	.30
❑ 38	Pete Mitchell	.50	.20
❑ 39	Derrick Thomas	1.25	.50
❑ 40	Dan Marino	4.00	1.50
❑ 41	Darnay Scott	.50	.20
❑ 42	Jake Reed	.75	.30
❑ 43	Chris Chandler	.75	.30
❑ 44	Dorsey Levens	1.25	.50
❑ 45	Kordell Stewart	.75	.30
❑ 46	Eddie George	1.25	.50
❑ 47	Corey Dillon	1.25	.50
❑ 48	Rich Gannon	1.25	.50
❑ 49	Chris Spielman	.50	.20
❑ 50	Jerry Rice	2.50	1.00
❑ 51	Trent Dilfer	.75	.30
❑ 52	Mark Chmura	.50	.20
❑ 53	Jimmy Smith	.75	.30
❑ 54	Isaac Bruce	1.25	.50
❑ 55	Karim Abdul-Jabbar	.75	.30
❑ 56	Sedrick Shaw	.50	.20
❑ 57	Jake Plummer	.75	.30
❑ 58	Tony Gonzalez	1.25	.50
❑ 59	Ben Coates	.75	.30
❑ 60	John Elway	4.00	1.50
❑ 61	Bruce Smith	.75	.30
❑ 62	Tim Brown	1.25	.50
❑ 63	Tim Dwight	1.25	.50
❑ 64	Yancey Thigpen	.50	.20
❑ 65	Terrell Owens	1.25	.50
❑ 66	Kyle Brady	.50	.20
❑ 67	Tony Martin	.75	.30
❑ 68	Michael Strahan	.75	.30
❑ 69	Deion Sanders	1.25	.50
❑ 70	Steve Young	1.50	.60
❑ 71	Dale Carter	.50	.20
❑ 72	Ty Law	.75	.30
❑ 73	Frank Wycheck	.50	.20
❑ 74	Marshall Faulk	1.50	.60
❑ 75	Vinny Testaverde	.75	.30
❑ 76	Chad Brown	.50	.20
❑ 77	Natrone Means	.75	.30
❑ 78	Bert Emanuel	.75	.30
❑ 79	Kerry Collins	.75	.30
❑ 80	Randall Cunningham	1.25	.50
❑ 81	Garrison Hearst	.75	.30
❑ 82	Curtis Enis	.50	.20
❑ 83	Steve Atwater	.50	.20
❑ 84	Kevin Greene	.50	.20
❑ 85	Steve McNair	1.25	.50
❑ 86	Andre Reed	.75	.30
❑ 87	J.J. Stokes	.75	.30
❑ 88	Eric Moulds	1.25	.50
❑ 89	Marvin Harrison	1.25	.50
❑ 90	Troy Aikman	2.50	1.00
❑ 91	Herman Moore	.75	.30
❑ 92	Michael Irvin	.75	.30
❑ 93	Frank Sanders	.75	.30
❑ 94	Duce Staley	1.25	.50
❑ 95	James Jett	.75	.30
❑ 96	Ricky Proehl	.50	.20
❑ 97	Andre Rison	.75	.30
❑ 98	Leslie Shepherd	.50	.20
❑ 99	Trent Green	1.25	.50
❑ 100	Terrell Davis	1.25	.50
❑ 101	Freddie Jones	.50	.20
❑ 102	Skip Hicks	.50	.20
❑ 103	Jeff Graham	.50	.20
❑ 104	Rob Moore	.75	.30
❑ 105	Torrance Small	.50	.20
❑ 106	Antonio Freeman	1.25	.50
❑ 107	Robert Brooks	.75	.30
❑ 108	Jon Kitna	1.25	.50
❑ 109	Curtis Conway	.75	.30
❑ 110	Brett Favre	4.00	1.50
❑ 111	Warrick Dunn	1.25	.50
❑ 112	Elvis Grbac	.75	.30
❑ 113	Corey Fuller	.50	.20
❑ 114	Rickey Dudley	.50	.20
❑ 115	Jamal Anderson	1.25	.50
❑ 116	Terry Glenn	1.25	.50
❑ 117	Rocket Ismail	.75	.30
❑ 118	John Randle	.75	.30
❑ 119	Chris Calloway	.50	.20
❑ 120	Peyton Manning	4.00	1.50
❑ 121	Keenan McCardell	.75	.30
❑ 122	O.J. McDuffie	.75	.30
❑ 123	Ed McCaffrey	.75	.30
❑ 124	Charlie Batch	1.25	.50
❑ 125	Jason Elam SH	.50	.20
❑ 126	Randy Moss SH	1.50	.60
❑ 127	John Elway SH	2.00	.75
❑ 128	Emmitt Smith SH	1.25	.50
❑ 129	Terrell Davis SH	1.25	.50
❑ 130	Jerris McPhail	.50	.20
❑ 131	Damon Gibson	.50	.20
❑ 132	Jim Pyne	.50	.20
❑ 133	Antonio Langham	.50	.20
❑ 134	Freddie Solomon	.50	.20
❑ 135	Ricky Williams RC	10.00	4.00
❑ 136	Daunte Culpepper RC	25.00	10.00
❑ 137	Chris Claiborne RC	2.00	.75
❑ 138	Amos Zereoue RC	5.00	2.00
❑ 139	Chris McAlister RC	4.00	1.50
❑ 140	Kevin Faulk RC	5.00	2.00
❑ 141	James Johnson RC	4.00	1.50
❑ 142	Mike Cloud RC	4.00	1.50
❑ 143	Jevon Kearse RC	10.00	4.00
❑ 144	Akili Smith RC	4.00	1.50
❑ 145	Edgerrin James RC	20.00	10.00
❑ 146	Cecil Collins RC	2.00	.75

- ❑ 147 Donovan McNabb RC 25.00 12.50
- ❑ 148 Kevin Johnson RC 5.00 2.00
- ❑ 149 Torry Holt RC 15.00 6.00
- ❑ 150 Rob Konrad RC 5.00 2.00
- ❑ 151 Tim Couch RC 5.00 2.00
- ❑ 152 David Boston RC 5.00 2.00
- ❑ 153 Karsten Bailey RC 4.00 1.50
- ❑ 154 Troy Edwards RC 4.00 1.50
- ❑ 155 Sedrick Irvin RC 2.00 .75
- ❑ 156 Shaun King RC 4.00 1.50
- ❑ 157 Peerless Price RC 5.00 2.00
- ❑ 158 Brock Huard RC 5.00 2.00
- ❑ 159 Cade McNown RC 4.00 1.50
- ❑ 160 Champ Bailey RC 8.00 3.00
- ❑ 161 D'Wayne Bates RC 4.00 1.50
- ❑ 162 Joe Germaine RC 4.00 1.50
- ❑ 163 Andy Katzenmoyer RC 4.00 1.50
- ❑ 164 Antoine Winfield RC 4.00 1.50
- ❑ 165 Checklist Card .50 .20

2000 Topps Chrome

- ❑ COMPLETE SET (270) 800.00 400.00
- ❑ COMP.SET w/o SPs (180) 50.00 25.00
- ❑ 1 Daunte Culpepper 1.50 .60
- ❑ 2 Troy Edwards .40 .15
- ❑ 3 Terrell Owens 1.25 .50
- ❑ 4 Ricky Proehl .40 .15
- ❑ 5 Shaun King .40 .15
- ❑ 6 Jeff George .60 .25
- ❑ 7 Champ Bailey .60 .25
- ❑ 8 Amani Toomer .40 .15
- ❑ 9 Stephen Boyd .40 .15
- ❑ 10 Thurman Thomas .60 .25
- ❑ 11 Patrick Jeffers 1.25 .50
- ❑ 12 Jake Plummer .60 .25
- ❑ 13 Peter Boulware .40 .15
- ❑ 14 Darrin Chiaverini .40 .15
- ❑ 15 Olandis Gary 1.25 .50
- ❑ 16 Peyton Manning 3.00 1.25
- ❑ 17 Joe Horn .60 .25
- ❑ 18 Wayne Chrebet .60 .25
- ❑ 19 Freddie Jones .40 .15
- ❑ 20 Kurt Warner 2.50 1.00
- ❑ 21 Mike Alstott 1.25 .50
- ❑ 22 Stephen Davis 1.25 .50
- ❑ 23 Tim Brown 1.25 .50
- ❑ 24 Damon Huard 1.25 .50
- ❑ 25 Terry Glenn .60 .25
- ❑ 26 Ricky Williams 1.25 .50
- ❑ 27 Tim Dwight 1.25 .50
- ❑ 28 Jay Riemersma .40 .15
- ❑ 29 Carl Pickens .60 .25
- ❑ 30 Brett Favre 4.00 1.50
- ❑ 31 Oronde Gadsden .60 .25
- ❑ 32 Steve McNair 1.25 .50
- ❑ 33 Michael Pittman .40 .15
- ❑ 34 Emmitt Smith 2.50 1.00
- ❑ 35 Mark Brunell 1.25 .50
- ❑ 36 Ed McCaffrey 1.25 .50
- ❑ 37 Tyrone Wheatley .60 .25
- ❑ 38 Sean Dawkins .40 .15
- ❑ 39 Jevon Kearse 1.25 .50
- ❑ 40 Tai Streets .40 .15
- ❑ 41 Keyshawn Johnson 1.25 .50
- ❑ 42 Germane Crowell .40 .15
- ❑ 43 Yatil Green .40 .15
- ❑ 44 Anthony Wright RC 4.00 1.50
- ❑ 45 Jerry Rice 2.50 1.00
- ❑ 46 Az-Zahir Hakim .60 .25
- ❑ 47 Stephen Alexander .40 .15
- ❑ 48 Zach Thomas 1.25 .50
- ❑ 49 Tony Simmons .40 .15
- ❑ 50 Jessie Armstead .40 .15
- ❑ 51 Kordell Stewart .60 .25
- ❑ 52 Cade McNown .40 .15
- ❑ 53 Tony Gonzalez .60 .25
- ❑ 54 John Randle .60 .25
- ❑ 55 Donovan McNabb 2.00 .75
- ❑ 56 Warrick Dunn 1.25 .50
- ❑ 57 Dorsey Levens .60 .25
- ❑ 58 Errict Rhett .60 .25
- ❑ 59 Priest Holmes 1.50 .60
- ❑ 60 Terrell Davis 1.25 .50
- ❑ 61 Natrone Means .40 .15
- ❑ 62 Brad Johnson 1.25 .50
- ❑ 63 Rickey Dudley .40 .15
- ❑ 64 Moses Moreno .40 .15
- ❑ 65 Randy Moss 2.50 1.00
- ❑ 66 Joe Montgomery .40 .15
- ❑ 67 Johnnie Morton .60 .25
- ❑ 68 Peerless Price .60 .25
- ❑ 69 Rocket Ismail .60 .25
- ❑ 70 David Boston 1.25 .50
- ❑ 71 Fred Taylor 1.25 .50
- ❑ 72 Jermaine Fazande .40 .15
- ❑ 73 Elvis Grbac .60 .25
- ❑ 74 Derrick Mayes .60 .25
- ❑ 75 Yancey Thigpen .40 .15
- ❑ 76 Ike Hilliard .60 .25
- ❑ 77 Muhsin Muhammad .60 .25
- ❑ 78 Shawn Jefferson .40 .15
- ❑ 79 Rod Smith .60 .25
- ❑ 80 Darnay Scott .60 .25
- ❑ 81 Cam Cleeland .40 .15
- ❑ 82 Steve Young 1.50 .60
- ❑ 83 E.G. Green .40 .15
- ❑ 84 Robert Smith 1.25 .50
- ❑ 85 Jermaine Lewis .60 .25
- ❑ 86 Tim Biakabutuka .60 .25
- ❑ 87 Jerome Pathon .60 .25
- ❑ 88 Kent Graham .40 .15
- ❑ 89 Bruce Smith .60 .25
- ❑ 90 Isaac Bruce 1.25 .50
- ❑ 91 Curtis Enis .40 .15
- ❑ 92 Bert Emanuel .40 .15
- ❑ 93 Keith Poole .40 .15
- ❑ 94 Troy Aikman 2.50 1.00
- ❑ 95 Rich Gannon 1.25 .50
- ❑ 96 Michael Westbrook .60 .25
- ❑ 97 Albert Connell .40 .15
- ❑ 98 James Johnson .40 .15
- ❑ 99 Jeff Blake .60 .25
- ❑ 100 Joey Galloway .60 .25
- ❑ 101 Rob Moore .60 .25
- ❑ 102 Chris Chandler .60 .25
- ❑ 103 Fred Lane .40 .15
- ❑ 104 Eddie Kennison .60 .25
- ❑ 105 Kevin Hardy .40 .15
- ❑ 106 Napoleon Kaufman .60 .25
- ❑ 107 Kevin Dyson .60 .25
- ❑ 108 Keenan McCardell .60 .25
- ❑ 109 Drew Bledsoe 1.50 .60
- ❑ 110 Kevin Johnson 1.25 .50
- ❑ 111 Terance Mathis .60 .25
- ❑ 112 Gus Frerotte .40 .15
- ❑ 113 Matthew Hatchette .40 .15
- ❑ 114 Herman Moore .60 .25
- ❑ 115 Curtis Martin 1.25 .50
- ❑ 116 Jacquez Green .40 .15
- ❑ 117 Jake Reed .60 .25
- ❑ 118 Antonio Freeman 1.25 .50
- ❑ 119 Jim Miller .40 .15
- ❑ 120 Frank Sanders .60 .25
- ❑ 121 Brian Griese 1.25 .50
- ❑ 122 Troy Brown .60 .25
- ❑ 123 Jeff Graham .40 .15
- ❑ 124 Marshall Faulk 1.50 .60
- ❑ 125 Vinny Testaverde .60 .25
- ❑ 126 Frank Wycheck .40 .15
- ❑ 127 Kerry Collins .60 .25
- ❑ 128 Jay Fiedler 1.25 .50
- ❑ 129 Cris Carter 1.25 .50
- ❑ 130 Jason Tucker .40 .15
- ❑ 131 Antowain Smith .60 .25
- ❑ 132 Tony Banks .60 .25
- ❑ 133 Terrence Wilkins .40 .15
- ❑ 134 Tony Martin .60 .25
- ❑ 135 Richard Huntley .40 .15
- ❑ 136 J.J. Stokes .60 .25
- ❑ 137 Ricky Watters .60 .25
- ❑ 138 Pete Mitchell .40 .15
- ❑ 139 Jimmy Smith .60 .25
- ❑ 140 Doug Flutie 1.25 .50
- ❑ 141 Corey Bradford .60 .25
- ❑ 142 Curtis Conway .60 .25
- ❑ 143 Pete Mitchell .40 .15
- ❑ 144 Torry Holt 1.25 .50
- ❑ 145 Warren Sapp .60 .25
- ❑ 146 Duce Staley 1.25 .50
- ❑ 147 Mikhael Ricks .40 .15
- ❑ 148 Edgerrin James 2.00 .75
- ❑ 149 Charlie Batch 1.25 .50
- ❑ 150 Rob Johnson .60 .25
- ❑ 151 Jamal Anderson 1.25 .50
- ❑ 152 Tim Couch .60 .25
- ❑ 153 O.J. McDuffie .60 .25
- ❑ 154 Charles Woodson .60 .25
- ❑ 155 Jake Delhomme RC 10.00 4.00
- ❑ 156 Eddie George 1.25 .50
- ❑ 157 Jim Harbaugh .60 .25
- ❑ 158 Jon Kitna 1.25 .50
- ❑ 159 Derrick Alexander .60 .25
- ❑ 160 Marvin Harrison 1.25 .50
- ❑ 161 James Stewart .60 .25
- ❑ 162 Qadry Ismail .60 .25
- ❑ 163 Wesley Walls .40 .15
- ❑ 164 Steve Beuerlein .60 .25
- ❑ 165 Marcus Robinson 1.25 .50
- ❑ 166 Bill Schroeder .60 .25
- ❑ 167 Charles Johnson .60 .25
- ❑ 168 Charlie Garner .60 .25
- ❑ 169 Eric Moulds 1.25 .50
- ❑ 170 Jerome Bettis 1.25 .50
- ❑ 171 Tai Streets .40 .15
- ❑ 172 Akili Smith .40 .15
- ❑ 173 Jonathan Linton .40 .15
- ❑ 174 Corey Dillon 1.25 .50
- ❑ 175 Junior Seau 1.25 .50
- ❑ 176 Jonathan Quinn .40 .15
- ❑ 177 Bobby Engram .40 .15
- ❑ 178 Shannon Sharpe .60 .25
- ❑ 179 Michael Basnight .40 .15
- ❑ 180 Sedrick Irvin .40 .15
- ❑ 181 Sammy Morris RC 10.00 4.00
- ❑ 182 Ron Dixon RC 10.00 4.00
- ❑ 183 Trevor Gaylor RC 10.00 4.00
- ❑ 184 Chris Cole RC 8.00 3.00
- ❑ 185 Deltha O'Neal RC 15.00 6.00
- ❑ 186 Sebastian Janikowski RC 15.00 6.00
- ❑ 187 Kwame Cavil RC 8.00 3.00
- ❑ 188 Chad Morton RC 15.00 6.00
- ❑ 189 Terrelle Smith RC 10.00 4.00
- ❑ 190 Frank Moreau RC 10.00 4.00
- ❑ 191 Kurt Warner HL 1.50 .60
- ❑ 192 Dan Marino HL 2.50 1.00
- ❑ 193 Cris Carter HL .60 .25
- ❑ 194 Brett Favre HL 2.50 1.00
- ❑ 195 Marshall Faulk HL 1.25 .50
- ❑ 196 Jevon Kearse HL .60 .25
- ❑ 197 Edgerrin James HL 1.50 .60
- ❑ 198 Emmitt Smith HL 1.50 .60
- ❑ 199 Andre Reed HL .40 .15
- ❑ 200 K.Dyson/F.Wycheck HL .40 .15
- ❑ 201 Olindo Mare MM .40 .15
- ❑ 202 Marcus Coleman MM .40 .15
- ❑ 203 James Johnson MM .40 .15
- ❑ 204 Ray Lucas MM .60 .25
- ❑ 205 Dedric Ward MM .40 .15
- ❑ 206 Richie Cunningham MM .40 .15
- ❑ 207 James Hasty MM .40 .15
- ❑ 208 Sedrick Shaw MM .40 .15
- ❑ 209 Kurt Warner MM 1.50 .60
- ❑ 210 Marshall Faulk MM 1.25 .50
- ❑ 211 Brian Shay EP 1.00 .40
- ❑ 212 L.C. Stevens EP 1.00 .40
- ❑ 213 Corey Thomas EP 1.00 .40
- ❑ 214 Scott Milanovich EP 1.50 .60
- ❑ 215 Pat Barnes EP 1.50 .60
- ❑ 216 Danny Wuerffel EP 1.50 .60
- ❑ 217 Kevin Daft EP 1.00 .40
- ❑ 218 Ron Powlus EP RC 2.00 .75
- ❑ 219 Eric Kresser EP 1.00 .40
- ❑ 220 Norman Miller EP RC 1.00 .40

❑ 221	Cory Sauter EP	1.00	.40
❑ 222	Marcus Crandell EP RC	1.50	.60
❑ 223	Sean Morey EP RC	1.50	.60
❑ 224	Jeff Ogden EP	1.50	.60
❑ 225	Ted White EP	1.00	.40
❑ 226	Jim Kubiak EP RC	1.50	.60
❑ 227	Aaron Stecker EP RC	2.00	.75
❑ 228	Ronnie Powell EP	1.00	.40
❑ 229	Matt Lytle EP RC	1.50	.60
❑ 230	Kendrick Nord EP RC	1.00	.40
❑ 231	Tim Rattay RC	15.00	6.00
❑ 232	Rob Morris RC	10.00	4.00
❑ 233	Chris Samuels RC	10.00	4.00
❑ 234	Todd Husak RC	15.00	6.00
❑ 235	Ahmed Plummer RC	15.00	6.00
❑ 236	Frank Murphy RC	8.00	3.00
❑ 237	Michael Wiley RC	10.00	4.00
❑ 238	Giovanni Carmazzi RC	8.00	3.00
❑ 239	Anthony Becht RC	15.00	6.00
❑ 240	John Abraham RC	20.00	7.50
❑ 241	Shaun Alexander RC	60.00	30.00
❑ 242	Thomas Jones RC	25.00	12.50
❑ 243	Courtney Brown RC	15.00	6.00
❑ 244	Curtis Keaton RC	10.00	4.00
❑ 245	Jerry Porter RC	25.00	10.00
❑ 246	Corey Simon RC	15.00	6.00
❑ 247	Dez White RC	15.00	6.00
❑ 248	Jamal Lewis RC	30.00	12.50
❑ 249	Ron Dayne RC	15.00	6.00
❑ 250	R.Jay Soward RC	10.00	4.00
❑ 251	Tee Martin RC	15.00	6.00
❑ 252	Shaun Ellis RC	15.00	6.00
❑ 253	Brian Urlacher RC	50.00	20.00
❑ 254	Reuben Droughns RC	15.00	6.00
❑ 255	Travis Taylor RC	15.00	6.00
❑ 256	Plaxico Burress RC	30.00	12.50
❑ 257	Chad Pennington RC	30.00	12.50
❑ 258	Sylvester Morris RC	10.00	4.00
❑ 259	Ron Dugans RC	8.00	3.00
❑ 260	Joe Hamilton RC	10.00	4.00
❑ 261	Chris Redman RC	10.00	4.00
❑ 262	Trung Canidate RC	10.00	4.00
❑ 263	J.R. Redmond RC	10.00	4.00
❑ 264	Danny Farmer RC	10.00	4.00
❑ 265	Todd Pinkston RC	15.00	6.00
❑ 266	Dennis Northcutt RC	15.00	6.00
❑ 267	Laveranues Coles RC	20.00	7.50
❑ 268	Bubba Franks RC	15.00	6.00
❑ 269	Travis Prentice RC	10.00	4.00
❑ 270	Peter Warrick RC	15.00	6.00

2001 Topps Chrome

❑	COMP.SET w/o SP's (210)	50.00	20.00
❑ 1	Randy Moss	2.50	1.00
❑ 2	Desmond Howard	.50	.20
❑ 3	Shawn Bryson	.50	.20
❑ 4	Lamar Smith	.75	.30
❑ 5	Peter Warrick	1.25	.50
❑ 6	Hines Ward	1.25	.50
❑ 7	J.R. Redmond	.50	.20
❑ 8	Reidel Anthony	.50	.20
❑ 9	Rich Gannon	1.25	.50
❑ 10	Ed McCaffrey	1.25	.50
❑ 11	Jamel White	.50	.20
❑ 12	Michael Pittman	.50	.20
❑ 13	Rob Johnson	.75	.30
❑ 14	Tim Couch	.75	.30
❑ 15	Stephen Alexander	.50	.20
❑ 16	Ricky Watters	.75	.30
❑ 17	Kerry Collins	.75	.30
❑ 18	Ricky Williams	1.25	.50
❑ 19	Joey Galloway	.75	.30
❑ 20	Chris Chandler	.75	.30
❑ 21	Marty Booker	.50	.20
❑ 22	Mark Brunell	1.25	.50
❑ 23	Antonio Freeman	1.25	.50
❑ 24	Richie Anderson	.50	.20
❑ 25	Amani Toomer	.75	.30
❑ 26	Trent Green	1.25	.50
❑ 27	Terrell Fletcher	.50	.20
❑ 28	Kevin Lockett	.50	.20
❑ 29	Ron Dixon	.50	.20
❑ 30	Charlie Batch	1.25	.50
❑ 31	Oronde Gadsden	.75	.30
❑ 32	Dorsey Levens	.75	.30
❑ 33	Jamal Lewis	2.00	.75
❑ 34	Craig Yeast	.50	.20
❑ 35	Muhsin Muhammad	.75	.30
❑ 36	Willie Jackson	.50	.20
❑ 37	Isaac Bruce	1.25	.50
❑ 38	Frank Wycheck	.50	.20
❑ 39	Troy Brown	.75	.30
❑ 40	Anthony Wright	.50	.20
❑ 41	Zach Thomas	1.25	.50
❑ 42	Qadry Ismail	.75	.30
❑ 43	Jake Plummer	.75	.30
❑ 44	Keenan McCardell	.50	.20
❑ 45	Charles Johnson	.50	.20
❑ 46	Brett Favre	4.00	1.50
❑ 47	Jacquez Green	.50	.20
❑ 48	Matt Hasselbeck	.75	.30
❑ 49	Tiki Barber	1.25	.50
❑ 50	Jeff Garcia	1.25	.50
❑ 51	Shawn Jefferson	.50	.20
❑ 52	Kevin Johnson	.75	.30
❑ 53	Terrence Wilkins	.50	.20
❑ 54	Mike Anderson	1.25	.50
❑ 55	Tim Brown	1.25	.50
❑ 56	Champ Bailey	1.25	.50
❑ 57	Jimmy Smith	.75	.30
❑ 58	Trent Dilfer	.75	.30
❑ 59	James Allen	.75	.30
❑ 60	David Boston	1.25	.50
❑ 61	Jeremiah Trotter	.75	.30
❑ 62	Freddie Jones	.50	.20
❑ 63	Deion Sanders	1.25	.50
❑ 64	Darrell Jackson	1.25	.50
❑ 65	David Patten	.50	.20
❑ 66	Jeremy McDaniel	.50	.20
❑ 67	Jay Fiedler	1.25	.50
❑ 68	Chad Lewis	.50	.20
❑ 69	Rocket Ismail	.75	.30
❑ 70	Cade McNown	.50	.20
❑ 71	Jevon Kearse	.75	.30
❑ 72	Jermaine Fazande	.50	.20
❑ 73	Junior Seau	1.25	.50
❑ 74	Rod Smith	.75	.30
❑ 75	Jermaine Lewis	.50	.20
❑ 76	Dennis Northcutt	.75	.30
❑ 77	Charlie Garner	.75	.30
❑ 78	Charles Woodson	.75	.30
❑ 79	Wayne Chrebet	.75	.30
❑ 80	Ahman Green	1.25	.50
❑ 81	Donald Hayes	.50	.20
❑ 82	Terance Mathis	.50	.20
❑ 83	Warrick Dunn	1.25	.50
❑ 84	Chris Sanders	.50	.20
❑ 85	Albert Connell	.50	.20
❑ 86	Robert Griffith	.50	.20
❑ 87	Germane Crowell	.50	.20
❑ 88	Tony Banks	.75	.30
❑ 89	Travis Taylor	.75	.30
❑ 90	Akili Smith	.50	.20
❑ 91	Michael Westbrook	.75	.30
❑ 92	Doug Flutie	1.25	.50
❑ 93	Ike Hilliard	.75	.30
❑ 94	Terry Glenn	.50	.20
❑ 95	Leslie Shepherd	.50	.20
❑ 96	Az-Zahir Hakim	.50	.20
❑ 97	La'Roi Glover	.50	.20
❑ 98	Peyton Manning	3.00	1.25
❑ 99	Jackie Harris	.50	.20
❑ 100	Edgerrin James	1.50	.60
❑ 101	Peerless Price	.75	.30
❑ 102	Jamal Anderson	1.25	.50
❑ 103	Keyshawn Johnson	1.25	.50
❑ 104	Derrick Mason	.75	.30
❑ 105	J.J. Stokes	.75	.30
❑ 106	Kevin Faulk	.75	.30
❑ 107	Tony Richardson	.50	.20
❑ 108	James Stewart	.75	.30
❑ 109	Tim Biakabutuka	.75	.30
❑ 110	Jon Kitna	1.25	.50
❑ 111	Thomas Jones	.75	.30
❑ 112	Steve McNair	1.25	.50
❑ 113	Sean Dawkins	.50	.20
❑ 114	Jerome Bettis	1.25	.50
❑ 115	Donovan McNabb	1.50	.60
❑ 116	Bill Schroeder	.75	.30
❑ 117	Rod Woodson	.75	.30
❑ 118	James McKnight	.75	.30
❑ 119	Daunte Culpepper	1.25	.50
❑ 120	Todd Husak	.50	.20
❑ 121	Shaun King	.50	.20
❑ 122	Tyrone Wheatley	.75	.30
❑ 123	Curtis Martin	1.25	.50
❑ 124	Terrell Davis	1.25	.50
❑ 125	Steve Beuerlein	.75	.30
❑ 126	Brad Johnson	1.25	.50
❑ 127	Joe Horn	.75	.30
❑ 128	Fred Taylor	1.25	.50
❑ 129	Brian Urlacher	2.00	.75
❑ 130	Ray Lewis	1.25	.50
❑ 131	Marshall Faulk	1.50	.60
❑ 132	Curtis Conway	.75	.30
❑ 133	Jason Sehorn	.50	.20
❑ 134	Jerome Pathon	.75	.30
❑ 135	Derrick Alexander	.75	.30
❑ 136	Jerry Rice	2.50	1.00
❑ 137	Jeff George	.75	.30
❑ 138	Johnnie Morton	.75	.30
❑ 139	Eric Moulds	.75	.30
❑ 140	Duce Staley	1.25	.50
❑ 141	Vinny Testaverde	.75	.30
❑ 142	Eddie George	1.25	.50
❑ 143	Shaun Alexander	1.50	.60
❑ 144	Drew Bledsoe	1.50	.60
❑ 145	Emmitt Smith	2.50	1.00
❑ 146	Marvin Harrison	1.25	.50
❑ 147	Frank Sanders	.50	.20
❑ 148	Aaron Shea	.50	.20
❑ 149	Cris Carter	1.25	.50
❑ 150	Tony Gonzalez	.75	.30
❑ 151	Marcus Robinson	1.25	.50
❑ 152	Danny Farmer	.50	.20
❑ 153	Warren Sapp	.75	.30
❑ 154	Kurt Warner	2.50	1.00
❑ 155	Jessie Armstead	.50	.20
❑ 156	Lawyer Milloy	.75	.30
❑ 157	Brian Griese	1.25	.50
❑ 158	Jason Taylor	.50	.20
❑ 159	Jeff Lewis	.50	.20
❑ 160	Travis Prentice	.50	.20
❑ 161	Tim Dwight	1.25	.50
❑ 162	Kyle Brady	.50	.20
❑ 163	Bubba Franks	.75	.30
❑ 164	James Thrash	.75	.30
❑ 165	Bobby Shaw	.50	.20
❑ 166	Ron Dayne	1.25	.50
❑ 167	Mike Alstott	1.25	.50
❑ 168	Bruce Smith	.50	.20
❑ 169	Jeff Graham	.50	.20
❑ 170	Jeff Blake	.75	.30
❑ 171	Laveranues Coles	1.25	.50
❑ 172	Herman Moore	.75	.30
❑ 173	Shannon Sharpe	.75	.30
❑ 174	Corey Dillon	1.25	.50
❑ 175	Ken Dilger	.50	.20
❑ 176	Eddie Kennison	.50	.20
❑ 177	Andre Rison	.75	.30
❑ 178	Stephen Davis	1.25	.50
❑ 179	Torry Holt	1.25	.50
❑ 180	Samari Rolle	.50	.20
❑ 181	Michael Strahan	.75	.30
❑ 182	Plaxico Burress	1.25	.50
❑ 183	Darnell Autry	.50	.20
❑ 184	Wesley Walls	.50	.20
❑ 185	Elvis Grbac	.75	.30
❑ 186	Marcus Pollard	.50	.20
❑ 187	Keith Poole	.50	.20
❑ 188	Ryan Leaf	.75	.30
❑ 189	Terrell Owens	1.25	.50
❑ 190	Dedric Ward	.50	.20

No.	Player	Hi	Lo
❑ 191	Donald Driver	.75	.30
❑ 192	Larry Foster	.50	.20
❑ 193	Priest Holmes	1.50	.60
❑ 194	Sammy Morris	.50	.20
❑ 195	Reggie Jones	.50	.20
❑ 196	Kordell Stewart	.75	.30
❑ 197	Sylvester Morris	.50	.20
❑ 198	Aaron Brooks	1.25	.50
❑ 199	Tai Streets	.50	.20
❑ 200	Chad Pennington	2.00	.75
❑ 201	Terrell Owens SH	1.25	.50
❑ 202	Marshall Faulk SH	1.25	.50
❑ 203	Mike Anderson SH	.75	.30
❑ 204	Cris Carter SH	1.25	.50
❑ 205	Corey Dillon SH	1.25	.50
❑ 206	Daunte Culpepper SH	1.25	.50
❑ 207	Peyton Manning SH	1.50	.60
❑ 208	Torry Holt SH	1.25	.50
❑ 209	Marvin Harrison SH	1.25	.50
❑ 210	Edgerrin James SH	1.25	.50
❑ 211	Sam Madison	.50	.20
❑ 212	Jonathan Quinn	.50	.20
❑ 213	Rob Morris	.50	.20
❑ 214	E.G. Green	.50	.20
❑ 215	David Sloan	.50	.20
❑ 216	Jason Tucker	.50	.20
❑ 217	Wali Rainer	.50	.20
❑ 218	Jerry Azumah	.50	.20
❑ 219	Dameyune Craig	.50	.20
❑ 220	Jammi German	.50	.20
❑ 221	LaDainian Tomlinson RC	175.00	100.00
❑ 222	Quincy Morgan RC	20.00	7.50
❑ 223	Steve Smith RC	40.00	20.00
❑ 224	Santana Moss RC	30.00	12.50
❑ 225	Koren Robinson RC	20.00	7.50
❑ 226	Kevin Kasper RC	20.00	7.50
❑ 227	Jamie Henderson RC	12.00	5.00
❑ 228	Adam Archuleta RC	20.00	7.50
❑ 229	Drew Brees RC	50.00	20.00
❑ 230	Michael Stone RC	8.00	3.00
❑ 231	Jamar Fletcher RC	12.00	5.00
❑ 232	Eric Westmoreland RC	12.00	5.00
❑ 233	Chris Barnes RC	12.00	5.00
❑ 234	Gerard Warren RC	20.00	7.50
❑ 235	Snoop Minnis RC	12.00	5.00
❑ 236	Chris Chambers RC	25.00	12.50
❑ 237	Damerien McCants RC	12.00	5.00
❑ 238	Kevan Barlow RC	20.00	7.50
❑ 239	Mike McMahon RC	20.00	7.50
❑ 240	Jabari Holloway RC	12.00	5.00
❑ 241	Travis Henry RC	20.00	7.50
❑ 242	Derrick Blaylock RC	20.00	7.50
❑ 243	Tim Hasselbeck RC	20.00	7.50
❑ 244	Andre Carter RC	20.00	7.50
❑ 245	Sage Rosenfels RC	20.00	7.50
❑ 246	Cedrick Wilson RC	20.00	7.50
❑ 247	Scotty Anderson RC	12.00	5.00
❑ 248	Ken-Yon Rambo RC	12.00	5.00
❑ 249	Marques Tuiasosopo RC	20.00	7.50
❑ 250	Reggie Wayne RC	30.00	15.00
❑ 251	Onomo Ojo RC	12.00	5.00
❑ 252	James Jackson RC	20.00	7.50
❑ 253	Moran Norris RC	8.00	3.00
❑ 254	Rashard Casey RC	12.00	5.00
❑ 255	Rudi Johnson RC	40.00	15.00
❑ 256	Willie Middlebrooks RC	12.00	5.00
❑ 257	Freddie Mitchell RC	20.00	7.50
❑ 258	Deuce McAllister RC	40.00	20.00
❑ 259	Chad Johnson RC	50.00	20.00
❑ 260	David Terrell RC	20.00	7.50
❑ 261	Jamal Reynolds RC	20.00	7.50
❑ 262	Michael Vick RC	200.00	75.00
❑ 263	Marcus Stroud RC	20.00	7.50
❑ 264	Dan Alexander RC	20.00	7.50
❑ 265	Jonathan Carter RC	12.00	5.00
❑ 266	Bobby Newcombe RC	12.00	5.00
❑ 267	Eddie Berlin RC	12.00	5.00
❑ 268	LaMont Jordan RC	40.00	20.00
❑ 269	Michael Bennett RC	30.00	12.50
❑ 270	Shaun Rogers RC	20.00	7.50
❑ 271	Travis Minor RC	12.00	5.00
❑ 272	Jesse Palmer RC	20.00	7.50
❑ 273	Derrick Gibson RC	12.00	5.00
❑ 274	Chris Weinke RC	20.00	7.50
❑ 275	Nate Clements RC	20.00	7.50
❑ 276	Eric Kelly RC	8.00	3.00
❑ 277	Justin Smith RC	20.00	7.50
❑ 278	Ryan Pickett RC	8.00	3.00
❑ 279	Anthony Thomas RC	20.00	7.50
❑ 280	Will Allen RC	12.00	5.00
❑ 281	Quincy Carter RC	20.00	7.50
❑ 282	Richard Seymour RC	20.00	7.50
❑ 283	Dan Morgan RC	20.00	7.50
❑ 284	Tay Cody RC	8.00	3.00
❑ 285	Alge Crumpler RC	25.00	12.50
❑ 286	Robert Ferguson RC	20.00	7.50
❑ 287	Will Peterson RC	12.00	5.00
❑ 288	Tony Dixon RC	12.00	5.00
❑ 289	Correll Buckhalter RC	20.00	7.50
❑ 290	Rod Gardner RC	20.00	7.50
❑ 291	Justin McCareins RC	20.00	7.50
❑ 292	Josh Heupel RC	20.00	7.50
❑ 293	Todd Heap RC	20.00	7.50
❑ 294	Damione Lewis RC	12.00	5.00
❑ 295	George Layne RC	12.00	5.00
❑ 296	Jamie Winborn RC	12.00	5.00
❑ 297	Billy Baber RC	8.00	3.00
❑ 298	T.J. Houshmandzadeh RC	20.00	7.50
❑ 299	Aaron Schobel RC	20.00	7.50
❑ 300	Gary Baxter RC	12.00	5.00
❑ 301	DeLawrence Grant RC	8.00	3.00
❑ 302	Morlon Greenwood RC	12.00	5.00
❑ 303	Shad Meier RC	12.00	5.00
❑ 304	Torrance Marshall RC	20.00	7.50
❑ 305	David Martin RC	12.00	5.00
❑ 306	Anthony Henry RC	20.00	7.50
❑ 307	Derrick Burgess RC	20.00	7.50
❑ 308	Andre Dyson RC	8.00	3.00
❑ 309	Ryan Helming RC	8.00	3.00
❑ 310	Fred Smoot RC	20.00	7.50
❑ 311	Arther Love RC	8.00	3.00
❑ 312	John Capel RC	12.00	5.00
❑ 313	Brandon Spoon RC	12.00	5.00
❑ 314	Karon Riley RC	8.00	3.00
❑ 315	Andre King RC	12.00	5.00
❑ 316	Quentin McCord RC	12.00	5.00
❑ 317	Zeke Moreno RC	20.00	7.50
❑ 318	Francis St. Paul RC	12.00	5.00
❑ 319	Richmond Flowers RC	12.00	5.00
❑ 320	Derek Combs RC	12.00	5.00

2002 Topps Chrome

No.	Player	Hi	Lo
❑	COMP.SET w/o SP's (165)	50.00	20.00
❑ 1	Anthony Thomas	.75	.30
❑ 2	Jake Plummer	.75	.30
❑ 3	Maurice Smith	.75	.30
❑ 4	Jamal Lewis	1.25	.50
❑ 5	Ray Lewis	1.25	.50
❑ 6	Alex Van Pelt	.50	.20
❑ 7	Chris Weinke	.75	.30
❑ 8	Corey Dillon	.75	.30
❑ 9	Quincy Morgan	.50	.20
❑ 10	Rocket Ismail	.75	.30
❑ 11	Brian Griese	1.25	.50
❑ 12	Johnnie Morton	.75	.30
❑ 13	Edgerrin James	1.50	.60
❑ 14	Keenan McCardell	.50	.20
❑ 15	Travis Minor	.75	.30
❑ 16	Sylvester Morris	.50	.20
❑ 17	Randy Moss	2.50	1.00
❑ 18	Drew Bledsoe	1.50	.60
❑ 19	Willie Jackson	.50	.20
❑ 20	Michael Strahan	.75	.30
❑ 21	Santana Moss	1.25	.50
❑ 22	Duce Staley	1.25	.50
❑ 23	Kendrell Bell	1.25	.50
❑ 24	LaDainian Tomlinson	2.00	.75
❑ 25	Terrell Owens	1.25	.50
❑ 26	Shaun Alexander	1.50	.60
❑ 27	Trung Canidate	.75	.30
❑ 28	Mike Alstott	1.25	.50
❑ 29	Kevin Dyson	.75	.30
❑ 30	Rod Gardner	.75	.30
❑ 31	David Boston	1.25	.50
❑ 32	Michael Vick	4.00	1.50
❑ 33	Qadry Ismail	.75	.30
❑ 34	Peerless Price	.75	.30
❑ 35	Rob Johnson	.75	.30
❑ 36	Marcus Robinson	.75	.30
❑ 37	Peter Warrick	.75	.30
❑ 38	Kevin Johnson	.75	.30
❑ 39	Ed McCaffrey	1.25	.50
❑ 40	Shaun Rogers	.50	.20
❑ 41	Marvin Harrison	1.25	.50
❑ 42	Priest Holmes	1.50	.60
❑ 43	Oronde Gadsden	.75	.30
❑ 44	Terry Glenn	.75	.30
❑ 45	Ike Hilliard	.75	.30
❑ 46	Charles Woodson	.75	.30
❑ 47	Freddie Mitchell	.75	.30
❑ 48	Drew Brees	1.25	.50
❑ 49	Jeff Garcia	1.25	.50
❑ 50	Kurt Warner	1.25	.50
❑ 51	Keyshawn Johnson	1.25	.50
❑ 52	Jevon Kearse	.75	.30
❑ 53	Stephen Davis	.75	.30
❑ 54	Shannon Sharpe	.75	.30
❑ 55	Eric Moulds	.75	.30
❑ 56	Muhsin Muhammad	.75	.30
❑ 57	Brian Urlacher	2.00	.75
❑ 58	Chad Johnson	1.25	.50
❑ 59	Tim Couch	.75	.30
❑ 60	Mike Anderson	1.25	.50
❑ 61	James Stewart	.75	.30
❑ 62	Corey Bradford	.50	.20
❑ 63	Reggie Wayne	1.25	.50
❑ 64	Mark Brunell	1.25	.50
❑ 65	Trent Green	.75	.30
❑ 66	Zach Thomas	1.25	.50
❑ 67	Michael Bennett	.75	.30
❑ 68	Troy Brown	.75	.30
❑ 69	Amani Toomer	.75	.30
❑ 70	Curtis Martin	1.25	.50
❑ 71	Tim Brown	1.25	.50
❑ 72	Correll Buckhalter	.75	.30
❑ 73	Kordell Stewart	.75	.30
❑ 74	Junior Seau	1.25	.50
❑ 75	Kevan Barlow	.75	.30
❑ 76	Matt Hasselbeck	.75	.30
❑ 77	Marshall Faulk	1.25	.50
❑ 78	Warren Sapp	.75	.30
❑ 79	Frank Wycheck	.50	.20
❑ 80	Michael Westbrook	.50	.20
❑ 81	Travis Henry	1.25	.50
❑ 82	David Terrell	1.25	.50
❑ 83	Jon Kitna	.75	.30
❑ 84	James Jackson	.50	.20
❑ 85	Joey Galloway	.75	.30
❑ 86	Rod Smith	.75	.30
❑ 87	Germane Crowell	.50	.20
❑ 88	Bill Schroeder	.75	.30
❑ 89	Dominic Rhodes	.75	.30
❑ 90	Fred Taylor	1.25	.50
❑ 91	Snoop Minnis	.50	.20
❑ 92	Chris Chambers	1.25	.50
❑ 93	Daunte Culpepper	1.25	.50
❑ 94	Deuce McAllister	1.50	.60
❑ 95	Kerry Collins	.75	.30
❑ 96	John Abraham	.75	.30
❑ 97	Rich Gannon	1.25	.50
❑ 98	Tiki Barber	1.25	.50
❑ 99	Hines Ward	1.25	.50
❑ 100	Tom Brady	3.00	1.25
❑ 101	Tim Dwight	.75	.30
❑ 102	Garrison Hearst	.75	.30
❑ 103	Darrell Jackson	.75	.30
❑ 104	Isaac Bruce	1.25	.50
❑ 105	Brad Johnson	.75	.30
❑ 106	Steve McNair	1.25	.50
❑ 107	Champ Bailey	.75	.30
❑ 108	Emmitt Smith	3.00	1.25
❑ 109	Mike McMahon	1.25	.50
❑ 110	Terrell Davis	1.25	.50

No.	Player	Price	Price
❑ 111	Antonio Freeman	1.25	.50
❑ 112	Jimmy Smith	.75	.30
❑ 113	Tony Gonzalez	.75	.30
❑ 114	Jay Fiedler	.75	.30
❑ 115	Cris Carter	1.25	.50
❑ 116	David Patten	.50	.20
❑ 117	Joe Horn	.75	.30
❑ 118	Laveranues Coles	.75	.30
❑ 119	Charlie Garner	.75	.30
❑ 120	Donovan McNabb	1.50	.60
❑ 121	Jerome Bettis	1.25	.50
❑ 122	Curtis Conway	.50	.20
❑ 123	Az-Zahir Hakim	.50	.20
❑ 124	Warrick Dunn	1.25	.50
❑ 125	Eddie George	1.25	.50
❑ 126	Quincy Carter	.75	.30
❑ 127	Ahman Green	1.25	.50
❑ 128	Peyton Manning	2.50	1.00
❑ 129	James McKnight	.50	.20
❑ 130	Antowain Smith	.75	.30
❑ 131	Ricky Williams	8.00	3.00
❑ 132	Chad Pennington	1.50	.60
❑ 133	Jerry Rice	2.50	1.00
❑ 134	Todd Pinkston	.75	.30
❑ 135	Plaxico Burress	.75	.30
❑ 136	Doug Flutie	1.25	.50
❑ 137	Koren Robinson	.75	.30
❑ 138	Torry Holt	1.25	.50
❑ 139	Aaron Brooks	1.25	.50
❑ 140	Ron Dayne	.75	.30
❑ 141	Vinny Testaverde	.75	.30
❑ 142	Brett Favre	3.00	1.25
❑ 143	James Thrash	.75	.30
❑ 144	Wayne Chrebet	.75	.30
❑ 145	Derrick Mason	.75	.30
❑ 146	Ahman Green WWU	.75	.30
❑ 147	Peyton Manning WWU	1.25	.50
❑ 148	Kurt Warner WWU	.75	.30
❑ 149	Daunte Culpepper WWU	.75	.30
❑ 150	Tom Brady WWU	1.50	.60
❑ 151	Rod Gardner WWU	.75	.30
❑ 152	Corey Dillon WWU	.75	.30
❑ 153	Priest Holmes WWU	1.00	.40
❑ 154	Shaun Alexander WWU	1.00	.40
❑ 155	Randy Moss WWU	1.25	.50
❑ 156	Eric Moulds WWU	.50	.20
❑ 157	Brett Favre WWU	1.50	.60
❑ 158	Todd Bouman WWU	.50	.20
❑ 159	Dominic Rhodes WWU	.50	.20
❑ 160	Marvin Harrison WWU	.75	.30
❑ 161	Torry Holt WWU	1.25	.50
❑ 162	Derrick Mason WWU	.50	.20
❑ 163	Jerry Rice WWU	1.25	.50
❑ 164	Donovan McNabb WWU	1.25	.50
❑ 165	Marshall Faulk WWU	1.25	.50
❑ 166	David Carr RC	30.00	12.50
❑ 167	Quentin Jammer RC	10.00	4.00
❑ 168	Mike Williams RC	8.00	3.00
❑ 169	Rocky Calmus RC	10.00	4.00
❑ 170	Travis Fisher RC	10.00	4.00
❑ 171	Dwight Freeney RC	12.00	5.00
❑ 172	Jeremy Shockey RC	40.00	15.00
❑ 173	Marquise Walker RC	8.00	3.00
❑ 174	Eric Crouch RC	10.00	4.00
❑ 175	DeShaun Foster RC	10.00	4.00
❑ 176	Roy Williams RC	25.00	12.50
❑ 177	Andre Davis RC	8.00	3.00
❑ 178	Alex Brown RC	10.00	4.00
❑ 179	Michael Lewis RC	10.00	4.00
❑ 180	Terry Charles RC	8.00	3.00
❑ 181	Clinton Portis RC	40.00	15.00
❑ 182	Dennis Johnson RC	5.00	2.00
❑ 183	Lito Sheppard RC	10.00	4.00
❑ 184	Ryan Sims RC	10.00	4.00
❑ 185	Raonall Smith RC	8.00	3.00
❑ 186	Albert Haynesworth RC	8.00	3.00
❑ 187	Eddie Freeman RC	5.00	2.00
❑ 188	Levi Jones RC	8.00	3.00
❑ 189	Josh McCown RC	12.00	5.00
❑ 190	Cliff Russell RC	8.00	3.00
❑ 191	Maurice Morris RC	10.00	4.00
❑ 192	Antwaan Randle El RC	15.00	6.00
❑ 193	Ladell Betts RC	10.00	4.00
❑ 194	Daniel Graham RC	10.00	4.00
❑ 195	David Garrard RC	10.00	4.00
❑ 196	Antonio Bryant RC	10.00	4.00
❑ 197	Patrick Ramsey RC	12.00	5.00
❑ 198	Kelly Campbell RC	8.00	3.00
❑ 199	Will Overstreet RC	5.00	2.00
❑ 200	Ryan Denney RC	8.00	3.00
❑ 201	John Henderson RC	10.00	4.00
❑ 202	Freddie Milons RC	8.00	3.00
❑ 203	Tim Carter RC	8.00	3.00
❑ 204	Kurt Kittner RC	8.00	3.00
❑ 205	Joey Harrington RC	30.00	12.50
❑ 206	Ricky Williams RC	8.00	3.00
❑ 207	Bryant McKinnie RC	8.00	3.00
❑ 208	Ed Reed RC	15.00	6.00
❑ 209	Josh Reed RC	10.00	4.00
❑ 210	Seth Burford RC	8.00	3.00
❑ 211	Javon Walker RC	20.00	7.50
❑ 212	Jamar Martin RC	8.00	3.00
❑ 213	Leonard Henry RC	8.00	3.00
❑ 214	Julius Peppers RC	20.00	7.50
❑ 215	Jabar Gaffney RC	10.00	4.00
❑ 216	Kalimba Edwards RC	10.00	4.00
❑ 217	Napoleon Harris RC	10.00	4.00
❑ 218	Ashley Lelie RC	20.00	7.50
❑ 219	Anthony Weaver RC	8.00	3.00
❑ 220	Bryan Thomas RC	8.00	3.00
❑ 221	Wendell Bryant RC	5.00	2.00
❑ 222	Damien Anderson RC	8.00	3.00
❑ 223	Travis Stephens RC	8.00	3.00
❑ 224	Rohan Davey RC	10.00	4.00
❑ 225	Mike Pearson RC	5.00	2.00
❑ 226	Marc Colombo RC	5.00	2.00
❑ 227	Phillip Buchanon RC	10.00	4.00
❑ 228	T.J. Duckett RC	15.00	6.00
❑ 229	Ron Johnson RC	8.00	3.00
❑ 230	Larry Tripplett RC	5.00	2.00
❑ 231	Randy Fasani RC	8.00	3.00
❑ 232	Keyuo Craver RC	8.00	3.00
❑ 233	Marquand Manuel RC	5.00	2.00
❑ 234	Jonathan Wells RC	10.00	4.00
❑ 235	Reche Caldwell RC	10.00	4.00
❑ 236	Luke Staley RC	8.00	3.00
❑ 237	Donte Stallworth RC	20.00	7.50
❑ 238	Levar Fisher RC	10.00	4.00
❑ 239	Lamar Gordon RC	10.00	4.00
❑ 240	William Green RC	10.00	4.00
❑ 241	Dusty Bonner RC	5.00	2.00
❑ 242	Craig Nall RC	10.00	4.00
❑ 243	Eric McCoo RC	5.00	2.00
❑ 244	David Thornton RC	5.00	2.00
❑ 245	Terry Jones RC	8.00	3.00
❑ 246	Lee Mays RC	10.00	4.00
❑ 247	Bryan Fletcher RC	5.00	2.00
❑ 248	Verron Haynes RC	10.00	4.00
❑ 249	Zak Kustok RC	10.00	4.00
❑ 250	Chad Hutchinson RC	8.00	3.00
❑ 251	Andra Davis RC	8.00	3.00
❑ 252	Wes Pate RC	5.00	2.00
❑ 253	Jon McGraw RC	5.00	2.00
❑ 254	Howard Green RC	5.00	2.00
❑ 255	Daryl Jones RC	8.00	3.00
❑ 256	David Priestley RC	8.00	3.00
❑ 257	Marques Anderson RC	10.00	4.00
❑ 258	Roosevelt Williams RC	5.00	2.00
❑ 259	Major Applewhite RC	10.00	4.00
❑ 260	Ronald Curry RC	10.00	4.00
❑ 261	Adrian Peterson RC	10.00	4.00
❑ 262	Tellis Redmon RC	8.00	3.00
❑ 263	Chester Taylor RC	10.00	4.00
❑ 264	Deion Branch RC	25.00	12.50
❑ 265	Tank Williams RC	5.00	2.00

2003 Topps Chrome

No.	Player	Price	Price
❑	COMP.SET w/o SP's (165)	40.00	15.00
❑ 1	Michael Vick	3.00	1.25
❑ 2	Josh Reed	.75	.30
❑ 3	James Stewart	.75	.30
❑ 4	Quincy Morgan	.75	.30
❑ 5	Corey Bradford	.50	.20
❑ 6	Fred Taylor	1.25	.50
❑ 7	David Patten	.50	.20
❑ 8	Jerome Bettis	1.25	.50
❑ 9	Jerry Porter	.75	.30
❑ 10	Steve McNair	1.25	.50
❑ 11	Stephen Davis	.75	.30
❑ 12	Frank Wycheck	.50	.20
❑ 13	Marcus Pollard	.50	.20
❑ 14	David Terrell	.75	.30
❑ 15	Bubba Franks	.75	.30
❑ 16	Trent Green	.75	.30
❑ 17	Mark Brunell	.75	.30
❑ 18	James Thrash	.50	.20
❑ 19	Mike Alstott	1.25	.50
❑ 20	Deuce McAllister	1.25	.50
❑ 21	Santana Moss	.75	.30
❑ 22	Jason Taylor	.50	.20
❑ 23	Corey Dillon	.75	.30
❑ 24	Jeff Blake	.50	.20
❑ 25	Ed McCaffrey	1.25	.50
❑ 26	Priest Holmes	1.50	.60
❑ 27	Tim Brown	1.25	.50
❑ 28	Curtis Martin	1.25	.50
❑ 29	Derrius Thompson	.50	.20
❑ 30	Jonathan Wells	.50	.20
❑ 31	William Green	.75	.30
❑ 32	Bill Schroeder	.75	.30
❑ 33	Amos Zereoue	.75	.30
❑ 34	Warren Sapp	.75	.30
❑ 35	Koren Robinson	.75	.30
❑ 36	Donovan McNabb	1.50	.60
❑ 37	Edgerrin James	1.25	.50
❑ 38	Kelly Holcomb	.75	.30
❑ 39	Daunte Culpepper	1.25	.50
❑ 40	Tommy Maddox	1.25	.50
❑ 41	Rod Gardner	.75	.30
❑ 42	T.J. Duckett	.75	.30
❑ 43	Drew Bledsoe	1.25	.50
❑ 44	Rod Smith	.75	.30
❑ 45	Peyton Manning	2.00	.75
❑ 46	Darrell Jackson	.75	.30
❑ 47	Brett Favre	3.00	1.25
❑ 48	Ashley Lelie	1.25	.50
❑ 49	Jeremy Shockey	2.00	.75
❑ 50	Hines Ward	1.25	.50
❑ 51	Jeff Garcia	1.25	.50
❑ 52	Eddie Kennison	.50	.20
❑ 53	Brian Urlacher	2.00	.75
❑ 54	Antwaan Randle El	1.25	.50
❑ 55	Eddie George	.75	.30
❑ 56	Derrick Brooks	.75	.30
❑ 57	Isaac Bruce	1.25	.50
❑ 58	Joe Horn	.75	.30
❑ 59	Jon Kitna	.75	.30
❑ 60	David Boston	.75	.30
❑ 61	Todd Heap	.75	.30
❑ 62	Lamar Smith	.50	.20
❑ 63	Germane Crowell	.50	.20
❑ 64	Kevin Johnson	.75	.30
❑ 65	Drew Brees	1.25	.50
❑ 66	Chad Lewis	.50	.20
❑ 67	Charlie Garner	.75	.30
❑ 68	Laveranues Coles	.75	.30
❑ 69	Shaun Alexander	1.25	.50
❑ 70	Kevan Barlow	.75	.30
❑ 71	Aaron Brooks	1.25	.50
❑ 72	Jake Plummer	.75	.30
❑ 73	Emmitt Smith	3.00	1.25
❑ 74	Terry Glenn	.50	.20
❑ 75	Michael Bennett	.75	.30
❑ 76	Deion Branch	1.25	.50
❑ 77	Keyshawn Johnson	1.25	.50
❑ 78	Marc Bulger	1.25	.50
❑ 79	Matt Hasselbeck	.75	.30
❑ 80	Garrison Hearst	.75	.30
❑ 81	Brian Griese	1.25	.50
❑ 82	Johnnie Morton	.75	.30
❑ 83	Patrick Ramsey	1.25	.50
❑ 84	Donald Driver	.75	.30
❑ 85	Joey Harrington	2.00	.75
❑ 86	Ricky Williams	1.25	.50

- ❑ 87 Jabar Gaffney .75 .30
- ❑ 88 Duce Staley .75 .30
- ❑ 89 Jimmy Smith .75 .30
- ❑ 90 Reggie Wayne .75 .30
- ❑ 91 Chad Johnson 1.25 .50
- ❑ 92 Steve Beuerlein .50 .20
- ❑ 93 Joey Galloway .75 .30
- ❑ 94 Curtis Conway .50 .20
- ❑ 95 Brad Johnson .75 .30
- ❑ 96 Jamal Lewis 1.25 .50
- ❑ 97 Terrell Owens 1.25 .50
- ❑ 98 Todd Pinkston .75 .30
- ❑ 99 Keenan McCardell .50 .20
- ❑ 100 Antonio Bryant .75 .30
- ❑ 101 Eric Moulds .75 .30
- ❑ 102 Jim Miller .50 .20
- ❑ 103 Troy Brown .75 .30
- ❑ 104 Rich Gannon .75 .30
- ❑ 105 Chad Pennington 1.50 .60
- ❑ 106 Michael Strahan .75 .30
- ❑ 107 Chris Chambers 1.25 .50
- ❑ 108 Antowain Smith .75 .30
- ❑ 109 Derrick Mason .75 .30
- ❑ 110 Michael Pittman .50 .20
- ❑ 111 Torry Holt 1.25 .50
- ❑ 112 Tony Gonzalez .75 .30
- ❑ 113 Marty Booker .75 .30
- ❑ 114 Shannon Sharpe .50 .20
- ❑ 115 Zach Thomas 1.25 .50
- ❑ 116 Plaxico Burress .75 .30
- ❑ 117 Kurt Warner 1.25 .50
- ❑ 118 Warrick Dunn .75 .30
- ❑ 119 Jay Fiedler .75 .30
- ❑ 120 LaMont Jordan 1.25 .50
- ❑ 121 Kerry Collins .75 .30
- ❑ 122 Jerry Rice 2.50 1.00
- ❑ 123 Randy Moss 2.00 .75
- ❑ 124 Tom Brady 3.00 1.25
- ❑ 125 Amani Toomer .75 .30
- ❑ 126 Travis Henry .75 .30
- ❑ 127 Chris Chandler .50 .20
- ❑ 128 Ray Lewis 1.25 .50
- ❑ 129 Donte Stallworth 1.25 .50
- ❑ 130 David Carr 2.00 .75
- ❑ 131 Andre Davis .50 .20
- ❑ 132 Travis Taylor .75 .30
- ❑ 133 Steve Smith 1.25 .50
- ❑ 134 Tiki Barber 1.25 .50
- ❑ 135 Chad Hutchinson .50 .20
- ❑ 136 Marshall Faulk 1.25 .50
- ❑ 137 Peerless Price .75 .30
- ❑ 138 Ahman Green 1.25 .50
- ❑ 139 Julius Peppers 1.25 .50
- ❑ 140 LaDainian Tomlinson 1.25 .50
- ❑ 141 Muhsin Muhammad .75 .30
- ❑ 142 Tim Couch .50 .20
- ❑ 143 Clinton Portis 2.00 .75
- ❑ 144 Anthony Thomas .75 .30
- ❑ 145 Marvin Harrison 1.25 .50
- ❑ 146 Priest Holmes WW .75 .30
- ❑ 147 Drew Bledsoe WW .75 .30
- ❑ 148 Tom Brady WW 1.25 .50
- ❑ 149 Shaun Alexander WW .75 .30
- ❑ 150 Brett Favre WW 1.25 .50
- ❑ 151 Travis Henry WW .50 .20
- ❑ 152 Marshall Faulk WW .75 .30
- ❑ 153 Terrell Owens WW .50 .20
- ❑ 154 Jeff Garcia WW .50 .20
- ❑ 155 Plaxico Burress WW .50 .20
- ❑ 156 Donovan McNabb WW .75 .30
- ❑ 157 Ricky Williams WW .75 .30
- ❑ 158 Michael Vick WW 1.50 .60
- ❑ 159 Steve Smith WW .75 .30
- ❑ 160 Marvin Harrison WW .50 .20
- ❑ 161 Chad Pennington WW .75 .30
- ❑ 162 Jeremy Shockey WW .75 .30
- ❑ 163 Tommy Maddox WW .50 .20
- ❑ 164 Steve McNair WW .50 .20
- ❑ 165 Rich Gannon WW .50 .20
- ❑ 166 Carson Palmer RC 30.00 15.00
- ❑ 167 J.R. Tolver RC 6.00 2.50
- ❑ 168 Michael Haynes RC 8.00 3.00
- ❑ 169 Terrell Suggs RC 12.00 5.00
- ❑ 170 Rashean Mathis RC 6.00 2.50
- ❑ 171 Chris Kelsay RC 8.00 3.00
- ❑ 172 Brad Banks RC 6.00 2.50
- ❑ 173 Jordan Gross RC 6.00 2.50
- ❑ 174 Lee Suggs RC 15.00 6.00
- ❑ 175 Kliff Kingsbury RC 6.00 2.50
- ❑ 176 William Joseph RC 8.00 3.00
- ❑ 177 Kelley Washington RC 8.00 3.00
- ❑ 178 Jerome McDougle RC 8.00 3.00
- ❑ 179 Keenan Howry RC 8.00 3.00
- ❑ 180 Chris Simms RC 12.00 5.00
- ❑ 181 Alonzo Jackson RC 6.00 2.50
- ❑ 182 L.J. Smith RC 8.00 3.00
- ❑ 183 Mike Doss RC 8.00 3.00
- ❑ 184 Bobby Wade RC 8.00 3.00
- ❑ 185 Ken Hamlin RC 8.00 3.00
- ❑ 186 Brandon Lloyd RC 10.00 4.00
- ❑ 187 Justin Fargas RC 8.00 3.00
- ❑ 188 DeWayne Robertson RC 8.00 3.00
- ❑ 189 Bryant Johnson RC 8.00 3.00
- ❑ 190 Boss Bailey RC 8.00 3.00
- ❑ 191 Onterrio Smith RC 8.00 3.00
- ❑ 192 Doug Gabriel RC 8.00 3.00
- ❑ 193 Jimmy Kennedy RC 8.00 3.00
- ❑ 194 B.J. Askew RC 8.00 3.00
- ❑ 195 Taylor Jacobs RC 6.00 2.50
- ❑ 196 Dallas Clark RC 8.00 3.00
- ❑ 197 DeWayne White RC 6.00 2.50
- ❑ 198 Arnaz Battle RC 8.00 3.00
- ❑ 199 Kareem Kelly RC 6.00 2.50
- ❑ 200 Talman Gardner RC 8.00 3.00
- ❑ 201 Billy McMullen RC 6.00 2.50
- ❑ 202 Travis Anglin RC 4.00 1.50
- ❑ 203 Anquan Boldin RC 20.00 10.00
- ❑ 204 Osi Umenyiora RC 12.00 5.00
- ❑ 205 Byron Leftwich RC 25.00 10.00
- ❑ 206 Marcus Trufant RC 8.00 3.00
- ❑ 207 Sam Aiken RC 6.00 2.50
- ❑ 208 LaBrandon Toefield RC 8.00 3.00
- ❑ 209 Terry Pierce RC 6.00 2.50
- ❑ 210 Charles Rogers RC 8.00 3.00
- ❑ 211 Chaun Thompson RC 4.00 1.50
- ❑ 212 Chris Brown RC 10.00 4.00
- ❑ 213 Justin Gage RC 8.00 3.00
- ❑ 214 Kevin Williams RC 8.00 3.00
- ❑ 215 Willis McGahee RC 20.00 7.50
- ❑ 216 Victor Hobson RC 8.00 3.00
- ❑ 217 Brian St.Pierre RC 8.00 3.00
- ❑ 218 Nate Burleson RC 10.00 4.00
- ❑ 219 Calvin Pace RC 6.00 2.50
- ❑ 220 Larry Johnson RC 30.00 15.00
- ❑ 221 Andre Woolfolk RC 8.00 3.00
- ❑ 222 Tyrone Calico RC 10.00 4.00
- ❑ 223 Seneca Wallace RC 8.00 3.00
- ❑ 224 Domanick Davis RC 12.00 5.00
- ❑ 225 Rex Grossman RC 12.00 5.00
- ❑ 226 Artose Pinner RC 8.00 3.00
- ❑ 227 Jason Witten RC 12.00 5.00
- ❑ 228 Bennie Joppru RC 8.00 3.00
- ❑ 229 Bethel Johnson RC 8.00 3.00
- ❑ 230 Kyle Boller RC 15.00 6.00
- ❑ 231 Shaun McDonald RC 8.00 3.00
- ❑ 232 Musa Smith RC 8.00 3.00
- ❑ 233 Ken Dorsey RC 8.00 3.00
- ❑ 234 Johnathan Sullivan RC 6.00 2.50
- ❑ 235 Andre Johnson RC 15.00 6.00
- ❑ 236 Nick Barnett RC 12.00 5.00
- ❑ 237 Teyo Johnson RC 8.00 3.00
- ❑ 238 Terence Newman RC 15.00 6.00
- ❑ 239 Kevin Curtis RC 8.00 3.00
- ❑ 240 Dave Ragone RC 8.00 3.00
- ❑ 241 Ty Warren RC 8.00 3.00
- ❑ 242 Walter Young RC 4.00 1.50
- ❑ 243 Kevin Walter RC 6.00 2.50
- ❑ 244 Carl Ford RC 4.00 1.50
- ❑ 245 Cecil Sapp RC 6.00 2.50
- ❑ 246 Sultan McCullough RC 6.00 2.50
- ❑ 247 Eugene Wilson RC 8.00 3.00
- ❑ 248 Ricky Manning RC 8.00 3.00
- ❑ 249 Andrew Williams RC 6.00 2.50
- ❑ 250 Juston Wood RC 4.00 1.50
- ❑ 251 Cory Redding RC 6.00 2.50
- ❑ 252 Charles Tillman RC 10.00 4.00
- ❑ 253 Terrence Edwards RC 6.00 2.50
- ❑ 254 Adrian Madise RC 6.00 2.50
- ❑ 255 David Kircus RC 6.00 2.50
- ❑ 256 Zuriel Smith RC 4.00 1.50
- ❑ 257 Earnest Graham RC 6.00 2.50
- ❑ 258 Ronald Bellamy RC 6.00 2.50
- ❑ 259 John Anderson RC 4.00 1.50
- ❑ 260 David Tyree RC 6.00 2.50
- ❑ 261 Malaefou MacKenzie RC 4.00 1.50
- ❑ 262 Ahmaad Galloway RC 6.00 2.50
- ❑ 263 Brooks Bollinger RC 8.00 3.00
- ❑ 264 Gibran Hamdan RC 4.00 1.50
- ❑ 265 Taco Wallace RC 6.00 2.50
- ❑ 266 LaTarence Dunbar RC 6.00 2.50
- ❑ 267 Justin Griffith RC 6.00 2.50
- ❑ 268 Bradie James RC 8.00 3.00
- ❑ 269 Danny Curley RC 4.00 1.50
- ❑ 270 Kenny Peterson RC 6.00 2.50
- ❑ 271 DeAndrew Rubin RC 4.00 1.50
- ❑ 272 Ryan Hoag RC 4.00 1.50
- ❑ 273 Rien Long RC 4.00 1.50
- ❑ 274 Troy Polamalu RC 30.00 15.00
- ❑ 275 Terrence Holt RC 6.00 2.50
- ❑ URB1 E.Smith/Payton/Sanders

2004 Topps Chrome

- ❑ COMP.SET w/o SP's (165) 30.00 12.50
- ❑ ROOKIE STATED ODDS 1:2
- ❑ RH38 STATED ODDS 1:24 HOB/RET
- ❑ 1 Peyton Manning 1.50 .60
- ❑ 2 Patrick Ramsey .60 .25
- ❑ 3 Justin McCareins .40 .15
- ❑ 4 Matt Hasselbeck .60 .25
- ❑ 5 Chris Chambers .60 .25
- ❑ 6 Bubba Franks .60 .25
- ❑ 7 Eric Moulds .60 .25
- ❑ 8 Anquan Boldin 1.00 .40
- ❑ 9 Brian Urlacher 1.25 .50
- ❑ 10 Stephen Davis .60 .25
- ❑ 11 Michael Vick 2.00 .75
- ❑ 12 Dante Hall 1.00 .40
- ❑ 13 Chad Pennington 1.00 .40
- ❑ 14 Kevan Barlow .60 .25
- ❑ 15 Tommy Maddox .60 .25
- ❑ 16 Domanick Davis 1.00 .40
- ❑ 17 Dwight Freeney .60 .25
- ❑ 18 LaVar Arrington 2.00 .75
- ❑ 19 Troy Hambrick .40 .15
- ❑ 20 Jake Plummer .60 .25
- ❑ 21 Willis McGahee 1.00 .40
- ❑ 22 Steve McNair 1.00 .40
- ❑ 23 Kerry Collins .60 .25
- ❑ 24 Hines Ward 1.00 .40
- ❑ 25 Terrell Owens 1.00 .40
- ❑ 26 Jerome Pathon .40 .15
- ❑ 27 Andre Johnson 1.00 .40
- ❑ 28 DeShaun Foster .60 .25
- ❑ 29 Terrell Suggs .60 .25
- ❑ 30 Marcel Shipp .60 .25
- ❑ 31 Kyle Boller 1.00 .40
- ❑ 32 Javon Walker .60 .25
- ❑ 33 Ahman Green 1.00 .40
- ❑ 34 Travis Henry .60 .25
- ❑ 35 Randy McMichael .40 .15
- ❑ 36 Jerry Rice 2.00 .75
- ❑ 37 Travis Taylor .40 .15
- ❑ 38 Fred Taylor .60 .25
- ❑ 39 Zach Thomas 1.00 .40
- ❑ 40 Marques Tuiasosopo .60 .25
- ❑ 41 Laveranues Coles .60 .25
- ❑ 42 Thomas Jones .60 .25
- ❑ 43 Jamie Sharper .40 .15
- ❑ 44 Quincy Morgan .60 .25
- ❑ 45 Troy Brown .60 .25
- ❑ 46 Joey Galloway .60 .25
- ❑ 47 Justin Fargas .60 .25

❑ 48 Daunte Culpepper 1.00 .40
❑ 49 Keenan McCardell .40 .15
❑ 50 Priest Holmes 1.25 .50
❑ 51 Chad Johnson 1.00 .40
❑ 52 Marty Booker .60 .25
❑ 53 Tim Rattay .40 .15
❑ 54 Brian Westbrook .60 .25
❑ 55 Ricky Williams 1.00 .40
❑ 56 Lee Suggs 1.00 .40
❑ 57 Keith Brooking .40 .15
❑ 58 Rex Grossman 1.00 .40
❑ 59 Dallas Clark .60 .25
❑ 60 Charles Rogers .60 .25
❑ 61 Donte' Stallworth .60 .25
❑ 62 Deion Branch 1.00 .40
❑ 63 Ike Hilliard .40 .15
❑ 64 Michael Strahan .60 .25
❑ 65 Randy Moss 1.25 .50
❑ 66 Isaac Bruce .60 .25
❑ 67 Brad Johnson .60 .25
❑ 68 Warrick Dunn .60 .25
❑ 69 Josh McCown .60 .25
❑ 70 Donovan McNabb 1.25 .50
❑ 71 Shaun Alexander 1.00 .40
❑ 72 William Green .60 .25
❑ 73 Carson Palmer 1.25 .50
❑ 74 Quentin Griffin 1.00 .40
❑ 75 LaDainian Tomlinson 1.25 .50
❑ 76 Edgerrin James 1.00 .40
❑ 77 Santana Moss .60 .25
❑ 78 Marshall Faulk 1.00 .40
❑ 79 Tyrone Calico .60 .25
❑ 80 Marvin Harrison 1.00 .40
❑ 81 Tony Gonzalez .60 .25
❑ 82 Deuce McAllister 1.00 .40
❑ 83 Drew Brees 1.00 .40
❑ 84 Todd Pinkston .40 .15
❑ 85 Jeff Garcia 1.00 .40
❑ 86 Darrell Jackson .60 .25
❑ 87 Ray Lewis 1.00 .40
❑ 88 Billy Volek 1.00 .40
❑ 89 Rudi Johnson .60 .25
❑ 90 Julius Peppers 1.00 .40
❑ 91 Peter Warrick .60 .25
❑ 92 Trent Green .60 .25
❑ 93 Onterrio Smith .60 .25
❑ 94 Jerome Bettis 1.00 .40
❑ 95 Keyshawn Johnson .60 .25
❑ 96 Jamal Lewis 1.00 .40
❑ 97 Alge Crumpler .60 .25
❑ 98 Michael Bennett .60 .25
❑ 99 Jimmy Smith .60 .25
❑ 100 Brett Favre 2.50 1.00
❑ 101 Jerry Porter .60 .25
❑ 102 Marc Bulger 1.00 .40
❑ 103 David Carr 1.00 .40
❑ 104 Mark Brunell .60 .25
❑ 105 Aaron Brooks .60 .25
❑ 106 Plaxico Burress .60 .25
❑ 107 Correll Buckhalter .60 .25
❑ 108 Jevon Kearse .60 .25
❑ 109 Michael Pittman .40 .15
❑ 110 Clinton Portis 1.00 .40
❑ 111 Corey Dillon .60 .25
❑ 112 Steve Smith 1.00 .40
❑ 113 Eddie Kennison .40 .15
❑ 114 Amani Toomer .60 .25
❑ 115 Kelly Holcomb .60 .25
❑ 116 Torry Holt 1.00 .40
❑ 117 Eddie George .60 .25
❑ 118 Jeremy Shockey 1.00 .40
❑ 119 Jon Kitna .60 .25
❑ 120 Todd Heap .60 .25
❑ 121 Ashley Lelie .60 .25
❑ 122 Byron Leftwich 1.25 .50
❑ 123 Duce Staley .60 .25
❑ 124 Rod Gardner .60 .25
❑ 125 Tom Brady 2.50 1.00
❑ 126 Reggie Wayne .60 .25
❑ 127 Joe Horn .60 .25
❑ 128 Curtis Martin 1.00 .40
❑ 129 Charlie Garner .60 .25
❑ 130 Derrick Mason .60 .25
❑ 131 Marcus Robinson .60 .25
❑ 132 David Boston .60 .25
❑ 133 Drew Bledsoe 1.00 .40
❑ 134 Anthony Thomas .60 .25
❑ 135 Tiki Barber 1.00 .40
❑ 136 Terry Glenn .40 .15
❑ 137 A.J. Feeley 1.00 .40
❑ 138 Peerless Price .60 .25
❑ 139 Jake Delhomme 1.00 .40
❑ 140 Kevin Faulk .40 .15
❑ 141 Quincy Carter .60 .25
❑ 142 Joey Harrington 1.00 .40
❑ 143 Donald Driver .60 .25
❑ 144 Koren Robinson .60 .25
❑ 145 Rod Smith .60 .25
❑ 146 Anquan Boldin WW .40 .15
❑ 147 Jamal Lewis WW .60 .25
❑ 148 Priest Holmes WW 1.00 .40
❑ 149 Peyton Manning WW 1.00 .40
❑ 150 Marvin Harrison WW .60 .25
❑ 151 Steve McNair WW .60 .25
❑ 152 Travis Henry WW .40 .15
❑ 153 Torry Holt WW .60 .25
❑ 154 Tom Brady WW 1.00 .40
❑ 155 Ahman Green WW .60 .25
❑ 156 Donovan McNabb WW 1.00 .40
❑ 157 Deuce McAllister WW .60 .25
❑ 158 Domanick Davis WW .60 .25
❑ 159 Clinton Portis WW 1.00 .40
❑ 160 Rudi Johnson WW .40 .15
❑ 161 Brett Favre WW 1.00 .40
❑ 162 LaDainian Tomlinson WW .75 .30
❑ 163 Steve Smith WW .60 .25
❑ 164 Edgerrin James WW .60 .25
❑ 165 Ty Law WW .40 .15
❑ 166 Ben Roethlisberger RC 50.00 25.00
❑ 167 Ahmad Carroll RC 6.00 2.50
❑ 168 Johnnie Morant RC 5.00 2.00
❑ 169 Greg Jones RC 5.00 2.00
❑ 170 Michael Clayton RC 10.00 4.00
❑ 171 Josh Harris RC 5.00 2.00
❑ 172 Tatum Bell RC 10.00 4.00
❑ 173 Robert Gallery RC 8.00 3.00
❑ 174 B.J. Symons RC 5.00 2.00
❑ 175 Roy Williams RC 21.00 5.00
❑ 176 DeAngelo Hall RC 6.00 2.50
❑ 177 Jeff Smoker RC 5.00 2.00
❑ 178 Lee Evans RC 6.00 2.50
❑ 179 Michael Jenkins RC 5.00 2.00
❑ 180 Steven Jackson RC 15.00 6.00
❑ 181 Will Smith RC 5.00 2.00
❑ 182 Vince Wilfork RC 6.00 2.50
❑ 183 Ben Troupe RC 5.00 2.00
❑ 184 Chris Gamble RC 6.00 2.50
❑ 185 Kevin Jones RC 15.00 6.00
❑ 186 Jonathan Vilma RC 5.00 2.00
❑ 187 Dontarrious Thomas RC 5.00 2.00
❑ 188 Michael Boulware RC 5.00 2.00
❑ 189 Mewelde Moore RC 6.00 2.50
❑ 190 Drew Henson RC 5.00 2.00
❑ 191 D.J. Williams RC 6.00 2.50
❑ 192 Ernest Wilford RC 5.00 2.00
❑ 193 John Navarre RC 5.00 2.00
❑ 194 Jerricho Cotchery RC 5.00 2.00
❑ 195 Derrick Hamilton RC 4.00 1.50
❑ 196 Carlos Francis RC 4.00 1.50
❑ 197 Ben Watson RC 5.00 2.00
❑ 198 Reggie Williams RC 6.00 2.50
❑ 199 Devard Darling RC 5.00 2.00
❑ 200 Chris Perry RC 8.00 3.00
❑ 201 Derrick Strait RC 5.00 2.00
❑ 202 Sean Taylor RC 6.00 2.50
❑ 203 Michael Turner RC 5.00 2.00
❑ 204 Keary Colbert RC 6.00 2.50
❑ 205 Eli Manning RC 30.00 15.00
❑ 206 Julius Jones RC 20.00 7.50
❑ 207 Jason Babin RC 5.00 2.00
❑ 208 Cody Pickett RC 5.00 2.00
❑ 209 Kenechi Udeze RC 5.00 2.00
❑ 210 Rashaun Woods RC 5.00 2.00
❑ 211 Matt Schaub RC 8.00 3.00
❑ 212 Tommie Harris RC 5.00 2.00
❑ 213 Dwan Edwards RC 2.50 1.00
❑ 214 Shawn Andrews RC 5.00 2.00
❑ 215 Larry Fitzgerald RC 15.00 6.00
❑ 216 P.K. Sam RC 4.00 1.50
❑ 217 Teddy Lehman RC 5.00 2.00
❑ 218 Darius Watts RC 5.00 2.00
❑ 219 D.J. Hackett RC 4.00 1.50
❑ 220 Cedric Cobbs RC 5.00 2.00
❑ 221 Antwan Odom RC 5.00 2.00
❑ 222 Marquise Hill RC 4.00 1.50
❑ 223 Luke McCown RC 5.00 2.00
❑ 224 Triandos Luke RC 5.00 2.00
❑ 225 Kellen Winslow RC 10.00 4.00
❑ 226 Derek Abney RC 5.00 2.00
❑ 227 Chris Cooley RC 5.00 2.00
❑ 228 Dunta Robinson RC 5.00 2.00
❑ 229 Sean Jones RC 4.00 1.50
❑ 230 Philip Rivers RC 15.00 7.50
❑ 231 Craig Krenzel RC 5.00 2.00
❑ 232 Daryl Smith RC 5.00 2.00
❑ 233 Samie Parker RC 5.00 2.00
❑ 234 Ben Hartsock RC 5.00 2.00
❑ 235 J.P. Losman RC 10.00 4.00
❑ 236 Karlos Dansby RC 5.00 2.00
❑ 237 Ricardo Colclough RC 5.00 2.00
❑ 238 Bernard Berrian RC 5.00 2.00
❑ 239 Junior Siavii RC 5.00 2.00
❑ 240 Devery Henderson RC 4.00 1.50
❑ 241 Adimchinobe Echemandu RC 4.001.50
❑ 242 Patrick Crayton RC 5.00 2.00
❑ 243 Marcus Tubbs RC 5.00 2.00
❑ 244 Jamaar Taylor RC 5.00 2.00
❑ 245 Andy Hall RC 4.00 1.50
❑ 246 Darnell Dockett RC 4.00 1.50
❑ 247 Darrion Scott RC 5.00 2.00
❑ 248 Jim Sorgi RC 5.00 2.00
❑ 249 Jeff Dugan RC 2.50 1.00
❑ 250 Ryan Krause RC 4.00 1.50
❑ 251 Nate Lawrie RC 4.00 1.50
❑ 252 Casey Bramlet RC 4.00 1.50
❑ 253 Donnell Washington RC 5.00 2.00
❑ 254 Jonathan Smith RC 4.00 1.50
❑ 255 Tank Johnson RC 4.00 1.50
❑ 256 Keith Smith RC 4.00 1.50
❑ 257 Brandon Miree RC 4.00 1.50
❑ 258 Michael Gaines RC 4.00 1.50
❑ 259 Keiwan Ratliff RC 4.00 1.50
❑ 260 Stuart Schweigert RC 5.00 2.00
❑ 261 Derrick Ward RC 2.50 1.00
❑ 262 Matt Ware RC 5.00 2.00
❑ 263 Tim Anderson RC 5.00 2.00
❑ 264 Bradlee Van Pelt RC 8.00 3.00
❑ 265 Shawntae Spencer RC 5.00 2.00
❑ 266 Joey Thomas RC 5.00 2.00
❑ 267 Maurice Mann RC 4.00 1.50
❑ 268 Tim Euhus RC 5.00 2.00
❑ 269 Matt Mauck RC 5.00 2.00
❑ 270 Sloan Thomas RC 4.00 1.50
❑ 271 Jeris McIntyre RC 4.00 1.50
❑ 272 Randy Starks RC 4.00 1.50
❑ 273 Clarence Moore RC 5.00 2.00
❑ 274 Drew Carter RC 5.00 2.00
❑ 275 Sean Ryan RC 4.00 1.50
❑ RH38 Tom Brady RH 5.00 2.00

2005 Topps Chrome

❑ COMPLETE SET (275) 200.00 100.00
❑ COMP.SET w/o RC's (165) 30.00 12.50
❑ ROOKIE STATED ODDS 1:2 HOB/RET
❑ RH STATED ODDS 1:288 HOB/RET
❑ RH REFRACT.ODDS 1:17,884 H, 1:22,080 R
❑ 1 Deuce McAllister 1.00 .40
❑ 2 Sean Taylor .60 .25
❑ 3 Koren Robinson .60 .25
❑ 4 Tiki Barber 1.00 .40
❑ 5 LaDainian Tomlinson 1.25 .50
❑ 6 Lee Evans .60 .25

❑	7	Aaron Brooks	.60	.25
❑	8	LaMont Jordan	1.00	.40
❑	9	Dante Hall	.60	.25
❑	10	Daunte Culpepper	1.00	.40
❑	11	Thomas Jones	.60	.25
❑	12	Warrick Dunn	.60	.25
❑	13	Willis McGahee	1.00	.40
❑	14	Ed Reed	.60	.25
❑	15	Derrick Mason	.60	.25
❑	16	Jason Witten	.60	.25
❑	17	Chad Johnson	1.00	.40
❑	18	Amani Toomer	.60	.25
❑	19	Joey Harrington	1.00	.40
❑	20	Brian Urlacher	1.00	.40
❑	21	Brian Westbrook	.60	.25
❑	22	Matt Hasselbeck	.60	.25
❑	23	Michael Vick	1.50	.60
❑	24	Kevin Jones	1.00	.40
❑	25	Julius Peppers	.60	.25
❑	26	Michael Clayton	1.00	.40
❑	27	Javon Walker	.60	.25
❑	28	Santana Moss	.60	.25
❑	29	Travis Henry	.60	.25
❑	30	Stephen Davis	.60	.25
❑	31	Larry Johnson	1.00	.40
❑	32	Terrell Owens	1.00	.40
❑	33	Ray Lewis	1.00	.40
❑	34	Jake Plummer	.60	.25
❑	35	Philip Rivers	1.00	.40
❑	36	Eli Manning	2.00	.75
❑	37	Tedy Bruschi	.60	.25
❑	38	Adam Vinatieri	1.00	.40
❑	39	J.P. Losman	1.00	.40
❑	40	Zach Thomas	1.00	.40
❑	41	Deion Branch	.60	.25
❑	42	Andre Johnson	.60	.25
❑	43	Marshall Faulk	1.00	.40
❑	44	Bertrand Berry	.50	.20
❑	45	Terrell Suggs	.60	.25
❑	46	Tom Brady	2.50	1.00
❑	47	Ashley Lelie	.60	.25
❑	48	Jonathan Wells	.50	.20
❑	49	Randy McMichael	.50	.20
❑	50	Charles Rogers	.60	.25
❑	51	Larry Fitzgerald	1.00	.40
❑	52	Hines Ward	1.00	.40
❑	53	Jason Taylor	.50	.20
❑	54	Ronde Barber	.50	.20
❑	55	T.J. Houshmandzadeh	.50	.20
❑	56	Keary Colbert	.60	.25
❑	57	DeAngelo Hall	.60	.25
❑	58	Chris Brown	.60	.25
❑	59	Chris Perry	.60	.25
❑	60	Steven Jackson	1.25	.50
❑	61	Kyle Boller	.60	.25
❑	62	Rudi Johnson	.60	.25
❑	63	Roy Williams S	.60	.25
❑	64	Onterrio Smith	.60	.25
❑	65	Roy Williams WR	1.00	.40
❑	66	Jerry Porter	.60	.25
❑	67	Edgerrin James	1.00	.40
❑	68	Randy Moss	1.00	.40
❑	69	Brian Griese	.60	.25
❑	70	Donovan McNabb	1.25	.50
❑	71	Joe Horn	.60	.25
❑	72	Muhsin Muhammad	.60	.25
❑	73	Johnnie Morton	.60	.25
❑	74	Chad Pennington	1.00	.40
❑	75	Torry Holt	1.00	.40
❑	76	Marc Bulger	1.00	.40
❑	77	Duce Staley	.60	.25
❑	78	Todd Heap	.60	.25
❑	79	Lee Suggs	.60	.25
❑	80	Patrick Ramsey	.60	.25
❑	81	Drew Bennett	.60	.25
❑	82	Michael Strahan	.60	.25
❑	83	Priest Holmes	1.00	.40
❑	84	DeShaun Foster	.60	.25
❑	85	Corey Dillon	.60	.25
❑	86	Antonio Gates	1.00	.40
❑	87	Trent Green	.60	.25
❑	88	Brandon Stokley	.60	.25
❑	89	Alge Crumpler	.60	.25
❑	90	Keyshawn Johnson	.60	.25
❑	91	Byron Leftwich	1.00	.40
❑	92	Dunta Robinson	.60	.25
❑	93	Ben Roethlisberger	2.50	1.00

❑	94	Rod Smith	.60	.25
❑	95	Robert Gallery	.60	.25
❑	96	Tony Gonzalez	.60	.25
❑	97	Steve McNair	1.00	.40
❑	98	Jeremy Shockey	1.00	.40
❑	99	Dominic Rhodes	.50	.20
❑	100	Michael Jenkins	.60	.25
❑	101	Jake Delhomme	1.00	.40
❑	102	Jerome Bettis	1.00	.40
❑	103	Jevon Kearse	.60	.25
❑	104	Plaxico Burress	.60	.25
❑	105	Dwight Freeney	.60	.25
❑	106	Marcus Robinson	.60	.25
❑	107	Rex Grossman	.60	.25
❑	108	Drew Henson	.60	.25
❑	109	Julius Jones	1.25	.50
❑	110	Jamal Lewis	1.00	.40
❑	111	Justin McCareins	.50	.20
❑	112	Billy Volek	.60	.25
❑	113	Curtis Martin	1.00	.40
❑	114	Tatum Bell	.60	.25
❑	115	Domanick Davis	.60	.25
❑	116	Marvin Harrison	1.00	.40
❑	117	Anquan Boldin	.60	.25
❑	118	Jimmy Smith	.60	.25
❑	119	Drew Brees	1.00	.40
❑	120	Donte Stallworth	.60	.25
❑	121	Nate Burleson	.60	.25
❑	122	Fred Taylor	.60	.25
❑	123	Takeo Spikes	.50	.20
❑	124	Jonathan Ogden	.50	.20
❑	125	Michael Bennett	.60	.25
❑	126	Clinton Portis	1.00	.40
❑	127	Ahman Green	1.00	.40
❑	128	Drew Bledsoe	1.00	.40
❑	129	Darrell Jackson	.60	.25
❑	130	Jonathan Vilma	.60	.25
❑	131	David Carr	1.00	.40
❑	132	Champ Bailey	.60	.25
❑	133	Derrick Blaylock	.50	.20
❑	134	T.J. Duckett	.60	.25
❑	135	Shaun Alexander	1.25	.50
❑	136	Peyton Manning	1.50	.60
❑	137	Isaac Bruce	.60	.25
❑	138	LaVar Arrington	1.00	.40
❑	139	Brett Favre	2.50	1.00
❑	140	Allen Rossum	.50	.20
❑	141	Eric Moulds	.60	.25
❑	142	Carson Palmer	1.00	.40
❑	143	Laveranues Coles	.60	.25
❑	144	Chester Taylor	.60	.25
❑	145	Reggie Wayne	.60	.25
❑	146	Curtis Martin LL	.60	.25
❑	147	Daunte Culpepper LL	.60	.25
❑	148	Muhsin Muhammad LL	.50	.20
❑	149	Shaun Alexander LL	1.00	.40
❑	150	Trent Green LL	.50	.20
❑	151	Joe Horn LL	.50	.20
❑	152	Corey Dillon LL	.50	.20
❑	153	Peyton Manning LL	1.00	.40
❑	154	Javon Walker LL	.50	.20
❑	155	Edgerrin James LL	.60	.25
❑	156	Jake Scott GM	.50	.20
❑	157	John Elway GM	2.00	.75
❑	158	Dwight Clark GM	.60	.25
❑	159	Lawrence Taylor GM	1.00	.40
❑	160	Joe Namath GM	1.25	.50
❑	161	Richard Dent GM	.60	.25
❑	162	Peyton Manning GM	1.00	.40
❑	163	Don Maynard GM	.50	.20
❑	164	Joe Greene GM	1.00	.40
❑	165	Roger Staubach GM	1.25	.50
❑	166	J.J. Arrington RC	8.00	3.00
❑	167	Cedric Benson RC	10.00	4.00
❑	168	Mark Bradley RC	5.00	2.00
❑	169	Reggie Brown RC	5.00	2.00
❑	170	Ronnie Brown RC	15.00	6.00
❑	171	Jason Campbell RC	8.00	3.00
❑	172	Maurice Clarett	5.00	2.00
❑	173	Mark Clayton RC	6.00	2.50
❑	174	Braylon Edwards RC	15.00	6.00
❑	175	Ciatrick Fason RC	5.00	2.00
❑	176	Charlie Frye RC	10.00	4.00
❑	177	Frank Gore RC	8.00	3.00
❑	178	David Greene RC	5.00	2.00
❑	179	Vincent Jackson RC	5.00	2.00
❑	180	Adam Jones RC	5.00	2.00

❑	181	Matt Jones RC	12.00	5.
❑	182	Stefan LeFors RC	5.00	2
❑	183	Heath Miller RC	12.00	5
❑	184	Ryan Moats RC	5.00	2
❑	185	Vernand Morency RC	5.00	2
❑	186	Terrence Murphy RC	5.00	2
❑	187	Kyle Orton RC	8.00	3.
❑	188	Roscoe Parrish RC	5.00	2.
❑	189	Courtney Roby RC	5.00	2.
❑	190	Aaron Rodgers RC	15.00	6.
❑	191	Carlos Rogers RC	6.00	2.
❑	192	Antrel Rolle RC	5.00	2.
❑	193	Eric Shelton RC	5.00	2.
❑	194	Alex Smith QB RC	20.00	7.
❑	195	Andrew Walter RC	8.00	3.
❑	196	Roddy White RC	5.00	2.
❑	197	Carnell Williams RC	25.00	10.
❑	198	Mike Williams	10.00	4.
❑	199	Troy Williamson RC	10.00	4.
❑	200	Taylor Stubblefield RC	2.50	1.
❑	201	Dan Cody RC	5.00	2.
❑	202	David Pollack RC	5.00	2.
❑	203	Craig Bragg RC	4.00	1.
❑	204	Alvin Pearman RC	5.00	2.
❑	205	Marcus Maxwell RC	4.00	1.
❑	206	Brock Berlin RC	4.00	1.
❑	207	Khalif Barnes RC	4.00	1.
❑	208	Eric King RC	4.00	1.
❑	209	Alex Smith TE RC	5.00	2.
❑	210	Dante Ridgeway RC	4.00	1.
❑	211	Shaun Cody RC	5.00	2.
❑	212	Donte Nicholson RC	5.00	2.
❑	213	DeMarcus Ware RC	8.00	3.
❑	214	Lionel Gates RC	4.00	1.
❑	215	Fabian Washington RC	5.00	2.
❑	216	Brandon Jacobs RC	6.00	2.
❑	217	Noah Herron RC	5.00	2.
❑	218	Derrick Johnson RC	8.00	3.
❑	219	J.R. Russell RC	4.00	1.
❑	220	Adrian McPherson RC	5.00	2.
❑	221	Marcus Spears RC	5.00	2.
❑	222	Justin Miller RC	4.00	1.
❑	223	Marion Barber RC	8.00	3.
❑	224	Anthony Davis RC	4.00	1.
❑	225	Chad Owens RC	5.00	2.
❑	226	Craphonso Thorpe RC	4.00	1.
❑	227	Travis Johnson RC	4.00	1.
❑	228	Erasmus James RC	5.00	2.
❑	229	Mike Patterson RC	5.00	2.0
❑	230	Airese Currie RC	5.00	2.0
❑	231	Justin Tuck RC	5.00	2.
❑	232	Dan Orlovsky RC	6.00	2.5
❑	233	Thomas Davis RC	5.00	2.
❑	234	Derek Anderson RC	5.00	2.
❑	235	Matt Roth RC	5.00	2.0
❑	236	Chris Henry RC	5.00	2.0
❑	237	Rasheed Marshall RC	5.00	2.0
❑	238	Bryant McFadden RC	5.00	2.0
❑	239	Darren Sproles RC	5.00	2.0
❑	240	Fred Gibson RC	4.00	1.5
❑	241	Barrett Ruud RC	5.00	2.0
❑	242	Kelvin Hayden RC	4.00	1.5
❑	243	Ryan Fitzpatrick RC	8.00	3.0
❑	244	Patrick Estes RC	4.00	1.5
❑	245	Zach Tuiasosopo RC	2.50	1.0
❑	246	Luis Castillo RC	5.00	2.0
❑	247	Lance Mitchell RC	4.00	1.5
❑	248	Ronald Bartell RC	4.00	1.5
❑	249	Jerome Mathis RC	5.00	2.0
❑	250	Marlin Jackson RC	5.00	2.0
❑	251	James Kilian RC	5.00	2.0
❑	252	Roydell Williams RC	5.00	2.0
❑	253	Joel Dreessen RC	4.00	1.5
❑	254	Paris Warren RC	4.00	1.5
❑	255	Dustin Fox RC	5.00	2.00
❑	256	Ellis Hobbs RC	5.00	2.00
❑	257	Mike Nugent RC	5.00	2.00
❑	258	Channing Crowder RC	5.00	2.00
❑	259	Kerry Rhodes RC	5.00	2.00
❑	260	Jerome Collins RC	4.00	1.50
❑	261	Stanford Routt RC	4.00	1.50
❑	262	Madison Hedgecock RC	5.00	2.00
❑	263	Rian Wallace RC	4.00	1.50
❑	264	Larry Brackins RC	4.00	1.50
❑	265	Manuel White RC	4.00	1.50
❑	266	Corey Webster RC	5.00	2.00
❑	267	Eric Moore RC	4.00	1.50

268	Kirk Morrison RC	5.00	2.00
269	Atiyyah Ellison RC	2.50	1.00
270	Travis Daniels RC	4.00	1.50
271	Boomer Grigsby RC	6.00	2.50
272	Alex Barron RC	2.50	1.00
273	Tab Perry RC	5.00	2.00
274	Cedric Houston RC	5.00	2.00
275	Kevin Burnett RC	5.00	2.00
RH39	Deion Branch RH	5.00	2.00
RH39R	Deion Branch RHR/100	15.00	6.00

2001 Topps Debut

	COMP.SET w/o SP's (100)	20.00	7.50
1	Marshall Faulk	1.25	.50
2	Ricky Watters	.60	.25
3	Bill Schroeder	.60	.25
4	Muhsin Muhammad	.60	.25
5	Peter Warrick	1.00	.40
6	Marvin Harrison	1.00	.40
7	Stephen Davis	1.00	.40
8	Cris Carter	1.00	.40
9	Charlie Batch	1.00	.40
10	David Boston	1.00	.40
11	Ike Hilliard	.60	.25
12	Steve McNair	1.00	.40
13	Kordell Stewart	.60	.25
14	Travis Prentice	.40	.15
15	Sammy Morris	.40	.15
16	Vinny Testaverde	.60	.25
17	Tyrone Wheatley	.60	.25
18	Jeff Garcia	1.00	.40
19	Brett Favre	3.00	1.25
20	Jake Plummer	.60	.25
21	Cade McNown	.40	.15
22	Rob Johnson	.60	.25
23	Tim Couch	.60	.25
24	Jerome Bettis	1.00	.40
25	Ricky Williams	1.00	.40
26	Darrell Jackson	1.00	.40
27	Troy Brown	.60	.25
28	Jamal Lewis	1.50	.60
29	Isaac Bruce	1.00	.40
30	Lamar Smith	.60	.25
31	Qadry Ismail	.60	.25
32	Elvis Grbac	.60	.25
33	Shaun Alexander	1.25	.50
34	Peyton Manning	2.50	1.00
35	Curtis Martin	1.00	.40
36	Jamal Anderson	1.00	.40
37	Mark Brunell	1.00	.40
38	Emmitt Smith	2.00	.75
39	Chad Lewis	.40	.15
40	Randy Moss	2.00	.75
41	Kurt Warner	2.00	.75
42	Terrence Wilkins	.40	.15
43	Corey Dillon	1.00	.40
44	Brian Griese	1.00	.40
45	Jon Kitna	1.00	.40
46	Eric Moulds	.60	.25
47	Steve Beuerlein	.60	.25
48	James Allen	.60	.25
49	Amani Toomer	.40	.15
50	Daunte Culpepper	1.00	.40
51	Michael Pittman	.40	.15
52	Warrick Dunn	1.00	.40
53	Terrell Owens	1.00	.40
54	Donald Hayes	.40	.15
55	Keenan McCardell	.40	.15
56	Tony Gonzalez	.60	.25
57	Freddie Jones	.40	.15
58	Charlie Garner	.60	.25
59	Shawn Jefferson	.40	.15
60	Brian Urlacher	1.50	.60
61	Donovan McNabb	1.25	.50
62	Az-Zahir Hakim	.40	.15
63	James Thrash	.60	.25
64	Hines Ward	1.00	.40
65	Shawn Bryson	.40	.15
66	Wayne Chrebet	.60	.25
67	Kevin Johnson	.60	.25
68	Eddie George	1.00	.40
69	Derrick Alexander	.60	.25
70	Tim Brown	1.00	.40
71	Jay Fiedler	1.00	.40
72	Aaron Brooks	1.00	.40
73	Torry Holt	1.00	.40
74	Edgerrin James	1.25	.50
75	Shannon Sharpe	.60	.25
76	Oronde Gadsden	.60	.25
77	Rod Smith	.60	.25
78	Rich Gannon	1.00	.40
79	Fred Taylor	1.00	.40
80	Derrick Mason	.60	.25
81	Joe Horn	.60	.25
82	Robert Smith	.60	.25
83	James Stewart	.60	.25
84	Jeff George	.60	.25
85	Troy Aikman	1.50	.60
86	Charles Johnson	.40	.15
87	Ahman Green	1.00	.40
88	Shaun King	.40	.15
89	Ray Lewis	1.00	.40
90	Trent Dilfer	.60	.25
91	Drew Bledsoe	1.25	.50
92	Jimmy Smith	.60	.25
93	Ed McCaffrey	1.00	.40
94	Kerry Collins	.60	.25
95	Terry Glenn	.60	.25
96	Ron Dayne	1.00	.40
97	Keyshawn Johnson	1.00	.40
98	Antonio Freeman	1.00	.40
99	Tiki Barber	1.00	.40
100	Mike Anderson	1.00	.40
101	Drew Brees AU RC	60.00	35.00
102	Chris Weinke AU RC	20.00	7.50
103	LaDain.Tomlinson AU RC	150.00	75.00
104	Michael Bennett AU RC	30.00	12.50
105	Anthony Thomas AU RC	20.00	7.50
106	LaMont Jordan AU RC	40.00	20.00
107	David Terrell AU RC	20.00	7.50
108	Michael Vick AU RC	200.00	75.00
109	Deuce McAllister AU RC	40.00	20.00
110	James Jackson AU RC	20.00	7.50
111	Mike McMahon JSY RC	15.00	6.00
112	Cedrick Wilson JSY RC	15.00	6.00
113	Ken Lucas JSY RC	15.00	6.00
114	Fred Smoot JSY RC	15.00	6.00
115	Alge Crumpler JSY RC	20.00	10.00
116	Sage Rosenfels JSY RC	15.00	6.00
117	Rashard Casey JSY RC	10.00	4.00
118	David Allen JSY RC	10.00	4.00
119	Bobby Newcombe JSY RC	10.00	4.00
120	Jesse Palmer JSY RC	15.00	6.00
121	Tommy Polley JSY RC	15.00	6.00
122	Kevan Barlow JSY RC	15.00	6.00
123	Scotty Anderson JSY RC	10.00	4.00
124	Travis Minor JSY RC	10.00	4.00
125	Snoop Minnis JSY RC	10.00	4.00
126	Moran Norris JSY RC	8.00	3.00
127	Alex Lincoln JSY RC	10.00	4.00
128	Chad Johnson JSY RC	40.00	20.00
129	Boo Williams JSY RC	10.00	4.00
130	Brian Natkin JSY RC	8.00	3.00
131	Orlando Huff JSY RC	8.00	3.00
132	Derrick Gibson JSY RC	10.00	4.00
133	Tony Driver JSY RC	15.00	6.00
134	Torrance Marshall JSY RC	15.00	6.00
135	Alex Bannister JSY RC	10.00	4.00
136	Morlon Greenwood JSY RC	8.00	3.00
137	Ennis Davis JSY RC	8.00	3.00
138	Mike Cerimele JSY RC	8.00	3.00
139	David Rivers JSY RC	10.00	4.00
140	Dustin McClintock JSY RC	10.00	4.00
141	Tay Cody JSY RC	8.00	3.00
142	Arther Love JSY RC	8.00	3.00
143	Sly Johnson JSY RC	10.00	4.00
144	Dan Alexander JSY RC	15.00	6.00
145	Will Allen JSY RC	10.00	4.00
146	Andre Dyson JSY RC	8.00	3.00
147	Margin Hooks JSY RC	8.00	3.00
148	Adam Archuleta JSY RC	15.00	6.00
149	Sedrick Hodge JSY RC	8.00	3.00
150	Kendrell Bell JSY RC	25.00	10.00
151	Reggie Wayne RC	12.00	5.00
152	Rod Gardner RC	6.00	2.50
153	Chris Chambers RC	10.00	4.00
154	Jamal Reynolds RC	6.00	2.50
155	Ben Hamilton RC	6.00	2.50
156	Dan Morgan RC	20.00	7.50
157	Quincy Morgan RC	6.00	2.50
158	Travis Henry RC	6.00	2.50
159	Ken-Yon Rambo RC	4.00	1.50
160	Josh Heupel RC	6.00	2.50
161	Marcus Stroud RC	6.00	2.50
162	Marques Tuiasosopo RC	6.00	2.50
163	Reggie Germany RC	4.00	1.50
164	Robert Ferguson RC	6.00	2.50
165	Jabari Holloway RC	4.00	1.50
166	Ben Leard RC	6.00	2.50
167	Bhawoh Jue RC	8.00	3.00
168	Freddie Mitchell RC	6.00	2.50
169	Vinny Sutherland RC	4.00	1.50
170	Jeff Backus RC	4.00	1.50
171	Correll Buckhalter RC	8.00	3.00
172	Mario Fatafehi RC	4.00	1.50
173	Rudi Johnson RC	12.00	5.00
174	Koren Robinson RC	6.00	2.50
175	Santana Moss RC	10.00	4.00

2002 Topps Debut

	COMP.SET w/o SP's (150)	25.00	10.00
1	Kurt Warner	1.00	.40
2	James Thrash	.60	.25
3	Aaron Brooks	1.00	.40
4	Mark Brunell	1.00	.40
5	Mike Anderson	1.00	.40
6	Benjamin Gay	.60	.25
7	Marvin Harrison	1.00	.40
8	Randy Moss	2.00	.75
9	Ron Dayne	.60	.25
10	Tim Brown	1.00	.40
11	Vinny Testaverde	.60	.25
12	Mike Alstott	1.00	.40
13	Tony Banks	.40	.15
14	Plaxico Burress	.60	.25
15	Chris Chambers	1.00	.40
16	Brett Favre	2.50	1.00
17	Quincy Carter	.60	.25
18	Brian Urlacher	1.50	.60
19	Byron Chamberlain	.40	.15
20	Tony Gonzalez	.60	.25
21	Troy Brown	.60	.25
22	Drew Brees	1.00	.40
23	Koren Robinson	.60	.25
24	Donald Hayes	.40	.15
25	Michael Vick	3.00	1.25
26	Travis Taylor	.60	.25
27	Peerless Price	.60	.25
28	Chad Johnson	1.00	.40
29	Tim Couch	.60	.25
30	Edgerrin James	1.25	.50
31	Willie Jackson	.40	.15
32	Hines Ward	1.00	.40
33	Terrell Owens	1.00	.40
34	Eddie George	1.00	.40

35	Michael Westbrook	.40	.15
36	Kerry Collins	.60	.25
37	Terrell Davis	1.00	.40
38	Marcus Robinson	.60	.25
39	Charlie Batch	.60	.25
40	Jake Plummer	.60	.25
41	Qadry Ismail	.60	.25
42	Snoop Minnis	.40	.15
43	Jimmy Smith	.60	.25
44	Charlie Garner	.60	.25
45	Jeff Graham	.40	.15
46	Torry Holt	1.00	.40
47	Kevin Dyson	.60	.25
48	Maurice Smith	.60	.25
49	Muhsin Muhammad	.60	.25
50	Curtis Martin	1.00	.40
51	Todd Pinkston	.60	.25
52	Matt Hasselbeck	.60	.25
53	Corey Dillon	.60	.25
54	Michael Pittman	.40	.15
55	Antonio Freeman	1.00	.40
56	Oronde Gadsden	.60	.25
57	Tiki Barber	1.00	.40
58	Isaac Bruce	1.00	.40
59	Rod Gardner	.60	.25
60	Derrick Mason	.60	.25
61	Joe Horn	.60	.25
62	Antowain Smith	.60	.25
63	Johnnie Morton	.60	.25
64	Kevin Johnson	.60	.25
65	Nick Goings	.40	.15
66	Jason Brookins	.40	.15
67	Travis Henry	1.00	.40
68	Brian Griese	1.00	.40
69	Priest Holmes	1.25	.50
70	Daunte Culpepper	1.00	.40
71	Amani Toomer	.60	.25
72	Rich Gannon	1.00	.40
73	Correll Buckhalter	.60	.25
74	Kevan Barlow	.60	.25
75	Stephen Davis	.60	.25
76	Keenan McCardell	.40	.15
77	Jon Kitna	.60	.25
78	Eric Moulds	.60	.25
79	Dez White	.40	.15
80	Rocket Ismail	.60	.25
81	Dominic Rhodes	.60	.25
82	Lamar Smith	.60	.25
83	David Patten	.40	.15
84	Duce Staley	1.00	.40
85	Curtis Conway	.40	.15
86	Kordell Stewart	.60	.25
87	Brad Johnson	.60	.25
88	Wayne Chrebet	.60	.25
89	Michael Bennett	.60	.25
90	Quincy Morgan	.40	.15
91	Steve Smith	1.00	.40
92	David Boston	1.00	.40
93	Shannon Sharpe	.60	.25
94	Mike McMahon	1.00	.40
95	Stacey Mack	.40	.15
96	Santana Moss	1.00	.40
97	Jeff Garcia	1.00	.40
98	Keyshawn Johnson	1.00	.40
99	Rod Smith	.60	.25
100	Jerome Bettis	1.00	.40
101	LaDainian Tomlinson	1.50	.60
102	Warrick Dunn	1.00	.40
103	Ray Lewis	1.00	.40
104	Chris Chandler	.60	.25
105	Jim Miller	.40	.15
106	Ahman Green	1.00	.40
107	Jay Fiedler	.60	.25
108	Tom Brady	2.50	1.00
109	Michael Strahan	.60	.25
110	James Jackson	.40	.15
111	Rob Johnson	.60	.25
112	Elvis Grbac	.60	.25
113	Troy Hambrick	.40	.15
114	Corey Bradford	.40	.15
115	Trent Green	.60	.25
116	Cris Carter	1.00	.40
117	Chris Fuamatu-Ma'afala	.40	.15
118	Chris Weinke	.60	.25
119	MarTay Jenkins	.40	.15
120	Laveranues Coles	.60	.25
121	Donovan McNabb	1.25	.50
122	Jerry Rice	2.00	.75
123	Garrison Hearst	.60	.25
124	Steve McNair	1.00	.40
125	Trung Canidate	.60	.25
126	Doug Flutie	1.00	.40
127	Ricky Williams		
128	Peyton Manning	2.00	.75
129	Kevin Kasper	.40	.15
130	Emmitt Smith	2.50	1.00
131	Peter Warrick	.60	.25
132	Anthony Thomas	.60	.25
133	Ike Hilliard	.40	.15
134	Kendrell Bell	1.00	.40
135	Shaun Alexander	1.25	.50
136	Wesley Walls	.40	.15
137	Gerard Warren	.40	.15
138	James Stewart	.60	.25
139	Drew Bledsoe	1.25	.50
140	Fred Taylor	1.00	.40
141	Marshall Faulk	1.00	.40
142	Marcus Pollard	.40	.15
143	Bill Schroeder	.60	.25
144	Marty Booker	.40	.15
145	Amos Zereoue	1.00	.40
146	Darrell Jackson	.60	.25
147	Brian Finneran	.40	.15
148	Alex Van Pelt	.60	.25
149	Andre Carter	.40	.15
150	Joey Galloway	.60	.25
151	Joey Harrington AU RC	30.00	15.00
152	Andre Davis AU RC	20.00	7.50
153	Eric Crouch AU RC	25.00	10.00
154	Kelly Campbell AU RC	15.00	6.00
155	Ron Johnson AU RC	15.00	6.00
156	David Carr JSY RC	25.00	10.00
157	Kurt Kittner JSY RC	12.00	5.00
158	Javon Walker JSY RC	25.00	12.50
159	DeShaun Foster JSY RC	12.00	5.00
160	Lamar Gordon JSY RC	15.00	6.00
161	Antwaan Randle El RC	5.00	2.00
162	Clinton Portis RC	12.00	5.00
163	Luke Staley RC	2.50	1.00
164	Daniel Graham RC	3.00	1.25
165	Ashley Lelie RC	6.00	2.50
166	Ladell Betts RC	3.00	1.25
167	Rocky Calmus RC	3.00	1.25
168	Ryan Sims RC	3.00	1.25
169	Jeremy Shockey RC	12.00	5.00
170	Damien Anderson RC	3.00	1.25
171	Bryant McKinnie RC	3.00	1.25
172	Kahlil Hill RC	2.50	1.00
173	John Henderson RC	3.00	1.25
174	Donte Stallworth RC	6.00	2.50
175	Kalimba Edwards RC	3.00	1.25
176	Freddie Milons RC	2.50	1.00
177	Antonio Bryant RC	3.00	1.25
178	Cliff Russell RC	2.50	1.00
179	T.J. Duckett RC	5.00	2.00
180	Roy Williams RC	8.00	3.00
181	Patrick Ramsey RC	4.00	1.50
182	Josh Reed RC	3.00	1.25
183	Wendell Bryant RC	1.50	.60
184	Jabar Gaffney RC	3.00	1.25
185	Napoleon Harris RC	3.00	1.25
186	Adrian Peterson RC	3.00	1.25
187	David Garrard RC	3.00	1.25
188	Levar Fisher RC	2.50	1.00
189	Quentin Jammer RC	3.00	1.25
190	Anthony Weaver RC	2.50	1.00
191	Dwight Freeney RC	4.00	1.50
192	Reche Caldwell RC	3.00	1.25
193	Larry Tripplett RC	2.50	1.00
194	Rohan Davey RC	3.00	1.25
195	Marquise Walker RC	2.50	1.00
196	William Green RC	3.00	1.25
197	Tracey Wistrom RC	2.50	1.00
198	Alan Harper RC	1.50	.60
199	Lito Sheppard RC	3.00	1.25
200	Albert Haynesworth RC	3.00	1.25

2003 Topps Draft Picks and Prospects

	COMPLETE SET (165)	50.00	25.00
1	Priest Holmes	1.25	.50
2	Tommy Maddox	1.00	.40
3	Donald Driver	.60	.25

4	Drew Bledsoe	1.00	.40
5	Tiki Barber	1.00	.40
6	Terrell Owens	1.00	.40
7	Rich Gannon	.60	.25
8	Isaac Bruce	1.00	.40
9	Stephen Davis	.60	.25
10	Peyton Manning	1.50	.60
11	Tony Gonzalez	.60	.25
12	Marty Booker	.60	.25
13	Warrick Dunn	.60	.25
14	Jimmy Smith	.60	.25
15	Troy Brown	.60	.25
16	Jerry Rice	2.00	.75
17	Curtis Conway	.40	.15
18	Kurt Warner	1.00	.40
19	Steve McNair	1.00	.40
20	Edgerrin James	1.00	.40
21	Aaron Brooks	1.00	.40
22	Joey Galloway	.60	.25
23	Peerless Price	.60	.25
24	Torry Holt	1.00	.40
25	Derrick Mason	.60	.25
26	Curtis Martin	1.00	.40
27	Daunte Culpepper	1.00	.40
28	Ahman Green	1.00	.40
29	Tim Couch	.40	.15
30	Ricky Williams	1.00	.40
31	Darrell Jackson	.60	.25
32	Keyshawn Johnson	1.00	.40
33	Jeff Garcia	1.00	.40
34	Charlie Garner	.60	.25
35	Randy Moss	1.50	.60
36	Rod Smith	.60	.25
37	Jamal Lewis	1.00	.40
38	Corey Dillon	.60	.25
39	Marvin Harrison	1.00	.40
40	Joe Horn	.60	.25
41	Laveranues Coles	.60	.25
42	Hines Ward	1.00	.40
43	Brad Johnson	.60	.25
44	Eddie George	.60	.25
45	Donovan McNabb	1.25	.50
46	Marshall Faulk	1.00	.40
47	Amani Toomer	.60	.25
48	Trent Green	.60	.25
49	Emmitt Smith	2.50	1.00
50	Brett Favre	2.50	1.00
51	Brian Griese	1.00	.40
52	Eric Moulds	.60	.25
53	Plaxico Burress	.60	.25
54	Fred Taylor	1.00	.40
55	Tom Brady	2.50	1.00
56	Michael Vick	2.50	1.00
57	Andre Davis	.40	.15
58	Chris Chambers	1.00	.40
59	Javon Walker	.60	.25
60	Marc Bulger	1.00	.40
61	LaDainian Tomlinson	1.00	.40
62	Chad Pennington	1.25	.50
63	Marc Boerigter	.60	.25
64	Rod Gardner	.60	.25
65	DeShaun Foster	.40	.15
66	Chris Redman	.40	.15
67	Chad Hutchinson	.40	.15
68	Deion Branch	1.00	.40
69	Jeremy Shockey	1.50	.60
70	Shaun Alexander	1.00	.40
71	Derrius Thompson	.40	.15
72	A.J. Feeley	.60	.25
73	Reggie Wayne	.60	.25

❏ 74 William Green	.60	.25
❏ 75 Julius Peppers	1.00	.40
❏ 76 Travis Henry	.60	.25
❏ 77 Marcel Shipp	.60	.25
❏ 78 Michael Bennett	.60	.25
❏ 79 Maurice Morris	.40	.15
❏ 80 Josh Reed	.60	.25
❏ 81 David Terrell	.60	.25
❏ 82 Drew Brees	1.00	.40
❏ 83 Jonathan Wells	.40	.15
❏ 84 Anthony Thomas	.60	.25
❏ 85 Quincy Morgan	.60	.25
❏ 86 Jerry Porter	.60	.25
❏ 87 Ron Johnson	.40	.15
❏ 88 Najeh Davenport	.40	.15
❏ 89 Lamar Gordon	.40	.15
❏ 90 Joey Harrington	1.50	.60
❏ 91 Donte Stallworth	1.00	.40
❏ 92 Kenny Watson	.40	.15
❏ 93 LaMont Jordan	1.00	.40
❏ 94 Antonio Bryant	.60	.25
❏ 95 Steve Smith	1.00	.40
❏ 96 T.J. Duckett	.60	.25
❏ 97 Patrick Ramsey	1.00	.40
❏ 98 Santana Moss	.60	.25
❏ 99 Chad Johnson	1.00	.40
❏ 100 Clinton Portis	1.50	.60
❏ 101 Reche Caldwell	.40	.15
❏ 102 Kevan Barlow	.60	.25
❏ 103 Deuce McAllister	1.00	.40
❏ 104 Koren Robinson	.40	.15
❏ 105 Todd Heap	.60	.25
❏ 106 Jabar Gaffney	.60	.25
❏ 107 Randy McMichael	.60	.25
❏ 108 Dwight Freeney	.60	.25
❏ 109 Antwaan Randle El	1.00	.40
❏ 110 David Carr	1.50	.60
❏ 111 Carson Palmer RC	6.00	2.50
❏ 112 Dahrran Diedrick RC	1.50	.60
❏ 113 Kyle Boller RC	3.00	1.25
❏ 114 Terrell Suggs RC	2.50	1.00
❏ 115 Rien Long RC	.75	.30
❏ 116 Justin Gage RC	1.50	.60
❏ 117 William Joseph RC	1.50	.60
❏ 118 Chris Simms RC	2.50	1.00
❏ 119 Avon Cobourne RC	.75	.30
❏ 120 Victor Hobson RC	1.50	.60
❏ 121 Jason Gesser RC	1.50	.60
❏ 122 Ronald Bellamy RC	1.25	.50
❏ 123 Terence Newman RC	3.00	1.25
❏ 124 Terrence Edwards RC	1.25	.50
❏ 125 Sultan McCullough RC	1.25	.50
❏ 126 Kareem Kelly RC	1.25	.50
❏ 127 Jason Witten RC	2.00	.75
❏ 128 Mike Doss RC	1.50	.60
❏ 129 Seneca Wallace RC	1.50	.60
❏ 130 Chris Brown RC	2.00	.75
❏ 131 Larry Johnson RC	6.00	3.00
❏ 132 Taylor Jacobs RC	1.25	.50
❏ 133 Jerome McDougle RC	1.50	.60
❏ 134 Kelley Washington RC	1.50	.60
❏ 135 Brad Banks RC	1.25	.50
❏ 136 DeWayne White RC	1.25	.50
❏ 137 LaBrandon Toefield RC	1.50	.60
❏ 138 Brian St.Pierre RC	1.50	.60
❏ 139 Kindal Moorehead RC	1.25	.50
❏ 140 Willis McGahee RC	4.00	1.50
❏ 141 Jimmy Kennedy RC	1.50	.60
❏ 142 Talman Gardner RC	1.50	.60
❏ 143 Chris Kelsay RC	1.50	.60
❏ 144 Cory Redding RC	1.25	.50
❏ 145 Dave Ragone RC	1.50	.60
❏ 146 Earnest Graham RC	1.25	.50
❏ 147 Andre Johnson RC	3.00	1.25
❏ 148 Boss Bailey RC	1.50	.60
❏ 149 Sam Aiken RC	1.25	.50
❏ 150 Byron Leftwich RC	5.00	2.00
❏ 151 Teyo Johnson RC	1.50	.60
❏ 152 Quentin Griffin RC	1.50	.60
❏ 153 Justin Fargas RC	1.50	.60
❏ 154 Bradie James RC	1.50	.60
❏ 155 Andre Woolfolk RC	1.50	.60
❏ 156 Marcus Trufant RC	1.50	.60
❏ 157 Ken Dorsey RC	1.50	.60
❏ 158 Onterrio Smith RC	1.50	.60
❏ 159 Bryant Johnson RC	1.50	.60
❏ 160 Charles Rogers RC	1.50	.60
❏ 161 Kliff Kingsbury RC	1.25	.50
❏ 162 Michael Haynes RC	1.50	.60
❏ 163 Bennie Joppru RC	1.50	.60
❏ 164 Brandon Lloyd RC	2.00	.75
❏ 165 Jarret Johnson RC	1.25	.50

2004 Topps Draft Picks and Prospects

❏ COMPLETE SET (165)	80.00	40.00
❏ 1 Steve McNair	1.00	.40
❏ 2 Stephen Davis	.60	.25
❏ 3 Chris Chambers	.60	.25
❏ 4 Curtis Martin	1.00	.40
❏ 5 Shaun Alexander	1.00	.40
❏ 6 Jon Kitna	.60	.25
❏ 7 Jimmy Smith	.60	.25
❏ 8 Travis Henry	.60	.25
❏ 9 Torry Holt	1.00	.40
❏ 10 Jamal Lewis	1.00	.40
❏ 11 Clinton Portis	1.00	.40
❏ 12 Aaron Brooks	.60	.25
❏ 13 Plaxico Burress	.60	.25
❏ 14 Trent Green	.60	.25
❏ 15 Chad Johnson	1.00	.40
❏ 16 Jake Delhomme	1.00	.40
❏ 17 David Boston	.60	.25
❏ 18 Joe Horn	.60	.25
❏ 19 Ahman Green	1.00	.40
❏ 20 Fred Taylor	.60	.25
❏ 21 Terrell Owens	1.00	.40
❏ 22 Brad Johnson	.60	.25
❏ 23 Laveranues Coles	.60	.25
❏ 24 Ricky Williams	1.00	.40
❏ 25 Peyton Manning	1.50	.60
❏ 26 Hines Ward	1.00	.40
❏ 27 Matt Hasselbeck	.60	.25
❏ 28 Marshall Faulk	1.00	.40
❏ 29 Tony Gonzalez	.60	.25
❏ 30 Marvin Harrison	1.00	.40
❏ 31 Eric Moulds	.60	.25
❏ 32 Chad Pennington	1.00	.40
❏ 33 Jerry Porter	.60	.25
❏ 34 Jeff Garcia	1.00	.40
❏ 35 Derrick Mason	.60	.25
❏ 36 Anthony Thomas	.60	.25
❏ 37 Drew Bledsoe	1.00	.40
❏ 38 Jake Plummer	.60	.25
❏ 39 Tiki Barber	1.00	.40
❏ 40 Brett Favre	2.50	1.00
❏ 41 Joey Harrington	1.00	.40
❏ 42 Daunte Culpepper	1.00	.40
❏ 43 LaVar Arrington	2.00	.75
❏ 44 Santana Moss	.60	.25
❏ 45 David Carr	1.00	.40
❏ 46 Randy Moss	1.25	.50
❏ 47 LaDainian Tomlinson	1.25	.50
❏ 48 Deuce McAllister	1.00	.40
❏ 49 Amani Toomer	.60	.25
❏ 50 Donovan McNabb	1.25	.50
❏ 51 Priest Holmes	1.25	.50
❏ 52 Corey Dillon	.60	.25
❏ 53 Tom Brady	2.50	1.00
❏ 54 Edgerrin James	1.00	.40
❏ 55 Michael Vick	2.00	.75
❏ 56 Anquan Boldin	1.00	.40
❏ 57 Robert Ferguson	.40	.15
❏ 58 Onterrio Smith	.60	.25
❏ 59 Marques Tuiasosopo	.60	.25
❏ 60 Rudi Johnson	.60	.25
❏ 61 Alge Crumpler	.60	.25
❏ 62 Antonio Bryant	.60	.25
❏ 63 LaMont Jordan	1.00	.40
❏ 64 Lamar Gordon	.40	.15
❏ 65 Tim Rattay	.40	.15
❏ 66 Antwaan Randle El	1.00	.40
❏ 67 Ladell Betts	.40	.15
❏ 68 LaBrandon Toefield	.40	.15
❏ 69 Ashley Lelie	.60	.25
❏ 70 Marc Bulger	1.00	.40
❏ 71 Reggie Wayne	.60	.25
❏ 72 William Green	.60	.25
❏ 73 Josh Reed	.40	.15
❏ 74 T.J. Duckett	.60	.25
❏ 75 Andre Johnson	1.00	.40
❏ 76 Deion Branch	1.00	.40
❏ 77 Tyrone Calico	.60	.25
❏ 78 Jeremy Shockey	1.00	.40
❏ 79 Najeh Davenport	.40	.15
❏ 80 Byron Leftwich	1.25	.50
❏ 81 Correll Buckhalter	.60	.25
❏ 82 Justin McCareins	.40	.15
❏ 83 Carson Palmer	1.25	.50
❏ 84 Bryant Johnson	.40	.15
❏ 85 Patrick Ramsey	.60	.25
❏ 86 Justin Fargas	.60	.25
❏ 87 Dallas Clark	.60	.25
❏ 88 Kelly Campbell	.40	.15
❏ 89 DeShaun Foster	.60	.25
❏ 90 Charles Rogers	.60	.25
❏ 91 Donte' Stallworth	.60	.25
❏ 92 Dante Hall	1.00	.40
❏ 93 Randy McMichael	.40	.15
❏ 94 Marcel Shipp	.60	.25
❏ 95 Kyle Boller	1.00	.40
❏ 96 Steve Smith	1.00	.40
❏ 97 Brian Westbrook	.60	.25
❏ 98 Kevan Barlow	.60	.25
❏ 99 Damerien McCants	.40	.15
❏ 100 Domanick Davis	1.00	.40
❏ 101 Andre' Davis	.40	.15
❏ 102 Nate Burleson	1.00	.40
❏ 103 Larry Johnson	1.25	.50
❏ 104 Drew Brees	1.00	.40
❏ 105 Koren Robinson	.60	.25
❏ 106 Quincy Carter	.60	.25
❏ 107 Javon Walker	.60	.25
❏ 108 Willis McGahee	1.00	.40
❏ 109 Chris Simms	.60	.25
❏ 110 Rex Grossman	1.00	.40
❏ 111 Steven Jackson RC	6.00	2.50
❏ 112 Greg Jones RC	2.00	.75
❏ 113 Brandon Everage RC	1.50	.60
❏ 114 DeAngelo Hall RC	2.50	1.00
❏ 115 Tatum Bell RC	4.00	1.50
❏ 116 B.J. Symons RC	2.00	.75
❏ 117 Michael Clayton RC	4.00	1.50
❏ 118 Jared Lorenzen RC	1.50	.60
❏ 119 Josh Harris RC	2.00	.75
❏ 120 Roy Williams RC	5.00	2.00
❏ 121 Mewelde Moore RC	2.50	1.00
❏ 122 Jeff Smoker RC	2.00	.75
❏ 123 Lee Evans RC	2.50	1.00
❏ 124 Michael Jenkins RC	2.00	.75
❏ 125 Drew Henson RC	2.00	.75
❏ 126 Ben Watson RC	2.00	.75
❏ 127 Jerricho Cotchery RC	2.00	.75
❏ 128 Ben Troupe RC	2.00	.75
❏ 129 Chris Gamble RC	2.50	1.00
❏ 130 Kevin Jones RC	6.00	2.50
❏ 131 Cody Pickett RC	2.00	.75
❏ 132 J.P. Losman RC	4.00	1.50
❏ 133 Michael Boulware RC	2.00	.75
❏ 134 Julius Jones RC	8.00	3.00
❏ 135 Keary Colbert RC	2.50	1.00
❏ 136 Vince Wilfork RC	2.50	1.00
❏ 137 Ernest Wilford RC	2.00	.75
❏ 138 John Navarre RC	2.00	.75
❏ 139 D.J. Williams RC	2.50	1.00
❏ 140 Larry Fitzgerald RC	6.00	2.50
❏ 141 Quincy Wilson RC	1.50	.60
❏ 142 James Newson RC	1.50	.60
❏ 143 Reggie Williams RC	2.50	1.00
❏ 144 Devard Darling RC	2.00	.75
❏ 145 Chris Perry RC	3.00	1.25
❏ 146 Derrick Strait RC	2.00	.75
❏ 147 Teddy Lehman RC	2.00	.75

❑ 148 Michael Turner RC 2.00 .75
❑ 149 Will Smith RC 2.00 .75
❑ 150 Eli Manning RC 12.00 5.00
❑ 151 Cedric Cobbs RC 2.00 .75
❑ 152 Ell Roberson UER RC 2.00 .75
❑ 153 Matt Schaub RC 3.00 1.25
❑ 154 Derrick Knight RC 1.50 .60
❑ 155 Rashaun Woods RC 2.00 .75
❑ 156 Jonathan Vilma RC 2.00 .75
❑ 157 Tommie Harris RC 2.00 .75
❑ 158 Dwan Edwards RC 1.50 .60
❑ 159 Will Poole RC 2.00 .75
❑ 160 Mike Williams RC 20.00 7.50
❑ 161 Philip Rivers RC 6.00 2.50
❑ 162 Sean Taylor RC 2.50 1.00
❑ 163 Darius Watts RC 2.00 .75
❑ 164 Casey Clausen RC 2.00 .75
❑ 165 Ben Roethlisberger RC 20.00 10.00

2005 Topps Draft Picks and Prospects

❑ COMP.SET w/o AU's (165) 40.00 15.00
❑ COMP.SET w/o RC's (110) 25.00 10.00
❑ ONE ROOKIE PER PACK
❑ DRAFT PICK AUTO ODDS 1:1179H, 1:1182R
❑ UNPRICED GOLD SUPERFRACTORS #'d TO 1
❑ UNPRICED PRINTING PLATES #'d TO 1
❑ 1 Marvin Harrison 1.00 .40
❑ 2 Rudi Johnson .60 .25
❑ 3 Matt Hasselbeck .60 .25
❑ 4 Plaxico Burress .60 .25
❑ 5 Chad Pennington 1.00 .40
❑ 6 Jamal Lewis 1.00 .40
❑ 7 Terrell Owens 1.00 .40
❑ 8 LaDainian Tomlinson 1.25 .50
❑ 9 Tiki Barber 1.00 .40
❑ 10 Dante Hall .60 .25
❑ 11 Peyton Manning 1.50 .60
❑ 12 Marshall Faulk 1.00 .40
❑ 13 Donovan McNabb 1.25 .50
❑ 14 Randy Moss 1.00 .40
❑ 15 Muhsin Muhammad .60 .25
❑ 16 Deuce McAllister 1.00 .40
❑ 17 Fred Taylor .60 .25
❑ 18 Jake Plummer .60 .25
❑ 19 Javon Walker .60 .25
❑ 20 Tony Gonzalez .60 .25
❑ 21 Michael Vick 1.50 .60
❑ 22 Brett Favre 2.50 1.00
❑ 23 Joe Horn .60 .25
❑ 24 Jeremy Shockey 1.00 .40
❑ 25 Laveranues Coles .60 .25
❑ 26 Trent Green .60 .25
❑ 27 Alge Crumpler .60 .25
❑ 28 Curtis Martin 1.00 .40
❑ 29 Torry Holt 1.00 .40
❑ 30 Daunte Culpepper 1.00 .40
❑ 31 Aaron Brooks .60 .25
❑ 32 Priest Holmes 1.00 .40
❑ 33 Eric Moulds .60 .25
❑ 34 Jerome Bettis 1.00 .40
❑ 35 David Carr 1.00 .40
❑ 36 Chad Johnson 1.00 .40
❑ 37 Ahman Green 1.00 .40
❑ 38 Clinton Portis 1.00 .40
❑ 39 Drew Brees 1.00 .40
❑ 40 Darrell Jackson .60 .25
❑ 41 Corey Dillon .60 .25
❑ 42 Reggie Wayne .60 .25
❑ 43 Shaun Alexander 1.25 .50
❑ 44 Hines Ward 1.00 .40
❑ 45 Tom Brady 2.50 1.00
❑ 46 Isaac Bruce .60 .25
❑ 47 Byron Leftwich 1.00 .40
❑ 48 Chris Chambers .60 .25
❑ 49 Marc Bulger 1.00 .40
❑ 50 Edgerrin James 1.00 .40
❑ 51 Jake Delhomme 1.00 .40
❑ 52 Koren Robinson .60 .25
❑ 53 Brian Westbrook .60 .25
❑ 54 Reuben Droughns .60 .25
❑ 55 Joey Harrington 1.00 .40
❑ 56 Eli Manning 2.00 .75
❑ 57 Julius Jones 1.25 .50
❑ 58 Nick Goings .50 .20
❑ 59 T.J. Houshmandzadeh .50 .20
❑ 60 Ben Roethlisberger 2.50 1.00
❑ 61 Charles Rogers .60 .25
❑ 62 Billy Volek .60 .25
❑ 63 Drew Henson .60 .25
❑ 64 Andre Johnson .60 .25
❑ 65 Carson Palmer 1.00 .40
❑ 66 Anquan Boldin .60 .25
❑ 67 Lee Suggs .60 .25
❑ 68 Jerry Porter .60 .25
❑ 69 J.P. Losman 1.00 .40
❑ 70 Nate Burleson .60 .25
❑ 71 Lee Evans .60 .25
❑ 72 Tatum Bell .60 .25
❑ 73 Chester Taylor .60 .25
❑ 74 Philip Rivers 1.00 .40
❑ 75 Rex Grossman .60 .25
❑ 76 Willis McGahee 1.00 .40
❑ 77 Antonio Gates 1.00 .40
❑ 78 Steven Jackson 1.25 .50
❑ 79 Roy Williams WR 1.00 .40
❑ 80 Chris Simms .60 .25
❑ 81 Najeh Davenport .50 .20
❑ 82 Kevin Jones 1.00 .40
❑ 83 Jason Witten .60 .25
❑ 84 Brandon Lloyd .50 .20
❑ 85 Larry Johnson 1.00 .40
❑ 86 Ronald Curry .60 .25
❑ 87 Chris Brown .60 .25
❑ 88 Kyle Boller .60 .25
❑ 89 Chris Perry .60 .25
❑ 90 Keary Colbert .60 .25
❑ 91 Sean Taylor .60 .25
❑ 92 Greg Jones .50 .20
❑ 93 Larry Fitzgerald 1.00 .40
❑ 94 Michael Clayton 1.00 .40
❑ 95 Mewelde Moore .60 .25
❑ 96 Drew Bennett .60 .25
❑ 97 Reggie Williams .60 .25
❑ 98 Quentin Griffin .60 .25
❑ 99 Josh McCown .60 .25
❑ 100 Santana Moss .60 .25
❑ 101 Kellen Winslow 1.00 .40
❑ 102 Michael Jenkins .60 .25
❑ 103 Dunta Robinson .60 .25
❑ 104 Luke McCown .50 .20
❑ 105 Brandon Stokley .60 .25
❑ 106 Derrick Blaylock .50 .20
❑ 107 Ernest Wilford .50 .20
❑ 108 Domanick Davis .60 .25
❑ 109 Jonathan Vilma .60 .25
❑ 110 Dwight Freeney .60 .25
❑ 111 Alex Smith QB AU RC 200.00 100.00
❑ 112 Derrick Johnson AU RC 120.00 60.00
❑ 113 Charlie Frye AU RC 120.00 60.00
❑ 114 Ronnie Brown AU RC 175.00 90.00
❑ 115 Mike Williams AU 100.00 40.00
❑ 116 Erasmus James RC 2.00 .75
❑ 117 Alex Smith TE RC 2.00 .75
❑ 118 Dan Orlovsky RC 2.50 1.00
❑ 119 Eric Shelton RC 2.00 .75
❑ 120 Reggie Brown RC 2.00 .75
❑ 121 Carlos Rogers RC 2.50 1.00
❑ 122 Dan Cody RC 2.00 .75
❑ 123 J.J. Arrington RC 2.50 1.00
❑ 124 Travis Johnson RC 1.50 .60
❑ 125 Antrel Rolle RC 2.00 .75
❑ 126 Andrew Walter RC 3.00 1.25
❑ 127 Craphonso Thorpe RC 1.50 .60
❑ 128 Bryan Randall RC 1.50 .60
❑ 129 Anttaj Hawthorne RC 1.50 .60
❑ 130 David Pollack RC 2.00 .75
❑ 131 Heath Miller RC 5.00 2.00
❑ 132 Charles Frederick RC 1.50 .60
❑ 133 Anthony Davis RC 1.50 .60
❑ 134 Chris Rix RC 1.50 .60
❑ 135 T.A. McLendon RC 1.50 .60
❑ 136 David Greene RC 2.00 .75
❑ 137 Timmy Chang RC 1.50 .60
❑ 138 Marcus Spears RC 2.00 .75
❑ 139 Airese Currie RC 2.00 .75
❑ 140 Chris Henry RC 2.00 .75
❑ 141 Josh Davis RC 1.50 .60
❑ 142 Jason Campbell RC 3.00 1.25
❑ 143 Barrett Ruud RC 2.00 .75
❑ 144 Courtney Roby RC 2.00 .75
❑ 145 Mike Patterson RC 2.00 .75
❑ 146 Jason White RC 2.00 .75
❑ 147 Fred Gibson RC 1.50 .60
❑ 148 Marion Barber RC 3.00 1.25
❑ 149 Braylon Edwards RC 6.00 2.50
❑ 150 Carnell Williams RC 10.00 4.00
❑ 151 Kyle Orton RC 3.00 1.25
❑ 152 Aaron Rodgers RC 6.00 2.50
❑ 153 Alvin Pearman RC 2.00 .75
❑ 154 Stefan LeFors RC 2.00 .75
❑ 155 Marlin Jackson RC 2.00 .75
❑ 156 Taylor Stubblefield RC 1.50 .60
❑ 157 Ciatrick Fason RC 2.00 .75
❑ 158 Kay-Jay Harris RC 1.50 .60
❑ 159 Frank Gore RC 3.00 1.25
❑ 160 Vernand Morency RC 2.00 .75
❑ 161 Adam Jones RC 2.00 .75
❑ 162 Troy Williamson RC 4.00 1.50
❑ 163 Roddy White RC 2.00 .75
❑ 164 Thomas Davis RC 2.00 .75
❑ 165 Mark Clayton RC 2.50 1.00
❑ 166 Craig Bragg RC 1.50 .60
❑ 167 Noah Herron RC 2.00 .75
❑ 168 Darren Sproles RC 2.00 .75
❑ 169 Terrence Murphy RC 2.00 .75
❑ 170 Walter Reyes RC 1.50 .60

2004 Topps Fan Favorites

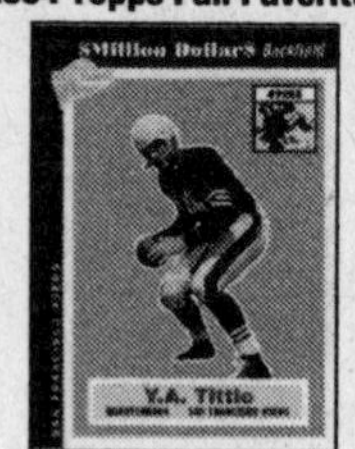

❑ COMPLETE SET (85) 40.00 15.00
❑ 1 Alan Page 1.25 .50
❑ 2 Abdul Salaam 1.00 .40
❑ 3 Bob Baumhower 1.00 .40
❑ 4 Bob Brudzinski 1.00 .40
❑ 5 Billy Johnson 1.00 .40
❑ 6 Cliff Branch 1.25 .50
❑ 7 Carl Banks 1.00 .40
❑ 8 Charles Bowser 1.00 .40
❑ 9 Clint Didier 1.00 .40
❑ 10 Carl Eller 1.00 .40
❑ 11 Charlie Joiner 1.00 .40
❑ 12 Dick Anderson 1.00 .40
❑ 13 Doug Betters 1.00 .40
❑ 14 Dave Casper 1.00 .40
❑ 15 Dwight Clark 1.25 .50
❑ 16 Dan Fouts 1.50 .60
❑ 17 Dave Foley 1.00 .40
❑ 18 Donnie Green 1.00 .40
❑ 19 Deacon Jones 1.25 .50
❑ 20 Don Maynard 1.25 .50
❑ 21 Dan Pastorini 1.00 .40
❑ 22 Drew Pearson 1.25 .50
❑ 23 Dwight White 1.00 .40
❑ 24 Emerson Boozer 1.00 .40

❑ 25	Earl Campbell	1.50	.60
❑ 26	Ernie Holmes	1.25	.50
❑ 27	Fred Biletnikoff	1.50	.60
❑ 28	Glenn Blackwood	1.00	.40
❑ 29	Gary Larsen	1.00	.40
❑ 30	Greg Lloyd	1.25	.50
❑ 31	George Martin	1.00	.40
❑ 32	Gene Upshaw	1.00	.40
❑ 33	Harry Carson	1.00	.40
❑ 34	Harold Jackson	1.00	.40
❑ 35	Hugh McElhenny	1.00	.40
❑ 36	Jeff Bostic	1.00	.40
❑ 37	Jim Burt	1.00	.40
❑ 38	Joe Greene	1.50	.60
❑ 39	John Hannah	1.00	.40
❑ 40	John Henry Johnson	1.00	.40
❑ 41	Joe Jacoby	1.00	.40
❑ 42	Jim Kiick	1.00	.40
❑ 43	Joe Klecko	1.00	.40
❑ 44	Joe Delamielleure	1.00	.40
❑ 45	Joe Montana	5.00	2.00
❑ 46	Jim Marshall	1.00	.40
❑ 47	Joe Namath	3.00	1.25
❑ 48	Jake Scott	1.00	.40
❑ 49	John Taylor	1.00	.40
❑ 50	Kim Bokamper	1.00	.40
❑ 51	Kevin Greene	1.25	.50
❑ 52	Karl Mecklenburg	1.00	.40
❑ 53	Ken Stabler	2.50	1.00
❑ 54	Kellen Winslow	1.25	.50
❑ 55	Lyle Blackwood	1.00	.40
❑ 56	Larry Csonka	1.50	.60
❑ 57	L.C. Greenwood	1.25	.50
❑ 58	Lamar Lundy	1.00	.40
❑ 59	Leonard Marshall	1.00	.40
❑ 60	Lawrence Taylor	1.50	.60
❑ 61	Mark Clayton	1.00	.40
❑ 62	Mark Duper	1.00	.40
❑ 63	Manny Fernandez	1.00	.40
❑ 64	Mark Gastineau	1.00	.40
❑ 65	Marty Lyons	1.00	.40
❑ 66	Mark May	1.00	.40
❑ 67	Mike Montler	1.00	.40
❑ 68	Merlin Olsen	1.25	.50
❑ 69	Matt Snell	1.00	.40
❑ 70	Ozzie Newsome	1.25	.50
❑ 71	Otis Sistrunk	1.00	.40
❑ 72	Phil Villapiano UER	1.00	.40
❑ 73	Roger Craig	1.25	.50
❑ 74	Richard Dent	1.00	.40
❑ 75	Randy Gradishar	1.00	.40
❑ 76	Russ Grimm	1.00	.40
❑ 77	Reggie McKenzie	1.00	.40
❑ 78	Roosevelt Grier	1.00	.40
❑ 79	Roger Staubach	3.00	1.25
❑ 80	Steve Grogan	1.00	.40
❑ 81	Stanley Morgan	1.00	.40
❑ 82	Tony Dorsett	1.50	.60
❑ 83	Ted Hendricks	1.00	.40
❑ 84	Tony Hill	1.00	.40
❑ 85	Y.A. Tittle	1.50	.60

1997 Topps Gallery

❑	COMPLETE SET (135)	30.00	12.50
❑ 1	Orlando Pace RC	.60	.25
❑ 2	Darrell Russell RC	.30	.10
❑ 3	Shawn Springs RC	.50	.20
❑ 4	Peter Boulware RC	.60	.25
❑ 5	Bryant Westbrook RC	.30	.10
❑ 6	Walter Jones RC	.60	.25
❑ 7	Ike Hilliard RC	2.00	.75
❑ 8	James Farrior RC	.60	.25
❑ 9	Tom Knight RC	.30	.10
❑ 10	Warrick Dunn RC	4.00	1.50
❑ 11	Tony Gonzalez RC	5.00	2.00
❑ 12	Reinard Wilson RC	.50	.20
❑ 13	Yatil Green RC	.50	.20
❑ 14	Reidel Anthony RC	.60	.25
❑ 15	Kenny Holmes RC	.60	.25
❑ 16	Dwayne Rudd RC	.60	.25
❑ 17	Renaldo Wynn RC	.30	.10
❑ 18	David LaFleur RC	1.00	.40
❑ 19	Antowain Smith RC	4.00	1.50
❑ 20	Jim Druckenmiller RC	.50	.20
❑ 21	Rae Carruth RC	.30	.10
❑ 22	Byron Hanspard RC	.50	.20
❑ 23	Jake Plummer RC	8.00	3.00
❑ 24	Corey Dillon RC	10.00	4.00
❑ 25	Darnell Autry RC	.50	.20
❑ 26	Kevin Lockett RC	.50	.20
❑ 27	Troy Davis RC	.50	.20
❑ 28	Mike Alstott	.60	.25
❑ 29	Napoleon Kaufman	.60	.25
❑ 30	Terrell Davis	.75	.30
❑ 31	Byron Bam Morris	.30	.10
❑ 32	Dana Stubblefield	.30	.10
❑ 33	Ki-Jana Carter	.30	.10
❑ 34	Hugh Douglas	.30	.10
❑ 35	Natrone Means	.50	.20
❑ 36	Marshall Faulk	.75	.30
❑ 37	Tyrone Wheatley	.50	.20
❑ 38	Tony Banks	.50	.20
❑ 39	Marvin Harrison	.60	.25
❑ 40	Eddie George	.60	.25
❑ 41	Eddie Kennison	.50	.20
❑ 42	Ray Mickens	.30	.10
❑ 43	Mike Mamula	.30	.10
❑ 44	Tamarick Vanover	.50	.20
❑ 45	Rashaan Salaam	.30	.10
❑ 46	Trent Dilfer	.60	.25
❑ 47	John Mobley	.30	.10
❑ 48	Gus Frerotte	.30	.10
❑ 49	Isaac Bruce	.60	.25
❑ 50	Mark Brunell	.75	.30
❑ 51	Jamal Anderson	.60	.25
❑ 52	Keyshawn Johnson	.60	.25
❑ 53	Curtis Conway	.50	.20
❑ 54	Zach Thomas	.60	.25
❑ 55	Simeon Rice	.50	.20
❑ 56	Lawrence Phillips	.30	.10
❑ 57	Ty Detmer	.50	.20
❑ 58	Bobby Engram	.50	.20
❑ 59	Joey Galloway	.50	.20
❑ 60	Curtis Martin	.75	.30
❑ 61	Kevin Hardy	.30	.10
❑ 62	Eric Moulds	.60	.25
❑ 63	Michael Westbrook	.50	.20
❑ 64	Robert Smith	.50	.20
❑ 65	Karim Abdul-Jabbar	.60	.25
❑ 66	Errict Rhett	.30	.10
❑ 67	Ray Lewis	1.00	.40
❑ 68	Terry Glenn	.60	.25
❑ 69	Leeland McElroy	.30	.10
❑ 70	Kerry Collins	.60	.25
❑ 71	Steve McNair	.75	.30
❑ 72	Kordell Stewart	.60	.25
❑ 73	Terry Allen	.60	.25
❑ 74	Michael Irvin	.60	.25
❑ 75	John Elway	2.50	1.00
❑ 76	Lamar Lathon	.30	.10
❑ 77	Rob Moore	.50	.20
❑ 78	Irving Fryar	.50	.20
❑ 79	Jim Everett	.30	.10
❑ 80	Steve Young	.75	.30
❑ 81	Bryan Cox	.30	.10
❑ 82	Dale Carter	.30	.10
❑ 83	Chris Warren	.50	.20
❑ 84	Shannon Sharpe	.50	.20
❑ 85	Reggie White	.60	.25
❑ 86	Deion Sanders	.60	.25
❑ 87	Hardy Nickerson	.30	.10
❑ 88	Edgar Bennett	.50	.20
❑ 89	Kent Graham	.30	.10
❑ 90	Dan Marino	2.50	1.00
❑ 91	Kevin Greene	.50	.20
❑ 92	Derrick Thomas	.60	.25
❑ 93	Carl Pickens	.50	.20
❑ 94	Neil O'Donnell	.50	.20
❑ 95	Drew Bledsoe	.75	.30
❑ 96	Michael Haynes	.30	.10
❑ 97	Tony Martin	.50	.20
❑ 98	Scott Mitchell	.50	.20
❑ 99	Rodney Hampton	.50	.20
❑ 100	Brett Favre	2.50	1.00
❑ 101	Darrell Green	.50	.20
❑ 102	Rod Woodson	.50	.20
❑ 103	Chris Spielman	.30	.10
❑ 104	Jake Reed	.50	.20
❑ 105	Jerry Rice	1.25	.50
❑ 106	Jeff Hostetler	.30	.10
❑ 107	Anthony Johnson	.30	.10
❑ 108	Keenan McCardell	.50	.20
❑ 109	Ben Coates	.50	.20
❑ 110	Emmitt Smith	2.00	.75
❑ 111	LeRoy Butler	.30	.10
❑ 112	Steve Atwater	.30	.10
❑ 113	Ricky Watters	.50	.20
❑ 114	Jim Harbaugh	.50	.20
❑ 115	Marcus Allen	.60	.25
❑ 116	Levon Kirkland	.30	.10
❑ 117	Jessie Tuggle	.30	.10
❑ 118	Ken Norton	.30	.10
❑ 119	Thurman Thomas	.60	.25
❑ 120	Junior Seau	.60	.25
❑ 121	Tim Brown	.60	.25
❑ 122	Michael Jackson	.50	.20
❑ 123	Eric Metcalf	.50	.20
❑ 124	Herman Moore	.50	.20
❑ 125	Bruce Smith	.50	.20
❑ 126	Cris Carter	.60	.25
❑ 127	Dave Brown	.30	.10
❑ 128	Jeff Blake	.50	.20
❑ 129	Robert Blackmon	.30	.10
❑ 130	Barry Sanders	2.00	.75
❑ 131	Blaine Bishop	.30	.10
❑ 132	Jerome Bettis	.60	.25
❑ 133	Stan Humphries	.50	.20
❑ 134	Vinny Testaverde	.50	.20
❑ 135	Troy Aikman	1.25	.50
❑ P54	Zach Thomas Promo	1.00	.40

2000 Topps Gallery

❑	COMPLETE SET (175)	50.00	20.00
❑	COMP.SET w/o SP's (125)	20.00	7.50
❑	UNPRICED PRESS PLATES EXIST		
❑ 1	Marshall Faulk	1.00	.40
❑ 2	Kordell Stewart	.50	.20
❑ 3	Priest Holmes	1.00	.40
❑ 4	James Johnson	.30	.10
❑ 5	Charlie Garner	.50	.20
❑ 6	Jeff Blake	.50	.20
❑ 7	Joey Galloway	.50	.20
❑ 8	Terrell Davis	.75	.30
❑ 9	Jerome Bettis	.75	.30
❑ 10	Bobby Engram	.50	.20
❑ 11	Muhsin Muhammad	.50	.20
❑ 12	Marcus Robinson	.75	.30
❑ 13	Kerry Collins	.50	.20
❑ 14	Jake Plummer	.50	.20
❑ 15	J.J. Stokes	.50	.20
❑ 16	Tim Couch	.50	.20
❑ 17	Napoleon Kaufman	.50	.20
❑ 18	Az-Zahir Hakim	.50	.20
❑ 19	Jimmy Smith	.50	.20

❑	20	Eddie George	.75	.30
❑	21	Jacquez Green	.30	.10
❑	22	Champ Bailey	.50	.20
❑	23	Wesley Walls	.30	.10
❑	24	Eric Moulds	.75	.30
❑	25	Corey Dillon	.75	.30
❑	26	Freddie Jones	.30	.10
❑	27	Jevon Kearse	.75	.30
❑	28	Ray Lucas	.50	.20
❑	29	Germane Crowell	.30	.10
❑	30	Randy Moss	1.50	.60
❑	31	Patrick Jeffers	.75	.30
❑	32	Zach Thomas	.75	.30
❑	33	Shannon Sharpe	.50	.20
❑	34	Derrick Mayes	.50	.20
❑	35	Antonio Freeman	.75	.30
❑	36	Terance Mathis	.50	.20
❑	37	Herman Moore	.50	.20
❑	38	Tony Banks	.50	.20
❑	39	Jerry Rice	1.50	.60
❑	40	Troy Aikman	1.50	.60
❑	41	Rickey Dudley	.30	.10
❑	42	Troy Edwards	.30	.10
❑	43	Curtis Martin	.75	.30
❑	44	Eddie Kennison	.50	.20
❑	45	Mark Brunell	.75	.30
❑	46	Shaun King	.30	.10
❑	47	Duce Staley	.75	.30
❑	48	Darnay Scott	.50	.20
❑	49	Sean Dawkins	.30	.10
❑	50	Edgerrin James	1.25	.50
❑	51	Olandis Gary	.75	.30
❑	52	Peerless Price	.50	.20
❑	53	Akili Smith	.30	.10
❑	54	Charlie Batch	.75	.30
❑	55	Tim Biakabutuka	.50	.20
❑	56	Rob Moore	.50	.20
❑	57	Keenan McCardell	.50	.20
❑	58	Dan Marino	2.50	1.00
❑	59	Tony Gonzalez	.50	.20
❑	60	Stephen Davis	.75	.30
❑	61	Ricky Watters	.50	.20
❑	62	Frank Wycheck	.30	.10
❑	63	Kevin Johnson	.75	.30
❑	64	Isaac Bruce	.75	.30
❑	65	Andre Reed	.50	.20
❑	66	Jamal Anderson	.75	.30
❑	67	Dorsey Levens	.50	.20
❑	68	Rocket Ismail	.50	.20
❑	69	Albert Connell	.30	.10
❑	70	Brett Favre	2.50	1.00
❑	71	Wayne Chrebet	.50	.20
❑	72	Jon Kitna	.75	.30
❑	73	Brian Griese	.75	.30
❑	74	Rob Johnson	.50	.20
❑	75	Qadry Ismail	.50	.20
❑	76	Derrick Alexander	.50	.20
❑	77	Tim Dwight	.75	.30
❑	78	Ike Hilliard	.50	.20
❑	79	Frank Sanders	.50	.20
❑	80	Fred Taylor	.75	.30
❑	81	Robert Smith	.75	.30
❑	82	Vinny Testaverde	.50	.20
❑	83	Steve Young	1.00	.40
❑	84	Tyrone Wheatley	.50	.20
❑	85	Mikhael Ricks	.30	.10
❑	86	Tony Martin	.50	.20
❑	87	Carl Pickens	.50	.20
❑	88	Warrick Dunn	.75	.30
❑	89	Emmitt Smith	1.50	.60
❑	90	Keyshawn Johnson	.75	.30
❑	91	James Stewart	.50	.20
❑	92	Doug Flutie	.75	.30
❑	93	Torry Holt	.75	.30
❑	94	Jeff Graham	.30	.10
❑	95	Steve McNair	.75	.30
❑	96	Errict Rhett	.50	.20
❑	97	Terrell Owens	.75	.30
❑	98	Terry Glenn	.50	.20
❑	99	Steve Beuerlein	.50	.20
❑	100	Kurt Warner	1.50	.60
❑	101	Jeff George	.50	.20
❑	102	Deion Sanders	.75	.30
❑	103	Johnnie Morton	.50	.20
❑	104	Antowain Smith	.50	.20
❑	105	O.J. McDuffie	.50	.20
❑	106	Rod Smith	.50	.20
❑	107	Jim Harbaugh	.50	.20
❑	108	Marvin Harrison	.75	.30
❑	109	Curtis Enis	.30	.10
❑	110	Drew Bledsoe	1.00	.40
❑	111	Mike Alstott	.75	.30
❑	112	Amani Toomer	.50	.20
❑	113	Elvis Grbac	.50	.20
❑	114	Tim Brown	.75	.30
❑	115	Cris Carter	.75	.30
❑	116	Donovan McNabb	1.25	.50
❑	117	Chris Chandler	.50	.20
❑	118	Kevin Dyson	.50	.20
❑	119	Rich Gannon	.75	.30
❑	120	Ricky Williams	.75	.30
❑	121	Brad Johnson	.75	.30
❑	122	Cade McNown	.30	.10
❑	123	Ed McCaffrey	.75	.30
❑	124	Michael Westbrook	.50	.20
❑	125	Peyton Manning	2.00	.75
❑	126	Brett Favre MAS	4.00	1.50
❑	127	Emmitt Smith MAS	2.50	1.00
❑	128	Tim Brown MAS	1.00	.40
❑	129	Troy Aikman MAS	2.50	1.00
❑	130	Jimmy Smith MAS	.75	.30
❑	131	Dan Marino MAS	4.00	1.50
❑	132	Cris Carter MAS	1.00	.40
❑	133	Jerry Rice MAS	2.50	1.00
❑	134	Steve Young MAS	1.50	.60
❑	135	Marshall Faulk MAS	1.50	.60
❑	136	Eddie George MAS	1.00	.40
❑	137	Drew Bledsoe MAS	1.50	.60
❑	138	Randy Moss ART	2.50	1.00
❑	139	Germane Crowell ART	.75	.30
❑	140	Akili Smith ART	.75	.30
❑	141	Tim Couch ART	.75	.30
❑	142	Marcus Robinson ART	1.00	.40
❑	143	Daunte Culpepper ART	1.50	.60
❑	144	Jevon Kearse ART	1.00	.40
❑	145	Edgerrin James ART	2.00	.75
❑	146	Tony Gonzalez ART	.75	.30
❑	147	Cade McNown ART	.75	.30
❑	148	Fred Taylor ART	1.00	.40
❑	149	Donovan McNabb ART	2.00	.75
❑	150	Ricky Williams ART	1.00	.40
❑	151	Jamal Lewis RC	5.00	2.00
❑	152	Tee Martin RC	2.00	.75
❑	153	Plaxico Burress RC	4.00	1.50
❑	154	Chad Pennington RC	5.00	2.00
❑	155	Curtis Keaton RC	1.50	.60
❑	156	Thomas Jones RC	3.00	1.25
❑	157	Courtney Brown RC	1.00	.40
❑	158	Ron Dayne RC	2.00	.75
❑	159	Shaun Alexander RC	10.00	4.00
❑	160	Travis Taylor RC	1.00	.40
❑	161	Sylvester Morris RC	1.50	.60
❑	162	Giovanni Carmazzi RC	1.50	.60
❑	163	Laveranues Coles RC	2.50	1.00
❑	164	Chris Redman RC	1.50	.60
❑	165	Bubba Franks RC	2.00	.75
❑	166	R.Jay Soward RC	1.50	.60
❑	167	Reuben Droughns RC	2.50	1.00
❑	168	Todd Pinkston RC	2.00	.75
❑	169	Trung Canidate RC	1.50	.60
❑	170	Danny Farmer RC	1.50	.60
❑	171	Ron Dugans RC	1.50	.60
❑	172	Dennis Northcutt RC	2.00	.75
❑	173	J.R. Redmond RC	1.50	.60
❑	174	Travis Prentice RC	1.50	.60
❑	175	Peter Warrick RC	2.00	.75

2001 Topps Gallery

❑		COMP.SET w/o SP's (100)	25.00	10.00
❑	1	Donovan McNabb	1.00	.40
❑	2	Jamal Anderson	.75	.30
❑	3	Steve McNair	.75	.30
❑	4	Peyton Manning	2.00	.75
❑	5	Curtis Martin	.75	.30
❑	6	Joey Galloway	.50	.20
❑	7	Daunte Culpepper	.75	.30
❑	8	Corey Dillon	.75	.30
❑	9	Brad Johnson	.75	.30
❑	10	Doug Flutie	.75	.30
❑	11	Jerome Bettis	.75	.30
❑	12	Elvis Grbac	.50	.20
❑	13	Aaron Brooks	.75	.30
❑	14	Ray Lewis	.75	.30
❑	15	Tim Dwight	.75	.30
❑	16	Robert Smith	.30	.10
❑	17	Jake Plummer	.50	.20
❑	18	Jay Fiedler	.75	.30
❑	19	Fred Taylor	.75	.30
❑	20	Jerry Rice	1.50	.60
❑	21	Shaun King	.30	.10
❑	22	Cade McNown	.30	.10
❑	23	Drew Bledsoe	1.00	.40
❑	24	Ricky Watters	.50	.20
❑	25	Muhsin Muhammad	.50	.20
❑	26	Shawn Jefferson	.30	.10
❑	27	Tiki Barber	.75	.30
❑	28	Derrick Alexander	.50	.20
❑	29	Stephen Davis	.75	.30
❑	30	James Stewart	.50	.20
❑	31	Terrell Owens	.75	.30
❑	32	Ed McCaffrey	.75	.30
❑	33	Jeff Graham	.30	.10
❑	34	Jamal Lewis	1.25	.50
❑	35	Edgerrin James	1.00	.40
❑	36	Tim Couch	.50	.20
❑	37	Marshall Faulk	1.00	.40
❑	38	Ike Hilliard	.50	.20
❑	39	Ahman Green	.75	.30
❑	40	Tim Biakabutuka	.50	.20
❑	41	Akili Smith	.30	.10
❑	42	David Boston	.75	.30
❑	43	Eddie George	.75	.30
❑	44	Hines Ward	.75	.30
❑	45	Chad Lewis	.30	.10
❑	46	Brian Urlacher	1.25	.50
❑	47	Eric Moulds	.50	.20
❑	48	Ricky Williams	.75	.30
❑	49	Warrick Dunn	.75	.30
❑	50	Kerry Collins	.50	.20
❑	51	Isaac Bruce	.75	.30
❑	52	Jimmy Smith	.50	.20
❑	53	Emmitt Smith	1.50	.60
❑	54	Cris Carter	.75	.30
❑	55	Jeff Garcia	.75	.30
❑	56	Mike Anderson	.75	.30
❑	57	Lamar Smith	.50	.20
❑	58	Brett Favre	2.50	1.00
❑	59	Steve Beuerlein	.50	.20
❑	60	Terry Glenn	.30	.10
❑	61	Tyrone Wheatley	.50	.20
❑	62	Charlie Batch	.75	.30
❑	63	Chris Chandler	.50	.20
❑	64	Sylvester Morris	.30	.10
❑	65	Joe Horn	.50	.20
❑	66	Kevin Johnson	.50	.20
❑	67	Rob Johnson	.50	.20
❑	68	Jeff George	.50	.20
❑	69	Keyshawn Johnson	.75	.30
❑	70	Wayne Chrebet	.50	.20
❑	71	Randy Moss	1.50	.60
❑	72	Marvin Harrison	.75	.30
❑	73	Peter Warrick	.75	.30
❑	74	Darrell Jackson	.75	.30
❑	75	Derrick Mason	.50	.20
❑	76	Oronde Gadsden	.50	.20
❑	77	Charles Johnson	.30	.10
❑	78	James Allen	.50	.20
❑	79	Torry Holt	.75	.30
❑	80	Troy Brown	.50	.20
❑	81	Amani Toomer	.50	.20
❑	82	Junior Seau	.75	.30
❑	83	Troy Aikman	1.25	.50
❑	84	Mark Brunell	.75	.30
❑	85	Brian Griese	.75	.30

❑ 86	Charlie Garner	.50	.20
❑ 87	Rich Gannon	.75	.30
❑ 88	Jeff Blake	.50	.20
❑ 89	Donald Hayes	.30	.10
❑ 90	Germane Crowell	.30	.10
❑ 91	Tony Gonzalez	.50	.20
❑ 92	Jon Kitna	.75	.30
❑ 93	Vinny Testaverde	.50	.20
❑ 94	Kordell Stewart	.50	.20
❑ 95	Keenan McCardell	.30	.10
❑ 96	Kurt Warner	1.50	.60
❑ 97	Bill Schroeder	.50	.20
❑ 98	Rod Smith	.50	.20
❑ 99	Tim Brown	.75	.30
❑ 100	Trent Dilfer	.50	.20
❑ 101	Michael Vick RC	12.00	5.00
❑ 102	Koren Robinson RC	1.50	.60
❑ 103	LaDainian Tomlinson RC	8.00	4.00
❑ 104	Todd Heap RC	1.50	.60
❑ 105	Correll Buckhalter RC	2.00	.75
❑ 106	Freddie Mitchell RC	1.50	.60
❑ 107	Josh Booty RC	1.50	.60
❑ 108	Chris Chambers RC	2.50	1.00
❑ 109	Chris Weinke RC	1.50	.60
❑ 110	Steve Smith RC	4.00	2.00
❑ 111	Travis Minor RC	1.00	.40
❑ 112	Ken-Yon Rambo RC	1.00	.40
❑ 113	Marques Tuiasosopo RC	1.50	.60
❑ 114	Bobby Newcombe RC	1.00	.40
❑ 115	Drew Brees RC	4.00	1.50
❑ 116	LaMont Jordan RC	3.00	1.25
❑ 117	Dan Morgan RC	1.50	.60
❑ 118	Reggie Wayne RC	3.00	1.25
❑ 119	Dan Alexander RC	1.50	.60
❑ 120	Alge Crumpler RC	2.00	.75
❑ 121	Robert Ferguson RC	1.50	.60
❑ 122	Rod Gardner RC	1.50	.60
❑ 123	Mike McMahon RC	1.50	.60
❑ 124	Kevan Barlow RC	1.50	.60
❑ 125	Snoop Minnis RC	1.00	.40
❑ 126	Sage Rosenfels RC	1.50	.60
❑ 127	Jesse Palmer RC	1.50	.60
❑ 128	Michael Bennett RC	2.50	1.00
❑ 129	Rudi Johnson RC	3.00	1.25
❑ 130	Deuce McAllister RC	3.00	1.25
❑ 131	Santana Moss RC	2.50	1.00
❑ 132	Josh Heupel RC	1.50	.60
❑ 133	Quincy Morgan RC	1.50	.60
❑ 134	Quincy Carter RC	1.50	.60
❑ 135	Anthony Thomas RC	1.50	.60
❑ 136	James Jackson RC	1.50	.60
❑ 137	Kevin Kasper RC	1.50	.60
❑ 138	Alex Bannister RC	1.00	.40
❑ 139	David Terrell RC	1.50	.60
❑ 140	Chad Johnson RC	4.00	1.50
❑ 141	Walter Payton	5.00	2.00
❑ 142	Bart Starr	3.00	1.25
❑ 143	Sonny Jurgensen	1.50	.60
❑ 144	Jim Brown	2.50	1.00
❑ 145A	Joe Namath HTA	10.00	4.00
❑ 145B	Joe Namath RETAIL	15.00	6.00
❑ NNO	Joe Namath Bucks	4.00	1.50

2002 Topps Gallery

❑ COMPLETE SET (200)	60.00	25.00
❑ COMP.SET w/o SP's (150)	40.00	15.00
❑ UNPRICED PRESS PLATES EXIST		
❑ FOUR DIFF.COLOR PP's MADE PER CARD		
❑ PRESS PLATE STATED ODDS 1:617		

❑ 1	Marshall Faulk	.75	.30
❑ 2	Mark Brunell	.75	.30
❑ 3	Jeff Garcia	.75	.30
❑ 4	David Terrell	.75	.30
❑ 5	Curtis Martin	.75	.30
❑ 6	Terrell Davis	.75	.30
❑ 7	Jake Plummer	.50	.20
❑ 8	Eric Moulds	.50	.20
❑ 9	Peyton Manning	1.50	.60
❑ 10	Hines Ward	.75	.30
❑ 11	Koren Robinson	.50	.20
❑ 12	Eddie George	.75	.30
❑ 13	Shane Matthews	.30	.10
❑ 14	Trent Green	.50	.20
❑ 15	Marcus Robinson	.50	.20
❑ 16	Michael Vick	2.50	1.00
❑ 17	Muhsin Muhammad	.50	.20
❑ 18	Rocket Ismail	.50	.20
❑ 19	Quincy Morgan	.30	.10
❑ 20	Mike McMahon	.75	.30
❑ 21	Randy Moss	1.50	.60
❑ 22	Willie Jackson	.30	.10
❑ 23	Freddie Mitchell	.50	.20
❑ 24	LaDainian Tomlinson	1.25	.50
❑ 25	Warrick Dunn	.75	.30
❑ 26	Zach Thomas	.75	.30
❑ 27	Bill Schroeder	.50	.20
❑ 28	Jon Kitna	.50	.20
❑ 29	Rob Johnson	.50	.20
❑ 30	Drew Bledsoe	1.00	.40
❑ 31	Ron Dayne	.50	.20
❑ 32	Tim Brown	.75	.30
❑ 33	Michael Westbrook	.30	.10
❑ 34	Terrell Owens	.75	.30
❑ 35	Santana Moss	.75	.30
❑ 36	Edgerrin James	1.00	.40
❑ 37	Ray Lewis	.75	.30
❑ 38	Chris Weinke	.50	.20
❑ 39	Brian Griese	.75	.30
❑ 40	Trent Dilfer	.50	.20
❑ 41	Jay Fiedler	.50	.20
❑ 42	Joe Horn	.50	.20
❑ 43	Chad Johnson	.75	.30
❑ 44	Plaxico Burress	.50	.20
❑ 45	Trung Canidate	.50	.20
❑ 46	Steve McNair	.75	.30
❑ 47	Curtis Conway	.30	.10
❑ 48	James Stewart	.50	.20
❑ 49	James Jackson	.30	.10
❑ 50	Tom Brady	2.00	.75
❑ 51	Emmitt Smith	2.00	.75
❑ 52	Michael Pittman	.30	.10
❑ 53	Tony Gonzalez	.50	.20
❑ 54	Daunte Culpepper	.75	.30
❑ 55	Michael Strahan	.50	.20
❑ 56	Keyshawn Johnson	.75	.30
❑ 57	Marvin Harrison	.75	.30
❑ 58	Brian Urlacher	1.25	.50
❑ 59	Jeff Blake	.30	.10
❑ 60	Chris Redman	.30	.10
❑ 61	James McKnight	.30	.10
❑ 62	Jerome Bettis	.75	.30
❑ 63	Shaun Alexander	1.00	.40
❑ 64	Rod Gardner	.50	.20
❑ 65	Jimmy Smith	.50	.20
❑ 66	Thomas Jones	.50	.20
❑ 67	Peter Warrick	.50	.20
❑ 68	Mike Anderson	.75	.30
❑ 69	Ahman Green	.75	.30
❑ 70	Amani Toomer	.50	.20
❑ 71	Rich Gannon	.75	.30
❑ 72	Vinny Testaverde	.50	.20
❑ 73	Isaac Bruce	.75	.30
❑ 74	Derrick Mason	.50	.20
❑ 75	John Abraham	.50	.20
❑ 76	Shannon Sharpe	.50	.20
❑ 77	Quincy Carter	.50	.20
❑ 78	Todd Pinkston	.50	.20
❑ 79	Drew Brees	.75	.30
❑ 80	Brad Johnson	.50	.20
❑ 81	Garrison Hearst	.50	.20
❑ 82	Anthony Thomas	.50	.20
❑ 83	Brett Favre	2.00	.75
❑ 84	Troy Brown	.50	.20
❑ 85	Charlie Garner	.50	.20
❑ 86	Kendrell Bell	.75	.30
❑ 87	Darrell Jackson	.50	.20
❑ 88	Ricky Williams	1.50	.60
❑ 89	Duce Staley	.75	.30
❑ 90	Stephen Davis	.50	.20
❑ 91	Dominic Rhodes	.50	.20
❑ 92	Travis Henry	.75	.30
❑ 93	David Boston	.75	.30
❑ 94	Deuce McAllister	1.00	.40
❑ 95	Ike Hilliard	.50	.20
❑ 96	Doug Flutie	.75	.30
❑ 97	Torry Holt	.75	.30
❑ 98	Keenan McCardell	.30	.10
❑ 99	Rod Smith	.50	.20
❑ 100	Donovan McNabb	1.00	.40
❑ 101	Corey Bradford	.30	.10
❑ 102	Germane Crowell	.30	.10
❑ 103	Michael Bennett	.50	.20
❑ 104	Wayne Chrebet	.50	.20
❑ 105	Mike Alstott	.75	.30
❑ 106	Kevin Dyson	.50	.20
❑ 107	Tim Couch	.50	.20
❑ 108	Donald Hayes	.30	.10
❑ 109	Maurice Smith	.50	.20
❑ 110	Snoop Minnis	.30	.10
❑ 111	Antowain Smith	.50	.20
❑ 112	Kordell Stewart	.50	.20
❑ 113	Kurt Warner	.75	.30
❑ 114	Jerry Rice	1.50	.60
❑ 115	Aaron Brooks	.75	.30
❑ 116	Tiki Barber	.75	.30
❑ 117	Marty Booker	.30	.10
❑ 118	Qadry Ismail	.50	.20
❑ 119	Peerless Price	.50	.20
❑ 120	Marcus Pollard	.30	.10
❑ 121	James Allen	.50	.20
❑ 122	Junior Seau	.75	.30
❑ 123	Fred Taylor	.75	.30
❑ 124	Corey Dillon	.50	.20
❑ 125	Lamar Smith	.50	.20
❑ 126	Laveranues Coles	.50	.20
❑ 127	James Thrash	.50	.20
❑ 128	Kevan Barlow	.50	.20
❑ 129	Matt Hasselbeck	.50	.20
❑ 130	David Patten	.30	.10
❑ 131	Antonio Freeman	.75	.30
❑ 132	Johnnie Morton	.50	.20
❑ 133	Priest Holmes	1.00	.40
❑ 134	Cris Carter	.75	.30
❑ 135	Kevin Johnson	.50	.20
❑ 136	Jim Miller	.30	.10
❑ 137	Kerry Collins	.50	.20
❑ 138	Joey Galloway	.50	.20
❑ 139	Correll Buckhalter	.50	.20
❑ 140	Chris Chambers	.75	.30
❑ 141	Travis Taylor	.50	.20
❑ 142	Ed McCaffrey	.75	.30
❑ 143	J.J. Stokes	.50	.20
❑ 144	Reggie Wayne	.75	.30
❑ 145	Az-Zahir Hakim	.30	.10
❑ 146	Tim Dwight	.50	.20
❑ 147	Jevon Kearse	.50	.20
❑ 148	Jamal Lewis	.75	.30
❑ 149	Warren Sapp	.50	.20
❑ 150	Jermaine Lewis	.30	.10
❑ 151	William Green RC	2.00	.75
❑ 152	Roy Williams RC	5.00	2.00
❑ 153	Kurt Kittner RC	1.50	.60
❑ 154	Daniel Graham RC	2.00	.75
❑ 155	Andre Davis RC	1.50	.60
❑ 156	Donte Stallworth RC	4.00	1.50
❑ 157	Josh Reed RC	2.00	.75
❑ 158	Rohan Davey RC	2.00	.75
❑ 159	Wendell Bryant RC	1.00	.40
❑ 160	Lito Sheppard RC	2.00	.75
❑ 161	Najeh Davenport RC	2.00	.75
❑ 162	Freddie Milons RC	1.50	.60
❑ 163	Patrick Ramsey RC	2.50	1.00
❑ 164	Luke Staley RC	1.50	.60
❑ 165	Maurice Morris RC	2.00	.75
❑ 166	Dwight Freeney RC	2.50	1.00
❑ 167	Jeremy Shockey RC	6.00	2.50
❑ 168	Jabar Gaffney RC	2.00	.75
❑ 169	DeShaun Foster RC	2.00	.75
❑ 170	Chad Hutchinson RC	1.50	.60
❑ 171	Tim Carter RC	1.50	.60
❑ 172	Napoleon Harris RC	2.00	.75
❑ 173	Kahlil Hill RC	1.50	.60
❑ 174	Josh McCown RC	3.00	1.25

175	Ron Johnson RC	1.50	.60
176	Marquise Walker RC	1.50	.60
177	Joey Harrington RC	5.00	2.00
178	Travis Stephens RC	1.50	.60
179	Julius Peppers RC	4.00	1.50
180	Ryan Sims RC	2.00	.75
181	Albert Haynesworth RC	1.50	.60
182	Phillip Buchanon RC	2.00	.75
183	Jonathan Wells RC	2.00	.75
184	Chester Taylor RC	2.00	.75
185	Antonio Bryant RC	2.00	.75
186	Adrian Peterson RC	2.00	.75
187	Clinton Portis RC	6.00	2.50
188	Lamar Gordon RC	2.00	.75
189	Reche Caldwell RC	2.00	.75
190	Ashley Lelie RC	4.00	1.50
191	T.J. Duckett RC	3.00	1.25
192	Eric Crouch RC	2.00	.75
193	David Garrard RC	2.00	.75
194	Quentin Jammer RC	2.00	.75
195	Ladell Betts RC	2.00	.75
196	Antwaan Randle El RC	3.00	1.25
197	Cliff Russell RC	1.50	.60
198	Javon Walker RC	4.00	1.50
199	John Henderson RC	2.00	.75
200	David Carr RC	5.00	2.00

2001 Topps Heritage

COMPLETE SET (146)		300.00	150.00
COMP.SET w/o SP's (110)		25.00	10.00
1	Ray Lewis	1.25	.50
2	Peter Warrick	1.25	.50
3	James Stewart	.75	.30
4	Junior Seau	1.25	.50
5	Jeff George	.75	.30
6	Amani Toomer	.50	.20
7	Elvis Grbac	.75	.30
8	David Boston	1.25	.50
9	Jimmy Smith	.75	.30
10	Warrick Dunn	1.25	.50
11	Hines Ward	1.25	.50
12	Joe Horn	.75	.30
13	Stephen Davis	1.25	.50
14	Tyrone Wheatley	.75	.30
15	Brian Urlacher	2.00	.75
16	Fred Taylor	1.25	.50
17	Jerry Rice	2.50	1.00
18	Keyshawn Johnson	1.25	.50
19	Jay Fiedler	1.25	.50
20	Jamal Anderson	1.25	.50
21	Emmitt Smith	2.50	1.00
22	Tiki Barber	1.25	.50
23	Daunte Culpepper	1.25	.50
24	Torry Holt	1.25	.50
25	Peyton Manning	3.00	1.25
26	Eddie George	1.25	.50
27	Jamal Lewis	2.00	.75
28	Ricky Williams	1.25	.50
29	Ahman Green	1.25	.50
30	Ed McCaffrey	1.25	.50
31	Curtis Martin	1.25	.50
32	Isaac Bruce	1.25	.50
33	Doug Flutie	1.25	.50
34	Steve McNair	1.25	.50
35	Donovan McNabb	1.50	.60
36	Keenan McCardell	.50	.20
37	Charlie Batch	1.25	.50
38	Cade McNown	.50	.20
39	Terrell Owens	1.25	.50
40	Brad Johnson	1.25	.50
41	Robert Smith	1.25	.50
42	Muhsin Muhammad	.75	.30
43	Kurt Warner	2.50	1.00
44	Lamar Smith	.75	.30
45	Brian Griese	1.25	.50
46	Trent Dilfer	.75	.30
47	Jeff Garcia	1.25	.50
48	Derrick Mason	.75	.30
49	Drew Bledsoe	1.50	.60
50	Marshall Faulk	1.50	.60
51	Corey Dillon	1.25	.50
52	Tony Gonzalez	.75	.30
53	Chad Lewis	.50	.20
54	Shaun Alexander	1.50	.60
55	Edgerrin James	1.50	.60
56	Eric Moulds	.75	.30
57	Aaron Brooks	1.25	.50
58	Zach Thomas	1.25	.50
59	Jerome Bettis	1.25	.50
60	Shannon Sharpe	.75	.30
61	Kerry Collins	.75	.30
62	Ricky Watters	.75	.30
63	Tim Couch	.75	.30
64	Marvin Harrison	1.25	.50
65	Tim Brown	1.25	.50
66	Mark Brunell	1.25	.50
67	Wayne Chrebet	.75	.30
68	Terry Glenn	.75	.30
69	Mike Anderson	1.25	.50
70	Randy Moss	2.50	1.00
71	Freddie Jones	.50	.20
72	Ike Hilliard	.75	.30
73	Derrick Alexander	.75	.30
74	Travis Prentice	.50	.20
75	Brett Favre	4.00	1.50
76	Rod Smith	.75	.30
77	Troy Aikman	2.00	.75
78	Cris Carter	1.25	.50
79	Rich Gannon	1.25	.50
80	Charlie Garner	.75	.30
81	Michael Pittman	.50	.20
82	Jeff Graham	.50	.20
83	Albert Connell	.50	.20
84	Bill Schroeder	.75	.30
85	Jeff Blake	.75	.30
86	Jon Kitna	1.25	.50
87	Qadry Ismail	.75	.30
88	Joey Galloway	.75	.30
89	Charles Johnson	.50	.20
90	Troy Brown	.75	.30
91	Johnnie Morton	.75	.30
92	Chris Chandler	.75	.30
93	Donald Hayes	.50	.20
94	Shaun King	.50	.20
95	Vinny Testaverde	.75	.30
96	James Allen	.75	.30
97	Jake Plummer	.75	.30
98	Antonio Freeman	1.25	.50
99	Sean Dawkins	.50	.20
100	Ron Dayne	1.25	.50
101	Rob Johnson	.75	.30
102	Kordell Stewart	.75	.30
103	Akili Smith	.50	.20
104	Shawn Jefferson	.50	.20
105	Germane Crowell	.50	.20
106	Kevin Johnson	.75	.30
107	Steve Beuerlein	.75	.30
108	Marcus Robinson	1.25	.50
109	Peerless Price	.75	.30
110	Jerome Pathon	.75	.30
111	Sage Rosenfels RC	8.00	3.00
112	Quincy Morgan RC	8.00	3.00
113	Chad Johnson RC	20.00	7.50
114	Josh Heupel RC	8.00	3.00
115	Anthony Thomas RC	8.00	3.00
116	Drew Brees RC	20.00	7.50
117	Kevan Barlow RC	8.00	3.00
118	Chris Chambers RC	12.00	5.00
119	Mike McMahon RC	8.00	3.00
120	Todd Heap RC	8.00	3.00
121	Leonard Davis RC	5.00	2.00
122	Richard Seymour RC	8.00	3.00
123	Robert Ferguson RC	8.00	3.00
124	Andre Carter RC	8.00	3.00
125	Jesse Palmer RC	8.00	3.00
126	Travis Minor RC	5.00	2.00
127	Rudi Johnson RC	15.00	6.00
128	Rod Gardner RC	8.00	3.00
129	Snoop Minnis RC	5.00	2.00
130	Koren Robinson RC	8.00	3.00
131	Chris Weinke RC	8.00	3.00
132	James Jackson RC	8.00	3.00
133	Michael Vick RC	50.00	25.00
134	Marques Tuiasosopo RC	8.00	3.00
135	Michael Bennett RC	12.00	5.00
136	LaDainian Tomlinson RC	40.00	20.00
137	Freddie Mitchell RC	8.00	3.00
138	Deuce McAllister RC	15.00	6.00
139	Quincy Carter RC	8.00	3.00
140	Santana Moss RC	12.00	5.00
141	David Terrell RC	8.00	3.00
142	Reggie Wayne RC	15.00	6.00
143	Justin Smith RC	8.00	3.00
144	Gerard Warren RC	8.00	3.00
145	Travis Henry RC	8.00	3.00
146	Dan Morgan RC	8.00	3.00
NNO	Checklist CL	.50	.20

2002 Topps Heritage

COMPLETE SET (194)		250.00	125.00
1	Jerome Bettis	1.25	.50
2	Jeff Blake SP	1.00	.40
3	Rod Smith	.75	.30
4	Eric Moulds	.75	.30
5	Michael Vick	4.00	1.50
6	Randy Moss	2.50	1.00
7	Todd Pinkston	.75	.30
8	Trung Canidate SP	1.50	.60
9	Steve McNair	1.25	.50
10	J.J. Stokes SP	1.50	.60
11	Ricky Williams	2.50	1.00
12	Germane Crowell SP	1.00	.40
13	Muhsin Muhammad SP	1.50	.60
14	Michael Pittman SP	1.00	.40
15	James Jackson SP	1.00	.40
16	Dominic Rhodes	.75	.30
17	Jay Fiedler	.75	.30
18	Marcus Robinson	.75	.30
19	Qadry Ismail SP	1.50	.60
20	Michael Strahan	.75	.30
21	Koren Robinson	.75	.30
22	James Allen SP	1.50	.60
23	Chad Pennington	1.50	.60
24	Fred Taylor	1.25	.50
25	Corey Dillon	.75	.30
26	Thomas Jones SP	1.50	.60
27	Anthony Thomas	.75	.30
28	Priest Holmes	1.50	.60
29	Troy Brown	.75	.30
30	Jerry Rice	2.50	1.00
31	Correll Buckhalter	.75	.30
32	Drew Brees	1.25	.50
33	Isaac Bruce	1.25	.50
34	Warrick Dunn SP	2.50	1.00
35	Chris Chambers	1.25	.50
36	Antonio Freeman	1.25	.50
37	Joey Galloway SP	1.50	.60
38	Rob Johnson SP	1.50	.60
39	Reggie Wayne	1.25	.50
40	Santana Moss	1.25	.50
41	Plaxico Burress	.75	.30
42	Frank Wycheck SP	1.00	.40
43	Johnnie Morton	.75	.30
44	Chris Weinke	.75	.30
45	Rocket Ismail SP	1.50	.60

❑ 46 Daunte Culpepper 1.25 .50
❑ 47 Deuce McAllister SP 3.00 1.25
❑ 48 Terrell Owens 1.25 .50
❑ 49 Michael Westbrook .50 .20
❑ 50 Tom Brady 3.00 1.25
❑ 51 Mike Anderson 1.25 .50
❑ 52 Jake Plummer .75 .30
❑ 53 Travis Taylor SP 1.50 .60
❑ 54 Marcus Pollard SP 1.00 .40
❑ 55 Zach Thomas 1.25 .50
❑ 56 Duce Staley 1.25 .50
❑ 57 Trent Dilfer .75 .30
❑ 58 Keyshawn Johnson 1.25 .50
❑ 59 Amani Toomer SP 1.50 .60
❑ 60 David Terrell 1.25 .50
❑ 61 Robert Ferguson SP 1.00 .40
❑ 62 Jeff Garcia 1.25 .50
❑ 63 Eddie George 1.25 .50
❑ 64 Marshall Faulk 1.25 .50
❑ 65 Travis Henry 1.25 .50
❑ 66 Tim Couch .75 .30
❑ 67 Mike McMahon 1.25 .50
❑ 68 John Abraham SP 1.50 .60
❑ 69 James Thrash .75 .30
❑ 70 Shaun Alexander 1.50 .60
❑ 71 Ike Hilliard SP 1.50 .60
❑ 72 Brian Griese 1.25 .50
❑ 73 Ray Lewis 1.25 .50
❑ 74 Jon Kitna .75 .30
❑ 75 Az-Zahir Hakim SP 1.00 .40
❑ 76 Oronde Gadsden SP 1.50 .60
❑ 77 Joe Horn .75 .30
❑ 78 Tim Brown 1.25 .50
❑ 79 Kendrell Bell 1.25 .50
❑ 80 LaDainian Tomlinson 2.00 .75
❑ 81 Brad Johnson .75 .30
❑ 82 Tony Gonzalez .75 .30
❑ 83 Bill Schroeder .75 .30
❑ 84 Quincy Carter .75 .30
❑ 85 Donald Hayes SP 1.00 .40
❑ 86 Peyton Manning 2.50 1.00
❑ 87 Drew Bledsoe 1.25 .50
❑ 88 Darrell Jackson .75 .30
❑ 89 Rod Gardner .75 .30
❑ 90 Derrick Mason .75 .30
❑ 91 Byron Chamberlain SP 1.00 .40
❑ 92 James Mcknight SP 1.00 .40
❑ 93 Kevin Johnson .75 .30
❑ 94 Terry Glenn .75 .30
❑ 95 Marty Booker SP 1.00 .40
❑ 96 Terrell Davis 1.25 .50
❑ 97 Vinny Testaverde .75 .30
❑ 98 Hines Ward 1.25 .50
❑ 99 Chad Lewis SP 1.00 .40
❑ 100 Kurt Warner 1.25 .50
❑ 101 Michael Bennett .75 .30
❑ 102 Edgerrin James 1.50 .60
❑ 103 Corey Bradford SP 1.00 .40
❑ 104 Chad Johnson SP 2.50 1.00
❑ 105 Alex Van Pelt .75 .30
❑ 106 Antowain Smith .75 .30
❑ 107 Rich Gannon 1.25 .50
❑ 108 Kevan Barlow SP 1.50 .60
❑ 109 Mike Alstott SP 2.50 1.00
❑ 110 Kerry Collins SP 1.50 .60
❑ 111 Jimmy Smith .75 .30
❑ 112 Jermaine Lewis SP 1.00 .40
❑ 113 Quincy Morgan SP 1.00 .40
❑ 114 Maurice Smith SP 1.50 .60
❑ 115 Willie Jackson .50 .20
❑ 116 Doug Flutie 1.25 .50
❑ 117 Matt Hasselbeck .75 .30
❑ 118 Amos Zereoue SP 2.50 1.00
❑ 119 Lamar Smith .75 .30
❑ 120 Snoop Minnis .50 .20
❑ 121 Troy Hambrick SP 1.00 .40
❑ 122 Shannon Sharpe SP 1.50 .60
❑ 123 Laveranues Coles .75 .30
❑ 124 Freddie Mitchell .75 .30
❑ 125 Kevin Dyson SP 1.50 .60
❑ 126 Torry Holt 1.25 .50
❑ 127 James Stewart SP 1.50 .60
❑ 128 Brian Urlacher 2.00 .75
❑ 129 David Boston 1.25 .50
❑ 130 Ron Dayne .75 .30
❑ 131 Garrison Hearst .75 .30
❑ 132 Stephen Davis .75 .30
❑ 133 Donovan McNabb 1.50 .60
❑ 134 David Patten .50 .20
❑ 135 Travis Minor SP 1.00 .40
❑ 136 Peerless Price SP 1.50 .60
❑ 137 Chris Redman SP 1.00 .40
❑ 138 Ahman Green 1.25 .50
❑ 139 Mark Brunell 1.25 .50
❑ 140 Charlie Garner .75 .30
❑ 141 Curtis Conway .50 .20
❑ 142 Wayne Chrebet .75 .30
❑ 143 Kordell Stewart .75 .30
❑ 144 Peter Warrick .75 .30
❑ 145 Emmitt Smith 3.00 1.25
❑ 146 Jim Miller SP 1.00 .40
❑ 147 Trent Green .75 .30
❑ 148 Cris Carter 1.25 .50
❑ 149 Aaron Brooks 1.25 .50
❑ 150 Curtis Martin 1.25 .50
❑ 151 Tiki Barber SP 2.50 1.00
❑ 152 Marvin Harrison 1.25 .50
❑ 153 Tyrone Wheatley SP 1.50 .60
❑ 154 Brett Favre 3.00 1.25
❑ 155 David Carr RC 8.00 3.00
❑ 156 Quentin Jammer RC 3.00 1.25
❑ 157 Julius Peppers RC 6.00 2.50
❑ 158 Mike Williams RC 2.50 1.00
❑ 159 Antwaan Randle El RC 5.00 2.00
❑ 160 Joey Harrington RC 8.00 3.00
❑ 161 Ashley Lelie RC 6.00 2.50
❑ 162 Marquise Walker RC 2.50 1.00
❑ 163 Rohan Davey RC 3.00 1.25
❑ 164 Patrick Ramsey RC 4.00 1.50
❑ 165 T.J. Duckett RC 5.00 2.00
❑ 166 DeShaun Foster RC 3.00 1.25
❑ 167 Donte Stallworth RC 6.00 2.50
❑ 168 William Green RC 3.00 1.25
❑ 169 Ron Johnson RC 2.50 1.00
❑ 170 Maurice Morris RC 3.00 1.25
❑ 171 Travis Stephens RC 2.50 1.00
❑ 172 Eric Crouch RC 3.00 1.25
❑ 173 David Garrard RC 3.00 1.25
❑ 174 Daniel Graham RC 3.00 1.25
❑ 175 Roy Williams RC 8.00 3.00
❑ 176 Jeremy Shockey RC 10.00 4.00
❑ 177 Josh McCown RC 4.00 1.50
❑ 178 Josh Reed RC 3.00 1.25
❑ 179 Andre Davis RC 2.50 1.00
❑ 180 Antonio Bryant RC 3.00 1.25
❑ 181 Clinton Portis RC 10.00 4.00
❑ 182 Javon Walker RC 6.00 2.50
❑ 183 Jabar Gaffney RC 3.00 1.25
❑ 184 Ladell Betts RC 3.00 1.25
❑ 185 Tim Carter RC 2.50 1.00
❑ 186 Reche Caldwell RC 3.00 1.25
❑ 187 Cliff Russell RC 2.50 1.00
❑ 188 Brian Westbrook SP RC 6.00 2.50
❑ 189 Freddie Milons RC 2.50 1.00
❑ 190 Phillip Buchanon RC 3.00 1.25
❑ 191 Lamar Gordon RC 3.00 1.25
❑ 192 Luke Staley RC 2.50 1.00
❑ 193 Albert Haynesworth RC 2.50 1.00
❑ 194 Kurt Kittner RC 2.50 1.00

2005 Topps Heritage

❑ COMPLETE SET (400) 175.00 100.00
❑ COMP.SET w/o SPs (300) 40.00 15.00
❑ 58T SP PRINTED WITH 1958 TOPPS DESIGN
❑ TBJ SP PRINTED W/THROWBACK JER.PHOTO

❑ 1 Curtis Martin 1.00 .40
❑ 2 Javon Walker .60 .25
❑ 3 Derrick Mason .60 .25
❑ 4 Julius Jones 1.25 .50
❑ 5 Marc Bulger 1.00 .40
❑ 6 Reggie Wayne .60 .25
❑ 7 Isaac Bruce .60 .25
❑ 8 Ray Lewis 1.00 .40
❑ 9 Drew Bledsoe 1.00 .40
❑ 10 Michael Vick 1.50 .60
❑ 11 Charles Rogers .60 .25
❑ 12 Lee Evans .60 .25
❑ 13 Jake Plummer .60 .25
❑ 14 Edgerrin James 1.00 .40
❑ 15 Hines Ward 1.00 .40
❑ 16 Peyton Manning 1.50 .60
❑ 17 Andre Johnson .60 .25
❑ 18 Trent Green .60 .25
❑ 19 Brian Westbrook .60 .25
❑ 20 Kevin Jones 1.00 .40
❑ 21 Deuce McAllister 1.00 .40
❑ 22 Marvin Harrison 1.00 .40
❑ 23 Dwight Freeney .60 .25
❑ 24 Ahman Green 1.00 .40
❑ 25 Plaxico Burress .60 .25
❑ 26 Daunte Culpepper 1.00 .40
❑ 27 Corey Dillon .60 .25
❑ 28 Joe Horn .60 .25
❑ 29 Torry Holt 1.00 .40
❑ 30 Randy Moss 1.00 .40
❑ 31 Drew Brees 1.00 .40
❑ 32 Jonathan Vilma .60 .25
❑ 33 Jerome Bettis 1.00 .40
❑ 34 Byron Leftwich 1.00 .40
❑ 35 Marshall Faulk 1.00 .40
❑ 36 Brett Favre 2.50 1.00
❑ 37 Steve McNair 1.00 .40
❑ 38 Rudi Johnson .60 .25
❑ 39 Tiki Barber 1.00 .40
❑ 40 Muhsin Muhammad .60 .25
❑ 41 Tony Gonzalez .60 .25
❑ 42 Chad Pennington 1.00 .40
❑ 43 Shaun Alexander 1.25 .50
❑ 44 Jamal Lewis 1.00 .40
❑ 45 Antonio Gates 1.00 .40
❑ 46 LaDainian Tomlinson 1.25 .50
❑ 47 Matt Hasselbeck .60 .25
❑ 48 Jake Delhomme 1.00 .40
❑ 49 Chad Johnson 1.00 .40
❑ 50 Willis McGahee 1.00 .40
❑ 51 Jason Witten .60 .25
❑ 52 J.P. Losman 1.00 .40
❑ 53 Donovan McNabb 1.25 .50
❑ 54A Eric Shelton RC 2.50 1.00
❑ 54B Eric Shelton 58T SP 3.00 1.25
❑ 55A Alex Smith QB RC 10.00 4.00
❑ 55B Alex Smith QB TBJ SP 12.00 5.00
❑ 56A Kyle Orton RC 4.00 1.50
❑ 56B Kyle Orton 58T SP 5.00 2.00
❑ 57A Andrew Walter RC 4.00 1.50
❑ 57B Andrew Walter TBJ SP 5.00 2.00
❑ 58A Ryan Moats RC 2.50 1.00
❑ 58B Ryan Moats 58T SP 3.00 1.25
❑ 59A Ciatrick Fason RC 2.50 1.00
❑ 59B Ciatrick Fason 58T SP 3.00 1.25
❑ 60A Vincent Jackson RC 2.50 1.00
❑ 60B Vincent Jackson 58T SP 3.00 1.25
❑ 61A Heath Miller RC 6.00 2.50
❑ 61B Heath Miller 58T SP 8.00 3.00
❑ 62A Carlos Rogers RC 3.00 1.25
❑ 62B Carlos Rogers TBJ SP 4.00 1.50
❑ 63A Terrence Murphy RC 2.50 1.00
❑ 63B Terrence Murphy 58T SP 3.00 1.25
❑ 64A Mike Williams 5.00 2.00
❑ 64B Mike Williams 58T SP 6.00 2.50
❑ 65A Vernand Morency RC 2.50 1.00
❑ 65B Vernand Morency 58T SP 3.00 1.25
❑ 66A Maurice Clarett 2.50 1.00
❑ 66B Maurice Clarett 58T SP 3.00 1.25
❑ 67A Roscoe Parrish RC 2.50 1.00
❑ 67B Roscoe Parrish 58T SP 3.00 1.25
❑ 68A Courtney Roby RC 2.50 1.00
❑ 68B Courtney Roby 58T SP 3.00 1.25
❑ 69 Tom Brady 2.50 1.00
❑ 70A David Greene RC 2.50 1.00
❑ 70B David Greene 58T SP 3.00 1.25

❑ 71A	Antrel Rolle RC	2.50	1.00
❑ 71B	Antrel Rolle 58T SP	3.00	1.25
❑ 72A	Mark Bradley RC	2.50	1.00
❑ 72B	Mark Bradley 58T SP	3.00	1.25
❑ 73A	Frank Gore RC	4.00	1.50
❑ 73B	Frank Gore 58T SP	5.00	2.00
❑ 74A	Cedric Benson RC	5.00	2.00
❑ 74B	Cedric Benson 58T SP	6.00	2.50
❑ 75A	Derrick Johnson 62T RC	4.00	1.50
❑ 75B	Derrick Johnson 58T SP	5.00	2.00
❑ 76A	Reggie Brown RC	2.50	1.00
❑ 76B	Reggie Brown 58T SP	3.00	1.25
❑ 77A	Ronnie Brown RC	8.00	3.00
❑ 77B	Ronnie Brown TBJ SP	10.00	4.00
❑ 78A	Jason Campbell RC	4.00	1.50
❑ 78B	Jason Campbell TBJ SP	5.00	2.00
❑ 79A	Charlie Frye RC	5.00	2.00
❑ 79B	Charlie Frye 58T SP	6.00	2.50
❑ 80	Jamie Sharper	.50	.20
❑ 81	Tony Romo	.50	.20
❑ 82	Rod Smith	.60	.25
❑ 83	Chester Taylor	.60	.25
❑ 84	Marcus Robinson	.60	.25
❑ 85	Terence Newman	.50	.20
❑ 86	Aaron Brooks	.60	.25
❑ 87	Kerry Collins	.60	.25
❑ 88	Brandon Lloyd	.50	.20
❑ 89	Michael Pittman	.50	.20
❑ 90	Sean Taylor	.60	.25
❑ 91	Michael Lewis	.50	.20
❑ 92	Jeremy Shockey	1.00	.40
❑ 93	Zach Thomas	1.00	.40
❑ 94	David Carr	1.00	.40
❑ 95	Champ Bailey	.60	.25
❑ 96	Julius Peppers	.60	.25
❑ 97	Brandon Stokley	.60	.25
❑ 98	Deion Branch	.60	.25
❑ 99	Charles Woodson	.60	.25
❑ 100	Darrell Jackson	.60	.25
❑ 101	Ronde Barber	.50	.20
❑ 102	Patrick Ramsey	.60	.25
❑ 103	Warrick Dunn	.60	.25
❑ 104	Takeo Spikes	.50	.20
❑ 105	Thomas Jones	.60	.25
❑ 106	T.J. Houshmandzadeh	.50	.20
❑ 107	Najeh Davenport	.50	.20
❑ 108	Nate Burleson	.60	.25
❑ 109	Kelly Campbell	.50	.20
❑ 110	LaVar Arrington	1.00	.40
❑ 111	Joey Harrington	1.00	.40
❑ 112	DeAngelo Hall	.60	.25
❑ 113	Derrick Blaylock	.50	.20
❑ 114	Michael Clayton	1.00	.40
❑ 115	Adam Archuleta	.50	.20
❑ 116	Jason Taylor	.50	.20
❑ 117	Donald Driver	.60	.25
❑ 118	Dan Morgan	.50	.20
❑ 119	Michael Jenkins	.60	.25
❑ 120	Drew Henson	.60	.25
❑ 121	Jay Fiedler	.50	.20
❑ 122	Ladell Betts	.50	.20
❑ 123	Jonathan Ogden	.50	.20
❑ 124	Domanick Davis	.60	.25
❑ 125	Sebastian Janikowski	.50	.20
❑ 126	Cedrick Wilson	.50	.20
❑ 127	Marcus Trufant	.50	.20
❑ 128	Santana Moss	.60	.25
❑ 129	Tatum Bell	.60	.25
❑ 130	Jonathan Wells	.50	.20
❑ 131	Laveranues Coles	.60	.25
❑ 132	Josh McCown	.60	.25
❑ 133	Antonio Bryant	.50	.20
❑ 134	John Lynch	.60	.25
❑ 135	Roy Williams WR	1.00	.40
❑ 136	Adam Vinatieri	1.00	.40
❑ 137	Dominic Rhodes	.50	.20
❑ 138	Tyrone Calico	.60	.25
❑ 139	Keenan McCardell	.50	.20
❑ 140	Antonio Pierce	.50	.20
❑ 141	Chris Chambers	.60	.25
❑ 142	Bubba Franks	.60	.25
❑ 143	Mike Vanderjagt	.50	.20
❑ 144	Ernest Wilford	.50	.20
❑ 145	Bertrand Berry	.50	.20
❑ 146	David Garrard	.50	.20
❑ 147	DeShaun Foster	.60	.25
❑ 148	Rashaun Woods	.60	.25
❑ 149	Wes Welker	.50	.20
❑ 150	Allen Rossum	.50	.20
❑ 151	Mike Anderson	.60	.25
❑ 152	Keyshawn Johnson	.60	.25
❑ 153	Alge Crumpler	.60	.25
❑ 154	Dunta Robinson	.60	.25
❑ 155	Kyle Boller	.60	.25
❑ 156	William Green	.50	.20
❑ 157	Peter Warrick	.50	.20
❑ 158	Doug Gabriel	.50	.20
❑ 159	Ashley Lelie	.60	.25
❑ 160	Ronald Curry	.60	.25
❑ 161	Keary Colbert	.60	.25
❑ 162	Shawn Bryson	.50	.20
❑ 163	Tim Rattay	.50	.20
❑ 164	Jabar Gaffney	.50	.20
❑ 165	Doug Jolley	.50	.20
❑ 166	Keith Brooking	.50	.20
❑ 167	Brian Urlacher	1.00	.40
❑ 168	Chris Gamble	.60	.25
❑ 169	Kurt Warner	.60	.25
❑ 170	Duce Staley	.60	.25
❑ 171	Steve Smith	.60	.25
❑ 172	Anquan Boldin	.60	.25
❑ 173	Fred Taylor	.60	.25
❑ 174	Donnie Edwards	.50	.20
❑ 175	Clarence Moore	.50	.20
❑ 176	Corey Bradford	.50	.20
❑ 177	Dante Hall	.60	.25
❑ 178	Warren Sapp	.60	.25
❑ 179	Todd Heap	.60	.25
❑ 180	Mewelde Moore	.60	.25
❑ 181	John Abraham	.50	.20
❑ 182	Rex Grossman	.60	.25
❑ 183	Stephen Davis	.60	.25
❑ 184	Greg Jones	.50	.20
❑ 185	Jeremiah Trotter	.50	.20
❑ 186	Carson Palmer	1.00	.40
❑ 187	Simeon Rice	.60	.25
❑ 188	A.J. Feeley	.60	.25
❑ 189	Matt Schaub	.60	.25
❑ 190	Jamaar Taylor	.50	.20
❑ 191	Joey Galloway	.60	.25
❑ 192	Quentin Griffin	.60	.25
❑ 193	Amani Toomer	.60	.25
❑ 194	Michael Strahan	.60	.25
❑ 195	Travis Henry	.60	.25
❑ 196	Billy Volek	.60	.25
❑ 197	Robert Ferguson	.50	.20
❑ 198	Reggie Williams	.60	.25
❑ 199	Jeff Garcia	.60	.25
❑ 200	Mark Brunell	.60	.25
❑ 201	Derrick Brooks	.60	.25
❑ 202	Tommy Maddox	.50	.20
❑ 203	William Henderson	.50	.20
❑ 204	Bryant Johnson	.50	.20
❑ 205	Philip Rivers	1.00	.40
❑ 206	James Farrior	.50	.20
❑ 207	Terrence McGee	.50	.20
❑ 208	Bernard Berrian	.50	.20
❑ 209	Gus Frerotte	.50	.20
❑ 210	Mike Alstott	.60	.25
❑ 211	Luke McCown	.50	.20
❑ 212	Michael Bennett	.60	.25
❑ 213	Kenechi Udeze	.50	.20
❑ 214	Chris Perry	.60	.25
❑ 215	Robert Gallery	.60	.25
❑ 216	Lito Sheppard	.50	.20
❑ 217	Brian Finneran	.50	.20
❑ 218	Brian Griese	.60	.25
❑ 219	Kevin Curtis	.60	.25
❑ 220	LaMont Jordan	1.00	.40
❑ 221	Jerry Porter	.60	.25
❑ 222	Reuben Droughns	.60	.25
❑ 223	Dallas Clark	.50	.20
❑ 224	Kevan Barlow	.60	.25
❑ 225	Ken Lucas	.50	.20
❑ 226	Lee Suggs	.60	.25
❑ 227	Marcus Pollard	.50	.20
❑ 228	David Givens	.60	.25
❑ 229	T.J. Duckett	.60	.25
❑ 230	Chris Simms	.60	.25
❑ 231	Maurice Morris	.50	.20
❑ 232	Chris McAllister	.50	.20
❑ 233	Justin Fargas	.50	.20
❑ 234	Jimmy Smith	.60	.25
❑ 235	Aaron Stecker	.50	.20
❑ 236	Donte Stallworth	.60	.25
❑ 237	Darren Sproles RC	2.50	1.00
❑ 238	Justin McCareins	.50	.20
❑ 239	Adrian McPherson RC	2.50	1.00
❑ 240	Brian Dawkins	.50	.20
❑ 241	Travis Taylor	.50	.20
❑ 242	Fabian Washington RC	2.50	1.00
❑ 243	Jerramy Stevens	.50	.20
❑ 244	Anthony Davis RC	2.00	.75
❑ 245	Alex Smith TE RC	2.50	1.00
❑ 246	Ricky Williams	.60	.25
❑ 247	Marion Barber RC	4.00	1.50
❑ 248	Marcus Spears RC	2.50	1.00
❑ 249	Mike Nugent RC	2.50	1.00
❑ 250	Dat Nguyen	.50	.20
❑ 251	Derek Anderson RC	2.50	1.00
❑ 252	Terrence Holt	.50	.20
❑ 253	Dane Looker	.50	.20
❑ 254	Randy McMichael	.50	.20
❑ 255	Craig Bragg RC	2.00	.75
❑ 256	James Kilian RC	2.50	1.00
❑ 257	Airese Currie RC	2.50	1.00
❑ 258	Noah Herron RC	2.50	1.00
❑ 259	Dan Cody RC	2.50	1.00
❑ 260	Willie Parker	10.00	4.00
❑ 261	Travis Johnson RC	2.00	.75
❑ 262	Dan Orlovsky RC	3.00	1.25
❑ 263	Chris Baker	.50	.20
❑ 264	Luis Castillo RC	2.50	1.00
❑ 265	Travis Daniels RC	2.00	.75
❑ 266	Justin Miller RC	2.00	.75
❑ 267	J.R. Russell RC	2.00	.75
❑ 268	Lance Mitchell RC	2.00	.75
❑ 269	T.A. McLendon RC	1.25	.50
❑ 270	Jerricho Cotchery	.50	.20
❑ 271	Chad Owens RC	2.50	1.00
❑ 272	Tab Perry RC	2.50	1.00
❑ 273	Corey Webster RC	2.50	1.00
❑ 274	Fred Gibson RC	2.00	.75
❑ 275	Brandon Jones RC	2.50	1.00
❑ 276	DeWayne Robertson	.50	.20
❑ 277	Brock Berlin RC	2.00	.75
❑ 278	Nehemiah Broughton RC	2.00	.75
❑ 279	Shaun Cody RC	2.50	1.00
❑ 280	Anthony Wright	.50	.20
❑ 281	Damien Nash RC	2.00	.75
❑ 282	Ryan Fitzpatrick RC	4.00	1.50
❑ 283	Paris Warren RC	2.00	.75
❑ 284	Justin Tuck RC	2.50	1.00
❑ 285	Cedric Houston RC	2.50	1.00
❑ 286	Odell Thurman RC	2.50	1.00
❑ 287	Kirk Morrison RC	2.50	1.00
❑ 288	Josh Davis RC	2.00	.75
❑ 289	Craphonso Thorpe RC	2.00	.75
❑ 290	Sam Aiken	.50	.20
❑ 291	Stanley Wilson RC	2.00	.75
❑ 292	Jonathan Babineaux RC	2.00	.75
❑ 293	Darryl Blackstock RC	2.00	.75
❑ 294	Roydell Williams RC	2.50	1.00
❑ 295	Channing Crowder RC	2.50	1.00
❑ 296	Deandra Cobb RC	2.00	.75
❑ 297	Larry Brackins RC	1.25	.50
❑ 298	Bryant McFadden RC	2.50	1.00
❑ 299	Kevin Burnett RC	2.50	1.00
❑ 300	Barrett Ruud RC	2.50	1.00
❑ 301	Terrell Owens SP	5.00	2.00
❑ 302	Ben Roethlisberger SP	12.00	5.00
❑ 303	Eric Moulds SP	3.00	1.25
❑ 304	Eli Manning SP	10.00	4.00
❑ 305	Ed Reed SP	3.00	1.25
❑ 306	Larry Fitzgerald SP	5.00	2.00
❑ 307	Clinton Portis SP	5.00	2.00
❑ 308	Priest Holmes SP	5.00	2.00
❑ 309	Drew Bennett SP	3.00	1.25
❑ 310	Steven Jackson SP	6.00	2.50
❑ 311	Roy Williams S SP	3.00	1.25
❑ 312	Marcel Shipp SP	2.50	1.00
❑ 313	Peerless Price SP	2.50	1.00
❑ 314	Troy Vincent SP	2.50	1.00
❑ 315	Justin Gage SP	2.50	1.00
❑ 316	Nick Goings SP	2.50	1.00
❑ 317	Dennis Northcutt SP	2.50	1.00
❑ 318	Quincy Morgan SP	2.50	1.00
❑ 319	Darius Watts SP	3.00	1.25
❑ 320	Jason Elam SP	2.50	1.00
❑ 321	Nick Barnett SP	2.50	1.00
❑ 322	Tony Hollings SP	2.50	1.00

❑	323 Samie Parker SP	2.50	1.00
❑	324 Kelly Campbell SP	2.50	1.00
❑	325 Kelly Holcomb SP	2.50	1.00
❑	326 Darren Sharper SP	2.50	1.00
❑	327 Tedy Bruschi SP	3.00	1.25
❑	328 Ernie Conwell SP	2.50	1.00
❑	329 Shaun Ellis SP	2.50	1.00
❑	330 Teyo Johnson SP	2.50	1.00
❑	331 Chris Brown SP	3.00	1.25
❑	332 Quentin Jammer SP	2.50	1.00
❑	333 Fred Smoot SP	2.50	1.00
❑	334 Eric Parker SP	2.50	1.00
❑	335 Steve Heiden SP	2.50	1.00
❑	336 Troy Polamalu SP	8.00	3.00
❑	337 Todd Pinkston SP	2.50	1.00
❑	338 L.J. Smith SP	2.50	1.00
❑	339 London Fletcher SP	2.50	1.00
❑	340 Devery Henderson SP	2.50	1.00
❑	341A Troy Williamson SP RC	6.00	2.50
❑	341B Troy Williamson TBJ SP	8.00	3.00
❑	342A J.J. Arrington SP RC	4.00	1.50
❑	342B J.J. Arrington 58T SP	5.00	2.00
❑	343A Carnell Williams SP RC	12.00	5.00
❑	343B Carnell Williams TBJ SP	15.00	6.00
❑	344A Aaron Rodgers SP RC	10.00	4.00
❑	344B Aaron Rodgers 58T SP	12.00	5.00
❑	345A Matt Jones SP RC	8.00	3.00
❑	345B Matt Jones 58T SP	10.00	4.00
❑	346A Roddy White SP RC	3.00	1.25
❑	346B Roddy White 58T SP	4.00	1.50
❑	347A Braylon Edwards SP RC	10.00	4.00
❑	347B Braylon Edwards TBJ SP	12.00	5.00
❑	348A Adam Jones SP RC	3.00	1.25
❑	348B Adam Jones TBJ SP	4.00	1.50
❑	349A Mark Clayton SP RC	4.00	1.50
❑	349B Mark Clayton TBJ SP	5.00	2.00
❑	350A Stefan LeFors SP RC	3.00	1.25
❑	350B Stefan LeFors 58T SP	4.00	1.50
❑	351 Alvin Pearman SP RC	3.00	1.25
❑	352 Erasmus James SP RC	3.00	1.25
❑	353 David Pollack SP RC	3.00	1.25
❑	354 Brandon Jacobs SP RC	4.00	1.50
❑	355 Chris Henry SP RC	3.00	1.25
❑	356 Thomas Davis SP RC	3.00	1.25
❑	357 Rasheed Marshall SP RC	3.00	1.25
❑	358 Matt Roth SP RC	3.00	1.25
❑	359 DeMarcus Ware SP RC	5.00	2.00
❑	360 Matt Cassell SP RC	5.00	2.00
❑	361 Stanford Routt SP RC	2.50	1.00
❑	362 Marlin Jackson SP RC	3.00	1.25
❑	363 Der.Johnson 59T SP ERR	5.00	2.00
❑	364 Jerome Mathis SP RC	3.00	1.25
❑	365 Lionel Gates SP RC	2.50	1.00

2002 Topps Pristine

❑	COMP.SET w/o SP's (50)	50.00	20.00
❑	1 Peyton Manning	5.00	2.00
❑	2 Darrell Jackson	1.50	.60
❑	3 Donovan McNabb	3.00	1.25
❑	4 Rod Smith	1.50	.60
❑	5 Daunte Culpepper	2.50	1.00
❑	6 Drew Brees	2.50	1.00
❑	7 Stephen Davis	1.50	.60
❑	8 Kurt Warner	2.50	1.00
❑	9 Eric Moulds	1.50	.60
❑	10 Jake Plummer	1.50	.60
❑	11 Chris Weinke	1.50	.60
❑	12 Brian Griese	2.50	1.00
❑	13 Corey Bradford	1.00	.40
❑	14 Trent Green	1.50	.60
❑	15 Tom Brady	6.00	2.50
❑	16 Jeff Garcia	2.50	1.00
❑	17 Tiki Barber	2.50	1.00
❑	18 Eddie George	2.50	1.00
❑	19 Jamal Lewis	2.50	1.00
❑	20 Troy Brown	1.50	.60
❑	21 Priest Holmes	3.00	1.25
❑	22 Jimmy Smith	1.50	.60
❑	23 Tim Brown	2.50	1.00
❑	24 Plaxico Burress	2.50	1.00
❑	25 Aaron Brooks	2.50	1.00
❑	26 Marshall Faulk	2.50	1.00
❑	27 Steve McNair	2.50	1.00
❑	28 Curtis Martin	2.50	1.00
❑	29 Corey Dillon	1.50	.60
❑	30 Tim Couch	1.50	.60
❑	31 Michael Vick	8.00	3.00
❑	32 David Boston	2.50	1.00
❑	33 Kordell Stewart	1.50	.60
❑	34 Jerome Bettis	2.50	1.00
❑	35 Keyshawn Johnson	2.50	1.00
❑	36 Torry Holt	2.50	1.00
❑	37 Shaun Alexander	3.00	1.25
❑	38 Brett Favre	6.00	2.50
❑	39 Marvin Harrison	2.50	1.00
❑	40 Randy Moss	5.00	2.00
❑	41 Jerry Rice	5.00	2.00
❑	42 LaDainian Tomlinson	4.00	1.50
❑	43 Terrell Owens	2.50	1.00
❑	44 Edgerrin James	3.00	1.25
❑	45 Anthony Thomas	1.50	.60
❑	46 Drew Bledsoe	3.00	1.25
❑	47 Ahman Green	2.50	1.00
❑	48 Ricky Williams	2.50	1.00
❑	49 Tony Gonzalez	1.50	.60
❑	50 Emmitt Smith	6.00	2.50
❑	51 Joey Harrington C RC	8.00	3.00
❑	52 Joey Harrington U	10.00	4.00
❑	53 Joey Harrington R	15.00	6.00
❑	54 Josh McCown C RC	4.00	1.50
❑	55 Josh McCown U	5.00	2.00
❑	56 Josh McCown R	8.00	3.00
❑	57 Antwaan Randle El C RC	5.00	2.00
❑	58 Antwaan Randle El U	6.00	2.50
❑	59 Antwaan Randle El R	10.00	4.00
❑	60 Reche Caldwell C RC	3.00	1.25
❑	61 Reche Caldwell U	4.00	1.50
❑	62 Reche Caldwell R	6.00	2.50
❑	63 Jason McAddley C RC	2.50	1.00
❑	64 Jason McAddley U	3.00	1.25
❑	65 Jason McAddley R	5.00	2.00
❑	66 Ashley Lelie C RC	6.00	2.50
❑	67 Ashley Lelie U	8.00	3.00
❑	68 Ashley Lelie R	12.00	5.00
❑	69 Travis Stephens C RC	2.50	1.00
❑	70 Travis Stephens U	3.00	1.25
❑	71 Travis Stephens R	5.00	2.00
❑	72 Chad Hutchinson C RC	2.50	1.00
❑	73 Chad Hutchinson U	3.00	1.25
❑	74 Chad Hutchinson R	5.00	2.00
❑	75 Quentin Jammer C RC	3.00	1.25
❑	76 Quentin Jammer U	4.00	1.50
❑	77 Quentin Jammer R	6.00	2.50
❑	78 Tim Carter C RC	2.50	1.00
❑	79 Tim Carter U	3.00	1.25
❑	80 Tim Carter R	5.00	2.00
❑	81 Antonio Bryant C RC	3.00	1.25
❑	82 Antonio Bryant U	4.00	1.50
❑	83 Antonio Bryant R	6.00	2.50
❑	84 Cliff Russell C RC	2.50	1.00
❑	85 Cliff Russell U	3.00	1.25
❑	86 Cliff Russell R	5.00	2.00
❑	87 Rohan Davey C RC	3.00	1.25
❑	88 Rohan Davey U	4.00	1.50
❑	89 Rohan Davey R	6.00	2.50
❑	90 Javon Walker C RC	6.00	2.50
❑	91 Javon Walker U	8.00	3.00
❑	92 Javon Walker R	10.00	4.00
❑	93 T.J. Duckett C RC	5.00	2.00
❑	94 T.J. Duckett U	6.00	2.50
❑	95 T.J. Duckett R	10.00	4.00
❑	96 Donte Stallworth C RC	6.00	2.50
❑	97 Donte Stallworth U	8.00	3.00
❑	98 Donte Stallworth R	12.00	5.00
❑	99 Andre Davis C RC	2.50	1.00
❑	100 Andre Davis U	3.00	1.25
❑	101 Andre Davis R	5.00	2.00
❑	102 Mike Williams C RC	2.50	1.00
❑	103 Mike Williams U	3.00	1.25
❑	104 Mike Williams R	5.00	2.00
❑	105 Freddie Milons C RC	2.50	1.00
❑	106 Freddie Milons U	3.00	1.25
❑	107 Freddie Milons R	5.00	2.00
❑	108 John Henderson C RC	3.00	1.25
❑	109 John Henderson U	3.00	1.25
❑	110 John Henderson R	6.00	2.50
❑	111 DeShaun Foster C RC	3.00	1.25
❑	112 DeShaun Foster U	4.00	1.50
❑	113 DeShaun Foster R	6.00	2.50
❑	114 Josh Reed C RC	3.00	1.25
❑	115 Josh Reed U	4.00	1.50
❑	116 Josh Reed R	6.00	2.50
❑	117 Jabar Gaffney C RC	3.00	1.25
❑	118 Jabar Gaffney U	4.00	1.50
❑	119 Jabar Gaffney R	6.00	2.50
❑	120 Clinton Portis C RC	10.00	4.00
❑	121 Clinton Portis U	12.00	5.00
❑	122 Clinton Portis R	20.00	7.50
❑	123 Jeremy Shockey C RC	10.00	4.00
❑	124 Jeremy Shockey U	12.00	5.00
❑	125 Jeremy Shockey R	20.00	7.50
❑	126 Dwight Freeney C RC	4.00	1.50
❑	127 Dwight Freeney U	5.00	2.00
❑	128 Dwight Freeney R	8.00	3.00
❑	129 Brian Westbrook C RC	5.00	2.00
❑	130 Brian Westbrook U	6.00	2.50
❑	131 Brian Westbrook R	10.00	4.00
❑	132 Randy Fasani C RC	2.50	1.00
❑	133 Randy Fasani U	3.00	1.25
❑	134 Randy Fasani R	5.00	2.00
❑	135 Julius Peppers C RC	6.00	2.50
❑	136 Julius Peppers U	8.00	3.00
❑	137 Julius Peppers R	12.00	5.00
❑	138 Patrick Ramsey C RC	6.00	2.50
❑	139 Patrick Ramsey U	5.00	2.00
❑	140 Patrick Ramsey R	8.00	3.00
❑	141 William Green C RC	3.00	1.25
❑	142 William Green U	5.00	2.00
❑	143 William Green R	8.00	3.00
❑	144 Daniel Graham C RC	3.00	1.25
❑	145 Daniel Graham U	4.00	1.50
❑	146 Daniel Graham R	6.00	2.50
❑	147 Ron Johnson C RC	2.50	1.00
❑	148 Ron Johnson U	3.00	1.25
❑	149 Ron Johnson R	5.00	2.00
❑	150 Maurice Morris C RC	3.00	1.25
❑	151 Maurice Morris U	4.00	1.50
❑	152 Maurice Morris R	6.00	2.50
❑	153 Eric Crouch C RC	3.00	1.25
❑	154 Eric Crouch U	5.00	2.00
❑	155 Eric Crouch R	8.00	3.00
❑	156 Roy Williams C RC	8.00	3.00
❑	157 Roy Williams U	10.00	4.00
❑	158 Roy Williams R	15.00	6.00
❑	159 Ladell Betts C RC	3.00	1.25
❑	160 Ladell Betts U	5.00	2.00
❑	161 Ladell Betts R	8.00	3.00
❑	162 David Garrard C RC	3.00	1.25
❑	163 David Garrard U	4.00	1.50
❑	164 David Garrard R	6.00	2.50
❑	165 Marquise Walker C RC	2.50	1.00
❑	166 Marquise Walker U	3.00	1.25
❑	167 Marquise Walker R	5.00	2.00
❑	168 David Carr C RC	8.00	3.00
❑	169 David Carr U	10.00	4.00
❑	170 David Carr R	15.00	6.00
❑	ESA1 Emmitt Smith AU	300.00	175.00
❑	ESJ1 Emmitt Smith JSY	40.00	15.00

2003 Topps Pristine

❑	COMP.SET w/o SP's (50)	40.00	15.00
❑	UNPRICED PRESS PLATES EXIST		
❑	FOUR DIFF.COLOR PP's MADE PER CARD		
❑	PRESS PLATES STATED ODDS 1:107		
❑	1 Brett Favre	6.00	2.50
❑	2 Rich Gannon	1.50	.60
❑	3 Randy Moss	4.00	1.50
❑	4 Travis Henry	1.50	.60
❑	5 Troy Brown	1.50	.60
❑	6 Darrell Jackson	1.50	.60
❑	7 Steve McNair	2.50	1.00
❑	8 Plaxico Burress	1.50	.60

❑ 9 Jerry Rice 5.00 2.00
❑ 10 Donovan McNabb 3.00 1.25
❑ 11 Marty Booker 1.50 .60
❑ 12 Joey Galloway 1.50 .60
❑ 13 Peerless Price 1.50 .60
❑ 14 Emmitt Smith 6.00 2.50
❑ 15 David Carr 4.00 1.50
❑ 16 Priest Holmes 3.00 1.25
❑ 17 LaDainian Tomlinson 2.50 1.00
❑ 18 Hines Ward 2.50 1.00
❑ 19 Tiki Barber 2.50 1.00
❑ 20 Fred Taylor 2.50 1.00
❑ 21 Marvin Harrison 2.50 1.00
❑ 22 Marshall Faulk 2.50 1.00
❑ 23 Terrell Owens 2.50 1.00
❑ 24 Patrick Ramsey 2.50 1.00
❑ 25 Michael Vick 6.00 2.50
❑ 26 Tom Brady 6.00 2.50
❑ 27 Shaun Alexander 2.50 1.00
❑ 28 Derrick Mason 1.50 .60
❑ 29 Keyshawn Johnson 2.50 1.00
❑ 30 Ricky Williams 2.50 1.00
❑ 31 Ahman Green 2.50 1.00
❑ 32 Joey Harrington 4.00 1.50
❑ 33 Corey Dillon 1.50 .60
❑ 34 Jamal Lewis 2.50 1.00
❑ 35 Drew Bledsoe 2.50 1.00
❑ 36 Tommy Maddox 2.50 1.00
❑ 37 Kurt Warner 2.50 1.00
❑ 38 Deuce McAllister 2.50 1.00
❑ 39 Curtis Martin 2.50 1.00
❑ 40 Chad Pennington 3.00 1.25
❑ 41 Trent Green 1.50 .60
❑ 42 Edgerrin James 2.50 1.00
❑ 43 Clinton Portis 4.00 1.50
❑ 44 Eric Moulds 1.50 .60
❑ 45 Peyton Manning 4.00 1.50
❑ 46 Jeff Garcia 2.50 1.00
❑ 47 Daunte Culpepper 2.50 1.00
❑ 48 Tim Couch 1.00 .40
❑ 49 Drew Brees 2.50 1.00
❑ 50 Aaron Brooks 2.50 1.00
❑ 51 Anquan Boldin C RC 8.00 3.00
❑ 52 Anquan Boldin U 10.00 4.00
❑ 53 Anquan Boldin R 15.00 6.00
❑ 54 Andre Johnson C RC 6.00 2.50
❑ 55 Andre Johnson U 8.00 3.00
❑ 56 Andre Johnson R 12.00 5.00
❑ 57 Artose Pinner C RC 3.00 1.25
❑ 58 Artose Pinner U 4.00 1.50
❑ 59 Artose Pinner R 6.00 2.50
❑ 60 Bryant Johnson C RC 3.00 1.25
❑ 61 Bryant Johnson U 4.00 1.50
❑ 62 Bryant Johnson R 6.00 2.50
❑ 63 Bethel Johnson C RC 3.00 1.25
❑ 64 Bethel Johnson U 4.00 1.50
❑ 65 Bethel Johnson R 6.00 2.50
❑ 66 Byron Leftwich C RC 10.00 4.00
❑ 67 Byron Leftwich U 12.00 5.00
❑ 68 Byron Leftwich R 20.00 7.50
❑ 69 Brian St.Pierre C RC 3.00 1.25
❑ 70 Brian St.Pierre U 4.00 1.50
❑ 71 Brian St.Pierre R 6.00 2.50
❑ 72 Chris Brown C RC 4.00 1.50
❑ 73 Chris Brown U 5.00 2.00
❑ 74 Chris Brown R 8.00 3.00
❑ 75 Carson Palmer C RC 12.00 5.00
❑ 76 Carson Palmer U 15.00 6.00
❑ 77 Carson Palmer R 25.00 10.00
❑ 78 Charles Rogers C RC 3.00 1.25
❑ 79 Charles Rogers U 4.00 1.50
❑ 80 Charles Rogers R 6.00 2.50
❑ 81 Chris Simms C RC 5.00 2.00
❑ 82 Chris Simms U 6.00 2.50
❑ 83 Chris Simms R 10.00 4.00
❑ 84 Dallas Clark C RC 3.00 1.25
❑ 85 Dallas Clark U 4.00 1.50
❑ 86 Dallas Clark R 6.00 2.50
❑ 87 Dave Ragone C RC 3.00 1.25
❑ 88 Dave Ragone U 4.00 1.50
❑ 89 Dave Ragone R 6.00 2.50
❑ 90 DeWayne Robertson C RC 3.00 1.25
❑ 91 DeWayne Robertson U 4.00 1.50
❑ 92 DeWayne Robertson R 6.00 2.50
❑ 93 Justin Fargas C RC 3.00 1.25
❑ 94 Justin Fargas U 4.00 1.50
❑ 95 Justin Fargas R 6.00 2.50
❑ 96 Kyle Boller C RC 6.00 2.50
❑ 97 Kyle Boller U 8.00 3.00
❑ 98 Kyle Boller R 12.00 5.00
❑ 99 Kevin Curtis C RC 3.00 1.25
❑ 100 Kevin Curtis U 4.00 1.50
❑ 101 Kevin Curtis R 6.00 2.50
❑ 102 Ken Dorsey C RC 3.00 1.25
❑ 103 Ken Dorsey U 4.00 1.50
❑ 104 Ken Dorsey R 6.00 2.50
❑ 105 Kelley Washington C RC 3.00 1.25
❑ 106 Kelley Washington U 4.00 1.50
❑ 107 Kelley Washington R 6.00 2.50
❑ 108 Kliff Kingsbury C RC 2.50 1.00
❑ 109 Kliff Kingsbury U 3.00 1.25
❑ 110 Kliff Kingsbury R 5.00 2.00
❑ 111 Larry Johnson C RC 12.00 6.00
❑ 112 Larry Johnson U 15.00 7.50
❑ 113 Larry Johnson R 25.00 12.50
❑ 114 Musa Smith C RC 3.00 1.25
❑ 115 Musa Smith U 4.00 1.50
❑ 116 Musa Smith R 6.00 2.50
❑ 117 Marcus Trufant C RC 3.00 1.25
❑ 118 Marcus Trufant U 4.00 1.50
❑ 119 Marcus Trufant R 6.00 2.50
❑ 120 Nate Burleson C RC 4.00 1.50
❑ 121 Nate Burleson U 6.00 2.50
❑ 122 Nate Burleson R 10.00 4.00
❑ 123 Onterrio Smith C RC 3.00 1.25
❑ 124 Onterrio Smith U 4.00 1.50
❑ 125 Onterrio Smith R 6.00 2.50
❑ 126 Rex Grossman C RC 5.00 2.00
❑ 127 Rex Grossman U 6.00 2.50
❑ 128 Rex Grossman R 10.00 4.00
❑ 129 Seneca Wallace C RC 3.00 1.25
❑ 130 Seneca Wallace U 4.00 1.50
❑ 131 Seneca Wallace R 6.00 2.50
❑ 132 Tyrone Calico C RC 4.00 1.50
❑ 133 Tyrone Calico U 5.00 2.00
❑ 134 Tyrone Calico R 8.00 3.00
❑ 135 Taylor Jacobs C RC 2.50 1.00
❑ 136 Taylor Jacobs U 3.00 1.25
❑ 137 Taylor Jacobs R 5.00 2.00
❑ 138 Teyo Johnson C RC 3.00 1.25
❑ 139 Teyo Johnson U 4.00 1.50
❑ 140 Teyo Johnson R 6.00 2.50
❑ 141 Terence Newman C RC 6.00 2.50
❑ 142 Terence Newman U 8.00 3.00
❑ 143 Terence Newman R 12.00 5.00
❑ 144 Terrell Suggs C RC 5.00 2.00
❑ 145 Terrell Suggs U 6.00 2.50
❑ 146 Terrell Suggs R 10.00 4.00
❑ 147 Willis McGahee C RC 8.00 3.00
❑ 148 Willis McGahee U 10.00 4.00
❑ 149 Willis McGahee R 15.00 6.00

2004 Topps Pristine

❑ COMP.SET w/o SP's (50) 40.00 15.00
❑ U/999 STATED ODDS 1:2
❑ R/499 STATED ODDS 1:4
❑ UNPRICED PRESS PLATES #'d OF 1
❑ 1 Michael Vick 5.00 2.00
❑ 2 Tony Gonzalez 1.50 .60
❑ 3 Terrell Owens 2.50 1.00
❑ 4 Brett Favre 6.00 2.50
❑ 5 Jamal Lewis 2.50 1.00
❑ 6 Tim Rattay 1.50 .60
❑ 7 Ricky Williams 2.50 1.00
❑ 8 Edgerrin James 2.50 1.00
❑ 9 Torry Holt 2.50 1.00

❑ 10 Randy Moss 3.00 1.25
❑ 11 Derrick Mason 1.50 .60
❑ 12 Joe Horn 1.50 .60
❑ 13 Marvin Harrison 2.50 1.00
❑ 14 Carson Palmer 3.00 1.25
❑ 15 Anquan Boldin 2.50 1.00
❑ 16 Quincy Carter 1.50 .60
❑ 17 Byron Leftwich 3.00 1.25
❑ 18 Eric Moulds 1.50 .60
❑ 19 Marc Bulger 2.50 1.00
❑ 20 Ahman Green 2.50 1.00
❑ 21 Jeff Garcia 2.50 1.00
❑ 22 Laveranues Coles 1.50 .60
❑ 23 Hines Ward 2.50 1.00
❑ 24 Santana Moss 1.50 .60
❑ 25 LaDainian Tomlinson 3.00 1.25
❑ 26 Domanick Davis 2.50 1.00
❑ 27 Stephen Davis 1.50 .60
❑ 28 Tiki Barber 2.50 1.00
❑ 29 Chris Chambers 1.50 .60
❑ 30 Priest Holmes 3.00 1.25
❑ 31 Chad Pennington 2.50 1.00
❑ 32 Shaun Alexander 2.50 1.00
❑ 33 Brad Johnson 1.50 .60
❑ 34 Marshall Faulk 2.50 1.00
❑ 35 Peyton Manning 4.00 1.50
❑ 36 Jake Plummer 1.50 .60
❑ 37 Clinton Portis 2.50 1.00
❑ 38 Matt Hasselbeck 1.50 .60
❑ 39 Amani Toomer 1.50 .60
❑ 40 Steve McNair 2.50 1.00
❑ 41 Daunte Culpepper 2.50 1.00
❑ 42 Fred Taylor 1.50 .60
❑ 43 Joey Harrington 2.50 1.00
❑ 44 Jake Delhomme 2.50 1.00
❑ 45 Deuce McAllister 2.50 1.00
❑ 46 Chad Johnson 2.50 1.00
❑ 47 Travis Henry 1.50 .60
❑ 48 Corey Dillon 1.50 .60
❑ 49 Tom Brady 6.00 2.50
❑ 50 Donovan McNabb 3.00 1.25
❑ 51 Ben Roethlisberger C RC 30.00 15.00
❑ 52 Ben Roethlisberger U 40.00 20.00
❑ 53 Ben Roethlisberger R 50.00 25.00
❑ 54 Ben Troupe C RC 3.00 1.25
❑ 55 Ben Troupe U 4.00 1.50
❑ 56 Ben Troupe R 5.00 2.00
❑ 57 Ben Watson C RC 3.00 1.25
❑ 58 Ben Watson U 4.00 1.50
❑ 59 Ben Watson R 5.00 2.00
❑ 60 Bernard Berrian C RC 3.00 1.25
❑ 61 Bernard Berrian U 4.00 1.50
❑ 62 Bernard Berrian R 5.00 2.00
❑ 63 Cedric Cobbs C RC 3.00 1.25
❑ 64 Cedric Cobbs U 4.00 1.50
❑ 65 Cedric Cobbs R 5.00 2.00
❑ 66 Chris Perry C RC 5.00 2.00
❑ 67 Chris Perry U 6.00 2.50
❑ 68 Chris Perry R 8.00 3.00
❑ 69 Darius Watts C RC 3.00 1.25
❑ 70 Darius Watts U 4.00 1.50
❑ 71 Darius Watts R 5.00 2.00
❑ 72 DeAngelo Hall C RC 4.00 1.50
❑ 73 DeAngelo Hall U 5.00 2.00
❑ 74 DeAngelo Hall R 6.00 2.50
❑ 75 Derrick Hamilton C RC 2.50 1.00
❑ 76 Derrick Hamilton U 3.00 1.25
❑ 77 Derrick Hamilton R 5.00 2.00
❑ 78 Devard Darling C RC 3.00 1.25
❑ 79 Devard Darling U 4.00 1.50

❑ 80 Devard Darling R 5.00 2.00
❑ 81 Devery Henderson C RC 2.50 1.00
❑ 82 Devery Henderson U 3.00 1.25
❑ 83 Devery Henderson R 4.00 1.50
❑ 84 Dunta Robinson C RC 3.00 1.25
❑ 85 Dunta Robinson U 4.00 1.50
❑ 86 Dunta Robinson R 5.00 2.00
❑ 87 Eli Manning C RC 15.00 7.50
❑ 88 Eli Manning U 20.00 7.50
❑ 89 Eli Manning R 25.00 10.00
❑ 90 Greg Jones C RC 3.00 1.25
❑ 91 Greg Jones U 4.00 1.50
❑ 92 Greg Jones R 5.00 2.00
❑ 93 J.P. Losman C RC 6.00 2.50
❑ 94 J.P. Losman U 8.00 3.00
❑ 95 J.P. Losman R 10.00 4.00
❑ 96 Julius Jones C RC 12.00 5.00
❑ 97 Julius Jones U 15.00 6.00
❑ 98 Julius Jones R 20.00 7.50
❑ 99 Keary Colbert C RC 4.00 1.50
❑ 100 Keary Colbert U 5.00 2.00
❑ 101 Keary Colbert R 6.00 2.50
❑ 102 Kellen Winslow C RC 6.00 2.50
❑ 103 Kellen Winslow U 8.00 3.00
❑ 104 Kellen Winslow R 10.00 4.00
❑ 105 Kevin Jones C RC 10.00 4.00
❑ 106 Kevin Jones U 12.00 5.00
❑ 107 Kevin Jones R 15.00 6.00
❑ 108 Larry Fitzgerald C RC 10.00 4.00
❑ 109 Larry Fitzgerald U 12.00 5.00
❑ 110 Larry Fitzgerald R 15.00 6.00
❑ 111 Lee Evans C RC 4.00 1.50
❑ 112 Lee Evans U 5.00 2.00
❑ 113 Lee Evans R 6.00 2.50
❑ 114 Luke McCown C RC 3.00 1.25
❑ 115 Luke McCown U 4.00 1.50
❑ 116 Luke McCown R 5.00 2.00
❑ 117 Matt Schaub C RC 5.00 2.00
❑ 118 Matt Schaub U 6.00 2.50
❑ 119 Matt Schaub R 8.00 3.00
❑ 120 Mewelde Moore C RC 4.00 1.50
❑ 121 Mewelde Moore U 5.00 2.00
❑ 122 Mewelde Moore R 6.00 2.50
❑ 123 Michael Clayton C RC 6.00 2.50
❑ 124 Michael Clayton U 8.00 3.00
❑ 125 Michael Clayton R 10.00 4.00
❑ 126 Michael Jenkins C RC 3.00 1.25
❑ 127 Michael Jenkins U 4.00 1.50
❑ 128 Michael Jenkins R 5.00 2.00
❑ 129 Philip Rivers C RC 10.00 4.00
❑ 130 Philip Rivers U 12.00 5.00
❑ 131 Philip Rivers R 15.00 6.00
❑ 132 Rashaun Woods C RC 3.00 1.25
❑ 133 Rashaun Woods U 4.00 1.50
❑ 134 Rashaun Woods R 5.00 2.00
❑ 135 Reggie Williams C RC 4.00 1.50
❑ 136 Reggie Williams U 5.00 2.00
❑ 137 Reggie Williams R 6.00 2.50
❑ 138 Robert Gallery C RC 5.00 2.00
❑ 139 Robert Gallery U 6.00 2.50
❑ 140 Robert Gallery R 8.00 3.00
❑ 141 Roy Williams C RC 8.00 3.00
❑ 142 Roy Williams U 10.00 4.00
❑ 143 Roy Williams R 12.00 5.00
❑ 144 Steven Jackson C RC 10.00 4.00
❑ 145 Steven Jackson U 12.00 5.00
❑ 146 Steven Jackson R 15.00 6.00
❑ 147 Tatum Bell C RC 6.00 2.50
❑ 148 Tatum Bell U 8.00 3.00
❑ 149 Tatum Bell R 10.00 4.00

2005 Topps Pristine

❑ COMP.SET w/o SP's (100) 60.00 25.00
❑ OVERALL JSY U STATED ODDS 1:6
❑ JSY U PRINT RUN 900 UNLESS NOTED
❑ AU R/100 STATED ODDS 1:37
❑ JSY AU S/25 STATED ODDS 1:675
❑ UNPRICED PRINT.PLATES PRINT RUN 1 SET
❑ 1 Tiki Barber C 2.50 1.00
❑ 2 LaDainian Tomlinson C 3.00 1.25
❑ 3 Drew Bennett C 1.50 .60
❑ 4 Jake Delhomme C 2.50 1.00
❑ 5 Deuce McAllister C 2.50 1.00
❑ 6 Jerome Bettis C 2.50 1.00
❑ 7 Javon Walker C 1.50 .60
❑ 8 Marshall Faulk C 2.50 1.00

❑ 9 Trent Green C 1.50 .60
❑ 10 Travis Henry C 1.50 .60
❑ 11 Eli Manning C 5.00 2.00
❑ 12 Donovan McNabb C 3.00 1.25
❑ 13 Priest Holmes C 2.50 1.00
❑ 14 Brandon Stokley C 1.50 .60
❑ 15 Curtis Martin C 2.50 1.00
❑ 16 Muhsin Muhammad C 1.50 .60
❑ 17 Corey Dillon C 1.50 .60
❑ 18 Fred Taylor C 1.50 .60
❑ 19 Michael Vick C 4.00 1.50
❑ 20 Michael Jenkins C 1.50 .60
❑ 21 Chris Brown C 1.50 .60
❑ 22 Willis McGahee C 2.50 1.00
❑ 23 Drew Bledsoe C 2.50 1.00
❑ 24 Michael Clayton C 2.50 1.00
❑ 25 Kerry Collins C 1.50 .60
❑ 26 Jason Witten C 1.50 .60
❑ 27 Clinton Portis C 2.50 1.00
❑ 28 Marc Bulger C 2.50 1.00
❑ 29 Julius Jones C 3.00 .40
❑ 30 Chad Pennington C 2.50 1.00
❑ 31 Kevin Jones C 2.50 1.00
❑ 32 Domanick Davis C 1.50 .60
❑ 33 Reggie Wayne C 1.50 .60
❑ 34 Jimmy Smith C 1.50 .60
❑ 35 Byron Leftwich C 2.50 1.00
❑ 36 Randy Moss C 2.50 1.00
❑ 37 Isaac Bruce C 1.50 .60
❑ 38 LaMont Jordan C 2.50 1.00
❑ 39 Edgerrin James C 2.50 1.00
❑ 40 Aaron Brooks C 1.50 .60
❑ 41 Steven Jackson C 3.00 1.25
❑ 42 Cedric Benson C RC 8.00 3.00
❑ 43 Brian Westbrook C 1.50 .60
❑ 44 Andrew Walter C RC 6.00 2.50
❑ 45 Andre Johnson C 1.50 .60
❑ 46 David Greene C RC 4.00 1.50
❑ 47 David Carr C 2.50 1.00
❑ 48 Marion Barber C RC 6.00 2.50
❑ 49 Warrick Dunn C 1.50 .60
❑ 50 Terrence Murphy C RC 4.00 1.50
❑ 51 Dante Hall C 1.50 .60
❑ 52 Willie Parker C 12.00 5.00
❑ 53 Laveranues Coles C 1.50 .60
❑ 54 DeMarcus Ware C RC 6.00 2.50
❑ 55 Santana Moss C 1.50 .60
❑ 56 Alvin Pearman C RC 4.00 1.50
❑ 57 Keary Colbert C 1.50 .60
❑ 58 Carlos Rogers C RC 5.00 2.00
❑ 59 Jeremy Shockey C 2.50 1.00
❑ 60 Craig Bragg C RC 3.00 1.25
❑ 61 Daunte Culpepper C 2.50 1.00
❑ 62 Charlie Frye C RC 8.00 3.00
❑ 63 DeShaun Foster C 1.50 .60
❑ 64 Chad Owens C RC 4.00 1.50
❑ 65 Dunta Robinson C 1.50 .60
❑ 66 Mike Nugent C RC 4.00 1.50
❑ 67 Jonathan Vilma C 1.50 .60
❑ 68 Erasmus James C RC 4.00 1.50
❑ 69 Randy McMichael C 1.25 .50
❑ 70 Stefan LeFors C RC 4.00 1.50
❑ 71 Ben Roethlisberger C 6.00 2.50
❑ 72 Tab Perry C RC 4.00 1.50
❑ 73 Joey Harrington C 2.50 1.00
❑ 74 Adrian McPherson C RC 4.00 1.50
❑ 75 Roy Williams WR C 2.50 1.00
❑ 76 Vincent Jackson C RC 4.00 1.50
❑ 77 Lee Suggs C 1.50 .60
❑ 78 Ryan Moats C RC 4.00 1.50
❑ 79 Plaxico Burress C 1.50 .60
❑ 80 Chris Henry C RC 4.00 1.50
❑ 81 Larry Fitzgerald C 2.50 1.00
❑ 82 Travis Johnson C RC 3.00 1.25
❑ 83 Terrell Owens C 2.50 1.00
❑ 84 Fabian Washington C RC 4.00 1.50
❑ 85 Stephen Davis C 1.50 .60
❑ 86 Odell Thurman C RC 4.00 1.50
❑ 87 Tatum Bell C 1.50 .60
❑ 88 Roddy White C RC 4.00 1.50
❑ 89 J.P. Losman C 2.50 1.00
❑ 90 J.J. Arrington C RC 5.00 2.00
❑ 91 Thomas Jones C 1.50 .60
❑ 92 Eric Shelton C RC 4.00 1.50
❑ 93 Charles Rogers C 1.50 .60
❑ 94 Matt Jones C RC 10.00 4.00
❑ 95 Chris Chambers C 1.50 .60
❑ 96 Jerome Mathis C RC 4.00 1.50
❑ 97 Darrell Jackson C 1.50 .60
❑ 98 Justin Miller C RC 3.00 1.25
❑ 99 Donte Stallworth C 1.50 .60
❑ 100 Brandon Jacobs C RC 5.00 2.00
❑ 101 Alex Smith QB JSY U RC 20.00 7.50
❑ 102 Mark Clayton JSY U RC 10.00 4.00
❑ 103 Antrel Rolle JSY U RC 8.00 3.00
❑ 104 Kyle Orton JSY/500 U RC 12.00 5.00
❑ 105 Roscoe Parrish JSY U RC 8.00 3.00
❑ 106 Vernand Morency JSY U RC 8.00 3.00
❑ 107 Maurice Clarett JSY U 8.00 3.00
❑ 108 Mark Bradley JSY U RC 8.00 3.00
❑ 109 Reg.Brown JSY/500 U RC 10.00 4.00
❑ 110 Ronnie Brown JSY U RC 15.00 6.00
❑ 111 B.Edwards JSY/500 U RC 12.00 5.00
❑ 112 T.Williamson JSY/500 U RC 10.00 4.00
❑ 113 Carnell Williams JSY U RC 20.00 7.50
❑ 114 Ricky Williams JSY/500 U 10.00 4.00
❑ 115 Jake Plummer JSY/500 U 10.00 4.00
❑ 116 Brian Urlacher JSY U 10.00 4.00
❑ 117 Joe Horn JSY/500 U 10.00 4.00
❑ 118 Anquan Boldin JSY/500 U 8.00 3.00
❑ 119 Carson Palmer JSY U 10.00 4.00
❑ 120 Rudi Johnson JSY/500 U 10.00 4.00
❑ 121 Matt Hasselbeck JSY/500 U 8.00 3.00
❑ 122 Warren Sapp JSY U
❑ 123 Steve McNair JSY/500 U 10.00 4.00
❑ 124 Shaun Alexander JSY U 12.00 5.00
❑ 125 Julius Peppers JSY/500 U 10.00 4.00
❑ 126 Dwight Freeney JSY/500 U 10.00 4.00
❑ 127 Patrick Kerney JSY U 8.00 3.00
❑ 128 Drew Brees JSY U 10.00 4.00
❑ 129 Tony Gonzalez JSY/500 U 8.00 3.00
❑ 130 Alge Crumpler JSY/500 U 8.00 3.00
❑ 131 Chad Johnson JSY/500 U 10.00 4.00
❑ 132 M.Muhammad JSY/500 U 8.00 3.00
❑ 133 Zach Thomas JSY/500 U 10.00 4.00
❑ 134 Marvin Harrison JSY U 10.00 4.00
❑ 135 LaVar Arrington JSY U 10.00 4.00
❑ 136 Eric Moulds JSY U 8.00 3.00
❑ 137 Michael Strahan JSY U 8.00 3.00
❑ 138 Jamal Lewis JSY/500 U 10.00 4.00
❑ 139 Ray Lewis JSY U 10.00 4.00
❑ 140 Hines Ward JSY/500 U 10.00 4.00
❑ 141 Peyton Manning JSY/500 U 15.00 6.00
❑ 142 Tom Brady JSY/500 U 15.00 6.00
❑ 143 Ahman Green JSY/500 U 10.00 4.00
❑ 144 Trent Green JSY/500 U 10.00 4.00
❑ 145 Brett Favre JSY/500 U 25.00 10.00
❑ 146 Aaron Rodgers AU R RC 80.00 30.00
❑ 147 Adam Jones AU R RC 20.00 7.50
❑ 148 Alex Smith QB AU R 100.00 50.00
❑ 149 Antrel Rolle AU R 25.00 10.00
❑ 150 Braylon Edwards AU R 60.00 30.00
❑ 151 Ciatrick Fason AU R RC 20.00 7.50
❑ 152 Courtney Roby AU R RC 20.00 7.50
❑ 153 Craphonso Thorpe AU R RC 20.00 7.50
❑ 154 Dan Cody AU R RC 20.00 7.50
❑ 155 Dan Orlovsky AU R RC 30.00 12.50
❑ 156 Darren Sproles AU R RC 20.00 7.50
❑ 157 David Pollack AU R RC 20.00 7.50
❑ 158 Derrick Johnson AU R RC 40.00 20.00
❑ 159 Frank Gore AU R RC 30.00 15.00
❑ 160 Heath Miller AU R RC 60.00 35.00
❑ 161 Jason Campbell AU R RC 40.00 20.00
❑ 162 Kyle Orton AU R 40.00 20.00
❑ 163 Mike Williams AU R 50.00 20.00
❑ 164 Ronnie Brown AU R 100.00 50.00
❑ 165 Troy Williamson AU R 40.00 20.00

166 Vernand Morency AU R	15.00	6.00
167 Deion Branch AU R	20.00	7.50
168 Brett Favre JSY AU S	250.00	150.00
169 Joe Montana JSY AU S	250.00	150.00
170 Barry Sanders JSY AU S	200.00	100.00
171 Tom Brady JSY AU S	200.00	100.00
172 Dan Marino JSY AU S	250.00	150.00

2004 Topps Signature

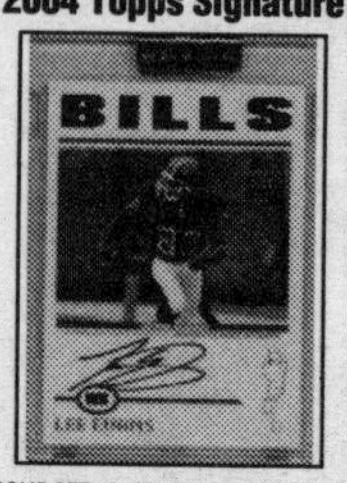

COMP.SET w/o SP's (55) 40.00 15.00
56-75 ROOKIE/499 STATED ODDS 1:3
ROOKIE AU/299 GROUP A ODDS 1:15
ROOKIE AU/999 GROUP B ODDS 1:11
ROOKIE AU/1099 GROUP C ODDS 1:4
ROOKIE AU/1499 GROUP D ODDS 1:3

1 Tom Brady	6.00	2.50
2 Chad Johnson	2.50	1.00
3 Amani Toomer	1.50	.60
4 Shaun Alexander	2.50	1.00
5 Terrell Owens	2.50	1.00
6 Jake Delhomme	2.50	1.00
7 Eric Moulds	1.50	.60
8 Fred Taylor	1.50	.60
9 Mark Brunell	1.50	.60
10 Priest Holmes	3.00	1.25
11 Marvin Harrison	2.50	1.00
12 Jeff Garcia	2.50	1.00
13 Brad Johnson	1.50	.60
14 Laveranues Coles	1.50	.60
15 LaDainian Tomlinson	3.00	1.25
16 Anquan Boldin	2.50	1.00
17 Curtis Martin	2.50	1.00
18 Joe Horn	1.50	.60
19 Domanick Davis	2.50	1.00
20 Jamal Lewis	2.50	1.00
21 Steve Smith	2.50	1.00
22 Aaron Brooks	1.50	.60
23 Hines Ward	2.50	1.00
24 Marc Bulger	2.50	1.00
25 Randy Moss	3.00	1.25
26 Jerry Rice	5.00	2.00
27 Tiki Barber	2.50	1.00
28 Jake Plummer	1.50	.60
29 Travis Henry	1.50	.60
30 Michael Vick	5.00	2.00
31 Matt Hasselbeck	1.50	.60
32 Santana Moss	1.50	.60
33 Corey Dillon	1.50	.60
34 Byron Leftwich	3.00	1.25
35 Clinton Portis	2.50	1.00
36 Derrick Mason	1.50	.60
37 Tim Rattay	1.50	.60
38 Chris Chambers	1.50	.60
39 Joey Harrington	2.50	1.00
40 Deuce McAllister	2.50	1.00
41 Tony Gonzalez	1.50	.60
42 Kurt Warner	2.50	1.00
43 Carson Palmer	3.00	1.25
44 Marshall Faulk	2.50	1.00
45 Peyton Manning	4.00	1.50
46 Ahman Green	2.50	1.00
47 Torry Holt	2.50	1.00
48 Chad Pennington	2.50	1.00
49 Trent Green	1.50	.60
50 Brett Favre	6.00	2.50
51 Stephen Davis	1.50	.60
52 Steve McNair	2.50	1.00
53 Daunte Culpepper	2.50	1.00
54 Edgerrin James	2.50	1.00
55 Donovan McNabb	3.00	1.25
56 Sean Taylor RC	8.00	3.00
57 Darius Watts RC	6.00	2.50
58 Ben Troupe RC	6.00	2.50
59 Josh Harris RC	6.00	2.50
60 Jeff Smoker RC	6.00	2.50
61 Mewelde Moore RC	8.00	3.00
62 Reggie Williams RC	8.00	3.00
63 Ben Watson RC	6.00	2.50
64 Rashaun Woods RC	6.00	2.50
65 Kellen Winslow RC	12.00	5.00
66 Robert Gallery RC	10.00	4.00
67 Steven Jackson RC	25.00	10.00
68 Craig Krenzel RC	6.00	2.50
69 DeAngelo Hall RC	8.00	3.00
70 Devard Darling RC	6.00	2.50
71 Julius Jones RC	25.00	10.00
72 Derrick Hamilton RC	5.00	2.00
73 Devery Henderson RC	5.00	2.00
74 Dunta Robinson RC	6.00	2.50
75 Larry Fitzgerald RC	20.00	7.50
76 Chris Perry AU/999 RC	30.00	12.50
77 J.P. Losman AU/1099 RC	30.00	12.50
78 Lee Evans AU/1099 RC	25.00	10.00
79 Cedric Cobbs AU/1499 RC	15.00	6.00
80 Philip Rivers AU/299 RC	80.00	50.00
81 Greg Jones AU/1499 RC	20.00	7.50
82 Michael Clayton AU/1099 RC	40.00	15.00
83 Jonathan Vilma AU/1099 RC	20.00	7.50
84 Jericho Cotchery AU/1499 RC	15.00	6.00
85 Roy Williams AU/299 RC	60.00	25.00
86 Keary Colbert AU/1499 RC	20.00	7.50
87 Luke McCown AU/1499 RC	15.00	6.00
88 Bernard Berrian AU/1499 RC	15.00	6.00
89 Michael Jenkins AU/1499 RC	20.00	7.50
90 Eli Manning AU/299 RC	200.00	125.00
91 Matt Schaub AU/1499 RC	25.00	12.50
92 Tatum Bell AU/1099 RC	30.00	12.50
93 Roethlisberger AU/299 RC	300.00	175.00
94 Kevin Jones AU/1099 RC	40.00	15.00
95 Cody Pickett AU/999 RC	20.00	7.50
96 Drew Henson AU/299 RC	40.00	15.00

2003 Topps Total

COMPLETE SET (550)	80.00	40.00
1 Rich Gannon	.50	.20
2 Travis Henry	.50	.20
3 Brian Finneran	.30	.10
4 Ed Hartwell	.30	.10
5 Az-Zahir Hakim	.30	.10
6 Rodney Peete	.30	.10
7 David Terrell	.50	.20
8 Matt Schobel	.30	.10
9 Andre Davis	.30	.10
10 Dexter Coakley	.30	.10
11 Rod Smith	.50	.20
12 Damerien McCants	.30	.10
13 Robert Ferguson	.30	.10
14 Kailee Wong	.30	.10
15 James Mungro	.30	.10
16 Fred Taylor	.75	.30
17 Tony Gonzalez	.50	.20
18 Randall Godfrey	.30	.10
19 Robert Thomas	.30	.10
20 Rohan Davey	.50	.20
21 Terrell Owens	.75	.30
22 Ron Dayne	.30	.10
23 Charlie Batch	.30	.10
24 Brian Westbrook	.50	.20
25 Plaxico Burress	.50	.20
26 Reche Caldwell	.30	.10
27 Fred Beasley	.30	.10
28 Anthony Simmons	.30	.10
29 Rod Woodson	.50	.20
30 Derrick Brooks	.50	.20
31 Shaun Ellis	.30	.10
32 Ladell Betts	.50	.20
33 Russell Davis	.30	.10
34 Warrick Dunn	.50	.20
35 Jeremy Shockey	1.25	.50
36 Alex Van Pelt	.30	.10
37 Todd Bouman	.30	.10
38 Kelly Campbell	.30	.10
39 Justin Smith	.30	.10
40 Jamel White	.30	.10
41 La'Roi Glover	.30	.10
42 Ian Gold	.30	.10
43 Robert Porcher	.30	.10
44 Jermaine Lewis	.30	.10
45 Marvin Harrison	.75	.30
46 Darren Sharper	.30	.10
47 Jamie Sharper	.30	.10
48 Tony Richardson	.30	.10
49 Moe Williams	.30	.10
50 Ricky Williams	.75	.30
51 Ty Law	.50	.20
52 Donte Stallworth	.75	.30
53 Shannon Sharpe	.50	.20
54 Santana Moss	.50	.20
55 Charlie Garner	.50	.20
56 Brian Dawkins	.50	.20
57 Dan Campbell	.30	.10
58 William Green	.50	.20
59 Ron Dugans	.30	.10
60 Darrell Jackson	.50	.20
61 Marc Bulger	.75	.30
62 Joe Jurevicius	.30	.10
63 Erron Kinney	.30	.10
64 Champ Bailey	.50	.20
65 Peerless Price	.50	.20
66 Gary Baxter	.30	.10
67 Chris Redman	.30	.10
68 London Fletcher	.30	.10
69 Dee Brown	.30	.10
70 Anthony Thomas	.50	.20
71 Jake Delhomme	.75	.30
72 Dorsey Levens	.30	.10
73 Roy Williams	.75	.30
74 Ashley Lelie	.75	.30
75 Joey Harrington	1.25	.50
76 William Henderson	.30	.10
77 Corey Bradford	.30	.10
78 Reggie Wayne	.50	.20
79 Kyle Brady	.30	.10
80 Trent Green	.50	.20
81 Bill Romanowski	.30	.10
82 Chike Okeafor RC	.75	.30
83 David Patten	.30	.10
84 Terrelle Smith	.30	.10
85 Kerry Collins	.50	.20
86 Derrick Mason	.50	.20
87 Trung Canidate	.50	.20
88 A.J. Feeley	.50	.20
89 Jason Gildon	.30	.10
90 Doug Flutie	.75	.30
91 Tai Streets	.30	.10
92 Keith Newman	.30	.10
93 Adam Archuleta	.30	.10
94 Simeon Rice	.50	.20
95 Eddie George	.50	.20
96 Frank Sanders	.30	.10
97 Freddie Jones	.30	.10
98 Charles Johnson	.30	.10
99 Keith Traylor	.30	.10
100 Drew Bledsoe	.75	.30
101 Muhsin Muhammad	.50	.20
102 Marques Anderson	.30	.10
103 Donald Hayes	.30	.10
104 Quincy Morgan	.50	.20
105 Chad Hutchinson	.30	.10
106 Mike Anderson	.50	.20
107 Randy McMichael	.50	.20
108 Vonnie Holliday	.30	.10
109 Marcus Coleman	.30	.10

- ❑ 110 Edgerrin James .75 .30
- ❑ 111 Michael Lewis .30 .10
- ❑ 112 Wayne Chrebet .50 .20
- ❑ 113 Antwaan Randle El .75 .30
- ❑ 114 Byron Chamberlain .30 .10
- ❑ 115 Jeff Garcia .75 .30
- ❑ 116 Kim Herring .30 .10
- ❑ 117 Kenny Holmes .30 .10
- ❑ 118 John Lynch .50 .20
- ❑ 119 Doug Jolley .30 .10
- ❑ 120 Duce Staley .50 .20
- ❑ 121 Kordell Stewart .50 .20
- ❑ 122 Stephen Alexander .30 .10
- ❑ 123 Andre Carter .30 .10
- ❑ 124 Bobby Engram .30 .10
- ❑ 125 Marshall Faulk .75 .30
- ❑ 126 Peter Simon RC .50 .20
- ❑ 127 Alge Crumpler .50 .20
- ❑ 128 Kenny Watson .30 .10
- ❑ 129 Duane Starks .30 .10
- ❑ 130 Jeff Blake .30 .10
- ❑ 131 Todd Heap .50 .20
- ❑ 132 Bobby Shaw .30 .10
- ❑ 133 Ricky Proehl .30 .10
- ❑ 134 John Abraham .30 .10
- ❑ 135 T.J. Houshmandzadeh .30 .10
- ❑ 136 Brian Urlacher 1.25 .50
- ❑ 137 Darren Woodson .30 .10
- ❑ 138 Steve Beuerlein .30 .10
- ❑ 139 Cory Schlesinger .30 .10
- ❑ 140 Ahman Green .75 .30
- ❑ 141 Jabar Gaffney .50 .20
- ❑ 142 Eddie Drummond .30 .10
- ❑ 143 Stacey Mack .30 .10
- ❑ 144 Johnnie Morton .50 .20
- ❑ 145 Chris Chambers .75 .30
- ❑ 146 Jim Kleinsasser .30 .10
- ❑ 147 Tebucky Jones .30 .10
- ❑ 148 Marcus Pollard .30 .10
- ❑ 149 Tony Brackens .30 .10
- ❑ 150 Chad Pennington 1.00 .40
- ❑ 151 Kevin Faulk .30 .10
- ❑ 152 Michael Lewis .30 .10
- ❑ 153 Mark Bruener .30 .10
- ❑ 154 Tim Dwight .50 .20
- ❑ 155 Jerry Rice 1.50 .60
- ❑ 156 Trent Dilfer .50 .20
- ❑ 157 Jon Ritchie .30 .10
- ❑ 158 Michael Pittman .30 .10
- ❑ 159 Lamar Gordon .30 .10
- ❑ 160 Rod Gardner .50 .20
- ❑ 161 Ken Dilger .30 .10
- ❑ 162 Doug Johnson .30 .10
- ❑ 163 Peter Boulware .30 .10
- ❑ 164 Jevon Kearse .50 .20
- ❑ 165 Julius Peppers .75 .30
- ❑ 166 Chris Chandler .30 .10
- ❑ 167 Lorenzo Neal .30 .10
- ❑ 168 Kevin Johnson .50 .20
- ❑ 169 Kevin Hardy .30 .10
- ❑ 170 KaRon Coleman .30 .10
- ❑ 171 James Stewart .50 .20
- ❑ 172 Tony Fisher .30 .10
- ❑ 173 Billy Miller .30 .10
- ❑ 174 Phillip Crosby .30 .10
- ❑ 175 Priest Holmes 1.00 .40
- ❑ 176 Elvis Joseph .30 .10
- ❑ 177 Bryan Gilmore .30 .10
- ❑ 178 D'Wayne Bates .30 .10
- ❑ 179 Quincy Carter .50 .20
- ❑ 180 Joe Horn .50 .20
- ❑ 181 Anthony Henry .30 .10
- ❑ 182 Anthony Becht .30 .10
- ❑ 183 Mike Peterson .30 .10
- ❑ 184 James Thrash .30 .10
- ❑ 185 Jerome Bettis .75 .30
- ❑ 186 Marcellus Wiley .30 .10
- ❑ 187 Tim Rattay .50 .20
- ❑ 188 Maurice Morris .30 .10
- ❑ 189 Jason Taylor .30 .10
- ❑ 190 Keyshawn Johnson .75 .30
- ❑ 191 John Simon .30 .10
- ❑ 192 Fred Smoot .30 .10
- ❑ 193 Wendell Bryant .30 .10
- ❑ 194 Brandon Stokley .50 .20
- ❑ 195 Kurt Warner .75 .30
- ❑ 196 Steve Smith .75 .30
- ❑ 197 Dez White .30 .10
- ❑ 198 Jim Miller .30 .10
- ❑ 199 Robert Griffith .30 .10
- ❑ 200 Michael Vick 2.00 .75
- ❑ 201 Antonio Bryant .50 .20
- ❑ 202 Laveranues Coles .50 .20
- ❑ 203 Kalimba Edwards .30 .10
- ❑ 204 Bubba Franks .50 .20
- ❑ 205 David Carr 1.25 .50
- ❑ 206 Dwight Freeney .50 .20
- ❑ 207 Eric Johnson .50 .20
- ❑ 208 Reggie Tongue .30 .10
- ❑ 209 Cam Cleeland .30 .10
- ❑ 210 Michael Bennett .50 .20
- ❑ 211 Antowain Smith .50 .20
- ❑ 212 Warren Sapp .50 .20
- ❑ 213 Ike Hilliard .30 .10
- ❑ 214 Olandis Gary .50 .20
- ❑ 215 Tim Brown .75 .30
- ❑ 216 Kevin Dyson .50 .20
- ❑ 217 Eddie Kennison .30 .10
- ❑ 218 Junior Seau .75 .30
- ❑ 219 Donnie Edwards .30 .10
- ❑ 220 Shaun Alexander .75 .30
- ❑ 221 Terrence Wilkins .30 .10
- ❑ 222 Garrison Hearst .50 .20
- ❑ 223 Keith Bulluck .30 .10
- ❑ 224 Zeron Flemister .30 .10
- ❑ 225 Jake Plummer .50 .20
- ❑ 226 Chad Johnson .75 .30
- ❑ 227 Travis Taylor .50 .20
- ❑ 228 Josh Reed .50 .20
- ❑ 229 James Farrior .30 .10
- ❑ 230 Marty Booker .50 .20
- ❑ 231 Todd Pinkston .50 .20
- ❑ 232 Dennis Northcutt .50 .20
- ❑ 233 Troy Hambrick .30 .10
- ❑ 234 Roland Williams .30 .10
- ❑ 235 Bill Schroeder .50 .20
- ❑ 236 Javon Walker .50 .20
- ❑ 237 Kevin Swayne .30 .10
- ❑ 238 Dominic Rhodes .50 .20
- ❑ 239 David Garrard .30 .10
- ❑ 240 Mike Maslowski RC .50 .20
- ❑ 241 Travis Minor .30 .10
- ❑ 242 Terry Glenn .30 .10
- ❑ 243 Deion Branch .75 .30
- ❑ 244 Adrian Peterson .30 .10
- ❑ 245 Tiki Barber .75 .30
- ❑ 246 Ray Lewis .75 .30
- ❑ 247 Marques Tuiasosopo .50 .20
- ❑ 248 Chad Lewis .30 .10
- ❑ 249 Takeo Spikes .30 .10
- ❑ 250 LaDainian Tomlinson .75 .30
- ❑ 251 Stephen Davis .50 .20
- ❑ 252 Koren Robinson .50 .20
- ❑ 253 Daylon McCutcheon .30 .10
- ❑ 254 Rob Johnson .50 .20
- ❑ 255 Donovan McNabb 1.00 .40
- ❑ 256 Derrius Thompson .30 .10
- ❑ 257 Marcel Shipp .50 .20
- ❑ 258 Keith Brooking .30 .10
- ❑ 259 Chris McAlister .30 .10
- ❑ 260 Eric Moulds .50 .20
- ❑ 261 Amos Zereoue .50 .20
- ❑ 262 Drew Brees .75 .30
- ❑ 263 Jon Kitna .50 .20
- ❑ 264 Brad Johnson .50 .20
- ❑ 265 Emmitt Smith 2.00 .75
- ❑ 266 Trevor Pryce .30 .10
- ❑ 267 Mike McMahon .50 .20
- ❑ 268 Patrick Ramsey .75 .30
- ❑ 269 Jonathan Wells .30 .10
- ❑ 270 Mark Brunell .50 .20
- ❑ 271 Marc Boerigter .50 .20
- ❑ 272 Rob Konrad .30 .10
- ❑ 273 Derrick Alexander .30 .10
- ❑ 274 Joey Galloway .50 .20
- ❑ 275 Peyton Manning 1.25 .50
- ❑ 276 Najeh Davenport .30 .10
- ❑ 277 Jesse Palmer .30 .10
- ❑ 278 LaMont Jordan .75 .30
- ❑ 279 Ernie Conwell .30 .10
- ❑ 280 Hines Ward .75 .30
- ❑ 281 Freddie Mitchell .50 .20
- ❑ 282 Curtis Conway .30 .10
- ❑ 283 Cedrick Wilson .30 .10
- ❑ 284 Troy Brown .50 .20
- ❑ 285 Torry Holt .75 .30
- ❑ 286 Mike Alstott .75 .30
- ❑ 287 Frank Wycheck .30 .10
- ❑ 288 Jeremiah Trotter .30 .10
- ❑ 289 Tyrone Wheatley .30 .10
- ❑ 290 David Boston .50 .20
- ❑ 291 Jay Fiedler .50 .20
- ❑ 292 Troy Walters .30 .10
- ❑ 293 Warrick Holdman .30 .10
- ❑ 294 Peter Warrick .50 .20
- ❑ 295 Tim Couch .30 .10
- ❑ 296 Aaron Glenn .30 .10
- ❑ 297 Deuce McAllister .75 .30
- ❑ 298 Michael Strahan .50 .20
- ❑ 299 Tom Brady 2.00 .75
- ❑ 300 Brett Favre 2.00 .75
- ❑ 301 Isaac Bruce .75 .30
- ❑ 302 Jimmy Smith .50 .20
- ❑ 303 Dante Hall .75 .30
- ❑ 304 James McKnight .30 .10
- ❑ 305 Daunte Culpepper .75 .30
- ❑ 306 Lawyer Milloy .50 .20
- ❑ 307 Jerome Pathon .30 .10
- ❑ 308 Steve McNair .75 .30
- ❑ 309 Vinny Testaverde .50 .20
- ❑ 310 Tommy Maddox .75 .30
- ❑ 311 Amani Toomer .50 .20
- ❑ 312 Aaron Brooks .75 .30
- ❑ 313 Gus Frerotte .30 .10
- ❑ 314 Kevan Barlow .50 .20
- ❑ 315 Matt Hasselbeck .50 .20
- ❑ 316 Clinton Portis 1.25 .50
- ❑ 317 Keenan McCardell .30 .10
- ❑ 318 Zach Thomas .75 .30
- ❑ 319 Curtis Martin .75 .30
- ❑ 320 Jamal Lewis .75 .30
- ❑ 321 T.J. Duckett .50 .20
- ❑ 322 Jerry Porter .50 .20
- ❑ 323 Randy Moss 1.25 .50
- ❑ 324 Rosevelt Colvin .30 .10
- ❑ 325 Corey Dillon .50 .20
- ❑ 326 Kelly Holcomb .50 .20
- ❑ 327 Josh McCown .50 .20
- ❑ 328 Ed McCaffrey .75 .30
- ❑ 329 Mikhael Ricks .30 .10
- ❑ 330 Donald Driver .50 .20
- ❑ 331 Darling/Thompson/McKinnon .30 .10
- ❑ 332 Hall/Carpenter/Buchanon .30 .10
- ❑ 333 Thomas/Weaver/Gregg RC .50 .20
- ❑ 334 Winfield/Wire/Clements .30 .10
- ❑ 335 Morgan/Fields/Witherspoon .50 .20
- ❑ 336 Brown/Robinson RC/Daniels .50 .20
- ❑ 337 Powell RC/Thornton/Williams RC .50 .20
- ❑ 338 Taylor RC/Little/Bentley .75 .30
- ❑ 339 Ekuban/Ellis/Myers .30 .10
- ❑ 340 Gard/Dalton RC/Berry RC .75 .30
- ❑ 341 Green/Curry RC/Holmes .50 .20
- ❑ 342 Hunt RC/KGB/Walker RC .75 .30
- ❑ 343 Walker/Deloach RC/Payne .30 .10
- ❑ 344 Bratzke/Washington/Morris .30 .10
- ❑ 345 Henderson/Coleman/Stroud .50 .20
- ❑ 346 Hicks/Browning RC/Sims .50 .20
- ❑ 347 A.Ogunleye RC/Chester RC 2.00 .75
- ❑ 348 Robbins/Mixon/Johnstone .30 .10
- ❑ 349 Phifer/Johnson/Bruschi .75 .30
- ❑ 350 Grant/Chase RC/Howard .50 .20
- ❑ 351 Short/Jones RC/Barrow .50 .20
- ❑ 352 Jones/Lewis/Cowart .30 .10
- ❑ 353 Barton/Parrella/Harris .30 .10
- ❑ 354 Whiting/Simon/Walker .30 .10
- ❑ 355 Smith/Hamp/von Oel 1.00 .40
- ❑ 356 Williams RC/Fisk/Johnson .50 .20
- ❑ 357 Smith/Ulbrich/Peterson .30 .10
- ❑ 358 Cochran RC/Eaton/Randle .50 .20
- ❑ 359 Lewis/Wistrom/Little .30 .10
- ❑ 360 Rudd/Spires/Quarles RC .75 .30
- ❑ 361 Haynesworth/Carter/Smith .30 .10
- ❑ 362 Smith/Armstead/Upshaw .30 .10
- ❑ 363 Ad.Wilson/Dex.Jackson RC .75 .30
- ❑ 364 F.Wakefield/K.Vanden .30 .10
- ❑ 365 K.Kasper/J.McAddley .30 .10
- ❑ 366 B.Smith/P.Kerney .30 .10
- ❑ 367 M.Jenkins/T.Gaylor .30 .10
- ❑ 368 C.Draft/M.Stewart .30 .10
- ❑ 369 J.Hunter/R.Johnson .30 .10
- ❑ 370 C.Fuller/E.Reed .50 .20

- ❑ 371 A.Schobel/J.Posey RC .50 .20
- ❑ 372 P.Williams/S.Adams .30 .10
- ❑ 373 D.Grant/M.Minter .30 .10
- ❑ 374 B.Buckner/K.Jenkins .30 .10
- ❑ 375 R.Howard RC/T.Cousin RC .50 .20
- ❑ 376 M.Brown/M.Green .50 .20
- ❑ 377 J.Azumah/R.W.McQuarters .30 .10
- ❑ 378 B.Simmons/S.Foley .30 .10
- ❑ 379 A.Hawkins/J.Burris .30 .10
- ❑ 380 Jo.Armour RC/M.Manuel .30 .10
- ❑ 381 G.Warren/O.Roye .30 .10
- ❑ 382 C.Brown/K.Lang .30 .10
- ❑ 383 D.Ross/M.Edwards .30 .10
- ❑ 384 A.Singleton RC/D.Nguyen .50 .20
- ❑ 385 A.Wilson/J.Mobley .30 .10
- ❑ 386 D.O'Neal/K.Kennedy .30 .10
- ❑ 387 L.Elliss/S.Rogers .30 .10
- ❑ 388 C.Cash/D.Bly .30 .10
- ❑ 389 B.Walker/C.Harris .30 .10
- ❑ 390 H.Navies RC/N.Diggs .30 .10
- ❑ 391 A.Harris/M.McKenzie .30 .10
- ❑ 392 C.Clemons/J.Foreman .30 .10
- ❑ 393 E.Brown/M.Stevens .30 .10
- ❑ 394 B.Scioli/L.Tripplett .30 .10
- ❑ 395 D.Macklin/W.Harris .30 .10
- ❑ 396 A.Ayodele/H.Douglas .30 .10
- ❑ 397 F.Bryant/J.Craft RC .30 .10
- ❑ 398 D.Darius/M.McCree .30 .10
- ❑ 399 S.Fujita/S.Barber .50 .20
- ❑ 400 E.Warfield RC/W.Bartee .75 .30
- ❑ 401 G.Wesley/J.Woods .30 .10
- ❑ 402 P.Surtain/S.Madison .30 .10
- ❑ 403 B.Marion/S.Knight .30 .10
- ❑ 404 G.Biekert/H.Crockett .30 .10
- ❑ 405 C.Claiborne/C.Hovan .30 .10
- ❑ 406 C.Chavous/K.Irvin .30 .10
- ❑ 407 C.Fauria/D.Graham .30 .10
- ❑ 408 O.Smith/R.Harrison .30 .10
- ❑ 409 A.Pleasant/R.Seymour .30 .10
- ❑ 410 D.Smith/S.Hodge .30 .10
- ❑ 411 A.Ambrose/D.Carter .30 .10
- ❑ 412 M.Mitchell/D.Rodgers .30 .10
- ❑ 413 W.Allen/W.Peterson .30 .10
- ❑ 414 C.Griffin/K.Hamilton .30 .10
- ❑ 415 O.Stoutmire/S.Williams .30 .10
- ❑ 416 A.Beasley/D.Abraham .30 .10
- ❑ 417 J.McGraw/S.Games .30 .10
- ❑ 418 C.Woodson/P.Buchanon .50 .20
- ❑ 419 T.Bryant/T.Armstrong .30 .10
- ❑ 420 B.Taylor/T.Vincent .30 .10
- ❑ 421 C.Emmons/N.Wayne .30 .10
- ❑ 422 B.Alexander/C.Hope .50 .20
- ❑ 423 J.Porter/K.Bell .75 .30
- ❑ 424 C.Scott/D.Washington .30 .10
- ❑ 425 B.Leber/R.McNeil .30 .10
- ❑ 426 Q.Jammer/T.Cody .30 .10
- ❑ 427 A.Plummer/J.Webster .30 .10
- ❑ 428 T.Parrish/Z.Bronson .30 .10
- ❑ 429 I.Mili/J.Stevens .30 .10
- ❑ 430 K.Lucas/S.Springs .30 .10
- ❑ 431 C.Brown/O.Huff .30 .10
- ❑ 432 J.Duncan/T.Polley .30 .10
- ❑ 433 A.Williams/T.Fisher .30 .10
- ❑ 434 B.Kelly/R.Barber .30 .10
- ❑ 435 A.Stecker/K.Williams .30 .10
- ❑ 436 D.Bennett/J.McCareins .50 .20
- ❑ 437 L.Schulters/T.Williams .30 .10
- ❑ 438 A.Dyson/S.Rolle .30 .10
- ❑ 439 I.Ohalete/M.Bowen .30 .10
- ❑ 440 B.Noble/D.Wilkinson .30 .10
- ❑ 441 Charles Rogers RC 1.25 .50
- ❑ 442 Jimmy Kennedy RC 1.25 .50
- ❑ 443 Kelley Washington RC 1.25 .50
- ❑ 444 Trent Smith RC 1.00 .40
- ❑ 445 Rashean Mathis RC 1.00 .40
- ❑ 446 Brian St.Pierre RC 1.25 .50
- ❑ 447 Bethel Johnson RC 1.25 .50
- ❑ 448 Alonzo Jackson RC 1.00 .40
- ❑ 449 Arnaz Battle RC 1.25 .50
- ❑ 450 Carson Palmer RC 6.00 2.50
- ❑ 451 Michael Haynes RC 1.25 .50
- ❑ 452 LaBrandon Toefield RC 1.25 .50
- ❑ 453 Earnest Graham RC 1.00 .40
- ❑ 454 Walter Young RC .60 .25
- ❑ 455 Terry Pierce RC 1.00 .40
- ❑ 456 Talman Gardner RC 1.25 .50
- ❑ 457 J.T. Wall RC .60 .25
- ❑ 458 DeWayne Robertson RC 1.25 .50
- ❑ 459 Bradie James RC 1.25 .50
- ❑ 460 Andre Johnson RC 2.50 1.00
- ❑ 461 Bobby Wade RC 1.25 .50
- ❑ 462 Chris Davis RC 1.00 .40
- ❑ 463 Kliff Kingsbury RC 1.00 .40
- ❑ 464 Osi Umenyiora RC 2.00 .75
- ❑ 465 Domanick Davis RC 2.00 .75
- ❑ 466 Sam Aiken RC 1.00 .40
- ❑ 467 Ty Warren RC 1.25 .50
- ❑ 468 Terence Newman RC 2.50 1.00
- ❑ 469 Zuriel Smith RC .60 .25
- ❑ 470 Willis McGahee RC 3.00 1.25
- ❑ 471 David Kircus RC 1.00 .40
- ❑ 472 Billy McMullen RC 1.00 .40
- ❑ 473 Antwoine Sanders RC .60 .25
- ❑ 474 Adrian Madise RC 1.00 .40
- ❑ 475 Byron Leftwich RC 4.00 1.50
- ❑ 476 Justin Gage RC 1.25 .50
- ❑ 477 Jason Witten RC 2.00 .75
- ❑ 478 Lee Suggs RC 2.50 1.00
- ❑ 479 Kareem Kelly RC 1.00 .40
- ❑ 480 Rex Grossman RC 2.00 .75
- ❑ 481 Nate Burleson RC 1.50 .60
- ❑ 482 Chris Brown RC 1.50 .60
- ❑ 483 Julian Battle RC 1.00 .40
- ❑ 484 Carl Ford RC .60 .25
- ❑ 485 Angelo Crowell RC 1.00 .40
- ❑ 486 Bennie Joppru RC 1.25 .50
- ❑ 487 Aaron Walker RC 1.00 .40
- ❑ 488 Brandon Green RC 1.00 .40
- ❑ 489 L.J. Smith RC 1.25 .50
- ❑ 490 Ken Dorsey RC 1.25 .50
- ❑ 491 Eugene Wilson RC 1.25 .50
- ❑ 492 Chaun Thompson RC .60 .25
- ❑ 493 Kevin Curtis RC 1.25 .50
- ❑ 494 Marcus Trufant RC 1.25 .50
- ❑ 495 Andrew Williams RC 1.00 .40
- ❑ 496 Visanthe Shiancoe RC 1.00 .40
- ❑ 497 Terrence Edwards RC 1.00 .40
- ❑ 498 Rien Long RC 1.00 .40
- ❑ 499 Nick Barnett RC 2.00 .75
- ❑ 500 Larry Johnson RC 6.00 3.00
- ❑ 501 Ken Hamlin RC 1.25 .50
- ❑ 502 Johnathan Sullivan RC 1.00 .40
- ❑ 503 Jeremi Johnson RC 1.00 .40
- ❑ 504 William Joseph RC 1.25 .50
- ❑ 505 Boss Bailey RC 1.25 .50
- ❑ 506 Anquan Boldin RC 3.00 1.25
- ❑ 507 Dave Ragone RC 1.25 .50
- ❑ 508 DeJuan Groce RC 1.25 .50
- ❑ 509 Rashad Moore RC 1.00 .40
- ❑ 510 Mike Doss RC 1.25 .50
- ❑ 511 Kenny Peterson RC 1.00 .40
- ❑ 512 Justin Griffith RC 1.00 .40
- ❑ 513 Jordan Gross RC 1.00 .40
- ❑ 514 Terrence Holt RC 1.00 .40
- ❑ 515 Seneca Wallace RC 1.25 .50
- ❑ 516 Ovie Mughelli RC .60 .25
- ❑ 517 Jerome McDougle RC 1.25 .50
- ❑ 518 Kevin Williams RC 1.25 .50
- ❑ 519 Musa Smith RC 1.25 .50
- ❑ 520 Teyo Johnson RC 1.25 .50
- ❑ 521 Victor Hobson RC 1.25 .50
- ❑ 522 Cory Redding RC 1.00 .40
- ❑ 523 Cecil Sapp RC 1.00 .40
- ❑ 524 Brandon Lloyd RC 1.50 .60
- ❑ 525 Chris Simms RC 2.00 .75
- ❑ 526 Artose Pinner RC 1.25 .50
- ❑ 527 DeWayne White RC 1.00 .40
- ❑ 528 Doug Gabriel RC 1.25 .50
- ❑ 529 Calvin Pace RC 1.00 .40
- ❑ 530 Onterrio Smith RC 1.25 .50
- ❑ 531 Terrell Suggs RC 2.00 .75
- ❑ 532 Ronald Bellamy RC 1.00 .40
- ❑ 533 Jimmy Wilkerson RC 1.00 .40
- ❑ 534 Travis Anglin RC .60 .25
- ❑ 535 Tyrone Calico RC 1.50 .60
- ❑ 536 Keenan Howry RC 1.25 .50
- ❑ 537 Gibran Hamdan RC .60 .25
- ❑ 538 Bryant Johnson RC 1.25 .50
- ❑ 539 Brad Banks RC 1.00 .40
- ❑ 540 Justin Fargas RC 1.25 .50
- ❑ 541 B.J. Askew RC 1.25 .50
- ❑ 542 J.R. Tolver RC 1.00 .40
- ❑ 543 Tully Banta-Cain RC 1.00 .40
- ❑ 544 Shaun McDonald RC 1.25 .50
- ❑ 545 Taylor Jacobs RC 1.00 .40
- ❑ 546 Ricky Manning RC 1.25 .50
- ❑ 547 Dallas Clark RC 1.25 .50
- ❑ 548 Juston Wood RC .60 .25
- ❑ 549 Andre Woolfolk RC 1.25 .50
- ❑ 550 Kyle Boller RC 2.50 1.00
- ❑ CL1 Checklist Card 1 .10 .02
- ❑ CL2 Checklist Card 2 .10 .02
- ❑ CL3 Checklist Card 3 .10 .02
- ❑ CL4 Checklist Card 4 .10 .02

2004 Topps Total

- ❑ COMPLETE SET (440) 80.00 40.00
- ❑ 1 Donovan McNabb 1.00 .40
- ❑ 2 Zach Thomas .75 .30
- ❑ 3 Randy Moss 1.00 .40
- ❑ 4 Kerry Collins .50 .20
- ❑ 5 Hines Ward .75 .30
- ❑ 6 Tyrone Calico .50 .20
- ❑ 7 Patrick Ramsey .50 .20
- ❑ 8 Jeff Garcia .75 .30
- ❑ 9 Aveion Cason .30 .10
- ❑ 10 Stephen Davis .50 .20
- ❑ 11 Marcel Shipp .50 .20
- ❑ 12 T.J. Duckett .50 .20
- ❑ 13 Chris McAlister .30 .10
- ❑ 14 Peter Warrick .50 .20
- ❑ 15 Ahman Green .75 .30
- ❑ 16 Deion Branch .75 .30
- ❑ 17 David Boston .50 .20
- ❑ 18 Wayne Chrebet .50 .20
- ❑ 19 Michael Strahan .50 .20
- ❑ 20 Arnaz Battle .50 .20
- ❑ 21 Darrell Jackson .50 .20
- ❑ 22 Chris Chandler .50 .20
- ❑ 23 Charlie Garner .50 .20
- ❑ 24 James Thrash .30 .10
- ❑ 25 LaDainian Tomlinson 1.00 .40
- ❑ 26 Jerry Porter .50 .20
- ❑ 27 Jerome Pathon .30 .10
- ❑ 28 Jerome Bettis .75 .30
- ❑ 29 Eddie George .50 .20
- ❑ 30 Jamal Lewis .75 .30
- ❑ 31 Ricky Proehl .30 .10
- ❑ 32 Josh Reed .30 .10
- ❑ 33 David Terrell .50 .20
- ❑ 34 Antonio Bryant .50 .20
- ❑ 35 Domanick Davis .75 .30
- ❑ 36 Artose Pinner .30 .10
- ❑ 37 Jed Weaver .30 .10
- ❑ 38 Johnnie Morton .50 .20
- ❑ 39 Troy Edwards .30 .10
- ❑ 40 Marvin Harrison .75 .30
- ❑ 41 Chris Hovan .30 .10
- ❑ 42 Boo Williams .30 .10
- ❑ 43 Ike Hilliard .30 .10
- ❑ 44 Sam Cowart .30 .10
- ❑ 45 Shaun Alexander .75 .30
- ❑ 46 Freddie Mitchell .50 .20
- ❑ 47 Garrison Hearst .50 .20
- ❑ 48 Joe Jurevicius .30 .10
- ❑ 49 Freddie Jones .30 .10
- ❑ 50 Michael Vick 1.50 .60
- ❑ 51 Mike Rucker .30 .10
- ❑ 52 Carson Palmer 1.00 .40
- ❑ 53 Az-Zahir Hakim .30 .10
- ❑ 54 Billy Miller .30 .10
- ❑ 55 Chad Pennington .75 .30
- ❑ 56 Charles Woodson .50 .20

57	Andre Carter	.30	.10
58	Maurice Morris	.30	.10
59	Leonard Little	.30	.10
60	Travis Henry	.50	.20
61	Thomas Jones	.50	.20
62	Dennis Northcutt	.30	.10
63	Quentin Griffin	.75	.30
64	Joey Harrington	.75	.30
65	Edgerrin James	.75	.30
66	Cortez Hankton	.30	.10
67	Jason Taylor	.30	.10
68	Eddie Kennison	.30	.10
69	Ty Law	.50	.20
70	Aaron Brooks	.50	.20
71	Antonio Gates	.75	.30
72	Antwaan Randle El	.75	.30
73	Kevan Barlow	.50	.20
74	Chris Brown	.75	.30
75	Clinton Portis	.75	.30
76	Rod Gardner	.50	.20
77	Isaac Bruce	.50	.20
78	Mike Alstott	.50	.20
79	Brian Westbrook	.50	.20
80	Amani Toomer	.50	.20
81	Justin Fargas	.50	.20
82	Michael Bennett	.50	.20
83	Dante Hall	.75	.30
84	Marcus Pollard	.30	.10
85	Fred Taylor	.50	.20
86	Tai Streets	.30	.10
87	Robert Ferguson	.30	.10
88	Roy Williams S	.50	.20
89	Lee Suggs	.75	.30
90	Chad Johnson	.75	.30
91	DeShaun Foster	.50	.20
92	Alge Crumpler	.50	.20
93	Travis Taylor	.30	.10
94	London Fletcher	.30	.10
95	Priest Holmes	1.00	.40
96	A.J. Feeley	.75	.30
97	Kevin Faulk	.30	.10
98	Shaun Ellis	.30	.10
99	Tim Dwight	.50	.20
100	Peyton Manning	1.25	.50
101	Dane Looker	.50	.20
102	Mark Brunell	.50	.20
103	Bryant Johnson	.30	.10
104	Kelley Washington	.30	.10
105	Rex Grossman	.75	.30
106	William Green	.50	.20
107	Keyshawn Johnson	.50	.20
108	Trevor Pryce	.30	.10
109	Donald Driver	.50	.20
110	David Carr	.75	.30
111	Marcus Robinson	.50	.20
112	Justin McCareins	.30	.10
113	Tim Brown	.75	.30
114	James Farrior	.30	.10
115	Deuce McAllister	.75	.30
116	Simeon Rice	.50	.20
117	Koren Robinson	.50	.20
118	Kassim Osgood	.30	.10
119	Tim Rattay	.30	.10
120	Laveranues Coles	.50	.20
121	Brian Finneran	.30	.10
122	Todd Heap	.50	.20
123	Bobby Shaw	.30	.10
124	Anthony Thomas	.50	.20
125	Brett Favre	2.00	.75
126	Dwight Freeney	.50	.20
127	Randy McMichael	.30	.10
128	David Givens	.50	.20
129	Rich Gannon	.50	.20
130	Tiki Barber	.75	.30
131	Terrell Owens	.75	.30
132	Drew Bennett	.50	.20
133	Shawn Bryson	.30	.10
134	Jabar Gaffney	.50	.20
135	Jake Delhomme	.75	.30
136	Warrick Dunn	.50	.20
137	Brandon Lloyd	.50	.20
138	Brad Johnson	.50	.20
139	Jon Kitna	.50	.20
140	Marshall Faulk	.75	.30
141	Javon Walker	.50	.20
142	Nate Burleson	.75	.30
143	Jimmy Smith	.50	.20
144	Adewale Ogunleye	.50	.20
145	Trent Green	.50	.20
146	Richard Seymour	.30	.10
147	Donte' Stallworth	.50	.20
148	Curtis Martin	.75	.30
149	Todd Pinkston	.30	.10
150	Steve McNair	.75	.30
151	Josh McCown	.50	.20
152	Ray Lewis	.75	.30
153	Muhsin Muhammad	.50	.20
154	Quincy Morgan	.50	.20
155	Jake Plummer	.50	.20
156	Jason Witten	.50	.20
157	Dallas Clark	.50	.20
158	Onterrio Smith	.50	.20
159	Jeremy Shockey	.75	.30
160	Ricky Williams	.75	.30
161	Jevon Kearse	.50	.20
162	Plaxico Burress	.50	.20
163	Drew Brees	.75	.30
164	Bobby Engram	.30	.10
165	Torry Holt	.75	.30
166	Ladell Betts	.30	.10
167	Kelly Holcomb	.50	.20
168	Vinny Testaverde	.50	.20
169	Marty Booker	.50	.20
170	Rudi Johnson	.50	.20
171	Andra Davis	.30	.10
172	Kurt Warner	.75	.30
173	Troy Brown	.50	.20
174	Jerry Rice	1.50	.60
175	Daunte Culpepper	.75	.30
176	Darren Sharper	.30	.10
177	Charles Rogers	.50	.20
178	Ashley Lelie	.50	.20
179	Correll Buckhalter	.50	.20
180	Anquan Boldin	.75	.30
181	Terrell Suggs	.50	.20
182	Reggie Wayne	.50	.20
183	Duce Staley	.50	.20
184	Donnie Edwards	.30	.10
185	Joe Horn	.50	.20
186	LaVar Arrington	1.50	.60
187	Keenan McCardell	.30	.10
188	Cedrick Wilson	.30	.10
189	Bubba Franks	.50	.20
190	Santana Moss	.50	.20
191	Peerless Price	.50	.20
192	Kyle Boller	.75	.30
193	Julius Peppers	.75	.30
194	Drew Bledsoe	.75	.30
195	Marc Bulger	.75	.30
196	Brian Urlacher	1.00	.40
197	Andre' Davis	.30	.10
198	Terry Glenn	.30	.10
199	Champ Bailey	.50	.20
200	Tom Brady	2.00	.75
201	Chris Chambers	.50	.20
202	Tommy Maddox	.50	.20
203	Derrick Brooks	.50	.20
204	Corey Dillon	.50	.20
205	Matt Hasselbeck	.50	.20
206	Keith Brooking	.30	.10
207	Steve Smith	.75	.30
208	Tony Gonzalez	.50	.20
209	Joey Galloway	.50	.20
210	Derrick Mason	.50	.20
211	Quincy Carter	.50	.20
212	Rod Smith	.50	.20
213	Andre Johnson	.75	.30
214	Rod Woodson	.50	.20
215	Byron Leftwich	1.00	.40
216	Kevin Dyson	.30	.10
217	Keith Bulluck	.30	.10
218	Eric Moulds	.50	.20
219	Jamie Sharper	.30	.10
220	Takeo Spikes	.30	.10
221	C.Pace/F.Wakefield	.30	.10
222	B.Smith/P.Kerney	.30	.10
223	E.Reed/G.Baxter	.50	.20
224	A.Schobel/J.Posey	.30	.10
225	K.Jenkins/B.Buckner	.30	.10
226	J.Smith/D.Clemons	.30	.10
227	M.Haynes/B.Robinson	.30	.10
228	C.Brown/G.Warren	.50	.20
229	T.Newman/D.Woodson	.50	.20
230	R.Johnson/M.Fatafehi	.30	.10
231	R.Porcher/J.Hall RC	.75	.30
232	K.Gbaja-Biamila/C.Hunt	.50	.20
233	A.Glenn/M.Coleman	.30	.10
234	N.Harper RC/J.Jefferson	.30	.10
235	H.Douglas/T.Brackens	.30	.10
236	V.Holliday/E.Hicks	.30	.10
237	S.Knight/A.Freeman	.30	.10
238	S.Martin/N.Rogers	.30	.10
239	R.Colvin/W.McGinest	.30	.10
240	O.Stoutmire/S.Williams	.30	.10
241	E.Barton/V.Hobson	.30	.10
242	W.Sapp/T.Washington	.50	.20
243	C.Simon/D.Walker	.50	.20
244	T.Polamalu/M.Logan	2.00	.75
245	J.Williams/A.Dingle RC	.30	.10
246	B.Young/B.Whiting	.30	.10
247	K.Hamlin/D.Robinson RC	.30	.10
248	D.Lewis/R.Pickett	.30	.10
249	A.McFarland/G.Spires	.30	.10
250	A.Haynesworth/R.Long	.30	.10
251	I.Ohalete/M.Bowen	.30	.10
252	B.Berry/K.King	.30	.10
253	E.Johnson/E.Jasper	.30	.10
254	C.Tillman/J.Azumah	.50	.20
255	M.Wiley/L.Glover	.30	.10
256	S.Rogers/D.Wilkinson	.30	.10
257	G.Walker/R.Smith	.30	.10
258	M.Doss/I.Bashir	.30	.10
259	M.Stroud/J.Henderson	.50	.20
260	R.Sims/J.Browning	.30	.10
261	J.Seau/M.Greenwood	.75	.30
262	K.Williams/K.Mixon	.30	.10
263	T.Warren/K.Traylor	.30	.10
264	W.Allen/W.Peterson	.30	.10
265	D.Barrett/R.Tongue	.30	.10
266	P.Buchanon/D.Gibson	.30	.10
267	L.Sheppard/S.Brown	.30	.10
268	B.Taylor/M.Trufant	.50	.20
269	M.Washington/M.Barrow	.30	.10
270	C.Draft/M.Stewart	.30	.10
271	M.Brown/M.Green	.50	.20
272	E.Brown/M.McCree	.30	.10
273	P.Surtain/S.Madison	.50	.20
274	B.Dawkins/M.Lewis	.50	.20
275	S.Springs/F.Smoot	.50	.20
276	McKinnon/Fisher/Thompson	.30	.10
277	Webster/McBride RC/Scott	.30	.10
278	Boulware/Hartwell/Thomas	.50	.20
279	Vincent/Milloy/Clements	.50	.20
280	Witherspoon/Morgan/Fields	.50	.20
281	Simmons/Hardy/Webster	.30	.10
282	Odom RC/Brown/Briggs	1.00	.40
283	Holdman/Thompson/Lang	.30	.10
284	Nguyen/Coakley/Singleton	.30	.10
285	Wilson/Spragan RC/Holland	.30	.10
286	Holmes/J.Davis RC/Bailey	.75	.30
287	Barnett/Diggs/Navies	.30	.10
288	Foreman/Peek/Wong	.30	.10
289	Brock RC/Reagor/Tripplett	.75	.30
290	Ayodele/Favors/Peterson	.50	.20
291	Barber/Maslowski/Fujita	.50	.20
292	Claiborne/Henderson/Nattiel	.50	.20
293	Bruschi/Phifer/Vrabel	.75	.30
294	Grant/Howard/Sullivan	.30	.10
295	Robbins/Joseph/Umenyiora	.75	.30
296	Abra/Rober/Fergus.RC	1.25	.50
297	Harris/Rudd/Brayton	.50	.20
298	Simoneau/Wayne/Jones	.30	.10
299	Porter/Bell/Haggans RC	2.00	.75
300	Jammer/Davis/Florence	.50	.20
301	Peterson/Ulbrich/Smith	.30	.10
302	Simmons/Huff/Brown	.30	.10
303	Tinoisamoa/Polley/Thomas	.30	.10
304	Quarles/Wyms/Nece	.30	.10
305	Carter/Hall/Simmon	.50	.20
306	Griffin/Daniels/Wynn	.30	.10
307	Jackson/Wilson/Macklin	.30	.10
308	Gregg/Douglas/Weaver	.30	.10
309	Williams/Denney/Adams	.30	.10
310	Hawkins/Minter/Manning	.30	.10
311	James/Herring/Beckett	.30	.10
312	Griffith/Little/Henry	.30	.10
313	Lynch/Ferg.RC/Hern.RC	.75	.30
314	Bly/Marion/Bryant	.30	.10
315	Harris/Roman/McKenzie	.30	.10
316	Thorn/Morris/Brackett RC	.75	.30
317	Mathis/Darius/Bolden RC	.50	.20

318	Warfield/Wesley/Woods	.30	.10
319	Winfield/Russell RC/Chavous	.50	.20
320	Harrison/Wilson/Poole	.50	.20
321	Rodgers/Ruff/Hodge	.30	.10
322	Green/Greisen/Emmons	.30	.10
323	Von Oelhoffen/Smith/Hampton	.75	.30
324	Godfrey/Foley/Leber	.30	.10
325	Plummer/Parrish/Rumph	.30	.10
326	Okeafor/Wistrom/Moore	.30	.10
327	Archuleta/Williams/Butler	.30	.10
328	Barber/Smith/Phillips	.50	.20
329	Dyson/Schulters/Williams	.30	.10
330	Thomas/Bellamy/Jones	.30	.10
331	Philip Rivers RC	5.00	2.00
332	Dwan Edwards RC	.75	.30
333	Ben Watson RC	1.50	.60
334	Karlos Dansby RC	1.50	.60
335	Cedric Cobbs RC	1.50	.60
336	Chris Perry RC	2.50	1.00
337	Darius Watts RC	1.50	.60
338	Ricardo Colclough RC	1.50	.60
339	Derrick Hamilton RC	1.25	.50
340	Devard Darling RC	1.50	.60
341	Daryl Smith RC	1.50	.60
342	Luke McCown RC	1.50	.60
343	Dunta Robinson RC	1.50	.60
344	Keith Smith RC	1.25	.50
345	Ben Hartsock RC	1.50	.60
346	J.P. Losman RC	3.00	1.25
347	Chris Cooley RC	1.50	.60
348	Keary Colbert RC	2.00	.75
349	Tommie Harris RC	1.50	.60
350	Eli Manning RC	8.00	4.00
351	Kevin Jones RC	5.00	2.00
352	Lee Evans RC	2.00	.75
353	D.J. Williams RC	2.00	.75
354	Ben Troupe RC	1.50	.60
355	Mewelde Moore RC	2.00	.75
356	Michael Clayton RC	3.00	1.25
357	Michael Jenkins RC	1.50	.60
358	Adimchinobe Echemandu RC	1.25	.50
359	Rashaun Woods RC	1.50	.60
360	Bernard Berrian RC	1.50	.60
361	Carlos Francis RC	1.25	.50
362	Roy Williams RC	4.00	1.50
363	Sean Taylor RC	2.00	.75
364	Steven Jackson RC	5.00	2.00
365	Tatum Bell RC	3.00	1.25
366	Jonathan Vilma RC	1.50	.60
367	Derrick Strait RC	2.00	.75
368	Andy Hall RC	1.25	.50
369	Jason Babin RC	1.50	.60
370	Will Smith RC	1.50	.60
371	Kenechi Udeze RC	1.50	.60
372	Vince Wilfork RC	2.00	.75
373	Ahmad Carroll RC	2.00	.75
374	Marquise Hill RC	1.25	.50
375	Ben Roethlisberger RC	15.00	7.50
376	Chris Gamble RC	2.00	.75
377	Junior Siavii RC	1.50	.60
378	Teddy Lehman RC	1.50	.60
379	Antwan Odom RC	1.50	.60
380	DeAngelo Hall RC	2.00	.75
381	Nathan Vasher RC	2.00	.75
382	B.J. Symons RC	1.50	.60
383	Reggie Williams RC	2.00	.75
384	Michael Boulware RC	1.50	.60
385	Matt Schaub RC	2.50	1.00
386	Sean Jones RC	1.25	.50
387	Courtney Watson RC	1.50	.60
388	Nathaniel Adibi RC	1.50	.60
389	Devery Henderson RC	1.25	.50
390	Greg Jones RC	1.50	.60
391	Joey Thomas RC	1.50	.60
392	Drew Carter RC	1.50	.60
393	Julius Jones RC	6.00	2.50
394	Keyaron Fox RC	1.25	.50
395	Darrion Scott RC	1.50	.60
396	Rich Gardner RC	1.25	.50
397	Jeff Smoker RC	1.50	.60
398	Will Poole RC	1.50	.60
399	Samie Parker RC	1.50	.60
400	Larry Fitzgerald RC	5.00	2.00
401	Jericho Cotchery RC	1.50	.60
402	Ernest Wilford RC	1.50	.60
403	Johnnie Morant RC	1.50	.60
404	Craig Krenzel RC	1.50	.60
405	Michael Turner RC	1.50	.60
406	D.J. Hackett RC	1.25	.50
407	P.K. Sam RC	1.25	.50
408	Triandos Luke RC	1.50	.60
409	Josh Harris RC	1.50	.60
410	Drew Henson RC	1.50	.60
411	John Navarre RC	1.50	.60
412	Cody Pickett RC	1.50	.60
413	Clarence Moore RC	1.50	.60
414	Michael Gaines RC	1.25	.50
415	Derek Abney RC	1.50	.60
416	Dontarrious Thomas RC	1.50	.60
417	Reggie Torbor RC	1.25	.50
418	Ryan Krause RC	1.25	.50
419	Travis LaBoy RC	1.50	.60
420	Kellen Winslow RC	3.00	1.25
421	Keiwan Ratliff RC	1.25	.50
422	Gilbert Gardner RC	1.25	.50
423	Jamaar Taylor RC	1.50	.60
424	Matt Ware RC	1.50	.60
425	Stuart Schweigert RC	1.50	.60
426	Marcus Tubbs RC	1.50	.60
427	Brandon Chillar RC	1.25	.50
428	Shawntae Spencer RC	1.50	.60
429	Marquis Cooper RC	1.25	.50
430	Derrick Ward RC	.75	.30
431	Tim Euhus RC	1.50	.60
432	Patrick Crayton RC	1.50	.60
433	Caleb Miller RC	1.25	.50
434	Donnell Washington RC	1.50	.60
435	Thomas Tapeh RC	1.25	.50
436	Randy Starks RC	1.25	.50
437	Sloan Thomas RC	1.25	.50
438	Maurice Mann RC	1.25	.50
439	Jim Sorgi RC	1.50	.60
440	Nate Lawrie RC	1.25	.50

2005 Topps Total

	COMPLETE SET (550)	80.00	30.00
	COMP.PACKERS TIN (20)	20.00	10.00
	COMP.STEELERS TIN (20)	20.00	10.00
1	Michael Vick	1.00	.40
2	O.Kreutz/Q.Mitchell RC	.40	.15
3	Re.Williams/Garrard/T.Edwards	.50	.20
4	Terence Newman	.40	.15
5	D.Jolley/C.Baker	.40	.15
6	D.Clark/S.Will.RC/B.Hamilton	.40	.15
7	Terrell Owens	.75	.30
8	I.Ohalete/A.Wilson	.40	.15
9	G.Walker/Payne/Rob.Smith	.40	.15
10	Quentin Jammer	.40	.15
11	Ke.Smith/D.Bly	.40	.15
12	C.Taylor/Ogden/B.Sams	.50	.20
13	Torry Holt	.75	.30
14	W.Henderson/N.Davenport	.40	.15
15	J.Slavii/Hicks/J.Allen	.50	.20
16	Keith Bulluck	.40	.15
17	K.Irvin/C.Chavous	.40	.15
18	F.Jackson/A.Bryant/A.Davis	.75	.30
19	Michael Pittman	.40	.15
20	Vanderjagt/H.Smith RC	.40	.15
21	J.Winborn/Ulbrich/D.Smith	.40	.15
22	Reggie Wayne	.50	.20
23	S.Lechler/Janikowski	.40	.15
24	K.Mathis RC/J.Webster/B.Scott	.40	.15
25	Daunte Culpepper	.75	.30
26	W.Peterson/W.Allen	.40	.15
27	T.Walter/F.Adams/L.Allen	.40	.15
28	Tauscher/M.Flanagan/Clifton RC	.40	.15
29	Jerome Bettis	.75	.30
30	M.Brown/R.McQuarters	.40	.15
31	Andre Johnson	.50	.20
32	Toefield/G.Jones/Fuamatu-Ma'Afala	.40	.15
33	G.Lewis/B.McMullen	.75	.30
34	Kyle Boller	.50	.20
35	Kacyvenski/T.White RC/Bates	.40	.15
36	Chris Brown	.50	.20
37	J.Phillips/B.Kelly	.40	.15
38	Saturday RC/Diem RC/Ta.Glenn	.40	.15
39	Clinton Portis	.75	.30
40	M.Scifres/N.Kaeding	.40	.15
41	Ke.Williams/Udeze/Johnstone	.40	.15
42	Tony Parrish	.40	.15
43	D.Armstrong/J.Gaffney	.40	.15
44	F.Bryant/C.Cash/Te.Holt	.40	.15
45	Kerry Collins	.50	.20
46	M.Strong/M.Morris	.50	.20
47	Robertson/J.Abraham/S.Ellis	.40	.15
48	Darrell Jackson	.50	.20
49	P.Price/A.Rossum	.40	.15
50	A.Henry/N.Jones RC/Frazier RC	.40	.15
51	Steven Jackson	1.00	.40
52	R.Sims/J.Browning	.40	.15
53	Robbins/Umenyiora/W.Joseph	.75	.30
54	Billy Volek	.50	.20
55	A.Ayodele/Da.Smith	.40	.15
56	I.Scott RC/Odom/T.Johnson	.40	.15
57	Onterrio Smith	.50	.20
58	M.Stover/D.Zastudil RC	.40	.15
59	Hunt/Gbaja-Biamila/Kampman RC	.50	.20
60	Dante Hall	.50	.20
61	J.Peterson/B.Young	.40	.15
62	Hardwick/Olivea RC/Oben	.40	.15
63	Chad Pennington	.75	.30
64	D.Clark/A.Moorehead	.40	.15
65	B.Taylor/K.Richard RC	.40	.15
66	K.Walker/J.Wade RC	.40	.15
67	Jeremy Shockey	.75	.30
68	Daylon McCutcheon	.40	.15
69	Coakley/Claiborne/Tinoisamoa	.40	.15
70	Roy Williams WR	.75	.30
71	L.Schulters/Ta.Williams	.40	.15
72	S.Brown/Hood RC/Wynn	.40	.15
73	Sean Taylor	.50	.20
74	L.Little/B.Chillar	.40	.15
75	Boiman/R.Starks/Clauss RC	.40	.15
76	Lee Suggs	.50	.20
77	P.Crayton/T.Glenn	.40	.15
78	Dansby/Darling/G.Hayes	.40	.15
79	Nick Barnett	.40	.15
80	R.Coleman/A.Lake RC	.40	.15
81	Berrian/J.Gage/D.Clark	.40	.15
82	Dominic Rhodes	.40	.15
83	C.Moore/R.Hymes	.40	.15
84	Fraley RC/Runyan/T.Thomas	.40	.15
85	Philip Rivers	.75	.30
86	A.Harris/A.Carroll	.40	.15
87	B.Sanders/Doss/J.Jefferson	1.25	.50
88	Cesaire RC/Ja.Will/Dingle	.40	.15
89	Eric Moulds	.50	.20
90	P.Zellner RC/R.Davis	.40	.15
91	K.Wong/Babin/A.Peek	.40	.15
92	Tony Richardson	.40	.15
93	G.Wesley/J.Woods	.40	.15
94	Fabini/Goodwin RC/K.Mawae	.40	.15
95	Tatum Bell	.50	.20
96	K.Lewis RC/C.Emmons	.40	.15
97	J.Galloway/W.Heller	.50	.20
98	Tom Brady	2.00	.75
99	R.Babers/B.Walker	.40	.15
100	Mickens/McGraw/Buckley	.40	.15
101	Zach Thomas	.75	.30
102	Co.Brown RC/A.Weaver	.40	.15
103	A.Will/J.Butler/K.Garrett	.40	.15
104	Troy Polamalu	1.25	.50
105	W.Sapp/T.Washington	.50	.20
106	T.Johnson/Crockett/Morant	.40	.15
107	Chris McAlister	.40	.15
108	C.Stanley RC/K.Brown	.40	.15
109	Drew Henson	.50	.20
110	James Hall	.40	.15
111	S.Player/N.Rackers	.40	.15
112	D.Watts/A.Lelie	.50	.20
113	J.David/N.Harper	.40	.15
114	R.Curry/D.Gabriel	.50	.20
115	R.Colclough/W.Williams	.50	.20

❑	116	C.Tillman/J.Azumah	.40	.15
❑	117	M.Kemoeatu RC/Ad.Thomas	.75	.30
❑	118	M.Roman/J.Thomas	.40	.15
❑	119	D.Henderson/M.Lewis	.40	.15
❑	120	M.Furrey/Manumaleuna	.40	.15
❑	121	R.Mahe/C.Buckhalter	.50	.20
❑	122	E.Kinney/T.Fleming	.40	.15
❑	123	W.Dunn/T.Duckett	.50	.20
❑	124	T.Euhus/M.Campbell	.40	.15
❑	125	P.Hunter/A.Glenn	.40	.15
❑	126	R.Tongue/D.Barrett	.40	.15
❑	127	S.Morris/L.Gordon	.40	.15
❑	128	R.Clark RC/S.Springs	.40	.15
❑	129	J.Miller/A.Vinatieri	.75	.30
❑	130	E.Warfield/W.Bartee	.40	.15
❑	131	Me.Moore/M.Bennett	.50	.20
❑	132	N.Goings/B.Hoover	.40	.15
❑	133	Q.Harris/D.Macklin	.40	.15
❑	134	E.Drummond/R.Swinton	.40	.15
❑	135	J.Fargas/A.Whitted	.40	.15
❑	136	N.Clements/T.McGee RC	.75	.30
❑	137	T.Hollings/J.Wells	.40	.15
❑	138	D.Cooper RC/K.Thomas RC	.40	.15
❑	139	P.Dawson/D.Frost RC	.40	.15
❑	140	J.McCown/J.Navarre	.50	.20
❑	141	G.Ellis/K.Coleman	.40	.15
❑	142	G.Wilson/B.Alexander	.40	.15
❑	143	A.Woolfolk/L.Thompson	.40	.15
❑	144	E.Conwell/B.Williams	.40	.15
❑	145	D.Akers/Di.Johnson RC	.40	.15
❑	146	Hillenmeyer RC/L.Briggs	2.00	.75
❑	147	R.Mathis RC/G.Brackett	1.50	.60
❑	148	J.Rice/R.Alexander	1.25	.50
❑	149	E.Coleman/D.Strait	.40	.15
❑	150	J.Hartwig RC/B.Troupe	.40	.15
❑	151	S.Davis/D.Florence	.40	.15
❑	152	P.Buchanon/M.Coleman	.40	.15
❑	153	S.Heiden/A.Shea	.40	.15
❑	154	T.Spikes/L.Fletcher	.40	.15
❑	155	T.Laboy/A.Odom	.40	.15
❑	156	A.Toomer/M.Cloud	.50	.20
❑	157	L.Tynes/C.Horn	.50	.20
❑	158	N.Diggs/P.Lenon RC	.40	.15
❑	159	R.Long/A.Haynesworth	.40	.15
❑	160	B.Askew/J.Sowell	.40	.15
❑	161	John Carney Mitch Berger	.40	.15
❑	162	K.Campbell/J.Wiggins	.40	.15
❑	163	Jerramy Stevens	.40	.15
❑	164	Willis McGahee	.75	.30
❑	165	Ed Reed	.50	.20
❑	166	Muhsin Muhammad	.50	.20
❑	167	Donovin Darius	.40	.15
❑	168	E.J. Henderson	.40	.15
❑	169	Tony Banks	.40	.15
❑	170	Fred Taylor	.50	.20
❑	171	Jeremiah Trotter	.40	.15
❑	172	Adam Archuleta	.40	.15
❑	173	Marcus Trufant	.40	.15
❑	174	Steve McNair	.75	.30
❑	175	Ben Roethlisberger	2.00	.75
❑	176	Derrick Blaylock	.40	.15
❑	177	Michael Strahan	.50	.20
❑	178	Robert Gallery	.50	.20
❑	179	Drew Brees	.75	.30
❑	180	David Kircus	.40	.15
❑	181	Robert Ferguson	.40	.15
❑	182	Jim Sorgi	.40	.15
❑	183	Alge Crumpler	.50	.20
❑	184	DeShaun Foster	.50	.20
❑	185	Reuben Droughns	.50	.20
❑	186	Charles Grant	.40	.15
❑	187	Jason Taylor	.40	.15
❑	188	James Thrash	.50	.20
❑	189	LaDainian Tomlinson	1.00	.40
❑	190	Tim Rattay	.40	.15
❑	191	Jeff Garcia	.50	.20
❑	192	Jerricho Cotchery	.40	.15
❑	193	Chris Simms	.50	.20
❑	194	Jevon Kearse	.50	.20
❑	195	Kyle Brady	.40	.15
❑	196	Trent Green	.50	.20
❑	197	Antoine Winfield	.40	.15
❑	198	Deion Branch	.50	.20
❑	199	Rudi Johnson	.50	.20
❑	200	Lee Evans	.50	.20
❑	201	Stephen Davis	.50	.20
❑	202	Darrell Dockett	.40	.15
❑	203	Kurt Warner	.50	.20
❑	204	Quincy Morgan	.40	.15
❑	205	Daimon Shelton	.40	.15
❑	206	Champ Bailey	.50	.20
❑	207	Jamal Lewis	.75	.30
❑	208	Brett Favre	2.00	.75
❑	209	Charles Woodson	.50	.20
❑	210	Koren Robinson	.50	.20
❑	211	Chris Chambers	.50	.20
❑	212	Dave Ragone	.40	.15
❑	213	Travis Minor	.40	.15
❑	214	Simeon Rice	.50	.20
❑	215	Tommy Maddox	.40	.15
❑	216	Aaron Stecker	.40	.15
❑	217	Dwight Freeney	.50	.20
❑	218	Thomas Jones	.50	.20
❑	219	Patrick Ramsey	.50	.20
❑	220	Travis Taylor	.40	.15
❑	221	Chris Weinke	.40	.15
❑	222	Marc Bulger	.75	.30
❑	223	James Farrior	.40	.15
❑	224	Billy Miller	.40	.15
❑	225	Mike Peterson	.40	.15
❑	226	Eddie Kennison	.40	.15
❑	227	Aaron Brooks	.50	.20
❑	228	Plaxico Burress	.50	.20
❑	229	Jerry Porter	.50	.20
❑	230	Joey Harrington	.75	.30
❑	231	Bubba Franks	.50	.20
❑	232	Michael Jenkins	.50	.20
❑	233	Larry Fitzgerald	.75	.30
❑	234	Troy Vincent	.40	.15
❑	235	Chad Johnson	.75	.30
❑	236	Roy Williams S	.50	.20
❑	237	Corey Dillon	.50	.20
❑	238	Donovan McNabb	1.00	.40
❑	239	Marcus Robinson	.50	.20
❑	240	Derrick Brooks	.50	.20
❑	241	David Bowens RC	.50	.20
❑	242	Renaldo Wynn	.40	.15
❑	243	Kevan Barlow	.50	.20
❑	244	Antonio Gates	.75	.30
❑	245	Duce Staley	.50	.20
❑	246	Ernest Wilford	.40	.15
❑	247	Kevin Jones	.75	.30
❑	248	Julius Peppers	.50	.20
❑	249	Terrell Suggs	.50	.20
❑	250	Bertrand Berry	.40	.15
❑	251	Brian Simmons	.40	.15
❑	252	Jake Plummer	.50	.20
❑	253	Brian Urlacher	.75	.30
❑	254	Justin McCareins	.40	.15
❑	255	L.J. Smith	.40	.15
❑	256	Matt Hasselbeck	.50	.20
❑	257	Rashaun Woods	.50	.20
❑	258	Rodney Harrison	.50	.20
❑	259	Brandon Stokley	.50	.20
❑	260	Tony Gonzalez	.50	.20
❑	261	J.P. Losman	.75	.30
❑	262	DeAngelo Hall	.50	.20
❑	263	Jake Delhomme	.75	.30
❑	264	Shaun Rogers	.40	.15
❑	265	Donald Driver	.50	.20
❑	266	Will Smith	.40	.15
❑	267	Brian Westbrook	.50	.20
❑	268	A.J. Feeley	.50	.20
❑	269	Marshall Faulk	.75	.30
❑	270	Marques Tuiasosopo	.40	.15
❑	271	Curtis Martin	.75	.30
❑	272	Jason Witten	.50	.20
❑	273	Kellen Winslow	.75	.30
❑	274	Corey Bradford	.40	.15
❑	275	Samari Rolle	.40	.15
❑	276	Anquan Boldin	.50	.20
❑	277	Adrian Peterson	.40	.15
❑	278	Javon Walker	.50	.20
❑	279	Fred Smoot	.40	.15
❑	280	Mike Alstott	.50	.20
❑	281	Randy McMichael	.40	.15
❑	282	Jay Fiedler	.40	.15
❑	283	Jamie Sharper	.40	.15
❑	284	Eli Manning	1.50	.60
❑	285	Todd Pinkston	.40	.15
❑	286	La'Roi Glover	.40	.15
❑	287	Chris Perry	.50	.20
❑	288	David Carr	.75	.30
❑	289	Bryant Johnson	.40	.15
❑	290	Ray Lewis	.75	.30
❑	291	Tommie Harris	.40	.15
❑	292	Joe Horn	.50	.20
❑	293	Rod Smith	.50	.20
❑	294	Michael Clayton	.75	.30
❑	295	Tyrone Calico	.50	.20
❑	296	Santana Moss	.50	.20
❑	297	Hines Ward	.75	.30
❑	298	Jonathan Vilma	.50	.20
❑	299	Randy Moss	.75	.30
❑	300	Donte Stallworth	.50	.20
❑	301	Isaac Bruce	.50	.20
❑	302	Brian Griese	.50	.20
❑	303	Dennis Northcutt	.40	.15
❑	304	Michael Green	.40	.15
❑	305	Marvin Harrison	.75	.30
❑	306	Jimmy Smith	.50	.20
❑	307	Patrick Kerney	.40	.15
❑	308	Todd Heap	.50	.20
❑	309	Dan Morgan	.40	.15
❑	310	Charles Rogers	.50	.20
❑	311	Dunta Robinson	.50	.20
❑	312	Deuce McAllister	.75	.30
❑	313	Ronde Barber	.40	.15
❑	314	Brandon Lloyd	.40	.15
❑	315	Tiki Barber	.75	.30
❑	316	LaMont Jordan	.75	.30
❑	317	Lito Sheppard	.40	.15
❑	318	Laveranues Coles	.50	.20
❑	319	Drew Bennett	.50	.20
❑	320	Julius Jones	1.00	.40
❑	321	Ahman Green	.75	.30
❑	322	Domanick Davis	.50	.20
❑	323	Byron Leftwich	.75	.30
❑	324	Nate Burleson	.50	.20
❑	325	David Givens	.50	.20
❑	326	Trent Dilfer	.50	.20
❑	327	T.J. Houshmandzadeh	.40	.15
❑	328	Keith Brooking	.40	.15
❑	329	Derrick Mason	.50	.20
❑	330	Ken Lucas	.40	.15
❑	331	Rex Grossman	.50	.20
❑	332	Edgerrin James	.75	.30
❑	333	Priest Holmes	.75	.30
❑	334	Donnie Edwards	.40	.15
❑	335	Pierson Prioleau RC	.75	.30
❑	336	Shaun Alexander	1.00	.40
❑	337	D.J. Williams	.40	.15
❑	338	Peyton Manning	1.25	.50
❑	339	Carson Palmer	.75	.30
❑	340	Keyshawn Johnson	.50	.20
❑	341	Tory James	.40	.15
❑	342	Drew Bledsoe	.75	.30
❑	343	Chris Gamble	.50	.20
❑	344	Mi.Lewis/B.Dawkins	.50	.20
❑	345	Forney/McClure RC/Weiner RC	.40	.15
❑	346	R.Smart/Kasay/J.Kyle	.40	.15
❑	347	J.Ferguson/Reeves/Nguyen	.40	.15
❑	348	Crocker/Lehan RC/M.Jameson	.40	.15
❑	349	Tyree/Ja.Taylor/T.Carter	.40	.15
❑	350	H.Thomas/D.Jones/Simoneau	.40	.15
❑	351	Royal/McCants/T.Jacobs	.40	.15
❑	352	Welker/D.Thompson/Gilmore	.40	.15
❑	353	D.Lewis/Pickett/Ty.Jackson	.40	.15
❑	354	F.Brown/F.Thomas/J.Bellamy	.40	.15
❑	355	Asomugha/M.Anderson/Schweigert	.40	.15
❑	356	M.Stroud/J.Hender/Favors	.40	.15
❑	357	W.Shields/Roaf/B.Waters RC	.40	.15
❑	358	Hamilton/Nalen/Lepsis	.40	.15
❑	359	J.Smith/Geathers/D.Clemons	.40	.15
❑	360	Wire/R.Baker/L.Milloy	.40	.15
❑	361	Ayanbadejo/J.Scobey/Hambrick	.40	.15
❑	362	St.Smith/Proehl/Colbert	.50	.20
❑	363	N.Harris/D.Thomas/Offord	.40	.15
❑	364	L.Neal/M.Turner/Pinnock	.50	.20
❑	365	Faneca/M.Smith RC/Hartings	1.25	.50
❑	366	E.Moore/Pope/Ayanbadejo RC	.75	.30
❑	367	A.Plummer/Jo.Hanson RC/Spencer	.40	.15
❑	368	L.Betts/Brunell/C.Morton	.50	.20
❑	369	Pace/Timmerman/McCollum	.40	.15
❑	370	B.Thomas/Barton/Hobson	.40	.15
❑	371	S.Barber/K.Fox/K.Mitchell	.40	.15
❑	372	K.Edwards/Wilkinson/Redding	.40	.15
❑	373	Co.Jackson RC/Lang/McKinley	.40	.15
❑	374	Bannan/R.Edwards/S.Adams	.40	.15
❑	375	M.Schaub/D.White/Finneran	.50	.20

❑ 376 Short/A.Wallace RC/K.Jenkins .40 .15
❑ 377 Leach/Carswell/Putzier .40 .15
❑ 378 Vrabel/T.Johnson/Bruschi .75 .30
❑ 379 Kiel/Je.Wilson RC/Fletcher .40 .15
❑ 380 Engelber/To.Brown RC/A.Adams .40 .15
❑ 381 Quarles/Gooch/D.White .40 .15
❑ 382 Madison/W.Poole/R.Howard .40 .15
❑ 383 Schneck RC/Gardocki/J.Reed .75 .30
❑ 384 J.Mitchell RC/Gross/Brzezinski RC .40 .15
❑ 385 Greisen/B.Green/A.Pierce .40 .15
❑ 386 C.Simon/D.Walker/McDougle .40 .15
❑ 387 D.Graham/Fauria/B.Watson .50 .20
❑ 388 E.Johnson/R.John/M.Coleman .40 .15
❑ 389 June/D.Thornton/Hutchins .50 .20
❑ 390 Teague/R.Tucker/M.Will.T .40 .15
❑ 391 M.Haynes/A.Brown/Ogunleye .75 .30
❑ 392 Ulmer RC/Br.Smith/De.Williams .40 .15
❑ 393 K.Faulk/Pass/Be.Johnson .50 .20
❑ 394 Tobeck RC/W.Jones/S.Hutchin .40 .15
❑ 395 V.Holliday/Y.Bell RC/K.Carter .40 .15
❑ 396 L.Foote/J.Porter/Al.Jackson .75 .30
❑ 397 Looker/K.Curtis/S.McDonald .50 .20
❑ 398 L.Marshall RC/C.Griffin/D.Evans .75 .30
❑ 399 D.Klecko/Izzo/R.Colvin .40 .15
❑ 400 M.Holland/Bentley/Gandy .40 .15
❑ 401 Pettigout/McKenzie RC/J.Whittle RC .40 .15
❑ 402 Sykes RC/Fatafehi/A.Wilson .40 .15
❑ 403 Meester RC/Ma.Will/Manuwai RC .40 .15
❑ 404 M.Schobel/K.Washing/Warrick .40 .15
❑ 405 M.Minter/R.Manning/C.Branch .40 .15
❑ 406 Jo.Reed/Jo.Smith/Aiken .40 .15
❑ 407 Birk/Liwienski/McKinnie .40 .15
❑ 408 Godfrey/Foley/Leber .40 .15
❑ 409 McFarland/Wyms/G.Spires .40 .15
❑ 410 E.Perry/Do.Lee/Booker .50 .20
❑ 411 Von Oelhoffen/Hoke RC/Aa.Smith .75 .30
❑ 412 B.Mitchell/Wistrom/Ra.Moore .40 .15
❑ 413 J.Green/Wilfork/T.Warren .50 .20
❑ 414 Middlebrooks/Lynch/N.Ferguson .40 .15
❑ 415 Reagor/R.Brock/Jo.Williams .40 .15
❑ 416 J.Dunn/S.Parker/La.Johnson .75 .30
❑ 417 La.Johnson/M.Wilkins RC/C.Miller .40 .15
❑ 418 Buckner/Moorehead/M.Rucker .40 .15
❑ 419 Denney/Kelsay/A.Schobel .40 .15
❑ 420 Singleton/B.James/K.O'Neil RC .40 .15
❑ 421 C.Thompson/Boyer/An.Davis .40 .15
❑ 422 D.Grant/Richardson RC/R.Mathis .40 .15
❑ 423 Schlesinger/Bryson/Pinner .40 .15
❑ 424 S.Johnson RC/R.Davis/Ru.Jones .40 .15
❑ 425 Phifer/Banta-Cain/McGinest .50 .20
❑ 426 McCardell/Osgood/E.Parker .40 .15
❑ 427 C.Woodard/Bernard/A.Cochran .40 .15
❑ 428 A.Battle/A.Walker/E.Johnson .40 .15
❑ 429 Salave'a RC/M.Wash/L.Arrington .75 .30
❑ 430 L.Mays/C.Wilson/Randle El .75 .30
❑ 431 D.Starks/E.Wilson/R.Gay .50 .20
❑ 432 Q.Griffin/M.Anderson/C.Sapp .50 .20
❑ 433 J.Thornton/L.Moore RC/Powell .40 .15
❑ 434 M.Gaines/Hankton/Seidman .40 .15
❑ 435 M.Haggan RC/Posey/A.Crowell .40 .15
❑ 436 O'Neal/M.Williams/K.Ratliff .40 .15
❑ 437 M.Light/Koppen RC/S.Neal RC .40 .15
❑ 438 C.Watson/D.Rodgers/J.Allen .50 .20
❑ 439 M.Boulware/Hamlin/Bierria RC .40 .15
❑ 440 T.Rogers RC/Unck RC/Roye .40 .15
❑ 441 Frank Gore RC 2.50 1.00
❑ 442 Mike Patterson RC 1.50 .60
❑ 443 DeMarcus Ware RC 2.50 1.00
❑ 444 Chris Henry RC 1.50 .60
❑ 445 Thomas Davis RC 1.50 .60
❑ 446 Justin Miller RC 1.25 .50
❑ 447 Shaun Cody RC 1.50 .60
❑ 448 Alex Barron RC .75 .30
❑ 449 Brock Berlin RC 1.25 .50
❑ 450 Travis Johnson RC 1.25 .50
❑ 451 Jerome Mathis RC 1.50 .60
❑ 452 Lance Mitchell RC 1.25 .50
❑ 453 Marlin Jackson RC 1.50 .60
❑ 454 Charlie Frye RC 3.00 1.25
❑ 455 Luis Castillo RC 1.50 .60
❑ 456 Fred Gibson RC 1.25 .50
❑ 457 Dustin Fox RC 1.50 .60
❑ 458 Ryan Fitzpatrick RC 2.50 1.00
❑ 459 Dan Orlovsky RC 2.00 .75
❑ 460 Justin Tuck RC 1.50 .60
❑ 461 Corey Webster RC 1.50 .60
❑ 462 Travis Daniels RC 1.25 .50
❑ 463 J.J. Arrington RC 2.00 .75
❑ 464 David Greene RC 1.50 .60
❑ 465 Alvin Pearman RC 1.50 .60
❑ 466 Manuel White RC 1.25 .50
❑ 467 Paris Warren RC 1.25 .50
❑ 468 Patrick Estes RC 1.25 .50
❑ 469 Cedric Houston RC 1.50 .60
❑ 470 David Pollack RC 1.50 .60
❑ 471 Craig Bragg RC 1.25 .50
❑ 472 Vincent Jackson RC 1.50 .60
❑ 473 Adam Jones RC 1.50 .60
❑ 474 Matt Jones RC 4.00 1.50
❑ 475 Stefan LeFors RC 1.50 .60
❑ 476 Heath Miller RC 4.00 1.50
❑ 477 Ryan Moats RC 1.50 .60
❑ 478 Vernand Morency RC 1.50 .60
❑ 479 Terrence Murphy RC 1.50 .60
❑ 480 Kyle Orton RC 2.50 1.00
❑ 481 Roscoe Parrish RC 1.50 .60
❑ 482 Courtney Roby RC 1.50 .60
❑ 483 Aaron Rodgers RC 5.00 2.00
❑ 484 Carlos Rogers RC 2.00 .75
❑ 485 Antrel Rolle RC 1.50 .60
❑ 486 Eric Shelton RC 1.50 .60
❑ 487 Alex Smith QB RC 6.00 2.50
❑ 488 Andrew Walter RC 2.50 1.00
❑ 489 Roddy White RC 1.50 .60
❑ 490 Carnell Williams RC 8.00 3.00
❑ 491 Mike Williams 3.00 1.25
❑ 492 Troy Williamson RC 3.00 1.25
❑ 493 Kirk Morrison RC 1.50 .60
❑ 494 Tab Perry RC 1.50 .60
❑ 495 Chad Owens RC 1.50 .60
❑ 496 Lofa Tatupu RC 2.00 .75
❑ 497 Craphonso Thorpe RC 1.25 .50
❑ 498 Ryan Riddle RC .75 .30
❑ 499 Marcus Maxwell RC 1.25 .50
❑ 500 Barrett Ruud RC 1.50 .60
❑ 501 Stanley Wilson RC 1.25 .50
❑ 502 Mike Nugent RC 1.50 .60
❑ 503 Eric King RC 1.25 .50
❑ 504 Darryl Blackstock RC 1.25 .50
❑ 505 Attiyah Ellison RC .75 .30
❑ 506 Donte Nicholson RC 1.50 .60
❑ 507 Airese Currie RC 1.50 .60
❑ 508 Larry Brackins RC .75 .30
❑ 509 Joel Dreessen RC 1.25 .50
❑ 510 Cedric Benson RC 3.00 1.25
❑ 511 Mark Bradley RC 1.50 .60
❑ 512 Reggie Brown RC 1.50 .60
❑ 513 Ronnie Brown RC 5.00 2.00
❑ 514 Jason Campbell RC 2.50 1.00
❑ 515 Maurice Clarett 1.50 .60
❑ 516 Mark Clayton RC 2.00 .75
❑ 517 Braylon Edwards RC 5.00 2.00
❑ 518 Ciatrick Fason RC 1.50 .60
❑ 519 Dan Cody RC 1.50 .60
❑ 520 Taylor Stubblefield RC .75 .30
❑ 521 J.R. Russell RC 1.25 .50
❑ 522 Rian Wallace RC .40 .15
❑ 523 Anthony Davis RC 1.25 .50
❑ 524 Derek Anderson RC 1.50 .60
❑ 525 Boomer Grigsby RC 2.00 .75
❑ 526 Rasheed Marshall RC 1.50 .60
❑ 527 Adrian McPherson RC 1.50 .60
❑ 528 Noah Herron RC 1.50 .60
❑ 529 Bryant McFadden RC 1.50 .60
❑ 530 Lionel Gates RC 1.25 .50
❑ 531 Matt Roth RC 1.50 .60
❑ 532 Derrick Johnson RC 2.50 1.00
❑ 533 Stanford Routt RC 1.25 .50
❑ 534 Brandon Jacobs RC 2.00 .75
❑ 535 Kevin Burnett RC 1.50 .60
❑ 536 Ryan Claridge RC 1.25 .50
❑ 537 James Kilian RC 1.50 .60
❑ 538 Oshiomogho Atogwe RC 1.25 .50
❑ 539 Fabian Washington RC 1.50 .60
❑ 540 Marion Barber RC 2.50 1.00
❑ 541 Anttaj Hawthorne RC 1.25 .50
❑ 542 Zach Tuiasosopo RC .75 .30
❑ 543 Ellis Hobbs RC 1.50 .60
❑ 544 Alex Smith TE RC 1.50 .60
❑ 545 Erasmus James RC 1.50 .60
❑ 546 Channing Crowder RC 1.50 .60
❑ 547 Kelvin Hayden RC 1.25 .50
❑ 548 Darren Sproles RC 1.50 .60
❑ 549 Marcus Spears RC 1.50 .60
❑ 550 Dante Ridgeway RC 1.25 .50
❑ CL1 Checklist 1 .10 .02
❑ CL2 Checklist 2 .10 .02
❑ CL3 Checklist 3 .10 .02
❑ CL4 Checklist 4 .10 .02
❑ VL1 Vince Lombardi Jumbo 6.00 3.00
❑ BR1 Ben Roethlisberger Jumbo 6.00 3.00

2005 Topps Turkey Red

❑ COMPLETE SET (299) 250.00 125.00
❑ COMP.SET w/o SP's (249) 60.00 25.00
❑ COMMON CARD (1-245) .50 .20
❑ SEMISTARS .60 .25
❑ UNLISTED STARS 1.00 .40
❑ COMMON ROOKIE (181-230)
❑ ROOKIE SEMISTARS
❑ COMMON SP (246-285) 4.00 1.50
❑ SP SEMISTARS 4.00 1.50
❑ SP UNL.STARS 5.00 2.00
❑ SP STATED ODDS 1:4
❑ UNPRICED WOOD/1 ODDS 1:2072H, 1:2089R
❑ 1A Eli Manning 2.00 .75
❑ 1B Eli Manning Ad Back 10.00 4.00
❑ 2 Clinton Portis 1.00 .40
❑ 3 Charles Woodson .60 .25
❑ 4A Ray Lewis 1.00 .40
❑ 4B Ray Lewis Ad Back 5.00 2.00
❑ 5 Michael Clayton 1.00 .40
❑ 6 Eric Moulds .60 .25
❑ 7 Derrick Blaylock .50 .20
❑ 8 Carson Palmer 1.00 .40
❑ 9 Zach Thomas 1.00 .40
❑ 10 Dallas Clark .50 .20
❑ 11 DeAngelo Hall .60 .25
❑ 12 Terrell Owens 1.00 .40
❑ 13 Brian Griese .60 .25
❑ 14 Dunta Robinson .60 .25
❑ 15 Kevan Barlow .60 .25
❑ 16 Jake Plummer .60 .25
❑ 17 James Farrior .50 .20
❑ 18A Peyton Manning 1.50 .60
❑ 18B Peyton Manning Ad Back 8.00 3.00
❑ 19 Michael Bennett .60 .25
❑ 20 Brian Urlacher 1.00 .40
❑ 21 Dante Hall .60 .25
❑ 22 Deion Branch .60 .25
❑ 23 Billy Volek .60 .25
❑ 24 Donald Driver .60 .25
❑ 25 LaDainian Tomlinson CL 1.00 .40
❑ 26 Donte Stallworth CL .50 .20
❑ 27 Joey Galloway .60 .25
❑ 28 Joey Harrington 1.00 .40
❑ 29 T.J. Houshmandzadeh .50 .20
❑ 30 LaDainian Tomlinson 1.25 .50
❑ 31 Darius Watts .60 .25
❑ 32 Chris Gamble .60 .25
❑ 33 Javon Walker .60 .25
❑ 34 Kevin Curtis .60 .25
❑ 35 Steven Jackson 1.25 .50
❑ 36 J.P. Losman 1.00 .40
❑ 37A Champ Bailey .60 .25
❑ 37B Champ Bailey Ad Back 3.00 1.25
❑ 38 Tiki Barber 1.00 .40
❑ 39 LaVar Arrington 1.00 .40
❑ 40 Byron Leftwich 1.00 .40
❑ 41 Edgerrin James 1.00 .40
❑ 42 DeShaun Foster .60 .25
❑ 43 Darrell Jackson .60 .25

❑ 44	Julius Peppers	.60	.25
❑ 45	David Carr	1.00	.40
❑ 46	Drew Bennett	.50	.20
❑ 47	Antonio Gates	1.00	.40
❑ 48A	Deuce McAllister	1.00	.40
❑ 48B	Deuce McAllister Ad Back	5.00	2.00
❑ 49	Patrick Ramsey	.60	.25
❑ 50	Antonio Bryant	.50	.20
❑ 51	Quentin Jammer	.50	.20
❑ 52	Chris Brown	.60	.25
❑ 53	Eddie Kennison	.50	.20
❑ 54	Steve McNair	1.00	.40
❑ 55	Corey Bradford	.50	.20
❑ 56	Chris Perry	.60	.25
❑ 57	Curtis Martin	1.00	.40
❑ 58	Mewelde Moore	.60	.25
❑ 59	Travis Taylor	.50	.20
❑ 60	Chad Pennington	1.00	.40
❑ 61	Chad Johnson	.60	.25
❑ 62	Kyle Boller	.60	.25
❑ 63	Tyrone Calico	.60	.25
❑ 64	Michael Pittman	.50	.20
❑ 65	Kerry Collins	.60	.25
❑ 66	Keary Colbert	.60	.25
❑ 67	LaMont Jordan CL	.50	.20
❑ 68	Robert Gallery	.60	.25
❑ 69	Derrick Mason	.60	.25
❑ 70	Brian Dawkins	.50	.20
❑ 71	Chris Simms	.60	.25
❑ 72	Marc Bulger	1.00	.40
❑ 73	Stephen Davis	.60	.25
❑ 74	Kurt Warner	.60	.25
❑ 75	Todd Heap	.60	.25
❑ 76	Domanick Davis CL	.50	.20
❑ 77	Shaun Alexander	1.00	.40
❑ 78	Jerry Porter	.60	.25
❑ 79	Chester Taylor	.60	.25
❑ 80A	Michael Vick	1.50	.60
❑ 80B	Michael Vick Ad Back	8.00	3.00
❑ 81	Justin McCareins	.50	.20
❑ 82	Fred Taylor	.60	.25
❑ 83	Laveranues Coles	.60	.25
❑ 84	Steve Smith	.50	.20
❑ 85	Sean Taylor	.60	.25
❑ 86	Marvin Harrison	1.00	.40
❑ 87	Ashley Lelie	.60	.25
❑ 88	Willis McGahee	1.00	.40
❑ 89	Terence Newman	.50	.20
❑ 90	Joe Horn	.60	.25
❑ 91	Lee Suggs	.60	.25
❑ 92	Keyshawn Johnson	.60	.25
❑ 93	Desmond Clark	.50	.20
❑ 94	T.J. Duckett	.60	.25
❑ 95	Reggie Wayne	.60	.25
❑ 96	Donte Stallworth	.60	.25
❑ 97	Clarence Moore	.50	.20
❑ 98	Jason Witten	.60	.25
❑ 99	Jake Delhomme	1.00	.40
❑ 100	Julius Jones	1.25	.50
❑ 101	Ben Troupe	.50	.20
❑ 102	Hines Ward	1.00	.40
❑ 103	Domanick Davis	.60	.25
❑ 104	B.J. Sams	.50	.20
❑ 105	Marcus Robinson	.60	.25
❑ 106	Devery Henderson	.50	.20
❑ 107	Matt Hasselbeck	.60	.25
❑ 108	Antonio Pierce	.50	.20
❑ 109	Santana Moss	.60	.25
❑ 110	Adam Vinatieri	1.00	.40
❑ 111	Michael Strahan	.60	.25
❑ 112	Greg Jones	.50	.20
❑ 113	Drew Brees	.60	.25
❑ 114	Marcus Robinson	.60	.25
❑ 115	Michael Jenkins	.60	.25
❑ 116	Randy McMichael	.50	.20
❑ 117	Jonathan Vilma	.60	.25
❑ 118	Greg Lewis	.50	.20
❑ 119	Ernest Wilford	.50	.20
❑ 120	Warrick Dunn	.60	.25
❑ 121	Shaun Alexander CL	.75	.30
❑ 122	Donnie Edwards	.50	.20
❑ 123	Antwaan Randle El	.60	.25
❑ 124	Rod Smith	.60	.25
❑ 125	Ed Reed	.60	.25
❑ 126	Muhsin Muhammad	.60	.25
❑ 127	L.J. Smith	.50	.20
❑ 128	Chris Chambers	.60	.25
❑ 129	Matt Schaub	.60	.25
❑ 130	Andre Johnson	.60	.25
❑ 131	Thomas Jones	.60	.25
❑ 132	Robert Ferguson	.50	.20
❑ 133	Jeremy Shockey	1.00	.40
❑ 134	William Green	.50	.20
❑ 135A	Ben Roethlisberger	2.50	1.00
❑ 135B	Ben Roethlisberger Ad Back	12.00	5.00
❑ 136A	Donovan McNabb	1.25	.50
❑ 136B	Donovan McNabb Ad Back	6.00	2.50
❑ 137	Duce Staley	.60	.25
❑ 138	Larry Fitzgerald	1.00	.40
❑ 139	Charles Rogers	.60	.25
❑ 140	Mark Brunell	.60	.25
❑ 141	Kevin Jones	1.25	.50
❑ 142	LaMont Jordan	.60	.25
❑ 143	Aaron Brooks	.60	.25
❑ 144	Brian Westbrook	.60	.25
❑ 145	Larry Johnson	1.00	.40
❑ 146	Tommy Maddox	.50	.20
❑ 147	Corey Dillon	.60	.25
❑ 148	William Henderson	.50	.20
❑ 149	Tony Hollings	.50	.20
❑ 150	Lee Evans	.60	.25
❑ 151	Kelly Holcomb	.50	.20
❑ 152	Reuben Droughns	.60	.25
❑ 153	Keenan McCardell	.50	.20
❑ 154	Ricky Williams	.60	.25
❑ 155	Rashaun Woods	.60	.25
❑ 156	D.J. Williams	.50	.20
❑ 157	Tom Brady	2.00	.75
❑ 158	Eric Parker	.50	.20
❑ 159	Mike Anderson	.60	.25
❑ 160	Roy Williams WR	1.00	.40
❑ 161	Mike Vanderjagt	.50	.20
❑ 162	Ronald Curry	.60	.25
❑ 163	Priest Holmes	1.00	.40
❑ 164	Bernard Berrian	.50	.20
❑ 165	Brian Finneran	.50	.20
❑ 166	Tony Gonzalez	.60	.25
❑ 167	Chris McAlister	.50	.20
❑ 168	Gus Frerotte	.50	.20
❑ 169	Bryant Johnson	.50	.20
❑ 170	Jay Fiedler	.50	.20
❑ 171	Bubba Franks	.60	.25
❑ 172	Tony Romo	.50	.20
❑ 173	Jamal Lewis	.60	.25
❑ 174	Torry Holt	.60	.25
❑ 175	Ladell Betts	.50	.20
❑ 176	Bertrand Berry	.50	.20
❑ 177	Josh McCown	.60	.25
❑ 178	Jonathan Wells	.50	.20
❑ 179	Plaxico Burress	.60	.25
❑ 180	Rudi Johnson	.60	.25
❑ 181	Cedric Benson RC	4.00	1.50
❑ 182	Carlos Rogers RC	2.50	1.00
❑ 183	Terrence Murphy RC	2.00	.75
❑ 184	Frank Gore RC	3.00	1.25
❑ 185	Vincent Jackson RC	2.00	.75
❑ 186	Ciatrick Fason RC	2.00	.75
❑ 187	Alex Smith QB RC	8.00	3.00
❑ 188	Mike Williams	4.00	1.50
❑ 189	Kyle Orton RC	3.00	1.25
❑ 190A	Ronnie Brown RC	6.00	2.50
❑ 190B	Ronnie Brown	10.00	4.00
❑ 191	Charlie Frye RC	4.00	1.50
❑ 192	Mark Bradley RC	2.00	.75
❑ 193	Antrel Rolle RC	2.00	.75
❑ 194	Roscoe Parrish RC	2.00	.75
❑ 195	Ryan Moats RC	2.00	.75
❑ 196	Andrew Walter RC	3.00	1.25
❑ 197	Troy Williamson RC	4.00	1.50
❑ 198	Carnell Williams RC	10.00	4.00
❑ 199	Adam Jones RC	2.00	.75
❑ 200	Braylon Edwards RC	6.00	2.50
❑ 201	Vernand Morency RC	2.00	.75
❑ 202	Ryan Fitzpatrick RC	3.00	1.25
❑ 203	Heath Miller RC	5.00	2.00
❑ 204	Eric Shelton RC	2.00	.75
❑ 205	Jason Campbell RC	2.50	1.00
❑ 206	David Pollack RC	2.50	1.00
❑ 207	Stefan LeFors RC	2.00	.75
❑ 208	DeMarcus Ware RC	3.00	1.25
❑ 209	J.J. Arrington RC	2.50	1.00
❑ 210	Marion Barber RC	3.00	1.25
❑ 211	Samkon Gado RC	12.00	5.00
❑ 212	Roddy White RC	2.00	.75
❑ 213	Brandon Jacobs RC	2.50	1.00
❑ 214	Mark Clayton RC	2.50	1.00
❑ 215	Alex Smith TE RC	2.00	.75
❑ 216	Darren Sproles RC	2.00	.75
❑ 217	Fabian Washington RC	2.00	.75
❑ 218	Brandon Jones RC	2.00	.75
❑ 219	Derrick Johnson RC	2.00	.75
❑ 220	Dan Orlovsky RC	2.50	1.00
❑ 221	Aaron Rodgers RC	6.00	2.50
❑ 222	Cedric Houston RC	2.00	.75
❑ 223	Reggie Brown RC	2.00	.75
❑ 224	Scottie Vines RC	2.00	.75
❑ 225	Willie Parker	8.00	3.00
❑ 226	Matt Jones RC	5.00	2.00
❑ 227	Odell Thurman RC	2.00	.75
❑ 228	Alvin Pearman RC	2.00	.75
❑ 229	Chris Henry RC	2.00	.75
❑ 230	Courtney Roby RC	2.00	.75
❑ 231	Isaac Bruce	.60	.25
❑ 232	Warrick Dunn CL	.50	.20
❑ 233	Willis McGahee CL	.75	.30
❑ 234	Marcus Pollard	.50	.20
❑ 235	Jason Taylor	.50	.20
❑ 236	Joe Namath	5.00	2.00
❑ 237	Joe Montana	10.00	4.00
❑ 238	Barry Sanders	6.00	2.50
❑ 239	Jim Brown	6.00	2.50
❑ 240	Terry Bradshaw	6.00	2.50
❑ 241	Ahman Green	1.00	.40
❑ 242	Tiki Barber CL	.75	.30
❑ 243	Julius Jones CL	1.00	.40
❑ 244	Daunte Culpepper	1.00	.40
❑ 245	Edgerrin James CL	.75	.30
❑ 246	Trent Green	5.00	2.00
❑ 247	Dwight Freeney	5.00	2.00
❑ 248A	Brett Favre	12.00	5.00
❑ 248B	Brett Favre Ad Back	15.00	6.00
❑ 249	Marshall Faulk	8.00	3.00
❑ 250	Jerome Bettis	8.00	3.00
❑ 251	Nate Burleson	5.00	2.00
❑ 252	Brandon Lloyd	5.00	2.00
❑ 253	Randy Moss	8.00	3.00
❑ 254	Drew Bledsoe	8.00	3.00
❑ 255	Brandon Stokley	5.00	2.00
❑ 256	Takeo Spikes	4.00	1.50
❑ 257	Philip Rivers	8.00	3.00
❑ 258	Lito Sheppard	4.00	1.50
❑ 259	Jimmy Smith	5.00	2.00
❑ 260	Tatum Bell	5.00	2.00
❑ 261	Allen Rossum	4.00	1.50
❑ 262	Amani Toomer	5.00	2.00
❑ 263	Jabar Gaffney	4.00	1.50
❑ 264	Jonathan Ogden	4.00	1.50
❑ 265	John Abraham	4.00	1.50
❑ 266	Aaron Stecker	4.00	1.50
❑ 267	Jason Elam	4.00	1.50
❑ 268	Najeh Davenport	4.00	1.50
❑ 269	Alge Crumpler	5.00	2.00
❑ 270	Roy Williams S	5.00	2.00
❑ 271	Trent Dilfer	5.00	2.00
❑ 272	Anquan Boldin	5.00	2.00
❑ 273	Artose Pinner	4.00	1.50
❑ 274	David Garrard	4.00	1.50
❑ 275	Terry Glenn	4.00	1.50
❑ 276	Adam Archuleta	4.00	1.50
❑ 277	Jeremiah Trotter	4.00	1.50
❑ 278	Travis Henry	5.00	2.00
❑ 279	Rex Grossman	5.00	2.00
❑ 280	Maurice Morris	4.00	1.50
❑ 281	Mike Alstott	5.00	2.00
❑ 282	Justin Gage	4.00	1.50
❑ 283	Dennis Northcutt	4.00	1.50
❑ 284	David Givens	5.00	2.00
❑ 285	Dominic Rhodes	4.00	1.50
❑ 286	Gerald Ford	5.00	2.00
❑ 287	Ronald Reagan	5.00	2.00
❑ 288	John F. Kennedy	5.00	2.00
❑ 289	Ulysses S. Grant	5.00	2.00
❑ CL1	Jumbo Checklist 1	1.00	.40
❑ CL2	Jumbo Checklist 2	1.00	.40

2004 UD Diamond All-Star

❑	COMP.SET w/o SP's (90)	20.00	7.50
❑	ROOKIE STATED ODDS 1:6		
❑ 1	Michael Vick	1.00	.40
❑ 2	Julius Peppers	.50	.20
❑ 3	Roy Williams S	.30	.10

❑ 4	Ahman Green	.50	.20
❑ 5	Trent Green	.30	.10
❑ 6	Tom Brady	1.25	.50
❑ 7	Rich Gannon	.30	.10
❑ 8	Drew Brees	.50	.20
❑ 9	Brad Johnson	.30	.10
❑ 10	Todd Heap	.30	.10
❑ 11	Chad Johnson	.50	.20
❑ 12	Ashley Lelie	.30	.10
❑ 13	Marvin Harrison	.50	.20
❑ 14	Daunte Culpepper	.50	.20
❑ 15	Amani Toomer	.30	.10
❑ 16	Terrell Owens	.50	.20
❑ 17	Shaun Alexander	.50	.20
❑ 18	Mark Brunell	.30	.10
❑ 19	Drew Bledsoe	.50	.20
❑ 20	Rudi Johnson	.30	.10
❑ 21	Charles Rogers	.30	.10
❑ 22	Edgerrin James	.50	.20
❑ 23	Randy Moss	.60	.25
❑ 24	Tiki Barber	.50	.20
❑ 25	Hines Ward	.50	.20
❑ 26	Koren Robinson	.30	.10
❑ 27	Laveranues Coles	.30	.10
❑ 28	Travis Henry	.30	.10
❑ 29	Carson Palmer	.60	.25
❑ 30	Joey Harrington	.50	.20
❑ 31	Byron Leftwich	.60	.25
❑ 32	Moe Williams	.20	.07
❑ 33	Chad Pennington	.50	.20
❑ 34	Duce Staley	.30	.10
❑ 35	Marshall Faulk	.50	.20
❑ 36	Clinton Portis	.50	.20
❑ 37	Marcel Shipp	.30	.10
❑ 38	Eric Moulds	.30	.10
❑ 39	Andre Davis	.20	.07
❑ 40	Brett Favre	1.25	.50
❑ 41	Fred Taylor	.30	.10
❑ 42	Ty Law	.30	.10
❑ 43	Santana Moss	.30	.10
❑ 44	Tommy Maddox	.30	.10
❑ 45	Torry Holt	.50	.20
❑ 46	Peerless Price	.30	.10
❑ 47	Stephen Davis	.30	.10
❑ 48	Quincy Carter	.30	.10
❑ 49	David Carr	.50	.20
❑ 50	Dante Hall	.50	.20
❑ 51	Deuce McAllister	.50	.20
❑ 52	Jerry Rice	1.00	.40
❑ 53	Tim Rattay	.20	.07
❑ 54	Derrick Brooks	.30	.10
❑ 55	Warrick Dunn	.30	.10
❑ 56	Anthony Thomas	.30	.10
❑ 57	Keyshawn Johnson	.30	.10
❑ 58	Domanick Davis	.50	.20
❑ 59	Ricky Williams	.50	.20
❑ 60	Aaron Brooks	.30	.10
❑ 61	Tim Brown	.50	.20
❑ 62	Brandon Lloyd	.30	.10
❑ 63	Steve McNair	.50	.20
❑ 64	Kyle Boller	.50	.20
❑ 65	Brian Urlacher	.60	.25
❑ 66	Jake Plummer	.30	.10
❑ 67	Peyton Manning	.75	.30
❑ 68	Chris Chambers	.30	.10
❑ 69	Jeremy Shockey	.50	.20
❑ 70	Brian Westbrook	.30	.10
❑ 71	Matt Hasselbeck	.30	.10
❑ 72	Derrick Mason	.30	.10
❑ 73	Anquan Boldin	.50	.20
❑ 74	Jake Delhomme	.50	.20
❑ 75	Jeff Garcia	.50	.20
❑ 76	Donald Driver	.30	.10
❑ 77	Priest Holmes	.60	.25
❑ 78	Corey Dillon	.30	.10
❑ 79	Curtis Martin	.50	.20
❑ 80	LaDainian Tomlinson	.60	.25
❑ 81	Marc Bulger	.50	.20
❑ 82	Jamal Lewis	.50	.20
❑ 83	Marty Booker	.30	.10
❑ 84	Quentin Griffin	.50	.20
❑ 85	Andre Johnson	.50	.20
❑ 86	Junior Seau	.50	.20
❑ 87	Joe Horn	.30	.10
❑ 88	Donovan McNabb	.60	.25
❑ 89	Kevan Barlow	.30	.10
❑ 90	Eddie George	.30	.10
❑ 91	Eli Manning RC	15.00	6.00
❑ 92	Larry Fitzgerald RC	10.00	4.00
❑ 93	Ben Roethlisberger RC	25.00	12.50
❑ 94	Roy Williams RC	8.00	3.00
❑ 95	Derrick Hamilton RC	2.50	1.00
❑ 96	Kellen Winslow RC	6.00	2.50
❑ 97	Bernard Berrian RC	3.00	1.25
❑ 98	Steven Jackson RC	10.00	4.00
❑ 99	DeAngelo Hall RC	4.00	1.50
❑ 100	Kevin Jones RC	10.00	4.00
❑ 101	Reggie Williams RC	4.00	1.50
❑ 102	Michael Clayton RC	6.00	2.50
❑ 103	Rashaun Woods RC	3.00	1.25
❑ 104	Devery Henderson RC	2.50	1.00
❑ 105	Ben Troupe RC	3.00	1.25
❑ 106	Cedric Cobbs RC	3.00	1.25
❑ 107	Lee Evans RC	4.00	1.50
❑ 108	Luke McCown RC	3.00	1.25
❑ 109	Chris Perry RC	5.00	2.00
❑ 110	J.P. Losman RC	6.00	2.50
❑ 111	Philip Rivers RC	10.00	4.00
❑ 112	Michael Jenkins RC	3.00	1.25
❑ 113	Greg Jones RC	3.00	1.25
❑ 114	Darius Watts RC	3.00	1.25
❑ 115	Tatum Bell RC	6.00	2.50
❑ 116	Ben Watson RC	3.00	1.25
❑ 117	Drew Henson RC	3.00	1.25
❑ 118	Keary Colbert RC	4.00	1.50
❑ 119	Matt Schaub RC	5.00	2.00
❑ 120	Julius Jones RC	12.00	5.00

2004 UD Diamond Pro Sigs

❑	COMP.SET w/o SP's (90)	20.00	7.50
❑	91-140 ROOKIE STATED ODDS 1:6		
❑ 1	Marcel Shipp	.40	.15
❑ 2	Anquan Boldin	.60	.25
❑ 3	Michael Vick	1.25	.50
❑ 4	Peerless Price	.40	.15
❑ 5	Warrick Dunn	.40	.15
❑ 6	Todd Heap	.40	.15
❑ 7	Kyle Boller	.60	.25
❑ 8	Jamal Lewis	.60	.25
❑ 9	Drew Bledsoe	.60	.25
❑ 10	Travis Henry	.40	.15
❑ 11	Eric Moulds	.40	.15
❑ 12	Julius Peppers	.60	.25
❑ 13	Stephen Davis	.40	.15
❑ 14	Jake Delhomme	.60	.25
❑ 15	Anthony Thomas	.40	.15
❑ 16	Brian Urlacher	.75	.30
❑ 17	Marty Booker	.40	.15
❑ 18	Chad Johnson	.60	.25
❑ 19	Rudi Johnson	.40	.15
❑ 20	Carson Palmer	.75	.30
❑ 21	Andre Davis	.25	.08
❑ 22	Jeff Garcia	.60	.25
❑ 23	Eddie George	.40	.15
❑ 24	Vinny Testaverde	.40	.15
❑ 25	Keyshawn Johnson	.40	.15
❑ 26	Ashley Lelie	.40	.15
❑ 27	Jake Plummer	.40	.15
❑ 28	Quentin Griffin	.60	.25
❑ 29	Charles Rogers	.40	.15
❑ 30	Joey Harrington	.60	.25
❑ 31	Ahman Green	.60	.25
❑ 32	Brett Favre	1.50	.60
❑ 33	Donald Driver	.40	.15
❑ 34	David Carr	.60	.25
❑ 35	Domanick Davis	.60	.25
❑ 36	Andre Johnson	.60	.25
❑ 37	Marvin Harrison	.60	.25
❑ 38	Edgerrin James	.60	.25
❑ 39	Peyton Manning	1.00	.40
❑ 40	Byron Leftwich	.75	.30
❑ 41	Fred Taylor	.40	.15
❑ 42	Trent Green	.40	.15
❑ 43	Dante Hall	.60	.25
❑ 44	Priest Holmes	.75	.30
❑ 45	Ricky Williams	.60	.25
❑ 46	Chris Chambers	.40	.15
❑ 47	Junior Seau	.60	.25
❑ 48	Daunte Culpepper	.60	.25
❑ 49	Randy Moss	.75	.30
❑ 50	Moe Williams	.25	.08
❑ 51	Tom Brady	1.50	.60
❑ 52	Deion Branch	.60	.25
❑ 53	Corey Dillon	.40	.15
❑ 54	Deuce McAllister	.60	.25
❑ 55	Aaron Brooks	.40	.15
❑ 56	Joe Horn	.40	.15
❑ 57	Michael Strahan	.40	.15
❑ 58	Tiki Barber	.60	.25
❑ 59	Jeremy Shockey	.60	.25
❑ 60	Chad Pennington	.60	.25
❑ 61	Santana Moss	.40	.15
❑ 62	Curtis Martin	.60	.25
❑ 63	Rich Gannon	.40	.15
❑ 64	Jerry Rice	1.25	.50
❑ 65	Jerry Porter	.40	.15
❑ 66	Terrell Owens	.60	.25
❑ 67	Brian Westbrook	.40	.15
❑ 68	Donovan McNabb	.75	.30
❑ 69	Hines Ward	.60	.25
❑ 70	Duce Staley	.40	.15
❑ 71	Tommy Maddox	.40	.15
❑ 72	Drew Brees	.60	.25
❑ 73	LaDainian Tomlinson	.75	.30
❑ 74	Tim Rattay	.25	.08
❑ 75	Brandon Lloyd	.40	.15
❑ 76	Kevan Barlow	.40	.15
❑ 77	Shaun Alexander	.60	.25
❑ 78	Koren Robinson	.40	.15
❑ 79	Matt Hasselbeck	.40	.15
❑ 80	Marshall Faulk	.60	.25
❑ 81	Torry Holt	.60	.25
❑ 82	Marc Bulger	.60	.25
❑ 83	Brad Johnson	.40	.15
❑ 84	Derrick Brooks	.40	.15
❑ 85	Steve McNair	.60	.25
❑ 86	Derrick Mason	.40	.15
❑ 87	Chris Brown	.60	.25
❑ 88	Mark Brunell	.40	.15
❑ 89	Laveranues Coles	.40	.15
❑ 90	Clinton Portis	.60	.25
❑ 91	Eli Manning RC	15.00	6.00
❑ 92	Larry Fitzgerald RC	10.00	4.00
❑ 93	Ben Roethlisberger RC	30.00	15.00
❑ 94	Roy Williams RC	8.00	3.00
❑ 95	Sean Taylor RC	4.00	1.50
❑ 96	Kellen Winslow RC	6.00	2.50
❑ 97	Chris Gamble RC	4.00	1.50
❑ 98	Steven Jackson RC	10.00	4.00
❑ 99	DeAngelo Hall RC	4.00	1.50
❑ 100	Kevin Jones RC	10.00	4.00
❑ 101	Reggie Williams RC	4.00	1.50
❑ 102	Michael Clayton RC	6.00	2.50
❑ 103	Rashaun Woods RC	3.00	1.25

❑ 104 D.J. Williams RC 4.00 1.50
❑ 105 Ben Troupe RC 3.00 1.25
❑ 106 Mewelde Moore RC 4.00 1.50
❑ 107 Lee Evans RC 4.00 1.50
❑ 108 Jonathan Vilma RC 3.00 1.25
❑ 109 Chris Perry RC 5.00 2.00
❑ 110 J.P. Losman RC 6.00 2.50
❑ 111 Philip Rivers RC 10.00 4.00
❑ 112 Michael Jenkins RC 3.00 1.25
❑ 113 Greg Jones RC 3.00 1.25
❑ 114 John Navarre RC 3.00 1.25
❑ 115 Jerricho Cotchery RC 3.00 1.25
❑ 116 Michael Turner RC 3.00 1.25
❑ 117 Drew Henson RC 3.00 1.25
❑ 118 Keary Colbert RC 4.00 1.50
❑ 119 Matt Schaub RC 5.00 2.00
❑ 120 Cody Pickett RC 3.00 1.25
❑ 121 Luke McCown RC 3.00 1.25
❑ 122 P.K. Sam RC 2.50 1.00
❑ 123 Ernest Wilford RC 3.00 1.25
❑ 124 Will Smith RC 3.00 1.25
❑ 125 Bernard Berrian RC 3.00 1.25
❑ 126 Robert Gallery RC 5.00 2.00
❑ 127 Ben Watson RC 3.00 1.25
❑ 128 Devery Henderson RC 2.50 1.00
❑ 129 Jeff Smoker RC 3.00 1.25
❑ 130 Josh Harris RC 3.00 1.25
❑ 131 Julius Jones RC 12.00 5.00
❑ 132 Dunta Robinson RC 3.00 1.25
❑ 133 Tatum Bell RC 6.00 2.50
❑ 134 Cedric Cobbs RC 3.00 1.25
❑ 135 Devard Darling RC 3.00 1.25
❑ 136 Johnnie Morant RC 3.00 1.25
❑ 137 Derrick Hamilton RC 2.50 1.00
❑ 138 Darius Watts RC 3.00 1.25
❑ 139 Tommie Harris RC 3.00 1.25
❑ 140 B.J. Symons RC 3.00 1.25

2005 UD Mini Jersey Collection

❑ COMPLETE SET (100) 50.00 25.00
❑ 1 Kurt Warner .75 .30
❑ 2 Anquan Boldin .75 .30
❑ 3 Michael Vick 2.00 .75
❑ 4 Warrick Dunn .75 .30
❑ 5 Kyle Boller .75 .30
❑ 6 Ray Lewis 1.25 .50
❑ 7 Jake Delhomme 1.25 .50
❑ 8 DeShaun Foster .75 .30
❑ 9 Carson Palmer 1.25 .50
❑ 10 Chad Johnson 1.25 .50
❑ 11 Rudi Johnson .75 .30
❑ 12 Kellen Winslow 1.25 .50
❑ 13 Lee Suggs .75 .30
❑ 14 Julius Jones 1.50 .60
❑ 15 Drew Bledsoe 1.25 .50
❑ 16 Tatum Bell .75 .30
❑ 17 Jake Plummer .75 .30
❑ 18 Roy Williams WR 1.25 .50
❑ 19 Kevin Jones 1.25 .50
❑ 20 Brett Favre 3.00 1.25
❑ 21 Ahman Green 1.25 .50
❑ 22 David Carr 1.25 .50
❑ 23 Andre Johnson .75 .30
❑ 24 Peyton Manning 2.00 .75
❑ 25 Edgerrin James 1.25 .50
❑ 26 Marvin Harrison 1.25 .50
❑ 27 Byron Leftwich 1.25 .50
❑ 28 Fred Taylor .75 .30
❑ 29 Priest Holmes 1.25 .50
❑ 30 Trent Green .75 .30
❑ 31 Tony Gonzalez .75 .30
❑ 32 A.J. Feeley .75 .30
❑ 33 Randy McMichael .60 .25
❑ 34 Daunte Culpepper 1.25 .50
❑ 35 Nate Burleson .75 .30
❑ 36 Tom Brady 3.00 1.25
❑ 37 Corey Dillon .75 .30
❑ 38 Aaron Brooks .75 .30
❑ 39 Joe Horn .75 .30
❑ 40 Deuce McAllister 1.25 .50
❑ 41 Eli Manning 2.50 1.00
❑ 42 Tiki Barber 1.25 .50
❑ 43 Jeremy Shockey 1.25 .50
❑ 44 Chad Pennington 1.25 .50
❑ 45 Curtis Martin 1.25 .50
❑ 46 Santana Moss .75 .30
❑ 47 Randy Moss 1.25 .50
❑ 48 Kerry Collins .75 .30
❑ 49 Donovan McNabb 1.50 .60
❑ 50 Terrell Owens 1.25 .50
❑ 51 Brian Westbrook .75 .30
❑ 52 Ben Roethlisberger 3.00 1.25
❑ 53 Jerome Bettis 1.25 .50
❑ 54 Drew Brees 1.25 .50
❑ 55 LaDainian Tomlinson 1.50 .60
❑ 56 Kevan Barlow .75 .30
❑ 57 Tim Rattay .60 .25
❑ 58 Matt Hasselbeck .75 .30
❑ 59 Shaun Alexander 1.50 .60
❑ 60 Darrell Jackson .75 .30
❑ 61 Marc Bulger 1.25 .50
❑ 62 Steven Jackson 1.50 .60
❑ 63 Torry Holt 1.25 .50
❑ 64 Michael Pittman .60 .25
❑ 65 Brian Griese .75 .30
❑ 66 Michael Clayton 1.25 .50
❑ 67 Steve McNair 1.25 .50
❑ 68 Drew Bennett .75 .30
❑ 69 Clinton Portis 1.25 .50
❑ 70 Patrick Ramsey .75 .30
❑ 71 Alex Smith QB RC 8.00 3.00
❑ 72 Aaron Rodgers RC 6.00 2.50
❑ 73 Jason Campbell RC 3.00 1.25
❑ 74 Ronnie Brown RC 6.00 2.50
❑ 75 Carnell Williams RC 10.00 4.00
❑ 76 Cedric Benson RC 4.00 1.50
❑ 77 J.J. Arrington RC 2.50 1.00
❑ 78 Braylon Edwards RC 6.00 2.50
❑ 79 Troy Williamson RC 4.00 1.50
❑ 80 Mike Williams 4.00 1.50
❑ 81 Matt Jones RC 5.00 2.00
❑ 82 Mark Clayton RC 2.50 1.00
❑ 83 Roddy White RC 2.00 .75
❑ 84 Reggie Brown RC 2.00 .75
❑ 85 Eric Shelton RC 2.00 .75
❑ 86 Peyton Manning SR 2.00 .75
❑ 87 Ben Roethlisberger SR 3.00 1.25
❑ 88 Julius Jones SR 1.50 .60
❑ 89 Michael Vick SR 2.00 .75
❑ 90 Tom Brady SR 3.00 1.25
❑ 91 Corey Dillon SR .75 .30
❑ 92 Terrell Owens SR 1.25 .50
❑ 93 Donovan McNabb SR 1.50 .60
❑ 94 Priest Holmes SR 1.25 .50
❑ 95 Kevin Jones SR 1.25 .50
❑ 96 Jerome Bettis SR 1.25 .50
❑ 97 Torry Holt SR 1.25 .50
❑ 98 Clinton Portis SR 1.25 .50
❑ 99 Drew Brees SR 1.25 .50
❑ 100 Tiki Barber SR 1.25 .50
❑ NNO Checklist Card .15 .05

2005 UD Portraits

❑ DRAFT PICK PRINT RUN 425 SER.#'d SETS
❑ 1 Larry Fitzgerald 3.00 1.25
❑ 2 Anquan Boldin 2.00 .75
❑ 3 Josh McCown 2.00 .75
❑ 4 Michael Vick 5.00 2.00
❑ 5 Alge Crumpler 2.00 .75
❑ 6 Peerless Price 1.50 .60
❑ 7 Ray Lewis 3.00 1.25
❑ 8 Jamal Lewis 2.00 .75
❑ 9 Todd Heap 2.00 .75
❑ 10 Derrick Mason 2.00 .75
❑ 11 J.P. Losman 3.00 1.25
❑ 12 Willis McGahee 3.00 1.25
❑ 13 Eric Moulds 2.00 .75
❑ 14 Jake Delhomme 3.00 1.25
❑ 15 DeShaun Foster 2.00 .75
❑ 16 Steve Smith 1.50 .60
❑ 17 Brian Urlacher 3.00 1.25
❑ 18 Rex Grossman 2.00 .75
❑ 19 Muhsin Muhammad 2.00 .75
❑ 20 Carson Palmer 3.00 1.25
❑ 21 Rudi Johnson 2.00 .75
❑ 22 Chad Johnson 2.00 .75
❑ 23 Julius Jones 4.00 1.50
❑ 24 Keyshawn Johnson 2.00 .75
❑ 25 Drew Bledsoe 3.00 1.25
❑ 26 Tatum Bell 2.00 .75
❑ 27 Jake Plummer 2.00 .75
❑ 28 Ashley Lelie 2.00 .75
❑ 29 Roy Williams WR 3.00 1.25
❑ 30 Kevin Jones 4.00 1.50
❑ 31 Joey Harrington 3.00 1.25
❑ 32 Brett Favre 8.00 3.00
❑ 33 Ahman Green 3.00 1.25
❑ 34 Javon Walker 2.00 .75
❑ 35 David Carr 3.00 1.25
❑ 36 Andre Johnson 2.00 .75
❑ 37 Domanick Davis 2.00 .75
❑ 38 Peyton Manning 5.00 2.00
❑ 39 Reggie Wayne 2.00 .75
❑ 40 Edgerrin James 3.00 1.25
❑ 41 Marvin Harrison 3.00 1.25
❑ 42 Byron Leftwich 3.00 1.25
❑ 43 Fred Taylor 2.00 .75
❑ 44 Jimmy Smith 2.00 .75
❑ 45 Priest Holmes 3.00 1.25
❑ 46 Larry Johnson 3.00 1.25
❑ 47 Trent Green 2.00 .75
❑ 48 A.J. Feeley 2.00 .75
❑ 49 Chris Chambers 2.00 .75
❑ 50 Randy McMichael 1.50 .60
❑ 51 Daunte Culpepper 3.00 1.25
❑ 52 Onterrio Smith 2.00 .75
❑ 53 Nate Burleson 2.00 .75
❑ 54 Tom Brady 6.00 2.50
❑ 55 Corey Dillon 2.00 .75
❑ 56 Deion Branch 2.00 .75
❑ 57 David Givens 2.00 .75
❑ 58 Aaron Brooks 2.00 .75
❑ 59 Deuce McAllister 3.00 1.25
❑ 60 Joe Horn 2.00 .75
❑ 61 Eli Manning 6.00 2.50
❑ 62 Jeremy Shockey 3.00 1.25
❑ 63 Tiki Barber 3.00 1.25
❑ 64 Chad Pennington 3.00 1.25
❑ 65 Curtis Martin 3.00 1.25
❑ 66 Jonathan Vilma 2.00 .75
❑ 67 Kerry Collins 2.00 .75
❑ 68 Jerry Porter 2.00 .75
❑ 69 Randy Moss 3.00 1.25
❑ 70 Donovan McNabb 4.00 1.50
❑ 71 Terrell Owens 3.00 1.25
❑ 72 Brian Dawkins 1.50 .60
❑ 73 Brian Westbrook 2.00 .75
❑ 74 Ben Roethlisberger 8.00 3.00
❑ 75 Jerome Bettis 3.00 1.25
❑ 76 Hines Ward 3.00 1.25
❑ 77 Duce Staley 2.00 .75
❑ 78 Drew Brees 2.00 .75
❑ 79 LaDainian Tomlinson 4.00 1.50
❑ 80 Antonio Gates 3.00 1.25

❑ 81 Eric Parker 1.50 .60
❑ 82 Tim Rattay 1.50 .60
❑ 83 Kevan Barlow 2.00 .75
❑ 84 Eric Johnson 2.00 .75
❑ 85 Shaun Alexander 3.00 1.25
❑ 86 Darrell Jackson 2.00 .75
❑ 87 Matt Hasselbeck 2.00 .75
❑ 88 Marc Bulger 3.00 1.25
❑ 89 Steven Jackson 4.00 1.50
❑ 90 Marshall Faulk 3.00 1.25
❑ 91 Torry Holt 2.00 .75
❑ 92 Michael Pittman 1.50 .60
❑ 93 Brian Griese 2.00 .75
❑ 94 Michael Clayton 3.00 1.25
❑ 95 Steve McNair 3.00 1.25
❑ 96 Billy Volek 2.00 .75
❑ 97 Chris Brown 2.00 .75
❑ 98 Clinton Portis 3.00 1.25
❑ 99 Patrick Ramsey 2.00 .75
❑ 100 Santana Moss 2.00 .75
❑ 101 Aaron Rodgers RC 15.00 6.00
❑ 102 Alex Smith QB RC 20.00 8.00
❑ 103 Charlie Frye RC 10.00 4.00
❑ 104 Andrew Walter RC 8.00 3.00
❑ 105 Jason Campbell RC 8.00 3.00
❑ 106 Dan Orlovsky RC 6.00 2.50
❑ 107 Derek Anderson RC 5.00 2.00
❑ 108 Kyle Orton RC 8.00 3.00
❑ 109 David Greene RC 5.00 2.00
❑ 110 James Kilian RC 4.00 1.50
❑ 111 Matt Jones RC 12.00 5.00
❑ 112 Cedric Benson RC 10.00 4.00
❑ 113 Ronnie Brown RC 15.00 6.00
❑ 114 Carnell Williams RC 25.00 10.00
❑ 115 Ciatrick Fason RC 5.00 2.00
❑ 116 Vernand Morency RC 5.00 2.00
❑ 117 Eric Shelton RC 5.00 2.00
❑ 118 Maurice Clarett 5.00 2.00
❑ 119 Marion Barber RC 8.00 3.00
❑ 120 Anthony Davis RC 4.00 1.50
❑ 121 J.J. Arrington RC 6.00 2.50
❑ 122 Ryan Moats RC 5.00 2.00
❑ 123 Frank Gore RC 8.00 3.00
❑ 124 Alvin Pearman RC 5.00 2.00
❑ 125 Darren Sproles RC 5.00 2.00
❑ 126 Cedric Houston RC 5.00 2.00
❑ 127 Braylon Edwards RC 15.00 6.00
❑ 128 Troy Williamson RC 10.00 4.00
❑ 129 Mark Clayton RC 6.00 2.50
❑ 130 Chris Henry RC 5.00 2.00
❑ 131 Roddy White RC 5.00 2.00
❑ 132 Fred Gibson RC 4.00 1.50
❑ 133 Craphonso Thorpe RC 4.00 1.50
❑ 134 Terrence Murphy RC 5.00 2.00
❑ 135 Roydell Williams RC 4.00 1.50
❑ 136 Roscoe Parrish RC 5.00 2.00
❑ 137 Reggie Brown RC 5.00 2.00
❑ 138 Craig Bragg RC 4.00 1.50
❑ 139 Larry Brackins RC 4.00 1.50
❑ 140 Rasheed Marshall RC 5.00 2.00
❑ 141 J.R. Russell RC 4.00 1.50
❑ 142 Vincent Jackson RC 5.00 2.00
❑ 143 Dante Ridgeway RC 4.00 1.50
❑ 144 Chad Owens RC 5.00 2.00
❑ 145 Airese Currie RC 4.00 1.50
❑ 146 Marcus Maxwell RC 4.00 1.50
❑ 147 Paris Warren RC 4.00 1.50
❑ 148 Tab Perry RC 5.00 2.00
❑ 149 Jerome Mathis RC 5.00 2.00
❑ 150 Courtney Roby RC 5.00 2.00
❑ 151 Heath Miller RC 12.00 5.00
❑ 152 Alex Smith TE RC 5.00 2.00
❑ 153 Kevin Everett RC 5.00 2.00
❑ 154 Travis Johnson RC 2.50 1.00
❑ 155 Mike Patterson RC 5.00 2.00
❑ 156 DeMarcus Ware RC 8.00 3.00
❑ 157 Erasmus James RC 4.00 1.50
❑ 158 Dan Cody RC 5.00 2.00
❑ 159 David Pollack RC 6.00 2.50
❑ 160 Shaun Cody RC 5.00 2.00
❑ 161 Matt Roth RC 5.00 2.00
❑ 162 Marcus Spears RC 5.00 2.00
❑ 163 Jonathan Babineaux RC 4.00 1.50
❑ 164 Justin Tuck RC 5.00 2.00
❑ 165 Channing Crowder RC 5.00 2.00
❑ 166 Odell Thurman RC 5.00 2.00
❑ 167 Barrett Ruud RC 5.00 2.00
❑ 168 Lance Mitchell RC 4.00 1.50
❑ 169 Derrick Johnson RC 5.00 2.00
❑ 170 Shawne Merriman RC 8.00 3.00
❑ 171 Kevin Burnett RC 5.00 2.00
❑ 172 Darryl Blackstock RC 4.00 1.50
❑ 173 Antrel Rolle RC 5.00 2.00
❑ 174 Adam Jones RC 5.00 2.00
❑ 175 Fabian Washington RC 5.00 2.00
❑ 176 Carlos Rogers RC 6.00 2.50
❑ 177 Corey Webster RC 4.00 1.50
❑ 178 Justin Miller RC 4.00 1.50
❑ 179 Eric Green RC 2.50 1.00
❑ 180 Marlin Jackson RC 5.00 2.00
❑ 181 Luis Castillo RC 5.00 2.00
❑ 182 Thomas Davis RC 4.00 1.50
❑ 183 Kirk Morrison RC 5.00 2.00
❑ 184 Vincent Fuller RC 4.00 1.50
❑ 185 Donte Nicholson RC 5.00 2.00
❑ 186 Brodney Pool RC 4.00 1.50
❑ 187 Mike Nugent RC 5.00 2.00
❑ 188 Timmy Chang RC 4.00 1.50
❑ 189 Matt Cassel RC 8.00 3.00
❑ 190 Adrian McPherson RC 5.00 2.00
❑ 191 Gino Guidugli RC 2.50 1.00
❑ 192 Stefan LeFors RC 5.00 2.00
❑ 193 Marcus Randall RC 4.00 1.50
❑ 194 Brandon Jacobs RC 6.00 2.50
❑ 195 Walter Reyes RC 2.50 1.00
❑ 196 Mark Bradley RC 5.00 2.00
❑ 197 Josh Bullocks RC 5.00 2.00
❑ 198 Chase Lyman RC 2.50 1.00
❑ 199 Harry Williams RC 4.00 1.50
❑ 200 Mike Williams

2003 Ultimate Collection

❑ 1 Peyton Manning 8.00 3.00
❑ 2 Aaron Brooks 5.00 2.00
❑ 3 Joey Harrington 8.00 3.00
❑ 4 Brett Favre 12.00 5.00
❑ 5 Donovan McNabb 6.00 2.50
❑ 6 Jeff Garcia 5.00 2.00
❑ 7 Michael Vick 12.00 5.00
❑ 8 David Carr 8.00 3.00
❑ 9 Drew Brees 5.00 2.00
❑ 10 Chad Pennington 6.00 2.50
❑ 11 Drew Bledsoe 5.00 2.00
❑ 12 Tom Brady 12.00 5.00
❑ 13 Kurt Warner 5.00 2.00
❑ 14 Brad Johnson 3.00 1.25
❑ 15 Jay Fiedler 3.00 1.25
❑ 16 Tim Couch 2.00 .75
❑ 17 Trent Green 3.00 1.25
❑ 18 Daunte Culpepper 5.00 2.00
❑ 19 Keyshawn Johnson 5.00 2.00
❑ 20 Garrison Hearst 3.00 1.25
❑ 21 LaDainian Tomlinson 5.00 2.00
❑ 22 Emmitt Smith 12.00 5.00
❑ 23 Steve McNair 5.00 2.00
❑ 24 Chris Redman 2.00 .75
❑ 25 Chad Hutchinson 2.00 .75
❑ 26 Deuce McAllister 5.00 2.00
❑ 27 Eddie George 3.00 1.25
❑ 28 Marshall Faulk 5.00 2.00
❑ 29 Ahman Green 5.00 2.00
❑ 30 Julius Peppers 5.00 2.00
❑ 31 Priest Holmes 6.00 2.50
❑ 32 Edgerrin James 5.00 2.00
❑ 33 Jerry Rice 10.00 4.00
❑ 34 Ricky Williams 5.00 2.00
❑ 35 Anthony Thomas 3.00 1.25
❑ 36 Jerome Bettis 5.00 2.00
❑ 37 Shaun Alexander 5.00 2.00
❑ 38 Randy Moss 8.00 3.00
❑ 39 Jeremy Shockey 8.00 3.00
❑ 40 Patrick Ramsey 5.00 2.00
❑ 41 Clinton Portis 8.00 3.00
❑ 42 Terrell Owens 5.00 2.00
❑ 43 Corey Dillon 3.00 1.25
❑ 44 Mark Brunell 3.00 1.25
❑ 45 Rich Gannon 3.00 1.25
❑ 46 Curtis Martin 5.00 2.00
❑ 47 Josh McCown 3.00 1.25
❑ 48 Kerry Collins 3.00 1.25
❑ 49 Peerless Price 3.00 1.25
❑ 50 David Boston 3.00 1.25
❑ 51 Plaxico Burress 3.00 1.25
❑ 52 Marvin Harrison 5.00 2.00
❑ 53 Travis Henry 3.00 1.25
❑ 54 Brian Urlacher 8.00 3.00
❑ 55 Jake Plummer 3.00 1.25
❑ 56 Dave Ragone/750 RC 10.00 4.00
❑ 57 Brian St.Pierre AU/250 RC 20.00 7.50
❑ 58 Tony Romo/750 RC 10.00 4.00
❑ 59 Dallas Clark/750 RC 10.00 4.00
❑ 60 Kirk Farmer/750 RC 8.00 3.00
❑ 61 Juston Wood/750 RC 8.00 3.00
❑ 62 Justin Gage/750 RC 10.00 4.00
❑ 63 Sam Aiken/750 RC 8.00 3.00
❑ 64 LaBrandon Toefield/750 RC 10.00 4.00
❑ 65 L.J. Smith/750 RC 10.00 4.00
❑ 66 Domanick Davis/750 RC 20.00 7.50
❑ 67 Artose Pinner/750 RC 10.00 4.00
❑ 68 Dahrran Diedrick/750 RC 10.00 4.00
❑ 69 Lee Suggs/750 RC 25.00 10.00
❑ 70 Bethel Johnson/750 RC 10.00 4.00
❑ 71 Tyrone Calico/750 RC 12.00 5.00
❑ 72 Kevin Curtis/750 RC 10.00 4.00
❑ 73 Bobby Wade/750 RC 10.00 4.00
❑ 74 Brandon Lloyd/750 RC 12.00 5.00
❑ 75 Bryant Johnson/750 RC 10.00 4.00
❑ 76 J.R. Tolver/750 RC 8.00 3.00
❑ 77 Billy McMullen/750 RC 8.00 3.00
❑ 78 Nate Burleson/750 RC 12.00 5.00
❑ 79 Jason Johnson AU/250 RC 20.00 7.50
❑ 80 Talman Gardner/250 RC 15.00 6.00
❑ 81 Anquan Boldin/250 RC 60.00 25.00
❑ 82 Musa Smith/250 RC 15.00 6.00
❑ 83 Teyo Johnson/250 RC 20.00 7.50
❑ 84 Kyle Boller AU/250 RC 60.00 25.00
❑ 85 Carson Palmer AU/250 RC 325.00 200.00
❑ 86 Byron Leftwich AU/250 RC 200.00 100.00
❑ 87 Earnest Graham AU/250 RC 30.00 12.50
❑ 88 Chris Brown AU/250 RC 60.00 30.00
❑ 89 Chris Simms AU/250 RC 80.00 50.00
❑ 90 Kliff Kingsbury AU/250 RC 30.00 12.50
❑ 91 Jason Gesser/750 RC 10.00 4.00
❑ 92 Brad Banks AU/250 RC 25.00 10.00
❑ 93 Ken Dorsey AU/250 RC 30.00 12.50
❑ 94 Rex Grossman AU/250 RC 80.00 40.00
❑ 95 Willis McGahee AU/250 RC 200.00 125.00
❑ 96 Larry Johnson AU/250 RC 350.00 250.00
❑ 97 Quentin Griffin AU/250 RC 30.00 12.50
❑ 98 Onterrio Smith AU/250 RC 40.00 15.00
❑ 99 Justin Fargas AU/250 RC 50.00 20.00
❑ 100 Kareem Kelly AU/250 RC 25.00 10.00
❑ 101 Arnaz Battle AU/250 RC 40.00 20.00
❑ 102 Kel Washington AU/250 RC 40.00 15.00
❑ 103 Seneca Wallace AU/250 RC 30.00 12.50
❑ 104 Taylor Jacobs AU/250 RC 25.00 10.00
❑ 105 Andre Johnson/750 RC 30.00 12.50
❑ 106 Charles Rogers/250 RC 15.00 6.00
❑ 107 Terrell Suggs AU/250 RC 60.00 25.00

2004 Ultimate Collection

❑ 1-65 PRINT RUN 750 SER.#'d SETS
❑ 66-91/99A/133-135 PRINT RUN 750 SETS
❑ 92-98 RC PRINT RUN 250 SER.#'d SETS
❑ 99B-124/131-132 AU RC PRINT RUN 250 SETS
❑ 125-130 AU RC PRINT RUN 150 SER.#'d SETS
❑ UNPRICED PLATINUM PRINT RUN 10 SETS
❑ 1 Emmitt Smith 10.00 4.00
❑ 2 Anquan Boldin 5.00 2.00
❑ 3 Michael Vick 10.00 4.00

❑ 4 Peerless Price 3.00 1.25
❑ 5 Kyle Boller 5.00 2.00
❑ 6 Jamal Lewis 5.00 2.00
❑ 7 Drew Bledsoe 5.00 2.00
❑ 8 Travis Henry 3.00 1.25
❑ 9 Stephen Davis 3.00 1.25
❑ 10 Jake Delhomme 5.00 2.00
❑ 11 Rex Grossman 5.00 2.00
❑ 12 Brian Urlacher 6.00 2.50
❑ 13 Carson Palmer 6.00 2.50
❑ 14 Chad Johnson 5.00 2.00
❑ 15 Jeff Garcia 5.00 2.00
❑ 16 Keyshawn Johnson 3.00 1.25
❑ 17 Roy Williams S 3.00 1.25
❑ 18 Jake Plummer 3.00 1.25
❑ 19 Joey Harrington 5.00 2.00
❑ 20 Charles Rogers 3.00 1.25
❑ 21 Ahman Green 5.00 2.00
❑ 22 Brett Favre 12.00 5.00
❑ 23 David Carr 5.00 2.00
❑ 24 Domanick Davis 5.00 2.00
❑ 25 Andre Johnson 5.00 2.00
❑ 26 Edgerrin James 5.00 2.00
❑ 27 Peyton Manning 8.00 3.00
❑ 28 Marvin Harrison 5.00 2.00
❑ 29 Byron Leftwich 6.00 2.50
❑ 30 Fred Taylor 3.00 1.25
❑ 31 Priest Holmes 6.00 2.50
❑ 32 Tony Gonzalez 3.00 1.25
❑ 33 Trent Green 3.00 1.25
❑ 34 Ricky Williams 5.00 2.00
❑ 35 Chris Chambers 3.00 1.25
❑ 36 Jay Fiedler 2.00 .75
❑ 37 Randy Moss 6.00 2.50
❑ 38 Daunte Culpepper 5.00 2.00
❑ 39 Tom Brady 12.00 5.00
❑ 40 Corey Dillon 3.00 1.25
❑ 41 Deuce McAllister 5.00 2.00
❑ 42 Aaron Brooks 3.00 1.25
❑ 43 Tiki Barber 5.00 2.00
❑ 44 Jeremy Shockey 5.00 2.00
❑ 45 Chad Pennington 5.00 2.00
❑ 46 Curtis Martin 5.00 2.00
❑ 47 Santana Moss 3.00 1.25
❑ 48 Jerry Rice 10.00 4.00
❑ 49 Rich Gannon 3.00 1.25
❑ 50 Donovan McNabb 6.00 2.50
❑ 51 Terrell Owens 5.00 2.00
❑ 52 Hines Ward 5.00 2.00
❑ 53 Plaxico Burress 3.00 1.25
❑ 54 LaDainian Tomlinson 6.00 2.50
❑ 55 Tim Rattay 2.00 .75
❑ 56 Matt Hasselbeck 3.00 1.25
❑ 57 Shaun Alexander 5.00 2.00
❑ 58 Marc Bulger 5.00 2.00
❑ 59 Marshall Faulk 5.00 2.00
❑ 60 Torry Holt 5.00 2.00
❑ 61 Brad Johnson 3.00 1.25
❑ 62 Steve McNair 5.00 2.00
❑ 63 Chris Brown 5.00 2.00
❑ 64 Mark Brunell 3.00 1.25
❑ 65 Clinton Portis 5.00 2.00
❑ 66 Michael Turner RC 10.00 4.00
❑ 67 Kris Wilson RC 10.00 4.00
❑ 68 Jeff Smoker RC 10.00 4.00
❑ 69 Adimchinobe Echemandu RC 8.00 3.00
❑ 71 Thomas Tapeh RC 8.00 3.00
❑ 72 Chris Cooley RC 10.00 4.00
❑ 73 Cody Pickett RC 10.00 4.00
❑ 74 P.K. Sam RC 8.00 3.00
❑ 75 Ben Hartsock RC 10.00 4.00
❑ 76 Tim Euhus RC 10.00 4.00
❑ 77 Jammal Lord RC 10.00 4.00
❑ 78 Ricardo Colclough RC 10.00 4.00
❑ 79 D.J. Hackett RC 8.00 3.00
❑ 80 Ahmad Carroll RC 12.00 5.00
❑ 81 Troy Fleming RC 8.00 3.00
❑ 82 John Navarre RC 10.00 4.00
❑ 83 Craig Krenzel RC 10.00 4.00
❑ 84 Johnnie Morant RC 10.00 4.00
❑ 85 D.J. Williams RC 12.00 5.00
❑ 86 Jarrett Payton RC 12.00 5.00
❑ 87 Quincy Wilson RC 8.00 3.00
❑ 88 B.J. Symons RC 10.00 4.00
❑ 89 Tommie Harris RC 10.00 4.00
❑ 90 Jonathan Vilma RC 10.00 4.00
❑ 91 Karlos Dansby RC 10.00 4.00
❑ 92 Jerricho Cotchery RC 12.00 5.00
❑ 93 Samie Parker RC 12.00 5.00
❑ 94 Carlos Francis RC 10.00 4.00
❑ 95 Jim Sorgi RC 12.00 5.00
❑ 96 Derrick Hamilton RC 10.00 4.00
❑ 97 Dunta Robinson RC 12.00 5.00
❑ 98 Chris Gamble RC 15.00 6.00
❑ 99A Josh Harris RC 10.00 4.00
❑ 99B Devery Henderson AU RC 25.00 10.00
❑ 100 Julius Jones AU RC 150.00 75.00
❑ 101 Cedric Cobbs AU RC 25.00 10.00
❑ 102 Greg Jones AU RC 40.00 15.00
❑ 103 Tatum Bell AU RC EXCH 100.00 50.00
❑ 104 Michael Jenkins AU RC 30.00 12.50
❑ 105 Devard Darling AU RC 25.00 10.00
❑ 106 Lee Evans AU RC 40.00 20.00
❑ 107 Keary Colbert AU RC 40.00 15.00
❑ 108 Bernard Berrian AU RC 25.00 10.00
❑ 109 Ben Watson AU RC 30.00 15.00
❑ 110 Matt Schaub AU RC 80.00 40.00
❑ 111 Darius Watts AU RC 25.00 10.00
❑ 112 Kevin Jones AU RC 120.00 50.00
❑ 113 Luke McCown AU RC 30.00 12.50
❑ 114 DeAngelo Hall AU RC 40.00 20.00
❑ 115 Rashaun Woods AU RC 25.00 10.00
❑ 116 Michael Clayton AU RC 80.00 30.00
❑ 117 Ben Troupe AU RC 25.00 10.00
❑ 118 B.J. Sams AU RC EXCH 25.00 10.00
❑ 119 Reggie Williams AU RC 30.00 15.00
❑ 120 Chris Perry AU RC 50.00 20.00
❑ 121 Roy Williams AU RC 100.00 50.00
❑ 122 Robert Gallery AU RC 30.00 12.50
❑ 123 J.P. Losman AU RC 60.00 30.00
❑ 124 Steven Jackson AU RC 120.00 60.00
❑ 125 Drew Henson AU RC 30.00 15.00
❑ 126 Kellen Winslow AU RC 60.00 30.00
❑ 127 B.Roethlisberger AU RC 600.00 350.00
❑ 128 Philip Rivers AU RC 200.00 125.00
❑ 129 Larry Fitzgerald AU RC 135.00 75.00
❑ 130 Eli Manning AU RC 400.00 250.00
❑ 131 Ernest Wilford AU RC 25.00 10.00
❑ 132 Mewelde Moore AU RC 30.00 15.00
❑ 133 Will Smith RC 10.00 4.00
❑ 134 Kenechi Udeze RC 10.00 4.00
❑ 135 Matt Mauck RC 10.00 4.00

2005 Ultimate Collection

❑ 1-100/270-289 PRINT RUN 550 SER.#'d SETS
❑ 101-200/250-269 PRINT RUN 235 SETS
❑ AUTO PRINT RUN 225 UNLESS NOTED
❑ 1 Larry Fitzgerald 5.00 2.00
❑ 2 Anquan Boldin 3.00 1.25
❑ 3 Kurt Warner 3.00 1.25
❑ 4 Michael Vick 8.00 3.00
❑ 5 Warrick Dunn 3.00 1.25
❑ 6 Alge Crumpler 3.00 1.25
❑ 7 Ray Lewis 5.00 2.00
❑ 8 Deion Sanders 5.00 2.00
❑ 9 Kyle Boller 3.00 1.25
❑ 10 Derrick Mason 3.00 1.25
❑ 11 J.P. Losman 5.00 2.00
❑ 12 Willis McGahee 5.00 2.00
❑ 13 Lee Evans 3.00 1.25
❑ 14 Eric Moulds 3.00 1.25
❑ 15 Jake Delhomme 5.00 2.00
❑ 16 Keary Colbert 3.00 1.25
❑ 17 DeShaun Foster 3.00 1.25
❑ 18 Brian Urlacher 5.00 2.00
❑ 19 Rex Grossman 3.00 1.25
❑ 20 Muhsin Muhammad 3.00 1.25
❑ 21 Carson Palmer 5.00 2.00
❑ 22 Rudi Johnson 3.00 1.25
❑ 23 Chad Johnson 5.00 2.00
❑ 24 Julius Jones 6.00 2.50
❑ 25 Keyshawn Johnson 3.00 1.25
❑ 26 Drew Bledsoe 5.00 2.00
❑ 27 Tatum Bell 3.00 1.25
❑ 28 Jake Plummer 3.00 1.25
❑ 29 Ashley Lelie 3.00 1.25
❑ 30 Roy Williams WR 5.00 2.00
❑ 31 Kevin Jones 5.00 2.00
❑ 32 Jeff Garcia 3.00 1.25
❑ 33 Brett Favre 12.00 5.00
❑ 34 Ahman Green 5.00 2.00
❑ 35 Javon Walker 3.00 1.25
❑ 36 David Carr 5.00 2.00
❑ 37 Andre Johnson 3.00 1.25
❑ 38 Domanick Davis 3.00 1.25
❑ 39 Peyton Manning 8.00 3.00
❑ 40 Reggie Wayne 3.00 1.25
❑ 41 Edgerrin James 5.00 2.00
❑ 42 Marvin Harrison 5.00 2.00
❑ 43 Byron Leftwich 5.00 2.00
❑ 44 Fred Taylor 3.00 1.25
❑ 45 Jimmy Smith 3.00 1.25
❑ 46 Priest Holmes 5.00 2.00
❑ 47 Larry Johnson 5.00 2.00
❑ 48 Trent Green 3.00 1.25
❑ 49 A.J. Feeley 3.00 1.25
❑ 50 Chris Chambers 3.00 1.25
❑ 51 Randy McMichael 2.50 1.00
❑ 52 Daunte Culpepper 5.00 2.00
❑ 53 Michael Bennett 3.00 1.25
❑ 54 Nate Burleson 3.00 1.25
❑ 55 Tom Brady 12.00 5.00
❑ 56 Corey Dillon 3.00 1.25
❑ 57 Deion Branch 3.00 1.25
❑ 58 David Givens 3.00 1.25
❑ 59 Aaron Brooks 3.00 1.25
❑ 60 Deuce McAllister 5.00 2.00
❑ 61 Joe Horn 3.00 1.25
❑ 62 Eli Manning 10.00 4.00
❑ 63 Jeremy Shockey 5.00 2.00
❑ 64 Tiki Barber 5.00 2.00
❑ 65 Chad Pennington 5.00 2.00
❑ 66 Curtis Martin 5.00 2.00
❑ 67 Laveranues Coles 3.00 1.25
❑ 68 Kerry Collins 3.00 1.25
❑ 69 LaMont Jordan 5.00 2.00
❑ 70 Randy Moss 5.00 2.00
❑ 71 Donovan McNabb 6.00 2.50
❑ 72 Terrell Owens 5.00 2.00
❑ 73 Brian Dawkins 2.50 1.00
❑ 74 Brian Westbrook 3.00 1.25
❑ 75 Ben Roethlisberger 12.00 5.00
❑ 76 Jerome Bettis 5.00 2.00
❑ 77 Hines Ward 5.00 2.00
❑ 78 Duce Staley 3.00 1.25
❑ 79 Drew Brees 5.00 2.00
❑ 80 LaDainian Tomlinson 6.00 2.50
❑ 81 Antonio Gates 5.00 2.00
❑ 82 Tim Rattay 2.50 1.00
❑ 83 Kevan Barlow 3.00 1.25
❑ 84 Eric Johnson 3.00 1.25
❑ 85 Shaun Alexander 6.00 2.50
❑ 86 Darrell Jackson 3.00 1.25
❑ 87 Matt Hasselbeck 3.00 1.25
❑ 88 Marc Bulger 5.00 2.00

- ❑ 89 Steven Jackson 6.00 2.50
- ❑ 90 Marshall Faulk 5.00 2.00
- ❑ 91 Torry Holt 5.00 2.00
- ❑ 92 Michael Pittman 2.50 1.00
- ❑ 93 Brian Griese 3.00 1.25
- ❑ 94 Michael Clayton 5.00 2.00
- ❑ 95 Steve McNair 5.00 2.00
- ❑ 96 Drew Bennett 3.00 1.25
- ❑ 97 Chris Brown 3.00 1.25
- ❑ 98 Clinton Portis 5.00 2.00
- ❑ 99 Patrick Ramsey 3.00 1.25
- ❑ 100 Santana Moss 3.00 1.25
- ❑ 101 James Kilian RC 10.00 4.00
- ❑ 102 Marlin Jackson RC 10.00 4.00
- ❑ 103 Corey Webster RC 10.00 4.00
- ❑ 104 Ryan Claridge RC 8.00 3.00
- ❑ 105 David Pollack RC 10.00 4.00
- ❑ 106 Deandra Cobb RC 8.00 3.00
- ❑ 107 Anttaj Hawthorne RC 8.00 3.00
- ❑ 108 Erasmus James RC 10.00 4.00
- ❑ 109 Dan Cody RC 10.00 4.00
- ❑ 110 Jerome Mathis RC 10.00 4.00
- ❑ 111 Barrett Ruud RC 10.00 4.00
- ❑ 112 Kevin Burnett RC 10.00 4.00
- ❑ 113 Jason White RC 10.00 4.00
- ❑ 114 Chase Lyman RC 8.00 3.00
- ❑ 115 Cedric Houston RC 10.00 4.00
- ❑ 116 Roydell Williams RC 10.00 4.00
- ❑ 117 Fred Gibson RC 8.00 3.00
- ❑ 118 Dustin Colquitt RC 8.00 3.00
- ❑ 119 Rasheed Marshall RC 10.00 4.00
- ❑ 120 Walter Reyes RC 8.00 3.00
- ❑ 121 Craig Bragg RC 8.00 3.00
- ❑ 122 Marcus Maxwell RC 8.00 3.00
- ❑ 123 LeRon McCoy RC 8.00 3.00
- ❑ 124 Harry Williams RC 8.00 3.00
- ❑ 125 Larry Brackins RC 8.00 3.00
- ❑ 126 J.R. Russell RC 8.00 3.00
- ❑ 127 Manuel White RC 8.00 3.00
- ❑ 128 Brandon Jones RC 10.00 4.00
- ❑ 129 Eric King RC 8.00 3.00
- ❑ 130 Travis Johnson RC 8.00 3.00
- ❑ 131 Mike Patterson RC 10.00 4.00
- ❑ 132 Marcus Spears RC 10.00 4.00
- ❑ 133 Darryl Blackstock RC 8.00 3.00
- ❑ 134 Michael Boley RC 8.00 3.00
- ❑ 135 Leroy Hill RC 10.00 4.00
- ❑ 136 Channing Crowder RC 10.00 4.00
- ❑ 137 Odell Thurman RC 10.00 4.00
- ❑ 138 Lance Mitchell RC 8.00 3.00
- ❑ 139 Jerome Collins RC 8.00 3.00
- ❑ 140 Stanford Routt RC 8.00 3.00
- ❑ 141 Justin Miller RC 8.00 3.00
- ❑ 142 Bryant McFadden RC 10.00 4.00
- ❑ 143 Eric Green RC 5.00 2.00
- ❑ 144 Fabian Washington RC 10.00 4.00
- ❑ 145 Antonio Perkins RC 8.00 3.00
- ❑ 146 Shaun Cody RC 10.00 4.00
- ❑ 147 Jonathan Babineaux RC 8.00 3.00
- ❑ 148 Ronald Bartell RC 8.00 3.00
- ❑ 149 Luis Castillo RC 10.00 4.00
- ❑ 150 Chris Carr RC 10.00 4.00
- ❑ 151 Justin Tuck RC 10.00 4.00
- ❑ 152 Brodney Pool RC 10.00 4.00
- ❑ 153 Matt Roth RC 10.00 4.00
- ❑ 154 DeMarcus Ware RC 15.00 6.00
- ❑ 155 Josh Bullocks RC 10.00 4.00
- ❑ 156 Vincent Fuller RC 8.00 3.00
- ❑ 157 Donte Nicholson RC 10.00 4.00
- ❑ 158 Rashied Davis RC 10.00 4.00
- ❑ 159 Nick Collins RC 10.00 4.00
- ❑ 160 Mike Nugent RC 10.00 4.00
- ❑ 161 Tyson Thompson RC 15.00 6.00
- ❑ 162 Darrent Williams RC 10.00 4.00
- ❑ 163 Kelvin Hayden RC 8.00 3.00
- ❑ 164 Oshiomogho Atogwe RC 8.00 3.00
- ❑ 165 Ryan Fitzpatrick RC 15.00 6.00
- ❑ 166 Stanley Wilson RC 8.00 3.00
- ❑ 167 Vonta Leach RC 10.00 4.00
- ❑ 168 Ellis Hobbs RC 10.00 4.00
- ❑ 169 Scott Starks RC 8.00 3.00
- ❑ 170 Lionel Gates RC 8.00 3.00
- ❑ 171 Alvin Pearman RC 10.00 4.00
- ❑ 172 Damien Nash RC 8.00 3.00
- ❑ 173 Noah Herron RC 10.00 4.00
- ❑ 174 Domonique Foxworth RC 10.00 4.00
- ❑ 175 Derrick Johnson CB RC 10.00 4.00
- ❑ 176 Lofa Tatupu RC 20.00 7.50
- ❑ 177 Daven Holly RC 10.00 4.00
- ❑ 178 Dante Ridgeway RC 8.00 3.00
- ❑ 179 Airese Currie RC 10.00 4.00
- ❑ 180 Adam Bergen RC 10.00 4.00
- ❑ 181 Kirk Morrison RC 10.00 4.00
- ❑ 182 Alfred Fincher RC 8.00 3.00
- ❑ 183 Jordan Beck RC 8.00 3.00
- ❑ 184 Sean Considine RC 10.00 4.00
- ❑ 185 Tab Perry RC 10.00 4.00
- ❑ 186 Travis Daniels RC 8.00 3.00
- ❑ 187 Paris Warren RC 8.00 3.00
- ❑ 188 Marviel Underwood RC 8.00 3.00
- ❑ 189 Jerome Carter RC 8.00 3.00
- ❑ 190 Kerry Rhodes RC 10.00 4.00
- ❑ 191 James Sanders RC 10.00 4.00
- ❑ 192 Stephen Spach RC 8.00 3.00
- ❑ 193 Bo Scaife RC 8.00 3.00
- ❑ 194 Andre Frazier RC 15.00 6.00
- ❑ 195 Alex Barron RC 5.00 2.00
- ❑ 196 Jammal Brown RC 10.00 4.00
- ❑ 197 Nehemiah Broughton RC 8.00 3.00
- ❑ 198 Elton Brown RC 5.00 2.00
- ❑ 199 David Baas RC 8.00 3.00
- ❑ 200 Joel Dreessen RC 8.00 3.00
- ❑ 201 Maurice Clarett AU/120 20.00 7.50
- ❑ 202 Craphonso Thorpe AU RC 15.00 6.00
- ❑ 203 Adam Jones AU RC 20.00 7.50
- ❑ 204 Mark Bradley AU RC 25.00 10.00
- ❑ 205 Vincent Jackson AU RC 25.00 10.00
- ❑ 206 Antrel Rolle AU RC 20.00 7.50
- ❑ 207 Heath Miller AU RC 80.00 40.00
- ❑ 208 Anthony Davis AU RC 15.00 6.00
- ❑ 209 Terrence Murphy AU RC 20.00 7.50
- ❑ 210 Chris Henry AU RC 25.00 12.50
- ❑ 211 Roscoe Parrish AU RC 20.00 7.50
- ❑ 212 Stefan LeFors AU RC 20.00 7.50
- ❑ 213 Derek Anderson AU RC 20.00 7.50
- ❑ 214 Darren Sproles AU RC 20.00 7.50
- ❑ 215 Adrian McPherson AU RC 20.00 7.50
- ❑ 216 Frank Gore AU RC 40.00 15.00
- ❑ 217 Marion Barber AU RC 40.00 15.00
- ❑ 218 Ryan Moats AU RC 25.00 12.50
- ❑ 219 Carlos Rogers AU RC 25.00 10.00
- ❑ 220 Vernand Morency AU RC 15.00 6.00
- ❑ 221 J.J. Arrington AU RC 25.00 10.00
- ❑ 222 Courtney Roby AU RC 20.00 7.50
- ❑ 223 Dan Orlovsky AU RC 25.00 10.00
- ❑ 224 Kyle Orton AU RC 40.00 15.00
- ❑ 225 David Greene AU RC 20.00 7.50
- ❑ 226 Roddy White AU/150 RC 30.00 12.50
- ❑ 227 Matt Jones AU/99 RC 80.00 40.00
- ❑ 228 Reggie Brown AU/150 RC 40.00 20.00
- ❑ 229 Mark Clayton AU/150 RC 40.00 20.00
- ❑ 230 Eric Shelton AU/150 RC 20.00 7.50
- ❑ 231 Ciatrick Fason AU/150 RC 20.00 7.50
- ❑ 232 Jason Campbell AU/150 RC 80.00 40.00
- ❑ 233 Charlie Frye AU/150 RC 80.00 40.00
- ❑ 234 Andrew Walter AU/150 RC 30.0015.00
- ❑ 235 Troy Williamson AU/120 RC 50.0025.00
- ❑ 236 Braylon Edwards AU/99 RC 120.00 60.00
- ❑ 237 Mike Williams AU/99 80.00 30.00
- ❑ 238 Cedric Benson AU/99 RC 120.00 70.00
- ❑ 239 Carnell Williams AU/99 RC 250.00 150.00
- ❑ 240 Ronnie Brown AU/99 RC 150.0075.00
- ❑ 241 Alex Smith QB AU/99 RC 175.0090.00
- ❑ 242 Aaron Rodgers AU/99 RC 175.00 100.00
- ❑ 243 Matt Cassel AU RC 40.00 15.00
- ❑ 244 Brandon Jacobs AU RC 25.00 10.00
- ❑ 245 Alex Smith TE AU RC 20.00 7.50
- ❑ 246 Derrick Johnson AU RC 40.00 15.00
- ❑ 247 Chad Owens AU RC 30.00 15.00
- ❑ 248 Thomas Davis AU RC 20.00 7.50
- ❑ 249 Shawne Merriman AU RC 50.00 25.00
- ❑ 250 Gino Guidugli RC 5.00 2.00
- ❑ 251 Timmy Chang RC 8.00 3.00
- ❑ 252 Todd Mortensen RC 8.00 3.00
- ❑ 253 Bryan Randall RC 8.00 3.00
- ❑ 254 Brock Berlin RC 8.00 3.00
- ❑ 255 T.A. McLendon RC 5.00 2.00
- ❑ 256 Kay-Jay Harris RC 8.00 3.00
- ❑ 257 Bobby Purify RC 8.00 3.00
- ❑ 258 Steve Savoy RC 5.00 2.00
- ❑ 259 Keron Henry RC 5.00 2.00
- ❑ 260 Josh Davis RC 8.00 3.00
- ❑ 261 Chauncey Stovall RC 5.00 2.00
- ❑ 262 Efrem Hill RC 8.00 3.00
- ❑ 263 Sione Pouha RC 10.00 4.00
- ❑ 264 Jesse Lumsden RC 5.00 2.00
- ❑ 265 Vincent Burns RC 8.00 3.00
- ❑ 266 Brady Poppinga RC 10.00 4.00
- ❑ 267 Boomer Grigsby RC 15.00 6.00
- ❑ 268 Robert McCune RC 8.00 3.00
- ❑ 269 Fred Amey RC 8.00 3.00
- ❑ 270 T.J. Duckett 3.00 1.25
- ❑ 271 Jamal Lewis 5.00 2.00
- ❑ 272 Rod Gardner 3.00 1.25
- ❑ 273 Thomas Jones 3.00 1.25
- ❑ 274 Jason Witten 3.00 1.25
- ❑ 275 Roy Williams S 3.00 1.25
- ❑ 276 Mike Anderson 3.00 1.25
- ❑ 277 Joey Harrington 5.00 2.00
- ❑ 278 Charles Rogers 3.00 1.25
- ❑ 279 Donald Driver 3.00 1.25
- ❑ 280 Jabar Gaffney 2.50 1.00
- ❑ 281 Reggie Williams 3.00 1.25
- ❑ 282 Tony Gonzalez 3.00 1.25
- ❑ 283 Ricky Williams 3.00 1.25
- ❑ 284 Mewelde Moore 2.50 1.00
- ❑ 285 Plaxico Burress 3.00 1.25
- ❑ 286 Jerry Porter 3.00 1.25
- ❑ 287 Brandon Lloyd 2.50 1.00
- ❑ 288 Isaac Bruce 3.00 1.25
- ❑ 289 LaVar Arrington 5.00 2.00

1991 Ultra

- ❑ COMPLETE SET (300) 20.00 7.50
- ❑ 1 Don Beebe .05 .01
- ❑ 2 Shane Conlan .05 .01
- ❑ 3 Pete Metzelaars .05 .01
- ❑ 4 Jamie Mueller .05 .01
- ❑ 5 Scott Norwood .05 .01
- ❑ 6 Andre Reed .10 .02
- ❑ 7 Leon Seals .05 .01
- ❑ 8 Bruce Smith .25 .08
- ❑ 9 Leonard Smith .05 .01
- ❑ 10 Thurman Thomas .25 .08
- ❑ 11 Lewis Billups .05 .01
- ❑ 12 Jim Breech .05 .01
- ❑ 13 James Brooks .10 .02
- ❑ 14 Eddie Brown .05 .01
- ❑ 15 Boomer Esiason .10 .02
- ❑ 16 David Fulcher .05 .01
- ❑ 17 Rodney Holman .05 .01
- ❑ 18 Bruce Kozerski .05 .01
- ❑ 19 Tim Krumrie .05 .01
- ❑ 20 Tim McGee .05 .01
- ❑ 21 Anthony Munoz .10 .02
- ❑ 22 Leon White .05 .01
- ❑ 23 Ickey Woods .05 .01
- ❑ 24 Carl Zander .05 .01
- ❑ 25 Brian Brennan .05 .01
- ❑ 26 Thane Gash .05 .01
- ❑ 27 Leroy Hoard .10 .02
- ❑ 28 Mike Johnson .05 .01
- ❑ 29 Reggie Langhorne .05 .01
- ❑ 30 Kevin Mack .05 .01
- ❑ 31 Clay Matthews .10 .02
- ❑ 32 Eric Metcalf .10 .02
- ❑ 33 Steve Atwater .05 .01
- ❑ 34 Melvin Bratton .05 .01
- ❑ 35 John Elway 1.25 .50
- ❑ 36 Bobby Humphrey .05 .01
- ❑ 37 Mark Jackson .05 .01
- ❑ 38 Vance Johnson .05 .01
- ❑ 39 Ricky Nattiel .05 .01
- ❑ 40 Steve Sewell .05 .01

❑ 41 Dennis Smith .05 .01
❑ 42 David Treadwell .05 .01
❑ 43 Michael Young .05 .01
❑ 44 Ray Childress .05 .01
❑ 45 Cris Dishman RC .05 .01
❑ 46 William Fuller .10 .02
❑ 47 Ernest Givins .10 .02
❑ 48 John Grimsley UER .05 .01
❑ 49 Drew Hill .05 .01
❑ 50 Haywood Jeffires .10 .02
❑ 51 Sean Jones .10 .02
❑ 52 Johnny Meads .05 .01
❑ 53 Warren Moon .25 .08
❑ 54 Al Smith .05 .01
❑ 55 Lorenzo White .05 .01
❑ 56 Albert Bentley .05 .01
❑ 57 Duane Bickett .05 .01
❑ 58 Bill Brooks .05 .01
❑ 59 Jeff George .25 .08
❑ 60 Mike Prior .05 .01
❑ 61 Rohn Stark .05 .01
❑ 62 Jack Trudeau .05 .01
❑ 63 Clarence Verdin .05 .01
❑ 64 Steve DeBerg .05 .01
❑ 65 Emile Harry .05 .01
❑ 66 Albert Lewis .05 .01
❑ 67 Nick Lowery UER .05 .01
❑ 68 Todd McNair .05 .01
❑ 69 Christian Okoye .05 .01
❑ 70 Stephone Paige .05 .01
❑ 71 Kevin Porter UER .05 .01
❑ 72 Derrick Thomas .25 .08
❑ 73 Robb Thomas .05 .01
❑ 74 Barry Word .05 .01
❑ 75 Marcus Allen .25 .08
❑ 76 Eddie Anderson .05 .01
❑ 77 Tim Brown .25 .08
❑ 78 Mervyn Fernandez .05 .01
❑ 79 Willie Gault .10 .02
❑ 80 Ethan Horton .05 .01
❑ 81 Howie Long .25 .08
❑ 82 Vance Mueller .05 .01
❑ 83 Jay Schroeder .05 .01
❑ 84 Steve Smith .05 .01
❑ 85 Greg Townsend .05 .01
❑ 86 Mark Clayton .10 .02
❑ 87 Jim C. Jensen .05 .01
❑ 88 Dan Marino 1.25 .50
❑ 89 Tim McKyer UER .05 .01
❑ 90 John Offerdahl .05 .01
❑ 91 Louis Oliver .05 .01
❑ 92 Reggie Roby .05 .01
❑ 93 Sammie Smith .05 .01
❑ 94 Hart Lee Dykes .05 .01
❑ 95 Irving Fryar .10 .02
❑ 96 Tommy Hodson .05 .01
❑ 97 Maurice Hurst .05 .01
❑ 98 John Stephens .05 .01
❑ 99 Andre Tippett .05 .01
❑ 100 Mark Boyer .05 .01
❑ 101 Kyle Clifton .05 .01
❑ 102 James Hasty .05 .01
❑ 103 Erik McMillan .05 .01
❑ 104 Rob Moore .25 .08
❑ 105 Joe Mott .05 .01
❑ 106 Ken O'Brien .05 .01
❑ 107 Ron Stallworth UER .05 .01
❑ 108 Al Toon .10 .02
❑ 109 Gary Anderson K .05 .01
❑ 110 Bubby Brister .05 .01
❑ 111 Thomas Everett .05 .01
❑ 112 Merril Hoge .05 .01
❑ 113 Louis Lipps .05 .01
❑ 114 Greg Lloyd .25 .08
❑ 115 Hardy Nickerson .10 .02
❑ 116 Dwight Stone .05 .01
❑ 117 Rod Woodson .25 .08
❑ 118 Tim Worley .05 .01
❑ 119 Rod Bernstine .05 .01
❑ 120 Marion Butts .10 .02
❑ 121 Gill Byrd .05 .01
❑ 122 Arthur Cox .05 .01
❑ 123 Burt Grossman .05 .01
❑ 124 Ronnie Harmon .05 .01
❑ 125 Anthony Miller .10 .02
❑ 126 Leslie O'Neal .10 .02
❑ 127 Gary Plummer .05 .01
❑ 128 Sam Seale .05 .01
❑ 129 Junior Seau .25 .08
❑ 130 Broderick Thompson .05 .01
❑ 131 Billy Joe Tolliver .05 .01
❑ 132 Brian Blades .10 .02
❑ 133 Jeff Bryant .05 .01
❑ 134 Derrick Fenner .05 .01
❑ 135 Jacob Green .05 .01
❑ 136 Andy Heck .05 .01
❑ 137 Patrick Hunter RC UER .05 .01
❑ 138 Norm Johnson .05 .01
❑ 139 Tommy Kane .05 .01
❑ 140 Dave Krieg .10 .02
❑ 141 John L. Williams .05 .01
❑ 142 Terry Wooden .05 .01
❑ 143 Steve Broussard .05 .01
❑ 144 Keith Jones .05 .01
❑ 145 Brian Jordan .10 .02
❑ 146 Chris Miller .10 .02
❑ 147 John Rade .05 .01
❑ 148 Andre Rison .10 .02
❑ 149 Mike Rozier .05 .01
❑ 150 Deion Sanders .40 .15
❑ 151 Neal Anderson .10 .02
❑ 152 Trace Armstrong .05 .01
❑ 153 Kevin Butler .05 .01
❑ 154 Mark Carrier DB .10 .02
❑ 155 Richard Dent .10 .02
❑ 156 Dennis Gentry .05 .01
❑ 157 Jim Harbaugh .25 .08
❑ 158 Brad Muster .05 .01
❑ 159 William Perry .10 .02
❑ 160 Mike Singletary .10 .02
❑ 161 Lemuel Stinson .05 .01
❑ 162 Troy Aikman .75 .30
❑ 163 Michael Irvin .25 .08
❑ 164 Mike Saxon .05 .01
❑ 165 Emmitt Smith 2.50 1.00
❑ 166 Jerry Ball .05 .01
❑ 167 Michael Cofer .05 .01
❑ 168 Rodney Peete .10 .02
❑ 169 Barry Sanders 1.25 .50
❑ 170 Robert Brown .05 .01
❑ 171 Anthony Dilweg .05 .01
❑ 172 Tim Harris .05 .01
❑ 173 Johnny Holland .05 .01
❑ 174 Perry Kemp .05 .01
❑ 175 Don Majkowski .05 .01
❑ 176 Brian Noble .05 .01
❑ 177 Jeff Query .05 .01
❑ 178 Sterling Sharpe .25 .08
❑ 179 Charles Wilson .05 .01
❑ 180 Keith Woodside .05 .01
❑ 181 Flipper Anderson UER .05 .01
❑ 182 Bern Brostek .05 .01
❑ 183 Pat Carter RC .05 .01
❑ 184 Aaron Cox .05 .01
❑ 185 Henry Ellard .10 .02
❑ 186 Jim Everett .10 .02
❑ 187 Cleveland Gary .05 .01
❑ 188 Jerry Gray .05 .01
❑ 189 Kevin Greene .10 .02
❑ 190 Mike Wilcher .05 .01
❑ 191 Alfred Anderson .05 .01
❑ 192 Joey Browner .05 .01
❑ 193 Anthony Carter .10 .02
❑ 194 Chris Doleman .05 .01
❑ 195 Rick Fenney .05 .01
❑ 196 Darrell Fullington .05 .01
❑ 197 Rich Gannon .25 .08
❑ 198 Hassan Jones .05 .01
❑ 199 Steve Jordan .05 .01
❑ 200 Mike Merriweather .05 .01
❑ 201 Al Noga .05 .01
❑ 202 Herschel Walker .10 .02
❑ 203 Wade Wilson .10 .02
❑ 204 Morten Andersen .05 .01
❑ 205 Gene Atkins .05 .01
❑ 206 Toi Cook RC .05 .01
❑ 207 Craig Heyward .10 .02
❑ 208 Dalton Hilliard .05 .01
❑ 209 Vaughan Johnson .05 .01
❑ 210 Eric Martin .05 .01
❑ 211 Brett Perriman .25 .08
❑ 212 Pat Swilling .10 .02
❑ 213 Steve Walsh .05 .01
❑ 214 Ottis Anderson .10 .02
❑ 215 Carl Banks .05 .01
❑ 216 Maurice Carthon .05 .01
❑ 217 Mark Collins .05 .01
❑ 218 Rodney Hampton .25 .08
❑ 219 Erik Howard .05 .01
❑ 220 Mark Ingram .10 .02
❑ 221 Pepper Johnson .05 .01
❑ 222 Dave Meggett .10 .02
❑ 223 Phil Simms .10 .02
❑ 224 Lawrence Taylor .25 .08
❑ 225 Lewis Tillman .05 .01
❑ 226 Everson Walls .05 .01
❑ 227 Fred Barnett .25 .08
❑ 228 Jerome Brown .05 .01
❑ 229 Keith Byars .05 .01
❑ 230 Randall Cunningham .25 .08
❑ 231 Byron Evans .05 .01
❑ 232 Wes Hopkins .05 .01
❑ 233 Keith Jackson .10 .02
❑ 234 Heath Sherman .05 .01
❑ 235 Anthony Toney .05 .01
❑ 236 Reggie White .25 .08
❑ 237 Rich Camarillo .05 .01
❑ 238 Ken Harvey .10 .02
❑ 239 Eric Hill .05 .01
❑ 240 Johnny Johnson .05 .01
❑ 241 Ernie Jones .05 .01
❑ 242 Tim McDonald .05 .01
❑ 243 Timm Rosenbach .05 .01
❑ 244 Jay Taylor .05 .01
❑ 245 Dexter Carter .05 .01
❑ 246 Mike Cofer .05 .01
❑ 247 Kevin Fagan .05 .01
❑ 248 Don Griffin .05 .01
❑ 249 Charles Haley .10 .02
❑ 250 Brent Jones .25 .08
❑ 251 Joe Montana UER 1.25 .50
❑ 252 Darryl Pollard .05 .01
❑ 253 Tom Rathman .05 .01
❑ 254 Jerry Rice .75 .30
❑ 255 John Taylor .10 .02
❑ 256 Steve Young .75 .30
❑ 257 Gary Anderson RB .05 .01
❑ 258 Mark Carrier WR .25 .08
❑ 259 Chris Chandler .25 .08
❑ 260 Reggie Cobb .05 .01
❑ 261 Reuben Davis .05 .01
❑ 262 Willie Drewrey .05 .01
❑ 263 Ron Hall .05 .01
❑ 264 Eugene Marve .05 .01
❑ 265 Winston Moss UER .05 .01
❑ 266 Vinny Testaverde .10 .02
❑ 267 Broderick Thomas .05 .01
❑ 268 Jeff Bostic .05 .01
❑ 269 Earnest Byner .05 .01
❑ 270 Gary Clark .25 .08
❑ 271 Darrell Green .05 .01
❑ 272 Jim Lachey .05 .01
❑ 273 Wilber Marshall .05 .01
❑ 274 Art Monk .10 .02
❑ 275 Gerald Riggs .05 .01
❑ 276 Mark Rypien .10 .02
❑ 277 Ricky Sanders .05 .01
❑ 278 Alvin Walton .05 .01
❑ 279 Nick Bell RC .05 .01
❑ 280 Eric Bieniemy RC .05 .01
❑ 281 Jarrod Bunch RC .05 .01
❑ 282 Mike Croel RC .05 .01
❑ 283 Brett Favre RC 10.00 5.00
❑ 284 Moe Gardner RC .05 .01
❑ 285 Pat Harlow RC .05 .01
❑ 286 Randal Hill RC .10 .02
❑ 287 Todd Marinovich RC .05 .01
❑ 288 Russell Maryland RC .25 .08
❑ 289 Dan McGwire RC .05 .01
❑ 290 Ernie Mills RC UER .10 .02
❑ 291 Herman Moore RC .25 .08
❑ 292 Godfrey Myles RC .05 .01
❑ 293 Browning Nagle RC .05 .01
❑ 294 Mike Pritchard RC .25 .08
❑ 295 Esera Tuaolo RC .05 .01
❑ 296 Mark Vander Poel RC .05 .01
❑ 297 Ricky Watters RC 1.50 .60
❑ 298 Chris Zorich RC .25 .08
❑ 299 Checklist Card .10 .02
❑ 300 Checklist Card .10 .02

1991 Ultra Update

❑ COMP.FACT.SET (100) 25.00 10.00
❑ U1 Brett Favre 20.00 7.50
❑ U2 Moe Gardner .10 .02
❑ U3 Tim McKyer .10 .02
❑ U4 Bruce Pickens RC .10 .02
❑ U5 Mike Pritchard .40 .15
❑ U6 Cornelius Bennett .20 .07
❑ U7 Phil Hansen RC .10 .02
❑ U8 Henry Jones RC .20 .07
❑ U9 Mark Kelso .10 .02
❑ U10 James Lofton .20 .07
❑ U11 Anthony Morgan RC .10 .02
❑ U12 Stan Thomas .10 .02
❑ U13 Chris Zorich .20 .07
❑ U14 Reggie Rembert .10 .02
❑ U15 Alfred Williams RC .10 .02
❑ U16 Michael Jackson RC WR .40 .15
❑ U17 Ed King RC .10 .02
❑ U18 Joe Morris .10 .02
❑ U19 Vince Newsome .10 .02
❑ U20 Tony Casillas .10 .02
❑ U21 Russell Maryland .40 .15
❑ U22 Jay Novacek .40 .15
❑ U23 Mike Croel .10 .02
❑ U24 Gaston Green .10 .02
❑ U25 Kenny Walker RC .10 .02
❑ U26 Melvin Jenkins RC .10 .02
❑ U27 Herman Moore .40 .15
❑ U28 Kelvin Pritchett RC .20 .07
❑ U29 Chris Spielman .20 .07
❑ U30 Vinnie Clark RC .10 .02
❑ U31 Allen Rice .10 .02
❑ U32 Vai Sikahema .10 .02
❑ U33 Esera Tuaolo .10 .02
❑ U34 Mike Dumas RC .10 .02
❑ U35 John Flannery RC .10 .02
❑ U36 Allen Pinkett .10 .02
❑ U37 Tim Barnett RC .10 .02
❑ U38 Dan Saleaumua .10 .02
❑ U39 Harvey Williams RC .40 .15
❑ U40 Nick Bell .10 .02
❑ U41 Roger Craig .20 .07
❑ U42 Ronnie Lott .20 .07
❑ U43 Todd Marinovich .10 .02
❑ U44 Robert Delpino .10 .02
❑ U45 Todd Lyght RC .10 .02
❑ U46 Robert Young RC .20 .07
❑ U47 Aaron Craver RC .10 .02
❑ U48 Mark Higgs RC .10 .02
❑ U49 Vestee Jackson .10 .02
❑ U50 Carl Lee .10 .02
❑ U51 Felix Wright .10 .02
❑ U52 Darrell Fullington .10 .02
❑ U53 Pat Harlow .10 .02
❑ U54 Eugene Lockhart .10 .02
❑ U55 Hugh Millen RC .10 .02
❑ U56 Leonard Russell RC .40 .15
❑ U57 Jon Vaughn RC .10 .02
❑ U58 Quinn Early .20 .07
❑ U59 Bobby Hebert .10 .02
❑ U60 Rickey Jackson .10 .02
❑ U61 Sam Mills .20 .07
❑ U62 Jarrod Bunch .10 .02
❑ U63 John Elliott .10 .02
❑ U64 Jeff Hostetler .20 .07
❑ U65 Ed McCaffrey RC 6.00 2.50
❑ U66 Kanavis McGhee RC .10 .02
❑ U67 Mo Lewis RC .20 .07
❑ U68 Browning Nagle .10 .02
❑ U69 Blair Thomas .10 .02
❑ U70 Antone Davis RC .10 .02
❑ U71 Brad Goebel RC .10 .02
❑ U72 Jim McMahon .20 .07
❑ U73 Clyde Simmons .10 .02
❑ U74 Randal Hill UER U71 .20 .07
❑ U75 Eric Swann RC .40 .15
❑ U76 Tom Tupa .10 .02
❑ U77 Jeff Graham RC WR .40 .15
❑ U78 Eric Green .10 .02
❑ U79 Neil O'Donnell RC .40 .15
❑ U80 Huey Richardson RC .10 .02
❑ U81 Eric Bieniemy .10 .02
❑ U82 John Friesz .40 .15
❑ U83 Eric Moten RC .10 .02
❑ U84 Stanley Richard RC .10 .02
❑ U85 Todd Bowles .10 .02
❑ U86 Merton Hanks RC .40 .15
❑ U87 Tim Harris .10 .02
❑ U88 Pierce Holt .10 .02
❑ U89 Ted Washington RC .10 .02
❑ U90 John Kasay RC .20 .07
❑ U91 Dan McGwire .10 .02
❑ U92 Lawrence Dawsey RC .20 .07
❑ U93 Charles McRae RC .10 .02
❑ U94 Jesse Solomon .10 .02
❑ U95 Robert Wilson RC .10 .02
❑ U96 Ricky Ervins RC .20 .07
❑ U97 Charles Mann .10 .02
❑ U98 Bobby Wilson RC .10 .02
❑ U99 Jerry Rice PV 1.50 .60
❑ U100 Nick Bell/J.McMahon CL .10 .02

1992 Ultra

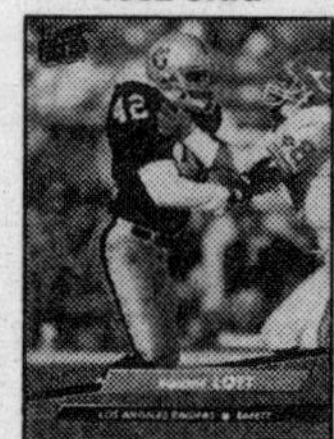

❑ COMPLETE SET (450) 15.00 6.00
❑ 1 Steve Broussard .10 .02
❑ 2 Rick Bryan .10 .02
❑ 3 Scott Case .10 .02
❑ 4 Darion Conner .10 .02
❑ 5 Bill Fralic .10 .02
❑ 6 Moe Gardner .10 .02
❑ 7 Tim Green .10 .02
❑ 8 Michael Haynes .20 .07
❑ 9 Chris Hinton .10 .02
❑ 10 Mike Kenn .10 .02
❑ 11 Tim McKyer .10 .02
❑ 12 Chris Miller .20 .07
❑ 13 Erric Pegram .20 .07
❑ 14 Mike Pritchard .20 .07
❑ 15 Andre Rison .20 .07
❑ 16 Jessie Tuggle .10 .02
❑ 17 Carlton Bailey RC .10 .02
❑ 18 Howard Ballard .10 .02
❑ 19 Cornelius Bennett .20 .07
❑ 20 Shane Conlan .10 .02
❑ 21 Kenneth Davis .10 .02
❑ 22 Kent Hull .10 .02
❑ 23 Mark Kelso .10 .02
❑ 24 James Lofton .20 .07
❑ 25 Keith McKeller .10 .02
❑ 26 Nate Odomes .10 .02
❑ 27 Jim Ritcher .10 .02
❑ 28 Leon Seals .10 .02
❑ 29 Darryl Talley .10 .02
❑ 30 Steve Tasker .20 .07
❑ 31 Thurman Thomas .40 .15
❑ 32 Will Wolford .10 .02
❑ 33 Jeff Wright .10 .02
❑ 34 Neal Anderson .10 .02
❑ 35 Trace Armstrong .10 .02
❑ 36 Mark Carrier DB .10 .02
❑ 37 Wendell Davis .10 .02
❑ 38 Richard Dent .20 .07
❑ 39 Shaun Gayle .10 .02
❑ 40 Jim Harbaugh .40 .15
❑ 41 Jay Hilgenberg .10 .02
❑ 42 Darren Lewis .10 .02
❑ 43 Steve McMichael .20 .07
❑ 44 Anthony Morgan .10 .02
❑ 45 Brad Muster .10 .02
❑ 46 William Perry .20 .07
❑ 47 John Roper .10 .02
❑ 48 Lemuel Stinson .10 .02
❑ 49 Tom Waddle .10 .02
❑ 50 Donnell Woolford .10 .02
❑ 51 Leo Barker RC .10 .02
❑ 52 Eddie Brown .10 .02
❑ 53 James Francis .10 .02
❑ 54 David Fulcher UER .10 .02
❑ 55 David Grant .10 .02
❑ 56 Harold Green .10 .02
❑ 57 Rodney Holman .10 .02
❑ 58 Lee Johnson .10 .02
❑ 59 Tim Krumrie .10 .02
❑ 60 Tim McGee .10 .02
❑ 61 Alonzo Mitz RC .10 .02
❑ 62 Anthony Munoz .20 .07
❑ 63 Alfred Williams .10 .02
❑ 64 Stephen Braggs .10 .02
❑ 65 Richard Brown RC .10 .02
❑ 66 Randy Hilliard RC .10 .02
❑ 67 Leroy Hoard .20 .07
❑ 68 Michael Jackson .20 .07
❑ 69 Mike Johnson .10 .02
❑ 70 James Jones DT .10 .02
❑ 71 Tony Jones T .10 .02
❑ 72 Ed King .10 .02
❑ 73 Kevin Mack .10 .02
❑ 74 Clay Matthews .20 .07
❑ 75 Eric Metcalf .20 .07
❑ 76 Vince Newsome .10 .02
❑ 77 Steve Beuerlein .20 .07
❑ 78 Larry Brown DB .10 .02
❑ 79 Tony Casillas .10 .02
❑ 80 Alvin Harper .20 .07
❑ 81 Issiac Holt .10 .02
❑ 82 Ray Horton .10 .02
❑ 83 Michael Irvin .40 .15
❑ 84 Daryl Johnston .40 .15
❑ 85 Kelvin Martin .10 .02
❑ 86 Ken Norton .20 .07
❑ 87 Jay Novacek .20 .07
❑ 88 Emmitt Smith 3.00 1.50
❑ 89 Vinson Smith RC .10 .02
❑ 90 Mark Stepnoski .20 .07
❑ 91 Tony Tolbert .10 .02
❑ 92 Alexander Wright .10 .02
❑ 93 Steve Atwater .10 .02
❑ 94 Tyrone Braxton .10 .02
❑ 95 Michael Brooks .10 .02
❑ 96 Mike Croel .10 .02
❑ 97 John Elway 2.50 1.00
❑ 98 Simon Fletcher .10 .02
❑ 99 Gaston Green .10 .02
❑ 100 Mark Jackson .10 .02
❑ 101 Keith Kartz .10 .02
❑ 102 Greg Kragen .10 .02
❑ 103 Greg Lewis .10 .02
❑ 104 Karl Mecklenburg .10 .02
❑ 105 Derek Russell .10 .02
❑ 106 Steve Sewell .10 .02
❑ 107 Dennis Smith .10 .02
❑ 108 David Treadwell .10 .02
❑ 109 Kenny Walker .10 .02
❑ 110 Michael Young .10 .02
❑ 111 Jerry Ball .10 .02
❑ 112 Bennie Blades .10 .02
❑ 113 Lomas Brown .10 .02
❑ 114 Scott Conover RC .10 .02
❑ 115 Ray Crockett .10 .02
❑ 116 Mel Gray .20 .07
❑ 117 Willie Green .10 .02
❑ 118 Erik Kramer .20 .07
❑ 119 Dan Owens .10 .02
❑ 120 Rodney Peete .20 .07

❑ 121 Brett Perriman .40 .15
❑ 122 Barry Sanders 2.50 1.00
❑ 123 Chris Spielman .20 .07
❑ 124 Marc Spindler .10 .02
❑ 125 William White .10 .02
❑ 126 Tony Bennett .10 .02
❑ 127 Matt Brock .10 .02
❑ 128 LeRoy Butler .10 .02
❑ 129 Chuck Cecil .10 .02
❑ 130 Johnny Holland .10 .02
❑ 131 Perry Kemp .10 .02
❑ 132 Don Majkowski .10 .02
❑ 133 Tony Mandarich .10 .02
❑ 134 Brian Noble .10 .02
❑ 135 Bryce Paup .40 .15
❑ 136 Sterling Sharpe .40 .15
❑ 137 Darrell Thompson .10 .02
❑ 138 Mike Tomczak .10 .02
❑ 139 Vince Workman .10 .02
❑ 140 Ray Childress .10 .02
❑ 141 Cris Dishman .10 .02
❑ 142 Curtis Duncan .10 .02
❑ 143 William Fuller .10 .02
❑ 144 Ernest Givins .20 .07
❑ 145 Haywood Jeffires .20 .07
❑ 146 Sean Jones .10 .02
❑ 147 Lamar Lathon .10 .02
❑ 148 Bruce Matthews .10 .02
❑ 149 Bubba McDowell .10 .02
❑ 150 Johnny Meads .10 .02
❑ 151 Warren Moon .40 .15
❑ 152 Mike Munchak .20 .07
❑ 153 Bo Orlando RC .10 .02
❑ 154 Al Smith .10 .02
❑ 155 Doug Smith .10 .02
❑ 156 Lorenzo White .10 .02
❑ 157 Chip Banks .10 .02
❑ 158 Duane Bickett .10 .02
❑ 159 Bill Brooks .10 .02
❑ 160 Eugene Daniel .10 .02
❑ 161 Jon Hand .10 .02
❑ 162 Jeff Herrod .10 .02
❑ 163 Jessie Hester .10 .02
❑ 164 Scott Radecic .10 .02
❑ 165 Rohn Stark .10 .02
❑ 166 Clarence Verdin .10 .02
❑ 167 John Alt .10 .02
❑ 168 Tim Barnett .10 .02
❑ 169 Tim Grunhard .10 .02
❑ 170 Dino Hackett .10 .02
❑ 171 Jonathan Hayes .10 .02
❑ 172 Bill Maas .10 .02
❑ 173 Chris Martin .10 .02
❑ 174 Christian Okoye .10 .02
❑ 175 Stephone Paige .10 .02
❑ 176 Jayice Pearson RC .10 .02
❑ 177 Kevin Porter .10 .02
❑ 178 Kevin Ross .10 .02
❑ 179 Dan Saleaumua .10 .02
❑ 180 Tracy Simien RC .10 .02
❑ 181 Neil Smith .40 .15
❑ 182 Derrick Thomas .40 .15
❑ 183 Robb Thomas .10 .02
❑ 184 Barry Word .10 .02
❑ 185 Marcus Allen .40 .15
❑ 186 Eddie Anderson .10 .02
❑ 187 Nick Bell .10 .02
❑ 188 Tim Brown .40 .15
❑ 189 Mervyn Fernandez .10 .02
❑ 190 Willie Gault .20 .07
❑ 191 Jeff Gossett .10 .02
❑ 192 Ethan Horton .10 .02
❑ 193 Jeff Jaeger .10 .02
❑ 194 Howie Long .40 .15
❑ 195 Ronnie Lott .20 .07
❑ 196 Todd Marinovich .10 .02
❑ 197 Don Mosebar .10 .02
❑ 198 Jay Schroeder .10 .02
❑ 199 Anthony Smith .10 .02
❑ 200 Greg Townsend .10 .02
❑ 201 Lionel Washington .10 .02
❑ 202 Steve Wisniewski .10 .02
❑ 203 Flipper Anderson .10 .02
❑ 204 Robert Delpino .10 .02
❑ 205 Henry Ellard .20 .07
❑ 206 Jim Everett .20 .07
❑ 207 Kevin Greene .20 .07
❑ 208 Darryl Henley .10 .02
❑ 209 Damone Johnson .10 .02
❑ 210 Larry Kelm .10 .02
❑ 211 Todd Lyght .10 .02
❑ 212 Jackie Slater .10 .02
❑ 213 Michael Stewart .10 .02
❑ 214 Pat Terrell .10 .02
❑ 215 Robert Young .10 .02
❑ 216 Mark Clayton .20 .07
❑ 217 Bryan Cox .20 .07
❑ 218 Jeff Cross .10 .02
❑ 219 Mark Duper .10 .02
❑ 220 Harry Galbreath .10 .02
❑ 221 David Griggs .10 .02
❑ 222 Mark Higgs .10 .02
❑ 223 Vestee Jackson .10 .02
❑ 224 John Offerdahl .10 .02
❑ 225 Louis Oliver .10 .02
❑ 226 Tony Paige .10 .02
❑ 227 Reggie Roby .10 .02
❑ 228 Pete Stoyanovich .10 .02
❑ 229 Richmond Webb .10 .02
❑ 230 Terry Allen .40 .15
❑ 231 Ray Berry .10 .02
❑ 232 Anthony Carter .20 .07
❑ 233 Cris Carter .75 .30
❑ 234 Chris Doleman .10 .02
❑ 235 Rich Gannon .40 .15
❑ 236 Steve Jordan .10 .02
❑ 237 Carl Lee .10 .02
❑ 238 Randall McDaniel .10 .02
❑ 239 Mike Merriweather .10 .02
❑ 240 Harry Newsome .10 .02
❑ 241 John Randle .20 .07
❑ 242 Henry Thomas .10 .02
❑ 243 Bruce Armstrong .10 .02
❑ 244 Vincent Brown .10 .02
❑ 245 Marv Cook .10 .02
❑ 246 Irving Fryar .20 .07
❑ 247 Pat Harlow .10 .02
❑ 248 Maurice Hurst .10 .02
❑ 249 Eugene Lockhart .10 .02
❑ 250 Greg McMurtry .10 .02
❑ 251 Hugh Millen .10 .02
❑ 252 Leonard Russell .20 .07
❑ 253 Chris Singleton .10 .02
❑ 254 Andre Tippett .10 .02
❑ 255 Jon Vaughn .10 .02
❑ 256 Morten Andersen .10 .02
❑ 257 Gene Atkins .10 .02
❑ 258 Wesley Carroll .10 .02
❑ 259 Jim Dombrowski .10 .02
❑ 260 Quinn Early .20 .07
❑ 261 Bobby Hebert .10 .02
❑ 262 Joel Hilgenberg .10 .02
❑ 263 Rickey Jackson .10 .02
❑ 264 Vaughan Johnson .10 .02
❑ 265 Eric Martin .10 .02
❑ 266 Brett Maxie .10 .02
❑ 267 Fred McAfee RC .10 .02
❑ 268 Sam Mills .10 .02
❑ 269 Pat Swilling .10 .02
❑ 270 Floyd Turner .10 .02
❑ 271 Steve Walsh .10 .02
❑ 272 Stephen Baker .10 .02
❑ 273 Jarrod Bunch .10 .02
❑ 274 Mark Collins .10 .02
❑ 275 John Elliott .10 .02
❑ 276 Myron Guyton .10 .02
❑ 277 Rodney Hampton .20 .07
❑ 278 Jeff Hostetler .20 .07
❑ 279 Mark Ingram .10 .02
❑ 280 Pepper Johnson .10 .02
❑ 281 Sean Landeta .10 .02
❑ 282 Leonard Marshall .10 .02
❑ 283 Kanavis McGhee .10 .02
❑ 284 Dave Meggett .20 .07
❑ 285 Bart Oates .10 .02
❑ 286 Phil Simms .20 .07
❑ 287 Reyna Thompson .10 .02
❑ 288 Lewis Tillman .10 .02
❑ 289 Brad Baxter .10 .02
❑ 290 Mike Brim RC .10 .02
❑ 291 Chris Burkett .10 .02
❑ 292 Kyle Clifton .10 .02
❑ 293 James Hasty .10 .02
❑ 294 Joe Kelly .10 .02
❑ 295 Jeff Lageman .10 .02
❑ 296 Mo Lewis .10 .02
❑ 297 Erik McMillan .10 .02
❑ 298 Scott Mersereau .10 .02
❑ 299 Rob Moore .20 .07
❑ 300 Tony Stargell .10 .02
❑ 301 Jim Sweeney .10 .02
❑ 302 Marvin Washington .10 .02
❑ 303 Lonnie Young .10 .02
❑ 304 Eric Allen .10 .02
❑ 305 Fred Barnett .40 .15
❑ 306 Keith Byars .10 .02
❑ 307 Byron Evans .10 .02
❑ 308 Wes Hopkins .10 .02
❑ 309 Keith Jackson .20 .07
❑ 310 James Joseph .10 .02
❑ 311 Seth Joyner .10 .02
❑ 312 Roger Ruzek .10 .02
❑ 313 Clyde Simmons .10 .02
❑ 314 William Thomas .10 .02
❑ 315 Reggie White .40 .15
❑ 316 Calvin Williams .20 .07
❑ 317 Rich Camarillo .10 .02
❑ 318 Jeff Faulkner .10 .02
❑ 319 Ken Harvey .10 .02
❑ 320 Eric Hill .10 .02
❑ 321 Johnny Johnson .10 .02
❑ 322 Ernie Jones .10 .02
❑ 323 Tim McDonald .10 .02
❑ 324 Freddie Joe Nunn .10 .02
❑ 325 Luis Sharpe .10 .02
❑ 326 Eric Swann .20 .07
❑ 327 Aeneas Williams .20 .07
❑ 328 Michael Zordich RC .10 .02
❑ 329 Gary Anderson K .10 .02
❑ 330 Bubby Brister .10 .02
❑ 331 Barry Foster .20 .07
❑ 332 Eric Green .10 .02
❑ 333 Bryan Hinkle .10 .02
❑ 334 Tunch Ilkin .10 .02
❑ 335 Carnell Lake .10 .02
❑ 336 Louis Lipps .10 .02
❑ 337 David Little .10 .02
❑ 338 Greg Lloyd .20 .07
❑ 339 Neil O'Donnell .20 .07
❑ 340 Rod Woodson .40 .15
❑ 341 Rod Bernstine .10 .02
❑ 342 Marion Butts .10 .02
❑ 343 Gill Byrd .10 .02
❑ 344 John Friesz .20 .07
❑ 345 Burt Grossman .10 .02
❑ 346 Courtney Hall .10 .02
❑ 347 Ronnie Harmon .10 .02
❑ 348 Shawn Jefferson .10 .02
❑ 349 Nate Lewis .10 .02
❑ 350 Craig McEwen RC .10 .02
❑ 351 Eric Moten .10 .02
❑ 352 Gary Plummer .10 .02
❑ 353 Henry Rolling .10 .02
❑ 354 Broderick Thompson .10 .02
❑ 355 Derrick Walker .10 .02
❑ 356 Harris Barton .10 .02
❑ 357 Steve Bono RC .40 .15
❑ 358 Todd Bowles .10 .02
❑ 359 Dexter Carter .10 .02
❑ 360 Michael Carter .10 .02
❑ 361 Keith DeLong .10 .02
❑ 362 Charles Haley .20 .07
❑ 363 Merton Hanks .20 .07
❑ 364 Tim Harris .10 .02
❑ 365 Brent Jones .20 .07
❑ 366 Guy McIntyre .10 .02
❑ 367 Tom Rathman .10 .02
❑ 368 Bill Romanowski .10 .02
❑ 369 Jesse Sapolu .10 .02
❑ 370 John Taylor .20 .07
❑ 371 Steve Young 1.50 .60
❑ 372 Robert Blackmon .10 .02
❑ 373 Brian Blades .20 .07
❑ 374 Jacob Green .10 .02
❑ 375 Dwayne Harper .10 .02
❑ 376 Andy Heck .10 .02
❑ 377 Tommy Kane .10 .02
❑ 378 John Kasay .10 .02
❑ 379 Cortez Kennedy .20 .07
❑ 380 Bryan Millard .10 .02
❑ 381 Rufus Porter .10 .02

❑	382 Eugene Robinson	.10	.02
❑	383 John L. Williams	.10	.02
❑	384 Terry Wooden	.10	.02
❑	385 Gary Anderson RB	.10	.02
❑	386 Ian Beckles	.10	.02
❑	387 Mark Carrier WR	.20	.07
❑	388 Reggie Cobb	.10	.02
❑	389 Tony Covington	.10	.02
❑	390 Lawrence Dawsey	.20	.07
❑	391 Ron Hall	.10	.02
❑	392 Keith McCants	.10	.02
❑	393 Charles McRae	.10	.02
❑	394 Tim Newton	.10	.02
❑	395 Jesse Solomon	.10	.02
❑	396 Vinny Testaverde	.20	.07
❑	397 Broderick Thomas	.10	.02
❑	398 Robert Wilson	.10	.02
❑	399 Earnest Byner	.10	.02
❑	400 Gary Clark	.40	.15
❑	401 Andre Collins	.10	.02
❑	402 Brad Edwards	.10	.02
❑	403 Kurt Gouveia	.10	.02
❑	404 Darrell Green	.10	.02
❑	405 Joe Jacoby	.10	.02
❑	406 Jim Lachey	.10	.02
❑	407 Chip Lohmiller	.10	.02
❑	408 Charles Mann	.10	.02
❑	409 Wilber Marshall	.10	.02
❑	410 Brian Mitchell	.20	.07
❑	411 Art Monk	.20	.07
❑	412 Mark Rypien	.10	.02
❑	413 Ricky Sanders	.10	.02
❑	414 Mark Schlereth RC	.10	.02
❑	415 Fred Stokes	.10	.02
❑	416 Bobby Wilson	.10	.02
❑	417 Corey Barlow RC	.10	.02
❑	418 Edgar Bennett RC	.40	.15
❑	419 Eddie Blake RC	.10	.02
❑	420 Terrell Buckley RC	.10	.02
❑	421 Willie Clay RC	.10	.02
❑	422 Rodney Culver RC	.10	.02
❑	423 Ed Cunningham RC	.10	.02
❑	424 Mark D'Onofrio RC	.10	.02
❑	425 Matt Darby RC	.10	.02
❑	426 Charles Davenport RC	.10	.02
❑	427 Will Furrer RC	.10	.02
❑	428 Keith Goganious RC	.10	.02
❑	429 Mario Bailey RC	.10	.02
❑	430 Chris Hakel RC	.10	.02
❑	431 Keith Hamilton RC	.20	.07
❑	432 Aaron Pierce RC	.10	.02
❑	433 Amp Lee RC	.10	.02
❑	434 Scott Lockwood RC	.10	.02
❑	435 Ricardo McDonald RC	.10	.02
❑	436 Dexter McNabb RC	.10	.02
❑	437 Chris Mims RC	.10	.02
❑	438 Mike Mooney RC	.10	.02
❑	439 Ray Roberts RC	.10	.02
❑	440 Patrick Rowe RC	.10	.02
❑	441 Leon Searcy RC	.10	.02
❑	442 Siran Stacy RC	.10	.02
❑	443 Kevin Turner RC	.10	.02
❑	444 Tommy Vardell RC	.10	.02
❑	445 Bob Whitfield RC	.10	.02
❑	446 Darryl Williams RC	.10	.02
❑	447 Checklist 1-110	.10	.02
❑	448 Checklist 111-224	.10	.02
❑	449 Checklist 230-340 UER	.10	.02
❑	450 Checklist 341-450	.10	.02
❑	AD Super Bowl XXVII Strip	2.00	.75

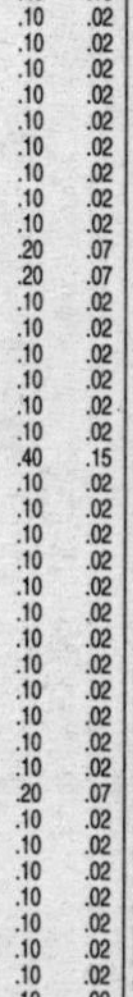

1993 Ultra

❑	COMPLETE SET (500)	20.00	7.50
❑	1 Vinnie Clark	.10	.02
❑	2 Darion Conner	.10	.02
❑	3 Eric Dickerson	.20	.07
❑	4 Moe Gardner	.10	.02
❑	5 Tim Green	.10	.02
❑	6 Roger Harper RC	.10	.02
❑	7 Michael Haynes	.20	.07
❑	8 Bobby Hebert	.10	.02
❑	9 Chris Hinton	.10	.02
❑	10 Pierce Holt	.10	.02
❑	11 Mike Kenn	.10	.02
❑	12 Lincoln Kennedy RC	.10	.02
❑	13 Chris Miller	.20	.07
❑	14 Mike Pritchard	.20	.07

❑	15 Andre Rison	.20	.07
❑	16 Deion Sanders	.75	.30
❑	17 Tony Smith RB	.10	.02
❑	18 Jessie Tuggle	.10	.02
❑	19 Howard Ballard	.10	.02
❑	20 Don Beebe	.10	.02
❑	21 Cornelius Bennett	.20	.07
❑	22 Bill Brooks	.10	.02
❑	23 Kenneth Davis	.10	.02
❑	24 Phil Hansen	.10	.02
❑	25 Henry Jones	.10	.02
❑	26 Jim Kelly	.40	.15
❑	27 Nate Odomes	.10	.02
❑	28 John Parrella RC	.10	.02
❑	29 Andre Reed	.20	.07
❑	30 Frank Reich	.20	.07
❑	31 Jim Ritcher	.10	.02
❑	32 Bruce Smith	.40	.15
❑	33 Thomas Smith RC	.20	.07
❑	34 Darryl Talley	.10	.02
❑	35 Steve Tasker	.20	.07
❑	36 Thurman Thomas	.40	.15
❑	37 Jeff Wright	.10	.02
❑	38 Neal Anderson	.10	.02
❑	39 Trace Armstrong	.10	.02
❑	40 Mark Carrier DB	.10	.02
❑	41 Curtis Conway RC	.75	.30
❑	42 Wendell Davis	.10	.02
❑	43 Richard Dent	.20	.07
❑	44 Shaun Gayle	.10	.02
❑	45 Jim Harbaugh	.40	.15
❑	46 Craig Heyward	.20	.07
❑	47 Darren Lewis	.10	.02
❑	48 Steve McMichael	.20	.07
❑	49 William Perry	.20	.07
❑	50 Carl Simpson RC	.10	.02
❑	51 Alonzo Spellman	.10	.02
❑	52 Keith Van Horne	.10	.02
❑	53 Tom Waddle	.10	.02
❑	54 Donnell Woolford	.10	.02
❑	55 John Copeland RC	.20	.07
❑	56 Derrick Fenner	.10	.02
❑	57 James Francis	.10	.02
❑	58 Harold Green	.10	.02
❑	59 David Klingler	.10	.02
❑	60 Tim Krumrie	.10	.02
❑	61 Ricardo McDonald	.10	.02
❑	62 Tony McGee RC	.20	.07
❑	63 Carl Pickens	.20	.07
❑	64 Lamar Rogers	.10	.02
❑	65 Jay Schroeder	.10	.02
❑	66 Daniel Stubbs	.10	.02
❑	67 Steve Tovar RC	.10	.02
❑	68 Alfred Williams	.10	.02
❑	69 Darryl Williams	.10	.02
❑	70 Jerry Ball	.10	.02
❑	71 David Brandon	.10	.02
❑	72 Rob Burnett	.10	.02
❑	73 Mark Carrier WR	.20	.07
❑	74 Steve Everitt RC	.10	.02
❑	75 Dan Footman RC	.10	.02
❑	76 Leroy Hoard	.20	.07
❑	77 Michael Jackson	.20	.07
❑	78 Mike Johnson	.10	.02
❑	79 Bernie Kosar	.20	.07
❑	80 Clay Matthews	.20	.07
❑	81 Eric Metcalf	.20	.07
❑	82 Michael Dean Perry	.20	.07
❑	83 Vinny Testaverde	.20	.07
❑	84 Tommy Vardell	.10	.02
❑	85 Troy Aikman	1.50	.60
❑	86 Larry Brown DB	.10	.02
❑	87 Tony Casillas	.10	.02
❑	88 Thomas Everett	.10	.02
❑	89 Charles Haley	.20	.07
❑	90 Alvin Harper	.20	.07
❑	91 Michael Irvin	.40	.15
❑	92 Jim Jeffcoat	.10	.02
❑	93 Daryl Johnston	.40	.15
❑	94 Robert Jones	.10	.02
❑	95 Leon Lett RC	.20	.07
❑	96 Russell Maryland	.10	.02
❑	97 Nate Newton	.20	.07
❑	98 Ken Norton	.20	.07
❑	99 Jay Novacek	.20	.07
❑	100 Darrin Smith RC	.20	.07
❑	101 Emmitt Smith	3.00	1.25
❑	102 Kevin Smith	.20	.07
❑	103 Mark Stepnoski	.10	.02
❑	104 Tony Tolbert	.10	.02
❑	105 Kevin Williams RC WR	.40	.15
❑	106 Steve Atwater	.10	.02
❑	107 Rod Bernstine	.10	.02
❑	108 Mike Croel	.10	.02
❑	109 Robert Delpino	.10	.02
❑	110 Shane Dronett	.10	.02
❑	111 John Elway	3.00	1.25
❑	112 Simon Fletcher	.10	.02
❑	113 Greg Kragen	.10	.02
❑	114 Tommy Maddox	.40	.15
❑	115 Arthur Marshall RC	.10	.02
❑	116 Karl Mecklenburg	.10	.02
❑	117 Glyn Milburn RC	.40	.15
❑	118 Reggie Rivers RC	.10	.02
❑	119 Shannon Sharpe	.40	.15
❑	120 Dennis Smith	.10	.02
❑	121 Kenny Walker	.10	.02
❑	122 Dan Williams RC	.10	.02
❑	123 Bennie Blades	.10	.02
❑	124 Lomas Brown	.10	.02
❑	125 Bill Fralic	.10	.02
❑	126 Mel Gray	.20	.07
❑	127 Willie Green	.10	.02
❑	128 Jason Hanson	.10	.02
❑	129 Antonio London RC	.10	.02
❑	130 Ryan McNeil RC	.40	.15
❑	131 Herman Moore	.40	.15
❑	132 Rodney Peete	.10	.02
❑	133 Brett Perriman	.40	.15
❑	134 Kelvin Pritchett	.10	.02
❑	135 Barry Sanders	2.50	1.00
❑	136 Tracy Scroggins	.10	.02
❑	137 Chris Spielman	.20	.07
❑	138 Pat Swilling	.10	.02
❑	139 Andre Ware	.10	.02
❑	140 Edgar Bennett	.40	.15
❑	141 Tony Bennett	.10	.02
❑	142 Matt Brock	.10	.02
❑	143 Terrell Buckley	.10	.02
❑	144 LeRoy Butler	.10	.02
❑	145 Mark Clayton	.10	.02
❑	146 Brett Favre	4.00	1.50
❑	147 Jackie Harris	.10	.02
❑	148 Johnny Holland	.10	.02
❑	149 Bill Maas	.10	.02
❑	150 Brian Noble	.10	.02
❑	151 Bryce Paup	.20	.07
❑	152 Ken Ruettgers	.10	.02
❑	153 Sterling Sharpe	.40	.15
❑	154 Wayne Simmons RC	.10	.02
❑	155 John Stephens	.10	.02
❑	156 George Teague RC	.20	.07
❑	157 Reggie White	.40	.15
❑	158 Micheal Barrow RC	.40	.15
❑	159 Cody Carlson	.10	.02
❑	160 Ray Childress	.10	.02
❑	161 Cris Dishman	.10	.02
❑	162 Curtis Duncan	.10	.02
❑	163 William Fuller	.10	.02
❑	164 Ernest Givins	.20	.07
❑	165 Brad Hopkins RC	.10	.02
❑	166 Haywood Jeffires	.20	.07
❑	167 Lamar Lathon	.10	.02
❑	168 Wilber Marshall	.10	.02
❑	169 Bruce Matthews	.10	.02
❑	170 Bubba McDowell	.10	.02
❑	171 Warren Moon	.40	.15

❑ 172 Mike Munchak .20 .07
❑ 173 Eddie Robinson .10 .02
❑ 174 Al Smith .10 .02
❑ 175 Lorenzo White .10 .02
❑ 176 Lee Williams .10 .02
❑ 177 Chip Banks .10 .02
❑ 178 John Baylor .10 .02
❑ 179 Duane Bickett .10 .02
❑ 180 Kerry Cash .10 .02
❑ 181 Quentin Coryatt .20 .07
❑ 182 Rodney Culver .10 .02
❑ 183 Steve Emtman .10 .02
❑ 184 Jeff George .40 .15
❑ 185 Jeff Herrod .10 .02
❑ 186 Jessie Hester .10 .02
❑ 187 Anthony Johnson .20 .07
❑ 188 Reggie Langhorne .10 .02
❑ 189 Roosevelt Potts RC .10 .02
❑ 190 Rohn Stark .10 .02
❑ 191 Clarence Verdin .10 .02
❑ 192 Will Wolford .10 .02
❑ 193 Marcus Allen .40 .15
❑ 194 John Alt .10 .02
❑ 195 Tim Barnett .10 .02
❑ 196 J.J.Birden .10 .02
❑ 197 Dale Carter .10 .02
❑ 198 Willie Davis .40 .15
❑ 199 Jaime Fields RC .10 .02
❑ 200 Dave Krieg .20 .07
❑ 201 Nick Lowery .10 .02
❑ 202 Charles Mincy RC .10 .02
❑ 203 Joe Montana 3.00 1.25
❑ 204 Christian Okoye .10 .02
❑ 205 Dan Saleaumua .10 .02
❑ 206 Will Shields RC .40 .15
❑ 207 Tracy Simien .10 .02
❑ 208 Neil Smith .40 .15
❑ 209 Derrick Thomas .40 .15
❑ 210 Harvey Williams .20 .07
❑ 211 Barry Word .10 .02
❑ 212 Eddie Anderson .10 .02
❑ 213 Patrick Bates RC .10 .02
❑ 214 Nick Bell .10 .02
❑ 215 Tim Brown .40 .15
❑ 216 Willie Gault .10 .02
❑ 217 Gaston Green .10 .02
❑ 218 Billy Joe Hobert RC .40 .15
❑ 219 Ethan Horton .10 .02
❑ 220 Jeff Hostetler .20 .07
❑ 221 James Lofton .20 .07
❑ 222 Howie Long .40 .15
❑ 223 Todd Marinovich .10 .02
❑ 224 Terry McDaniel .10 .02
❑ 225 Winston Moss .10 .02
❑ 226 Anthony Smith .10 .02
❑ 227 Greg Townsend .10 .02
❑ 228 Aaron Wallace .10 .02
❑ 229 Lionel Washington .10 .02
❑ 230 Steve Wisniewski .10 .02
❑ 231 Flipper Anderson .10 .02
❑ 232 Jerome Bettis RC 8.00 4.00
❑ 233 Marc Boutte .10 .02
❑ 234 Shane Conlan .10 .02
❑ 235 Troy Drayton RC .20 .07
❑ 236 Henry Ellard .20 .07
❑ 237 Jim Everett .20 .07
❑ 238 Cleveland Gary .10 .02
❑ 239 Sean Gilbert .20 .07
❑ 240 Darryl Henley .10 .02
❑ 241 David Lang .10 .02
❑ 242 Todd Lyght .10 .02
❑ 243 Anthony Newman .10 .02
❑ 244 Roman Phifer .10 .02
❑ 245 Gerald Robinson .10 .02
❑ 246 Henry Rolling .10 .02
❑ 247 Jackie Slater .10 .02
❑ 248 Keith Byars .10 .02
❑ 249 Marco Coleman .10 .02
❑ 250 Bryan Cox .10 .02
❑ 251 Jeff Cross .10 .02
❑ 252 Irving Fryar .20 .07
❑ 253 Mark Higgs .10 .02
❑ 254 Dwight Hollier RC .10 .02
❑ 255 Mark Ingram .10 .02
❑ 256 Keith Jackson .20 .07
❑ 257 Terry Kirby RC .40 .15
❑ 258 Dan Marino 3.00 1.25
❑ 259 O.J. McDuffie RC .40 .15
❑ 260 John Offerdahl .10 .02
❑ 261 Louis Oliver .10 .02
❑ 262 Pete Stoyanovich .10 .02
❑ 263 Troy Vincent .10 .02
❑ 264 Richmond Webb .10 .02
❑ 265 Jarvis Williams .10 .02
❑ 266 Terry Allen .40 .15
❑ 267 Anthony Carter .20 .07
❑ 268 Cris Carter .40 .15
❑ 269 Roger Craig .20 .07
❑ 270 Jack Del Rio .10 .02
❑ 271 Chris Doleman .10 .02
❑ 272 Qadry Ismail RC .40 .15
❑ 273 Steve Jordan .10 .02
❑ 274 Randall McDaniel .10 .02
❑ 275 Audray McMillian .10 .02
❑ 276 John Randle .20 .07
❑ 277 Sean Salisbury .10 .02
❑ 278 Todd Scott .10 .02
❑ 279 Robert Smith RC 2.50 1.00
❑ 280 Henry Thomas .10 .02
❑ 281 Ray Agnew .10 .02
❑ 282 Bruce Armstrong .10 .02
❑ 283 Drew Bledsoe RC 5.00 2.00
❑ 284 Vincent Brisby RC .40 .15
❑ 285 Vincent Brown .10 .02
❑ 286 Eugene Chung .10 .02
❑ 287 Marv Cook .10 .02
❑ 288 Pat Harlow .10 .02
❑ 289 Jerome Henderson .10 .02
❑ 290 Greg McMurtry .10 .02
❑ 291 Leonard Russell .20 .07
❑ 292 Chris Singleton .10 .02
❑ 293 Chris Slade RC .20 .07
❑ 294 Andre Tippett .10 .02
❑ 295 Brent Williams .10 .02
❑ 296 Scott Zolak .10 .02
❑ 297 Morten Andersen .10 .02
❑ 298 Gene Atkins .10 .02
❑ 299 Mike Buck .10 .02
❑ 300 Toi Cook .10 .02
❑ 301 Jim Dombrowski .10 .02
❑ 302 Vaughn Dunbar .10 .02
❑ 303 Quinn Early .20 .07
❑ 304 Joel Hilgenberg .10 .02
❑ 305 Dalton Hilliard .10 .02
❑ 306 Rickey Jackson .10 .02
❑ 307 Vaughan Johnson .10 .02
❑ 308 Reginald Jones .10 .02
❑ 309 Eric Martin .10 .02
❑ 310 Wayne Martin .10 .02
❑ 311 Sam Mills .10 .02
❑ 312 Brad Muster .10 .02
❑ 313 Willie Roaf RC .20 .07
❑ 314 Irv Smith RC .10 .02
❑ 315 Wade Wilson .10 .02
❑ 316 Carlton Bailey .10 .02
❑ 317 Michael Brooks .10 .02
❑ 318 Derek Brown TE .10 .02
❑ 319 Marcus Buckley RC .10 .02
❑ 320 Jarrod Bunch .10 .02
❑ 321 Mark Collins .10 .02
❑ 322 Eric Dorsey .10 .02
❑ 323 Rodney Hampton .20 .07
❑ 324 Mark Jackson .10 .02
❑ 325 Pepper Johnson .10 .02
❑ 326 Ed McCaffrey .40 .15
❑ 327 Dave Meggett .10 .02
❑ 328 Bart Oates .10 .02
❑ 329 Mike Sherrard .10 .02
❑ 330 Phil Simms .20 .07
❑ 331 Michael Strahan RC 2.00 .75
❑ 332 Lawrence Taylor .40 .15
❑ 333 Brad Baxter .10 .02
❑ 334 Chris Burkett .10 .02
❑ 335 Kyle Clifton .10 .02
❑ 336 Boomer Esiason .20 .07
❑ 337 James Hasty .10 .02
❑ 338 Johnny Johnson .10 .02
❑ 339 Marvin Jones RC .10 .02
❑ 340 Jeff Lageman .10 .02
❑ 341 Mo Lewis .10 .02
❑ 342 Ronnie Lott .20 .07
❑ 343 Leonard Marshall .10 .02
❑ 344 Johnny Mitchell .10 .02
❑ 345 Rob Moore .20 .07
❑ 346 Browning Nagle .10 .02
❑ 347 Coleman Rudolph RC .10 .02
❑ 348 Blair Thomas .10 .02
❑ 349 Eric Thomas .10 .02
❑ 350 Brian Washington .10 .02
❑ 351 Marvin Washington .10 .02
❑ 352 Eric Allen .10 .02
❑ 353 Victor Bailey RC .10 .02
❑ 354 Fred Barnett .20 .07
❑ 355 Mark Bavaro .10 .02
❑ 356 Randall Cunningham .40 .15
❑ 357 Byron Evans .10 .02
❑ 358 Andy Harmon RC .20 .07
❑ 359 Tim Harris .10 .02
❑ 360 Lester Holmes .10 .02
❑ 361 Seth Joyner .10 .02
❑ 362 Keith Millard .10 .02
❑ 363 Leonard Renfro RC .10 .02
❑ 364 Heath Sherman .10 .02
❑ 365 Vai Sikahema .10 .02
❑ 366 Clyde Simmons .10 .02
❑ 367 William Thomas .10 .02
❑ 368 Herschel Walker .20 .07
❑ 369 Andre Waters .10 .02
❑ 370 Calvin Williams .20 .07
❑ 371 Johnny Bailey .10 .02
❑ 372 Steve Beuerlein .20 .07
❑ 373 Rich Camarillo .10 .02
❑ 374 Chuck Cecil .10 .02
❑ 375 Chris Chandler .20 .07
❑ 376 Gary Clark .20 .07
❑ 377 Ben Coleman RC .10 .02
❑ 378 Ernest Dye RC .10 .02
❑ 379 Ken Harvey .10 .02
❑ 380 Garrison Hearst RC 1.50 .60
❑ 381 Randal Hill .10 .02
❑ 382 Robert Massey .10 .02
❑ 383 Freddie Joe Nunn .10 .02
❑ 384 Ricky Proehl .10 .02
❑ 385 Luis Sharpe .10 .02
❑ 386 Tyronne Stowe .10 .02
❑ 387 Eric Swann .20 .07
❑ 388 Aeneas Williams .10 .02
❑ 389 Chad Brown RC LB .20 .07
❑ 390 Dermontti Dawson .10 .02
❑ 391 Donald Evans .10 .02
❑ 392 Deon Figures RC .10 .02
❑ 393 Barry Foster .20 .07
❑ 394 Jeff Graham .20 .07
❑ 395 Eric Green .10 .02
❑ 396 Kevin Greene .20 .07
❑ 397 Carlton Haselrig .10 .02
❑ 398 Andre Hastings RC .20 .07
❑ 399 D.J. Johnson .10 .02
❑ 400 Carnell Lake .10 .02
❑ 401 Greg Lloyd .20 .07
❑ 402 Neil O'Donnell .40 .15
❑ 403 Darren Perry .10 .02
❑ 404 Mike Tomczak .10 .02
❑ 405 Rod Woodson .40 .15
❑ 406 Eric Bieniemy .10 .02
❑ 407 Marion Butts .10 .02
❑ 408 Gill Byrd .10 .02
❑ 409 Darren Carrington RC .10 .02
❑ 410 Darrien Gordon RC .10 .02
❑ 411 Burt Grossman .10 .02
❑ 412 Courtney Hall .10 .02
❑ 413 Ronnie Harmon .10 .02
❑ 414 Stan Humphries .20 .07
❑ 415 Nate Lewis .10 .02
❑ 416 Natrone Means RC .40 .15
❑ 417 Anthony Miller .20 .07
❑ 418 Chris Mims .10 .02
❑ 419 Leslie O'Neal .20 .07
❑ 420 Gary Plummer .10 .02
❑ 421 Stanley Richard .10 .02
❑ 422 Junior Seau .40 .15
❑ 423 Harry Swayne .10 .02
❑ 424 Jerrol Williams .10 .02
❑ 425 Harris Barton .10 .02
❑ 426 Steve Bono .20 .07
❑ 427 Kevin Fagan .10 .02
❑ 428 Don Griffin .10 .02
❑ 429 Dana Hall .10 .02
❑ 430 Adrian Hardy .10 .02
❑ 431 Brent Jones .20 .07
❑ 432 Todd Kelly RC .10 .02

❑ 433	Amp Lee	.10	.02
❑ 434	Tim McDonald	.10	.02
❑ 435	Guy McIntyre	.10	.02
❑ 436	Tom Rathman	.10	.02
❑ 437	Jerry Rice	2.00	.75
❑ 438	Bill Romanowski	.10	.02
❑ 439	Dana Stubblefield RC	.40	.15
❑ 440	John Taylor	.20	.07
❑ 441	Steve Wallace	.10	.02
❑ 442	Michael Walter	.10	.02
❑ 443	Ricky Watters	.40	.15
❑ 444	Steve Young	1.50	.60
❑ 445	Robert Blackmon	.10	.02
❑ 446	Brian Blades	.20	.07
❑ 447	Jeff Bryant	.10	.02
❑ 448	Ferrell Edmunds	.10	.02
❑ 449	Carlton Gray RC	.10	.02
❑ 450	Dwayne Harper	.10	.02
❑ 451	Andy Heck	.10	.02
❑ 452	Tommy Kane	.10	.02
❑ 453	Cortez Kennedy	.20	.07
❑ 454	Kelvin Martin	.10	.02
❑ 455	Dan McGwire	.10	.02
❑ 456	Rick Mirer RC	.40	.15
❑ 457	Rufus Porter	.10	.02
❑ 458	Ray Roberts	.10	.02
❑ 459	Eugene Robinson	.10	.02
❑ 460	Chris Warren	.20	.07
❑ 461	John L. Williams	.10	.02
❑ 462	Gary Anderson RB	.10	.02
❑ 463	Tyji Armstrong	.10	.02
❑ 464	Reggie Cobb	.10	.02
❑ 465	Eric Curry RC	.10	.02
❑ 466	Lawrence Dawsey	.10	.02
❑ 467	Steve DeBerg	.10	.02
❑ 468	Santana Dotson	.20	.07
❑ 469	Demetrius DuBose RC	.10	.02
❑ 470	Paul Gruber	.10	.02
❑ 471	Ron Hall	.10	.02
❑ 472	Courtney Hawkins	.10	.02
❑ 473	Hardy Nickerson	.20	.07
❑ 474	Ricky Reynolds	.10	.02
❑ 475	Broderick Thomas	.10	.02
❑ 476	Mark Wheeler	.10	.02
❑ 477	Jimmy Williams	.10	.02
❑ 478	Carl Banks	.10	.02
❑ 479	Reggie Brooks RC	.20	.07
❑ 480	Earnest Byner	.10	.02
❑ 481	Tom Carter RC	.20	.07
❑ 482	Andre Collins	.10	.02
❑ 483	Brad Edwards	.10	.02
❑ 484	Ricky Ervins	.10	.02
❑ 485	Kurt Gouveia	.10	.02
❑ 486	Darrell Green	.10	.02
❑ 487	Desmond Howard	.20	.07
❑ 488	Jim Lachey	.10	.02
❑ 489	Chip Lohmiller	.10	.02
❑ 490	Charles Mann	.10	.02
❑ 491	Tim McGee	.10	.02
❑ 492	Brian Mitchell	.20	.07
❑ 493	Art Monk	.20	.07
❑ 494	Mark Rypien	.10	.02
❑ 495	Ricky Sanders	.10	.02
❑ 496	Checklist 1-126	.10	.02
❑ 497	Checklist 127-254	.10	.02
❑ 498	Checklist 255-382	.10	.02
❑ 499	Checklist 383-500	.10	.02
❑ 500	Inserts Checklist	.10	.02

1994 Ultra

❑	COMPLETE SET (525)	25.00	10.00
❑	COMP.SERIES 1 (325)	12.00	5.00
❑	COMP.SERIES 2 (200)	12.00	5.00
❑ 1	Steve Beuerlein	.20	.07
❑ 2	Gary Clark	.20	.07
❑ 3	Randal Hill	.10	.02
❑ 4	Seth Joyner	.10	.02
❑ 5	Jamir Miller RC	.20	.07
❑ 6	Ronald Moore	.10	.02
❑ 7	Luis Sharpe	.10	.02
❑ 8	Clyde Simmons	.10	.02
❑ 9	Eric Swann	.20	.07
❑ 10	Aeneas Williams	.10	.02
❑ 11	Chris Doleman	.10	.02
❑ 12	Bert Emanuel RC	.40	.15
❑ 13	Moe Gardner	.10	.02
❑ 14	Jeff George	.40	.15
❑ 15	Roger Harper	.10	.02
❑ 16	Pierce Holt	.10	.02
❑ 17	Lincoln Kennedy	.10	.02
❑ 18	Erric Pegram	.10	.02
❑ 19	Andre Rison	.20	.07
❑ 20	Deion Sanders	.75	.30
❑ 21	Jessie Tuggle	.10	.02
❑ 22	Cornelius Bennett	.20	.07
❑ 23	Bill Brooks	.10	.02
❑ 24	Jeff Burris RC	.20	.07
❑ 25	Kent Hull	.10	.02
❑ 26	Henry Jones	.10	.02
❑ 27	Jim Kelly	.40	.15
❑ 28	Marvcus Patton	.10	.02
❑ 29	Andre Reed	.20	.07
❑ 30	Bruce Smith	.40	.15
❑ 31	Thomas Smith	.10	.02
❑ 32	Thurman Thomas	.40	.15
❑ 33	Jeff Wright	.10	.02
❑ 34	Trace Armstrong	.10	.02
❑ 35	Mark Carrier DB	.10	.02
❑ 36	Dante Jones	.10	.02
❑ 37	Erik Kramer	.20	.07
❑ 38	Terry Obee	.10	.02
❑ 39	Alonzo Spellman	.10	.02
❑ 40	John Thierry RC	.10	.02
❑ 41	Tom Waddle	.10	.02
❑ 42	Donnell Woolford	.10	.02
❑ 43	Tim Worley	.10	.02
❑ 44	Chris Zorich	.10	.02
❑ 45	John Copeland	.10	.02
❑ 46	Harold Green	.10	.02
❑ 47	David Klingler	.10	.02
❑ 48	Ricardo McDonald	.10	.02
❑ 49	Tony McGee	.10	.02
❑ 50	Louis Oliver	.10	.02
❑ 51	Carl Pickens	.20	.07
❑ 52	Darnay Scott RC	.75	.30
❑ 53	Steve Tovar	.10	.02
❑ 54	Dan Wilkinson RC	.20	.07
❑ 55	Darryl Williams	.10	.02
❑ 56	Derrick Alexander WR RC	.40	.15
❑ 57	Michael Jackson	.20	.07
❑ 58	Tony Jones T	.10	.02
❑ 59	Antonio Langham RC	.20	.07
❑ 60	Eric Metcalf	.20	.07
❑ 61	Stevon Moore	.10	.02
❑ 62	Michael Dean Perry	.20	.07
❑ 63	Anthony Pleasant	.10	.02
❑ 64	Vinny Testaverde	.20	.07
❑ 65	Eric Turner	.10	.02
❑ 66	Tommy Vardell	.10	.02
❑ 67	Troy Aikman	1.50	.60
❑ 68	Larry Brown DB	.10	.02
❑ 69	Shante Carver RC	.10	.02
❑ 70	Charles Haley	.20	.07
❑ 71	Michael Irvin	.40	.15
❑ 72	Leon Lett	.10	.02
❑ 73	Nate Newton	.10	.02
❑ 74	Jay Novacek	.20	.07
❑ 75	Darrin Smith	.10	.02
❑ 76	Emmitt Smith	2.50	1.00
❑ 77	Tony Tolbert	.10	.02
❑ 78	Erik Williams	.10	.02
❑ 79	Kevin Williams WR	.20	.07
❑ 80	Steve Atwater	.10	.02
❑ 81	Rod Bernstine	.10	.02
❑ 82	Ray Crockett	.10	.02
❑ 83	Mike Croel	.10	.02
❑ 84	Shane Dronett	.10	.02
❑ 85	Jason Elam	.20	.07
❑ 86	John Elway	3.00	1.25
❑ 87	Simon Fletcher	.10	.02
❑ 88	Glyn Milburn	.20	.07
❑ 89	Anthony Miller	.20	.07
❑ 90	Shannon Sharpe	.20	.07
❑ 91	Gary Zimmerman	.10	.02
❑ 92	Bennie Blades	.10	.02
❑ 93	Lomas Brown	.10	.02
❑ 94	Mel Gray	.10	.02
❑ 95	Jason Hanson	.10	.02
❑ 96	Ryan McNeil	.10	.02
❑ 97	Scott Mitchell	.20	.07
❑ 98	Herman Moore	.40	.15
❑ 99	Johnnie Morton RC	1.50	.60
❑ 100	Robert Porcher	.10	.02
❑ 101	Barry Sanders	2.50	1.00
❑ 102	Chris Spielman	.20	.07
❑ 103	Pat Swilling	.10	.02
❑ 104	Edgar Bennett	.40	.15
❑ 105	Terrell Buckley	.10	.02
❑ 106	Reggie Cobb	.10	.02
❑ 107	Brett Favre	3.00	1.25
❑ 108	Sean Jones	.10	.02
❑ 109	Ken Ruettgers	.10	.02
❑ 110	Sterling Sharpe	.20	.07
❑ 111	Wayne Simmons	.10	.02
❑ 112	Aaron Taylor RC	.10	.02
❑ 113	George Teague	.10	.02
❑ 114	Reggie White	.40	.15
❑ 115	Micheal Barrow	.10	.02
❑ 116	Gary Brown	.10	.02
❑ 117	Cody Carlson	.10	.02
❑ 118	Ray Childress	.10	.02
❑ 119	Cris Dishman	.10	.02
❑ 120	Henry Ford RC	.10	.02
❑ 121	Haywood Jeffires	.20	.07
❑ 122	Bruce Matthews	.10	.02
❑ 123	Bubba McDowell	.10	.02
❑ 124	Marcus Robertson	.10	.02
❑ 125	Eddie Robinson	.10	.02
❑ 126	Webster Slaughter	.10	.02
❑ 127	Trev Alberts RC	.20	.07
❑ 128	Tony Bennett	.10	.02
❑ 129	Ray Buchanan	.10	.02
❑ 130	Quentin Coryatt	.10	.02
❑ 131	Eugene Daniel	.10	.02
❑ 132	Steve Emtman	.10	.02
❑ 133	Marshall Faulk RC	6.00	2.50
❑ 134	Jim Harbaugh	.40	.15
❑ 135	Roosevelt Potts	.10	.02
❑ 136	Rohn Stark	.10	.02
❑ 137	Marcus Allen	.40	.15
❑ 138	Donnell Bennett RC	.40	.15
❑ 139	Dale Carter	.10	.02
❑ 140	Tony Casillas	.10	.02
❑ 141	Mark Collins	.10	.02
❑ 142	Willie Davis	.20	.07
❑ 143	Tim Grunhard	.10	.02
❑ 144	Greg Hill RC	.40	.15
❑ 145	Joe Montana	3.00	1.25
❑ 146	Tracy Simien	.10	.02
❑ 147	Neil Smith	.20	.07
❑ 148	Derrick Thomas	.40	.15
❑ 149	Tim Brown	.40	.15
❑ 150	James Folston RC	.10	.02
❑ 151	Rob Fredrickson RC	.20	.07
❑ 152	Jeff Hostetler	.20	.07
❑ 153	Rocket Ismail	.20	.07
❑ 154	James Jett	.10	.02
❑ 155	Terry McDaniel	.10	.02
❑ 156	Winston Moss	.10	.02
❑ 157	Greg Robinson	.10	.02
❑ 158	Anthony Smith	.10	.02
❑ 159	Steve Wisniewski	.10	.02
❑ 160	Flipper Anderson	.10	.02
❑ 161	Jerome Bettis	.60	.25
❑ 162	Isaac Bruce RC	4.00	2.00
❑ 163	Shane Conlan	.10	.02
❑ 164	Wayne Gandy RC	.10	.02
❑ 165	Sean Gilbert	.10	.02
❑ 166	Todd Lyght	.10	.02
❑ 167	Chris Miller	.10	.02
❑ 168	Anthony Newman	.10	.02
❑ 169	Roman Phifer	.10	.02
❑ 170	Jackie Slater	.10	.02
❑ 171	Gene Atkins	.10	.02

❑ 172 Aubrey Beavers RC .10 .02
❑ 173 Tim Bowens RC .20 .07
❑ 174 J.B. Brown .10 .02
❑ 175 Marco Coleman .10 .02
❑ 176 Bryan Cox .10 .02
❑ 177 Irving Fryar .20 .07
❑ 178 Terry Kirby .40 .15
❑ 179 Dan Marino 3.00 1.25
❑ 180 Troy Vincent .10 .02
❑ 181 Richmond Webb .10 .02
❑ 182 Terry Allen .20 .07
❑ 183 Cris Carter .75 .30
❑ 184 Jack Del Rio .10 .02
❑ 185 Vencie Glenn .10 .02
❑ 186 Randall McDaniel .10 .02
❑ 187 Warren Moon .40 .15
❑ 188 David Palmer RC .40 .15
❑ 189 John Randle .20 .07
❑ 190 Todd Scott .10 .02
❑ 191 Todd Steussie RC .20 .07
❑ 192 Henry Thomas .10 .02
❑ 193 Dewayne Washington RC .20 .07
❑ 194 Bruce Armstrong .10 .02
❑ 195 Harlon Barnett .10 .02
❑ 196 Drew Bledsoe 1.00 .40
❑ 197 Vincent Brisby .20 .07
❑ 198 Vincent Brown .10 .02
❑ 199 Marion Butts .10 .02
❑ 200 Ben Coates .20 .07
❑ 201 Todd Collins .10 .02
❑ 202 Maurice Hurst .10 .02
❑ 203 Willie McGinest RC .40 .15
❑ 204 Ricky Reynolds .10 .02
❑ 205 Chris Slade .10 .02
❑ 206 Mario Bates RC .40 .15
❑ 207 Derek Brown RBK .10 .02
❑ 208 Vince Buck .10 .02
❑ 209 Quinn Early .20 .07
❑ 210 Jim Everett .20 .07
❑ 211 Michael Haynes .20 .07
❑ 212 Tyrone Hughes .20 .07
❑ 213 Joe Johnson RC .10 .02
❑ 214 Vaughan Johnson .10 .02
❑ 215 Willie Roaf .10 .02
❑ 216 Renaldo Turnbull .10 .02
❑ 217 Michael Brooks .10 .02
❑ 218 Dave Brown .20 .07
❑ 219 Howard Cross .10 .02
❑ 220 Stacey Dillard .10 .02
❑ 221 Jumbo Elliott .10 .02
❑ 222 Keith Hamilton .10 .02
❑ 223 Rodney Hampton .20 .07
❑ 224 Thomas Lewis RC .20 .07
❑ 225 Dave Meggett .10 .02
❑ 226 Corey Miller .10 .02
❑ 227 Thomas Randolph RC .10 .02
❑ 228 Mike Sherrard .10 .02
❑ 229 Kyle Clifton .10 .02
❑ 230 Boomer Esiason .20 .07
❑ 231 Aaron Glenn RC .40 .15
❑ 232 James Hasty .10 .02
❑ 233 Bobby Houston .10 .02
❑ 234 Johnny Johnson .10 .02
❑ 235 Mo Lewis .10 .02
❑ 236 Ronnie Lott .20 .07
❑ 237 Rob Moore .20 .07
❑ 238 Marvin Washington .10 .02
❑ 239 Ryan Yarborough RC .10 .02
❑ 240 Eric Allen .10 .02
❑ 241 Victor Bailey .10 .02
❑ 242 Fred Barnett .20 .07
❑ 243 Mark Bavaro .10 .02
❑ 244 Randall Cunningham .40 .15
❑ 245 Byron Evans .10 .02
❑ 246 William Fuller .10 .02
❑ 247 Andy Harmon .10 .02
❑ 248 William Perry .20 .07
❑ 249 Herschel Walker .20 .07
❑ 250 Bernard Williams RC .10 .02
❑ 251 Dermontti Dawson .10 .02
❑ 252 Deon Figures .10 .02
❑ 253 Barry Foster .10 .02
❑ 254 Kevin Greene .20 .07
❑ 255 Charles Johnson RC .40 .15
❑ 256 Levon Kirkland .10 .02
❑ 257 Greg Lloyd .20 .07
❑ 258 Neil O'Donnell .40 .15
❑ 259 Darren Perry .10 .02
❑ 260 Dwight Stone .10 .02
❑ 261 Rod Woodson .20 .07
❑ 262 John Carney .10 .02
❑ 263 Isaac Davis RC .10 .02
❑ 264 Courtney Hall .10 .02
❑ 265 Ronnie Harmon .10 .02
❑ 266 Stan Humphries .20 .07
❑ 267 Vance Johnson .10 .02
❑ 268 Natrone Means .40 .15
❑ 269 Chris Mims .10 .02
❑ 270 Leslie O'Neal .10 .02
❑ 271 Stanley Richard .10 .02
❑ 272 Junior Seau .40 .15
❑ 273 Harris Barton .10 .02
❑ 274 Dennis Brown .10 .02
❑ 275 Eric Davis .10 .02
❑ 276 William Floyd RC .40 .15
❑ 277 John Johnson .10 .02
❑ 278 Tim McDonald .10 .02
❑ 279 Ken Norton Jr. .20 .07
❑ 280 Jerry Rice 1.50 .60
❑ 281 Jesse Sapolu .10 .02
❑ 282 Dana Stubblefield .20 .07
❑ 283 Ricky Watters .20 .07
❑ 284 Bryant Young RC .40 .15
❑ 285 Steve Young 1.00 .40
❑ 286 Sam Adams RC .20 .07
❑ 287 Brian Blades .20 .07
❑ 288 Ferrell Edmunds .10 .02
❑ 289 Patrick Hunter .10 .02
❑ 290 Cortez Kennedy .20 .07
❑ 291 Rick Mirer .40 .15
❑ 292 Nate Odomes .10 .02
❑ 293 Ray Roberts .10 .02
❑ 294 Eugene Robinson .10 .02
❑ 295 Rod Stephens .10 .02
❑ 296 Chris Warren .20 .07
❑ 297 Marty Carter .10 .02
❑ 298 Horace Copeland .10 .02
❑ 299 Eric Curry .10 .02
❑ 300 Santana Dotson .20 .07
❑ 301 Craig Erickson .10 .02
❑ 302 Paul Gruber .10 .02
❑ 303 Courtney Hawkins .10 .02
❑ 304 Martin Mayhew .10 .02
❑ 305 Hardy Nickerson .20 .07
❑ 306 Errict Rhett RC .40 .15
❑ 307 Vince Workman .10 .02
❑ 308 Reggie Brooks .20 .07
❑ 309 Tom Carter .10 .02
❑ 310 Andre Collins .10 .02
❑ 311 Brad Edwards .10 .02
❑ 312 Kurt Gouveia .10 .02
❑ 313 Darrell Green .10 .02
❑ 314 Ethan Horton .10 .02
❑ 315 Desmond Howard .20 .07
❑ 316 Tre Johnson RC .10 .02
❑ 317 Sterling Palmer RC .10 .02
❑ 318 Heath Shuler RC .40 .15
❑ 319 Tyronne Stowe .10 .02
❑ 320 NFL 75th Anniversary .10 .02
❑ 321 Checklist .10 .02
❑ 322 Checklist .10 .02
❑ 323 Checklist .10 .02
❑ 324 Checklist .10 .02
❑ 325 Checklist .10 .02
❑ 326 Garrison Hearst .40 .15
❑ 327 Eric Hill .10 .02
❑ 328 Seth Joyner .10 .02
❑ 329 Jim McMahon .20 .07
❑ 330 Jamir Miller .10 .02
❑ 331 Ricky Proehl .10 .02
❑ 332 Clyde Simmons .10 .02
❑ 333 Chris Doleman .10 .02
❑ 334 Bert Emanuel .40 .15
❑ 335 Jeff George .40 .15
❑ 336 D.J. Johnson .10 .02
❑ 337 Terance Mathis .20 .07
❑ 338 Clay Matthews .10 .02
❑ 339 Tony Smith RB .10 .02
❑ 340 Don Beebe .10 .02
❑ 341 Bucky Brooks RC .10 .02
❑ 342 Jeff Burris .20 .07
❑ 343 Kenneth Davis .10 .02
❑ 344 Phil Hansen .10 .02
❑ 345 Pete Metzelaars .10 .02
❑ 346 Darryl Talley .10 .02
❑ 347 Joe Cain .10 .02
❑ 348 Curtis Conway .40 .15
❑ 349 Shaun Gayle .10 .02
❑ 350 Chris Gedney .10 .02
❑ 351 Erik Kramer .20 .07
❑ 352 Vinson Smith .10 .02
❑ 353 John Thierry .10 .02
❑ 354 Lewis Tillman .10 .02
❑ 355 Mike Brim .10 .02
❑ 356 Derrick Fenner .10 .02
❑ 357 James Francis .10 .02
❑ 358 Louis Oliver .10 .02
❑ 359 Darnay Scott .40 .15
❑ 360 Dan Wilkinson .20 .07
❑ 361 Alfred Williams .10 .02
❑ 362 Derrick Alexander WR .40 .15
❑ 363 Rob Burnett .10 .02
❑ 364 Mark Carrier WR .20 .07
❑ 365 Steve Everitt .10 .02
❑ 366 Leroy Hoard .10 .02
❑ 367 Pepper Johnson .10 .02
❑ 368 Antonio Langham .20 .07
❑ 369 Shante Carver .10 .02
❑ 370 Alvin Harper .20 .07
❑ 371 Daryl Johnston .20 .07
❑ 372 Russell Maryland .10 .02
❑ 373 Kevin Smith .10 .02
❑ 374 Mark Stepnoski .10 .02
❑ 375 Darren Woodson .20 .07
❑ 376 Allen Aldridge RC .10 .02
❑ 377 Ray Crockett .10 .02
❑ 378 Karl Mecklenburg .10 .02
❑ 379 Anthony Miller .20 .07
❑ 380 Mike Pritchard .10 .02
❑ 381 Leonard Russell .10 .02
❑ 382 Dennis Smith .10 .02
❑ 383 Anthony Carter .20 .07
❑ 384 Van Malone RC .10 .02
❑ 385 Robert Massey .10 .02
❑ 386 Scott Mitchell .20 .07
❑ 387 Johnnie Morton .60 .25
❑ 388 Brett Perriman .20 .07
❑ 389 Tracy Scroggins .10 .02
❑ 390 Robert Brooks .40 .15
❑ 391 LeRoy Butler .10 .02
❑ 392 Reggie Cobb .10 .02
❑ 393 Sean Jones .10 .02
❑ 394 George Koonce .10 .02
❑ 395 Steve McMichael .20 .07
❑ 396 Bryce Paup .20 .07
❑ 397 Aaron Taylor .10 .02
❑ 398 Henry Ford .10 .02
❑ 399 Ernest Givins .20 .07
❑ 400 Jeremy Nunley RC .10 .02
❑ 401 Bo Orlando .10 .02
❑ 402 Al Smith .10 .02
❑ 403 Barron Wortham RC .10 .02
❑ 404 Trev Alberts .20 .07
❑ 405 Tony Bennett .10 .02
❑ 406 Kerry Cash .10 .02
❑ 407 Sean Dawkins RC .40 .15
❑ 408 Marshall Faulk 2.00 .75
❑ 409 Jim Harbaugh .40 .15
❑ 410 Jeff Herrod .10 .02
❑ 411 Kimble Anders .20 .07
❑ 412 Donnell Bennett .20 .07
❑ 413 J.J. Birden .10 .02
❑ 414 Mark Collins .10 .02
❑ 415 Lake Dawson RC .20 .07
❑ 416 Greg Hill .40 .15
❑ 417 Charles Mincy .10 .02
❑ 418 Greg Biekert .10 .02
❑ 419 Rob Fredrickson .20 .07
❑ 420 Nolan Harrison .10 .02
❑ 421 Jeff Jaeger .10 .02
❑ 422 Albert Lewis .10 .02
❑ 423 Chester McGlockton .10 .02
❑ 424 Tom Rathman .10 .02
❑ 425 Harvey Williams .20 .07
❑ 426 Isaac Bruce 1.50 .60
❑ 427 Troy Drayton .10 .02
❑ 428 Wayne Gandy .10 .02
❑ 429 Fred Stokes .10 .02
❑ 430 Robert Young .10 .02
❑ 431 Gene Atkins .10 .02
❑ 432 Aubrey Beavers .10 .02

❑ 433 Tim Bowens .20 .07
❑ 434 Keith Byars .10 .02
❑ 435 Jeff Cross .10 .02
❑ 436 Mark Ingram .10 .02
❑ 437 Keith Jackson .10 .02
❑ 438 Michael Stewart .10 .02
❑ 439 Chris Hinton .10 .02
❑ 440 Qadry Ismail .40 .15
❑ 441 Carlos Jenkins .10 .02
❑ 442 Warren Moon .40 .15
❑ 443 David Palmer .20 .07
❑ 444 Jake Reed .20 .07
❑ 445 Robert Smith .40 .15
❑ 446 Todd Steussie .20 .07
❑ 447 Dewayne Washington .20 .07
❑ 448 Marion Butts .10 .02
❑ 449 Tim Goad .10 .02
❑ 450 Myron Guyton .10 .02
❑ 451 Kevin Lee RC .10 .02
❑ 452 Willie McGinest .40 .15
❑ 453 Ricky Reynolds .10 .02
❑ 454 Michael Timpson .10 .02
❑ 455 Morten Andersen .10 .02
❑ 456 Jim Everett .20 .07
❑ 457 Michael Haynes .20 .07
❑ 458 Joe Johnson .10 .02
❑ 459 Wayne Martin .10 .02
❑ 460 Sam Mills .10 .02
❑ 461 Irv Smith .10 .02
❑ 462 Carlton Bailey .10 .02
❑ 463 Chris Calloway .10 .02
❑ 464 Mark Jackson .10 .02
❑ 465 Thomas Lewis .20 .07
❑ 466 Thomas Randolph .10 .02
❑ 467 Stevie Anderson RC .10 .02
❑ 468 Brad Baxter .10 .02
❑ 469 Aaron Glenn .20 .07
❑ 470 Jeff Lageman .10 .02
❑ 471 Johnny Mitchell .10 .02
❑ 472 Art Monk .20 .07
❑ 473 William Fuller .10 .02
❑ 474 Charlie Garner RC 1.25 .50
❑ 475 Vaughn Hebron .10 .02
❑ 476 Bill Romanowski .10 .02
❑ 477 William Thomas .10 .02
❑ 478 Greg Townsend .10 .02
❑ 479 Bernard Williams .10 .02
❑ 480 Calvin Williams .20 .07
❑ 481 Eric Green .10 .02
❑ 482 Charles Johnson .40 .15
❑ 483 Carnell Lake .10 .02
❑ 484 Byron Bam Morris RC .20 .07
❑ 485 John L. Williams .10 .02
❑ 486 Darren Carrington .10 .02
❑ 487 Andre Coleman RC .10 .02
❑ 488 Isaac Davis .10 .02
❑ 489 Dwayne Harper .10 .02
❑ 490 Tony Martin .40 .15
❑ 491 Mark Seay RC .40 .15
❑ 492 Richard Dent .20 .07
❑ 493 William Floyd .40 .15
❑ 494 Rickey Jackson .10 .02
❑ 495 Brent Jones .20 .07
❑ 496 Ken Norton Jr. .20 .07
❑ 497 Gary Plummer .10 .02
❑ 498 Deion Sanders .75 .30
❑ 499 John Taylor .20 .07
❑ 500 Lee Woodall RC .10 .02
❑ 501 Bryant Young .40 .15
❑ 502 Sam Adams .20 .07
❑ 503 Howard Ballard .10 .02
❑ 504 Michael Bates .10 .02
❑ 505 Robert Blackmon .10 .02
❑ 506 John Kasay .10 .02
❑ 507 Kelvin Martin .10 .02
❑ 508 Kevin Mawae RC .40 .15
❑ 509 Rufus Porter .10 .02
❑ 510 Lawrence Dawsey .10 .02
❑ 511 Trent Dilfer RC 1.25 .50
❑ 512 Thomas Everett .10 .02
❑ 513 Jackie Harris .10 .02
❑ 514 Errict Rhett .20 .07
❑ 515 Henry Ellard .20 .07
❑ 516 John Friesz .20 .07
❑ 517 Ken Harvey .10 .02
❑ 518 Ethan Horton .10 .02
❑ 519 Tre Johnson .10 .02
❑ 520 Jim Lachey .10 .02
❑ 521 Heath Shuler .40 .15
❑ 522 Tony Woods .10 .02
❑ 523 Checklist .10 .02
❑ 524 Checklist .10 .02
❑ 525 Checklist .10 .02

1995 Ultra

❑ COMPLETE SET (550) 50.00 20.00
❑ COMP.SERIES 1 (350) 25.00 10.00
❑ COMP.SERIES 2 (200) 25.00 10.00
❑ 1 Michael Bankston .10 .02
❑ 2 Larry Centers .20 .07
❑ 3 Garrison Hearst .40 .15
❑ 4 Eric Hill .10 .02
❑ 5 Seth Joyner .10 .02
❑ 6 Lorenzo Lynch .10 .02
❑ 7 Jamir Miller .10 .02
❑ 8 Clyde Simmons .10 .02
❑ 9 Eric Swann .20 .07
❑ 10 Aeneas Williams .10 .02
❑ 11 Devin Bush RC .10 .02
❑ 12 Ron Davis RC .10 .02
❑ 13 Chris Doleman .10 .02
❑ 14 Bert Emanuel .40 .15
❑ 15 Jeff George .20 .07
❑ 16 Roger Harper .10 .02
❑ 17 Craig Heyward .20 .07
❑ 18 Pierce Holt .10 .02
❑ 19 D.J. Johnson .10 .02
❑ 20 Terance Mathis .20 .07
❑ 21 Chuck Smith .10 .02
❑ 22 Jessie Tuggle .10 .02
❑ 23 Cornelius Bennett .20 .07
❑ 24 Ruben Brown RC .40 .15
❑ 25 Jeff Burris .10 .02
❑ 26 Matt Darby .10 .02
❑ 27 Phil Hansen .10 .02
❑ 28 Henry Jones .10 .02
❑ 29 Jim Kelly .40 .15
❑ 30 Mark Maddox RC .10 .02
❑ 31 Andre Reed .20 .07
❑ 32 Bruce Smith .40 .15
❑ 33 Don Beebe .10 .02
❑ 34 Kerry Collins RC 1.50 .60
❑ 35 Darion Conner .10 .02
❑ 36 Pete Metzelaars .10 .02
❑ 37 Sam Mills .20 .07
❑ 38 Tyrone Poole RC .40 .15
❑ 39 Joe Cain .10 .02
❑ 40 Mark Carrier DB .10 .02
❑ 41 Curtis Conway .40 .15
❑ 42 Jeff Graham .10 .02
❑ 43 Raymont Harris .10 .02
❑ 44 Erik Kramer .10 .02
❑ 45 Rashaan Salaam RC .20 .07
❑ 46 Lewis Tillman .10 .02
❑ 47 Donnell Woolford .10 .02
❑ 48 Chris Zorich .10 .02
❑ 49 Jeff Blake RC .75 .30
❑ 50 Mike Brim .10 .02
❑ 51 Ki-Jana Carter RC .40 .15
❑ 52 James Francis .10 .02
❑ 53 Carl Pickens .20 .07
❑ 54 Darnay Scott .20 .07
❑ 55 Steve Tovar .10 .02
❑ 56 Dan Wilkinson .20 .07
❑ 57 Alfred Williams .10 .02
❑ 58 Darryl Williams .10 .02
❑ 59 Derrick Alexander WR .40 .15
❑ 60 Rob Burnett .10 .02
❑ 61 Steve Everitt .10 .02
❑ 62 Leroy Hoard .10 .02
❑ 63 Michael Jackson .20 .07
❑ 64 Pepper Johnson .10 .02
❑ 65 Tony Jones T .10 .02
❑ 66 Antonio Langham .10 .02
❑ 67 Anthony Pleasant .10 .02
❑ 68 Craig Powell RC .10 .02
❑ 69 Vinny Testaverde .20 .07
❑ 70 Eric Turner .10 .02
❑ 71 Troy Aikman 1.50 .60
❑ 72 Charles Haley .20 .07
❑ 73 Michael Irvin .40 .15
❑ 74 Daryl Johnston .20 .07
❑ 75 Robert Jones .10 .02
❑ 76 Leon Lett .10 .02
❑ 77 Russell Maryland .10 .02
❑ 78 Jay Novacek .20 .07
❑ 79 Darrin Smith .10 .02
❑ 80 Emmitt Smith 2.50 1.25
❑ 81 Kevin Smith .10 .02
❑ 82 Erik Williams .10 .02
❑ 83 Kevin Williams WR .20 .07
❑ 84 Sherman Williams RC .10 .02
❑ 85 Darren Woodson .20 .07
❑ 86 Elijah Alexander RC .10 .02
❑ 87 Steve Atwater .10 .02
❑ 88 Ray Crockett .10 .02
❑ 89 Shane Dronett .10 .02
❑ 90 Jason Elam .20 .07
❑ 91 John Elway 3.00 1.25
❑ 92 Simon Fletcher .10 .02
❑ 93 Glyn Milburn .10 .02
❑ 94 Anthony Miller .20 .07
❑ 95 Leonard Russell .10 .02
❑ 96 Shannon Sharpe .20 .07
❑ 97 Bennie Blades .10 .02
❑ 98 Lomas Brown .10 .02
❑ 99 Willie Clay .10 .02
❑ 100 Luther Elliss RC .10 .02
❑ 101 Mike Johnson .10 .02
❑ 102 Robert Massey .10 .02
❑ 103 Scott Mitchell .20 .07
❑ 104 Herman Moore .40 .15
❑ 105 Brett Perriman .20 .07
❑ 106 Robert Porcher .10 .02
❑ 107 Barry Sanders 2.50 1.00
❑ 108 Chris Spielman .20 .07
❑ 109 Edgar Bennett .20 .07
❑ 110 Robert Brooks .40 .15
❑ 111 LeRoy Butler .10 .02
❑ 112 Brett Favre 3.00 1.50
❑ 113 Sean Jones .10 .02
❑ 114 John Jurkovic .10 .02
❑ 115 George Koonce .10 .02
❑ 116 Wayne Simmons .10 .02
❑ 117 George Teague .10 .02
❑ 118 Reggie White .40 .15
❑ 119 Micheal Barrow .10 .02
❑ 120 Gary Brown .10 .02
❑ 121 Cody Carlson .10 .02
❑ 122 Ray Childress .10 .02
❑ 123 Cris Dishman .10 .02
❑ 124 Bruce Matthews .10 .02
❑ 125 Steve McNair RC 3.00 1.25
❑ 126 Marcus Robertson .10 .02
❑ 127 Webster Slaughter .10 .02
❑ 128 Al Smith .10 .02
❑ 129 Tony Bennett .10 .02
❑ 130 Ray Buchanan .10 .02
❑ 131 Quentin Coryatt .20 .07
❑ 132 Sean Dawkins .20 .07
❑ 133 Marshall Faulk 2.00 .75
❑ 134 Stephen Grant RC .10 .02
❑ 135 Jim Harbaugh .20 .07
❑ 136 Jeff Herrod .10 .02
❑ 137 Ellis Johnson RC .10 .02
❑ 138 Tony Siragusa .10 .02
❑ 139 Steve Beuerlein .20 .07
❑ 140 Tony Boselli RC .40 .15
❑ 141 Darren Carrington .10 .02
❑ 142 Reggie Cobb .10 .02
❑ 143 Kelvin Martin .10 .02
❑ 144 Kelvin Pritchett .10 .02
❑ 145 Joel Smeenge .10 .02

❑ 146 James O. Stewart RC 1.25 .50
❑ 147 Marcus Allen .40 .15
❑ 148 Kimble Anders .20 .07
❑ 149 Dale Carter .20 .07
❑ 150 Mark Collins .10 .02
❑ 151 Willie Davis .20 .07
❑ 152 Lake Dawson .20 .07
❑ 153 Greg Hill .20 .07
❑ 154 Trezelle Jenkins RC .10 .02
❑ 155 Darren Mickell .10 .02
❑ 156 Tracy Simien .10 .02
❑ 157 Neil Smith .20 .07
❑ 158 William White .10 .02
❑ 159 Joe Aska RC .10 .02
❑ 160 Greg Biekert .10 .02
❑ 161 Tim Brown .40 .15
❑ 162 Rob Fredrickson .10 .02
❑ 163 Andrew Glover RC .10 .02
❑ 164 Jeff Hostetler .20 .07
❑ 165 Rocket Ismail .20 .07
❑ 166 Napoleon Kaufman RC 1.25 .50
❑ 167 Terry McDaniel .10 .02
❑ 168 Chester McGlockton .20 .07
❑ 169 Anthony Smith .10 .02
❑ 170 Harvey Williams .10 .02
❑ 171 Steve Wisniewski .10 .02
❑ 172 Gene Atkins .10 .02
❑ 173 Aubrey Beavers .10 .02
❑ 174 Tim Bowens .10 .02
❑ 175 Bryan Cox .10 .02
❑ 176 Jeff Cross .10 .02
❑ 177 Irving Fryar .20 .07
❑ 178 Dan Marino 3.00 1.25
❑ 179 O.J. McDuffie .40 .15
❑ 180 Billy Milner RC .10 .02
❑ 181 Bernie Parmalee .20 .07
❑ 182 Troy Vincent .10 .02
❑ 183 Richmond Webb .10 .02
❑ 184 Derrick Alexander DE RC .10 .02
❑ 185 Cris Carter .40 .15
❑ 186 Jack Del Rio .10 .02
❑ 187 Qadry Ismail .20 .07
❑ 188 Ed McDaniel .10 .02
❑ 189 Randall McDaniel .10 .02
❑ 190 Warren Moon .20 .07
❑ 191 John Randle .20 .07
❑ 192 Jake Reed .20 .07
❑ 193 Fuad Reveiz .10 .02
❑ 194 Korey Stringer RC .20 .07
❑ 195 Dewayne Washington .20 .07
❑ 196 Bruce Armstrong .10 .02
❑ 197 Drew Bledsoe 1.00 .40
❑ 198 Vincent Brisby .10 .02
❑ 199 Vincent Brown .10 .02
❑ 200 Marion Butts .10 .02
❑ 201 Ben Coates .20 .07
❑ 202 Myron Guyton .10 .02
❑ 203 Maurice Hurst .10 .02
❑ 204 Mike Jones .10 .02
❑ 205 Ty Law RC 1.50 .60
❑ 206 Willie McGinest .20 .07
❑ 207 Chris Slade .10 .02
❑ 208 Mario Bates .20 .07
❑ 209 Quinn Early .20 .07
❑ 210 Jim Everett .10 .02
❑ 211 Mark Fields RC .40 .15
❑ 212 Michael Haynes .20 .07
❑ 213 Tyrone Hughes .20 .07
❑ 214 Joe Johnson .10 .02
❑ 215 Wayne Martin .10 .02
❑ 216 Willie Roaf .10 .02
❑ 217 Irv Smith .10 .02
❑ 218 Jimmy Spencer .10 .02
❑ 219 Winfred Tubbs .10 .02
❑ 220 Renaldo Turnbull .10 .02
❑ 221 Michael Brooks .10 .02
❑ 222 Dave Brown .20 .07
❑ 223 Chris Calloway .10 .02
❑ 224 Howard Cross .10 .02
❑ 225 John Elliott .10 .02
❑ 226 Keith Hamilton .10 .02
❑ 227 Rodney Hampton .20 .07
❑ 228 Thomas Lewis .20 .07
❑ 229 Thomas Randolph .10 .02
❑ 230 Mike Sherrard .10 .02
❑ 231 Michael Strahan .40 .15
❑ 232 Tyrone Wheatley RC 1.25 .50
❑ 233 Brad Baxter .10 .02
❑ 234 Kyle Brady RC .40 .15
❑ 235 Kyle Clifton .10 .02
❑ 236 Hugh Douglas RC .40 .15
❑ 237 Boomer Esiason .20 .07
❑ 238 Aaron Glenn .10 .02
❑ 239 Bobby Houston .10 .02
❑ 240 Johnny Johnson .10 .02
❑ 241 Mo Lewis .10 .02
❑ 242 Johnny Mitchell .10 .02
❑ 243 Marvin Washington .10 .02
❑ 244 Fred Barnett .20 .07
❑ 245 Randall Cunningham .40 .15
❑ 246 William Fuller .10 .02
❑ 247 Charlie Garner .40 .15
❑ 248 Andy Harmon .10 .02
❑ 249 Greg Jackson .10 .02
❑ 250 Mike Mamula RC .10 .02
❑ 251 Bill Romanowski .10 .02
❑ 252 Bobby Taylor RC .40 .15
❑ 253 William Thomas .10 .02
❑ 254 Calvin Williams .20 .07
❑ 255 Michael Zordich .10 .02
❑ 256 Chad Brown .20 .07
❑ 257 Mark Bruener RC .20 .07
❑ 258 Dermontti Dawson .20 .07
❑ 259 Barry Foster .20 .07
❑ 260 Kevin Greene .20 .07
❑ 261 Charles Johnson .20 .07
❑ 262 Carnell Lake .10 .02
❑ 263 Greg Lloyd .20 .07
❑ 264 Byron Bam Morris .10 .02
❑ 265 Neil O'Donnell .20 .07
❑ 266 Darren Perry .10 .02
❑ 267 Ray Seals .10 .02
❑ 268 Kordell Stewart RC 1.50 .60
❑ 269 John L. Williams .10 .02
❑ 270 Rod Woodson .20 .07
❑ 271 Jerome Bettis .40 .15
❑ 272 Isaac Bruce .75 .30
❑ 273 Kevin Carter RC .40 .15
❑ 274 Shane Conlan .10 .02
❑ 275 Troy Drayton .10 .02
❑ 276 Sean Gilbert .20 .07
❑ 277 Todd Lyght .10 .02
❑ 278 Chris Miller .10 .02
❑ 279 Anthony Newman .10 .02
❑ 280 Roman Phifer .10 .02
❑ 281 Robert Young .10 .02
❑ 282 John Carney .10 .02
❑ 283 Andre Coleman .10 .02
❑ 284 Courtney Hall .10 .02
❑ 285 Ronnie Harmon .10 .02
❑ 286 Dwayne Harper .10 .02
❑ 287 Stan Humphries .20 .07
❑ 288 Shawn Jefferson .10 .02
❑ 289 Tony Martin .20 .07
❑ 290 Natrone Means .20 .07
❑ 291 Chris Mims .10 .02
❑ 292 Leslie O'Neal .20 .07
❑ 293 Junior Seau .40 .15
❑ 294 Mark Seay .20 .07
❑ 295 Eric Davis .10 .02
❑ 296 William Floyd .20 .07
❑ 297 Merton Hanks .10 .02
❑ 298 Brent Jones .10 .02
❑ 299 Ken Norton Jr. .20 .07
❑ 300 Gary Plummer .10 .02
❑ 301 Jerry Rice 1.50 .60
❑ 302 Deion Sanders 1.00 .40
❑ 303 Jesse Sapolu .10 .02
❑ 304 J.J. Stokes RC .40 .15
❑ 305 Dana Stubblefield .20 .07
❑ 306 John Taylor .10 .02
❑ 307 Steve Wallace .10 .02
❑ 308 Lee Woodall .10 .02
❑ 309 Bryant Young .20 .07
❑ 310 Steve Young 1.25 .50
❑ 311 Sam Adams .10 .02
❑ 312 Howard Ballard .10 .02
❑ 313 Robert Blackmon .10 .02
❑ 314 Brian Blades .20 .07
❑ 315 Joey Galloway RC 1.50 .60
❑ 316 Carlton Gray .10 .02
❑ 317 Cortez Kennedy .20 .07
❑ 318 Rick Mirer .20 .07
❑ 319 Eugene Robinson .10 .02
❑ 320 Chris Warren .20 .07
❑ 321 Terry Wooden .10 .02
❑ 322 Derrick Brooks RC 1.50 .60
❑ 323 Lawrence Dawsey .10 .02
❑ 324 Trent Dilfer .40 .15
❑ 325 Santana Dotson .10 .02
❑ 326 Thomas Everett .10 .02
❑ 327 Paul Gruber .10 .02
❑ 328 Jackie Harris .10 .02
❑ 329 Courtney Hawkins .10 .02
❑ 330 Martin Mayhew .10 .02
❑ 331 Hardy Nickerson .10 .02
❑ 332 Errict Rhett .20 .07
❑ 333 Warren Sapp RC 1.50 .60
❑ 334 Charles Wilson .10 .02
❑ 335 Reggie Brooks .20 .07
❑ 336 Tom Carter .10 .02
❑ 337 Henry Ellard .20 .07
❑ 338 Ricky Ervins .10 .02
❑ 339 Darrell Green .10 .02
❑ 340 Ken Harvey .10 .02
❑ 341 Brian Mitchell .10 .02
❑ 342 Cory Raymer RC .10 .02
❑ 343 Heath Shuler .20 .07
❑ 344 Michael Westbrook RC .40 .15
❑ 345 Tony Woods .10 .02
❑ 346 Checklist .10 .02
❑ 347 Checklist .10 .02
❑ 348 Checklist .10 .02
❑ 349 Checklist .10 .02
❑ 350 Checklist .10 .02
❑ 351 Checklist .10 .02
❑ 352 Checklist .10 .02
❑ 353 Dave Krieg .10 .02
❑ 354 Rob Moore .20 .07
❑ 355 J.J. Birden .10 .02
❑ 356 Eric Metcalf .20 .07
❑ 357 Bryce Paup .20 .07
❑ 358 Willie Green .20 .07
❑ 359 Derrick Moore .10 .02
❑ 360 Michael Timpson .10 .02
❑ 361 Eric Bieniemy .10 .02
❑ 362 Keenan McCardell .40 .15
❑ 363 Andre Rison .20 .07
❑ 364 Lorenzo White .10 .02
❑ 365 Deion Sanders 1.00 .40
❑ 366 Wade Wilson .10 .02
❑ 367 Aaron Craver .10 .02
❑ 368 Michael Dean Perry .10 .02
❑ 369 Rod Smith WR RC 12.00 5.00
❑ 370 Henry Thomas .10 .02
❑ 371 Mark Ingram .10 .02
❑ 372 Chris Chandler .20 .07
❑ 373 Mel Gray .10 .02
❑ 374 Flipper Anderson .10 .02
❑ 375 Craig Erickson .10 .02
❑ 376 Mark Brunell 1.00 .40
❑ 377 Ernest Givins .10 .02
❑ 378 Randy Jordan .10 .02
❑ 379 Webster Slaughter .10 .02
❑ 380 Tamarick Vanover RC .40 .15
❑ 381 Gary Clark .10 .02
❑ 382 Steve Emtman .10 .02
❑ 383 Eric Green .10 .02
❑ 384 Louis Oliver .10 .02
❑ 385 Robert Smith .40 .15
❑ 386 Dave Meggett .10 .02
❑ 387 Eric Allen .10 .02
❑ 388 Wesley Walls .20 .07
❑ 389 Herschel Walker .20 .07
❑ 390 Ronald Moore .10 .02
❑ 391 Adrian Murrell .20 .07
❑ 392 Charles Wilson .10 .02
❑ 393 Derrick Fenner .10 .02
❑ 394 Pat Swilling .10 .02
❑ 395 Kelvin Martin .10 .02
❑ 396 Rodney Peete .10 .02
❑ 397 Ricky Watters .20 .07
❑ 398 Erric Pegram .20 .07
❑ 399 Leonard Russell .10 .02
❑ 400 Alexander Wright .10 .02
❑ 401 Darrien Gordon .10 .02
❑ 402 Alfred Pupunu .10 .02
❑ 403 Elvis Grbac .40 .15
❑ 404 Derek Loville .10 .02
❑ 405 Steve Broussard .10 .02
❑ 406 Ricky Proehl .10 .02

❑ 407 Bobby Joe Edmonds .10 .02
❑ 408 Alvin Harper .10 .02
❑ 409 Dave Moore RC .10 .02
❑ 410 Terry Allen .20 .07
❑ 411 Gus Frerotte .20 .07
❑ 412 Leslie Shepherd RC .20 .07
❑ 413 Stoney Case RC .10 .02
❑ 414 Frank Sanders RC .40 .15
❑ 415 Roell Preston RC .20 .07
❑ 416 Lorenzo Styles RC .10 .02
❑ 417 Justin Armour RC .10 .02
❑ 418 Todd Collins RC .20 .07
❑ 419 Darick Holmes RC .20 .07
❑ 420 Kerry Collins .60 .25
❑ 421 Tyrone Poole .20 .07
❑ 422 Rashaan Salaam .20 .07
❑ 423 Todd Sauerbrun RC .10 .02
❑ 424 Ki-Jana Carter .40 .15
❑ 425 David Dunn RC .10 .02
❑ 426 Ernest Hunter RC .10 .02
❑ 427 Eric Zeier RC .40 .15
❑ 428 Eric Bjornson RC .10 .02
❑ 429 Sherman Williams .10 .02
❑ 430 Terrell Davis RC 2.50 1.00
❑ 431 Luther Elliss .10 .02
❑ 432 Kez McCorvey RC .10 .02
❑ 433 Antonio Freeman RC 1.25 .50
❑ 434 Craig Newsome RC .10 .02
❑ 435 Steve McNair 1.50 .60
❑ 436 Chris Sanders RC .20 .07
❑ 437 Zack Crockett RC .20 .07
❑ 438 Ellis Johnson .10 .02
❑ 439 Tony Boselli .40 .15
❑ 440 James O. Stewart .40 .15
❑ 441 Trezelle Jenkins .10 .02
❑ 442 Tamarick Vanover .40 .15
❑ 443 Derrick Alexander DE .10 .02
❑ 444 Chad May RC .10 .02
❑ 445 James A.Stewart RC .10 .02
❑ 446 Ty Law .40 .15
❑ 447 Curtis Martin RC 3.00 1.25
❑ 448 Will Moore RC .10 .02
❑ 449 Mark Fields .20 .07
❑ 450 Ray Zellars RC .20 .07
❑ 451 Charles Way RC .10 .02
❑ 452 Tyrone Wheatley .40 .15
❑ 453 Kyle Brady .40 .15
❑ 454 Wayne Chrebet RC 2.50 1.00
❑ 455 Hugh Douglas .20 .07
❑ 456 Chris T.Jones RC .10 .02
❑ 457 Mike Mamula .10 .02
❑ 458 Fred McCrary RC .10 .02
❑ 459 Bobby Taylor .40 .15
❑ 460 Mark Bruener .20 .07
❑ 461 Kordell Stewart .60 .25
❑ 462 Kevin Carter .20 .07
❑ 463 Lovell Pinkney RC .10 .02
❑ 464 Johnny Thomas WR RC .10 .02
❑ 465 Terrell Fletcher RC .10 .02
❑ 466 Jimmy Oliver RC .10 .02
❑ 467 J.J. Stokes .40 .15
❑ 468 Christian Fauria RC .20 .07
❑ 469 Joey Galloway .60 .25
❑ 470 Derrick Brooks .60 .25
❑ 471 Warren Sapp .40 .15
❑ 472 Michael Westbrook .40 .15
❑ 473 Garrison Hearst ES .40 .15
❑ 474 Jeff George ES .20 .07
❑ 475 Terance Mathis ES .20 .07
❑ 476 Andre Reed ES .20 .07
❑ 477 Bruce Smith ES .40 .15
❑ 478 Lamar Lathon ES .10 .02
❑ 479 Curtis Conway ES .40 .15
❑ 480 Jeff Blake ES .40 .15
❑ 481 Carl Pickens ES .20 .07
❑ 482 Eric Turner ES .10 .02
❑ 483 Troy Aikman ES .75 .30
❑ 484 Michael Irvin ES .40 .15
❑ 485 Emmitt Smith ES 1.25 .50
❑ 486 John Elway ES 1.50 .60
❑ 487 Shannon Sharpe ES .20 .07
❑ 488 Herman Moore ES .40 .15
❑ 489 Barry Sanders ES 1.25 .50
❑ 490 Brett Favre ES 1.50 .60
❑ 491 Reggie White ES .40 .15
❑ 492 Haywood Jeffires ES .10 .02
❑ 493 Sean Dawkins ES .10 .02
❑ 494 Marshall Faulk ES 1.00 .40
❑ 495 Desmond Howard ES .20 .07
❑ 496 Steve Bono ES .20 .07
❑ 497 Derrick Thomas ES .40 .15
❑ 498 Irving Fryar ES .20 .07
❑ 499 Terry Kirby ES .20 .07
❑ 500 Dan Marino ES 1.50 .60
❑ 501 O.J. McDuffie ES .40 .15
❑ 502 Cris Carter ES .40 .15
❑ 503 Warren Moon ES .20 .07
❑ 504 Jake Reed ES .20 .07
❑ 505 Drew Bledsoe ES .40 .15
❑ 506 Ben Coates ES .20 .07
❑ 507 Jim Everett ES .10 .02
❑ 508 Rodney Hampton ES .20 .07
❑ 509 Mo Lewis ES .10 .02
❑ 510 Tim Brown ES .40 .15
❑ 511 Jeff Hostetler ES .20 .07
❑ 512 Rocket Ismail ES .20 .07
❑ 513 Chester McGlockton ES .20 .07
❑ 514 Fred Barnett ES .20 .07
❑ 515 Greg Lloyd ES .20 .07
❑ 516 Byron Bam Morris ES .10 .02
❑ 517 Rod Woodson ES .20 .07
❑ 518 Jerome Bettis ES .40 .15
❑ 519 Isaac Bruce ES .40 .15
❑ 520 Stan Humphries ES .20 .07
❑ 521 Natrone Means ES .20 .07
❑ 522 Junior Seau ES .40 .15
❑ 523 William Floyd ES .20 .07
❑ 524 Jerry Rice ES .75 .30
❑ 525 Steve Young ES .60 .25
❑ 526 Cortez Kennedy ES .20 .07
❑ 527 Rick Mirer ES .20 .07
❑ 528 Chris Warren ES .20 .07
❑ 529 Trent Dilfer ES .40 .15
❑ 530 Errict Rhett ES .20 .07
❑ 531 Darrell Green ES .10 .02
❑ 532 Heath Shuler ES .20 .07
❑ 533 Stoney Case RO .10 .02
❑ 534 Eric Zeier RO .20 .07
❑ 535 Kerry Collins RO .20 .07
❑ 536 Steve McNair RO 1.25 .50
❑ 537 Kordell Stewart RO .60 .25
❑ 538 Rob Johnson RO RC 1.00 .40
❑ 539 Eric Ball EE .10 .02
❑ 540 Darrick Brownlow EE .10 .02
❑ 541 Paul Butcher EE .10 .02
❑ 542 Carlester Crumpler EE .10 .02
❑ 543 Maurice Douglas EE .10 .02
❑ 544 Keith Elias EE RC .10 .02
❑ 545 Kenneth Gant EE .10 .02
❑ 546 Corey Harris EE .10 .02
❑ 547 Andre Hastings EE .20 .07
❑ 548 Thomas Homco EE .10 .02
❑ 549 Lenny McGill EE .10 .02
❑ 550 Mark Pike EE .10 .02
❑ P1 Promo Sheet 2.00 .75
❑ P264 Byron Bam Morris Prototype 1.00 .40

1996 Ultra

❑ COMPLETE SET (200) 25.00 10.00
❑ 1 Larry Centers .25 .08
❑ 2 Garrison Hearst .25 .08
❑ 3 Rob Moore .25 .08
❑ 4 Eric Swann .10 .02
❑ 5 Aeneas Williams .10 .02
❑ 6 Bert Emanuel .25 .08
❑ 7 Jeff George .25 .08
❑ 8 Craig Heyward .10 .02
❑ 9 Terance Mathis .10 .02
❑ 10 Eric Metcalf .10 .02
❑ 11 Cornelius Bennett .10 .02
❑ 12 Darick Holmes .10 .02
❑ 13 Jim Kelly .50 .20
❑ 14 Bryce Paup .10 .02
❑ 15 Bruce Smith .25 .08
❑ 16 Mark Carrier WR .10 .02
❑ 17 Kerry Collins .50 .20
❑ 18 Lamar Lathon .10 .02
❑ 19 Derrick Moore .10 .02
❑ 20 Tyrone Poole .10 .02
❑ 21 Curtis Conway .50 .20
❑ 22 Jeff Graham .10 .02
❑ 23 Raymont Harris .25 .08
❑ 24 Erik Kramer .10 .02
❑ 25 Rashaan Salaam .25 .08
❑ 26 Jeff Blake .50 .20
❑ 27 Ki-Jana Carter .25 .08
❑ 28 Carl Pickens .25 .08
❑ 29 Darnay Scott .25 .08
❑ 30 Dan Wilkinson .10 .02
❑ 31 Leroy Hoard .10 .02
❑ 32 Michael Jackson .25 .08
❑ 33 Andre Rison .25 .08
❑ 34 Vinny Testaverde .25 .08
❑ 35 Eric Turner .10 .02
❑ 36 Troy Aikman 1.25 .50
❑ 37 Charles Haley .25 .08
❑ 38 Michael Irvin .50 .20
❑ 39 Daryl Johnston .25 .08
❑ 40 Jay Novacek .10 .02
❑ 41 Deion Sanders .75 .30
❑ 42 Emmitt Smith 2.00 .75
❑ 43 Steve Atwater .10 .02
❑ 44 Terrell Davis 1.00 .40
❑ 45 John Elway 2.50 1.00
❑ 46 Anthony Miller .25 .08
❑ 47 Shannon Sharpe .25 .08
❑ 48 Scott Mitchell .25 .08
❑ 49 Herman Moore .25 .08
❑ 50 Johnnie Morton .25 .08
❑ 51 Brett Perriman .10 .02
❑ 52 Barry Sanders 2.00 .75
❑ 53 Chris Spielman .10 .02
❑ 54 Edgar Bennett .25 .08
❑ 55 Robert Brooks .50 .20
❑ 56 Mark Chmura .25 .08
❑ 57 Brett Favre 2.50 1.00
❑ 58 Reggie White .50 .20
❑ 59 Mel Gray .10 .02
❑ 60 Haywood Jeffires .10 .02
❑ 61 Steve McNair 1.00 .40
❑ 62 Chris Sanders .25 .08
❑ 63 Rodney Thomas .10 .02
❑ 64 Quentin Coryatt .10 .02
❑ 65 Sean Dawkins .10 .02
❑ 66 Ken Dilger .25 .08
❑ 67 Marshall Faulk .60 .25
❑ 68 Jim Harbaugh .25 .08
❑ 69 Tony Boselli .10 .02
❑ 70 Mark Brunell .75 .30
❑ 71 Desmond Howard .25 .08
❑ 72 Jimmy Smith .50 .20
❑ 73 James O. Stewart .25 .08
❑ 74 Marcus Allen .50 .20
❑ 75 Steve Bono .10 .02
❑ 76 Lake Dawson .10 .02
❑ 77 Neil Smith .25 .08
❑ 78 Derrick Thomas .50 .20
❑ 79 Tamarick Vanover .25 .08
❑ 80 Bryan Cox .10 .02
❑ 81 Irving Fryar .25 .08
❑ 82 Eric Green .10 .02
❑ 83 Dan Marino 2.50 1.00
❑ 84 O.J. McDuffie .25 .08
❑ 85 Bernie Parmalee .10 .02
❑ 86 Cris Carter .50 .20
❑ 87 Qadry Ismail .25 .08
❑ 88 Warren Moon .25 .08
❑ 89 Jake Reed .25 .08
❑ 90 Robert Smith .25 .08
❑ 91 Drew Bledsoe .75 .30
❑ 92 Vincent Brisby .10 .02
❑ 93 Ben Coates .25 .08
❑ 94 Curtis Martin 1.00 .40

❑ 95	Willie McGinest	.10	.02
❑ 96	Dave Meggett	.10	.02
❑ 97	Mario Bates	.25	.08
❑ 98	Quinn Early	.10	.02
❑ 99	Jim Everett	.10	.02
❑ 100	Michael Haynes	.10	.02
❑ 101	Renaldo Turnbull	.10	.02
❑ 102	Dave Brown	.10	.02
❑ 103	Rodney Hampton	.25	.08
❑ 104	Mike Sherrard	.10	.02
❑ 105	Phillippi Sparks	.10	.02
❑ 106	Tyrone Wheatley	.25	.08
❑ 107	Hugh Douglas	.25	.08
❑ 108	Boomer Esiason	.25	.08
❑ 109	Aaron Glenn	.10	.02
❑ 110	Mo Lewis	.10	.02
❑ 111	Johnny Mitchell	.10	.02
❑ 112	Tim Brown	.50	.20
❑ 113	Jeff Hostetler	.10	.02
❑ 114	Rocket Ismail	.10	.02
❑ 115	Chester McGlockton	.10	.02
❑ 116	Harvey Williams	.10	.02
❑ 117	Fred Barnett	.10	.02
❑ 118	William Fuller	.10	.02
❑ 119	Charlie Garner	.25	.08
❑ 120	Ricky Watters	.25	.08
❑ 121	Calvin Williams	.10	.02
❑ 122	Kevin Greene	.25	.08
❑ 123	Greg Lloyd	.25	.08
❑ 124	Byron Bam Morris	.10	.02
❑ 125	Neil O'Donnell	.25	.08
❑ 126	Erric Pegram	.10	.02
❑ 127	Kordell Stewart	.50	.20
❑ 128	Yancey Thigpen	.25	.08
❑ 129	Rod Woodson	.25	.08
❑ 130	Jerome Bettis	.50	.20
❑ 131	Isaac Bruce	.50	.20
❑ 132	Troy Drayton	.10	.02
❑ 133	Sean Gilbert	.10	.02
❑ 134	Chris Miller	.10	.02
❑ 135	Andre Coleman	.10	.02
❑ 136	Ronnie Harmon	.10	.02
❑ 137	Aaron Hayden RC	.10	.02
❑ 138	Stan Humphries	.25	.08
❑ 139	Natrone Means	.25	.08
❑ 140	Junior Seau	.50	.20
❑ 141	William Floyd	.25	.08
❑ 142	Merton Hanks	.10	.02
❑ 143	Brent Jones	.10	.02
❑ 144	Derek Loville	.10	.02
❑ 145	Jerry Rice	1.25	.50
❑ 146	J.J. Stokes	.50	.20
❑ 147	Steve Young	1.00	.40
❑ 148	Brian Blades	.10	.02
❑ 149	Joey Galloway	.50	.20
❑ 150	Cortez Kennedy	.10	.02
❑ 151	Rick Mirer	.25	.08
❑ 152	Chris Warren	.25	.08
❑ 153	Derrick Brooks	.50	.20
❑ 154	Trent Dilfer	.50	.20
❑ 155	Alvin Harper	.10	.02
❑ 156	Jackie Harris	.10	.02
❑ 157	Hardy Nickerson	.10	.02
❑ 158	Errict Rhett	.25	.08
❑ 159	Terry Allen	.25	.08
❑ 160	Henry Ellard	.10	.02
❑ 161	Brian Mitchell	.10	.02
❑ 162	Heath Shuler	.25	.08
❑ 163	Michael Westbrook	.50	.20
❑ 164	Tim Biakabutuka RC	.50	.20
❑ 165	Tony Brackens RC	.50	.20
❑ 166	Rickey Dudley RC	.50	.20
❑ 167	Bobby Engram RC	.50	.20
❑ 168	Daryl Gardener RC	.10	.02
❑ 169	Eddie George RC	1.50	.60
❑ 170	Terry Glenn RC	1.25	.50
❑ 171	Kevin Hardy RC	.50	.20
❑ 172	Keyshawn Johnson RC	1.25	.50
❑ 173	Cedric Jones RC	.10	.02
❑ 174	Leeland McElroy RC	.25	.08
❑ 175	Jonathan Ogden RC	.50	.20
❑ 176	Lawrence Phillips RC	.50	.20
❑ 177	Simeon Rice RC	1.25	.50
❑ 178	Regan Upshaw RC	.10	.02
❑ 179	Justin Armour FI	.10	.02
❑ 180	Kyle Brady FI	.10	.02
❑ 181	Devin Bush FI	.10	.02
❑ 182	Kevin Carter FI	.10	.02
❑ 183	Wayne Chrebet FI	.75	.30
❑ 184	Napoleon Kaufman FI	.50	.20
❑ 185	Frank Sanders FI	.25	.08
❑ 186	Warren Sapp FI	.10	.02
❑ 187	Eric Zeier FI	.10	.02
❑ 188	Ray Zellars FI	.10	.02
❑ 189	Bill Brooks SW	.10	.02
❑ 190	Chris Calloway SW	.10	.02
❑ 191	Zack Crockett SW	.10	.02
❑ 192	Antonio Freeman SW	.50	.20
❑ 193	Tyrone Hughes SW	.10	.02
❑ 194	Daryl Johnston SW	.25	.08
❑ 195	Tony Martin SW	.10	.02
❑ 196	Keenan McCardell SW	.50	.20
❑ 197	Glyn Milburn SW	.10	.02
❑ 198	David Palmer SW	.10	.02
❑ 199	Checklist	.10	.02
❑ 200	Checklist	.10	.02
❑ P1	Promo Sheet	2.00	.75

1997 Ultra

❑	COMPLETE SET (350)	80.00	40.00
❑	COMP.SERIES 1 (200)	30.00	15.00
❑	COMP.SERIES 2 (150)	50.00	25.00
❑ 1	Brett Favre	2.50	1.25
❑ 2	Ricky Watters	.40	.15
❑ 3	Dan Marino	2.50	1.00
❑ 4	Bryan Still	.25	.08
❑ 5	Chester McGlockton	.25	.08
❑ 6	Tim Biakabutuka	.40	.15
❑ 7	Dave Brown	.25	.08
❑ 8	Mike Alstott	.60	.25
❑ 9	O.J. McDuffie	.40	.15
❑ 10	Mark Brunell	.75	.30
❑ 11	Michael Bates	.25	.08
❑ 12	Tyrone Wheatley	.40	.15
❑ 13	Eddie George	.60	.25
❑ 14	Kevin Greene	.40	.15
❑ 15	Jerris McPhail	.25	.08
❑ 16	Harvey Williams	.25	.08
❑ 17	Eric Swann	.25	.08
❑ 18	Carl Pickens	.40	.15
❑ 19	Terrell Davis	.75	.30
❑ 20	Charles Way	.25	.08
❑ 21	Jamie Asher	.25	.08
❑ 22	Qadry Ismail	.40	.15
❑ 23	Lawrence Phillips	.25	.08
❑ 24	John Friesz	.25	.08
❑ 25	Dorsey Levens	.60	.25
❑ 26	Willie McGinest	.25	.08
❑ 27	Chris T. Jones	.25	.08
❑ 28	Cortez Kennedy	.25	.08
❑ 29	Raymont Harris	.25	.08
❑ 30	William Roaf	.25	.08
❑ 31	Ted Johnson	.25	.08
❑ 32	Tony Martin	.40	.15
❑ 33	Jim Everett	.25	.08
❑ 34	Ray Zellars	.25	.08
❑ 35	Derrick Alexander WR	.40	.15
❑ 36	Leonard Russell	.25	.08
❑ 37	William Thomas	.25	.08
❑ 38	Karim Abdul-Jabbar	.40	.15
❑ 39	Kevin Turner	.25	.08
❑ 40	Robert Brooks	.40	.15
❑ 41	Kent Graham	.25	.08
❑ 42	Tony Brackens	.25	.08
❑ 43	Rodney Hampton	.40	.15
❑ 44	Drew Bledsoe	.75	.30
❑ 45	Barry Sanders	2.00	.75
❑ 46	Tim Brown	.60	.25
❑ 47	Reggie White	.60	.25
❑ 48	Terry Allen	.60	.25
❑ 49	Jim Harbaugh	.40	.15
❑ 50	John Elway	2.50	1.00
❑ 51	William Floyd	.40	.15
❑ 52	Michael Jackson	.40	.15
❑ 53	Larry Centers	.40	.15
❑ 54	Emmitt Smith	2.00	.75
❑ 55	Bruce Smith	.40	.15
❑ 56	Terrell Owens	.75	.30
❑ 57	Deion Sanders	.60	.25
❑ 58	Neil O'Donnell	.40	.15
❑ 59	Kordell Stewart	.60	.25
❑ 60	Bobby Engram	.40	.15
❑ 61	Keenan McCardell	.40	.15
❑ 62	Ben Coates	.40	.15
❑ 63	Curtis Martin	.75	.30
❑ 64	Hugh Douglas	.25	.08
❑ 65	Eric Moulds	.60	.25
❑ 66	Derrick Thomas	.60	.25
❑ 67	Byron Bam Morris	.25	.08
❑ 68	Bryan Cox	.25	.08
❑ 69	Rob Moore	.40	.15
❑ 70	Michael Haynes	.25	.08
❑ 71	Brian Mitchell	.25	.08
❑ 72	Alex Molden	.25	.08
❑ 73	Steve Young	.75	.30
❑ 74	Andre Reed	.40	.15
❑ 75	Michael Westbrook	.40	.15
❑ 76	Eric Metcalf	.40	.15
❑ 77	Tony Banks	.40	.15
❑ 78	Ken Dilger	.25	.08
❑ 79	John Henry Mills RC	.25	.08
❑ 80	Ashley Ambrose	.25	.08
❑ 81	Jason Dunn	.25	.08
❑ 82	Trent Dilfer	.60	.25
❑ 83	Wayne Chrebet	.60	.25
❑ 84	Ty Detmer	.40	.15
❑ 85	Aeneas Williams	.25	.08
❑ 86	Frank Wycheck	.25	.08
❑ 87	Jessie Tuggle	.25	.08
❑ 88	Steve McNair	.75	.30
❑ 89	Chris Slade	.25	.08
❑ 90	Anthony Johnson	.25	.08
❑ 91	Simeon Rice	.40	.15
❑ 92	Mike Tomczak	.25	.08
❑ 93	Sean Jones	.25	.08
❑ 94	Wesley Walls	.40	.15
❑ 95	Thurman Thomas	.60	.25
❑ 96	Scott Mitchell	.40	.15
❑ 97	Desmond Howard	.40	.15
❑ 98	.Chris Warren	.40	.15
❑ 99	Glyn Milburn	.25	.08
❑ 100	Vinny Testaverde	.40	.15
❑ 101	James O.Stewart	.40	.15
❑ 102	Iheanyi Uwaezuoke	.25	.08
❑ 103	Stan Humphries	.40	.15
❑ 104	Terance Mathis	.40	.15
❑ 105	Thomas Lewis	.25	.08
❑ 106	Eddie Kennison	.40	.15
❑ 107	Rashaan Salaam	.25	.08
❑ 108	Curtis Conway	.40	.15
❑ 109	Chris Sanders	.25	.08
❑ 110	Marcus Allen	.60	.25
❑ 111	Gilbert Brown	.40	.15
❑ 112	Jason Sehorn	.40	.15
❑ 113	Zach Thomas	.60	.25
❑ 114	Bobby Hebert	.25	.08
❑ 115	Herman Moore	.40	.15
❑ 116	Ray Lewis	1.00	.40
❑ 117	Darnay Scott	.40	.15
❑ 118	Jamal Anderson	.60	.25
❑ 119	Keyshawn Johnson	.60	.25
❑ 120	Adrian Murrell	.40	.15
❑ 121	Sam Mills	.25	.08
❑ 122	Irving Fryar	.40	.15
❑ 123	Ki-Jana Carter	.25	.08
❑ 124	Gus Frerotte	.25	.08
❑ 125	Terry Glenn	.60	.25
❑ 126	Quentin Coryatt	.25	.08
❑ 127	Robert Smith	.40	.15
❑ 128	Jeff Blake	.40	.15
❑ 129	Natrone Means	.40	.15
❑ 130	Isaac Bruce	.60	.25
❑ 131	Lamar Lathon	.25	.08

❑ 132 Johnnie Morton .40 .15
❑ 133 Jerry Rice 1.25 .50
❑ 134 Errict Rhett .25 .08
❑ 135 Junior Seau .60 .25
❑ 136 Joey Galloway .40 .15
❑ 137 Napoleon Kaufman .60 .25
❑ 138 Troy Aikman 1.25 .50
❑ 139 Kevin Hardy .25 .08
❑ 140 Jimmy Smith .40 .15
❑ 141 Edgar Bennett .40 .15
❑ 142 Hardy Nickerson .25 .08
❑ 143 Greg Lloyd .25 .08
❑ 144 Dale Carter .25 .08
❑ 145 Jake Reed .40 .15
❑ 146 Cris Carter .60 .25
❑ 147 Todd Collins .25 .08
❑ 148 Mel Gray .25 .08
❑ 149 Lawyer Milloy .40 .15
❑ 150 Kimble Anders .40 .15
❑ 151 Darick Holmes .25 .08
❑ 152 Bert Emanuel .40 .15
❑ 153 Marshall Faulk .75 .30
❑ 154 Frank Sanders .40 .15
❑ 155 Leeland McElroy .25 .08
❑ 156 Rickey Dudley .40 .15
❑ 157 Tamarick Vanover .40 .15
❑ 158 Kerry Collins .60 .25
❑ 159 Jeff Graham .25 .08
❑ 160 Jerome Bettis .60 .25
❑ 161 Greg Hill .25 .08
❑ 162 John Mobley .25 .08
❑ 163 Michael Irvin .60 .25
❑ 164 Marvin Harrison .60 .25
❑ 165 Jim Schwantz RC .25 .08
❑ 166 Jermaine Lewis .60 .25
❑ 167 Levon Kirkland .25 .08
❑ 168 Nilo Silvan .25 .08
❑ 169 Ken Norton .25 .08
❑ 170 Yancey Thigpen .40 .15
❑ 171 Antonio Freeman .60 .25
❑ 172 Terry Kirby .40 .15
❑ 173 Brad Johnson .60 .25
❑ 174 Reidel Anthony RC .60 .25
❑ 175 Tiki Barber RC 5.00 2.00
❑ 176 Pat Barnes RC .60 .25
❑ 177 Michael Booker RC .25 .08
❑ 178 Peter Boulware RC .60 .25
❑ 179 Rae Carruth RC .25 .08
❑ 180 Troy Davis RC .40 .15
❑ 181 Corey Dillon RC 5.00 2.00
❑ 182 Jim Druckenmiller RC .40 .15
❑ 183 Warrick Dunn RC 2.00 .75
❑ 184 James Farrior RC .60 .25
❑ 185 Yatil Green RC .40 .15
❑ 186 Walter Jones RC .60 .25
❑ 187 Tom Knight RC .25 .08
❑ 188 Sam Madison RC .60 .25
❑ 189 Tyrus McCloud RC .25 .08
❑ 190 Orlando Pace RC .60 .25
❑ 191 Jake Plummer RC 4.00 1.50
❑ 192 Dwayne Rudd RC .60 .25
❑ 193 Darrell Russell RC .25 .08
❑ 194 Sedrick Shaw RC .40 .15
❑ 195 Shawn Springs RC .40 .15
❑ 196 Bryant Westbrook RC .25 .08
❑ 197 Danny Wuerffel RC .60 .25
❑ 198 Reinard Wilson RC .40 .15
❑ 199 Checklist .25 .08
❑ 200 Checklist .60 .25
❑ 201 Rick Mirer .25 .08
❑ 202 Torrance Small .25 .08
❑ 203 Ricky Proehl .25 .08
❑ 204 Will Blackwell RC .40 .15
❑ 205 Warrick Dunn 1.00 .40
❑ 206 Rob Johnson .60 .25
❑ 207 Jim Schwantz .25 .08
❑ 208 Ike Hilliard RC 1.25 .50
❑ 209 Chris Canty RC .25 .08
❑ 210 Chris Boniol .25 .08
❑ 211 Jim Druckenmiller .25 .08
❑ 212 Tony Gonzalez RC 2.50 1.00
❑ 213 Scottie Graham .25 .08
❑ 214 Byron Hanspard RC .40 .15
❑ 215 Gary Brown .25 .08
❑ 216 Darrell Russell .25 .08
❑ 217 Sedrick Shaw .40 .15
❑ 218 Boomer Esiason .40 .15
❑ 219 Peter Boulware .40 .15
❑ 220 Willie Green .25 .08
❑ 221 Dietrich Jells .25 .08
❑ 222 Freddie Jones RC .40 .15
❑ 223 Eric Metcalf .40 .15
❑ 224 John Henry Mills .25 .08
❑ 225 Michael Timpson .25 .08
❑ 226 Danny Wuerffel .60 .25
❑ 227 Daimon Shelton RC .25 .08
❑ 228 Henry Ellard .25 .08
❑ 229 Flipper Anderson .25 .08
❑ 230 Hunter Goodwin RC .25 .08
❑ 231 Jay Graham RC .40 .15
❑ 232 Duce Staley RC 6.00 2.50
❑ 233 Lamar Thomas .25 .08
❑ 234 Rod Woodson .40 .15
❑ 235 Zack Crockett .25 .08
❑ 236 Ernie Mills .25 .08
❑ 237 Kyle Brady .25 .08
❑ 238 Jesse Campbell .25 .08
❑ 239 Anthony Miller .25 .08
❑ 240 Michael Haynes .25 .08
❑ 241 Qadry Ismail .40 .15
❑ 242 Tom Knight .25 .08
❑ 243 Brian Manning RC .25 .08
❑ 244 Derrick Mayes .40 .15
❑ 245 Jamie Sharper RC .40 .15
❑ 246 Sherman Williams .25 .08
❑ 247 Yatil Green .40 .15
❑ 248 Howard Griffith .25 .08
❑ 249 Brian Blades .25 .08
❑ 250 Mark Chmura .40 .15
❑ 251 Chris Darkins .25 .08
❑ 252 Willie Davis .25 .08
❑ 253 Quinn Early .25 .08
❑ 254 Marc Edwards RC .25 .08
❑ 255 Charlie Jones .25 .08
❑ 256 Jake Plummer 1.50 .60
❑ 257 Heath Shuler .25 .08
❑ 258 Fred Barnett .25 .08
❑ 259 William Henderson .40 .15
❑ 260 Michael Booker .25 .08
❑ 261 Chad Brown .25 .08
❑ 262 Garrison Hearst .40 .15
❑ 263 Leon Johnson RC .40 .15
❑ 264 Antowain Smith RC 2.00 .75
❑ 265 Darnell Autry RC .40 .15
❑ 266 Craig Heyward .25 .08
❑ 267 Walter Jones .25 .08
❑ 268 Dexter Coakley RC .60 .25
❑ 269 Mercury Hayes .25 .08
❑ 270 Brett Perriman .25 .08
❑ 271 Chris Spielman .25 .08
❑ 272 Kevin Greene .40 .15
❑ 273 Kevin Lockett RC .40 .15
❑ 274 Troy Davis .40 .15
❑ 275 Brent Jones .25 .08
❑ 276 Chris Chandler .40 .15
❑ 277 Bryant Westbrook .25 .08
❑ 278 Desmond Howard .40 .15
❑ 279 Tyrone Hughes .25 .08
❑ 280 Kez McCorvey .25 .08
❑ 281 Stephen Davis .60 .25
❑ 282 Steve Everitt .25 .08
❑ 283 Andre Hastings .25 .08
❑ 284 Marcus Robinson RC 5.00 2.00
❑ 285 Donnell Woolford .25 .08
❑ 286 Mario Bates .25 .08
❑ 287 Corey Dillon 2.00 .75
❑ 288 Jackie Harris .25 .08
❑ 289 Lorenzo Neal .25 .08
❑ 290 Anthony Pleasant .25 .08
❑ 291 Andre Rison .40 .15
❑ 292 Amani Toomer .40 .15
❑ 293 Eric Turner .25 .08
❑ 294 Elvis Grbac .40 .15
❑ 295 Cris Dishman .25 .08
❑ 296 Tom Carter .25 .08
❑ 297 Mark Carrier DB .25 .08
❑ 298 Orlando Pace .40 .15
❑ 299 Jay Riemersma RC .25 .08
❑ 300 Daryl Johnston .40 .15
❑ 301 Joey Kent RC .60 .25
❑ 302 Ronnie Harmon .25 .08
❑ 303 Rocket Ismail .40 .15
❑ 304 Terrell Davis .75 .30
❑ 305 Sean Dawkins .25 .08
❑ 306 Jeff George .40 .15
❑ 307 David Palmer .25 .08
❑ 308 Dwayne Rudd .25 .08
❑ 309 J.J. Stokes .40 .15
❑ 310 James Farrior .40 .15
❑ 311 William Fuller .25 .08
❑ 312 George Jones RC .40 .15
❑ 313 John Allred RC .25 .08
❑ 314 Tony Graziani RC .60 .25
❑ 315 Jeff Hostetler .25 .08
❑ 316 Keith Poole RC .60 .25
❑ 317 Neil Smith .40 .15
❑ 318 Steve Tasker .25 .08
❑ 319 Mike Vrabel RC 10.00 4.00
❑ 320 Pat Barnes .60 .25
❑ 321 James Hundon RC .60 .25
❑ 322 O.J. Santiago RC .40 .15
❑ 323 Billy Davis RC .25 .08
❑ 324 Shawn Springs .40 .15
❑ 325 Reinard Wilson .25 .08
❑ 326 Charles Johnson .40 .15
❑ 327 Micheal Barrow .25 .08
❑ 328 Derrick Mason RC 3.00 1.25
❑ 329 Muhsin Muhammad .40 .15
❑ 330 David LaFleur RC .25 .08
❑ 331 Reidel Anthony .40 .15
❑ 332 Tiki Barber 2.00 .75
❑ 333 Ray Buchanan .25 .08
❑ 334 John Elway 2.50 1.00
❑ 335 Alvin Harper .25 .08
❑ 336 Damon Jones RC .25 .08
❑ 337 Dedric Ward RC .40 .15
❑ 338 Jim Everett .25 .08
❑ 339 Jon Harris .25 .08
❑ 340 Warren Moon .60 .25
❑ 341 Rae Carruth .25 .08
❑ 342 John Mobley .25 .08
❑ 343 Tyrone Poole .25 .08
❑ 344 Mike Cherry RC .25 .08
❑ 345 Horace Copeland .25 .08
❑ 346 Deon Figures .25 .08
❑ 347 Antwuan Wyatt RC .25 .08
❑ 348 Tommy Vardell .25 .08
❑ 349 Checklist (201-324) .25 .08
❑ 350 Checklist (325-350/inserts) .25 .08
❑ S1A T.Davis Sample AU 80.00 40.00
❑ AU3 Dan Marino AU 100.00 40.00
❑ S1 Terrell Davis Sample 3.00 1.25

1998 Ultra

❑ COMPLETE SET (425) 120.00 50.00
❑ COMP.SERIES 1 (225) 80.00 30.00
❑ COMP.SERIES 2 (200) 50.00 25.00
❑ 1 Barry Sanders 2.50 1.00
❑ 2 Brett Favre 3.00 1.50
❑ 3 Napoleon Kaufman .75 .30
❑ 4 Robert Smith .75 .30
❑ 5 Terry Allen .75 .30
❑ 6 Vinny Testaverde .50 .20
❑ 7 William Floyd .30 .10
❑ 8 Carl Pickens .50 .20
❑ 9 Antonio Freeman .75 .30
❑ 10 Ben Coates .50 .20
❑ 11 Elvis Grbac .50 .20
❑ 12 Kerry Collins .50 .20
❑ 13 Orlando Pace .30 .10
❑ 14 Steve Broussard .30 .10
❑ 15 Terance Mathis .50 .20
❑ 16 Tiki Barber .75 .30

❑ 17 Cris Carter .75 .30
❑ 18 Eric Green .30 .10
❑ 19 Eric Metcalf .30 .10
❑ 20 Jeff George .50 .20
❑ 21 Leslie Shepherd .30 .10
❑ 22 Natrone Means .50 .20
❑ 23 Scott Mitchell .50 .20
❑ 24 Adrian Murrell .50 .20
❑ 25 Gilbert Brown .30 .10
❑ 26 Jimmy Smith .50 .20
❑ 27 Mark Bruener .30 .10
❑ 28 Troy Aikman 1.50 .60
❑ 29 Warrick Dunn .75 .30
❑ 30 Jay Graham .30 .10
❑ 31 Craig Whelihan RC .30 .10
❑ 32 Ed McCaffrey .50 .20
❑ 33 Jamie Asher .30 .10
❑ 34 John Randle .50 .20
❑ 35 Michael Jackson .30 .10
❑ 36 Rickey Dudley .30 .10
❑ 37 Sean Dawkins .30 .10
❑ 38 Andre Rison .50 .20
❑ 39 Bert Emanuel .50 .20
❑ 40 Jeff Blake .50 .20
❑ 41 Curtis Conway .50 .20
❑ 42 Eddie Kennison .50 .20
❑ 43 James McKnight .75 .30
❑ 44 Rae Carruth .30 .10
❑ 45 Tito Wooten RC .30 .10
❑ 46 Cris Dishman .30 .10
❑ 47 Ernie Conwell .30 .10
❑ 48 Fred Lane .30 .10
❑ 49 Jamal Anderson .75 .30
❑ 50 Lake Dawson .30 .10
❑ 51 Michael Strahan .50 .20
❑ 52 Reggie White .75 .30
❑ 53 Trent Dilfer .75 .30
❑ 54 Troy Brown .50 .20
❑ 55 Wesley Walls .50 .20
❑ 56 Chidi Ahanotu .30 .10
❑ 57 Dwayne Rudd .30 .10
❑ 58 Jerry Rice 1.50 .60
❑ 59 Johnnie Morton .50 .20
❑ 60 Sherman Williams .30 .10
❑ 61 Steve McNair .75 .30
❑ 62 Will Blackwell .30 .10
❑ 63 Chris Chandler .50 .20
❑ 64 Dexter Coakley .30 .10
❑ 65 Horace Copeland .30 .10
❑ 66 Jerald Moore .30 .10
❑ 67 Leon Johnson .30 .10
❑ 68 Mark Chmura .50 .20
❑ 69 Micheal Barrow .30 .10
❑ 70 Muhsin Muhammad .50 .20
❑ 71 Terry Glenn .75 .30
❑ 72 Tony Brackens .30 .10
❑ 73 Chad Scott .30 .10
❑ 74 Glenn Foley .50 .20
❑ 75 Keenan McCardell .50 .20
❑ 76 Peter Boulware .30 .10
❑ 77 Reidel Anthony .50 .20
❑ 78 William Henderson .50 .20
❑ 79 Tony Martin .50 .20
❑ 80 Tony Gonzalez .75 .30
❑ 81 Charlie Jones .30 .10
❑ 82 Chris Gedney .30 .10
❑ 83 Chris Calloway .30 .10
❑ 84 Dale Carter .30 .10
❑ 85 Ki-Jana Carter .30 .10
❑ 86 Shawn Springs .30 .10
❑ 87 Antowain Smith .75 .30
❑ 88 Eric Turner .30 .10
❑ 89 John Mobley .30 .10
❑ 90 Ken Dilger .30 .10
❑ 91 Bobby Hoying .50 .20
❑ 92 Curtis Martin .75 .30
❑ 93 Drew Bledsoe 1.25 .50
❑ 94 Gary Brown .30 .10
❑ 95 Marvin Harrison .75 .30
❑ 96 Todd Collins .30 .10
❑ 97 Chris Warren .50 .20
❑ 98 Danny Kanell .50 .20
❑ 99 Tony McGee .30 .10
❑ 100 Rod Smith .50 .20
❑ 101 Frank Sanders .50 .20
❑ 102 Irving Fryar .50 .20
❑ 103 Marcus Allen .75 .30
❑ 104 Marshall Faulk 1.00 .40
❑ 105 Bruce Smith .50 .20
❑ 106 Charlie Garner .50 .20
❑ 107 Paul Justin .30 .10
❑ 108 Randal Hill .30 .10
❑ 109 Erik Kramer .30 .10
❑ 110 Rob Moore .50 .20
❑ 111 Shannon Sharpe .50 .20
❑ 112 Warren Moon .75 .30
❑ 113 Zach Thomas .75 .30
❑ 114 Dan Marino 3.00 1.50
❑ 115 Duce Staley 1.00 .40
❑ 116 Eric Swann .30 .10
❑ 117 Kenny Holmes .30 .10
❑ 118 Merton Hanks .30 .10
❑ 119 Raymont Harris .30 .10
❑ 120 Terrell Davis .75 .30
❑ 121 Thurman Thomas .75 .30
❑ 122 Wayne Martin .30 .10
❑ 123 Charles Way .30 .10
❑ 124 Chuck Smith .30 .10
❑ 125 Corey Dillon .75 .30
❑ 126 Darnell Autry .30 .10
❑ 127 Isaac Bruce .75 .30
❑ 128 Joey Galloway .50 .20
❑ 129 Kimble Anders .50 .20
❑ 130 Aeneas Williams .30 .10
❑ 131 Andre Hastings .30 .10
❑ 132 Chad Lewis .50 .20
❑ 133 J.J. Stokes .50 .20
❑ 134 John Elway 3.00 1.25
❑ 135 Karim Abdul-Jabbar .75 .30
❑ 136 Ken Harvey .30 .10
❑ 137 Robert Brooks .50 .20
❑ 138 Rodney Thomas .30 .10
❑ 139 James Stewart .50 .20
❑ 140 Billy Joe Hobert .30 .10
❑ 141 Frank Wycheck .30 .10
❑ 142 Jake Plummer .75 .30
❑ 143 Jerris McPhail .30 .10
❑ 144 Kordell Stewart .75 .30
❑ 145 Terrell Owens .75 .30
❑ 146 Willie Green .30 .10
❑ 147 Anthony Miller .30 .10
❑ 148 Courtney Hawkins .30 .10
❑ 149 Larry Centers .30 .10
❑ 150 Gus Frerotte .30 .10
❑ 151 O.J. McDuffie .50 .20
❑ 152 Ray Zellars .30 .10
❑ 153 Terry Kirby .30 .10
❑ 154 Tommy Vardell .30 .10
❑ 155 Willie Davis .30 .10
❑ 156 Chris Canty .30 .10
❑ 157 Byron Hanspard .30 .10
❑ 158 Chris Penn .30 .10
❑ 159 Damon Jones .30 .10
❑ 160 Derrick Mayes .50 .20
❑ 161 Emmitt Smith 2.50 1.25
❑ 162 Keyshawn Johnson .75 .30
❑ 163 Mike Alstott .75 .30
❑ 164 Tom Carter .30 .10
❑ 165 Tony Banks .50 .20
❑ 166 Bryant Westbrook .30 .10
❑ 167 Chris Sanders .30 .10
❑ 168 Deion Sanders .75 .30
❑ 169 Garrison Hearst .75 .30
❑ 170 Jason Taylor .50 .20
❑ 171 Jerome Bettis .75 .30
❑ 172 John Lynch .50 .20
❑ 173 Troy Davis .30 .10
❑ 174 Freddie Jones .30 .10
❑ 175 Herman Moore .50 .20
❑ 176 Jake Reed .50 .20
❑ 177 Mark Brunell .75 .30
❑ 178 Ray Lewis .75 .30
❑ 179 Stephen Davis .30 .10
❑ 180 Tim Brown .75 .30
❑ 181 Willie McGinest .30 .10
❑ 182 Andre Reed .50 .20
❑ 183 Darrien Gordon .30 .10
❑ 184 David Palmer .30 .10
❑ 185 James Jett .50 .20
❑ 186 Junior Seau .75 .30
❑ 187 Zack Crockett .30 .10
❑ 188 Brad Johnson .75 .30
❑ 189 Charles Johnson .30 .10
❑ 190 Eddie George .75 .30
❑ 191 Jermaine Lewis .50 .20
❑ 192 Michael Irvin .75 .30
❑ 193 Reggie Brown LB .30 .10
❑ 194 Steve Young 1.00 .40
❑ 195 Warren Sapp .50 .20
❑ 196 Wayne Chrebet .75 .30
❑ 197 David Dunn .30 .10
❑ 198 Dorsey Levens CL .50 .20
❑ 199 Troy Aikman CL .75 .30
❑ 200 John Elway CL .75 .30
❑ 201 Peyton Manning RC 30.00 12.50
❑ 202 Ryan Leaf RC 3.00 1.25
❑ 203 Charles Woodson RC 4.00 1.50
❑ 204 Andre Wadsworth RC 2.50 1.00
❑ 205 Brian Simmons RC 2.50 1.00
❑ 206 Curtis Enis RC 1.50 .60
❑ 207 Randy Moss RC 20.00 7.50
❑ 208 Germane Crowell RC 2.50 1.00
❑ 209 Greg Ellis RC 1.50 .60
❑ 210 Kevin Dyson RC 3.00 1.25
❑ 211 Skip Hicks RC 2.50 1.00
❑ 212 Alonzo Mayes RC 1.50 .60
❑ 213 Robert Edwards RC 2.50 1.00
❑ 214 Fred Taylor RC 5.00 2.00
❑ 215 Robert Holcombe RC 2.50 1.00
❑ 216 John Dutton RC 1.50 .60
❑ 217 Vonnie Holliday RC 2.50 1.00
❑ 218 Tim Dwight RC 3.00 1.25
❑ 219 Tavian Banks RC 2.50 1.00
❑ 220 Marcus Nash RC 1.50 .60
❑ 221 Jason Peter RC 1.50 .60
❑ 222 Michael Myers RC 1.50 .60
❑ 223 Takeo Spikes RC 3.00 1.25
❑ 224 Kivuusama Mays RC 1.50 .60
❑ 225 Jacquez Green RC 2.50 1.00
❑ 226 Doug Flutie .75 .30
❑ 227 Ike Hilliard .50 .20
❑ 228 Craig Heyward .30 .10
❑ 229 Kevin Hardy .30 .10
❑ 230 Jason Dunn .30 .10
❑ 231 Billy Davis .30 .10
❑ 232 Chester McGlockton .30 .10
❑ 233 Sean Gilbert .30 .10
❑ 234 Bert Emanuel .50 .20
❑ 235 Keith Byars .30 .10
❑ 236 Tyrone Wheatley .50 .20
❑ 237 Ricky Proehl .30 .10
❑ 238 Michael Bates .30 .10
❑ 239 Derrick Alexander .50 .20
❑ 240 Harvey Williams .30 .10
❑ 241 Mike Pritchard .30 .10
❑ 242 Paul Justin .30 .10
❑ 243 Jeff Hostetler .30 .10
❑ 244 Eric Moulds .75 .30
❑ 245 Jeff Burris .30 .10
❑ 246 Gary Brown .30 .10
❑ 247 Anthony Johnson .30 .10
❑ 248 Dan Wilkinson .30 .10
❑ 249 Chris Warren .50 .20
❑ 250 Chris Darkins .30 .10
❑ 251 Eric Metcalf .30 .10
❑ 252 Pat Swilling .30 .10
❑ 253 Lamar Smith .50 .20
❑ 254 Quinn Early .30 .10
❑ 255 Carlester Crumpler .30 .10
❑ 256 Eric Bieniemy .30 .10
❑ 257 Aaron Bailey .30 .10
❑ 258 Neil O'Donnell .50 .20
❑ 259 Rod Woodson .50 .20
❑ 260 Ricky Whittle .30 .10
❑ 261 Iheanyi Uwaezuoke .30 .10
❑ 262 Heath Shuler .30 .10
❑ 263 Darren Sharper .50 .20
❑ 264 John Henry Mills .30 .10
❑ 265 Marco Battaglia .30 .10
❑ 266 Yancey Thigpen .30 .10
❑ 267 Irv Smith .30 .10
❑ 268 Jamie Sharper .30 .10
❑ 269 Marcus Robinson 5.00 2.00
❑ 270 Dorsey Levens .75 .30
❑ 271 Qadry Ismail .50 .20
❑ 272 Desmond Howard .50 .20
❑ 273 Webster Slaughter .30 .10
❑ 274 Eugene Robinson .30 .10
❑ 275 Bill Romanowski .30 .10
❑ 276 Vincent Brisby .30 .10
❑ 277 Errict Rhett .50 .20

❑	278	Albert Connell	.30	.10
❑	279	Thomas Lewis	.30	.10
❑	280	John Farquhar RC	.30	.10
❑	281	Marc Edwards	.30	.10
❑	282	Tyrone Davis	.30	.10
❑	283	Eric Allen	.30	.10
❑	284	Aaron Glenn	.30	.10
❑	285	Roosevelt Potts	.30	.10
❑	286	Kez McCorvey	.30	.10
❑	287	Joey Kent	.50	.20
❑	288	Jim Druckenmiller	.30	.10
❑	289	Sean Dawkins	.30	.10
❑	290	Edgar Bennett	.30	.10
❑	291	Vinny Testaverde	.50	.20
❑	292	Chris Slade	.30	.10
❑	293	Lamar Lathon	.30	.10
❑	294	Jackie Harris	.30	.10
❑	295	Jim Harbaugh	.50	.20
❑	296	Rob Fredrickson	.30	.10
❑	297	Ty Detmer	.50	.20
❑	298	Karl Williams	.30	.10
❑	299	Troy Drayton	.30	.10
❑	300	Curtis Martin	.75	.30
❑	301	Tamarick Vanover	.30	.10
❑	302	Lorenzo Neal	.30	.10
❑	303	John Hall	.30	.10
❑	304	Kevin Greene	.50	.20
❑	305	Bryan Still	.30	.10
❑	306	Neil Smith	.50	.20
❑	307	Greg Lloyd	.30	.10
❑	308	Shawn Jefferson	.30	.10
❑	309	Aaron Taylor	.30	.10
❑	310	Sedrick Shaw	.30	.10
❑	311	O.J. Santiago	.30	.10
❑	312	Kevin Abrams	.30	.10
❑	313	Dana Stubblefield	.30	.10
❑	314	Daryl Johnston	.50	.20
❑	315	Bryan Cox	.30	.10
❑	316	Jeff Graham	.30	.10
❑	317	Mario Bates	.50	.20
❑	318	Adrian Murrell	.50	.20
❑	319	Greg Hill	.30	.10
❑	320	Jahine Arnold	.30	.10
❑	321	Justin Armour	.30	.10
❑	322	Ricky Watters	.50	.20
❑	323	Lamont Warren	.30	.10
❑	324	Mack Strong	.75	.30
❑	325	Darnay Scott	.50	.20
❑	326	Brian Mitchell	.30	.10
❑	327	Rob Johnson	.50	.20
❑	328	Kent Graham	.30	.10
❑	329	Hugh Douglas	.30	.10
❑	330	Simeon Rice	.50	.20
❑	331	Rick Mirer	.30	.10
❑	332	Randall Cunningham	.75	.30
❑	333	Steve Atwater	.30	.10
❑	334	Latario Rachal	.30	.10
❑	335	Tony Martin	.50	.20
❑	336	Leroy Hoard	.30	.10
❑	337	Howard Griffith	.30	.10
❑	338	Kevin Lockett	.30	.10
❑	339	William Floyd	.30	.10
❑	340	Jerry Ellison	.30	.10
❑	341	Kyle Brady	.30	.10
❑	342	Michael Westbrook	.50	.20
❑	343	Kevin Turner	.30	.10
❑	344	David LaFleur	.30	.10
❑	345	Robert Jones	.30	.10
❑	346	Dave Brown	.30	.10
❑	347	Kevin Williams	.30	.10
❑	348	Amani Toomer	.50	.20
❑	349	Amp Lee	.30	.10
❑	350	Bryce Paup	.30	.10
❑	351	Dewayne Washington	.30	.10
❑	352	Mercury Hayes	.30	.10
❑	353	Tim Biakabutuka	.50	.20
❑	354	Ray Crockett	.30	.10
❑	355	Ted Washington	.30	.10
❑	356	Pete Mitchell	.30	.10
❑	357	Billy Jenkins RC	.30	.10
❑	358	Troy Aikman CL	.75	.30
❑	359	Drew Bledsoe CL	.75	.30
❑	360	Steve Young CL	.75	.30
❑	361	Antonio Freeman NG	.50	.20
❑	362	Antowain Smith NG	.50	.20
❑	363	Barry Sanders NG	1.50	.60
❑	364	Bobby Hoying NG	.30	.10
❑	365	Brett Favre NG	2.00	.75
❑	366	Corey Dillon NG	.50	.20
❑	367	Dan Marino NG	2.00	.75
❑	368	Drew Bledsoe NG	.75	.30
❑	369	Eddie George NG	.50	.20
❑	370	Emmitt Smith NG	1.50	.60
❑	371	Herman Moore NG	.50	.20
❑	372	Jake Plummer NG	.50	.20
❑	373	Jerome Bettis NG	.50	.20
❑	374	Jerry Rice NG	1.00	.40
❑	375	Joey Galloway NG	.50	.20
❑	376	John Elway NG	2.00	.75
❑	377	Kordell Stewart NG	.50	.20
❑	378	Mark Brunell NG	.75	.30
❑	379	Keyshawn Johnson NG	.50	.20
❑	380	Steve Young NG	.75	.30
❑	381	Steve McNair NG	.50	.20
❑	382	Terrell Davis NG	.75	.30
❑	383	Tim Brown NG	.50	.20
❑	384	Troy Aikman NG	1.00	.40
❑	385	Warrick Dunn NG	.75	.30
❑	386	Ryan Leaf	3.00	1.25
❑	387	Tony Simmons RC	2.00	.75
❑	388	Rodney Williams RC	1.25	.50
❑	389	John Avery RC	2.00	.75
❑	390	Shaun Williams RC	2.00	.75
❑	391	Anthony Simmons RC	2.00	.75
❑	392	Rashaan Shehee RC	2.00	.75
❑	393	Robert Holcombe	2.00	.75
❑	394	Larry Shannon RC	1.25	.50
❑	395	Skip Hicks	2.00	.75
❑	396	Rod Rutledge RC	1.25	.50
❑	397	Donald Hayes RC	2.00	.75
❑	398	Curtis Enis	1.25	.50
❑	399	Mikhael Ricks RC	2.00	.75
❑	400	Brian Griese RC	6.00	2.50
❑	401	Michael Pittman RC	4.00	1.50
❑	402	Jacquez Green	2.00	.75
❑	403	Jerome Pathon RC	3.00	1.25
❑	404	Ahman Green RC	15.00	6.00
❑	405	Marcus Nash	1.25	.50
❑	406	Randy Moss	15.00	6.00
❑	407	Terry Fair RC	2.00	.75
❑	408	Jammi German RC	1.25	.50
❑	409	Stephen Alexander RC	2.00	.75
❑	410	Grant Wistrom RC	2.00	.75
❑	411	Charlie Batch RC	3.00	1.25
❑	412	Fred Taylor	4.00	1.50
❑	413	Pat Johnson RC	2.00	.75
❑	414	Robert Edwards	2.00	.75
❑	415	Keith Brooking RC	3.00	1.25
❑	416	Peyton Manning	25.00	12.50
❑	417	Duane Starks RC	1.25	.50
❑	418	Andre Wadsworth	2.00	.75
❑	419	Brian Alford RC	1.25	.50
❑	420	Brian Kelly RC	2.00	.75
❑	421	Joe Jurevicius RC	3.00	1.25
❑	422	Tebucky Jones RC	1.25	.50
❑	423	R.W. McQuarters RC	2.00	.75
❑	424	Kevin Dyson	2.50	1.00
❑	425	Charles Woodson	3.00	1.25
❑	R1	Reggie White COMM	.60	.25
❑	P20	Jeff George Promo	.75	.30

1999 Ultra

	#	Player		
❑		COMPLETE SET (300)	100.00	40.00
❑		COMP.SET w/o SP's (250)	20.00	10.00
❑	1	Terrell Davis	.75	.30
❑	2	Courtney Hawkins	.30	.10
❑	3	Cris Carter	.75	.30
❑	4	Darnay Scott	.30	.10
❑	5	Darrell Green	.50	.20
❑	6	Jimmy Smith	.50	.20
❑	7	Doug Flutie	.75	.30
❑	8	Michael Jackson	.30	.10
❑	9	Warren Sapp	.50	.20
❑	10	Greg Hill	.30	.10
❑	11	Karim Abdul-Jabbar	.50	.20
❑	12	Greg Ellis	.30	.10
❑	13	Dan Marino	2.50	1.00
❑	14	Napoleon Kaufman	.75	.30
❑	15	Peyton Manning	2.50	1.00
❑	16	Simeon Rice	.50	.20
❑	17	Tony Simmons	.30	.10
❑	18	Carlester Crumpler	.30	.10
❑	19	Charles Johnson	.30	.10
❑	20	Derrick Alexander	.30	.10
❑	21	Kent Graham	.30	.10
❑	22	Randall Cunningham	.75	.30
❑	23	Trent Green	.75	.30
❑	24	Chris Spielman	.30	.10
❑	25	Carl Pickens	.50	.20
❑	26	Bill Romanowski	.30	.10
❑	27	Jermaine Lewis	.50	.20
❑	28	Ahman Green	.75	.30
❑	29	Bryan Still	.30	.10
❑	30	Dorsey Levens	.75	.30
❑	31	Frank Wycheck	.30	.10
❑	32	Jerome Bettis	.75	.30
❑	33	Reidel Anthony	.50	.20
❑	34	Robert Jones	.30	.10
❑	35	Terry Glenn	.75	.30
❑	36	Tim Brown	.75	.30
❑	37	Eric Metcalf	.30	.10
❑	38	Kevin Greene	.50	.20
❑	39	Takeo Spikes	.30	.10
❑	40	Brian Mitchell	.30	.10
❑	41	Duane Starks	.30	.10
❑	42	Eddie George	.75	.30
❑	43	Joe Jurevicius	.50	.20
❑	44	Kimble Anders	.50	.20
❑	45	Kordell Stewart	.50	.20
❑	46	Leroy Hoard	.30	.10
❑	47	Rod Smith	.50	.20
❑	48	Terrell Owens	.75	.30
❑	49	Ty Detmer	.50	.20
❑	50	Charles Woodson	.75	.30
❑	51	Andre Rison	.50	.20
❑	52	Chris Slade	.30	.10
❑	53	Frank Sanders	.50	.20
❑	54	Michael Irvin	.50	.20
❑	55	Jerome Pathon	.30	.10
❑	56	Desmond Howard	.50	.20
❑	57	Billy Davis	.30	.10
❑	58	Anthony Simmons	.30	.10
❑	59	James Jett	.50	.20
❑	60	Jake Plummer	.50	.20
❑	61	John Avery	.30	.10
❑	62	Marvin Harrison	.75	.30
❑	63	Merton Hanks	.30	.10
❑	64	Ricky Proehl	.30	.10
❑	65	Steve Beuerlein	.30	.10
❑	66	Willie McGinest	.30	.10
❑	67	Bryce Paup	.30	.10
❑	68	Brett Favre	2.50	1.00
❑	69	Brian Griese	.75	.30
❑	70	Curtis Martin	.75	.30
❑	71	Drew Bledsoe	1.00	.40
❑	72	Jim Harbaugh	.50	.20
❑	73	Joey Galloway	.50	.20
❑	74	Natrone Means	.50	.20
❑	75	O.J. McDuffie	.50	.20
❑	76	Tiki Barber	.75	.30
❑	77	Wesley Walls	.50	.20
❑	78	Will Blackwell	.30	.10
❑	79	Bert Emanuel	.50	.20
❑	80	J.J. Stokes	.50	.20
❑	81	Steve McNair	.75	.30
❑	82	Adrian Murrell	.50	.20
❑	83	Dexter Coakley	.30	.10
❑	84	Jeff George	.50	.20
❑	85	Marshall Faulk	1.00	.40
❑	86	Tim Biakabutuka	.50	.20
❑	87	Troy Drayton	.30	.10
❑	88	Ty Law	.50	.20
❑	89	Brian Simmons	.30	.10

❑ 90 Eric Allen	.30	.10
❑ 91 Jon Kitna	.75	.30
❑ 92 Junior Seau	.75	.30
❑ 93 Kevin Turner	.30	.10
❑ 94 Larry Centers	.30	.10
❑ 95 Robert Edwards	.30	.10
❑ 96 Rocket Ismail	.50	.20
❑ 97 Sam Madison	.30	.10
❑ 98 Stephen Alexander	.30	.10
❑ 99 Trent Dilfer	.50	.20
❑ 100 Vonnie Holliday	.30	.10
❑ 101 Charlie Garner	.50	.20
❑ 102 Deion Sanders	.75	.30
❑ 103 Jamal Anderson	.75	.30
❑ 104 Mike Vanderjagt	.30	.10
❑ 105 Aeneas Williams	.30	.10
❑ 106 Daryl Johnston	.50	.20
❑ 107 Hugh Douglas	.30	.10
❑ 108 Torrance Small	.30	.10
❑ 109 Amani Toomer	.30	.10
❑ 110 Amp Lee	.30	.10
❑ 111 Germane Crowell	.30	.10
❑ 112 Marco Battaglia	.30	.10
❑ 113 Michael Westbrook	.50	.20
❑ 114 Randy Moss	2.00	.75
❑ 115 Ricky Watters	.50	.20
❑ 116 Rob Johnson	.50	.20
❑ 117 Tony Gonzalez	.75	.30
❑ 118 Charles Way	.30	.10
❑ 119 Chris Penn	.30	.10
❑ 120 Eddie Kennison	.50	.20
❑ 121 Elvis Grbac	.50	.20
❑ 122 Eric Moulds	.75	.30
❑ 123 Terry Fair	.30	.10
❑ 124 Tony Banks	.50	.20
❑ 125 Chris Chandler	.50	.20
❑ 126 Emmitt Smith	1.50	.60
❑ 127 Herman Moore	.50	.20
❑ 128 Irv Smith	.30	.10
❑ 129 Kyle Brady	.30	.10
❑ 130 Lamont Warren	.30	.10
❑ 131 Troy Davis	.30	.10
❑ 132 Andre Reed	.50	.20
❑ 133 Justin Armour	.30	.10
❑ 134 James Hasty	.30	.10
❑ 135 Johnnie Morton	.50	.20
❑ 136 Reggie Barlow	.30	.10
❑ 137 Robert Holcombe	.30	.10
❑ 138 Sean Dawkins	.30	.10
❑ 139 Steve Atwater	.30	.10
❑ 140 Tim Dwight	.75	.30
❑ 141 Wayne Chrebet	.50	.20
❑ 142 Alonzo Mayes	.30	.10
❑ 143 Mark Brunell	.75	.30
❑ 144 Antowain Smith	.75	.30
❑ 145 Byron Bam Morris	.30	.10
❑ 146 Isaac Bruce	.75	.30
❑ 147 Bryan Cox	.30	.10
❑ 148 Bryant Westbrook	.30	.10
❑ 149 Duce Staley	.75	.30
❑ 150 Barry Sanders	2.50	1.00
❑ 151 La'Roi Glover RC	.75	.30
❑ 152 Ray Crockett	.30	.10
❑ 153 Tony Brackens	.30	.10
❑ 154 Roy Barker	.30	.10
❑ 155 Kerry Collins	.50	.20
❑ 156 Andre Wadsworth	.30	.10
❑ 157 Cameron Cleeland	.30	.10
❑ 158 Koy Detmer	.30	.10
❑ 159 Marcus Pollard	.30	.10
❑ 160 Patrick Jeffers RC	6.00	2.50
❑ 161 Aaron Glenn	.30	.10
❑ 162 Andre Hastings	.30	.10
❑ 163 Bruce Smith	.50	.20
❑ 164 David Palmer	.30	.10
❑ 165 Erik Kramer	.50	.20
❑ 166 Orlando Pace	.30	.10
❑ 167 Robert Brooks	.50	.20
❑ 168 Shawn Springs	.30	.10
❑ 169 Terance Mathis	.50	.20
❑ 170 Chris Calloway	.30	.10
❑ 171 Gilbert Brown	.30	.10
❑ 172 Charlie Jones	.30	.10
❑ 173 Curtis Enis	.30	.10
❑ 174 Eugene Robinson	.30	.10
❑ 175 Garrison Hearst	.50	.20
❑ 176 Jason Elam	.30	.10
❑ 177 John Randle	.50	.20
❑ 178 Keith Poole	.30	.10
❑ 179 Kevin Hardy	.30	.10
❑ 180 Keyshawn Johnson	.75	.30
❑ 181 O.J. Santiago	.30	.10
❑ 182 Jacquez Green	.30	.10
❑ 183 Bobby Engram	.50	.20
❑ 184 Damon Jones	.30	.10
❑ 185 Freddie Jones	.30	.10
❑ 186 Jake Reed	.50	.20
❑ 187 Jerry Rice	1.50	.60
❑ 188 Joey Kent	.30	.10
❑ 189 Lamar Smith	.50	.20
❑ 190 John Elway	2.50	1.00
❑ 191 Leon Johnson	.30	.10
❑ 192 Mark Chmura	.50	.20
❑ 193 Peter Boulware	.30	.10
❑ 194 Zach Thomas	.75	.30
❑ 195 Marc Edwards	.30	.10
❑ 196 Mike Alstott	.75	.30
❑ 197 Yancey Thigpen	.30	.10
❑ 198 Oronde Gadsden	.50	.20
❑ 199 Rae Carruth	.30	.10
❑ 200 Troy Aikman	1.50	.60
❑ 201 Shawn Jefferson	.30	.10
❑ 202 Rob Moore	.50	.20
❑ 203 Rickey Dudley	.30	.10
❑ 204 Jason Taylor	.30	.10
❑ 205 Curtis Conway	.50	.20
❑ 206 Darrien Gordon	.30	.10
❑ 207 Eric Green	.30	.10
❑ 208 Jessie Armstead	.30	.10
❑ 209 Keenan McCardell	.50	.20
❑ 210 Robert Smith	.75	.30
❑ 211 Mo Lewis	.30	.10
❑ 212 Ryan Leaf	.75	.30
❑ 213 Steve Young	1.00	.40
❑ 214 Tyrone Davis	.30	.10
❑ 215 Chad Brown	.30	.10
❑ 216 Ike Hilliard	.30	.10
❑ 217 Jimmy Hitchcock	.30	.10
❑ 218 Kevin Dyson	.50	.20
❑ 219 Levon Kirkland	.30	.10
❑ 220 Neil O'Donnell	.50	.20
❑ 221 Ray Lewis	.75	.30
❑ 222 Shannon Sharpe	.50	.20
❑ 223 Skip Hicks	.30	.10
❑ 224 Brad Johnson	.75	.30
❑ 225 Charlie Batch	.75	.30
❑ 226 Corey Dillon	.75	.30
❑ 227 Dale Carter	.30	.10
❑ 228 John Mobley	.30	.10
❑ 229 Hines Ward	.75	.30
❑ 230 Leslie Shepherd	.30	.10
❑ 231 Michael Strahan	.50	.20
❑ 232 R.W. McQuarters	.30	.10
❑ 233 Mike Pritchard	.30	.10
❑ 234 Antonio Freeman	.75	.30
❑ 235 Ben Coates	.50	.20
❑ 236 Michael Bates	.30	.10
❑ 237 Ed McCaffrey	.50	.20
❑ 238 Gary Brown	.30	.10
❑ 239 Mark Bruener	.30	.10
❑ 240 Mikhael Ricks	.30	.10
❑ 241 Muhsin Muhammad	.50	.20
❑ 242 Priest Holmes	1.25	.50
❑ 243 Stephen Davis	.75	.30
❑ 244 Vinny Testaverde	.50	.20
❑ 245 Warrick Dunn	.75	.30
❑ 246 Derrick Mayes	.30	.10
❑ 247 Fred Taylor	.75	.30
❑ 248 Drew Bledsoe CL	.50	.20
❑ 249 Eddie George CL	.50	.20
❑ 250 Steve Young CL	.50	.20
❑ 251 Jamal Anderson BB	.60	.25
❑ 252 D.Gordon/Romanowski BB	.30	.10
❑ 253 Shannon Sharpe BB	.30	.10
❑ 254 Terrell Davis BB	1.00	.40
❑ 255 Rod Smith BB	.30	.10
❑ 256 Rod Smith BB	.30	.10
❑ 257 John Elway BB	5.00	2.00
❑ 258 Tim Dwight BB	.60	.25
❑ 259 Elway/McC/Griff/Dav.BB	3.00	1.25
❑ 260 John Elway BB	5.00	2.00
❑ 261 Ricky Williams RC	6.00	2.50
❑ 262 Tim Couch RC	3.00	1.25
❑ 263 Chris Claiborne RC	1.50	.60
❑ 264 Champ Bailey RC	5.00	2.00
❑ 265 Torry Holt RC	8.00	3.00
❑ 266 Donovan McNabb RC	15.00	6.00
❑ 267 David Boston RC	3.00	1.25
❑ 268 Chris McAlister RC	2.50	1.00
❑ 269 Brock Huard RC	3.00	1.25
❑ 270 Daunte Culpepper RC	12.00	5.00
❑ 271 Matt Stinchcomb RC	1.50	.60
❑ 272 Edgerrin James RC	12.00	5.00
❑ 273 Jevon Kearse RC	6.00	2.50
❑ 274 Ebenezer Ekuban RC	2.50	1.00
❑ 275 Kris Farris RC	1.50	.60
❑ 276 Chris Terry RC	1.50	.60
❑ 277 Jerame Tuman RC	3.00	1.25
❑ 278 Akili Smith RC	2.50	1.00
❑ 279 Aaron Gibson RC	1.50	.60
❑ 280 Rahim Abdullah RC	2.50	1.00
❑ 281 Peerless Price RC	3.00	1.25
❑ 282 Antoine Winfield RC	2.50	1.00
❑ 283 Antuan Edwards RC	1.50	.60
❑ 284 Rob Konrad RC	3.00	1.25
❑ 285 Troy Edwards RC	2.50	1.00
❑ 286 John Thornton RC	1.50	.60
❑ 287 James Johnson RC	2.50	1.00
❑ 288 Gary Stills RC	1.50	.60
❑ 289 Mike Peterson RC	2.50	1.00
❑ 290 Kevin Faulk RC	3.00	1.25
❑ 291 Jared DeVries RC	1.50	.60
❑ 292 Martin Gramatica RC	1.50	.60
❑ 293 Montae Reagor RC	1.50	.60
❑ 294 Andy Katzenmoyer RC	2.50	1.00
❑ 295 Sedrick Irvin RC	1.50	.60
❑ 296 D'Wayne Bates RC	2.50	1.00
❑ 297 Amos Zereoue RC	3.00	1.25
❑ 298 Dre' Bly RC	3.00	1.25
❑ 299 Kevin Johnson RC	3.00	1.25
❑ 300 Cade McNown RC	2.50	1.00
❑ P247 Fred Taylor Promo	2.00	.75

2000 Ultra

Card		
❑ COMPLETE SET (249)	100.00	40.00
❑ COMP.SET w/o SP's (220)	20.00	7.50
❑ 1 Kurt Warner	1.50	.60
❑ 2 Derrick Alexander	.50	.20
❑ 3 Aaron Craver	.30	.10
❑ 4 Kevin Faulk	.50	.20
❑ 5 Marcus Robinson	.75	.30
❑ 6 Tony Banks	.50	.20
❑ 7 Jon Ritchie	.30	.10
❑ 8 Torry Holt	.75	.30
❑ 9 Joe Horn	.50	.20
❑ 10 Eddie George	.75	.30
❑ 11 Michael Westbrook	.50	.20
❑ 12 Gus Frerotte	.30	.10
❑ 13 Tim Brown	.75	.30
❑ 14 Tamarick Vanover	.30	.10
❑ 15 David Sloan	.30	.10
❑ 16 Darnay Scott	.30	.10
❑ 17 Junior Seau	.75	.30
❑ 18 Warren Sapp	.50	.20
❑ 19 Priest Holmes	1.00	.40
❑ 20 Jerry Rice	1.50	.60
❑ 21 Cade McNown	.30	.10
❑ 22 Johnnie Morton	.50	.20
❑ 23 Vinny Testaverde	.50	.20
❑ 24 James Jett	.30	.10
❑ 25 Tony Gonzalez	.50	.20
❑ 26 Charlie Batch	.75	.30
❑ 27 Tony Simmons	.30	.10

❑ 28	James Stewart	.50	.20
❑ 29	Corey Dillon	.75	.30
❑ 30	Ricky Williams	.75	.30
❑ 31	Ryan Leaf	.50	.20
❑ 32	Terry Allen	.50	.20
❑ 33	Freddie Jones	.30	.10
❑ 34	Terry Kirby	.30	.10
❑ 35	Charles Johnson	.50	.20
❑ 36	William Henderson	.50	.20
❑ 37	Stephen Alexander	.30	.10
❑ 38	Moe Williams	.50	.20
❑ 39	David Boston	.75	.30
❑ 40	Emmitt Smith	1.50	.60
❑ 41	Ken Oxendine	.30	.10
❑ 42	Byron Hanspard	.30	.10
❑ 43	Dwight Stone	.30	.10
❑ 44	Jim Harbaugh	.50	.20
❑ 45	Curtis Enis	.30	.10
❑ 46	Peerless Price	.50	.20
❑ 47	Terance Mathis	.50	.20
❑ 48	Mike Alstott	.75	.30
❑ 49	Rod Smith	.50	.20
❑ 50	Marshall Faulk	1.00	.40
❑ 51	Derrick Mayes	.50	.20
❑ 52	Keenan McCardell	.50	.20
❑ 53	Curtis Martin	.75	.30
❑ 54	Bobby Engram	.30	.10
❑ 55	Carl Pickens	.50	.20
❑ 56	Robert Smith	.75	.30
❑ 57	Ike Hilliard	.50	.20
❑ 58	Reidel Anthony	.50	.20
❑ 59	Jeff Graham	.30	.10
❑ 60	Mark Brunell	.75	.30
❑ 61	Joe Montgomery	.30	.10
❑ 62	Ed McCaffrey	.75	.30
❑ 63	Kenny Bynum	.30	.10
❑ 64	Curtis Conway	.50	.20
❑ 65	Trent Dilfer	.50	.20
❑ 66	Jake Reed	.50	.20
❑ 67	Jake Plummer	.50	.20
❑ 68	Tony Martin	.50	.20
❑ 69	Yatil Green	.30	.10
❑ 70	Keyshawn Johnson	.75	.30
❑ 71	Leroy Hoard	.30	.10
❑ 72	Skip Hicks	.30	.10
❑ 73	Marvin Harrison	.75	.30
❑ 74	Steve Beuerlein	.50	.20
❑ 75	Will Blackwell	.30	.10
❑ 76	Derek Loville	.30	.10
❑ 77	Warrick Dunn	.75	.30
❑ 78	Amos Zereoue	.75	.30
❑ 79	Ray Lucas	.50	.20
❑ 80	Randy Moss	1.50	.60
❑ 81	Wesley Walls	.30	.10
❑ 82	Jimmy Smith	.50	.20
❑ 83	Kordell Stewart	.50	.20
❑ 84	Brian Griese	.75	.30
❑ 85	Martin Gramatica	.30	.10
❑ 86	Chris Chandler	.50	.20
❑ 87	Reggie Barlow	.30	.10
❑ 88	Jeff George	.50	.20
❑ 89	Tavian Banks	.30	.10
❑ 90	Mushin Muhammad	.50	.20
❑ 91	Steve McNair	.75	.30
❑ 92	Hines Ward	.75	.30
❑ 93	Brian Mitchell	.30	.10
❑ 94	Daunte Culpepper	1.00	.40
❑ 95	Tim Dwight	.75	.30
❑ 96	Terrence Wilkins	.30	.10
❑ 97	Fred Lane	.30	.10
❑ 98	Brett Favre	2.50	1.00
❑ 99	Richie Anderson	.50	.20
❑ 100	Jamal Anderson	.75	.30
❑ 101	Doug Flutie	.75	.30
❑ 102	Charles Woodson	.50	.20
❑ 103	Jacquez Green	.30	.10
❑ 104	Olandis Gary	.75	.30
❑ 105	Steve Young	1.00	.40
❑ 106	Wayne Chrebet	.50	.20
❑ 107	Karim Abdul-Jabbar	.50	.20
❑ 108	Andre Rison	.50	.20
❑ 109	Eddie Kennison	.30	.10
❑ 110	Jevon Kearse	.75	.30
❑ 111	Tony Richardson RC	.50	.20
❑ 112	Jake Delhomme RC	3.00	1.25
❑ 113	Errict Rhett	.50	.20
❑ 114	Akili Smith	.30	.10
❑ 115	Tyrone Wheatley	.50	.20
❑ 116	Corey Bradford	.50	.20
❑ 117	J.J. Stokes	.50	.20
❑ 118	Simeon Rice	.50	.20
❑ 119	Brad Johnson	.75	.30
❑ 120	Edgerrin James	1.25	.50
❑ 121	Amani Toomer	.30	.10
❑ 122	O.J. McDuffie	.50	.20
❑ 123	Az-Zahir Hakim	.50	.20
❑ 124	Troy Edwards	.30	.10
❑ 125	Tim Biakabutuka	.50	.20
❑ 126	Jason Tucker	.30	.10
❑ 127	Charles Way	.30	.10
❑ 128	Terrell Davis	.75	.30
❑ 129	Garrison Hearst	.50	.20
❑ 130	Fred Taylor	.75	.30
❑ 131	Robert Holcombe	.30	.10
❑ 132	Frank Sanders	.50	.20
❑ 133	Morten Andersen	.30	.10
❑ 134	Cris Carter	.75	.30
❑ 135	Patrick Jeffers	.75	.30
❑ 136	Antonio Freeman	.75	.30
❑ 137	Jonathan Linton	.30	.10
❑ 138	Rashaan Shehee	.30	.10
❑ 139	Luther Broughton RC	.50	.20
❑ 140	Tim Couch	.50	.20
❑ 141	Keith Poole	.30	.10
❑ 142	Champ Bailey	.50	.20
❑ 143	Yancey Thigpen	.30	.10
❑ 144	Joey Galloway	.50	.20
❑ 145	Mac Cody	.30	.10
❑ 146	Damon Huard	.75	.30
❑ 147	Dorsey Levens	.50	.20
❑ 148	Donovan McNabb	1.25	.50
❑ 149	Jamie Asher	.30	.10
❑ 150	Peyton Manning	2.00	.75
❑ 151	Leslie Shepherd	.30	.10
❑ 152	Charlie Rogers	.30	.10
❑ 153	Tony Horne	.30	.10
❑ 154	Jim Miller	.30	.10
❑ 155	Richard Huntley	.30	.10
❑ 156	Germane Crowell	.30	.10
❑ 157	Natrone Means	.30	.10
❑ 158	Justin Armour	.30	.10
❑ 159	Drew Bledsoe	1.00	.40
❑ 160	Dedric Ward	.30	.10
❑ 161	Allen Rossum	.30	.10
❑ 162	Ricky Watters	.50	.20
❑ 163	Kerry Collins	.50	.20
❑ 164	James Johnson	.30	.10
❑ 165	Elvis Grbac	.50	.20
❑ 166	Larry Centers	.30	.10
❑ 167	Rob Moore	.50	.20
❑ 168	Jay Riemersma	.30	.10
❑ 169	Bill Schroeder	.50	.20
❑ 170	Deion Sanders	.75	.30
❑ 171	Jerome Bettis	.75	.30
❑ 172	Dan Marino	2.50	1.00
❑ 173	Terrell Owens	.75	.30
❑ 174	Kevin Carter	.30	.10
❑ 175	Lamar Smith	.50	.20
❑ 176	Ken Dilger	.30	.10
❑ 177	Napoleon Kaufman	.50	.20
❑ 178	Kevin Williams	.30	.10
❑ 179	Tremain Mack	.30	.10
❑ 180	Troy Aikman	1.50	.60
❑ 181	Glyn Milburn	.30	.10
❑ 182	Pete Mitchell	.30	.10
❑ 183	Cameron Cleeland	.30	.10
❑ 184	Qadry Ismail	.50	.20
❑ 185	Michael Pittman	.30	.10
❑ 186	Kevin Dyson	.50	.20
❑ 187	Matt Hasselbeck	.50	.20
❑ 188	Kevin Johnson	.75	.30
❑ 189	Rich Gannon	.75	.30
❑ 190	Stephen Davis	.75	.30
❑ 191	Frank Wycheck	.30	.10
❑ 192	Eric Moulds	.75	.30
❑ 193	Jon Kitna	.75	.30
❑ 194	Mario Bates	.30	.10
❑ 195	Na Brown	.30	.10
❑ 196	Jeff Blake	.50	.20
❑ 197	Charles Evans	.30	.10
❑ 198	Oronde Gadsden	.50	.20
❑ 199	Donnell Bennett	.30	.10
❑ 200	Isaac Bruce	.75	.30
❑ 201	Olindo Mare	.30	.10
❑ 202	Darnell McDonald	.30	.10
❑ 203	Charlie Garner	.50	.20
❑ 204	Shawn Jefferson	.30	.10
❑ 205	Adrian Murrell	.50	.20
❑ 206	Peter Boulware	.30	.10
❑ 207	LeShon Johnson	.30	.10
❑ 208	Herman Moore	.50	.20
❑ 209	Duce Staley	.75	.30
❑ 210	Sean Dawkins	.30	.10
❑ 211	Antowain Smith	.50	.20
❑ 212	Albert Connell	.30	.10
❑ 213	Jeff Garcia	.75	.30
❑ 214	Kimble Anders	.30	.10
❑ 215	Shaun King	.30	.10
❑ 216	Rocket Ismail	.50	.20
❑ 217	Andrew Glover	.30	.10
❑ 218	Rickey Dudley	.30	.10
❑ 219	Michael Basnight	.30	.10
❑ 220	Terry Glenn	.50	.20
❑ 221	Peter Warrick RC	3.00	1.25
❑ 222	Ron Dayne RC	3.00	1.25
❑ 223	Thomas Jones RC	5.00	2.00
❑ 224	Joe Hamilton RC	2.50	1.00
❑ 225	Tim Rattay RC	3.00	1.25
❑ 226	Chad Pennington RC	8.00	3.00
❑ 227	Dennis Northcutt RC	3.00	1.25
❑ 228	Troy Walters RC	3.00	1.25
❑ 229	Travis Prentice RC	2.50	1.00
❑ 230	Shaun Alexander RC	15.00	6.00
❑ 231	J.R. Redmond RC	2.50	1.00
❑ 232	Chris Redman RC	2.50	1.00
❑ 233	Tee Martin RC	3.00	1.25
❑ 234	Tom Brady RC	30.00	15.00
❑ 235	Travis Taylor RC	3.00	1.25
❑ 236	R.Jay Soward RC	2.50	1.00
❑ 237	Jamal Lewis RC	8.00	3.00
❑ 238	Giovanni Carmazzi RC	2.00	.75
❑ 239	Dez White RC	3.00	1.25
❑ 240	LaVar Arrington RC SP	120.00	60.00
❑ 241	Laveranues Coles RC	4.00	1.50
❑ 242	Sherrod Gideon RC	2.00	.75
❑ 243	Trung Canidate RC	2.50	1.00
❑ 244	Michael Wiley RC	2.50	1.00
❑ 245	Anthony Lucas RC	2.00	.75
❑ 246	Darrell Jackson RC	6.00	2.50
❑ 247	Plaxico Burress RC	6.00	2.50
❑ 248	Reuben Droughns RC	4.00	1.50
❑ 249	Marc Bulger RC	6.00	2.50
❑ 250	Danny Farmer RC	2.50	1.00

2001 Ultra

❑	COMP.SET w/o SP's (250)	25.00	10.00
❑ 1	Daunte Culpepper	.75	.30
❑ 2	Kurt Warner	1.50	.60
❑ 3	Emmitt Smith	1.50	.60
❑ 4	Eddie George	.75	.30
❑ 5	Ron Dayne	.75	.30
❑ 6	Zach Thomas	.75	.30
❑ 7	Itula Mili	.30	.10
❑ 8	Jake Reed	.50	.20
❑ 9	James Stewart	.50	.20
❑ 10	Terrence Wilkins	.30	.10
❑ 11	Jeff Blake	.50	.20
❑ 12	Kerry Collins	.50	.20
❑ 13	Christian Fauria	.30	.10
❑ 14	Jackie Harris	.30	.10
❑ 15	Kevin Johnson	.50	.20
❑ 16	Tony Martin	.30	.10
❑ 17	Joey Galloway	.50	.20

❑ 18	Junior Seau	.75	.30
❑ 19	Jason Tucker	.30	.10
❑ 20	Steve Beuerlein	.30	.10
❑ 21	Mike Cloud	.30	.10
❑ 22	Kevin Faulk	.50	.20
❑ 23	Az-Zahir Hakim	.30	.10
❑ 24	Charles Johnson	.30	.10
❑ 25	Curtis Martin	.75	.30
❑ 26	Eric Moulds	.50	.20
❑ 27	Bill Schroeder	.50	.20
❑ 28	Amani Toomer	.30	.10
❑ 29	Obafemi Ayanbadejo	.30	.10
❑ 30	Aaron Shea	.30	.10
❑ 31	Ken Dilger	.30	.10
❑ 32	Terry Glenn	.30	.10
❑ 33	Rocket Ismail	.50	.20
❑ 34	Dorsey Levens	.30	.10
❑ 35	Brian Mitchell	.30	.10
❑ 36	Tony Richardson	.30	.10
❑ 37	Sam Madison	.30	.10
❑ 38	Darren Sharper	.30	.10
❑ 39	Derrick Alexander	.50	.20
❑ 40	Aaron Brooks	.75	.30
❑ 41	Casey Crawford	.30	.10
❑ 42	Terrell Fletcher	.30	.10
❑ 43	William Henderson	.30	.10
❑ 44	Thomas Jones	.50	.20
❑ 45	Keenan McCardell	.30	.10
❑ 46	Chad Pennington	1.25	.50
❑ 47	Akili Smith	.30	.10
❑ 48	Hines Ward	.75	.30
❑ 49	Champ Bailey	.50	.20
❑ 50	Cris Carter	.75	.30
❑ 51	Corey Dillon	.75	.30
❑ 52	Tony Gonzalez	.50	.20
❑ 53	Darrell Jackson	.75	.30
❑ 54	Chad Lewis	.30	.10
❑ 55	Dave Moore	.30	.10
❑ 56	Jay Riemersma	.30	.10
❑ 57	J.J. Stokes	.50	.20
❑ 58	Frank Wycheck	.30	.10
❑ 59	Tiki Barber	.75	.30
❑ 60	Tony Carter	.30	.10
❑ 61	Rickey Dudley	.30	.10
❑ 62	John Lynch	.50	.20
❑ 63	Larry Foster	.30	.10
❑ 64	Willie Jackson	.30	.10
❑ 65	Jamal Lewis	1.25	.50
❑ 66	Herman Moore	.50	.20
❑ 67	Andre Rison	.50	.20
❑ 68	Michael Strahan	.50	.20
❑ 69	Charlie Batch	.75	.30
❑ 70	Larry Centers	.30	.10
❑ 71	Ron Dugans	.30	.10
❑ 72	Jeff Graham	.30	.10
❑ 73	Edgerrin James	1.00	.40
❑ 74	Jermaine Lewis	.30	.10
❑ 75	Charles Woodson	.50	.20
❑ 76	Chris Redman	.30	.10
❑ 77	Jon Ritchie	.30	.10
❑ 78	Fred Taylor	.75	.30
❑ 79	Jamal Anderson	.75	.30
❑ 80	Isaac Bruce	.75	.30
❑ 81	Terrell Davis	.75	.30
❑ 82	Rich Gannon	.75	.30
❑ 83	Joe Horn	.50	.20
❑ 84	Eddie Kennison	.50	.20
❑ 85	Steve McNair	.75	.30
❑ 86	Travis Prentice	.30	.10
❑ 87	Rod Smith	.50	.20
❑ 88	Ricky Watters	.50	.20
❑ 89	Michael Bates	.30	.10
❑ 90	Byron Chamberlain	.30	.10
❑ 91	Warrick Dunn	.75	.30
❑ 92	Elvis Grbac	.50	.20
❑ 93	Patrick Jeffers	.50	.20
❑ 94	Ray Lewis	.75	.30
❑ 95	Sammy Morris	.30	.10
❑ 96	Marcus Robinson	.75	.30
❑ 97	Travis Taylor	.50	.20
❑ 98	Fred Beasley	.30	.10
❑ 99	Chris Chandler	.50	.20
❑ 100	Tim Dwight	.75	.30
❑ 101	Ahman Green	.75	.30
❑ 102	Shawn Jefferson	.30	.10
❑ 103	Jeremy McDaniel	.30	.10
❑ 104	Sylvester Morris	.30	.10
❑ 105	John Randle	.30	.10
❑ 106	Vinny Testaverde	.50	.20
❑ 107	Anthony Becht	.30	.10
❑ 108	Wayne Chrebet	.50	.20
❑ 109	Stephen Boyd	.30	.10
❑ 110	Jacquez Green	.30	.10
❑ 111	MarTay Jenkins	.30	.10
❑ 112	Jason Gildon	.30	.10
❑ 113	Chad Morton	.30	.10
❑ 114	Deion Sanders	.75	.30
❑ 115	Yancey Thigpen	.30	.10
❑ 116	Marty Booker	.30	.10
❑ 117	Curtis Conway	.50	.20
❑ 118	Jermaine Fazande	.30	.10
❑ 119	Matthew Hatchette	.30	.10
❑ 120	Pat Johnson	.30	.10
❑ 121	Terance Mathis	.50	.20
❑ 122	Terrell Owens	.75	.30
❑ 123	Corey Simon	.50	.20
❑ 124	Darrick Vaughn	.30	.10
❑ 125	Drew Bledsoe	1.00	.40
❑ 126	Albert Connell	.30	.10
❑ 127	Brett Favre	2.50	1.00
❑ 128	Marvin Harrison	.75	.30
❑ 129	Keyshawn Johnson	.75	.30
❑ 130	Derrick Mason	.50	.20
❑ 131	Dennis Northcutt	.50	.20
❑ 132	Shannon Sharpe	.50	.20
❑ 133	Brian Urlacher	1.25	.50
❑ 134	Mike Anderson	.75	.30
❑ 135	Mark Bruener	.30	.10
❑ 136	Sean Dawkins	.30	.10
❑ 137	Jeff Garcia	.75	.30
❑ 138	Tony Horne	.30	.10
❑ 139	Shaun King	.30	.10
❑ 140	Cade McNown	.30	.10
❑ 141	Peerless Price	.50	.20
❑ 142	R.Jay Soward	.30	.10
❑ 143	Tyrone Wheatley	.50	.20
❑ 144	Richie Anderson	.30	.10
❑ 145	Mark Brunell	.75	.30
❑ 146	JaJuan Dawson	.30	.10
❑ 147	Charlie Garner	.50	.20
❑ 148	Desmond Howard	.30	.10
❑ 149	Jon Kitna	.50	.20
❑ 150	Duane Starks	.30	.10
❑ 151	J.R. Redmond	.30	.10
❑ 152	Duce Staley	.75	.30
❑ 153	Dez White	.30	.10
❑ 154	David Boston	.75	.30
❑ 155	Tim Couch	.50	.20
❑ 156	Jay Fiedler	.75	.30
❑ 157	Jessie Armstead	.30	.10
❑ 158	Rob Johnson	.50	.20
❑ 159	Brad Johnson	.75	.30
❑ 160	Derrick Mayes	.30	.10
❑ 161	Jerome Pathon	.50	.20
❑ 162	David Sloan	.30	.10
❑ 163	Wesley Walls	.30	.10
❑ 164	Shaun Alexander	1.00	.40
❑ 165	Derrick Brooks	.75	.30
❑ 166	Germane Crowell	.30	.10
❑ 167	Doug Flutie	.75	.30
❑ 168	Ike Hilliard	.50	.20
❑ 169	Hugh Douglas	.30	.10
❑ 170	Wane McGarity	.30	.10
❑ 171	Michael Pittman	.30	.10
❑ 172	Shawn Bryson	.30	.10
❑ 173	Richard Huntley	.30	.10
❑ 174	Darnell Autry	.30	.10
❑ 175	Plaxico Burress	.75	.30
❑ 176	Trent Dilfer	.50	.20
❑ 177	Jeff George	.50	.20
❑ 178	Qadry Ismail	.50	.20
❑ 179	Ryan Leaf	.50	.20
❑ 180	Jim Miller	.30	.10
❑ 181	Jerry Rice	1.50	.60
❑ 182	Kordell Stewart	.50	.20
❑ 183	Ricky Williams	.75	.30
❑ 184	James Allen	.50	.20
❑ 185	Courtney Brown	.50	.20
❑ 186	Reidel Anthony	.30	.10
❑ 187	Bubba Franks	.50	.20
❑ 188	Priest Holmes	1.00	.40
❑ 189	Napoleon Kaufman	.30	.10
❑ 190	Trevor Pryce	.30	.10
❑ 191	Jake Plummer	.50	.20
❑ 192	Jimmy Smith	.50	.20
❑ 193	Michael Wiley	.30	.10
❑ 194	Brock Huard	.30	.10
❑ 195	Troy Brown	.50	.20
❑ 196	Stephen Davis	.75	.30
❑ 197	Oronde Gadsden	.50	.20
❑ 198	Brad Hoover	.30	.10
❑ 199	La'Roi Glover	.30	.10
❑ 200	Donovan McNabb	1.00	.40
❑ 201	Jerry Porter	.50	.20
❑ 202	Robert Smith	.50	.20
❑ 203	Justin Watson	.30	.10
❑ 204	Tim Biakabutuka	.50	.20
❑ 205	Laveranues Coles	.75	.30
❑ 206	Marshall Faulk	1.00	.40
❑ 207	Jim Harbaugh	.50	.20
❑ 208	Doug Johnson	.30	.10
❑ 209	Tee Martin	.50	.20
❑ 210	Muhsin Muhammad	.50	.20
❑ 211	Darnay Scott	.30	.10
❑ 212	Jeremiah Trotter	.50	.20
❑ 213	Troy Aikman	1.25	.50
❑ 214	Kyle Brady	.30	.10
❑ 215	Sam Cowart	.30	.10
❑ 216	Darren Howard	.30	.10
❑ 217	Donald Hayes	.30	.10
❑ 218	Freddie Jones	.30	.10
❑ 219	Ed McCaffrey	.75	.30
❑ 220	David Patten	.30	.10
❑ 221	Brian Griese	.75	.30
❑ 222	Dedric Ward	.30	.10
❑ 223	Jerome Bettis	.75	.30
❑ 224	Greg Clark	.30	.10
❑ 225	Bobby Engram	.30	.10
❑ 226	Matt Hasselbeck	.50	.20
❑ 227	James Jett	.30	.10
❑ 228	Peyton Manning	2.00	.75
❑ 229	Randy Moss	1.50	.60
❑ 230	Warren Sapp	.50	.20
❑ 231	James Thrash	.50	.20
❑ 232	Mike Alstott	.75	.30
❑ 233	Tim Brown	.75	.30
❑ 234	Randall Cunningham	.75	.30
❑ 235	Antonio Freeman	.75	.30
❑ 236	Torry Holt	.75	.30
❑ 237	Jevon Kearse	.50	.20
❑ 238	James McKnight	.50	.20
❑ 239	Marcus Pollard	.30	.10
❑ 240	Lamar Smith	.50	.20
❑ 241	Peter Warrick	.75	.30
❑ 242	Donnell Bennett	.30	.10
❑ 243	Joe Johnson	.30	.10
❑ 244	Troy Edwards	.30	.10
❑ 245	Trent Green	.75	.30
❑ 246	Jason Taylor	.30	.10
❑ 247	Aeneas Williams	.30	.10
❑ 248	Johnnie Morton	.50	.20
❑ 249	Frank Sanders	.30	.10
❑ 250	Jason Sehorn	.30	.10
❑ 251	Chris Weinke RC	6.00	2.50
❑ 252	Bobby Newcombe RC	4.00	1.50
❑ 253	LaDainian Tomlinson RC	30.00	15.00
❑ 254	Chad Johnson RC	15.00	6.00
❑ 255	Derrick Gibson RC	4.00	1.50
❑ 256	Sage Rosenfels RC	6.00	2.50
❑ 257	LaMont Jordan RC	12.00	5.00
❑ 258	Mike McMahon RC	6.00	2.50
❑ 259	Vinny Sutherland RC	4.00	1.50
❑ 260	Drew Brees RC	15.00	6.00
❑ 261	Deuce McAllister RC	12.00	5.00
❑ 262	Kevan Barlow RC	6.00	2.50
❑ 263	Jamar Fletcher RC	4.00	1.50
❑ 264	Gerard Warren RC	6.00	2.50
❑ 265	Todd Heap RC	6.00	2.50
❑ 266	Travis Henry RC	6.00	2.50
❑ 267	Quincy Morgan RC	6.00	2.50
❑ 268	Anthony Thomas RC	6.00	2.50
❑ 269	Andre Carter RC	6.00	2.50
❑ 270	Freddie Mitchell RC	6.00	2.50
❑ 271	Richard Seymour RC	6.00	2.50
❑ 272	Josh Booty RC	6.00	2.50
❑ 273	Robert Ferguson RC	6.00	2.50
❑ 274	Marques Tuiasosopo RC	6.00	2.50
❑ 275	Reggie Wayne RC	12.00	5.00
❑ 276	Jabari Holloway RC	4.00	1.50
❑ 277	Rudi Johnson RC	12.00	5.00
❑ 278	Michael Bennett RC	10.00	4.00

❑ 279 Snoop Minnis RC 4.00 1.50
❑ 280 Dan Morgan RC 6.00 2.50
❑ 281 Rod Gardner RC 6.00 2.50
❑ 282 Jesse Palmer RC 6.00 2.50
❑ 283 Michael Vick RC 40.00 20.00
❑ 284 Chris Chambers RC 10.00 4.00
❑ 285 James Jackson RC 6.00 2.50
❑ 286 David Terrell RC 6.00 2.50
❑ 287 Koren Robinson RC 6.00 2.50
❑ 288 Travis Minor RC 4.00 1.50
❑ 289 Santana Moss RC 10.00 4.00
❑ 290 Josh Heupel RC 6.00 2.50
❑ 291 Jamal Reynolds RC 6.00 2.50
❑ 292 Ken-Yon Rambo RC 4.00 1.50
❑ 293 Cedrick Wilson RC 6.00 2.50
❑ 294 Alge Crumpler RC 8.00 4.00
❑ 295 Fred Smoot RC 6.00 2.50
❑ 296 Dan Alexander RC 6.00 2.50
❑ 297 Tim Hasselbeck RC 6.00 2.50
❑ 298 Will Allen RC 4.00 1.50
❑ 299 Keith Adams RC 4.00 1.50
❑ 300 Heath Evans RC 4.00 1.50
❑ U301 Quincy Carter RC 6.00 2.50
❑ U302 Derrick Blaylock RC 6.00 2.50
❑ U303 Correll Buckhalter RC 8.00 3.00
❑ U304 A.J. Feeley RC 6.00 2.50
❑ U305 Milton Wynn RC 4.00 1.50
❑ U306 Kevin Kasper RC 6.00 2.50
❑ U307 Justin McCareins RC 6.00 2.50
❑ U308 Dave Dickenson RC 4.00 1.50
❑ U309 Steve Smith RC 15.00 7.50
❑ U310 Moran Norris RC 2.50 1.00

2002 Ultra

❑ COMP.SET w/o SP's (200) 25.00 10.00
❑ 1 Donovan McNabb 1.00 .40
❑ 2 Chad Pennington 1.00 .40
❑ 3 Shaun Alexander 1.00 .40
❑ 4 Corey Dillon .50 .20
❑ 5 Kurt Warner .75 .30
❑ 6 Ed McCaffrey .75 .30
❑ 7 Hugh Douglas .30 .10
❑ 8 Tony Gonzalez .50 .20
❑ 9 Travis Taylor .50 .20
❑ 10 Tony Boselli .30 .10
❑ 11 Chad Scott .30 .10
❑ 12 Ernie Conwell .30 .10
❑ 13 Brad Johnson .50 .20
❑ 14 Donald Hayes .30 .10
❑ 15 Emmitt Smith 2.00 .75
❑ 16 Jimmy Smith .50 .20
❑ 17 Anthony Becht .30 .10
❑ 18 Rod Gardner .50 .20
❑ 19 Muhsin Muhammad .50 .20
❑ 20 Troy Hambrick .30 .10
❑ 21 Keenan McCardell .30 .10
❑ 22 Laveranues Coles .50 .20
❑ 23 Kevin Dyson .50 .20
❑ 24 Grant Wistrom .30 .10
❑ 25 Eric Moulds .50 .20
❑ 26 Nate Clements .30 .10
❑ 27 Terrell Davis .75 .30
❑ 28 Aaron Glenn .30 .10
❑ 29 Eric Hicks .30 .10
❑ 30 Tiki Barber .75 .30
❑ 31 Jake Plummer .50 .20
❑ 32 Junior Seau .75 .30
❑ 33 Marshall Faulk .75 .30
❑ 34 Warrick Dunn .75 .30
❑ 35 Bill Gramatica .30 .10
❑ 36 Tim Couch .50 .20
❑ 37 Kabeer Gbaja-Biamila .50 .20
❑ 38 Kailee Wong .30 .10
❑ 39 David Patten .30 .10
❑ 40 Correll Buckhalter .50 .20
❑ 41 Troy Brown .50 .20
❑ 42 Drew Bledsoe 1.00 .40
❑ 43 Travis Henry .75 .30
❑ 44 Jim Miller .30 .10
❑ 45 Rod Smith .50 .20
❑ 46 Tai Streets .30 .10
❑ 47 Snoop Minnis .30 .10
❑ 48 Ron Dayne .50 .20
❑ 49 Tyrone Wheatley .50 .20
❑ 50 LaDainian Tomlinson 1.25 .50
❑ 51 Akili Smith .30 .10
❑ 52 Warren Sapp .50 .20
❑ 53 Adam Archuleta .30 .10
❑ 54 Chris Fuamatu-Ma'afala .30 .10
❑ 55 Marty Booker .30 .10
❑ 56 Trevor Pryce .30 .10
❑ 57 Peyton Manning 1.50 .60
❑ 58 Lamar Smith .50 .20
❑ 59 Amani Toomer .50 .20
❑ 60 Greg Biekert .30 .10
❑ 61 Marcellus Wiley .30 .10
❑ 62 Ahmed Plummer .30 .10
❑ 63 Mike Alstott .75 .30
❑ 64 Gary Walker .30 .10
❑ 65 Champ Bailey .50 .20
❑ 66 Chris Redman .30 .10
❑ 67 David Terrell .75 .30
❑ 68 Mike McMahon .75 .30
❑ 69 Marvin Harrison .75 .30
❑ 70 Jay Fiedler .50 .20
❑ 71 JaJuan Dawson .30 .10
❑ 72 Charlie Garner .50 .20
❑ 73 Curtis Conway .30 .10
❑ 74 J.J. Stokes .50 .20
❑ 75 Ronde Barber .30 .10
❑ 76 Alge Crumpler .50 .20
❑ 77 Jamir Miller .30 .10
❑ 78 Brett Favre 2.00 .75
❑ 79 Randy Moss 1.50 .60
❑ 80 Joe Horn .50 .20
❑ 81 Hines Ward .75 .30
❑ 82 Lawyer Milloy .50 .20
❑ 83 Aeneas Williams .30 .10
❑ 84 Chris McAlister .30 .10
❑ 85 Anthony Thomas .50 .20
❑ 86 Johnnie Morton .50 .20
❑ 87 Edgerrin James 1.00 .40
❑ 88 Chris Chambers .75 .30
❑ 89 Michael Strahan .50 .20
❑ 90 Charles Woodson .50 .20
❑ 91 Tim Dwight .50 .20
❑ 92 Kevan Barlow .50 .20
❑ 93 Donnie Abraham .30 .10
❑ 94 Peter Boulware .30 .10
❑ 95 Marcus Robinson .50 .20
❑ 96 Shaun Rogers .30 .10
❑ 97 Dominic Rhodes .50 .20
❑ 98 Zach Thomas .75 .30
❑ 99 Kerry Collins .50 .20
❑ 100 Tim Brown .75 .30
❑ 101 Garrison Hearst .50 .20
❑ 102 Steve McNair .75 .30
❑ 103 Fred Smoot .30 .10
❑ 104 Isaac Bruce .75 .30
❑ 105 Jamal Lewis .75 .30
❑ 106 Brian Urlacher 1.25 .50
❑ 107 Takeo Spikes .30 .10
❑ 108 Marcus Pollard .30 .10
❑ 109 Jason Taylor .30 .10
❑ 110 Deuce McAllister 1.00 .40
❑ 111 Jerry Rice 1.50 .60
❑ 112 Terrell Owens .75 .30
❑ 113 Eddie George .75 .30
❑ 114 Rob Morris .30 .10
❑ 115 Mike Brown .75 .30
❑ 116 Joey Galloway .50 .20
❑ 117 Fred Taylor .75 .30
❑ 118 Rich Gannon .75 .30
❑ 119 Chris Chandler .50 .20
❑ 120 Koren Robinson .50 .20
❑ 121 Dan Morgan .30 .10
❑ 122 Rocket Ismail .50 .20
❑ 123 Mark Brunell .75 .30
❑ 124 John Abraham .50 .20
❑ 125 Stephen Davis .50 .20
❑ 126 Patrick Kerney .30 .10
❑ 127 Anthony Henry .30 .10
❑ 128 Scotty Anderson .30 .10
❑ 129 Oronde Gadsden .30 .10
❑ 130 Willie Jackson .30 .10
❑ 131 Kendrell Bell .75 .30
❑ 132 Ray Lewis .75 .30
❑ 133 Quincy Carter .50 .20
❑ 134 James Stewart .50 .20
❑ 135 Travis Minor .30 .10
❑ 136 Kyle Turley .30 .10
❑ 137 Jason Gildon .30 .10
❑ 138 David Boston .75 .30
❑ 139 Justin Smith .30 .10
❑ 140 Jamie Sharper .30 .10
❑ 141 Antowain Smith .50 .20
❑ 142 Freddie Mitchell .50 .20
❑ 143 Frank Sanders .30 .10
❑ 144 Kevin Johnson .50 .20
❑ 145 Darren Sharper .30 .10
❑ 146 Eric Johnson .30 .10
❑ 147 Ty Law .50 .20
❑ 148 James Thrash .50 .20
❑ 149 Matt Hasselbeck .50 .20
❑ 150 Peerless Price .50 .20
❑ 151 T.J. Houshmandzadeh .50 .20
❑ 152 Mike Anderson .75 .30
❑ 153 Jermaine Lewis .30 .10
❑ 154 Trent Green .50 .20
❑ 155 Ron Dixon .30 .10
❑ 156 Duce Staley .75 .30
❑ 157 Drew Brees .75 .30
❑ 158 Torry Holt .75 .30
❑ 159 Keyshawn Johnson .75 .30
❑ 160 Michael Vick 2.50 1.00
❑ 161 Benjamin Gay .30 .10
❑ 162 Bill Schroeder .50 .20
❑ 163 Byron Chamberlain .30 .10
❑ 164 Tedy Bruschi .75 .30
❑ 165 Kordell Stewart .50 .20
❑ 166 Deltha O'Neal .30 .10
❑ 167 Quincy Morgan .30 .10
❑ 168 Bubba Franks .50 .20
❑ 169 Daunte Culpepper .75 .30
❑ 170 Ricky Williams 4.00 1.50
❑ 171 Plaxico Burress .50 .20
❑ 172 Trent Dilfer .50 .20
❑ 173 Steve Smith .75 .30
❑ 174 Greg Ellis .30 .10
❑ 175 Tony Brackens .30 .10
❑ 176 Santana Moss .75 .30
❑ 177 Frank Wycheck .30 .10
❑ 178 Michael Pittman .30 .10
❑ 179 Peter Warrick .50 .20
❑ 180 Antonio Freeman .75 .30
❑ 181 Tom Brady 2.00 .75
❑ 182 Bobby Taylor .30 .10
❑ 183 Jeff Garcia .75 .30
❑ 184 Darrell Jackson .50 .20
❑ 185 Chris Weinke .50 .20
❑ 186 Darren Woodson .30 .10
❑ 187 Hardy Nickerson .30 .10
❑ 188 Wayne Chrebet .50 .20
❑ 189 Samari Rolle .30 .10
❑ 190 Jamal Anderson .50 .20
❑ 191 James Jackson .30 .10
❑ 192 Ahman Green .75 .30
❑ 193 Michael Bennett .50 .20
❑ 194 Aaron Brooks .75 .30
❑ 195 Jerome Bettis .75 .30
❑ 196 Jay Riemersma .30 .10
❑ 197 Brian Griese .75 .30
❑ 198 Priest Holmes 1.00 .40
❑ 199 Curtis Martin .75 .30
❑ 200 Derrick Mason .50 .20
❑ 201 Antonio Bryant RC 5.00 2.00
❑ 202 David Carr RC 12.00 5.00
❑ 203 Eric Crouch RC 5.00 2.00
❑ 204 Freddie Milons RC 4.00 1.50
❑ 205 Najeh Davenport RC 5.00 2.00
❑ 206 Rohan Davey RC 5.00 2.00
❑ 207 T.J. Duckett RC 8.00 3.00
❑ 208 DeShaun Foster RC 5.00 2.00

❑ 209	Jabar Gaffney RC	5.00	2.00
❑ 210	William Green RC	5.00	2.00
❑ 211	Joey Harrington RC	12.00	5.00
❑ 212	Travis Stephens RC	4.00	1.50
❑ 213	Julius Peppers RC	10.00	4.00
❑ 214	Adrian Peterson RC	5.00	2.00
❑ 215	Josh Reed RC	5.00	2.00
❑ 216	Mike Williams RC	5.00	2.00
❑ 217	Javon Walker RC	10.00	4.00
❑ 218	Marquise Walker RC	4.00	1.50
❑ 219	Patrick Ramsey RC	6.00	2.50
❑ 220	Lamar Gordon RC	5.00	2.00
❑ 221	David Garrard RC	5.00	2.00
❑ 222	Major Applewhite RC	5.00	2.00
❑ 223	Andre Davis RC	4.00	1.50
❑ 224	Roy Williams RC	12.00	5.00
❑ 225	Tim Carter RC	4.00	1.50
❑ 226	Ron Johnson RC	4.00	1.50
❑ 227	Randy Fasani RC	4.00	1.50
❑ 228	Ashley Lelie RC	10.00	4.00
❑ 229	Ladell Betts RC	5.00	2.00
❑ 230	Antwaan Randle El RC	8.00	3.00
❑ 231	Jonathan Wells RC	5.00	2.00
❑ 232	Brian Westbrook RC	8.00	3.00
❑ 233	Clinton Portis RC	15.00	6.00
❑ 234	Luke Staley RC	4.00	1.50
❑ 235	Cliff Russell RC	4.00	1.50
❑ 236	Jeremy Shockey RC	15.00	6.00
❑ 237	Donte Stallworth RC	10.00	4.00
❑ 238	Daniel Graham RC	5.00	2.00
❑ 239	Reche Caldwell RC	5.00	2.00
❑ 240	Ryan Sims RC	5.00	2.00

2003 Ultra

❑	COMP.SET w/o SP's (160)	30.00	12.50
❑ 1	Rich Gannon	.50	.20
❑ 2	Warren Sapp	.50	.20
❑ 3	Steve McNair	.75	.30
❑ 4	Donovan McNabb	1.00	.40
❑ 5	Chad Pennington	1.00	.40
❑ 6	Michael Vick	2.00	.75
❑ 7	Hines Ward	.75	.30
❑ 8	Terrell Owens	.75	.30
❑ 9	Brett Favre	2.00	.75
❑ 10	Jeremy Shockey	1.25	.50
❑ 11	William Green	.50	.20
❑ 12	Marvin Harrison	.75	.30
❑ 13	Mark Brunell	.50	.20
❑ 14	Todd Heap	.50	.20
❑ 15	Tim Couch	.30	.10
❑ 16	Javon Walker	.50	.20
❑ 17	Zach Thomas	.50	.20
❑ 18	Brian Westbrook	.50	.20
❑ 19	Matt Hasselbeck	.50	.20
❑ 20	Jevon Kearse	.50	.20
❑ 21	David Boston	.50	.20
❑ 22	Michael Bennett	.50	.20
❑ 23	James Mungro	.30	.10
❑ 24	Antowain Smith	.50	.20
❑ 25	Laveranues Coles	.50	.20
❑ 26	Curtis Conway	.30	.10
❑ 27	Peerless Price	.50	.20
❑ 28	Michael Strahan	.50	.20
❑ 29	Tommy Maddox	.75	.30
❑ 30	Dennis Northcutt	.50	.20
❑ 31	Rod Gardner	.50	.20
❑ 32	Marcel Shipp	.50	.20
❑ 33	Quincy Morgan	.50	.20
❑ 34	Reggie Wayne	.50	.20
❑ 35	Troy Brown	.50	.20
❑ 36	John Abraham	.30	.10
❑ 37	Tim Dwight	.50	.20
❑ 38	Jamal Lewis	.75	.30
❑ 39	Chad Hutchinson	.30	.10
❑ 40	Jerramy Stevens	.30	.10
❑ 41	Deion Branch	.75	.30
❑ 42	Jake Plummer	.50	.20
❑ 43	Junior Seau	.75	.30
❑ 44	T.J. Duckett	.50	.20
❑ 45	Emmitt Smith	2.00	.75
❑ 46	Edgerrin James	.75	.30
❑ 47	David Patten	.30	.10
❑ 48	Charlie Garner	.50	.20
❑ 49	Quentin Jammer	.30	.10
❑ 50	Corey Dillon	.50	.20
❑ 51	Rod Smith	.50	.20
❑ 52	Marc Boerigter	.50	.20
❑ 53	Michael Lewis	.30	.10
❑ 54	Kendrell Bell	.50	.20
❑ 55	Isaac Bruce	.75	.30
❑ 56	Warrick Dunn	.50	.20
❑ 57	Antonio Bryant	.50	.20
❑ 58	Peyton Manning	1.25	.50
❑ 59	Ty Law	.50	.20
❑ 60	Jerry Rice	1.50	.60
❑ 61	Jeff Garcia	.75	.30
❑ 62	Joey Galloway	.50	.20
❑ 63	Aaron Glenn	.30	.10
❑ 64	Aaron Brooks	.75	.30
❑ 65	Tim Brown	.75	.30
❑ 66	David Terrell	.50	.20
❑ 67	Fred Smoot	.30	.10
❑ 68	Brian Finneran	.30	.10
❑ 69	Roy Williams	.75	.30
❑ 70	Corey Bradford	.30	.10
❑ 71	Deuce McAllister	.75	.30
❑ 72	Jerry Porter	.50	.20
❑ 73	Kevan Barlow	.50	.20
❑ 74	Keith Brooking	.30	.10
❑ 75	Brian Urlacher	1.25	.50
❑ 76	Jabar Gaffney	.50	.20
❑ 77	Randy Moss	1.25	.50
❑ 78	Charles Woodson	.50	.20
❑ 79	Darrell Jackson	.50	.20
❑ 80	John Lynch	.50	.20
❑ 81	Chester Taylor	.30	.10
❑ 82	Anthony Thomas	.50	.20
❑ 83	Jonathan Wells	.30	.10
❑ 84	Daunte Culpepper	.75	.30
❑ 85	Phillip Buchanon	.30	.10
❑ 86	Koren Robinson	.30	.10
❑ 87	Ronde Barber	.30	.10
❑ 88	Julius Peppers	.75	.30
❑ 89	Clinton Portis	1.25	.50
❑ 90	Jay Fiedler	.50	.20
❑ 91	Donte Stallworth	.75	.30
❑ 92	Marc Bulger	.75	.30
❑ 93	Joe Jurevicius	.30	.10
❑ 94	Jon Kitna	.50	.20
❑ 95	Ricky Williams	.75	.30
❑ 96	Joe Horn	.50	.20
❑ 97	Jerome Bettis	.75	.30
❑ 98	Kurt Warner	.75	.30
❑ 99	Travis Henry	.50	.20
❑ 100	Ahman Green	.75	.30
❑ 101	Jimmy Smith	.50	.20
❑ 102	Curtis Martin	.75	.30
❑ 103	Simeon Rice	.50	.20
❑ 104	Patrick Ramsey	.75	.30
❑ 105	Josh Reed	.50	.20
❑ 106	James Stewart	.50	.20
❑ 107	Trent Green	.50	.20
❑ 108	Randy McMichael	.50	.20
❑ 109	Amos Zereoue	.50	.20
❑ 110	Keyshawn Johnson	.75	.30
❑ 111	DeShaun Foster	.30	.10
❑ 112	Kevin Johnson	.50	.20
❑ 113	Dwight Freeney	.50	.20
❑ 114	Tom Brady	2.00	.75
❑ 115	Santana Moss	.50	.20
❑ 116	LaDainian Tomlinson	.75	.30
❑ 117	Joey Harrington	1.25	.50
❑ 118	Priest Holmes	1.00	.40
❑ 119	Amani Toomer	.50	.20
❑ 120	Plaxico Burress	.50	.20
❑ 121	Brad Johnson	.50	.20
❑ 122	Champ Bailey	.50	.20
❑ 123	Muhsin Muhammad	.50	.20
❑ 124	Ashley Lelie	.75	.30
❑ 125	Tony Gonzalez	.50	.20
❑ 126	Kerry Collins	.50	.20
❑ 127	Antwaan Randle El	.75	.30
❑ 128	Torry Holt	.75	.30
❑ 129	Ladell Betts	.50	.20
❑ 130	Travis Taylor	.30	.10
❑ 131	Marty Booker	.50	.20
❑ 132	Patrick Surtain	.30	.10
❑ 133	Duce Staley	.50	.20
❑ 134	Shaun Alexander	.75	.30
❑ 135	Eddie George	.50	.20
❑ 136	Eric Moulds	.50	.20
❑ 137	David Carr	1.25	.50
❑ 138	Fred Taylor	.75	.30
❑ 139	Wayne Chrebet	.50	.20
❑ 140	Bobby Taylor	.30	.10
❑ 141	Derrick Brooks	.50	.20
❑ 142	Stephen Davis	.50	.20
❑ 143	Ray Lewis	.75	.30
❑ 144	Kelly Holcomb	.50	.20
❑ 145	Terry Glenn	.30	.10
❑ 146	Jason Taylor	.30	.10
❑ 147	Todd Pinkston	.50	.20
❑ 148	Derrick Mason	.50	.20
❑ 149	Chad Johnson	.75	.30
❑ 150	Ed McCaffrey	.50	.20
❑ 151	Tiki Barber	.75	.30
❑ 152	Drew Brees	.75	.30
❑ 153	Marshall Faulk	.75	.30
❑ 154	Drew Bledsoe	.75	.30
❑ 155	Andre Davis	.30	.10
❑ 156	Donald Driver	.50	.20
❑ 157	Chris Chambers	.75	.30
❑ 158	Brian Dawkins	.50	.20
❑ 159	Garrison Hearst	.50	.20
❑ 160	Frank Wycheck	.30	.10
❑ 161	Carson Palmer RC	15.00	6.00
❑ 162	Byron Leftwich RC	12.00	5.00
❑ 163	Charles Rogers RC	4.00	1.50
❑ 164	Andre Johnson RC	8.00	3.00
❑ 165	Chris Simms RC	6.00	2.50
❑ 166	Rex Grossman RC	6.00	2.50
❑ 167	Brandon Lloyd RC	5.00	2.00
❑ 168	Lee Suggs RC	8.00	3.00
❑ 169	Larry Johnson RC	15.00	7.50
❑ 170	Onterrio Smith RC	4.00	1.50
❑ 171	Dave Ragone RC	4.00	1.50
❑ 172	Taylor Jacobs RC	3.00	1.25
❑ 173	Kelley Washington RC	4.00	1.50
❑ 174	Bryant Johnson RC	4.00	1.50
❑ 175	Kyle Boller RC	8.00	3.00
❑ 176	Ken Dorsey RC	4.00	1.50
❑ 177	Kliff Kingsbury RC	3.00	1.25
❑ 178	Jason Gesser RC	4.00	1.50
❑ 179	Brian St.Pierre RC	4.00	1.50
❑ 180	Brad Banks RC	3.00	1.25
❑ 181	Seneca Wallace RC	4.00	1.50
❑ 182	Tony Romo RC	4.00	1.50
❑ 183	Terrell Suggs RC	6.00	2.50
❑ 184	Terence Newman RC	8.00	3.00
❑ 185	Willis McGahee RC	10.00	4.00
❑ 186	Justin Fargas RC	4.00	1.50
❑ 187	Musa Smith RC	4.00	1.50
❑ 188	Earnest Graham RC	3.00	1.25
❑ 189	Chris Brown RC	5.00	2.00
❑ 190	LaBrandon Toefield RC	4.00	1.50
❑ 191	Bennie Joppru RC	4.00	1.50
❑ 192	Jason Witten RC	6.00	2.50
❑ 193	Anquan Boldin RC	10.00	4.00
❑ 194	Talman Gardner RC	4.00	1.50
❑ 195	Justin Gage RC	4.00	1.50
❑ 196	Sam Aiken RC	3.00	1.25
❑ 197	Kevin Curtis RC	4.00	1.50
❑ 198	Terrence Edwards RC	3.00	1.25
❑ U199	DeWayne Robertson RC	4.00	1.50
❑ U200	Kevin Williams RC	4.00	1.50
❑ U201	Marcus Trufant RC	4.00	1.50
❑ U202	Jimmy Kennedy RC	4.00	1.50
❑ U203	Ty Warren RC	4.00	1.50
❑ U204	Michael Haynes RC	4.00	1.50
❑ U205	Jerome McDougle RC	4.00	1.50
❑ U206	Dallas Clark RC	4.00	1.50
❑ U207	William Joseph RC	4.00	1.50
❑ U208	Andre Woolfolk RC	4.00	1.50

	Card		
❑ U209	Bethel Johnson RC	4.00	1.50
❑ U210	Teyo Johnson RC	4.00	1.50
❑ U211	Tyrone Calico RC	5.00	2.00
❑ U212	L.J. Smith RC	4.00	1.50
❑ U213	Nate Burleson RC	5.00	2.00
❑ U214	B.J. Askew RC	4.00	1.50
❑ U215	Billy McMullen RC	4.00	1.50
❑ U216	Domanick Davis RC	6.00	2.50
❑ U217	Doug Gabriel RC	4.00	1.50
❑ U218	Quentin Griffin RC	4.00	1.50

2004 Ultra

❑ COMP.SET w/o L13's (218) 60.00 25.00
❑ COMP.SET w/o SP's (200) 30.00 12.50
❑ COMP.UPDATE SET (21) 40.00 15.00
❑ L13 201-213 ROOKIE ODDS 1:100H,1:530R
❑ L13 ROOKIE PRINT RUN 500 SER.#'d SETS
❑ 214-232 ROOKIE STATED ODDS 1:4H,1:6R
❑ U234-U254 ODDS 2:1 TRADITION HOT PACK

	Card		
❑ 1	Michael Vick	1.50	.60
❑ 2	Kelley Washington	.30	.10
❑ 3	Rex Grossman	.75	.30
❑ 4	Boss Bailey	.50	.20
❑ 5	Johnnie Morton	.50	.20
❑ 6	Michael Strahan	.50	.20
❑ 7	Joey Porter	.50	.20
❑ 8	Keenan McCardell	.30	.10
❑ 9	Quincy Carter	.50	.20
❑ 10	Travis Henry	.50	.20
❑ 11	Bertrand Berry	.30	.10
❑ 12	Marvin Harrison	.75	.30
❑ 13	Ty Law	.50	.20
❑ 14	Phillip Buchanon	.30	.10
❑ 15	Kevan Barlow	.50	.20
❑ 16	Eddie George	.50	.20
❑ 17	Drew Bledsoe	.75	.30
❑ 18	Antonio Bryant	.50	.20
❑ 19	Marcus Pollard	.30	.10
❑ 20	Brian Russell RC	.75	.30
❑ 21	Santana Moss	.50	.20
❑ 22	Julian Peterson	.30	.10
❑ 23	Justin McCareins	.30	.10
❑ 24	Ed Reed	.50	.20
❑ 25	Charles Tillman	.50	.20
❑ 26	Dat Nguyen	.30	.10
❑ 27	Ricky Manning	.30	.10
❑ 28	Dwight Freeney	.50	.20
❑ 29	Zach Thomas	.75	.30
❑ 30	Tiki Barber	.75	.30
❑ 31	Jay Riemersma	.30	.10
❑ 32	Joe Jurevicius	.30	.10
❑ 33	Marcel Shipp	.50	.20
❑ 34	Justin Gage	.50	.20
❑ 35	Charles Rogers	.50	.20
❑ 36	Eddie Kennison	.30	.10
❑ 37	Deion Branch	.75	.30
❑ 38	Matt Hasselbeck	.50	.20
❑ 39	L.J. Smith	.50	.20
❑ 40	Jamal Lewis	.75	.30
❑ 41	Muhsin Muhammad	.50	.20
❑ 42	Terence Newman	.50	.20
❑ 43	Jabar Gaffney	.50	.20
❑ 44	Junior Seau	.75	.30
❑ 45	Jeremy Shockey	.75	.30
❑ 46	Hines Ward	.75	.30
❑ 47	Brad Johnson	.50	.20
❑ 48	Kyle Boller	.75	.30

	Card		
❑ 49	Steve Smith	.75	.30
❑ 50	Quincy Morgan	.50	.20
❑ 51	Corey Bradford	.30	.10
❑ 52	Ricky Williams	.75	.30
❑ 53	Amani Toomer	.50	.20
❑ 54	Plaxico Burress	.50	.20
❑ 55	Derrick Brooks	.50	.20
❑ 56	Dre Bly	.30	.10
❑ 57	Terrell Suggs	.50	.20
❑ 58	DeShaun Foster	.50	.20
❑ 59	Andre Davis	.30	.10
❑ 60	Rod Smith	.50	.20
❑ 61	Andre Johnson	.75	.30
❑ 62	Randy McMichael	.30	.10
❑ 63	Ike Hilliard	.30	.10
❑ 64	Antwaan Randle El	.75	.30
❑ 65	Warren Sapp	.50	.20
❑ 66	LaBrandon Toefield	.30	.10
❑ 67	Chad Johnson	.75	.30
❑ 68	Javon Walker	.50	.20
❑ 69	Jimmy Smith	.50	.20
❑ 70	Donte Stallworth	.50	.20
❑ 71	Brian Dawkins	.50	.20
❑ 72	Leonard Little	.30	.10
❑ 73	Ladell Betts	.30	.10
❑ 74	Ray Lewis	.75	.30
❑ 75	Stephen Davis	.50	.20
❑ 76	Dennis Northcutt	.30	.10
❑ 77	Ashley Lelie	.50	.20
❑ 78	Billy Miller	.30	.10
❑ 79	Chris Chambers	.50	.20
❑ 80	John Abraham	.30	.10
❑ 81	Quentin Jammer	.30	.10
❑ 82	Isaac Bruce	.50	.20
❑ 83	Peerless Price	.50	.20
❑ 84	Jake Delhomme	.75	.30
❑ 85	Lee Suggs	.75	.30
❑ 86	Shannon Sharpe	.50	.20
❑ 87	Domanick Davis	.75	.30
❑ 88	Daunte Culpepper	.75	.30
❑ 89	Shaun Ellis	.30	.10
❑ 90	Drew Brees	.75	.30
❑ 91	Torry Holt	.75	.30
❑ 92	Alge Crumpler	.50	.20
❑ 93	Mike Rucker	.50	.20
❑ 94	Tim Couch	.30	.10
❑ 95	Quentin Griffin	.75	.30
❑ 96	David Carr	.75	.30
❑ 97	Moe Williams	.30	.10
❑ 98	Chad Pennington	.75	.30
❑ 99	LaDainian Tomlinson	1.00	.40
❑ 100	Adam Archuleta	.30	.10
❑ 101	Julius Peppers	.75	.30
❑ 102	Clinton Portis	.75	.30
❑ 103	Marcus Stroud	.30	.10
❑ 104	Tom Brady	2.00	.75
❑ 105	Teyo Johnson	.30	.10
❑ 106	Terrell Owens	.75	.30
❑ 107	Keith Bulluck	.30	.10
❑ 108	Eric Moulds	.50	.20
❑ 109	Jake Plummer	.50	.20
❑ 110	Reggie Wayne	.50	.20
❑ 111	Tedy Bruschi	.50	.20
❑ 112	Rich Gannon	.50	.20
❑ 113	Tony Parrish	.30	.10
❑ 114	Steve McNair	.75	.30
❑ 115	T.J. Duckett	.50	.20
❑ 116	Peter Warrick	.50	.20
❑ 117	Donald Driver	.50	.20
❑ 118	Fred Taylor	.50	.20
❑ 119	Joe Horn	.50	.20
❑ 120	Jerry Porter	.50	.20
❑ 121	Marc Bulger	.75	.30
❑ 122	Trung Canidate	.30	.10
❑ 123	Warrick Dunn	.50	.20
❑ 124	Kelly Holcomb	.50	.20
❑ 125	Robert Ferguson	.30	.10
❑ 126	Byron Leftwich	1.00	.40
❑ 127	Michael Lewis	.30	.10
❑ 128	Jerry Rice	1.50	.60
❑ 129	Marshall Faulk	.75	.30
❑ 130	Patrick Ramsey	.50	.20
❑ 131	Josh McCown	.50	.20
❑ 132	Anthony Thomas	.50	.20
❑ 133	Joey Harrington	.75	.30
❑ 134	Dante Hall	.75	.30
❑ 135	Daniel Graham	.30	.10

	Card		
❑ 136	Richard Seymour	.30	.10
❑ 137	Brandon Lloyd	.50	.20
❑ 138	Anquan Boldin	.75	.30
❑ 139	Jon Kitna	.50	.20
❑ 140	Nick Barnett	.50	.20
❑ 141	Priest Holmes	1.00	.40
❑ 142	Bethel Johnson	.50	.20
❑ 143	Shaun Alexander	.75	.30
❑ 144	Todd Heap	.50	.20
❑ 145	Brian Urlacher	1.00	.40
❑ 146	Peyton Manning	1.25	.50
❑ 147	Jason Taylor	.30	.10
❑ 148	Kerry Collins	.50	.20
❑ 149	Tommy Maddox	.50	.20
❑ 150	Charles Lee	.30	.10
❑ 151	Tim Rattay	.30	.10
❑ 152	Carson Palmer	1.00	.40
❑ 153	Brett Favre	2.00	.75
❑ 154	Trent Green	.50	.20
❑ 155	Aaron Brooks	.50	.20
❑ 156	Brian Westbrook	.50	.20
❑ 157	Itula Mili	.30	.10
❑ 158	Keith Brooking	.30	.10
❑ 159	Rudi Johnson	.50	.20
❑ 160	Najeh Davenport	.30	.10
❑ 161	Kevin Johnson	.30	.10
❑ 162	Boo Williams	.30	.10
❑ 163	Corey Simon	.50	.20
❑ 164	Darrell Jackson	.50	.20
❑ 165	Damerien McCants	.30	.10
❑ 166	Willis McGahee	.75	.30
❑ 167	Terry Glenn	.30	.10
❑ 168	Dallas Clark	.50	.20
❑ 169	Randy Moss	1.00	.40
❑ 170	Charles Woodson	.50	.20
❑ 171	Jeff Garcia	.75	.30
❑ 172	Chris Brown	.75	.30
❑ 173	Emmitt Smith	1.50	.60
❑ 174	Marty Booker	.50	.20
❑ 175	Artose Pinner	.30	.10
❑ 176	Tony Gonzalez	.50	.20
❑ 177	Troy Brown	.50	.20
❑ 178	Freddie Mitchell	.50	.20
❑ 179	Marcus Trufant	.30	.10
❑ 180	London Fletcher	.30	.10
❑ 181	Roy Williams S	.50	.20
❑ 182	Edgerrin James	.75	.30
❑ 183	Michael Bennett	.50	.20
❑ 184	Jerald Sowell	.30	.10
❑ 185	David Boston	.50	.20
❑ 186	Derrick Mason	.50	.20
❑ 187	Bryant Johnson	.30	.10
❑ 188	Corey Dillon	.50	.20
❑ 189	Ahman Green	.75	.30
❑ 190	Vonnie Holliday	.30	.10
❑ 191	Deuce McAllister	.75	.30
❑ 192	Donovan McNabb	1.00	.40
❑ 193	Koren Robinson	.50	.20
❑ 194	Laveranues Coles	.50	.20
❑ 195	Takeo Spikes	.30	.10
❑ 196	Richie Anderson	.30	.10
❑ 197	Onterrio Smith	.50	.20
❑ 198	Curtis Martin	.75	.30
❑ 199	Antonio Gates	.75	.30
❑ 200	Champ Bailey	.50	.20
❑ 201	Eli Manning L13 RC	80.00	30.00
❑ 202	Philip Rivers L13 RC	50.00	25.00
❑ 203	Roy Williams L13 RC	50.00	20.00
❑ 204	Drew Henson L13 RC	20.00	7.50
❑ 205	Chris Perry L13 RC	25.00	10.00
❑ 206	Larry Fitzgerald L13 RC	50.00	20.00
❑ 207	Rashaun Woods L13 RC	20.00	7.50
❑ 208	Reggie Williams L13 RC	30.00	12.50
❑ 209	Mike Williams L13 RC	60.00	25.00
❑ 210	Kellen Winslow L13 RC	30.00	12.50
❑ 211	Steven Jackson L13 RC	50.00	20.00
❑ 212	Kevin Jones L13 RC	50.00	20.00
❑ 213	Ben Roethlisberger L13 RC	120.00	60.00
❑ 214	Michael Turner RC	4.00	1.50
❑ 215	Tatum Bell RC	8.00	3.00
❑ 216	Quincy Wilson RC	2.50	1.00
❑ 217	Devery Henderson RC	2.50	1.00
❑ 218	Ernest Wilford RC	4.00	1.50
❑ 219	Cody Pickett RC	4.00	1.50
❑ 220	Ryan Dinwiddie RC	2.50	1.00
❑ 221	J.P. Losman RC	8.00	3.00
❑ 222	Derrick Knight RC	2.50	1.00

❑ 223 Michael Jenkins RC 4.00 1.50
❑ 224 Greg Jones RC 4.00 1.50
❑ 225 Cedric Cobbs RC 4.00 1.50
❑ 226 Will Poole RC 4.00 1.50
❑ 227 Michael Clayton RC 8.00 3.00
❑ 228 Sean Taylor RC 6.00 2.50
❑ 229 Will Smith RC 4.00 1.50
❑ 230 Jonathan Vilma RC 4.00 1.50
❑ 231 Lee Evans RC 5.00 2.00
❑ 232 Julius Jones RC 15.00 6.00
❑ U234 D.J. Williams RC 6.00 2.50
❑ U235 Mewelde Moore RC 6.00 2.50
❑ U236 Ben Watson RC 5.00 2.00
❑ U237 Robert Gallery RC 8.00 3.00
❑ U238 DeAngelo Hall RC 6.00 2.50
❑ U239 Luke McCown RC 5.00 2.00
❑ U240 Ben Troupe RC 5.00 2.00
❑ U241 Keary Colbert RC 6.00 2.50
❑ U242 Matt Schaub RC 8.00 3.00
❑ U243 Kenechi Udeze RC 5.00 2.00
❑ U244 Jeff Smoker RC 5.00 2.00
❑ U245 Derrick Hamilton RC 4.00 1.50
❑ U246 Bernard Berrian RC 5.00 2.00
❑ U247 Devard Darling RC 5.00 2.00
❑ U248 Johnnie Morant RC 5.00 2.00
❑ U249 Vince Wilfork RC 6.00 2.50
❑ U250 Jerricho Cotchery RC 5.00 2.00
❑ U251 Darius Watts RC 5.00 2.00
❑ U252 Carlos Francis RC 4.00 1.50
❑ U253 P.K. Sam RC 4.00 1.50

2005 Ultra

❑ COMP.SET w/o RC's (200) 30.00 12.50
❑ 201-213 L13 PRINT RUN 599 SER.#'d SETS
❑ OVERALL ROOKIE STATED ODDS 1:4
❑ 1 Peyton Manning 1.25 .50
❑ 2 Brian Westbrook .50 .20
❑ 3 Daunte Culpepper .75 .30
❑ 4 Marvin Harrison .75 .30
❑ 5 Edgerrin James .75 .30
❑ 6 Reggie Wayne .50 .20
❑ 7 Michael Vick 1.25 .50
❑ 8 Donte Stallworth .50 .20
❑ 9 Brian Urlacher .75 .30
❑ 10 Hines Ward .75 .30
❑ 11 Charles Rogers .50 .20
❑ 12 Roy Williams WR .75 .30
❑ 13 Julius Peppers .50 .20
❑ 14 Eric Moulds .50 .20
❑ 15 Ray Lewis .75 .30
❑ 16 Byron Leftwich .75 .30
❑ 17 Fred Taylor .50 .20
❑ 18 Andre Johnson .50 .20
❑ 19 Travis Henry .50 .20
❑ 20 Tom Brady 2.00 .75
❑ 21 Drew Bledsoe .75 .30
❑ 22 Tiki Barber .75 .30
❑ 23 Larry Fitzgerald .75 .30
❑ 24 Jeff Garcia .50 .20
❑ 25 Rex Grossman .50 .20
❑ 26 Larry Johnson .75 .30
❑ 27 Curtis Martin .75 .30
❑ 28 Chad Pennington .75 .30
❑ 29 Dwight Freeney .50 .20
❑ 30 Peerless Price .40 .15
❑ 31 Rich Gannon .50 .20
❑ 32 Matt Hasselbeck .50 .20
❑ 33 Clinton Portis .75 .30
❑ 34 Jerry Rice 1.25 .50
❑ 35 Jeremy Shockey .75 .30
❑ 36 Tony Gonzalez .50 .20
❑ 37 Deuce McAllister .75 .30
❑ 38 Shaun Alexander 1.00 .40
❑ 39 Peter Warrick .50 .20
❑ 40 Isaac Bruce .50 .20
❑ 41 Antonio Bryant .40 .15
❑ 42 Mike Alstott .50 .20
❑ 43 Domanick Davis .50 .20
❑ 44 Jake Delhomme .75 .30
❑ 45 Santana Moss .50 .20
❑ 46 Ahman Green .75 .30
❑ 47 David Carr .75 .30
❑ 48 Kyle Boller .50 .20
❑ 49 Chris Chambers .50 .20
❑ 50 Quentin Griffin .40 .15
❑ 51 Donovan McNabb 1.00 .40
❑ 52 Eli Manning 1.50 .60
❑ 53 Julius Jones 1.00 .40
❑ 54 Sean Taylor .50 .20
❑ 55 Javon Walker .50 .20
❑ 56 Randy Moss .75 .30
❑ 57 Thomas Jones .50 .20
❑ 58 Joey Harrington .75 .30
❑ 59 Michael Boulware .40 .15
❑ 60 Marshall Faulk .75 .30
❑ 61 Tony Parrish .40 .15
❑ 62 Bertrand Berry .40 .15
❑ 63 Alge Crumpler .50 .20
❑ 64 Aaron Brooks .50 .20
❑ 65 Muhsin Muhammad .50 .20
❑ 66 Simeon Rice .50 .20
❑ 67 Corey Dillon .50 .20
❑ 68 Willis McGahee .75 .30
❑ 69 Ben Roethlisberger 2.00 .75
❑ 70 Chad Johnson .75 .30
❑ 71 Jamal Lewis .75 .30
❑ 72 Drew Brees .75 .30
❑ 73 LaDainian Tomlinson 1.00 .40
❑ 74 Reuben Droughns .50 .20
❑ 75 Priest Holmes .75 .30
❑ 76 Jerry Porter .50 .20
❑ 77 Chris Brown .50 .20
❑ 78 Steve McNair .75 .30
❑ 79 Troy Brown .50 .20
❑ 80 Jerome Bettis .75 .30
❑ 81 Patrick Kerney .40 .15
❑ 82 Terrell Owens .75 .30
❑ 83 Brett Favre 2.00 .75
❑ 84 Carson Palmer .75 .30
❑ 85 Jake Plummer .50 .20
❑ 86 Tedy Bruschi .50 .20
❑ 87 Plaxico Burress .50 .20
❑ 88 Jonathan Vilma .50 .20
❑ 89 Ed Reed .50 .20
❑ 90 Brian Dawkins .40 .15
❑ 91 Anquan Boldin .50 .20
❑ 92 Vinny Testaverde .50 .20
❑ 93 David Givens .50 .20
❑ 94 Rudi Johnson .50 .20
❑ 95 Philip Rivers .75 .30
❑ 96 Jimmy Smith .50 .20
❑ 97 Emmitt Smith 3.00 1.25
❑ 98 Eric Johnson .50 .20
❑ 99 Jeremiah Trotter .40 .15
❑ 100 Duce Staley .50 .20
❑ 101 Warrick Dunn .50 .20
❑ 102 Nate Burleson .50 .20
❑ 103 Marc Bulger .75 .30
❑ 104 Joe Horn .50 .20
❑ 105 Rodney Harrison .40 .15
❑ 106 Zach Thomas .50 .20
❑ 107 Michael Clayton .75 .30
❑ 108 Derrick Brooks .50 .20
❑ 109 Michael Lewis .40 .15
❑ 110 Kurt Warner .50 .20
❑ 111 Jason Witten .50 .20
❑ 112 Roy Williams S .50 .20
❑ 113 Kabeer Gbaja-Biamila .50 .20
❑ 114 Torry Holt .75 .30
❑ 115 Tim Rattay .40 .15
❑ 116 Josh McCown .50 .20
❑ 117 Brian Griese .50 .20
❑ 118 Patrick Ramsey .50 .20
❑ 119 A.J. Feeley .50 .20
❑ 120 Kerry Collins .50 .20
❑ 121 Trent Green .50 .20
❑ 122 Billy Volek .50 .20
❑ 123 Travis Taylor .40 .15
❑ 124 T.J. Houshmandzadeh .40 .15
❑ 125 James Farrior .40 .15
❑ 126 Bryan Scott .40 .15
❑ 127 Lito Sheppard .40 .15
❑ 128 David Patten .40 .15
❑ 129 Antwaan Randle El .50 .20
❑ 130 Antonio Gates .75 .30
❑ 131 Brandon Stokley .40 .15
❑ 132 Keyshawn Johnson .50 .20
❑ 133 Amani Toomer .50 .20
❑ 134 Shawn Springs .40 .15
❑ 135 Eddie George .50 .20
❑ 136 Kevin Jones .75 .30
❑ 137 Darrell Jackson .50 .20
❑ 138 Ricky Manning .40 .15
❑ 139 Laveranues Coles .50 .20
❑ 140 Champ Bailey .50 .20
❑ 141 Rod Smith .50 .20
❑ 142 Ashley Lelie .50 .20
❑ 143 Charles Woodson .50 .20
❑ 144 Drew Bennett .50 .20
❑ 145 Derrick Mason .50 .20
❑ 146 Donovin Darius .40 .15
❑ 147 Dennis Northcutt .40 .15
❑ 148 Jamie Sharper .40 .15
❑ 149 Steven Jackson 1.00 .40
❑ 150 David Terrell .40 .15
❑ 151 Onterrio Smith .40 .15
❑ 152 Donald Driver .50 .20
❑ 153 Antoine Winfield .40 .15
❑ 154 Michael Pittman .40 .15
❑ 155 Dan Morgan .40 .15
❑ 156 Troy Polamalu 1.25 .50
❑ 157 Willie McGinest .40 .15
❑ 158 Justin McCareins .40 .15
❑ 159 Allen Rossum .40 .15
❑ 160 Deion Branch .50 .20
❑ 161 Deion Sanders .75 .30
❑ 162 Josh Reed .40 .15
❑ 163 Lee Evans .50 .20
❑ 164 Lee Suggs .50 .20
❑ 165 Dante Hall .50 .20
❑ 166 Eddie Kennison .40 .15
❑ 167 Ken Dorsey .40 .15
❑ 168 Andre Dyson .40 .15
❑ 169 Keith Bulluck .40 .15
❑ 170 Todd Pinkston .40 .15
❑ 171 Jevon Kearse .50 .20
❑ 172 Dunta Robinson .40 .15
❑ 173 Steve Smith .50 .20
❑ 174 Koren Robinson .40 .15
❑ 175 Freddie Mitchell .40 .15
❑ 176 L.J. Smith .40 .15
❑ 177 Kevin Curtis .40 .15
❑ 178 Marcus Robinson .40 .15
❑ 179 Kellen Winslow .75 .30
❑ 180 Reggie Williams .50 .20
❑ 181 Bubba Franks .50 .20
❑ 182 J.P. Losman .75 .30
❑ 183 Chris Perry .50 .20
❑ 184 Michael Jenkins .50 .20
❑ 185 T.J. Duckett .50 .20
❑ 186 Rashaun Woods .40 .15
❑ 187 Ben Watson .50 .20
❑ 188 Bryant Johnson .40 .15
❑ 189 Dallas Clark .40 .15
❑ 190 William Green .40 .15
❑ 191 Daniel Graham .40 .15
❑ 192 Jerramy Stevens .40 .15
❑ 193 DeShaun Foster .50 .20
❑ 194 Nick Goings .40 .15
❑ 195 Ronald Curry .40 .15
❑ 196 Kevan Barlow .50 .20
❑ 197 Kevin Faulk .40 .15
❑ 198 Eric Parker .40 .15
❑ 199 Keenan McCardell .40 .15
❑ 200 LaMont Jordan .75 .30
❑ 201 Alex Smith QB L13 RC 60.00 30.00
❑ 202 Aaron Rodgers L13 RC 60.00 25.00
❑ 203 Cedric Benson L13 RC 40.00 20.00
❑ 204 Braylon Edwards L13 RC 40.00 20.00
❑ 205 Ronnie Brown L13 RC 60.00 30.00
❑ 206 Carnell Williams L13 RC 80.00 40.00
❑ 207 Troy Williamson L13 RC 25.00 12.50

❑ 208 Mark Clayton L13 RC	25.00	12.50
❑ 209 Charlie Frye L13 RC	30.00	15.00
❑ 210 Mike Williams L13	30.00	12.50
❑ 211 Marion Barber L13 RC	25.00	12.50
❑ 212 Eric Shelton L13 RC	20.00	7.50
❑ 213 Antrel Rolle L13 RC	20.00	7.50
❑ 214 Heath Miller RC	12.00	5.00
❑ 215 Dan Cody RC	5.00	2.00
❑ 216 Adam Jones RC	5.00	2.00
❑ 217 Derrick Johnson RC	8.00	3.00
❑ 218 Alex Smith TE RC	5.00	2.00
❑ 219 Kyle Orton RC	8.00	3.00
❑ 220 David Pollack RC	5.00	2.00
❑ 221 Erasmus James RC	5.00	2.00
❑ 222 Justin Tuck RC	5.00	2.00
❑ 223 Jason Campbell RC	8.00	3.00
❑ 224 Dan Orlovsky RC	6.00	2.50
❑ 225 Thomas Davis RC	5.00	2.00
❑ 226 J.J. Arrington RC	6.00	2.50
❑ 227 Roddy White RC	5.00	2.00
❑ 228 David Greene RC	5.00	2.00
❑ 229 Ciatrick Fason RC	5.00	2.00
❑ 230 Chris Henry RC	5.00	2.00
❑ 231 Reggie Brown RC	5.00	2.00
❑ 232 Vernand Morency RC	5.00	2.00
❑ 233 Carlos Rogers RC	6.00	2.50
❑ 234 Ryan Moats RC	5.00	2.00
❑ 235 Roscoe Parrish RC	5.00	2.00
❑ 236 Terrence Murphy RC	5.00	2.00
❑ 237 Shawne Merriman RC	8.00	3.00
❑ 238 Courtney Roby RC	5.00	2.00
❑ 239 Mark Bradley RC	5.00	2.00
❑ 240 Marcus Spears RC	5.00	2.00
❑ 241 Justin Miller RC	4.00	1.50
❑ 242 Matt Jones RC	12.00	5.00
❑ 243 DeMarcus Ware RC	8.00	3.00
❑ 244 Fabian Washington RC	5.00	2.00
❑ 245 Marlin Jackson RC	5.00	2.00
❑ 246 Corey Webster RC	5.00	2.00
❑ 247 Brandon Jacobs RC	6.00	2.50
❑ 248 Frank Gore RC	8.00	3.00

1991 Upper Deck

❑ COMPLETE SET (700)	15.00	6.00
❑ COMP.FACT.SET (700)	25.00	10.00
❑ COMP.SERIES 1 SET (500)	10.00	4.00
❑ COMP.SERIES 2 SET (200)	5.00	2.00
❑ COMP.FACT.SERIES 2 (200)	6.00	2.50
❑ 1 Dan McGwire CL	.05	.01
❑ 2 Eric Bieniemy RC	.05	.01
❑ 3 Mike Dumas RC	.05	.01
❑ 4 Mike Croel RC	.05	.01
❑ 5 Russell Maryland RC	.25	.08
❑ 6 Charles McRae RC	.05	.01
❑ 7 Dan McGwire RC	.05	.01
❑ 8 Mike Pritchard RC	.25	.08
❑ 9 Ricky Watters RC	1.50	.60
❑ 10 Chris Zorich RC	.25	.08
❑ 11 Browning Nagle RC	.05	.01
❑ 12 Wesley Carroll RC	.05	.01
❑ 13 Brett Favre RC	10.00	5.00
❑ 14 Rob Carpenter RC WR	.05	.01
❑ 15 Eric Swann RC	.25	.08
❑ 16 Stanley Richard RC	.05	.01
❑ 17 Herman Moore RC	.25	.08
❑ 18 Todd Marinovich RC	.05	.01
❑ 19 Aaron Craver RC	.05	.01
❑ 20 Chuck Webb RC	.05	.01
❑ 21 Todd Lyght RC	.05	.01
❑ 22 Greg Lewis RC	.05	.01
❑ 23 Eric Turner RC	.10	.02
❑ 24 Alvin Harper RC	.25	.08
❑ 25 Jarrod Bunch RC	.05	.01
❑ 26 Bruce Pickens RC	.05	.01
❑ 27 Harvey Williams RC	.25	.08
❑ 28 Randal Hill RC	.10	.02
❑ 29 Nick Bell RC	.05	.01
❑ 30 Jim Everett AT	.10	.02
❑ 31 R.Cunningham/Jackson AT	.05	.01
❑ 32 Steve DeBerg AT	.05	.01
❑ 33 Warren Moon/D.Hill AT	.10	.02
❑ 34 D.Marino/M.Clayton AT	.50	.20
❑ 35 J.Montana/J.Rice AT	.50	.20
❑ 36 Percy Snow	.05	.01
❑ 37 Kelvin Martin	.05	.01
❑ 38 Scott Case	.05	.01
❑ 39 John Gesek RC	.05	.01
❑ 40 Barry Word	.05	.01
❑ 41 Cornelius Bennett	.10	.02
❑ 42 Mike Kenn	.05	.01
❑ 43 Andre Reed	.10	.02
❑ 44 Bobby Hebert	.05	.01
❑ 45 William Perry	.10	.02
❑ 46 Dennis Byrd	.05	.01
❑ 47 Martin Mayhew	.05	.01
❑ 48 Issiac Holt	.05	.01
❑ 49 William White	.05	.01
❑ 50 JoJo Townsell	.05	.01
❑ 51 Jarvis Williams	.05	.01
❑ 52 Joey Browner	.05	.01
❑ 53 Pat Terrell	.05	.01
❑ 54 Joe Montana 3X UER	1.25	.50
❑ 55 Jeff Herrod	.05	.01
❑ 56 Cris Carter	.50	.20
❑ 57 Jerry Rice	.75	.30
❑ 58 Brett Perriman	.25	.08
❑ 59 Kevin Fagan	.05	.01
❑ 60 Wayne Haddix	.05	.01
❑ 61 Tommy Kane	.05	.01
❑ 62 Pat Beach	.05	.01
❑ 63 Jeff Lageman	.05	.01
❑ 64 Hassan Jones	.05	.01
❑ 65 Bennie Blades	.05	.01
❑ 66 Tim McGee	.05	.01
❑ 67 Robert Blackmon	.05	.01
❑ 68 Fred Stokes RC	.05	.01
❑ 69 Barney Bussey RC	.05	.01
❑ 70 Eric Metcalf	.10	.02
❑ 71 Mark Kelso	.05	.01
❑ 72 Neal Anderson TC	.05	.01
❑ 73 Boomer Esiason TC	.05	.01
❑ 74 Thurman Thomas TC	.25	.08
❑ 75 John Elway TC	.50	.20
❑ 76 Eric Metcalf TC	.10	.02
❑ 77 Vinny Testaverde TC	.10	.02
❑ 78 Johnny Johnson TC	.05	.01
❑ 79 Anthony Miller TC	.10	.02
❑ 80 Derrick Thomas TC	.10	.02
❑ 81 Jeff George TC	.10	.02
❑ 82 Troy Aikman TC	.40	.15
❑ 83 Dan Marino TC	.50	.20
❑ 84 Randall Cunningham TC	.10	.02
❑ 85 Deion Sanders TC	.05	.01
❑ 86 Jerry Rice TC	.40	.15
❑ 87 Lawrence Taylor TC	.10	.02
❑ 88 Al Toon TC	.05	.01
❑ 89 Barry Sanders TC	.50	.20
❑ 90 Warren Moon TC	.10	.02
❑ 91 Don Majkowski TC	.05	.01
❑ 92 Andre Tippett TC	.05	.01
❑ 93 Bo Jackson TC	.30	.10
❑ 94 Jim Everett TC	.10	.02
❑ 95 Art Monk TC	.10	.02
❑ 96 Morten Andersen TC	.05	.01
❑ 97 John L. Williams TC	.05	.01
❑ 98 Rod Woodson TC	.10	.02
❑ 99 Herschel Walker TC	.10	.02
❑ 100 Checklist 1-100	.05	.01
❑ 101 Steve Young	.75	.30
❑ 102 Jim Lachey	.05	.01
❑ 103 Tom Rathman	.05	.01
❑ 104 Earnest Byner	.05	.01
❑ 105 Karl Mecklenburg	.05	.01
❑ 106 Wes Hopkins	.05	.01
❑ 107 Michael Irvin	.25	.08
❑ 108 Burt Grossman	.05	.01
❑ 109 Jay Novacek UER	.25	.08
❑ 110 Ben Smith	.05	.01
❑ 111 Rod Woodson	.25	.08
❑ 112 Ernie Jones	.05	.01
❑ 113 Bryan Hinkle	.05	.01
❑ 114 Vai Sikahema	.05	.01
❑ 115 Bubby Brister	.05	.01
❑ 116 Brian Blades	.10	.02
❑ 117 Don Majkowski	.05	.01
❑ 118 Rod Bernstine	.05	.01
❑ 119 Brian Noble	.05	.01
❑ 120 Eugene Robinson	.05	.01
❑ 121 John Taylor	.10	.02
❑ 122 Vance Johnson	.05	.01
❑ 123 Art Monk	.10	.02
❑ 124 John Elway	1.25	.50
❑ 125 Dexter Carter	.05	.01
❑ 126 Anthony Miller	.10	.02
❑ 127 Keith Jackson	.10	.02
❑ 128 Albert Lewis	.05	.01
❑ 129 Billy Ray Smith	.05	.01
❑ 130 Clyde Simmons	.05	.01
❑ 131 Merril Hoge	.05	.01
❑ 132 Ricky Proehl	.05	.01
❑ 133 Tim McDonald	.05	.01
❑ 134 Louis Lipps	.05	.01
❑ 135 Ken Harvey	.10	.02
❑ 136 Sterling Sharpe	.10	.02
❑ 137 Gill Byrd	.05	.01
❑ 138 Tim Harris	.05	.01
❑ 139 Derrick Fenner	.05	.01
❑ 140 Johnny Holland	.05	.01
❑ 141 Ricky Sanders	.05	.01
❑ 142 Bobby Humphrey	.05	.01
❑ 143 Roger Craig	.10	.02
❑ 144 Steve Atwater	.05	.01
❑ 145 Ickey Woods	.05	.01
❑ 146 Randall Cunningham	.25	.08
❑ 147 Marion Butts	.10	.02
❑ 148 Reggie White	.25	.08
❑ 149 Ronnie Harmon	.05	.01
❑ 150 Mike Saxon	.05	.01
❑ 151 Greg Townsend	.05	.01
❑ 152 Troy Aikman	.75	.30
❑ 153 Shane Conlan	.05	.01
❑ 154 Deion Sanders	.40	.15
❑ 155 Bo Jackson	.30	.10
❑ 156 Jeff Hostetler	.10	.02
❑ 157 Albert Bentley	.05	.01
❑ 158 James Williams	.05	.01
❑ 159 Bill Brooks	.05	.01
❑ 160 Nick Lowery	.05	.01
❑ 161 Ottis Anderson	.10	.02
❑ 162 Kevin Greene	.10	.02
❑ 163 Neil Smith	.25	.08
❑ 164 Jim Everett	.10	.02
❑ 165 Derrick Thomas	.25	.08
❑ 166 John L. Williams	.05	.01
❑ 167 Timm Rosenbach	.05	.01
❑ 168 Leslie O'Neal	.10	.02
❑ 169 Clarence Verdin	.05	.01
❑ 170 Dave Krieg	.10	.02
❑ 171 Steve Broussard	.05	.01
❑ 172 Emmitt Smith	2.50	1.00
❑ 173 Andre Rison	.10	.02
❑ 174 Bruce Smith	.25	.08
❑ 175 Mark Clayton	.10	.02
❑ 176 Christian Okoye	.05	.01
❑ 177 Duane Bickett	.05	.01
❑ 178 Stephone Paige	.05	.01
❑ 179 Fredd Young	.05	.01
❑ 180 Mervyn Fernandez	.05	.01
❑ 181 Phil Simms	.10	.02
❑ 182 Pete Holohan	.05	.01
❑ 183 Pepper Johnson	.05	.01
❑ 184 Jackie Slater	.05	.01
❑ 185 Stephen Baker	.05	.01
❑ 186 Frank Cornish	.05	.01
❑ 187 Dave Waymer	.05	.01
❑ 188 Terance Mathis	.10	.02
❑ 189 Darryl Talley	.05	.01
❑ 190 James Hasty	.05	.01
❑ 191 Jay Schroeder	.05	.01
❑ 192 Kenneth Davis	.05	.01
❑ 193 Chris Miller	.10	.02
❑ 194 Scott Davis	.05	.01
❑ 195 Tim Green	.05	.01

❑ 196 Dan Saleaumua .05 .01
❑ 197 Rohn Stark .05 .01
❑ 198 John Alt .05 .01
❑ 199 Steve Tasker .10 .02
❑ 200 Checklist 101-200 .05 .01
❑ 201 Freddie Joe Nunn .05 .01
❑ 202 Jim Breech .05 .01
❑ 203 Roy Green .05 .01
❑ 204 Gary Anderson RB .05 .01
❑ 205 Rich Camarillo .05 .01
❑ 206 Mark Bortz .05 .01
❑ 207 Eddie Brown .05 .01
❑ 208 Brad Muster .05 .01
❑ 209 Anthony Munoz .10 .02
❑ 210 Dalton Hilliard .05 .01
❑ 211 Erik McMillan .05 .01
❑ 212 Perry Kemp .05 .01
❑ 213 Jim Thornton .05 .01
❑ 214 Anthony Dilweg .05 .01
❑ 215 Cleveland Gary .05 .01
❑ 216 Leo Goeas .05 .01
❑ 217 Mike Merriweather .05 .01
❑ 218 Courtney Hall .05 .01
❑ 219 Wade Wilson .10 .02
❑ 220 Billy Joe Tolliver .05 .01
❑ 221 Harold Green .10 .02
❑ 222 Al(Bubba) Baker .10 .02
❑ 223 Carl Zander .05 .01
❑ 224 Thane Gash .05 .01
❑ 225 Kevin Mack .05 .01
❑ 226 Morten Andersen .05 .01
❑ 227 Dennis Gentry .05 .01
❑ 228 Vince Buck .05 .01
❑ 229 Mike Singletary .10 .02
❑ 230 Rueben Mayes .05 .01
❑ 231 Mark Carrier WR .25 .08
❑ 232 Tony Mandarich .05 .01
❑ 233 Al Toon .10 .02
❑ 234 Renaldo Turnbull .05 .01
❑ 235 Broderick Thomas .05 .01
❑ 236 Anthony Carter .10 .02
❑ 237 Flipper Anderson .05 .01
❑ 238 Jerry Robinson .05 .01
❑ 239 Vince Newsome .05 .01
❑ 240 Keith Millard .05 .01
❑ 241 Reggie Langhorne .05 .01
❑ 242 James Francis .05 .01
❑ 243 Felix Wright .05 .01
❑ 244 Neal Anderson .10 .02
❑ 245 Boomer Esiason .10 .02
❑ 246 Pat Swilling .10 .02
❑ 247 Richard Dent .10 .02
❑ 248 Craig Heyward .10 .02
❑ 249 Ron Morris .05 .01
❑ 250 Eric Martin .05 .01
❑ 251 Jim C. Jensen .05 .01
❑ 252 Anthony Toney .05 .01
❑ 253 Sammie Smith .05 .01
❑ 254 Calvin Williams .10 .02
❑ 255 Dan Marino 1.25 .50
❑ 256 Warren Moon .25 .08
❑ 257 Tommie Agee .05 .01
❑ 258 Haywood Jeffires .10 .02
❑ 259 Eugene Lockhart .05 .01
❑ 260 Drew Hill .05 .01
❑ 261 Vinny Testaverde .10 .02
❑ 262 Jim Arnold .05 .01
❑ 263 Steve Christie .05 .01
❑ 264 Chris Spielman .10 .02
❑ 265 Reggie Cobb .05 .01
❑ 266 John Stephens .05 .01
❑ 267 Jay Hilgenberg .05 .01
❑ 268 Brent Williams .05 .01
❑ 269 Rodney Hampton .25 .08
❑ 270 Irving Fryar .10 .02
❑ 271 Terry McDaniel .05 .01
❑ 272 Reggie Roby .05 .01
❑ 273 Allen Pinkett .05 .01
❑ 274 Tim McKyer .05 .01
❑ 275 Bob Golic .05 .01
❑ 276 Wilber Marshall .05 .01
❑ 277 Ray Childress .05 .01
❑ 278 Charles Mann .05 .01
❑ 279 Cris Dishman RC .05 .01
❑ 280 Mark Rypien .10 .02
❑ 281 Michael Cofer .05 .01
❑ 282 Keith Byars .05 .01
❑ 283 Mike Rozier .05 .01
❑ 284 Seth Joyner .10 .02
❑ 285 Jessie Tuggle .05 .01
❑ 286 Mark Bavaro .05 .01
❑ 287 Eddie Anderson .05 .01
❑ 288 Sean Landeta .05 .01
❑ 289 Howie Long/George Brett .25 .08
❑ 290 Reyna Thompson .05 .01
❑ 291 Ferrell Edmunds .05 .01
❑ 292 Willie Gault .10 .02
❑ 293 John Offerdahl .05 .01
❑ 294 Tim Brown .25 .08
❑ 295 Bruce Matthews .10 .02
❑ 296 Kevin Ross .05 .01
❑ 297 Lorenzo White .05 .01
❑ 298 Dino Hackett .05 .01
❑ 299 Curtis Duncan .05 .01
❑ 300 Checklist 201-300 .05 .01
❑ 301 Andre Ware .10 .02
❑ 302 David Little .05 .01
❑ 303 Jerry Ball .05 .01
❑ 304 Dwight Stone UER .05 .01
❑ 305 Rodney Peete .10 .02
❑ 306 Mike Baab .05 .01
❑ 307 Tim Worley .05 .01
❑ 308 Paul Farren .05 .01
❑ 309 Carnell Lake .05 .01
❑ 310 Clay Matthews .10 .02
❑ 311 Alton Montgomery .05 .01
❑ 312 Ernest Givins .10 .02
❑ 313 Mike Horan .05 .01
❑ 314 Sean Jones .10 .02
❑ 315 Leonard Smith .05 .01
❑ 316 Carl Banks .05 .01
❑ 317 Jerome Brown .05 .01
❑ 318 Everson Walls .05 .01
❑ 319 Ron Heller .05 .01
❑ 320 Mark Collins .05 .01
❑ 321 Eddie Murray .05 .01
❑ 322 Jim Harbaugh .25 .08
❑ 323 Mel Gray .10 .02
❑ 324 Keith Van Horne .05 .01
❑ 325 Lomas Brown .05 .01
❑ 326 Carl Lee .05 .01
❑ 327 Ken O'Brien .05 .01
❑ 328 Dermontti Dawson .05 .01
❑ 329 Brad Baxter .05 .01
❑ 330 Chris Doleman .05 .01
❑ 331 Louis Oliver .05 .01
❑ 332 Frank Stams .05 .01
❑ 333 Mike Munchak .10 .02
❑ 334 Fred Strickland .05 .01
❑ 335 Mark Duper .10 .02
❑ 336 Jacob Green .05 .01
❑ 337 Tony Paige .05 .01
❑ 338 Jeff Bryant .05 .01
❑ 339 Lemuel Stinson .05 .01
❑ 340 David Wyman .05 .01
❑ 341 Lee Williams .05 .01
❑ 342 Trace Armstrong .05 .01
❑ 343 Junior Seau .25 .08
❑ 344 John Roper .05 .01
❑ 345 Jeff George .25 .08
❑ 346 Herschel Walker .10 .02
❑ 347 Sam Clancy .05 .01
❑ 348 Steve Jordan .05 .01
❑ 349 Nate Odomes .05 .01
❑ 350 Martin Bayless .05 .01
❑ 351 Brent Jones .25 .08
❑ 352 Ray Agnew .05 .01
❑ 353 Charles Haley .10 .02
❑ 354 Andre Tippett .05 .01
❑ 355 Ronnie Lott .10 .02
❑ 356 Thurman Thomas .25 .08
❑ 357 Fred Barnett .25 .08
❑ 358 James Lofton .10 .02
❑ 359 William Frizzell RC .05 .01
❑ 360 Keith McKeller .05 .01
❑ 361 Rodney Holman .05 .01
❑ 362 Henry Ellard .10 .02
❑ 363 David Fulcher .05 .01
❑ 364 Jerry Gray .05 .01
❑ 365 James Brooks .10 .02
❑ 366 Tony Stargell .05 .01
❑ 367 Keith McCants .05 .01
❑ 368 Lewis Billups .05 .01
❑ 369 Ervin Randle .05 .01
❑ 370 Pat Leahy .05 .01
❑ 371 Bruce Armstrong .05 .01
❑ 372 Steve DeBerg .05 .01
❑ 373 Guy McIntyre .05 .01
❑ 374 Deron Cherry .05 .01
❑ 375 Fred Marion .05 .01
❑ 376 Michael Haddix .05 .01
❑ 377 Kent Hull .05 .01
❑ 378 Jerry Holmes .05 .01
❑ 379 Jim Ritcher .05 .01
❑ 380 Ed West .05 .01
❑ 381 Richmond Webb .05 .01
❑ 382 Mark Jackson .05 .01
❑ 383 Tom Newberry .05 .01
❑ 384 Ricky Nattiel .05 .01
❑ 385 Keith Sims .05 .01
❑ 386 Ron Hall .05 .01
❑ 387 Ken Norton .10 .02
❑ 388 Paul Gruber .05 .01
❑ 389 Daniel Stubbs .05 .01
❑ 390 Ian Beckles .05 .01
❑ 391 Hoby Brenner .05 .01
❑ 392 Tory Epps .05 .01
❑ 393 Sam Mills .05 .01
❑ 394 Chris Hinton .05 .01
❑ 395 Steve Walsh .05 .01
❑ 396 Simon Fletcher .05 .01
❑ 397 Tony Bennett .10 .02
❑ 398 Aundray Bruce .05 .01
❑ 399 Mark Murphy .05 .01
❑ 400 Checklist 301-400 .05 .01
❑ 401 Barry Sanders SL .50 .20
❑ 402 Jerry Rice SL .40 .15
❑ 403 Warren Moon SL .10 .02
❑ 404 Derrick Thomas SL .10 .02
❑ 405 Nick Lowery LL .05 .01
❑ 406 Mark Carrier DB LL .10 .02
❑ 407 Michael Carter .05 .01
❑ 408 Chris Singleton .05 .01
❑ 409 Matt Millen .10 .02
❑ 410 Ronnie Lippett .05 .01
❑ 411 E.J. Junior .05 .01
❑ 412 Ray Donaldson .05 .01
❑ 413 Keith Willis .05 .01
❑ 414 Jessie Hester .05 .01
❑ 415 Jeff Cross .05 .01
❑ 416 Greg Jackson RC .05 .01
❑ 417 Alvin Walton .05 .01
❑ 418 Bart Oates .05 .01
❑ 419 Chip Lohmiller .05 .01
❑ 420 John Elliott .05 .01
❑ 421 Randall McDaniel .05 .01
❑ 422 Richard Johnson CB RC .05 .01
❑ 423 Al Noga .05 .01
❑ 424 Lamar Lathon .05 .01
❑ 425 Rick Fenney .05 .01
❑ 426 Jack Del Rio .10 .02
❑ 427 Don Mosebar .05 .01
❑ 428 Luis Sharpe .05 .01
❑ 429 Steve Wisniewski .05 .01
❑ 430 Jimmie Jones .05 .01
❑ 431 Freeman McNeil .05 .01
❑ 432 Ron Rivera .05 .01
❑ 433 Hart Lee Dykes .05 .01
❑ 434 Mark Carrier DB .10 .02
❑ 435 Rob Moore .25 .08
❑ 436 Gary Clark .25 .08
❑ 437 Heath Sherman .05 .01
❑ 438 Darrell Green .05 .01
❑ 439 Jessie Small .05 .01
❑ 440 Monte Coleman .05 .01
❑ 441 Leonard Marshall .05 .01
❑ 442 Richard Johnson .05 .01
❑ 443 Dave Meggett .10 .02
❑ 444 Barry Sanders 1.25 .50
❑ 445 Lawrence Taylor .25 .08
❑ 446 Marcus Allen .25 .08
❑ 447 Johnny Johnson .05 .01
❑ 448 Aaron Wallace .05 .01
❑ 449 Anthony Thompson .05 .01
❑ 450 D.Marino/S.DeBerg CL .40 .15
❑ 451 Andre Rison TM .10 .02
❑ 452 Thurman Thomas TM .10 .02
❑ 453 Neal Anderson MVP .05 .01
❑ 454 Boomer Esiason MVP .05 .01
❑ 455 Eric Metcalf MVP .10 .02
❑ 456 Emmitt Smith TM 1.25 .50

❑ 457	Bobby Humphrey MVP	.05	.01
❑ 458	Barry Sanders TM	.50	.20
❑ 459	Sterling Sharpe TM	.10	.02
❑ 460	Warren Moon TM	.10	.02
❑ 461	Albert Bentley MVP	.05	.01
❑ 462	Steve DeBerg MVP	.05	.01
❑ 463	Greg Townsend MVP	.05	.01
❑ 464	Henry Ellard MVP	.10	.02
❑ 465	Dan Marino TM	.50	.20
❑ 466	Anthony Carter MVP	.10	.02
❑ 467	John Stephens MVP	.05	.01
❑ 468	Pat Swilling MVP	.05	.01
❑ 469	Ottis Anderson MVP	.10	.02
❑ 470	Dennis Byrd MVP	.05	.01
❑ 471	Randall Cunningham TM	.10	.02
❑ 472	Johnny Johnson TM	.05	.01
❑ 473	Rod Woodson TM	.10	.02
❑ 474	Anthony Miller MVP	.10	.02
❑ 475	Jerry Rice TM	.40	.15
❑ 476	John L.Williams MVP	.05	.01
❑ 477	Wayne Haddix MVP	.05	.01
❑ 478	Earnest Byner MVP	.05	.01
❑ 479	Doug Widell	.05	.01
❑ 480	Tommy Hodson	.05	.01
❑ 481	Shawn Collins	.05	.01
❑ 482	Rickey Jackson	.05	.01
❑ 483	Tony Casillas	.05	.01
❑ 484	Vaughan Johnson	.05	.01
❑ 485	Floyd Dixon	.05	.01
❑ 486	Eric Green	.05	.01
❑ 487	Harry Hamilton	.05	.01
❑ 488	Gary Anderson K	.05	.01
❑ 489	Bruce Hill	.05	.01
❑ 490	Gerald Williams	.05	.01
❑ 491	Cortez Kennedy	.25	.08
❑ 492	Chet Brooks	.05	.01
❑ 493	Dwayne Harper RC	.05	.01
❑ 494	Don Griffin	.05	.01
❑ 495	Andy Heck	.05	.01
❑ 496	David Treadwell	.05	.01
❑ 497	Irv Pankey	.05	.01
❑ 498	Dennis Smith	.05	.01
❑ 499	Marcus Dupree	.05	.01
❑ 500	Checklist 401-500	.05	.01
❑ 501	Wendell Davis	.05	.01
❑ 502	Matt Bahr	.05	.01
❑ 503	Rob Burnett RC	.10	.02
❑ 504	Maurice Carthon	.05	.01
❑ 505	Donnell Woolford	.05	.01
❑ 506	Howard Ballard	.05	.01
❑ 507	Mark Boyer	.05	.01
❑ 508	Eugene Marve	.05	.01
❑ 509	Joe Kelly	.05	.01
❑ 510	Will Wolford	.05	.01
❑ 511	Robert Clark	.05	.01
❑ 512	Matt Brock RC	.05	.01
❑ 513	Chris Warren	.25	.08
❑ 514	Ken Willis	.05	.01
❑ 515	George Jamison RC	.05	.01
❑ 516	Rufus Porter	.05	.01
❑ 517	Mark Higgs RC	.05	.01
❑ 518	Thomas Everett	.05	.01
❑ 519	Robert Brown	.05	.01
❑ 520	Gene Atkins	.05	.01
❑ 521	Hardy Nickerson	.10	.02
❑ 522	Johnny Bailey	.05	.01
❑ 523	William Frizzell	.05	.01
❑ 524	Steve McMichael	.10	.02
❑ 525	Kevin Porter	.05	.01
❑ 526	Carwell Gardner	.05	.01
❑ 527	Eugene Daniel	.05	.01
❑ 528	Vestee Jackson	.05	.01
❑ 529	Chris Goode	.05	.01
❑ 530	Leon Seals	.05	.01
❑ 531	Darion Conner	.05	.01
❑ 532	Stan Brock	.05	.01
❑ 533	Kirby Jackson RC	.05	.01
❑ 534	Marv Cook	.05	.01
❑ 535	Bill Fralic	.05	.01
❑ 536	Keith Woodside	.05	.01
❑ 537	Hugh Green	.05	.01
❑ 538	Grant Feasel	.05	.01
❑ 539	Bubba McDowell	.05	.01
❑ 540	Vai Sikahema	.05	.01
❑ 541	Aaron Cox	.05	.01
❑ 542	Roger Craig	.10	.02
❑ 543	Robb Thomas	.05	.01
❑ 544	Ronnie Lott	.10	.02
❑ 545	Robert Delpino	.05	.01
❑ 546	Greg McMurtry	.05	.01
❑ 547	Jim Morrissey RC	.05	.01
❑ 548	Johnny Rembert	.05	.01
❑ 549	Markus Paul RC	.05	.01
❑ 550	Karl Wilson RC	.05	.01
❑ 551	Gaston Green	.05	.01
❑ 552	Willie Drewrey	.05	.01
❑ 553	Michael Young	.05	.01
❑ 554	Tom Tupa	.05	.01
❑ 555	John Friesz	.25	.08
❑ 556	Cody Carlson RC	.05	.01
❑ 557	Eric Allen	.05	.01
❑ 558	Thomas Benson	.05	.01
❑ 559	Scott Mersereau RC	.05	.01
❑ 560	Lionel Washington	.05	.01
❑ 561	Brian Brennan	.05	.01
❑ 562	Jim Jeffcoat	.05	.01
❑ 563	Jeff Jaeger	.05	.01
❑ 564	D.J. Johnson	.05	.01
❑ 565	Danny Villa	.05	.01
❑ 566	Don Beebe	.05	.01
❑ 567	Michael Haynes	.25	.08
❑ 568	Brett Faryniarz RC	.05	.01
❑ 569	Mike Prior	.05	.01
❑ 570	John Davis RC	.05	.01
❑ 571	Vernon Turner RC	.05	.01
❑ 572	Michael Brooks	.05	.01
❑ 573	Mike Gann	.05	.01
❑ 574	Ron Holmes	.05	.01
❑ 575	Gary Plummer	.05	.01
❑ 576	Bill Romanowski	.05	.01
❑ 577	Chris Jacke	.05	.01
❑ 578	Gary Reasons	.05	.01
❑ 579	Tim Jorden RC	.05	.01
❑ 580	Tim McKyer	.05	.01
❑ 581	Johnnie Jackson RC	.05	.01
❑ 582	Ethan Horton	.05	.01
❑ 583	Pete Stoyanovich	.05	.01
❑ 584	Jeff Query	.05	.01
❑ 585	Frank Reich	.10	.02
❑ 586	Riki Ellison	.05	.01
❑ 587	Eric Hill	.05	.01
❑ 588	Anthony Shelton RC	.05	.01
❑ 589	Steve Smith	.05	.01
❑ 590	Garth Jax RC	.05	.01
❑ 591	Greg Davis RC	.05	.01
❑ 592	Bill Maas	.05	.01
❑ 593	Henry Rolling RC	.05	.01
❑ 594	Keith Jones	.05	.01
❑ 595	Tootie Robbins	.05	.01
❑ 596	Brian Jordan	.10	.02
❑ 597	Derrick Walker RC	.05	.01
❑ 598	Jonathan Hayes	.05	.01
❑ 599	Nate Lewis RC	.05	.01
❑ 600	Checklist 501-600	.05	.01
❑ 601	Croel/Lewis/Tray/Walk CL	.05	.01
❑ 602	James Jones RC DT	.05	.01
❑ 603	Tim Barnett RC	.05	.01
❑ 604	Ed King RC	.05	.01
❑ 605	Shane Curry RF	.05	.01
❑ 606	Mike Croel	.05	.01
❑ 607	Bryan Cox RC	.25	.08
❑ 608	Shawn Jefferson RC	.10	.02
❑ 609	Kenny Walker RC	.05	.01
❑ 610	Michael Jackson RC WR	.25	.08
❑ 611	Jon Vaughn RC	.05	.01
❑ 612	Greg Lewis	.05	.01
❑ 613	Joe Valerio RF	.05	.01
❑ 614	Pat Harlow RC	.05	.01
❑ 615	Henry Jones RC	.10	.02
❑ 616	Jeff Graham RC WR	.25	.08
❑ 617	Darryll Lewis RC	.10	.02
❑ 618	Keith Traylor RC	.05	.01
❑ 619	Scott Miller RF	.05	.01
❑ 620	Nick Bell	.05	.01
❑ 621	John Flannery RC	.05	.01
❑ 622	Leonard Russell RC	.10	.02
❑ 623	Alfred Williams RC	.05	.01
❑ 624	Browning Nagle	.05	.01
❑ 625	Harvey Williams	.10	.02
❑ 626	Dan McGwire	.05	.01
❑ 627	Favre/Pritchard/Pegram CL	.50	.20
❑ 628	William Thomas RC	.05	.01
❑ 629	Lawrence Dawsey RC	.10	.02
❑ 630	Aeneas Williams RC	.25	.08
❑ 631	Stan Thomas RF	.05	.01
❑ 632	Randal Hill	.05	.01
❑ 633	Moe Gardner RC	.05	.01
❑ 634	Alvin Harper	.10	.02
❑ 635	Esera Tuaolo RC	.05	.01
❑ 636	Russell Maryland	.10	.02
❑ 637	Anthony Morgan RC	.05	.01
❑ 638	Erric Pegram RC	.25	.08
❑ 639	Herman Moore	.25	.08
❑ 640	Ricky Ervins RC	.10	.02
❑ 641	Kelvin Pritchett RC	.10	.02
❑ 642	Roman Phifer RC	.05	.01
❑ 643	Antone Davis RC	.05	.01
❑ 644	Mike Pritchard	.10	.02
❑ 645	Vinnie Clark RC	.05	.01
❑ 646	Jake Reed RC	.50	.20
❑ 647	Brett Favre	4.00	1.50
❑ 648	Todd Lyght	.05	.01
❑ 649	Bruce Pickens	.05	.01
❑ 650	Darren Lewis RC	.05	.01
❑ 651	Wesley Carroll	.05	.01
❑ 652	James Joseph RC	.10	.02
❑ 653	Robert Delpino AR	.05	.01
❑ 654	Deion Sanders/V.Glenn AR	.05	.01
❑ 655	J.Rice/T.McDaniels AR	.30	.10
❑ 656	B.Sanders/D.Thomas AR	.50	.20
❑ 657	Ken Tippins AR	.05	.01
❑ 658	Christian Okoye AR	.05	.01
❑ 659	Rich Gannon	.25	.08
❑ 660	Johnny Meads	.05	.01
❑ 661	J.J.Birden RC	.10	.02
❑ 662	Bruce Kozerski	.05	.01
❑ 663	Felix Wright	.05	.01
❑ 664	Al Smith	.05	.01
❑ 665	Stan Humphries	.25	.08
❑ 666	Alfred Anderson	.05	.01
❑ 667	Nate Newton	.10	.02
❑ 668	Vince Workman RC	.10	.02
❑ 669	Ricky Reynolds	.05	.01
❑ 670	Bryce Paup RC	.25	.08
❑ 671	Gill Fenerty	.05	.01
❑ 672	Darrell Thompson	.05	.01
❑ 673	Anthony Smith	.05	.01
❑ 674	Darryl Henley RC	.05	.01
❑ 675	Brett Maxie	.05	.01
❑ 676	Craig Taylor RC	.05	.01
❑ 677	Steve Wallace	.10	.02
❑ 678	Jeff Feagles RC	.05	.01
❑ 679	James Washington RC	.05	.01
❑ 680	Tim Harris	.05	.01
❑ 681	Dennis Gibson	.05	.01
❑ 682	Toi Cook RC	.05	.01
❑ 683	Lorenzo Lynch	.05	.01
❑ 684	Brad Edwards RC	.05	.01
❑ 685	Ray Crockett RC	.05	.01
❑ 686	Harris Barton	.05	.01
❑ 687	Byron Evans	.05	.01
❑ 688	Eric Thomas	.05	.01
❑ 689	Jeff Criswell	.05	.01
❑ 690	Eric Ball	.05	.01
❑ 691	Brian Mitchell	.10	.02
❑ 692	Quinn Early	.10	.02
❑ 693	Aaron Jones	.05	.01
❑ 694	Jim Dombrowski	.05	.01
❑ 695	Jeff Bostic	.05	.01
❑ 696	Tony Casillas	.05	.01
❑ 697	Ken Lanier	.05	.01
❑ 698	Henry Thomas	.05	.01
❑ 699	Steve Beuerlein	.10	.02
❑ 700	Checklist 601-700	.05	.01
❑ P1	Joe Montana Promo	2.50	1.00
❑ P2	Barry Sanders Promo	2.00	.75
❑ SP1	Darrell Green Fastest	.50	.20
❑ SP2	Don Shula 300th Win	2.00	.75

1992 Upper Deck

❑	COMPLETE SET (620)	15.00	6.00
❑	COMP.SERIES 1 (400)	10.00	4.00
❑	COMP.SERIES 2 (220)	5.00	2.50
❑ 1	Bennett/Buckley/McNabb C	.10	.02
❑ 2	Edgar Bennett RC	.25	.08
❑ 3	Eddie Blake RC	.05	.01
❑ 4	Brian Bollinger RC	.05	.01
❑ 5	Joe Bowden RC	.05	.01
❑ 6	Terrell Buckley RC	.05	.01
❑ 7	Willie Clay RC	.05	.01
❑ 8	Ed Cunningham RC	.05	.01

Card	Price 1	Price 2
☐ 9 Matt Darby RC	.05	.01
☐ 10 Will Furrer RC	.05	.01
☐ 11 Chris Hakel RC	.05	.01
☐ 12 Carlos Huerta	.05	.01
☐ 13 Amp Lee RC	.05	.01
☐ 14 Ricardo McDonald RC	.05	.01
☐ 15 Dexter McNabb RC	.05	.01
☐ 16 Chris Mims RC	.05	.01
☐ 17 Derrick Moore RC	.10	.02
☐ 18 Mark D'Onofrio RC	.05	.01
☐ 19 Patrick Rowe RC	.05	.01
☐ 20 Leon Searcy RC	.05	.01
☐ 21 Torrance Small RC	.10	.02
☐ 22 Jimmy Smith RC	3.00	1.25
☐ 23 Tony Smith RC WR	.05	.01
☐ 24 Siran Stacy RC	.05	.01
☐ 25 Kevin Turner RC	.05	.01
☐ 26 Tommy Vardell RC	.05	.01
☐ 27 Bob Whitfield RC	.05	.01
☐ 28 Darryl Williams RC	.05	.01
☐ 29 Jeff Sydner RC	.05	.01
☐ 30 Mike Croel/L.Russell CL	.05	.01
☐ 31 Todd Marinovich ART	.05	.01
☐ 32 Leonard Russell ART	.05	.01
☐ 33 Nick Bell ART	.05	.01
☐ 34 Alvin Harper ART	.05	.01
☐ 35 Mike Pritchard ART	.05	.01
☐ 36 Lawrence Dawsey AR	.05	.01
☐ 37 Tim Barnett AR	.05	.01
☐ 38 John Flannery AR	.05	.01
☐ 39 Stan Thomas AR	.05	.01
☐ 40 Ed King AR	.05	.01
☐ 41 Charles McRae AR	.05	.01
☐ 42 Eric Moten AR	.05	.01
☐ 43 Moe Gardner AR	.05	.01
☐ 44 Kenny Walker AR	.05	.01
☐ 45 Esera Tuaolo AR	.05	.01
☐ 46 Alfred Williams AR	.05	.01
☐ 47 Bryan Cox AR	.05	.01
☐ 48 Mo Lewis AR	.05	.01
☐ 49 Mike Croel ART	.05	.01
☐ 50 Stanley Richard AR	.05	.01
☐ 51 Tony Covington AR	.05	.01
☐ 52 Larry Brown DB AR	.05	.01
☐ 53 Aeneas Williams AR	.05	.01
☐ 54 John Kasay AR	.05	.01
☐ 55 Jon Vaughn ART	.05	.01
☐ 56 David Fulcher	.05	.01
☐ 57 Barry Foster	.10	.02
☐ 58 Terry Wooden	.05	.01
☐ 59 Gary Anderson K	.05	.01
☐ 60 Alfred Williams	.05	.01
☐ 61 Robert Blackmon	.05	.01
☐ 62 Brian Noble	.05	.01
☐ 63 Terry Allen	.25	.08
☐ 64 Darrell Green	.05	.01
☐ 65 Darren Comeaux	.05	.01
☐ 66 Rob Burnett	.05	.01
☐ 67 Jarrod Bunch	.05	.01
☐ 68 Michael Jackson	.10	.02
☐ 69 Greg Lloyd	.10	.02
☐ 70 Richard Brown RC	.05	.01
☐ 71 Harold Green	.05	.01
☐ 72 William Fuller	.05	.01
☐ 73 Mark Carrier DB TC	.05	.01
☐ 74 David Fulcher TC	.05	.01
☐ 75 Cornelius Bennett TC	.05	.01
☐ 76 Steve Atwater TC	.05	.01
☐ 77 Kevin Mack TC	.05	.01
☐ 78 Mark Carrier WR TC	.05	.01
☐ 79 Tim McDonald TC	.05	.01
☐ 80 Marion Butts TC	.05	.01
☐ 81 Christian Okoye TC	.05	.01
☐ 82 Jeff Herrod TC	.05	.01
☐ 83 Emmitt Smith TC	.60	.25
☐ 84 Mark Duper TC	.05	.01
☐ 85 Keith Jackson TC	.05	.01
☐ 86 Andre Rison TC	.10	.02
☐ 87 John Taylor TC	.05	.01
☐ 88 Rodney Hampton TC	.10	.02
☐ 89 Rob Moore TC	.05	.01
☐ 90 Chris Spielman TC	.05	.01
☐ 91 Haywood Jeffires TC	.05	.01
☐ 92 Sterling Sharpe TC	.10	.02
☐ 93 Irving Fryar TC	.05	.01
☐ 94 Marcus Allen TC	.10	.02
☐ 95 Henry Ellard TC	.05	.01
☐ 96 Mark Rypien TC	.05	.01
☐ 97 Pat Swilling TC	.05	.01
☐ 98 Brian Blades TC	.05	.01
☐ 99 Eric Green TC	.05	.01
☐ 100 Anthony Carter TC	.05	.01
☐ 101 Burt Grossman	.05	.01
☐ 102 Gary Anderson RB	.05	.01
☐ 103 Neil Smith	.25	.08
☐ 104 Jeff Feagles	.05	.01
☐ 105 Shane Conlan	.05	.01
☐ 106 Jay Novacek	.10	.02
☐ 107 Bill Brooks	.05	.01
☐ 108 Mark Ingram	.05	.01
☐ 109 Anthony Munoz	.10	.02
☐ 110 Wendell Davis	.05	.01
☐ 111 Jim Everett	.10	.02
☐ 112 Bruce Matthews	.05	.01
☐ 113 Mark Higgs	.05	.01
☐ 114 Chris Warren	.10	.02
☐ 115 Brad Baxter	.05	.01
☐ 116 Greg Townsend	.05	.01
☐ 117 Al Smith	.05	.01
☐ 118 Jeff Cross	.05	.01
☐ 119 Terry McDaniel	.05	.01
☐ 120 Ernest Givins	.10	.02
☐ 121 Fred Barnett	.10	.02
☐ 122 Flipper Anderson	.05	.01
☐ 123 Floyd Turner	.05	.01
☐ 124 Stephen Baker	.05	.01
☐ 125 Tim Johnson	.05	.01
☐ 126 Brent Jones	.10	.02
☐ 127 Leonard Marshall	.05	.01
☐ 128 Jim Price	.05	.01
☐ 129 Jessie Hester	.05	.01
☐ 130 Mark Carrier WR	.10	.02
☐ 131 Bubba McDowell	.05	.01
☐ 132 Andre Tippett	.05	.01
☐ 133 James Hasty	.05	.01
☐ 134 Mel Gray	.10	.02
☐ 135 Christian Okoye	.05	.01
☐ 136 Earnest Byner	.05	.01
☐ 137 Ferrell Edmunds	.05	.01
☐ 138 Henry Ellard	.10	.02
☐ 139 Rob Moore	.10	.02
☐ 140 Brian Jordan	.10	.02
☐ 141 Clarence Verdin	.05	.01
☐ 142 Cornelius Bennett	.10	.02
☐ 143 John Taylor	.10	.02
☐ 144 Derrick Thomas	.25	.08
☐ 145 Thurman Thomas	.25	.08
☐ 146 Warren Moon	.25	.08
☐ 147 Vinny Testaverde	.10	.02
☐ 148 Steve Bono RC	.25	.08
☐ 149 Robb Thomas	.05	.01
☐ 150 John Friesz	.10	.02
☐ 151 Richard Dent	.10	.02
☐ 152 Eddie Anderson	.05	.01
☐ 153 Kevin Greene	.10	.02
☐ 154 Marion Butts	.05	.01
☐ 155 Barry Sanders	1.25	.50
☐ 156 Andre Rison	.10	.02
☐ 157 Ronnie Lott	.10	.02
☐ 158 Eric Allen	.05	.01
☐ 159 Mark Clayton	.10	.02
☐ 160 Terance Mathis	.10	.02
☐ 161 Darryl Talley	.05	.01
☐ 162 Eric Metcalf	.10	.02
☐ 163 Reggie Cobb	.05	.01
☐ 164 Ernie Jones	.05	.01
☐ 165 David Griggs	.05	.01
☐ 166 Tom Rathman	.05	.01
☐ 167 Bubby Brister	.10	.02
☐ 168 Broderick Thomas	.05	.01
☐ 169 Chris Doleman	.05	.01
☐ 170 Charles Haley	.10	.02
☐ 171 Michael Haynes	.10	.02
☐ 172 Rodney Hampton	.10	.02
☐ 173 Nick Bell	.05	.01
☐ 174 Gene Atkins	.05	.01
☐ 175 Mike Merriweather	.05	.01
☐ 176 Reggie Roby	.05	.01
☐ 177 Bennie Blades	.05	.01
☐ 178 John L. Williams	.05	.01
☐ 179 Rodney Peete	.10	.02
☐ 180 Greg Montgomery	.05	.01
☐ 181 Vince Newsome	.05	.01
☐ 182 Andre Collins	.05	.01
☐ 183 Erik Kramer	.10	.02
☐ 184 Bryan Hinkle	.05	.01
☐ 185 Reggie White	.25	.08
☐ 186 Bruce Armstrong	.05	.01
☐ 187 Anthony Carter	.10	.02
☐ 188 Pat Swilling	.05	.01
☐ 189 Robert Delpino	.05	.01
☐ 190 Brent Williams	.05	.01
☐ 191 Johnny Johnson	.05	.01
☐ 192 Aaron Craver	.05	.01
☐ 193 Vincent Brown	.05	.01
☐ 194 Herschel Walker	.10	.02
☐ 195 Tim McDonald	.05	.01
☐ 196 Gaston Green	.05	.01
☐ 197 Brian Blades	.10	.02
☐ 198 Rod Bernstine	.05	.01
☐ 199 Brett Perriman	.10	.02
☐ 200 John Elway	1.25	.50
☐ 201 Michael Carter	.05	.01
☐ 202 Mark Carrier DB	.05	.01
☐ 203 Cris Carter	.50	.20
☐ 204 Kyle Clifton	.05	.01
☐ 205 Alvin Wright	.05	.01
☐ 206 Andre Ware	.05	.01
☐ 207 Dave Waymer	.05	.01
☐ 208 Darren Lewis	.05	.01
☐ 209 Joey Browner	.05	.01
☐ 210 Rich Miano	.05	.01
☐ 211 Marcus Allen	.25	.08
☐ 212 Steve Broussard	.05	.01
☐ 213 Joel Hilgenberg	.05	.01
☐ 214 Bo Orlando RC	.05	.01
☐ 215 Clay Matthews	.10	.02
☐ 216 Chris Hinton	.05	.01
☐ 217 Al Edwards	.05	.01
☐ 218 Tim Brown	.25	.08
☐ 219 Sam Mills	.05	.01
☐ 220 Don Majkowski	.05	.01
☐ 221 James Francis	.05	.01
☐ 222 Steve Hendrickson RC	.05	.01
☐ 223 James Thornton	.05	.01
☐ 224 Byron Evans	.05	.01
☐ 225 Pepper Johnson	.05	.01
☐ 226 Darryl Henley	.05	.01
☐ 227 Simon Fletcher	.05	.01
☐ 228 Hugh Millen	.05	.01
☐ 229 Tim McGee	.05	.01
☐ 230 Richmond Webb	.05	.01
☐ 231 Tony Bennett	.05	.01
☐ 232 Nate Odomes	.05	.01
☐ 233 Scott Case	.05	.01
☐ 234 Dalton Hilliard	.05	.01
☐ 235 Paul Gruber	.05	.01
☐ 236 Jeff Lageman	.05	.01
☐ 237 Tony Mandarich	.05	.01
☐ 238 Cris Dishman	.05	.01
☐ 239 Steve Walsh	.05	.01
☐ 240 Moe Gardner	.05	.01
☐ 241 Bill Romanowski	.05	.01
☐ 242 Chris Zorich	.10	.02
☐ 243 Stephone Paige	.05	.01
☐ 244 Mike Croel	.05	.01
☐ 245 Leonard Russell	.10	.02
☐ 246 Mark Rypien	.05	.01
☐ 247 Aeneas Williams	.10	.02
☐ 248 Steve Atwater	.05	.01
☐ 249 Michael Stewart	.05	.01
☐ 250 Pierce Holt	.05	.01
☐ 251 Kevin Mack	.05	.01
☐ 252 Sterling Sharpe	.25	.08

❑ 253	Lawrence Dawsey	.10	.02
❑ 254	Emmitt Smith	1.50	.60
❑ 255	Todd Marinovich	.05	.01
❑ 256	Neal Anderson	.05	.01
❑ 257	Mo Lewis	.05	.01
❑ 258	Vance Johnson	.05	.01
❑ 259	Rickey Jackson	.05	.01
❑ 260	Esera Tuaolo	.05	.01
❑ 261	Wilber Marshall	.05	.01
❑ 262	Keith Henderson	.05	.01
❑ 263	William Thomas	.05	.01
❑ 264	Rickey Dixon	.05	.01
❑ 265	Dave Meggett	.10	.02
❑ 266	Gerald Riggs	.05	.01
❑ 267	Tim Harris	.05	.01
❑ 268	Ken Harvey	.05	.01
❑ 269	Clyde Simmons	.05	.01
❑ 270	Irving Fryar	.10	.02
❑ 271	Darion Conner	.05	.01
❑ 272	Vince Workman	.05	.01
❑ 273	Jim Harbaugh	.25	.08
❑ 274	Lorenzo White	.05	.01
❑ 275	Bobby Hebert	.05	.01
❑ 276	Duane Bickett	.05	.01
❑ 277	Jeff Bryant	.05	.01
❑ 278	Scott Stephen	.05	.01
❑ 279	Bob Golic	.05	.01
❑ 280	Steve McMichael	.10	.02
❑ 281	Jeff Graham	.25	.08
❑ 282	Keith Jackson	.10	.02
❑ 283	Howard Ballard	.05	.01
❑ 284	Michael Brooks	.05	.01
❑ 285	Freeman McNeil	.10	.02
❑ 286	Rodney Holman	.05	.01
❑ 287	Eric Bieniemy	.05	.01
❑ 288	Seth Joyner	.05	.01
❑ 289	Carwell Gardner	.05	.01
❑ 290	Brian Mitchell	.10	.02
❑ 291	Chris Miller	.10	.02
❑ 292	Ray Berry	.05	.01
❑ 293	Matt Brock	.05	.01
❑ 294	Eric Thomas	.05	.01
❑ 295	John Kasay	.05	.01
❑ 296	Jay Hilgenberg	.05	.01
❑ 297	Darrell Thompson	.05	.01
❑ 298	Rich Gannon	.25	.08
❑ 299	Steve Young	.60	.25
❑ 300	Mike Kenn	.05	.01
❑ 301	Emmitt Smith SL	.60	.25
❑ 302	Haywood Jeffires SL	.05	.01
❑ 303	Michael Irvin SL	.25	.08
❑ 304	Warren Moon SL	.10	.02
❑ 305	Chip Lohmiller SL	.05	.01
❑ 306	Barry Sanders SL	.50	.20
❑ 307	Ronnie Lott SL	.10	.02
❑ 308	Pat Swilling SL	.05	.01
❑ 309	Thurman Thomas SL	.10	.02
❑ 310	Reggie Roby SL	.05	.01
❑ 311	Moon/Irvin/T.Thomas CL	.10	.02
❑ 312	Jacob Green	.05	.01
❑ 313	Stephen Braggs	.05	.01
❑ 314	Haywood Jeffires	.10	.02
❑ 315	Freddie Joe Nunn	.05	.01
❑ 316	Gary Clark	.10	.02
❑ 317	Tim Barnett	.05	.01
❑ 318	Mark Duper	.05	.01
❑ 319	Eric Green	.05	.01
❑ 320	Robert Wilson	.05	.01
❑ 321	Michael Ball	.05	.01
❑ 322	Eric Martin	.05	.01
❑ 323	Alexander Wright	.05	.01
❑ 324	Jessie Tuggle	.05	.01
❑ 325	Ronnie Harmon	.05	.01
❑ 326	Jeff Hostetler	.10	.02
❑ 327	Eugene Daniel	.05	.01
❑ 328	Ken Norton Jr.	.10	.02
❑ 329	Reyna Thompson	.05	.01
❑ 330	Jerry Ball	.05	.01
❑ 331	Leroy Hoard	.10	.02
❑ 332	Chris Martin	.05	.01
❑ 333	Keith McKeller	.05	.01
❑ 334	Brian Washington	.05	.01
❑ 335	Eugene Robinson	.05	.01
❑ 336	Maurice Hurst	.05	.01
❑ 337	Dan Saleaumua	.05	.01
❑ 338	Neil O'Donnell	.10	.02
❑ 339	Dexter Davis	.05	.01
❑ 340	Keith McCants	.05	.01
❑ 341	Steve Beuerlein	.10	.02
❑ 342	Roman Phifer	.05	.01
❑ 343	Bryan Cox	.10	.02
❑ 344	Art Monk	.10	.02
❑ 345	Michael Irvin	.25	.08
❑ 346	Vaughan Johnson	.05	.01
❑ 347	Jeff Herrod	.05	.01
❑ 348	Stanley Richard	.05	.01
❑ 349	Michael Young	.05	.01
❑ 350	Rod.Hampton/R.Cobb CL	.10	.02
❑ 351	Jim Harbaugh MVP	.10	.02
❑ 352	David Fulcher MVP	.05	.01
❑ 353	Thurman Thomas MVP	.10	.02
❑ 354	Gaston Green MVP	.05	.01
❑ 355	Leroy Hoard MVP	.05	.01
❑ 356	Reggie Cobb MVP	.05	.01
❑ 357	Tim McDonald MVP	.05	.01
❑ 358	Ronnie Harmon MVP UER	.05	.01
❑ 359	Derrick Thomas MVP	.10	.02
❑ 360	Jeff Herrod MVP	.05	.01
❑ 361	Michael Irvin MVP	.25	.08
❑ 362	Mark Higgs MVP	.05	.01
❑ 363	Reggie White MVP	.10	.02
❑ 364	Chris Miller MVP	.05	.01
❑ 365	Steve Young MVP	.30	.10
❑ 366	Rodney Hampton MVP	.10	.02
❑ 367	Jeff Lageman MVP	.05	.01
❑ 368	Barry Sanders MVP	.50	.20
❑ 369	Haywood Jeffires MVP	.05	.01
❑ 370	Tony Bennett MVP	.05	.01
❑ 371	Leonard Russell MVP	.05	.01
❑ 372	Jeff Jaeger MVP	.05	.01
❑ 373	Robert Delpino MVP	.05	.01
❑ 374	Mark Rypien MVP	.05	.01
❑ 375	Pat Swilling MVP	.05	.01
❑ 376	Cortez Kennedy MVP	.10	.02
❑ 377	Eric Green MVP	.05	.01
❑ 378	Cris Carter MVP	.10	.02
❑ 379	John Roper	.05	.01
❑ 380	Barry Word	.05	.01
❑ 381	Shawn Jefferson	.05	.01
❑ 382	Tony Casillas	.05	.01
❑ 383	John Baylor RC	.05	.01
❑ 384	Al Noga	.05	.01
❑ 385	Charles Mann	.05	.01
❑ 386	Gill Byrd	.05	.01
❑ 387	Chris Singleton	.05	.01
❑ 388	James Joseph	.05	.01
❑ 389	Larry Brown DB	.05	.01
❑ 390	Chris Spielman	.10	.02
❑ 391	Anthony Thompson	.05	.01
❑ 392	Karl Mecklenburg	.05	.01
❑ 393	Joe Kelly	.05	.01
❑ 394	Kanavis McGhee	.05	.01
❑ 395	Bill Maas	.05	.01
❑ 396	Marv Cook	.05	.01
❑ 397	Louis Lipps	.05	.01
❑ 398	Marty Carter RC	.05	.01
❑ 399	Louis Oliver	.05	.01
❑ 400	Eric Swann	.10	.02
❑ 401	Troy Auzenne RC	.05	.01
❑ 402	Kurt Barber	.05	.01
❑ 403	Marc Boutte RC	.05	.01
❑ 404	Dale Carter	.10	.02
❑ 405	Marco Coleman	.05	.01
❑ 406	Quentin Coryatt	.05	.01
❑ 407	Shane Dronett RC	.05	.01
❑ 408	Vaughn Dunbar	.05	.01
❑ 409	Steve Emtman	.05	.01
❑ 410	Dana Hall RC	.05	.01
❑ 411	Jason Hanson RC	.10	.02
❑ 412	Courtney Hawkins RC	.10	.02
❑ 413	Terrell Buckley	.05	.01
❑ 414	Robert Jones RC	.05	.01
❑ 415	David Klingler	.05	.01
❑ 416	Tommy Maddox	1.50	.60
❑ 417	Johnny Mitchell RC	.05	.01
❑ 418	Carl Pickens	.10	.02
❑ 419	Tracy Scroggins	.05	.01
❑ 420	Tony Sacca RC	.05	.01
❑ 421	Kevin Smith DB	.05	.01
❑ 422	Alonzo Spellman	.10	.02
❑ 423	Troy Vincent RC	.05	.01
❑ 424	Sean Gilbert RC	.10	.02
❑ 425	Larry Webster RC	.05	.01
❑ 426	Carl Pickens/Klingler CL	.10	.02
❑ 427	Bill Fralic	.05	.01
❑ 428	Kevin Murphy	.05	.01
❑ 429	Lemuel Stinson	.05	.01
❑ 430	Harris Barton	.05	.01
❑ 431	Dino Hackett	.05	.01
❑ 432	John Stephens	.05	.01
❑ 433	Keith Jennings RC	.05	.01
❑ 434	Derrick Fenner	.05	.01
❑ 435	Kenneth Gant RC	.05	.01
❑ 436	Willie Gault	.10	.02
❑ 437	Steve Jordan	.05	.01
❑ 438	Charles Haley	.10	.02
❑ 439	Keith Kartz	.05	.01
❑ 440	Nate Lewis	.05	.01
❑ 441	Doug Widell	.05	.01
❑ 442	William White	.05	.01
❑ 443	Eric Hill	.05	.01
❑ 444	Melvin Jenkins	.05	.01
❑ 445	David Wyman	.05	.01
❑ 446	Ed West	.05	.01
❑ 447	Brad Muster	.05	.01
❑ 448	Ray Childress	.05	.01
❑ 449	Kevin Ross	.05	.01
❑ 450	Johnnie Jackson S	.05	.01
❑ 451	Tracy Simien RC	.05	.01
❑ 452	Don Mosebar	.05	.01
❑ 453	Jay Hilgenberg	.05	.01
❑ 454	Wes Hopkins	.05	.01
❑ 455	Jay Schroeder	.05	.01
❑ 456	Jeff Bostic	.05	.01
❑ 457	Bryce Paup	.25	.08
❑ 458	Dave Waymer	.05	.01
❑ 459	Toi Cook	.05	.01
❑ 460	Anthony Smith	.05	.01
❑ 461	Don Griffin	.05	.01
❑ 462	Bill Hawkins	.05	.01
❑ 463	Courtney Hall	.05	.01
❑ 464	Jeff Uhlenhake	.05	.01
❑ 465	Mike Sherrard	.05	.01
❑ 466	James Jones DT	.05	.01
❑ 467	Jerrol Williams	.05	.01
❑ 468	Eric Ball	.05	.01
❑ 469	Randall McDaniel	.05	.01
❑ 470	Alvin Harper	.10	.02
❑ 471	Tom Waddle	.05	.01
❑ 472	Tony Woods	.05	.01
❑ 473	Kelvin Martin	.05	.01
❑ 474	Jon Vaughn	.05	.01
❑ 475	Gill Fenerty	.05	.01
❑ 476	Aundray Bruce	.05	.01
❑ 477	Morten Andersen	.05	.01
❑ 478	Lamar Lathon	.05	.01
❑ 479	Steve DeOssie	.05	.01
❑ 480	Marvin Washington	.05	.01
❑ 481	Herschel Walker	.10	.02
❑ 482	Howie Long	.25	.08
❑ 483	Calvin Williams	.10	.02
❑ 484	Brett Favre	2.50	1.25
❑ 485	Johnny Bailey	.05	.01
❑ 486	Jeff Gossett	.05	.01
❑ 487	Carnell Lake	.05	.01
❑ 488	Michael Zordich RC	.05	.01
❑ 489	Henry Rolling	.05	.01
❑ 490	Steve Smith	.05	.01
❑ 491	Vestee Jackson	.05	.01
❑ 492	Ray Crockett	.05	.01
❑ 493	Dexter Carter	.05	.01
❑ 494	Nick Lowery	.05	.01
❑ 495	Cortez Kennedy	.10	.02
❑ 496	Cleveland Gary	.05	.01
❑ 497	Kelly Stouffer	.05	.01
❑ 498	Carl Carter	.05	.01
❑ 499	Shannon Sharpe	.25	.08
❑ 500	Roger Craig	.10	.02
❑ 501	Willie Drewrey	.05	.01
❑ 502	Mark Schlereth RC	.05	.01
❑ 503	Tony Martin	.10	.02
❑ 504	Tom Newberry	.05	.01
❑ 505	Ron Hall	.05	.01
❑ 506	Scott Miller	.05	.01
❑ 507	Donnell Woolford	.05	.01
❑ 508	Dave Krieg	.10	.02
❑ 509	Eric Pegram	.10	.02
❑ 510	Checklist 401-510	.05	.01
❑ 511	Barry Sanders SBK	.60	.25
❑ 512	Thurman Thomas SBK	.10	.02
❑ 513	Warren Moon SBK	.10	.02

❑	514 John Elway SBK	.50	.20
❑	515 Ronnie Lott SBK	.10	.02
❑	516 Emmitt Smith SBK	.60	.25
❑	517 Andre Rison SBK	.10	.02
❑	518 Steve Atwater SBK	.05	.01
❑	519 Steve Young SBK	.30	.10
❑	520 Mark Rypien SBK	.05	.01
❑	521 Rich Camarillo	.05	.01
❑	522 Mark Bavaro	.05	.01
❑	523 Brad Edwards	.05	.01
❑	524 Chad Hennings RC	.10	.02
❑	525 Tony Paige	.05	.01
❑	526 Shawn Moore	.05	.01
❑	527 Sidney Johnson RC	.05	.01
❑	528 Sanjay Beach RC	.05	.01
❑	529 Kelvin Pritchett	.05	.01
❑	530 Jerry Holmes	.05	.01
❑	531 Al Del Greco	.05	.01
❑	532 Bob Gagliano	.05	.01
❑	533 Drew Hill	.05	.01
❑	534 Donald Frank RC	.05	.01
❑	535 Pio Sagapolutele RC	.05	.01
❑	536 Jackie Slater	.05	.01
❑	537 Vernon Turner	.05	.01
❑	538 Bobby Humphrey	.05	.01
❑	539 Audray McMillian	.05	.01
❑	540 Gary Brown RC	.25	.08
❑	541 Wesley Carroll	.05	.01
❑	542 Nate Newton	.05	.01
❑	543 Vai Sikahema	.05	.01
❑	544 Chris Chandler	.25	.08
❑	545 Nolan Harrison RC	.05	.01
❑	546 Mark Green	.05	.01
❑	547 Ricky Watters	.25	.08
❑	548 J.J. Birden	.05	.01
❑	549 Cody Carlson	.05	.01
❑	550 Tim Green	.05	.01
❑	551 Mark Jackson	.05	.01
❑	552 Vince Buck	.05	.01
❑	553 George Jamison	.05	.01
❑	554 Anthony Pleasant	.05	.01
❑	555 Reggie Johnson	.05	.01
❑	556 John Jackson WR	.05	.01
❑	557 Ian Beckles	.05	.01
❑	558 Buford McGee	.05	.01
❑	559 Fuad Reveiz UER	.05	.01
❑	560 Joe Montana	1.25	.50
❑	561 Phil Simms	.10	.02
❑	562 Greg McMurtry	.05	.01
❑	563 Gerald Williams	.05	.01
❑	564 Dave Cadigan	.05	.01
❑	565 Rufus Porter	.05	.01
❑	566 Jim Kelly	.25	.08
❑	567 Deion Sanders	.50	.20
❑	568 Mike Singletary	.10	.02
❑	569 Boomer Esiason	.10	.02
❑	570 Andre Reed	.10	.02
❑	571 James Washington	.05	.01
❑	572 Jack Del Rio	.05	.01
❑	573 Gerald Perry	.05	.01
❑	574 Vinnie Clark	.05	.01
❑	575 Mike Piel	.05	.01
❑	576 Michael Dean Perry	.10	.02
❑	577 Ricky Proehl	.05	.01
❑	578 Leslie O'Neal	.10	.02
❑	579 Russell Maryland	.05	.01
❑	580 Eric Dickerson	.10	.02
❑	581 Fred Strickland	.05	.01
❑	582 Nick Lowery	.05	.01
❑	583 Joe Milinichik RC	.05	.01
❑	584 Mark Vlasic	.05	.01
❑	585 James Lofton	.10	.02
❑	586 Bruce Smith	.25	.08
❑	587 Harvey Williams	.10	.02
❑	588 Bernie Kosar	.10	.02
❑	589 Carl Banks	.05	.01
❑	590 Jeff George	.25	.08
❑	591 Fred Jones RC	.05	.01
❑	592 Todd Scott	.05	.01
❑	593 Keith Jones	.05	.01
❑	594A Tootie Robbins ERR	.05	.01
❑	594B Tootie Robbins COR	.05	.01
❑	595 Todd Philcox RC	.05	.01
❑	596 Browning Nagle	.05	.01
❑	597 Troy Aikman	.75	.30
❑	598 Dan Marino	1.25	.50
❑	599 Lawrence Taylor	.25	.08
❑	600 Webster Slaughter	.05	.01
❑	601 Aaron Cox	.05	.01
❑	602 Matt Stover	.05	.01
❑	603 Keith Sims	.05	.01
❑	604 Dennis Smith	.05	.01
❑	605 Kevin Porter	.05	.01
❑	606 Anthony Miller	.10	.02
❑	607 Ken O'Brien	.05	.01
❑	608 Randall Cunningham	.25	.08
❑	609 Timm Rosenbach	.05	.01
❑	610 Junior Seau	.25	.08
❑	611 Johnny Rembert	.05	.01
❑	612 Rick Tuten	.05	.01
❑	613 Willie Green	.05	.01
❑	614 Sean Salisbury RC**/C	.05	.01
❑	615 Martin Bayless	.05	.01
❑	616 Jerry Rice	.75	.30
❑	617 Randal Hill	.05	.01
❑	618 Dan McGwire	.05	.01
❑	619 Merril Hoge	.05	.01
❑	620 Checklist 571-620	.05	.01
❑	A560 Joe Montana Blowup UDA	15.00	6.00
❑	A598 Dan Marino Blowup UDA	15.00	6.00
❑	SP3 James Lofton Yardage	.75	.30
❑	SP4 Art Monk Catches	.50	.20

1992 Upper Deck Gold

❑	COMPLETE SET (50)	12.00	5.00
❑	G1 Steve Emtman RC	.10	.02
❑	G2 Carl Pickens RC	.30	.10
❑	G3 Dale Carter RC	.30	.10
❑	G4 Greg Skrepenak RC	.10	.02
❑	G5 Kevin Smith RC DB	.15	.05
❑	G6 Marco Coleman RC	.15	.05
❑	G7 David Klingler RC	.15	.05
❑	G8 Phillippi Sparks RC	.10	.02
❑	G9 Tommy Maddox RC	1.50	.60
❑	G10 Quentin Coryatt RC	.15	.05
❑	G11 Ty Detmer	.30	.10
❑	G12 Vaughn Dunbar RC	.10	.02
❑	G13 Ashley Ambrose RC	.30	.10
❑	G14 Kurt Barber RC	.10	.02
❑	G15 Chester McGlockton RC	.30	.10
❑	G16 Todd Collins RC	.10	.02
❑	G17 Steve Israel RC	.10	.02
❑	G18 Marquez Pope RC	.10	.02
❑	G19 Alonzo Spellman RC	.15	.05
❑	G20 Tracy Scroggins RC	.10	.02
❑	G21 Jim Kelly QC	.30	.10
❑	G22 Troy Aikman QC	.60	.25
❑	G23 Randall Cunningham QC	.30	.10
❑	G24 Bernie Kosar QC	.15	.05
❑	G25 Dan Marino QC	1.00	.40
❑	G26 Andre Reed	.15	.05
❑	G27 Deion Sanders	.50	.20
❑	G28 Randal Hill	.10	.02
❑	G29 Eric Dickerson	.15	.05
❑	G30 Jim Kelly	.30	.10
❑	G31 Bernie Kosar	.15	.05
❑	G32 Mike Singletary	.15	.05
❑	G33 Anthony Miller	.15	.05
❑	G34 Harvey Williams	.30	.10
❑	G35 Randall Cunningham	.30	.10
❑	G36 Joe Montana	1.25	.50
❑	G37 Dan McGwire	.10	.02
❑	G38 Al Toon	.15	.05
❑	G39 Carl Banks	.10	.02
❑	G40 Troy Aikman	.75	.30
❑	G41 Junior Seau	.30	.10
❑	G42 Jeff George	.30	.10
❑	G43 Michael Dean Perry	.15	.05
❑	G44 Lawrence Taylor	.30	.10
❑	G45 Dan Marino	1.25	.50
❑	G46 Jerry Rice	.75	.30
❑	G47 Boomer Esiason	.15	.05
❑	G48 Bruce Smith	.30	.10
❑	G49 Leslie O'Neal	.15	.05
❑	G50 Checklist Card	.10	.02

1993 Upper Deck

❑	COMPLETE SET (530)	25.00	10.00
❑	1 Mirer/Hearst/Con/Ken CL	.25	.08
❑	2 Eric Curry RC	.05	.01
❑	3 Rick Mirer RC	.25	.08
❑	4 Dan Williams RC	.05	.01
❑	5 Marvin Jones RC	.05	.01
❑	6 Willie Roaf RC	.10	.02
❑	7 Reggie Brooks RC	.10	.02
❑	8 Horace Copeland RC	.10	.02
❑	9 Lincoln Kennedy RC	.05	.01
❑	10 Curtis Conway RC	.40	.15
❑	11 Drew Bledsoe RC	2.50	1.00
❑	12 Patrick Bates RC	.05	.01
❑	13 Wayne Simmons RC	.05	.01
❑	14 Irv Smith RC	.05	.01
❑	15 Robert Smith RC	1.25	.50
❑	16 O.J.McDuffie RC	.25	.08
❑	17 Darrien Gordon RC	.05	.01
❑	18 John Copeland RC	.10	.02
❑	19 Derek Brown RC RBK	.05	.01
❑	20 Jerome Bettis RC	5.00	2.50
❑	21 Deon Figures RC	.05	.01
❑	22 Glyn Milburn RC	.25	.08
❑	23 Garrison Hearst RC	.75	.30
❑	24 Qadry Ismail RC	.25	.08
❑	25 Terry Kirby RC	.25	.08
❑	26 Lamar Thomas RC	.05	.01
❑	27 Tom Carter RC	.10	.02
❑	28 Andre Hastings RC	.10	.02
❑	29 George Teague RC	.10	.02
❑	30 Tommy Maddox CL	.10	.02
❑	31 David Klingler ART	.05	.01
❑	32 Tommy Maddox ART	.10	.02
❑	33 Vaughn Dunbar ART	.05	.01
❑	34 Rodney Culver ART	.05	.01
❑	35 Carl Pickens ART	.10	.02
❑	36 Courtney Hawkins ART	.05	.01
❑	37 Tyji Armstrong ART	.05	.01
❑	38 Ray Roberts ART	.05	.01
❑	39 Troy Auzenne ART	.05	.01
❑	40 Shane Dronett ART	.05	.01
❑	41 Chris Mims ART	.05	.01
❑	42 Sean Gilbert ART	.05	.01
❑	43 Steve Emtman ART	.05	.01
❑	44 Robert Jones ART	.05	.01
❑	45 Marco Coleman ART	.05	.01
❑	46 Ricardo McDonald ART	.05	.01
❑	47 Quentin Coryatt ART	.10	.02
❑	48 Dana Hall ART	.05	.01
❑	49 Darren Perry ART	.05	.01
❑	50 Darryl Williams ART	.05	.01
❑	51 Kevin Smith ART	.05	.01
❑	52 Terrell Buckley ART	.05	.01
❑	53 Troy Vincent ART	.05	.01
❑	54 Lin Elliott ART	.05	.01
❑	55 Dale Carter ART	.05	.01
❑	56 Steve Atwater HIT	.05	.01
❑	57 Junior Seau HIT	.10	.02

❑	58	Ronnie Lott HIT	.05	.01
❑	59	Louis Oliver HIT	.05	.01
❑	60	Cortez Kennedy HIT	.05	.01
❑	61	Pat Swilling HIT	.05	.01
❑	62	Hitmen Checklist	.05	.01
❑	63	Curtis Conway TC	.25	.08
❑	64	Alfred Williams TC	.05	.01
❑	65	Jim Kelly TC	.10	.02
❑	66	Simon Fletcher TC	.05	.01
❑	67	Eric Metcalf TC	.05	.01
❑	68	Lawrence Dawsey TC	.05	.01
❑	69	Garrison Hearst TC	.25	.08
❑	70	Anthony Miller TC	.05	.01
❑	71	Neil Smith TC	.05	.01
❑	72	Jeff George TC	.10	.02
❑	73	Emmitt Smith TC	.75	.30
❑	74	Dan Marino TC	.75	.30
❑	75	Clyde Simmons TC	.05	.01
❑	76	Deion Sanders TC	.25	.08
❑	77	Ricky Watters TC	.10	.02
❑	78	Rodney Hampton TC	.10	.02
❑	79	Brad Baxter TC	.05	.01
❑	80	Barry Sanders TC	.60	.25
❑	81	Warren Moon TC	.10	.02
❑	82	Brett Favre TC	1.00	.40
❑	83	Drew Bledsoe TC	1.25	.50
❑	84	Eric Dickerson TC	.10	.02
❑	85	Cleveland Gary TC	.05	.01
❑	86	Earnest Byner TC	.05	.01
❑	87	Wayne Martin TC	.05	.01
❑	88	Rick Mirer TC	.25	.08
❑	89	Barry Foster TC	.05	.01
❑	90	Terry Allen TC	.10	.02
❑	91	Vinnie Clark	.05	.01
❑	92	Howard Ballard	.05	.01
❑	93	Eric Ball	.05	.01
❑	94	Marc Boutte	.05	.01
❑	95	Larry Centers RC	.25	.08
❑	96	Gary Brown	.05	.01
❑	97	Hugh Millen	.05	.01
❑	98	Anthony Newman RC	.05	.01
❑	99	Darrell Thompson	.05	.01
❑	100	George Jamison	.05	.01
❑	101	James Francis	.05	.01
❑	102	Leonard Harris	.05	.01
❑	103	Lomas Brown	.05	.01
❑	104	James Lofton	.10	.02
❑	105	Jamie Dukes	.05	.01
❑	106	Quinn Early	.10	.02
❑	107	Ernie Jones	.05	.01
❑	108	Torrance Small	.05	.01
❑	109	Michael Carter	.05	.01
❑	110	Aeneas Williams	.05	.01
❑	111	Renaldo Turnbull	.05	.01
❑	112	Al Smith	.05	.01
❑	113	Troy Auzenne	.05	.01
❑	114	Stephen Baker	.05	.01
❑	115	Daniel Stubbs	.05	.01
❑	116	Dana Hall	.05	.01
❑	117	Lawrence Taylor	.25	.08
❑	118	Ron Hall	.05	.01
❑	119	Derrick Fenner	.05	.01
❑	120	Martin Mayhew	.05	.01
❑	121	Jay Schroeder	.05	.01
❑	122	Michael Zordich	.05	.01
❑	123	Ed McCaffrey	.25	.08
❑	124	John Stephens	.05	.01
❑	125	Brad Edwards	.05	.01
❑	126	Don Griffin	.05	.01
❑	127	Broderick Thomas	.05	.01
❑	128	Ted Washington	.05	.01
❑	129	Haywood Jeffires	.10	.02
❑	130	Gary Plummer	.05	.01
❑	131	Mark Wheeler	.05	.01
❑	132	Ty Detmer	.25	.08
❑	133	Derrick Walker	.05	.01
❑	134	Henry Ellard	.10	.02
❑	135	Neal Anderson	.05	.01
❑	136	Bruce Smith	.25	.08
❑	137	Cris Carter	.25	.08
❑	138	Vaughn Dunbar	.05	.01
❑	139	Dan Marino	1.50	.60
❑	140	Troy Aikman	.75	.30
❑	141	Randall Cunningham	.25	.08
❑	142	Daryl Johnston	.25	.08
❑	143	Mark Clayton	.05	.01
❑	144	Rich Gannon	.25	.08
❑	145	Nate Newton	.10	.02
❑	146	Willie Gault	.05	.01
❑	147	Brian Washington	.05	.01
❑	148	Fred Barnett	.10	.02
❑	149	Gill Byrd	.05	.01
❑	150	Art Monk	.10	.02
❑	151	Stan Humphries	.10	.02
❑	152	Charles Mann	.05	.01
❑	153	Greg Lloyd	.10	.02
❑	154	Marvin Washington	.05	.01
❑	155	Bernie Kosar	.10	.02
❑	156	Pete Metzelaars	.05	.01
❑	157	Chris Hinton	.05	.01
❑	158	Jim Harbaugh	.25	.08
❑	159	Willie Davis	.25	.08
❑	160	Leroy Thompson	.05	.01
❑	161	Scott Miller	.05	.01
❑	162	Eugene Robinson	.05	.01
❑	163	David Little	.05	.01
❑	164	Pierce Holt	.05	.01
❑	165	James Hasty	.05	.01
❑	166	Dave Krieg	.10	.02
❑	167	Gerald Williams	.05	.01
❑	168	Kyle Clifton	.05	.01
❑	169	Bill Brooks	.05	.01
❑	170	Vance Johnson	.05	.01
❑	171	Greg Townsend	.05	.01
❑	172	Jason Belser	.05	.01
❑	173	Brett Perriman	.25	.08
❑	174	Steve Jordan	.05	.01
❑	175	Kelvin Martin	.05	.01
❑	176	Greg Kragen	.05	.01
❑	177	Kerry Cash	.05	.01
❑	178	Chester McGlockton	.10	.02
❑	179	Jim Kelly	.25	.08
❑	180	Todd McNair	.05	.01
❑	181	Leroy Hoard	.10	.02
❑	182	Seth Joyner	.05	.01
❑	183	Sam Gash RC	.25	.08
❑	184	Joe Nash	.05	.01
❑	185	Lin Elliott RC	.05	.01
❑	186	Robert Porcher	.05	.01
❑	187	Tommy Hodson	.05	.01
❑	188	Greg Lewis	.05	.01
❑	189	Dan Saleaumua	.05	.01
❑	190	Chris Goode	.05	.01
❑	191	Henry Thomas	.05	.01
❑	192	Bobby Hebert	.05	.01
❑	193	Clay Matthews	.10	.02
❑	194	Mark Carrier WR	.10	.02
❑	195	Anthony Pleasant	.05	.01
❑	196	Eric Dorsey	.05	.01
❑	197	Clarence Verdin	.05	.01
❑	198	Marc Spindler	.05	.01
❑	199	Tommy Maddox	.25	.08
❑	200	Wendell Davis	.05	.01
❑	201	John Fina	.05	.01
❑	202	Alonzo Spellman	.05	.01
❑	203	Darryl Williams	.05	.01
❑	204	Mike Croel	.05	.01
❑	205	Ken Norton Jr.	.10	.02
❑	206	Mel Gray	.10	.02
❑	207	Chuck Cecil	.05	.01
❑	208	John Flannery	.05	.01
❑	209	Chip Banks	.05	.01
❑	210	Chris Martin	.05	.01
❑	211	Dennis Brown	.05	.01
❑	212	Vinny Testaverde	.10	.02
❑	213	Nick Bell	.05	.01
❑	214	Robert Delpino	.05	.01
❑	215	Mark Higgs	.05	.01
❑	216	Al Noga	.05	.01
❑	217	Andre Tippett	.05	.01
❑	218	Pat Swilling	.05	.01
❑	219	Phil Simms	.10	.02
❑	220	Ricky Proehl	.05	.01
❑	221	William Thomas	.05	.01
❑	222	Jeff Graham	.10	.02
❑	223	Darion Conner	.05	.01
❑	224	Mark Carrier DB	.05	.01
❑	225	Willie Green	.05	.01
❑	226	Reggie Rivers RC	.05	.01
❑	227	Andre Reed	.10	.02
❑	228	Deion Sanders	.50	.20
❑	229	Chris Doleman	.05	.01
❑	230	Jerry Ball	.05	.01
❑	231	Eric Dickerson	.10	.02
❑	232	Carlos Jenkins	.05	.01
❑	233	Mike Johnson	.05	.01
❑	234	Marco Coleman	.05	.01
❑	235	Leslie O'Neal	.10	.02
❑	236	Browning Nagle	.05	.01
❑	237	Carl Pickens	.10	.02
❑	238	Steve Emtman	.05	.01
❑	239	Alvin Harper	.10	.02
❑	240	Keith Jackson	.10	.02
❑	241	Jerry Rice	1.00	.40
❑	242	Cortez Kennedy	.10	.02
❑	243	Tyji Armstrong	.05	.01
❑	244	Troy Vincent	.05	.01
❑	245	Randal Hill	.05	.01
❑	246	Robert Blackmon	.05	.01
❑	247	Junior Seau	.25	.08
❑	248	Sterling Sharpe	.25	.08
❑	249	Thurman Thomas	.25	.08
❑	250	David Klingler	.05	.01
❑	251	Jeff George	.25	.08
❑	252	Anthony Miller	.10	.02
❑	253	Earnest Byner	.05	.01
❑	254	Eric Swann	.10	.02
❑	255	Jeff Herrod	.05	.01
❑	256	Eddie Robinson	.05	.01
❑	257	Eric Allen	.05	.01
❑	258	John Taylor	.10	.02
❑	259	Sean Gilbert	.10	.02
❑	260	Ray Childress	.05	.01
❑	261	Michael Haynes	.10	.02
❑	262	Greg McMurtry	.05	.01
❑	263	Bill Romanowski	.05	.01
❑	264	Todd Lyght	.05	.01
❑	265	Clyde Simmons	.05	.01
❑	266	Webster Slaughter	.05	.01
❑	267	J.J. Birden	.05	.01
❑	268	Aaron Wallace	.05	.01
❑	269	Carl Banks	.05	.01
❑	270	Ricardo McDonald	.05	.01
❑	271	Michael Brooks	.05	.01
❑	272	Dale Carter	.05	.01
❑	273	Mike Pritchard	.10	.02
❑	274	Derek Brown TE	.05	.01
❑	275	Burt Grossman	.05	.01
❑	276	Mark Schlereth	.05	.01
❑	277	Karl Mecklenburg	.05	.01
❑	278	Rickey Jackson	.05	.01
❑	279	Ricky Ervins	.05	.01
❑	280	Jeff Bryant	.05	.01
❑	281	Eric Martin	.05	.01
❑	282	Carlton Haselrig	.05	.01
❑	283	Kevin Mack	.05	.01
❑	284	Brad Muster	.05	.01
❑	285	Kelvin Pritchett	.05	.01
❑	286	Courtney Hawkins	.05	.01
❑	287	Levon Kirkland	.05	.01
❑	288	Steve DeBerg	.05	.01
❑	289	Edgar Bennett	.25	.08
❑	290	Michael Dean Perry	.10	.02
❑	291	Richard Dent	.10	.02
❑	292	Howie Long	.25	.08
❑	293	Chris Mims	.05	.01
❑	294	Kurt Barber	.05	.01
❑	295	Wilber Marshall	.05	.01
❑	296	Ethan Horton	.05	.01
❑	297	Tony Bennett	.05	.01
❑	298	Johnny Johnson	.05	.01
❑	299	Craig Heyward	.10	.02
❑	300	Steve Israel	.05	.01
❑	301	Kenneth Gant	.05	.01
❑	302	Eugene Chung	.05	.01
❑	303	Harvey Williams	.10	.02
❑	304	Jarrod Bunch	.05	.01
❑	305	Darren Perry	.05	.01
❑	306	Steve Christie	.05	.01
❑	307	John Randle	.10	.02
❑	308	Warren Moon	.25	.08
❑	309	Charles Haley	.10	.02
❑	310	Tony Smith RB	.05	.01
❑	311	Steve Broussard	.05	.01
❑	312	Alfred Williams	.05	.01
❑	313	Terrell Buckley	.05	.01
❑	314	Trace Armstrong	.05	.01
❑	315	Brian Mitchell	.10	.02
❑	316	Steve Atwater	.05	.01
❑	317	Nate Lewis	.05	.01
❑	318	Richard Brown	.05	.01

❑ 319 Rufus Porter .05 .01
❑ 320 Pat Harlow .05 .01
❑ 321 Anthony Smith .05 .01
❑ 322 Jack Del Rio .05 .01
❑ 323 Darryl Talley .05 .01
❑ 324 Sam Mills .05 .01
❑ 325 Chris Miller .10 .02
❑ 326 Ken Harvey .05 .01
❑ 327 Rod Woodson .25 .08
❑ 328 Tony Tolbert .05 .01
❑ 329 Todd Kinchen .05 .01
❑ 330 Brian Noble .05 .01
❑ 331 Dave Meggett .05 .01
❑ 332 Chris Spielman .10 .02
❑ 333 Barry Word .05 .01
❑ 334 Jessie Hester .05 .01
❑ 335 Michael Jackson .10 .02
❑ 336 Mitchell Price .05 .01
❑ 337 Michael Irvin .25 .08
❑ 338 Simon Fletcher .05 .01
❑ 339 Keith Jennings .05 .01
❑ 340 Vai Sikahema .05 .01
❑ 341 Roger Craig .10 .02
❑ 342 Ricky Watters .25 .08
❑ 343 Reggie Cobb .05 .01
❑ 344 Kanavis McGhee .05 .01
❑ 345 Barry Foster .10 .02
❑ 346 Marion Butts .05 .01
❑ 347 Bryan Cox .05 .01
❑ 348 Wayne Martin .05 .01
❑ 349 Jim Everett .10 .02
❑ 350 Nate Odomes .05 .01
❑ 351 Anthony Johnson .10 .02
❑ 352 Rodney Hampton .10 .02
❑ 353 Terry Allen .25 .08
❑ 354 Derrick Thomas .25 .08
❑ 355 Calvin Williams .10 .02
❑ 356 Pepper Johnson .05 .01
❑ 357 John Elway 1.50 .60
❑ 358 Steve Young .75 .30
❑ 359 Emmitt Smith 1.50 .60
❑ 360 Brett Favre 2.00 .75
❑ 361 Cody Carlson .05 .01
❑ 362 Vincent Brown .05 .01
❑ 363 Gary Anderson RB .05 .01
❑ 364 Jon Vaughn .05 .01
❑ 365 Todd Marinovich .05 .01
❑ 366 Carnell Lake .05 .01
❑ 367 Kurt Gouveia .05 .01
❑ 368 Lawrence Dawsey .05 .01
❑ 369 Neil O'Donnell .25 .08
❑ 370 Duane Bickett .05 .01
❑ 371 Ronnie Harmon .05 .01
❑ 372 Rodney Peete .05 .01
❑ 373 Cornelius Bennett .10 .02
❑ 374 Brad Baxter .05 .01
❑ 375 Ernest Givins .10 .02
❑ 376 Keith Byars .05 .01
❑ 377 Eric Bieniemy .05 .01
❑ 378 Mike Brim .05 .01
❑ 379 Darren Lewis .05 .01
❑ 380 Heath Sherman .05 .01
❑ 381 Leonard Russell .10 .02
❑ 382 Brent Jones .10 .02
❑ 383 David Whitmore .05 .01
❑ 384 Ray Roberts .05 .01
❑ 385 John Offerdahl .05 .01
❑ 386 Keith McCants .05 .01
❑ 387 John Baylor .05 .01
❑ 388 Amp Lee .05 .01
❑ 389 Chris Warren .10 .02
❑ 390 Herman Moore .25 .08
❑ 391 Johnny Bailey .05 .01
❑ 392 Tim Johnson .05 .01
❑ 393 Eric Metcalf .10 .02
❑ 394 Chris Chandler .10 .02
❑ 395 Mark Rypien .05 .01
❑ 396 Christian Okoye .05 .01
❑ 397 Shannon Sharpe .25 .08
❑ 398 Eric Hill .05 .01
❑ 399 David Lang .05 .01
❑ 400 Bruce Matthews .05 .01
❑ 401 Harold Green .05 .01
❑ 402 Mo Lewis .05 .01
❑ 403 Terry McDaniel .05 .01
❑ 404 Wesley Carroll .05 .01
❑ 405 Richmond Webb .05 .01
❑ 406 Andre Rison .10 .02
❑ 407 Lonnie Young .05 .01
❑ 408 Tommy Vardell .05 .01
❑ 409 Gene Atkins .05 .01
❑ 410 Sean Salisbury .05 .01
❑ 411 Kenneth Davis .05 .01
❑ 412 John L. Williams .05 .01
❑ 413 Roman Phifer .05 .01
❑ 414 Bennie Blades .05 .01
❑ 415 Tim Brown .25 .08
❑ 416 Lorenzo White .05 .01
❑ 417 Tony Casillas .05 .01
❑ 418 Tom Waddle .05 .01
❑ 419 David Fulcher .05 .01
❑ 420 Jessie Tuggle .05 .01
❑ 421 Emmitt Smith SL .75 .30
❑ 422 Clyde Simmons SL .05 .01
❑ 423 Sterling Sharpe SL .10 .02
❑ 424 Sterling Sharpe SL .10 .02
❑ 425 Emmitt Smith SL .75 .30
❑ 426 Dan Marino SL .75 .30
❑ 427 Henry Jones SL .05 .01
❑ 428 Thurman Thomas SL .10 .02
❑ 429 Greg Montgomery SL .05 .01
❑ 430 Pete Stoyanovich SL .05 .01
❑ 431 Emmitt Smith CL .40 .15
❑ 432 Steve Young BB .40 .15
❑ 433 Jerry Rice BB .50 .20
❑ 434 Ricky Watters BB .10 .02
❑ 435 Barry Foster BB .05 .01
❑ 436 Cortez Kennedy BB .05 .01
❑ 437 Warren Moon BB .10 .02
❑ 438 Thurman Thomas BB .10 .02
❑ 439 Brett Favre BB 1.00 .40
❑ 440 Andre Rison BB .10 .02
❑ 441 Barry Sanders BB .60 .25
❑ 442 Chris Berman CL .05 .01
❑ 443 Moe Gardner .05 .01
❑ 444 Robert Jones .05 .01
❑ 445 Reggie Langhorne .05 .01
❑ 446 Flipper Anderson .05 .01
❑ 447 James Washington .05 .01
❑ 448 Aaron Craver .05 .01
❑ 449 Jack Trudeau .05 .01
❑ 450 Neil Smith .25 .08
❑ 451 Chris Burkett .05 .01
❑ 452 Russell Maryland .05 .01
❑ 453 Drew Hill .05 .01
❑ 454 Barry Sanders 1.25 .50
❑ 455 Jeff Cross .05 .01
❑ 456 Bennie Thompson .05 .01
❑ 457 Marcus Allen .25 .08
❑ 458 Tracy Scroggins .05 .01
❑ 459 LeRoy Butler .05 .01
❑ 460 Joe Montana 1.50 .60
❑ 461 Eddie Anderson .05 .01
❑ 462 Tim McDonald .05 .01
❑ 463 Ronnie Lott .10 .02
❑ 464 Gaston Green .05 .01
❑ 465 Shane Conlan .05 .01
❑ 466 Leonard Marshall .05 .01
❑ 467 Melvin Jenkins .05 .01
❑ 468 Don Beebe .05 .01
❑ 469 Johnny Mitchell .05 .01
❑ 470 Darryl Henley .05 .01
❑ 471 Boomer Esiason .10 .02
❑ 472 Mark Kelso .05 .01
❑ 473 John Booty .05 .01
❑ 474 Pete Stoyanovich .05 .01
❑ 475 Thomas Smith RC .10 .02
❑ 476 Carlton Gray RC .05 .01
❑ 477 Dana Stubblefield RC .25 .08
❑ 478 Ryan McNeil RC .25 .08
❑ 479 Natrone Means RC .25 .08
❑ 480 Carl Simpson RC .05 .01
❑ 481 Robert O'Neal RC .05 .01
❑ 482 Demetrius DuBose RC .05 .01
❑ 483 Darrin Smith RC .10 .02
❑ 484 Micheal Barrow RC .25 .08
❑ 485 Chris Slade RC .10 .02
❑ 486 Steve Tovar RC .05 .01
❑ 487 Ron George RC .05 .01
❑ 488 Steve Tasker .10 .02
❑ 489 Will Furrer .05 .01
❑ 490 Reggie White .25 .08
❑ 491 Sean Jones .05 .01
❑ 492 Gary Clark .10 .02
❑ 493 Donnell Woolford .05 .01
❑ 494 Steve Beuerlein .10 .02
❑ 495 Anthony Carter .10 .02
❑ 496 Louis Oliver .05 .01
❑ 497 Chris Zorich .05 .01
❑ 498 David Brandon .05 .01
❑ 499 Bubba McDowell .05 .01
❑ 500 Adrian Cooper .05 .01
❑ 501 Bill Johnson .05 .01
❑ 502 Shawn Jefferson .05 .01
❑ 503 Siran Stacy .05 .01
❑ 504 James Jones DT .05 .01
❑ 505 Tom Rathman .05 .01
❑ 506 Vince Buck .05 .01
❑ 507 Kent Graham RC .25 .08
❑ 508 Darren Carrington RC .05 .01
❑ 509 Rickey Dixon .05 .01
❑ 510 Toi Cook .05 .01
❑ 511 Steve Smith .05 .01
❑ 512 Eric Green .05 .01
❑ 513 Phillippi Sparks .05 .01
❑ 514 Lee Williams .05 .01
❑ 515 Gary Reasons .05 .01
❑ 516 Shane Dronett .05 .01
❑ 517 Jay Novacek .10 .02
❑ 518 Kevin Greene .10 .02
❑ 519 Derek Russell .05 .01
❑ 520 Quentin Coryatt .10 .02
❑ 521 Santana Dotson .10 .02
❑ 522 Donald Frank .05 .01
❑ 523 Mike Prior .05 .01
❑ 524 Dwight Hollier RC .05 .01
❑ 525 Eric Davis .05 .01
❑ 526 Dalton Hilliard .05 .01
❑ 527 Rodney Culver .05 .01
❑ 528 Jeff Hostetler .10 .02
❑ 529 Ernie Mills .05 .01
❑ 530 Craig Erickson .10 .02
❑ P231 Eric Dickerson Promo 1.25 .50

1994 Upper Deck

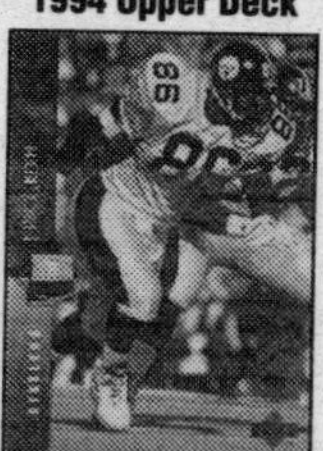

❑ COMPLETE SET (330) 25.00 12.50
❑ 1 Dan Wilkinson RC .20 .07
❑ 2 Antonio Langham RC .20 .07
❑ 3 Derrick Alexander WR RC .40 .15
❑ 4 Charles Johnson RC .40 .15
❑ 5 Bucky Brooks RC .10 .02
❑ 6 Trev Alberts RC .20 .07
❑ 7 Marshall Faulk RC 6.00 2.50
❑ 8 Willie McGinest RC .40 .15
❑ 9 Aaron Glenn RC .40 .15
❑ 10 Ryan Yarborough RC .10 .02
❑ 11 Greg Hill RC .40 .15
❑ 12 Sam Adams RC .20 .07
❑ 13 John Thierry RC .10 .02
❑ 14 Johnnie Morton RC .75 .30
❑ 15 LeShon Johnson RC .20 .07
❑ 16 David Palmer RC .40 .15
❑ 17 Trent Dilfer RC 1.25 .50
❑ 18 Jamir Miller RC .20 .07
❑ 19 Thomas Lewis RC .20 .07
❑ 20 Heath Shuler RC .40 .15
❑ 21 Wayne Gandy .10 .02
❑ 22 Isaac Bruce RC 4.00 2.00
❑ 23 Joe Johnson RC .10 .02
❑ 24 Mario Bates RC .40 .15
❑ 25 Bryant Young RC .40 .15
❑ 26 William Floyd RC .40 .15
❑ 27 Errict Rhett RC .40 .15

❑ 28 Chuck Levy RC .10 .02
❑ 29 Darnay Scott RC .75 .30
❑ 30 Rob Fredrickson RC .20 .07
❑ 31 Jamir Miller HW .10 .02
❑ 32 Thomas Lewis HW .10 .02
❑ 33 John Thierry HW .10 .02
❑ 34 Sam Adams HW .10 .02
❑ 35 Joe Johnson HW .10 .02
❑ 36 Bryant Young HW .20 .07
❑ 37 Wayne Gandy HW .10 .02
❑ 38 LeShon Johnson HW .10 .02
❑ 39 Mario Bates HW .20 .07
❑ 40 Greg Hill HW .20 .07
❑ 41 Andy Heck .10 .02
❑ 42 Warren Moon .40 .15
❑ 43 Jim Everett .20 .07
❑ 44 Bill Romanowski .10 .02
❑ 45 Michael Haynes .20 .07
❑ 46 Chris Doleman .10 .02
❑ 47 Merril Hoge .10 .02
❑ 48 Chris Miller .10 .02
❑ 49 Clyde Simmons .10 .02
❑ 50 Jeff George .40 .15
❑ 51 Jeff Burris RC .20 .07
❑ 52 Ethan Horton .10 .02
❑ 53 Scott Mitchell .20 .07
❑ 54 Howard Ballard .10 .02
❑ 55 Lewis Tillman .10 .02
❑ 56 Marion Butts .10 .02
❑ 57 Erik Kramer .20 .07
❑ 58 Ken Norton Jr. .20 .07
❑ 59 Anthony Miller .20 .07
❑ 60 Chris Hinton .10 .02
❑ 61 Ricky Proehl .10 .02
❑ 62 Craig Heyward .20 .07
❑ 63 Darryl Talley .10 .02
❑ 64 Tim Worley .10 .02
❑ 65 Derrick Fenner .10 .02
❑ 66 Jerry Ball .10 .02
❑ 67 Darrin Smith .10 .02
❑ 68 Mike Croel .10 .02
❑ 69 Ray Crockett .10 .02
❑ 70 Tony Bennett .10 .02
❑ 71 Webster Slaughter .10 .02
❑ 72 Anthony Johnson .20 .07
❑ 73 Charles Mincy .10 .02
❑ 74 Calvin Jones RC .10 .02
❑ 75 Henry Ellard .20 .07
❑ 76 Troy Vincent .10 .02
❑ 77 Sean Salisbury .10 .02
❑ 78 Pat Harlow .10 .02
❑ 79 James Williams RC LB .10 .02
❑ 80 Dave Brown .20 .07
❑ 81 Kent Graham .20 .07
❑ 82 Seth Joyner .10 .02
❑ 83 Deon Figures .10 .02
❑ 84 Stanley Richard .10 .02
❑ 85 Tom Rathman .10 .02
❑ 86 Rod Stephens .10 .02
❑ 87 Ray Seals .10 .02
❑ 88 Andre Collins .10 .02
❑ 89 Cornelius Bennett .20 .07
❑ 90 Richard Dent .20 .07
❑ 91 Louis Oliver .10 .02
❑ 92 Rodney Peete .10 .02
❑ 93 Jackie Harris .10 .02
❑ 94 Tracy Simien .10 .02
❑ 95 Greg Townsend .10 .02
❑ 96 Michael Stewart .10 .02
❑ 97 Irving Fryar .20 .07
❑ 98 Todd Collins .10 .02
❑ 99 Irv Smith .10 .02
❑ 100 Chris Calloway .10 .02
❑ 101 Kevin Greene .20 .07
❑ 102 John Friesz .20 .07
❑ 103 Steve Bono .20 .07
❑ 104 Brian Blades .20 .07
❑ 105 Reggie Cobb .10 .02
❑ 106 Eric Swann .20 .07
❑ 107 Mike Pritchard .10 .02
❑ 108 Bill Brooks .10 .02
❑ 109 Jim Harbaugh .40 .15
❑ 110 David Whitmore .10 .02
❑ 111 Eddie Anderson .10 .02
❑ 112 Ray Crittenden RC .10 .02
❑ 113 Mark Collins .10 .02
❑ 114 Brian Washington .10 .02
❑ 115 Barry Foster .10 .02
❑ 116 Gary Plummer .10 .02
❑ 117 Marc Logan .10 .02
❑ 118 John L. Williams .10 .02
❑ 119 Marty Carter .10 .02
❑ 120 Kurt Gouveia .10 .02
❑ 121 Ronald Moore .10 .02
❑ 122 Pierce Holt .10 .02
❑ 123 Henry Jones .10 .02
❑ 124 Donnell Woolford .10 .02
❑ 125 Steve Tovar .10 .02
❑ 126 Anthony Pleasant .10 .02
❑ 127 Jay Novacek .20 .07
❑ 128 Dan Williams .10 .02
❑ 129 Barry Sanders 2.50 1.00
❑ 130 Robert Brooks .40 .15
❑ 131 Lorenzo White .10 .02
❑ 132 Kerry Cash .10 .02
❑ 133 Joe Montana 3.00 1.25
❑ 134 Jeff Hostetler .20 .07
❑ 135 Jerome Bettis .60 .25
❑ 136 Dan Marino 3.00 1.25
❑ 137 Vencie Glenn .10 .02
❑ 138 Vincent Brown .10 .02
❑ 139 Rickey Jackson .10 .02
❑ 140 Carlton Bailey .10 .02
❑ 141 Jeff Lageman .10 .02
❑ 142 William Thomas .10 .02
❑ 143 Neil O'Donnell .40 .15
❑ 144 Shawn Jefferson .10 .02
❑ 145 Steve Young 1.00 .40
❑ 146 Chris Warren .20 .07
❑ 147 Courtney Hawkins .10 .02
❑ 148 Brad Edwards .10 .02
❑ 149 O.J.McDuffie .40 .15
❑ 150 David Lang .10 .02
❑ 151 Chuck Cecil .10 .02
❑ 152 Norm Johnson .10 .02
❑ 153 Pete Metzelaars .10 .02
❑ 154 Shaun Gayle .10 .02
❑ 155 Alfred Williams .10 .02
❑ 156 Eric Turner .10 .02
❑ 157A Emmitt Smith ERR 1900 2.50 1.00
❑ 157B Emmitt Smith COR 2.50 1.00
❑ 158 Steve Atwater .10 .02
❑ 159 Robert Porcher .10 .02
❑ 160 Edgar Bennett .40 .15
❑ 161 Bubba McDowell .10 .02
❑ 162 Jeff Herrod .10 .02
❑ 163 Keith Cash .10 .02
❑ 164 Patrick Bates .10 .02
❑ 165 Todd Lyght .10 .02
❑ 166 Mark Higgs .10 .02
❑ 167 Carlos Jenkins .10 .02
❑ 168 Drew Bledsoe 1.00 .40
❑ 169 Wayne Martin .10 .02
❑ 170 Mike Sherrard .10 .02
❑ 171 Ronnie Lott .20 .07
❑ 172 Fred Barnett .20 .07
❑ 173 Eric Green .10 .02
❑ 174 Leslie O'Neal .10 .02
❑ 175 Brent Jones .20 .07
❑ 176 Jon Vaughn .10 .02
❑ 177 Vince Workman .10 .02
❑ 178 Ron Middleton .10 .02
❑ 179 Terry McDaniel .10 .02
❑ 180 Willie Davis .20 .07
❑ 181 Gary Clark .20 .07
❑ 182 Bobby Hebert .10 .02
❑ 183 Russell Copeland .10 .02
❑ 184 Chris Gedney .10 .02
❑ 185 Tony McGee .10 .02
❑ 186 Rob Burnett .10 .02
❑ 187 Charles Haley .20 .07
❑ 188 Shannon Sharpe .20 .07
❑ 189 Mel Gray .10 .02
❑ 190 George Teague .10 .02
❑ 191 Ernest Givins .20 .07
❑ 192 Ray Buchanan .10 .02
❑ 193 J.J. Birden .10 .02
❑ 194 Tim Brown .40 .15
❑ 195 Tim Lester .10 .02
❑ 196 Marco Coleman .10 .02
❑ 197 Randall McDaniel .10 .02
❑ 198 Bruce Armstrong .10 .02
❑ 199 Willie Roaf .10 .02
❑ 200 Greg Jackson .10 .02
❑ 201 Johnny Mitchell .10 .02
❑ 202 Calvin Williams .20 .07
❑ 203 Jeff Graham .10 .02
❑ 204 Darren Carrington .10 .02
❑ 205 Jerry Rice 1.50 .60
❑ 206 Cortez Kennedy .20 .07
❑ 207 Charles Wilson .10 .02
❑ 208 James Jenkins TE RC .10 .02
❑ 209 Ray Childress .10 .02
❑ 210 LeRoy Butler .10 .02
❑ 211 Randal Hill .10 .02
❑ 212 Lincoln Kennedy .10 .02
❑ 213 Kenneth Davis .10 .02
❑ 214 Terry Obee .10 .02
❑ 215 Ricardo McDonald .10 .02
❑ 216 Pepper Johnson .10 .02
❑ 217 Alvin Harper .20 .07
❑ 218 John Elway 3.00 1.25
❑ 219 Derrick Moore .10 .02
❑ 220 Terrell Buckley .10 .02
❑ 221 Haywood Jeffires .20 .07
❑ 222 Jessie Hester .10 .02
❑ 223 Kimble Anders .20 .07
❑ 224 Rocket Ismail .20 .07
❑ 225 Roman Phifer .10 .02
❑ 226 Bryan Cox .10 .02
❑ 227 Cris Carter .75 .30
❑ 228 Sam Gash .10 .02
❑ 229 Renaldo Turnbull .10 .02
❑ 230 Rodney Hampton .20 .07
❑ 231 Johnny Johnson .10 .02
❑ 232 Tim Harris .10 .02
❑ 233 Leroy Thompson .10 .02
❑ 234 Junior Seau .40 .15
❑ 235 Tim McDonald .10 .02
❑ 236 Eugene Robinson .10 .02
❑ 237 Lawrence Dawsey .10 .02
❑ 238 Tim Johnson .10 .02
❑ 239 Jason Elam .20 .07
❑ 240 Willie Green .10 .02
❑ 241 Larry Centers .40 .15
❑ 242 Erric Pegram .10 .02
❑ 243 Bruce Smith .40 .15
❑ 244 Alonzo Spellman .10 .02
❑ 245 Carl Pickens .20 .07
❑ 246 Michael Jackson .20 .07
❑ 247 Kevin Williams WR .20 .07
❑ 248 Glyn Milburn .20 .07
❑ 249 Herman Moore .40 .15
❑ 250 Brett Favre 3.00 1.25
❑ 251 Al Smith .10 .02
❑ 252 Roosevelt Potts .10 .02
❑ 253 Marcus Allen .40 .15
❑ 254 Anthony Smith .10 .02
❑ 255 Sean Gilbert .10 .02
❑ 256 Keith Byars .10 .02
❑ 257 Scottie Graham RC .20 .07
❑ 258 Leonard Russell .10 .02
❑ 259 Eric Martin .10 .02
❑ 260 Jarrod Bunch .10 .02
❑ 261 Rob Moore .20 .07
❑ 262 Herschel Walker .20 .07
❑ 263 Levon Kirkland .10 .02
❑ 264 Chris Mims .10 .02
❑ 265 Ricky Watters .20 .07
❑ 266 Rick Mirer .40 .15
❑ 267 Santana Dotson .20 .07
❑ 268 Reggie Brooks .20 .07
❑ 269 Garrison Hearst .40 .15
❑ 270 Thurman Thomas .40 .15
❑ 271 Johnny Bailey .10 .02
❑ 272 Andre Rison .20 .07
❑ 273 Jim Kelly .40 .15
❑ 274 Mark Carrier DB .10 .02
❑ 275 David Klingler .10 .02
❑ 276 Eric Metcalf .20 .07
❑ 277 Troy Aikman UER 1.50 .60
❑ 278 Simon Fletcher .10 .02
❑ 279 Pat Swilling .10 .02
❑ 280 Sterling Sharpe .20 .07
❑ 281 Cody Carlson .10 .02
❑ 282 Steve Emtman .10 .02
❑ 283 Neil Smith .20 .07
❑ 284 James Jett .10 .02
❑ 285 Shane Conlan .10 .02
❑ 286 Keith Jackson .10 .02
❑ 287 Qadry Ismail .40 .15

❑ 288 Chris Slade	.10	.02
❑ 289 Derek Brown RBK	.10	.02
❑ 290 Phil Simms	.20	.07
❑ 291 Boomer Esiason	.20	.07
❑ 292 Eric Allen	.10	.02
❑ 293 Rod Woodson	.20	.07
❑ 294 Ronnie Harmon	.10	.02
❑ 295 John Taylor	.20	.07
❑ 296 Ferrell Edmunds	.10	.02
❑ 297 Craig Erickson	.10	.02
❑ 298 Brian Mitchell	.10	.02
❑ 299 Dante Jones	.10	.02
❑ 300 John Copeland	.10	.02
❑ 301 Steve Beuerlein	.20	.07
❑ 302 Deion Sanders	.75	.30
❑ 303 Andre Reed	.20	.07
❑ 304 Curtis Conway	.40	.15
❑ 305 Harold Green	.10	.02
❑ 306 Vinny Testaverde	.20	.07
❑ 307 Michael Irvin	.40	.15
❑ 308 Rod Bernstine	.10	.02
❑ 309 Chris Spielman	.20	.07
❑ 310 Reggie White	.40	.15
❑ 311 Gary Brown	.10	.02
❑ 312 Quentin Coryatt	.10	.02
❑ 313 Derrick Thomas	.40	.15
❑ 314 Greg Robinson	.10	.02
❑ 315 Troy Drayton	.10	.02
❑ 316 Terry Kirby	.40	.15
❑ 317 John Randle	.20	.07
❑ 318 Ben Coates	.20	.07
❑ 319 Tyrone Hughes	.20	.07
❑ 320 Corey Miller	.10	.02
❑ 321 Brad Baxter	.10	.02
❑ 322 Randall Cunningham	.40	.15
❑ 323 Greg Lloyd	.20	.07
❑ 324 Stan Humphries	.20	.07
❑ 325 Dana Stubblefield	.20	.07
❑ 326 Kelvin Martin	.10	.02
❑ 327 Hardy Nickerson	.20	.07
❑ 328 Desmond Howard	.20	.07
❑ 329 Mark Carrier WR	.20	.07
❑ 330 Daryl Johnston	.20	.07
❑ P19 Joe Montana Promo	2.50	1.00

1995 Upper Deck

❑ COMPLETE SET (300)	30.00	12.50
❑ 1 Ki-Jana Carter RC	.40	.15
❑ 2 Tony Boselli RC	.40	.15
❑ 3 Steve McNair RC	4.00	1.50
❑ 4 Michael Westbrook RC	.40	.15
❑ 5 Kerry Collins RC	2.00	.75
❑ 6 Kevin Carter RC	.40	.15
❑ 7 James A.Stewart RC	.10	.02
❑ 8 Joey Galloway RC	2.00	.75
❑ 9 Kyle Brady RC	.40	.15
❑ 10 J.J. Stokes RC	.40	.15
❑ 11 Derrick Alexander DE RC	.10	.02
❑ 12 Warren Sapp RC	2.00	.75
❑ 13 Mark Fields RC	.40	.15
❑ 14 Tyrone Wheatley RC	1.50	.60
❑ 15 Napoleon Kaufman RC	1.50	.60
❑ 16 James O. Stewart RC	1.50	.60
❑ 17 Luther Elliss RC	.10	.02
❑ 18 Rashaan Salaam RC	.20	.07
❑ 19 Jimmy Oliver RC	.10	.02
❑ 20 Mark Bruener RC	.20	.07
❑ 21 Derrick Brooks RC	2.00	.75
❑ 22 Christian Fauria RC	.20	.07
❑ 23 Ray Zellars RC	.20	.07
❑ 24 Todd Collins RC	.20	.07
❑ 25 Sherman Williams RC	.10	.02
❑ 26 Frank Sanders RC	.40	.15
❑ 27 Rodney Thomas RC	.20	.07
❑ 28 Rob Johnson RC	1.25	.50
❑ 29 Steve Stenstrom RC	.10	.02
❑ 30 Curtis Martin RC	4.00	1.50
❑ 31 Gary Clark	.10	.02
❑ 32 Troy Aikman	1.50	.60
❑ 33 Mike Sherrard	.10	.02
❑ 34 Fred Barnett	.20	.07
❑ 35 Henry Ellard	.20	.07
❑ 36 Terry Allen	.20	.07
❑ 37 Jeff Graham	.10	.02
❑ 38 Herman Moore	.40	.15
❑ 39 Brett Favre	3.00	1.25
❑ 40 Trent Dilfer	.40	.15
❑ 41 Derek Brown RBK	.10	.02
❑ 42 Andre Rison	.20	.07
❑ 43 Flipper Anderson	.10	.02
❑ 44 Jerry Rice	1.50	.60
❑ 45 Andre Reed	.20	.07
❑ 46 Sean Dawkins	.20	.07
❑ 47 Irving Fryar	.20	.07
❑ 48 Vincent Brisby	.10	.02
❑ 49 Rob Moore	.20	.07
❑ 50 Carl Pickens	.20	.07
❑ 51 Vinny Testaverde	.20	.07
❑ 52 Ray Childress	.10	.02
❑ 53 Eric Green	.10	.02
❑ 54 Anthony Miller	.20	.07
❑ 55 Lake Dawson	.20	.07
❑ 56 Tim Brown	.40	.15
❑ 57 Stan Humphries	.20	.07
❑ 58 Rick Mirer	.20	.07
❑ 59 Randal Hill	.10	.02
❑ 60 Charles Haley	.20	.07
❑ 61 Chris Calloway	.10	.02
❑ 62 Calvin Williams	.20	.07
❑ 63 Ethan Horton	.10	.02
❑ 64 Cris Carter	.40	.15
❑ 65 Curtis Conway	.40	.15
❑ 66 Scott Mitchell	.20	.07
❑ 67 Edgar Bennett	.20	.07
❑ 68 Craig Erickson	.10	.02
❑ 69 Jim Everett	.10	.02
❑ 70 Terance Mathis	.20	.07
❑ 71 Robert Young	.10	.02
❑ 72 Brent Jones	.10	.02
❑ 73 Bill Brooks	.20	.07
❑ 74 Marshall Faulk	2.00	.75
❑ 75 O.J. McDuffie	.40	.15
❑ 76 Ben Coates	.20	.07
❑ 77 Johnny Mitchell	.10	.02
❑ 78 Darnay Scott	.20	.07
❑ 79 Derrick Alexander WR	.40	.15
❑ 80 Lorenzo White	.10	.02
❑ 81 Charles Johnson	.20	.07
❑ 82 John Elway	3.00	1.25
❑ 83 Willie Davis	.20	.07
❑ 84 James Jett	.20	.07
❑ 85 Mark Seay	.20	.07
❑ 86 Brian Blades	.20	.07
❑ 87 Ronald Moore	.10	.02
❑ 88 Alvin Harper	.10	.02
❑ 89 Dave Brown	.20	.07
❑ 90 Randall Cunningham	.40	.15
❑ 91 Heath Shuler	.20	.07
❑ 92 Jake Reed	.20	.07
❑ 93 Donnell Woolford	.10	.02
❑ 94 Barry Sanders	2.50	1.00
❑ 95 Reggie White	.40	.15
❑ 96 Lawrence Dawsey	.10	.02
❑ 97 Michael Haynes	.20	.07
❑ 98 Bert Emanuel	.40	.15
❑ 99 Troy Drayton	.10	.02
❑ 100 Steve Young	1.25	.50
❑ 101 Bruce Smith	.40	.15
❑ 102 Roosevelt Potts	.10	.02
❑ 103 Dan Marino	3.00	1.25
❑ 104 Michael Timpson	.10	.02
❑ 105 Boomer Esiason	.20	.07
❑ 106 David Klingler	.20	.07
❑ 107 Eric Metcalf	.20	.07
❑ 108 Gary Brown	.10	.02
❑ 109 Neil O'Donnell	.20	.07
❑ 110 Shannon Sharpe	.20	.07
❑ 111 Joe Montana	3.00	1.25
❑ 112 Jeff Hostetler	.20	.07
❑ 113 Ronnie Harmon	.10	.02
❑ 114 Chris Warren	.20	.07
❑ 115 Larry Centers	.20	.07
❑ 116 Michael Irvin	.40	.15
❑ 117 Rodney Hampton	.20	.07
❑ 118 Herschel Walker	.20	.07
❑ 119 Reggie Brooks	.20	.07
❑ 120 Qadry Ismail	.20	.07
❑ 121 Chris Zorich	.10	.02
❑ 122 Chris Spielman	.20	.07
❑ 123 Sean Jones	.10	.02
❑ 124 Errict Rhett	.20	.07
❑ 125 Tyrone Hughes	.20	.07
❑ 126 Jeff George	.20	.07
❑ 127 Chris Miller	.10	.02
❑ 128 Ricky Watters	.20	.07
❑ 129 Jim Kelly	.40	.15
❑ 130 Tony Bennett	.10	.02
❑ 131 Terry Kirby	.20	.07
❑ 132 Drew Bledsoe	1.00	.40
❑ 133 Johnny Johnson	.10	.02
❑ 134 Dan Wilkinson	.20	.07
❑ 135 Leroy Hoard	.10	.02
❑ 136 Darryll Lewis	.10	.02
❑ 137 Barry Foster	.20	.07
❑ 138 Shane Dronett	.10	.02
❑ 139 Marcus Allen	.40	.15
❑ 140 Harvey Williams	.10	.02
❑ 141 Tony Martin	.20	.07
❑ 142 Rod Stephens	.10	.02
❑ 143 Eric Swann	.20	.07
❑ 144 Daryl Johnston	.20	.07
❑ 145 Dave Meggett	.10	.02
❑ 146 Charlie Garner	.40	.15
❑ 147 Ken Harvey	.10	.02
❑ 148 Warren Moon	.20	.07
❑ 149 Steve Walsh	.10	.02
❑ 150 Pat Swilling	.10	.02
❑ 151 Terrell Buckley	.10	.02
❑ 152 Courtney Hawkins	.10	.02
❑ 153 Willie Roaf	.10	.02
❑ 154 Chris Doleman	.10	.02
❑ 155 Jerome Bettis	.40	.15
❑ 156 Dana Stubblefield	.20	.07
❑ 157 Cornelius Bennett	.20	.07
❑ 158 Quentin Coryatt	.20	.07
❑ 159 Bryan Cox	.10	.02
❑ 160 Marion Butts	.10	.02
❑ 161 Aaron Glenn	.10	.02
❑ 162 Louis Oliver	.10	.02
❑ 163 Eric Turner	.10	.02
❑ 164 Cris Dishman	.10	.02
❑ 165 John L. Williams	.10	.02
❑ 166 Simon Fletcher	.10	.02
❑ 167 Neil Smith	.20	.07
❑ 168 Chester McGlockton	.20	.07
❑ 169 Natrone Means	.20	.07
❑ 170 Sam Adams	.10	.02
❑ 171 Clyde Simmons	.10	.02
❑ 172 Jay Novacek	.20	.07
❑ 173 Keith Hamilton	.10	.02
❑ 174 William Fuller	.10	.02
❑ 175 Tom Carter	.10	.02
❑ 176 John Randle	.20	.07
❑ 177 Lewis Tillman	.10	.02
❑ 178 Mel Gray	.10	.02
❑ 179 George Teague	.10	.02
❑ 180 Hardy Nickerson	.10	.02
❑ 181 Mario Bates	.20	.07
❑ 182 D.J. Johnson	.10	.02
❑ 183 Sean Gilbert	.20	.07
❑ 184 Bryant Young	.20	.07
❑ 185 Jeff Burris	.10	.02
❑ 186 Floyd Turner	.10	.02
❑ 187 Troy Vincent	.10	.02
❑ 188 Willie McGinest	.20	.07
❑ 189 James Hasty	.10	.02
❑ 190 Jeff Blake RC	1.00	.40
❑ 191 Stevon Moore	.10	.02
❑ 192 Ernest Givins	.10	.02
❑ 193 Byron Bam Morris	.10	.02
❑ 194 Ray Crockett	.10	.02
❑ 195 Dale Carter	.20	.07
❑ 196 Terry McDaniel	.10	.02

❑ 197	Leslie O'Neal	.20	.07
❑ 198	Cortez Kennedy	.20	.07
❑ 199	Seth Joyner	.10	.02
❑ 200	Emmitt Smith	2.50	1.00
❑ 201	Thomas Lewis	.20	.07
❑ 202	Andy Harmon	.10	.02
❑ 203	Ricky Ervins	.10	.02
❑ 204	Fuad Reveiz	.10	.02
❑ 205	John Thierry	.10	.02
❑ 206	Bennie Blades	.10	.02
❑ 207	LeShon Johnson	.20	.07
❑ 208	Charles Wilson	.10	.02
❑ 209	Joe Johnson	.10	.02
❑ 210	Chuck Smith	.10	.02
❑ 211	Roman Phifer	.10	.02
❑ 212	Ken Norton Jr.	.20	.07
❑ 213	Bucky Brooks	.10	.02
❑ 214	Ray Buchanan	.10	.02
❑ 215	Tim Bowens	.10	.02
❑ 216	Vincent Brown	.10	.02
❑ 217	Marcus Turner	.10	.02
❑ 218	Derrick Fenner	.10	.02
❑ 219	Antonio Langham	.10	.02
❑ 220	Cody Carlson	.10	.02
❑ 221	Greg Lloyd	.20	.07
❑ 222	Steve Atwater	.10	.02
❑ 223	Donnell Bennett	.20	.07
❑ 224	Rocket Ismail	.20	.07
❑ 225	John Carney	.10	.02
❑ 226	Eugene Robinson	.10	.02
❑ 227	Aeneas Williams	.10	.02
❑ 228	Darrin Smith	.10	.02
❑ 229	Phillippi Sparks	.10	.02
❑ 230	Eric Allen	.10	.02
❑ 231	Brian Mitchell	.10	.02
❑ 232	David Palmer	.20	.07
❑ 233	Mark Carrier DB	.10	.02
❑ 234	Dave Krieg	.10	.02
❑ 235	Robert Brooks	.40	.15
❑ 236	Eric Curry	.10	.02
❑ 237	Wayne Martin	.10	.02
❑ 238	Craig Heyward	.20	.07
❑ 239	Isaac Bruce	.75	.30
❑ 240	Deion Sanders	1.00	.40
❑ 241	Steve Tasker	.20	.07
❑ 242	Jim Harbaugh	.20	.07
❑ 243	Aubrey Beavers	.10	.02
❑ 244	Chris Slade	.10	.02
❑ 245	Mo Lewis	.10	.02
❑ 246	Alfred Williams	.10	.02
❑ 247	Michael Dean Perry	.10	.02
❑ 248	Marcus Robertson	.10	.02
❑ 249	Kevin Greene	.20	.07
❑ 250	Leonard Russell	.10	.02
❑ 251	Greg Hill	.20	.07
❑ 252	Rob Fredrickson	.10	.02
❑ 253	Junior Seau	.40	.15
❑ 254	Rick Tuten	.10	.02
❑ 255	Garrison Hearst	.40	.15
❑ 256	Russell Maryland	.10	.02
❑ 257	Michael Brooks	.10	.02
❑ 258	Bernard Williams	.10	.02
❑ 259	Reggie Roby	.10	.02
❑ 260	Dewayne Washington	.20	.07
❑ 261	Raymont Harris	.10	.02
❑ 262	Brett Perriman	.20	.07
❑ 263	LeRoy Butler	.10	.02
❑ 264	Santana Dotson	.10	.02
❑ 265	Irv Smith	.10	.02
❑ 266	Ron George	.10	.02
❑ 267	Marquez Pope	.10	.02
❑ 268	William Floyd	.20	.07
❑ 269	Matt Darby	.10	.02
❑ 270	Jeff Herrod	.10	.02
❑ 271	Bernie Parmalee	.20	.07
❑ 272	Leroy Thompson	.10	.02
❑ 273	Ronnie Lott	.20	.07
❑ 274	Steve Tovar	.10	.02
❑ 275	Michael Jackson	.20	.07
❑ 276	Al Smith	.10	.02
❑ 277	Rod Woodson	.20	.07
❑ 278	Glyn Milburn	.10	.02
❑ 279	Kimble Anders	.20	.07
❑ 280	Anthony Smith	.10	.02
❑ 281	Andre Coleman	.10	.02
❑ 282	Terry Wooden	.10	.02
❑ 283	Mickey Washington	.10	.02
❑ 284	Steve Beuerlein	.20	.07
❑ 285	Mark Brunell	1.00	.40
❑ 286	Keith Goganious	.10	.02
❑ 287	Desmond Howard	.20	.07
❑ 288	Darren Carrington	.10	.02
❑ 289	Derek Brown TE	.10	.02
❑ 290	Reggie Cobb	.10	.02
❑ 291	Jeff Lageman	.10	.02
❑ 292	Lamar Lathon	.10	.02
❑ 293	Sam Mills	.20	.07
❑ 294	Carlton Bailey	.10	.02
❑ 295	Mark Carrier WR	.20	.07
❑ 296	Willie Green	.20	.07
❑ 297	Frank Reich	.10	.02
❑ 298	Don Beebe	.10	.02
❑ 299	Tim McKyer	.10	.02
❑ 300	Pete Metzelaars	.10	.02
❑ A19	Joe Montana	15.00	6.00
❑ A103	Dan Marino	15.00	6.00
❑ P1	Joe Montana Promo	2.00	.75
❑ P2	Joe Montana Promo Numbered 19	2.00	.75
❑ P3	Marshall Faulk Promo	1.00	.40

1996 Upper Deck

❑	COMPLETE SET (300)	30.00	12.50
❑ 1	Keyshawn Johnson RC	1.25	.50
❑ 2	Kevin Hardy RC	.50	.20
❑ 3	Simeon Rice RC	1.25	.50
❑ 4	Jonathan Ogden RC	.50	.20
❑ 5	Cedric Jones RC	.10	.02
❑ 6	Lawrence Phillips RC	.50	.20
❑ 7	Tim Biakabutuka RC	.50	.20
❑ 8	Terry Glenn RC	1.25	.50
❑ 9	Rickey Dudley RC	.50	.20
❑ 10	Willie Anderson RC	.10	.02
❑ 11	Alex Molden RC	.10	.02
❑ 12	Regan Upshaw RC	.10	.02
❑ 13	Walt Harris RC	.10	.02
❑ 14	Eddie George RC	1.50	.60
❑ 15	John Mobley RC	.10	.02
❑ 16	Duane Clemons RC	.10	.02
❑ 17	Eddie Kennison RC	.50	.20
❑ 18	Marvin Harrison RC	3.00	1.25
❑ 19	Daryl Gardener RC	.10	.02
❑ 20	Leeland McElroy RC	.25	.08
❑ 21	Eric Moulds RC	1.50	.60
❑ 22	Alex Van Dyke RC	.25	.08
❑ 23	Mike Alstott RC	1.25	.50
❑ 24	Jeff Lewis RC	.25	.08
❑ 25	Bobby Engram RC	.50	.20
❑ 26	Derrick Mayes RC	.50	.20
❑ 27	Karim Abdul-Jabbar RC	.50	.20
❑ 28	Bobby Hoying RC	.50	.20
❑ 29	Stepfret Williams RC	.25	.08
❑ 30	Chris Darkins RC	.10	.02
❑ 31	Stephen Davis RC	2.00	.75
❑ 32	Danny Kanell RC	.50	.20
❑ 33	Tony Brackens RC	.50	.20
❑ 34	Leslie O'Neal	.10	.02
❑ 35	Chris Doleman	.10	.02
❑ 36	Larry Brown	.10	.02
❑ 37	Ronnie Harmon	.10	.02
❑ 38	Chris Spielman	.10	.02
❑ 39	John Jurkovic	.10	.02
❑ 40	Shawn Jefferson	.10	.02
❑ 41	William Floyd	.25	.08
❑ 42	Eric Davis	.10	.02
❑ 43	Willie Clay	.10	.02
❑ 44	Marco Coleman	.10	.02
❑ 45	Lorenzo White	.10	.02
❑ 46	Neil O'Donnell	.25	.08
❑ 47	Natrone Means	.25	.08
❑ 48	Cornelius Bennett	.10	.02
❑ 49	Steve Walsh	.10	.02
❑ 50	Jerome Bettis	.50	.20
❑ 51	Boomer Esiason	.25	.08
❑ 52	Glyn Milburn	.10	.02
❑ 53	Kevin Greene	.25	.08
❑ 54	Seth Joyner	.10	.02
❑ 55	Jeff Graham	.10	.02
❑ 56	Darren Woodson	.25	.08
❑ 57	Dale Carter	.10	.02
❑ 58	Lorenzo Lynch	.10	.02
❑ 59	Tim Brown	.50	.20
❑ 60	Jerry Rice	1.25	.50
❑ 61	Garrison Hearst	.25	.08
❑ 62	Eric Metcalf	.10	.02
❑ 63	Leroy Hoard	.10	.02
❑ 64	Thurman Thomas	.50	.20
❑ 65	Sam Mills	.10	.02
❑ 66	Curtis Conway	.50	.20
❑ 67	Carl Pickens	.25	.08
❑ 68	Deion Sanders	.75	.30
❑ 69	Shannon Sharpe	.25	.08
❑ 70	Herman Moore	.25	.08
❑ 71	Robert Brooks	.50	.20
❑ 72	Rodney Thomas	.10	.02
❑ 73	Ken Dilger	.25	.08
❑ 74	Mark Brunell	.75	.30
❑ 75	Marcus Allen	.50	.20
❑ 76	Dan Marino	2.50	1.00
❑ 77	Robert Smith	.25	.08
❑ 78	Drew Bledsoe	.75	.30
❑ 79	Jim Everett	.10	.02
❑ 80	Rodney Hampton	.25	.08
❑ 81	Adrian Murrell	.25	.08
❑ 82	Daryl Hobbs RC	.10	.02
❑ 83	Ricky Watters	.25	.08
❑ 84	Yancey Thigpen	.25	.08
❑ 85	Roman Phifer	.10	.02
❑ 86	Tony Martin	.25	.08
❑ 87	Dana Stubblefield	.25	.08
❑ 88	Joey Galloway	.50	.20
❑ 89	Errict Rhett	.25	.08
❑ 90	Terry Allen	.25	.08
❑ 91	Aeneas Williams	.10	.02
❑ 92	Craig Heyward	.10	.02
❑ 93	Vinny Testaverde	.25	.08
❑ 94	Bryce Paup	.10	.02
❑ 95	Kerry Collins	.50	.20
❑ 96	Rashaan Salaam	.25	.08
❑ 97	Dan Wilkinson	.10	.02
❑ 98	Jay Novacek	.10	.02
❑ 99	John Elway	2.50	1.00
❑ 100	Bennie Blades	.10	.02
❑ 101	Edgar Bennett	.25	.08
❑ 102	Darryll Lewis	.10	.02
❑ 103	Marshall Faulk	.60	.25
❑ 104	Bryan Schwartz	.10	.02
❑ 105	Tamarick Vanover	.25	.08
❑ 106	Terry Kirby	.25	.08
❑ 107	John Randle	.25	.08
❑ 108	Ted Johnson RC	.50	.20
❑ 109	Mario Bates	.25	.08
❑ 110	Phillippi Sparks	.10	.02
❑ 111	Marvin Washington	.10	.02
❑ 112	Terry McDaniel	.10	.02
❑ 113	Bobby Taylor	.10	.02
❑ 114	Carnell Lake	.10	.02
❑ 115	Troy Drayton	.10	.02
❑ 116	Darren Bennett	.10	.02
❑ 117	J.J. Stokes	.50	.20
❑ 118	Rick Mirer	.25	.08
❑ 119	Jackie Harris	.10	.02
❑ 120	Ken Harvey	.10	.02
❑ 121	Rob Moore	.25	.08
❑ 122	Jeff George	.25	.08
❑ 123	Andre Rison	.25	.08
❑ 124	Darick Holmes	.10	.02
❑ 125	Tim McKyer	.10	.02
❑ 126	Alonzo Spellman	.10	.02
❑ 127	Jeff Blake	.50	.20
❑ 128	Kevin Williams	.10	.02
❑ 129	Anthony Miller	.25	.08
❑ 130	Barry Sanders	2.00	.75

❑ 131 Brett Favre 2.50 1.25
❑ 132 Steve McNair 1.00 .40
❑ 133 Jim Harbaugh .25 .08
❑ 134 Desmond Howard .25 .08
❑ 135 Steve Bono .10 .02
❑ 136 Bernie Parmalee .10 .02
❑ 137 Warren Moon .25 .08
❑ 138 Curtis Martin 1.00 .40
❑ 139 Irv Smith .10 .02
❑ 140 Thomas Lewis .10 .02
❑ 141 Kyle Brady .10 .02
❑ 142 Napoleon Kaufman .50 .20
❑ 143 Mike Mamula .10 .02
❑ 144 Erric Pegram .10 .02
❑ 145 Isaac Bruce .50 .20
❑ 146 Andre Coleman .10 .02
❑ 147 Merton Hanks .10 .02
❑ 148 Brian Blades .10 .02
❑ 149 Hardy Nickerson .10 .02
❑ 150 Michael Westbrook .50 .20
❑ 151 Larry Centers .25 .08
❑ 152 Morten Andersen .10 .02
❑ 153 Michael Jackson .25 .08
❑ 154 Bruce Smith .25 .08
❑ 155 Derrick Moore .10 .02
❑ 156 Mark Carrier DB .10 .02
❑ 157 John Copeland .10 .02
❑ 158 Emmitt Smith 2.00 .75
❑ 159 Jason Elam .25 .08
❑ 160 Scott Mitchell .25 .08
❑ 161 Mark Chmura .25 .08
❑ 162 Blaine Bishop .10 .02
❑ 163 Tony Bennett .10 .02
❑ 164 Pete Mitchell .25 .08
❑ 165 Dan Saleaumua .10 .02
❑ 166 Pete Stoyanovich .10 .02
❑ 167 Cris Carter .50 .20
❑ 168 Vince Brisby .10 .02
❑ 169 Wayne Martin .10 .02
❑ 170 Tyrone Wheatley .25 .08
❑ 171 Mo Lewis .10 .02
❑ 172 Harvey Williams .10 .02
❑ 173 Calvin Williams .10 .02
❑ 174 Norm Johnson .10 .02
❑ 175 Mark Rypien .10 .02
❑ 176 Stan Humphries .25 .08
❑ 177 Derek Loville .10 .02
❑ 178 Christian Fauria .10 .02
❑ 179 Warren Sapp .10 .02
❑ 180 Henry Ellard .10 .02
❑ 181 Jamir Miller .10 .02
❑ 182 Jessie Tuggle .10 .02
❑ 183 Stevon Moore .10 .02
❑ 184 Jim Kelly .50 .20
❑ 185 Mark Carrier .10 .02
❑ 186 Chris Zorich .10 .02
❑ 187 Harold Green .10 .02
❑ 188 Chris Boniol .10 .02
❑ 189 Allen Aldridge .10 .02
❑ 190 Brett Perriman .10 .02
❑ 191 Chris Jacke .10 .02
❑ 192 Todd McNair .10 .02
❑ 193 Floyd Turner .10 .02
❑ 194 Jeff Lageman .10 .02
❑ 195 Derrick Thomas .50 .20
❑ 196 Eric Green .10 .02
❑ 197 Orlando Thomas .10 .02
❑ 198 Ben Coates .25 .08
❑ 199 Tyrone Hughes .10 .02
❑ 200 Dave Brown .10 .02
❑ 201 Brad Baxter .10 .02
❑ 202 Chester McGlockton .10 .02
❑ 203 Rodney Peete .10 .02
❑ 204 Willie Williams .10 .02
❑ 205 Kevin Carter .10 .02
❑ 206 Aaron Hayden RC .10 .02
❑ 207 Steve Young 1.00 .40
❑ 208 Chris Warren .25 .08
❑ 209 Eric Curry .10 .02
❑ 210 Brian Mitchell .10 .02
❑ 211 Frank Sanders .25 .08
❑ 212 Terance Mathis UER .10 .02
❑ 213 Eric Turner .10 .02
❑ 214 Bill Brooks .10 .02
❑ 215 John Kasay .10 .02
❑ 216 Erik Kramer .10 .02
❑ 217 Darnay Scott .25 .08
❑ 218 Charles Haley .25 .08
❑ 219 Steve Atwater .10 .02
❑ 220 Jason Hanson .10 .02
❑ 221 LeRoy Butler .10 .02
❑ 222 Cris Dishman .10 .02
❑ 223 Sean Dawkins .10 .02
❑ 224 James O. Stewart .25 .08
❑ 225 Greg Hill .25 .08
❑ 226 Jeff Cross .10 .02
❑ 227 Qadry Ismail .25 .08
❑ 228 Dave Meggett .10 .02
❑ 229 Eric Allen .10 .02
❑ 230 Chris Calloway .10 .02
❑ 231 Wayne Chrebet .75 .30
❑ 232 Jeff Hostetler .10 .02
❑ 233 Andy Harmon .10 .02
❑ 234 Greg Lloyd .25 .08
❑ 235 Toby Wright .10 .02
❑ 236 Junior Seau .50 .20
❑ 237 Bryant Young .25 .08
❑ 238 Robert Blackmon .10 .02
❑ 239 Trent Dilfer .50 .20
❑ 240 Leslie Shepherd .10 .02
❑ 241 Eric Swann .10 .02
❑ 242 Bert Emanuel .25 .08
❑ 243 Antonio Langham .10 .02
❑ 244 Steve Christie .10 .02
❑ 245 Tyrone Poole .10 .02
❑ 246 Jim Flanigan .10 .02
❑ 247 Tony McGee .10 .02
❑ 248 Michael Irvin .50 .20
❑ 249 Byron Bam Morris .10 .02
❑ 250 Terrell Davis 1.00 .40
❑ 251 Johnnie Morton .25 .08
❑ 252 Sean Jones .10 .02
❑ 253 Chris Sanders .25 .08
❑ 254 Quentin Coryatt .10 .02
❑ 255 Willie Jackson .25 .08
❑ 256 Mark Collins .10 .02
❑ 257 Randal Hill .10 .02
❑ 258 David Palmer .10 .02
❑ 259 Will Moore .10 .02
❑ 260 Michael Haynes .10 .02
❑ 261 Mike Sherrard .10 .02
❑ 262 William Thomas .10 .02
❑ 263 Kordell Stewart .50 .20
❑ 264 D'Marco Farr .10 .02
❑ 265 Terrell Fletcher .10 .02
❑ 266 Lee Woodall .10 .02
❑ 267 Eugene Robinson .10 .02
❑ 268 Alvin Harper .10 .02
❑ 269 Gus Frerotte .25 .08
❑ 270 Antonio Freeman .50 .20
❑ 271 Clyde Simmons .10 .02
❑ 272 Chuck Smith .10 .02
❑ 273 Steve Tasker .10 .02
❑ 274 Kevin Butler .10 .02
❑ 275 Steve Tovar .10 .02
❑ 276 Troy Aikman 1.25 .50
❑ 277 Aaron Craver .10 .02
❑ 278 Henry Thomas .10 .02
❑ 279 Craig Newsome .10 .02
❑ 280 Brent Jones .10 .02
❑ 281 Micheal Barrow .10 .02
❑ 282 Ray Buchanan .10 .02
❑ 283 Jimmy Smith .50 .20
❑ 284 Neil Smith .25 .08
❑ 285 O.J. McDuffie .25 .08
❑ 286 Jake Reed .25 .08
❑ 287 Ty Law .50 .20
❑ 288 Torrance Small .10 .02
❑ 289 Hugh Douglas .25 .08
❑ 290 Pat Swilling .10 .02
❑ 291 Charlie Garner .25 .08
❑ 292 Ernie Mills .10 .02
❑ 293 John Carney .10 .02
❑ 294 Ken Norton .10 .02
❑ 295 Cortez Kennedy .10 .02
❑ 296 Derrick Brooks .50 .20
❑ 297 Heath Shuler .25 .08
❑ 298 Reggie White .50 .20
❑ 299 Kimble Anders .25 .08
❑ 300 Willie McGinest .10 .02
❑ P96 Dan Marino Promo 2.00 .75
❑ MS1 Dan Marino 5.00 2.00
❑ MS2 Dan Marino 5.00 2.00
❑ P13 Dan Marino Promo 2.50 1.00

1997 Upper Deck

❑ COMPLETE SET (300) 40.00 20.00
❑ 1 Orlando Pace RC .60 .25
❑ 2 Darrell Russell RC .25 .08
❑ 3 Shawn Springs RC .40 .15
❑ 4 Bryant Westbrook RC .25 .08
❑ 5 Ike Hilliard RC 1.25 .50
❑ 6 Peter Boulware RC .60 .25
❑ 7 Tom Knight RC .25 .08
❑ 8 Yatil Green RC .40 .15
❑ 9 Tony Gonzalez RC 2.50 1.00
❑ 10 Reidel Anthony RC .60 .25
❑ 11 Warrick Dunn RC 2.00 .75
❑ 12 Kenny Holmes RC .60 .25
❑ 13 Jim Druckenmiller RC .40 .15
❑ 14 James Farrior RC .60 .25
❑ 15 David LaFleur RC .25 .08
❑ 16 Antowain Smith RC 2.00 .75
❑ 17 Rae Carruth RC .25 .08
❑ 18 Dwayne Rudd RC .60 .25
❑ 19 Jake Plummer RC 4.00 1.50
❑ 20 Reinard Wilson RC .40 .15
❑ 21 Byron Hanspard RC .40 .15
❑ 22 Will Blackwell RC .40 .15
❑ 23 Troy Davis RC .40 .15
❑ 24 Corey Dillon RC 5.00 2.00
❑ 25 Joey Kent RC .60 .25
❑ 26 Renaldo Wynn RC .25 .08
❑ 27 Pat Barnes RC .60 .25
❑ 28 Kevin Lockett RC .40 .15
❑ 29 Darnell Autry RC .40 .15
❑ 30 Walter Jones RC .60 .25
❑ 31 Trevor Pryce RC .60 .25
❑ 32 Dan Marino SRF 1.25 .50
❑ 33 Steve Young SRF .25 .08
❑ 34 John Elway SRF 1.25 .50
❑ 35 Jerry Rice SRF .60 .25
❑ 36 Tim Brown SRF .60 .25
❑ 37 Deion Sanders SRF .60 .25
❑ 38 Troy Aikman SRF .60 .25
❑ 39 Barry Sanders SRF 1.00 .40
❑ 40 Emmitt Smith SRF 1.00 .40
❑ 41 Junior Seau SRF .60 .25
❑ 42 Neil Smith .40 .15
❑ 43 Brett Perriman .25 .08
❑ 44 Jim Everett .25 .08
❑ 45 Qadry Ismail .40 .15
❑ 46 Dana Stubblefield .25 .08
❑ 47 Bryant Young .25 .08
❑ 48 Ken Norton Jr. .25 .08
❑ 49 Terrell Owens .75 .30
❑ 50 Jerry Rice 1.25 .50
❑ 51 Steve Young .75 .30
❑ 52 Terry Kirby .40 .15
❑ 53 Chris Doleman .25 .08
❑ 54 Lee Woodall .25 .08
❑ 55 Merton Hanks .25 .08
❑ 56 Garrison Hearst .40 .15
❑ 57 Rashaan Salaam .25 .08
❑ 58 Raymont Harris .25 .08
❑ 59 Curtis Conway .40 .15
❑ 60 Bobby Engram .40 .15
❑ 61 Bryan Cox .25 .08
❑ 62 Walt Harris .25 .08
❑ 63 Tyrone Hughes .25 .08
❑ 64 Rick Mirer .25 .08
❑ 65 Jeff Blake .40 .15
❑ 66 Carl Pickens .40 .15
❑ 67 Darnay Scott .40 .15

❑ 68	Tony McGee	.25	.08
❑ 69	Ki-Jana Carter	.25	.08
❑ 70	Ashley Ambrose	.25	.08
❑ 71	Dan Wilkinson	.25	.08
❑ 72	Chris Spielman	.25	.08
❑ 73	Todd Collins	.25	.08
❑ 74	Andre Reed	.40	.15
❑ 75	Quinn Early	.25	.08
❑ 76	Eric Moulds	.60	.25
❑ 77	Darick Holmes	.25	.08
❑ 78	Thurman Thomas	.60	.25
❑ 79	Bruce Smith	.40	.15
❑ 80	Bryce Paup	.25	.08
❑ 81	John Elway	2.50	1.00
❑ 82	Terrell Davis	.75	.30
❑ 83	Anthony Miller	.25	.08
❑ 84	Shannon Sharpe	.40	.15
❑ 85	Alfred Williams	.25	.08
❑ 86	John Mobley	.25	.08
❑ 87	Tory James	.25	.08
❑ 88	Steve Atwater	.25	.08
❑ 89	Darrien Gordon	.25	.08
❑ 90	Mike Alstott	.60	.25
❑ 91	Errict Rhett	.25	.08
❑ 92	Trent Dilfer	.60	.25
❑ 93	Courtney Hawkins	.25	.08
❑ 94	Warren Sapp	.40	.15
❑ 95	Regan Upshaw	.25	.08
❑ 96	Hardy Nickerson	.25	.08
❑ 97	Donnie Abraham RC	.60	.25
❑ 98	Larry Centers	.40	.15
❑ 99	Aeneas Williams	.25	.08
❑ 100	Kent Graham	.25	.08
❑ 101	Rob Moore	.40	.15
❑ 102	Frank Sanders	.40	.15
❑ 103	Leeland McElroy	.25	.08
❑ 104	Eric Swann	.25	.08
❑ 105	Simeon Rice	.40	.15
❑ 106	Seth Joyner	.25	.08
❑ 107	Stan Humphries	.40	.15
❑ 108	Tony Martin	.40	.15
❑ 109	Charlie Jones	.25	.08
❑ 110	Andre Coleman UER 103	.25	.08
❑ 111	Terrell Fletcher	.25	.08
❑ 112	Junior Seau	.60	.25
❑ 113	Eric Metcalf	.40	.15
❑ 114	Chris Penn	.25	.08
❑ 115	Marcus Allen	.60	.25
❑ 116	Greg Hill	.25	.08
❑ 117	Tamarick Vanover	.40	.15
❑ 118	Lake Dawson	.25	.08
❑ 119	Derrick Thomas	.60	.25
❑ 120	Dale Carter	.25	.08
❑ 121	Elvis Grbac	.40	.15
❑ 122	Aaron Bailey	.25	.08
❑ 123	Jim Harbaugh	.40	.15
❑ 124	Marshall Faulk	.75	.30
❑ 125	Sean Dawkins	.25	.08
❑ 126	Marvin Harrison	.60	.25
❑ 127	Ken Dilger	.25	.08
❑ 128	Tony Bennett	.25	.08
❑ 129	Jeff Herrod	.25	.08
❑ 130	Chris Gardocki	.25	.08
❑ 131	Cary Blanchard	.25	.08
❑ 132	Troy Aikman	1.25	.50
❑ 133	Emmitt Smith	2.00	.75
❑ 134	Sherman Williams	.25	.08
❑ 135	Michael Irvin	.60	.25
❑ 136	Eric Bjornson	.25	.08
❑ 137	Herschel Walker	.40	.15
❑ 138	Tony Tolbert	.25	.08
❑ 139	Deion Sanders	.60	.25
❑ 140	Daryl Johnston	.40	.15
❑ 141	Dan Marino	2.50	1.00
❑ 142	O.J. McDuffie	.40	.15
❑ 143	Troy Drayton	.25	.08
❑ 144	Karim Abdul-Jabbar	.40	.15
❑ 145	Stanley Pritchett	.25	.08
❑ 146	Fred Barnett	.25	.08
❑ 147	Zach Thomas	.60	.25
❑ 148	Shawn Wooden RC	.25	.08
❑ 149	Ty Detmer	.40	.15
❑ 150	Derrick Witherspoon	.25	.08
❑ 151	Ricky Watters	.40	.15
❑ 152	Charlie Garner	.40	.15
❑ 153	Chris T. Jones	.25	.08
❑ 154	Irving Fryar	.40	.15
❑ 155	Mike Mamula	.25	.08
❑ 156	Troy Vincent	.25	.08
❑ 157	Bobby Taylor	.25	.08
❑ 158	Chris Boniol	.25	.08
❑ 159	Devin Bush	.25	.08
❑ 160	Bert Emanuel	.40	.15
❑ 161	Jamal Anderson	.60	.25
❑ 162	Terance Mathis	.40	.15
❑ 163	Cornelius Bennett	.25	.08
❑ 164	Ray Buchanan	.25	.08
❑ 165	Chris Chandler	.40	.15
❑ 166	Dave Brown	.25	.08
❑ 167	Danny Kanell	.25	.08
❑ 168	Rodney Hampton	.40	.15
❑ 169	Tyrone Wheatley	.40	.15
❑ 170	Amani Toomer	.40	.15
❑ 171	Chris Calloway	.25	.08
❑ 172	Thomas Lewis	.25	.08
❑ 173	Phillippi Sparks	.25	.08
❑ 174	Mark Brunell	.75	.30
❑ 175	Keenan McCardell	.40	.15
❑ 176	Willie Jackson	.25	.08
❑ 177	Jimmy Smith	.40	.15
❑ 178	Pete Mitchell	.25	.08
❑ 179	Natrone Means	.40	.15
❑ 180	Kevin Hardy	.25	.08
❑ 181	Tony Brackens	.25	.08
❑ 182	James O. Stewart	.40	.15
❑ 183	Wayne Chrebet	.60	.25
❑ 184	Keyshawn Johnson	.60	.25
❑ 185	Adrian Murrell	.40	.15
❑ 186	Neil O'Donnell	.40	.15
❑ 187	Hugh Douglas	.25	.08
❑ 188	Mo Lewis	.25	.08
❑ 189	Marvin Washington	.25	.08
❑ 190	Aaron Glenn	.25	.08
❑ 191	Barry Sanders	2.00	.75
❑ 192	Scott Mitchell	.40	.15
❑ 193	Herman Moore	.40	.15
❑ 194	Johnnie Morton	.40	.15
❑ 195	Glyn Milburn	.25	.08
❑ 196	Reggie Brown LB	.40	.15
❑ 197	Jason Hanson	.25	.08
❑ 198	Steve McNair	.75	.30
❑ 199	Eddie George	.60	.25
❑ 200	Ronnie Harmon	.25	.08
❑ 201	Chris Sanders	.25	.08
❑ 202	Willie Davis	.25	.08
❑ 203	Frank Wycheck	.25	.08
❑ 204	Darryll Lewis	.25	.08
❑ 205	Blaine Bishop	.25	.08
❑ 206	Robert Brooks	.40	.15
❑ 207	Brett Favre	2.50	1.25
❑ 208	Edgar Bennett	.40	.15
❑ 209	Dorsey Levens	.60	.25
❑ 210	Derrick Mayes	.40	.15
❑ 211	Antonio Freeman	.60	.25
❑ 212	Mark Chmura	.40	.15
❑ 213	Reggie White	.60	.25
❑ 214	Gilbert Brown	.40	.15
❑ 215	LeRoy Butler	.25	.08
❑ 216	Craig Newsome	.25	.08
❑ 217	Kerry Collins	.60	.25
❑ 218	Wesley Walls	.40	.15
❑ 219	Muhsin Muhammad	.40	.15
❑ 220	Anthony Johnson	.25	.08
❑ 221	Tim Biakabutuka	.40	.15
❑ 222	Kevin Greene	.40	.15
❑ 223	Sam Mills	.25	.08
❑ 224	John Kasay	.25	.08
❑ 225	Micheal Barrow	.25	.08
❑ 226	Drew Bledsoe	.75	.30
❑ 227	Curtis Martin	.75	.30
❑ 228	Terry Glenn	.60	.25
❑ 229	Ben Coates	.40	.15
❑ 230	Shawn Jefferson	.25	.08
❑ 231	Willie McGinest	.25	.08
❑ 232	Ted Johnson	.25	.08
❑ 233	Lawyer Milloy	.40	.15
❑ 234	Ty Law	.40	.15
❑ 235	Willie Clay	.25	.08
❑ 236	Tim Brown	.60	.25
❑ 237	Rickey Dudley	.40	.15
❑ 238	Napoleon Kaufman	.60	.25
❑ 239	Chester McGlockton	.25	.08
❑ 240	Rob Fredrickson	.25	.08
❑ 241	Terry McDaniel	.25	.08
❑ 242	Desmond Howard	.40	.15
❑ 243	Jeff George	.40	.15
❑ 244	Isaac Bruce	.60	.25
❑ 245	Tony Banks	.40	.15
❑ 246	Lawrence Phillips UER 247	.25	.08
❑ 247	Kevin Carter	.25	.08
❑ 248	Roman Phifer	.25	.08
❑ 249	Keith Lyle	.25	.08
❑ 250	Eddie Kennison	.40	.15
❑ 251	Craig Heyward	.25	.08
❑ 252	Vinny Testaverde	.40	.15
❑ 253	Derrick Alexander WR	.40	.15
❑ 254	Michael Jackson	.40	.15
❑ 255	Byron Bam Morris	.25	.08
❑ 256	Eric Green	.25	.08
❑ 257	Ray Lewis	1.00	.40
❑ 258	Antonio Langham	.25	.08
❑ 259	Michael McCrary	.25	.08
❑ 260	Gus Frerotte	.25	.08
❑ 261	Terry Allen	.60	.25
❑ 262	Brian Mitchell	.25	.08
❑ 263	Michael Westbrook	.40	.15
❑ 264	Sean Gilbert	.25	.08
❑ 265	Rich Owens	.25	.08
❑ 266	Ken Harvey	.25	.08
❑ 267	Jeff Hostetler	.25	.08
❑ 268	Michael Haynes	.25	.08
❑ 269	Mario Bates	.25	.08
❑ 270	Renaldo Turnbull UER 273	.25	.08
❑ 271	Ray Zellars	.25	.08
❑ 272	Joe Johnson	.25	.08
❑ 273	Eric Allen	.25	.08
❑ 274	Heath Shuler	.25	.08
❑ 275	Daryl Hobbs	.25	.08
❑ 276	John Friesz	.25	.08
❑ 277	Brian Blades	.25	.08
❑ 278	Joey Galloway	.40	.15
❑ 279	Chris Warren	.40	.15
❑ 280	Lamar Smith	.60	.25
❑ 281	Cortez Kennedy	.25	.08
❑ 282	Chad Brown	.25	.08
❑ 283	Warren Moon	.60	.25
❑ 284	Jerome Bettis	.60	.25
❑ 285	Charles Johnson	.40	.15
❑ 286	Kordell Stewart	.60	.25
❑ 287	Erric Pegram	.25	.08
❑ 288	Norm Johnson	.25	.08
❑ 289	Levon Kirkland	.25	.08
❑ 290	Greg Lloyd	.25	.08
❑ 291	Carnell Lake	.25	.08
❑ 292	Brad Johnson	.60	.25
❑ 293	Cris Carter	.60	.25
❑ 294	Jake Reed	.40	.15
❑ 295	Robert Smith	.40	.15
❑ 296	Derrick Alexander DE	.25	.08
❑ 297	John Randle	.40	.15
❑ 298	Dixon Edwards	.25	.08
❑ 299	Orlanda Thomas	.25	.08
❑ 300	Dewayne Washington	.25	.08

1998 Upper Deck

❑	COMPLETE SET (255)	200.00	75.00
❑	COMP.SET w/o SP's (213)	25.00	12.50
❑ 1	Peyton Manning RC	50.00	20.00
❑ 2	Ryan Leaf RC	5.00	2.00
❑ 3	Andre Wadsworth RC	3.00	1.25
❑ 4	Charles Woodson RC	6.00	2.50
❑ 5	Curtis Enis RC	2.50	1.00
❑ 6	Grant Wistrom RC	3.00	1.25

❑	7 Greg Ellis RC	2.50	1.00
❑	8 Fred Taylor RC	8.00	3.00
❑	9 Duane Starks RC	2.50	1.00
❑	10 Keith Brooking RC	5.00	2.00
❑	11 Takeo Spikes RC	5.00	2.00
❑	12 Jason Peter RC	2.50	1.00
❑	13 Anthony Simmons RC	3.00	1.25
❑	14 Kevin Dyson RC	5.00	2.00
❑	15 Brian Simmons RC	3.00	1.25
❑	16 Robert Edwards RC	3.00	1.25
❑	17 Randy Moss RC	30.00	12.50
❑	18 John Avery RC	3.00	1.25
❑	19 Marcus Nash RC	2.50	1.00
❑	20 Jerome Pathon RC	5.00	2.00
❑	21 Jacquez Green RC	3.00	1.25
❑	22 Robert Holcombe RC	3.00	1.25
❑	23 Pat Johnson RC	3.00	1.25
❑	24 Germane Crowell RC	3.00	1.25
❑	25 Joe Jurevicius RC	5.00	2.00
❑	26 Skip Hicks RC	3.00	1.25
❑	27 Ahman Green RC	25.00	10.00
❑	28 Brian Griese RC	10.00	4.00
❑	29 Hines Ward RC	20.00	10.00
❑	30 Tavian Banks RC	3.00	1.25
❑	31 Tony Simmons RC	3.00	1.25
❑	32 Victor Riley RC	2.50	1.00
❑	33 Rashaan Shehee RC	3.00	1.25
❑	34 R.W. McQuarters RC	3.00	1.25
❑	35 Flozell Adams RC	2.50	1.00
❑	36 Tra Thomas RC	2.50	1.00
❑	37 Greg Favors RC	3.00	1.25
❑	38 Jon Ritchie RC	3.00	1.25
❑	39 Jesse Haynes RC	2.50	1.00
❑	40 Ryan Sutter RC	2.50	1.00
❑	41 Mo Collins RC	2.50	1.00
❑	42 Tim Dwight RC	5.00	2.00
❑	43 Chris Chandler	.40	.15
❑	44 Byron Hanspard	.25	.08
❑	45 Jessie Tuggle	.25	.08
❑	46 Jamal Anderson	.60	.25
❑	47 Terance Mathis	.40	.15
❑	48 Morten Andersen	.25	.08
❑	49 Jake Plummer	.60	.25
❑	50 Mario Bates	.40	.15
❑	51 Frank Sanders	.40	.15
❑	52 Adrian Murrell	.40	.15
❑	53 Simeon Rice	.40	.15
❑	54 Aeneas Williams	.25	.08
❑	55 Eric Swann UER	.25	.08
❑	56 Jim Harbaugh	.40	.15
❑	57 Michael Jackson	.25	.08
❑	58 Peter Boulware	.25	.08
❑	59 Errict Rhett	.40	.15
❑	60 Jermaine Lewis	.40	.15
❑	61 Eric Zeier	.40	.15
❑	62 Rod Woodson	.40	.15
❑	63 Rob Johnson	.60	.25
❑	64 Antowain Smith	.60	.25
❑	65 Bruce Smith	.40	.15
❑	66 Eric Moulds	.60	.25
❑	67 Andre Reed	.40	.15
❑	68 Thurman Thomas	.60	.25
❑	69 Lonnie Johnson	.25	.08
❑	70 Kerry Collins	.40	.15
❑	71 Kevin Greene	.40	.15
❑	72 Fred Lane	.25	.08
❑	73 Rae Carruth	.25	.08
❑	74 Michael Bates	.25	.08
❑	75 William Floyd	.25	.08
❑	76 Sean Gilbert	.25	.08
❑	77 Erik Kramer	.25	.08
❑	78 Edgar Bennett	.25	.08
❑	79 Curtis Conway	.40	.15
❑	80 Darnell Autry	.25	.08
❑	81 Ryan Wetnight RC	.25	.08
❑	82 Walt Harris	.25	.08
❑	83 Bobby Engram	.40	.15
❑	84 Jeff Blake	.40	.15
❑	85 Carl Pickens	.40	.15
❑	86 Darnay Scott	.40	.15
❑	87 Corey Dillon	.60	.25
❑	88 Reinard Wilson	.25	.08
❑	89 Ashley Ambrose	.25	.08
❑	90 Troy Aikman	1.25	.50
❑	91 Michael Irvin	.60	.25
❑	92 Emmitt Smith	2.00	.75
❑	93 Deion Sanders	.60	.25
❑	94 David LaFleur	.25	.08
❑	95 Chris Warren	.40	.15
❑	96 Darren Woodson	.25	.08
❑	97 John Elway	2.50	1.00
❑	98 Terrell Davis	.60	.25
❑	99 Rod Smith	.40	.15
❑	100 Shannon Sharpe	.40	.15
❑	101 Ed McCaffrey	.40	.15
❑	102 Steve Atwater	.25	.08
❑	103 John Mobley	.25	.08
❑	104 Darrien Gordon	.25	.08
❑	105 Barry Sanders	2.00	.75
❑	106 Scott Mitchell	.40	.15
❑	107 Herman Moore	.40	.15
❑	108 Johnnie Morton	.40	.15
❑	109 Robert Porcher	.25	.08
❑	110 Bryant Westbrook	.25	.08
❑	111 Tommy Vardell	.25	.08
❑	112 Brett Favre	2.50	1.00
❑	113 Dorsey Levens	.60	.25
❑	114 Reggie White	.60	.25
❑	115 Antonio Freeman	.60	.25
❑	116 Robert Brooks	.40	.15
❑	117 Mark Chmura	.40	.15
❑	118 Derrick Mayes	.40	.15
❑	119 Gilbert Brown	.25	.08
❑	120 Marshall Faulk	.75	.30
❑	121 Jeff Burris	.25	.08
❑	122 Marvin Harrison	.60	.25
❑	123 Quentin Coryatt	.25	.08
❑	124 Ken Dilger	.25	.08
❑	125 Zack Crockett	.25	.08
❑	126 Mark Brunell	.60	.25
❑	127 Bryce Paup	.25	.08
❑	128 Tony Brackens	.25	.08
❑	129 Renaldo Wynn	.25	.08
❑	130 Keenan McCardell	.40	.15
❑	131 Jimmy Smith	.40	.15
❑	132 Kevin Hardy	.25	.08
❑	133 Elvis Grbac	.40	.15
❑	134 Tamarick Vanover	.25	.08
❑	135 Chester McGlockton	.25	.08
❑	136 Andre Rison	.40	.15
❑	137 Derrick Alexander	.40	.15
❑	138 Tony Gonzalez	.60	.25
❑	139 Derrick Thomas	.60	.25
❑	140 Dan Marino	2.50	1.00
❑	141 Karim Abdul-Jabbar	.60	.25
❑	142 O.J. McDuffie	.40	.15
❑	143 Yatil Green	.25	.08
❑	144 Charles Jordan	.25	.08
❑	145 Brock Marion	.25	.08
❑	146 Zach Thomas	.60	.25
❑	147 Brad Johnson	.60	.25
❑	148 Cris Carter	.60	.25
❑	149 Jake Reed	.40	.15
❑	150 Robert Smith	.60	.25
❑	151 John Randle	.40	.15
❑	152 Dwayne Rudd	.25	.08
❑	153 Randall Cunningham	.60	.25
❑	154 Drew Bledsoe	1.00	.40
❑	155 Terry Glenn	.60	.25
❑	156 Ben Coates	.40	.15
❑	157 Willie Clay	.25	.08
❑	158 Chris Slade	.25	.08
❑	159 Derrick Cullors RC	.25	.08
❑	160 Ty Law	.40	.15
❑	161 Danny Wuerffel	.40	.15
❑	162 Andre Hastings	.25	.08
❑	163 Troy Davis	.25	.08
❑	164 Billy Joe Hobert	.25	.08
❑	165 Eric Guliford	.25	.08
❑	166 Mark Fields	.25	.08
❑	167 Alex Molden	.25	.08
❑	168 Danny Kanell	.40	.15
❑	169 Tiki Barber	.60	.25
❑	170 Charles Way	.25	.08
❑	171 Amani Toomer	.40	.15
❑	172 Michael Strahan	.40	.15
❑	173 Jessie Armstead	.25	.08
❑	174 Jason Sehorn	.40	.15
❑	175 Glenn Foley	.40	.15
❑	176 Curtis Martin	.60	.25
❑	177 Aaron Glenn	.25	.08
❑	178 Keyshawn Johnson	.60	.25
❑	179 James Farrior	.25	.08
❑	180 Wayne Chrebet	.60	.25
❑	181 Keith Byars	.25	.08
❑	182 Jeff George	.40	.15
❑	183 Napoleon Kaufman	.60	.25
❑	184 Tim Brown	.60	.25
❑	185 Darrell Russell	.25	.08
❑	186 Rickey Dudley	.25	.08
❑	187 James Jett	.40	.15
❑	188 Desmond Howard	.40	.15
❑	189 Bobby Hoying	.40	.15
❑	190 Charlie Garner	.40	.15
❑	191 Irving Fryar	.40	.15
❑	192 Chris T. Jones	.25	.08
❑	193 Mike Mamula	.25	.08
❑	194 Troy Vincent	.25	.08
❑	195 Kordell Stewart	.60	.25
❑	196 Jerome Bettis	.60	.25
❑	197 Will Blackwell	.25	.08
❑	198 Levon Kirkland	.25	.08
❑	199 Carnell Lake	.25	.08
❑	200 Charles Johnson	.25	.08
❑	201 Greg Lloyd	.25	.08
❑	202 Donnell Woolford	.25	.08
❑	203 Tony Banks	.40	.15
❑	204 Amp Lee	.25	.08
❑	205 Isaac Bruce	.60	.25
❑	206 Eddie Kennison	.40	.15
❑	207 Ryan McNeil	.25	.08
❑	208 Mike Jones	.25	.08
❑	209 Ernie Conwell	.25	.08
❑	210 Natrone Means	.40	.15
❑	211 Junior Seau	.60	.25
❑	212 Tony Martin	.40	.15
❑	213 Freddie Jones	.25	.08
❑	214 Bryan Still	.25	.08
❑	215 Rodney Harrison	.40	.15
❑	216 Steve Young	.75	.30
❑	217 Jerry Rice	1.25	.50
❑	218 Garrison Hearst	.60	.25
❑	219 J.J. Stokes	.40	.15
❑	220 Ken Norton	.25	.08
❑	221 Greg Clark	.25	.08
❑	222 Terrell Owens	.60	.25
❑	223 Bryant Young	.25	.08
❑	224 Warren Moon	.60	.25
❑	225 Jon Kitna	.60	.25
❑	226 Ricky Watters	.40	.15
❑	227 Chad Brown	.25	.08
❑	228 Joey Galloway	.40	.15
❑	229 Shawn Springs	.25	.08
❑	230 Cortez Kennedy	.25	.08
❑	231 Trent Dilfer	.60	.25
❑	232 Warrick Dunn	.60	.25
❑	233 Mike Alstott	.60	.25
❑	234 Warren Sapp	.40	.15
❑	235 Bert Emanuel	.40	.15
❑	236 Reidel Anthony	.40	.15
❑	237 Hardy Nickerson	.25	.08
❑	238 Derrick Brooks	.60	.25
❑	239 Steve McNair	.60	.25
❑	240 Yancey Thigpen	.25	.08
❑	241 Anthony Dorsett	.25	.08
❑	242 Blaine Bishop	.25	.08
❑	243 Kenny Holmes	.25	.08
❑	244 Eddie George	.60	.25
❑	245 Chris Sanders	.25	.08
❑	246 Gus Frerotte	.25	.08
❑	247 Terry Allen	.60	.25
❑	248 Dana Stubblefield	.25	.08
❑	249 Michael Westbrook	.40	.15
❑	250 Darrell Green	.40	.15
❑	251 Brian Mitchell	.25	.08
❑	252 Ken Harvey	.25	.08
❑	CL1 Troy Aikman CL	.60	.25
❑	CL2 Dan Marino CL	.75	.30
❑	CL3 Herman Moore CL	.40	.15

1999 Upper Deck

❑	COMPLETE SET (270)	100.00	50.00
❑	COMP.SET w/o SP's (225)	25.00	12.50
❑	1 Jake Plummer	.50	.20
❑	2 Adrian Murrell	.50	.20
❑	3 Rob Moore	.50	.20
❑	4 Larry Centers	.30	.10
❑	5 Simeon Rice	.50	.20
❑	6 Andre Wadsworth	.30	.10
❑	7 Frank Sanders	.50	.20
❑	8 Tim Dwight	.75	.30

9	Ray Buchanan	.30	.10
10	Chris Chandler	.50	.20
11	Jamal Anderson	.75	.30
12	O.J. Santiago	.30	.10
13	Danny Kanell	.30	.10
14	Terance Mathis	.50	.20
15	Priest Holmes	1.25	.50
16	Tony Banks	.50	.20
17	Ray Lewis	.75	.30
18	Patrick Johnson	.30	.10
19	Michael Jackson	.30	.10
20	Michael McCrary	.30	.10
21	Jermaine Lewis	.50	.20
22	Eric Moulds	.75	.30
23	Doug Flutie	.75	.30
24	Antowain Smith	.75	.30
25	Rob Johnson	.50	.20
26	Bruce Smith	.50	.20
27	Andre Reed	.50	.20
28	Thurman Thomas	.50	.20
29	Fred Lane	.30	.10
30	Wesley Walls	.50	.20
31	Tim Biakabutuka	.50	.20
32	Kevin Greene	.30	.10
33	Steve Beuerlein	.30	.10
34	Muhsin Muhammad	.50	.20
35	Rae Carruth	.30	.10
36	Bobby Engram	.50	.20
37	Curtis Enis	.30	.10
38	Edgar Bennett	.30	.10
39	Erik Kramer	.30	.10
40	Steve Stenstrom	.30	.10
41	Alonzo Mayes	.30	.10
42	Curtis Conway	.50	.20
43	Tony McGee	.30	.10
44	Darnay Scott	.30	.10
45	Jeff Blake	.50	.20
46	Corey Dillon	.75	.30
47	Ki-Jana Carter	.30	.10
48	Takeo Spikes	.30	.10
49	Carl Pickens	.50	.20
50	Ty Detmer	.50	.20
51	Leslie Shepherd	.30	.10
52	Terry Kirby	.30	.10
53	Marquez Pope	.30	.10
54	Antonio Langham	.30	.10
55	Jamir Miller	.30	.10
56	Derrick Alexander DT	.30	.10
57	Troy Aikman	1.50	.60
58	Rocket Ismail	.50	.20
59	Emmitt Smith	1.50	.60
60	Michael Irvin	.50	.20
61	David LaFleur	.30	.10
62	Chris Warren	.30	.10
63	Deion Sanders	.75	.30
64	Greg Ellis	.30	.10
65	John Elway	2.50	1.00
66	Bubby Brister	.30	.10
67	Terrell Davis	.75	.30
68	Ed McCaffrey	.50	.20
69	John Mobley	.30	.10
70	Bill Romanowski	.30	.10
71	Rod Smith	.50	.20
72	Shannon Sharpe	.50	.20
73	Charlie Batch	.75	.30
74	Germane Crowell	.30	.10
75	Johnnie Morton	.30	.10
76	Barry Sanders	2.50	1.00
77	Robert Porcher	.30	.10
78	Stephen Boyd	.30	.10
79	Herman Moore	.50	.20
80	Brett Favre	2.50	1.00
81	Mark Chmura	.30	.10
82	Antonio Freeman	.75	.30
83	Robert Brooks	.50	.20
84	Vonnie Holliday	.30	.10
85	Bill Schroeder	.75	.30
86	Dorsey Levens	.75	.30
87	Santana Dotson	.30	.10
88	Peyton Manning	2.50	1.00
89	Jerome Pathon	.30	.10
90	Marvin Harrison	.75	.30
91	Ellis Johnson	.30	.10
92	Ken Dilger	.30	.10
93	E.G. Green	.30	.10
94	Jeff Burris	.30	.10
95	Mark Brunell	.75	.30
96	Fred Taylor	.75	.30
97	Jimmy Smith	.50	.20
98	James Stewart	.50	.20
99	Kyle Brady	.30	.10
100	Dave Thomas RC	.30	.10
101	Keenan McCardell	.50	.20
102	Elvis Grbac	.50	.20
103	Tony Gonzalez	.75	.30
104	Andre Rison	.50	.20
105	Donnell Bennett	.30	.10
106	Derrick Thomas	.75	.30
107	Warren Moon	.75	.30
108	Derrick Alexander WR	.50	.20
109	Dan Marino	2.50	1.00
110	O.J. McDuffie	.50	.20
111	Karim Abdul-Jabbar	.50	.20
112	John Avery	.30	.10
113	Sam Madison	.30	.10
114	Jason Taylor	.30	.10
115	Zach Thomas	.75	.30
116	Randall Cunningham	.75	.30
117	Randy Moss	2.00	.75
118	Cris Carter	.75	.30
119	Jake Reed	.50	.20
120	Matthew Hatchette	.30	.10
121	John Randle	.50	.20
122	Robert Smith	.75	.30
123	Drew Bledsoe	1.00	.40
124	Ben Coates	.50	.20
125	Terry Glenn	.75	.30
126	Ty Law	.50	.20
127	Tony Simmons	.30	.10
128	Ted Johnson	.30	.10
129	Tony Carter	.30	.10
130	Willie McGinest	.30	.10
131	Danny Wuerffel	.30	.10
132	Cameron Cleeland	.30	.10
133	Eddie Kennison	.50	.20
134	Joe Johnson	.30	.10
135	Andre Hastings	.30	.10
136	La'Roi Glover RC	.75	.30
137	Kent Graham	.30	.10
138	Tiki Barber	.75	.30
139	Gary Brown	.30	.10
140	Ike Hilliard	.30	.10
141	Jason Sehorn	.30	.10
142	Michael Strahan	.50	.20
143	Amani Toomer	.30	.10
144	Kerry Collins	.50	.20
145	Vinny Testaverde	.50	.20
146	Wayne Chrebet	.50	.20
147	Curtis Martin	.75	.30
148	Mo Lewis	.30	.10
149	Aaron Glenn	.30	.10
150	Steve Atwater	.30	.10
151	Keyshawn Johnson	.75	.30
152	James Farrior	.30	.10
153	Rich Gannon	.75	.30
154	Tim Brown	.75	.30
155	Darrell Russell	.30	.10
156	Rickey Dudley	.30	.10
157	Charles Woodson	.75	.30
158	James Jett	.50	.20
159	Napoleon Kaufman	.75	.30
160	Duce Staley	.75	.30
161	Doug Pederson	.30	.10
162	Bobby Hoying	.50	.20
163	Koy Detmer	.30	.10
164	Kevin Turner	.30	.10
165	Charles Johnson	.30	.10
166	Mike Mamula	.30	.10
167	Jerome Bettis	.75	.30
168	Courtney Hawkins	.30	.10
169	Will Blackwell	.30	.10
170	Kordell Stewart	.50	.20
171	Richard Huntley	.50	.20
172	Levon Kirkland	.30	.10
173	Hines Ward	.75	.30
174	Trent Green	.75	.30
175	Marshall Faulk	1.00	.40
176	Az-Zahir Hakim	.30	.10
177	Amp Lee	.30	.10
178	Robert Holcombe	.30	.10
179	Isaac Bruce	.75	.30
180	Kevin Carter	.30	.10
181	Jim Harbaugh	.50	.20
182	Junior Seau	.75	.30
183	Natrone Means	.50	.20
184	Ryan Leaf	.75	.30
185	Charlie Jones	.30	.10
186	Rodney Harrison	.30	.10
187	Mikhael Ricks	.30	.10
188	Steve Young	1.00	.40
189	Terrell Owens	.75	.30
190	Jerry Rice	1.50	.60
191	J.J. Stokes	.50	.20
192	Irv Smith	.30	.10
193	Bryant Young	.30	.10
194	Garrison Hearst	.50	.20
195	Jon Kitna	.75	.30
196	Ahman Green	.75	.30
197	Joey Galloway	.50	.20
198	Ricky Watters	.50	.20
199	Chad Brown	.30	.10
200	Shawn Springs	.30	.10
201	Mike Pritchard	.30	.10
202	Trent Dilfer	.50	.20
203	Reidel Anthony	.50	.20
204	Bert Emanuel	.50	.20
205	Warrick Dunn	.75	.30
206	Jacquez Green	.30	.10
207	Hardy Nickerson	.30	.10
208	Mike Alstott	.75	.30
209	Eddie George	.75	.30
210	Steve McNair	.75	.30
211	Kevin Dyson	.50	.20
212	Frank Wycheck	.30	.10
213	Jackie Harris	.30	.10
214	Blaine Bishop	.30	.10
215	Yancey Thigpen	.30	.10
216	Brad Johnson	.75	.30
217	Rodney Peete	.30	.10
218	Michael Westbrook	.50	.20
219	Skip Hicks	.30	.10
220	Brian Mitchell	.30	.10
221	Dan Wilkinson	.30	.10
222	Dana Stubblefield	.30	.10
223	Kordell Stewart CL	.50	.20
224	Fred Taylor CL	.75	.30
225	Warrick Dunn CL	.50	.20
226	Champ Bailey RC	3.00	1.25
227	Chris McAlister RC	1.50	.60
228	Jevon Kearse RC	4.00	1.50
229	Ebenezer Ekuban RC	1.50	.60
230	Chris Claiborne RC	1.00	.40
231	Andy Katzenmoyer RC	1.50	.60
232	Tim Couch RC	2.00	.75
233	Daunte Culpepper RC	10.00	4.00
234	Akili Smith RC	1.50	.60
235	Donovan McNabb RC	12.00	5.00
236	Sean Bennett RC	1.00	.40
237	Brock Huard RC	2.00	.75
238	Cade McNown RC	1.50	.60
239	Shaun King RC	1.50	.60
240	Joe Germaine RC	1.50	.60
241	Ricky Williams RC	5.00	2.00
242	Edgerrin James RC	10.00	4.00
243	Sedrick Irvin RC	1.00	.40
244	Kevin Faulk RC	2.00	.75
245	Rob Konrad RC	2.00	.75
246	James Johnson RC	1.50	.60
247	Amos Zereoue RC	2.00	.75
248	Torry Holt RC	6.00	2.50
249	D'Wayne Bates RC	1.50	.60
250	David Boston RC	2.00	.75
251	Dameane Douglas RC	2.00	.75
252	Troy Edwards RC	1.50	.60

❑ 253 Kevin Johnson RC 2.00 .75
❑ 254 Peerless Price RC 2.00 .75
❑ 255 Antoine Winfield RC 1.50 .60
❑ 256 Mike Cloud RC 1.50 .60
❑ 257 Joe Montgomery RC 1.50 .60
❑ 258 Jermaine Fazande RC 1.50 .60
❑ 259 Scott Covington RC 2.00 .75
❑ 260 Aaron Brooks RC 5.00 2.00
❑ 261 Patrick Kerney RC 2.00 .75
❑ 262 Cecil Collins RC 1.00 .40
❑ 263 Chris Greisen RC 1.50 .60
❑ 264 Craig Yeast RC 1.50 .60
❑ 265 Karsten Bailey RC 1.50 .60
❑ 266 Reginald Kelly RC 1.00 .40
❑ 267 Al Wilson RC 1.50 .60
❑ 268 Jeff Paulk RC 1.00 .40
❑ 269 Jim Kleinsasser RC 2.00 .75
❑ 270 Darrin Chiaverini RC 1.50 .60

2000 Upper Deck

❑ COMPLETE SET (1-270) 120.00 60.00
❑ COMP.SET w/o SPs (222) 30.00 12.50
❑ 1 Jake Plummer .50 .20
❑ 2 Michael Pittman .30 .10
❑ 3 Rob Moore .50 .20
❑ 4 David Boston .75 .30
❑ 5 Frank Sanders .50 .20
❑ 6 Aeneas Williams .30 .10
❑ 7 Kwamie Lassiter .30 .10
❑ 8 Rob Fredrickson .30 .10
❑ 9 Tim Dwight .75 .30
❑ 10 Chris Chandler .50 .20
❑ 11 Jamal Anderson .75 .30
❑ 12 Shawn Jefferson .30 .10
❑ 13 Ken Oxendine .30 .10
❑ 14 Terance Mathis .50 .20
❑ 15 Bob Christian .30 .10
❑ 16 Qadry Ismail .50 .20
❑ 17 Jermaine Lewis .50 .20
❑ 18 Rod Woodson .50 .20
❑ 19 Michael McCrary .30 .10
❑ 20 Tony Banks .50 .20
❑ 21 Peter Boulware .30 .10
❑ 22 Shannon Sharpe .50 .20
❑ 23 Peerless Price .50 .20
❑ 24 Rob Johnson .50 .20
❑ 25 Eric Moulds .75 .30
❑ 26 Doug Flutie .75 .30
❑ 27 Jay Riemersma .30 .10
❑ 28 Antowain Smith .50 .20
❑ 29 Jonathan Linton .30 .10
❑ 30 Muhsin Muhammad .50 .20
❑ 31 Patrick Jeffers .75 .30
❑ 32 Steve Beuerlein .50 .20
❑ 33 Natrone Means .30 .10
❑ 34 Tim Biakabutuka .50 .20
❑ 35 Michael Bates .30 .10
❑ 36 Chuck Smith .30 .10
❑ 37 Wesley Walls .30 .10
❑ 38 Cade McNown .30 .10
❑ 39 Curtis Enis .30 .10
❑ 40 Marcus Robinson .75 .30
❑ 41 Eddie Kennison .50 .20
❑ 42 Bobby Engram .50 .20
❑ 43 Glyn Milburn .30 .10
❑ 44 Marty Booker .50 .20
❑ 45 Akili Smith .30 .10
❑ 46 Corey Dillon .75 .30
❑ 47 Darnay Scott .50 .20
❑ 48 Tremain Mack .30 .10
❑ 49 Damon Griffin .30 .10
❑ 50 Takeo Spikes .30 .10
❑ 51 Tony McGee .30 .10
❑ 52 Tim Couch .50 .20
❑ 53 Kevin Johnson .75 .30
❑ 54 Darrin Chiaverini .30 .10
❑ 55 Jamir Miller .30 .10
❑ 56 Errict Rhett .50 .20
❑ 57 Terry Kirby .30 .10
❑ 58 Marc Edwards .30 .10
❑ 59 Troy Aikman 1.50 .60
❑ 60 Emmitt Smith 1.50 .60
❑ 61 Rocket Ismail .50 .20
❑ 62 Jason Tucker .30 .10
❑ 63 Dexter Coakley .30 .10
❑ 64 Joey Galloway .50 .20
❑ 65 Wane McGarity .30 .10
❑ 66 Terrell Davis .75 .30
❑ 67 Olandis Gary .75 .30
❑ 68 Brian Griese .75 .30
❑ 69 Gus Frerotte .30 .10
❑ 70 Byron Chamberlain .30 .10
❑ 71 Ed McCaffrey .75 .30
❑ 72 Rod Smith .50 .20
❑ 73 Al Wilson .30 .10
❑ 74 Charlie Batch .75 .30
❑ 75 Germane Crowell .30 .10
❑ 76 Sedrick Irvin .30 .10
❑ 77 Johnnie Morton .50 .20
❑ 78 Robert Porcher .30 .10
❑ 79 Herman Moore .50 .20
❑ 80 James Stewart .50 .20
❑ 81 Brett Favre 2.50 1.00
❑ 82 Antonio Freeman .75 .30
❑ 83 Bill Schroeder .50 .20
❑ 84 Dorsey Levens .50 .20
❑ 85 Corey Bradford .50 .20
❑ 86 De'Mond Parker .30 .10
❑ 87 Vonnie Holliday .30 .10
❑ 88 Peyton Manning 2.00 .75
❑ 89 Edgerrin James 1.25 .50
❑ 90 Marvin Harrison .75 .30
❑ 91 Ken Dilger .30 .10
❑ 92 Terrence Wilkins .30 .10
❑ 93 Marcus Pollard .30 .10
❑ 94 Fred Lane .30 .10
❑ 95 Mark Brunell .75 .30
❑ 96 Fred Taylor .75 .30
❑ 97 Jimmy Smith .50 .20
❑ 98 Keenan McCardell .50 .20
❑ 99 Carnell Lake .30 .10
❑ 100 Tavian Banks .30 .10
❑ 101 Kyle Brady .30 .10
❑ 102 Hardy Nickerson .30 .10
❑ 103 Elvis Grbac .50 .20
❑ 104 Tony Gonzalez .50 .20
❑ 105 Derrick Alexander WR .50 .20
❑ 106 Donnell Bennett .30 .10
❑ 107 Mike Cloud .30 .10
❑ 108 Donnie Edwards .30 .10
❑ 109 Jay Fiedler .75 .30
❑ 110 James Johnson .30 .10
❑ 111 Tony Martin .50 .20
❑ 112 Damon Huard .75 .30
❑ 113 O.J. McDuffie .50 .20
❑ 114 Thurman Thomas .50 .20
❑ 115 Zach Thomas .75 .30
❑ 116 Oronde Gadsden .50 .20
❑ 117 Randy Moss 1.50 .60
❑ 118 Robert Smith .75 .30
❑ 119 Cris Carter .75 .30
❑ 120 Matthew Hatchette .30 .10
❑ 121 Daunte Culpepper 1.00 .40
❑ 122 Leroy Hoard .30 .10
❑ 123 Drew Bledsoe 1.00 .40
❑ 124 Terry Glenn .50 .20
❑ 125 Troy Brown .50 .20
❑ 126 Kevin Faulk .30 .10
❑ 127 Lawyer Milloy .50 .20
❑ 128 Ricky Williams .75 .30
❑ 129 Keith Poole .30 .10
❑ 130 Jake Reed .50 .20
❑ 131 Cam Cleeland .30 .10
❑ 132 Jeff Blake .50 .20
❑ 133 Andrew Glover .30 .10
❑ 134 Kerry Collins .50 .20
❑ 135 Amani Toomer .50 .20
❑ 136 Joe Montgomery .30 .10
❑ 137 Ike Hilliard .50 .20
❑ 138 Tiki Barber .75 .30
❑ 139 Pete Mitchell .30 .10
❑ 140 Ray Lucas .50 .20
❑ 141 Mo Lewis .30 .10
❑ 142 Curtis Martin .75 .30
❑ 143 Vinny Testaverde .50 .20
❑ 144 Wayne Chrebet .50 .20
❑ 145 Dedric Ward .30 .10
❑ 146 Tim Brown .75 .30
❑ 147 Rich Gannon .75 .30
❑ 148 Tyrone Wheatley .50 .20
❑ 149 Napoleon Kaufman .50 .20
❑ 150 Charles Woodson .50 .20
❑ 151 Darrell Russell .30 .10
❑ 152 James Jett .30 .10
❑ 153 Rickey Dudley .30 .10
❑ 154 Jon Ritchie .30 .10
❑ 155 Duce Staley .75 .30
❑ 156 Donovan McNabb 1.25 .50
❑ 157 Torrance Small .30 .10
❑ 158 Allen Rossum .30 .10
❑ 159 Mike Mamula .30 .10
❑ 160 Na Brown .30 .10
❑ 161 Charles Johnson .50 .20
❑ 162 Kent Graham .30 .10
❑ 163 Troy Edwards .30 .10
❑ 164 Jerome Bettis .75 .30
❑ 165 Hines Ward .75 .30
❑ 166 Kordell Stewart .50 .20
❑ 167 Levon Kirkland .30 .10
❑ 168 Richard Huntley .30 .10
❑ 169 Marshall Faulk 1.00 .40
❑ 170 Kurt Warner 1.50 .60
❑ 171 Torry Holt .75 .30
❑ 172 Isaac Bruce .75 .30
❑ 173 Kevin Carter .30 .10
❑ 174 Az-Zahir Hakim .50 .20
❑ 175 Ricky Proehl .30 .10
❑ 176 Jermaine Fazande .30 .10
❑ 177 Curtis Conway .50 .20
❑ 178 Freddie Jones .30 .10
❑ 179 Junior Seau .75 .30
❑ 180 Jeff Graham .30 .10
❑ 181 Jim Harbaugh .50 .20
❑ 182 Rodney Harrison .30 .10
❑ 183 Steve Young 1.00 .40
❑ 184 Jerry Rice 1.50 .60
❑ 185 Charlie Garner .50 .20
❑ 186 Terrell Owens .75 .30
❑ 187 Jeff Garcia .75 .30
❑ 188 Fred Beasley .30 .10
❑ 189 J.J. Stokes .50 .20
❑ 190 Ricky Watters .50 .20
❑ 191 Jon Kitna .75 .30
❑ 192 Derrick Mayes .50 .20
❑ 193 Sean Dawkins .30 .10
❑ 194 Charlie Rogers .30 .10
❑ 195 Mike Pritchard .30 .10
❑ 196 Cortez Kennedy .30 .10
❑ 197 Christian Fauria .30 .10
❑ 198 Warrick Dunn .75 .30
❑ 199 Shaun King .30 .10
❑ 200 Mike Alstott .75 .30
❑ 201 Warren Sapp .50 .20
❑ 202 Jacquez Green .30 .10
❑ 203 Reidel Anthony .30 .10
❑ 204 Dave Moore .30 .10
❑ 205 Keyshawn Johnson .75 .30
❑ 206 Eddie George .75 .30
❑ 207 Steve McNair .75 .30
❑ 208 Kevin Dyson .50 .20
❑ 209 Jevon Kearse .75 .30
❑ 210 Yancey Thigpen .30 .10
❑ 211 Frank Wycheck .30 .10
❑ 212 Isaac Byrd .30 .10
❑ 213 Neil O'Donnell .30 .10
❑ 214 Brad Johnson .75 .30
❑ 215 Stephen Davis .75 .30
❑ 216 Michael Westbrook .50 .20
❑ 217 Albert Connell .30 .10
❑ 218 Brian Mitchell .30 .10
❑ 219 Bruce Smith .50 .20
❑ 220 Stephen Alexander .30 .10
❑ 221 Jeff George .50 .20

❑ 222	Adrian Murrell	.30	.10
❑ 223	Courtney Brown RC	4.00	1.50
❑ 224	John Engelberger RC	2.50	1.00
❑ 225	Deltha O'Neal RC	4.00	1.50
❑ 226	Corey Simon RC	4.00	1.50
❑ 227	R.Jay Soward RC	2.50	1.00
❑ 228	Marc Bulger RC	8.00	3.00
❑ 229	Raynoch Thompson RC	2.50	1.00
❑ 230	Deon Grant RC	2.50	1.00
❑ 231	Darrell Jackson RC	8.00	3.00
❑ 232	Chris Cole RC	2.50	1.00
❑ 233	Trevor Gaylor RC	2.50	1.00
❑ 234	John Abraham RC	4.00	1.50
❑ 235	Chris Redman RC	2.50	1.00
❑ 236	Joe Hamilton RC	2.50	1.00
❑ 237	Chad Pennington RC	10.00	4.00
❑ 238	Tee Martin RC	4.00	1.50
❑ 239	Giovanni Carmazzi RC	2.00	.75
❑ 240	Tim Rattay RC	4.00	1.50
❑ 241	Ron Dayne RC	4.00	1.50
❑ 242	Shaun Alexander RC	20.00	7.50
❑ 243	Thomas Jones RC	6.00	2.50
❑ 244	Reuben Droughns RC	4.00	1.50
❑ 245	Jamal Lewis RC	10.00	4.00
❑ 246	Michael Wiley RC	2.50	1.00
❑ 247	J.R. Redmond RC	2.50	1.00
❑ 248	Travis Prentice RC	2.50	1.00
❑ 249	Todd Husak RC	4.00	1.50
❑ 250	Trung Canidate RC	2.50	1.00
❑ 251	Brian Urlacher RC	15.00	6.00
❑ 252	Anthony Becht RC	4.00	1.50
❑ 253	Bubba Franks RC	4.00	1.50
❑ 254	Tom Brady RC	40.00	20.00
❑ 255	Peter Warrick RC	4.00	1.50
❑ 256	Plaxico Burress RC	8.00	3.00
❑ 257	Sylvester Morris RC	2.50	1.00
❑ 258	Dez White RC	4.00	1.50
❑ 259	Travis Taylor RC	4.00	1.50
❑ 260	Todd Pinkston RC	4.00	1.50
❑ 261	Dennis Northcutt RC	4.00	1.50
❑ 262	Jerry Porter RC	5.00	2.00
❑ 263	Laveranues Coles RC	5.00	2.00
❑ 264	Danny Farmer RC	2.50	1.00
❑ 265	Curtis Keaton RC	2.50	1.00
❑ 266	Sherrod Gideon RC	2.00	.75
❑ 267	Ron Dugans RC	2.00	.75
❑ 268	Steve McNair CL	.50	.20
❑ 269	Jake Plummer CL	.50	.20
❑ 270	Antonio Freeman CL	.50	.20

2001 Upper Deck

❑	COMPLETE SET (280)	300.00	150.00
❑	COMP.SET w/o SP's (180)	25.00	10.00
❑ 1	Jake Plummer	.50	.20
❑ 2	David Boston	.75	.30
❑ 3	Thomas Jones	.50	.20
❑ 4	Frank Sanders	.30	.10
❑ 5	Eric Zeier	.30	.10
❑ 6	Jamal Anderson	.75	.30
❑ 7	Chris Chandler	.50	.20
❑ 8	Shawn Jefferson	.30	.10
❑ 9	Darrick Vaughn	.30	.10
❑ 10	Terance Mathis	.50	.20
❑ 11	Jamal Lewis	1.25	.50
❑ 12	Shannon Sharpe	.50	.20
❑ 13	Elvis Grbac	.50	.20
❑ 14	Ray Lewis	.75	.30
❑ 15	Qadry Ismail	.50	.20
❑ 16	Chris Redman	.30	.10
❑ 17	Rob Johnson	.75	.30
❑ 18	Eric Moulds	.50	.20
❑ 19	Sammy Morris	.30	.10
❑ 20	Shawn Bryson	.30	.10
❑ 21	Jeremy McDaniel	.30	.10
❑ 22	Muhsin Muhammad	.50	.20
❑ 23	Brad Hoover	.30	.10
❑ 24	Tim Biakabutuka	.50	.20
❑ 25	Steve Beuerlein	.30	.10
❑ 26	Jeff Lewis	.30	.10
❑ 27	Wesley Walls	.30	.10
❑ 28	Cade McNown	.30	.10
❑ 29	James Allen	.50	.20
❑ 30	Marcus Robinson	.75	.30
❑ 31	Brian Urlacher	1.25	.50
❑ 32	Bobby Engram	.30	.10
❑ 33	Peter Warrick	.75	.30
❑ 34	Corey Dillon	.75	.30
❑ 35	Akili Smith	.30	.10
❑ 36	Danny Farmer	.30	.10
❑ 37	Ron Dugans	.30	.10
❑ 38	Jon Kitna	.75	.30
❑ 39	Tim Couch	.50	.20
❑ 40	Kevin Johnson	.50	.20
❑ 41	Travis Prentice	.30	.10
❑ 42	Spergon Wynn	.30	.10
❑ 43	Errict Rhett	.30	.10
❑ 44	Dennis Northcutt	.50	.20
❑ 45	Courtney Brown	.50	.20
❑ 46	Tony Banks	.30	.10
❑ 47	Emmitt Smith	1.50	.60
❑ 48	Joey Galloway	.50	.20
❑ 49	Rocket Ismail	.50	.20
❑ 50	Randall Cunningham	.75	.30
❑ 51	James McKnight	.50	.20
❑ 52	Terrell Davis	.75	.30
❑ 53	Mike Anderson	.75	.30
❑ 54	Brian Griese	.75	.30
❑ 55	Rod Smith	.50	.20
❑ 56	Ed McCaffrey	.75	.30
❑ 57	Eddie Kennison	.50	.20
❑ 58	Olandis Gary	.50	.20
❑ 59	Charlie Batch	.75	.30
❑ 60	Germane Crowell	.30	.10
❑ 61	James O. Stewart	.50	.20
❑ 62	Johnnie Morton	.50	.20
❑ 63	Brett Favre	2.50	1.00
❑ 64	Antonio Freeman	.75	.30
❑ 65	Dorsey Levens	.50	.20
❑ 66	Ahman Green	.75	.30
❑ 67	Bill Schroeder	.50	.20
❑ 68	Peyton Manning	2.00	.75
❑ 69	Edgerrin James	1.00	.40
❑ 70	Marvin Harrison	.75	.30
❑ 71	Jerome Pathon	.50	.20
❑ 72	Ken Dilger	.30	.10
❑ 73	Mark Brunell	.75	.30
❑ 74	Fred Taylor	.75	.30
❑ 75	Jimmy Smith	.50	.20
❑ 76	Keenan McCardell	.30	.10
❑ 77	R.Jay Soward	.30	.10
❑ 78	Todd Collins	.30	.10
❑ 79	Tony Gonzalez	.50	.20
❑ 80	Derrick Alexander	.50	.20
❑ 81	Tony Richardson	.30	.10
❑ 82	Sylvester Morris	.30	.10
❑ 83	Oronde Gadsden	.50	.20
❑ 84	Lamar Smith	.50	.20
❑ 85	Jay Fiedler	.75	.30
❑ 86	Jason Taylor	.30	.10
❑ 87	Ray Lucas	.30	.10
❑ 88	O.J. McDuffie	.30	.10
❑ 89	Randy Moss	1.50	.60
❑ 90	Cris Carter	.75	.30
❑ 91	Daunte Culpepper	.75	.30
❑ 92	Moe Williams	.50	.20
❑ 93	Troy Walters	.30	.10
❑ 94	Drew Bledsoe	1.00	.40
❑ 95	Terry Glenn	.50	.20
❑ 96	Kevin Faulk	.50	.20
❑ 97	J.R. Redmond	.30	.10
❑ 98	Troy Brown	.50	.20
❑ 99	Ricky Williams	.75	.30
❑ 100	Jeff Blake	.50	.20
❑ 101	Joe Horn	.50	.20
❑ 102	Albert Connell	.30	.10
❑ 103	Aaron Brooks	.75	.30
❑ 104	Chad Morton	.30	.10
❑ 105	Kerry Collins	.50	.20
❑ 106	Amani Toomer	.50	.20
❑ 107	Ron Dayne	.75	.30
❑ 108	Tiki Barber	.75	.30
❑ 109	Ike Hilliard	.50	.20
❑ 110	Ron Dixon	.30	.10
❑ 111	Jason Sehorn	.30	.10
❑ 112	Vinny Testaverde	.50	.20
❑ 113	Wayne Chrebet	.50	.20
❑ 114	Curtis Martin	.75	.30
❑ 115	Dedric Ward	.30	.10
❑ 116	Laveranues Coles	.75	.30
❑ 117	Windrell Hayes	.30	.10
❑ 118	Tim Brown	.75	.30
❑ 119	Rich Gannon	.75	.30
❑ 120	Tyrone Wheatley	.50	.20
❑ 121	Charlie Garner	.50	.20
❑ 122	Andre Rison	.50	.20
❑ 123	Charles Woodson	.50	.20
❑ 124	Trace Armstrong	.30	.10
❑ 125	Duce Staley	.75	.30
❑ 126	Donovan McNabb	1.00	.40
❑ 127	Darnell Autry	.30	.10
❑ 128	Charles Johnson	.30	.10
❑ 129	Torrance Small	.30	.10
❑ 130	Kordell Stewart	.50	.20
❑ 131	Jerome Bettis	.75	.30
❑ 132	Plaxico Burress	.75	.30
❑ 133	Bobby Shaw	.30	.10
❑ 134	Troy Edwards	.30	.10
❑ 135	Marshall Faulk	1.00	.40
❑ 136	Kurt Warner	1.50	.60
❑ 137	Isaac Bruce	.75	.30
❑ 138	Torry Holt	.75	.30
❑ 139	Trent Green	.75	.30
❑ 140	Az-Zahir Hakim	.30	.10
❑ 141	Junior Seau	.75	.30
❑ 142	Curtis Conway	.50	.20
❑ 143	Doug Flutie	.75	.30
❑ 144	Jeff Graham	.30	.10
❑ 145	Freddie Jones	.30	.10
❑ 146	Marcellus Wiley	.30	.10
❑ 147	Jeff Garcia	.75	.30
❑ 148	Jerry Rice	1.50	.60
❑ 149	Fred Beasley	.30	.10
❑ 150	Terrell Owens	.75	.30
❑ 151	J.J. Stokes	.50	.20
❑ 152	Garrison Hearst	.50	.20
❑ 153	Ricky Watters	.30	.10
❑ 154	Shaun Alexander	1.00	.40
❑ 155	Matt Hasselbeck	.50	.20
❑ 156	Brock Huard	.30	.10
❑ 157	Darrell Jackson	.75	.30
❑ 158	John Randle	.30	.10
❑ 159	Warrick Dunn	.75	.30
❑ 160	Shaun King	.30	.10
❑ 161	Ryan Leaf	.50	.20
❑ 162	Mike Alstott	.75	.30
❑ 163	Jacquez Green	.30	.10
❑ 164	Brad Johnson	.75	.30
❑ 165	Keyshawn Johnson	.75	.30
❑ 166	Eddie George	.75	.30
❑ 167	Steve McNair	.75	.30
❑ 168	Neil O'Donnell	.30	.10
❑ 169	Derrick Mason	.50	.20
❑ 170	Frank Wycheck	.30	.10
❑ 171	Kevin Dyson	.50	.20
❑ 172	Jevon Kearse	.50	.20
❑ 173	Jeff George	.50	.20
❑ 174	Stephen Davis	.75	.30
❑ 175	Larry Centers	.30	.10
❑ 176	Michael Westbrook	.50	.20
❑ 177	Stephen Alexander	.50	.20
❑ 178	Ron Dayne	.75	.30
❑ 179	Donovan McNabb	1.00	.40
❑ 180	Jimmy Smith	.50	.20
❑ 181	Adam Archuleta RC	5.00	2.00
❑ 182	A.J. Feeley RC	5.00	2.00
❑ 183	Alex Bannister RC	3.00	1.25
❑ 184	Alge Crumpler RC	6.00	3.00
❑ 185	Andre Carter RC	5.00	2.00
❑ 186	Andre Dyson RC	2.00	.75
❑ 187	Anthony Thomas RC	5.00	2.00
❑ 188	Arther Love RC	2.00	.75
❑ 189	Bobby Newcombe RC	3.00	1.25
❑ 190	Brandon Spoon RC	5.00	2.00

❑ 191	Carlos Polk RC	2.00	.75
❑ 192	Casey Hampton RC	5.00	2.00
❑ 193	Cedrick Wilson RC	5.00	2.00
❑ 194	Chad Johnson RC	12.00	5.00
❑ 195	Chris Chambers RC	8.00	3.00
❑ 196	Chris Taylor RC	3.00	1.25
❑ 197	Chris Weinke RC	5.00	2.00
❑ 198	Correll Buckhalter RC	6.00	2.50
❑ 199	Damione Lewis RC	3.00	1.25
❑ 200	Dan Alexander RC	5.00	2.00
❑ 201	Dan Morgan RC	5.00	2.00
❑ 202	Willie Middlebrooks RC	3.00	1.25
❑ 203	David Terrell RC	5.00	2.00
❑ 204	Derrick Gibson RC	3.00	1.25
❑ 205	Deuce McAllister RC	10.00	4.00
❑ 206	Drew Brees RC	12.00	5.00
❑ 207	Edgerton Hartwell RC	2.00	.75
❑ 208	Fred Smoot RC	5.00	2.00
❑ 209	Freddie Mitchell RC	5.00	2.00
❑ 210	Gary Baxter RC	3.00	1.25
❑ 211	Gerard Warren RC	5.00	2.00
❑ 212	Hakim Akbar RC	2.00	.75
❑ 213	Heath Evans RC	3.00	1.25
❑ 214	Jabari Holloway RC	3.00	1.25
❑ 215	Jamal Reynolds RC	5.00	2.00
❑ 216	Jamar Fletcher RC	3.00	1.25
❑ 217	James Jackson RC	5.00	2.00
❑ 218	Jamie Winborn RC	3.00	1.25
❑ 219	Jesse Palmer RC	5.00	2.00
❑ 220	Josh Booty RC	5.00	2.00
❑ 221	Josh Heupel RC	5.00	2.00
❑ 222	Justin Smith RC	5.00	2.00
❑ 223	Karon Riley RC	2.00	.75
❑ 224	Ken Lucas RC	3.00	1.25
❑ 225	Kenyatta Walker RC	2.00	.75
❑ 226	Ken-Yon Rambo RC	3.00	1.25
❑ 227	Kevan Barlow RC	5.00	2.00
❑ 228	Kevin Kasper RC	5.00	2.00
❑ 229	Koren Robinson RC	5.00	2.00
❑ 230	LaDainian Tomlinson RC	25.00	12.50
❑ 231	LaMont Jordan RC	10.00	4.00
❑ 232	Leonard Davis RC	3.00	1.25
❑ 233	Marcus Stroud RC	5.00	2.00
❑ 234	Marques Tuiasosopo RC	5.00	2.00
❑ 235	Snoop Minnis RC	3.00	1.25
❑ 236	Michael Bennett RC	8.00	3.00
❑ 237	Michael Stone RC	2.00	.75
❑ 238	Mike McMahon RC	5.00	2.00
❑ 239	Michael Vick RC	30.00	12.50
❑ 240	Moran Norris RC	2.00	.75
❑ 241	Morlon Greenwood RC	3.00	1.25
❑ 242	Nate Clements RC	5.00	2.00
❑ 243	Orlando Huff RC	2.00	.75
❑ 244	Quincy Morgan RC	5.00	2.00
❑ 245	Reggie Wayne RC	10.00	4.00
❑ 246	Richard Seymour RC	5.00	2.00
❑ 247	Robert Ferguson RC	5.00	2.00
❑ 248	Rod Gardner RC	5.00	2.00
❑ 249	Rudi Johnson RC	10.00	4.00
❑ 250	Sage Rosenfels RC	5.00	2.00
❑ 251	Santana Moss RC	8.00	3.00
❑ 252	Scotty Anderson RC	3.00	1.25
❑ 253	Sedrick Hodge RC	2.00	.75
❑ 254	Shaun Rogers RC	5.00	2.00
❑ 255	Steve Hutchinson RC	3.00	1.25
❑ 256	T.J. Houshmandzadeh RC	5.00	2.00
❑ 257	Tay Cody RC	2.00	.75
❑ 258	George Layne RC	3.00	1.25
❑ 259	Todd Heap RC	5.00	2.00
❑ 260	Tommy Polley RC	5.00	2.00
❑ 261	Tony Dixon RC	3.00	1.25
❑ 262	Brian Allen RC	2.00	.75
❑ 263	Torrance Marshall RC	5.00	2.00
❑ 264	Travis Henry RC	5.00	2.00
❑ 265	Travis Minor RC	3.00	1.25
❑ 266	Vinny Sutherland RC	3.00	1.25
❑ 267	Will Allen RC	3.00	1.25
❑ 268	Derrick Blaylock RC	5.00	2.00
❑ 269	Zeke Moreno RC	5.00	2.00
❑ 270	Chris Barnes RC	3.00	1.25
❑ 271	Dee Brown RC	5.00	2.00
❑ 272	Reggie White RC	3.00	1.25
❑ 273	Derek Combs RC	3.00	1.25
❑ 274	Steve Smith RC	12.00	6.00
❑ 275	John Capel RC	3.00	1.25
❑ 276	Justin McCareins RC	5.00	2.00
❑ 277	Damerien McCants RC	3.00	1.25
❑ 278	Eddie Berlin RC	3.00	1.25
❑ 279	Francis St. Paul RC	3.00	1.25
❑ 280	Quincy Carter RC	5.00	2.00

2002 Upper Deck

❑	COMP.SET w/o SP's (180)	25.00	10.00
❑ 1	Jake Plummer	.50	.20
❑ 2	Marcel Shipp	.75	.30
❑ 3	David Boston	.75	.30
❑ 4	Arnold Jackson	.30	.10
❑ 5	Frank Sanders	.30	.10
❑ 6	Freddie Jones	.30	.10
❑ 7	Michael Vick	2.50	1.00
❑ 8	Jamal Anderson	.50	.20
❑ 9	Warrick Dunn	.75	.30
❑ 10	Maurice Smith	.30	.10
❑ 11	Shawn Jefferson	.30	.10
❑ 12	Chris Redman	.30	.10
❑ 13	Jeff Blake	.30	.10
❑ 14	Jamal Lewis	.75	.30
❑ 15	Travis Taylor	.50	.20
❑ 16	Ray Lewis	.75	.30
❑ 17	Chris McAlister	.30	.10
❑ 18	Drew Bledsoe	1.00	.40
❑ 19	Travis Henry	.75	.30
❑ 20	Larry Centers	.30	.10
❑ 21	Eric Moulds	.50	.20
❑ 22	Reggie Germany	.30	.10
❑ 23	Peerless Price	.50	.20
❑ 24	Chris Weinke	.50	.20
❑ 25	Lamar Smith	.50	.20
❑ 26	Nick Goings	.30	.10
❑ 27	Muhsin Muhammad	.50	.20
❑ 28	Isaac Byrd	.30	.10
❑ 29	Wesley Walls	.30	.10
❑ 30	Jim Miller	.30	.10
❑ 31	Anthony Thomas	.50	.20
❑ 32	Dez White	.30	.10
❑ 33	David Terrell	.75	.30
❑ 34	Marty Booker	.50	.20
❑ 35	Brian Urlacher	1.25	.50
❑ 36	Jon Kitna	.50	.20
❑ 37	Corey Dillon	.50	.20
❑ 38	Peter Warrick	.50	.20
❑ 39	Darnay Scott	.30	.10
❑ 40	Chad Johnson	.75	.30
❑ 41	Tim Couch	.50	.20
❑ 42	James Jackson	.30	.10
❑ 43	JaJuan Dawson	.30	.10
❑ 44	Kevin Johnson	.50	.20
❑ 45	Quincy Morgan	.30	.10
❑ 46	Courtney Brown	.50	.20
❑ 47	Quincy Carter	.50	.20
❑ 48	Emmitt Smith	2.00	.75
❑ 49	Joey Galloway	.50	.20
❑ 50	Rocket Ismail	.50	.20
❑ 51	Ken-Yon Rambo	.30	.10
❑ 52	Brian Griese	.75	.30
❑ 53	Terrell Davis	.75	.30
❑ 54	Mike Anderson	.75	.30
❑ 55	Shannon Sharpe	.50	.20
❑ 56	Ed McCaffrey	.75	.30
❑ 57	Rod Smith	.50	.20
❑ 58	Mike McMahon	.75	.30
❑ 59	James Stewart	.50	.20
❑ 60	Az-Zahir Hakim	.30	.10
❑ 61	Desmond Howard	.30	.10
❑ 62	Germane Crowell	.30	.10
❑ 63	Brett Favre	2.00	.75
❑ 64	Ahman Green	.75	.30
❑ 65	Antonio Freeman	.75	.30
❑ 66	Terry Glenn	.50	.20
❑ 67	Kabeer Gbaja-Biamila	.50	.20
❑ 68	Kent Graham	.30	.10
❑ 69	James Allen	.50	.20
❑ 70	Corey Bradford	.30	.10
❑ 71	Jermaine Lewis	.30	.10
❑ 72	Jamie Sharper	.30	.10
❑ 73	Peyton Manning	1.50	.60
❑ 74	Edgerrin James	1.00	.40
❑ 75	Dominic Rhodes	.50	.20
❑ 76	Marvin Harrison	.75	.30
❑ 77	Qadry Ismail	.50	.20
❑ 78	Mark Brunell	.75	.30
❑ 79	Fred Taylor	.75	.30
❑ 80	Stacey Mack	.30	.10
❑ 81	Jimmy Smith	.50	.20
❑ 82	Keenan McCardell	.30	.10
❑ 83	Trent Green	.50	.20
❑ 84	Priest Holmes	1.00	.40
❑ 85	Derrick Alexander	.50	.20
❑ 86	Johnnie Morton	.50	.20
❑ 87	Snoop Minnis	.30	.10
❑ 88	Tony Gonzalez	.50	.20
❑ 89	Jay Fiedler	.50	.20
❑ 90	Ricky Williams	2.50	1.00
❑ 91	Chris Chambers	.75	.30
❑ 92	Oronde Gadsden	.30	.10
❑ 93	Zach Thomas	.75	.30
❑ 94	Daunte Culpepper	.75	.30
❑ 95	Michael Bennett	.50	.20
❑ 96	Randy Moss	1.50	.60
❑ 97	Sean Dawkins	.30	.10
❑ 98	Tom Brady	2.00	.75
❑ 99	Antowain Smith	.50	.20
❑ 100	David Patten	.30	.10
❑ 101	Troy Brown	.50	.20
❑ 102	Adam Vinatieri	.75	.30
❑ 103	Aaron Brooks	.75	.30
❑ 104	Deuce McAllister	1.00	.40
❑ 105	Jake Reed	.50	.20
❑ 106	Jerome Pathon	.50	.20
❑ 107	Joe Horn	.50	.20
❑ 108	Kyle Turley	.30	.10
❑ 109	Kerry Collins	.50	.20
❑ 110	Ron Dayne	.50	.20
❑ 111	Tiki Barber	.75	.30
❑ 112	Amani Toomer	.50	.20
❑ 113	Ike Hilliard	.50	.20
❑ 114	Michael Strahan	.50	.20
❑ 115	Vinny Testaverde	.50	.20
❑ 116	Chad Pennington	1.00	.40
❑ 117	Curtis Martin	.75	.30
❑ 118	Santana Moss	.75	.30
❑ 119	Laveranues Coles	.50	.20
❑ 120	Wayne Chrebet	.50	.20
❑ 121	Rich Gannon	.75	.30
❑ 122	Charlie Garner	.50	.20
❑ 123	Jerry Rice	1.50	.60
❑ 124	Tim Brown	.75	.30
❑ 125	Charles Woodson	.50	.20
❑ 126	Donovan McNabb	1.00	.40
❑ 127	Duce Staley	.75	.30
❑ 128	Correll Buckhalter	.50	.20
❑ 129	Freddie Mitchell	.50	.20
❑ 130	James Thrash	.50	.20
❑ 131	Todd Pinkston	.50	.20
❑ 132	Kordell Stewart	.50	.20
❑ 133	Jerome Bettis	.75	.30
❑ 134	Chris Fuamatu-Ma'afala	.30	.10
❑ 135	Hines Ward	.75	.30
❑ 136	Plaxico Burress	.50	.20
❑ 137	Kendrell Bell	.75	.30
❑ 138	Doug Flutie	.75	.30
❑ 139	Drew Brees	.75	.30
❑ 140	LaDainian Tomlinson	1.25	.50
❑ 141	Curtis Conway	.30	.10
❑ 142	Tim Dwight	.50	.20
❑ 143	Junior Seau	.75	.30
❑ 144	Jeff Garcia	.75	.30
❑ 145	Garrison Hearst	.50	.20
❑ 146	Kevan Barlow	.50	.20
❑ 147	Terrell Owens	.75	.30
❑ 148	J.J. Stokes	.50	.20
❑ 149	Trent Dilfer	.50	.20
❑ 150	Shaun Alexander	1.00	.40

❑ 151 Ricky Watters .50 .20
❑ 152 Bobby Engram .30 .10
❑ 153 Koren Robinson .50 .20
❑ 154 Kurt Warner .75 .30
❑ 155 Marshall Faulk .75 .30
❑ 156 Isaac Bruce .75 .30
❑ 157 Ricky Proehl .30 .10
❑ 158 Terrence Wilkins .30 .10
❑ 159 Torry Holt .75 .30
❑ 160 Brad Johnson .50 .20
❑ 161 Shaun King .30 .10
❑ 162 Rob Johnson .50 .20
❑ 163 Mike Alstott .75 .30
❑ 164 Michael Pittman .30 .10
❑ 165 Keyshawn Johnson .75 .30
❑ 166 Steve McNair .75 .30
❑ 167 Eddie George .75 .30
❑ 168 Derrick Mason .50 .20
❑ 169 Kevin Dyson .50 .20
❑ 170 Frank Wycheck .30 .10
❑ 171 Jevon Kearse .50 .20
❑ 172 Danny Wuerffel .50 .20
❑ 173 Stephen Davis .50 .20
❑ 174 Michael Westbrook .30 .10
❑ 175 Rod Gardner .50 .20
❑ 176 Champ Bailey .50 .20
❑ 177 Darrell Green .30 .10
❑ 178 Kurt Warner CL .50 .20
❑ 179 Brett Favre CL 1.00 .40
❑ 180 Randy Moss CL .75 .30
❑ 181 David Boston SS 4.00 1.50
❑ 182 Jake Plummer SS 2.50 1.00
❑ 183 Michael Vick SS 12.00 5.00
❑ 184 Drew Bledsoe SS 5.00 2.00
❑ 185 Anthony Thomas SS 2.50 1.00
❑ 186 Tim Couch SS 2.50 1.00
❑ 187 Emmitt Smith SS 10.00 4.00
❑ 188 Ahman Green SS 4.00 1.50
❑ 189 Brett Favre SS 10.00 4.00
❑ 190 Edgerrin James SS 5.00 2.00
❑ 191 Peyton Manning SS 8.00 3.00
❑ 192 Mark Brunell SS 4.00 1.50
❑ 193 Daunte Culpepper SS 4.00 1.50
❑ 194 Randy Moss SS 8.00 3.00
❑ 195 Tom Brady SS 10.00 4.00
❑ 196 Aaron Brooks SS 4.00 1.50
❑ 197 Ricky Williams SS 4.00 1.50
❑ 198 Curtis Martin SS 4.00 1.50
❑ 199 Jerry Rice SS 8.00 3.00
❑ 200 Donovan McNabb SS 5.00 2.00
❑ 201 Jerome Bettis SS 4.00 1.50
❑ 202 Kordell Stewart SS 2.50 1.00
❑ 203 LaDainian Tomlinson SS 6.00 2.50
❑ 204 Jeff Garcia SS 4.00 1.50
❑ 205 Terrell Owens SS 4.00 1.50
❑ 206 Shaun Alexander SS 5.00 2.00
❑ 207 Kurt Warner SS 4.00 1.50
❑ 208 Marshall Faulk SS 4.00 1.50
❑ 209 Keyshawn Johnson SS 4.00 1.50
❑ 210 Steve McNair SS 4.00 1.50
❑ 211 Damien Anderson RC 5.00 2.00
❑ 212 Jason McAddley RC 5.00 2.00
❑ 213 Josh McCown RC 8.00 3.00
❑ 214 Josh Scobey RC 4.00 1.50
❑ 215 Preston Parsons RC 3.00 1.25
❑ 216 Dusty Bonner RC 3.00 1.25
❑ 217 Kahlil Hill RC 5.00 2.00
❑ 218 Kurt Kittner RC 5.00 2.00
❑ 219 T.J. Duckett RC 10.00 4.00
❑ 220 Chester Taylor RC 6.00 2.50
❑ 221 Kalimba Edwards RC 6.00 2.50
❑ 223 Ron Johnson RC 5.00 2.00
❑ 224 Tellis Redmon RC 5.00 2.00
❑ 225 Wes Pate RC 3.00 1.25
❑ 226 David Priestley RC 5.00 2.00
❑ 227 Josh Reed RC 6.00 2.50
❑ 228 Mike Williams RC 5.00 2.00
❑ 229 Ryan Denney RC 5.00 2.00
❑ 230 DeShaun Foster RC 6.00 2.50
❑ 231 Julius Peppers RC 12.00 5.00
❑ 232 Randy Fasani RC 5.00 2.00
❑ 233 Adrian Peterson RC 6.00 2.50
❑ 234 Alex Brown RC 6.00 2.50
❑ 235 Gavin Hoffman RC 3.00 1.25
❑ 236 Levi Jones RC 5.00 2.00
❑ 237 Andra Davis RC 5.00 2.00
❑ 238 Andre Davis RC 5.00 2.00
❑ 239 William Green RC 6.00 2.50
❑ 240 Antonio Bryant RC 6.00 2.50
❑ 241 Chad Hutchinson RC 5.00 2.00
❑ 242 Roy Williams RC 15.00 6.00
❑ 243 Woody Dantzler RC 5.00 2.00
❑ 244 Ashley Lelie RC 12.00 5.00
❑ 245 Clinton Portis RC 20.00 7.50
❑ 246 Lamont Thompson RC 5.00 2.00
❑ 247 James Mungro RC 6.00 2.50
❑ 248 Joey Harrington RC 15.00 6.00
❑ 249 Luke Staley RC 5.00 2.00
❑ 250 Craig Nall RC 6.00 2.50
❑ 251 Javon Walker RC 12.00 5.00
❑ 252 Najeh Davenport RC 6.00 2.50
❑ 253 David Carr RC 15.00 6.00
❑ 254 Saleem Rasheed RC 6.00 2.50
❑ 255 Mike Rumph RC 6.00 2.50
❑ 256 Jabar Gaffney RC 6.00 2.50
❑ 257 Jonathan Wells RC 6.00 2.50
❑ 258 Dwight Freeney RC 8.00 3.00
❑ 259 Larry Tripplett RC 3.00 1.25
❑ 260 David Garrard RC 6.00 2.50
❑ 261 John Henderson RC 6.00 2.50
❑ 262 Ryan Sims RC 6.00 2.50
❑ 263 Leonard Henry RC 5.00 2.00
❑ 264 Brian Allen RC 5.00 2.00
❑ 265 Atrews Bell RC 3.00 1.25
❑ 266 Bryant McKinnie RC 5.00 2.00
❑ 267 Kelly Campbell RC 5.00 2.00
❑ 268 Raonall Smith RC 5.00 2.00
❑ 269 Antwoine Womack RC 5.00 2.00
❑ 270 Daniel Graham RC 6.00 2.50
❑ 271 Deion Branch RC 12.00 5.00
❑ 272 Sam Simmons RC 3.00 1.25
❑ 273 Rohan Davey RC 6.00 2.50
❑ 274 Charles Grant RC 6.00 2.50
❑ 275 Derrick Lewis RC 3.00 1.25
❑ 276 Donte Stallworth RC 12.00 5.00
❑ 277 J.T. O'Sullivan RC 5.00 2.00
❑ 278 Keyuo Craver RC 5.00 2.00
❑ 279 Ricky Williams RC 5.00 2.00
❑ 280 Bryan Thomas RC 5.00 2.00
❑ 281 Jeremy Shockey RC 20.00 7.50
❑ 282 Tim Carter RC 5.00 2.00
❑ 283 Larry Ned RC 2.50 1.00
❑ 284 Napoleon Harris RC 4.00 1.50
❑ 285 Phillip Buchanon RC 6.00 2.50
❑ 286 Ronald Curry RC 6.00 2.50
❑ 287 Brian Westbrook RC 10.00 4.00
❑ 288 Freddie Milons RC 5.00 2.00
❑ 289 Lito Sheppard RC 6.00 2.50
❑ 290 Antwaan Randle El RC 10.00 4.00
❑ 291 Lee Mays RC 2.50 1.00
❑ 292 Daryl Jones RC 5.00 2.00
❑ 293 Justin Peelle RC 3.00 1.25
❑ 294 Quentin Jammer RC 4.00 1.50
❑ 295 Reche Caldwell RC 6.00 2.50
❑ 296 Seth Burford RC 5.00 2.00
❑ 297 Terry Charles RC 5.00 2.00
❑ 298 Brandon Doman RC 5.00 2.00
❑ 299 Maurice Morris RC 6.00 2.50
❑ 300 Eric Crouch RC 6.00 2.50
❑ 301 Lamar Gordon RC 6.00 2.50
❑ 302 Marquise Walker RC 5.00 2.00
❑ 303 Tracey Wistrom RC 5.00 2.00
❑ 304 Travis Stephens RC 5.00 2.00
❑ 305 Herb Haygood RC 3.00 1.25
❑ 306 Albert Haynesworth RC 5.00 2.00
❑ 307 Rocky Calmus RC 6.00 2.50
❑ 308 Cliff Russell RC 5.00 2.00
❑ 309 Ladell Betts RC 6.00 2.50
❑ 310A Patrick Ramsey RC 8.00 3.00
❑ 310B Ed Reed RC 10.00 4.00

2003 Upper Deck

❑ COMP.SET w/o SP's (180) 25.00 10.00
❑ 1 Brad Johnson .50 .20
❑ 2 Derrick Brooks .50 .20
❑ 3 Simeon Rice .50 .20
❑ 4 Warren Sapp .50 .20
❑ 5 Thomas Jones .50 .20
❑ 6 Mike Alstott .75 .30
❑ 7 Michael Pittman .30 .10
❑ 8 Tim Brown .75 .30
❑ 9 Rich Gannon .50 .20
❑ 10 Charlie Garner .50 .20
❑ 11 Jerry Porter .50 .20
❑ 12 Phillip Buchanon .30 .10
❑ 13 Charles Woodson .50 .20
❑ 14 James Thrash .30 .10
❑ 15 Duce Staley .50 .20
❑ 16 Brian Westbrook .50 .20
❑ 17 Correll Buckhalter .50 .20
❑ 18 Koy Detmer .30 .10
❑ 19 Brian Dawkins .50 .20
❑ 20 Jon Ritchie .30 .10
❑ 21 Ahman Green .75 .30
❑ 22 Donald Driver .50 .20
❑ 23 Bubba Franks .50 .20
❑ 24 Javon Walker .50 .20
❑ 25 Kabeer Gbaja-Biamila .50 .20
❑ 26 Robert Ferguson .30 .10
❑ 27 Eddie George .50 .20
❑ 28 Jevon Kearse .50 .20
❑ 29 Billy Volek .75 .30
❑ 30 Frank Wycheck .30 .10
❑ 31 Derrick Mason .50 .20
❑ 32 Tommy Maddox .75 .30
❑ 33 Jerome Bettis .75 .30
❑ 34 Antwaan Randle El .75 .30
❑ 35 Amos Zereoue .50 .20
❑ 36 Hines Ward .75 .30
❑ 37 Jeff Garcia .75 .30
❑ 38 Terrell Owens .75 .30
❑ 39 Tim Rattay .50 .20
❑ 40 Brandon Doman .30 .10
❑ 41 Tai Streets .30 .10
❑ 42 Garrison Hearst .50 .20
❑ 43 Kerry Collins .50 .20
❑ 44 Tiki Barber .75 .30
❑ 45 Amani Toomer .50 .20
❑ 46 Jesse Palmer .30 .10
❑ 47 Tim Carter .30 .10
❑ 48 Michael Strahan .50 .20
❑ 49 Ike Hilliard .30 .10
❑ 50 Marvin Harrison .75 .30
❑ 51 Peyton Manning 1.25 .50
❑ 52 Marcus Pollard .30 .10
❑ 53 James Mungro .30 .10
❑ 54 Reggie Wayne .50 .20
❑ 55 Peerless Price .50 .20
❑ 56 Warrick Dunn .50 .20
❑ 57 T.J. Duckett .50 .20
❑ 58 Keith Brooking .30 .10
❑ 59 Doug Johnson .30 .10
❑ 60 Brian Finneran .30 .10
❑ 61 Chad Pennington 1.00 .40
❑ 62 Curtis Martin .75 .30
❑ 63 Marvin Jones .30 .10
❑ 64 Wayne Chrebet .50 .20
❑ 65 LaMont Jordan .75 .30
❑ 66 Curtis Conway .30 .10
❑ 67 Vinny Testaverde .50 .20
❑ 68 Tim Couch .30 .10
❑ 69 William Green .50 .20
❑ 70 Andre Davis .30 .10
❑ 71 Quincy Morgan .50 .20
❑ 72 Dennis Northcutt .50 .20
❑ 73 Kelly Holcomb .50 .20
❑ 74 Jake Plummer .50 .20
❑ 75 Mike Anderson .75 .30
❑ 76 Ashley Lelie .75 .30
❑ 77 Ed McCaffrey .75 .30
❑ 78 Shannon Sharpe .30 .10
❑ 79 Rod Smith .50 .20
❑ 80 Terrell Davis .75 .30
❑ 81 Antowain Smith .50 .20

❑ 82 Kevin Faulk	.30	.10
❑ 83 David Patten	.30	.10
❑ 84 Deion Branch	.75	.30
❑ 85 Troy Brown	.50	.20
❑ 86 Rohan Davey	.50	.20
❑ 87 Jay Fiedler	.50	.20
❑ 88 Randy McMichael	.50	.20
❑ 89 Derrius Thompson	.30	.10
❑ 90 Jason Taylor	.30	.10
❑ 91 Zach Thomas	.75	.30
❑ 92 Ricky Williams	.75	.30
❑ 93 Deuce McAllister	.75	.30
❑ 94 Donte Stallworth	.75	.30
❑ 95 Jerome Pathon	.30	.10
❑ 96 Michael Lewis	.30	.10
❑ 97 Joe Horn	.50	.20
❑ 98 Priest Holmes	1.00	.40
❑ 99 Johnnie Morton	.50	.20
❑ 100 Eddie Kennison	.30	.10
❑ 101 Dante Hall	.75	.30
❑ 102 Tony Gonzalez	.50	.20
❑ 103 Marc Boerigter	.50	.20
❑ 104 Drew Brees	.75	.30
❑ 105 David Boston	.50	.20
❑ 106 Reche Caldwell	.30	.10
❑ 107 Tim Dwight	.50	.20
❑ 108 Doug Flutie	.75	.30
❑ 109 Drew Bledsoe	.75	.30
❑ 110 Eric Moulds	.50	.20
❑ 111 Alex Van Pelt	.30	.10
❑ 112 Charles Johnson	.30	.10
❑ 113 Takeo Spikes	.30	.10
❑ 114 Josh Reed	.50	.20
❑ 115 Ladell Betts	.50	.20
❑ 116 Laveranues Coles	.50	.20
❑ 117 Champ Bailey	.50	.20
❑ 118 Trung Canidate	.50	.20
❑ 119 Kenny Watson	.30	.10
❑ 120 Rod Gardner	.50	.20
❑ 121 Kurt Warner	.75	.30
❑ 122 Lamar Gordon	.30	.10
❑ 123 Shaun McDonald RC	.75	.30
❑ 124 Marc Bulger	.75	.30
❑ 125 Isaac Bruce	.75	.30
❑ 126 Torry Holt	.75	.30
❑ 127 Matt Hasselbeck	.50	.20
❑ 128 Maurice Morris	.30	.10
❑ 129 Bobby Engram	.30	.10
❑ 130 Darrell Jackson	.50	.20
❑ 131 Koren Robinson	.50	.20
❑ 132 Chris Redman	.30	.10
❑ 133 Todd Heap	.50	.20
❑ 134 Travis Taylor	.50	.20
❑ 135 Ron Johnson	.30	.10
❑ 136 Ray Lewis	.75	.30
❑ 137 Jake Delhomme	.75	.30
❑ 138 Muhsin Muhammad	.50	.20
❑ 139 Stephen Davis	.50	.20
❑ 140 Julius Peppers	.75	.30
❑ 141 Rodney Peete	.30	.10
❑ 142 Mark Brunell	.50	.20
❑ 143 Jimmy Smith	.50	.20
❑ 144 Kyle Brady	.30	.10
❑ 145 Kevin Lockett	.30	.10
❑ 146 David Garrard	.30	.10
❑ 147 Fred Taylor	.75	.30
❑ 148 Michael Bennett	.50	.20
❑ 149 Ronald Bellamy RC	1.00	.40
❑ 150 Randy Moss	1.25	.50
❑ 151 D'Wayne Bates	.30	.10
❑ 152 Josh McCown	.50	.20
❑ 153 Marquise Walker	.30	.10
❑ 154 Jeff Blake	.30	.10
❑ 155 Freddie Jones	.30	.10
❑ 156 Marcel Shipp	.50	.20
❑ 157 Troy Hambrick	.30	.10
❑ 158 Joey Galloway	.50	.20
❑ 159 Terry Glenn	.30	.10
❑ 160 Roy Williams	.75	.30
❑ 161 Antonio Bryant	.50	.20
❑ 162 Quincy Carter	.50	.20
❑ 163 Anthony Thomas	.50	.20
❑ 164 Marty Booker	.50	.20
❑ 165 Dez White	.30	.10
❑ 166 Adrian Peterson	.30	.10
❑ 167 Kordell Stewart	.50	.20
❑ 168 David Terrell	.50	.20
❑ 169 Jabar Gaffney	.50	.20
❑ 170 Bennie Joppru RC	1.00	.40
❑ 171 Corey Bradford	.30	.10
❑ 172 David Carr	1.25	.50
❑ 173 James Stewart	.50	.20
❑ 174 Ty Detmer	.30	.10
❑ 175 Az-Zahir Hakim	.30	.10
❑ 176 Bill Schroeder	.50	.20
❑ 177 Jon Kitna	.50	.20
❑ 178 Chad Johnson	.75	.30
❑ 179 Ron Dugans	.30	.10
❑ 180 Peter Warrick	.50	.20
❑ 181 Brett Favre SS	10.00	4.00
❑ 182 Emmitt Smith SS	12.00	5.00
❑ 183 LaDainian Tomlinson SS	5.00	2.00
❑ 184 Joey Harrington SS	8.00	3.00
❑ 185 Brian Urlacher SS	8.00	3.00
❑ 186 Daunte Culpepper SS	5.00	2.00
❑ 187 Jamal Lewis SS	5.00	2.00
❑ 188 Shaun Alexander SS	5.00	2.00
❑ 189 Marshall Faulk SS	5.00	2.00
❑ 190 Travis Henry SS	4.00	1.50
❑ 191 Trent Green SS	4.00	1.50
❑ 192 Aaron Brooks SS	5.00	2.00
❑ 193 Chris Chambers SS	5.00	2.00
❑ 194 Tom Brady SS	10.00	4.00
❑ 195 Clinton Portis SS	8.00	3.00
❑ 196 Kevin Johnson SS	4.00	1.50
❑ 197 Santana Moss SS	4.00	1.50
❑ 198 Michael Vick SS	12.00	5.00
❑ 199 Edgerrin James SS	.75	.30
❑ 200 Jeremy Shockey SS	8.00	3.00
❑ 201 Kevan Barlow SS	4.00	1.50
❑ 202 Plaxico Burress SS	4.00	1.50
❑ 203 Steve McNair SS	5.00	2.00
❑ 204 Donovan McNabb SS	6.00	2.50
❑ 205 Jerry Rice SS	10.00	4.00
❑ 206 Keyshawn Johnson SS	5.00	2.00
❑ 207 Patrick Ramsey SS	5.00	2.00
❑ 208 Stephen Davis SS	4.00	1.50
❑ 209 Corey Dillon SS	4.00	1.50
❑ 210 Chad Hutchinson SS	4.00	1.50
❑ 211 Brad Banks RC	4.00	1.50
❑ 212 Kliff Kingsbury RC	4.00	1.50
❑ 213 Jason Gesser RC	5.00	2.00
❑ 214 Jason Johnson RC	3.00	1.25
❑ 215 Brian St.Pierre RC	5.00	2.00
❑ 216 Ken Dorsey RC	5.00	2.00
❑ 217 Seneca Wallace RC	5.00	2.00
❑ 218 Brooks Bollinger RC	5.00	2.00
❑ 219 Chris Brown RC	6.00	2.50
❑ 220 B.J Askew RC	5.00	2.00
❑ 221 Earnest Graham RC	4.00	1.50
❑ 222 Quentin Griffin RC	5.00	2.00
❑ 223 Musa Smith RC	5.00	2.00
❑ 224 Artose Pinner RC	5.00	2.00
❑ 225 Domanick Davis RC	8.00	3.00
❑ 226 Anquan Boldin RC	12.00	5.00
❑ 227 Talman Gardner RC	5.00	2.00
❑ 228 Brandon Lloyd RC	6.00	2.50
❑ 229 Bryant Johnson RC	5.00	2.00
❑ 230 Kareem Kelly RC	4.00	1.50
❑ 231 Arnaz Battle RC	5.00	2.00
❑ 232 Keenan Howry RC	5.00	2.00
❑ 233 Justin Gage RC	5.00	2.00
❑ 234 Tyrone Calico RC	8.00	3.00
❑ 235 Teyo Johnson RC	5.00	2.00
❑ 236 Malaefou MacKenzie RC	3.00	1.25
❑ 237 Terence Newman RC	10.00	5.00
❑ 238 Marcus Trufant RC	5.00	2.00
❑ 239 Mike Doss RC	5.00	2.00
❑ 240 Terrell Suggs RC	8.00	3.00
❑ 241 Carson Palmer RC	30.00	12.50
❑ 242 Byron Leftwich RC	25.00	10.00
❑ 243 Rex Grossman RC	12.00	5.00
❑ 244 Kyle Boller RC	15.00	6.00
❑ 245 Dave Ragone RC	8.00	3.00
❑ 246 Chris Simms RC	12.00	5.00
❑ 247 Larry Johnson RC	30.00	15.00
❑ 248 Lee Suggs RC	15.00	6.00
❑ 249 Justin Fargas RC	8.00	3.00
❑ 250 Onterrio Smith RC	8.00	3.00
❑ 251 Willis McGahee RC	20.00	7.50
❑ 252 Charles Rogers RC	5.00	2.00
❑ 253 Andre Johnson RC	15.00	6.00
❑ 254 Taylor Jacobs RC	8.00	3.00
❑ 255 Kelley Washington RC	8.00	3.00
❑ 256 Tony Romo RC	6.00	2.50
❑ 257 Jerel Myers RC	4.00	1.50
❑ 258 Kirk Farmer RC	4.00	1.50
❑ 259 Kevin Walter RC	5.00	2.00
❑ 260 Gibran Hamdan RC	4.00	1.50
❑ 261 Juston Wood RC	4.00	1.50
❑ 262 Travis Anglin RC	4.00	1.50
❑ 263 Marquel Blackwell RC	4.00	1.50
❑ 264 Jason Thomas RC	5.00	2.00
❑ 265 Carl Ford RC	4.00	1.50
❑ 266 Walter Young RC	4.00	1.50
❑ 267 Sultan McCullough RC	5.00	2.00
❑ 268 Dahrran Diedrick RC	6.00	2.50
❑ 269 Cecil Sapp RC	5.00	2.00
❑ 270 Doug Gabriel RC	6.00	2.50
❑ 271 LaBrandon Toefield RC	6.00	2.50
❑ 272 Adrian Madise RC	5.00	2.00
❑ 273 J.R. Tolver RC	5.00	2.00
❑ 274 Kevin Curtis RC	6.00	2.50
❑ 275 Bobby Wade RC	6.00	2.50
❑ 276 Sam Aiken RC	5.00	2.00
❑ 277 Mike Bush RC	4.00	1.50
❑ 278 Billy McMullen RC	5.00	2.00
❑ 279 Bethel Johnson RC	5.00	2.00
❑ 280 David Kircus RC	5.00	2.00
❑ 281 Zuriel Smith RC	4.00	1.50
❑ 282 LaTarence Dunbar RC	5.00	2.00
❑ 283 Nate Burleson RC	8.00	3.00
❑ 284 Antwone Savage RC	4.00	1.50
❑ 285 Terrence Edwards RC	5.00	2.00

2004 Upper Deck

❑ COMPLETE SET (275) 135.00 75.00
❑ COMP.SET w/o SP's (250) 60.00 30.00
❑ COMP.SET w/o RC's (200) 25.00 10.00
❑ 201-225 ROOKIE STATED ODDS 1:8
❑ 226-275 ROOKIE STATED ODDS 1:1
❑ UNPRICED PRINT PLATE PRINT RUN 1 SET

❑ 1 Anquan Boldin	.75	.30
❑ 2 Josh McCown	.50	.20
❑ 3 Emmitt Smith	1.50	.60
❑ 4 Freddie Jones	.30	.10
❑ 5 Marcel Shipp	.50	.20
❑ 6 Shaun King	.30	.10
❑ 7 Michael Vick	1.50	.60
❑ 8 T.J. Duckett	.50	.20
❑ 9 Peerless Price	.50	.20
❑ 10 Warrick Dunn	.50	.20
❑ 11 Keith Brooking	.30	.10
❑ 12 Brian Finneran	.30	.10
❑ 13 Anthony Wright	.30	.10
❑ 14 Kyle Boller	.75	.30
❑ 15 Jamal Lewis	.75	.30
❑ 16 Todd Heap	.50	.20
❑ 17 Ray Lewis	.75	.30
❑ 18 Terrell Suggs	.50	.20
❑ 19 Travis Taylor	.30	.10
❑ 20 Drew Bledsoe	.75	.30
❑ 21 Willis McGahee	.75	.30
❑ 22 Eric Moulds	.50	.20
❑ 23 Travis Henry	.50	.20
❑ 24 Takeo Spikes	.30	.10
❑ 25 Josh Reed	.30	.10
❑ 26 Lawyer Milloy	.50	.20
❑ 27 Stephen Davis	.50	.20
❑ 28 Jake Delhomme	.75	.30
❑ 29 Steve Smith	.75	.30
❑ 30 DeShaun Foster	.50	.20

❑ 31 Dan Morgan .30 .10
❑ 32 Julius Peppers .75 .30
❑ 33 Rod Smart .30 .10
❑ 34 Rex Grossman .75 .30
❑ 35 Thomas Jones .50 .20
❑ 36 Marty Booker .50 .20
❑ 37 Anthony Thomas .50 .20
❑ 38 Brian Urlacher 1.00 .40
❑ 39 Justin Gage .50 .20
❑ 40 Chad Johnson .75 .30
❑ 41 Carson Palmer 1.00 .40
❑ 42 Peter Warrick .50 .20
❑ 43 Jon Kitna .50 .20
❑ 44 Kelley Washington .30 .10
❑ 45 Rudi Johnson .50 .20
❑ 46 Jeff Garcia .75 .30
❑ 47 Dennis Northcutt .30 .10
❑ 48 Lee Suggs .75 .30
❑ 49 Andre Davis .30 .10
❑ 50 Quincy Morgan .50 .20
❑ 51 Kelly Holcomb .50 .20
❑ 52 Keyshawn Johnson .50 .20
❑ 53 Quincy Carter .50 .20
❑ 54 Antonio Bryant .50 .20
❑ 55 Terry Glenn .30 .10
❑ 56 Terence Newman .50 .20
❑ 57 Roy Williams S .50 .20
❑ 58 Champ Bailey .50 .20
❑ 59 Jake Plummer .50 .20
❑ 60 Quentin Griffin .75 .30
❑ 61 John Lynch .50 .20
❑ 62 Rod Smith .50 .20
❑ 63 Ashley Lelie .50 .20
❑ 64 Joey Harrington .75 .30
❑ 65 Az-Zahir Hakim .30 .10
❑ 66 Charles Rogers .50 .20
❑ 67 Tai Streets .30 .10
❑ 68 Shawn Bryson .30 .10
❑ 69 Artose Pinner .30 .10
❑ 70 Brett Favre 2.00 .75
❑ 71 Nick Barnett .50 .20
❑ 72 Ahman Green .75 .30
❑ 73 Kabeer Gbaja-Biamila .50 .20
❑ 74 Javon Walker .50 .20
❑ 75 Donald Driver .50 .20
❑ 76 Tim Couch .30 .10
❑ 77 David Carr .75 .30
❑ 78 Corey Bradford .30 .10
❑ 79 J.J. Moses .30 .10
❑ 80 Domanick Davis .75 .30
❑ 81 Jabar Gaffney .50 .20
❑ 82 Andre Johnson .75 .30
❑ 83 Marvin Harrison .75 .30
❑ 84 Peyton Manning 1.25 .50
❑ 85 Dallas Clark .50 .20
❑ 86 Edgerrin James .75 .30
❑ 87 Reggie Wayne .50 .20
❑ 88 Dwight Freeney .50 .20
❑ 89 Byron Leftwich 1.00 .40
❑ 90 LaBrandon Toefield .30 .10
❑ 91 Fred Taylor .50 .20
❑ 92 Troy Edwards .30 .10
❑ 93 Jimmy Smith .50 .20
❑ 94 Kyle Brady .30 .10
❑ 95 Trent Green .50 .20
❑ 96 Tony Gonzalez .50 .20
❑ 97 Dante Hall .75 .30
❑ 98 Priest Holmes 1.00 .40
❑ 99 Eddie Kennison .30 .10
❑ 100 Johnnie Morton .50 .20
❑ 101 Jay Fiedler .30 .10
❑ 102 Junior Seau .75 .30
❑ 103 Ricky Williams .75 .30
❑ 104 Chris Chambers .50 .20
❑ 105 Zach Thomas .75 .30
❑ 106 David Boston .50 .20
❑ 107 A.J. Feeley .75 .30
❑ 108 Daunte Culpepper .75 .30
❑ 109 Onterrio Smith .50 .20
❑ 110 Randy Moss 1.00 .40
❑ 111 Moe Williams .30 .10
❑ 112 Michael Bennett .50 .20
❑ 113 Jim Kleinsasser .30 .10
❑ 114 Tom Brady 2.00 .75
❑ 115 Kevin Faulk .30 .10
❑ 116 Deion Branch .75 .30
❑ 117 Corey Dillon .50 .20
❑ 118 Troy Brown .50 .20
❑ 119 Adam Vinatieri .75 .30
❑ 120 Tedy Bruschi .50 .20
❑ 121 Aaron Brooks .50 .20
❑ 122 Deuce McAllister .75 .30
❑ 123 Donte' Stallworth .50 .20
❑ 124 Joe Horn .50 .20
❑ 125 Jerome Pathon .30 .10
❑ 126 Boo Williams .30 .10
❑ 127 Jeremy Shockey .75 .30
❑ 128 Kurt Warner .75 .30
❑ 129 Amani Toomer .50 .20
❑ 130 Tiki Barber .75 .30
❑ 131 Ike Hilliard .30 .10
❑ 132 Michael Strahan .50 .20
❑ 133 Chad Pennington .75 .30
❑ 134 Santana Moss .50 .20
❑ 135 Wayne Chrebet .50 .20
❑ 136 Curtis Martin .75 .30
❑ 137 LaMont Jordan
❑ 138 Justin McCareins .30 .10
❑ 139 Jerry Rice 1.50 .60
❑ 140 Rich Gannon .50 .20
❑ 141 Tim Brown .75 .30
❑ 142 Jerry Porter .50 .20
❑ 143 Warren Sapp .50 .20
❑ 144 Charles Woodson .50 .20
❑ 145 Donovan McNabb 1.00 .40
❑ 146 Brian Westbrook .50 .20
❑ 147 Todd Pinkston .30 .10
❑ 148 Jevon Kearse .50 .20
❑ 149 Freddie Mitchell .50 .20
❑ 150 Correll Buckhalter .50 .20
❑ 151 Terrell Owens .75 .30
❑ 152 Tommy Maddox .50 .20
❑ 153 Duce Staley .50 .20
❑ 154 Plaxico Burress .50 .20
❑ 155 Hines Ward .75 .30
❑ 156 Antwaan Randle El .75 .30
❑ 157 Jerome Bettis .75 .30
❑ 158 Kendrell Bell .50 .20
❑ 159 LaDainian Tomlinson 1.00 .40
❑ 160 Doug Flutie .75 .30
❑ 161 Quentin Jammer .30 .10
❑ 162 Drew Brees .75 .30
❑ 163 Reche Caldwell .30 .10
❑ 164 Tim Dwight .50 .20
❑ 165 Tim Rattay .30 .10
❑ 166 Kevan Barlow .50 .20
❑ 167 Brandon Lloyd .50 .20
❑ 168 Cedrick Wilson .30 .10
❑ 169 Julian Peterson .30 .10
❑ 170 Ahmed Plummer .30 .10
❑ 171 Matt Hasselbeck .50 .20
❑ 172 Koren Robinson .50 .20
❑ 173 Shaun Alexander .75 .30
❑ 174 Darrell Jackson .50 .20
❑ 175 Marcus Trufant .30 .10
❑ 176 Bobby Engram .30 .10
❑ 177 Marc Bulger .75 .30
❑ 178 Torry Holt .75 .30
❑ 179 Marshall Faulk .75 .30
❑ 180 Orlando Pace .30 .10
❑ 181 Isaac Bruce .50 .20
❑ 182 Kyle Turley .30 .10
❑ 183 Brad Johnson .50 .20
❑ 184 Charlie Garner .50 .20
❑ 185 Keenan McCardell .30 .10
❑ 186 Mike Alstott .50 .20
❑ 187 Derrick Brooks .50 .20
❑ 188 Brian Griese .50 .20
❑ 189 Steve McNair .75 .30
❑ 190 Chris Brown .75 .30
❑ 191 Eddie George .50 .20
❑ 192 Tyrone Calico .50 .20
❑ 193 Derrick Mason .50 .20
❑ 194 Drew Bennett .50 .20
❑ 195 Mark Brunell .50 .20
❑ 196 LaVar Arrington 1.50 .60
❑ 197 Clinton Portis .75 .30
❑ 198 Laveranues Coles .50 .20
❑ 199 Patrick Ramsey .50 .20
❑ 200 Rod Gardner .50 .20
❑ 201 Eli Manning RC 30.00 12.50
❑ 202 Larry Fitzgerald RC 15.00 6.00
❑ 203 Michael Jenkins RC 5.00 2.00
❑ 204 Ben Roethlisberger RC 50.00 25.00
❑ 025 Philip Rivers RC 15.00 7.50
❑ 206 Kellen Winslow RC 10.00 4.00
❑ 207 Kevin Jones RC 15.00 6.00
❑ 208 Steven Jackson RC 15.00 6.00
❑ 209 Reggie Williams RC 6.00 2.50
❑ 210 Chris Perry RC 8.00 3.00
❑ 211 Roy Williams RC 12.00 5.00
❑ 212 Rashaun Woods RC 5.00 2.00
❑ 213 Chris Gamble RC 6.00 2.50
❑ 214 Sean Taylor RC 6.00 2.50
❑ 215 Robert Gallery RC 8.00 3.00
❑ 216 Ben Troupe RC 5.00 2.00
❑ 217 Lee Evans RC 6.00 2.50
❑ 218 Michael Clayton RC 10.00 4.00
❑ 219 J.P. Losman RC 10.00 4.00
❑ 220 Devery Henderson RC 4.00 1.50
❑ 221 Drew Henson RC 5.00 2.00
❑ 222 DeAngelo Hall RC 6.00 2.50
❑ 223 Julius Jones RC 20.00 7.50
❑ 224 Ben Watson RC 5.00 2.00
❑ 225 Greg Jones RC 5.00 2.00
❑ 226 D.J. Williams RC 2.50 1.00
❑ 227 Tommie Harris RC 1.50 .60
❑ 228 Shawn Andrews RC 1.50 .60
❑ 229 Vince Wilfork RC 2.50 1.00
❑ 230 Dunta Robinson RC 1.50 .60
❑ 231 Will Smith RC 1.50 .60
❑ 232 Jonathan Vilma RC 1.50 .60
❑ 233 Ricardo Colclough RC 1.50 .60
❑ 234 Ahmad Carroll RC 2.50 1.00
❑ 235 Karlos Dansby RC 1.50 .60
❑ 236 Matt Ware RC 1.50 .60
❑ 237 Jim Sorgi RC 1.50 .60
❑ 238 Will Poole RC 1.50 .60
❑ 239 Derrick Strait RC 1.50 .60
❑ 240 Andy Hall RC 1.25 .50
❑ 241 Nathan Vasher RC 2.00 .75
❑ 242 D.J. Hackett RC 1.25 .50
❑ 243 Jason Babin RC 1.50 .60
❑ 244 Derrick Hamilton RC 1.25 .50
❑ 245 Michael Boulware RC 1.50 .60
❑ 246 Michael Turner RC 1.50 .60
❑ 247 Sean Jones RC 1.25 .50
❑ 248 Ernest Wilford RC 1.50 .60
❑ 249 Cedric Cobbs RC 1.50 .60
❑ 250 Tatum Bell RC 4.00 1.50
❑ 251 Bernard Berrian RC 1.50 .60
❑ 252 Vernon Carey RC 1.25 .50
❑ 253 Kenechi Udeze RC 1.50 .60
❑ 254 P.K. Sam RC 1.25 .50
❑ 255 Ben Hartsock RC 1.50 .60
❑ 256 Chris Cooley RC 1.50 .60
❑ 257 Josh Harris RC 1.50 .60
❑ 258 Cody Pickett RC 1.50 .60
❑ 259 Carlos Francis RC 1.25 .50
❑ 260 Devard Darling RC 1.50 .60
❑ 261 Johnnie Morant RC 1.50 .60
❑ 262 John Navarre RC 1.50 .60
❑ 263 Kris Wilson RC 1.50 .60
❑ 264 Jerricho Cotchery RC 1.50 .60
❑ 265 Darius Watts RC 1.50 .60
❑ 266 Quincy Wilson RC 1.25 .50
❑ 267 Maurice Mann RC 1.25 .50
❑ 268 Samie Parker RC 1.50 .60
❑ 269 B.J. Symons RC 1.50 .60
❑ 270 Matt Schaub RC 3.00 1.25
❑ 271 Jeff Smoker RC 1.50 .60
❑ 272 Craig Krenzel RC 1.50 .60
❑ 273 Luke McCown RC 1.50 .60
❑ 274 Mewelde Moore RC 2.00 .75
❑ 275 Keary Colbert RC 2.50 1.00

2005 Upper Deck

❑ COMPLETE SET (275) 250.00 125.00
❑ COMP.SET w/o SP's (250) 60.00 30.00
❑ COMP.SET w/o RC's (200) 30.00 12.50
❑ 201-225 ROOKIE STATED ODDS 1:8
❑ 226-275 ROOKIE STATED ODDS 1:1
❑ 1 Larry Fitzgerald .75 .30
❑ 2 Anquan Boldin .50 .20
❑ 3 Kurt Warner .50 .20
❑ 4 Josh McCown .50 .20
❑ 5 Bryant Johnson .40 .15
❑ 6 Duane Starks .40 .15
❑ 7 Michael Vick 1.25 .50
❑ 8 Warrick Dunn .50 .20

❑ 9 T.J. Duckett .50 .20
❑ 10 Peerless Price .40 .15
❑ 11 Alge Crumpler .50 .20
❑ 12 Patrick Kerney .40 .15
❑ 13 Ed Reed .50 .20
❑ 14 Ray Lewis .75 .30
❑ 15 Kyle Boller .50 .20
❑ 16 Ma'Ake Kemoeatu RC .75 .30
❑ 17 Jamal Lewis .75 .30
❑ 18 Derrick Mason .50 .20
❑ 19 J.P. Losman .75 .30
❑ 20 Willis McGahee .75 .30
❑ 21 Lawyer Milloy .40 .15
❑ 22 Lee Evans .50 .20
❑ 23 Eric Moulds .50 .20
❑ 24 Takeo Spikes .40 .15
❑ 25 Jake Delhomme .75 .30
❑ 26 DeShaun Foster .50 .20
❑ 27 Keary Colbert .50 .20
❑ 28 Stephen Davis .50 .20
❑ 29 Nick Goings .40 .15
❑ 30 Julius Peppers .50 .20
❑ 31 Rex Grossman .50 .20
❑ 32 Brian Urlacher .75 .30
❑ 33 Thomas Jones .50 .20
❑ 34 Muhsin Muhammad .50 .20
❑ 35 Anthony Thomas .50 .20
❑ 36 Bernard Berrian .40 .15
❑ 37 Carson Palmer .75 .30
❑ 38 Chad Johnson .75 .30
❑ 39 Peter Warrick .40 .15
❑ 40 T.J. Houshmandzadeh .40 .15
❑ 41 Rudi Johnson .50 .20
❑ 42 Justin Smith .40 .15
❑ 43 Jeff Garcia .50 .20
❑ 44 Lee Suggs .50 .20
❑ 45 William Green .40 .15
❑ 46 Kellen Winslow .75 .30
❑ 47 Dennis Northcutt .40 .15
❑ 48 Antonio Bryant .40 .15
❑ 49 Julius Jones 1.00 .40
❑ 50 Drew Bledsoe .75 .30
❑ 51 Keyshawn Johnson .50 .20
❑ 52 Al Johnson .40 .15
❑ 53 Jason Witten .50 .20
❑ 54 Roy Williams S .50 .20
❑ 55 Jake Plummer .50 .20
❑ 56 Champ Bailey .50 .20
❑ 57 Tatum Bell .50 .20
❑ 58 Reuben Droughns .50 .20
❑ 59 Ashley Lelie .50 .20
❑ 60 Rod Smith .50 .20
❑ 61 Kevin Jones .75 .30
❑ 62 Roy Williams WR .75 .30
❑ 63 Charles Rogers .50 .20
❑ 64 Joey Harrington .75 .30
❑ 65 Az-Zahir Hakim .40 .15
❑ 66 Dre Bly .40 .15
❑ 67 Brett Favre 2.00 .75
❑ 68 Javon Walker .50 .20
❑ 69 Ahman Green .75 .30
❑ 70 Donald Driver .50 .20
❑ 71 Robert Ferguson .40 .15
❑ 72 Nick Barnett .40 .15
❑ 73 David Carr .75 .30
❑ 74 Domanick Davis .50 .20
❑ 75 Andre Johnson .50 .20
❑ 76 Jabar Gaffney .40 .15
❑ 77 Dunta Robinson .50 .20
❑ 78 Jamie Sharper .40 .15
❑ 79 Peyton Manning 1.25 .50
❑ 80 Edgerrin James .75 .30
❑ 81 Marvin Harrison .75 .30
❑ 82 Reggie Wayne .50 .20
❑ 83 Brandon Stokley .50 .20
❑ 84 Dwight Freeney .50 .20
❑ 85 Byron Leftwich .75 .30
❑ 86 Fred Taylor .50 .20
❑ 87 Jimmy Smith .50 .20
❑ 88 Greg Jones .40 .15
❑ 89 Donovin Darius .40 .15
❑ 90 Reggie Williams .50 .20
❑ 91 Priest Holmes .75 .30
❑ 92 Larry Johnson .75 .30
❑ 93 Tony Gonzalez .50 .20
❑ 94 Trent Green .50 .20
❑ 95 Eddie Kennison .40 .15
❑ 96 Johnnie Morton .50 .20
❑ 97 Jason Taylor .40 .15
❑ 98 A.J. Feeley .50 .20
❑ 99 Sammy Morris .40 .15
❑ 100 Chris Chambers .50 .20
❑ 101 Randy McMichael .40 .15
❑ 102 Zach Thomas .75 .30
❑ 103 Antoine Winfield .40 .15
❑ 104 Daunte Culpepper .75 .30
❑ 105 Michael Bennett .50 .20
❑ 106 Nate Burleson .50 .20
❑ 107 Onterrio Smith .50 .20
❑ 108 Marcus Robinson .50 .20
❑ 109 Tom Brady 2.00 .75
❑ 110 Corey Dillon .50 .20
❑ 111 David Givens .50 .20
❑ 112 David Patten .40 .15
❑ 113 Adam Vinatieri .75 .30
❑ 114 Troy Brown .50 .20
❑ 115 Aaron Brooks .50 .20
❑ 116 Deuce McAllister .75 .30
❑ 117 Joe Horn .50 .20
❑ 118 Donte Stallworth .50 .20
❑ 119 Charles Grant .40 .15
❑ 120 Jerome Pathon .40 .15
❑ 121 Eli Manning 1.50 .60
❑ 122 Tiki Barber .75 .30
❑ 123 Amani Toomer .50 .20
❑ 124 Jeremy Shockey .75 .30
❑ 125 Michael Strahan .50 .20
❑ 126 Plaxico Burress .50 .20
❑ 127 Chad Pennington .75 .30
❑ 128 Curtis Martin .75 .30
❑ 129 Laveranues Coles .50 .20
❑ 130 Wayne Chrebet .50 .20
❑ 131 Jonathan Vilma .50 .20
❑ 132 Justin McCareins .40 .15
❑ 133 Kerry Collins .50 .20
❑ 134 Jerry Porter .50 .20
❑ 135 LaMont Jordan .75 .30
❑ 136 Randy Moss .75 .30
❑ 137 Barry Sims .40 .15
❑ 138 Warren Sapp .50 .20
❑ 139 Donovan McNabb 1.00 .40
❑ 140 Brian Westbrook .50 .20
❑ 141 Terrell Owens .75 .30
❑ 142 Jevon Kearse .50 .20
❑ 143 Brian Dawkins .50 .20
❑ 144 Ben Roethlisberger 2.00 .75
❑ 145 Jerome Bettis .75 .30
❑ 146 Duce Staley .50 .20
❑ 147 Cedrick Wilson .40 .15
❑ 148 Hines Ward .75 .30
❑ 149 Antwaan Randle El .50 .20
❑ 150 Troy Polamalu 1.25 .50
❑ 151 Philip Rivers .75 .30
❑ 152 Drew Brees .75 .30
❑ 153 LaDainian Tomlinson 1.00 .40
❑ 154 Antonio Gates .75 .30
❑ 155 Reche Caldwell .40 .15
❑ 156 Eric Parker .40 .15
❑ 157 Kevan Barlow .50 .20
❑ 158 Tim Rattay .40 .15
❑ 159 Eric Johnson .50 .20
❑ 160 Rashaun Woods .50 .20
❑ 161 Brandon Lloyd .40 .15
❑ 162 Julian Peterson .40 .15
❑ 163 Matt Hasselbeck .50 .20
❑ 164 Shaun Alexander 1.00 .40
❑ 165 Michael Boulware .40 .15
❑ 166 Darrell Jackson .50 .20
❑ 167 Koren Robinson .50 .20
❑ 168 Marcus Trufant .40 .15
❑ 169 Marc Bulger .75 .30
❑ 170 Steven Jackson 1.00 .40
❑ 171 Marshall Faulk .75 .30
❑ 172 Issac Bruce .50 .20
❑ 173 Torry Holt .75 .30
❑ 174 Michael Clayton .75 .30
❑ 175 Michael Pittman .40 .15
❑ 176 Brian Griese .50 .20
❑ 177 Joey Galloway .50 .20
❑ 178 Derrick Brooks .50 .20
❑ 179 Josh Savage RC .50 .20
❑ 180 Steve McNair .75 .30
❑ 181 Chris Brown .50 .20
❑ 182 Billy Volek .50 .20
❑ 183 Ben Troupe .40 .15
❑ 184 Drew Bennett .50 .20
❑ 185 Clinton Portis .75 .30
❑ 186 Mark Brunell .50 .20
❑ 187 Patrick Ramsey .50 .20
❑ 188 Sean Taylor .50 .20
❑ 189 LaVar Arrington .75 .30
❑ 190 Santana Moss .50 .20
❑ 191 David Terrell .50 .20
❑ 192 Deion Branch .50 .20
❑ 193 Chester Taylor .50 .20
❑ 194 Derrick Blaylock .40 .15
❑ 195 Shaun Ellis .40 .15
❑ 196 Terrell Suggs .50 .20
❑ 197 Charles Woodson .50 .20
❑ 198 Jason Elam .40 .15
❑ 199 Lawrence Tynes RC .50 .20
❑ 200 David Akers .40 .15
❑ 201 Alex Smith QB RC 25.00 10.00
❑ 202 Aaron Rodgers RC 20.00 7.50
❑ 203 Ronnie Brown RC 20.00 7.50
❑ 204 Carnell Williams RC 25.00 12.50
❑ 205 Braylon Edwards RC 20.00 7.50
❑ 206 Antrel Rolle RC 6.00 2.50
❑ 207 Cedric Benson RC 12.00 5.00
❑ 208 Troy Williamson RC 12.00 5.00
❑ 209 Mark Clayton RC 8.00 3.00
❑ 210 Matt Jones RC 15.00 6.00
❑ 211 Reggie Brown RC 6.00 2.50
❑ 212 Charlie Frye RC 12.00 5.00
❑ 213 Heath Miller RC 15.00 6.00
❑ 214 Vincent Jackson RC 6.00 2.50
❑ 215 Andrew Walter RC 10.00 4.00
❑ 216 Roddy White RC 6.00 2.50
❑ 217 Adam Jones RC 6.00 2.50
❑ 218 J.J. Arrington RC 8.00 3.00
❑ 219 Eric Shelton RC 6.00 2.50
❑ 220 Terrence Murphy RC 6.00 2.50
❑ 221 Frank Gore RC 10.00 4.00
❑ 222 Roscoe Parrish RC 6.00 2.50
❑ 223 Jason Campbell RC 10.00 4.00
❑ 224 Carlos Rogers RC 8.00 3.00
❑ 225 Mike Williams 12.00 5.00
❑ 226 Erasmus James RC 6.00 2.50
❑ 227 Travis Johnson RC 1.50 .60
❑ 228 Dan Cody RC 2.00 .75
❑ 229 Thomas Davis RC 2.00 .75
❑ 230 David Pollack RC 2.00 .75
❑ 231 David Greene RC 2.00 .75
❑ 232 Alex Smith TE RC 2.00 .75
❑ 233 Ryan Moats RC 2.00 .75
❑ 234 Ciatrick Fason RC 2.00 .75
❑ 235 Vernand Morency RC 2.00 .75
❑ 236 Fred Gibson RC 6.00 2.50
❑ 237 Craphonso Thorpe RC 1.50 .60
❑ 238 Kevin Everett RC 2.00 .75
❑ 239 Kyle Orton RC 3.00 1.25
❑ 240 Derek Anderson RC 2.00 .75
❑ 241 Derrick Johnson RC 3.00 1.25
❑ 242 Mark Bradley RC 2.00 .75
❑ 243 Chris Henry RC 2.00 .75
❑ 244 DeMarcus Ware RC 3.00 1.25
❑ 245 Luis Castillo RC 2.00 .75
❑ 246 Mike Patterson RC 2.00 .75
❑ 247 Brodney Pool RC 2.00 .75
❑ 248 Barrett Ruud RC 2.00 .75
❑ 249 Darren Sproles RC 2.00 .75
❑ 250 Stefan LeFors RC 2.00 .75
❑ 251 Josh Bullocks RC 2.00 .75
❑ 252 Kevin Burnett RC 2.00 .75

253	Lofa Tatupu RC	2.50	1.00
254	Matt Roth RC	2.00	.75
255	Shaun Cody RC	2.00	.75
256	Shawne Merriman RC	3.00	1.25
257	Corey Webster RC	2.00	.75
258	Channing Crowder RC	2.00	.75
259	Justin Miller RC	1.50	.60
260	Eric Green RC	1.00	.40
261	Marcus Spears RC	2.00	.75
262	Marlin Jackson RC	2.00	.75
263	Odell Thurman RC	2.00	.75
264	Mike Nugent RC	2.00	.75
265	Marion Barber RC	3.00	1.25
266	Anttaj Hawthorne RC	1.50	.60
267	Dan Orlovsky RC	2.50	1.00
268	Fabian Washington RC	2.00	.75
269	Justin Tuck RC	2.00	.75
270	Jerome Mathis RC	2.00	.75
271	Ronald Bartell RC	1.50	.60
272	Kirk Morrison RC	2.00	.75
273	Adrian McPherson RC	2.00	.75
274	Matt Cassel RC	6.00	2.50
275	Maurice Clarett	2.00	.75

2005 Upper Deck AFL

	COMPLETE SET (90)	40.00	20.00
1	Hunkie Cooper	.75	.30
2	Siaha Burley	.75	.30
3	Sherdrick Bonner	.75	.30
4	Bo Kelly	.50	.20
5	Evan Hlavacek	.50	.20
6	Tacoma Fontaine	.50	.20
7	Troy Bergeron	1.00	.40
8	Darrin Chiaverini	.75	.30
9	Bobby Pesavento	.50	.20
10	Tom Pace	.50	.20
11	Raymond Philyaw	.75	.30
12	Bob McMillen	.75	.30
13	Etu Molden	.75	.30
14	Jeremy McDaniel	.75	.30
15	Todd Hammel	.75	.30
16	John Dutton	.75	.30
17	Damian Harrell	1.00	.40
18	Kevin McKenzie	.50	.20
19	Willis Marshall	.50	.20
20	Rashad Floyd	.50	.20
21	Andy McCullough	.50	.20
22	Damien Groce	.75	.30
23	Chad Salisbury	.50	.20
24	Sedrick Robinson	.50	.20
25	Cornelius White	.50	.20
26	Wilmont Perry	.50	.20
27	Clint Stoerner	2.00	.75
28	Will Pettis	.75	.30
29	Bobby Sippio	.75	.30
30	Jason Shelley	.50	.20
31	Duke Pettijohn	.50	.20
32	Robert Thomas	.50	.20
33	Jim Kubiak	.75	.30
34	Dialleo Burks	.75	.30
35	Matt Nagy	1.50	.60
36	Kevin Gaines	.50	.20
37	Josh Bush	.50	.20
38	Michael Bishop	1.00	.40
39	Anthony Hines	.50	.20
40	Chris Jackson	.75	.30
41	Jerome Riley	.50	.20
42	Josh Jeffries	.50	.20
43	Clint Dolezel	.75	.40
44	Marcus Nash	1.00	.40
45	Coco Blalock	.75	.30
46	Cornelius Bonner	.50	.20
47	Frank Carter	.50	.20
48	John Kaleo	.75	.30
49	Kevin Ingram	.50	.20
50	Greg Hopkins	.75	.30
51	Lonnie Ford	.50	.20
52	Brian Sump	.50	.20
53	Leon Murray	.50	.20
54	Darryl Hammond	.50	.20
55	Fred Coleman	.50	.20
56	Ahmad Hawkins	.50	.20
57	Gabe Amey	.50	.20
58	Andy Kelly	.75	.30
59	Chris Pointer	.50	.20
60	Aaron Bailey	.75	.30
61	Dan Curran	.50	.20
62	Lamont Moore	.50	.20
63	Thabiti Davis	.75	.30
64	Aaron Garcia	1.00	.40
65	Lincoln DuPree	.50	.20
66	William Holder	.50	.20
67	Chris Anthony	.50	.20
68	Markeith Cooper	.50	.20
69	Cory Fleming	.75	.30
70	Kenny McEntyre	.75	.30
71	Bret Cooper	.50	.20
72	Travis McGriff	.75	.30
73	Joe Hamilton	.75	.30
74	Tony Graziani	1.00	.40
75	Takuya Furutani	.50	.20
76	Chris Ryan	.50	.20
77	Joseph Todd	.50	.20
78	Sean Scott	.75	.30
79	Mark Grieb	1.00	.40
80	James Hundon	.75	.30
81	James Roe	.75	.30
82	Omarr Smith	.75	.30
83	Rashied Davis	.75	.30
84	Calvin Schexnayder	.50	.20
85	Shane Stafford	.75	.40
86	Lawrence Samuels	.75	.30
87	T.T. Toliver	.50	.20
88	Freddie Solomon	.75	.30
89	Cliff Dell	.50	.20
90	Rich Young	.50	.20

2006 Upper Deck AFL

	COMPLETE SET (190)	60.00	30.00
1	Sherdrick Bonner	.75	.30
2	Clarence Coleman	.50	.20
3	Randy Gatewood	.50	.20
4	Tom Pace	.50	.20
5	Vince Amey	.50	.20
6	Evan Hlavacek	.50	.20
7	Josh Jeffries	.50	.20
8	Gary Kral	.50	.20
9	Bo Kelly	.50	.20
10	Clarence Lawson	.50	.20
11	Damien Groce	.75	.30
12	John Fitzgerald	.50	.20
13	Kevin Nickerson	.75	.30
14	Tom Briggs	.50	.20
15	Darrin Chiaverini	.75	.30
16	Ira Gooch	.50	.20
17	Tacoma Fontaine	.75	.30
18	Lindsay Fleshman	.50	.20
19	Tim Seder	.50	.20
20	Henry Bryant	.50	.20
21	Sedrick Robinson	.50	.20
22	Damon Mason	.50	.20
23	Raymond Philyaw	.75	.30
24	John Moyer	.50	.20
25	Etu Molden	.75	.30
26	Henry Douglas	.50	.20
27	Bob McMillen	.75	.30
28	Todd Hammel	.75	.30
29	Jeremy McDaniel	.75	.30
30	Keith Gispert	.50	.20
31	Russell Shaw	.50	.20
32	C.J. Johnson	.50	.20
33	Cornelius White	.50	.20
34	John Dutton	.75	.30
35	Damian Harrell	1.00	.40
36	Willis Marshall	.50	.20
37	Clay Rush	.50	.20
38	Andy McCullough	.75	.30
39	Kevin McKenzie	.50	.20
40	Rich Young	.50	.20
41	Ahmad Hawkins	.50	.20
42	Rashad Floyd	.50	.20
43	Delvin Hughley	.50	.20
44	Saul Patu	.50	.20
45	Matt D'Orazio	.75	.30
46	Lenzie Jackson	.50	.20
47	B.J. Barre	.50	.20
48	Mike Sutton	.50	.20
49	Gillis Wilson	.50	.20
50	Randall Lane	.50	.20
51	Frank Carter	.50	.20
52	Bobby Olive	.50	.20
53	Jamarr Ward	.50	.20
54	Thabiti Davis	.75	.30
55	John Kaleo	.75	.30
56	Clint Dolezel	1.00	.40
57	Jason Shelley	.50	.20
58	Will Pettis	.75	.30
59	Hamin Milligan	.50	.20
60	Duke Pettijohn	.50	.20
61	Carlos Martinez	.50	.20
62	Lucas Yarnell	.50	.20
63	Jermaine Lewis	.50	.20
64	Joe Minucci	.50	.20
65	Jermaine Jones	.50	.20
66	Scottie Montgomery	.50	.20
67	Jim Kubiak	.75	.30
68	Matt Nagy	1.00	.40
69	Troy Bergeron	1.00	.40
70	Chris Jackson	.75	.30
71	Derek Lee	1.00	.40
72	Robert Thomas	.50	.20
73	Kevin Aldridge	.50	.20
74	Nelson Garner	.50	.20
75	Nick Ward	.50	.20
76	Ricky Parker	.50	.20
77	Willie Gary	.50	.20
78	Michael Bishop	1.00	.40
79	Anthony Hines	.75	.30
80	Chris Avery	.75	.30
81	Josh Bush	.50	.20
82	Rupert Grant	.50	.20
83	Bryant Shaw	.50	.20
84	Dennison Robinson	.50	.20
85	Kahlil Carter	.50	.20
86	Chris Ryan	.50	.20
87	Marvin Taylor	.50	.20
88	Timon Marshall	.50	.20
89	Traco Rachal	.50	.20
90	Marcus Nash	1.00	.40
91	Coco Blalock	.75	.30
92	Joe Douglass	.50	.20
93	Ricky Ross	.50	.20
94	Sunungura Rusununguko	.50	.20
95	Marlion Jackson	.50	.20
96	Jerome Riley	.50	.20
97	Wilky Bazile	.50	.20
98	Dameon Porter	.50	.20
99	Rodney Filer	.50	.20
100	Cornelius Bonner	.50	.20
101	Brian Mann	.50	.20
102	Silas Demary	.75	.30
103	Tony Locke	.50	.20
104	Kevin Ingram	.50	.20
105	Lonnie Ford	.50	.20
106	Greg Hopkins	.75	.30
107	Remy Hamilton	.50	.20
108	Brian Sump	.50	.20
109	Antuan Simmons	.50	.20
110	Jerald Brown	.50	.20
111	Anthony Derricks	.50	.20
112	Leon Murray	.50	.20
113	James Baron	.50	.20
114	Clint Stoerner	1.25	.50
115	T.T. Toliver	.75	.30
116	Jarrick Hillery	.50	.20
117	Darryl Hammond	.50	.20
118	Tony Dodson	.50	.20
119	Hardy Mitchell	.50	.20
120	Levelle Brown	.50	.20
121	DeRon Jenkins	.50	.20
122	Cory Fleming	.75	.30
123	Andy Kelly	.75	.30
124	Aaron Bailey	.75	.30

- ❑ 125 B.J. Cohen .50 .20
- ❑ 126 Carl Bond .50 .20
- ❑ 127 Nyle Wiren .50 .20
- ❑ 128 Jermaine Miles .50 .20
- ❑ 129 Stacy Evans .50 .20
- ❑ 130 Terrance Joseph .50 .20
- ❑ 131 Nikia Adderson .50 .20
- ❑ 132 Calvin Spears .50 .20
- ❑ 133 Chris Pointer .50 .20
- ❑ 134 Steve Smith .50 .20
- ❑ 135 Aaron Garcia 1.00 .40
- ❑ 136 Mike Horacek .75 .30
- ❑ 137 Chris Anthony .50 .20
- ❑ 138 Ernest Certain .50 .20
- ❑ 139 Josh White .50 .20
- ❑ 140 Rob Bironas .50 .20
- ❑ 141 Lynaris Elpheage .50 .20
- ❑ 142 Corey Johnson .50 .20
- ❑ 143 Marcus Owen .50 .20
- ❑ 144 Sir Mawn Wilson .50 .20
- ❑ 145 Chris Angel .50 .20
- ❑ 146 Billy Parker .50 .20
- ❑ 147 Joe Hamilton .75 .30
- ❑ 148 E.J. Burt .50 .20
- ❑ 149 Jimmy Fryzel .50 .20
- ❑ 150 Wes Ours .50 .20
- ❑ 151 Idris Price .50 .20
- ❑ 152 Kenny McEntyre .75 .30
- ❑ 153 Chris Sanders .50 .20
- ❑ 154 Jerrian James .50 .20
- ❑ 155 Jonathan Ordway .50 .20
- ❑ 156 Tony Graziani 1.00 .40
- ❑ 157 Marcus Knight .75 .30
- ❑ 158 Sean Scott .75 .30
- ❑ 159 Kevin Gaines .50 .20
- ❑ 160 Tyronne Jones .50 .20
- ❑ 161 Rob Milanese .50 .20
- ❑ 162 Chris Brown .50 .20
- ❑ 163 Eddie Moten .50 .20
- ❑ 164 Calvin Coleman .50 .20
- ❑ 165 Mark Grieb 1.00 .40
- ❑ 166 James Roe .75 .30
- ❑ 167 Rashied Davis .75 .30
- ❑ 168 James Hundon .75 .30
- ❑ 169 Barry Wagner .50 .20
- ❑ 170 Rodney Wright .50 .20
- ❑ 171 Shalon Baker .50 .20
- ❑ 172 Dan Frantz .50 .20
- ❑ 173 Calvin Schexnayder .50 .20
- ❑ 174 Clevan Thomas .50 .20
- ❑ 175 Fred Coleman .50 .20
- ❑ 176 Shane Stafford 1.00 .40
- ❑ 177 Lawrence Samuels .75 .30
- ❑ 178 Freddie Solomon .75 .30
- ❑ 179 Ronney Daniels .50 .20
- ❑ 180 Bobby Sippio .75 .30
- ❑ 181 Matt George .50 .20
- ❑ 182 Jarrod Penright .50 .20
- ❑ 183 Demetris Bendross .50 .20
- ❑ 184 Tramain Jones .50 .20
- ❑ 185 Khori Ivy .50 .20
- ❑ 186 Kelvin Hunter .50 .20
- ❑ 187 Siaha Burley .75 .30
- ❑ 188 Justin Skaggs .50 .20
- ❑ 189 Orshawante Bryant .50 .20
- ❑ 190 Joe Germaine .75 .30

2005 Upper Deck ESPN

- ❑ COMP.SET w/o RC's (100) 25.00 10.00
- ❑ DRAFT PICK STATED ODDS 1:4
- ❑ 1 Larry Fitzgerald .75 .30
- ❑ 2 Josh McCown .50 .20
- ❑ 3 Anquan Boldin .50 .20
- ❑ 4 Michael Vick 1.25 .50
- ❑ 5 Warrick Dunn .50 .20
- ❑ 6 Peerless Price .40 .15
- ❑ 7 Alge Crumpler .50 .20
- ❑ 8 Jamal Lewis .75 .30
- ❑ 9 Kyle Boller .50 .20
- ❑ 10 Derrick Mason .50 .20
- ❑ 11 Willis McGahee .75 .30
- ❑ 12 J.P. Losman .75 .30
- ❑ 13 Eric Moulds .50 .20
- ❑ 14 Jake Delhomme .75 .30
- ❑ 15 Steve Smith .50 .20
- ❑ 16 DeShaun Foster .50 .20
- ❑ 17 Muhsin Muhammad .50 .20
- ❑ 18 Thomas Jones .50 .20
- ❑ 19 Rex Grossman .50 .20
- ❑ 20 Chad Johnson .75 .30
- ❑ 21 Carson Palmer .75 .30
- ❑ 22 Rudi Johnson .50 .20
- ❑ 23 Lee Suggs .50 .20
- ❑ 24 Kellen Winslow .75 .30
- ❑ 25 Luke McCown .40 .15
- ❑ 26 Julius Jones 1.00 .40
- ❑ 27 Keyshawn Johnson .50 .20
- ❑ 28 Drew Bledsoe .75 .30
- ❑ 29 Tatum Bell .50 .20
- ❑ 30 Jake Plummer .50 .20
- ❑ 31 Rod Smith .50 .20
- ❑ 32 Roy Williams WR .75 .30
- ❑ 33 Kevin Jones .75 .30
- ❑ 34 Joey Harrington .75 .30
- ❑ 35 Jeff Garcia .50 .20
- ❑ 36 Brett Favre 2.00 .75
- ❑ 37 Javon Walker .50 .20
- ❑ 38 Ahman Green .75 .30
- ❑ 39 David Carr .75 .30
- ❑ 40 Andre Johnson .50 .20
- ❑ 41 Domanick Davis .50 .20
- ❑ 42 Peyton Manning 1.25 .50
- ❑ 43 Edgerrin James .75 .30
- ❑ 44 Marvin Harrison .75 .30
- ❑ 45 Byron Leftwich .75 .30
- ❑ 46 Fred Taylor .50 .20
- ❑ 47 Jimmy Smith .50 .20
- ❑ 48 Priest Holmes .75 .30
- ❑ 49 Trent Green .50 .20
- ❑ 50 Tony Gonzalez .50 .20
- ❑ 51 Larry Johnson .75 .30
- ❑ 52 Chris Chambers .50 .20
- ❑ 53 A.J. Feeley .50 .20
- ❑ 54 Randy McMichael .40 .15
- ❑ 55 Daunte Culpepper .75 .30
- ❑ 56 Nate Burleson .50 .20
- ❑ 57 Michael Bennett .50 .20
- ❑ 58 Tom Brady 2.00 .75
- ❑ 59 Deion Branch .50 .20
- ❑ 60 Corey Dillon .50 .20
- ❑ 61 Aaron Brooks .50 .20
- ❑ 62 Deuce McAllister .75 .30
- ❑ 63 Joe Horn .50 .20
- ❑ 64 Eli Manning 1.50 .60
- ❑ 65 Jeremy Shockey .75 .30
- ❑ 66 Tiki Barber .75 .30
- ❑ 67 Plaxico Burress .50 .20
- ❑ 68 Chad Pennington .75 .30
- ❑ 69 Curtis Martin .75 .30
- ❑ 70 Laveranues Coles .50 .20
- ❑ 71 Jerry Porter .50 .20
- ❑ 72 Randy Moss .75 .30
- ❑ 73 Kerry Collins .50 .20
- ❑ 74 Donovan McNabb 1.00 .40
- ❑ 75 Brian Westbrook .50 .20
- ❑ 76 Terrell Owens .75 .30
- ❑ 77 Ben Roethlisberger 2.00 .75
- ❑ 78 Jerome Bettis .75 .30
- ❑ 79 Hines Ward .75 .30
- ❑ 80 Drew Brees .75 .30
- ❑ 81 LaDainian Tomlinson 1.00 .40
- ❑ 82 Antonio Gates .75 .30
- ❑ 83 Tim Rattay .40 .15
- ❑ 84 Eric Johnson .50 .20
- ❑ 85 Rashaun Woods .50 .20
- ❑ 86 Matt Hasselbeck .50 .20
- ❑ 87 Shaun Alexander 1.00 .40
- ❑ 88 Darrell Jackson .50 .20
- ❑ 89 Marc Bulger .75 .30
- ❑ 90 Marshall Faulk .75 .30
- ❑ 91 Torry Holt .75 .30
- ❑ 92 Brian Griese .50 .20
- ❑ 93 Michael Pittman .40 .15
- ❑ 94 Michael Clayton .75 .30
- ❑ 95 Steve McNair .75 .30
- ❑ 96 Chris Brown .50 .20
- ❑ 97 Drew Bennett .50 .20
- ❑ 98 Clinton Portis .75 .30
- ❑ 99 Patrick Ramsey .50 .20
- ❑ 100 Santana Moss .50 .20
- ❑ 101 Aaron Rodgers RC 8.00 3.00
- ❑ 102 Alex Smith QB RC 10.00 4.00
- ❑ 103 Charlie Frye RC 5.00 2.00
- ❑ 104 Andrew Walter RC 4.00 1.50
- ❑ 105 David Greene RC 2.50 1.00
- ❑ 106 Dan Orlovsky RC 3.00 1.25
- ❑ 107 Derek Anderson RC 2.50 1.00
- ❑ 108 Carnell Williams RC 12.00 5.00
- ❑ 109 Ronnie Brown RC 8.00 3.00
- ❑ 110 Ciatrick Fason RC 2.50 1.00
- ❑ 111 Cedric Benson RC 5.00 2.00
- ❑ 112 Vincent Jackson RC 2.50 1.00
- ❑ 113 Eric Shelton RC 2.50 1.00
- ❑ 114 Frank Gore RC 4.00 1.50
- ❑ 115 Braylon Edwards RC 8.00 3.00
- ❑ 116 Roddy White RC 2.50 1.00
- ❑ 117 Troy Williamson RC 5.00 2.00
- ❑ 118 Craphonso Thorpe RC 2.00 .75
- ❑ 119 Mark Clayton RC 3.00 1.25
- ❑ 120 Fred Gibson RC 2.00 .75
- ❑ 121 Reggie Brown RC 2.50 1.00
- ❑ 122 Matt Jones RC 6.00 2.50
- ❑ 123 David Pollack RC 2.50 1.00
- ❑ 124 Derrick Johnson RC 4.00 1.50
- ❑ 125 Erasmus James RC 2.50 1.00
- ❑ 126 Antrel Rolle RC 2.50 1.00
- ❑ 127 Thomas Davis RC 2.50 1.00
- ❑ 128 Adam Jones RC 2.50 1.00
- ❑ 129 Corey Webster RC 2.50 1.00
- ❑ 130 Marlin Jackson RC 2.50 1.00
- ❑ 131 Brodney Pool RC 2.50 1.00
- ❑ 132 Mark Bradley RC 2.50 1.00
- ❑ 133 Stefan LeFors RC 2.50 1.00
- ❑ 134 Alex Smith TE RC 2.50 1.00
- ❑ 135 Heath Miller RC 6.00 2.50
- ❑ 136 Jason Campbell RC 4.00 1.50
- ❑ 137 Kyle Orton RC 5.00 1.50
- ❑ 138 Vernand Morency RC 2.50 1.00
- ❑ 139 Carlos Rogers RC 3.00 1.25
- ❑ 140 J.J. Arrington RC 3.00 1.25
- ❑ 141 Ryan Moats RC 2.50 1.00
- ❑ 142 Chris Henry RC 2.50 1.00
- ❑ 143 Terrence Murphy RC 2.50 1.00
- ❑ 144 Fabian Washington RC 2.50 1.00
- ❑ 145 Roscoe Parrish RC 2.50 1.00
- ❑ 146 Kevin Everett RC 2.50 1.00
- ❑ 147 Travis Johnson RC 2.00 .75
- ❑ 148 Mike Williams 5.00 2.00
- ❑ 149 Maurice Clarett 2.50 1.00
- ❑ 150 Channing Crowder RC 2.50 1.00
- ❑ 151 Odell Thurman RC 2.00 .75
- ❑ 152 DeMarcus Ware RC 4.00 1.50
- ❑ 153 Shawne Merriman RC 4.00 1.50
- ❑ 154 Jerome Mathis RC 2.50 1.00
- ❑ 155 Marcus Spears RC 2.50 1.00
- ❑ 156 Luis Castillo RC 2.50 1.00
- ❑ 157 Darren Sproles RC 2.50 1.00
- ❑ 158 Marion Barber RC 4.00 1.50
- ❑ 159 Justin Tuck RC 2.50 1.00
- ❑ 160 Courtney Roby RC 2.50 1.00

2004 Upper Deck Foundations

- ❑ COMP.SET w/o SP's (100) 20.00 7.50
- ❑ 101-240 RC PRINT RUN 350 SER.#'d SETS
- ❑ 241-257 RC JSY PRINT RUN 1299 SETS
- ❑ 258-263 RC JSY PRINT RUN 499 SER.#'d SETS
- ❑ 1 Josh McCown .50 .20
- ❑ 2 Emmitt Smith 1.50 .60
- ❑ 3 Anquan Boldin .75 .30

❑	4	T.J. Duckett	.50	.20
❑	5	Peerless Price	.50	.20
❑	6	Michael Vick	1.50	.60
❑	7	Todd Heap	.50	.20
❑	8	Kyle Boller	.75	.30
❑	9	Jamal Lewis	.75	.30
❑	10	Travis Henry	.50	.20
❑	11	Eric Moulds	.50	.20
❑	12	Drew Bledsoe	.75	.30
❑	13	Steve Smith	.75	.30
❑	14	Stephen Davis	.50	.20
❑	15	Jake Delhomme	.75	.30
❑	16	Rex Grossman	.75	.30
❑	17	Brian Urlacher	1.00	.40
❑	18	Anthony Thomas	.50	.20
❑	19	Rudi Johnson	.50	.20
❑	20	Chad Johnson	.75	.30
❑	21	Carson Palmer	1.00	.40
❑	22	Quincy Morgan	.50	.20
❑	23	Jeff Garcia	.75	.30
❑	24	Andre Davis	.30	.10
❑	25	Roy Williams S	.50	.20
❑	26	Eddie George	.50	.20
❑	27	Keyshawn Johnson	.50	.20
❑	28	Jake Plummer	.50	.20
❑	29	Champ Bailey	.50	.20
❑	30	Ashley Lelie	.50	.20
❑	31	Joey Harrington	.75	.30
❑	32	Charles Rogers	.50	.20
❑	33	Az-Zahir Hakim	.30	.10
❑	34	Javon Walker	.50	.20
❑	35	Brett Favre	2.00	.75
❑	36	Ahman Green	.75	.30
❑	37	Domanick Davis	.75	.30
❑	38	David Carr	.75	.30
❑	39	Andre Johnson	.75	.30
❑	40	Peyton Manning	1.25	.50
❑	41	Marvin Harrison	.75	.30
❑	42	Edgerrin James	.75	.30
❑	43	Jimmy Smith	.50	.20
❑	44	Fred Taylor	.50	.20
❑	45	Byron Leftwich	1.00	.40
❑	46	Trent Green	.50	.20
❑	47	Tony Gonzalez	.50	.20
❑	48	Priest Holmes	1.00	.40
❑	49	Dante Hall	.75	.30
❑	50	Ricky Williams	.75	.30
❑	51	David Boston	.50	.20
❑	52	Chris Chambers	.50	.20
❑	53	A.J. Feeley	.75	.30
❑	54	Randy Moss	1.00	.40
❑	55	Michael Bennett	.50	.20
❑	56	Daunte Culpepper	.75	.30
❑	57	Troy Brown	.50	.20
❑	58	Tom Brady	2.00	.75
❑	59	Corey Dillon	.50	.20
❑	60	Donte' Stallworth	.50	.20
❑	61	Deuce McAllister	.75	.30
❑	62	Aaron Brooks	.50	.20
❑	63	Kurt Warner	.75	.30
❑	64	Jeremy Shockey	.75	.30
❑	65	Santana Moss	.50	.20
❑	66	Curtis Martin	.75	.30
❑	67	Chad Pennington	.75	.30
❑	68	Amani Toomer	.50	.20
❑	69	Tim Brown	.75	.30
❑	70	Rich Gannon	.50	.20
❑	71	Jerry Rice	1.50	.60
❑	72	Jerry Porter	.50	.20
❑	73	Terrell Owens	.75	.30
❑	74	Jevon Kearse	.50	.20
❑	75	Donovan McNabb	1.00	.40
❑	76	Tommy Maddox	.50	.20
❑	77	Plaxico Burress	.50	.20
❑	78	Hines Ward	.75	.30
❑	79	Duce Staley	.50	.20
❑	80	LaDainian Tomlinson	1.00	.40
❑	81	Drew Brees	.75	.30
❑	82	Donnie Edwards	.30	.10
❑	83	Tim Rattay	.30	.10
❑	84	Kevan Barlow	.50	.20
❑	85	Brandon Lloyd	.50	.20
❑	86	Shaun Alexander	.75	.30
❑	87	Matt Hasselbeck	.50	.20
❑	88	Koren Robinson	.50	.20
❑	89	Torry Holt	.75	.30
❑	90	Marshall Faulk	.75	.30
❑	91	Marc Bulger	.75	.30
❑	92	Keenan McCardell	.30	.10
❑	93	Derrick Brooks	.50	.20
❑	94	Brad Johnson	.50	.20
❑	95	Steve McNair	.75	.30
❑	96	Derrick Mason	.50	.20
❑	97	Chris Brown	.75	.30
❑	98	Mark Brunell	.50	.20
❑	99	LaVar Arrington	1.50	.60
❑	100	Clinton Portis	.75	.30
❑	101	Brandon Chillar RC	8.00	3.00
❑	102	Mike Karney RC	8.00	3.00
❑	103	Jamaar Taylor RC	10.00	4.00
❑	104	Casey Clausen RC	10.00	4.00
❑	105	Drew Carter RC	10.00	4.00
❑	106	Travis LaBoy RC	10.00	4.00
❑	107	Jonathan Vilma RC	10.00	4.00
❑	108	Tramon Douglas RC	5.00	2.00
❑	109	Bob Sanders RC	20.00	7.50
❑	110	Mewelde Moore RC	12.00	5.00
❑	111	Randy Starks RC	8.00	3.00
❑	112	Tank Johnson RC	8.00	3.00
❑	113	Triandos Luke RC	10.00	4.00
❑	114	Dexter Reid RC	5.00	2.00
❑	115	Cedric Cobbs RC	10.00	4.00
❑	116	Darius Watts RC	10.00	4.00
❑	117	Ryan Krause RC	8.00	3.00
❑	118	Igor Olshansky RC	10.00	4.00
❑	119	Adimchinobe Echemandu RC	8.00	3.00
❑	120	Jason Fife RC	8.00	3.00
❑	121	Justin Smiley RC	10.00	4.00
❑	122	Marcus Tubbs RC	10.00	4.00
❑	123	Nathan Vasher RC	12.00	5.00
❑	124	Troy Fleming RC	8.00	3.00
❑	125	Ben Troupe RC	10.00	4.00
❑	126	Jammal Lord RC	10.00	4.00
❑	127	Jared Lorenzen RC	8.00	3.00
❑	128	Shawntae Spencer RC	10.00	4.00
❑	129	Darnell Dockett RC	8.00	3.00
❑	130	Derrick Strait RC	10.00	4.00
❑	131	Clarence Moore RC	10.00	4.00
❑	132	Jason Babin RC	10.00	4.00
❑	133	Jerricho Cotchery RC	10.00	4.00
❑	134	Karlos Dansby RC	10.00	4.00
❑	135	Marquise Hill RC	8.00	3.00
❑	136	Niko Koutouvides RC	8.00	3.00
❑	137	Andy Hall RC	8.00	3.00
❑	138	Teddy Lehman RC	10.00	4.00
❑	139	Will Smith RC	10.00	4.00
❑	140	Bernard Berrian RC	10.00	4.00
❑	141	Chris Cooley RC	10.00	4.00
❑	142	Landon Johnson RC	8.00	3.00
❑	143	Devard Darling RC	10.00	4.00
❑	144	Mark Jones RC	8.00	3.00
❑	145	Jake Grove RC	5.00	2.00
❑	146	John Navarre RC	10.00	4.00
❑	147	Keary Colbert RC	12.00	5.00
❑	148	Gilbert Gardner RC	8.00	3.00
❑	149	P.K. Sam RC	8.00	3.00
❑	150	Richard Seigler RC	8.00	3.00
❑	151	Marquis Cooper RC	8.00	3.00
❑	152	Tommie Harris RC	10.00	4.00
❑	153	Thomas Tapeh RC	8.00	3.00
❑	154	Ben Utecht RC	5.00	2.00
❑	155	Chris Gamble RC	12.00	5.00
❑	156	Daryl Smith RC	10.00	4.00
❑	157	Sean Taylor RC	12.00	5.00
❑	158	Caleb Miller RC	8.00	3.00
❑	159	Johnnie Morant RC	10.00	4.00
❑	160	Keith Smith RC	8.00	3.00
❑	161	Matt Mauck RC	10.00	4.00
❑	162	Matt Ware RC	10.00	4.00
❑	163	Quincy Wilson RC	8.00	3.00
❑	164	Samie Parker RC	10.00	4.00
❑	165	Kendrick Starling RC	5.00	2.00
❑	166	Antwan Odom RC	10.00	4.00
❑	167	Brandon Miree RC	8.00	3.00
❑	168	Casey Bramlet RC	8.00	3.00
❑	169	Cody Pickett RC	10.00	4.00
❑	170	Demorrio Williams RC	10.00	4.00
❑	171	Dunta Robinson RC	10.00	4.00
❑	172	D.J. Hackett RC	8.00	3.00
❑	173	Josh Harris RC	10.00	4.00
❑	174	Kenechi Udeze RC	10.00	4.00
❑	175	Michael Boulware RC	10.00	4.00
❑	176	Ricardo Colclough RC	10.00	4.00
❑	177	Shawn Andrews RC	10.00	4.00
❑	178	Jeris McIntyre RC	8.00	3.00
❑	179	Jim Sorgi RC	10.00	4.00
❑	180	Clarence Farmer RC	8.00	3.00
❑	181	Courtney Watson RC	10.00	4.00
❑	182	Derek Abney RC	10.00	4.00
❑	183	Dwan Edwards RC	5.00	2.00
❑	184	Ryan Dinwiddie RC	8.00	3.00
❑	185	B.J. Johnson RC	8.00	3.00
❑	186	Ben Watson RC	10.00	4.00
❑	187	Kris Wilson RC	10.00	4.00
❑	188	Michael Turner RC	10.00	4.00
❑	189	Derrick Ward RC	5.00	2.00
❑	190	Jonathan Smith RC	8.00	3.00
❑	191	Vernon Carey RC	8.00	3.00
❑	192	Ben Hartsock RC	10.00	4.00
❑	193	Rich Gardner RC	8.00	3.00
❑	194	D.J. Williams RC	12.00	5.00
❑	195	Derrick Hamilton RC	8.00	3.00
❑	196	Drew Henson RC	10.00	4.00
❑	197	Jeff Smoker RC	10.00	4.00
❑	198	Joey Thomas RC	10.00	4.00
❑	199	Keyaron Fox RC	8.00	3.00
❑	200	Nate Lawrie RC	8.00	3.00
❑	201	Sloan Thomas RC	8.00	3.00
❑	202	Justin Jenkins RC	8.00	3.00
❑	203	Stuart Schweigert RC	10.00	4.00
❑	204	Ran Carthon RC	8.00	3.00
❑	205	Ahmad Carroll RC	12.00	5.00
❑	206	Bradlee Van Pelt RC	15.00	6.00
❑	207	Patrick Crayton RC	10.00	4.00
❑	208	Chris Snee RC	8.00	3.00
❑	209	Fred Russell RC	10.00	4.00
❑	210	Dontarrious Thomas RC	10.00	4.00
❑	211	Will Poole RC	10.00	4.00
❑	212	Jarrett Payton RC	12.00	5.00
❑	213	Keiwan Ratliff RC	8.00	3.00
❑	214	Nate Kaeding RC	10.00	4.00
❑	215	Tim Euhus RC	10.00	4.00
❑	216	Sean Jones RC	8.00	3.00
❑	217	Will Allen RC	10.00	4.00
❑	218	B.J. Symons RC	10.00	4.00
❑	219	Carlos Francis RC	8.00	3.00
❑	220	Craig Krenzel RC	10.00	4.00
❑	221	Andrae Thurman RC	5.00	2.00
❑	222	Ernest Wilford RC	10.00	4.00
❑	223	Glenn Earl RC	8.00	3.00
❑	224	Jeremy LeSueur RC	8.00	3.00
❑	225	Junior Siavii RC	10.00	4.00
❑	226	Maurice Mann RC	8.00	3.00
❑	227	Michael Waddell RC	5.00	2.00
❑	228	Jason Wright RC	8.00	3.00
❑	229	Sean Ryan RC	8.00	3.00
❑	230	Vince Wilfork RC	12.00	5.00
❑	231	Matt Kegel RC	10.00	4.00
❑	232	Chris Collins RC	8.00	3.00
❑	233	Jonathan Smith RC	8.00	3.00
❑	234	Renaldo Works RC	10.00	4.00
❑	235	Matt Kranchick RC	10.00	4.00
❑	236	J.R. Reed RC	8.00	3.00
❑	237	Jason Shivers RC	8.00	3.00
❑	238	Donnell Washington RC	10.00	4.00
❑	239	Jorge Cordova RC	5.00	2.00
❑	240	Wes Welker RC	10.00	4.00
❑	241	Robert Gallery JSY RC	10.00	4.00
❑	242	Luke McCown JSY RC	6.00	2.50
❑	243	Roy Williams JSY RC	15.00	6.00
❑	244	Julius Jones JSY RC	25.00	10.00
❑	245	Tatum Bell JSY RC	12.00	5.00
❑	246	Steven Jackson JSY RC	20.00	7.50
❑	247	Reggie Williams JSY RC	8.00	3.00

❑ 248 Devery Henderson JSY RC 5.00 2.00
❑ 249 DeAngelo Hall JSY RC 8.00 3.00
❑ 250 Rashaun Woods JSY RC 6.00 2.50
❑ 251 Chris Perry JSY RC 10.00 4.00
❑ 252 Matt Schaub JSY RC 10.00 4.00
❑ 253 Lee Evans JSY RC 12.00 5.00
❑ 254 Michael Jenkins JSY RC 6.00 2.50
❑ 255 J.P. Losman JSY RC 12.00 5.00
❑ 256 Kevin Jones JSY RC 20.00 7.50
❑ 257 Michael Clayton JSY RC 12.00 5.00
❑ 258 Eli Manning JSY RC 30.00 15.00
❑ 259 Roethlisberger JSY RC 60.00 30.00
❑ 260 Larry Fitzgerald JSY RC 20.00 7.50
❑ 261 Philip Rivers JSY RC 20.00 10.00
❑ 262 Greg Jones JSY RC 10.00 4.00
❑ 263 Kellen Winslow JSY RC 12.00 5.00

2005 Upper Deck Foundations

❑ COMP.SET w/o RCs (100) 20.00 7.50
❑ 101-200 RC PRINT RUN 399 SER.#'d SETS
❑ ROOKIE AU STATED ODDS 1:12
❑ UNPRICED ROOKIE FOUNDATIONS #'d TO 1
❑ CARD #233 WAS NOT RELEASED
❑ 1 Larry Fitzgerald .75 .30
❑ 2 Anquan Boldin .50 .20
❑ 3 Kurt Warner .50 .20
❑ 4 Michael Vick 1.25 .50
❑ 5 T.J. Duckett .50 .20
❑ 6 Peerless Price .40 .15
❑ 7 Todd Heap .50 .20
❑ 8 Jamal Lewis .75 .30
❑ 9 Kyle Boller .50 .20
❑ 10 Derrick Mason .50 .20
❑ 11 J.P. Losman .75 .30
❑ 12 Willis McGahee .75 .30
❑ 13 Lee Evans .50 .20
❑ 14 Eric Moulds .50 .20
❑ 15 Jake Delhomme .75 .30
❑ 16 Keary Colbert .50 .20
❑ 17 DeShaun Foster .50 .20
❑ 18 Brian Urlacher .75 .30
❑ 19 Rex Grossman .50 .20
❑ 20 Muhsin Muhammad .50 .20
❑ 21 Carson Palmer .75 .30
❑ 22 Rudi Johnson .50 .20
❑ 23 Chad Johnson .75 .30
❑ 24 Julius Jones 1.00 .40
❑ 25 Keyshawn Johnson .50 .20
❑ 26 Drew Bledsoe .75 .30
❑ 27 Tatum Bell .50 .20
❑ 28 Jake Plummer .50 .20
❑ 29 Ashley Lelie .50 .20
❑ 30 Roy Williams WR .75 .30
❑ 31 Kevin Jones .75 .30
❑ 32 Jeff Garcia .50 .20
❑ 33 Brett Favre 2.00 .75
❑ 34 Ahman Green .75 .30
❑ 35 Javon Walker .50 .20
❑ 36 David Carr .75 .30
❑ 37 Andre Johnson .50 .20
❑ 38 Domanick Davis .50 .20
❑ 39 Peyton Manning 1.25 .50
❑ 40 Reggie Wayne .50 .20
❑ 41 Edgerrin James .75 .30
❑ 42 Marvin Harrison .75 .30
❑ 43 Byron Leftwich .75 .30
❑ 44 Fred Taylor .50 .20
❑ 45 Jimmy Smith .50 .20
❑ 46 Priest Holmes .75 .30
❑ 47 Tony Gonzalez .50 .20
❑ 48 Trent Green .50 .20
❑ 49 A.J. Feeley .50 .20
❑ 50 Chris Chambers .50 .20
❑ 51 Randy McMichael .40 .15
❑ 52 Daunte Culpepper .75 .30
❑ 53 Michael Bennett .50 .20
❑ 54 Nate Burleson .50 .20
❑ 55 Tom Brady 2.00 .75
❑ 56 Corey Dillon .50 .20
❑ 57 Deion Branch .50 .20
❑ 58 Richard Seymour .50 .20
❑ 59 Aaron Brooks .50 .20
❑ 60 Deuce McAllister .75 .30
❑ 61 Joe Horn .50 .20
❑ 62 Eli Manning 1.50 .60
❑ 63 Jeremy Shockey .75 .30
❑ 64 Tiki Barber .75 .30
❑ 65 Chad Pennington .75 .30
❑ 66 Curtis Martin .75 .30
❑ 67 Laveranues Coles .50 .20
❑ 68 Kerry Collins .50 .20
❑ 69 LaMont Jordan .75 .30
❑ 70 Randy Moss .75 .30
❑ 71 Donovan McNabb 1.00 .40
❑ 72 Terrell Owens .75 .30
❑ 73 Jeremiah Trotter .40 .15
❑ 74 Brian Westbrook .50 .20
❑ 75 Ben Roethlisberger 2.00 .75
❑ 76 Jerome Bettis .75 .30
❑ 77 Hines Ward .75 .30
❑ 78 Antwaan Randle El .50 .20
❑ 79 Drew Brees .75 .30
❑ 80 LaDainian Tomlinson 1.00 .40
❑ 81 Antonio Gates .75 .30
❑ 82 Tim Rattay .40 .15
❑ 83 Brandon Lloyd .40 .15
❑ 84 Eric Johnson .50 .20
❑ 85 Shaun Alexander 1.00 .40
❑ 86 Darrell Jackson .50 .20
❑ 87 Matt Hasselbeck .50 .20
❑ 88 Marc Bulger .75 .30
❑ 89 Steven Jackson 1.00 .40
❑ 90 Marshall Faulk .75 .30
❑ 91 Torry Holt .75 .30
❑ 92 Joey Galloway .50 .20
❑ 93 Brian Griese .50 .20
❑ 94 Michael Clayton .75 .30
❑ 95 Steve McNair .75 .30
❑ 96 Drew Bennett .50 .20
❑ 97 Chris Brown .50 .20
❑ 98 Clinton Portis .75 .30
❑ 99 Patrick Ramsey .50 .20
❑ 100 Santana Moss .50 .20
❑ 101 Gino Guidugli RC 4.00 1.50
❑ 102 James Kilian RC 8.00 3.00
❑ 103 Matt Cassel RC 12.00 5.00
❑ 104 Adrian McPherson RC 8.00 3.00
❑ 105 Timmy Chang RC 6.00 2.50
❑ 106 Chris Rix RC 6.00 2.50
❑ 107 Lionel Gates RC 6.00 2.50
❑ 108 Alvin Pearman RC 8.00 3.00
❑ 109 Damien Nash RC 6.00 2.50
❑ 110 Noah Herron RC 8.00 3.00
❑ 111 Steve Savoy RC 4.00 1.50
❑ 112 Craig Bragg RC 6.00 2.50
❑ 113 Larry Brackins RC 6.00 2.50
❑ 114 Nick Collins RC 8.00 3.00
❑ 115 Josh Davis RC 6.00 2.50
❑ 116 Chad Owens RC 8.00 3.00
❑ 117 Dante Ridgeway RC 6.00 2.50
❑ 118 Airese Currie RC 8.00 3.00
❑ 119 Chauncey Stovall RC 4.00 1.50
❑ 120 Harry Williams RC 6.00 2.50
❑ 121 Alex Smith TE RC 8.00 3.00
❑ 122 Jerome Collins RC 6.00 2.50
❑ 123 Rick Razzano RC 8.00 3.00
❑ 124 Derrick Johnson RC 12.00 5.00
❑ 125 Mike Patterson RC 8.00 3.00
❑ 126 Jonathan Babineaux RC 6.00 2.50
❑ 127 Matt Roth RC 8.00 3.00
❑ 128 Shaun Cody RC 8.00 3.00
❑ 129 Justin Tuck RC 8.00 3.00
❑ 130 Vincent Burns RC 6.00 2.50
❑ 131 DeMarcus Ware RC 12.00 5.00
❑ 132 Jerome Mathis RC 8.00 3.00
❑ 133 Darryl Blackstock RC 6.00 2.50
❑ 134 Robert McCune RC 6.00 2.50
❑ 135 Channing Crowder RC 8.00 3.00
❑ 136 Odell Thurman RC 8.00 3.00
❑ 137 Marcus Maxwell RC 6.00 2.50
❑ 138 Lance Mitchell RC 6.00 2.50
❑ 139 Jordan Beck RC 6.00 2.50
❑ 140 Alfred Fincher RC 6.00 2.50
❑ 141 Kirk Morrison RC 8.00 3.00
❑ 142 Kelvin Hayden RC 6.00 2.50
❑ 143 Justin Miller RC 6.00 2.50
❑ 144 Bryant McFadden RC 8.00 3.00
❑ 145 Eric Green RC 4.00 1.50
❑ 146 Fabian Washington RC 8.00 3.00
❑ 147 Ellis Hobbs RC 8.00 3.00
❑ 148 Ronald Bartell RC 6.00 2.50
❑ 149 Brodney Pool RC 8.00 3.00
❑ 150 Josh Bullocks RC 8.00 3.00
❑ 151 Vincent Fuller RC 6.00 2.50
❑ 152 Donte Nicholson RC 8.00 3.00
❑ 153 Sean Considine RC 8.00 3.00
❑ 154 Oshiomogho Atogwe RC 6.00 2.50
❑ 155 Dustin Fox RC 8.00 3.00
❑ 156 Mike Nugent RC 8.00 3.00
❑ 157 Shane Boyd RC 4.00 1.50
❑ 158 Ryan Fitzpatrick RC 12.00 5.00
❑ 159 Brock Berlin RC 6.00 2.50
❑ 160 Bryan Randall RC 6.00 2.50
❑ 161 Matt Jones RC 20.00 7.50
❑ 162 Todd Mortensen RC 6.00 2.50
❑ 163 Darian Durant RC 8.00 3.00
❑ 164 Stanley Wilson RC 6.00 2.50
❑ 165 Nehemiah Broughton RC 6.00 2.50
❑ 166 Manuel White RC 6.00 2.50
❑ 167 Zach Tuiasosopo RC 4.00 1.50
❑ 168 Deandra Cobb RC 6.00 2.50
❑ 169 Charles Frederick 6.00 2.50
❑ 170 Efrem Hill RC 6.00 2.50
❑ 171 Jason Anderson RC 6.00 2.50
❑ 172 Rasheed Marshall RC 8.00 3.00
❑ 173 Tab Perry RC 8.00 3.00
❑ 174 Paris Warren RC 6.00 2.50
❑ 175 Roydell Williams RC 8.00 3.00
❑ 176 Fred Amey RC 6.00 2.50
❑ 177 Kerry Wright RC 6.00 2.50
❑ 178 Joel Dreessen RC 6.00 2.50
❑ 179 Bo Scaife RC 6.00 2.50
❑ 180 Alex Barron RC 4.00 1.50
❑ 181 Jammal Brown RC 8.00 3.00
❑ 182 Michael Roos RC 4.00 1.50
❑ 183 Khalif Barnes RC 6.00 2.50
❑ 184 Logan Mankins RC 10.00 4.00
❑ 185 Elton Brown RC 4.00 1.50
❑ 186 David Baas RC 6.00 2.50
❑ 187 Chris Spencer RC 8.00 3.00
❑ 188 Marcus Spears RC 8.00 3.00
❑ 189 Trent Cole RC 8.00 3.00
❑ 190 Luis Castillo RC 8.00 3.00
❑ 191 Bill Swancutt RC 6.00 2.50
❑ 192 Jesse Lumsden RC 4.00 1.50
❑ 193 Lofa Tatupu RC 10.00 4.00
❑ 194 Boomer Grigsby RC 10.00 4.00
❑ 195 Domonique Foxworth RC 8.00 3.00
❑ 196 Travis Daniels RC 6.00 2.50
❑ 197 Darrent Williams RC 8.00 3.00
❑ 198 Kerry Rhodes RC 8.00 3.00
❑ 199 Mark Bradley RC 8.00 3.00
❑ 200 Bobby Purify RC 6.00 2.50
❑ 201 Dan Orlovsky AU/699 RC 12.00 5.00
❑ 202 David Greene AU/699 RC 10.00 4.00
❑ 203 Anthony Davis AU/699 RC 8.00 3.00
❑ 204 Taylor Stubblefield AU/699 RC 8.00 3.00
❑ 205 Walter Reyes AU/699 RC 8.00 3.00
❑ 206 Darren Sproles AU/699 RC 10.00 4.00
❑ 207 Courtney Roby AU/375 RC 12.00 5.00
❑ 208 Marlin Jackson AU/699 RC 10.00 4.00
❑ 209 Corey Webster AU/699 RC 10.00 4.00
❑ 210 Ryan Moats AU/699 RC 15.00 6.00
❑ 211 Marion Barber AU/375 RC 25.00 12.50
❑ 212 Frank Gore AU/699 RC 20.00 7.50
❑ 213 Kay-Jay Harris AU/699 RC 8.00 3.00
❑ 214 Anttaj Hawthorne AU/699 RC 8.00 3.00
❑ 215 Adam Jones AU/699 RC 10.00 4.00
❑ 216 Stefan LeFors AU/375 RC 12.00 5.00
❑ 217 Barrett Ruud AU/699 RC 10.00 4.00
❑ 218 Kevin Burnett AU/699 RC 10.00 4.00
❑ 219 T.A. McLendon AU/699 RC 8.00 3.00

❑ 220 James Butler AU/699 RC 8.00 3.00
❑ 221 J.R. Russell AU/699 RC 8.00 3.00
❑ 222 Vincent Jackson AU/300 RC 12.00 5.00
❑ 223 J.J. Arrington AU/699 RC 20.00 7.50
❑ 224 Maurice Clarett AU/175 20.00 7.50
❑ 225 Brandon Jacobs AU/699 RC 12.00 5.00
❑ 226 Craphonso Thorpe AU/699 RC 8.00 3.00
❑ 227 Fred Gibson AU/575 RC 8.00 3.00
❑ 228 Travis Johnson AU/699 RC 8.00 3.00
❑ 229 Kyle Orton AU/575 RC 30.00 15.00
❑ 230 Jason White AU/575 RC 10.00 4.00
❑ 231 Terrence Murphy AU/575 RC 10.00 4.00
❑ 232 Mark Clayton AU/375 RC 20.00 7.50
❑ 234 David Pollack AU/575 RC 12.00 5.00
❑ 235 Erasmus James AU/575 RC 10.00 4.00
❑ 236 Dan Cody AU/575 RC 10.00 4.00
❑ 237 Thomas Davis AU/575 RC 10.00 4.00
❑ 238 Carlos Rogers AU/575 RC 12.00 5.00
❑ 239 Derek Anderson AU/699 RC 10.00 4.00
❑ 240 Antrel Rolle AU/575 RC 10.00 4.00
❑ 241 Shawne Merriman AU/575 RC 20.00 10.00
❑ 242 Reggie Brown AU/699 RC 12.00 5.00
❑ 243 Heath Miller AU/699 RC 40.00 20.00
❑ 244 Roscoe Parrish AU/375 RC 12.00 5.00
❑ 245 Roddy White AU/375 RC 12.00 5.00
❑ 246 Eric Shelton AU/699 RC 10.00 4.00
❑ 247 Vernand Morency AU/575 RC 10.00 4.00
❑ 248 Ciatrick Fason AU/375 RC 12.00 5.00
❑ 249 Andrew Walter AU/375 RC 20.00 7.50
❑ 250 Jason Campbell AU/375 RC 40.00 25.00
❑ 251 Charles Frederick AU/699 RC 8.00 3.00
❑ 252 Troy Williamson AU/175 RC 30.00 12.50
❑ 253 Braylon Edwards AU/175 RC 80.00 30.00
❑ 254 Mike Williams AU/175 60.00 25.00
❑ 255 Cedric Benson AU/50 RC 100.00 50.00
❑ 256 Carnell Williams AU/175 RC 120.00 60.00
❑ 257 Ro.Brown AU/175 RC EXCH 100.00 50.00
❑ 258 Charlie Frye AU/175 RC 50.00 25.00
❑ 259 Alex Smith QB AU/175 RC 100.00 50.00
❑ 260 Aaron Rodgers AU/175 RC 80.00 40.00
❑ P1 Ben Roethlisberger Promo

2005 Upper Deck Kickoff

❑ COMPLETE SET (135) 50.00 20.00
❑ COMP.SET w/o RC's (90) 20.00 7.50
❑ COMMON CARD (1-90) .25 .08
❑ SEMISTARS .30 .10
❑ UNLISTED STARS .50 .20
❑ COMMON ROOKIE (91-135) 1.25 .50
❑ ROOKIE SEMISTARS 1.25 .50
❑ ROOKIE UNL.STARS 1.25 .50
❑ ONE DRAFT PICK PER PACK
❑ 1 Larry Fitzgerald .50 .20
❑ 2 Anquan Boldin .30 .10
❑ 3 Josh McCown .30 .10
❑ 4 Michael Vick .75 .30
❑ 5 Alge Crumpler .30 .10
❑ 6 Peerless Price .25 .08
❑ 7 Ray Lewis .50 .20
❑ 8 Kyle Boller .30 .10
❑ 9 Derrick Mason .30 .10
❑ 10 J.P. Losman .50 .20
❑ 11 Willis McGahee .50 .20
❑ 12 Eric Moulds .30 .10
❑ 13 Jake Delhomme .50 .20
❑ 14 DeShaun Foster .30 .10
❑ 15 Steve Smith .30 .10
❑ 16 Thomas Jones .30 .10
❑ 17 Rex Grossman .30 .10
❑ 18 Muhsin Muhammad .30 .10
❑ 19 Carson Palmer .50 .20
❑ 20 Rudi Johnson .30 .10
❑ 21 Chad Johnson .50 .20
❑ 22 Julius Jones .60 .25
❑ 23 Keyshawn Johnson .30 .10
❑ 24 Drew Bledsoe .50 .20
❑ 25 Tatum Bell .30 .10
❑ 26 Jake Plummer .30 .10
❑ 27 Ashley Lelie .30 .10
❑ 28 Roy Williams WR .50 .20
❑ 29 Kevin Jones .50 .20
❑ 30 Joey Harrington .50 .20
❑ 31 Brett Favre 1.25 .50
❑ 32 Ahman Green .50 .20
❑ 33 Javon Walker .30 .10
❑ 34 David Carr .50 .20
❑ 35 Andre Johnson .30 .10
❑ 36 Domanick Davis .30 .10
❑ 37 Peyton Manning .75 .30
❑ 38 Reggie Wayne .30 .10
❑ 39 Marvin Harrison .50 .20
❑ 40 Byron Leftwich .50 .20
❑ 41 Fred Taylor .30 .10
❑ 42 Jimmy Smith .30 .10
❑ 43 Priest Holmes .50 .20
❑ 44 Larry Johnson .50 .20
❑ 45 Trent Green .30 .10
❑ 46 A.J. Feeley .30 .10
❑ 47 Chris Chambers .30 .10
❑ 48 Randy McMichael .25 .08
❑ 49 Daunte Culpepper .50 .20
❑ 50 Michael Bennett .30 .10
❑ 51 Nate Burleson .30 .10
❑ 52 Tom Brady 1.25 .50
❑ 53 Corey Dillon .30 .10
❑ 54 Deion Branch .30 .10
❑ 55 Aaron Brooks .30 .10
❑ 56 Deuce McAllister .50 .20
❑ 57 Joe Horn .30 .10
❑ 58 Eli Manning 1.00 .40
❑ 59 Jeremy Shockey .50 .20
❑ 60 Tiki Barber .50 .20
❑ 61 Chad Pennington .50 .20
❑ 62 Curtis Martin .50 .20
❑ 63 Kerry Collins .30 .10
❑ 64 Jerry Porter .30 .10
❑ 65 Randy Moss .50 .20
❑ 66 Donovan McNabb .60 .25
❑ 67 Terrell Owens .50 .20
❑ 68 Brian Westbrook .30 .10
❑ 69 Ben Roethlisberger 1.25 .50
❑ 70 Jerome Bettis .50 .20
❑ 71 Hines Ward .50 .20
❑ 72 Drew Brees .50 .20
❑ 73 LaDainian Tomlinson .60 .25
❑ 74 Antonio Gates .50 .20
❑ 75 Kevan Barlow .30 .10
❑ 76 Eric Johnson .30 .10
❑ 77 Shaun Alexander .60 .25
❑ 78 Matt Hasselbeck .30 .10
❑ 79 Marc Bulger .50 .20
❑ 80 Steven Jackson .60 .25
❑ 81 Torry Holt .50 .20
❑ 82 Michael Pittman .25 .08
❑ 83 Brian Griese .30 .10
❑ 84 Michael Clayton .50 .20
❑ 85 Steve McNair .50 .20
❑ 86 Drew Bennett .30 .10
❑ 87 Chris Brown .30 .10
❑ 88 Clinton Portis .50 .20
❑ 89 Patrick Ramsey .30 .10
❑ 90 Santana Moss .30 .10
❑ 91 Aaron Rodgers RC 4.00 1.50
❑ 92 Alex Smith QB RC 5.00 2.00
❑ 93 Charlie Frye RC 2.50 1.00
❑ 94 Andrew Walter RC 2.00 .75
❑ 95 Jason Campbell RC 2.00 .75
❑ 96 Derek Anderson RC 1.25 .50
❑ 97 David Greene RC 1.25 .50
❑ 98 Ronnie Brown RC 4.00 1.50
❑ 99 Carnell Williams RC 6.00 2.50
❑ 100 Cedric Benson RC 2.50 1.00
❑ 101 Ciatrick Fason RC 1.25 .50
❑ 102 Vernand Morency RC 1.25 .50
❑ 103 Matt Jones RC 3.00 1.25
❑ 104 Maurice Clarett 1.25 .50
❑ 105 Mike Williams 2.50 1
❑ 106 Braylon Edwards RC 4.00 1
❑ 107 Mark Clayton RC 1.50
❑ 108 Reggie Brown RC 1.25
❑ 109 Troy Williamson RC 2.50 1
❑ 110 Roddy White RC 1.25
❑ 111 Jerome Mathis RC 1.25
❑ 112 Heath Miller RC 3.00 1
❑ 113 Antrel Rolle RC 1.25
❑ 114 Adam Jones RC 1.25
❑ 115 Vincent Jackson RC 1.25
❑ 116 Alex Smith TE RC 1.25
❑ 117 Marcus Spears RC 1.25
❑ 118 Courtney Roby RC 1.25
❑ 119 Stefan LeFors RC 1.25
❑ 120 Derrick Johnson RC 2.00
❑ 121 Shawne Merriman RC 2.00
❑ 122 Thomas Davis RC 1.25
❑ 123 Marlin Jackson RC 1.25
❑ 124 Ryan Moats RC 1.25
❑ 125 Dan Orlovsky RC 1.50
❑ 126 Kyle Orton RC 2.00
❑ 127 Adrian McPherson RC 1.25
❑ 128 Eric Shelton RC 1.25
❑ 129 Chris Henry RC 1.25
❑ 130 Carlos Rogers RC 1.50
❑ 131 Roscoe Parrish RC 1.25
❑ 132 J.J. Arrington RC 1.50
❑ 133 Mark Bradley RC 1.25
❑ 134 Frank Gore RC 2.00
❑ 135 Terrence Murphy RC 1.25

1997 Upper Deck Legenc

❑ COMPLETE SET (208) 60.00 25.
❑ 1 Bart Starr 2.50 1.
❑ 2 Jim Brown 2.50 1.
❑ 3 Joe Namath 3.00 1.
❑ 4 Walter Payton 5.00 2.
❑ 5 Terry Bradshaw 3.00 1.
❑ 6 Franco Harris .60
❑ 7 Dan Fouts .60
❑ 8 Steve Largent .60
❑ 9 Johnny Unitas 2.50 1.
❑ 10 Gale Sayers 1.50
❑ 11 Roger Staubach 3.00 1.
❑ 12 Tony Dorsett .60
❑ 13 Fran Tarkenton 1.50 .6
❑ 14 Charley Taylor .40
❑ 15 Ray Nitschke .60 .2
❑ 16 Jim Ringo .40
❑ 17 Dick Butkus 1.50 .6
❑ 18 Fred Biletnikoff .60
❑ 19 Lenny Moore .40
❑ 20 Len Dawson .60
❑ 21 Lance Alworth .40
❑ 22 Chuck Bednarik .40
❑ 23 Raymond Berry .40
❑ 24 Donnie Shell .25 .0
❑ 25 Mel Blount .40
❑ 26 Willie Brown .40
❑ 27 Ken Houston .25 .0
❑ 28 Larry Csonka .60 .2
❑ 29 Mike Ditka 1.25 .5
❑ 30 Art Donovan .40 .1
❑ 31 Sam Huff .40 .1
❑ 32 Lem Barney .25 .0
❑ 33 Hugh McElhenny .40 .1
❑ 34 Otto Graham .75 .3
❑ 35 Joe Greene .60 .2

❑ 36	Mike Rozier	.25	.08
❑ 37	Lou Groza	.40	.15
❑ 38	Ted Hendricks	.25	.08
❑ 39	Elroy Hirsch	.40	.15
❑ 40	Paul Hornung	.75	.30
❑ 41	Charlie Joiner	.40	.15
❑ 42	Deacon Jones	.40	.15
❑ 43	Bill Bradley	.25	.08
❑ 44	Floyd Little	.25	.08
❑ 45	Willie Lanier	.25	.08
❑ 46	Bob Lilly	.40	.15
❑ 47	Sid Luckman	.40	.15
❑ 48	John Mackey	.25	.08
❑ 49	Don Maynard	.40	.15
❑ 50	Mike McCormack	.25	.08
❑ 51	Bobby Mitchell	.40	.15
❑ 52	Ron Mix	.40	.15
❑ 53	Marion Motley	.25	.08
❑ 54	Leo Nomellini	.40	.15
❑ 55	Mark Duper	.25	.08
❑ 56	Mel Renfro	.25	.08
❑ 57	Jim Otto	.40	.15
❑ 58	Alan Page	.40	.15
❑ 59	Joe Perry	.40	.15
❑ 60	Andy Robustelli	.25	.08
❑ 61	Lee Roy Selmon	.40	.15
❑ 62	Jackie Smith	.40	.15
❑ 63	Art Shell	.40	.15
❑ 64	Jan Stenerud	.25	.08
❑ 65	Gene Upshaw	.40	.15
❑ 66	Y.A. Tittle	.60	.25
❑ 67	Paul Warfield	.60	.25
❑ 68	Kellen Winslow	.25	.08
❑ 69	Randy White	.40	.15
❑ 70	Larry Wilson	.25	.08
❑ 71	Willie Wood	.40	.15
❑ 72	Jack Ham	.40	.15
❑ 73	Jack Youngblood	.25	.08
❑ 74	Dan Abramowicz	.25	.08
❑ 75	Dick Anderson	.25	.08
❑ 76	Ken Anderson	.40	.15
❑ 77	Steve Bartkowski	.25	.08
❑ 78	Bill Bergey	.25	.08
❑ 79	Rocky Bleier	.40	.15
❑ 80	Cliff Branch	.40	.15
❑ 81	John Brodie	.25	.08
❑ 82	Bobby Bell	.25	.08
❑ 83	Billy Cannon	.25	.08
❑ 84	Gino Cappelletti	.25	.08
❑ 85	Harold Carmichael	.25	.08
❑ 86	Dave Casper	.25	.08
❑ 87	Wes Chandler	.25	.08
❑ 88	Todd Christensen	.25	.08
❑ 89	Dwight Clark	.40	.15
❑ 90	Mark Clayton	.25	.08
❑ 91	Cris Collinsworth	.25	.08
❑ 92	Roger Craig	.40	.15
❑ 93	Randy Cross	.25	.08
❑ 94	Isaac Curtis	.25	.08
❑ 95	Mike Curtis	.25	.08
❑ 96	Ben Davidson	.25	.08
❑ 97	Fred Dean	.25	.08
❑ 98	Tom Dempsey	.25	.08
❑ 99	Eric Dickerson	.40	.15
❑ 100	Lynn Dickey	.25	.08
❑ 101	John McKay LL	.25	.08
❑ 102	Carl Eller	.25	.08
❑ 103	Chuck Foreman	.25	.08
❑ 104	Russ Francis	.25	.08
❑ 105	Joe Gibbs LL	.40	.15
❑ 106	Gary Garrison	.25	.08
❑ 107	Randy Gradishar	.25	.08
❑ 108	L.C. Greenwood	.40	.15
❑ 109	Rosey Grier	.25	.08
❑ 110	Steve Grogan	.25	.08
❑ 111	Ray Guy	.25	.08
❑ 112	John Hadl	.25	.08
❑ 113	Jim Hart	.25	.08
❑ 114	George Halas LL	.40	.15
❑ 115	Mike Haynes	.25	.08
❑ 116	Charlie Hennigan	.25	.08
❑ 117	Chuck Howley	.25	.08
❑ 118	Harold Jackson	.25	.08
❑ 119	Tom Jackson	.25	.08
❑ 120	Ron Jaworski	.25	.08
❑ 121	John Jefferson	.25	.08
❑ 122	Billy Johnson	.25	.08
❑ 123	Ed Too Tall Jones	.40	.15
❑ 124	Jack Kemp	1.50	.60
❑ 125	Jim Kiick	.25	.08
❑ 126	Billy Kilmer	.40	.15
❑ 127	Jerry Kramer	.40	.15
❑ 128	Paul Krause	.25	.08
❑ 129	Daryle Lamonica	.25	.08
❑ 130	Bill Walsh LL	.40	.15
❑ 131	James Lofton	.25	.08
❑ 132	Hank Stram LL	.25	.08
❑ 133	Archie Manning	.40	.15
❑ 134	Jim Marshall	.25	.08
❑ 135	Harvey Martin	.25	.08
❑ 136	Tommy McDonald	.25	.08
❑ 137	Max McGee	.40	.15
❑ 138	Reggie McKenzie	.25	.08
❑ 139	Karl Mecklenburg	.25	.08
❑ 140	Tom Landry LL	.60	.25
❑ 141	Terry Metcalf	.25	.08
❑ 142	Matt Millen	.25	.08
❑ 143	Earl Morrall	.25	.08
❑ 144	Mercury Morris	.25	.08
❑ 145	Chuck Noll LL	.40	.15
❑ 146	Joe Morris	.25	.08
❑ 147	Mark Moseley	.25	.08
❑ 148	Haven Moses	.25	.08
❑ 149	Chuck Muncie	.25	.08
❑ 150	Anthony Munoz	.40	.15
❑ 151	Tommy Nobis	.25	.08
❑ 152	Babe Parilli	.25	.08
❑ 153	Drew Pearson	.40	.15
❑ 154	Ozzie Newsome	.25	.08
❑ 155	Jim Plunkett	.40	.15
❑ 156	William Perry	.25	.08
❑ 157	Johnny Robinson	.25	.08
❑ 158	Ahmad Rashad	.40	.15
❑ 159	George Rogers	.25	.08
❑ 160	Sterling Sharpe	.40	.15
❑ 161	Billy Sims	.25	.08
❑ 162	Sid Gillman LL	.25	.08
❑ 163	Mike Singletary	.25	.08
❑ 164	Charlie Sanders	.25	.08
❑ 165	Bubba Smith	.25	.08
❑ 166	Ken Stabler	2.00	.75
❑ 167	Freddie Solomon	.25	.08
❑ 168	John Stallworth	.40	.15
❑ 169	Dwight Stephenson	.40	.15
❑ 170	Vince Lombardi LL	1.00	.40
❑ 171	Weeb Ewbank LL	.25	.08
❑ 172	Lionel Taylor	.25	.08
❑ 173	Otis Taylor	.25	.08
❑ 174	Joe Theismann	.60	.25
❑ 175	Bob Trumpy	.25	.08
❑ 176	Mike Webster	.25	.08
❑ 177	Jim Zorn	.25	.08
❑ 178	Joe Montana	5.00	2.00
❑ 179	Packers Superbowl SM	.40	.15
❑ 180	Bart Starr SM	1.25	.50
❑ 181	Max McGee SM	.40	.15
❑ 182	Joe Namath SM	1.50	.60
❑ 183	Johnny Unitas SM	1.25	.50
❑ 184	Len Dawson SM	.40	.15
❑ 185	Chuck Howley SM	.25	.08
❑ 186	Roger Staubach SM	1.50	.60
❑ 187	Paul Warfield SM	.40	.15
❑ 188	Larry Csonka SM	.40	.15
❑ 189	Fran Tarkenton SM	.60	.25
❑ 190	Terry Bradshaw SM	1.50	.60
❑ 191	Ken Stabler SM	.75	.30
❑ 192	Fred Biletnikoff SM	.40	.15
❑ 193	Chuck Foreman SM	.25	.08
❑ 194	Harvey Martin SM	.25	.08
❑ 195	Tony Dorsett SM	.40	.15
❑ 196	Terry Bradshaw SM	1.50	.60
❑ 197	John Stallworth SM	.25	.08
❑ 198	Franco Harris SM	.40	.15
❑ 199	Ken Anderson SM	.25	.08
❑ 200	Joe Theismann SM	.40	.15
❑ 201	Jim Plunkett SM	.25	.08
❑ 202	Roger Craig SM	.25	.08
❑ 203	William Perry SM	.25	.08
❑ 204	Steve Grogan SM	.25	.08
❑ 205	Joe Montana SM	2.50	1.00
❑ 206	Russ Francis SM	.25	.08
❑ 207	Joe Montana SM	2.50	1.00
❑ 208	Joe Montana SM	2.50	1.00

2000 Upper Deck Legends

❑	COMPLETE SET (132)	400.00	200.00
❑	COMP.SET w/o SP's (90)	20.00	7.50
❑ 1	Jake Plummer	.30	.10
❑ 2	Jamal Anderson	.50	.20
❑ 3	Doug Flutie	.50	.20
❑ 4	Jim Kelly	.60	.25
❑ 5	Dick Butkus	1.00	.40
❑ 6	Mike Singletary	.50	.20
❑ 7	Gale Sayers	1.00	.40
❑ 8	Boomer Esiason	.30	.10
❑ 9	Anthony Munoz	.30	.10
❑ 10	Otto Graham	.30	.10
❑ 11	Jim Brown	1.25	.50
❑ 12	Ozzie Newsome	.20	.07
❑ 13	Bob Lilly	.30	.10
❑ 14	Troy Aikman	1.25	.50
❑ 15	Emmitt Smith	1.25	.50
❑ 16	Roger Staubach	1.25	.50
❑ 17	Deion Sanders	.50	.20
❑ 18	Tony Dorsett	.50	.20
❑ 19	Terrell Davis	.50	.20
❑ 20	John Elway	2.00	.75
❑ 21	Charlie Batch	.50	.20
❑ 22	Brett Favre	2.00	.75
❑ 23	Bart Starr	1.50	.60
❑ 24	Reggie White	.50	.20
❑ 25	Earl Campbell	.50	.20
❑ 26	Peyton Manning	1.50	.60
❑ 27	Edgerrin James	1.00	.40
❑ 28	Johnny Unitas	1.25	.50
❑ 29	Marvin Harrison	.50	.20
❑ 30	Mark Brunell	.50	.20
❑ 31	Fred Taylor	.50	.20
❑ 32	Len Dawson	.50	.20
❑ 33	Dan Marino	2.00	.75
❑ 34	Bob Griese	.50	.20
❑ 35	Mark Duper	.20	.07
❑ 36	Thurman Thomas	.30	.10
❑ 37	Fran Tarkenton	1.00	.40
❑ 38	Randy Moss	1.25	.50
❑ 39	Cris Carter	.50	.20
❑ 40	Gary Anderson	.20	.07
❑ 41	John Randle	.30	.10
❑ 42	Drew Bledsoe	.75	.30
❑ 43	Archie Manning	.30	.10
❑ 44	Ricky Williams	.50	.20
❑ 45	Frank Gifford	.50	.20
❑ 46	Kerry Collins	.30	.10
❑ 47	Phil Simms	.30	.10
❑ 48	Vinny Testaverde	.30	.10
❑ 49	Curtis Martin	.50	.20
❑ 50	Keyshawn Johnson	.50	.20
❑ 51	Joe Namath	1.25	.50
❑ 52	Marcus Allen	.60	.25
❑ 53	Bruce Smith	.30	.10
❑ 54	Ken Stabler	1.25	.50
❑ 55	Fred Biletnikoff	.50	.20
❑ 56	Howie Long	.60	.25
❑ 57	Ron Jaworski	.20	.07
❑ 58	Harold Carmichael	.20	.07
❑ 59	Kordell Stewart	.30	.10
❑ 60	Levon Kirkland	.20	.07
❑ 61	Mel Blount	.30	.10
❑ 62	Jerome Bettis	.50	.20
❑ 63	John Stallworth	.30	.10
❑ 64	Franco Harris	.60	.25
❑ 65	Jim Harbaugh	.30	.10
❑ 66	Kellen Winslow	.30	.10

❑	67	Charlie Joiner	.20	.07
❑	68	Junior Seau	.50	.20
❑	69	Jerry Rice	1.25	.50
❑	70	Steve Young	1.00	.40
❑	71	Joe Montana	2.50	1.00
❑	72	Roger Craig	.30	.10
❑	73	Ronnie Lott	.30	.10
❑	74	Jon Kitna	.50	.20
❑	75	Steve Largent	.50	.20
❑	76	Ricky Watters	.30	.10
❑	77	Kurt Warner	1.25	.50
❑	78	Marshall Faulk	.75	.30
❑	79	Isaac Bruce	.50	.20
❑	80	Merlin Olsen	.30	.10
❑	81	Lee Roy Selmon	.20	.07
❑	82	Tim Brown	.50	.20
❑	83	Tim Couch	.30	.10
❑	84	Mike Alstott	.50	.20
❑	85	Eddie George	.50	.20
❑	86	Steve McNair	.50	.20
❑	87	Brad Johnson	.50	.20
❑	88	Sonny Jurgensen	.50	.20
❑	89	Art Monk	.30	.10
❑	90	Joe Theismann	.50	.20
❑	91	Ray Nitschke TCL	10.00	4.00
❑	92	Doak Walker TCL	10.00	4.00
❑	93	Thurman Thomas TCL	10.00	4.00
❑	94	Jim Brown TCL	12.00	5.00
❑	95	Sammy Baugh TCL	15.00	6.00
❑	96	Reggie White TCL	10.00	4.00
❑	97	Eric Dickerson TCL	10.00	4.00
❑	98	Paul Hornung TCL	10.00	4.00
❑	99	Deion Sanders TCL	12.00	5.00
❑	100	Bronko Nagurski TCL	10.00	4.00
❑	101	Walter Payton TCL	25.00	12.50
❑	102	Jim Thorpe TCL	12.00	5.00
❑	103	Ron Dayne RC	6.00	2.50
❑	104	Tim Rattay RC	6.00	2.50
❑	105	Brian Urlacher RC	25.00	10.00
❑	106	Bubba Franks RC	6.00	2.50
❑	107	Chad Pennington RC	15.00	6.00
❑	108	Chris Cole RC	5.00	2.00
❑	109	Chris Redman RC	5.00	2.00
❑	110	Courtney Brown RC	6.00	2.50
❑	111	Curtis Keaton RC	5.00	2.00
❑	112	Dennis Northcutt RC	10.00	4.00
❑	113	Dez White RC	6.00	2.50
❑	114	Giovanni Carmazzi RC	10.00	4.00
❑	115	J.R. Redmond RC	5.00	2.00
❑	116	JaJuan Dawson RC	10.00	4.00
❑	117	Jamal Lewis RC	15.00	6.00
❑	118	Jerry Porter RC	8.00	3.00
❑	119	Laveranues Coles RC	8.00	3.00
❑	120	Peter Warrick RC	6.00	2.50
❑	121	Plaxico Burress RC	12.00	5.00
❑	122	R.Jay Soward RC	5.00	2.00
❑	123	Reuben Droughns RC	8.00	3.00
❑	124	Ron Dixon RC	5.00	2.00
❑	125	Ron Dugans RC	10.00	4.00
❑	126	Shaun Alexander RC	30.00	12.50
❑	127	Sylvester Morris RC	5.00	2.00
❑	128	Thomas Jones RC	10.00	4.00
❑	129	Todd Pinkston RC	6.00	2.50
❑	130	Travis Prentice RC	5.00	2.00
❑	131	Travis Taylor RC	10.00	4.00
❑	132	Trung Canidate RC	5.00	2.00

2001 Upper Deck Legends

❑		COMP.SET w/o SP's (90)	30.00	12.50
❑	1	Jake Plummer	.50	.20
❑	2	Jamal Anderson	.75	.30
❑	3	Ray Lewis	.75	.30
❑	4	Johnny Unitas	1.50	.60
❑	5	Jamal Lewis	1.50	.60
❑	6	Andre Reed	.50	.20
❑	7	Jim Kelly	1.25	.50
❑	8	Thurman Thomas	.50	.20
❑	9	Rob Johnson	.50	.20
❑	10	Brian Urlacher	1.50	.60
❑	11	Dick Butkus	1.50	.60
❑	12	Gale Sayers	1.50	.60
❑	13	James Allen	.50	.20
❑	14	Corey Dillon	.75	.30
❑	15	Jim Brown	1.50	.60
❑	16	Tim Couch	.50	.20
❑	17	Joey Galloway	.50	.20
❑	18	Emmitt Smith	2.00	.75
❑	19	Randy White	.50	.20
❑	20	Roger Staubach	1.50	.60
❑	21	Troy Aikman	1.50	.60
❑	22	Tony Dorsett	.75	.30
❑	23	Brian Griese	.75	.30
❑	24	Floyd Little	.30	.10
❑	25	John Elway	3.00	1.25
❑	26	Mike Anderson	.75	.30
❑	27	Terrell Davis	.75	.30
❑	28	Barry Sanders	2.00	.75
❑	29	Charlie Batch	.75	.30
❑	30	Bart Starr	2.00	.75
❑	31	Paul Hornung	.75	.30
❑	32	Reggie White	.75	.30
❑	33	Warren Moon	.75	.30
❑	34	Edgerrin James	1.25	.50
❑	35	Peyton Manning	2.50	1.00
❑	36	Mark Brunell	.75	.30
❑	37	Tony Gonzalez	.50	.20
❑	38	Eric Dickerson	.50	.20
❑	39	Jack Youngblood	.30	.10
❑	40	Jay Fiedler	.75	.30
❑	41	Lamar Smith	.50	.20
❑	42	Dan Marino	3.00	1.25
❑	43	Oronde Gadsden	.50	.20
❑	44	Cris Carter	.75	.30
❑	45	Fran Tarkenton	1.25	.50
❑	46	Daunte Culpepper	.75	.30
❑	47	Randy Moss	2.00	.75
❑	48	Robert Smith	.30	.10
❑	49	Drew Bledsoe	1.25	.50
❑	50	Archie Manning	.50	.20
❑	51	Jeff Blake	.50	.20
❑	52	Ricky Williams	.75	.30
❑	53	Kerry Collins	.50	.20
❑	54	Ron Dayne	.75	.30
❑	55	Lawrence Taylor	.75	.30
❑	56	Wayne Chrebet	.50	.20
❑	57	Vinny Testaverde	.50	.20
❑	58	Joe Namath	1.50	.60
❑	59	Jim Plunkett	.50	.20
❑	60	George Blanda	.75	.30
❑	61	Tim Brown	.75	.30
❑	62	Jerry Rice	2.00	.75
❑	63	Ken Stabler	1.50	.60
❑	64	Marcus Allen	1.25	.50
❑	65	Donovan McNabb	1.25	.50
❑	66	Harold Carmichael	.30	.10
❑	67	Franco Harris	1.25	.50
❑	68	Jerome Bettis	.75	.30
❑	69	Terry Bradshaw	1.50	.60
❑	70	Doug Flutie	.75	.30
❑	71	Lance Alworth	.50	.20
❑	72	Junior Seau	.75	.30
❑	73	Kellen Winslow	.50	.20
❑	74	Dan Fouts	.75	.30
❑	75	Joe Montana	5.00	2.00
❑	76	Terrell Owens	.75	.30
❑	77	Jeff Garcia	.75	.30
❑	78	Steve Young	1.25	.50
❑	79	Matt Hasselbeck	.50	.20
❑	80	Kurt Warner	2.00	.75
❑	81	Marshall Faulk	1.25	.50
❑	82	Brad Johnson	.75	.30
❑	83	Eddie George	.75	.30
❑	84	Charley Taylor	.50	.20
❑	85	Stephen Davis	.75	.30
❑	86	Jeff George	.50	.20
❑	87	John Riggins	1.25	.50
❑	88	Joe Theismann	.75	.30
❑	89	Michael Westbrook	.50	.20
❑	90	Sonny Jurgensen	.75	.30
❑	91	Andre Carter RC	8.00	3.00
❑	92	Cedrick Wilson RC	8.00	3.00
❑	93	Kevan Barlow RC	8.00	3.00
❑	94	Anthony Thomas RC	8.00	3.00
❑	95	David Terrell RC	8.00	3.00
❑	96	Chad Johnson RC	20.00	7.50
❑	97	Justin Smith RC	8.00	3.00
❑	98	Rudi Johnson RC	15.00	6.00
❑	99	T.J. Houshmandzadeh RC	8.00	3.00
❑	100	Brandon Spoon RC	8.00	3.00
❑	101	Nate Clements RC	8.00	3.00
❑	102	Travis Henry RC	8.00	3.00
❑	103	Kevin Kasper RC	8.00	3.00
❑	104	Willie Middlebrooks RC	5.00	2.00
❑	105	Gerard Warren RC	8.00	3.00
❑	106	James Jackson RC	8.00	3.00
❑	107	Quincy Morgan RC	8.00	3.00
❑	108	Bobby Newcombe RC	5.00	2.00
❑	109	Arnold Jackson RC	5.00	2.00
❑	110	Carlos Polk RC	3.00	1.25
❑	111	Drew Brees RC	20.00	7.50
❑	112	LaDainian Tomlinson RC	40.00	20.00
❑	113	Tay Cody RC	3.00	1.25
❑	114	Zeke Moreno RC	8.00	3.00
❑	115	Snoop Minnis RC	5.00	2.00
❑	116	George Layne RC	5.00	2.00
❑	117	Derrick Blaylock RC	8.00	3.00
❑	118	Reggie Wayne RC	15.00	6.00
❑	119	Tony Dixon RC	5.00	2.00
❑	120	Quincy Carter RC	8.00	3.00
❑	121	Chris Chambers RC	12.00	5.00
❑	122	Jamar Fletcher RC	5.00	2.00
❑	123	Josh Heupel RC	8.00	3.00
❑	124	Travis Minor RC	5.00	2.00
❑	125	A.J. Feeley RC	8.00	3.00
❑	126	Correll Buckhalter RC	10.00	4.00
❑	127	Freddie Mitchell RC	8.00	3.00
❑	128	Alge Crumpler RC	10.00	5.00
❑	129	Michael Vick RC	50.00	20.00
❑	130	Vinny Sutherland RC	5.00	2.00
❑	131	Marcus Stroud RC	8.00	3.00
❑	132	Mike McMahon RC	8.00	3.00
❑	133	Scotty Anderson RC	5.00	2.00
❑	134	Shaun Rogers RC	8.00	3.00
❑	135	Jesse Palmer RC	8.00	3.00
❑	136	Will Allen RC	5.00	2.00
❑	137	LaMont Jordan RC	15.00	6.00
❑	138	Santana Moss RC	12.00	5.00
❑	139	Reggie White RC	5.00	2.00
❑	140	Jamal Reynolds RC	8.00	3.00
❑	141	Robert Ferguson RC	8.00	3.00
❑	142	Torrance Marshall RC	8.00	3.00
❑	143	Chris Weinke RC	8.00	3.00
❑	144	Dan Morgan RC	8.00	3.00
❑	145	Steve Smith RC	20.00	10.00
❑	146	Dee Brown RC	8.00	3.00
❑	147	Arther Love RC	3.00	1.25
❑	148	Hakim Akbar RC	3.00	1.25
❑	149	Jabari Holloway RC	5.00	2.00
❑	150	Derek Combs RC	5.00	2.00
❑	151	Derrick Gibson RC	5.00	2.00
❑	152	Ken-Yon Rambo RC	5.00	2.00
❑	153	Marques Tuiasosopo RC	8.00	3.00
❑	154	Adam Archuleta RC	8.00	3.00
❑	155	Tommy Polley RC	8.00	3.00
❑	156	Brian Allen RC	3.00	1.25
❑	157	Milton Wynn RC	5.00	2.00
❑	158	Francis St.Paul RC	5.00	2.00
❑	159	Edgerton Hartwell RC	3.00	1.25
❑	160	Gary Baxter RC	5.00	2.00
❑	161	Todd Heap RC	8.00	3.00
❑	162	Chris Barnes RC	5.00	2.00
❑	163	Fred Smoot RC	8.00	3.00
❑	164	Rod Gardner RC	8.00	3.00
❑	165	Sage Rosenfels RC	8.00	3.00
❑	166	Damerien McCants RC	5.00	2.00
❑	167	Deuce McAllister RC	15.00	6.00
❑	168	Moran Norris RC	3.00	1.25
❑	169	Sedrick Hodge RC	3.00	1.25
❑	170	Alex Bannister RC	5.00	2.00
❑	171	Heath Evans RC	5.00	2.00
❑	172	Josh Booty RC	8.00	3.00
❑	173	Ken Lucas RC	5.00	2.00

❑ 174 Koren Robinson RC	8.00	3.00
❑ 175 Chris Taylor RC	5.00	2.00
❑ 176 Andre Dyson RC	3.00	1.25
❑ 177 Dan Alexander RC	8.00	3.00
❑ 178 Justin McCareins RC	8.00	3.00
❑ 179 Eddie Berlin RC	5.00	2.00
❑ 180 Michael Bennett RC	12.00	5.00

2004 Upper Deck Legends

❑ COMP.SET w/o SP's (90)	20.00	7.50
❑ 91-110 LEGENDS/1250 ODDS 1:24		
❑ 111-190 ROOKIE/650 ODDS 1:12		
❑ 1 Josh McCown	.50	.20
❑ 2 Emmitt Smith	1.50	.60
❑ 3 Michael Vick	1.50	.60
❑ 4 Peerless Price	.50	.20
❑ 5 Ray Lewis	.75	.30
❑ 6 Kyle Boller	.75	.30
❑ 7 Deion Sanders	.75	.30
❑ 8 Drew Bledsoe	.75	.30
❑ 9 Travis Henry	.50	.20
❑ 10 Eric Moulds	.50	.20
❑ 11 Steve Smith	.75	.30
❑ 12 Stephen Davis	.50	.20
❑ 13 Jake Delhomme	.75	.30
❑ 14 Rex Grossman	.75	.30
❑ 15 Brian Urlacher	1.00	.40
❑ 16 Thomas Jones	.50	.20
❑ 17 Chad Johnson	.75	.30
❑ 18 Rudi Johnson	.50	.20
❑ 19 Carson Palmer	1.00	.40
❑ 20 William Green	.50	.20
❑ 21 Andre Davis	.30	.10
❑ 22 Jeff Garcia	.75	.30
❑ 23 Roy Williams S	.50	.20
❑ 24 Eddie George	.50	.20
❑ 25 Keyshawn Johnson	.50	.20
❑ 26 Reuben Droughns	.50	.20
❑ 27 Jake Plummer	.50	.20
❑ 28 Champ Bailey	.50	.20
❑ 29 Charles Rogers	.50	.20
❑ 30 Joey Harrington	.75	.30
❑ 31 Ahman Green	.75	.30
❑ 32 Brett Favre	2.00	.75
❑ 33 Javon Walker	.50	.20
❑ 34 David Carr	.75	.30
❑ 35 Domanick Davis	.75	.30
❑ 36 Andre Johnson	.75	.30
❑ 37 Marvin Harrison	.75	.30
❑ 38 Edgerrin James	.75	.30
❑ 39 Peyton Manning	1.25	.50
❑ 40 Byron Leftwich	1.00	.40
❑ 41 Fred Taylor	.50	.20
❑ 42 Trent Green	.50	.20
❑ 43 Tony Gonzalez	.50	.20
❑ 44 Priest Holmes	1.00	.40
❑ 45 Zach Thomas	.75	.30
❑ 46 Chris Chambers	.50	.20
❑ 47 Jay Fiedler	.30	.10
❑ 48 Daunte Culpepper	.75	.30
❑ 49 Randy Moss	1.00	.40
❑ 50 Onterrio Smith	.50	.20
❑ 51 Tom Brady	2.00	.75
❑ 52 Deion Branch	.75	.30
❑ 53 Corey Dillon	.50	.20
❑ 54 Deuce McAllister	.75	.30
❑ 55 Aaron Brooks	.50	.20
❑ 56 Joe Horn	.50	.20
❑ 57 Tiki Barber	.75	.30
❑ 58 Kurt Warner	.75	.30
❑ 59 Jeremy Shockey	.75	.30
❑ 60 Chad Pennington	.75	.30
❑ 61 Santana Moss	.50	.20
❑ 62 Curtis Martin	.75	.30
❑ 63 Kerry Collins	.50	.20
❑ 64 Jerry Rice	1.50	.60
❑ 65 Jerry Porter	.50	.20
❑ 66 Terrell Owens	.75	.30
❑ 67 Jevon Kearse	.50	.20
❑ 68 Donovan McNabb	1.00	.40
❑ 69 Hines Ward	.75	.30
❑ 70 Plaxico Burress	.50	.20
❑ 71 Duce Staley	.50	.20
❑ 72 Drew Brees	.75	.30
❑ 73 LaDainian Tomlinson	1.00	.40
❑ 74 Tim Rattay	.30	.10
❑ 75 Brandon Lloyd	.50	.20
❑ 76 Kevan Barlow	.50	.20
❑ 77 Shaun Alexander	.75	.30
❑ 78 Koren Robinson	.50	.20
❑ 79 Matt Hasselbeck	.50	.20
❑ 80 Marshall Faulk	.75	.30
❑ 81 Torry Holt	.75	.30
❑ 82 Marc Bulger	.75	.30
❑ 83 Brian Griese	.50	.20
❑ 84 Derrick Brooks	.50	.20
❑ 85 Steve McNair	.75	.30
❑ 86 Derrick Mason	.50	.20
❑ 87 Chris Brown	.75	.30
❑ 88 Mark Brunell	.50	.20
❑ 89 Laveranues Coles	.50	.20
❑ 90 Clinton Portis	.75	.30
❑ 91 Dick Butkus	8.00	3.00
❑ 92 Gale Sayers	6.00	2.50
❑ 93 Mike Ditka	5.00	2.00
❑ 94 Jim Brown	8.00	3.00
❑ 95 Roger Staubach	8.00	3.00
❑ 96 Troy Aikman	6.00	2.50
❑ 97 John Elway	8.00	3.00
❑ 98 Barry Sanders	8.00	3.00
❑ 99 Bart Starr	10.00	4.00
❑ 100 Paul Hornung	5.00	2.00
❑ 101 Len Dawson	5.00	2.00
❑ 102 Dan Marino	10.00	4.00
❑ 103 Fran Tarkenton	6.00	2.50
❑ 104 Archie Manning	5.00	2.00
❑ 105 Joe Namath	8.00	3.00
❑ 106 Ken Stabler	6.00	2.50
❑ 107 Lynn Swann	6.00	2.50
❑ 108 Terry Bradshaw	8.00	3.00
❑ 109 Joe Montana	12.00	5.00
❑ 110 Joe Theismann	5.00	2.00
❑ 111 Bernard Berrian RC	5.00	2.00
❑ 112 Ben Hartsock RC	5.00	2.00
❑ 113 Karlos Dansby RC	5.00	2.00
❑ 114 Thomas Tapeh RC	4.00	1.50
❑ 115 Keary Colbert RC	6.00	2.50
❑ 116 Ben Troupe RC	5.00	2.00
❑ 117 Jonathan Vilma RC	5.00	2.00
❑ 118 Jamaar Taylor RC	5.00	2.00
❑ 119 Ben Roethlisberger RC	50.00	25.00
❑ 120 Samie Parker RC	5.00	2.00
❑ 121 Dunta Robinson RC	5.00	2.00
❑ 122 Dontarrious Thomas RC	5.00	2.00
❑ 123 Adimchinobe Echemandu RC	4.00	1.50
❑ 124 Darius Watts RC	5.00	2.00
❑ 125 Ben Watson RC	5.00	2.00
❑ 126 Terry Johnson RC	4.00	1.50
❑ 127 D.J. Hackett RC	4.00	1.50
❑ 128 Devery Henderson RC	4.00	1.50
❑ 129 Kellen Winslow Jr. RC	10.00	4.00
❑ 130 Travis LaBoy RC	5.00	2.00
❑ 131 Maurice Mann RC	4.00	1.50
❑ 132 Rashaun Woods RC	5.00	2.00
❑ 133 Michael Turner RC	5.00	2.00
❑ 134 Junior Siavii RC	5.00	2.00
❑ 135 Johnnie Morant RC	5.00	2.00
❑ 136 Larry Fitzgerald RC	15.00	6.00
❑ 137 Kevin Jones RC	15.00	6.00
❑ 138 Will Smith RC	5.00	2.00
❑ 139 Robert Gallery RC	8.00	3.00
❑ 140 Michael Jenkins RC	5.00	2.00
❑ 141 Cedric Cobbs RC	5.00	2.00
❑ 142 Igor Olshansky RC	5.00	2.00
❑ 143 Josh Harris RC	5.00	2.00
❑ 144 Michael Clayton RC	10.00	4.00
❑ 145 Mewelde Moore RC	6.00	2.50
❑ 146 Jason Babin RC	5.00	2.00
❑ 147 Cody Pickett RC	5.00	2.00
❑ 148 Lee Evans RC	6.00	2.50
❑ 149 Greg Jones RC	5.00	2.00
❑ 150 Marcus Tubbs RC	5.00	2.00
❑ 151 Craig Krenzel RC	5.00	2.00
❑ 152 Roy Williams RC	12.00	5.00
❑ 153 Tatum Bell RC	10.00	4.00
❑ 154 Kenechi Udeze RC	5.00	2.00
❑ 155 Shawn Andrews RC	5.00	2.00
❑ 156 Reggie Williams RC	6.00	2.50
❑ 157 Julius Jones RC	20.00	7.50
❑ 158 Vince Wilfork RC	6.00	2.50
❑ 159 Vernon Carey RC	4.00	1.50
❑ 160 Eli Manning RC	25.00	12.50
❑ 161 Devard Darling RC	5.00	2.00
❑ 162 Sean Taylor RC	6.00	2.50
❑ 163 Teddy Lehman RC	5.00	2.00
❑ 164 Jammal Lord RC	5.00	2.00
❑ 165 J.P. Losman RC	10.00	4.00
❑ 166 Jerricho Cotchery RC	5.00	2.00
❑ 167 Ahmad Carroll RC	6.00	2.50
❑ 168 Michael Boulware RC	5.00	2.00
❑ 169 Quincy Wilson RC	4.00	1.50
❑ 170 Derrick Hamilton RC	4.00	1.50
❑ 171 Kris Wilson RC	5.00	2.00
❑ 172 D.J. Williams RC	6.00	2.50
❑ 173 P.K. Sam RC	4.00	1.50
❑ 174 Matt Schaub RC	8.00	3.00
❑ 175 Ernest Wilford RC	5.00	2.00
❑ 176 Chris Gamble RC	6.00	2.50
❑ 177 Courtney Watson RC	5.00	2.00
❑ 178 Drew Henson RC	5.00	2.00
❑ 179 Chris Perry RC	8.00	3.00
❑ 180 Tommie Harris RC	5.00	2.00
❑ 181 Marquis Cooper RC	4.00	1.50
❑ 182 Philip Rivers RC	15.00	6.00
❑ 183 Carlos Francis RC	4.00	1.50
❑ 184 DeAngelo Hall RC	6.00	2.50
❑ 185 Daryl Smith RC	5.00	2.00
❑ 186 Troy Fleming RC	4.00	1.50
❑ 187 Luke McCown RC	5.00	2.00
❑ 188 Steven Jackson RC	15.00	6.00
❑ 189 Ricardo Colclough RC	5.00	2.00
❑ 190 Gilbert Gardner RC	4.00	1.50

2005 Upper Deck Legends

❑ COMP.SET w/o SP's (100)	20.00	7.50
❑ ROOKIE PRINT RUN 725 SER.#'d SETS		
❑ 166-195 LEG.PRINT RUN 1025 SER.#'d SETS		
❑ 1 Charley Taylor	.50	.20
❑ 2 Roger Craig	.50	.20
❑ 3 Ozzie Newsome	.50	.20
❑ 4 Rocky Bleier	.75	.30
❑ 5 Russ Francis	.40	.15
❑ 6 Jerry Rice	1.50	.60
❑ 7 Pat Haden	.40	.15
❑ 8 Brett Favre	2.00	.75
❑ 9 Joe Ferguson	.40	.15
❑ 10 Ed Jones	.50	.20
❑ 11 Joe Washington	.40	.15
❑ 12 John Brodie	.40	.15
❑ 13 Peyton Manning	1.25	.50
❑ 14 Mark Van Eeghen	.40	.15
❑ 15 William Perry	.50	.20
❑ 16 Bob Brown	.40	.15
❑ 17 Herb Adderley	.40	.15

❑ 18 Deion Sanders	1.00	.40
❑ 19 Lenny Moore	.50	.20
❑ 20 Tom Mack	.40	.15
❑ 21 Jim McMahon	.75	.30
❑ 22 Bobby Mitchell	.50	.20
❑ 23 John Mackey	.40	.15
❑ 24 Curtis Martin	.75	.30
❑ 25 Junior Seau	.50	.20
❑ 26 Harold Jackson	.40	.15
❑ 27 Jim Zorn	.40	.15
❑ 28 Chuck Foreman	.40	.15
❑ 29 Willie Brown	.40	.15
❑ 30 Cliff Branch	.50	.20
❑ 31 Jerry Kramer	.50	.20
❑ 32 Harry Carson	.40	.15
❑ 33 Chuck Noll	.50	.20
❑ 34 Len Hauss	.40	.15
❑ 35 Jim Plunkett	.50	.20
❑ 36 Ollie Matson	.50	.20
❑ 37 Billy Kilmer	.50	.20
❑ 38 Jim Marshall	.40	.15
❑ 39 Dan Dierdorf	.40	.15
❑ 40 Jim Kelly	1.00	.40
❑ 41 Vince Ferragamo	.40	.15
❑ 42 Ottis Anderson	.40	.15
❑ 43 Charlie Joiner	.40	.15
❑ 44 George Blanda	.75	.30
❑ 45 Drew Pearson	.50	.20
❑ 46 Andre Reed	.50	.20
❑ 47 Merlin Olsen	.50	.20
❑ 48 Paul Warfield	.50	.20
❑ 49 James Lofton	.40	.15
❑ 50 Art Donovan	.50	.20
❑ 51 Dwight Clark	.50	.20
❑ 52 Raymond Berry	.50	.20
❑ 53 L.C. Greenwood	.50	.20
❑ 54 Dave Casper	.40	.15
❑ 55 Don Maynard	.50	.20
❑ 56 Bud Grant	.40	.15
❑ 57 Roman Gabriel	.50	.20
❑ 58 Cris Collinsworth	.50	.20
❑ 59 Joe Theismann	.75	.30
❑ 60 Paul Hornung	.75	.30
❑ 61 Alan Page	.50	.20
❑ 62 Deacon Jones	.50	.20
❑ 63 Steve Largent	.75	.30
❑ 64 Phil Simms	.50	.20
❑ 65 Floyd Little	.40	.15
❑ 66 Archie Manning	.75	.30
❑ 67 Ken Stabler	1.00	.40
❑ 68 Fran Tarkenton	1.00	.40
❑ 69 Len Dawson	.75	.30
❑ 70 Mike Ditka	.75	.30
❑ 71 Conrad Dobler	.40	.15
❑ 72 Jack Lambert	.75	.30
❑ 73 Marcus Allen	.75	.30
❑ 74 Bo Jackson	1.00	.40
❑ 75 Jerome Bettis	.75	.30
❑ 76 Jack Ham	.50	.20
❑ 77 Marshall Faulk	.75	.30
❑ 78 Mike Singletary	.75	.30
❑ 79 Bob Griese	.75	.30
❑ 80 Dick Butkus	1.25	.50
❑ 81 Gale Sayers	1.00	.40
❑ 82 Earl Campbell	.75	.30
❑ 83 Dan Fouts	.75	.30
❑ 84 Franco Harris	1.00	.40
❑ 85 Steve Young	1.00	.40
❑ 86 Tony Dorsett	.75	.30
❑ 87 Jim Brown	1.25	.50
❑ 88 Roger Staubach	1.25	.50
❑ 89 Troy Aikman	1.00	.40
❑ 90 Barry Sanders	1.25	.50
❑ 91 Bernie Kosar	.50	.20
❑ 92 Dan Marino	2.00	.75
❑ 93 John Elway	1.25	.50
❑ 94 Randy Moss	.75	.30
❑ 95 Joe Montana	2.50	1.00
❑ 96 Joe Montana CL	1.25	.50
❑ 97 Dan Marino CL	1.00	.40
❑ 98 John Elway CL	.75	.30
❑ 99 Gale Sayers CL	.50	.20
❑ 100 Paul Hornung CL	.50	.20
❑ 101 Aaron Rodgers RC	15.00	6.00
❑ 102 Alex Smith QB RC	20.00	7.50
❑ 103 Carnell Williams RC	25.00	10.00
❑ 104 Ronnie Brown RC	15.00	6.00
❑ 105 Ciatrick Fason RC	5.00	2.00
❑ 106 Charlie Frye RC	10.00	4.00
❑ 107 Derek Anderson RC	5.00	2.00
❑ 108 Braylon Edwards RC	15.00	6.00
❑ 109 Roddy White RC	5.00	2.00
❑ 110 Thomas Davis RC	5.00	2.00
❑ 111 Jason Campbell RC	8.00	3.00
❑ 112 Andrew Walter RC	8.00	3.00
❑ 113 Kyle Orton RC	8.00	3.00
❑ 114 David Greene RC	5.00	2.00
❑ 115 Cedric Benson RC	10.00	4.00
❑ 116 Vernand Morency RC	5.00	2.00
❑ 117 Eric Shelton RC	5.00	2.00
❑ 118 Maurice Clarett	5.00	2.00
❑ 119 Brandon Jacobs RC	6.00	2.50
❑ 120 Anthony Davis RC	4.00	1.50
❑ 121 Marion Barber RC	8.00	3.00
❑ 122 J.J. Arrington RC	6.00	2.50
❑ 123 Ryan Moats RC	5.00	2.00
❑ 124 Frank Gore RC	8.00	3.00
❑ 125 Stefan LeFors RC	5.00	2.00
❑ 126 Darren Sproles RC	5.00	2.00
❑ 127 Cedric Houston RC	5.00	2.00
❑ 128 Troy Williamson RC	10.00	4.00
❑ 129 Mark Clayton RC	6.00	2.50
❑ 130 Chris Henry RC	5.00	2.00
❑ 131 Fred Gibson RC	4.00	1.50
❑ 132 Craphonso Thorpe RC	4.00	1.50
❑ 133 Terrence Murphy RC	5.00	2.00
❑ 134 Dan Orlovsky RC	6.00	2.50
❑ 135 Roscoe Parrish RC	5.00	2.00
❑ 136 Reggie Brown RC	5.00	2.00
❑ 137 Craig Bragg RC	4.00	1.50
❑ 138 Larry Brackins RC	2.50	1.00
❑ 139 Adrian McPherson RC	5.00	2.00
❑ 140 Matt Jones RC	12.00	5.00
❑ 141 Heath Miller RC	12.00	5.00
❑ 142 Alex Smith TE RC	5.00	2.00
❑ 143 Kevin Everett RC	5.00	2.00
❑ 144 Jerome Mathis RC	5.00	2.00
❑ 145 Travis Johnson RC	4.00	1.50
❑ 146 Channing Crowder RC	5.00	2.00
❑ 147 Mike Williams	10.00	4.00
❑ 148 Barrett Ruud RC	5.00	2.00
❑ 149 Marcus Spears RC	5.00	2.00
❑ 150 Derrick Johnson RC	8.00	3.00
❑ 151 Shawne Merriman RC	8.00	3.00
❑ 152 Kevin Burnett RC	5.00	2.00
❑ 153 Erasmus James RC	5.00	2.00
❑ 154 Dan Cody RC	5.00	2.00
❑ 155 David Pollack RC	5.00	2.00
❑ 156 Antrel Rolle RC	5.00	2.00
❑ 157 Adam Jones RC	5.00	2.00
❑ 158 Mark Bradley RC	5.00	2.00
❑ 159 Carlos Rogers RC	6.00	2.50
❑ 160 Vincent Jackson RC	5.00	2.00
❑ 161 DeMarcus Ware RC	8.00	3.00
❑ 162 Corey Webster RC	5.00	2.00
❑ 163 Justin Miller RC	4.00	1.50
❑ 164 Eric Green RC	2.50	1.00
❑ 165 Marlin Jackson RC	5.00	2.00
❑ 166 Herb Adderley LH	3.00	1.25
❑ 167 Fran Tarkenton LH	6.00	2.50
❑ 168 Troy Aikman LH	6.00	2.50
❑ 169 Charlie Joiner LH	3.00	1.25
❑ 170 George Blanda LH	5.00	2.00
❑ 171 Jim Kelly LH	6.00	2.50
❑ 172 Joe Montana LH	12.00	5.00
❑ 173 Jack Ham LH	4.00	1.50
❑ 174 Marcus Allen LH	5.00	2.00
❑ 175 Tony Dorsett LH	5.00	2.00
❑ 176 Barry Sanders LH	8.00	3.00
❑ 177 Paul Warfield LH	4.00	1.50
❑ 178 Dan Marino LH	10.00	4.00
❑ 179 John Elway LH	8.00	3.00
❑ 180 Franco Harris LH	6.00	2.50
❑ 181 Mike Singletary LH	5.00	2.00
❑ 182 Gale Sayers LH	6.00	2.50
❑ 183 Bob Griese LH	5.00	2.00
❑ 184 Dan Fouts LH	5.00	2.00
❑ 185 Earl Campbell LH	5.00	2.00
❑ 186 Jim Brown LH	8.00	3.00
❑ 187 Dick Butkus LH	8.00	3.00
❑ 188 Paul Hornung LH	5.00	2.00
❑ 189 Roger Staubach LH	8.00	3.00
❑ 190 Steve Largent LH	5.00	2.00
❑ 191 Ryan Fitzpatrick RC	8.00	3.00
❑ 192 Alvin Pearman RC	5.00	2.00
❑ 193 Courtney Roby RC	5.00	2.00
❑ 194 Chase Lyman RC	4.00	1.50
❑ 195 Roydell Williams RC	5.00	2.00

2000 Upper Deck Pros and Prospects

❑ COMPLETE SET (126)	600.00	300.00
❑ COMP.SET w/o SP's (84)	20.00	7.50
❑ 1 Jake Plummer	.30	.10
❑ 2 Michael Pittman	.20	.07
❑ 3 Tim Dwight	.50	.20
❑ 4 Chris Chandler	.30	.10
❑ 5 Qadry Ismail	.30	.10
❑ 6 Shannon Sharpe	.30	.10
❑ 7 Peerless Price	.30	.10
❑ 8 Rob Johnson	.30	.10
❑ 9 Eric Moulds	.50	.20
❑ 10 Muhsin Muhammad	.30	.10
❑ 11 Patrick Jeffers	.50	.20
❑ 12 Steve Beuerlein	.30	.10
❑ 13 Cade McNown	.20	.07
❑ 14 Curtis Enis	.20	.07
❑ 15 Marcus Robinson	.50	.20
❑ 16 Akili Smith	.20	.07
❑ 17 Corey Dillon	.50	.20
❑ 18 Tim Couch	.30	.10
❑ 19 Kevin Johnson	.50	.20
❑ 20 Errict Rhett	.30	.10
❑ 21 Troy Aikman	1.00	.40
❑ 22 Emmitt Smith	1.00	.40
❑ 23 Rocket Ismail	.30	.10
❑ 24 Terrell Davis	.50	.20
❑ 25 Olandis Gary	.50	.20
❑ 26 Brian Griese	.50	.20
❑ 27 Ed McCaffrey	.50	.20
❑ 28 Charlie Batch	.50	.20
❑ 29 Germane Crowell	.20	.07
❑ 30 James O. Stewart	.30	.10
❑ 31 Brett Favre	1.50	.60
❑ 32 Antonio Freeman	.50	.20
❑ 33 Dorsey Levens	.30	.10
❑ 34 Peyton Manning	1.25	.50
❑ 35 Edgerrin James	.75	.30
❑ 36 Marvin Harrison	.50	.20
❑ 37 Mark Brunell	.50	.20
❑ 38 Fred Taylor	.50	.20
❑ 39 Jimmy Smith	.30	.10
❑ 40 Elvis Grbac	.30	.10
❑ 41 Tony Gonzalez	.30	.10
❑ 42 Damon Huard	.50	.20
❑ 43 James Johnson	.20	.07
❑ 44 Jay Fiedler	.50	.20
❑ 45 Randy Moss	1.00	.40
❑ 46 Robert Smith	.50	.20
❑ 47 Cris Carter	.50	.20
❑ 48 Drew Bledsoe	.60	.25
❑ 49 Terry Glenn	.30	.10
❑ 50 Ricky Williams	.50	.20
❑ 51 Jeff Blake	.30	.10
❑ 52 Keith Poole	.20	.07
❑ 53 Kerry Collins	.30	.10
❑ 54 Amani Toomer	.20	.07
❑ 55 Vinny Testaverde	.30	.10
❑ 56 Keyshawn Johnson	.50	.20
❑ 57 Curtis Martin	.50	.20
❑ 58 Tim Brown	.50	.20
❑ 59 Rich Gannon	.50	.20
❑ 60 Tyrone Wheatley	.30	.10

❑ 61 Duce Staley .50 .20
❑ 62 Donovan McNabb .75 .30
❑ 63 Troy Edwards .20 .07
❑ 64 Jerome Bettis .50 .20
❑ 65 Marshall Faulk .60 .25
❑ 66 Kurt Warner 1.00 .40
❑ 67 Torry Holt .50 .20
❑ 68 Isaac Bruce .50 .20
❑ 69 Junior Seau .50 .20
❑ 70 Jeff Graham .20 .07
❑ 71 Steve Young .60 .25
❑ 72 Jerry Rice 1.00 .40
❑ 73 Charlie Garner .30 .10
❑ 74 Ricky Watters .30 .10
❑ 75 Jon Kitna .50 .20
❑ 76 Warrick Dunn .50 .20
❑ 77 Shaun King .20 .07
❑ 78 Mike Alstott .50 .20
❑ 79 Eddie George .50 .20
❑ 80 Steve McNair .50 .20
❑ 81 Kevin Dyson .30 .10
❑ 82 Brad Johnson .50 .20
❑ 83 Stephen Davis .50 .20
❑ 84 Michael Westbrook .30 .10
❑ 85 Peter Warrick RC 12.00 5.00
❑ 86 LaVar Arrington RC 60.00 30.00
❑ 87 Chris Redman RC 10.00 4.00
❑ 88 Courtney Brown RC 12.00 5.00
❑ 89 Plaxico Burress RC 25.00 10.00
❑ 90 Corey Simon RC 12.00 5.00
❑ 91 Bubba Franks RC 12.00 5.00
❑ 92 Deon Grant RC 10.00 4.00
❑ 93 Brian Urlacher RC 40.00 15.00
❑ 94 Ron Dayne RC 12.00 5.00
❑ 95 Sylvester Morris RC 10.00 4.00
❑ 96 Shaun Alexander RC 50.00 25.00
❑ 97 Dez White RC 12.00 5.00
❑ 98 Thomas Jones RC 20.00 7.50
❑ 99 Travis Taylor RC 12.00 5.00
❑ 100 Kwame Cavil RC 6.00 2.50
❑ 101 Jamal Lewis RC 25.00 10.00
❑ 102 Chad Pennington RC 25.00 10.00
❑ 103 J.R. Redmond RC 10.00 4.00
❑ 104 Sebastian Janikowski RC 12.00 5.00
❑ 105 Anthony Lucas RC 6.00 2.50
❑ 106 Travis Prentice RC 10.00 4.00
❑ 107 Danny Farmer RC 10.00 4.00
❑ 108 Sherrod Gideon RC 6.00 2.50
❑ 109 Todd Pinkston RC 12.00 5.00
❑ 110 Dennis Northcutt RC 12.00 5.00
❑ 111 Tim Rattay RC 12.00 5.00
❑ 112 Troy Walters RC 12.00 5.00
❑ 113 Michael Wiley RC 10.00 4.00
❑ 114 R.Jay Soward RC 10.00 4.00
❑ 115 Trung Canidate RC 10.00 4.00
❑ 116 Reuben Droughns RC 15.00 6.00
❑ 117 Rondell Mealey RC 6.00 2.50
❑ 118 Chris Coleman RC 12.00 5.00
❑ 119 Giovanni Carmazzi RC 10.00 4.00
❑ 120 Trevor Insley RC 10.00 4.00
❑ 121 Shyrone Stith RC 10.00 4.00
❑ 122 Gari Scott RC 6.00 2.50
❑ 123 Tee Martin RC 12.00 5.00
❑ 124 Tom Brady RC 120.00 60.00
❑ 125 Marcus Knight RC 10.00 4.00
❑ 126 Jerry Porter RC 25.00 10.00
❑ 127 Brad Hoover RC 5.00 2.00
❑ 128 Chad Morton RC 8.00 3.00
❑ 129 Charles Lee RC 5.00 2.00
❑ 130 Damon Hodge RC 5.00 2.00
❑ 131 Darrell Jackson RC 15.00 6.00
❑ 132 Doug Johnson RC 8.00 3.00
❑ 133 Frank Moreau RC 5.00 2.00
❑ 134 JaJuan Dawson RC 5.00 2.00
❑ 135 Jake Delhomme RC 30.00 15.00
❑ 136 Jarious Jackson RC 5.00 2.00
❑ 137 Joe Hamilton RC 5.00 2.00
❑ 138 Larry Foster RC 5.00 2.00
❑ 139 Laveranues Coles RC 10.00 4.00
❑ 140 Aaron Shea RC 8.00 3.00
❑ 141 Matt Lytle RC 5.00 2.00
❑ 142 Mike Anderson RC 15.00 6.00
❑ 143 Ron Dixon RC 5.00 2.00
❑ 144 Ronney Jenkins RC 5.00 2.00
❑ 145 Sammy Morris RC 5.00 2.00
❑ 146 Shockmain Davis RC 5.00 2.00
❑ 147 Spergon Wynn RC 5.00 2.00
❑ 148 Todd Husak RC 8.00 3.00
❑ 149 Trevor Gaylor RC 5.00 2.00
❑ 150 Tywan Mitchell RC 5.00 2.00
❑ 151 Windrell Hayes RC 5.00 2.00
❑ 152 Bobby Shaw RC 5.00 2.00

2001 Upper Deck Pros and Prospects

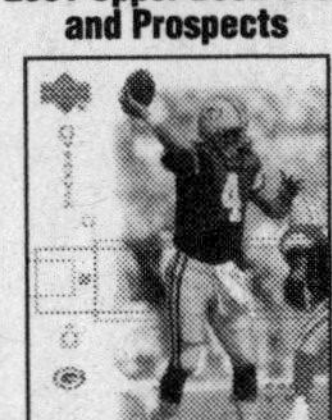

❑ COMP.SET w/o SP's (90) 15.00 6.00
❑ 1 Jake Plummer .30 .10
❑ 2 David Boston .50 .20
❑ 3 Jamal Anderson .50 .20
❑ 4 Doug Johnson .20 .07
❑ 5 Maurice Smith .30 .10
❑ 6 Jamal Lewis .75 .30
❑ 7 Shannon Sharpe .30 .10
❑ 8 Trent Dilfer .30 .10
❑ 9 Doug Flutie .50 .20
❑ 10 Rob Johnson .30 .10
❑ 11 Eric Moulds .50 .20
❑ 12 Muhsin Muhammad .30 .10
❑ 13 Brad Hoover .20 .07
❑ 14 Tim Biakabutuka .30 .10
❑ 15 Cade McNown .20 .07
❑ 16 James Allen .30 .10
❑ 17 Marcus Robinson .50 .20
❑ 18 Brian Urlacher .75 .30
❑ 19 Peter Warrick .50 .20
❑ 20 Corey Dillon .50 .20
❑ 21 Tim Couch .30 .10
❑ 22 Kevin Johnson .30 .10
❑ 23 Travis Prentice .20 .07
❑ 24 Troy Aikman .75 .30
❑ 25 Emmitt Smith 1.00 .40
❑ 26 Terrell Davis .50 .20
❑ 27 Mike Anderson .50 .20
❑ 28 Brian Griese .50 .20
❑ 29 Charlie Batch .50 .20
❑ 30 Germane Crowell .20 .07
❑ 31 James Stewart .30 .10
❑ 32 Brett Favre 1.50 .60
❑ 33 Antonio Freeman .50 .20
❑ 34 Dorsey Levens .30 .10
❑ 35 Ahman Green .50 .20
❑ 36 Peyton Manning 1.25 .50
❑ 37 Edgerrin James .60 .25
❑ 38 Marvin Harrison .50 .20
❑ 39 Mark Brunell .50 .20
❑ 40 Fred Taylor .50 .20
❑ 41 Jimmy Smith .30 .10
❑ 42 Elvis Grbac .30 .10
❑ 43 Tony Gonzalez .30 .10
❑ 44 Derrick Alexander .30 .10
❑ 45 Oronde Gadsden .30 .10
❑ 46 Lamar Smith .30 .10
❑ 47 Jay Fiedler .50 .20
❑ 48 Randy Moss 1.00 .40
❑ 49 Moe Williams .30 .10
❑ 50 Cris Carter .50 .20
❑ 51 Daunte Culpepper .50 .20
❑ 52 Drew Bledsoe .60 .25
❑ 53 Terry Glenn .30 .10
❑ 54 Ricky Williams .50 .20
❑ 55 Jeff Blake .30 .10
❑ 56 Joe Horn .30 .10
❑ 57 Aaron Brooks .50 .20
❑ 58 La'Roi Glover .20 .07
❑ 59 Kerry Collins .30 .10
❑ 60 Amani Toomer .30 .10
❑ 61 Ron Dayne .50 .20
❑ 62 Vinny Testaverde .30 .10
❑ 63 Wayne Chrebet .30 .10
❑ 64 Curtis Martin .50 .20
❑ 65 Tim Brown .50 .20
❑ 66 Rich Gannon .50 .20
❑ 67 Tyrone Wheatley .30 .10
❑ 68 Duce Staley .50 .20
❑ 69 Donovan McNabb .60 .25
❑ 70 Kordell Stewart .30 .10
❑ 71 Jerome Bettis .50 .20
❑ 72 Marshall Faulk .60 .25
❑ 73 Kurt Warner 1.00 .40
❑ 74 Isaac Bruce .50 .20
❑ 75 Junior Seau .50 .20
❑ 76 Curtis Conway .30 .10
❑ 77 Jeff Garcia .50 .20
❑ 78 Jerry Rice 1.00 .40
❑ 79 Charlie Garner .30 .10
❑ 80 Terrell Owens .50 .20
❑ 81 Ricky Watters .20 .07
❑ 82 Shaun Alexander .60 .25
❑ 83 Warrick Dunn .50 .20
❑ 84 Shaun King .20 .07
❑ 85 Derrick Brooks .50 .20
❑ 86 Eddie George .50 .20
❑ 87 Steve McNair .50 .20
❑ 88 Brad Johnson .50 .20
❑ 89 Jeff George .30 .10
❑ 90 Stephen Davis .50 .20
❑ 91 Jamal Reynolds RC 12.00 5.00
❑ 92 Justin Smith RC 12.00 5.00
❑ 93 Dan Morgan RC 12.00 5.00
❑ 94 Deuce McAllister RC 30.00 15.00
❑ 95 Drew Brees RC 40.00 15.00
❑ 96 Josh Booty RC 12.00 5.00
❑ 97 Mike McMahon RC 12.00 5.00
❑ 98 Sage Rosenfels RC 12.00 5.00
❑ 99 Marques Tuiasosopo RC 12.00 5.00
❑ 100 Josh Heupel RC 12.00 5.00
❑ 101 Heath Evans RC 8.00 3.00
❑ 102 Reggie White RC 8.00 3.00
❑ 103 Tim Hasselbeck RC 12.00 5.00
❑ 104 LaDainian Tomlinson RC 60.00 30.00
❑ 105 Kevan Barlow RC 12.00 5.00
❑ 106 LaMont Jordan RC 25.00 10.00
❑ 107 James Jackson RC 12.00 5.00
❑ 108 Anthony Thomas RC 12.00 5.00
❑ 109 Correll Buckhalter RC 15.00 6.00
❑ 110 Travis Henry RC 12.00 5.00
❑ 111 Dan Alexander RC 12.00 5.00
❑ 112 Travis Minor RC 8.00 3.00
❑ 113 Rudi Johnson RC 30.00 12.50
❑ 114 Michael Bennett RC 25.00 10.00
❑ 115 Todd Heap RC 12.00 5.00
❑ 116 Snoop Minnis RC 8.00 3.00
❑ 117 Santana Moss RC 25.00 10.00
❑ 118 Reggie Wayne RC 25.00 10.00
❑ 119 Koren Robinson RC 12.00 5.00
❑ 120 Chris Chambers RC 20.00 7.50
❑ 121 David Terrell RC 12.00 5.00
❑ 122 Rod Gardner RC 12.00 5.00
❑ 123 Quincy Morgan RC 12.00 5.00
❑ 124 Ken-Yon Rambo RC 8.00 3.00
❑ 125 Ronney Daniels RC 5.00 2.00
❑ 126 Ja'Mar Toombs RC 8.00 3.00
❑ 127 Bobby Newcombe RC 8.00 3.00
❑ 128 Cedrick Wilson RC 12.00 5.00
❑ 129 Chad Johnson RC 40.00 15.00
❑ 130 Shaun Rogers RC 12.00 5.00
❑ 131 Robert Ferguson RC 12.00 5.00
❑ 132 Kevin Kasper RC 12.00 5.00
❑ 133 Chris Weinke JSY RC 25.00 10.00
❑ 134 Freddie Mitchell JSY RC 15.00 6.00
❑ 135 Michael Vick JSY RC 100.00 40.00
❑ 136 Chris Taylor RC 8.00 3.00
❑ 137 Vinny Sutherland RC 8.00 3.00
❑ 138 Gerard Warren RC 12.00 5.00
❑ 139 Torrance Marshall RC 12.00 5.00
❑ 140 Jesse Palmer RC 12.00 5.00

2003 Upper Deck Pros and Prospects

❑ COMP.SET w/o SP's (90) 20.00 7.50
❑ 1 Jake Plummer .60 .25
❑ 2 David Boston .60 .25

❑ 3 Warrick Dunn .60 .25
❑ 4 T.J. Duckett .60 .25
❑ 5 Chris Redman .40 .15
❑ 6 Jamal Lewis 1.00 .40
❑ 7 Drew Bledsoe 1.00 .40
❑ 8 Travis Henry .60 .25
❑ 9 Eric Moulds .60 .25
❑ 10 Peerless Price .60 .25
❑ 11 Rodney Peete .60 .25
❑ 12 Julius Peppers 1.00 .40
❑ 13 Anthony Thomas .60 .25
❑ 14 Brian Urlacher 1.50 .60
❑ 15 Marty Booker .60 .25
❑ 16 David Terrell .60 .25
❑ 17 Corey Dillon .60 .25
❑ 18 Peter Warrick .60 .25
❑ 19 Jon Kitna .60 .25
❑ 20 Tim Couch .40 .15
❑ 21 Andre Davis .40 .15
❑ 22 Quincy Morgan .60 .25
❑ 23 Dennis Northcutt .60 .25
❑ 24 Roy Williams 1.00 .40
❑ 25 Emmitt Smith 2.50 1.00
❑ 26 Joey Galloway .60 .25
❑ 27 Antonio Bryant .60 .25
❑ 28 Brian Griese 1.00 .40
❑ 29 Clinton Portis 1.50 .60
❑ 30 Shannon Sharpe .60 .25
❑ 31 Joey Harrington 1.50 .60
❑ 32 Az-Zahir Hakim .40 .15
❑ 33 Brett Favre 2.50 1.00
❑ 34 Robert Ferguson .40 .15
❑ 35 Donald Driver .60 .25
❑ 36 David Carr 1.50 .60
❑ 37 Jabar Gaffney .60 .25
❑ 38 Edgerrin James 1.00 .40
❑ 39 Marvin Harrison 1.00 .40
❑ 40 Reggie Wayne .60 .25
❑ 41 Mark Brunell .60 .25
❑ 42 Fred Taylor 1.00 .40
❑ 43 Priest Holmes 1.25 .50
❑ 44 Trent Green .60 .25
❑ 45 Marc Boerigter .60 .25
❑ 46 Jay Fiedler .60 .25
❑ 47 Chris Chambers 1.00 .40
❑ 48 Randy McMichael .60 .25
❑ 49 Randy Moss 1.50 .60
❑ 50 Daunte Culpepper 1.00 .40
❑ 51 Michael Bennett .60 .25
❑ 52 Antowain Smith .60 .25
❑ 53 David Patten .40 .15
❑ 54 Troy Brown .60 .25
❑ 55 Aaron Brooks 1.00 .40
❑ 56 Joe Horn .60 .25
❑ 57 Donte Stallworth 1.00 .40
❑ 58 Amani Toomer .60 .25
❑ 59 Kerry Collins .60 .25
❑ 60 Tiki Barber 1.00 .40
❑ 61 Santana Moss .60 .25
❑ 62 Curtis Martin 1.00 .40
❑ 63 Wayne Chrebet .60 .25
❑ 64 Rich Gannon .60 .25
❑ 65 Charlie Garner .60 .25
❑ 66 Tim Brown 1.00 .40
❑ 67 Donovan McNabb 1.25 .50
❑ 68 Duce Staley .60 .25
❑ 69 Hines Ward 1.00 .40
❑ 70 Antwaan Randle El 1.00 .40
❑ 71 Plaxico Burress .60 .25
❑ 72 Jerome Bettis 1.00 .40
❑ 73 Junior Seau 1.00 .40
❑ 74 LaDainian Tomlinson 1.00 .40
❑ 75 Tai Streets .40 .15
❑ 76 Kevan Barlow .60 .25
❑ 77 Garrison Hearst .60 .25
❑ 78 Jeff Garcia 1.00 .40
❑ 79 Shaun Alexander 1.00 .40
❑ 80 Matt Hasselbeck .60 .25
❑ 81 Marshall Faulk 1.00 .40
❑ 82 Marc Bulger 1.00 .40
❑ 83 Torry Holt 1.00 .40
❑ 84 Isaac Bruce 1.00 .40
❑ 85 Brad Johnson .60 .25
❑ 86 Keyshawn Johnson 1.00 .40
❑ 87 Steve McNair 1.00 .40
❑ 88 Kevin Dyson .60 .25
❑ 89 Patrick Ramsey 1.00 .40
❑ 90 Ladell Betts .60 .25
❑ 91 Marcel Shipp SP 2.50 1.00
❑ 92 Michael Vick SP 8.00 3.00
❑ 93 Ray Lewis SP 3.00 1.25
❑ 94 Josh Reed SP 2.50 1.00
❑ 95 Josh McCown SP 2.50 1.00
❑ 96 Kelly Holcomb SP 2.50 1.00
❑ 97 William Green SP 2.50 1.00
❑ 98 Chad Hutchinson SP 1.50 .60
❑ 99 Rod Smith SP 2.50 1.00
❑ 100 James Stewart SP 2.50 1.00
❑ 101 Ahman Green SP 3.00 1.25
❑ 102 Peyton Manning SP 5.00 2.00
❑ 103 Jimmy Smith SP 2.50 1.00
❑ 104 Tony Gonzalez SP 2.50 1.00
❑ 105 Ricky Williams SP 3.00 1.25
❑ 106 Jason Taylor SP 1.50 .60
❑ 107 Tom Brady SP 6.00 2.50
❑ 108 Deuce McAllister SP 3.00 1.25
❑ 109 Jeremy Shockey SP 5.00 2.00
❑ 110 Chad Pennington SP 4.00 1.50
❑ 111 Jerry Rice SP 6.00 2.50
❑ 112 A.J. Feeley SP 2.50 1.00
❑ 113 Tommy Maddox SP 3.00 1.25
❑ 114 Drew Brees SP 3.00 1.25
❑ 115 Terrell Owens SP 3.00 1.25
❑ 116 Maurice Morris SP 1.50 .60
❑ 117 Kurt Warner SP 3.00 1.25
❑ 118 Derrick Brooks SP 2.50 1.00
❑ 119 Eddie George SP 2.50 1.00
❑ 120 Rod Gardner SP 2.50 1.00
❑ 121 Leftwich AU RC/Pnn.AU/250 80.00 30.00
❑ 122 Dorsey AU RC/Test/2000 20.00 7.50
❑ 123 Palmer AU RC/Mnn.AU/250 250.00 150.00
❑ 124 Simms AU RC/Bru.AU/250 50.0030.00
❑ 125 A.Johnson RC/S.Moss 20.00 7.50
❑ 126 Banks AU RC/Brks.AU/250 30.0012.50
❑ 127 J.R. Tolver RC/Hakim 4.00 1.50
❑ 128 J.Myers RC/J.Reed 2.50 1.00
❑ 129 R.Bellamy RC/A.Toomer 4.00 1.50
❑ 130 J.Gesser RC/D.Bledsoe 5.00 2.00
❑ 131 Kingsbury AU RC/S.Baugh 20.00 7.50
❑ 132 K.Boller RC/Brees AU/500 50.00 20.00
❑ 133 L.Johnson RC/Thomas AU 40.0020.00
❑ 134 K.Kelly AU RC/Morton/2000 20.007.50
❑ 135 B.Johnson RC/Gard.AU/500 20.007.50
❑ 136 Johnson RC/Couch AU/500 25.0010.00
❑ 137 T.Suggs AU RC/Nmll/2000 20.00 7.50
❑ 138 Ragone RC/Brnli AU/500 40.00 15.00
❑ 139 M.Smith RC/C.Trippi 5.00 2.00
❑ 140 J.Wood RC/J.Harrington 4.00 1.50
❑ 141 J.Thomas RC/Michael Vick 5.00 2.00
❑ 142 Graham AU RC/E.Smt/2000 30.00 12.50
❑ 143 McGahee AU RC/Jms/2000 50.0020.00
❑ 144 R.Lee RC/Alexander AU/500 30.00 15.00
❑ 145 A.Boldin RC/J.Walker 12.00 5.00
❑ 146 Jacobs AU RC/Cald AU/250 30.00 12.50
❑ 147 T.Gardner RC/L.Coles 5.00 2.00
❑ 148 B.Wade RC/D.Northcutt 5.00 2.00
❑ 149 McMullen RC/Bruce AU/500 20.007.50
❑ 150 A.Cobourne RC/A.Zereoue 2.50 1.00
❑ 151 B.James RC/F.Kinard 5.00 2.00
❑ 152 Washing AU RC/Prc/2000 25.00 10.00
❑ 153 E.Steinbach RC/J.Parker 4.00 1.50
❑ 154 J.Kennedy RC/E.Stautner 5.00 2.00
❑ 155 R.Long RC/A.Weinmeister 2.50 1.00
❑ 156 C.Brown AU RC/Andr/2000 25.0010.00
❑ 157 T.Johnson RC/T.Gonzalez 5.00 2.00
❑ 158 O.Smith RC/M.Morris 8.00 3.00
❑ 159 Fargas AU RC/Portis/2000 20.00 7.50
❑ 160 S.Wallace RC/A.Randle El 5.00 2.00
❑ 161 St.Pierre RC/Mann AU/500 80.0040.00
❑ 162 Toefield RC/Tmln AU/500 50.00 25.00
❑ 163 M.Blackwell RC/Culpepper 2.50 1.00
❑ 164 K.Howry RC/A.J.Feeley 5.00 2.00
❑ 165 J.Gage RC/K.Farmer RC 5.00 2.00
❑ 166 S.Witten RC/A.Davis 2.50 1.00
❑ 167 Weathersby RC/A.Williams 2.50 1.00
❑ 168 B.Bailey RC/C.Bailey 6.00 2.50
❑ 169 B.Lloyd RC/K.Kittner 6.00 2.50
❑ 170 D.Gabriel RC/C.Chambers 5.00 2.00
❑ 171 A.Gbaja-Biamila RC/KGB 5.00 2.00
❑ 172 D.Diedrick RC/A.Green 5.00 2.00
❑ 173 K.Curtis RC/K.Dyson 5.00 2.00
❑ 174 McCull RC/McAll.AU/500 25.00 12.50
❑ 175 M.Bush RC/M.Trufant RC 5.00 2.00
❑ 176 Z.Hilton RC/S.Aiken RC 4.00 1.50
❑ 177 Newman RC/Woolfolk RC 12.00 6.00
❑ 178 T.Calico RC/K.Holcomb 8.00 3.00
❑ 179 J.T. Wall RC/T.Edwards RC 8.00 3.00
❑ 180 C.Paus RC/M.Seidman RC 8.00 3.00
❑ 181 L.J. Smith RC/M.Battaglia 5.00 2.00
❑ 182 Griffin AU RC/Sav.RC/2000 20.00 7.50
❑ 183 L.Suggs RC/M.Vick 15.00 6.00
❑ 184 B.Askew RC/B.Joppru RC 5.00 2.00
❑ 185 M.Pinkard RC/Todd Heap 2.50 1.00
❑ 186 A.Battle RC/Tim Brown 5.00 2.00
❑ 187 C.Rogers RC/P.Burress 5.00 2.00
❑ 188 A.Pinnock RC/D.Staley 4.00 1.50
❑ 189 Grossman RC/Mnn.AU/500 80.0040.00
❑ 190 G.Wrighster RC/J.Peelle 4.00 1.50
❑ KBBF K.Boller/B.Favre AU/25 200.00125.00
❑ RGBF Grossman/Favre AU/25 200.00 100.00

2005 Upper Deck Rookie Debut

❑ COMP.SET w/o SP's (100) 20.00 10.00
❑ ROOKIE STATED ODDS 1:3
❑ UNPRICED BLUE PRINT RUN 15 SETS
❑ 1 Larry Fitzgerald .75 .30
❑ 2 Kurt Warner .50 .20
❑ 3 Anquan Boldin .50 .20
❑ 4 Michael Vick 1.25 .50
❑ 5 Warrick Dunn .50 .20
❑ 6 Peerless Price .40 .15
❑ 7 Jamal Lewis .75 .30
❑ 8 Derrick Mason .50 .20
❑ 9 Kyle Boller .50 .20
❑ 10 Willis McGahee .75 .30
❑ 11 J.P. Losman .75 .30
❑ 12 Eric Moulds .50 .20
❑ 13 Stephen Davis .50 .20
❑ 14 Jake Delhomme .75 .30
❑ 15 Steve Smith .50 .20
❑ 16 Thomas Jones .50 .20
❑ 17 Brian Urlacher .75 .30
❑ 18 Rex Grossman .50 .20
❑ 19 Carson Palmer .75 .30
❑ 20 Rudi Johnson .50 .20
❑ 21 Chad Johnson .75 .30
❑ 22 Kellen Winslow .75 .30
❑ 23 Luke McCown .40 .15
❑ 24 Lee Suggs .50 .20
❑ 25 Drew Bledsoe .75 .30
❑ 26 Keyshawn Johnson .50 .20
❑ 27 Julius Jones 1.00 .40
❑ 28 Roy Williams S .50 .20

❑ 29 Jake Plummer .50 .20
❑ 30 Tatum Bell .50 .20
❑ 31 Rod Smith .50 .20
❑ 32 Roy Williams WR .75 .30
❑ 33 Joey Harrington .75 .30
❑ 34 Kevin Jones .75 .30
❑ 35 Brett Favre 2.00 .75
❑ 36 Javon Walker .50 .20
❑ 37 Ahman Green .75 .30
❑ 38 David Carr .75 .30
❑ 39 Andre Johnson .50 .20
❑ 40 Domanick Davis .50 .20
❑ 41 Peyton Manning 1.25 .50
❑ 42 Marvin Harrison .75 .30
❑ 43 Edgerrin James .75 .30
❑ 44 Reggie Wayne .50 .20
❑ 45 Byron Leftwich .75 .30
❑ 46 Jimmy Smith .50 .20
❑ 47 Fred Taylor .50 .20
❑ 48 Priest Holmes .75 .30
❑ 49 Trent Green .50 .20
❑ 50 Tony Gonzalez .50 .20
❑ 51 Chris Chambers .50 .20
❑ 52 Sammy Morris .40 .15
❑ 53 A.J. Feeley .50 .20
❑ 54 Daunte Culpepper .75 .30
❑ 55 Nate Burleson .50 .20
❑ 56 Michael Bennett .50 .20
❑ 57 Tom Brady 2.00 .75
❑ 58 David Givens .50 .20
❑ 59 Corey Dillon .50 .20
❑ 60 Ty Law .50 .20
❑ 61 Aaron Brooks .50 .20
❑ 62 Joe Horn .50 .20
❑ 63 Deuce McAllister .75 .30
❑ 64 Eli Manning 1.50 .60
❑ 65 Tiki Barber .75 .30
❑ 66 Amani Toomer .50 .20
❑ 67 Chad Pennington .75 .30
❑ 68 Curtis Martin .75 .30
❑ 69 Santana Moss .50 .20
❑ 70 Jerry Porter .50 .20
❑ 71 Randy Moss .75 .30
❑ 72 Kerry Collins .50 .20
❑ 73 Donovan McNabb 1.00 .40
❑ 74 Terrell Owens .75 .30
❑ 75 Brian Westbrook .50 .20
❑ 76 Ben Roethlisberger 2.00 .75
❑ 77 Hines Ward .75 .30
❑ 78 Jerome Bettis .75 .30
❑ 79 Duce Staley .50 .20
❑ 80 Drew Brees .75 .30
❑ 81 LaDainian Tomlinson 1.00 .40
❑ 82 Antonio Gates .75 .30
❑ 83 Tim Rattay .40 .15
❑ 84 Kevan Barlow .50 .20
❑ 85 Eric Johnson .50 .20
❑ 86 Matt Hasselbeck .50 .20
❑ 87 Shaun Alexander 1.00 .40
❑ 88 Darrell Jackson .50 .20
❑ 89 Marc Bulger .75 .30
❑ 90 Marshall Faulk .75 .30
❑ 91 Torry Holt .75 .30
❑ 92 Chris Simms .50 .20
❑ 93 Michael Clayton .75 .30
❑ 94 Michael Pittman .40 .15
❑ 95 Steve McNair .75 .30
❑ 96 Drew Bennett .50 .20
❑ 97 Chris Brown .50 .20
❑ 98 Clinton Portis .75 .30
❑ 99 Patrick Ramsey .50 .20
❑ 100 Laveranues Coles .50 .20
❑ 101 Gino Guidugli RC 1.50 .60
❑ 102 Kyle Orton RC 5.00 2.00
❑ 103 David Greene RC 3.00 1.25
❑ 104 Charlie Frye RC 6.00 2.50
❑ 105 Andrew Walter RC 5.00 2.00
❑ 106 Dan Orlovsky RC 4.00 1.50
❑ 107 Jason White RC 3.00 1.25
❑ 108 Sonny Cumbie RC 2.50 1.00
❑ 109 Ronnie Brown RC 10.00 4.00
❑ 110 Carnell Williams RC 15.00 6.00
❑ 111 Anthony Davis RC 2.50 1.00
❑ 112 Kay-Jay Harris RC 2.50 1.00
❑ 113 Walter Reyes RC 2.50 1.00
❑ 114 Darren Sproles RC 3.00 1.25
❑ 115 Mark Clayton RC 4.00 1.50
❑ 116 Braylon Edwards RC 10.00 4.00
❑ 117 Charles Frederick RC 2.50 1.00
❑ 118 Fred Gibson RC 2.50 1.00
❑ 119 Craphonso Thorpe RC 2.50 1.00
❑ 120 Terrence Murphy RC 3.00 1.25
❑ 121 Antrel Rolle RC 3.00 1.25
❑ 122 Marlin Jackson RC 3.00 1.25
❑ 123 Corey Webster RC 3.00 1.25
❑ 124 Travis Johnson RC 2.50 1.00
❑ 125 Shawne Merriman RC 5.00 2.00
❑ 126 Aaron Rodgers RC 10.00 4.00
❑ 127 Alex Smith QB RC 12.00 5.00
❑ 128 T.A. McLendon RC 1.50 .60
❑ 129 Troy Williamson RC 6.00 2.50
❑ 130 Ryan Moats RC 3.00 1.25
❑ 131 Vernand Morency RC 3.00 1.25
❑ 132 Brock Berlin RC 2.50 1.00
❑ 133 J.J. Arrington RC 4.00 1.50
❑ 134 Frank Gore RC 5.00 2.00
❑ 135 Chris Henry RC 3.00 1.25
❑ 136 Roscoe Parrish RC 3.00 1.25
❑ 137 Alex Smith TE RC 3.00 1.25
❑ 138 Ciatrick Fason RC 3.00 1.25
❑ 139 Marion Barber RC 5.00 2.00
❑ 140 J.R. Russell RC 2.50 1.00
❑ 141 Heath Miller RC 8.00 3.00
❑ 142 Marcus Spears RC 3.00 1.25
❑ 143 Alvin Pearman RC 3.00 1.25
❑ 144 David Pollack RC 3.00 1.25
❑ 145 Erasmus James RC 3.00 1.25
❑ 146 Noah Herron RC 3.00 1.25
❑ 147 Dan Cody RC 3.00 1.25
❑ 148 Eric Shelton RC 3.00 1.25
❑ 149 Anttaj Hawthorne RC 2.50 1.00
❑ 150 Steve Savoy RC 1.50 .60
❑ 151 Mike Patterson RC 3.00 1.25
❑ 152 Kirk Morrison RC 3.00 1.25
❑ 153 Airese Currie RC 3.00 1.25
❑ 154 Derrick Johnson RC 5.00 2.00
❑ 155 Darryl Blackstock RC 2.50 1.00
❑ 156 Mike Williams 6.00 2.50
❑ 157 Ernest Shazor RC 3.00 1.25
❑ 158 James Butler RC 2.50 1.00
❑ 159 Thomas Davis RC 3.00 1.25
❑ 160 Carlos Rogers RC 4.00 1.50
❑ 161 Mark Bradley RC 3.00 1.25
❑ 162 Jerome Mathis RC 3.00 1.25
❑ 163 Justin Miller RC 2.50 1.00
❑ 164 Donte Nicholson RC 3.00 1.25
❑ 165 Derek Anderson RC 3.00 1.25
❑ 166 Brandon Browner RC 2.50 1.00
❑ 167 Domonique Foxworth RC 3.00 1.25
❑ 168 Kevin Burnett RC 3.00 1.25
❑ 169 Lorenzo Alexander RC 2.50 1.00
❑ 170 Oshiomogho Atogwe RC 2.50 1.00
❑ 171 Dustin Fox RC 3.00 1.25
❑ 172 Jamaal Brimmer RC 1.50 .60
❑ 173 Ryan Fitzpatrick RC 5.00 2.00
❑ 174 Bill Swancutt RC 2.50 1.00
❑ 175 Barrett Ruud RC 3.00 1.25
❑ 176 Channing Crowder RC 3.00 1.25
❑ 177 Timmy Chang RC 2.50 1.00
❑ 178 Chris Rix RC 2.50 1.00
❑ 179 Justin Tuck RC 3.00 1.25
❑ 180 Adam Jones RC 3.00 1.25
❑ 181 Bryant McFadden RC 3.00 1.25
❑ 182 Taylor Stubblefield RC 1.50 .60
❑ 183 Vincent Jackson RC 3.00 1.25
❑ 184 Craig Bragg RC 2.50 1.00
❑ 185 Reggie Brown RC 3.00 1.25
❑ 186 Roddy White RC 3.00 1.25
❑ 187 Jason Campbell RC 5.00 2.00
❑ 188 Derek Wake RC 3.00 1.25
❑ 189 Josh Davis RC 2.50 1.00
❑ 190 Mike Nugent RC 3.00 1.25
❑ 191 Maurice Clarett 3.00 1.25
❑ 192 Brandon Jacobs RC 4.00 1.50
❑ 193 Matt Jones RC 8.00 3.00
❑ 194 Chad Owens RC 3.00 1.25
❑ 195 Paris Warren RC 2.50 1.00
❑ 196 Tab Perry RC 3.00 1.25
❑ 197 Jovan Haye RC 2.50 1.00
❑ 198 Cedric Benson RC 6.00 2.50
❑ 199 Bobby Purify RC 2.50 1.00
❑ 200 Stefan LeFors RC 3.00 1.25

2005 Upper Deck Rookie Materials

❑ COMP.SET w/o RC's (90) 25.00 10.00
❑ DRAFT PICK STATED ODDS 1:3
❑ 1 Larry Fitzgerald .75 .30
❑ 2 Kurt Warner .50 .20
❑ 3 Michael Vick 1.25 .50
❑ 4 Peerless Price .40 .15
❑ 5 Todd Heap .50 .20
❑ 6 Jamal Lewis .75 .30
❑ 7 Kyle Boller .50 .20
❑ 8 J.P. Losman .75 .30
❑ 9 Willis McGahee .75 .30
❑ 10 Lee Evans .50 .20
❑ 11 Eric Moulds .50 .20
❑ 12 Jake Delhomme .75 .30
❑ 13 Keary Colbert .50 .20
❑ 14 DeShaun Foster .50 .20
❑ 15 Brian Urlacher .75 .30
❑ 16 Rex Grossman .50 .20
❑ 17 Muhsin Muhammad .50 .20
❑ 18 Carson Palmer .75 .30
❑ 19 Rudi Johnson .50 .20
❑ 20 Chad Johnson .75 .30
❑ 21 Julius Jones 1.00 .40
❑ 22 Keyshawn Johnson .50 .20
❑ 23 Drew Bledsoe .75 .30
❑ 24 Tatum Bell .50 .20
❑ 25 Jake Plummer .50 .20
❑ 26 Ashley Lelie .50 .20
❑ 27 Roy Williams WR .75 .30
❑ 28 Kevin Jones .75 .30
❑ 29 Jeff Garcia .50 .20
❑ 30 Brett Favre 2.00 .75
❑ 31 Ahman Green .75 .30
❑ 32 Javon Walker .50 .20
❑ 33 David Carr .75 .30
❑ 34 Andre Johnson .50 .20
❑ 35 Domanick Davis .50 .20
❑ 36 Peyton Manning 1.25 .50
❑ 37 Edgerrin James .75 .30
❑ 38 Marvin Harrison .75 .30
❑ 39 Byron Leftwich .75 .30
❑ 40 Fred Taylor .50 .20
❑ 41 Jimmy Smith .50 .20
❑ 42 Priest Holmes .75 .30
❑ 43 Tony Gonzalez .50 .20
❑ 44 Trent Green .50 .20
❑ 45 A.J. Feeley .50 .20
❑ 46 Chris Chambers .50 .20
❑ 47 Randy McMichael .40 .15
❑ 48 Daunte Culpepper .75 .30
❑ 49 Michael Bennett .50 .20
❑ 50 Nate Burleson .50 .20
❑ 51 Tom Brady 2.00 .75
❑ 52 Corey Dillon .50 .20
❑ 53 Deion Branch .50 .20
❑ 54 Aaron Brooks .50 .20
❑ 55 Deuce McAllister .75 .30
❑ 56 Joe Horn .50 .20
❑ 57 Eli Manning 1.50 .60
❑ 58 Jeremy Shockey .75 .30
❑ 59 Tiki Barber .75 .30
❑ 60 Chad Pennington .75 .30
❑ 61 Curtis Martin .75 .30
❑ 62 Laveranues Coles .50 .20
❑ 63 Kerry Collins .50 .20
❑ 64 LaMont Jordan .75 .30

❑ 65	Randy Moss	.75	.30
❑ 66	Donovan McNabb	1.00	.40
❑ 67	Terrell Owens	.75	.30
❑ 68	Brian Westbrook	.50	.20
❑ 69	Ben Roethlisberger	2.00	.75
❑ 70	Jerome Bettis	.75	.30
❑ 71	Hines Ward	.75	.30
❑ 72	Drew Brees	.75	.30
❑ 73	LaDainian Tomlinson	1.00	.40
❑ 74	Antonio Gates	.75	.30
❑ 75	Tim Rattay	.40	.15
❑ 76	Eric Johnson	.50	.20
❑ 77	Shaun Alexander	1.00	.40
❑ 78	Darrell Jackson	.50	.20
❑ 79	Matt Hasselbeck	.50	.20
❑ 80	Marc Bulger	.75	.30
❑ 81	Steven Jackson	1.00	.40
❑ 82	Torry Holt	.75	.30
❑ 83	Joey Galloway	.50	.20
❑ 84	Brian Griese	.50	.20
❑ 85	Michael Clayton	.75	.30
❑ 86	Steve McNair	.75	.30
❑ 87	Chris Brown	.50	.20
❑ 88	Clinton Portis	.75	.30
❑ 89	Patrick Ramsey	.50	.20
❑ 90	Santana Moss	.50	.20
❑ 91	Aaron Rodgers RC	10.00	4.00
❑ 92	Alex Smith QB RC	12.00	5.00
❑ 93	Jason Campbell RC	5.00	2.00
❑ 94	Charlie Frye RC	6.00	2.50
❑ 95	David Greene RC	3.00	1.25
❑ 96	Dan Orlovsky RC	4.00	1.50
❑ 97	Adrian McPherson RC	3.00	1.25
❑ 98	Kyle Orton RC	5.00	2.00
❑ 99	Andrew Walter RC	5.00	2.00
❑ 100	Cedric Benson RC	6.00	2.50
❑ 101	Carnell Williams RC	15.00	6.00
❑ 102	Ronnie Brown RC	10.00	4.00
❑ 103	Vernand Morency RC	3.00	1.25
❑ 104	Ciatrick Fason RC	3.00	1.25
❑ 105	Maurice Clarett	3.00	1.25
❑ 106	Eric Shelton RC	3.00	1.25
❑ 107	J.J. Arrington RC	4.00	1.50
❑ 108	Frank Gore RC	5.00	2.00
❑ 109	Stefan LeFors RC	3.00	1.25
❑ 110	Troy Williamson RC	6.00	2.50
❑ 111	Braylon Edwards RC	10.00	4.00
❑ 112	Mike Williams	6.00	2.50
❑ 113	Vincent Jackson RC	3.00	1.25
❑ 114	Courtney Roby RC	3.00	1.25
❑ 115	Roddy White RC	3.00	1.25
❑ 116	Matt Jones RC	8.00	3.00
❑ 117	Ryan Moats RC	3.00	1.25
❑ 118	Mark Bradley RC	3.00	1.25
❑ 119	Mark Clayton RC	4.00	1.50
❑ 120	Terrence Murphy RC	3.00	1.25
❑ 121	Roscoe Parrish RC	3.00	1.25
❑ 122	Carlos Rogers RC	4.00	1.50
❑ 123	Antrel Rolle RC	3.00	1.25
❑ 124	Adam Jones RC	3.00	1.25
❑ 125	Heath Miller RC	8.00	3.00
❑ 126	Reggie Brown RC	3.00	1.25
❑ 127	Shawne Merriman RC	5.00	2.00
❑ 128	Marcus Spears RC	3.00	1.25
❑ 129	DeMarcus Ware RC	5.00	2.00
❑ 130	Mike Nugent RC	3.00	1.25

2004 Upper Deck Rookie Premiere

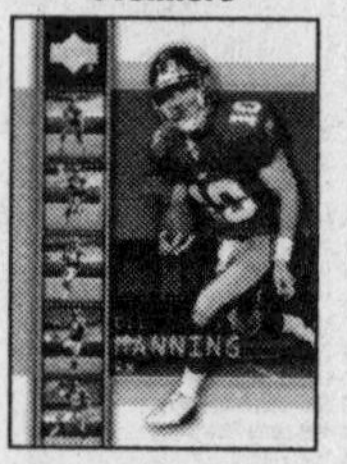

❑	COMPLETE SET (30)	30.00	18.00
❑ 1	Eli Manning	8.00	3.00
❑ 2	Ben Roethlisberger	15.00	7.50
❑ 3	Philip Rivers	3.00	1.25
❑ 4	Roy Williams WR	2.50	1.00
❑ 5	Larry Fitzgerald	3.00	1.25
❑ 6	Tatum Bell	2.00	.75
❑ 7	J.P. Losman	2.00	.75
❑ 8	Steven Jackson	3.00	1.25
❑ 9	Ben Watson	1.00	.40
❑ 10	Devery Henderson	.75	.30
❑ 11	Kevin Jones	3.00	1.25
❑ 12	Chris Perry	1.50	.60
❑ 13	Kellen Winslow Jr.	2.00	.75
❑ 14	Lee Evans	1.25	.50
❑ 15	Reggie Williams	1.25	.50
❑ 16	Ben Troupe	1.00	.40
❑ 17	Michael Clayton	2.00	.75
❑ 18	Michael Jenkins	1.00	.40
❑ 19	Rashaun Woods	1.00	.40
❑ 20	DeAngelo Hall	1.25	.50
❑ 21	Cedric Cobbs	1.00	.40
❑ 22	Luke McCown	1.00	.40
❑ 23	Robert Gallery	1.50	.60
❑ 24	Julius Jones	4.00	1.50
❑ 25	Matt Schaub	1.00	.40
❑ 26	Keary Colbert	1.25	.50
❑ 27	Bernard Berrian	1.00	.40
❑ 28	Greg Jones	1.25	.50
❑ 29	Darius Watts	1.00	.40
❑ 30	Checklist Card	1.00	.40

2005 Upper Deck Rookie Premiere

❑	COMPLETE SET (30)	25.00	10.00
❑ 1	Ciatrick Fason	.75	.30
❑ 2	Alex Smith QB	3.00	1.25
❑ 3	Antrel Rolle	.75	.30
❑ 4	Carnell Williams	4.00	1.50
❑ 5	Ronnie Brown	2.50	1.00
❑ 6	Charlie Frye	1.50	.60
❑ 7	Roddy White	.75	.30
❑ 8	Braylon Edwards	2.50	1.00
❑ 9	Mark Bradley	.75	.30
❑ 10	Vincent Jackson	.75	.30
❑ 11	Matt Jones	2.00	.75
❑ 12	Stefan LeFors	.75	.30
❑ 13	Kyle Orton	1.25	.50
❑ 14	Troy Williamson	1.50	.60
❑ 15	Mark Clayton	1.00	.40
❑ 16	Aaron Rodgers	2.50	1.00
❑ 17	Cedric Benson	1.50	.60
❑ 18	Mike Williams	1.50	.60
❑ 19	Adam Jones	.75	.30
❑ 20	Reggie Brown	.75	.30
❑ 21	J.J. Arrington	1.00	.40
❑ 22	Andrew Walter	1.25	.50
❑ 23	David Greene	.75	.30
❑ 24	Roscoe Parrish	.75	.30
❑ 25	Terrence Murphy	.75	.30
❑ 26	Jason Campbell	1.25	.50
❑ 27	Maurice Clarett	.75	.30
❑ 28	Frank Gore	1.25	.50
❑ 29	Ryan Moats	.75	.30
❑ 30	Checklist Card	.75	.30

1995 Zenith

❑	COMPLETE SET (150)	20.00	7.50
❑ Z1	Emmitt Smith	2.00	.75
❑ Z2	Chris Spielman	.25	.08
❑ Z3	Johnny Mitchell	.15	.05
❑ Z4	Boomer Esiason	.25	.08
❑ Z5	Jackie Harris	.15	.05
❑ Z6	Warren Moon	.25	.08
❑ Z7	Harvey Williams	.15	.05
❑ Z8	Steve Walsh	.15	.05
❑ Z9	Cris Carter	.40	.15
❑ Z10	Natrone Means	.25	.08
❑ Z11	Art Monk	.25	.08
❑ Z12	Leslie O'Neal	.25	.08
❑ Z13	Adrian Murrell	.25	.08
❑ Z14	John Elway	2.50	1.00
❑ Z15	Larry Centers	.25	.08
❑ Z16	Ricky Ervins	.15	.05
❑ Z17	Jeff Graham	.15	.05
❑ Z18	Ricky Watters	.25	.08
❑ Z19	Eric Green	.15	.05
❑ Z20	Curtis Conway	.40	.15
❑ Z21	Jake Reed	.25	.08
❑ Z22	Michael Timpson	.15	.05
❑ Z23	Marcus Allen	.40	.15
❑ Z24	Andre Rison	.25	.08
❑ Z25	Terry Kirby	.25	.08
❑ Z26	Reggie White	.40	.15
❑ Z27	Randall Cunningham	.40	.15
❑ Z28	Jim Kelly	.40	.15
❑ Z29	Robert Brooks	.40	.15
❑ Z30	Terance Mathis	.25	.08
❑ Z31	Anthony Miller	.25	.08
❑ Z32	Neil O'Donnell	.25	.08
❑ Z33	Jeff Hostetler	.25	.08
❑ Z34	Drew Bledsoe	.75	.30
❑ Z35	Irving Spikes	.25	.08
❑ Z36	Keith Byars	.15	.05
❑ Z37	Rod Woodson	.25	.08
❑ Z38	Rob Moore	.25	.08
❑ Z39	Scott Mitchell	.25	.08
❑ Z40	Cody Carlson	.15	.05
❑ Z41	Alvin Harper	.15	.05
❑ Z42	Chris Warren	.25	.08
❑ Z43	Ben Coates	.25	.08
❑ Z44	Jim Everett	.15	.05
❑ Z45	Vinny Testaverde	.25	.08
❑ Z46	Glyn Milburn	.15	.05
❑ Z47	Calvin Williams	.25	.08
❑ Z48	Fred Barnett	.25	.08
❑ Z49	Tim Brown	.40	.15
❑ Z50	Lorenzo White	.15	.05
❑ Z51	Brent Jones	.15	.05
❑ Z52	Henry Ellard	.25	.08
❑ Z53	Rick Mirer	.25	.08
❑ Z54	Junior Seau	.40	.15
❑ Z55	Jeff Blake RC	1.00	.40
❑ Z56	Desmond Howard	.25	.08
❑ Z57	Jerry Rice	1.25	.50
❑ Z58	Lewis Tillman	.15	.05
❑ Z59	Roosevelt Potts	.15	.05
❑ Z60	Rocket Ismail	.25	.08
❑ Z61	Eric Hill	.15	.05
❑ Z62	Brett Favre	2.50	1.00
❑ Z63	Haywood Jeffires	.15	.05
❑ Z64	Barry Foster	.25	.08
❑ Z65	Flipper Anderson	.15	.05
❑ Z66	Troy Aikman	1.25	.50
❑ Z67	Herschel Walker	.25	.08

- ❑ Z68 Sean Dawkins .25 .08
- ❑ Z69 Erric Pegram .25 .08
- ❑ Z70 Irving Fryar .25 .08
- ❑ Z71 Thurman Thomas .40 .15
- ❑ Z72 Eric Metcalf .25 .08
- ❑ Z73 John Taylor .15 .05
- ❑ Z74 Jeff George .25 .08
- ❑ Z75 Courtney Hawkins .15 .05
- ❑ Z76 Carl Pickens .25 .08
- ❑ Z77 Mike Sherrard .15 .05
- ❑ Z78 Rodney Hampton .25 .08
- ❑ Z79 Joe Montana 2.50 1.00
- ❑ Z80 Willie Davis .25 .08
- ❑ Z81 Chris Penn .15 .05
- ❑ Z82 Dave Brown .25 .08
- ❑ Z83 Gary Brown .15 .05
- ❑ Z84 Andre Reed .25 .08
- ❑ Z85 Michael Irvin .40 .15
- ❑ Z86 Vincent Brisby .15 .05
- ❑ Z87 Barry Sanders 2.00 .75
- ❑ Z88 Qadry Ismail .25 .08
- ❑ Z89 Reggie Brooks .25 .08
- ❑ Z90 Bruce Smith .40 .15
- ❑ Z91 David Klingler .25 .08
- ❑ Z92 Michael Haynes .25 .08
- ❑ Z93 Derek Russell .15 .05
- ❑ Z94 Steve Young 1.00 .40
- ❑ Z95 Terry Allen .25 .08
- ❑ Z96 Mark Seay .25 .08
- ❑ Z97 Dan Marino 2.50 1.00
- ❑ Z98 Jerry Rice RW 1.25 .50
- ❑ Z99 Cris Carter RW .40 .15
- ❑ Z100 Art Monk RW .25 .08
- ❑ Z101 Cortez Kennedy .25 .08
- ❑ Z102 Stan Humphries .25 .08
- ❑ Z103 Herman Moore .40 .15
- ❑ Z104 Ronald Moore .15 .05
- ❑ Z105 Greg Lloyd .25 .08
- ❑ Z106 Jerome Bettis .40 .15
- ❑ Z107 Craig Erickson .15 .05
- ❑ Z108 Keith Jackson .15 .05
- ❑ Z109 Sterling Sharpe .25 .08
- ❑ Z110 Ronnie Harmon .15 .05
- ❑ Z111 Deion Sanders .75 .30
- ❑ Z112 Charles Haley .25 .08
- ❑ Z113 Bernie Parmalee .25 .08
- ❑ Z114 Leroy Hoard .15 .05
- ❑ Z115 O.J. McDuffie .40 .15
- ❑ Z116 Garrison Hearst .40 .15
- ❑ Z117 Kevin Greene .25 .08
- ❑ Z118 Derek Brown .15 .05
- ❑ Z119 Mark Brunell .75 .30
- ❑ Z120 Kevin Williams .25 .08
- ❑ Z121 Dan Wilkinson .25 .08
- ❑ Z122 Chuck Levy .15 .05
- ❑ Z123 Derrick Alexander WR .40 .15
- ❑ Z124 Aaron Bailey RC .15 .05
- ❑ Z125 Thomas Lewis .25 .08
- ❑ Z126 Antonio Langham .15 .05
- ❑ Z127 Bryan Reeves .15 .05
- ❑ Z128 William Floyd .25 .08
- ❑ Z129 Lake Dawson .25 .08
- ❑ Z130 Bert Emanuel .40 .15
- ❑ Z131 Marshall Faulk 1.50 .60
- ❑ Z132 Heath Shuler .25 .08
- ❑ Z133 David Palmer .25 .08
- ❑ Z134 Willie McGinest .25 .08
- ❑ Z135 Mario Bates .25 .08
- ❑ Z136 Byron Bam Morris .15 .05
- ❑ Z137 Tim Bowens .15 .05
- ❑ Z138 Errict Rhett .25 .08
- ❑ Z139 Charlie Garner .40 .15
- ❑ Z140 Darnay Scott .25 .08
- ❑ Z141 Greg Hill .25 .08
- ❑ Z142 LeShon Johnson .25 .08
- ❑ Z143 Charles Johnson .25 .08
- ❑ Z144 Trent Dilfer .40 .15
- ❑ Z145 Gus Frerotte .25 .08
- ❑ Z146 Johnnie Morton .25 .08
- ❑ Z147 Glenn Foley .15 .05
- ❑ Z148 Perry Klein .15 .05
- ❑ Z149 Ryan Yarborough .25 .08
- ❑ Z150 Tydus Winans .15 .05

1996 Zenith

- ❑ COMPLETE SET (150) 25.00 10.00
- ❑ 1 Dan Marino 3.00 1.25

- ❑ 2 Yancey Thigpen .25 .08
- ❑ 3 Marcus Allen .50 .20
- ❑ 4 Curtis Conway .50 .20
- ❑ 5 Troy Aikman 1.50 .60
- ❑ 6 William Floyd .25 .08
- ❑ 7 Ricky Watters .25 .08
- ❑ 8 Herman Moore .25 .08
- ❑ 9 Jim Harbaugh .25 .08
- ❑ 10 Isaac Bruce .50 .20
- ❑ 11 Drew Bledsoe 1.00 .40
- ❑ 12 Jeff Blake .50 .20
- ❑ 13 Tim Brown .50 .20
- ❑ 14 Deion Sanders 1.00 .40
- ❑ 15 Greg Hill .25 .08
- ❑ 16 Ben Coates .25 .08
- ❑ 17 Errict Rhett .25 .08
- ❑ 18 Barry Sanders 2.50 1.00
- ❑ 19 Erik Kramer .10 .02
- ❑ 20 Emmitt Smith 2.50 1.00
- ❑ 21 Brett Favre 3.00 1.25
- ❑ 22 Jerome Bettis .50 .20
- ❑ 23 Garrison Hearst .25 .08
- ❑ 24 Michael Irvin .50 .20
- ❑ 25 Chris Warren .25 .08
- ❑ 26 Steve Young 1.25 .50
- ❑ 27 Cris Carter .50 .20
- ❑ 28 Carl Pickens .25 .08
- ❑ 29 Lake Dawson .10 .02
- ❑ 30 Marshall Faulk .60 .25
- ❑ 31 Vincent Brisby .10 .02
- ❑ 32 Jerry Rice 1.50 .60
- ❑ 33 Eric Metcalf .10 .02
- ❑ 34 Natrone Means .25 .08
- ❑ 35 Steve Bono .10 .02
- ❑ 36 John Elway 3.00 1.25
- ❑ 37 Jeff Hostetler .10 .02
- ❑ 38 Scott Mitchell .25 .08
- ❑ 39 Andre Rison .25 .08
- ❑ 40 Daryl Johnston .25 .08
- ❑ 41 Mark Brunell 1.00 .40
- ❑ 42 Jeff George .25 .08
- ❑ 43 Mario Bates .25 .08
- ❑ 44 Erric Pegram .10 .02
- ❑ 45 Brent Jones .10 .02
- ❑ 46 Trent Dilfer .50 .20
- ❑ 47 Larry Centers .25 .08
- ❑ 48 Anthony Miller .25 .08
- ❑ 49 Reggie White .50 .20
- ❑ 50 Bill Brooks .10 .02
- ❑ 51 Chris Zorich .10 .02
- ❑ 52 Jim Kelly .50 .20
- ❑ 53 Junior Seau .50 .20
- ❑ 54 Chris Miller .10 .02
- ❑ 55 Gus Frerotte .25 .08
- ❑ 56 Andre Reed .25 .08
- ❑ 57 Darnay Scott .25 .08
- ❑ 58 Brett Perriman .10 .02
- ❑ 59 Edgar Bennett .25 .08
- ❑ 60 Warren Moon .25 .08
- ❑ 61 Neil O'Donnell .25 .08
- ❑ 62 Jay Novacek .10 .02
- ❑ 63 Byron Bam Morris .10 .02
- ❑ 64 Jim Everett .10 .02
- ❑ 65 Ken Norton, Jr. .10 .02
- ❑ 66 Tony Martin .25 .08
- ❑ 67 Steve Atwater .10 .02
- ❑ 68 Henry Ellard .10 .02
- ❑ 69 Rodney Hampton .25 .08
- ❑ 70 Derrick Thomas .50 .20
- ❑ 71 Stan Humphries .25 .08
- ❑ 72 Harvey Williams .10 .02
- ❑ 73 Greg Lloyd .25 .08
- ❑ 74 Jake Reed .25 .08
- ❑ 75 Charles Haley .25 .08
- ❑ 76 Quinn Early .10 .02
- ❑ 77 Rodney Peete .10 .02
- ❑ 78 Brian Blades .10 .02
- ❑ 79 Robert Brooks .50 .20
- ❑ 80 Terry Allen .25 .08
- ❑ 81 Dave Brown .10 .02
- ❑ 82 Derrick Alexander WR .25 .08
- ❑ 83 Terance Mathis .10 .02
- ❑ 84 Rick Mirer .25 .08
- ❑ 85 Herschel Walker .25 .08
- ❑ 86 Charlie Garner .25 .08
- ❑ 87 Jeff Graham .10 .02
- ❑ 88 Bruce Smith .25 .08
- ❑ 89 Terry Kirby .25 .08
- ❑ 90 Craig Heyward .10 .02
- ❑ 91 Bernie Parmalee .10 .02
- ❑ 92 Adrian Murrell .25 .08
- ❑ 93 Derek Loville .10 .02
- ❑ 94 Heath Shuler .25 .08
- ❑ 95 Shannon Sharpe .25 .08
- ❑ 96 Bert Emanuel .25 .08
- ❑ 97 Hugh Douglas .25 .08
- ❑ 98 Lovell Pinkney .10 .02
- ❑ 99 Sherman Williams .10 .02
- ❑ 100 Tony Boselli .10 .02
- ❑ 101 Wayne Chrebet .50 .20
- ❑ 102 Orlando Thomas .10 .02
- ❑ 103 Darick Holmes .10 .02
- ❑ 104 Tyrone Wheatley .25 .08
- ❑ 105 Christian Fauria .10 .02
- ❑ 106 Frank Sanders .25 .08
- ❑ 107 Chad May .10 .02
- ❑ 108 James O. Stewart .25 .08
- ❑ 109 Ken Dilger .25 .08
- ❑ 110 Kyle Brady .10 .02
- ❑ 111 Todd Collins .25 .08
- ❑ 112 Terrell Fletcher .10 .02
- ❑ 113 Eric Bjornson .10 .02
- ❑ 114 Justin Armour .10 .02
- ❑ 115 Rob Johnson .50 .20
- ❑ 116 Terrell Davis 1.00 .40
- ❑ 117 J.J. Stokes .50 .20
- ❑ 118 Rashaan Salaam .25 .08
- ❑ 119 Chris Sanders .25 .08
- ❑ 120 Kerry Collins .50 .20
- ❑ 121 Michael Westbrook .50 .20
- ❑ 122 Eric Zeier .10 .02
- ❑ 123 Curtis Martin 1.00 .40
- ❑ 124 Rodney Thomas .10 .02
- ❑ 125 Kordell Stewart .50 .20
- ❑ 126 Joey Galloway .50 .20
- ❑ 127 Steve McNair 1.00 .40
- ❑ 128 Napoleon Kaufman .50 .20
- ❑ 129 Tamarick Vanover .25 .08
- ❑ 130 Stoney Case .10 .02
- ❑ 131 James A. Stewart .10 .02
- ❑ 132 Carl Pickens PP .25 .08
- ❑ 133 Jim Harbaugh PP .25 .08
- ❑ 134 Yancey Thigpen PP .25 .08
- ❑ 135 Ricky Watters PP .25 .08
- ❑ 136 Isaac Bruce PP .50 .20
- ❑ 137 Kordell Stewart PP .50 .20
- ❑ 138 Jeff Blake PP .25 .08
- ❑ 139 Terrell Davis PP .50 .20
- ❑ 140 Scott Mitchell PP .10 .02
- ❑ 141 Rodney Thomas PP .10 .02
- ❑ 142 Robert Brooks PP .50 .20
- ❑ 143 Joey Galloway PP .50 .20
- ❑ 144 Brett Favre PP 1.50 .60
- ❑ 145 Kerry Collins PP .50 .20
- ❑ 146 Herman Moore PP .25 .08
- ❑ 147 E.Smith/Aikman/Irvin 1.50 .60
- ❑ 148 Dan Marino CL .50 .20
- ❑ 149 Jerry Rice CL .50 .20
- ❑ 150 Emmitt Smith CL .50 .20

1997 Zenith

❑ COMPLETE SET (150)		25.00	10.00
❑ 1	Brett Favre	3.00	1.25
❑ 2	Jerry Rice	1.50	.60
❑ 3	Shannon Sharpe	.50	.20
❑ 4	Dan Marino	3.00	1.25
❑ 5	James O.Stewart	.50	.20
❑ 6	Warren Moon	.75	.30
❑ 7	Emmitt Smith	2.50	1.00
❑ 8	Kordell Stewart	.75	.30
❑ 9	Kerry Collins	.75	.30
❑ 10	Ricky Watters	.50	.20
❑ 11	Gus Frerotte	.30	.10
❑ 12	Barry Sanders	2.50	1.00
❑ 13	Joey Galloway	.50	.20
❑ 14	Marshall Faulk	1.00	.40
❑ 15	Todd Collins	.30	.10
❑ 16	Steve McNair	1.00	.40
❑ 17	Tyrone Wheatley	.50	.20
❑ 18	Isaac Bruce	.75	.30
❑ 19	Troy Aikman	1.50	.60
❑ 20	Larry Centers	.50	.20
❑ 21	Alvin Harper	.30	.10
❑ 22	Rashaan Salaam	.30	.10
❑ 23	Eric Metcalf	.50	.20
❑ 24	Jim Everett	.30	.10
❑ 25	Ken Dilger	.30	.10
❑ 26	Curtis Martin	1.00	.40
❑ 27	Neil O'Donnell	.50	.20
❑ 28	Thurman Thomas	.75	.30
❑ 29	Andre Rison	.50	.20
❑ 30	Steve Bono	.50	.20
❑ 31	Garrison Hearst	.50	.20
❑ 32	Junior Seau	.75	.30
❑ 33	Napoleon Kaufman	.75	.30
❑ 34	Jerome Bettis	.75	.30
❑ 35	Frank Wycheck	.30	.10
❑ 36	Lamar Smith	.75	.30
❑ 37	Derrick Alexander WR	.50	.20
❑ 38	Steve Young	1.00	.40
❑ 39	Cris Carter	.75	.30
❑ 40	O.J. McDuffie	.50	.20
❑ 41	Deion Sanders	.75	.30
❑ 42	Robert Brooks	.50	.20
❑ 43	Jeff Blake	.50	.20
❑ 44	Marcus Allen	.75	.30
❑ 45	Herman Moore	.50	.20
❑ 46	Ray Zellars	.30	.10
❑ 47	Tim Brown	.75	.30
❑ 48	John Elway	3.00	1.25
❑ 49	Charles Johnson	.50	.20
❑ 50	Rodney Peete	.30	.10
❑ 51	Curtis Conway	.50	.20
❑ 52	Kevin Greene	.50	.20
❑ 53	Andre Reed	.50	.20
❑ 54	Mark Brunell	1.00	.40
❑ 55	Tony Martin	.50	.20
❑ 56	Elvis Grbac	.50	.20
❑ 57	Wayne Chrebet	.75	.30
❑ 58	Vinny Testaverde	.50	.20
❑ 59	Terry Allen	.75	.30
❑ 60	Dave Brown	.30	.10
❑ 61	LeShon Johnson	.30	.10
❑ 62	Trent Dilfer	.75	.30
❑ 63	Chris Warren	.50	.20
❑ 64	Chris Sanders	.30	.10
❑ 65	Kevin Carter	.30	.10
❑ 66	Jim Harbaugh	.50	.20
❑ 67	Terance Mathis	.50	.20
❑ 68	Ben Coates	.50	.20
❑ 69	Robert Smith	.50	.20
❑ 70	Drew Bledsoe	1.00	.40
❑ 71	Henry Ellard	.30	.10
❑ 72	Scott Mitchell	.50	.20
❑ 73	Andre Hastings	.30	.10
❑ 74	Rodney Hampton	.50	.20
❑ 75	Michael Jackson	.50	.20
❑ 76	Jeff Hostetler	.30	.10
❑ 77	Reggie White	.75	.30
❑ 78	Desmond Howard	.50	.20
❑ 79	Adrian Murrell	.50	.20
❑ 80	Carl Pickens	.50	.20
❑ 81	Erik Kramer	.30	.10
❑ 82	Terrell Davis	1.00	.40
❑ 83	Sean Dawkins	.30	.10
❑ 84	Jamal Anderson	.75	.30
❑ 85	Stan Humphries	.50	.20
❑ 86	Chris T. Jones	.30	.10
❑ 87	Hardy Nickerson	.30	.10
❑ 88	Anthony Johnson	.30	.10
❑ 89	Michael Haynes	.30	.10
❑ 90	Irving Spikes	.30	.10
❑ 91	Bruce Smith	.50	.20
❑ 92	Keenan McCardell	.50	.20
❑ 93	Chris Chandler	.50	.20
❑ 94	Tamarick Vanover	.50	.20
❑ 95	Dorsey Levens	.75	.30
❑ 96	Roman Phifer	.30	.10
❑ 97	Michael Irvin	.75	.30
❑ 98	Tim Biakabutuka	.50	.20
❑ 99	Stepfret Williams	.30	.10
❑ 100	Eddie George	.75	.30
❑ 101	Karim Abdul-Jabbar	.75	.30
❑ 102	Amani Toomer	.50	.20
❑ 103	Tony Banks	.50	.20
❑ 104	Regan Upshaw	.30	.10
❑ 105	Leeland McElroy	.30	.10
❑ 106	Jason Dunn	.30	.10
❑ 107	Keyshawn Johnson	.75	.30
❑ 108	Winslow Oliver	.30	.10
❑ 109	Walt Harris	.30	.10
❑ 110	Stanley Pritchett	.30	.10
❑ 111	Eddie Kennison	.50	.20
❑ 112	Terrell Owens	1.00	.40
❑ 113	Duane Clemons	.30	.10
❑ 114	John Mobley	.30	.10
❑ 115	Simeon Rice	.50	.20
❑ 116	Tony Brackens	.30	.10
❑ 117	Eric Moulds	.75	.30
❑ 118	Marvin Harrison	.75	.30
❑ 119	Rickey Dudley	.50	.20
❑ 120	Mike Alstott	.75	.30
❑ 121	Terry Glenn	.75	.30
❑ 122	Brian Dawkins	.75	.30
❑ 123	Kevin Hardy	.30	.10
❑ 124	Bobby Engram	.50	.20
❑ 125	Alex Van Dyke	.30	.10
❑ 126	Zach Thomas	.75	.30
❑ 127	Bryan Still	.30	.10
❑ 128	Detron Smith	.30	.10
❑ 129	Jerome Woods	.30	.10
❑ 130	Muhsin Muhammad	.50	.20
❑ 131	Lawrence Phillips	.30	.10
❑ 132	Alex Molden	.30	.10
❑ 133	Steve Young SH	.30	.10
❑ 134	Troy Aikman SH	.75	.30
❑ 135	Junior Seau SH	.30	.10
❑ 136	John Elway SH	1.50	.60
❑ 137	Dan Marino SH	1.50	.60
❑ 138	Desmond Howard SH	.50	.20
❑ 139	Brett Favre SH	1.50	.60
❑ 140	Jerry Rice SH	.75	.30
❑ 141	Kerry Collins SH	.50	.20
❑ 142	Barry Sanders SH	1.25	.50
❑ 143	Mark Brunell SH	.75	.30
❑ 144	Drew Bledsoe SH	.75	.30
❑ 145	Eddie Kennison SH	.50	.20
❑ 146	Marvin Harrison SH	.75	.30
❑ 147	Emmitt Smith SH	1.25	.50
❑ 148	E.George/Glenn/Dudl/Hoy.	.75	.30
❑ 149	Emmitt Smith CL	.75	.30
❑ 150	Dan Marino CL	.75	.30

2005 Zenith

❑ COMP.SET w/o RCs (100)		25.00	10.00
❑ ROOKIE/999 STATED ODDS 1:24 RETAIL			
❑ 101-150 AU PRINT RUN 99 SER.#'d SETS			
❑ 1	Larry Fitzgerald	.75	.30
❑ 2	Anquan Boldin	.50	.20
❑ 3	Kurt Warner	.50	.20
❑ 4	Alge Crumpler	.50	.20
❑ 5	Michael Vick	1.25	.50
❑ 6	Warrick Dunn	.50	.20
❑ 7	Jamal Lewis	.75	.30
❑ 8	Kyle Boller	.50	.20
❑ 9	Derrick Mason	.50	.20
❑ 10	Ray Lewis	.75	.30
❑ 11	Willis McGahee	.75	.30
❑ 12	J.P. Losman	.75	.30
❑ 13	Lee Evans	.50	.20
❑ 14	Eric Moulds	.50	.20
❑ 15	Jake Delhomme	.75	.30
❑ 16	Steve Smith	.50	.20
❑ 17	DeShaun Foster	.50	.20
❑ 18	Rex Grossman	.50	.20
❑ 19	Muhsin Muhammad	.50	.20
❑ 20	Brian Urlacher	.75	.30
❑ 21	Carson Palmer	.75	.30
❑ 22	Chad Johnson	.75	.30
❑ 23	Rudi Johnson	.50	.20
❑ 24	Lee Suggs	.50	.20
❑ 25	Reuben Droughns	.50	.20
❑ 26	Trent Dilfer	.50	.20
❑ 27	Drew Bledsoe	.75	.30
❑ 28	Julius Jones	1.00	.40
❑ 29	Keyshawn Johnson	.50	.20
❑ 30	Roy Williams S	.50	.20
❑ 31	Ashley Lelie	.50	.20
❑ 32	Jake Plummer	.50	.20
❑ 33	Tatum Bell	.50	.20
❑ 34	Joey Harrington	.75	.30
❑ 35	Roy Williams WR	.75	.30
❑ 36	Kevin Jones	.75	.30
❑ 37	Ahman Green	.75	.30
❑ 38	Brett Favre	2.00	.75
❑ 39	Javon Walker	.50	.20
❑ 40	David Carr	.75	.30
❑ 41	Domanick Davis	.50	.20
❑ 42	Andre Johnson	.50	.20
❑ 43	Marvin Harrison	.75	.30
❑ 44	Edgerrin James	.75	.30
❑ 45	Peyton Manning	1.25	.50
❑ 46	Fred Taylor	.50	.20
❑ 47	Byron Leftwich	.75	.30
❑ 48	Jimmy Smith	.50	.20
❑ 49	Priest Holmes	.75	.30
❑ 50	Trent Green	.50	.20
❑ 51	Tony Gonzalez	.50	.20
❑ 52	Chris Chambers	.50	.20
❑ 53	A.J. Feeley	.50	.20
❑ 54	Daunte Culpepper	.75	.30
❑ 55	Michael Bennett	.50	.20
❑ 56	Nate Burleson	.50	.20
❑ 57	Tom Brady	2.00	.75
❑ 58	Deion Branch	.50	.20

❑ 59 Tedy Bruschi	.50	.20
❑ 60 Corey Dillon	.50	.20
❑ 61 Aaron Brooks	.50	.20
❑ 62 Deuce McAllister	.75	.30
❑ 63 Joe Horn	.50	.20
❑ 64 Eli Manning	1.50	.60
❑ 65 Tiki Barber	.75	.30
❑ 66 Plaxico Burress	.50	.20
❑ 67 Jeremy Shockey	.75	.30
❑ 68 Chad Pennington	.75	.30
❑ 69 Curtis Martin	.75	.30
❑ 70 Laveranues Coles	.50	.20
❑ 71 Kerry Collins	.50	.20
❑ 72 LaMont Jordan	.75	.30
❑ 73 Randy Moss	.75	.30
❑ 74 Brian Westbrook	.50	.20
❑ 75 Terrell Owens	.75	.30
❑ 76 Donovan McNabb	1.00	.40
❑ 77 Ben Roethlisberger	2.00	.75
❑ 78 Duce Staley	.50	.20
❑ 79 Jerome Bettis	.75	.30
❑ 80 Hines Ward	.75	.30
❑ 81 Drew Brees	.75	.30
❑ 82 Antonio Gates	.75	.30
❑ 83 LaDainian Tomlinson	1.00	.40
❑ 84 Kevan Barlow	.50	.20
❑ 85 Brandon Lloyd	.40	.15
❑ 86 Matt Hasselbeck	.50	.20
❑ 87 Shaun Alexander	1.00	.40
❑ 88 Darrell Jackson	.50	.20
❑ 89 Torry Holt	.75	.30
❑ 90 Marc Bulger	.75	.30
❑ 91 Steven Jackson	1.00	.40
❑ 92 Brian Griese	.50	.20
❑ 93 Michael Clayton	.75	.30
❑ 94 Steve McNair	.75	.30
❑ 95 Chris Brown	.50	.20
❑ 96 Drew Bennett	.50	.20
❑ 97 Patrick Ramsey	.50	.20
❑ 98 Clinton Portis	.75	.30
❑ 99 Santana Moss	.50	.20
❑ 100 LaVar Arrington	.75	.30
❑ 101 Adrian McPherson RC	5.00	2.00
❑ 102 Airese Currie RC	5.00	2.00
❑ 103 Alvin Pearman RC	5.00	2.00
❑ 104 Anthony Davis RC	4.00	1.50
❑ 105 Brandon Jacobs RC	6.00	2.50
❑ 106 Brandon Jones RC	5.00	2.00
❑ 107 Bryant McFadden RC	5.00	2.00
❑ 108 Cedric Houston RC	5.00	2.00
❑ 109 Chad Owens RC	5.00	2.00
❑ 110 Chris Henry RC	5.00	2.00
❑ 111 Craig Bragg RC	4.00	1.50
❑ 112 Craphonso Thorpe RC	4.00	1.50
❑ 113 Damien Nash RC	4.00	1.50
❑ 114 Dan Cody RC	5.00	2.00
❑ 115 Dan Orlovsky RC	6.00	2.50
❑ 116 Dante Ridgeway RC	4.00	1.50
❑ 117 Darren Sproles RC	5.00	2.00
❑ 118 David Greene RC	5.00	2.00
❑ 119 David Pollack RC	5.00	2.00
❑ 120 Deandra Cobb RC	4.00	1.50
❑ 121 DeMarcus Ware RC	8.00	3.00
❑ 122 Derek Anderson RC	5.00	2.00
❑ 123 Derrick Johnson RC	8.00	3.00
❑ 124 Erasmus James RC	5.00	2.00
❑ 125 Fabian Washington RC	5.00	2.00
❑ 126 Fred Gibson RC	4.00	1.50
❑ 127 Harry Williams RC	4.00	1.50
❑ 128 Heath Miller RC	12.00	5.00
❑ 129 J.R. Russell RC	4.00	1.50
❑ 130 James Kilian RC	5.00	2.00
❑ 131 Jerome Mathis RC	5.00	2.00
❑ 132 Larry Brackins RC	2.50	1.00
❑ 133 LeRon McCoy RC	4.00	1.50
❑ 134 Lionel Gates RC	4.00	1.50
❑ 135 Marcus Maxwell RC	4.00	1.50
❑ 136 Marcus Spears RC	5.00	2.00
❑ 137 Marion Barber RC	8.00	3.00
❑ 138 Marlin Jackson RC	6.00	2.50
❑ 139 Matt Cassel RC	8.00	3.00
❑ 140 Matt Roth RC	5.00	2.00
❑ 141 Mike Williams	10.00	4.00
❑ 142 Noah Herron RC	5.00	2.00
❑ 143 Paris Warren RC	4.00	1.50
❑ 144 Rasheed Marshall RC	5.00	2.00
❑ 145 Roydell Williams RC	5.00	2.00
❑ 146 Ryan Fitzpatrick RC	8.00	3.00
❑ 147 Shaun Cody RC	5.00	2.00
❑ 148 Shawne Merriman RC	8.00	3.00
❑ 149 Tab Perry RC	5.00	2.00
❑ 150 Thomas Davis RC	5.00	2.00
❑ 151 Adam Jones AU RC	40.00	15.00
❑ 152 Alex Smith QB AU RC	175.00	100.00
❑ 153 Antrel Rolle AU RC	50.00	20.00
❑ 154 Andrew Walter AU RC	80.00	40.00
❑ 155 Braylon Edwards AU RC	120.00	60.00
❑ 156 Carnell Williams AU RC	200.00	100.00
❑ 157 Carlos Rogers AU RC	50.00	20.00
❑ 158 Charlie Frye AU RC	80.00	50.00
❑ 159 Ciatrick Fason AU RC	40.00	15.00
❑ 160 Courtney Roby AU RC	40.00	15.00
❑ 161 Eric Shelton AU RC	40.00	15.00
❑ 162 Frank Gore AU RC	50.00	20.00
❑ 163 J.J. Arrington AU RC	50.00	25.00
❑ 164 Kyle Orton AU RC	60.00	30.00
❑ 165 Jason Campbell AU RC	60.00	35.00
❑ 166 Mark Bradley AU RC	40.00	15.00
❑ 167 Mark Clayton AU RC	50.00	25.00
❑ 168 Matt Jones AU RC	80.00	40.00
❑ 169 Maurice Clarett AU	40.00	15.00
❑ 170 Reggie Brown AU RC	50.00	25.00
❑ 171 Ronnie Brown AU RC	175.00	90.00
❑ 172 Roddy White AU RC	40.00	15.00
❑ 173 Ryan Moats AU RC	50.00	25.00
❑ 174 Roscoe Parrish AU RC	40.00	15.00
❑ 175 Stefan LeFors AU RC	40.00	15.00
❑ 176 Terrence Murphy AU RC	40.00	15.00
❑ 177 Troy Williamson AU RC	80.00	40.00
❑ 178 Vernand Morency AU RC	40.00	15.00
❑ 179 Vincent Jackson AU RC	40.00	15.00
❑ 180 Aaron Rodgers AU RC	175.00	90.00
❑ 181 Cedric Benson AU RC	120.00	60.00

1996 Press Pass

❑ COMPLETE SET (55)	20.00	7.50
❑ 1 Keyshawn Johnson	1.50	.60
❑ 2 Jonathan Ogden	.60	.25
❑ 3 Duane Clemons	.20	.07
❑ 4 Kevin Hardy	.20	.07
❑ 5 Eddie George	2.50	1.00
❑ 6 Karim Abdul-Jabbar	.60	.25
❑ 7 Terry Glenn	.60	.25
❑ 8 Leeland McElroy	.40	.15
❑ 9 Simeon Rice	.75	.30
❑ 10 Roman Oben	.20	.07
❑ 11 Daryl Gardener	.20	.07
❑ 12 Marcus Coleman	.20	.07
❑ 13 Christian Peter	.20	.07
❑ 14 Tim Biakabutuka	.60	.25
❑ 15 Eric Moulds	1.50	.60
❑ 16 Chris Darkins	.20	.07
❑ 17 Andre Johnson	.20	.07
❑ 18 Lawyer Milloy	.60	.25
❑ 19 Jon Runyan	.20	.07
❑ 20 Mike Alstott	1.50	.60
❑ 21 Jeff Hartings	.60	.25
❑ 22 Amani Toomer	1.25	.50
❑ 23 Danny Kanell	.60	.25
❑ 24 Marco Battaglia	.20	.07
❑ 25 Stephen Davis	1.50	.60
❑ 26 Johnny McWilliams	.20	.07
❑ 27 Israel Ifeanyi	.20	.07
❑ 28 Scott Slutzker	.20	.07
❑ 29 Bryant Mix	.20	.07
❑ 30 Brian Roche	.20	.07
❑ 31 Stanley Pritchett	.20	.07
❑ 32 Jerome Woods	.20	.07
❑ 33 Tommie Frazier	.40	.15
❑ 34 Stepfret Williams	.20	.07
❑ 35 Ray Mickens	.20	.07
❑ 36 Alex Van Dyke	.20	.07
❑ 37 Bobby Hoying	.60	.25
❑ 38 Tony Brackens	.60	.25
❑ 39 Dietrich Jells	.20	.07
❑ 40 Jason Odom	.20	.07
❑ 41 Randall Godfrey	.20	.07
❑ 42 Willie Anderson	.20	.07
❑ 43 Tony Banks	.60	.25
❑ 44 Michael Cheever	.20	.07
❑ 45 Je'Rod Cherry	.20	.07
❑ 46 Chris Doering	.20	.07
❑ 47 Steve Taneyhill	.20	.07
❑ 48 Kyle Wachholtz	.20	.07
❑ 49 Dusty Zeigler	.20	.07
❑ 50 Derrick Mayes	.40	.15
❑ 51 Orpheus Roye	.20	.07
❑ 52 Sedric Clark	.20	.07
❑ 53 Richard Huntley	.40	.15
❑ 54 Donnie Edwards	.60	.25
❑ 55 Zach Thomas CL	.60	.25
❑ RED Lawrence Phillips	6.00	2.50
❑ P1 Tim Biakabutuka Promo	1.00	.40

1996 Press Pass Paydirt

❑ COMPLETE SET (75)	25.00	12.50
❑ 1 Keyshawn Johnson	2.00	.75
❑ 2 Jonathan Ogden	.75	.30
❑ 3 Duane Clemons	.10	.02
❑ 4 Kevin Hardy	.30	.10
❑ 5 Eddie George	2.50	1.00
❑ 6 Karim Abdul-Jabbar	.75	.30
❑ 7 Terry Glenn	1.50	.60
❑ 8 Leeland McElroy	.30	.10
❑ 9 Simeon Rice	1.00	.40
❑ 10 Roman Oben	.10	.02
❑ 11 Daryl Gardener	.10	.02
❑ 12 Marcus Coleman	.10	.02
❑ 13 Christian Peter UER Chris Doering stamp on front	.10	.02
❑ 14 Tim Biakabutuka	.75	.30
❑ 15 Eric Moulds	.75	.30
❑ 16 Chris Darkins	.10	.02
❑ 17 Andre Johnson	.10	.02
❑ 18 Lawyer Milloy	.75	.30
❑ 19 Jon Runyan	.10	.02
❑ 20 Mike Alstott	1.50	.60
❑ 21 Jeff Hartings	.75	.30
❑ 22 Amani Toomer	1.25	.50
❑ 23 Danny Kanell	.75	.30
❑ 24 Marco Battaglia	.10	.02
❑ 25 Stephen Davis	1.50	.60
❑ 26 Johnny McWilliams	.10	.02
❑ 27 Israel Ifeanyi	.10	.02
❑ 28 Scott Slutzker	.10	.02
❑ 29 Bryant Mix	.10	.02
❑ 30 Brian Roche	.10	.02
❑ 31 Stanley Pritchett	.10	.02
❑ 32 Jerome Woods	.10	.02
❑ 33 Tommie Frazier	.30	.10
❑ 34 Stepfret Williams	.10	.02
❑ 35 Ray Mickens	.10	.02
❑ 36 Alex Van Dyke	.10	.02
❑ 37 Bobby Hoying	.75	.30

❑ 38	Tony Brackens	.75	.30
❑ 39	Dietrich Jells	.10	.02
❑ 40	Jason Odom	.10	.02
❑ 41	Randall Godfrey	.10	.02
❑ 42	Willie Anderson	.10	.02
❑ 43	Tony Banks	.75	.30
❑ 44	Michael Cheever	.10	.02
❑ 45	Je'Rod Cherry	.10	.02
❑ 46	Chris Doering	.10	.02
❑ 47	Steve Taneyhill	.10	.02
❑ 48	Kyle Wachholtz	.10	.02
❑ 49	Dusty Zeigler	.10	.02
❑ 50	Derrick Mayes	.30	.10
❑ 51	Orpheus Roye	.10	.02
❑ 52	Sedric Clark	.10	.02
❑ 53	Richard Huntley	.30	.10
❑ 54	Donnie Edwards	.75	.30
❑ 55	Zach Thomas	1.25	.50
❑ 56	Alex Molden	.10	.02
❑ 57	Jimmy Herndon	.10	.02
❑ 58	Mike Alstott	1.50	.60
❑ 59	Scott Greene	.10	.02
❑ 60	Danny Kanell	.75	.30
❑ 61	Jonathan Ogden	.75	.30
❑ 62	Simeon Rice	1.00	.40
❑ 63	Kevin Hardy	.30	.10
❑ 64	Jon Runyan	.10	.02
❑ 65	Stephen Davis	1.50	.60
❑ 66	Tim Biakabutuka	.75	.30
❑ 67	Terry Glenn	1.50	.60
❑ 68	Leeland McElroy	.30	.10
❑ 69	Eric Moulds	2.00	.75
❑ 70	Karim Abdul-Jabbar	.75	.30
❑ 71	Lawyer Milloy	.30	.10
❑ 72	Derrick Mayes	.75	.30
❑ 73	Tommie Frazier	.30	.10
❑ 74	Bobby Hoying	.75	.30
❑ 75	Kyle Wachholtz CL	.10	.02
❑ RED	Lawrence Phillips	6.00	2.50

1997 Press Pass

❑	COMPLETE SET (49)	20.00	7.50
❑ 1	Orlando Pace	.50	.20
❑ 2	Warrick Dunn	1.00	.40
❑ 3	Danny Wuerffel	.50	.20
❑ 4	Darnell Autry	.20	.07
❑ 5	Troy Davis	.20	.07
❑ 6	Jake Plummer	2.00	.75
❑ 7	Corey Dillon	2.50	1.00
❑ 8	Reidel Anthony	.50	.20
❑ 9	Byron Hanspard	.30	.10
❑ 10	Tiki Barber	2.50	1.00
❑ 11	Ike Hilliard	.50	.20
❑ 12	Rae Carruth	.20	.07
❑ 13	Yatil Green	.30	.10
❑ 14	Peter Boulware	.50	.20
❑ 15	Jim Druckenmiller	.30	.10
❑ 16	Pat Barnes	.20	.07
❑ 17	Trevor Pryce	.50	.20
❑ 18	Kevin Lockett	.20	.07
❑ 19	Koy Detmer	.50	.20
❑ 20	Bryant Westbrook	.20	.07
❑ 21	Darrell Russell	.20	.07
❑ 22	Tony Gonzalez	1.25	.50
❑ 23	Shawn Springs	.30	.10
❑ 24	Chris Canty	.20	.07
❑ 25	David LaFleur	.20	.07
❑ 26	Dwayne Rudd	.20	.07
❑ 27	Bob Sapp	.50	.20
❑ 28	Mike Vrabel	2.00	.75
❑ 29	Antowain Smith	1.00	.40
❑ 30	Keith Poole	.20	.07
❑ 31	Sedrick Shaw	.30	.10
❑ 32	Tremain Mack	.20	.07
❑ 33	Matt Russell	.20	.07
❑ 34	Reinard Wilson	.30	.10
❑ 35	Marc Edwards	.30	.10
❑ 36	Greg Jones	.20	.07
❑ 37	Michael Booker	.20	.07
❑ 38	James Farrior	.50	.20
❑ 39	Danny Wuerffel HL	.30	.10
❑ 40	Troy Davis HL	.20	.07
❑ 41	Corey Dillon HL	1.00	.40
❑ 42	Jake Plummer HL	.75	.30
❑ 43	Peter Boulware HL	.30	.10
❑ 44	Eddie Robinson CO	.50	.20
❑ 45	Bobby Bowden CO	.75	.30
❑ 46	Steve Spurrier CO	1.25	.50
❑ 47	Gary Barnett CO	.20	.07
❑ 48	Joe Paterno CO SP	50.00	20.00
❑ 49	Tom Osborne CO	1.25	.50
❑ 50	Jarrett Irons CL	.20	.07

1998 Press Pass

❑	COMPLETE SET (50)	20.00	7.50
❑ 1	Peyton Manning	6.00	2.50
❑ 2	Ryan Leaf	.50	.20
❑ 3	Charles Woodson	.75	.30
❑ 4	Andre Wadsworth	.30	.10
❑ 5	Randy Moss	4.00	1.50
❑ 6	Curtis Enis	.25	.08
❑ 7	Tra Thomas	.25	.08
❑ 8	Flozell Adams	.25	.08
❑ 9	Jason Peter	.25	.08
❑ 10	Brian Simmons	.30	.10
❑ 11	Takeo Spikes	.50	.20
❑ 12	Michael Myers	.25	.08
❑ 13	Kevin Dyson	.50	.20
❑ 14	Grant Wistrom	.30	.10
❑ 15	Fred Taylor	1.25	.50
❑ 16	Germane Crowell	.30	.10
❑ 17	Sam Cowart	.30	.10
❑ 18	Anthony Simmons LB	.30	.10
❑ 19	Robert Edwards	.30	.10
❑ 20	Shaun Williams	.30	.10
❑ 21	Phil Savoy	.25	.08
❑ 22	Leonard Little	.50	.20
❑ 23	Saladin McCullough	.25	.08
❑ 24	Duane Starks	.25	.08
❑ 25	John Avery	.30	.10
❑ 26	Vonnie Holliday	.50	.20
❑ 27	Tim Dwight	.50	.20
❑ 28	Donovin Darius	.30	.10
❑ 29	Alonzo Mayes	.25	.08
❑ 30	Jerome Pathon	.50	.20
❑ 31	Brian Kelly	.30	.10
❑ 32	Hines Ward	2.50	1.25
❑ 33	Jacquez Green	.30	.10
❑ 34	Marcus Nash	.25	.08
❑ 35	Ahman Green	2.50	1.00
❑ 36	Joe Jurevicius	.50	.20
❑ 37	Tavian Banks	.30	.10
❑ 38	Donald Hayes	.30	.10
❑ 39	Robert Holcombe	.30	.10
❑ 40	E.G. Green	.30	.10
❑ 41	John Dutton	.25	.08
❑ 42	Skip Hicks	.30	.10
❑ 43	Pat Johnson	.30	.10
❑ 44	Keith Brooking	.50	.20
❑ 45	Alan Faneca	1.00	.40
❑ 46	Steve Spurrier CO	1.00	.40
❑ 47	Mike Price CO	.25	.08
❑ 48	Bobby Bowden CO	.30	.10
❑ 49	Tom Osborne CO	1.00	.40
❑ 50	Peyton Manning CL	1.50	.60
❑ P1	Randy Moss Promo	3.00	1.25

1999 Press Pass

❑	COMPLETE SET (45)	20.00	7.50
❑ 1	Ricky Williams	1.25	.50
❑ 2	Tim Couch	.60	.25
❑ 3	Champ Bailey	1.00	.40
❑ 4	Chris Claiborne	.30	.10
❑ 5	Donovan McNabb	3.00	1.25
❑ 6	Edgerrin James	2.50	1.00
❑ 7	Akili Smith	1.00	.40
❑ 8	John Tait	.30	.10
❑ 9	Jevon Kearse	1.50	.60
❑ 10	Torry Holt	1.50	.60
❑ 11	Troy Edwards	.40	.15
❑ 12	Chris McAlister	.40	.15
❑ 13	Daunte Culpepper	2.50	1.00
❑ 14	Andy Katzenmoyer	.40	.15
❑ 15	David Boston	.60	.25
❑ 16	Ebenezer Ekuban	.40	.15
❑ 17	Peerless Price	.60	.25
❑ 18	Shaun King	.40	.15
❑ 19	Joe Germaine	.40	.15
❑ 20	Brock Huard	.60	.25
❑ 21	Michael Bishop	.60	.25
❑ 22	Amos Zereoue	.60	.25
❑ 23	Sedrick Irvin	.30	.10
❑ 24	Autry Denson	.40	.15
❑ 25	Kevin Faulk	.60	.25
❑ 26	James Johnson	.40	.15
❑ 27	D'Wayne Bates	.40	.15
❑ 28	Kevin Johnson	1.00	.40
❑ 29	Tai Streets	.60	.25
❑ 30	Craig Yeast	.40	.15
❑ 31	Dre' Bly	.60	.25
❑ 32	Anthony Poindexter	.30	.10
❑ 33	Jared DeVries	.30	.10
❑ 34	Rob Konrad	.60	.25
❑ 35	Dat Nguyen	.60	.25
❑ 36	Cade McNown	.40	.15
❑ 37	Scott Covington	.60	.25
❑ 38	Jon Jansen	.30	.10
❑ 39	Rufus French	.30	.10
❑ 40	Mike Rucker	.60	.25
❑ 41	Aaron Gibson	.30	.10
❑ 42	Kris Farris	.30	.10
❑ 43	Anthony McFarland	.30	.10
❑ 44	Matt Stinchcomb	.40	.15
❑ 45	Dee Miller CL	.30	.10

2000 Press Pass

❑ COMPLETE SET (45)	20.00	7.50
❑ 1 Peter Warrick	.50	.20
❑ 2 Travis Claridge	.25	.08
❑ 3 Courtney Brown	.60	.25
❑ 4 Plaxico Burress	1.00	.40
❑ 5 Chad Pennington	1.00	.40
❑ 6 Thomas Jones	.75	.30
❑ 7 Ron Dayne	.50	.20
❑ 8 Brian Urlacher	2.00	.75
❑ 9 Corey Simon	.60	.25
❑ 10 Chris Samuels	.40	.15
❑ 11 Stockar McDougle	.25	.08
❑ 12 Deon Grant	.40	.15
❑ 13 Cosey Coleman	.25	.08
❑ 14 Sylvester Morris	.40	.15
❑ 15 Shyrone Stith	.40	.15
❑ 16 Shaun Alexander	2.50	1.00
❑ 17 Dez White	.50	.20
❑ 18 John Engelberger	.40	.15
❑ 19 Tim Rattay	.50	.20
❑ 20 Todd Pinkston	.50	.20
❑ 21 John Abraham	.50	.20
❑ 22 R.Jay Soward	.40	.15
❑ 23 Shaun Ellis	.50	.20
❑ 24 Keith Bulluck	.50	.20
❑ 25 Jerry Porter	.60	.25
❑ 26 Darren Howard	.40	.15
❑ 27 Joe Hamilton	.40	.15
❑ 28 Deltha O'Neal	.50	.20
❑ 29 Chris Redman	.40	.15
❑ 30 Deon Dyer	.40	.15
❑ 31 Jamal Lewis	1.00	.40
❑ 32 Chris Hovan	.40	.15
❑ 33 Raynoch Thompson	.40	.15
❑ 34 Travis Taylor	.50	.20
❑ 35 Sebastian Janikowski	.50	.20
❑ 36 Travis Prentice	.40	.15
❑ 37 Tom Brady	12.00	5.00
❑ 38 Tee Martin	.50	.20
❑ 39 J.R. Redmond	.40	.15
❑ 40 Dennis Northcutt	.50	.20
❑ 41 Laveranues Coles	.60	.25
❑ 42 Danny Farmer	.40	.15
❑ 43 Darrell Jackson	1.00	.40
❑ 44 Chris McIntosh	.25	.08
❑ 45 Peter Warrick CL	.40	.15
❑ P1 Peter Warrick Promo	2.00	.75

2001 Press Pass

❑ COMPLETE SET (50)	25.00	10.00
❑ COMP.FACTORY SET (46)	25.00	10.00
❑ COMP.SET w/o SP's (45)	20.00	7.50
❑ 1 Michael Vick CL	2.50	1.00
❑ 2 Drew Brees	2.00	.75
❑ 3 Michael Vick	6.00	2.50
❑ 4 Chris Weinke	.75	.30
❑ 5 Marques Tuiasosopo	.75	.30
❑ 6 Josh Booty	.75	.30
❑ 7 Josh Heupel	.75	.30
❑ 8 Sage Rosenfels	.75	.30
❑ 9 Mike McMahon	.75	.30
❑ 10 Deuce McAllister	1.50	.60
❑ 11 LaDainian Tomlinson	5.00	2.00
❑ 12 LaMont Jordan	1.50	.60
❑ 13 James Jackson	.75	.30
❑ 14 Travis Henry	.75	.30
❑ 15 Anthony Thomas	.75	.30
❑ 16 Travis Minor	.60	.25
❑ 17 Michael Bennett	1.25	.50
❑ 18 Kevan Barlow	.75	.30
❑ 19 Rudi Johnson	1.50	.60
❑ 20 Santana Moss	1.50	.60
❑ 21 Quincy Morgan	.75	.30
❑ 22 Rod Gardner	.75	.30
❑ 23 David Terrell	.75	.30
❑ 24 Chris Chambers	1.50	.60
❑ 25 Reggie Wayne	2.00	.75
❑ 26 Ken-Yon Rambo	.60	.25
❑ 27 Chad Johnson	2.00	.75
❑ 28 Snoop Minnis	.60	.25
❑ 29 Freddie Mitchell	.75	.30
❑ 30 Koren Robinson	.75	.30
❑ 31 Bobby Newcombe	.60	.25
❑ 32 Robert Ferguson	.75	.30
❑ 33 Todd Heap	.75	.30
❑ 34 Steve Hutchinson	.60	.25
❑ 35 Leonard Davis	.60	.25
❑ 36 Kenyatta Walker	.40	.15
❑ 37 Justin Smith	.75	.30
❑ 38 Jamal Reynolds	.75	.30
❑ 39 Richard Seymour	.75	.30
❑ 40 Shaun Rogers	.75	.30
❑ 41 Gerard Warren	.75	.30
❑ 42 Jamar Fletcher	.60	.25
❑ 43 Gary Baxter	.60	.25
❑ 44 Nate Clements	.75	.30
❑ 45 Derrick Gibson	.60	.25
❑ 46 Drew Brees PP	5.00	2.00
❑ 47 Michael Vick PP	10.00	4.00
❑ 48 Deuce McAllister PP	4.00	1.50
❑ 49 LaDainian Tomlinson PP	8.00	3.00
❑ 50 David Terrell PP	1.00	.40

2002 Press Pass

❑ COMPLETE SET (50)	40.00	15.00
❑ COMP.SET w/o SP's (45)	25.00	10.00
❑ 1 David Carr	3.00	1.25
❑ 2 Eric Crouch	1.00	.40
❑ 3 Rohan Davey	1.00	.40
❑ 4 David Garrard	1.00	.40
❑ 5 Joey Harrington	3.00	1.25
❑ 6 Kurt Kittner	.75	.30
❑ 7 David Neill	.75	.30
❑ 8 Patrick Ramsey	1.25	.50
❑ 9 Antwaan Randle El	1.50	.60
❑ 10 Damien Anderson	.75	.30
❑ 11 T.J. Duckett	2.00	.75
❑ 12 DeShaun Foster	1.00	.40
❑ 13 Lamar Gordon	1.00	.40
❑ 14 William Green	1.00	.40
❑ 15 Leonard Henry	.75	.30
❑ 16 Adrian Peterson	1.00	.40
❑ 17 Clinton Portis	4.00	1.50
❑ 18 Jonathan Wells	1.00	.40
❑ 19 Brian Westbrook	2.00	.75
❑ 20 Antonio Bryant	1.00	.40
❑ 21 Reche Caldwell	1.00	.40
❑ 22 Kelly Campbell	.75	.30
❑ 23 Andre Davis	.75	.30
❑ 24 Jabar Gaffney	1.00	.40
❑ 25 Ron Johnson	.75	.30
❑ 26 Ashley Lelie	2.00	.75
❑ 27 Josh Reed	1.00	.40
❑ 28 Cliff Russell	.75	.30
❑ 29 Donte Stallworth	2.00	.75
❑ 30 Javon Walker	2.00	.75
❑ 31 Marquise Walker	.75	.30
❑ 32 Daniel Graham	1.00	.40
❑ 33 Jeremy Shockey	4.00	1.50
❑ 34 Bryant McKinnie	.75	.30
❑ 35 Mike Pearson	.50	.20
❑ 36 Mike Williams	.75	.30
❑ 37 Phillip Buchanon	1.00	.40
❑ 38 Quentin Jammer	1.00	.40
❑ 39 Kalimba Edwards	1.00	.40
❑ 40 Julius Peppers	2.00	.75
❑ 41 Wendell Bryant	.50	.20
❑ 42 John Henderson	1.00	.40
❑ 43 Ryan Sims	1.00	.40
❑ 44 Roy Williams	2.50	1.00
❑ 45 David Carr CL	1.25	.50
❑ 46 David Carr PP	6.00	2.50
❑ 47 Joey Harrington PP	6.00	2.50
❑ 48 T.J. Duckett PP	4.00	1.50
❑ 49 Donte Stallworth PP	4.00	1.50
❑ 50 William Green PP	2.50	1.00

2003 Press Pass

❑ COMPLETE SET (50)	50.00	20.00
❑ COMP.SET w/o SP's (45)	25.00	10.00
❑ 1 Brad Banks	.75	.30
❑ 2 Kyle Boller	2.00	.75
❑ 3 Ken Dorsey	1.00	.40
❑ 4 Jason Gesser	1.00	.40
❑ 5 Rex Grossman	1.50	.60
❑ 6 Kliff Kingsbury	.75	.30
❑ 7 Byron Leftwich	3.00	1.25
❑ 8 Carson Palmer	4.00	1.50
❑ 9 Dave Ragone	1.00	.40
❑ 10 Chris Simms	1.50	.60
❑ 11 Brian St.Pierre	1.00	.40
❑ 12 Chris Brown	1.25	.50
❑ 13 Avon Cobourne	.50	.20
❑ 14 Dahrran Diedrick	1.00	.40
❑ 15 Justin Fargas	1.00	.40
❑ 16 Earnest Graham	.75	.30
❑ 17 Larry Johnson	4.00	2.00
❑ 18 Willis McGahee	2.50	1.00
❑ 19 Musa Smith	1.00	.40
❑ 20 Onterrio Smith	1.00	.40
❑ 21 Lee Suggs	2.00	.75
❑ 22 Anquan Boldin	2.50	1.00
❑ 23 Talman Gardner	1.00	.40
❑ 24 Taylor Jacobs	.75	.30
❑ 25 Andre Johnson	2.00	.75
❑ 26 Bryant Johnson	1.00	.40
❑ 27 Brandon Lloyd	1.25	.50

- ❑ 28 Charles Rogers 1.00 .40
- ❑ 29 Kelley Washington 1.00 .40
- ❑ 30 Teyo Johnson 1.00 .40
- ❑ 31 Bennie Joppru 1.00 .40
- ❑ 32 Jason Witten 1.50 .60
- ❑ 33 Andrew Pinnock .75 .30
- ❑ 34 Jordan Gross .75 .30
- ❑ 35 Kwame Harris .75 .30
- ❑ 36 Eric Steinbach .75 .30
- ❑ 37 Brett Williams .50 .20
- ❑ 38 Terence Newman 2.00 .75
- ❑ 39 Marcus Trufant 1.00 .40
- ❑ 40 Andre Woolfolk 1.00 .40
- ❑ 41 Terrell Suggs 1.50 .60
- ❑ 42 Jimmy Kennedy 1.00 .40
- ❑ 43 Boss Bailey 1.00 .40
- ❑ 44 Mike Doss 1.00 .40
- ❑ 45 Carson Palmer CL 1.50 .60
- ❑ 46 Carson Palmer PP 8.00 3.00
- ❑ 47 Byron Leftwich PP 6.00 2.50
- ❑ 48 Charles Rogers PP 2.00 .75
- ❑ 49 Kyle Boller PP 4.00 1.50
- ❑ 50 Andre Johnson PP 4.00 1.50

2004 Press Pass

- ❑ COMPLETE SET (50) 50.00 20.00
- ❑ COMP.SET w/o SP's (45) 30.00 12.50
- ❑ 1 Casey Clausen 1.00 .40
- ❑ 2 Craig Krenzel 1.00 .40
- ❑ 3 J.P. Losman 2.00 .75
- ❑ 4 Eli Manning 5.00 2.00
- ❑ 5 Luke McCown 1.00 .40
- ❑ 6 John Navarre 1.00 .40
- ❑ 7 Cody Pickett 1.00 .40
- ❑ 8 Philip Rivers 3.00 1.25
- ❑ 9 Ben Roethlisberger 8.00 4.00
- ❑ 10 Matt Schaub 1.50 .60
- ❑ 11 Cedric Cobbs 1.00 .40
- ❑ 12 Steven Jackson 3.00 1.25
- ❑ 13 Kevin Jones 3.00 1.25
- ❑ 14 Greg Jones 1.00 .40
- ❑ 15 Julius Jones 4.00 1.50
- ❑ 16 Jarrett Payton 1.25 .50
- ❑ 17 Chris Perry 1.50 .60
- ❑ 18 Michael Turner 1.00 .40
- ❑ 19 Quincy Wilson .75 .30
- ❑ 20 Jason Wright .50 .20
- ❑ 21 Bernard Berrian 1.00 .40
- ❑ 22 Michael Clayton 2.00 .75
- ❑ 23 Devard Darling 1.00 .40
- ❑ 24 Lee Evans 1.25 .50
- ❑ 25 Larry Fitzgerald 3.00 1.25
- ❑ 26 Devery Henderson .75 .30
- ❑ 27 Michael Jenkins 1.00 .40
- ❑ 28 Darius Watts 1.00 .40
- ❑ 29 Mike Williams 6.00 3.00
- ❑ 30 Roy Williams WR 2.50 1.00
- ❑ 31 Rashaun Woods 1.00 .40
- ❑ 32 Ben Troupe 1.00 .40
- ❑ 33 Shawn Andrews 1.00 .40
- ❑ 34 Robert Gallery 1.50 .60
- ❑ 35 Tommie Harris 1.00 .40
- ❑ 36 Vince Wilfork 1.25 .50
- ❑ 37 Will Smith 1.00 .40
- ❑ 38 Teddy Lehman 1.00 .40
- ❑ 39 Jonathan Vilma 1.00 .40
- ❑ 40 D.J. Williams 1.25 .50
- ❑ 41 DeAngelo Hall 1.25 .50
- ❑ 42 Dunta Robinson 1.00 .40
- ❑ 43 Derrick Strait 1.00 .40
- ❑ 44 Keith Smith .75 .30
- ❑ 45 Eli Manning CL 3.00 1.25
- ❑ 46 Eli Manning PP 10.00 4.00
- ❑ 47 Ben Roethlisberger PP 15.00 7.50
- ❑ 48 Larry Fitzgerald PP 6.00 2.50
- ❑ 49 Roy Williams PP 5.00 2.00
- ❑ 50 Philip Rivers PP 6.00 2.50

2005 Press Pass

- ❑ COMPLETE SET (50) 50.00 25.00
- ❑ COMP.SET w/o PP'S (45) 30.00 12.50
- ❑ POWER PICK STATED ODDS 1:14 H/R
- ❑ UNPRICED HOBBY SOLO PRINT RUN 1 SET
- ❑ 1 Derek Anderson 1.00 .40
- ❑ 2 Brock Berlin .75 .30
- ❑ 3 Charlie Frye 2.00 .75
- ❑ 4 Gino Guidugli .50 .20
- ❑ 5 David Greene 1.00 .40
- ❑ 6 Stefan LeFors 1.00 .40
- ❑ 7 Dan Orlovsky 1.25 .50
- ❑ 8 Kyle Orton 1.50 .60
- ❑ 9 Aaron Rodgers 3.00 1.25
- ❑ 10 Alex Smith QB 4.00 1.50
- ❑ 11 Andrew Walter 1.50 .60
- ❑ 12 Jason White 1.00 .40
- ❑ 13 J.J. Arrington 1.25 .50
- ❑ 14 Ronnie Brown 3.00 1.25
- ❑ 15 Anthony Davis .75 .30
- ❑ 16 Kay-Jay Harris .75 .30
- ❑ 17 T.A. McLendon .50 .20
- ❑ 18 Ryan Moats 1.00 .40
- ❑ 19 Vernand Morency 1.00 .40
- ❑ 20 Carnell Williams 5.00 2.00
- ❑ 21 Mark Bradley 1.00 .40
- ❑ 22 Reggie Brown 1.00 .40
- ❑ 23 Mark Clayton 1.25 .50
- ❑ 24 Braylon Edwards 3.00 1.25
- ❑ 25 Fred Gibson .75 .30
- ❑ 26 Terrence Murphy 1.00 .40
- ❑ 27 J.R. Russell .75 .30
- ❑ 28 Craphonso Thorpe .75 .30
- ❑ 29 Roddy White 1.00 .40
- ❑ 30 Mike Williams 2.50 1.00
- ❑ 31 Troy Williamson 2.00 .75
- ❑ 32 Heath Miller 2.50 1.00
- ❑ 33 Alex Smith TE 1.00 .40
- ❑ 34 Khalif Barnes .75 .30
- ❑ 35 Jammal Brown 1.00 .40
- ❑ 36 Brandon Browner .75 .30
- ❑ 37 Marlin Jackson 1.00 .40
- ❑ 38 Carlos Rogers 1.25 .50
- ❑ 39 Antrel Rolle 1.00 .40
- ❑ 40 Dan Cody 1.00 .40
- ❑ 41 Erasmus James 1.00 .40
- ❑ 42 David Pollack 1.00 .40
- ❑ 43 Anttaj Hawthorne .75 .30
- ❑ 44 Derrick Johnson 1.50 .60
- ❑ 45 Ronnie Brown CL 1.50 .60
- ❑ 46 Carnell Williams PP 10.00 4.00
- ❑ 47 Aaron Rodgers PP 6.00 2.50
- ❑ 48 Alex Smith QB PP 8.00 3.00
- ❑ 49 Braylon Edwards PP 6.00 3.00
- ❑ 50 Mike Williams PP 5.00 2.00

2006 Press Pass

- ❑ COMPLETE SET (50) 50.00 25.00
- ❑ COMP.SET w/o SP's (45) 25.00 10.00
- ❑ POWER PICK ODDS 1:14
- ❑ UNPRICED SOLO SER.#'d TO 1
- ❑ 1 Brodie Croyle 2.50 1.00
- ❑ 2 Jay Cutler 3.00 1.25
- ❑ 3 Omar Jacobs 1.25 .50
- ❑ 4 Matt Leinart 4.00 1.50
- ❑ 5 Drew Olson 1.00 .40
- ❑ 6 Michael Robinson 2.00 .75
- ❑ 7 D.J. Shockley 1.00 .40
- ❑ 8 Brad Smith 1.00 .40
- ❑ 9 Marcus Vick 1.00 .40
- ❑ 10 Charlie Whitehurst 1.25 .50
- ❑ 11 Vince Young 4.00 1.50
- ❑ 12 Joseph Addai 1.50 .60
- ❑ 13 Reggie Bush 6.00 2.50
- ❑ 14 Jerome Harrison .75 .30
- ❑ 15 Laurence Maroney 2.50 1.00
- ❑ 16 Leon Washington .75 .30
- ❑ 17 LenDale White 3.00 1.25
- ❑ 18 DeAngelo Williams 3.00 1.25
- ❑ 19 Jason Avant 1.00 .40
- ❑ 20 Derek Hagan .75 .30
- ❑ 21 Chris Hannon .75 .30
- ❑ 22 Santonio Holmes 3.00 1.25
- ❑ 23 Chad Jackson 2.00 .75
- ❑ 24 Greg Lee .75 .30
- ❑ 25 Sinorice Moss 2.00 .75
- ❑ 26 Martin Nance .50 .20
- ❑ 27 Maurice Stovall 1.25 .50
- ❑ 28 Travis Wilson .75 .30
- ❑ 29 Dominique Byrd 1.25 .50
- ❑ 30 Vernon Davis 2.50 1.00
- ❑ 31 Marcedes Lewis 1.25 .50
- ❑ 32 Leonard Pope 1.25 .50
- ❑ 33 Jimmy Williams 1.25 .50
- ❑ 34 Darnell Bing 1.00 .40
- ❑ 35 Michael Huff 1.25 .50
- ❑ 36 Mathias Kiwanuka 1.00 .40
- ❑ 37 Mario Williams 2.50 1.00
- ❑ 38 Haloti Ngata 1.25 .50
- ❑ 39 Gabe Watson .75 .30
- ❑ 40 Rodrique Wright .50 .20
- ❑ 41 D'Brickashaw Ferguson 1.50 .60
- ❑ 42 Chad Greenway 1.50 .60
- ❑ 43 A.J. Hawk 3.00 1.25
- ❑ 44 DeMeco Ryans 1.25 .50
- ❑ 45 Reggie Bush CL 3.00 1.25
- ❑ 46 Reggie Bush PP 12.00 5.00
- ❑ 47 Matt Leinart PP 8.00 3.00
- ❑ 48 Vince Young PP 8.00 3.00
- ❑ 49 A.J. Hawk PP 6.00 2.50
- ❑ 50 DeAngelo Williams PP 6.00 2.50

2002 Press Pass JE

❑ COMPLETE SET (45)	25.00	10.00
❑ 1 David Carr	3.00	1.25
❑ 2 Julius Peppers	2.00	.75
❑ 3 Joey Harrington	3.00	1.25
❑ 4 Mike Williams	.75	.30
❑ 5 Quentin Jammer	1.00	.40
❑ 6 Ryan Sims	1.00	.40
❑ 7 Bryant McKinnie	.75	.30
❑ 8 Roy Williams	2.50	1.00
❑ 9 John Henderson	1.00	.40
❑ 10 Wendell Bryant	.50	.20
❑ 11 Donte Stallworth	2.00	.75
❑ 12 Jeremy Shockey	4.00	1.50
❑ 13 William Green	1.00	.40
❑ 14 Phillip Buchanon	1.00	.40
❑ 15 T.J. Duckett	2.00	.75
❑ 16 Ashley Lelie	2.00	.75
❑ 17 Javon Walker	2.00	.75
❑ 18 Daniel Graham	1.00	.40
❑ 19 Jerramy Stevens	1.00	.40
❑ 20 Patrick Ramsey	1.25	.50
❑ 21 Jabar Gaffney	1.00	.40
❑ 22 DeShaun Foster	1.00	.40
❑ 23 Kalimba Edwards	1.00	.40
❑ 24 Josh Reed	1.00	.40
❑ 25 Mike Pearson	.50	.20
❑ 26 Andre Davis	.75	.30
❑ 27 Reche Caldwell	1.00	.40
❑ 28 Clinton Portis	4.00	1.50
❑ 29 Maurice Morris	1.00	.40
❑ 30 Ladell Betts	1.00	.40
❑ 31 Antwaan Randle El	1.50	.60
❑ 32 Antonio Bryant	1.00	.40
❑ 33 Josh McCown	1.25	.50
❑ 34 Lamar Gordon	1.00	.40
❑ 35 Marquise Walker	.75	.30
❑ 36 Cliff Russell	.75	.30
❑ 37 Brian Westbrook	2.00	.75
❑ 38 Eric Crouch	1.00	.40
❑ 39 Jonathan Wells	1.00	.40
❑ 40 David Garrard	1.00	.40
❑ 41 Rohan Davey	1.00	.40
❑ 42 Ron Johnson	.75	.30
❑ 43 Kurt Kittner	.75	.30
❑ 44 Adrian Peterson	1.00	.40
❑ 45 David Carr CL	1.25	.50

2003 Press Pass JE

❑ COMPLETE SET (45)	25.00	10.00
❑ 1 Boss Bailey	1.00	.40
❑ 2 Brad Banks	.75	.30
❑ 3 Anquan Boldin	2.50	1.00
❑ 4 Kyle Boller	2.00	.75
❑ 5 Chris Brown	1.25	.50
❑ 6 Avon Cobourne	.50	.20
❑ 7 Ken Dorsey	1.00	.40
❑ 8 Justin Fargas	1.00	.40
❑ 9 Talman Gardner	1.00	.40
❑ 10 Jason Gesser	1.00	.40
❑ 11 Earnest Graham	.75	.30
❑ 12 Jordon Gross	.75	.30
❑ 13 Rex Grossman	1.50	.60
❑ 14 Kwame Harris	.75	.30
❑ 15 Taylor Jacobs	.75	.30
❑ 16 Larry Johnson	4.00	2.00
❑ 17 Bryant Johnson	1.00	.40
❑ 18 Andre Johnson	2.00	.75
❑ 19 Teyo Johnson	1.00	.40
❑ 20 William Joseph	1.00	.40
❑ 21 Bennie Joppru	1.00	.40
❑ 22 Jimmy Kennedy	1.00	.40
❑ 23 Kliff Kingsbury	.75	.30
❑ 24 Byron Leftwich	3.00	1.25
❑ 25 Brandon Lloyd	1.25	.50
❑ 26 Jerome McDougle	1.00	.40
❑ 27 Willis McGahee	2.50	1.00
❑ 28 Terence Newman	2.00	.75
❑ 29 Carson Palmer	4.00	1.50
❑ 30 Terry Pierce	.75	.30
❑ 31 Dave Ragone	1.00	.40
❑ 32 DeWayne Robertson	1.00	.40
❑ 33 Charles Rogers	1.00	.40
❑ 34 Chris Simms	1.50	.60
❑ 35 Musa Smith	1.00	.40
❑ 36 Onterrio Smith	1.00	.40
❑ 37 Brian St.Pierre	1.00	.40
❑ 38 Lee Suggs	2.00	.75
❑ 39 Terrell Suggs	1.50	.60
❑ 40 Marcus Trufant	1.00	.40
❑ 41 Seneca Wallace	1.00	.40
❑ 42 Kelley Washington	1.00	.40
❑ 43 Jason Witten	1.50	.60
❑ 44 Andre Woolfolk	1.00	.40
❑ 45 Byron Leftwich CL	2.00	.75

2001 Press Pass SE

❑ COMPLETE SET (45)	40.00	20.00
❑ 1 Michael Vick	6.00	2.50
❑ 2 Drew Brees	2.00	.75
❑ 3 Quincy Carter	.75	.30
❑ 4 Marques Tuiasosopo	.75	.30
❑ 5 Chris Weinke	.75	.30
❑ 6 Sage Rosenfels	.75	.30
❑ 7 Jesse Palmer	.75	.30
❑ 8 Mike McMahon	.75	.30
❑ 9 Josh Booty	.75	.30
❑ 10 Josh Heupel	.75	.30
❑ 11 LaDainian Tomlinson	5.00	2.00
❑ 12 Deuce McAllister	1.50	.60
❑ 13 Michael Bennett	1.25	.50
❑ 14 Anthony Thomas	.75	.30
❑ 15 LaMont Jordan	1.50	.60
❑ 16 Travis Henry	.75	.30
❑ 17 James Jackson	.75	.30
❑ 18 Kevan Barlow	.75	.30
❑ 19 Travis Minor	.60	.25
❑ 20 Rudi Johnson	1.50	.60
❑ 21 David Terrell	.75	.30
❑ 22 Koren Robinson	.75	.30
❑ 23 Rod Gardner	.75	.30
❑ 24 Santana Moss	1.50	.60
❑ 25 Freddie Mitchell	.75	.30
❑ 26 Reggie Wayne	2.00	.75
❑ 27 Quincy Morgan	.75	.30
❑ 28 Chris Chambers	1.50	.60
❑ 29 Robert Ferguson	.75	.30
❑ 30 Chad Johnson	2.00	.75
❑ 31 Snoop Minnis	.60	.25
❑ 32 Todd Heap	.75	.30
❑ 33 Steve Hutchinson	.60	.25
❑ 34 Leonard Davis	.60	.25
❑ 35 Kenyatta Walker	.40	.15
❑ 36 Justin Smith	.75	.30
❑ 37 Andre Carter	.75	.30
❑ 38 Jamal Reynolds	.75	.30
❑ 39 Gerard Warren	.75	.30
❑ 40 Richard Seymour	.75	.30
❑ 41 Damione Lewis	.60	.25
❑ 42 Jamar Fletcher	.60	.25
❑ 43 Nate Clements	.75	.30
❑ 44 Derrick Gibson	.60	.25
❑ 45 David Terrell CL	.60	.25

2004 Press Pass SE

❑ COMPLETE SET (40)	30.00	15.00
❑ MANN.MINI EXCH EXPIRATION 6/1/2005		
❑ 1 Shawn Andrews	1.00	.40
❑ 2 Casey Clausen	1.00	.40
❑ 3 Michael Clayton	2.00	.75
❑ 4 Cedric Cobbs	1.00	.40
❑ 5 Devard Darling	1.00	.40
❑ 6 Lee Evans	1.25	.50
❑ 7 Larry Fitzgerald	3.00	1.25
❑ 8 Robert Gallery	1.50	.60
❑ 9 DeAngelo Hall	1.25	.50
❑ 10 Tommie Harris	1.00	.40
❑ 11 Ben Hartsock	1.00	.40
❑ 12 Devery Henderson	.75	.30
❑ 13 Steven Jackson	3.00	1.25
❑ 14 Michael Jenkins	1.00	.40
❑ 15 Greg Jones	1.00	.40
❑ 16 Kevin Jones	3.00	1.25
❑ 17 Teddy Lehman	1.00	.40
❑ 18 J.P. Losman	2.00	.75
❑ 19 Eli Manning	5.00	2.00
❑ 20 Mewelde Moore	1.25	.50
❑ 21 John Navarre	1.00	.40
❑ 22 Jarrett Payton	1.25	.50
❑ 23 Chris Perry	1.50	.60
❑ 24 Cody Pickett	1.00	.40
❑ 25 Philip Rivers	3.00	1.25

❑ 26 Ben Roethlisberger 8.00 4.00
❑ 27 Matt Schaub 1.50 .60
❑ 28 Will Smith 1.00 .40
❑ 29 Ben Troupe 1.00 .40
❑ 30 Michael Turner 1.00 .40
❑ 31 Ben Watson 1.00 .40
❑ 32 Darius Watts 1.00 .40
❑ 33 Vince Wilfork 1.25 .50
❑ 34 Mike Williams 6.00 3.00
❑ 35 Reggie Williams 1.25 .50
❑ 36 Roy Williams WR 2.50 1.00
❑ 37 Quincy Wilson .75 .30
❑ 38 Rashaun Woods 1.00 .40
❑ 39 Jason Wright .75 .30
❑ 40 Eli Manning CL 3.00 1.25
❑ NNO Eli Manning Mini Helmet 120.00 60.00

2005 Press Pass SE

❑ COMPLETE SET (40) 25.00 10.00
❑ 1 Charlie Frye 2.00 .75
❑ 2 David Greene 1.00 .40
❑ 3 Gino Guidugli .50 .20
❑ 4 Stefan LeFors 1.00 .40
❑ 5 Dan Orlovsky 1.25 .50
❑ 6 Kyle Orton 1.50 .60
❑ 7 Aaron Rodgers 3.00 1.25
❑ 8 Alex Smith QB 4.00 1.50
❑ 9 Andrew Walter 1.50 .60
❑ 10 Jason White 1.00 .40
❑ 11 J.J. Arrington 1.25 .50
❑ 12 Marion Barber 1.50 .60
❑ 13 Ronnie Brown 3.00 1.25
❑ 14 Anthony Davis .75 .30
❑ 15 Ciatrick Fason 1.00 .40
❑ 16 T.A. McLendon .50 .20
❑ 17 Vernand Morency 1.00 .40
❑ 18 Walter Reyes .75 .30
❑ 19 Carnell Williams 5.00 2.00
❑ 20 Mark Bradley 1.00 .40
❑ 21 Reggie Brown 1.00 .40
❑ 22 Mark Clayton 1.25 .50
❑ 23 Braylon Edwards 3.00 1.25
❑ 24 Fred Gibson .75 .30
❑ 25 Chris Henry 1.00 .40
❑ 26 Terrence Murphy 1.00 .40
❑ 27 J.R. Russell .75 .30
❑ 28 Craphonso Thorpe .75 .30
❑ 29 Roddy White 1.00 .40
❑ 30 Mike Williams 2.50 1.00
❑ 31 Troy Williamson 2.00 .75
❑ 32 Heath Miller 2.50 1.00
❑ 33 Alex Smith TE 1.00 .40
❑ 34 Jammal Brown 1.00 .40
❑ 35 Marlin Jackson 1.00 .40
❑ 36 Antrel Rolle 1.00 .40
❑ 37 Dan Cody 1.00 .40
❑ 38 Derrick Johnson 1.50 .60
❑ 39 Thomas Davis 1.00 .40
❑ 40 Aaron Rodgers CL 2.00 .75

2006 Press Pass SE

❑ 1 Joseph Addai
❑ 2 Jason Avant
❑ 3 Reggie Bush
❑ 4 Dominique Byrd
❑ 5 Brodie Croyle
❑ 6 Jay Cutler
❑ 7 Vernon Davis
❑ 8 Maurice Drew
❑ 9 Anthony Fasano
❑ 10 D'Brickashaw Ferguson
❑ 11 Bruce Gradkowski
❑ 12 Darrell Hackney
❑ 13 Derek Hagan
❑ 14 Jerome Harrison
❑ 15 A.J. Hawk
❑ 16 Santonio Holmes
❑ 17 Michael Huff
❑ 18 Chad Jackson
❑ 19 Omar Jacobs
❑ 20 Matt Leinart
❑ 21 Marcedes Lewis
❑ 22 Laurence Maroney
❑ 23 Reggie McNeal
❑ 24 Sinorice Moss
❑ 25 Martin Nance
❑ 26 Haloti Ngata
❑ 27 Leonard Pope
❑ 28 Michael Robinson
❑ 29 D.J. Shockley
❑ 30 Maurice Stovall
❑ 31 Marcus Vick
❑ 32 Leon Washington
❑ 33 LenDale White
❑ 34 Charlie Whitehurst
❑ 35 Jimmy Williams
❑ 36 Mario Williams
❑ 37 DeAngelo Williams
❑ 38 Demetrius Williams
❑ 39 Vince Young
❑ 40 Vince Young CL

1999 SAGE

❑ COMPLETE SET (50) 30.00 15.00
❑ 1 Rahim Abdullah .60 .25
❑ 2 Jerry Azumah .60 .25
❑ 3 Champ Bailey 1.25 .50
❑ 4 D'Wayne Bates .60 .25
❑ 5 Michael Bishop 1.00 .40
❑ 6 David Boston 1.00 .40
❑ 7 Fernando Bryant .60 .25
❑ 8 Tony Bryant .60 .25
❑ 9 Chris Claiborne .40 .15
❑ 10 Mike Cloud .60 .25
❑ 11 Cecil Collins .40 .15
❑ 12 Tim Couch 1.00 .40
❑ 13 Daunte Culpepper 4.00 1.50
❑ 14 Jared DeVries .60 .25
❑ 15 Adrian Dingle .60 .25
❑ 16 Antuan Edwards .60 .25
❑ 17 Troy Edwards .60 .25
❑ 18 Kevin Faulk 1.00 .40
❑ 19 Rufus French .40 .15
❑ 20 Martin Gramatica .40 .15
❑ 21 Torry Holt 2.50 1.00
❑ 22 Sedrick Irvin .40 .15
❑ 23 Edgerrin James 4.00 1.50
❑ 24 Jon Jansen .40 .15
❑ 25 Andy Katzenmoyer .60 .25
❑ 26 Jevon Kearse 2.50 1.00
❑ 27 Patrick Kerney 1.00 .40
❑ 28 Lamar King .60 .25
❑ 29 Shaun King .60 .25
❑ 30 Jim Kleinsasser 1.00 .40
❑ 31 Rob Konrad 1.00 .40
❑ 32 Brian Kuklick .60 .25
❑ 33 Chris McAlister .60 .25
❑ 34 Darnell McDonald .60 .25
❑ 35 Reggie McGrew .60 .25
❑ 36 Donovan McNabb 5.00 2.00
❑ 37 Cade McNown .60 .25
❑ 38 Dat Nguyen 1.00 .40
❑ 39 Solomon Page .40 .15
❑ 40 Mike Peterson 1.00 .40
❑ 41 Anthony Poindexter .60 .25
❑ 42 Peerless Price 1.00 .40
❑ 43 Mike Rucker 1.00 .40
❑ 44 L.J. Shelton .40 .15
❑ 45 Akili Smith 1.50 .60
❑ 46 John Tait .40 .15
❑ 47 Fred Vinson .60 .25
❑ 48 Al Wilson 1.00 .40
❑ 49 Antoine Winfield .60 .25
❑ 50 Damien Woody .60 .25

2000 SAGE

❑ COMPLETE SET (50) 15.00 6.00
❑ 1 John Abraham .75 .30
❑ 2 Shaun Alexander 4.00 1.50
❑ 3 LaVar Arrington 3.00 1.25
❑ 4 Courtney Brown 1.00 .40
❑ 5 Keith Bulluck .75 .30
❑ 6 Plaxico Burress 1.50 .60
❑ 7 Giovanni Carmazzi .40 .15
❑ 8 Kwame Cavil .40 .15
❑ 9 Cosey Coleman .40 .15
❑ 10 Laveranues Coles 1.00 .40
❑ 11 Tim Couch .75 .30
❑ 12 Ron Dayne .75 .30
❑ 13 Reuben Droughns 1.00 .40
❑ 14 Shaun Ellis .75 .30
❑ 15 John Engelberger .60 .25
❑ 16 Danny Farmer .60 .25
❑ 17 Dwayne Goodrich .75 .30
❑ 18 Deon Grant .60 .25
❑ 19 Chris Hovan .60 .25
❑ 20 Darren Howard .60 .25
❑ 21 Todd Husak .75 .30
❑ 22 Thomas Jones 1.25 .50
❑ 23 Curtis Keaton .60 .25
❑ 24 Jamal Lewis 1.50 .60
❑ 25 Anthony Lucas .40 .15
❑ 26 Tee Martin .75 .30
❑ 27 Stockar McDougle .40 .15
❑ 28 Corey Moore .40 .15
❑ 29 Rob Morris .60 .25
❑ 30 Sammy Morris .60 .25
❑ 31 Sylvester Morris .60 .25
❑ 32 Chad Pennington 2.00 .75
❑ 33 Todd Pinkston .75 .30
❑ 34 Ahmed Plummer .75 .30
❑ 35 Jerry Porter 1.00 .40

❑ 36 Travis Prentice .60 .25
❑ 37 Tim Rattay .75 .30
❑ 38 Chris Redman .60 .25
❑ 39 J.R. Redmond .60 .25
❑ 40 Chris Samuels .60 .25
❑ 41 Brandon Short .60 .25
❑ 42 Corey Simon 1.00 .40
❑ 43 R.Jay Soward .60 .25
❑ 44 Shyrone Stith .60 .25
❑ 45 Raynoch Thompson .60 .25
❑ 46 Brian Urlacher 3.00 1.25
❑ 47 Todd Wade .40 .15
❑ 48 Troy Walters .75 .30
❑ 49 Dez White .75 .30
❑ 50 Michael Wiley .60 .25

2001 SAGE

❑ COMPLETE SET (50) 20.00 7.50
❑ 1 Will Allen .60 .25
❑ 2 Adam Archuleta .75 .30
❑ 3 Jeff Backus .60 .25
❑ 4 Alex Bannister .60 .25
❑ 5 Gary Baxter .60 .25
❑ 6 Michael Bennett 1.25 .50
❑ 7 Josh Booty .75 .30
❑ 8 Drew Brees 2.00 .75
❑ 9 Correll Buckhalter 1.25 .50
❑ 10 Quincy Carter .75 .30
❑ 11 Chris Chambers 1.50 .60
❑ 12 Alge Crumpler 1.00 .40
❑ 13 Andre Dyson .40 .15
❑ 14 Robert Ferguson .75 .30
❑ 15 Jamar Fletcher .60 .25
❑ 16 Rod Gardner .75 .30
❑ 17 Reggie Germany .60 .25
❑ 18 Derrick Gibson .60 .25
❑ 19 Casey Hampton .75 .30
❑ 20 Tim Hasselbeck .75 .30
❑ 21 Todd Heap .75 .30
❑ 22 Travis Henry .75 .30
❑ 23 Josh Heupel .75 .30
❑ 24 Willie Howard .60 .25
❑ 25 Steve Hutchinson .60 .25
❑ 26 James Jackson .75 .30
❑ 27 Rudi Johnson 1.50 .60
❑ 28 LaMont Jordan 1.50 .60
❑ 29 Torrance Marshall .75 .30
❑ 30 Deuce McAllister 1.50 .60
❑ 31 Willie Middlebrooks .60 .25
❑ 32 Quincy Morgan .75 .30
❑ 33 Santana Moss 1.50 .60
❑ 34 Jesse Palmer .75 .30
❑ 35 Carlos Polk .40 .15
❑ 36 Ken-Yon Rambo .60 .25
❑ 37 Jamal Reynolds .75 .30
❑ 38 Koren Robinson .75 .30
❑ 39 Richard Seymour .75 .30
❑ 40 Justin Smith .75 .30
❑ 41 Fred Smoot .75 .30
❑ 42 Marcus Stroud .75 .30
❑ 43 David Terrell .75 .30
❑ 44 LaDainian Tomlinson 5.00 2.00
❑ 45 Ja'Mar Toombs .60 .25
❑ 46 Michael Vick 6.00 2.50
❑ 47 Kenyatta Walker .40 .15
❑ 48 Gerard Warren .75 .30
❑ 49 Reggie Wayne 2.00 .75
❑ 50 Jamie Winborn .60 .25

2002 SAGE

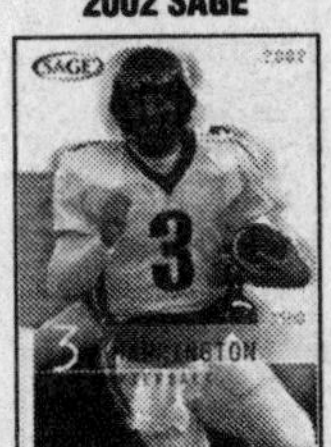

❑ COMPLETE SET (45) 40.00 15.00
❑ 1 Ladell Betts 1.50 .60
❑ 2 Antonio Bryant 1.50 .60
❑ 3 Reche Caldwell 1.50 .60
❑ 4 Kelly Campbell 1.25 .50
❑ 5 David Carr 5.00 2.00
❑ 6 Tim Carter 1.25 .50
❑ 7 Eric Crouch 1.50 .60
❑ 8 Ronald Curr 1.50 .60
❑ 9 Rohan Davey 1.50 .60
❑ 10 Andre Davis 1.25 .50
❑ 11 T.J. Duckett 3.00 1.25
❑ 12 Randy Fasani 1.25 .50
❑ 13 DeShaun Foster 1.50 .60
❑ 14 Dwight Freeney 2.00 .75
❑ 15 Jabar Gaffney 1.50 .60
❑ 16 Lamar Gordon 1.50 .60
❑ 17 Daniel Graham 1.50 .60
❑ 18 Joey Harrington 5.00 2.00
❑ 19 Napoleon Harri 1.50 .60
❑ 20 Albert Haynesworth 1.25 .50
❑ 21 John Henderson 5.00 2.00
❑ 22 Chad Hutchinson 1.25 .50
❑ 23 Quentin Jammer 1.50 .60
❑ 24 Ron Johnson 1.25 .50
❑ 25 Kurt Kittner 1.25 .50
❑ 26 Ashley Lelie 3.00 1.25
❑ 27 Bryant McKinnie 1.25 .50
❑ 28 Maurice Morris 1.50 .60
❑ 29 David Neill 1.25 .50
❑ 30 J.T. O'Sullivan 1.25 .50
❑ 31 Brian Poli-Dixon 1.25 .50
❑ 32 Clinton Portis 6.00 2.50
❑ 33 Patrick Ramsey 2.00 .75
❑ 34 Josh Reed 1.50 .60
❑ 35 Cliff Russell 1.25 .50
❑ 36 Lito Sheppard 1.50 .60
❑ 37 Jeremy Shockey 6.00 2.50
❑ 38 Luke Staley 1.25 .50
❑ 39 Donte Stallworth 3.00 1.25
❑ 40 Travis Stephens 1.25 .50
❑ 41 Chester Taylor 1.50 .60
❑ 42 Larry Tripplett .75 .30
❑ 43 Javon Walker 3.00 1.25
❑ 44 Marquise Walker 1.25 .50
❑ 45 Jonathan Wells 1.50 .60

2003 SAGE

❑ COMPLETE SET (45) 25.00 10.00
❑ 1 Sam Aiken 1.25 .50
❑ 2 Boss Bailey 1.50 .60
❑ 3 Brad Banks 2.00 .75
❑ 4 Tully Banta-Cain 1.25 .50
❑ 5 Amaz Battle 1.50 .60
❑ 6 Ronald Bellamy 1.25 .50
❑ 7 Kyle Boller 3.00 1.25
❑ 8 Chris Brown 2.00 .75
❑ 9 Tyrone Calico 2.00 .75
❑ 10 Dallas Clark 1.50 .60
❑ 11 Kevin Curtis 1.50 .60
❑ 12 Sammy Davis 1.50 .60
❑ 13 Dahrran Diedrick 1.50 .60
❑ 14 Ken Dorsey 1.50 .60
❑ 15 Justin Fargas 1.50 .60
❑ 16 Justin Gage 1.50 .60
❑ 17 Jason Gesser 1.50 .60
❑ 18 Cie Grant 1.50 .60
❑ 19 Rex Grossman 2.50 1.00
❑ 20 E.J. Henderson 1.50 .60
❑ 21 Taylor Jacobs 1.25 .50
❑ 22 Bryant Johnson 1.50 .60
❑ 23 Larry Johnson 6.00 3.00
❑ 24 Teyo Johnson 1.50 .60
❑ 25 Kliff Kingsbury 1.25 .50
❑ 26 Brandon Lloyd 2.00 .75
❑ 27 Rashean Mathis 1.25 .50
❑ 28 Jerome McDougle 1.50 .60
❑ 29 Willis McGahee 4.00 1.50
❑ 30 Billy McMullen 1.25 .50
❑ 31 Terence Newman 3.00 1.25
❑ 32 Donnie Nickey 1.25 .50
❑ 33 Terry Pierce 1.25 .50
❑ 34 Dave Ragone 1.50 .60
❑ 35 Charles Rogers 1.50 .60
❑ 36 Chris Simms 2.50 1.00
❑ 37 Musa Smith 1.50 .60
❑ 38 Lee Suggs 3.00 1.25
❑ 39 Terrell Suggs 2.50 1.00
❑ 40 Marcus Trufant 1.50 .60
❑ 41 Seneca Wallace 1.50 .60
❑ 42 Kelley Washington 1.50 .60
❑ 43 Matt Wilhelm 1.50 .60
❑ 44 Jason Witten 2.50 1.00
❑ 45 George Wrighster 1.25 .50

2004 SAGE

❑ COMPLETE SET (46) 30.00 12.50
❑ STATED PRINT RUN 3200 SETS
❑ 1 Tatum Bell 2.50 1.00
❑ 2 Bernard Berrian 1.25 .50
❑ 3 Michael Boulware 1.25 .50
❑ 4 Drew Carter 1.25 .50
❑ 5 Maurice Clarett 1.50 .60
❑ 6 Casey Clausen 1.25 .50
❑ 7 Michael Clayton 2.50 1.00
❑ 8 Chris Collins 1.00 .40

9	Karlos Dansby	1.25	.50
10	Devard Darling	1.25	.50
11	Lee Evans	1.50	.60
12	Clarence Farmer	1.00	.40
13	Chris Gamble	1.50	.60
14	Jake Grove	1.00	.40
15	DeAngelo Hall	1.50	.60
16	Josh Harris	1.25	.50
17	Tommie Harris	1.25	.50
18	Devery Henderson	1.00	.40
19	Steven Jackson	4.00	1.50
20	Michael Jenkins	1.25	.50
21	Greg Jones	1.25	.50
22	Kevin Jones	4.00	1.50
23	Sean Jones	1.00	.40
24	Derrick Knight	1.00	.40
25	Craig Krenzel	1.25	.50
26	Jared Lorenzen	1.00	.40
27	Eli Manning	6.00	2.50
28	John Navarre	1.25	.50
29	Chris Perry	1.50	.60
30	Cody Pickett	1.25	.50
31	Will Poole	1.25	.50
32	Philip Rivers	4.00	1.50
33	Ell Roberson	1.25	.50
34	Dunta Robinson	1.25	.50
35	Ben Roethlisberger	10.00	5.00
36	Rod Rutherford	1.00	.40
37	P.K. Sam	1.00	.40
38	Matt Schaub	2.00	.75
39	Will Smith	1.25	.50
40	Jeff Smoker	1.25	.50
41	Ben Troupe	1.25	.50
42	Ernest Wilford	1.25	.50
43	Reggie Williams	1.50	.60
44	Roy Williams WR	3.00	1.25
45	Quincy Wilson	1.00	.40
46	Rashaun Woods	1.25	.50

2005 SAGE

	COMPLETE SET (54)	30.00	12.50
1	Derek Anderson	1.25	.50
2	J.J. Arrington	1.50	.60
3	Marion Barber	2.00	.75
4	Brock Berlin	1.00	.40
5	Jammal Brown	1.25	.50
6	Reggie Brown	1.25	.50
7	Ronnie Brown	4.00	1.50
8	Jason Campbell	2.00	.75
9	Mark Clayton	1.50	.60
10	Channing Crowder	1.25	.50
11	Anthony Davis	1.00	.40
12	Josh Davis	1.00	.40
13	Thomas Davis	1.25	.50
14	Ciatrick Fason	1.25	.50
15	Ryan Fitzpatrick	1.25	.50
16	Charlie Frye	2.50	1.00
17	Fred Gibson	1.00	.40
18	Johnathan Goddard	1.00	.40
19	Frank Gore	2.00	.75
20	David Greene	1.25	.50
21	Kay-Jay Harris	1.00	.40
22	Marlin Jackson	1.25	.50
23	Brandon Jacobs	1.50	.60
24	Derrick Johnson	1.50	.60
25	Matt Jones	3.00	1.25
26	T.A. McLendon	1.00	.40
27	Adrian McPherson	1.25	.50
28	Justin Miller	1.00	.40
29	Vernand Morency	1.25	.50
30	Terrence Murphy	1.25	.50
31	Dan Orlovsky	1.50	.60
32	Kyle Orton	2.00	.75
33	Roscoe Parrish	1.25	.50
34	Brodney Pool	1.25	.50
35	Dante Ridgeway	1.00	.40
36	Chris Rix	1.00	.40
37	Aaron Rodgers	4.00	1.50
38	Carlos Rogers	1.50	.60
39	J.R. Russell	1.00	.40
40	Alex Smith TE	1.25	.50
41	Alex Smith QB	5.00	2.00
42	Taylor Stubblefield	1.00	.40
43	Craphonso Thorpe	1.00	.40
44	Andrew Walter	2.00	.75
45	DeMarcus Ware	2.00	.75
46	Fabian Washington	1.25	.50
47	Corey Webster	1.25	.50
48	Jason White	1.25	.50
49	Roddy White	1.25	.50
50	Carnell Williams	6.00	2.50
51	Troy Williamson	2.50	1.00
52	Maurice Clarett	1.25	.50
53	Ben Roethlisberger	4.00	1.50
54	Antrel Rolle	1.25	.50

2000 SAGE HIT

	COMPLETE SET (50)	25.00	10.00
1	Jerry Porter	1.00	.40
2	Tim Couch	.75	.30
3	Chris Samuels	.60	.25
4	Plaxico Burress	1.50	.60
5	Michael Wiley	.60	.25
6	Thomas Jones	1.25	.50
7	Chris Redman	.60	.25
8	Anthony Lucas	.40	.15
9	Kwame Cavil	.40	.15
10	Chad Pennington	2.00	.75
11	LaVar Arrington	4.00	1.50
12	Giovanni Carmazzi	.40	.15
13	Tim Rattay	.75	.30
14	Laveranues Coles	1.00	.40
15	Mario Edwards	.60	.25
16	John Engelberger	.60	.25
17	Tee Martin	.75	.30
18	R.Jay Soward	.60	.25
19	Ahmed Plummer	.75	.30
20	Na'il Diggs	.60	.25
21	J.R. Redmond	.60	.25
22	Dez White	.75	.30
23	Reuben Droughns	1.00	.40
24	Sylvester Morris	.60	.25
25	Cosey Coleman	.40	.15
26	Corey Moore	.40	.15
27	Curtis Keaton	.60	.25
28	Danny Farmer	.60	.25
29	Travis Claridge	.40	.15
30	Troy Walters	.75	.30
31	Jamal Lewis	1.50	.60
32	Shaun King	.40	.15
33	Ron Dayne	.75	.30
34	Keith Bulluck	.75	.30
35	Corey Simon	1.00	.40
36	Deon Dyer	.60	.25
37	Shaun Alexander	4.00	1.50
38	Shyrone Stith	.60	.25
39	Shaun Ellis	.75	.30
40	Todd Pinkston	.75	.30
41	Travis Prentice	.60	.25
42	Chris Hovan	.60	.25
43	Brandon Short	.60	.25
44	Brian Urlacher	3.00	1.25
45	Rob Morris	.75	.30
46	Raynoch Thompson	.60	.25
47	Deon Grant	.60	.25
48	Stockar McDougle	.40	.15
49	Darren Howard	.60	.25
50	Courtney Brown	1.00	.40

2001 SAGE HIT

	COMPLETE SET (50)	25.00	10.00
1	David Terrell	.75	.30
2	Jamar Fletcher	.60	.25
3	Koren Robinson	.75	.30
4	Ken-Yon Rambo	.60	.25
5	LaDainian Tomlinson	5.00	2.00
6	Santana Moss	1.50	.60
7	Michael Vick	6.00	2.50
8	Steve Hutchinson	.60	.25
9	Robert Ferguson	.75	.30
10	Torrance Marshall	.75	.30
11	Scotty Anderson	.75	.30
12	Derrick Gibson	.60	.25
13	Marcus Stroud	.75	.30
14	Josh Heupel	.75	.30
15	Drew Brees	2.00	.75
16	Gerard Warren	.75	.30
17	Quincy Carter	.75	.30
18	Gary Baxter	.60	.25
19	Alex Bannister	.60	.25
20	Travis Henry	.75	.30
21	Andre Dyson	.40	.15
22	Deuce McAllister	1.50	.60
23	Rod Gardner	.75	.30
24	Jamie Winborn	.60	.25
25	Will Allen	.60	.25
26	Kenyatta Walker	.40	.15
27	Tim Hasselbeck	.75	.30
28	Alge Crumpler	1.00	.40
29	Michael Bennett	1.25	.50

30 LaMont Jordan	1.50	.60
31 Jeff Backus	.60	.25
32 Rudi Johnson	1.50	.60
33 Willie Howard	.60	.25
34 Josh Booty	.75	.30
35 Todd Heap	.75	.30
36 Correll Buckhalter	1.25	.50
37 Jesse Palmer	.75	.30
38 Carlos Polk	.40	.15
39 Richard Seymour	.75	.30
40 Adam Archuleta	.75	.30
41 James Jackson	.75	.30
42 Willie Middlebrooks	.60	.25
43 Ja'Mar Toombs	.60	.25
44 Chris Chambers	1.50	.60
45 Reggie Germany	.60	.25
46 Casey Hampton	.75	.30
47 Reggie Wayne	2.00	.75
48 Jamal Reynolds	.75	.30
49 Justin Smith	.75	.30
50 Quincy Morgan	.75	.30

2002 SAGE HIT

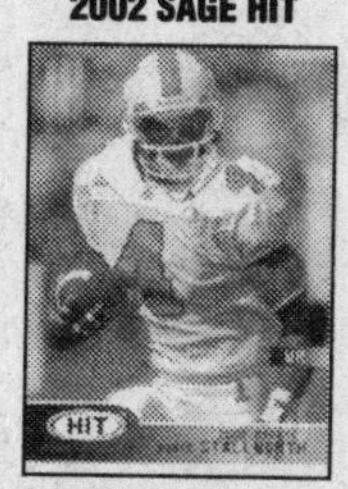

COMPLETE SET (48)	30.00	12.50
1 John Henderson	1.25	.50
2 Tim Carter	1.00	.40
3 Joey Harrington	4.00	1.50
4 Marquise Walker	1.00	.40
5 Quentin Jammer	1.25	.50
6 Rohan Davey	1.25	.50
7A Eric Crouch QB	1.25	.50
7B Eric Crouch RB	1.25	.50
8 David Carr	4.00	1.50
9 Maurice Morris	1.25	.50
10 Jabar Gaffney	1.25	.50
11 David Neill	1.00	.40
12 Randy Fasani	1.00	.40
13 Alex Brown	1.25	.50
14 J.T. O'Sullivan	1.00	.40
15 Kurt Kittner	1.00	.40
16 Ashley Lelie	2.50	1.00
17 Reche Caldwell	1.25	.50
18 T.J. Duckett	2.50	1.00
19 Chester Taylor	1.25	.50
20 Jonathan Wells	1.25	.50
21 Kelly Campbell	1.00	.40
22 Bryant McKinnie	1.00	.40
23 Lito Sheppard	1.25	.50
24 Donte Stallworth	2.50	1.00
25 Josh Reed	1.25	.50
26 DeShaun Foster	1.25	.50
27 Patrick Ramsey	1.50	.60
28 Clinton Portis	5.00	2.00
29 Albert Haynesworth	1.00	.40
31 Cliff Russell	1.00	.40
32 Luke Staley	1.00	.40
33 Ron Johnson	1.00	.40
34 Travis Stephens	1.00	.40
35 Chad Hutchinson	1.00	.40
36 Lamar Gordon	1.25	.50
37 Larry Tripplett	.60	.25
38 Napoleon Harris	1.25	.50
39 Daniel Graham	1.25	.50
40 Antonio Bryant	1.25	.50
41 Javon Walker	2.50	1.00
42 Brian Poli-Dixon	1.00	.40
43 Jeremy Shockey	5.00	2.00
44 Andre Davis	1.00	.40
45 Ladell Betts	1.25	.50
46 Michael Vick	2.00	.75
NNO David Carr CL	1.50	.60

2003 SAGE HIT

COMPLETE SET (48)	25.00	10.00
1 Charles Rogers	1.00	.40
2 Willis McGahee	2.50	1.00
3 Arnaz Battle	1.00	.40
4 Terence Newman	2.00	.75
5 Larry Johnson	4.00	2.00
6 Taylor Jacobs	.75	.30
7 Kyle Boller	2.00	.75
8 Rex Grossman	1.50	.60
9 Jerome McDougle	1.00	.40
10 Jason Witten	1.50	.60
11 Ken Dorsey	1.00	.40
12 Justin Gage	1.00	.40
13 Andy Groom	.75	.30
14 Seneca Wallace	1.00	.40
15 Dave Ragone	1.00	.40
16 Kliff Kingsbury	.75	.30
17 Jason Gesser	1.00	.40
18 George Wrighster	.75	.30
19 Ronald Bellamy	.75	.30
20 Donnie Nickey	.75	.30
21 Billy McMullen	.75	.30
22 Lee Suggs	2.00	.75
23 Chris Brown	1.25	.50
24 Bryant Johnson	1.00	.40
25 Justin Fargas	1.00	.40
26 Brandon Lloyd	1.25	.50
27 Tyrone Calico	1.25	.50
28 Sam Aiken	.75	.30
29 Cie Grant	1.00	.40
30 Dahrran Diedrick	1.00	.40
31 Kelley Washington	1.00	.40
32 Musa Smith	1.00	.40
33 Kevin Curtis	1.00	.40
34 Terry Pierce	.75	.30
35 Matt Wilhelm	1.00	.40
36 Rashean Mathis	.75	.30
37 Brad Banks	.75	.30
38 Tully Banta-Cain	.75	.30
39 Sammy Davis	1.00	.40
40 Teyo Johnson	1.00	.40
41 Chris Simms	1.50	.60
42 E.J. Henderson	1.00	.40
43 Terrell Suggs	1.50	.60
44 Dallas Clark	1.00	.40
45 Marcus Trufant	1.00	.40
46 Boss Bailey	1.00	.40
47 David Carr	1.50	.60
NNO Charles Rogers CL	1.00	.40

2004 SAGE HIT

COMPLETE SET (46)	30.00	12.50
1 Reggie Williams	1.25	.50
2 Bernard Berrian	1.00	.40
3 Lee Evans	1.25	.50
4 Roy Williams WR	2.50	1.00
5 Josh Harris	1.00	.40
6 Greg Jones	1.00	.40
7 Ben Roethlisberger	8.00	4.00
8 Drew Carter	1.00	.40
9 Devery Henderson	.75	.30
10 Eli Manning	5.00	2.00
11 Karlos Dansby	1.00	.40
12 Michael Jenkins	1.00	.40
13 Maurice Clarett	1.25	.50
14 Michael Clayton	2.00	.75
15 Casey Clausen	1.00	.40
16 John Navarre	1.00	.40
17 Philip Rivers	3.00	1.50
18 Jeff Smoker	1.00	.40
19 Ernest Wilford	1.00	.40
20 Derrick Knight	.75	.30
21 Chris Gamble	1.25	.50
22 Jared Lorenzen	.75	.30
23 Chris Perry	1.50	.60
24 Rod Rutherford	.75	.30
25 Kevin Jones	3.00	1.25
26 Michael Boulware	1.00	.40
27 Tatum Bell	2.00	.75
28 Will Poole	1.00	.40
29 Jake Grove	.75	.30
30 Ell Roberson	1.00	.40
31 Devard Darling	1.00	.40
32 Dunta Robinson	1.00	.40
33 Cody Pickett	1.00	.40
34 Steven Jackson	3.00	1.25
35 Matt Schaub	1.50	.60
36 Sean Jones	.75	.30
37 Tommie Harris	1.00	.40
38 Chris Collins	.75	.30
39 Will Smith	1.00	.40
40 DeAngelo Hall	1.25	.50
41 Rashaun Woods	1.00	.40
42 Ben Troupe	1.00	.40
43 Quincy Wilson	.75	.30
44 P.K. Sam	.75	.30
45 Clarence Farmer	.75	.30
NNO Eli Manning CL	3.00	1.25
EM Eli Manning SEC/30	50.00	20.00

2005 SAGE HIT

❑ COMPLETE SET (50)	25.00	10.00
❑ 1 Craphonso Thorpe	.75	.30
❑ 2 Derrick Johnson	1.50	.60
❑ 3 Frank Gore SP	2.00	.75
❑ 4 Ciatrick Fason	1.00	.40
❑ 5 Charlie Frye	2.00	.75
❑ 6 Antrel Rolle	1.00	.40
❑ 7 Dan Orlovsky	1.25	.50
❑ 8 Aaron Rodgers	3.00	1.25
❑ 9 Mark Clayton	1.25	.50
❑ 10 Thomas Davis	1.00	.40
❑ 11 Alex Smith QB	4.00	1.50
❑ 12 Fred Gibson SP	1.00	.40
❑ 13 Maurice Clarett SP	1.25	.50
❑ 14 David Greene	1.00	.40
❑ 15 Carlos Rogers	1.25	.50
❑ 16 Andrew Walter	1.50	.60
❑ 17 Jason Campbell	1.50	.60
❑ 18 Jason White	1.00	.40
❑ 19 Matt Jones	2.50	1.00
❑ 20 Marion Barber SP	2.00	.75
❑ 21 Taylor Stubblefield	.75	.30
❑ 22 Jammal Brown SP	1.25	.50
❑ 23 Ronnie Brown	3.00	1.25
❑ 24 Carnell Williams	5.00	2.00
❑ 25 Kay-Jay Harris	.75	.30
❑ 26 Reggie Brown	1.00	.40
❑ 27 Troy Williamson	2.00	.75
❑ 28 Anthony Davis	.75	.30
❑ 29 Josh Davis SP	1.00	.40
❑ 30 J.J. Arrington	1.25	.50
❑ 31 Alex Smith TE	1.00	.40
❑ 32 Corey Webster SP	1.25	.50
❑ 33 Vernand Morency	1.00	.40
❑ 34 Derek Anderson	1.00	.40
❑ 35 DeMarcus Ware SP	2.00	.75
❑ 36 Kyle Orton	1.50	.60
❑ 37 Brock Berlin	.75	.30
❑ 38 Marlin Jackson	1.00	.40
❑ 39 Channing Crowder	1.00	.40
❑ 40 Roddy White	1.00	.40
❑ 41 Roscoe Parrish	1.00	.40
❑ 42 Adrian McPherson	1.00	.40
❑ 43 Brodney Pool	1.00	.40
❑ 44 T.A. McLendon	.75	.30
❑ 45 Terrence Murphy	1.00	.40
❑ 46 Chris Rix	.75	.30
❑ 47 Ben Roethlisberger SP	4.00	1.50
❑ 48 Dante Ridgeway SP	1.00	.40
❑ 49 Justin Miller	.75	.30
❑ 50 Johnathan Goddard SP	1.00	.40
❑ BRJ Roethlisberger MAC JSY/7		
❑ EMJ Eli Manning SEC JSY/10		
❑ PRJ Philip Rivers AAC JSY/17		
❑ ROY Roethlisberger ROY/100	20.00	7.50

2006 SAGE HIT

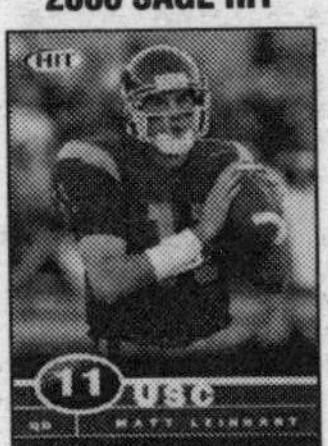

❑ COMPLETE SET (55)	25.00	10.00
❑ 1 Reggie McNeal	1.00	.40
❑ 2 Jimmy Williams SP	1.25	.50
❑ 3 D.J. Shockley SP	1.00	.40
❑ 4 Omar Jacobs	1.25	.50
❑ 5 Reggie Bush	6.00	2.50
❑ 6 Charlie Whitehurst	1.25	.50
❑ 7 Michael Huff	1.25	.50
❑ 8 Tye Hill	1.00	.40
❑ 9 Mario Williams	2.50	1.00
❑ 10 Vince Young	4.00	1.50
❑ 11 Matt Leinart UER	4.00	1.50
❑ 12 Brodie Croyle	2.50	1.00
❑ 13 Paul Pinegar	.75	.30
❑ 14 Drew Olson	1.00	.40
❑ 15 Martin Nance	.50	.20
❑ 16 David Thomas	1.00	.40
❑ 17 Dwayne Slay SP	.75	.30
❑ 18 Vernon Davis	2.50	1.00
❑ 19 Taurean Henderson SP	1.00	.40
❑ 20 Maurice Drew	1.50	.60
❑ 21 LenDale White	3.00	1.25
❑ 22 Laurence Maroney	2.50	1.00
❑ 23 Leon Washington	.75	.30
❑ 24 Erik Meyer SP	.75	.30
❑ 25 Maurice Stovall	1.25	.50
❑ 26 Ashton Youboty	1.00	.40
❑ 27 Devin Aromashodu	.75	.30
❑ 28 Mike Hass	1.00	.40
❑ 29 Jonathan Orr	.75	.30
❑ 30 Joseph Addai	1.50	.60
❑ 31 Leonard Pope	1.25	.50
❑ 32 Michael Robinson	2.00	.75
❑ 33 Mike Bell	.75	.30
❑ 34 Ernie Sims SP	1.50	.60
❑ 35 Skyler Green	1.00	.40
❑ 36 Demetrius Williams	1.00	.40
❑ 37 Winston Justice	1.25	.50
❑ 38 Sinorice Moss	2.00	.75
❑ 39 Charles Gordon SP	.75	.30
❑ 40 Gerald Riggs	.75	.30
❑ 41 Jerome Harrison	.75	.30
❑ 42 Bobby Carpenter	1.50	.60
❑ 43 Dominique Byrd	1.25	.50
❑ 44 Bruce Gradkowski	.75	.30
❑ 45 Rodrique Wright	.50	.20
❑ 46 D'Brickashaw Ferguson	1.50	.60
❑ 47 Daniel Bullocks SP	1.00	.40
❑ 48 Jason Avant	1.00	.40
❑ 49 Will Blackmon	.75	.30
❑ 50 Devin Hester SP	1.00	.40
❑ 51 Alan Zemaitis SP	1.00	.40
❑ 52 Hank Baskett	.75	.30
❑ 53 Carnell Williams ROY SP	3.00	1.25
❑ 54 Bush/Leinart CL SP	3.00	1.25
❑ 55 Vince Young CL SP	2.00	.75

2004 SAGE Jersey Update

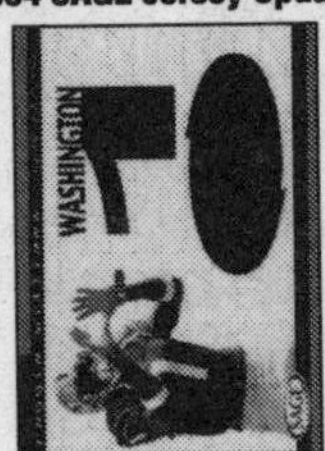

❑ PREMIUM SWATCH/10 NOT PRICED		
❑ 1 Tatum Bell	15.00	6.00
❑ 2 Maurice Clarett	12.00	5.00
❑ 3 Casey Clausen	10.00	4.00
❑ 4 Lee Evans	12.00	5.00
❑ 5 Josh Harris	10.00	4.00
❑ 6 Devery Henderson	8.00	3.00
❑ 7 Michael Jenkins	12.00	5.00
❑ 8 Greg Jones	10.00	4.00
❑ 9 Kevin Jones	20.00	7.50
❑ 10 Jared Lorenzen	8.00	3.00
❑ 11 Eli Manning	30.00	12.50
❑ 12 John Navarre	10.00	4.00
❑ 13 Chris Perry	12.00	5.00
❑ 14 Cody Pickett	12.00	5.00
❑ 15 Philip Rivers	20.00	7.50
❑ 16 Ell Roberson	10.00	4.00
❑ 17 Ben Roethlisberger	50.00	25.00
❑ 18 Rod Rutherford	8.00	3.00
❑ 19 Matt Schaub	15.00	6.00
❑ 20 Jeff Smoker	10.00	4.00
❑ 21 Reggie Williams	15.00	6.00
❑ 22 Roy Williams WR	20.00	7.50
❑ 23 Quincy Wilson	8.00	3.00
❑ 24 Rashaun Woods	10.00	4.00

2005 SAGE Premium Action Autographs Gold

❑ GOLD PRINT RUN 50 SER.#'d SETS
❑ *BLACK PORTRAIT: .5X TO 1.2X GOLD ACT.
❑ BLACK PORTRAIT PRINT RUN 25 SETS

❑ A1 Aaron Rodgers	50.00	20.00
❑ A2 Adrian McPherson	15.00	6.00
❑ A3 Alex Smith QB		
❑ A4 Alex Smith TE	15.00	6.00
❑ A5 Andrew Walter	25.00	10.00
❑ A6 Anthony Davis	12.00	5.00
❑ A7 Brandon Jacobs	20.00	8.00
❑ A8 Brock Berlin	12.00	5.00
❑ A9 Brodney Pool	12.00	5.00
❑ A10 Carnell Williams	80.00	30.00
❑ A11 Carlos Rogers	20.00	8.00
❑ A12 Channing Crowder	15.00	6.00

❑ A13	Charlie Frye	30.00	12.00
❑ A14	Chris Rix	12.00	5.00
❑ A15	Ciatrick Fason	15.00	6.00
❑ A16	Corey Webster	12.00	5.00
❑ A17	Craphonso Thorpe	12.00	5.00
❑ A18	Dan Orlovsky	20.00	8.00
❑ A19	Dante Ridgeway	12.00	5.00
❑ A20	David Greene	15.00	6.00
❑ A21	DeMarcus Ware	25.00	10.00
❑ A22	Derek Anderson	15.00	6.00
❑ A23	Derrick Johnson	25.00	10.00
❑ A24	Fabian Washington	20.00	8.00
❑ A25	Frank Gore	25.00	10.00
❑ A26	Fred Gibson	12.00	5.00
❑ A27	J.J. Arrington	20.00	8.00
❑ A28	J.R. Russell	12.00	5.00
❑ A29	Jammal Brown	15.00	6.00
❑ A30	Jason Campbell	25.00	10.00
❑ A31	Jason White	15.00	6.00
❑ A32	Johnathan Goddard	12.00	5.00
❑ A33	Josh Davis	12.00	5.00
❑ A34	Justin Miller	12.00	5.00
❑ A35	Kay-Jay Harris	12.00	5.00
❑ A36	Kyle Orton	25.00	10.00
❑ A37	Mark Clayton	20.00	8.00
❑ A38	Marlin Jackson	15.00	6.00
❑ A39	Matt Jones	40.00	15.00
❑ A40	Reggie Brown	15.00	6.00
❑ A41	Roddy White	15.00	6.00
❑ A42	Ronnie Brown	50.00	20.00
❑ A43	Roscoe Parrish	15.00	6.00
❑ A44	Ryan Fitzpatrick	25.00	10.00
❑ A45	T.A. McLendon	8.00	3.00
❑ A46	Taylor Stubblefield	8.00	3.00
❑ A47	Terrence Murphy	15.00	6.00
❑ A48	Thomas Davis	12.00	5.00
❑ A49	Troy Williamson	30.00	12.00
❑ A50	Vernand Morency	15.00	6.00

1991 Wild Card Draft

❑ COMPLETE SET (160) 8.00 3.00
❑ *5 STRIPES: 1.2X TO 3X BASIC CARDS
❑ *10 STRIPES: 2X TO 5X BASIC CARDS
❑ *20 STRIPES: 3X TO 8X BASIC CARDS
❑ *50 STRIPES: 5X TO 12X BASIC CARDS
❑ *100 STRIPES: 10X TO 25X BASIC CARDS
❑ *1000 STRIPES: 40X TO 100X BASIC CARDS

❑ 1A	Wild Card 1	.05	.01
❑ 1B	Todd Lyght	.05	.01
❑ 2	Kelvin Pritchett	.05	.01
❑ 3	Robert Young	.05	.01
❑ 4	Reggie Johnson	.05	.01
❑ 5	Eric Turner	.10	.02
❑ 6	Pat Tyrance	.05	.01
❑ 7	Curvin Richards	.05	.01
❑ 8	Calvin Stephens	.05	.01
❑ 9	Corey Miller	.05	.01
❑ 10	Michael Jackson	.10	.02
❑ 11	Simmie Carter	.05	.01
❑ 12	Roland Smith	.05	.01
❑ 13	Pat O'Hara	.05	.01
❑ 14	Scott Conover	.05	.01
❑ 15A	Wild Card 2	.05	.01
❑ 15B	Russell Maryland	.05	.01
❑ 16	Greg Amsler	.05	.01
❑ 17	Moe Gardner	.05	.01
❑ 18	Howard Griffith	.05	.01
❑ 19	David Daniels	.05	.01
❑ 20	Henry Jones	.05	.01
❑ 21	Don Davey	.05	.01
❑ 22A	Wild Card 3	.05	.01
❑ 22B	Rocket Ismail	.40	.15
❑ 23	Richie Andrews	.05	.01
❑ 24	Shawn Moore	.05	.01
❑ 25	Anthony Moss	.05	.01
❑ 26	Vince Moore	.05	.01
❑ 27	Leroy Thompson	.05	.01
❑ 28	Darrick Brown	.05	.01
❑ 29	Mel Agee	.05	.01
❑ 30	Darryll Lewis	.05	.01
❑ 31	Hyland Hickson	.05	.01
❑ 32	Leonard Russell	.05	.01
❑ 33	Floyd Fields	.05	.01
❑ 34	Esera Tuaolo	.05	.01
❑ 35	Todd Marinovich	.05	.01
❑ 36	Gary Wellman	.05	.01
❑ 37	Ricky Ervins	.05	.01
❑ 38	Pat Harlow	.05	.01
❑ 39	Mo Lewis	.05	.01
❑ 40	John Kasay	.05	.01
❑ 41	Phil Hansen	.05	.01
❑ 42	Kevin Donnalley	.05	.01
❑ 43	Dexter Davis	.05	.01
❑ 44	Vance Hammond	.05	.01
❑ 45	Chris Gardocki RC	.25	.08
❑ 46	Bruce Pickens	.05	.01
❑ 47	Godfrey Myles	.05	.01
❑ 48	Ernie Mills	.10	.02
❑ 49	Derek Russell	.05	.01
❑ 50	Chris Zorich	.05	.01
❑ 51	Alfred Williams	.05	.01
❑ 52	Jon Vaughn	.05	.01
❑ 53	Adrian Cooper	.05	.01
❑ 54	Eric Bieniemy	.05	.01
❑ 55	Robert Bailey	.05	.01
❑ 56	Ricky Watters	.60	.25
❑ 57	Mark Vander Poel	.05	.01
❑ 58	James Joseph	.05	.01
❑ 59	Darren Lewis	.05	.01
❑ 60	Wesley Carroll	.10	.02
❑ 61	Dave Key	.05	.01
❑ 62	Mike Pritchard	.10	.02
❑ 63	Craig Erickson	.10	.02
❑ 64	Browning Nagle	.05	.01
❑ 65	Mike Dumas	.05	.01
❑ 66	Andre Jones	.05	.01
❑ 67	Herman Moore	.25	.08
❑ 68	Greg Lewis	.05	.01
❑ 69	James Goode	.05	.01
❑ 70	Stan Thomas	.05	.01
❑ 71	Jerome Henderson	.05	.01
❑ 72	Doug Thomas	.05	.01
❑ 73	Tony Covington	.05	.01
❑ 74	Charles Mincy	.05	.01
❑ 75	Kanavis McGhee	.05	.01
❑ 76	Tom Backes	.05	.01
❑ 77	Fernandus Vinson	.05	.01
❑ 78	Marcus Robertson	.05	.01
❑ 79	Eric Harmon	.05	.01
❑ 80	Rob Selby	.05	.01
❑ 81	Ed King	.05	.01
❑ 82	William Thomas	.05	.01
❑ 83	Mike Jones DE	.05	.01
❑ 84	Paul Justin	.05	.01
❑ 85	Robert Wilson	.05	.01
❑ 86	Jesse Campbell	.05	.01
❑ 87	Hayward Haynes	.05	.01
❑ 88	Mike Croel	.05	.01
❑ 89	Jeff Graham	.10	.02
❑ 90	Vinnie Clark	.05	.01
❑ 91	Keith Cash	.05	.01
❑ 92	Tim Ryan	.05	.01
❑ 93	Jarrod Bunch	.05	.01
❑ 94	Stanley Richard	.05	.01
❑ 95	Alvin Harper	.05	.01
❑ 96	Bob Dahl	.05	.01
❑ 97	Mark Gunn	.05	.01
❑ 98	Frank Blevins	.05	.01
❑ 99	Harvey Williams	.10	.02
❑ 100	Dixon Edwards	.05	.01
❑ 101	Blake Miller	.05	.01
❑ 102	Bobby Wilson	.05	.01
❑ 103	Chuck Webb	.05	.01
❑ 104	Randal Hill	.10	.02
❑ 105	Shane Curry	.05	.01
❑ 106	Barry Sanders	1.00	.40
❑ 107	Richard Fain	.05	.01
❑ 108	Joe Garten	.05	.01
❑ 109	Dean Dingman	.05	.01
❑ 110	Mark Tucker	.05	.01
❑ 111	Dan McGwire	.05	.01
❑ 112	Paul Glonek	.05	.01
❑ 113	Tom Dohring	.05	.01
❑ 114	Joe Sims	.05	.01
❑ 115	Bryan Cox	.05	.01
❑ 116	Bobby Olive	.05	.01
❑ 117	Blaise Bryant	.05	.01
❑ 118	Charles Johnson	.05	.01
❑ 119	Brett Favre	6.00	2.50
❑ 120	Luis Cristobal	.05	.01
❑ 121	Don Gibson	.05	.01
❑ 122	Scott Ross	.05	.01
❑ 123	Huey Richardson	.05	.01
❑ 124	Chris Smith	.05	.01
❑ 125	Duane Young	.05	.01
❑ 126	Eric Swann	.10	.02
❑ 127	Jeff Fite	.05	.01
❑ 128	Eugene Williams	.05	.01
❑ 129	Harlan Davis	.05	.01
❑ 130	James Bradley	.05	.01
❑ 131	Rob Carpenter	.05	.01
❑ 132	Dennis Ransom	.05	.01
❑ 133	Mike Arthur	.05	.01
❑ 134	Chuck Weatherspoon	.05	.01
❑ 135	Darrell Malone	.05	.01
❑ 136	George Thornton	.05	.01
❑ 137	Lamar McGriggs	.05	.01
❑ 138	Alex Johnson	.05	.01
❑ 139	Eric Moten	.05	.01
❑ 140	Joe Valerio	.05	.01
❑ 141	Jake Reed	.25	.08
❑ 142	Ernie Thompson	.05	.01
❑ 143	Roland Poles	.05	.01
❑ 144	Randy Bethel	.05	.01
❑ 145	Terry Bagsby	.05	.01
❑ 146	Tim James	.05	.01
❑ 147	Kenny Walker	.05	.01
❑ 148	Nolan Harrison	.05	.01
❑ 149	Keith Traylor	.05	.01
❑ 150	Nick Subis	.05	.01
❑ 151	Scott Zolak	.05	.01
❑ 152	Pio Sagapolutele	.05	.01
❑ 153	James Jones	.05	.01
❑ 154	Mike Sullivan	.05	.01
❑ 155	Joe Johnson	.05	.01
❑ 156	Todd Scott	.05	.01
❑ 157	Checklist 1	.05	.01
❑ 158	Checklist 2	.05	.01
❑ 159	Checklist 3	.05	.01
❑ 160	Checklist 4	.05	.01

Acknowledgments

Every year we make active solicitations for expert input. We are particularly appreciative of the help (however extensive or cursory) provided for this volume. We receive many inquiries, comments, and questions regarding material within this book. In fact, each and every one is read and digested. Time constraints, however, prevent us from personally replying. But keep sharing your knowledge. Even though we cannot respond to each letter, you are making significant contributions to the hobby through your interest and comments.

The effort to continually refine and improve our books also involves a growing number of people and types of expertise on our home team. Our company boasts a substantial Sports Data Publishing team, which strengthens our ability to provide comprehensive analysis of the marketplace.

Our football analysts played a major part in compiling this year s book, traveling thousands of miles during the past year to attend sportscard shows and visit card shops around the United States and Canada. The Beckett Football specialists are Brian Fleischer and Dan Hitt (Senior Manager of SDP).

Bill Sutherland s coordination of input as BFCM editor this past year helped immeasurably; Rich Klein as research analyst and primary proofer also added many hours of painstaking work.

The effort was ably assisted by the rest of the SDP Team: Clint Hall, Gabe Haro, Keith Hower, Beverly Mills, Grant Sandground (Senior Price Guide Editor), and Tim Trout.

The price-gathering and analytical talents of this fine group of hobbyists have helped make our Beckett team stronger, while making this guide and its companion monthly Price Guide more widely recognized as the hobby s most reliable and relied-upon source of pricing information.

In addition, Andrew Taylor contributed many programming improvements to make this process smoother. Also this book could not produced without the fine work of our prepress team. Under the leadership of Pete Adauto, Gean Paul Figari was responsible for the layout and general presentation of this book.

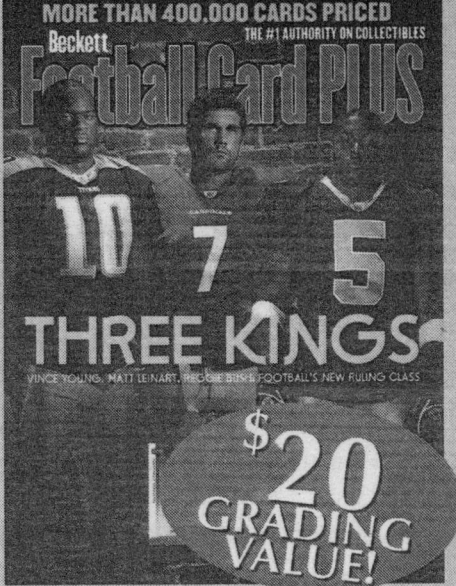

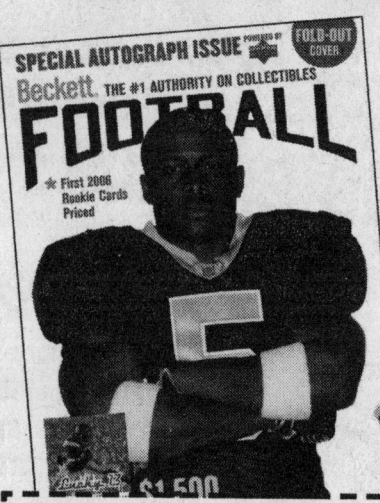